THE WORLD ALMANAC®

AND BOOK OF FACTS

2015

WORLD ALMANAC BOOKS

THE WORLD ALMANAC
AND BOOK OF FACTS
2015

Senior Editor: Sarah Janssen
Editor: M. L. Liu **Associate Editor:** Shmuel Ross
Index Editor: Nan Badgett
Contributors: Jeremy Eagle, Robert Famighetti, Marshall Gerometta, Jacqueline Laks Gorman, Richard Hantula, Sarah Hilliard, Michael J. Kaufman, Donhae Koo, John Mastroberardino, William A. McGeveran Jr., Lynn M. Messina, Janet M. Olson, Lisa Renaud, John Rosenthal, Helene Salmon, Peter J. Schmidtke, George W. Smith, Edward A. Thomas, Lori P. Wiesenfeld

Production: Newgen North America
Design and Production, Year in Pictures: Q2A/Bill Smith
Design, Cover: Takeshi Takahashi
Photo Research: Edward A. Thomas

For Infobase Learning:
Editorial Director: Laurie E. Likoff
Project Editor: Edward A. Thomas

Front cover: Jennifer Lawrence: Newscom, nfusla-52/Karl Larsen/INFphoto.com; Derek Jeter: Newscom: John Angelillo/UPI; Kevin Durant: Newscom: Armando Arorizo/EFE. **Back cover/tabs:** Shutterstock (unless otherwise noted); Tarantula Nebula: NASA/JPL/PSU. **Interior pages:** Photos are from AP Images unless otherwise noted. **Alaska Resources Library and Information Services:** *Exxon Valdez*, 476. **Jimmy Carter Library and Museum:** Carter, 511. **Everett Collection:** Kiner, 816. **Federal Emergency Management Agency:** 9/11 attack: Andrea Booher, 478; Hurricane Katrina: Liz Roll, 479; Joplin tornado: Jace Anderson, 481. **Federal Reserve System:** Yellen, 196. **Gerald R. Ford Presidential Library and Museum:** Gerald R. Ford, 511. **iStockphoto:** Great Wall, 649. **Lyndon Baines Johnson Library and Museum:** Vietnam War protesters, 473; Johnson, 510. **Library of Congress:** 447-53; 504-13 (U.S. presidents, unless otherwise noted); 661; 662; 666. **NASA:** Moon landing, 667. **Natl. Archives and Records Administration:** 454, 455, 485, 487; Grant, 507. **Newscom:** California drought: John G. Mabanglo/EPA, 194; Mondale and Ferraro: Dennis Brack, 475; Angelou: Jerome Ware/ZUMA Press, 815; Bacall: picture-alliance, 815; Caesar, Garner, and Rooney: PF1 WENN Photos, 815, 816; Dee: JT Vintage/ZUMA Press, 815; Gywnn: Cliff Welch/Icon SMI 357, 815; Kasem: s_bukley, 815; O'Toole: GINIES/SIPA, 816; Wallach: Sven Arnstein/Stay Still/Photoshot, 816. **Richard Nixon Library and Museum:** Nixon resignation, 474. **Public domain:** 446; Adams, 505; Taylor, 506; McKinley, 508; 654; 655; 659; 664. **Reuters:** Yazidi: Rodi Said, 198; ISIS: Stringer, 198. **David Rydevik:** 2004 tsunami, 672. **Shutterstock:** George Washington Bridge, 197; 648; 650; 651; 653; 656; 658; Stritch and Williams, 816. **U.S. Army:** Little Rock Nine, 456. **U.S. Dept. of Defense:** Oklahoma City bombing: Staff Sgt. Preston Chasteen, 477. **U.S. Marine Corps:** Iraq surge, 480; Iraq war: Lance Cpl. Kevin C. Quihuis Jr., 673. **U.S. Strategic Bombing Survey:** 665. **Washington Natl. Guard:** Washington landslide: Army Sgt. Virginia Owens, 122nd Public Affairs Operations Center, 331. **White House:** George W. Bush: Eric Draper, 512; Obama: Pete Souza, 513. **White House Historical Society:** Madison, 504. **Wikipedia Commons:** 497, 498, 647.

World Almanac® Books
An imprint of Infobase Learning
132 West 31st Street
New York, NY 10001

Hardcover	International Standard Serial Number	Paperback
ISBN-13: 978-1-60057-188-6	0084-1382	ISBN-13: 978-1-60057-190-9
ISBN-10: 1-60057-188-3		ISBN-10: 1-60057-190-5

The World Almanac® and Book of Facts is distributed to the trade by Simon & Schuster, and in paperback and hardcover to schools and libraries at special discounts by Infobase Learning. For further information, contact (800) 322-8755 or visit www.Infobase.com.

You can find The World Almanac® and Book of Facts on the Internet at www.worldalmanac.com.
Email: almanac@infobaselearning.com

The World Almanac® and Book of Facts 2015
Book printed and bound by RR Donnelly, Crawfordsville, IN
Date printed: November 2014
Printed in the United States of America
RRD 10 9 8 7 6 5 4 3 2 1

CONTENTS

2014: SPECIAL FEATURES AND YEAR IN REVIEW

2014: YEAR IN PICTURES

THE WORLD ALMANAC
AND BOOK OF FACTS 2015

Top 10 News Topics of 2014

1. As Syria's Civil War Continues, ISIS Gains Control of Large Areas of Syria and Iraq. In the fourth year of Syria's civil war, the forces of Pres. Bashar al-Assad continued to battle a wide range of opposition groups, including the Sunni extremist Islamic State in Iraq and Syria (ISIS). The UN estimated in Aug. that more than 191,000 people had been killed in the conflict. More than 3.2 mil refugees had fled the country by the end of Oct., and another 6.5 mil were displaced within Syria. ISIS seized control of large areas of northern and eastern Syria, including oil installations to fund its operations. In an offensive beginning in June, ISIS forces captured large parts of northern and central Iraq and set up a self-proclaimed caliphate. A U.S.-led campaign of air attacks on ISIS fighters in Iraq began Aug. 8, and U.S.-led air and cruise missile attacks against ISIS forces and other Sunni extremists in Syria began the night of Sept. 22-23. Pres. Barack Obama announced Sept. 10 that the U.S. would send more military advisers to Iraq and would provide training and weapons to Syrian rebel groups fighting ISIS and Assad's forces. A further increase in U.S. troop presence was announced Nov. 7.

2. Ebola Outbreak Kills Thousands. The worst outbreak of Ebola virus disease since the illness was first identified in humans in 1976 apparently originated in Guinea in Dec. 2013 and devastated parts of West Africa in 2014. In Guinea, Liberia, and Sierra Leone, the epidemic overwhelmed health-care systems and disrupted daily life and commerce. Other nations and nongovernmental organizations sent health-care workers and equipment, but as of the end of Oct., the World Health Organization (WHO) did not consider the epidemic to be under control. By Oct. 29, more than 13,500 West African cases had been reported to WHO; 4,950 victims had died. The first person diagnosed in the U.S., a man who had traveled from Liberia to Texas, died in a Dallas hospital Oct. 8. Two of his nurses tested positive for Ebola within a week. Later that month, an American doctor who had returned from treating Ebola patients in Guinea became New York City's first Ebola case.

3. Shooting of a Black Teenager Sparks Violent Protests. Unarmed black teenager Michael Brown was fatally shot by a white police officer Aug. 9 in the St. Louis suburb of Ferguson, MO. Accounts differed as to whether 18-year-old Brown had acted aggressively or had put his hands up and represented no apparent threat when killed. Protests over the shooting were met by heavily armed police in riot gear. An Aug. 10 demonstration and others in the following days turned violent, and some looting occurred. The state highway patrol, led by a black officer, took control of security in Ferguson Aug. 14, and National Guard troops were called in four days later. Protests occurred in the following weeks, as a St. Louis County investigation continued into whether charges should be brought against Darren Wilson, the officer involved. The U.S. Dept. of Justice also opened a civil rights investigation into the incident.

4. Republicans Win Senate Majority in Midterm Elections. The Republican Party made major gains in U.S. Senate, House of Representatives, and gubernatorial elections held Nov. 4. In what many analysts saw as discontent with the country's course and the leadership of Pres. Barack Obama, voters unseated several incumbent Democratic senators and gave GOP candidates gubernatorial victories in such traditionally Democratic states as Massachusetts and Maryland. Picking up at least seven Senate seats (pending final results in Alaska and Louisiana), the GOP won control of the Senate for the first time in eight years. Increasing its majority in the House, the Republican Party will control both houses of Congress in Jan. 2015, as well as more than 60% of governorships.

5. Tens of Thousands of Central American Children Apprehended at U.S. Border. From Oct. 2013 to July 2014, some 60,000 children and teenagers, most unaccompanied by an adult, were caught trying to cross into the U.S. from Mexico. Most were apparently fleeing drug-related violence, other crime, and extreme poverty in Honduras, Guatemala, and El Salvador. The influx strained resources, as thousands of minors had to be sheltered. Under 2008 anti-trafficking legislation, undocumented minors from countries not bordering the U.S. must receive a hearing before they can be deported. On Sept. 30, Pres. Obama approved a plan to allow Central American children to apply for refugee status while in their home countries, to discourage risky journeys through Mexico. Broader revision of U.S. immigration policy remained stalled.

6. Israel-Hamas Conflict in Gaza Leaves Thousands Dead. The fiercest fighting in five years between Israel and Hamas in Gaza erupted in 2014. After nine months of intensive diplomacy by U.S. Sec. of State John Kerry, Israeli-Palestinian peace talks were suspended in Apr. over issues including prisoner releases, Israeli settlements, and the inclusion of Hamas in a Palestinian unity government. The June 12 killing of three Israeli teenagers in the West Bank and the July 2 killing of a Palestinian teenager heightened tensions, and rocket attacks from Gaza into Israel increased. Israel launched an air campaign July 8 against rocket-launch sites and other Hamas targets in Gaza, including tunnels under the border. It sent ground troops into the territory July 17 (they withdrew Aug. 5). Some Israeli attacks caused high civilian casualties. An Aug. 26 ceasefire essentially restored the status quo. Palestinian deaths in the conflict were estimated at more than 2,100, and Israel reported about 70 soldiers and civilians were killed.

7. Ukraine Battles Pro-Russian Separatists and Loses Crimea. Pro-European and pro-Russian factions in Ukraine battled each other politically and militarily in 2014. After violent protests in Kiev against pro-Russian Pres. Viktor Yanukovych, parliament removed him from office Feb. 22. Less than a week later, pro-Russian rebels in Ukraine's Crimean Peninsula began seizing government facilities. Russia sent troops into Crimea and annexed the territory Mar. 18. Fighting erupted the next month in eastern Ukraine between government forces and pro-Russian separatists, widely reported to be aided by Russian military equipment and troops. As the conflict continued, Petro Poroshenko, an advocate of closer ties with Europe, won Ukraine's May 25 presidential election. On July 17, a Malaysia Airlines jet was shot down over eastern Ukraine by a missile believed to have been fired by separatist forces; all 298 on board were killed. A Sept. 5 ceasefire reduced the level of violence somewhat, but clashes continued.

8. Afghanistan Elects New Leadership as the U.S. Draws Down Troops. As fighting continued between government forces and the Taliban and other insurgents in 2014, Afghanistan held elections for a new president. Former Foreign Min. Abdullah Abdullah and former Finance Min. Ashraf Ghani received the most votes in the Apr. 5 first round and competed in a June 14 runoff marred by widespread allegations of fraud. Under a U.S.-negotiated recount and power-sharing agreement, Ghani was declared the winner Sept. 21 but agreed to appoint Abdullah to the new post of chief executive officer. Both took office Sept. 29. The U.S. and its allies continued to draw down troops in 2014. As of Oct. 6, NATO's Intl. Security Assistance Force totaled just over 34,500 troops, including about 24,000 from the U.S. Pres. Barack Obama announced, May 27, that the U.S. force level would fall below 10,000 by year's end, and that all U.S. forces would leave by the end of 2016.

9. Revelations Raise Concerns About Data Security and Privacy. In separate attacks, hackers gained access to private data on tens of millions of people. Retail chain Target announced Jan. 10 that a security breach first revealed in Dec. may have allowed hackers to steal data on upwards of 70 mil consumers. A flaw known as the Heartbleed bug, found in Apr. in the OpenSSL encryption software used to secure most websites may have allowed hackers access to passwords and other protected data. In an attack beginning in June, hackers obtained the names, addresses, phone numbers, and email addresses of 83 mil customers of JPMorgan Chase, which the largest U.S. bank reported Oct. 2. Edward Snowden's revelations about U.S. Natl. Security Agency (NSA) surveillance continued to make news. The Obama administration in Mar. announced plans to limit NSA collection of Americans' telephone records. On May 31, the *NY Times* reported, based on Snowden's documents, that NSA monitoring of communications included collecting millions of images that had been emailed, texted, or posted on social media.

10. Germany Wins the World Cup; Russia Hosts the Winter Olympics. Brazil hosted the FIFA men's World Cup championship June 12-July 13, with more than 3.4 mil fans attending the tournament's 64 matches. In the July 13 final, Germany's Mario Götze scored a goal in extra time for a 1-0 victory over Argentina and Germany's fourth men's World Cup title. Sochi, Russia, was the host city for the XXII Olympic Winter Games, Feb. 7-23. Russia led in the overall medal count (33), followed by the U.S. (28) and Norway (26).

THE WORLD
AT A GLANCE

Number Ones

World's most populous country . . . . China, 1.36 billion population in 2014 *(p. 734)*

World's most populous urban area. . . . . Tokyo, Japan, 37.8 million population in 2014 *(p. 734)*

World's wealthiest person. . . . . .Carlos Slim Helú, Mexico, $79.2 billion net worth as of Oct. 2014 *(p. 57)*

Wealthiest American. . . . . Bill Gates, $79.0 billion net worth as of Oct. 2014 *(p. 57)*

Most-visited U.S. social networking website. . . . . Facebook, 200.4 million unique visitors in June 2014 *(p. 305)*

Most-used U.S. search engine . . . . Google, 12.3 billion searches in June 2014 *(p. 305)*

U.S. airline that carried the most passengers. . . . . American/US Airways, 143.8 million in 2013 *(p. 97)*

World's busiest airport by passenger traffic . . . . . .Hartsfield-Jackson Atlanta Intl. Airport, 94.4 million passengers in 2013 *(p. 97)*

Top U.S. state by traveler spending . . . . California, $110.8 billion in 2012 *(p. 95)*

Nation with the most paid days off of work per year. . . . . .Austria, 38 paid days off *(p. 98)*

Most popular recording artist by digital sales . . . . Katy Perry, 72 million units sold as of Aug. 2014 *(p. 259)*

Surprising Facts

An insurance analysis of "weather-related loss events" (natural disasters) found that occurrences on every continent had increased by at least 150% between 1980 and 2011. *(p. 326)*

The average U.S. movie ticket price surpassed $8 for the first time in 2013. *(p. 252)*

In 1950, the U.S. produced 75.7% of the world's motor vehicles; by 2013, that number had dropped to 12.7%. *(p. 88)*

Only two U.S. states (Arizona and Montana) have no laws in place that address texting while behind the wheel for at least some drivers. *(p. 92)*

Visitors to the U.S. from Mexico in 2013 spent an average of $733 per person; from Canada, $1,156; from France, $3,907; from Brazil, $5,085. *(p. 95)*

Americans paid an average of 24.6% of their gross wage earnings in income tax and Social Security contributions in 2013; Belgians, who had some of the highest personal-income tax rates, paid 42.6%. *(p. 736)*

Even before U.S. health-care reform went into effect, the U.S. was by far the top spender on health expenses among the 50 most populous nations, at $8,467 per capita in 2011. Australia came closest to matching U.S. spending, at $5,991 per capita. *(p. 150)*

California had the highest student-to-teacher ratio of any state in the 2012-13 school year, with 24.9 pupils for every teacher; the U.S. average was 15.9. *(p. 392)*

21% of female high school students reported being bullied electronically in 2013; the rate for high school boys was 8.5%. *(p. 393)*

Milestone Birthdays, 2015

90
Yogi Berra, May 12
Barbara Bush, June 8
B.B. King, Sept. 16
Angela Lansbury, Oct. 16
Doris Roberts, Nov. 4
Dick Van Dyke, Dec. 13

80
Dalai Lama, July 6
Ron Paul, Aug. 20
Frank Robinson, Aug. 31
Jerry Lee Lewis, Sept. 29
Julie Andrews, Oct. 1
Woody Allen, Dec. 1
Sandy Koufax, Dec. 30

70
Tom Selleck, Jan. 29
Eric Clapton, Mar. 30
Helen Mirren, July 26

70
Steve Martin, Aug. 14
Van Morrison, Aug. 31
Phil Jackson, Sept. 17
John Lithgow, Oct. 19
Henry Winkler, Oct. 30
Neil Young, Nov. 12
Bette Midler, Dec. 1
Diane Sawyer, Dec. 22

60
Kevin Costner, Jan. 18
John Roberts, Jan. 27
Kelsey Grammer, Feb. 21
Bruce Willis, Mar. 19
Tim Berners-Lee, June 8
Mike Huckabee, Aug. 24
Yo-Yo Ma, Oct. 7
Bill Gates, Oct. 28
Whoopi Goldberg, Nov. 13

50
Diane Lane, Jan. 22
Chris Rock, Feb. 7
Sarah Jessica Parker, Mar. 25
Robert Downey Jr., Apr. 4
Jon Cryer, Apr. 16
Martin Lawrence, Apr. 16
Kevin James, Apr. 26
Brooke Shields, May 31
J. K. Rowling, July 31
Viola Davis, Aug. 11
Charlie Sheen, Sept. 3
Ben Stiller, Nov. 30

40
Bradley Cooper, Jan. 5
Drew Barrymore, Feb. 22
Johnny Galecki, Apr. 30
David Beckham, May 2
Angelina Jolie, June 4

40
Tobey Maguire, June 27
Alex Rodriguez, July 27
Charlize Theron, Aug. 7
Kate Winslet, Oct. 5
Jesse Tyler Ferguson, Oct. 22
Tiger Woods, Dec. 30

30
Reggie Bush, Mar. 2
Keira Knightley, Mar. 26
Michael Phelps, June 30
Kaley Cuoco, Nov. 30
Amanda Seyfried, Dec. 3

21
Harry Styles, Feb. 1
Dakota Fanning, Feb. 23
Justin Bieber, Mar. 1

18
Malala Yousafzai, July 12

EBOLA OUTBREAK FACTS

Ebola is a historically rare, deadly disease caused by infection with one of five identified Ebola virus strains (four of which are known to cause the disease in humans). The virus was first identified in 1976 near the Ebola River, in the Democratic Republic of the Congo.

The 2014 Ebola epidemic is the largest in history, with three West African nations (Guinea, Liberia, and Sierra Leone) experiencing widespread outbreaks of the Zaire strain of the virus. Mali identified its first case of Ebola on Oct. 23, 2014. The World Health Organization (WHO) declared that outbreaks in Senegal and Nigeria were contained by mid-Oct. 2014.

The average fatality rate for Ebola virus in the 2014 outbreak is around 50%. Many past Ebola outbreaks occurred in remote villages and were more easily contained, but the 2014 outbreak involved major urban areas and spread quickly.

The first case of Ebola to be diagnosed in the U.S. was identified on Sept. 30, 2014; the patient, Thomas Eric Duncan, had recently traveled from Liberia to Dallas, TX. He died Oct. 8, 2014.

Signs and Symptoms

Symptoms can appear 2 to 21 days after exposure to the virus and include the following:

- Diarrhea
- Fever
- Headache
- Muscle pain
- Rash
- Stomach pain
- Unexplained bleeding or bruising
- Vomiting
- Weakness

On average, symptoms begin to show 8-10 days after exposure. The earliest symptoms are flu-like: headache, fever, and aches and pains, followed by gastrointestinal distress. More severe symptoms develop in about half of Ebola patients. Patients can begin to hemorrhage, bleeding internally or from eyes and mouths; some victims pass blood as vomit or urine. When internal hemorrhaging is severe, blood pressure can fall so low that organs begin to fail.

Transmission

It is not certain how Ebola outbreaks begin, but many epidemiologists believe that it is transmitted through contact with an infected animal, such as a bat or primate. It appears that only mammals can transmit the disease. During the outbreak in West Africa in 2014, the public was urged to reduce the risk of transmission by avoiding contact with bats, monkeys, and apes and not eating their meat unless thoroughly cooked.

Ebola can only be spread to others after symptoms appear. The virus does not spread through the air or through water supplies. Once symptoms manifest, Ebola is transmitted through direct-contact exposure to infected bodily fluids, contaminated objects (like syringes or bedding), or the body of someone who died of the virus. The fluids or contamination must bypass a person's natural skin barrier through a mucous membrane (eyes, nose, or mouth) or broken skin. Infectious body fluids include the following:

- Blood
- Breast milk
- Feces
- Saliva
- Semen
- Sweat
- Tears
- Urine
- Vomit

Ebola can only survive on dry surfaces—like doors or shelves—for a few hours, and it can be killed with household bleach. However, the virus can live in bodily fluids for up to a few days, even at room temperature.

Diagnosis

Diagnosing Ebola is difficult at the onset of the disease because the earliest symptoms, like fever, are not specific to Ebola. In combination with known exposure to Ebola or travel in an area where an outbreak is occurring, symptoms may point to immediate isolation and notification of public health authorities. Laboratory testing can then confirm or exclude the diagnosis of Ebola.

Treatment

No vaccination or medication was available specifically to treat Ebola in 2014, though some were in development. Instead, health care workers treat symptoms in Ebola patients and can significantly improve patient outcomes with rehydration techniques (oral and IV fluids and balancing electrolytes), monitoring blood pressure and oxygen levels, and treating any infections.

Exposure Risk and Prevention

Health care workers and family and friends caring for Ebola patients are the most likely to be exposed to body fluids and are thus at the highest risk of exposure. In an area affected by an Ebola outbreak, hygiene should be practiced conscientiously, especially proper hand-washing and sanitation procedures.

Other prevention procedures, especially for health care workers, include:

- Isolation of patients with Ebola
- Proper use of protective clothing (including masks, gloves, gowns, and goggles or face shields)
- Proper infection-control measures (including equipment sterilization, disinfectant use, and safe burial practices)

Another public health measure used to prevent single cases from turning into outbreaks is contact tracing. Contact tracing seeks to identify and locate every person who has been in direct contact with a sick Ebola patient. Contacts are then watched for 21 days for any signs of developing Ebola. If they have a fever or show other symptoms, they are isolated, and the cycle starts again with their contacts. Contact tracing identifies new cases more quickly, so they can be isolated earlier and stop further spread.

Website: www.cdc.gov/vhf/ebola/

Ebola Outbreaks, 1976-2012
Source: World Health Organization (WHO)

Year	Country	Ebolavirus species	Cases	Deaths	Fatality rate	Year	Country	Ebolavirus species	Cases	Deaths	Fatality rate
1976	Dem. Rep. of Congo	Zaire	318	280	88%	2001-02	Congo Rep.	Zaire	59	44	75%
1976	Sudan	Sudan	284	151	53	2003[1]	Congo Rep.	Zaire	143	128	90
1977	Dem. Rep. of Congo	Zaire	1	1	100	2003[2]	Congo Rep.	Zaire	35	29	83
1979	Sudan	Sudan	34	22	65	2004	Sudan	Sudan	17	7	41
1994	Gabon	Zaire	52	31	60	2005	Congo Rep.	Zaire	12	10	83
1994	Côte d'Ivoire	Taï Forest	1	0	0	2007	Dem. Rep. of Congo	Zaire	264	187	71
1995	Dem. Rep. of Congo	Zaire	315	254	81	2007	Uganda	Bundibugyo	149	37	25
1996	South Africa (ex-Gabon)	Zaire	1	1	100	2008	Dem. Rep. of Congo	Zaire	32	14	44
1996	Gabon	Zaire	60	45	75	2011	Uganda	Sudan	1	1	100
1996	Gabon	Zaire	31	21	68	2012	Dem. Rep. of Congo	Bundibugyo	57	29	51
2000	Uganda	Sudan	425	224	53	2012	Uganda	Sudan	24	17	71
2001-02	Gabon	Zaire	65	53	82	2012	Uganda	Sudan	7	4	57

(1) Jan.-Apr. (2) Nov.-Dec.

AMERICAN VETERANS: A STATUS REPORT

In 2014, almost 22 mil Americans were veterans of service in the U.S. armed forces. Three-quarters of them had served during wartime—from World War II to the 21st-century conflicts in southwest Asia. More than 3.7 mil people were what the U.S. Dept. of Veterans Affairs (VA) terms post-9/11 Gulf War-era veterans, who served after the terrorist attacks of Sept. 11, 2001. About half of those were involved in the conflicts in Afghanistan and Iraq that began in 2001 and 2003, respectively.

Veterans are eligible for a wide range of benefits to recognize and reward their service, help them reintegrate into civilian life, and assist them with service-related problems. Those problems may be severe, including medical, social, and economic challenges. In addition, many veterans have had difficulty utilizing some services or accessing some benefits to which they are entitled.

A History of Honoring Service

Over the centuries, the U.S. has run programs that have helped millions of veterans, but failures in those programs have denied or delayed help to many. As early as 1636, Plymouth Colony enacted a law requiring it to support disabled soldiers who were injured fighting the Pequot Indians. During the American Revolution, the Continental Congress voted to provide pensions to disabled veterans. However, because payment of the pensions was initially left to the states, many eligible former soldiers never received them.

The Civil War increased the number of American veterans from 80,000 to almost 2 mil (counting only Union soldiers). In accordance with Pres. Abraham Lincoln's policy "to care for him who shall have borne the battle and for his widow, and his orphan" (now the VA motto), Congress approved pensions for those disabled in the war and later expanded coverage to all veterans over a certain age. (The federal government did not recognize Confederate soldiers as veterans until a 1958 Congressional pardon.)

Some 4.6 mil veterans returned from World War I, resulting in dramatic expansions of veterans' programs. The Veterans Bureau, a forerunner of today's VA, was established in 1921. Three years later, Congress voted to give cash bonuses to World War I veterans, but most were not payable for 20 years. In 1932, as the Great Depression worsened, a "Bonus Army" of thousands of veterans gathered in Washington, DC, demanding immediate payment. The use of Army troops to forcibly remove protesters from the city was a low point in the treatment of U.S. war veterans.

The 16 mil veterans of World War II benefited from the most comprehensive legislation to date to assist former soldiers. The 1944 Servicemen's Readjustment Act, popularly known as the GI Bill, has been called one of the most important pieces of legislation in U.S. history. One key provision provided government payments to enable veterans to get a 4-year college degree or comparable training. Another provided low-cost government-guaranteed mortgage loans for veterans, as well as loans to start or build a business. The GI Bill transformed the lives of tens of millions and greatly contributed to the country's dramatic economic growth in the postwar decades.

Subsequent legislation and programs for veterans have been based on types of benefits in the GI Bill and its predecessors. Today's post-9/11 veterans are eligible for education, health care, pensions, and other benefits.

New GI Bill for Education

In 2008, Congress passed a measure popularly known as the Post-9/11 GI Bill, with enhancements to benefits signed into law in Jan. 2011. This new GI Bill provides a variety of education benefits for veterans who served after Sept. 10, 2001, including tuition (usually in the form of payments made directly to the school), housing allowances, and payments to offset the cost of books and other supplies. Veterans must have served on active duty for 36 months (or 30 days before a disability discharge) to be eligible for maximum benefits, which are prorated for people who served less time. The program covers up to 36 months of college education or the equivalent in a wide variety of occupational and other training programs. People attending in-state public institutions may have up to 100% of tuition costs paid for by the federal government; tuition coverage is often less comprehensive for out-of-state or private-institution students.

The program had some growing pains when it first went into effect in Aug. 2009—many veterans complained of long delays in processing their applications. However, by Nov. 2013, the VA reported that average processing time was 23 days.

In the first full fiscal year (2010) that the new GI Bill was in effect, more than 350,000 people received education benefits. The number of participants in the program increased to more than 750,000 by 2013. In Nov. 2013, the VA reported that its total post-9/11 GI Bill education spending had passed $30 bil.

Members of Congress questioned whether some for-profit institutions receiving payments from the VA were providing poor-quality education. A 2014 Congressional Research Service report found that relatively little data had been collected on the number of veterans completing their educational programs, as well as on how their education or training affected subsequent employment. One survey of students who used some form of VA education benefit between 2002 and 2010 found that 52% had earned a post-secondary degree or certificate. The VA announced plans in 2012 to begin collecting more comprehensive data on educational outcomes.

VA Health Care System

The VA operates a large health care system that includes 820 outpatient clinics and 150 hospitals throughout the U.S. Most veterans who served on active duty for two years or the full period for which they were called up are eligible for VA health care.

Veterans Using the VA Health Care System, 2002-13

Source: Veterans Health Administration Office of Policy and Planning, U.S. Dept. of Veterans Affairs

Note: Data are for fiscal year.

Veterans With Service-Related Disabilities, 2000-13
Source: Veterans Benefits Administration, U.S. Dept. of Veterans Affairs

Degree of disability
- 0%-20%
- 30%-40%
- 50%-60%
- 70%-100%

Number (mil): values by year — 2.31 (2000), 2.32 (2001), 2.40 (2002), 2.49 (2003), 2.56 (2004), 2.64 (2005), 2.73 (2006), 2.84 (2007), 2.95 (2008), 3.07 (2009), 3.21 (2010), 3.36 (2011), 3.54 (2012), 3.74 (2013)

Note: Data are for fiscal year.

With veterans returning from Afghanistan and Iraq, the number of patients using VA health care increased sharply in the post-9/11 years. More than 8.9 mil people were enrolled in the system as of fiscal year 2013, a 30% increase since 2002. The VA cared for 5.7 mil patients in 2013, 35% more than in 2002. The number of unique outpatient visits in 2013 was 86.4 mil—86% higher than 12 years earlier.

VA health care spending more than doubled, from $23 bil in 2002 to almost $56 bil in 2013. However, the spending increase may not have been sufficient for the services needed. In Apr. 2014, news reports based on whistleblower accounts maintained that staff at the Phoenix VA Health Care System routinely falsified records to conceal the fact that large numbers of patients waited far longer than the VA standard of two weeks for an appointment; 40 patients were said to have died while awaiting care. An Aug. 2014 report from the VA Office of the Inspector General confirmed that intentional records falsification at the Phoenix facility left thousands of patients at risk of never receiving an appointment, that senior staff were aware of the practice, that some patients had apparently died as a result of appointment delays (though it could not confirm the figure of 40), and that record falsification was also occurring at dozens of other VA facilities around the country.

Legislation signed by Pres. Barack Obama Aug. 7, 2014, provided funding to allow VA facilities to hire more doctors and other staff, permitted veterans facing long treatment delays to use other providers at VA expense, and made it easier for the VA to dismiss poorly performing staff.

Growing Numbers of Disabled Veterans

Post-9/11 veterans have presented the health care system—and other branches of the VA—with the need for wide-ranging services. The U.S. Bureau of Labor Statistics (BLS) reported that as of Aug. 2013, 29% of post-9/11 veterans had service-related disabilities, compared to 15% of all veterans. VA statistics showed that between fiscal years 2000 and 2013, the number of disabled veterans increased by 62%, from 2.3 mil to 3.7 mil. The greatest rate of increase (more than 240%) was among veterans with the most severe disabilities.

The increased incidence of service-related disabilities may reflect, in part, better diagnosis of conditions that in earlier periods might have gone unreported. In addition, with improvements in battlefield and other emergency care, severely injured troops now have a greater chance of survival.

The VA rates the severity of disabilities in 10% increments, on a scale from 0% to 100%. A rating generally represents a disabled veteran's estimated loss in earning capacity. Besides medical care, disabled veterans are eligible for monthly cash payments in accordance with their disability rating. These payments can be critically important to the economic well-being of veterans, especially those unable to work. However, many veterans have experienced long waits for a VA decision on their application for benefits. In Apr. 2013, when the VA implemented new procedures to streamline claims processing, the average wait time was 286 days. In its 2014 annual members survey, the organization Iraq and Afghanistan Veterans of America (IAVA) found that 29% of respondents who applied for disability waited more than a year. However, by late 2014, the VA reported that the average wait time was below 150 days for veterans using its new filing process.

Brain Injuries and Mental Health

The incidence of traumatic brain injury (TBI) among members of the armed forces has been increasing in the post-9/11 era. From 12,407 in 2002, the number of annual TBI cases peaked at 32,668 in 2011 before declining slightly in 2012 and 2013. TBI can be combat or noncombat related. Many post-9/11 cases are the result of vehicle crashes, falls, military training accidents, or sports injuries. Of the total 307,000 cases diagnosed from 2000 through the first half of 2014, most were mild with apparently only short-term effects. However, more than 10% were moderate, severe, or penetrating brain injuries (in which the membrane covering the brain is pierced). These more serious cases of TBI can have long-term effects, which may include Parkinson's disease, seizures, dementia, depression, and certain hormone-deficiency diseases. New VA regulations that went into effect in Jan. 2014 made it easier for veterans who suffered moderate or worse TBI and had one of those five conditions to qualify for free medical care and disability payments.

The stress of combat or service in a combat zone can lead to post-traumatic stress disorder (PTSD) and other mental-health issues. In a 2011 Pew Research Center survey of post-9/11 veterans, 16% said they had been severely injured, 60% served with someone who had been badly injured, and 47% served with someone who had been killed. Among respondents exposed to casualties, 42% said they suffered from PTSD (compared to 27% of those not exposed to casualties).

Of the 1,089,668 Afghanistan or Iraq war veterans receiving VA health care from Oct. 1, 2001, through June 30, 2014, 31% (337,285 patients) were diagnosed with PTSD; 25% (270,005) were diagnosed with depression (some patients received both diagnoses). In the IAVA 2014 members' survey, 53% of respondents said they had some type of mental health injury as a result of service in Iraq or Afghanistan, 35% reported taking antidepressants, and 32% said they took anti-anxiety medication.

Military service in time of war may increase the risk of suicide. In the IAVA survey, 40% of respondents reported knowing a fellow veteran who committed suicide, and 31% said they had considered suicide. A report released by the VA in 2014 concluded that suicide rates among men using the VA health care system decreased slightly in 2001-11. However, the report found a significant increase (almost 44%) from 2009 to 2011 in the suicide rates of younger male veterans (between the ages of 18 and

29), including a more than 71% increase among men age 24 or younger. The suicide rate among women using VA health care rose by about 50% between 2001 and 2011. The VA operates a Veterans Crisis Line that can provide emergency intervention or counseling referrals to callers. The department also has 300 Vet Centers that offer a variety of counseling services and suicide prevention referrals.

Victims of Sexual Assault

A large number of veterans are coping with trauma resulting from sexual assault while in the armed forces. The VA uses the term military sexual trauma (MST) for incidents of sexual assault during military service or sexual harassment that is repeated and threatening. About 1 in 4 women and 1 in 100 men in the VA health care system reported having been victims of MST. (Because 85% of all service members, depending on the branch of service, are male, the response rate among men indicates a large number of MST cases.) In the IAVA 2014 survey, 30% of female respondents and 1% of males said they were military sexual assault victims. The adequacy of the military's response to the problem has been questioned. Only 35% of female and 36% of male victims in the IAVA survey said they reported the assault. The main reason given by women for not reporting (59%) was that they did not think anything would be done in response; for men, it was concern that they would be treated differently by their peers (69%). A majority of both groups also expressed fears that reporting would have impacted their careers. A 2013 American Civil Liberties Union study found that disability claims for PTSD stemming from MST were rejected by the VA at a far higher rate than disability claims for PTSD from other causes.

Family and Other Individual Challenges

For many veterans, separation from family and experiences during service continue to impact family life after they return. The challenges may be increased by multiple deployments to war zones, experienced by almost half of Afghanistan and Iraq veterans. A 2011 report from Brown University's Watson Institute for International Studies' Cost of War project found alcohol and drug abuse, reckless driving, divorce, domestic violence, and children's emotional problems among Afghanistan or Iraq veterans and their families. In a 2014 Washington Post-Kaiser Family Foundation survey of Afghanistan or Iraq veterans, 50% of respondents no longer on active duty said their transition to civilian life was somewhat or very difficult; 45% often or sometimes experienced relationship problems with their spouse or partner as a result of military service; and 55% reported feeling disconnected from civilian life. In the IAVA 2014 survey, 56% of married veterans said deployment led to "major strains on the relationship"; 34% of respondents with children said their "anger issues" affected their relationship with their children.

Joblessness and Homelessness

Service in the armed forces often postpones or interrupts nonmilitary education, job training, and career pursuit. The time away from school or work can impact veterans economically when they leave the military. BLS data for 2013 showed the unemployment rate for post-9/11 veterans was 9%, almost 2 percentage points higher than for the entire civilian labor force. Both male and female post-9/11 veterans had higher unemployment rates than all veterans, nonveterans, and all civilian workers. In the IAVA 2014 survey, 77% of respondents said they went through a period of unemployment after leaving the military; 64% reported some difficulty each month paying their bills; 7% said they had lived in their car for some period of time, and 2% reported having lived in a shelter.

Homelessness is a problem among both post-9/11 veterans and those who served earlier. Nearly half of homeless veterans served during the Vietnam War era. About half of homeless veterans have disabilities; half have serious mental health problems, and more than two-thirds have substance abuse problems. The VA National Center on Homelessness Among Veterans was established in 2009 to assist the homeless, prevent homelessness in at-risk veterans, and study the issue. The center's 2013 annual point-in-time count found almost 58,000 homeless veterans on a single Jan. night. That figure represented a 23.5% decline since 2009. However, homeless veterans still made up about 12% of homeless Americans (while veterans make up about 7% of the total U.S. population). VA spending in fiscal year 2014 included $1.4 bil for programs to reduce homelessness.

Service and Sacrifice

Although many post-9/11 veterans risked their lives, suffered injuries, and have had a difficult transition to civilian life, a sizable majority apparently feel they did the right thing. In the 2014 Washington Post-Kaiser survey, 89% of respondents said that, if they had the chance to make the decision again, they would still join the military, and 71% believed Americans appreciated their service. A far higher proportion said they did something in Iraq or Afghanistan that made them feel proud (87%) than said they did something that made them feel guilty (25%). The IAVA 2014 survey showed similar results; 74% of that poll's participants said they would recommend military service to a family member or close friend.

However, 70% of the IAVA respondents also said they did not think Americans understood the sacrifices made by Afghanistan and Iraq veterans. Given the high incidence of disability and medical problems, family difficulties, and economic hardship, the sacrifices have been significant. A wide range of VA and other programs have been put in place to help veterans return to and succeed in civilian life. Whether these programs are enough—and whether they are run well enough—continues to be debated.

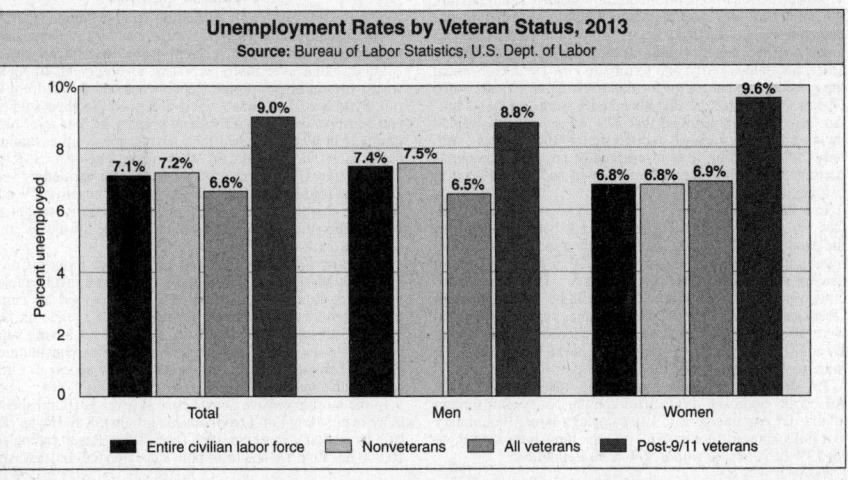

Unemployment Rates by Veteran Status, 2013
Source: Bureau of Labor Statistics, U.S. Dept. of Labor

Total: Entire civilian labor force 7.1%, Nonveterans 7.2%, All veterans 6.6%, Post-9/11 veterans 9.0%

Men: Entire civilian labor force 7.4%, Nonveterans 7.5%, All veterans 6.5%, Post-9/11 veterans 8.8%

Women: Entire civilian labor force 6.8%, Nonveterans 6.8%, All veterans 6.9%, Post-9/11 veterans 9.6%

Percent unemployed

■ Entire civilian labor force   ▢ Nonveterans   ▨ All veterans   ■ Post-9/11 veterans

ELECTION 2014

Republicans Take Senate Majority and Strengthen Hold on House

Republicans dominated the midterm elections, Nov. 4, 2014, gaining control of the U.S. Senate while substantially increasing their majority in the House of Representatives, and adding to their strong advantage in control of the nation's statehouses.

The Republican Victory

The Republicans had the advantage of being the opposition party in an off-year election, but every path to winning a majority required them to win or hold onto a number of seats expected to be contested in close races. In the end, the GOP picked up at least seven seats in the Senate previously held by Democrats, one more than needed for a majority. They won seats Democrats had hoped to retain in Arkansas, Colorado, Iowa, and North Carolina, in addition to Democratic seats in Montana, West Virginia, and South Dakota, where Republican victories had been anticipated. Republicans also had a seemingly insurmountable lead in Alaska, where some ballots still remained to be counted as of Nov. 5, and were favored to defeat the incumbent Democrat in Louisiana, where a runoff election was scheduled for Dec. 6. No incumbent Republican senators were unseated in the election.

In the House, where many seats for both parties were not seriously at risk, Republicans added a net total of 12 seats, as of Nov. 7, with some results oustanding. In the governors' races, Republicans lost only one state they had previously held (Pennsylvania), held onto contested states like Florida and Georgia, and won the traditionally Democratic states of Illinois, Maryland, and Massachusetts. Based on preliminary results, Republicans were also expected to have secured control of a record 67 of the 98 state legislative chambers.

Voter turnout was considered a key factor for both parties in the election. Democratic parties and interest groups spent tens of millions of dollars on technocentric get-out-the-vote operations, aimed especially at African American and other heavily Democratic blocs in key states. But Republicans, who in the past had lagged in their voter turnout outreach, made strong efforts to catch up. It was not yet clear what effect controversial voter identification laws, newly enacted in many states, had on voter turnout.

The results were widely considered to amount to a Republican wave, and a setback for the administration of Democratic Pres. Barack Obama. Obama acknowledged "Republicans had a good night" and indicated he would cooperate with efforts to make Washington work better. But he did not indicate any change in policy and reiterated his intention to issue an executive order on immigration before the year's end.

Electorate Issues and Concerns

A CNN/Opinion Research Corp. poll in late Oct. found that 38% of Americans were "somewhat angry" and another 30% "very angry" over the state of the nation. Pre-election Gallup polls showed Obama's approval rating hovering around 42%. The national Republican election strategy sought to turn the midterms into a referendum on Obama's performance and competence. While tactics varied between states, Republicans focused much of their election advertising on Obamacare, national security, and terrorism. Few Democrats asked the president to campaign for them, but GOP TV ads noted Obama's Oct. 2 remark that his policies were "on the ballot." An Oct. Gallup poll found that 32% of respondents wanted their vote to be a message in opposition to the president, with only 20% intending it as a message of support. Democrats portrayed GOP hopefuls as anti-women and uninterested in helping the middle class.

In a Pew Research poll of registered voters taken in mid-Oct., more believed Republicans would do better dealing with the economy (the biggest issue according to most polls) and immigration. Respondents gave the GOP a 17-point edge in dealing with terrorism and budget deficits. However, Democrats were given a six-point advantage in health care (though Obamacare remained unpopular according to most polls) and were also favored on education and abortion/contraception. By a 50%-28% margin, respondents believed Democrats were more willing to work with the other party.

Pre-election polls found that only about one-third of Americans approved of Obama's foreign policy. But foreign affairs did not emerge as a key campaign issue. Preliminary exit polls showed foreign policy as the most important issue for 13% of voters, of whom 56% were Republican.

Election Spending

The nonpartisan Center for Responsive Politics (CRP) projected that reportable total spending on the 2014 congressional elections would exceed $3.67 bil, slightly more than the $3.63 bil spent on the 2010 midterms. According to their estimates, "Team Red" (GOP candidates, parties, committees, and sympathetic outside groups) would slightly outspend "Team Blue" (their Democratic counterparts), 51%-49%. The CRP estimated that outside groups (funded mostly by a handful of mega-donors) would account for about $500 mil in spending, or around 13% of the election money spent, compared to 8.5% in 2010. The biggest outside contributors supporting Republicans were the Karl Rove-associated American Crossroads/ Crossroads GPS groups, U.S. Chamber of Commerce, and National Rifle Assn.; the biggest Democrat-supporting outside contributors were the Senate Majority PAC and House Majority PAC.

Republican Primaries and the Tea Party

After the 2012 elections, when the GOP lost Senate seats that had appeared within reach because of gaffes by Tea Party candidates like Todd Akin in Missouri and Richard Mourdock in Indiana, the Republican establishment began recruiting viable new candidates and working to support struggling incumbents in primary challenges. Business groups like the Chamber of Commerce also intervened to put money behind establishment candidates. Insurgents did not topple a single GOP senator in the Republican primaries, though Ben Sasse, a conservative academic and government consultant backed by the Tea Party movement, won a heavily contested May 13 GOP primary for Nebraska's open Senate seat.

The Tea Party claimed credit for victories in a few House primary races. The year's biggest primary upset was the June 10 defeat of House Majority Leader Eric Cantor (R, VA), 56%-44% by a little known conservative economics professor, David Brat. Brat's campaign, never regarded as promising, did not actually attract much financial support from national Tea Party groups before the primary. Pundits offered many reasons in retrospect for Cantor's defeat, including his ties to Wall Street and Washington, DC, and his willingness to make deals with Democrats. His loss may have influenced other Republican candidates to be more careful about alienating their conservative base. Even if the Tea Party produced few upsets in the 2014 primaries, its presence may have motivated Republican candidates to move rightward.

Key Senate Results

The Republicans easily picked up seats in Montana, West Virginia, and South Dakota, where incumbent Democrats were retiring and most polls had projected Republican wins.

Other gains were more surprising to observers. In Iowa, where several higher-profile Republicans had decided not to run, State Sen. Joni Ernst, a self-described "mother, soldier, and conservative," won a five-way primary in June after running ads in which she said that, having grown up castrating hogs, she could cut pork in Washington. Facing U.S. Rep. Bruce Braley (D), in a race for the seat being vacated by veteran Sen. Tom Harkin (D), she was hit with negative TV ads for some sharply conservative positions. But Ernst sought to portray herself as a pragmatist promoting "the Iowa way" and won by a comfortable margin.

In a close Senate race flooded with outside money, Colorado Sen. Mark Udall (D), initially considered invulnerable, faced U.S. Rep. Cory Gardner (R). Udall focused his campaign attention, too narrowly in the view of critics, on the issues of abortion and conception. Attacked for having supported a "personhood" amendment to the state constitution, Gardner reversed himself, called for broader access to birth control, and defeated Udall by a few points.

In the most expensive Senate contest (over $110 mil spent, more than $80 mil of it from outside groups), Kay Hagan (D, NC) faced State House Speaker Thom Tillis (R); an estimated 10,800 negative TV ads from both sides flooded the airwaves during just one week in Oct. In the end, Hagan lost the seat by a small margin.

In Alaska, incumbent Sen. Mark Begich (D), who had come to office in a 2008 election held days after his GOP opponent was convicted of corruption, faced former state Atty. Gen. Dan Sullivan (R). Begich stressed an intention to work across the aisle and campaigned widely in the sprawling state, but he appeared to be losing the race. In Virginia, on the other hand, Sen. Mark Warner (D) won reelection by a razor-thin margin after leading challenger Ed Gillespie, a former Republican Natl. Committee chair, by as much as 20 points in polls.

In Louisiana, Sen. Mary Landrieu (D) failed to win 50% or more of the Nov. 4 vote, and so would have to face her closest opponent, U.S. Rep. Bill Cassidy (R), in a runoff.

Democrats had a major win in New Hampshire, where Sen. Jeanne Shaheen (D) was able to fend off a challenge from former Massachusetts Sen. Scott Brown (R), who was recruited by national Republicans for the race but apparently was unable to overcome charges of carpetbagging. In other competitive races, U.S. Rep. Gary Peters (D) easily defeated former Sec. of State Terri Lynn Land (R) to fill the vacancy left by retiring Michigan Sen. Carl Levin (D). And in Minnesota, Sen. Al Franken (D) won reelection by a large margin.

Democrats fell short in three states where they had hoped to capture a GOP seat. Senate Minority Leader Mitch McConnell (R, KY) easily defeated Kentucky Sec. of State Alison Lundergan Grimes (D). Grimes had blamed McConnell for partisanship and gridlock in Washington but drew attention for repeatedly refusing to say whether she had voted for Obama. In Georgia, businessman David Perdue (R) outpolled Michelle Nunn (D), daughter of former Sen. Sam Nunn (D, GA), with more than the 50% vote needed to avoid a runoff. In Kansas, the seat of veteran Sen. Pat Roberts (R) appeared threatened after Chad Taylor (D) bowed out of the race to the benefit of independent candidate Greg Orman. Orman, a multimillionaire investor, campaigned as a "problem-solver" who did not commit to either party. But Roberts turned the race around and won by a large margin.

Notable House Races

As in 2006 and 2010, about 99% of House incumbents seeking renomination were successful. Other than Eric Cantor, only three incumbents were defeated in primaries. But a number of incumbent Democrats fell to Republican challengers, most notably veteran West Virginia Rep. Nick Rahall, whose 38-year House tenure was ended by state Sen. Evan Jenkins. It appeared that—when all undecided races were settled—the Republicans would pick up enough seats to give them their biggest House majority since the early 1930s.

Among the races that drew attention, Rep. Ron Barber (D, AZ), former aide to U.S. Rep. Gabrielle Giffords who was wounded with her in a 2011 shooting, trailed Martha McSally (R), a former Air Force combat veteran heavily supported by Republican groups, but the race was too close to call as of Nov. 8. In New York, Rep. Michael Grimm easily kept his solidly Republican seat, despite a federal indictment and an incident where he threatened to throw a journalist off a Capitol Hill balcony.

In early Oct., the national Democratic Party shifted TV advertising funds to increase support for several Democratic incumbents, including Brad Schneider (IL) and Bill Enyart (IL), who both lost, and Rick Nolan (MN) and Sean Patrick Maloney (NY), both of whom won. Democrats also boosted spending in Nebraska, where GOP Rep. Lee Terry, criticized for an ad said to be racially charged, lost to state legislator Brad Ashford (D).

The most expensive House race (close to $20 mil raised on both sides, over $13 mil of which was from outside sources) was in California's 7th District, where former U.S. Rep. Doug Ose (R) was leading incumbent Ami Bera (D).

Governors' Races

Of the 36 state governorships at stake in 2014, Republicans defended 22 to the Democrats' 14. A few incumbents, such as Democrats Jerry Brown (CA) and Andrew Cuomo (NY) and Republicans John Kasich (OH), Terry Brandstad (IA), Susana Martinez (NM), and Nikki Haley (SC), coasted to victory, but many had a harder time.

Weighed down by unpopular education cuts and his position on the Penn State scandal, Pennsylvania Gov. Tom Corbett was defeated by businessman Tom Wolf (D); he was the only Republican incumbent to lose (pending a final result in Alaska). But some Democratic incumbents had trouble even in traditionally Democratic states. Illinois Gov. Pat Quinn was defeated by Bruce Rauner, despite campaign appearances by Pres. Obama and First Lady Michelle Obama on his behalf. Among nonincumbents, former Massachusetts Atty. Gen. Martha Coakley (D), who lost a 2010 special election to fill the seat held by the late Sen. Ted Kennedy (D), was defeated by former health-care CEO Charlie Baker (R). Lieutenant Gov. Anthony Brown (D), under attack for tax increases under outgoing Gov. Martin O'Malley (D) in Maryland, failed in his bid to become the nation's third elected African-American governor, losing to real-estate magnate Larry Hogan (R).

In Connecticut, Gov. Dannel Malloy (D), under fire on economic issues, narrowly defeated businessman Tom Foley (R). Colorado Gov. John Hickenlooper, who easily won office in 2010 as a centrist Democrat, scrambled to come out ahead of former U.S. Rep. Bob Beauprez (R).

Wisconsin Gov. Scott Walker (R), known for his controversial fight with teachers' unions and for surviving a 2012 recall election, defeated businesswoman Mary Burke (D) by a comfortable margin. Kansas Gov. Sam Brownback (R), whose experiment in strongly conservative economic and tax policies alienated many moderate Republicans, defeated state Rep. Paul Davis (D). Georgia Gov. Nathan Deal (R) outpolled state Sen. Jason Carter (D), grandson of former Pres. Jimmy Carter. Michigan Gov. Rick Snyder (R) defeated former U.S. Rep. Mark Schauer (D). In Alaska, the race remained too close to call, with Gov. Sean Parnell (R) slightly behind independent Bill Walker; the Democratic nominee for governor had bowed out of the race to join Walker as lieutenant governor on a "unity" ticket.

In Maine, Gov. Paul LePage (R), a combative Tea Party favorite, bested Mike Michaud (D), who would have been the first openly gay U.S. governor. In the costliest governor's race, Florida Gov. Rick Scott (R) narrowly defeated Charlie Crist, a former Republican governor seeking a return to office as a Democrat. Each unleashed a barrage of negative TV ads, and both had high unfavorability ratings.

Republicans easily retained the governorship in Texas, where state Sen. Wendy Davis (D), known for her filibuster of a bill restricting abortion access, waged a scattershot campaign against state Atty. Gen. Greg Abbott (R).

Ballot Issues

There were some 150 statewide measures on Nov. 4 ballots. Four states that voted Republican in the 2012 presidential election—Alaska, Arkansas, Nebraska, and South Dakota—approved increases in the state minimum wage. Tennessee voted for a constitutional provision to bar any future state income tax, and Georgia approved an amendment prohibiting personal state income tax increases above the 2015 top rate, set at 6%. Massachusetts voters agreed to eliminate an automatic annual gas tax increase enacted in 2013.

Voters rejected anti-abortion provisions in North Dakota and Colorado, while Tennessee by a large margin approved a measure giving lawmakers the power to restrict abortions. A Missouri proposition that would have tied teachers' pay to student performance and other measurements failed.

Arkansas rejected a measure to legalize alcohol statewide. Voters in Alaska, Oregon, and Washington, DC, all agreed to allow legalized recreational marijuana, but in Florida a measure that would have permitted the use of marijuana for medical purposes failed. On a local level, voters in Berkeley, CA, approved a tax on sugary soft drinks, but a similar measure in San Francisco fell short of the required two-thirds majority.

Balance of Power, 2014

	Senate		House		Governors	
	Before	After	Before[1]	After	Before	After
Dem.	53	44	199	184	21	17
Rep.	45	52	233	244	29	31
Ind.	2	2	0	0	0	0

Note: After figures exclude 2 Senate seats, 7 House seats, and 2 gubernatorial races that were undecided as of Nov. 9, 2014. (1) Excludes 3 vacant House seats.

Members of the 114th Congress: U.S. Senate

Source: © Associated Press; all rights reserved. 2014 results are preliminary as of Nov. 5, 2014.

52 Republicans, 44 Democrats, 2 independents (who were expected to caucus with Democrats), 2 undecided. Boldface denotes the 2014 election winner. * = Incumbent. Third-party or independent candidates receiving fewer than 50,000 votes are not necessarily listed.

Terms are for six years and end Jan. 3 of the year preceding the senator's name in the following table. Annual salary, $174,000; President Pro Tempore, Majority Leader, and Minority Leader, $193,400. To be eligible to serve in the Senate, a person must be at least 30 years old, a U.S. citizen for at least nine years, and a resident of the state from which elected.

D = Democrat; **R** = Republican; **CP** = Constitution Party; **DFL** = Dem.-Farmer-Labor; **I** = Independent; **IP** = Independence Party; **LB** = Libertarian; **NPA** = No party affiliation; **NPL** = Nonpartisan League.

Term ends	Senator/candidate (party); service from[1]	2014 election results
Alabama		
2017	Richard Shelby (R); 1/6/1987	
2021	**Jeff Sessions* (R); 1/7/1997**	Unopposed
Alaska		
2017	Lisa Murkowski (R); 12/20/2002	
2021	Dan Sullivan (R)	110,203
	Mark Begich* (D); 1/6/2009	102,054
Arizona		
2017	John McCain (R); 1/6/1987	
2019	Jeff Flake (R); 2013	
Arkansas		
2017	John Boozman (R); 1/5/2011	
2021	**Tom Cotton (R)**	476,309
	Mark Pryor* (D); 1/7/2003	332,669
California		
2017	Barbara Boxer (D); 1993	
2019	Dianne Feinstein (D); 11/10/1992	
Colorado		
2017	Michael F. Bennet (D); 1/22/2009	
2021	**Cory Gardner (R)**	930,742
	Mark Udall* (D); 1/6/2009	853,496
Connecticut		
2017	Richard Blumenthal (D); 1/5/2011	
2019	Christopher S. Murphy (D); 2013	
Delaware		
2019	Thomas R. Carper (D); 2001	
2021	**Christopher Coons* (D); 11/15/2010**	130,645
	Kevin Wade (R)	98,819
Florida		
2017	Marco Rubio (R); 1/5/2011	
2019	Bill Nelson (D); 2001	
Georgia		
2017	Johnny Isakson (R); 2005	
2021	**David Perdue (R)**	1,355,392
	Michelle Nunn (D)	1,154,388
Hawaii		
2017	**Brian Schatz* (D); 12/26/2012[2]**	246,720
	Cam Cavasso (R)	97,972
2019	Mazie K. Hirono (D); 2013	
Idaho		
2017	Mike Crapo (R); 1/6/1999	
2021	**Jim Risch* (R); 1/6/2009**	285,322
	Nels Mitchell (D)	151,697
Illinois		
2017	Mark Kirk (R); 11/29/2010	
2021	**Richard J. Durbin* (D); 1/7/1997**	1,841,590
	Jim Oberweis (R)	1,497,908
	Sharon Hansen (LB)	130,229
Indiana		
2017	Dan Coats (R); 1/5/2011	
2019	Joe Donnelly (D); 2013	
Iowa		
2017	Chuck Grassley (R); 1981	
2021	**Joni Ernst (R)**	586,921
	Bruce Braley (D)	491,708
Kansas		
2017	Jerry Moran (R); 1/5/2011	
2021	**Pat Roberts* (R); 1/7/1997**	449,974
	Greg Orman (I)	358,898
Kentucky		
2017	Rand Paul (R); 1/5/2011	
2021	**Mitch McConnell* (R); 1985**	806,689
	Alison Lundergan Grimes (D)	584,625
Louisiana		
2017	David Vitter (R); 2005	
2021[3]	Mary L. Landrieu* (D); 1/7/1997	618,840
	Bill Cassidy (R)	602,439
	Rob Maness (R)	202,413
Maine		
2019	Angus King (I); 2013	
2021	**Susan M. Collins* (R); 1/7/1997**	409,663
	Shenna Bellows (D)	189,069
Maryland		
2017	Barbara Ann Mikulski (D); 1/6/1987	
2019	Benjamin L. Cardin (D); 2007	
Massachusetts		
2019	Elizabeth A. Warren (D); 2013	
2021	**Ed Markey* (D); 7/16/2013**	1,285,736
	Brian Herr (R)	789,378
Michigan		
2019	Debbie Stabenow (D); 2001	
2021	**Gary Peters (D)**	1,693,781
	Terri Lynn Land (R)	1,283,850
	Jim Fulner (LB)	62,504
Minnesota		
2019	Amy Klobuchar (DFL); 2007	
2021	**Al Franken* (DFL); 7/7/2009**	1,052,784
	Mike McFadden (R)	849,898
Mississippi		
2019	Roger F. Wicker (R); 12/31/2007	
2021	**Thad Cochran* (R); 12/27/1978**	370,208
	Travis Childers (D)	228,974
Missouri		
2017	Roy Blunt (R); 1/5/2011	
2019	Claire McCaskill (D); 2007	
Montana		
2019	Jon Tester (D); 2007	
2021	**Steve Daines (R)**	210,863
	Amanda Curtis (D)	145,601
Nebraska		
2019	Deb Fischer (R); 2013	
2021	**Ben Sasse (R)**	339,868
	Dave Domina (D)	162,874
Nevada		
2017	Harry Reid (D); 1/6/1987	
2019	Dean Heller (R); 5/9/2011	
New Hampshire		
2017	Kelly Ayotte (R); 1/5/2011	
2021	**Jeanne Shaheen* (D); 1/6/2009**	250,722
	Scott Brown (R)	234,846

Term ends	Senator/candidate (party); service from[1]	2014 election results
New Jersey		
2019	Robert Menendez (D); 1/18/2006	
2021	**Cory Booker* (D); 10/31/2013**	968,320
	Jeff Bell (R)	722,879
New Mexico		
2019	Martin Heinrich (D); 2013	
2021	**Tom Udall* (D); 1/6/2009**	280,074
	Allen E. Weh (R)	225,706
New York		
2017	Charles E. Schumer (D); 1/6/1999	
2019	Kirsten E. Gillibrand (D); 1/27/2009	
North Carolina		
2017	Richard Burr (R); 2005	
2021	**Thom Tillis (R)**	1,413,269
	Kay Hagan* (D); 1/6/2009	1,364,758
	Sean Haugh (LB)	108,183
North Dakota		
2017	John Hoeven (R); 1/5/2011	
2019	Heidi Heitkamp (D-NPL); 2013	
Ohio		
2017	Rob Portman (R); 1/5/2011	
2019	Sherrod Brown (D); 2007	
Oklahoma		
2017[4]	**James Lankford (R)**	556,382
	Connie Johnson (D)	237,531
2021	**James M. Inhofe* (R); 11/21/1994**	557,537
	Matt Silverstein (D)	233,932
Oregon		
2017	Ron Wyden (D); 2/6/1996	
2021	**Jeff Merkley* (D); 1/6/2009**	732,666
	Monica Wehby (R)	496,680
Pennsylvania		
2017	Pat Toomey (R); 1/5/2011	
2019	Bob Casey Jr. (D); 2007	
Rhode Island		
2019	Sheldon Whitehouse (D); 2007	
2021	**Jack Reed* (D); 1/7/1997**	211,513
	Mark Zaccaria (R)	88,426
South Carolina		
2017[5]	**Tim Scott* (R); 1/3/2013**	749,266
	Joyce Dickerson (D)	454,279
2021	**Lindsey Graham* (R); 1/7/2003**	665,605
	Brad Hutto (D)	475,532

Term ends	Senator/candidate (party); service from[1]	2014 election results
South Dakota		
2017	John Thune (R); 2005	
2021	**Mike Rounds (R)**	140,721
	Rick Weiland (D)	82,408
Tennessee		
2019	Bob Corker (R); 2007	
2021	**Lamar Alexander* (R); 1/7/2003**	849,748
	Gordon Ball (D)	437,175
Texas		
2019	Ted Cruz (R); 2013	
2021	**John Cornyn* (R); 12/2/2002**	2,848,903
	David Alameel (D)	1,592,060
	Rebecca Paddock (LB)	133,313
	Emily Sanchez (Green)	54,558
Utah		
2017	Mike Lee (R); 1/5/2011	
2019	Orrin G. Hatch (R); 1977	
Vermont		
2017	Patrick Leahy (D); 1975	
2019	Bernard Sanders (I); 2007	
Virginia		
2019	Timothy M. Kaine (D); 2013	
2021	**Mark Warner* (D); 1/6/2009**	1,071,283
	Ed Gillespie (R)	1,054,556
	Robert Sarvis (LB)	53,396
Washington		
2017	Patty Murray (D); 1993	
2019	Maria Cantwell (D); 2001	
West Virginia		
2019	Joe Manchin III (D); 11/15/2010	
2021	**Shelley Moore Capito (R)**	280,123
	Natalie Tennant (D)	155,456
Wisconsin		
2017	Ron Johnson (R); 1/5/2011	
2019	Tammy Baldwin (D); 2013	
Wyoming		
2019	John Barrasso (R); 6/22/2007	
2021	**Michael B. Enzi* (R); 1/7/1997**	119,534
	Charlie Hardy (D)	29,043

(1) Jan. 3, unless otherwise noted. (2) Sen. Daniel Inouye (D) died in office Dec. 17, 2012; Schatz was appointed to fill the seat until the 2014 general election, when a special election was held. (3) No candidate won the required majority; a runoff between the top two vote recipients was scheduled for Dec. 6, 2014. (4) Sen. Tom Coburn (R) announced Jan. 16, 2014, that he would retire when the 113th Congress expired. The special election held on the date of the 2014 general election filled the seat for the two years remaining in his term. (5) Sen. Jim DeMint (R) resigned effective Jan. 1, 2013; Scott was appointed to fill the seat until the 2014 general election, when a special election was held.

Members of the 114th Congress: U.S. House of Representatives

Source: © Associated Press; all rights reserved. 2014 results are preliminary as of Nov. 5, 2014.

244 Republicans, 184 Democrats, 7 undecided. Boldface denotes the 2014 election winner. * = Incumbent. Third-party or independent candidates receiving fewer than 10,000 votes are not necessarily listed.

Terms are for two years ending on Jan. 3, 2015. Annual salary, $174,000; Majority Leader and Minority Leader, $196,400; Speaker of the House, $223,500. To be eligible for membership, a person must be at least 25 years of age, a U.S. citizen for at least seven years, and a resident of the state from which elected.

D = Democrat; **R** = Republican; **Amer. Elect** = Americans Elect; **CP** = Constitution Party; **DFL** = Dem.-Farmer-Labor; **I** = Independent; **Indep. Amer.** = Independent American Party; **IP** = Independence Party; **LB** = Libertarian; **NPA** = No party affiliation; **NPD** = No party designation; **NPL** = Nonpartisan League; **PFP** = Peace and Freedom Party; **Prog.** = Progressive.

Dist.	Representative/candidate (party)	2014 election results
Alabama		
1	**Bradley Byrne* (R)**	103,320
	Burton LeFlore (D)	47,913
2	**Martha Roby* (R)**	95,073
	Erick Wright (D)	48,789
3	**Mike Rogers* (R)**	102,303
	Jesse Smith (D)	53,641
4	**Robert B. Aderholt* (R)**	Unopposed
5	**Mo Brooks* (R)**	115,212
	Mark Bray (I)	38,830

Dist.	Representative/candidate (party)	2014 election results
6	**Gary Palmer (R)**	135,711
	Mark Lester (D)	42,172
7	**Terri A. Sewell* (D)**	Unopposed
Alaska		
	Don Young* (R)	115,848
	Forrest Dunbar (D)	90,534
	Jim McDermott (LB)	16,791
Arizona		
1	**Ann Kirkpatrick* (D)**	77,184
	Andy Tobin (R)	67,838

Dist.	Representative/candidate (party)	2014 election results
2	Martha McSally (R)	78,799
	Ron Barber* (R)	78,763
3	Raúl M. Grijalva* (D)	42,880
	Gabriela Saucedo Mercer (R)	35,498
4	Paul A. Gosar* (R)	101,672
	Mike Weisser (D)	37,391
5	Matt Salmon* (R)	92,442
	James Woods (D)	42,155
6	David Schweikert* (R)	99,591
	W. John Williamson (D)	54,161
7	Ruben Gallego (D)	39,716
	Joe Cobb (LB)	8,557
8	Trent Franks* (R)	101,249
	Stephen Dolgos (Amer. Elect)	32,303
9	Kyrsten Sinema* (D)	65,343
	Wendy Rogers (R)	51,309

Arkansas

Dist.	Representative/candidate (party)	2014 election results
1	Rick Crawford* (R)	122,722
	Jackie McPherson (D)	62,902
2	French Hill (R)	123,014
	Patrick Henry Hays (D)	103,379
	Debbie Standiford (LB)	10,581
3	Steve Womack* (R)	151,093
	Grant Brand (LB)	39,143
4	Bruce Westerman (R)	110,163
	James Lee Witt (D)	87,335

California

Dist.	Representative/candidate (party)	2014 election results
1	Doug La Malfa* (R)	95,003
	Heidi Hall (D)	59,127
2	Jared Huffman* (D)	113,241
	Dale K. Mensing (R)	40,612
3	John Garamendi* (D)	58,213
	Dan Logue (R)	52,145
4	Tom McClintock* (R)	92,383
	Art Moore (R)	61,297
5	Mike Thompson* (D)	87,865
	James Hinton (I)	28,595
6	Doris O. Matsui* (D)	57,708
	Joseph McCray Sr. (R)	22,504
7	Doug Ose (R)	56,284
	Ami Bera* (D)	53,273
8	Paul Cook* (R)	62,778
	Bob Conaway (D)	30,151
9	Jerry McNerney* (D)	40,244
	Antonio C. "Tony" Amador (R)	37,847
10	Jeff Denham* (R)	47,315
	Michael Eggman (D)	36,609
11	Mark DeSaulnier (D)	70,947
	Tue Phan (R)	36,276
12	Nancy Pelosi* (D)	111,720
	John Dennis (R)	23,861
13	Barbara Lee* (D)	99,800
	Dakin Sundeen (R)	14,523
14	Jackie Speier* (D)	78,828
	Robin Chew (R)	25,030
15	Eric Swalwell* (D)	65,054
	Hugh Bussell (R)	29,180
16	Johnny Tacherra (R)	35,207
	Jim Costa* (D)	34,471
17	Mike Honda* (D)	41,480
	Ro Khanna (D)	37,931
18	Anna G. Eshoo* (D)	79,577
	Richard Fox (R)	40,386
19	Zoe Lofgren* (D)	50,555
	Robert Murray (D)	25,167
20	Sam Farr* (D)	65,087
	Ronald Paul Kabat (NPD)	22,385
21	David G. Valadao* (R)	37,657
	Amanda Renteria (D)	25,886
22	Devin Nunes* (R)	69,139
	Suzanna "Sam" Aguilera-Marrero (D)	26,671
23	Kevin McCarthy* (R)	78,716
	Raul Garcia (D)	25,785
24	Lois Capps* (D)	75,307
	Chris Mitchum (R)	70,673
25	Steve Knight (R)	46,610
	Tony Strickland (R)	40,491
26	Julia Brownley* (D)	63,811
	Jeff Gorell (R)	63,281

Dist.	Representative/candidate (party)	2014 election results
27	Judy Chu* (D)	57,489
	Jack Orswell (R)	40,674
28	Adam B. Schiff* (D)	69,944
	Steve Stokes (NPD)	22,083
29	Tony Cárdenas* (D)	38,092
	Will Leader (R)	13,066
30	Brad Sherman* (D)	64,830
	Mark S. Reed (R)	35,130
31	Pete Aguilar (D)	40,123
	Paul Chabot (R)	38,488
32	Grace F. Napolitano* (D)	39,691
	Arturo Alas (R)	27,167
33	Ted Lieu (D)	79,708
	Elan Carr (R)	56,854
34	Xavier Becerra* (D)	34,032
	Adrienne Edwards (D)	12,411
35	Norma J. Torres (D)	30,710
	Christina Gagnier (D)	17,838
36	Raul Ruiz* (D)	54,985
	Brian Nestande (R)	48,153
37	Karen Bass* (D)	70,900
	Adam King (R)	13,660
38	Linda T. Sánchez* (D)	45,117
	Benjamin Campos (R)	31,718
39	Ed Royce* (R)	69,045
	Peter Anderson (D)	31,646
40	Lucille Roybal-Allard* (D)	24,227
	David Sanchez (D)	15,249
41	Mark Takano* (D)	32,960
	Steve Adams (R)	26,841
42	Ken Calvert* (R)	54,772
	Tim Sheridan (D)	28,277
43	Maxine Waters* (D)	53,433
	John Wood Jr. (R)	22,478
44	Janice Hahn* (D)	46,802
	Adam Shbeita (PFP)	6,982
45	Mimi Walters (R)	78,080
	Drew E. Leavens (D)	41,224
46	Loretta Sanchez* (D)	31,642
	Adam Nick (R)	24,204
47	Alan Lowenthal* (D)	49,763
	Andy Whallon (R)	40,737
48	Dana Rohrabacher* (R)	83,431
	Suzanne Joyce Savary (D)	46,351
49	Darrell E. Issa* (R)	73,447
	Dave Peiser (D)	47,398
50	Duncan D. Hunter* (R)	83,379
	James Kimber (D)	33,135
51	Juan Vargas* (D)	38,440
	Stephen Meade (R)	18,852
52	Scott Peters* (D)	92,410
	Carl DeMaio (R)	87,919
53	Susan A. Davis* (D)	62,906
	Larry A. Wilske (R)	45,771

Colorado

Dist.	Representative/candidate (party)	2014 election results
1	Diana DeGette* (D)	161,691
	Martin Walsh (R)	72,841
2	Jared Polis* (D)	176,866
	George Leing (R)	143,075
3	Scott R. Tipton* (R)	158,477
	Abel J. Tapia (D)	96,252
	Tisha Casida (I)	10,730
4	Ken Buck (R)	177,217
	Vic Meyers (D)	77,831
5	Doug Lamborn* (R)	156,749
	Irv Halter (D)	105,373
6	Mike Coffman* (R)	131,146
	Andrew Romanoff (D)	104,887
7	Ed Perlmutter* (D)	126,352
	Don Ytterberg (R)	105,421

Connecticut

Dist.	Representative/candidate (party)	2014 election results
1	John B. Larson* (D)	134,980
	Matthew Corey (R)	78,112
2	Joe Courtney* (D)	140,924
	Lori Hopkins-Cavanagh (R)	80,199
3	Rosa L. DeLauro* (D)	136,610
	James Brown (R)	68,035
4	Jim Himes* (D)	93,994
	Dan Debicella (R)	89,310

Dist.	Representative/candidate (party)	2014 election results
5	**Elizabeth Esty* (D)**	**107,929**
	Mark Greenberg (R)	93,961
Delaware		
	John C. Carney Jr.* (D)	**137,245**
	Rose Izzo (R)	85,142
Florida		
1	**Jeff Miller* (R)**	**164,897**
	Jim Bryan (D)	54,892
	Mark Wichern (NPA)	15,257
2	**Gwen Graham (D)**	**125,132**
	Steve Southerland II* (R)	122,939
3	**Ted Yoho* (R)**	**148,483**
	Marihelen Wheeler (D)	73,695
4	**Ander Crenshaw* (R)**	**177,565**
	Paula Moser-Bartlett (NPA)	35,549
	Gary L. Koniz (NPA)	13,644
5	**Corrine Brown* (D)**	**112,092**
	Glo Smith (R)	59,152
6	**Ron DeSantis* (R)**	**166,101**
	David Cox (D)	99,463
7	**John L. Mica* (R)**	**144,370**
	Wes Neuman (D)	72,925
8	**Bill Posey* (R)**	**180,541**
	Gabriel Rothblatt (D)	93,588
9	**Alan Grayson* (D)**	**93,739**
	Carol Platt (R)	74,903
10	**Daniel Webster* (R)**	**142,967**
	Michael McKenna (D)	89,267
11	**Richard B. Nugent* (R)**	**181,398**
	Dave Koller (D)	90,706
12	**Gus M. Bilirakis* (R)**	**Unopposed**
13	**David W. Jolly* (R)**	**168,092**
	Lucas Overby (LB)	55,273
14	**Kathy Castor* (D)**	**Unopposed**
15	**Dennis A. Ross* (R)**	**128,533**
	Alan Cohn (D)	84,620
16	**Vern Buchanan* (R)**	**168,990**
	Henry Lawrence (D)	105,357
17	**Tom Rooney* (R)**	**141,310**
	Will Bronson (D)	82,126
18	**Patrick Murphy* (D)**	**151,253**
	Carl Domino (R)	101,778
19	**Curt Clawson* (R)**	**159,038**
	April Freeman (D)	80,607
20	**Alcee L. Hastings* (D)**	**128,217**
	Jay Bonner (R)	28,900
21	**Ted Deutch* (D)**	**Unopposed**
22	**Lois Frankel* (D)**	**125,071**
	Paul Spain (R)	90,452
23	**Debbie Wasserman Schultz* (D)**	**103,034**
	Joe Kaufman (R)	61,428
24	**Frederica S. Wilson* (D)**	**129,065**
	Dufirstson Neree (R)	15,220
25	**Mario Diaz-Balart* (R)**	**Unopposed**
26	**Carlos Curbelo (R)**	**82,780**
	Joe Garcia* (D)	77,958
27	**Ileana Ros-Lehtinen* (R)**	**Unopposed**
Georgia		
1	**Buddy Carter (R)**	**93,882**
	Brian Reese (D)	59,594
2	**Sanford D. Bishop Jr.* (D)**	**96,215**
	Greg Duke (R)	66,474
3	**Lynn A. Westmoreland* (R)**	**Unopposed**
4	**Henry "Hank" Johnson* (D)**	**Unopposed**
5	**John Lewis* (D)**	**Unopposed**
6	**Tom Price* (R)**	**138,616**
	Robert Montigel (D)	71,140
7	**Rob Woodall* (R)**	**113,260**
	Thomas Wight (D)	59,740
8	**Austin Scott* (R)**	**Unopposed**
9	**Doug Collins* (R)**	**145,856**
	David Vogel (D)	34,866
10	**Jody Hice (R)**	**130,572**
	Ken Dious (D)	65,676
11	**Barry Loudermilk (R)**	**Unopposed**
12	**Rick W. Allen (R)**	**90,987**
	John Barrow* (D)	75,123
13	**David Scott* (D)**	**Unopposed**
14	**Tom Graves* (R)**	**Unopposed**

Dist.	Representative/candidate (party)	2014 election results
Hawaii		
1	**Mark Takai (D)**	**93,331**
	Charles K. Djou (R)	86,409
2	**Tulsi Gabbard* (D)**	**141,978**
	Kawika Crowley (R)	33,621
Idaho		
1	**Raul R. Labrador* (R)**	**143,558**
	Shirley Ringo (D)	77,352
2	**Mike Simpson* (R)**	**131,465**
	Richard Stallings (D)	82,728
Illinois		
1	**Bobby L. Rush* (D)**	**150,904**
	Jimmy Lee Tillman (R)	57,453
2	**Robin L. Kelly* (D)**	**152,037**
	Eric M. Wallace (R)	42,946
3	**Daniel Lipinski* (D)**	**110,806**
	Sharon Brannigan (R)	61,047
4	**Luis V. Gutierrez* (D)**	**74,581**
	Hector Concepcion (R)	20,990
5	**Mike Quigley* (D)**	**109,530**
	Vince Kolber (R)	53,341
	Nancy Wade (Green)	10,536
6	**Peter J. Roskam* (R)**	**152,655**
	Michael Mason (D)	74,583
7	**Danny K. Davis* (D)**	**143,604**
	Robert Bumpers (R)	25,346
8	**Tammy Duckworth* (D)**	**79,015**
	Larry Kaifesh (R)	63,555
9	**Janice D. Schakowsky* (D)**	**133,275**
	Susanne Atanus (R)	69,042
10	**Robert Dold (R)**	**93,569**
	Brad Schneider* (D)	87,465
11	**Bill Foster* (D)**	**87,764**
	Darlene Senger (R)	77,230
12	**Mike Bost (R)**	**106,435**
	William L. Enyart* (D)	84,136
	Paula Bradshaw (Green)	11,474
13	**Rodney Davis* (R)**	**122,661**
	Ann Callis (D)	86,126
14	**Randy Hultgren* (R)**	**143,354**
	Dennis Anderson (D)	75,229
15	**John Shimkus* (R)**	**165,824**
	Eric Thorsland (D)	55,314
16	**Adam Kinzinger* (R)**	**151,464**
	Randall Olsen (D)	62,695
17	**Cheri Bustos* (D)**	**108,228**
	Bobby Schilling (R)	88,004
18	**Aaron Schock* (R)**	**182,696**
	Darrel Miller (D)	61,652
Indiana		
1	**Peter J. Visclosky* (D)**	**86,572**
	Mark Leyva (R)	51,034
2	**Jackie Walorski* (R)**	**85,119**
	Joe Bock (D)	55,331
3	**Marlin A. Stutzman* (R)**	**102,565**
	Justin Kuhnle (D)	39,629
4	**Todd Rokita* (R)**	**94,919**
	John Dale (D)	47,025
5	**Susan Brooks* (R)**	**105,238**
	Shawn Denney (D)	49,705
6	**Luke Messer* (R)**	**101,006**
	Susan Hall Heitzman (D)	45,062
7	**André Carson* (D)**	**60,870**
	Catherine "Cat" Ping (R)	46,588
8	**Larry Bucshon* (R)**	**103,234**
	Tom Spangler (D)	61,309
9	**Todd C. Young* (R)**	**99,810**
	Bill Bailey (D)	52,659
Iowa		
1	**Rod Blum (R)**	**147,153**
	Pat Murphy (D)	140,086
2	**David Loebsack* (D)**	**142,566**
	Mariannette Miller-Meeks (R)	129,157
3	**David Young (R)**	**148,652**
	Staci Appel (D)	118,938
4	**Steve King* (R)**	**169,141**
	Jim Mowrer (D)	104,873

Dist.	Representative/candidate (party)	2014 election results
Kansas		
1	**Tim Huelskamp* (R)**	**132,140**
	James "Jim" Sherow (D)	63,577
2	**Lynn Jenkins* (R)**	**126,627**
	Margie Wakefield (D)	85,076
3	**Kevin Yoder* (R)**	**132,501**
	Kelly Kultala (D)	87,781
4	**Mike Pompeo* (R)**	**135,993**
	Perry Schuckman (D)	67,643
Kentucky		
1	**Ed Whitfield* (R)**	**173,020**
	Charles Hatchett (D)	63,595
2	**S. Brett Guthrie* (R)**	**156,936**
	Ron Leach (D)	69,898
3	**John A. Yarmuth* (D)**	**157,045**
	Michael Macfarlane (R)	87,972
4	**Thomas Massie* (R)**	**150,463**
	Peter Newberry (D)	71,693
5	**Harold "Hal" Rogers* (R)**	**171,080**
	Kenneth Stepp (D)	47,617
6	**Garland "Andy" Barr* (R)**	**147,285**
	Elisabeth Jensen (D)	98,383
Louisiana		
1	**Steve Scalise* (R)**	**188,455**
	M. V. "Vinny" Mendoza (D)	24,685
	Lee A. Dugas (D)	21,205
2	**Cedric L. Richmond* (D)**	**152,103**
	Gary Landrieu (D)	37,775
	David Brooks (NPA)	16,321
	Samuel Davenport (LB)	15,227
3	**Charles W. Boustany Jr.* (R)**	**185,835**
	Russell Richard (NPA)	28,330
	Bryan Barrilleaux (R)	22,056
4	**John Fleming* (R).**	**152,670**
	Randall Lord (LB)	55,224
5[1]	Jamie Mayo (D)	67,610
	Ralph Abraham (R)	55,487
	Zach Dasher (R)	53,627
	Vance McAllister* (R)	26,605
	Clyde C. Holloway (R)	17,875
6[1]	Edwin Edwards (D)	77,852
	Garrett Graves (R)	70,706
	Paul Dietzel (R).	35,013
	Dan Claitor (R)	26,520
	Lenar Whitney (R).	19,146
Maine		
1	**Chellie Pingree* (D)**	**185,474**
	Isaac Misiuk (R)	94,343
	Richard Murphy (I)	27,511
2	**Bruce Poliquin (R)**	**132,407**
	Emily Cain (D).	117,588
	Blaine Richardson (I)	30,979
Maryland		
1	**Andy Harris* (R)**	**170,504**
	Bill Tilghman (D)	70,532
2	**C. A. Dutch Ruppersberger* (D)**	**115,586**
	David Banach (R)	67,995
3	**John P. Sarbanes* (D).**	**122,066**
	Charles Long (R)	83,279
4	**Donna F. Edwards* (D)**	**126,633**
	Nancy Hoyt (R)	51,721
5	**Steny H. Hoyer* (D)**	**138,284**
	Chris Chaffee (R)	77,451
6	**John Delaney* (D).**	**89,318**
	Dan Bongino (R)	87,152
7	**Elijah E. Cummings* (D).**	**136,913**
	Corrogan R. Vaughn (R)	53,718
8	**Chris Van Hollen* (D)**	**127,260**
	Dave Wallace (R)	83,711
Massachusetts		
1	**Richard E. Neal* (D)**	**Unopposed**
2	**James P. McGovern* (D).**	**Unopposed**
3	**Niki Tsongas* (D)**	**138,120**
	Ann Wofford (R)	81,167
4	**Joseph P. Kennedy III* (D)**	**Unopposed**
5	**Katherine M. Clark* (D).**	**Unopposed**
6	**Seth W. Moulton* (D)**	**149,449**
	Richard R. Tisei (R).	111,848
	Chris Stockwell (I).	12,175

Dist.	Representative/candidate (party)	2014 election results
7	**Michael E. Capuano* (D)**	**Unopposed**
8	**Stephen F. Lynch* (D).**	**Unopposed**
9	**Bill Keating* (D)**	**140,100**
	John Chapman (R)	114,670
Michigan		
1	**Dan Benishek* (R)**	**130,410**
	Jerry Cannon (D)	113,259
2	**Bill Huizenga* (R)**	**135,949**
	Dean Vanderstelt (D)	71,022
3	**Justin Amash* (R).**	**125,747**
	Bob Goodrich (D)	84,713
4	**John Moolenaar (R)**	**124,300**
	Jeff Holmes (D).	86,133
5	**Daniel T. Kildee* (D)**	**140,939**
	Allen Hardwick (R)	65,404
6	**Fred Upton* (R).**	**116,601**
	Paul Clements (D)	84,391
7	**Tim Walberg* (R).**	**118,715**
	Pam Byrnes (D)	91,403
8	**Mike Bishop (R)**	**132,445**
	Eric Schertzing (D)	101,191
9	**Sander M. Levin* (D).**	**136,334**
	George Brikho (R)	81,467
10	**Candice S. Miller* (R).**	**156,678**
	Chuck Stadler (D).	67,061
11	**Dave Trott (R).**	**138,229**
	Bobby McKenzie (D).	100,665
12	**Debbie Dingell (D).**	**133,323**
	Terry Bowman (R).	64,112
13	**John Conyers Jr.* (D)**	**130,905**
	Jeff Gorman (R)	26,406
14	**Brenda Lawrence (D)**	**165,116**
	Christina Barr (R)	41,801
Minnesota		
1	**Tim Walz* (DFL).**	**122,641**
	Jim Hagedorn (R)	103,356
2	**John Kline* (R).**	**137,781**
	Mike Obermueller (DFL).	95,562
	Paula Overby (IP)	12,319
3	**Erik Paulsen* (R).**	**167,517**
	Sharon Sund (DFL)	101,847
4	**Betty McCollum* (DFL).**	**147,842**
	Sharna Wahlgren (R)	79,482
	Dave Thomas (IP)	14,058
5	**Keith Ellison* (DFL)**	**167,079**
	Doug Daggett (R)	56,577
	Lee Bauer (IP)	12,001
6	**Tom Emmer (R)**	**133,324**
	Joe Perske (DFL)	90,921
	John Denney (IP)	12,459
7	**Collin C. Peterson* (DFL)**	**130,538**
	Torrey Westrom (R).	109,953
8	**Richard Nolan* (DFL)**	**128,920**
	Stewart Mills (R)	125,225
	Ray Sandman (Green)	11,442
Mississippi		
1	**Alan Nunnelee* (R).**	**101,451**
	Ron Dickey (D)	43,039
2	**Bennie G. Thompson* (D)**	**96,631**
	Troy Ray (I)	35,317
	Shelley Shoemake (Reform).	11,109
3	**Gregg Harper* (R).**	**115,396**
	Douglas Magee (D)	46,506
4	**Steven M. Palazzo* (R)**	**106,274**
	Matt Moore (D)	36,858
Missouri		
1	**Wm. Lacy Clay* (D).**	**118,005**
	Dan Elder (R)	34,965
2	**Ann Wagner* (R).**	**147,025**
	Arthur Lieber (D)	74,807
3	**Blaine Luetkemeyer* (R)**	**130,859**
	Courtney Denton (D)	51,990
4	**Vicky Hartzler* (R)**	**119,995**
	Nate Irvin (D)	46,438
5	**Emanuel Cleaver* (D)**	**79,094**
	Jacob Turk (R)	69,012
6	**Sam Graves* (R).**	**124,547**
	W. A. "Bill" Hedge (D)	55,132

Dist.	Representative/candidate (party)	2014 election results
7	Billy Long* (R)	104,027
	Jim Evans (D)	47,267
	Kevin Craig (LB)	12,583
8	Jason T. Smith* (R)	106,105
	Barbara Stocker (D)	38,702
Montana		
	Ryan Zinke (R)	201,004
	John Lewis (D)	146,187
	Mike Fellows (LB)	15,044
Nebraska		
1	Jeff Fortenberry* (R)	122,259
	Dennis Crawford (D)	54,995
2	Brad Ashford (D)	76,354
	Lee Terry* (R)	72,222
3	Adrian Smith* (R)	139,994
	Mark Sullivan (D)	45,426
Nevada		
1	Dina Titus* (D)	45,618
	Annette Teijeiro (R)	30,400
2	Mark E. Amodei* (R)	122,575
	Kristen Spees (D)	52,033
	Janine Hansen (Indep. Amer.)	11,798
3	Joe Heck* (R)	88,502
	Erin Bilbray (D)	52,615
4	Cresent Hardy (R)	63,435
	Steven A. Horsford* (D)	59,800
New Hampshire		
1	Frank Guinta (R)	125,321
	Carol Shea-Porter* (D)	116,626
2	Ann McLane Kuster* (D)	130,428
	Marilinda Garcia (R)	106,635
New Jersey		
1	Donald Norcross (D)	91,834
	Garry Cobb (R)	63,363
2	Frank A. LoBiondo* (R)	104,166
	Bill Hughes (D)	62,288
3	Tom MacArthur (R)	95,166
	Aimee Belgard (D)	75,972
4	Chris Smith* (R)	78,016
	Ruben M. Scolavino (D)	33,906
5	Scott Garrett* (R)	100,355
	Roy Cho (D)	77,559
6	Frank Pallone Jr.* (D)	59,244
	Anthony E. Wilkinson (R)	35,448
7	Leonard Lance* (R)	102,919
	Janice Kovach (D)	67,253
8	Albio Sires* (D)	57,954
	Jude Anthony Tiscornia (R)	14,315
9	Bill Pascrell Jr.* (D)	76,690
	Dierdre Paul (R)	33,918
10	Donald M. Payne Jr.* (D)	93,395
	Yolanda Dentley (R)	13,842
11	Rodney P. Frelinghuysen* (R)	105,506
	Mark Dunec (D)	63,070
12	Bonnie Watson Coleman (D)	86,578
	Alieta Eck (R)	52,672
New Mexico		
1	Michelle Lujan Grisham* (D)	102,471
	Mike Frese (R)	72,566
2	Steve Pearce* (R)	94,607
	Roxanne "Rocky" Lara (D)	51,976
3	Ben Ray Luján* (D)	110,497
	Jefferson L. Byrd (R)	70,009
New York		
1	Lee M. Zeldin (R)	89,564
	Timothy H. Bishop* (D)	73,860
2	Peter T. King* (R)	91,701
	Patricia Maher (D)	40,009
3	Steve Israel* (D)	85,310
	Grant M. Lally (R)	71,212
4	Kathleen M. Rice (D)	137,294
	Bruce Blakeman (R)	76,515
5	Gregory W. Meeks* (D)	72,454
	Allen Steinhardt (I)	3,618
6	Grace Meng* (D)	Unopposed
7	Nydia M. Velázquez* (D)	53,283
	Jose Luis Fernandez (R)	5,299
8	Hakeem S. Jeffries* (D)	71,280
	Alan Bellone (Conservative)	6,286

Dist.	Representative/candidate (party)	2014 election results
9	Yvette D. Clarke* (D)	78,157
	Daniel Cavanagh (Conservative)	9,149
10	Jerrold Nadler* (D)	82,880
	Ross Brady (Conservative)	11,284
11	Michael G. Grimm* (R)	56,221
	Domenic M. Recchia (D)	42,786
12	Carolyn B. Maloney* (D)	83,870
	Nick Di Iorio (R)	21,160
13	Charles B. Rangel* (D)	64,142
	Daniel Vila Rivera (Green)	9,231
14	Joseph Crowley* (D)	47,370
	Elizabeth Perri (Conservative)	6,318
15	José E. Serrano* (D)	51,665
	Eduardo Ramirez (Conservative)	972
16	Eliot L. Engel* (D)	Unopposed
17	Nita M. Lowey* (D)	93,001
	Chris E. Day (R)	72,363
18	Sean Patrick Maloney* (D)	84,415
	Nan Hayworth (R)	81,625
19	Christopher P. Gibson* (R)	124,428
	Sean Eldridge (D)	67,024
20	Paul Tonko* (D)	118,993
	Jim Fischer (R)	75,491
21	Elise Stefanik* (R)	89,776
	Aaron Woolf (D)	54,593
	Matthew Funiciello (Green)	18,362
22	Richard L. Hanna* (R)	Unopposed
23	Thomas Reed* (R)	105,623
	Martha Robertson (D)	63,229
24	John Katko* (R)	112,469
	Daniel B. Maffei* (D)	75,286
25	Louise McIntosh Slaughter* (D)	93,053
	Mark W. Assini (R)	92,471
26	Brian Higgins* (D)	79,344
	Kathleen A. Weppner (R)	35,894
27	Chris Collins* (R)	125,178
	Jim O'Donnell (D)	49,423
North Carolina		
1	G. K. Butterfield* (D)	150,529
	Arthur Rich (R)	54,692
2	Renee L. Ellmers* (R)	121,336
	Clay Aiken (D)	84,826
3	Walter B. Jones* (R)	138,307
	Marshall Adame (D)	65,548
4	David E. Price* (D)	168,005
	Paul Wright (R)	56,792
5	Virginia Foxx* (R)	138,905
	Josh Brannon (D)	88,670
6	Mark Walker (R)	146,329
	Laura Fjeld (D)	103,085
7	David Rouzer (R)	134,026
	Jonathan Barfield Jr. (D)	83,676
8	Richard Hudson* (R)	120,444
	Antonio Blue (D)	65,172
9	Robert Pittenger* (R)	Unopposed
10	Patrick T. McHenry* (R)	132,936
	Tate MacQueen (D)	84,921
11	Mark Meadows* (R)	143,833
	Tom Hill (D)	84,723
12	Alma Adams (D)	129,178
	Vince Coakley (R)	42,128
13	George Holding* (R)	152,430
	Brenda Cleary (D)	113,481
North Dakota		
	Kevin Cramer* (R)	137,569
	George Sinner (Dem.-NPL)	95,355
	Robert J. "Jack" Seaman (LB)	14,476
Ohio		
1	Steve Chabot* (R)	122,721
	Fred Kundrata (D)	70,644
2	Brad Wenstrup* (R)	130,479
	Marek Tyszkiewicz (D)	66,933
3	Joyce Beatty* (D)	89,048
	John Adams (R)	50,295
4	Jim Jordan* (R)	124,215
	Janet Garrett (D)	59,112
5	Robert "Bob" Latta* (R)	132,448
	Robert Fry (D)	57,328

Dist.	Representative/candidate (party)	2014 election results
6	Bill Johnson* (R)	109,829
	Jennifer Garrison (D)	72,779
7	Bob Gibbs* (R)	Unopposed
8	John Boehner* (R)	124,925
	Tom Poetter (D)	50,622
	Jim Condit (CP)	10,041
9	Marcy Kaptur* (D)	106,338
	Richard May (R)	50,792
10	Mike Turner* (R)	128,758
	Robert Klepinger (D)	61,720
11	Marcia Fudge* (D)	132,396
	Mark Zetzer (R)	34,769
12	Pat Tiberi* (R)	147,871
	David Tibbs (D)	60,026
13	Tim Ryan* (D)	118,650
	Thomas Pekarek (R)	54,610
14	David P. Joyce* (R)	133,520
	Michael Wager (D)	69,510
15	Steve Stivers* (R)	126,457
	Scott Wharton (D)	64,714
16	Jim Renacci* (R)	130,463
	Pete Crossland (D)	74,158
Oklahoma		
1	Jim Bridenstine* (R)	Unopposed
2	Markwayne Mullin* (R)	110,819
	Earl E. Everett (D)	38,924
3	Frank D. Lucas* (R)	133,070
	Frankie Robbins (D)	36,112
4	Tom Cole* (R)	117,649
	Bert Smith (D)	40,956
5	Steve Russell (R)	95,557
	Al McAffrey (D)	57,721
Oregon		
1	Suzanne Bonamici* (D)	135,244
	Jason Yates (R)	81,336
2	Greg Walden* (R)	197,920
	Aelea Christofferson (D)	71,387
	Sharon Durbin (LB)	10,071
3	Earl Blumenauer* (D)	181,441
	James Buchal (R)	50,303
4	Peter A. DeFazio* (D)	172,550
	Art Robinson (R)	111,932
5	Kurt Schrader* (D)	137,657
	Tootie Smith (R)	100,762
Pennsylvania		
1	Robert A. Brady* (D)	128,669
	Megan Ann Rath (R)	26,584
2	Chaka Fattah* (D)	177,648
	Armond James (R)	24,987
3	Mike Kelly* (R)	112,406
	Dan LaVallee (D)	73,240
4	Scott Perry* (R)	146,317
	Linda D. Thompson (D)	49,983
5	Glenn W. Thompson* (R)	113,485
	Kerith Strano Taylor (D)	65,041
6	Ryan A. Costello (R)	118,450
	Manan Trivedi (D)	92,193
7	Patrick Meehan* (R)	143,265
	Mary Ellen Balchunis (D)	87,783
8	Michael G. Fitzpatrick* (R)	137,676
	Kevin Strouse (D)	84,705
9	Bill Shuster* (R)	108,587
	Alanna K. Hartzok (D)	62,193
10	Tom Marino* (R)	111,547
	Scott Brion (D)	44,221
	Nick Troiano (I)	22,611
11	Lou Barletta* (R)	121,618
	Andy Ostrowski (D)	61,832
12	Keith J. Rothfus* (R)	126,567
	Erin McClelland (D)	86,977
13	Brendan Boyle (D)	122,651
	Dee Adcock (R)	60,163
14	Mike Doyle* (D)	Unopposed
15	Charles W. Dent* (R)	Unopposed
16	Joseph R. Pitts* (R)	101,083
	Tom Houghton (D)	73,921
17	Matthew Cartwright (D)	93,177
	David Moylan (R)	70,919
18	Tim Murphy* (R)	Unopposed

Dist.	Representative/candidate (party)	2014 election results
Rhode Island		
1	David N. Cicilline* (D)	82,334
	Cormick Lynch (R)	55,797
2	Jim Langevin* (D)	100,187
	Rhue Reis (R)	60,949
South Carolina		
1	Mark Sanford* (R)	Unopposed
2	Joe Wilson* (R)	121,379
	Phil Black (D)	68,438
3	Jeff Duncan* (R)	116,021
	Barbara Jo Mullis (D)	46,556
4	Trey Gowdy* (R)	125,930
	Curtis McLaughlin (LB)	21,849
5	Mick Mulvaney* (R)	102,017
	Tom Adams (D)	71,119
6	James E. Clyburn* (D)	125,172
	Anthony Culler (R)	43,658
7	Tom Rice* (R)	102,576
	Gloria Bromell-Tinubu (D)	68,412
South Dakota		
	Kristi L. Noem* (R)	183,796
	Corinna Robinson (D)	92,438
Tennessee		
1	Phil Roe* (R)	115,276
	Robert Franklin (I)	9,892
2	John J. Duncan Jr.* (R)	120,853
	Bob Scott (D)	37,599
3	Chuck Fleischmann* (R)	97,301
	Mary M. Headrick (D)	53,943
4	Scott DesJarlais* (R)	84,781
	Lenda Sherrell (D)	51,338
5	Jim Cooper* (D)	95,635
	Bob Ries (R)	54,939
6	Diane Black* (R)	115,190
	Amos Powers (D)	37,215
7	Marsha Blackburn* (R)	110,498
	Daniel Cramer (D)	42,260
8	Stephen Fincher* (R)	122,205
	Wes Bradley (D)	42,403
	Steve Cohen* (D)	87,308
	Charlotte Bergmann (R)	27,163
Texas		
1	Louie Gohmert* (R)	108,703
	Shirley J. McKellar (D)	31,072
2	Ted Poe* (R)	101,795
	Niko Letsos (D)	44,349
3	Sam Johnson* (R)	112,726
	Paul Blair (Green)	24,759
4	John Ratcliffe (R)	Unopposed
5	Jeb Hensarling* (R)	89,638
	Ken Ashby (LB)	15,252
6	Joe Barton* (R)	92,285
	David Cozad (D)	54,986
7	John Culberson* (R)	90,422
	James Cargas (D)	49,341
8	Kevin Brady* (R)	124,897
	Ken Petty (LB)	14,930
9	Al Green* (D)	77,979
	Johnny Johnson (LB)	7,886
10	Michael T. McCaul* (R)	109,311
	Tawana Walter-Cadien (D)	60,020
11	Mike Conaway* (R)	107,752
	Ryan Lange (LB)	11,607
12	Kay Granger* (R)	113,105
	Mark Greene (D)	41,720
13	Mac Thornberry* (R)	110,636
	Mike Minter (D)	16,803
14	Randy Weber* (R)	89,876
	Don Brown (D)	52,420
15	Rubén Hinojosa* (D)	48,561
	Eddie Zamora (R)	38,551
16	Beto O'Rourke* (D)	49,257
	Corey Roen (R)	21,293
17	Bill Flores* (R)	85,085
	Nick Haynes (D)	42,696
18	Sheila Jackson Lee* (D)	75,963
	Sean Seibert (R)	26,194
19	Randy Neugebauer* (R)	89,701
	Neal Marchbanks (D)	21,350

Dist.	Representative/candidate (party)	2014 election results
20	**Joaquin Castro* (D)**	66,538
	Jeffrey Blunt (LB)	21,400
21	**Lamar Smith* (R)**	135,513
	Antonio Diaz (Green)	27,782
	Ryan Shields (LB)	25,483
22	**Pete Olson* (R)**	100,780
	Frank Briscoe (D)	47,789
23	**Will Hurd (R)**	57,901
	Pete P. Gallego* (D)	55,436
24	**Kenny Marchant* (R)**	93,446
	Patrick McGehearty (D)	46,360
25	**Roger Williams* (R)**	106,929
	Marco Montoya (D)	64,341
26	**Michael C. Burgess* (R)**	116,758
	Mark Boler (LB)	24,490
27	**Blake Farenthold* (R)**	83,270
	Wesley Reed (D)	44,112
28	**Henry Cuellar* (D)**	62,471
	William Aikens (LB)	10,146
29	**Gene Green* (D)**	41,229
	James Stanczak (LB)	4,818
30	**Eddie Bernice Johnson* (D)**	92,971
	Max Koch (LB)	7,149
31	**John R. Carter* (R)**	91,484
	Louie Minor (D)	45,634
32	**Pete Sessions* (R)**	96,420
	Frank Perez (D)	55,281
33	**Marc Veasey* (D)**	43,728
	Jason Reeves (R)	6,822
34	**Filemon Vela* (D)**	47,457
	Larry Smith (R)	30,617
35	**Lloyd Doggett* (D)**	60,027
	Susan Narvaiz (R)	31,985
36	**Brian Babin (R)**	100,933
	Michael K. Cole (D)	29,291
Utah		
1	**Rob Bishop* (R)**	70,240
	Donna McAleer (D)	31,668
2	**Chris Stewart* (R)**	76,966
	Luz Robles (D)	42,356
3	**Jason Chaffetz* (R)**	94,571
	Brian Wonnacott (D)	29,575
4	**Mia Love (R)**	64,390
	Doug Owens (D)	60,165
Vermont		
	Peter Welch* (D)	123,896
	Mark Donka (R)	59,903
Virginia		
1	**Robert J. Wittman* (R)**	131,596
	Norm Mosher (D)	72,053
2	**Scott Rigell* (R)**	138,149
	Suzanne Patrick (D)	100,585
3	**Bobby Scott* (D)**	Unopposed
4	**J. Randy Forbes* (R)**	121,134
	Elliott Fausz (D)	75,214
5	**Robert Hurt* (R)**	124,381
	Lawrence Gaughan (D)	72,905
6	**Bob Goodlatte* (R)**	133,202
	Will Hammer (LB)	22,008
	Elaine Hildebrandt (Indep. Green)	21,159

Dist.	Representative/candidate (party)	2014 election results
7	**David Brat (R)**	147,897
	Jack Trammell (D)	89,793
8	**Donald S. Beyer Jr.* (D)**	127,981
	Micah Edmond (R)	64,477
9	**H. Morgan Griffith* (R)**	117,032
	William Carr (I)	39,309
10	**Barbara Comstock (R)**	125,864
	John Foust (D)	89,896
11	**Gerry Connolly* (D)**	106,726
	Suzanne Scholte (R)	75,760
Washington		
1	**Suzan DelBene* (D)**	65,431
	Pedro Celis (R)	54,076
2	**Rick Larsen* (D)**	67,812
	B.J. Guillot (R)	41,889
3	**Jaime Herrera Beutler* (R)**	80,764
	Bob Dingethal (D)	52,460
4	**Dan Newhouse (R)**	47,755
	Clint Didier (R)	44,605
5	**Cathy McMorris Rodgers* (R)**	84,551
	Joseph Pakootas (D)	57,721
6	**Derek Kilmer* (D)**	91,692
	Marty McClendon (R)	53,901
7	**Jim McDermott* (D)**	97,258
	Craig Keller (R)	25,745
8	**Dave Reichert* (R)**	73,592
	Jason Ritchie (D)	42,856
9	**Adam Smith* (D)**	63,613
	Doug Basler (R)	28,072
10	**Denny Heck* (D)**	60,203
	Joyce McDonald (R)	48,913
West Virginia		
1	**David B. McKinley* (R)**	91,941
	Glen Gainer (D)	51,755
2	**Alex Mooney (R)**	72,237
	Nick Casey (D)	67,325
3	**Evan Jenkins (R)**	77,170
	Nick J. Rahall II* (D)	62,309
Wisconsin		
1	**Paul Ryan* (R)**	182,118
	Rob Zerban (D)	105,465
2	**Mark Pocan* (D)**	224,548
	Peter Theron (R)	103,303
3	**Ron Kind* (D)**	155,221
	Tony Kurtz (R)	118,669
4	**Gwen Moore* (D)**	178,838
	Dan Sebring (R)	68,404
5	**F. James Sensenbrenner Jr.* (R)**	230,725
	Chris Rockwood (D)	101,065
6	**Glenn Grothman (R)**	169,625
	Mark Harris (D)	122,146
7	**Sean P. Duffy* (R)**	169,299
	Kelly Westlund (D)	112,825
8	**Reid J. Ribble* (R)**	188,370
	Ron Gruett (D)	101,045
Wyoming		
	Cynthia M. Lummis* (R)	111,129
	Richard Grayson (D)	37,365

(1) No candidate won the required majority; a runoff between the top two vote recipients was scheduled for Dec. 6, 2014.

Members of the 114th Congress: Nonvoting Members

Representative/candidate (party)	2014 election results
American Samoa	
Aumua Amata (R)	4,306
Eni F.H. Faleomavaega* (D)	3,157
District of Columbia	
Eleanor Holmes Norton* (D)	122,155
Nelson Rimensnyder (R)	9,655
Guam	
Madeleine Z. Bordallo* (D)	20,550
Margaret Metcalfe (R)	14,866

Representative/candidate (party)	2014 election results
Northern Mariana Islands	
Gregorio Kilili Camacho Sablan* (D)	8,549
Andrew Sablan Salas (R)	4,547
Puerto Rico—Resident Commissioner[1]	
Pedro R. Pierluisi (New Prog./D)	
Virgin Islands	
Stacey Plaskett (D)	15,333
Vince Danet (R)	1,550

(1) The resident commissioner of Puerto Rico is the only member of the House of Representatives who serves a four-year term. Pierluisi was elected in Nov. 2012.

Governors of the 50 States

Source: © Associated Press; all rights reserved. 2014 results are preliminary as of Nov. 5, 2014.

Boldface denotes the 2014 election winner. * = Incumbent. Third-party or independent candidates receiving fewer than 50,000 votes are not necessarily listed. Governors of states not holding elections in Nov. 2014 are shown for reference with date of term end in place of results.

Terms are for four years, with the exception of two-year terms for governors of New Hampshire and Vermont.

D = Democrat; **R** = Republican; **CP** = Constitution Party; **DFL** = Dem.-Farmer-Labor; **I** = Independent; **IP** = Independence Party; **LB** = Libertarian; **NPA** = No party affiliation.

State	Governor/candidate (party)	2014 election results	State	Governor/candidate (party)	2014 election results
Alabama	**Robert Bentley* (R)**	**747,357**	Mississippi	Phil Bryant (R)	NA (Jan. 2016)
	Parker Griffith (D)	427,218	Missouri	Jay Nixon (D)	NA (Jan. 2017)
Alaska	**Bill Walker (NPA)**	**107,395**	Montana	Steve Bullock (D)	NA (Jan. 2017)
	Sean Parnell* (R)	104,230	Nebraska	**Pete Ricketts (R)**	**301,646**
Arizona	**Doug Ducey (R)**	**619,791**		Chuck Hassebrook (D)	203,968
	Fred DuVal (D)	475,577	Nevada	**Brian Sandoval* (R)**	**386,535**
Arkansas	**Asa Hutchinson (R)**	**468,017**		Robert Goodman (D)	130,742
	Mike Ross (D)	350,535	New Hampshire	**Maggie Hassan* (D)**	**255,229**
California	**Jerry Brown* (D)**	**3,049,385**		Walt Havenstein (R)	230,305
	Neel Kashkari (R)	2,147,271	New Jersey	Chris Christie (R)	NA (Jan. 2018)
Colorado	**John Hickenlooper* (D)**	**914,641**	New Mexico	**Susana Martinez* (R)**	**288,482**
	Bob Beauprez (R)	888,156		Gary K. King (D)	214,614
Connecticut	**Dan Malloy* (D)**	**547,372**	New York	**Andrew Cuomo* (D)**	**1,918,644**
	Tom Foley (R)	517,458		Rob Astorino (R)	1,442,392
Delaware	Jack A. Markell (D)	NA (Jan. 2017)		Howie Hawkins (Green)	173,510
Florida	**Rick Scott* (R)**	**2,861,390**	North Carolina	Pat McCrory (R)	NA (Jan. 2017)
	Charlie Crist (D)	2,795,262	North Dakota	Jack Dalrymple (R)	NA (Dec. 2016)
	Adrian Wyllie (LB)	222,878	Ohio	**John Kasich* (R)**	**1,922,436**
Georgia	**J. Nathan Deal* (R)**	**1,341,161**		Edward FitzGerald (D)	989,201
	Jason Carter (D)	1,138,476		Anita Rios (Green)	99,415
	Andrew Hunt (LB)	60,151	Oklahoma	**Mary Fallin* (R)**	**459,788**
Hawaii	**David Ige (D)**	**181,065**		Joe Dorman (D)	337,728
	Duke Aiona (R)	135,742	Oregon	**John Kitzhaber* (D)**	**657,436**
Idaho	**C. L. "Butch" Otter* (R)**	**235,349**		Dennis Richardson (R)	598,407
	A. J. Balukoff (D)	169,497	Pennsylvania	**Tom Wolf (D)**	**1,899,318**
Illinois	**Bruce Rauner (R)**	**1,773,665**		Tom Corbett* (R)	1,560,057
	Patrick Quinn* (D)	1,601,059	Rhode Island	**Gina M. Raimondo (D)**	**123,460**
	Chad Grimm (LB)	117,644		Allan Fung (R)	111,291
Indiana	Mike Pence (R)	NA (Jan. 2017)		Bob Healey (Moderate)	67,707
Iowa	**Terry Branstad* (R)**	**664,806**	South Carolina	**Nikki R. Haley* (R)**	**689,319**
	Jack Hatch (D)	419,258		Vincent Sheheen (D)	510,230
Kansas	**Sam Brownback* (R)**	**423,666**	South Dakota	**Dennis Daugaard* (R)**	**195,373**
	Paul Davis (D)	390,614		Susan Wismer (D)	70,508
Kentucky	Steven L. Beshear (D)	NA (Dec. 2015)	Tennessee	**Bill Haslam* (R)**	**950,968**
Louisiana	Bobby Jindal (R)	NA (Jan. 2016)		Charles V. "Charlie" Brown (D)	308,754
Maine	**Paul LePage* (R)**	**291,274**	Texas	**Greg Abbott (R)**	**2,784,134**
	Mike Michaud (D)	261,770		Wendy Davis (D)	1,829,828
	Eliot Cutler (I)	50,909		Kathie Glass (LB)	66,328
Maryland	**Larry Hogan (R)**	**847,107**	Utah	Gary R. Herbert (R)	NA (Jan. 2017)
	Anthony G. Brown (D)	770,511	Vermont[1]	**Peter Shumlin* (D)**	**89,883**
Massachusetts	**Charles D. Baker (R)**	**1,041,640**		Scott Milne (R)	87,788
	Martha Coakley (D)	1,001,279	Virginia	Terry McAuliffe (D)	NA (Jan. 2018)
	Evan Falchuk (United Indep.)	71,144	Washington	Jay Inslee (D)	NA (Jan. 2017)
Michigan	**Rick Snyder* (R)**	**1,598,922**	West Virginia	Earl Ray Tomblin (D)	NA (Jan. 2017)
	Mark Schauer (D)	1,469,375	Wisconsin	**Scott Walker* (R)**	**1,259,031**
Minnesota	**Mark Dayton* (DFL)**	**988,710**		Mary Burke (D)	1,121,490
	Jeff Johnson (R)	878,940	Wyoming	**Matthew Mead* (R)**	**98,029**
	Hannah Nicollet (IP)	56,883		Peter Gosar (D)	45,326

NA = Not applicable. **Note:** Kentucky, Massachusetts, Pennsylvania, and Virginia are self-designated commonwealths. (1) No candidate won the required majority; state law requires the legislature to select the governor.

Governors of U.S. Commonwealths and Territories

D = Democrat; **R** = Republican; **I** = Independent; **PDP** = Popular Democratic Party. Governors of areas not holding elections in Nov. 2014 are shown for reference with date of term end in place of results.

Area	Governor/candidate (party)	2014 election results	Area	Governor/candidate (party)	2014 election results
American Samoa	Lolo Matalasi Moliga (I)	NA (Jan. 2017)	Guam	**Eddie Calvo* (R)**	**22,365**
N. Mariana Isls.	**Eloy Songao Inos* (R)**	**6,342**		Carl Gutierrez (D)	12,632
	Heinz Sablan Hofschneider (I)	4,501	Puerto Rico	Alejandro García Padilla (PDP)	NA (Jan. 2017)
	Juan Nekai Babauta (I)	2,414	Virgin Isls.	**Kenneth Mapp (I)**	**9,441**
	Edward M. Deleon Guerrero (D)	541		Donna M. Christensen (D)	7,442
				Soraya Diase Coffelt (I)	1,539
				Mona Barnes (I)	1,302

NA = Not applicable.

Nov. 1, 2013, to Oct. 31, 2014

The Chronology of Events reports the top National, International, and General news stories, month by month.

November 2013

National

Gunman Opens Fire at LAX, Killing Officer—A gunman Nov. 1 shot three security workers and an airline passenger, one of them fatally, at Terminal 3 in Los Angeles Intl. Airport. Carrying a .223-caliber assault rifle and hundreds of rounds of ammunition, the gunman shot and killed 39-year-old Transportation Safety Admin. (TSA) officer Gerardo I. Hernandez at point-blank range and appeared to seek out other TSA employees as he roamed the airport. Some bystanders suffered minor injuries. Paul Ciancia, the alleged shooter, was critically injured by police in a gunfight before being taken into custody. The 23-year-old Ciancia had no known history of mental illness, but a note found in his belongings threatened the TSA and contained antigovernment rants. He was charged with the murder of a federal officer and commission of violence in an international airport. Hernandez was the first TSA officer to die in the line of duty. The incident affected about 746 flights nationwide Nov. 1.

Two States Approve Same-Sex Marriage Bills—Hawaii and Illinois both legalized same-sex marriage, as each state's governor signed a bill reforming the institution in Nov. After the U.S. Supreme Court ruled in June that parts of the federal Defense of Marriage Act was unconstitutional, Hawaii Gov. Neil Abercrombie (D) worked out a compromise bill with state legislators that made same-sex marriage legal in the state but included a provision exempting religious and affiliated nonprofit groups from having to perform—or provide goods, services, or facilities for—same-sex weddings. He signed the bill Nov. 13. Illinois Gov. Pat Quinn (D) signed a similar law Nov. 20. The Illinois law, set to go into effect June 1, 2014, would allow those in existing civil unions to convert them into marriages, as well as legalize same-sex marriage ceremonies.

JPMorgan Agrees to Record Fine; Twitter Makes IPO; Other Economic News—JPMorgan Chase Nov. 19 reached a $13-bil agreement with the Justice Dept. to settle a number of investigations into its mortgage products. As part of the agreement, JPMorgan acknowledged misrepresenting mortgage-backed securities to the public and unsuspecting investors prior to the 2008 financial crisis. Earlier in the month, a hedge fund group unrelated to JPMorgan, SAC Capital Advisors, had agreed to plead guilty to insider trading Nov. 4 and pay a then-record $1.8-bil fine.

The social media site Twitter had its initial public offering on the New York Stock Exchange Nov. 7. Prices were set at $26 a share as the market opened but rose to a high of $50.09 before closing its first day of trading at $44.90. The Dow Jones Industrial Average reached an all-time high Nov. 27, closing at 16,097.33. The S&P 500 reached an all-time high the same day, closing at 1,807.23. The Dow finished the month at 16,086.41, up 3.5% over Oct.; the S&P ended at 1,805.81, up 2.8%; and the Nasdaq Composite Index was at 4,059.89, a difference of 3.6%.

The jobs report issued Nov. 8 revealed that 204,000 jobs were added to payrolls in Oct. 2013, far exceeding the predicted 120,000. Unemployment rose to 7.3% from Sept.'s figure of 7.2%, and 4.1 mil people remained in the ranks of the long-term unemployed. The unemployment figures included an increase of 448,000 people on temporary layoff during Oct. Many were federal government workers furloughed during the shutdown, which had delayed the release of the report by nearly a week. The labor force participation rate was at its lowest point since Mar. 1978, falling to 62.8% from 63.2% in Sept. Job figures for prior months were revised upward, with jobs created in Aug. tallying 238,000, up from 193,000, and in Sept. totaling 163,000, rather than 148,000.

Senate Democrats Limit Minority Filibusters With "Nuclear Option"—Led by Majority Leader Harry Reid (D, NV), the U.S. Senate voted Nov. 21, 52-48, to reform Senate filibuster rules. The rules change permits a simple majority vote—as opposed to a supermajority of 60—to end filibusters preventing votes on most executive and judicial nominees (excluding those to the U.S. Supreme Court). This implementation of the so-called nuclear option allowed dozens of Obama nominees, who had been held up by filibusters due to the Senate's 55-45 party split, to proceed towards Senate confirmation. Senate Minority Leader Mitch McConnell (R, KY) called it "a sad day in the history of the Senate," but Sen. Jeff Merkley (D, OR) praised the action as "clearing the decks of the Senate" to address important legislation.

International

Iraqi Insurgent Violence Continues—Iraqi Pres. Nouri al-Maliki met Oct. 30-Nov. 1 with Pres. Barack Obama and other U.S. officials in Washington, DC, and reportedly asked for increased military aid to combat almost daily insurgent attacks—many by Sunni militias linked to al-Qaeda—on police and civilians throughout Iraq. Insurgents used car bombs, suicide bombers, and roadside bombs to carry out attacks, which had escalated since the U.S. withdrew its forces in Dec. 2011, and since Apr. 2013, when the government raided a Sunni protest camp. The UN attributed the persistence of the violence in part to disunity within the government, which has failed to agree on a strategy for securing the peace.

UN's Assistance Mission for Iraq reported Jan. 1, 2014, that 659 were killed in insurgent violence in Nov. and another 759 in Dec. More than 7,800 Iraqis died in acts of terrorism and violence in Iraq in 2013, making 2013 the country's deadliest year since 2008.

Toronto Mayor Admits Drug Use, Refuses to Step Down—Rob Ford, the mayor of Toronto, ON, Canada, admitted Nov. 5 to using crack cocaine and to hiding the truth from his family and staff. After months of denying similar charges, Ford made the admission when he learned the Toronto police department had a video of him smoking crack, which Ford said he probably did when he was in "one of [his] drunken stupors." The news prompted many Toronto citizens and government officials to call for Ford's resignation. Ford admitted to making mistakes and apologized to his staff, colleagues, and the city but refused to step down. The city council voted Nov. 18 to reduce Ford's budget by 60%, resulting in severe cuts to his staff, and to revoke much of his authority, including his ability to select committee chairs and oversee emergencies. Much of Ford's budget and many of his responsibilities were taken over by Deputy Mayor Norm Kelly.

Typhoon Haiyan Devastates the Philippines—Shortly before dawn Nov. 8, Typhoon Haiyan—also known as Yolanda—made landfall in the Philippines, bringing waves as high as 25 ft and winds of up to 195 mph. The storm destroyed large portions of the country, ripping apart buildings and power lines, flooding roads, and washing away homes and their inhabitants. Early warnings had been issued ahead of the Category 5 storm, and many of the more than 12 mil people thought to be in its path were able to evacuate, but more than 6,200 died, and about 4.1 mil were displaced, according to the national disaster management council (NDRRMC) as of Mar. 6, 2014. Tacloban, the capital city of Leyte Province with a population of 220,000 before the storm, was particularly hard hit, as was the island of Samar.

It was the deadliest natural disaster in the modern history of the Philippines, which is located in the world's most active typhoon belt. In the storm's wake, Pres. Benigno "Noynoy" Aquino III declared a "state of national calamity" Nov. 11, but the government struggled to deliver relief supplies to remote areas where roads, airports, and other critical infrastructure were damaged or destroyed. The international community also mobilized financial, medical, and military aid to the devastated country. The U.S. sent the aircraft carrier USS *George Washington*, which arrived off the Samar coast Nov. 14 to provide logistical support and supplies, and pledged $20 mil to the relief effort.

China's Reform Agenda Intrigues International Investors—After Chinese Pres. Xi Jinping and top Communist Party officials met in Beijing Nov. 9-12 for the 18th Central Committee's third plenary session, China announced a

60-point reform agenda Nov. 15. Among the reforms were landmark economic and social-policy changes to increase the Chinese economy's private sector, relax the one-child policy, and eliminate "re-education" labor camps. The Hong Kong and Shanghai stock markets gained almost 3% on Nov. 18, the first day of trading after the announcement, but some international observers were skeptical that the reforms could be accomplished by 2020 or that the leadership was motivated to do so.

Multination Talks Yield Landmark Iranian Nuclear Deal—After four days of marathon negotiations in Geneva, Switzerland, European Union foreign policy chief Catherine Ashton announced Nov. 24 that Iranian Foreign Min. Mohammad Javad Zarif had agreed to a deal with representatives from the P5+1 nations (China, France, Germany, Russia, UK, and U.S.). The terms of the six-month agreement restrict Iran's nuclear enrichment capabilities and give extensive access to international weapons inspectors while allowing the possession of nuclear technology to generate energy. Iran agreed to suspend development at their Arak reactor and to dilute medium-grade uranium—previously enriched to within 20% of weapons grade—to prevent its use in weapons production. In exchange, some $7 bil in sanctions would be lifted for six months. Secret talks between the U.S. and Iran were said to have helped negotiations move forward, and the more open attitude of Iranian Pres. Hassan Rouhani toward the West was credited with making the talks possible. Israel remained skeptical of the agreement, with Israeli Pres. Benjamin Netanyahu calling it "a historic mistake."

General

Mucho Macho Man Wins Breeders' Cup in Thrilling Style—Mucho Macho Man fought off the surging Will Take Charge and Declaration of War to win the $5-mil prize at the 2013 Breeders' Cup Classic at Santa Anita Park in Arcadia, CA, Nov. 2. Slow-motion replay showed jockey Gary Stevens and Mucho Macho Man, last year's second-place finisher, won by a nose. Will Take Charge finished second, and Declaration of War was a close third.

One World Trade Center Named Tallest U.S. Building—The Council on Tall Buildings and Urban Habitat Nov. 12 declared One World Trade Center (1 WTC) in New York, NY, to be the tallest skyscraper in the U.S. and third tallest in the world. The building, at 1,776 ft tall, surpassed the Willis (formerly Sears) Tower in Chicago, IL, which is 1,451 ft in height. A controversial ruling determined that a 408-ft spire on top of 1 WTC was part of the building's construction and "completes the architectural expression" of the tower and could thus be included in its official height.

Church of England Approves Ordination of Female Bishops—By a vote of 378-8, with 25 abstentions, the Church of England's General Synod Nov. 20 supported proposals for the ordination of women as bishops beginning as early as 2014. The measures included "guidance" for parishes not in favor of female ministry and proposed appointing an ombudsman to settle disputes between those who support and those who oppose newly elevated women bishops. Final approval of the proposals would occur in July 2014. British Prime Min. David Cameron suggested that women bishops could be put on an accelerated path to become members of the House of Lords, joining other senior bishops.

New World Chess Champion Crowned—Twenty-two-year-old Magnus Carlsen of Norway defeated the reigning World Chess Champion, India's Viswanathan Anand, in a 10-game match Nov. 9-22 in Chennai, India, 6½-3½. In the best-of-12 match, Carlsen won three games, tied seven, and lost none. Anand failed to press his advantage early in the contest, then fell behind in games 5-6 and never recovered. Carlsen, a grandmaster since the age of 13, ended Anand's six-year reign as champion after winning a chance to play him in the eight-player Candidates Tournament, which took place Mar. 15-Apr. 1, 2013. Carlsen won $1.5 mil and Anand $1.0 mil in the match, which was widely viewed by television audiences in Norway and India.

Pacquiao Victorious in Return to the Ring—Filipino boxer Manny Pacquiao defeated American Brandon "Bam Bam" Rios Nov. 23 and became the World Boxing Organization's international welterweight champion. The judges' unanimous decision was 120-108, 119-109, and 118-110 in favor of Pacquiao, who claimed his 55th career victory. Pacquiao's previous bout, 11 months prior, had disappointed fans when he was knocked out by Juan Manuel Márquez.

December 2013
National

Two Major Airlines Merge; GM Selects Woman CEO; Markets Soar—The merger of American Airlines and US Airways became official Dec. 9, resulting in the formation of the world's largest airline, American Airlines Group Inc. The process of integrating the two airlines and their more than 100,000 collective employees, reservation systems, and websites would take up to two years. American Airlines and its parent company, AMR Corp., officially emerged from bankruptcy on the day the deal closed. In other transportation industry news, Mary Barra was named the next CEO of General Motors (GM) Dec. 10, to replace the retiring Dan Akerson Jan. 15, 2014. A 33-year employee of the largest U.S. auto manufacturer, Barra had most recently led GM's global product development group. The appointment made her the first woman to lead a major auto company and one of only 23 women to head a Fortune 500 company.

The end-of-year financial indicators mostly showed 2013 as a year of progress. The last day of 2013 was a record day on Wall Street, as the Dow Jones Industrial Average closed at an all-time high of 16,576.66, the S&P 500 closed at a record 1,848.36, and the Nasdaq Composite Index closed at 4,176.59, its highest level in 13 years. All three benchmark indexes were up substantially in 2013: the Dow gained 26.5%, the S&P 500 was up 29.6%, and the Nasdaq climbed 38.3% from year-end 2012. The Dept. of Labor's Dec. 6 jobs report showed that the economy added 203,000 jobs in Nov., and the 7.0% unemployment rate was the lowest since Nov. 2008. Gold prices declined 28% in 2013—the first annual loss since 2000—as investors continued to speculate over when the Federal Reserve would begin tapering its $85-bil monthly asset purchase program. The Fed announced Dec. 18 that monthly asset purchases would be reduced to $75 bil in Jan. 2014.

NSA Scandal Developments Include New Surveillance Revelations, Conflicting Federal Rulings, Panel Recommendations—Documents leaked by former Natl. Security Agency (NSA) contractor Edward Snowden were revealed Dec. 9 to contain evidence that intelligence agencies were using online games in their hunt for terrorists. In addition to collecting data from the Xbox Live network, intelligence agents from the UK and U.S. had joined *World of Warcraft*, the most popular online video game in the world, and the online virtual world *Second Life* as part of their surveillance efforts. Intelligence officials believed the games could be used by terrorists or other criminals to communicate, transfer money, or plan future attacks, but there was no indication that any terrorist plots had been foiled by such surveillance.

A panel of outside advisers Dec. 18 presented 46 recommendations to Pres. Barack Obama to curb NSA spying activities, in particular the agency's collection and storage of telephone metadata. The panel called for either the phone companies or another outside organization to collect the data and for warrants to be issued for the information they contained. The panel's recommendations followed the release of an opinion by U.S. District Court Judge Richard Leon in Washington, DC, who ruled Dec. 16 that the data collection program was "probably unconstitutional." Leon was contradicted Dec. 27 by federal judge William Pauley in New York City, who ruled that the same program was legal. The American Civil Liberties Union, which initiated the latter case, announced it would appeal that ruling.

Gay Rights Advocates See Setbacks Overseas, Progress in U.S.—Pres. Barack Obama Dec. 18 appointed tennis legend Billie Jean King and former hockey Olympian Caitlin Cahow to the official U.S. delegation to the Winter Olympic Games in Sochi, Russia. The appointments of Cahow and King, who are both openly gay, were seen as an attempt to make a statement about human rights in Russia, where discriminatory laws against homosexuals are often enforced. Russian Pres. Vladimir Putin insisted that LGBT athletes and visitors would suffer no discrimination during the games. Meanwhile, India's Supreme Court, Dec. 11, overturned a 2009 lower court ruling that had struck down a colonial law that criminalized homosexual activity. Uganda passed a law Dec. 20 stiffening the punishment for homosexuality to include the possibility of life in prison.

The right to same-sex marriage was affirmed in two more states with decisions handed down by the New Mexico Supreme Court Dec. 19 and a federal judge in Utah Dec. 20. On Jan. 6, 2014, the U.S. Supreme Court stayed the judicial order legalizing same-sex marriage in Utah pending appeal.

Data Breach Affects Millions of Target Customers— The discount superstore Target announced Dec. 19 that about 40 mil customers who used credit or debit cards at their stores Nov. 27-Dec. 15, 2013, could have had their account information stolen. The hackers were believed to have stolen customer names, card numbers, expiration dates, and security codes. Target offered free credit-monitoring services for one year to anyone who had shopped in its U.S. stores. Further investigation, reported Jan. 10, found that information such as the names, phone numbers, and email addresses of up to 70 mil customers had been taken in one of the largest-ever known thefts of retail data.

International

Massive Protests in Ukraine Over EU Pact; Latvia Joins Eurozone—Weeks of demonstrations that began in late Nov. in favor of an EU-Ukraine trade pact culminated in an estimated crowd of 800,000 gathering Dec. 8 in the Ukranian capital of Kiev. Ukrainian Pres. Viktor Yanukovych said that the trade agreement would hurt the country by forcing it to cut ties with Russia while EU leaders claimed it would improve the Ukrainian economy. Instead, Yanukovych announced that he planned to expand Ukraine's partnership agreements with Russia, which had lobbied against Ukraine's pending EU pact using threats of trade sanctions.

News of Yanukovych's decision prompted anger and calls for the president's resignation. Protests in Kiev's Independence Square began to turn violent by Nov. 30. Several thousand protesters attempted Dec. 1 to breach fortifications in front of the presidential administration building but were turned back with tear gas, truncheons, and flash grenades. Dozens of protesters and about 100 police officers were injured in the melee. Demonstrators also occupied Kiev City Hall and blockaded the Cabinet Ministry, preventing top government officials from entering.

Another Russian neighbor, Latvia, became the 18th EU member nation to adopt the euro, Jan 1, 2014.

World Mourns Death of Nelson Mandela—Former South African Pres. Nelson Mandela, whose life and 27-year imprisonment made him a symbol for the anti-apartheid movement and other human-rights causes, died Dec. 5 in Johannesburg at age 95. F. W. de Klerk, who freed Mandela from prison and was the country's last president under apartheid, praised him as a great "unifier." More than 100 past and present heads of state attended a memorial service Dec. 10 at FNB Stadium in Soweto with thousands of spectators. U.S. Pres. Barack Obama, Archbishop Desmond Tutu, and others spoke in tribute to Mandela. His body lay in state Dec. 11-13 in Pretoria, where an estimated 100,000 paid their respects. Mandela received a state funeral Dec. 15 in his ancestral home of Qunu and was laid to rest in his family's plot after a private service.

Controversy arose when it was revealed Dec. 12 that a man hired to provide sign-language interpretation at the memorial service, Thamsanqa Jantjie, was not signing intelligibly during the service; Jantjie was reported to have had a history of mental health issues.

UN Approves Military Operations in Central African Republic—A UN Security Council vote Dec. 5 authorized military intervention in the Central African Republic (CAR) to stop sectarian violence between Christians, who make up about 85% of the population, and Muslims. That evening, French Pres. François Hollande announced that the total

number of French troops in the CAR, a former French colony, would double to more than 1,200, while African Union troop strength would increase Dec. 7 from 3,500 to 6,000.

The Muslim rebel alliance, led by current interim Pres. Michel Djotodia, ousted Pres. François Bozizé in a Mar. 2013 coup. Bozizé loyalists joined with existing Christian militias—including Christian groups organized in the wake of the coup who call themselves the anti-Balaka—to try to oust the rebels. In the week following the Security Council vote, some 450 people were killed in attacks in and around Bangui, the nation's capital, with about 150 killed elsewhere in the country. The UN High Commissioner for Refugees announced Dec. 17 that the conflict had internally displaced more than 710,000 people, including 210,000 Bangui residents in just the previous two weeks. The first French deaths in the conflict occurred Dec. 10, when two soldiers were killed.

Uruguay Is First Nation to Legalize Marijuana—In an effort to diminish drug trafficking across its borders, Uruguay's parliament voted 16-13 to legalize marijuana Dec. 10, becoming the first country to do so on a national basis. The law, regulating the growth, sale, and use of the drug, would take effect in 120 days, at which time a drug control board would be established to determine cultivation standards and set prices. Under the legislation's terms, Uruguayan residents over 18 would be permitted to own up to six marijuana plants a year or as much as 480 g (about 17 oz.) and to form 15-45-member smoking clubs, which would be allowed to grow up to 99 plants per year. Marijuana users would be required to register with the government, and the control board would track their marijuana purchases. Sales would be restricted to licensed pharmacies. The law faced opposition from those who feared decriminalizing the drug would increase its use; opinion polls showed that 58% of Uruguayans were against legalization.

High-Ranking North Korean Official Executed—The state-controlled Korean Central News Agency reported Dec. 13 that North Korean leader Kim Jong Un had ordered the execution of his 67-year-old uncle Jang Song Thaek following a special military tribunal. Jang was vice chairman of North Korea's top military body and supposed second-in-command to Kim. In the news agency's reports, Jang was accused of forming a faction to challenge the 30-year-old leader's authority and undermining the country's economy and infrastructure, as well as leading a "dissolute and depraved life." He was also said to have maintained a secret account from which he spent at least $6.3 mil in 2009.

Jailed Activists Freed by Russian Amnesty Law—Two members of the Russian activist punk band Pussy Riot, jailed in Aug. 2012 for "hooliganism motivated by religious hatred," were freed Dec. 23 in accordance with the terms of an amnesty law passed the previous week. The band was arrested after performing a profanity-filled song called "Punk Prayer," protesting the Russian government, in Moscow's Christ the Savior cathedral in Feb. 2012. Nadezhda Tolokonnikova and Maria Alekhina were due to be released in Mar. 2014 but were freed, per the terms of the amnesty law, because they were mothers of small children. About 20,000 other prisoners were also set to be released. Many observers, including the two freed women, believed the amnesty law had been passed to improve Russia's human rights image leading up to the Winter Olympic Games in Sochi.

Suicide Bombings Shake Russia as Olympic Games Approach—Two separate suicide bombings in Volgograd, Russia, killed 34 people Dec. 29-30. In the first incident, a suicide bomber detonated explosives when approaching a train station metal detector; the resulting fireball killed 18 people. Less than 24 hours later, on Dec. 30, another bomber detonated explosives on a crowded bus, resulting in 16 more deaths. The Muslim insurgency group Vilayat Dagestan from the North Caucasus region claimed responsibility in Jan. 2014 and warned that additional violence would follow. Volgograd (formerly Stalingrad) is located about 560 mi southeast of Moscow and about 400 mi northeast of Sochi, where the 2014 Winter Olympic Games were scheduled to open Feb. 7. Many observers expressed concern that the bombings were meant as a warning of imminent violence at the Games. Russian Pres. Vladimir Putin ordered increased security, especially in the areas close to Sochi.

General

Bronx Train Derailment Kills Four, Injures Dozens— A Metro-North commuter train carrying about 115 people derailed at around 7:20 AM Dec. 1 as it traveled through a curve near the Spuyten Duyvil station in the Bronx, NY. Four people, three of whom had been thrown from the train, died in the derailment, and 59 people were injured. The train was found to have been traveling 82 mph through a 30-mph zone at the time of the crash. No criminal charges were filed against the train's engineer, who failed to slow the train to its designated speed before the curve, but Metro-North instituted precautions against such accidents in the future.

Pope Francis Approves Commission on Sex Abuse, Is Named *Time* Person of the Year—On the third day of meetings with his Council of Cardinals, Pope Francis approved a proposal Dec. 5 to establish a commission on the sexual abuse of children by Catholic clergy. According to a Council spokesman, its purpose was to help the Vatican "study the present programs in place for the protection of children, and to come up with suggestions for new initiatives." The Congregation for the Doctrine of the Faith would still have responsibility for disciplining offending clergy and religious personnel. For this action and others since taking office in Mar. 2013, the editorial board of *Time* magazine named Pope Francis its Person of the Year Dec. 11. In explaining the board's decision, the magazine's managing editor, Nancy Gibbs, credited Pope Francis with "pulling the papacy out of the palace and into the streets."

Sporting Kansas City Wins MLS Championship— Sporting Kansas City won the Major League Soccer (MLS) Cup title over Real Salt Lake Dec. 7 at Sporting Park in Kansas City, KS. After the 120-min. regulation game ended in a 1-1 draw, Sporting KC won its second title in the longest shootout in MLS playoff history, 7-6. SKC defender Aurelien Collin scored what turned out to be the winning penalty on the team's ninth shot; RSL's Lovel Palmer's answering shot was deflected by the crossbar. Collin, who'd also scored Kansas City's tying goal in regulation, was named the MVP of the MLS Cup.

Chang'e 3 Mission Makes China Third Country to Land on the Moon—China became the first country in 37 years to land a spacecraft on the moon when the *Chang'e 3* probe—named for a Chinese lunar goddess—touched down Dec. 14 on Mare Imbrium, or Sea of Rains crater. *Chang'e 3* had been launched Dec. 1 and made China the third country, after the U.S. and former Soviet Union, to complete an unmanned soft landing on the moon. (In a hard landing, the equipment crashes into the moon.) Later that day, the Yutu (Jade Rabbit) rover emerged from the craft. Both the *Chang'e 3* and the Yutu were expected to photograph the landing area and study the chemical composition of the lunar surface with X-ray and infrared spectrometers.

January 2014
National

Yellen Confirmed as Federal Reserve Chair; Other Economic News—The Senate Jan. 6 voted, 56-26, to confirm Janet Yellen's nomination to succeed Ben Bernanke as chair of the Federal Reserve. Yellen, who had served as the Fed's vice chair since 2010, is the first woman to lead the policymaking bank. She assumed the post Feb. 3 as the financial body was beginning to scale back its stimulus strategy of purchasing bonds to galvanize the economy and lower unemployment.

The Labor Dept. reported Jan. 10 that 74,000 new nonagricultural jobs were added to the national economy in Dec., which was far less than the 2013 monthly average of 182,000 new jobs. While the unemployment rate dropped to 6.7% in Dec. from 7.0% in Nov., the reduction was attributed to people dropping out of the workforce. The stock market was off to a slow start, with the Dow Jones Industrial Average closing at 15,698.85, down 5.3% for the month. The S&P 500 closed at 1,782.59, 3.6% down from Dec. 2013. The Nasdaq Composite

Index finished the month at 4,103.88, down 1.7% from the end of 2013.

Aides to Republican Presidential Hopeful Accused of Orchestrating Traffic Fiasco—Documents published Jan. 8 implicated a senior member of the administration of New Jersey Gov. Chris Christie (R) in engineering unannounced and unnecessary road lane closures Sept. 9-13, 2013, as an act of political retribution. The closures snarled traffic for hours at New Jersey entrances to the highly traveled George Washington Bridge between Fort Lee, NJ, and New York City. The newly released personal emails and text messages included evidence that Bridget Anne Kelley, a deputy chief of staff for Christie, and David Wildstein, a Christie appointee at the Port Authority of NY and NJ, had orchestrated the severe traffic gridlock to punish Fort Lee Mayor Mark Sokolich (D) for not backing Christie in his 2013 reelection race. Christie fired Kelley and apologized in a news conference Jan. 9, claiming he had no prior knowledge of the scheme, but Wildstein's attorney asserted Jan. 31 that Christie knew about the nature of the closings as they occurred. Wildstein had resigned his post Dec. 6 when details of the bridge scandal began coming to light.

Christie, who had often been named as a 2016 Republican presidential contender, found his political future threatened. In the wake of the bridge scandal, more people came forth to accuse the Christie administration of having abused its power. Hoboken Mayor Dawn Zimmer (D) claimed Jan. 19 that the Christie administration had threatened to withhold Hurricane Sandy recovery aid unless she approved a development project. An outside legal team, retained by Christie to conduct an investigation of his office, concluded Mar. 27 that the governor had no involvement in the lane closures, but other investigations were ongoing.

Chemical Spill in West Virginia Leaves 300,000 Without Safe Water—A chemical leak in West Virginia's Kanawha Valley Jan. 9 led to a nine-county ban on tap water use for some 300,000 residents. Authorities determined that approximately 7,500 gallons of crude MCHM, a chemical mixture used in coal processing, leaked from a storage tank owned by Freedom Industries into the Elk River, 2.5 mi upstream of Charleston, WV, and just 1 mi from a major water plant. Gov. Earl Ray Tomblin (D) declared a state of emergency and ordered a ban on drinking, cooking, and bathing with tap water for West Virginia American Water customers in nine area counties; Pres. Barack Obama declared a federal emergency Jan. 10. The ban lasted up to 10 days for some residents. State officials Jan. 18 confirmed 20 people had been hospitalized and more than 400 had been treated for exposure to the chemicals, which can cause skin and eye irritation, headaches, breathing difficulties, and nausea. The spill generated criticism of lax governmental regulations—the company had largely been allowed to operate without oversight, with its last governmental inspection in 1991—and U.S. Sen. Joe Manchin III (D, WV) introduced a bill to establish new chemical storage standards. Freedom Industries filed for bankruptcy protection Jan. 17 in the wake of some two dozen lawsuits.

Obama Announces Changes to National Surveillance Programs—In an effort to address widespread privacy concerns, Pres. Barack Obama outlined reforms to current Natl. Security Agency (NSA) surveillance strategy in a speech at the Justice Dept. Jan. 17. He defended the NSA's current far-reaching operations, which were revealed in part when classified documents were leaked in 2013 by former NSA contractor Edward Snowden, but promised to reform the handling of bulk domestic phone records. The proposed reforms also included requiring that agencies seek approval from the Foreign Intelligence Surveillance Act (FISA) court before conducting database searches (except in certain emergency cases) and shifting management of the database away from the NSA. Obama also urged Congress to form a nongovernmental panel of privacy advocates to weigh in on FISA cases and promised that the government would not spy on allies without a compelling reason. The American Civil Liberties Union acknowledged Obama's efforts but criticized the president for not ending the collection of bulk phone data.

The Obama administration and major Internet firms including Facebook, Google, Microsoft, and Yahoo resolved a legal dispute Jan. 27 concerning the level of detail companies can publicly reveal about intelligence agency requests for information. Under the settlement, companies can divulge in rough numbers how many requests were made and customer accounts affected.

State of the Union Proposes Ambitious Economic Agenda, Defends Iran Nuclear Negotiations—In his State of the Union address Jan. 28, Pres. Barack Obama outlined economic measures to help reduce income inequality across the country. These included executive actions raising the minimum wage received by federal contract employees and establishing federally guaranteed retirement-savings accounts. He called for congressional action to reform corporate tax codes and reinstate long-term unemployment benefits, and to pass measures ensuring equal pay for women and greater access to preschool. The address also urged legislators to revisit gun control, immigration reform, and infrastructure investment, issues that had seen little congressional action, and defended the Affordable Care Act, major provisions of which went into effect Jan. 1. Pledging to move the nation away from a "permanent war footing," Obama touted plans to remove most U.S. troops from Afghanistan by the end of 2014 and defended efforts to negotiate with Iran over its nuclear program without the passage of additional economic sanctions.

The official Republican response, delivered by Rep. Cathy McMorris Rodgers (R, WA) the same night, criticized the Affordable Care Act and promoted conservative economic traditions.

International

Sunni Militants Capture Strategic Iraqi Cities—Sunni militants with the Islamic State of Iraq and Syria (ISIS)—an insurgent group that evolved from al-Qaeda in Iraq—wrested control of Fallujah away from Iraqi security forces Jan. 3, more than two years after the U.S. withdrew its combat forces. Located in Anbar province in central Iraq, Fallujah was the site of the U.S. military's bloodiest battle since the Vietnam War; close to 100 coalition troops died during a Nov. 2004 confrontation with insurgents there. The militants, who also captured parts of the nearby provincial capital of Ramadi the same week, appealed to the almost exclusively Sunni Muslim population to take up arms against the largely Shiite government of Prime Min. Nouri al-Maliki.

The United Nations reported Jan. 1 that violent attacks killed 8,868 people in Iraq during 2013, including at least 7,818 civilians, for the highest annual toll since 2008.

Egypt Passes Revised Constitution; Opposition Boycotts Vote—The Supreme Electoral Commission of Egypt reported that an amended draft of its constitution passed in a Jan. 14-15 referendum with the support of 98.1% of those who voted. Voter turnout stood at just 38.6% of eligible voters, however, and some who campaigned against the new constitution were allegedly arrested. Supporters of the banned Muslim Brotherhood, which the military-led government has suppressed since it overthrew Brotherhood-supported Pres. Mohammed Morsi in July 2013, rejected the referendum outcome after boycotting the vote. The new constitution expanded the rights of women and minorities, but critics opposed provisions giving the military the right to appoint the nation's defense secretary and to try civilians in military courts, a provision that had been criticized in the previous constitution.

Central African Republic Chooses Neutral Interim Leader—Catherine Samba-Panza was elected interim president of the Central African Republic Jan. 20 by a transitional assembly working to end sectarian violence that had claimed some 2,000 lives and, according to a Jan. 3 United Nations report, displaced close to 1 mil people. Samba-Panza, mayor of the capital city of Bangui and the country's first female leader, is unaffiliated with either of the nation's two warring groups—Muslim rebels known as Seleka, who led a Mar. 2013 coup and committed atrocities against the majority Christian population, and the anti-Balaka Christian militias that have carried out revenge attacks on rebel groups and Muslim residents. While working to end the violence, Samba-Panza will prepare for elections to choose a successor to Michel Djotodia,

who was installed in the 2013 coup but resigned Jan. 10. The European Union voted Jan. 20 to commit 500 soldiers to operate alongside 1,600 French troops and 4,000 African peacekeepers already working in the country. International donors pledged $496 mil in assistance.

Temporary Armistice in South Sudan Signed But Sporadic Fighting Continues—The government of South Sudan and a rebel alliance agreed to a temporary ceasefire Jan. 23 following clashes that left over 450,000 displaced and close to 10,000 dead, including nearly 200 refugees whose boat overturned on the White Nile River. The government agreed to accelerate the release of 11 rebels it had been holding since fighting began five weeks earlier in the country's capital of Juba, when Pres. Salva Kiir accused ousted Vice Pres. Riek Machar and his rebel group of attempting a coup. The United Nations reported Jan. 29 that isolated skirmishes were still occurring but said that fighting had decreased since the ceasefire.

Multination Syrian Peace Talks Stalemate; War Spills Into Lebanon—The Syrian government of Pres. Bashar al-Assad and the opposition Syrian National Coalition failed to agree on steps toward political transition during negotiations attended by some 40 countries Jan. 22-31 in Montreux and Geneva, Switzerland. The talks were the first formal meeting of the two sides in the three-year-old war, which the UK-based Syrian Observatory for Human Rights (SOHR) reported has claimed the lives of more than 136,000 as of Jan. 31. Syrian negotiators rejected Coalition demands that Assad step down from power. The two sides also disagreed on steps to alleviate suffering in the besieged central western city of Homs. Assad has forbidden aid to the city, but the government said during the peace talks that it would allow women and children to evacuate. In the leadup to the summit, the UN retracted Iran's invitation to attend the talks because it would not publicly support the formation of a Syrian transitional government, a precondition demanded by the U.S.

At least 482 were killed in clashes Jan. 3-10 between Syrian rebels and the anti-Assad, Sunni militant group ISIS. In evidence of the war's spread to Lebanon, one person was killed and six were wounded Jan. 5 during fighting between Tripoli districts that support opposing sides in the Syrian conflict, and at least 7 people were killed and 15 wounded by a rocket that crossed from Syria into the anti-Assad border city of Arsal, Jan. 17.

General

Florida State Defeats Auburn to Claim College Football Championship—The Florida State Seminoles won a third national title Jan. 6, narrowly defeating the Auburn Tigers, 34-31, in Pasadena, CA. Heisman Trophy-winning quarterback Jameis Winston, the game's offensive MVP, completed 20 of 35 passes for two touchdowns and 237 yards. The Seminoles rebounded from an 18-point deficit, the largest ever overcome in a BCS national championship game. It was the 16th and final BCS title game; the 2014 season will introduce a four-team playoff.

Three Elected to Baseball Hall of Fame—The Baseball Writers' Assn. of America elected pitchers Greg Maddux and Tom Glavine and slugger Frank Thomas to the Natl. Baseball Hall of Fame Jan. 8. All three were in their first year of eligibility. Maddux, a four-time Cy Young Award-winner, was elected with 97.2% of the vote, the eighth highest in history. Glavine, a 10-time All-Star who achieved the fourth-highest number of wins among left-handed pitchers, received 91.9%. Thomas, who won MVP awards in 1993 and 1994 and concluded his career with 521 career home runs, received 83.7% of the votes. Career home-run record-holder Barry Bonds, who was widely suspected of using performance enhancing drugs (PEDs), received just 34.7% in his second year of eligibility.

Arrest Made in Decades-Old Lufthansa Heist—An alleged senior member of the Bonanno crime family, 78-year-old Vincent Asaro, was charged Jan. 23 with participating in the 1978 robbery of $6 mil in cash and jewels from JFK Intl. Airport in New York, NY. The so-called Lufthansa heist was then the largest cash robbery in U.S. history and was a key plot element of the film *Goodfellas* (1990). Although a Lufthansa cargo agent indicted in 1979 was the only person convicted, authorities long suspected the mastermind to be now-deceased James "Jimmy the Gent" Burke. Asaro was also charged with the 1969 murder of suspected informant Paul Katz, whose remains FBI agents discovered in the basement of a home owned by Burke's daughter in Queens, NY.

Na, Wawrinka Win Australian Open Titles—In her third Australian Open final in four years, Li Na of China defeated Dominika Cibulkova of Slovakia (7-6 (7-3), 6-0) at Rod Laver Arena in Melbourne, Jan. 25. The 31-year-old Na became the oldest women's champion in Australia in the Open era. The next evening, Switzerland's Stanislas Wawrinka won his first Grand Slam title against Spain's Rafael Nadal (6-3, 6-2, 3-6, 6-3). Nadal, who had prevailed over eighth-seed Wawrinka in all 12 of their prior matches, received treatment after injuring his back in the second set of the 2-hr., 21-min. match.

Daft Punk, Macklemore and Ryan Lewis "Get Lucky" at the Grammy Awards—French electronic music duo Daft Punk won five Grammy Awards and the duo of rapper Macklemore and producer Ryan Lewis won four awards at the ceremony held in Los Angeles, CA, on Jan. 26. Daft Punk won album of the year and record of the year for *Random Access Memories* and "Get Lucky," respectively. Macklemore and Ryan Lewis nearly swept the rap categories in addition to winning the best new artist Grammy. The rap duo performed "Same Love" with singers Madonna and Mary Lambert while rapper and actress Queen Latifah officiated at the onstage weddings of 33 same-sex couples.

February 2014
National

Stock Market Recovers Early Losses; Other Economic News—The Dow Jones Industrial Average Feb. 3 experienced its greatest daily point drop since June 2013, falling 326 points, or –2.1%, to close at 15,372.80. Similarly, the S&P 500 closed Feb. 3 at 1,741.89, down 2.3% from the previous trading day. But both rebounded strongly; the S&P finished the month at 1,859.45, up 4.3% from Jan., and the Dow closed Feb. at 16,321.71, up 4.0% over the previous month. The Nasdaq Composite Index ended Feb. at 4,308.12, up 5.0% from Jan. According to the Labor Dept.'s Feb. 7 report, the U.S. economy gained 113,000 jobs in Jan., trimming the monthly unemployment rate to 6.6% from 6.7% in Dec. 2013, while adding 499,000 people to the workforce.

Comcast Feb. 13 announced a $45-bil deal to acquire media firm Time Warner Cable that would merge the country's largest and second-largest cable TV providers. The merger was expected to be scrutinized by antitrust regulators. One of the world's largest bitcoin exchanges, Mt. Gox, filed for bankruptcy protection Feb. 28 four days after the debt-ridden company discovered the disappearance of almost 850,000 bitcoin from its virtual coffers. Tokyo-based Mt. Gox halted trading and prevented investors from withdrawing money after it learned that hackers had infiltrated its online platform Feb. 7. Investor confidence in the largely unregulated five-year-old digital currency fell sharply after the shutdown, with bitcoin prices dropping to $550 per coin from about $800 at the start of Feb.

Pentagon Proposes Reducing Army to Pre-WWII Numbers—In a Feb. 2 news conference, Defense Sec. Chuck Hagel announced that the Pentagon's 2015 budget recommendations, which took into account sequestration cuts, included plans to shrink the size of the U.S. Army to its lowest active troop levels since 1940. The department's proposed $496-bil budget for fiscal year 2015 called for the Army's active troop levels to drop to 440,000-450,000 by 2019—down from 570,000 during the peak of the wars in Afghanistan and Iraq. The Pentagon acknowledged the reduction could expose troops to greater risks and would not allow for long-term foreign occupations, but argued the military needed to shift strategy away from large-scale land wars as it prepares for nearly a trillion dollars in budget cuts over the next decade. In a joint statement, Sens. Lindsey Graham (R, SC) and John McCain (R, AZ) vowed to block the proposal, which they said would weaken the nation's security.

Obama Signs $956-Billion Farm Bill, Debt Limit Suspension—Pres. Barack Obama Feb. 7 signed into law a five-year "farm bill" that cut $16.6 bil from agricultural subsidies and food assistance programs, following four years of contentious congressional debate. The bill, which was expected to cost the federal government an estimated $956 bil over the next decade, was passed by the House Jan. 29, 251-166, and by the Senate Feb. 4, 68-32. The legislation discontinued some federal subsidies, including the practice of giving farmers per-acre fixed payments regardless of crop yield. The government will continue to pay approximately 62% of farmers' crop insurance premiums in lieu of direct payments, which totaled some $5 bil. In addition to subsidies, legislators clashed over funding the U.S. Dept. of Agriculture's Supplemental Nutritional Assistance Program, better known as the food stamp program, which constitutes nearly 80% of the farm bill budget. The final bill trimmed some $8 bil from that program over 10 years—far less than the $40 bil cut in the House's version of the bill. The food stamp funding cuts prompted criticism from anti-poverty advocates, as the Congressional Budget Office estimated that approximately 850,000 households nationwide would see benefits reduced.

Pres. Obama signed legislation Feb. 15 suspending the federal government's borrowing limit through Mar. 15, 2015. The country's debt ceiling had been restored on Feb. 7 at $17.2 trillion after its previous suspension in Oct. 2013 at $16.7 trillion. The bill passed the House Feb. 11, 221-201, with 28 Republicans joining 193 Democrats, and cleared the Senate Feb. 12, 55-43, on party lines. The Congressional Budget Office Feb. 4 projected a $514-bil deficit for fiscal year 2014, down from $680 bil in 2013.

International

Ukrainian Revolution Turns Violent; Parliament Impeaches President—Demonstrations in the Ukrainian capital of Kiev claimed the lives of dozens in Feb. and drove Ukrainian Pres. Viktor Yanukovych from power. Anti-government demonstrations had begun in late Nov. 2013 in opposition to the pro-Russian Yanukovych's abandonment of a free trade agreement with the European Union. Protesters staged largely peaceful demonstrations of up to 800,000 people in Kiev, but two protesters were killed Jan. 22, six days before Ukrainian Prime Min. Mykola Azarov resigned and parliament annulled a new anti-protest law. In mid-Feb., demonstrators abandoned City Hall—which they had occupied since Dec. 2013—after the government offered amnesty to over 230 jailed protesters. But clashes in Kiev's Independence Square between protesters and security forces ignited Feb. 18, killing at least 18, including 7 police officers. Protesters took over the square Feb. 20 in rioting that killed at least 40. The EU, despite criticism from Russia, imposed economic sanctions on Ukrainian officials thought to be responsible for escalating the violence. A deal signed Feb. 21 between opposition leaders and the government called for Yanukovych to hold early presidential elections, form a unity government, and establish constitutional reforms. But Yanukovych fled as protesters took control of the capital. Parliament formally removed him from power Feb. 22 and named Oleksandr Turchynov as acting president. Yanukovych, who later surfaced in Russia, denounced the events as a coup, and the new government issued an arrest warrant Feb. 24 for his role in protesters' deaths.

China and Taiwan Hold First Meetings in 65 Years—Representatives from China and Taiwan met in Nanjing, China, Feb. 11 for their first formal talks since 1949, when Nationalists led by Chiang Kai-shek fled mainland China for Taiwan after their defeat by Communist forces loyal to Mao Zedong. Officials discussed building upon economic ties, establishing lines of communication between governments, and opening offices in one another's country. While the talks resulted in few substantive changes, observers noted their symbolic importance—China does not officially recognize the government of Taiwan, and the two countries previously communicated only through semiofficial agencies. Taiwanese Pres. Ma Ying-jeou has worked to develop closer economic ties with China, and trade between the two countries has doubled since he took office in 2008, to $197 bil in 2013.

Protests Spark Violence in Venezuela—More than a week of demonstrations both for and against Venezuelan Pres. Nicolás Maduro Moros in cities across the country descended into violence that killed three in Caracas Feb. 12, sparking the country's worst strife in a decade. Activists opposed to Maduro, who was narrowly elected in Apr. 2013, had organized the demonstrations to protest widespread poverty, increasing crime, and alleged state-sponsored repression and human rights violations. As the protests spread, counterdemonstrations by Maduro supporters also grew. Maduro accused three U.S. consular officials of working with the opposition and ordered their expulsion Feb. 16. Tens of thousands of demonstrators advocating both sides assembled Feb. 22 in Caracas, where some activists called for Maduro to disarm vigilante groups who they asserted were responsible for increasing violence. As of May 2, at least 41 people had died in the unrest and the government had arrested more than 2,000.

Political Unrest in Thailand Turns Violent; Prime Minister Faces Corruption Charges—Attacks Feb. 22-23 on protesters calling for the resignation of Thai Prime Min. Yingluck Shinawatra left four dead, including three children, and more than 50 injured. Shinawatra refused to resign and condemned the attacks, which the opposition People's Democratic Reform Committee blamed on her regime. The demonstrations were a continuation of large-scale protests that have embroiled Thailand since Nov., when tens of thousands of largely middle-class activists from Bangkok and the southern region of the country objected to a government-backed amnesty bill that would have allowed Shinawatra's billionaire brother, former prime minister Thaksin Shinawatra, to return to Thailand without serving a two-year prison term for corruption charges. Critics contend that he continued to run the government from exile. Shinawatra imposed wide-ranging security measures in Jan. and her government retained the support of rural northern residents, who benefited from welfare measures instituted by the former prime minister before his 2006 ouster. Thailand's anti-corruption agency charged Prime Min. Shinawatra Feb. 27 with negligently handling a rice-subsidy program.

General

Seahawks Crush Broncos in Super Bowl XLVIII; Other NFL News—The Seattle Seahawks routed the Denver Broncos, 43-8, at MetLife Stadium in East Rutherford, NJ, Feb. 2 to win Super Bowl XLVIII. Seahawks defensive end Cliff Avril chalked up a two-point safety just 12 sec. into the game—the quickest score in Super Bowl history—and Seattle held their opponents scoreless until the Broncos completed a touchdown on the final play of the third quarter. The win marked the Seahawks' first Super Bowl title and their 35-point victory was the largest Super Bowl win margin since 1993. Seahawks lineman Malcolm Smith, who returned an interception 69 yards for a touchdown, was the game's MVP. An average 112.2 mil viewers tuned in, making it the most watched game in history; the halftime show, starring Bruno Mars and the Red Hot Chili Peppers, also set an all-time high, with 115.3 mil viewers.

Six-time All-Pro punter and 14-season Oakland Raider Ray Guy became the first punter ever elected to the Pro Football Hall of Fame Feb. 1. Defensive lineman Michael Sam of the Univ. of Missouri Tigers publicly declared Feb. 9 that he was gay, paving the way for the 2013 Southeastern Conference Defensive Player of the Year to become the first openly gay player drafted into the NFL. (Sam was drafted by St. Louis in the 7th and final round of the 2014 NFL Draft, May 10.)

According to an NFL report released Feb. 14, Miami Dolphins guard Richie Incognito and two teammates subjected Dolphins offensive tackle Jonathan Martin to almost daily harassment and bullying, including sexual taunts and racial slurs. Incognito was suspended for the final eight games of the season—two without pay—the week after Martin left the team in Oct. 2013. The Dolphins Mar. 11 traded Martin to the San Francisco 49ers.

XXII Winter Olympics Held in Sochi, Russia—More than 2,800 athletes from 88 countries competed in 98 events at the XXII Olympic Winter Games hosted Feb. 7-23 by Sochi, Russia. Russia led in gold medals with 13, including victories in the inaugural team figure skating event, the two- and four-man bobsled races, and pairs figure skating. Russia also led in the overall medal count with 33 (13 gold, 11 silver, 9 bronze), followed by the U.S. with 28 (9-7-12) and Norway with 26 (11-5-10). Belarusian biathlonist Darya Domracheva was the only athlete to win three individual gold medals, and Norway's cross-country skier Marit Bjoergen won three gold medals in 2014, giving her 10 career medals, the most ever for a female athlete in the Winter Olympics. Forty-year-old biathlete Ole Einar Bjoerndalen of Norway became the oldest Winter Olympic gold medalist in an individual event by winning the men's 10k sprint Feb. 8; he also tied the career overall record for Winter Olympic medals with 12 medals. U.S. ice dancers Meryl Davis and Charlie White became the first U.S. pair to win gold in the ice dancing competition Feb. 17. Other standout performers included Russia's short-track speed skater Viktor Ahn (3-0-1); and Ireen Wust (2-3-0), one of several Dutch speed skaters who collectively earned gold in 8 of 12 events and won 23 of 36 possible medals.

Sochi also hosted the Paralympic Games, Mar. 7-16, in which 45 countries were represented by nearly 550 athletes with disabilities. The Russian team finished first with 80 medals (30 gold, 28 silver, 22 bronze), followed by Ukraine with 25 (5-9-11) and the U.S. with 18 (2-7-9).

Storm Kills Dozens in U.S.; UK Hit With Flooding—A major ice storm struck the U.S. Feb. 11 in Texas and moved eastward, leaving more than 500,000 in Georgia and the Carolinas without power. The same storm system dumped up to 15 in. of snow in Washington, DC, and pummeled the Northeast. In total, the storm system caused at least 26 deaths in the U.S. Meteorologists attributed frequent storms and bitterly cold temperatures in Jan. and Feb. in parts of the U.S. and Canada to a southerly shifting of the Arctic polar vortex air mass. The polar vortex was also thought to be responsible for high winds and record winter rainfall, which caused severe flooding across Wales and southern and central England from early Dec. to late Feb. and contributed to the deaths of at least 11 people. Parts of Ireland and Wales were hit Feb. 12 with winds of up to 108 mph.

Mexican Drug Cartel Boss Captured—Mexican marines Feb. 22 apprehended Joaquin "El Chapo" Guzman Loera, the apparent leader of the Sinaloa Cartel, the world's dominant drug trafficking organization. Guzman had eluded authorities since 2001 following his escape in a laundry cart from a maximum security prison where he was serving a 20-year sentence on charges that included murder, racketeering, and money laundering. Despite facing indictments from at least six U.S. and four Mexican states, Guzman received public support from at least 1,000 people who demonstrated in the Sinaloa state capital to demand his release. Since 2007, more than 80,000 people have died in Mexico's drug war.

March 2014
National

Recalls Plague General Motors, Toyota—The Justice Dept. initiated a criminal investigation, reported Mar. 11, into why General Motors (GM) waited more than a decade to start recalls for vehicles with defective ignition switches, manufactured by Delphi, linked to at least 13 deaths and 32 accidents. The switches could turn off engines mid-use, thereby disabling power steering and airbag systems even if a car was in motion. In a Mar. 12 filing with federal safety regulators, GM admitted to having known about the safety issue as far back as 2001, though it asserted its belief that the problem had been fixed. GM began recalling vehicles with the defective switches Feb. 7; the initial recall covered about 800,000 vehicles, but this number rose to 2.6 mil by the end of Mar. Newly appointed GM CEO Mary Barra apologized publicly to families of the victims at an Apr. 1 House subcommittee hearing and later confirmed that GM would set up a fund to compensate victims and affected families. The National Highway Traffic Safety Administration May 16 fined GM $35 mil for its failure to act. The automaker's troubles continued May 20, as it issued four unrelated recalls; by June 30, it had recalled more than 27 mil vehicles in the U.S., at an estimated cost of $2.5 bil.

Toyota agreed Mar. 19 to admit wrongdoing and pay a $1.2-bil criminal fine—the largest ever for an automaker in the U.S.—to end a U.S. government probe into charges that the company hid information about defective parts that caused sudden acceleration in several models. Toyota had recalled more than 10 mil vehicles in 2009-10 and faced several hundred wrongful death lawsuits. On Apr. 9, Toyota announced it was recalling nearly 6.4 mil vehicles for steering and other issues.

Indicators Paint Mixed Picture; Other Economic News—The Bureau of Economic Analysis's revised figures for the fourth quarter of 2013, released Mar. 27, showed that real GDP grew by only 2.6% compared to 4.1% in the third quarter. In addition to a 12.8% decrease in federal spending over the fourth quarter, residential investment fell sharply, declining by 7.9%. GDP growth for 2013 was 1.9%, down from the 2012 growth of 2.8%. The Dow Jones Industrial Average remained above 16,000 throughout Mar., closing the month at 16,457.66, up 0.8% from Feb. The S&P 500 also held steady, finishing Mar. at 1,872.34, up 0.7% from Feb., while the Nasdaq Composite Index closed the month at 4,198.99, down 2.5% from Feb. The Labor Dept. reported Mar. 7 that the economy had added 175,000 jobs in Feb. and the unemployment rate had edged up to 6.7% from 6.6% in Jan. as more people entered the workforce.

Obama Unveils 2015 Federal Budget—Pres. Barack Obama Mar. 4 proposed a $3.9-tril federal budget for fiscal year 2015 (which begins Oct. 1, 2014) that would increase infrastructure spending and continue deficit reduction, projecting a $564-bil deficit for 2015 that would fall to $413 bil in 2018. The budget was not expected to pass Congress but rather to serve as an outline of the administration's policy agenda. The proposal differed only slightly from Obama's 2014 budget, most notably by dropping a modest entitlement reform that had been seen as a gesture of compromise that would curb Social Security spending by changing the inflation measure used to calculate cost-of-living. In opposition to automatic spending reductions imposed by the 2013 budget sequestration, the new budget would provide $56 bil to climate research, job training, and other selected programs. In addition to $651 bil in new revenue from wealthy taxpayers, the proposal sought to expand the earned income tax credit and increase tobacco taxes to finance $76 bil in early childhood education improvements over the next decade. Congressional Republicans rebuffed the proposal, which exceeded spending limits put in place in the Dec. 2013 budget deal.

CIA Misconduct Alleged in Senate; Obama Outlines NSA Reforms—Sen. Dianne Feinstein (D, CA), the chair of the Senate Intelligence Committee, accused the Central Intelligence Agency Mar. 11 of hacking into Senate staff members' computers and secretly deleting classified files during the course of an investigation into post-9/11 interrogation techniques. Feinstein objected on the Senate floor to CIA Dir. John Brennan's claim that personnel removed files they believed her staff was not authorized to view. The senator said she believed the CIA had violated federal domestic spying laws by removing documents to which she said her staff had been granted access. The *Washington Post* Mar. 31 reported the committee's conclusion that the CIA had systematically deceived the government by burying details about the harshness of its enhanced interrogation program and overstating its effectiveness.

Pres. Obama Mar. 27 proposed plans to discontinue the Natl. Security Agency's bulk collection and storage of telephone data, conducted since the Patriot Act became law in 2001. The government instead would need to secure separate court orders to search records stored by telephone companies for 18 months. The proposal must pass Congress, which was considering a similar plan that would end bulk collection of data and require a court order—based on reasonable suspicion—to access data within two degrees of separation of a suspected terrorist.

Obamacare Enrollment Deadline Passes; HHS Secretary Resigns—Mar. 31 marked the end of the six-month enrollment period for private individual health insurance plans offered in accordance with the 2010 Patient Protection and Affordable Care Act (ACA), informally referred to as Obamacare. Pres. Obama said Apr. 1 that 7.1 mil had signed up through state and federal health care exchanges, slightly exceeding the initial enrollment target.

The enrollment period was not without complications, especially on the insurance exchanges, which were bogged down by many technical bugs, particularly at the beginning of the enrollment period. (Due to issues with the enrollment websites, the administration extended the deadline to mid-Apr. for people who had started applications but were unable to complete enrollment by the Mar. deadline.) The Treasury Dept. Feb. 10 had pushed back to the start of 2016 the date by which companies with 50-99 full-time employees must provide insurance plans or face fines. The administration Mar. 5 announced that consumers could continue on plans that did not meet ACA minimum requirements through Oct. 2016.

Health and Human Services Sec. Kathleen Sebelius announced her resignation Apr. 10. She had served in the post since Apr. 2009 and faced criticism for mishandling the rollout of many Obamacare measures, including the issues with the insurance exchanges. The Senate June 5 confirmed Office of Management and Budget director Sylvia Mathews Burwell as the new HHS secretary.

International

Russia Annexes Crimea Amid International Criticism—After pro-Russia gunmen seized airports and government buildings Feb. 27-28 in Crimea in southern Ukraine, Russia's parliament Mar. 1 unanimously approved Pres. Vladimir Putin's request to use force there to protect Russian interests. Russia's UN envoy claimed that it had deployed troops to the semiautonomous peninsula at the request of former Ukrainian Pres. Viktor Yanukovych, who was ousted in Feb. after months of popular unrest. The Crimean parliament announced Mar. 6 that the region would hold a referendum on whether to formally secede and join Russia, which had held the region until 1954. According to the official results of the Mar. 16 referendum, voter turnout was more than 80% of eligible Crimeans, and 96.8% voted to secede and unite with Russia. A day earlier, the UN Security Council attempted to pass a resolution declaring the referendum invalid; Russia vetoed that resolution, but the European Union and U.S. imposed individual sanctions Mar. 17. Russian forces continued seizing military bases in the region, resulting in the death Mar. 18 of a Ukrainian soldier at a facility in Simferopol. Putin Mar. 18 signed a treaty annexing Crimea, which was ratified by the Russian Parliament Mar. 20-21. Ukraine Mar. 21 ordered the evacuation of all of its military personnel from Crimea three days later.

The Group of Eight (G8) industrialized countries voted to expel Russia Mar. 24, and the Intl. Monetary Fund announced Mar. 27 that it would extend up to $18 bil in rescue loans to Ukraine. Russia deployed some 40,000 military personnel along its western border with Ukraine, which Putin told German Chancellor Angela Merkel Mar. 31 that he would partially withdraw.

Boko Haram Violence Kills Scores in Nigeria—Staggered bomb blasts engineered by Boko Haram insurgents killed about 50 people Mar. 1 at a soccer facility in Maiduguri in northeastern Nigeria. Boko Haram agents later that day wiped out the village of Mainok, killing 47, and killed at least 29 more in the town of Mafa the next day, sending government troops fleeing. Dedicated to establishing a strict Islamist state, the 12-year-old group first launched attacks in 2009 on police stations and government buildings. Boko Haram has since escalated its campaign of violence—including a Feb. 25 arson attack on a school that killed dozens and a Mar. 14 attack on a military barracks—and was designated a terrorist organization by the U.S. in 2010. Nigerian Pres. Goodluck Jonathan declared a state of emergency for three northeastern states in May 2013 in response to growing violence.

Malaysian Airliner Vanishes; Extensive Search Inconclusive—Air traffic controllers Mar. 8 permanently lost contact with Malaysia Airlines Flight 370 about 40 min. after its departure from Kuala Lumpur, Malaysia, bound for Beijing, China, carrying 227 passengers and 12 crewmembers. Malaysian Prime Min. Najib Razak announced Mar. 24 that the plane was presumed lost in the southern Indian Ocean, with no survivors. The search, which involved more than 25 nations, significantly shifted locations several times and was criticized as mishandled and confused from the start, with much of the blame from victims' families landing on the Malaysian government. Satellite images of objects resembling floating wreckage failed to lead to the plane. Searchers attempting to locate the plane's signal-emitting flight-data recorder, or black box, before its batteries expired detected, in early Apr., two sets of underwater pings that Australian officials discounted in late May. The search—reportedly the most expensive in aviation history—expanded in mid-Apr. to include a seafloor-sweeping robotic submersible.

French Socialists Fall at Polls, Appoint New Prime Minister—In municipal elections marked by record-low turnout Mar. 23 and 30, France's Socialist Party experienced huge losses, failing to retain control in more than 150 cities. Support shifted to the center-right UMP, the party of former Pres. Nicolas Sarkozy, which together with its allies captured 46% of the vote. Socialists, Greens, and other left-wing parties won 40% of the vote. The far-right Natl. Front party won about 7% of the vote and control in 11 towns for its best poll showing yet. Socialists retained leadership in Paris, which elected Anne Hidalgo as its first female mayor. French Pres. François Hollande named centrist socialist Manuel Valls, previously the government's interior minister, to replace Jean-Marc Ayrault, whose government resigned in the wake of the results Mar. 31, as prime minister.

Rebel Group Signs Philippine Peace Pact After Decades of Unrest—The Philippines government and the Moro Islamic Liberation Front (MILF), the country's largest militant Islamist group, signed a long sought-after peace agreement Mar. 27 creating a semi-autonomous region in Mindano, home to a majority of the country's 5 mil Muslims. The deal, set to take effect in 2015, grants greater political autonomy and allows the region to retain a large share of natural resource revenues. In exchange, MILF will disband its guerrilla forces. The pact was an effort to end 45 years of violent conflict that has claimed the lives of more than 120,000 people and displaced some 2 mil. Several other groups remain opposed to the peace process, including Abu Sayyaf, which lost 25 fighters when it clashed with government forces in late Apr. during an attempt to take control of a training camp.

General

12 Years a Slave, Gravity **Big Winners at Oscars**—The antebellum drama *12 Years a Slave* received the Oscar for best picture at the 86th Academy Awards ceremony in Los Angeles, CA, Mar. 2. Best director went to Alfonso Cuarón for his space thriller *Gravity*, which won seven Oscars. Golden Globe-winner Matthew McConaughey won his first Oscar for best actor in a leading role for his portrayal of AIDS activist Ron Woodroof in *Dallas Buyers Club*; Jared Leto won best supporting actor for the same film. Australian Cate Blanchett received best actress for Woody Allen's *Blue Jasmine*, and Mexican-Kenyan Lupita Nyong'o won best supporting actress for *12 Years a Slave*. Second-time Oscar host Ellen DeGeneres helped the broadcast draw 43.7 mil viewers, the most since the 2000 ceremony.

Cosmic Inflation Evidence Strengthens Big Bang Theory—Dr. John Kovac of the Harvard-Smithsonian Center for Astrophysics announced Mar. 17 that a team of astronomers had identified light wave patterns that are considered evidence that the universe rapidly expanded some 13.8 bil years ago, just after its formation from the so-called Big Bang. Using a telescope located at the ultra-arid South Pole, researchers spent three years scanning a small portion of the sky for faint light ripples (known as gravitational waves) remaining from the origins of the universe. Although it has been generally accepted for decades that the universe underwent "cosmic inflation" just after its birth, Kovac's team was the first to document the twisting light pattern considered to be its signature. (The evidence required further analysis and confirmation to ascertain its exact significance.)

Washington State Mudslide Kills 43—A deadly landslide Mar. 22 engulfed 49 houses and buildings along Washington state's Stillaguamish River, killing 43. Destabilized by twice the average rainfall over the previous 45 days, a section of a 600-ft hill collapsed into a rapidly moving, mile-wide wall of mud, trees, and other debris near the town of Oso, approximately 55 mi northeast of Seattle. Hundreds of search-and-rescue personnel converged on the site, rescuing at least eight survivors from the muck, which was up to 40 ft deep. The state's lieutenant governor declared a state of emergency that evening and Pres. Obama Apr. 2 declared a major disaster, paving the way for displaced residents to receive federal aid. A county official's comments about the "completely unforeseen" nature of the slide generated criticism from geologists who pointed to seven notable slides in the area since 1937—most recently in 2006.

Obama Visits Pope at Vatican; Francis Canonizes Predecessors—Pres. Obama Mar. 27 met Pope Francis in Vatican City for the first time since the pontiff's election a year earlier. The two discussed poverty, immigration policy, and human trafficking, in addition to "religious freedom, life, and conscientious objection," a likely reference to the ongoing battle over the U.S. church leadership's objection to an Affordable Care Act provision mandating that employers offer insurance covering contraceptives.

In an unprecedented dual ceremony a month later, Pope Francis Apr. 27 declared two of his 20th-century predecessors, Pope John Paul II and Pope John XXIII, to be saints. More than 800,000 people crowded St. Peter's Square and the surrounding area in Vatican City to watch the canonizations, at which Pope Emeritus Benedict XVI made a rare public appearance.

April 2014
National

Home Lending Plummets; Other Economic News—The first quarter of 2014 saw mortgage lending sink to its lowest level since 1997, with homeowners borrowing $235 bil in Jan.-Mar., a 58% drop from the same period the year before and a 23% decrease from fourth quarter 2013. Analysts attributed the trend to stricter credit requirements and rising average interest rates, which the Federal Home Loan Mortgage Corp. Apr. 3 reported at 4.41% for a 30-year loan, up nearly a percentage point from Apr. 2013.

In contrast to the sluggish mortgage market, the Dow Jones Industrial Average closed Apr. at a record-high 16,580.84, up 0.7% from Mar., while the S&P 500 finished the month at a near-record 1,883.95, a 0.6% increase from Mar. The Nasdaq Composite Index fell 2.0% in Apr., closing the month at 4,114.56. The Dept. of Labor Apr. 4 reported that the economy had added 192,000 jobs in Mar. According to the government, unemployment for Mar. remained fixed at Feb.'s rate of 6.7%, with 503,000 additional people entering the labor force.

U.S. regulators Apr. 9 ordered Bank of America to pay $727 mil to consumers for misleading marketing and unfair billing practices relating to add-ons including identify-theft and payment-protection products. According to the Consumer Financial Protection Bureau, the company had misled 1.4 mil consumers and unfairly billed 1.9 mil.

House Republicans Propose Budget, Spending Cuts—House Budget Committee Chair Paul Ryan (R, WI) Apr. 1 unveiled the Republican's $3.7-tril budget plan for fiscal year 2015, which would cut $5.1 tril from projected federal spending over 10 years. In contrast to Pres. Barack Obama's $3.9-tril proposal, which did not include major changes to entitlement programs, Ryan's blueprint aimed to repeal Obamacare and transform Medicare coverage by giving future recipients the option to use government subsidies to buy private insurance plans. Ryan, the 2012 Republican vice-presidential nominee and a likely 2016 presidential contender, forecast that his plan would balance the budget over the course of a decade, though some analysts called that conclusion into question due to the methodology used. The House Apr. 10 voted 219-205 to pass Ryan's plan. The Senate was expected to reject it.

Supreme Court Ends Overall Limits on Campaign Donations—The U.S. Supreme Court Apr. 2 ruled, 5-4, in *McCutcheon v. Federal Election Commission*, to overturn caps to limit the total aggregate dollar amount individuals can contribute to candidates and political parties in a two-year election cycle. The case against the limits, in place since the 1970s, was brought by Alabama businessman Shaun McCutcheon, who was joined in the suit by the Republican Natl. Committee. The court's ruling left in place caps on donations to individual candidates, parties, and political action committees. Writing for the majority, Chief Justice John Roberts said that political contributions are tantamount to free speech and should therefore be regulated only to safeguard against "a direct exchange of an official act for money," or the appearance of such, not to lessen the amount of money in politics. Associate Justice Stephen Breyer wrote the dissent, which argued the decision defined corruption too narrowly and, by allowing the political process to be influenced by too much money, would damage the "marketplace of ideas" protected by the First Amendment.

Fort Hood Shooting Kills Four; Other Incidents of Mass Violence—A shooter at Fort Hood military base in Texas shot and killed three people and injured 16 others Apr. 2 before taking his own life. Officials did not establish a clear motive for the gunman, identified as Army specialist Ivan Lopez, but confirmed that, minutes before the shooting, he had been in a heated argument over the handling of his request for a leave of absence. Fort Hood was also the site of a shooting that killed 13 in 2009.

Brandishing two eight-inch kitchen knives, a 16-year-old student reportedly stabbed 20 students and a security guard Apr. 9 at a high school in Murrysville, PA. A 73-year-old former Ku Klux Klan leader was accused of fatally shooting three people Apr. 13 at a Jewish community center and retirement village in Overland Park, KS. A package handler at a suburban Atlanta FedEx facility Apr. 29 shot and wounded six people—three critically—before fatally shooting himself.

Oklahoma Inmate Dies During Botched Lethal Injection—Clayton Lockett, convicted and sentenced to death in 2000 for the 1999 rape and murder of a 19-year-old woman, died of cardiac arrest Apr. 29 shortly after a doctor at the Oklahoma State Penitentiary in McAlester determined that, due to complications stemming from a collapsed vein, Lockett had not received a lethal dose of the drugs intended to execute him. Although state officials reported Lockett became unconscious several minutes after the first injection, a sedative meant to render him unconscious, multiple witnesses said that he writhed, mumbled, and lifted his head until officials closed the blinds in the execution chamber 16 min. into the procedure. He was pronounced dead 43 min. after the first injection. Oklahoma Gov. Mary Fallin (R) stayed the execution of another inmate scheduled that same day and instructed the Dept. of Corrections to review the state's execution procedures.

A nationwide shortage of the drugs typically used to carry out lethal injections had called Oklahoma's execution procedures into question, with the state Supreme Court ruling for a delay but ultimately lifting a stay on the execution after weeks of political maneuvering by Fallin's office and the legislature. Pres. Obama described the incident as deeply troubling and asked the federal Justice Dept. to investigate death penalty programs nationwide.

International

Crimean Separatism Spreads to Eastern Ukraine; De-escalation Pact Stalls—Demonstrations in eastern Ukrainian cities continued into Apr. as protesters seeking union with Russia demanded Crimea-style referendums on self-determination. Activists in Donetsk, Kharkiv, and Luhansk stormed government buildings Apr. 6; Ukrainian authorities claimed armed separatists in Luhansk held nearly 60 people hostage for several days. Donetsk protesters established a self-proclaimed republic Apr. 7, but a regional poll released Apr. 9 showed just 4.7% of Donetsk residents wanted the region to secede. Countering Russia's claim that Ukraine was fomenting civil war, U.S. Sec. of State John Kerry and others in the international community asserted Apr. 8 that Russia had sent agents across the border to destabilize Ukraine. Under an agreement reached Apr. 17 in Geneva, Switzerland, the U.S., EU, Russia, and Ukraine agreed all parties needed to refrain

from violence and support disarming and disbanding separatist groups, but protesters did not disband and Ukraine and Russia each accused the other of breaking the pact.

Ukrainian forces held off some 100 pro-Russia attackers at a military base in Artemivsk Apr. 24, the same day its military killed up to five separatists near the pro-Russia stronghold of Sloviansk. Claiming Russia's right to protect ethnic Russians living in eastern Ukraine, the Russian military conducted training exercises along the Ukrainian border. The Group of Seven (G7) industrialized countries formally condemned Russia Apr. 25, and the U.S. announced new sanctions against Russia Apr. 28.

Nigerian Militants Abduct Hundreds of Schoolgirls—Agents of the al-Qaeda–linked Islamist group Boko Haram seized 276 mostly Christian teenage girls from a school in northeastern Nigeria, Apr. 14. Fifty-seven of the girls escaped by early May, while the group continued using its terror tactic, abducting at least 11 more girls from other Nigerian villages May 4. In response to perceived inaction from the Nigerian government in response to Boko Haram, parents of the missing girls and other concerned parties held demonstrations, pleaded with the international community, and raised awareness online; their #BringBackOurGirls campaign went viral. Boko Haram released a video May 5 in which the alleged Boko Haram leader threatened to sell the girls and demanded the release of imprisoned militants.

Nigerian Pres. Goodluck Jonathan scuttled a prisoner exchange deal in mid-May; later that month, an official of Nigeria's widely criticized military claimed that it knew the girls' whereabouts but considered rescue attempts to be too risky. According to the Council on Foreign Relations as of the end of Apr., Boko Haram had killed more than 4,000 people since 2011.

Israel Halts Peace Talks With Palestinians—The Israeli government suspended U.S.-brokered negotiations with the Palestinian Authority Apr. 24, a day after the Palestinians' ruling Fatah Party and the militant organization Hamas agreed to form a unity government. With the deadline on the nine-month-old peace talks set to expire, Israeli Prime Min. Benjamin Netanyahu said Israel would not resume talks with any government that includes Hamas, which Israel, the U.S., and the European Union consider a terrorist organization. The talks had been on the verge of collapse since Apr. 1 when Palestinian Authority Pres. Mahmoud Abbas signed accession letters to 15 conventions and treaties, breaking a pledge to not join world bodies during the negotiations. The Palestinians said the move was in response to Israel failing to carry out a planned release of prisoners Mar. 29.

Egyptian Court Sentences Morsi Supporters to Death—An Egyptian judge Apr. 28 handed down a preliminary sentence of death to Muslim Brotherhood leader Mohammed Badie and 682 others for alleged participation in Aug. 2013 riots in the central Egyptian city of Minya that killed a police officer. The Brotherhood said the government incited violence when military and police killed hundreds of supporters of ousted president Mohammed Morsi participating in sit-ins. The defendants were mostly in hiding and were barred from attending the trial. In a separate ruling the same day, the court commuted to life imprisonment 492 of 529 death sentences delivered the month before on identical charges. A court June 21 acquitted 496 of the 683 defendants while upholding death sentences for Badie and 182 alleged supporters and substituting life sentences for four others.

Obama Emphasizes Security and Trade on Asia Tour—At the start of a weeklong trip to Asia that wrapped up Apr. 29, Pres. Obama publicly declared the U.S. would defend Japan in its dispute with China over the resource-rich Senkaku Islands in the East China Sea. Further rankling China, the U.S. Apr. 28 signed a 10-year agreement with the Philippines. It provides the U.S. a substantial military footprint in the country for the first time since the early 1990s and will provide leverage against Chinese claims on islands the Philippines insists are within its exclusive economic zone. Obama also facilitated the final agreement of a binational defense team that would transfer control of South Korean troops to the U.S. in the event of war. U.S. efforts to recruit Japan and Malaysia to participate in a Trans-Pacific Partnership deal that would require the two countries to lower tariffs on imports remained fruitless.

General

Heartbleed Bug Leaves Users Vulnerable Online—OpenSSL, a developer of encryption tools used by the majority of Internet servers, posted an advisory on its website Apr. 7 regarding a two-year-old flaw in its software known as the Heartbleed bug, which allowed access to users' passwords and personal information. Although the company released patched software the same day, an estimated 600,000 websites were determined to be immediately vulnerable. Many companies and institutions quickly updated their sites, but over 300,000 had not yet installed the more secure software one month later. The Natl. Security Agency denied an Apr. 12 Bloomberg news report claiming the intelligence service had exploited the bug since 2012.

UConn Men and Women Win NCAA Basketball Tournaments—The Univ. of Connecticut Huskies defeated the Univ. of Kentucky Wildcats, 60-54, to win the school's fourth NCAA men's basketball championship Apr. 7 at AT&T Stadium in Arlington, TX. The victory—coach Kevin Ollie's first—for the 7th seed team came just a year after UConn was shut out of the postseason by the NCAA for poor academic performance. The Huskies led the Wildcats the entire game, with senior guard Shabazz Napier scoring 22 points; he was named the most outstanding player of the men's Final Four.

At the women's tournament final Apr. 8, the Univ. of Connecticut Huskies defeated the Notre Dame Fighting Irish, 79-58, at Bridgestone Arena in Nashville, TN, in the first NCAA basketball championship game to feature two undefeated teams. Sophomore Breanna Stewart led the Huskies with 21 points and was named most outstanding player of the women's Final Four for the second straight year. UConn head coach Geno Auriemma claimed his record ninth tournament victory. UConn's win marked the second time it won the men's and women's basketball championships in the same year; it is the only Division I school to have done so.

Bubba Watson Wins Second Masters Tournament—Bubba Watson donned the green Masters title jacket for the second time in three years after defeating 20-year-old Masters rookie Jordan Spieth at the Augusta Natl. Golf Club in Augusta, GA, Apr. 13. Spieth led most of the first half of the final round until Watson tied with a birdie on the eighth hole, and took the lead with another on the ninth. Watson finished the day with 69 strokes and 8-under-280 for the tournament, three shots ahead of both Spieth and Sweden's Jonas Blixt.

South Korean Ferry Accident Kills Hundreds—A 479-ft-long ferry capsized and sank Apr. 16 in calm waters off the southern coast of South Korea, killing 304 of 476 people on board. The passengers were mostly high school students. Officials attributed the disaster to insufficient ballast and improperly stowed cargo of more than three times the legal weight limit, which caused the ship to turn abruptly at high speed. Prosecutors charged the captain and three members of his crew with murder and other members of the crew with lesser charges. The CEO and other officials of Cheonghaejin Marine Co., which operated the ferry, were also arrested. The government received widespread criticism for responding slowly to the accident and providing inaccurate information. Prime Min. Chung Hongwon submitted his resignation Apr. 27, and Pres. Park Geun Hye announced plans to disband the Coast Guard May 19. After two nominees for prime minister withdrew amid controversy, Pres. Park retroactively rejected Chung's resignation June 26.

Avalanche Overtakes 16 on Everest—An avalanche swept down Mount Everest Apr. 18, killing 16 Nepali guides, most of them ethnic Sherpas, who had been preparing ropes approximately 19,000 ft up the mountain. Nine more were injured. The disaster marked the greatest loss of life in a single day on the 29,035-ft-tall peak, which straddles the border between Nepal and Tibet. Everest expedition companies canceled trips throughout the climbing season as Sherpas boycotted Everest and engaged in a dispute with the Nepalese government over regulations, insurance, and compensation for victims' families.

Deadly Tornadoes Hit Great Plains, Southeast—Some 75 tornadoes touched down Apr. 27-30 from Nebraska to North Carolina, killing at least 35 people. Central Arkansas was hit Apr. 27 by an EF-4 tornado that unleashed 180-190 mph winds on a 41-mi path. The tornado, which killed 16, was the deadliest tornado to hit Arkansas since 1968. The following day, 10 people were killed by another EF-4 funnel in Louisville, MS. At least seven EF-3 tornadoes with wind speeds of 136-165 mph struck Alabama, Mississippi, and Tennessee.

NBA Bans Team Owner for Racist Comments—Los Angeles Clippers team owner Donald Sterling was banned for life from the National Basketball Association Apr. 29 after TMZ Sports released a recording of Sterling asking his alleged mistress to refrain from bringing African Americans to Clippers games. In addition to the ban, which included a prohibition on his attending NBA games, NBA commissioner Adam Silver fined Sterling the maximum penalty of $2.5 mil. The NBA appointed an interim chief executive to the team May 9, three days before Sterling apologized during an interview on CNN. Shelly Sterling, Donald Sterling's estranged wife, negotiated the sale of the team May 29 for a record $2 bil to former Microsoft CEO Steve Ballmer. Donald Sterling sued to stop the sale in June, and also filed a $1-bil lawsuit against the NBA. A county superior court decision July 28, 2014, allowed the sale to move forward even if Sterling continued to appeal.

May 2014
National

AT&T and DirecTV Propose Merger; Other Business and Economic News—Telecom giant AT&T May 18 announced plans to acquire satellite TV provider DirecTV in a $48.5-bil stock-and-cash transaction. The merger required government approval in the U.S. and Latin America, but the companies hoped to close the deal within the next year. Testifying before Congress June 24, AT&T CEO Randall Stephenson claimed the merger would enable continued competition in the cable and broadband arenas, given the pending Comcast-Time Warner Cable merger, but lawmakers at the hearing voiced concern over industry consolidation.

Credit Suisse May 19 pleaded guilty to criminal charges and admitted that it had helped thousands of Americans evade taxes for decades. Under the terms of the plea deal, the Switzerland-based bank would pay $2.6 bil in penalties but was not required to turn over individual account records.

The Apr. jobs report, released May 2 by the Labor Dept., showed that 288,000 jobs were added to the U.S. economy, the strongest monthly showing since Jan. 2012. The report also showed the unemployment rate for Apr. had fallen to 6.3% but attributed the difference to 806,000 fewer people in the workforce. Revisions to earlier figures showed greater job growth during the first quarter of 2014, with an additional 36,000 jobs added during Feb. and Mar. The Dow Jones Industrial Average and the S&P 500 both finished May at record highs, giving both indices four straight months of growth. The Dow closed at 16,717.17 May 30, up 0.8% from Apr. The S&P 500 finished the month at 1,923.57, up 2.1%, and the Nasdaq Composite Index closed May at 4,242.62, up 3.1%.

Veterans Affairs Secretary Resigns in Midst of Health Care Scandal—Dept. of Veterans Affairs Sec. Eric Shinseki resigned May 30 in the wake of revelations that VA hospitals had routinely manipulated schedules to disguise patient waiting times exceeding three months. Following allegations of deadly delays made public by House Committee on Veterans' Affairs chair Rep. Jeff Miller (R, FL) Apr. 9, CNN reported Apr. 23 that at least 40 veterans in the Phoenix VA Health Care System had died awaiting treatment. The VA inspector general's office announced May 28 that 1,700 patients in the Phoenix system, including 35 who died, had been relegated to unofficial waiting lists. The inspector's office cited the practice as systemic within the organization and longstanding; patients waited an average of 115 days for appointments; A VA audit released June 9 revealed that more than 57,000 veterans waited at least 90 days for an appointment and another 64,000 never received an appointment.

The House June 10 unanimously passed a bill allowing veterans to receive treatment at non-VA hospitals under certain conditions; the Senate June 11 voted 93-3 to pass a similar bill, the same day the FBI launched a criminal investigation. The legislation was signed into law Aug. 7. Pres. Barack Obama June 30 nominated former Procter & Gamble CEO Bob McDonald as VA secretary; he was unanimously confirmed by the Senate July 29.

U.S. Exchanges Five Taliban Detainees for Imprisoned Soldier; Obama Outlines Afghanistan Transition—Pakistani militants linked to the Taliban freed U.S. Army Sgt. Bowe Bergdahl May 31 in exchange for five Taliban members detained in Guantánamo Bay, Cuba. Held for five years, Bergdahl was the only U.S. soldier known to be held captive in the war in Afghanistan. Critics of the exchange claimed the agreement would embolden militants to capture more soldiers and questioned whether Qatar, which took custody of the five detainees, would honor its pledge to enforce a one-year ban on their travel beyond its borders. Some lawmakers also asserted that the Obama administration had acted illegally when it failed to notify Congress 30 days in advance of the transfer. The administration contended that the "acute urgency" of the situation justified sidestepping Congress.

The circumstances of Bergdahl's capture came under renewed scrutiny following his release. Military officials confirmed that he had voluntarily left his unit's post, and personal letters and emails in which he had described his disillusionment with the Army's mission received further review.

Pres. Obama May 27 announced a new timetable to pull out all but 9,800 troops from Afghanistan by the end of 2014 and to reduce that number by half in 2015. The remainder would depart at the end of 2016.

International

Ukraine Digs in Against Separatists Amid Escalating Violence—Nearly 40 separatists fighting for union with Russia died in a building fire during clashes in Odesa May 2, one day after acting Ukrainian Pres. Olexander Turchynov reinstated military conscription to counter pro-Russian groups active in the eastern and southern portions of the country. In protest over the deaths, separatists stormed a government office in Odesa May 4 and caused the release of 67 separatists detained in the unrest. Ukrainian forces killed 30 rebels May 5 during an assault to retake the eastern city of Slovyansk. Russian Pres. Vladimir Putin May 7 urged separatists, who were widely believed to be backed by Russia, to postpone referendums on independence and engage in talks with the government. Despite public polls showing limited backing for secession, leaders of the "People's Republics" of Donetsk and Luhansk held unmonitored referendums May 11 and announced support for independence at 89% and 96%, respectively. The Ukrainian government and international officials dismissed the referenda as an illegal farce.

Separatists boycotted national reconciliation talks May 14 and further discussions held May 17. The United Nations issued a report May 16 outlining human rights violations perpetrated primarily by separatists. Continuing violence in eastern regions impeded participation in the May 25 presidential election, won by the pro-EU candidate Petro Poroshenko. Ukrainian forces May 27 initiated a successful assault to recapture the main airport in Donetsk, killing at least 40. Pro-Moscow rebels May 29 shot down a Ukrainian military helicopter—killing at least 14 people, including a general—using a rocket launcher believed to be Russian-made. U.S. Defense Sec. Chuck Hagel announced May 30 that Russia, publicly critical of Ukraine's military actions, had moved most of its troops away from the Ukrainian border.

Military Leader Wins Egyptian Presidential Election—Former general and defense minister Abdel Fattah al-Sisi claimed victory in Egypt's presidential election held May 26-28 with 97% of the vote. It was the first election held since Sisi led the ousting of democratically elected Islamist president Mohammed Morsi in July 2013. With Morsi's Muslim Brotherhood banned and its supporters vowing to boycott the election, Sisi faced only one opponent, leftist politician Hamdeen Sabahy. Critics questioned the government's claim that 47% of Egypt's 54 mil voters had participated in the election, which was extended by one day due to low voter turnout.

European Union observers and the U.S.-funded Democracy Intl. criticized the election process as falling short of international standards. More than 1,400 people—mostly Morsi supporters—have died in political violence in Egypt since July 2013.

South China Sea Dispute Spurs Deadly Riots in Vietnam—Demonstrators protesting China's installation of an oil rig in disputed waters claimed by both China and Vietnam attacked Chinese targets in and around Ho Chi Minh City, May 13-15, sparking violence that killed at least four people and injured 100. Dozens of foreign-owned factories were destroyed, including those owned by companies based in Taiwan and South Korea. China evacuated 3,000 citizens from the country by May 18 and sent ships to withdraw more.

China July 16 announced it was moving the rig away from the contested Paracel Islands. China and Vietnam also both claim sovereignty of the nearby Spratly Islands, parts of which the Philippines claim.

Hindu Nationalists Rout India's Ruling Party in Largest-Ever Election—Results announced May 16 confirmed India's Hindu nationalist Bharatiya Janata Party (BJP) won 282 of 543 seats in the lower house of parliament in a general election victory that unseated the governing Indian Natl. Congress Party. Two-thirds of registered voters cast 551 mil votes during the five-week-long balloting, which was both the nation's longest and the world's largest democratic election. The election also marked the first time in 30 years that a political party in India won a majority large enough to lead without forming a coalition. The Indian Natl. Congress won 44 seats, a loss of 162 seats and the lowest tally ever for the party, which had governed India for much of its 67 years of independence. The BJP's Narendra Modi, who campaigned on a pledge to implement business reforms and boost the economy, was sworn in as prime minister May 26.

China and Russia Sign 30-Year Energy Deal; U.S. Charges China With Hacking—China solidified its future access to cleaner energy May 21 when it signed a $400+ bil deal with Russia's state-operated energy company Gazprom. Under the agreement, China will buy 38 bil cubic meters of natural gas annually for 30 years beginning in 2018, at prices believed to be lower than what Russia charges in Europe, but higher than what China paid its current Turkmenistan suppliers. Gazprom, the world's largest natural gas provider, currently supplies 30% of the gas needs of Europe, which has attempted to diversify its supply and has, along with the U.S., adopted sanctions against Russia in response to Russia's alleged support for the separatists in Ukraine. The deal, a decade in the making, strengthens ties between Russia and China and adds tension to the strained U.S. relationship with both nations.

The U.S. announced May 19 that it had charged five Chinese army officers with hacking into the electronic records of U.S. companies and a labor union in the solar, nuclear power, and metals industries to gain business intelligence. According to the FBI, the alleged illegal espionage occurred 2006-14 and targeted Alcoa Inc., Allegheny Technologies, SolarWorld, U.S. Steel, USW, and Westinghouse Electric.

Military Ousts Government, Assumes Control in Thailand—Two days after declaring martial law, Thai military leaders May 22 suspended the constitution and detained more than 200 politicians and other individuals. The military takeover was the latest development in more than six months of unrest that broke out when then-Prime Min. Yingluck Shinawatra of the Pheu Thai party introduced a bill granting amnesty to her brother, ousted former Prime Min. Thaksin Shinawatra. Antigovernment activists staged ongoing demonstrations, occupying government buildings in Bangkok and forcing the cancellation of elections, which they expected Pheu Thai to win. A constitutional court removed Prime Min. Shinawatra from office May 7 on unrelated corruption charges, and the country's election commission May 15 postponed July elections to elect her successor. Three protesters were killed by unidentified attackers May 15, bringing the total number of deaths associated with the unrest to at least 28 since Nov. 2013. Coup leader Gen. Prayuth Chan-ocha announced May 26 that the military had the support of Thai monarch King Bhumibol and revealed plans May 30 for the junta to stay in power until at least mid-2015.

Iraq Holds First National Election Since U.S. Pullout—According to results published May 26, the Shiite State of Law coalition of Iraqi Prime Min. Nouri al-Maliki won 92 of 328 seats in Apr. 30 parliamentary elections. Maliki was seeking a third four-year term in office but still faced significant challenges. About 62% of 22 mil eligible voters turned out for the first national election in Iraq since the U.S. withdrew combat troops in Dec. 2011. Security was tight amid fears of violence—31 people had been killed at an Apr. election rally in Baghdad—and at least 14 people were killed at northern and western polling stations. Officials canceled polling in parts of Anbar province, including Fallujah and Ramadi, due to clashes with Islamist militants.

General

Mudslides Bury Hundreds in Afghanistan—Authorities confirmed that hundreds of people were killed May 2 by two landslides that buried some 300 homes in up to 200 ft of mud in the northeast Afghan village of Abi Barak in remote Badakhshan province. Estimates of the death toll varied significantly, from 500 to more than 2,000, with little hope of recovering missing bodies. The Afghan military the following day flew rescue teams there to provide aid to more than 4,000 displaced persons from the village. U.S.-led coalition forces delivered 15 tons of food and supplies to the region.

California Chrome Sweeps Kentucky Derby and Preakness Stakes—California Chrome, a three-year-old chestnut colt, won the 140th running of the Kentucky Derby at Churchill Downs in Louisville, KY. Ridden by Victor Espinoza, the 5-2 favorite broke away from the pack on the final turn of the 1¼ mi race and crossed the finish line at 2:03.66. At age 77, Art Sherman became the oldest trainer to win the Derby. California Chrome became the first California-born horse to win the race since 1962.

California Chrome stayed on course to win the Triple Crown after clinching the 139th Preakness Stakes May 17 at Pimlico Race Course in Baltimore, MD. Espinoza accelerated on the final turn past early leader Pablo Del Monte and late-race pacesetters Ria Antonia and Social Inclusion to finish in 1:54.84. Ride On Curlin finished 1.5 lengths behind, with Social Inclusion taking third.

Hundreds Die in Turkish Mining Accident—A May 13 explosion at Soma mine complex in western Turkey led to the deaths of 301 out of 787 miners, most due to carbon monoxide released by the ensuing fire. Trade unions held strikes throughout the country May 15, the same day police in Izmir used tear gas and water cannons to disperse 20,000 demonstrators protesting both alleged safety violations by the mine's operator, Soma Komur Isletmeleri A.S., and Prime Min. Recep Tayyip Erdogan's perceived insensitivity to the worst mining accident in the nation's history. Protests continued in a half-dozen major cities, and three mining company executives were arrested May 18 and charged with negligence. Miners and residents claimed safety conditions had deteriorated at the Soma mine since the government privatized it in 2005.

Paleontologists Excavate Biggest Dinosaur Yet Known—Researchers in Argentina announced May 16 the discovery of fossilized bones of the largest dinosaur yet, a 130-ft-long herbivore estimated at 85 tons, some 8 tons heavier than the previous contender, *Argentinosaurus*. Based on its 7.9-ft femur, lead researcher Jose Luis Carballido from the Museum of Paleontology Egidio Feruglio estimated the dinosaur stood 65 ft tall with its neck extended. Working in desert terrain in the southern region of Patagonia, archaeologists had excavated about 150 bones from seven partial 95- to 100-mil-year-old skeletons of the yet-unnamed species.

Violent Rampage Kills 6, Injures 13 at UCSB—A heavily armed man killed six people and injured 13 others near the Univ. of California-Santa Barbara (UCSB) in Isla Vista, CA, May 23. After stabbing two of his roommates and a third man—all UCSB undergraduates—to death in his apartment, the 22-year-old attacker fatally shot two female students outside of a sorority house and a male student inside of a deli. Driving away from the spree, he injured a number of

pedestrians and twice engaged in gunfire with sheriff's deputies before fatally shooting himself. The attacker, identified as Elliot Rodger, a former community college student, had communicated his intentions in a video uploaded to YouTube the night before the attack.

June 2014
National

Obama Administration Proposes New Power Plant Emission Rules, Marine Sanctuary Expansion—The Environmental Protection Agency June 2 proposed new regulations requiring states to reduce carbon dioxide emissions from existing power plants by an average of 30% below 2005 levels by 2030. Regulators touted the flexibility of the new rules, which would set individual goals for states to allow each to create policies to reach its reduction goal, but critics noted the rules could force the closure of many of the nation's 557 coal-fired plants, which generate 39% of the country's electricity but emit large amounts of carbon dioxide and other atmospheric pollutants. The agency estimated the proposal would cost $7.3-$8.8 bil per year to implement but claimed it would produce up to $55-$93 bil in annual economic benefits and prevent up to 6,600 premature deaths yearly. Environmentalists lauded the proposal, but the U.S. Chamber of Commerce and coal industry advocates said it would damage the economy and raise energy costs.

Pres. Obama June 17 proposed greatly expanding the Pacific Remote Islands Marine National Monument, which surrounds a group of islands between American Samoa and Hawaii. The expansion of the sanctuary, created in 2009 by Pres. George W. Bush, would double the area of the world's waters protected from fishing and oil drilling and create the world's largest marine sanctuary.

House Majority Leader Loses Primary, Announces Resignation—House majority leader Rep. Eric Cantor (R, VA) was defeated in Virginia's Republican primary June 10 by Dave Brat, a Tea Party-backed economics professor. Brat, a political novice with campaign finances of just over $230,000 to Cantor's $5.7 mil, defeated the seven-term congressman 56%-44%. Brat had accused Cantor—often viewed as a link between the establishment GOP and the Tea Party—of being soft on immigration by supporting a measure that would grant legal status to immigrants who had come to the U.S. illegally as children. The day after his loss, Cantor announced his resignation as majority leader; House Republicans June 19 elected majority whip Kevin McCarthy (R, CA) to replace him. Cantor resigned from Congress effective Aug. 18 and called for a special election to be held to fill his seat.

U.S. Captures Suspected Leader of Benghazi Attack—U.S. military commandos and FBI agents June 15 apprehended Ahmed Abu Khattala, an alleged ringleader of the Sept. 11, 2012, attack by Islamist militants on the U.S. consulate in Benghazi, Libya, that killed U.S. Amb. J. Christopher Stevens and three other Americans. Officials detained Khattala in an overnight raid on a Benghazi-area residence and interrogated him aboard the USS *New York* in the Mediterranean Sea. Khattala pleaded not guilty to a single charge of conspiracy June 28 in federal court in Washington, DC.

The House May 8 had voted 232-186 to assemble a select committee to further investigate the Benghazi matter—the eighth such probe. The committee was charged with determining whether the administration had mishandled the attack or attempted any cover-up for political gain.

First Quarter Economy Shrinks; Other Economic News—The Commerce Dept. June 25 announced it had underestimated the amount by which the U.S. economy was shrinking when it revised its first-quarter gross domestic product growth estimate from –1% to –2.9% (the estimate was further revised July 30, to –2.1%). The greatest economic contraction in five years was attributed to factors that included severe winter weather, a decrease in health-care spending, and the expiration of unemployment benefits. Other reports showed reasons for economic optimism, including an increase in business equipment orders in May, signaling a growth in corporate investment, and the Labor Dept.'s June 6 jobs report, which showed 217,000 new jobs were added to payrolls in May. The new jobs marked the fourth straight month of 200,000+ job gains, but the unemployment rate remained flat at 6.3%. In other labor news, the city council of Seattle, WA, voted June 2 to raise the city's minimum wage from $9.32 to $15 per hour over the next few years, the highest of any major city in the U.S.

French bank BNP Paribas pleaded guilty June 30 to violating U.S. sanctions against Cuba, Iran, and Sudan and agreed to pay $8.9-bil penalty. The fine was a record for a bank accused of transacting with sanctioned nations. The Dow Jones Industrial Average remained above 16,700 throughout June, closing the month at 16,826.60, up 0.7% from May. The S&P 500 finished June at 1,960.23, up 1.9% from the month before, while the Nasdaq Composite Index closed June at 4,408.18, up 3.9%.

Obama Vows Action on Immigration Amid Influx of Migrant Children—In response to a surge in illegal border crossings by unaccompanied children, Pres. Barack Obama June 30 pledged to take unspecified executive action to carry out immigration reform without congressional approval. Obama also asked Congress to expand the government's authority to speed up deportations of children from outside of Mexico, generating criticism from human rights groups, who claimed the children were refugees. The influx of minors traveling alone across the southern border of the U.S. from Central American countries with high levels of violence and poverty—some 52,000 between Oct. 1, 2013, and June 15—was straining immigration authorities' resources. Obama blamed House Republicans for derailing immigration reform efforts following the Senate's passage of a bipartisan bill in July 2013. Republicans claimed that a 2012 executive order that deferred deportations of those who had come to the country illegally as children before 2007 contributed to the influx by generating misinformation south of the border. Obama July 8 asked Congress to appropriate $3.7 bil in emergency funding to cope with the surge.

Supreme Court Ends Term With Rulings on Religious Liberty, Digital Privacy—The Supreme Court June 30 concluded its 2013-14 term with a landmark decision concerning the right of for-profit corporations to refuse to pay for insurance covering contraceptives for employees as required by the Affordable Care Act. Restricting its decision to "closely held corporations," the court in *Burwell v. Hobby Lobby Stores, Inc.* sided 5-4 with Hobby Lobby and Conestoga Wood—both family-run companies reportedly operated according to Christian principles. Writing for the majority, Associate Justice Samuel Alito said the Obama administration had failed to uphold the Religious Freedom Restoration Act by mandating that such companies pay for coverage. Associate Justice Ruth Bader Ginsberg, in a strongly worded dissent, said the decision would allow companies to "opt out of any law … they judge incompatible with their sincerely held religious beliefs."

In another major decision June 25, the court in *Riley v. California* ruled that police may not search the contents of a cell phone following an arrest without a warrant. Writing for the unanimous court, Chief Justice John Roberts said that cell phones "hold for many Americans 'the privacies of life'" and as such are "worthy of the protection for which the Founders fought."

International

Palestinians Form Unity Government; Kidnapped Israelis Found Dead—Palestinian Authority Pres. Mahmoud Abbas June 2 swore in an interim unity government that included both Abbas's Fatah party and rival movement Hamas. The two factions were united as one governing authority for the first time since 2007, when Hamas took control of the Gaza Strip away from Fatah. In the wake of the rift, the Fatah party retained power in the West Bank and negotiated directly with Israel in peace talks, including the latest round of discussions that had faltered in Apr. The same day the government was sworn in, the Israeli security cabinet declared its refusal to negotiate with any government that included Hamas—which denies Israel's right to exist—and voted to authorize new sanctions against the Palestinian Authority and hold it responsible for any rocket or other attacks emanating from Hamas-controlled Gaza.

The bodies of three Israeli teenagers abducted June 12 from a West Bank Jewish settlement were found June 30 in the West Bank after a massive search that resulted in the arrests of more than 150 Palestinians. Throughout the month, the Israeli military and Gaza militants exchanged airstrikes and rocket fire across the Israeli border. Hamas denied responsibility for the kidnappings.

Ukraine Holds Peace Talks as Fighting Rages—Fighting between Ukrainian military forces and pro-Russian rebel separatists continued through June, with rebels capturing two military bases June 4 in the eastern region of Luhansk. The following day, U.S. Pres. Barack Obama and UK Prime Min. David Cameron threatened Russia with additional sanctions if it continued to support the separatists, a charge Russian Pres. Vladimir Putin continued to deny. Sworn in on June 7, Ukrainian Pres. Petro Poroshenko ordered the creation June 10 of humanitarian corridors to allow for the relocation of displaced civilians, whom the United Nations estimated at 10,000. Heavy fighting in Kramatorsk, Slovyansk, and Luhansk killed two Ukrainian soldiers and about 40 rebels June 10, four days before rebels shot down a Ukrainian military transport plane, killing all 49 aboard. Russia's state-owned Gazprom effectively cut off all natural gas supplies to Ukraine June 16 after Ukraine declined an offer priced above pre-crisis levels. Despite Russia's earlier promises of de-escalation, NATO June 19 reported a renewed buildup of Russian troops along the Ukrainian border. Poroshenko declared a weeklong ceasefire June 20, which separatist leaders agreed to observe at June 23 peace talks attended by Russia and the EU. In defiance of the ceasefire, rebels the next day shot down a military helicopter, killing nine. Poroshenko June 27 signed a landmark EU trade pact, which ousted former Ukrainian Pres. Viktor Yanukovych had declined to sign in Nov. The UN estimated June 24 that 423 people had been killed in clashes in eastern Ukraine, Apr. 15-June 20.

Assad Wins Syrian Presidential Election; Other Developments—Syrian Pres. Bashar al-Assad proclaimed a landslide victory in June 3 voting that secured the leader of the civil war-torn country a third seven-year term in office. Government officials said Assad received nearly 89% of the vote in the election, which a Syrian court claimed was participated in by 73% of eligible voters despite boycotts by opposition groups. The European Union and other observers declared the election illegitimate.

The Organization for the Prohibition of Chemical Weapons (OPCW) released a report June 16 claiming the Syrian regime was most likely continuing to use toxic chemicals, including chlorine gas, in attacks on rebels. Syria June 23 surrendered the last 100 of 1,300 tons of toxic materials it had declared, nearly two months past the Apr. 27 deadline set by the United Nations, with OPCW calling the Syrian regime's cooperation "satisfactory." According to the UK-based Syrian Observatory for Human Rights, as of May 19 more than 162,000 people had died in Syria's 3.5-year-old conflict.

ISIS Overruns Mosul, Captures Parts of Five Iraq Provinces—Sunni Islamic militants formerly affiliated with al-Qaeda June 10 overtook the northern Iraqi city of Mosul, the country's second largest city, occupying the airport, military bases, and government facilities. The Islamic State of Iraq and Syria, also known as the Islamic State of Iraq and the Levant but more popularly as ISIS, took Mosul after battling security forces for four days. ISIS had also taken control of Fallujah in Jan. 2014 and claimed other territories in Iraq and Syria. According to the International Organization for Migration, up to 500,000 people—including large numbers of security personnel—fled Mosul in ISIS's wake. Kurdish security forces June 12 took over Kirkuk to keep the oil-rich city out of ISIS control. After the Mosul takeover, ISIS pressed south toward Baghdad, capturing cities whose forces had fled without resistance. Security personnel June 17 repelled militants in three areas less than 40 mi from Baghdad. Iraq reported June 14 that Iran had sent 2,000 troops to help security forces and Shiite militias battle ISIS, and Pres. Barack Obama June 19 announced the U.S. would send up to 300 military advisers.

The UN reported that more than 2,400 Iraqis were killed in acts of terror or violence in June, the highest monthly death toll since 2007.

On June 29, ISIS declared it had established a "caliphate" of territory stretching from Aleppo, Syria, to Iraq's Diyala province, and announced it was changing its name to "the Islamic State."

General

Tonalist Wins Belmont Stakes; California Chrome Fails in Triple Crown Bid—In the third event in horse racing's Triple Crown, Tonalist, a 9-1 long shot ridden by jockey Joel Rosario, won the 146th Belmont Stakes June 7 at Belmont Park in Elmont, NY. The horse, which had run neither the Kentucky Derby nor the Preakness, beat Commissioner by a head; Medal Count took third a length behind. Derby and Preakness winner California Chrome tied for fourth alongside Wicked Strong.

Couple Kill Police in Las Vegas Restaurant; Other Shootings—Armed with hundreds of rounds of ammunition, a married couple ambushed and shot to death two police officers in a Las Vegas pizzeria, June 8. The couple placed a "Don't Tread on Me" flag and a swastika-stamped anti-government note on the officers' bodies, then fled to a Walmart store, where they killed a man who was attempting to use a handgun to fight back. Police responders engaged the couple in a gunfight that killed the husband; the wife fatally shot herself.

A gunman June 4 shot five members of the Royal Canadian Mounted Police in Moncton, NB, Canada, killing three. After a two-day search, police apprehended and charged a 24-year-old suspect in the killings. A 26-year-old man was accused of shooting three students, one fatally, at Seattle Pacific Univ. June 5 before he was tackled by a student security guard. At a high school outside of Portland, OR, a 15-year-old June 10 shot and killed a fellow student and wounded a teacher before killing himself. Ten people in New Orleans were injured June 29 when they were caught in a gun battle between two shooters on Bourbon Street. One of the injured died July 2.

Sharapova, Nadal Win French Open Titles—Russian Maria Sharapova defeated Romanian Simona Halep (6-4, 6-7 (5-7), 6-4) June 7 at a steamy Roland Garros in Paris, France, to win her second French Open title and her fifth Grand Slam title. The next day, Spaniard Rafael Nadal beat Serbian Novak Djokovic (3-6, 7-5, 6-2, 6-4) and became the first player to win five consecutive French Open titles and the only man to win nine titles at the same Grand Slam tournament. Nadal's record for match victories at the French Open improved to a near-perfect 66-1.

L.A. Kings Hoist Stanley Cup for Second Championship in Three Years—The Los Angeles Kings defeated the New York Rangers in five games to win the NHL's Stanley Cup Championship June 13 at the Staples Center in Los Angeles. The series featured three overtime games including a tense final contest that the Kings won on a goal 14 min., 43 sec. into double overtime. Los Angeles forward Justin Williams won the Conn Smythe Trophy as the most valuable player in the playoffs.

San Antonio Spurs Capture NBA Finals—The San Antonio Spurs defeated the defending champion Miami Heat in five games to win the franchise's fifth NBA Finals June 15 at San Antonio's AT&T Center. The Spurs, who had lost the championship to Miami in 2013, outscored their opponents by 70 points throughout the series, the largest cumulative point differential in NBA Finals history. Spurs forward Kawhi Leonard led the team in scoring in the last three games and was named the NBA Finals MVP; the 22-year-old Leonard was the youngest player to receive the award since 1982.

Kaymer Takes Golf's U.S. Open—Germany's Martin Kaymer won the 114th U.S. Open golf tournament June 15 at Pinehurst Resort's No. 2 course in Pinehurst, NC. Kaymer maintained at least a four-shot lead throughout the last 48 holes to finish atop the leaderboard with a 9-under-par 271. Americans Eric Compton and Rickie Fowler each finished eight strokes back. The 29-year-old Kaymer became the fifth golfer ever to win two majors and be number-one ranked before the age of 30.

July 2014
National

Federal Reserve to End Bond-Buying Stimulus Program; Other Economic News—In a show of optimism about economic prospects, the Federal Reserve July 9 signaled that it would likely end in Oct. its bond-buying program known as quantitative easing, which it instituted to boost economic recovery. The stimulus, which began in Sept. 2012, was the Federal Reserve's third and largest bond-buying program since the 2008 economic crisis. On July 31, the Dow Jones Industrial Average plunged 316.99 points in its steepest one-day drop in six months. Closing the month at 16,563.3, the Dow dropped 1.6% from June and the S&P 500 finished July at 1,930.67, down 1.5% for the month. The Nasdaq Composite Index closed July at 4,369.77, down 0.9% from June. The Labor Dept. July 3 announced the economy gained 288,000 jobs in June, with the unemployment rate, falling to 6.1% from 6.3% in May.

Citigroup agreed July 14 to pay $7 bil in fines for misleading investors about unsound mortgage-backed securities, the collapse of which helped fuel the 2007-09 financial crisis. The Justice Dept. settlement included a record $4 bil in civil penalties.

Reynolds American and Lorillard, the second and third largest U.S. cigarette makers, respectively, announced a $27.4-bil merger July 15. The move would create a stronger firm behind Marlboro-purveyor Altria and would bring together the Camel and Newport tobacco brands. The agreement came three days before a Florida jury ordered a Reynolds subsidiary to pay $23.6 bil in damages—the largest individual death payout in Florida history—to the widow of a smoker. Microsoft July 17 reported it would slash up to 18,000 jobs—14% of its workforce—mostly from the phone and tablet business acquired from Nokia in Apr. Real estate websites Zillow and Trulia agreed July 28 to merge; together, they would own around half of the traffic to online real estate listings.

CDC Shuts Two Labs After Safety Mishaps—Centers for Disease Control and Prevention Dir. Thomas Frieden announced July 11 that the agency would temporarily close flu and anthrax labs at its Atlanta, GA, headquarters following two serious safety lapses. A CDC lab May 23 was found to have mistakenly contaminated a more benign flu sample with potent H5N1 "bird flu" virus before sending it to another lab. On June 19, the CDC announced that up to 75 scientists in Atlanta could have been exposed to live anthrax bacteria, though no employees had shown signs of infection as of July 11. The CDC suspended shipment of infectious agents pending a review of safety procedures with external advisors. Researchers in early July discovered 60-year-old vials containing the lethal smallpox virus unsecured at the National Institutes of Health in Maryland.

Appeals Courts Deliver Contradictory Rulings on Obamacare Financing—Within hours of one another July 22, two federal appeals court panels handed down opposing rulings on the legality of subsidies received by more than 4.5 mil consumers who purchased insurance under the Affordable Care Act. A three-judge panel for the District of Columbia Circuit was split in saying that the federal government cannot award insurance subsidies in the 36 states that failed to establish their own exchanges. Another appeals court in Richmond, VA, decided unanimously that tax credits could be issued in all states. The plaintiffs in both suits contended the law awards subsidies to consumers specifically "enrolled through an Exchange established by the State." The Obama administration was expected to ask for further review of the DC Circuit ruling.

International

Outbreak of Ebola Virus Accelerates in West Africa—The worst recorded outbreak of the deadly Ebola virus continued to spread throughout West Africa, killing some 729 victims in Guinea, Liberia, Nigeria, and Sierra Leone as of July 31. It was thought to have started in Guinea in Dec. 2013. Although Liberia instituted desperate measures including quarantining communities, health officials partially attributed the rapid outbreak of the extremely infectious virus—spread by contact with bodily fluids—to a scarcity of latex gloves and sanitary medical supplies and a lack of public understanding. Two American missionaries, physician Kent Brantly and aide Nancy Writebol, were treated with an experimental Ebola drug never before tested on humans after they contracted the virus in late July while caring for patients in Liberia. Brantly and Writebol were evacuated to the U.S. and released after doctors determined they were not contagious. Doctors were not able to determine if the drug had contributed to their recovery. The World Health Organization declared the outbreak an international public-health emergency Aug. 8.

Japan Sheds Pacifist Stance—Shifting the country away from more than 60 years of post-WWII pacifism, the cabinet of Japanese Prime Min. Shinzo Abe July 1 adopted a resolution ending the country's constitutional ban on "collective self-defense," or defending an ally under attack. In advance of the change, which was expected to be approved by the national legislature, thousands of demonstrators in Tokyo demanded a public referendum. While the U.S. and Philippines welcomed the action, the move threatened to sour relations with South Korea and China. In recent years, Japan has edged away from its pacifist stance by refueling war ships and transporting cargo for Western countries engaged in wars in Iraq and Afghanistan.

Pro-Democracy Activists March in Hong Kong—Some 150,000 demonstrators marched from Victoria Park to Hong Kong's financial district July 1, the 17th anniversary of Hong Kong's return to Chinese sovereignty, demanding the right to nominate candidates for the 2017 election for Hong Kong's chief executive. Police the following day arrested more than 500 mostly student activists who staged a sit-in. The demonstrations followed the release several weeks earlier by Chinese officials of a white paper affirming Beijing's "comprehensive jurisdiction" over Hong Kong.

Israel Launches Gaza Strip Offensive—Israeli forces July 8 initiated a campaign known as Operation Protective Edge in the densely populated Gaza Strip against Hamas militants who had launched rocket strikes against Israel. The rocket strikes were sparked in part by the killing of a Palestinian teen and by crackdowns that occurred during and following a search that uncovered the bodies of three kidnapped Israeli teens in the West Bank. Calling up 40,000 reservists, the Israeli military struck alleged Hamas targets in Gaza, including underground tunnels leading to Israel and alleged command centers in residential buildings. Hamas leaders July 15 rejected an Egyptian ceasefire proposal accepted by Israel and continued to wage attacks. Two days later, Israel sent ground troops into Gaza, triggering clashes that killed scores of Palestinians, including more than 100 on July 20 alone. U.S. Pres. Barack Obama supported Israel's right to defend itself, but voiced concern over rising civilian casualties in Gaza, especially over 16 people killed and 200 injured July 24 by a blast that struck a school used as a shelter by the United Nations. According to the UN, more than 1,800 Palestinians had been killed in the operation as of Aug. 5, including more than 1,300 civilians (408 of whom were children); nearly 70 Israelis were killed.

German Government Requests Expulsion of U.S. Intelligence Official—In a sign of Germany's continued displeasure with U.S. espionage practices, the German government July 10 requested that the top Central Intelligence Agency official leave the country after two new cases of U.S. spying on Germany were alleged. German law enforcement raided Berlin locations July 9 while investigating a defense ministry employee it suspected of spying for the CIA, less than a week after German officials charged a foreign intelligence service employee with selling information to the U.S. Diplomatic relations between the two nations had been strained since Oct. 2013, when documents leaked by former U.S. National Security Agency contractor Edward Snowden revealed that the NSA had tapped the cellphone of German Chancellor Angela Merkel.

Libyan Militias Clash in Tripoli; U.S. Evacuates Embassy—In the bloodiest fighting in Libya since the 2011 overthrow of dictator Muammar Qaddafi, rival militias battling for control of Tripoli's main airport killed at least 236 people over a three-week span beginning July 13. At least 23 Egyptian workers were killed by rockets July 26, the same day the U.S. State Dept. announced it had evacuated embassy staff. The fighting caused significant damage to the airport's infrastructure and nearly 1.6 mil gallons of fuel were burned.

In the eastern Libyan city of Benghazi, at least 38 people, mostly soldiers, were killed July 26-29 in clashes between the army and Islamist fighters who seized a military base. The U.S. House Intelligence Committee voted July 31 to declassify its report on the 2012 attack by Islamist terrorists on U.S. diplomatic facilities in Benghazi that killed four U.S. personnel. The committee inquiry—the fourth of its kind—did not find evidence suggesting a failure in intelligence that would have prevented the attack or evidence of a willful cover-up by administration officials following the attack.

Airliner Downed Over Ukraine, Killing 298; New Sanctions, Other Developments—Pro-Russia separatists were widely suspected of shooting down Malaysia Airlines Flight 17, killing all 298 people onboard, on July 17 as it traveled from Amsterdam to Kuala Lumpur some 33,000 ft above a portion of eastern Ukraine controlled by rebels. The Ukrainian government and separatists blamed one another for the incident, and Ukrainian officials also accused rebels of tampering with evidence at the crash site. Insurgent leaders handed over the plane's two flight recorders July 21. U.S. investigators July 22 said that evidence including shrapnel markings and social media data and photos indicated that rebels had shot down the aircraft with a surface-to-air missile system obtained from Russia. Previously reluctant to enact stricter sanctions against Russia, the European Union July 29 announced it had passed measures targeting its energy, banking, and defense sectors; the U.S. passed similar sanctions the same day.

Ukrainian Pres. Petro Poroshenko ended a ceasefire with insurgents at the beginning of July and launched operations to reclaim rebel-controlled areas. Ukraine's military July 5 took back the separatist stronghold of Slovyansk. Despite losing roughly half of their territory, rebels waged a missile attack against troops in Zelenopilya July 11, killing at least 19 and injuring 93. Government forces July 21 struck rebels in Donetsk, sparking accusations that Ukraine had launched rockets at civilian areas. U.S. officials July 24 reported they had evidence confirming the Russian military was firing across the border at targets in Ukraine.

Reform Candidate Wins Indonesian Presidential Election—Indonesia's election commission announced July 22 that Jakarta Gov. Joko Widodo, known popularly as Jokowi, had won Indonesia's presidential election over retired Gen. Prabowo Subianto, 53%-47%. Joko, of the Indonesian Democratic Party of Struggle, was widely seen as a populist and reformer; he pledged to make Indonesia, the world's fourth most populous nation, more "people-centric" in its governance. The Great Indonesia Movement Party's Prabowo, the son-in-law of former Pres. Suharto, filed an appeal of the results July 25, alleging fraud in the election, in which more than 130 mil people voted July 9. Analysts did not expect the appeal to change the election result, and Joko was sworn in Oct. 20.

General

Kvitova and Djokovic Take Wimbledon Championships—In the shortest women's Wimbledon final in 31 years, No. 6-seed Petra Kvitova of the Czech Republic defeated No. 13-seed Eugenie Bouchard of Canada (6-3, 6-0) in 55 min. at the All-England Club in London July 5. The next day, Serbian Novak Djokovic, the No. 1 seed, edged No. 4-seed Roger Federer (6-7, 6-4, 7-6, 5-7, 6-4) of Switzerland to win his second men's Wimbledon title. In a grueling 3-hr., 56-min. match, Djokovic came back from a five-straight game loss in the fourth set to defeat the seven-time champion.

Martin, McIlroy Win Respective British Opens—Mo Martin shot 1-under-287 to win the 39th Women's British Open golf championship July 13 at Royal Birkdale Golf Club in Southport, England. It was the first Major victory for Martin, who entered the tournament 99th in the Rolex World Rankings. Martin scored an eagle on the last hole of the final round to defeat Suzann Pettersen of Norway and Shanshan Feng of China by one shot. A week later, 25-year-old Rory McIlroy of Northern Ireland shot 17-under-271 to win the 143rd British Open at the Royal Liverpool Golf Club in Hoylake, England. McIlroy finished two shots ahead of American Rickie Fowler and Spain's Sergio García to become the third youngest golfer behind Jack Nicklaus and Tiger Woods to win three of the four major tournaments.

Germany Triumphs in World Cup Soccer—Germany's national soccer team won its fourth FIFA World Cup title July 13 in Rio de Janeiro, Brazil, defeating Argentina 1-0 on an overtime goal by Mario Götze. The final match capped a month-long, 64-game championship round that was the first played in South America since 1978. Despite the U.S. team's 2-1 loss to Belgium before the quarterfinals, a record 26.5 mil American television viewers tuned in to watch the final game. In addition to winning the title, Germany reached the final for a record eighth time and became the first country to compete in four straight World Cup semifinals. In one of the tournament's odder moments, Uruguay's Luis Suárez was suspended for four months for biting Italy's Giorgio Chiellini.

Church of England Votes to Allow Women Bishops—Twenty years after it began ordaining women as priests, the General Synod of the Church of England passed a measure July 14 allowing women to become bishops. Passing by an overall vote of 351-72, the measure included a provision allowing individual parishes to request a male bishop. Anglican provinces in the U.S., Canada, Ireland, and Australia already permitted women bishops; with more than 26 mil baptized members, the Church of England is the largest in the Anglican Communion.

Typhoon Rammasun Kills at Least 139 in Southeast Asia—Typhoon Rammasun July 15 hit the island of Luzon in the Philippines, pounding shanty dwellings housing thousands of people in Manila. At least 94 people were killed in the island nation; in all, the Philippine government evacuated 370,000 people. The storm strengthened to Category 5 over the South China Sea before unleashing 155 mph winds on China's island province of Hainan July 18, killing 18 in the region. Rammasun made final landfall in China the next day, causing flash flooding that killed 27 people.

Algerian Airliner Crashes, Killing All Onboard—Air Algérie Flight 5017 crashed July 24 en route to Algeria from Burkina Faso, killing all 116 onboard. Officials lost radar contact with the aircraft 50 min. after takeoff, soon after the crew requested permission to divert the plane to avoid storms. Later that day, Burkina Faso forces located wreckage of the aircraft in the northern Mali desert. The incident came less than 24 hr. after TransAsia Airways Flight 222 crashed in Taiwan's Penghu Islands, killing 48.

Italian Nibali Wins Tour de France—Vincenzo Nibali, a 29-year-old Italian, won the 101st Tour de France July 27. It was the first Tour victory for Nibali, who placed third overall in 2012. Slovakian Peter Sagan claimed the green jersey as the race's best sprinter for the third year in a row. Nibali finished the Tour in 89 hr., 59 min., 6 sec., beating France's Jean-Christophe Péraud by 7 min., 37 sec., the widest margin of victory in the Tour since 1997.

August 2014
National

Bank of America to Pay Record Fine; Other Economic News—Bank of America, the nation's second largest bank, agreed Aug. 21 to pay $16.65 bil to settle charges from the U.S. Dept. of Justice and six states that it misled investors into buying toxic mortgage-backed securities preceding the 2008 financial crisis. The agreement was the largest-ever civil settlement between the U.S. government and a single company and provided $7 bil for financially distressed homeowners. Accounting for most of the allegations was home-loan giant Countrywide Financial, which Bank of America acquired in 2008. The settlement pushed the bank's total penalties for the crisis to nearly $74 bil.

The world's leading smartphone makers, Apple and Samsung, agreed Aug. 5 to drop all patent lawsuits against each other outside of the U.S. Burger King announced plans

Aug. 26 to acquire Canadian doughnut chain Tim Hortons for $11.4 bil, a move that would create the world's third-largest fast-food company. The agreement, which would move Burger King's headquarters to Canada in order to save on taxes in a maneuver known as an inversion, generated backlash from consumers and politicians.

The Commerce Dept. July 30 announced a 4% increase in GDP over the second quarter of 2014, an improvement over first quarter performance which the government the same day revised to –2.1% from –2.9%. The Labor Dept. Aug 1. reported the economy added 209,000 jobs in July, and July's jobless rate rose slightly to 6.2%. The Dow Jones Industrial Average finished Aug. at 17,098.45, up 3.2% from the month before while the S&P 500 closed the month at a record 2,003.37, a 3.8% gain from July. The Nasdaq Composite Index finished Aug. at 4,580.27, its highest level since 2000 and up 4.8% from July.

Government Overhauls Medical Care for Vets—Pres. Barack Obama Aug. 7 signed a $16.3-bil bill revamping the Dept. of Veterans Affairs medical system in response to revelations that VA staff had manipulated schedules to conceal long wait times for appointments. The overhaul provided $10 bil over three years to allow veterans to visit a private physician or medical facility under certain conditions. The bipartisan bill, which the Senate July 31 passed, 91-3, a day after the House cleared it, 420-5, also allocated funds to open 27 new clinics and hire thousands of additional doctors and nurses as well as made it easier for the VA's secretary to terminate poorly performing executives. The Senate July 29 had voted unanimously to confirm Robert McDonald, a West Point graduate and former corporate executive, as VA secretary to replace Gen. Eric Shinseki.

Fatal Police Shooting of Black Missouri Teen Sparks Protests—A white police officer in Ferguson, MO, shot and killed an unarmed black teen Aug. 9, inciting almost two weeks of sometimes-violent protests. While the county police chief said the following day that 18-year-old Michael Brown had assaulted the officer and reached for his gun, a witness who had been with Brown said that the officer repeatedly fired upon Brown without provocation. A candlelight vigil met by armed police in riot gear the night of Aug. 10 turned violent, leaving several businesses looted and two officers injured. Ferguson police arrested 32 people Aug. 10 and fired tear gas and rubber bullets at crowds Aug. 11, allegedly in response to protesters throwing rocks. Despite the FBI's announcement Aug. 11 of a civil rights investigation into the incident, tense protests continued. Missouri Gov. Jay Nixon (D) Aug. 14 transferred control of security operations in Ferguson to the state highway patrol under the command of an African American officer. Ferguson police the next day released the name of the officer involved in Brown's shooting, Darren Wilson, along with video footage implicating the teen in a robbery immediately preceding the shooting. Nixon Aug. 16 declared a state of emergency and called in National Guard troops Aug. 18. A grand jury convened Aug. 20 to determine whether to charge Wilson.

After more than three weeks of relative calm, protests resumed in the streets of Ferguson Sept. 23 after a fire destroyed a Brown memorial. Protesters later called for the resignation of Ferguson Police Chief Thomas Jackson for his handling of events after the shooting. Demonstrations continued into Oct., with more than 50 arrested Oct. 13 during heightened tensions following the fatal police shooting of black teen Vonderitt Myers Jr. in St. Louis Oct. 8.

Judges Block Restrictive Abortion Laws in Four States—A Louisiana federal judge Aug. 31 temporarily blocked enforcement of a state law mandating abortion doctors obtain admitting privileges at nearby hospitals. Plaintiffs claimed doctors did not have sufficient time to secure the privileges and that the new law would likely force the closure of the state's five clinics that provided abortions and other women's health services. Admitting privileges laws have been passed by 11 states and a federal judge temporarily barred a similar state law in Alabama from going into effect Aug. 4. A Mississippi federal appeals court July 29 had voted 2-1 to block the state's admitting privileges law, ruling it could not be used to force the closure of the state's sole abortion clinic. A Texas judge Aug. 29 said that a 2013 state law that required facilities providing abortion services to adhere to the same standards as hospital surgical facilities was unconstitutional.

International

Ukrainian Military Squeezes Rebel Strongholds; Russian Convoy Crosses Border—Ukraine's military advanced on the pro-Russian separatist strongholds of Donetsk and Luhansk in Aug., almost completely surrounding the latter by Aug. 3. Despite reportedly amassing some 20,000 troops at its border with Ukraine, Russia said it would not aid the separatists but responded to Western sanctions by enacting a year-long ban on food imports from the European Union, U.S., and three other countries. The United Nations Aug. 13 reported the death toll in the crisis through Aug. 10 had nearly doubled since late July, to at least 2,086. Ukraine Aug. 10 rejected a ceasefire request from encircled Donetsk rebels, demanding a full surrender. A stalled convoy of some 220 Russian trucks purportedly delivering humanitarian aid but feared to contain weapons crossed the border Aug. 22 into rebel-held territory without Ukraine's permission. Citing support for the separatists among some of its members, Ukrainian Pres. Petro Poroshenko Aug. 25 dissolved parliament and called for Oct. elections.

Poroshenko met Russian Pres. Vladimir Putin Aug. 26 in Minsk, Belarus, for peace talks that failed to produce a resolution. Ukrainian officials the same day released footage of 10 Russian paratroopers captured in Ukraine that Russia claimed had entered the country in error. Ukraine in defiance of Russia announced Aug. 29 that it would seek NATO membership.

Afghan Soldier Kills Visiting U.S. General—The first American general to die in the war in Afghanistan and the highest ranking U.S. military officer to be killed in combat since the Vietnam War was fatally shot Aug. 5 in an attack by an Afghan soldier at a military academy in Kabul. Maj. Gen. Harold J. Greene was killed and 15 others, including eight Americans, were injured. Despite a sharp drop in "green-on-blue" insider attacks since 2012—green-on-blue attacks killed 53 coalition troops in 2012 and 16 in 2013—the shooting, which was the third such incident in 2014, underscored the ongoing threat. As of Sept. 25, at least 2,342 U.S. military personnel had been killed in the war in Afghanistan since late 2001, along with 1,127 coalition troops from outside the U.S., including 453 from the United Kingdom. Since the beginning of 2014, 47 U.S. personnel had died in the conflict, down from 132 in 2013 and 313 in 2012.

Tribunal Sentences Cambodian Leaders for Crimes Against Humanity—A United Nations-backed tribunal Aug. 7 sentenced two former senior Cambodian leaders to life imprisonment for their role in atrocities committed during the first years of dictator Pol Pot's Khmer Rouge regime, which is thought to have killed at least 1.7 mil Cambodians, 1975-79. The now-elderly men, Nuon Chea and Khieu Samphan, served as deputy communist party secretary and national president, respectively, and were arrested in 2007 on charges including crimes against humanity, murder, kidnapping, and political persecution. The two were the last members of the regime declared fit to stand trial in this case and face additional charges of genocide. The eight-year-old tribunal has handed down one other verdict, a life sentence in 2012, but Nuon and Khieu are the first top-level leaders to be sentenced. Pol Pot died in 1998 while under house arrest.

U.S. Carries Out Airstrikes in Iraq; ISIS Beheads American Journalist; Iraq Leadership Dispute Settled—Pres. Barack Obama Aug. 7 authorized open-ended airstrikes to disrupt the extremist Sunni group known as ISIS, which was attempting to capture the northern Iraqi Kurdish capital of Erbil. Obama also authorized strikes and humanitarian drops to aid tens of thousands of members of the Yazidi religious sect who had fled to a mountain outside of Sinjar to avoid execution by ISIS militants. ISIS was known to persecute non-Sunnis, particularly Christians and Yazidi, demanding they convert, flee, pay a nonbeliever tax, or face execution. Kurdish forces Aug. 10 retook two cities and later regained control of Mosul Dam with the help of Iraqi security forces. Obama

Aug. 13 announced the breaking of ISIS's siege on Yazidis on Mount Sinjar, a claim Yazidi leaders and the United Nations disputed. The UN Aug. 13 declared its highest level of emergency for ISIS's bloody campaign in Iraq, and the UN Assistance Mission in Iraq said Sept. 2 that 1,420 civilians were killed in Iraq in Aug. with another 1.8 mil displaced since Jan.

A protracted leadership dispute following Iraqi parliamentary election results announced in May was resolved Aug. 15, when Iraqi Prime Min. Nouri al-Maliki Aug. 14 announced he would relinquish power to fellow Islamic Dawa party member Haider al-Abadi rather than seek a third term. Criticized for his autocratic rule, Maliki had lost the support of many U.S. officials and Shiite backers.

ISIS released a video Aug. 19 showing the beheading of *GlobalPost* journalist James Foley, kidnapped Nov. 22 in northwestern Syria. The video, authenticated by U.S. officials Aug. 20, also shows American-Israeli *Time* magazine contributor Steven Sotloff, whom the onscreen masked militant threatened with death if the U.S continued airstrikes against ISIS. An administration official Aug. 22 confirmed Obama was considering airstrikes against ISIS targets in northern Syria, where reports indicated roughly two-thirds of the group's 20,000-31,000 fighters were located. ISIS forces took control of large swaths of northern Syrian territory—including oilfields—since 2013. Syria's three-year-old civil war, which the UN in Aug. estimated had killed over 191,000, was ongoing. ISIS fighters by mid-Aug. had seized villages 30 mi northeast of Syria's largest city of Aleppo and on Aug. 24 took control of Tabqa airbase, the Syrian government's sole remaining military stronghold in the northeastern province of Raqqa.

Turkey Holds First Direct Presidential Election—Turkish Prime Min. Recep Tayyip Erdogan was proclaimed the victor Aug. 10 of the country's first popular presidential election, in which 74% of eligible voters participated. Erdogan, who was prohibited from seeking a fourth term as prime minister, won 52% of the vote and avoided a runoff election. Campaigning on a plan to create a new national constitution, he also pledged to facilitate peace with the country's Kurds. Despite the five-year position's largely ceremonial role, analysts said Erdogan was likely to fully use and even expand the presidential powers, which included appointing judges, vetoing bills, and convening cabinet and national security meetings. Erdogan had weathered large-scale protests in the summer of 2013 over his alleged authoritarian rule and Islamist agenda, and in Feb. 2014 had pushed through measures—later overturned—that limited judiciary oversight in the midst of a corruption scandal that threatened to ensnare him and fellow party members.

Peace Deal Ends Seven-Week-Old Fighting in Gaza—Israeli and Palestinian officials Aug. 26 agreed to an open-ended ceasefire halting 50 days of bloody conflict in Gaza that had killed over 2,100 Palestinians—mostly civilians—and some 70 Israelis. Initially rejected six weeks earlier by Gaza's governing faction Hamas, the Egypt-brokered deal called on Israel to open border crossings to Gaza to allow in humanitarian aid and construction materials. Negotiators deferred discussion of many other issues, including Hamas's disarmament, demands for a Gazan seaport and airport, and an end to Israel's economic blockade. Following the collapse of multiple ceasefires, the truce essentially returned the two sides to terms first agreed upon in Nov. 2012. The conflict, the third major round of Israeli-Hamas hostilities in five years, began in July with Hamas firing rockets into Israeli territory after Israelis allegedly killed a Palestinian teen in retribution for the murder of three Israeli teens. Israel Aug. 5 had ended its first large-scale ground assault on Gaza in more than five years after officials said they had largely dismantled Hamas's network of tunnels from which it staged attacks on Israel. The conflict displaced some 600,000 Palestinians and destroyed more than 11,000 homes.

General

Earthquake Strikes Southwestern China—A 6.1-magnitude earthquake struck China Aug. 3, killing at least 589 in the country's southwestern province of Yunnan. The quake also injured more than 2,400 and damaged or destroyed tens of thousands of homes and sent tremors felt nearly 200 mi from its epicenter in the mountainous village of Longtoushan. Poor weather and hundreds of aftershocks slowed rescue teams, and narrow roads buried by landslides prevented aid workers from easily reaching smaller villages. Officials said nearly 230,000 people were relocated.

Hackers Amass Over 1 Billion Passwords—The *New York Times* Aug. 5 reported a group of hackers believed to be in south-central Russia had accumulated some 1.2 bil stolen Internet usernames and passwords in the largest known collection of illegally obtained online credentials. U.S.-based Hold Security, which uncovered the massive database, also said that the criminals had collected about 542 mil unique email addresses. According to the security firm, the hackers breached and gained data from some 420,000 websites, most of which it said remained vulnerable.

European Spacecraft *Rosetta* Rendezvous With Comet—More than 4 bil mi and nearly 10.5 years into its mission, the European Space Agency's unmanned *Rosetta* probe Aug. 6 became the first spacecraft to reach and orbit a comet. The probe flew along with the mass of ice and dust known as Comet 67P/Churyumov-Gerasimenko at a distance of 62 mi as it traveled at more than 30,000 mph some 250 mil mi from Earth, roughly halfway between the orbits of Jupiter and Mars. The ESA said it expected the probe's landing craft to touch down on the comet in Nov. 2014.

September 2014
National

Alibaba Debuts in Largest-Ever IPO; Other Economic News—The Chinese e-commerce firm Alibaba raised a U.S.-high $21.8 bil in its Sept. 19 initial public offering on the New York Stock Exchange. Bankers for the company exercised an option to buy additional shares, revaluing the offering at $25 bil, making it the largest IPO in history over the Agriculture Bank of China's $22.1-bil debut in 2010. Alibaba's market value of $231.4 bil after the first day of trading Sept. 19 placed it among top-tier U.S. tech firms Microsoft ($385 bil), Facebook ($200 bil), and Amazon ($150 bil). The Dow Jones Industrial Average closed at a record high 17,279.74 Sept. 19 but finished the month at 17,042.90, down 0.3% from Aug. The S&P 500 closed Sept. at 1,972.29, slipping 1.6% from the month before. The Nasdaq Composite Index finished Sept. at 4,493.39, falling 1.9%. All three indexes were still up for the quarter and year over year.

A federal judge in New Orleans ruled Sept. 4 that BP's "conscious disregard of known risks" made it responsible for the 2010 blowout of the *Deepwater Horizon* rig that killed 11 workers and spewed oil into the Gulf of Mexico for nearly three months. The ruling opened BP up to nearly $18 bil in potential civil penalties beyond the $28+ bil it had already paid in damages and cleanup.

After half a year of 200,000+ jobs growth per month, the Labor Dept. Sept. 5 reported job gains slipped to 142,000 in Aug., while the unemployment rate edged downward to 6.1% from 6.2%, mostly due to people leaving the workforce. The Commerce Dept. Aug. 28 bumped up its estimate of the growth of the country's second-quarter GDP to 4.2% from the July figure of 4.0%.

Multiple Security Breaches Blemish Secret Service—An unauthorized man armed with a knife entered the White House in Washington, DC, Sept. 19, sparking a congressional inquiry on security procedures. The man—an Iraq War veteran reportedly suffering from post-traumatic stress disorder—jumped a fence, sprinted 70 yds to the building, and made his way through the unlocked exterior door and several interior rooms before being subdued. (Pres. Barack Obama was not in the building at the time.) Secret Service Dir. Julia Pierson testified Sept. 30 in congressional hearings that she had briefed the president on only one security breach in 2014—the Sept. 19 incident. But the *Washington Examiner* reported that same day that an armed contractor with a criminal record had ridden in an elevator with Obama two weeks earlier in Atlanta, GA. The *Washington Post* Sept. 27 reported the Secret Service was unaware for four days in Nov. 2011 that a gunman had fired seven bullets into the White House, one of which broke a second-story window. Pierson, the first woman to lead the Secret Service, resigned Oct. 1.

Attorney General Eric Holder Announces Resignation—Eric Holder, the nation's first African-American attorney general and one of three remaining members of Pres. Obama's original cabinet, announced Sept. 25 that he would step down after a replacement was confirmed. Holder had been lauded by civil rights advocates for using his position as head of the Dept. of Justice to defend gay marriage and minority voting rights, reduce prison terms for nonviolent drug offenders, and initiate 20 investigations into police abuses. But he was criticized by some for his support for U.S. counterterrorism policies, including killing U.S. citizens living abroad with links to al-Qaeda, and for his failure to prosecute banking executives in connection with the 2008 financial crisis. Holder also clashed with lawmakers over his refusal to turn over documents related to the mishandled gunrunning sting Operation Fast and Furious. The House in June 2012 voted to hold Holder in contempt—the first time it had taken such an action against a U.S. attorney general—for refusing to comply.

International

Ebola Deaths Surge in West Africa—Health officials worked throughout Sept. to contain the ongoing outbreak in West Africa of the deadly Ebola virus, which the World Health Organization (WHO) said had killed at least 3,338 people out of 7,178 cases as of Sept. 28. With a health-care system in a state of near collapse, 1,998 deaths were in Liberia alone. Sierra Leone ordered additonal quarantine areas Sept. 24, restricting the movement of about one-third of the nation's population, just three days after the end of a controversial 72-hr. nationwide lockdown. WHO officials said the outbreak—fatal in about 70% of cases—was still spreading in Sierra Leone but appeared to be stabilizing in Guinea, where it had originated in Dec. 2013.

The U.S. Sept. 16 announced it would send 3,000 military personnel to West Africa to help coordinate the response and to build 17 treatment centers. The CDC Sept. 30 announced that a Liberian man, who had recently traveled to Dallas, TX, on a passenger jet, had the first case of Ebola to be diagnosed in the U.S. The facility that treated the man—Texas Health Presbyterian Hospital Dallas—came under fire for initially misdiagnosing and discharging him, thereby potentially exposing others to the virus, which is highly contagious through contact with bodily fluids. The hospital announced the man's death Oct. 8.

Islamist Militias Seize Libyan Capital—A coalition of Islamist militias known variously as Operation Dawn, Libya Dawn, or Dawn of Libya took control of the Libyan capital of Tripoli by Sept. 1 after fighters captured the city's international airport Aug. 23 in fierce clashes with pro-government forces and entered a residential annex of the U.S. embassy Aug. 31. (U.S. personnel had been evacuated in July due to the increasingly unstable security situation in the country.) Empowered by weak transitional governments following the 2011 ouster of Muammar al-Qaddafi and galvanized by Islamist factions losing power in parliament, the militias have played a key role in plunging Libya into its worst round of violence in three years and displacing some 100,000 Libyans during Aug. alone.

Ukraine Signs Ceasefire Deal With Separatists; Other Developments—Ukrainian officials Sept. 5 signed a ceasefire agreement with pro-Russia separatists waging a five-month-old insurgency in eastern Ukraine. The truce—forged largely by Russian Pres. Vladimir Putin—followed allegations by Ukrainian and NATO officials that Russian troops in late Aug. and early Sept. had assisted the separatists in a counteroffensive that delivered key gains, including the Donetsk-region town of Ilovaisk, where Russian forces Aug. 29 reportedly killed some 100 Ukrainian soldiers. Cementing these gains, the ceasefire called on both sides to withdraw all heavy weapons and release more than 2,000 prisoners combined. The Ukrainian parliament Sept. 16 ratified the country's association agreement with the EU, with concessions to Moscow in the form of delayed implementation of trade provisions until at least 2016. In the wake of truce violations that had killed nearly 40 people, representatives met Sept. 19-20 in Minsk for another round of talks. A NATO official Sept. 24 reported that Russia had withdrawn a large number of its troops from Ukraine. The EU said the following week that the development, while encouraging, did not warrant reversing sanctions. The end of the month saw continued fighting for control of Donetsk airport. As of Oct. 6, the UN reported deaths in the conflict at 3,660.

NATO officials agreed Sept. 5 to create a 4,000-troop force to respond to Russian threats against Baltic member states.

Iraq Gets New Prime Minister; U.S. Launches Airstrikes Against ISIS in Syria—Hailed for his potential to better unite Iraqis, Shiite Haider al-Abadi was sworn in as the country's new prime minister Sept. 8. Iraq's minority Sunnis and Kurds had been increasingly alienated by former Shiite Iraqi Prime Min. Nouri al-Maliki's autocratic rule. Abadi pledged to unify Iraqis, especially in the fight against the Sunni Islamic extremist group calling itself the Islamic State (popularly known as ISIS).

Vowing to destroy ISIS forces, Pres. Barack Obama Sept. 10 said he would expand U.S. airstrikes against militants in Iraq and initiate strikes on ISIS targets in northern Syria. Obama said he would send 475 more noncombat personnel to Iraq to serve in a support capacity, putting the total U.S. troop level there at about 1,600. The U.S. House Sept. 17 approved, 273-156, a bill authorizing $500 mil to arm and train Syrian rebels and the Senate passed the legislation, 78-22, Sept. 18; Pres. Obama signed it the next day. U.S. officials announced the formation of a core coalition against ISIS that included Germany, which armed and trained Kurdish forces in Iraq, and France, which initiated airstrikes in Iraq four days before the U.S. began targeting ISIS in Syria Sept. 23. Five Arab countries, including Saudi Arabia and Jordan, were also participating in strikes. The expanded military action followed ISIS propaganda videos released earlier in the month showing the purported beheadings of American-Israeli journalist Steven Sotloff and British aid worker David Haines. ISIS launched an assault Sept. 16 on the strategic border city of Kobani in northern Syria, capturing dozens of villages and forcing more than 160,000 Kurdish refugees to flee into neighboring Turkey by the end of Sept.

Scotland Chooses to Stay in the UK—In a Sept. 18 referendum addressing Scotland's sovereignty, more than 2 mil people—55% of those who cast votes—voted to remain part of the UK instead of becoming an independent nation. Participated in by 85% of eligible voters, the referendum capped a divisive debate over whether to sever more than 300 years of union with England. Those in favor of independence cited more government control, especially over offshore oil reserves; those behind the "No" campaign argued taxes would have to be increased to recreate nationalized services, such as national defense. British officials had said they would not permit Scotland to use the British pound as its currency, and economists had raised concerns about its ability to join the European Union. British Prime Min. David Cameron said post-referendum that increased-autonomy legislation—giving Scotland greater control over spending, taxes, and welfare in exchange for staying with the UK—would be enacted by Jan. 2015.

Afghan Presidential Candidates Strike Power-Sharing Deal—Three months after Afghanistan's June 14 presidential runoff election, the rival candidates agreed Sept. 21 to form a unity government, ending a long dispute over voting results in which both candidates accused the other's supporters of fraud. The deal called for former Finance Min. Ashraf Ghani to replace outgoing Pres. Hamid Karzai and past Foreign Min. Abdullah Abdullah—who narrowly survived an assassination attempt June 6—to assume the newly created role of chief executive. The power-sharing deal also specified parity in high-level economic and security appointments and called for electoral reforms.

Taliban forces in the six months preceding the agreement had carried out 700 ground attacks that killed 1,368 police personnel and 800 soldiers—more than in any other corresponding time frame. Just three days before Ghani and Abdullah were sworn in Sept. 29, Taliban forces killed about 70 villagers after seizing a strategic district in Ghazni province. Afghan and U.S. officials Sept. 30 signed the U.S.-Afghan Bilateral Security Agreement, which provided for 9,800 American and at least 2,000 NATO troops to stay in Afghanistan through 2024 after the formal end of the combat mission Dec. 31, 2014.

General

Williams and Cilic Victorious at U.S. Open—American tennis great Serena Williams won her sixth U.S. Open singles championship Sept. 7 against No. 10-ranked Caroline Wozniacki of Denmark (6-3, 6-3) at the Billie Jean King Natl. Tennis Center in Flushing Meadows Corona Park in New York City. It was Williams's 18th Grand Slam singles title, which tied her with legends Chris Evert and Martina Navratilova. Croatia's Marin Cilic, the No. 14 seed, claimed his first grand slam title when he defeated (6-3, 6-3, 6-3) 10th-seeded Kei Nishikori of Japan, also playing in his first major final.

Domestic Abuse Scandals Tarnish NFL—Exacerbating extant criticism of the National Football League's handling of an assault case involving Baltimore Ravens running back Ray Rice, the website TMZ Sept. 8 released graphic video footage of the 27-year-old Rice punching his then-fiancée in a hotel elevator. Within hours of the video's release, the Ravens terminated Rice's contract and the NFL suspended him indefinitely. The assault had first become public when Rice was arrested Feb. 15; video footage showing Rice dragging Palmer out of the elevator had circulated widely. But Rice had avoided trial on aggravated assault charges by participating in a pre-trial intervention program, and NFL Commissioner Roger Goodell July 24 imposed a two-game suspension as a penalty. Facing widespread criticism over the relatively mild punishment, Goodell in late Aug. announced a six-game penalty for future first-time domestic violence offenders and said Rice's punishment had been too lenient. Goodell said league officials had not received the more graphic video released in Sept., a claim disputed by some. The NFL Sept. 10 announced an investigation into the matter would be led by former FBI Dir. Robert Mueller.

Minnesota Vikings running back Adrian Peterson surrendered himself to authorities Sept. 13 on charges of reckless or negligent injury to a child. Peterson allegedly used a tree branch to strike and discipline his four-year-old son. After initially reactivating Peterson, the Vikings placed him on the exempt list and suspended him from all team activities Sept. 17, amid outcry and threats from sponsors. That same day, the Carolina Panthers suspended defensive end Greg Hardy, who was convicted in a bench trial in July of assaulting and threatening to kill his then-girlfriend; he was appealing the conviction.

Phoenix Sweeps Chicago in WNBA Finals—The defending champion Phoenix Mercury defeated the Chicago Sky, 87-82, in Game 3 Sept. 12 at the UIC Pavilion in Chicago to take the WNBA championship for the second straight year. Veteran Mercury guard Diana Taurasi averaged 20.3 points in the Finals and was named the WNBA Finals MVP.

Blade Runner Convicted of Homicide—South African sprinter Oscar Pistorius was found guilty of culpable homicide Sept. 12 after a judge ruled he acted negligently when he fired shots through a door, killing his girlfriend, whom he claimed to have mistaken for an intruder. Pistorius was acquitted on the more serious charge of premeditated murder. He was sentenced Oct. 21 to five years in prison, in addition to a suspended three-year sentence for a firearms charge. The first amputee to win a World Championship track medal, he also became the first double amputee to participate in the Olympics when he competed in the 2012 games.

Multiple Shipwrecks May Have Drowned 700—According to the Intl. Organization for Migration, human traffickers Sept. 10 off the coast of Malta allegedly rammed and sank a ship carrying about 500 undocumented migrants heading to Europe, drowning all but nine on board. Another migrant boat sank off the coast of Libya Sept. 14, killing over 200 and bringing the sea-based death toll for European-bound migrants to nearly 3,000 for the year.

Flooding in India and Pakistan Kills Hundreds—About 550 people in Pakistan, India, and India-controlled Kashmir were killed during the first three weeks of Sept. in flooding and mudslides from seasonal monsoon rains. The governments were criticized for failing to warn residents and for lack of disaster preparedness. Millions were affected by the floods, the worst in the region in 60 years, and hundreds of thousands were evacuated.

Indian Spacecraft Reaches Mars—India's unmanned Mars Orbiter Mission entered the Red Planet's orbit Sept. 24, making the Indian Space Research Organization (ISRO) the first agency to succeed on its maiden attempt and the fourth program to send a spacecraft to Mars. The ISRO completed the 10-month-long mission at a cost of $74 mil, a fraction of the $671 mil NASA spent on its 10th Mars-orbiting probe MAVEN, which had reached the planet three days earlier.

Japanese Volcano Overcomes Hikers—Japan's Mt. Ontake erupted without warning Sept. 27, spewing ash and toxic gases that killed at least 56 hikers and injured dozens more. Officials estimated as many as 250 people were at the summit of the volcano—located about 125 mi west of Tokyo—at the time of the flare-up. The eruption was Japan's deadliest in 90 years, surpassing a 1991 eruption of Mt. Unzen that killed 43.

October 2014
National

Jobless Rate Lowest Since Recession, Other Economic/ Business News—The Labor Dept. Oct. 3 reported that the unemployment rate in Sept. fell to 5.9% from 6.1% in Aug. The rate was the lowest since July 2008, but labor force participation in Sept. dipped to a 36-year low of 62.7%. The economy added 248,000 jobs in Sept. and revised its jobs growth numbers for July and Aug. a combined 69,000 jobs upward, to 243,000 and 180,000, respectively. Wall Street saw its steepest intraday drop in more than three years Oct. 15, with the Dow Jones Industrial Average plunging 460 points before rebounding to close 173 points down from the day before. The Dow finished Oct. at 17,390.52, up 2.0% from Aug. while the S&P 500 closed the month at 2,018.05, gaining 2.3% from the month before. The Nasdaq Composite Index finished Oct. at 4,630.74, climbing 3.1% during the same period. Despite the volatile stock market, the Conference Board Oct. 28 reported consumer confidence hit a seven-year high during the month.

Banking giant JPMorgan Chase announced Oct. 2 that hackers had accessed contact information from 76 mil household accounts and 7 mil business accounts—one of the largest personal data thefts in history. Less than three weeks later, JPMorgan received more than $92 mil in fines from the European Union for colluding with the Royal Bank of Scotland on interest rates.

U.S. Supreme Court Begins Session With Same-Sex Marriage, Voter ID Law—The U.S. Supreme Court opened its annual term Oct. 6 and declined to hear appeals from five states with same-sex marriage bans that had been struck down by federal appellate court rulings. The Court's announcement had the effect of legalizing same-sex marriages in Indiana, Oklahoma, Utah, Virginia, and Wisconsin and paving the way for same-sex unions in six more states under the jurisdiction of those appellate courts.

The Court Oct. 18 rejected an emergency request by the Justice Dept. and civil rights groups to prevent Texas from applying a voter ID law—widely described as the nation's toughest—in the upcoming Nov. 4 election. A federal judge had ruled it unconstitutional Oct. 9, but an appeals court the next week declared it was too late to change the state's voting requirements. Associate Justice Ruth Bader Ginsberg, one of three dissenting justices, said that the Texas law risked disenfranchising hundreds of thousands of mostly black and Hispanic voters. The Court Oct. 9 prevented Wisconsin from enforcing its new voter ID law.

Midterm Elections Projected as Most Expensive Ever—Projections released Oct. 22 and revised Oct. 29 by the nonpartisan Center for Responsive Politics (CRP) predicted about $3.7 bil would be spent on the Nov. 2014 election, making it the most expensive midterm election in U.S. history. Most of the sum ($2.7 bil) was projected to come from candidates and political parties, while almost $700 mil was expected from outside groups, including super PACs and nonprofit organizations. The revised spending forecast exceeded 2010's midterm contest by about $40 mil, and the center noted that very large donors to outside groups were having more of an impact than on past elections. It expected the trend to continue in the 2016 election cycle, with more money coming from fewer people. The CRP projection came less than five years after the U.S. Supreme Court's decision in *Citizens United v. Federal Election Commission* removed caps on political spending by unions and corporations.

International

Belgian Lawmakers Form "Kamikaze" Coalition—After more than four months without an elected government in linguistically and culturally divided Belgium, three Dutch-speaking parties Oct. 7 formed a center-right coalition with the free market liberal Reformist Movement (MR) the lone French-speaking party in the alliance. With the MR party's Charles Michel serving as prime minister, the coalition was the first in 26 years of not to include the Socialist party and the first to include ministers from the separatist New Flemish Alliance, which won 32% of votes in May 25 elections. The coalition planned to tighten immigration and asylum requirements and balance the national budget by 2018. Belgium spent 541 days, 2010-11, forming its previous government, 2010-11.

ISIS Gains Ground in Spite of Coalition Efforts; Jury Convicts Blackwater Guards—The Sunni extremist group known as the Islamic State of Iraq and Syria (ISIS) succeeded Oct. 10 in capturing territory within eight mi. of the Baghdad airport. By mid-Oct., ISIS had seized 80% of Iraq's largest province of Anbar—including multiple military bases—and continued to carry out acts of terror in line with a triple-suicide bombing northeast of Baghdad that killed 26 people Oct. 12. ISIS Oct. 3 released a video showing the apparent beheading of British aid worker Alan Henning, the fourth Western worker to be beheaded on camera by the group. Fighting in the northern Syrian city of Kobani continued to rage through Oct., killing more than 800 in 40 days as U.S. airstrikes and weapon drops helped Kurdish fighters retake portions of the city. The United Nations Oct 2 reported that more than 5,500 people had been killed in Iraq since ISIS began its offensive in June.

A U.S. federal jury Oct. 22 convicted four former guards employed by the Blackwater security firm (now known as Acadmi) for their role in 2007 shootings that killed 17 Iraqi civilians and injured 20 others. The jury pronounced Nicholas Slatten guilty of first-degree murder and found three others guilty of multiple counts of voluntary and attempted manslaughter. In addition to creating an international outrage, the incident had raised questions about the U.S. military's increased reliance on defense contractors.

Ukrainian Crisis Talks Stall; Pro-Western Parties Claim Victory at Polls—Diplomatic talks in Milan, Italy, Oct. 17 involving Ukrainian Pres. Petro Poroshenko and Russian Pres. Vladimir Putin failed to create a roadmap for ending more than six months of fighting which the United Nations said had killed at least 4,035 people in eastern Ukraine as of Oct. 29. The two leaders nevertheless agreed to let aerial drones monitor conflict zones and international borders. They also reached a preliminary agreement on Russia supplying natural gas to Ukraine; the deal was finalized Oct. 30. Ahead of the talks, Putin had ordered the withdrawal of Russia's troops along its border with Ukraine. The United Nations Oct. 8 reported that 331 people had been killed since the start of a ceasefire signed Sept. 5. Vowing to take control of more cities, separatist leaders Oct. 23 announced they would no longer observe the ceasefire and stepped up attacks at the Donetsk airport while launching assaults on Ukrainian forces in the Donbass region. On Oct. 26, 52% of eligible Ukrainian voters elected a parliament dominated by pro-European parties. Poroshenko's party finished second with 21.8% of the vote, just slightly below the People's Front's 22.2%; the sole pro-Russian party won 9.4%, coming in fourth.

Democracy Talks Stalemate Amid Massive Protests in Hong Kong—Discussions deadlocked Oct. 21 between senior members of Hong Kong's government and representatives of a student group organizing large-scale demonstrations aimed at forcing China to allow the public to nominate candidates for Hong Kong's 2017 election for chief executive. The 2017 election would be the first for the post voted on by the people. Officials said they could not supersede the Chinese government, which issued a directive Aug 31 affirming nomination by a reportedly pro-China committee. Student leaders began protesting in late Sept. outside government offices in the territory. Joined by members of the pro-democracy group Occupy Central, demonstrators succeeded in blocking key roadways but clashed throughout much of Oct. with police and anti-Occupy protesters alleged to be from organized crime "triads." In addition to electoral reform, protesters called for the resignation of Hong Kong's current chief executive, Leung Chunying, whom they accused of allegiance to China.

Secularists Win Control in Tunisian Elections—Tunisia's secular Nidaa Tounes party defeated the governing moderate Islamic Ennahda movement Oct. 26 in the country's second parliamentary election—and first under a new constitution—since protesters ousted autocratic president Zine al-Abidine Ben Ali in 2011, setting off Arab Spring uprisings across much of the Middle East. According to official results, the secularists won 39% of the seats, while the Islamists won just under 32%, down from 42% in the outgoing parliament. Critics had accused the Islamists of economic mismanagement and leniency towards terrorists. Foreign observers said the election, which about 60% of eligible voters participated in and which featured some 100 parties, was largely free of irregularities.

Largest Ever Ebola Outbreak Continues; Virus Spreads to U.S., Sparks Debate—According to an Oct. 29 report from the World Health Organization, the ongoing outbreak of the Ebola virus in the West African countries of Guinea, Liberia, and Sierra Leone had infected at least 13,700. Although agency officials reported the virus was still out of control in Liberia—where more than half of deaths in the outbreak had occurred—they said new cases in the country appeared to be declining. U.S. researchers Oct. 9 announced that the first trial of an Ebola vaccine had begun in Mali. Drawing criticism from most public health authorities, Australia and Canada later in the month became the first industrialized countries to ban entry to persons from nations where the outbreak was widespread.

A week after the death of Thomas Eric Duncan—the first Ebola patient to be diagnosed in the U.S.—officials Oct. 15 reported that a second nurse who treated Duncan had contracted the Ebola virus despite following safety procedures (both nurses were declared virus-free by Oct. 28). The news triggered calls from some politicians for the U.S. to enact a travel ban, and the U.S. Centers for Disease Control enacted stricter treatment and monitoring procedures. Following the Oct. 23 Ebola diagnosis of a New York City doctor who had just returned from volunteering in Guinea, returning nurse Kaci Hickox drew national attention after she became the first person subjected to state-mandated quarantine in New Jersey. Hickox had twice tested negative for the virus and criticized the decision to quarantine as against accepted medical procedure. Released early, she defied a quarantine policy in her home state of Maine by taking a bike ride, before a state judge ruled in her favor.

Uprising Ends Burkina Faso Presidency—Burkina Faso Pres. Blaise Compaore resigned Oct. 31 in the wake of mass demonstrations over efforts to extend his 27-year rule. The day before, protesters in the capital city of Ouagadougou, objecting to a proposed constitutional amendment that would allow Compaore to seek a fifth term, set fire to government buildings including the nation's parliament. Military leaders assumed control following Compaore's resignation, prompting activists to stage rallies against a feared coup attempt.

General

Cave Paintings Challenge Art History Beliefs—A study published Oct. 8 in the journal *Nature* dated a painting of a human hand on a cave wall on the Indonesian island of Sulawesi to at least 39,900 years ago, comparable to the world's oldest known cave art (at least 40,800 years old) at Spain's El Castillo site. According to the joint Australian-Indonesian research team, the seven caves studied also contain paintings of animals created at least 35,000 years ago, roughly the same age as well-known images in Chauvet Cave in France. The study opens up the possibility that humans carried a tradition of cave painting with them when they migrated out of Africa some 70,000 years ago.

Catholic Bishops Debate Approaches to Homosexuality, Divorce—A Vatican assembly on family issues convened Oct. 5-19, opening discussions to be addressed in a larger meeting of bishops in Oct. 2015. The "extraordinary general assembly" of 191 bishops gained widespread attention when a preliminary draft collecting the ideas of those present tentatively raised the possibilities of a more welcoming approach toward homosexuals and allowing some divorced and remarried Catholics to take communion. The final report was worded more conservatively, calling for further consideration of these matters. Even so, passages related to the two groups were approved only by a simple majority of those present and not the two-thirds majority required for a consensus. Pope Francis, warning both of "the temptation of hostile rigidity" by "so-called traditionalists" and of "deceptive mercy" by "so-called progressives," urged further debate on the issues. Francis also beatified Pope Paul VI, who led the Church in 1963-78.

Gunman Attacks Canadian Parliament—A man fired shots in Canada's national parliament building in Ottawa Oct. 22, shortly after fatally shooting a soldier guarding the country's National War Memorial. The shooter, a recent convert to Islam, was killed by the sergeant-at-arms of the House of Commons. The attack came two days after another recent convert to Islam ran over two Canadian soldiers with his car, killing one, near Montréal, QC. Officials labeled the Oct. 20 incident a terrorist act; it was the first deadly attack in Canada by Islamic militants.

School Shooting Kills Five in WA—A 15-year-old student opened fire at a high school in Marysville, WA on Oct. 24 shooting five students, four fatally. According to the local sheriff's office, Jaylen Fryberg had sent text messages to his five victims—two cousins, and three reportedly close friends—requesting they meet him in the cafeteria, where the shooting occurred. Witnesses said that a teacher confronted the shooter, an American Indian who was named a prince on the school's homecoming court the week before, but he fatally turned the gun on himself.

San Francisco Giants Win Third World Series in Five Years—The San Francisco Giants won the 2014 World Series over the Kansas City Royals in seven games that ended Oct. 29 at Kauffman Stadium in Kansas City, MO. Both teams were Wild Card winners and it was the only time in Series history that both teams had fewer than 90 regular-season wins (excluding seasons cut short). The final game brought several dramatic moments, including the first World Series play to be reversed under new video replay rules, and a Royals runner reaching third base with two out in the ninth inning, representing what could have been the winning run. Giants pitcher Madison Bumgarner was the Series MVP, with a 117-pitch, complete-game shutout to his credit in Game 5 and five final scoreless innings in relief in Game 7.

Accidents Befall Two Spacecraft in Same Week—In a setback to space tourism and commercial space travel, *SpaceShipTwo*, developed by British billionaire Richard Branson's Virgin Galactic venture to be a passenger spacecraft, crashed Oct. 31 in California's Mojave Desert during its 55th test flight, killing one pilot and seriously injuring another. As of the incident date, more than 700 people had paid deposits for future flights of up to $250,000. Three days earlier, an unmanned commercial Antares rocket carrying supplies to the International Space Station (ISS) exploded about 15 sec. after liftoff at a Virginia facility. The incident spawned questions about NASA's dependence on commercial contractors to ferry supplies. In Sept., NASA had selected Boeing and SpaceX to transport astronauts to the ISS by as early as 2017.

OBITUARIES

A

Abbado, Claudio, 80, Italian opera conductor at La Scala (Milan), 1968-86; Bologna, Italy, Jan. 20, 2014.

Albanese, Licia, 105, Italian-born soprano who sang title role in Puccini's *Madama Butterfly* over 300 times; New York, NY, Aug. 15, 2014.

Albrecht, Karl, 94, German businessman who cofounded the supermarket chain Aldi with brother Theo; Essen, Germany, July 16, 2014.

Angelou, Maya, 86, author and poet best known for memoir *I Know Why the Caged Bird Sings* (1969); Winston-Salem, NC, May 28, 2014.

Askew, Reubin, 85, Florida governor (D, 1971-79) who worked on desegregation, the environment, and fiscal responsibility; Tallahassee, FL, Mar. 13, 2014.

Attenborough, Richard, 90, British actor, Academy Award-winning director, and producer best known for directing *Gandhi* (1982); London, Eng., UK, Aug. 24, 2014.

B

Bacall, Lauren, 89, actress known for *To Have and Have Not* (1944) and *The Big Sleep* (1946) with husband Humphrey Bogart; New York, NY, Aug. 12, 2014.

Baker, Howard, 88, U.S. senator (R, TN, 1967-85) who investigated Pres. Nixon and served as majority leader (1981-85); White House chief of staff (1987-88); Huntsville, TN, June 26, 2014.

Baraka, Amiri (Everett LeRoi Jones), 79, poet and playwright who wrote about the black experience; Newark, NJ, Jan. 9, 2014.

Beck, Marilyn, 85, Hollywood columnist; Oceanside, CA, May 31, 2014.

Becker, Gary, 83, Nobel Prize-winning economist known for human behavioral studies; Chicago, IL, May 3, 2014.

Bellamy, Walter, 74, Hall of Fame basketball player and Olympic gold medalist (1960); College Park, GA, Nov. 2, 2013.

Bendjelloul, Malik, 36, Swedish documentarian who won an Academy Award for *Searching for Sugar Man* (2012); Stockholm, Sweden, May 13, 2014.

Bergen, Polly, 84, Emmy Award-winning actress best known for *Cape Fear* (1962); Southbury, CT, Sept. 20, 2014.

Berger, Thomas, 89, satirical novelist best known for *Little Big Man* (1964); Nyack, NY, July 13, 2014.

Bergonzi, Carlo, 90, Italian tenor known for Verdi operas; Milan, Italy, July 25, 2014.

Berns, Sam, 17, student who became the face of premature aging disease progeria; Boston, MA, Jan. 10, 2014.

Biggs, Ronnie, 84, British criminal known for the Great Train Robbery (1963) and prison escape (1965); London, Eng., UK, Dec. 18, 2013.

Bradlee, Benjamin, 93, *Washington Post* editor (1968-91) who oversaw the Watergate story, which led to the resignation of Pres. Richard Nixon; Washington, DC, Oct. 21, 2014.

Brady, James, 73, press secretary to Pres. Ronald Reagan who was wounded in assassination attempt on Reagan and later became gun control advocate; Alexandria, VA, Aug. 4, 2014.

Brenner, David, 78, comedian who appeared on *The Tonight Show* over 150 times; New York, NY, Mar. 15, 2014.

Brinkley, Joel, 61, Pulitzer Prize-winning journalist for *NY Times* (1983-2006); Washington, DC, Mar. 11, 2014.

Bronfman, Edgar, Sr., 84, Canadian-born businessman and philanthropist who led family business, Seagram; New York, NY, Dec. 21, 2013.

Browne, Sylvia, 77, author and TV personality who claimed psychic abilities; San Jose, CA, Nov. 20, 2013.

Burns, James MacGregor, 95, Pulitzer Prize-winning historian and political scientist known for books on Franklin D. Roosevelt; Williamstown, MA, July 15, 2014.

C

Caesar, Sid, 91, Emmy Award-winning actor and writer best known for pioneering TV variety series *Your Show of Shows* (1950-54); Beverly Hills, CA, Feb. 12, 2014.

Carter, Rubin "Hurricane", 76, boxer whose conviction for triple homicide was later overturned; Toronto, ON, Canada, Apr. 20, 2014.

Cashen, Frank, 88, NY Mets general manager (1980-91) who helped win the 1986 World Series; Easton, MD, June 30, 2014.

Cathy, S(amuel) Truett, 93, Chick-fil-A fast-food restaurant founder; Clayton County, GA, Sept. 8, 2014.

Cavendish, Deborah, 94, Dowager Duchess of Devonshire; one of the famed Mitford sisters; Eng., UK, Sept. 24, 2014.

Clapp, Louise Brough, 91, tennis player who won 35 Grand Slam titles; Vista, CA, Feb. 3, 2014.

Coachman, Alice, 90, high jumper who was the first black woman to win an Olympic gold medal (1948); Albany, GA, July 14, 2014.

Coleman, Jerry, 89, NY Yankees second baseman (1949-57) and broadcaster for NY Yankees and San Diego Padres; San Diego, CA, Jan. 5, 2014.

Crewe, Bob, 83, songwriter and producer who cowrote "Big Girls Don't Cry" (1962) and "Lady Marmalade" (1975); Scarborough, ME, Sept. 11, 2014.

D

Dahl, Robert, 98, political scientist regarded for views on power and democracy; Hamden, CT, Feb. 5, 2014.

Davis, Ann B., 88, actress best known as housekeeper Alice on *The Brady Bunch* (1969-74); San Antonio, TX, June 1, 2014.

DeCrow, Karen, 76, activist who led the National Organization of Women (1974-77); Jamesville, NY, June 6, 2014.

Dee, Ruby, 89, actress and activist best known for *A Raisin in the Sun* (1961) and for collaborations with husband Ossie Davis; New Rochelle, NY, June 11, 2014.

de la Renta, Oscar, 82, Dominican Republic-born fashion designer who dressed famous women, including first ladies; Kent, CT, Oct. 20, 2014.

Dickson Wright, Clarissa, 66, English chef best known as one of *Two Fat Ladies* in a 1990s cooking show; Edinburgh, Scotland, UK, Mar. 15, 2014.

Douglas, Hal, 89, voiceover artist known for movie trailers; Lovettsville, VA, Mar. 7, 2014.

Duvalier, Jean-Claude, 63, former president of Haiti (1971-86) known as "Baby Doc," whose ruthless regime followed his father's example; Port-au-Prince, Haiti, Oct. 4, 2014.

E

Eisenhower, John, 91, U.S. Army brigadier general and military historian; son of Pres. Dwight D. Eisenhower; Trappe, MD, Dec. 21, 2013.

Everly, Phil, 74, singer who performed with brother Don as the Everly Brothers; Burbank, CA, Jan. 3, 2014.

DJ E-Z Rock (Rodney Bryce), 46, hip-hop producer known for "It Takes Two" (1998); Apr. 27, 2014.

F

Feldstein, Al, 88, writer, artist, and editor of *Mad* magazine (1956-85); Paradise Valley, MT, Apr. 29, 2014.

Field, Syd, 77, teacher and author of *Screenplay: The Foundations of Screenwriting* (1979), a definitive resource on its subject; Beverly Hills, CA, Nov. 17, 2013.

Foley, James, 40, American photojournalist beheaded by Sunni militant group ISIS in an online propaganda film; Syria, death reported Aug. 19, 2014.

Fontaine, Joan, 96, British-American Academy Award-winning actress; Carmel, CA, Dec. 15, 2013.

Ford, Eileen, 92, cofounder of Ford Modeling Agency; Morristown, NJ, July 9, 2014.

Ford, William Clay, 88, Ford Motor Co. executive; Detroit Lions owner (1963-2014); Grosse Point, MI, Mar. 9, 2014.

Forst, Donald H., 81, journalist who led *New York Newsday*, *Village Voice*, and *Boston Herald*; Albany, NY, Jan. 4, 2014.

Fraser, Ian, 81, Emmy Award-winning British composer and conductor best known for collaborations with Julie Andrews; Los Angeles, CA, Oct. 31, 2014.

G

García Márquez, Gabriel, 87, Nobel Prize-winning Colombian author known for "magical realism" in *One Hundred Years of Solitude* (1967) and *Love in the Time of Cholera* (1985); Mexico City, Mexico, Apr. 17, 2014.

Garner, James, 86, actor known for TV shows *Maverick* (1957-62) and *The Rockford Files* (1974-80); Los Angeles, CA, July 19, 2014.

Gaskin, Stephen, 79, Marine-turned-hippie who cofounded "The Farm," a commune; Summertown, TN, July 1, 2014.

Gelb, Arthur, Jr., 90, editor and *NY Times* executive who diversified the paper's content in new sections; New York, NY, May 20, 2014.

Geldof, Peaches, 25, British writer and TV personality; Kent, Eng., UK, Apr. 7, 2014.

Glazer, Malcolm, 85, businessman; owner of Tampa Bay Buccaneers and Manchester United; May 28, 2014.

Goffin, Gerry, 75, lyricist who with wife Carole King wrote hit songs, including "Will You Love Me Tomorrow?" (1960) and "One Fine Day" (1963); Los Angeles, CA, June 19, 2014.

Gola, Tom, 81, Hall of Fame basketball player for La Salle Univ. and Philadelphia Warriors; Meadowbrook, PA, Jan. 26, 2014.

Golan, Menahem, 85, Israeli director and movie producer; Jaffa, Israel, Aug. 8, 2014.

Goldstein, Al, 77, cofounder of adult magazine *Screw*; Brooklyn, NY, Dec. 19, 2013.

Goodman, George, 83, author and economics commentator who wrote under the pseudonym Adam Smith; Miami, FL, Jan. 3, 2014.

Gordimer, Nadine, 90, Nobel Prize-winning South African writer whose works examined apartheid South Africa; Johannesburg, South Africa, July 13, 2014.

Grant, Bob, 84, conservative radio host known for combative style; Hillsborough, NJ, Dec. 31, 2013.

Greenglass, David, 92, spy for the Soviet Union who testified against his sister and brother-in-law, Ethel and Julius Rosenberg, which led to their convictions and executions; NY, July 1, 2014.

Guralnik, Gerald, 77, one of six physicists who theorized the Higgs boson; Providence, RI, Apr. 26, 2014.

Gwynn, Tony, 54, San Diego Padres slugger who was eight-time National League batting champion; Poway, CA, June 16, 2014.

H

Haden, Charlie, 76, jazz bassist with the Ornette Coleman Quartet who then led the Liberation Music Orchestra; Los Angeles, CA, July 11, 2014.

Hall, Jim, 83, jazz guitarist and composer; New York, NY, Dec. 10, 2013.

Hamilton, (Foreststorn) "Chico," 92, jazz drummer and bandleader who pioneered West Coast cool jazz; New York, NY, Nov. 25, 2013.

Hellwig, James, 54, WWE pro wrestler known as the Ultimate Warrior; Scottsdale, AZ, Apr. 8, 2014.

Hernández, Melba, 92, Cuban revolutionary with Fidel Castro who later served as ambassador to Vietnam and Cambodia; Havana, Cuba, Mar. 9, 2014.

Hoffman, Philip Seymour, 46, Academy Award-winning actor and director known for *Capote* (2005) and *Doubt* (2008); New York, NY, Feb. 2, 2014.

Hogwood, Christopher, 73, British conductor and founder of the Academy of Ancient Music ensemble; Cambridge, Eng., UK, Sept. 24, 2014.

Holder, Geoffrey, 84, Trinidadian actor, dancer, and choreographer who won Tony Awards for *The Wiz* (1975); New York, NY, Oct. 5, 2014.

Hollein, Hans, 80, Austrian Pritzker Prize-winning postmodern architect and designer; Vienna, Austria, Apr. 24, 2014.

Holt, Nancy, 75, artist known for public installations and land art; New York, NY, Feb. 8, 2014.

Hoskins, Bob, 71, British actor known for *Who Framed Roger Rabbit?* (1988); Apr. 29, 2014.

I

Iyengar, B(ellur) K(rishnamachar) S(undararaja), 95, Indian guru and author whose *Light on Yoga* (1966) popularized yoga practice; Pune, India, Aug. 20, 2014.

J

Jancsó, Miklós, 92, Hungarian film director known for political epics; Hungary, Jan. 31, 2014.

Jaruzelski, Wojciech, 90, Polish general who was the nation's last Communist leader (1981-90) and first president (1989-90); Warsaw, Poland, May 25, 2014.

Jeffords, Jim, 80, U.S. senator (VT, 1989-2007) who switched from Republican to independent in 2001, giving Democrats control of Congress; Washington, DC, Aug. 18, 2014.

Jemison, T(heodore) J(udson), 95, minister and civil rights activist; Natl. Baptist Convention president (1982-94); Baton Rouge, LA, Nov. 15, 2013.

Jobe, Frank, 88, surgeon who developed Tommy John procedure to fix pitchers' elbows; Santa Monica, CA, Mar. 6, 2014.

Johnson, Russell, 89, actor known as "the Professor" on TV series *Gilligan's Island* (1964-67); Bainbridge Isl., WA, Jan. 16, 2014.

Jones, (Wallace) "Wah Wah," 88, multisport star at Univ. of Kentucky; Olympic gold medalist in basketball (1948); Lexington, KY, July 27, 2014.

K

Kalashnikov, Mikhail, 94, Russian general who invented the AK-47 rifle; Izhevsk, Russia, Dec. 23, 2013.

Kaplan, Justin, 88, Pulitzer Prize-winning biographer of Mark Twain; Cambridge, MA, Mar. 2, 2014.

Kaplan, Peter, 59, editor of *NY Observer* (1994-2009), a weekly paper that incubated journalists and chronicled the elite; New York, NY, Nov. 29, 2013.

Kasem, Casey, 82, radio personality and voice actor who hosted *America's Top 40* (1970-2004) and voiced Shaggy in animated *Scooby Doo* series; Gig Harbor, WA, June 15, 2014.

Kaufman, Bel, 103, German-born teacher and writer whose debut novel, *Up the Down Staircase* (1965), depicted an urban school; New York, NY, July 25, 2014.

Keating, Charles, 90, financier whose fraud epitomized the 1980s savings-and-loan crisis; Phoenix, AZ, Mar. 31, 2014.

Keyes, Daniel, 86, author known for sci-fi story (1959) and subsequent novel (1966) *Flowers for Algernon;* Boca Raton, FL, June 15, 2014.

Kimes, Sante, 79, criminal convicted of murder and many other crimes with son; Bedford Hills, NY, May 19, 2014.

Kiner, Ralph, 91, National League slugger who hit 369 home runs in 10 seasons; longtime NY Mets broadcaster (1962-2013); Rancho Mirage, CA, Feb. 6, 2014.

Kinnell, Galway, 87, Pulitzer Prize-winning poet whose work dealt with social issues; Sheffield, VT, Oct. 28, 2014.

Kinzler, Jack, 94, NASA engineer, known as "Mr. Fix It," who helped repair the damaged *Skylab* (1973); Taylor Lake Village, TX, Mar. 4, 2014.

Kizer, Carolyn, 89, Pulitzer Prize-winning poet whose work focused on women's experiences; Sonoma, CA, Oct. 9, 2014.

Knuckles, Frankie, 59, producer and DJ who pioneered house music; Chicago, IL, Mar. 31, 2014.

Kochiyama, Yuri, 93, Japanese-American internment camp survivor and civil rights activist; Berkeley, CA, June 1, 2014.

Koenig, Julian, 93, advertising copywriter who coined "Earth Day" and created the VW Beetle tagline, "Think small"; New York, NY, June 12, 2014.

Kumin, Maxine, 88, Pulitzer Prize-winning poet; U.S. poet laureate (1981-82); Warner, NH, Feb. 6, 2014.

Kwolek, Stephanie, 90, chemist who invented the bulletproof material Kevlar for DuPont; Wilmington, DE, June 18, 2014.

L

Lange, Jim, 81, host of TV show *The Dating Game* (1965-80); Mill Valley, CA, Feb. 25, 2014.

Laughlin, Tom, 82, actor, writer, and director best known for 1970s Billy Jack films; Thousand Oaks, CA, Dec. 12, 2013.

Leigh, Mitch, 86, Tony Award-winning composer of *Man of La Mancha* (1965); New York, NY, Mar. 16, 2014.

Leiter, Saul, 89, photographer best known for New York City images; New York, NY, Nov. 26, 2013.

Lessing, Doris, 94, British Nobel Prize-winning author who wrote about the experiences of women; best known for *The Golden Notebook* (1962); London, Eng., UK, Nov. 17, 2013.

Lorch, Lee, 98, activist who helped desegregate New York City's Stuyvesant Town housing complex; Toronto, ON, Canada, Feb. 28, 2014.

Lurie, Dan, 90, bodybuilding pioneer; Roslyn, NY, Nov. 6, 2013.

M

Maazel, Lorin, 84, child prodigy and conductor for the New York Philharmonic, Cleveland Orchestra, and Vienna State Opera; Castleton, VA, July 13, 2014.

MacLeod, Alistair, 77, Canadian writer known for short stories and novel *No Great Mischief* (1999); Windsor, ON, Canada, Apr. 20, 2014.

Magruder, Jeb Stuart, 79, Nixon aide who served seven months in prison for Watergate role; Danbury, CT, May 11, 2014.

Mandela, Nelson, 95, South African anti-apartheid leader who went from prison imprisonment (1962-90) to South Africa's first black president (1994-99); Houghton, South Africa, Dec. 5, 2013.

Matthiessen, Peter, 86, novelist and naturalist known for *The Snow Leopard* (1978); cofounder of *Paris Review;* Sagaponack, NY, Apr. 5, 2014.

Mazursky, Paul, 84, filmmaker who focused on social trends in *Bob & Carol & Ted & Alice* (1969) and *An Unmarried Woman* (1978); Los Angeles, CA, June 20, 2014.

McCain, Franklin, 73, civil rights activist; desegregated Woolworth's lunch counter; Greensboro, NC, Jan. 9, 2014.

McGinniss, Joe, 71, writer known for *The Selling of the President 1968* (1969) and *Fatal Vision* (1983); Worcester, MA, Mar. 10, 2014.

Mellon, Rachel "Bunny," 103, heiress noted for horticulture, philanthropy, and art collecting; Upperville, VA, Mar. 17, 2014.

Menino, Thomas, 71, Boston mayor (D, 1993-2014) who helped transform downtown; Boston, MA, Oct. 30, 2014.

Mikkelsen, Vern, 85, Hall of Fame forward for Minneapolis Lakers (1949-59); Wayzata, MN, Nov. 21, 2013.

Mock, Jerrie, 88, pilot who was the first woman to fly solo around the world (1964); Quincy, FL, Sept. 30, 2014.

Mondale, Joan, 83, promoted fine arts as wife of Vice Pres. Walter Mondale (1977-81); Minneapolis, MN, Feb. 3, 2014.

Mortier, Gérard, 70, Belgian opera director whose innovations made him controversial; Brussels, Belgium, Mar. 8, 2014.

Mowat, Farley, 92, Canadian writer whose *Never Cry Wolf* (1963) changed perceptions of wolves, which he had studied; Pope Hope, ON, Canada, May 6, 2014.

Myers, Walter Dean, 76, children's and young adult writer whose *Fallen Angels* (1988) was frequently challenged for realism and language; New York, NY, July 1, 2014.

N

Nez, Chester, 93, Marine veteran who was the last of the original Navajo code talkers; Albuquerque, NM, June 4, 2014.

Noll, Chuck, 82, NFL coach who led the Pittsburgh Steelers (1969-91) to four Super Bowl victories; Sewickley, PA, June 13, 2014.

Nuland, Sherwin B., 83, surgeon who wrote *How We Die* (1994), which addressed end-of-life decisions; Hamden, CT, Mar. 3, 2014.

O

Onoda, Hiroo, 91, last World War II Japanese Army officer to surrender; he hid out in the Philippines until 1974; Tokyo, Japan, Jan. 16, 2014.

O'Toole, Peter, 81, Irish-born actor who gained fame playing title character in *Lawrence of Arabia* (1962); London, Eng., UK, Dec. 14, 2013.

P

Paisley, Ian, 88, Irish Democratic Unionist Party leader and Protestant minister who agreed to power sharing in Northern Ireland (2007); Belfast, N. Ireland, UK, Sept. 12, 2014.

Pardo, Don, 96, announcer best known for work on *Saturday Night Live* (1975-2014); Tucson, AZ, Aug. 18, 2014.

Park, Barbara, 66, children's book author known for the Junie B. Jones series; Scottsdale, AZ, Nov. 15, 2013.

Parker, Clarence "Ace," 101, Hall of Fame quarterback with the Brooklyn Dodgers (NFL, 1937-41); Portsmouth, VA, Nov. 6, 2013.

Parker, Eleanor, 91, actress best known as the baroness in *The Sound of Music* (1965); Palm Springs, CA, Dec. 9, 2013.

Phelps, Fred, Sr., 84, founder of Westboro Baptist Church, known for staging high-profile anti-gay protests; Topeka, KS, Mar. 19, 2014.

Price, Ray, 87, country singer-songwriter who developed a signature sound named for him; Mount Pleasant, TX, Dec. 16, 2013.

Q

Quigley, Joan, 87, astrologer known for giving readings to First Lady Nancy Reagan; San Francisco, CA, Oct. 21, 2014.

R

Ramis, Harold, 69, actor and filmmaker known for *Caddyshack* (1980), *Ghostbusters* (1984), and *Groundhog Day* (1993); Chicago, IL, Feb. 24, 2014.

Ramone, Tommy (Tom Erdelyi), 65, Hungarian-born musician who was a founding member of the Ramones; Ridgewood, NY, July 11, 2014.

Ramsay, Jack, 89, Hall of Fame basketball coach who led the Portland Trail Blazers to an NBA title (1977); Naples, FL, Apr. 28, 2014.

Rankin, Arthur, Jr., 89, animator who helped create the stop-motion *Rudolph the Red-Nosed Reindeer* (1964); Harrington Sound, Bermuda, Jan. 30, 2014.

Rechelbacher, Horst, 72, Austrian-born hairstylist who founded Aveda skin- and hair-care company; Osceola, WI, Feb. 15, 2014.

Reid, Alec, 82, Irish Catholic priest who played a role in the Northern Ireland peace accord; Dublin, Ireland, Nov. 22, 2013.

Resnais, Alain, 91, French filmmaker known for Holocaust documentary *Night and Fog* (1955); Paris, France, Mar. 1, 2014.

Rivers, Joan, 81, comedian known for unapologetic biting wit; hosted *Fashion Police* (2010-14) with daughter Melissa; New York, NY, Sept. 4, 2014.

Rodgers, Mary, 83, writer and composer known for *Once Upon a Mattress* (1959); New York, NY, June 26, 2014

Rooney, Mickey, 93, actor whose 90-year career included hundreds of roles; best known for playing Andy Hardy in more than a dozen films; Los Angeles, CA, Apr. 6, 2014.

Rowley, Janet, 88, geneticist who was first to link chromosomal abnormalities and cancer; Chicago, IL, Dec. 17, 2013.

Rózewicz, Tadeusz, 92, Polish poet and playwright who drew on his WWII experiences; Wroclaw, Poland, Apr. 24, 2014.

S

Sanger, Frederick, 95, two-time Nobel Prize-winning British biochemist who pioneered genome sequencing; Cambridge, Eng., UK, Nov. 19, 2013.

Schell, Maximilian, 83, Austrian-Swiss Academy Award-winning actor best known for *Judgment at Nuremberg* (1961); Innsbruck, Austria, Feb. 1, 2014.

Schiffrin, André, 78, French-born publisher who cofounded the nonprofit publishing house New Press; Paris, France, Dec. 1, 2013.

Schlesinger, James R., 85, economist who served as secretary of defense (1973-75) and as the first energy secretary (1977-79); Baltimore, MD, Mar. 27, 2014.

Scott, Jimmy, 88, jazz singer with rare genetic condition, which left him with a voice that never changed; Las Vegas, NV, June 12, 2014.

Scott, L'Wren (Luann Bambrough), 49, fashion model and designer; New York, NY, Mar. 17, 2014.

Seeger, Pete, 94, singer-songwriter and activist who wrote "Where Have All the Flowers Gone?" and "If I Had a Hammer"; New York, NY, Jan. 27, 2014.

Seldes, Marian, 86, Tony Award-winning actress known for Edward Albee performances; New York, NY, Oct. 6, 2014.

Sharon, Ariel, 85, Israeli general who served many roles in Israeli government, including prime minister; Tel Aviv, Israel, Jan. 1, 2014.

Shaw, Run Run, 106, Chinese movie mogul who created Hong Kong action movie industry; Hong Kong, Dec. 31, 2013.

Shevardnadze, Eduard, 89, Georgian politician who served as USSR foreign min. (1985-90) and president of Georgia (1995-2003); Tblisi, Georgia, July 7, 2014.

Silver, Horace, 85, jazz pianist and composer who pioneered hard bop style; New Rochelle, NY, June 18, 2014.

Singh, Khushwant, 99, Indian journalist and novelist known for *Train to Pakistan* (1956) which explored Pakistan's independence; New Delhi, India, Mar. 20, 2014.

Speakes, Larry, 74, deputy press secretary under Pres. Ronald Reagan (1981-87); Cleveland, MS, Jan. 10, 2014.

Sperling, John, 93, founder of Univ. of Phoenix (1973) as a for-profit school for working adults; Marin County, CA, Aug. 22, 2014.

Stewart, Mary, 97, British writer known for romantic and fantasy novels; Loch Awe, Scotland, UK, May 9, 2014.

Stone, Chuck, 89, Tuskegee airman and later a noted editor and columnist; cofounded Natl. Assn. of Black Journalists; Chapel Hill, NC, Apr. 6, 2014.

Strauss, Robert, 95, lawyer and political strategist who served as U.S. ambassador to USSR/Russia (1991-92); Washington, DC, Mar. 19, 2014.

Stritch, Elaine, 89, Tony- and Emmy Award-winning singer and actress with unfiltered opinions; well known for TV guest roles (*30 Rock*) and cabaret appearances; Birmingham, MI, July 17, 2014.

Sturtevant, Elaine, 89, artist who gained recognition for recreating other artists' work; Paris, France, May 7, 2014.

Suárez, Adolfo, 81, Spanish prime minister (1976-81) who was first democratically elected leader after Franco dictatorship; Madrid, Spain, Mar. 23, 2014.

T

Tavener, John, 69, British composer of religious music; Child Okeford, Eng., UK, Nov. 12, 2013.

Temple Black, Shirley, 85, iconic child star who acted, sang, and danced; later ambassador to Ghana and Czechoslovakia; Woodside, CA, Feb. 10, 2014.

Tianming, Wu, 74, Chinese film director, producer, and studio executive who helped reshape Chinese filmmaking; Beijing, China, Mar. 4, 2014.

Townsend, Sue, 68, British writer best known for character Adrian Mole; Leicester, Eng., UK, Apr. 10, 2014.

Traficant, James, Jr., 73, U.S. representative (D, OH, 1985-2002) who was convicted of bribery and expelled from Congress; Youngstown, OH, Sept. 27, 2014.

Trotter, Charlie, 54, chef known for Chicago restaurant and TV cooking show; Chicago, IL, Nov. 5, 2013.

Turner, Morrie, 90, cartoonist whose comic strip *Wee Pals* featured the first integrated cast of characters; Sacramento, CA, Jan. 25, 2014.

U

Ultra Violet (Isabelle Dufresne), 78, French-born artist known as a regular of Andy Warhol's Factory films; New York, NY, June 14, 2014.

Utley, Garrick, 74, TV journalist best known for Vietnam War coverage; New York, NY, Feb. 20, 2014.

V

Vale, Jerry, 81, crooning singer known for "You Don't Know Me" (1956); Palm Desert, CA, May 18, 2014.

Van Kirk, Theodore, 93, navigator and last living crew member of *Enola Gay*, which dropped an atomic bomb on Hiroshima, Japan; Stone Mountain, GA, July 28, 2014.

Vignelli, Massimo, 83, graphic designer known for NYC subway map (1972) and Bloomingdale's iconic brown bags; New York, NY, May 27, 2014.

von Trapp, Maria Franziska, 99, Austrian-born member of the Trapp Family Singers, whose story inspired *The Sound of Music*; Stowe, VT, Feb. 18, 2014.

W

Waite, Ralph, 85, actor best known as patriarch in TV series *The Waltons* (1972-80); Palm Desert, CA, Feb. 13, 2014.

Walker, Paul, 40, actor known for *Fast and Furious* movies; Valencia, CA, Nov. 30, 2013.

Wallach, Eli, 98, character actor remembered for *The Magnificent Seven* (1960) and *The Good, the Bad and the Ugly* (1966); New York, NY, June 24, 2014.

Walsh, Lawrence, 102, lawyer appointed as independent counsel in the Iran-Contra affair (1986); Oklahoma City, OK, Mar. 19, 2014.

Welch, Bob, 57, pitcher who won the AL Cy Young Award (1990); Seal Point, CA, June 9, 2014.

Williams, Robin, 63, Academy Award-winning actor and comedian whose many films included *Good Morning, Vietnam* (1987) and *Good Will Hunting* (1997); Tiburon, CA, Aug. 11, 2014.

Willis, Gordon, 82, cinematographer on Academy Award-winning *Godfather* films; North Falmouth, MA, May 18, 2014.

Wilson, Ralph, 95, owner of the Buffalo Bills (1960-2014); Grosse Pointe Shores, MI, Mar. 25, 2014.

Winter, Johnny, 70, guitarist and producer; Zurich, Switzerland, July 16, 2014.

Womack, Bobby, 70, Rock and Roll Hall of Fame singer-songwriter; Tarzana, CA, June 27, 2014.

Y

Yeager, Linnea "Bunny," 85, model-turned-photographer known for Bettie Page pin-up shots; North Miami, FL, May 25, 2014.

Young, (Johnnie) Mae, 90, Hall of Fame professional wrestler for over seven decades; Columbia, SC, Jan. 14, 2014.

Z

Zaentz, Saul, 92, Academy Award-winning producer for *One Flew Over the Cuckoo's Nest* (1975), *Amadeus* (1984), and *The English Patient* (1996); San Francisco, CA, Jan. 3, 2014.

Zamperini, Louis, 97, airman who survived 47 days adrift in a raft and two years as a Japanese POW; story told in Laura Hillenbrand's book *Unbroken* (2010); Los Angeles, CA, July 2, 2014.

Zimbalist, Efrem, Jr., 95, actor known for *77 Sunset Strip* (1958-64) and *The F.B.I.* (1965-74); Solvang, CA, May 2, 2014.

Zimmer, Don, 83, infielder (1954-65) who also managed, coached, and advised MLB teams for decades; Dunedin, FL, June 4, 2014.

CONGRESS

Key Information on the 113th Congress

The 113th Congress convened Jan. 3, 2013, with the Senate under Democratic control (53-45, 2 ind.) and the House of Representatives led by Republicans (233-206, 2 vacant seats). A record 101 women were serving in Congress, of whom 81 (including three nonvoting delegates) were in the House and 20 in the Senate. Congress also had a record number of Hispanic members, with 34 (including one nonvoting delegate and a resident commissioner) serving in the House and four in the Senate. The House had 43 African-American members (including two nonvoting delegates), 12 Americans of Asian or Pacific Islander heritage (including two nonvoting delegates), and two American Indians. Among Senate members were two African Americans and one Asian American. The Senate's oldest member, Frank Lautenberg (D, NJ), died June 3, 2013, at age 89. The Senate Nov. 21, 2013, voted 52-48 to end filibusters of most executive and judicial branch appointments—except for nominees to the Supreme Court—through a simple majority rather than a 60-vote supermajority.

Leadership. John Boehner (R, OH) retained his office of speaker of the House when the 113th Congress convened. Majority Leader Eric Cantor (R, VA) held his post through July 31, 2014, when he resigned following a June primary loss; Majority Whip Kevin McCarthy (R, CA) took over Cantor's position, and Steve Scalise (R, LA) became majority whip. Other leading House members were Minority Leader Nancy Pelosi (D, CA) and Minority Whip Steny Hoyer (D, MD). The all-time longest continuously serving member of the House was John Dingell (D, MI), in office since 1955. The top-ranking members of the Senate were Majority Leader Harry Reid (D, NV), Minority Leader Mitch McConnell (R, KY), Majority Whip Richard Durbin (D, IL), and Minority Whip John Cornyn (R, TX).

Ethics. First-term representative Trey Radel (R, FL) resigned Jan. 27, 2014, after pleading guilty the previous Nov. to misdemeanor possession of cocaine; he was the first active U.S. representative to plead guilty to a drug charge in 31 years. Elected to serve in the current Congress, 7-term representative Jesse Jackson Jr. resigned Nov. 20, 2012; less than three months later, federal officials charged him with misusing $750,000 in campaign funds. Jackson, who cited health reasons for his departure, was sentenced in Aug. 2013 to 2½ years in prison.

Unfinished Business. The Senate Sept. 18, 2014, and House Sept. 19, 2014, adjourned for the election campaign season. Congress's failure to pass legislation addressing immigration and a surge in illegal crossings of the country's southern border prompted Pres. Obama to pledge executive action on the matter, but he announced in Sept. any action would be delayed until after the election. Congress also failed to agree on long-term transportation infrastructure funding.

For Further Information. Detailed legislative information can be accessed at www.congress.gov.

Major Actions of the 113th Congress

Major actions taken by the 113th Congress through Oct. 2014. Laws are identified by their Public Law (PL) number.

Safety for Women, Others. Violence Against Women Reauthorization Act of 2013 renews an expired measure first signed into law in 1994 providing legal assistance and other support to victims of rape and domestic abuse; adds protection for student, lesbian, gay, transgender, and immigrant victims; expands authority of tribal courts to prosecute non-Native Americans accused of abuse. Passed by the Senate Feb. 12, 78-22; passed by the House Feb. 28, 286-138; signed by Pres. Obama Mar. 7 (PL 113-4).

Student Loans. Bipartisan Student Loan Certainty Act of 2013 lowers federally subsidized undergraduate Stafford loan interest rates, which had doubled July 1, 2013, almost to previous levels; ties student loans to the financial marketplace, which could increase rates to a cap of 8.25% and 9.5% for undergraduate and graduate students, respectively. Passed by the Senate July 24, 81-18; passed by the House (as amended) July 31, 392-31; signed by Pres. Obama Aug. 9 (PL 113-28).

Federal Budget. Bipartisan Budget Act of 2013 provides over $2 tril for discretionary federal spending through Sept. 2015. Eliminates $63 bil in forced budget cuts by increasing airline fees, reducing certain benefits to military and federal retirees, and lowering payments to Medicare providers. Passed by the House (as amended) Dec. 12, 332-94; passed by the Senate Dec. 18, 64-36; signed by Pres. Obama Dec. 26 (PL 113-67).

Farm Aid, Nutritional Assistance. Agriculture Act of 2014 renews a bill that expired in 2013 with appropriation of $956 bil over 10 years; trims $16.6 bil from farm subsidies and food stamp programs (the latter of which totals $756 bil); replaces direct payments to farmers with subsidized crop insurance. Passed by the House (as amended) Jan. 29, 251-166; passed by the Senate (as amended) Feb. 4, 68-32; signed by Pres. Obama Feb. 7 (PL 113-79).

Open Records. Digital Accountability and Transparency Act of 2014 requires the government to standardize federal financial data; mandates publishing of additional financial information on usaspending.gov. Passed by the Senate Apr. 10, unanimous consent; passed by the House Apr. 28, voice vote; signed by Pres. Obama May 9 (PL 113-101).

Veterans Health Care. Veterans Access, Choice, and Accountability Act of 2014 provides $16.3 bil to open 27 new VA medical facilities, hire additional doctors and nurses, and allow vets unable to receive timely care at VA facilities to seek treatment at non-VA clinics; expands authority of VA secretary to terminate managers. Passed by the House (as amended) July 30, 420-5; passed by the Senate (as amended) July 31, 91-3; signed by Pres. Obama Aug. 7 (PL 113-146).

Congressional Activity, 1947-2014

Source: *Congressional Record,* U.S. Govt. Printing Office; THOMAS database, Library of Congress

The recent session of Congress has been widely perceived as being less productive than previous sessions. The data below shows the number of public laws passed in every session of Congress since 1947.

Congress (years)	Public laws passed	Measures passed	Congress (years)	Public laws passed	Measures passed
80th (1947-48)	906	4,132	97th (1981-82)	473	2,267
81st (1949-50)	921	5,764	98th (1983-84)	623	2,670
82nd (1951-52)	594	4,593	99th (1985-86)	664	2,698
83rd (1953-54)	781	5,201	100th (1987-88)	713	2,932
84th (1955-56)	1,028	5,713	101st (1989-90)	650	2,691
85th (1957-58)	936	5,126	102nd (1991-92)	590	2,615
86th (1959-60)	800	4,165	103rd (1993-94)	465	2,054
87th (1961-62)	885	4,769	104th (1995-96)	333	1,834
88th (1963-64)	666	3,425	105th (1997-98)	394	2,077
89th (1965-66)	810	4,116	106th (1999-00)	580	2,779
90th (1967-68)	640	3,390	107th (2001-02)	377	2,163
91st (1969-70)	695	3,318	108th (2003-04)	498	2,674
92nd (1971-72)	607	2,840	109th (2005-06)	482	2,684
93rd (1973-74)	649	3,088	110th (2007-08)	460	3,336
94th (1975-76)	588	3,176	111th (2009-10)	383	2,939
95th (1977-78)	633	3,211	112th (2011-12)	283	1,744
96th (1979-80)	613	2,960	113th (2013-14)	184[1]	1,383[2]

Note: Measures passed refers to bills, joint resolutions, concurrent resolutions, or simple resolutions passed by the House or Senate. Public laws must be signed into law by the president. (1) As of Oct. 2014. (2) As of Aug. 31, 2014.

U.S. SUPREME COURT

The U.S. Supreme Court's 2013-14 term began Oct. 7, 2013, and concluded June 30, 2014, for its summer recess. The justices decided 73 cases (67 of which carried signed opinions) and issued 10 rulings (14%) by a 5-4 majority. The court decided an unusually high 48 cases (66%) unanimously, though in many cases the justices' individual reasoning varied widely.

Chief Justice John G. Roberts Jr. presided over his ninth full term. The eight associate justices, by order of seniority, were Antonin Scalia, Anthony M. Kennedy, Clarence Thomas, Ruth Bader Ginsburg, Stephen G. Breyer, Samuel A. Alito Jr., Sonia Sotomayor, and Elena Kagan.

Roberts, Scalia, Thomas, and Alito tended to vote as a conservative bloc, while Ginsburg, Breyer, Sotomayor, and Kagan composed the court's liberal wing. Associate Justice Kennedy was in the majority on all 10 of this term's 5-4 split decisions.

Notable Supreme Court Decisions, 2013-14

Note: The columns on the right provide information on how each justice voted. Gray shading indicates a justice who was part of the majority; black indicates a justice recused himself or herself. MO = justice authored majority opinion; CO = justice authored concurring opinion; COJ = justice authored opinion concurring in judgment but not its reasoning; DO = justice authored dissenting opinion; CD in part = justice authored opinion containing both concurring and dissenting opinions.

Affirmative Action

The Supreme Court Apr. 22 ruled in *Schuette v. Coalition to Defend Affirmative Action* that an amendment to Michigan's state constitution barring public colleges and universities from preferential treatment based on race or gender did not violate the U.S. Constitution. In opinions on three separate lines of reasoning, six justices agreed that the amendment did not violate the constitutional rights of underrepresented groups in Michigan.

Kagan	Sotomayor	Breyer	Ginsburg	Kennedy	Scalia	Thomas	Roberts	Alito
(recused)	DO	COJ		MO	COJ	CO		

Campaign Finance

The court Apr. 2 struck down as unconstitutional limits that capped the total dollar amount that individuals could contribute to all political candidates and parties during a single two-year electoral cycle. The 5-4 ruling left intact the caps on the amount of money donors were allowed to contribute to individual candidates or parties. The case was *McCutcheon v. Federal Election Commission*.

Kagan	Sotomayor	Breyer	Ginsburg	Kennedy	Scalia	Thomas	Roberts	Alito
		DO				COJ	MO	

Copyright

The Supreme Court June 25 ruled in *ABC Inc. v. Aereo Inc.* that a service provided by technology firm Aereo Inc. violated the 1976 Copyright Act, because it acted like a cable company in transmitting broadcast TV content to subscribers' digital devices without permission from the originating broadcast networks.

Kagan	Sotomayor	Breyer	Ginsburg	Kennedy	Scalia	Thomas	Roberts	Alito
		MO			DO			

Criminal Justice

In a decision laying out broad protections for digital privacy, the court June 25 unanimously decided that police generally could not search the cellular telephones of arrested individuals without first obtaining a search warrant. The ruling concerned two cases, *Riley v. California* and *U.S. v. Wurie*.

Kagan	Sotomayor	Breyer	Ginsburg	Kennedy	Scalia	Thomas	Roberts	Alito
							MO	CO

The Supreme Court May 27 struck down, 5-4, a Florida law requiring proof that a person's intelligence quotient (IQ) was 70 or below before additional evidence of intellectual disability could be presented to exempt the person from the death penalty under a 2002 Supreme Court ruling. The case was *Hall v. Florida*.

Kagan	Sotomayor	Breyer	Ginsburg	Kennedy	Scalia	Thomas	Roberts	Alito
				MO				DO

Environment

The court June 23 ruled in *Utility Air Regulatory Group v. EPA* that the Environmental Protection Agency could require fixed sources of pollution—such as factories and power plants—that were already under federal scrutiny for emissions of other pollutants to obtain permits related to their emission of greenhouse gases. However, the court sharply rebuked the EPA for the reasoning the agency had used to design the carbon regulatory measures for such sources, rejecting the broad authority to interpret legislation claimed by the agency.

Kagan	Sotomayor	Breyer	Ginsburg	Kennedy	Scalia	Thomas	Roberts	Alito
	CD in part				MO			CD in part

Executive Power

The court June 26 unanimously ruled in *National Labor Relations Board v. Noel Canning* that Pres. Barack Obama's appointment of three people to the National Labor Relations Board during a congressional recess in Jan. 2012 was unconstitutional. However, the justices in a 5-4 split decision upheld the president's power to make such appointments during congressional recesses of at least 10 days.

Kagan	Sotomayor	Breyer	Ginsburg	Kennedy	Scalia	Thomas	Roberts	Alito
		MO			COJ			

Free Speech

The Supreme Court June 26 in *McCullen v. Coakley* unanimously struck down as unconstitutional a 2007 Massachusetts law establishing 35-ft zones around the entrances to clinics that provided abortions as places where protesters were not allowed to stand. Despite the unanimity of the ruling, the court was deeply split over the reasoning behind it.

Kagan	Sotomayor	Breyer	Ginsburg	Kennedy	Scalia	Thomas	Roberts	Alito
					COJ		MO	COJ

Labor

The Supreme Court June 30 decided, 5-4, in *Harris v. Quinn* that nonunionized home health care workers in Illinois who were paid by Medicaid, the joint state-federal health insurance program, could not be compelled to pay fees to the labor union that engaged in collective bargaining with the state on their behalf.

Kagan	Sotomayor	Breyer	Ginsburg	Kennedy	Scalia	Thomas	Roberts	Alito
DO								MO

Religion

The Supreme Court June 30 ruled, 5-4, that some closely held corporations could claim an exemption based on their owners' religious beliefs to a 2010 Patient Protection and Affordable Care Act mandate requiring many businesses to provide health insurance that covers all forms of contraception. The ruling was based on the 1993 Religious Freedom Restoration Act, which allows exemptions from participation in federal laws that substantially burden religious freedoms in circumstances where the government could find a less restrictive means of meeting its goals. The ruling came in the cases of *Burwell v. Hobby Lobby Stores* and *Conestoga Wood Specialties Corp. v. Burwell*.

Kagan	Sotomayor	Breyer	Ginsburg	Kennedy	Scalia	Thomas	Roberts	Alito
DO				DO	CO			MO

The Supreme Court May 5 ruled, 5-4, that a New York town's practice of opening town board meetings with prayers that were almost always given by Christian clerics and often contained explicitly sectarian content did not violate the First Amendment. The case was *Town of Greece v. Galloway*.

Kagan	Sotomayor	Breyer	Ginsburg	Kennedy	Scalia	Thomas	Roberts	Alito
DO		DO		MO		COJ		CO

NOTABLE QUOTES, 2014

Around the World

"The analogy we use around here sometimes, and I think is accurate, is if a jayvee team puts on Lakers uniforms that doesn't make them Kobe Bryant."

—Pres. Barack Obama, referring to certain jihadist groups after the capture of Fallujah by the Sunni militant group known commonly as ISIS or ISIL, in the Jan. 27 issue of *The New Yorker*.

"If we see that disorder spreading to the eastern regions, and if people ask us for help … then we reserve the right to use all means at our disposal to protect those citizens."

—Russian Pres. Vladimir Putin, Mar. 4, referring to Ukraine, in response to a popular revolt that had toppled a pro-Russian president there.

"This is theft on an international scale, when under the cover of troops, one country has just come and robbed a part of an independent state."

—Ukrainian Prime Min. Arseniy Yatsenyuk, Mar. 18, after Russia annexed Crimea, having occupied it with troops.

"We're not searching for a needle in a haystack—we're still trying to define where the haystack is."

—Mark Binskin, Australia's deputy defense chief, Mar. 25, on the search in the southern Indian Ocean for a Malaysian jetliner that went missing Mar. 8.

"There is a market for selling humans. Allah says I should sell. He commands me to sell. I will sell women."

—Alleged leader of Boko Haram militants, who kidnapped more than 200 girls from a school in rural Nigeria, in a video May 5.

"They were children. They just want to play and study and live a good life."

—Aunt of one of four Palestinian boys killed by Israeli missiles on a Gaza beach July 16.

"It's not a pleasant thought that you sit one day on the patio drinking coffee with your wife and a bunch of terrorists will rise from the ground."

—Eyal Brandies, a political scientist living in an Israeli kibbutz near where 13 Gaza militants emerged from a tunnel July 17.

"Great nations need organizing principles, and 'don't do stupid stuff' is not an organizing principle."

—Former Sec. of State Hillary Clinton, criticizing aspects of the Obama administration's foreign policy, in an interview published online Aug. 10 by *The Atlantic*.

"Our objective is clear: we will degrade, and ultimately destroy, ISIL through a comprehensive and sustained counterterrorism strategy."

—Pres. Barack Obama, in a Sept. 10 speech to the nation outlining U.S. plans to intervene in Iraq and Syria.

"We have chosen unity over division. … Today is a momentous result for Scotland, but also for the United Kingdom as a whole."

—Alistair Darling, "No" campaign head, after Scottish voters rejected independence from the UK in a Sept. 18 referendum.

"We are trying to treat as many people as we can, but there are not nearly enough treatment centers and patient beds. We have to turn people away. And they are dying at our front door."

—Jackson K.P. Naimah, team leader for Doctors Without Borders in Monrovia, Liberia, in a statement on the Ebola outbreak at an emergency meeting of the UN Security Council Sept. 18.

"I would dance in the streets, but I am too afraid."

—Opposition activist inside the ISIS "capital" of Raqqa, Syria, hit in the first U.S. air strikes against targets in Syria, Sept. 23.

National News

"Time for some traffic problems in Fort Lee."

—Bridget Anne Kelly, deputy chief of staff to Gov. Chris Christie (R, NJ), calling for disruptive lane closings near the George Washington Bridge in apparent political retaliation against a local mayor, in an email made public Jan. 8.

"The recovery still feels like a recession to many Americans."

—Janet Yellen, Mar. 31, in her first public speech after having been named Federal Reserve chair.

"The Government may no more restrict how many candidates or causes a donor may support than it may tell a newspaper how many candidates it may endorse."

—Chief Justice John G. Roberts, Apr. 2, writing for the majority in *McCutcheon v. FEC*, in which the U.S. Supreme Court declared limits on overall contributions in a two-year election cycle unconstitutional.

"Where enough money calls the tune, the general public will not be heard."

—Associate Justice Stephen Breyer, Apr. 2, in his dissenting opinion in *McCutcheon v. FEC*.

"Literally, silence can kill. GM did not act and did not alert us in a timely manner. What GM did was break the law."

—Transportation Sec. Anthony Foxx, May 16, after General Motors was fined a record $35 mil for taking more than a decade to disclose an ignition-switch defect in its cars that was linked to at least 29 deaths.

"Whether amnesty or clemency ever becomes a possibility is not for me to say. … But, if I could go anywhere in the world, that place would be home."

—Former Natl. Security Agency contractor Edward Snowden, who was granted asylum in Russia after leaking classified information about NSA surveillance activities, in an interview with NBC's Brian Williams that aired May 28.

"If Mr. Snowden wants to come back to the United States, we'll have him on a flight today."

—Sec. of State John Kerry, on NBC's *Today* show, May 28.

"We did a whole lot of things that were right, but we tortured some folks. We did some things that were contrary to our values."

—Pres. Barack Obama, Aug. 1, referring to U.S. interrogations of al-Qaeda detainees.

"Hands up, don't shoot!"

—Refrain of protesters after the Aug. 9 police shooting of Michael Brown, an unarmed black teenager, in Ferguson, MO.

"Twenty-one days, in your home, with your friends and your family, and you'll be compensated … Read a book—read my book."

—New York Gov. Andrew Cuomo, Oct. 27, on the potential benefits of a home quarantine for health care workers returning from treating Ebola patients in West Africa. (Cuomo's book, a memoir, sold under 1,000 copies in its first week.)

People

"I just want to make sure I could tell my story the way I want to tell it. I just want to own my truth."

—Michael Sam, in a *NY Times* interview, Feb. 9; he became the first NFL player to be drafted after coming out publicly as gay.

"I am Jimmy Fallon and I will be your host—for now."

—Jimmy Fallon, in his debut Feb. 17 at the helm of NBC's *The Tonight Show*, after former host Jay Leno departed the show for a second time.

"It doesn't escape me for one moment that so much joy in my life is thanks to so much pain in someone else's. And so I want to salute the spirit of Patsey for her guidance."

—Lupita Nyong'o, Mar. 2, accepting the Oscar for Best Supporting Actress, for playing the slave Patsey in *12 Years a Slave*.

"I will not look at a picture where I'm tormented by what I saw and felt that night."

—South African double-amputee sprinter Oscar Pistorius, Apr. 9, at his trial in the shooting death of his girlfriend.

"It's true that anything could happen, but let's face it, at my age I don't have much to lose."

—Pope Francis, rejecting use of the specially protected Popemobile, in an interview with a Barcelona newspaper published June 13.

"I lost my balance, making my body unstable and falling on top of my opponent. At that moment I hit my face against the player leaving a small bruise on my cheek and a strong pain in my teeth."

—Uruguay striker Luis Suárez attempting to explain his biting of Italy defender Giorgio Chiellini at the World Cup, June 24.

"I looked at other teams, but I wasn't going to leave Miami for anywhere except Cleveland. The more time passed, the more it felt right. This is what makes me happy."

—NBA superstar LeBron James, July 11, on his decision to return to the Cleveland Cavaliers.

"Both men and women should feel free to be sensitive. Both men and women should feel free to be strong. It is time that we all perceive gender on a spectrum, instead of two sets of opposing ideals."

—Actress and UN Women Goodwill Ambassador Emma Watson, in a speech at the UN, Sept. 20.

"I am not satisfied with the way we handled it."

—NFL Commissioner Roger Goodell, Sept. 19, referring to the league's widely criticized response to a domestic abuse scandal involving Baltimore running back Ray Rice.

Like *People*, Only Papal

Pope Francis has refused many of the trappings of his predecessors since his 2013 election as leader of the world's 1.2 bil Roman Catholics. He wears simple clothes, the Popemobile is in storage, and he has yet to move into the luxurious papal apartments, preferring to live in a Vatican guesthouse. The seeming humility demonstrated by his actions makes it all the more odd that he now has his own fan magazine. Italy's Mondadori publishing house, known for celebrity gossip magazines, launched *Il Mio Papa* (My Pope) on Mar. 5, 2014, with an initial run of 3 mil copies and a price of half a euro (about 65¢). The glossy weekly was "designed to report on and share the words and actions of Pope Francis," said editor Aldo Vitali. Each issue includes a free pinup of the Pope, ideal for hanging in a school locker beside other celebrity magazine subjects, such as One Direction and Justin Bieber.

Fox News Discomfits the White House

The federal government shutdown of 2013 had many minor and major consequences. One of those was that federal employees—including most National Park Service groundskeepers—were furloughed. The White House gardens were left unattended. The blog Obama Foodorama, quoted by Huffington Post Oct. 16, 2013, reported, "The wildlife that lives on the historic 18-acre campus—including a newly arrived fox now making a home at the White House—are having a field day." The shutdown ended after 16 days, and most visiting animals were chased away. But the fox (which showed up on the grounds earlier in 2013) must have decided it liked it there. The *Wall Street Journal* reported Apr. 17, 2014, that the White House groundskeepers had been trying to capture it for relocation, but it so far had eluded them at every turn.

This is not the first time Washington institutions have had to deal with local wildlife. Pres. George H.W. Bush's goldfish pond was briefly a sushi bar for raccoons, and a different fox was hunted through the U.S. Supreme Court building in 2002. But this fox has been an unusually wily opponent, slipping out of multiple humane traps. It has been sighted in the White House vegetable garden, Rose Garden, South Lawn, and other areas on the grounds, but no one has found its den—some have theorized that it's actually multiple foxes. As Danny Kaye put it in the movie *The Court Jester*: you'll never outfox the fox.

Reckless Recovery

At the end of Oct. 2012, the James family home in Keansburg, NJ, was badly damaged by Hurricane Sandy. The family's situation only got worse when the family dog, a terrier-pitbull mix named Reckless, escaped through a gap in a storm-mangled fence, leaving his collar behind. The family went on searches, reported Reckless missing to animal control, and called local shelters, but they couldn't find their pet. Eighteen months later, in early May 2014, the family decided to adopt a new dog, and there was Reckless, inside the first cage they approached at the Monmouth County SPCA. He recognized them immediately and jumped three feet into the air. They were able to confirm it was him due to a distinctive scar on the top of his head. Shelter records showed Reckless was picked up as a stray in Nov. 2013, a year after he had gone missing. He appeared to be well fed, so the shelter guessed that someone had been caring for him for at least part of the time he was gone. Reckless is now happily living again with the James family, and his days as an escape artist are presumably over—he has an implanted tracking microchip.

I've Been Shirking on the Railroad

If a train leaves Paris going east at 120 km per hr and another train leaves Strasbourg going west at 170 km per hr, how long will it take before the two are in danger of colliding? An expensive miscalculation on the part of the two companies responsible for France's railway system made that a less-than-hypothetical question this year. The weekly newspaper *Le Canard Enchaîné* reported May 21, 2014, that France's national railway company,

SNCF, had ordered 1,860 new trains using track information supplied by France's national railway network operator, RFF. RFF provided specifications in line with current international standards. Unfortunately, neither company took into account the system's older platforms, built more than 50 years ago, that were not in line with contemporary standards. The result? The train cars were 20 cm (about 8 in.) too wide for some 1,300 platforms (out of 8,700). In some tight places, trains on adjacent tracks would have brushed against each other. Officials concluded that platforms needed to be trimmed and tracks adjusted, at an estimated cost of more than $60 mil.

Black and White and Red All Over

Working in a newspaper office would not rank highly on anyone's list of hazardous occupations. Perhaps it carries an increased risk of paper cuts. But as *Baltimore Sun* journalist Mike Dresser learned, every job has hidden drawbacks.

For about a decade, the 60-year-old Dresser had experienced skin and eye troubles. As he described in an interview with ABC News May 22, 2014, "I'd wake up in the morning with my eyes swollen to the point where I couldn't see through the slits." Doctors didn't know what was wrong, but eventually somebody suggested a patch test for allergies. As Dresser wrote in a memo to his colleagues, "The next time you see me in the newsroom, you may see me wearing the type of rubber gloves used by a doctor or a crime scene technician ... I found out this week after nearly 38 years at *The Sun* that I am allergic to newspaper ink." More specifically, he was allergic to the pine resin used to make newsprint. He also discovered that he was allergic to a blue dye commonly used in dark-colored clothing, adding, "So if a new colleague asks why the old guy always wears white or cream even in winter, that's the reason. This transition may take some time because of the expense involved. I'm looking at Mark Twain as a possible role model."

Old Man's War

In the U.S., men ages 18-25 are required to register with the Selective Service System. If a military draft were authorized, in the event of a national emergency, registrants could be called on to serve in the armed forces. The U.S. military is currently all-volunteer, and the last draft was held in 1973, so the last thing one might expect is to get a conscription notice for one's great-grandfather. But that happened in many Pennsylvania households this year when 14,215 notices went out beginning June 30 demanding that men born in the late 19th century register for Selective Service or face serious consequences. The Associated Press reported July 10 that 73-year-old Chuck Huey received a letter making that demand of his late grandfather, a WWI vet who died in 1995 at the age of 100. The clerk responsible for notifying young men of their need to register had meant to send notifications to those born between 1993 and 1997 but inadvertently also notified those born in 1893-97. The Selective Service System apologized for the error.

Gambling Council Loses Its Bet

To Singapore's Natl. Council on Problem Gambling, established when the nation legalized casinos in 2005, it must have seemed like a sure thing. They produced a TV advertisement to dissuade gambling on upcoming World Cup matches, showing children discussing the competition. One expected Brazil to win, another was rooting for Spain, and a third, called Andy, said, "I hope Germany wins. My dad bet all my savings on them." The ad was meant to dramatize the harmful impact of excessive gambling on families. Unfortunately, the message was muted when Germany won the World Cup July 13, and much fun was had with the ad. "Looks like the boy's father who bet all his savings on Germany will be laughing all the way to the bank!" said Singapore's minister of manpower and parliament member Tan Chuan-Jin on Facebook. The council went into damage-control mode and rushed out a follow-up ad in which Andy was asked if he got his savings back, and he replied, "No, Dad never stops. He wants to bet one more time."

HISTORICAL ANNIVERSARIES

1915 – 100 Years Ago

The U.S. House of Representatives Jan. 12 votes 204-174 against a constitutional amendment that would give women the right to vote.

An earthquake in Avezzano, Italy, kills 30,000+ Jan. 13.

Alexander Graham Bell in New York City calls former assistant Thomas Watson in San Francisco for the first transcontinental phone call Jan. 25.

Ottoman Empire begins a policy of forced deportation of Armenians in Apr. that escalates to mass executions; an estimated 1 mil Armenians die in the genocide.

Germans deploy poisonous chlorine gas on French and Canadian troops in the Second Battle of Ypres Apr. 22-May 25.

A German submarine sinks the British ocean liner *Lusitania* May 7, killing 1,198 aboard, including 128 Americans.

The steamship *Eastland* capsized in the Chicago River July 24; 844 people were trapped or trampled below deck and drowned not far from shore in 20 ft of water.

Major hurricanes make landfall in Galveston, TX, in Aug. and New Orleans, LA, in Sept., killing 550.

Haiti became virtual U.S. protectorate under Sept. 16 treaty after U.S. troops occupied the country to quell a revolt.

After 100,000 deaths and an eight-month battle, Allies Dec. 15 begin to retreat from the Turkish peninsula of Gallipoli.

Art. Marc Chagall's *Birthday*; Carl Larsson's *Midvinterblot*; Amedeo Modigliani's *Portrait of Juan Gris*; Diego Rivera's *Table on a Café Terrace*. Erté begins designing *Harper's Bazaar* covers.

Film. D. W. Griffith's *The Birth of a Nation* premieres as *The Clansman*; it is considered the first feature film and first blockbuster but is strongly criticized for its depiction of slavery and Reconstruction. Theda Bara's *A Fool There Was*; Reginald Barker's *The Italian* and *The Coward*; Charlie Chaplin's *The Tramp* and *The Bank*.

Literature. John Buchan's *The Thirty-Nine Steps*; T. S. Eliot's "The Love Song of J. Alfred Prufrock"; Ford Madox Ford's *The Good Soldier*; Charlotte Perkins Gilman's *Herland*; Franz Kafka's *The Metamorphosis*; D. H. Lawrence's *The Rainbow*; W. Somerset Maugham's *Of Human Bondage*; John McCrae's "In Flanders Fields."

Music. Max Reger's *Requiem*; Richard Strauss's *An Alpine Symphony*.

Nonfiction. Van Wyck Brooks's *America's Coming-of-Age*.

Pop music. George Asaf and Felix Powell's "Pack Up Your Troubles in Your Old Kit-Bag, and Smile, Smile, Smile"; Alfred Bryan and Al Piantadosi's "I Didn't Raise My Boy to Be a Soldier"; George L. Cobb and Jack Yellen's "Alabama Jubilee."

Science and technology. Albert Einstein completes general theory of relativity. Alfred Wegener publishes "The Origin of Continents and Oceans," his theory of continental drift.

Sports. Jess Willard defeats Jack Johnson for heavyweight title in Cuba.

Theater. *The Blue Paradise*, *The Princess Pat*, *The Shadow*, and *Very Good Eddie* debut on Broadway.

Miscellaneous. NAACP presents first Spingarn Medal to Howard Univ. professor Ernest E. Just.

1965 – 50 Years Ago

Pres. Lyndon B. Johnson outlines "Great Society" program of civil rights, poverty, and health care legislation Jan. 4 in State of the Union address.

Civil rights leader Malcolm X is assassinated in New York City Feb. 21.

U.S. begins bombing North Vietnam Feb. 24 and sends its first 3,500 combat troops to the country Mar. 8.

The Selma-to-Montgomery march for voting rights begins Mar. 7 and is halted by state and local law enforcement attacks on demonstrators. Marchers are given federal protection and successfully complete it Mar. 21-25.

U.S. intervenes in Dominican Republic civil war Apr. 28, sending 42,000 troops to prevent the installation of a Communist regime.

On July 28, Pres. Johnson more than doubles the monthly draft call to 35,000 and sends another 50,000 combat troops to Vietnam, bringing the total U.S. troop strength there to 125,000.

The Medicare and Medicaid programs are signed into law, July 30; the Voting Rights Act is signed into law Aug. 6.

Riots erupt in south-central Los Angeles, Aug. 11-16, resulting in 34 deaths and $40 mil in property damages.

Pres. Johnson signs the Immigration Act of 1965 Oct. 3, abolishing the national origins quota system.

Paul VI is the first pope to visit the U.S. Oct. 4.

A coup in Indonesia Sept. 30 attempts to remove President-for-Life Sukarno from office.

More than 30 mil people are affected by a blackout in NE U.S. and Canada Nov. 9-10.

Joseph Mobutu (later known as Mobutu Sese Seko) takes power in the Congo Nov. 24, beginning a 32-year dictatorship.

Art. Judy Chicago's *Rainbow Pickett*; James Gill's *The Machines*; Robert Indiana's *The Confederacy* series; Roy Lichtenstein's *Big Painting No. 6*; James Rosenquist's *F-111*. Yoko Ono performs *Cut Piece* at Carnegie Hall.

Film. *Cat Ballou*; *Darling* starring Julie Christie; *Doctor Zhivago* starring Omar Sharif and Julie Christie; Sergio Leone's *For a Few Dollars More* starring Clint Eastwood; Blake Edwards's *The Great Race* starring Tony Curtis, Jack Lemmon, and Natalie Wood; *The Greatest Story Ever Told*; *Help!* starring The Beatles; *A Patch of Blue* starring Sidney Poitier and Shelley Winters; *The Sound of Music* starring Julie Andrews and Christopher Plummer; *A Thousand Clowns*; *What's New Pussycat?*

Health and medicine. Congress passes legislation requiring cigarette warning labels for the first time. The artificial sweetener aspartame is discovered.

Literature. Frank Herbert's *Dune*; Bel Kaufman's *Up the Down Staircase*; James Michener's *The Source*; Katherine Anne Porter's *Collected Stories*.

Music. Jack Beeson's *Lizzie Borden*; Karlheinz Stockhausen's *Mikrophonie II*.

Nonfiction. *The Autobiography of Malcolm X*; Daniel Patrick Moynihan's *The Negro Family*; Ralph Nader's *Unsafe at Any Speed*; Arthur M. Schlesinger's *A Thousand Days*. Truman Capote's *In Cold Blood* is serialized in *The New Yorker*.

Pop music. The Beatles release *Help* and *Rubber Soul* and have six consecutive number-one singles, including "Yesterday." Bob Dylan goes electric at Newport Folk Festival and releases *Highway 61 Revisited*. John Coltrane's *A Love Supreme*; The Righteous Brothers' "You've Lost That Lovin' Feelin'"; Rolling Stones' "I Can't Get No (Satisfaction)"; Sam the Sham and the Pharoahs' "Wooly Bully."

Science and technology. First spacewalk is conducted by Soviet cosmonaut Alexei A. Leonov. Gordon Moore theorizes exponential computing power growth in what becomes known as Moore's Law.

Sports. Astrodome, the first multipurpose domed sports stadium, opens in Houston, TX. Muhammad Ali KOs Sonny Liston via "phantom punch" in first round of heavyweight championship rematch.

Television. *A Charlie Brown Christmas* is broadcast for the first time; *Bonanza* is highest-rated program. *I Spy* and *Days of Our Lives* debut. NBC leads the network color-TV transition, announcing a nearly all-color fall lineup for the first time.

Theater. On Broadway, *Man of La Mancha* begins a 6-year run and Neil Simon's *The Odd Couple* debuts. LeRoi Jones (later known as Amiri Baraka) founds Black Arts Repertory in Harlem.

Miscellaneous. Second Vatican Council adjourns. Construction on Eero Saarinen's Gateway Arch in St. Louis, MO, is completed.

1990 – 25 Years Ago

Soviet Union's Central Committee abandons political monopoly Feb. 7, and all 15 Soviet republics hold relatively open elections for the first time since 1917.

After more than 25 years in prison, South African anti-apartheid activist Nelson Mandela is released Feb. 11.

An arson fire Mar. 25 at Happy Land social club in Bronx, NY, kills 87.

A 7.4-magnitude earthquake strikes Iran June 20, killing at least 40,000 people.

A stampede during the Hajj in Mecca, Saudi Arabia, kills 1,426 pilgrims July 2.

David Souter is nominated to fill William Brennan's seat on the U.S. Supreme Court July 25 and sworn in Oct. 9.

Pres. George H.W. Bush July 26 signs into law the Americans With Disabilities Act.

Iraq invades Kuwait Aug. 2, and Pres. Bush orders Operation Desert Shield in Saudi Arabia Aug. 7. The UN Nov. 29 authorizes military force after Jan. 15, 1991.

East and West Germany are formally reunited as one nation Oct. 3.

UK Prime Min. Margaret Thatcher, in office since 1979, resigns Nov. 28.

Mary Robinson is inaugurated Dec. 3 as the first woman president of Ireland.

Solidarity trade union leader Lech Walesa Dec. 9 is elected president of Poland.

Art. Damien Hirst's *A Thousand Years*; Jeff Koons's *Made in Heaven* series; Faith Ringgold's *Freedom of Speech*; Rachel Whiteread's *Ghost*.

Film. Kevin Costner's *Dances With Wolves*; Tim Burton's *Edward Scissorhands*; *Ghost* starring Demi Moore and Patrick Swayze; Martin Scorsese's *Goodfellas*; *Home Alone*; *House Party*; *The Hunt for Red October* starring Alec Baldwin and Sean Connery; *Kindergarten Cop* starring Arnold Schwarzenegger; the Coen Brothers' *Miller's Crossing*; *Misery* starring Kathy Bates and James Caan; *Pretty Woman* starring Richard Gere and Julia Roberts; *Reversal of Fortune*; David Lynch's *Wild at Heart*.

Health and medicine. A four-year-old girl becomes the first person ever to receive human gene therapy. The international Human Genome Project is launched.

Literature. Jean M. Auel's *The Plains of Passage*; A. S. Byatt's *Possession*; Charles Johnson's *Middle Passage*;

Tim O'Brien's *The Things They Carried*; Dr. Seuss's *Oh, the Places You'll Go!*; John Updike's *Rabbit at Rest*.

Music. Gerald Barry's *The Intelligence Park*; Paul Lansky's *Smalltalk*; John Zorn's *Naked City*. José Carreras, Plácido Domingo, and Luciano Pavaroti perform for the first time as the Three Tenors.

Nonfiction. Judith Butler's *Gender Trouble*; Ron Chernow's *The House of Morgan*; Camille Paglia's *Sexual Personae*; William Styron's *Darkness Visible*; Laurel Thatcher Ulrich's *A Midwife's Tale*.

Pop music. Vocal duo Milli Vanilli wins best new artist Grammy in Feb.; the award is rescinded in Nov. when the record's producer admits the duo did not sing on the recordings. Depeche Mode's *Violator*; LL Cool J's *Mama Said Knock You Out*; Madonna's "Vogue"; MC Hammer's "U Can't Touch This"; Megadeath's *Rust in Peace*; Sinead O'Connor's "Nothing Compares 2 U"; Pixies' *Bossanova*; Public Enemy's *Fear of a Black Planet*; Vanilla Ice's "Ice Ice Baby."

Science and technology. Hubble Space Telescope is deployed Apr. 24; NASA announces it has serious defect and needs repair June 27. Tim Berners-Lee creates first prototype World Wide Web server, browser, and Web pages. The Intergovernmental Panel on Climate Change releases its first assessment report.

Sports. Buster Douglas KOs Mike Tyson for heavyweight championship in Feb. but loses title to Evander Holyfield eight months later. Martina Navratilova wins ninth Wimbledon singles championship.

Television. New TV series include *Beverly Hills 90210*, *Law & Order*, *Northern Exposure*, and *Twin Peaks*. Highest-rated series include *Cheers* and *Roseanne*.

Theater. On Broadway, *The Grapes of Wrath*, Neil Simon's *Lost in Yonkers*, and August Wilson's *The Piano Lesson* debut. *A Chorus Line* closes after a record 6,237 performances.

Miscellaneous. Mayor of Washington, DC, Marion Barry, is arrested for drug possession. After one of the most expensive investigations/prosecutions to date, the McMartin preschool (CA) sexual abuse trial ends with no convictions and all charges dropped. McDonald's opens its first franchise in the Soviet Union.

WORLD ALMANAC EDITORS' PICKS
2014 Time Capsule

The editors of *The World Almanac* have selected the following items as representative of the year 2014.

- A biohazard suit intended to protect a medical worker from contact with the highly contagious bodily fluids of a patient diagnosed with the Ebola virus.

- The distinctive Vivienne Westwood hat worn by Pharrell Williams in his performance of the chart-topping single "Happy" during the Grammy Awards ceremony Jan. 26.

- The black box from Malaysia Airlines Flight 370, which disappeared Mar. 8 with 239 people aboard.

- An assortment of ballots cast—to opposite results—in the Crimea independence referendum Mar. 16 and the Scotland independence referendum Sept. 18.

- Digital evidence from 2014's many sports scandals, including the recording released Apr. 25 of L.A. Clippers owner Donald Sterling making racist remarks to a friend and the video released Sept. 8 of Baltimore Ravens running back Ray Rice striking his then-fiancée in a casino elevator.

- Italian defender Giorgio Chiellini's World Cup jersey, with the bite mark on its shoulder courtesy of Uruguay's Luis Suárez in group-stage play June 24.

- A large vessel of ice and water, to be used in yet another "ice bucket challenge" video; the viral campaign raised $115 mil in donations to the ALS Assn. July-Oct.

- A dancing baby Groot toy to represent *Guardians of the Galaxy*, which earned $94.3 mil at the box office during its opening weekend in Aug. on its way to becoming the summer's highest grossing film.

- A collection of protesters' signs and law enforcement riot gear from the demonstrations in the aftermath of the Aug. 9 shooting of unarmed black teenager Michael Brown in Ferguson, MO.

- Banners carried during the People's Climate March in New York City, which sought to call attention to international action on global climate change Sept. 21.

- The bat that NY Yankee Derek Jeter used to hit a game-winning single in the final home game of his 20-year career Sept. 25.

- A ballot from each of the states that elected a Republican to a seat formerly held by a Democrat in the U.S. Senate Nov. 4, giving the GOP a majority of both chambers in the next Congress.

ECONOMICS

Index of Leading Economic Indicators

Source: The Conference Board

The index of leading economic indicators is used to project the U.S. economy's performance. The index is made up of 10 measurements of economic activity that tend to change direction in advance of the overall economy. The index has predicted economic downturns from 8 to 20 months in advance and recoveries from 1 to 10 months in advance. It can be inconsistent, however, and has occasionally shown false signals of recessions. In 2012, the Conference Board made significant changes to the composition of the Leading Economic Index for the first time since 1996. As a result, data from 2012 forward are not directly comparable with those from prior years. The components are listed below.

- Average weekly hours of production workers in manufacturing
- Average weekly initial claims for unemployment insurance
- Manufacturers' new orders for consumer goods and materials, adjusted for inflation
- Institute for Supply Management index of new orders
- Manufacturers' new orders for nondefense capital goods, excluding aircraft, adjusted for inflation

- Building permits for new private housing units
- Stock prices of the Standard & Poors 500 stock index
- Leading Credit Index, a proprietary Conference Board measure of credit conditions
- Interest rate spread (10-yr Treasury bonds less federal funds)
- Average consumer expectations for business and economic conditions (surveys by Conference Board and Reuters/Univ. of Michigan)

U.S. Gross Domestic Product, Gross National Product, Net National Product, National Income, and Personal Income, 1970-2013

Source: Bureau of Economic Analysis, U.S. Dept. of Commerce
(in billions of current dollars, revised)

	1970	1980	1990	2000	2005	2010	2012	2013
Gross domestic product	$1,075.9	$2,862.5	$5,979.6	$10,289.7	$13,095.4	$14,958.3	$16,244.6	$16,799.7
Gross national product	1,082.3	2,896.7	6,014.3	10,326.8	13,189.0	15,164.2	16,497.4	17,057.5
Less: Consumption of fixed capital...	136.8	426.0	886.8	1,514.2	1,982.0	2,381.6	2,542.9	2,646.6
Equals: Net national product	945.5	2,470.7	5,127.4	8,812.5	11,207.0	12,782.6	13,954.6	14,410.9
Less: Statistical discrepancy	5.3	43.9	91.3	−94.5	−33.8	43.1	−17.0	−131.4
Equals: National income	940.1	2,426.8	5,036.1	8,907.0	11,240.8	12,739.5	13,971.6	14,542.4
Less: Corporate profits with inventory valuation and capital consumption adjustments	86.2	223.6	417.2	781.2	1,477.7	1,740.6	2,009.5	2,102.1
Taxes on production and imports less subsidies[1]	86.6	190.5	398.0	662.7	873.6	1,001.2	1,065.6	1088.0
Contributions for government social insurance	46.4	166.2	410.1	705.8	873.3	984.1	950.7	1106.0
Net interest and miscellaneous payments on assets	40.5	186.2	450.1	565.0	496.8	489.4	439.6	469.2
Business current transfer payments (net)	4.4	14.0	39.2	85.3	93.9	128.5	106.9	124.4
Current surplus of government enterprises	−1.2	−5.1	3.2	10.7	−6.4	−22.9	−27.7	−40.1
Plus: Personal income receipts on assets	112.7	386.0	991.2	1,453.5	1,666.5	1,739.6	1,958.5	1,997.7
Personal current transfer receipts	74.7	279.5	594.9	1,083.0	1,512.0	2,276.9	2,358.3	2,444.3
Equals: Personal income	864.6	2,316.8	4,904.5	8,632.8	10,610.3	12,435.2	13,743.8	14,134.7
Addenda:								
Gross domestic income	1,070.5	2,818.6	5,888.2	10,384.3	13,129.2	14,915.2	16,261.6	16,931.2
Gross national income	1,076.9	2,852.8	5,922.9	10,421.3	13,222.7	15,121.1	16,514.5	17,188.9

Note: Numbers may not add up to totals due to rounding. (1) Subsidies are included net of the current surplus of government enterprises.

U.S. Gross Domestic Product, 2000-13

Source: Bureau of Economic Analysis, U.S. Dept. of Commerce

	Billions of current dollars				Billions of constant (2009) dollars			
	2000	2005	2012	2013	2000	2005	2012	2013
Gross domestic product	$10,289.7	$13,095.4	$16,244.6	$16,799.7	$12,565.2	$14,235.6	$15,470.7	$15,761.3
Personal consumption expenditures	6,801.6	8,790.3	11,149.6	11,501.5	8,182.1	9,527.8	10,517.6	10,727.9
Goods	2,452.9	3,080.3	3,769.7	3,885.9	2,588.3	3,177.2	3,534.1	3,659.4
Durable goods	912.6	1,127.2	1,202.7	1,263.0	758.3	1,046.9	1,246.7	1,333.3
Nondurable goods	1,540.3	1,953.1	2,567.0	2,622.9	1,863.6	2,132.3	2,296.8	2,342.0
Services	4,348.8	5,710.1	7,379.9	7,615.7	5,611.6	6,349.4	6,982.7	7,067.1
Gross private domestic investment	2,033.8	2,527.1	2,475.2	2,670.0	2,375.5	2,672.6	2,436.0	2,566.4
Fixed investment	1,979.2	2,467.5	2,409.1	2,564.0	2,316.2	2,611.0	2,365.3	2,470.9
Nonresidential	1,493.8	1,611.5	1,970.0	2,047.1	1,647.7	1,717.4	1,931.8	1,984.4
Structures	318.1	345.6	437.3	456.4	533.5	421.2	421.6	426.9
Equipment	766.1	790.7	907.6	939.7	726.9	801.6	905.9	934.4
Intellectual property products	409.5	475.1	625.0	651.0	426.1	495.0	605.8	624.8
Residential	485.4	856.1	439.2	516.9	637.9	872.6	433.7	486.6
Change in inventories	54.5	59.6	66.1	106.1	66.2	64.3	57.6	81.5
Net exports of goods and services	−380.1	−715.7	−547.2	−497.3	−482.7	−777.1	−430.8	−412.3
Exports	1,094.3	1,310.4	2,195.9	2,259.9	1,272.4	1,388.4	1,957.4	2,010.0
Goods	797.1	925.3	1,536.0	1,567.0	902.0	969.2	1,353.2	1,385.0
Services	297.2	385.1	659.9	692.9	368.2	418.4	603.7	624.8
Imports	1,474.4	2,026.1	2,743.1	2,757.2	1,755.1	2,165.5	2,388.2	2,422.3
Goods	1,250.4	1,716.2	2,295.4	2,296.0	1,454.4	1,814.7	1,964.3	1,988.3
Services	224.0	309.9	447.7	461.2	297.2	346.1	422.8	433.5
Government consumption expenditures and gross investment	1,834.4	2,493.7	3,167.0	3,125.5	2,498.2	2,826.2	2,963.1	2,896.9
Federal	632.4	946.3	1,295.7	1,245.9	817.7	1,034.8	1,220.3	1,157.4
National defense	391.7	608.3	817.1	770.7	512.3	665.5	769.1	715.0
Nondefense	240.7	338.1	478.6	475.1	305.4	369.4	451.2	442.5
State and local	1,202.0	1,547.4	1,871.3	1,879.6	1,689.1	1,792.3	1,742.8	1,739.2

U.S. Gross Domestic Product, 1930-2013
Source: Bureau of Economic Analysis, U.S. Dept. of Commerce
(in billions of current dollars)

1930	1935	1940	1945	1950	1960	1965	1970	1975	1980	1985	1990	1995	2000	2005	2010	2012	2013
92	74	103	228	300	543	744	1,076	1,689	2,863	4,347	5,980	7,664	10,285	13,094	14,964	16,245	16,800

U.S. National Income by Type, 1930-2013
Source: Bureau of Economic Analysis, U.S. Dept. of Commerce
(in billions of current dollars)

	1930	1940	1950	1970	1980	1990	2000	2010	2012	2013
NATIONAL INCOME[1]	$83.1	$91.6	$267.0	$940.1	$2,426.8	$5,036.1	$8,907.0	$12,739.5	$13,971.6	$14,542.4
Employee compensation	47.2	52.8	158.5	625.1	1,626.2	3,342.7	5,856.6	7,967.3	8,611.6	8,859.4
Wages and salaries	46.2	49.9	147.3	551.6	1,373.4	2,741.2	4,825.9	6,377.5	6,926.8	7,137.5
Government	5.2	8.5	22.6	117.2	261.5	519.0	779.8	1,191.1	1,197.3	1,195.0
Other	41.0	41.4	124.6	1,112.0	2,222.2	4,046.1	5,186.4	5,077.1	5,729.4	5,942.5
Supplements to wages and salaries	1.0	2.9	11.2	73.6	252.8	601.5	1,030.7	1,589.8	1,684.9	1,721.9
Employer contributions for employee pension and insurance funds	1.0	1.6	7.8	49.7	163.9	395.0	685.5	1,120.4	1,170.6	1,190.6
Employer contributions for government social insurance	0.0	1.4	3.4	23.8	88.9	206.5	345.2	469.4	514.3	531.2
Proprietors' income with inventory valuation and capital consumption adjustments	10.9	12.2	37.5	77.8	171.6	354.4	757.8	1,032.7	1,224.9	1,348.8
Farm	3.9	4.1	12.9	12.9	11.7	32.2	31.5	46.0	75.4	127.6
Nonfarm	7.0	8.2	24.6	64.9	159.9	322.3	726.3	986.7	1,149.6	1,221.2
Rental income of persons with capital consumption adjustments	5.4	3.8	8.8	20.7	19.7	31.4	187.7	402.8	541.2	590.6
Corporate profits with inventory valuation and capital consumption adjustments	7.5	9.9	36.1	86.2	223.6	417.2	781.2	1,740.6	2,009.5	2,102.1
Taxes on corporate income	0.8	2.8	17.9	34.8	87.2	145.4	265.1	370.6	434.8	418.9
Profits after tax with inventory valuation and capital consumption adjustments	6.7	7.0	18.1	51.5	136.4	271.7	516.1	1,370.0	1,574.7	1,683.2
Net dividends	5.5	4.0	8.8	24.3	64.1	169.1	384.7	563.9	770.3	902.0
Undistributed profits with inventory valuation and capital consumption adjustments	1.2	3.0	9.3	27.2	72.3	102.7	131.4	806.0	804.3	781.2
Net interest and miscellaneous payments	4.8	3.3	3.2	40.5	186.2	450.1	565.0	489.4	439.6	469.2

Note: Numbers may not add up to totals because of rounding and incomplete enumeration. (1) National income is the aggregate of labor and property earnings that arise in the production of goods and services. It is the sum of employee compensation, proprietors' income, rental income, adjusted corporate profits, and net interest. It measures the total factor costs of goods and services produced by the economy. Income is measured before deduction of taxes. Total national income figures include adjustments not itemized.

U.S. National Income by Industry, 2000-13
Source: Bureau of Economic Analysis, U.S. Dept. of Commerce
(in billions of current dollars)

	2000	2005	2009	2010	2011	2012	2013
National income without capital consumption adjustment	$8,817.5	$11,339.8	$12,088.3	$12,662.6	$13,130.0	$14,016.0	$14,576.0
Domestic industries	8,780.5	11,246.3	11,941.1	12,456.7	12,869.2	13,763.2	14,318.2
Private industries	7,729.4	9,865.5	10,318.1	10,776.9	11,182.4	12,070.5	12,637.5
Agriculture, forestry, fishing, and hunting	73.8	94.0	104.4	120.9	150.1	159.4	219.2
Mining	90.7	175.0	149.2	185.3	233.0	254.5	253.4
Utilities	137.3	162.1	177.0	190.8	171.8	202.0	214.0
Construction	470.7	648.9	545.7	521.0	541.1	586.9	634.0
Manufacturing	1,243.1	1,326.7	1,216.5	1,356.9	1,412.0	1,561.5	1,584.5
Durable goods	758.2	753.2	651.3	757.1	785.7	879.7	897.9
Nondurable goods	485.0	573.5	565.2	599.8	626.3	681.8	686.4
Wholesale trade	570.6	685.2	704.6	737.9	772.0	852.8	878.7
Retail trade	666.7	857.0	840.0	872.2	898.6	959.0	991.4
Transportation and warehousing	268.5	333.4	342.3	369.0	380.6	423.7	441.5
Information	306.8	423.0	436.7	443.3	442.8	487.2	505.3
Finance, insurance, real estate, rental, and leasing	1,472.6	1,969.1	2,135.5	2,139.9	2,176.4	2,312.8	2,479.1
Professional and business services[1]	1,115.7	1,428.1	1,591.0	1,695.8	1,779.1	1,920.3	2,005.0
Educational services, health care, and social assistance	689.4	988.4	1,252.4	1,292.5	1,334.3	1,396.9	1,440.0
Arts, entertainment, recreation, accommodation, and food services	340.1	437.2	463.0	483.3	508.9	554.5	581.0
Other services, except government	283.3	337.4	359.8	368.0	381.8	399.0	411.1
Government	1,051.0	1,380.8	1,623.0	1,679.8	1,686.8	1,692.7	1,680.7
Rest of the world	37.0	93.5	147.2	206.0	260.8	252.8	257.8

Note: Estimates in this table are based on the 2002 North American Industry Classification System (NAICS). (1) Consists of professional, scientific, and technical services; management of companies and enterprises; and administrative and waste management services.

Distribution of U.S. Total Personal Income, 1930-2013

Source: Bureau of Economic Analysis, U.S. Dept. of Commerce
(in billions of current dollars, except for per capita figures)

Year	Personal income	Personal current taxes	Disposable personal income	Personal outlays	Personal savings	Savings as % of income[1]	Disposable personal income per capita Current dollars	Disposable personal income per capita Constant (2009) dollars
1930	$76.5	$1.6	$74.9	$71.6	$3.3	4.4%	$608	$6,411
1940	79.4	1.7	77.7	72.4	5.3	6.8	588	7,464
1950	233.9	18.9	215.0	195.0	20.0	9.3	1,417	10,033
1960	422.5	46.1	376.5	338.6	37.8	10.0	2,083	11,877
1970	864.6	103.1	761.5	665.5	96.1	12.6	3,713	16,643
1980	2,316.8	298.9	2,018.0	1,804.8	213.2	10.6	8,861	20,159
1990	4,904.5	592.7	4,311.8	3,976.3	335.4	7.8	17,235	25,556
2000	8,632.8	1,232.3	7,400.5	7,102.6	297.9	4.0	26,206	31,525
2005	10,610.3	1,208.5	9,401.8	9,159.1	242.7	2.6	31,763	34,428
2007	11,995.7	1,487.9	10,507.9	10,190.6	317.2	3.0	34,829	35,870
2008	12,430.6	1,435.2	10,995.4	10,444.0	551.3	5.0	36,104	36,082
2009	12,082.1	1,144.9	10,937.2	10,266.5	670.7	6.1	35,598	35,598
2010	12,435.2	1,191.5	11,243.7	10,609.5	634.2	5.6	36,296	35,706
2011	13,191.3	1,404.0	11,787.4	11,119.1	668.2	5.7	37,776	36,293
2012	13,743.8	1,498.0	12,245.8	11,558.4	687.4	5.6	38,965	36,756
2013	14,134.7	1,658.5	12,476.2	11,914.9	561.3	4.5	39,424	36,772

Note: Personal income minus current taxes equals disposable income; disposable income minus outlays equals savings. Figures may not add up to totals because of rounding. (1) Personal savings as a percentage of disposable personal income.

Consumer Price Index

The Consumer Price Index (CPI) is a measure of the change in prices over time of one or more kinds of basic consumer goods and services. Beginning in Jan. 1978, the Bureau of Labor Statistics began publishing CPIs for two population groups: (1) all urban consumers (CPI-U, which covers about 87% of the total U.S. population); and (2) urban wage earners and clerical workers (CPI-W, which covers about 32% of the total U.S. population). The CPI-U also includes professional, managerial, and technical workers; the self-employed; short-term workers; the unemployed; retirees; and others not in the labor force.

The CPI is based on the price of food, clothing, shelter, and fuels; transportation fares; charges for doctors' and dentists' services; drug prices; and the cost of other goods and services bought for day-to-day living. The index currently measures price changes from a designated reference period, 1982-84, which equals 100.0. Use of this reference period began in Jan. 1988.

U.S. Consumer Price Index by Major Group, 1915-2013

Source: Bureau of Labor Statistics, U.S. Dept. of Labor
For all urban consumers. **1982-84 = 100**, unless otherwise noted.

Year	All items	Apparel	Food & beverages	Housing	Transportation	Medical care	Entertainment & recreation[1]	Educ. & communication[1]	Other goods & services
1915	10.1	15.3	—	—	—	—	—	—	—
1920	20.0	43.1	—	—	—	—	—	—	—
1930	16.7	24.2	—	—	—	—	—	—	—
1940	14.0	21.8	—	—	14.2	10.4	—	—	—
1945	18.0	31.4	—	—	15.9	11.9	—	—	—
1950	24.1	40.3	—	—	22.7	15.1	—	—	—
1955	26.8	42.9	—	—	25.8	18.2	—	—	—
1960	29.6	45.7	—	—	29.8	22.3	—	—	—
1965	31.5	47.8	—	—	31.9	25.2	—	—	—
1970	38.8	59.2	40.1	36.4	37.5	34.0	—	—	40.9
1975	53.8	72.5	60.2	50.7	50.1	47.5	—	—	53.9
1980	82.4	90.9	86.7	81.1	83.1	74.9	—	—	75.2
1985	107.6	105.0	105.6	107.7	106.4	113.5	—	—	114.5
1990	130.7	124.1	132.1	128.5	120.5	162.8	—	—	159.0
1995	152.4	132.0	148.9	148.5	139.1	220.5	94.5	92.2	206.9
2000	172.2	129.6	168.4	169.6	153.3	260.8	103.3	102.5	271.1
2005	195.3	119.5	191.2	195.7	173.9	323.2	109.4	113.7	313.4
2009	214.5	120.0	218.2	217.1	179.3	375.6	114.3	127.4	368.6
2010	218.1	119.5	220.0	216.3	193.4	388.4	113.3	129.9	381.3
2011	224.9	122.1	227.9	219.1	212.4	400.3	113.4	131.5	387.2
2012	229.6	126.3	233.7	222.7	217.3	414.9	114.7	133.8	394.4
2013	233.0	127.4	237.0	227.4	217.4	425.1	115.3	135.9	401.0

— = Comparable data not available. (1) Dec. 1997 = 100. Entertainment was reclassified as Recreation in 1997. Data is not seasonally adjusted.

U.S. Consumer Price Index, 1915-2013

Source: Bureau of Labor Statistics, U.S. Dept. of Labor

Excluding 2009, prices as measured by the U.S. Consumer Price Index have risen steadily since World War II. What cost $1.00 in 1982-84 cost about $0.10 in 1913, $0.18 in 1945, and nearly $2.33 in 2013.

(Annual averages of monthly figures, for all urban consumers. **1982-84 = 100**.)

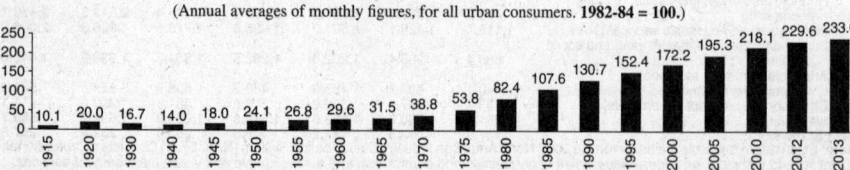

U.S. Consumer Price Indexes for Selected Items and Groups, 1970-2013

Source: Bureau of Labor Statistics, U.S. Dept. of Labor
Annual averages of monthly figures, for all urban consumers. 1982-84 = 100, unless otherwise noted.

	1970	1975	1980	1985	1990	1995	2000	2005	2010	2012	2013
ALL ITEMS	38.8	53.8	82.4	107.6	130.7	152.4	172.2	195.3	218.1	229.6	233.0
Food and beverages	40.1	60.2	86.7	105.6	132.1	148.9	168.4	191.2	220.0	233.7	237.0
Food	39.2	59.8	86.8	105.6	132.4	148.4	167.8	190.7	219.6	233.8	237.0
Food at home	39.9	61.8	88.4	104.3	132.3	148.8	167.9	189.8	215.8	231.8	233.9
Cereals and bakery products	37.1	62.9	83.9	107.9	140.0	167.5	188.3	209.0	250.4	267.7	270.4
Meats, poultry, fish, eggs	44.6	67.0	92.0	100.1	130.0	138.8	154.5	184.7	207.7	231.0	236.0
Dairy products	44.7	62.6	90.9	103.2	126.5	132.8	160.7	182.4	199.2	217.3	217.6
Fruits and vegetables	37.8	56.9	82.1	108.4	149.0	177.7	204.6	241.4	273.5	282.8	290.0
Nonalcoholic beverages	27.1	41.3	91.4	104.3	113.5	131.7	137.8	144.4	161.6	168.6	166.9
Sugar and sweets	30.5	65.3	90.5	105.8	124.7	137.5	154.0	165.2	201.2	214.7	211.0
Fats and oils	39.2	73.5	89.3	108.9	126.3	137.3	147.4	167.7	200.6	232.6	229.3
Other foods	39.6	58.9	83.6	106.4	131.2	151.1	172.2	182.5	204.6	216.6	217.7
Food away from home	37.5	54.5	83.4	108.3	133.4	149.0	169.0	193.4	226.1	238.0	243.1
Alcoholic beverages	52.1	65.9	86.4	106.4	129.3	153.9	174.7	195.9	223.3	230.8	234.6
Housing	36.4	50.7	81.1	107.7	128.5	148.5	169.6	195.7	216.3	222.7	227.4
Shelter	35.5	48.8	81.0	109.8	140.0	165.7	193.4	224.4	248.4	257.1	263.1
Rent of primary residence	46.5	58.0	80.9	111.8	138.4	157.8	183.9	217.3	249.4	260.4	267.7
Fuels and utilities	29.1	45.4	75.4	106.5	111.6	123.7	137.9	179.0	214.2	219.0	225.2
Household furnishings and operations	46.8	63.4	86.3	103.8	113.3	123.0	128.2	126.1	125.5	125.7	124.8
Apparel	59.2	72.5	90.9	105.0	124.1	132.0	129.6	119.5	119.5	126.3	127.4
Men's and boys'	62.2	75.5	89.4	105.0	120.4	126.2	129.7	116.1	111.9	119.5	121.6
Women's and girls'	71.8	85.5	96.0	104.9	122.6	126.9	121.5	110.8	107.1	113.0	113.3
Footwear	56.8	69.6	91.8	102.3	117.4	125.4	123.8	122.6	128.0	131.8	135.0
Transportation	37.5	50.1	83.1	106.4	120.5	139.1	153.3	173.9	193.4	217.3	217.4
Private transportation	37.5	50.6	84.2	106.2	118.8	136.3	149.1	170.2	188.7	212.8	212.4
New vehicles	53.1	63.0	88.5	106.1	121.4	141.0	142.8	137.9	138.0	144.2	145.8
Used cars and trucks	31.2	43.8	62.3	113.7	117.6	156.5	155.8	139.4	143.1	150.3	149.9
Gasoline	27.9	45.1	97.5	98.6	101.0	99.8	128.6	194.7	238.6	311.5	302.6
Public transportation	35.2	43.5	69.0	110.5	142.6	175.9	209.6	217.3	251.4	271.4	278.9
Medical care	34.0	47.5	74.9	113.5	162.8	220.5	260.8	323.2	388.4	414.9	425.1
Recreation[1]	NA	NA	NA	NA	NA	94.5	103.3	109.4	113.3	114.7	115.3
Other goods and services	40.9	53.9	75.2	114.5	159.0	206.9	271.1	313.4	381.3	394.4	401.0
Tobacco products	43.1	54.7	72.0	116.7	181.5	225.7	394.9	502.8	807.3	853.5	876.8
Personal care	43.5	57.9	81.9	108.3	130.4	147.1	165.6	185.6	206.6	212.1	215.0
Personal care products	42.7	58.0	79.6	107.6	128.2	143.1	153.7	154.4	161.1	162.2	161.8
Personal care services	44.2	57.7	83.7	108.9	132.8	151.5	178.1	203.9	229.6	234.2	238.8

NA = Not available. **Note:** Data is not seasonally adjusted. (1) Dec. 1997 = 100.

Consumer Price Indexes by Region and Major Cities, 1990-2013

Source: Bureau of Labor Statistics, U.S. Dept. of Labor
For all urban consumers; % change not annualized. 1982-84 = 100, unless otherwise noted.

Region and city	1990	1995	2000	2005	2009	2010	2011	2012	2013
U.S. city average	130.7	152.4	172.2	195.3	214.5	218.1	224.9	229.6	233.0
Northeast urban	136.3	159.1	179.4	207.5	229.3	233.9	241.0	245.7	249.0
Boston-Brockton-Nashua, MA-NH-ME-CT	138.9	158.6	183.6	216.4	233.8	237.4	243.9	247.7	251.1
New York-Northern New Jersey-Long Island, NY-NJ-CT-PA	138.5	162.2	182.5	212.7	236.8	240.9	247.7	252.6	256.8
Philadelphia-Wilmington-Atlantic City, PA-NJ-DE-MD	135.8	158.7	176.5	204.2	223.3	227.7	233.8	238.1	240.9
Pittsburgh, PA	126.2	149.2	168.0	189.8	212.1	215.4	225.1	232.9	235.9
Midwest urban	127.4	148.4	168.3	188.4	204.1	208.0	214.7	219.1	222.2
Chicago-Gary-Kenosha, IL-IN-WI	131.7	153.3	173.8	194.3	210.0	212.9	218.7	222.0	224.5
Cincinnati-Hamilton, OH-KY-IN	126.5	146.2	164.8	181.6	200.6	204.7	211.1	216.3	220.0
Cleveland-Akron, OH	129.0	147.9	168.0	187.9	200.5	204.6	211.0	214.7	217.5
Detroit-Ann Arbor-Flint, MI	128.6	148.6	169.8	190.8	203.5	205.1	211.8	216.1	219.5
Kansas City, MO-KS	126.0	145.3	166.6	185.3	201.0	205.4	213.5	218.5	221.6
Milwaukee-Racine, WI	126.2	151.0	168.6	185.2	203.0	209.6	216.9	221.1	225.1
Minneapolis-St. Paul, MN-WI	127.0	147.0	170.1	193.1	207.9	211.7	219.3	224.5	228.8
St. Louis, MO-IL	128.1	145.2	163.1	186.2	198.5	203.2	209.8	214.8	218.0
South urban	127.9	149.0	167.2	188.3	207.8	211.3	218.6	223.2	226.7
Atlanta, GA	131.7	150.9	170.6	188.9	201.0	203.5	209.1	212.8	216.3
Dallas-Fort Worth, TX	125.1	144.9	164.7	184.7	200.5	201.6	207.9	212.2	216.0
Houston-Galveston-Brazoria, TX	120.6	139.8	154.2	175.6	190.5	194.2	200.5	204.2	207.6
Miami-Fort Lauderdale, FL	128.0	148.9	167.8	194.3	221.4	223.1	230.9	235.2	238.2
Tampa-St. Petersburg-Clearwater, FL[1]	111.7	129.7	145.7	168.5	189.9	193.5	198.9	203.6	206.8
Washington-Baltimore, DC-MD-VA-WV[2]	NA	NA	107.6	124.3	139.8	142.2	147.0	150.2	152.5
West urban	131.5	153.5	174.8	198.9	218.8	221.2	227.5	232.4	235.8
Anchorage, AK	118.6	138.9	150.9	171.8	191.7	195.1	201.4	205.9	212.4
Denver-Boulder-Greeley, CO	120.9	147.9	173.2	190.9	208.5	212.4	220.3	224.6	230.8
Honolulu, HI	138.1	166.1	176.3	197.8	230.0	234.9	243.6	249.5	253.9
Los Angeles-Riverside-Orange County, CA	135.9	154.6	171.6	201.8	223.2	225.9	231.9	236.6	239.2
Phoenix-Mesa, AZ[3]	NA	NA	NA	108.3	117.6	118.2	121.5	124.2	125.8
Portland-Salem, OR-WA	127.4	153.2	178.0	196.0	215.6	218.3	224.6	229.8	235.5
San Diego, CA	138.4	156.8	182.8	220.6	242.3	245.5	252.9	257.0	260.3
San Francisco-Oakland-San Jose, CA	132.1	151.6	180.2	202.7	224.4	227.5	233.4	239.6	245.0
Seattle-Tacoma-Bremerton, WA	126.8	152.3	179.2	200.2	226.0	226.7	232.8	238.7	241.6

NA = Not available. **Note:** Data is not seasonally adjusted. (1) 1987 = 100. (2) Nov. 1996 = 100. (3) Dec. 2001 = 100.

Median Income by Race, Hispanic Origin, and Sex, 1948-2013

Source: *Current Population Survey*, U.S. Census Bureau, U.S. Dept. of Commerce

Race, Hispanic origin, and year		Male			Female		
		Number with income (thous.)	Median income Current dollars	2013 dollars	Number with income (thous.)	Median income Current dollars	2013 dollars
All races	2013	108,706	$35,228	$35,228	109,956	$22,063	$22,063
	2012	107,534	33,904	34,397	109,383	21,520	21,833
	2010	105,191	32,205	34,408	107,220	20,775	22,196
	2000	98,504	28,343	38,340	101,704	16,063	21,729
	1990	88,220	20,293	35,062	92,245	10,070	17,399
	1980	78,661	12,530	33,726	80,826	4,920	13,243
	1970	65,008	6,670	35,709	51,647	2,237	11,976
	1960	55,172	4,080	28,084	36,526	1,261	8,680
	1950	47,585	2,570	21,709	24,651	953	8,050
	1948	47,370	2,396	20,239	22,725	1,009	8,523
White	2013	89,758	36,398	36,398	88,344	22,358	22,358
	2012	89,220	35,557	36,074	88,174	21,756	22,072
	2010	87,829	34,045	36,373	86,999	20,864	22,291
	2000	83,372	29,797	40,307	84,123	16,079	21,750
	1990	76,480	21,170	36,577	78,566	10,317	17,825
	1980	69,420	13,328	35,873	70,573	4,947	13,315
	1970	58,447	7,011	37,535	45,288	2,266	12,131
	1960	49,788	4,296	29,571	32,001	1,352	9,306
	1950	NA	2,709	22,883	NA	1,060	8,954
	1948	NA	2,510	21,202	NA	1,133	9,570
White, not Hispanic	2013	73,333	40,122	40,122	74,382	23,780	23,780
	2012	73,240	38,751	39,314	74,529	22,902	23,235
	2010	72,723	37,154	39,695	73,995	21,715	23,200
	2000	72,530	31,508	42,621	75,206	16,665	22,543
	1990	69,987	21,958	37,939	72,939	10,581	18,282
	1980	65,564	13,681	36,824	67,084	4,980	13,404
Black	2013	12,311	24,643	24,643	15,038	19,955	19,955
	2012	11,961	24,959	25,322	14,722	19,925	20,215
	2010	11,433	23,086	24,665	14,212	19,548	20,885
	2000	9,905	21,343	28,871	12,461	15,881	21,482
	1990	8,820	12,868	22,233	10,687	8,328	14,389
	1980	7,387	8,009	21,557	8,596	4,580	12,327
	1970	5,844	4,157	22,255	5,844	2,063	11,045
	1960	5,384	2,260	15,556	4,525	837	5,761
	1950	NA	1,471	12,425	NA	474	4,004
	1948	NA	1,363	11,513	NA	492	4,156
Asian	2013	6,162	39,204	39,204	6,043	24,734	24,734
	2012	5,810	39,606	40,182	5,972	23,290	23,628
	2010	5,406	35,121	37,523	5,604	23,552	25,163
	2000	4,303	30,833	41,708	4,192	17,356	23,478
	1990	2,235	19,394	33,509	2,333	11,086	19,154
Hispanic	2013	16,484	25,411	25,411	14,034	17,762	17,762
	2012	16,005	24,592	24,949	13,689	16,725	16,968
	2010	15,106	22,420	23,953	12,947	16,292	17,406
	2000	11,343	19,498	26,375	9,431	12,248	16,568
	1990	6,767	13,470	23,273	5,903	7,532	13,014
	1980	3,996	9,659	25,998	3,617	4,405	11,856

NA = Not available. **Note:** Income for persons 15 years of age and over beginning in Mar. 1980; 14 years of age and over as of Mar. of the following year for previous years. Beginning in 2010, totals for White, Black, and Asian include those who identified themselves as being that race in combination with some other race. Before 2010, Asian category includes Pacific Islanders. Hispanic persons may be of any race.

Consumer Credit Outstanding, 2010-13

Source: Federal Reserve System

(in billions of dollars as of Dec. of year shown, not seasonally adjusted)

	2010	2012	2013		2010	2012	2013
TOTAL	$2,522.2	$2,923.6	$3,097.9	Federal government[1]	—	—	—
Major holders				Nonfinancial business	$26.0	$28.8	$23.1
Depository institutions	1,185.5	1,218.6	1,271.6	Pools of securitized assets[2] . . .	31.4	31.2	30.5
Finance companies	705.0	679.8	679.1				
Credit unions	226.5	243.6	265.6	**Nonrevolving[3]**	1,807.4	2,076.9	2,240.3
Federal government[1]	356.2	616.8	729.8	Depository institutions	520.8	542.1	578.1
Nonfinancial business	45.5	49.2	43.5	Finance companies	623.5	608.4	612.1
Pools of securitized assets[2] . . .	50.3	50.0	49.2	Credit unions	190.1	204.8	222.2
Major types of credit, by holder				Federal government[1]	356.2	616.8	729.8
Revolving	840.0	846.7	857.6	Nonprofit and educational institutions[4]	78.4	65.6	59.1
Depository institutions	664.7	676.5	693.5	Nonfinancial business	19.5	20.4	20.4
Finance companies	81.5	71.4	67.1	Pools of securitized assets[2] . . .	19.0	18.8	18.6
Credit unions	36.3	38.9	43.4				

— = Not available. (1) Includes student loans originated by the Dept. of Education under the Federal Direct Loan Program and the Perkins Loan Program, as well as Federal Family Education Program loans that the government purchased under the Ensuring Continued Access to Student Loans Act. (2) Outstanding balances of pools on which securities have been issued; these balances are no longer carried on the balance sheets of the loan originators. (3) Includes motor vehicle loans and all other loans not included in revolving credit, such as loans for mobile homes, education, boats, trailers, or vacations. These loans may be secured or unsecured. (4) Includes student loans originated under the Federal Family Education Loan Program and held by educational institutions and nonprofit organizations that are affiliated with state governments.

Financial Assets of U.S. Families, 1989-2013

Source: *Survey of Consumer Finances* (triennial), Federal Reserve System

Category	1989	1992	1995	1998	2001	2004	2007	2010	2013
Median net worth (thous.)	$46.9	$49.5	$57.8	$71.7	$86.6	$93.1	$120.6	$77.3	$81.2
Average net worth (thous.)	185.9	186.6	212.1	282.9	397.4	449.4	557.8	498.8	534.6
Financial assets					Percent of families holding asset				
Transaction accounts	19.0%	17.4%	13.9%	11.4%	11.4%	13.1%	10.9%	13.3%	13.3%
Certificates of deposit	10.2	8.0	5.6	4.3	3.1	3.7	4.0	3.9	2.0
Savings bonds	1.5	1.1	1.3	0.7	0.7	0.5	0.4	0.3	0.3
Bonds	10.2	8.4	6.3	4.3	4.5	5.3	4.1	4.4	3.2
Stocks	15.0	16.5	15.6	22.7	21.5	17.5	17.8	14.0	15.9
Pooled investment funds (excluding money market funds)	5.3	7.6	12.7	12.4	12.1	14.6	15.8	15.0	14.8
Retirement accounts	21.5	25.8	28.3	27.8	29.0	32.4	35.0	38.1	38.8
Cash value life insurance	6.0	5.9	7.2	6.3	5.3	2.9	3.2	2.5	2.7
Other managed assets	6.5	5.4	5.8	8.5	10.5	7.9	6.5	6.2	7.6
Other	4.8	3.8	3.3	1.7	1.9	2.1	2.1	2.3	1.5
Financial assets as % of total assets	30.5	31.6	36.8	40.7	42.2	35.8	34.0	37.9	40.8

World's Wealthiest Individuals, 2014

Source: *Forbes* magazine
(as of Oct. 15, 2014)

Rank	Name, country	Source of wealth	Net worth (bil)
1.	Carlos Slim Helú, Mexico	Telecom	$79.2
2.	Bill Gates, U.S.	Microsoft	79.0
3.	Warren Buffett, U.S.	Berkshire Hathaway	66.3
4.	Amancio Ortega, Spain	Inditex	55.5
5.	Larry Ellison, U.S.	Oracle	47.7
6.	Charles Koch, U.S.	Manufacturing, energy	39.7
6.	David Koch, U.S.	Manufacturing, energy	39.7
8.	Christy Walton, U.S.	Wal-Mart	37.3
9.	Jim C. Walton, U.S.	Wal-Mart	36.0
10.	Alice Walton, U.S.	Wal-Mart	34.6
11.	S. Robson Walton, U.S.	Wal-Mart	34.6
12.	Liliane Bettencourt, France	L'Oreal	33.9
13.	Michael Bloomberg, U.S.	Bloomberg, LP	32.7
14.	Mark Zuckerberg, U.S.	Facebook	32.3
15.	Sheldon Adelson, U.S.	Sands casinos	31.2
16.	Li Ka-shing, Hong Kong	Hutchison Whampoa	30.8
17.	Stefan Persson, Sweden	H&M	30.0
18.	Larry Page, U.S.	Google	29.5
19.	Bernard Arnault, France	LVMH-Moët Hennessy	29.1
20.	Sergey Brin, U.S.	Google	$29.0
21.	Jeff Bezos, U.S.	Amazon.com	28.5
22.	Carl Icahn, U.S.	Investments	24.6
23.	Michele Ferrero, Italy	Chocolate	24.4
24.	George Soros, U.S.	Hedge funds	24.0
25.	Aliko Dangote, Nigeria	Cement, sugar, flour	23.6
26.	David Thomson, Canada	Media, publishing	23.3
27.	Lee Shau Kee, Hong Kong	Real estate	22.6
28.	Forrest Mars Jr., U.S.	Candy	22.4
28.	Jacqueline Mars, U.S.	Candy	22.4
28.	John Mars, U.S.	Candy	22.4
31.	Mukesh Ambani, India	Petrochemicals, oil, gas	22.2
32.	Steve Ballmer, U.S.	Microsoft	21.3
33.	Al-Waleed bin Talal, Saudi Arabia	Investments	21.1
34.	Jorge Paulo Lemann, Brazil	Beer	20.8
35.	Michael Dell, U.S.	Dell Computers	20.6
36.	Phil Knight, U.S.	Nike	20.4
37.	Jack Ma, China	Alibaba	19.4
38.	Len Blavatnik, U.S.	Investments	19.1
39.	Alisher Usmanov, Russia	Steel, mining, telecom	17.8
40.	Dilip Shanghvi, India	Pharmaceuticals	17.8

Persons Below Poverty Level, 1960-2013

Source: U.S. Census Bureau, U.S. Dept. of Commerce

Year	Number below poverty level (mil)					% of subgroup below poverty level					Avg. income cut-off, family of 4 at poverty level[4]
	All races[1]	Asian[2]	White	Black[2]	Hispanic[3]	All races[1]	Asian[2]	White	Black[2]	Hispanic[3]	
1960	39.9	NA	28.3	NA	NA	22.2%	NA	17.8%	NA	NA	$3,022
1970	25.4	NA	17.5	7.5	NA	12.6	NA	9.9	33.5%	NA	3,968
1980	29.3	NA	19.7	8.6	3.5	13.0	NA	10.2	32.5	25.7%	8,414
1990	33.6	0.9	22.3	9.8	6.0	13.5	12.2%	10.7	31.9	28.1	13,359
1995	36.4	1.4	24.4	9.9	8.6	13.8	14.6	11.2	29.3	30.3	15,569
2000	31.6	1.3	21.6	8.0	7.7	11.3	9.9	9.5	22.5	21.5	17,604
2001	32.9	1.3	22.7	8.1	8.0	11.7	10.2	9.9	22.7	21.4	18,104
2002	34.6	1.2	23.5	8.9	8.6	12.1	10.0	10.2	23.9	21.8	18,392
2003	35.9	1.5	24.3	9.1	9.1	12.5	11.8	10.5	24.3	22.5	18,810
2004	37.0	1.3	25.3	9.4	9.1	12.7	9.7	10.8	24.7	21.9	19,307
2005	37.0	1.5	24.9	9.5	9.4	12.6	10.9	10.6	24.7	21.8	19,971
2006	36.5	1.4	24.4	9.5	9.2	12.3	10.1	10.3	24.2	20.6	20,614
2007	37.3	1.5	25.1	9.7	9.9	12.5	10.2	10.5	24.4	21.5	21,203
2008	39.8	1.7	27.0	9.9	11.0	13.2	11.6	11.2	24.6	23.2	22,025
2009	43.6	1.9	29.8	10.6	12.4	14.3	12.4	12.3	25.9	25.3	21,954
2010	46.3	2.1	31.1	11.6	13.5	15.1	12.0	13.0	27.4	26.5	22,315
2011	46.2	2.2	30.8	11.7	13.2	15.0	12.3	12.8	27.5	25.3	23,021
2012	46.5	2.1	30.8	11.8	13.6	15.0	11.4	12.7	27.1	25.6	23,492
2013	45.3	2.0	29.9	12.0	12.7	14.5	10.4	12.3	27.1	23.5	23,834

NA = Not available. **Note:** Because of a change in the definition of poverty, data prior to 1980 are not directly comparable to data since 1980. (1) Includes other races not shown separately. (2) Beginning in 2002, numbers include those who identified themselves as being Asian or black in combination with some other race. For 1990-2000, Asian includes Pacific Islanders. (3) Persons of Hispanic origin may be of any race. (4) Figures for 1960-80 for nonfarm families only.

Poverty Thresholds by Family Size, 1980-2013
Source: U.S. Census Bureau, U.S. Dept. of Commerce

	1980	1990	2000	2010	2013		1980	1990	2000	2010	2013
1 person	$4,190	$6,652	$8,791	$11,137	$11,888	3 people	$6,565	$10,419	$13,740	$17,373	$18,552
Under age 65. . . .	4,290	6,800	8,959	11,344	12,119	4 people	8,414	13,359	17,604	22,315	23,834
Age 65 or older . .	3,949	6,268	8,259	10,458	11,173	5 people	9,966	15,792	20,815	26,442	28,265
2 people	5,363	8,509	11,235	14,216	15,142	6 people	11,269	17,839	23,533	29,904	31,925
Householder						7 people	12,761	20,241	26,750	34,019	36,384
under age 65 . .	5,537	8,794	11,589	14,676	15,679	8 people	14,199	22,582	29,701	37,953	40,484
Householder age						9 or more people . .	16,896	26,848	35,150	45,224	48,065
65 or older.	4,983	7,905	10,418	13,194	14,095						

Note: Weighted averages; not used for computing poverty data.

Families Below Poverty Level by Status, Race, and Sex, 1980-2013
Source: U.S. Census Bureau, U.S. Dept. of Commerce
(numbers in thousands)

Year and race	All families			Married-couple families			Male householder, no wife present			Female householder, no husband present		
		Below poverty level			Below poverty level			Below poverty level			Below poverty level	
	Total	Number	Percent	Total	Number	Percent	Total	Number	Percent	Total	Number	Percent
All races												
1980	60,309	6,217	10.3%	49,294	3,032	6.2%	1,933	213	11.0%	9,082	2,972	32.7%
1990	66,322	7,098	10.7	52,147	2,981	5.7	2,907	349	12.0	11,268	3,768	33.4
2000	73,778	6,400	8.7	56,598	2,637	4.7	4,277	485	11.3	12,903	3,278	25.4
2010	79,559	9,400	11.8	58,667	3,681	6.3	5,649	892	15.8	15,243	4,827	31.7
2011	80,529	9,497	11.8	58,963	3,652	6.2	5,888	950	16.1	15,678	4,894	31.2
2012	80,944	9,520	11.8	59,224	3,705	6.3	6,231	1,023	16.4	15,489	4,793	30.9
2013	81,217	9,130	11.2	59,692	3,476	5.8	6,330	1,008	15.9	15,195	4,646	30.6
White[1]												
1980	52,710	4,195	8.0	44,860	2,437	5.4	1,584	149	9.4	6,266	1,609	25.7
1990	56,803	4,622	8.1	47,014	2,386	5.1	2,277	226	9.9	7,512	2,010	26.8
2000	61,330	4,333	7.1	49,473	2,181	4.4	3,283	332	10.1	8,574	1,820	21.2
2010	63,976	6,305	9.9	50,016	2,921	5.8	4,176	563	13.5	9,784	2,822	28.8
2011	64,625	6,334	9.8	50,061	2,863	5.7	4,348	614	14.1	10,216	2,857	28.0
2012	64,735	6,299	9.7	50,171	2,875	5.7	4,592	651	14.2	9,972	2,774	27.8
2013	64,702	6,032	9.3	50,206	2,677	5.3	4,635	649	14.0	9,862	2,706	27.4
Black[1]												
1980	6,317	1,826	28.9	3,392	474	14.0	291	52	17.7	2,634	1,301	49.4
1990	7,471	2,193	29.3	3,569	448	12.6	472	97	20.6	3,430	1,648	48.1
2000	8,731	1,686	19.3	4,214	266	6.3	732	120	16.3	3,785	1,300	34.3
2010	9,571	2,311	24.1	4,267	377	8.8	916	236	25.7	4,387	1,698	38.7
2011	9,656	2,334	24.2	4,362	408	9.4	956	234	24.4	4,338	1,693	39.0
2012	9,823	2,327	23.7	4,483	440	9.8	1,040	262	25.2	4,300	1,624	37.8
2013	9,923	2,267	22.8	4,676	416	8.9	1,102	255	23.1	4,145	1,596	38.5

(1) Data are for one race only. The Census Bureau revised race categories in 2002, so data after 2002 are not directly comparable with data for previous years.

Poverty Rates by State, 1990-2013
Source: U.S. Census Bureau, U.S. Dept. of Commerce

The poverty rate is the proportion of the population with income below the government's official poverty level, which is adjusted each year for inflation. The national poverty rate declined to 14.5% in 2013, from 15.0% in 2012. More than 45 mil people in the U.S. were living in poverty in 2013, up from 31.6 mil in 2000.

State	1990	2000	2005	2010	2013	State	1990	2000	2005	2010	2013
Alabama	19.2%	13.3%	16.7%	17.2%	16.7%	Montana	16.3%	14.1%	13.8%	14.5%	14.5%
Alaska	11.4	7.6	10.0	12.5	10.9	Nebraska	10.3	8.6	9.5	10.2	11.0
Arizona	13.7	11.7	15.2	18.8	20.2	Nevada	9.8	8.8	10.6	16.6	17.4
Arkansas	19.6	16.5	13.8	15.3	17.1	New Hampshire . .	6.3	4.5	5.6	6.5	9.0
California	13.9	12.7	13.2	16.3	14.9	New Jersey	9.2	7.3	6.8	11.1	11.1
Colorado	13.7	9.8	11.4	12.3	10.6	New Mexico	20.9	17.5	17.9	18.3	21.7
Connecticut.	6.0	7.7	9.3	8.6	11.3	New York	14.3	13.9	14.5	16.0	14.5
Delaware	6.9	8.4	9.2	12.2	14.0	North Carolina . . .	13.0	12.5	13.1	17.4	18.6
Dist. of Columbia	21.1	15.2	21.3	19.5	21.3	North Dakota	13.7	10.4	11.2	12.6	9.9
Florida	14.4	11.0	11.1	16.0	14.9	Ohio	11.5	10.0	12.3	15.4	13.7
Georgia	15.8	12.1	14.4	18.8	16.3	Oklahoma	15.6	14.9	15.6	16.3	14.0
Hawaii	11.0	8.9	8.6	12.4	11.1	Oregon	9.2	10.9	12.0	14.3	15.1
Idaho	14.9	12.5	9.9	13.8	12.9	Pennsylvania . . .	11.0	8.6	11.2	12.2	12.4
Illinois	13.7	10.7	11.5	14.1	13.3	Rhode Island . . .	7.5	10.2	12.1	14.0	13.5
Indiana	13.0	8.5	12.6	16.3	11.6	South Carolina . .	16.2	11.1	15.0	16.9	15.9
Iowa	10.4	8.3	11.3	10.3	10.8	South Dakota . . .	13.3	10.7	11.8	13.6	10.3
Kansas	10.3	8.0	12.5	14.5	13.2	Tennessee	16.9	13.5	14.9	16.7	18.1
Kentucky	17.3	12.6	14.8	17.7	20.0	Texas	15.9	15.5	16.2	18.4	16.8
Louisiana	23.6	17.2	18.3	21.5	19.2	Utah	8.2	7.6	9.2	10.0	8.3
Maine	13.1	10.1	12.6	12.6	12.3	Vermont	10.9	10.0	7.6	10.8	8.7
Maryland	9.9	7.4	9.7	10.9	10.3	Virginia	11.1	8.3	9.2	10.7	10.4
Massachusetts . .	10.7	9.8	10.1	10.9	11.9	Washington	8.9	10.8	10.2	11.6	12.0
Michigan	14.3	9.9	12.0	15.7	14.5	West Virginia . . .	18.1	14.7	15.4	16.8	17.3
Minnesota	12.0	5.7	8.1	10.8	12.0	Wisconsin	9.3	9.3	10.2	10.1	11.0
Mississippi	25.7	14.9	20.1	22.5	22.5	Wyoming	11.0	10.8	10.6	9.6	11.8
Missouri	13.4	9.2	11.6	15.0	13.7	**United States** . .	**13.5**	**11.3**	**12.6**	**15.1**	**14.5**

Selected Personal Consumption Expenditures in the U.S., 1990-2013

Source: Bureau of Economic Analysis, U.S. Dept. of Commerce

(in billions of dollars)

	1990	1995	2000	2005	2010	2012	2013
Personal consumption expenditures	$3,825.6	$4,984.2	$6,792.4	$8,794.1	$10,202.2	$11,083.1	$11,484.3
Goods	1,491.3	1,815.5	2,452.9	3,080.3	3,362.8	3,741.9	3,851.2
Durable goods	497.1	635.7	912.6	1,127.2	1,070.7	1,192.1	1,249.3
Motor vehicles and parts	205.1	255.7	363.2	410.0	342.0	395.1	417.7
New motor vehicles	134.7	147.5	210.7	248.9	182.3	237.2	250.3
Net purchases of used motor vehicles	42.2	72.9	110.7	110.5	104.2	96.4	104.7
Motor vehicle parts and accessories	28.3	35.4	41.8	50.6	55.5	61.5	62.6
Furnishings, durable household equip.	120.9	146.7	208.1	271.3	250.4	271.1	280.9
Furniture and furnishings	69.2	83.4	121.7	160.6	148.4	160.5	165.6
Household appliances	23.7	26.6	34.1	45.1	41.7	44.2	45.7
Glassware, tableware, and household utensils	18.4	23.7	35.3	44.6	42.7	47.2	50.0
Recreational goods and vehicles	105.6	153.7	230.9	305.0	312.7	334.8	348.7
Video, audio, photo equip.	56.1	84.7	127.7	172.7	194.1	203.6	210.6
Sporting equipment, guns, ammunition	19.9	27.2	39.1	50.9	51.3	58.6	61.6
Sports and recreational vehicles	16.6	22.5	34.9	49.1	35.6	40.7	43.7
Other durable goods	65.5	79.6	110.4	141.0	165.6	191.1	202.0
Jewelry and watches	30.3	37.8	49.1	59.8	62.6	72.3	76.9
Therapeutic appliances and equipment	18.4	21.0	32.2	43.2	55.6	61.7	63.2
Nondurable goods	994.2	1,179.8	1,540.3	1,953.1	2,292.1	2,549.8	2,601.9
Food and beverages purchased for off-premises consumption	391.2	443.7	540.6	668.2	788.9	854.9	872.2
Food and nonalcoholic beverages	341.2	388.3	463.1	575.3	675.9	732.1	747.0
Alcoholic beverages	49.3	55.0	77.1	92.6	112.6	122.4	124.7
Clothing and footwear	195.2	231.2	280.8	310.7	320.6	353.7	360.7
Women's and girls' clothing	94.5	108.9	132.7	149.6	152.8	168.9	172.6
Men's and boys' clothing	57.4	72.2	85.9	86.3	84.9	93.8	95.1
Children's and infants' clothing	8.1	9.0	11.4	15.4	17.7	18.9	19.1
Other clothing materials and footwear	35.3	41.2	50.8	59.3	65.2	72.2	73.9
Gasoline and other energy goods	124.2	133.4	184.5	283.8	333.4	415.5	408.3
Other nondurable goods	283.6	371.4	534.4	690.4	849.2	925.7	960.7
Pharmaceutical and other medical products	59.1	85.1	159.0	248.5	334.1	369.3	388.6
Recreational items	50.9	68.9	91.9	112.6	127.7	138.3	142.6
Household supplies	54.2	70.4	86.7	102.0	108.3	116.2	119.5
Personal care products	39.3	50.2	68.5	88.0	104.7	114.0	118.0
Tobacco	41.0	49.2	68.5	76.7	106.3	108.9	108.0
Magazines, newspapers, and stationery	36.5	46.1	56.6	58.0	62.8	72.7	78.7
Services	2,334.3	3,168.6	4,339.5	5,713.8	6,839.4	7,341.3	7,633.2
Housing and utilities	696.5	913.7	1,198.6	1,583.6	1,909.0	2,009.0	2,086.3
Housing	570.6	756.1	1,010.5	1,332.5	1,609.7	1,718.2	1,780.9
Rental of tenant-occupied nonfarm housing	150.8	186.6	227.9	268.3	372.6	429.0	445.5
Imputed rental of owner-occupied nonfarm housing	412.8	559.4	768.9	1,044.3	1,214.5	1,264.2	1,309.1
Household utilities	125.9	157.6	188.1	251.1	299.3	290.8	305.5
Water supply and sanitation	27.1	39.3	50.4	61.3	78.0	83.0	85.8
Electricity	71.8	87.6	98.4	128.5	166.8	163.3	168.5
Natural gas	27.0	30.7	39.3	61.3	54.6	44.5	51.1
Health care	506.2	719.9	918.4	1,322.3	1,690.7	1,854.7	1,920.3
Outpatient services	232.1	336.6	436.6	626.2	767.9	835.8	864.5
Physician services	134.8	177.8	229.2	333.9	402.8	438.2	456.3
Dental services	32.4	45.4	63.6	87.9	104.5	109.0	109.3
Paramedical services	64.9	113.4	143.8	204.4	260.6	288.6	298.9
Hospitals	228.8	318.4	393.9	577.2	770.5	857.3	893.0
Nursing homes	45.3	64.8	87.9	119.0	152.3	161.6	162.8
Transportation services	126.4	177.9	263.5	289.4	292.9	319.9	332.6
Motor vehicle services	87.2	129.1	189.3	211.8	211.9	229.3	237.7
Motor vehicle maintenance and repair	73.9	93.5	127.4	155.1	154.2	165.6	169.0
Public transportation	39.2	48.8	74.3	77.6	81.0	90.6	95.0
Recreation services	121.8	181.1	254.4	328.9	385.1	418.4	436.0
Clubs, sports centers, parks, theaters, museums	49.7	69.5	91.9	117.9	141.8	155.0	160.9
Gambling	23.7	45.4	67.6	96.5	105.6	113.6	117.7
Food services and accommodations	262.7	316.1	408.8	530.6	617.7	685.0	714.7
Purchased meals and beverages	228.3	271.8	344.9	446.0	516.9	571.0	594.0
Accommodations	27.6	36.6	55.0	72.5	85.5	96.8	103.3
Financial services and insurance	247.4	366.4	566.3	689.6	763.2	788.4	826.7
Financial services	135.7	212.9	360.0	417.4	473.3	488.0	517.1
Insurance	111.7	153.5	206.3	272.2	290.0	300.5	309.6
Other services	297.5	391.2	571.5	759.1	905.4	977.4	1,010.9
Telecommunication services	60.7	85.2	126.4	137.7	152.1	158.9	165.1
Postal and delivery services	7.5	9.2	9.9	10.4	11.7	10.4	10.4
Internet access	0.1	1.6	16.4	29.7	63.0	82.1	91.1
Higher education	34.7	51.9	76.8	110.9	158.3	172.7	182.4
Nursery, elementary, and secondary schools	14.8	19.2	24.1	29.6	35.3	37.6	38.1
Commercial and vocational schools	11.1	14.4	24.3	30.3	42.0	45.6	47.3
Professional and other services	67.7	82.8	113.0	148.4	163.3	170.9	173.2
Personal care and clothing services	44.5	57.1	80.4	103.3	114.9	125.8	127.3
Social services and religious activities	41.2	58.1	81.1	110.2	138.9	147.5	154.1
Household maintenance	25.4	34.5	48.6	57.9	58.6	64.6	67.9

Note: Subtotals may not add up to totals due to rounding or incomplete enumeration.

Leading U.S. Businesses, 2014

Source: *Financial Times 500*, based on data from Thomson ONE Banker, Thomson Reuters Datastream, and individual companies
(ranked by market value, in millions of dollars; as of Mar. 31, 2014)

Aerospace and defense
Company (rank)	Market value
United Technologies (35)	$107,077.3
Boeing (39)	92,495.8
Lockheed Martin (85)	52,117.4
General Dynamics (115)	37,478.0
Precision Castparts (118)	36,707.8
Raytheon (142)	31,070.3
Northrop Grumman (172)	26,741.0
Textron (198)	10,940.9
Rockwell Collins (388)	10,788.7
L3 Communications (401)	10,218.0
Transdigm (419)	9,772.6
B/E Aerospace (446)	9,121.5

Automobiles and parts
Company (rank)	Market value
Ford Motor Co. (68)	$60,553.9
General Motors (80)	54,720.5
Johnson Controls (141)	31,421.8
Tesla Motors (175)	25,679.4
Delphi Automotive (216)	20,765.2
Harley-Davidson (307)	14,655.0
BorgWarner (323)	14,034.8
Genuine Parts (337)	13,351.2
Autoliv (429)	9,428.3
TRW Automotive (448)	9,040.1
LKG (495)	7,951.5

Banks
Company (rank)	Market value
Wells Fargo (7)	$261,217.5
JP Morgan Chase (10)	229,897.9
Bank of America (18)	181,086.3
Citigroup (22)	144,627.3
US Bancorp (48)	78,007.5
PNC Financial Services (96)	46,463.6
BB&T (157)	28,569.7
SunTrust Banks (209)	21,274.6
Fifth Third Bancorp (224)	19,547.2
M&T Bank (288)	15,909.7
Regions Financial (298)	15,315.5
KeyCorp (349)	12,665.0
Credicorp (385)	11,000.5
Comerica (428)	9,432.2
Huntington Bancshares (485)	8,302.9

Beverages
Company (rank)	Market value
Coca-Cola (19)	$170,331.6
PepsiCo (28)	128,267.9
Brown-Forman (233)	19,067.6
Constellation Brands (281)	16,127.3
Coca Cola Enterprises (357)	12,104.9
Monster Beverage (368)	11,589.6
Dr Pepper Snapple Group (387)	10,811.9
Molson Coors Brewing (431)	9,402.1

Chemicals
Company (rank)	Market value
E I Du Pont de Nemours (65)	$61,482.1
Dow Chemical (73)	58,768.8
LyondellBasell Industries (93)	48,292.1
Praxair (112)	38,432.5
Ecolab (138)	32,492.6
PPG Industries (170)	26,828.1
Air Products & Chemicals (180)	25,197.5
Mosaic (264)	17,008.5
CF Industries (315)	14,456.6
Eastman Chemical (343)	13,030.5
Sigma Aldrich (382)	11,094.7
FMC (404)	10,188.2
Celanese (464)	8,655.8
Airgas (499)	7,877.7

Construction and materials
Company (rank)	Market value
Sherwin-Williams (221)	$19,735.6
Fluor (352)	12,429.3
Chicago Bridge & Iron (430)	9,406.9
Vulcan Materials (463)	8,685.6
Jacobs Engineering (478)	8,375.9
Masco (496)	7,944.2
Quanta Services (500)	7,872.7

Electricity
Company (rank)	Market value
Nextera Energy (102)	$41,631.3
Dominion Resources (103)	41,288.1
Southern (110)	39,016.1
Exelon (154)	$28,775.0
American Electric Power (187)	24,713.0
PPL (214)	20,902.0
PG&E (220)	19,773.9
Public Service Enterprise (229)	19,305.1
Edison International (243)	18,444.1
Consolidated Edison (292)	15,714.2
Xcel Energy (301)	15,128.0
Northeast Utilities (318)	14,361.2
FirstEnergy (319)	14,249.5
DTE Energy (341)	13,150.7
Entergy (359)	12,004.3
NRG Energy (399)	10,344.3
AES (400)	10,337.7
Calpine (457)	8,843.9

Electronic and electrical equipment
Company (rank)	Market value
Emerson Electric (95)	$46,959.4
TE Connectivity (186)	24,719.1
Agilent Technologies (239)	18,644.9
Amphenol (311)	14,499.0
Roper Industries (339)	13,290.6
Ametek (351)	12,626.7
Trimble Navigation (407)	10,135.2

Financial services
Company (rank)	Market value
Visa (34)	$108,859.5
American Express (37)	95,396.9
Mastercard (45)	85,253.9
Goldman Sachs (51)	74,183.4
Morgan Stanley (66)	61,481.0
Blackrock (82)	52,678.1
Capital One Financial (97)	44,193.9
Bank of New York Mellon (105)	40,062.9
Charles Schwab (123)	35,541.5
Franklin Resources (127)	34,179.2
State Street (147)	30,020.2
Discover Financial Services (165)	27,324.0
CME Group (183)	24,848.1
Intercontinental Exchange (196)	22,769.2
T Rowe Price (208)	21,624.2
Ameriprise Financial (212)	20,978.7
McGraw Hill Financial (215)	20,879.2
TD Ameritrade Holding (238)	18,723.4
Moody's (267)	16,973.5
Invesco (284)	15,966.5
Northern Trust (293)	15,558.0
Affiliated Managers (383)	11,038.6
SLM (393)	10,494.5
CIT Group (422)	9,578.4
Voya Financial (437)	9,227.8
Western Union (451)	8,964.2
Fidelity National Financial (462)	8,687.8
Equifax (486)	8,290.4

Fixed-line telecommunications
Company (rank)	Market value
Verizon Communications (15)	$196,939.7
AT&T (16)	182,604.1
CenturyLink (235)	18,980.0
Level 3 Communications (439)	9,207.2

Food and drug retailers
Company (rank)	Market value
CVS Caremark (41)	$88,972.4
Walgreen (62)	63,014.5
McKesson (104)	40,633.5
Cardinal Health (191)	23,995.3
Kroger (202)	22,174.2
Sysco (210)	21,134.9
Whole Foods Market (236)	18,862.6
AmerisourceBergen (302)	15,033.3
Safeway (386)	8,507.3

Food producers
Company (rank)	Market value
Monsanto (69)	$59,718.9
Mondelez International (74)	58,768.7
Kraft Foods Group (131)	33,448.4
General Mills (148)	31,843.0
Archer Daniels Midland (158)	28,453.6
Kellogg (199)	22,524.9
The Hershey Company (266)	16,993.8
Mead Johnson Nutrition (270)	16,800.3
Keurig Green Mountain (291)	15,721.4
Campbell Soup (322)	$14,080.9
ConAgra Foods (342)	13,045.2
Hormel Foods (344)	13,006.8
Tyson Foods (361)	11,894.8
Bunge (364)	11,728.7
Leucadia National (403)	10,195.7
J M Smucker (408)	10,082.7
McCormick (470)	8,487.9

Forestry and paper
Company (rank)	Market value
International Paper (219)	$20,132.2

Gas, water, and multi-utilities
Company (rank)	Market value
Duke Energy (89)	$50,349.3
Spectra Energy (184)	24,756.1
Sempra Energy (193)	23,720.9
Oneok (354)	12,313.0
NiSource (381)	11,156.1
Wisconsin Energy (392)	10,513.9
Centerpoint Energy (406)	10,160.2
Ameren (411)	9,996.5
American Water Works (489)	8,113.0

General industrials
Company (rank)	Market value
General Electric (8)	$259,547.3
3M (40)	89,238.2
Honeywell International (52)	72,537.6
Danaher (83)	52,386.1
Eaton (122)	35,754.2

General retailers
Company (rank)	Market value
Wal-Mart Stores (9)	$246,805.7
Amazon.com (21)	154,480.4
Home Depot (32)	109,306.3
eBay (55)	71,516.7
Lowe's Companies (91)	49,818.1
Costco Wholesale (92)	49,125.5
TJX Cos (100)	43,134.2
Target (113)	38,313.4
Macy's (207)	21,634.9
Netflix (211)	21,053.9
Gap (247)	17,906.9
AutoZone (250)	17,845.7
Dollar General (256)	17,398.4
L Brands (276)	16,520.9
O'Reilly Automotive (289)	15,788.5
Ross Stores (297)	15,381.5
Bed Bath & Beyond (308)	14,649.4
Nordstrom (362)	11,846.3
Kohl's (363)	11,846.1
Tiffany & Co (384)	11,031.4
Dollar Tree (390)	10,760.8
Carmax (394)	10,446.9
Tractor Supply (417)	9,797.8
Advance Auto Participations (438)	9,225.2
Best Buy (443)	9,165.4
Signet Jewelers (469)	8,495.5
H&R Block (487)	8,278.6

Health care equipment and services
Company (rank)	Market value
UnitedHealth Group (47)	$81,103.8
Medtronic (64)	61,590.1
Express Scripts (76)	58,233.2
Thermo Fisher Scientific (94)	47,109.1
Baxter International (106)	39,802.1
Covidien (135)	33,170.3
Stryker (143)	30,811.9
WellPoint (161)	28,118.8
Aetna (168)	27,191.6
HCA Holdings (194)	23,297.2
Cigna (197)	22,727.1
Becton Dickinson (198)	22,598.9
St. Jude Medical (240)	18,564.4
Boston Scientific (248)	17,893.3
Humana (255)	17,440.4
Intuitive Surgical (271)	16,790.4
Zimmer (286)	15,942.2
Davita Healthcare Partners (306)	14,678.8
C R Bard (376)	11,460.4
Henry Schein (402)	10,199.0
Waters (436)	9,233.9
Varian Medical Systems (460)	8,697.4

Company (rank)	Market value
CareFusion (476)	$8,381.2
Laboratory Corp. of America (477)	8,377.3
Quest Diagnostics (480)	8,358.3

Household goods and home construction

Company (rank)	Market value
Procter & Gamble (12)	$218,539.4
Stanley Black & Decker (350)	12,652.4
Whirlpool (369)	11,580.4
Clorox (377)	11,433.7
Mohawk Industries (414)	9,886.4
Church & Dwight (426)	9,481.0
Newell Rubbermaid (481)	8,339.1
Jarden (493)	7,960.3

Industrial engineering

Company (rank)	Market value
Caterpillar (61)	$63,380.4
Illinois Tool Works (128)	34,146.5
Deere (129)	33,568.9
Cummins (164)	27,396.1
Paccar (192)	23,917.1
Parker-Hannifin (249)	17,852.2
Rockwell Automation (259)	17,285.2
Ingersoll-Rand (287)	15,914.8
Pentair (296)	15,493.5
Dover (324)	13,900.6
Flowserve (389)	10,778.6
Pall (416)	9,821.6

Industrial metals and mining

Company (rank)	Market value
Freeport-McMoRan Copper & Gold (125)	$34,340.5
Southern Copper (190)	24,264.6
Nucor (285)	16,095.0
Alcoa (325)	13,873.4

Industrial transportation

Company (rank)	Market value
Union Pacific (44)	$85,396.1
United Parcel Service (58)	69,094.1
FedEx (107)	39,173.6
Norfolk Southern (145)	30,099.2
CSX (151)	29,126.0
Kansas City Southern (379)	11,261.1
Hunt JB Transport Services (474)	8,432.4
Expeditor International of Washington (492)	7,968.2

Leisure goods

Company (rank)	Market value
Activision Blizzard (310)	$14,560.8
Mattel (330)	13,651.9
Polaris Industries (440)	9,203.9
Electronic Arts (450)	8,981.2

Life insurance

Company (rank)	Market value
MetLife (70)	$59,492.2
Prudential Financial (109)	39,021.9
Aflac (155)	28,669.5
Principal Financial (331)	13,591.0
Lincoln National (336)	13,361.7
Unum Group (444)	9,161.1
Genworth Financial (458)	8,782.7

Media

Company (rank)	Market value
Walt Disney (23)	$140,287.3
Comcast (26)	129,376.1
21st Century Fox (56)	71,469.8
Viacom (57)	70,105.9
Time Warner (75)	58,317.5
Liberty Global (108)	39,024.3
DirecTV (111)	38,970.6
Time Warner Cable (114)	38,060.7
CBS (126)	34,256.5
Sirius XM Radio (226)	19,511.4
Liberty (230)	19,197.3
Omnicom (237)	18,745.7
Discovery Communications (245)	18,301.0
Nielsen (268)	16,908.8
Liberty Media (303)	14,945.1
Dish Network (329)	13,680.5
Charter Communications (338)	13,311.8
News (405)	9,866.8
Scripps Networks Interactive (468)	8,499.9
IHS (488)	8,268.5

Mining

Company (rank)	Market value
Newmont Mining (367)	$11,671.4
Consol Energy (441)	9,179.4

Mobile telecommunications

Company (rank)	Market value
Sprint (120)	$36,170.7
T-Mobile US (173)	$26,505.1
SBA Communications (366)	11,711.9

Non-life insurance

Company (rank)	Market value
Berkshire Hathaway (5)	$308,090.6
American International Group (53)	72,466.6
ACE (133)	33,349.3
Travelers Cos. (148)	29,983.0
Marsh & McLennan (169)	27,084.0
Aon (178)	25,376.7
Allstate (179)	25,296.9
Chubb (205)	21,893.0
Loews (263)	17,060.5
Hartford Financial Services (290)	15,742.5
Progressive Ohio (317)	14,393.6
CNA Financial (371)	11,528.4
Everest Re (461)	8,689.5
XL Group (465)	8,647.6
Markel (482)	8,334.4
Cincinnati Financial (494)	7,957.0
Willis Group (498)	7,900.2

Oil and gas producers

Company (rank)	Market value
Exxon Mobil (2)	$422,098.3
Chevron (11)	227,014.7
ConocoPhillips (42)	86,358.3
Occidental Petroleum (49)	75,289.4
EOG Resources (81)	53,579.5
Phillips 66 (98)	43,708.3
Anadarko Petroleum (99)	43,403.6
Apache (136)	32,742.4
Valero Energy (160)	28,286.7
Devon Energy (166)	27,267.3
Pioneer Natural Resources (171)	26,745.4
Hess (174)	26,116.2
Noble Energy (176)	25,620.6
Marathon Petroleum (177)	25,490.1
Marathon Oil (189)	24,572.9
Continental Resources (195)	23,067.3
Chesapeake Energy (262)	17,068.4
Antero Resources (278)	16,404.3
Southwestern Energy (280)	16,238.3
EQT (305)	14,733.0
Cabot Oil & Gas (320)	14,137.7
Range Resources (332)	13,581.1
Cheniere Energy (340)	13,179.2
Concho Resources (347)	12,882.3
Murphy Oil (378)	11,279.3
Cimarex Energy (398)	10,364.0
Hollyfrontier (427)	9,467.3
Linn Energy (432)	9,385.7
Whiting Petroleum (479)	8,370.1

Oil equipment and services

Company (rank)	Market value
Schlumberger (29)	$127,377.9
Halliburton (90)	50,107.5
Kinder Morgan (130)	33,486.7
National Oilwell Varco (132)	33,369.3
Baker Hughes (159)	28,360.4
Williams Cos. (162)	27,773.6
Cameron International (333)	13,390.6
Weatherford International (335)	13,387.7
FMC Technologies (353)	12,341.1
Helmerich & Payne (370)	11,566.4
Core Laboratories (453)	8,903.2
Buckeye Partners (466)	8,647.4
Noble (484)	8,320.5

Personal goods

Company (rank)	Market value
Colgate-Palmolive (71)	$59,463.6
Nike (84)	52,257.9
Kimberly-Clark (101)	41,749.9
V F (167)	27,250.0
Michael Kors (234)	19,020.2
Estee Lauder (285)	15,952.4
Coach (328)	13,784.7
PVH (405)	10,184.0
Under Armour (412)	9,949.9
Ralph Lauren (421)	9,608.4

Pharmaceuticals and biotechnology

Company (rank)	Market value
Johnson & Johnson (6)	$277,826.2
Pfizer (13)	205,359.9
Merck (20)	166,938.9
Gilead Sciences (33)	108,972.2
Amgen (38)	93,122.5
Bristol Myers Squibb (43)	$86,079.7
AbbVie (46)	82,036.9
Biogen Idec (54)	72,305.7
Eli Lilly (59)	65,908.8
Abbott Laboratories (72)	59,423.6
Celgene (77)	56,680.4
Allergan (117)	37,119.4
Actavis (121)	35,919.7
Alexion Pharmaceuticals (146)	30,095.9
Regeneron Pharmaceuticals (150)	29,399.8
Forest Laboratories (182)	25,001.6
Perrigo (217)	20,685.4
Illumina (232)	19,073.1
Mylan (246)	18,160.5
Vertex Pharmaceuticals (272)	16,697.9
Zoetis (312)	14,491.1
Endo International (395)	10,419.1
Biomarin Pharmaceutical (418)	9,796.5
Incyte (456)	8,859.5
Jazz Pharmaceuticals (490)	8,052.9

Real estate investment and services

Company (rank)	Market value
CBRE Group (447)	$9,105.8

Real estate investment trusts

Company (rank)	Market value
Simon Property Group (86)	$51,537.1
American Tower (139)	32,340.1
Public Storage (152)	29,031.6
Crown Castle International (188)	24,647.3
Equity Residential Trust Properties (213)	20,939.0
Prologis (218)	20,400.7
General Growth Properties (227)	19,440.9
Vornado Realty Trust (242)	18,458.8
Ventas (251)	17,824.6
HCP (252)	17,767.5
Boston Properties (254)	17,523.8
Health Care Reit (258)	17,336.1
Weyerhaeuser (261)	17,156.8
AvalonBay Communities (265)	16,995.1
Host Hotels & Resorts (300)	15,186.6
Annaly Capital Management (396)	10,393.7
SL Green Realty (423)	9,563.7
Kimco Realty (449)	8,981.6
Macerich (459)	8,760.7
Realty Income (471)	8,483.0

Software and computer services

Company (rank)	Market value
Microsoft (3)	$340,216.8
Google (4)	313,003.9
IBM (14)	200,447.6
Oracle (17)	182,412.9
Facebook (30)	119,943.2
Yahoo (119)	36,237.2
Salesforce.com (124)	34,830.6
Adobe Systems (137)	32,720.8
Cognizant Technology Solutions (144)	30,735.6
Twitter (163)	27,459.6
Intuit (203)	22,022.0
Cerner (228)	19,347.0
VMware (321)	14,127.0
CA (326)	13,871.9
Symantec (327)	13,810.3
Check Point Software Technologies (345)	13,002.7
Autodesk (380)	11,173.0
Citrix Systems (391)	10,554.8
Akamai Technologies (397)	10,392.6
Red Hat (409)	10,041.7
Equinix (445)	9,131.8
FireEye (454)	8,874.5
Computer Sciences (455)	8,861.0
ServiceNow (473)	8,454.7
Splunk (475)	8,429.0
Workday (483)	8,329.3

Support services

Company (rank)	Market value
Accenture (48)	$50,468.3
Automatic Data Processing (116)	37,225.8
Waste Management (223)	19,570.6
Tyco International (225)	19,517.1

Company (rank)	Market value	Company (rank)	Market value	Company (rank)	Market value
LinkedIn (231)	$19,153.7	Western Digital (206)	$21,693.5	**Travel and leisure**	
W.W. Grainger (257)	17,348.2	Seagate Technology (241)	18,462.9	McDonald's (36)	$97,038.0
Fidelity Natl. Info. Services (294)	15,536.2	SanDisk (244)	18,308.9	Las Vegas Sands (60)	65,639.1
Paychex (295)	15,495.3	Broadcom (269)	16,832.4	Priceline.com (63)	62,147.9
Fastenal (309)	14,630.9	Analog Devices (273)	16,607.7	Starbucks (79)	55,467.9
Alliance Data Systems (313)	14,486.9	Motorola Solutions (279)	16,335.1	Yum! Brands (134)	33,317.9
Fiserv (316)	14,426.8	Avago Technologies (283)	16,091.6	Delta Air Lines (149)	29,431.0
Xerox (334)	13,389.9	NXP Semiconductors (304)	14,805.5	Wynn Resorts (200)	22,494.3
Republic Services (355)	12,249.9	Xilinx (314)	14,482.2	Carnival (201)	22,422.2
Verisk Analytics (410)	10,003.5	Juniper Networks (346)	12,908.9	Hilton Worldwide (204)	21,897.8
Stericycle (420)	9,675.7	NetApp (356)	12,224.0	Chipotle Mexican Grill (253)	17,660.2
Fleetcor Technologies (425)	9,493.4	KLA Tencor (372)	11,517.1	American Airlines (260)	17,257.5
United Rentals (442)	9,176.3	Altera (373)	11,506.9	United Continental (274)	16,582.5
Towers Watson (491)	8,043.6	Garmin (374)	11,498.3	Southwest Airlines (275)	16,574.0
Technology hardware and equipment		Linear Technology (375)	11,487.0	Marriott International (277)	16,516.0
Apple (1)	$478,766.1	NVIDIA (413)	9,926.5	Starwood Hotels & Restaurants	
Qualcomm (24)	133,358.4	Microchip Technology (424)	9,510.7	Worldwide (299)	15,277.2
Intel (27)	128,347.1	Maxim Integrated Products (434)	9,342.0	MGM Resorts International (348)	12,682.5
Cisco Systems (31)	115,465.9	Lam Research (452)	8,927.2	Royal Caribbean Cruises (358)	12,069.5
Hewlett-Packard (67)	61,326.1	Marvell Technology (497)	7,928.6	Hertz Global (360)	11,926.1
EMC (78)	55,570.9	**Tobacco**		TripAdvisor (365)	11,725.3
Texas Instruments (87)	51,014.9	Philip Morris International (25)	$129,387.9	Wyndham Worldwide (433)	9,383.9
Corning (153)	28,957.5	Altria Group (50)	74,592.4	Burger King Worldwide (435)	9,340.7
Micron Technology (181)	25,100.4	Reynolds American (156)	28,658.6	Expedia (472)	8,457.7
Applied Materials (185)	24,724.0	Lorillard (222)	19,588.1		

World's Largest Companies, 2014

Source: *FT Global 500*, based on data from Thomson ONE Banker, Thomson Reuters Datastream, and individual companies
(ranked by market value, in millions of dollars; as of Mar. 31, 2014)

Rank	Company (2013 rank), country	Market value	Rank	Company (2013 rank), country	Market value
1.	Apple (1), U.S.	$478,766.1	52.	Bank of China (40), China	$118,616.7
2.	Exxon Mobil (2), U.S.	422,098.3	53.	Siemens (63), Germany	118,567.5
3.	Microsoft (7), U.S.	340,216.8	54.	Ambev (41), Brazil	117,679.2
4.	Google (15), U.S.	313,003.9	55.	Commonwealth Bank of Australia (47),	
5.	Berkshire Hathaway (3), U.S.	308,090.6		Australia	115,695.0
6.	Johnson & Johnson (12), U.S.	277,826.2	56.	Cisco Systems (50), U.S.	115,465.9
7.	Wells Fargo (23), U.S.	261,217.5	57.	Bayer (73), Germany	112,126.2
8.	General Electric (6), U.S.	259,547.3	58.	Banco Santander (96), Spain	110,278.0
9.	Roche (20), Switzerland	258,542.1	59.	Home Depot (54), U.S.	109,306.3
10.	Wal-Mart Stores (5), U.S.	246,805.7	60.	Gilead Sciences (89), U.S.	108,972.2
11.	Nestle (9), Switzerland	242,954.9	61.	Visa (66), U.S.	108,859.5
12.	Royal Dutch Shell (17), UK	238,993.5	62.	United Technologies (72), U.S.	107,077.3
13.	JP Morgan Chase (25), U.S.	229,897.9	63.	British American Tobacco (55), UK	104,634.8
14.	Novartis (24), Switzerland	229,770.4	64.	Rio Tinto (64), Australia/UK	104,308.8
15.	Chevron (10), U.S.	227,014.7	65.	BASF (80), Germany	102,105.5
16.	PetroChina (4), China	220,893.7	66.	Daimler (126), Germany	101,624.0
17.	Procter & Gamble (16), U.S.	218,539.4	67.	Taiwan Semiconductor Manufacturing (70),	
18.	Samsung Electronics (13), South Korea	208,518.6		Taiwan	100,899.1
19.	Pfizer (18), U.S.	205,359.9	68.	Novo Nordisk (91), Denmark	100,804.4
20.	IBM (8), U.S.	200,447.6	69.	SAP (61), Germany	99,642.7
21.	Industrial & Commercial Bank of China (11),		70.	Westpac Banking (60), Australia	99,587.5
	China	200,179.4	71.	L'Oreal (62), France	99,197.5
22.	Verizon Communications (32), U.S.	196,939.7	72.	Vodafone Group (34), UK	97,106.8
23.	Toyota Motor (27), Japan	195,057.4	73.	McDonald's (58), U.S.	97,038.0
24.	HSBC (22), UK	191,251.3	74.	Sinopec (53), China	96,667.8
25.	China Mobile (14), Hong Kong	184,573.4	75.	BNP Paribas (112), France	96,085.6
26.	AT&T (21), U.S.	182,604.1	76.	American Express (90), U.S.	95,396.9
27.	Oracle (30), U.S.	182,412.9	77.	Royal Bank Canada (69), Canada	95,246.2
28.	Bank of America (39), U.S.	181,086.3	78.	Saudi Basic Industries (83), Saudi Arabia	93,991.1
29.	China Construction Bank (19), China	174,465.7	79.	Inditex (76), Spain	93,555.3
30.	BHP Billiton (28), Australia/UK	173,490.4	80.	Amgen (86), U.S.	93,122.5
31.	Coca-Cola (26), U.S.	170,331.6	81.	Boeing (107), U.S.	92,495.8
32.	Anheuser-Busch InBev (29), Belgium	168,640.3	82.	LVMH (68), France	92,323.7
33.	Merck (38), U.S.	166,938.9	83.	Gazprom (57), Russia	91,289.4
34.	Total (48), France	155,984.8	84.	Eni (78), Italy	91,209.2
35.	Amazon.com (43), U.S.	154,480.4	85.	SoftBank (141), Japan	90,937.0
36.	BP (37), U.S.	147,771.1	86.	Statoil (84), Norway	90,007.9
37.	Citigroup (36), U.S.	144,627.3	87.	3M (93), U.S.	89,238.2
38.	Agricultural Bank of China (33)	141,661.8	88.	CVS Caremark (104), U.S.	88,972.4
39.	Walt Disney (56), U.S.	140,287.3	89.	Lloyds Banking Group (150), UK	88,822.7
40.	Sanofi (35), France	138,132.8	90.	Petrobras (49), Brazil	88,517.8
41.	Qualcomm (45), U.S.	133,358.4	91.	Toronto-Dominion Bank (85), Canada	86,509.0
42.	Tencent Holdings (122), Hong Kong	129,640.5	92.	ConocoPhillips (92), U.S.	86,358.3
43.	Philip Morris Intl. (31), U.S.	129,387.9	93.	Bristol Myers Squibb (105), U.S.	86,079.7
44.	Comcast (51), U.S.	129,376.1	94.	Union Pacific (106), U.S.	85,396.1
45.	GlaxoSmithKline (46), UK	128,915.8	95.	Mastercard (113), U.S.	85,253.9
46.	Intel (52), U.S.	128,347.1	96.	ANZ Banking (79), Australia	84,053.1
47.	PepsiCo (42), U.S.	128,267.9	97.	AbbVie (109), U.S.	82,036.9
48.	Schlumberger (59), U.S.	127,377.9	98.	AstraZeneca (116), UK	81,492.6
49.	Facebook (193), U.S.	119,943.2	99.	BMW (136), Germany	81,192.2
50.	Volkswagen (67), Germany	119,119.8	100.	UnitedHealth Group (124), U.S.	81,103.8
51.	Unilever (44), Netherlands/UK	118,795.6			

Note: Revenue figures rounded at source.

Top U.S. Franchises, 2014

Source: *Entrepreneur* magazine

Rank	Company (2013 Rank)	Type of business	Locations	Startup costs[1]
1.	Anytime Fitness (6)	Fitness center	2,539	$56,290-353,890
2.	Hampton Hotels (1)	Mid-price hotels	1,944	$3.69 mil-6.57 mil
3.	Subway (2)	Submarine sandwiches, salads	42,210	$85,690-262,850
4.	Supercuts (5)	Hair salon	2,390	$113,750-233,600
5.	Jimmy John's Gourmet Sandwiches (12)	Gourmet sandwiches	1,954	$330,500-519,500
6.	7-Eleven Inc. (4)	Convenience stores	53,049	$50,000-1.63 mil
7.	Servpro (7)	Insurance/disaster restoration and cleaning	1,649	$138,550-187,190
8.	Denny's Inc. (8)	Family restaurant	1,696	$1.12 mil-2.61 mil
9.	Pizza Hut Inc. (10)	Pizza, pasta, wings	14,967	$297,000-2.1 mil
10.	Dunkin' Donuts (13)	Coffee, doughnuts, baked goods	10,862	$294,000-1.51 mil
11.	Hardee's (14)	Burgers, chicken, biscuits	1,960	$1.14 mil-1.53 mil
12.	Jan-Pro Franchising Intl. Inc. (19)	Commercial cleaning	11,532	$3,150-50,900
13.	Days Inn (17)	Hotels	1,812	$198,860-7.3 mil
14.	KFC Corp. (15)	Chicken	18,198	$1.25 mil-2.53 mil
15.	H&R Block (11)	Tax preparation, electronic filing	11,315	$31,500-148,690
16.	McDonald's (9)	Burgers, chicken, salads, beverages	35,493	$1 mil-2.33 mil
17.	Aaron's (18)	Furniture, electronics, computer, and appliance leasing and sales	2,135	$275,610-707,400
18.	Kumon Math & Reading Centers (16)	Supplemental education	25,437	$72,190-149,320
19.	Cruise Planners-American Express Travel (34)	Cruise and tour travel agency	1,734	$2,090-21,980
20.	Taco Bell (NA)	Mexican food	5,980	$1.19 mil-2.47 mil
21.	Liberty Tax Service (28)	Tax preparation	4,406	$56,790-69,900
22.	The UPS Store (32)	Postal, business, and communications services	4,789	$150,140-420,290
23.	Vanguard Cleaning Systems (25)	Commercial cleaning	2,946	$9,850-35,830
24.	Snap-on Tools (26)	Professional tools and equipment	4,805	$152,690-318,980
25.	Midas Intl. Corp. (31)	Auto repair and maintenance	2,165	$203,130-424,510

NA = Not available. **Note:** Franchises are ranked by a combination of factors, including financial strength and stability, growth rate, number of locations, startup costs, and whether the company provides financing. (1) Does not include franchise fees, which vary.

United States Mint

Source: United States Mint, U.S. Dept. of the Treasury

The United States Mint was created on Apr. 2, 1792, by an act of Congress, which established the U.S. national coinage system. In 1799, the mint became an independent agency reporting directly to the president. It was made a statutory bureau of the Treasury Department in 1873, with a director appointed by the president.

The mint manufactures and ships all U.S. coins for circulation to Federal Reserve banks and branches, which in turn issue coins to the public and business community through depository institutions. The mint also safeguards the Treasury Department's stored gold and silver, as well as other monetary assets.

The composition of dimes, quarters, and half dollars, traditionally produced from silver, was changed by the Coinage Act of 1965, which mandated that these coins from then on be minted from a cupronickel-clad alloy. In 1970, legislative action mandated that the half dollar and a dollar coin be minted from the same alloy.

Mint headquarters are in Washington, DC. Mint production facilities are in Philadelphia, Denver, San Francisco, and West Point, NY. In addition, the mint is responsible for the U.S. Bullion Depository at Fort Knox, KY.

Contact information: (800) USA-MINT.

Website: www.usmint.gov.

New Circulating and Commemorative Coins

Source: United States Mint, U.S. Dept. of the Treasury

Dollar coins. A large, unwieldy dollar coin featuring the likeness of Pres. Dwight D. Eisenhower was minted 1971-78. The smaller Susan B. Anthony dollar, minted 1979-81, marked the first time that a woman other than a mythical figure appeared on a generally circulated U.S. coin. A golden dollar coin was first minted in 2000. It depicts Sacagawea, a Shoshone woman who helped guide explorers Lewis and Clark, on the obverse. In 2007, the mint began issuing a series of golden dollar coins featuring U.S. presidents on the front and the Statue of Liberty on the back. Each includes the president's name, likeness, and years of service. Four are to be issued each year in the order in which the presidents served. The 2014 set featured Warren G. Harding, Calvin Coolidge, Herbert Hoover, and Franklin D. Roosevelt; the 2015 set includes Harry S. Truman, Dwight D. Eisenhower, John F. Kennedy, and Lyndon B. Johnson. Only presidents deceased more than two years will be honored, so the program is currently slated to end in 2016 with coins commemorating Richard Nixon and Gerald Ford. The mint also issues golden dollar coins whose reverse sides celebrate the important contributions made by American Indian tribes to the development of the U.S. The 2012 coin commemorated trade routes of the 17th century; the 2013 coin celebrated the treaty with the Delaware tribe of Native Americans; and the 2014 coin commemorated the

hospitality that ensured the success of the Lewis and Clark exhibition.

America the Beautiful quarters. In 2010, the U.S. Mint began an initiative to honor 56 national parks and other sites of national importance. Five new reverse designs appear on the quarter-dollar each year in 2010-21; the order of issuance corresponds to the order in which the featured site was first established. The 2013 coins commemorated White Mountain National Forest, NH; Perry's Victory and International Peace Memorial, OH; Great Basin National Park, NV; Fort McHenry National Monument and Historic Shrine, MD; and Mount Rushmore National Memorial, SD. The 2014 coins commemorated Great Smoky Mountains National Park, TN; Shenandoah National Park, VA; Arches National Park, UT; Great Sand Dunes National Park, CO, and Everglades National Park, FL. The 2015 coins will commemorate Homestead National Monument of America, NE;, Kisatchie National Forest, LA; Blue Ridge Parkway, NC; Bombay Hook National Wildlife Refuge, DE; and Saratoga National Historical Park, NY.

Commemorative coins. From 1892 to 1954, and again since 1982, Congress has authorized the mint to produce more than 50 different commemorative coins. Recent issues include the 2009 Louis Braille Bicentennial-Braille Literacy silver dollar, the 2014 Civil Rights Act of 1964 silver dollar, and the 2014 National Baseball Hall of Fame Coins.

Bureau of Engraving and Printing

Source: Bureau of Engraving and Printing, U.S. Dept. of the Treasury

The Bureau of Engraving and Printing manufactures the financial and other securities of the U.S. It designs and prints a variety of products, including Federal Reserve notes (bills in various denominations), Treasury securities, identification cards, naturalization certificates, and other special security documents. The bureau produces printings in denominations ranging from a 1/5-cent wine stamp to a $100,000,000 Intl. Monetary Fund special note. It also produces all hand-engraved invitations issued by the White House.

The first general circulation of paper money by the federal government dates back to 1861, prior to the establishment of the bureau, when Congress authorized the U.S. Treasury to issue non-interest-bearing demand notes, nicknamed "greenbacks" because of their color, to finance the Civil War. A portrait of Pres. Abraham Lincoln appeared on the face of the first $10 notes. By 1862, the design of U.S. currency incorporated fine-line engraving, intricate geometric lathe work patterns, a Treasury seal, and engraved signatures to aid in counterfeit deterrence. All U.S. currency issued since 1861 remain valid and redeemable at full face value.

The Bureau of Engraving and Printing began operations by 1862, originally separating and sealing bank notes that were printed by private companies. In 1877, the bureau became the sole producer of U.S. currency. The Federal Reserve Act of 1913 created the Federal Reserve as the nation's central bank and provided for currency called Federal Reserve notes. The first notes, issued the following year, were $10 notes bearing a portrait of Pres. Andrew Jackson. In 1929, the look of U.S. currency was standardized. The national motto, "In God We Trust," was added to paper money in 1957.

On Oct. 9, 2003, the Treasury began a major currency redesign, beginning with the introduction of a new $20 note. The bills are the first since 1905 to use background colors other than green and black. Other security features include color-shifting ink in the number 20 in the lower right corner on the note's face. A new $50 note with similar security features was released Sept. 28, 2004, followed by a $10 note on Mar. 2, 2006, and a $5 note Mar. 13, 2008. The $100 bill was the last note to be redesigned. The new hundreds went into circulation Oct. 8, 2013. Their security and anti-counterfeiting features include a blue 3-D security ribbon and the image of a bell in an inkwell on the face. The bell changes color from copper to green when the note is tilted. All older notes remain legal tender, but will gradually be withdrawn from circulation. For more information, see www.newmoney.gov.

The Bureau of Engraving and Printing currently operates two facilities, one in Washington, DC, opened in 1914, and one in Fort Worth, TX, which began operations in 1991.

Denominations of U.S. Currency

Since 1969 the largest denomination of U.S. currency that has been issued is the $100 bill. As larger-denomination bills reach the Federal Reserve Bank, they are removed from circulation. Because some discontinued currency is expected to be in the hands of holders for many years, the description of the various denominations below is continued.

Note	Portrait	Embellishment on back	Note	Portrait	Embellishment on back
$1	George Washington	Great Seal of U.S.	$500	William McKinley	Ornate denominational marking
2	Thomas Jefferson	Signers of Declaration	1,000	Grover Cleveland	Ornate denominational marking
5	Abraham Lincoln	Lincoln Memorial	5,000	James Madison	Washington resigning as Army commander
10	Alexander Hamilton	U.S. Treasury			
20	Andrew Jackson	White House	10,000	Salmon Chase	Embarkation of the Pilgrims
50	Ulysses S. Grant	U.S. Capitol	100,000*	Woodrow Wilson	Ornate denominational marking
100	Benjamin Franklin	Independence Hall			

* = For use only in transactions between Federal Reserve System and Treasury Department.

The U.S. $1 Bill

Plate position: Shows where on the 32-note plate this bill was printed.

Serial number: Each bill has its own.

Federal Reserve District number: Shows which district issued the bill.

Federal Reserve District seal: The name of the Federal Reserve Bank that issued the bill is printed in the seal. The letter tells you where the bill is from. Here are the letter codes for the 12 Federal Reserve Districts:

A: Boston
B: New York
C: Philadelphia
D: Cleveland
E: Richmond
F: Atlanta
G: Chicago
H: St. Louis
I: Minneapolis
J: Kansas City
K: Dallas
L: San Francisco

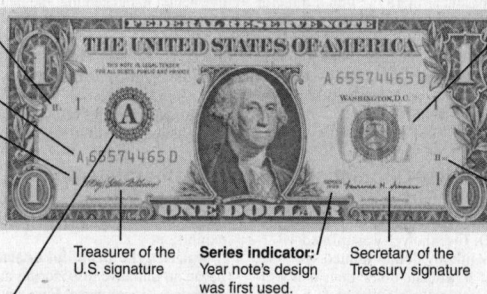

Treasury Department seal: The balancing scales represent justice. The pointed stripe across the middle has 13 stars for the original 13 colonies. The key represents authority.

Plate serial number: Shows which printing plate was used for the face of the bill.

Treasurer of the U.S. signature

Series indicator: Year note's design was first used.

Secretary of the Treasury signature

Plate serial number: Shows which plate was used for the back.

Front of the Great Seal of the United States: The bald eagle is the national bird. The shield has 13 stripes for the 13 original colonies. The eagle holds 13 arrows (symbol of war) and an olive branch (symbol of peace). Above the eagle is the motto "E Pluribus Unum," Latin for "out of many, one," and a constellation of 13 stars.

Reverse of the Great Seal of the United States: The pyramid symbolizes something that endures for ages. The eye, known as the Eye of Providence, probably comes from an ancient Egyptian symbol. The pyramid has 13 levels; at its base are the Roman numerals for 1776, the year of American independence. "Annuit Coeptis" is Latin for "God has favored our undertaking." "Novus Ordo Seclorum" is Latin for "a new order of the ages." Both phrases are from the works of the Roman poet Virgil.

U.S. Currency and Coin

Source: Bureau of the Fiscal Service, U.S. Dept. of the Treasury

Total Money in Circulation, 1955-2014

Date	Dollars (mil)	Per capita[1]	Date	Dollars (mil)	Per capita[1]	Date	Dollars (mil)	Per capita[1]
June 30, 1955.....	$30,229	$183	Sept. 30, 1985	$187,337	$782	June 30, 2009......	$909,697	$2,963
June 30, 1960.....	32,064	177	Sept. 30, 1990	278,903	1,105	June 30, 2010......	945,138	3,051
June 30, 1965.....	39,719	204	Sept. 30, 1995	409,272	1,553	June 30, 2011......	1,028,910	3,302
June 30, 1970.....	54,351	265	Sept. 30, 2000	568,614	2,061	June 30, 2012......	1,111,901	3,540
June 30, 1975.....	81,196	380	Sept. 30, 2005	766,487	2,578	June 30, 2013......	1,193,771	3,774
Sept. 30, 1980	129,916	581	June 30, 2008	826,314	2,676	June 30, 2014......	1,282,431	4,027

(1) Based on U.S. Census Bureau population estimates.

Currency in Circulation by Denomination, 2014

(in millions of dollars)

Denomination	$1	$2	$5	$10	$20	$50	$100	$500	$1,000	$5,000	$10,000	Total currency[2]
Total currency in circulation ...	$10,699	$2,102	$12,453	$17,980	$153,736	$73,739	$967,973	$142	$165	$2	$3	$1,238,995
Federal Reserve notes[1]........	10,557	1,970	12,320	17,960	153,716	73,728	967,951	142	165	2	3	1,238,514
U.S. notes.......	—	132	108	—	—	—	—	—	—	—	—	240
Currency no longer issued. ..	141	—	25	20	20	11	22	—	—	—	—	240

NA = Not applicable. — = Less than $1 million. (1) Issued on or after July 1, 1929. (2) Includes fractional notes and the value of partial denominations not presented for redemption.

Budget Receipts and Outlays, 1789-1940

Source: U.S. Dept. of the Treasury

(in thousands of dollars; annual statements for years ending June 30, unless otherwise noted)

Yearly average	Receipts	Outlays	Yearly average	Receipts	Outlays	Yearly average	Receipts	Outlays
1789-1800[1].....	$5,717	$5,776	1866-1870	$447,301	$377,642	1906-1910	$628,507	$639,178
1801-1810[2].....	13,056	9,086	1871-1875	336,830	287,460	1911-1915	710,227	720,252
1811-1820[2].....	21,032	23,943	1876-1880	288,124	255,598	1916-1920	3,483,652	8,065,333
1821-1830[2].....	21,928	16,162	1881-1885	366,961	257,691	1921-1925	4,306,673	3,578,989
1831-1840[2].....	30,461	24,495	1886-1890	375,448	279,134	1926-1930	4,069,138	3,182,807
1841-1850[2].....	28,545	34,097	1891-1895	352,891	363,599	1931-1935	2,770,973	5,214,874
1851-1860	60,237	60,163	1896-1900	434,877	457,451	1936-1940	4,960,614	10,192,367
1861-1865 160,907	160,907	683,785	1901-1905	559,481	535,559			

(1) Average for period Mar. 4, 1789, to Dec. 31, 1800. (2) Years 1801-42 end Dec. 31; average for 1841-50 is for the period Jan. 1, 1841, to June 30, 1850.

U.S. Budget Receipts and Outlays, Fiscal Years 2000-13

Source: Congressional Budget Office; *Budget of the U.S. Government*, Office of Mgmt. and Budget, Exec. Office of the President

A $236 bil surplus in 2000 turned into a $1.4 tril deficit by 2009; estimates for 2014 show the deficit reduced by half. Over the past decade, the total amount of money the government receives in taxes has varied little, while outlays have more than doubled for national defense, Medicare, and other health and income security programs.

(in millions of current dollars; numbers may not add up to totals because of independent rounding or omitted subcategories, including some subcategories with negative values)

Function and subfunction	2000	2005	2010	2011	2012	2013
NET RECEIPTS.............................	$2,025,191	$2,153,611	$2,162,706	$2,303,466	$2,450,164	$2,775,103
Individual income taxes.....................	1,004,462	927,222	898,549	1,091,473	1,132,206	1,316,405
Corporation income taxes...................	207,289	278,282	191,437	181,085	242,289	273,506
Social insurance and retirement receipts	652,852	794,125	864,814	818,792	845,314	947,820
Employment and general retirement	620,451	747,664	815,894	758,516	774,927	887,445
Old-age and survivors insurance (off-budget)	411,677	493,646	539,996	483,683	486,783	575,555
Disability insurance (off-budget)............	68,907	83,830	91,691	82,105	82,718	97,719
Hospital insurance	135,529	166,068	180,068	188,490	201,143	209,270
Railroad retirement/pension fund	2,688	2,284	2,285	2,415	2,519	2,791
Railroad social security equivalent account ...	1,650	1,836	1,854	1,823	1,764	2,110
Unemployment insurance	27,640	42,002	44,823	56,241	66,647	56,811
Other retirement	4,761	4,459	4,097	4,035	3,740	3,564
Excise taxes	68,865	73,094	66,909	72,381	79,061	84,007
Federal funds	22,692	22,547	18,256	18,904	20,359	28,330
Alcohol	8,140	8,111	9,229	9.294	9,765	9,253
Tobacco	7,221	7,920	17,160	16,685	16,351	15,083
Telephone..............................	5,670	6,047	993	930	757	733
Transportation fuels	819	−770	−11,030	−8,644	−5,751	−2,681
Trust funds	46,173	50,547	48,653	53,477	58,702	55,677
Transportation..........................	34,972	37,892	34,992	36,906	40,169	36,462
Airport and airway	9,739	10,314	10,612	11,532	12,532	12,854
Black lung disability	518	610	595	623	629	531
Inland waterway	101	91	74	84	90	75
Oil spill liability	182	—	476	501	497	410
Aquatic resources.......................	342	429	580	593	614	539
Leaking underground storage tank..........	184	189	169	152	170	162
Tobacco assessments	—	899	937	932	939	947
Vaccine injury compensation	133	123	218	278	254	204
Other receipts............................	91,723	80,888	140,997	139,735	151,294	153,365

Function and subfunction	2000	2005	2010	2011	2012	2013
OUTLAYS	$1,788,950	$2,471,957	$3,457,079	$3,603,059	$3,537,127	$3,454,605
National defense	294,363	495,294	693,485	705,554	677,852	633,385
Department of Defense—Military	281,029	474,071	666,703	678,064	650,851	607,795
Military personnel	75,950	127,463	155,690	161,608	152,266	150,825
Operation and maintenance	105,812	188,118	275,988	291,038	282,297	259,662
Procurement	51,696	82,294	133,603	128,003	124,712	114,912
Research, development, test, and evaluation	37,602	65,694	76,990	74,871	70,396	66,892
Military construction	5,109	5,331	21,169	19,917	14,553	12,318
Family housing	3,413	3,720	3,173	3,432	2,331	1,829
Atomic energy defense activities	12,138	18,031	19,308	20,410	19,246	17,573
Defense-related activities	1,196	3,192	7,474	7,080	7,755	8,017
International affairs	17,213	34,565	45,195	45,685	47,189	46,418
International development and humanitarian assistance	6,516	17,696	19,014	21,255	21,882	22,824
International security assistance	6,387	7,895	11,363	12,042	11,464	9,868
Conduct of foreign affairs	4,708	9,148	13,557	12,486	13,553	13,038
Foreign information and exchange activities	817	1,129	1,485	1,575	1,556	1,519
International financial programs	−1,215	−1,303	−224	−1,673	−1,266	−831
General science, space, and technology	18,594	23,597	30,100	29,466	29,060	28,908
General science and basic research	6,167	8,819	11,730	12,434	12,458	12,479
Space flight, research, and supporting activities	12,427	14,778	18,370	17,032	16,602	16,429
Energy	−761	440	11,618	12,174	14,858	11,042
Energy supply	−1,818	−929	5,801	8,084	9,017	9,038
Energy conservation	666	883	4,997	6,736	4,941	1,240
Emergency energy preparedness	162	162	199	−3,263	375	217
Energy information, policy, and regulation	229	324	621	617	525	547
Natural resources and environment	25,003	27,983	43,667	45,473	41,631	38,145
Water resources	5,078	5,724	11,662	11,621	9,178	7,675
Conservation and land management	6,762	6,226	10,783	11,955	11,101	10,723
Recreational resources	2,540	2,990	3,911	4,157	3,752	3,506
Pollution control and abatement	7,395	8,065	10,841	10,946	10,813	9,624
Agriculture	36,458	26,565	21,356	20,662	17,791	29,492
Farm income stabilization	33,446	22,048	16,604	16,017	13,173	25,049
Agricultural research and services	3,012	4,517	4,752	4,645	4,618	4,443
Commerce and housing credit	3,207	7,566	−82,316	−12,573	40,823	−83,199
Mortgage credit	−3,335	−862	35,804	14,158	−8,143	−87,854
Postal Service	2,129	−1,223	−682	909	2,744	−1,839
Deposit insurance	−3,053	−1,371	−32,033	−8,697	6,666	4,292
Transportation	46,853	67,894	91,972	92,966	93,019	91,673
Ground transportation	31,697	42,317	60,784	60,902	61,308	60,005
Air transportation	10,571	18,807	21,431	21,353	21,725	21,464
Water transportation	4,394	6,439	9,351	10,359	9,650	9,774
Community and regional development	10,623	26,262	23,894	23,883	25,132	32,336
Community development	5,480	5,861	9,901	9,605	8,769	7,814
Area and regional development	2,538	2,745	3,249	4,050	4,424	1,540
Disaster relief and insurance	2,605	17,656	10,744	10,228	11,939	22,982
Education, training, employment, and social services	53,764	97,555	128,598	101,233	90,823	72,808
Elementary, secondary, and vocational education	20,578	38,271	73,261	66,476	47,492	42,407
Higher education	10,115	31,442	20,908	1,108	12,113	−525
Research and general education aids	2,543	3,124	3,631	3,710	3,704	3,705
Training and employment	6,777	6,852	9,854	9,139	7,779	7,271
Social services	12,557	16,251	19,119	18,931	17,867	18,062
Health	154,504	250,548	369,068	372,504	346,742	358,315
Health care services	136,201	219,559	330,710	332,210	308,160	321,849
Health research and training	15,979	28,050	34,214	36,198	34,502	32,881
Consumer and occupational health and safety	2,324	2,939	4,144	4,096	4,080	3,585
Medicare	197,113	298,638	451,636	485,653	471,793	497,826
Income security	253,724	345,847	622,210	597,352	541,344	536,511
General retirement and disability insurance (excl. social security)	5,189	6,976	6,564	6,697	7,760	6,969
Federal employee retirement and disability	77,152	93,351	119,867	124,450	122,388	131,739
Unemployment compensation	23,012	35,435	160,145	120,556	93,771	70,729
Housing assistance	28,949	37,899	58,651	55,440	47,948	46,687
Food and nutrition assistance	32,483	50,833	95,110	103,199	106,871	109,706
Social security	409,423	523,305	706,737	730,811	773,290	813,551
Veterans benefits and services	46,989	70,120	108,384	127,189	124,595	138,938
Income security for veterans	24,907	35,767	49,163	58,747	55,899	65,890
Veterans education, training, and rehabilitation	1,285	2,790	8,089	10,683	10,402	12,893
Hospital and medical care for veterans	19,516	28,754	45,714	50,062	50,588	52,544
Veterans housing	364	860	540	1,262	1,413	1,328
Administration of justice	28,499	40,019	54,383	56,056	56,277	52,601
Federal law enforcement activities	12,121	19,912	28,713	29,802	28,977	27,295
Federal litigative and judicial activities	7,762	9,641	13,073	13,565	14,670	14,633
Federal correctional activities	3,707	5,862	7,748	8,057	8,294	6,892
Criminal justice assistance	4,909	4,604	4,849	4,632	4,336	3,781
General government	13,013	16,997	23,014	27,476	28,036	27,755
Legislative functions	2,227	3,460	4,100	3,974	3,908	3,747
Executive direction and management	456	569	528	446	628	478
Central fiscal operations	8,285	9,515	11,906	11,631	11,985	12,051
General property and records management	−32	472	1,194	2,304	2,247	−10
Central personnel management	184	101	338	124	67	372
General purpose fiscal assistance	2,084	3,333	5,082	7,475	7,787	7,852
Deductions for offsetting receipts	−2,383	−2,841	−1,721	−1,479	−2,011	−2,692
Net interest	222,949	183,986	196,194	229,962	220,408	220,885
Undistributed offsetting receipts	−42,581	−65,224	−82,116	−88,467	−103,536	−92,785
Employer share, employee retirement (on-budget)	−30,214	−47,977	−62,100	−64,581	−68,347	−65,155
TOTAL SURPLUS/DEFICIT	236,241	−318,346	−1,294,373	−1,299,593	−1,086,963	−679,502

Federal Receipts, Outlays, and Surpluses or Deficits, 1901-2014

Source: *Budget of the U.S. Government, Fiscal Year 2015*, Office of Management and Budget, Exec. Office of the President
(in millions of current dollars)

Fiscal year	Receipts	Outlays	Surplus or deficit (–)	Fiscal year	Receipts	Outlays	Surplus or deficit (–)	Fiscal year	Receipts	Outlays	Surplus or deficit (–)
1901	$588	$525	**$63**	1939	$6,295	$9,141	–$2,846	1977	$355,559	$409,218	–$53,659
1902	562	485	**77**	1940	6,548	9,468	–2,920	1978	399,561	458,746	–59,185
1903	562	517	**45**	1941	8,712	13,653	–4,941	1979	463,302	504,028	–40,726
1904	541	584	–43	1942	14,634	35,137	–20,503	1980	517,112	590,941	–73,830
1905	544	567	–23	1943	24,001	78,555	–54,554	1981	599,272	678,241	–78,968
1906	595	570	**25**	1944	43,747	91,304	–47,557	1982	617,766	745,743	–127,977
1907	666	579	**87**	1945	45,159	92,712	–47,553	1983	600,562	808,364	–207,802
1908	602	659	–57	1946	39,296	55,232	–15,936	1984	666,438	851,805	–185,367
1909	604	694	–89	1947	38,514	34,496	**4,018**	1985	734,037	946,344	–212,308
1910	676	694	–18	1948	41,560	29,764	**11,796**	1986	769,155	990,382	–221,227
1911	702	691	**11**	1949	39,415	38,835	**580**	1987	854,288	1,004,017	–149,730
1912	693	690	**3**	1950	39,443	42,562	–3,119	1988	909,238	1,064,416	–155,178
1913	714	715	—	1951	51,616	45,514	**6,102**	1989	991,105	1,143,744	–152,639
1914	725	726	—	1952	66,167	67,686	–1,519	1990	1,031,958	1,252,994	–221,036
1915	683	746	–63	1953	69,608	76,101	–6,493	1991	1,054,988	1,324,226	–269,238
1916	761	713	**48**	1954	69,701	70,855	–1,154	1992	1,091,208	1,381,529	–290,321
1917	1,101	1,954	–853	1955	65,451	68,444	–2,993	1993	1,154,335	1,409,386	–255,051
1918	3,645	12,677	–9,032	1956	74,587	70,640	**3,947**	1994	1,258,566	1,461,753	–203,186
1919	5,130	18,493	–13,363	1957	79,990	76,578	**3,412**	1995	1,351,790	1,515,742	–163,952
1920	6,649	6,358	**291**	1958	79,636	82,405	–2,769	1996	1,453,053	1,560,484	–107,431
1921	5,571	5,062	**509**	1959	79,249	92,098	–12,849	1997	1,579,232	1,601,116	–21,884
1922	4,026	3,289	**736**	1960	92,492	92,191	**301**	1998	1,721,728	1,652,458	**69,270**
1923	3,853	3,140	**713**	1961	94,388	97,723	–3,335	1999	1,827,452	1,701,842	**125,610**
1924	3,871	2,908	**963**	1962	99,676	106,821	–7,146	2000	2,025,191	1,788,950	**236,241**
1925	3,641	2,924	**717**	1963	106,560	111,316	–4,756	2001	1,991,082	1,862,846	**128,236**
1926	3,795	2,930	**865**	1964	112,613	118,528	–5,915	2002	1,853,136	2,010,894	–157,758
1927	4,013	2,857	**1,155**	1965	116,817	118,228	–1,411	2003	1,782,314	2,159,899	–377,585
1928	3,900	2,961	**939**	1966	130,835	134,532	–3,698	2004	1,880,114	2,292,841	–412,727
1929	3,862	3,127	**734**	1967	148,822	157,464	–8,643	2005	2,153,611	2,471,957	–318,346
1930	4,058	3,320	**738**	1968	152,973	178,134	–25,161	2006	2,406,869	2,655,050	–248,181
1931	3,116	3,577	–462	1969	186,882	183,640	**3,242**	2007	2,567,985	2,728,686	–160,701
1932	1,924	4,659	–2,735	1970	192,807	195,649	–2,842	2008	2,523,991	2,982,544	–458,553
1933	1,997	4,598	–2,602	1971	187,139	210,172	–23,033	2009	2,104,989	3,517,677	–1,412,688
1934	2,955	6,541	–3,586	1972	207,309	230,681	–23,373	2010	2,162,706	3,457,079	–1,294,373
1935	3,609	6,412	–2,803	1973	230,799	245,707	–14,908	2011	2,303,466	3,603,059	–1,299,593
1936	3,923	8,228	–4,304	1974	263,224	269,359	–6,135	2012	2,450,164	3,537,127	–1,086,963
1937	5,387	7,580	–2,193	1975	279,090	332,332	–53,242	2013	2,775,103	3,454,605	–679,502
1938	6,751	6,840	–89	1976	298,060	371,792	–73,732	2014[1]	3,001,721	3,650,526	–648,805

— = $500,000 or less. Figures in **bold** denote annual surplus. **Note:** Budget figures prior to 1933 are based on "Administrative Budget" concepts rather than "Unified Budget" concepts. Through 1976, fiscal year ends June 30; after 1976, fiscal year ends Sept. 30. Surplus or deficit column may not equal difference between figures because of rounding. (1) Estimate as of Feb. 1, 2014.

Budget Deficits as Percent of GDP in Selected Countries, 1995-2015

Source: *OECD Economic Outlook*, Organization for Economic Cooperation and Development (OECD)

Country/area	1995	2000	2005	2009	2010	2011	2012	2013	2014	2015
Australia	–3.9%	0.4%	1.2%	–4.7%	–5.1%	–3.6%	–2.9%	–1.4%	–2.5%	–1.4%
Austria	–5.9	–1.9	–1.8	–4.1	–4.5	–2.4	–2.6	–1.5	–2.8	–1.3
Canada	–5.3	2.9	1.5	–4.5	–4.9	–3.7	–3.4	–3.0	–2.1	–1.2
Czech Republic	–13.4	–3.7	–3.6	–5.8	–4.7	–3.2	–4.2	–1.5	–2.1	–2.6
Denmark	–2.9	2.2	5.0	–2.8	–2.7	–2.0	–3.9	–0.9	–1.5	–3.0
Estonia	1.1	–0.2	1.6	–2.0	0.2	1.1	–0.2	–0.2	–0.2	–0.1
Finland	–6.2	6.8	2.5	–2.7	–2.8	–1.0	–2.2	–2.5	–2.2	–0.9
France	–5.5	–1.5	–3.0	–7.5	–7.0	–5.2	–4.9	–4.3	–3.8	–3.1
Germany	–9.7	1.3	–3.3	–3.1	–4.2	–0.8	0.1	0.0	–0.2	0.2
Greece	–9.1	–3.7	–5.3	–15.6	–11.0	–9.6	–8.9	–12.7	–2.5	–1.4
Hungary	–8.7	–3.0	–7.9	–4.5	–4.4	4.2	–2.2	–2.3	–2.9	–2.9
Iceland	–3.0	1.7	4.9	–9.9	–10.1	–5.6	–3.8	–2.1	–2.0	–2.1
Ireland	–2.1	4.8	1.6	–13.7	–30.6	–13.0	–8.1	–7.0	–4.7	–3.1
Israel	NA	–4.0	–4.9	–3.9	–4.6	–3.9	–5.1	–4.3	–3.9	–3.6
Italy	–7.4	–0.9	–4.4	–5.4	–4.4	–3.6	–2.9	–2.8	–2.7	–2.1
Japan	–4.7	–7.6	–6.7	–8.8	–8.3	–8.8	–8.7	–9.3	–8.4	–6.7
Korea, South	3.5	5.4	3.4	–1.0	1.0	1.0	1.0	–0.4	0.1	0.5
Luxembourg	2.4	6.0	0.0	–0.7	–0.8	0.2	0.0	0.1	0.3	–0.9
Netherlands	–9.2	2.0	–0.3	–5.6	–5.0	–4.3	–4.0	–2.4	–2.7	–2.0
New Zealand	2.5	1.8	4.7	–2.7	–7.4	–4.4	–2.1	–0.3	0.1	0.7
Norway	3.2	15.4	15.1	10.5	11.1	13.6	13.9	11.1	10.7	10.2
Poland	–4.4	–3.0	–4.1	–7.5	–7.8	–5.1	–3.9	–4.3	5.6	–2.9
Portugal	–5.0	–2.9	–5.9	–10.2	–9.9	–4.3	–6.5	–5.0	–4.0	–2.4
Slovakia	–3.4	–12.3	–2.8	–8.0	–7.5	–4.8	–4.5	–2.8	–2.7	–2.6
Slovenia	–8.4	–3.7	–1.5	–6.3	–5.9	–6.4	–4.0	–14.7	–4.1	–2.6
Spain	–6.5	–1.0	1.0	–11.1	–9.6	–9.6	–10.6	–7.1	–5.5	–4.5
Sweden	–7.3	3.6	1.9	–1.0	0.0	0.0	–0.7	–1.3	–1.5	–0.8
Switzerland	–2.0	0.1	–0.7	0.8	0.3	0.7	–0.2	0.1	0.3	0.3
United Kingdom	–5.8	3.7	–3.3	–11.2	–10.0	–7.9	–6.3	–5.9	–5.3	–4.1
United States	–3.3	1.5	–3.3	–12.8	–12.2	–10.7	–9.3	–6.4	–5.8	–4.6
Total OECD	–4.8	0.1	–2.8	–8.4	–8.0	–6.5	–5.9	–4.6	–3.9	–3.2
Brazil	NA	NA	NA	–3.3	–2.5	–2.6	–2.5	–3.3	–3.4	–3.1
China	NA	NA	NA	–1.1	–0.7	0.1	–0.3	–0.7	–1.2	–1.2
India	NA	NA	NA	–9.6	–7.4	–7.4	–7.5	–7.1	–6.5	–5.9
Indonesia	NA	NA	NA	–1.6	–0.7	–1.1	–1.9	–2.2	–2.2	–2.0
Russia	NA	NA	NA	–4.0	–1.2	4.2	0.5	–0.5	0.0	0.2
South Africa	NA	NA	NA	–5.2	–6.0	–5.6	6.2	–6.1	–5.8	–5.5

NA = Not available.

Public Debt of the U.S., 1946-2018

Source: *Budget of the U.S. Government,* Office of Management and Budget, Exec. Office of the President

Year	Debt held by public Current dollars (bil)	Debt held by public FY2013 dollars (bil)	Debt held by public As % of GDP	Interest on public debt as % of— Total federal outlays	Interest on public debt as % of— GDP	Year	Debt held by public Current dollars (bil)	Debt held by public FY2013 dollars (bil)	Debt held by public As % of GDP	Interest on public debt as % of— Total federal outlays	Interest on public debt as % of— GDP
1946	$241.9	$2,342.9	106.1%	7.4%	1.8%	2006	$4,829.0	$5,440.0	35.3%	8.9%	1.7%
1950	219.0	1,716.3	78.5	11.4	1.7	2007	5,035.1	5,522.6	35.1	9.2	1.8
1955	226.6	1,560.7	55.7	7.6	1.3	2008	5,803.1	6,236.3	39.3	8.7	1.8
1960	236.8	1,445.1	44.3	8.5	1.5	2009	7,544.7	8,013.8	52.3	5.7	1.4
1965	260.8	1,490.4	36.7	8.1	1.3	2010	9,018.9	9,497.1	61.0	6.6	1.5
1970	283.2	1,348.6	27.0	7.9	1.5	2011	10,128.2	10,460.6	65.8	7.4	1.7
1975	394.7	1,385.0	24.5	7.5	1.6	2012	11,281.1	11,450.9	70.1	6.6	1.4
1980	711.9	1,738.5	25.5	10.6	2.2	2013	11,982.6	11,982.6	72.1	7.5	1.6
1985	1,507.3	2,809.4	35.3	16.2	3.6	2014[1]	12,902.7	12,712.4	74.4	7.4	1.6
1990	2,411.6	3,864.7	40.8	16.2	3.4	2015[1]	13,591.8	13,164.6	74.6	7.7	1.7
1995	3,604.4	5,097.4	47.5	15.8	3.2	2016[1]	14,256.6	13,557.4	74.3	8.8	1.9
2000	3,409.8	4,445.6	33.6	13.0	2.3	2017[1]	14,843.5	13,840.9	73.5	10.3	2.2
2005	4,592.2	5,341.4	35.6	7.7	1.5	2018[1]	15,370.5	14,051.0	72.4	11.9	2.5

Note: As of end of fiscal year. Through 1976, the fiscal year ended June 30. For 1977 on, the fiscal year ended Sept. 30. (1) Estimate.

State Finances: Revenues, Taxes, Expenditures, and Debt, 2012

Source: U.S. Census Bureau, U.S. Dept. of Commerce

(in thousands of dollars)

State	Revenues Total revenue	Revenues General revenues	Revenues Intergovt. revenue	Taxes	Total expenditures	Debt at end of fiscal year
Alabama	$28,970,138	$22,226,197	$8,227,630	$9,049,294	$27,730,899	$8,719,430
Alaska	15,050,413	14,324,470	2,866,427	7,049,398	11,729,460	5,909,456
Arizona	30,947,615	27,324,259	10,752,958	12,973,265	31,232,561	14,182,905
Arkansas	18,439,297	17,121,229	5,909,693	8,284,500	19,618,284	3,568,702
California	250,882,537	199,269,940	57,426,009	115,089,654	267,017,700	152,821,830
Colorado	25,675,544	21,871,252	6,396,060	10,250,628	28,238,168	16,329,530
Connecticut	27,307,921	24,488,058	5,798,580	15,401,018	28,370,101	31,965,511
Delaware	8,015,377	7,417,356	1,881,424	3,346,952	8,315,681	5,796,853
Florida	82,823,985	71,230,368	23,256,254	32,997,012	79,482,176	38,171,049
Georgia	40,505,805	36,240,927	14,082,843	16,576,903	44,751,105	13,400,514
Hawaii	10,600,634	9,988,555	2,357,724	5,516,146	11,565,554	8,398,012
Idaho	8,308,086	7,104,084	2,497,542	3,374,304	8,301,262	3,945,615
Illinois	68,901,523	60,986,400	15,999,360	36,257,762	72,622,240	64,301,765
Indiana	35,284,647	31,675,739	10,515,088	15,704,507	35,832,998	22,511,518
Iowa	20,979,691	18,257,359	6,362,157	7,832,388	20,407,524	6,166,080
Kansas	16,144,318	15,068,811	4,099,551	7,418,341	16,747,356	6,860,094
Kentucky	25,683,865	22,574,396	8,088,953	10,505,794	29,349,094	15,103,515
Louisiana	26,942,887	25,336,717	11,213,427	8,994,053	31,685,604	15,415,488
Maine	8,342,043	7,899,821	2,893,782	3,777,130	9,047,755	5,605,606
Maryland	36,004,081	33,161,450	10,375,250	17,038,494	41,030,733	25,741,733
Massachusetts	48,981,548	44,842,219	13,254,940	22,805,644	56,487,432	79,800,278
Michigan	64,021,268	52,910,694	18,054,809	23,919,741	61,726,982	30,823,672
Minnesota	38,553,800	34,160,246	9,725,219	20,560,540	38,612,582	13,230,223
Mississippi	18,765,201	17,034,874	7,809,467	6,953,362	20,051,298	7,194,251
Missouri	31,065,599	26,487,433	10,814,599	10,802,052	31,360,850	20,385,537
Montana	7,727,604	5,725,954	2,206,636	2,459,324	7,062,896	3,995,366
Nebraska	9,781,249	9,147,193	3,194,260	4,332,757	9,525,518	2,073,385
Nevada	14,317,867	10,982,789	3,018,419	6,775,112	13,477,122	3,896,718
New Hampshire	7,153,139	5,838,148	1,871,733	2,208,201	7,423,747	8,029,849
New Jersey	57,582,037	51,103,196	14,069,932	27,456,175	68,121,744	64,851,557
New Mexico	15,195,673	14,124,922	5,353,495	5,093,142	17,018,829	7,550,084
New York	179,604,728	148,573,219	56,075,971	71,545,745	181,226,180	135,884,070
North Carolina	56,470,410	45,700,056	15,498,419	22,713,357	53,624,402	18,291,688
North Dakota	9,246,488	8,541,288	1,797,141	5,620,036	6,315,436	2,083,611
Ohio	72,465,759	59,312,201	21,275,467	25,924,024	76,524,453	36,521,981
Oklahoma	23,263,487	20,715,240	7,500,174	8,839,299	22,598,865	9,979,234
Oregon	25,059,234	21,699,120	7,846,393	8,699,626	26,862,451	13,782,071
Pennsylvania	78,539,490	66,864,534	20,668,328	32,949,917	87,346,336	46,205,176
Rhode Island	7,946,561	6,803,391	2,345,553	2,827,503	8,325,783	9,211,790
South Carolina	26,106,015	21,243,078	7,327,090	8,036,482	27,791,485	14,854,263
South Dakota	4,351,161	3,991,132	1,657,561	1,521,477	4,424,154	3,607,615
Tennessee	30,803,108	27,302,757	11,268,836	11,982,345	31,497,959	6,167,659
Texas	137,723,090	108,125,353	37,985,130	48,596,548	125,532,786	45,626,393
Utah	15,600,624	14,176,003	4,487,061	5,809,953	17,109,026	7,067,149
Vermont	6,348,888	5,474,067	1,908,390	2,757,370	5,959,250	3,390,961
Virginia	43,130,206	39,431,718	9,784,138	18,137,586	46,761,727	27,799,760
Washington	40,665,155	34,073,722	10,010,901	17,624,715	45,501,471	29,090,132
West Virginia	13,247,295	12,294,552	4,359,169	5,285,773	13,222,912	7,306,756
Wisconsin	35,880,592	31,410,686	9,087,593	15,995,335	36,446,089	22,995,708
Wyoming	8,645,489	6,147,228	2,442,146	2,550,991	5,773,573	1,321,804
United States	**1,912,253,172**	**1,627,804,381**	**533,699,688**	**798,221,675**	**1,976,789,593**	**1,147,933,947**

Note: Figures may not add up to totals because of rounding.

State and Local Government Receipts and Current Expenditures, 1960-2013

Source: Bureau of Economic Analysis, U.S. Dept. of Commerce

(in billions of current dollars; as of July 2014)

	1960	1970	1980	1990	2000	2010	2011	2012	2013
Receipts	**$44.2**	**$118.9**	**$335.3**	**$729.6**	**$1,303.1**	**$1,998.5**	**$2,030.5**	**$2,061.2**	**$2,125.6**
Current tax receipts	37.0	91.3	230.0	519.1	893.2	1,305.6	1,368.3	1,424.8	1,471.8
Personal current taxes	4.2	14.2	48.9	122.6	236.7	297.6	324.1	354.7	375.0
Income taxes	2.5	10.9	42.6	109.6	217.4	267.1	292.9	322.7	342.7
Other.......................	1.7	3.3	6.3	13.0	19.4	30.5	31.2	31.9	32.3
Taxes on production and imports	31.5	73.3	166.7	374.1	621.3	960.4	994.0	1,017.0	1,041.6
Sales taxes...................	12.2	31.6	82.9	184.3	316.8	446.0	466.7	482.0	501.1
Property taxes.................	16.2	36.7	68.8	161.5	254.7	435.0	439.2	443.7	446.4
Other........................	3.1	5.0	15.0	28.3	49.8	79.4	88.1	91.2	94.1
Taxes on corporate income	1.2	3.7	14.5	22.5	35.2	47.7	50.2	53.2	55.3
Contributions for government social insurance	0.5	1.1	3.6	10.0	10.8	18.1	18.2	17.7	17.7
Income receipts on assets	1.3	5.2	26.3	68.5	93.9	82.6	79.2	78.6	79.7
Interest receipts	1.0	4.3	23.1	64.1	86.3	69.1	64.8	63.0	63.2
Dividends	—	—	0.1	0.2	1.4	2.3	2.6	3.4	3.7
Rents and royalties................	0.3	0.8	3.1	4.2	6.3	11.2	11.7	12.3	12.7
Current transfer receipts..............	4.3	20.1	76.9	126.4	299.7	612.0	582.1	556.2	570.8
Federal grants-in-aid.............	3.8	18.3	69.7	104.4	233.1	505.3	472.5	444.4	450.0
From business (net)	0.2	0.6	2.5	7.1	28.6	43.4	44.2	43.2	49.9
From persons	0.3	1.2	4.7	14.9	38.0	63.2	65.4	68.6	70.9
Current surplus of government enterprises	1.2	1.3	−1.4	5.6	5.4	−19.8	−17.4	−16.2	−14.3
Expenditures....................	**41.6**	**115.9**	**329.9**	**736.0**	**1,293.2**	**2,235.8**	**2,246.4**	**2,293.8**	**2,350.8**
Consumption expenditures	34.1	92.1	252.8	546.2	969.1	1,518.3	1,524.8	1,546.1	1,584.5
Government social benefit payments to persons	4.6	16.1	51.2	127.7	271.4	523.8	530.4	540.6	565.4
Interest payments..................	3.0	7.7	25.6	61.8	52.1	192.1	190.7	206.6	200.3
Subsidies	0.0	0.0	0.4	0.4	0.5	1.6	0.5	0.5	0.5
Net state and local government saving	**2.6**	**3.0**	**5.4**	**−6.5**	**9.9**	**−237.3**	**−215.9**	**−232.6**	**−225.1**
Social insurance funds	0.0	0.2	1.3	2.0	2.0	3.2	4.4	4.5	4.3
Other...........................	2.5	2.8	4.1	−8.4	7.9	−240.5	−220.4	−237.0	−229.5
Addenda:									
Total receipts.....................	**47.2**	**125.1**	**353.9**	**754.6**	**1,347.3**	**2,075.2**	**2,104.3**	**2,135.5**	**2,197.2**
Current receipts	44.2	118.9	335.3	729.6	1,303.1	1,998.5	2030.5	2,061.2	2,125.6
Capital transfer receipts	3.0	6.2	18.6	25.0	44.2	76.7	73.8	74.2	71.6
Total expenditures	**52.0**	**135.4**	**364.7**	**807.2**	**1,418.5**	**2,385.5**	**2,374.0**	**2,402.3**	**2,449.2**
Current expenditures	41.6	115.9	329.9	736	1,293.2	2,235.8	2,246.4	2,293.8	2,350.8
Gross government investment	14.1	29.3	65.7	132.2	232.9	351.9	340.5	331.6	327.8
Capital transfer payments...........	—	—	—	0.0	0.0	0.0	0.0	0.0	0.0
Net purchases of nonproduced assets	0.9	1.1	2.2	5.7	8.6	10.6	9.2	8.7	9.0
Less: Consumption of fixed capital....	4.5	10.9	33.1	66.7	116.2	212.7	222.2	231.8	238.4
Net lending or net borrowing (−)......	**−4.8**	**−10.3**	**−10.8**	**−52.7**	**−71.2**	**−310.3**	**−269.6**	**−266.9**	**−252.0**

Federal Deposit Insurance Corporation (FDIC)

The Federal Deposit Insurance Corporation (FDIC) was created by Congress during the height of the Depression to maintain stability and public confidence in the nation's banking system. It covered depositors for up to $2,500 in case of bank failure in 1934; the limit today is 100 times that much, or $250,000. In its unique role as deposit insurer of banks and savings associations, and in cooperation with other federal and state bank regulatory agencies, the FDIC seeks to promote the safety and soundness of insured depository institutions in the U.S. financial system.

The quarterly premiums on deposit insurance are paid by the banks rather than by consumers. The amount of the premium is based on the institution's balance of insured deposits for the preceding quarter and the institution's risk to the insurance fund. In 2009, Congress permanently increased the limit that the FDIC may borrow from the U.S. Treasury from $30 bil to $100 bil.

U.S. Banks, 1935-2014

Source: *Summary of Deposits*, Federal Deposit Insurance Corp.

Comprises all FDIC-insured commercial and savings banks, including savings and loan institutions (S&Ls).

	Number of banks					Deposits (in mil dollars)				
		Commercial banks[1]			Savings		Commercial banks[1]			Savings
Year	All banks[2]	National charter	State charter	Non-members	banks, total	All deposits[2]	National charter	State charter	Non-members	banks, total
1935[3]	15,295	5,386	1,001	7,735	1,173	$45,102	$24,802	$13,653	$5,669	$978
1940	15,772	5,144	1,342	6,956	2,330	67,494	35,787	20,642	7,040	4,025
1950	16,500	4,958	1,912	6,576	3,054	171,963	84,941	41,602	19,726	25,694
1960	17,549	4,530	1,641	6,955	4,423	310,262	120,242	65,487	34,369	90,164
1970	18,205	4,621	1,147	7,743	4,694	686,901	285,436	101,512	95,566	204,367
1980	18,763	4,425	997	9,013	4,328	1,832,716	656,752	191,183	344,311	640,470
1990	15,158	3,979	1,009	7,355	2,815	3,637,292	1,558,915	397,797	693,438	987,142
1995	12,289	2,941	995	6,230	2,082	3,214,678	1,337,105	439,430	696,108	735,856
2000	10,119	2,302	996	5,180	1,622	4,003,744	1,792,773	707,562	793,275	706,461
2005	8,855	1,864	906	4,779	1,293	5,933,742	2,946,589	765,673	1,191,977	1,023,620
2007	8,605	1,676	888	4,786	1,244	6,702,053	3,273,531	831,116	1,425,412	1,165,119
2008	8,441	1,585	874	4,744	1,227	7,025,791	3,596,712	857,003	1,432,614	1,132,356
2009	8,185	1,505	858	4,632	1,180	7,559,590	4,141,792	962,232	1,512,677	936,101
2010	7,821	1,427	836	4,413	1,135	7,676,878	4,305,697	1,002,425	1,464,022	891,159
2011	7,523	1,349	824	4,240	1,100	8,249,233	4,708,210	1,120,747	1,491,112	909,912
2012	7,255	1,285	836	4,101	1,023	8,947,239	5,250,842	1,220,930	1,576,616	874,850
2013	6,950	1,194	849	3,937	960	9,433,525	5,667,790	1,281,662	1,648,350	806,933
2014	6,669	1,110	860	3,789	900	10,112,716	6,089,894	1,445,246	1,729,789	807,157

Note: Figures are for the end of the year shown through 1990 and for June 30 thereafter. (1) Nonmembers are banks that are not members of the Federal Reserve System; national charter and state charter institutions are Federal Reserve members. (2) Includes U.S. branches of foreign banks not listed separately. (3) Figures for 1935 do not include S&Ls, the data for which are not available.

U.S. Bank Failures, 1934-2014
Source: Federal Deposit Insurance Corp.

Covers all FDIC-insured commercial and savings banks, including savings and loan institutions (S&Ls) 1980 and after. As of Aug. 14, 2014.

Year	Closed or assisted	Year	Closed or assisted	Year	Closed or assisted	Year	Closed or assisted	Year	Closed or assisted
1934.....	9	1960-69 ..	44	1988.....	470	1998	3	2008	30
1935.....	25	1970-79 ..	79	1989.....	534	1999	8	2009	148
1936.....	69	1980.....	22	1990.....	382	2000	7	2010	157
1937.....	75	1981.....	40	1991.....	271	2001	4	2011	92
1938.....	74	1982.....	119	1992.....	181	2002	11	2012	51
1939.....	60	1983.....	99	1993.....	50	2003	3	2013	24
1940.....	43	1984.....	106	1994.....	15	2004	4	2014	14
1941.....	15	1985.....	180	1995.....	8	2005	0	**Total,**	
1942.....	20	1986.....	204	1996.....	6	2006	0	**1934-2014**	**4,071**
1950-59 ..	28	1987.....	262	1997.....	1	2007	3		

Largest U.S. Bank Holding Companies, 2014
Source: National Information Center, Federal Financial Institutions Examination Council
(ranked by total assets, in billions of dollars; as of June 30, 2014)

Rank	Institution name, location	Assets	Rank	Institution name, location	Assets
1.	JPMorgan Chase & Co., New York, NY	$2,520.3	20.	Charles Schwab Corp., San Francisco, CA ..	$143.4
2.	Bank of America Corp., Charlotte, NC	2,172.0	21.	State Farm Mutual Automobile Insurance Co.,	
3.	Citigroup Inc., New York, NY	1,909.7		Bloomington, IL........................	135.5
4.	Wells Fargo & Co., San Francisco, CA	1,598.9	22.	Fifth Third Bancorp, Cincinnati, OH	132.6
5.	Goldman Sachs Group, Inc., New York, NY....	860.0	23.	Citizens Financial Group, Inc., Providence, RI ...	130.6
6.	Morgan Stanley, New York, NY..............	826.6	24.	United Services Auto Assn., San Antonio, TX....	129.1
7.	General Electric Capital Corp., Norwalk, CT	516.3	25.	Regions Financial Corp., Birmingham, AL	119.0
8.	Bank of New York Mellon Corp.,		26.	BMO Financial Corp., Wilmington, DE	116.2
	New York, NY	400.7	27.	Santander Holdings USA, Inc., Boston, MA....	112.5
9.	U.S. Bancorp, Minneapolis, MN	389.1	28.	Unionbancal Corp., San Francisco, CA	108.8
10.	PNC Financial Services Group, Inc.,		29.	Northern Trust Corp., Chicago, IL............	105.8
	Pittsburgh, PA	327.3	30.	Keycorp, Cleveland, OH	91.9
11.	Capital One Financial Corp., McLean, VA......	298.7	31.	M&T Bank Corp., Buffalo, NY	90.8
12.	HSBC North America Holdings Inc.,		32.	Bancwest Corp., Honolulu, HI	86.6
	New York, NY	289.6	33.	Discover Financial Services, Riverwoods, IL	78.9
13.	State Street Corp., Boston, MA	282.3	34.	BBVA Compass Bancshares, Inc., Houston, TX	75.7
14.	Teachers Insurance & Annuity Assn. of		35.	Deutsche Bank Trust Corp., New York, NY.....	69.4
	America, New York, NY...................	256.9	36.	Comerica Incorporated, Dallas, TX...........	65.4
15.	TD Bank US Holding Co., Cherry Hill, NJ......	236.0	37.	Huntington Bancshares Inc., Columbus, OH ...	63.8
16.	BB&T Corp., Winston Salem, NC	188.0	38.	Zions BanCorp., Salt Lake City, UT	55.1
17.	Suntrust Banks, Inc., Atlanta, GA	182.6	39.	New York Community Bancorp, Inc., Westbury, NY	48.6
18.	American Express Co., New York, NY	152.4	40.	E*Trade Financial Corp., New York, NY	45.7
19.	Ally Financial Inc., Detroit, MI	149.9			

Note: Includes foreign-owned banks with a strong presence in the U.S.

Status of Top Recipients of Treasury Department "Bailout" Funds, 2014
Source: ProPublica

Since Oct. 2008, the federal government has spent more than $600 bil to bail out more than 900 institutions severely affected by the financial crisis. As of Aug. 12, 2014, the government had recouped $388 bil in loans and $265 bil in dividends, interest, and other returns, leading to an overall profit of more than $41 bil. Companies that have failed to repay the government, resulting in a loss to the taxpayers, are listed in bold italics.
(in billions of dollars, ranked by amount disbursed; as of Aug. 12, 2014)

Recipient	Disbursed	Repaid[1]	Net profit or amount outstanding[2]	Recipient	Disbursed	Repaid[1]	Net profit or amount outstanding[2]
Fannie Mae............	$116.1	$126.7	$10.6	BB&T	$3.1	$3.3	$0.2
Freddie Mac	71.3	86.3	14.9	Bank of New York Mellon ..	3.0	3.2	0.2
AIG Insurance	67.8	72.9	5.0	KeyCorp	2.5	2.9	0.4
General Motors	*50.7*	*39.3*	*–11.4*	*CIT Group*	*2.3*	*0.04*	*–2.3*
Bank of America	45.0	49.6	4.6	Comerica Incorporated....	2.3	2.6	0.3
Citigroup..............	45.0	58.4	13.4	State Street............	2.0	2.1	0.1
JPMorgan Chase	25.0	26.7	1.7	RLJ Western Asset Public/			
Wells Fargo............	25.0	27.3	2.3	Private Master Fund, L.P.	1.9	2.3	0.5
GMAC (now Ally Financial) .	16.3	17.9	1.6	Invesco Legacy Securities			
Chrysler	*10.7*	*9.4*	*–1.3*	Master Fund, L.P.	1.7	2.3	0.6
Goldman Sachs	10.0	11.4	1.4	Marshall & Ilsley	1.7	1.9	0.2
Morgan Stanley.........	10.0	11.3	1.3	Oaktree PPIP Fund, L.P. ..	1.7	2.0	0.3
PNC Financial Services ...	7.6	8.3	0.7	*JPMorgan Chase*			
U.S. Bancorp	6.6	6.9	0.3	*subsidiaries*	*1.6*	*0.0*	*–1.6*
SunTrust..............	4.9	5.4	0.5	Blackrock PPIF, L.P.	1.6	2.0	0.4
Capital One Financial Corp.	3.6	3.8	0.3	Northern Trust..........	1.6	1.7	0.1
Regions Financial Corp. ...	3.5	4.1	0.6	Chrysler Financial Services	1.5	1.5	—
Wellington Management				Marathon Legacy Securities			
Legacy Securities PPIF				Public-Private Investment			
Master Fund, L.P	3.4	4.2	0.7	Partnership, L.P.	1.4	1.8	0.4
Fifth Third Bancorp	3.4	4.0	0.6	*Bank of America subsids.*			
Hartford Financial Services				*(incl. Countrywide)*	*1.4*	*0.0*	*–1.4*
Insurance	3.4	4.2	0.8	Zions Bancorp	1.4	1.7	0.3
American Express Financial				Huntington Bancshares ...	1.4	1.6	0.2
Services	3.4	3.8	0.4	Wells Fargo Bank, NA	1.3	0.0	–1.3
AG GECC PPIF Master				Discover Financial Services	1.2	1.5	0.2
Fund, L.P.	3.4	4.3	0.9	*Ocwen Financial Corp.,*			
AllianceBernstein Legacy				*Inc.*	*1.1*	*0.0*	*–1.1*
Securities Master Fund, L.P.	3.2	3.8	0.6	Total.................	611.8	653.2	41.3

— = less than $0.1 bil. **Note:** Total includes other disbursements not shown. Figures may not add up to totals due to rounding. (1) Amounts repaid include principal, dividends, interest, warrants, and other proceeds. (2) Negative number represents outstanding debt.

Federal Reserve System

The Federal Reserve System is the central bank for the U.S. The system was established on Dec. 23, 1913, originally to give the country an elastic currency, provide facilities for discounting commercial paper, and improve the supervision of banking. Since then, the system's responsibilities have been broadened. Over the years, stability and growth of the economy, a high level of employment, stability in the purchasing power of the dollar, and reasonable balance in transactions with other countries have come to be recognized as primary objectives of governmental economic policy.

The Federal Reserve System consists of the Board of Governors, the 12 District Reserve Banks and their branch offices, and the Federal Open Market Committee. Several advisory councils help the board meet its varied responsibilities.

The hub of the system is the 7-member Board of Governors in Washington, DC. The members of the board are appointed by the president and confirmed by the Senate to 14-year terms. The president also appoints the chairman and vice chairman of the board from among the board members for 4-year terms. As of Aug. 2014, the board members were: Janet L. Yellen, chair; Stanley Fischer, vice-chair; Daniel K. Tarullo; Jerome H. Powell; and Lael Brainard. There were two vacancies.

The 12 **District Reserve Banks** and their branch offices serve as the decentralized portion of the system, carrying out day-to-day operations such as circulating currency and coin and providing fiscal agency functions and payments mechanism services. The 12 are in Boston, New York, Philadelphia, Cleveland, Richmond, Atlanta, Chicago, St. Louis, Minneapolis, Kansas City, Dallas, and San Francisco.

The system's principal function is monetary policy, which it controls using three tools: reserve requirements, the discount rate, and open market operations.

Uniform **reserve requirements**, set by the board, are applied to the transaction accounts and nonpersonal time deposits of all depository institutions. Responsibility for setting the **discount rate** (the interest rate at which depository institutions can borrow money from the Reserve Banks) is shared by the Board of Governors and the Reserve Banks. Changes in the discount rate are recommended by the individual boards of directors of the Reserve Banks and are subject to approval by the Board of Governors.

The most important tool of monetary policy is **open market operations**, or the purchase and sale of government securities. Responsibility for influencing the cost and availability of money and credit through the purchase and sale of government securities lies with the **Federal Open Market Committee** (FOMC), which is composed of the seven members of the Board of Governors, the president of the Federal Reserve Bank of New York, and four other Federal Reserve Bank presidents, who each serve one-year terms on a rotating basis. The committee bases its decisions on economic and financial developments and outlook, setting yearly growth objectives for key measures of money supply and credit. The decisions of the committee are carried out by the domestic trading desk of the Federal Reserve Bank of New York.

A Federal Advisory Council meets with the Federal Reserve Board four times a year to discuss business and financial conditions, as well as to make recommendations.

Website: www.federalreserve.gov

Federal Reserve Board Discount Rates, 1955-2014

The interest rate that the Federal Reserve charges its member banks to borrow money overnight is often referred to as the discount rate. On Jan. 9, 2003, the Fed divided the discount window into two categories: primary credit, for banks in sound financial condition, and secondary credit, for banks that do not qualify for primary credit. The secondary credit rate is ½ a percentage point higher than the primary credit rate. Banks typically raise or lower the rates they extend to their customers to track changes in the discount rate.

Effective date	Rate	Effective date	Rate	Effective date	Rate	Effective date	Rate	Effective date	Rate
1955:		**1970:**		**1979:**		**1990:**		**2003:**	
Jan. 3	1½	Nov. 13	5¾	July 20	10	Dec. 18	6½	Jan. 9	2¼[1]
Apr. 15	1¾	Dec. 4	5½	Aug. 17	10½	**1991:**		June 25	2
Aug. 5	2	**1971:**		Sept. 19	11	Apr. 30	5½	**2004:**	
Sept. 9	2¼	Jan. 8	5¼	Oct. 8	12	Sept. 13	5	June 30	2¼
Nov. 18	2½	Jan. 22	5	**1980:**		Nov. 6	4½	Aug. 10	2½
1956:		Feb. 19	4¾	Feb. 15	13	Dec. 20	3½	Sept. 21	2¾
Apr. 13	2¾	July 16	5	May 30	12	**1992:**		Nov. 10	3
Aug. 24	3	Nov. 19	4¾	June 13	11	July 2	3	Dec. 14	3¼
1957:		Dec. 17	4½	July 28	10	**1994:**		**2005:**	
Aug. 23	3½	**1973:**		Sept. 26	11	May 17	3½	Feb. 2	3½
Nov. 15	3	Jan. 15	5	Nov. 17	12	Aug. 16	4	Mar. 22	3¾
1958:		Feb. 26	5½	Dec. 5	13	Nov. 15	4¾	May 3	4
Jan. 24	2¾	May 4	5¾	**1981:**		**1995:**		June 30	4¼
Mar. 7	2¼	May 11	6	May 5	14	Feb. 1	5	Aug. 9	4½
Apr. 18	1¾	June 11	6½	Nov. 2	13	**1996:**		Sept. 20	4¾
Sept. 12	2	July 2	7	Dec. 4	12	Jan. 31	5	Nov. 1	5
Nov. 7	2½	Aug. 14	7½	**1982:**		**1998:**		Dec. 13	5¼
1959:		**1974:**		July 20	11½	Oct. 15	4¾	**2006:**	
Mar. 6	3	Apr. 25	8	Aug. 2	11	Nov. 17	4½	Jan. 31	5½
May 29	3½	Dec. 9	7¾	Aug. 16	10	**1999:**		Mar. 28	5¾
Sept. 11	4	**1975:**		Aug. 27	10	Aug. 24	4¾	May 10	6
1960:		Jan. 10	7¼	Oct. 12	9½	Nov. 16	5	June 29	6¼
June 10	3½	Feb. 5	6¾	Dec. 15	8½	**2000:**		**2007:**	
Aug. 12	3	Mar. 19	6¼	**1984:**		Feb. 2	5¼	Aug. 17	5¾
1963:		May 16	6	Apr. 9	9	Mar. 21	5½	Sept.18	5¼
July 17	3½	**1976:**		Nov. 21	8½	May 16	6	Nov. 1	5
1964:		Jan. 19	5½	Dec. 24	8	**2001:**		Dec. 12	4¾
Nov. 24	4	Nov. 22	5¼	**1985:**		Jan. 3	5¾	**2008:**	
1965:		**1977:**		May 20	7½	Jan. 31	5	Jan. 22	4
Dec. 6	4½	Aug. 31	5¾	**1986:**		Mar. 20	4½	Jan. 30	3½
1967:		Oct. 26	6	Mar. 7	7	Apr. 18	4	Mar. 17	3¼
Apr. 7	4	**1978:**		Apr. 21	6½	May 15	3½	Mar. 18	2½
Nov. 20	4½	Jan. 9	6½	July 11	6	June 27	3¼	Apr. 30	2¼
1968:		May 11	7	Aug. 21	5½	Aug. 21	3	Oct. 8	1¾
Mar. 22	5	July 3	7¼	**1987:**		Sept. 17	2½	Oct. 29	1¼
Apr. 19	5½	Aug. 21	7¾	Sept. 4	6	Oct. 2	2	Dec. 16	½
Aug. 30	5¼	Sept. 22	8	**1988:**		Dec. 11	1¼	**2010:**	
Dec. 18	5½	Oct. 16	8½	Aug. 9	6½	**2002:**		Feb. 19	¾
1969:		Nov. 1	9½	**1989:**		Nov. 6	¾		
Apr. 4	6			Feb. 24	7				

Note: As of Oct. 15, 2014, rate effective Feb. 19, 2010, was unchanged. (1) Adjustment credit rate replaced with primary credit rate. See note above.

Standard & Poor's 500 Index, 1998-2014
Monthly closing levels beginning with Oct. 1998; record high daily closing was 2,011.36 on Sept. 18, 2014.

U.S. Holdings of Foreign Securities, 2006-13
Source: *U.S. Portfolio Holdings of Foreign Securities*, U.S. Dept. of the Treasury
(in billions of dollars; countries within a region ranked by 2013 figure)

	2006	2010	2011	2012	2013[1]		2006	2010	2011	2012	2013[1]
Europe	$3,129	$3,154	$2,978	$3,562	$4,433	**Latin America and**					
United						**Caribbean**	$946	$1,064	$1,393	$1,598	$1,715
Kingdom	1,076	1,001	989	1,129	1,341	Cayman Islands . .	376	366	709	797	902
France	402	366	306	375	465	Brazil	110	235	196	216	180
Switzerland.	264	327	292	333	443	Bermuda.	208	159	161	178	211
Germany.	292	299	266	330	391	Mexico	108	109	108	157	153
Netherlands	234	233	242	286	386	Curaçao[2]	58	83	70	70	86
Ireland	121	132	149	181	281	**Asia**	1,166	1,342	1,232	1,426	1,640
Sweden.	102	122	115	122	165	Japan	596	519	509	521	686
Spain	111	87	76	99	133	South Korea	124	148	146	175	183
Luxembourg	60	100	93	105	125	Hong Kong	88	135	116	145	140
Italy.	106	66	62	110	124	China, mainland	75	102	77	120	135
Canada.	478	695	736	808	826	Taiwan	74	95	72	88	98
Africa	57	99	88	110	103	India	49	91	59	79	86
South Africa	43	78	71	86	77	**Total holdings**	5,991	6,763	6,841	7,941	9,156
Australia	173	323	334	351	337						

(1) Preliminary. (2) Figures are for Netherlands Antilles prior to 2012.

Record One-Day Gains and Losses of the Dow Jones Industrial Average
Source: Dow Jones & Co., Inc.
(ranked by largest one-day losses and gains for two terms; as of Oct. 15, 2014)

		Greatest % losses					Greatest point losses		
Rank	**Date**	**Close**	**Net chg.**	**% chg.**	**Rank**	**Date**	**Close**	**Net chg.**	**% chg.**
1.	10/19/1987	1,738.74	−508.00	−22.61%	1.	9/29/2008	10,365.45	−777.68	−6.98%
2.	10/28/1929	260.64	−38.33	−12.82	2.	10/15/2008	8,577.91	−733.08	−7.87
3.	10/29/1929	230.07	−30.57	−11.73	3.	9/17/2001	8,920.70	−684.81	−7.13
4.	11/6/1929	232.13	−25.55	−9.92	4.	12/1/2008	8,149.09	−679.95	−7.70
5.	12/18/1899	58.27	−5.57	−8.72	5.	10/9/2008	8,579.19	−678.92	−7.33

		Greatest % gains					Greatest point gains		
Rank	**Date**	**Close**	**Net chg.**	**% chg.**	**Rank**	**Date**	**Close**	**Net chg.**	**% chg.**
1.	3/15/1933	62.10	8.26	15.34%	1.	10/13/2008	9,387.61	936.42	11.08%
2.	10/6/1931	99.34	12.86	14.87	2.	10/28/2008	9,065.12	889.35	10.88
3.	10/30/1929	258.47	28.40	12.34	3.	11/13/2008	8,835.25	552.60	6.67
4.	9/21/1932	75.16	7.67	11.36	4.	3/16/2000	10,630.61	499.19	4.93
5.	10/13/2008	9,387.61	936.42	11.08	5.	3/23/2009	7,775.86	497.48	6.84

Dow Jones Industrial Average, 1965-2014
Source: Dow Jones & Co., Inc.
(as of Oct. 15, 2014)

Year	Highest close		Lowest close		Year	Highest close		Lowest close	
1965	Dec. 31	969.26	June 28	840.59	2000	Jan. 14	11,722.98	Mar. 7	9,796.03
1970	Dec. 29	842.00	May 6	631.16	2001	May 21	11,337.92	Sept. 21	8,235.81
1975	July 15	881.81	Jan. 2	632.04	2002	Mar. 19	10,635.25	Oct. 9	7,286.27
1980	Nov. 20	1,000.17	Apr. 21	759.13	2003	Dec. 31	10,453.90	Mar. 11	7,524.06
1985	Dec. 16	1,553.10	Jan. 4	1,184.96	2004	Dec. 28	10,854.54	Oct. 25	9,749.99
1990	July 16	2,999.75	Oct. 11	2,365.10	2005	Mar. 4	10,940.50	Apr. 20	10,012.36
1991	Dec. 31	3,168.83	Jan. 9	2,470.30	2006	Dec. 27	12,510.57	Jan. 20	10,667.39
1992	June 1	3,413.21	Oct. 9	3,136.58	2007	Oct. 9	14,164.53	Mar. 5	12,050.41
1993	Dec. 29	3,794.33	Jan. 20	3,241.95	2008	Jan. 3	13,056.72	Nov. 20	7,552.29
1994	Jan. 31	3,978.36	Apr. 4	3,593.35	2009	Dec. 30	10,548.51	Mar. 9	6,547.05
1995	Dec. 13	5,216.47	Jan. 30	3,832.08	2010	Dec. 29	11,585.38	July 2	9,686.48
1996	Dec. 27	6,560.91	Jan. 10	5,032.94	2011	Apr. 29	12,810.54	Oct. 3	10,655.30
1997	Aug. 6	8,259.31	Apr. 11	6,391.69	2012	Oct. 5	13,610.15	June 4	12,101.46
1998	Nov. 23	9,374.27	Aug. 31	7,539.07	2013	Dec. 31	16,576.66	Jan. 8	13,328.85
1999	Dec. 31	11,497.12	Jan. 22	9,120.67	2014	Sept. 19	17,279.74*	Feb. 3	15,372.80

* = Record high closing.

Milestones of the Dow Jones Industrial Average
(as of Oct. 15, 2014)

First close over—	First close over—	First close over—	First close over—	First close over—
100 Jan. 12, 1906	3,000 Apr. 17, 1991	6,000 Oct. 14, 1996	9,000 Apr. 6, 1998	12,000 Oct. 19, 2006
500 Mar. 12, 1956	3,500 May 19, 1993	6,500 Nov. 25, 1996	9,500 Jan. 6, 1999	13,000 Apr. 25, 2007
1,000 Nov. 14, 1972	4,000 Feb. 23, 1995	7,000 Feb. 13, 1997	10,000 Mar. 29, 1999	14,000 July 19, 2007
1,500 Dec. 11, 1985	4,500 June 16, 1995	7,500 June 10, 1997	10,500 Apr. 21, 1999	15,000 June 27, 2013
2,000 Jan. 8, 1987	5,000 Nov. 21, 1995	8,000 July 16, 1997	11,000 May 3, 1999	16,000 Nov. 21, 2013
2,500 July 17, 1987	5,500 Feb. 8, 1996	8,500 Feb. 27, 1998	11,500 Jan. 7, 2000	17,000 July 3, 2014

Components of the Dow Jones Averages
(as of Oct. 15, 2014)

Dow Jones Industrial Average

Company name (ticker symbol)	Company name (ticker symbol)	Company name (ticker symbol)
American Express Co. (AXP)	Home Depot Inc. (HD)	Pfizer Inc. (PFE)
AT&T Inc. (T)	Intel Corp. (INTC)	Procter & Gamble Co. (PG)
Boeing Co. (BA)	International Business Machines	3M Co. (MMM)
Caterpillar Inc. (CAT)	Corp. (IBM)	Travelers Companies, Inc. (TRV)
Chevron Corp. (CVX)	Johnson & Johnson (JNJ)	United Technologies Corp. (UTX)
Cisco Systems, Inc. (CSCO)	JPMorgan Chase & Co. (JPM)	UnitedHealth Group Inc. (UNH)
Coca-Cola Co. (KO)	McDonald's Corp. (MCD)	Verizon Communications Inc. (VZ)
E. I. DuPont de Nemours & Co. (DD)	Merck & Co., Inc. (MRK)	Visa Inc. (V)
Exxon Mobil Corp. (XOM)	Microsoft Corp. (MSFT)	Wal-Mart Stores Inc. (WMT)
General Electric Co. (GE)	Nike (NKE)	Walt Disney Co. (DIS)
Goldman Sachs Group (GS)		

Dow Jones Utility Average

Company name (ticker symbol)	Company name (ticker symbol)	Company name (ticker symbol)
AES Corp. (AES)	Dominion Resources Inc. (Virginia) (D)	NiSource Inc. (NI)
American Electric Power Co.	Duke Energy Corp. (DUK)	PG&E Corp. (PCG)
Inc. (AEP)	Edison International (EIX)	Public Service Enterprise Group
American Water Works Co. (AWK)	Exelon Corp. (EXC)	Inc. (PEG)
CenterPoint Energy (CNP)	FirstEnergy Corp. (FE)	Southern Co. (SO)
Consolidated Edison Inc. (ED)	NextEra Energy, Inc. (NEE)	

Dow Jones Transportation Average

Company name (ticker symbol)	Company name (ticker symbol)	Company name (ticker symbol)
Alaska Air Group, Inc. (ALK)	FedEx Corp. (FDX)	Matson Inc. (MATX)
Avis Budget Group Inc. (CAR)	J.B. Hunt Transport Services Inc.	Norfolk Southern Corp. (NSC)
C.H. Robinson Worldwide Inc.	(JBHT)	Ryder System Inc. (R)
(CHRW)	JetBlue Airways Corp. (JBLU)	Southwest Airlines Co. (LUV)
Con-way Inc. (CNW)	Kansas City Southern (KSU)	Union Pacific Corp. (UNP)
CSX Corp. (CSX)	Kirby Corp. (KEX)	United Continental Holdings (UAL)
Delta Air Lines, Inc. (DAL)	Landstar System Inc. (LSTR)	United Parcel Service Inc. CIB (UPS)
Expeditors Intl. of Washington		
Inc. (EXPD)		

Record One-Day Gains and Losses on the Nasdaq Stock Market
Source: Nasdaq Stock Market
(ranked by largest one-day losses and gains for two terms; as of Oct. 15, 2014)

	Greatest point gains			Greatest % gains			Greatest point losses			Greatest % losses	
Rank	Date	Change	Rank	Date	% change	Rank	Date	Change	Rank	Date	% change
1.	1/3/2001	324.83	1.	1/3/2001	14.17%	1.	4/14/2000	−355.49	1.	10/19/1987	−11.35%
2.	12/5/2000	274.05	2.	10/13/2008	11.81	2.	4/3/2000	−349.15	2.	4/14/2000	−9.67
3.	4/18/2000	254.41	3.	12/5/2000	10.48	3.	4/12/2000	−286.27	3.	10/26/1987	−9.14
4.	5/30/2000	254.37	4.	10/28/2008	9.53	4.	4/10/2000	−258.25	4.	10/20/1987	−9.00
5.	10/19/2000	247.04	5.	4/5/2001	8.92	5.	1/4/2000	−229.46	5.	10/26/1987	−9.00
6.	10/13/2008	242.09	6.	4/18/2001	8.12	6.	3/14/2000	−200.61	6.	12/1/2008	−8.95
7.	6/2/2000	230.88	7.	5/30/2000	7.94	7.	5/10/2000	−200.28	7.	8/31/1998	−8.56
8.	4/25/2000	228.75	8.	10/13/2000	7.87	8.	5/23/2000	−199.66	8.	10/15/2008	−8.47
9.	4/17/2000	217.87	9.	10/19/2000	7.79	9.	9/29/2008	−199.61	9.	4/3/2000	−7.64
10.	10/13/2008	194.74	10.	5/8/2002	7.78	10.	10/25/2000	−190.22	10.	1/2/2001	−7.23

Nasdaq Stock Market Closing Prices, 1971-2014
Source: Nasdaq Stock Market

Year	High	Low	Year	High	Low	Year	High	Low	Year	High	Low
1971	114.12	99.68	1982	241.63	158.92	1993	790.56	645.02	2004	2,178.00	1,752.00
1972	135.15	113.65	1983	329.11	229.88	1994	803.93	691.23	2005	2,273.37	1,904.18
1973	136.84	88.67	1984	288.41	223.91	1995	1,072.82	740.53	2006	2,465.98	2,020.39
1974	96.53	54.87	1985	325.53	245.82	1996	1,328.45	978.17	2007	2,811.61	2,340.68
1975	88.00	60.70	1986	411.21	322.14	1997	1,748.62	1,194.39	2008	2,609.63	1,505.90
1976	97.88	78.06	1987	456.27	288.49	1998	2,200.63	1,357.09	2009	2,167.70	1,265.52
1977	105.05	93.66	1988	397.54	329.00	1999	4,090.61	2,193.13	2010	2,671.48	2,091.79
1978	139.25	99.09	1989	487.60	376.87	2000	5,048.62*	2,332.78	2011	2,873.54	2,335.83
1979	152.29	117.84	1990	470.30	322.93	2001	2,892.36	1,387.06	2012	3,183.95	2,648.36
1980	208.29	124.09	1991	586.35	352.85	2002	2,059.38	1,114.11	2013	4,176.59	3,091.81
1981	223.96	170.80	1992	676.95	545.85	2003	2,009.88	1,271.47	2014	4,598.19	3,996.96

* = Record high closing, Mar. 10, 2000; as of Oct. 15, 2014.

Average Yields of Treasury, Corporate, and State and Local Bonds, 1986-2014

Source: Office of Market Finance, U.S. Dept. of the Treasury; Federal Reserve System

Period	Treasury 30-year bonds[1]	New Aa corporate bonds[2]	State and local bonds[3]	Period	Treasury 30-year bonds[1]	New Aa corporate bonds[2]	State and local bonds[3]	Period	Treasury 30-year bonds[1]	New Aa corporate bonds[2]	State and local bonds[3]
1986				**1996**				**2005**			
June	7.57%	9.39%	7.87%	June	7.06%	8.00%	6.02%	June	4.35%	4.96%	4.23%
Dec.	7.37	8.87	6.87	Dec.	6.55	7.45	5.64	Dec.	4.73	5.37	4.46
1987				**1997**				**2006**			
June	8.57	9.64	7.79	June	6.77	7.71	5.53	June	5.15	5.89	4.60
Dec.	9.12	10.22	7.96	Dec.	5.99	6.68	5.19	Dec.	4.68	5.32	4.11
1988				**1998**				**2007**			
June	9.00	10.08	7.78	June	5.70	6.43	5.12	June	5.20	5.79	4.60
Dec.	9.01	10.05	7.61	Dec.	5.06	6.13	4.98	Dec.	4.53	5.49	4.42
1989				**1999**				**2008**			
June	8.27	9.24	7.02	June	6.04	7.21	5.37	June	4.69	5.68	4.69
Dec.	7.90	9.23	6.98	Dec.	6.35	7.55	5.95	Dec.	2.87	5.05	5.56
1990				**2000**				**2009**			
June	8.46	9.69	7.24	June	5.93	7.75	5.80	June	4.52	5.61	4.81
Dec.	8.24	9.55	7.09	Dec.	5.49	7.21	5.22	Dec.	4.49	5.26	4.21
1991				**2001**				**2010**			
June	8.47	9.37	7.13	June	5.67	7.11	5.20	June	4.13	4.88	4.36
Dec.	7.70	8.55	6.69	Dec.	5.48	6.80	5.25	Dec.	4.42	5.02	4.92
1992				**2002**				**2011**			
June	7.84	8.45	6.49	June	5.65	6.57	5.09	June	4.23	4.99	4.51
Dec.	7.44	8.12	6.22	Dec.	5.01	5.93	4.85	Dec.	2.98	3.93	3.95
1993				**2003**				**2012**			
June	6.81	7.48	5.63	June	4.34	4.97	4.33	June	2.70	3.64	3.94
Dec.	6.25	7.22	5.35	Dec.	5.11	5.62	4.65	Dec.	2.88	3.65	3.48
1994				**2004**				**2013**			
June	7.40	8.16	6.11	June	5.45	6.01	5.05	June	3.40	4.27	4.27
Dec.	7.87	8.66	6.80	Dec.	4.88	5.47	4.49	Dec.	3.89	4.62	4.73
1995								**2014**			
June	6.57	7.42	5.84					June	3.42	4.25	4.35
Dec.	6.06	7.02	5.45								

(1) On Feb. 18, 2002, the U.S. treasury discontinued the 30-year constant maturity yield and reintroduced it on Feb. 9, 2006; rates in the interim are for 20-year yields. (2) Treasury series based on 3-week moving average of reoffering yields of new corporate bonds rated Aa by Moody's Investors Service with an original maturity of at least 20 years. Treasury discontinued yield index after Jan. 31, 2003. Rates thereafter are for Moody's seasoned Aaa corporate bonds as listed by Federal Reserve. (3) Index of new reoffering yields on 20-year general obligations rated Aa by Moody's Investors Service; discontinued by Treasury Jan. 31, 2003; rates thereafter are from Bond Buyer Index of general obligation, 20-year-to-maturity, mixed quality state and local bonds.

Ownership of U.S. Treasury Securities, 2001-13

Source: *Treasury Bulletin, June 2014*, Financial Management Service, U.S. Dept. of the Treasury

In 2001, just over 17% of U.S. treasury securities were held by foreign and international investors. By 2013, the total public debt had nearly tripled, while the portion held by investors outside the U.S. had nearly doubled, to 33.9%.

(in billions of dollars)

	2001	2005	2006	2007	2008	2009	2010	2011	2012	2013
Total public debt	$5,943	$8,170	$8,680	$9,229	$10,700	$12,311	$14,025	$15,223	$16,433	$17,352
Federal Reserve and intra-governmental holdings ..	3,124	4,200	4,558	4,834	4,806	5,277	5,656	6,440	6,524	7,205
Total privately held	2,819	3,971	4,122	4,396	5,893	7,034	8,369	8,783	9,909	10,147
Depository institutions	181	129	115	130	105	202	319	280	349	324
U.S. savings bonds.	190	205	202	196	194	191	188	185	182	179
Private pension funds[1]	146	184	216	229	260	302	346	397	457	510
Pension funds of state and local governments.	155	154	153	144	130	152	160	173	215	225
Insurance companies	106	202	198	142	171	222	248	272	270	273
Mutual funds.	262	254	248	344	758	669	721	905	1,043	1,135
State and local governments.	328	512	571	648	601	584	591	545	533	494
Foreign and international . .	1,040	2,034	2,103	2,353	3,077	3,685	4,436	5,007	5,574	5,802
Other investors[2]	411	295	316	210	597	1,026	1,360	1,019	1,288	1,205

(1) Includes securities held by the Federal Employees Retirement System Thrift Savings Plan "G Fund." (2) Includes individuals, government-sponsored enterprises, brokers and dealers, bank personal trusts and estates, corporate and noncorporate businesses, and other investors.

Federal Corporate Tax Rates, 2014

Personal service corporations (used by incorporated professionals such as attorneys and doctors) pay a flat rate of 35%.

Taxable income amount	Tax rate	Taxable income amount	Tax rate
Not more than $50,000.	15%	$335,001 to $10,000,000	34%
$50,001 to $75,000.	25	$10,000,001 to $15,000,000.	35
$75,001 to $100,000.	34	$15,000,001 to $18,333,333.	38
$100,001 to $335,000.	39	More than $18,333,333	35

Characteristics of Mutual Fund Investors, 2013

Source: *The Investment Company Fact Book 2014*, Investment Company Institute

Median age.	52	Married or living with a partner.	76%
Median annual household income	$80,000	Four-year college degree or more.	47%
Median household financial assets.	$200,000	Own Individual Retirement Accounts (IRAs).	63%
Median mutual fund assets.	$100,000	Hold more than half their financial assets in mutual	
Median number of funds owned	3	funds.	66%
Employed	69%		

Performance of Mutual Funds by Type, 2014

Source: *Kiplinger's Personal Finance* magazine analysis of Morningstar data
(as of Aug. 31, 2014)

Fund type/fund objective	Average annual return 1-year	3-year	5-year	Fund type/fund objective	Average annual return 1-year	3-year	5-year
Large-Company				**Sector**			
Growth	24.43%	18.56%	16.10%	Equity Precious Metals	−0.46%	−22.32%	−4.35%
Blend	23.27	19.07	15.43	Financial	18.76	19.16	10.87
Value	22.17	19.16	14.97	Health	34.44	29.11	21.48
Midsize-Company				Natural Resources	18.54	4.77	9.40
Growth	19.94	17.42	16.98	Real Estate	23.24	13.63	17.91
Blend	22.17	19.14	17.13	Technology	28.44	18.13	16.23
Value	23.45	20.31	17.17	Utilities	23.26	14.93	13.84
Small-Company				**Multialternative Funds**			
Growth	14.40	17.33	17.45	International	5.81	3.54	4.47
Blend	18.38	18.45	16.74	Diversified Emerging Markets	19.15	4.18	7.46
Value	19.15	18.83	16.27	Miscellaneous Region	15.15	6.97	8.61
Taxable Government Bond				World Bond	7.57	2.81	4.95
Short-Term	1.07	0.43	1.38	World Stock	19.51	13.95	12.34
Intermediate-Term	4.14	1.56	3.31	**Corporate Bond**			
Long-Term	14.70	5.76	8.07	High Yield	9.30	9.54	10.93
Tax-Free Government Bond				Short-Term	2.21	1.78	2.71
Short-Term	2.42	1.41	1.96	Intermediate-Term	6.19	3.67	5.30
Intermediate-Term	7.89	3.88	4.59	Long-Term	9.43	5.00	6.70
Long-Term Municipal	11.28	5.38	5.55				

Mutual Fund Ownership, 1940-2013

Source: *The Investment Company Fact Book 2014*, Investment Company Institute

Year	Mutual funds	Mutual fund accounts (thous.)	Households owning mutual funds Number (thous.)	Percent of all households	Total net assets (bil)	Exchange-traded funds (ETFs) Number of funds	Total net assets (bil)
1940	68	296	NA	NA	$0.45	NA	NA
1950	98	939	NA	NA	2.53	NA	NA
1960	161	4,898	NA	NA	17.03	NA	NA
1970	361	10,690	NA	NA	47.62	NA	NA
1980	564	12,088	4,600	5.7%	134.76	NA	NA
1990	3,079	61,948	23,400	25.1	1,065.19	NA	NA
2000	8,155	244,705	48,600	45.7	6,964.63	80	$65.58
2005	7,974	275,479	50,300	44.4	8,891.11	204	300.82
2008	8,019	264,597	52,500	45.0	9,602.57	728	531.29
2009	7,659	269,449	50,400	43.0	11,112.67	797	777.13
2010	7,548	291,299	53,200	45.3	11,831.33	923	991.99
2011	7,580	272,628	52,900	44.1	11,626.49	1,134	1,048.13
2012	7,582	257,074	53,800	44.4	13,043.67	1,194	1,337.11
2013	7,707	264,848	56,700	46.3	15,017.68	1,294	1,674.61

NA = Not available. **Note:** Does not include data for funds that invest primarily in other mutual funds. Mutual fund accounts data include both individual and omnibus accounts.

Chicago Futures and Options, 2012-13

Source: CME Group, Inc.

Futures group	2012	2013	% change, 2012-13	Futures group	2012	2013	% change, 2012-13
Futures	2,451,973,414	2,639,333,848	7.6%	Equity Index	59,141,790	91,588,208	54.9%
Commodities & alternative investments	228,866,989	212,291,673	-7.2	FX Products	10,458,884	15,182,579	45.2
Energy	358,446,263	358,817,207	0.1	Interest Rate	227,833,251	285,915,903	25.5
Equity Index	588,508,170	574,250,115	-2.4	Metals–CMX	11,393,005	12,999,887	14.1
FX Products	203,302,545	208,013,568	2.3	**Combined futures and options**	2,890,036,506	3,161,817,548	9.4
Interest Rate	995,269,254	1,201,664,860	20.7	Commodities & alternative investments	288,701,777	264,239,923	-8.5
Metals–CMX	77,580,193	84,296,425	8.7	Energy	427,847,637	423,666,080	-1.0
Options	438,063,092	522,483,700	19.3	Equity Index	647,649,960	665,838,323	2.8
Commodities & alternative investments	59,834,788	51,948,250	-13.2	FX Products	213,761,429	223,196,147	4.4
Energy	69,401,374	64,848,873	-6.6	Interest Rate	1,223,102,505	1,487,580,763	21.6
				Metals–CMX	88,973,198	97,296,312	9.4

Gold Owned by the U.S., 2014

Source: *Status Report of U.S. Treasury-Owned Gold*, Bureau of the Fiscal Service, U.S. Dept. of the Treasury
(as of July 31, 2014)

	Fine troy ounces	Book value		Fine troy ounces	Book value
Total Treasury-owned gold	261,498,926	$11,041,059,958	**Held by the Federal Reserve Bank**	13,452,811	$568,007,258
Gold bullion	258,641,878	10,920,429,099	Gold bullion	13,378,981	564,890,013
Gold coins, blanks, miscellaneous	2,857,048	120,630,859	Federal Reserve Banks– NY vault	13,376,988	564,805,850
Held by the U.S. Mint	248,046,116	10,473,052,701	Federal Reserve Banks–display	1,993	84,162
Denver, CO, deep storage	43,853,707	1,851,599,996	Gold coins	73,830	3,117,245
Fort Knox, KY, deep storage	147,341,858	6,221,097,413	Federal Reserve Banks– NY vault	73,452	3,101,307
West Point, NY, deep storage	54,067,331	2,282,841,677	Federal Reserve Banks–display	377	15,937
Gold coins, blanks, miscellaneous	2,783,219	117,513,615			

World's Leading Gold Producers, 1980-2013

Source: *Mineral Commodity Summaries 2014*, U.S. Geological Survey, U.S. Dept. of the Interior

(ranked by 2013 production; in thousands of troy ounces)

Country	1980	1990	2000	2005	2008	2009	2010	2011	2012	2013[1]
China	225	3,215	5,787	7,234	9,163	10,288	11,092	11,639	12,957	13,503
Australia	548	7,845	9,530	8,423	6,912	7,202	8,391	8,295	8,038	8,198
United States	970	9,452	11,349	8,231	7,491	7,170	7,427	7,523	7,555	7,298
Russia[2]	8,300	9,710	4,598	5,279	5,531	6,200	6,173	6,430	7,009	7,073
Peru[3]	134	293	4,263	6,682	5,783	5,864	5,273	5,272	5,176	4,823
South Africa	21,669	19,451	13,767	9,474	6,840	6,354	6,076	5,819	5,144	4,662
Canada	1,627	5,433	5,022	3,844	3,054	3,130	2,926	3,119	3,344	3,858
Mexico	196	311	848	976	1,619	1,652	2,347	2,701	3,119	3,215
Uzbekistan	NA	NA	2,733	2,894	2,733	2,894	2,894	2,926	2,990	2,990
Ghana	353	540	2,318	2,149	2,346	2,568	2,637	2,572	2,797	2,733
Brazil	NA	NA	NA	NA	1,608	1,929	1,865	1,993	2,090	2,411
Indonesia[4]	60	360	4,006	4,200	2,070	4,180	3,858	3,087	1,897	1,929
World	39,197	70,089	82,949	79,412	73,304	79,091	82,306	85,520	86,485	89,057

NA = Not available. **Note:** One kg is equal to 32.1507 troy oz. (1) Estimated. (2) Russia figures for 1980-90 refer to the former USSR. Includes gold recovered as a byproduct but excludes secondary production. (3) Includes documented production from placer artisanal production. (4) Excludes production from "people's mines," which may add more than 600,000 troy oz. to the total.

Prices of Precious Metals, 1990-2013

Source: *Mineral Commodity Summaries 2014*, U.S. Geological Survey, U.S. Dept. of the Interior

Year	Dollars per troy ounce			Dollars per pound			
	Platinum[1]	Gold	Silver	Copper[2]	Lead	Tin[3]	Zinc[4]
1990	$467	$385	$4.82	$1.23	$0.46	$3.86	$0.75
1995	425	386	5.15	1.38	0.42	4.16	0.56
1998	375	295	5.54	0.79	0.45	3.73	0.51
1999	379	280	5.25	0.76	0.44	3.66	0.53
2000	549	280	5.00	0.88	0.44	3.70	0.56
2001	533	272	4.39	0.77	0.44	3.15	0.44
2002	543	311	4.62	0.76	0.44	2.92	0.39
2003	694	365	4.91	0.85	0.44	3.40	0.41
2004	849	411	6.69	1.34	0.55	5.47	0.52
2005	900	446	7.34	1.74	0.61	4.83	0.67
2006	1,144	606	11.57	3.15	0.77	5.65	1.59
2007	1,308	699	13.41	3.28	1.24	8.99	1.54
2008	1,578	874	15.00	3.19	1.20	11.29	0.89
2009	1,208	975	14.69	2.41	0.87	8.37	0.78
2010	1,616	1,228	20.20	3.48	1.09	12.40	1.02
2011	1,725	1,572	35.26	4.06	1.22	15.75	1.06
2012	1,555	1,673	31.21	3.67	1.14	12.83	0.96
2013[5]	1,511	1,400	23.80	3.40	1.14	13.40	0.96

P = Preliminary. (1) Average annual dealer prices. (2) U.S. producer price for cathode copper. (3) Platt's Metals Week price. (4) Platt's Metals Week price for North American special high grade zinc except for 1990, which shows average price for high grade zinc. (5) Estimated.

Economic and Financial Glossary

Reviewed by William M. Gentry, Graduate School of Business, Columbia University.

Annuity contract: An investment vehicle sold by insurance companies. Annuity buyers can elect to receive periodic payments for the rest of their lives. Annuities provide insurance against outliving one's wealth.

Arbitrage: A form of hedged investment meant to capture slight differences in the prices of two related securities—for example, buying gold in London and selling it at a higher price in New York.

Balance of payments: The difference between all payments, for some categories of transactions, made to and from foreign countries over a set period of time. A favorable balance of payments exists when more payments are coming in than going out; an unfavorable balance of payments obtains when the reverse is true. Payments may include gold, the cost of merchandise and services, interest and dividend payments, money spent by travelers, and repayment of principal on loans.

Balance of trade (trade gap): The difference between exports and imports, in both actual funds and credit. A nation's balance of trade is favorable when exports exceed imports and unfavorable when the reverse is true.

Balanced budget: A budget is balanced when receipts equal expenditures. When receipts exceed expenditures, there is a **surplus**; when they fall short of expenditures, there is a **deficit**.

Bear market: A market in which prices are falling.

Bearer bond: A bond issued in bearer form rather than being registered in a specific owner's name. Ownership is determined by possession.

Bond: A written promise, or IOU, by the issuer to repay a fixed amount of borrowed money on a specified date and generally to pay interest at regular intervals in the interim.

Bull market: A market in which prices are on the rise.

Capital gain (or loss): An increase (or decrease) in the market value of an asset over some period of time. For tax purposes, capital gains are typically calculated from when an asset is bought to when it is sold.

Collateralized debt obligation (CDO): A financial security backed by a pool of assets that generate cash, such as mortgages, bonds, or loans. CDOs are typically sliced into tranches, or sections, whose reward is commensurate with their risk of default.

Commercial paper: An extremely short-term corporate IOU, generally due in 270 days or less.

Consumer price index (CPI): A statistical measure of the change in the price of consumer goods.

Convertible bond: A corporate bond (see below) that may be converted to a stated number of shares of common stock. Its price tends to fluctuate along with fluctuations in the price of the stock and with changes in interest rates.

Corporate bond: A bond issued by a corporation. The bond normally has a stated life and pays a fixed rate of interest. Considered safer than the common or preferred stock of the same company.

Cost of living: The cost of maintaining a standard of living measured in terms of purchased goods and services. Inflation typically measures changes in the cost of living.

Cost-of-living adjustments: Changes in promised payments, such as retirement benefits, to account for changes in the cost of living.

Credit crunch (liquidity crisis): A situation in which cash for lending is in short supply.

Debenture: An unsecured bond backed only by the general credit of the issuing corporation.

Deficit spending: Government spending in excess of revenues, generally financed with the sale of bonds. A deficit increases the government debt.

Deflation: A decrease in the level of prices.

Depression: A long period of economic decline marked by low prices, high unemployment, and many business failures.

Derivatives: Financial contracts, such as options, whose values are based on, or derived from, the price of an underlying financial asset or indicator such as a stock or an interest rate.

Devaluation: The official lowering of a nation's currency, decreasing its value in relation to foreign currencies.

Discount rate: The rate of interest set by the Federal Reserve that member banks are charged when borrowing money through the Federal Reserve System.

Disposable income: Income after taxes that is available to persons for spending and saving.

Diversification: Investing in more than one asset in order to reduce the riskiness of the overall asset portfolio. By holding more than one asset, losses on some assets may be offset by gains realized on other assets.

Dividend: Discretionary payment by a corporation to its shareholders, usually in the form of cash or stock shares.

Dow Jones Industrial Average: An index of stock market prices, based on the prices of 30 companies, 27 of which are on the New York Stock Exchange.

Econometrics: The use of statistical methods to study economic and financial data.

Exchange-traded fund (ETF): A security whose price tracks a pool of assets or an index, such as the S&P 500. ETFs are not managed, and therefore have no management fees like a mutual fund. ETF prices vary throughout the day as they are bought and sold. See also **Mutual fund**.

Federal Deposit Insurance Corp. (FDIC): A U.S. government-sponsored corporation that insures accounts in national banks and other qualified institutions against bank failures.

Federal Reserve System: The entire banking system of the U.S., incorporating 12 Federal Reserve banks (one in each of 12 Federal Reserve districts), 25 Federal Reserve branch banks, all national banks, and state-chartered commercial banks and trust companies that have been admitted to its membership. The governors of the system greatly influence the nation's monetary and credit policies.

Full employment: The economy is said to be at full employment when everyone who wishes to work at the going wage-rate for his or her type of labor is employed, save only for the small amount of unemployment due to the time it takes to switch from one job to another.

Futures: A futures contract is an agreement to buy or sell a specific amount of a commodity or financial instrument at a particular price at a set date in the future. For example, futures based on a stock index (such as the Dow Jones Industrial Average) are bets on the future price of that group of stocks.

Golden parachute: Provisions in contracts of some high-level executives guaranteeing substantial severance benefits if they lose their position in a corporate takeover.

Government bond: A bond issued by the U.S. Treasury, considered a safe investment. These are divided into two categories—marketable and not marketable. Savings bonds cannot be bought and sold once the original purchase is made. Marketable bonds fall into several categories. Treasury bills are short-term U.S. obligations, maturing in 3, 6, or 12 months. Treasury notes mature in up to 10 years. Treasury bonds mature in 10 to 30 years. Indexed bonds are adjusted for inflation.

Greenmail: A company buying back its own shares for more than the going market price to avoid a threatened hostile takeover.

Gross domestic product (GDP): The market value of all goods and services that have been bought for final use during a period of time. It became the official measure of the size of the U.S. economy in 1991, replacing **gross national product (GNP)**, in use since 1941. GDP covers workers and capital employed within the nation's borders. GNP covers production by U.S. residents regardless of where it takes place. The switch aligned U.S. terminology with that of most other industrialized countries.

Hedge fund: A flexible investment fund for a limited number of large investors (the minimum investment is typically $1 mil). Hedge funds use a variety of investment techniques, including those forbidden to mutual funds, such as short-selling and heavy leveraging.

Hedging: Taking two positions whose gains and losses will offset each other if prices change, in order to limit risk.

Individual retirement account (IRA): A self-funded tax-advantaged retirement plan that allows employed individuals to contribute up to a maximum yearly sum. With a traditional IRA, individuals contribute pre-tax earnings and defer income taxes until retirement. With a Roth IRA, individuals contribute after-tax earnings but do not pay taxes on future withdrawals (the interest is never taxed). **401(k) plans** are employer-sponsored plans similar to traditional IRAs but having higher contribution limits.

Inflation: An increase in the level of prices.

Insider information: Important facts about the condition or plans of a corporation that have not been released to the general public.

Interest: The cost of borrowing money.

Investment bank: A financial institution that arranges the initial issuance of stocks and bonds and offers companies advice about acquisitions and divestitures.

Junk bonds: Bonds issued by companies with low credit ratings. They typically pay relatively high interest rates because of the fear of default.

Leading indicators: A series of 11 indicators from different segments of the economy used by the U.S. Commerce Dept. to predict when changes in economic activity might occur.

Leverage: The extent to which a purchase was paid for with borrowed money. Amplifies the potential gain or loss for the purchaser.

Leveraged buyout (LBO): An acquisition of a company in which much of the purchase price is borrowed, with the debt to be repaid from future profits or by subsequently selling off company assets. A leveraged buyout is typically carried out by a small group of investors, often including incumbent management.

Liquid assets: Assets consisting of cash and/or items that are easily converted into cash.

Margin account: A brokerage account that allows a person to trade securities on credit. A **margin call** is a demand for more collateral on the account.

Money supply: The currency held by the public, plus checking accounts in commercial banks and savings institutions.

Mortgage-backed securities: Created when a bank, builder, or government agency gathers a group of mortgages and then sells bonds to other institutions and the public. The investors receive their proportionate share of the interest payments on the loans as well as the principal payments. Usually, the mortgages in question are guaranteed by the government.

Municipal bond: Issued by governmental units such as states, cities, local taxing authorities, and other agencies. Interest is exempt from U.S.—and sometimes state and local—income tax. Municipal bond unit investment trusts offer a portfolio of many different municipal bonds chosen by professionals. The income is exempt from federal income taxes.

Mutual fund: A portfolio of professionally bought and managed financial assets whose share price is based on the net asset value, i.e. the value of all the investments owned by the funds, less any debt, and divided by the total number of shares. Mutual funds are a way for investors to diversify their holdings, rather than hold individual stocks. **Bond funds** are mutual funds whose assets are exclusively bonds. See also Exchange-traded fund (ETFs).

National debt: The debt of the national government, as distinguished from the debts of political subdivisions of the nation and of private business and individuals.

National debt ceiling: Total borrowing limit set by Congress beyond which the U.S. national debt cannot rise. This limit is periodically raised by congressional vote.

Option: A contractual agreement between a buyer and seller to buy or sell shares of a specific security at a stated price within a given period of time. A **call** option gives one party the right to buy shares; a **put** option affords the right to sell shares.

Prime interest rate: The rate charged by banks on short-term loans to large commercial customers with the highest credit rating.

Producer price index: A statistical measure of the change in the price of wholesale goods. It is reported for 3 different stages of the production chain: crude, intermediate, and finished goods.

Program trading: Trading techniques involving large numbers and large blocks of stocks, usually used in conjunction with computer programs. Techniques include index arbitrage, in which traders profit from price differences between stocks and futures contracts on stock indexes, and portfolio insurance, which is the use of stock-index futures to protect stock investors from potentially large losses when the market drops.

Public debt: The total of a nation's debts owed by state, local, and national government. Increases in this sum, reflected in public-sector deficits, indicate how much of the nation's spending is being financed by borrowing rather than by taxation.

Recession: A mild decrease in economic activity marked by a decline in real (inflation-adjusted) GDP, employment, and trade, usually lasting from six months to a year, and marked by widespread decline in many sectors of the economy.

Savings Association Insurance Fund (SAIF): Created in 1989 to insure accounts in savings and loan associations up to $100,000.

Seasonal adjustment: Statistical changes made to compensate for regular fluctuations in data that are so great they tend to distort data and make comparisons meaningless. For instance, seasonal adjustments are made for a slowdown in housing construction in midwinter and for the rise in farm income in the fall after summer crops are harvested.

Short-selling: Borrowing shares of stock from a brokerage firm and selling them, hoping to buy the shares back at a lower price, return them, and realize a profit from the decline in prices.

Stagnation: Economic slowdown in which there is little growth in the GDP, capital investment, and real income.

Stock: Common stocks are shares of ownership in a corporation. For publicly held firms, the stock typically trades on an exchange, such as the New York Stock Exchange; for closely held firms, the founders and managers own most of the stock. There can be wide swings in the prices of this kind of stock. **Preferred** stock is a type of stock on which a fixed dividend must be paid before holders of common stock are issued their share of the issuing corporation's earnings. Preferred stock is less risky than common stock. **Convertible preferred** stock can be converted into the common stock of the company that issued the preferred. **Over-the-counter** stock is not traded on the major or regional exchanges but bought directly from dealers. **Blue-chip** stocks are so called because they have been leading stocks for a long time. **Growth** stocks are from companies that reinvest their earnings, rather than pay dividends, with the expectation of future stock price appreciation.

Supply-side economics: A school of thinking about economic policy holding that lowering income tax rates will inevitably lead to enhanced economic growth and general revitalization of the economy.

Takeover: Acquisition of one company by another company or group by sale or merger. A friendly takeover occurs when the acquired company's management is agreeable to the merger; when management is opposed to the merger, it is a hostile takeover.

Tender offer: A public offer to buy a company's stock; usually priced at a premium above the market.

Zero coupon bond: A corporate or government bond that is issued at a deep discount from the maturity value and pays no interest during the life of the bond. It is redeemable at face value.

Top Brands in Selected Categories, 2013-14

Source: Information Resources, Inc., a Chicago-based marketing research company

Figures for 52-week period ending Aug. 10, 2014. Percent change represents dollar sales change in 2013-14 over same period in 2012-13.

Product	Sales (mil)	% change	Market share
Baby food, total	**$1,019,947,135**	**0.7%**	
Gerber Second Foods Nature Select	133,194,951	1.8	13.1%
Gerber Second Foods	80,858,927	2.8	7.9
Gerber	72,381,063	-8.0	7.1
Gerber Graduates	61,556,201	-2.1	6.0
Plum Organics Yum	41,187,703	-2.3	4.0
Batteries (alkaline), total	**$1,067,182,489**	**-6.5%**	
Duracell Coppertop	406,314,455	-14.2	38.1%
Energizer Max	349,601,367	0.4	32.8
Private label	205,285,940	-5.4	19.2
Duracell	50,685,659	123.1	4.8
Ray O Vac	11,760,632	-37.7	1.1
Beer, domestic, total	**$8,666,999,780**	**4.3%**	
Bud Light	1,451,277,663	1.4	16.7%
Coors Light	795,312,872	-0.2	9.2
Miller Lite	645,294,036	0.4	7.5
Budweiser	556,236,581	-1.5	6.4
Michelob Ultra	286,020,027	9.8	3.3
Beer, imported, total	**$2,165,835,954**	**3.9%**	
Corona Extra	462,855,170	5.8	21.4%
Heineken	272,477,283	0.0	12.6
Modelo Especial	199,045,943	24.7	9.2
Corona Light	141,169,580	4.7	6.5
Stella Artois Lager	133,182,671	10.8	6.2
Bottled water, total	**$4,113,330,527**	**1.4%**	
Private label	1,134,022,988	6.4	27.6%
Dasani	375,877,589	6.3	9.1
Aquafina	291,844,365	-4.2	7.1
Poland Spring	269,151,514	2.2	6.5
Nestle Pure Life	263,574,840	12.0	6.4
Cat food (dry), total	**$1,090,912,051**	**-0.9%**	
Iams Proactive Health	95,087,478	29.5	8.7%
Meow Mix Original Choice	80,220,469	0.4	7.4
Purina Cat Chow	74,675,612	0.5	6.9
Purina Kit & Kaboodle	71,442,831	-1.4	6.6
Private label	66,871,482	-9.1	6.1
Cereal (ready-to-eat), total	**$5,997,867,099**	**-4.3%**	
Private label	578,240,180	-7.7	9.6%
General Mills Honey Nut Cheerios	320,170,259	-3.3	5.3
Post Honey Bunches Of Oats	264,661,224	2.3	4.4
Kellogg's Frosted Flakes	249,690,274	-3.6	4.2
General Mills Cheerios	237,382,203	-4.2	4.0
Chocolate candy, total	**$2,551,642,838**	**5.0%**	
M&M's	311,133,069	-2.6	12.2%
Hershey's	173,424,386	3.0	6.8
Reese's	125,473,577	-0.1	4.9
Dove Promises	109,269,186	-0.2	4.3
Private label	106,723,652	12.9	4.2
Coffee (ground), total	**$2,596,360,687**	**-6.5%**	
Folger's	689,411,226	-8.8	26.6%
Maxwell House	382,833,186	-10.5	14.7
Starbuck's	267,071,348	0.4	10.3
Private label	261,692,791	-9.7	10.1
Dunkin' Donuts	185,999,269	0.0	7.2

Product	Sales (mil)	% change	Market share
Coffee (ground decaffeinated), total	**$224,915,059**	**-7.0%**	
Folger's	49,838,770	-10.5	22.2%
Private label	36,974,520	-7.3	16.4
Starbucks	22,290,680	-2.0	9.9
Dunkin' Donuts	20,605,818	-4.6	9.2
Maxwell House	17,394,302	-11.2	7.7
Cookies, total	**$4,607,401,493**	**1.8%**	
Private label	671,486,482	0.0	14.6%
Nabisco Oreo	423,987,118	12.7	9.2
Nabisco Chips Ahoy	398,839,252	6.8	8.7
Nabisco Oreo Double Stuf	180,648,495	3.0	3.9
Lofthouse	118,291,536	-7.8	2.6
Dog food (dry), total	**$2,081,118,963**	**-3.2%**	
Iams Proactive Health	165,445,176	34.1	8.0%
Private label	160,854,725	-13.9	7.7
Purina One Smart Blend	152,736,858	1.5	7.3
Pedigree	143,944,778	-10.3	6.9
Purina Dog Chow	142,855,891	-3.3	6.9
Ice cream, total	**$4,001,207,434**	**1.9%**	
Private label	973,540,241	-2.6	24.3%
Blue Bell	395,044,325	5.9	9.9
Haagen Dazs	330,056,139	5.4	8.3
Ben & Jerry's	289,270,325	4.0	7.2
Breyer's	269,752,457	-8.8	6.7
Pizza (frozen), total	**$3,007,865,763**	**0.4%**	
Di Giorno	617,206,829	-7.6	20.5%
Private label	329,306,057	2.5	11.0
Red Baron	241,513,032	-1.6	8.0
Totino's Party Pizza	191,271,541	3.5	6.4
Tombstone	190,137,340	-6.2	6.3
Potato chips, total	**$3,886,495,143**	**2.9%**	
Lay's	1,108,005,835	4.1	28.5%
Wavy Lay's	370,994,958	13.9	9.6
Ruffles	311,187,545	-0.1	8.0
Private label	295,193,845	5.5	7.6
Pringles	278,414,731	6.9	7.2
Salad dressing, total	**$1,352,531,559**	**-1.1%**	
Kraft	255,834,775	-4.2	18.9%
Hidden Valley Ranch	237,512,997	-1.1	17.6
Private label	205,312,471	2.9	15.2
Wishbone	166,862,421	-5.0	12.3
Ken's Steak House	163,393,632	1.8	12.1
Soft drinks, total	**$8,005,091,054**	**-1.1%**	
Coca Cola	1,904,765,660	1.8	23.8%
Pepsi	1,179,373,877	-1.5	14.7
Mountain Dew	771,742,849	-1.8	9.6
Dr. Pepper	633,812,792	-0.1	7.9
Sprite	579,472,098	3.6	7.2
Soft drinks (low-calorie), total	**$4,173,309,197**	**-7.3%**	
Diet Coke	1,040,185,615	-5.6	24.9%
Diet Pepsi	579,118,328	-5.4	13.9
Coke Zero	353,881,456	-0.2	8.5
Diet Mountain Dew	321,659,468	-4.9	7.7
Diet Dr. Pepper	263,332,478	-7.7	6.3

Note: "Private label" represents the aggregated sales figures for store-branded products in that category. Total category sales include other brands not listed here.

Who Owns What: Familiar Consumer Products and Services

The following is a partial list of well-known consumer brands with their (U.S.) parent companies as of Sept. 2014. Among brands not listed are many whose parent companies have the same or a similar name (e.g., Colgate is owned by Colgate-Palmolive Co.).

ABC broadcasting: Walt Disney
Advil: Pfizer
Ajax cleanser: Colgate-Palmolive
Altoids mints: Mars
Amana appliances: Whirlpool
American Girl: Mattel
Aquafina water: PepsiCo
Arm & Hammer: Church & Dwight
Band-Aid bandages: Johnson & Johnson
Barbie dolls: Mattel
Bejeweled video game: PopCap
Ben & Jerry's ice cream: Unilever
Betty Crocker products: General Mills
Bounty paper towels: Procter & Gamble
Braun appliances: Procter & Gamble
Brita water systems: Clorox
Cadbury chocolates: Mondelēz International
Calphalon cookware: Newell Rubbermaid
Canada Dry ginger ale: Dr Pepper Snapple Group
ChapStick: Pfizer
Charmin toilet tissue: Procter & Gamble
Cheer detergent: Procter & Gamble
Cheez Whiz: Kraft Foods
Chips Ahoy!: Mondelēz International
Clairol hair products: Procter & Gamble
Claritin allergy products: Merck
Contadina tomatoes: Del Monte
Coppertone sunscreen: Merck
Crest toothpaste: Procter & Gamble
Crisco shortening: J.M. Smucker
Dasani water: Coca-Cola
Doritos chips: PepsiCo
Dove soap: Unilever
Dreyer's ice cream: Nestlé
Duracell batteries: Procter & Gamble
Febreze: Procter & Gamble
Fisher-Price toys: Mattel
Folger's coffee: J.M. Smucker
Formula 409 spray cleaner: Clorox
Friskies cat food: Nestlé
Frito-Lay's snacks: PepsiCo
Fruit of the Loom apparel: Berkshire Hathaway
Gatorade: PepsiCo
GEICO auto insurance: Berkshire Hathaway
Gerber baby food: Nestlé
Gillette: Procter & Gamble
Glad products: Clorox
Glade air fresheners: S.C. Johnson

Green Giant vegetables: General Mills
Halls cough drops: Mondelēz International
Head & Shoulders shampoo: Procter & Gamble
Healthy Choice meals: ConAgra
Hebrew National meats: ConAgra
Hellmann's mayonnaise: Unilever
Hot Wheels/Matchbox cars: Mattel
Huggies diapers: Kimberly-Clark
Hunt's tomatoes: ConAgra
Iams pet food: Procter & Gamble
Irish Spring soap: Colgate-Palmolive
Ivory soap: Procter & Gamble
Jell-O: Kraft Foods
Jennie-O turkey: Hormel
Jif peanut butter: J.M. Smucker
Jimmy Dean sausages: Hillshire Brands
Keebler cookies: Kellogg Co.
KFC restaurants: Yum! Brands
Kibbles 'n Bits pet food: Del Monte
Kingsford charcoal: Clorox
Kit Kat candy: Hershey
KitchenAid appliances: Whirlpool
Kiwi shoe products: S.C. Johnson
Kleenex: Kimberly-Clark
Knorr soups: Unilever
Kool-Aid: Kraft Foods
Lipton tea: Unilever
Listerine mouthwash: Johnson & Johnson
Maxwell House coffee: Kraft Foods
Maytag appliances: Whirlpool
Minute Maid juices: Coca-Cola
Mr. Clean: Procter & Gamble
Monopoly board game: Hasbro
Mountain Dew soda: PepsiCo
Neosporin: Johnson & Johnson
Neutrogena soap: Johnson & Johnson
9 Lives cat food: Del Monte
OFF! insect repellents: S.C. Johnson
Olay: Procter & Gamble
Old Navy clothing: Gap
Oreo cookies: Mondelēz International
Oscar Mayer meats: Kraft Foods
Pampers: Procter & Gamble
Pantene shampoo: Procter & Gamble
Paper Mate pens: Newell Rubbermaid
Pedigree pet food: Mars
Pepperidge Farm prods.: Campbell Soup
Pepto-Bismol: Procter & Gamble
Perrier water: Nestlé
Pillsbury: General Mills
Pine-Sol cleaner: Clorox

Pizza Hut restaurants: Yum! Brands
Planters nuts: Kraft Foods
Post-it notes: 3M
Prego pasta sauce: Campbell Soup
Pringles snacks: Kellogg Co.
Purina pet foods: Nestlé
Q-Tips: Unilever
Quaker Oats: PepsiCo
Ragu sauce: Unilever
Raid insecticide: S.C. Johnson
Reese's candy: Hershey
Rice-A-Roni: PepsiCo
Right Guard deodorant: Henkel
Ritz crackers: Mondelēz International
Robitussin: Pfizer
Rogaine hair-growth aide: Johnson & Johnson
Saran wrap: S.C. Johnson
Schick razors: Energizer
Scope mouthwash: Procter & Gamble
Scotch tape: 3M
Scott tissue: Kimberly-Clark
Skippy peanut butter: Hormel
SlimFast: Unilever
S.O.S. soap pads: Clorox
S&W canned vegetables: Del Monte
Splenda sweetener: Johnson & Johnson
Sprite soda: Coca-Cola
Sudafed: Johnson & Johnson
Swanson broth: Campbell Soup
Taco Bell restaurants: Yum! Brands
Tampax tampons: Procter & Gamble
Tide detergent: Procter & Gamble
Timberland apparel: V.F. Corp.
Trident gum: Mondelēz International
Trojan condoms: Church & Dwight
Tropicana: PepsiCo
Twizzlers candy: Hershey
Tylenol: Johnson & Johnson
V8 vegetable juice: Campbell Soup
Vans apparel: V.F. Corp.
Vaseline: Unilever
Velveeta cheese products: Kraft Foods
Viagra: Pfizer
Vicks cold medicines: Procter & Gamble
Visine eye drops: Johnson & Johnson
Windex: S.C. Johnson
Wrigley's candy and gum: Mars
Xanax: Pfizer
Yoplait yogurt: General Mills
Ziploc storage bags: S.C. Johnson

U.S. Home Ownership Rates, by Selected Characteristics, 2005, 2014

Source: U.S. Census Bureau, U.S. Dept. of Commerce

Region	2005	2014	Age	2005	2014	Race/ethnicity[1]	2005	2014	Income	2005	2014
Northeast	64.7%	62.1%	Under 35	42.8%	35.9%	White, non-			Median family		
Midwest	73.4	69.6	35-44	68.7	60.2	Hispanic	75.6%	72.9%	income or more	84.0%	79.8%
South	70.4	65.9	45-54	76.3	70.7	Black	48.0	43.5	Below median		
West	63.8	59.6	55-64	81.3	76.4	Hispanic	49.2	45.8	family income	52.7	49.8
			65+	80.3	80.1	Other	58.0	54.7	Total U.S.	68.6	64.7

Note: Figures are for 2nd quarter of year shown. Not seasonally adjusted. (1) Hispanic householders may be of any race. "Other" includes householders self-identifying as Asian, Native Hawaiian/Pacific Islander, and Native American/Alaska Native, as well as combinations of two or more races/ethnicities.

U.S. Housing Affordability, 1990-2014

Source: National Association of REALTORS®

Year	Median-priced existing home	Avg. mortgage rate[1]	Monthly principal & interest payment	Payment as % of median monthly income	Year	Median-priced existing home	Avg. mortgage rate[1]	Monthly principal & interest payment	Payment as % of median monthly income
1990	$92,000	10.04%	$648	22.0%	2009	$172,100	5.14%	$751	14.8%
1995	110,500	7.85	639	18.9	2010	173,100	4.89	734	14.5
2000	139,000	8.03	818	19.3	2011	166,200	4.67	687	13.4
2005	219,000	5.91	1,040	22.4	2012	177,200	3.83	663	12.9
2006	221,900	6.58	1,131	23.2	2013	197,400	4.00	754	14.2
2007	217,900	6.52	1,104	21.7	2014[2]	212,000	4.34	843	15.6
2008	196,600	6.15	958	18.1					

(1) All figures assume a down payment of 20% of the home price. Based on effective rate on loans closed on existing homes for the period shown. (2) Figures are for May, the latest available.

Median Price of Existing Single-Family Homes, by Metropolitan Area, 2010-14

Source: National Association of REALTORS®

Median prices are in thousands of dollars and based on all transactions within time period shown. 2nd qtr. 2014 figures are preliminary.

Metropolitan area	2010	2013	2014
Akron, OH	$108.9	$118.5	$119.5
Albany-Schenectady-Troy, NY	195.7	202.6	198.5
Albuquerque, NM	178.7	174.3	178.7
Allentown-Bethlehem-Easton, PA-NJ	224.0	179.5	181.0
Amarillo, TX	124.7	138.4	141.9
Anaheim-Santa Ana-Irvine, CA	546.4	651.6	691.9
Atlanta-Sandy Springs-Marietta, GA	114.8	139.5	166.2
Atlantic City, NJ	226.4	218.3	207.9
Austin-Round Rock, TX	193.6	222.9	247.5
Baltimore-Towson, MD	246.1	251.9	255.6
Barnstable Town, MA	326.0	335.1	346.4
Baton Rouge, LA	169.6	170.0	172.1
Beaumont-Port Arthur, TX	125.1	135.5	138.6
Birmingham-Hoover, AL	143.0	165.1	170.3
Bismarck, ND	163.4	217.7	233.5
Bloomington-Normal, IL	157.9	154.0	151.0
Boise City-Nampa, ID	136.2	163.7	174.6
Boston-Cambridge-Quincy, MA-NH	357.3	375.9	398.1
Boulder, CO	358.1	371.8	448.8
Bridgeport-Stamford-Norwalk, CT	408.6	403.0	427.4
Buffalo-Niagara Falls, NY	121.2	131.0	127.3
Burlington-South Burlington, VT	261.2	280.3	273.4
Canton-Massillon, OH	90.9	104.0	115.9
Cape Coral-Fort Myers, FL	88.9	166.1	199.8
Cedar Rapids, IA	144.7	155.8	156.3
Champaign-Urbana, IL	141.9	143.1	142.8
Charleston-North Charleston, SC	200.5	221.7	233.8
Charleston, WV	129.1	134.0	131.1
Charlotte-Gastonia-Concord, NC-SC	143.3	174.2	203.6
Chattanooga, TN-GA	121.4	132.3	143.3
Chicago-Naperville-Joliet, IL	191.4	191.3	218.0
Cincinnati-Middletown, OH-KY-IN	128.0	135.5	147.3
Cleveland-Elyria-Mentor, OH	114.5	117.7	127.9
Colorado Springs, CO	195.5	216.8	222.5
Columbia, MO	146.3	155.2	161.8
Columbia, SC	142.6	146.8	156.7
Columbus, OH	136.4	142.8	162.6
Corpus Christi, TX	135.1	152.6	168.7
Cumberland, MD-WV	100.3	102.2	99.4
Dallas-Fort Worth-Arlington, TX	143.8	175.6	191.3
Davenport-Moline-Rock Island, IA-IL	112.2	114.6	118.3
Dayton, OH	103.6	106.5	120.9
Deltona-Daytona Beach-Ormond Beach, FL	115.6	117.1	131.2
Denver-Aurora, CO	232.4	280.6	316.3
Des Moines, IA	150.9	170.4	175.5
Detroit-Warren-Livonia, MI[1]	NA	NA	NA
Dover, DE	193.3	178.4	181.3
Durham, NC	158.3	192.7	203.8
El Paso, TX	134.3	141.2	141.3
Erie, PA	107.7	113.3	118.0
Eugene-Springfield, OR	196.3	200.9	213.1
Fargo, ND-MN	NA	164.6	169.8
Gainesville, FL	161.6	167.3	173.0
Gary-Hammond, IN	122.9	130.1	135.6
Grand Rapids, MI	91.5	128.4	142.0
Green Bay, WI	130.4	134.7	147.9
Greensboro-High Point, NC	129.8	131.0	137.4
Greenville, SC	145.3	159.2	165.2
Gulfport-Biloxi, MS	125.0	107.8	113.0
Hartford-West Hartford-East Hartford, CT	235.8	227.0	225.9
Honolulu, HI	607.6	661.5	678.5
Houston-Baytown-Sugar Land, TX	155.0	181.3	204.0
Indianapolis, IN	123.3	136.7	148.7
Jackson, MS	133.2	148.2	157.8
Jacksonville, FL	137.7	160.8	185.0
Kansas City, MO-KS	141.6	154.8	164.3
Knoxville, TN	140.9	146.7	152.0
Lansing-East Lansing, MI	84.4	102.2	121.7
Las Vegas-Paradise, NV	138.0	173.8	196.2
Lexington-Fayette, KY	143.2	143.8	148.5
Lincoln, NE	133.6	143.3	145.7
Little Rock-North Little Rock, AR	132.5	137.0	135.6
Los Angeles-Long Beach-Santa Ana, CA	323.3	405.6	420.3
Louisville, KY-IN	134.6	139.5	143.3
Madison, WI	217.7	221.5	224.7
Manchester-Nashua, NH	232.0	229.2	237.4
Memphis, TN-MS-AR	120.2	129.4	142.1
Miami-Fort Lauderdale-Miami Beach, FL	201.9	246.0	270.0
Milwaukee-Waukesha-West Allis, WI	205.9	200.7	207.7
Minneapolis-St. Paul-Bloomington, MN-WI	170.6	196.2	212.9
Mobile, AL	121.0	108.4	122.1
Montgomery, AL	129.0	133.4	136.9
Nashville-Davidson--Murfreesboro, TN	153.8	176.4	184.9
New Haven-Milford, CT	231.0	226.5	229.6
New Orleans-Metairie-Kenner, LA	159.7	164.7	168.9
New York-Northern New Jersey-Long Island, NY-NJ-PA	393.7	391.8	396.7
Norwich-New London, CT	204.7	186.6	184.3
Oklahoma City, OK	145.7	153.1	146.1
Omaha, NE-IA	137.3	145.7	150.8
Orlando, FL	134.7	160.4	182.0
Palm Bay-Melbourne-Titusville, FL	103.0	126.2	137.0
Pensacola-Ferry Pass-Brent, FL	141.0	152.4	156.3
Peoria, IL	116.9	114.4	126.0
Philadelphia-Camden-Wilmington, PA-NJ-DE-MD	214.9	220.3	227.2
Phoenix-Mesa-Scottsdale, AZ	139.2	183.6	198.6
Pittsfield, MA	195.5	183.4	176.0
Portland-South Portland-Biddeford, ME	218.0	228.9	227.4
Portland-Vancouver-Beaverton, OR-WA	237.3	265.5	286.2
Providence-New Bedford-Fall River, RI-MA	228.5	230.8	245.5
Raleigh-Cary, NC	190.4	196.9	211.6
Reading, PA	153.3	148.2	150.6
Reno-Sparks, NV	179.5	218.4	244.1
Richmond, VA	NA	207.5	221.5
Riverside-San Bernardino-Ontario, CA	179.3	241.6	274.6
Rochester, NY	118.9	126.3	128.1
Rockford, IL	NA	86.6	85.3
Sacramento-Arden-Arcade-Roseville, CA	184.2	239.5	271.0
Saint Louis, MO-IL	131.1	134.3	149.9
Salem, OR	173.5	168.5	200.4
Salt Lake City, UT	206.5	230.6	242.1
San Antonio, TX	151.0	171.0	184.2
San Diego-Carlsbad-San Marcos, CA	385.7	464.3	504.2
San Francisco-Oakland-Fremont, CA	525.6	679.2	769.6
San Jose-Sunnyvale-Santa Clara, CA	595.0	780.0	899.5
Sarasota-Bradenton-Venice, FL	164.6	203.9	224.2
Seattle-Tacoma-Bellevue, WA	295.7	336.3	357.4
Shreveport-Bossier City, LA	156.6	162.4	156.6
Sioux Falls, SD	143.3	155.5	162.4
Spartanburg, SC	118.2	128.2	128.8
Spokane, WA	172.2	174.2	178.5
Springfield, IL	124.0	116.9	126.8
Springfield, MA	190.0	189.8	199.0
Springfield, MO	109.1	117.1	123.3
Syracuse, NY	125.1	125.5	124.6
Tallahassee, FL	152.8	171.9	165.0
Tampa-St. Petersburg-Clearwater, FL	134.2	142.8	156.0
Toledo, OH	81.5	81.7	95.9
Topeka, KS	107.2	109.0	120.7
Trenton-Ewing, NJ	250.7	257.5	271.8
Tucson, AZ	156.6	169.6	176.9
Tulsa, OK	132.3	143.1	146.9
Virginia Beach-Norfolk-Newport News, VA-NC	205.0	193.0	200.0
Washington-Arlington-Alexandria, DC-VA-MD-WV	325.3	381.9	403.6
Wichita, KS	118.7	122.2	128.4
Wilmington, NC	NA	207.2	217.2
Winston-Salem, NC	NA	128.7	137.4
Worcester, MA	223.3	231.3	240.5

NA = Not available. (1) $53,800 in 2011, and $63,400 in 2012.

Characteristics of American Housing Units, 2011

Source: *American Housing Survey, 2011*, U.S. Dept. of Housing and Urban Development

Characteristic	Number of homes (thous.)	% of all homes	Characteristic	Number of homes (thous.)	% of all homes
Total units	132,419	100.0%	**Number of bedrooms**		
Units in structure			None	1,413	1.1%
1, detached	82,974	62.7	1	14,924	11.3
1, attached	7,768	5.9	2	35,083	26.5
2-4	10,678	8.1	3	54,245	41.0
5-9	6,354	4.8	4 or more	26,755	20.2
10-19	6,028	4.6	**Number of complete bathrooms**		
20-49	4,474	3.4	None	1,808	1.4
50 or more	5,096	3.8	1	46,800	35.3
Manufactured/mobile home/trailer	9,049	6.8	1-1/2	16,666	12.6
Cooperatives	896	0.7	2 or more	67,145	50.7
Condominiums	9,363	7.1	**Location**		
Year built			Inside metropolitan statistical areas	104,017	78.6
2010-14	720	0.5	Outside metropolitan statistical areas	28,402	21.4
2005-09	8,267	6.2	Northeast	23,717	17.9
2000-04	9,250	7.0	Midwest	29,545	22.3
1995-99	8,948	6.8	South	50,381	38.0
1990-94	7,206	5.4	West	28,776	21.7
1985-89	9,014	6.8	**Lot size[2]**		
1980-84	7,715	5.8	Less than 1/8 acre	15,638	16.2
1975-79	13,579	10.3	1/8-1/4 acre	25,011	25.9
1970-74	11,176	8.4	1/4-1/2 acre	17,705	18.4
1960-69	15,405	11.6	1/2-1 acre	11,321	11.7
1950-59	13,455	10.2	1-5 acres	19,076	19.8
1940-49	7,836	5.9	5-10 acres	3,037	3.2
1930-39	5,536	4.2	10+ acres	4,599	4.8
1920-29	5,323	4.0	Median lot size (acres)	0.25	—
1919 or earlier	8,989	6.8	**Equipment**		
Median year built	1974	—	Dishwasher	85,831	64.8
Square footage of unit[1]			Kitchen sink disposal	65,976	49.8
Less than 500	973	1.1	Trash compactor	4,349	3.3
500-749	2,678	2.9	Washing machine	103,435	78.1
750-999	6,529	7.1	Clothes dryer	100,642	76.0
1,000-1,499	20,919	22.7	Lacking full kitchen facilities	5,875	4.4
1,500-1,999	20,560	22.3	Air conditioning	113,558	85.8
2,000-2,499	14,343	15.6	**Main heating source[3]**		
2,500-2,999	7,553	8.2	Piped gas	63,791	48.6
3,000-3,999	7,225	7.9	Electricity	48,330	36.8
4,000 or more	4,479	4.9	Fuel oil	8,867	6.7
Not reported/Don't know	6,762	7.3	Bottled gas	6,780	5.2
Median square footage	1,700	—	Wood	2,442	1.9

— = Not applicable. (1) Percentages based on 92,023 single detached homes and trailers. (2) Percentages based on 96,386 total single-unit structures. (3) Percentages based on 131,368 homes with heat.

Fair Market Rents for Select Metropolitan Areas, 2014

Source: *Fair Market Rents 2014*, U.S. Dept. of Housing and Urban Development

Metropolitan area	Number of bedrooms 0	1	2	3	4	Metropolitan area	Number of bedrooms 0	1	2	3	4
Atlanta, GA	$708	$773	$916	$1,213	$1474	Minneapolis-St. Paul, MN-WI	$641	$796	$996	$1,403	$1,656
Austin, TX	681	834	1,050	1,421	1,723	Nashville-Davidson, TN	616	710	850	1,130	1,213
Baltimore-Towson, MD	833	985	1,232	1,574	1,713	New Orleans-Metairie, LA	648	767	950	1,192	1,443
Birmingham-Hoover, AL	545	652	773	1,015	1,142	New York, NY	1,196	1,249	1,481	1,904	2,134
Boston-Cambridge-Quincy, MA-NH	1,071	1,196	1,494	1,861	2,023	Oklahoma City, OK	503	584	748	1,024	1,229
Buffalo-Niagara Falls, NY	581	617	768	982	1,111	Orlando-Kissimmee-Sanford, FL	707	836	997	1,330	1,608
Charlotte-Gastonia-Rock Hill, NC-SC	636	701	831	1,120	1,389	Philadelphia-Camden-Wilmington, PA-NJ-DE-MD	814	959	1,156	1,440	1,546
Chicago-Joliet-Naperville, IL	812	922	1,093	1,393	1,624	Phoenix-Mesa-Glendale, AZ	582	735	908	1,338	1,563
Cincinnati-Middleton, OH-KY-IN	463	579	769	1,065	1,173	Pittsburgh, PA	549	630	786	987	1,050
Cleveland-Elyria-Mentor, OH	502	603	764	1,023	1,057	Portland-Vancouver, OR-WA	682	793	944	1,391	1,672
Columbus, OH	501	624	811	1,046	1,209	Providence-Fall River, RI-MA	686	773	944	1,176	1,407
Dallas, TX	607	728	921	1,229	1,484	Richmond, VA	797	838	993	1,306	1,582
Denver-Aurora-Broomfield, CO	723	893	1,156	1,696	1,967	Riverside-San Bernardino-Ontario, CA	788	908	1,153	1,629	1,987
Detroit-Warren-Livonia, MI	510	648	846	1,128	1,233	Sacramento-Arden-Arcade-Roseville, CA	676	806	1,012	1,491	1,792
Hartford, CT	732	918	1,144	1,425	1,655	St. Louis, MO-IL	533	633	816	1,063	1,206
Honolulu, HI	1,260	1,374	1,810	2,667	3,061	Salt Lake City, UT	606	727	901	1,285	1,513
Houston-Baytown-Sugar Land, TX	599	721	890	1,215	1,502	San Antonio, TX	551	695	872	1,137	1,247
Indianapolis, IN	516	637	792	1,056	1,232	San Diego-Carlsbad-San Marcos, CA	964	1,060	1,390	2,021	2,462
Jacksonville, FL	628	775	931	1,228	1,502	San Francisco, CA	1,256	1,635	2,062	2,801	3,386
Kansas City, MO-KS	559	719	891	1,221	1,360	San Jose-Santa Clara, CA	1,213	1,419	1,809	2,551	2,892
Las Vegas-Paradise, NV	630	787	969	1,428	1,695	San Juan-Guaynabo, PR	464	502	601	810	975
Los Angeles-Long Beach, CA	913	1,103	1,424	1,926	2,145	Seattle-Bellevue, WA	811	959	1,180	1,739	2,090
Louisville, KY-IN	507	592	737	1,020	1,154	Tampa-St. Petersburg, FL	610	765	959	1,280	1,533
Memphis, TN-MS-AR	614	702	832	1,137	1,267	Washington-Arlington-Alexandria, DC-VA-MD	1,167	1,230	1,458	1,951	2,451
Miami-Miami Beach, FL	745	907	1,162	1,594	1,863						
Milwaukee, WI	579	713	896	1,143	1,236						

Note: Figures are projections made in the previous fiscal year. Metropolitan area may include individual cities not shown.

TRADE

U.S. Trade With Selected Countries and Major Areas, 2013

Source: U.S. Census Bureau, U.S. Bureau of Economic Analysis, U.S. Dept. of Commerce
(in millions of dollars; top 25 countries as ranked by amount of total trade with U.S.)

Rank	Country	Total trade with U.S.	U.S. exports to	Rank[1]	U.S. imports from	Rank[1]	U.S. trade balance with	Rank[2]
1.	Canada	$634,162.4	$301,609.6	1	$332,552.8	2	−30,943.2	6
2.	China[3]	562,184.1	121,736.4	3	440,447.7	1	−318,711.3	1
3.	Mexico	506,607.9	226,079.1	2	280,528.8	3	−54,449.7	4
4.	Japan	203,779.1	65,205.8	4	138,573.3	4	−73,367.5	2
5.	Germany	161,706.1	47,361.6	5	114,344.5	5	−66,982.9	3
6.	South Korea	104,101.1	41,714.7	10	62,386.4	6	−20,671.6	9
7.	United Kingdom	100,170.3	47,353.2	6	52,817.1	7	−5,463.9	24
8.	France	77,452.6	31,744.8	12	45,707.8	9	−13,963.0	16
9.	Brazil	71,752.3	44,118.5	7	27,633.8	16	16,484.7	230
10.	Saudi Arabia	70,763.2	18,956.5	19	51,806.7	8	−32,850.2	5
11.	India	63,687.6	21,842.3	18	41,845.3	10	−20,003.0	10
12.	Taiwan	63,412.1	25,472.2	16	37,939.9	12	−12,467.7	17
13.	Netherlands	61,802.2	42,571.6	8	19,230.6	23	23,341.0	233
14.	Italy	55,446.5	16,754.9	22	38,691.6	11	−21,936.8	8
15.	Switzerland	55,048.9	26,772.8	14	28,276.1	15	−1,503.2	44
16.	Belgium	50,952.5	31,940.5	11	19,012.0	24	12,928.5	229
17.	Singapore	48,514.8	30,671.8	13	17,843.0	26	12,828.9	228
18.	Hong Kong	48,026.3	42,341.9	9	5,684.4	44	36,657.5	234
19.	Venezuela	45,200.9	13,203.5	24	31,997.4	13	−18,793.8	12
20.	Malaysia	40,296.7	13,007.4	25	27,289.3	17	−14,281.9	15
21.	Colombia	40,017.3	18,391.7	20	21,625.6	22	−3,234.0	32
22.	Russia	38,222.7	11,136.5	28	27,086.2	18	−15,949.8	13
23.	Ireland	38,135.8	6,639.6	39	31,496.2	14	−24,856.6	7
24.	Thailand	37,970.3	11,797.1	27	26,173.2	19	−14,376.1	14
25.	Israel	36,555.8	13,747.1	23	22,808.7	21	−9,061.6	21

Major area/group

Country	Total trade with U.S.	U.S. exports to	U.S. imports from	U.S. trade balance with
North America	$1,140,770.3	$527,688.7	$613,081.6	−$85,392.9
Europe	787,390.5	326,726.8	460,663.7	−133,937.0
Euro Area	500,136.3	198,078.0	302,058.3	−103,980.3
EU	649,741.9	262,150.6	387,591.3	−125,440.7
Africa	85,236.3	35,175.3	50,061.0	−14,885.7
OECD	2,215,535.4	966,131.0	1,249,404.4	−283,273.3
Pacific Rim Countries	1,159,394.4	388,084.8	771,309.6	−383,224.8
Asia-Near East	180,476.7	73,284.4	107,192.3	−33,907.9
Asia-South	79,414.0	25,950.2	53,463.8	−27,513.7
Asia-NICs	264,054.2	140,200.6	123,853.6	16,347.0
ASEAN	205,942.8	78,985.7	126,957.1	−47,971.4
APEC	2,451,727.6	971,008.9	1,480,718.7	−509,709.8
South/Central America	342,911.0	184,398.5	158,512.5	25,886.0
Twenty Latin American Republics	823,761.4	393,959.0	429,802.4	−35,843.4
CAFTA-DR	59,773.9	29,643.9	30,130.0	−486.1
Central American Common Market	48,355.3	22,485.0	25,870.3	−3,385.3
Latin American Free Trade Area	750,542.2	352,165.1	398,377.1	−46,212.1
NATO Allies	1,239,950.0	563,136.3	676,813.7	−113,677.4
OPEC	237,369.2	84,679.3	152,689.9	−68,010.6
WORLD TOTAL	**$3,847,914.2**	**$1,579,592.9**	**$2,268,321.3**	**−$688,728.4**

Note: Figures shown are on Census Bureau basis and are not seasonally adjusted. Figures may not equal totals due to rounding. Country grouping data reflect groups at the time of reporting. (1) Rank shown is for column to the left. Ranking includes territories as well as nations. (2) Rank by size of U.S. trade deficit. Ranking includes territories as well as nations. (3) Not incl. Hong Kong, Macao, and Taiwan. **Definitions of major areas/groups used in table, as provided by source: North America**—Canada, Mexico. **Europe**—Albania, Andorra, Armenia, Austria, Azerbaijan, Belarus, Belgium, Bosnia-Herzegovina, Bulgaria, Croatia, Cyprus, Czech Republic, Denmark, Estonia, Faroe Isls., Finland, France, Georgia, Germany, Gibraltar, Greece, Hungary, Iceland, Ireland, Italy, Kazakhstan, Kosovo, Kyrgyzstan, Latvia, Liechtenstein, Lithuania, Luxembourg, Macedonia, Malta, Moldova, Monaco, Montenegro, Netherlands, Norway, Poland, Portugal, Romania, Russia, San Marino, Serbia, Slovakia, Slovenia, Spain, Svalbard-Jan Mayen Isl., Sweden, Switzerland, Tajikistan, Turkey, Turkmenistan, Ukraine, United Kingdom, Uzbekistan, Vatican City. **Euro Area**—Austria, Belgium, Cyprus, Estonia, Finland, France, Germany, Greece, Ireland, Italy, Latvia, Luxembourg, Malta, Netherlands, Portugal, Slovakia, Slovenia, Spain. **EU (European Union)**—Euro Area plus Bulgaria, Croatia, Czech Republic, Denmark, Hungary, Lithuania, Poland, Romania, Sweden, United Kingdom. **Africa**—Algeria, Angola, Benin, Botswana, British Indian Ocean Territories, Burkina Faso, Burundi, Cabo Verde, Cameroon, Central African Republic, Chad, Comoros, Congo (Brazzaville), Congo (Kinshasa), Djibouti, Egypt, Equatorial Guinea, Eritrea, Ethiopia, French Southern and Antarctic Lands, Gabon, Gambia, Ghana, Guinea, Guinea-Bissau, Ivory Coast, Kenya, Lesotho, Liberia, Libya, Madagascar, Malawi, Mali, Mauritania, Mauritius, Mayotte, Morocco, Mozambique, Namibia, Niger, Nigeria, Réunion, Rwanda, St. Helena, São Tomé and Príncipe, Senegal, Seychelles, Sierra Leone, Somalia, South Africa, South Sudan, Sudan, Swaziland, Tanzania, Togo, Tunisia, Uganda, Western Sahara, Zambia, Zimbabwe. **OECD (Org. for Economic Cooperation and Development)**—Australia, Austria, Belgium, Canada, Chile, Czech Republic, Denmark, Estonia, Finland, France, Germany, Greece, Hungary, Iceland, Ireland, Israel, Italy, Japan, Korea (South), Luxembourg, Mexico, Netherlands, New Zealand, Norway, Poland, Portugal, Slovakia, Slovenia, Spain, Sweden, Switzerland, Turkey, United Kingdom, U.S. **Pacific Rim Countries**—Australia, Brunei, China, Hong Kong, Indonesia, Japan, Korea (South), Macao, Malaysia, New Zealand, Papua New Guinea, Philippines, Singapore, Taiwan. **Asia-Near East**—Bahrain, Gaza Strip Administered by Israel, Iran, Iraq, Israel, Jordan, Kuwait, Lebanon, Oman, Qatar, Saudi Arabia, Syria, United Arab Emirates, West Bank Administered by Israel, Yemen. **Asia-South**—Afghanistan, Bangladesh, India, Nepal, Pakistan, Sri Lanka. **Asia-NICs (Newly Industrialized Countries)**—Hong Kong, Korea (South), Singapore, Taiwan. **ASEAN (Assn. of South East Asia Nations)**—Brunei, Cambodia, Indonesia, Laos, Malaysia, Myanmar, Philippines, Singapore, Thailand, Vietnam. **APEC (Asia-Pacific Economic Cooperation)**—Australia, Brunei, Canada, Chile, China, Hong Kong, Indonesia, Japan, Korea (South), Malaysia, Mexico, New Zealand, Papua New Guinea, Peru, Philippines, Russia, Singapore, Taiwan, Thailand, U.S., Vietnam. **South/Central America**—Anguilla, Antigua and Barbuda, Argentina, Aruba, Bahamas, Barbados, Belize, Bermuda, Bolivia, Brazil, British Virgin Isls., Cayman Isls., Chile, Colombia, Costa Rica, Curaçao, Cuba, Dominica, Dominican Republic, Ecuador, El Salvador, Falkland Isls., French Guiana, Grenada, Guadeloupe, Guatemala, Guyana, Haiti, Honduras, Jamaica, Martinique, Montserrat, Netherlands Antilles, Nicaragua, Panama, Paraguay, Peru, Sint Marten, St. Kitts and Nevis, St. Lucia, St. Vincent and the Grenadines, Suriname, Trinidad and Tobago, Turks and Caicos Isls., Uruguay, Venezuela. **Twenty Latin American Republics**—Argentina, Bolivia, Brazil, Chile, Colombia, Costa Rica, Cuba, Dominican Republic, Ecuador, El Salvador, Guatemala, Haiti, Honduras, Mexico, Nicaragua, Panama, Paraguay, Peru, Uruguay, Venezuela. **CAFTA-DR (Dominican Republic-Central America United States Free Trade Agreement)**—Costa Rica, Dominican Republic, El Salvador, Guatemala, Honduras, Nicaragua. **Central American Common Market**—Costa Rica, El Salvador, Guatemala, Honduras, Nicaragua. **Latin American Free Trade Area**—Argentina, Bolivia, Brazil, Chile, Colombia, Ecuador, Mexico, Paraguay, Peru, Uruguay, Venezuela. **NATO (North Atlantic Treaty Org.) Allies**—Belgium, Bulgaria, Canada, Czech Republic, Denmark, Estonia, France, Germany, Greece, Hungary, Iceland, Italy, Latvia, Lithuania, Luxembourg, Netherlands, Norway, Poland, Portugal, Romania, Slovakia, Slovenia, Spain, Turkey, United Kingdom. **OPEC (Org. of Petroleum Exporting Countries)**—Algeria, Angola, Ecuador, Iran, Iraq, Kuwait, Libya, Nigeria, Qatar, Saudi Arabia, United Arab Emirates, Venezuela.

U.S. Exports and Imports by Principal Commodities, 2013

Source: U.S. Census Bureau, U.S. Bureau of Economic Analysis, U.S. Dept. of Commerce

(in millions of dollars)

Item[1]	Exports	Imports	Item	Exports	Imports
Total[1]	$1,579,593	$2,268,321	Essential oil and reinoids	$14,854	$12,480
Manufactured goods	1,183,359	1,830,128	Fertilizers	4,083	7,959
Agricultural commodities	144,363	104,373	Plastics in primary forms	34,530	14,000
			Plastics in nonprimary forms	12,094	8,944
Food and live animals	103,214	88,239	Chemical materials and products	30,610	14,976
Live animals other than fish	968	2,634	Manufactured goods by material	115,839	234,806
Meat and preparations	17,911	6,508	Leather and leather manufactures	1,346	1,280
Dairy products and birds	5,899	1,768	Rubber manufactures	9,938	21,075
Fish and preparations	5,248	17,865	Cork and wood manufactures	2,182	9,058
Cereals and preparations	24,277	9,690	Paper and paperboard	16,139	15,978
Vegetables and fruits	21,687	26,413	Textile yarn, fabrics	12,857	25,814
Sugar, preparations, and honey	2,429	4,307	Nonmetallic mineral manufactures	12,550	41,908
Coffee, tea, cocoa, and spices	3,093	11,798	Iron and steel	18,444	36,626
Feeding stuff for animals	13,164	2,883	Nonferrous metals	15,718	38,270
Miscellaneous edible products	8,537	4,374	Manufactures of metals	26,665	44,797
Beverages and tobacco	6,452	20,800	Machinery and transport		
Beverages	4,829	18,626	equipment	513,919	886,782
Tobacco and manufactures	1,623	2,175	Power generating machinery	38,417	60,649
Crude materials except fuels	85,209	34,855	Specialized industrial machinery	49,203	42,273
Hides, skins, and furskins (raw)	3,136	288	Metalworking machinery	6,046	9,920
Oil seeds and oleaginuos fruits	24,108	1,645	General industrial machinery	66,629	83,464
Crude rubber	3,257	4,248	Office machinery	21,553	117,460
Cork and wood	6,524	6,402	Telecommunications equipment	23,652	146,199
Pulp and waste paper	8,665	3,619	Electrical machinery	78,499	149,917
Textile fibers including waste	8,228	1,294	Road vehicles	118,658	244,451
Crude fertilizers	2,478	2,598	Transport equipment	111,283	32,447
Metalliferous ores and metal scrap	25,814	8,291	Miscellaneous manufactured		
Crude animal and vegetable			articles	121,692	333,247
materials	3,000	6,469	Prefabricated buildings	3,141	10,402
Mineral fuels and lubricants	147,693	379,770	Furniture	6,129	38,002
Coal, coke, and briquettes	11,455	1,019	Travel goods	583	10,585
Petroleum products and preparations	123,368	363,152	Apparel and clothing accessories	3,425	87,924
Gas, natural, and manufactured	12,514	13,169	Footwear	789	24,810
Electric current	356	2,429	Scientific and controlling equipment	50,139	47,452
Animal and vegetable oils	3,179	5,669	Photographic equipment	6,556	13,511
Animal oil and fat	765	260	Miscellaneous manufactured articles	50,930	100,560
Fixed vegetable fats and oil (crude)	1,987	5,255	Miscellaneous commodities	75,419	88,676
Animal or vegetable fats, processed	428	153	Special transactions	7,191	56,781
Chemicals and related products	198,816	195,477	Coin, including gold coin	397	2,459
Organic chemicals	42,503	52,314	Coin, other than gold	47	35
Inorganic chemicals	11,205	14,194	Gold, nonmonetary	33,194	15,958
Dyeing, tanning, and coloring			Low value estimate	34,588	13,443
materials	7,550	3,813	Re-exports	208,161	NA
Medicinal and pharmaceutical			Agricultural commodities	4,316	NA
products	41,386	66,799	Manufactured goods	199,297	NA

NA = Not available. **Note:** Commodity group totals include products not listed here. Figures may not equal totals due to rounding. (1) Total on Census Bureau basis; includes re-exports.

Trends in U.S. Foreign Trade, 1790-2013

Source: U.S. Census Bureau, U.S. Bureau of Economic Analysis, U.S. Dept. of Commerce

In 1790, U.S. exports and imports combined came to $43 mil, and there was a $3 mil trade deficit. By 2011, the deficit had ballooned to more than half a trillion dollars. In 2012, the trade deficit declined for the first time since 2009.

(in millions of dollars)

Year	Exports	Imports	Trade balance	Year	Exports	Imports	Trade balance	Year	Exports	Imports	Trade balance
1790	$20	$23	–$3	1890	$858	$789	$69	1990	$535,233	$616,097	–$80,864
1795	48	70	–22	1895	808	732	76	1995	794,387	890,771	–96,384
1800	71	91	–20	1900	1,394	850	545	1996	851,602	955,667	–104,065
1805	96	121	–25	1905	1,519	1,118	401	1997	934,453	1,042,726	–108,273
1810	67	85	–19	1910	1,745	1,557	188	1998	933,174	1,099,314	–166,140
1815	53	113	–60	1915	2,769	1,674	1,094	1999	967,008	1,230,764	–263,755
1820	70	74	–5	1920	8,228	5,278	2,950	2000	1,072,782	1,450,119	–377,337
1825	91	90	1	1925	4,910	4,227	683	2001	1,007,725	1,370,065	–362,339
1830	72	63	9	1930	3,843	3,061	782	2002	980,879	1,399,044	–418,165
1835	115	137	–22	1935	2,283	2,047	235	2003	1,023,937	1,514,482	–490,545
1840	124	98	25	1940	4,021	2,625	1,396	2004	1,163,724	1,768,622	–604,897
1845	106	113	–7	1945	9,806	4,159	5,646	2005	1,288,257	1,996,171	–707,914
1850	144	174	–29	1950	9,997	8,954	1,043	2006	1,460,792	2,213,191	–752,399
1855	219	258	–39	1955	14,298	11,566	2,732	2007	1,652,859	2,351,925	–699,065
1860	334	354	–20	1960	25,940	22,432	3,508	2008	1,840,332	2,542,634	–702,302
1865	166	239	–73	1965	35,285	30,621	4,664	2009	1,578,187	1,961,844	–383,657
1870	393	436	–43	1970	56,640	54,386	2,254	2010	1,844,468	2,343,847	–499,379
1875	513	533	–20	1975	132,585	120,181	12,404	2011	2,112,825	2,669,663	–556,838
1880	836	668	168	1980	271,834	291,241	–19,407	2012	2,210,585	2,745,240	–534,656
1885	742	578	165	1985	289,070	410,950	–121,880	2013	2,271,385	3,746,249	–474,864

Note: Figures shown using balance of payments basis.

World Trade Organization (WTO)

The World Trade Organization is an international body that seeks to promote free trade by eliminating barriers to trade. Founded in 1995, the WTO had grown to 160 member countries as of June 26, 2014, with 24 others, including Belarus and Iran, granted observer status. International intergovernmental organizations, such as the International Monetary Fund and the World Bank, may also be granted observer status. With the exception of Vatican City, observers must start accession negotiations within five years of becoming observers.

U.S. Trade in Goods and Services, 2013

Source: U.S. Census Bureau, U.S. Bureau of Economic Analysis, U.S. Dept. of Commerce
(in millions of dollars; top five countries as ranked by amount of total trade with U.S.)

Country and category	Food and live animals	Beverages and tobacco	Crude materials, except fuels	Mineral fuels, lubricants	Chemicals	Manu-factured goods	Machinery and transport equip-ment	Misc. manufac-tured	Commo-dities and transac-tions[1]	Total
Canada										
U.S. exports to	$21,931	$1,797	$7,171	$24,574	$32,945	$38,799	$130,909	$30,663	$10,885	$300,245
U.S. imports fr.	−20,795	−982	−12,890	−112,898	−27,753	−40,032	−90,867	−12,829	−17,367	−338,233
Trade balance	1,136	815	−5,719	−88,324	5,192	1,233	40,042	17,834	−6,482	−37,988
China										
U.S. exports to	8,819	294	32,684	2,745	13,449	5,994	47,558	8,771	1,530	122,016
U.S. imports fr.	−6,152	−69	−2,196	−385	−15,576	−51,697	−233,791	−145,439	−4,730	−460,090
Trade balance	2,667	225	30,488	2,360	−2,127	−45,703	−186,233	−136,668	−3,200	−338,074
Mexico										
U.S. exports to	13,925	583	7,661	23,023	26,684	29,513	100,994	16,053	6,965	226,153
U.S. imports fr.	−16,098	−3,385	−1,598	−35,152	−5,562	−19,308	−161,769	−28,822	−11,272	−283,059
Trade balance	−2,173	−2,802	6,063	−12,129	21,122	10,205	−60,775	−12,769	−4,307	−56,906
Japan										
U.S. exports to	11,237	635	3,988	2,602	11,174	3,684	20,397	10,319	1,055	65,145
U.S. imports fr.	−632	−87	−600	−705	−9,509	−10,775	−105,814	−10,445	−3,536	−142,149
Trade balance	10,605	548	3,388	1,897	1,665	−7,091	−85,417	−126	−2,481	−77,004
Germany										
U.S. exports to	1,248	341	2,261	862	7,205	3,356	22,925	6,801	2,361	47,442
U.S. imports fr.	1,203	486	953	445	21,141	10,029	68,237	10,651	3,761	116,925
Trade balance	45	−145	1,308	417	−13,936	−6,673	−45,312	−3,850	−1,400	−69,483

Note: Figures for exports are "free alongside ship" values; figures for imports are "cost, insurance, and freight" values. Neither is directly comparable with the Census Bureau basis shown in other tables in this section. Trade balance is with U.S. Total includes categories not shown here. (1) Not classified elsewhere.

Foreign Exchange Rates, 1970-2013

Source: Federal Reserve Board

One U.S. dollar was worth the following amounts in each country's national currency; exchange rates are annual averages.

Year	Australia (dollar)	Austria (schilling; euro)	Belgium (franc; euro)	Canada (dollar)	China (yuan)	Denmark (krone)	France (franc; euro)	Germany[1] (deutsche mark; euro)	Greece (drachma; euro)
1970	0.8980	25.8800	49.6800	1.0103	NA	7.4890	5.5200	3.6480	30.0000
1980	0.8772	12.9450	29.2370	1.1693	NA	5.6340	4.2250	1.8175	42.6200
1990	1.2799	11.3700	33.4180	1.1668	NA	6.1890	5.4453	1.6157	158.5100
1995	1.3486	10.0810	29.4800	1.3724	8.3700	5.6020	4.9915	1.4331	231.6600
2000	1.7197	1.0832	1.0832	1.4855	8.2784	8.0950	1.0832	1.0832	365.9200
2005	1.3111	0.8033	0.8033	1.2115	8.1936	5.9953	0.8033	0.8033	0.8033
2008	1.1714	0.6791	0.6791	1.0660	6.9477	5.0885	0.6791	0.6791	0.6791
2009	1.2615	0.7176	0.7176	1.1412	6.8307	5.3574	0.7176	0.7176	0.7176
2010	1.0870	0.7541	0.7541	1.0298	6.7696	5.6266	0.7541	0.7541	0.7541
2011	0.9679	0.7178	0.7178	0.9887	6.4630	5.3535	0.7178	0.7178	0.7178
2012	0.9653	0.7777	0.7777	0.9995	6.3093	5.7922	0.7777	0.7777	0.7777
2013	1.0327	0.7530	0.7530	1.0300	6.1478	5.6170	0.7530	0.7530	0.7530

Year	Hong Kong (dollar)	India (rupee)	Ireland (pound; euro)	Italy (lira; euro)	Japan (yen)	Malaysia (ringgit)	Mexico (new peso)	Netherlands (guilder; euro)	Norway (krone)
1970	NA	7.576	2.3959	623.0000	357.60	3.0900	NA	3.5970	7.1400
1980	NA	7.887	2.0577	856.0000	226.63	2.1767	1.9875	1.9875	4.9381
1990	NA	17.504	1.6585	1,198.0000	144.79	2.7049	2.812	1.8209	6.2597
1995	7.7357	32.427	1.6038	1,628.9000	94.06	2.5044	6.419	1.6057	6.3352
2000	7.7925	45.000	1.0832	1.0832	107.80	3.8000	9.459	1.0832	8.8131
2005	7.7775	44.000	0.8033	0.8033	110.11	3.7869	10.894	0.8033	6.4412
2008	7.7862	43.390	0.6791	0.6791	103.39	3.3292	11.143	0.6791	5.6365
2009	7.7514	48.330	0.7176	0.7176	93.68	3.5231	13.498	0.7176	6.2908
2010	7.7687	45.65	0.7541	0.7541	87.78	3.2175	12.623	0.7541	6.0451
2011	7.7841	46.58	0.7178	0.7178	79.70	3.0564	12.427	0.7178	5.6022
2012	7.7569	53.37	0.7777	0.7777	79.82	3.0862	13.154	0.7777	5.8181
2013	7.7565	58.51	0.7530	0.7530	97.60	3.1488	12.758	0.7530	5.8772

Year	Portugal (escudo; euro)	Singapore (dollar)	South Korea (won)	Spain (peseta; euro)	Sweden (krona)	Switzerland (franc)	Taiwan (dollar)	Thailand (baht)	UK (pound)
1970	28.7500	3.0800	310.57	69.7200	5.1700	4.3160	NA	21.000	0.4174
1980	50.0800	2.1412	607.43	71.7600	4.2309	1.6772	NA	20.476	0.4302
1990	142.5500	1.8125	707.76	101.9300	5.9188	1.3892	NA	25.585	0.5603
1995	151.1100	1.4174	771.27	124.6900	7.1333	1.1825	26.495	24.915	0.6335
2000	1.0832	1.7250	1,130.90	1.0832	9.1735	1.6904	31.260	40.210	0.6598
2005	0.8033	1.6639	1,023.75	0.8033	7.4710	1.2459	32.131	40.252	0.5493
2008	0.6791	1.4140	1,098.71	0.6791	6.5846	1.0816	31.521	32.962	0.5392
2009	0.7176	1.4543	1,274.63	0.7176	7.6539	1.0860	33.020	34.310	0.6385
2010	0.7541	1.3629	1,155.74	0.7541	7.2053	1.0432	31.498	31.700	0.6472
2011	0.7178	1.2565	1,106.94	0.7178	6.4878	0.8862	29.382	30.462	0.6233
2012	0.7777	1.2492	1,126.16	0.7777	6.7721	0.9377	29.558	31.055	0.6308
2013	0.7530	1.2511	1,094.67	0.7530	6.5124	0.9269	29.680	30.696	0.6393

NA = Not available. **Note:** The euro, the European Union's single currency, replaced the national currencies in the EU nations shown above. Since 1999 (or 2001 in the case of Greece), the euro has been fixed at the following conversion rates: 13.7603 Austrian schillings, 40.3399 Belgian francs, 6.55957 French francs, 1.95583 German marks, 340.750 Greek drachmas, 0.787564 Irish pounds, 1,936.27 Italian lire, 2.20371 Netherlands guilders, 200.482 Portuguese escudos, and 166.386 Spanish pesetas. (1) West Germany before 1991.

Top U.S. Trading Partners, 1995-2013

Source: U.S. Census Bureau, U.S. Dept. of Commerce
(in millions of dollars; top five trade partners as ranked by amount of total trade with U.S. in 2013)

Country/category	1995	2000	2005	2009	2010	2011	2012	2013
Canada								
U.S. exports	$127,226.0	$178,940.9	$211,898.7	$204,658.0	$249,256.5	$281,291.5	$292,539.7	$300,346.9
U.S. imports from	144,369.9	230,838.3	290,384.3	226,248.4	277,636.7	315,366.5	323,936.5	332,077.9
Trade balance..........	−17,143.9	−51,897.4	−78,485.6	−21,590.5	−28,380.3	−34,075.0	−31,396.8	−31,731.0
China								
U.S. exports to	11,753.7	16,185.2	41,192.0	69,496.7	91,911.1	103,986.5	110,483.6	122,016.3
U.S. imports from	45,543.2	100,018.2	243,470.1	296,373.9	364,952.6	399,378.9	425,578.9	440,433.5
Trade balance..........	−33,789.5	−83,833.0	−202,278.1	−226,877.2	−273,041.6	−295,392.4	−315,095.3	−318,417.2
Mexico								
U.S. exports to	46,292.1	111,349.0	120,247.6	128,892.1	163,664.6	198,068.6	215,931.2	226,152.9
U.S. imports from	62,100.4	135,926.3	170,108.6	176,654.4	229,985.6	262,873.9	277,569.8	280,455.5
Trade balance..........	−15,808.3	−24,577.3	−49,861.0	−47,762.2	−66,321.0	−64,805.3	−61,638.6	−54,302.6
Japan								
U.S. exports to	64,342.7	64,924.4	54,680.6	51,134.2	60,471.9	65,686.4	69,955.0	65,144.8
U.S. imports from	123,479.4	146,479.4	138,003.7	95,803.7	120,552.1	128,927.9	146,392.2	138,533.5
Trade balance..........	−59,136.6	−81,555.0	−83,323.1	−44,669.5	−60,080.3	−63,241.5	−76,437.2	−73,388.7
Germany								
U.S. exports to	22,394.3	29,448.4	34,183.7	43,306.3	48,155.3	49,146.8	48,797.1	47,442.2
U.S. imports from	36,843.9	58,512.9	84,750.9	71,498.2	82,450.4	98,687.9	108,708.1	114,644.4
Trade balance..........	−14,449.6	−29,064.5	−50,567.2	−28,191.9	−34,295.1	−49,541.1	−59,911.0	−67,202.2

Note: Trade balance is with U.S. Figures shown are on Census Bureau basis.

Busiest U.S. Ports, 2012

Source: U.S. Army Corps of Engineers, Dept. of the Army, U.S. Dept. of Defense
(figures in tons; ranked by total tonnage handled)

Rank	Port	Total	Domestic	Foreign	Imports	Exports
1.	South Louisiana, LA	252,069,033	132,719,721	119,349,312	35,133,596	84,215,716
2.	Houston, TX	238,185,582	75,742,260	162,443,322	83,816,269	78,627,053
3.	New York, NY and NJ	132,039,959	45,074,986	86,964,973	62,799,784	24,165,189
4.	New Orleans, LA	79,342,141	42,856,439	36,485,702	17,271,856	19,213,846
5.	Beaumont, TX.................	78,515,010	28,830,962	49,684,048	40,615,037	9,069,011
6.	Long Beach, CA	77,385,055	11,585,070	65,799,985	41,215,516	24,584,469
7.	Corpus Christi, TX	69,001,357	23,300,339	45,701,018	30,878,967	14,822,051
8.	Los Angeles, CA..............	61,819,495	6,950,011	54,869,484	32,894,905	21,974,579
9.	Baton Rouge, LA	59,992,818	36,669,020	23,323,798	15,182,279	8,141,519
10.	Plaquemines, LA	58,280,348	33,638,082	24,642,266	1,668,182	22,974,084
11.	Texas City, TX................	56,721,627	20,761,770	35,959,857	27,660,191	8,299,666
12.	Mobile, AL....................	54,887,669	25,067,682	29,819,987	13,308,382	16,511,605
13.	Lake Charles, LA	54,382,331	23,117,141	31,265,190	23,421,496	7,843,694
14.	Huntington-Tristate, WV	52,911,517	52,911,517	0	0	0
15.	Norfolk Harbor, VA	46,219,206	5,769,190	40,450,016	8,899,896	31,550,120
16.	Baltimore, MD.................	42,102,106	5,278,153	36,823,953	12,830,987	23,992,966
17.	Pittsburgh, PA................	35,154,800	35,154,800	0	0	0
18.	St. Louis, MO and IL...........	34,985,453	34,985,453	0	0	0
19.	Duluth-Superior, MN and WI......	34,672,105	26,897,959	7,774,146	423,347	7,350,799
20.	Savannah, GA	34,132,066	2,206,984	31,925,082	15,440,141	16,484,941
21.	Pascagoula, MS	33,784,810	8,969,915	24,814,895	17,339,620	7,475,275
22.	Tampa, FL...................	31,650,258	21,583,215	10,067,043	5,310,235	4,756,808
23.	Port Arthur, TX	30,618,123	10,745,809	19,872,314	10,694,732	9,177,582
24.	Newport News, VA	30,508,064	1,259,341	29,248,723	188,444	29,060,279
25.	Philadelphia, PA	28,539,476	11,998,639	16,540,837	15,848,753	692,084
26.	Valdez, AK	27,899,959	27,893,332	6,627	6,627	0
27.	Portland, OR.................	25,549,283	8,303,855	17,245,428	3,372,942	13,872,486
28.	Tacoma, WA	24,918,310	5,883,802	19,034,508	6,602,527	12,431,981
29.	Seattle, WA..................	23,748,337	5,323,174	18,425,163	8,287,335	10,137,828
30.	Richmond, CA	22,555,921	9,903,050	12,652,871	9,805,091	2,847,780
31.	Freeport, TX.................	22,084,551	5,607,875	16,476,676	14,374,246	2,102,430
32.	Port Everglades, FL	21,104,883	10,044,265	11,060,618	7,315,739	3,744,879
33.	Charleston, SC	19,105,017	2,068,285	17,036,732	10,600,174	6,436,558
34.	Oakland, CA.................	18,728,247	2,332,289	16,395,958	6,275,286	10,120,672
35.	Paulsboro, NJ	17,372,629	5,825,136	11,547,493	10,250,657	1,296,836
36.	Chicago, IL..................	17,090,171	15,622,293	1,467,878	1,351,976	115,902
37.	Boston, MA..................	16,315,050	4,719,300	11,595,750	10,136,281	1,459,469
38.	Two Harbors, MN	16,210,087	15,416,006	794,081	0	794,081
39.	Jacksonville, FL	15,415,144	6,215,925	9,199,219	6,966,270	2,232,949
40.	Honolulu, HI	14,320,504	13,352,311	968,193	820,821	147,372
41.	Memphis, TN	13,564,063	13,564,063	0	0	0
42.	Indiana Harbor, IN	13,164,061	12,903,020	261,041	214,191	46,850
43.	Detroit, MI...................	12,929,325	10,339,481	2,589,844	2,494,492	95,352
44.	Portland, ME.................	12,821,501	1,003,924	11,817,577	11,789,239	28,338
45.	Longview, WA................	12,192,962	1,713,902	10,479,060	866,088	9,612,972
46.	Anacortes, WA...............	11,743,390	7,795,133	3,948,257	1,870,669	2,077,588
47.	Galveston, TX................	11,618,368	6,851,348	4,767,020	1,872,763	2,894,257
48.	Matagorda, TX	11,589,123	3,436,744	8,152,379	5,800,442	2,351,937
49.	Kalama, WA	11,523,061	1,059,572	10,463,489	565,840	9,897,649
50.	Cleveland, OH	11,313,415	9,924,890	1,388,525	1,371,686	16,839

U.S. Railroad Freight and Miles, 1890-2012

Source: Assn. of Amer. Railroads; Bureau of Transportation Statistics, Research and Innovative Tech. Admin., U.S. Dept. of Transportation
(freight figures in billion ton-miles)

Year	Class I freight[1]	All freight	Miles[2]	Year	Class I freight[1]	All freight	Miles[2]	Year	Class I freight[1]	All freight	Miles[2]
1890 ...	NA	76	163,597	1960 ...	572	575	217,552	2007 ...	1,771	1,820	140,695
1900 ...	NA	142	193,346	1970 ...	765	771	205,782	2008 ...	1,777	1,730	139,326
1910 ...	NA	255	240,293	1980 ...	919	932	178,056	2009 ...	1,532	1,582	139,118
1920 ...	410	414	252,845	1990 ...	1,034	1,064	145,979	2010 ...	1,691	NA	138,623
1930 ...	383	386	249,052	2000 ...	1,466	1,546	144,473	2011 ...	1,729	NA	138,565
1940 ...	373	375	233,670	2005 ...	1,696	1,733	140,810	2012 ...	1,713	NA	138,524
1950 ...	589	592	223,779	2006 ...	1,772	1,856	140,490				

NA = Not available. **Note:** A ton-mile equals one ton of freight transported one statute mile. (1) Largest class of freight railroad companies, determined by annual operating revenue. (2) Aggregate length of operating roadway in U.S., excluding yard tracks, sidings, and parallel tracks.

Merchant Fleets of the World, 2013

Source: Maritime Administration, U.S. Dept. of Transportation
(oceangoing, self-propelled, privately-owned cargo vessels of 10,000 gross deadweight tons or more for top 25 flags of registry, ranked by total tons)

Flag of registry	Total[1] No.	Total[1] Tons (thous.)	Dry bulk No.	Dry bulk Tons (thous.)	Container No.	Container Tons (thous.)	General cargo No.	General cargo Tons (thous.)	Tanker No.	Tanker Tons (thous.)
Panama	6,158	328,206	2,604	199,557	706	38,105	1,103	10,846	1,331	73,728
Liberia.	2,974	193,408	785	63,205	1,010	47,839	235	3,779	910	78,132
Marshall Islands	1,876	136,328	753	59,229	237	8,700	92	1,894	772	66,196
Hong Kong	1,855	127,077	930	76,864	330	17,910	219	4,476	362	27,668
Singapore	1,776	92,513	349	31,191	378	15,451	121	2,473	852	42,156
Bahamas, The	1,029	63,125	256	14,794	57	1,748	247	4,245	394	41,072
Malta.	1,587	69,065	549	34,527	130	6,015	321	2,356	537	25,503
Greece	704	72,480	250	24,289	33	2,392	28	65	383	45,655
China[2].	1,416	49,384	553	27,898	160	5,985	286	2,662	389	12,707
Cyprus	788	31,438	290	18,781	208	4,894	153	1,344	123	6,335
Japan	577	22,696	183	12,988	2	101	37	243	247	8,480
United Kingdom	397	17,661	37	4,219	153	9,842	75	580	80	2,277
Isle of Man	332	23,343	80	9,947	8	743	56	540	177	12,067
Italy.	483	20,254	111	8,624	15	820	45	502	242	8,980
Norway (NIS)[3].	383	17,657	66	4,358	0	0	59	1,634	210	10,600
Germany.	288	14,622	2	326	218	13,518	41	269	24	487
Antigua and Barbuda	1,221	13,798	40	1,534	390	6,723	751	5,241	21	169
South Korea	764	17,232	180	12,475	82	1,053	259	1,576	221	1,897
Denmark (DIS)[4]	307	13,373	4	401	90	7,430	34	82	167	5,328
Indonesia	1,396	12,856	120	2,894	156	1,461	671	2,770	398	5,597
Bermuda.	118	10,874	26	3,986	17	745	4	56	71	6,086
U.S.	185	7,887	6	260	75	3,357	22	238	48	3,340
Malaysia	269	8,188	8	258	23	225	66	316	159	7,315
Turkey.	546	9,388	105	4,978	44	747	261	1,419	112	2,003
Netherlands	749	7,171	9	693	57	1,084	575	4,353	89	812
Top 25 registries.	**28,178**	**1,380,025**	**8,296**	**618,276**	**4,579**	**196,889**	**5,761**	**53,959**	**8,319**	**494,591**
Total	**36,307**	**1,508,939**	**9,307**	**654,966**	**4,909**	**206,547**	**9,908**	**74,617**	**10,499**	**552,645**

Note: As of Jan. 31, 2013. (1) Includes roll-on/roll-off cargo not shown separately. (2) Excludes Hong Kong. (3) Norwegian Intl. Shipping Registry. (4) Danish Intl. Shipping Registry.

U.S. International Transactions, 1970-2013

Source: U.S. Bureau of Economic Analysis, U.S. Dept. of Commerce
(in millions of dollars; revised as of June 2014)

CURRENT ACCOUNT	1970	1980	1990	2000	2005	2010	2012	2013
Exports of goods and services and income payments (credits)	$68,388	$344,440	$712,128	$1,471,532	$1,895,983	$2,630,799	$3,085,260	$3,178,744
Goods	42,469	224,250	387,401	784,940	913,016	1,290,273	1,561,689	1,592,784
Services	14,171	47,585	147,833	290,381	373,006	563,333	654,850	687,410
Primary income receipts	11,748	72,605	176,894	358,822	543,982	684,915	762,885	780,120
Imports of goods and services and income payments (debits)	66,055	342,124	791,097	1,882,288	2,641,418	3,074,729	3,546,009	3,578,998
Goods	39,866	249,750	498,438	1,231,722	1,695,820	1,938,950	2,303,785	2,294,453
Services	14,519	41,492	117,660	216,115	304,448	409,313	450,360	462,134
Primary income payments.	5,514	42,533	148,345	339,643	476,349	507,254	559,892	580,466
Secondary income payments (current transfers)[1]	6,156	8,349	26,654	94,808	164,801	219,212	231,972	241,945
CAPITAL ACCOUNT								
Capital transfer receipts and other credits.	NA	NA	0	35	15462	0	7,668	0
Capital transfer payments and other debits	NA	NA	7,220	36	2346	157	764	412
Net U.S. acquisition of financial assets[2]	9,336	86,968	103,985	589,315	572,317	963,449	171,418	644,763
Net U.S. incurrence of liabilities[2]....	7,226	62,036	162,109	1,067,016	1,273,038	1,386,345	601,973	1,017,669
Balance on current account	**2,331**	**2,318**	**−78,969**	**−410,756**	**−745,434**	**−443,930**	**−460,749**	**−400,254**
Balance on capital account	**NA**	**NA**	**−7,221**	**−1**	**13,116**	**−157**	**6,904**	**−412**
Net lending (+) or net borrowing (−) from financial-acct. transactions[3] ..	2,110	24,932	−58,124	−477,701	−700,721	−436,972	−423,492	−370,658

NA = Not available or applicable. (1) Includes U.S. government and private transfers, such as U.S. government grants and pensions, fines and penalties, withholding taxes, personal transfers (remittances), insurance-related transfers, and other current transfers. (2) Excludes financial derivatives. (3) Net lending means that U.S. residents are net suppliers of funds to foreign residents, and net borrowing means the opposite. Net lending or net borrowing can be computed from current- and capital-account transactions or from financial-account transactions.

U.S. International Direct Investments, 1990-2013

Source: U.S. Bureau of Economic Analysis, U.S. Dept. of Commerce
(in millions of dollars)

	U.S. direct investment abroad					Foreign direct investment in U.S.				
	1990	2000	2010	2012	2013	1990	2000	2010	2012	2013
All countries	$430,521	$1,316,247	$3,741,910	$4,384,671	$4,660,906	$394,911	$1,256,867	$2,280,044	$2,605,755	$2,763,956
Canada	69,508	132,472	295,206	346,080	368,297	29,544	114,309	192,463	217,800	237,921
Europe	214,739	687,320	2,034,559	2,443,287	2,607,204	247,320	887,014	1,659,774	1,857,270	1,933,589
Austria	1,113	2,872	11,485	14,367	16,719	625	3,007	4,532	5,330	5,948
Belgium	9,464	17,973	43,975	46,137	47,951	3,900	14,787	69,565	87,142	65,135
Czech Rep.	NA	1,228	5,268	5,956	6,196	NA	NA	-65	-223	82
Denmark	1,726	5,270	11,802	13,627	13,533	819	4,025	7,772	7,582	10,076
Finland	544	1,342	1,597	2,008	1,966	1,504	8,875	4,943	6,296	7,597
France	19,164	42,628	78,320	76,874	77,964	18,650	125,740	189,763	230,205	226,131
Germany	27,609	55,508	103,319	118,168	118,361	28,232	122,412	203,077	201,121	208,841
Greece	282	795	1,775	1,024	1,049	NA	NA	-41	-265	-332
Hungary	NA	1,920	4,237	7,493	6,007	NA	NA	39,266	20,223	20,116
Ireland	5,894	35,903	158,851	207,263	239,631	1,340	25,523	24,097	21,138	26,219
Italy	14,063	23,484	27,137	27,530	27,560	1,524	6,576	20,142	22,132	25,384
Luxembourg	1,697	27,849	272,206	391,359	416,278	2,195	58,930	170,309	191,011	201,603
Netherlands	19,120	115,429	514,689	669,331	722,786	64,671	138,894	234,408	274,879	273,884
Norway	4,209	4,379	28,541	44,938	44,289	773	2,665	10,478	19,030	26,075
Poland	NA	3,884	13,152	13,342	13,464	NA	NA	4,386	220	251
Portugal	897	2,664	2,612	2,058	1,985	NA	NA	204	373	363
Russia	NA	1,147	10,040	14,834	14,631	NA	NA	5,689	5,774	6,197
Spain	7,868	21,236	52,390	29,890	31,380	792	5,068	43,095	47,173	48,528
Sweden	1,787	25,959	23,275	34,485	36,472	5,484	21,991	38,780	43,926	44,397
Switzerland	25,099	55,377	119,891	123,131	129,769	17,674	64,719	180,642	195,652	209,397
Turkey	522	1,826	4,155	5,430	5,302	NA	NA	749	NA	838
UK	72,707	230,762	501,247	535,671	570,987	98,676	277,613	400,435	472,561	518,643
Latin America[1]	71,413	266,576	752,788	845,186	884,402	20,168	53,691	62,130	84,352	99,701
Argentina	2,531	17,488	11,747	14,596	15,171	NA	NA	464	178	119
Bahamas	NA	NA	28,501	33,002	34,747	1,535	1,254	1,753	378	876
Barbados	252	2,141	7,524	12,438	13,911	NA	NA	706	1,126	839
Bermuda	20,169	60,114	265,524	282,353	287,004	1,550	18,336	365	-12,045	-11,773
Brazil	14,384	36,717	66,963	79,054	78,094	377	882	1,357	3,309	1,054
Chile	1,896	10,052	30,747	37,827	41,110	NA	NA	391	403	487
Colombia	1,677	3,693	6,181	7,371	7,819	NA	NA	382	765	609
Costa Rica	251	1,716	1,827	1,024	969	NA	NA	-48	-110	-55
Curaçao[2]	NA	NA	NA	4,504	5,075	12,974	3,807	NA	3,246	3,168
Dominican Rep.	529	1,143	1,432	1,244	1,342	NA	NA	-142	87	15
Ecuador	280	832	1,283	449	427	NA	NA	77	40	8
Honduras	262	399	936	849	901	NA	NA	7	-35	-22
Mexico	10,313	39,352	85,751	98,377	101,454	575	7,462	10,970	14,458	17,610
Panama	9,289	30,758	5,156	5,194	5,796	4,188	3,819	952	1,125	1,231
Peru	599	3,130	7,196	8,667	10,061	NA	NA	182	121	100
UK isls. in Caribbean	5,929	33,451	191,680	213,269	234,206	-2,979	15,191	38,477	66,187	80,106
Venezuela	1,087	10,531	10,255	13,458	14,487	496	792	3,122	4,512	4,718
Africa	3,650	11,891	54,816	58,639	60,427	505	2,700	2,265	3,810	1,968
Egypt	1,231	1,998	12,599	17,341	19,321	NA	NA	-277	-106	-100
Nigeria	-401	470	5,058	8,402	8,067	NA	NA	23	20	-3
South Africa	775	3,562	6,017	5,510	5,207	10	704	699	1,066	1,052
Middle East	3,959	10,863	34,431	39,911	45,299	4,425	6,506	16,808	20,181	21,166
Israel	746	3,735	9,464	8,676	9,539	640	3,012	8,714	9,053	9,471
Saudi Arabia	1,899	3,661	7,436	9,488	10,550	NA	NA	NA	NA	NA
UAE	409	683	4,935	8,335	10,765	99	64	747	2,514	1,804
Asia and Pacific	64,718	207,125	570,111	651,569	695,278	92,948	192,647	346,605	422,341	469,610
Australia	15,110	34,838	125,421	143,253	158,996	6,542	18,775	35,632	48,407	44,742
China	354	11,140	58,996	53,740	61,534	NA	NA	3,300	6,943	8,073
Hong Kong	6,055	27,447	41,264	54,899	58,828	1,511	1,493	4,440	8,856	5,860
India	372	2,379	24,666	22,822	24,318	NA	NA	4,102	6,365	7,118
Indonesia	3,207	8,904	10,558	13,556	12,777	NA	NA	138	-31	-55
Japan	22,599	57,091	113,523	125,286	123,174	83,091	159,690	255,012	299,121	342,327
Malaysia	1,466	7,910	26,233	30,929	32,807	56	310	338	679	635
New Zealand	3,156	4,271	11,791	14,080	16,409	157	395	584	995	972
Philippines	1,355	3,638	6,724	9,457	7,919	77	47	103	266	268
Singapore	3,975	24,133	5,399	4,097	4,376	1,289	5,087	21,517	18,310	19,760
South Korea	2,695	8,968	102,778	139,708	154,438	-1,009	3,110	15,746	25,502	32,456
Taiwan	2,226	7,836	22,188	17,683	16,905	836	3,174	4,642	5,412	6,420
Thailand	1,790	5,824	12,999	14,320	14,428	NA	NA	158	366	439
EU[3]	180,491	609,674	2,036,631	2,239,580	NA	220,874	814,033	1,457,842	1,647,567	NA
OPEC[4]	7,145	28,545	53,114	63,369	NA	4,216	4,330	11,282	15,487	NA

NA = Not available. **Note:** On a historical cost basis for comparison purposes. Direct investment in all industries. Book value of foreign direct investors' equity in, and net outstanding loans to, their U.S. affiliates. A U.S. affiliate is a U.S. business enterprise in which a single foreign direct investor owns at least 10% of the voting securities or the equivalent. Regional totals include counties or territories not shown. (1) Latin America incl. the Caribbean and other Western Hemisphere. (2) Figures before 2010 are for the entire Netherlands Antilles, a confederation that ended in 2010. (3) European Union members in 2013: Austria, Belgium, Bulgaria, Croatia, Cyprus, Czech Rep., Denmark, Estonia, Finland, France, Germany, Greece, Hungary, Ireland, Italy, Latvia, Lithuania, Luxembourg, Malta, Netherlands, Poland, Portugal, Romania, Slovakia, Slovenia, Spain, Sweden, UK. (4) Org. of Petroleum Exporting Countries in 2013: Algeria, Angola, Ecuador, Iran, Iraq, Kuwait, Libya, Nigeria, Qatar, Saudi Arabia, United Arab Emirates, Venezuela.

TRANSPORTATION AND TRAVEL

Top Motor Vehicle Producing Nations, 2013

Source: International Organization of Motor Vehicle Manufacturers (OICA)
(in thousands of units; ranked by total production)

Nation	Total motor vehicles	Cars	Light commercial vehicles[1]	% change, 2012-13[2]	Nation	Total motor vehicles	Cars	Light commercial vehicles[1]	% change, 2012-13[2]
China[3]	22,117	18,085	4,032	14.8%	Malaysia	596	540	56	4.7
U.S.	11,046	4,347	6,699	6.9	Poland	583	475	108	-10.9
Japan	9,630	8,189	1,441	-3.1	South Africa	546	265	281	1.2
Germany	5,718	5,440	278	1.2	Belgium	480	450	31	-10.8
South Korea	4,521	4,123	399	-0.9	Romania	411	411	0	21.7
India	3,881	3,139	742	-7.0	Taiwan	339	291	48	-0.1
Brazil	3,740	2,742	998	9.9	Hungary	222	220	2	2.1
Mexico	3,052	1,772	1,280	1.7	Australia	216	185	30	-4.7
Thailand	2,533	1,123	1,410	4.3	Austria	171	148	23	20.0
Canada	2,380	965	1,415	-3.4	Sweden	161	161	NA	-1.1
Russia	2,175	1,920	256	-2.6	Uzbekistan	155	134	21	-5.7
Spain	2,163	1,720	444	9.3	Portugal	154	110	44	-5.8
France	1,740	1,460	280	-11.6	Slovenia	94	89	4	-28.4
U.K.	1,597	1,510	88	1.3	Ukraine	50	46	5	-33.9
Indonesia	1,208	925	283	13.4	Egypt	39	26	13	-30.9
Czech Rep.	1,133	1,128	4	-3.9	Serbia	11	10	1	-1.2
Turkey	1,126	634	492	4.9	Finland	3	3	0	14.8
Slovakia	975	975	0	5.2	Others	602	474	128	0.4
Argentina	791	507	284	3.5	**NAFTA**	**16,478**	**NA**	**NA**	**4.3**
Iran	744	631	113	-25.6	**World total**	**87,300**	**65,433**	**21,867**	**3.7**
Italy	658	388	270	-2.0%					

NA = Not available. **Note:** Numbers may not add up to totals due to rounding. (1) Pickup trucks and vans. (2) Percent change in number of total motor vehicles. (3) Not including Taiwan.

World Motor Vehicle Production, 1950-2013

Source: For 1950-97, American Automobile Manufacturers Assn.; 2000-12, Automotive News Data Center and R.L. Polk; 2013, OICA
(in thousands of units)

Year	United States	Canada	Europe[1]	Japan	Other	World total	U.S. % of world total
1950	8,006	388	1,991	32	160	10,577	75.7%
1960	7,905	398	6,837	482	866	16,488	47.9
1970	8,284	1,160	13,049	5,289	1,637	29,419	28.2
1980	8,010	1,324	15,496	11,043	2,692	38,565	20.8
1990	9,783	1,928	18,866	13,487	4,496	48,554	20.1
2000	12,832	2,952	17,678	10,145	16,098	59,704	21.5
2001	11,518	2,535	17,825	9,777	16,170	57,705	19.7
2002	12,328	2,624	17,419	10,240	16,975	59,587	20.7
2003	12,145	2,547	16,943	10,286	19,641	61,562	19.7
2004	12,021	2,698	20,850	10,512	16,573	65,654	18.3
2005	12,018	2,665	20,855	10,800	20,691	67,892	17.7
2006	11,351	2,545	21,490	11,486	23,180	70,992	16.0
2007	10,611	2,602	22,858	11,596	26,019	74,647	14.2
2008	8,503	2,046	21,608	10,969	31,224	67,602	12.6
2009	5,591	1,476	17,075	7,648	32,374	59,096	9.5
2010	7,632	2,074	19,371	9,197	35,036	73,311	10.4
2011	8,462	2,127	20,709	7,901	36,828	76,027	11.1
2012	10,142	2,454	22,324	9,448	36,714	81,082	12.5
2013	11,046	2,380	19,726	9,630	44,518	87,300	12.7

Note: Data may not be fully comparable across all years because they are derived from different sources. Number of units may not add up to totals because of rounding. (1) Prior to 2004, numbers exclude Eastern European production.

New and Used Passenger Cars Imported Into the U.S. by Country of Origin, 1970-2013

Source: Foreign Trade Division, U.S. Census Bureau
(in number of units)

Year	Japan	Germany[1]	Italy	UK	Sweden	France	S. Korea	Mexico	Canada	Total[2]
1970	381,338	674,945	42,523	76,257	57,844	37,114	NA	NA	692,783	2,013,420
1975	695,573	370,012	102,344	67,106	51,993	15,647	NA	0	733,766	2,074,653
1980	1,991,502	338,711	46,899	32,517	61,496	47,386	NA	1	594,770	3,116,448
1985	2,527,467	473,110	8,689	24,474	142,640	42,882	NA	13,647	1,144,805	4,397,679
1990	1,867,794	245,286	11,045	27,271	93,084	1,976	201,475	215,986	1,220,221	3,944,602
1995	1,114,360	204,932	1,031	42,450	82,593	14	131,718	462,800	1,552,691	3,624,428
2000	1,839,093	488,323	3,125	81,196	86,707	134	568,121	934,000	2,138,811	6,324,284
2005	1,832,534	547,191	5,377	184,716	93,736	412	730,500	693,149	1,967,985	6,564,844
2006	2,347,532	532,022	5,469	148,014	81,008	567	697,061	947,824	1,963,922	7,380,077
2007	2,300,913	466,458	5,650	108,576	92,600	1,746	676,594	889,474	1,912,744	7,220,792
2008	2,190,013	502,971	5,783	110,737	59,638	28,198	612,300	928,273	1,609,005	6,525,836
2009	1,238,773	348,093	3,067	78,999	27,017	16,909	476,912	649,740	1,164,849	4,276,163
2010	1,569,220	506,053	4,298	96,689	38,749	4,153	515,601	902,565	1,741,493	5,668,111
2011	1,421,750	537,158	5,372	95,742	26,884	3,580	587,574	953,514	1,835,819	5,673,139
2012	1,723,014	629,579	11,767	114,073	24,653	10,949	705,089	1,052,212	2,094,793	6,590,863
2013	1,722,119	657,829	14,289	115,326	21,617	12,694	759,964	1,126,825	2,009,140	6,682,004

NA = Not available. **Note:** Excludes cars assembled in U.S. foreign trade zones. (1) Figures prior to 1991 are for West Germany. (2) Includes units imported from countries not shown in table.

Passenger Car Production in U.S. Plants, 2011-13

Source: WardsAuto Group, a division of Penton
(in number of units)

	2013	2012	2011		2013	2012	2011
FLAT ROCK ASSEMBLY[1]				**HONDA TOTAL**	733,998	639,108	349,969
TOTAL	—	133,004	117,836	Acura ILX	17,196	30,244	—
Ford Mustang	—	95,438	78,286	Acura TL	25,714	39,421	35,763
Mazda6	—	37,566	39,550	**Acura total**	42,910	69,665	35,763
				Honda Accord	466,695	400,143	229,439
CHRYSLER TOTAL	343,204	334,825	250,417	Honda Civic	224,393	169,300	84,767
Chrysler 200 Series	129,685	150,321	122,625	**Honda total**	691,088	569,443	314,206
Chrysler total	129,685	150,321	122,625				
Dodge Avenger	121,944	113,541	75,951	**HYUNDAI TOTAL**	399,495	361,348	338,127
Dodge Caliber	—	—	51,841	Hyundai Elantra	194,059	138,997	112,665
Dodge Dart	88,973	69,645	—	Hyundai Sonata	205,436	222,351	225,462
Dodge Viper	1,501	—	—				
Dodge total	212,418	183,186	127,792	**KIA MOTORS TOTAL**	133,946	128,536	35,132
Lancia Flavia	1,101	1,318	—	Kia Optima	133,946	128,536	35,132
FORD TOTAL	553,446	419,907	311,814	**MITSUBISHI TOTAL**	—	13,716	26,583
Ford C-Max	38,532	19,890	—	Mitsubishi Eclipse	—	—	7,142
Ford Focus	292,809	283,447	221,514	Mitsubishi Galant	—	13,716	19,441
Ford Fusion	29,277	—	—				
Ford Mustang	88,020	—	—	**NISSAN TOTAL**	470,232	406,782	385,109
Ford Taurus	93,115	101,875	77,664	Nissan Altima	383,818	334,710	319,203
Ford total	541,753	405,212	299,178	Nissan Leaf	26,387	192	—
Lincoln MKS	11,693	14,695	12,636	Nissan Maxima	48,247	71,877	65,906
				Nissan Sentra	11,780	3	—
GENERAL MOTORS TOTAL	831,854	840,700	721,501				
Buick LaCrosse	53,484	56,561	64,729	**SUBARU**[2] **TOTAL**	137,803	143,529	125,738
Buick Lucerne	—	—	15,882	Subaru Legacy	40,800	50,403	46,568
Buick Verano	53,646	57,435	4,471	Toyota Camry	97,003	93,126	79,170
Buick total	107,130	113,996	85,082				
Cadillac ATS	47,650	26,278	—	**TESLA TOTAL**	24,093	3,139	720
Cadillac CTS	34,956	48,247	64,935	Tesla Model S	24,093	3,139	—
Cadillac DTS	—	—	6,515	Tesla Roadster	—	—	720
Cadillac ELR	271	—	—				
Cadillac STS	—	—	1,907	**TOYOTA TOTAL**	607,623	531,876	268,314
Cadillac total	82,877	74,525	73,357	Toyota Avalon	100,006	42,442	38,684
Chevrolet Corvette	15,726	14,960	13,222	Toyota Camry	348,970	359,832	227,663
Chevrolet Cruze	282,946	279,382	281,810	Toyota Corolla	158,647	129,602	1,967
Chevrolet Impala	36,210	—	—				
Chevrolet Malibu	189,870	229,170	214,388	**VOLKSWAGEN TOTAL**	133,141	152,543	46,451
Chevrolet Sonic	94,038	97,840	36,527	Volkswagen Passat	133,141	152,543	46,451
Chevrolet Volt	22,507	24,196	14,510				
Chevrolet total	641,297	645,548	560,457	**TOTAL CARS**	4,368,835	4,109,013	2,977,711
Opel Ampera	550	6,631	2,605				

— = No production. (1) AutoAlliance Intl., a joint venture between Ford and Mazda, produced cars for both automakers (1992-2012). The joint agreement changed in Sept. 2012, after which Ford renamed the operation Flat Rock Assembly. (2) SIA (Subaru of Indiana Automotive) also builds the Toyota Camry in collaboration with Toyota.

Domestic and Imported Retail Car Sales in the U.S., 1980-2013

Source: WardsAuto Group, a division of Penton
(in number of units)

	Cars			Light trucks			All vehicles		
Year	Domestic[1]	Imports	Total cars	Domestic[1]	Imports	Total light trucks	Domestic[1]	Imports	Total vehicles
1980	6,579,778	2,369,457	8,949,235	1,750,735	478,887	2,229,622	8,330,513	2,848,344	11,178,857
1985	8,204,670	2,774,517	10,979,187	3,629,080	832,186	4,461,266	12,109,999	3,615,292	15,725,291
1986	8,215,017	3,189,222	11,404,239	3,675,914	977,920	4,653,834	12,145,084	4,177,937	16,323,021
1987	7,085,279	3,106,598	10,191,877	3,791,882	921,698	4,713,580	11,144,275	4,048,671	15,192,946
1988	7,543,116	3,003,692	10,546,808	4,199,643	710,661	4,910,304	12,054,181	3,737,363	15,791,544
1989	7,098,098	2,680,419	9,778,517	4,113,441	641,387	4,754,828	11,503,384	3,341,877	14,845,261
1990	6,918,869	2,384,346	9,303,215	3,956,756	611,941	4,568,697	11,135,513	3,013,865	14,149,378
1991	6,161,523	2,023,406	8,184,979	3,605,633	538,008	4,143,641	9,975,798	2,573,725	12,549,523
1992	6,285,916	1,927,197	8,213,113	4,247,097	408,003	4,655,100	10,767,685	2,349,759	13,117,444
1993	6,741,667	1,776,192	8,517,859	5,000,482	377,639	5,378,121	12,029,051	2,169,803	14,198,854
1994	7,255,303	1,735,214	8,990,517	5,658,302	409,759	6,068,061	13,251,198	2,160,176	15,411,374
1995	7,113,902	1,506,257	8,620,159	5,705,708	402,181	6,107,889	13,192,861	1,923,464	15,116,325
1996	7,206,349	1,272,196	8,478,545	6,179,881	438,757	6,618,638	13,732,379	1,723,733	15,456,112
1997	6,862,175	1,355,305	8,217,480	6,324,758	579,483	6,904,241	13,549,251	1,948,609	15,497,860
1998	6,705,208	1,379,781	8,084,989	6,802,016	656,002	7,458,018	13,913,028	2,054,259	15,967,287
1999	6,918,781	1,718,927	8,637,708	7,480,607	775,223	8,255,830	14,901,266	2,513,462	17,414,728
2000	6,761,603	2,016,120	8,777,723	7,719,707	852,325	8,572,032	14,922,648	2,889,025	17,811,673
2001	6,254,371	2,097,629	8,352,000	7,789,089	981,280	8,770,369	14,372,624	3,099,754	17,472,378
2002	5,816,671	2,225,584	8,042,255	7,707,738	1,066,375	8,774,113	13,829,568	3,309,084	17,138,652
2003	5,472,500	2,083,051	7,555,551	7,856,322	1,227,180	9,083,502	13,638,351	3,329,091	16,967,442
2004	5,333,496	2,149,059	7,482,555	8,138,107	1,246,258	9,384,365	13,880,251	3,418,322	17,298,573
2005	5,473,450	2,186,533	7,659,983	8,072,456	1,215,315	9,287,771	14,020,528	3,423,801	17,444,329
2006	5,416,828	2,344,764	7,761,592	7,396,058	1,346,750	8,742,808	13,334,843	3,714,138	17,048,981
2007	5,197,271	2,365,063	7,562,334	7,138,803	1,388,085	8,526,888	12,687,016	3,773,299	16,460,315
2008	4,490,863	2,278,271	6,769,134	5,329,165	1,096,469	6,425,634	10,107,753	3,385,439	13,493,192
2009	3,558,283	1,843,282	5,401,565	4,116,550	884,242	5,000,792	7,867,766	2,734,277	10,602,043
2010	3,791,499	1,844,240	5,635,739	5,020,441	898,644	5,919,085	9,020,088	2,752,438	11,772,526
2011	4,142,811	1,946,897	6,089,708	5,662,578	982,443	6,645,021	10,101,294	2,939,624	13,040,918
2012	5,118,329	2,125,325	7,243,654	6,137,440	1,060,720	7,198,160	11,549,851	3,197,708	14,787,690
2013	5,431,885	2,153,982	7,585,867	6,707,097	1,239,268	7,946,365	12,479,757	3,404,212	15,883,969

Note: Vehicles are cars and light trucks belonging to gross vehicle weight (GWV) classes 1-3 (under 14,001 lbs). (1) Includes the U.S., Canada, and Mexico.

U.S. Vehicle Sales, 2000-13
Source: WardsAuto Group, a division of Penton

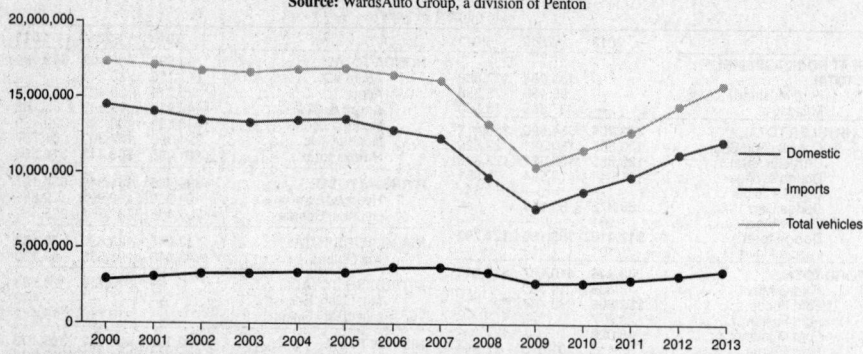

Note: Vehicles are cars and light trucks belonging to gross vehicle weight (GVW) classes 1-3 (under 14,001 lbs). Domestic sales include the U.S., Canada, and Mexico.

U.S. Sales of Hybrid and Electric Vehicles, 2000-13
Source: WardsAuto Group, a division of Penton; in number of units

Power type	2000	2005	2006	2007	2008	2009	2010	2011	2012	2013
Hybrid car	9,350	151,253	177,674	282,790	250,462	237,263	231,819	231,075	407,628	478,031
Hybrid light truck	0	54,575	75,844	70,072	65,226	53,477	42,286	30,432	24,170	20,023
Total hybrid	**9,350**	**205,828**	**253,518**	**352,862**	**315,688**	**290,740**	**274,105**	**261,507**	**431,798**	**498,054**
Electric car	463	0	0	0	27	675	326	10,447	14,517	46,913
Electric light truck	0	0	0	0	0	0	0	0	192	1,096
Total electric	**463**	**0**	**0**	**0**	**27**	**675**	**326**	**10,447**	**14,709**	**48,009**
Plug-in hybrid car	0	0	0	0	0	0	326	7,671	38,585	49,043

Top-Selling Passenger Cars in the U.S., 2010-13
Source: WardsAuto Group, a division of Penton
(ranked by number of vehicles sold)

Car	2013 sales	Car	2013 sales	Car	2013 sales
1. Toyota Camry	408,484	8. Hyundai Elantra	247,912	15. Kia Optima	155,893
2. Honda Accord	366,678	9. Ford Focus	234,570	16. Nissan Sentra	129,143
3. Honda Civic	336,180	10. Hyundai Sonata	203,648	17. Chrysler 200-Series	122,480
4. Nissan Altima	320,723	11. Chevrolet Malibu	200,594	18. Kia Soul	118,079
5. Toyota Corolla	302,180	12. Toyota Prius	192,249	19. Nissan Versa	117,352
6. Ford Fusion	295,280	13. Volkswagen Jetta	163,793	20. BMW 3-Series	113,718
7. Chevrolet Cruze	248,224	14. Chevrolet Impala	156,797		

Car	2012 sales	Car	2011 sales	Car	2010 sales
1. Toyota Camry	404,886	1. Toyota Camry	308,510	1. Toyota Camry	327,804
2. Honda Accord	331,872	2. Nissan Altima	268,981	2. Honda Accord	282,530
3. Honda Civic	317,909	3. Ford Fusion	248,067	3. Toyota Corolla/Matrix	266,082
4. Nissan Altima	302,934	4. Toyota Corolla/Matrix	240,259	4. Honda Civic	260,218
5. Toyota Corolla/Matrix	290,947	5. Honda Accord	235,625	5. Nissan Altima	229,263
6. Ford Focus	245,922	6. Chevrolet Cruze	231,732	6. Ford Fusion	219,219
7. Ford Fusion	241,263	7. Hyundai Sonata	225,961	7. Chevrolet Malibu	198,770
8. Chevrolet Cruze	237,758	8. Honda Civic	221,235	8. Hyundai Sonata	196,623
9. Hyundai Sonata	230,605	9. Chevrolet Malibu	204,808	9. Ford Focus	172,421
10. Chevrolet Malibu	210,951	10. Hyundai Elantra	186,361	10. Chevrolet Impala	172,078

U.S. Retail Car Sales by Vehicle Size, 1985-2013
Source: WardsAuto Group, a division of Penton
(as percent of total U.S. sales)

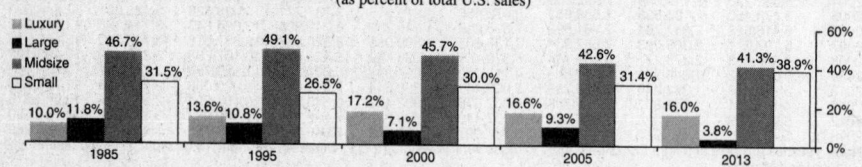

U.S. Light Truck Sales by Type, 1985-2013

Source: WardsAuto Group, a division of Penton
(as percent of total U.S. sales)

NA = Not applicable. **Note:** Comm. chassis sales (not shown) were 1.0% (for 1985), 0.7% (1995), 0.2% (2000), 0.1% (2005), 0.0% (2013).

Top-Selling Light Trucks in the U.S., 2011-13

Source: WardsAuto Group, a division of Penton
(ranked by number of vehicles sold)

Truck	2013 sales	Truck	2012 sales	Truck	2011 sales
1. Ford F-Series	713,960	1. Ford F-Series	607,854	1. Ford F-Series	552,647
2. Chevrolet Silverado	480,414	2. Chevrolet Silverado	418,312	2. Chevrolet Silverado	415,130
3. Ram Pickup	344,772	3. Ram Pickup	283,056	3. Ford Escape	254,293
4. Honda CR-V	303,904	4. Honda CR-V	281,652	4. Ram Pickup	237,236
5. Ford Escape	295,993	5. Ford Escape	261,008	5. Honda CR-V	218,373
6. Chevrolet Equinox	238,192	6. Chevrolet Equinox	218,621	6. Chevrolet Equinox	193,274
7. Toyota RAV4	218,249	7. Toyota RAV4	171,877	7. GMC Sierra	149,170
8. Ford Explorer	192,397	8. Ford Explorer	164,207	8. Ford Explorer	135,704
9. GMC Sierra	184,389	9. GMC Sierra	157,185	9. Toyota RAV4	132,237
10. Jeep Grand Cherokee	174,275	10. Jeep Grand Cherokee	154,734	10. Kia Sorento	130,235

Most Popular Colors, by Vehicle Type, 2013

Source: WardsAuto Group, a division of Penton; DuPont Automotive Products; for 2013 model year

Luxury cars/SUVs		Intermediate cars/CUVs		Compact/sports cars		Light trucks	
Color	Percent	Color	Percent	Color	Percent	Color	Percent
Black/black effect	33%	White/white pearl	24%	White/white pearl	21%	White/white pearl	35%
White/white pearl	21	Black/black effect	20	Black/black effect	20	Black/black effect	20
Gray	13	Silver	16	Silver	14	Silver	11
Silver	13	Gray	14	Gray	14	Red	10
Red	8	Red	8	Red	11	Gray	8
Beige/brown	5	Blue	6	Blue	9	Blue	7
Yellow/gold	3	Beige/brown	4	Beige/brown	5	Beige/brown	5
Blue	3	Green	3	Yellow/gold	3	Yellow/gold	2
Green	1	Yellow/gold	2	Green	1	Green	1
Other	<1	Other	3	Other	2	Other	1

U.S. Light-Duty Vehicle Fuel Efficiency, 1975-2013

Source: Natl. Vehicle and Fuel Emissions Laboratory, Office of Transportation and Air Quality, U.S. Environmental Protection Agency

Cars and light-duty trucks (SUVs, minivans, passenger vans, and pickup trucks) showed significant fuel-efficiency improvements from 1975 through 1987, when the fuel economy for both reached a high of 22 miles per gallon (mpg). The fuel economy value mainly declined, 1988-2004, but since 2005, fuel economy has generally increased, reaching a new all-time high of 24 mpg in 2013.

Year[1]	Cars (mpg)	Light-duty trucks (mpg)	All light-duty vehicles (mpg)	Year[1]	Cars (mpg)	Light-duty trucks (mpg)	All light-duty vehicles (mpg)
1975	13.5	11.6	13.1	2003	23.0	16.7	19.6
1980	20.0	15.8	19.2	2004	22.9	16.5	19.3
1985	23.0	17.5	21.3	2005	23.1	16.9	19.9
1990	23.3	17.4	21.2	2006	23.0	17.2	20.1
1995	23.3	17.0	20.5	2007	23.7	17.4	20.6
1996	23.1	17.2	20.4	2008	23.9	17.8	21.0
1997	23.2	16.8	20.2	2009	25.0	18.5	22.4
1998	23.0	17.1	20.1	2010	25.7	18.8	22.6
1999	22.7	16.6	19.7	2011	25.6	19.1	22.4
2000	22.5	16.8	19.8	2012	27.0	19.3	23.6
2002	22.8	16.5	19.5	2013	27.4	19.7	24.0

Note: Adjusted mpg composite values (city and highway fuel efficiency combined in a 55%/45% ratio) are used for all vehicles and are intended to reflect real-world use. (1) Because of changes in methodology, mpg figures prior to 1986 are not entirely comparable with later values.

Registered Cars in the U.S., 1900-2012

Source: Office of Highway Policy Information, Federal Highway Administration, U.S. Dept. of Transportation
(number of automobiles for public and private use)

Year	Reg. cars	Year	Reg. cars	Year	Reg. cars	Year	Reg. cars	Year	Reg. cars
1900	8,000	1945	25,796,985	1985	127,885,193	1997	129,748,704	2005	136,568,083
1905	77,400	1950	40,339,077	1990	133,700,497	1998	131,838,538	2006	135,399,945
1910	458,377	1955	52,144,739	1991	128,299,601	1999	132,432,044	2007	135,932,930
1915	2,332,426	1960	61,671,390	1992	126,581,148	2000	133,621,420	2008	137,079,843
1920	8,131,522	1965	75,257,588	1993	127,327,189	2001	137,633,467	2009	134,879,600
1925	17,481,001	1970	89,243,557	1994	127,883,469	2002	135,920,677	2010	130,892,240
1930	23,034,753	1975	106,705,934	1995	128,386,775	2003	135,669,897	2011	125,656,528
1935	22,567,827	1980	121,600,843	1996	129,728,311	2004	136,430,651	2012	111,289,906
1940	27,465,826								

Note: There were no publicly owned vehicles before 1925; statistics also exclude military vehicles for all years. Alaska and Hawaii data included since 1960.

Licensed Drivers, by Age and Sex, 1980-2012

Source: Office of Highway Policy Information, Federal Highway Administration, U.S. Dept. of Transportation
(numbers in thousands)

Age (years)	1980 Total	1990 Total	2000 Total	2010 Male	2010 Female	2010 Total	2012 Male	2012 Female	2012 Total	% total drivers
Under 16	93	43	27	199	198	398	65	63	127	0.1%
16	1,823	1,443	1,470	608	605	1,213	590	589	1,179	0.6
17	2,790	2,132	2,331	1,025	1,004	2,028	982	963	1,944	0.9
18	3,247	2,595	2,839	1,408	1,323	2,731	1,319	1,251	2,570	1.2
19	3,542	3,037	3,077	1,641	1,546	3,187	1,551	1,458	3,009	1.4
19 and under.......	**11,496**	**9,249**	**9,744**	**4,880**	**4,676**	**9,556**	**4,506**	**4,324**	**8,830**	**4.2**
20	3,636	3,229	3,140	1,744	1,682	3,426	1,662	1,590	3,252	1.5
21	3,733	3,249	3,172	1,756	1,717	3,474	1,729	1,678	3,407	1.6
22	3,811	3,262	3,182	1,757	1,725	3,483	1,814	1,777	3,591	1.7
23	3,938	3,398	3,247	1,767	1,748	3,515	1,815	1,793	3,608	1.7
24	3,915	3,758	3,225	1,792	1,779	3,571	1,817	1,806	3,623	1.7
20-24	**19,032**	**16,897**	**15,966**	**8,817**	**8,651**	**17,469**	**8,836**	**8,645**	**17,481**	**8.3**
25-29	18,925	19,895	17,586	9,179	9,253	18,431	9,142	9,214	18,357	8.7
30-34	17,369	20,578	19,155	8,934	8,915	17,849	9,088	9,242	18,331	8.7
35-39	13,696	19,055	21,059	9,079	9,082	18,161	8,668	8,758	17,426	8.2
40-44	11,134	16,905	21,093	9,613	9,565	19,178	9,533	9,568	19,101	9.0
45-49	10,076	13,020	19,154	10,381	10,433	20,814	9,893	9,943	19,837	9.4
50-54	10,090	10,484	16,868	10,241	10,388	20,628	10,299	10,459	20,758	9.8
55-59	9,770	9,438	12,760	9,127	9,313	18,440	9,503	9,739	19,242	9.1
60-64	8,232	9,235	9,915	7,847	8,011	15,858	8,129	8,379	16,508	7.8
65-69	6,580	8,375	8,386	5,652	5,816	11,468	6,311	6,516	12,827	6.1
70-74	NA	NA	7,468	4,029	4,202	8,231	4,349	4,557	8,907	4.2
75-79	NA	NA	5,911	2,966	3,192	6,158	3,041	3,255	6,296	3.0
80-84	NA	NA	3,511	2,090	2,373	4,464	2,097	2,338	4,435	2.1
85 and over........	NA	NA	2,050	1,541	1,870	3,411	1,590	1,890	3,480	1.6
Total..............	**145,295**	**167,015**	**190,625**	**104,374**	**105,740**	**210,115**	**104,985**	**106,830**	**211,815**	**100.0**

NA = Not available. **Note:** Numbers may not add up to totals due to rounding.

Handheld Phone and Texting Device Laws for Drivers, 2014

Source: Insurance Institute for Highway Safety; as of Aug. 2014

State	Handheld ban	Texting ban	Enforcement	State	Handheld ban	Texting ban	Enforcement	State	Handheld ban	Texting ban	Enforcement
AL	No[1]	Yes	P[2]	KY	No[4]	Yes	P	ND	No[4]	Yes	P
AK	No	Yes	P	LA	No[4,5,7]	Yes	P[8]	OH	No[4]	Yes	P[2]
AZ	No	No	NA	ME	No[5]	Yes	P	OK	No[5]	No[5]	P
AR	No[3]	Yes	P[2]	MD	Yes	Yes	P	OR	Yes	Yes	P
CA	Yes	Yes	P[2]	MA	No[4]	Yes	P	PA	No	Yes	P
CO	No[4]	Yes	P	MI	No[5]	Yes	P	RI	No[4]	Yes	P
CT	Yes	Yes	P	MN	No[9]	Yes	P	SC	No	Yes	P
DE	Yes	Yes	P	MS	No	No[5]	P	SD	No[5]	Yes	S
DC	Yes	Yes	P	MO	No	No[10]	P	TN	No[5]	Yes	P
FL	No	Yes	S	MT	No	No	NA	TX	No[4]	No[4]	P
GA	No[4]	Yes	P	NE	No[11]	Yes	S	UT	No[4]	Yes	P
HI	Yes	Yes	P	NV	Yes	Yes	P	VT	Yes	Yes	P
ID	No	Yes	P	NH	No[4,12]	Yes	P	VA	No[4]	Yes	P
IL	Yes	Yes	P	NJ	Yes	Yes	P	WA	Yes	Yes	P
IN	No[4]	Yes	P	NM	No[5]	Yes	P	WV	Yes	Yes	P
IA	No[5]	Yes	S[6]	NY	Yes	Yes	P	WI	No[5]	Yes	P
KS	No[5]	Yes	P	NC	No[4]	Yes	P	WY	No	Yes	P

NA = Not applicable. P = Officer may stop vehicle for violation (primary); S = Officer may issue citation only when vehicle is stopped for another moving violation (secondary). **Note:** Laws shown for licensed passenger car drivers. Different laws and regulations apply to school bus, municipal transit, and other mass transit operators. Different laws may apply in school zones, construction zones, or other such areas. (1) Yes for 16-year-old drivers and for 17-year-old drivers who have held an intermediate license for fewer than 6 months. (2) Secondary for cell phone use by young drivers. (3) Yes for drivers under 21 years of age. (4) Yes for drivers under 18. (5) Yes for learner's permit and intermediate license holders. (6) Primary for learner's permit and intermediate license holders. (7) Yes for drivers in the year after getting their first license. (8) Secondary for cell phone use by novice drivers. (9) Yes for learner's permit and provisional license holders in their first year after licensing. (10) Yes for drivers 21 and younger. (11) Yes for learner's permit and intermediate license holders under 18. (12) Ban for all drivers to go into effect 7/1/15.

Selected Motor Vehicle Statistics

Source: Federal Highway Admin., U.S. Dept. of Transportation; Insurance Inst. for Highway Safety; American Petroleum Inst.

Driver's license age requirements, state gas tax, and safety belt use laws (incl. laws passed, but not in effect) as of 2014. Other figures are for 2012.

STATE	Driver's license age requirements: Learner's permit	Regular[1]	Gas taxes (cents/gal)[5]	Safety belt use law[6]	Licensed drivers: Per 1,000 resident pop.	Per reg. motor vehicle	Reg. motor vehicles per 1,000 pop.	Fuel use per reg. motor vehicle (gal)	Annual miles driven: Per gal used	Per reg. vehicle	Per lic. driver
Alabama	15	17	39.3	P	794	0.82	1,005	683	19.64	13,408	16,972
Alaska	14	16y, 6m	30.8	P	720	0.72	1,060	576	10.73	6,181	9,104
Arizona	15y, 6m	16y, 6m	37.4	S	717	0.95	788	655	17.77	11,646	12,800
Arkansas	14	18	40.2	P	746	0.94	841	823	16.42	13,517	15,243
California	15y, 6m	17[2]	68.2	P	636	0.92	728	624	18.89	11,778	13,482
Colorado	15	17	40.4	P	734	0.88	879	591	17.35	10,252	12,283
Connecticut	16	18[2,3]	67.7	P	692	0.96	754	635	18.19	11,554	12,580
Delaware	16	17[2]	41.4	P	785	0.80	1,029	527	18.46	9,734	12,753
Dist. of Columbia	16	18[4]	41.9	P	634	1.34	510	358	30.91	11,081	8,907
Florida	15	18	54.4	P	719	0.93	811	607	20.12	12,216	13,771
Georgia	15	18[2]	45.9	P	663	0.90	771	761	18.46	14,056	16,332
Hawaii	15y, 6m	17[2]	66.9	P	657	0.78	885	406	20.08	8,159	10,983
Idaho	14y, 6m	16[2]	43.4	S	685	0.70	1,030	586	16.94	9,922	14,927
Illinois	15	18[2]	57.5	P	640	0.85	787	600	17.21	10,322	12,698
Indiana	15	18	60.2	P	822	0.94	918	713	18.44	13,144	14,681
Iowa	14	17[2]	40.4	P	721	0.67	1,142	654	13.77	8,999	14,250
Kansas	14	16y, 6m	42.4	P(a)	699	0.87	849	728	17.15	12,482	15,150
Kentucky	16	17[2]	50.9	P	681	0.85	838	794	16.24	12,898	15,859
Louisiana	15	17[2]	38.4	P	635	0.78	845	752	16.04	12,056	16,037
Maine	15	16y, 9m[2]	48.4	P	758	0.91	888	732	16.45	12,032	14,083
Maryland	15y, 9m	18	45.8	P(a)	697	1.08	677	812	17.45	14,180	13,767
Massachusetts	16	18[2]	44.9	S	712	0.99	745	647	17.46	11,301	11,817
Michigan	14y, 9m	17[2]	60.4	P	710	0.94	789	680	17.84	12,124	13,471
Minnesota	15	17[2]	47.0	P	618	0.69	948	641	17.43	11,176	17,156
Mississippi	15	16y, 6m	36.8	P	656	0.98	688	1,090	17.29	18,842	19,748
Missouri	15	17y, 11m	35.7	S(b)	712	0.79	944	718	16.79	12,051	15,974
Montana	14y, 6m	16[2]	46.2	S	754	0.58	1,481	516	15.47	7,984	15,683
Nebraska	15	17	45.7	S	735	0.76	1,018	669	15.26	10,207	14,137
Nevada	15y, 6m	18[2]	51.6	S	626	0.85	772	649	17.45	11,335	13,974
New Hampshire	15y, 6m	18[2]	42.2	None	806	0.88	986	608	16.28	9,900	12,111
New Jersey	16	18	32.9	P(a)	681	0.81	892	613	15.31	9,382	12,290
New Mexico	15	16y, 6m[2]	37.3	P	686	0.84	866	822	17.22	14,155	17,869
New York	16	17[2]	68.9	P	575	1.13	534	650	18.88	12,271	11,399
North Carolina	15	16y, 6m[2]	55.2	P(a)	685	0.89	799	677	19.90	13,468	15,716
North Dakota	14	16	41.4	S	719	0.66	1,158	1,008	12.34	12,445	20,050
Ohio	15y, 6m	18[2]	46.4	S	694	0.83	876	637	17.48	11,142	14,079
Oklahoma	15y, 6m	16y, 6m	35.4	P	629	0.73	902	797	17.46	13,916	19,944
Oregon	15	17[2,3]	49.5	P	710	0.81	905	562	16.74	9,405	11,977
Pennsylvania	16	17	60.2	S(b)	693	0.89	820	627	15.05	9,443	11,183
Rhode Island	16	17y, 6m[2]	51.4	P	714	0.93	813	495	18.46	9,138	10,413
South Carolina	15	16y, 6m	35.2	P	732	0.93	825	848	14.85	12,584	14,189
South Dakota	14	16	40.4	S	728	0.67	1,204	691	13.14	9,081	15,019
Tennessee	15	17	39.8	P	708	0.89	835	751	17.57	13,197	15,559
Texas	15	18[2]	38.4	P	585	0.79	777	834	14.08	11,752	15,594
Utah	15	17[2]	42.9	S(b)	626	0.95	694	764	17.52	13,389	14,830
Vermont	15	16y, 6m[2]	51.4	S	846	0.93	970	621	19.15	11,889	13,627
Virginia	15y, 6m	18[2]	35.7	S	677	0.81	869	694	16.40	11,376	14,617
Washington	15	17[2]	55.9	P	758	0.94	848	567	17.13	9,703	10,858
West Virginia	15	17	54.1	P	669	0.91	786	756	17.44	13,179	15,485
Wisconsin	15y, 6m	16y, 9m[2]	51.3	P	708	0.84	911	625	18.12	11,330	14,566
Wyoming	15	16y, 6m[2]	51.3	S	731	0.56	1,387	919	12.61	11,597	21,991
U.S. AVERAGE			49.6		675	0.88	808	680	17.21	11,705	14,016

Note: Most states have graduated licensing systems that phase in full driving privileges. During the learner's stage, driving generally is not permitted without adult supervision. In an intermediate stage, young licensees may be allowed to drive unsupervised under certain conditions. (1) Min. age at which all restrictions may be lifted on private passenger car operation. (2) Applicants under a specified age (typically between 17 and 19) must complete driver education. (3) Home training (CT) or more hours of supervised driving (OR) may be substituted for driver ed. (4) Learner's stage mandatory for all license applicants regardless of age. (5) Some values rounded. Includes 18.4 cents per gallon in federal excise taxes. (6) P = Officer may stop vehicle for violation (primary); S = Officer may issue seat belt citation only when vehicle is stopped for another moving violation (secondary). (a) Secondary enforcement for rear seat occupants; (b) Primary enforcement for children under a specified age.

International Tourism Receipts, 2000-13

Source: World Tourism Organization (UNWTO), ©UNWTO

(in billions of U.S. dollars; ranked by most recent figures available)

Rank Country	2000	2005	2010	2011	2012	2013*	Rank Country	2000	2005	2010	2011	2012	2013*
1. U.S.	82.9	82.2	103.5	115.6	126.2	139.6	28. Sweden	4.1	6.8	8.7	10.4	10.8	11.5
2. Spain	30.0	48.0	52.5	60.0	56.3	60.4	29. Poland	5.7	6.3	9.5	10.7	10.9	10.9
3. France	33.0	44.0	47.0	54.8	53.6	56.1	30. United Arab						
4. China	16.2	29.3	45.8	48.5	50.0	51.7	Emirates	1.1	3.2	8.6	9.2	10.4	NA
5. Macao	3.2	7.9	27.8	38.5	43.7	51.6	31. Croatia	2.8	7.4	8.3	9.2	8.8	9.6
6. Italy	27.5	35.4	38.8	43.0	41.2	43.9	32. Indonesia	5.0	4.5	7.0	8.0	8.3	9.3
7. Thailand	7.5	9.6	20.1	27.2	33.8	42.1	33. South Africa	2.7	7.5	9.1	9.5	10.0	9.2
8. Germany	18.7	29.2	34.7	38.9	38.1	41.2	34. Saudi Arabia	NA	4.6	6.7	8.5	7.4	7.7
9. UK	21.9	30.7	32.4	35.1	36.2	40.6	35. Vietnam	NA	2.3	4.5	5.7	6.8	7.5
10. Hong Kong	5.9	10.3	22.2	28.5	33.1	38.9	36. New Zealand	2.9	6.5	6.5	7.3	7.1	7.5
11. Australia	9.4	16.7	28.4	31.3	31.7	31.0	37. Czech Republic	3.0	4.8	7.1	7.6	7.0	7.1
12. Turkey	7.6	19.2	22.6	25.1	25.3	28.0	38. Denmark	3.7	5.3	5.9	6.8	6.6	7.0
13. Malaysia	5.0	8.8	18.1	19.7	20.2	21.0	39. Morocco	2.0	4.6	6.7	7.3	6.7	6.9
14. Austria	9.8	16.1	18.6	19.9	18.9	20.1	40. Brazil	1.8	3.9	5.7	6.6	6.6	6.7
15. Singapore	5.1	6.2	14.2	18.1	19.0	19.0	41. Egypt	4.3	6.9	12.5	8.7	9.9	6.0
16. India	3.5	7.5	14.5	17.7	18.0	18.4	42. Lebanon	NA	5.5	7.9	6.5	6.0	NA
17. Canada	10.8	13.7	15.8	16.8	17.4	17.7	43. Israel	4.1	2.9	5.1	5.3	5.5	5.7
18. Switzerland	6.6	10.0	14.7	17.1	16.0	16.5	44. Norway	2.2	3.5	4.7	5.3	5.4	5.7
19. Greece	9.2	13.3	12.7	14.6	13.4	15.9	45. Dominican						
20. Netherlands	7.2	10.5	12.9	14.3	13.7	15.6	Republic	2.9	3.5	4.2	4.4	4.7	5.1
21. Japan	3.4	6.6	13.2	11.0	14.6	14.9	46. Hungary	3.8	4.1	5.4	5.6	4.8	5.1
22. South Korea	6.8	5.8	10.3	12.5	13.4	14.3	47. Ukraine	0.4	3.1	3.8	4.3	4.8	5.1
23. Mexico	8.3	11.8	12.0	11.9	12.7	13.8	48. Luxembourg	1.8	3.6	4.1	4.8	4.6	4.8
24. Belgium	6.6	9.9	12.1	13.1	13.0	13.5	49. Philippines	2.2	2.3	2.6	3.2	4.1	4.7
25. Taiwan	3.7	5.0	8.7	11.1	11.8	12.7	50. Ireland	2.6	4.8	4.1	4.2	3.9	4.4
26. Portugal	5.2	7.7	10.1	11.3	11.1	12.3	World	476	681	931	1,042	1,078	1,159
27. Russia	3.4	5.9	8.8	11.3	10.8	12.0							

NA = Not available. * = Preliminary.

International Tourist Arrivals by Country of Destination, 2000-13

Source: World Tourism Organization (UNWTO), ©UNWTO

(visitors in millions; ranked by most recent figures available)

Rank Country	2000	2005	2010	2011	2012	2013*	% change, 2012-13	Rank Country	2000	2005	2010	2011	2012	2013*	% change, 2012-13
1. France	77.2	75.0	77.6	81.6	83.0	NA	NA	28. Morocco	4.3	5.8	9.3	9.3	9.4	10.0	7.2%
2. U.S.	51.2	49.2	60.0	62.7	66.7	69.8	4.7%	29. Dubai	3.1	5.8	7.4	8.1	9.0	10.0	11.3
3. Spain	46.4	55.9	52.7	56.2	57.5	60.7	5.6	30. South Africa	5.9	7.4	8.1	8.3	9.2	9.5	3.5
4. China	31.2	46.8	55.7	57.6	57.7	55.7	-3.5	31. Egypt	5.1	8.2	14.1	9.5	11.2	9.2	-18.1
5. Italy	41.2	36.5	43.6	46.1	46.4	47.7	2.9	32. Czech							
6. Turkey	9.6	24.2	31.4	34.7	35.7	37.8	5.9	Republic	4.8	9.4	8.6	9.0	9.5	9.0	-4.8
7. Germany	19.0	21.5	26.9	28.4	30.4	31.5	3.7	33. Switzerland	7.8	7.2	8.6	8.5	8.6	9.0	4.7
8. UK	23.2	28.0	28.3	29.3	29.3	31.2	6.4	34. Denmark	3.5	9.2	8.7	7.9	8.1	NA	NA
9. Russia	19.2	19.9	20.3	22.7	25.7	28.4	10.2	35. Indonesia	5.1	5.0	7.0	7.6	8.0	8.8	9.4
10. Thailand	9.6	11.6	15.9	19.2	22.4	26.5	18.8	36. Portugal	5.7	6.0	6.8	7.4	7.7	8.3	8.3
11. Malaysia	10.2	16.4	24.6	24.7	25.0	25.7	2.7	37. Belgium	6.5	6.7	7.2	7.5	7.6	7.6	0.7
12. Hong Kong	8.8	14.8	20.1	22.3	23.8	25.7	8.0	38. Ireland	6.6	7.3	7.1	7.6	7.6	NA	NA
13. Austria	18.0	20.0	22.0	23.0	24.2	24.8	2.7	39. Taiwan	2.6	3.4	5.6	6.1	7.3	8.0	9.6
14. Ukraine	6.4	17.6	21.2	21.4	23.0	24.7	7.2	40. Vietnam	2.1	3.5	5.0	6.3	6.8	7.6	10.6
15. Mexico	20.6	21.9	23.3	23.4	23.4	23.7	1.4	41. Bulgaria	2.8	4.8	6.0	6.3	6.5	6.9	5.5
16. Greece	13.1	14.8	15.0	16.4	15.5	17.9	15.5	42. India	2.6	3.9	5.8	6.3	6.6	6.8	4.1
17. Canada	19.6	18.8	16.2	16.0	16.3	16.6	1.5	43. Australia	4.9	5.5	5.8	5.8	6.0	6.4	5.8
18. Poland	17.4	15.2	12.5	13.4	14.8	15.8	6.8	44. Tunisia	5.1	6.4	6.9	4.8	6.0	6.3	5.3
19. Macao	5.2	9.0	11.9	12.9	13.6	14.3	5.1	45. Brazil	5.3	5.4	5.2	5.4	5.7	NA	NA
20. Saudi Arabia	6.6	8.0	10.9	17.5	14.3	13.2	-7.4	46. Argentina	2.9	3.8	5.3	5.7	5.6	5.6	-0.3
21. Netherlands	10.0	10.0	10.9	11.3	12.2	12.8	4.9	47. Kazakhstan	1.5	3.1	3.4	4.1	4.4	4.9	11.0
22. South Korea	5.3	6.0	8.8	9.8	11.1	12.2	9.3	48. Norway	3.1	3.8	4.8	5.0	4.4	4.7	8.2
23. Singapore	6.1	7.1	9.2	10.4	11.1	NA	NA	49. Dominican							
24. Croatia	5.3	7.7	9.1	9.9	10.4	11.0	5.7	Republic	3.0	3.7	4.1	4.3	4.6	4.7	2.8
25. Sweden	3.8	4.9	5.0	10.0	10.9	NA	NA	50. Philippines	2.0	2.6	3.5	3.9	4.3	4.7	9.6
26. Hungary	3.0	10.0	9.5	10.3	10.4	10.7	3.1	World	677	807	948	995	1,035	1,087	5.0
27. Japan	4.8	6.7	8.6	6.2	8.4	10.4	24.0								

NA = Not available or not applicable. * = Preliminary.

World Tourism Receipts, 1990-2013

Source: World Tourism Organization (UNWTO), © UNWTO

(in billions of U.S. dollars)

Year	Receipts[1]	Year	Receipts[1]	Year	Receipts[1]	Year	Receipts[1]	Year	Receipts[1]	Year	Receipts[1]
1990	$262	1994	$356	1998	$443	2002	$486	2006	$747	2010	$931
1991	278	1995	403	1999	458	2003	533	2007	861	2011	1,042
1992	317	1996	437	2000	476	2004	635	2008	944	2012	1,078
1993	323	1997	436	2001	466	2005	681	2009	856	2013	1,159*

* = Provisional. (1) Total of all transactions made by or on behalf of visitors for the duration of their visit. Does not include receipts from international passenger transport contracted from companies outside a traveler's country of residence.

International Travel to the U.S., 1990-2013

Source: Office of Travel and Tourism Industries, Intl. Trade Admin., U.S. Dept. of Commerce; World Tourism Organization
(number of visitors in millions)

* = Preliminary.

U.S. Domestic Leisure Travel Volume, 1995-2013

Source: U.S. Travel Assn.
(in billions of person-trips of 50 mi or more, one-way)

Note: Method of collecting travel data has been revised; data for earlier years have been adjusted to maintain comparability.

Top 10 U.S. States by Traveler Spending, 2012

Source: U.S. Travel Assn.
(domestic and international traveler spending within state, in billions of dollars)

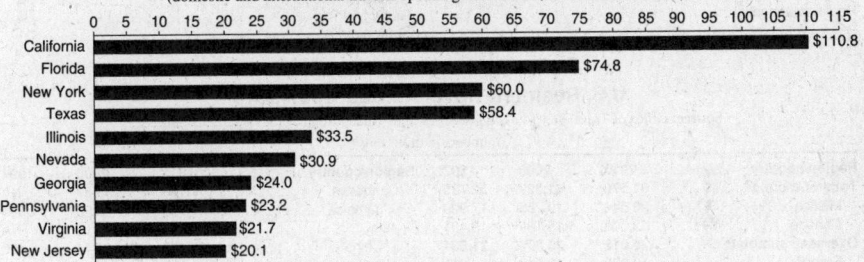

State	Spending
California	$110.8
Florida	$74.8
New York	$60.0
Texas	$58.4
Illinois	$33.5
Nevada	$30.9
Georgia	$24.0
Pennsylvania	$23.2
Virginia	$21.7
New Jersey	$20.1

International Visitors to the U.S. by Top Countries of Origin, 2013

Source: Office of Travel and Tourism Industries, Intl. Trade Admin., U.S. Dept. of Commerce
(ranked by number of visitors)

Country of origin	Visitors	Expenditures (mil)	Expenditures per visitor	Country of origin	Visitors	Expenditures (mil)	Expenditures per visitor
1. Canada	23,387,275	$27,033	$1,155.88	12. Italy	838,883	4,143	$4,938.71
2. Mexico	14,342,722	10,509	732.71	13. Venezuela	788,069	3,567	4,526.25
3. United Kingdom	3,835,308	13,715	3,575.98	14. Colombia	748,116	NA	NA
4. Japan	3,730,287	17,973	4,818.13	15. Argentina	686,098	3,503	5,105.68
5. Brazil	2,060,291	10,476	5,084.72	16. Spain	619,860	NA	NA
6. Germany	1,916,471	7,538	3,933.27	17. Netherlands	589,296	2,467	4,186.35
7. China[1]	1,806,553	9,797	5,423.03	18. Sweden	476,571	1,482	3,109.72
8. France	1,504,654	5,879	3,907.21	19. Switzerland	473,064	NA	NA
9. South Korea	1,359,924	4,617	3,395.04	20. Taiwan	384,581	1,380	3,588.32
10. Australia	1,205,060	6,070	5,037.09	All countries	69,768,455	180,700	2,590.00
11. India	859,156	5,550	6,459.83				

NA = Not available. Note: Expenditures include passenger fares. (1) Not including Hong Kong, Macao, and Taiwan.

Traveler Spending in the U.S., 1987-2013

Source: Office of Travel and Tourism Industries, Intl. Trade Admin., U.S. Dept. of Commerce; U.S. Travel Assn.
(in billions of dollars by origin of traveler)

Year	Domestic	International	Year	Domestic	International	Year	Domestic	International
1987	$235	$31	1996	$385	$70	2005	572	$82
1988	258	38	1997	406	73	2006	610	86
1989	273	47	1998	425	71	2007	641	97
1990	291	43	1999	458	75	2008	662	110
1991	296	48	2000	503	82	2009	606	94
1992	306	55	2001	484	72	2010	644	104
1993	323	58	2002	478	67	2011	697	116
1994	340	58	2003	496	65	2012	728	126
1995	360	63	2004	532	75	2013	748	140

Characteristics of U.S. Travelers Visiting Overseas Destinations, 2013

Source: Survey of Intl. Air Travelers, Office of Travel and Tourism Industries, Intl. Trade Admin., U.S. Dept. of Commerce

Total U.S. resident travelers	29,015,000
Males (adults)	51%
Females (adults)	49%
Avg. age of males (yrs.)	45.1
Avg. age of females (yrs.)	43.6
Median annual household income	$100,000
Avg. total trip expend. per visitor (incl. airfare)	$3,127
Avg. expend. outside the U.S. per visitor per day	$86
Median number of nights	10

Region of residence	% of travelers
Middle Atlantic	25%
South Atlantic (incl. Florida, DC metro area)	20
Pacific (incl. California, Washington)	15
West South Central (incl. Texas)	11
East North Central (incl. Illinois, Ohio)	10
West North Central	6
Mountain	5
New England	5
East South Central	3
Pacific Islands	1

Main purpose of trip	% of travelers
Vacation/holiday	50%
Visit friends/relatives	27
Business	11
Education	5
Convention/conference/trade show	3
Religion/pilgrimages	2
Health treatment	1

Occupation	% of travelers
Management, business, science, arts	43%
Retired	15
Service occupations	11
Student	11
Sales and office	6
Homemaker	6
Military/government	3
Production, transportation, material moving	2
National resources, construction, maintenance	2

Leisure/recreational activities[1]	% of travelers
Sightseeing	79%
Shopping	76
Small towns/countryside	43
Experience fine dining	40
Historical locations	40
Guided tours	37
Art galleries/museums	32
Cultural/ethnic heritage sights	31
National parks/monuments	28
Nightclubbing/dancing	24
Water sports	20
Concert/play/musical	14
Casino/gamble	10
Amusement/theme parks	9
Camping/hiking	7
Environmental/ecological excursions	7
Sporting event	7
Golfing/tennis	4
Hunting/fishing	4
Snow sports	1

(1) Percentages based on multiple responses.

U.S. Resident Travel Abroad, 1997-2013

Source: Office of Travel and Tourism Industries, Intl. Trade Admin., U.S. Dept. of Commerce

(numbers in thousands)

Region/country[1]	2013	2000	1997	Region/country[1]	2013	2000	1997
Total outbound[2]	61,570	61,327	52,735	Caribbean	7,196	3,867	NA
Mexico	20,546	19,285	17,909	Jamaica	1,799	886	1,341
Canada	12,008	15,189	13,401	Asia	5,455	4,914	NA
Overseas subtotal[3]	29,015	26,853	21,634	China[4]	1,132	644	476
Europe	10,039	13,373	NA	India	1,045	457	368
United Kingdom	2,640	4,189	3,570	South America	2,118	2,095	NA
France	2,002	2,927	2,098	Central America	2,002	886	NA
Italy	1,799	2,148	1,471	Middle East	1,712	1,370	NA
Germany	1,741	2,309	1,796	Africa	899	483	NA
Spain	1,045	1,262	714	Oceania	551	1,047	NA

NA = Not available. = Visits of one or more nights. Visitation estimates for Canada and Mexico include all modes of transportation used. Estimates for all other countries are available only for air travel to that country and are based upon data from the airlines that voluntarily provided it. (1) Only individual countries that received more than 1 mil visitors in 2013 are shown. Region figures include U.S. resident travelers to all countries in region. (2) To Canada, Mexico, and overseas. (3) To all countries except Canada and Mexico. (4) Not including Hong Kong, Macao, and Taiwan.

Airline Safety, U.S. Scheduled Commercial Carriers, 1985-2013

Source: National Transportation Safety Board; Federal Aviation Administration, U.S. Dept. of Transportation

Year	Departures (mil)	Fatal accidents	Fatalities[1]	Rate of fatal accidents[2]	Year	Departures (mil)	Fatal accidents	Fatalities[1]	Rate of fatal accidents[2]
1985	6.1	4	197	0.066	2004	10.8	1	13	0.009
1990	7.8	4	11	0.051	2005	10.9	3	22	0.027
1995	8.1	1	160	0.012	2006	10.6	2	50	0.019
1996	7.9	3	342	0.038	2007	10.7	0	0	—
1997	9.9	3	3	0.030	2008	10.3	0	0	—
1998	10.5	1	1	0.009	2009	9.6	1	50	0.010
1999	10.9	2	12	0.018	2010	9.5	0	0	—
2000	11.1	2	89	0.018	2011	9.4	0	0	—
2001[3]	10.6	6	531	0.019	2012	9.2	0	0	—
2002	10.3	0	0	—	2013*	8.9	1	2	0.011
2003	10.2	2	22	0.020					

— = Not applicable. * = Preliminary. (1) Includes deaths that occurred on the ground as a result of an accident, except for fatalities resulting from the Sept. 11, 2001, terrorist attacks. (2) Per 100,000 departures. (3) The Sept. 11, 2001, terrorist attacks have been included among the number of fatal accidents but have been excluded when calculating the accident rate.

U.S. Airline Statistics, 2000-13

Source: Airlines for America
(in millions, except where otherwise noted)

	2000	2005	2007	2008	2009	2010	2011	2012	2013
Passengers enplaned[1] ...	666.1	738.6	769.6	743.3	703.9	720.5	730.8	736.7	743.1
Revenue passenger miles[1,2]	692,757	779,035	829,441	812,377	769,412	798,043	814,354	823,182	840,423
Available seat miles[1,3] ...	956,950	1,003,364	1,037,691	1,021,330	957,105	972,601	992,672	994,546	1,011,152
Cargo revenue ton miles[1,2]	23,888	28,039	29,571	28,119	24,970	27,885	28,123	27,790	26,441
% of seating utilized[1]	72.4%	77.6%	79.9%	79.5%	80.4%	82.1%	82.0%	82.8%	83.1%
Passenger revenue[4]....	$94,307	$94,340	$108,172	$112,228	$91,977	$104,431	$114,820	$116,909	$121,330
Net profit[4]	$2,238	−$28,647	$6,306	−$24,500	−$2,905	$2,245	$527	$132	$12,257
Total employment[4,5]	520.6	421.2	413.1	407.6	385.9	378.1	386.0	387.8	380.8

(1) Scheduled service only. (2) One fare-paying passenger or one ton of revenue cargo transported one mile. (3) One seat transported one mile. (4) Passenger carriers only. (5) Figures are of avg. full-time equivalents (FTE), i.e., the number of full-time employees that could have been employed if the reported number of hours worked by part-time employees had been worked by full-time employees. In this table, part-time employees are treated as 0.5 FTEs.

Top 25 U.S. Passenger Airlines, 2013

Source: Airlines for America
(in millions; ranked by number of passengers enplaned in scheduled service)

	Airline	Passengers		Airline	Passengers		Airline	Passengers		Airline	Passengers
1.	American/US Airways	143.8	6.	JetBlue Airways	30.4	13.	Republic Airlines	10.0	20.	Shuttle America	6.1
2.	Southwest/AirTran	133.1	7.	SkyWest Airlines	27.1	14.	Hawaiian Airlines	9.9	21.	Chautauqua Airlines	5.0
3.	Delta Air Lines	120.4	8.	Alaska Airlines	19.7	15.	Mesa Airlines	8.5	22.	PSA Airlines	4.9
4.	United Airlines	90.1	9.	Envoy Air	17.7	16.	Allegiant Air	7.1	23.	GoJet Airlines	4.3
5.	ExpressJet Airlines	33.0	10.	Endeavor Air	13.2	17.	Horizon Air	7.1	24.	Compass Airlines	3.8
			11.	Spirit Airlines	12.1	18.	Virgin America	6.3	25.	Piedmont Airlines	3.1
			12.	Frontier Airlines	10.2	19.	Air Wisconsin	6.1			

Note: Includes domestic and international passengers on U.S. airlines.

Top North American Airports by Passenger Traffic, 2013

Source: 2013 World Annual Traffic Report, Airports Council Intl.

City/airport name (airport code)	Total passengers[1]
1. Hartsfield-Jackson Atlanta Intl. (ATL)	94,431,224
2. Chicago O'Hare Intl. (ORD)	66,777,161
3. Los Angeles Intl. (LAX)	66,667,619
4. Dallas/Ft. Worth Intl. (DFW)	60,470,507
5. Denver Intl. (DEN)	52,556,359
6. New York John F. Kennedy Intl. (JFK)	50,423,765
7. San Francisco Intl. (SFO)	44,945,760
8. Charlotte Douglas Intl. (CLT)	43,457,471
9. Las Vegas McCarran Intl. (LAS)	40,933,037
10. Miami Intl. (MIA)	40,562,948
11. Phoenix Sky Harbor Intl. (PHX)	40,341,614
12. Houston George Bush Intercontinental (IAH)	39,799,414
13. Toronto Pearson Intl. (YYZ)	36,109,469
14. Newark Liberty Intl. (EWR)	35,016,236
15. Seattle-Tacoma Intl. (SEA)	34,776,666
16. Orlando Intl. (MCO)	34,768,945
17. Minneapolis/St. Paul Intl. (MSP)	33,892,074
18. Detroit Metro Wayne County (DTW)	32,389,544
19. Philadelphia Intl. (PHL)	30,504,112
20. Boston Logan Intl. (BOS)	30,235,850
21. New York LaGuardia (LGA)	26,722,183
22. Ft. Lauderdale-Hollywood Intl. (FLL)	23,559,779
23. Baltimore/Wash. Intl. Thurgood Marshall (BWI)	22,498,353
24. Washington Dulles Intl. (IAD)	21,796,326
25. Ronald Reagan Wash. National (DCA)	20,392,671

Top World Airports by Passenger Traffic, 2013

Source: 2013 World Annual Traffic Report, Airports Council Intl.

City/airport name (country; airport code)	Total passengers[1]
1. Beijing Capital Intl. (China; PEK)	83,712,355
2. London Heathrow (UK; LHR)	72,368,061
3. Tokyo Haneda Intl. (Japan; HND)	68,906,509
4. Dubai Intl. (United Arab Emirates; DXB)	66,431,533
5. Paris Charles de Gaulle (France; CDG)	62,052,917
6. Jakarta Soekarno-Hatta Intl. (Indonesia; CGK).	60,137,347
7. Hong Kong Intl. (China; HKG)	59,588,081
8. Frankfurt Intl. (Germany; FRA)	58,036,948
9. Singapore Changi (Singapore; SIN)	53,726,087
10. Amsterdam Schiphol (Netherlands; AMS)	52,569,200
11. Guangzhou Baiyun Intl. (China; CAN)	52,450,262
12. Bangkok Suvarnabhumi (Thailand; BKK)	51,363,451
13. Istanbul Atatürk Intl. (Turkey; IST)	51,304,654
14. Kuala Lumpur Intl. (Malaysia; KUL)	47,498,127
15. Shanghai Pudong Intl. (China; PVG)	47,189,849
16. Seoul Incheon Intl. (South Korea; ICN)	41,679,758
17. Madrid-Barajas (Spain; MAD)	39,717,850
18. Munich (Germany; MUC)	38,672,644
19. Sydney Intl. (Australia; SYD)	38,254,039
20. Delhi Indira Gandhi Intl. (India; DEL)	36,712,455
21. São Paulo/Guarulhos Intl. (Brazil; GRU)	36,190,251
22. Rome Leonardo da Vinci-Fiumicino (Italy; FCO)	36,165,762
23. Shanghai Hongqiao Intl. (China; SHA)	35,599,643
24. London Gatwick (UK; LGW)	35,463,238
25. Tokyo Narita Intl. (Japan; NRT)	35,314,750

Note: World list excludes North American airports and airports that do not participate in Airports Council Intl.'s Airport Traffic Statistics collection. (1) Arriving and departing passengers and direct transit passengers counted once.

Busiest Amtrak Stations, 2013

Source: Amtrak National Fact Sheet, Amtrak; ranked by total ridership

Station	Tickets from	Tickets to	Total ridership	Station	Tickets from	Tickets to	Total ridership
New York, NY	4,790,862	4,765,562	9,556,424	San Diego, CA	343,187	343,766	686,953
Washington, DC	2,520,472	2,512,920	5,033,392	Providence, RI	326,123	334,144	660,267
Philadelphia, PA	2,062,369	2,063,134	4,125,503	Newark, NJ	331,047	325,775	656,822
Chicago, IL	1,762,317	1,760,071	3,522,388	Portland, OR	323,731	328,724	652,455
Los Angeles, CA....	822,981	820,725	1,643,706	Seattle, WA........	322,428	317,626	640,054
Boston South Station, MA....	723,221	710,927	1,434,148	Milwaukee, WI......	310,729	306,424	617,153
Sacramento, CA	571,836	560,914	1,132,750	Emeryville, CA	301,677	297,182	598,859
Baltimore, MD.......	533,746	531,830	1,065,576	Lancaster, PA	290,027	288,704	578,731
Albany-Rensselaer, NY....	382,179	382,719	764,898	Harrisburg, PA......	287,821	284,119	571,940
				Bakersfield, CA.....	275,000	271,439	546,439
New Haven, CT	374,670	370,860	745,530	Boston Back Bay, MA	277,344	263,426	540,770
Wilmington, DE......	369,654	368,659	738,313	Boston North Station, MA.............	238,242	237,205	475,447
BWI Airport, MD.....	350,822	359,691	710,513	Martinez, CA........	235,080	238,756	473,836

Top Travel Websites, 2014

Source: comScore Media Metrix, Inc.; ranked by number of visitors

Rank	Website	Visitors (thous.)[1]	Rank	Website	Visitors (thous.)[1]
1.	TripAdvisor Inc.	29,669	12.	Delta Airlines	8,754
2.	Expedia Inc.	25,114	13.	Marriott	8,355
3.	Priceline.com Incorporated	23,001	14.	Hilton Worldwide	8,287
4.	Southwest Airlines Co.	13,494	15.	Kayak.com Network	7,760
5.	HomeAway	12,612	16.	American Airlines	7,409
6.	Travelocity	10,442	17.	United Airlines	7,316
7.	Orbitz Worldwide	10,099	18.	Fareportal Media Group	7,186
8.	MediaShift	10,056	19.	InterContinental Hotels Group	6,227
9.	USATODAY Travel	9,637	20.	Disney Parks & Travel	5,820
10.	Yahoo Travel	9,364		Total travel audience[2]	152,465
11.	About.com Travel	8,891		Total Internet audience[2]	250,403

(1) Number of unique visitors, in thousands, who visited website at least once in June 2014. (2) Audience comprises all persons older than two years of age, at U.S. home/work locations.

Number of Paid Days Off Per Year in Selected Countries

Source: No-Vacation Nation Revisited, May 2013, Center for Economic and Policy Research

The figures are based on statutory entitlements for an employee working five days a week. Ranked by total paid days off.

Country	Paid vacation days	Paid holidays	Total paid days off	Country	Paid vacation days	Paid holidays	Total paid days off	Country	Paid vacation days	Paid holidays	Total paid days off
Austria	25	13	38	New Zealand	20	10	30	Finland	25	0	25
Portugal	22	13	35	Ireland	20	9	29	Sweden	25	0	25
Spain	22	12	34	Australia	20	8	28	Netherlands	20	0	20
France	30	1	31	UK	28	0	28	Switzerland	20	0	20
Italy	20	10	30	Norway	25	2	27	Canada	10	9	19
Belgium	20	10	30	Greece	20	6	26	Japan	10	0	10
Germany	20	10	30	Denmark	25	0	25	U.S.	0	0	0

Note: The U.S. has no nationwide statutory entitlement that mandates paid days off.

Record-Breaking Roller Coasters

Source: UltimateRollerCoaster.com; speed measured in mph, length and height in ft

Steel-Tracked Roller Coasters

Fastest

	Roller coaster	Theme park, location
149.1 mph	Formula Rossa	Ferrari World Abu Dhabi, United Arab Emirates
128	Kingda Ka	Six Flags Great Adventure, Jackson, NJ
120	Top Thrill Dragster	Cedar Point, Sandusky, OH
106.8	Dodonpa	Fuji-Q High Land, Fujiyoshida-shi, Japan
100	Tower of Terror	Dreamworld, Gold Coast, Australia
100	Superman: Escape From Krypton	Six Flags Magic Mountain, Valencia, CA

Tallest

456 ft	Kingda Ka	Six Flags Great Adventure, Jackson, NJ
420	Top Thrill Dragster	Cedar Point, Sandusky, OH
415	Superman: Escape From Krypton	Six Flags Magic Mountain, Valencia, CA
377	Tower of Terror	Dreamworld, Gold Coast, Australia
318	Steel Dragon 2000	Nagashima Spa Land, Mie, Japan

Largest drop

418 ft	Kingda Ka	Six Flags Great Adventure, Jackson, NJ
400	Top Thrill Dragster	Cedar Point, Sandusky, OH
306.8	Steel Dragon 2000	Nagashima Spa Land, Mie, Japan
306	Leviathan	Canada's Wonderland, Vaughan, ON, Canada

Longest

8,133 ft	Steel Dragon 2000	Nagashima Spa Land, Mie, Japan
7,450	The Ultimate	Lightwater Valley, UK
6,709	Fujiyama	Fuji-Q High Land, Fujiyoshida-shi, Japan
6,595	Millennium Force	Cedar Point, Sandusky, OH
6,562	Formula Rossa	Ferrari World Abu Dhabi, United Arab Emirates

Wood-Tracked Roller Coasters

Fastest

	Roller coaster	Theme park, location
72 mph	Goliath	Six Flags Great America, Gurnee, IL
70	El Toro	Six Flags Great Adventure, Jackson, NJ
68.4	Colossos	Heide Park, Soltau, Germany
68	Outlaw Run	Silver Dollar City, Branson, MO
67.4	The Voyage	Holiday World & Splashin' Safari, Santa Claus, IN

Tallest

197 ft	Colossos	Heide Park, Soltau, Germany
183	T Express	Everland, Yongin, S. Korea
181	El Toro	Six Flags Great Adventure, Jackson, NJ
165	Goliath	Six Flags Great America, Gurnee, IL
163	The Voyage	Holiday World & Splashin' Safari, Santa Claus, IN

Largest drop

180 ft	Goliath	Six Flags Great America, Gurnee, IL
176	El Toro	Six Flags Great Adventure, Jackson, NJ
162	Outlaw Run	Silver Dollar City, Branson, MO
159	Colossos	Heide Park, Soltau, Germany
155	Mean Streak	Cedar Point, Sandusky, OH

Longest

7,400 ft	The Beast	Kings Island, Cincinnati, OH
6,442	The Voyage	Holiday World & Splashin' Safari, Santa Claus, IN
5,578	White Cyclone	Nagashima Spa Land, Mie, Japan
5,427	Mean Streak	Cedar Point, Sandusky, OH
5,384	Shivering Timbers	Michigan's Adventure, Muskegon, MI

Passports, Health Regulations, and Travel Warnings for Foreign Travel

Source: Bureau of Consular Affairs, U.S. Dept. of State; Centers for Disease Control and Prevention (CDC), U.S. Dept. of Health and Human Services; World Health Organization (WHO); Transportation Security Administration (TSA), U.S. Dept. of Homeland Security

Passports, Visas

Passports are issued by the Dept. of State to U.S. citizens and nationals to provide documentation for foreign travel. As of Oct. 2014, the fees for a new passport book and passport card for persons ages 16 and over total $165; provided certain criteria are met, these can be renewed for $140. For a passport book alone, fees are $135 for a new passport and $110 for passport renewal.

In July 2008, the U.S. government began issuing passport cards. Travelers arriving by land or sea from Canada, Mexico, the Caribbean, and Bermuda may present a passport card to enter the U.S. Passport cards may not be used for air travel, however. The fees for a new passport card for persons ages 16 and over $55.

A U.S. passport is often sufficient for U.S. citizens to gain admission for a limited stay in another country. Some countries also require an entry visa. Each country has its own specific guidelines concerning length and purpose of visit, among other considerations. Visitors may need to provide proof of sufficient funds for their intended stay, onward/return tickets, and/or at least six months remaining validity on their U.S. passports.

All persons traveling by air outside of the U.S. (excluding direct travel to and from a U.S. territory) are required to present a passport or other valid document upon reentering the U.S.

For up-to-date passport and international travel information, visit the Consular Affairs website (travel.state.gov) or call the National Passport Information Center at 1-877-4USA-PPT (1-877-487-2778).

Health Regulations

Under WHO regulations, first instituted in 1969, member countries agree to abide by resolutions meant to contain the spread of disease. For example, some countries require travelers to provide proof of vaccination against yellow fever before entering.

Detailed information can be found in *Health Information for International Travel*, or the "yellow book," published every two years by the CDC. The book is written primarily for health care providers but may be of use to other travelers. The CDC also issues travel notices on outbreaks, health precautions, and health warnings. For current notices and more on travelers' health, visit wwwnc.cdc.gov/travel/.

WHO publishes a more technical guide, *International Travel and Health*, which can be found online at www.who.int/ith/.

Travel Warnings and Alerts

The State Dept. issues travel warnings as recommendations that Americans avoid travel to certain countries. Long-term conditions in such countries may be dangerous or unstable; because of an embassy closure or limited personnel, the U.S. government's ability to assist U.S. citizens may be reduced. As of Oct. 2014, travel warnings were in effect for the following countries: Afghanistan, Algeria, Burundi, Cameroon, Central African Republic, Chad, Colombia, Dem. Rep. of the Congo, Djibouti, El Salvador, Eritrea, Haiti, Honduras, Iran, Iraq, Israel (incl. West Bank and Gaza), Kenya, Lebanon, Lesotho, Liberia, Libya, Mali, Mauritania, Mexico, Niger, Nigeria, North Korea, Pakistan, Philippines, Saudi Arabia, Sierra Leone, Somalia, South Sudan, Sudan, Syria, Ukraine, Venezuela, and Yemen.

The department issues travel alerts when it has concerns about short-term conditions—natural disasters, terrorist attacks, anniversaries of attacks, election-related demonstrations, and regional sporting events, among others. For the latest travel warnings and alerts, see travel.state.gov.

Summary of TSA Regulations

Airplane carry-ons. TSA promotes the "3-1-1" rule regarding carry-on items. Containers with liquids, gels, aerosols, creams, or pastes must hold **3.4** oz or less; these containers should be packed inside a single **1**-quart, clear plastic, zip-top bag; and this **1** bag must be X-rayed when going through security. Exceptions to the 3-1-1 rule include medication, baby formula and food, and breast milk. Travelers must declare any exceptions at security.

Security checkpoint identification. Adult travelers (18 years of age and over) must present a photo ID. Acceptable documents include a U.S. passport or passport card; foreign government-issued passport; state-issued driver's license; permanent resident card; or U.S. military ID, among others.

Screening process. Travelers may wear loose fitting or religious garments (incl. head coverings) through security. They may be subject to additional screening if clothing could conceal prohibited items. Travelers may request a private area if selected for personal screening. Travelers will be screened by someone of the same gender.

Disability-related permitted carry-on items:

- Wheelchairs
- Crutches, canes, and walkers
- Personal supplemental oxygen (though not permitted by all airlines)
- Slate and stylus
- Medications and associated supplies
- Service animals

Permitted carry-on items:

- Disposable razors
- Eye drops and saline solution (amounts greater than 3.4 oz must be declared)
- Nail clippers, tweezers
- Metal scissors with pointed tips and blades shorter than 4 inches
- Mobile phones
- Umbrellas (must be inspected at security)
- Beverages (any size) purchased after security screening
- Musical instruments (one per traveler going through security, though some airlines prohibit musical instruments as carry-ons)

Prohibited carry-on items:

- Knives (except for plastic or round-bladed butter knives), incl. knives that are religious objects
- Baseball bats, golf clubs
- Flares
- Firearms or realistic firearm replicas, ammunition, firearm parts
- Hammers, screwdrivers, wrenches, pliers, and other tools more than 7 in. in length
- Brass knuckles
- Lighter fluid
- Liquid bleach, turpentine, paint thinner
- Spray paint
- Self-defense sprays

For complete travel information, visit www.tsa.gov/traveler-information.

Air Distances Between Selected World Cities

Point-to-point measurements, in miles, are usually from City Hall or its equivalent.

	Bangkok	Beijing	Berlin	Cairo	Cape Town	Caracas	Chicago	Hong Kong	Honolulu	Lima
Bangkok	...	2,046	5,352	4,523	6,300	10,555	8,570	1,077	6,609	12,244
Beijing	2,046	...	4,584	4,698	8,044	8,950	6,604	1,217	5,077	10,349
Berlin	5,352	4,584	...	1,797	5,961	5,238	4,414	5,443	7,320	6,896
Cairo	4,523	4,698	1,797	...	4,480	6,342	6,141	5,066	8,848	7,726
Cape Town	6,300	8,044	5,961	4,480	...	6,366	8,491	7,376	11,535	6,072
Caracas	10,555	8,950	5,238	6,342	6,366	...	2,495	10,165	6,021	1,707
Chicago	8,570	6,604	4,414	6,141	8,491	2,495	...	7,797	4,256	3,775
Hong Kong	1,077	1,217	5,443	5,066	7,376	10,165	7,797	...	5,556	11,418
Honolulu	6,609	5,077	7,320	8,848	11,535	6,021	4,256	5,556	...	5,947
London	5,944	5,074	583	2,185	5,989	4,655	3,958	5,990	7,240	6,316
Los Angeles	7,637	6,250	5,782	7,520	9,969	3,632	1,745	7,240	2,557	4,171
Madrid	6,337	5,745	1,165	2,087	5,308	4,346	4,189	6,558	7,872	5,907
Melbourne	4,568	5,643	9,918	8,675	6,425	9,717	9,673	4,595	5,505	8,059
Mexico City	9,793	7,753	6,056	7,700	8,519	2,234	1,690	8,788	3,789	2,639
Montreal	8,338	6,519	3,740	5,427	7,922	2,438	745	7,736	4,918	3,970
Moscow	4,389	3,607	1,006	1,803	6,279	6,177	4,987	4,437	7,047	7,862
New York, NY	8,669	6,844	3,979	5,619	7,803	2,120	714	8,060	4,969	3,639
Paris	5,877	5,120	548	1,998	5,786	4,732	4,143	5,990	7,449	6,370
Rio de Janeiro	9,994	10,768	6,209	6,143	3,781	2,804	5,282	11,009	8,288	2,342
Rome	5,494	5,063	737	1,326	5,231	5,195	4,824	5,774	8,040	6,750
San Francisco	7,931	5,918	5,672	7,466	10,248	3,902	1,859	6,905	2,398	4,518
Singapore	883	2,771	6,164	5,137	6,008	11,402	9,372	1,605	6,726	11,689
Stockholm	5,089	4,133	528	2,096	6,423	5,471	4,331	5,063	6,875	7,166
Tokyo	2,865	1,307	5,557	5,958	9,154	6,314	5,063	1,791	3,859	9,631
Warsaw	5,033	4,325	322	1,619	5,935	5,559	4,679	5,147	7,366	7,215
Washington, DC	8,807	6,942	4,181	5,822	7,895	2,047	596	8,155	4,838	3,509

	London	Los Angeles	Madrid	Melbourne	Mexico City	Montreal	Moscow	New Delhi	New York, NY	Paris
Bangkok	5,944	7,637	6,337	4,568	9,793	8,338	4,389	1,813	8,669	5,877
Beijing	5,074	6,250	5,745	5,643	7,753	6,519	3,607	2,353	6,844	5,120
Berlin	583	5,782	1,165	9,918	6,056	3,740	1,006	3,598	3,979	548
Cairo	2,185	7,520	2,087	8,675	7,700	5,427	1,803	2,758	5,619	1,998
Cape Town	5,989	9,969	5,308	6,425	8,519	7,922	6,279	5,769	7,803	5,786
Caracas	4,655	3,632	4,346	9,717	2,234	2,438	6,177	8,833	2,120	4,732
Chicago	3,958	1,745	4,189	9,673	1,690	745	4,987	7,486	714	4,143
Hong Kong	5,990	7,240	6,558	4,595	8,788	7,736	4,437	2,339	8,060	5,990
Honolulu	7,240	2,557	7,872	5,505	3,789	4,918	7,047	7,412	4,969	7,449
London	...	5,439	785	10,500	5,558	3,254	1,564	4,181	3,469	214
Los Angeles	5,439	...	5,848	7,931	1,542	2,427	6,068	7,011	2,451	5,601
Madrid	785	5,848	...	10,758	5,643	3,448	2,147	4,530	3,593	655
Melbourne	10,500	7,931	10,758	...	8,426	10,395	8,950	6,329	10,359	10,430
Mexico City	5,558	1,542	5,643	8,426	...	2,317	6,676	9,120	2,090	5,725
Montreal	3,254	2,427	3,448	10,395	2,317	...	4,401	7,012	331	3,432
Moscow	1,564	6,068	2,147	8,950	6,676	4,401	...	2,698	4,683	1,554
New York, NY	3,469	2,451	3,593	10,359	2,090	331	4,683	7,318	...	3,636
Paris	214	5,601	655	10,430	5,725	3,432	1,554	4,102	3,636	...
Rio de Janeiro	5,750	6,330	5,045	8,226	4,764	5,078	7,170	8,753	4,801	5,684
Rome	895	6,326	851	9,929	6,377	4,104	1,483	3,684	4,293	690
San Francisco	5,367	347	5,803	7,856	1,887	2,543	5,885	7,691	2,572	5,577
Singapore	6,747	8,767	7,080	3,759	10,327	9,203	5,228	2,571	9,534	6,673
Stockholm	942	5,454	1,653	9,630	6,012	3,714	716	3,414	3,986	1,003
Tokyo	5,959	5,470	6,706	5,062	7,035	6,471	4,660	3,638	6,757	6,053
Warsaw	905	5,922	1,427	9,598	6,337	4,022	721	3,277	4,270	852
Washington, DC	3,674	2,300	3,792	10,180	1,885	489	4,876	7,500	205	3,840

	Rio de Janeiro	Rome	San Francisco	Singapore	Stockholm	Tehran	Tokyo	Vienna	Warsaw	Wash., DC
Bangkok	9,994	5,494	7,931	883	5,089	3,391	2,865	5,252	5,033	8,807
Beijing	10,768	5,063	5,918	2,771	4,133	3,490	1,307	4,648	4,325	6,942
Berlin	6,209	737	5,672	6,164	528	2,185	5,557	326	322	4,181
Cairo	6,143	1,326	7,466	5,137	2,096	1,234	5,958	1,481	1,619	5,822
Cape Town	3,781	5,231	10,248	6,008	6,423	5,241	9,154	5,656	5,935	7,895
Caracas	2,804	5,195	3,902	11,402	5,471	7,320	8,808	5,372	5,559	2,047
Chicago	5,282	4,824	1,859	9,372	4,331	6,502	6,314	4,698	4,679	596
Hong Kong	11,009	5,774	6,905	1,605	5,063	3,843	1,791	5,431	5,147	8,155
Honolulu	8,288	8,040	2,398	6,726	6,875	8,070	3,859	7,632	7,366	4,838
London	5,750	895	5,367	6,747	942	2,743	5,959	771	905	3,674
Los Angeles	6,330	6,326	347	8,767	5,454	7,682	5,470	6,108	5,922	2,300
Madrid	5,045	851	5,803	7,080	1,653	2,978	6,706	1,128	1,427	3,792
Melbourne	8,226	9,929	7,856	3,759	9,630	7,826	5,062	9,790	9,598	10,180
Mexico City	4,764	6,377	1,887	10,327	6,012	8,184	7,035	6,320	6,337	1,885
Montreal	5,078	4,104	2,543	9,203	3,714	5,880	6,471	4,009	4,022	489
Moscow	7,170	1,483	5,885	5,228	716	1,532	4,660	1,043	721	4,876
New York, NY	4,801	4,293	2,572	9,534	3,986	6,141	6,757	4,234	4,270	205
Paris	5,684	690	5,577	6,673	1,003	2,625	6,053	645	852	3,840
Rio de Janeiro	...	5,707	6,613	9,785	6,683	7,374	11,532	6,127	6,455	4,779
Rome	5,707	...	6,259	6,229	1,245	2,127	6,142	477	820	4,497
San Francisco	6,613	6,259	...	8,448	5,399	7,362	5,150	5,994	5,854	2,441
Singapore	9,785	6,229	8,448	...	5,936	4,103	3,300	6,035	5,843	9,662
Stockholm	6,683	1,245	5,399	5,936	...	2,173	5,053	780	494	4,183
Tehran	7,374	2,127	7,362	4,103	2,173	...	4,775	1,532	1,879	6,341
Tokyo	11,532	6,142	5,150	3,300	5,053	4,775	...	5,689	5,347	6,791
Warsaw	6,455	820	5,854	5,843	494	1,879	5,347	347	...	4,472
Washington, DC	4,779	4,497	2,441	9,662	4,183	6,341	6,791	4,438	4,472	...

AGRICULTURE

Number and Acreage of Farms by State, 2000, 2013

Source: National Agricultural Statistics Service, U.S. Dept. of Agriculture

State	No. of farms (thous.) 2013	No. of farms (thous.) 2000	Acreage in farms (mil) 2013	Acreage in farms (mil) 2000	Acreage per farm 2013	Acreage per farm 2000	State	No. of farms (thous.) 2013	No. of farms (thous.) 2000	Acreage in farms (mil) 2013	Acreage in farms (mil) 2000	Acreage per farm 2013	Acreage per farm 2000
AL	43.5	47.0	9.0	9.0	207	191	NE	49.6	46.1	45.3	46.1	913	887
AK	0.8	0.6	0.8	0.9	1,092	1,569	NV	4.2	3.1	6.0	6.4	1,434	2,065
AZ	19.6	10.7	26.2	26.9	1,337	2,518	NH	4.4	3.3	0.5	0.4	107	133
AR	44.6	48.0	13.8	14.6	309	304	NJ	9.1	9.7	0.7	0.8	79	86
CA	77.9	83.1	25.5	28.0	327	337	NM	24.8	18.0	43.2	44.9	1,742	2,494
CO	35.6	30.0	31.7	31.6	890	1,060	NY	35.5	37.5	7.2	7.7	203	205
CT	6.0	4.2	0.4	0.4	73	86	NC	50.0	55.5	8.4	9.2	168	166
DE	2.5	2.6	0.5	0.6	204	215	ND	30.8	30.8	39.3	39.4	1,276	1,279
FL	48.0	44.0	9.6	10.4	199	238	OH	75.0	79.0	14.0	14.8	187	187
GA	42.3	49.1	9.5	10.9	225	223	OK	80.1	84.5	34.4	33.8	429	401
HI	7.0	5.5	1.1	1.4	160	251	OR	35.0	40.0	16.5	17.3	471	433
ID	24.5	24.5	11.8	11.9	482	486	PA	59.3	59.0	7.7	7.7	130	130
IL	75.1	77.0	26.9	27.5	358	357	RI	1.3	0.8	0.1	0.1	56	75
IN	58.7	63.4	14.7	15.2	250	240	SC	24.8	24.2	5.0	4.9	200	203
IA	88.5	94.0	30.6	32.5	346	346	SD	32.0	32.4	43.3	44.0	1,353	1,358
KS	61.8	64.5	46.1	47.5	746	736	TN	68.0	88.0	10.9	11.8	160	134
KY	76.5	90.0	13.0	13.7	170	152	TX	248.5	228.3	130.1	130.9	524	573
LA	27.3	29.0	7.9	8.0	288	277	UT	18.2	15.5	11.0	11.6	604	747
ME	8.2	7.1	1.5	1.4	183	190	VT	7.3	6.6	1.3	1.3	171	192
MD	12.4	12.4	2.1	2.1	165	172	VA	46.0	48.5	8.3	8.7	180	180
MA	7.8	6.1	0.5	0.5	67	89	WA	37.0	37.0	14.8	15.6	400	420
MI	52.0	53.0	10.0	10.2	191	192	WV	21.4	20.8	3.6	3.6	168	173
MN	74.4	81.0	25.9	27.9	348	344	WI	69.8	77.5	14.6	16.0	209	206
MS	37.3	42.0	10.9	11.2	292	266	WY	11.5	9.2	30.2	34.5	2,626	3,750
MO	99.4	109.0	28.4	30.2	286	277	U.S.	2,103.2	2,166.8	914.2	945.1	435	436
MT	28.1	27.8	59.7	59.3	2,125	2,133							

Supplemental Nutrition Assistance Program (SNAP), 1969-2013

Source: Food and Nutrition Service (FNS), U.S. Dept. of Agriculture

Fiscal year	Avg. participation (thous.)	Avg. monthly benefit per person	Total benefits (mil)	All other costs (mil)[1]	Total costs (mil)	Fiscal year	Avg. participation (thous.)	Avg. monthly benefit per person	Total benefits (mil)	All other costs (mil)[1]	Total costs (mil)
1969	2,878	$6.63	$228.8	$21.7	$250.5	2002	19,096	$79.67	$18,256.2	$2,380.8	$20,637.0
1970	4,340	10.55	549.7	27.2	576.9	2003	21,250	83.94	21,404.3	2,412.0	23,816.3
1975	17,064	21.40	4,385.5	233.2	4,618.7	2004	23,811	86.16	24,618.9	2,480.1	27,099.0
1980	21,082	34.47	8,720.9	485.6	9,206.5	2005	25,628	92.89	28,567.9	2,504.2	31,072.1
1985	19,899	44.99	10,743.6	959.6	11,703.2	2006	26,549	94.75	30,187.4	2,715.7	32,903.1
1990	20,049	58.78	14,142.8	1,304.5	15,447.3	2007	26,316	96.18	30,373.3	2,800.3	33,173.5
1995	26,619	71.27	22,764.1	1,856.3	24,620.4	2008	28,223	102.19	34,608.4	3,033.6	37,642.0
1996	25,543	73.21	22,440.1	1,890.9	24,331.0	2009	33,490	125.31	50,359.9	3,260.1	53,620.0
1997	22,858	71.27	19,548.9	1,958.7	21,507.6	2010	40,302	133.79	64,702.2	3,581.8	68,283.9
1998	19,791	71.12	16,890.5	2,097.8	18,988.3	2011	44,709	133.85	71,810.9	3,876.3	75,687.2
1999	18,183	72.27	15,769.4	2,051.5	17,820.9	2012	46,609	133.41	74,619.3	3,823.4	78,442.7
2000	17,194	72.62	14,983.3	2,070.7	17,054.0	2013	47,636	133.07	76,066.3	3,857.5	79,923.8
2001	17,318	74.81	15,547.4	2,242.0	17,789.4						

(1) Includes the federal share of state administrative expenses, nutrition education, and employment and training programs, in addition to other federal costs (e.g., benefit and retailer redemption and monitoring, payment accuracy, EBT [electronic benefit transfer] systems, program evaluation and modernization, program access, health and nutrition pilot projects).

U.S. Federal Food Assistance Programs, 1990-2013

Source: Food and Nutrition Service (FNS), U.S. Dept. of Agriculture
(in millions of dollars; for fiscal years ending on Sept. 30)

Program	1990	1995	2000	2005	2009	2010	2011	2012	2013
Supplemental Nutrition Assistance Program (SNAP)[1]	$15,491	$24,620	$17,054	$31,073	$53,620	$68,284	$75,687	$78,443	$79,924
Puerto Rico nutrition assistance[2]	937	1,131	1,268	1,495	2,001	2,001	2,001	2,001	2,001
Natl. school lunch[3]	3,834	5,160	6,149	8,031	9,994	10,880	11,300	11,579	12,221
School breakfast[3,4]	596	1,048	1,393	1,927	2,583	2,859	3,034	3,277	3,514
WIC (Women, Infants, and Children)[5]	2,122	3,440	3,982	4,994	6,472	6,680	7,170	6,798	6,453
Summer food service[6]	164	237	267	267	347	359	373	398	428
Child and adult care[7]	813	1,464	1,683	2,111	2,534	2,638	2,724	2,855	2,994
Special milk[4]	19	17	15	16	14	12	12	12	11
Nutrition for the elderly (NSIP)[8]	142	148	137	4	2	3	2	3	2
Food distrib. to Indian reserv.[9]	66	65	76	76	100	95	94	97	100
Commodity supplemental food prog.[9]	85	99	98	156	155	165	198	209	203
Food distrib. to charitable insts.[10]	104	64	2	4	0	1	0	0	0
Emergency food assistance (TEFAP)[11]	334	135	225	373	617	631	532	444	691
Total	24,707	37,628	32,349	50,527	78,439	94,608	103,128	106,116	108,542

Note: 2013 data are preliminary. All data subject to revision by the FNS. (1) Formerly known as the Food Stamp Program. Includes benefits and admin. expenses. (2) Provides benefits analogous to SNAP. (3) Data are nine-month averages (summer months excluded). (4) Figures are cash payments based on federal reimbursement rates to states. (5) Includes food benefits, nutrition services and admin. funds, Farmers' Market Nutrition Program, infrastructure, breastfeeding promotion and peer counseling, program evaluation, and technical assistance. (6) Includes cash payments, commodity costs, and admin. costs for services similar to natl. school lunch and breakfast programs. (7) Includes cash payments, entitlement and bonus commodities, cash-in-lieu of commodities, sponsor admin. costs, start-up costs, and audits. (8) For 2003 and on, program administered by the Agency on Aging; FNS costs limited to value of commodities distributed. (9) Includes cost of commodities and distrib. and admin. expenses. (10) Includes summer camps. (11) Includes cost of commodities to hunger relief orgs. (e.g., food banks, soup kitchens) and admin. expenses.

U.S. Cost of Food, 2014

Source: Center for Nutrition Policy and Promotion (CNPP), U.S. Dept. of Agriculture (USDA)

Age-gender group	Weekly cost[1]				Monthly cost[1]			
	Thrifty plan	Low-cost plan	Mod.-cost plan	Liberal plan	Thrifty plan	Low-cost plan	Mod.-cost plan	Liberal plan
Individual child[2]								
1 year	$22.00	$29.30	$33.20	$40.70	$95.20	$127.00	$143.80	$176.20
2-3 years	23.90	30.70	37.00	45.00	103.70	133.20	160.20	195.10
4-5 years	25.30	31.70	39.30	48.00	109.40	137.40	170.30	207.90
6-8 years	32.00	44.60	53.70	63.60	138.80	193.30	232.60	275.50
9-11 years	36.20	48.30	62.20	72.40	157.00	209.10	269.40	313.90
Individual male[2]								
12-13 years	38.90	55.00	69.00	81.00	168.60	238.50	299.00	351.00
14-18 years	40.10	55.90	71.30	81.90	173.80	242.20	308.80	354.90
19-50 years	43.20	55.70	69.90	86.00	187.20	241.50	302.70	372.40
51-70 years	39.40	52.70	65.50	79.00	170.90	228.20	284.00	342.20
71+ years	39.80	52.30	64.50	79.80	172.20	226.50	279.60	345.70
Individual female[2]								
12-13 years	39.00	47.60	57.30	70.30	169.10	206.50	248.10	304.40
14-18 years	38.30	47.60	57.70	71.00	166.20	206.20	250.00	307.60
19-50 years	38.40	48.40	59.70	76.40	166.60	209.80	258.80	330.90
51-70 years	38.00	47.20	58.80	71.00	164.60	204.50	254.80	307.60
71+ years	36.90	46.80	58.10	70.10	159.90	202.80	251.60	303.50
2-person family								
19-50 years	89.80	114.60	142.60	178.50	389.10	496.40	617.70	773.60
51-70 years	85.20	109.80	136.80	165.00	369.10	475.90	592.70	714.80
4-person family[3] with 2 children ages—								
2-3 and 4-5 years	130.80	166.60	205.90	255.30	566.90	721.90	892.10	1,106.30
6-8 and 9-11 years	149.90	197.00	245.40	298.30	649.50	853.70	1,063.50	1,292.70

Note: The official USDA food plans represent a nutritious diet at four different cost levels. The nutritional bases are the 1997-2005 Dietary Reference Intakes, 2005 Dietary Guidelines for Americans, and 2005 MyPyramid food intake recommendations. In addition to cost, differences among plans are in specific foods and quantities of foods. Another basis of the food plans is that all meals and snacks are prepared at home. For specific foods and quantities, see *Thrifty Food Plan, 2006* and *The Low-Cost, Moderate-Cost, and Liberal Food Plans, 2007* from the CNPP. All four food plans are based on 2001-02 data and updated to current dollars using the consumer price index for specific food items. (1) All costs are rounded to nearest 10 cents. (2) The costs given are for individuals in 4-person families. (3) Defined as a couple, 19-50 years old, and two children.

Direct Government Payments to Farmers, by State, 1950-2012

Source: Economic Research Service, U.S. Dept. of Agriculture

(in millions of dollars)

State	1950	1960	1970	1980	1990	2000	2010	2011	2012
Alabama	$8.1	$13.0	$79.5	$23.0	$82.2	$171.0	$134.6	$115.8	$118.0
Alaska	NA	0.1	0.1	0.2	1.1	1.7	9.6	11.3	12.4
Arizona	1.7	2.2	52.0	5.1	43.3	107.2	70.2	58.1	50.2
Arkansas	5.7	13.4	87.7	34.5	312.7	976.8	389.4	364.8	365.1
California	13.6	21.9	131.9	14.1	252.3	689.0	363.7	259.1	287.5
Colorado	11.9	24.8	68.0	18.0	236.7	351.4	271.6	235.4	215.7
Connecticut	0.5	0.6	0.8	0.9	2.1	18.1	15.5	10.5	8.9
Delaware	0.4	0.6	1.7	1.0	3.2	25.1	24.3	21.0	15.4
Florida	3.2	7.1	18.5	7.0	37.2	114.1	93.0	175.1	69.1
Georgia	10.6	22.9	83.6	28.9	130.6	385.1	262.3	222.3	256.7
Hawaii	NA	9.2	11.1	0.7	0.5	11.9	16.2	16.9	11.4
Idaho	3.5	13.3	48.0	7.9	133.4	264.1	163.6	113.4	126.7
Illinois	10.1	17.9	166.6	35.7	506.6	2,010.4	697.9	627.4	630.8
Indiana	5.7	16.8	111.0	15.0	244.2	939.9	372.5	300.5	323.0
Iowa	10.9	20.8	235.8	44.6	753.7	2,303.2	1,024.8	811.8	855.4
Kansas	9.1	28.5	227.6	93.3	834.7	1,233.9	631.8	542.8	518.6
Kentucky	7.4	15.8	45.8	10.0	81.6	449.5	319.6	273.8	303.4
Louisiana	11.4	15.1	55.1	20.0	154.6	471.0	209.7	209.8	219.1
Maine	1.0	2.7	1.7	3.4	7.0	13.9	48.8	17.4	21.9
Maryland	1.3	2.8	8.0	3.5	17.4	104.4	54.3	41.1	56.2
Massachusetts	0.6	0.7	0.6	0.7	3.0	11.0	20.1	20.9	17.0
Michigan	7.2	18.0	65.7	10.7	168.8	381.3	184.6	156.6	175.4
Minnesota	8.2	31.7	151.8	69.6	511.8	1,504.4	566.1	487.9	534.7
Mississippi	9.9	12.5	146.5	18.8	186.0	464.9	251.2	245.6	219.1
Missouri	10.4	23.7	153.9	78.9	299.1	872.3	435.6	367.1	396.0
Montana	6.1	15.6	85.4	58.5	299.6	490.4	327.1	298.6	239.3
Nebraska	8.8	22.1	203.0	82.9	624.6	1,407.8	509.4	470.3	480.3
Nevada	0.2	0.9	2.1	1.3	5.3	3.9	9.8	10.4	12.9
New Hampshire	0.6	0.7	0.5	0.7	1.9	4.8	20.1	12.9	14.9
New Jersey	0.9	1.8	4.3	0.9	15.7	22.5	22.0	17.1	11.9
New Mexico	2.4	11.2	43.1	20.9	63.8	79.8	91.5	88.1	97.7
New York	5.7	12.7	22.0	5.8	59.3	160.2	66.0	57.4	104.3
North Carolina	8.8	12.8	59.7	13.2	73.3	449.1	438.4	401.1	430.4
North Dakota	5.9	38.6	167.2	116.6	545.4	1,178.0	844.8	460.8	409.1
Ohio	7.3	19.2	89.6	9.4	197.0	678.3	373.2	256.7	279.8
Oklahoma	8.8	24.9	118.0	34.9	319.0	440.1	318.7	341.8	295.6

State	1950	1960	1970	1980	1990	2000	2010	2011	2012
Oregon	$3.4	$8.7	$23.1	$5.9	$89.1	$137.6	$150.4	$110.8	$118.0
Pennsylvania	6.3	11.8	25.2	8.3	41.4	147.9	81.3	73.8	119.3
Rhode Island	0.1	0.1	0.1	0.1	0.2	1.2	6.4	3.9	3.9
South Carolina	3.8	14.2	54.4	13.4	62.6	144.9	125.5	113.6	110.2
South Dakota	5.4	28.9	91.7	65.3	332.9	795.7	401.0	303.4	330.8
Tennessee	6.7	14.9	71.0	18.7	91.0	300.8	153.3	140.2	176.2
Texas	24.9	72.5	543.2	231.8	974.7	1,670.4	1,018.3	917.4	838.1
Utah	2.4	6.6	11.1	5.1	34.9	36.3	39.2	35.1	39.5
Vermont	1.3	1.6	4.1	1.3	5.8	26.1	21.1	17.8	22.2
Virginia	5.0	7.1	20.0	13.3	32.4	153.0	110.9	100.4	139.9
Washington	3.3	9.7	57.9	9.5	205.4	352.8	313.8	231.1	203.7
West Virginia	2.1	3.0	3.6	2.5	6.0	23.5	16.5	14.3	25.2
Wisconsin	7.7	16.9	51.7	12.4	181.2	603.8	259.3	196.0	281.8
Wyoming	3.0	9.9	15.2	7.3	31.3	37.3	42.7	41.3	42.6
U.S.	**283.5**	**702.4**	**3,717.4**	**1,285.7**	**9,298.0**	**23,221.6**	**12,391.7**	**10,420.5**	**10,635.1**

NA = Not available. **Note:** Direct federal government payments to farmers are for eligible historic production of wheat, corn, barley, grain sorghum, oats, upland cotton, long/medium grain rice, soybeans, other oilseeds, and peanuts. Producers enroll annually to receive payments based on rates specified in the Farm Act and on their historic program payment acres and yields.

U.S. Annual Per Capita Consumption of Selected Foods, 1970-2012

Source: Economic Research Service, U.S. Dept. of Agriculture; Distilled Spirits Council of the U.S.; Beer Institute; Wine Institute
(fruits and vegetables in pounds, beverages in gallons)

	1970	1990	2012	% change, 1970-2012		1970	1990	2012	% change, 1970-2012
Fresh fruit	96.3	111.4	124.5	29.3%	**Fresh vegetables**	144.4	163.9	176.8	22.5%
Apples	16.5	19.0	15.5	–6.6	Bell peppers	2.0	5.4	10.7	439.8
Avocados	0.4	1.3	5.0	1,081.7	Broccoli	0.5	3.1	5.8	1,083.6
Bananas	17.4	24.3	25.4	46.2	Cabbage	8.1	7.8	6.3	–22.4
Grapes	2.7	7.2	7.2	169.2	Carrots	5.8	8.0	7.6	31.0
Melons	19.4	22.3	21.7	11.9	Celery	6.8	6.7	5.5	–18.0
Oranges	15.7	12.0	10.4	–33.8	Cucumbers	2.6	4.3	7.1	173.1
Peaches/nectarines	5.5	5.3	3.7	–32.6	Garlic	0.4	1.1	1.9	419.0
Pears	1.8	3.1	2.7	46.9	Head lettuce	20.8	25.8	13.2	–36.4
Pineapples	0.7	1.9	6.1	818.0	Onions	9.5	14.2	18.6	95.5
Strawberries	1.6	3.0	7.2	352.0	Potatoes	59.3	44.9	34.1	–42.5
Canned vegetables	93.0	110.3	93.0	0.0	Sweet corn	7.2	6.2	9.0	25.7
Green peas	0.9	2.0	0.8	–15.0	Tomatoes	10.3	13.2	17.3	68.0
Snap beans	1.1	3.7	3.0	167.4	**Beverages**				
Sweet corn	14.3	11.0	5.9	–59.0	Bottled water	NA	8.8	NA	NA
Tomatoes	62.1	75.3	66.4	6.9	Carbonated soft drinks	24.3	46.2	NA	NA
Frozen vegetables	43.7	66.7	72.2	65.1	Regular	22.2	35.6	NA	NA
Broccoli	1.0	2.2	2.6	165.4	Diet	2.1	10.7	NA	NA
Carrots	1.4	2.3	1.2	–17.0	Coffee	33.4	26.8	24.7	–25.9
Green peas	1.9	2.2	1.8	–5.5	Fruit juice	5.5	7.0	6.0	9.3
Potatoes	28.5	46.4	49.8	74.6	Beer	18.5	23.9	28.2	52.4
Sweet corn	5.7	8.6	9.7	68.7	Wine	1.3	2.1	2.7	108.4
					Distilled spirits	1.8	1.5	1.6	–12.8

NA = Not available. **Note:** All figures are rounded; percent change is calculated based on unrounded original data.

U.S. Meat Production and Consumption, 1940-2014

Source: Economic Research Service, U.S. Dept. of Agriculture
(in millions of pounds)

Year	Beef Prod.	Beef Cons.	Veal Prod.	Veal Cons.	Lamb and mutton Prod.	Lamb and mutton Cons.	Pork Prod.	Pork Cons.	All red meats[1] Prod.	All red meats[1] Cons.	All poultry Prod.	All poultry Cons.
1940	7,175	7,257	981	981	876	873	10,044	9,701	19,076	18,812	NA	NA
1950	9,534	9,529	1,230	1,206	597	596	10,714	10,390	22,075	21,721	3,174	3,097
1960	14,728	15,465	1,109	1,118	769	857	13,905	14,057	30,511	31,497	6,310	6,168
1970	21,684	23,451	588	613	551	669	14,699	14,957	37,522	39,689	10,193	9,981
1980	21,643	23,560	400	420	318	351	16,617	16,838	38,978	41,170	14,173	13,525
1990	22,743	24,030	327	325	363	397	15,354	16,025	38,787	40,778	23,468	22,152
1995	25,222	25,534	319	319	285	346	17,849	17,768	43,675	43,967	30,393	25,944
2000	26,888	27,338	225	225	234	354	18,952	18,643	46,299	46,560	36,073	30,508
2008	26,663	27,302	152	150	180	343	23,367	19,415	50,361	47,210	43,235	35,379
2009	25,965	26,904	147	147	177	338	22,999	19,839	49,274	47,227	41,673	34,116
2010	26,304	26,392	145	150	168	317	22,437	19,072	49,039	45,931	43,058	35,201
2011	26,195	25,545	138	139	153	295	22,758	18,384	49,232	44,363	43,513	35,548
2012	25,913	25,752	126	123	161	299	23,253	18,604	49,439	44,779	43,523	34,870
2013	25,720	25,483	120	119	161	324	23,187	19,095	49,174	45,020	44,159	35,630
2014*	24,538	24,671	107	108	159	318	22,760	18,788	47,552	43,887	44,479	36,107

NA = Not available. * = Preliminary. (1) Numbers may not add up to totals because of rounding.

U.S. Annual Per Capita Consumption of Meat and Dairy, 1910-2012

Source: Economic Research Service, U.S. Dept. of Agriculture

(in pounds per capita per year, unless otherwise noted)

	1910	1930	1950	1970	1990	2000	2010	2012	% change, 1910-2012
Meat									
Beef....................	48.5	33.7	44.6	79.6	63.9	64.5	56.7	54.5	12.4%
Chicken................	11.0	11.1	14.3	27.4	42.4	54.2	58.0	56.6	416.0
Fish/shellfish..........	11.2	10.2	11.9	11.7	14.9	15.2	15.8	14.2	26.8
Pork...................	38.2	41.1	43.0	48.1	46.4	47.8	44.4	42.6	11.3
Red meat..............	96.0	83.6	95.8	131.9	112.2	113.7	102.1	98.0	2.1
Dairy									
Butter.................	18.4	17.6	10.9	5.4	4.4	4.5	5.0	5.6	−69.8
Cheese, American......	2.8	3.2	5.5	7.0	11.1	12.7	13.3	13.2	378.6
Cheese, other.........	1.5	1.5	2.2	4.4	13.5	17.2	19.6	20.3	1,237.4
Ice cream.............	1.9	9.3	16.4	16.7	14.8	15.6	13.5	12.9	564.9
Milk, skim/lower fat (gallons)...........	7.1	5.0	2.9	5.8	15.2	14.4	14.7	14.1	100.6
Milk, whole (gallons).................	25.2	28.2	34.2	25.3	10.5	8.0	5.6	5.4	−78.4

U.S. Organic Farmland and Animals, 1995-2011

Source: Economic Research Service, U.S. Dept. of Agriculture

Crop	Organic acreage[1]						% change, 1995-2011	% change, 2005-11	Total U.S. farmland[2]
	1995	2000	2004	2005	2008	2011			
Total cropland	638,500	1,218,905	1,452,353	1,723,271	2,655,382	3,084,989	383.2%	79.0%	370,653,755
Grains									
Corn......	32,650	77,912	99,111	130,672	194,637	234,470	618.1	79.4	93,600,000
Wheat...	120,820	206,474	214,244	293,824	415,902	344,644	185.3	17.3	60,433,000
Oats.....	13,250	29,771	42,616	46,465	57,374	62,015	368.0	33.5	3,760,000
Barley	17,150	41,904	26,629	39,271	46,954	63,903	272.6	62.7	4,020,000
Rice......	8,400	26,870	22,173	26,428	49,638	48,533	477.8	83.6	2,761,000
Beans									
Soybeans	47,200	136,071	114,239	122,217	125,621	132,411	180.5	8.3	63,631,000
Dry beans	NA	14,010	7,642	10,561	16,465	28,656	NA	171.3	1,526,900
Dry peas & lentils ...	5,900	10,144	15,893	17,757	16,987	17,887	203.2	0.7	571,000
Hay & silage	84,100	231,207	356,590	411,342	793,442	785,970	834.6	91.1	61,625,000
All vegetables	NA	62,342	86,822	98,525	177,049	147,446	NA	49.7	2,045,020
All fruits.....	NA	43,481	80,707	97,277	121,066	131,498	NA	35.2	3,839,300
Other crops									
Cotton	32,850	15,027	9,213	9,537	15,377	12,030	−63.4	26.1	10,830,300
Peanuts ...	NA	2,085	9,514	11,940	16,776	13,258	NA	11.0	1,230,000
Potatoes ..	NA	5,433	7,300	6,581	8,273	13,258	NA	101.5	1,148,800
Trees for maple syrup	10,200	11,965	13,357	12,247	31,340	43,831	329.7	257.9	NA
Fallow land ..	NA	57,688	116,582	198,650	194,428	271,644	NA	36.7	37,968,749
Total pasture & rangeland...	276,300	557,167	1,592,756	2,331,158	2,160,577	2,298,130	731.8	−1.4	473,212,960
Total farmland	914,800	1,776,073	3,045,109	4,054,429	4,815,959	5,383,119	488.4	32.8	843,866,715

Animal	Number of organic animals[1]					% change, 2000-11	% change, 2005-11	Total U.S. animals
	1995	2000	2004	2005	2008	2011			
Total livestock	NA	56,028	157,253	196,506	475,829	492,353	778.8%	150.6%	167,512,858
Beef cows ...	NA	13,829	36,662	36,113	63,680	106,181	667.8	194.0	32,834,801
Milk cows ...	NA	38,196	74,840	87,082	249,766	254,771	567.0	192.6	9,266,574
Other cows[3] ..	NA	NA	36,598	58,822	144,817	113,114	NA	92.3	54,246,483
Hogs & pigs..	NA	1,724	4,883	10,018	10,111	12,373	617.7	23.5	65,110,000
Sheep & lambs..	NA	2,279	4,270	4,471	7,455	5,914	159.5	32.3	6,055,000
Total poultry ..	NA	3,159,050	7,304,566	13,757,270	15,518,075	37,028,242	1,072.1	169.2	9,632,362,000
Layer hens ..	NA	1,113,746	1,787,901	2,415,056	5,538,011	6,663,278	498.3	175.9	377,492,000
Broilers	NA	1,924,807	4,769,104	10,405,879	9,015,984	28,644,354	1,388.2	175.3	8,882,000,000
Turkeys	NA	9,138	164,292	144,086	398,531	504,315	5,418.9	250.0	262,460,000
Other/ unclassified	NA	111,359	583,269	792,249	565,549	1,216,295	992.2	53.5	110,410,000

NA = Not available. (1) Based on information from USDA-accredited state and private organic certifiers. (2) Total acreage of organic and nonorganic land used for agricultural purposes. (3) Includes breeding stock, replacement heifers, and unclassified cows.

Livestock on Farms in the U.S., 1900-2014

Source: National Agricultural Statistics Service, U.S. Dept. of Agriculture

(in thousands)

Year (on Jan. 1)	All cattle[1]	Milk cows	Sheep and lambs	Hogs and pigs[2]	Year (on Jan. 1)	All cattle[1]	Milk cows	Sheep and lambs	Hogs and pigs[2]
1900........	59,739	16,544	48,105	51,055	1995........	102,755	9,487	8,886	57,150
1910........	58,993	19,450	50,239	48,072	2000........	98,199	9,183	7,036	59,335
1920........	70,400	21,455	40,743	60,159	2003........	96,100	9,142	6,321	59,554
1930........	61,003	23,032	51,565	55,705	2004........	94,888	8,990	6,105	60,444
1940........	68,309	24,940	52,107	61,165	2005........	95,838	9,005	6,135	60,975
1950........	77,963	23,853	29,826	58,937	2006........	96,702	9,063	6,230	61,449
1955........	96,592	23,462	31,582	50,474	2007........	97,003	9,132	6,165	62,490
1960........	96,236	19,527	33,170	59,026	2008........	96,035	9,257	5,950	66,963
1965........	109,000	16,981	25,127	56,106	2009........	94,521	9,333	5,747	66,768
1970........	112,369	12,091	20,423	57,046	2010........	93,881	9,086	5,620	65,327
1975........	132,028	11,220	14,515	54,693	2011........	100,000	9,200	5,480	64,625
1980........	111,242	10,758	12,699	67,318	2012........	90,769	9,230	5,365	66,361
1985........	109,582	10,777	10,716	54,073	2013........	89,300	9,218	5,335	66,373
1990........	95,816	10,015	11,358	53,788	2014........	87,730	9,209	5,210	64,775

(1) For 1970 and on, includes milk cows and heifers that have calved. (2) As of Dec. 1 of preceding year.

Production of Principal U.S. Crops, 1990-2013

Source: National Agricultural Statistics Service, U.S. Dept. of Agriculture

Year	Corn for grain (1,000 bu)	Oats (1,000 bu)	Barley (1,000 bu)	Sorghum for grain (1,000 bu)	All wheat (1,000 bu)	Rye (1,000 bu)	Flaxseed (1,000 bu)	Cotton (upland) (1,000 b)	Cottonseed (1,000 t)
1990	7,934,028	357,654	422,196	573,303	2,729,778	10,176	3,812	15,505.4	5,968.5
1995	7,373,876	162,027	359,562	460,373	2,182,591	10,064	2,211	17,532.2	6,848.7
2000	9,915,051	149,545	318,728	470,526	2,232,460	8,386	10,730	16,799.2	6,435.6
2002	8,966,787	116,002	226,906	360,713	1,605,878	6,488	11,863	16,530.3	6,183.9
2003	10,089,222	144,383	278,283	411,237	2,344,760	8,634	10,516	17,822.9	6,664.6
2004	11,807,086	115,695	279,743	453,654	2,158,245	8,255	10,368	22,505.1	8,242.1
2005	11,114,082	114,878	211,896	392,933	2,104,690	7,537	19,695	23,259.7	8,172.1
2006	10,534,868	93,638	180,165	277,538	1,812,036	7,193	11,019	20,822.4	7,347.9
2007	13,037,875	90,430	210,110	497,445	2,051,088	6,311	5,896	18,355.1	6,588.7
2008	12,091,648	89,135	240,193	472,342	2,499,164	7,979	5,716	12,384.5	4,300.3
2009	13,091,862	93,081	227,323	382,983	2,218,061	6,993	7,423	11,787.6	4,148.8
2010	12,446,865	81,190	180,268	345,625	2,206,916	7,431	9,056	17,600.0	6,098.1
2011	12,359,612	53,649	155,780	214,443	1,999,347	6,326	2,791	14,722.0	5,370.0
2012	10,780,296	64,024	220,284	246,932	2,266,027	6,944	5,709	16,535.0	5,666.0
2013	13,925,147	65,879	215,078	389,046	2,129,695	7,669	3,356	12,551.0	4,406.0

Year	Tobacco (1,000 lb)	All hay (1,000 t)	Beans, dry edible (1,000 cwt)	Peas, dry edible (1,000 cwt)	Peanuts[1] (1,000 lb)	Soybeans[2] (1,000 bu)	Potatoes (1,000 cwt)	Sweet potatoes (1,000 cwt)
1990	1,626,380	146,212	32,379	2,372	3,602,770	1,925,947	402,110	12,594
1995	1,268,538	154,166	30,812	4,765	4,247,455	2,176,814	443,606	12,906
2000	1,052,999	151,921	26,409	3,474	3,265,505	2,757,810	513,621	13,794
2002	871,122	149,467	30,312	4,727	3,321,040	2,756,147	458,171	12,799
2003	802,560	157,585	22,492	5,202	4,144,150	2,453,665	457,814	15,891
2004	881,973	158,247	17,788	11,419	4,288,200	3,123,686	456,041	16,112
2005	645,015	151,017	26,772	14,003	4,869,860	3,063,237	423,926	15,730
2006	727,347	142,336	24,247	13,203	3,464,250	3,188,247	441,348	16,248
2007	787,653	146,901	25,586	16,287	3,672,250	2,667,117	444,875	18,070
2008	800,504	146,270	25,558	12,270	5,162,400	2,967,007	415,055	18,443
2009	822,581	147,700	25,427	17,137	3,691,650	3,359,011	432,601	19,469
2010	718,190	145,624	31,801	14,221	4,156,840	3,329,181	404,273	23,845
2011	598,252	131,216	19,890	5,625	3,658,590	3,093,524	429,647	26,964
2012	762,709	119,878	31,925	10,872	6,763,300	3,033,581	462,766	26,482
2013	724,709	135,946	24,486	15,620	4,174,180	3,288,833	437,483	24,785

Year	Rice (1,000 cwt)	Sugarcane (1,000 t)	Sugar beets (1,000 t)	Pecans[3] (1,000 lb)	Apples (1,000 t)	Grapes (1,000 t)	Peaches (1,000 t)	Oranges[4] (1,000 bx)	Grapefruit[4] (1,000 bx)
1990	156,088	28,136	27,513	205,000	4,828	5,660	1,121	184,415	49,300
1995	173,871	30,944	27,954	268,000	5,293	5,922	1,150	263,605	71,050
2000	190,872	36,114	32,541	209,850	5,291	7,688	1,276	299,760	66,980
2002	210,960	35,553	27,707	172,900	4,262	7,339	1,268	283,760	58,660
2003	199,897	33,858	30,710	282,100	4,397	6,664	1,260	267,040	50,080
2004	232,362	29,013	30,021	185,800	5,220	6,240	1,307	294,620	52,540
2005	223,235	26,606	27,433	280,250	4,853	7,814	1,185	216,500	25,640
2006	193,736	29,564	34,064	207,300	4,912	6,378	1,010	210,750	30,600
2007	198,388	29,969	31,834	387,305	4,545	7,057	1,127	177,280	39,900
2008	203,733	27,603	26,881	202,080	4,817	7,319	1,135	234,376	37,900
2009	219,850	30,432	29,783	302,020	4,853	7,307	1,104	210,709	32,025
2010	243,104	27,360	32,034	293,740	4,646	7,471	1,150	192,835	30,400
2011	184,941	29,224	28,896	269,700	4,713	7,448	1,072	204,949	30,360
2012	199,546	32,227	35,224	302,800	4,491	7,527	977	206,119	27,650
2013	189,886	32,235	32,837	266,435	5,026	8,658	902	191,888	28,450

b = bale; bu = bushel; bx = box; cwt = hundred weight; lb = pounds; t = tons. **Note:** Some 2013 figures are preliminary estimates. (1) Harvested for nuts. (2) Harvested for beans. (3) Utilized production only. (4) Crop year ending in year cited.

Animal Products: Average Prices Received by U.S. Farmers, 1940-2013

Source: National Agricultural Statistics Service, U.S. Dept. of Agriculture

Figures represent dollars per 100 lb for beef cattle, veal calves, hogs, lambs, milk (wholesale), and sheep; dollars per head for milk cows; cents per lb for broilers, chickens, turkeys, and wool; and cents per dozen for eggs. Weighted calendar year prices for livestock and livestock products other than wool. For 1943-63, wool prices were weighted on marketing year basis. The marketing year was changed in 1964 from a calendar year to a Dec.-Nov. basis for broilers, chickens, eggs, and hogs.

Year	Broilers	Calves (veal)	Cattle (beef)	Chickens (excl. broilers)	Eggs	Hogs	Lambs[1]	Milk cows	Milk	Sheep[1]	Turkeys	Wool
1940	17.3	8.83	7.56	13.0	18.0	5.39	8.10	61	1.82	3.95	15.2	28.4
1950	27.4	26.30	23.30	22.2	36.3	18.00	25.10	198	3.89	11.60	32.8	62.1
1960	16.9	22.90	20.40	12.2	36.1	15.30	17.90	223	4.21	5.61	25.4	42.0
1970	13.6	34.50	27.10	9.1	39.1	22.70	26.40	332	5.71	7.51	22.6	35.4
1980	27.7	76.80	62.40	11.0	56.3	38.00	63.60	1,190	13.05	21.30	41.3	88.1
1990	32.6	95.60	74.60	9.3	70.9	53.70	55.50	1,160	13.74	23.20	39.4	80.0
2000	33.6	104.00	68.60	5.7	61.8	42.30	79.80	1,340	12.40	34.30	40.7	33.0
2001	39.3	106.00	71.30	4.5	62.2	44.30	66.90	1,500	15.04	34.60	39.0	36.0
2002	30.5	96.40	66.50	4.8	58.9	33.40	73.80	1,600	12.18	27.90	36.5	53.0
2003	34.6	102.00	79.70	4.9	73.2	37.20	94.40	1,340	12.55	34.90	36.1	73.0
2004	44.6	119.00	85.80	5.8	71.4	49.30	101.00	1,580	16.13	38.80	42.0	80.0
2005	43.6	135.00	89.70	6.5	54.0	50.20	110.00	1,770	15.19	45.10	44.9	71.0
2006	36.3	133.00	87.20	5.8	58.2	46.00	95.50	1,730	12.96	35.20	47.9	68.0
2007	43.6	119.00	89.90	5.6	88.5	46.60	98.50	1,830	19.21	31.00	52.3	87.0

Year	Broilers	Calves (veal)	Cattle (beef)	Chickens (excl. broilers)	Eggs	Hogs	Lambs[1]	Milk cows	Milk	Sheep[1]	Turkeys	Wool
2008	45.8	110.00	89.10	6.6	109.0	47.00	99.60	1,950	18.45	27.20	56.5	99.0
2009	45.7	105.00	80.30	7.2	81.7	41.60	99.60	1,390	12.93	32.50	50.0	79.0
2010	48.2	117.00	92.20	8.1	85.7	54.10	125.00	1,330	16.35	49.70	61.5	115.0
2011	46.6	142.00	113.00	8.7	95.6	65.30	NA	1,420	20.25	NA	68.2	167.0
2012	50.0	168.00	122.00	8.8	101.1	64.20	NA	1,430	18.56	NA	72.1	153.0
2013	60.6	181.00	125.00	9.5	107.2	67.20	NA	1,380	20.12	NA	66.5	145.0

NA = Not available. (1) Prices not calculated after 2010.

Crops: Average Prices Received by U.S. Farmers, 1940-2013

Source: National Agricultural Statistics Service, U.S. Dept. of Agriculture

Figures represent cents per lb for apples, cotton, and peanuts; dollars per bushel for barley, corn, oats, soybeans, and wheat; dollars per 100 lb for potatoes, rice, and sorghum; and dollars per ton for cottonseed and baled hay. Weighted crop year prices. The marketing year is described as follows: apples, June-May; barley, hay, oats, potatoes, and wheat, July-June; cotton, cottonseed, peanuts, and rice, Aug.-July; soybeans, Sept.-Aug.; and corn and sorghum grain, Oct.-Sept.

Year	Apples	Barley	Corn	Cotton-seed	Cotton (upland)*	Hay	Oats	Peanuts	Pota-toes	Rice	Sor-ghum	Soy-beans	Wheat
1940	NA	0.39	0.62	21.70	9.8	9.78	0.30	3.7	0.85	1.80	0.87	0.89	0.67
1950	NA	1.19	1.52	86.60	39.9	21.10	0.79	10.9	1.50	5.09	1.88	2.47	2.00
1960	2.7	0.84	1.00	42.50	30.1	21.70	0.60	10.0	2.00	4.55	1.49	2.13	1.74
1970	6.5	0.97	1.33	56.40	21.9	26.10	0.62	12.8	2.21	5.17	2.04	2.85	1.33
1980	12.1	2.86	3.11	129.00	74.4	71.00	1.79	25.1	6.55	12.80	5.25	7.57	3.91
1990	20.9	2.14	2.28	121.00	67.1	80.60	1.14	34.7	6.08	6.68	3.79	5.74	2.61
2000	17.8	2.11	1.85	105.00	49.8	84.60	1.10	27.4	5.08	5.61	3.37	4.54	2.62
2001	22.9	2.22	1.97	90.50	29.8	96.50	1.59	23.4	6.99	4.25	4.25	4.38	2.78
2002	25.6	2.72	2.32	101.00	44.5	92.40	1.81	18.2	6.69	4.49	4.14	5.53	3.56
2003	29.4	2.83	2.42	117.00	61.8	85.50	1.48	19.3	5.89	8.08	4.26	7.34	3.40
2004	21.8	2.48	2.06	107.00	41.6	92.00	1.48	18.9	5.67	7.33	3.19	5.74	3.40
2005	24.4	2.53	2.00	96.00	47.7	98.20	1.63	17.3	7.06	7.65	3.33	5.66	3.42
2006	31.7	2.85	3.04	111.00	46.5	110.00	1.87	17.7	7.33	9.96	5.88	6.43	4.26
2007	28.8	4.02	4.20	162.00	59.3	128.00	2.63	20.5	7.51	12.80	7.28	10.10	6.48
2008	23.2	5.37	4.06	223.00	47.8	152.00	3.15	23.0	9.09	16.80	5.72	9.97	6.78
2009	23.1	4.66	3.55	158.00	62.9	108.00	2.02	21.7	8.25	14.40	5.75	9.59	4.87
2010	25.1	3.86	5.18	161.00	81.5	114.00	2.52	22.5	9.20	12.70	8.96	11.30	5.70
2011	30.3	5.35	6.22	260.00	88.3	178.00	3.49	31.8	9.41	14.50	10.70	12.50	7.24
2012	37.1	6.43	6.89	252.00	72.5	187.00	3.89	30.1	8.65	15.10	11.30	14.40	7.77
2013[1]	31.1	6.05	4.50	247.00	76.4	179.00	3.70	25.7	9.79	16.00	7.60	12.70	6.80

*Beginning in 1964, 480-lb net weight bales. NA = Not available. (1) Preliminary data.

World Meat Production, 2000, 2012

Source: UN Food and Agriculture Organization; in thousands of metric tons; ranked by top producers in 2012

Top beef producers

Rank	Country	2000	2012
1.	U.S.	12,298	11,849
2.	Brazil	6,579	9,307
3.	China[1]	4,988	6,560
4.	India	2,237	2,626
5.	Argentina	2,718	2,500
6.	Australia	1,988	2,125
7.	Mexico	1,409	1,821
8.	Russia	1,894	1,642
9.	Pakistan	886	1,587
10.	France	1,528	1,492
11.	Canada	1,263	1,205
12.	Germany	1,304	1,146
13.	Italy	1,153	982
14.	UK	705	885
15.	Egypt	544	865
16.	Colombia	745	854
17.	South Africa	625	844
18.	Turkey	359	801
19.	Uzbekistan	390	780
20.	New Zealand	572	603
21.	Spain	651	591
22.	Indonesia	386	541
23.	Japan	530	519
24.	Uruguay	453	500
	Venezuela	429	500
	Africa	4,312	5,883
	Asia	12,858	17,356
	Central America	1,766	2,303
	Europe	11,768	10,429
	North America	13,561	13,053
	Oceania	2,581	2,748
	South America	11,846	14,880
	World total	**58,916**	**66,886**

Top pork producers

Rank	Country	2000	2012
1.	China[1]	35,694	49,000
2.	U.S.	8,597	10,555
3.	Germany	3,982	5,474
4.	Spain	2,905	3,466
5.	Brazil	2,600	3,465
6.	Vietnam	1,409	3,160
7.	Russia	1,569	2,559
8.	France	2,312	2,180
9.	Canada	1,640	1,998
10.	Poland	1,923	1,836
11.	Philippines	1,213	1,678
12.	Denmark	1,625	1,669
13.	Italy	1,479	1,651
14.	Netherlands	1,623	1,332
15.	Japan	1,256	1,297
16.	Mexico	1,030	1,239
17.	Belgium	1,042	1,150
18.	South Korea	916	982
19.	Thailand	693	886
20.	Taiwan	921	878
21.	UK	899	825
22.	Indonesia	413	729
23.	Ukraine	676	701
24.	Myanmar	123	620
25.	Chile	261	540
	Africa	769	1,199
	Asia	44,041	60,593
	Central America	1,140	1,421
	Europe	25,258	27,227
	North America	10,237	12,554
	Oceania	489	500
	South America	3,774	5,289
	World total	**85,917**	**109,122**

Top poultry producers

Rank	Country	2000	2012
1.	U.S.	16,416	19,796
2.	China[1]	11,890	18,230
3.	Brazil	6,125	12,051
4.	Russia	775	3,346
5.	Mexico	1,868	2,833
6.	India	904	2,258
7.	Iran	815	1,962
8.	Indonesia	818	1,781
9.	Turkey	661	1,737
10.	France	2,220	1,720
11.	Argentina	1,000	1,711
12.	UK	1,513	1,612
13.	Poland	589	1,546
14.	South Africa	821	1,496
15.	Japan	1,195	1,445
16.	Germany	790	1,428
17.	Thailand	1,149	1,348
18.	Malaysia	714	1,324
19.	Italy	1,092	1,261
20.	Canada	1,065	1,233
21.	Myanmar	248	1,193
22.	Peru	542	1,171
23.	Spain	987	1,165
24.	Colombia	504	1,112
25.	Australia	643	1,077
	Africa	2,955	4,958
	Asia	22,899	37,977
	Central America	2,371	3,657
	Europe	11,864	17,722
	North America	17,480	21,029
	Oceania	767	1,275
	South America	9,733	18,422
	World total	**68,560**	**105,636**

(1) Not including Hong Kong or Macao.

World Corn, Rice, and Wheat Production, 2000, 2013

Source: UN Food and Agriculture Organization; in millions of metric tons; ranked by top producers in 2013

Top corn producers

Rank	Country	2000	2013
1.	U.S.	251.9	353.7
2.	China	106.2	217.8
3.	Brazil	31.9	80.5
4.	Argentina	16.8	32.1
5.	Ukraine	3.8	30.9
6.	India	12.0	23.3
7.	Mexico	17.6	22.7
8.	Indonesia	9.7	18.5
9.	France	16.0	15.1
10.	Canada	7.0	14.2
11.	South Africa	11.4	12.4
12.	Russia	1.5	11.6
13.	Romania	4.9	11.3
14.	Nigeria	4.1	10.4
15.	Philippines	4.5	7.4
16.	Hungary	5.0	6.7
17.	Ethiopia	2.7	6.7
18.	Italy	10.1	6.5
19.	Egypt	6.5	6.5
20.	Turkey	2.3	5.9
21.	Serbia	NA	5.9
22.	Vietnam	2.0	5.2
23.	Thailand	4.5	5.1
24.	Spain	4.0	4.9
25.	Pakistan	1.6	4.8
	Africa	44.3	71.0
	Asia	149.1	304.3
	Central America	20.3	26.6
	Europe	63.5	117.5
	North America	258.8	367.9
	Oceania	0.6	0.7
	South America	55.4	127.6
	World total	**592.5**	**1,016.4**

Top rice producers

Rank	Country	2000	2013
1.	China	189.8	205.0
2.	India	127.5	159.2
3.	Indonesia	51.9	71.3
4.	Bangladesh	37.6	51.5
5.	Vietnam	32.5	44.1
6.	Thailand	25.8	38.8
7.	Myanmar	21.3	28.0
8.	Philippines	12.4	18.4
9.	Brazil	11.1	11.8
10.	Japan	9.4	10.8
11.	Pakistan	7.2	9.8
12.	Cambodia	4.0	9.3
13.	U.S.	8.7	8.6
14.	Egypt	6.0	6.8
15.	South Korea	7.2	5.6
16.	Nigeria	3.3	4.7
17.	Nepal	4.2	4.5
18.	Sri Lanka	2.9	4.5
19.	Madagascar	2.5	3.6
20.	Laos	2.2	3.3
21.	Peru	1.9	3.1
22.	North Korea	1.7	2.9
23.	Malaysia	2.1	2.6
24.	Iran	2.0	2.5
25.	Colombia	2.7	2.4
	Africa	17.5	29.0
	Asia	543.1	674.7
	Central America	1.2	1.2
	Europe	3.2	3.9
	North America	8.7	8.6
	Oceania	1.1	1.2
	South America	20.9	24.9
	World total	**596.9**	**745.2**

Top wheat producers

Rank	Country	2000	2013
1.	China	99.6	121.7
2.	India	76.4	93.5
3.	U.S.	60.6	58.0
4.	Russia	34.5	52.1
5.	France	37.4	38.6
6.	Canada	26.5	37.5
7.	Germany	21.6	25.0
8.	Pakistan	21.1	24.2
9.	Australia	22.1	22.9
10.	Ukraine	10.2	22.8
11.	Turkey	21.0	22.1
12.	Iran	8.1	14.0
13.	Kazakhstan	9.1	13.9
14.	UK	16.7	11.9
15.	Poland	8.5	9.5
16.	Egypt	6.6	9.5
17.	Argentina	16.1	8.0
18.	Spain	7.3	7.6
19.	Romania	4.5	7.3
20.	Italy	7.5	7.0
21.	Morocco	1.4	6.9
22.	Uzbekistan	3.5	6.8
23.	Brazil	1.7	5.7
24.	Afghanistan	1.5	5.2
25.	Bulgaria	2.8	5.1
	Africa	14.3	28.1
	Asia	254.5	318.8
	Central America	3.5	3.4
	Europe	183.6	225.5
	North America	87.2	95.5
	Oceania	22.4	23.3
	South America	20.2	18.6
	World total	**585.7**	**713.2**

NA = Not available.

Value of U.S. Agricultural Exports and Imports, 1978-2013

Source: Economic Research Service, U.S. Dept. of Agriculture
(in billions of dollars, unless otherwise noted)

Year[1]	Agric. trade surplus	Agric. exports	% of all exports	Agric. imports	% of all imports	Year[1]	Agric. trade surplus	Agric. exports	% of all exports	Agric. imports	% of all imports
1978	$13.4	$27.3	21%	$13.9	8%	1997	$21.7	$57.3	9%	$35.7	4%
1980	23.2	40.5	19	17.3	7	1998	16.8	53.7	8	36.8	4
1982	23.6	39.1	18	15.5	6	1999	11.8	49.1	8	37.3	4
1983	18.5	34.8	18	16.3	7	2000	11.9	50.8	7	38.9	3
1984	19.1	38.0	18	18.9	6	2001	13.7	52.7	8	39.0	3
1985	11.5	31.2	15	19.7	6	2002	12.4	53.3	8	41.0	4
1986	5.4	26.3	13	20.9	6	2003	10.3	56.0	9	45.7	4
1987	7.2	27.9	12	20.7	5	2004	9.7	62.4	9	52.7	4
1988	14.3	35.3	12	21.0	5	2005	4.8	62.5	8	57.7	4
1989	18.1	39.7	12	21.6	5	2006	4.6	68.6	8	64.0	4
1990	16.6	39.5	11	22.9	5	2007	12.2	82.2	8	70.1	4
1991	16.4	39.3	10	22.9	5	2008	35.6	114.9	10	79.3	4
1992	18.3	43.1	10	24.8	5	2009	22.9	96.3	10	73.4	5
1993	17.7	42.9	10	25.1	4	2010	29.6	108.6	10	79.0	4
1994	19.2	46.2	10	27.0	4	2011	42.9	137.4	11	94.5	4
1995	26.0	56.3	10	30.3	4	2012	32.4	135.8	10	103.4	5
1996	26.8	60.3	10	33.5	4	2013	37.1	140.9	10	103.8	5

(1) Fiscal year (Oct.-Sept.).

Crop Consumption Per Capita in Selected Nations, 1980-2011

Source: UN Food and Agriculture Organization
(in kilograms per capita per year, unless otherwise noted)

	Corn				Rice				Wheat			
Country	1980	1990	2011	% change, 1980-2011	1980	1990	2011	% change, 1980-2011	1980	1990	2011	% change, 1980-2011
Afghanistan	33	24	3	-92.4%	20	17	16	-16.8%	162	140	162	0.2%
Argentina	6	5	10	65.0	3	6	8	212.0	115	114	103	-9.9
Australia	2	4	5	121.7	8	8	11	42.1	29	21	17	-39.7
Bangladesh	0	0	0	NA	144	159	173	19.7	50	44	54	7.9
Brazil	22	22	24	9.5	39	41	34	-12.8	76	78	70	-8.8
Canada	4	3	19	421.6	3	5	10	185.3	59	77	63	7.7
China	5	4	7	51.0	76	81	79	4.6	33	33	40	20.8
Congo Republic	5	3	4	-23.4	2	5	20	1,064.7	33	33	40	20.8
Cuba	0	0	24	NA	51	47	64	25.1	78	74	52	-33.5
Egypt	49	57	63	30.2	26	31	40	49.6	129	151	146	13.0
France	2	3	11	533.3	4	4	6	62.9	96	92	106	11.4
Germany	3	6	10	212.9	2	2	3	57.9	69	67	85	24.5
India	8	8	7	-17.5	64	78	72	12.4	45	41	59	31.2
Indonesia	24	29	34	43.5	125	131	133	6.4	10	9	24	142.3
Iran	1	1	0	316.7	30	30	29	-1.7	154	164	152	-1.1
Iraq	0	3	0	NA	31	37	30	-2.9	144	185	140	-3.3
Israel	12	23	17	46.1	6	8	9	53.3	138	124	122	-11.6

Country	Corn 1980	1990	2011	% change, 1980-2011	Rice 1980	1990	2011	% change, 1980-2011	Wheat 1980	1990	2011	% change, 1980-2011
Italy	5	3	4	-16.0%	5	5	5	13.0%	174	149	146	-16.2%
Japan	15	19	11	-24.7	59	53	43	-26.7	44	44	49	11.0
Kenya	114	88	77	-32.4	2	1	10	329.2	20	23	34	70.5
Korea, North	43	56	45	6.3	71	70	75	4.9	32	22	23	-26.3
Korea, South	2	13	13	700.0	138	97	86	-37.8	49	48	52	5.3
Mexico	118	124	116	-1.8	5	4	6	21.3	42	42	34	-20.4
New Zealand	1	3	4	200.0	2	4	7	191.7	78	69	76	-3.2
Nigeria	6	33	31	409.8	15	21	30	104.8	16	3	25	57.1
Pakistan	7	6	14	113.4	23	14	12	-44.9	114	128	114	0.0
Philippines	22	19	31	40.5	97	94	119	22.7	17	20	15	-12.5
Russia	NA	NA	1	NA	NA	NA	5	NA	NA	NA	131	NA
Saudi Arabia	12	13	22	93.9	33	18	37	12.0	88	104	91	3.4
South Africa	120	108	100	-16.5	4	8	17	288.6	56	57	61	7.7
Thailand	5	5	10	117.4	137	114	112	-18.6	4	4	12	195.0
Turkey	9	21	18	110.6	4	7	10	149.2	210	223	174	-17.3
Ukraine	NA	NA	12	NA	NA	NA	4	NA	NA	NA	106	NA
United Arab Emirates	1	1	1	-22.2	43	34	50	16.5	NA	NA	NA	NA
UK	3	3	3	-9.4	2	3	7	263.2	63	65	96	52.5
U.S.	8	13	13	58.2	4	7	8	92.3	70	81	80	13.2
Venezuela	55	54	57	3.4	21	13	27	28.2	50	51	55	8.5
Vietnam	7	7	11	58.2	128	133	145	13.2	17	3	9	-47.6
Africa	37	41	43	16.7	15	17	23	57.4	48	48	49	3.8
Asia	8	9	10	26.3	76	82	78	2.0	54	61	63	17.0
Central America	107	113	103	-4.6	8	7	10	33.3	38	38	34	-10.6
Europe	4	5	7	94.6	5	4	5	-2.0	118	117	108	-8.5
North America	8	12	13	74.7	4	7	8	102.6	71	81	79	10.9
Oceania	2	4	5	136.8	9	10	13	50.6	79	69	70	-11.2
South America	22	23	26	19.0	30	32	30	0.0	58	58	58	0.2
World per capita consumption	13	15	18	36.2	49	54	54	9.8	65	68	65	0.8

NA = Not available or not applicable. **Note:** All figures are rounded. Percent change based on unrounded raw data.

Meat Consumption Per Capita in Selected Nations, 1980-2011

Source: UN Food and Agriculture Organization

(in kilograms per capita per year, unless otherwise noted)

Country	Beef 1980	1990	2011	% change, 1980-2011	Pork 1980	1990	2011	% change, 1980-2011	Poultry 1980	1990	2011	% change, 1980-2011
Afghanistan	5	7	5	-5.9	NA	NA	NA	NA	1	1	3	188.9%
Argentina	85	64	55	-35.4	10	4	9	-5.3%	11	11	35	215.2
Australia	53	47	41	-22.8	15	18	23	58.2	21	24	45	116.8
Bangladesh	2	1	1	-13.3	0	0	0	NA	1	1	1	133.3
Brazil	23	28	39	73.8	8	7	13	57.5	10	14	41	302.0
Canada	40	36	30	-26.1	35	28	24	-29.5	22	28	37	67.9
China	0	1	5	1,100.0	12	20	36	200.8	2	3	13	652.9
Congo Republic	4	1	3	-25.0	1	2	3	257.1	2	5	22	1,015.0
Cuba	15	13	6	-58.4	5	10	19	306.4	9	12	17	81.9
Egypt	7	8	13	88.6	0	0	0	NA	4	5	12	205.3
France	33	33	25	-22.3	38	34	34	-10.7	16	21	23	44.4
Germany	23	22	13	-41.7	60	60	54	-11.0	10	11	18	85.6
India	2	2	1	-43.5	0	1	0	-25.0	0	1	2	800.0
Indonesia	2	2	3	38.9	1	3	3	150.0	1	3	7	483.3
Iran	6	6	6	-6.5	0	0	0	NA	6	7	26	346.6
Iraq	5	7	3	-43.5	0	0	0	NA	9	11	14	67.4
Israel	13	14	28	111.5	3	2	3	0.0	35	39	70	97.5
Italy	26	27	22	-17.9	25	32	40	61.0	18	20	18	0.0
Japan	5	8	9	80.0	14	15	21	51.9	10	14	19	89.1
Kenya	12	9	11	-7.6	0	0	0	NA	2	1	1	-75.0
Korea, North	2	2	1	-50.0	10	11	5	-51.6	2	3	2	-19.0
Korea, South	3	6	15	461.5	8	13	31	296.2	3	6	16	556.0
Mexico	11	14	16	50.9	18	9	14	-22.5	6	10	30	368.3
New Zealand	57	39	48	-17.1	12	14	19	68.7	10	17	36	269.8
Nigeria	5	2	2	-57.4	1	1	2	200.0	2	2	2	0.0
Pakistan	5	6	9	79.2	0	0	0	NA	1	2	4	633.3
Philippines	3	2	4	57.1	9	12	18	110.3	5	4	11	129.2
Russia	NA	NA	16	NA	NA	NA	23	NA	NA	NA	23	NA
Saudi Arabia	6	5	6	-1.6	NA	NA	NA	NA	24	29	48	100.8
South Africa	20	17	16	-19.8	3	4	5	50.0	8	15	35	346.2
Thailand	6	6	3	-55.2	6	6	13	128.6	7	9	12	78.3
Turkey	3	7	10	221.9	0	0	0	NA	6	8	19	233.3
Ukraine	NA	NA	9	NA	NA	NA	18	NA	NA	NA	22	NA
United Arab Emirates	14	13	5	-63.1	NA	NA	NA	NA	43	39	39	-9.2
UK	23	21	19	-17.2	26	25	27	1.1	14	19	31	126.5
U.S.	47	43	37	-21.8	33	28	28	-15.5	26	39	51	94.7
Venezuela	22	18	20	-8.6	6	5	7	18.3	17	13	45	159.8
Vietnam	2	2	7	278.9	5	10	34	549.1	2	3	16	766.7
Africa	7	6	6	-12.5	1	1	1	100.0	3	3	6	148.0
Asia	2	3	4	120.0	6	9	15	144.3	2	3	9	327.3
Central America	10	12	14	35.6	14	8	12	-17.6	6	9	27	365.5
Europe	23	25	15	-35.0	32	35	35	7.8	12	15	22	85.5
North America	47	43	36	-22.3	33	28	28	-16.6	26	38	50	92.3
Oceania	50	43	39	-22.1	14	17	22	58.1	18	22	42	135.2
South America	28	27	31	11.3	7	6	11	50.0	9	12	35	275.0
World per capita consumption	11	10	9	-11.3	12	13	16	31.4	6	8	14	148.3

NA = Not available or not applicable. **Note:** All figures are rounded. Percent change based on unrounded raw data.

World Capture of Fish, Crustaceans, and Mollusks, 2003-12

Source: UN Food and Agriculture Organization

(in thousands of metric tons; ranked by 2012 captures; total includes nations not shown)

Country	2003	2005	2010	2011	2012	Country	2003	2005	2010	2011	2012
China	14,347	14,589	15,415	15,769	16,167	Norway	2,549	2,393	2,680	2,283	2,151
Indonesia	4,584	4,684	5,375	5,701	5,814	Thailand	2,850	2,814	1,811	1,835	1,835
U.S.	4,939	4,893	4,426	5,153	5,128	South Korea	1,657	1,647	1,733	1,748	1,670
India	3,712	3,691	4,689	4,311	4,863	Mexico	1,357	1,319	1,527	1,566	1,575
Peru	6,086	9,388	4,261	8,248	4,842	Bangladesh	1,141	1,334	1,727	1,601	1,536
Russia	3,282	3,198	4,070	4,255	4,331	Malaysia	1,287	1,214	1,433	1,379	1,477
Japan	4,688	4,334	4,066	3,776	3,644	Iceland	1,987	1,665	1,061	1,138	1,450
Myanmar	1,344	1,732	3,063	3,333	3,579	Morocco	919	1,026	1,136	959	1,171
Vietnam	1,856	1,988	2,414	2,514	2,622	Spain	889	853	971	1,005	930
Chile	3,612	4,328	2,680	3,063	2,573	World total	88,287	92,492	89,086	93,734	91,336
Philippines	2,166	2,270	2,612	2,363	2,323						

World Aquaculture Production, 2003-12

Source: UN Food and Agriculture Organization; ranked by 2012 production volume

Country	Metric tons (thous.)					Value (mil)				
	2003	2005	2010	2011	2012	2003	2005	2010	2011	2012
China	25,083	28,121	36,734	38,621	41,108	$25,983	$30,204	$58,822	$61,756	$66,213
India	2,316	2,967	3,786	3,673	4,209	2,591	3,763	7,339	7,933	9,248
Vietnam	938	1,437	2,672	2,846	3,086	1,968	2,931	5,150	5,596	5,808
Indonesia	997	1,197	2,305	2,718	3,068	1,699	1,999	4,895	6,315	6,715
Bangladesh	857	882	1,309	1,524	1,726	1,243	1,246	2,840	3,378	3,911
Norway	584	662	1,020	1,144	1,321	1,352	2,136	5,087	5,161	5,167
Thailand	1,064	1,304	1,286	1,201	1,234	1,465	1,741	2,817	3,362	3,316
Chile	567	724	701	955	1,071	2,152	3,229	3,753	6,314	5,993
Egypt	445	540	920	987	1,018	615	792	1,546	1,964	2,011
Myanmar	252	485	851	817	885	645	959	956	1,071	1,501
Philippines	460	557	745	767	791	601	794	1,563	1,723	1,955
Brazil	273	258	480	630	707	478	445	950	1,368	1,502
Japan	824	746	718	557	633	2,831	2,892	3,792	3,949	4,102
South Korea	388	437	476	507	484	889	1,195	1,482	1,555	1,394
U.S.	546	514	497	397	420	823	896	1,023	1,105	1,006
Taiwan	352	305	310	314	344	906	969	1,116	1,372	1,238
Ecuador	95	139	272	309	322	423	610	1,247	1,429	1,510
Iran	92	112	220	247	297	274	320	638	721	867
Malaysia	167	176	373	287	284	300	339	839	758	832
Spain	268	219	252	272	264	307	308	520	571	493
World total[1]	38,916	44,297	59,037	62,012	66,633	54,036	65,631	117,805	130,207	137,732

Note: Does not include production of aquatic plants or marine mammals. (1) Includes nations not shown.

U.S. Commercial Landings of Fish and Shellfish, 1990-2012

Source: Natl. Marine Fisheries Service, Natl. Oceanic and Atmospheric Admin., U.S. Dept. of Commerce

Year	Landings for human food		Landings for industrial purposes[1]		Total	
	Weight (mil lbs)	Value (mil)	Weight (mil lbs)	Value (mil)	Weight (mil lbs)	Value (mil)
1990	7,041	$3,366	2,363	$156	9,404	$3,522
1995	7,667	3,625	2,121	145	9,788	3,770
2000	6,912	3,398	2,157	152	9,069	3,550
2001	7,311	3,064	2,178	154	9,489	3,218
2002	7,205	2,940	2,192	152	9,397	3,092
2003	7,521	3,185	1,986	157	9,507	3,347
2004	7,794	3,611	1,889	145	9,683	3,756
2005	7,997	3,825	1,710	117	9,707	3,942
2006	7,842	3,911	1,641	113	9,483	4,024
2007	7,490	4,015	1,819	177	9,309	4,192
2008	6,633	4,231	1,692	152	8,325	4,383
2009	6,198	3,733	1,833	158	8,031	3,891
2010	6,526	4,356	1,705	164	8,231	4,520
2011	7,909	5,108	1,949	181	9,858	5,289
2012[1]	7,477	4,923	2,157	180	9,634	5,103

Note: Does not include products of aquaculture, except oysters and clams. Landings reported in round (live) weight for all items except univalve and bivalve mollusks (e.g., clams, oysters, and scallops), which are reported in weight of meats (excluding the shell). Incl. landings by U.S.-flag vessels outside of the 50 states. (1) Processed into meal, oil, solubles, and shell products or used as bait or animal food. (2) Preliminary.

U.S. Domestic Landings by Region, 2005, 2012

Source: Natl. Marine Fisheries Service, Natl. Oceanic and Atmospheric Admin., U.S. Dept. of Commerce

Region	2005		2012[1]	
	Weight (thous. lbs)	Value (thous.)	Weight (thous. lbs)	Value (thous.)
New England	684,090	$971,663	664,243	$1,191,359
Middle Atlantic[2]	199,937	221,505	750,987	487,232
Chesapeake[2]	508,953	218,933	NA[2]	NA[2]
South Atlantic	122,422	125,117	108,013	171,594
Gulf	1,196,355	620,987	1,643,480	754,200
Pacific Coast (incl. Alaska)	6,950,647	1,700,927	6,418,346	2,365,937
Great Lakes[3]	16,732	12,434	18,347	19,956
Hawaii	28,139	70,811	31,048	112,300
Total	9,707,275	3,942,376	9,634,464	5,102,578

NA = Not available. Note: Landings reported in round (live) weight for all items except univalve and bivalve mollusks (e.g., clams, oysters, scallops), which are reported in weight of meats (excluding the shell). (1) Preliminary. (2) Chesapeake Region states (Maryland and Virginia) included with Middle Atlantic in 2012. (3) Data for the Great Lakes states lag by one year (i.e., figures are for 2004 and 2011).

EMPLOYMENT

Employment and Unemployment in the U.S., 1900-2013

Source: Bureau of Labor Statistics, U.S. Dept. of Labor

(civilian labor force, persons 16 years of age and older unless otherwise noted; annual averages, in thousands)

Year	Employed	Unemployed Number	Rate	Year	Employed	Unemployed Number	Rate	Year	Employed	Unemployed Number	Rate
1900[1] ...	26,956	1,420	5.0%	1987	112,440	7,425	6.2%	2001	136,933	6,801	4.7%
1910[1] ...	34,599	2,150	5.9	1988	114,968	6,701	5.5	2002	136,485	8,378	5.8
1920[1] ...	39,208	2,132	5.2	1989	117,342	6,528	5.3	2003	137,736	8,774	6.0
1930[1] ...	44,183	4,340	8.9	1990	118,793	7,047	5.6	2004	139,252	8,149	5.5
1940[1] ...	47,520	8,120	14.6	1991	117,718	8,628	6.8	2005	141,730	7,591	5.1
1950	58,918	3,288	5.0	1992	118,492	9,613	7.5	2006	144,427	7,001	4.6
1955	62,170	2,852	4.4	1993	120,259	8,940	6.9	2007	146,047	7,078	4.6
1960	65,778	3,852	5.5	1994	123,060	7,996	6.1	2008	145,362	8,924	5.8
1965	71,088	3,366	4.5	1995	124,900	7,404	5.6	2009	139,877	14,265	9.3
1970	78,678	4,093	4.9	1996	126,708	7,236	5.4	2010	139,064	14,825	9.6
1975	85,846	7,929	8.5	1997	129,558	6,739	4.9	2011	139,869	13,747	8.9
1980	99,303	7,637	7.1	1998	131,463	6,210	4.5	2012	142,469	12,506	8.1
1985	107,150	8,312	7.2	1999	133,488	5,880	4.2	2013	143,929	11,460	7.4
1986	109,597	8,237	7.0	2000	136,891	5,692	4.0				

Note: Because of revisions in population controls, data for a given year may not be strictly comparable to other years. **Other unemployment rates (1905-45)**, persons 14 years of age and older: 1905, 4.3%; 1915, 8.5%; 1925, 3.2%; 1935, 20.3%; 1936, 16.9%; 1937, 14.3%; 1938, 19.0%; 1939, 17.2%; 1945, 1.9%. (1) Persons 14 years of age and older.

Unemployment Insurance Data by State, 2013

Source: Employment and Training Admin., U.S. Dept. of Labor; state programs only

State/ terr.	Unemployment rate	Monetarily eligible claimants	Number of first payments	Number of final payments	Initial claims	Benefits paid	Average weekly benefit	Employers subject to state law
AL	6.5%	142,247	87,327	37,580	249,773	$272,687,548	$207	82,945
AK	6.5	52,035	34,219	19,560	81,330	141,209,493	250	17,931
AZ	8.0	153,809	103,262	49,049	257,584	332,181,089	221	122,655
AR	7.5	113,994	75,052	31,180	185,171	259,378,503	289	68,190
CA	8.9	1,411,280	1,227,461	634,651	2,939,862	5,725,095,722	301	1,271,053
CO	6.8	136,276	107,561	56,243	170,725	547,714,230	356	151,655
CT	7.8	161,143	146,208	59,719	250,931	731,504,861	345	98,018
DE	6.7	33,198	20,684	10,013	51,620	106,871,145	245	26,244
DC	8.3	31,556	27,947	13,945	24,452	143,686,691	299	30,243
FL	7.2	422,549	225,849	171,898	718,019	948,972,873	231	484,568
GA	8.2	319,613	227,804	109,469	540,216	622,222,150	267	207,448
HI	4.8	40,719	31,573	11,489	93,305	198,516,367	424	30,707
ID	6.2	60,358	46,254	16,701	101,616	130,889,860	264	46,798
IL	9.2	388,123	400,043	170,393	725,979	2,076,368,917	324	306,421
IN	7.5	200,624	142,481	49,056	316,095	526,009,687	243	128,303
IA	4.6	118,938	94,474	31,347	175,253	400,768,278	337	74,626
KS	5.4	82,713	66,002	30,694	154,079	247,954,788	341	68,716
KY	8.3	146,433	70,938	34,964	248,013	407,517,703	292	88,175
LA	6.2	105,597	62,082	22,436	141,690	194,780,820	207	100,913
ME	6.7	50,749	38,585	15,025	80,031	151,444,730	285	41,419
MD	6.6	172,903	134,124	60,517	299,429	696,358,367	329	138,823
MA	7.1	279,861	226,751	106,347	371,521	1,464,986,851	424	194,235
MI	8.8	360,175	297,198	145,392	639,539	1,153,443,117	293	199,537
MN	5.1	188,726	138,824	58,183	264,260	742,266,087	376	129,104
MS	8.6	88,013	58,334	24,248	134,196	160,769,228	194	52,946
MO	6.5	202,781	137,718	66,682	379,374	442,799,255	242	142,230
MT	5.6	40,755	27,400	13,055	66,446	114,553,375	290	37,201
NE	3.9	53,143	34,399	14,740	81,827	105,340,816	276	57,429
NV	9.8	83,955	83,383	41,626	190,395	425,661,948	308	57,937
NH	5.3	37,839	24,539	7,246	58,731	99,972,384	287	40,559
NJ	8.2	378,475	333,301	172,941	582,949	2,176,898,333	398	228,762
NM	6.9	38,382	38,988	19,450	68,206	220,537,961	303	44,774
NY	7.7	750,161	569,645	257,350	1,197,227	2,807,534,501	308	510,539
NC	8.0	309,355	210,584	129,530	500,684	861,974,128	290	198,547
ND	2.9	25,264	19,115	7,893	27,190	99,790,608	396	25,064
OH	7.4	330,772	232,147	89,517	541,837	1,099,951,607	318	218,787
OK	5.4	87,238	53,154	28,896	114,534	246,034,438	293	84,661
OR	7.7	168,014	114,355	54,531	347,271	667,098,340	316	112,275
PA	7.4	487,908	442,654	172,727	1,195,021	2,482,248,639	360	305,660
PR	14.3	100,558	88,404	52,957	140,549	211,043,915	119	47,160
RI	9.5	45,007	36,995	16,329	79,389	199,860,821	351	33,044
SC	7.6	149,055	83,081	37,103	250,996	248,809,384	248	99,399
SD	3.8	12,076	7,315	1,322	17,213	30,107,695	276	26,083
TN	8.2	183,449	126,742	58,583	297,662	447,643,468	235	114,445
TX	6.3	641,323	450,061	220,944	879,653	2,170,058,407	341	483,588
UT	4.4	72,136	49,669	17,854	93,324	196,153,000	345	70,921
VT	4.4	26,584	21,454	4,406	42,286	77,305,326	313	21,600
VA	5.5	208,293	123,969	61,789	290,236	555,209,309	295	199,386
VI	NA	2,908	2,751	1,994	3,333	14,381,571	337	3,390
WA	7.0	263,922	195,029	70,084	460,572	1,067,106,630	387	226,118
WV	6.5	68,091	51,736	18,256	82,426	214,073,443	275	36,004
WI	6.7	267,853	214,125	74,736	552,383	783,235,611	276	132,898
WY	4.6	21,589	15,311	6,124	26,850	75,174,058	359	22,041
U.S.	**7.4**	**10,318,518**	**7,879,061**	**3,688,764**	**17,783,253**	**39,356,722,583**	**310**	**7,742,168**

NA = Not available.

U.S. Unemployment Duration by Industry and Occupation, 2013
Source: Bureau of Labor Statistics, U.S. Dept. of Labor

Occupation	Total	Number of unemployed persons (thous.)				Weeks of unemployment	
		Less than 5 weeks	5 to 14 weeks	15 to 26 weeks	27 weeks and over	Average (mean) duration	Median duration
Management, professional, and related	2,036	447	473	315	801	37.5	18.0
Management, business, and financial operations	831	149	186	141	355	41.2	21.0
Professional and related	1,205	298	287	174	446	35.0	15.6
Service	2,444	588	596	364	896	34.4	15.7
Sales and office	2,575	546	583	404	1,042	39.6	19.2
Sales and related	1,212	275	288	185	463	37.7	17.2
Office and administrative support	1,363	270	295	218	579	41.4	20.9
Natural resources, construction, and maintenance	1,423	353	355	228	487	34.7	14.7
Farming, fishing, and forestry	124	33	38	22	30	26.7	11.8
Construction and extraction	1,016	259	254	161	342	34.7	14.3
Installation, maintenance, and repair	284	61	63	45	115	38.5	19.4
Production, transportation, and material moving	1,690	351	396	288	656	37.9	18.3
Production	792	153	176	136	327	40.5	19.9
Transportation and material moving	898	197	219	153	329	35.6	16.9
Industry[1]							
Agriculture and related industries	148	37	46	30	35	25.2	12.4
Mining, quarrying, and oil and gas extraction	66	18	22	12	15	20.9	11.1
Construction	957	237	244	151	324	35.0	14.4
Manufacturing	1,031	190	230	172	439	42.4	20.6
Durable goods	619	112	140	95	273	43.5	21.5
Nondurable goods	412	78	90	77	166	40.8	19.7
Wholesale and retail trade	1,487	312	341	230	604	39.0	19.1
Transportation and utilities	452	94	109	68	180	37.6	18.3
Information	185	40	36	32	77	41.2	20.4
Financial activities	440	84	95	76	185	42.6	20.7
Professional and business services	1,321	271	311	221	518	36.9	18.5
Education and health services	1,447	342	334	211	561	35.5	17.2
Leisure and hospitality	1,421	368	370	211	472	32.1	13.6
Other services	449	108	104	75	161	35.9	16.3
Public administration	237	50	46	40	101	40.5	21.8
No previous work experience	1,247	295	347	202	404	32.6	13.9
Total unemployed	**11,460**	**2,584**	**2,759**	**1,807**	**4,310**	**36.5**	**17.0**

Note: Persons 16 years of age and older. (1) Includes wage and salary workers only.

Persons Not in the U.S. Labor Force, 2013
Source: Bureau of Labor Statistics, U.S. Dept. of Labor

The Labor Dept.'s unemployment rate, based on its household survey, shows the number of people out of work as a percentage of U.S. adults age 16 and older in the labor force. That rate excludes the millions of adults considered to be not in the labor force.

(in thousands)

	Number	Age in years			Sex	
		16 to 24	25 to 54	55 and over	Men	Women
Total not in the labor force	90,290	17,458	23,630	49,201	35,889	54,401
Do not want a job now[1]	83,901	15,362	20,898	47,641	32,947	50,953
Want a job[1]	6,390	2,096	2,733	1,561	2,941	3,448
Did not search for work in previous year	3,402	1,079	1,327	996	1,479	1,923
Searched in previous year but not previous 4 weeks[2]	2,988	1,017	1,406	565	1,463	1,525
Not available to work now	628	286	272	70	239	390
Available to work now	2,360	731	1,134	495	1,224	1,135
Reason not currently looking[3]						
Discouragement over job prospects[4]	861	213	431	218	510	351
Reasons other than discouragement	1,498	518	703	277	714	784
Family responsibilities	229	33	148	48	61	169
In school or training	294	234	56	4	159	135
Ill health or disability	151	18	74	58	74	77
Other[5]	823	232	425	166	420	403

(1) Includes some persons who are not asked if they want a job. (2) Persons who had a job in the prior 12 months must have searched since the end of that job to be considered unemployed. (3) Of those available to work now. (4) Includes believing no work is available, not being able to find work, lacking necessary schooling or training, thought of as too young or old by employers, and other types of discrimination. (5) Includes those who did not actively look for work in the prior four weeks for such reasons as child care and transportation problems, as well as a small number for which reason for nonparticipation was not ascertained.

U.S. Displaced Workers, 2014
Source: Bureau of Labor Statistics, U.S. Dept. of Labor

	Number (thous.)	Reason for job loss		
		Plant or company closed down or moved	Insufficient work	Position or shift abolished
Total displaced workers	**4,292**	**35.3%**	**32.6%**	**32.1%**
Age: 20 to 24 years	91	45.6	33.1	21.3
25 to 54 years	2,897	35.1	34.6	30.3
55 to 64 years	1,004	34.2	28.8	37.0
65 years and over	301	37.1	25.8	37.1
Sex: Men	2,390	35.0	37.8	27.2
Women	1,902	35.5	26.1	38.4
Race: White	3,499	35.4	31.1	33.6
Black	465	40.1	38.0	21.8
Asian	192	36.2	28.4	35.4
Hispanic or Latino	685	41.5	40.0	18.4

Note: As of Jan. 2014. Displaced workers are persons age 20 or older who lost or left jobs they had held for at least three years. Workers in this table were displaced between Jan. 2011 and Dec. 2013. Hispanic or Latino persons may be of any race.

U.S. Unemployment Rates by Selected Characteristics, 1995-2014
Source: Bureau of Labor Statistics, U.S. Dept. of Labor

	1995	2000	2005	2009	2010	2011	2012	2013 Jan.	2013 June	2013 Yr.	2014 Jan.	2014 June
Total (all civilian workers)	5.6%	4.0%	5.1%	9.3%	9.6%	8.9%	8.1%	8.5%	7.8%	7.4%	7.0%	6.3%
Men, 20 years and older	4.8	3.3	4.4	9.6	9.8	8.7	7.5	8.4	6.8	7.0	7.0	5.5
Women, 20 years and older	4.9	3.6	4.6	7.5	8.0	7.9	7.3	7.4	7.0	6.5	6.0	5.5
Both sexes, 16 to 19 years	17.3	13.1	16.6	24.3	25.9	24.4	24.0	24.2	26.6	22.9	21.0	23.9
White	4.9	3.5	4.4	8.5	8.7	7.9	7.2	7.6	6.8	6.5	6.2	5.5
Black	10.4	7.6	10.0	14.8	16.0	15.8	13.8	14.3	14.3	13.1	12.6	11.1
Asian	—	3.6	4.0	7.3	7.5	7.0	5.9	6.5	5.0	5.2	4.8	5.1
Hispanic or Latino (any race)	9.3	5.7	6.0	12.1	12.5	11.5	10.3	10.5	9.1	9.1	9.1	7.8
Married men, spouse present	3.3	—	—	6.6	6.8	5.8	4.9	4.6	4.3	4.3	3.8	3.4
Married women, spouse present	3.9	—	—	5.5	5.9	5.6	5.3	5.2	4.6	4.6	3.9	3.8
Women who maintain families, spouse absent	8.0	5.9	7.8	11.5	12.3	12.4	11.4	11.3	10.7	10.2	9.1	8.1
Occupation												
Management, professional, and related	2.4	1.8	2.3	4.6	4.7	4.5	4.1	3.9	4.2	3.6	3.1	3.5
Service	7.5	5.2	6.4	9.6	10.3	9.9	9.1	10.0	9.3	8.6	8.5	6.9
Sales and office	5.0	3.8	4.8	8.5	9.0	8.7	7.7	8.5	6.9	7.2	7.1	5.8
Natural resources, constr., and maintenance	—	5.3	6.5	15.6	16.1	13.3	11.5	13.3	8.9	9.8	10.2	7.3
Production, transp., and material moving	—	5.1	6.5	13.3	12.8	11.3	9.8	11.1	8.7	9.1	9.0	6.9
Industry												
Nonagricultural, private wage, and salary workers	5.8	4.1	5.2	9.8	9.9	9.0	7.9	8.6	7.2	7.2	7.0	5.8
Mining	5.2	4.4	3.1	11.6	9.4	6.1	6.0	9.6	6.4	5.8	6.5	2.5
Construction	11.5	6.2	7.4	19.0	20.6	16.4	13.9	16.1	9.8	11.3	12.3	8.2
Manufacturing	4.9	3.5	4.9	12.1	10.6	9.0	7.3	7.9	6.4	6.6	5.6	4.4
Durable goods	4.4	3.2	4.6	12.9	11.2	9.2	7.2	7.1	5.9	6.3	5.1	4.0
Nondurable goods	5.7	4.0	5.3	10.6	9.6	8.5	7.5	9.1	7.1	7.1	6.4	5.1
Wholesale and retail trade	6.5	4.3	5.4	9.0	9.5	8.9	8.1	8.2	7.0	7.3	7.8	5.8
Transportation and utilities	4.5	3.4	4.1	8.9	8.4	8.2	6.9	7.7	6.3	6.6	6.8	5.4
Information	—	3.2	5.0	9.2	9.7	7.3	7.6	8.2	5.6	6.2	6.6	5.2
Financial activities	3.3	2.4	2.9	6.4	6.4	5.1	5.5	5.5	4.7	4.5	3.8	4.4
Professional and business services	—	4.8	6.2	10.8	10.8	9.7	8.9	10.4	8.2	8.3	8.4	6.6
Education and health services	—	2.5	3.4	5.3	5.8	5.6	5.5	5.4	5.6	4.9	4.1	4.5
Leisure and hospitality	—	6.6	7.8	11.7	12.2	11.6	10.4	12.0	10.7	10.0	9.5	8.6
Other services	8.4	3.9	4.8	7.5	8.5	8.8	7.2	7.9	6.3	6.9	7.4	5.9
Agriculture and related	11.1	9.0	8.3	14.3	13.9	12.5	12.4	13.1	8.2	10.1	13.0	4.7
Government	2.9	2.1	2.6	3.6	4.4	4.7	4.3	4.2	5.2	4.0	3.4	3.6
Self-employed and unpaid family workers	—	2.1	2.7	5.5	5.9	6.0	5.4	5.8	5.0	5.3	5.2	4.6

— = Not available. **Note:** All monthly rates are unadjusted, except for married men and women, which are seasonally adjusted.

Employed Persons in the U.S. by Occupation and Sex, 2012-13
Source: Bureau of Labor Statistics, U.S. Dept. of Labor
(persons 16 years of age and older; numbers in thousands)

	Total 2012	Total 2013	Men 2012	Men 2013	Women 2012	Women 2013
Total	142,469	143,929	75,555	76,353	66,914	67,577
Management, professional, and related occupations	54,043	54,712	26,208	26,597	27,834	28,114
Management, business, and financial operations	22,678	22,794	12,779	12,898	9,899	9,896
Management	16,042	16,037	9,849	9,906	6,194	6,131
Business and financial operations	6,636	6,757	2,931	2,992	3,705	3,765
Professional and related	31,365	31,917	13,429	13,699	17,936	18,218
Computer and mathematical	3,816	3,980	2,841	2,941	976	1,039
Architecture and engineering	2,846	2,806	2,457	2,410	390	396
Life, physical, and social science	1,316	1,307	720	705	596	602
Community and social services	2,265	2,332	819	879	1,446	1,453
Legal	1,786	1,809	885	891	901	918
Education, training, and library	8,543	8,623	2,253	2,261	6,290	6,362
Arts, design, entertainment, sports, and media	2,814	2,879	1,456	1,520	1,358	1,359
Healthcare practitioner and technical	7,977	8,182	1,998	2,092	5,979	6,090
Service occupations	25,459	25,929	11,135	11,260	14,324	14,669
Healthcare support	3,496	3,537	434	393	3,062	3,145
Protective service	3,096	3,130	2,449	2,469	647	661
Food preparation and serving related	8,018	8,209	3,648	3,721	4,370	4,488
Building and grounds cleaning and maintenance	5,591	5,661	3,430	3,473	2,160	2,188
Personal care and service	5,258	5,392	1,173	1,205	4,085	4,187
Sales and office occupations	33,152	33,246	12,653	12,680	20,500	20,566
Sales and related	15,457	15,444	7,922	7,935	7,535	7,509
Office and administrative support	17,695	17,802	4,730	4,745	12,965	13,057
Natural resources, construction, and maintenance occupations	12,821	13,058	12,266	12,461	554	598
Farming, fishing, and forestry	994	964	768	755	226	209
Construction and extraction	7,005	7,130	6,832	6,948	173	182
Installation, maintenance, and repair	4,821	4,964	4,666	4,757	156	207
Production, transportation, and material moving occupations	16,994	16,984	13,294	13,354	3,701	3,630
Production	8,455	8,275	6,109	5,991	2,346	2,284
Transportation and material moving	8,540	8,709	7,185	7,363	1,355	1,346

Note: Numbers may not add up to totals because of independent rounding.

Projected Openings for Selected High-Paying Occupations, 2012-22

Source: Employment Projections Program, Bureau of Labor Statistics, U.S. Dept. of Labor

Job openings shown below represent the average number expected each year, from 2012 to 2022, for workers in the U.S. who are entering these occupations for the first time.

Occupation	Annual avg. job openings[1]	Median annual earnings[2]	Occupation	Annual avg. job openings[1]	Median annual earnings[2]
Registered nurses	1,052,600	$65,470	Sales reps, wholesale and manuf.[5]	420,700	$54,230
General and operations mgrs.	613,100	98,460	First-line retail supervisors	419,800	36,820
Secretaries and administrative assistants[3]	587,600	32,410	Gen. maintenance and repair workers	379,700	35,210
Accountants and auditors	544,200	63,550	Bookkeeping, accounting, auditing clerks	370,000	35,170
First-line office and admin. support			Lic. practical and vocational nurses	363,100	41,540
supervisors	508,000	49,330	Carpenters	329,200	39,940
Elementary school teachers[4]	467,400	53,400	Secondary school teachers[6]	312,600	55,050
Truck drivers, heavy and tractor-trailer	464,700	38,200	Sales reps, services, all other	302,000	50,850

(1) As a result of growth and replacement needs. (2) For 2012. (3) Except legal, medical, and executive. (4) Except special education. (5) Except technical and scientific products. (6) Except special and career/technical education.

Highest Average Weekly Wages by County, 2013

Source: Bureau of Labor Statistics, U.S. Dept. of Labor

County	Avg. weekly wage	% change, 2012-13	County	Avg. weekly wage	% change, 2012-13
San Mateo, CA	$2,724	−15.8%	Fairfax, VA	$1,558	−2.0%
New York, NY	2,041	−3.3	Morris, NJ	1,553	5.0
Santa Clara, CA	1,972	3.4	Somerset, NJ	1,484	2.8
San Francisco, CA	1,753	3.0	Middlesex, MA	1,437	0.1
Suffolk, MA	1,741	0.6	Alexandria City, VA	1,414	−3.2
Fairfield, CT	1,653	−3.3	Westchester, NY	1,348	−0.3
Washington, DC	1,638	−3.9	Montgomery, MD	1,316	−2.3
Arlington, VA	1,588	−2.4	**United States**	**1,000**	**0.0**

Note: Figures shown are for the 4th quarter, from among the 335 largest U.S. counties, which comprise 71.7% of total covered workers. Horry County, SC, recorded the lowest average weekly earnings among the largest counties, with an average weekly wage of $587 in the 4th quarter of 2013. It was followed by Cameron County, TX ($598); Hidalgo County, TX ($620); Lake County, FL ($668); Webb County, TX ($670); and El Paso County, TX ($686). Data include all workers covered by state and federal unemployment insurance programs.

Federal Minimum Hourly Wage Rates

Source: Bureau of Labor Statistics, U.S. Dept. of Labor

Effective date	Minimum wage	% avg. earnings[1]	In 2014 dollars	Effective date	Minimum wage	% avg. earnings[1]	In 2014 dollars
Oct. 24, 1938	$0.25	40%	$4.19	Jan. 1, 1978	$2.65	43%	$9.60
Oct. 24, 1939	0.30	48	5.10	Jan. 1, 1979	2.90	43	9.44
Oct. 24, 1945	0.40	39	5.25	Jan. 1, 1980	3.10	43	8.89
Jan. 25, 1950	0.75	52	7.35	Jan. 1, 1981	3.35	42	8.71
Mar. 1, 1956	1.00	51	8.69	Apr. 1, 1990	3.80	35	6.87
Sept. 3, 1961	1.15	50	9.09	Apr. 1, 1991	4.25	38	7.37
Sept. 3, 1963	1.25	51	9.65	Oct. 1, 1996	4.75	37	7.15
Feb. 1, 1967	1.40	49	9.90	Sept. 1, 1997	5.15	39	7.58
Feb. 1, 1968	1.60	53	10.86	July 24, 2007	5.85	34	6.67
May 1, 1974	2.00	45	9.59	July 24, 2008	6.55	37	7.19
Jan. 1, 1975	2.10	43	9.22	July 24, 2009	7.25	40	7.99
Jan. 1, 1976	2.30	44	9.55				

Note: Before 1961, the minimum wage applied primarily to employees engaged in, or producing goods for, interstate commerce. Coverage was added 1961-64 primarily to employees in large retail and service enterprises and to local transit, construction, and gas station employees. Coverage was added 1966-77 (at reduced rates) to farm workers; federal, state, and local government employees; workers in various retail and service trades; and certain domestic workers. Starting in 1978, the minimum wage applied equally to all covered, nonexempt workers. At present, exceptions apply under specific circumstances to workers with disabilities, full-time students, persons under age 20 in their first 90 consecutive calendar days of employment, tipped employees, and student-learners. (1) Percent of gross hourly earnings of production workers in manufacturing.

Fatal Occupational Injuries, 2013

Source: Census of Fatal Occupational Injuries, Bureau of Labor Statistics, U.S. Dept. of Labor, in cooperation with other agencies

Event or exposure	Fatalities Number	%	Event or exposure	Fatalities Number	%
Total	4,405	100%	**Contact with objects and equipment**	**717**	**16%**
Transportation incidents	**1,740**	**40**	Struck by object or equipment	503	11
Roadway, involving motorized land vehicles	991	22	Struck by falling object or equipment	245	6
Collision between vehicles	517	12	Struck by flying object	29	1
Vehicle struck object on side of road	270	6	Caught in or compressed by equipment or objects	131	3
Noncollision	182	4	Caught in running equipment or machinery	105	2
Jackknifed or overturned	157	4	Caught in or crushed in collapsing materials	78	2
Nonroadway	223	5	**Falls, slips, trips**	**699**	**16**
Jackknifed or overturned	116	3	Fall to lower level	574	13
Pedestrian vehicular incident	284	6	Fall on same level	106	2
Rail vehicle incident	41	1			
Water vehicle incident	60	1	**Exposure to harmful substances or environments**	**330**	**7**
Aircraft incident	133	3	Exposure to electricity	139	3
			Exposure to temperature extremes	38	1
Violence by persons or animals	**753**	**17**	Exposure to other harmful substances	121	3
Homicides	397	9	Inhalation of harmful substance	37	1
Shooting	316	7			
Stabbing	38	1	**Fires and explosions**	**148**	**3**
Self-inflicted injuries	270	6			

Note: Totals for categories may include subcategories not shown separately. Percentages show incidence rate per total fatalities. Numbers are preliminary.

U.S. Occupational Injuries and Illnesses Involving Days Away From Work, 2012

Source: Bureau of Labor Statistics, U.S. Dept. of Labor

Characteristic	Illnesses/ injuries[2]	Percent of days-away-from-work cases[1] involving—							Median days away from work
		1 day	2 days	3-5 days	6-10 days	11-20 days	21-30 days	31 days or more	
Total	905,690	14.1%	10.7%	17.2%	12.0%	11.5%	6.4%	28.0%	8
Gender									
Male	559,830	13.5	10.0	17.1	11.8	11.6	6.8	29.2	10
Female	342,640	15.2	11.9	17.4	12.3	11.4	5.8	26.0	7
Age[3]									
14-15	120	16.7	58.3	NA	NA	NA	NA	NA	2
16-19	21,170	22.4	14.7	21.6	13.0	14.1	4.0	10.2	4
20-24	89,590	19.9	14.9	20.0	12.9	11.0	5.1	16.1	4
25-34	202,200	16.3	12.9	19.4	12.2	11.5	5.8	21.9	6
35-44	195,270	13.7	9.8	17.0	12.6	11.3	6.6	29.0	9
45-54	219,150	11.9	9.0	15.4	11.5	11.5	7.2	33.6	12
55-64	136,880	10.4	8.7	15.2	11.7	11.8	7.0	35.1	14
65 and over	27,260	11.0	9.0	14.1	9.8	12.4	7.3	36.3	14
Occupation(s)									
Management	22,460	17.0	11.8	15.3	12.9	12.2	5.5	25.3	7
Business, financial operations	5,810	20.7	13.4	15.5	10.7	10.2	6.2	23.4	6
Computer and mathematical	2,820	26.2	7.8	11.0	10.6	14.9	4.3	25.2	8
Architecture, engineering	2,910	17.5	9.6	10.3	13.4	11.0	15.8	22.3	10
Life, physical, social science	1,490	18.8	8.1	16.8	15.4	12.8	10.1	18.8	6
Community, social services	7,350	16.7	12.9	18.5	17.4	10.1	4.2	20.3	7
Legal	550	18.2	12.7	9.10	7.3	43.6	5.5	3.6	12
Education, training, library	8,550	21.1	11.2	21.4	12.3	10.2	5.3	18.6	5
Arts, design, entertainment, sports, media	4,580	14.8	12.7	15.5	12.2	15.7	7.4	21.6	7
Health care practitioners	50,400	15.0	11.5	19.0	12.6	11.7	7.4	22.9	7
Health care support	57,080	14.9	12.8	19.5	14.7	10.5	5.4	22.2	6
Protective service	9,310	14.9	11.5	16.1	10.3	11.5	5.6	30.0	8
Food preparation, serving	69,800	17.1	13.4	20.9	13.0	10.9	5.3	19.4	5
Building and grounds cleaning, maintenance	58,360	14.9	10.7	18.7	12.8	11.3	6.0	25.5	7
Personal care, service	25,600	14.6	13.1	16.7	12.7	12.3	6.7	23.9	7
Sales	57,530	15.7	12.1	16.0	11.0	10.7	5.6	28.9	7
Office administrative support	64,280	15.3	11.0	16.9	11.1	11.6	6.2	27.7	8
Farming, fishing, forestry	14,480	13.3	8.8	21.4	14.8	10.2	6.8	24.6	7
Construction, extraction	67,940	11.8	9.5	15.5	11.6	11.2	6.3	34.1	12
Installation, maintenance, repair	83,860	12.7	10.4	16.5	10.9	12.6	6.5	30.4	10
Production	109,880	14.9	10.4	16.9	11.7	12.2	6.7	27.2	9
Transportation, material moving	177,760	10.9	8.3	15.9	11.4	11.4	7.3	34.8	13
Length of service with employer									
Less than 3 months	95,670	16.8	13.6	18.4	11.3	11.3	6.1	22.4	6
3-11 months	171,540	16.5	11.9	18.0	12.8	11.0	5.6	24.1	7
1-5 years	300,490	14.6	11.4	17.6	12.2	11.4	6.8	26.0	7
More than 5 years	325,220	11.5	8.6	16.1	11.8	12.1	6.5	33.3	12
Race or ethnic origin[4]									
White	362,480	16.1	50.7	17.1	11.4	11.5	6.0	26.4	7
Hispanic or Latino	118,940	13.3	10.3	19.0	12.1	10.4	7.4	27.4	8
Black	70,710	13.5	11.9	18.6	11.7	11.7	4.8	27.9	7
Asian	13,770	15.3	14.4	14.0	14.7	11.8	7.3	22.5	7
American Indian or Alaskan Native	4,200	11.7	14.3	21.7	10.7	10.0	5.2	26.2	6
Native Hawaiian or Pacific Islander	2,940	11.6	11.9	21.1	21.8	10.5	5.1	18.4	6
More than one race	1,130	11.5	8.0	35.4	6.2	8.8	1.8	29.2	4
Hispanic or Latino and other race	710	50.7	5.6	12.7	5.6	8.5	5.6	11.3	1
Not reported	330,830	12.3	9.6	16.3	12.6	11.9	6.9	30.4	10

NA = Not available. (1) Cases include those that resulted in days away from work, some of which also included job transfers or restrictions. (2) Number of nonfatal occupational injuries and illnesses involving days away from work for private industry workers; excludes farms with fewer than 11 employees. (3) Information is not shown separately for injured workers under age 14; they accounted for fewer than 50 cases. (4) Of those reporting only one race. Some cases may be counted as both "More than one race" and another category. Hispanic persons may be of any race.

Civilian Employment of the Executive Branch, 1940-2012

Source: U.S. Office of Personnel Management

(numbers in thousands)

Year	Total executive branch	Dept. of Defense	Civilian agencies/depts.									
			Total employees	Agriculture	HHS, Education, Social Sec.[1]	Homeland Sec.	Interior	Justice	Transportation	Treasury	Veterans Affairs	Other
1940	699	256	443	98	9	18	46	11	NA	45	40	176
1945	3,370	2,635	736	82	11	20	45	19	NA	84	65	409
1950	1,439	753	686	84	13	20	66	20	NA	76	188	219
1955	1,860	1,187	673	86	40	21	54	24	NA	65	178	206
1960	1,808	1,047	761	99	62	21	56	24	NA	62	172	265
1965	1,901	1,034	867	113	87	21	71	27	NA	74	167	307
1970	2,203	1,219	983	118	112	23	75	33	62	84	169	308
1975	2,149	1,042	1,107	121	147	31	80	47	69	101	213	297
1980	2,161	960	1,201	129	163	40	77	48	66	102	228	346
1985	2,252	1,107	1,145	122	147	40	80	55	56	110	247	286
1990	2,250	1,034	1,216	123	129	49	78	71	61	132	248	326
1991	2,243	1,013	1,230	126	135	50	82	77	64	139	256	302
1992	2,225	952	1,274	128	136	56	85	82	64	133	260	329
1993	2,157	891	1,266	124	135	56	85	82	63	127	268	326
1994	2,085	850	1,235	120	133	55	81	83	59	128	262	315
1995	2,012	802	1,210	113	132	56	76	87	58	128	264	297
2000	1,778	651	1,127	104	126	70	74	98	58	113	220	265
2001	1,792	647	1,145	109	129	73	76	99	59	117	226	258
2002	1,818	645	1,173	98	130	76	77	96	96	118	223	258
2003	1,867	636	1,231	100	131	153	72	102	58	132	226	257
2004	1,882	644	1,238	111	130	153	77	104	57	111	236	257
2005	1,872	649	1,224	108	131	147	76	105	56	108	235	258
2006	1,880	653	1,227	105	129	154	72	107	54	107	239	260
2007	1,888	651	1,237	103	129	159	72	107	54	104	254	254
2008	1,960	670	1,289	104	132	172	76	109	55	106	274	261
2009	2,094	737	1,357	104	139	180	75	113	57	109	297	283
2010	2,133	773	1,360	107	144	183	70	118	58	110	305	265
2011	2,146	774	1,372	104	143	194	77	117	58	108	314	257
2012	2,104	730	1,374	99	143	191	77	117	57	112	323	255

NA = Not available. **Note:** End-of-fiscal-year count; U.S. Postal Service excluded. (1) Estimated, 1940-50.

Median Earnings by Industry and Sex, 2013

Source: American Community Survey, U.S. Census Bureau, U.S. Dept. of Commerce

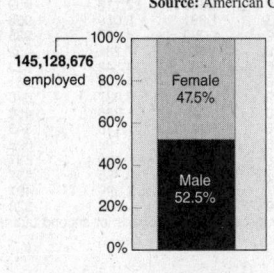

145,128,676 employed — Female 47.5%, Male 52.5%

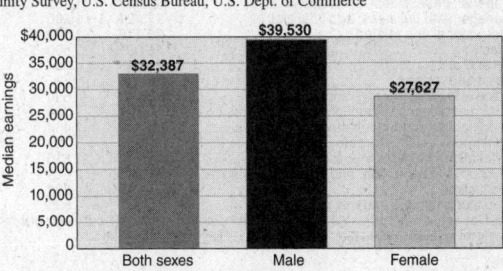

Both sexes $32,387 — Male $39,530 — Female $27,627

Industry	Number employed	Male (%)	Female (%)	Median earnings	Median earnings (male)	Median earnings (female)
Agriculture; forestry; fishing, hunting; mining	2,883,101	81.5%	18.5%	$32,053	$35,789	$20,740
Arts, entertainment, recreation; accommodation, food services	14,019,659	48.8	51.2	15,380	18,038	12,754
Construction	8,930,742	90.8	9.2	34,195	34,770	31,683
Educational services; health care, social assistance	33,440,184	25.8	74.2	34,049	42,604	31,492
Finance, insurance; real estate, rental, leasing	9,562,287	45.3	54.7	44,935	57,245	38,543
Information	3,086,265	58.3	41.7	47,328	54,788	37,794
Manufacturing	15,226,643	71.1	28.9	41,458	46,102	32,047
Other services, except public administration	7,203,232	47.0	53.0	22,135	30,233	17,143
Professional, scientific, management; administrative, waste management services	16,038,857	58.1	41.9	40,834	48,404	33,561
Public administration	6,864,026	55.9	44.1	50,793	57,294	42,617
Retail trade	16,844,787	50.7	49.3	21,284	26,041	17,300
Transportation, warehousing; utilities	7,083,841	76.2	23.8	42,183	45,911	35,309
Wholesale trade	3,944,833	70.5	29.5	41,259	44,553	35,150

Note: For the civilian employed population 16 years of age and over including workers not employed full-time.

U.S. Median Weekly Earnings, 2014
Source: Bureau of Labor Statistics, U.S. Dept. of Labor

AGE, RACE, AND ETHNICITY	Total		Men		Women	
	Number of workers (thous.)	Median weekly earnings	Number of workers (thous.)	Median weekly earnings	Number of workers (thous.)	Median weekly earnings
All workers, by age						
16 years and over	106,555	$780	59,714	$857	46,840	$716
16 to 24 years	9,858	464	5,663	481	4,195	449
16 to 19 years	1,241	365	766	372	475	356
20 to 24 years	8,616	483	4,897	499	3,720	465
25 years and over	96,697	831	54,052	914	42,645	750
25 to 54 years	75,371	818	42,560	892	32,811	744
25 to 34 years	25,436	711	14,585	732	10,851	685
35 to 44 years	24,436	875	13,980	958	10,456	769
45 to 54 years	25,499	903	13,995	1,009	11,504	783
55 years and over	21,326	881	11,492	993	9,834	768
55 to 64 years	17,586	896	9,464	1,012	8,122	770
65 years and over	3,740	807	2,028	913	1,712	758
White						
16 years and over	84,544	802	48,509	884	36,035	725
16 to 24 years	7,938	478	4,648	495	3,290	455
25 years and over	76,606	855	43,862	942	32,745	758
25 to 54 years	58,842	841	34,067	919	24,775	752
55 years and over	17,765	907	9,795	1,017	7,970	772
Black						
16 years and over	12,736	649	6,056	667	6,680	631
16 to 24 years	1,122	404	565	403	556	406
25 years and over	11,615	680	5,491	696	6,124	663
25 to 54 years	9,429	671	4,491	683	4,938	653
55 years and over	2,186	731	999	751	1,186	698
Asian						
16 years and over	6,320	954	3,512	1,139	2,807	855
16 to 24 years	376	474	209	492	168	468
25 years and over	5,943	1,000	3,304	1,176	2,639	895
25 to 54 years	4,893	1,026	2,775	1,204	2,118	908
55 years and over	1,051	919	529	1,011	522	808
Hispanic[1]						
16 years and over	17,599	583	10,840	609	6,759	532
16 to 24 years	2,182	420	1,359	424	823	414
25 years and over	15,417	609	9,481	637	5,936	565
25 to 54 years	13,340	607	8,230	637	5,110	562
55 years and over	2,077	625	1,251	637	826	593
OCCUPATION						
Managerial, professional, and related	43,003	1,135	20,887	1,343	22,116	969
Management, business, and financial	17,424	1,200	9,335	1,391	8,090	1,038
Professional and related	25,578	1,078	11,552	1,299	14,026	935
Service	15,051	500	7,820	580	7,231	452
Sales and office	23,543	667	9,200	759	14,342	623
Sales and related	9,854	683	5,448	806	4,406	561
Office and administrative support	13,689	659	3,752	714	9,937	646
Natural resources, construction, and maintenance	10,726	740	10,360	748	366	460
Farming, fishing, and forestry	749	454	605	499	145	345
Construction and extraction	5,827	728	5,736	729	92	699
Installation, maintenance, and repair	4,149	815	4,020	820	130	637
Production, transportation, and material moving	14,232	629	11,447	677	2,785	497
Production	7,245	632	5,347	699	1,898	491
Transportation and material moving	6,987	625	6,100	646	887	528

Note: Not seasonally adjusted; figures are median usual weekly earnings of full-time wage and salary workers for second quarter 2014. Total includes races not shown here. (1) May be of any race.

Average Hours and Earnings of U.S. Production Workers, 1969-2013
Source: Bureau of Labor Statistics, U.S. Dept. of Labor
(annual averages)

Year	Weekly hours	Hourly earnings	Weekly earnings	Year	Weekly hours	Hourly earnings	Weekly earnings	Year	Weekly hours	Hourly earnings	Weekly earnings
1969	37.5	$3.22	$120.70	1984	35.1	$8.49	$298.26	1999	34.3	$13.49	$463.15
1970	37.0	3.40	125.79	1985	34.9	8.74	304.62	2000	34.3	14.02	480.99
1971	36.7	3.63	133.22	1986	34.7	8.93	309.78	2001	34.0	14.54	493.74
1972	36.9	3.90	143.87	1987	34.7	9.14	317.39	2002	33.9	14.97	506.60
1973	36.9	4.14	152.59	1988	34.6	9.44	326.48	2003	33.7	15.37	517.82
1974	36.4	4.43	161.61	1989	34.5	9.80	338.34	2004	33.7	15.69	528.89
1975	36.0	4.73	170.29	1990	34.3	10.20	349.63	2005	33.8	16.12	544.05
1976	36.1	5.06	182.65	1991	34.1	10.51	358.46	2006	33.9	16.75	567.39
1977	35.9	5.44	195.58	1992	34.2	10.77	368.20	2007	33.8	17.42	589.27
1978	35.8	5.88	210.29	1993	34.3	11.05	378.89	2008	33.6	18.07	607.53
1979	35.6	6.34	225.69	1994	34.5	11.34	391.17	2009	33.1	18.61	616.01
1980	35.2	6.85	241.07	1995	34.3	11.65	400.04	2010	33.4	19.05	636.25
1981	35.2	7.44	261.53	1996	34.3	12.04	413.25	2011	33.6	19.44	653.19
1982	34.7	7.87	273.10	1997	34.5	12.51	431.86	2012	33.7	19.74	665.82
1983	34.9	8.20	286.43	1998	34.5	13.01	448.59	2013	33.7	20.13	677.67

Note: Data refer to production workers in natural resources, mining, and manufacturing; construction workers; and non-supervisory workers in the service industries.

Elderly in U.S. Labor Force, 1890-2013

Source: U.S. Census Bureau, U.S. Dept. of Commerce

(labor force participation rate of persons age 65 and older; 1910 figures not available)

Median Weekly Earnings of U.S. Workers by Union Affiliation, 2000, 2013

Source: Bureau of Labor Statistics, U.S. Dept. of Labor

Sex and age	Total	2000 Union member[1]	2000 Represented by unions[2]	2000 Non-union	Total	2013 Union member[1]	2013 Represented by unions[2]	2013 Non-union
Total, 16 years and older ..	$576	$696	$691	$542	$776	$950	$944	$750
16 to 24 years..........	361	437	436	355	454	576	565	445
25 years and older	611	709	705	592	827	966	961	797
25 to 34 years........	550	627	624	529	708	877	871	683
35 to 44 years........	631	716	712	614	874	1,008	1,001	844
45 to 54 years........	671	755	752	639	883	999	996	857
55 to 64 years........	617	727	723	592	904	998	992	882
65 years and older	442	577	565	422	801	871	866	786
Men, 16 years and older...	646	739	737	620	860	991	985	831
16 to 24 years..........	376	458	457	370	479	577	573	473
25 years and older	700	753	752	682	912	1,010	1,005	891
25 to 34 years........	603	678	675	591	744	902	897	722
35 to 44 years........	731	776	774	718	956	1,060	1,052	936
45 to 54 years........	777	801	799	769	994	1,073	1,067	978
55 to 64 years........	738	755	757	729	1,011	1,039	1,035	1,002
65 years and older	537	613	613	514	937	896	897	944
Women, 16 years and older	491	616	613	472	706	898	893	676
16 to 24 years..........	342	406	405	339	423	575	542	420
25 years and older	515	627	623	497	740	911	907	716
25 to 34 years........	493	579	578	483	665	845	843	642
35 to 44 years........	520	605	604	506	767	958	951	743
45 to 54 years........	565	697	692	522	761	924	923	738
55 to 64 years........	505	659	647	481	779	928	923	757
65 years and older	378	485	484	365	691	841	832	670

Note: Data refer to the sole or principal job of full- and part-time workers. Excludes self-employed workers regardless of whether or not their businesses are incorporated. (1) Includes members of an employee association similar to a union. (2) Includes members of a labor union or employee association similar to a union as well as those whose jobs are covered by a union or an employee-association contract.

Work Stoppages (Strikes and Lockouts) in the U.S., 1950-2013

Source: Bureau of Labor Statistics, U.S. Dept. of Labor; involving 1,000 workers or more

Year	No.	Workers (thous.)	Days idle (thous.)	Year	No.	Workers (thous.)	Days idle (thous.)	Year	No.	Workers (thous.)	Days idle (thous.)
1950	424	1,698	30,390	1985	54	324	7,079	2000	39	394	20,419
1955	363	2,055	21,180	1986	69	533	11,861	2001	29	99	1,151
1960	222	896	13,260	1987	46	174	4,481	2002	19	46	660
1965	268	999	15,140	1988	40	118	4,381	2003	14	129	4,091
1970	381	2,468	52,761	1989	51	452	16,996	2004	17	171	3,344
1975	235	965	17,563	1990	44	185	5,926	2005	22	100	1,736
1976	231	1,519	23,962	1991	40	392	4,584	2006	20	70	2,688
1977	298	1,212	21,258	1992	35	364	3,989	2007	21	189	1,265
1978	219	1,006	23,774	1993	35	182	3,981	2008	15	72	1,954
1979	235	1,021	20,409	1994	45	322	5,020	2009	5	13	124
1980	187	795	20,844	1995	31	192	5,771	2010	11	45	302
1981	145	729	16,908	1996	37	273	4,889	2011	19	113	1,020
1982	96	656	9,061	1997	29	339	4,497	2012	19	148	1,131
1983	81	909	17,461	1998	34	387	5,116	2013	15	55	290
1984	62	376	8,499	1999	17	73	1,996				

Note: Numbers cover stoppages that began in the year indicated. Workers are counted more than once if they are involved in more than one stoppage during the year. For work stoppages ongoing at the end of a calendar year, days idle include only the days for the calendar year.

U.S. Union Membership, 1930-2013

Source: Bureau of Labor Statistics, U.S. Dept. of Labor

(numbers in thousands)

Year	Total employed[1]	% in union	Union members[2]	Year	Total employed[1]	% in union	Union members[2]	Year	Total employed[1]	% in union	Union members[2]
1930	29,424	11.6%	3,401	1970	70,920	27.3%	19,381	2006	128,237	12.0%	15,359
1935	27,053	13.2	3,584	1975	76,945	25.5	19,611	2007	129,767	12.1	15,670
1940	32,376	26.9	8,717	1980	90,564	21.9	19,843	2008	129,377	12.4	16,098
1945	40,394	35.5	14,322	1985	94,521	18.0	16,996	2009	124,490	12.3	15,327
1950	45,222	31.5	14,267	1990	103,905	16.1	16,740	2010	124,073	11.9	14,715
1955	50,675	33.2	16,802	1995	110,038	14.9	16,360	2011	125,187	11.8	14,764
1960	54,234	31.4	17,049	2000	120,786	13.5	16,258	2012	127,577	11.3	14,366
1965	60,815	28.4	17,299	2005	125,889	12.5	15,685	2013	129,110	11.3	14,528

(1) Does not include agricultural employment; from 1985 on, does not include self-employed or unemployed persons. (2) From 1930 to 1980, includes dues-paying members of traditional trade unions, regardless of employment status; after 1980, includes employed only. From 1985 on, includes members of employee associations that engage in collective bargaining with employers.

ENERGY

U.S. Energy Overview, 1960-2013

Source: *Monthly Energy Review*, Aug. 2014, Energy Information Administration (EIA), U.S. Dept. of Energy; in quadrillion Btu

	1960	1970	1980	1985	1990	1995	2000	2005	2010	2012	2013
Production	**42.80**	**63.50**	**67.23**	**67.80**	**70.70**	**71.17**	**71.33**	**69.43**	**74.76**	**79.23**	**81.68**
Fossil fuels	39.87	59.19	59.01	57.54	58.56	57.54	57.37	55.04	58.20	62.35	64.12
Coal[1]	10.82	14.61	18.60	19.33	22.49	22.13	22.74	23.19	22.04	20.68	19.99
Natural gas (dry)	12.66	21.67	19.91	16.98	18.33	19.08	19.66	18.56	21.81	24.64	24.89
Crude oil[2]	14.93	20.40	18.25	18.99	15.57	13.89	12.36	10.97	11.58	13.79	15.77
Natural gas plant liquids (NGPL)	1.46	2.51	2.25	2.24	2.17	2.44	2.61	2.33	2.78	3.25	3.47
Nuclear electric power	0.01	0.24	2.74	4.08	6.10	7.08	7.86	8.16	8.43	8.06	8.27
Renewable energy	2.93	4.08	5.49	6.18	6.04	6.56	6.10	6.23	8.13	8.83	9.30
Conventional hydroelectric power[3]	1.61	2.63	2.90	2.97	3.05	3.21	2.81	2.70	2.54	2.63	2.56
Biomass[4]	1.32	1.43	2.48	3.02	2.74	3.10	3.01	3.10	4.33	4.42	4.61
Geothermal energy	—	0.01	0.11	0.20	0.17	0.15	0.16	0.18	0.21	0.21	0.22
Solar	NA	NA	NA	—	0.06	0.07	0.07	0.06	0.13	0.23	0.31
Wind	NA	NA	NA	—	0.03	0.03	0.06	0.18	0.92	1.34	1.60
Imports	**4.19**	**8.34**	**15.80**	**11.78**	**18.82**	**22.26**	**28.97**	**34.71**	**29.88**	**27.08**	**24.54**
Coal	0.01	—	0.03	0.05	0.07	0.24	0.31	0.76	0.48	0.21	0.21
Natural gas	0.16	0.85	1.01	0.95	1.55	2.90	3.87	4.45	3.83	3.22	2.96
All petroleum prods.[5]	4.00	7.47	14.66	10.61	17.12	18.88	24.53	29.25	25.37	23.37	21.09
Electricity[6]	0.02	0.02	0.09	0.16	0.06	0.15	0.17	0.15	0.15	0.20	0.22
Exports	**1.48**	**2.63**	**3.69**	**4.20**	**4.75**	**4.51**	**4.01**	**4.56**	**8.23**	**11.36**	**11.80**
Coal	1.02	1.94	2.42	2.44	2.77	2.32	1.53	1.27	2.10	3.09	2.90
Natural gas	0.01	0.07	0.05	0.06	0.09	0.16	0.25	0.74	1.15	1.63	1.59
All petroleum prods.[5]	0.43	0.55	1.16	1.66	1.82	1.99	2.15	2.44	4.84	6.35	6.93
Electricity[6]	—	0.01	0.01	0.02	0.06	0.01	0.05	0.07	0.06	0.04	0.04
Consumption	**45.09**	**67.84**	**78.12**	**76.49**	**84.49**	**91.03**	**98.81**	**100.28**	**98.02**	**95.00**	**97.53**
Fossil fuels	42.14	63.52	69.83	66.09	72.33	77.26	84.73	85.79	81.41	77.99	79.80
Coal	9.84	12.26	15.42	17.48	19.17	20.09	22.58	22.80	20.83	17.33	18.08
Natural gas[7]	12.39	21.80	20.24	17.70	19.60	22.67	23.82	22.57	24.57	26.09	26.63
Petroleum[8]	19.92	29.52	34.20	30.92	33.55	34.44	38.26	40.39	36.01	34.58	35.10
Nuclear electric power	0.01	0.24	2.74	4.08	6.10	7.08	7.86	8.16	8.43	8.06	8.27
Renewable energy	2.93	4.08	5.49	6.18	6.04	6.56	6.11	6.24	8.08	8.79	9.29
Conventional hydroelectric power[3]	1.61	2.63	2.90	2.97	3.05	3.21	2.81	2.70	2.54	2.63	2.56
Biomass[4]	1.32	1.43	2.48	3.02	2.74	3.10	3.01	3.12	4.29	4.38	4.61
Geothermal energy	—	0.01	0.11	0.20	0.17	0.15	0.16	0.18	0.21	0.21	0.22
Solar	NA	NA	NA	—	0.06	0.07	0.07	0.06	0.13	0.23	0.31
Wind	NA	NA	NA	—	0.03	0.03	0.06	0.02	0.92	1.34	1.60

NA = Not available. — = Less than 0.005 quadrillion Btu. **Note:** Numbers may not add up to totals because of rounding. (1) Incl. waste coal supplied beginning in 1989 and refuse recovery beginning in 2001. (2) Incl. lease condensate. (3) Starting in 1990, pumped storage was removed and expanded coverage of industrial use of hydroelectric power was included. (4) Category known as "wood, waste, and alcohol" for years prior to 2000. Includes wood, waste, and alcohol fuels (ethanol blended into motor gasoline). Ethanol is included in both Petroleum and Biomass categories but is only counted once in totals. (5) Incl. imports of crude oil for the Strategic Petroleum Reserve, which began in 1977; excl. biofuels. (6) Small amts. transmitted across borders with Canada and Mexico. (7) Incl. supplemental gaseous fuels. (8) Petroleum products supplied, incl. natural gas plant liquids and crude oil burned as fuel.

World's Largest Energy Producers and Consumers, 1980-2012

Source: Energy Information Administration (EIA), U.S. Dept. of Energy

(primary energy in quadrillion Btu; ranked by top producers/consumers in 2011)

Production	1980	1985	1990	1995	2000	2005	2010	2011	2012
1. China	18.12	24.30	29.37	34.88	37.71	60.41	84.23	90.57	NA
2. United States	67.18	67.70	70.70	71.17	71.33	69.43	74.77	78.00	79.20
3. Russia	NA	NA	NA	41.42	41.70	51.05	53.74	54.63	NA
4. Saudi Arabia	22.43	8.64	15.92	20.66	21.59	25.44	24.93	26.40	NA
5. Canada	10.28	12.02	13.41	16.83	18.13	18.89	18.36	18.83	19.22
6. India	3.10	5.27	6.82	9.48	9.83	11.74	15.44	15.89	NA
7. Iran	3.94	5.59	7.67	9.35	10.40	13.12	14.61	14.86	NA
8. Indonesia	4.23	4.20	5.30	6.95	7.69	9.06	13.78	14.40	NA
9. Australia	3.24	5.00	6.16	7.43	9.66	10.97	12.91	12.35	12.85
10. Brazil	1.90	3.38	3.76	4.47	6.36	7.66	9.47	9.91	NA
Consumption	**1980**	**1985**	**1990**	**1995**	**2000**	**2005**	**2010**	**2011**	**2012**
1. China	17.29	22.01	26.99	34.59	39.76	64.20	95.74	103.72	NA
2. United States	78.07	76.39	84.49	91.03	98.81	100.28	98.02	97.46	94.95
3. Russia	NA	NA	NA	27.94	26.14	27.89	29.73	29.96	NA
4. India	4.04	5.91	7.88	11.54	13.33	16.33	22.71	23.47	NA
5. Japan	15.20	15.69	18.77	20.94	22.41	22.57	21.85	21.11	20.43
6. Canada	9.80	10.15	10.98	12.21	13.02	13.84	12.95	13.54	13.29
7. Germany[1]	14.86	14.83	14.86	14.39	14.26	14.10	14.03	13.45	13.51
8. Brazil	4.02	4.59	5.75	7.02	8.53	9.35	11.30	12.13	NA
9. Korea, South	1.76	2.31	3.84	6.36	7.84	9.21	10.82	11.32	11.45
10. France	8.39	8.35	9.13	10.05	10.05	10.86	11.38	11.02	10.67

NA = Not available. (1) Data for 1980-90 represent sum of figures for East and West Germany and may not be directly comparable with data for other years.

U.S. Energy Consumption by Source, 1949-2013

Source: *Monthly Energy Review*, Aug. 2014, Energy Information Administration (EIA), U.S. Dept. of Energy

Gasoline Retail Prices in Selected Countries, 1990-2013

Source: *Energy Prices and Taxes*, International Energy Agency
(average price in dollars per gallon, including taxes)

Country	1990	1995	2000	2002	2003	2004	2005	2006	2007	2008	2009	2010	2011	2012	2013
							Regular unleaded								
Australia	NA	$1.93	$1.93	$1.78	$2.20	$2.73	$3.22	$3.52	$3.86	$4.47	$3.79	$4.35	$5.60	$5.60	$5.30
Canada	$1.85	1.51	1.85	1.70	2.01	2.35	2.88	3.26	3.60	4.09	3.14	3.79	4.77	4.81	4.69
Germany	2.65	3.97	3.44	3.67	4.58	5.26	5.64	6.02	6.89	7.76	6.81	7.12	NA	NA	NA
Japan	3.14	4.43	3.63	3.14	3.48	3.94	4.28	4.47	4.50	5.75	4.85	5.72	6.93	6.97	6.06
South Korea	2.04	2.95	4.16	3.82	4.13	4.50	5.26	5.91	6.21	5.83	4.69	5.60	6.59	6.66	6.66
Mexico	1.02	1.10	2.01	2.23	2.04	2.04	2.23	2.31	2.42	2.46	2.12	2.46	2.80	2.95	3.37
United States	1.17	1.10	1.48	1.36	1.55	1.85	2.27	2.57	2.80	3.26	2.35	2.76	3.52	3.63	3.52
China	NA	NA	NA	1.21	1.32	1.48	1.70	2.12	2.31	3.10	3.26	3.71	NA	NA	NA
Taiwan	2.46	2.23	2.16	1.93	2.16	2.46	2.76	3.07	3.22	3.52	3.03	3.56	4.05	NA	NA
							Premium unleaded								
France	$3.63	$4.28	$3.79	$3.63	$4.35	$5.00	$5.45	$5.87	$6.59	$7.50	$6.36	$6.74	$7.91	$7.61	$7.72
Germany	2.76	4.09	3.56	3.75	4.69	5.34	5.75	6.13	6.97	7.76	6.81	7.12	8.21	8.03	8.03
Italy	4.58	4.01	3.79	3.75	4.54	5.30	5.75	6.09	6.74	7.65	6.47	6.85	8.18	8.71	8.78
Mexico	NA	NA	2.23	2.50	2.31	2.38	2.57	2.73	2.95	3.03	2.65	2.95	3.14	3.14	3.56
Spain	NA	3.26	2.84	2.91	3.48	4.09	4.50	4.85	5.38	6.13	5.26	5.83	6.97	6.93	7.19
United Kingdom	2.84	3.22	4.58	4.16	4.69	5.56	5.98	6.36	7.15	7.42	5.87	6.85	8.10	8.14	7.95
United States	NA	1.21	1.59	1.44	1.67	1.97	2.38	2.69	2.91	3.37	2.46	2.91	3.63	3.75	3.67
South Africa	NA	NA	1.78	1.40	1.93	2.57	3.07	3.41	3.63	4.13	3.22	4.09	NA	NA	NA
Thailand	NA	1.25	1.36	1.36	1.51	1.78	2.23	2.76	3.22	4.01	4.13	4.85	NA	NA	NA

NA = Not available. **Note:** Premium unleaded refers to fuels with a research octane number of 95.

Average U.S. Gasoline Prices, 1950-2013

Source: *Monthly Energy Review*, Aug. 2014; *Short-Term Energy Outlook*, Aug. 2014; Energy Information Administration (EIA), U.S. Dept. of Energy

(in dollars per gallon, including taxes; constant dollars is price in Aug. 2014 dollars)

Year	Current dollars — Leaded regular	Current dollars — Unleaded regular	Current dollars — Unleaded premium	Current dollars — All types[1]	Constant dollars, unleaded regular[2]	Year	Current dollars — Leaded regular	Current dollars — Unleaded regular	Current dollars — Unleaded premium	Current dollars — All types[1]	Constant dollars, unleaded regular[2]
1950	$0.27	NA	NA	NA	NA	1996	NA	$1.23	$1.41	$1.29	$1.82
1955	0.29	NA	NA	NA	NA	1997	NA	1.23	1.42	1.29	1.78
1960	0.31	NA	NA	NA	NA	1998	NA	1.06	1.25	1.12	1.50
1965	0.31	NA	NA	NA	NA	1999	NA	1.17	1.36	1.22	1.63
1970	0.36	NA	NA	NA	NA	2000	NA	1.51	1.69	1.56	2.06
1975	0.57	NA	NA	NA	NA	2001	NA	1.46	1.66	1.53	1.92
1980	1.19	$1.25	NA	$1.22	$3.60	2002	NA	1.36	1.56	1.44	1.78
1985	1.12	1.20	$1.34	1.20	2.58	2003	NA	1.59	1.78	1.64	2.02
1986	0.86	0.93	1.09	0.93	1.92	2004	NA	1.88	2.07	1.92	2.33
1987	0.90	0.95	1.09	0.96	1.91	2005	NA	2.30	2.49	2.34	2.77
1988	0.90	0.95	1.11	0.96	1.83	2006	NA	2.59	2.81	2.64	3.04
1989	1.00	1.02	1.20	1.06	1.90	2007	NA	2.80	3.03	2.85	3.22
1990	1.15	1.16	1.35	1.22	2.06	2008	NA	3.27	3.52	3.32	3.60
1991	NA	1.14	1.32	1.20	1.93	2009	NA	2.35	2.61	2.40	2.61
1992	NA	1.13	1.32	1.19	1.84	2010	NA	2.79	3.05	2.84	3.04
1993	NA	1.11	1.30	1.17	1.76	2011	NA	3.53	3.79	3.58	3.73
1994	NA	1.11	1.31	1.17	1.73	2012	NA	3.64	3.92	3.70	3.76
1995	NA	1.15	1.34	1.21	1.74	2013	NA	3.53	3.84	3.58	3.58

NA = Not applicable. **Note:** Until unleaded gas became available in 1976, leaded was the only type used in automobiles. (1) Includes types of motor gasoline not shown separately. Includes gasohol starting in 1985. (2) Base prices vary slightly from unleaded regular column at left.

Energy Consumption, Total and Per Capita, by State, 2012

Source: State Energy Data System, Energy Information Administration (EIA), U.S. Dept. of Energy

Total Consumption

Rank, state	Btu (tril)	Rank, state	Btu (tril)
1. Texas	12,281.9	27. Maryland	1,386.4
2. California	7,640.7	28. Massachusetts	1,386.0
3. Florida	4,064.9	29. Mississippi	1,133.4
4. Louisiana	3,908.6	30. Kansas	1,126.6
5. Illinois	3,863.8	31. Arkansas	1,064.3
6. Ohio	3,686.4	32. Oregon	985.9
7. Pennsylvania	3,630.8	33. Nebraska	860.6
8. New York	3,513.4	34. Utah	792.2
9. Georgia	2,790.8	35. Connecticut	730.3
10. Indiana	2,785.6	36. West Virginia	722.7
11. Michigan	2,704.5	37. New Mexico	687.0
12. North Carolina	2,482.9	38. Nevada	640.0
13. Virginia	2,355.6	39. Alaska	637.3
14. New Jersey	2,271.9	40. North Dakota	552.9
15. Tennessee	2,097.2	41. Wyoming	546.9
16. Washington	2,056.7	42. Idaho	519.2
17. Alabama	1,904.7	43. Montana	391.7
18. Kentucky	1,870.6	44. Maine	379.1
19. Minnesota	1,824.3	45. South Dakota	376.4
20. Missouri	1,812.6	46. New Hampshire	283.9
21. Wisconsin	1,733.9	47. Hawaii	280.3
22. South Carolina	1,571.2	48. Delaware	273.6
23. Oklahoma	1,568.8	49. Rhode Island	181.6
24. Colorado	1,452.4	50. District of Columbia	169.3
25. Iowa	1,449.6	51. Vermont	128.9
26. Arizona	1,407.0	**United States**	**94,970.9**

Note: U.S. total includes 4.0 trillion Btu of net imports of coal coke not allocated to the states.

Consumption per Capita

Rank, state	Btu (mil)	Rank, state	Btu (mil)
1. Wyoming	948.5	27. Delaware	298.3
2. Alaska	872.7	28. Washington	298.3
3. Louisiana	849.3	29. Virginia	287.7
4. North Dakota	788.4	30. Maine	285.4
5. Iowa	471.4	31. Pennsylvania	284.4
6. Texas	471.3	32. Georgia	281.5
7. Nebraska	463.8	33. Colorado	279.9
8. South Dakota	451.3	34. Utah	277.5
9. Kentucky	427.1	35. Michigan	273.7
10. Indiana	426.1	36. District of Columbia	267.2
11. Oklahoma	411.1	37. New Jersey	256.2
12. Alabama	395.4	38. North Carolina	254.7
13. Kansas	390.4	39. Oregon	252.8
14. Montana	389.5	40. Maryland	235.6
15. West Virginia	389.2	41. Nevada	232.4
16. Mississippi	379.5	42. New Hampshire	214.8
17. Arkansas	360.8	43. Arizona	214.8
18. Minnesota	339.1	44. Florida	210.4
19. South Carolina	332.6	45. Massachusetts	208.6
20. New Mexico	329.7	46. Vermont	205.9
21. Idaho	325.4	47. Connecticut	203.3
22. Tennessee	324.9	48. Hawaii	201.6
23. Ohio	319.1	49. California	201.1
24. Wisconsin	302.9	50. New York	179.5
25. Missouri	300.9	51. Rhode Island	172.9
26. Illinois	300.3	**United States**	**302.6**

U.S. Production of Crude Oil by State, 2013

Source: *Petroleum Supply Annual 2013*, Energy Information Administration (EIA), U.S. Dept. of Energy

Oil production in North Dakota nearly tripled between 2010 and 2013 through the use of hydraulic fracturing, or fracking, a process by which water, sand, and chemicals are injected at high pressure to create fractures in shale rock, releasing the oil within.

(in thousands of barrels)

Rank, state	Total	Rank, state	Total	Rank, state	Total	Rank, state	Total
1. Texas	929,820	9. Wyoming	63,230	17. Arkansas	6,640	25. South Dakota	1,811
2. North Dakota	313,275	10. Kansas	46,817	18. West Virginia	6,386	26. New York	352
3. California	199,406	11. Utah	35,056	19. Ohio	5,184	27. Nevada	334
4. Alaska	187,910	12. Montana	29,093	20. Pennsylvania	4,905	28. Tennessee	309
5. Oklahoma	116,288	13. Mississippi	24,056	21. Kentucky	2,893	29. Missouri	199
6. New Mexico	99,552	14. Alabama	10,391	22. Nebraska	2,778	30. Arizona	59
7. Louisiana	71,878	15. Illinois	8,585	23. Indiana	2,399	31. Virginia	9
8. Colorado	64,313	16. Michigan	7,658	24. Florida	2,174	**U.S. total**	**2,719,559**

Note: One barrel is equal to 42 U.S. gallons. U.S. total includes 475,798 thousand barrels of federal offshore oil production.

Fracking in the U.S.

Hydraulic fracturing, more commonly known as fracking, is a process by which water, sand, and chemicals are injected at high pressure to create fractures in shale rock, releasing the oil and/or natural gas within. Enormous shale deposits in Pennsylvania, California, and other parts of North America have inspired predictions that the U.S. could some day be a net energy exporting nation. However, the most recent U.S. Dept. of Energy estimates significantly reduced the estimates of oil that can realistically be derived from some of those shale deposits. Fracking also involves numerous environmental concerns, including pollution of groundwater, use of freshwater in drought-prone areas, and effects on seismicity in earthquake-prone areas.

Shale Oil and Gas Resources in the U.S., 2012

Source: *Oil and Gas Module, Assumptions to the Annual Energy Outlook, 2014*, Energy Information Administration (EIA), U.S. Dept. of Energy

Region/basin	Technically recoverable resources			Region/basin	Technically recoverable resources		
	Crude oil (bil barrels)	Dry natural gas (tril cu ft)	Natural gas plant liquids (bil barrels)		Crude oil (bil barrels)	Dry natural gas (tril cu ft)	Natural gas plant liquids (bil barrels)
East				**Rocky Mountain**			
Appalachian	1.5	194.1	3.7	Denver	0.4	14.2	0.1
Illinois	—	41.7	7.5	Greater Green R.	0.9	10.6	0.5
Michigan	—	23.4	2.9	MT Thrust Belt	0.6	0.4	—
Gulf Coast				North Central MT	—	0.3	—
Black Warrior	—	4.3	—	Paradox	1.0	0.8	—
TX-LA-MS Salt	0.9	223.6	—	Powder River	2.1	2.4	0.1
Western Gulf	24.3	113.3	1.4	San Juan	—	21.9	—
Midcontinent				SW Wyoming	1.6	48.5	3.6
Anadarko	0.9	24.4	1.2	Uinta-Piceance	0.5	44.0	—
Arkoma	—	37.6	0.6	Williston	9.3	10.7	0.5
Black Warrior	—	1.6	—	Wind R.	—	4.4	0.2
Southwest				**West Coast**			
Fort Worth	—	20.3	0.8	Columbia	—	12.2	—
Permian	14.6	47.9	4.0	San Joaquin/L.A.	0.6	0.6	—
				Total	**59.2**	**903.2**	**27.6**

— = Less than 500 mil barrels.

U.S. Petroleum Trade, 1976-2014

Source: *Monthly Energy Review*, Aug. 2014, Energy Information Administration (EIA), U.S. Dept. of Energy
(in thousands of barrels per day; average for the year)

Year	Imports from Persian Gulf[1]	Total imports	Total exports	Net imports[2]	Petroleum products supplied[3]	Year	Imports from Persian Gulf[1]	Total imports	Total exports	Net imports[2]	Petroleum products supplied[3]
1976	1,840	7,313	223	7,090	17,461	2001	2,761	11,871	971	10,900	19,649
1980	1,519	6,909	544	6,365	17,056	2002	2,269	11,530	984	10,546	19,761
1985	311	5,067	781	4,286	15,726	2003	2,501	12,264	1,027	11,238	20,034
1990	1,966	8,018	857	7,161	16,988	2004	2,493	13,145	1,048	12,097	20,731
1991	1,845	7,627	1,001	6,626	16,714	2005	2,334	13,714	1,165	12,549	20,802
1992	1,778	7,888	950	6,938	17,033	2006	2,211	13,707	1,317	12,390	20,687
1993	1,782	8,620	1,003	7,618	17,237	2007	2,163	13,468	1,433	12,036	20,680
1994	1,728	8,996	942	8,054	17,718	2008	2,370	12,915	1,802	11,114	19,498
1995	1,573	8,835	949	7,886	17,725	2009	1,689	11,691	2,024	9,667	18,771
1996	1,604	9,478	981	8,498	18,309	2010	1,711	11,793	2,353	9,441	19,180
1997	1,755	10,162	1,003	9,158	18,620	2011	1,861	11,436	2,986	8,450	18,882
1998	2,136	10,708	945	9,764	18,917	2012	2,156	10,598	3,205	7,393	18,490
1999	2,464	10,852	940	9,912	19,519	2013	2,008	9,794	3,594	6,200	18,887
2000	2,488	11,459	1,040	10,419	19,701	2014[4]	NA	9,251	3,783	5,468	18,879

NA = Not available. **Note:** U.S. exports include shipments to U.S. territories; imports include receipts from U.S. territories. Numbers may not add up to totals because of rounding. (1) Bahrain, Iran, Iraq, Kuwait, Qatar, Saudi Arabia, United Arab Emirates, and the Neutral Zone between Kuwait and Saudi Arabia. (2) Total imports minus total exports. (3) Includes domestic production and imports minus change in stocks, refinery imports, and exports. (4) Estimated annualized 7-month average, for Jan.-July.

World Fossil Fuel Reserves

Source: International Energy Statistics Database, Energy Information Administration (EIA), U.S. Dept. of Energy

	Crude oil (bil barrels), 2014	Natural gas (tril cu ft), 2014	Coal (mil short tons), 2011		Crude oil (bil barrels), 2014	Natural gas (tril cu ft), 2014	Coal (mil short tons), 2011
North America[1]	213.9	393.8	267,411	Middle East	804.1	2,828.1	1,237
Canada	173.2	66.7	7,255	Bahrain	0.1	3.3	NA
Greenland	0.0	0.0	202	Iran	157.3	1,193.0	1,237
Mexico	10.1	17.1	1,335	Iraq	140.3	111.5	NA
United States[1]	30.5	308.4	258,619	Israel	0.0	10.1	NA
Central & South America	326.4	275.1	16,139	Kuwait	104.0	63.5	NA
Argentina	2.8	13.4	606	Oman	5.5	30.0	NA
Bolivia	0.2	9.9	1	Qatar	25.2	885.3	NA
Brazil	13.2	13.7	7,308	Saudi Arabia	268.4	290.8	NA
Chile	0.2	3.5	171	Syria	2.5	8.5	NA
Colombia	2.4	7.0	7,436	UAE	97.8	215.0	NA
Cuba	0.1	2.5	NA	Yemen	3.0	16.9	NA
Ecuador	8.2	0.2	26	Africa	126.7	606.0	35,069
Peru	0.6	15.4	49	Algeria	12.2	159.1	65
Trinidad and Tobago	0.7	13.1	NA	Angola	9.1	9.7	NA
Venezuela	297.7	196.4	528	Congo, Dem. Rep.	0.2	0.0	97
Europe	12.4	142.2	90,743	Congo Rep.	1.6	3.2	NA
Albania	0.2	0.0	875	Egypt	4.4	77.2	18
Bosnia & Herz.	0.0	0.0	3,145	Libya	48.5	54.7	NA
Bulgaria	0.0	0.2	2,608	Mozambique	0.0	100.0	234
Czech Republic	0.0	0.2	1,160	Namibia	0.0	2.2	NA
Germany	0.2	4.1	44,697	Niger	0.2	0.0	77
Greece	0.0	0.0	3,329	Nigeria	37.1	180.7	209
Hungary	0.0	0.3	1,830	South Africa	0.0	NA	33,241
Italy	0.6	2.1	55	Sudan[2]	5.0	3.0	NA
Macedonia	0.0	0.0	366	Swaziland	0.0	0.0	159
Montenegro	0.0	0.0	157	Tanzania	0.0	0.2	220
Netherlands	0.3	39.9	NA	Zimbabwe	0.0	0.0	553
Norway	5.8	73.8	6	Asia & Oceania	45.9	539.2	317,827
Poland	0.2	3.2	6,024	Afghanistan	0.0	1.8	73
Romania	0.6	3.7	321	Australia	1.4	43.0	84,217
Serbia	0.1	1.7	14,783	Bangladesh	0.0	9.3	323
Slovakia	0.0	0.5	289	Brunei	1.1	13.8	NA
Slovenia	0.0	0.0	246	China	24.4	155.4	126,215
Spain	0.2	0.1	584	India	5.7	47.0	66,800
Turkey	0.3	0.2	9,592	Indonesia	3.6	104.4	30,883
United Kingdom	3.0	8.6	251	Japan	0.0	0.7	383
Eurasia	118.9	2,177.8	251,364	Korea, North	0.0	0.0	661
Armenia	0.0	0.0	180	Korea, South	NA	0.2	139
Azerbaijan	7.0	35.0	NA	Laos	0.0	0.0	554
Belarus	0.2	0.1	110	Malaysia	4.0	83.0	4
Georgia	0.0	0.3	222	Mongolia	NA	0.0	2,778
Kazakhstan	30.0	85.0	37,038	Myanmar	0.1	10.0	2
Kyrgyzstan	0.0	0.2	895	New Zealand	0.1	1.0	629
Russia	80.0	1,688.0	173,074	Pakistan	0.3	26.7	2,282
Tajikistan	0.0	0.2	413	Philippines	0.1	3.5	348
Turkmenistan	0.6	265.0	NA	Thailand	0.4	9.0	1,366
Ukraine	0.4	39.0	37,339	Vietnam	4.4	24.7	165
Uzbekistan	0.6	65.0	2,094	World[1]	1,646.0	6,845.6	979,791

NA = Not reported separately but included in regional and world totals. **Note:** Regional and world totals may include countries not shown. Proved reserves only. Some countries omitted for lack of appreciable reserves. (1) Figures for crude oil and natural gas are from 2013, the latest year available. (2) Includes South Sudan.

U.S. Crude Oil Imports by Selected Countries, 1975-2013

Source: *Petroleum Supply Annual*, Energy Information Administration (EIA), U.S. Dept. of Energy

The United States' dependence on foreign oil continues to decline thanks to increased production of crude oil, natural gas, and domestic biofuels like ethanol and biodiesel. Imports fell to just 7.7 mil barrels a day in 2013, down from a peak of more than 10 mil barrels per day a decade ago. And imports from the Oil Producing and Exporting Countries (OPEC) declined to 3.5 mil barrels daily, an amount not seen in two decades. Net imports account for just 40% of U.S. petroleum use. Since 2005, Canada has been the largest supplier of U.S. oil by far, responsible for more than a third of all U.S. imports. Sanctions do not permit the U.S. to import oil from Iran.

(in thousands of barrels per day; ranked by 2013 imports)

Country	1975	1980	1985	1990	1995	2000	2005	2010	2012	2013
Canada	600	199	468	643	1,040	1,348	1,633	1,970	2,425	2,569
Saudi Arabia#	701	1,250	132	1,195	1,260	1,523	1,445	1,082	1,361	1,325
Mexico	70	507	715	689	1,027	1,313	1,556	1,152	975	850
Venezuela#	395	156	306	666	1,151	1,223	1,241	912	912	755
Colombia	0	0	0	140	207	318	156	338	403	367
Iraq#	2	28	46	514	0	620	527	415	476	341
Kuwait#	4	27	4	79	213	263	227	195	303	326
Nigeria#	746	841	280	784	621	875	1,077	983	406	239
Ecuador#[1]	0	0	0	0	96	125	276	210	177	228
Angola#[2]	71	37	104	236	360	295	456	383	222	202
Brazil	0	1	0	0	0	5	94	255	189	109
Chad	NA	NA	NA	NA	NA	NA	74	18	28	66
Russia[3]	0	0	0	1	14	7	199	269	101	45
Libya#	223	548	0	0	0	0	44	43	56	43
Algeria#	264	456	84	63	27	1	228	328	120	29
Azerbaijan	NA	NA	NA	NA	NA	NA	NA	55	24	29
Gabon[4]	NA	NA	NA	NA	229	143	127	47	42	24
United Kingdom	0	173	278	155	341	291	224	120	18	21
Congo Republic	NA	NA	NA	NA	20	42	25	70	29	18
Indonesia	379	314	292	98	64	36	19	33	6	18
Equatorial Guinea	NA	NA	NA	NA	NA	6	68	50	41	17
Norway	12	144	31	96	258	302	119	25	26	17
Argentina	NA	NA	NA	NA	44	53	56	29	21	13
Vietnam	NA	NA	NA	NA	1	9	31	12	10	13
Peru	NA	NA	NA	NA	21	4	4	14	8	11
Thailand	NA	NA	NA	NA	1	3	2	13	20	9
Trinidad and Tobago	115	115	98	76	62	56	64	45	27	8
Non-OPEC countries[1,2,4]	NA	NA	NA	NA	3,660	4,526	5,310	4,661	4,495	4,229
OPEC countries[1,2,4]	3,211	3,864	1,312	3,514	3,570	4,544	4,816	4,553	4,031	3,490
Persian Gulf countries	1,121	1,508	244	1,801	1,479	2,409	2,207	1,694	2,140	1,994
TOTAL	4,105	5,263	3,201	5,894	7,230	9,071	10,126	9,213	8,527	7,719

= OPEC member. NA = Not available. (1) Ecuador suspended its OPEC membership Dec.1992-Nov. 2007. Ecuador's imports in 1993-2007 appear in non-OPEC totals. (2) Angola became a member of OPEC as of Jan. 1, 2007, and is not included in OPEC totals from before that year. (3) May include oil from USSR states before 1992. (4) Gabon withdrew from OPEC Dec. 31, 1994. Imports from Jan. 1, 1995, on appear in non-OPEC totals.

U.S. Coal Production and Consumption, 1950-2013

Source: *Monthly Energy Review*, Aug. 2014; *Annual Coal Report, 2012*; Energy Information Administration (EIA), U.S. Dept. of Energy

(in thousand short tons)

Year	Coal production[1] Surface mining	Coal production[1] Underground mining	Coal production[1] Total production	Coal consumption Residential	Coal consumption Commercial	Coal consumption Industrial	Coal consumption Electric power[2]	Coal consumption Total consumption
1950	139,388	421,000	560,388	51,562	63,021	224,637	91,871	494,102
1960	141,745	292,584	434,329	24,159	16,789	177,402	176,685	398,081
1970	272,131	340,530	612,661	9,024	7,090	186,637	320,182	523,231
1975	361,174	293,467	654,641	2,823	6,587	147,244	405,962	562,640
1980	492,192	337,508	829,700	1,355	5,097	127,004	569,274	702,730
1985	532,838	350,800	883,638	1,711	6,068	116,429	693,841	818,049
1990	604,529	424,546	1,029,076	1,345	5,379	115,207	782,567	904,498
1995	636,725	396,249	1,032,974	755	5,052	106,067	850,230	962,104
2000	699,953	373,659	1,073,612	454	3,673	94,147	985,821	1,084,095
2005	762,887	368,612	1,131,498	378	4,342	83,774	1,037,485	1,125,978
2006	803,728	359,022	1,162,750	290	2,936	82,429	1,026,636	1,112,292
2007	794,845	351,790	1,146,635	353	3,173	79,331	1,045,141	1,127,998
2008	814,729	357,079	1,171,809	351	3,506	76,463	1,040,580	1,120,548
2009	742,862	332,062	1,074,923	353	3,210	60,641	933,627	997,478
2010	745,357	337,155	1,084,368	339	3,081	70,381	975,052	1,048,514
2011	748,372	345,606	1,095,628	307	2,793	67,671	932,484	1,002,948
2012	672,748	342,387	1,016,458	NA	2,045	63,589	823,551	889,185
2013	NA	NA	983,964	NA	1,951	64,805	858,351	925,106

NA = Not available. (1) A small amount of refuse recovery has been included in coal production figures since 2001. (2) Electricity-only and combined-heat-and-power (CHP) plants whose primary business is to sell electricity or electricity and heat to the public. Through 1988, data are for electric utilities only; beginning in 1989, data are for electric utilities and independent power producers.

World Nuclear Power Summary, 2013

Source: *Nuclear Power Reactors in the World*, International Atomic Energy Agency; as of Dec. 31, 2013

Country	Reactors in operation No. of units	Reactors in operation Total MW(e)	Reactors under construction No. of units	Reactors under construction Total MW(e)	Nuclear electricity supplied in 2012 TW(e).h[1]	Nuclear electricity supplied in 2012 % of nation's total	Total operating experience[2] Years	Total operating experience[2] Months
Argentina	2	935	1	692	5.7	4.4%	70	7
Armenia	1	375	—	—	2.2	29.2	39	8
Belgium	7	5,927	—	—	40.6	52.1	261	7
Brazil	2	1,884	1	1,245	13.8	2.8	45	3
Bulgaria	2	1,906	—	—	13.3	30.7	155	3
Canada	19	13,500	—	—	94.3	16.0	655	7
China	20	15,977	29	28,774	104.8	2.1	160	0
Czech Republic	6	3,884	—	—	29.0	35.9	134	10
Finland	4	2,752	1	1,600	22.7	33.3	139	4
France	58	63,130	1	1,630	405.9	73.3	1,932	3
Germany	9	12,068	—	—	92.1	15.4	799	1
Hungary	4	1,889	—	—	14.5	50.7	114	2
India	21	5,308	6	3,907	30.0	3.5	397	6
Iran	1	915	—	—	3.9	1.5	2	4
Japan	48	42,388	2	1,325	13.9	1.7	1,646	4
Korea, South	23	20,721	5	6,370	132.5	27.6	427	1
Mexico	2	1,330	—	—	11.4	4.6	43	11
Netherlands	1	482	—	—	2.7	2.8	69	0
Pakistan	3	690	2	630	4.4	4.4	58	8
Romania	2	1,300	—	—	10.7	19.8	23	11
Russia	33	23,643	10	8,382	161.7	17.5	1,124	2
Slovakia	4	1,815	2	880	14.6	51.7	148	7
Slovenia	1	688	—	—	5.0	33.6	32	3
South Africa	2	1,860	—	—	13.6	5.7	58	7
Spain	7	7,121	—	—	54.3	19.7	301	1
Sweden	10	9,474	—	—	63.7	42.7	412	6
Switzerland	5	3,308	—	—	25.0	36.4	194	11
Taiwan	6	5032	2	2,600	39.8	19.1	194	1
Ukraine	15	13,107	2	1,900	78.2	43.6	412	6
United Kingdom	16	9,243	—	—	64.1	18.3	1,527	7
United States	100	99,081	5	5,633	790.2	19.4	3,912	4
Total	**434**	**371,733**	**72**	**69,367**	**2,358.9**		**15,660**	**7**

— = Not applicable. MW(e) = Megawatt electricity. (1) 1 terawatt-hour [TW(e).h] = 106 megawatt-hour [MW(e).h]. For an average power plant, 1 TW(e).h = 0.39 megaton of coal equivalent (input) and 0.23 megaton of oil equivalent (input). (2) Total includes shutdown plants for countries not listed here: Italy (80 years, 8 months), Kazakhstan (25 years, 10 months), and Lithuania (43 years, 6 months).

Nations Most Reliant on Nuclear Energy, 2013

Source: *Nuclear Power Reactors in the World*, International Atomic Energy Agency (IAEA)
(nuclear electricity generation as % of total electricity generated within country)

Rank	Country	Nuclear share	Rank	Country	Nuclear share	Rank	Country	Nuclear share	Rank	Country	Nuclear share
1.	France	73.3%	9.	Slovenia	33.6%	17.	Taiwan	19.1%	24.	Pakistan	4.4%
2.	Belgium	52.1	10.	Finland	33.3	18.	United Kingdom	18.3	25.	India	3.5
3.	Slovakia	51.7	11.	Bulgaria	30.7	19.	Russia	17.5	26.	Brazil	2.8
4.	Hungary	50.7	12.	Armenia	29.2	20.	Canada	16.0		Netherlands	2.8
5.	Ukraine	43.6	13.	Korea, South	27.6	21.	Germany	15.5	28.	China	2.1
6.	Sweden	42.7	14.	Romania	19.8	22.	South Africa	5.7	29.	Japan	1.7
7.	Switzerland	36.4	15.	Spain	19.7	23.	Mexico	4.6	30.	Iran	1.5
8.	Czech Republic	35.9	16.	United States	19.4	24.	Argentina	4.4			

U.S. Nuclear Reactors and Power Plant Operations, 1953-2013

Source: *Monthly Energy Review*, Aug. 2014, Energy Information Administration (EIA), U.S. Dept. of Energy

Years	Number of reactor units Ordered[1]	Number of reactor units Cancelled	Number of reactor units Construction permits issued[2]	Number of reactor units Low-power licenses issued[3]	Number of reactor units Full-power licenses issued[4]	Number of reactor units Shutdown[5]	Operable units[6]	Capacity factor[6,7]	Nuclear electricity generation (bil net kWh)[6]	Nuclear share of domestic electricity generation[6]
1953-59	14	0	8	2	2	0	2	NA	0.2	NA
1960-64	7	0	12	13	12	2	13	NA	3.3	0.3%
1965-69	81	0	50	8	9	4	17	NA	13.9	1.0
1970-74	143	16	59	41	41	5	55	47.8%	114.0	6.1
1975-79	13	43	48	17	17	3	69	58.4	255.2	11.3
1980-84	0	54	0	24	19	1	87	56.3	327.6	13.5
1985-89	0	7	0	24	28	4	111	62.2	529.4	17.8
1990-94	0	2	0	2	3	3	109	73.8	640.4	19.7
1995-99	0	2	0	1	1	6	104	85.3	728.3	19.7
2000-04	0	0	0	0	0	0	104	90.1	788.5	19.9
2005-09	0	0	0	0	0	0	104	90.3	798.9	20.2
2010-13	0	0	0	0	0	4	100	90.1	789.0	19.4
Total	**259**	**124**	**177**	**132**	**132**	**32**	**NA**	**NA**	**NA**	**NA**

NA = Not applicable. **Note:** The permit/license categories shown here are historic. The Nuclear Regulatory Commission anticipates 16 or more new combined license applications under current regulations over the next few years—the first of which was submitted in Sept. 2007—which may amount to 25 or more new reactor units. (1) Order placed by a utility or government agency for a nuclear steam supply system. (2) Permits issued in a given period, not extant permits. (3) Permission to conduct testing but not operate at full power. (4) Permission to operate at full power. (5) Permanently ceased operation. (6) As of the end of the designated period. (7) The ratio of electric energy produced to the amount that could be produced at continuous full-power operation.

U.S. Nuclear Reactors Generating the Most Electricity, 2010

Source: U.S. Nuclear Statistics Database, Energy Information Administration (EIA), U.S. Dept. of Energy

(in thousand net megawatt-hours)

Rank	Reactor, location	Electricity generated	Capacity[1]	Rank	Reactor, location	Electricity generated	Capacity[1]
1.	Palo Verde-2, Wintersburg, AZ	11,652,972	101%	14.	LaSalle-2, Seneca, IL	9,925,542	101%
2.	South Texas-1, Bay City, TX	11,304,107	101	15.	Catawba-1, Lake Wylie, SC	9,889,074	100
3.	Seabrook-1, Portsmouth, NH	10,910,055	100	16.	Limerick-2, Pottstown, PA	9,879,131	99
4.	Perry-1, Dothan, OH	10,619,711	98	17.	South Texas-2, Bay City, TX	9,822,674	88
5.	Comanche Peak-2, Glen Rose, TX	10,531,748	104	18.	Peach Bottom-3, Lancaster, PA	9,759,275	100
6.	Byron-1, Byron, IL	10,337,288	101	19.	Diablo Canyon-2, San Luis Obispo, CA	9,752,476	100
7.	Waterford-3, Taft, LA	10,276,184	100	20.	Watts Bar-1, Spring City, TN	9,738,457	99
8.	Vogtle-1, Waynesboro, GA	10,247,423	102	21.	Comanche Peak-1, Glen Rose, TX	9,676,719	91
9.	Palo Verde-3, Wintersburg, AZ	10,238,992	89	22.	Grand Gulf-1, Port Gibson, MS	9,643,241	88
10.	Susquehanna-2, Berwick, PA	10,221,221	98	23.	Wolf Creek-1, Burlington, KS	9,555,712	94
11.	McGuire-2, Cowens Ford Dam, NC	10,014,695	104	24.	Sequoyah-2, Chattanooga, TN	9,536,672	97
12.	Braidwood-2, Braidwood, IL	10,003,246	99	25.	Byron-2, Byron, IL	9,518,424	96
13.	Salem-2, Salem, NJ	9,954,772	98				

(1) The ratio of power generated to the maximum potential generation expressed as a percentage.

Renewable Energy Sources

Source: U.S. Dept. of Energy

Concern over the environmental impact of burning fossil fuels has helped spur interest in alternative fuels that are less polluting. And because the supply of fossil fuels is finite and diminishing, there is interest in "renewable" sources that do not deplete existing supplies. However, renewable energy sources still make up only a small share of U.S. domestic energy production (about 11% in 2013). The main reason for this is their relatively higher cost (in some cases two to four times that of power obtained from traditional fuels). The following are the major renewable energy sources available.

Biomass is plant-derived material usable as an energy source. It includes wood energy crops such as hybrid poplars and willow trees, agricultural crops including soybeans and corn, and animal and other wastes. Biomass is one of the two most common renewable energy sources in the U.S. today, along with hydropower. Biomass such as wood can be burned to produce heat and generate electricity. Agricultural crops can be chemically converted into fuels such as ethanol and biodiesel; these are the only known renewable liquid energy sources and may one day replace petroleum and fossil-fuel-produced diesel. But bringing ethanol and biodiesel into wide use would require more energy-efficient methods of production and transportation. Overall, biomass fuels burn much cleaner than fossil fuels, though biomass fuels still produce carbon dioxide and other pollutants.

Geothermal energy is generated from heat inside of the Earth. This form of energy is both clean and renewable. The technology has caught on in countries with substantial geothermal activity such as Iceland, where it accounted for 66% of primary energy use in 2011. In the U.S., the best sources for geothermal power are in the West, where there are many heated underground lakes. Large-scale access would require drilling. A major goal in this field is to find a way to harness energy directly from magma (molten rock material), which has great potential because of its high temperatures.

Hydrogen is the third most abundant element on Earth. It does not naturally occur on Earth as a pure gas or liquid but is always combined with other elements (such as oxygen, to form water, or carbon, to form methane). If hydrogen is to be used for energy, it must be separated from these other elements. That can be achieved through methods involving heat, photosynthesis, sunlight, or electricity.

Hydrogen batteries, or fuel cells, were used by NASA's space shuttles. Within a fuel cell, a chemical reaction occurs in which electrons are released from hydrogen atoms. These electrons flow through an external circuit as electricity. The hydrogen atoms' protons combine with oxygen (and some of the electrons in the electric current) to produce heat and water suitable for drinking. Fuel cells do not run down but work as long as hydrogen is supplied. Some experts think hydrogen will be the power source of the future. An infrastructure would need to be created for safe and cost-effective transportation and storage of hydrogen.

Hydropower, or hydroelectric power, is generated by water flowing through turbines. Along with biomass fuels, it is one of the two most common renewable energy sources in the U.S. today. A dam on a river is a common hydropower producer. No harmful greenhouse gases are produced, but the dams needed to generate power can harm river ecosystems. Researchers are working on turbine technologies to maximize use of hydropower and reduce adverse environmental effects.

Ocean energy can be generated in two ways. Thermal ocean energy uses heat that the ocean absorbs from the sun to power generators, sometimes producing drinkable desalinated water as a byproduct. Mechanical ocean energy is generated by the movement of tides and waves through turbines. In both cases, power generation is not very efficient with current technology. Much more research is needed. Mechanical ocean energy requires the building of large dams or breakwater-type structures called tidal barrages, which could harm coastal ecosystems.

Solar energy is generated using heat and light from the sun. Solar energy is an increasingly common source of electricity. Photovoltaic (PV) solar cells are made of semiconducting materials that can directly convert sunlight to electricity without producing any harmful waste. Arrays of mirrors can concentrate the sun's rays onto PV panels, making solar collectors more efficient. Sunlight can also be used to heat water directly. According to the Dept. of Energy, homes incorporating solar heating designs can save as much as 50% on heating bills. The downside to solar energy is that it depends heavily on a range of factors including location, time of year, and weather.

Wind energy uses wind turbines to produce energy. They are perched on high towers, usually 100 ft tall or higher, and often placed in large groups ("farms"). Farmers and homeowners sometimes use stand-alone turbines to generate supplemental electricity. Tax credits for wind energy producers and government incentives for homeowners have significantly lowered the price of wind power. But some object to wind farms because of their appearance or the noise the turbines make. Wind power raises few other environmental problems, but the turbines can pose a danger to birds. In addition, because weather is involved, consistent energy generation can be a challenge.

CRIME

Measuring Crime

Source: Federal Bureau of Investigation (FBI) and Bureau of Justice Statistics (BJS), U.S. Dept. of Justice

The U.S. Dept. of Justice administers two statistical programs to measure trends in crime in the U.S. Because of differences in focus and methodology, their results are not strictly comparable.

The Federal Bureau of Investigation (FBI) conducts the **Uniform Crime Report (UCR)** program, which aims to provide statistics for law enforcement administration, operation, and management. It collects actual counts on the crimes of homicide, forcible rape, robbery, aggravated assault, burglary, larceny-theft, motor vehicle theft, and arson as they are reported to law enforcement agencies. Each year, the program releases a preliminary report in the spring, followed by a more detailed, final report in the fall.

The **National Crime Victimization Survey (NCVS)** is conducted annually by the Bureau of Justice Statistics through interviews with members of a nationally representative sample of households about their experiences with crime. The survey complements the UCR by providing alternative and previously unavailable data, including details about the victims of crime and their offenders (e.g., age, sex, ethnicity, victim-offender relationship) and information on crimes not reported to law enforcement. In contrast to the UCR, the NCVS does not cover homicide, arson, commercial crimes, or crimes against children under age 12.

Further explanation of the UCR and NCVS is available at www.bjs.gov/content/pub/html/ntcm.cfm.

Crime in the U.S., 1989-2012

Source: *Crime in the United States, 2012*, Federal Bureau of Investigation (FBI), U.S. Dept. of Justice

In the FBI's Uniform Crime Report (UCR) Program, offenses are classified as **violent crimes** if they involve force or the threat of force: murder and nonnegligent manslaughter, forcible rape, robbery, and aggravated assault. The following offenses are considered **property crimes**: burglary, larceny-theft, motor vehicle theft, and arson. Arson data is excluded from this table because of variations in the level of participation by reporting agencies. That data is presented separately online at www.fbi.gov/about-us/cjis/ucr/.

Year(s)	Population[1]	Violent crime					Property crime			
		All violent crimes	Murder and nonnegligent manslaughter	Forcible rape[2]	Robbery	Aggravated assault[3]	All property crimes	Burglary	Larceny-theft[4]	Motor vehicle theft
NUMBER OF OFFENSES										
1989	246,819,230	1,646,037	21,500	94,504	578,326	951,707	12,605,412	3,168,170	7,705,872	7,872,442
1990	249,464,396	1,820,127	23,438	102,555	639,271	1,054,863	12,655,486	3,073,909	7,945,670	1,635,907
1995	262,803,276	1,798,792	21,606	97,470	580,509	1,099,207	12,063,935	2,593,784	7,997,710	1,472,441
2000	281,421,906	1,425,486	15,586	90,178	408,016	911,706	10,182,584	2,050,992	6,971,590	1,160,002
2001[5]	285,317,559	1,439,480	16,037	90,863	423,557	909,023	10,437,189	2,116,531	7,092,267	1,228,391
2002	287,973,924	1,423,677	16,229	95,235	420,806	891,407	10,455,277	2,151,252	7,057,379	1,246,646
2003	290,788,976	1,383,676	16,528	93,883	414,235	859,030	10,442,862	2,154,834	7,026,802	1,261,226
2004	293,656,842	1,360,088	16,148	95,089	401,470	847,381	10,319,386	2,144,446	6,937,089	1,237,851
2005	296,507,061	1,390,745	16,740	94,347	417,438	862,220	10,174,754	2,155,448	6,783,447	1,235,859
2006	299,398,484	1,435,123	17,309	94,472	449,246	874,096	10,019,601	2,194,993	6,626,363	1,198,245
2007	301,621,157	1,422,970	17,128	92,160	447,324	866,358	9,882,212	2,190,198	6,591,542	1,100,472
2008	304,059,724	1,394,461	16,465	90,750	443,563	843,683	9,774,152	2,228,887	6,586,206	959,059
2009	307,006,550	1,325,896	15,399	89,241	408,742	812,514	9,337,060	2,203,313	6,338,095	795,652
2010	309,330,219	1,251,248	14,722	85,593	369,089	781,844	9,112,625	2,168,459	6,204,601	739,565
2011	311,587,816	1,206,005	14,661	84,175	354,746	752,423	9,052,743	2,185,140	6,151,095	716,508
2012	313,914,040	1,214,462	14,827	84,376	354,520	760,739	8,975,438	2,103,787	6,150,598	721,053
PERCENT CHANGE: NUMBER OF OFFENSES										
2012/2011........	0.7%	1.1%	0.2%	-0.1%	1.1%	-0.9%	-3.7%	—	0.6%	
2012/2008........	-12.9	-9.9	-7.0	-20.1	-9.8	-8.2	-5.6	-6.6%	-24.8	
2012/2003........	-12.2	-10.3	-10.1	-14.4	-11.4	-14.1	-2.4	-12.5	-42.8	
RATE PER 100,000 RESIDENTS										
1989.............	666.9	8.7	38.3	234.3	385.6	5,107.1	1,283.6	3,189.6	634.0	
1990.............	729.6	9.4	41.1	256.3	422.9	5,073.1	1,232.2	3,185.1	655.8	
1995.............	684.5	8.2	37.1	220.9	418.3	4,590.5	987.0	3,043.2	560.3	
2000.............	506.5	5.5	32.0	145.0	324.0	3,618.3	728.8	2,477.3	412.2	
2001[5]...........	504.5	5.6	31.8	148.5	318.6	3,658.1	741.8	2,485.7	430.5	
2002.............	494.4	5.6	33.1	146.1	309.5	3,630.6	747.0	2,450.7	432.9	
2003.............	475.8	5.7	32.3	142.5	295.4	3,591.2	741.0	2,416.5	433.7	
2004.............	463.2	5.5	32.4	136.7	288.6	3,514.1	730.3	2,362.3	421.5	
2005.............	469.0	5.6	31.8	140.8	290.8	3,431.5	726.9	2,287.8	416.8	
2006.............	479.3	5.8	31.6	150.0	292.0	3,346.6	733.1	2,213.2	400.2	
2007.............	471.8	5.7	30.6	148.3	287.2	3,276.4	726.1	2,185.4	364.9	
2008.............	458.6	5.4	29.8	145.9	277.5	3,214.6	733.0	2,166.1	315.4	
2009.............	431.9	5.0	29.1	133.1	264.7	3,041.3	717.7	2,064.5	259.2	
2010.............	404.5	4.8	27.7	119.3	252.8	2,945.9	701.0	2,005.8	239.1	
2011.............	387.1	4.7	27.0	113.9	241.5	2,905.4	701.3	1,974.1	230.0	
2012.............	386.9	4.7	26.9	112.9	242.3	2,859.2	670.2	1,959.3	229.7	
PERCENT CHANGE: RATE PER 100,000 RESIDENTS										
2012/2011........	—	0.4%	-0.5%	-0.8%	0.4%	-1.6%	-4.4%	-0.7%	-0.1%	
2012/2008........	-15.6%	-12.8	-9.9	-22.6	-12.7	-11.1	-8.6	-9.5	-27.2	
2012/2003........	-18.7	-16.9	-16.7	-20.7	-18.0	-20.4	-9.6	-18.9	-47.0	

— = Less than 0.1%. (1) U.S. Census Bureau estimates for July 1 of each year except for 1990, 2000, and 2010, which show Apr. 1 decennial census counts. (2) Does not include statutory rape (i.e., rape not involving force) and other offenses of a sexual nature. Also does not include sexual attacks on males, which are considered aggravated assaults or sex offenses, depending on circumstances and extent of injuries. (The FBI revised its definition of rape in 2012 to be more inclusive.) (3) Attack upon another with the intent of doing serious bodily harm; usually accompanied by the use of a weapon or other means likely to produce death or great bodily harm. (4) The unlawful taking of another's property not involving force or fraud (e.g., theft of motor vehicle parts, shoplifting). Excludes crimes such as embezzlement and check fraud. (5) The murder and nonnegligent homicides that occurred as a result of the Sept. 11, 2001, terrorist attacks are not included.

U.S. Crime Rates by Region, Geographic Division, and State, 2012
Source: *Crime in the United States, 2012*, Federal Bureau of Investigation (FBI), U.S. Dept. of Justice
(per 100,000 residents, as estimated by U.S. Census Bureau for July 1 of year)

	Violent crime					Property crime[1]			
	All violent crimes	Murder and nonnegligent manslaughter	Forcible rape[2]	Robbery	Aggravated assault[3]	All property crimes	Burglary	Larceny-theft[4]	Motor vehicle theft
Total U.S.[5]	386.9	4.7	26.9	112.9	242.3	2,859.2	670.2	1,959.3	229.7
Northeast	349.0	3.8	19.7	121.4	204.1	2,080.5	422.9	1,532.8	124.9
New England	307.4	2.4	26.0	82.1	196.9	2,238.7	494.9	1,601.2	142.6
Connecticut	283.0	4.1	25.6	102.7	150.6	2,140.0	409.7	1,550.7	179.6
Maine	122.7	1.9	28.0	31.8	61.0	2,509.9	561.3	1,873.7	74.9
Massachusetts	405.5	1.8	24.7	98.6	280.4	2,153.0	519.7	1,494.4	138.9
New Hampshire	187.9	1.1	34.0	35.7	117.0	2,324.0	412.2	1,834.3	77.5
Rhode Island	252.4	3.2	27.4	67.9	153.9	2,572.3	566.4	1,755.7	250.2
Vermont	142.6	1.3	19.3	17.9	104.2	2,398.7	633.4	1,695.8	69.5
Middle Atlantic	363.7	4.3	17.5	135.2	206.7	2,024.6	397.5	1,508.6	118.6
New Jersey	290.2	4.4	11.7	128.4	145.7	2,047.3	477.6	1,383.7	185.9
New York	406.8	3.5	14.6	146.4	242.3	1,922.0	329.9	1,503.5	88.6
Pennsylvania	348.7	5.4	26.1	122.8	194.4	2,166.3	445.5	1,603.1	117.7
Midwest	354.6	4.7	31.7	103.2	215.0	2,764.8	644.5	1,921.1	199.2
East North Central	368.5	5.2	31.6	121.0	210.7	2,749.9	678.0	1,873.9	198.0
Illinois	414.8	5.8	27.7	151.2	230.0	2,578.7	552.2	1,826.9	199.5
Indiana	345.7	4.7	25.5	100.9	214.6	3,029.2	728.3	2,092.0	209.0
Michigan	454.5	7.0	46.4	105.6	295.5	2,530.5	664.4	1,612.0	254.1
Ohio	299.7	4.3	31.7	132.0	131.7	3,117.4	895.9	2,052.5	169.0
Wisconsin	280.5	3.0	21.3	80.7	175.5	2,453.8	488.0	1,822.3	143.5
West North Central	323.5	3.5	32.0	63.3	224.7	2,798.3	569.1	2,027.2	202.1
Iowa	263.9	1.5	28.3	31.3	202.8	2,271.8	556.1	1,584.8	130.9
Kansas	354.6	2.9	36.5	52.0	263.2	3,143.2	650.3	2,258.0	234.9
Minnesota	230.9	1.8	30.5	64.6	134.0	2,568.3	471.8	1,939.3	157.2
Missouri	450.9	6.5	25.1	96.0	323.4	3,314.4	705.2	2,338.4	270.8
Nebraska	259.4	2.9	38.3	60.9	157.4	2,754.9	470.8	2,060.7	223.5
North Dakota	244.7	4.0	38.0	18.7	183.1	2,010.1	339.8	1,505.8	164.5
South Dakota	321.8	3.0	70.2	19.0	229.7	2,060.1	391.0	1,541.4	127.8
South[5]	423.7	5.5	27.1	112.5	278.6	3,226.8	806.8	2,206.3	213.7
South Atlantic[5]	416.6	5.4	23.9	116.8	270.5	3,145.6	768.4	2,170.3	206.9
Delaware	547.4	6.2	26.5	162.7	352.0	3,340.9	803.7	2,380.6	156.6
District of Columbia[5]	1,243.7	13.9	37.3	638.3	554.1	4,860.8	556.5	3,725.3	579.0
Florida	487.1	5.2	27.2	123.7	330.9	3,276.7	794.9	2,288.6	193.2
Georgia	378.9	5.9	21.4	125.6	226.0	3,410.6	874.9	2,248.0	287.7
Maryland	476.8	6.3	21.0	172.3	277.2	2,753.5	573.2	1,924.9	255.3
North Carolina	353.4	4.9	20.3	96.3	231.8	3,369.5	1,018.5	2,185.7	165.3
South Carolina	558.8	6.9	35.5	95.0	421.4	3,822.2	954.5	2,588.3	279.5
Virginia	190.1	3.8	17.7	57.5	111.1	2,162.1	360.5	1,690.7	110.9
West Virginia	316.3	3.9	22.7	45.2	244.6	2,364.9	608.5	1,637.3	119.1
East South Central	433.3	6.1	29.1	102.0	296.1	3,123.2	865.3	2,076.3	181.5
Alabama	449.9	7.1	26.9	104.1	311.8	3,502.2	984.7	2,312.8	204.8
Kentucky	222.6	4.5	29.0	80.7	108.4	2,552.9	675.4	1,725.2	152.2
Mississippi	260.8	7.4	27.5	76.5	149.4	2,811.0	940.6	1,725.6	144.8
Tennessee	643.6	6.0	31.5	126.5	479.6	3,371.4	870.2	2,300.1	201.0
West South Central	430.4	5.4	31.3	110.6	283.1	3,411.3	840.5	2,329.8	240.9
Arkansas	469.1	5.9	42.3	78.7	342.3	3,660.1	1,081.3	2,384.7	194.1
Louisiana	496.9	10.8	25.2	119.0	342.0	3,540.6	915.7	2,453.7	171.3
Oklahoma	469.3	5.7	41.6	84.7	337.3	3,401.0	936.6	2,161.3	303.1
Texas	408.6	4.4	29.6	116.6	258.0	3,361.8	785.9	2,326.4	249.4
West	386.5	4.2	27.5	116.2	238.5	2,949.8	663.3	1,924.0	362.5
Mountain	378.7	3.9	36.4	84.6	253.7	3,006.8	657.6	2,099.9	249.2
Arizona	428.9	5.5	34.7	112.7	276.0	3,539.2	807.8	2,439.1	292.3
Colorado	308.9	3.1	40.7	65.4	199.6	2,684.7	504.2	1,947.4	233.1
Idaho	207.9	1.8	30.0	15.2	160.9	1,983.5	450.3	1,447.7	85.5
Montana	272.2	2.7	37.7	19.0	212.8	2,583.7	387.4	2,028.3	168.0
Nevada	607.6	4.5	33.7	178.3	391.1	2,809.4	801.8	1,644.6	363.1
New Mexico	559.1	5.6	45.9	88.6	419.1	3,600.7	1,025.3	2,313.4	261.9
Utah	205.8	1.8	33.0	38.5	132.5	2,991.8	453.3	2,328.4	210.1
Wyoming	201.4	2.4	26.7	10.6	161.7	2,293.8	368.7	1,823.9	101.3
Pacific	390.0	4.4	23.6	130.2	231.7	2,924.5	665.8	1,845.9	412.7
Alaska	603.2	4.1	79.7	86.1	433.2	2,739.4	403.3	2,128.0	208.1
California	423.1	5.0	20.6	148.6	248.9	2,758.7	646.1	1,669.5	443.2
Hawaii	239.2	2.1	20.5	74.7	141.9	3,075.2	573.1	2,243.2	258.9
Oregon	247.6	2.4	29.2	61.9	154.1	3,224.2	561.7	2,400.9	261.7
Washington	295.6	3.0	31.8	83.3	177.5	3,658.6	880.5	2,395.3	382.8
Puerto Rico	273.8	26.7	0.9	171.7	74.5	1,409.3	416.9	833.0	159.4

Note: Offense totals are based on all reporting agencies and estimates for unreported areas. Figures may not add up to totals due to rounding. (1) Data for arson, considered a property crime, are not included in this table. (2) Does not include statutory rape (i.e., rape not involving force) and other offenses of a sexual nature. Also does not include sexual attacks on males, which are considered aggravated assaults or sex offenses, depending on circumstances and extent of injuries. (3) Attack upon another with the intent of doing serious bodily harm; usually accompanied by the use of a weapon or other means likely to produce death or great bodily harm. (4) The unlawful taking of another's property not involving force or fraud (e.g., theft of motor vehicle parts, shoplifting). Excludes crimes such as embezzlement and check fraud. (5) Includes offenses reported by National Zoological Park Police and Washington Metro Transit Police.

Crime Rates in the Largest U.S. Metropolitan Areas, 2012

Source: *Crime in the United States, 2012,* Federal Bureau of Investigation, U.S. Dept. of Justice
(per 100,000 population, as estimated by U.S. Census Bureau for July 1 of year)

Memphis was the U.S. metropolitan statistical area (MSA) with the highest rate of violent crime in 2012, with more than 1,000 violent crimes per 100,000 people; it was 50% higher than in the Las Vegas MSA, which had the second-highest rate of 696.5. San Juan, PR, had the highest murder rate, with 32 per 100,000 residents; New Orleans had the second-highest, of 20.6, followed by Memphis with 11.5. Among MSAs with populations over 1 mil, Raleigh, NC, had the lowest murder rate (1.8) and Richmond, VA, had the lowest overall violent crime rate (243.4).

Metropolitan statistical area (MSA)	MSA pop. (mil)	All violent crimes	Violent crime				Property crime			
			Murder and nonnegligent manslaughter	Forcible rape	Robbery	Aggravated assault	All property crimes	Burglary	Larceny-theft	Motor vehicle theft
Atlanta-Sandy Springs-Roswell, GA	5.4	408.6	6.1	20.1	154.2	228.2	3,383.4	871.9	2,136.4	375.1
Baltimore-Columbia-Towson, MD	2.8	621.2	9.5	24.4	214.2	373.2	2,984.3	634.5	2,089.7	260.1
Boston-Cambridge-Newton, MA-NH	4.6	355.2	2.1	22.4	93.2	237.6	1,983.9	398.3	1,453.2	132.3
Chicago-Naperville-Elgin, IL-IN-WI.................	9.5	NA	7.1	NA	184.2	202.6	2,677.0	533.8	1,888.6	254.6
Cincinnati, OH-KY-IN	2.1	284.5	3.5	32.2	131.8	117.1	3,318.9	794.3	2,391.6	133.0
Dallas-Fort Worth-Arlington, TX	6.7	344.7	4.1	28.3	119.9	192.4	3,175.9	783.5	2,128.5	264.0
Denver-Aurora-Lakewood, CO	2.6	337.5	3.9	43.6	84.4	205.6	2,746.6	499.5	1,950.4	296.8
Detroit-Warren-Dearborn, MI ..	4.3	574.4	10.9	34.2	163.5	365.8	2,730.0	696.5	1,583.1	450.4
Houston-The Woodlands-Sugar Land, TX............	6.2	561.5	5.7	24.4	219.9	311.6	NA	NA	2,299.3	378.4
Kansas City, MO-KS.........	2.0	488.2	7.7	33.8	119.1	327.7	3,475.6	753.0	2,335.0	387.6
Las Vegas-Henderson-Paradise, NV.....................	2.0	696.5	4.8	37.0	221.6	433.2	2,966.0	878.8	1,675.3	411.8
Los Angeles-Long Beach-Anaheim, CA.............	13.1	393.0	5.0	18.2	161.2	208.7	2,296.9	466.3	1,465.8	364.8
Miami-Fort Lauderdale-West Palm Beach, FL	5.7	565.2	6.3	23.6	197.0	338.3	3,929.7	850.0	2,792.6	287.0
Minneapolis-St. Paul-Bloomington, MN-WI.......	3.4	NA	2.2	NA	90.5	141.4	NA	NA	2,101.5	193.7
New York-Newark-Jersey City, NY-NJ-PA	19.8	NA	3.8	10.8	160.7	NA	1,704.5	291.9	1,288.0	124.6
Orlando-Kissimmee-Sanford, FL	2.2	546.1	5.0	30.7	121.4	389.0	3,485.0	968.5	2,277.6	238.9
Philadelphia-Camden-Wilmington, PA-NJ-DE-MD ..	6.0	NA	8.6	27.7	210.4	NA	2,665.7	563.0	1,904.3	198.4
Phoenix-Mesa-Scottsdale, AZ..	4.3	406.8	5.3	27.6	127.3	246.6	NA	820.0	2,284.3	NA
Pittsburgh, PA	2.4	NA	4.2	15.2	89.9	NA	1,900.5	398.5	1,425.6	76.4
Portland-Vancouver-Hillsboro, OR-WA	2.3	266.5	2.4	31.8	78.1	154.3	3,164.3	528.8	2,299.3	336.1
Riverside-San Bernardino-Ontario, CA	4.3	368.7	4.1	17.1	121.3	226.2	3,021.3	872.1	1,672.8	476.4
Sacramento-Roseville-Arden-Arcade, CA	2.2	441.1	3.8	24.1	132.9	280.2	2,925.7	695.6	1,787.3	442.8
St. Louis, MO-IL	2.8	463.6	7.3	27.1	111.5	317.7	2,881.8	606.9	2,026.0	248.9
San Antonio-New Braunfels, TX	2.2	390.7	5.1	36.4	95.1	254.1	4,688.1	924.5	3,424.0	339.5
San Diego-Carlsbad, CA	3.2	373.6	3.4	21.8	101.0	247.4	2,196.9	444.2	1,369.8	382.9
San Francisco-Oakland-Hayward, CA	4.4	550.8	6.5	20.1	271.7	252.5	NA	NA	NA	628.0
San Juan-Carolina-Caguas, Puerto Rico..............	2.3	336.4	32.0	0.7	224.4	79.2	1,575.1	411.4	941.6	222.1
Seattle-Tacoma-Bellevue, WA	3.5	336.8	2.9	28.7	110.7	194.4	NA	NA	2,496.0	453.4
Tampa-St. Petersburg-Clearwater, FL	2.9	409.3	3.9	24.5	94.7	286.2	2,862.8	676.7	2,032.7	153.3
Washington-Arlington-Alexandria, DC-VA-MD-WV	5.8	332.7	3.6	16.9	150.6	161.6	2,282.1	312.3	1,751.6	218.2

NA = Not available.

Criminal Victimization, 2003-12

Source: *Criminal Victimization, 2012,* Bureau of Justice Statistics, U.S. Dept. of Justice

A crime committed against an individual or single household counts as one **victimization**. Because a personal crime may involve more than one victim, the number of victimizations may be greater than the number of personal crime incidents.

Victimization rates measure the frequency with which victimizations occured. Personal crime victimization rates are based on the number of victimizations per 1,000 persons in the total population age 12 and over.

Type of crime	Number of victimizations			Rate per 1,000 persons		
	2003	2011	2012	2003	2011	2012
Violent crime[1]	7,679,050	5,812,520	6,842,590	32.1	22.6	26.1
Rape/sexual assault...................	325,310	244,190	346,830	1.4	0.9	1.3
Robbery	708,380	557,260	741,760	3.0	2.2	2.8
Assault	6,645,360	5,011,080	5,754,010	27.8	19.5	22.0
Aggravated assault................	1,362,270	1,053,390	996,110	5.7	4.1	3.8
Simple assault....................	5,283,100	3,957,690	4,757,900	22.1	15.4	18.2
Domestic violence[2].................	1,480,920	1,354,910	1,259,390	6.2	5.3	4.8
Intimate partner violence[3]........	1,040,290	850,770	810,790	4.3	3.3	3.1
Violent crime involving injury	2,029,200	1,450,650	1,573,460	8.5	5.6	6.0
Serious violent crime[4]..............	2,395,950	1,854,840	2,084,690	10.0	7.2	8.0
Serious domestic violence[2]	650,650	369,040	411,080	2.7	1.4	1.6
Serious intimate partner violence[3]	498,470	262,660	270,240	2.1	1.0	1.0
Serious violent crime involving weapons ...	1,695,680	1,194,420	1,415,120	7.1	4.6	5.4
Serious violent crime involving injury	953,740	689,810	762,170	4.0	2.7	2.6

Note: Details may not add up to totals due to rounding. (1) Includes rape or sexual assault, robbery, aggravated assault, and simple assault but excludes murder because victimization data are based on interviews with victims. (2) Victimization by intimate partners and family members. (3) Victimization by current or former spouses, boyfriends, or girlfriends. (4) Includes rape or sexual assault, robbery, and aggravated assault.

State and Federal Prison Population; Death Penalty, 2000-12

Source: *Prisoners in 2012; Capital Punishment, 2012;* Bureau of Justice Statistics, U.S. Dept. of Justice

After rising for four decades, the prison population declined in 2012 for the third straight year. As of Dec. 31, 2012, 1,570,397 prisoners were under the jurisdiction, or legal authority, of state (86.1%) or federal (13.8%) correctional authorities. The federal prison population increased by 0.7%. Under orders from the U.S. Supreme Court to reduce inmate overcrowding to 137.5% of the state's prison capacity, California decreased its prison population by more than 15,000 for the second straight year. That represented more than half of the total decline. Arkansas, Colorado, North Carolina, and Maryland all reduced their prison populations by more than 1,000 inmates. New Hampshire's prison population increased by more than 1,000 inmates. Jails, which are locally operated, typically hold persons awaiting trial or sentencing as well as those sentenced to one year or less.

The imprisonment rate, or number of prisoners per 100,000 U.S. residents, also declined in 2012, from 492 to 480. The rate is still significantly higher than the rate of 470 at year-end 2001. Black males were incarcerated at 6.1 times the rate of white males (2,841 per 100,000 U.S. residents vs. 463 per 100,000) and more than twice as often as Hispanic males (1,158 per 100,000).

For the 12th straight year, the number of persons under sentence of death declined; there were 3,033 inmates on death row at year-end 2012. Nine states executed a total of 43 inmates; Texas executed more than a third of the total. Seventeen death row inmates died of other causes, and 51 had their sentences commuted or overturned. Seventy-nine inmates were added to death row in 2012, the lowest number since 1973. Since 2000, the death row population has decreased every year, but the composition has changed little: 98% were male, 56% were white, and 42% were black. The average time between sentencing and execution declined from 16 years and 6 months to 15 years and 10 months.

As of mid-2014, 33 states and the federal government authorized the death penalty. Maryland repealed the death penalty for offenses committed after May 2, 2013; Connecticut did likewise for crimes after Apr. 25, 2012; New Mexico repealed capital sentences for crimes committed after July 1, 2009. Illinois abolished the death penalty July 1, 2011. All death penalty states authorize lethal injection as a method of execution; eight also permit electrocution; three permit the gas chamber, three hanging, and two (Oklahoma and Utah) authorize firing squads.

| | Prisoners | | | | Death penalty[1] | | | Executed, as of 2012[2]— | |
Jurisdiction	Year-end 2000	Year-end 2011	Year-end 2012	% change, 2011-12	Death penalty statute?	Under sentence of death, year-end 2012	Executed in 2012	Since 1930	Since 1977
U.S. total	1,391,261	1,598,968	1,570,397	-1.8%	—	3,033	43	5,179[3]	1,320[3]
Federal[4]	145,416	216,362	217,815	0.7	Y	56	0	36	3
State	1,245,845	1,382,606	1,352,582	-2.2	33[5]	2,977	43	5,143	1,317
Alabama	26,332	32,270	32,431	0.5	Y	191	0	190	55
Alaska[6]	4,173	5,597	5,633	0.6	N	—	—	—	—
Arizona[7]	26,510	40,020	40,080	0.1	Y	125	6	72	34
Arkansas	11,915	16,108	14,654	-9.0	Y	38	0	145	27
California	163,001	149,569	134,534	-10.1	Y	712	0	305	13
Colorado	16,833	21,978	20,462	-6.9	Y	3	0	48	1
Connecticut[6]	18,355	18,324	17,530	-4.3	N	10	0	22	1
Delaware[6]	6,921	6,739	6,914	2.6	Y	17	1	28	16
Florida	71,319	103,055	101,930	-1.1	Y	403	3	244	74
Georgia[7]	44,232	55,944	55,457	-0.9	Y	95	0	418	52
Hawaii[6]	5,053	6,037	5,831	-3.4	N	—	—	—	—
Idaho	5,535	7,739	7,985	3.2	Y	12	1	6	3
Illinois	45,281	48,427	49,348	1.9	N	—	—	102	12
Indiana	20,125	28,906	28,831	-0.3	Y	12	0	61	20
Iowa[7]	7,955	9,116	8,733	-4.2	N	—	—	18	—
Kansas	8,344	9,327	9,682	3.8	Y	9	0	15	0
Kentucky	14,919	21,545	22,110	2.6	Y	34	0	106	3
Louisiana	35,207	39,710	40,172	1.2	Y	85	0	162	28
Maine	1,679	2,145	2,108	-1.7	N	—	—	—	—
Maryland	23,538	22,558	21,522	-4.6	N	5	0	73	5
Massachusetts	10,722	11,623	11,308	-2.7	N	—	—	27	—
Michigan	47,718	42,940	43,636	1.6	N	—	—	—	—
Minnesota	6,238	9,800	9,938	1.4	N	—	—	—	—
Mississippi	20,241	21,386	22,319	4.4	Y	49	6	175	21
Missouri	27,543	30,833	31,247	1.3	Y	47	0	130	68
Montana	3,105	3,678	3,609	-1.9	Y	2	0	9	3
Nebraska	3,895	4,616	4,705	1.9	Y	11	0	7	3
Nevada	10,063	12,778	12,883	0.8	Y	81	0	41	12
New Hampshire	2,257	2,614	2,790	6.7	Y	1	0	1	0
New Jersey	29,784	23,834	23,225	-2.6	N	—	—	74	0
New Mexico	5,342	6,998	6,727	-3.9	N	2	0	9	1
New York	70,199	55,436	54,210	-2.2	N	0	0	329	0
North Carolina	31,266	39,440	37,136	-5.8	Y	152	0	306	43
North Dakota	1,076	1,423	1,512	6.3	N	—	—	—	—
Ohio	45,833	50,964	50,876	-0.2	Y	139	3	221	49
Oklahoma	23,181	25,977	25,225	-2.9	Y	55	6	161	102
Oregon	10,580	14,510	14,840	2.3	Y	35	0	20	2
Pennsylvania	36,847	51,578	51,125	-0.9	Y	200	0	155	3
Rhode Island[6]	3,286	3,337	3,318	-0.6	N	—	—	—	—
South Carolina	21,778	22,914	22,388	-2.3	Y	50	0	205	43
South Dakota	2,616	3,535	3,650	3.3	Y	3	2	4	3
Tennessee	22,166	28,479	28,411	-0.2	Y	83	0	99	6
Texas	166,719	172,224	166,372	-3.4	Y	290	15	789	492
Utah	5,637	6,879	6,962	1.2	Y	8	0	21	7
Vermont[6]	1,697	2,053	2,034	-0.9	N	—	—	4	—
Virginia	30,168	38,130	37,044	-2.8	Y	9	0	201	109
Washington	14,915	17,847	17,271	-3.2	Y	8	0	52	5
West Virginia	3,856	6,826	7,070	3.6	N	—	—	40	0
Wisconsin	20,754	22,657	22,600	-0.3	N	—	—	—	—
Wyoming	1,680	2,183	2,204	1.0	Y	1	0	8	1

— = Not available or applicable. (1) Figures do not include persons held under Armed Forces jurisdiction with a military death sentence for murder. (2) Data do not include 160 executions carried out by military authorities between 1930 and 1961. (3) Total executed includes 40 executions performed under the District of Columbia's jurisdiction since 1930. (4) Prisoners sentenced under DC's criminal code are housed in federal facilities. (5) As of mid-2014. Connecticut, Maryland, and New Mexico continue to hold prisoners on death row for crimes committed before each state repealed capital punishment. (6) Prisons and jails form one integrated system. Data includes total jail and prison population. (7) Prisoner population based on custody count.

Prison Situation Under Correctional Authorities' Jurisdiction, 2012

Source: *Prisoners in 2012*, Bureau of Justice Statistics, U.S. Dept. of Justice

Largest prison populations		Imprisonment rate of sentenced prisoners		% change in prison population, 2011-12		Prison population as % of maximum prison capacity	
Jurisdiction	Number	Jurisdiction	Rate[1]	Jurisdiction	% change	Jurisdiction	% max. capacity
U.S. total	1,570,397	U.S. total	480	U.S. total	–1.8%	U.S. total	NA
Federal[2]	217,815	Federal[2]	62	Federal[2]	0.7	Federal[2]	137.3%
State	1,352,582	State	418	State	–2.2	State	NA
1. Texas	166,372	1. Louisiana	893	1. California	–10.1	1. Alaska	142.7
2. California	134,534	2. Mississippi	717	2. Arkansas......	–9.0	2. Massachusetts	138.6
3. Florida.......	101,930	3. Alabama......	650	3. Colorado......	–6.9	3. North Dakota[5]..	135.3
4. Georgia[3]	55,457	4. Oklahoma	648	4. North Carolina	–5.8	4. Wisconsin[5]	130.7
5. New York	54,210	5. Texas	601	5. Maryland......	–4.6	5. Iowa	121.2
6. Pennsylvania ..	51,125	6. Arizona[3]	583	6. Connecticut[4]..	–4.3	6. Nebraska[5].....	118.9
7. Ohio	50,876	7. Georgia[3]	542	7. Iowa[3].........	–4.2	7. Delaware[5].....	118.7
8. Illinois	49,348	8. Florida........	524	8. New Mexico ...	–3.9	8. Ohio	118.4
9. Michigan......	43,636	9. Missouri	518	9. Hawaii[4].......	–3.4	9. Colorado......	115.2
10. Louisiana	40,172	10. Idaho.........	499	Texas	–3.4	10. Nevada........	110.2
11. Arizona.......	40,080	11. Arkansas......	494	11. Washington....	–3.2	11. Hawaii.........	110.0
12. North Carolina	37,136	12. Kentucky......	489	12. Oklahoma	–2.9	12. California[5].....	107.8
13. Virginia	37,044	13. South Carolina	458	13. Virginia	–2.8	13. Idaho[5,6].......	103.7
14. Alabama	32,431	14. Virginia	451	14. Massachusetts	–2.7	14. Minnesota.....	103.5
15. Missouri	31,247	15. Delaware[4]....	448	15. New Jersey....	–2.6	15. Washington....	103.0
16. Indiana	28,831	16. Michigan......	441	16. South Carolina	–2.3	16. Kansas	102.0
17. Tennessee	28,411	17. Indiana	440	17. New York	–2.2	17. North Carolina	101.9
18. Oklahoma	25,225	Ohio	440	18. Montana	–1.9	18. Pennsylvania[5]..	100.9
19. New Jersey....	23,225	19. Tennessee	438	19. Maine	–1.7	19. New Hampshire[5]	100.0
20. Wisconsin.....	22,600	20. South Dakota ..	434	20. Florida........	–1.1	New York	100.0

NA = Not applicable. **Note:** Excludes jail population unless otherwise noted. (1) Prisoners sentenced to more than one year. Rates are per 100,000 population, based upon U.S. Census Bureau population estimates. (2) Federal totals include prisoners sentenced under DC's criminal code. (3) Population based on custody count (number of prisoners held in its facilities) as opposed to jurisdiction count (number of prisoners under its legal authority). Some states are unable to provide both counts. (4) Prisons and jails form one integrated system. Data includes total jail and prison population. (5) State defines capacity in a way that differs from standard definition. (6) Includes prisoners held in private facilities.

Imprisonment Rate by Gender, Race, Hispanic Origin, and Age, 2012

Source: *Prisoners in 2012*, Bureau of Justice Statistics, U.S. Dept. of Justice

(number of prisoners sentenced to more than one year per 100,000 of each group in the U.S. resident population)

	Male					Female			
Age	Total[1]	White	Black	Hispanic	Age	Total[1]	White	Black	Hispanic
Total[2]	909	463	2,841	1,158	Total[2]	63	49	115	64
18-19	428	148	1,393	458	18-19	18	11	35	22
20-24	1,476	654	4,284	1,726	20-24	100	78	163	101
25-29	2,032	998	6,138	2,412	25-29	166	138	263	165
30-34	2,213	1,098	6,932	2,594	30-34	175	147	287	163
35-39	1,975	992	6,258	2,338	35-39	149	128	251	130
40-44	1,682	927	5,148	1,986	40-44	130	108	230	113
45-49	1,451	814	4,433	1,731	45-49	107	82	204	97
50-54	1,031	581	3,219	1,352	50-54	65	49	128	66
55-59	636	360	2,016	983	55-59	34	24	71	42
60-64	386	238	1,144	687	60-64	16	12	32	22
65 or older	146	99	423	280	65 or older	4	3	6	7

Note: Rates are based on U.S. Census Bureau population estimates. Hispanics may be of any race but are not included in white and black populations here. (1) Includes racial categories not shown here. (2) Includes persons under age 18.

Law Enforcement Officers and Civilian Employees, 2012

Source: *Crime in the United States, 2012*; *Law Enforcement Officers Killed and Assaulted, 2012*; Federal Bureau of Investigation (FBI), U.S. Dept. of Justice

As of Oct. 31, 2012, 14,006 city, county, state, college and university, and tribal agencies around the country collectively employed 956,322 full-time law enforcement workers. About two-thirds of these employees were sworn officers. The FBI's UCR program defines a sworn law enforcement officer as a person who ordinarily carries a firearm and badge, has full arrest powers, and is paid from government funds specifically dedicated to law enforcement. Civilians (e.g., clerks, radio dispatchers, correctional officers) made up the remainder.

Altogether, they provided service to an estimated 285 mil people around the country, meaning there were 3.4 full-time law enforcement employees (civilian and sworn officers) and 2.4 sworn officers per 1,000 residents.

The great majority of sworn officers (88.1 %) were male, but females made up 60.3% of civilian employees. Not surprisingly, the most populous state, California, employed the greatest number of full-time law enforcement workers (117,268). The nation's capital, Washington, DC, had the highest rate, with 7.9 full-time law enforcement employees (and 6.8 sworn officers) for every 1,000 residents in its population.

Nationwide, 48 law enforcement officers were killed in the line of duty in 2012, down dramatically from 72 in 2011. Of that number, 12 died while attempting to make arrests, 6 in ambush situations, 8 while performing traffic stops, 5 during tactical situations, and 4 while answering disturbance calls. Eight died while investigating suspicious persons or circumstances. Almost all (44 of the 48 officers) were killed with firearms, even though 24 of those officers were wearing body armor. Handguns were responsible for the great majority (32) of officer murders.

Arrests by Race, 2012

Source: *Crime in the United States, 2012*, Federal Bureau of Investigation, U.S. Dept. of Justice

Each instance in which a person is arrested, cited, or summoned for an offense is counted as one arrest. The figures below therefore do not represent the number of individuals arrested but the number of times persons were arrested, as an individual may be arrested multiple times in one year. Arrest estimates are based on statistics from law enforcement agencies that reported 12 months of arrest data.

Offense charged	Total	Number of arrests where arrestee was—				% distrib. for offense charged[1]			
		White	Black	Amer. Indian/ Alaska Native	Asian/ Pacific Islander	White	Black	Amer. Indian/ Alaska Native	Asian/ Pacific Islander
Total arrests	9,390,473	6,502,919	2,640,067	135,165	112,322	69.3%	28.1%	1.4%	1.2%
Violent crime.	402,470	236,394	155,088	5,198	5,790	58.7	38.5	1.3	1.4
Murder and nonnegligent manslaughter.	8,506	4,101	4,203	102	100	48.2	49.4	1.2	1.2
Forcible rape.	13,886	9,027	4,512	183	164	65.0	32.5	1.3	1.2
Robbery	80,135	34,761	44,002	601	771	43.4	54.9	0.7	1.0
Aggravated assault.	299,943	188,505	102,371	4,312	4,755	62.8	34.1	1.4	1.6
Property crime	1,275,315	866,802	373,963	17,804	16,746	68.0	29.3	1.4	1.3
Burglary	219,232	147,156	67,554	1,966	2,556	67.1	30.8	0.9	1.2
Larceny-theft.	994,304	677,895	288,025	15,052	13,332	68.2	29.0	1.5	1.3
Motor vehicle theft	52,952	35,251	16,301	645	755	66.6	30.8	1.2	1.4
Arson	8,827	6,500	2,083	141	103	73.6	23.6	1.6	1.2
Other assaults[2]	924,839	606,048	294,678	13,898	10,215	65.5	31.9	1.5	1.1
Forgery and counterfeiting	51,759	33,950	16,900	239	670	65.6	32.7	0.5	1.3
Fraud	117,706	78,331	37,171	1,143	1,061	66.5	31.6	1.0	0.9
Embezzlement	12,371	7,994	4,103	74	200	64.6	33.2	0.6	1.6
Stolen property: buying, receiving, possessing	75,516	50,144	23,787	615	970	66.4	31.5	0.8	1.3
Vandalism.	175,243	125,987	44,650	2,845	1,761	71.9	25.5	1.6	1.0
Weapons: carrying, possessing, etc.	114,979	66,909	45,842	764	1,464	58.2	39.9	0.7	1.3
Prostitution and commercialized vice	43,216	23,172	18,486	175	1,383	53.6	42.8	0.4	3.2
Sex offenses (except forcible rape and prostitution)	52,354	38,063	12,850	628	813	72.7	24.5	1.2	1.6
Drug abuse violations	1,194,956	801,198	372,914	8,299	12,545	67.0	31.2	0.7	1.0
Gambling	5,951	1,707	4,008	22	214	28.7	67.4	0.4	3.6
Offenses against the family and children	81,762	53,760	25,698	1,740	564	65.8	31.4	2.1	0.7
Driving under the influence. . . .	981,110	830,498	118,557	13,313	18,742	84.6	12.1	1.4	1.9
Liquor laws	337,687	275,457	46,355	11,314	4,561	81.6	13.7	3.4	1.4
Drunkenness	398,600	324,209	62,944	7,218	4,229	81.3	15.8	1.8	1.1
Disorderly conduct	418,960	262,810	145,183	7,751	3,216	62.7	34.7	1.9	0.8
Vagrancy	20,698	13,034	7,080	389	195	63.0	34.2	1.9	0.9
All other offenses (except traffic violations)	2,649,909	1,773,792	808,609	41,206	26,302	66.9	30.5	1.6	1.0
Suspicion[3].	1,160	610	535	4	11	52.6	46.1	0.3	0.9
Curfew and loitering law violations.	53,912	32,050	20,666	526	670	59.4	38.3	1.0	1.2

(1) Percentages may not add up to 100 due to rounding. (2) Simple assaults, where no weapons were used and where the victim did not sustain serious injury (e.g., stalking). (3) Arrested for no specific offense and released without formal charges being placed against a person.

Sentenced Prisoners by Offense, Race, and Hispanic Origin, 2011

Source: *Prisoners in 2012*, Bureau of Justice Statistics, U.S. Dept. of Justice

Offense	All inmates		White[1]		Black[1]		Hispanic	
	Number	% of total	Number	% of total	Number	% of total	Number	% of total
Total	1,341,804	100.0%	465,180	100.0%	509,677	100.0%	282,353	100.0%
All violent crimes	710,875	53.0	228,782	49.2	284,631	55.8	162,489	57.5
Murder[2]	163,762	12.2	45,369	9.8	65,568	12.9	37,956	13.4
Manslaughter	21,051	1.6	8,107	1.7	7,408	1.5	3,456	1.2
Rape/sexual assault	165,656	12.3	79,282	17.0	39,975	7.8	35,863	12.7
Robbery	181,415	13.5	38,312	8.2	99,096	19.4	36,694	13.0
Aggravated or simple assault	138,574	10.3	42,375	9.1	56,281	11.0	38,252	13.5
Other violent crimes	40,416	3.0	15,336	3.3	16,304	3.2	10,270	3.6
All property crimes	245,351	18.3	108,560	23.3	78,197	15.3	38,264	13.6
Burglary.	128,823	9.6	53,547	11.5	46,795	9.2	22,038	7.8
Larceny-theft	42,029	3.1	19,617	4.2	12,679	2.5	5,679	2.0
Motor vehicle theft	14,703	1.1	6,596	1.4	3,330	0.7	4,132	1.5
Fraud	30,333	2.3	14,738	3.2	8,256	1.6	2,628	0.9
Other property crimes	29,463	2.2	14,063	3.0	7,137	1.4	3,786	1.3
Drug offenses[3]	225,242	16.8	67,271	14.5	91,775	18.0	47,479	16.8
Public-order offenses[4]	141,803	10.6	54,834	11.8	50,489	9.9	32,275	11.4
Other/unspecified[5]	18,534	1.4	5,733	1.2	4,585	0.9	1,846	0.7

Note: Counts based on state prisoners with a sentence of more than one year. Details may not add up to totals due to rounding and missing offense data, and because "All inmates" includes race categories not shown here. (1) White and black totals exclude Hispanics and persons of two or more races. (2) Includes nonnegligent manslaughter. (3) Includes trafficking, possession, and other drug offenses. (4) Includes weapons, drunk driving, and court offenses; commercialized vice, morals, and decency offenses; liquor law violations; and other public-order offenses. (5) Includes juvenile offenses and other unspecified offense categories.

Firearm Violence, 1993-2011

Source: *Firearm Violence, 1993-2011*, Bureau of Justice Statistics, U.S. Dept. of Justice

The number of homicides due to firearms has declined by nearly 40% since 1993, the year Congress passed the Brady Handgun Violence Prevention Act. The Brady Act required licensed dealers to conduct background checks on individuals seeking to purchase firearms. As of Dec. 31, 2009, federal, state, and local authorities had denied more than 1.9 mil of 108 mil applications to purchase firearms; the most common reason for denial was a previous felony conviction or indictment. (The Federal Assault Weapons Ban, which Congress passed in 1994 to prohibit the manufacture of certain semi-automatic weapons, expired in 2004.)

	Homicides				Nonfatal victimizations			
Year	By handgun	By other type of firearm	Total	Rate[1]	By handgun	By other type of firearm	Total	Rate[2]
1993	NA	NA	18,253	7.0	NA	NA	1,529,700	730
1994	13,510	2,830	17,527	6.7	1,387,100	150,200	1,568,500	740
1995	12,090	2,670	15,551	5.8	1,240,200	132,800	1,193,200	550
1996	10,800	2,510	14,037	5.2	999,600	141,000	1,100,800	510
1997	9,750	2,630	13,252	4.9	894,200	159,800	1,024,100	470
1998	8,870	2,160	11,798	4.3	783,400	141,100	835,400	380
1999	8,010	2,150	10,828	3.9	659,600	74,100	640,900	290
2000	8,020	2,190	10,801	3.8	555,800	65,300	610,200	270
2001	7,820	2,220	11,348	4.0	506,600	65,900	563,100	250
2002	8,230	2,620	11,829	4.1	471,600	63,200	540,000	230
2003	8,890	2,180	11,920	4.1	436,100	53,200	467,300	200
2004	8,330	2,350	11,624	4.0	391,700	53,400	456,500	190
2005	8,550	2,840	12,352	4.2	410,600	56,200	503,500	210
2006	9,060	2,700	12,791	4.3	497,400	47,600	614,400	250
2007	8,570	3,080	12,632	4.2	509,700	65,600	554,800	220
2008	7,930	3,120	12,179	4.0	400,700	57,400	371,300	150
2009	7,370	2,970	11,493	3.8	348,700	37,600	410,100	160
2010	6,920	3,030	11,078	3.6	382,100	26,700	415,000	160
2011	7,230	2,690	11,101	3.6	389,400	49,700	467,300	180

NA = Not available. **Note:** Numbers may not add up to totals because of small differences in sample sizes. (1) Per 100,000 persons. (2) Per 100,000 persons age 12 or older.

Hate Crimes by Offense Type, Bias Motivation, 2012

Source: *Hate Crime Statistics, 2012*, Federal Bureau of Investigation (FBI), U.S. Dept. of Justice

Hate crimes are defined as crimes in which victims are chosen because of one or more personal characteristics, such as race, ethnicity, or religion. Congress enacted the Hate Crime Statistics Act of 1990, which led to the collection of hate crime data as part of the FBI's Uniform Crime Report (UCR) program beginning in 1992. Not all agencies that participate in the UCR program submit hate crime data, so the data presented is not representative of the nation as a whole.

Bias motivation	Incidents	Crimes against persons					Crimes against property						Total crimes against society[3]
		Aggravated assault	Simple assault	Intimidation	Other[1]	Total crimes against persons[1]	Robbery	Burglary	Larceny-theft	Destruction/damage/vandalism	Other[2]	Total crimes against property[2]	
SINGLE-BIAS INCIDENTS	6,705	853	1,564	1,487	55	3,959	126	141	258	1,904	114	2,543	203
Race	3,297	448	754	829	15	2,046	50	69	136	787	52	1,094	157
Anti-white	739	95	199	121	8	423	23	29	85	94	33	264	52
Anti-black	2,180	317	481	635	1	1,434	20	28	22	574	10	654	92
Anti-American Indian/ Alaskan Native	109	10	22	8	6	46	3	6	21	18	5	53	10
Anti-Asian/Pacific Islander	134	18	29	33	0	80	3	3	6	38	4	54	0
Anti-multiple races, group	135	8	23	32	0	63	1	3	2	63	0	69	3
Religion	1,166	44	128	158	11	341	4	18	64	692	32	810	15
Anti-Jewish	696	11	72	87	1	171	2	10	17	486	8	523	2
Anti-Catholic	79	10	4	7	1	22	0	0	11	38	5	54	3
Anti-Protestant	34	0	1	1	0	2	1	1	9	16	4	31	1
Anti-Islamic	149	14	41	43	3	101	0	1	4	39	4	48	0
Anti-other religion	107	8	4	16	6	34	0	2	2	63	4	71	2
Anti-multiple religions, group	89	1	4	0	4	9	1	3	18	48	6	76	4
Anti-atheism/ agnosticism/etc.	12	0	2	0	0	2	0	1	3	2	1	7	3
Sexual orientation	1,318	211	453	262	22	948	50	23	24	249	14	360	10
Anti-male homosexual	720	114	285	141	9	549	39	8	5	112	7	171	0
Anti-female homosexual	162	14	45	43	5	107	1	2	5	43	2	53	2
Anti-homosexual	369	75	111	70	1	257	10	8	6	84	2	110	2
Anti-heterosexual	26	1	3	3	6	13	0	1	2	6	2	11	2
Anti-bisexual	41	7	9	5	1	22	0	4	6	4	1	15	4
Ethnicity/national origin	822	131	196	230	6	563	21	28	21	165	9	244	15
Anti-Hispanic	488	89	127	127	4	347	16	15	13	81	5	130	11
Anti-other ethnicity/ national origin	334	42	69	103	2	216	5	13	8	84	4	114	4
Disability	102	19	33	8	1	61	1	3	13	11	7	35	6
Anti-physical	20	4	9	3	0	16	0	1	0	2	3	3	1
Anti-mental	82	15	24	5	1	45	1	3	12	11	5	32	5
MULTIPLE-BIAS INCIDENTS[4]	13	1	6	2	0	9	0	1	0	2	1	4	0
TOTAL OFFENSES	6,718	854	1,570	1,489	55	3,968	126	142	258	1,906	115	2,547	203

(1) Includes murder, nonnegligent manslaughter, forcible rape, and additional offenses not shown here in detail. (2) Includes arson, motor vehicle theft, and additional offenses not shown here in detail. (3) Includes drug or narcotic offenses, gambling and prostitution offenses, and weapon law violations where society as a whole is considered the victim. (4) More than one offense type must occur and at least two offense types must be motivated by different biases to count as a multiple-bias incident.

Notable Assassinations Since 1865

1865—Apr. 14: U.S. Pres. Abraham Lincoln shot by John Wilkes Booth, well-known actor with Confederate sympathies, at Ford's Theater in Washington, DC; died Apr. 15.

1881—Mar. 13: Alexander II of Russia. **July 2:** U.S. Pres. James A. Garfield shot by Charles J. Guiteau, disappointed office seeker, in Washington, DC; died Sept. 19.

1894—June 24: French Pres. Sadi Carnot by Sante Caserio, Italian anarchist, in Lyon.

1898—Sept. 10: Empress Elizabeth of Austria stabbed by Luigi Luccheni, Italian anarchist.

1900—July 29: Umberto I, king of Italy, by an anarchist.

1901—Sept. 6: U.S. Pres. William McKinley shot by Leon Czolgosz, anarchist, in Buffalo, NY; died Sept. 14.

1908—Feb. 1: King Carlos I of Portugal and his son Luís Filipe, in Lisbon.

1913—Feb. 23: Mexican Pres. Francisco I. Madero and Vice Pres. José María Pino Suárez. **Mar. 18:** King George of Greece.

1914—June 28: Archduke Franz Ferdinand of Austria-Hungary and his wife shot by Gavrilo Princip, Serb nationalist, in Sarajevo, Bosnia.

1916—Dec. 30: Grigory Rasputin, Russian mystic and court figure, by group of aristocrats.

1918—July 12: Grand Duke Michael of Russia, at Perm. **July 16:** Nicholas II, former (abdicated) czar of Russia; his wife, Czarina Alexandra; their son, Czarevitch Alexis; their daughters, Grand Duchesses Olga, Tatiana, Marie, Anastasia; and 4 members of household executed by Bolsheviks at Ekaterinburg.

1920—May 20: Mexican Pres. Gen. Venustiano Carranza, in Tlaxcalantongo.

1922—Aug. 22: Michael Collins, Irish revolutionary, in West Cork. **Dec. 16:** Polish Pres. Gabriel Narutowicz in Warsaw.

1923—July 20: Gen. Francisco "Pancho" Villa, ex-rebel leader, in Parral, Mexico.

1928—July 17: Gen. Alvaro Obregon, president-elect of Mexico, in San Angel.

1932—May 6: French Pres. Paul Doumer shot by Russian émigré, Pavel Gorgulov, in Paris.

1934—July 25: Austrian Chancellor Engelbert Dollfuss by Nazis, in Vienna.

1935—Sept. 8: Sen. Huey P. Long, former Louisiana governor, shot by Dr. Carl Austin Weiss, son-in-law of political opponent, in Baton Rouge; died Sept. 10.

1940—Aug. 20: Leon Trotsky (Lev Bronstein), exiled Soviet commissar of war, fatally wounded with ice ax by Soviet agent nr. Mexico City.

1948—Jan. 30: Leader of movement for Indian independence Mohandas K. Gandhi (Mahatma) shot by Hindu fanatic in New Delhi. **Sept. 17:** Count Folke Bernadotte, UN mediator for Palestine, by Jewish extremists in Jerusalem.

1951—July 20: Jordanian King Abdullah ibn Hussein. **Oct. 16:** Prime Min. Liaquat Ali Khan of Pakistan shot, in Rawalpindi.

1956—Sept. 21: Pres. Anastasio Somoza of Nicaragua shot in Leon by a young poet; died Sept. 29.

1957—July 26: Guatemalan Pres. Carlos Castillo Armas, in Guatemala City by one of his guards.

1958—July 14: King Faisal of Iraq, Crown Prince Abdullah, and **July 15,** Prem. Nuri as-Said, by rebels in Baghdad.

1959—Sept. 25: Prime Min. Solomon Bandaranaike of Ceylon (Sri Lanka), by Buddhist monk in Colombo.

1961—Jan. 17: First elected prime min. of the Congo, Patrice Lumumba, in Katanga Prov. by political rivals. **May 30:** Dominican dictator Rafael Leónidas Trujillo Molina, nr. Ciudad Trujillo.

1963—June 12: Medgar Evers, NAACP's Mississippi field secretary, shot by Byron De La Beckwith in Jackson, MS. **Nov. 2:** Pres. Ngo Dinh Diem of South Vietnam and his brother, Ngo Dinh Nhu, in military coup. **Nov. 22:** U.S. Pres. John F. Kennedy shot while riding in motorcade through downtown Dallas, TX; accused gunman Lee Harvey Oswald murdered by nightclub owner Jack Ruby while awaiting trial.

1965—Jan. 21: Iranian Prem. Hassan Ali Mansour, in Tehran. **Feb. 21:** Malcolm X, black nationalist leader, shot by 3 men linked to Nation of Islam at New York City rally.

1966—Sept. 6: Prime Min. Hendrik F. Verwoerd of South Africa stabbed to death in parliament at Cape Town.

1968—Apr. 4: Rev. Martin Luther King Jr. fatally shot in Memphis, TN; James Earl Ray convicted of crime. **June 5:** Sen. Robert F. Kennedy (D, NY) shot in Los Angeles; died June 6. Sirhan Sirhan convicted of crime.

1971—Nov. 28: Jordanian Prime Min. Wasfi Tal by Palestinian guerrillas, in Cairo, Egypt.

1973—Mar. 2: U.S. Amb. Cleo A. Noel Jr., U.S. Charge d'Affaires George C. Moore, and Belgian Charge d'Affaires Guy Eid by Palestinian guerrillas, in Khartoum, Sudan. **Dec. 20:** Spanish Prem. Luis Carrero Blanco in car bombing by Basque separatist group ETA, in Madrid.

1974—Aug. 19: U.S. Amb. to Cyprus, Rodger P. Davies, by sniper's bullet in Nicosia.

1975—Feb. 11: Pres. Richard Ratsimandrava of Madagascar shot in Tananarive. **Mar. 25:** Saudi Arabian King Faisal shot by

nephew Prince Musad Abdel Aziz, in Riyadh. **Aug. 15:** Bangladesh Pres. Sheik Mujibur Rahman killed in coup.

1976—Feb. 13: Nigerian head of state, Gen. Murtala Ramat Mohammed, by self-styled young revolutionaries.

1977—Mar. 16: Kamal Jumblat, Lebanese Druse chieftain, shot nr. Beirut. **Mar. 18:** Rep. of the Congo Pres. Marien Ngouabi shot in Brazzaville.

1978—May 9: Former Italian Prem. Aldo Moro killed by Red Brigades terrorists who had abducted him Mar. 16 in Rome and held him hostage. **July 9:** Former Iraqi Prem. Abdul Razak Al-Naif shot in London.

1979—Feb. 14: U.S. Amb. Adolph Dubs shot by Afghan Muslim extremists in Kabul. **Aug. 27:** Lord Mountbatten, WWII hero, and 2 others when a bomb exploded on his fishing boat off coast of Co. Sligo, Ireland. IRA claimed responsibility. **Oct. 26:** S. Korean Pres. Park Chung Hee and 6 bodyguards fatally shot by Kim Jae Kyu, head of S. Korean intelligence agency.

1980—Apr. 12: Liberian Pres. William R. Tolbert, in military coup. **Sept. 17:** Former Nicaraguan Pres. Anastasio Somoza Debayle shot in Paraguay.

1981—Oct. 6: Egyptian Pres. Anwar al-Sadat shot by commandos while reviewing military parade in Cairo; 7 others killed, 28 wounded.

1982—Sept. 14: Lebanese Pres.-elect Bashir Gemayel killed by bomb in east Beirut.

1983—Aug. 21: Philippine opposition leader Benigno Aquino Jr. shot at Manila Intl. Airport.

1984—Oct. 31: Indian Prime Min. Indira Gandhi shot by 2 Sikh bodyguards in New Delhi.

1986—Feb. 28: Swedish Prime Min. Olof Palme shot on Stockholm street; case still unsolved

1987—June 1: Lebanese Prem. Rashid Karami killed when bomb exploded aboard helicopter.

1988—Apr. 16: PLO military chief Khalil Wazir (Abu Jihad) gunned down by Israeli commandos in Tunisia.

1989—Aug. 18: Colombian pres. candidate Luis Carlos Galán killed by Medellín cartel drug traffickers at campaign rally in Bogotá. **Nov. 22:** Lebanese Pres. Rene Moawad killed when bomb exploded next to his motorcade.

1990—Mar. 22: Colombian pres. candidate Bernardo Jaramillo Ossa shot at airport in Bogotá.

1991—May 21: Former Indian Prime Min. Rajiv Gandhi killed by bomb during election rally in Madras.

1992—June 29: Algerian Pres. Mohammed Boudiaf shot in Annaba.

1993—May 1: Sri Lankan Pres. Ranasinghe Premadasa killed by bomb in Colombo.

1994—Apr. 6: Burundian Pres. Cyprien Ntaryamira and Rwandan Pres. Juvénal Habyarimana killed with 8 others when their plane was shot down, precipitating Rwandan genocide.

1995—Nov. 4: Israeli Prime Min. Yitzhak Rabin shot by Yigal Amir, Jewish extremist, at peace rally in Tel Aviv.

1996—Oct. 2: Andrei Lukanov, former Bulgarian prime min., shot outside home by unidentified assailant.

1998—Feb. 6: Prefect of Corsica, Claude Erignac, shot in back by 2 men while walking to concert. **Apr. 26:** Guatemalan Roman Catholic Bishop Juan Gerardi Conedera, human rights champion, found beaten to death in Guatemala City.

1999—Mar. 23: Paraguayan Vice Pres. Luis María Argaña ambushed and shot to death along with his driver by 4 unidentified assailants, in Asunción. **Apr. 9:** Niger Pres. Ibrahim Bare Mainassara ambushed and killed by dissident soldiers. **Oct. 27:** Armenian Prime Min. Vazgen Sarkissian, along with 7 others, shot during session of parliament.

2000—Jan. 15: Serbian paramilitary leader Zeljko Raznjatovic (Arkan), with 2 others, shot in Belgrade. **June 8:** Brig. Gen. Stephen Saunders, Britain's senior military rep. in Greece, fatally shot by 2 men on motorcycle while driving in Athens suburb.

2001—Jan. 16: Dem. Rep. of the Congo Pres. Laurent Kabila shot to death by bodyguard at pres. palace in Kinshasa. **June 1:** Nepal's King Birendra, Queen Aiswarya, and 7 other royals fatally shot by Crown Prince Dipendra, who also killed himself. **Oct. 14:** Abdel Rahman Hamad, a leader of Palestinian militant group Hamas, shot by Israeli military snipers. **Oct. 17:** Israeli tourism min. Rehavam Zeevi fatally shot; Popular Front for the Liberation of Palestine claimed responsibility.

2002—Mar. 16: Colombian cleric Isaías Duarte Cancino, critic of Colombian guerrillas and drug traffickers, shot outside of church in Cali. **May 6:** Dutch right-wing politician Pim Fortuyn shot outside radio station in Hilversum. **July 6:** Afghan Vice Pres. Haji Abdul Qadir shot outside his office in Kabul.

2003—Mar. 12: Serbian Prime Min. Zoran Djindjic shot by paramilitary snipers outside govt. headquarters in Belgrade. **Apr. 10:** Shiite Muslim cleric Abdul Majid al-Khoei attacked by crowd, hacked to death at Imam Ali mosque, Najaf, Iraq. **Apr. 17:** Sergei Yushenkov, former Russian legislator and Liberal Party head, shot outside apartment in Moscow.

Sept. 10: Swedish Foreign Min. Anna Lindh stabbed in Stockholm dept. store by mentally ill man; died Sept. 11.

2004—Feb. 13: Former Chechen Pres. Zelimkhan Yandarbiyev killed after car exploded in Qatar. **Mar. 22:** Sheik Ahmed Yassin, spiritual leader of Hamas, by Israeli missile attack in Gaza City. **Apr. 17:** Hamas leader Abdel Aziz Rantisi by Israeli missile strike, in Gaza City. **May 9:** Chechen Pres. Akhmad Kadyrov by bomb at WWII memorial service in Grozny. **May 17:** Iraqi Gov. Council Pres. Ezzedine Salim by car bomb at Green Zone checkpoint in Baghdad. **Nov. 2:** Filmmaker Theo van Gogh, critic of Islam and great-grandnephew of painter Vincent van Gogh, shot and stabbed by Muslim militant in Amsterdam.

2005—Jan. 4: Baghdad Gov. Ali al-Haidari gunned down by insurgents in Baghdad, Iraq. **Feb. 14:** Former Lebanese Prime Min. Rafik al-Hariri killed when motorcade bombed in Beirut. **Mar. 8:** Former Chechen pres. Aslan Maskhadov killed in raid by Russian special forces, in village outside Grozny.

2006—Feb. 11: Leading Kazakhstan opposition politician Altynbek Sarsenbayev (Sarsenbaiuly) kidnapped, found murdered outside Almaty. **Sept. 14:** Andrei Kozlov, Russian central banker active in reforming industry, shot in Moscow. **Oct. 7:** Anna Politkovskaya, reporter critical of Kremlin's Chechnya policies, fatally shot in apartment building in Moscow.

2007—June 13: Walid Eido, Lebanese parliament member who was part of anti-Syria coalition, killed by car bomb in Beirut. **Aug. 2:** *Oakland Post* editor Chauncey Bailey, who was investigating financial status of black Muslim organization, shot in Oakland, CA. **Dec. 27:** Benazir Bhutto, former Pakistani prime min. and first female elected leader of a Muslim state, by bomb and gunman later linked to then-Pres. Pervez Musharraf.

2008—Feb. 12: Imad Mughniyeh, top Hezbollah commander and reputed mastermind of the 1983 bombing of U.S. embassy in Beirut, by car bomb in Damascus, Syria. Mughniyeh had been on FBI's Most Wanted Terrorist list. **May 8:** Edgar Eusebio Millán Gómez, Mexico's acting national police chief, by gunmen outside his Mexico City home. **Aug. 1:** Syrian brig. gen. and top aide Mohammed Suleiman reportedly shot by sniper nr. Tartus. **Oct. 23:** Ivo Pukanic, editor-in-chief of Croatian political newspaper *Nacional*, killed in Zagreb when bomb exploded nr. his car.

2009—Mar. 2: Guinea-Bissau's longtime Pres. João Bernardo Vieira shot by army troops outside his home in Bissau. **Mar. 31:** Sulim Yamadayev, former Chechen gen. and enemy of the Kremlin-installed pres., shot in Dubai, UAE. **May 31:** Dr. George Tiller, one of the few doctors in the U.S. to perform abortions late in pregnancy, shot to death in his Wichita, KS, church by anti-abortion activist. **June 12:** Harith al-Obaidi, Sunni member of Iraq's parliament, shot at a Baghdad mosque. **July 15:** Natalya Estemirova, Russian journalist who reported on human rights abuses in Chechnya, found shot in Ingushetia. **Sept. 27:** Two officials from the Russian republic of Dagestan, Alim-Sultan Alkhamatov and Alim-Sultan Atuyev, shot dead in separate incidents.

2010—Jan. 19: Mahmoud al-Mabhouh, a senior commander for Hamas, found drugged and suffocated in his Dubai, UAE, hotel room; Israel's Mossad spy agency suspected. **Aug. 2:** Raza Haider, member of Pakistan's parliament, shot by 4 gunmen in a mosque in Karachi.

2011—July 12: Ahmed Wali Karzai, power-wielding half-brother of Afghan Pres. Hamid Karzai, shot dead in his Kandahar home by a longtime confidant. Two other Karzai allies, including Kandahar mayor Ghulam Hamidi, assassinated over the next 2 weeks. **July 28:** Gen. Abdul Fattah Younes, Libya's rebel commander, and 2 officers killed in Benghazi. **Sept. 20:** Burhanuddin Rabbani, leader of Afghanistan's High Peace Council and a former pres., killed in his Kabul home by assassin with explosives hidden in his turban.

2012—Jan. 11: Iranian nuclear scientist Mostafa Ahmadi Roshan killed by car bomb. **July 18:** Three senior Syrian officials, including Defense Min. Dawoud Rajiha and Assef Shawkat, brother-in-law to Pres. Bashar al-Assad, killed by bomb.

2013—Feb. 6: Chokri Belaid, vocal critic of Tunisian Prime Min. Hamadi Jebali, shot in front of his home, sparking violent demonstrations against the Islamist govt. **May 3:** Gunmen on motorbikes killed Sadiq Zaman Khattak, an anti-Taliban candidate for Pakistan's National Assembly, and his 4-year-old son in Karachi. **July 25:** Tunisian secular opposition lawmaker, Mohamed Brahmi, shot to death outside his home in the Tunis suburbs, by unidentified assailants on a motorcycle.

Notable Assassination Attempts Since 1912

1912—Oct. 14: Former U.S. Pres. Theodore Roosevelt shot and wounded by mentally ill man in Milwaukee, WI.

1933—Feb. 15: In Miami, FL, anarchist Joseph Zangara shot at Pres.-elect Franklin D. Roosevelt, but a woman seized Zangara's arm; bullet fatally wounded Chicago Mayor Anton J. Cermak, who died Mar. 6.

1944—July 20: Adolf Hitler injured when bomb, planted by German officer, exploded in his headquarters; one aide killed,12 injured.

1950—Nov. 1: In attempt to assassinate Pres. Harry Truman, 2 members of Puerto Rican nationalist movement—Griselio Torresola and Oscar Collazo—tried to shoot their way into Blair House, across the street from White House. Torresola killed. Pvt. Leslie Coffelt, White House policeman, fatally shot.

1970—Nov. 27: Pope Paul VI unharmed by knife-wielding assailant who attempted to attack him in airport in Manila, Philippines.

1972—May 15: Alabama Gov. George Wallace seriously wounded when shot in Laurel, MD, by fame-seeking Arthur Bremer.

1975—Sept. 5: Pres. Gerald R. Ford unharmed when Secret Service agent grabbed pistol aimed at him by Lynette "Squeaky" Fromme, follower of cult leader Charles Manson, in Sacramento, CA. **Sept. 22:** Pres. Ford unharmed when bystander grabbed arm of Sara Jane Moore as she fired upon Ford in San Francisco.

1980—May 29: Civil rights leader Vernon E. Jordan Jr. shot and wounded in Ft. Wayne, IN.

1981—Mar. 30: Pres. Ronald Reagan, along with Press Sec. James Brady, Secret Service agent Timothy J. McCarthy, and Wash., DC, policeman Thomas Delahanty shot and seriously wounded by John W. Hinckley Jr. in DC. **May 13:** Pope John Paul II and 2 bystanders shot and wounded by Mehmet Ali Agca, escaped Turkish prisoner, in St. Peter's Square, Vatican City.

1982—May 12: Pope John Paul II wounded by ultra-conservative priest wielding bayonet, in Fatima, Portugal.

1984—Oct. 12: British Prime Min. Margaret Thatcher unharmed when a bomb, said to have been planted by the IRA, exploded at the Grand Hotel in Brighton, Eng., during a Party conference; 4 died, incl. a member of Parliament.

1986—Sept. 7: Chilean Pres. Gen. Augusto Pinochet Ugarte unharmed after motorcade was attacked by rebels.

1995—June 26: Egyptian Pres. Hosni Mubarak unharmed when shots fired at his motorcade in Addis Ababa, Ethiopia; 4 died, incl. 2 Ethiopian police officers.

1997—Feb. 12: Colombian Pres. Ernesto Samper Pizano unharmed when bomb exploded on runway in Barranquilla as his plane was preparing to land. **Apr. 30:** Tajik Pres. Imamali Rakhmanov injured when a grenade was thrown at him.

1998—Feb. 9: Georgian Pres. Eduard A. Shevardnadze unharmed when gunmen fired on his motorcade in Tbilisi.

2002—Apr. 14: Leading Colombian pres. candidate Álvaro Uribe Vélez unharmed after bomb exploded under parked bus as his motorcade passed in Barranquilla; 3 bystanders killed. **July 14:** French Pres. Jacques Chirac unharmed when Maxime Brunerie, gunman with ties to neo-Nazi groups, fired at his open-top vehicle during Bastille Day parade in Paris. **Sept. 5:** Afghan Pres. Hamid Karzai unharmed after militant shot at car in Kandahar. **Nov. 25:** Turkmenistan Pres. Saparmurat Niyazov unharmed after gunmen opened fire on his motorcade in Ashgabat.

2003—Dec. 14: Pakistani Pres. Pervez Musharraf unharmed after bomb detonated on bridge in Rawalpindi seconds after his motorcade crossed.

2004—Mar. 19: Taiwanese Pres. Chen Shui-bian shot while campaigning in motorcade; minor injuries. **July 13:** Separatists bombed motorcade of Sergei Abramov, Chechnya's acting pres. **Sept. 5:** Ukrainian opposition presidential candidate Viktor Yushchenko, who later won office, fell ill after meeting; diagnosed with dioxin poisoning. **Sept. 16:** Rocket fired at helicopter carrying Afghan Pres. Hamid Karzai, nr. Gardez.

2005—Mar. 15: Kosovo Pres. Ibrahim Rugova survived bombing of his motorcade as it traveled through Pristina.

2008—Feb. 11: Pres. José Ramos-Horta in attack led by fugitive former army official in Dili, Timor-Leste. Ambush of Prime Min. Xanana Gusmão's motorcade a short time later unsuccessful. **Apr. 27:** Afghan Pres. Hamid Karzai unharmed after Taliban fired on military parade in Kabul where Karzai was in attendance.

2009—June 22: Yunus-Bek Yevkurov, pres. of Ingushetia region of Russia, seriously wounded when suicide bomber in car packed with explosives crashed into his motorcade.

2010—Sept. 23: Alexander Ankvab, vice pres. of Georgian region of Ankhazia, survived 4th assassination attempt in 5 years, a grenade fired with his Gudauta home.

2011—Jan. 8: U.S. Rep. Gabrielle Giffords (D, AZ) severely wounded by lone gunman at public meeting nr. Arizona supermarket; 6 others killed, including a federal judge. **June 3:** Yemeni Pres. Ali Abdullah Saleh survived presidential palace bombing.

2012—May 18: Taliban killed 7 in assassination attempt on gov. of the Afghanistan prov. of Farah. **Sept. 12:** Hassan Sheik Mohamud survived suicide bombing attack on his home 2 days after being elected Somalia's president.

2013—Apr. 29: Syrian Prime Min. Wael Nader al-Halqi survived car bombing of his motorcade in Damascus.

Notable U.S. Kidnappings Since 1924

Bobby Franks, 14, in Chicago, May 21, 1924, by 2 youths from wealthy families—Richard Loeb, 18, and Nathan Leopold, 19—who killed boy. Demand for $10,000 ignored. Loeb killed in prison; Leopold paroled 1958.

Charles A. Lindbergh Jr., 20 months old, nr. Hopewell, NJ, Mar. 1, 1932; found dead May 12. Ransom of $50,000 paid to man identified as Bruno Richard Hauptmann, 35, paroled German convict who entered U.S. illegally. Hauptmann convicted, electrocuted in Trenton, NJ, prison, Apr. 3, 1936.

William A. Hamm Jr., 39, brewing company pres. in St. Paul, MN, June 15, 1933, by Karpis-Barker gang. $100,000 paid. Alvin Karpis given life sentence, paroled in 1969.

Charles F. Urschel, in Oklahoma City, July 22, 1933. Released July 31 after $200,000 paid. George "Machine Gun" Kelly and 5 others sentenced to life.

Brooke L. Hart, 22, in San Jose, CA. Thomas Thurmond and John Holmes arrested after demanding $40,000. When Hart's body was found in San Francisco Bay, Nov. 26, 1933, a mob forced its way into jail and lynched the 2 kidnappers.

June Robles, 6, abducted in Tucson, AZ, Apr. 25, 1934. Missing for 19 days after ransom note sent to parents. Found alive in iron cage buried in desert. No arrests ever made.

George Weyerhaeuser, 9, of Weyerhaeuser lumber company, in Tacoma, WA, May 24, 1935. Returned home June 1 after $200,000 paid. Kidnappers given 20 to 60 years.

Robert C. Greenlease, 6, son of wealthy car dealer, taken from Kansas City, MO, school Sept. 28, 1953; held for $600,000. Body found Oct. 7. Bonnie Brown Heady and Carl A. Hall pleaded guilty, were executed.

Lee Crary, 8, in Everett, WA, Sept. 22, 1957; $10,000 ransom not paid. Crary escaped after 3 days and led police to George E. Collins, who was convicted.

Frank Sinatra Jr., 19, from hotel room in Lake Tahoe, CA, Dec. 8, 1963. Released Dec. 11 after his father paid $240,000 ransom. Three men sentenced to prison.

Barbara Jane Mackle, 20, abducted Dec. 17, 1968, from Atlanta, GA, motel; found unharmed 3 days later, buried in coffin-like box 18 in. underground, after her father paid $500,000 ransom. Gary Steven Krist sentenced to life, Ruth Eisenmann-Schier to 7 years.

Virginia Piper, 49, abducted July 27, 1972, from her home in suburban Minneapolis, MN; found unharmed nr. Duluth 2 days later after husband, retired banker, paid $1 mil ransom.

J. Paul Getty III, 17, grandson of the oil billionaire, disappeared July 10, 1973, in Rome, Italy. Ransom of $2.8 mil paid after abductors sent one of Getty's ears to an Italian newspaper with a warning that other parts of his body would be mutilated. Released Dec. 15.

Patricia "Patty" Hearst, 19, taken from her Berkeley, CA, apartment Feb. 4, 1974; "Symbionese Liberation Army" captors demanded her father, publisher Randolph Hearst, give millions to area poor. Patty implicated in San Francisco bank holdup, Apr. 15. The FBI, Sept. 18, 1975, captured her and others. She was convicted of bank robbery, Mar. 20, 1976; released from prison under executive clemency, Feb. 1, 1979. In 1978, William and Emily Harris were sentenced to 10 years to life for the kidnapping; both were paroled in 1983.

J. Reginald Murphy, 40, an editor of *Atlanta Constitution* (GA), kidnapped Feb. 20, 1974; freed Feb. 22 after newspaper paid $700,000 ransom. William A. H. Williams later convicted.

Jack Teich, Kings Point, NY, steel executive, seized Nov. 12, 1974; released Nov. 19 after payment of $750,000.

Adam Walsh, 6, abducted from Hollywood, FL, dept. store, July 27, 1981. Severed head found 2 weeks later. John Walsh, Adam's father, became active in raising awareness about missing children. Case officially closed in 2008; drifter who had died in prison while serving life sentences for murder found responsible.

Terry Anderson, 37, Middle East bureau chief for Associated Press, in Beirut, Lebanon, by members of Islamic fundamentalist group Hezbollah on Mar. 16, 1985. Freed Dec. 4, 1991. Anderson had been held hostage with **William Buckley**, 55, CIA station chief in Beirut who was kidnapped Mar. 16, 1984, and died in captivity.

Jaycee Dugard, 11, kidnapped nr. her home in South Lake Tahoe, CA, June 10, 1991; held for 18 years by Nancy and Philip Garrido, who fathered 2 girls with Dugard during her captivity. Dugard, along with her 11- and 15-year-old daughters, was reunited with her family Aug. 27, 2009, after police arrested the Garridos.

Sidney J. Reso, oil company exec., seized Apr. 29, 1992; died May 3. Arthur D. Seale—former security official at oil company—and his wife, Irene, arrested June 19. Arthur sentenced to life in prison; Irene sentenced to 20-year prison term.

Polly Klaas, 12, Petaluma, CA, abducted at knife point, Oct. 1, 1993, during slumber party at her home. Police arrested Richard Allen Davis on Nov. 30; he led them to her body, found Dec. 4 in wooded area of Cloverdale, CA. Davis found guilty June 18, 1996, and sentenced to death Sept. 26.

Tionda Z. Bradley, 10, and sister **Diamond Yvette Bradley**, 3, went missing July 6, 2001, in Chicago. Note left by Tionda at home stated the 2 girls were going to the store and playground. Disappearance still unsolved.

Daniel Pearl, 38, reporter for *Wall Street Journal*, disappeared Jan. 23, 2002, while researching story in Karachi, Pakistan. British-born militant Ahmad Omar Saeed Sheikh Feb. 14 admitted to organizing the kidnapping and said Pearl was dead. Sheikh and 3 others convicted July 15 of kidnapping and murder by judge in Hyderabad.

Elizabeth Smart, 14, abducted from her home in Salt Lake City, UT, June 5, 2002, by Brian D. Mitchell, and forced to live with Mitchell and wife Wanda for 9 months in various U.S. cities; found walking down street with captors in Sandy, UT, 15 mi from Smart family home, Mar. 12, 2003.

Michelle Knight, 21, abducted Aug. 23, 2002; **Amanda Berry**, 17, seized Apr. 21, 2003; and **Gina DeJesus**, 14, kidnapped Apr. 2, 2004. All 3 women escaped from the Cleveland, OH, home of Ariel Castro, May 6, 2013, after a decade in captivity during which Berry gave birth to a daughter.

Jill Carroll, 28, freelance journalist on assignment for *Christian Science Monitor*, seized in Baghdad by group called the Revenge Brigade, Jan. 7, 2006. She was released Mar. 30; 4 Iraqis arrested in connection with her kidnapping.

Steve Centanni, 60, Fox News reporter released Aug. 26, 2006 (along with a colleague), after being held hostage for 13 days by Palestinian militant group Holy Jihad Brigades. The group had demanded U.S. release of all Muslims in its prisons.

Reigh Storrow Mills, 7, abducted July 27, 2008, by her father, Christian Gerhartsreiter (alias Clark Rockefeller); reunited with her mother Aug. 2, 2008, by FBI agents who took Gerhartsreiter into custody.

Felix Batista, 55, Cuban-American security expert who negotiated the release of numerous kidnapping victims in Latin America, abducted in Mexico Dec. 10, 2008.

David Rohde, 41, *NY Times* reporter captured by the Taliban in Afghanistan Nov. 10, 2008; escaped June 19, 2009.

Jessica Buchanan, 32, aid worker for Danish Refugee Council, taken hostage by Somali pirates Oct. 25, 2011; rescued by U.S. Navy SEALs Jan. 25, 2012.

James Foley, 39, freelance journalist, taken hostage during civil war in Syria's Idlib province, Nov. 22, 2012. ISIS militants released video Aug. 19, 2014, showing execution of Foley.

Richard Engel, 39, NBC News foreign correspondent in Syria and his crew held captive, Dec. 13, 2012; freed by rebel militia 5 days later.

Hannah Anderson, 16, abducted Aug. 3, 2013, by James DiMaggio, a family friend who killed her mother and brother at his California home before fleeing with her to Idaho; freed Aug. 10 when FBI agents shot and killed DiMaggio.

Notable Terrorist Incidents Worldwide Since 1971

Source: U.S. Dept. of State; *Facts On File World News Digest*; World Almanac research

Selected noteworthy incidents, excluding most assassinations, kidnappings, and military targets. Does not include all incidents in Iraq or Afghanistan, 2001-present; see also Chronology of the Year's Events.

1971—Mar. 1: Senate wing of U.S. Capitol Building in Wash., DC, bombed by Weather Underground; no deaths.

1972—July 21: "Bloody Friday." Provisional IRA exploded 20+ bombs across Belfast, N. Ireland; 9 killed, hundreds injured. **Sept. 5:** Palestinian group Black September killed 2 Israeli athletes and seized 9 others at Olympic Village in Munich, W. Germany, during Summer Olympics; 9 hostages, 5 militants, 1 Ger. officer died in botched rescue.

1973—Dec. 17: Palestinian gunman attacked Rome airport and bombed plane on tarmac; hijacked Lufthansa plane with 5 Italian hostages to Athens, Greece, then to Kuwait; 31 killed in all.

1974—June 17: Houses of Parliament in London, England, bombed by Provisional IRA; 11 injured.

1975—Jan. 27: Puerto Rican FALN nationalists bombed Fraunces Tavern in New York City; 4 killed, 53 injured. **Jan. 29:** U.S. State Dept. building in Wash., DC, bombed by Weather Underground; no deaths.

1976—June 27: Palestinian and Baader-Meinhof militants forced Air France jet to land in Entebbe, Uganda. Israeli army rescued 103 hostages from airport terminal in battle with terrorists and Ugandan troops, July 3-4; 32 killed in all.

1978—Mar. 11: Palestinian militants shot civilians and hijacked bus with hostages from Haifa to Tel Aviv, Israel. Bus exploded during firefight with police at a roadblock; 38 killed.

1979—Nov. 4: Iranian radicals seized U.S. embassy in Tehran, taking 66 Americans hostage. 52 were held until Jan. 20, 1981.

Nov. 20: 200 Islamic terrorists seized Grand Mosque in Mecca, Saudi Arabia, and held hundreds of pilgrims hostage. Saudi forces retook mosque Dec. 4; about 250 died.
1980—Feb. 27: Members of leftist guerrilla group April 19 Movement (M-19) seized Dominican Republic embassy in Bogota, Colombia; 80 hostages taken, 18 held until Apr. 27.
1983—Apr. 18: Hezbollah suicide truck bomb at U.S. embassy in Beirut, Lebanon, killed 63. **Oct. 9:** N. Korean agents ambushed a S. Korean govt. delegation in Rangoon, Burma, killing 21. **Oct. 23:** Hezbollah suicide truck bombings of U.S. and French military bases, Beirut, Lebanon; 242 Americans, 58 French killed.
1984—Sept. 20: U.S. embassy annex nr. Beirut, Lebanon, bombed, killing approx. 20.
1985—Apr. 12: Bomb blast at restaurant nr. U.S. air base in Torrejon, Spain; 18 killed. **June 14:** Hezbollah members hijacked TWA Flight 847 with 153 passengers and crew to Beirut, Lebanon; 39 held for 17 days, 1 U.S. Navy sailor killed. **June 23:** Air India Flight 182 destroyed by bomb off coast of Ireland; 329 killed. Blamed on Sikh terrorists. **Oct. 7:** Four Palestinians hijacked Italian cruise ship *Achille Lauro*; 1 passenger killed. **Nov. 23:** EgyptAir Flight 648 from Athens, Greece, to Cairo hijacked to Malta by Palestinian group Abu Nidal; 60 killed in rescue. **Dec. 27:** Palestinian militants opened fire at El-Al airline counters at Rome and Vienna airports; 19 killed.
1986—Apr. 5: Nightclub in Berlin, W. Germany, bombed; 3 killed, incl. 2 U.S. service personnel, 200+ hurt. 3 Libyan embassy workers in Germany convicted.
1987—Apr. 17: Bomb in Sri Lankan capital killed 100+; blamed on Tamil rebels who, 4 days later, attacked Sinhalese travelers on highway, killing 127. **June 19:** Basque group ETA bombed supermarket garage in Barcelona, Spain; 21 killed, 45 injured. **Nov. 29:** Bomb planted by N. Korean agents exploded on Korean Air Lines Flight 858 over Indian Ocean; 115 killed.
1988—Dec. 21: Pan Am Flight 103 exploded over Lockerbie, Scotland, killing all 259 aboard and 11 on ground; Libya took responsibility for bombing in Aug. 2003.
1989—Sept. 19: French UTA Flight 722 from Congo Republic to Paris destroyed by bomb in midair over Niger; 171 killed.
1992—Mar. 17: Israeli embassy in Buenos Aires, Argentina, bombed; 28 killed, 200+ injured. Hezbollah suspected.
1993—Feb. 26: Truck bomb exploded in World Trade Center garage in New York City; 6 killed. Blast later linked to al- Qaeda. **Mar. 12-19:** At least 11 bombs ripped through Bombay and Calcutta, India; 300+ killed.
1994—Feb. 25: U.S.-born Israeli settler Baruch Goldstein opened fire in mosque in Hebron, West Bank; about 30 Muslim worshippers killed. **July 18:** Buenos Aires, Argentina, Jewish center bombed; 87 killed. Blamed on Hezbollah.
1995—Mar. 20: Twelve killed and over 5,000 injured when Japanese Aum Shinri-kyu cult members released sarin nerve gas in several Tokyo subway cars. **Apr. 19:** Murrah Federal Building in Oklahoma City bombed, killing 168 and injuring 500+. Timothy McVeigh and Terry Nichols convicted. McVeigh executed in 2001; Nichols sentenced to life in prison. **Nov. 13:** U.S. military compound in Riyadh, Saudi Arabia, bombed by Islamic Movement of Change; 7 killed.
1996—Jan. 31: Tamil Tigers drove explosives-laden truck into Central Bank in Colombo, Sri Lanka; 90 killed. **June 25:** Bombladen fuel truck exploded outside Khobar Towers, U.S. military complex in Dhahran, Saudi Arabia; killed 19. **July 27:** Bomb exploded at Centennial Olympic Park in Atlanta, GA, during Summer Games; killed 2, injured 100+. Extremist Eric Robert Rudolph sentenced to life in prison, 2005. **Dec. 3:** Bomb exploded on subway train in Paris; 4 killed, 86 injured. Algerian extremists suspected.
1997—Nov. 17: Gamaa al-Islamiya militants killed 58 tourists and 4 Egyptians in Valley of the Kings nr. Luxor, Egypt.
1998—Aug. 7: U.S. embassies in Nairobi, Kenya, and Dar-es-Salaam, Tanzania, bombed; 257 people killed. Al-Qaeda blamed. **Aug. 15:** IRA car bomb exploded outside courthouse in Omagh, N. Ireland; killed 29, injured 300+. **Oct. 18:** National Liberation Army of Colombia blew up Ocensa oil pipeline; about 71 killed, 100+ injured.
1999—Sept. 9-16: Three buildings bombed in Moscow and Volgodonsk, Russia; about 300 killed. Chechen rebels blamed.
2000—Oct. 12: Small boat assisting in docking of U.S.S. *Cole* exploded while alongside it in Aden, Yemen; 17 U.S. sailors killed, 39 injured. Blamed on al-Qaeda.
2001—Sept. 11: 19 al-Qaeda terrorists hijacked 4 U.S. domestic flights, including 2 planes that crashed into New York City's World Trade Center towers and 1 into Pentagon. Total dead minus hijackers: 2,973; deadliest terrorist attack yet on U.S. soil. **Sept.-Nov. 7:** Letters tainted with deadly anthrax bacteria mailed through U.S. postal system killed 5, sickened 17; investigation concluded in 2010 that microbiologist Bruce Ivins, who committed suicide in 2008, was responsible.
2002—Mar. 27: Suicide bombing at hotel in Netanya, Israel, during Passover celebration; 27 killed. **Oct 12:** Resort in Bali, Indonesia, bombed; 202 dead. Jemaah Islamiah blamed.

Oct. 23: Chechen guerrillas seized theater in Moscow, held 700+ hostages. Russian authorities gassed theater; most guerrillas and about 128 hostages killed. **Dec. 27:** Chechen rebels plowed truck bomb into pro-Russian govt. headquarters in Grozny, Chechnya; 80 killed, 152 injured.
2003—May 12-13: Al-Qaeda militants detonated car bombs at 3 residential complexes used by Westerners in Riyadh, Saudi Arabia; 34 killed. **May 16:** Five explosions in Casablanca, Morocco; 44 killed, 100+ wounded. Blamed on al-Qaeda. **Aug. 19:** UN headquarters in Baghdad bombed by truck; 22 killed, incl. UN envoy to Iraq. **Aug. 25:** 2 bombs exploded in taxis in Mumbai, India; 46 killed, 100+ injured. Islamic militants suspected. **Nov. 15:** Two synagogues in Istanbul, Turkey, bombed; 25 killed. **Nov. 20:** British consulate and offices of British bank HSBC bombed in Istanbul, Turkey; 27 killed. Blamed on al-Qaeda. **Dec. 5:** Suicide bombing on commuter train in Yessentuki, Russia; 44 killed, 150 injured. Blamed on Chechen rebels.
2004—Feb. 6: Bomb exploded in Moscow subway; 39 killed, 130 injured. Chechen rebels blamed. **Mar. 11:** Al-Qaeda cell bombed 4 commuter trains during morning rush hour in Madrid, Spain; 191 killed, about 1,200 injured. **May 29:** Al-Qaeda militants stormed foreigner compound in Khobar, Saudi Arabia, taking hostages; 22 killed. **Aug. 24:** Two Russian passenger planes crashed nearly simultaneously in diff. parts of Russia; 90 killed. Blamed on Chechen rebels. **Sept. 1:** Chechen militants seized school in Beslan, in North Ossetia, Russia; held 1,000+ hostage for 3 days before Russian troops stormed school. About 330 killed, incl. 27 hostage-takers.
2005—July 7: Four bombs exploded on 3 separate subways and 1 bus in central London, Eng.; 52 killed, about 700 injured. **July 21:** Four bombs placed on 3 subways and 1 bus in London malfunction. No deaths reported. **July 23:** Three car bombs explode nr. resorts at Sharm el Sheik, Egypt; about 90 killed. **Nov. 9:** 3 suicide bombings targeted hotels in Amman, Jordan; killed 56+, injured about 100. Al-Qaeda in Iraq took responsibility.
2006—July 11: 8 explosions struck 7 different trains and 1 station of public commuter rail system in Mumbai, India; 207 killed, 700+ wounded. Lashkar-e-Qahhar (Army of Terror) claimed responsibility.
2007—Feb. 19: Train traveling between New Delhi and border with Pakistan caught fire, 68 killed; Indian ministers blamed Muslim militants for trying to disrupt peace talks between India and Pakistan. **Dec. 11:** Two coordinated car bombs went off outside govt. building and UN office building in Algiers, Algeria; 41 killed, incl. 17 UN employees, 170 wounded.
2008—Sept. 20: Suicide bomber in truck set off explosion outside of Marriott Hotel in Islamabad, Pakistan. Hotel was popular among foreigners, wealthy residents and was located nr. prime min.'s house and parliament building; 53 killed, 271 wounded. **Nov. 26-29:** Series of attacks and bombings on luxury hotels and high-profile targets in Mumbai, India; 171 killed, 300 injured.
2009—Feb. 20: Suicide bomber targeted Shiite funeral in Dera Ismail Khan, Pakistan; 30 killed, 50+ wounded. **Dec. 25:** Umar Farouk Abdulmutallab, 23-year-old Nigerian, failed to blow up a Northwest Airlines flight from Amsterdam to Detroit with bomb hidden in his underpants.
2010—Jan. 1: Taliban suicide bomber killed more than 100 on a playground in NW Pakistan. **Mar. 29:** Two female Chechen separatists detonated suicide bombs at two landmark subway stations in Moscow, killing at least 40. **July 9:** Suicide bombers targeted tribal elders in Mohmand, Pakistan, killing more than 100. **July 11:** Several bombs exploded simultaneously in Kampala, Uganda, killing more than 70 people who had gathered to watch the broadcast of the World Cup final.
2011—Jan. 24: Suicide bomber killed 35 in Moscow's Domodedovo Airport, location chosen to maximize deaths of foreigners. **July 22:** Anders Behring Breivik, a right-wing Norwegian extremist, set off car bomb outside govt. buildings in Oslo, then massacred dozens of young people at a summer camp on Tyrifjorden Lake, bringing death toll to 77.
2012—Jan. 21: Series of attacks by Islamist extremist group Boko Haram killed more than 185 in Kano, Nigeria. **May 21:** Suicide bomber claimed by al-Qaeda in the Arabian Peninsula killed more than 100 soldiers, wounded 200 during military parade rehearsal nr. Yemeni presidential palace. **Sept. 11:** Terrorists stormed U.S. embassy in Benghazi, Libya, killing 4 Americans, including U.S. Amb. J. Christopher Stevens.
2013—Apr. 15: Two bombs exploded nr. Boston Marathon finish line, killing 3 and injuring 264; 4-day search ended in death of 1 bomber, Tamerlan Tsarnaev, and capture of the other, his brother Dzhokhar, a naturalized Chechen immigrant. **May 22:** Off-duty soldier Lee Rigby stabbed to death in London by 2 British citizens of Nigerian descent. **Sept. 21:** Al-Shabaab, a Somali militant group, killed more than 70 people and wounded at least 200 at a Nairobi, Kenya, shopping mall.
2014—Apr.-May: Islamist extremist group Boko Haram kidnapped more than 250 girls from schools in Nigeria.

MILITARY AFFAIRS

Chairmen of the Joint Chiefs of Staff, 1949-2014

Chairman	Service
Gen. of the Army Omar N. Bradley, USA	8/16/1949-8/15/1953
Adm. Arthur W. Radford, USN.	8/15/1953-8/15/1957
Gen. Nathan F. Twining, USAF.	8/15/1957-9/30/1960
Gen. Lyman L. Lemnitzer, USA.	10/1/1960-9/30/1962
Gen. Maxwell D. Taylor, USA	10/1/1962-7/1/1964
Gen. Earle G. Wheeler, USA.	7/3/1964-7/2/1970
Adm. Thomas H. Moorer, USN	7/2/1970-7/1/1974
Gen. George S. Brown, USAF.	7/1/1974-6/20/1978
Gen. David C. Jones, USAF	6/21/1978-6/18/1982

Chairman	Service
Gen. John W. Vessey Jr., USA	6/18/1982-9/30/1985
Adm. William J. Crowe Jr., USN	10/1/1985-9/30/1989
Gen. Colin L. Powell, USA.	10/1/1989-9/30/1993
Gen. John M. Shalikashvili, USA.	10/25/1993-9/30/1997
Gen. Henry H. Shelton, USA.	9/30/1997-9/30/2001
Gen. Richard B. Myers, USAF.	10/1/2001-9/30/2005
Gen. Peter Pace, USMC	9/30/2005-9/30/2007
Adm. Michael G. Mullen, USN.	10/1/2007-9/30/2011
Gen. Martin E. Dempsey, USA	10/1/2011-

Chief Commanding Officers of the U.S. Military

Chairman, Joint Chiefs of Staff: Gen. Martin E. Dempsey (U.S. Army)
Vice Chairman: Adm. James A. Winnefeld Jr. (U.S. Navy)

Date of rank is date when the individual achieved his or her current rank. While serving in any of these positions, or as commander of a unified or specified combatant command, basic pay is $21,147.30 per month. Officers hold positions listed as of Oct. 1, 2014.

Army

Chief of Staff (CSA)	Date of rank
Odierno, Raymond T.	Sept. 16, 2008

Other Generals

Allyn, Daniel	Apr. 26, 2013
Austin, Lloyd J., III	Sept. 1, 2010
Brooks, Vincent K.	July 2, 2013
Campbell, John F.	Mar. 8, 2013
Dempsey, Martin E.	Dec. 8, 2008
Grass, Frank J.	Sept. 7, 2012
Jacoby, Charles H., Jr.	Aug. 3, 2011
Milley, Mark A.	Aug. 15, 2014
Perkins, David G.	Mar. 14, 2014
Rodriguez, David M.	Aug. 15, 2011
Scaparrotti, Curtis M.	Oct. 2, 2013
Via, Dennis L.	Aug. 7, 2012
Votel, Joseph L., III	Aug. 28, 2014

Air Force

Chief of Staff (CSAF or AF/CC)	Date of rank
Welsh III, Mark A.	Dec. 13, 2010

Other Generals

Breedlove, Philip M.	Jan. 14, 2011
Carlisle, Herbert J.	Aug. 3, 2012
Gorenc, Frank	Aug. 2, 2013
Hostage, Gilmary M., III.	Sept. 13, 2011
Hyten, John E.	Aug. 15, 2014
McDew, Darren W.	May 5, 2014
Rand, Robin.	Oct. 10, 2013
Selva, Paul J.	Nov. 30, 2012

Air Force

Spencer, Larry O.	July 27, 2012
Wolfenbarger, Janet C.	June 5, 2012

Navy

Chief of Naval Operations (CNO)	Date of rank
Greenert, Jonathan W. (submariner).	Sept. 29, 2007

Other Admirals

Ferguson, Mark E., III (surface warfare)	Aug. 2, 2011
Gortney, William E. (aviator)	May 24, 2012
Haney, Cecil D. (surface warfare)	Jan. 20, 2012
Harris, Harry B., Jr. (aviator)	Oct. 16, 2013
Howard, Michelle J. (surface warfare)	July 1, 2014
Locklear, Samuel J., III (surface warfare)	Mar. 9, 2012
Richardson, John M. (submariner)	July 26, 2012
Rogers, Michael S. (information warfare)	Mar. 31, 2014
Winnefeld, James A. "Sandy," Jr. (aviator)	May 7, 2010

Marine Corps

Commandant of the Marine Corps (CMC)	Date of rank
Amos, James F.	July 2, 2008

Other Generals

Dunford, Joseph F., Jr.	Aug. 4, 2010
Kelly, John F.	July 26, 2012
Paxton, John M., Jr.	Dec. 15, 2012

Coast Guard

Commandant, with rank of Admiral	Date of rank
Zukunft, Paul F.	May 30, 2014

Vice Commandant, with rank of Vice Admiral	
Neffenger, Peter V.	May 20, 2014

Unified Combatant Commands Commanders-in-Chief

U.S. European Command, Stuttgart-Vaihingen, Germany:
Gen. Philip M. Breedlove (USAF)
U.S. Pacific Command, Honolulu, Hawaii:
Adm. Samuel J. Locklear III (USN)
U.S. Special Operations Command, MacDill AFB, Florida:
Gen. Joseph L. Votel III (U.S. Army)
U.S. Transportation Command, Scott AFB, Illinois:
Gen. Paul J. Selva (USAF)
U.S. Central Command, MacDill AFB, Florida:
Gen. Lloyd J. Austin III (U.S. Army)

U.S. Southern Command, Doral, Florida:
Gen. John F. Kelly (USMC)
U.S. Northern Command, Peterson AFB, Colorado:
Gen. Charles H. Jacoby Jr. (U.S. Army)
U.S. Strategic Command, Offutt AFB, Nebraska:
Adm. Cecil D. Haney (USN)
U.S. Africa Command, Kelley Barracks, Stuttgart, Germany:
Gen. David M. Rodriguez (U.S. Army)

North Atlantic Treaty Organization (NATO) International Commands

NATO Headquarters: Chairman, NATO Military Committee:
Gen. Knud Bartels (Danish Army)
ACO Subordinate Commands:
Joint Force Command Brunssum (JFC Brunssum):
Gen. Hans-Lothar Domröse (German Army), Commander
Joint Force Command Naples (JFC Naples): Adm. Mark
Ferguson (USN), Commander

Strategic Commands:
Allied Command Operations (ACO): Gen. Philip M. Breedlove (USAF), Supreme Allied Commander, Europe
Allied Command Transformation (ACT): Gen. Jean-Paul Paloméros (French Air Force), Supreme Allied Commander Transformation

Directors of the Central Intelligence Agency, 1946-2014

In 1942, Pres. Franklin D. Roosevelt established the Office of Strategic Services (OSS); it was disbanded in 1945. In 1946, Pres. Harry Truman established the Central Intelligence Group (CIG) to operate under the National Intelligence Authority (NIA). A 1947 law replaced the NIA with the National Security Council (NSC) and the CIG with the Central Intelligence Agency (CIA).

Director	Served	Appointed by President
Adm. Sidney W. Souers	1946	Truman
Gen. Hoyt S. Vandenberg	1946-1947	Truman
Adm. Roscoe H. Hillenkoetter	1947-1950	Truman
Gen. Walter Bedell Smith	1950-1953	Truman
Allen W. Dulles	1953-1961	Eisenhower
John A. McCone	1961-1965	Kennedy
Adm. William F. Raborn Jr.	1965-1966	Johnson, L. B.
Richard Helms	1966-1973	Johnson, L. B.
James R. Schlesinger	1973	Nixon
William E. Colby	1973-1976	Nixon
George H. W. Bush	1976-1977	Ford
Adm. Stansfield Turner	1977-1981	Carter

Director	Served	Appointed by President
William J. Casey	1981-1987	Reagan
William H. Webster	1987-1991	Reagan
Robert M. Gates	1991-1993	Bush, G. H. W.
R. James Woolsey	1993-1995	Clinton
John M. Deutch	1995-1997	Clinton
George J. Tenet	1997-2004	Clinton
Porter Goss	2004-2006	Bush, G. W.
Gen. Michael V. Hayden	2006-2009	Bush, G. W.
Leon E. Panetta	2009-2011	Obama
Gen. David H. Petraeus	2011-2012	Obama
John O. Brennan	2013-	Obama

U.S. Army and Air Force Units

Army Units. Squad: In infantry, usually 8-16 enlisted personnel under a staff sergeant. **Platoon:** In infantry, 2-4 squads under a lieutenant. **Company:** Headquarters and 3-5 platoons under a captain. (Company-size unit in the artillery is a battery; in the cavalry, a troop.) **Battalion:** HQ and 4-6 companies under a lieutenant colonel. (Battalion-size unit in the cavalry is a squadron.) **Brigade:** HQ and 2-5 battalions under a colonel. (Brigade-size unit in the cavalry and rangers is a regiment; in the special forces, a group.) **Division:** HQ and 3 brigades with artillery, combat support, and combat service support units under a major general. **Corps:** Two or more divisions with corps troops under a lieutenant general. **Army:** HQ and 2 or more corps with operational and support responsibilities under a general.

Air Force Units. Flight: Numerically designated flights are the lowest level unit. They are used primarily where there is a need for small mission elements to be incorporated into an organized unit. **Squadron:** The basic unit. Designates specific operational or support capability like mission units in operational commands. **Group:** Flexible unit composed of 2 or more squadrons whose functions may be operational, support, or administrative in nature. **Wing:** Primary group with supporting groups on a distinct mission with significant scope such as combat, flying training, or airlift. **Numbered Air Force (NAF):** Normally operationally oriented, the numbered air force is designed for the control of subordinate units with the same mission and/or geographical location. **Major Command (MAJCOM):** A major subdivision with full staff that manages a major segment of the USAF mission. Major command is composed of 3 or more numbered air forces.

Active Duty U.S. Military Personnel Strength Worldwide, 2014

Source: U.S. Dept. of Defense

(as of June 30, 2014)

TOTAL WORLDWIDE[1] **1,347,187**	**EUROPE**		**EAST ASIA AND PACIFIC**
	Belgium	1,194	Australia 180
U.S. TERRITORIES AND	Germany	40,463	British Indian Ocean Territory
SPEC. LOCATIONS	Greece	383	(Diego Garcia) 548
U.S., 48 contiguous states 1,107,883	Greenland	131	Japan 49,996
Alaska 20,040	Italy	11,324	South Korea . . . . NA
Guam 5,521	Netherlands	378	Philippines 33
Hawaii 50,763	Portugal	704	Singapore 183
Puerto Rico 143	Spain	2,107	Thailand 289
Regional total[2] **1,184,356**	Turkey	1,539	**Regional total[2]** **51,363**
	United Kingdom	9,551	
OTHER WESTERN HEMISPHERE	**Regional total[2]**	**68,147**	**NORTH AFRICA, NEAR EAST, AND**
Canada 128	**SUB-SAHARAN AFRICA**		**SOUTH ASIA***
Colombia 50	South Africa	215	Afghanistan[3] 44,492
Cuba (Guantánamo) 754	**Regional total[2]**	**378**	Bahrain 3,227
Haiti 6	**FORMER SOVIET UNION**		Egypt 267
Honduras 372	**Total**	82	Iraq[3] 560
Regional total[2] **1,627**			Qatar 592
			Saudi Arabia 332
			United Arab Emirates 313
			Regional total[2,4] **4,889**

NA = Not available. *Special Forces personnel involved in Operation Enduring Freedom (OEF) in Afghanistan were not reported by Dept. of Defense. (1) Includes undistributed personnel. (2) Most countries and areas with fewer than 100 assigned U.S. military members not listed; regional totals include personnel stationed in countries and areas not shown. (3) Includes troops in surrounding areas and deployed Reserve/National Guard. (4) Excludes troops deployed for OEF/Operation New Dawn.

U.S. Army Personnel on Active Duty, 1940-2014

Source: Dept. of the Army, U.S. Dept. of Defense

(as of midyear, except where noted)

Date	Total strength[1]	Commissioned officers			Warrant officers[3]		Enlisted personnel		
		Total	Male	Female[2]	Male	Female	Total	Male	Female
1940	267,767	17,563	16,624	939	763	—	249,441	249,441	—
1942	3,074,184	203,137	190,662	12,475	3,285	—	2,867,762	2,867,762	—
1943	6,993,102	557,657	521,435	36,222	21,919	—	6,413,526	6,358,200	55,325
1944	7,992,868	740,077	692,351	47,726	36,893	10	7,215,888	7,144,601	71,287
1945	8,266,373	835,403	772,511	62,892	56,216	44	7,374,710	7,283,930	90,780
1946	1,889,690	257,300	240,658	16,642	9,826	18	1,622,546	1,605,847	16,699
1950	591,487	67,784	63,375	4,409	4,760	22	518,921	512,370	6,551
1955	1,107,606	111,347	106,196	5,151	10,552	48	985,659	977,943	7,716
1960	871,348	91,056	86,832	4,224	10,141	39	770,112	761,833	8,279
1965	967,049	101,812	98,029	3,783	10,285	23	854,929	846,409	8,520
1970	1,319,735	143,704	138,469	5,235	23,005	13	1,153,013	1,141,537	11,476
1975	781,316	89,756	85,184	4,572	13,214	22	678,324	640,621	37,703
1980 (Sept. 30) . . .	772,661	85,339	77,843	7,496	13,265	113	673,944	612,593	61,351
1985 (Sept. 30) . . .	776,244	94,103	83,563	10,540	15,296	288	666,557	598,639	67,918
1990 (Mar. 31) . . .	746,220	91,330	79,520	11,810	15,177	470	639,713	567,015	72,698
1995	521,036	72,646	62,250	10,396	12,053	599	435,807	377,832	57,975
2000	471,633	66,344	56,391	9,953	10,608	781	393,900	333,947	59,953
2005 (Sept. 30) . . .	492,728	69,174	57,675	11,499	11,506	976	406,923	346,194	57,354
2006 (Sept. 30) . . .	505,402	68,742	57,318	11,424	11,931	1,035	419,353	361,528	57,825
2007 (Sept. 30) . . .	522,017	70,657	58,854	11,803	13,844	1,160	433,109	374,989	58,120
2008 (Sept. 30) . . .	539,170	72,650	60,357	12,293	13,428	1,246	451,846	392,163	59,683
2009 (Sept. 30) . . .	553,044	75,337	63,146	12,191	13,815	1,348	457,980	398,579	59,401
2010 (Sept. 30) . . .	566,045	78,588	64,952	13,636	14,106	1,434	467,248	406,871	60,377
2011 (Sept. 30) . . .	565,463	81,395	67,140	14,255	14,373	1,472	463,605	403,381	60,224
2012 (Sept. 30) . . .	550,064	82,538	68,021	14,517	14,401	1,484	447,075	389,646	57,429
2013 (Sept. 30) . . .	532,043	82,916	68,219	14,697	14,229	1,489	428,923	373,263	55,660
2014 (July 31)	512,107	83,090	68,245	14,845	14,113	1,470	408,996	354,817	54,179

— = Not applicable. **Note:** Represents strength of active Army, including Philippine Scouts (1940-46), ret. Regular Army personnel on extended active duty, and National Guard and Reserve personnel on extended active duty; excl. U.S. Military Academy cadets, contract surgeons, and National Guard and Reserve personnel not on extended active duty. (1) Includes categories not listed, e.g., West Point cadets. Data for 1940-46 include personnel in the Army Air Forces and its predecessors (Air Service and Air Corps). (2) Includes Army Nurse Corps for all years, Women's Army Corps (1942-78), and Medical Specialists Corps (1949 and after). (3) Act of Congress approved Apr. 27, 1926, directed the appointment as warrant officers of field clerks still in active service. Includes flight officers as follows: 1943, 5,700; 1944, 13,615; 1945, 31,117; 1946, 2,580.

U.S. Navy Personnel on Active Duty, 1940-2014
Source: U.S. Dept. of Defense
(as of midyear, except where noted)

Year	Officers	Nurses[1]	Enlisted	Officer candidates[1]	Total[2]	Year	Officers	Nurses[1]	Enlisted	Officer candidates[1]	Total[2]
1940	13,162	442	144,824	2,569	160,997	2000 (Oct.)	53,698	—	320,212	—	373,910
1945	320,293	11,086	2,988,207	61,231	3,380,817	2005	54,039	—	305,368	—	363,858
1950	42,687	1,964	331,860	5,037	381,538	2006	53,209	—	295,773	—	353,496
1960	67,456	2,103	544,040	4,385	617,984	2007 (Sept.)	51,385	—	281,772	—	337,547
1970	78,488	2,273	605,899	6,000	692,660	2008	52,184	—	276,346	—	331,785
1980	63,100	—	464,100	—	527,200	2009	52,233	—	274,858	—	331,637
1990 (Sept.)	74,429	—	530,133	—	604,562	2010	53,071	—	273,609	—	330,065
1995 (May)	61,075	—	402,626	—	463,701	2011	53,620	—	270,425	—	328,648
1996	60,013	—	376,595	—	436,608	2012 (Mar.)	52,558	—	263,928	—	320,961
1997	57,341	—	340,616	—	397,957	2013 (Feb.)	52,450	—	260,581	—	317,464
1998 (Sept.)	55,007	—	326,196	—	381,203	2014 (July)	54,760	—	266,268	—	325,513
1999	55,726	—	322,372	—	378,098						

— = Not applicable. (1) Starting in 1980, "Nurses" are included with "Officers," and "Officer candidates" are included with "Enlisted." (2) May include categories not shown, e.g., midshipmen.

U.S. Air Force Personnel on Active Duty, 1918-2014
Source: U.S. Dept. of Defense
(as of midyear, except where noted)

Year[1]	Strength	Year[1]	Strength	Year[1]	Strength	Year[1]	Strength	Year[1]	Strength	Year[1]	Strength
1918	195,023	1943	2,197,114	1980	557,969	1994	426,327	2000	357,777	2010	337,505
1920	9,050	1944	2,372,292	1986	608,200	1995	400,051	2005	358,705	2011	333,729
1930	13,531	1945	2,282,259	1990	535,233	1996	389,400	2006	352,620	2012[2]	332,709
1940	51,165	1950	411,277	1991	510,432	1997	378,681	2007	340,596	2013[3]	334,157
1941	152,125	1960	814,213	1992	470,315	1998	363,479	2008	328,771	2014[4]	327,747
1942	764,415	1970	791,078	1999	444,351	1999	357,929	2009	334,009		

(1) Prior to 1950, data are for U.S. Army Air Corps and Air Service of the Signal Corps. (2) In Mar. (3) In Feb. (4) In July.

U.S. Marine Corps Personnel on Active Duty, 1940-2014
Source: U.S. Dept. of Defense
(as of midyear, except where noted)

Year	Officers	Enlisted	Total	Year	Officers	Enlisted	Total	Year	Officers	Enlisted	Total
1940	1,800	26,545	28,345	1995	18,017	153,929	171,946	2007	19,456	162,085	181,541
1945	37,067	437,613	474,680	1996	18,146	154,141	172,287	2008	20,137	172,903	193,040
1950	7,254	67,025	74,279	1997	18,089	154,240	172,329	2009	21,031	183,243	204,274
1960	16,203	154,418	170,621	1998	17,984	154,648	172,632	2010	21,680	179,446	201,126
1970	24,941	234,796	259,737	1999	17,892	155,250	173,142	2011	22,281	178,546	200,827
1980	18,198	170,271	188,469	2000	17,897	154,744	172,641	2012 (Mar.)	22,253	176,174	198,427
1990	19,958	176,694	196,652	2005	19,118	159,113	178,231	2013 (Feb.)	21,907	173,222	195,129
1993	18,878	161,205	180,083	2006	19,218	159,705	178,923	2014 (July)	21,314	167,923	189,237
1994	18,430	159,949	178,379								

U.S. Coast Guard Personnel on Active Duty, 1970-2014
Source: U.S. Dept. of Defense
(as of midyear, except where noted)

Year	Officers	Cadets	Enlisted	Total	Year	Officers	Cadets	Enlisted	Total
1970	5,512	653	31,524	37,689	2007	8,231	720	32,314	41,265
1980	6,463	877	32,041	39,381	2008	8,282	1,005	33,137	42,424
1985	6,775	733	31,087	38,595	2009	8,497	993	34,024	43,514
1990	6,475	820	29,860	37,308	2010	8,678	744	33,713	43,135
1995	7,489	841	28,401	36,731	2011	8,659	1,053	33,615	43,327
2000	7,154	863	27,695	35,712	2012 (Mar.)	8,316	988	33,758	43,062
2005	7,908	1,006	31,900	40,814	2013 (Jan.)	8,376	1,010	32,971	42,357
2006	8,032	1,004	32,001	40,639	2014 (July)	8,467	896	31,273	40,636

Women in the U.S. Armed Forces
Source: U.S. Dept. of Defense; U.S. Census Bureau, U.S. Dept. of Commerce; U.S. Coast Guard, U.S. Dept. of Homeland Security
Women in the Army, Navy, Air Force, Marines, and Coast Guard are fully integrated with male personnel. All enlisted jobs were opened to women when the draft ended June 30, 1973. Admission to service academies began in 1976. Under rules instituted in 1993, women were allowed to fly combat aircraft and serve aboard warships. By the mid-1990s, 80% of all jobs and more than 90% of all career fields had been opened to women. The first woman achieved the rank of four-star general in 2009. In Apr. 2010, the Navy announced that women would be placed on submarine crews by Jan. 2012. The Pentagon in 2013 lifted its ban on women serving in direct ground combat units.

Women Active Duty Troops, 2014

Service	% women
Army	13.9%
Navy	17.8
Marines	7.6
Air Force	18.9
Coast Guard	15.1

Women on Active Duty, All Services, 1973-2014

Year	% women	Year	% women
1973	2.5%	2000	14.4%
1975	4.6	2005	14.6
1981	8.9	2011	14.6
1987	10.2	2012	14.6
1993	11.6	2013	14.9
1997	13.6	2014	15.2

Women Veterans by Period of Service, 2014

Period of service[1]	% of women vets
Gulf War era[2]	57.3%
Vietnam era	11.9
Korean War	2.3
World War II	2.5
Peacetime only	26.0

Note: Numbers on active duty are as of Sept. 30 in previous years and July 31 in 2014. (1) Includes women who served in multiple periods. (2) Includes women who served both pre- and post-9/11 but not in peacetime only.

Average Age and Length of Service of Active Enlisted Personnel, 1973-2012
Source: U.S. Dept. of Defense

Year	Avg. age	Avg. months of service	Year	Avg. age	Avg. months of service	Year	Avg. age	Avg. months of service
1973	25.0	69.8	1987	26.1	74.8	2000	27.1	85.5
1974	25.0	69.6	1988	26.3	76.7	2001	27.0	84.4
1975	24.9	68.2	1989	26.4	78.0	2002	27.1	84.1
1976	24.9	67.6	1990	26.7	81.8	2003	27.0	83.3
1977	24.9	66.5	1991	27.0	84.8	2004	27.0	82.6
1978	25.0	67.3	1992	27.1	86.4	2005	27.1	83.2
1979	25.1	67.7	1992	27.1	86.4	2006	27.1	82.0
1980	25.0	66.5	1993	27.2	87.7	2007	27.1	81.0
1981	25.1	67.1	1994	27.3	89.6	2008	27.1	80.3
1982	25.4	68.6	1995	27.4	89.3	2009	27.2	80.4
1983	25.6	70.0	1996	27.4	89.6	2010	27.3	80.9
1984	25.7	71.1	1997	27.4	89.2	2011	27.4	81.1
1985	25.8	72.3	1998	27.3	88.4	2012	27.4	NA
1986	25.9	73.1	1999	27.3	87.3			

NA = Not available.

Monthly Military Pay Scale
Source: U.S. Dept. of Defense
(effective Jan. 1, 2014; salaries rounded to nearest dollar)

	<2	2	3	4	6	8	10	12	14	16	18	20	22	24	26
Commissioned officers															
O-10	NA	NA	NA	NA	NA	NA	NA	NA	NA	NA	NA	16,072	16,151	16,487	17,072
O-9	NA	NA	NA	NA	NA	NA	NA	NA	NA	NA	NA	14,057	14,552	14,552	15,062
O-8	9,946	10,272	10,488	10,549	10,819	11,269	11,374	11,802	11,925	12,293	12,827	13,319	13,647	13,647	13,647
O-7	8,264	8,648	8,826	8,967	9,223	9,476	9,768	10,059	10,351	11,269	12,044	12,044	12,044	12,044	12,106
O-6	6,125	6,730	7,171	7,171	7,199	7,507	7,548	7,548	7,977	8,735	9,180	9,625	9,878	10,135	10,632
O-5	5,107	5,753	6,151	6,226	6,474	6,623	6,950	7,190	7,500	7,974	8,199	8,422	8,676	8,676	8,676
O-4	4,406	5,100	5,441	5,516	5,832	6,171	6,593	6,921	7,150	7,281	7,357	7,357	7,357	7,357	7,357
O-3	3,874	4,391	4,740	5,168	5,415	5,687	5,863	6,152	6,302	6,302	6,302	6,302	6,302	6,302	6,302
O-2	3,347	3,812	4,391	4,539	4,632	4,632	4,632	4,632	4,632	4,632	4,632	4,632	4,632	4,632	4,632
O-1	2,905	3,024	3,656	3,656	3,656	3,656	3,656	3,656	3,656	3,656	3,656	3,656	3,656	3,656	3,656
Commissioned officers with over 4 years of active duty service as enlisted member or warrant officer															
O-3	NA	NA	NA	5,168	5,415	5,687	5,863	6,152	6,395	6,536	6,726	6,726	6,726	6,726	6,726
O-2	NA	NA	NA	4,539	4,632	4,780	5,029	5,221	5,364	5,364	5,364	5,364	5,364	5,364	5,364
O-1	NA	NA	NA	3,656	3,903	4,048	4,195	4,340	4,539	4,539	4,539	4,539	4,539	4,539	4,539
Warrant officers															
W-5	NA	NA	NA	NA	NA	NA	NA	NA	NA	NA	NA	7,118	7,480	7,748	8,046
W-4	4,004	4,307	4,430	4,552	4,761	4,968	5,178	5,494	5,771	6,034	6,249	6,459	6,768	7,022	7,311
W-3	3,656	3,808	3,965	4,016	4,180	4,502	4,837	4,995	5,178	5,366	5,705	5,933	6,070	6,215	6,413
W-2	3,235	3,541	3,635	3,700	3,910	4,236	4,397	4,556	4,751	4,903	5,041	5,205	5,314	5,400	5,400
W-1	2,840	3,145	3,227	3,401	3,607	3,909	4,051	4,248	4,442	4,595	4,736	4,907	4,907	4,907	4,907
Enlisted members															
E-9	NA	NA	NA	NA	NA	NA	4,837	4,946	5,085	5,247	5,411	5,674	5,896	6,129	6,487
E-8	NA	NA	NA	NA	NA	3,959	4,134	4,243	4,373	4,514	4,768	4,896	5,115	5,237	5,536
E-7	2,753	3,004	3,119	3,272	3,391	3,595	3,710	3,914	4,084	4,200	4,324	4,372	4,532	4,619	4,947
E-6	2,381	2,620	2,735	2,848	2,965	3,229	3,332	3,530	3,591	3,636	3,687	3,687	3,687	3,687	3,687
E-5	2,181	2,327	2,440	2,555	2,735	2,922	3,076	3,095	3,095	3,095	3,095	3,095	3,095	3,095	3,095
E-4	2,000	2,102	2,216	2,328	2,427	2,427	2,427	2,427	2,427	2,427	2,427	2,427	2,427	2,427	2,427
E-3	1,805	1,919	2,035	2,035	2,035	2,035	2,035	2,035	2,035	2,035	2,035	2,035	2,035	2,035	2,035
E-2	1,717	1,717	1,717	1,717	1,717	1,717	1,717	1,717	1,717	1,717	1,717	1,717	1,717	1,717	1,717
E-1[1]	1,532	1,532	1,532	1,532	1,532	1,532	1,532	1,532	1,532	1,532	1,532	1,532	1,532	1,532	1,532

NA = Not applicable. **Note:** Basic pay rate for Academy cadets/midshipmen and ROTC members/applicants is $1,017. See Dept. of Defense Financial Management Regulations for details on payscale limitations and eligibility requirements. **Over 30 years**—O-10: 17,925; O-9: 15,816; O-8: 13,989; O-7: 12,348; O-6: 10,844; W-5: 8,449; W-4: 7,457; E-9: 6,811; E-8: 5,647. **Over 34 years**—O-10: 18,821; O-9: 16,607; O-8: 14,339; W-5: 8,871; E-9: 7,152. **Over 38 years**—O-10: 19,763; O-9: 17,437; W-5: 9,315; E-9: 7,510. (1) Applicable to E-1 with 4 months or more of active duty. Basic pay for an E-1 with less than 4 months of active duty is $1,416.30.

U.S. Veteran Population, 2014
Source: U.S. Dept. of Veterans Affairs
(projected population, in thousands, as of Sept. 30)

Period of service	Vet. pop.
Total peacetime veterans[1]	5,413.8
Service between Vietnam era and Gulf War era	3,310.0
Service between Korean War and Vietnam era	2,005.0
Service between WWII and Korean War	85.5
Pre-WWII service	13.3
Total wartime veterans[2]	16,205.9
Total World War II[3]	1,111.6
WWII only	1,002.5
Total Korean War[3]	1,878.3
Korean War with no other wartime service	1,606.8
Korean War with service in WWII	79.6
Total Vietnam era[3]	7,154.0
Vietnam era with no other wartime service	6,631.4
Vietnam era with service in Korea	162.3
Vietnam era with service in Korea and WWII	29.6
Total Gulf War era[3]	6,693.8
Gulf War era pre-9/11 with service in Vietnam era	286.7
Gulf War era pre-9/11, post-9/11, and with service in Vietnam era	44.1
Gulf War era pre-9/11	2,686.1
Gulf War era pre-9/11 and post-9/11	1,337.1
Gulf War era post-9/11	2,339.8
TOTAL VETERANS IN CIVILIAN LIFE	21,619.7

Note: Figures are for U.S. veterans worldwide. Includes those who served on active duty in Army, Navy, Air Force, Marines, Coast Guard, uniformed Public Health Service and NOAA, and reservists called to federal active duty. Excludes those dishonorably discharged, those whose only active duty was training, and those currently on active duty. (1) Veterans with both wartime and peacetime service are counted only as "wartime veterans." (2) Veterans serving in more than one period are counted only once in total. (3) Total includes veterans who also served in other periods.

African American Service in U.S. Wars
Source: U.S. Dept. of Defense; U.S. Census Bureau; U.S. Dept. of Commerce

American Revolution. About 5,000 served in the Continental Army, mostly in integrated units, some in all-black combat units.
Civil War. Some 180,000 served in 163 units of the Union Army's U.S. Colored Troops, and 200,000 worked in service units—10% of the Union Army in all; about 37,000 died, 31,000 wounded.
World War I. 350,000-400,000 served in the armed forces, 100,000 in France. Some 40,000 fought.
World War II. Some 1 mil served in the armed forces—8% of all troops—mostly in Army service units; all-black fighter and bomber Army Air Force units and infantry divisions gave distinguished service.

Korean War. More than 600,000 served in the military; 3,075 lost their lives in combat. By 1954, armed forces were completely desegregated.
Vietnam War. 274,937 served in the armed forces (1965-74)—9.8% of all troops; 7,243 were killed in combat.
Persian Gulf War. About 104,000 served in the Kuwaiti theater—20% of all U.S. troops; 66 died in combat.
Operation Enduring Freedom. 191 military deaths and 1,400 wounded in Afghanistan and elsewhere (as of Aug. 29, 2014).
Operation Iraqi Freedom/Operation New Dawn. 444 military deaths and 2,766 wounded.

Outlays for Individual Payments to Veterans, 1940-2015
Source: White House Office of Management and Budget
(in millions of dollars)

Year	Total	Compensation	Pensions	Hospital, medical	Education	Insurance & burial	Year	Total	Compensation	Pensions	Hospital, medical	Education	Insurance & burial
1940 ..	$578	$244	$185	$69	—	$80	2005 ..	$62,206	$30,877	$3,663	$23,073	$3,224	$1,369
1950 ..	8,827	1,533	476	764	$2,739	3,315	2006 ..	63,658	30,991	3,547	24,445	3,325	1,350
1960 ..	5,355	2,049	1,263	931	392	720	2007 ..	69,740	31,055	3,376	30,537	3,427	1,345
1970 ..	8,808	2,980	2,255	1,723	1,002	848	2008 ..	76,113	36,256	3,790	31,096	3,607	1,364
1980 ..	20,927	7,446	3,585	6,290	2,418	1,188	2009 ..	85,501	40,399	4,161	35,264	4,308	1,369
1990 ..	28,545	10,735	3,594	12,021	795	1,400	2010 ..	95,997	43,377	4,359	38,216	8,727	1,318
2000 ..	46,086	20,775	2,969	19,343	1,636	1,363	2011 ..	111,100	52,762	4,664	41,299	11,088	1,287
2001 ..	45,435	18,579	2,760	20,966	1,783	1,347	2012 ..	108,214	50,050	4,537	41,688	10,696	1,243
2002 ..	50,969	22,418	3,166	22,384	1,681	1,320	2013 ..	122,582	59,386	5,173	43,618	13,175	1,230
2003 ..	55,792	24,696	3,229	24,487	2,049	1,331	2014*	133,378	66,300	5,448	46,494	13,731	1,405
2004 ..	55,021	26,297	3,334	21,590	2,408	1,392	2015*	142,419	71,850	5,802	48,950	14,485	1,332

— = Not available. *Estimate. **Note:** Compensation is service-connected; pension is not.

Veterans Health Administration Characteristics, 2002-13
Source: U.S. Dept. of Veterans Affairs

Fiscal year	Total enrollees[1] (mil)	Outpatient visits[2] (mil)	Inpatient admissions (thous.)	Fiscal year	Total enrollees[1] (mil)	Outpatient visits[2] (mil)	Inpatient admissions (thous.)
2002	6.8	46.5	564.7	2008	7.8	67.7	641.4
2003	7.1	49.8	567.3	2009	8.1	74.9	662.0
2004	7.3	54.0	589.8	2010	8.3	80.2	682.3
2005	7.7	57.5	585.8	2011	8.6	79.8	692.1
2006	7.9	59.1	568.9	2012	8.8	83.6	703.5
2007	7.8	62.3	589.0	2013	8.9	86.4	694.7

(1) Includes non-enrolled veteran patients. (2) Includes fee visits.

Employment Status of Veterans With Service-Connected Disabilities, 2013
Source: Bureau of Labor Statistics, U.S. Dept. of Labor; as of Aug. 2013

Veteran status, presence of disability, and period of service	Employed (thous.) Total	Men	Women	Unemployed (thous.) Total	Men	Women	Unemployment rate (%) Total	Men	Women	Not in labor force (thous.) Total	Men	Women
Total veterans	10,139	8,878	1,260	671	566	105	6.2%	6.0%	7.7%	10,550	9,687	863
With service-connected disability	1,379	1,204	175	91	67	24	6.2	5.3	12.2	1,723	1,599	124
Without service-connected disability ..	6,710	5,859	851	473	422	51	6.6	6.7	5.7	6,934	6,422	512
Gulf War era, total	4,428	3,682	746	366	295	71	7.6	7.4	8.7	1,188	858	330
With service-connected disability	2,611	2,160	451	243	209	34	8.5	8.8	7.0	458	329	129
Without service-connected disability ..	2,036	1,664	372	226	183	43	10.0	9.9	10.3	621	432	188
Gulf War era II	2,036	1,664	372	226	183	43	10.0	9.9	10.3	621	432	188
With service-connected disability	533	439	94	50	31	19	8.6	6.6	17.1	244	170	73
Without service-connected disability ..	1,109	892	216	138	124	14	11.1	12.2	6.1	213	142	71
Gulf War era I	2,392	2,018	374	140	111	28	5.5	5.2	7.1	568	426	142
With service-connected disability	403	338	64	17	16	2	4.1	4.4	NA	169	144	25
Without service-connected disability ..	1,502	1,268	234	104	85	20	6.5	6.3	7.8	245	187	58
WWII, Korean War, and Vietnam era ...	2,705	2,614	91	147	139	8	5.1	5.0	7.8	6,906	6,633	273
With service-connected disability	208	202	5	17	17	NA	7.6	7.8	NA	1,116	1,110	7
Without service-connected disability ..	1,924	1,856	68	108	104	4	5.3	5.3	NA	4,684	4,479	205
Other service periods	3,005	2,582	423	158	132	26	5.0	4.9	5.8	2,455	2,196	259
With service-connected disability	236	224	11	7	3	3	2.7	1.4	NA	194	176	18
Without service-connected disability ..	2,175	1,843	332	123	109	14	5.3	5.6	3.9	1,792	1,614	177

NA = Not available. **Note:** Veterans in survey were on active duty in the U.S. Armed Forces during these periods of service: Gulf War era II (Sept. 2001-present), Gulf War era I (Aug. 1990-Aug. 2001), Vietnam era (Aug.1964-Apr. 1975), Korean War (July 1950-Jan. 1955), World War II (Dec. 1941-Dec. 1946), and other service periods. Veterans who served in more than one wartime period are classified in the most recent period only. A service-connected disability is a health condition or impairment caused or made worse by military service.

Nations With Largest Armed Forces, by Active-Duty Troop Strength

Source: *The Military Balance 2014*, International Institute for Strategic Studies, published by Routledge Journals, Taylor & Francis, UK (as of Nov. 2013 except troop strength data, which is as of 2014)

| | | Troop strength | | | | Navy | | Combat aircraft | |
| | | Active troops | Reserve troops | Defense expend. | Tanks (MBT) | Cruisers/ frigates/ destroyers | Sub-marines | (air force only) | |
Rank	Country	(thous.)		(mil)	(army only)			FGA	FTR
1.	China	2,333	510	$112,173	6,840	54F/15D*	70	543+	842
2.	United States	1,492	844	600,400	5,838	22C/13F/62D*	72	823	275
3.	India	1,325	1,155	36,297	2,874+	13F/11D*	14	738	62
4.	North Korea	1,190	600	—	3,500+	3F	72	48	441+
5.	Russia	845	20,000	68,163	2,550	5C/9F/18D*	64	343	580
6.	South Korea	655	4,500	31,846	2,414	3C/13F/6D	23	294	174
7.	Pakistan	644	0	5,890	2,501+	11F	8	174	199
8.	Iran	523	350	17,749	1,663+	0	29	111	184+
9.	Turkey	511	379	10,742	2,504	19F	14	299	53
10.	Vietnam	482	5,000	3,800	1,270	2F	2	97	0
11.	Egypt	439	479	5,278	2,497	8F	4	310	62
12.	Myanmar	406	0	2,400	185+	4F	0	0	89
13.	Indonesia	396	400	8,366	2+	11F	2	16	22
14.	Thailand	361	200	6,213	283	10F*	0	12	79
15.	Brazil	318	1,340	34,730	393	11F/3D*	5	61	57
16.	Taiwan	290	1,657	10,316	565	4C/22F	4	128	288
17.	Colombia	281	62	7,016	0	4F	4	22	0
18.	Iraq	271	0	16,897	336+	0	0	0	0
19.	Mexico	270	87	5,775	0	7F	0	0	10
20.	Japan	247	56	50,977	777	2C/11F/32D*	18	139	201
21.	Sudan	244	0	1,516	445	0	0	0	22
22.	Saudi Arabia	234	0	59,560	600	4F/3D	0	172	81
23.	France	222	30	52,352	254	11F/12D*	10	169	67
24.	South Sudan	210	0	714	110+	0	0	0	0
25.	Eritrea	202	120	78[1]	270	0	0	10	6
26.	Morocco	196	150	3,730	434	5F	0	51	22
27.	Germany	186	40	44,201	322	11F/7D	4	83	101
	Afghanistan	186	0	2,898	0	0	0	0	0
29.	Syria	178	0	—	4,950	0	0	205	70
30.	Israel	177	465	15,163	480	0	3	251	143

— = Not available. * = Navy with aircraft carrier(s), as follows: Brazil 1, China 1, France 1, India 1, Italy 2, Japan 2, Russia 1, Thailand 1, U.S. 10. FGA = Fighter, ground attack. FTR = Fighter. MBT = Main battle tank. (1) As of 2011.

Budget for Global War on Terror Operations, 2001-11

Source: Congressional Research Service, Library of Congress

(in billions of dollars)

	2001/02[1]	2003	2004	2005	2006	2007	2008	2009	2010	2011[2]	Total
Total: All missions	$33.8	$81.1	$94.1	$107.6	$121.5	$170.9	$185.6	$155.1	$165.3	$168.1	$1,283.3
Dept. of Defense.	33.0	77.4	72.4	102.6	116.8	164.9	179.2	148.3	154.3	159.1	1,208.1
Foreign aid and diplomacy[3]	0.8	3.7	21.7	4.8	4.3	5.0	5.4	5.4	9.1	6.5	66.7
Veterans Affairs medical. . . .	0.0	0.0	0.0	0.2	0.4	1.0	1.0	1.5	1.9	2.4	8.4
Op. Iraqi Freedom/New Dawn[4]	0.0	53.0	75.9	85.6	101.7	131.3	142.1	95.5	71.3	49.3	805.5
Dept. of Defense.	0.0	50.0	56.4	83.4	98.1	127.2	138.5	92.0	66.5	45.7	757.8
Foreign aid and diplomacy[3]	0.0	3.0	19.5	2.0	3.2	3.2	2.7	2.2	3.3	2.3	41.4
Veterans Affairs medical. . . .	0.0	0.0	0.0	0.2	0.4	0.9	0.9	1.2	1.5	1.3	6.3
Op. Enduring Freedom[5]	20.8	14.7	14.6	20.0	19.0	39.2	43.4	59.5	93.8	118.6	443.5
Dept. of Defense.	20.0	14.0	12.4	17.2	17.9	37.2	40.6	56.1	87.7	113.3	416.2
Foreign aid and diplomacy[3]	0.8	0.7	2.2	2.8	1.1	1.9	2.7	3.1	5.7	4.1	25.1
Veterans Affairs medical. . . .	0.0	0.0	0.0	0.0	0.0	0.1	0.1	0.2	0.5	1.1	2.1
Op. Noble Eagle[6].	13.0	8.0	3.7	2.1	0.8	0.5	0.1	0.1	0.1	0.1	28.6
Dept. of Defense unallocated	0.0	5.5	0.0	0.0	0.0	0.0	0.0	0.0	0.0	0.0	5.5

(1) Fiscal year (FY) 2001 and FY2002 funds combined because most were obligated in FY2002 after the Sept. 11, 2001, attacks at the end of FY2001, on Sept. 30, 2001. (2) FY2011 Continuing Resolution, signed by Pres. Obama Mar. 18, 2011, extended funding for all agencies through Apr. 8, 2011. (3) Includes monies for reconstruction, development and humanitarian aid, embassy operations, counternarcotics, initial training of the Afghan and Iraqi armies, foreign military sales credits, and Economic Support Funds. (4) Began in fall 2002 with the buildup of troops for the Mar. 2003 invasion of Iraq and continued with counterinsurgency and stability operations. (5) Covers Afghanistan and other ongoing Global War on Terror operations, ranging from the Philippines to Djibouti, that began immediately after the Sept. 11, 2001, attacks. (6) Dept. of Defense funds that rebuilt the Pentagon and provided higher security at U.S. military bases and other homeland security, including combat air patrol.

Leading Purchasers of U.S. Defense Articles and Services

Source: Congressional Research Service, Library of Congress

	Worldwide deliveries, 2004-07						Worldwide deliveries, 2008-11				
Rank	Country	Value	Rank	Country	Value	Rank	Country	Value	Rank	Country	Value
1.	Israel.	$5.7 bil	6.	South Korea . . .	$2.5 bil	1.	Saudi Arabia. . .	$5.9 bil	6.	Iraq	$2.6 bil
2.	Egypt	5.2 bil	7.	Japan	2.4 bil	2.	Egypt	3.9 bil	7.	Japan	2.5 bil
3.	Saudi Arabia . .	4.3 bil	8.	Poland	1.9 bil	3.	Israel.	3.8 bil	8.	South Korea . . .	2.5 bil
4.	Taiwan	4.3 bil	9.	Australia	1.7 bil	4.	Australia	2.9 bil	9.	Greece	2.1 bil
5.	Greece	2.8 bil	10.	UK.	1.6 bil	5.	Taiwan	2.9 bil	10.	Turkey.	2.0 bil

Note: Total dollar value of all U.S. defense articles and services actually delivered to top 10 purchasers worldwide. Figures include government-to-government sales through the Foreign Military Sales system (which accounts for the overwhelming majority of U.S. conventional arms deliveries) concluded in calendar years listed, as well as commercially licensed exports concluded in pertinent fiscal years.

U.S. Foreign Military Financing, 2005-13

Source: Defense Security Cooperation Agency, U.S. Dept. of Defense
(in thousands of U.S. dollars)

	2005	2010	2013		2005	2010	2013
Western Hemisphere	$108,155	$89,720	$54,442	**Europe**	$220,274	$151,696	$100,824
Colombia	99,200	55,000	28,862	Bosnia and			
El Salvador	1,488	1,000	1,709	Herzegovina	8,480	4,000	4,272
Mexico	0	5,250	6,646	Bulgaria	6,944	9,000	7,406
Near East and				Czech Republic	5,952	6,000	4,747
South Asia	4,541,843	4,666,797	4,616,855	Georgia	11,904	16,000	13,672
Afghanistan	396,800	0	0	Macedonia	5,208	4,000	3,418
Bahrain	18,847	19,000	12,575	Poland	76,470	47,000	18,989
Egypt	1,289,600	1,300,000	1,234,259	Romania	13,412	12,999	11,391
Israel	2,202,240	2,775,000	2,943,234	Turkey	33,728	0	0
Jordan	304,352	300,000	284,829	Ukraine	2,976	11,000	6,646
Lebanon	0	0	71,207	**Africa**	49,453	45,370	43,924
Oman	19,840	8,847	7,595	Djibouti	4,468	2,000	949
Pakistan	298,000	248,000	0	Liberia	2,976	6,000	4,421
Yemen	10,420	12,500	18,989	Morocco	15,128	9,000	7,595
East Asia and				Tunisia	10,407	18,000	20,554
Pacific	36,537	59,100	53,316	**World total**	4,956,262	5,015,952	4,874,146
Indonesia	0	20,000	13,292				
Mongolia	2,778	4,500	3,048				
Philippines	29,760	29,000	25,483				

Note: Regional subtotals include countries not listed. Grants extended to foreign governments in a fiscal year to pay for military equipment and services. May be from U.S. Dept. of Defense (DOD) or, for specific countries, negotiated directly with U.S. commercial suppliers with DOD approval.

Defense Contracts, 2013

Source: U.S. Dept. of Defense
(in millions of U.S. dollars)

Listed are the 50 companies or organizations receiving the largest dollar volume of prime contract awards from the U.S. Dept. of Defense during fiscal year 2013 (Oct. 1, 2012-Sept. 30, 2013).

Rank Contractor	Contracts awarded[1]	% of total	Rank Contractor	Contracts awarded[1]	% of total
1. Lockheed Martin Corp.	$37,241.7	12.08%	27. Oshkosh Corp.	$1,728.7	0.56%
2. The Boeing Co.	19,980.1	6.48	28. Hewlett-Packard Co.	1,671.3	0.54
3. Raytheon Co.	12,954.9	4.20	29. CACI International Inc.	1,534.2	0.50
4. General Dynamics Corp.	11,680.4	3.79	30. Sierra Nevada Corp.	1,450.1	0.47
5. Huntington Ingalls Industries Inc.	5,630.7	1.83	31. AmerisourceBergen Corp.	1,416.8	0.46
6. United Technologies Corp.	5,491.0	1.78	32. Harris Corp.	1,351.0	0.44
7. L-3 Communications Holdings Inc.	5,446.4	1.77	33. Refinery Associates of Texas Inc.	1,340.1	0.43
8. BAE Systems PLC	4,753.1	1.54	34. Miscellaneous foreign contractors	1,322.8	0.43
9. Northrop Grumman Corp.	4,693.7	1.52	35. Alliant Techsystems Inc.	1,288.5	0.42
10. SAIC Inc.	4,252.9	1.38	36. United Launch Alliance LLC	1,260.0	0.41
11. Humana Inc.	3,463.0	1.12	37. URS Corp.	1,235.5	0.40
12. Veritas Capital Fund II LP	2,997.4	0.97	38. Honeywell International Inc.	1,226.1	0.40
13. Health Net Inc.	2,907.7	0.94	39. ManTech International Corp.	1,183.2	0.38
14. Textron Inc.	2,712.4	0.88	40. UnitedHealth Group Inc.	1,026.7	0.33
15. Northrop Grumman Corp.	2,595.5	0.84	41. A.P. Moller-Marsk A/S	957.3	0.31
16. Bechtel Group Inc.	2,507.7	0.81	42. Cardinal Health Inc.	956.2	0.31
17. General Electric Co.	2,308.5	0.75	43. National Fuel Inc.	914.5	0.30
18. Northrop Grumman Systems Corp.	2,297.3	0.74	44. Atlantic Diving Supply Inc.	894.3	0.29
19. Fluor Corp.	2,134.2	0.69	45. Rockwell Collins Inc.	879.8	0.29
20. Bell Boeing Joint Project Office	2,096.4	0.68	46. FedEx Corp.	870.1	0.28
21. General Atomic Technologies Corp.	2,093.1	0.68	47. ITT Corp.	855.0	0.28
22. Booz Allen Hamilton Holding Corp.	2,054.6	0.67	48. The Aerospace Corp.	812.8	0.26
23. Supreme Group Holding SARL	2,027.7	0.66	49. Massachusetts Institute of Tech.	808.0	0.26
24. TriWest Healthcare Alliance Corp.	1,819.3	0.59	50. Total S.A.	794.0	0.26
25. Computer Sciences Corp.	1,797.6	0.58	Other	132,575.0	42.80
26. Exelis Inc.	1,729.3	0.56	**Total**	**310,018.7**	

Note: Contractors listed more than once represent different company locations or facilities. Amounts given are as reported by Oct. 1, 2014. Total is sum of all contracts to top 50,000 contractors. (1) Amounts include contracts awarded to subsidiaries of each company.

Arms Transfer Agreements With the World by Supplier, 2004-11

Source: Congressional Research Service, Library of Congress
(in millions of current U.S. dollars)

Supplier	2004	2005	2006	2007	2008	2009	2010	2011	2004-11
United States	$12,368	$12,099	$15,435	$23,691	$36,323	$22,002	$21,103	$66,274	$209,295
Russia	8,800	8,400	15,400	10,400	6,600	13,300	8,800	4,800	76,500
France	2,900	6,300	7,700	2,200	3,800	9,600	1,800	4,400	38,700
United Kingdom	4,200	2,900	4,100	9,500	300	1,400	1,500	400	24,300
China	1,000	2,700	2,000	2,500	2,100	2,500	1,600	2,100	16,500
Germany	4,100	2,000	2,800	1,800	5,500	3,600	100	100	20,000
Italy	400	1,500	1,200	1,400	4,100	1,600	1,900	1,200	13,300
All other European	5,200	7,400	5,600	6,700	5,300	6,500	4,200	3,300	44,200
All others	3,300	1,900	3,400	2,800	3,100	5,000	2,900	2,700	25,100
Total	42,268	45,199	57,635	60,991	67,123	65,502	43,903	85,274	467,895

Note: All data are for the calendar year given except for U.S. MAP (Military Assistance Program), IMET (International Military Education, and Training), and Excess Defense Article data, which are included with the particular fiscal year. All amounts given include the values of all categories of weapons, spare parts, construction, all associated services, military assistance, excess defense articles, and training programs. Statistics for foreign countries are based upon estimated selling prices. All foreign data are rounded to the nearest $100 mil.

Personal Salutes and Honors

The U.S. **national salute**, 21 guns, is also the salute to a national flag. U.S. independence is commemorated by the salute to the Union—one gun for each state—fired at noon July 4, at all military posts provided with suitable artillery.

A 21-gun salute on arrival and departure, with 4 ruffles and flourishes, is rendered to the **president**, to a former president, and to a president-elect. The national anthem or "Hail to the Chief," as appropriate, is played for the president, and the national anthem for the others. A 21-gun salute on arrival and departure, with 4 ruffles and flourishes, also is rendered to the **sovereign or chief of state of a foreign country** or a member of a reigning royal family, and the national anthem of his or her country is played. The music is considered an inseparable part of the salute and immediately follows the ruffles and flourishes without pause. For the Honors March, generals receive the "General's March," admirals receive the "Flag Officer's March," and all others receive the 32-bar medley of "The Stars and Stripes Forever."

GRADE, TITLE, OR OFFICE	SALUTE (IN GUNS) Arriving	SALUTE (IN GUNS) Leaving	Ruffles and flourishes	Music
Vice President of U.S.	19	—	4	Hail, Columbia
Speaker of the House	19	—	4	Honors March
U.S. or foreign ambassador in country to which accredited	19	—	4	Natl. anthem of official
Premier or prime minister	19	—	4	Natl. anthem of official
Secretary of Defense, Army, Navy, or Air Force	19	19	4	Honors March
Other cabinet members, Senate president pro tempore, governor, or chief justice of U.S.	19	—	4	Honors March
Chairman, Joint Chiefs of Staff	19	19	4	Honors March
Army chief of staff, chief of naval operations, Air Force chief of staff, Marine commandant	19	19	4	Honors March
General of the Army, general of the Air Force, fleet admiral	19	19	4	Honors March
Generals, admirals	17	17	4	Honors March
Assistant secretaries of Defense, Army, Navy, or Air Force	17	17	4	Honors March
Chair of a committee of Congress	17	—	4	Honors March

Medal of Honor

Source: Congressional Medal of Honor Society; U.S. Army, U.S. Dept. of Defense
(as of Sept. 4, 2014)

The Medal of Honor is the highest military award for bravery that can be given to any individual in the U.S. The first Army Medals of Honor were awarded on Mar. 25, 1863; the first Navy medals went to sailors and Marines on Apr. 3, 1863.

On Dec. 21, 1861, Pres. Abraham Lincoln signed a bill to create the Navy Medal of Honor. Lincoln, on July 14, 1862, approved a resolution providing for the presentation of Medals of Honor to enlisted men of the Army and Voluntary Forces. The law was amended on Mar. 3, 1863, so that officers as well as enlisted men were eligible.

The Medal of Honor is awarded in the name of Congress to a person who, while a member of the armed forces, distinguishes himself or herself conspicuously by gallantry and intrepidity at the risk of life above and beyond the call of duty while engaged in an action against any enemy of the U.S.; while engaged in military operations involving conflict with an opposing foreign force; or while serving with friendly foreign forces engaged in an armed conflict against an opposing armed force in which the U.S. is not a belligerent party.

The deed performed must have been one of personal bravery or self-sacrifice so conspicuous as to clearly distinguish the individual above his or her comrades and must have involved risk of life. Incontestable proof of the performance of service is required, and each recommendation for award of this decoration is considered on the standard of extraordinary merit.

Prior to World War I, the 2,625 Army Medal of Honor awards up to that time were reviewed to determine which met new stringent criteria. The Army removed 911 names from the list, most of them former members of a Civil War volunteer infantry group who had been induced to extend their enlistments when they were promised the medal. However, the medal was restored to Dr. Mary Walker in 1977 and to Buffalo Bill Cody and seven other Indian scouts in 1989.

Seven African American soldiers were awarded Medals of Honor for service in World War II (six of them posthumously) in Jan. 1997. Previously, no black soldier had received the medal for World War II service; an Army inquiry begun in 1993 concluded that the prevailing political climate and Army practices of the time had prevented proper recognition of heroism on the part of black soldiers in that war. In 1996, Congress authorized a review of Asian American and Pacific Islander recipients of the Distinguished Service Cross whose award should be upgraded. Twenty-two Asian Americans received the Medal of Honor for World War II service in June 2000.

In one of the largest Medal of Honor ceremonies in U.S. history, Pres. Barack Obama Mar. 18, 2014, awarded 24 mostly Hispanic, Jewish, and African-American veterans with the nation's highest military decoration for valor displayed in World War II, the Korean War, and Vietnam. The recipients, three of whom were alive to receive the award, had been found deserving following a congressionally mandated review of the records of service members who may have been overlooked due to discrimination.

Medal of Honor Recipients From Recent Conflicts

Honoree; rank (branch of service)	Date of action	Date of award
Somalia Campaign		
Gordon, Gary I.; Master Sgt. (U.S. Army)*	10/3/1993	5/23/1994
Shughart, Randall D.; Sgt. First Class (U.S. Army)*	10/3/1993	5/23/1994
War in Iraq		
Dunham, Jason L.; Cpl. (USMC)*	4/14/2004	1/11/2007
McGinnis, Ross A.; Pvt. First Class (U.S. Army)*	12/4/2006	6/5/2008
Monsoor, Michael A.; Petty Officer Second Class (U.S. Navy)*	9/29/2006	4/8/2008
Smith, Paul R.; Sgt. First Class (U.S. Army)*	4/4/2003	4/5/2005
War in Afghanistan		
Carpenter, William Kyle; Lance Cpl. (USMC)	11/21/2010	6/19/2014
Carter, Ty M.; Specialist (U.S. Army)	10/3/2009	8/26/2013
Giunta, Salvatore A.; Specialist (U.S. Army)	10/25/2007	11/16/2010
Meyer, Dakota; Sgt. (USMC)	9/8/2009	9/15/2011
Miller, Robert J.; Staff Sgt. (U.S. Army)*	1/25/2008	10/6/2010
Monti, Jared C.; Sgt. First Class (U.S. Army)*	6/21/2006	9/17/2009
Murphy, Michael P.; Lt. (U.S. Navy)*	6/28/2005	10/22/2007
Petry, Leroy A.; Staff Sgt. (U.S. Army)	5/26/2008	7/12/2011
Pitts, Ryan M.; Sgt. (U.S. Army)	7/13/2008	7/21/2014
Romesha, Clinton L.; Staff Sgt. (U.S. Army)	10/3/2009	2/11/2013
Swenson, William D.; Capt. (U.S. Army)	9/8/2009	10/15/2013
White, Kyle J.; Sgt. (U.S. Army)	11/9/2007	5/13/2014

* = Awarded posthumously.

Other Selected Awards

Source: U.S. Army Institute of Heraldry; Navy Department Awards Web Service; Air Force Personnel Center

Distinguished Service Cross

Established by Congress July 9, 1918, on recommendation of Gen. John J. "Black Jack" Pershing, and awarded for extraordinary heroism not justifying the award of a Medal of Honor. The act or acts of heroism must have been so notable and have involved risk of life so extraordinary as to set the individual apart from his or her comrades.

Silver Star

Third-highest military combat honor. An earlier version of this award, the Citation Star, was established by Congress on July 19, 1918, and retroactively awarded to soldiers for "gallantry in action," back to the Spanish-American War. The Silver Star medal replaced the Citation Star in 1932 and is awarded for gallantry in action which, while of a lesser degree than that required for award of the Distinguished Service Cross, must nevertheless have been performed with marked distinction.

Legion of Merit

Established by Congress on July 20, 1942, and awarded to individuals who have distinguished themselves by exceptionally meritorious conduct in the performance of outstanding services. There are different designs depending on the level of command of the award recipient.

Distinguished Flying Cross

Established by Congress July 2, 1926, and awarded for heroism or extraordinary achievement while participating in aerial flight. Awards are made only to recognize single acts of heroism or extraordinary achievement, not sustained operational activities against an armed enemy. Initial awards were given to persons who made record-breaking long-distance and endurance flights or who set altitude records. The first DFC was awarded to Cpt. Charles A. Lindbergh on May 31, 1927. DFCs were awarded retroactively to Orville and Wilbur Wright.

Soldier's Medal

Established by Congress July 2, 1926, to recognize acts of heroism not involving actual conflict with an enemy. The same degree of heroism is required as for the award of the Distinguished Flying Cross. The performance must have involved personal hazard or danger and the voluntary risk of life under conditions not involving conflict with an armed enemy. Awards are not made solely on the basis of having saved a life.

Bronze Star

Established by Executive Order Feb. 4, 1944, largely to raise the morale of ground troops in WWII, on the recommendation of Gen. George C. Marshall. It is awarded to any person who, while serving in any capacity in or with the U.S. military, distinguishes himself or herself by heroic or meritorious achievement or service not involving participation in aerial flight.

Purple Heart

The original Purple Heart, designated as the Badge of Military Merit, was established by Gen. George Washington on Aug. 7, 1782. Following the American Revolution, the badge fell into disuse until 1932, the 200th anniversary of Washington's birth. During WWII, the Order of the Purple Heart was awarded for both wounds received in action and for meritorious service. Following the introduction of the Legion of Merit, the Purple Heart was awarded only for combat wounds. Today, it is awarded to any armed forces member who, while serving with the U.S. Armed Services, has been wounded or killed, or who has died or may hereafter die after being wounded in action against an enemy of the U.S. or in an armed conflict in which the U.S. or friendly foreign forces are engaged; as the result of an act of any hostile foreign force; as a result of an international terrorist attack against the U.S. or a friendly foreign nation; or as a result of military operations outside the U.S. as part of a peacekeeping force. Wounds must be inflicted by weapon fire while directly engaged in armed conflict, regardless of the fire causing the wound, or while held as a prisoner of war or while being taken captive.

Air Medal

Authorized by Pres. Franklin D. Roosevelt on May 11, 1942, and awarded for heroism or meritorious achievement while participating in aerial flight. Awards may be made to recognize single acts of merit or heroism or for meritorious service. Awards are not made to individuals who use air transportation solely for the purpose of moving members from a point in a combat zone.

Army Commendation

Established Dec. 18, 1945, and awarded for heroism, meritorious achievement, or meritorious service. It may also be awarded to a member of the armed forces of a friendly foreign nation who distinguishes him- or herself by an act of heroism, extraordinary achievement, or meritorious service which has been of mutual benefit to a friendly nation and the U.S.

U.S. Military Awards in Selected Wars and Conflicts

Source: U.S. Army Human Resources Command, U.S. Dept. of Defense; Congressional Medal of Honor Society

Award	Civil War	WWI	WWII	Korea	Vietnam	Gulf War	OEF[1]	Iraq[2]
Medal of Honor	1,522	119	474	146	259	0	12	4
Distinguished Service Cross	NA	6,430	4,427	715	840	0	13	15
Silver Star	NA	NA	73,654	10,061	21,634	75	365	355
Legion of Merit	NA	NA	20,273	NA	10,356	158	200	133
Distinguished Flying Cross	NA	NA	126,318	NA	21,697	108	207	118
Soldier's Medal	NA	NA	12,485	581	5,402	43	43	111
Bronze Star (total)[3]	NA	NA	395,380	30,359	719,968	27,967	64,843	111,474
Purple Heart	NA	NA	NA	NA	220,516	504	8,965	22,313
Air Medal (total)[3]	NA	NA	1,166,471	0	1,039,124	6,399	16,188	21,887
Army Commendation (total)[3]	NA	NA	0	0	837,037	81,979	168,672	388,208

NA = Not available or applicable. **Note:** Numbers for the individual decorations shown here represent only those awards that were properly processed and reported to Dept. of the Army Headquarters. The actual number of individual decorations awarded under combat conditions, when award approval authority is delegated to field commanders, cannot be stated with absolute certainty. Numbers here reflect the current statistics recorded by the Military Awards Branch, as of June 30, 2014, except for MOH, which is as reported by the Congressional Medal of Honor Society as of Oct. 1, 2014. (1) Operation Enduring Freedom (primarily Afghanistan). (2) Operation Iraqi Freedom and Operation New Dawn. (3) Includes awards for valor/heroism and for meritorious service or achievement.

Federal Service Academies

U.S. Military Academy, West Point, NY. Founded 1802. Awards BS degree and Army commission for a 5-year service obligation. **Website:** www.usma.edu

U.S. Naval Academy, Annapolis, MD. Founded 1845. Awards BS degree and Navy or Marine Corps commission for a 5-year service obligation. **Website:** www.usna.edu

U.S. Air Force Academy, Colorado Springs, CO. Founded 1954. Awards BS degree and Air Force commission for a 6-year service obligation. **Website:** www.usafa.edu

U.S. Coast Guard Academy, New London, CT. Founded 1876. Awards BS degree and Coast Guard commission for a 5-year service obligation. **Website:** www.cga.edu

U.S. Merchant Marine Academy, Kings Point, NY. Founded 1943. Awards BS degree; a license as a deck, engineer, or dual officer; and a U.S. Naval Reserve commission. Service obligations vary according to options taken by the graduate. **Website:** www.usmma.edu

U.S. Army, Navy, Air Force, Marine Corps, and Coast Guard Insignia

Source: Dept. of the Army, Dept. of the Navy, Dept. of the Air Force, U.S. Dept. of Defense; U.S. Coast Guard, U.S. Dept. of Homeland Security

Army

General of the Armies—Gen. John J. Pershing (1860-1948), the only person to have held this rank while living, was authorized to prescribe his own insignia but never wore in excess of four stars. Congress established the rank in 1799 to be bestowed posthumously on George Washington; Washington was finally promoted to the rank by joint resolution of Congress, approved by Pres. Gerald Ford, Oct. 19, 1976.

General of the Army—Five silver stars fastened together in a circle and the coat of arms of the U.S. in gold color metal with shield and crest enameled. Reserved for wartime use only.

Rank	Insignia
General of the Army*	Five silver stars
General	Four silver stars
Lieutenant General	Three silver stars
Major General	Two silver stars
Brigadier General	One silver star
Colonel	Silver eagle
Lieutenant Colonel	Silver oak leaf
Major	Gold oak leaf
Captain	Two silver bars
First Lieutenant	One silver bar
Second Lieutenant	One gold bar

Warrant Officers

Grade Five—Silver bar with enamel black line.
Grade Four—Silver bar with 4 enamel black squares.
Grade Three—Silver bar with 3 enamel black squares.
Grade Two—Silver bar with 2 enamel black squares.
Grade One—Silver bar with 1 enamel black square.

Noncommissioned Officers

Sergeant Major of the Army (E-9)—Three chevrons above 3 arcs, with a U.S. coat of arms centered on the chevrons, flanked by 2 stars—1 star on each side of the eagle. Also distinctive red-and-white shield collar insignia.

Command Sergeant Major (E-9)—Three chevrons above 3 arcs with a 5-pointed star with a wreath around the star between the chevrons and arcs.

Sergeant Major (E-9)—Three chevrons above 3 arcs with a 5-pointed star between the chevrons and arcs.

First Sergeant (E-8)—Three chevrons above 3 arcs with a lozenge between the chevrons and arcs.

Master Sergeant (E-8)—Three chevrons above 3 arcs.
Sergeant First Class (E-7)—Three chevrons above 2 arcs.
Staff Sergeant (E-6)—Three chevrons above 1 arc.
Sergeant (E-5)—Three chevrons.
Corporal (E-4)—Two chevrons.

Specialists

Specialist (E-4)—Eagle device only.

Other Enlisted

Private First Class (E-3)—One chevron above 1 arc.
Private (E-2)—One chevron.
Private (E-1)—None.
*Rank reserved for wartime use only.

Air Force

Insignia for Air Force officers are identical to those of the Army. Insignia for enlisted personnel are worn on both sleeves and consist of 1 star and an appropriate number of rockers. Chevrons appear above 5 rockers for the top three noncommissioned officer ranks, as follows (in ascending order): Master Sergeant, 1 chevron; Senior Master Sergeant, 2 chevrons; Chief Master Sergeant, 3 chevrons. The insignia of the Chief Master Sergeant of the Air Force has 3 chevrons and a wreath around the star design. General of the Air Force is reserved for wartime use only.

Navy

The following stripes are worn on the lower sleeves of the Service Dress Blue uniform. They are of gold embroidery.

Rank	Insignia
Fleet Admiral*	1 two inch with 4 one-half inch
Admiral	1 two inch with 3 one-half inch
Vice Admiral	1 two inch with 2 one-half inch
Rear Admiral (upper half)	1 two inch with 1 one-half inch
Rear Admiral (lower half)	1 two inch
Captain	4 one-half inch
Commander	3 one-half inch
Lieutenant Commander	2 one-half inch with 1 one-quarter inch between
Lieutenant	2 one-half inch
Lieutenant (jr. grade)	1 one-half inch with 1 one-quarter inch above
Ensign	1 one-half inch
Warrant Officer W-4	½" stripe with 1 break
Warrant Officer W-3	½" stripe with 2 breaks, 2" apart
Warrant Officer W-2	½" stripe with 3 breaks, 2" apart

Enlisted personnel (noncommissioned petty officers)—Rating badge worn on the upper left sleeve consisting of a spread eagle, appropriate number of chevrons, and centered specialty mark.

*Rank reserved for wartime use only.

Marine Corps

Marine Corps' distinctive cap and collar ornament is the Marine Corps emblem—a combination of the American eagle, a globe, and an anchor. Marine Corps and Army officer insignia are similar. Marine Corps enlisted insignia, although basically similar to the Army's, feature crossed rifles beneath the chevrons. Marine Corps enlisted rank insignia are as follows:

Sergeant Major of the Marine Corps (E-9)—Same as Sergeant Major (below) but with Marine Corps emblem in the center with a 5-pointed star on both sides of the emblem.

Sergeant Major (E-9)—Three chevrons above 4 rockers with a 5-pointed star in the center.

Master Gunnery Sergeant (E-9)—Three chevrons above 4 rockers with a bursting bomb insignia in the center.

First Sergeant (E-8)—Three chevrons above 3 rockers with a diamond in the middle.

Master Sergeant (E-8)—Three chevrons above 3 rockers with crossed rifles in the middle.

Gunnery Sergeant (E-7)—Three chevrons above 2 rockers with crossed rifles in the middle.

Staff Sergeant (E-6)—Three chevrons above 1 rocker with crossed rifles in the middle.

Sergeant (E-5)—Three chevrons above crossed rifles.

Corporal (E-4)—Two chevrons above crossed rifles.

Lance Corporal (E-3)—One chevron above crossed rifles.

Private First Class (E-2)—One chevron.

Private (E-1)—None.

Coast Guard

Coast Guard insignia follow Navy custom, with certain minor changes such as the officer cap insignia. The Coast Guard shield is worn on both sleeves of officers and on the right sleeve of all enlisted personnel.

U.S. Armed Forces Contact Information

Additional information on all the U.S. Armed Forces branches, as well as many other related organizations, can be accessed through the official website of the Dept. of Defense: www.defense.gov.

Army—Office of the Chief of Public Affairs, Media Relations Division—MRD, 1500 Army Pentagon, Washington, DC 20310-1500. **Website:** www.army.mil

Navy—Chief of Information, 1200 Navy Pentagon, Washington, DC 20350-1200. **Website:** www.navy.mil

Air Force—Office of Public Affairs, 1690 Air Force Pentagon, Washington, DC 20330-1690. **Website:** www.af.mil

Marine Corps—Marine Corps Headquarters, Division of Public Affairs, 3000 Marine Corps, Pentagon, Washington, DC 20350-3000. **Website:** www.usmc.mil

Coast Guard—Commandant (CG-09222), Attn: Chief of Media Relations, U.S. Coast Guard, 2100 2nd St. SW, Stop 7362, Washington, DC 20593-7362. **Website:** www.uscg.mil

Casualties in Principal Wars of the U.S.

Source: U.S. Dept. of Defense; U.S. Coast Guard, U.S. Dept. of Homeland Security

Data prior to World War I are based on incomplete records in many cases. Casualty data are confined to dead and wounded personnel and, therefore, exclude personnel captured or missing in action who were subsequently returned to military control.

	Branch of service	Number serving	CASUALTIES Battle deaths	Other deaths	Wounds not mortal[1]	Total[2]
Revolutionary War	Total	—	**4,435**	—	**6,188**	**10,623**
1775-83	Army	184,000	4,044	—	6,004	10,048
	Navy	to	342	—	114	456
	Marines	250,000[13]	49	—	70	119
War of 1812	Total	286,730[14]	**2,260**	—	**4,505**	**6,765**
1812-15	Army	—	1,950	—	4,000	5,950
	Navy	—	265	—	439	704
	Marines	—	45	—	66	111
Mexican War	Total	78,718[14]	**1,733**	**11,550**	**4,152**	**17,435**
1846-48	Army	—	1,721	11,550	4,102	17,373
	Navy	—	1	—	3	4
	Marines	—	11	—	47	58
	Coast Guard[8]	71 off.	—	—	—	—
Civil War						
1861-65						
Union forces[3]	Total	**2,213,363**	**140,414**	**224,097**	**281,881**	**646,392**
	Army	2,128,948[14]	138,154	221,374	280,040	639,568
	Navy	84,415	2,112	2,411	1,710	6,233
	Marines	(in Navy total)	148	312	131	591
	Coast Guard[8]	219 off.	1	—	—	1
Confederate forces (estimate)[3]	Total	—	**74,524**	**59,297**	—	**133,821**
	Army	600,000	—	—	—	—
	Navy	to	—	—	—	—
	Marines	1,500,000	—	—	—	—
Spanish-American War	Total	**306,760**	**385**	**2,061**	**1,662**	**4,108**
1898	Army[9]	280,564	369	2,061	1,594	4,024
	Navy	22,875	10	—	47	57
	Marines	3,321	6	—	21	27
	Coast Guard[8]	660	0	—	—	—
World War I	Total	**4,734,991**	**53,402**	**63,114**	**204,002**	**320,518**
Apr. 6, 1917-Nov. 11, 1918	Army[10]	4,057,101	50,510	55,868	193,663	300,041
	Navy	599,051	431	6,856	819	8,106
	Marines	78,839	2,461	390	9,520	12,371
	Coast Guard	8,835	111	81	—	192
World War II[4]	Total	**16,112,566**	**291,557**	**113,842**	**670,846**	**1,076,245**
Dec. 7, 1941-Dec. 31, 1946	Army[11]	11,260,000	234,874	83,400	565,861	884,135
	Navy[12]	4,183,466	36,950	25,664	37,778	100,392
	Marines	669,100	19,733	4,778	67,207	91,718
	Coast Guard	241,093	574	1,343	—	1,917
Korean War[5]	Total	**5,720,000**	**33,739**	**2,835**	**103,284**	**139,858**
June 25, 1950-July 27, 1953	Army	2,834,000	27,731	2,125	77,596	107,452
	Navy	1,177,000	503	154	1,576	2,233
	Marines	424,000	4,267	242	23,744	28,253
	Air Force	1,285,000	1,238	314	368	1,920
	Coast Guard	44,143	—	—	—	—
Vietnam War[6]	Total	**8,744,000**	**47,434**	**10,786**	**153,303**	**211,523**
Aug. 4, 1964-Jan. 27, 1973	Army	4,368,000	30,963	7,261	96,802	135,026
	Navy	1,842,000	1,631	935	4,178	6,744
	Marines	794,000	13,095	1,749	51,392	66,236
	Air Force	1,740,000	1,745	841	931	3,517
	Coast Guard	8,000	7	2	60	69
Persian Gulf War	Total	**2,225,000**	**148**	**235**	**467**	**850**
1991	Army	782,000	98	126	354	578
	Navy	669,000	6	50	12	68
	Marines	213,000	24	44	92	160
	Air Force	561,000	20	15	9	44
	Coast Guard	400	—	—	—	—
Iraq War[7]	Total	**269,363[15]**	**3,520**	**958**	**32,242**	**36,720**
Mar. 19, 2003-Dec. 15, 2011	Army	99,664[15]	2,575	719	22,522	25,816
	Navy	61,018[15]	63	41	642	746
	Marines	66,166[15]	852	171	8,626	9,649
	Air Force	42,515[15]	29	27	452	508
	Coast Guard	1,250[15]	1	—	—	1

— = Not available. Off. = Officers. **Note:** As of Sept. 3, 2014, there have been 1,833 battle deaths, 506 non-hostile deaths, and 19,982 wounded in Op. Enduring Freedom, mostly in Afghanistan and the Persian Gulf area. (1) Marine Corps data for Iraq War, World War II, the Spanish-American War, and prior wars represent the number of individuals wounded, whereas all other data in this column represent the total number (incidence) of wounds. (2) Totals for all branches do not include categories for which no data are listed. (3) From the final report of the Provost Marshal General, 1863-66. Authoritative statistics for the Confederate forces are not available. In addition, an estimated 26,000-31,000 Confederate personnel died in Union prisons. New estimates published in *Civil War History* in 2012 recalculated the death toll for both sides and determined that it was 20% higher than previously thought, at 750,000. (4) Data are for Dec. 1, 1941, through Dec. 31, 1946, when hostilities were officially terminated by presidential proclamation; few battle deaths or wounds not mortal were incurred after Japanese acceptance of Allied peace terms on Aug. 14, 1945. Numbers serving Dec. 1, 1941-Aug. 31, 1945: Total—14,903,213; Army—10,420,000; Navy—3,883,520; Marine Corps—599,693. (5) As a result of an ongoing Dept. of Defense review of available Korean War casualty record information, updates have been made to previously reported figures for battle deaths and other deaths. (6) Number serving Aug. 5, 1964-Jan. 27, 1973 (date of cease-fire). Includes casualties incurred in Mayagüez incident. Wounds not mortal exclude 150,341 persons not requiring hospital care. (7) Military deaths during the invasion phase, which ended Apr. 30, 2003, totaled 115 combat-related and 23 other. (8) Then known as the U.S. Revenue Cutter Services, predecessor to the U.S. Coast Guard. (9) Number serving Apr. 21-Aug. 13, 1898, while dead and wounded data are for May 1-Aug. 31, 1898. Active hostilities ceased on Aug. 13, 1898, but the U.S. and Spain did not exchange ratifications of the treaty of peace until Apr. 11, 1899. (10) Includes Army Air Forces battle deaths and wounds not mortal, as well as casualties suffered by American forces in northern Russia to Aug. 25, 1919, and in Siberia to Apr. 1, 1920. Other deaths cover Apr. 1, 1917-Dec. 31, 1918. (11) Includes Army Air Forces. (12) Battle deaths and wounds not mortal include casualties incurred in Oct. 1941 due to hostile action. (13) Estimated. (14) As reported by Commissioner of Pensions in his Annual Report for Fiscal Year 1903. (15) Number serving as of Mar. 31, 2003, i.e., does not include numbers of troops deployed since then.

Timeline of Major Wars Since 1066

Norman Conquest
1066-71
William I, duke of Normandy, landed on the English coast near Hastings on Sept. 28, 1066, and defeated Harold II, Saxon king of England, at Battle of Hastings Oct. 14. William crowned king Dec. 25 in Westminster Abbey. Most revolts were suppressed by 1071. **Conquest linked England's interests with those of the continent and led to its rise as a powerful monarchy.**

Crusades
1095-1270/1291
Military expeditions undertaken by **Western European Christians**, usually at the behest of the **papacy**, to recover **Jerusalem** and other Biblical places of pilgrimage from **Muslim** control. In the long term, stimulated trade and flow of ideas between East and West. Pope Urban II called Nov. 27, 1095, for the **First Crusade**; Crusaders took Jerusalem on July 15, 1099, massacred inhabitants, and founded four temporary states: Antioch, Edessa, Jerusalem, and Tripoli. The failed **Second Crusade** was prompted by Muslims' capture of Edessa in 1144. Jerusalem was captured by Ayyubid sultan Saladin on Oct. 2, 1187, leading to the **Third Crusade**, which involved the Holy Roman emperor, Frederick I (Barbarossa); the French king, Philip II (Augustus); and the English king, Richard I (Lion-Heart) but did not lead to a Crusader victory. The **Fourth Crusade** sacked Constantinople on Apr. 13, 1204. The **Fifth Crusade** began with capture of Damietta in Egypt (1219) but failed at Cairo. A **Sixth Crusade** led to the Treaty of Jaffa in 1229, giving Jerusalem to the Crusaders until 1244, when its seizure by the Khwarezmians led to the launch of a **Seventh Crusade**. The last crusade abruptly ended when its leader, French King Louis IX, died in 1270. The last major Crusader stronghold, Acre, was lost on May 18, 1291.

Hundred Years War
1337-1453
Series of armed conflicts over rival claims to the French throne, broken by a number of truces and peace treaties. Edward III declared self king of France in 1338 and invaded, with victories at Crécy (1346) and Poitiers (1356). **Treaty of Brétigny** signed May 8, 1360, but French king Charles V renewed fighting in 1369. Truce from 1396 until **Henry V** of England invaded in 1415 and **defeated French army at Agincourt**, capturing land north of Loire River, including Paris. Treaty of Troyes in 1420 made Henry VI heir of both thrones. The siege of French stronghold Orléans, lifted in 1429 with help from **Joan of Arc**, turned tide in favor of French, who won last battle (1453). **War ended English claims to France, paved way for French absolute monarchy.**

Wars of the Roses
1455-85
Series of dynastic civil wars for the throne in England fought by the **rival houses of Lancaster and York**. Richard, third duke of York, in conflict with the Lancastrian King **Henry VI**, won victories at St. Albans (1455) and Northampton (1460); Richard died at battle of Wakefield on Dec. 30, 1460, before coronation, leaving his son to become King Edward IV. Henry VI imprisoned in Tower of London, 1465. Edward died in 1483; his brother became **Richard III** after usurping throne from Edward V, nephew. Henry Tudor defeated Richard III at the Battle of Bosworth Field (1485). As Henry VII, he married Edward IV's daughter Elizabeth, 1486, **uniting the houses.**

Thirty Years' War
1618-48
A series of religious and political conflicts involving **most countries of Western Europe**; majority of fighting in Germany, devastating it. Protestants stormed Hapsburg palace in the "Defenestration of Prague" (May 23, 1618). Major conflicts included defeat of King Christian IV of Denmark and Norway by Catholic League (1626); victories by Lutheran King Gustav II Adolph of Sweden at Breitenfeld (1631) and Lützen (1632). France, under cardinal and statesman **Richelieu**, chief minister of King Louis XIII, declared war on the Hapsburgs in May 1635; defeated Austro-Bavarian army (Aug. 3, 1645), leading to Truce of Ulm. **Peace of Westphalia** signed at Münster on Oct. 24, 1648, bringing peace by recognizing the rulers' sovereignty within their lands and their right to determine the religious beliefs of their subjects.

English Civil Wars
1638-60
Series of conflicts between followers of King Charles I (Cavaliers) and of Parliament (Roundheads), over divine right of king versus Parliament's right to control national finances. Presbyterian Scots, allied with Parliament, rioted and in 1640 occupied the northern counties of England. **Oliver Cromwell**, second in command of Parliament's New Model Army, destroyed the king's army at Battle of Naseby (June 14, 1645); first civil war ended May 1646 when Charles surrendered to the Scots. Charles later allied with Scots but was defeated by Cromwell at Preston Aug. 17-19, 1648, and executed Jan. 30, 1649. Parliament abolished monarchy and House of Lords. Cromwell suppressed Irish and Scottish rebellions, was briefly succeeded by son Richard after death (1658). **Charles II restored to the throne** by the "Long Parliament," May 1660.

War of the Spanish Succession
1701-14
War fought by the Grand Alliance (originally England, Netherlands, Denmark, and Austria; later also Portugal), against coalition of France, Spain, and a number of small Italian and German principalities to preserve balance of power after death of Spanish king Charles II. Opened with invasion of Italy, via Venice, by an Austrian army under Prince Eugène of Savoy in May 1701. French forced to withdraw from Netherlands and Italy in 1706 and were finally defeated in 1709 in bloodiest battle of the war at French village of Malplaquet. Treaty of Rastatt and Baden signed in 1714; **Austria given control of Spanish Netherlands, and peace settled between Austria and France.**

War of the Austrian Succession
1740-48
Conflict over rival claims for the **hereditary dominions of the Habsburg family**, following death (1740) of Charles VI, Holy Roman emperor and archduke of Austria. An alliance of Bavaria, France, Spain, Sardinia, Prussia, and Saxony fought against Austria, allied with Holland and Great Britain. King Frederick the Great of Prussia captured Silesia from Austria in the First (1740-42) and Second (1744-45) Silesian Wars. British king George II defeated French army at Battle of Dettingen am Main (June 27, 1743). French conquered Austrian Netherlands (1745-46). Treaty of Aix-la-Chapelle Oct. 18, 1748, **restored most original borders; Prussia became significant force.**

Seven Years' War
1756-63
Worldwide conflicts fought for **control of Germany** and for **supremacy in colonial N America and India**. French defeated British Gen. Edward Braddock in Battle of Monongahela in 1754, leading to formal declaration of **French-Indian War**, May 1756. Frederick II of Prussia invaded Saxony on Aug. 29, 1756; defeated French at Rossbach (1757), Austrians at Leuthen (1757), Russians at Zorndorf (1758). By 1760, British conquered French Canada. Peter III of Russia signed armistice with Prussia, 1762. Treaty of Paris signed Feb. 10, 1763; Peace of Hubertusburg Feb. 15, 1763, between Prussia and Austria. **England emerged as leading world naval power.**

American Revolution
1775-83
Conflict between Great Britain and 13 British colonies in eastern N America. George Washington took command of the Continental Army, July 2, 1775, and King George III declared colonies traitors on Aug. 23. **Declaration of Independence of colonies adopted July 4, 1776**. France recognized the colonies' independence Feb. 6, 1778, followed by Spain on June 21, 1779; both pledged support. French fleet drove British fleet under Adm. Thomas Graves from Chesapeake Bay on Sept. 5, 1781. French and Americans laid siege to Yorktown, VA, Sept. 28-Oct. 19, forcing British Gen. Cornwallis to surrender. **Treaty of Paris** (Sept. 3, 1783) recognized U.S. independence.

Wars of French Revolution and Napoleonic Wars
1792-1815
Large-scale wars fought between France and two multinational coalitions. France declared war on the Austrian part of the Holy Roman Empire, Apr. 20, 1792. Newly created French Republic declared war on monarchs of Britain and Holland, Feb. 1, 1793, and Spain, Mar. 7. **Napoleon Bonaparte** defeated Austria in N Italy (1796-97), captured Egypt from Britain (1798-99; Battle of the Pyramids, July 21, 1798), and became First Consul after coup d'état of Nov. 9-10, 1799. French Grande Armée later swept through Europe using innovative and aggressive tactics. French navy defeated by British under Adm. Horatio Nelson at **Trafalgar** (Oct. 21, 1805), but Napoleon defeated Austro-Russian forces at Austerlitz (Dec. 2) and controlled most of Europe except Russia and Great Britain by 1808. France suffered its first major defeat by Austria at Aspern-Essling, May 21-22, 1809. **Napoleon invaded Russia**, captured Moscow Sept. 14, 1812, but fled the bitter Russian winter and abandoned Germany after defeat at Leipzig, Oct. 16-19, 1813. Paris captured by Allied armies Mar. 30-31, 1814. Napoleon exiled to Elba May 4 but returned for "Hundred Days" reign, Mar. 20-June 28, 1815; **final defeat at Waterloo** by British and Prussian troops (June 18). The **Bourbon monarchy was restored under Louis XVIII**, and Britain, Prussia, Russia, and Austria maintained European peace.

Crimean War
1853-56

Conflict between **Russia** and coalition of **Great Britain, France, Sardinia, and Turkey for influence over Balkans** and the straits between the Black Sea and Mediterranean. Russia destroyed Turkish fleet at Sinope on Nov. 30, 1853. Britain and France declared war in Mar. 1854 and with Turkish troops defeated Russians at Battle of Alma River, Sept. 20. Lord Lucan of Britain prevented Russia from capturing Balaklava on Oct. 25 ("Charge of the Light Brigade" led by Lord Cardigan). Siege of Sevastopol ended when Russia evacuated Sept. 8, 1855. Treaty of Paris signed Mar. 30, 1856; **curbed Russian expansion and loosened European power alignments.**

American Civil War
1861-65

Conflict between the U.S. (the Union) and 11 secessionist Southern states, organized as the Confederate States of America. Union garrison at Fort Sumter in harbor of Charleston, SC, surrendered to Brig. Gen. Pierre Beauregard (Apr. 12-13, 1861). 22,000 Confederates under Beauregard repelled 35,000 Union troops under Gen. Irvin McDowell along Bull Run stream near Manassas, VA (July 21). The *Merrimack* (renamed the *Virginia*) battled the *Monitor* Mar. 9, 1862. In **Battle of Antietam** (Sept. 17), some 12,000 Northerners and 12,700 Southerners were killed or wounded. Pres. Abraham Lincoln announced **Emancipation Proclamation** on Sept. 22. Confederate Gen. Robert E. Lee's forces numbering 75,000 battled 88,000 Union troops under Gen. George Meade at **Gettysburg** July 1-3, 1863; Lee's army forced back across the Potomac River. Lee surrendered to Ulysses S. Grant at **Appomattox Court House** (Apr. 9, 1865). **The Union was preserved and slavery abolished.**

Franco-Prussian War
1870-71

German states led by Prussia defeated France, seizing Alsace and part of Lorraine. French defeated in several major battles, culminating at **Sedan** Sept. 1, 1870, when Prussian forces decisively defeated the French army and captured emperor Napoleon III. Prussian king crowned William I, emperor of unified Germany, Jan 18, 1871. **France surrendered** Jan. 28. Final treaty signed May 10; set the stage for later **German imperialistic expansion.**

Spanish-American War
1898

War waged by the U.S. to **liberate Cuba from Spanish rule**. A mysterious explosion, blamed on Spain by American newspapers, sank the U.S. battleship *Maine* in Havana's harbor (Feb. 15, 1898), killing 260. The U.S. called for Spain's withdrawal from Cuba, and Spain declared war (Apr. 24). Rufus Shafter led 17,000 U.S. troops from Daiquirí to Santiago de Cuba, taking **San Juan Hill** with help of the Rough Riders under Teddy Roosevelt. Santiago de Cuba surrendered July 17. The Treaty of Paris (Dec. 10, 1898) provided for the **independence of Cuba** and the cession by Spain to the U.S. of **Puerto Rico, Guam, and for a $20 mil payment, the Philippine Islands.**

World War I
1914-18

Local European war that grew into a global war involving 32 nations: the Allies and the Associated Powers—28 nations including Great Britain, France, Russia, Italy, and the U.S.—versus the Central Powers of Germany, Austria-Hungary, Turkey, and Bulgaria. Archduke Francis Ferdinand of Austria assassinated in Sarajevo, Bosnia (June 28, 1914). Germany invaded France through Belgium; advance on Paris halted by the French under Gen. Joseph Jacques Césaire Joffre at the **First Battle of the Marne**, Sept. 5-12. Germany checked the Russian army at the Battle of Tannenberg, Aug. 26-30. The British suffered 57,470 casualties (19,240 dead) in the opening day of the **First Battle of the Somme** (July 1-Nov. 18, 1916), first of 12 battles that forced Germany back to Hindenburg Line. **U.S. declared war on Germany Apr. 6, 1917.** Russian involvement ended when Bolshevik party seized power on Nov. 7; signed armistice Dec. 15. German offensive halted by U.S. and French troops at **Second Battle of the Marne** (July 15-Aug. 5, 1918), turning point of the war. Allied counteroffensive broke the Hindenburg Line, and an armistice was signed Nov. 11.

World War II
1939-45

Global military conflict stemming from European unrest after World War I and Japan's aggressive expansion into Asia and the Pacific. **War in Europe:** Nazi-Soviet nonaggression pact (Aug. 23, 1939) freed Germany and the Soviet Union to attack Poland in Sept. **Britain and France declared war on Germany** Sept. 3. German forces raced through Europe (Apr.-June 1940), captured Paris June 14. **Italy declared war on France and Britain** June 10. German-Italian campaigns won the Balkans and N Africa by June 1941. U.S. entered war Dec. 1941. Three million Axis troops invaded Russia June 22, 1941, but Russian counterthrusts stopped the German advance (**Stalingrad**, Aug. 20, 1942-Feb. 2, 1943), and Allies took N Africa (Nov. 8, 1942-May 13, 1943), Italy (July 10, 1943-May 2, 1945). Normandy invaded on **D-Day**, June 6, 1944; Paris liberated Aug. 25. Leaders at Yalta Conference (Feb. 4-11, 1945) discussed defeat and division of Germany into four. Adolf Hitler committed suicide Apr. 30. **Germany surrendered unconditionally** May 7. **War in the Pacific:** Japan invaded China (July 7, 1937), joined alliance with Germany and Italy (Sept. 27, 1940), and signed nonaggression pact with Russia (Apr. 13, 1941); attacked Hawaii's Pearl Harbor, Dec. 7, 1941; U.S. declared war on Japan Dec. 8. **Battle of Midway** (June 4-7, 1942) repulsed Japanese advance. Marines landed on Guadalcanal Aug. 7. Navy defeated Japanese fleet at **Leyte Gulf**, Oct. 23-26, 1944. B-29 bombing raids on Japan began in Nov. Marines invaded Iwo Jima (Feb. 19-Mar. 16, 1945) with heavy casualties, then Okinawa (Apr. 1-June 21). **U.S. atom bombs dropped** on Hiroshima (Aug. 6) and Nagasaki (Aug. 9) and Soviet invasion of Manchuria (Aug. 8) **forced Japan to agree, on Aug. 14, to surrender;** formal surrender on Sept. 2.

Korean War
1950-53

Military struggle fought on the Korean Peninsula between the Democratic Peoples' Republic of Korea (N Korea) and the Republic of Korea (S Korea) that developed into an international war involving China allied with N Korea against the U.S. and other nations under the UN flag. DPRK army crossed the 38th parallel and invaded S Korea (June 25, 1950), entering Seoul (June 26). Amphibious assault launched at **Inchon** by Gen. Douglas MacArthur (Sept. 15) helped U.S. forces rout DPRK close to Yalu River by Nov. 24. Chinese counterattack retook Seoul (Jan. 4, 1951) but were forced back to the 38th parallel by Apr. 22. Armistice was signed (July 27, 1953) by the UN, DPRK, and China, but not ROK, **leaving the peninsula partitioned at about the 38th parallel.**

Vietnam War
1959-75

Struggle primarily in S Vietnam that widened into a war between S Vietnam supported mainly by the U.S. and N Vietnam supported by the USSR and China. Viet Minh, led by Communist leader Ho Chi Minh, formed the Democratic Republic of Vietnam (Sept. 2, 1945). Colonial power France withdrew after fortress at Dien Bien Phu fell (May 8, 1954). Pres. John F. Kennedy pledged U.S. commitment to S Vietnamese independence Dec. 14, 1961. USS *Maddox* destroyer damaged in **Gulf of Tonkin** (Aug. 2, 1964), prompting Congress to increase involvement. Regular bombing of N Vietnam began (Feb. 24, 1965), and the first U.S. combat ground forces arrived (Mar. 6). N Vietnamese Army siege of **Khe Sanh** (Jan. 21-Apr. 7, 1968) and the **"Tet" offensive** (Jan. 30) aimed to cause insurrection in the S. **My Lai Massacre** by U.S. soldiers of civilians (Mar. 16, 1968) created scandal, fueled U.S. disaffection with war. U.S. forces peaked at 543,400 in Apr. 1969. NVA **"Easter Offensive"** (Mar. 30, 1972) rebuffed, and U.S. responded with aerial bombings in May and Dec. U.S. withdrew after ceasefire, Jan. 1973. **NVA offensive captured Saigon, Apr. 30, 1975, and unified Vietnam under Communist rule.**

Persian Gulf Wars
1991, 2003-10

Conflicts fought principally between Iraq and the U.S. concerning Iraq's influence in the Middle East and its development of weapons of mass destruction. **First Gulf War:** Iraq under dictator Saddam Hussein invaded Kuwait Aug 2, 1990, and annexed it; UN Security Council ordered Iraqi forces to withdraw by Jan. 15, 1991. Beginning Jan. 17, a U.S.-led multinational force (**Operation Desert Storm**) bombed military targets in Iraq and Kuwait. A coordinated air-land offensive (**Operation Desert Sabre**, begun Feb. 24) retook Kuwait City Feb. 26, and permanent ceasefire was signed on Apr. 6. Iraq was ordered to pay reparations to Kuwait, reveal locations of biological and chemical weapons, and eliminate weapons of mass destruction. **Second Gulf War:** The U.S. and UK mistakenly claimed that Iraq was still producing WMDs and posed an imminent threat. The UN passed Resolution 1441, Nov. 8, 2002, warning Iraq of "serious consequences" if it failed to cooperate fully and unconditionally with UN weapons inspectors. Iraq rejected a Mar. 17, 2003, U.S. ultimatum demanding Hussein and his sons leave Iraq. U.S. launched **Operation Iraqi Freedom** Mar. 19, 2003, with support from UK and other allies, but without full UN Security Council support. Baghdad fell Apr. 9, and major combat operations declared over May 1. Hussein was captured Dec. 13, 2003, but guerrilla opposition to U.S. troops and insurgent violence continued. U.S. combat operations in Iraq formally ended Aug. 31, 2010.

HEALTH

U.S. Health Expenditures, 1960-2011

Source: *Health, United States, 2013*, National Center for Health Statistics, Centers for Disease Control and Prevention

	1960	1970	1980	1990	2000	2005	2010	2011
					Amount in billions			
National health expenditures	$27.4	$74.9	$255.8	$724.3	$1,377.2	$2,030.5	$2,600.0	$2,700.7
					Percent distribution			
Health consumption expenditures	90.6%	89.6%	92.1%	93.3%	93.6%	93.8%	94.3%	94.3%
Personal health care	85.4	84.3	84.9	85.2	84.6	83.6	84.2	84.4
Hospital care	32.8	36.3	39.3	34.6	30.2	30.0	31.4	31.5
Professional services	29.3	26.4	25.3	28.7	28.3	27.4	26.7	26.8
Physician and clinical services	20.6	19.1	18.7	21.9	21.1	20.5	20.0	20.0
Other professional services	1.4	1.0	1.4	2.4	2.7	2.6	2.7	2.7
Dental services	7.3	6.3	5.2	4.4	4.5	4.3	4.0	4.0
Other personal care	1.6	1.8	3.3	3.4	4.7	4.8	4.9	4.9
Home health care[1]	0.2	0.3	0.9	1.7	2.4	2.4	2.7	2.8
Nursing care facilities and retirement communities[1]	3.0	5.4	6.0	6.2	6.2	5.5	5.5	5.5
Retail outlet sales of medical products	18.4	14.1	10.1	10.6	12.9	13.5	13.0	12.9
Prescription drugs	9.8	7.3	4.7	5.6	8.8	10.1	9.8	9.7
Durable medical equipment	2.7	2.3	1.6	1.9	1.8	1.5	1.4	1.4
Nondurable medical products	5.9	4.4	3.8	3.1	2.3	1.8	1.7	1.7
Government administration	0.2	1.0	1.1	1.0	1.2	1.4	1.2	1.2
Net cost of health insurance	3.7	2.5	3.6	4.4	4.7	6.0	5.8	5.8
Government public health activities[2]	1.4	1.8	2.5	2.8	3.1	2.8	3.1	2.9
Investment	9.4	10.4	7.9	6.7	6.4	6.2	5.7	5.7
Research[3]	2.5	2.6	2.1	1.8	1.8	2.0	1.9	1.8
Structures and equipment	6.8	7.8	5.7	5.0	4.5	4.2	3.9	3.8
					Average annual percent change from previous year shown			
National health expenditures	—	10.6%	13.1%	11.0%	6.6%	8.1%	5.1%	3.9%
Health consumption expenditures	—	10.5	13.4	11.1	6.7	8.1	5.2	3.9
Personal health care	—	10.4	13.2	11.0	6.6	7.8	5.2	4.1
Hospital care	—	11.7	14.0	9.6	5.2	8.0	6.0	4.3
Professional services	—	9.5	12.6	12.4	6.5	7.4	4.5	4.2
Physician and clinical services	—	9.8	12.8	12.8	6.2	7.5	4.5	4.3
Other professional services	—	6.4	17.0	17.5	7.8	7.3	5.8	4.9
Dental services	—	9.0	11.0	9.0	7.0	6.9	3.9	3.0
Other personal care	—	11.4	20.4	11.1	10.3	8.4	5.8	4.0
Home health care[1]	—	14.5	26.9	18.1	9.9	8.5	7.9	4.5
Nursing care facilities and retirement communities[1]	—	17.4	14.2	11.4	6.6	5.7	4.9	4.4
Retail outlet sales of medical products	—	7.7	9.4	11.4	8.8	9.0	4.3	3.3
Prescription drugs	—	7.5	8.2	12.8	11.6	11.1	4.5	2.9
Durable medical equipment	—	9.0	8.8	13.0	6.2	4.4	3.4	5.3
Nondurable medical products	—	7.4	11.4	8.6	3.5	3.4	4.0	4.0
Government administration	—	29.9	14.1	10.0	9.1	10.6	1.9	4.7
Net cost of health insurance	—	6.4	17.3	13.1	7.3	13.8	4.2	4.0
Government public health activities[2]	—	13.8	16.9	12.0	8.0	5.4	7.2	-0.5
Investment	—	11.7	10.0	9.2	6.0	7.6	3.3	2.9
Research[3]	—	10.9	10.8	8.9	7.2	9.6	4.0	1.7
Structures and equipment	—	12.0	9.7	9.4	5.6	6.8	3.0	3.6

— = Not applicable. **Note:** Numbers may not add up to totals because of rounding. (1) Freestanding facilities only. Additional services of this type provided in hospital-based facilities are counted as hospital care. (2) Includes personal care services delivered by government public health agencies. (3) Excludes research and development expenditures of drug companies and other mfrs. and providers of medical equipment and supplies. They are included in the consumption expenditure class in which a product falls.

Health Coverage for Persons Under 65, 1984-2012

Source: *Health, United States, 2013*, National Center for Health Statistics, Centers for Disease Control and Prevention

	Private insurance				Medicaid[1]				Not covered[2]			
	1984[3]	1995[3]	2000	2012	1984[3]	1995[3]	2000	2012	1984[3]	1995[3]	2000	2012
					Percent of each population group							
Total	76.8%	71.3%	71.5%	61.8%	6.8%	11.5%	9.5%	18.0%	14.5%	16.1%	17.0%	16.9%
Age												
Under 18 years	72.6	65.2	66.6	53.4	11.9	21.5	19.6	38.9	13.9	13.4	12.6	6.6
18-44 years	76.5	70.9	70.5	61.4	5.1	7.8	5.6	11.6	17.1	20.4	22.4	24.8
45-64 years	83.3	80.1	78.7	70.0	3.4	5.6	4.5	8.0	9.6	10.9	12.6	15.6
Race and Hispanic origin[4]												
White, non-Hispanic	82.4	78.6	79.5	72.6	3.7	7.1	6.1	11.5	11.9	13.0	12.5	12.7
Black, non-Hispanic	58.2	53.4	56.0	46.4	20.7	28.1	21.0	31.3	19.7	17.9	19.5	17.8
Hispanic, any race	55.7	46.4	47.8	36.7	13.3	21.9	15.5	30.5	29.5	31.4	35.6	30.4
Percent of poverty level												
Below 100%	32.2	22.6	25.2	16.5	33.0	48.4	38.4	52.5	33.9	29.6	34.2	28.2
100%-199%	70.3	55.3	50.1	36.7	5.3	14.4	16.2	30.1	21.8	28.3	31.0	29.3
200%-399%	89.3	86.4	78.1	71.3	0.8	2.3	4.0	9.0	7.6	10.0	15.4	16.2
400% or more	95.4	93.2	91.9	90.6	0.2	0.4	0.9	1.7	3.2	5.4	5.9	4.9
Geographic region												
Northeast	80.5	75.4	76.3	67.2	8.6	11.7	10.6	19.3	10.2	13.3	12.2	11.5
Midwest	80.6	77.3	78.8	68.4	7.4	10.5	8.0	16.3	11.3	12.2	12.3	13.6
South	74.3	66.9	66.8	57.3	5.1	11.3	9.4	17.8	17.7	19.4	20.5	20.3
West	71.9	67.5	66.5	58.5	7.0	12.9	10.4	19.1	18.2	17.9	20.7	19.0

Note: Data based on household interviews of a sample of the civilian noninstitutionalized population. Percents may not add up to 100 because other types of health insurance (e.g., Medicare, military) are not shown, and persons with both private insurance and Medicaid appear in both sections. (1) Includes Medicaid and other public assistance. (2) Includes persons not covered by private insurance, Medicaid or other public assistance, Medicare, or military plans. (3) A change in the questionnaire in 1997 prevents direct comparison with later years. (4) Changed reporting methods make race data before 1999 not strictly comparable with those from 1999 on.

Spending on Health in the 50 Most Populous Countries, 2011

Source: *World Health Statistics 2014*, World Health Organization

Country	As % of GDP	Per capita[1]	Country	As % of GDP	Per capita[1]	Country	As % of GDP	Per capita[1]	Country	As % of GDP	Per capita[1]
Afghanistan...	8.4%	$48	Germany.....	11.3%	$4,996	Mozambique..	6.4%	$33	Sudan.......	6.7%	$119
Algeria	4.4	233	Ghana......	5.3	83	Myanmar			Tanzania.....	7.4	38
Argentina ...	7.9	866	India.......	3.9	62	(Burma)....	1.8	19	Thailand	4.1	214
Australia	9.0	5,991	Indonesia ...	2.9	99	Nepal	6.1	41	Turkey.......	6.1	644
Bangladesh...	3.8	27	Iran........	4.6	326	Nigeria	5.7	85	Uganda......	9.3	41
Brazil.......	8.9	1,119	Iraq[2]......	2.7	160	Pakistan	3.0	36	Ukraine.....	7.3	262
Canada.....	10.9	5,656	Italy........	9.2	3,339	Peru	4.7	283	UK..........	9.4	3,659
China	5.1	274	Japan.......	10.0	4,656	Philippines ...	4.4	105	U.S.........	17.7	8,467
Colombia	6.5	466	Kenya	4.4	35	Poland.......	6.9	920	Uzbekistan ..	5.6	91
Congo, Dem.			Korea, South..	7.4	1,652	Russia.......	6.1	803	Venezuela....	4.5	487
Rep. of the..	6.1	15	Malaysia	3.8	384	Saudi Arabia..	3.5	721	Vietnam	6.8	93
Egypt	4.9	137	Mexico	6.0	609	South Africa..	8.7	670	Yemen.......	5.0	63
Ethiopia.....	4.1	14	Morocco	6.3	195	Spain	9.3	2,978	World[3]	9.1	1,007
France......	11.6	4,968									

(1) At average exchange rate. (2) Not including expenditures for Northern Iraq. (3) Includes other nations not shown.

Population Not Covered by Health Insurance by State, 1990-2013

Source: American Community Survey, U.S. Census Bureau, U.S. Dept. of Commerce

(numbers in thousands)

	1990 No. not covered	1990 % pop. not covered	2000 No. not covered	2000 % pop. not covered	2013 No. not covered	2013 % pop. not covered		1990 No. not covered	1990 % pop. not covered	2000 No. not covered	2000 % pop. not covered	2013 No. not covered	2013 % pop. not covered
AL	710	17.4%	557	12.7%	645	13.6%	MT	115	14.0%	146	16.4%	165	16.5%
AK	77	15.4	114	18.3	132	18.5	NE	138	8.5	140	8.3	209	11.3
AZ	547	15.5	834	16.0	1,118	17.1	NV	201	16.5	336	16.4	570	20.7
AR	421	17.4	367	13.8	465	16.0	NH	107	9.9	99	8.0	140	10.7
CA	5,683	19.1	6,154	18.1	6,500	17.2	NJ	773	10.0	985	11.7	1,160	13.2
CO	495	14.7	598	13.8	729	14.1	NM	339	22.2	426	23.7	382	18.6
CT	226	6.9	313	9.3	333	9.4	NY	2,176	12.1	3,001	16.0	2,070	10.7
DE	96	13.9	69	8.9	83	9.1	NC	883	13.8	1,046	13.1	1,509	15.6
DC	109	19.2	75	13.6	42	6.7	ND	40	6.3	66	10.7	73	10.4
FL	2,376	18.0	2,727	17.0	3,853	20.0	OH	1,123	10.3	1,191	10.7	1,258	11.0
GA	971	15.3	1,145	14.1	1,846	18.8	OK	574	18.6	624	18.4	666	17.7
HI	81	7.3	110	9.1	91	6.7	OR	360	12.4	417	12.2	571	14.7
ID	159	15.2	194	15.0	257	16.2	PA	1,218	10.1	963	8.0	1,222	9.7
IL	1,272	10.9	1,632	13.3	1,618	12.7	RI	105	11.1	74	7.1	120	11.6
IN	587	10.7	650	10.8	903	14.0	SC	550	16.2	473	11.9	739	15.8
IA	225	8.1	239	8.4	248	8.1	SD	81	11.6	77	10.5	93	11.3
KS	272	10.8	274	10.3	348	12.3	TN	673	13.7	585	10.4	887	13.9
KY	480	13.2	521	13.0	616	14.3	TX	3,569	21.1	4,650	22.4	5,748	22.1
LA	797	19.7	755	17.3	751	16.6	UT	156	9.0	259	11.5	402	14.0
ME	139	11.2	135	10.6	147	11.2	VT	54	9.5	50	8.3	45	7.2
MD	601	12.7	511	9.7	593	10.2	VA	996	15.7	747	10.7	991	12.3
MA	530	9.1	527	8.4	247	3.7	WA	557	11.4	772	13.2	960	14.0
MI	865	9.4	838	8.5	1,072	11.0	WV	249	13.8	247	13.9	255	14.0
MN	389	8.9	368	7.5	440	8.2	WI	321	6.7	398	7.5	518	9.1
MS	531	19.9	361	12.9	500	17.1	WY	58	12.5	74	15.3	77	13.4
MO	665	12.7	511	9.3	773	13.0	U.S.	34,719	13.9	38,426	13.7	45,181	14.5

Persons Not Covered by Health Insurance by Selected Characteristics, 2013

Source: Annual Social and Economic Supplement, Current Population Survey, U.S. Census Bureau, U.S. Dept. of Commerce

(numbers in thousands)

	Number not covered	% of pop. specified at left		Number not covered	% of pop. specified at left
Race and Hispanic origin			**Marital status**		
White	31,053	12.8%	Married......................	13,451	13.3%
White, not Hispanic	19,132	9.8	Widowed.....................	703	21.2
Black........................	6,475	15.9	Divorced.....................	4,397	21.7
Asian	2,471	14.5	Separated....................	1,282	26.0
Hispanic, any race	13,203	24.3	Never married................	15,986	24.6
Nativity			**Household income**		
Native born	30,587	11.2	Less than $25,000	12,052	21.6
Foreign born	11,366	27.7	$25,000 to $49,999...........	13,125	18.7
Naturalized citizen...........	3,043	15.9	$50,000 to $74,999...........	7,480	13.1
Not a citizen.................	8,324	38.1	$75,000 to $99,999...........	4,153	9.7
Age			$100,000 to $149,999..........	3,020	6.3
Under age 65	41,260	15.3	$150,000 or more.............	2,123	5.3
Under age 18................	5,441	7.3	**Work experience[1]**		
Under age 19................	5,907	7.6	All workers	24,952	17.1
Aged 19 to 25	6,864	22.6	Worked full time, year round ...	14,043	13.9
Aged 26 to 34	8,948	23.5	Less than full time, year round	10,908	24.0
Aged 35 to 44	7,556	19.0	Did not work at least one week...	10,867	22.4
Aged 45 to 64	11,985	14.5	**Total ....**	**41,953**	**13.4**
Aged 65 and older...........	693	1.6			

(1) Persons aged 18 to 64 only.

Health Insurance Marketplace Plan Enrollment by Selected Characteristics

Source: Centers for Medicare and Medicaid Services (CMS), U.S. Dept. of Health and Human Services (cumulative enrollment-related activity for Oct. 1, 2013-Mar. 31, 2014, incl. additional special enrollment period activity through Apr. 19, 2014; as of Apr. 29, 2014)

	Marketplace total		State marketplaces[1]		Federal marketplace[2]	
	Number[3]	Percent	Number[3]	Percent	Number[3]	Percent
Number who have selected a plan	8,019,763	NA	2,573,585	32%	5,446,178	68%
By known age	8,005,702	100%	2,559,531	100	5,446,171	100
0 to 34 years of age	2,746,465	34	852,497	33	1,893,968	35
18 years of age and younger	497,522	6	141,906	6	355,616	7
18 to 25 years of age	869,476	11	264,453	10	605,023	11
18 to 34 years of age	2,248,943	28	710,591	28	1,538,352	28
26 to 34 years of age	1,379,467	17	446,138	17	933,329	17
35 to 44 years of age	1,371,645	17	431,243	17	940,402	17
45 to 54 years of age	1,814,837	23	595,921	23	1,218,916	22
55 to 64 years of age	2,036,251	25	664,208	26	1,372,043	25
65 years of age and older	36,504	0	15,662	1	20,842	0
Age unknown	14,063	NA	14,056	NA	7	NA
By known financial assistance status[4]	6,670,458	100	2,425,385	100	5,446,178	100
With financial assistance	6,670,458	85	1,987,196	82	4,683,262	86
Without financial assistance	1,201,105	15	438,189	18	762,916	14
Financial assistance status unknown	148,200	NA	148,200	NA	0	NA

NA = Not applicable. **Note:** Numbers and percentages may not add up to totals due to rounding. (1) For states implementing their own marketplaces, known as state-based marketplaces. (2) For states with marketplaces supported or fully run by the Dept. of Health and Human Services, or the federally facilitated marketplace. (3) Includes individuals whether or not a first premium payment has been made. (4) Advance premium tax credit with or without cost-sharing reduction.

Federal Health Insurance Marketplace Average Monthly Premiums, 2014

Source: Centers for Medicare and Medicaid Services (CMS), U.S. Dept. of Health and Human Services (based on enrollment-related activity for Oct. 1, 2013-May 12, 2014)

In states with health insurance marketplaces supported or fully run by the federal government, 87% of those who selected a plan chose one with tax credits based on projected income. Comparable data for states that implemented their own marketplaces are not available.

State	Avg. premium after tax credits	Avg. % reduction in premium after tax credits	Avg. premium before tax credits	Avg. tax credit	State	Avg. premium after tax credits	Avg. % reduction in premium after tax credits	Avg. premium before tax credits	Avg. tax credit
Alabama	$76	77%	$334	$258	New Hampshire	$100	74%	$390	$290
Alaska	94	81	507	413	New Jersey	148	68	465	317
Arizona	113	58	272	159	New Mexico	120	64	334	214
Arkansas	94	76	387	293	North Carolina	81	79	381	300
Delaware	130	67	392	263	North Dakota	132	62	350	218
Florida	68	80	347	278	Ohio	121	67	372	250
Georgia	54	84	341	287	Oklahoma	75	73	277	202
Idaho	68	75	276	207	Pennsylvania	84	74	330	246
Illinois	114	64	316	202	South Carolina	84	77	367	283
Indiana	88	79	424	336	South Dakota	101	73	372	271
Iowa	108	69	350	242	Tennessee	86	69	281	195
Kansas	67	77	290	223	Texas	72	76	305	233
Louisiana	83	79	397	314	Utah	84	66	243	159
Maine	99	78	443	344	Virginia	77	77	331	254
Michigan	97	72	342	246	West Virginia	113	73	415	302
Mississippi	23	95	438	415	Wisconsin	112	74	427	316
Missouri	59	83	344	286	Wyoming	113	79	536	422
Montana	99	71	345	246	**Federal total**	**82**	**76**	**346**	**264**
Nebraska	94	69	308	214					

Health Care Visits by Selected Characteristics, 1997-2012

Source: National Health Interview Survey; *Health, United States*; National Center for Health Statistics; Centers for Disease Control and Prevention; U.S. Dept. of Health and Human Services

Characteristic	Zero visits			1-3 visits			4-9 visits			10 or more visits		
	1997	2000	2012	1997	2000	2012	1997	2000	2012	1997	2000	2012
						Percent distribution						
All persons	16.5%	16.7%	16.0%	46.2%	45.4%	47.6%	23.6%	24.6%	23.6%	13.7%	13.3%	12.8%
Age												
Under 6 years	5.0	6.3	4.2	44.9	44.5	50.8	37.0	38.1	35.6	13.0	11.1	9.4
6-17 years	15.3	15.2	10.0	58.7	58.2	62.5	19.3	20.6	21.2	6.8	6.0	6.3
18-44 years	21.7	23.5	24.7	46.7	45.2	45.9	19.0	19.1	18.0	12.6	12.2	11.4
45-64 years	16.9	15.0	15.1	42.9	43.4	44.6	24.7	25.7	25.1	15.5	15.9	15.1
65-74 years	9.8	9.0	6.9	36.9	34.5	39.3	31.6	34.5	32.9	21.6	22.1	20.8
75 years and over	7.7	5.8	5.0	31.8	29.3	30.9	33.8	39.3	35.5	26.6	25.6	28.6
Sex												
Male	21.3	21.7	20.8	47.1	45.9	48.2	20.6	22.3	20.6	11.0	10.1	10.3
Female	11.8	11.9	11.4	45.4	44.8	47.0	26.5	27.0	26.5	16.3	16.3	15.1
Race and Hispanic origin												
White, not Hispanic	14.7	14.5	13.5	46.6	45.4	47.7	24.4	25.9	25.0	14.3	14.1	13.8
Black, not Hispanic	16.9	17.1	15.1	46.1	46.8	49.1	23.1	23.5	23.2	13.8	12.6	12.6
Hispanic[1]	24.9	26.8	24.1	42.3	41.8	44.5	20.3	19.8	21.1	12.5	11.6	10.3
Health insurance status[2]												
Insured continuously	14.1	14.0	12.5	49.2	48.8	51.4	23.6	24.6	23.9	13.0	12.6	12.2
Uninsured for any period	18.9	20.6	20.3	46.0	44.5	46.9	20.8	20.8	20.6	14.4	14.1	12.1
Uninsured	39.0	43.2	44.0	41.4	39.6	41.6	13.2	12.1	10.6	6.4	5.1	3.9

Note: Totals include persons of races not shown separately and of unknown health insurance status. (1) Persons of Hispanic origin may be of any race. (2) In 12 months prior to interview, for under-65 population only.

Reasons Given by Patients for Outpatient Visits, 2010

Source: National Hospital Ambulatory Medical Care Survey, National Center for Health Statistics, Centers for Disease Control and Prevention, U.S. Dept. of Health and Human Services

Rank	Reason	Number of visits (thous.)	% of all visits	Rank	Reason	Number of visits (thous.)	% of all visits
1.	Progress visit, not otherwise specified	11,960	11.9%	11.	Well-baby examination	1,226	1.2%
2.	General medical examination	5,275	5.2	12.	Earache or ear infection	1,164	1.2
3.	Prenatal examination, routine	3,015	3.0	13.	Knee symptoms	1,151	1.1
4.	Diabetes mellitus	2,831	2.8	14.	Hypertension	1,146	1.1
5.	Medication, other and unspecified kinds	2,436	2.4	15.	Other special examination	1,126	1.1
				16.	Back symptoms	1,002	1.0
6.	Cough	2,253	2.2	17.	Gynecological examination	942	0.9
7.	Counseling, not otherwise specified	2,235	2.2	18.	Skin rash	940	0.9
8.	Postoperative visit	2,233	2.2	19.	Headache, pain in head	927	0.9
9.	Stomach pain, cramps, and spasms	1,655	1.6	20.	Fever	915	0.9
10.	Symptoms referable to throat	1,585	1.6		All other reasons	54,725	54.3
					All visits	100,742	100.0

Emergency Room Visits by Diagnosis, 2010

Source: National Hospital Ambulatory Medical Care Survey, National Center for Health Statistics, Centers for Disease Control and Prevention, U.S. Dept. of Health and Human Services

Rank	Principal diagnosis group	Number of visits (thous.)	% of all visits	Rank	Principal diagnosis group	Number of visits (thous.)	% of all visits
1.	Heart disease, excluding ischemic	1,100	6.4%	11.	Chronic and unspecified bronchitis	294	1.7%
2.	Chest pain	1,001	5.8	12.	Fractures, excluding lower limb	287	1.7
3.	Pneumonia	784	4.5	13.	Fracture of the lower limb	264	1.5
4.	Ischemic heart disease	505	2.9	14.	Asthma	260	1.5
5.	Cerebrovascular disease	457	2.7	15.	Disorder of gallbladder and biliary tract	236	1.4
6.	Psychoses, excluding major depressive disorder	455	2.6	16.	Malignant neoplasms	230	1.3
				17.	Diabetes mellitus	225	1.3
7.	Cellulitis and abscess	368	2.1	18.	Noninfectious enteritis and colitis	210	1.2
8.	Abdominal pain	344	2.0	19.	Anemias	209	1.2
9.	Syncope and collapse	308	1.8	20.	Gastrointestinal hemmorrhage	186	1.1
10.	Urinary tract infection, site not specified	299	1.7		All other diagnoses[1]	9,217	53.5
					All visits	17,239	100.0

(1) Includes blanks and discharges in which diagnosis was unknown.

Most Frequently Mentioned Drugs at Outpatient Department Visits, 2010

Source: National Hospital Ambulatory Medical Care Survey, National Center for Health Statistics, Centers for Disease Control and Prevention, U.S. Dept. of Health and Human Services

Rank	Therapeutic drug category[1]	No. of mentions (thous.)	% of total[2]	Rank	Therapeutic drug category[1]	No. of mentions (thous.)	% of total[2]
1.	Analgesics	31,287	11.0%	11.	Diuretics	8,817	3.1%
2.	Antidiabetic agents	14,549	5.1	12.	ACE[3] inhibitors	8,144	2.9
3.	Antihyperlipidemic agents	13,380	4.7	13.	Proton pump inhibitors	7,826	2.7
4.	Antidepressants	12,828	4.5	14.	Dermatological agents	7,736	2.7
5.	Anxiolytics, sedatives, and hypnotics	11,233	3.9	15.	Vitamins	7,576	2.7
6.	Immunostimulants	9,996	3.5	16.	Antihistamines	6,917	2.4
7.	Bronchodilators	9,978	3.5	17.	Antiemetic/antivertigo agents	6,206	2.2
8.	Antiplatelet agents	9,726	3.4	18.	Vitamin and mineral combinations	5,695	2.0
9.	Beta-adrenergic blocking agents	9,710	3.4	19.	Calcium channel blocking agents	5,645	2.0
10.	Anticonvulsants	9,695	3.4	20.	Thyroid hormones	4,936	1.7

Note: A mention is a documentation in a patient's record of a drug provided, prescribed, or continued. (1) Based on the Multum Lexicon second-level therapeutic drug category. (2) Based on an estimated 285,056,000 drugs provided, prescribed, or continued at outpatient department visits in 2010. (3) Angiotensin-converting enzyme.

U.S. Organ Transplants

Source: Organ Procurement and Transplantation Network (OPTN), United Network for Organ Sharing (UNOS)

Waiting List, June 2014			Transplants Performed, 2013		
Type of transplant	Patients waiting	% of total	Type of transplant	Number	% of total
Any organ	134,161	—	Any organ	28,953	—
Kidney	108,393	80.8%	Kidney	16,894	58.3%
Liver	16,391	12.2	Liver	6,455	22.3
Heart	4,041	3.0	Heart	2,531	8.7
Kidney-pancreas	2,114	1.6	Lung	1,923	6.6
Lung	1,697	1.3	Kidney-pancreas	762	2.6
Pancreas	1,206	0.9	Pancreas	256	0.9
Intestine	264	0.2	Intestine	109	0.4
Heart-lung	55	0.0	Heart-lung	23	0.1

Note: Waiting list as of June 6, 2014.

Drug Use in the General U.S. Population, 2012

Source: Substance Abuse and Mental Health Services Administration (SAMHSA), U.S. Dept. of Health and Human Services

According to the 2012 results of SAMHSA's annual survey, an estimated 124.8 mil Americans 12 years of age and older (or 48.0% of that population) had used an illicit drug at least once in their lifetimes. Of that number, an estimated 78.0 mil (30.0% of persons 12 or older) had used an illicit drug other than marijuana at least once in their lives. About 16.0% of the 12-and-older population had used an illicit drug in the previous year; 9.2% had used one in the month prior to their participation in the survey.

The rate of current illicit drug use (i.e., within the past month) in 2012 was 11.6% for men and 6.9% for women.

SAMHSA's Drug Abuse Warning Network (DAWN) reported 2.5 mil drug abuse or misuse-related visits to hospital emergency departments in 2011. Just over half (51%) of all visits involved illicit drugs, with the highest rates for cocaine and marijuana. About 25% of all visits associated with drug misuse or abuse also involved alcohol.

Illicit Drug Use Among Persons 12 or Older, 2005-12

Source: National Survey on Drug Use and Health, Substance Abuse and Mental Health Services Admin. (SAMHSA), U.S. Dept. of Health and Human Services

(numbers in thousands)

	2005 No.	2005 %	2008 No.	2008 %	2009 No.	2009 %	2010 No.	2010 %	2011 No.	2011 %	2012 No.	2012 %
Used in lifetime												
Illicit drugs[1]	112,085	46.1	117,325	47.0	118,705	47.1	119,508	47.1	121,078	47.0	124,808	48.0
Illicit drugs other than marijuana[1]	71,822	29.5	75,573	30.3	75,780	30.1	76,203	30.0	75,447	29.3	78,034	30.0
Used in past month												
Illicit drugs[1]	19,720	8.1	20,077	8.0	21,813	8.7	22,622	8.9	22,454	8.7	23,863	9.2
Illicit drugs other than marijuana[1]	8,963	3.7	8,565	3.4	9,157	3.6	9,017	3.6	8,020	3.1	8,883	3.4
Used in past year												
Illicit drugs[1]	35,041	14.4	35,525	14.2	37,954	15.1	38,806	15.3	38,287	14.9	41,479	16.0
Marijuana and hashish	25,375	10.4	25,768	10.3	28,521	11.3	29,206	11.5	29,739	11.5	31,513	12.1
Illicit drugs other than marijuana[1]	20,109	8.3	19,990	8.0	21,000	8.3	20,576	8.1	18,959	7.4	21,267	8.2
Cocaine	5,523	2.3	5,255	2.1	4,797	1.9	4,499	1.8	3,857	1.5	4,671	1.8
Crack	1,381	0.6	1,109	0.4	1,016	0.4	871	0.3	625	0.2	921	0.4
Heroin	379	0.2	453	0.2	605	0.2	618	0.2	620	0.2	669	0.3
Hallucinogens	3,809	1.6	3,678	1.5	4,509	1.8	4,517	1.8	4,069	1.6	4,306	1.7
LSD	563	0.2	802	0.3	779	0.3	874	0.3	880	0.3	1,057	0.4
PCP	164	0.1	99	0.0	122	0.0	95	0.0	119	0.0	172	0.1
Ecstasy	1,960	0.8	2,139	0.9	2,799	1.1	2,645	1.0	2,422	0.9	2,610	1.0
Inhalants	2,187	0.9	2,047	0.8	2,090	0.8	2,030	0.8	1,861	0.7	1,693	0.7
Nonmedical use of psychotherapeutics[2]	15,346	6.3	15,166	6.1	16,006	6.4	16,031	6.3	14,657	5.7	16,666	6.4
Pain relievers	11,815	4.9	11,885	4.8	12,405	4.9	12,213	4.8	11,143	4.3	12,489	4.8
OxyContin®	1,226	0.5	1,459	0.6	1,677	0.7	1,869	0.7	1,623	0.6	1,477	0.6
Tranquilizers	5,249	2.2	5,103	2.0	5,460	2.2	5,581	2.2	5,109	2.0	6,073	2.3
Stimulants	3,088	1.3	2,639	1.1	3,060	1.2	2,887	1.1	2,700	1.0	3,317	1.3
Sedatives	750	0.3	621	0.2	811	0.3	907	0.4	526	0.2	590	0.2

(1) Illicit drugs include marijuana/hashish, cocaine (including crack), heroin, hallucinogens, inhalants, or prescription-type psycho-therapeutics used nonmedically. (2) Includes the nonmedical use of pain relievers, tranquilizers, stimulants, or sedatives but not over-the-counter drugs.

Lifetime Prevalence of Drug Use in 12th Graders, 1975-2013

Source: Monitoring the Future study, Univ. of Michigan Inst. for Social Research; National Institute on Drug Abuse

(percent who have ever used)

Drug	1975	1980	1985	1990	1995	2000	2005	2009	2010	2011	2012	2013	2012-13 change
Any illicit drug[1]	55.2%	65.4%	60.6%	47.9%	48.4%	54.0%	50.4%	46.7%	48.2%	49.9%	49.1%	50.4%	1.3%
Marijuana/hashish	47.3	60.3	54.2	40.7	41.7	48.8	44.8	42.0	43.8	45.5	45.2	45.5	0.3
Inhalants[2]	—	17.3	18.1	18.5	17.8	14.6	11.9	10.2	9.0	8.1	7.9	6.9	−1.0
Amyl/butyl nitrites	—	11.1	7.9	2.1	1.5	0.8	1.1	1.1	—	—	—	—	—
Hallucinogens[3]	—	15.6	12.1	9.7	13.1	13.6	9.3	8.0	8.6	8.3	7.5	7.6	0.1
LSD	11.3	9.3	7.5	8.7	11.7	11.1	3.5	3.1	4.0	4.0	3.8	3.9	0.1
PCP	—	9.6	4.9	2.8	2.7	3.4	2.4	1.7	1.8	2.3	1.6	1.3	−0.3
Ecstasy (MDMA)	—	—	—	—	—	11.0	5.4	6.5	7.3	8.0	7.2	7.1	−0.1
Cocaine	9.0	15.7	17.3	9.4	6.0	8.6	8.0	6.0	5.5	5.2	4.9	4.5	−0.4
Crack	—	—	—	3.5	3.0	3.9	3.5	2.4	2.4	1.9	2.1	1.8	−0.3
Heroin (with and without a needle)	2.2	1.1	1.2	1.3	1.6	2.4	1.5	1.2	1.6	1.4	1.1	1.0	−0.1
Narcotics other than heroin[4]	9.0	9.8	10.2	8.3	7.2	10.6	12.8	13.2	13.0	13.0	12.2	11.1	−1.1
Amphetamines[4]	22.3	26.4	26.2	17.5	15.3	15.6	13.1	9.9	11.1	12.2	12.0	12.4	0.3
Methamphetamine	—	—	—	—	—	7.9	4.5	2.4	2.3	2.1	1.7	1.5	−0.2
Crystal meth. (ice)	—	—	—	2.7	3.9	4.0	4.0	2.1	1.8	2.1	1.7	2.0	0.3
Sedatives (barbiturates)[4]	18.2	14.9	11.8	7.5	7.6	9.3	11.0	8.4	7.5	7.0	6.9	7.5	0.6
Methaqualone[4]	8.1	9.5	6.7	2.3	1.2	0.8	1.3	0.7	0.4	0.6	0.8	—	—
Tranquilizers[4]	17.0	15.2	11.9	7.2	7.1	8.9	9.9	9.3	8.5	8.7	8.5	7.7	−0.8
Alcohol	90.4	93.2	92.2	89.5	80.7	80.3	75.1	72.3	71.0	70.0	69.4	68.2	−1.2
Cigarettes	73.6	71.0	68.8	64.4	64.2	62.5	50.0	43.6	42.2	40.0	39.5	38.1	−1.4
Smokeless tobacco	—	—	—	—	30.9	23.1	17.5	16.3	17.6	16.9	17.4	17.2	−0.2
Steroids[4]	—	—	—	2.9	2.3	2.5	2.6	2.2	2.0	1.8	1.8	2.1	0.3

— = Not available. **Note:** Because of changes to question wording, some data may not be directly comparable to data from previous years. (1) Includes marijuana, LSD, other hallucinogens, crack, other cocaine, or heroin; or any use of narcotics other than heroin, amphetamines, sedatives (barbiturates), or tranquilizers not under a doctor's orders. (2) Not adjusted for underreporting of amyl and butyl nitrites. (3) Not adjusted for underreporting of PCP. (4) Includes only drug use not under a doctor's orders.

Cigarette Use in the U.S., 1985-2012

Source: National Survey on Drug Use and Health, Substance Abuse and Mental Health Services Admin. (SAMHSA), U.S. Dept. of Health and Human Services

(percentage reporting use in the month prior to the survey)

	1985	2000	2005	2010	2011	2012		1985	2000	2005	2010	2011	2012
Total[1]	38.7	24.9	24.9	23.0	22.1	22.1	**Race/ethnicity**						
							White, not Hispanic	38.9	25.9	26.0	24.3	23.5	23.7
Sex							Black, not Hispanic	38.0	23.3	24.5	22.6	21.5	23.0
Male	43.4	26.9	27.4	25.4	24.3	24.6	Hispanic	40.0	20.7	22.1	20.1	18.5	16.8
Female	34.5	23.1	22.5	20.7	19.9	19.8	**Education[2]**						
Age group							Non-high school graduate	37.3	32.4	34.8	34.3	33.7	33.7
12-17 years	29.4	13.4	10.8	8.3	7.8	6.6	High school graduate	37.0	31.1	31.8	29.6	28.3	29.4
18-25 years	47.4	38.3	39.0	34.2	33.5	31.8	Some college	32.6	27.7	28.1	25.8	25.9	25.5
26 years and older	45.7[3]	24.2	24.3	22.8	21.9	22.4	College graduate	23.0	13.9	13.8	12.8	11.7	11.5

(1) Persons 12 years of age and older. (2) Persons aged 18 and older. (3) Persons aged 26 to 34 only.

Daily Use of Cigarettes by 8th, 10th, and 12th Graders, 1995-2013

Source: Monitoring the Future study, Univ. of Michigan Inst. for Social Research; National Institute on Drug Abuse

(percent who smoked daily in last 30 days)

	8th grade					% change, 2010-13	10th grade					% change, 2010-13	12th grade					% change, 2010-13
	1995	2000	2005	2010	2013		1995	2000	2005	2010	2013		1995	2000	2005	2010	2013	
Total	9.3	7.4	4.0	2.9	1.8	-37.9%	16.3	14.0	7.5	6.6	4.4	-33.3%	21.6	20.6	13.6	10.7	8.5	-20.6%
Sex																		
Male	9.2	7.0	3.9	3.5	1.7	-51.4	16.3	13.7	7.2	7.2	5.4	-25.0	21.7	20.9	14.6	12.3	9.7	-21.1
Female	9.2	7.5	4.0	2.3	1.8	-21.7	16.1	14.1	7.7	5.9	3.4	-42.4	20.8	19.7	11.9	8.7	6.5	-25.3
College plans																		
None or under 4 yrs.	22.5	21.7	14.4	12.8	8.3	-35.2	32.7	28.8	19.2	19.1	13.4	-29.8	33.7	31.7	24.9	21.6	18.8	-13.0
Complete 4 yrs.	7.5	5.6	2.9	2.0	1.4	-30.0	13.3	11.6	5.9	5.0	3.4	-32.0	17.4	16.6	10.5	8.2	5.8	-29.3
Region																		
Northeast	9.2	6.9	3.2	2.4	1.3	-45.8	15.8	14.1	7.6	5.7	3.6	-36.8	22.5	22.8	13.3	10.3	9.8	-4.9
Midwest	11.0	9.0	4.8	3.3	1.5	-54.5	17.6	16.3	8.6	7.3	4.9	-32.9	25.7	23.6	16.3	12.5	8.4	-32.8
South	9.4	7.8	5.0	3.8	2.6	-31.6	19.3	15.7	8.8	7.9	5.7	-27.8	21.7	19.4	15.4	12.3	10.5	-14.6
West	7.0	4.9	2.4	1.4	1.2	-14.3	9.4	7.8	4.0	4.4	3.1	-29.5	14.5	16.9	7.6	6.7	4.6	-31.3
Race/ethnicity[1]																		
White	10.5	9.0	4.6	3.2	2.0	-37.5	23.9	25.7	17.1	7.4	5.7	-23.0	23.9	25.7	17.1	13.5	10.9	-19.3
Black	2.8	3.2	2.1	1.9	1.5	-21.1	6.1	8.0	5.6	3.5	2.6	-25.7	6.1	8.0	5.6	5.3	5.3	0.0
Hispanic	9.2	7.1	3.1	2.3	1.4	-39.1	11.6	15.7	7.7	4.4	2.6	-40.9	11.6	15.7	7.7	5.7	4.7	-17.5

Note: Figures may not add up to totals because of rounding. (1) For each of these groups, data for the specified year and previous year have been combined to increase sample size and thus provide a more reliable estimate.

Alcohol Use by 8th and 12th Graders, 1980-2013

Source: Monitoring the Future study, Univ. of Michigan Inst. for Social Research; National Inst. on Drug Abuse

	1980	1990	1995	2000	2005	2009	2010	2011	2012	2013	2012-13 change
Alcohol use[1]				Percent using in the month before the survey							
All 12th graders	72.0%	57.1%	51.3%	50.0%	47.0%	43.5%	41.2%	40.0%	41.5%	39.2%	-2.3%
Male	77.4	61.3	55.7	54.0	50.7	47.8	44.2	42.1	43.8	41.8	-2.0
Female	66.8	52.3	47.0	46.1	43.3	38.9	37.9	37.5	38.8	36.3	-2.5
White	75.4	63.8	54.5	55.1	52.3	47.2	45.4	43.8	43.8	43.6	-0.2
Black	47.6	35.8	35.2	30.0	29.0	30.5	31.4	30.1	29.6	28.4	-1.1
Hispanic	63.6	49.1	48.7	51.2	43.3	40.1	40.1	39.7	39.8	39.0	-0.8
All 8th graders	—	—	24.6	22.4	17.1	14.9	13.8	12.7	11.0	10.2	-0.8
Male	—	—	25.0	22.5	16.2	14.7	13.2	12.1	10.3	9.3	-1.0
Female	—	—	24.0	22.0	17.9	14.9	14.3	12.8	11.6	11.2	-0.4
White	—	—	25.4	24.7	17.9	15.4	13.9	12.3	10.7	9.5	-1.3
Black	—	—	18.7	16.0	14.9	12.3	11.8	11.6	10.0	9.7	-0.3
Hispanic	—	—	32.4	26.7	20.6	19.2	18.1	18.0	17.5	14.3	-3.2
Heavy alcohol use[2]				Percent heavily using in the two weeks before the survey							
All 12th graders	41.2%	32.2%	29.8%	30.0%	27.1%	25.2%	23.2%	21.6%	23.7%	22.1%	-1.6%
Male	52.1	39.1	36.9	36.7	32.6	30.5	28.0	25.5	27.2	26.1	-1.1
Female	30.5	24.4	23.0	23.5	21.6	20.2	18.4	17.6	19.7	18.1	-1.6
White	44.3	36.6	32.3	34.6	32.5	29.0	27.6	25.9	25.7	25.6	-0.1
Black	17.7	14.4	14.9	11.5	11.3	12.0	13.1	11.3	11.3	12.5	1.2
Hispanic	33.1	25.6	26.6	31.0	23.9	22.6	22.1	20.8	21.8	22.4	0.7
All 8th graders	—	—	12.3	11.7	8.4	7.8	7.2	6.4	5.1	5.1	0.0
Male	—	—	12.5	11.7	8.2	7.8	6.5	6.1	4.6	4.5	-0.1
Female	—	—	12.1	11.3	8.6	7.7	7.8	6.5	5.5	5.7	0.2
White	—	—	12.1	13.0	9.0	7.7	7.1	6.2	4.9	4.2	-0.6
Black	—	—	8.3	7.3	6.1	5.2	5.3	5.1	4.3	4.5	0.2
Hispanic	—	—	18.4	16.0	12.1	11.5	10.8	10.4	9.9	7.8	-2.1

— = Not available. (1) Since 1993 the alcohol question has indicated that a "drink" is defined as "more than a few sips." (2) Five or more drinks in a row.

Acquired Immune Deficiency Syndrome (AIDS)

Source: Centers for Disease Control and Prevention (CDC), U.S. Dept. of Health and Human Services

AIDS (Acquired Immune Deficiency Syndrome) is caused by the human immunodeficiency virus (HIV). HIV kills or disables crucial immune cells, progressively destroying the body's ability to fight disease.

HIV is commonly spread through unprotected sexual contact with an infected partner's semen or vaginal fluids. It is also spread through contact with infected blood. Where modern screening techniques are used, it is rare to contract HIV from transfusion or organ/tissue transplants. But it can be contracted when intravenous drug users share syringes and similar equipment with others. A woman can also transmit HIV to her child during pregnancy or delivery or through breastfeeding. With treatment, a woman can reduce her transmission rate from 15%-45% to less than 1%. There is no evidence HIV can spread through saliva or casual contact such as in the sharing of food utensils, towels and bedding, telephones, or toilet seats.

Some people experience flu-like symptoms within a few weeks of being infected with HIV. Even when symptoms are not present, HIV is active in the body, multiplying, infecting, and killing crucial CD4+ T cells, also known as T-lymphocytes or T-helper cells, which signal other immune cells to perform their functions.

The term AIDS applies to the most advanced stages of HIV infection. According to the official case definition issued by the CDC, an HIV-infected person with fewer than 200 CD4+ T cells per cubic millimeter of blood can be said to have AIDS. (Healthy adults usually have 500-1,600 per cubic millimeter.) An HIV-infected person, regardless of T cell count, is diagnosed with AIDS if he or she develops one of 20+ conditions that typically affect people with advanced HIV. Most of these conditions are opportunistic infections that occur when the immune system is so ravaged by HIV that the body cannot fight off certain bacteria, viruses, and microbes.

Months or years prior to the onset of AIDS, people may experience such symptoms as swollen glands, lack of energy, fevers and sweats, and skin rashes. People diagnosed with AIDS may develop infections of the intestinal tract, lungs, brain, eyes, and other organs and become severely debilitated. They also are prone to developing certain cancers, especially those caused by viruses, such as Kaposi's sarcoma, cervical cancer, and lymphoma. Children with AIDS may have delayed development or fail to thrive.

HIV is primarily detected by testing a person's blood for the presence of antibodies (disease-fighting proteins of the immune system) to HIV. In very rare cases, HIV antibodies may take more than six months after exposure to reach detectable levels. But in 97% of infected individuals, the antibodies are detectable in the first three months. HIV testing may also be performed on oral fluid and urine samples. Rapid HIV tests can provide preliminary results in about 20 minutes.

Patients receiving antiretroviral therapy typically take a combination of drugs. Taking more than one drug reduces the chance of the virus becoming resistant to any single one. While these drugs extend the period between HIV infection and the development of serious illness, they do not prevent the spread of the disease to others and can have severe side effects.

In 1987, a drug called zidovudine (commonly known as AZT) became the first approved treatment for HIV disease. Since then, the U.S. Food and Drug Administration has approved approximately 35 drugs to treat people living with HIV/AIDS. These drugs belong in different classes: Nucleoside/Nucleotide Reverse Transcriptase Inhibitors (NRTIs), Non-Nucleoside Reverse Transcriptase Inhibitors (NNRTIs), Protease Inhibitors (PIs), Entry Inhibitors, Fusion Inhibitors, and Integrase Inhibitors. Each class of drug attacks the virus at a different point in its life cycle. Patients generally take three different antiretrovirals (ARVs) from two different classes.

There are also fixed-dose combinations of drugs. These are not a separate class of HIV medications but combinations of two or more medications, with specific fixed doses, from one or more different classes. These ARVs are combined into a single pill.

Since there is no vaccine or cure for AIDS, the best way to prevent HIV is to avoid activities that carry a risk. The CDC recommends abstinence (the only certain protection), mutual monogamy with an uninfected partner, limiting the number of one's sexual partners, never sharing needles, and using condoms correctly and consistently. Pre-exposure prophylaxis, or PrEP, is a prevention option for people who are at high risk of getting HIV. It is meant to be used consistently, as a pill taken every day, and to be used with other prevention options. PrEP has been shown to greatly reduce the risk of HIV infection. PEP, or post-exposure prophylaxis, is the use of ARVs after a single high-risk event to stop HIV from making copies of itself and spreading throughout the body. PEP must be started no more than 72 hours after the exposure to HIV, and it is not always effective.

New AIDS Diagnoses in the U.S., by Transmission Category, 1985-2011

Source: *HIV Surveillance Report, 2011*; National Center for HIV/AIDS, Viral Hepatitis, STD, and TB Prevention; CDC

Transmission category	All years[1]	1985	1990	2000	2005	2008	2009	2010	2011
All males 13 years of age and older	913,368	7,504	36,193	30,251	27,436	24,015	23,226	22,030	24,088
Male-to-male sexual contact	555,032	5,348	23,658	13,648	16,824	15,427	15,458	14,934	16,694
Injection drug use	187,938	1,103	6,923	5,554	4,350	2,985	2,563	2,323	2,346
Male-to-male sexual contact and injection drug use	80,902	661	2,943	1,587	2,085	1,714	1,491	1,393	1,392
Heterosexual contact[2]	77,521	32	715	2,537	3,920	3,724	3,581	3,256	3,526
Other[3]	11,975	—	—	—	256	165	134	123	131
All females 13 years of age and older	228,541	524	4,547	9,979	9,799	8,593	7,971	7,410	7,949
Injection drug use	73,382	287	2,347	2,545	2,724	2,041	1,776	1,582	1,615
Heterosexual contact[2]	104,037	119	1,538	4,025	6,856	6,432	6,073	5,697	6,206
Other[3]	51,122	—	—	—	219	119	122	130	129
All children, under 13 years of age	9,483	—	—	—	55	37	14	24	15
Perinatal	8,623	—	—	—	50	32	13	19	12
Other[4]	860	—	—	—	5	5	1	5	2

— = Not available. **Note:** The definition of AIDS cases for reporting purposes was expanded in 1985, 1987, and 1993, as more was learned about the spectrum of human immunodeficiency virus-associated diseases. (1) Includes number of diagnoses for years not shown, from the beginning of the epidemic (1981) through 2011. (2) Heterosexual contact with a person known to have or be at high risk for HIV infection. (3) Includes hemophilia, blood transfusion, perinatal exposure, and risk factors not reported or not identified. (4) Includes hemophilia, blood transfusion, and risk factors not reported or not identified.

New HIV Diagnoses in the U.S., 2008-11

Source: *Health, United States*, National Center for Health Statistics, Centers for Disease Control and Prevention

Characteristic	Male				Female			
	2008	2009	2010	2011	2008	2009	2010	2011
Total diagnoses, age 13 and over	38,104	36,392	35,918	38,825	12,146	10,804	10,125	10,257
Race/Hispanic origin								
White	12,206	11,583	11,355	12,041	2,046	1,772	1,680	1,776
Black or African American	16,277	15,491	15,293	16,447	7,967	6,977	6,592	6,595
Asian[1]	685	612	646	821	123	134	132	153
Native Hawaiian or other Pacific Islander	68	62	53	70	10	18	9	8
American Indian or Alaska Native	179	151	161	161	44	53	61	51
Hispanic or Latino[2]	7,979	7,825	7,725	8,605	1,681	1,635	1,463	1,530
Multiple race	710	667	686	679	274	214	188	144
Age diagnosed								
13-14 years	13	11	20	27	30	20	25	26
15-24 years	7,113	7,480	8,093	8,680	1,835	1,704	1,563	1,615
25-34 years	10,127	9,990	9,933	11,107	3,206	2,687	2,581	2,586
35-44 years	10,319	9,146	8,371	8,527	3,242	2,898	2,562	2,511
45-54 years	7,352	6,787	6,547	7,220	2,618	2,388	2,229	2,295
55-64 years	2,503	2,363	2,357	2,551	966	874	944	990
65 years and over	677	616	597	713	249	234	221	235

Note: Data are based on reporting by 50 states and DC. Subpopulations were calculated independent of total and may not equal totals. Children under age 13 made up fewer than 300 cases per year and are not shown. (1) Includes Asian and Pacific Islander legacy cases. (2) May be of any race.

U.S. Deaths of Persons With HIV Ever Classified as AIDS, 1981-2010

Source: *HIV Surveillance Report, 2011*; National Center for HIV/AIDS, Viral Hepatitis, STD, and TB Prevention; CDC

Age at death	Deaths	% of total
Under 13 years old	4,961	0.8%
13-14	293	0.0
15-19	1,249	0.2
20-24	9,414	1.5
25-29	45,966	7.4
30-34	100,003	16.1
35-39	125,079	20.2
40-44	116,708	18.8
45-49	87,154	14.1
50-54	56,584	9.1
55-59	33,799	5.5
60-64	19,283	3.1
65 years and over	19,555	3.2
Race/ethnicity		
White	259,858	41.9
Black	252,826	40.8
Hispanic/Latino (any race)	94,042	15.2
Asian[1]	3,131	0.5
American Indian/Alaska Native	1,882	0.3
Native Hawaiian/other Pacific Islander	357	0.1
Multiple races	7,879	1.3

Transmission category	Deaths	% of total
Male adult or adolescent	506,942	81.8%
Male-to-male sexual contact	277,095	44.7
Injection drug use	112,647	18.2
Male-to-male sexual contact and injection drug use	44,456	7.2
Heterosexual contact[2]	24,963	4.0
Perinatal	277	0.0
Other[3]	47,504	7.7
Female adult or adolescent	108,145	17.4
Injection drug use	46,596	7.5
Heterosexual contact[2]	41,769	6.7
Perinatal	379	0.1
Other[3]	19,401	3.1
Child (under 13 years old at death)	4,961	0.8
Perinatal	4,498	0.7
Other[3]	463	0.1
Region of residence		
Northeast	199,628	32.2
Midwest	62,670	10.1
South	233,893	37.7
West	123,857	20.0
Total[4]	620,048	

Note: Deaths of persons with diagnosed HIV infection may be due to any cause. (1) Includes Asian/Pacific Islander legacy cases. (2) Heterosexual contact with a person known to have or to be at high risk for HIV infection. (3) Includes hemophilia, blood transfusion, and risk factor not reported or not identified. (4) Includes persons of unknown race/ethnicity. Because estimated totals were calculated independently, subpopulation values may not add up to the total.

Allergies and Asthma

Source: Asthma and Allergy Foundation of America

An estimated one in five Americans suffers from allergies. People with allergies have immune systems that overreact to a foreign protein substance ("allergen") that is eaten, breathed into the lungs, injected, or touched. Common allergens include plant pollens, dust mites, or animal dander; plants such as poison ivy; certain drugs, such as penicillin; and foods such as eggs, milk, wheat, nuts, or seafood.

The tendency to develop allergies is usually inherited. While allergies typically manifest in childhood, they can show up at any age. Food allergies and eczema (patches of dry skin) are common allergies among infants. Older children and adults may develop allergic rhinitis, or hay fever, in reaction to an inhaled allergen. Allergic rhinitis symptoms include nasal congestion, runny nose, and sneezing.

People with allergies should avoid contact with an allergen, if feasible. Medications, such as antihistamines and nasal steroids, may be used to decrease an allergic reaction. Other effective allergy treatments include decongestants, eye drops, and ointments. There are also treatments aimed at gradually desensitizing a patient to an allergen.

Some allergy sufferers also have asthma. Asthma, which can develop at any age, is a chronic inflammation disease affecting the passageways that carry air into and out of the lungs. About 20 mil Americans have asthma. During what is known as an asthma attack, these inflamed, supersensitive airways tighten and fill with mucus. A person may experience wheezing, difficulty breathing, tightening of the chest, and coughing. Exposure to an allergen can set off an attack. Asthma can become life-threatening if not controlled in its early stages. The following symptoms may be indicative of an emergency: the patient shows no improvement minutes after initial treatment; struggles to breathe while hunched over with his or her chest and neck pulled in; has trouble walking or talking; and develops gray or blue lips or fingernails.

Besides common allergens, tobacco smoke, cold air, and expressing strong emotion can trigger an asthma attack, as can respiratory infections or physical exercise. An accurate diagnosis by a physician is important. Although there is no cure for asthma or allergies, they can be controlled through lifestyle changes and medications (including quick-relief and long-term control).

Website: www.aafa.org

Alzheimer's Disease

Source: Alzheimer's Association

Alzheimer's disease, the most common form of dementia, is a progressive, degenerative brain disease in which nerve cells deteriorate and die. The most common early symptom is forgetting newly learned information. As the disease advances, it leads to disorientation and mood/behavior changes; confusion about events, time, and place; suspicions about family, friends, and caregivers; more serious memory loss; and difficulty speaking, swallowing, and walking.

The rate of progression of Alzheimer's varies, ranging from 4 to 20 years. The average length of time from onset of symptoms until death is eight years. As they become progressively debilitated, affected individuals grow increasingly susceptible to infections of the lungs, urinary tract, and other organs.

Alzheimer's disease affects an estimated 5.2 mil Americans, striking men and women of all races and ethnicities. Almost two-thirds of all Americans living with Alzheimer's are women. Although most people are older than age 65 when diagnosed with Alzheimer's, younger-onset, or early-onset, cases occur in people in their 40s and 50s. An estimated 11% of the U.S. population over age 65 has Alzheimer's.

Diagnosis involves a comprehensive evaluation that may include a complete health history, physical examination, neurological and mental status assessments, and other tests. Skilled health care professionals can generally diagnose Alzheimer's with more than 90% accuracy. Depression, drug interactions, nutritional imbalances, and infections such as AIDS, meningitis, and syphilis can cause similar symptoms. Other forms of dementia, such as those associated with Huntington's disease, Parkinson's disease, frontotemporal dementia, and vascular disease, can also appear to be Alzheimer's. Absolute confirmation of a diagnosis requires a brain biopsy or autopsy.

Treatments for cognitive and behavioral symptoms are available, but no intervention has yet been developed to prevent Alzheimer's or reverse its course. The U.S. Food and Drug Administration has approved five drugs that temporarily slow worsening of symptoms for about six to twelve months.

They are effective for only about half of the individuals who take them. Some research suggests that risk factors for heart disease, such as high blood pressure, elevated cholesterol, diabetes, and excess body weight, may increase a person's risk of developing Alzheimer's. Staying physically and mentally active and socially connected may be associated with a lower risk for the disease.

Providing care for people with Alzheimer's is physically and psychologically demanding. About 60%-70% of affected individuals live at home, where family or friends tend to them without pay. In the disease's advanced stages, many individuals require long-term residential care. Nearly half of all nursing home residents in the U.S. have Alzheimer's.

The U.S. cost of diagnosing, treating, and providing long-term care for Alzheimer's patients is estimated to be $214 bil in 2014. People with Alzheimer's need a safe, stable environment and a regular daily schedule offering appropriate stimulation. Physical exercise and social interaction are important, as are proper nutrition and adequate pain management. Security is also a consideration, because many people with Alzheimer's tend to wander. An identification bracelet with the person's name, address, and condition can help ensure the safe return of an individual who wanders.

Website: www.alz.org

Warning Signs of Alzheimer's Disease

- Memory loss that disrupts daily life
- Challenges in planning or solving problems
- Difficulty completing familiar tasks at home, at work, or at leisure
- Confusion with time or place
- Trouble understanding visual images and spatial relationships
- New problems with words in speaking or writing
- Misplacing things and losing the ability to retrace steps
- Decreased or poor judgment
- Withdrawal from work or social activities
- Changes in mood and personality

Arthritis

Source: Arthritis Foundation; Centers for Disease Control and Prevention (CDC), U.S. Dept. of Health and Human Services

The term arthritis refers to more than 100 different diseases that cause pain, aching, stiffness, and swelling in or around the joints. The condition is usually chronic. The CDC estimates that 50 mil adults in the United States report being told by a doctor that they have arthritis. Arthritis annually results in 44.2 mil ambulatory care visits and an estimated 992,000 hospitalizations. The cause for most types of arthritis is unknown; scientists are studying the roles played by genetics, lifestyle, and environment.

Symptoms may develop gradually or suddenly. A visit to the doctor is indicated when pain, stiffness, swelling in a joint, or difficulty in moving a joint persists for three days or more. To diagnose arthritis, the doctor records the patient's symptoms and examines his or her joints, looking for any swelling or limited movement. In addition, the doctor checks for other signs often seen with arthritis, such as rashes, mouth sores, or eye involvement. The doctor may test blood, urine, or joint fluid, or take X-rays of the joints.

Of the three most prevalent forms of arthritis, **osteoarthritis** is the most common, affecting approximately 27 mil Americans. It usually occurs after age 40. In patients with osteoarthritis, also called degenerative arthritis, the protective cartilage of joints is lost and changes occur in the bone, leading to pain and stiffness. The joints most commonly affected are the lower back, hips, knees, and feet.

Fibromyalgia, another common arthritis condition, affects about 5 mil Americans. People suffering from fibromyalgia

experience widespread pain, abnormal pain processing, sleep disturbance, fatigue, and psychological distress. Other symptoms include morning stiffness, tingling or numbness in hands and feet, headaches, or problems with thinking and memory. More women than men are afflicted with this type of arthritis.

Rheumatoid arthritis, which affects an estimated 1.5 mil in the U.S., is one of the most serious and disabling forms of the disease. In this type—which is also more common and more degenerative in women—inflammation of the joints leads to cartilage and bone damage. The hands, wrists, feet, knees, ankles, and elbows can be affected.

Other forms of arthritis and related conditions include lupus, gout, psoriatic arthritis, and Sjögren's syndrome. Bursitis and tendinitis, which may result from injuring or overusing a joint, are also related.

Medications that relieve pain and swelling, such as analgesics, anti-inflammatory drugs, biologic response modifiers, glucocorticoids, and antirheumatic drugs, can be used to treat arthritis. They also tend to slow the disease process. Most treatment programs call for exercise, use of heat or cold, and joint-protection techniques, such as avoidance of excess stress on the joints, the use of assistive devices, and weight loss and control. In some cases, surgery may help.

Website: www.arthritis.org

Attention Deficit Hyperactivity Disorder (ADHD)

Source: Centers for Disease Control and Prevention; Natl. Institute of Mental Health

Attention deficit hyperactivity disorder, or ADHD, is one of the most common neurobehavioral disorders of childhood. It is usually first diagnosed in childhood and often lasts into adulthood. Children with ADHD may have trouble paying attention, controlling impulsive behaviors, or be overly active.

Signs and Symptoms of ADHD

- Daydreaming a lot
- Forgetting or losing things a lot
- Squirming or fidgeting
- Talking too much
- Making careless mistakes or taking unnecessary risks
- Having a hard time resisting temptation or taking turns
- Having difficulty getting along with others

There are three different types of ADHD, depending on which types of symptoms are strongest in the individual. A person who is **predominantly inattentive** is easily distracted or forgets details of daily routines. Someone who is **predominantly hyperactive-impulsive** may fidget and talk a lot and find it hard to sit still for long. In the third type, **combined presentation**, the individual displays symptoms of the first two types equally. The cause of ADHD is unknown, but current research shows that genetics plays an important role.

The average age of onset is 7 years old. ADHD affects about 4.1% of American adults age 18 years and older in a given year. The disorder affects 9.0% of American children age 13 to 18 years. Boys are four times more at risk than girls. Studies show that the number of children being diagnosed with ADHD is increasing, but it is unclear why. Rates of ADHD diagnosis increased an average of 3% per year from 1997 to 2006 and an average of 5% per year from 2003 to 2011. In addition, a 2013 survey found that in 2011, 11% of children aged 4-17 years had ever received an ADHD diagnosis and that 8.8% currently had ADHD.

In most cases, ADHD is treated with a combination of medication and behavior therapy. Stimulants are the most widely used medication. Nonstimulants, approved for treating ADHD in 2003, have fewer side effects than stimulants and can last up to 24 hours.

Breast Cancer

Source: American Cancer Society, Inc.

In 2014, an estimated 232,670 women and 2,360 men in the U.S. will be newly diagnosed with breast cancer, and about 40,000 women and 430 men will die from it. Currently, nearly 3.0 mil women are living with a history of breast cancer, the second biggest cause of cancer death for women in the U.S. (lung cancer ranks first). But mortality rates have been declining, especially among younger women, probably because of earlier detection and improved treatment.

The risk for breast cancer increases with age. It is higher for women with a personal or family history of cancer (particularly breast cancer), a long menstrual history (menstrual periods that started early and ended later in life), recent use of birth control pills, use of menopausal hormone therapy containing estrogen and progestin, and in those who have no children or had no live birth until age 30 or older. Other risk factors include alcohol consumption and being overweight or obese. Inherited mutations such as in the BRCA1 and BRCA2 genes greatly increase risk, but these probably account for 5% to 10% of all breast cancers. By far the majority of women who develop breast cancer have no family history of it.

Breast cancer often manifests first as an abnormality on a mammogram X-ray. Physical symptoms that show up later, which may be detectable by a woman or her doctor, include a breast lump and, less commonly, persistent changes to the breast, such as thickening, swelling, distortion, tenderness, skin irritation, redness, scaliness, or nipple abnormalities, such as ulceration, retraction, or spontaneous discharge. Breast pain is more likely to be caused by benign conditions and is not a common symptom of breast cancer.

Studies show that early detection increases survival and treatment options. Although most detected breast lumps are noncancerous, any suspicious lump should be biopsied.

Treatment for breast cancer may involve breast-conserving surgery (removal of the tumor and surrounding tissue), mastectomy (surgical removal of the breast), radiation therapy, chemotherapy, hormone therapy, and/or targeted therapy. The five-year survival rate for female invasive breast cancer patients has improved from 75% in the mid-1970s to 84% today. The five-year survival for women diagnosed with localized breast cancer (cancer that has not spread to lymph nodes or other locations outside the breast) is 99%.

Website: www.cancer.org

Prostate Cancer

Source: Prostate Cancer Foundation; American Cancer Society, Inc.

The prostate is a male gland located between the bladder and scrotum that secretes seminal fluid. Prostate cancer is the most common non-skin cancer in the U.S., and the second-most common cause, after lung cancer, of cancer deaths in American men. In 2014, an estimated 233,000 men will be diagnosed with prostate cancer, and about 29,480 will die from the disease. Currently, nearly 3.0 mil men in the U.S. are living with a history of prostate cancer.

The exact cause of prostate cancer is unknown. The most identifiable risk factors are age, family history, and race. About 60% of all prostate cancers are diagnosed in men over the age of 65, and the chances of developing the disease rise dramatically with age. Having a single first-degree relative with a history of prostate cancer more than doubles a man's risk of developing the disease, and those with several affected relatives have a much higher risk. African-American men are much more likely to develop prostate cancer than non-Hispanic white men and are more than twice as likely to die from it. The cause for this disparity remains unclear.

Usually, the disease has no symptoms in its early stages. As the disease advances, a man may experience weak or interrupted urine flow; inability to urinate or difficulty starting or stopping the urine flow; the need to urinate frequently, especially at night; blood in the urine; or pain or burning with urination. Advanced prostate cancer commonly spreads to the bones, which can cause pain in the hips, spine, ribs, or other areas.

The American Cancer Society recommends that once they reach 50, men at average risk of prostate cancer should speak with their health care provider about the benefits and limitations of prostate-specific antigen (PSA) testing. African-American men or those with a family history of the disease should be aware of their screening options beginning at age 40 or 45. Men under 40 seldom get prostate cancer.

Prostate cancer treatment may include surgery, radiation, hormonal therapy, chemotherapy, or some combination. If caught early on, while tumor cells are localized within the prostate, the five-year relative survival rate approaches 100%.

Websites: www.pcf.org; www.cancer.org

Cancer Risk Factors

Source: American Cancer Society, Inc., www.cancer.org

Alcohol: Alcohol consumption increases the risk of cancers of the mouth, pharynx, larynx, esophagus, liver, colorectum, breast, and possibly pancreas. Alcohol consumption combined with tobacco use increases the risk of cancers of the mouth, larynx, and esophagus far more than either drinking or smoking alone.

Diet and physical activity: Overweight and obesity are associated with increased risk for developing many cancers, including cancers of the breast in postmenopausal women, colon and rectum, endometrium, kidney, pancreas, and adenocarcinoma of the esophagus. Overweight and obesity may also be associated with increased risk of aggressive prostate cancer, non-Hodgkin lymphoma, multiple myeloma, and cancers of the liver, cervix, ovary, and gallbladder. It's not yet known for certain how diet, nutrition intake, and the amount and distribution of body fat factor into the development of certain cancers.

Environmental hazards: Exposure to various chemicals (including benzene, asbestos, vinyl chloride, arsenic, and aflatoxin) increases risk of various cancers. Risk of lung cancer from asbestos is greatly increased among smokers.

Estrogen: Menopausal hormone therapy (MHT, formerly called hormone replacement therapy) without the use of progestin can increase the risk of endometrial and ovarian cancer. Combining progestin with estrogen MHT may help minimize that risk. Studies, however, suggest that use of MHT increases the risk of breast cancer. The benefits and risks of the use of estrogen should be discussed carefully with one's doctor.

HPV infection: There are two vaccines (Gardasil and Cervarix) approved for use in females ages 9-26 for the prevention of the most common types of HPV infection that cause cervical cancer. Gardasil is also approved for use in males ages 9-26 for the prevention of anal and penile cancers, and the prevention of anal, vaginal, and vulvar cancers (and precancers) in women.

Radiation: Excessive exposure to ionizing radiation can increase cancer risk. Medical and dental X-rays are adjusted to deliver the lowest dose possible without sacrificing image quality. Excessive radon exposure in the home may increase lung cancer risk, especially in cigarette smokers.

Smokeless tobacco: Use of chewing tobacco, snuff, and other tobacco products that are not smoked causes oral, esophageal, and pancreatic cancers. The excess risk of cancer of the cheek and gum is especially high among long-term snuff users.

Smoking: The risk of developing lung cancer is about 23 times higher for current male smokers and 13 times higher for current female smokers than for those who have never smoked. Smoking accounts for at least 30% of all U.S. cancer deaths. Tobacco use is responsible for nearly 1 in 5 deaths in the U.S. Smoking increases the risk of the following types of cancer: nasopharynx, nasal cavity and paranasal sinuses, lip, oral cavity (mouth, tongue, lips), pharynx, larynx, lung, esophagus, pancreas, cervix, ovary (mucinous), kidney, bladder, stomach, colorectum, and acute myeloid leukemia.

Sunlight: Many of the 3.5 mil skin cancers diagnosed annually in the U.S. could have been prevented by protection from the sun's rays and avoiding indoor tanning. Epidemiological evidence shows that sun exposure is a major factor in the development of melanoma and that incidence rates are increasing worldwide.

Screening Guidelines for Early Detection of Cancer

Cancer site	Population	Test or procedure	Frequency
Breast	Women, age 20+	Breast self-examination (BSE)	Beginning in their early 20s: women should be told about BSE. Reporting any new breast symptoms to a health professional should be emphasized. Women should receive instruction and have their technique reviewed at a periodic health exam.
		Clinical breast examination (CBE)	Women in their 20s and 30s: CBE should be part of a periodic health exam, preferably at least every 3 years. Asymptomatic women aged 40+ should continue to receive a CBE as part of a periodic health exam, preferably annually.
		Mammography	At age 40: begin annual mammography. A CBE should be performed prior to mammography.
Cervix	Women, ages 21-65	Pap test, HPV DNA test	All women should begin screening by age 21. Women ages 21-29 should have a Pap test every 3 years. From ages 30-65, the preferred way to screen is with a Pap test combined with an HPV test every 5 years. Another option is to get tested every 3 years with just the Pap test. Some women age 65 or over who have had a certain number of negative consecutive tests in the previous 10 years should consult a physician; health history may allow them to stop cervical cancer screening. Women who have had a total hysterectomy may stop screening. Women should not be screened annually by any method at any age.
Colorectal	Men and women, age 50+	Fecal occult blood test (FOBT) with at least 50% test sensitivity for cancer, or fecal immunochemical test (FIT) with at least 50% test sensitivity for cancer, **or**	Annual, starting at age 50. Testing at home with adherence to manufacturer's recommendation for collection techniques and number of samples is recommended. FOBT with the single stool sample collected on the clinician's fingertip during a digital rectal examination in a health care setting is not recommended. Guaiac-based toilet bowl FOBT tests also are not recommended. In comparison with guaiac-based tests for the detection of occult blood, immunochemical tests are more patient-friendly and are likely to be equal or better in sensitivity and specificity. There is no need to repeat an FOBT in response to an initial positive finding.
		Stool DNA test, **or**	Interval uncertain, starting at age 50. The stool DNA test approved for colorectal cancer screening in 2008 is no longer commercially available. As of 2014, new stool DNA tests were undergoing evaluation.
		Flexible sigmoidoscopy (FSIG), **or**	Every 5 years, starting at age 50. FSIG can be performed alone, or consideration can be given to combining FSIG performed every 5 years with a highly sensitive guaiac FOBT or FIT performed annually.
		Double contrast barium enema (DCBE), **or**	Every 5 years, starting at age 50
		Colonoscopy	Every 10 years, starting at age 50
		CT colonography	Every 5 years, starting at age 50
Endometrial	Women, at menopause		Women at average risk should be informed about risks and symptoms of endometrial cancer and strongly encouraged to report any unexpected bleeding or spotting to their physicians.
Lung	Current or former smokers, ages 55-74	Low dose helical CT (LDCT)	Apparently healthy patients who currently smoke or have quit within the past 15 years should discuss lung-cancer screening with a clinician. Informed and shared decision making related to the potential benefits, limitations, and harms associated with screening for lung cancer with LDCT should occur before any decision is made.
Prostate	Men, age 50+	Digital rectal examination (DRE) and prostate-specific antigen test (PSA)	Men who have at least a 10-year life expectancy should make an informed decision with their health care provider about whether to be screened for prostate cancer after receiving information about the potential benefits, risks, and uncertainties associated with prostate cancer screening.

New U.S. Cancer Cases and Deaths for Leading Sites, 2014

Source: *Cancer Facts & Figures 2014*, American Cancer Society, Inc.

The following estimates exclude basal cell and squamous cell skin cancers and in situ carcinomas (i.e., noninvasive cancers), except of the urinary bladder. In 2014, an estimated 62,570 new cases of carcinoma in situ of the female breast and 63,770 cases of melanoma in situ are expected to be diagnosed. More than 3 mil cases of basal cell and squamous cell skin cancer are diagnosed yearly; most cases are highly curable.

Estimated New Cases

Both sexes		Male		Female	
Breast	235,030	Prostate	233,000	Breast	232,670
Prostate	233,000	Lung and bronchus	116,000	Lung and bronchus	108,210
Lung and bronchus	224,210	Urinary bladder	56,390	Uterine corpus	52,630
Colon	96,830	Colon	48,450	Colon	48,380
Melanoma—skin	76,100	Melanoma—skin	43,890	Thyroid	47,790
Urinary bladder	74,690	Kidney and renal pelvis	39,140	Non-Hodgkin lymphoma	32,530
Non-Hodgkin lymphoma	70,800	Non-Hodgkin lymphoma	38,270	Melanoma—skin	32,210
Kidney and renal pelvis	63,920	Liver and intrahepatic bile duct	24,600	Kidney and renal pelvis	24,780
Thyroid	62,980	Pancreas	23,530	Pancreas	22,890
Uterine corpus	52,630	Rectum	23,380	Ovary	21,980
All sites	**1,665,540**	**All sites**	**855,220**	**All sites**	**810,320**

Estimated Deaths

Both sexes		Male		Female	
Lung and bronchus	159,260	Lung and bronchus	86,930	Lung and bronchus	72,330
Colon and rectum	50,310	Prostate	29,480	Breast	40,000
Breast	40,430	Colon and rectum	26,270	Colon and rectum	24,040
Pancreas	39,590	Pancreas	20,170	Pancreas	19,420
Prostate	29,480	Liver and intrahepatic bile duct	15,870	Ovary	14,270
Liver and intrahepatic bile duct	23,000	Esophagus	12,450	Uterine corpus	8,590
Non-Hodgkin lymphoma	18,990	Urinary bladder	11,170	Non-Hodgkin lymphoma	8,520
Urinary bladder	15,580	Non-Hodgkin lymphoma	10,470	Liver and intrahepatic bile duct	7,130
Esophagus	15,450	Kidney and renal pelvis	8,900	Brain and other nervous system	6,230
Brain and other nervous system	14,320	Brain and other nervous system	8,090	Myeloma	4,980
All sites	**585,720**	**All sites**	**310,010**	**All sites**	**275,710**

U.S. Cancer Survival Rates by Year of Diagnosis, 1960-2010

Source: SEER (Surveillance, Epidemiology, and End Results) Cancer Statistics Review, 1975-2011, National Cancer Institute, National Institutes of Health

Year of diagnosis	All races % total	% male	% female	White % total	% male	% female	Black % total	% male	% female
1960-63	—	—	—	39.0%	—	—	27.0%	—	—
1970-73	—	—	—	43.0	—	—	31.0	—	—
1975-77	48.9%	41.7%	55.9%	49.8	42.7%	56.5%	39.0	32.7%	46.2%
1978-80	49.0	43.1	54.9	50.0	44.3	55.6	38.9	33.3	45.6
1981-83	50.2	45.2	55.1	51.3	46.6	56.0	38.7	34.1	44.4
1984-86	52.4	47.1	57.6	53.6	48.6	58.5	40.1	35.4	45.5
1987-89	55.3	51.1	59.6	56.7	52.8	60.6	42.9	38.8	47.7
1990-92	59.9	59.1	60.9	61.4	60.8	62.0	47.7	47.5	48.1
1993-96	61.3	60.8	61.8	62.4	62.0	62.8	52.7	54.4	50.5
1996-98	63.3	63.0	63.6	64.4	64.1	64.7	55.1	57.8	51.9
1999-2003	66.4	66.8	66.0	67.7	68.1	67.2	58.4	61.9	54.3
2004-10	68.3	69.0	67.6	69.4	70.0	68.7	61.5	64.9	57.7

— = Statistic could not be calculated. **Note:** The geographic areas of surveillance may vary for different years. Rates are five-year relative (estimated) survival rates for all invasive cancer sites; based on follow-up of patients into 2011.

U.S. Cancer Survival Rates by Age at Diagnosis, 2004-10

Source: SEER (Surveillance, Epidemiology, and End Results) Cancer Statistics Review, 1975-2011, National Cancer Institute, National Institutes of Health

Age at diagnosis	All races % total	% male	% female	White % total	% male	% female	Black % total	% male	% female
Under age 45	81.1%	76.4%	84.1%	82.7%	78.3%	85.6%	69.7%	63.3%	73.5%
Ages 45-54	73.0	67.6	77.5	74.5	68.8	79.1	62.6	61.1	64.2
Ages 55-64	69.8	69.7	69.9	70.7	70.3	71.1	62.8	65.6	58.5
Under age 65	73.1	70.2	76.0	74.3	71.2	77.4	64.1	63.9	64.3
Ages 65-74	65.6	68.8	61.0	66.1	68.9	62.0	60.4	66.6	51.4
Ages 65 and older	58.6	62.9	53.4	59.0	62.9	54.3	53.4	61.1	44.2
Ages 75 and older	51.3	55.7	47.1	51.9	55.8	48.2	43.1	50.7	36.7

Note: Rates are five-year relative (estimated) survival rates for all invasive cancer sites; based on follow-up of patients into 2011.

Skin Cancer

Source: American Cancer Society, Inc.

Skin cancer is generally divided into two main classes, **nonmelanomas** and **melanomas**, both types affecting different types of skin cells. Melanoma develops in skin cells called melanocytes, which produce melanin, a pigment that gives skin a tan or brown color and helps to protect the deeper layers of skin from some of the harmful effects of the sun.

Melanoma is the most dangerous type of skin cancer because it can easily spread to other parts of the body.

Although skin cancer is the most common type of cancer diagnosed in the U.S., melanoma accounts for less than 2% of all skin cancers. The American Cancer Society estimates that in 2014, 76,100 new cases of melanoma will be diagnosed in the U.S., and about 9,710 people will die from melanoma, while 12,980 will die from any skin cancer.

The exact causes of melanoma are unclear, but there are several risk factors that have been associated with the disease:

- Overexposure to UV light (sunlight or tanning booths)
- Multiple or unusual moles
- Fair skin, freckling, and light hair
- Family history or personal history of skin cancers
- Occupational exposure to coal tar, pitch, creosote, arsenic compounds, or radium
- Past history of severe sunburns

Melanomas generally look like abnormal moles on the surface of the skin. Normal moles are most often an evenly colored brown, tan, or black spot on the skin that can be flat or raised. They normally have a distinct border that separates them from normal skin cells. Moles can be present at birth, form over time, or even disappear. Abnormal moles differ from regular skin cells and may be a sign of skin cancer. An irregular mole should be examined as soon as possible. Irregular moles generally have the following characteristics:

- Asymmetry: one half does not match the other half
- Border: edges are irregular, ragged, notched, or blurred
- Color: not uniform; may be shades of brown or black, and patches of pink, red, blue, or white
- Diameter: moles wider than ¼ inch are abnormal (however, melanomas can be smaller)
- Evolving: mole changes size, shape, or color

If a melanoma is suspected, the doctor will perform a biopsy using cells extracted from the suspected cancer or by removing the whole mass and examining it. If a melanoma is found, doctors will often check to see if the cancer has spread to other parts of the body. This is called staging and is represented by Roman numerals I through IV (1-4). The lower the number, the less the cancer has spread. This will determine what course of treatment is necessary.

If caught early, melanoma is highly curable. The overall five-year survival rate for melanoma is 91%. For localized melanoma, the five-year survival rate is 98%; survival rates for regional and distant stage diseases are 62% and 16%, respectively. About 84% of melanomas are diagnosed at a localized stage.

Treatment may include simple removal of the melanoma; amputation if the cancer is found on a finger or toe; or chemotherapy, immunotherapy, and/or radiation if the melanoma has spread to other parts of the body.

Website: www.cancer.org

Depression

Source: National Institute of Mental Health (NIMH), National Institutes of Health, U.S. Dept. of Health and Human Services

Depression is a serious illness that affects thoughts, feelings, and the ability to function in everyday life. It strikes all age groups and often goes unrecognized or is inadequately treated. The NIMH estimates that about 20.9 mil American adults age 18 and older suffer from depression or some other mood or depressive disorder in any given year; more than 16% of all Americans will have had depression at some point in life. Young people are at particular risk; in a one-year period, persons aged 18 to 29 years were 200% more likely to have experienced depression than those who were 60 or older.

Women are 70% more likely than men to experience depression during their lifetime. Although conventional wisdom holds that depression is most closely associated with menopause, the childbearing years, followed by the years prior to menopause, are marked by the highest rates of depression. The influence of hormones on depression in women has been an active area of NIMH research.

Available treatments can alleviate symptoms, and with awareness growing, more people with depression are seeking help. But many depressed people—and those around them—still fail to realize that they have an illness or could benefit from medical help.

Symptoms and Types of Depression

- Persistent sad, anxious, or "empty" feelings
- Feelings of hopelessness or pessimism
- Feelings of guilt, worthlessness, or helplessness
- Irritability, restlessness
- Loss of interest in activities or hobbies once pleasurable, including sex
- Fatigue and decreased energy
- Difficulty concentrating, remembering details, and making decisions
- Insomnia, early-morning wakefulness, or excessive sleeping
- Overeating or appetite loss
- Thoughts of suicide, suicide attempts
- Aches or pains, headaches, cramps, or digestive problems that do not ease even with treatment

A diagnosis of **major depressive disorder** (or **major depression**) is made if an individual reports experiencing five or more of these symptoms in the same two-week period.

Bipolar disorder (or **manic-depressive illness**) is characterized by episodes of major depression alternating with periods of mania, when a person experiences a persistent, abnormally elevated mood or irritability, accompanied by feelings of inflated self-esteem, less need for sleep, increased talkativeness, racing thoughts, distractibility, agitation, and excessive involvement in pleasurable activities that have a high potential for painful consequences. While it shares some of the features of major depression, bipolar disorder is a distinct illness.

Treatments for Depression

A variety of medicines are used to treat depression. These drugs influence the functioning of certain neurotransmitters in the brain, primarily serotonin and norepinephrine. Older drugs—tricyclic antidepressants (TCAs) and monoamine oxidase inhibitors (MAOIs)—affect the functioning of both of these neurotransmitters. But they can have strong side effects or, in the case of MAOIs, require dietary restrictions. Newer medications, such as selective serotonin reuptake inhibitors (SSRIs), have fewer side effects. All of these medications can be effective, but some people respond to one type and not another.

NIMH research has shown that certain types of psychotherapy, particularly cognitive-behavioral therapy (CBT) and interpersonal therapy (IPT), can help relieve depression. CBT helps patients change the negative thinking and behaving patterns often associated with depression. IPT focuses patients on working through personal relationships that may contribute to depression. Studies of adults have shown that a combination of psychotherapy and antidepressant medication is most effective in treating moderate-to-severe depression.

Electroconvulsive therapy (ECT) has been found effective in treating some cases of severe depression, particularly those that have not responded to other forms of treatment. ECT involves producing a seizure in the brain of a patient under general anesthesia by applying electrical stimulation through electrodes placed on the scalp. Memory loss and other cognitive problems, though common side effects, are typically short-lived.

Website: www.nimh.nih.gov

Diabetes

Source: American Diabetes Association; Centers for Disease Control and Prevention, U.S. Dept. of Health and Human Services

Diabetes is a chronic disease in which the body does not produce or properly use the hormone **insulin**. Insulin is needed to convert sugar, starches, and other foods into energy. Both genetics and environment appear to play roles in the onset of diabetes. This disease, which has no cure, is the seventh leading cause of death by disease in the U.S. According to death certificate data, 73,932 people in the U.S. died as a result of diabetes in 2012. In 2012, an estimated 29.1 mil Americans had diabetes, 8.1 mil of whom were undiagnosed.

The American Diabetes Association supports studies proving that detection at an earlier stage and modest lifestyle changes, such as eating better and exercising more, will help prevent or delay complications.

There are two major types of diabetes:

Type 1 (formerly known as insulin-dependent or juvenile diabetes). The body does not produce insulin; the disease is usually diagnosed in children and young adults. People with type 1 diabetes must take daily insulin to stay alive.

Type 2 (formerly known as non-insulin dependent or adult-onset diabetes). The body does not produce enough or cannot properly use insulin. It is the most common form of the disease (90%-95% of diabetes cases in people over age 20) and often begins later in life.

Prediabetes

In 2012, 86 mil Americans age 20 and older had prediabetes, the state that occurs when a person's blood glucose levels are higher than normal but not high enough for a diagnosis of diabetes. According to the Centers for Disease Control and Prevention, 15%-30% of people with prediabetes will develop type 2 diabetes within five years unless lifestyle changes are made.

Complications From Diabetes

People often have diabetes for many years before it is diagnosed. During that time, serious complications may develop. Potential complications include the following:

Blindness. Diabetes is the leading cause of new cases of blindness in people ages 20-74. Each year, 12,000 to 24,000 people lose their eyesight because of diabetes.

Kidney disease. About 30% of patients with type 1 diabetes and 10%-40% of those with type 2 diabetes eventually suffer from kidney failure. In 2011, a total of 49,677 people in the U.S. initiated treatment for kidney failure due to diabetes.

Amputations. Diabetes is the most frequent cause for nontraumatic lower-limb amputations. The risk of a leg amputation is 15-40 times greater for a person with diabetes than for the average American. In 2010, approximately 73,000 lower-limb amputations were performed as a result of complications brought on by diabetes.

Heart disease and stroke. People with diabetes are about 1.7 times more likely to die of heart disease. They are 1.5 times more likely to suffer a stroke.

Common Diabetes Symptoms

- Frequent urination
- Thirst
- Hunger
- Extreme fatigue
- Blurry vision
- Cuts/bruises that are slow to heal
- Weight loss, even with increased caloric intake (type 1)
- Tingling, pain, or numbness in the hands/feet (type 2)

Gestational Diabetes

Gestational diabetes is a form of diabetes that affects about 18% of pregnant women. Usually there are no symptoms, or the symptoms are mild. Because the condition usually appears around the 24th week, it is recommended that all pregnant women receive a glucose tolerance test between the 24th and 28th week. Pregnancy hormones can cause insulin resistance, making blood glucose levels rise. The goal of treatment is to keep blood glucose levels within normal limits, mainly through diet and exercise; treatment may also include daily blood glucose testing and insulin injections. Women with gestational diabetes tend to have larger babies at birth, which can increase the chance of problems at the time of delivery. Glucose levels usually return to normal after delivery, but odds of recurrence in future pregnancies and development of type 2 diabetes later in life increase.
Website: www.diabetes.org

Eating Disorders

Source: National Institute of Mental Health, National Institutes of Health, U.S. Dept. of Health and Human Services

Eating disorders involve serious disturbances in eating behavior, usually in the forms of extreme and unhealthy reduction of food intake or severe overeating. They are not due to a failure of will; rather, they are real and treatable medical illnesses in which certain behavior patterns get out of control. The main types are anorexia nervosa, bulimia nervosa, and binge-eating disorder (technically categorized with "eating disorders not otherwise specified"). These disorders usually develop in adolescence or early adulthood and often occur with other illnesses such as depression, substance abuse, and anxiety disorders. They are much more common among females; about 5%-10% of anorexia patients, 20% of bulimia patients, and 40% of binge eaters are male.

If not treated, eating disorders can lead to serious complications, including heart conditions and kidney failure, which may result in death.

Anorexia nervosa affects an estimated 0.9% of all females. Symptoms include resistance to maintaining weight at minimally healthy levels, intense fear of gaining weight, exaggerated importance of body weight or shape in one's self image, and infrequent or absent menstrual periods. Anorexics see themselves as overweight even when they are dangerously thin. In response, they avoid food and take other extreme measures to lose weight, such as exercising compulsively or purging by means of vomiting or laxatives and enemas. While some anorexics fully recover after a single episode, others may relapse frequently or experience chronic deterioration.

Bulimia nervosa affects an estimated 0.5% of females. It is characterized by recurrent uncontrolled binge-eating episodes followed by what is believed to be compensatory behavior to prevent weight gain, such as self-induced vomiting, use of laxatives or diuretics, exercising excessively, or fasting. Persons with bulimia can weigh within the normal range for their age and height, but they still fear gaining weight and are intensely dissatisfied with their bodies. They often perform their behaviors in secret, feeling shame when they binge and relief when they purge.

Binge-eating disorder affects an estimated 2%-3.5% of males and females in the U.S. As with bulimia, a binge-eating disorder involves episodes of excessive eating during which the sufferer may feel a complete lack of control. But individuals with this disorder do not compensate by purging, exercising, or fasting. Many are thus overweight or obese, and the shame they feel can lead to further binge-eating.

Eating disorder sufferers may not admit they are ill. Early diagnosis and a comprehensive treatment program are essential to recovery. Some patients may need immediate hospitalization. For anorexia, treatment usually follows three established steps: weight restoration, usually in an inpatient hospital setting; treatment of any accompanying psychological disturbances, including the use of medications; and achieving long-term remission or recovery by reducing or eliminating negative thoughts and behaviors.

Heart and Blood Vessel Disease

Source: American Heart Association; National Center for Chronic Disease Prevention and Health Promotion, Centers for Disease Control and Prevention; National Heart, Blood, and Lung Institute, National Institutes of Health, U.S. Dept. of Health and Human Services

Warning Signs of Heart Attack

- Chest discomfort. Most heart attacks involve discomfort in the center of the chest that lasts more than a few minutes or that goes away and then returns. It can feel like uncomfortable pressure, squeezing, fullness, or pain.
- Discomfort in other areas of the upper body. Symptoms can include pain or discomfort in one or both arms, the back, neck, jaw, or stomach.
- Shortness of breath. This feeling may occur with or without chest discomfort.
- Other signs may include breaking out in a cold sweat, nausea, or lightheadedness.

The American Heart Association advises immediate action at onset of symptoms, as more than half of heart attack victims die within an hour of symptoms first manifesting. Call 9-1-1. Get to a hospital right away.

Warning Signs of Stroke

- Sudden numbness or weakness of the face, arm, or leg, especially on one side of the body.
- Sudden confusion, trouble speaking, or understanding.
- Sudden trouble seeing in one or both eyes.
- Sudden trouble walking, dizziness, loss of balance or coordination.
- Sudden severe headache with no known cause.

Prompt treatment of a stroke can be a major factor in controlling the effects. If you have one or more stroke symptoms that last more than a few minutes, call 9-1-1 or the emergency medical service number immediately so an ambulance, ideally one with advanced life support, can be sent for you quickly.

Major Modifiable Risk Factors

High blood pressure. High blood pressure, or hypertension, increases the risk of stroke, heart attack, kidney failure, and congestive heart failure. It affects men and women of all races, ethnic origins, and ages. Obesity, physical inactivity, and an unhealthy diet can contribute to this often symptomless disease. Individuals should have a blood pressure reading at least once every two years or more often if advised by a physician.

A blood pressure reading consists of two measurements, with one value written above the other, such as 122/78 mmHg (millimeters of mercury). The upper number (systolic pressure) represents the amount of pressure in the arteries when the heart contracts (beats) and pushes blood through the circulatory system. The lower number (diastolic pressure) represents the pressure in the arteries between beats, when the heart is resting. According to National Institutes of Health (NIH) guidelines, a blood pressure reading below 120/80 is considered normal, while readings from 120/80 to 139/89 are considered prehypertension.

There are two stages of high blood pressure:

Stage 1 is 140-159 (systolic) over 90-99 (diastolic);

Stage 2 is 160+ (systolic) over 100+ (diastolic).

The diagnosis can be based on either the systolic or the diastolic reading.

High blood pressure usually cannot be cured, but it can be controlled in a variety of ways, including lifestyle modifications and medication. Treatment always should be at the direction and under the supervision of a physician. The treatment goal for patients with hypertension is blood pressure below 140/90. Individuals with hypertension and diabetes or chronic kidney disease should aim for blood pressure lower than 130/80.

High blood cholesterol. Cholesterol is a waxy fat-like substance found in all cells of the body. It is produced by the body and also comes in some foods. The body needs some cholesterol, but excess levels increase the risk of heart disease. High cholesterol in itself usually does not cause symptoms, so many people are unaware that they have a problem.

There are two major kinds of cholesterol: LDL (low-density lipoprotein), often called "bad" cholesterol, leads to narrowing of the arteries. HDL (high-density lipoprotein), known as "good" cholesterol, helps reduce that risk.

NIH guidelines classify total cholesterol levels (determined by a blood test) of less than 200 mg/dl as desirable, 200-239 as borderline high, and 240 and higher as high. About 13% of Americans have a cholesterol level of 240 mg/dl or higher. LDL levels of less than 100 are considered optimal, 130-159 as borderline high, 160-189 as high, and 190 and higher as very high. For HDL, levels of 60 mg/dl and higher are considered protective against heart disease, while levels under 40 mg/dl are considered a risk factor.

As with high blood pressure, high blood cholesterol can be controlled by lifestyle changes and medication and should be treated by a physician.

Triglycerides, another form of fat in the blood, can also raise the risk of heart disease. Levels that are borderline high (150-199) or high (200 or more) may need treatment.

Diabetes. Diabetes is a major risk factor for heart disease; at least 65% of people with diabetes mellitus die of some form of heart or blood vessel disease.

Smoking. Cigarette smokers are two to four times more likely to develop coronary heart disease (CHD). Smoking is also associated with the risk of sudden cardiac death.

Obesity. Using a body mass index (BMI) of 25 and higher for overweight and 30 and higher for obesity, about 69% of Americans aged 20 and over are either overweight or obese, and 35% are obese.

Physical inactivity. A sedentary lifestyle is a risk factor for CHD. The risk increase is comparable to that observed for high blood cholesterol, high blood pressure, or cigarette smoking.

Women and Cardiovascular Disease

The American Heart Association reports that heart disease, stroke, and other cardiovascular diseases are the number one cause of death in American women. (Cancer is the second leading cause.) One in three women died of some form of cardiovascular disease in 2010. Because heart disease was long viewed as a "man's" disease, many of the major cardiovascular studies were conducted only on men. Recent attention has been directed toward understanding the influence of gender on cardiovascular disease risk and prevention, but important gaps in knowledge remain.

Women often present some of the same classic symptoms of heart attack as men, such as chest pain that spreads to the shoulders and arms. But women may more often report atypical chest pain, abdominal pain, difficulty breathing (dyspnea), and nausea. Another problem in **diagnosis** is that women tend to have heart attacks later in life than men, so symptoms may be masked by other age-related diseases such as arthritis or osteoporosis. Even certain diagnostic tests and procedures such as the exercise stress test may not be as accurate in women, with the result that the disease process leading to heart attack or stroke may not be detected early on, with potentially serious consequences.

Website: www.heart.org

Irritable Bowel Syndrome

Source: National Institute of Diabetes and Digestive and Kidney Diseases, National Institutes of Health

Irritable bowel syndrome (IBS)—a functional disorder, not a disease, in the gastrointestinal tract—is one of the most common disorders diagnosed by physicians. An estimated 10%-15% of Americans have IBS symptoms; however, less than one-third of people with the condition see a health care provider for diagnosis. IBS occurs more frequently in women than in men, and it is most often found in people younger than 45 years. Though IBS causes discomfort and may even be painful, it does not damage the bowel.

Many people are uncomfortable discussing IBS because of its symptoms. They may include the following:

- Bowel movements occurring more or less often than usual
- Abdominal pain
- Bloating
- Discomfort
- Constipation
- Mucus in the stool
- Diarrhea

For most people, IBS is a chronic condition, and there will likely be times when the symptoms may worsen or disappear altogether only to reappear in the future. Most complications are derived from the symptoms, such as hemorrhoids, which may form as a result of diarrhea and constipation. People with chronic IBS may also go through periods of depression because of the constant discomfort and the symptoms' interference in work and personal relationships.

The specific causes for IBS are unknown. The walls of the intestines are lined with layers of muscle that contract and relax in a coordinated manner as they move food through the digestive system. When a person has IBS, the contractions cause food to either speed up or slow down as it moves through the bowel, subsequently causing gas, bloating, diarrhea, or constipation. Some researchers believe that people who suffer from IBS have a colon that is particularly sensitive to certain foods. Foods rich in carbohydrates, spicy or fatty foods, coffee, and alcohol in particular can trigger IBS symptoms. Another common factor is a low tolerance for stretching of the large intestine. Women tend to have more severe symptoms during menstrual periods, leading researchers to believe that IBS may have a hormonal trigger. Recent research has shown that serotonin, a neurotransmitter hormone, may be linked with gastrointestinal functioning.

IBS can sometimes result from infection or other problems in the body. Researchers have found that people who have had gastroenteritis later develop IBS. But because IBS symptoms can match those of many serious diseases, it is important for chronic sufferers to consult their doctors. If symptoms began early in life and have remained stable, one may need to get a colonoscopy to rule out inflammatory bowel disease, such as Crohn's disease or ulcerative colitis, or even colon cancer. Those with IBS over 50 years of age should be regularly screened for colon cancer.

Despite the uncertainty over what causes IBS, there are known precautionary measures that people with sensitive digestive systems can take. Keeping a well-balanced diet is the best possible preventive. Eating foods with dietary fiber, such as whole-grain bread and cereal, as well as vegetables and beans as part of a daily diet can reduce IBS symptoms, although high-fiber diets may cause gas and bloating. Eating large meals has been shown to worsen the condition, so IBS sufferers may want to eat several smaller meals.

There is no cure for IBS. Treatment usually involves lessening the symptoms so that they don't interfere as much in a person's life.

Common Infectious Diseases

Source: National Institutes of Health, Centers for Disease Control and Prevention, U.S. Dept. of Health and Human Services; World Health Organization

The following is a list of major infectious diseases. It is meant to be used for reference purposes only and not as a tool for diagnosis. Statistics may appear uneven because of the different reporting methods used by the various agencies and because not all diseases are surveyed in the same year.

Chicken pox

(*Varicella simplex*) Usually nonthreatening viral disease commonly associated with children. In adults, the disease can be serious. **Transmission:** highly contagious. Transmitted by direct contact with rash, coughing, or sneezing of infected persons. **Symptoms:** blister-like rash, discomfort, high fever. Infected people may develop shingles later in life. **Vaccine:** available since 1995. **Treatment:** none; antibiotics in some severe cases. **Annual U.S. cases:** before 1995, about 4 mil, mostly children; 13,447 reported in 2012.

Chlamydia

(*Chlamydia trachomatis*) One of the most widely spread sexually transmitted diseases (STDs). **Transmission:** sexually transmitted. **Symptoms:** about 70% of those infected show no symptoms. In women, vaginal discharge, infection of the cervix and urinary tract; can cause pelvic inflammatory disease. In men, infection of urinary tract and epididymitis (inflammation of testicular duct); can also infect the throat, rectum, and eyes. **Treatment:** curable with antibiotics. **Annual U.S. cases:** 1,422,976 in 2012.

Common cold

(More than 200 different viruses) An upper respiratory viral infection. **Transmission:** touching one's nose, eyes, or mouth after touching something contaminated by the virus; inhalation of airborne virus. **Symptoms:** irritated nose or scratchy throat, sneezing and watery green or yellow nasal discharge, coughing, muscle aches, headaches, postnasal drip, decreased appetite. **Treatment:** no cure. Over-the-counter remedies can relieve symptoms; effectiveness of antiviral drugs uncertain. **Est. annual U.S. cases:** about 1 bil.

Gonorrhea

(*Neisseria gonorrhoeae*) Common bacterial STD. **Transmission:** sexually transmitted. **Symptoms:** in men, discomfort in urethra, yellow or green discharge, burning during urination. In women, pelvic pain, bleeding associated with intercourse, burning during urination, yellow or bloody discharge. **Treatment:** highly curable with antibiotics. **Annual U.S. cases:** 334,826 in 2012.

Hepatitis

A viral disease that causes inflammation of the liver. In the U.S., five forms are endemic: A, B, C, D, and E. Forms A, B, and C are the most common. **Symptoms:** all forms have generally similar symptoms including jaundice, fatigue, abdominal pain, loss of appetite, nausea, mild flu-like symptoms. Many cases cause no symptoms. In extreme cases, liver transplants may be necessary.

Hepatitis A (*Hepatovirus picornaviridae*). **Transmission:** consuming food or water contaminated with feces from infected persons. **Vaccine:** effective; travelers are advised to not drink tap water in countries where disease is common. **Treatment:** disease usually resolves on its own; alcohol consumption should be avoided. **Est. annual U.S. cases:** 2,700 infections in 2011; 1,562 acute lab-confirmed cases reported in 2012.

Hepatitis B (*Orthohepadnavirus hepadnaviridae*). **Transmission:** unsterilized needle sharing; contaminated blood transfusions; sexual contact. **Vaccine:** highly effective. **Treatment:** for chronic cases, drug treatment is necessary. For acute cases, disease usually resolves itself. Severe cases treated with lamivudine. **Est. annual U.S. cases:** 18,800 infections in 2011; 2,895 acute lab-confirmed cases reported in 2012.

Hepatitis C (*Hepacivirus flavinviridae*). **Transmission:** unsterilized needle sharing; contaminated blood transfusions; sexual contact. **Vaccine:** none. **Treatment:** chronic cases treated with drugs, which eliminates virus in about 50% of patients. For acute cases, treatment recommended if disease present after two to three months. **Est. annual U.S. cases:** 16,500 infections in 2011; 1,782 acute lab-confirmed cases reported in 2012.

HPV

(More than 100 strains of human papillomavirus) Common viral infection; leading cause of cervical cancer. **Transmission:** sexually transmitted. **Symptoms:** most of those infected have no symptoms but can still transmit virus. In some cases, genital warts and precancerous bumps on anus, cervix or vulva, or penis. **Vaccine:** Gardasil and Cervarix. **Treatment:** while there is no cure, a healthy immune system can usually fight off HPV on its own. Women with HPV should have a Pap smear and pelvic exam every six months. **Est. annual U.S. cases:** 14 mil new cases; approximately 79 mil currently infected with HPV.

Influenza

(Various influenza viruses) Highly contagious viral respiratory infection. **Transmission:** airborne; contact with face after touching infected surface. **Symptoms:** chills, fatigue, fever, headaches, sore throat, sinus congestion, coughing. ("Stomach flu" is not influenza.) **Vaccine:** yearly vaccinations recommended; available as injection or nasal spray. **Treatment:** antiviral drugs; disease normally runs its course in a matter of days. **Est. annual U.S. cases:** 5%-20% of population; more than 200,000 flu-related hospitalizations, 3,000-49,000 flu-related deaths.

Lyme disease

(*Borrelia burgdorferi*) Bacterial inflammatory disease, first identified 1975 in Old Lyme, CT. Found across the U.S., usually in areas with large deer populations. **Transmission:** bite from infected deer tick. Mice and deer are most common tick hosts. **Symptoms:** mimic those of other diseases. Flu-like symptoms: fatigue, stiff neck, joint inflammation; skin rash may appear at site of tick bite. **Treatment:** antibiotics in early stages; anti-inflammatory drugs to relieve symptoms. Without treatment, long-term complications (some fatal) involving joints, heart, and nervous system. **Annual U.S. cases:** from 9,895 reported cases in 1992 to 30,831 confirmed and probable cases in 2012.

Malaria

(*Plasmodium* parasite) Infectious disease known from as early as 2700 BCE. Virtually eradicated in developed countries; still a major killer in tropical regions. **Transmission:** bite from infected mosquito. **Symptoms:** high fever, shaking chills, heavy sweating, headaches, fatigue, enlarged spleen. If left untreated, organ damage and death. **Treatment:** antimalarial drugs, including chloroquine, for treatment and prevention. **Annual cases:** 1,503 in the U.S. in 2012; worldwide, an estimated 207 mil cases and 627,000 deaths, mostly young children in sub-Saharan Africa, in 2012.

Measles

(*Rubeola* virus) Once-common viral infection; occurs sporadically in U.S. **Transmission:** airborne transmission by infected persons. **Symptoms:** itchy and raised rash, sore throat, cough, pink eye, high fever. In rare cases, encephalitis, seizures, permanent deafness, death. **Vaccine:** highly effective. **Treatment:** no specific treatment; symptoms relieved with bed rest, acetaminophen, humidified air. **Annual U.S. cases:** 55 in 2012.

Mumps

(Mumps virus) Acute and contagious viral infection. **Transmission:** direct contact with mucus or saliva of infected persons. **Symptoms:** painful, visible swelling of the salivary or parotid glands in the face. Chills, headaches, fever, painful swallowing. In some cases, inflammation of testes, pancreas, ovaries. In severe cases, brain swelling and symptoms ranging from nausea and drowsiness to seizures and permanent deafness. **Vaccine:** MMR (measles, mumps, and

rubella) vaccine is effective. **Treatment:** no specific treatment; symptoms may be relieved by applying ice or heat to swollen glands. **Annual U.S. cases:** 229 in 2012.

Peptic ulcer

(Most from *Helicobacter pylori* [*H. pylori*] bacteria; also overuse of aspirin or other anti-inflammatory drugs) Weakening of the stomach's protective mucous coating, allowing stomach acid and bacteria to irritate stomach lining. **Transmission:** *H. pylori* may be transmitted through food and water. **Symptoms:** indigestion; bloating; dull, transient abdominal pain or discomfort; nausea; vomiting. **Treatment:** antibiotics, acid-suppressing drugs. **Est. annual U.S. cases:** about 20% of the population under 40 years of age and half of those over 60 may be infected with *H. pylori*. An estimated 500,000 to 850,000 develop peptic ulcers each year.

Pertussis or Whooping cough

(*Bordetella pertussis* or *B. parepertussis*) Upper respiratory bacterial infection. **Transmission:** airborne transmission by infected persons; highly contagious. **Symptoms:** initially, mild cold-like symptoms, fever, diarrhea, difficulty breathing; later, violent coughing with characteristic "whooping" sound when patient tries to breathe between coughs, vomiting. In severe cases, apnea, pneumonia, seizures, encephalopathy. **Vaccine:** available as part of combination vaccine that also prevents diphtheria and tetanus. **Treatment:** antibiotics in early cases; otherwise, disease must run its course. **Annual U.S. cases:** 48,277 in 2012.

Salmonella or Salmonellosis

(*Salmonella enteritidis*) Bacterial infection. **Transmission:** eating foods contaminated by feces carrying the bacteria or eating undercooked meats or raw eggs contaminated by bacteria. Contact with feces of infected animal or pet. **Symptoms:** fever, diarrhea, abdominal cramps 12 to 72 hours after infection. **Treatment:** no standard treatment. Runs its course in four to seven days. Antibiotics in severe cases. **Annual U.S. cases:** 53,800 in 2012.

Shigellosis

(Four species of *Shigella: boydii, dysenteriae, flexneri,* and *sonnei*) Bacterial infection and a form of dysentery, an intestinal disease. **Transmission:** consuming food contaminated by infected feces or eating vegetables grown in fields containing contaminated sewage. Swimming in contaminated water. **Symptoms:** watery or bloody diarrhea one to four days after infection, high fever, vomiting, painful bowel movements. In extreme cases, seizures in children, intestinal perforation. **Treatment:** mild infection allowed to run its course; replacement of fluids and salts lost through excessive diarrhea. Antibiotics in severe cases. Although severe diarrhea is symptomatic, antidiarrheal medicines may make illness worse. **Annual U.S. cases:** 15,283 in 2012.

Syphilis

(*Treponema pallidum*) Bacterial infection known since ancient times that spread rampantly throughout Europe in the Middle Ages. **Transmission:** sexually transmitted. **Symptoms:** primary stage: painless sore, called a chancre, where bacteria enters the body; usually heals in 3 to 12 weeks with or without treatment. Without treatment, disease enters secondary stage: skin rash as chancre is healing or weeks after it is healed. Without treatment, enters tertiary stage: mouth sores, fever, fatigue, loss of appetite, weight loss, hair loss, jaundice, syphilitic meningitis, aortic aneurysms, lesions, damage to nervous system, heart, and eyes. Most infected do not progress beyond primary or secondary stage. **Treatment:** curable with antibiotics (mostly penicillin). **Annual U.S. cases:** 49,903 in 2012; 15,667 primary and secondary.

Tetanus or Lockjaw

(*Clostridium tetani*) Bacterial infection. **Transmission:** bacteria, found in soil, entering body through broken skin. **Symptoms:** muscle stiffness and spasms or "locking" of muscles of the jaw, neck, and limbs. **Vaccine:** four forms of immunization. **Treatment:** tetanus immune globulin to fight infection. With treatment, less than 10% of cases are fatal. **Annual U.S. cases:** 37 in 2012.

Tuberculosis

(*Mycobacterium tuberculosis*) Bacterial infection that primarily affects the lungs. **Transmission:** airborne transmission by persons with active TB infection. **Symptoms:** weight loss, fever, cough with discharge (sometimes with bloody sputum), night sweats, growing shortness of breath over time, chest pains. **Vaccine/treatment:** BCG (Bacille Calmette Guerin) vaccine only effective in protecting young children and used where TB is prevalent. Not recommended by health experts for use in the U.S. because of the low risk of infection and its variable effectiveness. **Annual U.S. cases:** 9,945 in 2012.

Yellow fever

(Yellow fever virus, in *flavivirus* group) Viral infection that has caused large epidemics in South America, the Caribbean, and Africa. **Transmission:** bite from mosquito carrying the virus. **Symptoms:** headaches, muscle aches, fever, jaundice (yellowing skin), nausea and vomiting, kidney failure, severe generalized pain. In severe cases, shock, coma, and death. **Vaccine:** available, safe, and effective. **Treatment:** symptoms treated until disease runs its course. **Annual cases:** none in the U.S.; an estimated 200,000 new cases and 30,000 deaths worldwide.

U.S. Reported Cases and Deaths From Vaccine-Preventable Diseases, 1950-2011

Source: Centers for Disease Control and Prevention, U.S. Dept. of Health and Human Services

Year	Diphtheria Cases	Diphtheria Deaths	Tetanus Cases	Tetanus Deaths	Pertussis Cases	Pertussis Deaths	Polio (paralytic) Cases	Polio (paralytic) Deaths	Measles Cases	Measles Deaths	Mumps Cases	Mumps Deaths	Rubella Cases	Rubella Deaths
1950	5,796	410	486	336	120,718	1,118	33,300	1,904	319,124	468	NR		NR	
1960	918	69	368	231	14,809	118	3,190	230	441,703	380	NR	42	NR	12
1970	435	30	148	79	4,249	12	33	7	47,351	89	104,953	16	56,552	31
1980	3	1	95	28	1,730	11	9	2	13,506	11	8,576	2	3,904	1
1990	4	1	64	11	4,570	12	6	0	27,786	64	5,292	1	1,125	8
2000	1	0	35	5	7,867	12	0	0	86	1	338	2	176	0
2001	2	0	37	5	7,580	17	0	0	116	1	266	0	23	2
2002	1	0	25	5	9,771	18	0	0	44	0	270	1	18	0
2003	1	1	20	4	11,647	11	0	0	56	1	231	0	7	0
2004	0	0	34	4	25,827	16	0	0	37	0	258	0	10	1
2005	0	0	27	1	25,616	31	1[1]	0	66	1	314	0	11	0
2006	0	0	41	4	15,632	9	0	0	55	0	6,584	1	11	0
2007	0	0	28	5	10,454	9	0	0	43	0	800	0	11	1
2008	0	NA	19	NA	13,278	NA	0	NA	140	NA	454	NA	16	NA
2009	0	NA	18	NA	16,858	NA	1[1]	NA	71	NA	1,991	NA	3	NA
2010	0	NA	26	NA	27,550	NA	0	NA	63	NA	2,612	NA	5	NA
2011[2]	0	NA	9	NA	15,216	NA	0	NA	212	NA	370	NA	4	NA

NA = Not available. NR = Not nationally reportable. (1) Vaccine-associated/derived paralytic polio. 2005 case acquired outside the U.S. 2009 case apparently acquired in MN. (2) Provisional data.

Dietary Guidelines for Americans, 2010: Key Recommendations

Source: *Dietary Guidelines for Americans, 2010*, U.S. Dept. of Agriculture; U.S. Dept. of Health and Human Services

Balancing Calories to Manage Weight

- Prevent and/or reduce overweight and obesity through improved eating and physical activity behaviors.
- Control total calorie intake to manage body weight.
- Increase physical activity and reduce time spent in sedentary behaviors.
- Maintain appropriate calorie balance during each stage of life.

Foods and Food Components to Reduce

- Reduce daily sodium intake to less than 2,300 mg. Further reduce intake to 1,500 mg among persons who are 51 and older and those of any age who are African American or have hypertension, diabetes, or chronic kidney disease.
- Consume less than 10% of calories from saturated fatty acids by replacing them with monounsaturated and polyunsaturated fatty acids.
- Consume less than 300 mg per day of dietary cholesterol.
- Keep trans fatty acid consumption as low as possible by limiting foods that contain synthetic sources of trans fats, such as partially hydrogenated oils.
- Reduce the intake of calories from solid fats and added sugars.
- Limit the consumption of foods that contain refined grains, especially refined grain foods that contain solid fats, added sugars, and sodium.
- If alcohol is consumed, it should be consumed in moderation—up to one drink per day for women and two drinks per day for men.

Foods and Nutrients to Increase

- Increase vegetable and fruit intake.
- Eat a variety of vegetables (especially dark-green, red, and orange vegetables), beans, and peas.
- Consume at least half of all grains as whole grains. Replace refined grains with whole grains.
- Increase intake of fat-free or low-fat milk and milk products, such as milk, yogurt, cheese, or fortified soy beverages.
- Choose a variety of protein foods, which include seafood, lean meat/poultry, eggs, beans and peas, soy products, and unsalted nuts and seeds.
- Increase seafood consumed by choosing seafood in place of some meat and poultry.
- Replace protein foods that are higher in solid fats with choices that are lower in solid fats and calories and/or are sources of oils.
- Use oils to replace solid fats where possible.
- Choose foods that provide more potassium, dietary fiber, calcium, and vitamin D, which are nutrients of concern in American diets. These foods include vegetables, fruits, whole grains, and milk and milk products.

Building Healthy Eating Patterns

- Select an eating pattern that meets nutrient needs over time at an appropriate calorie level.
- Account for all foods and beverages consumed and assess how they fit within a total healthy eating pattern.
- Follow food safety recommendations when preparing and eating foods to reduce the risk of foodborne illnesses.

Website: www.health.gov/dietaryguidelines/

Dietary Requirements

The Food and Nutrition Board of the National Academy of Sciences' Institute of Medicine, in reports published between 1997 and 2010, established **Dietary Reference Intakes (DRIs)**. DRIs establish daily consumption values for vitamins and elements (often called minerals) that aim to optimize health, not just guard against nutritional deficiencies, at all stages of life.

There are four DRI categories. The **Recommended Dietary Allowance (RDA)** gives intake values that meet the nutrient requirements of almost all (97%-98%) individuals in a specified group. The **Estimated Average Requirement (EAR)** specifies the average daily nutrient intake level

estimated to meet the requirement of half the healthy individuals in a specified group. **Adequate Intake (AI)** values are given when there is inadequate scientific evidence to calculate an RDA. For healthy breastfed infants, the AI is the mean intake; for other life stage groups, the AI is thought to cover the needs of all group individuals, but lack of data or uncertainty in the data prevents the percentage of individuals covered from being specified with confidence. The **Tolerable Upper Intake Level (UL)** designates the maximum intake amount that is unlikely to pose a risk of adverse health effects in almost all healthy individuals in a group. RDAs and AIs may both be used as individual intake goals.

Estimated Calorie Requirements

Source: *Dietary Guidelines for Americans, 2010*, U.S. Dept. of Agriculture; U.S. Dept. of Health and Human Services
Estimated amount of calories, rounded to the nearest 200, needed to maintain energy balance by sex, for various age groups and levels of physical activity.

	Age (years)	Sedentary[1]	Moderately active[2]	Active[3]		Age (years)	Sedentary[1]	Moderately active[2]	Active[3]
Child	2-3	1,000-1,200	1,000-1,400	1,000-1,400	Male	4-8	1,200-1,400	1,400-1,600	1,600-2,000
Female[4]	4-8	1,200-1,400	1,400-1,600	1,400-1,800		9-13	1,600-2,000	1,800-2,200	2,000-2,600
	9-13	1,400-1,600	1,600-2,000	1,800-2,200		14-18	2,000-2,400	2,400-2,800	2,800-3,200
	14-18	1,800	2,000	2,400		19-30	2,400-2,600	2,600-2,800	3,000
	19-30	1,800-2,000	2,000-2,200	2,400		31-50	2,200-2,400	2,400-2,600	2,800-3,000
	31-50	1,800	2,000	2,200		51+	2,000-2,200	2,200-2,400	2,400-2,800
	51+	1,600	1,800	2,000-2,200					

Note: Based on Estimated Energy Requirements (EER) equations, using reference heights (average) and reference weights (healthy) for each age/gender group. For children and adolescents, reference height and weight vary. For adults, the reference man is 5 ft 10 in. tall and weighs 154 lbs. The reference woman is 5 ft 4 in. tall and weighs 126 lbs. (1) Engaging only in the light activities associated with ordinary day-to-day life. (2) Includes physical activity equivalent to walking 1.5 to 3 miles per day at 3-4 mph. (3) Includes physical activity equivalent to walking more than 3 miles per day at 3-4 mph. (4) Excludes women who are pregnant or breastfeeding.

Understanding Food Components

Proteins, composed of amino acids, are essential to good nutrition. They build, maintain, and repair the body. Best sources: eggs, milk, fish, meat, poultry, soybeans, nuts. High-quality proteins such as eggs, meat, or fish supply all eight amino acids needed in a diet. Plant-sourced foods can be combined to meet protein needs as well.

Fats provide energy by furnishing calories to the body. They also help the body absorb vitamins A, D, E, and K. Best sources of polyunsaturated and monounsaturated fats: vegetable/plant oils, nuts. Concentrated sources of saturated fats: meats, cheeses, butter, cream, egg yolks, lard.

Carbohydrates are the most important source of energy for the body. The digestive system changes carbohydrates into glucose, which the body uses for energy for cells, tissues, and organs. The body stores extra sugar in the liver and muscles. Best sources: grains, legumes, potatoes, vegetables, fruits.

Fiber is the portion of plant foods that our bodies cannot digest. There are two basic types: insoluble and soluble. Insoluble fibers move food materials through the digestive tract; soluble fibers tend to slow them down. Both types absorb water, thus preventing and treating constipation. Soluble fibers may also be helpful in reducing blood cholesterol levels. Best sources: beans, bran, fruits, whole grains, vegetables.

Water dissolves and transports other nutrients throughout the body, aiding in the processes of digestion, absorption, circulation, and excretion. It helps regulate body temperature.

Vitamins

Vitamin A promotes good eyesight; helps keep skin and mucous membranes resistant to infection. Best sources: liver, sweet potatoes, carrots, kale, cantaloupe, turnip greens, collard greens, broccoli, fortified milk.

Vitamin B$_1$ (thiamine) prevents beriberi. Essential to carbohydrate metabolism and nervous system health. Best sources: eggs, enriched bread and flour, nuts, seeds, organ meats, whole grains.

Vitamin B$_2$ (riboflavin) protects the skin, mouth, eyes, and mucous membranes. Essential to growth, red blood cell production, and energy metabolism. Best sources: dairy products, meat, poultry, broccoli, spinach, eggs, nuts.

Vitamin B$_6$ (pyridoxine) is important in the regulation of the central nervous system and in protein metabolism. Best sources: whole grains, meat, fish, nuts, avocado, bananas.

Vitamin B$_{12}$ (cobalamin) is needed to form red blood cells. Best sources: meat, shellfish, poultry, eggs, dairy products.

Niacin maintains health of skin, nerves, and the digestive system. Best sources: poultry, nuts, fish, eggs.

Folic acid (folacin) is required for new cell formation, growth, and reproduction and for important chemical reactions in body cells. Best sources: leafy green vegetables, fruits, dried beans, peas, nuts, enriched bread, cereals.

Other B vitamins include biotin and pantothenic acid.

Vitamin C (ascorbic acid) maintains collagen, a protein necessary for the formation of skin, ligaments, and bones. Helps heal wounds and mend fractures. Best sources: citrus fruits and juices, cantaloupe, broccoli, Brussels sprouts, potatoes and sweet potatoes, tomatoes, cabbage.

Vitamin D is important for bone development. Best sources: sunlight, milk products, tuna, salmon, oysters.

Vitamin E (tocopherol) helps protect red blood cells. Best sources: vegetable oils, wheat germ, whole grains, eggs, peanuts, margarine, green leafy vegetables.

Vitamin K is necessary for formation of prothrombin, which helps blood to clot. Also made by intestinal bacteria. Best dietary sources: green leafy vegetables, tomatoes.

Minerals

Calcium works with phosphorus to build and maintain bones and teeth. Best sources: dairy, leafy green vegetables.

Phosphorus's main function is in the formation of bones and teeth, but it performs more functions than any other mineral and plays a part in nearly every chemical reaction in the body. Best sources: cheese, milk, meats, poultry, fish, tofu.

Iron is necessary for the formation of myoglobin, a reservoir of oxygen for muscle tissue, and hemoglobin, which transports oxygen within blood. Best sources: lean meats, beans, green leafy vegetables, shellfish, whole grains.

Other minerals include chloride, chromium, cobalt, copper, fluoride, iodine, magnesium, manganese, molybdenum, potassium, selenium, sodium, sulfur, zinc.

Understanding Food Label Claims

Source: Center for Food Safety and Applied Nutrition, FDA, U.S. Dept. of Health and Human Services; Food Safety and Inspection Service, Agricultural Marketing Service, U.S. Dept. of Agriculture (USDA)

Nutrition Packaging Terms

Manufacturers can make certain claims on processed food labels only if they meet the definitions specified here.

SUGAR. Sugar free: less than 0.5 g per serving; **No added sugars; Without added sugars:** no sugars or sugar-containing ingredients added during processing; must state if food is not "low calorie" or "reduced calorie"; **Unsweetened; No added sweeteners:** remain as factual statements; **Reduced sugar:** at least 25% less sugar than reference food.

FAT. Fat free: less than 0.5 g of fat per serving; **Saturated fat free:** less than 0.5 g of saturated fat and less than 0.5 g of trans fatty acids per serving; **Low fat:** 3 g or less per serving and, if the serving is 30 g or less or 2 tbs or less, per 50 g of the food; **Low saturated fat:** 1 g or less per serving and not more than 15% of calories from saturated fat; **Reduced fat; Less fat:** at least 25% less per serving than reference food.

FIBER. High fiber: 5 g or more per serving (must also meet low-fat definition or state level of total fat); **Good source**

of fiber: 2.5 g to 4.9 g per serving; More fiber; Added fiber: at least 2.5 g more per serving than reference food.

SODIUM. Sodium free: less than 5 mg per serving; Low sodium: 140 mg or less per serving and, if the serving is 30 g or less or 2 tbs or less, per 50 g of the food; Very low sodium: 35 mg or less per serving and, if the serving is 30 g or less or 2 tbs or less, per 50 g of the food; Reduced sodium; Less sodium: at least 25% less per serving than reference food.

CALORIES. Calorie free: less than 5 calories per serving; Low calorie: 40 calories or less per serving; if the serving is 30 g or less or 2 tbs or less, 40 calories or less per 50 g of the food; Reduced calories; Fewer calories: at least 25% less calories than reference food.

CHOLESTEROL. Cholesterol free: less than 2 mg of cholesterol and 2 g or less of saturated fat per serving; Low cholesterol: 20 mg or less of cholesterol and 2 g or less of saturated fat per serving and, if the serving is 30 g or less or 2 tbs or less, per 50 g of the food; Reduced cholesterol; Less cholesterol: at least 25% less than reference food.

Other Packaging Terms

The FDA allows food producers and marketers to use language on their packaging that advertises the health benefits and production methods of their products. Products marked certified have been formally evaluated for class, grade, or other quality characteristics by the USDA's Food Safety and Inspection Service. Below are some common packaging terms and their meanings.

Organic: Produced by farmers who use environmentally friendly methods to raise their crops or animals. Before a product can be labeled organic, the farm where the food is grown must pass a special inspection by a USDA official. Organic foods must be produced without irradiation, sewage sludge, synthetic fertilizers, prohibited pesticides, and genetically modified organisms.

The official USDA organic label may appear on vegetables, fruit, packages of meat, cartons of milk, eggs, cheese, and other single-ingredient foods. Foods that contain 100% organic ingredients may advertise "100 percent certified organic" on the front of the packaging along with the organic seal. Foods with at least 95% organic ingredients may be called "organic" and may place the official seal on their packaging. Products with at least 70% organic ingredients may advertise "made with organic" prominently on the front of the package that the item contains organic ingredients. Products with less than 70% organic ingredients may not make any organic claims on the front of the package but may list organic ingredients on the side panel.

Natural: The FDA has not developed a definition for use of the term natural or its derivatives. However, the agency has not objected to the use of the term if the food does not contain added color, artificial flavors, or synthetic substances.

Free range or free roaming: Producers must demonstrate to the USDA that the poultry has been allowed access to the outside.

Fresh poultry: Whole poultry and cuts that have never been below 26°F.

Frozen poultry: Temperature of raw, frozen poultry is 0°F or below.

Gluten free: Products with a gluten limit of 20 parts per million.

Halal and Zabiah Halal: Produced in federally inspected meat packing plants and handled in accordance with Islamic law and under Islamic authority.

Kosher: Meat and poultry products prepared under rabbinical supervision.

No hormones added: Hormones are not allowed in the raising of hogs or poultry, so those products may not make this claim. If sufficient documentation is provided to the USDA, this term may appear on packages of beef.

No antibiotics added: Claim may be made on a package (red meat and poultry) if sufficient documentation is provided to the USDA showing that the animals were raised without antibiotics.

Recommended Levels for Elements (Minerals)

Source: Food and Nutrition Board, Institute of Medicine, National Academy of Sciences, 2010

(in milligrams per day (mg/d) or micrograms per day (µg/d); asterisk denotes level defined as "adequate intake" (AI))

Life stage group		Calcium (mg/d)	Chromium (µg/d)	Copper (µg/d)	Fluoride (mg/d)	Iodine (µg/d)	Iron (mg/d)	Magnesium (mg/d)	Manganese (mg/d)	Molybdenum (µg/d)	Phosphorus (mg/d)	Selenium (µg/d)	Zinc (mg/d)
Infants	0-6 mos.	200*	0.2*	200*	0.01*	110*	0.27*	30*	0.003*	2*	100*	15*	2*
	6-12 mos.	260*	5.5*	220*	0.5*	130*	11	75*	0.6*	3*	275*	20*	3
Children	1-3 yrs.	700	11*	340	0.7*	90	7	80	1.2*	17	460	20	3
	4-8 yrs.	1,000	15*	440	1*	90	10	130	1.5*	22	500	30	5
Males	9-13 yrs.	1,300	25*	700	2*	120	8	240	1.9*	34	1,250	40	8
	14-18 yrs.	1,300	35*	890	3*	150	11	410	2.2*	43	1,250	55	11
	19-30 yrs.	1,000	35*	900	4*	150	8	400	2.3*	45	700	55	11
	31-50 yrs.	1,000	35*	900	4*	150	8	420	2.3*	45	700	55	11
	51-70 yrs.	1,000	30*	900	4*	150	8	420	2.3*	45	700	55	11
	over 70 yrs.	1,200	30*	900	4*	150	8	420	2.3*	45	700	55	11
Females	9-13 yrs.	1,300	21*	700	2*	120	8	240	1.6*	34	1,250	40	8
	14-18 yrs.	1,300	24*	890	3*	150	15	360	1.6*	43	1,250	55	9
	19-30 yrs.	1,000	25*	900	3*	150	18	310	1.8*	45	700	55	8
	31-50 yrs.	1,000	25*	900	3*	150	18	320	1.8*	45	700	55	8
	51-70 yrs.	1,200	20*	900	3*	150	8	320	1.8*	45	700	55	8
	over 70 yrs.	1,200	20*	900	3*	150	8	320	1.8*	45	700	55	8
Pregnancy	14-18 yrs.	1,300	29*	1,000	3*	220	27	400	2.0*	50	1,250	60	12
	19-30 yrs.	1,000	30*	1,000	3*	220	27	350	2.0*	50	700	60	11
	31-50 yrs.	1,000	30*	1,000	3*	220	27	360	2.0*	50	700	60	11
Lactation	14-18 yrs.	1,300	44*	1,300	3*	290	10	360	2.6*	50	1,250	70	13
	19-30 yrs.	1,000	45*	1,300	3*	290	9	310	2.6*	50	700	70	12
	31-50 yrs.	1,000	45*	1,300	3*	290	9	320	2.6*	50	700	70	12

Note: For healthy breastfed infants, the AI is the mean intake. The AI for other life stage and gender groups is believed to cover the needs of all healthy individuals in the group, but lack of data or uncertainty in the data prevents the percentage of individuals covered by this intake from being specified with confidence.

Recommended Levels for Vitamins

Source: Food and Nutrition Board, Institute of Medicine, National Academy of Sciences, 2010
(in milligrams per day (mg/d) or micrograms per day (µg/d); asterisk denotes level defined as "adequate intake" (AI))

Life stage group		Vitamin A (µg/d)	Vitamin C (mg/d)	Vitamin D (µg/d)	Vitamin E (mg/d)	Vitamin K (µg/d)	Thiamin (mg/d)	Riboflavin (mg/d)	Niacin (mg/d)	Vitamin B6 (mg/d)	Folate (µg/d)	Vitamin B12 (µg/d)	Pantothenic acid (mg/d)	Biotin (µg/d)	Choline (mg/d)
Infants	0-6 mos.	400*	40*	10	4*	2.0*	0.2*	0.3*	2*	0.1*	65*	0.4*	1.7*	5*	125*
	6-12 mos.	500*	50*	10	5*	2.5*	0.3*	0.4*	4*	0.3*	80*	0.5*	1.8*	6*	150*
Children	1-3 yrs.	300	15	15	6	30*	0.5	0.5	6	0.5	150	0.9	2*	8*	200*
	4-8 yrs.	400	25	15	7	55*	0.6	0.6	8	0.6	200	1.2	3*	12*	250*
Males	9-13 yrs.	600	45	15	11	60*	0.9	0.9	12	1.0	300	1.8	4*	20*	375*
	14-18 yrs.	900	75	15	15	75*	1.2	1.3	16	1.3	400	2.4	5*	25*	550*
	19-30 yrs.	900	90	15	15	120*	1.2	1.3	16	1.3	400	2.4	5*	30*	550*
	31-50 yrs.	900	90	15	15	120*	1.2	1.3	16	1.3	400	2.4	5*	30*	550*
	51-70 yrs.	900	90	15	15	120*	1.2	1.3	16	1.7	400	2.4	5*	30*	550*
	over 70 yrs.	900	90	20	15	120*	1.2	1.3	16	1.7	400	2.4	5*	30*	550*
Females	9-13 yrs.	600	45	15	11	60*	0.9	0.9	12	1.0	300	1.8	4*	20*	375*
	14-18 yrs.	700	65	15	15	75*	1.0	1.0	14	1.2	400	2.4	5*	25*	400*
	19-30 yrs.	700	75	15	15	90*	1.1	1.1	14	1.3	400	2.4	5*	30*	425*
	31-50 yrs.	700	75	15	15	90*	1.1	1.1	14	1.3	400	2.4	5*	30*	425*
	51-70 yrs.	700	75	15	15	90*	1.1	1.1	14	1.5	400	2.4	5*	30*	425*
	over 70 yrs.	700	75	20	15	90*	1.1	1.1	14	1.5	400	2.4	5*	30*	425*
Pregnancy	14-18 yrs.	750	80	15	15	75*	1.4	1.4	18	1.9	600	2.6	6*	30*	450*
	19-30 yrs.	770	85	15	15	90*	1.4	1.4	18	1.9	600	2.6	6*	30*	450*
	31-50 yrs.	770	85	15	15	90*	1.4	1.4	18	1.9	600	2.6	6*	30*	450*
Lactation	14-18 yrs.	1,200	115	15	19	75*	1.4	1.6	17	2.0	500	2.8	7*	35*	550*
	19-30 yrs.	1,300	120	15	19	90*	1.4	1.6	17	2.0	500	2.8	7*	35*	550*
	31-50 yrs.	1,300	120	15	19	90*	1.4	1.6	17	2.0	500	2.8	7*	35*	550*

Note: For healthy breastfed infants, the AI is the mean intake. The AI for other life stage and gender groups is believed to cover the needs of all healthy individuals in the group, but lack of data or uncertainty in the data prevents the percentage of individuals covered by this intake from being specified with confidence.

Top 10 Calorie Sources in American Diets

Source: *Dietary Guidelines for Americans, 2010*, U.S. Dept. of Agriculture

Rank	All Americans (ages 2+)	Children and adolescents (ages 2-18)	All adults (ages 19+)
1.	Grain-based desserts	Grain-based desserts	Grain-based desserts
2.	Yeast breads	Pizza	Yeast breads
3.	Chicken dishes	Soda/energy/sports drinks	Chicken dishes
4.	Soda/energy/sports drinks	Yeast breads	Soda/energy/sports drinks
5.	Pizza	Chicken dishes	Alcoholic beverages
6.	Alcoholic beverages	Pasta dishes	Pizza
7.	Pasta dishes	Reduced-fat milk	Tortillas, burritos, tacos
8.	Tortillas, burritos, tacos	Dairy desserts	Pasta dishes
9.	Beef dishes	Potato/corn/other chips	Beef dishes
10.	Dairy desserts	Ready-to-eat cereals	Dairy desserts

Note: Data are drawn from analyses of usual dietary intakes conducted by the Natl. Cancer Institute. Foods and beverages consumed were divided into 97 categories and ranked according to calorie contribution to the diet. Average total daily calorie intake was 2,157 overall, 2,027 for children and adolescents (ages 2-18), and 2,199 for adults (ages 19+).

Weight Guidelines for Adults

Source: *Dietary Guidelines for Americans, 2010*, U.S. Dept. of Agriculture; National Center for Health Statistics, CDC

Guidelines on identification, evaluation, and treatment of overweight and obesity in adults were released in June 1998 by the National Heart, Lung, and Blood Institute (NHLBI), in cooperation with the National Institute of Diabetes and Digestive and Kidney Diseases (NIDDK). The guidelines, based on research into risk factors contributing to heart disease, stroke, and other conditions, define overweight and obesity in terms of **body mass index (BMI)**. BMI is based on a person's weight and height and is strongly correlated with total body fat content. A BMI of 25-29 is said to indicate **overweight**; a BMI of 30 or higher indicates **obesity**. Weight reduction is advised for persons with a BMI of 25 or higher. Factors such as a large waist circumference, high blood pressure or cholesterol, and family medical history may increase a person's risk of developing an obesity-related disease.

The National Center for Health Statistics notes that in 2011-12, 34.9% of American adults were obese. Over the past four decades, childhood obesity rates in America have more than tripled, and in 2011-12, 16.9% of children (ages 2-19) were obese. Based on directly measured weight and height, between 1988-94 and 2011-12, the proportion of adults ages 20 years and over who were obese rose by 52.4%, from 22.9%. During the same period, obesity increased by 56.6% in children ages 6-11, from 11.3% to 17.7%, and by 95.2% in adolescents ages 12-19, from 10.5% to 20.5%.

A high prevalence of overweight and obesity is a public health concern because excess body fat has been associated with type 2 diabetes, hypertension, dyslipidemia, cardiovascular disease, stroke, gallbladder disease, respiratory dysfunction, gout, osteoarthritis, and certain kinds of cancers.

Body Mass Index (BMI) by Height and Weight

Weight (lbs)

Height	NORMAL						OVERWEIGHT					OBESE									
4'10"	91	96	100	105	110	115	119	124	129	134	138	143	148	153	158	162	167	172	177	181	186
4'11"	94	99	104	109	114	119	124	128	133	138	143	148	153	158	163	168	173	178	183	188	193
5'0"	97	102	107	112	118	123	128	133	138	143	148	153	158	163	168	174	179	184	189	194	199
5'1"	100	106	111	116	122	127	132	137	143	148	153	158	164	169	174	180	185	190	195	201	206
5'2"	104	109	115	120	126	131	136	142	147	153	158	164	169	175	180	186	191	196	202	207	213
5'3"	107	113	118	124	130	135	141	146	152	158	163	169	175	180	186	191	197	203	208	214	220
5'4"	110	116	122	128	134	140	145	151	157	163	169	174	180	186	192	197	204	209	215	221	227
5'5"	114	120	126	132	138	144	150	156	162	168	174	180	186	192	198	204	210	216	222	228	234
5'6"	118	124	130	136	142	148	155	161	167	173	179	186	192	198	204	210	216	223	229	235	241
5'7"	121	127	134	140	146	153	159	166	172	178	185	191	198	204	211	217	223	230	236	242	249
5'8"	125	131	138	144	151	158	164	171	177	184	190	197	203	210	216	223	230	236	243	249	256
5'9"	128	135	142	149	155	162	169	176	182	189	196	203	209	216	223	230	236	243	250	257	263
5'10"	132	139	146	153	160	167	174	181	188	195	202	209	216	222	229	236	243	250	257	264	271
5'11"	136	143	150	157	165	172	179	186	193	200	208	215	222	229	236	243	250	257	265	272	279
6'0"	140	147	154	162	169	177	184	191	199	206	213	221	228	235	242	250	258	265	272	279	287
6'1"	144	151	159	166	174	182	189	197	204	212	219	227	235	242	250	257	265	272	280	288	295
6'2"	148	155	163	171	179	186	194	202	210	218	225	233	241	249	256	264	272	280	287	295	303
6'3"	152	160	168	176	184	192	200	208	216	224	232	240	248	256	264	272	279	287	295	303	311
6'4"	156	164	172	180	189	197	205	213	221	230	238	246	254	263	271	279	287	295	304	312	320
BMI[1]	19	20	21	22	23	24	25	26	27	28	29	30	31	32	33	34	35	36	37	38	39

(1) The BMI numbers apply to both men and women. Some very muscular people may have a high BMI without health risks.

Calories Used During Physical Activity

Source: Center for Nutrition Policy and Promotion, U.S. Dept. of Agriculture

Amount of calories burned during physical activities are estimates for a man who is 5 ft 10 in. tall and weighs 154 lbs. The more an individual weighs, the more calories he or she will burn by exercising at the same intensity.

Moderate physical activities	In 1 hr.	In 30 min.	Vigorous physical activities	In 1 hr.	In 30 min.
Hiking	370	185	Running/jogging (5 miles per hour)	590	295
Light gardening/yard work	330	165	Bicycling (more than 10 miles per hour)	590	295
Dancing	330	165	Swimming (slow freestyle laps)	510	255
Golf (walking and carrying clubs)	330	165	Aerobics	480	240
Bicycling (less than 10 miles per hour)	290	145	Walking (4½ miles per hour)	460	230
Walking (3½ miles per hour)	280	140	Heavy yard work (e.g., chopping wood)	440	220
Weight training (general light workout)	220	110	Weight lifting (vigorous effort)	440	220
Stretching	180	90	Basketball (vigorous)	440	220

Obesity Among Adults in the U.S., 2011-12

Source: National Health and Nutrition Examination Survey, National Center for Health Statistics, CDC

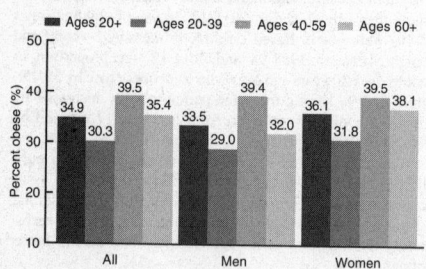

Obesity Among Children and Adolescents in the U.S., 2011-12

Source: National Health and Nutrition Examination Survey, National Center for Health Statistics, CDC

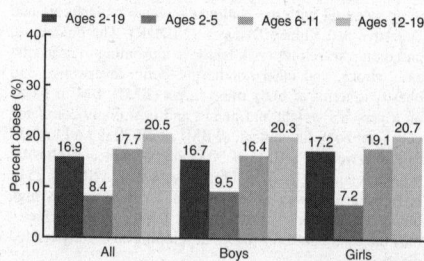

Basic First Aid

Note: This information is not intended to be a substitute for formal training. It is recommended that you contact your local American Red Cross chapter to sign up for a First Aid/CPR/AED (automated external defibrillator) course.

In an emergency, it is important to get medical assistance as soon as possible, but knowing what to do until a doctor or other trained person gets to the scene can save a life, especially in cases of severe bleeding, choking, poisoning, and shock.

People with special medical problems, such as diabetes, cardiovascular disease, epilepsy, or allergies, are urged to wear some sort of emblem identifying the problem as a safeguard against receiving medication that might be harmful or even fatal. Emblems may be obtained from MedicAlert Foundation, 2323 Colorado Ave., Turlock, CA 95382; (888) 633-4298; www. medicalert.org.

Animal bite: Call 9-1-1 or the local emergency number if the wound is bleeding seriously or if you suspect the animal might have rabies. Control any bleeding. Wash minor wounds with soap under running water and apply antibiotic ointment and a dressing. When possible, proper authorities should test the animal for rabies.

Asphyxiation: Call 9-1-1 or the local emergency number.

Bleeding: Use a barrier between your hand and the wound to help prevent infection. Cover wound with a sterile dressing. Apply direct pressure until bleeding stops. Cover compress with a bandage. Call 9-1-1 or the local emergency number if bleeding is severe.

Burn: Check for life-threatening conditions. If the burn is mild, with skin unbroken and no blisters, flush with cold running water for at least 20 minutes. Gently wash with soap and water and pat dry. Apply a thin layer of antibiotic ointment. Apply a loose, sterile dry dressing to prevent infection. If the burn is severe, call 9-1-1 or the local emergency number. Care for shock (see separate entry). Keep the person from getting chilled or overheated until advanced medical assistance arrives. Do not try to clean a severe burn or break blisters.

Chemical in eye: Call 9-1-1 or the local emergency number. Turn the person's head to the side so that the affected eye is lower than the unaffected eye. Flush the affected eye with large amounts of water for at least 20 minutes.

Choking: See **First Aid for Choking** below.

Convulsions (seizures): Remove nearby objects that might cause injury. Protect the person's head by placing a thin folded towel or item of clothing under it. Roll him or her on one side to drain fluids from the mouth. Do not place anything between the person's teeth. Stay with the person until he or she is fully conscious. If convulsions do not stop, get medical attention immediately.

Cut (minor): Use a clean barrier between your hand and the wound to prevent infection. Apply direct pressure for a few minutes to control any bleeding. Wash the wound thoroughly with soap and water and apply a thin layer of antibiotic ointment or a microthin film dressing. Cover the wound with a sterile dressing and a bandage.

Foreign object in eye: If an object is impaled in someone's eye, do not remove it. If not impaled, try to remove the object by having the person blink several times. If the object doesn't come out, gently flush the eye with saline solution or water. Do not rub the eye. If the object still doesn't come out, the person should receive professional medical attention.

Frostbite: Handle the frostbitten area gently. Do not rub. If there is no danger of the affected area refreezing, soak it in warm water (not warmer than 105°F). Do not allow the frostbitten area to touch the side of the water container. Keep the frostbitten part in the water until normal color returns and it feels warm. Loosely bandage the area with dry, sterile dressings. If fingers or toes are frostbitten, put cotton or gauze between them. Do not break any blisters. Call 9-1-1 or seek emergency help as soon as possible.

Heart attack and stroke: See **Heart and Blood Vessel Disease** earlier in chapter.

Heat stroke: Remove the person from the heat. Loosen any tight clothing. Immerse person in cold water until he or she becomes alert. If a large enough source of water is not available, drench the person with cold water and fan constantly. If the person is conscious, have him or her slowly drink some cool water. Call 9-1-1 if the person's condition does not improve.

Hypothermia: Call 9-1-1 or the local emergency number. For mild hypothermia, cover all exposed skin. Replace wet clothes with something dry. If the person is alert, give him or her simple carbohydrates to eat and warm, nonalcoholic and decaffeinated liquids to drink. Apply heat pads or other heat sources if available but do not place against bare skin.

Loss of limb: Call 9-1-1 or the local emergency number and care for any life-threatening conditions. If a limb is severed, it is important to properly protect the limb so that it can possibly be reattached. After the victim is cared for, the limb should be wrapped in sterile gauze and placed in a plastic bag. Place bag in a larger bag or container of an ice and water slurry, not ice alone. Be sure the limb is taken to the hospital with the person.

Poisoning: Care for any life-threatening conditions. Call the National Capital Poison Center (800-222-1222), 9-1-1, or the local emergency number and follow their directions. Do not give the person any food or drink or induce vomiting unless specified to do so by medical professionals.

Shock (injury-related): Monitor breathing and consciousness. Have the person lie down and keep him or her as comfortable as possible. Maintain an open airway. Give sips of cool water if he or she tolerates fluids. Elevate his or her legs about 12 inches unless you suspect injuries to the head or lower extremities. Maintain normal body temperature. If the weather is cold or damp, place blankets or extra clothing over and under the person; if the weather is hot, provide shade.

Snakebite: Call 9-1-1 or the local emergency number. Gently wash the injury. Splint bitten extremities, and keep the area at approximately the level of the heart. Keep the person calm. Do not cut, suck, apply a constricting band, or apply cold to a bite from a pit viper (such as a rattlesnake, copperhead, or cottonmouth). For a bite from an elapid snake, such as a coral snake, apply an elastic roller bandage after washing the wound.

Sprains and strains: Splint any injured bone or joint that the person cannot use.

Sting from bee or wasp: If possible, remove the stinger by scraping it away with your finger or a plastic card (like a credit card) or using tweezers. If you use tweezers, grasp the stinger, not the venom sac. Wash the area with soap and water. Cover it to keep it clean. Apply cold to the area. Call 9-1-1 or the local emergency number immediately if the wound does not stop swelling, the person collapses, or he or she is known to be allergic to the sting.

Unconsciousness: Call 9-1-1 or the local emergency number immediately. Do not move the person if a spinal injury is suspected.

First Aid for Choking

The recommended first aid for a conscious choking victim who is unable to speak, cough, or breathe is to deliver a series of five blows to the back and five thrusts to the abdomen. Have another person call 9-1-1 or the local emergency number. Obtain consent from the victim to treat him or her. Lean the victim forward and apply five blows to his or her back with the heel of your hand. Then stand or kneel behind the victim and wrap your arms around his or her waist. Make a fist with one hand and place the thumb side against the middle of the person's abdomen, just above the navel and well below the lower tip of the breastbone. Grasp your fist in your other hand and quickly thrust upwards into the abdomen five times. Continue back blows and abdominal thrusts until the object is dislodged, and the person can breathe or cough forcefully, or the person loses consciousness.

VITAL STATISTICS

Births and Deaths in the U.S., 1960-2013

Source: National Center for Health Statistics (NCHS), U.S. Dept. of Health and Human Services

Year	BIRTHS Total number	Rate	DEATHS Total number	Rate	Year	BIRTHS Total number	Rate	DEATHS Total number	Rate
1960	4,257,850	23.7	1,711,982	9.5	2002	4,021,726	13.9	2,443,387	8.5
1970	3,731,386	18.4	1,921,031	9.5	2003	4,089,950	14.1	2,448,288	8.4
1980	3,612,258	15.9	1,989,841	8.8	2004	4,112,052	14.0	2,397,615	8.2
1990	4,092,994	16.7	2,148,463	8.6	2005	4,138,349	14.0	2,448,017	8.3
1994	3,952,767	15.0	2,278,994	8.7	2006	4,265,555	14.2	2,426,264	8.1
1995	3,899,589	14.6	2,312,132	8.7	2007	4,316,233	14.3	2,423,712	8.0
1996	3,891,494	14.4	2,314,690	8.6	2008	4,247,694	14.0	2,471,984	8.1
1997	3,880,894	14.2	2,314,245	8.5	2009	4,130,665	13.5	2,437,163	7.9
1998	3,941,553	14.3	2,337,256	8.5	2010	3,999,386	13.0	2,468,435	8.0
1999	3,959,417	14.2	2,391,399	8.6	2011	3,953,590	12.7	2,515,458	8.1
2000	4,058,814	14.4	2,403,351	8.5	2012[1]	3,958,000	12.6	2,539,000	8.1
2001	4,025,933	14.1	2,416,425	8.5	2013[1]	3,940,000	12.5	2,594,000	8.2

Note: Statistics cover only events occurring within the U.S. and exclude fetal deaths. Rates per 1,000 population; enumerated as of Apr. 1 for decennial census years; estimated as of July 1 for all other years. Beginning in 1970, statistics exclude births and deaths among nonresidents of the U.S. (1) Provisional.

Marriage and Divorce Rates in the U.S., 1920-2011

Source: National Center for Health Statistics (NCHS), U.S. Dept. of Health and Human Services

(Per 1,000 total population. Divorce rates for 2005-11 were calculated excluding data and populations from the nonreporting states California, Georgia, Hawaii, Indiana, Louisiana, and Minnesota. Some data are provisional.)

The U.S. marriage rate dipped during the Depression and peaked sharply just after World War II; the trend after that has been more gradual. The divorce rate generally rose from the 1920s through 1981, when it peaked at 5.3 per 1,000 population, before declining somewhat. The graph below shows marriage and divorce rates since 1920.

U.S. Median Age at First Marriage, 1890-2013

Source: U.S. Census Bureau, U.S. Dept. of Commerce

Year[1]	Men	Women	Year[1]	Men	Women	Year[1]	Men	Women	Year[1]	Men	Women	Year[1]	Men	Women
1890	26.1	22.0	1950	22.8	20.3	1985	25.5	23.3	2003	27.1	25.3	2009	28.1	25.9
1900	25.9	21.9	1960	22.8	20.3	1990	26.1	23.9	2004	27.4	25.3	2010	28.2	26.1
1910	25.1	21.6	1965	22.8	20.6	1995	26.9	24.5	2005	27.1	25.3	2011	28.4	26.4
1920	24.6	21.2	1970	23.2	20.8	2000	26.8	25.1	2006	27.5	25.5	2012	28.6	26.6
1930	24.3	21.3	1975	23.5	21.1	2001	26.9	25.1	2007	27.5	25.6	2013	29.0	26.6
1940	24.3	21.5	1980	24.7	22.0	2002	26.9	25.3	2008	27.6	25.9			

(1) Figures after 1947 based on Current Population Survey data; earlier figures based on decennial censuses.

Divorce Rates by State, 2011

Source: National Center for Health Statistics (NCHS), U.S. Dept. of Health and Human Services

State	Divorce rate	State	Divorce rate	State	Divorce rate
Alabama	4.3	Louisiana	NA	Ohio	3.4
Alaska	4.8	Maine	4.2	Oklahoma	5.2
Arizona	3.9	Maryland	2.9	Oregon	3.8
Arkansas	5.3	Massachusetts	2.7	Pennsylvania	2.8
California	NA	Michigan	3.4	Rhode Island	3.2
Colorado	4.4	Minnesota	NA	South Carolina	3.2
Connecticut	3.1	Mississippi	4.0	South Dakota	3.3
Delaware	3.6	Missouri	3.9	Tennessee	4.3
District of Columbia	2.9	Montana	4.0	Texas	3.2
Florida	4.5	Nebraska	3.5	Utah	3.7
Georgia	NA	Nevada	5.6	Vermont	3.6
Hawaii	NA	New Hampshire	3.8	Virginia	3.8
Idaho	4.9	New Jersey	2.9	Washington	4.1
Illinois	2.6	New Mexico	3.3	West Virginia	5.2
Indiana	NA	New York	2.9	Wisconsin	2.9
Iowa	2.4	North Carolina	3.7	Wyoming	4.8
Kansas	3.9	North Dakota	2.7	**United States**	**3.6**
Kentucky	4.4				

NA = Not available. **Note:** Rate per 1,000 population. Rate includes annulments and may also include divorce petitions filed and legal separations in some counties and states.

Birth Rates and Fertility Rates by Age of Mother, 1950-2013

Source: National Center for Health Statistics (NCHS), U.S. Dept. of Health and Human Services

Live births per 1,000 women by age of mother

Year	Birth rate[1]	Fertility rate[2]	10-14 years	15-19 years	15-17 years	18-19 years	20-24 years	25-29 years	30-34 years	35-39 years	40-44 years	45-49 years
1950	24.1	106.2	1.0	81.6	40.7	132.7	196.6	166.1	103.7	52.9	15.1	1.2
1960	23.7	118.0	0.8	89.1	43.9	166.7	258.1	197.4	112.7	56.2	15.5	0.9
1970	18.4	87.9	1.2	68.3	38.8	114.7	167.8	145.1	73.3	31.7	8.1	0.5
1980	15.9	68.4	1.1	53.0	32.5	82.1	115.1	112.9	61.9	19.8	3.9	0.2
1990	16.7	70.9	1.4	59.9	37.5	88.6	116.5	120.2	80.8	31.7	5.5	0.2
1995	14.6	64.6	1.3	56.0	35.5	87.7	107.5	108.8	81.1	34.0	6.6	0.3
1996	14.4	64.1	1.2	53.5	33.3	84.7	107.8	108.6	82.1	34.9	6.8	0.3
1997	14.2	63.6	1.1	51.3	31.4	82.1	107.3	108.3	83.0	35.7	7.1	0.4
1998	14.3	64.3	1.0	50.3	29.9	80.9	108.4	110.2	85.2	36.9	7.4	0.4
1999	14.2	64.4	0.9	48.8	28.2	79.1	107.9	111.2	87.1	37.8	7.4	0.4
2000	14.4	65.9	0.9	47.7	26.9	78.1	109.7	113.5	91.2	39.7	8.0	0.5
2001	14.1	65.3	0.8	45.3	24.7	76.1	106.2	113.4	91.9	40.6	8.1	0.5
2002	13.9	64.8	0.7	43.0	23.2	72.8	103.6	113.6	91.5	41.4	8.3	0.5
2003	14.1	66.1	0.6	41.6	22.4	70.7	102.6	115.6	95.1	43.8	8.7	0.5
2004	14.0	66.3	0.7	41.1	22.1	70.0	101.7	115.5	95.3	45.4	8.9	0.5
2005	14.0	66.7	0.7	40.5	21.4	69.9	102.2	115.5	95.8	46.3	9.1	0.6
2006	14.2	68.5	0.6	41.9	22.0	73.0	105.9	116.7	97.7	47.3	9.4	0.6
2007	14.3	69.5	0.6	42.5	22.1	73.9	106.3	117.5	99.9	47.5	9.5	0.6
2008	14.0	68.6	0.6	41.5	21.7	70.6	103.0	115.1	99.3	46.9	9.8	0.7
2009	13.5	66.2	0.5	37.9	19.6	64.0	96.2	111.5	97.5	46.1	10.0	0.7[4]
2010	13.0	64.1	0.4	34.2	17.3	58.2	90.0	108.3	96.5	45.9	10.2	0.7[4]
2011	12.7	63.2	0.4	31.3	15.4	54.1	85.3	107.2	96.5	47.2	10.3	0.7
2012	12.6	63.0	0.4	29.4	14.1	51.4	83.1	106.5	97.3	48.3	10.4	0.7
2013[3]	12.5	62.9	0.3	26.6	12.3	47.3	81.2	106.2	98.7	49.6	10.5	0.8

(1) Live births per 1,000 population. (2) Live births per 1,000 women 15-44 years of age. (3) Preliminary. (4) Women 45-54 years of age.

Cesarean Delivery Rates by State, 1990-2013

Source: National Center for Health Statistics (NCHS), U.S. Dept. of Health and Human Services

State	1990	2000	2010	2013[1]	Percent change, 1990-2013	State	1990	2000	2010	2013[1]	Percent change, 1990-2013
Alabama	25.9%	26.3%	35.3%	35.8%	38.2%	Missouri	22.8%	22.3%	31.9%	31.1%	36.4%
Alaska	15.1	17.0	21.5	24.1	59.6	Montana	20.5	19.0	30.3	29.7	44.9
Arizona	18.3	18.6	27.0	27.4	49.7	Nebraska	19.1	22.5	31.1	30.3	58.6
Arkansas	27.6	26.3	34.8	34.5	25.0	Nevada	19.6	21.7	34.8	34.9	78.1
California	22.3	23.4	33.0	33.2	48.9	New Hampshire	21.8	21.0	30.4	30.0	37.6
Colorado	17.0	18.3	25.9	26.0	52.9	New Jersey	24.7	27.3	38.4	38.4	55.5
Connecticut	17.4	21.6	35.1	34.8	100.0	New Mexico	18.3	17.1	22.8	24.3	32.8
Delaware	24.9	24.8	33.9	31.5	26.5	New York	23.1	24.6	34.5	34.3	48.5
District of Columbia	25.9	22.6	33.0	34.2	32.0	North Carolina	22.7	23.0	30.8	30.4	33.9
Florida	25.2	24.9	37.8	37.7	49.6	North Dakota	19.3	20.6	27.7	28.6	48.2
Georgia	22.5	22.5	33.8	34.3	52.4	Ohio	23.7	20.0	30.7	31.1	31.2
Hawaii	20.2	14.6	27.2	25.4	25.7	Oklahoma	0.9	21.0	34.7	33.8	3,655.6
Idaho	18.8	18.3	24.8	24.9	32.4	Oregon	19.0	19.4	29.4	28.0	47.4
Illinois	22.2	20.9	31.1	31.7	42.8	Pennsylvania	22.2	21.7	31.3	31.4	41.4
Indiana	21.3	21.5	30.3	30.5	43.2	Rhode Island	18.4	21.9	33.0	31.2	69.6
Iowa	20.6	20.8	30.3	30.8	49.5	South Carolina	22.4	25.2	35.0	35.1	56.7
Kansas	23.1	22.2	30.5	30.2	30.7	South Dakota	19.6	22.8	26.6	25.5	30.1
Kentucky	23.7	23.6	35.4	36.6	54.4	Tennessee	24.3	24.8	34.2	33.4	37.4
Louisiana	27.0	26.6	39.6	38.9	44.1	Texas	22.3	24.7	35.1	35.2	57.8
Maine	21.2	22.8	29.8	30.0	41.5	Utah	17.7	16.8	23.1	22.4	26.6
Maryland	21.1	24.1	34.5	35.1	66.4	Vermont	19.3	17.3	27.5	27.2	40.9
Massachusetts	22.2	23.3	33.0	31.5	41.9	Virginia	23.4	23.1	34.3	33.8	44.4
Michigan	21.8	21.9	32.6	32.6	49.5	Washington	17.8	20.6	29.5	28.3	59.0
Minnesota	17.5	19.4	27.1	26.9	53.7	West Virginia	26.7	25.4	36.0	35.9	34.5
Mississippi	26.6	28.2	37.0	38.5	44.7	Wisconsin	17.6	17.5	26.0	26.2	48.9
						Wyoming	19.8	19.4	27.9	28.9	46.0
						United States	**22.0**	**22.8**	**32.7**	**32.7**	**48.6**

Note: The cesarean rate is the percentage of all live births by cesarean delivery. (1) Preliminary.

Use of Infertility Services by Selected Characteristics, 2006-10

Source: National Center for Health Statistics (NCHS), U.S. Dept. of Health and Human Services

Characteristic	Total[1]	Age in years				Prior live births		Current fertility problems[2]	
		25-29	30-34	35-39	40-44	None	One or more	Yes	No
Number (thous.)	40,912	10,535	9,188	10,538	10,652	10,340	30,572	5,791	35,121
					Percent				
Any infertility service	16.8%	12.5%	14.4%	20.7%	19.3%	17.6%	16.5%	41.0%	12.8%
Any medical help to get pregnant	12.5	7.7	11.1	16.4	14.5	13.6	12.1	36.3	8.6
Advice	9.4	6.2	7.8	13.3	9.9	11.4	8.7	28.9	6.1
Tests on either partner	7.3	3.3	6.3	10.4	9.0	8.5	6.9	27.4	4.0
Ovulation drugs	5.8	2.4	5.5	8.6	6.5	5.6	5.8	19.5	3.5
Surgery or treatment of blocked tubes	1.3	0.3	0.5	2.0	2.3	1.8	1.1	3.2	1.0
Artificial insemination	1.7	0.3	0.9	2.9	2.8	2.3	1.5	7.4	0.8
Assisted reproductive technology	0.7	NA	0.2	1.5	0.9	0.9	0.6	3.1	0.3
Any medical help to prevent miscarriage	6.8	6.1	5.7	8.1	7.3	2.7	8.2	12.8	5.8

NA = Not available. Note: Data is for women or their partners who have ever used service shown. Respondents could report one or more types of medical help, so sum of figures will not equal totals. (1) Women aged 25-44. (2) Impaired fecundity (physical difficulty in either getting pregnant or carrying a pregnancy to live birth) or 12-month infertility at time of interview.

Numbers of Multiple Births in the U.S., 1990-2012

Source: National Center for Health Statistics (NCHS), U.S. Dept. of Health and Human Services

The general upward trend in multiple births reflects greater numbers of births to older women and increased use of fertility drugs.

Year	Twins	Triplets	Quadruplets	Quintuplets[1]	Year	Twins	Triplets	Quadruplets	Quintuplets[1]
1990	93,865	2,830	185	13	2006	137,085	6,118	355	67
1995	96,736	4,551	365	57	2007	138,961	5,967	369	91
2000	118,916	6,742	506	77	2008	138,660	5,877	345	46
2001	121,246	6,885	501	85	2009	137,217	5,905	355	80
2002	125,134	6,898	434	69	2010	132,562	5,153	313	37
2003	128,665	7,110	468	85	2011	131,269	5,137	239	41
2004	132,219	6,750	439	86	2012	131,024	4,598	276	45
2005	133,122	6,208	418	68					

(1) Quintuplets and other multiple births of five or more.

Origin Countries for U.S. Foreign Adoptions, 2000-13

Source: Office of Immigration Statistics, U.S. Dept. of Homeland Security
(ranked by 2013 adoptions)

Country	2013	2012	2011	2010	2009	2008	2007	2006	2005	2002	2000
China	2,306	2,697	2,589	3,401	2,990	3,852	5,453	6,493	7,906	6,119	5,053
Ethiopia	993	1,568	1,727	2,513	2,221	1,666	1,255	732	441	105	95
Ukraine	438	395	632	445	605	487	606	460	821	1,106	659
Haiti	388	154	33	133[1]	336	300	190	309	234	187	131
Congo, Dem. Rep. of the	313	240	133	41	21	9	10	4	11	0	1
Uganda	276	238	207	62	69	55	54	12	17	18	1
Russia	250	748	970	1,082	1,580	1,859	2,310	3,706	4,639	4,939	4,269
Nigeria	183	197	149	189	109	148	33	62	65	45	4
Philippines	178	125	230	214	292	279	265	245	271	221	173
Ghana	170	171	100	117	104	100	33	28	16	11	13
Total[2]	7,094	8,668	9,320	11,059[1]	12,782	17,229	19,741	20,705	22,710	20,100	18,120

(1) Does not reflect approximately 1,090 Haitian children admitted as part of the Special Humanitarian Parole following the 2010 earthquake in Haiti. (2) Includes countries not shown.

Leading Causes of Infant Death in the U.S., 2012

Source: National Center for Health Statistics (NCHS), U.S. Dept. of Health and Human Services

Cause	Number	Percent of total deaths	Mortality rate[1]
Congenital malformations, deformations, and chromosomal abnormalities	4,939	20.9%	124.9
Disorders related to short gestation and low birth weight, not elsewhere classified	4,202	17.8	106.3
Sudden infant death syndrome	1,679	7.1	42.5
Newborn affected by maternal complications of pregnancy	1,507	6.4	38.1
Accidents (unintentional injuries)	1,169	4.9	29.6
Newborn affected by complications of placenta, cord, and membranes	1,018	4.3	25.8
Bacterial sepsis[2] of newborn	566	2.4	14.3
Respiratory distress of newborn	504	2.1	12.8
Diseases of the circulatory system	492	2.1	12.4
Neonatal hemorrhage	422	1.8	10.7
All other causes	7,131	30.2	—
All causes	**23,629**	**100.0**	**597.8**

(1) Infant deaths during the first year of life per 100,000 live births. (2) Toxic condition resulting from the spread of bacteria.

Nonmarital Childbearing in the U.S., 1970-2011

Source: National Center for Health Statistics (NCHS), U.S. Dept. of Health and Human Services

	1970	1975	1980	1985	1990	1995	2000	2005	2008	2009	2010	2011
Births to unmarried mothers (thous.)	399	448	666	828	1,165	1,254	1,347	1,527	1,727	1,694	1,633	1,608
Race/Hispanic origin of mother	*Percent of live births to unmarried mothers*											
All races and origins	10.7%	14.3%	18.4%	22.0%	28.0%	32.2%	33.2%	36.9%	40.6%	41.0%	40.8%	40.7%
White	5.5	7.1	11.2	14.7	20.4	25.3	27.1	31.7	35.7	36.0	35.9	35.7
Black	37.5	49.5	56.1	61.2	66.5	69.9	68.5	69.3	71.8	72.3	72.1	71.8
American Indian or Alaska Native	22.4	32.7	39.2	46.8	53.6	57.2	58.4	63.5	65.8	65.4	65.6	66.2
Asian or Pacific Islander	—	—	7.3	9.5	13.2	16.3	14.8	16.2	16.9	17.2	17.0	17.2
Hispanic origin (selected states)[1,2]	—	—	23.6	29.5	36.7	40.8	42.7	48.0	52.6	53.2	53.4	53.3
Maternal age	*Percent distribution of live births to unmarried mothers*											
Under 20 years	50.1%	52.1%	40.8%	33.8%	30.9%	30.9%	28.0%	23.1%	22.2%	21.4%	20.1%	18.4%
20-24 years	31.8	29.9	35.6	36.3	34.7	34.5	37.4	38.3	37.1	36.9	36.8	36.9
25 years and over	18.1	18.0	23.5	29.9	34.4	34.7	34.6	38.6	40.7	41.7	43.1	44.8
Race/Hispanic origin of mother	*Live births per 1,000 unmarried women 15-44 years of age[3]*											
All races and origins	26.4	24.5	29.4	32.8	43.8	44.3	44.0	47.5	52.5	50.5	47.6	46.0
White[4]	13.9	12.4	18.1	22.5	32.9	37.0	38.2	43.0	48.2	46.3	44.5	42.7
Black[4]	95.5	84.2	81.1	77.0	90.5	74.5	70.5	67.8	72.5	69.9	65.3	63.7
Hispanic origin (selected states)[1,2]	—	—	—	—	89.6	88.7	87.2	100.3	105.1	96.8	80.6	75.1

— = Not available. (1) Hispanic origin data prior to 1995 is not directly comparable with data for more recent years due to differences in reporting area. (2) Hispanics may be of any race. (3) Rates computed by relating births to unmarried mothers, regardless of mother's age, to unmarried women 15-44 years of age. (4) For 1970 and 1975, birth rates are by race of child.

Number, Ratio, and Rate of Legal Abortions in U.S., 1970-2010

Source: *Abortion Surveillance—United States, 2010*, Centers for Disease Control and Prevention, U.S. Dept. of Health and Human Services

Year	Legal abortions	Ratio[1]	Rate[2]	Year	Legal abortions	Ratio[1]	Rate[2]	Year	Legal abortions	Ratio[1]	Rate[2]
1970	193,491	52	5	1993	1,330,414	333	23	2002	854,122	250	16
1971	485,816	137	11	1994	1,267,415	321	21	2003	848,163	245	16
1972	586,760	180	13	1995	1,210,883	311	20	2004	839,226	241	16
1973	615,831	196	14	1996	1,225,937	315	21	2005	820,151	236	16
1974	763,476	242	17	1997	1,186,039	306	20	2006	852,385	237	16
1975	854,853	272	18	1998	884,273	270	17	2007	827,609	230	16
1980	1,297,606	359	25	1999	861,789	261	17	2008	825,564	232	16
1990	1,429,247	344	24	2000	857,475	251	16	2009	789,116	227	15
1991	1,388,937	338	24	2001	853,485	249	16	2010	765,651	228	15
1992	1,359,146	334	23								

Note: After 1998, reporting area varies. (1) Number of abortions per 1,000 live births. (2) Number of abortions per 1,000 women aged 15-44 years.

Reported U.S. Abortions by Age, Race, and Marital Status, 2010

Source: *Abortion Surveillance—United States, 2010*, Centers for Disease Control and Prevention, U.S. Dept. of Health and Human Services

Characteristic	White No.	%	Race Black No.	%	Other No.	%	Total, all races No.	%
Age[1]								
Under 15 years	569	0.4%	843	0.7%	91	0.4%	1,503	0.5%
15-19 years	22,029	14.6	18,465	15.3	2,799	11.8	43,293	14.7
20-24 years	50,708	33.5	41,222	34.2	6,952	29.3	98,882	33.5
25-29 years	36,136	23.9	30,222	25.1	5,871	24.7	72,229	24.4
30-34 years	22,034	14.6	18,266	15.1	4,176	17.6	44,476	15.1
35-39 years	13,890	9.2	9,080	7.5	2,742	11.6	25,712	8.7
40 years and over	5,790	3.8	2,530	2.1	1,100	4.6	9,420	3.2
Total	**151,156**	**100.0**	**120,628**	**100.0**	**23,731**	**100.0**	**295,515**	**100.0**
Marital status[2]								
Married	22,937	16.7	7,851	8.3	6,167	28.8	36,955	14.6
Unmarried	114,795	83.3	86,765	91.7	15,277	71.2	216,837	85.4
Total	**137,732**	**100.0**	**94,616**	**100.0**	**21,444**	**100.0**	**253,792**	**100.0**

Note: The CDC requests data annually from the central health agencies of 52 reporting areas (all states, DC, and NYC). Reporting is voluntary. (1) Data from 30 reporting areas; excludes 22 (AZ, CA, CT, FL, HI, IL, KY, MD, MA, NE, NV, NH, NM, NYC, NY state, PA, TX, UT, VT, WA, WI, WY) that did not report, did not report by race/age, or did not meet reporting standards. (2) Data from 28 reporting areas; excludes 24 (AZ, CA, CT, FL, GA, HI, IL, KY, LA, MD, MA, NE, NV, NH, NM, NYC, NY state, PA, TX, UT, VT, WA, WI, WY) that did not report, did not report by race/marital status, or did not meet reporting standards.

Number of Sexual Partners for U.S. Adults by Age and Race, 2008

Source: *Sexual Behavior, Sexual Attraction, and Sexual Identity in the United States*, National Center for Health Statistics (NCHS), U.S. Dept. of Health and Human Services

	No. of opposite-sex partners in lifetime, % distrib. 0	1	2	3-6	7-14	15+	Median no.[2]		No. of opposite-sex partners in lifetime, % distrib. 0	1	2	3-6	7-14	15+	Median no.[2]
Male, 15-44 years[1]	11.4	15.0	7.6	26.5	18.1	21.4	5.1	**Female, 15-44 years[1]**	11.3	22.2	10.7	31.6	16.0	8.3	3.2
Age								**Age**							
15-19 years	43.3	21.2	9.4	17.6	5.4	3.1	1.8	15-19 years	48.1	22.7	8.2	15.7	4.1	1.1	1.4
20-24 years	14.4	19.1	8.0	26.1	18.1	14.2	4.1	20-24 years	12.6	24.5	12.5	31.6	11.7	7.2	2.6
25-44 years	2.4	12.3	7.0	28.9	21.5	27.9	6.1	25-44 years	1.6	21.4	10.9	35.6	20.1	10.4	3.6
Race/ethnicity[3]								**Race/ethnicity[3]**							
White	11.6	16.1	7.3	25.7	18.4	20.9	5.1	White	11.7	19.2	9.7	31.4	18.9	8.9	3.7
Black	9.6	8.3	5.0	25.6	21.6	30.0	6.9	Black	10.5	12.3	8.3	40.9	16.7	11.3	4.4
Hispanic	7.9	12.5	10.2	32.6	17.8	19.1	4.6	Hispanic	10.7	35.0	16.7	26.6	6.6	4.4	1.6

(1) Includes people of other or multiple races and origin groups, not shown separately. (2) Excludes people who have never had sex with a partner. (3) Figures are for whites and blacks who are not Hispanic. Hispanics may be of any race.

Sexual Orientation Among U.S. Adults, 2013

Source: *National Health Interview Survey, 2013*, National Center for Health Statistics (NCHS), U.S. Dept. of Health and Human Services

Sexual orientation	Gay or lesbian[1] Number (thous.)	% of group	Straight[2] Number (thous.)	% of group	Bisexual Number (thous.)	% of group
Overall	3,729	1.6%	224,163	97.7%	1,514	0.7%
Sex						
Men..................	2,000	1.8	108,093	97.8	481	0.4
Women	1,729	1.5	116,071	97.7	1,033	0.9
Age						
18-44 years	2,028	1.9	104,947	97.1	1,153	1.1
45-64 years............	1,422	1.8	77,686	97.8	289	0.4
65 years and older	278	0.7	41,531	99.2	73	0.2

Note: Percent distributions may not total 100 because of rounding. (1) Response option provided was "gay" for men and "gay or lesbian" for women. (2) Response option provided was "straight, that is, not gay" for men and "straight, that is, not gay or lesbian" for women.

Number of Opposite-Sex Partners in Past Year, 2008

Source: *Sexual Behavior, Sexual Attraction, and Sexual Identity in the United States*, National Center for Health Statistics, USDHHS (U.S. males and females 15-44 years of age)

Number of Opposite-Sex Partners in Lifetime by Age, 2008

Source: *Sexual Behavior, Sexual Attraction, and Sexual Identity in the United States*, National Center for Health Statistics, USDHSS (U.S. males and females 15-44 years of age)

Contraceptive Use in the U.S. by Age and Race, 2006-10

Source: National Survey of Family Growth, National Center for Health Statistics (NCHS), U.S. Dept. of Health and Human Services

	All women	Age in years 15-19	20-24	25-29	30-34	35-39	40-44	Race and ethnicity[1] White	Black	Asian	Hispanic
All women (thous.)	61,755	10,478	10,365	10,535	9,188	10,538	10,652	37,384	8,451	2,456	10,474
Contraceptive status and method					*Percent distribution*						
Using contraception	62.2%	30.5%	58.3%	65.3%	69.7%	74.6%	75.3%	65.6%	54.2%	58.5%	59.7%
Female sterilization	16.5	—	1.5	10.7	20.9	27.9	38.1	15.5	20.2	6.6	18.9
Male sterilization	6.2	—	0.5	2.7	6.6	12.4	15.1	8.7	0.9	4.0	3.3
Pill	17.1	16.2	27.4	21.5	17.7	12.7	7.4	21.0	9.9	12.3	11.8
Other hormonal methods	4.5	4.9	7.1	7.4	3.9	2.0	1.4	3.5	7.2	2.2	5.5
Implant, Lunelle™, or patch	0.9	0.7	1.1	1.5	0.9	0.5	—	0.5	1.0	—	1.5
3-month injectable (Depo-Provera™)	2.3	3.5	3.3	3.4	1.7	1.0	0.6	1.6	4.6	—	2.9
Contraceptive ring	1.3	0.7	2.7	2.4	1.4	0.5	0.4	1.4	1.6	—	1.0
Intrauterine device (IUD)	3.5	0.8	3.3	4.7	4.9	4.8	2.4	3.6	2.6	2.7	4.0
Condom	10.2	6.1	14.9	13.6	10.8	9.0	6.8	9.2	10.5	23.6	10.8
Periodic abstinence, calendar rhythm	0.6	—	0.2	0.5	0.8	1.0	1.1	0.6	0.2	1.8	0.8
Periodic abstinence, natural family planning	0.1	0.0	0.0	0.0	0.4	—	—	0.1	—	—	—
Withdrawal	3.2	2.1	3.3	4.1	3.2	4.1	2.6	3.1	2.4	4.9	3.4
Other methods[2]	0.3	0.2	—	0.3	0.5	0.6	0.4	0.3	0.1	—	0.7
Not using contraception[3]	37.8	69.5	41.7	34.7	30.3	25.4	24.7	34.4	45.8	41.6	40.3
Surgically sterile, female (noncontraceptive)	0.4	—	—	0.2	—	0.4	1.5	0.3	0.4	0.0	0.7
Nonsurgically sterile, female or male	1.7	0.5	1.4	1.4	1.8	2.0	3.1	1.5	2.3	1.5	1.6
Pregnant or postpartum	5.0	3.2	8.1	8.4	7.2	2.3	1.4	4.5	6.1	3.6	6.7
Seeking pregnancy	4.0	0.6	4.0	6.3	6.0	4.8	2.4	3.6	4.7	3.4	4.5
Never had intercourse	11.8	51.4	11.6	3.1	1.9	1.1	0.6	11.3	11.8	17.6	12.4
No intercourse in 3 months before interview	7.3	7.1	7.9	7.0	6.6	6.5	8.6	6.4	9.2	8.8	7.5
Had intercourse in 3 months before interview	7.7	6.7	8.7	8.4	6.7	8.4	7.1	6.9	11.2	6.7	7.0

— = Figure does not meet standard of reliability or precision. **Note:** Data was collected in interviews with women aged 15-44, in 2006-10. For all methods shown, the reported standard error was less than 3.9%. (1) Hispanics may be of any race. Other columns below are for non-Hispanic persons. (2) Includes diaphragm (with or without jelly or cream), emergency contraception, female condom or vaginal pouch, foam, cervical cap, Today™ sponge, suppository or insert, jelly or cream (without diaphragm), and other methods. (3) Includes male sterilization unknown reason and male surgical sterilization for noncontraceptive reasons, not shown separately.

Sexual Activity of Older Adults, 1999-2009

Source: *Sex, Romance, and Relationships–AARP Survey of Midlife and Older Adults*, Apr. 2010

Sexual activity[1]	Total 1999	2004	2009	Men 1999	2004	2009	Women 1999	2004	2009
Kissing and hugging	65%	69%	58%	74%	76%	67%	58%	62%	49%
Sexual touching or caressing	55	53	44	63	61	54	47	46	35
Sexual intercourse	38	36	28	42	41	33	35	31	23
Oral sex	13	14	16	14	19	20	11	10	12
Anal sex	—	—	3	—	—	4	—	—	2
Self stimulation	12	20	22	23	34	34	3	8	12

(1) Sexual activities engaged in at least once a week by persons ages 45 and older in the six months prior to the survey.

Sexual Activity of U.S. High School Students, 2013

Source: *Youth Risk Behavior Surveillance—United States, 2013*, Centers for Disease Control and Prevention, U.S. Dept. of Health and Human Services

Race/ethnicity	Ever had sexual intercourse Female	Male	Total	First sexual intercourse before age 13 Female	Male	Total	Currently sexually active[1] Female	Male	Total	Condom use during last sexual intercourse[2] Female	Male	Total
White[3]	45.3%	42.2%	43.7%	2.1%	4.4%	3.3%	35.9%	29.7%	32.8%	53.2%	61.8%	57.1%
Black[3]	53.4	68.4	60.6	4.9	24.0	14.0	37.6	47.0	42.1	55.3	73.0	64.7
Hispanic	46.9	51.7	49.2	3.8	9.2	6.4	34.7	34.7	34.7	50.7	66.5	58.3
Grade												
9	28.1	32.0	30.0	2.9	8.7	5.8	19.8	19.3	19.6	56.5	69.5	62.7
10	41.7	41.1	41.4	3.2	8.7	6.0	31.8	27.0	29.4	55.5	69.3	61.7
11	53.9	54.3	54.1	3.3	8.0	5.6	40.7	39.6	40.2	54.8	70.6	62.3
12	62.8	65.4	64.1	2.5	7.4	4.9	50.7	47.8	49.3	48.4	58.0	53.0
Total	46.0	47.5	46.8	3.1	8.3	5.6	35.2	32.7	34.0	53.1	65.8	59.1

(1) Sexual intercourse during the 3 months preceding the survey. (2) Among the 34.0% who were sexually active. (3) Non-Hispanic.

Risk Behaviors in U.S. High School Students, 2013

Source: *Youth Risk Behavior Surveillance—United States, 2013*, Centers for Disease Control and Prevention, U.S. Dept. of Health and Human Services

		Percent rarely or never wore seat belts[1] Female	Male	Total	Percent rarely or never wore bicycle helmets[2] Female	Male	Total	Percent who rode with a driver who had been drinking alcohol[3] Female	Male	Total
Race/ethnicity	White, non-Hispanic	4.7%	8.5%	6.6%	85.7%	85.8%	85.7%	19.9%	19.6%	19.7%
	Black, non-Hispanic	7.1	11.8	9.5	90.6	96.2	93.9	24.8	18.9	21.9
	Hispanic	8.7	8.9	8.8	90.9	93.7	92.4	29.2	28.9	29.1
Grade	9	7.1	9.8	8.5	85.4	87.4	86.5	20.8	18.1	19.4
	10	5.7	8.4	7.1	87.6	89.3	88.5	23.8	19.9	21.8
	11	6.3	9.7	8.0	87.2	90.2	88.9	21.8	23.4	22.6
	12	5.1	8.3	6.7	88.2	87.8	88.0	23.2	25.3	24.2
Total		6.1	9.1	7.6	87.0	88.6	87.9	22.4	21.4	21.9

(1) When riding in a car driven by someone else. (2) Among the 67.0% of students who rode a bicycle during the 12 months preceding the survey. (3) In a car or other vehicle one or more times in the 30 days preceding the survey.

Risky Driving Behaviors by U.S. High School Students, 2013

Source: *Youth Risk Behavior Surveillance–United States, 2013*, Centers for Disease Control and Prevention, U.S. Dept. of Health and Human Services

		Percent who drove when drinking alcohol[1] Female	Male	Total	Percent who texted or emailed while driving[2] Female	Male	Total
Race/ethnicity	White, non-Hispanic	8.2%	12.4%	10.4%	46.7%	45.1%	45.8%
	Black, non-Hispanic	5.4	6.9	6.2	26.5	31.5	29.1
	Hispanic	8.4	14.5	11.6	32.1	39.5	36.0
Grade	9	6.1	9.6	8.0	15.1	18.3	16.9
	10	4.6	7.4	6.2	25.0	27.8	26.5
	11	8.0	14.0	11.0	48.7	49.6	49.0
	12	10.5	15.7	13.1	59.5	61.0	60.3
Total		7.8	12.0	10.0	40.9	41.8	41.4

(1) Among the 64.3% of students who had driven a car or other vehicle one or more times during the 30 days before the survey. (2) Among the 64.7% of students who drove a car or other vehicle on at least one day during the 30 days before the survey.

U.S. Motor Vehicle Crashes, 2012

Source: National Safety Council (NSC); Natl. Highway Traffic Safety Admin. (NHTSA)

An estimated 36,300 people in the U.S. were killed in motor vehicle crashes in 2012, up 5% from the total for 2011. Both the number of drivers (213 mil) and the vehicle miles driven (3.0 tril) increased in 2012; the death rate per 100 mil vehicle miles also increased (4%) to 1.23, the highest level since 2008.

Although motor vehicle deaths per 10,000 registered vehicles rose 5% from 1.37 in 2011 to 1.44 in 2012, they were down from 1.89 in 2003, a decrease of 24% over nine years. The rate of fatalities per 100,000 population declined 25% between 2003 and 2012 but increased 5% between 2011 and 2012.

Male drivers were involved in about 5.5 mil crashes, whereas female drivers were in 4.3 mil. Male drivers were also involved in 74% of fatal crashes, or about 33,124, compared with 11,509 incidents involving female drivers.

In 2012, 10,322 traffic fatalities, or 31%, involved an intoxicated (blood alcohol concentration of 0.08 or greater) driver or motorcycle operator, an increase of 4.6% from 2011.

Seat belt use was 87% in 2013. In 2012, safety belts and child restraints saved an estimated 12,458 lives. Another 2,213 lives were saved by frontal air bags. Women used safety belts (88%) more often than men (84%). In 2013, the least likely safety belt users were in pickup trucks (78%) or traveling in light traffic (74%).

Crashes	Deaths	Injuries
All motor vehicle crashes	36,300	3,900,000
Collision between motor vehicles	13,500	2,900,000
Collision with fixed object	11,500	530,000
Collision with pedestrian	6,100	170,000
Noncollision accidents (e.g., rollovers)	4,000	170,000
Collision with pedalcycle	1,000	115,000
Collision with railroad train	100	1,000
Other (mostly collisions with animals)	100	14,000

Note: NSC numbers are rounded and preliminary.

Improper Driving Reported in U.S. Crashes, 2000-12

Source: National Safety Council

Type	Percent of fatal crashes			Percent of injury crashes			Percent of all crashes		
	2012	2005	2000	2012	2005	2000	2012	2005	2000
Improper driving	51.0%	62.7%	61.6%	48.3%	62.7%	60.3%	51.0%	58.5%	57.8%
Speed too fast or unsafe	12.7	18.1	23.7	9.4	15.0	16.3	8.7	12.7	13.6
Right of way	9.0	12.2	18.6	12.8	17.5	19.9	11.7	14.3	12.7
Failed to yield	5.9	8.0	10.1	8.5	12.5	12.5	8.7	10.8	12.7
Disregarded signal	1.3	1.4	4.6	2.1	2.5	3.6	1.5	1.7	5.3
Passed stop sign	1.8	2.8	3.8	2.2	2.5	1.3	1.5	1.8	2.2
Drove left of center	5.2	8.0	8.2	0.8	2.2	1.1	0.8	1.6	1.0
Made improper turn	1.1	4.5	0.7	1.9	4.2	2.0	2.1	4.5	2.4
Improper overtaking	0.9	1.4	0.9	0.6	0.6	0.6	0.8	0.8	0.9
Followed too closely	0.8	1.0	0.5	4.7	6.8	4.3	7.1	8.7	5.0
Other improper driving	21.3	17.5	9.0	18.1	16.4	16.1	19.8	15.9	14.1
No improper driving stated	49.0	37.3	38.4	51.7	37.3	39.7	49.0	41.5	42.2

Note: Based on reports from state traffic authorities. When a driver was under the influence of alcohol or drugs, the crash was considered a result of the driver's physical condition, not a driving error. Percents may not add up to totals due to rounding.

U.S. Passenger Deaths and Death Rates, 1999-2011

Source: National Safety Council

Year	Light duty vehicles[1]		Vans, SUVs, pickup trucks		Buses[2]		Railroad passenger trains		Scheduled airlines[3]	
	Deaths	Rate[4]	Deaths	Rate[4]	Deaths	Rate[4]	Deaths	Rate[4]	Deaths	Rate[4]
1999	20,851	0.84	11,295	0.76	40	0.07	14	0.10	24	0.005
2000	20,689	0.81	11,545	0.76	3	0.01	4	0.03	94	0.02
2001	20,310	0.78	11,736	0.76	11	0.02	3	0.02	279	0.06
2002	20,564	0.78	12,278	0.78	36	0.06	7	0.05	0	0.00
2003	19,723	0.74	12,551	0.78	30	0.05	3	0.02	24	0.005
2004	19,183	0.71	12,678	0.75	27	0.05	3	0.02	13	0.002
2005	18,509	0.68	13,043	0.76	43	0.07	16	0.10	22	0.004
2006	17,792	0.66	12,723	0.72	15	0.02	2	0.01	52	0.01
2007	29,075	0.66	NA	NA	18	0.03	5	0.03	0	0.00
2008	25,457	0.59	NA	NA	50	0.08	24	0.13	0	0.00
2009	23,441	0.53	NA	NA	21	0.04	3	0.02	49	0.01
2010	22,271	0.50	NA	NA	28	0.05	3	0.02	0	0.00
2011	21,221	0.48	NA	NA	35	0.06	6	0.03	0	0.00

NA = Not available. (1) From 2007 on, includes passenger cars, light trucks, vans, and SUVs, which are shown separately in previous years. Drivers of light duty vehicles are considered passengers. Includes taxi passengers. (2) Excludes school buses. (3) Excludes charter, cargo, and on-demand service and deaths due to suicide/sabotage. (4) Deaths per 100 mil passenger miles.

U.S. Death Rates for Suicide at Selected Ages, 1960-2010

Source: *Health, United States, 2012*, National Center for Health Statistics (NCHS), U.S. Dept. of Health and Human Services

Age	2010			2000			1980			1960		
	Both sexes	Male	Female	Both sexes	Male	Female	Both sexes	Male	Female	Both sexes	Male	Female
15-24 years	10.5	16.9	3.9	10.2	17.1	3.0	12.3	20.2	4.3	5.2	8.2	2.2
25-44 years	15.0	23.6	6.4	13.4	21.3	5.4	15.6	24.0	7.7	12.2	17.9	6.6
45-64 years	18.6	29.2	8.6	13.5	21.3	6.2	15.9	23.7	8.9	22.0	34.4	10.2
65 years and older	14.9	29.0	4.2	15.2	31.1	4.0	17.6	35.0	6.1	24.5	44.0	8.4
All ages	12.1	19.8	5.0	10.4	17.7	4.0	12.2	19.9	5.7	12.5	20.0	5.6

Note: Rate is per 100,000 population. Rates for all ages include ages not shown here.

U.S. Fires, 2013

Source: National Fire Protection Association

Fires

- Public fire departments responded to 1,240,000 fires in 2013, a decrease of 9.8% from 2012.

- Every 25 seconds, a fire department responds to a fire somewhere in the United States.

- There were 487,500 structure fires in 2013, a slight increase of 1.5% from 2012. Of those fires, 76% (369,000 fires) occurred in homes.

- Fires in highway vehicles decreased 4.9% from the previous year, totaling 164,000 in 2013.

- There were 564,500 fires in outside properties, a significant decrease of 19.3% from 2012.

Intentionally set fires

- There were an estimated 22,500 intentionally set structure fires in 2013, a decrease of 13.5% from 2012.

- Intentionally set structure fires are believed to have resulted in 150 civilian deaths in 2013, a decrease of 16.7% from the year before. Property damage from intentionally set structure fires totaled $577 mil, a slight decrease of 0.7% from the 2012 figure.

Civilian deaths

- There were an estimated 3,240 civilian fire deaths in 2013. This was a 13.5% increase from the year before.

- The number of civilian fire deaths that occurred in home structure fires increased 15.7% to 2,755, and fires in the home caused 85% of all fire deaths.

- Fires caused an average of one civilian death every 162 minutes.

Civilian injuries

- There were an estimated 15,925 civilian fire injuries reported in 2013, a 3.5% decrease from 2012. Nationwide, a civilian was injured in a fire every 33 minutes; a civilian fire injury occurred in a home fire every 43 minutes.

- Home structure fires were the site of 12,200 civilian fire injuries in 2013. Non-home structure fires accounted for 3,725 civilian injuries.

Property damage

- Direct property damage from fires amounted to an estimated $11.5 bil in 2013, a decrease of 7.3% from 2012. Structure fires accounted for $9.5 bil of property damage.

- Property loss associated with home fires came to $6.8 bil for 2013.

Leading Causes of Death in the U.S., 2012

Source: National Center for Health Statistics (NCHS), U.S. Dept. of Health and Human Services

	Number	% of total deaths	Death rate[1]		Number	% of total deaths	Death rate[1]
All causes	2,543,279	100.0%	732.8	6. Alzheimer's diseases	83,637	3.3%	23.8
1. Diseases of the heart	599,711	23.6	170.5	7. Diabetes	73,932	2.9	21.2
2. Cancer	582,623	22.9	166.5	8. Influenza and pneumonia	50,636	2.0	14.4
3. Chronic lower respiratory diseases	143,489	5.6	41.5	9. Kidney disease	45,622	1.8	13.1
4. Stroke	128,546	5.1	36.9	10. Intentional self-harm (suicide)	40,600	1.6	12.6
5. Accidents (unintentional injuries)	127,792	5.0	39.1	All other causes (residual)	666,691	26.2	—

(1) Per 100,000 population.

Principal Types of Accidental Deaths in the U.S., 1970-2012

Source: National Safety Council; National Center for Health Statistics, U.S. Dept. of Health and Human Services

Year[1]	Total	Motor vehicle	Falls	Poisoning	Drowning	Fires, flames, smoke	Choking: inhalation of food, object	Firearms	Mechanical suffocation
1970	NA	54,633	16,926	5,299	7,860	6,718	2,753	2,406	NA
1980	105,718	53,172	13,294	4,331	7,257	5,822	3,249	1,955	NA
1985	93,457	45,901	12,001	5,170	5,316	4,938	3,551	1,649	NA
1990	91,983	46,814	12,313	5,803	4,685	4,175	3,303	1,416	NA
1995	93,320	43,363	13,986	9,072	4,350	3,761	3,185	1,225	NA
2000	97,900	43,354	13,322	12,757	3,482	3,377	4,313	776	1,335
2003	109,277	44,757	17,229	19,457	3,306	3,369	4,272	730	1,309
2004	112,012	44,933	18,807	20,950	3,308	3,229	4,470	649	1,421
2005	117,809	45,343	19,656	23,617	3,582	3,197	4,386	789	1,514
2006	121,599	45,316	20,823	27,531	3,579	3,109	4,332	642	1,580
2007	123,706	43,945	22,631	29,846	3,443	3,286	4,344	613	1,653
2008	121,902	39,790	24,013	31,116	3,548	2,912	4,366	592	1,759
2009	118,046	36,216	24,792	31,758	3,517	2,756	4,370	554	1,569
2010	120,859	35,332	26,009	33,041	3,782	2,782	4,570	606	1,595
2011[2]	123,300	34,700	26,700	35,100	3,800	2,900	4,600	850	1,800
2012[2,3]	127,200	36,300	27,800	36,900	3,900	3,000	4,700	600	2,100
Death rates per 100,000 population									
1970	NA	26.8	8.3	2.6	3.9	3.3	1.4	1.2	NA
1980	46.5	23.4	5.9	1.9	3.2	2.6	1.4	0.9	NA
1985	39.3	19.3	5.0	2.2	2.2	2.1	1.5	0.7	NA
1990	36.9	18.8	4.9	2.3	1.9	1.7	1.3	0.6	NA
1995	35.5	16.5	5.3	3.4	1.7	1.4	1.2	0.5	NA
2000	35.6	15.7	4.8	4.6	1.3	1.2	1.6	0.3	0.5
2003	37.6	15.4	5.9	6.7	1.1	1.2	1.5	0.3	0.4
2004	38.1	15.3	6.4	7.1	1.1	1.1	1.5	0.2	0.5
2005	39.7	15.3	6.6	8.0	1.2	1.1	1.5	0.3	0.5
2006	40.8	15.2	7.0	9.2	1.2	1.0	1.5	0.2	0.5
2007	41.1	14.6	7.5	9.9	1.1	1.1	1.4	0.2	0.5
2008	40.0	13.1	7.9	10.2	1.2	1.0	1.4	0.2	0.6
2009	38.5	11.8	8.1	10.3	1.1	0.9	1.4	0.2	0.5
2010	39.0	11.4	8.4	10.7	1.2	0.9	1.5	0.9	0.5
2011[2]	39.6	11.1	8.6	11.3	1.2	0.9	1.5	0.9	0.6
2012[2,3]	40.5	11.6	8.9	11.8	1.2	1.0	1.5	1.0	0.7

NA = Not available. **Note:** All figures include on-the-job deaths. (1) Data after 1999 are not comparable with earlier data because of classification changes. (2) Preliminary. (3) Total includes 12,500 other accidental deaths.

Deaths in the U.S. Involving Firearms by Age and Sex, 2010

Source: National Safety Council

Type and sex	All ages	Under 5	5-14	15-19	20-24	25-44	45-64	65-74	75 & older
Total firearms deaths	31,672	82	298	2,331	3,870	10,962	9,419	2,316	2,394
Male	27,356	56	232	2,081	3,504	9,396	7,891	2,016	2,180
Female	4,316	26	66	250	366	1,566	1,528	300	214
Unintentional	606	25	37	72	73	198	139	38	24
Male	515	21	30	63	64	166	116	32	23
Female	91	4	7	9	9	32	23	6	1
Suicide	19,392	—	81	668	1,378	5,508	7,479	2,053	2,225
Male	16,962	—	69	601	1,243	4,733	6,382	1,844	2,090
Female	2,430	—	12	67	135	775	1,097	209	135
Homicide	11,078	54	165	1,554	2,335	5,004	1,630	207	129
Male	9,340	33	121	1,384	2,117	4,264	1,242	126	53
Female	1,738	21	44	170	218	740	388	81	76
Legal intervention	344	0	1	16	52	172	94	8	1
Male	336	0	1	15	51	168	92	8	1
Female	8	0	0	1	1	4	2	0	0
Undetermined[1]	252	3	14	21	32	80	77	10	15
Male	203	2	11	18	29	65	59	6	13
Female	49	1	3	3	3	15	18	4	2

— = Not applicable. (1) The intention involved (whether accident, suicide, or homicide) could not be determined.

U.S. Infant Mortality Rates by Race and Sex, 1960-2011

Source: National Center for Health Statistics (NCHS), U.S. Dept. of Health and Human Services

Year	All races[1] Both sexes	Male	Female	White Both sexes	Male	Female	Black Both sexes	Male	Female
1960	26.0	29.3	22.6	22.9	26.0	19.6	44.3	49.1	39.4
1970	20.0	22.4	17.5	17.8	20.0	15.4	32.6	36.2	29.0
1980	12.6	13.9	11.2	11.0	12.3	9.6	21.4	23.3	19.4
1990	9.2	10.3	8.1	7.6	8.5	6.6	18.0	19.6	16.2
1995	7.6	8.3	6.8	6.3	7.0	5.6	15.1	16.3	13.9
1996	7.3	8.0	6.6	6.1	6.7	5.4	14.7	16.0	13.3
1997	7.2	8.0	6.5	6.0	6.7	5.4	14.2	15.5	12.8
1998	7.2	7.8	6.5	6.0	6.5	5.4	14.3	15.7	12.8
1999	7.1	7.7	6.4	5.8	6.4	5.2	14.6	15.9	13.2
2000	6.9	7.6	6.2	5.7	6.2	5.1	14.1	15.5	12.6
2001	6.8	7.5	6.1	5.7	6.2	5.1	14.0	15.5	12.5
2002	7.0	7.6	6.3	5.8	6.4	5.1	14.4	15.4	13.3
2003	6.9	7.6	6.1	5.7	6.3	5.0	14.0	15.5	12.4
2004	6.8	7.5	6.1	5.7	6.2	5.1	13.8	15.2	12.3
2005	6.9	7.6	6.2	5.7	6.3	5.1	13.7	15.2	12.3
2006	6.7	7.3	6.0	5.6	6.1	5.0	13.3	14.4	12.2
2007	6.8	7.4	6.1	5.6	6.2	5.1	13.2	14.5	11.9
2008	6.6	7.2	6.0	5.6	6.1	5.0	12.7	13.9	11.5
2009	6.4	7.0	5.8	5.3	5.8	4.8	12.6	14.1	11.2
2010	6.2	6.7	5.6	5.2	5.7	4.7	11.6	12.7	10.5
2011[2]	6.1	NA	NA	5.1	NA	NA	11.4	NA	NA

NA = Not available. **Note:** Rates per 1,000 live births in specified group. (1) Includes races other than white and black. (2) Preliminary.

Years of Life Expected at Birth in U.S., 1900-2011

Source: National Center for Health Statistics (NCHS), U.S. Dept. of Health and Human Services

Year[2]	All races[1] Both sexes	Male	Female	White Both sexes	Male	Female	Black Both sexes	Male	Female
1900	47.3	46.3	48.3	47.6	46.6	48.7	NA	NA	NA
1910	50.0	48.4	51.8	50.3	48.6	52.0	NA	NA	NA
1920	54.1	53.6	54.6	54.9	54.4	55.6	NA	NA	NA
1930	59.7	58.1	61.6	61.4	59.7	63.5	NA	NA	NA
1940	62.9	60.8	65.2	64.2	62.1	66.6	NA	NA	NA
1950	68.2	65.6	71.1	69.1	66.5	72.2	NA	NA	NA
1960	69.7	66.6	73.1	70.6	67.4	74.1	NA	NA	NA
1970	70.8	67.1	74.7	71.7	68.0	75.6	64.1	60.0	68.3
1980	73.7	70.0	77.5	74.4	70.7	78.1	68.1	63.8	72.5
1985	74.7	71.2	78.2	75.3	71.9	78.7	69.3	65.0	73.4
1990	75.4	71.8	78.8	76.1	72.7	79.4	69.1	64.5	73.6
1995	75.8	72.5	78.9	76.5	73.4	79.6	69.6	65.2	73.9
1996	76.1	73.1	79.1	76.8	73.9	79.7	70.2	66.1	74.2
1997	76.5	73.6	79.4	77.1	74.3	79.9	71.1	67.2	74.7
1998	76.7	73.8	79.5	77.3	74.5	80.0	71.3	67.6	74.8
1999	76.7	73.9	79.4	77.3	74.6	79.9	71.4	67.8	74.7
2000	76.8	74.1	79.3	77.3	74.7	79.9	71.8	68.2	75.1
2001	76.9	74.2	79.4	77.4	74.8	79.9	72.0	68.4	75.2
2002	76.9	74.3	79.5	77.4	74.9	79.9	72.1	68.6	75.4
2003	77.1	74.5	79.6	77.6	75.0	80.0	72.3	68.8	75.6
2004	77.5	74.9	79.9	77.9	75.4	80.4	72.8	69.3	76.0
2005	77.4	74.9	79.9	77.9	75.4	80.4	72.8	69.3	76.1
2006	77.7	75.1	80.2	78.2	75.7	80.6	73.2	69.7	76.5
2007	77.9	75.4	80.4	78.4	75.9	80.8	73.6	70.0	76.8
2008	78.1	75.6	80.6	78.5	76.1	80.9	74.0	70.6	77.2
2009	78.6	76.0	80.9	78.8	76.4	81.2	74.7	71.4	77.7
2010	78.7	76.2	81.0	78.9	76.5	81.3	75.1	71.8	78.0
2011[3]	78.7	76.3	81.1	79.0	76.6	81.3	75.3	72.1	78.2

NA = Not available. (1) Includes races other than white and black. (2) Data prior to 1940 does not include all states. (3) Preliminary.

U.S. Life Expectancy at Selected Ages, 2011

Source: National Center for Health Statistics (NCHS), U.S. Dept. of Health and Human Services

Exact age in years	All races[1] Both sexes	Male	Female	White Both sexes	Male	Female	Black Both sexes	Male	Female
0	78.7	76.3	81.1	79.0	76.6	81.3	75.3	72.1	78.2
1	78.2	75.8	80.5	78.4	76.0	80.7	75.2	72.0	78.0
5	74.3	71.9	76.6	74.4	72.1	76.7	71.3	68.2	74.1
10	69.3	66.9	71.6	69.5	67.1	71.8	66.3	63.2	69.1
15	64.4	62.0	66.7	64.5	62.2	66.8	61.4	58.3	64.2
20	59.5	57.2	61.8	59.7	57.4	61.9	56.6	53.6	59.3
25	54.8	52.5	56.9	54.9	52.7	57.0	51.9	49.0	54.4
30	50.0	47.9	52.0	50.2	48.0	52.2	47.3	44.5	49.6
35	45.3	43.2	47.2	45.4	43.4	47.4	42.6	40.0	44.9
40	40.6	38.6	42.5	40.7	38.7	42.6	38.0	35.5	40.2
45	36.0	34.0	37.8	36.1	34.2	37.9	33.6	31.0	35.7
50	31.5	29.6	33.2	31.6	29.8	33.3	29.3	26.8	31.3
55	27.2	25.5	28.8	27.3	25.6	28.9	25.2	22.9	27.1
60	23.1	21.5	24.5	23.2	21.6	24.5	21.5	19.3	23.2
65	19.2	17.8	20.4	19.2	17.8	20.4	18.0	16.1	19.4
70	15.5	14.3	16.5	15.5	14.3	16.5	14.7	13.1	15.8
75	12.1	11.0	12.9	12.1	11.0	12.9	11.7	10.3	12.5
80	9.1	8.2	9.7	9.1	8.2	9.6	9.0	7.9	9.6
85	6.5	5.9	6.9	6.5	5.8	6.9	6.8	5.9	7.2
90	4.6	4.1	4.8	4.5	4.0	4.8	5.0	4.4	5.3
95	3.2	2.9	3.3	3.2	2.8	3.3	3.7	3.3	3.8
100	2.3	2.1	2.3	2.3	2.0	2.3	2.8	2.5	2.8

Note: Data is preliminary. (1) Includes races other than white and black.

NOTED PERSONALITIES

Widely Known Americans of the Present

Political leaders, journalists, other prominent living persons. As of Oct. 2014. Excludes most who fall in categories listed elsewhere in Noted Personalities, such as Writers of the Present and Entertainment Personalities of the Present. Includes some figures who are active in American life but are not U.S. citizens.

Roger Ailes, b 5/15/40 (Warren, OH), TV exec.

Madeleine K. Albright, b 5/15/37 (Prague, Czech.), former sec. of state.

Edwin "Buzz" Aldrin, b 1/20/30 (Montclair, NJ), former astronaut, second person to walk on the Moon.

Samuel A. Alito Jr., b 4/1/50 (Trenton, NJ), Supreme Court justice.

Paul Allen, b 1/21/53 (Seattle, WA), co-founder of Microsoft.

Christiane Amanpour, b 1/12/58 (London, Eng., UK), TV journalist.

Marc Andreessen, b 7/9/71 (New Lisbon, IA), co-author of web browser Mosaic, cofounder of Netscape.

David Axelrod, b 2/22/55 (New York, NY), political strategist; former sr. adviser to Pres. Obama.

Michele Bachmann, b 4/6/56 (Waterloo, IA), U.S. rep. (R, MN), 2012 pres. contender.

F. Lee Bailey, b 6/10/33 (Waltham, MA), attorney.

Russell Baker, b 8/14/25 (Morrisonville, VA), columnist.

Mary Barra, b 12/24/61 (Waterford, MI), General Motors CEO.

Dave Barry, b 7/3/47 (Armonk, NY), humorist.

Marion Barry, b 3/6/36 (Itta Bena, MS), DC city council member; former Washington, DC, mayor (D).

Max Baucus, b 12/11/41 (Helena, MT), U.S. ambassador to China, former senator (D, MT).

Gary Bauer, b 5/4/46 (Covington, KY), domestic policy adviser to Pres. Reagan; founder, Campaign for Working Families.

Glenn Beck, b 2/10/64 (Mount Vernon, WA), political commentator.

Chris Berman, b 5/10/55 (Greenwich, CT), sportscaster.

Ben Bernanke, b 12/13/53 (Augusta, GA), former Federal Reserve chair.

Carl Bernstein, b 2/14/44 (Washington, DC); journalist; with Bob Woodward cracked Watergate scandal.

Jeff Bezos, b 1/12/64 (Albuquerque, NM), founder and CEO of Amazon.com.

Jill Biden, b 6/5/51 (Hammonton, NJ), English college professor, wife of U.S. vice pres. Joe Biden.

Joseph R. Biden Jr., b 11/20/42 (Scranton, PA), U.S. vice pres.; former sen. (D, DE).

James H. Billington, b 6/1/29 (Bryn Mawr, PA), librarian of U.S. Congress.

Lloyd Blankfein, b 9/20/54 (Bronx, NY), CEO and chairman of Goldman Sachs.

Wolf Blitzer, b 3/22/48 (Augsburg, Germany), TV journalist.

Harold Bloom, b 7/11/30 (New York, NY), literary critic.

Michael R. Bloomberg, b 2/14/42 (Brighton, MA), former NYC mayor, financial information/media entrepreneur.

John Boehner, b 11/17/49 (Cincinnati, OH), U.S. rep. (R, OH), speaker of the House.

Charles F. Bolden, b 8/19/46 (Columbia, SC), NASA head.

Julian Bond, b 1/14/40 (Nashville, TN), civil rights leader, former NAACP chair.

Cory Booker, b 4/27/69 (Washington, DC), U.S. sen. (D, NJ), former Newark mayor.

Barbara Boxer, b 11/11/40 (Brooklyn, NY), U.S. senator (D, CA).

L. Paul Bremer III, b 9/30/41 (Hartford, CT), diplomat, former top U.S. civilian administrator in Iraq.

John O. Brennan, b 9/22/55 (North Bergen, NJ), CIA director.

Jimmy Breslin, b 10/17/30 (Jamaica, Queens, NY), columnist, author.

Stephen Breyer, b 8/15/38 (San Francisco, CA), Supreme Court justice.

Sergey Brin, b 8/21/73 (Moscow, Russia), cofounder of Google.

Roslyn M. Brock, b 5/30/65 (Fort Pierce, FL), NAACP chair.

Tom Brokaw, b 2/6/40 (Webster, SD), TV journalist, retired NBC anchor.

David Brooks, b 8/11/61 (Toronto, ON, Can.), columnist, political commentator.

Aaron Brown, b 11/10/48 (Hopkins, MN), broadcast journalist.

Jerry (Edmund G.) Brown Jr., b 4/7/38 (San Francisco, CA), CA gov. (1975-83, 2011-) (D), former pres. candidate.

Scott Brown, b 9/12/59 (Wakefield, MA), 2014 U.S. sen. (R, NH) candidate, former senator (R, MA).

Pat Buchanan, b 11/2/38 (Washington, DC), journalist, former pres. candidate.

Warren Buffett, b 8/30/30 (Omaha, NE), investor, leading philanthropist.

Sylvia Mathews Burwell, b 6/1/65 (Hinton, WV), health and human services sec.

Barbara Bush, b 6/8/25 (Flushing, NY), former first lady.

Barbara Bush, b 11/25/81 (Dallas, TX), daughter of former Pres. George W. Bush.

George H. W. Bush, b 6/12/24 (Milton, MA), former U.S. president.

George W. Bush, b 7/6/46 (New Haven, CT), former U.S. president.

Laura Bush, b 11/4/46 (Midland, TX), former first lady.

Herman Cain, b 12/13/45 (Memphis, TN), former chairman and CEO of Godfather's Pizza; 2012 pres. contender.

Eric Cantor, b 6/6/63 (Richmond, VA), former U.S. rep. (R, VA), former House majority leader.

Tucker Carlson, b 5/16/69 (San Francisco, CA), journalist, TV commentator.

Jay Carney, b 5/22/65 (Washington, DC), CNN political commentator, former White House press secretary.

Jimmy Carter, b 10/1/24 (Plains, GA), former U.S. president; 2002 Nobel Peace Prize winner.

Rosalynn Carter, b 8/18/27 (Plains, GA), former first lady.

James Carville Jr., b 10/25/44 (Fort Benning, GA), TV political commentator.

Steve Case, b 8/21/58 (Honolulu, HI), former AOL Time Warner chairman.

Joaquin Castro, b 9/16/74 (San Antonio, TX), U.S. rep. (D, TX).

Julian Castro, b 9/16/74 (San Antonio, TX), housing and urban development sec., former San Antonio mayor.

Dick Cheney, b 1/30/41 (Lincoln, NE), former U.S. vice president.

Lynne Cheney, b 8/14/41 (Casper, WY), political commentator, wife of former U.S. vice pres. Dick Cheney.

Noam Chomsky, b 12/7/28 (Philadelphia, PA), linguist, activist.

Chris Christie, b 9/6/62 (Newark, NJ), NJ governor (R).

Connie Chung, b 8/20/46 (Washington, DC), TV journalist.

James R. Clapper Jr., b 1941, director of national intelligence.

Bill Clinton, b 8/19/46 (Hope, AR), former U.S. president.

Chelsea Clinton, b 2/27/80 (Little Rock, AR), daughter of former pres. Bill Clinton and Hillary Rodham Clinton.

Hillary Rodham Clinton, b 10/26/47 (Chicago, IL), former sec. of state, U.S. sen. (D, NY), first lady; 2008 pres. contender.

Kate Clinton, b 11/9/47 (Buffalo, NY), political humorist.

Kenneth Cole, b 3/23/54 (Brooklyn, NY), fashion designer.

Gail Collins, b 11/25/45 (Cincinnati, OH), newspaper columnist, writer.

Jason Collins, b 12/2/78 (Northridge, CA), first openly gay NBA player.

James Comey, b 12/14/60 (Yonkers, NY), FBI director.

Tim Cook, b 11/1/60 (Robertdale, AZ), CEO of Apple, Inc.

Anderson Cooper, b 6/3/67 (New York, NY), CNN anchor.

John Cornyn, b 2/2/52 (Houston, TX), U.S. sen. (R, TX), minority whip.

Jon Corzine, b 1/1/47 (Willey's Station, IL), former U.S. sen. (D, NJ) and NJ governor.

Bob Costas, b 3/22/52 (Astoria, Queens, NY), TV sports journalist.

Ann Coulter, b 12/8/61 (New Canaan, CT), political commentator, author.

Katie Couric, b 1/7/57 (Arlington, VA), journalist, anchor for Yahoo! News; former *Today* show, *CBS Evening News* anchor.

Candy Crowley, b 12/12/48 (Kalamazoo, MI), CNN senior political correspondent.

Ted Cruz, b 12/22/70 (Calgary, AB, Can.), U.S. sen. (R, TX).

Mark Cuban, b 7/31/58 (Pittsburgh, PA), entrepreneur, Dallas Mavericks (NBA) owner.

Andrew Cuomo, b 12/6/57 (New York, NY), NY governor (D), former state atty. gen.

Mario Cuomo, b 6/15/32 (Jamaica, Queens, NY), former NY governor (D).

Ann Curry, b 11/19/56 (Guam), former *Today* show news anchor.

Richard M. Daley, b 4/24/42 (Chicago, IL), former Chicago mayor (D).

Howard Dean, b 11/17/48 (New York, NY), former VT gov., former Dem. Natl. Committee chair.

Bill de Blasio, b 5/8/61 (New York, NY), NYC mayor (D).

Michael Dell, b 2/23/65 (Houston, TX), founder, chairman, and CEO of Dell computers.

Martin Dempsey, b 3/14/52 (Bayonne, NJ) chairman, Joint Chiefs of Staff.

Alan Dershowitz, b 9/1/38 (Brooklyn, NY), attorney, political commentator.

Barry Diller, b 2/2/42 (San Francisco, CA), media exec.

Jamie Dimon, b 3/13/56 (New York, NY), chairman, CEO of JPMorgan Chase.

Lou Dobbs, b 9/24/45 (Childress, TX), TV journalist.

James Dobson, b 4/21/36 (Shreveport, LA), evangelical Christian leader, chairman of Focus on the Family.

Christopher Dodd, b 5/27/44 (Willimantic, CT), Motion Picture Assn. of America chair/CEO; former U.S. sen. (D, CT).

Timothy Dolan, b 2/6/50 (St. Louis, MO), Rom. Cath. cardinal, archbishop of NY.

Elizabeth Hanford Dole, b 7/29/36 (Salisbury, NC), former U.S. sen. (R, NC), Red Cross pres., cabinet member.

Robert Dole, b 7/22/23 (Russell, KS), former U.S. Senate majority leader (R, KS), 1996 pres. nominee.

Sam Donaldson, b 3/11/34 (El Paso, TX), TV journalist.

Elizabeth Drew, b 11/16/35 (Cincinnati, OH), journalist.

Matt Drudge, b 10/27/66 (Takoma Park, MD), Internet journalist.

Michael S. Dukakis, b 11/3/33 (Brookline, MA), former MA gov. (D), 1988 pres. nominee.

Arne Duncan, b 11/6/64 (Chicago, IL), education secretary.

Dick Durbin, b 11/21/44 (East St. Louis, IL), U.S. Senate majority whip (D, IL).

Josh Earnest, b 5/2/77 (Kansas City, MO), White House press secretary.

Bernard Ebbers, b 8/27/41 (Edmonton, AB, Can.), former WorldCom CEO; jailed for fraud.

Marian Wright Edelman, b 6/6/39 (Bennettsville, SC), pres. and founder of Children's Defense Fund.

John Edwards, b 6/10/53 (Seneca, SC), former U.S. sen. (D, NC), 2004 vice-pres. candidate, 2008 pres. contender.

Edward Egan, b 4/2/32 (Oak Park, IL), Rom. Cath. cardinal, archbishop emeritus of New York.

Michael Eisner, b 3/7/42 (Mt. Kisco, NY), former Disney Co. CEO.

Lawrence J. Ellison, b 8/17/44 (New York, NY), Oracle Corp. founder, CEO.

Rahm Emanuel, b 11/29/59 (Chicago, IL), Chicago mayor; former White House chief of staff, U.S. rep. (D, IL).

Myrlie Evers-Williams, b 3/17/33 (Vicksburg, MS), civil rights activist.

Louis Farrakhan, b 5/11/33 (Roxbury, MA), Nation of Islam leader.

Dianne Feinstein, b 6/22/33 (San Francisco, CA), U.S. sen. (D, CA).

Larry Flynt, b 11/1/42 (Lakeville, KY), publisher.

Steve (Malcolm) Forbes Jr., b 7/18/47 (Morristown, NJ), publisher, former pres. contender.

Tom Ford, b 8/27/61 (Austin, TX), fashion designer.

Barney Frank, b 3/31/40 (Bayonne, NJ), attorney, former U.S. rep. (D, MA).

Al Franken, b 5/21/51 (New York, NY), U.S. sen. (D, MN); humorist, political writer.

Thomas Friedman, b 7/20/53 (Minneapolis, MN), columnist, author.

Bill Gates, b 10/28/55 (Seattle, WA), software pioneer; Microsoft exec.

Henry Louis Gates Jr., b 9/16/50 (Keyser, WV), African American studies scholar.

Robert M. Gates, b 9/25/43 (Wichita, KS), former sec. of defense.

David Geffen, b 2/21/43 (Brooklyn, NY), entertainment exec.

Timothy Geithner, b 8/18/61 (New York, NY), former Treasury secretary.

Robert Gibbs, b 3/29/71 (Auburn, AL), former White House press sec.

Charles Gibson, b 3/4/43 (Evanston, IL), TV journalist, former host of ABC's *World News*.

Gabrielle Giffords, b 6/8/70 (Tucson, AZ), former U.S. rep. (D, AZ); shot in 2011 assassination attempt.

Kirsten Gillibrand, b 12/9/66 (Albany, NY), U.S. sen. (D, NY), attorney.

Newt Gingrich, b 6/17/43 (Harrisburg, PA), former House speaker (R, GA), 2012 pres. contender.

Ruth Bader Ginsburg, b 3/15/33 (Brooklyn, NY), U.S. Supreme Court justice.

Rudolph Giuliani, b 5/28/44 (Brooklyn, NY), former NYC mayor (R).

John Glenn, b 7/18/21 (Cambridge, OH), former U.S. sen. (D, OH), astronaut.

Alberto Gonzales, b 8/4/55 (San Antonio, TX), former U.S. attorney general.

Roger Goodell, b 2/19/59 (Jamestown, NY), NFL commissioner.

Ellen Goodman, b 4/11/41 (Newton, MA), columnist.

Doris Kearns Goodwin, b 1/4/43 (Brooklyn, NY), historian, TV commentator.

Berry Gordy, b 11/28/29 (Detroit, MI), Motown record label founder.

Al Gore Jr., b 3/31/48 (Washington, DC), former U.S. sen. (D, TN), vice pres., 2000 pres. nominee; 2007 Nobel Peace Prize winner.

Rev. Billy Graham, b 11/7/18 (Charlotte, NC), evangelist.

(William) Franklin Graham III, b 7/14/52 (Asheville, NC), evangelist, son of Billy Graham.

Temple Grandin, b 8/29/47 (Boston, MA), animal behavioral scientist, autism activist.

Jeff Greenfield, b 6/10/43 (New York, NY), TV journalist.

Alan Greenspan, b 3/6/26 (New York, NY), former Federal Reserve chairman.

Chuck Hagel, b 10/4/46 (North Platte, NE), defense sec., former U.S. sen. (R, NE).

Jenna Bush Hager, b 11/25/81 (Dallas, TX), daughter of former Pres. George W. Bush.

Pete Hamill, b 6/24/35 (Brooklyn, NY), journalist, author.

Sean Hannity, b 12/30/61 (New York, NY), radio and TV host, author, political commentator.

Kamala Harris, b 10/20/64 (Oakland, CA), atty. gen. (CA).

Reed Hastings, b 10/8/60 (Boston, MA), founder, pres., CEO and board chair, Netflix, Inc.

Orrin Hatch, b 3/22/34 (Homestead Park, PA), U.S. sen. (R, UT).

Hugh Hefner, b 4/9/26 (Chicago, IL), publisher.

Tommy Hilfiger, b 3/24/51 (Elmira, NY), fashion designer.

Anita Hill, b 7/30/56 (Morris, OK), legal scholar; complainant against Supreme Court justice nominee Clarence Thomas.

Paris Hilton, b 2/17/81 (New York, NY), heiress, actress.

Perez Hilton, b 3/23/78 (Miami, FL), gossip columnist.

James P. Hoffa, b 5/19/41 (Detroit, MI), Teamsters Union head.

Eric Holder Jr., b 1/21/51 (Bronx, NY), first African American U.S. atty. gen.

David Horowitz, b 1/10/39 (New York, NY), consumer advocate, columnist, author.

Steny H. Hoyer, b 6/14/39 (New York, NY), House minority whip, former majority leader (D, MD).

Mike Huckabee, b 8/24/55 (Hope, AR), former gov. (R, AR), minister, 2008 pres. contender, TV host.

Arianna Huffington, b 7/15/50 (Athens, Greece), political commentator.

H. Wayne Huizenga, b 12/29/39 (Evergreen Park, IL), entrepreneur, sports exec.

Brit Hume, b 6/22/43 (Washington, DC), TV journalist on FOX.

Jon Huntsman Jr., b 3/26/60 (Palo Alto, CA), former UT gov. (R), ambassador to China, 2012 pres. contender.

Lee Iacocca, b 10/15/24 (Allentown, PA), former auto exec. (Ford, Chrysler).

Carl Icahn, b 2/16/36 (Queens, NY), financier.

Gwen Ifill, b 9/29/55 (Queens, NY), TV journalist, moderator on PBS.

Don Imus, b 7/23/40 (Riverside, CA), talk-show host.

Patricia Ireland, b 10/19/45 (Oak Park, IL), feminist leader.

Rev. Jesse Jackson, b 10/8/41 (Greenville, SC), civil rights leader, former pres. contender.

Marc Jacobs, b 4/9/64 (New York, NY), fashion designer.

Valerie Jarrett, b 11/14/56 (Shiraz, Iran), sr. adviser to Pres. Obama.

Bobby Jindal, b 6/10/71 (Baton Rouge, LA), LA governor (R), first elected Indian American governor.

Jasper Johns, b 5/15/30 (Augusta, GA), artist.

Gary Johnson, b 1/1/53 (Minot, ND), former NM governor (R); 2012 Libertarian pres. nominee.

Robert L. Johnson, b 4/8/46 (Hickory, MS), Black Entertainment Television founder.

Vernon E. Jordan Jr., b 8/15/35 (Atlanta, GA), attorney, former pres. adviser, civil rights leader.

Elena Kagan, b 4/28/60 (New York, NY), Supreme Court justice.

Tim Kaine, b 2/26/58 (St. Paul, MN), former Dem Natl. Committee chair, VA governor.

Donna Karan, b 10/2/48 (Forest Hills, Queens, NY), fashion designer.

Jeffrey Katzenberg, b 12/21/50 (New York, NY), entertainment exec.

Thomas Kean, b 4/21/35 (New York, NY), 9/11 commission chair, former Drew Univ. pres., former NJ gov (R).

Garrison Keillor, b 8/7/42 (Anoka, MN), author, broadcaster.

Mark Kelly, b 2/21/64 (Orange, NJ), U.S. Navy capt., former NASA shuttle commander.

Megyn Kelly, b 11/18/70 (Syracuse, NY), TV commentator, host.

Anthony M. Kennedy, b 7/23/36 (Sacramento, CA), Supreme Court justice.

Kirk Kerkorian, b 6/6/17 (Fresno, CA), pres. and CEO of investment firm Tracinda Corp.

John Kerry, b 12/11/43 (Aurora, CO), sec. of state, former U.S. sen. (D, MA), 2004 pres. nominee.

Larry King, b 11/19/33 (Brooklyn, NY), TV talk-show host.

Michael Kinsley, b 3/9/51 (Detroit, MI), editor, political commentator.

Calvin Klein, b 11/19/42 (Bronx, NY), fashion designer.

Philip H. Knight, b 2/24/38 (Portland, OR), founder and chairman of the board of Nike.

Charles G. Koch, b 5/3/40 (Wichita, KS), Koch Industries exec.; philanthropist.

David H. Koch, b 11/1/35 (Wichita, KS), Koch Industries exec.; philanthropist.

Ted Koppel, b 2/8/40 (Lancashire, Eng., UK), former TV journalist.

Michael Kors, b 8/9/59 (Merrick, NY), fashion designer.

Larry Kramer, b 6/25/35 (Bridgeport, CT), AIDS activist, writer.

Nicholas D. Kristof, b 4/27/59 (Chicago, IL), columnist, author.

William Kristol, b 12/23/52 (New York, NY), editor, columnist.

Steve Kroft, b 8/22/45 (Kokomo, IN), TV journalist.

Paul Krugman, b 2/28/53 (Long Island, NY), economist, columnist.

Brian Lamb, b 10/9/41 (Lafayette, IN), cable TV exec., journalist.

Wayne LaPierre Jr., b 11/8/49 (NY), National Rifle Assn. exec. VP.

Matt Lauer, b 12/30/57 (New York, NY), TV journalist, NBC *Today* show co-host.

Ralph Lauren, b 10/14/39 (Bronx, NY), fashion designer.

Bernard F. Law, b 11/4/31 (Torreon, Mexico), cardinal archbishop emeritus of Boston.

Patrick Leahy, b 3/31/40 (Montpelier, VT), U.S. sen. (D, VT), president pro tempore.

Norman Lear, b 7/27/22 (New Haven, CT), TV producer, political activist.

Jim Lehrer, b 5/19/34 (Wichita, KS), TV journalist, author.

Carl Levin, b 6/28/34 (Detroit, MI), U.S. sen. (D, MI), Armed Services Committee chair.

Jacob Lew, b 8/29/55 (New York, NY), sec. of treasury, former White House chief of staff.

Monica Lewinsky, b 7/23/73 (San Francisco, CA), former White House intern.

Joseph Lieberman, b 2/24/42 (Stamford, CT), former U.S. sen. (I, CT), 2000 vice-pres. nominee (D).

Rush Limbaugh, b 1/12/51 (Cape Girardeau, MO), radio talk-show host.

Gary Locke, b 1/21/50 (Seattle, WA), former U.S. ambassador to China, commerce sec., WA gov. (D).

Trent Lott, b 10/9/41 (Grenada, MS), former U.S. sen. (R, MS) and majority leader.

Shannon Lucid, b 1/14/43 (Shanghai, China), NASA scientist, astronaut.

Rachel Maddow, b 4/1/73 (Castro Valley, CA), TV/radio host, political commentator.

Bernie Madoff, b 4/29/38 (Queens, NY), financier who swindled investors; sentenced to 150 years in prison.

Chelsea (fmr. Bradley) Manning, b 12/17/87 (Crescent, OK), Army pvt. convicted on espionage charges for providing classified information to WikiLeaks.

Susana Martinez, b 7/14/59 (El Paso, TX), NM governor (R).

Mary Matalin, b 8/19/53 (Chicago, IL), political commentator.

Chris Matthews, b 12/17/45 (Philadelphia, PA), TV journalist.

Marissa Mayer, b 5/30/75 (Wausau, WI), Yahoo! CEO.

John McCain, b 8/29/36 (Panama Canal Zone), U.S. sen. (R, AZ), 2008 Republican presidential candidate.

Kevin McCarthy, b 1/26/65 (Bakersfield, CA), U.S. rep. (R, CA), House majority leader.

Mitch McConnell, b 2/20/42 (Tuscumbia, AL), U.S. sen. (R, KY), minority leader.

David McCullough, b 7/7/33 (Pittsburgh, PA), historian, biographer.

Denis McDonough, b 12/2/69 (Stillwater, MN), White House chief of staff.

Dr. Phil McGraw, b 9/1/50 (Vinita, OK), talk-show host, motivational speaker, author.

John McLaughlin, b 3/29/27 (Providence, RI), TV journalist.

Kate Michelman, b 8/4/42 (NJ), abortion-rights activist.

Kate Millett, b 9/14/34 (St. Paul, MN), author, feminist.

George Mitchell, b 8/20/33, (Waterville, ME), former spec. envoy for Middle East peace, U.S. Sen. majority leader (D, ME), diplomat, Disney Co. chair.

Walter Mondale, b 1/5/28 (Ceylon, MN), former vice pres., U.S. sen. (D, MN), 1984 pres. nominee.

Ernest Moniz, b 12/22/44 (Fall River, MA), energy sec., nuclear physicist.

Michael Moore, b 4/23/54 (Davison, MI), activist, documentary filmmaker, author.

Bill Moyers, b 6/5/34 (Hugo, OK), TV journalist, author.

Robert S. Mueller III, b 8/7/44 (New York, NY), former FBI director.

David Muir, b 11/8/73 (Syracuse, NY), ABC World News anchor.

Michael Mullen, b 10/4/46 (Los Angeles, CA), former chairman of Joint Chiefs of Staff.

Rupert Murdoch, b 3/11/31 (Melbourne, Vic., Aust.), media exec.

Ralph Nader, b 2/27/34 (Winsted, CT), consumer advocate, independent pres. cand. in 1996, 2000, 2004, and 2008.

Janet Napolitano, b 11/29/57 (New York, NY), Univ. of Calif. pres.; former homeland security sec., AZ governor (D).

Craig Newmark, b 12/6/52 (Morristown, NJ), founder of Craigslist.com.

Peggy Noonan, b 9/7/50 (Brooklyn, NY), columnist, speechwriter.

Oliver North, b 10/7/43 (San Antonio, TX), talk-show host, former Natl. Sec. Council aide, figure in Iran-contra scandal.

Eleanor Holmes Norton, b 6/13/37 (Washington, DC), U.S. House delegate for Washington, DC (D).

Barack Obama, b 8/4/61 (Honolulu, HI), U.S. president, former U.S. sen. (D, IL).

Michelle Obama, b 1/17/64 (Chicago, IL), first lady, lawyer.

Soledad O'Brien, b 9/19/66 (Smithtown, NY), TV journalist.

Sandra Day O'Connor, b 3/26/30 (El Paso, TX), former Supreme Court justice.

Keith Olbermann, b 1/27/59 (New York, NY), political commentator, former ESPN/MSNBC host.

Todd Oldham, b 11/22/61 (Corpus Christi, TX), fashion designer.

Bill O'Reilly, b 9/10/49 (New York, NY), TV commentator, host.

Joel Osteen, b 3/5/63 (Houston, TX), televangelist, author.

Michael Ovitz, b 12/14/46 (Encino, CA), entertainment exec.

Clarence Page, b 6/2/47 (Dayton, OH), journalist, TV commentator.

Lawrence Page, b 3/26/73 (East Lansing, MI), cofounder of Google.

Camille Paglia, b 4/2/47 (Endicott, NY), scholar, author.

Sarah Palin, b 2/11/64 (Sandpoint, ID), former AK governor (R), 2008 vice-pres. nominee.

Leon E. Panetta, b 6/28/38 (Monterey, CA), former sec. of defense, CIA director, White House chief of staff, and U.S. rep. (D, CA).

Sean Parker, b 12/3/79 (Herndon, VA), cofounder of Napster, Facebook.

Richard Parsons, b 4/4/48 (Brooklyn, NY), former Citigroup chairman, Time Warner CEO.

David Paterson, b 5/20/54 (Brooklyn, NY), attorney, former NY governor (D).

Rand Paul, b 1/7/63 (Pittsburgh, PA), U.S. sen. (R, KY).

Ron Paul, b 8/20/35 (Pittsburgh, PA), physician, former U.S. rep. (R, TX), pres. contender (2008, 2012).

Jane Pauley, b 10/31/50 (Indianapolis, IN), TV journalist.

Henry Paulson, b 3/28/46 (Palm Beach, FL), former sec. of treasury, former CEO/chairman of Goldman Sachs.

Nancy Pelosi, b 3/26/40 (Baltimore, MD), U.S. rep. (D, CA), House minority leader, former House speaker.

Ross Perot, b 6/27/30 (Texarkana, TX), entrepreneur, former pres. nominee.

Rick Perry, b 3/4/50 (Paint Creek, TX), TX governor (R), 2012 pres. contender.

David Petraeus, b 11/7/52 (Cornwall-on-Hudson, NY), former CIA director, U.S. Forces Afghanistan cmdr., CENTCOM cmdr.

Colin Powell, b 4/5/37 (New York, NY), former sec. of state, natl. security adviser, Joint Chiefs of Staff chairman.

Samantha Power, b 9/21/70 (Dublin, Ire.), U.S. ambassador to UN.

Reince Priebus, b 3/18/72 (Kenosha, WI), Rep. Natl. Committee chair.

Dan Quayle, b 2/4/47 (Indianapolis, IN), former U.S. vice pres., U.S. sen. (R, IN).

Anna Quindlen, b 7/8/53 (Philadelphia, PA), author, columnist.

Martha Raddatz, b 1953 (Idaho Falls, ID), ABC news correspondent.

Dan Rather, b 10/31/31 (Wharton, TX), TV journalist, retired CBS anchor.

Nancy Reagan, b 7/6/21 (Flushing, Queens, NY), former first lady.

Sumner Redstone, b 5/27/23 (Boston, MA), Viacom/CBS chairman.

Ralph Reed Jr., b 6/24/61 (Portsmouth, VA), political adviser.

Robert B. Reich, b 6/24/46 (Scranton, PA), economist, author, former labor sec.

Harry Reid, b 12/2/39 (Searchlight, NV), U.S. Sen. majority leader (D, NV).

Janet Reno, b 7/21/38 (Miami, FL), former U.S. attorney gen.

Condoleezza Rice, b 11/14/54 (Birmingham, AL), former sec. of state, former natl. security adviser.

Susan Rice, b 11/17/64 (Washington, DC), national security adviser, former U.S. ambassador to UN.

Frank Rich, b 6/2/49 (Washington, DC), essayist, columnist.

Cecile Richards, b 1957 (Waco, TX), pres. of Planned Parenthood.

Bill Richardson, b 11/15/47 (Pasadena, CA), former energy sec., UN rep., U.S. rep. (D, NM), NM gov. (D); 2008 pres. contender.

Tom Ridge, b 8/26/45 (Munhall, PA), former homeland security sec., PA gov. (R).

Geraldo Rivera, b 7/4/43 (New York, NY), TV journalist.

Cokie Roberts, b 12/27/43 (New Orleans, LA), TV journalist.

John G. Roberts, b 1/27/55 (Buffalo, NY), Supreme Court chief justice.

Robin Roberts, b 11/23/60 (Tuskegee, AL), Good Morning America co-host.

Rev. Pat Robertson, b 3/22/30 (Lexington, VA), religious broadcasting exec., former pres. contender.

V. Gene Robinson, b 5/29/47 (Lexington, KY), first openly gay Episcopal bishop (retired).

David Rockefeller, b 6/12/15 (New York, NY), banker.

Buddy Roemer, b 10/4/43 (Shreveport, LA), former LA governor, U.S. rep. (D); 2012 pres. contender.

Al Roker, b 8/20/54 (Queens, NY), TV weather person.

Mitt Romney, b 3/12/47 (Detroit, MI), 2012 pres. nominee, former MA gov. (R).

Charlie Rose, b 1/5/42 (Henderson, NC), TV journalist.

Karl Rove, b 12/25/50 (Denver, CO), former adviser to Pres. G. W. Bush, political commentator.

Marco Rubio, b 5/28/71 (Miami, FL), U.S. sen. (R, FL).

Donald Rumsfeld, b 7/9/32 (Chicago, IL), former sec. of defense.

Edward Ruscha, b 12/16/37 (Omaha, NE), pop artist.

Paul Ryan, b 1/29/70 (Janesville, WI), 2012 vice-pres. nominee, U.S. rep. (R, WI).

Morley Safer, b 11/8/31 (Toronto, ON, Can.), TV journalist.

Rick Santorum, b 5/10/58 (Winchester, VA), former U.S. sen. (R, PA); 2012 pres. contender.

Diane Sawyer, b 12/22/45 (Glasgow, KY), TV journalist, former anchor of ABC World News.

Antonin Scalia, b 3/11/36 (Trenton, NJ), Supreme Court justice.

Stephen Scalise, b 10/6/65 (New Orleans, LA), U.S. rep. (R, LA), House majority whip.

Bob Schieffer, b 2/25/37 (Austin, TX), CBS TV news anchor.

Phyllis Schlafly, b 8/15/24 (St. Louis, MO), political activist.

Caroline Kennedy Schlossberg, b 11/27/57 (New York, NY), ambassador to Japan, author, daughter of Pres. Kennedy.

Eric Schmidt, b 4/27/55 (Washington, DC), former Google CEO.

Rev. Robert Schuller, b 9/16/26 (Alton, IA), TV evangelist.

Charles Schumer, b 11/23/50 (Brooklyn, NY), U.S. sen. (D, NY).

Arnold Schwarzenegger, b 7/30/47 (Thal, Styria, Austria), actor, former CA gov. (R).

Willard Scott, b 3/7/34 (Alexandria, VA), former TV weather person.

Kathleen Sebelius, b 5/15/58 (Cincinnati, OH), former health and human services sec., KS governor (D).

Richard Serra, b 11/2/39 (San Francisco, CA), sculptor.

Rev. Al Sharpton, b 10/3/54 (Brooklyn, NY), activist, civil rights leader, TV personality.

Eric Shinseki, b 11/28/42 (Lihue, HI), former veterans affairs sec., Army chief of staff.

Will Shortz, b 8/26/52 (Crawfordsville, IN), puzzle editor.

Maria Shriver, b 11/6/55 (Chicago, IL), TV journalist, former CA first lady.

George P. Shultz, b 12/13/20 (New York, NY), former sec. of state, other cabinet posts.

Michelangelo Signorile, b 12/19/60 (Brooklyn, NY), journalist, author.

Adam Silver, b 4/25/62 (Rye, NY), NBA commissioner.

Nate Silver, b 1/13/78 (E. Lansing, MI), statistician.

Russell Simmons, b 10/4/57 (Queens, NY), music producer.

Bob Simon, b 5/29/41 (Bronx, NY), TV journalist.

O. J. Simpson, b 7/9/47 (San Francisco, CA), former football star, murder defendant.

Harry Smith, b 8/21/51 (Lansing, IL), NBC TV journalist, former CBS morning anchor.

Liz Smith, b 2/2/23 (Ft. Worth, TX), gossip columnist.

Edward Snowden, b 6/21/83 (Elizabeth City, NC), computer specialist accused of leaking classified information about U.S. and UK govt. surveillance.

George Soros, b 8/12/30 (Budapest, Hung.), financier, philanthropist.

Sonia Sotomayor, b 6/25/54 (Bronx, NY), Supreme Court justice.

David H. Souter, b 9/17/39 (Melrose, MA), former Supreme Court justice.

Kate Spade, b 1962 (Kansas City, MO), fashion designer.

Steven Spielberg, b 12/18/46 (Cincinnati, OH), movie director, producer.

Eliot Spitzer, b 6/10/59 (Bronx, NY), former NY gov. (D); resigned after involvement with prostitutes exposed.

Lesley Stahl, b 12/16/41 (Swampscott, MA), TV journalist.

Michael Steele, b 10/19/58 (Prince George's Co., MD), former Rep. Natl. Committee chair, MD lt. gov.

Shelby Steele, b 1/1/46 (Chicago, IL), scholar, critic.

Ben Stein, b 11/25/44 (Washington, DC), attorney, columnist, former speechwriter, actor, TV personality.

Gloria Steinem, b 3/25/34 (Toledo, OH), author, feminist.

Frank Stella, b 5/12/36 (Malden, MA), painter.

George Stephanopoulos, b 2/10/61 (Fall River, MA), TV journalist, *Good Morning America* co-host; former pres. adviser.

Howard Stern, b 1/12/54 (Roosevelt, NY), radio talk-show host.

John Paul Stevens, b 4/20/20 (Chicago, IL), former Supreme Court justice.

Martha Stewart, b 8/3/41 (Nutley, NJ), homemaking adviser, entrepreneur, TV personality.

Biz Stone, b 3/10/74 (Boston, MA), cofounder of Twitter.

Chesley Sullenberger III, b 1/23/51 (Denison, TX), pilot who safely landed a passenger jet in the Hudson River.

Andrew Sullivan, b 8/10/63 (Eng., UK), political commentator and blogger.

Arthur Ochs Sulzberger Jr., b 9/22/51 (Mt. Kisco, NY), newspaper publisher.

Lawrence H. Summers, b 11/30/54 (New Haven, CT), economist; former Natl. Economic Council dir., Harvard Univ. pres., sec. of treasury.

George Tenet, b 1/5/53 (Flushing, Queens, NY), former CIA director.

Clarence Thomas, b 6/23/48 (Savannah, GA), Supreme Court justice.

Chuck Todd, b 4/8/72 (Miami, FL), TV journalist, *Meet the Press* moderator.

Richard Trumka, b 7/24/49 (Waynesburg, PA), pres. of AFL-CIO.

Donald Trump, b 6/14/46 (Jamaica, Queens, NY), real estate exec., TV personality.

Ted Turner, b 11/19/38 (Cincinnati, OH), TV exec., philanthropist.

Neil deGrasse Tyson, b 10/5/58 (New York, NY), astrophysicist, director of NYC's Hayden Planetarium, author, TV host.

Urvashi Vaid, b 10/8/58 (New Delhi, India), LGBT rights activist.

Gloria Vanderbilt, b 2/20/24 (New York, NY), fashion designer, heiress.

Greta Van Susteren, b 6/11/54 (Appleton, WI), attorney, TV journalist.

Jesse Ventura, b 7/15/51 (Minneapolis, MN), former wrestler, MN governor (I).

Meredith Vieira, b 12/30/53 (Providence, RI), former *Today* show co-host.

Paul Volcker, b 9/5/27 (Cape May, NJ), economist, former Federal Reserve chairman.

Jimmy Wales, b 8/8/66 (Huntsville, AL), cofounder of Wikipedia.

Barbara Walters, b 9/25/29 (Boston, MA), TV journalist.

Vera Wang, b 6/27/49 (New York, NY), fashion designer.

Rick Warren, b 1/28/54 (San Jose, CA), evangelical Christian pastor, founder of Saddleback Church, author.

Debbie Wasserman Schultz, b 9/27/66 (Forest Hills, NY), U.S. rep. (D, FL), Dem. Natl. Committee chair.

James Watson, b 4/6/28 (Chicago, IL), biochemist, DNA pioneer, co-winner of the 1962 Nobel Prize.

Dr. Andrew Weil, b 6/8/42 (Philadelphia, PA), health adviser.

Anthony Weiner, b 9/4/64 (Brooklyn, NY), former U.S. rep. (D, NY); resigned after 2011 scandal.

Harvey Weinstein, b 3/19/52 (Flushing, Queens, NY), movie exec.

Jack Welch, b 11/19/35 (Peabody, MA), former General Electric CEO.

Jann Wenner, b 1/7/46 (New York, NY), publisher, founder of *Rolling Stone*.

Cornel West, b 6/23/53 (Tulsa, OK), African American scholar, critic.

Ruth Westheimer, b 6/4/28 (Frankfurt am Main, Germany), human sexuality expert.

Mary Jo White, b 12/27/47 (Kansas City, MO), Securities and Exchange Commission chair.

Meg Whitman, b 8/4/56 (Cold Spring Harbor, NY), 2010 CA gubernatorial candidate (R), former eBay CEO; HP CEO.

Elie Wiesel, b 9/30/28 (Sighet, Romania), scholar, author, 1986 Nobel Peace Prize winner.

George Will, b 5/4/41 (Champaign, IL), journalist, author.

Brian Williams, b 5/5/59 (Ridgewood, NJ), NBC TV news anchor.

Evan Williams, b 3/31/72 (Clarks, NE), cofounder and CEO of Twitter.

Jody Williams, b 10/9/50 (Brattleboro, VT), peace activist, 1997 Nobel Peace Prize winner.

Edie (Edith) Windsor, b 6/20/29 (Philadelphia, PA), LGBT activist.

Oprah Winfrey, b 1/29/54 (Kosciusko, MS), TV and media personality, businesswoman, actress.

Bob Woodward, b 3/26/43 (Geneva, IL), journalist; with Carl Bernstein cracked Watergate scandal.

Steve Wozniak, b 8/11/50 (Sunnyvale, CA), inventor, cofounder of Apple.

Steve Wynn, b 1/27/42 (New Haven, CT), casino developer.

Chuck Yeager, b 2/13/23 (Myra, WV), test pilot, first man to break sound barrier.

Janet Yellen, b 8/13/46 (New York, NY), Federal Reserve chair.

Paula Zahn, b 2/24/56 (Omaha, NE), TV journalist.

Mark Zuckerberg, b 5/14/84 (Dobbs Ferry, NY), founder of Facebook.

Mortimer Zuckerman, b 6/4/37 (Montréal, QC, Can.), publisher, columnist.

Widely Known World Personalities of the Present

Living non-Americans only. Generally excludes current heads of state or government (see Nations chapter) and excludes most others covered elsewhere, such as in Widely Known Americans, Writers, and Entertainment or Sports Personalities.

Mahmoud Abbas (Abu Mazen), b 3/26/35 (Safed, Palestine [now Israel]), president of the Palestinian National Authority.

Gerry Adams, b 10/6/48 (Belfast, N. Ireland, UK), Sinn Fein leader.

Mahmoud Ahmadinejad, b 10/28/56 (Garmsar, Iran), former Iranian pres.

Albert II, b 6/6/34 (Brussels, Belgium), former king (1993-2013).

Viswanathan Anand, b 12/11/69 (Chennai, Madras, India), former world chess champion.

Prince Andrew (Duke of York), b 2/19/60 (London, Eng., UK), second son of Queen Elizabeth II.

Kofi Annan, b 4/8/38 (Kumasi, Ghana), former UN sec.-gen.; 2001 Nobel laureate.

Princess Anne (Princess Royal), b 8/15/50 (London, Eng., UK), daughter of Queen Elizabeth II.

Michael Arad, b 1969 (London, Eng., UK), designer of the Natl. 9/11 Memorial in NYC.

Oscar Arias Sánchez, b 9/13/41 (Heredia, Costa Rica), former Costa Rican pres., peace negotiator, 1987 Nobel laureate.

Giorgio Armani, b 7/30/34 (Piacenza, Italy), fashion designer.

Hanan Ashrawi, b 10/8/46 (Nablus, Israel), Palestinian activist.

Julian Assange, b 7/3/71 (Townsville, Qld., Australia), founder of WikiLeaks media org.

Ban Ki-moon, b 6/13/44 (Umsong, [now] South Korea), UN sec.-gen.

Ehud Barak, b 2/12/42 (Mishmar Ha-Sharon Kibbutz, Israel), former Israeli minister of defense, former Israeli prime min.

Beatrix, b 1/31/38 (Netherlands), former queen (1980-2013).

Benedict XVI (Joseph Ratzinger), b 4/16/27 (Marktl am Inn, Germany), pope emeritus of Rom. Cath. Church, elected 2005.

Boris Berezovsky, b 1/23/46 (Moscow, USSR), businessman, politician.

Tim Berners-Lee, b 6/8/55 (London, Eng., UK), World Wide Web inventor.

Tony Blair, b 5/6/53 (Edinburgh, Scot., UK), former British prime min.

Hans Blix, b 6/28/28 (Uppsala, Swed.), former UN weapons inspector.

Bono (Paul David Hewson), b 5/20/60 (Glasnevin, Dublin, Ire.), musician, social activist, philanthropist.

Fernando Botero, b 4/19/32 (Medellín, Colombia), artist.

Boutros Boutros-Ghali, b 11/14/22 (Cairo, Egypt), former UN sec.-gen.

Richard Branson, b 7/18/50 (S. London, Eng., UK), British Virgin Records and Airways founder.

Gordon Brown, b 2/20/51 (Glasgow, Scot., UK), former British prime min.

Tina Brown, b 11/21/53 (Maidenhead, Eng., UK), journalist, author.

Carla Bruni, b 12/23/67 (Turin, Italy), former first lady of France, musician, actress, model.

Mark Burnett, b 7/17/60 (Myland, Eng., UK), reality TV producer.

Rhonda Byrne, b 3/12/51 (Australia), author, TV writer and producer.

Kim Campbell, b 3/10/47 (Port Alberni, BC, Can.), former Canadian prime min.

Pierre Cardin, b 7/7/22 (San Biaggio di Callalta, Italy), fashion designer.

Magnus Carlsen, b 11/30/90 (Tonsberg, Norway), world chess champion.

Princess Caroline, b 1/23/57 (Monte Carlo, Monaco), Monaco royal (eldest daughter of Prince Rainier and Princess Grace).

Fidel Castro, b 8/13/26 (Birán, Cuba), former prime min., pres. of Cuba.

Prince Charles (of Wales), b 11/14/48 (London, Eng., UK), eldest son of Queen Elizabeth II; heir to British throne.

Chen Guangcheng, b 11/12/71 (Dongshigu, China), civil rights activist.

Yao Chen, b 10/5/79 (Nanping, Fujian, China), actress, microblogger.

Jacques Chirac, b 11/29/32 (Paris, France), former French pres.

Deepak Chopra, b 1946 (New Delhi, India), New Age writer.

Jean Chrétien, b 1/11/34 (Shawinigan, QC, Can.), former Canadian prime min.

Christo (Javacheff), b 6/13/35 (Gabrovo, Bulg.), artist.

Joe (Charles Joseph) Clark, b 6/5/39 (High River, AB, Can.), former Canadian prime min.

King Constantine II, b 6/2/40 (Psychiko, Greece), former king of Greece.

Simon Cowell, b 10/7/59 (Brighton, East Sussex, Eng., UK), music exec., TV producer, former *American Idol* host.

Dalai Lama, 14th (Tenzin Gyatso), b 7/6/35 (Taktser, Amdo, Tibet), Buddhist leader; 1989 Nobel Peace Prize laureate.

Richard Dawkins, b 3/26/41 (Nairobi, Kenya), ethologist, evolutionary biologist, author.

F. W. (Frederik Willem) de Klerk, b 3/18/36 (Johannesburg, S. Afr.), former S. African pres.; 1993 Nobel Peace Prize winner.

Mario Draghi, b 9/3/47 (Rome, Italy), European Central Bank pres.

Shirin Ebadi, b 6/21/47 (Hamadan, Iran), human rights activist, 2003 Nobel Peace Prize winner.

Prince Edward (Earl of Essex), b 3/10/64 (London, Eng., UK), third son of Queen Elizabeth II.

Mohamed ElBaradei, b 6/17/42 (Cairo, Egypt), former director general of the International Atomic Energy Agency (IAEA); 2005 Nobel Peace Prize winner.

Sarah Ferguson, b 10/15/58 (London, Eng., UK), Duchess of York, ex-wife of Prince Andrew.

Francis (Jorge Mario Bergoglio), b 12/17/36 (Buenos Aires, Argentina), pope of Rom. Cath. Church.

John Galliano, b 11/28/60 (Gibraltar, UK), fashion designer.

Prince George Alexander Louis (of Cambridge), b 7/22/13 (London, Eng., UK), third in line to British throne.

Wael Ghonim, b 12/23/80 (Cairo, Egypt), computer engineer and Internet activist.

Valery Giscard d'Estaing, b 2/2/26 (Koblenz, Ger.), former French pres.

Jane Goodall, b 4/3/34 (London, Eng., UK), anthropologist, primatologist.

Mikhail Gorbachev, b 3/2/31 (Privolnoye, USSR), former Soviet pres.; 1990 Nobel Peace Prize winner.

Jürgen Habermas, b 6/18/29 (Dusseldorf, Ger.), philosopher.

Stephen Hawking, b 1/8/42 (Oxford, Eng., UK), physicist, author.

Prince Henry (Harry) (of Wales), b 9/15/84 (London, Eng., UK), son of Prince Charles.

Damien Hirst, b 6/7/65 (Bristol, Eng., UK), artist.

David Hockney, b 7/9/37 (Bradford, Eng., UK), artist.

Hu Jintao, b 12/21/42 (Shanghai, China), former pres. of China.

Jiang Zemin, b 8/17/26 (Yangzhou, Jiangsu Prov., China), former pres. of China.

Juan Carlos I, b 1/5/38 (Rome, Italy), former king of Spain (1975-2014).

Garry Kasparov, b 4/13/63 (Baku, Azerbaijan, USSR), former world chess champion; Russian pro-democracy leader.

Ayatollah Ali Khamenei, b 7/17/39 (Mashhad, Iran), Supreme Leader and former president of Iran, cleric, author.

Helmut Kohl, b 4/3/30 (Ludwigshafen, Ger.), former German chancellor.

Hans Kung, b 3/19/28 (Sursee, Switz.), Rom. Cath. theologian.

Christine Lagarde, b 1/1/56 (Paris, France), Intl. Monetary Fund managing dir.

Karl Lagerfeld, b 9/10/38 (Hamburg, Germany), fashion designer.

Richard Leakey, b 12/19/44 (Nairobi, Kenya), anthropologist, paleontologist, conservationist.

Jean-Marie Le Pen, b 6/20/28 (LaTrinité-sur-Mer, Fr.), French right-wing politician.

Marine Le Pen, b 8/5/68 (Neuilly-sur-Seine, Fr.), head of France's National Front.

Tzipi Livni, b 7/5/58 (Tel Aviv, Isr.), attorney, Israeli justice minister.

John Major, b 3/29/43 (Wimbledon, Eng., UK), former British prime min.

Nouri al-Malaki, b 7/1/50 (Iraq), former prime min. of Iraq.

Imelda Marcos, b 7/2/29 (Manila, Philip.), former first lady of the Philippines.

Paul Martin, b 8/28/38 (Windsor, ON, Can.), former prime min. of Canada.

Peter Max, b 10/19/37 (Berlin, Ger.), artist, designer.

Stella McCartney, b 9/13/71 (London, Eng., UK), fashion designer.

Angela Merkel, b 7/17/54 (Hamburg, Ger.), first woman chancellor of Germany.

Jean-Marie Messier, b 12/13/56 (Grenoble, Fr.), former CEO of Vivendi Universal.

Empress Michiko, b 10/20/34 (Tokyo, Japan), empress of Japan.

Catherine (Kate) Middleton (Duchess of Cambridge), b 1/9/82 (Reading, Eng., UK), wife of Prince William.

Maryam Mirzakhani, b 5/1977 (Tehran, Iran), mathematician.

Mohammed Morsi, b 8/8/51 (Edwa, Egypt), first democratically elected pres. of Egypt; deposed July 2013.

Kate Moss, b 1/16/74 (Addiscombe, Surrey, Eng., UK), model.

Hosni Mubarak, b 5/4/28 (Kafre al-Musailha, Egypt), deposed Egyptian president.

Brian Mulroney, b 3/20/39 (Baie-Corneau, QC, Can.), former Canadian prime min.

Prince Naruhito, b 2/23/60 (Tokyo, Japan), crown prince of Japan.

Hassan Nasrallah, b 8/31/60 (Qarantina, Lebanon), sec.-gen. of Hezbollah.

Queen Noor (Lisa Halaby), b 8/23/51 (Washington, DC), American-born widow of Jordan's King Hussein.

Ehud Olmert, b 9/30/45 (Binyamina, Palestine), former prime min. of Israel.

Daniel Ortega Saavedra, b 11/11/45 (La Libertad, Nicar.), Nicaraguan pres., Sandinista leader.

Camilla Parker-Bowles (Duchess of Cornwall), b 7/17/47 (London, Eng., UK), wife of Prince Charles.

Javier Perez de Cuellar, b 1/19/20 (Lima, Peru), former UN sec.-gen.

Prince Philip (Duke of Edinburgh), b 6/10/21 (Corfu, Greece), husband of Queen Elizabeth II.

Gerhard Richter, b 2/9/32 (Dresden, Ger.), artist.

Mary Robinson, b 5/21/44 (Ballina, Co. Mayo, Ireland), former Irish pres., former UN High Commissioner for Human Rights.

Arundhati Roy, b 11/24/61 (Shillong, Meghalaya, India), author, political activist.

Ségolène Royal, b 9/22/53 (Dakar, Senegal), French socialist politician.

Muqtada al-Sadr, b 8/12/73? (Najaf, Iraq), extremist Shiite cleric.

Nicolas Sarkozy, b 1/28/55 (Paris, France), former French pres.

Helmut Schmidt, b 12/23/18 (Hamburg, Germany), former German chancellor.

Gerhard Schröder, b 4/7/44 (Mossenburg, Germany), former German chancellor.

Ayatollah Ali al-Sistani, b 8/4/30 (Mashhad, Iran), major Iraqi Shiite religious leader.

Carlos Slim Helú, b 1/28/40 (Mexico City, Mexico), chairman and CEO of Telmex, Telcel and América Móvil.

Princess Stephanie, b 2/1/65 (Monte Carlo, Monaco), youngest child of Prince Rainier and Princess Grace.

Dominique Strauss-Kahn, b 4/25/49 (Neuilly-sur-Seine, France), former Intl. Monetary Fund managing dir.

Aung San Suu Kyi, b 6/19/45 (Rangoon, Myanmar), member of parliament, pro-democracy political activist, 1991 Nobel Peace Prize winner.

Valentina Tereshkova, b 3/6/37 (Maslennikovo, Russia, USSR), first woman in space.

John Napier Turner, b 6/7/29 (Richmond, Surrey, Eng., UK), former Canadian prime min.

Desmond Tutu, b 10/7/31 (Klerksdorp, Transvaal, S. Afr.), former S. African archbishop; 1984 Nobel Peace Prize winner.

Lech Walesa, b 9/29/43 (Popowo, Pol.), Solidarity leader, former pres. of Poland; 1983 Nobel Peace Prize winner.

Justin Welby, b 1/6/56 (London, Eng., UK), archbishop of Canterbury.

Prince William (Duke of Cambridge), b 6/21/82 (London, Eng., UK), son of Prince Charles; 2nd in line to British throne.

Rowan Williams, b 6/14/50 (Ystradgynlais, Wales, UK), former archbishop of Canterbury.

Malala Yousafzai, b 7/12/97 (Mingora, Pakistan), education activist.

Muhammad Yunus, b 6/28/40 (Chittagong, India), economist, 2006 Nobel Peace Prize winner.

Mohammad Javad Zarif, b 1/8/60 (Tehran, Iran), Irani minister of foreign affairs.

Ayman al-Zawahiri, b 6/19/51 (Cairo, Egypt), reputed high-ranking al-Qaeda leader.

Architects

Alvar Aalto, 1898-1976, Säynätsalo, Jyväskylä, Finland; Vuoksenniska Church, Vuoksenniska, Finland.

Max Abramovitz, 1908-2004, Avery Fisher Hall, New York, NY; U.S. Steel Bldg. (now USX Towers), Pittsburgh, PA.

Tadao Ando, b 1941, Modern Art Museum, Ft. Worth, TX; Stone Hill Center, MA.

Michael Arad, b 1969, World Trade Center Memorial, New York, NY.

Henry Bacon, 1866-1924, Lincoln Memorial, Washington, DC.

Benjamin Banneker, 1731-1806, African American inventor, astronomer, mathematician; helped design and lay out Washington, DC.

Pietro Belluschi, 1899-1994, Juilliard School, Lincoln Center, Pan Am Bldg. (now MetLife Bldg.) with Walter Gropius, New York, NY.

Marcel Breuer, 1902-81, Whitney Museum of American Art (with Hamilton Smith), New York, NY.

Charles Bulfinch, 1763-1844, State House, Boston, MA; Capitol (part), Wash., DC.

Gordon Bunshaft, 1909-90, Lever House, New York, NY; Hirshhorn Museum, Washington, DC.

Daniel H. Burnham, 1846-1912, Union Station, Washington, DC; Flatiron Bldg., New York, NY.

Irwin Chanin, 1892-1988, theaters, skyscrapers, New York, NY.

David Childs, b 1941, Washington Mall Master Plan/Constitution Gardens, Washington, DC; One World Trade Center, New York, NY.

Lucio Costa, 1902-98, master plan for city of Brasilia, Brazil (with Oscar Niemeyer).

Ralph Adams Cram, 1863-1942, Cath. of St. John the Divine, New York, NY; U.S. Military Acad. (part), West Point, NY.

Norman Foster, b 1935, Commerzbank Headquarters, Frankfurt-am-Main, Ger.; London Millennium Bridge, 30 St. Mary Axe, London, UK.

James Ingo Freed, 1930-2005, Holocaust Memorial, Washington, DC; Jacob K. Javits Center, New York, NY.

R. Buckminster Fuller, 1895-1983, U.S. Pavilion (geodesic domes), Expo 67, Montreal, QC, Can.

Frank O. Gehry, b 1929, Guggenheim Museum, Bilbao, Spain; Experience Music Project, Seattle, WA; Walt Disney Concert Hall, Los Angeles, CA.

Cass Gilbert, 1859-1934, Custom House, Woolworth Bldg., New York, NY; Supreme Court Bldg., Washington, DC.

Bertram G. Goodhue, 1869-1924, Capitol, Lincoln, NE; St. Thomas's Church, St. Bartholomew's Church, New York, NY.

Michael Graves, b 1934, Portland Bldg., Portland, OR; Humana Bldg., Louisville, KY.

Walter Gropius, 1883-1969, Pan Am Bldg. (now MetLife Bldg.) (with Pietro Belluschi), New York, NY.

Zaha Hadid, b 1950, Rosenthal Center for Contemporary Art, Cincinnati, OH; London Aquatics Centre, Eng., UK.

Lawrence Halprin, 1916-2009, Ghirardelli Sq., San Francisco, CA; Nicollet Mall, Minneapolis, MN; FDR Memorial, Wash., DC.

Peter Harrison, 1716-75, Touro Synagogue, Redwood Library, Newport, RI.

Wallace K. Harrison, 1895-1981, Metropolitan Opera House, Lincoln Center, New York, NY.

Thomas Hastings, 1860-1929, NY Public Library (with John Carrère), Frick Mansion, New York, NY.

James Hoban, 1762-1831, White House, Washington, DC.

Raymond Hood, 1881-1934, Rockefeller Center (part), Daily News Bldg., New York, NY; Tribune Tower, Chicago, IL.

Richard M. Hunt, 1827-95, Metropolitan Museum (part), New York, NY; Biltmore Estate, Asheville, NC.

Helmut Jahn, b 1940, United Airlines Terminal, O'Hare Airport, Chicago, IL.

William Le Baron Jenney, 1832-1907, Home Insurance Bldg. (demolished 1931), Chicago, IL.

Philip C. Johnson, 1906-2005, AT&T headquarters (now 550 Madison Ave.), New York, NY; Transco (now Williams) Tower, Houston, TX.

Albert Kahn, 1869-1942, General Motors Bldg., Detroit, MI.

Louis Kahn, 1901-74, Salk Laboratory, La Jolla, CA; Yale Art Gallery, New Haven, CT.

Rem Koolhaas, b 1944, Seattle Central Library, Seattle, WA.

Christopher Grant LaFarge, 1862-1938, Roman Catholic Chapel, West Point, NY.

Benjamin H. Latrobe, 1764-1820, Capitol (part), Washington, DC; State Capitol Bldg., Richmond, VA.

Le Corbusier (Charles-Edouard Jeanneret), 1887-1965, Salvation Army Hostel, Swiss Dormitory, Paris, France; master plan for cities of Algiers and Buenos Aires.

William Lescaze, 1896-1969, Philadelphia Savings Fund Society, PA; Borg-Warner Bldg., Chicago, IL.

Daniel Libeskind, b 1946, primary architect for the rebuilding of World Trade Center site, New York, NY.

Maya Lin, b 1959, Vietnam Veterans Mem., Washington, DC.

Charles Rennie Mackintosh, 1868-1928, Glasgow School of Art; Hill House, Helensburgh, Scot., UK.

Bernard R. Maybeck, 1862-1957, Hearst Hall, Univ. of CA, Berkeley; First Church of Christ Scientist, Berkeley, CA.

Charles F. McKim, 1847-1909, Boston Public Library; Columbia Univ. (part), New York, NY.

Charles M. McKim, b 1920, KUHT-TV Transmitter Bldg., Lutheran Church of the Redeemer, Houston, TX.

Richard Meier, b 1934, Getty Center Museum, Los Angeles, CA; High Museum of Art, Atlanta, GA.

Ludwig Mies van der Rohe, 1886-1969, Seagram Bldg. (with Philip C. Johnson), New York, NY; National Gallery, Berlin, Ger.

Robert Mills, 1781-1855, Washington Monument, Washington, DC.

Charles Moore, 1925-93, Sea Ranch, nr. San Francisco, CA; Piazza d'Italia, New Orleans, LA.

Julia Morgan, 1872-1957, San Simeon, CA.

John Nash, 1752-1835, Buckingham Palace, London, Eng., UK.

Richard J. Neutra, 1892-1970, Mathematics Park, Princeton, NJ; Orange Co. Courthouse, Santa Ana, CA.

Oscar Niemeyer, 1907-2012, government buildings, Brasilia Palace Hotel, Brasilia, Braz.

Gyo Obata, b 1923, Natl. Air and Space Museum, Smithsonian Inst., Washington, DC; Dallas-Ft. Worth Airport, TX.

Frederick L. Olmsted, 1822-1903, Central Park, New York, NY; Fairmount Park, Philadelphia, PA.

I(eoh) M(ing) Pei, b 1917, East Wing, Natl. Gallery of Art, Washington, DC; Pyramid, The Louvre, Paris, Fr.; Rock & Roll Hall of Fame and Museum, Cleveland, OH.

Cesar Pelli, b 1926, World Financial Center, Carnegie Hall Tower, New York, NY; Petronas Twin Towers, Malaysia.

William Pereira, 1909-85, Cape Canaveral, FL; Transamerica Pyramid, San Francisco, CA.

Renzo Piano, b 1937, Pompidou Centre, Paris, Fr.; New York Times Bldg., New York, NY; The Shard, London.

John Russell Pope, 1874-1937, National Gallery, Jefferson Memorial, Wash., DC.

John Portman, b 1924, Peachtree Center, Atlanta, GA.

George Browne Post, 1837-1913, NY Stock Exchange, New York, NY; Capitol, Madison, WI.

James Renwick Jr., 1818-95, Grace Church, St. Patrick's Cathedral, New York, NY; Smithsonian Institution (Castle), Washington, DC.

Henry H. Richardson, 1838-86, Trinity Church, Boston, MA.

Kevin Roche, b 1922, Oakland Museum, Oakland, CA; Fine Arts Center, Univ. of Massachusetts, Amherst, MA.

James Gamble Rogers, 1867-1947, Columbia-Presbyterian Medical Ctr.,

New York, NY; Northwestern Univ., Evanston, IL.

John Wellborn Root, 1887-1963, Palmolive Bldg., Chicago, IL; Hotel Statler, Wash., DC.

Paul Rudolph, 1918-97, Jewitt Art Center, Wellesley College, MA; Art & Architecture Bldg., Yale Univ., New Haven, CT.

Eero Saarinen, 1910-61, Gateway to the West Arch, St. Louis, MO; TWA Flight Center, JFK Airport, New York, NY.

Kazuyo Sejima, b 1956, 21st Century Museum of Contemporary Art (with Ryue Nishizawa), Kanazawa, Japan.

Louis Skidmore, 1897-1962, Atomic Energy Commission town site, Oak Ridge, TN; Terrace Plaza Hotel, Cincinnati, OH.

Norma Merrick Sklarek, 1928-2012, Terminal One, Los Angeles International Airport, CA.

Clarence S. Stein, 1882-1975, Temple Emanu-El, New York, NY.

Edward Durell Stone, 1902-78, interior of Radio City Music Hall, Museum of Modern Art, New York, NY.

Louis H. Sullivan, 1856-1924, Auditorium Bldg., Chicago, IL.

Kenzo Tange, 1913-2005, Hiroshima Peace Park, 1964 Tokyo Olympic stadiums, Japan.

Richard Upjohn, 1802-78, Trinity Church, New York, NY.

Max O. Urbahn, 1912-95, Vehicle Assembly Bldg., Cape Canaveral, FL.

Joern Utzon, 1918-2008, Sydney Opera House, NSW, Australia.

William Van Alen, 1883-1954, Chrysler Building, New York, NY.

Robert Venturi, b 1925, Gordon Wu Hall, Princeton, NJ; Mielparque Nikko Kirifuri Resort, Japan.

Ralph T. Walker, 1889-1973, NY Telephone Bldg., New York, NY; IBM Research Lab, Poughkeepsie, NY.

Wang Shu, 1963, Ningbo Museum, China.

Roland A. Wank, 1898-1970, Cincinnati Union Terminal, OH; head architect, 1933-44, Tennessee Valley Authority.

Stanford White, 1853-1906, Washington Arch in Washington Square Park, first Madison Square Garden, New York, NY.

Christopher Wren, 1632-1723, St. Paul's Cathedral, London, Eng., UK.

Frank Lloyd Wright, 1867-1959, Imperial Hotel, Tokyo, Jpn.; Guggenheim Museum, New York, NY; Kaufmann "Fallingwater" house, Mill Run, PA; Taliesin West, Scottsdale, AZ.

Thomas Wright, b 1957, Burj Al Arab hotel, Dubai, UAE.

William Wurster, 1895-1973, Ghirardelli Sq., San Francisco, CA.

Minoru Yamasaki, 1912-86, World Trade Center (destroyed 2001), New York, NY.

Artists, Photographers, and Sculptors of the Past

Artists are painters unless otherwise indicated.

Berenice Abbott, 1898-1991, (U.S.) photographer. Documentary of New York City, *Changing New York* (1939).

Ansel Easton Adams, 1902-84, (U.S.) photographer. Landscapes of the American Southwest.

Washington Allston, 1779-1843, (U.S.) landscapist. *Belshazzar's Feast.*

Albrecht Altdorfer, 1480-1538, (Ger.) landscapist.

Fra Angelico, c. 1400-55, (It.) Renaissance muralist. *Madonna of the Linen Drapers' Guild.*

Diane Arbus, 1923-71, (U.S.) photographer. Disturbing images.

Alexsandr Archipenko, 1887-1964, (U.S.) sculptor. *Boxing Match, Medranos.*

Jean Arp, 1887-1966, (Fr.) sculptor and painter. Founder of Dada movement.

Richard Artschwager, 1923-2013, (U.S.) painter and sculptor. *Table With Pink Tablecloth.*

Eugène Atget, 1856-1927, (Fr.) photographer. Paris life.

John James Audubon, 1785-1851, (U.S.) *Birds of America.*

Richard Avedon, 1923-2004, (U.S.) fashion and celebrity photographer.

Hans Baldung-Grien, 1484-1545, (Ger.) *Todentanz.*

Ernst Barlach, 1870-1938, (Ger.) Expressionist sculptor. *Man Drawing a Sword.*

Frédéric-Auguste Bartholdi, 1834-1904, (Fr.) sculptor. *Liberty Enlightening the World* (Statue of Liberty).

Fra Bartolommeo, 1472-1517, (It.) *Vision of St. Bernard.*

Romare Bearden, 1911-88, (U.S.) collage and other media. *The Visitation.*

Aubrey Beardsley, 1872-98, (Br.) illustrator. *Salome, Lysistrata, Morte d'Arthur, Volpone.*

Cecil Beaton, 1904-80, (Br.) fashion and celebrity photographer.

Max Beckmann, 1884-1950, (Ger.) Expressionist. *The Descent From the Cross.*

Gentile Bellini, 1426-1507, (It.) Renaissance. *Procession in St. Mark's Square.*

Giovanni Bellini, 1428-1516, (It.) Renaissance. *St. Francis in Ecstasy.*

Jacopo Bellini, 1400-70, (It.) Renaissance. *Crucifixion.*

George Wesley Bellows, 1882-1925, (U.S.) sports artist, portraitist, landscapist. *Stag at Sharkey's, Edith Clavell.*

Thomas Hart Benton, 1889-1975, (U.S.) American regionalist. *Threshing Wheat, Arts of the West.*

Ruth Bernhard, 1905-2006, (Ger.-U.S.) photographer. Black-and-white studies of female nudes.

Gianlorenzo Bernini, 1598-1680, (It.) Baroque sculptor. *The Assumption.*

Albert Bierstadt, 1830-1902, (U.S.) landscapist. *The Rocky Mountains, Mount Corcoran.*

George Caleb Bingham, 1811-79, (U.S.) American frontier. *Fur Traders Descending the Missouri.*

William Blake, 1757-1827, (Br.) engraver. *Book of Job, Songs of Innocence, Songs of Experience.*

Rosa Bonheur, 1822-99, (Fr.) Realist. *The Horse Fair.*

Pierre Bonnard, 1867-1947, (Fr.) Intimist. *The Breakfast Room, Girl in a Straw Hat.*

Gutzon Borglum, 1867-1941, (U.S.) sculptor. Mt. Rushmore Memorial.

Hieronymus Bosch, 1450-1516, (Flem.) religious allegories. *The Crowning With Thorns.*

Sandro Botticelli, 1444-1510, (It.) Renaissance. *Birth of Venus, Adoration of the Magi, Guiliano de'Medici.*

Louise Bourgeois, 1911-2010, (Fr.) sculptor. *Maman.*

Margaret Bourke-White, 1904-71, (U.S.) photographer, photojournalist. WWII, USSR, rural South during the Depression.

Mathew Brady, c. 1823-96, (U.S.) official photographer of the Civil War.

Constantin Brancusi, 1876-1957, (Romania-Fr.) Nonobjective sculptor. *Flying Turtle, The Kiss.*

Georges Braque, 1882-1963, (Fr.) Cubist. *Violin and Palette.*

Pieter Bruegel the Elder, c. 1525-69, (Flem.) Renaissance. *The Peasant Dance, Hunters in the Snow, Magpie on the Gallows.*

Pieter Bruegel the Younger, 1564-1638, (Flem.) Baroque. *Village Fair, The Crucifixion.*

Edward Burne-Jones, 1833-98, (Br.) Pre-Raphaelite artist-craftsman. *The Mirror of Venus.*

Alexander Calder, 1898-1976, (U.S.) sculptor. *Lobster Trap and Fish Tail.*

Julia Margaret Cameron, 1815-79, (Br.) photographer, prominent portraitist.

Robert Capa (Endre Friedmann), 1913-54, (Hung.-U.S.) photographer, war photojournalist. Invasion of Normandy.

Michelangelo Merisi da Caravaggio, 1573-1610, (It.) Baroque. *The Supper at Emmaus.*

Emily Carr, 1871-1945, (Can.) landscapist. *Blunden Harbour, Big Raven, Rushing Sea of Undergrowth.*

Carlo Carrà, 1881-1966, (It.) Metaphysical school. *Lot's Daughters, The Enchanted Room.*

Leonora Carrington, 1917-2011, (Br.) Surrealist. *The Inn of the Dawn Horse (Self-Portrait).*

Henri Cartier-Bresson, 1908-2004, (Fr.) photographer. *Imagenes à la sauvette.*

Mary Cassatt, 1844-1926, (U.S.) Impressionist. *The Cup of Tea, Woman Bathing, The Boating Party.*

George Catlin, 1796-1872, (U.S.) American Indian life. *Gallery of Indians, Buffalo Dance.*

Benvenuto Cellini, 1500-71, (It.) Mannerist sculptor, goldsmith. *Perseus and Medusa.*

Paul Cézanne, 1839-1906, (Fr.) Post-Impressionist. *Card Players, Mont-Sainte-Victoire With Large Pine Trees.*

Marc Chagall, 1887-1985, (Russ.) Jewish life and folklore. *I and the Village, The Praying Jew.*

John Chamberlain, 1927-2011, (U.S.) sculptor of automobile metal.

Jean Simeon Chardin, 1699-1779, (Fr.) still lifes. *The Kiss, The Grace.*

Giorgio de Chirico, 1888-1978, (It.) founded the Metaphysical school. *Enigma of an Autumn Night.*

Frederick Church, 1826-1900, (U.S.) Hudson River school. *Niagara, Andes of Ecuador.*

Giovanni Cimabue, 1240-1302, (It.) Byzantine mosaicist. *Madonna Enthroned With St. Francis.*

Claude (Lorrain) (Claude Gellée), 1600-82, (Fr.) Ideal-landscapist. *The Enchanted Castle.*

Thomas Cole, 1801-48, (U.S.) Hudson River school. *The Ox-Bow, In the Catskills.*

John Constable, 1776-1837, (Br.) landscapist. *Salisbury Cathedral From the Bishop's Grounds.*

John Singleton Copley, 1738-1815, (U.S.) portraitist. *Samuel Adams, Watson and the Shark.*

Lovis Corinth, 1858-1925, (Ger.) Expressionist. *Apocalypse.*

Jean-Baptiste-Camille Corot, 1796-1875, (Fr.) landscapist. *Souvenir de Mortefontaine, Pastorale.*

Correggio, 1494-1534, (It.) Renaissance muralist. *Mystic Marriages of St. Catherine.*

Gustave Courbet, 1819-77, (Fr.) Realist. *The Artist's Studio.*

Lucas Cranach the Elder, 1472-1553, (Ger.) Protestant Reformation portraitist. *Luther.*

Imogen Cunningham, 1883-1976, (U.S.) photographer, portraitist. Plants.

Nathaniel Currier, 1813-88, and **James M. Ives**, 1824-95, (both U.S.) lithographers. *A Midnight Race on the Mississippi, American Forest Scene — Maple Sugaring.*

John Steuart Curry, 1897-1946, (U.S.) Americana, murals. *Baptism in Kansas.*

Edward S. Curtis, 1868-1952, (U.S.) photographer. *The Native American Indian.*

Salvador Dalí, 1904-89, (Sp.) Surrealist. *Persistence of Memory, The Crucifixion.*

Honoré Daumier, 1808-79, (Fr.) caricaturist. *The Third-Class Carriage.*

Jacques-Louis David, 1748-1825, (Fr.) Neoclassicist. *The Oath of the Horatii.*

Arthur Davies, 1862-1928, (U.S.) Romantic landscapist. *Unicorns, Leda and the Dioscuri.*

Edgar Degas, 1834-1917, (Fr.) Realist/Impressionist. *The Ballet Class.*

Willem de Kooning, 1904-97, (Neth.-U.S.) Abstract Expressionist. *Excavation, Woman I, Door to the River.*

Eugène Delacroix, 1798-1863, (Fr.) Romantic. *Massacre at Chios, Liberty Leading the People.*

Paul Delaroche, 1797-1856, (Fr.) historical themes. *Children of Edward IV.*

Luca Della Robbia, 1400-82, (It.) Renaissance terra-cotta. *Cantoria* (singing gallery), Florence cathedral.

Donatello, 1386-1466, (It.) Renaissance sculptor. *David, Gattamelata.*

Aaron Douglas, 1899-79, (U.S.) Harlem Renaissance illustrator and muralist.

Jean Dubuffet, 1902-85, (Fr.) painter, sculptor, printmaker. *Group of Four Trees.*

Marcel Duchamp, 1887-1968, (Fr.) Dadaist. *Nude Descending a Staircase, No. 2.*

Raoul Dufy, 1877-1953, (Fr.) Fauvist. *Chateau and Horses.*

Asher Brown Durand, 1796-1886, (U.S.) Hudson River school. *Kindred Spirits.*

Albrecht Dürer, 1471-1528, (Ger.) Renaissance painter, engraver, woodcuts. *St. Jerome in His Study, Melencolia I.*

Anthony van Dyck, 1599-1641, (Flem.) Baroque portraitist. *Portrait of Charles I Hunting.*

Thomas Eakins, 1844-1916, (U.S.) Realist. *The Gross Clinic.*

Alfred Eisenstaedt, 1898-1995, (Ger.-U.S.) photographer, photojournalist. Famous photo, V-J Day, Aug. 14, 1945.

Peter Henry Emerson, 1856-1936, (Br.) photographer. Promoted photography as an independent art form.

Jacob Epstein, 1880-1959, (Br.) religious and allegorical sculptor. *Genesis, Ecce Homo.*

Erté (Romain de Tiertoff), 1892-1990, (Fr.) painter, fashion and stage designer.

Walker Evans, 1903-75, (U.S.) photographer. Documented Great Depression.

Jan van Eyck, c. 1390-1441, (Flem.) naturalistic panels. *Adoration of the Lamb.*

Horst Faas, 1933-2012, (Ger.) Vietnam War photographer.

Roger Fenton, 1819-69, (Br.) photographer. Crimean War.

Anselm Feuerbach, 1829-80, (Ger.) Romantic Classicist. *Judgment of Paris, Iphigenia.*

John Bernard Flannagan, 1895-1942, (U.S.) animal sculptor. *Triumph of the Egg.*

Jean-Honoré Fragonard, 1732-1806, (Fr.) Rococo. *The Swing.*

Helen Frankenthaler, 1928-2011, (U.S.) Abstract Expressionist. *Mountains and Sea.*

Daniel Chester French, 1850-1931, (U.S.) sculptor. *The Minute Man of Concord*; seated *Lincoln*, Lincoln Memorial, Washington, DC.

Lucian Freud, 1922-2011, (Ger.-Br.) portraitist. *Girl With Roses.*

Caspar David Friedrich, 1774-1840, (Ger.) Romantic landscapist. *Man and Woman Gazing at the Moon.*

Thomas Gainsborough, 1727-88, (Br.) portraitist. *The Blue Boy, The Watering Place, Orpin the Parish Clerk.*

Alexander Gardner, 1821-82, (U.S.) photographer. Civil War, railroad construction, Great Plains Indians.

Paul Gauguin, 1848-1903, (Fr.) Post-Impressionist. *The Tahitians, Spirit of the Dead Watching.*

Lorenzo Ghiberti, 1378-1455, (It.) Renaissance sculptor. "Gates of Paradise" baptistery doors, Florence, It.

Alberto Giacometti, 1901-66, (Switz.) attenuated sculptures of solitary figures. *Man Pointing.*

Giorgione, c. 1477-1510, (It.) Renaissance. *The Tempest.*

Giotto di Bondone, 1267-1337, (It.) Renaissance. *Presentation of Christ in the Temple.*

François Girardon, 1628-1715, (Fr.) Baroque sculptor of classical themes. *Apollo Tended by the Nymphs.*

Edward Gorey, 1925-2000, (U.S.) illustrator. *The Doubtful Guest.*

Arshile Gorky, 1905-48, (U.S.) Surrealist. *The Liver Is the Cock's Comb.*

Francisco de Goya y Lucientes, 1746-1828, (Sp.) painter, printmaker. *The Naked Maja, The Disasters of War* (etchings).

El Greco (Domenikos Theotokopoulos), 1541-1614, (Gr.-Sp.) painter, sculptor. *View of Toledo, Assumption of the Virgin.*

Horatio Greenough, 1805-52, (U.S.) Neoclassical sculptor.

Matthias Grünewald, 1480-1528, (Ger.) mystical religious themes. *The Resurrection.*

Frans Hals, c. 1580-1666, (Neth.) portraitist. *Laughing Cavalier, Gypsy Girl.*

Richard Hamilton, 1922-2011, (Br.) Pop Art. *Just What Is It That Makes Today's Homes So Different, So Appealing?*

Austin Hansen, 1910-96, (U.S.) photographer. Harlem, NY, life.

Childe Hassam, 1859-1935, (U.S.) Impressionist. *Southwest Wind, July 14 Rue Daunon.*

Edward Hicks, 1780-1849, (U.S.) folk. *The Peaceable Kingdom.*

Lewis Wickes Hine, 1874-1940, (U.S.) photographer. Studies of immigrants, children in industry.

Hans Hofmann, 1880-1966, (U.S.) early Abstract Expressionist. *Spring, The Gate.*

William Hogarth, 1697-1764, (Br.) caricaturist. *The Rake's Progress.*

Katsushika Hokusai, 1760-1849, (Jpn.) printmaker. *Crabs.*

Hans Holbein the Elder, 1460-1524, (Ger.) late Gothic. *Presentation of Christ in the Temple.*

Hans Holbein the Younger, 1497-1543, (Ger.) portraitist. *Henry VIII, The French Ambassadors.*

Winslow Homer, 1836-1910, (U.S.) naturalist, marine themes. *Marine Coast, High Cliff.*

Edward Hopper, 1882-1967, (U.S.) realistic urban scenes. *Nighthawks, House by the Railroad.*

Horst P. Horst, 1906-99, (Ger.) fashion, celebrity photographer.

Jean-Auguste-Dominique Ingres, 1780-1867, (Fr.) Classicist. *Valpincon Bather.*

George Inness, 1825-94, (U.S.) luminous landscapist. *Delaware Water Gap.*

William Henry Jackson, 1843-1942, (U.S.) photographer. American West, building of Union Pacific Railroad.

Jeanne-Claude (Javacheff), 1935-2009, (Moroc.), created large-scale, temporary installations in public places with her husband, Christo.

Donald Judd, 1928-94, (U.S.) sculptor, major Minimalist.

Frida Kahlo, 1907-54, (Mex.) folkloric stylist. *Self-Portrait With Monkey.*

Wassily Kandinsky, 1866-1944, (Russ.) Abstractionist. *Capricious Forms, Improvisation 28 (second version).*

Paul Klee, 1879-1940, (Switz.) Abstractionist. *Twittering Machine, Pastoral, Death and Fire.*

Gustav Klimt, 1862-1918, (Austria) cofounder of Vienna Secession Movement. *The Kiss.*

Oscar Kokoschka, 1886-1980, (Austria) Expressionist. *View of Prague, Harbor of Marseilles.*

Kathe Kollwitz, 1867-1945, (Ger.) printmaker, social justice themes. *The Peasant War.*

Gaston Lachaise, 1882-1935, (U.S.) figurative sculptor. *Standing Woman.*

John La Farge, 1835-1910, (U.S.) muralist. *Red and White Peonies, The Ascension.*

Sir Edwin (Henry) Landseer, 1802-73, (Br.) painter, sculptor. *Shoeing, Rout of Comus.*

Dorothea Lange, 1895-1965, (U.S.) photographer. Great Depression, migrant farm workers.

Fernand Léger, 1881-1955, (Fr.) Machine art. *The Cyclists.*

Saul Leiter, 1923-2013, (U.S) photographer.

Leonardo da Vinci, 1452-1519, (It.) Renaissance. *Mona Lisa, Last Supper, The Annunciation.*

Emanuel Leutze, 1816-68, (U.S.) historical themes. *Washington Crossing the Delaware.*

Roy Lichtenstein, 1923-97, (U.S.) Pop Art.

Jacques Lipchitz, 1891-1973, (Fr.) Cubist sculptor. *Harpist.*

Filippino Lippi, 1457-1504, (It.) Renaissance. *Adoration of the Magi.*

Fra Filippo Lippi, 1406-69, (It.) Renaissance. *Coronation of the Virgin, Madonna and Child With Angels.*

Morris Louis, 1912-62, (U.S.) Abstract Expressionist. *Signa, Stripes, Alpha-Phi.*

René Magritte, 1898-1967, (Belg.) Surrealist. *The Descent of Man, The Betrayal of Images.*

Aristide Maillol, 1861-1944, (Fr.) sculptor. *L'Harmonie.*

Édouard Manet, 1832-83, (Fr.) forerunner of Impressionism. *Luncheon on the Grass, Olympia.*

Andrea Mantegna, 1431-1506, (It.) Renaissance frescoes. *Triumph of Caesar.*

Robert Mapplethorpe, 1946-89, (U.S.) photographer.

Franz Marc, 1880-1916, (Ger.) Expressionist. *Blue Horses.*

John Marin, 1870-1953, (U.S.) Expressionist seascapes. *Maine Island.*

Reginald Marsh, 1898-1954, (U.S.) satire. *Tattoo and Haircut.*

Agnes Martin, 1912-2004, (U.S.) abstract artist. *Night Sea.*

Masaccio, 1401-28, (It.) Renaissance. *The Tribute Money.*

Henri Matisse, 1869-1954, (Fr.) Fauvist. *Woman With the Hat.*

John McCracken, 1934-2011, (U.S.) minimalist sculptor.

Michelangelo Buonarroti, 1475-1564, (It.) Renaissance. *Pietà, David, Moses, The Last Judgment*, Sistine Chapel ceiling.

Jean-Francois Millet, 1814-75, (Fr.) peasants. *The Gleaners, The Man With a Hoe.*

Joan Miró, 1893-1983, (Sp.) exuberant colors, playful images. Catalan landscape. *Dutch Interior.*

Amedeo Modigliani, 1884-1920, (It.) figurative works. *Reclining Nude.*

Piet Mondrian, 1872-1944, (Neth.) Abstractionist. *Composition With Red, Yellow and Blue.*

Claude Monet, 1840-1926, (Fr.) Impressionist. *The Bridge at Argenteuil, Haystacks, Bridge Over a Pond of Water Lillies.*

Henry Moore, 1898-1986, (Br.) sculptor of large-scale, abstract works. *Reclining Figure* (several).

Gustave Moreau, 1826-98, (Fr.) Symbolist. *The Apparition, Dance of Salome.*

James Wilson Morrice, 1865-1924, (Can.) landscapist. *The Ferry, Quebec, Venice, Looking Over the Lagoon.*

William Morris, 1834-96, (Br.) decorative artist, leader of Arts and Crafts movement.

Grandma Moses (Anna Mary Robertson Moses), 1860-1961, (U.S.) folk. *Out for the Christmas Tree, Catching the Thanksgiving Turkey.*

Edvard Munch, 1863-1944, (Nor.) Expressionist. *The Cry.*

Bartolome Murillo, 1618-82, (Sp.) Baroque religious artist. *Vision of St. Anthony, The Two Trinities.*

Elizabeth Murray, 1940-2007, (U.S.) abstract colors. *Kitchen Party.*

Eadweard Muybridge, 1830-1904, (Br.-U.S.) photographer. Studies of motion, *Animal Locomotion.*

Nadar (Gaspar-Félix Tournachon), 1820-1910, (Fr.) photographer, caricaturist, portraitist. Invented photo-essay.

LeRoy Neiman, 1921-2012, (U.S.) sports expressionist painter.

Arnold Newman, 1918-2006, (U.S.) portrait photographer.

Barnett Newman, 1905-70, (U.S.) Abstract Expressionist. *Stations of the Cross.*

Isamu Noguchi, 1904-88, (U.S.) abstract sculptor, designer. *Kouros, BirdC(MU)*, sculptural gardens.

Kenneth Noland, 1924-2010, (U.S.) Color Field, abstract.

Georgia O'Keeffe, 1887-1986, (U.S.) Southwest motifs. *Cow's Skull: Red, White, and Blue; The Shelton With Sunspots.*

José Clemente Orozco, 1883-1949, (Mex.) frescoes. *House of Tears, Pre-Columbian Golden Age.*

Timothy H. O'Sullivan, 1840-82, (U.S.) Civil War photographer.

Gordon Parks, 1912-2006, (U.S.) African American photographer, filmmaker. *Life* photographer, 1948-68.

Charles Willson Peale, 1741-1827, (U.S.) Amer. Revolutionary portraitist. *The Staircase Group*, U.S. presidents.

Rembrandt Peale, 1778-1860, (U.S.) portraitist. *Thomas Jefferson.*

Irving Penn, 1917-2009, (U.S.) portraitist, fashion photographer.

Pietro Perugino, 1446-1523, (It.) Renaissance. *Delivery of the Keys to St. Peter.*

Pablo Picasso, 1881-1973, (Sp.) painter, sculptor. *Guernica, Dove, Head of a Woman, Head of a Bull, Metamorphosis.*

Piero della Francesca, c. 1415-92, (It.) Renaissance. *Duke of Urbino, Flagellation of Christ.*

Camille Pissarro, 1830-1903, (Fr.) Impressionist. *Boulevard des Italiens, Morning, Sunlight; Bather in the Woods.*

Jackson Pollock, 1912-56, (U.S.) Abstract Expressionist. *Autumn Rhythm.*

Nicolas Poussin, 1594-1665, (Fr.) Baroque pictorial classicism. *St. John on Patmos.*

Maurice B. Prendergast, c. 1860-1924, (U.S.) Postimpressionist watercolorist. *Umbrellas in the Rain.*

Pierre-Paul Prud'hon, 1758-1823, (Fr.) Romanticist. *Crime Pursued by Vengeance and Justice.*

Pierre Cecile Puvis de Chavannes, 1824-98, (Fr.) muralist. *The Poor Fisherman.*

Raphael Sanzio, 1483-1520, (It.) Renaissance. *Disputa, School of Athens, Sistine Madonna.*

Robert Rauschenberg, 1925-2008, (U.S.) printmaker. *Combine, Bed, Revolvers, Outpost.*

Man Ray (Emmanuel Radnitsky), 1890-1976, (U.S.) Dadaist and Surrealist. *Observing Time, The Lovers, Marquis de Sade.*

Odilon Redon, 1840-1916, (Fr.) Symbolist painter, lithographer. *In the Dream, Vase of Flowers.*

Rembrandt van Rijn, 1606-69, (Neth.) painter, printmaker. *The Bridal Couple, The Night Watch.*

Frederic Remington, 1861-1909, (U.S.) painter, sculptor. Portrayer of the American West, *Bronco Buster.*

Pierre-Auguste Renoir, 1841-1919, (Fr.) Impressionist. *The Luncheon of the Boating Party, Dance in the Country.*

Joshua Reynolds, 1723-92, (Br.) portraitist. *Mrs. Siddons as the Tragic Muse.*

Herb Ritts, 1952-2002, (U.S.) photographer. Nudes, celebrities.

Diego Rivera, 1886-1957, (Mex.) frescoes. *The Fecund Earth.*

Larry Rivers, 1923-2002, (U.S.) painter, sculptor, often realistic. Dutch Masters series.

Henry Peach Robinson, 1830-1901, (Br.) photographer. A leader of "high art" photography.

Norman Rockwell, 1894-1978, (U.S.) painter, illustrator. *Saturday Evening Post* covers.

Auguste Rodin, 1840-1917, (Fr.) sculptor. *The Thinker.*

Milton Rogovin, 1909-2011, (U.S.) documentary photographer.

Willy Ronis, 1910-2009, (Fr.) photographer. Post-war Paris.

Joe Rosenthal, 1911-2006, (U.S.) photojournalist; photographed six Marines raising the U.S. flag over Iwo Jima in WWII.

Mark Rothko, 1903-70, (U.S.) Abstract Expressionist. *Light, Earth and Blue.*

Georges Rouault, 1871-1958, (Fr.) Expressionist. *Three Judges.*

Henri Rousseau, 1844-1910, (Fr.) primitive exotic themes. *The Snake Charmer.*

Theodore Rousseau, 1812-67, (Switz.-Fr.) landscapist. *Under the Birches, Evening.*

Peter Paul Rubens, 1577-1640, (Flem.) Baroque. *Mystic Marriage of St. Catherine.*

Jacob van Ruisdael, c. 1628-82, (Neth.) landscapist. *Jewish Cemetery.*

Charles M. Russell, 1866-1926, (U.S.) Western life.

Salomon van Ruysdael, c. 1600-70, (Neth.) landscapist. *River With Ferry-Boat.*

Albert Pinkham Ryder, 1847-1917, (U.S.) seascapes, allegories. *Toilers of the Sea.*

Augustus Saint-Gaudens, 1848-1907, (U.S.) memorial statues. *Farragut, Mrs. Henry Adams (Grief).*

Niki de Saint Phalle, 1930-2002, (Fr.) paintings, sculptures, prints, large public installations.

Andrea Sansovino, 1460-1529, (It.) Renaissance sculptor. *Baptism of Christ.*

Jacopo Sansovino, 1486-1570, (It.) Renaissance sculptor. *St. John the Baptist.*

John Singer Sargent, 1856-1925, (U.S.) Edwardian society portraitist. *The Wyndham Sisters, Madam X.*

Andrea del Sarto, 1486-1530, (It.) frescoes. *Madonna of the Harpies.*

George Segal, 1924-2000, (U.S.) sculptor. Life-sized figures realistically depicting daily life.

Georges Seurat, 1859-91, (Fr.) Pointillist. *Sunday Afternoon on the Island of La Grande Jatte.*

Gino Severini, 1883-1966, (It.) Futurist and Cubist. *Dynamic Hieroglyph of the Bal Tabarin.*

Ben Shahn, 1898-1969, (U.S.) social and political themes. *Sacco and Vanzetti* series, *Seurat's Lunch, Handball.*

Charles Sheeler, 1883-1965, (U.S.) abstractionist.

David Alfaro Siqueiros, 1896-1974, (Mex.) political muralist. *March of Humanity.*

David Smith, 1906-65, (U.S.) welded metal sculpture. *Hudson River Landscape, Zig, Cubi* series.

Edward Steichen, 1879-1973, (U.S.) photographer. Credited with transforming photography into an art form.

Alfred Stieglitz, 1864-1946, (U.S.) photographer, editor. Helped create acceptance of photography as art.

Paul Strand, 1890-1976, (U.S.) photographer. People, nature, landscapes.

Gilbert Stuart, 1755-1828, (U.S.) portraitist. George Washington, Thomas Jefferson, James Madison.

Thomas Sully, 1783-1872, (U.S.) portraitist. *Col. Thomas Handasyd Perkins, The Passage of the Delaware.*

William Henry Fox Talbot, 1800-77, (Br.) photographer. *Pencil of Nature*, early photographically illustrated book.

George Tames, 1919-94, (U.S.) photographer. Presidents, political leaders.

Yves Tanguy, 1900-55, (Fr.) Surrealist. *Rose of the Four Winds; Mama, Papa Is Wounded!*

Giovanni Battista Tiepolo, 1696-1770, (It.) Rococo frescoes. *The Crucifixion.*

Jacopo Tintoretto, 1518-94, (It.) Mannerist. *The Last Supper.*

Titian (Tiziano Vecellio), c. 1488-1576, (It.) Renaissance. *Venus and the Lute Player, The Bacchanal.*

Jose Rey Toledo, 1916-94, (U.S.) Native American life. Tribal dances.

George Tooker, 1920-2011, (U.S.) Magic Realist. *Subway.*

Henri de Toulouse-Lautrec, 1864-1901, (Fr.) Postimpressionist. *At the Moulin Rouge.*

John Trumbull, 1756-1843, (U.S.) historical themes. *The Declaration of Independence.*

Deborah Turbeville, 1937-2013, (U.S.) fashion photographer.

J(oseph) M(allord) W(illiam) Turner, 1775-1851, (Br.) Romantic landscapist. *Snow Storm.*

Cy Twombly, 1928-2011, (U.S.) painter and sculptor. *Leda and the Swan.*

Paolo Uccello, 1397-1475, (It.) Gothic-Renaissance. *The Rout of San Romano.*

Maurice Utrillo, 1883-1955, (Fr.) Impressionist. *Sacre-Coeur de Montmartre.*

Vincent van Gogh, 1853-90, (Neth.) *The Starry Night, L'Arlesienne, Bedroom at Arles, Self-Portrait.*

John Vanderlyn, 1775-1852, (U.S.) Neoclassicist. *Ariadne Asleep on the Island of Naxos.*

Diego Velázquez, 1599-1660, (Sp.) Baroque. *Las Meninas, Portrait of Juan de Pareja.*

Jan Vermeer, 1632-75, (Neth.) interior genre subjects. *Young Woman With a Water Jug.*

Paolo Veronese, 1528-88, (It.) devotional themes, vastly peopled canvases. *The Temptation of St. Anthony.*

Andrea del Verrocchio, 1435-88, (It.) sculptor. *Colleoni.*

Maurice de Vlaminck, 1876-1958, (Fr.) Fauvist landscapist. *Red Trees.*

Andy Warhol, 1928-87, (U.S.) Pop Art. *Campbell's Soup Cans, Marilyn Diptych.*

Antoine Watteau, 1684-1721, (Fr.) Rococo "scenes of gallantry." *The Embarkation for Cythera.*

George Frederic Watts, 1817-1904, (Br.) painter and sculptor. Grandiose allegorical themes. *Hope.*

Benjamin West, 1738-1820, (U.S.) realistic historical themes. *Death of General Wolfe.*

Edward Weston, 1886-1958, (U.S.) photographer. Landscapes of American West.

James Abbott McNeill Whistler, 1834-1903, (U.S.) *Arrangement in Grey and Black No. 1 (Portrait of the Artist's Mother).*

Archibald M. Willard, 1836-1918, (U.S.) murals. *The Spirit of '76.*

Grant Wood, 1891-1942, (U.S.) Midwestern regionalist. *American Gothic, Daughters of Revolution.*

Andrew Wyeth, 1917-2009, (U.S.) regionalist. *Christina's World.*

Ossip Zadkine, 1890-1967, (Russ.) School of Paris sculptor. *The Destroyed City, Musicians, Christ.*

Business Leaders and Philanthropists of the Past

Giovanni Agnelli, 1921-2003, (It.) industrialist; principal shareholder of Fiat.

Karl Albrecht, 1920-2014, and **Theo Albrecht**, 1922-2010, (both Ger.) cofounders of Aldi supermarkets

Walter Annenberg, 1908-2002, (U.S.) publisher, founder of *TV Guide*, philanthropist.

Elizabeth Arden (F. N. Graham), 1884-1966, (U.S.) Canadian-born founder of cosmetics empire.

Philip D. Armour, 1832-1901, (U.S.) industrialist; streamlined meatpacking.

Brooke Astor, 1902-2007, (U.S.) philanthropist; pres. of Vincent Astor Foundation.

John Jacob Astor, 1763-1848, (U.S.) German-born fur trader, banker, real estate magnate; at death, richest in U.S.

Francis W. Ayer, 1848-1923, (U.S.) ad industry pioneer.

August Belmont, 1816-90, (U.S.) German-born financier.

James B. (Diamond Jim) Brady, 1856-1917, (U.S.) financier, philanthropist, legendary bon vivant.

Adolphus Busch, 1839-1913, (U.S.) German-born businessman; established brewery empire.

Asa Candler, 1851-1929, (U.S.) founded Coca-Cola Co.

Andrew Carnegie, 1835-1919, (U.S.) Scottish-born industrialist, philanthropist; founded Carnegie Steel Co.

Tom Carvel, 1908-89, (Gr.-U.S.) founded ice cream chain.

William Colgate, 1783-1857, (Br.-U.S.) businessman, philanthropist; founded soap-making empire.

Jay Cooke, 1821-1905, (U.S.) financier.

Peter Cooper, 1791-1883, (U.S.) industrialist, inventor, philanthropist; founded Cooper Union (1859).

Ezra Cornell, 1807-74, (U.S.) businessman, philanthropist; headed Western Union.

Erastus Corning, 1794-1872, (U.S.) financier; headed New York Central Railroad.

Charles Crocker, 1822-88, (U.S.) railroad builder, financier.

Samuel Cunard, 1787-1865, (Can.) pioneered transatlantic steam navigation.

Marcus Daly, 1841-1900, (U.S.) Irish-born copper magnate.

W. Edwards Deming, 1900-93, (U.S.) quality-control expert who revolutionized Japanese manufacturing.

Walt Disney, 1901-66, (U.S.) pioneer in cinema animation; built entertainment empire.

Herbert H. Dow, 1866-1930, (U.S.) founder of chemical co.

Anthony Drexel, 1826-93, (U.S.) banker, philanthropist, university founder.

James Duke, 1856-1925, (U.S.) founded American Tobacco, Duke Univ.

Eleuthere I. du Pont, 1771-1834, (Fr.-U.S.) gunpowder manufacturer; founded one of the largest business empires.

Thomas C. Durant, 1820-85, (U.S.) railroad official, financier.

William C. Durant, 1861-1947, (U.S.) industrialist; formed General Motors.

George Eastman, 1854-1932, (U.S.) inventor; manufacturer of photographic equipment.

Marshall Field, 1834-1906, (U.S.) merchant; founded Chicago's largest department store.

Harvey Firestone, 1868-1938, (U.S.) founded tire company.

Avery Fisher, 1906-94, (U.S.) industrialist, philanthropist; founded Fisher Electronics.

Henry M. Flagler, 1830-1913, (U.S.) financier; helped form Standard Oil, developed FL as resort state.

Malcolm Forbes, 1919-90, (U.S.) magazine publisher.

Henry Ford, 1863-1947, (U.S.) automaker; developed first popular low-priced car.

Henry Ford II, 1917-87, (U.S.) headed auto company founded by grandfather.

Henry C. Frick, 1849-1919, (U.S.) steel and coke magnate; had prominent role in development of U.S. Steel.

Jakob Fugger (Jakob the Rich), 1459-1525, (Ger.) headed leading banking, trading house in 16th-cent. Europe.

Alfred C. Fuller, 1885-1973, (U.S.) Canadian-born businessman; founded brush company.

Elbert H. Gary, 1846-1927, (U.S.) chaired board of U.S. Steel, 1903-27.

Jean Paul Getty, 1892-1976, (U.S.) founded oil empire.

Amadeo Giannini, 1870-1949, (U.S.) founded Bank of America.

Stephen Girard, 1750-1831, (U.S.) French-born financier, philanthropist; richest man in U.S. at time of death.

Leonard H. Goldenson, 1905-99, (U.S.) turned ABC into major TV network.

Jay Gould, 1836-92, (U.S.) railroad magnate, financier.

Hetty Green, 1834-1916, (U.S.) financier, the "witch of Wall St."; richest woman in U.S. in her day.

William Gregg, 1800-67, (U.S.) launched textile industry in the South.

Meyer Guggenheim, 1828-1905, (U.S.) Swiss-born merchant, philanthropist; built merchandising, mining empires.

Armand Hammer, 1898-1990, (U.S.) headed Occidental Petroleum, promoted U.S.-Soviet ties.

Elliot Handler, 1916-2011, (U.S.) cofounder of Mattel; introduced the Barbie doll.

Edward H. Harriman, 1848-1909, (U.S.) railroad financier; headed Union Pacific.

Henry J. Heinz, 1844-1919, (U.S.) founded food empire.

Leona Helmsley, 1920-2007, (U.S.) real estate magnate, philanthropist.

Milton Snavely Hershey, 1857-1945, (U.S.) chocolate co. founder, philanthropist.

James J. Hill, 1838-1916, (U.S.) Canadian-born railroad magnate, financier; founded Great Northern Railway.

Conrad N. Hilton, 1888-1979, (U.S.) hotel chain founder.

Howard Hughes, 1905-76, (U.S.) industrialist, aviator, filmmaker.

H. L. Hunt, 1889-1974, (U.S.) oil magnate.

Collis P. Huntington, 1821-1900, (U.S.) railroad magnate.

Henry E. Huntington, 1850-1927, (U.S.) railroad builder, philanthropist.

Walter L. Jacobs, 1898-1985, (U.S.) founder of the first rental car agency.

Steve Jobs, 1955-2011, (U.S.) Apple cofounder and exec.; Pixar exec.

Howard Johnson, 1896-1972, (U.S.) founded restaurants.

John H. Johnson, 1918-2005, (U.S.) built publishing empire based on *Ebony* and *Jet.*

Samuel Curtis Johnson, 1928-2004, (U.S.) headed S.C. Johnson & Sons.

Henry J. Kaiser, 1882-1967, (U.S.) industrialist; built empire in steel, aluminum.

Minor C. Keith, 1848-1929, (U.S.) railroad magnate; founded United Fruit Co.

Will K. Kellogg, 1860-1951, (U.S.) businessman, philanthropist; founded breakfast food co.

Richard King, 1825-85, (U.S.) cattle farmer; founded King Ranch in Texas.

John W. Kluge, 1914-2010, (Ger.-U.S.) Metromedia chair; philanthropist.

William S. Knudsen, 1879-1948, (U.S.) Danish-born auto industry executive.

Samuel H. Kress, 1863-1955, (U.S.) businessman, art collector, philanthropist; founded "dime store" chain.

Ray A. Kroc, 1902-84, (U.S.) original CEO of McDonald's Corp.; oversaw company's vast expansion.

Alfred Krupp, 1812-87, (Ger.) armaments magnate.

Estée Lauder, 1908-2004, (U.S.) cofounder of Estée Lauder companies.

Kenneth L. Lay, 1942-2006, (U.S.) former CEO of Enron; indicted on fraud charges.

William Levitt, 1907-94, (U.S.) industrialist; "suburb maker."

Thomas Lipton, 1850-1931, (Scot.) merchant; tea empire.

James McGill, 1744-1813, (Scot.-Can.) founded university.

Andrew W. Mellon, 1855-1937, (U.S.) financier, industrialist, philanthropist.

Charles E. Merrill, 1885-1956, (U.S.) financier; developed firm of Merrill Lynch.

J(ohn) P(ierpont) Morgan, 1837-1913, (U.S.) most powerful figure in finance and industry at turn of 20th cent.

Akio Morita, 1921-99, (Jpn.) cofounded Sony Corp.

Malcolm Muir, 1885-1979, (U.S.) created *Business Week* magazine; headed *Newsweek*, 1937-61.

Roy Neuberger, 1903-2010, (U.S.) financier, art patron.

Samuel Newhouse, 1895-1979, (U.S.) publishing and broadcasting magnate.

Aristotle Onassis, 1906-75, (Gr.) shipping magnate.

William S. Paley, 1901-90, (U.S.) built CBS communications empire.
Frederick D. Patterson, 1901-88, (U.S.) founder of United Negro College Fund, 1944.
George Peabody, 1795-1869, (U.S.) merchant, financier, philanthropist.
James C. Penney, 1875-1971, (U.S.) businessman; developed department store.
Frank Perdue, 1920-2005, (U.S.) founder of Perdue Farms, chicken-processing company.
William C. Procter, 1862-1934, (U.S.) headed soap co.
John D. Rockefeller, 1839-1937, (U.S.) industrialist; established Standard Oil.
John D. Rockefeller Jr., 1874-1960, (U.S.) philanthropist; provided land for UN.
Laurance S. Rockefeller, 1910-2004, (U.S.) philanthropist, conservationist.
Meyer A. Rothschild, 1743-1812, (Ger.) founded international banking house.
Thomas Fortune Ryan, 1851-1928, (U.S.) financier; a founder of American Tobacco.
Edmond J. Safra, 1932-99, (U.S.) banker.
David Sarnoff, 1891-1971, (U.S.) broadcasting pioneer; established first radio network, NBC.
Richard Sears, 1863-1914, (U.S.) founded mail-order co.

Werner von Siemens, 1816-92, (Ger.) industrialist, inventor.
Alfred P. Sloan, 1875-1966, (U.S.) industrialist, philanthropist; headed General Motors.
A. Leland Stanford, 1824-93, (U.S.) railroad official, philanthropist; founded university.
Frank Stanton, 1908-2006, (U.S.) president of CBS network, 1946-71.
Nathan Straus, 1848-1931, (U.S.) German-born merchant, philanthropist; headed Macy's dept. stores.
Levi Strauss, c. 1829-1902, (U.S.) pants manufacturer.
Clement Studebaker, 1831-1901, (U.S.) wagon, carriage maker.
Gustavus Swift, 1839-1903, (U.S.) pioneer meatpacker.
Gerard Swope, 1872-1957, (U.S.) industrialist, economist; headed General Electric.
Dave Thomas, 1932-2002, (U.S.) Wendy's founder.
James Walter Thompson, 1847-1928, (U.S.) ad executive, founder of ad agency.
Alice Tully, 1902-93, (U.S.) philanthropist, arts patron.
Theodore N. Vail, 1845-1920, (U.S.) organized Bell Telephone system, headed AT&T.
Cornelius Vanderbilt, 1794-1877, (U.S.) financier; established steamship, railroad empires.

Henry Villard, 1835-1900, (U.S.) German-born railroad executive, financier.
Charles R. Walgreen, 1873-1939, (U.S.) founded drugstore chain.
Madame C. J. Walker, 1867-1919, (U.S.) African-American hair care entrepreneur, philanthropist.
DeWitt Wallace, 1889-1981, and **Lila Wallace**, 1889-1984, (both U.S.) cofounders of *Reader's Digest* magazine.
Sam Walton, 1918-92, (U.S.) founder of Wal-Mart stores.
John Wanamaker, 1838-1922, (U.S.) department-store merchandising pioneer.
Aaron Montgomery Ward, 1843-1913, (U.S.) established first mail-order firm.
Thomas J. Watson, 1874-1956, (U.S.) IBM head, 1914-56.
George Westinghouse, 1846-1914, (U.S.) inventor, manufacturer; organized Westinghouse Electric Co., 1886.
John Hay Whitney, 1905-82, (U.S.) publisher, sportsman, philanthropist.
Charles E. Wilson, 1890-1961, (U.S.) auto exec., public official.
Frank W. Woolworth, 1852-1919, (U.S.) created five-and-dime chain.
William Wrigley Jr., 1861-1932, (U.S.) founded Wrigley chewing gum company.

American Cartoonists

Reviewed by Lucy Shelton Caswell, Professor and Curator, Cartoon Research Library, Ohio State University.

Scott Adams, b 1957, Dilbert.
Charles Addams, 1912-88, macabre cartoons.
Brad Anderson, b 1924, Marmaduke.
Sergio Aragones, b 1937, *MAD* magazine.
Peter Arno, 1904-68, *The New Yorker*.
Tex Avery, 1908-80, animator; Bugs Bunny, Porky Pig.
George Baker, 1915-75, The Sad Sack.
Carl Barks, 1901-2000, Donald Duck comic books.
C. C. Beck, 1910-89, Captain Marvel.
Dave Berg, 1920-2002, *Mad* magazine.
Jim Berry, b 1932, Berry's World.
Herb Block (Herblock), 1909-2001, political cartoonist.
George Booth, b 1926, *The New Yorker*.
Berkeley Breathed, b 1957, Bloom County.
Dik Browne, 1917-89, Hi & Lois, Hagar the Horrible.
Marjorie Buell, 1904-93, Little Lulu.
Ernie Bushmiller, 1905-82, Nancy.
Milton Caniff, 1907-88, Terry & the Pirates, Steve Canyon.
Al Capp, 1909-79, Li'l Abner.
Roz Chast, b 1954, *The New Yorker*.
Gene Colan, 1926-2011, Daredevil.
Paul Conrad, 1924-2010, political cartoonist.
Roy Crane, 1901-77, Captain Easy, Buz Sawyer.
R(obert) Crumb, b 1943, underground cartoonist.
Shamus Culhane, 1908-96, animator.
Jay N. "Ding" Darling, 1876-1962, political cartoonist.
Jack Davis, b 1924, *MAD* magazine.
Jim Davis, b 1945, Garfield.
Billy DeBeck, 1890-1942, Barney Google.
Rudolph Dirks, 1877-1968, The Katzenjammer Kids.
Walt Disney, 1901-66, produced animated cartoons; created Mickey Mouse, Donald Duck.
Steve Ditko, b 1927, Spider-Man.
Mort Drucker, b 1929, *MAD* magazine.
Will Eisner, 1917-2005, the Spirit.
Jules Feiffer, b 1929, political cartoonist.
Bud Fisher, 1884-1954, Mutt & Jeff.
Ham Fisher, 1900-55, Joe Palooka.
Max Fleischer, 1883-1972, Betty Boop.
Hal Foster, 1892-1982, Tarzan, Prince Valiant.
Fontaine Fox, 1884-1964, Toonerville Folks.
Isadore "Friz" Freleng, 1905-95, animator; Yosemite Sam, Porky Pig, Sylvester and Tweety Bird.
Rube Goldberg, 1883-1970, Boob McNutt.
Chester Gould, 1900-85, Dick Tracy.
Harold Gray, 1894-1968, Little Orphan Annie.
Matt Groening, b 1954, Life in Hell, The Simpsons.

Cathy Guisewite, b 1950, Cathy.
Bill Hanna, 1910-2001, and **Joe Barbera**, 1911-2006, animators; Tom & Jerry, Yogi Bear, Flintstones.
Oliver Harrington, 1912-95, Bootsie.
Johnny Hart, 1931-2007, BC, Wizard of Id.
Alfred Harvey, 1913-94, created Casper the Friendly Ghost.
Jimmy Hatlo, 1898-1963, Little Iodine.
John Held Jr., 1889-1958, Jazz Age.
George Herriman, 1881-1944, Krazy Kat.
Harry Hershfield, 1885-1974, Abie the Agent.
Stephen Hillenburg, b 1961, SpongeBob SquarePants.
Al Hirschfeld, 1903-2003, *NY Times* theater caricaturist.
Burne Hogarth, 1911-96, Tarzan.
Helen Hokinson, 1900-49, *The New Yorker*.
Nicole Hollander, b 1939, Sylvia.
Lynn Johnston, b 1947 (Can.), For Better or For Worse.
Oliver Johnston, 1912-2008, Disney animator.
Chuck Jones, 1912-2002, animator; Bugs Bunny, Porky Pig.
Mike Judge, b 1962, Beavis and Butt-head, King of the Hill.
Bob Kane, 1916-98, Batman.
Bil Keane, 1922-2011, The Family Circus.
Walt Kelly, 1913-73, Pogo.
Hank Ketcham, 1920-2001, Dennis the Menace.
Ted Key, 1912-2008, Hazel.
Frank King, 1883-1969, Gasoline Alley.
Jack Kirby, 1917-94, Fantastic Four, The Incredible Hulk.
Rollin Kirby, 1875-1952, political cartoonist.
B(ernard) Kliban, 1935-90, cat books.
Edward Koren, b 1935, *The New Yorker*.
John Kricfalusi, b 1955, Ren & Stimpy.
Joe Kubert, 1926-2012, Sgt. Rock.
Harvey Kurtzman, 1921-93, *MAD* magazine.
Walter Lantz, 1900-94, Woody Woodpecker.
Gary Larson, b 1950, The Far Side.
Mell Lazarus, b 1927, Momma, Miss Peach.
Stan Lee, b 1922, Marvel Comics.
David Levine, 1926-2009, *NY Review of Books* caricatures.
Seth MacFarlane, b 1973, Family Guy.
Jeff MacNelly, 1947-2000, political cartoonist; Shoe.
Doug Marlette, 1949-2007, political cartoonist; Kudzu.
Don Martin, 1931-2000, *MAD* magazine.
Bill Mauldin, 1921-2003, political cartoonist.
Winsor McCay, 1872-1934, Little Nemo.
John T. McCutcheon, 1870-1949, political cartoonist.
Dwayne McDuffie, 1962-2011, *Justice League*.
Aaron McGruder, b 1974, The Boondocks.

George McManus, 1884-1954, Bringing Up Father.
Dale Messick, 1906-2005, Brenda Starr.
Norman Mingo, 1896-1980, Alfred E. Neuman.
Bob Montana, 1920-75, Archie.
Dick Moores, 1909-86, Gasoline Alley.
Willard Mullin, 1902-78, sports cartoonist; Dodgers "Bum," Mets "Kid."
Russell Myers, b 1938, Broom Hilda.
Thomas Nast, 1840-1902, political cartoonist; Republican elephant, Democratic donkey.
Pat Oliphant, b 1935, political cartoonist.
Frederick Burr Opper, 1857-1937, Happy Hooligan.
Richard Outcault, 1863-1928, Yellow Kid, Buster Brown.
Brant Parker, 1920-2007, Wizard of Id.
Trey Parker, b 1969, animator, co-creator of South Park.
Harvey Pekar, 1939-2010, American Splendor.
Mike Peters, b 1943, Mother Goose & Grimm.
George Price, 1901-95, *The New Yorker*.
Antonio Prohias, 1921-98, Spy vs. Spy.
Alex Raymond, 1909-56, Flash Gordon, Jungle Jim.
Forrest (Bud) Sagendorf, 1915-94, Popeye.
Art Sansom, 1920-91, The Born Loser.
Charles Schulz, 1922-2000, Peanuts.
Elzie C. Segar, 1894-1938, Popeye.
Joe Shuster, 1914-92, and **Jerry Siegel**, 1914-96, Superman.
Sidney Smith, 1887-1935, The Gumps.
Otto Soglow, 1900-75, Little King.
Art Spiegelman, b 1948, Raw, Maus.
William Steig, 1907-2003, *The New Yorker*.
Matt Stone, b 1971, animator, co-creator of South Park.
James Swinnerton, 1875-1974, Little Jimmy, Canyon Kiddies.
Paul Szep, b 1941, political cartoonist.
Paul Terry, 1887-1971, animator of Mighty Mouse.
Bob Thaves, 1924-2006, Frank and Ernest.
James Thurber, 1894-61, *The New Yorker*.
Garry Trudeau, b 1948, Doonesbury.
Jim Unger, 1937-2012, Herman.
Mort Walker, b 1923, Beetle Bailey.
Bill Watterson, b 1958, Calvin and Hobbes.
Russ Westover, 1887-1966, Tillie the Toiler.
Signe Wilkinson, b 1950, political cartoonist.
Frank Willard, 1893-1958, Moon Mullins.
J. R. Williams, 1888-1957, The Willets Family, Out Our Way.
Gahan Wilson, b 1930, *The New Yorker*.
Tom Wilson, 1931-2011, Ziggy.
Art Young, 1866-1943, political cartoonist.
Chic Young, 1901-73, Blondie.

Economists, Educators, Historians, and Social Scientists of the Past

For psychologists, see Scientists of the Past.

Brooks Adams, 1848-1927, (U.S.) historian, political theoretician; *The Law of Civilization and Decay*.

Henry Adams, 1838-1918, (U.S.) historian, autobiographer; *The Education of Henry Adams*.

Stephen Ambrose, 1936-2002, (U.S.) historian; *Eisenhower*.

Francis Bacon, 1561-1626, (Eng.) philosopher, essayist, statesman; championed observation and induction.

George Bancroft, 1800-91, (U.S.) historian; 10-volume *History of the United States*.

Jack Barbash, 1910-94, (U.S.) labor economist; helped create the AFL-CIO.

Henry Barnard, 1811-1900, (U.S.) public school reformer.

Charles A. Beard, 1874-1948, (U.S.) historian; *The Economic Basis of Politics*.

(St.) Bede (the Venerable), c. 673-735, (Br.) scholar, historian; *Ecclesiastical History of the English People*.

Daniel Bell, 1919-2011, (U.S.) sociologist; *The End of Ideology*.

Ruth Benedict, 1887-1948, (U.S.) anthropologist; studied Indian tribes of the Southwest.

Sir Isaiah Berlin, 1909-97, (Br.) philosopher, historian; *The Age of Enlightenment*.

Leonard Bloomfield, 1887-1949, (U.S.) linguist; *Language*.

Franz Boas, 1858-1942, (U.S.) German-born anthropologist; studied American Indians.

Van Wyck Brooks, 1886-1963, (U.S.) historian; critic of New England culture, especially literature.

Edmund Burke, 1729-97, (Ire.) British parliamentarian and political philosopher; *Reflections on the Revolution in France*.

Nicholas Murray Butler, 1862-1947, (U.S.) educator; headed Columbia Univ., 1902-45; Nobel Peace Prize, 1931.

James MacGregor Burns, 1918-2014, (U.S.) historian, political theorist.

Joseph Campbell, 1904-87, (U.S.) author, editor, teacher; wrote books on mythology, folklore.

Thomas Carlyle, 1795-1881, (Scot.) historian, critic; *Sartor Resartus*, *Past and Present*, *The French Revolution*.

(Charles) Bruce Catton, 1899-1978, (U.S.) historian; *A Stillness at Appomattox*.

Edward Channing, 1856-1931, (U.S.) historian; 6-volume *History of the United States*.

Henry Steele Commager, 1902-98, (U.S.) historian, educator; *The Growth of the American Republic*.

John R. Commons, 1862-1945, (U.S.) economist, labor historian; *Legal Foundations of Capitalism*.

James B. Conant, 1893-1978, (U.S.) educator, diplomat; *The American High School Today*.

Benedetto Croce, 1866-1952, (It.) philosopher, statesman, historian; *Philosophy of the Spirit*.

Bernard A. De Voto, 1897-1955, (U.S.) historian; wrote trilogy on American West, edited Mark Twain manuscripts.

Melvil Dewey, 1851-1931, (U.S.) devised decimal system of library-book classification.

Donald Herbert Donald, 1920-2009, (U.S.) Pulitzer Prize-winning Civil War and Lincoln historian.

St. Clair Drake, 1911-90, (U.S.) sociologist, black studies pioneer; *Black Metropolis* (1945), with Horace R. Cayton.

W(illiam) E(dward) B(urghardt) Du Bois, 1868-1963, (U.S.) historian, sociologist; NAACP founder, 1909.

Will(iam), 1885-1981, (U.S.) and **Ariel Durant**, 1898-1981, (Ukraine), historians; *The Story of Civilization*.

Emile Durkheim, 1858-1917, (Fr.) a founder of modern sociology; *The Rules of Sociological Method*.

Jean Baptiste Point du Sable, c. 1750-1818, (U.S.) pioneer trader and first settler of Chicago, 1779.

Charles Eliot, 1834-1926, (U.S.) educator, Harvard president.

Friedrich Engels, 1820-95, (Ger.) political writer; with Marx wrote the *Communist Manifesto*.

Irving Fisher, 1867-1947, (U.S.) economist; contributed to the development of modern monetary theory.

John Fiske, 1842-1901, (U.S.) historian and lecturer; popularized Darwinian theory of evolution.

Charles Fourier, 1772-1837, (Fr.) utopian socialist.

John Hope Franklin, 1915-2009, (U.S.) historian; *From Slavery to Freedom: A History of African Americans*.

Sir James George Frazer, 1854-1941, (Br.) anthropologist; studied myth in religion; *The Golden Bough*.

Milton Friedman, 1912-2006, (U.S.) economist.

Paul Fussell, 1924-2012, (U.S.) literary historian; *The Great War and Modern Memory*.

John Kenneth Galbraith, 1908-2006, (Can.-U.S.) economist, author, professor, former amb. to India.

Giovanni Gentile, 1875-1944, (It.) philosopher, educator; reformed Italian educational system.

Henry George, 1839-97, (U.S.) economist, reformer; led single-tax movement.

Edward Gibbon, 1737-94, (Br.) historian; *The History of the Decline and Fall of the Roman Empire*.

Andrew Greeley, 1928-2013, (U.S.) Rom. Cath priest; sociologist.

Francesco Guicciardini, 1483-1540, (It.) historian; *Storia d'Italia*, principal historical work of the 16th cent.

Thomas Hobbes, 1588-1679, (Eng.) philosopher, political theorist; *Leviathan*.

Richard Hofstadter, 1916-70, (U.S.) historian; *The Age of Reform*.

Charles Hamilton Houston, 1895-1950, (U.S.) African American lawyer, Howard University instructor; champion of minority rights.

Samuel Huntington, 1927-2008, (U.S.), political scientist, Harvard University professor; *The Clash of Civilizations*.

Alfred Kahn, 1917-2010, (U.S.) economist; deregulated the U.S. airline industry.

John Keegan, 1934-2012, (Br.) war historian; *The Face of Battle*.

George F. Kennan, 1904-2005, (U.S.) diplomat, historian; main architect of U.S. Cold War "containment" strategy.

John Maynard Keynes, 1883-1946, (Br.) economist; principal advocate of deficit spending.

Alfred Kinsey, 1894-1956, (U.S.) zoologist; pioneering human sex researcher.

Russell Kirk, 1918-94, (U.S.) social philosopher; *The Conservative Mind*.

Alfred L. Kroeber, 1876-1960, (U.S.) cultural anthropologist; studied Indians of North and South America.

Elisabeth Kubler-Ross, 1926-2004, (Switz.) psychiatrist, author; *On Death and Dying*.

Christopher Lasch, 1932-94, (U.S.) social critic, historian; *The Culture of Narcissism*.

James L. Laughlin, 1850-1933, (U.S.) economist; helped establish Federal Reserve System.

Margaret Leech, 1893-1974, (U.S.) historian; *Reveille in Washington, 1860-1865*.

Lucien Lévy-Bruhl, 1857-1939, (Fr.) philosopher; studied the psychology of primitive societies; *Primitive Mentality*.

John Locke, 1632-1704, (Eng.) philosopher, political theorist; *Two Treatises of Government*.

Thomas B. Macaulay, 1800-59, (Br.) historian, statesman.

Niccolò Machiavelli, 1469-1527, (It.) writer, statesman; *The Prince*.

Bronislaw Malinowski, 1884-1942, (Pol.) considered the father of social anthropology.

Thomas R. Malthus, 1766-1834, (Br.) economist; *Essay on the Principle of Population*.

Horace Mann, 1796-1859, (U.S.) pioneered modern public school system.

Karl Mannheim, 1893-1947, (Hung.) sociologist, historian; *Ideology and Utopia*.

Harriet Martineau, 1802-76, (Eng.) writer, feminist; *Society in America*.

Karl Marx, 1818-83, (Ger.) political theorist, proponent of Communism; *Communist Manifesto*, *Das Kapital*.

Benjamin Mays, 1895-1984, (U.S.) minister, educator, civil rights leader; headed Morehouse College, 1940-67.

Giuseppe Mazzini, 1805-72, (It.) political philosopher.

William H. McGuffey, 1800-73, (U.S.) his *Reader* was a mainstay of 19th-cent. U.S. public education.

George H. Mead, 1863-1931, (U.S.) philosopher, social psychologist.

Margaret Mead, 1901-78, (U.S.) cultural anthropologist; popularized field; *Coming of Age in Samoa*.

Alexander Meiklejohn, 1872-1964, (U.S.) Br.-born educator; championed academic freedom and experimental curricula.

James Mill, 1773-1836, (Scot.) philosopher, historian, economist; a proponent of utilitarianism.

John Stuart Mill, 1806-73, (Eng.) philosopher, economist; *Utilitarianism*. Eldest son of James Mill.

Perry G. Miller, 1905-63, (U.S.) historian; interpreted 17th-cent. New England.

Theodor Mommsen, 1817-1903, (Ger.) historian; *The History of Rome*.

Ashley Montagu, 1905-99, (Eng.) anthropologist; *The Natural Superiority of Women*.

Charles-Louis Montesquieu, 1689-1755, (Fr.) social philosopher; *The Spirit of Laws*.

Maria Montessori, 1870-1952, (It.) educator, physician; started Montessori method of student self-motivation.

Samuel Eliot Morison, 1887-1976, (U.S.) historian; chronicled voyages of early explorers.

Lewis Mumford, 1895-1990, (U.S.) sociologist, critic; *The Culture of Cities*.

Gunnar Myrdal, 1898-1987, (Swed.) economist, social scientist; *Asian Drama: An Inquiry Into the Poverty of Nations*.

Allan Nevins, 1890-1971, (U.S.) historian, biographer; *The Ordeal of the Union*.

José Ortega y Gasset, 1883-1955, (Sp.) philosopher; advocated control by elite; *The Revolt of the Masses*.

Elinor Ostrom, 1933-2012, (U.S.) political economist.

Robert Owen, 1771-1858, (Br.) political philosopher, reformer; pioneer in cooperative movement.

Thomas Paine, 1737-1809, (Br.-U.S.) political theorist, writer; *Common Sense*.

Vilfredo Pareto, 1848-1923, (It.) economist, sociologist.

Francis Parkman, 1823-93, (U.S.) historian; *France and England in North America*.

Elizabeth P. Peabody, 1804-94, (U.S.) education pioneer; founded first kindergarten in U.S., 1860.

William Prescott, 1796-1859, (U.S.) early American historian; *The Conquest of Peru*.

Pierre Joseph Proudhon, 1809-65, (Fr.) social theorist; father of anarchism; *The Philosophy of Property*.

François Quesnay, 1694-1774, (Fr.) economic theorist.

Robert V. Remini, 1921-2013, (U.S.) historian; *The Life of Andrew Jackson*.

David Ricardo, 1772-1823, (Br.) economic theorist; advocated free international trade.

David Riesman, 1909-2002, (U.S.) sociologist; co-author, *The Lonely Crowd*.

Jacqueline de Romilly, 1913-2010, (Fr.) scholar of Greek civilization and language.

Theodore Roszak, 1933-2011, (U.S.) historian; *The Making of a Counter Culture*.

Jean-Jacques Rousseau, 1712-78, (Fr.) social philosopher; the father of romantic sensibility; *Confessions*.

Paul Samuelson, 1915-2009, (U.S.) economist, famed for modern mathematical approach to economics.

Edward Sapir, 1884-1939, (Ger.-U.S.) anthropologist; studied ethnology and linguistics of U.S. Indian groups.

Ferdinand de Saussure, 1857-1913, (Switz.) a founder of modern linguistics.

Arthur Schlesinger Jr., 1917-2007, (U.S.) historian, author; *The Imperial Presidency*.

Joseph Schumpeter, 1883-1950, (Czech.-U.S.) economist, sociologist.

Elizabeth Seton, 1774-1821, (U.S.) nun; est. parochial school education in U.S., first native-born American saint.

Georg Simmel, 1858-1918, (Ger.) sociologist, philosopher; helped establish German sociology.

Robert Sklar, 1936-2011, (U.S.) film scholar.

Adam Smith, 1723-90, (Br.) economist; advocated laissez-faire economy, free trade; *The Wealth of Nations*.

Jared Sparks, 1789-1866, (U.S.) historian, educator, editor; *The Library of American Biography*.

Oswald Spengler, 1880-1936, (Ger.) philosopher, historian; *The Decline of the West*.

Leo Steinberg, 1920-2011, (Russ.-U.S.) art historian.

William G. Sumner, 1840-1910, (U.S.) social scientist, economist; laissez-faire economy, Social Darwinism.

Hippolyte Taine, 1828-93, (Fr.) historian, basis of naturalistic school; *The Origins of Contemporary France*.

A(lan) J(ohn) P(ercivale) Taylor, 1906-90, (Br.) historian; *The Origins of the Second World War*.

Nikolaas Tinbergen, 1907-88, (Neth.-Br.) ethologist; pioneer in study of animal behavior.

Alexis de Tocqueville, 1805-59, (Fr.) political scientist, historian; *Democracy in America*.

Francis E. Townsend, 1867-1960, (U.S.) led old-age pension movement, 1933.

Arnold Toynbee, 1889-1975, (Br.) historian; *A Study of History*, sweeping analysis of hist. of civilizations.

George Trevelyan, 1876-1962, (Br.) historian, statesman. Favored "literary" over "scientific" history; *History of England*.

Henri Troyat, 1911-2007, (Russ.-Fr.), biographies of major figures in Russian history.

Frederick J. Turner, 1861-1932, (U.S.) historian, educator; *The Frontier in American History*.

Thorstein B. Veblen, 1857-1929, (U.S.) economist, social philosopher; *The Theory of the Leisure Class*.

Giovanni Vico, 1668-1744, (It.) historian, biographer; regarded by many as first modern historian; *New Science*.

Izaak Walton, 1593-1683, (Eng.) biographer; political-philosophical study of fishing, *The Compleat Angler*.

Booker T. Washington, 1856-1915, (U.S.) founder, 1881, and first pres. of Tuskegee Institute; *Up From Slavery*.

Sidney J., 1859-1947, and **Beatrice Webb**, 1858-1943, (both Br.) leading figures in Fabian Society and Labor Party.

Max Weber, 1864-1920, (Ger.) sociologist; *The Protestant Ethic and the Spirit of Capitalism*.

Walter White, 1893-1955, (U.S.) exec. sec., NAACP, 1931-55.

Roy Wilkins, 1901-81, (U.S.) exec. director, NAACP, 1955-77.

Emma Hart Willard, 1787-1870, (U.S.) pioneered higher education for women.

James Q. Wilson, 1931-2012, (U.S.) political scientist; co-authored broken windows theory.

Carter G. Woodson, 1875-1950, (U.S.) historian; founded Assn. for the Study of Negro Life and History.

C. Vann Woodward, 1908-99, (U.S.) historian; *The Strange Career of Jim Crow*.

Howard Zinn, 1922-2010, (U.S.) historian; *A People's History of the United States*.

American Journalists of the Past

Reviewed by Dean Mills, Dean, Missouri School of Journalism.

See also Business Leaders and Philanthropists, American Cartoonists, and Writers of the Past.

Franklin P. Adams (F.P.A.), 1881-1960, humorist; wrote column "The Conning Tower."

Joseph W. Alsop, 1910-89, and **Stewart Alsop**, 1914-74, Washington-based political analysts, columnists.

Jack Anderson, 1922-2006, muckraking Washington, DC, syndicated columnist.

Brooks Atkinson, 1894-1984, theater critic.

Robert L. Bartley, 1937-2003, editorial-page editor for *Wall Street Journal*.

James Gordon Bennett, 1795-1872, editor and publisher; founded *NY Herald*.

James Gordon Bennett, 1841-1918, succeeded father, financed expeditions, founded afternoon paper.

Nellie Bly (Elizabeth Cochrane), 1867-1922, pioneer woman journalist, investigative reporter; noted for series on trip around the world.

Elias Boudinot, c. 1803-39, founding editor of first Native American newspaper in U.S., *Cherokee Phoenix* (1828-34).

Ed Bradley, 1941-2006, TV journalist (*60 Minutes*); one of the first African American journalists to report on the Vietnam War.

Andrew Breitbart, 1969-2012, conservative commentator and blogger.

David Brinkley, 1920-2003, co-anchor of NBC's *Huntley-Brinkley Report*, host of ABC's *This Week With David Brinkley*.

Arthur Brisbane, 1864-1936, editor; helped introduce "yellow journalism" with sensational, simply written articles.

David Broder, 1929-2011, political journalist for *The Washington Post*.

Joyce Brothers, 1927-2013, psychologist, columnist.

Heywood Broun, 1888-1939, author, columnist; founded American Newspaper Guild.

Helen Gurley Brown, 1922-2012, author; editor-in-chief of *Cosmopolitan* magazine (1965-97).

Art Buchwald, 1925-2007, journalist, humorist, syndicated columnist.

William F. Buckley Jr., 1925-2008, columnist and commentator; founder of *National Review*.

Herb Caen, 1916-97, longtime columnist for *San Francisco Chronicle* and *Examiner*.

John Campbell, 1653-1728, published *Boston News-Letter*, first continuing newspaper in the American colonies.

Jimmy Cannon, 1909-73, syndicated sports columnist.

John Chancellor, 1927-96, NBC reporter, anchor.

Harry Chandler, 1864-1944, *Los Angeles Times* publisher (1917-41); made it a dominant force.

Otis Chandler, 1928-2006, *Los Angeles Times* publisher (1960-80).

Marquis Childs, 1903-90, reporter and columnist for *St. Louis Post-Dispatch* and United Feature syndicate.

Craig Claiborne, 1920-2000, *NY Times* food editor and critic; key in internationalizing American tastes.

Alexander Cockburn, 1941-2012, left-wing journalist.

Charles Collingwood, 1917-85, CBS news correspondent.

Alistair Cooke, 1908-2004, journalist, TV narrator; naturalized American citizen, "Letter From America" series.

Howard Cosell, 1920-95, TV and radio sportscaster.

Gardner Cowles, 1861-1946, founded newspaper chain.

Judith Crist, 1922-2012, film critic.

Walter Cronkite, 1916-2009, CBS evening news anchor, TV journalist.

Evelyn Cunningham, 1916-2010, African American civil rights reporter.

Cyrus Curtis, 1850-1933, publisher of *Saturday Evening Post*, *Ladies' Home Journal*, *Country Gentleman*.

John Charles Daly, 1914-91, war correspondent, TV journalist; Voice of America head.

Charles Anderson Dana, 1819-97, editor, publisher; made *NY Sun* famous for its news reporting.

Elmer (Holmes) Davis, 1890-1958, *NY Times* editorial writer, radio commentator.

Richard Harding Davis, 1864-1916, war correspondent, travel writer, fiction writer.

Benjamin Day, 1810-89, published *NY Sun* beginning in 1833, introducing penny press to the U.S.

Dorothy Dix (Elizabeth Meriwether Gilmer), 1861-1951, reporter; pioneer of the advice column genre.

Finley Peter Dunne, 1867-1936, humorist, social critic; wrote "Mr. Dooley" columns.

Roger Ebert, 1942-2013, film critic.

Mary Baker Eddy, 1821-1910, founded Christian Science movement and *Christian Science Monitor*.

Rowland Evans Jr., 1921-2001, Washington columnist.

Fanny Fern (Sara Willis Parton), 1811-72, newspaper columnist, author.

Marshall Field III, 1893-1956, retail magnate, *Chicago Sun* founder.

Doris Fleeson, 1901-70, war correspondent, columnist.

Benjamin Franklin, 1706-90, publisher of *Poor Richard's Almanack*.

James Franklin, 1697-1735, printer, pioneer journalist; publisher of *New England Courant* and *Rhode Island Gazette*.

Fred W. Friendly, 1915-98, radio, TV reporter, producer, executive; collaborator with Edward R. Murrow.

Margaret Fuller, 1810-50, social reformer, transcendentalist, critic and foreign correspondent for *NY Tribune*.

Frank E. Gannett, 1876-1957, founded newspaper chain.

Mary Ellen Garber, 1916-2008, sports journalist.

William Lloyd Garrison, 1805-79, abolitionist; publisher of *The Liberator*.

Jack Germond, 1928-2013, political reporter.

Edwin Lawrence Godkin, 1831-1902, founder of *The Nation*, editor of *NY Evening Post*.

Katharine Graham, 1917-2001, *Washington Post* publisher.

Sheilah Graham, 1904-89, Hollywood gossip columnist.

Horace Greeley, 1811-72, editor, politician; founded *NY Tribune*.

Meg Greenfield, 1930-99, *Newsweek* columnist, *Washington Post* editorial page editor.

Gilbert Hovey Grosvenor, 1875-1966, longtime editor of *National Geographic* magazine.

John Gunther, 1901-70, *Chicago Daily News* foreign correspondent, author.

David Halberstam, 1934-2007, journalist, sports reporter, author; *The Best and the Brightest*, *Summer of '49*.

2014 YEAR IN PICTURES

Deadly Landslide A hill collapse Mar. 22, 2014, sent a landslide of mud and debris nearly a mile wide surging near Oso, WA, killing 43 people.

Ferguson Protests The fatal police shooting Aug. 9, 2014, of an unarmed 18-year-old black man sparked large-scale protests in Ferguson, MO, in which demonstrators often clashed with police.

Migration Spikes The Dept. of Homeland Security reported that more than 52,000 unaccompanied children, most from Honduras, Guatemala, and El Salvador, had been caught crossing the U.S.-Mexico border Oct. 1, 2013-June 15, 2014.

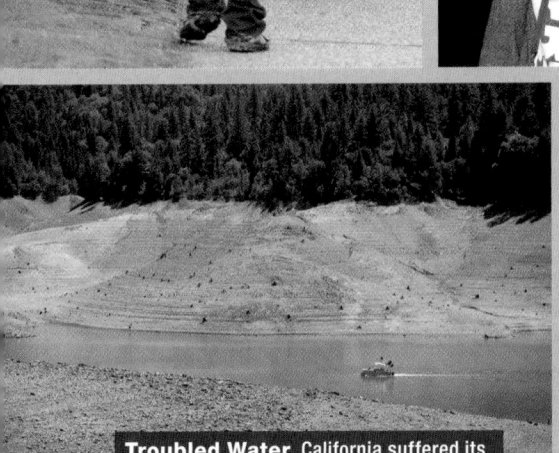

Prisoner Swap U.S. Army Sgt. Bowe Bergdahl, a five-year captive of a Pakistani group linked to the Taliban, was released May 31, 2014, as part of a prisoner exchange that sent five Guantánamo Bay detainees to Qatar.

Troubled Water California suffered its third year of severe drought conditions in 2014, depleting water resources statewide.

Green Wednesday Colorado opened legal marijuana retail stores Jan. 1, 2014; on the basis of ballot initiatives passed in 2012, Colorado and Washington were the first states to decriminalize recreational marijuana use.

Total Recalls In the wake of crashes linked to 21 deaths, U.S. automaker General Motors issued more than 50 vehicle recalls in 2014, affecting 26 mil vehicles; GM CEO Mary Barra testified before Congress Apr. 1-2.

Hobby Lobby The U.S. Supreme Court ruled, June 30, 2014, that some closely held corporations could claim a religious exemption to a federal health care regulation that mandated contraception coverage.

Rule Change The Environmental Protection Agency proposed new power plant emission rules June 2, 2014, which seek to reduce carbon emissions but threaten the survival of the nation's 557 coal-fired power plants.

195

Chairwoman of the Board Janet Yellen was sworn in as chair of the Federal Reserve Board Feb. 3, 2014; she was the first woman ever to hold the powerful financial post.

Spies Spied Central Intelligence Agency Director John Brennan apologized July 31, 2014, when an agency inquiry found that the CIA had improperly searched Senate Intelligence Committee files.

VA in Crisis Dept. of Veterans Affairs Sec. Eric Shinseki resigned May 30, 2014, following revelations that the Phoenix, AZ, VA health care system routinely covered up lengthy waiting periods that prevented patients from receiving timely care.

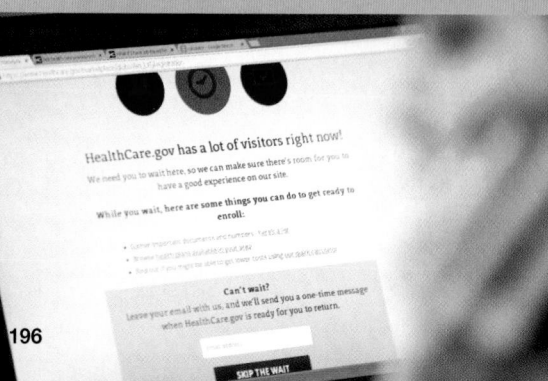

HealthCare.gov has a lot of visitors right now!

We need you to wait here, so we can make sure there's room for you to have a good experience on our site.

While you wait, here are some things you can do to get ready to enroll:

Can't wait?
Leave your email with us, and we'll send you a one-time message when HealthCare.gov is ready for you to return.

SKIP THE WAIT

Signing Up In spite of the troubled launch of health insurance marketplaces mandated by the Affordable Care Act, the Obama administration announced Apr. 17, 2014, that 8 mil people had enrolled in new private insurance plans.

Bridgegate In documents published Jan. 8, 2014, officials in the administration of New Jersey Gov. Chris Christie (R) appeared to orchestrate massive traffic gridlock as political retribution. Christie apologized Jan. 9, claiming no prior knowledge of the actions.

Leadership Upset Eric Cantor (R, VA) became the first sitting House majority leader ever to lose a primary June 10, 2014.

Balance of Power Republicans hoped to emerge from 2014 midterm elections with a Senate majority. Among those senators seeking reelection was Minority Leader Mitch McConnell (R, KY), who was challenged by Kentucky Sec. of State Alison Lundergan Grimes (D).

>WORLD

ISIS Offensive Islamic State in Iraq and Syria (ISIS) made territorial gains throughout 2014 and declared an Islamic "caliphate."

Afghanistan in Transition Afghan Pres. Ashraf Ghani Ahmadzai (right) and chief executive Abdullah Abdullah (left) were sworn in Sept. 29, 2014; the pair represented the first democratic transfer of power in Afghanistan since the Taliban regime was toppled in 2001.

Conflict in Ukraine Pro-Russian separatists deployed as militias in eastern Ukrainian cities beginning in Apr. 2014, reportedly aided by Russian military resources.

Fleeing Violence ISIS's offensive in northern Iraq forced tens of thousands of Yazidis, Christians, and other minorities to flee their homes in Aug. 2014.

Bring Back Our Girls Terrorist group Boko Haram kidnapped 276 girls from a Nigerian school Apr. 14, 2014; a campaign to save them went viral, but most of the girls remained missing months later.

Civil Disobedience Thousands of pro-democracy activists took to the streets in Hong Kong Sept.-Oct. 2014 to demand reforms in China's semi-autonomous former British colony.

Ebola Outbreak The Ebola outbreak had killed more than 3,000 in West Africa as of Oct. 2, 2014; World Health Organization officials believed the outbreak could exceed 20,000 cases.

Humanitarian Crisis The UN refugee agency estimated in Aug. 2014 that there were nearly 3 mil Syrian refugees in neighboring nations and 6.5 mil displaced in Syria.

50-Day War More than 2,200 died in the summer conflict between Israel and Gaza before a lasting cease-fire was agreed to Aug. 26, 2014.

>WORLD

Thai Coup A military coup in Thailand May 22, 2014, was the latest development in the country's political crisis; many demonstrators ignored Gen. Prayuth Chan-ocha's warning against participating in anti-coup protests.

President Jokowi Populist Jakarta Gov. Joko Widodo was declared the winner of Indonesia's presidential election July 22, 2014.

***Sewol* Sinks** The *Sewol*, a ferry en route to a resort island off the South Korean coast, capsized Apr. 16, 2014, killing at least 300 people, most of them high school students.

Lost Flight Malaysia Airlines Flight 370 disappeared Mar. 8, 2014, with 239 people aboard; a search aided by 26 nations had still turned up no sign of the flight six months later.

Democracy in Action More than 550 mil votes were cast Apr.-May 2014 in India's parliamentary elections; the opposition Bharatiya Janata Party won a large majority.

Sarah Josepha Buell Hale, 1788-1879, first female magazine editor; *Ladies' Magazine*, later *Godey's Lady's Book*.

Paul Harvey, 1918-2009, radio broadcaster and commentator.

William Randolph Hearst, 1863-1951, founder of Hearst newspaper chain, one of the pioneers of yellow journalism.

Gabriel Heatter, 1890-1972, radio commentator.

John Hersey, 1914-98, foreign correspondent for *Time*, *Life*, and *The New Yorker*; author.

Marguerite Higgins, 1920-66, reporter, war correspondent.

Christopher Hitchens, 1949-2011, columnist and literary critic.

Hedda Hopper, 1885-1966, Hollywood gossip columnist.

Roy Howard, 1883-1964, editor, executive; Scripps-Howard papers and United Press (later United Press International).

Chet (Chester Robert) Huntley), 1911-74, co-anchor of NBC's *Huntley-Brinkley Report*.

Ada Louise Huxtable, 1921-2013, architecture critic.

Ralph Ingersoll, 1900-85, editor; *Fortune*, *Time*, *Life* exec.

Molly Ivins, 1944-2007, author, syndicated political columnist.

Peter Jennings, 1938-2005, ABC correspondent, anchor.

Pauline Kael, 1919-2001, film critic.

H. V. (Hans von) Kaltenborn, 1878-1965, radio commentator, reporter.

Murray Kempton, 1917-97, reporter, columnist for magazines and newspapers, including *NY Post*.

Dorothy Kilgallen, 1913-65, crime reporter, columnist.

James J. Kilpatrick, 1920-2010, political columnist, author and television personality.

John S. Knight, 1894-1981, editor, publisher; founded Knight newspaper group, which merged into Knight-Ridder.

Joseph Kraft, 1942-86, foreign policy columnist.

Irving Kristol, 1920-2009, columnist, commentator.

Arthur Krock, 1886-1974, *NY Times* political writer, Washington bureau chief.

Charles Kuralt, 1934-97, TV anchor; host of CBS "On the Road" featuring stories about life in the U.S.

Ann Landers (Eppie Lederer), 1918-2002, advice columnist.

David Lawrence, 1888-1973, reporter, columnist, publisher; founded *U.S. News & World Report*.

Frank Leslie, 1821-80, engraver, publisher of newspapers and magazines, notably *Leslie's Illustrated Newspaper*.

Anthony Lewis, 1927-2013, legal journalist.

Alexander Liberman, 1912-99, editorial director for Condé Nast magazines.

A(bbott) J(oseph) Liebling, 1904-63, foreign correspondent, critic; principally with *The New Yorker*.

Walter Lippmann, 1889-1974, political analyst, social critic, columnist, author.

Peter Lisagor, 1915-76, Washington bureau chief, *Chicago Daily News*; broadcast commentator.

David Ross Locke, 1833-88, humorist, satirist under pseudonym P.V. Nasby; owned *Toledo (Ohio) Blade*.

Elijah Parish Lovejoy, 1802-37, abolitionist editor in St. Louis and in Alton, IL; killed by proslavery mob.

Clare Booth Luce, 1903-87, war correspondent for *Life*, diplomat, playwright.

Henry R. Luce, 1898-1967, founded *Time*, *Fortune*, *Life*, *Sports Illustrated*.

Dwight Macdonald, 1906-82, reporter, social critic.

Don Marquis, 1878-1937, humor columnist for *NY Sun* and *NY Tribune*; wrote "Archy and Mehitabel" stories.

Nancy Hicks Maynard, 1946-2008, African American publisher, journalist.

Robert Maynard, 1937-97, first African American editor and then owner of major U.S. paper, the *Oakland Tribune*.

C(harles) K(enny) McClatchy, 1858-1936, founder of McClatchy newspaper chain.

Sarah McClendon, 1910-2003, veteran White House correspondent.

Samuel McClure, 1857-1949, founder (1893) of *McClure's Magazine*, famous for its investigative reporting.

Anne O'Hare McCormick, 1889-1954, foreign correspondent; first woman on *NY Times* editorial board.

Robert R. McCormick, 1880-1955, editor, publisher, executive of *Chicago Tribune* and *NY Daily News*.

Ralph McGill, 1893-1969, crusading editor, publisher of *Atlanta Constitution*.

Mary McGrory, 1918-2004, Washington columnist.

O(scar) O(dd) McIntyre, 1884-1938, feature writer, syndicated columnist on everyday life in New York City.

Joseph Medill, 1823-99, longtime editor of the *Chicago Tribune*.

H(enry) L(ouis) Mencken, 1880-1956, reporter, editor, columnist with *Baltimore Sun* papers; anti-establishment viewpoint.

Edwin Meredith, 1876-1928, founder of magazine company.

Frank A. Munsey, 1854-1925, owner, editor, and publisher of newspapers and magazines, including *Munsey's Magazine*.

Edward R. Murrow, 1908-65, broadcast reporter, executive; reported from Britain in WWII; hosted *See It Now*, *Person to Person*.

Allen Neuharth, 1924-2013, *USA Today* founder.

Edwin Newman, 1919-2010, NBC news correspondent.

Louella Parsons, 1881-1972, Hollywood gossip columnist.

Ethel L. Payne, 1911-91, African American civil rights reporter.

Daniel Pearl, 1963-2002, American journalist; kidnapped and murdered in Pakistan.

Drew (Andrew Russell) Pearson, 1897-1969, investigative reporter, columnist.

(James) Westbrook Pegler, 1894-1969, reporter, columnist.

Shirley Povich, 1905-98, sports columnist.

Joseph Pulitzer, 1847-1911, *NY World* publisher; founded Columbia Journalism School, Pulitzer Prizes.

Joseph Pulitzer II, 1885-1955, longtime *St. Louis Post-Dispatch* editor, publisher; built it into major paper.

Ernie Pyle, 1900-45, reporter, war correspondent; killed in WWII.

William Raspberry, 1935-2012, public affairs columnist.

Henry Raymond, 1820-69, cofounder, editor, *NY Times*.

Harry Reasoner, 1923-91, ABC and CBS news reporter, anchor.

John Reed, 1887-1920, reporter; foreign correspondent famous for coverage of Bolshevik Revolution; buried at the Kremlin.

Whitelaw Reid, 1837-1912, longtime editor, *NY Tribune*.

James Reston, 1909-95, *NY Times* political reporter, columnist.

Frank Reynolds, 1923-83, ABC reporter, anchor.

(Henry) Grantland Rice, 1880-1954, sportswriter.

Jacob Riis, 1849-1914, reporter, photographer; exposed slum conditions in *How the Other Half Lives*.

Max Robinson, 1939-88, first African American to anchor network news (ABC), 1978.

Andy Rooney, 1919-2011, radio and TV commentator (*60 Minutes*).

A. M. Rosenthal, 1922-2006, reporter, editor for *NY Times* (1943-99).

Harold Ross, 1892-1951, founder, editor, *The New Yorker*.

Carl T. Rowan, 1925-2000, reporter, columnist, author.

Mike Royko, 1932-97, Chicago newspaper columnist; wrote *Boss*, biography of Mayor Richard J. Daley (1902-76).

Louis Rukeyser, 1933-2006, TV journalist, financial analyst; hosted *Wall Street Week* on public television.

(Alfred) Damon Runyon, 1884-1946, sportswriter, columnist; stories collected in *Guys and Dolls*.

Tim Russert, 1950-2008, TV journalist; moderator of *Meet the Press* (NBC).

John B. Russwurm, 1799-1851, cofounded (1827) nation's first black newspaper, *Freedom's Journal*, in New York, NY.

William Safire, 1929-2009, Pulitzer Prize-winning columnist, *NY Times*.

Adela Rogers St. Johns, 1894-1988, reporter, sportswriter for Hearst newspapers.

Pierre Salinger, 1925-2004, press sec. under Pres. Kennedy and Johnson, foreign correspondent.

Harrison Salisbury, 1908-93, reporter, foreign correspondent; Soviet specialist.

Andrew Sarris, 1928-2012, film critic, *Village Voice*.

Daniel Schorr, 1916-2010, broadcast and print journalist.

E(dward) W(illis) Scripps, 1854-1926, founded first large U.S. newspaper chain, pioneered syndication.

Eric Sevareid, 1912-92, war correspondent, radio newscaster, CBS commentator.

Anthony Shadid, 1968-2012, foreign correspondent.

Randy Shilts, 1951-94, journalist; author of *And the Band Played On*.

William L. Shirer, 1904-93, broadcaster, foreign correspondent; wrote *The Rise and Fall of the Third Reich*.

Howard K. Smith, 1914-2002, ABC news reporter, anchor.

Red (Walter) Smith, 1905-82, sportswriter.

Edgar P. Snow, 1905-71, correspondent; expert on Chinese Communist movement.

Tony Snow, 1955-2008, columnist, radio/TV journalist, White House press sec.

Tom Snyder, 1936-2007, television journalist.

Lawrence Spivak, 1900-94, co-creator, moderator, producer of *Meet the Press*.

(Joseph) Lincoln Steffens, 1866-1936, muckraking journalist.

I(sidor) F(einstein) Stone, 1907-89, one-man editor of *I. F. Stone's Weekly*.

Arthur Hays Sulzberger, 1891-1968, long-time publisher of *NY Times* (1935-61).

Arthur Ochs "Punch" Sulzberger, 1926-2012, long-time publisher of *NY Times* (1963-92).

C(yrus) L(eo) Sulzberger, 1912-93, *NY Times* foreign correspondent, columnist.

David Susskind, 1920-87, TV producer, public affairs talk-show host (*Open End*).

John Cameron Swayze, 1906-95, early TV newscaster (NBC).

Herbert Bayard Swope, 1882-1958, war correspondent, editor of *NY World*.

Ida Tarbell, 1857-1944, muckraking journalist.

Helen Thomas, 1920-2013, White House correspondent, 1959-2010.

Isaiah Thomas, 1750-1831, printer, publisher; cofounder of revolutionary journal, *Massachusetts Spy*.

Lowell Thomas, 1892-1981, radio newscaster, world traveler.

Dorothy Thompson, 1894-1961, foreign correspondent, columnist, radio commentator.

Hunter S. Thompson, 1937-2005, political journalist, author; *Fear and Loathing on the Campaign Trail* (1972).

Kenneth Thompson, 1923-2006, Canadian media magnate; owned Toronto *Globe and Mail* newspapers.

Abigail Van Buren (Pauline Phillips), 1918-2013, advice columnist.

Mike Wallace, 1918-2012, TV journalist (*60 Minutes*).

Ida Bell Wells-Barnett, 1862-1931, African American reporter, editor, anti-lynching crusader.

William Allen White, 1868-1944, newspaper editor, publisher.

Tom Wicker, 1926-2011, *NY Times* political reporter, columnist.

Walter Winchell, 1897-1972, reporter, columnist, broadcaster of celebrity news.

John Peter Zenger, 1697-1746, printer, journalist; acquitted in precedent-setting libel suit (1735).

Military and Naval Leaders of the Past

Reviewed by Alan C. Aimone, U.S. Military Academy Library.

Alexander the Great, 356-323 BCE, (Maced.) conquered Persia and much of the world known to Europeans.

Harold Alexander, 1891-1969, (Br.) led Allied invasion of Italy, 1943, WWII.

Ethan Allen, 1738-89, (U.S.) headed Green Mountain Boys; captured Ft. Ticonderoga, 1775, Amer. Rev.

Edmund Allenby, 1861-1936, (Br.) in Boer War, WWI; led Egyptian expeditionary force, 1917-18.

Benedict Arnold, 1741-1801, (U.S.) victorious at Saratoga; tried to betray West Point to British, Amer. Rev.

Henry "Hap" Arnold, 1886-1950, (U.S.) commanded Army Air Force in WWII.

Ashurnasirpal II, 884-859 BCE, (Assyria) king; began Assyrian conquest of Middle East.

John Barry, 1745-1803, (U.S.) won numerous sea battles during Amer. Rev.

Pierre Beauregard, 1818-93, (U.S.) Confed. general; ordered bombardment of Ft. Sumter that began Civil War.

Belisarius, c. 505-565, (Byzant.) won remarkable victories for Byzantine emperor Justinian I.

Gebhard von Blücher, 1742-1819, (Ger.) helped defeat Napoleon at Waterloo.

Simón Bolívar, 1783-1830, (Venez.) S. Amer. revolutionary who liberated much of the continent from Spanish rule.

Napoleon Bonaparte, 1769-1821, (Fr.) defeated Russia and Austria at Austerlitz, 1805; invaded Russia, 1812; defeated at Waterloo, 1815.

Edward Braddock, 1695-1755, (Br.) commanded forces in French and Indian War.

Omar N. Bradley, 1893-1981, (U.S.) headed U.S. ground troops in Normandy invasion, 1944, WWII.

John Burgoyne, 1722-92, (Br.) general; defeated at Saratoga, Amer. Rev.

Julius Caesar, 100-44 BCE, (Rom.) general and politician; conquered northern Gaul, overthrew Roman Republic.

Charlemagne, 742-814, (Fr.) king of the Franks, Holy Roman Emperor; conquered most of Western Europe.

Claire Lee Chennault, 1893-1958, (U.S.) headed Flying Tigers in WWII.

El Cid (Rodrigo Díaz de Vivar), 1040-99, (Sp.) renowned knight; captured Valencia (1094), hero of "Song of Cid" epic.

Mark W. Clark, 1896-1984, (U.S.) helped plan N African invasion in WWII; commander of UN forces, Korean War.

Karl von Clausewitz, 1780-1831, (Prus.) military theorist.

Lucius D. Clay, 1897-1978, (U.S.) led Berlin airlift, 1948-49.

Henry Clinton, 1738-95, (Br.) commander of forces in Amer. Rev., 1778-81.

Cochise, c. 1815-74, (Amer. Ind.) chief of Chiricahua band of Apache Indians in Southwest U.S.

Charles Cornwallis, 1738-1805, (Br.) victorious at Brandywine, 1777; surrendered at Yorktown, Amer. Rev.

Hernán Cortés, 1485-1547, (Sp.) led Spanish conquistadors in the defeat of the Aztec empire, 1519-28.

Crazy Horse, 1849-77, (Amer. Ind.) Sioux war chief victorious at Battle of Little Bighorn.

George Armstrong Custer, 1839-76, (U.S.) army officer defeated and killed at Battle of Little Bighorn.

Benjamin O. Davis Jr., 1912-2002, (U.S.) leader of WWII black aviators; first African American general in U.S. Air Force.

Benjamin O. Davis Sr., 1877-1970, (U.S.) first African American general in U.S. Army, 1940.

Moshe Dayan, 1915-81, (Isr.) directed campaigns in the 1967, 1973 Arab-Israeli wars.

Stephen Decatur, 1779-1820, (U.S.) naval hero of Barbary wars, War of 1812.

Anton Denikin, 1872-1947, (Russ.) led White forces in Russian civil war.

George Dewey, 1837-1917, (U.S.) destroyed Spanish fleet at Manila, 1898, Span.-Amer. War.

Karl Doenitz, 1891-1980, (Ger.) submarine cmdr. in chief and naval cmdr., WWII; last pres. of Third Reich.

Jimmy Doolittle, 1896-1993, (U.S.) led 1942 air raid on Tokyo and other Japanese cities in WWII.

Hugh Dowding, 1882-1970, (Br.) headed RAF Fighter Command, 1936-40, WWII.

Jubal Early, 1816-94, (U.S.) Confed. general; led raid on Washington, DC, 1864, Civil War.

Dwight D. Eisenhower, 1890-1969, (U.S.) commanded Allied forces in Europe, WWII.

Erich von Falkenhayn, 1861-1922, (Ger.) minister of war, general, commander at Verdun in WWI.

David Farragut, 1801-70, (U.S.) Union admiral; captured New Orleans, Mobile Bay, Civil War.

John Arbuthnot Fisher, 1841-1920, (Br.) WWI admiral; naval reformer.

Ferdinand Foch, 1851-1929, (Fr.) headed victorious Allied armies, 1918, WWI.

Nathan Bedford Forrest, 1821-77, (U.S.) Confed. general; led raids against Union supply lines, Civil War.

Frederick the Great, 1712-86, (Prus.) led Prussia in Seven Years' War.

Horatio Gates, 1728-1806, (U.S.) commanded army at Saratoga, Amer. Rev.

Genghis Khan, 1162-1227, (Mongol) unified Mongol tribes, subjugated much of Asia, 1206-21.

Geronimo, 1829-1909, (Amer. Ind.) leader of Chiricahua band of Apache Indians.

Vo Nguyen Giap, 1911?-2013, (Viet.) commanded People's Army of Vietnam against U.S.

Charles G. Gordon, 1833-85, (Br.) led forces in China, Crimean War; killed at Khartoum.

Ulysses S. Grant, 1822-85, (U.S.) headed Union army, Civil War, 1864-65; forced Robert E. Lee's surrender, 1865.

Nathanael Greene, 1742-86, (U.S.) defeated British in Southern campaign, 1780-81, Amer. Rev.

Heinz Guderian, 1888-1954, (Ger.) tank theorist; led panzer forces in Poland, France, Russia, WWII.

Gustavus Adolphus, 1594-1632, (Swed.) king, military tactician, reformer; led forces in Thirty Years' War.

Douglas Haig, 1861-1928, (Br.) led British armies in France, 1915-18, WWI.

William F. Halsey, 1882-1959, (U.S.) defeated Japanese fleet at Leyte Gulf, 1944, WWII.

Hannibal, 247-183 BCE, (Carthage) invaded Rome, crossing Alps, in Second Punic War, 218-201 BCE.

Sir Arthur Travers Harris, 1895-1984, (Br.) led Britain's WWII bomber command.

Paul von Hindenburg, 1847-1934, (Ger.) chief of general staff, WWI; second pres. of Weimar Republic.

Richard Howe, 1726-99, (Br.) commanded navy in Amer. Rev., 1776-78; June 1 victory against French, 1794.

William Howe, 1729-1814, (Br.) commanded forces in Amer. Rev., 1776-78.

Isaac Hull, 1773-1843, (U.S.) sunk British frigate *Guerriere*, War of 1812.

Thomas "Stonewall" Jackson, 1824-63, (U.S.) Confed. general; led Shenandoah Valley campaign, Civil War.

Daniel James Jr., 1920-78, (U.S.) first black 4-star general, 1975; commander, N. American Air Defense Command.

Joseph Joffre, 1852-1931, (Fr.) headed Allied armies; won Battle of the Marne, 1914, WWI.

John Paul Jones, 1747-92, (U.S.) commanded *Bonhomme Richard* in victory over *Serapis*, Amer. Rev., 1779.

Chief Joseph, c. 1840-1904, (Amer. Ind.) chief of the Nez Percé; forced by U.S. army to retreat and surrender.

Stephen Kearny, 1794-1848, (U.S.) headed Army of the West in Mexican War.

Albert Kesselring, 1885-1960, (Ger.) field marshal who led the defense of Italy in WWII.

Ernest J. King, 1878-1956, (U.S.) key WWII naval strategist.

Horatio H. Kitchener, 1850-1916, (Br.) led forces in Boer War, victorious at Khartoum, organized army in WWI.

Henry Knox, 1750-1806, (U.S.) general in Amer. Rev.; first sec. of war under U.S. Constitution.

Lavrenti Kornilov, 1870-1918, (Russ.) commander-in-chief, 1917; led counterrevolutionary march on Petrograd.

Thaddeus Kosciusko, 1746-1817, (Pol.) aided Amer. Rev.

Walter Krueger, 1881-1967, (U.S.) led Sixth Army in WWII in Southwest Pacific.

Mikhail Kutuzov, 1745-1813, (Russ.) fought at Borodino, Napol. Wars, 1812; abandoned Moscow, forced French retreat.

Marquis de Lafayette, 1757-1834, (Fr.) fought in, secured French aid for Amer. Rev.

T(homas) E. Lawrence (of Arabia), 1888-1935, (Br.) organized revolt of Arabs against Turks in WWI.

William Daniel Leahy, 1875-1959, (U.S.) chief of staff to Pres. Roosevelt in WWII, Fleet Admiral.

Henry (Light-Horse Harry) Lee, 1756-1818, (U.S.) cavalry officer in Amer. Rev.

Robert E. Lee, 1807-70, (U.S.) Confed. general; defeated at Gettysburg, Civil War; surrendered to Grant, 1865.

Curtis LeMay, 1906-90, (U.S.) Air Force cmdr. in WWII, Korean War, Vietnam War.

Lyman Lemnitzer, 1899-1988, (U.S.) WWII hero; later general, chairman of Joint Chiefs of Staff.

James Longstreet, 1821-1904, (U.S.) aided Lee at Gettysburg, Civil War.

Erich Ludendorff, 1865-1937, (Ger.) general; victor at Tannenberg, WWI.

Douglas MacArthur, 1880-1964, (U.S.) commanded forces in SW Pacific in WWII; headed occupation forces in Japan, 1945-51; UN commander in Korean War.

Carl Gustaf Mannerheim, 1867-1951, (Fin.) army officer and pres. of Finland, 1944-46.

Erich von Manstein, 1887-1973, (Ger.) served WWI, WWII; planned invasion of France (1940); convicted of war crimes.

Francis Marion, 1733-95, (U.S.) led guerrilla actions in South Carolina during Amer. Rev.

Duke of Marlborough, 1650-1722, (Br.) led forces against Louis XIV in War of the Spanish Succession.

George C. Marshall, 1880-1959, (U.S.) chief of staff in WWII; authored Marshall Plan.

Maurice, Count of Nassau, 1567-1625, (Neth.) military innovator; led forces in Thirty Years' War.

George B. McClellan, 1826-85, (U.S.) Union general; commanded Army of the Potomac, 1861-62, Civil War.

George Meade, 1815-72, (U.S.) commanded Union forces at Gettysburg, Civil War.

Doris "Dorie" Miller, 1919-43, (U.S.) Navy hero of Pearl Harbor attack; first African American awarded Navy Cross.

Billy Mitchell, 1879-1936, (U.S.) WWI air-power advocate; court-martialed for insubordination, later indicated.

Helmuth von Moltke, 1800-91, (Ger.) victorious in Austro-Prussian, Franco-Prussian wars.

Louis de Montcalm, 1712-59, (Fr.) headed troops in Canada, French and Indian War; defeated at Quebec, 1759.

Bernard Law Montgomery, 1887-1976, (Br.) stopped German offensive at Alamein, 1942, WWII; helped plan Normandy invasion.

Daniel Morgan, 1736-1802, (U.S.) victorious at Cowpens, 1781, Amer. Rev.

Louis Mountbatten, 1900-79, (Br.) Supreme Allied Commander of SE Asia, 1943-46, WWII.

Joachim Murat, 1767-1815, (Fr.) led cavalry at Marengo, Austerlitz, and Jena, Napoleonic Wars.

Horatio Nelson, 1758-1805, (Br.) naval cmdr.; destroyed French fleet at Trafalgar.

Michel Ney, 1769-1815, (Fr.) commanded forces in Switz., Austria, Russ., Napoleonic Wars; defeated at Waterloo.

Chester Nimitz, 1885-1966, (U.S.) cmdr. of naval forces in Pacific in WWII.

George S. Patton, 1885-1945, (U.S.) led assault on Sicily, 1943, Third Army invasion of Europe, WWII.

Oliver Perry, 1785-1819, (U.S.) won Battle of Lake Erie in War of 1812.

John Pershing, 1860-1948, (U.S.) commanded Mexican border campaign, 1916; Amer. Expeditionary Force, WWI.

Henri Philippe Pétain, 1856-1951, (Fr.) defended Verdun, 1916; headed Vichy government in WWII.

George E. Pickett, 1825-75, (U.S.) Confed. general famed for "charge" at Gettysburg, Civil War.

Charles Portal, 1893-1971, (Br.) chief of staff, Royal Air Force, 1940-45; led in Battle of Britain.

Manfred Freiherr von Richthofen (Red Baron), 1892-1918, (Ger.) WWI flying ace, led elite fighter squadron.

Hyman Rickover, 1900-86, (U.S.) father of nuclear navy.

Matthew Bunker Ridgway, 1895-1993, (U.S.) commanded Allied ground forces in Korean War.

Erwin Rommel, 1891-1944, (Ger.) headed Afrika Korps, WWII.

Gerd von Rundstedt, 1875-1953, (Ger.) supreme cmdr. in West, 1942-45, WWII.

Saladin, 1138-93, (Kurdish Muslim) recaptured Jerusalem from Crusaders.

Aleksandr Samsonov, 1859-1914, (Russ.) led invasion of E Prussia, WWI; defeated at Tannenberg, 1914.

Antonio Lopez de Santa Anna, 1794-1876, (Mex.) defeated Texans at the Alamo; defeated in Mexican War.

Maurice, Count of Saxe, 1696-1750, (Fr.) general, noted tactician; War of Austrian Succession, War of Pol. Succession.

H. Norman Schwarzkopf, 1934-2012, (U.S.) army general; led Persian Gulf War, 1991.

Scipio Africanus the Elder, 234?-183 BCE, (Rom.) hero of Second Punic War; defeated Hannibal, invaded N Africa.

Winfield Scott, 1786-1866, (U.S.) hero of War of 1812; headed forces in Mexican War, took Mexico City.

Philip Sheridan, 1831-88, (U.S.) Union cavalry officer; headed Army of the Shenandoah, 1864-65, Civil War.

William T. Sherman, 1820-91, (U.S.) Union general; sacked Atlanta during "march to the sea," 1864, Civil War.

Sitting Bull, c. 1831-90, (Amer. Ind.) Hunkpapa Sioux chief; victorious at Battle of the Little Big Horn.

Carl Spaatz, 1891-1974, (U.S.) directed strategic bombing against Germany, later Japan, in WWII.

Raymond Spruance, 1886-1969, (U.S.) victorious at Midway Island, 1942, WWII.

Joseph W. Stilwell, 1883-1946, (U.S.) headed forces in the China, Burma, India theater in WWII.

J.E.B. Stuart, 1833-64, (U.S.) Confed. cavalry commander, Civil War.

Sun Tzu, 6th? cent. BCE, (China) general; author of *The Art of War*.

Aleksandr Suvorov, 1729-1800, (Russ.) commanded Allied Russian and Austrian armies, Russo-Turkish War.

Tamerlane, 1336-1405, (Turkoman Mongol) conqueror; established empire from India to Mediterranean Sea.

Tecumseh, 1768-1813, (Amer. Ind.) Shawnee chief; led Indian confederation opposing colonists.

George H. Thomas, 1816-70, (U.S.) saved Union army at Chattanooga, 1863; won at Nashville, 1864, Civil War.

Semyon Timoshenko, 1895-1970, (USSR) defended Moscow, Stalingrad, WWII; led winter offensive, 1942-43.

Alfred von Tirpitz, 1849-1930, (Ger.) responsible for submarine blockade in WWI.

Henri de la Tour d'Auvergne, Viscount of Turenne, 1611-75, (Fr.) marshal; Thirty Years' War, Fronde, War of Devolution.

Sebastien Le Prestre de Vauban, 1633-1707, (Fr.) innovative military engineer, theorist.

Jonathan M. Wainwright, 1883-1953, (U.S.) forced to surrender on Corregidor, Philippines, 1942, WWII.

George Washington, 1732-99, (U.S.) led Continental army, 1775-83, Amer. Rev.

Archibald Wavell, 1883-1950, (Br.) commanded forces in N and E Africa, SE Asia in WWII.

Anthony Wayne, 1745-96, (U.S.) captured Stony Point, NY, 1779, Amer. Rev.

Duke of Wellington, 1769-1852, (Br.) defeated Napoleon at Waterloo, 1815.

William Westmoreland, 1914-2005, (U.S.) commanded forces in Vietnam, 1964-68.

William I (The Conqueror), 1027-87, (Br.) victor, Battle of Hastings, 1066; became first Norman king of England.

James Wolfe, 1727-59, (Br.) captured Quebec from French, 1759, French and Indian War.

Isoroku Yamamoto, 1884-1943, (Jpn.) cmdr. in chief of Japanese fleet, naval planner before and during WWII.

Georgi Zhukov, 1895-1974, (Russ.) defended Moscow, 1941; led assault on Berlin, 1945, WWII.

Philosophers and Religious Figures of the Past

Excludes biblical figures and popes (see Religion chapter). For Greeks and Romans, see also Historical Figures chapter.

Lyman Abbott, 1835-1922, (U.S.) clergyman, reformer; advocate of Christian Socialism.

Pierre Abelard, 1079-1142, (Fr.) philosopher, theologian, teacher; used dialectic method to support Christian beliefs.

Felix Adler, 1851-1933, (U.S.) German-born founder of the Ethical Culture Soc.

Mortimer Adler, 1902-2001, (U.S.) philosopher; helped create "Great Books" program.

(St.) Anselm, c. 1033-1109, (It.) philosopher-theologian, church leader; "ontological argument" for God's existence.

(St.) Thomas Aquinas, 1225-74, (It.) pre-eminent medieval philosopher-theologian; *Summa Theologica*.

Aristotle, 384-322 BCE, (Gr.) pioneering wide-ranging philosopher, logician, ethician, naturalist.

(St.) Augustine, 354-430, (N Africa) philosopher, theologian, bishop; *Confessions, City of God, On the Trinity*.

J. L. Austin, 1911-60, (Br.) ordinary-language philosopher.

Averroes (Ibn Rushd), 1126-98, (Sp.) Islamic philosopher, physician.

Avicenna (Ibn Sina), 980-1037, (Iran) Islamic philosopher, scientist.

A(lfred) J(ules) Ayer, 1910-89, (Br.) philosopher, logical positivist; *Language, Truth, and Logic*.

Roger Bacon, c. 1214-94, (Eng.) philosopher, scientist.

Bahá'u'lláh (Mirza Husayn Ali), 1817-92, (Pers.) founder of Bahá'í faith.

Karl Barth, 1886-1968, (Switz.) theologian; a leading force in 20th-cent. Protestantism.

Thomas à Becket, 1118-70, (Eng.) archbishop of Canterbury; opposed Henry II, murdered by king's men.

(St.) Benedict, c. 480-547, (It.) founded the Benedictines.

Jeremy Bentham, 1748-1832, (Br.) philosopher, reformer; enunciated utilitarianism.

Henri Bergson, 1859-1941, (Fr.) philosopher of evolution.

George Berkeley, 1685-1753, (Ire.) idealist philosopher, bishop.

John Biddle, 1615-62, (Eng.) founder of English Unitarianism.

Jakob Boehme, 1575-1624, (Ger.) theosophist, mystic.

Dietrich Bonhoeffer, 1906-45, (Ger.) Lutheran theologian, pastor; executed as opponent of Nazis.

William Brewster, 1567-1644, (Eng.) led Pilgrims.

Emil Brunner, 1889-1966, (Switz.) Protestant theologian.

Giordano Bruno, 1548-1600, (It.) philosopher, pantheist.

Martin Buber, 1878-1965, (Ger.) Jewish philosopher, theologian; *I and Thou*.

Buddha (Siddhartha Gautama), c. 563-c. 483 BCE, (India) philosopher; founded Buddhism.

John Calvin, 1509-64, (Fr.) theologian; a key figure in the Protestant Reformation.

Rudolph Carnap, 1891-1970, (U.S.) German-born analytic philosopher; a founder of logical positivism.

William Ellery Channing, 1780-1842, (U.S.) clergyman; early spokesman for Unitarianism.

Auguste Comte, 1798-1857, (Fr.) philosopher; originated positivism.

Confucius, 551-479 BCE, (China) founder of Confucianism.

John Cotton, 1584-1652, (Eng.) Puritan theologian.

Thomas Cranmer, 1489-1556, (Eng.) Anglican churchman; wrote much of *Book of Common Prayer*.

Jacques Derrida, 1930-2004, (Fr.) deconstructionist philosopher.

René Descartes, 1596-1650, (Fr.) philosopher, mathematician; "father of modern philosophy"; *Discourse on Method, Meditations on First Philosophy*.

John Dewey, 1859-1952, (U.S.) philosopher, educator; instrumentalist theory of knowledge, progressive education.

Denis Diderot, 1713-84, (Fr.) philosopher, encyclopedist.

John Duns Scotus, c. 1266-1308, (Scot.) Franciscan philosopher, theologian.

Mary Baker Eddy, 1821-1910, (U.S.) founder of Christian Science; *Science and Health*.

Jonathan Edwards, 1703-58, (U.S.) preacher, theologian; "Sinners in the Hands of an Angry God."

(Desiderius) Erasmus, c. 1466-1536, (Neth.) Renaissance humanist; *On the Freedom of the Will*.

Jerry Falwell, 1933-2007, (U.S.) TV evangelist, religious commentator.

Johann Fichte, 1762-1814, (Ger.) idealist philosopher.

Michel Foucault, 1926-84, (Fr.) structuralist philosopher, historian.

George Fox, 1624-91, (Br.) founder of Society of Friends (Quakers).

(St.) Francis of Assisi, 1182-1226, (It.) espoused voluntary poverty, founded Franciscans.

al-Ghazali, 1058-1111, (Iran) Islamic philosopher.

Billy James Hargis, 1925-2004, (U.S.) anti-Communist televangelist; founder of the Church of the Christian Crusade.

Georg W. F. Hegel, 1770-1831, (Ger.) idealist philosopher; *Phenomenology of Mind*.

Martin Heidegger, 1889-1976, (Ger.) existentialist philosopher; affected many fields; *Being and Time*.

Johann G. Herder, 1744-1803, (Ger.) philosopher, cultural historian; a founder of German Romanticism.

Thomas Hobbes, 1588-1679, (Eng.) philosopher, political theorist; *Leviathan*.

David Hume, 1711-76, (Scot.) empiricist philosopher; *Enquiry Concerning Human Understanding*.

Jan Hus, 1369-1415, (Czech.) religious reformer.

Edmund Husserl, 1859-1938, (Ger.) philosopher; founded the phenomenological movement.

Thomas Huxley, 1825-95, (Br.) philosopher, educator.

William Ralph Inge, 1860-1954, (Br.) theologian; explored mystic aspects of Christianity.

William James, 1842-1910, (U.S.) philosopher, psychologist, pragmatist; studied religious experience.

Karl Jaspers, 1883-1969, (Ger.) existentialist philosopher.

Joan of Arc, 1412-31, (Fr.) national heroine, a patron saint of France; key figure in the Hundred Years' War.

Immanuel Kant, 1724-1804, (Ger.) philosopher; founder of modern critical philosophy; *Critique of Pure Reason*.

Thomas à Kempis, c. 1380-1471, (Ger.) monk, devotional writer; *Imitation of Christ* attributed to him.

Soren Kierkegaard, 1813-55, (Den.) religious philosopher, pre-existentialist; *Either/Or, The Sickness Unto Death*.

John Knox, 1505-72, (Scot.) leader of Protestant Reformation in Scotland.

Lao-Tzu, 604-531 BCE, (China) philosopher; considered the founder of the Taoist religion.

Gottfried von Leibniz, 1646-1716, (Ger.) rationalistic philosopher, logician, mathematician.

John Locke, 1632-1704, (Eng.) political theorist, empiricist philosopher; *Essay Concerning Human Understanding*.

(St.) Ignatius Loyola, 1491-1556, (Sp.) founder of the Jesuits; *Spiritual Exercises*.

Martin Luther, 1483-1546, (Ger.) leader of the Protestant Reformation; founded Lutheran church.

Jean-Francois Lyotard, 1924-98, (Fr.) postmodern philosopher, lecturer; *The Post-Modern Condition*.

Maimonides, 1135-1204, (Sp.) major Jewish philosopher.

Gabriel Marcel, 1889-1973, (Fr.) Rom. Cath. existentialist philosopher, dramatist.

Jacques Maritain, 1882-1973, (Fr.) neo-Thomist philosopher.

Cotton Mather, 1663-1728, (U.S.) defender of orthodox Puritanism; founded Yale, 1701.

Aimee Semple McPherson, 1890-1944, (Can.) Pentecostal evangelist.

Philipp Melanchthon, 1497-1560, (Ger.) theologian, humanist; an important voice in the Reformation.

Maurice Merleau-Ponty, 1908-61, (Fr.) existentialist philosopher; *Phenomenology of Perception*.

Thomas Merton, 1915-68, (U.S.) Trappist monk, spiritual writer; *The Seven Storey Mountain*.

Dwight Moody, 1837-99, (U.S.) evangelist.

Rev. Sun Myung Moon, 1920-2012, (N. Kor.) Unification Church founder.

G(eorge) E(dward) Moore, 1873-1958, (Br.) philosopher; *Principia Ethica*, "A Defense of Common Sense."

Muhammad, c. 570-632, (Arab.) prophet of Islam.

Elijah Muhammad, 1897-1975, (U.S.) founder of Black Muslim group, Nation of Islam.

Heinrich Muhlenberg, 1711-87, (Ger.) organized the Lutheran Church in America.

John H. Newman, 1801-90, (Br.) Rom. Cath. convert, cardinal; led Oxford Movement; *Apologia pro Vita Sua*.

Reinhold Niebuhr, 1892-1971, (U.S.) Protestant theologian.

Richard Niebuhr, 1894-1962, (U.S.) Protestant theologian.

Friedrich Nietzsche, 1844-1900, (Ger.) philosopher; *The Birth of Tragedy, Beyond Good and Evil, Thus Spake Zarathustra*.

Robert Nozick, 1938-2002, (U.S.) political philosopher; *Anarchy, State, and Utopia*.

Blaise Pascal, 1623-62, (Fr.) philosopher, mathematician; *Pensées*.

(St.) Patrick, c. 389-c. 461, (Br.) brought Christianity to Ireland.

Norman Vincent Peale, 1898-1993, (U.S.) minister, author; *The Power of Positive Thinking*.

C(harles) S. Peirce, 1839-1914, (U.S.) philosopher, logician; originated concept of pragmatism, 1878.

Plato, c. 428-347 BCE, (Gr.) philosopher; wrote Socratic dialogues; argued for immortality of soul, indep. reality of ideas or forms; *Republic, Meno, Phaedo, Apology*.

Plotinus, 205-70, (Rom.) a founder of neo-Platonism; *Enneads*.

W(illard) V(an) O(rman) Quine, 1908-2001, (U.S.) philosopher, logician; "On What There Is."

John Rawls, 1922-2002, (U.S.) political philosopher; *A Theory of Justice*.

Oral Roberts, 1918-2009, (U.S.) televangelist, university founder.

Moishe Rosen, 1932-2010, (U.S.) Jews for Jesus founder.

Josiah Royce, 1855-1916, (U.S.) idealist philosopher.

Bertrand Russell, 1872-1970, (Br.) philosopher, logician; one of the founders of modern logic; prolific popular writer.

Charles T. Russell, 1852-1916, (U.S.) founder of Jehovah's Witnesses.

Gilbert Ryle, 1900-76, (Br.) analytic philosopher; *The Concept of Mind*.

George Santayana, 1863-1952, (U.S.) philosopher, writer, critic; *The Sense of Beauty, The Realms of Being*.

Jean-Paul Sartre, 1905-80, (Fr.) philosopher, novelist, playwright; *Nausea, No Exit, Being and Nothingness*.

Friedrich von Schelling, 1775-1854, (Ger.) philosopher of romantic movement.

Friedrich Schleiermacher, 1768-1834, (Ger.) theologian; a founder of modern Protestant theology.

Arthur Schopenhauer, 1788-1860, (Ger.) philosopher; *The World as Will and Idea*.

Albert Schweitzer, 1875-1965, (Ger.) theologian, social philosopher, medical missionary.

Joseph Smith, 1805-44, (U.S.) founded Latter-Day Saints (Mormon) movement, 1830.

Socrates, 469-399 BCE, (Gr.) philosopher immortalized by Plato.

Herbert Spencer, 1820-1903, (Br.) philosopher of evolution.

Herbert Spiegel, 1914-2009, (U.S.) psychiatrist who popularized hypnosis.

Baruch de Spinoza, 1632-77, (Neth.) rationalist philosopher; *Ethics*.

John Stott, 1921-2011, (Br.) evangelical Anglican cleric.

Billy Sunday, 1862-1935, (U.S.) evangelist.

Daisetz Teitaro Suzuki, 1870-1966, (Jpn.) Buddhist scholar.

Emanuel Swedenborg, 1688-1772, (Swed.) philosopher, mystic; *Principia*.

Pierre Teilhard de Chardin, 1881-1955, (Fr.) Jesuit priest, paleontologist, philosopher-theologian; *The Divine Milieu*.

(St.) Therese of Lisieux, 1873-97, (Fr.) Carmelite nun ("Little Flower"), revered for everyday sanctity; *The Story of a Soul*.

Paul Tillich, 1886-1965, (U.S.) German-born philosopher, theologian; brought depth psychology to Protestantism.

John Wesley, 1703-91, (Br.) theologian, evangelist; founded Methodism.

Alfred North Whitehead, 1861-1947, (Br.) philosopher, mathematician; *Process and Reality*.

William of Occam, c. 1285-c. 1349, (Eng.) medieval scholastic philosopher, nominalist.

Roger Williams, c. 1603-83, (U.S.) clergyman; championed religious freedom and separation of church and state.

Ludwig Wittgenstein, 1889-1951, (Austria) philosopher; major influence on contemporary language philosophy; *Tractatus Logico-Philosophicus*, *Philosophical Investigations*.

John Woolman, 1720-72, (U.S.) Quaker social reformer, abolitionist, writer; *The Journal*.

John Wycliffe, 1320-84, (Eng.) theologian, reformer.

(St.) Francis Xavier, 1506-52, (Sp.) Jesuit missionary; "Apostle of the Indies."

Brigham Young, 1801-77, (U.S.) Mormon leader after Joseph Smith's assassination; colonized Utah.

Huldrych Zwingli, 1484-1531, (Switz.) theologian; led Swiss Protestant Reformation.

Political Leaders of the Past

U.S. presidents, vice presidents, Supreme Court justices, and signers of the Declaration of Independence listed elsewhere.

Abu Bakr, 573-634, (Arab.) Muslim leader, first caliph, chosen successor to Muhammad.

Dean Acheson, 1893-1971, (U.S.) sec. of state; architect of Cold War foreign policy.

Samuel Adams, 1722-1803, (U.S.) patriot; Boston Tea Party firebrand.

Konrad Adenauer, 1876-1967, (Ger.) first West German chancellor.

Emilio Aguinaldo, 1869-1964, (Philip.) revolutionary; fought against Spain and the U.S.

Corazon Aquino, 1933-2009, (Philip.) pres. of the Philippines, 1986-92.

Akbar, 1542-1605, Mogul emperor of India.

Carl Albert, 1908-2000, (U.S.) House rep. (D, OK), Speaker, 1971-76.

Salvador Allende Gossens, 1908-73, (Chile) Marxist pres., 1970-73; ousted and died in coup.

Idi Amin, 1925-2003, (Uganda) Ugandan ruler, 1971-79; blamed for hundreds of thousands of deaths.

Yasir Arafat, 1929-2004, (Egypt) leader of the Palestine Liberation Organization (PLO).

Herbert H. Asquith, 1852-1928, (Br.) Liberal prime min.; instituted major social reforms.

Hafez al Assad, 1930-2000, (Syr.) Syrian ruler from 1970.

Atahualpa, 1500?-33, (Inca) ruling chief of Peru.

Kemal Ataturk, 1881-1938, (Turk.) founded modern Turkey.

Clement Attlee, 1883-1967, (Br.) Labour party leader, prime min.; enacted natl. health care system, nationalized many industries.

Stephen F. Austin, 1793-1836, (U.S.) led Texas colonization.

Mikhail Bakunin, 1814-76, (Russ.) revolutionary; leading exponent of anarchism.

Arthur J. Balfour, 1848-1930, (Br.) foreign sec. under Lloyd George; issued Balfour Declaration backing Zionism.

Bernard M. Baruch, 1870-1965, (U.S.) financier, govt. adviser.

Fulgencio Batista y Zaldívar, 1901-73, (Cub.) Cuban pres., 1940-44, 1952-59; overthrown by Castro.

Lord Beaverbrook, 1879-1964, (Br.) financier, statesman, newspaper owner.

Menachem Begin, 1913-92, (Isr.) Israeli prime min.; shared 1978 Nobel Peace Prize.

Ahmed Ben Bella, 1918-2012, (Alg.) first Algerian pres., 1963-65.

Eduard Benes, 1884-1948, (Czech.) pres. during interwar and post-WWII eras.

David Ben-Gurion, 1886-1973, (Isr.) first prime min. of Israel, 1948-53, 1955-63.

Thomas Hart Benton, 1782-1858, (U.S.) MO senator; championed agrarian interests and westward expansion.

Aneurin Bevan, 1897-1960, (Br.) Labour party leader.

Ernest Bevin, 1881-1951, (Br.) Labour party leader, foreign minister; helped lay foundation for NATO.

Benazir Bhutto, 1953-2007, (Pak.) former prime min. of Pakistan.

Otto von Bismarck, 1815-98, (Ger.) statesman known as the Iron Chancellor; uniter of Germany, 1870.

James G. Blaine, 1830-93, (U.S.) Republican politician, diplomat; influential in Pan-American movement.

Léon Blum, 1872-1950, (Fr.) socialist leader, writer; headed first Popular Front government.

William E. Borah, 1865-1940, (U.S.) isolationist senator (R, ID); helped block U.S. membership in League of Nations.

Cesare Borgia, 1476-1507, (It.) soldier, politician; an outstanding figure of the Italian Renaissance.

P. W. Botha, 1916-2006, (S. Afr.) S. African president, prime min.

Tom Bradley, 1917-98, (U.S.) first African American mayor of L.A.

Willy Brandt, 1913-92, (Ger.) statesman, chancellor of West Germany, 1969-74; promoted East/West peace, *Ostpolitik*.

Leonid Brezhnev, 1906-82, (USSR) Soviet leader, 1964-82.

Aristide Briand, 1862-1932, (Fr.) foreign min.; chief architect of Locarno Pact and anti-war Kellogg-Briand Pact.

William Jennings Bryan, 1860-1925, (U.S.) Democratic, populist leader, orator; three times lost race for presidency.

Ralph Bunche, 1904-71, (U.S.) first black person to win the Nobel Peace Prize, 1950; undersecretary of the UN, 1950.

Robert Byrd, 1917-2010, (U.S.) longest serving U.S. senator (D, WV).

John C. Calhoun, 1782-1850, (U.S.) political leader; champion of states' rights and a symbol of the Old South.

James Callaghan (Baron Callaghan), 1912-2005, (Br.) Labour party politician, prime min., 1976-79.

Robert Castlereagh, 1769-1822, (Br.) foreign sec.; guided Grand Alliance against Napoleon.

Camillo Benso Cavour, 1810-61, (It.) statesman; largely responsible for uniting Italy under the House of Savoy.

Nicolae Ceausescu, 1918-89, (Roman.) Communist leader, head of state, 1967-89; executed.

Austen Chamberlain, 1863-1937, (Br.) statesman; helped finalize Locarno Treaties, both 1925.

Neville Chamberlain, 1869-1940, (Br.) Conservative prime min. whose appeasement of Hitler led to Munich Pact.

Hugo Chávez, 1954-2013, (Venez.) socialist Venezuelan pres., 1999-2013.

Chiang Kai-shek, 1887-1975, (China) Nationalist Chinese pres. whose government was driven from mainland to Taiwan.

Madame Chiang Kai-shek (Mayling Soong), 1898-2003, (China) highly influential wife of Nationalist Chinese leader Chiang Kai-shek.

Shirley Chisholm, 1924-2005, (U.S.) first black woman elected to U.S. House (1968, D, NY); pres. contender, 1972.

Warren Christopher, 1925-2011, (U.S.) secretary of state, diplomat.

Winston Churchill, 1874-1965, (Br.) prime min., soldier, author; guided Britain through WWII.

Galeazzo Ciano, 1903-44, (It.) Fascist foreign minister; helped create Rome-Berlin Axis; executed by Benito Mussolini.

Henry Clay, 1777-1852, (U.S.) "The Great Compromiser"; one of the most influential pre-Civil War political leaders.

Georges Clemenceau, 1841-1929, (Fr.) twice prem.; Woodrow Wilson's antagonist at Paris Peace Conference after WWI.

DeWitt Clinton, 1769-1828, (U.S.) political leader; responsible for promoting the Erie Canal.

Robert Clive, 1725-74, (Br.) first administrator of Bengal; laid foundation for British Empire in India.

Jean Baptiste Colbert, 1619-83, (Fr.) statesman; influential under Louis XIV; created the French navy.

Bettino Craxi, 1934-2000, (It.) Italy's first post-WWII Socialist prem.

David Crockett, 1786-1836, (U.S.) frontiersman, congressman; died defending the Alamo.

Oliver Cromwell, 1599-1658, (Br.) Lord Protector of England; led parliamentary forces during Civil War.

Curzon of Kedleston, 1859-1925, (Br.) viceroy of India, foreign sec.; major force in post-WWI world.

Édouard Daladier, 1884-1970, (Fr.) Radical Socialist politician, arrested by Vichy, interned by Germans until 1945.

Richard J. Daley, 1902-76, (U.S.) Chicago mayor.

Georges Danton, 1759-94, (Fr.) leading French Rev. figure.

Jefferson Davis, 1808-89, (U.S.) pres. of the Confederacy.

Charles G. Dawes, 1865-1951, (U.S.) statesman, banker; advanced plan to stabilize post-WWI German finances.

William L. Dawson, 1886-1970, (U.S.) IL congressman; first black chairman of a major U.S. House committee.

Alcide De Gasperi, 1881-1954, (It.) prime min.; founder of Christian Democratic party.

Charles De Gaulle, 1890-1970, (Fr.) general, statesman; first pres. of the Fifth Republic.

Deng Xiaoping, 1904-97, (China) "paramount leader" of China; backed economic modernization.

Eamon De Valera, 1882-1975, (Ire.-U.S.) statesman; led fight for Irish independence.

Thomas E. Dewey, 1902-71, (U.S.) NY governor (R); twice lost in try for presidency.

Ngo Dinh Diem, 1901-63, (Viet.) South Vietnamese pres.; assassinated in government takeover.

Everett M. Dirksen, 1896-1969, (U.S.) Senate Republican minority leader, orator.

Benjamin Disraeli, 1804-81, (Br.) prime min.; considered founder of modern Conservative party.

Anatoly Dobrynin, 1919-2010, (Russ.) diplomat and Soviet amb. to U.S. (1962-86).

Engelbert Dollfuss, 1892-1934, (Austria) chancellor; assassinated by Austrian Nazis.

Andrea Doria, 1466-1560, (It.) Genoese admiral, statesman; called "Father of Peace" and "Liberator of Genoa."

Stephen A. Douglas, 1813-61, (U.S.) Democratic leader, orator; ran against Lincoln for IL sen. seat, presidency.

Alexander Dubcek, 1921-92, (Czech.) statesman whose attempted liberalization was crushed, 1968.

John Foster Dulles, 1888-1959, (U.S.) sec. of state under Eisenhower; Cold War policy maker.

Lawrence Eagleburger, 1930-2011, (U.S.) diplomat and foreign policy advisor.

Abba Eban, 1915-2002, (Isr.) diplomat; foreign min., 1966-74.

Friedrich Ebert, 1871-1925, (Ger.) Social Democratic movement leader; first pres., Weimar Republic, 1919-25.

Sir Anthony Eden, 1897-1977, (Br.) foreign sec., prime min. during Suez invasion of 1956.

Ludwig Erhard, 1897-1977, (Ger.) economist, West German chancellor; led nation's economic rise after WWII.

King Fahd, 1923-2005, (Saudi Arabia) monarch from 1982 but inactive after 1995 stroke; encouraged U.S. relations.

Geraldine Ferraro, 1935-2011, (U.S.) former U.S. rep. (D, NY), vice-pres. nominee.

Joao Baptista de Figueiredo, 1918-99, (Braz.) president of Brazil; restored the nation's democracy.

Hamilton Fish, 1808-93, (U.S.) sec. of state; successfully mediated disputes with Great Britain, Latin America.

James V. Forrestal, 1892-1949, (U.S.) sec. of navy, first sec. of defense.

Francisco Franco, 1892-1975, (Sp.) leader of rebel forces during Spanish Civil War, longtime ruler of Spain.

Benjamin Franklin, 1706-90, (U.S.) printer, publisher, author, inventor, scientist, diplomat.

Louis de Frontenac, 1620-98, (Fr.) governor of New France (Canada); encouraged explorations, fought Iroquois.

J. William Fulbright, 1905-95, (U.S.) senator (D, AR); leading figure in U.S. foreign policy during Cold War years.

Hugh Gaitskell, 1906-63, (Br.) Labour party leader; major force in reversing its stand for unilateral disarmament.

Albert Gallatin, 1761-1849, (U.S.) sec. of treasury; instrumental in negotiating end of War of 1812.

Léon Gambetta, 1838-82, (Fr.) statesman, politician; one of the founders of the Third Republic.

Indira Gandhi, 1917-84, (India) daughter of Jawaharlal Nehru; prime min. of India, 1966-77, 1980-84; assassinated.

Mohandas K. Gandhi, 1869-1948, (India) political leader, ascetic; led movement against British rule; assassinated.

Giuseppe Garibaldi, 1807-82, (It.) patriot, soldier; a leader in the Risorgimento, Italian unification movement.

William E. Gladstone, 1809-98, (Br.) prime min.; dominant force of Liberal party 1868-94.

Paul Joseph Goebbels, 1897-1945, (Ger.) Nazi propagandist; master of mass psychology.

Barry Goldwater, 1909-98, (U.S.) conservative U.S. senator (R, AZ), 1964 pres. nominee.

Klement Gottwald, 1896-1953, (Czech.) Communist leader; ushered Communism into his country.

Alexander Hamilton, 1755-1804, (U.S.) first treasury sec.; champion of strong central government.

Dag Hammarskjold, 1905-61, (Swed.) statesman; UN sec.-general.

King Hassan II, 1929-99, (Moroc.) ruler of Morocco,1962-99.

Vaclav Havel, 1936-2011, (Czech.) first president of Czech Republic, 1989-92.

John Hay, 1838-1905, (U.S.) sec. of state; primarily associated with Open Door Policy toward China.

Sir Edward Heath, 1916-2005, (Br.) Conservative prime min., 1970-74; promoted European unity.

Jesse Helms, 1921-2008, (U.S.) conservative senator (R, NC).

Patrick Henry, 1736-99, (U.S.) major Revolutionary War figure, orator.

Édouard Herriot, 1872-1957, (Fr.) Radical Socialist leader; twice prem., pres. of National Assembly.

Theodor Herzl, 1860-1904, (Hung.) founded modern Zionism.

Heinrich Himmler, 1900-45, (Ger.) head of Nazi SS and Gestapo.

Paul von Hindenburg, 1847-1934, (Ger.) field marshal, WWI; second pres. of Weimar Republic, 1925-34.

Adolf Hitler, 1889-1945, (Ger.) dictator; built Nazism, launched WWII, presided over the Holocaust.

Ho Chi Minh, 1890-1969, (Viet.) N. Vietnamese pres., Vietnamese Communist leader.

Harry L. Hopkins, 1890-1946, (U.S.) New Deal administrator; closest adviser to Franklin D. Roosevelt during WWII.

Edward M. House, 1858-1938, (U.S.) diplomat; confidential adviser to Woodrow Wilson.

Samuel Houston, 1793-1863, (U.S.) leader of struggle for Texas independence.

Cordell Hull, 1871-1955, (U.S.) sec. of state, 1933-44; initiated reciprocal trade to lower tariffs, helped organize UN.

Hubert H. Humphrey, 1911-78, (U.S.) senator (D, MN), vice pres., pres. candidate.

King Hussein, 1935-99, (Jordan) peacemaker; ruler of Jordan, 1952-99.

Saddam Hussein, 1937-2006, (Iraq) Iraqi ruler; put to death for crimes against humanity.

Muhammad Ali Jinnah, 1876-1948, (Pak.) founder, first gov.-gen. of Pakistan.

Barbara Jordan, 1936-96, (U.S.) congresswoman, orator, educator; first black woman to win a seat in the TX senate, 1966.

Benito Juarez, 1806-72, (Mex.) rallied his country against foreign threats; sought to create democratic, federal republic.

Constantine Karamanlis, 1907-98, (Gr.) Greek prime min.; restored democracy, later president.

Frank B. Kellogg, 1856-1937, (U.S.) sec. of state; negotiated Kellogg-Briand Pact to outlaw war.

Jack Kemp, 1935-2009, (U.S.) sec. of HUD, U.S. rep. (R, NY), football player.

Edward M. Kennedy, 1932-2009, (U.S.) senator (D, MA); championed progressive causes.

Robert F. Kennedy, 1925-68, (U.S.) attorney general, sen. (D, NY); assassinated while seeking presidency.

Aleksandr Kerensky, 1881-1970, (Russ.) headed provisional government after Feb. 1917 revolution.

Ayatollah Ruhollah Khomeini, 1900-89, (Iran), religious-political leader; spearheaded overthrow of Shah, 1979.

Nikita Khrushchev, 1894-1971, (USSR) prem., first sec. of Communist party; initiated de-Stalinization.

Kim Dae Jung, 1925-2009, (Korea) S. Korean dissident, opposition leader, pres.; 2000 Nobel Peace Prize winner.

Kim Il Sung, 1912-94, (Korea) N. Korean dictator, 1948-94.

Kim Jong Il, 1942-2011, (Korea) N. Korean dictator, 1994-2011.

Edward I. Koch, 1924-2013, (U.S.) New York City mayor, 1978-89.

Lajos Kossuth, 1802-94, (Hung.) principal figure in 1848 Hungarian revolution.

Pyotr Kropotkin, 1842-1921, (Russ.) anarchist; counseled the peasants but opposed Bolshevism.

Kublai Khan, c. 1215-94, (Mongol) emperor; founder of Yüan dynasty in China.

Béla Kun, 1886-c. 1939, (Hung.) member of Third Communist International; tried to foment worldwide revolution.

Robert M. LaFollette, 1855-1925, (U.S.) WI public official; leader of progressive movement.

Fiorello La Guardia, 1882-1947, (U.S.) New York City reform mayor, 1933-45.

Pierre Laval, 1883-1945, (Fr.) politician; Vichy foreign min.; executed for treason.

Andrew Bonar Law, 1858-1923, (Br.) Conservative party politician; led opposition to Irish home rule.

Vladimir Ilyich Lenin (Ulyanov), 1870-1924, (Russ.) revolutionary; founded Bolshevism; Soviet leader, 1917-24.

Ferdinand de Lesseps, 1805-94, (Fr.) diplomat, engineer; conceived idea of Suez Canal.

Rene Levesque, 1922-87, (Can.) prem. of Quebec, 1976-85; led unsuccessful separatist campaign.

Trygve Lie, 1896-1968, (Nor.) first UN sec.-gen.

Maxim Litvinov, 1876-1951, (Pol.-Russ.) revolutionary, commissar of foreign affairs; favored cooperation with West.

Liu Shaoqi, c. 1898-1969, (China) Communist leader; fell from grace during Cultural Revolution.

David Lloyd George, 1863-1945, (Br.) Liberal party prime min.; laid foundations for modern welfare state.

Henry Cabot Lodge, 1850-1924, (U.S.) senator (R, MA); led opposition to participation in League of Nations.

Huey P. Long, 1893-1935, (U.S.) Louisiana political demagogue, governor, U.S. senator; assassinated.

Rosa Luxemburg, 1871-1919, (Ger.) revolutionary; leader of the German Social Democratic party and Spartacus party.

J. Ramsay MacDonald, 1866-1937, (Br.) first Labour party prime min. of Great Britain.

Harold Macmillan, 1895-1986, (Br.) prime min. of Great Britain, 1957-63.

Makarios III, 1913-77, (Cyprus) Greek Orthodox archbishop; first pres. of Cyprus.

Nelson Mandela, 1918-2013, (S. Afr.) antiapartheid leader; 1st black pres. of S. Africa, 1994-99.

Wilma Mankiller, 1945-2010, (U.S.) first female chief of the Cherokee Nation.

Mao Zedong, 1893-1976, (China) chief Chinese Marxist theorist, revolutionary, political leader; led revolution establishing his nation as Communist state.

Jean Paul Marat, 1743-93, (Fr.) revolutionary, politician; identified with radical Jacobins; assassinated.

Thurgood Marshall, 1908-93, (U.S.) first black U.S. solicitor general, 1965; first black justice of U.S. Supreme Court, 1967-91.

José Martí, 1853-95, (Cub.) patriot, poet; independence leader.

Jan Masaryk, 1886-1948, (Czech.) foreign min.; died under mysterious circumstances, allegedly committed suicide following Communist coup.

Thomas G. Masaryk, 1850-1937, (Czech.) statesman, philosopher; first pres. of Czechoslovakia.

Jules Mazarin, 1602-61, (Fr.) cardinal, statesman; prime min. under Louis XIII and queen regent Anne of Austria.

Giuseppe Mazzini, 1805-72, (It.) reformer dedicated to Risorgimento movement for renewal of Italy.

Tom Mboya, 1930-69, (Kenya) political leader; instrumental in securing independence for Kenya.

Eugene McCarthy, 1916-2005, (U.S.) political leader, author; 1968 Dem. presidential contender.

Joseph R. McCarthy, 1908-57, (U.S.) senator (R, WI); extremist in searching out alleged Communists and pro-Communists.

George McGovern, 1922-2012, (U.S.) liberal senator (D, SD), 1972 pres. nominee.

Cosimo I de' Medici, 1519-74, (It.) Duke of Florence, grand duke of Tuscany.

Lorenzo de' Medici (the Magnificent), 1449-92, (It.) merchant prince; a towering figure in Italian Renaissance.

Catherine de Médicis, 1519-89, (Fr.) queen consort of Henry II, regent of France; influential in Catholic-Huguenot wars.

Golda Meir, 1898-1978, (Isr.) a founder of the state of Israel; prime min., 1969-74.

Klemens W. N. L. Metternich, 1773-1859, (Austria) statesman; arbiter of post-Napoleonic Europe.

Slobodan Milosevic, 1941-2006, (Serb./Yugo.) former Yugoslav pres.; tried for war crimes.

François Mitterrand, 1916-96, (Fr.) pres. of France, 1981-95.

Mobutu Sese Seko, 1930-97, (Zaire) longtime ruler of Zaire (now Dem. Rep. of Congo), 1965-97; exiled after rebellion.

Guy Mollet, 1905-75, (Fr.) socialist politician, resistance leader.

Henry Morgenthau Jr., 1891-1967, (U.S.) sec. of treasury; fundraiser for New Deal and U.S. WWII activities.

Gouverneur Morris, 1752-1816, (U.S.) statesman, diplomat, financial expert; helped plan decimal coinage.

Daniel Patrick Moynihan, 1927-2003, (U.S.) senator (D, NY), diplomat, social scientist, author.

Benito Mussolini, 1883-1945, (It.) leader of the Italian fascist state; assassinated.

Imre Nagy, c. 1896-1958, (Hung.) Communist prem.; assassinated after Soviets crushed 1956 uprising.

Gamal Abdel Nasser, 1918-70, (Egypt) leader of Arab unification, second Egyptian pres.

Jawaharlal Nehru, 1889-1964, (India) prime min.; guided India through its early years of independence.

Kwame Nkrumah, 1909-72, (Ghana) first prime min., 1957-60; pres., 1960-66, of Ghana.

Frederick North, 1732-92, (Br.) prime min.; his policies led to loss of American colonies.

Julius K. Nyerere, 1922-99, (Tanz.) founding father; first pres., 1962-85, of Tanzania.

Daniel O'Connell, 1775-1847, (Ire.) nationalist political leader; known as The Liberator.

Omar, c. 581-644, (Arab.) Muslim leader; second caliph, led Islam to become an imperial power.

Thomas P. (Tip) O'Neill Jr., 1912-94, (U.S.) U.S. rep. (D, MA), Speaker of the House, 1977-86.

Ignace Paderewski, 1860-1941, (Pol.) statesman, pianist, composer, briefly prime min.; ardent patriot.

Ian Paisley, 1926-2014, (Ire.) Unionist Party leader who agreed to power sharing in N. Ireland.

Viscount Palmerston, 1784-1865, (Br.) Whig-Liberal prime min., foreign min.; embodied British nationalism.

Andreas George Papandreou, 1919-96, (Gr.) leftist politician; served as prem., 1981-89, 1993-96.

Georgios Papandreou, 1888-1968, (Gr.) Republican politician; served 3 times as prime min.

Franz von Papen, 1879-1969, (Ger.) politician; major role in overthrow of Weimar Republic and rise of Hitler.

Charles Stewart Parnell, 1846-1891, (Ire.) nationalist leader; "uncrowned king of Ireland."

Lester Pearson, 1897-1972, (Can.) diplomat, Liberal party leader, prime min.

Robert Peel, 1788-1850, (Br.) reformist prime min.; founder of Conservative party.

Frances Perkins, 1882-1965, (U.S.) first female cabinet member (sec. of labor).

Eva (Evita) Perón, 1919-52, (Arg.) highly influential second wife of Juan Perón.

Juan Perón, 1895-1974, (Arg.) dynamic pres. of Argentina, 1946-55, 1973-74.

Joseph Pilsudski, 1867-1935, (Pol.) statesman; instrumental in reestablishing Polish state in the 20th cent.

Charles Pinckney, 1757-1824, (U.S.) founding father; his Pinckney plan largely incorporated into Constitution.

Christian Pineau, 1905-95, (Fr.) leader of French Resistance during WWII; French foreign min., 1956-58.

Augusto Pinochet (Ugarte), 1915-2006, (Chile) former Chilean ruler; indicted for human rights abuses while in office.

William Pitt the Elder, 1708-78, (Br.) statesman; the "Great Commoner," transformed Britain into imperial power.

William Pitt the Younger, 1759-1806, (Br.) prime min. during French Revolutionary wars.

Georgi Plekhanov, 1857-1918, (Russ.) revolutionary, social philosopher; called "father of Russian Marxism."

Raymond Poincaré, 1860-1934, (Fr.) French pres.; advocated harsh punishment of Germany after WWI.

Pol Pot, 1925-98, (Camb.) leader of Khmer Rouge; ruled Cambodia, 1975-79; responsible for mass deaths.

Georges Pompidou, 1911-74, (Fr.) Gaullist political leader; pres., 1969-74.

Grigori Potemkin, 1739-91, (Russ.) field marshal; favorite of empress Catherine II.

Adam Clayton Powell Jr., 1908-72, (U.S.) civil rights leader; U.S. rep. (D, NY), 1945-69.

Muammar al-Qaddafi, 1942-2011, (Libya) Libyan ruler, 1969-2011.

Yitzhak Rabin, 1922-95, (Isr.) military, political leader; prime min. of Israel, 1974-77, 1992-95; assassinated.

Joseph H. Rainey, 1832-87, (U.S.) first black person elected to U.S. House (1869), from SC.

Edmund Randolph, 1753-1813, (U.S.) attorney; prominent in drafting, ratification of Constitution.

John Randolph, 1773-1833, (U.S.) southern planter; strong advocate of states' rights.

Jeannette Rankin, 1880-1973, (U.S.) pacifist; first woman member of U.S. Congress (R, MT).

Walter Rathenau, 1867-1922, (Ger.) industrialist, statesman.

Sam Rayburn, 1882-1961, (U.S.) U.S. rep. (D, TX) for 47 years, House Speaker for 17.

Hiram R. Revels, 1822-1901, (U.S.) first African American U.S. senator; elected in MS, served 1870-71.

Paul Reynaud, 1878-1966, (Fr.) statesman; prem. in 1940 at time of France's defeat by Germany.

Syngman Rhee, 1875-1965, (Korea) first pres. of S. Korea.

Cecil Rhodes, 1853-1902, (Br.) imperialist, industrial magnate; established Rhodes scholarships in his will.

Ann Richards, 1933-2006, (U.S.) former TX gov.

Cardinal de Richelieu, 1585-1642, (Fr.) statesman, known as "red eminence"; chief minister to Louis XIII.

Maximilien Robespierre, 1758-94, (Fr.) leading figure in French Revolution and Reign of Terror.

Nelson Rockefeller, 1908-79, (U.S.) Republican governor of NY, 1959-73; U.S. vice pres., 1974-77.

Eleanor Roosevelt, 1884-1962, (U.S.) influential first lady, humanitarian, UN diplomat.

Elihu Root, 1845-1937, (U.S.) lawyer, statesman, diplomat; leading Republican supporter of the League of Nations.

Dean Rusk, 1909-95, (U.S.) statesman; sec. of state, 1961-69.

John Russell, 1792-1878, (Br.) Liberal prime min. during the Irish potato famine.

Anwar al-Sadat, 1918-81, (Egypt) pres., 1970-81; promoted peace with Israel; Nobel laureate; assassinated.

António de Oliveira Salazar, 1889-1970, (Port.) longtime dictator.

José de San Martin, 1778-1850, S. Amer. revolutionary; protector of Peru.

Eisaku Sato, 1901-75, (Jpn.) prime min.; presided over Japan's post-WWII emergence as major world power.

Abdul Aziz Ibn Saud, c.1880-1953, (Saudi Arabia) king of Saudi Arabia, 1932-53.

Robert Schuman, 1886-1963, (Fr.) statesman; founded European Coal and Steel Community.

Carl Schurz, 1829-1906, (U.S.) German-American political leader, journalist, orator, dedicated reformer.

Kurt Schuschnigg, 1897-1977, (Austria) chancellor; unsuccessful in stopping Austria's annexation by Germany.

William H. Seward, 1801-72, (U.S.) anti-slavery activist; as U.S. sec. of state purchased Alaska.

Carlo Sforza, 1872-1952, (It.) foreign min., anti-Fascist.

Yitzhak Shamir, 1915-2012, (Isr.) prime min. of Israel, 1983-84, 1986-92.

Ariel Sharon, 1928-2014, (Isr.) prime min. of Israel, 2001-06.

Eduard Shevardnadze, 1928-2014, (Geo.) Georgian pres., 1995-2003.

Norodom Sihanouk, 1922-2012, (Camb.) King of Cambodia (1941-55, 1993-2004).

Sitting Bull, c.1831-90, (Amer. Ind.) Sioux leader in Battle of Little Bighorn against George A. Custer, 1876.

Alfred E. Smith, 1873-1944, (U.S.) NY Democratic governor; first Roman Catholic to run for president.

Margaret Chase Smith, 1897-1995, (U.S.) congresswoman, senator (R, ME); first woman elected to both houses of Congress.

Jan C. Smuts, 1870-1950, (S. Afr.) statesman, philosopher, soldier, prime min.

Paul Henri Spaak, 1899-1972, (Belg.) statesman, socialist leader.

Joseph Stalin, 1879-1953, (USSR) Soviet dictator, 1924-53; instituted forced collectivization, massive purges, and labor camps, causing millions of deaths.

Edwin M. Stanton, 1814-69, (U.S.) sec. of war, 1862-68.

Alexander Stephens, 1812-83, (U.S.) vice pres. of the Confederacy.

Edward R. Stettinius Jr., 1900-49, (U.S.) industrialist; sec. of state who coordinated aid to WWII allies.

Adlai E. Stevenson, 1900-65, (U.S.) Democratic leader, diplomat, governor (IL), presidential candidate.

Henry L. Stimson, 1867-1950, (U.S.) statesman; served in 5 administrations, foreign policy adviser in 1930s and 1940s.

Carl Stokes, 1927-96, (U.S.) first black mayor of a major American city (Cleveland, 1967-72).

Suharto, 1921-2008, (Indon.) former longtime Indonesian ruler.

Sukarno, 1901-70, (Indon.) dictatorial first pres. of the Indonesian republic.

Sun Yat-sen, 1866-1925, (China) revolutionary; leader of Kuomintang political party, regarded as father of modern China.

Robert A. Taft, 1889-1953, (U.S.) conservative Senate leader (OH); called "Mr. Republican."

Charles de Talleyrand, 1754-1838, (Fr.) statesman, diplomat; the major force of the Congress of Vienna of 1814-15.

U Thant, 1909-74, (Burma) statesman, UN sec.-general.

Margaret Thatcher, 1925-2013, (Br.) conservative British prime min., 1979-90; first woman UK prime min.

Norman M. Thomas, 1884-1968, (U.S.) social reformer; six times Socialist party presidential candidate.

Josip Broz Tito, 1892-1980, (Yugo.) pres. of Yugoslavia from 1953; WWII guerrilla chief, postwar rival of Stalin.

Palmiro Togliatti, 1893-1964, (It.) major Italian Communist leader.

Hideki Tojo, 1885-1948, (Jpn.) statesman, soldier; prime min. during most of WWII.

François Toussaint L'Ouverture, c.1744-1803, (Haiti) patriot, martyr; thwarted French colonial aims.

Leon Trotsky, 1879-1940, (Russ.) revolutionary; founded Red Army, expelled from party in conflict with Stalin; assassinated.

Pierre Elliott Trudeau, 1919-2000, (Can.) longtime liberal prime min. of Canada, 1968-79, 1980-84; achieved native Canadian constitution.

Rafael L. Trujillo Molina, 1891-1961, (Dom. Rep.) dictator of Dominican Republic, 1930-61; assassinated.

Moise K. Tshombe, 1919-69, (Congo) pres. of secessionist Katanga prov., prem. of Congo (now Dem. Rep. of the Congo).

William M. Tweed, 1823-78, (U.S.) political boss of Tammany Hall, New York City's Democratic political machine.

Walter Ulbricht, 1893-1973, (Ger.) Communist leader of German Democratic Republic.

Arthur H. Vandenberg, 1884-1951, (U.S.) senator (R, MI); proponent of bipartisan anti-Communist foreign policy.

Eleutherios Venizelos, 1864-1936, (Gr.) most prominent Greek statesman of early 20th cent.

Hendrik F. Verwoerd, 1901-66, (S. Afr.) prime min.; rigorously applied apartheid policy despite protest.

Kurt Waldheim, 1918-2007, (Austria) UN sec.-gen., Austrian pres.

George Wallace, 1919-98, (U.S.) former segregationist governor of Alabama, pres. candidate.

Robert Walpole, 1676-1745, (Br.) statesman; generally considered Britain's first prime min.

Harold Washington, 1922-87, (U.S.) first black mayor of Chicago.

Robert C. Weaver, 1907-97, (U.S.) first African American appointed to cabinet; sec. of Housing and Urban Development.

Daniel Webster, 1782-1852, (U.S.) orator, politician; advocate of business interests during Jacksonian agrarianism.

Caspar Weinberger, 1917-2006, (U.S.) business exec., former defense sec., other cabinet posts.

Chaim Weizmann, 1874-1952, (Russ.-Isr.) Zionist leader, scientist; first Israeli pres.

Kevin White, 1929-2012, (U.S.) Boston mayor, 1967-84.

Wendell L. Willkie, 1892-1944, (U.S.) Republican who tried to unseat Franklin D. Roosevelt when he ran for his third term.

Harold Wilson, 1916-95, (Br.) Labour party leader; prime min., 1964-70, 1974-76.

Boris Yeltsin, 1931-2007, (Russ.) first freely elected pres. of post-Soviet Russia.

Coleman A. Young, 1918-97, (U.S.) first African-American mayor of Detroit, 1974-93.

Emiliano Zapata, c.1879-1919, (Mex.) revolutionary; major influence on modern Mexico.

Todor Zhivkov, 1911-98, (Bulg.) Communist ruler of Bulgaria from 1954 until ousted in a 1989 coup.

Zhou Enlai, 1898-1976, (China) diplomat, prime min.; a leading figure of the Chinese Communist party.

Scientists of the Past

Revised by Peter Barker, Prof. and Chair, Dept. of the History of Science, Univ. of Oklahoma.

For pre-modern scientists, see also Philosophers and Religious Figures of the Past and the Historical Figures chapter.

Albertus Magnus, c.1200-80, (Ger.) theologian, philosopher; helped found medieval study of natural science.

Alhazen (Ibn al-Haytham), c. 965-c. 1040, mathematician, astronomer, optical theorist.

Andre-Marie Ampère, 1775-1836, (Fr.) mathematician, chemist; founder of electrodynamics.

Neil Armstrong, 1930-2012, (U.S.) astronaut, first man to walk on the Moon.

John V. Atanasoff, 1903-95, (U.S.) physicist; co-invented Atanasoff-Berry electronic digital computer (1939-41).

Amedeo Avogadro, 1776-1856, (It.) chemist, physicist; proposed that equal volumes of gas contain equal numbers of molecules, permitting determination of molecular weights.

John Bardeen, 1908-91, (U.S.) double Nobel laureate in physics (transistor, 1956; superconductivity, 1972).

A. H. Becquerel, 1852-1908, (Fr.) physicist; discovered radioactivity in uranium (1896).

Alexander Graham Bell, 1847-1922, (U.S.) inventor; first to patent and commercially exploit the telephone (1876).

Daniel Bernoulli, 1700-82, (Switz.) mathematician; developed fluid dynamics and kinetic theory of gases.

Clifford Berry, 1918-63, (U.S.) collaborated with John V. Atanasoff on the ABC electronic digital computer (1939-41).

Jöns Jakob Berzelius, 1779-1848, (Swed.) chemist; developed modern chemical symbols and formulas.

Henry Bessemer, 1813-98, (Br.) engineer; invented Bessemer steel-making process.

Hans Bethe, 1906-2005, (Ger.-U.S.) physicist; won Nobel Prize in 1967 for describing how stars generate energy.

Bruno Bettelheim, 1903-90, (Austria-U.S.) psychoanalyst; studied disturbed children; *Uses of Enchantment* (1976).

Louis Blériot, 1872-1936, (Fr.) engineer; monoplane pioneer, first Channel flight (1909).

Franz Boas, 1858-1942, (Ger.-U.S.) founded modern anthropology; studied Pacific Coast tribes.

Niels Bohr, 1885-1962, (Den.) atomic and nuclear physicist; founded quantum mechanics.

Norman Borlaug, 1914-2009, (U.S.) plant pathologist and geneticist; father of "green" (agricultural) revolution.

Max Born, 1882-1970, (Ger.) atomic and nuclear physicist; helped develop quantum mechanics.

Satyendranath Bose, 1894-1974, (India) physicist; forerunner of modern quantum theory for integral-spin particles.

Louis de Broglie, 1892-1987, (Fr.) physicist; proposed quantum wave-particle duality.

Robert Bunsen, 1811-99, (Ger.) chemist; pioneered spectroscopic analysis; discovered rubidium, caesium.

Luther Burbank, 1849-1926, (U.S.) naturalist; developed plant breeding into a modern science.

Vannevar Bush, 1890-1974, (U.S.) electrical engineer; developed differential analyzer, an early analogue computer; headed WWII Office of Scientific Res. and Dev.

Marvin Camras, 1916-95, (U.S.) inventor, electrical engineer; invented magnetic tape recording.

Alexis Carrel, 1873-1944, (Fr.) surgeon, biologist; developed methods of suturing blood vessels, transplanting organs.

Rachel Carson, 1907-64, (U.S.) marine biologist, environmentalist; *Silent Spring* (1962).

George Washington Carver, 1864-1943, (U.S.) chemist and botanist; promoted alternative crops.

James Chadwick, 1891-1974, (Br.) physicist; discovered the neutron (1932); led Brit. Manhattan Project group in U.S.

Albert Claude, 1898-1983, (Belg.-U.S.) a founder of modern cell biology; determined role of mitochondria.

Samuel Cohen, 1921-2010, (U.S.) physicist who invented the neutron bomb.

Barry Commoner, 1917-2012, biologist; noted environmentalist.

Nicolaus Copernicus, 1473-1543, (Pol.) first modern astronomer to propose Sun as center of the planets' motions.

Jacques Yves Cousteau, 1910-97, (Fr.) oceanographer; co-inventor, with Emile Gagnan, of the Aqualung (1943).

Seymour Cray, 1925-96, (U.S.) computer industry pioneer; developed supercomputers.

Francis Crick, 1916-2004, (Br.) biophysicist; co-discoverer of genetic code; shared 1962 Nobel Prize.

Marie, 1867-1934, (Pol.-Fr.) and **Pierre Curie**, 1859-1906, (Fr.) physical chemists; pioneer investigators of radioactivity; discovered radium and polonium (1898).

Gottlieb Daimler, 1834-1900, (Ger.) engineer, inventor; pioneer automobile manufacturer.

John Dalton, 1766-1844, (Br.) chemist, physicist; formulated atomic theory, made first table of atomic weights.

Charles Darwin, 1809-82, (Br.) naturalist; established theory of organic evolution; *Origin of Species* (1859).

Lee De Forest, 1873-1961, (U.S.) inventor of triode; pioneer in wireless telegraphy, sound pictures, television.

Pierre-Gilles de Gennes, 1932-2007, (Fr.) physicist whose research aided development of liquid-crystal display (LCD); awarded Nobel Prize for Physics, 1991.

Max Delbruck, 1906-81, (Ger.-U.S.) founded molecular biology.

Rudolf Diesel, 1858-1913, (Ger.) mechanical engineer; patented Diesel engine (1892).

Theodosius Dobzhansky, 1900-75, (Russ.-U.S.) biologist; reconciled genetics and natural selection.

Christian Doppler, 1803-53, (Austria) physicist; showed change in wave frequency caused by motion of source, now known as Doppler effect.

J. Presper Eckert Jr., 1919-95, (U.S.) co-inventor, with John W. Mauchly, of the ENIAC computer (1943-45).

Thomas A. Edison, 1847-1931, (U.S.) inventor; held more than 1,000 patents, including incandescent electric lamp.

Robert Edwards, 1925-2013, (Br.) physiologist; pioneered in vitro fertilization.

Paul Ehrlich, 1854-1915, (Ger.) medical researcher in immunology and bacteriology; pioneered antitoxin production.

Albert Einstein, 1879-1955, (Ger.) theoretical physicist; founded relativity theory.

John F. Enders, 1897-1985, (U.S.) virologist; helped discover vaccines against polio, measles, mumps and chicken pox.

Erik Erikson, 1902-94, (U.S.) psychoanalyst, author; theory of developmental stages of life; *Childhood and Society* (1950).

Leonhard Euler, 1707-83, (Switz.) mathematician, physicist; pioneer of calculus, revived ideas of Fermat.

Gabriel Fahrenheit, 1686-1736, (Ger.) physicist; improved thermometers and introduced Fahrenheit temperature scale.

Michael Faraday, 1791-1867, (Br.) chemist, physicist; discovered electrical induction and invented dynamo (1831).

Philo T. Farnsworth, 1906-71, (U.S.) inventor; built first television system (San Francisco, 1928).

Pierre de Fermat, 1601-65, (Fr.) mathematician; founded modern theory of numbers.

Enrico Fermi, 1901-54, (It.-U.S.) nuclear physicist; demonstrated first controlled chain reaction (Chicago, 1942).

Richard Feynman, 1918-88, (U.S.) theoretical physicist, author; founder of Quantum Electrodynamics (QED).

Alexander Fleming, 1881-1955, (Br.) bacteriologist; discovered penicillin (1928).

Jean B. J. Fourier, 1768-1830, (Fr.) introduced Fourier Series, method of analysis in math and physics.

Sigmund Freud, 1856-1939, (Austria) psychiatrist; founder of psychoanalysis; *Interpretation of Dreams* (1901).

Erich Fromm, 1900-80, (U.S.) psychoanalyst; *Man for Himself* (1947).

Galileo Galilei, 1564-1642, (It.) physicist; used telescope to vindicate Copernicus, founded modern science of motion.

Carl Friedrich Gauss, 1777-1855, (Ger.) mathematician; completed work of Fermat and Euler in number theory.

Josiah W. Gibbs, 1839-1903, (U.S.) theoretical physicist, chemist; founded chemical thermodynamics.

Robert H. Goddard, 1882-1945, (U.S.) physicist; invented liquid fuel rocket (1926).

George W. Goethals, 1858-1928, (U.S.) chief engineer who completed Panama Canal (1907-14).

William C. Gorgas, 1854-1920, (U.S.) physician; pioneer in prevention of yellow fever and malaria.

Stephen Jay Gould, 1941-2002, (U.S.) paleontologist, evolutionary biologist, writer.

Ernst Haeckel, 1834-1919, (Ger.) zoologist, evolutionist; early Darwinist, introduced concept of "ecology."

Otto Hahn, 1879-1968, (Ger.) chemist; with Lise Meitner discovered nuclear fission (1938).

Edmund Halley, 1656-1742, (Br.) astronomer; predicted return of 1682 comet (Halley's Comet) in 1759.

William Harvey, 1578-1657, (Br.) physician, anatomist; discovered circulation of the blood (1628).

Werner Heisenberg, 1901-76, (Ger.) physicist; developed matrix mechanics and uncertainty principle (1927).

Hermann von Helmholtz, 1821-94, (Ger.) physicist, physiologist; formulated principle of conservation of energy.

William Herschel, 1738-1822, (Ger.-Br.) astronomer; discovered Uranus (1781).

Heinrich Hertz, 1857-94, (Ger.) physicist; discovered radio waves and photo-electric effect (1886-87).

David Hilbert, 1862-1943, (Ger.) mathematician; contributed to algebra, calculus, and foundational studies (formalism).

Albert Hofmann, 1906-2008, (Switz.) chemist; father of LSD.

Edwin P. Hubble, 1889-1953, (U.S.) astronomer; discovered observational evidence of expanding universe.

Alexander von Humboldt, 1769-1859, (Ger.) naturalist; explored S. America, created ecology.

Edward Jenner, 1749-1823, (Br.) physician; pioneered vaccination, introduced term "virus."

James Joule, 1818-89, (Br.) physicist; found relation between heat and mechanical energy (conservation of energy).

Carl Jung, 1875-1961, (Switz.) psychiatrist; founder of analytical psychology.

Ernest Everett Just, 1883-1941, (U.S.) marine biologist; studied egg development; *Biology of Cell Surfaces* (1941).

Johannes Kepler, 1571-1630, (Ger.) astronomer; discovered laws of planetary motion.

Al-Khawarizmi, early 9th cent., (Arab.) mathematician; regarded as founder of algebra.

Robert Koch, 1843-1910, (Ger.) bacteriologist; isolated bacterial causes of tuberculosis and other diseases.

Georges Köhler, 1946-95, (Ger.) immunologist; with Cesar Milstein, developed monoclonal antibody technique.

Willem Kolff, 1911-2009, (Neth.-U.S.) physician, biomedical engineer; developed first practical kidney dialysis machine; considered the "father of artificial organs."

Jacques Lacan, 1901-81, (Fr.) influential psychoanalyst.

Joseph Lagrange, 1736-1813, (Fr.) geometer, astronomer; showed that gravity of Earth and Moon cancel, creating stable points in space around them.

Jean B. Lamarck, 1744-1829, (Fr.) naturalist; forerunner of Darwin in evolutionary theory.

Pierre Simon de Laplace, 1749-1827, (Fr.) astronomer, physicist; proposed nebular origin for solar system.

Lewis H. Latimer, 1848-1928, (U.S.) African American scientist; associate of Edison; supervised installation of first electric street lighting in New York City.

Antoine Lavoisier, 1743-94, (Fr.) a founder of modern chemistry.

Ernest O. Lawrence, 1901-58, (U.S.) physicist; invented the cyclotron.

Louis, 1903-72, and **Mary Leakey**, 1913-96, (both Br.) early hominid paleoanthropologists; discovered remains in Africa.

Anton van Leeuwenhoek, 1632-1723, (Neth.) founder of microscopy.

Jerome Lejeune, 1927-94, (Fr.) geneticist; discovered chromosomal cause of Down syndrome (1959).

Claude Levi-Strauss, 1908-2009, (Belg.-Fr.) cultural anthropologist, sociologist, philosopher.

Kurt Lewin, 1890-1947, (Ger.-U.S.) social psychologist; studied human motivation and group dynamics.

Justus von Liebig, 1803-73, (Ger.) founded quantitative organic chemistry.

Joseph Lister, 1827-1912, (Br.) physician; pioneered antiseptic surgery.

Hendrik Lorentz, 1853-1928, (Neth.) physicist; developed electron theory of matter, contributed to relativity theory.

Konrad Lorenz, 1903-89, (Austria) ethologist; pioneer in study of animal behavior.

Bernard Lovell, 1913-2012, (Br.) physicist and radio astronomer.

Percival Lowell, 1855-1916, (U.S.) astronomer; predicted the existence of Pluto.

Louis, 1864-1948, and **Auguste Lumière**, 1862-1954, (both Fr.) invented cinematograph, made first motion picture (1895).

Theodore H. Maiman, 1927-2007, (U.S.) physicist; invented the first workable laser, which he displayed in 1960.

Guglielmo Marconi, 1874-1937, (It.) physicist; developed wireless telegraphy.

John W. Mauchly, 1907-80, (U.S.) co-inventor, with J. Presper Eckert Jr., of computer ENIAC (1943-45).

James Clerk Maxwell, 1831-79, (Br.) physicist; unified electricity and magnetism, electromagnetic theory of light.

Maria Goeppert Mayer, 1906-72, (Ger.-U.S.) physicist; developed shell model of atomic nuclei.

Barbara McClintock, 1902-92, (U.S.) geneticist; showed that some genetic elements are mobile.

Lise Meitner, 1878-1968, (Austria) co-discoverer, with Otto Hahn, of nuclear fission (1938).

Gregor J. Mendel, 1822-84, (Austria) botanist, monk; his experiments became the foundation of modern genetics.

Dmitri Mendeleyev, 1834-1907, (Russ.) chemist; established Periodic Table of the Elements.

Bruce R. Merrifield, 1921-2006, (U.S.) chemist; discovered how to synthesize proteins quickly and efficiently.

Franz Mesmer, 1734-1815, (Ger.) physician; introduced hypnotherapy.

Albert A. Michelson, 1852-1931, (U.S.) physicist; invented interferometer.

Robert A. Millikan, 1868-1953, (U.S.) physicist; measured electronic charge.

Thomas Hunt Morgan, 1866-1945, (U.S.) geneticist, embryologist; established role of chromosomes in heredity.

Isaac Newton, 1642-1727, (Br.) natural philosopher; discovered laws of gravitation, motion; with Gottfried Wilhelm Leibniz, founded calculus.

Robert N. Noyce, 1927-90, (U.S.) invented microchip.

J. Robert Oppenheimer, 1904-67, (U.S.) physicist; scientific director of Manhattan Project.

Wilhelm Ostwald, 1853-1932, (Ger.) chemist, philosopher; main founder of modern physical chemistry.

Louis Pasteur, 1822-95, (Fr.) chemist; showed that germs cause disease and fermentation; originated pasteurization.

Linus C. Pauling, 1901-94, (U.S.) chemist; studied chemical bonds; campaigned for nuclear disarmament.

Jean Piaget, 1896-1980, (Switz.) psychologist; four-stage theory of intellectual development in children.

Max Planck, 1858-1947, (Ger.) physicist; introduced quantum hypothesis (1900).

Jules Henri Poincaré, 1854-1912, (Fr.) mathematician; founded algebraic topology, many other discoveries.

Walter S. Reed, 1851-1902, (U.S.) Army physician; proved mosquitoes transmit yellow fever.

Theodor Reik, 1888-1969, (Austria-U.S.) psychoanalyst; major Freudian disciple.

Sally Ride, 1951-2012, (U.S.) astronaut; 1st U.S. woman in space.

Bernhard Riemann, 1826-66, (Ger.) mathematician; developed non-Euclidean geometry used by Einstein.

Norbert Rillieux, 1806-94, (U.S.) African American inventor of a vacuum pan evaporator (1846); revolutionized sugar-refining industry.

Wilhelm Roentgen, 1845-1923, (Ger.) physicist; discovered X-rays (1895).

Carl Rogers, 1902-87, (U.S.) psychotherapist, author; originated nondirective therapy.

Ernest Rutherford, 1871-1937, (Br.) physicist; pioneer investigator of radioactivity, identified the atomic nucleus.

Albert B. Sabin, 1906-93, (Russ.-U.S.) developed oral polio live-virus vaccine.

Carl Sagan, 1934-96, (U.S.) astronomer, author.

Jonas Salk, 1914-95, (U.S.) developed first successful polio vaccine, widely used in U.S. after 1955.

Allan Sandage, 1926-2010, (U.S.) astronomer; refined the Hubble Constant, a measure of the universe's expansion.

Frederick Sanger, 1918-2013, (Br.) biochemist; detailed molecular structure of insulin.

Giovanni Schiaparelli, 1835-1910, (It.) astronomer; reported canals on Mars.

Erwin Schrödinger, 1887-1961, (Austria) physicist; developed wave equation for quantum systems.

Glenn T. Seaborg, 1912-99, (U.S.) chemist; Nobel Prize winner (1951); co-discoverer of plutonium.

Harlow Shapley, 1885-1972, (U.S.) astronomer; mapped galactic clusters and position of Sun in our galaxy.

Norman E. Shumway, 1923-2006, (U.S.) surgeon; performed world's first successful heart-lung transplant.

B. F. Skinner, 1904-90, (U.S.) psychologist; leading advocate of behaviorism.

Richard E. Smalley, 1943-2005, (U.S.) chemist; with three other scientists, discovered buckminsterfullerenes, a previously unknown class of carbon molecules.

Roger W. Sperry, 1913-94, (U.S.) neurobiologist; established different functions of right and left sides of brain.

Benjamin Spock, 1903-98, (U.S.) pediatrician, child care expert; *Common Sense Book of Baby and Child Care*.

Charles P. Steinmetz, 1865-1923, (Ger.-U.S.) electrical engineer; developed basic ideas on alternating current.

Ernst Stuhlinger, 1913-2008, (Ger.) rocket scientist; electric propulsion for NASA in early space age.

Leo Szilard, 1898-1964, (Hung.-U.S.) physicist; helped on Manhattan Project, later opposed nuclear weapons.

Edward Teller, 1908-2003, (Hung.-U.S.) physicist; aided on Manhattan Project, had key role in development of H-bomb.

Nikola Tesla, 1856-1943, (Serb.-U.S.) invented electrical devices including AC dynamos, transformers, and motors.

William Thomson (Lord Kelvin), 1824-1907, (Br.) physicist; aided in success of transatlantic telegraph cable (1865); proposed Kelvin absolute temperature scale.

Alan Turing, 1912-54, (Br.) mathematician; helped develop basis for computers.

James Van Allen, 1914-2006, (U.S.) physicist; discovered the presence of radiation belts around Earth (Van Allen belts).

Rudolf Virchow, 1821-1902, (Ger.) pathologist; pioneered the modern theory that diseases affect the body through cells.

Alessandro Volta, 1745-1827, (It.) physicist; electricity pioneer.

Wernher von Braun, 1912-77, (Ger.-U.S.) developed rockets for warfare and space exploration.

John von Neumann, 1903-57, (Hung.-U.S.) mathematician; originated game theory; basic design for modern computers.

Alfred Russell Wallace, 1823-1913, (Br.) naturalist; proposed concept of evolution independently of Darwin.

John B. Watson, 1878-1958, (U.S.) psychologist; a founder of behaviorism.

James E. Watt, 1736-1819, (Br.) mechanical engineer, inventor; invented modern steam engine (1765).

Alfred L. Wegener, 1880-1930, (Ger.) meteorologist, geophysicist; postulated continental drift.

Norbert Wiener, 1894-1964, (U.S.) mathematician; founder of cybernetics.

Daniel Hale Williams, 1858-1931, (U.S.) African American surgeon; performed one of first two open-heart operations (1893).

Sewall Wright, 1889-1988, (U.S.) evolutionary theorist; helped found population genetics.

Wilhelm Wundt, 1832-1920, (Ger.) founder of experimental psychology.

Qian Xuesen, 1911-2009, (China) rocket scientist; helped found Jet Propulsion Lab, father of China's space program.

Rosalyn Yalow, 1921-2011, (U.S.) physicist; co-developer of radioimmunoassay.

Ferdinand von Zeppelin, 1838-1917, (Ger.) soldier, aeronaut, airship designer.

Social Reformers, Activists, and Humanitarians of the Past

Ralph David Abernathy, 1926-90, (U.S.) black civil rights activist; pres., 1968, Southern Christian Leadership Conf.

Jane Addams, 1860-1935, (U.S.) cofounder of Hull House; won Nobel Peace Prize, 1931.

Susan B. Anthony, 1820-1906, (U.S.) a leader in temperance, antislavery, and woman suffrage movements.

Thomas Barnardo, 1845-1905, (Br.) social reformer; pioneer in care of destitute children.

Clara Barton, 1821-1912, (U.S.) organized American Red Cross.

Daisy Bates, 1914-99, (U.S.) black civil rights leader who fought for integration; advocate for the "Little Rock 9" during Arkansas desegregation crisis in 1957.

Henry Ward Beecher, 1813-87, (U.S.) clergyman, abolitionist.

Peter Benenson, 1921-2005, (Br.) activist; founded Amnesty International, 1961.

Mary McLeod Bethune, 1875-1955, (U.S.) black educator, civil rights activist; adviser to FDR and Truman; founder, pres., Bethune-Cookman College.

Amelia Bloomer, 1818-94, (U.S.) suffragette, social reformer.

Yelena Bonner, 1923-2011, (Russ.) human rights activist in former Soviet Union.

William Booth, 1829-1912, (Br.) founded Salvation Army.

James Brady, 1940-2014, (U.S.) gun control advocate; Reagan press sec.

John Brown, 1800-59, (U.S.) abolitionist who led murder of five pro-slavery men; hanged.

Frances Xavier (Mother) Cabrini, 1850-1917, (It.-U.S.) nun; founded charitable institutions; first American canonized as a saint, 1946.

Stokely Carmichael (Kwame Toure), 1941-98, (Trinidad-U.S.) black power activist; major proponent of Pan-Africanism; prime min. of Black Panthers.

Carrie Chapman Catt, 1859-1947, (U.S.) suffragette.

Cesar Chavez, 1927-93, (U.S.) labor leader; helped establish United Farm Workers of America.

Eldridge Cleaver, 1935-98, (U.S.) revolutionary social critic; former minister of information for Black Panthers; *Soul on Ice*.

Clarence Darrow, 1857-1938, (U.S.) lawyer; defender of underdog, opponent of capital punishment.

Ossie Davis, 1917-2005, (U.S.) black civil rights activist, actor, director.

Dorothy Day, 1897-1980, (U.S.) founder of Catholic Worker movement.

Eugene V. Debs, 1855-1926, (U.S.) labor leader; led Pullman strike, 1894; 4-time Socialist presidential candidate.

Vine Deloria Jr., 1933-2005, (U.S.) Native American activist, author; *Custer Died for Your Sins*.

Dorothea Dix, 1802-87, (U.S.) crusader for mentally ill.

Thomas Dooley, 1927-61, (U.S.) "jungle doctor"; noted for efforts to supply medical aid to developing countries.

Marjory Stoneman Douglas, 1890-1998, (U.S.) writer, environmentalist; campaigned to save Florida Everglades.

Frederick Douglass, 1817-95, (U.S.) slave, author, editor, orator, diplomat; edited abolitionist weekly *The North Star*.

Andrea Dworkin, 1946-2005, (U.S.) radical feminist, antipornography crusader.

Medgar Evers, 1925-63, (U.S.) black civil rights leader; campaigned to register black voters; assassinated.

James Farmer, 1920-99, (U.S.) black civil rights leader; founded Congress of Racial Equality (CORE).

Betty Friedan, 1921-2006, (U.S.) author, feminist; *The Feminine Mystique*.

Millard Fuller, 1935-2009, (U.S.) founder of Habitat for Humanity.

William Lloyd Garrison, 1805-79, (U.S.) abolitionist.

Miep Gies, 1909-2010, (Neth.) protector of Anne Frank and her family during WWII.

Emma Goldman, 1869-1940, (Russ.-U.S.) published anarchist *Mother Earth*; birth-control advocate.

Samuel Gompers, 1850-1924, (U.S.) labor leader; first president of the American Federation of Labor (AFL).

Prince Hall, 1735-1807, (U.S.) activist; founded black Freemasonry; served in American Revolutionary War.

Michael Harrington, 1928-89, (U.S.) exposed poverty in affluent U.S. in *The Other America*, 1963.

Dorothy Height, 1912-2010, (U.S.) civil rights activist; pres. of the National Council of Negro Women, 1957-97.

Sidney Hillman, 1887-1946, (U.S.) labor leader; helped organize CIO.

Benjamin Hooks, 1925-2010, (U.S.) civil rights activist; exec. dir. NAACP, 1977-92.

Samuel G. Howe, 1801-76, (U.S.) social reformer; changed public attitudes toward the blind, deaf, mentally challenged.

Franklin Kameny, 1925-2011, (U.S.) gay rights activist.

Helen Keller, 1880-1968, (U.S.) crusader for better treatment for the disabled; deaf and blind herself.

Jack Kevorkian 1928-2011, (U.S.) pathologist; assisted-suicide activist.

Coretta Scott King, 1927-2006, (U.S.) black civil rights leader; wife of Rev. Martin Luther King Jr.

Rev. Martin Luther King Jr., 1929-68, (U.S.) civil rights leader; led 1955-56 Montgomery, AL, boycott; founder, pres., Southern Christian Leadership Conference, 1957; Nobel peace laureate, 1964; assassinated.

Maggie Kuhn, 1905-95, (U.S.) founded Gray Panthers, 1970.

William Kunstler, 1919-95, (U.S.) civil liberties attorney.

John L. Lewis, 1880-1969, (U.S.) labor leader; headed United Mine Workers, 1920-60.

Almena Lomax, 1915-2011, (U.S.) civil rights activist; journalist who founded *The Los Angeles Tribune*.

Clara Luper, 1923-2011, (U.S.) civil rights activist.

Wangari Maathai, 1940-2011, (Kenya), environmental activist; 2004 Nobel Peace Prize winner.

Robert Macauley, 1923-2010, (U.S.) founder of AmeriCares.

Malcolm X (Little), 1925-65, (U.S.) Black Muslim, black nationalist leader; promoted black pride; assassinated.

Russell Means, 1939-2012, (U.S.) American Indian activist.

Karl Menninger, 1893-1990, (U.S.) with brother William, founded Menninger Clinic and Menninger Foundation.

Lucretia Mott, 1793-1880, (U.S.) reformer, pioneer feminist.

Philip Murray, 1886-1952, (U.S.) Scottish-born labor leader.

Huey P. Newton, 1942-89, (U.S.) co-founded Black Panther Party, 1966.

Florence Nightingale, 1820-1910, (Br.) founder of modern nursing.

Emmeline Pankhurst, 1858-1928, (Br.) suffragette.

Rosa Parks, 1913-2005, (U.S.) black civil rights activist; her actions sparked 1955-56 Montgomery, AL, bus boycott.

A. Philip Randolph, 1889-1979, (U.S.) organized Brotherhood of Sleeping Car Porters, 1925; an organizer of 1941 and 1963 March on Washington movements.

Walter Reuther, 1907-70, (U.S.) labor leader; headed United Auto Workers.

Jacob Riis, 1849-1914, (U.S.) crusader for urban reforms.

Paul Robeson, 1898-1976, (U.S.) actor, singer, black civil rights activist.

Bayard Rustin, 1910-87, (U.S.) an organizer of the 1963 March on Washington; exec. director, A. Philip Randolph Institute.

Margaret Sanger, 1883-1966, (U.S.) social reformer; pioneered the birth-control movement.

Earl of Shaftesbury (A. A. Cooper), 1801-85, (Br.) social reformer.

Eunice Kennedy Shriver, 1921-2009, (U.S.) cofounder of Special Olympics for mentally challenged athletes.

Sargent Shriver, 1915-2011, (U.S.) founding director of Peace Corps; founder of Job Corps, Head Start.

Fred Shuttlesworth, 1922-2011, (U.S.) civil rights activist.

Albertina Sisulu, 1918-2011, (S. Africa), anti-apartheid activist.

Elizabeth Cady Stanton, 1815-1902, (U.S.) woman suffrage pioneer.

Lucy Stone, 1818-93, (U.S.) feminist, abolitionist.

Mother Teresa of Calcutta, 1910-97, (Alban.) nun; founded order to care for sick, dying poor; 1979 Nobel Peace Prize.

Willard Townsend, 1895-1957, (U.S.) organized the United Transport Service Employees (Red Caps), 1935.

Sojourner Truth (Isabella Baumfree), 1797-1883, (U.S.) preacher, abolitionist; worked for black educ. opportunity.

Harriet Tubman, 1823-1913, (U.S.) prominent figure in the Underground Railroad, which helped runaway slaves in the South reach safety in the North; nurse, spy for Union Army in the Civil War.

Nat Turner, 1800-31, (U.S.) slave who led the most significant of more than 200 slave revolts in U.S., in Southampton, VA; hanged.

Philip Vera Cruz, 1905-94, (Philip.-U.S.) helped found the United Farm Workers Union.

Edgar Wayburn, 1906-2010, (U.S.) conservationist; Sierra Club pres.

William Wilberforce, 1759-1833, (Br.) social reformer; prominent in struggle to abolish slave trade.

Frances E. Willard, 1839-98, (U.S.) temperance, women's rights leader.

Mary Wollstonecraft, 1759-97, (Br.) *Vindication of the Rights of Women*.

Sports Personalities of the Past and Present

Henry (Hank) Aaron, b 1934, Milwaukee-Atlanta outfielder; hit record 755 home runs, led NL 4 times; record 2,297 RBI.

Kareem Abdul-Jabbar, b 1947, Milwaukee, L.A. Lakers center; MVP 6 times; all-time leading NBA scorer, 38,387 points.

Andre Agassi, b 1970, tennis player; won Wimbledon (1992); U.S. Open ('94, '99), Austral. Open ('95, 2000-01, '03), French Open ('99).

Troy Aikman, b 1966, quarterback; led Dallas Cowboys to Super Bowl wins in 1993-94, '96; Super Bowl MVP, 1993.

Ben Ainslie, b 1977, (Br.) most decorated Olympic sailor; gold, 2000, '04, '08, '12. silver, 1996.

Amy Alcott, b 1956, golfer; 33 career wins (5 majors); inducted into Hall of Fame, 1999.

Grover Cleveland "Pete" Alexander, 1887-1950, pitcher; won 373 NL games; pitched 16 shutouts, 1916.

Muhammad Ali, b 1942, 3-time heavyweight champion.

Fernando Alonso, b 1981, (Sp.) Formula 1 racer; youngest ever to win a World Grand Prix championship, 2005; defended title, 2006.

Morten Andersen, b 1960, (Den.) kicker; NFL's career points leader, with 2,544 (1982-2007).

Gary Anderson, b 1959, (S. Afr.) kicker; NFL's 2nd in career points, with 2,434.

Sparky Anderson, 1934-2010, first manager to win World Series in the NL (Cincinnati, 1975-76) and AL (Detroit, 1984).

Mario Andretti, b 1940, (It.) race-car driver; won Daytona 500 (1967), Indy 500 (1969); Formula 1 world title (1978).

Earl Anthony, 1938-2001, bowler; won record 6 PBA Championships (1973-75, '81-'83), 43 career PBA tournaments.

Eddie Arcaro, 1916-97, only jockey to win racing's Triple Crown twice, 1941, '48; rode to 4,779 wins in his career.

Lance Armstrong, b 1971, cyclist; record 7-time winner of Tour de France (1999-2005); stripped of victories in 2012 for use of performance-enhancing drugs.

Arthur Ashe, 1943-93, tennis player; won U.S. Open (1968); Wimbledon (1975).

Evelyn Ashford, b 1957, sprinter; won 100m gold (1984) and silver (1988); member of 5 U.S. Olympic teams.

Red Auerbach, 1917-2006, coached Boston to 9 NBA titles.

Tracy Austin, b 1962, youngest player to win U.S. Open tennis title (age 16 in 1979).

Victoria Azarenka, b 1989, (Belarus) tennis player; won Australian Open (2012-13).

Ernie Banks, b 1931, Chicago Cubs slugger; hit 512 NL homers; twice MVP.

Roger Bannister, b 1929, (Br.) physician; ran 1st sub-4-min. mile, May 6, 1954 (3 min. 59.4 sec.).

Charles Barkley, b 1963, NBA MVP, 1993; 4th player ever to surpass 20,000 points, 10,000 rebounds, 4,000 assists.

Rick Barry, b 1944, NBA scoring leader, 1967; ABA scoring leader, 1969.

Sammy Baugh, 1914-2008, Washington Redskins quarterback; held numerous records upon retirement after 16 seasons.

Elgin Baylor, b 1934, L.A. Lakers forward; 11-time all-star.

Bob Beamon, b 1946, Olympic long jump gold medalist, 1968; world record jump of 29 ft 2½ in. stood until 1991.

Boris Becker, b 1967, (Ger.) tennis star; won U.S. Open 1989; Wimbledon champ 1985-86, '89.

David Beckham, b 1975, (Br.) soccer star; joined L.A. Galaxy, 2007-12, with record-breaking $250-mil contract.

Bill Belichick, b 1952, NFL coach; led New England Patriots to 3 Super Bowl wins (2001, '03-'04); best all-time post-season coaching record.

Jean Béliveau, b 1931, (Can.) Montréal Canadiens center; scored 507 goals; twice MVP.

Johnny Bench, b 1947, Cincinnati Reds catcher; twice MVP; led league in home runs twice, RBIs 3 times.

Patty Berg, 1918-2006, 80+ golf tournament wins; AP Woman Athlete of the Year 3 times.

Chris Berman, b 1955, sportscaster, anchor for ESPN and ABC Sports.

Yogi Berra, b 1925, Yankee catcher (1946-63); 3-time MVP.

Abebe Bikila, 1932-73, (Eth.) runner; won consecutive Olympic marathon gold medals in 1960 (barefoot), '64.

Matt Biondi, b 1965, swimmer; won 5 golds, 1988 Olympics.

Larry Bird, b 1956, Boston Celtics forward (1979-92); NBA MVP, 1984-86; 1998 coach of the year with Indiana Pacers.

Bonnie Blair, b 1964, speed skater; won 5 individual gold medals in 3 Olympics (1988, '92, '94).

George Blanda, 1927-2010, quarterback, kicker; 26 years as active player, scored 2,002 career points.

Fanny Blankers-Koen, 1918-2004, (Neth.) track star; won 4 golds in 1948 Olympics.

Wade Boggs, b 1958, AL batting champ, 1983, '85-'88; reached 3,000 career hits, 1999 (3,010).

Usain Bolt, b 1986, (Jam.) Olympic sprinter, gold medalist, 2008, '12; world record for men's 100m, 200m runs.

Barry Bonds, b 1964, outfielder; hit record 73 homers, 2001; NL MVP, 1990, '92-'93, 2001-04; 1st all-time in HRs (762); indicted in steroid scandal, 2007; convicted of obstruction of justice, 2011.

Björn Borg, b 1956, (Swed.) led Sweden to first Davis Cup, 1975; 6-time French Open, 5-time Wimbledon champion.

Ray Bourque, b 1960, (Can.) Boston defenseman,1979-2000; 5-time Norris Trophy winner; won Stanley Cup with Colorado, 2001.

Bill Bradley, b 1943, All-American at Princeton; led NY Knicks to 2 NBA titles (1970, '73); U.S. senator, 1979-97.

Donald Bradman, 1908-2001, (Austral.) widely regarded as greatest cricketer ever; set several batting records.

Terry Bradshaw, b 1948, quarterback; led Pittsburgh to 4 Super Bowl wins, 1975-76, '79-'80; NFL MVP, 1978.

Tom Brady, b 1977, quarterback; led New England Patriots to 3 Super Bowl titles, 2002, '04-'05; Super Bowl MVP, 2002, '04; NFL MVP, 2007, '11.

Ryan Braun, b 1983, Milwaukee Brewers left fielder; NL MVP, 2011.

Drew Brees, b 1979, New Orleans Saints quarterback; Super Bowl MVP, 2010.

Christine Brennan, b 1958, sports journalist for *USA Today*, radio and TV commentator specializing in figure skating.

George Brett, b 1953, Kansas City Royals infielder; led AL in batting, 1976, '80, '90; MVP, 1980.

Lou Brock, b 1939, St. Louis Cardinals outfielder; stole NL single-season record 118 bases, 1974; led NL 8 times.

Jim Brown, b 1936, Cleveland fullback; 12,312 career yds; NFL MVP 1957-58, '65.

Paul Brown, 1908-91, football team-owner, coach; led eponymous Cleveland Browns to 3 NFL championships.

Bob Bryan and **Mike Bryan,** b 1978, doubles tennis players; won French Open (2003, '13); U.S. Open, (2005, '08, '10, '12, '14); Wimbledon, (2006, '11, '13); Austral. Open (2006-07, '09-'12); Olympic gold, 2012.

Kobe Bryant, b 1978, NBA guard; won 3 straight titles with Lakers (2000-02); leading NBA scorer, 2005-06 and '06-'07; NBA MVP, 2007-08; NBA Finals MVP, 2009-10; member of U.S. Olympic gold medal teams (2008, '12).

Paul "Bear" Bryant, 1913-83, college football coach with 323 wins; led Alabama to 6 national titles (1961, '64-'65, '73, '78-'79).

Sergei Bubka, b 1963, (Ukr.) pole vaulter; first to clear 20 ft; gold medal, 1988 Olympics.

Don Budge, 1915-2000, won numerous amateur and pro tennis titles; Grand Slam, 1938.

Reggie Bush, b 1985, NFL running back; helped USC to 2 national titles (2003-04) ('04 vacated).

Dick Butkus, b 1942, Chicago Bears linebacker; NFL defensive player of the year (1969-70).

Dick Button, b 1929, figure skater; won 1948, '52 Olympic gold medals; world titleholder, 1948-52.

Miguel Cabrera, b 1983, (Venez.) 9-time All-Star; won AL triple crown (2012); AL MVP 2013.

Walter Camp, 1859-1925, Yale football player, coach, athletic director; established many rules for modern football.

Roy Campanella, 1921-93, Hall of Fame catcher for the Brooklyn Dodgers (1948-57); 3-time NL MVP.

Earl Campbell, b 1955, NFL running back; MVP 1978-79.

Jose Canseco, b 1964, outfielder; led Oakland A's to the World Series, 1988; wrote book about steroids in baseball, 2005.

Eric Cantona, b 1966, (Fr.) soccer star; Manchester United (1992-97).

Rod Carew, b 1945, AL infielder; 7 batting titles, 1977 MVP.

Steve Carlton, b 1944, NL pitcher; won 20 games 6 times, Cy Young award 4 times; 4,136 career strikeouts.

Pete Carroll, b 1951, college and pro football coach; coached the USC Trojans to 2 championships (2003-04).

Billy Casper, b 1931, PGA Player of the Year 2 times; U.S. Open champion twice.

Tamika Catchings, b 1979, Indiana Fever forward; 3-time Olympic gold medalist (2004, '08, '12); WNBA MVP, 2011.

Wilt Chamberlain, 1936-99, center; NBA leading scorer 7 times, MVP 4 times; scored 100 pts. in a game, 1962.

Bobby Clarke, b 1949, (Can.) Philadelphia Flyers center; led team to 2 Stanley Cup championships; MVP 3 times.

Roger Clemens, b 1962, pitcher; 1986 AL MVP; only 7-time Cy Young winner (1986-87, '91, '97-'98, 2001, '04); twice recorded record 20 Ks in a game; 354 wins, 4,672 Ks (3rd all-time); accused of lying to Congress about steroids, 2010.

Roberto Clemente, 1934-72, Pittsburgh Pirates outfielder; won 4 batting titles; MVP, 1966; 3,000 career hits; killed in plane crash.

Kim Clijsters, b 1983, (Belg.) tennis player; U.S. Open winner (2005, '09-'10); Austral. Open (2011).

Ty Cobb, 1886-1961, Detroit Tigers outfielder; record .367 lifetime batting average, 12 batting titles.

Sebastian Coe, b 1956, (Br.) runner; won Olympic 1,500m gold medal and 800m silver medal in 1980 and '84.

Nadia Comaneci, b 1961, (Rom.) gymnast; won 3 gold medals, achieved 7 perfect scores, 1976 Olympics; 9 Olympic medals overall.

Maureen Connolly, 1934-69, won tennis Grand Slam, 1953; AP Woman Athlete of the Year 3 times.

Jimmy Connors, b 1952, tennis player; 5 U.S. Open, 2 Wimbledon titles.

Alberto Contador, b 1982, (Sp.) cyclist; won Tour de France 2007, '09; stripped of 2010 title because of doping offense.

Cynthia Cooper, b 1963, basketball; 4-time MVP of WNBA finals; 2-time league MVP for the Houston Comets.

James J. Corbett, 1866-1933, heavyweight champion, 1892-97; credited with being the first "scientific" boxer.

Angel Cordero Jr., b 1942, jockey; leading money winner, 1976, '82-'83; rode 3 Kentucky Derby winners.

Margaret Smith Court, b 1942, (Austral.) tennis great; won 24 Grand Slam events.

Bob Cousy, b 1928, Boston guard; 6 NBA titles, 1957 MVP.

Sidney Crosby, b 1987, (Can.) hockey player; Art Ross Trophy (2007, '14), Olympic gold medal (2010).

Mark Cuban, b 1958, Dallas Mavericks owner; known for outspokenness.

Bjoern Daehlie, b 1967, (Nor.) cross-country skier; won record 8 Winter Olympic gold medals.

Lindsay Davenport, b 1976, tennis player; won Olympic gold, 1996; U.S. Open, 1998; Wimbledon, 1999; Austral. Open, 2000.

Al Davis, 1929-2011, Oakland Raiders owner, former coach.

Oscar De La Hoya, b 1973, won IBF lightweight (1995); WBC super lightweight (1996); welterweight (1997-99, 2000) titles.

Donna de Varona, b 1947, swimmer; won 2 Olympic golds, 1964; 1st female sportscaster at a major network, 1965.

Dizzy Dean, 1910-74, pitcher; St. Louis Cardinals' "Gashouse Gang" in the '30s.

Mary Decker Slaney, b 1958, runner; has held 6 separate American records from the 800m to 10,000m.

Frank Deford, b 1938, sr. contributing writer for *Sports Illustrated*; author, commentator.

Juan Martin del Potro, b 1988, (Arg.) tennis player; won U.S. Open, 2009.

Jack Dempsey, 1895-1983, heavyweight champ, 1919-26.

Gail Devers, b 1966, Olympic 100m gold medalist (1992, '96).

Joe DiMaggio, 1914-99, NY Yankees outfielder; hit safely in record 56 consecutive games, 1941; AL MVP 3 times.

Novak Djokovic, b 1987, (Serb.) tennis player; won Austral. Open (2008, '11-'13), Wimbledon (2011, '14), U.S. Open (2011).

Landon Donovan, b 1982, soccer forward; all-time leading U.S. men's intl. goal scorer with 57; MLS MVP, 2009.

Tony Dorsett, b 1954, Heisman winner who led the Dallas Cowboys to an NFL title in his rookie year, 1977.

Gabrielle Douglas, b 1995, first African-American gymnast to win Olympic gold in all-around (2012).

Tim Duncan, b 1976, San Antonio center; 3-time NBA Finals MVP, 1999, 2003, '05; NBA MVP, 2002-03.

Roberto Duran, b 1951, (Pan.) boxer; held titles at 3 weights; lost 1980 "no mas" fight to Sugar Ray Leonard.

Kevin Durant, b 1988, NBA forward; Olympic gold medalist, 2012; NBA MVP, 2014.

Leo Durocher, 1905-91, manager; won 3 NL pennants (Brooklyn, 1941; NY Giants, 1951, '54), 1954 World Series.

Dale Earnhardt Jr., b 1974, stock car racer; Daytona 500 winner (2004, '14).

Dale Earnhardt Sr., 1951-2001, 7-time NASCAR Winston Cup champ; died in a last-lap crash at 2001 Daytona 500.

Stefan Edberg, b 1966, (Swed.) tennis player; U.S. Open (1991-92), Wimbledon (1988, '90), Austral. Open (1985, '87).

Gertrude Ederle, 1905-2003, first woman to swim English Channel; broke existing men's record, 1926.

Teresa Edwards, b 1964, 5-time basketball Olympian; gold medalist, 1984, '88, '96, 2000; bronze medalist, 1992.

Hicham El Guerrouj, b 1974, (Morocco) runner; holds world records in mile (3:43.13) and 1,500m (3:26); won gold medals in 1,500m and 5,000m, 2004 Olympics.

John Elway, b 1960, quarterback; led Denver Broncos to 2 Super Bowl wins, 1998-99; NFL MVP, 1987; Super Bowl MVP, 1999.

Julius "Dr. J" Erving, b 1950, 3-time ABA MVP, 1981 NBA MVP.

Phil Esposito, b 1942, (Can.) NHL scoring leader 5 times.

Janet Evans, b 1971, 4 Olympic swimming golds, 1988, '92.

Lee Evans, b 1947, Olympic 400m gold medalist in 1968 with 43.86-sec. world record not broken until 1988.

Chris Evert, b 1954, 6-time U.S. tennis champ, 3-time Wimbledon champ.

Ray Ewry, 1873-1937, track-and-field star; won 8 Olympics gold medals (1900, '04, '08).

Nick Faldo, b 1957, (Br.) golfer; won Masters, British Open 3 times each.

Juan Manuel Fangio, 1911-95 (Arg.), 5-time World Grand Prix driving champ (1951, '54-'57).

Marshall Faulk, b 1973, 2000 NFL MVP; scored then-record 26 TDs, 2001; 3-time Off. Player of the Year (1999-2001).

Brett Favre, b 1969, quarterback; led Green Bay to Super Bowl win, 1997; NFL MVP, 1995-96; co-MVP, 1997; left retirement to play for NY Jets, 2008; Minnesota Vikings, 2009-10.

Roger Federer, b 1981, (Switz.) tennis star; won Austral. Open (2004, '06-'07, '10), Wimbledon (2003-07, '09, '12), U.S. Open (2004-08), French Open (2009).

Bob Feller, 1918-2010, Cleveland Indians pitcher; won 266 games; pitched 3 no-hitters, 12 one-hitters.

Rollie Fingers, b 1946, pitcher; 341 career saves; AL MVP, Cy Young Award, 1981; World Series MVP, 1974.

Peggy Fleming, b 1948, world figure skating champion, 1966-68; gold medalist, 1968 Olympics.

Whitey Ford, b 1928, NY Yankees pitcher; won record 10 World Series games.

George Foreman, b 1949, heavyweight champion, 1973-74, '94-'95; at 45, oldest to win a heavyweight title; gold medalist, 1968 Olympics.

Dick Fosbury, b 1947, high jumper; won 1968 Olympic gold medal; developed the "Fosbury Flop."

Jimmie Foxx, 1907-67, Red Sox, Athletics slugger; MVP 3 times; triple crown, 1933.

A. J. Foyt, b 1935, won Indy 500 4 times; U.S. Auto Club champ 7 times.

Dario Franchitti, b 1973, (Scot.) 3-time Indy 500 winner, 2007, '10, '12.

Missy Franklin, b 1995, won 4 Olympic swimming golds, 2012.

Joe Frazier, 1944-2011, heavyweight champion, 1970-73; gold medalist, 1964 Olympics.

Walt Frazier, b 1945, Hall of Fame guard for NY Knicks' NBA championship teams (1970, '73).

Peter Gammons, b 1945, sportswriter, broadcaster; named to Baseball Hall of Fame.

Lou Gehrig, 1903-41, NY Yankees 1st baseman; MVP, 1927, '36; triple crown, 1934; AL record 184 RBIs, 1931; played in 2,130 straight games (1925-39), a record that stood until 1995.

Althea Gibson, 1927-2003, 2-time U.S. Nationals and Wimbledon champ.

Bob Gibson, b 1935, St. Louis Cardinals pitcher; won Cy Young award twice; struck out 3,117 batters.

Josh Gibson, 1911-47, Hall of Fame catcher; known as "Babe Ruth of the Negro Leagues"; credited with as many as 84 homers in 1 season, about 800 in his career.

Marc Girardelli, b 1963, (Lux.) skier; won 5 World Cup titles.

Raul Gonzalez, b 1977, (Sp.) soccer player; led Real Madrid to 3 Champions League titles (1998, 2000, '02); all-time top UEFA goal scorer (71).

Jeff Gordon, b 1971, race-car driver; youngest to win NASCAR title 4 times (1995, '97-'98, 2001).

Steffi Graf, b 1969, (Ger.) won tennis Grand Slam 1988; U.S. Open champ 5 times; Wimbledon, 7 times; Austral. 4 times; French 6 times.

Otto Graham, 1921-2003, Cleveland quarterback; 4-time all-pro.

Red Grange, 1903-91, All-American at Univ. of Illinois, 1923-25; played for Chicago Bears, 1925-35.

"Mean" Joe Greene, b 1946, Pittsburgh Steelers lineman; twice NFL outstanding defensive player.

Wayne Gretzky, b 1961, (Can.) top scorer in NHL history with record 894 goals, 1,963 assists, 2,857 points; MVP, 1980-87, '89.

Bob Griese, b 1945, All-Pro quarterback; led Miami Dolphins to undefeated 17-0 season, 1972, 2 Super Bowl titles, 1973-74.

Ken Griffey Jr., b 1969, outfielder; led AL in homers 1994, '97-'99; 1997 AL MVP; 10 gold gloves.

Archie Griffin, b 1954, Ohio State running back; only 2-time winner of the Heisman Trophy (1974-75).

Florence Griffith Joyner, 1959-98, sprinter; won 3 gold medals at 1988 Olympics; world and Olympic record for 100m.

Lefty Grove, 1900-75, pitcher; won 300 AL games.

Vladimir Guerrero, b 1975, (Dom. Rep.) right fielder; 2004 AL MVP award.

Janet Guthrie, b 1938, 1st woman driver in Indy 500 (1977).

Tony Gwynn, 1960-2014, 8-time NL batting champ (1984, '87-'89, '94-'97); 3,141 career hits.

Walter Hagen, 1892-1969, golfer; 5 PGA, 4 British Open titles.

Mika Hakkinen, b 1968, (Fin.) Formula One racing driver; Formula One champion, 1998-99.

George Halas, 1895-1983, founder/player/coach of Chicago Bears; won 6 NFL championships as coach.

Roy Halladay, b 1977, pitcher; Cy Young Award, 2003, '10; pitched perfect game, 2010.

Dorothy Hamill, b 1956, figure skater; gold medalist at the Olympics and World championships, 1976.

Josh Hamilton, b 1981, Texas Rangers outfielder; AL MVP, 2010.

Scott Hamilton, b 1958, U.S. and world figure skating champion, 1981-84; Olympic gold medalist, 1984.

Mia Hamm, b 1972, soccer player; led U.S. teams to World Cup victories (1991, '99) and Olympic gold (1996, 2004).

Franco Harris, b 1950, running back; 4 Super Bowls with Steelers (1975-76, '79-'80); 1,000+ yds in a season 8 times.

Marvin Harrison, b 1972, Indianapolis Colts wide receiver; NFL record for single-season receptions (143), 2002.

Bill Hartack, 1932-2007, jockey; rode 5 Kentucky Derby winners.

Dominik Hasek b 1965, (Czech.) NHL goaltender; won Vezina Trophy, 1994-95, '97-'99, 2001; NHL MVP, 1997-98.

John Havlicek, b 1940, Boston Celtics forward; scored 26,395 career pts.

Eric Heiden, b 1958, speed skater; won 5 Olympic golds, 1980.

Rickey Henderson, b 1958, outfielder; 1990 AL MVP; record 130 stolen bases, 1982; all-time leader in steals, runs.

Sonja Henie, 1912-69, (Nor.) world champion figure skater, 1927-36; Olympic medalist, 1928, '32, '36.

Martina Hingis, b 1980, (Switz.) won Austral. and U.S. Opens, Wimbledon; youngest number one player (16 yrs., 6 mos.), 1997.

Ben Hogan, 1912-97, golfer; won 4 U.S. Open titles, 2 PGA Championships, 2 Masters.

Santonio Holmes, b 1984, wide receiver; Super Bowl MVP, 2009.

Evander Holyfield, b 1962, 4-time heavyweight champion.

Rogers Hornsby, 1896-1963, NL 2nd baseman; batted record .424, 1924; twice won triple crown.

Paul Hornung, b 1935, Green Bay Packers running back, placekicker; scored record 176 points, 1960.

Ryan Howard, b 1979, first baseman for Philadelphia Phillies; known for his hitting; 2006 NL MVP.

Gordie Howe, b 1928, (Can.) hockey forward; NHL MVP 6 times; scored 801 goals in 26 NHL seasons.

Carl Hubbell, 1903-88, NY Giants pitcher; 20-game winner 5 consecutive years, 1933-37.

Bobby Hull, b 1939, (Can.) NHL all-star 10 times; MVP, 1965-66.

Brett Hull, b 1964, (Can.) St. Louis Blues forward; led NHL in goals, 1990-92; MVP, 1991.

Catfish Hunter, 1946-99, pitched perfect game, 1968; 20-game winners 5 times.

Don Hutson, 1913-97, Packers receiver; caught 99 TD passes; 2-time NFL MVP.

Juli Inkster, b 1960, Hall of Fame golfer; 2nd to win all 4 of LPGA's modern majors; won 7 career major titles.

Bo Jackson, b 1962, NFL running back (1987-90) and MLB outfielder (1986-91, '93-'94); 1985 Heisman Trophy winner.

Phil Jackson, b 1945, won 11 NBA titles as coach of Bulls and Lakers; 1970, '73 title as player with NY Knicks.

Reggie Jackson, b 1946, slugger; led AL in home runs 4 times; MVP, 1973; hit 5 World Series home runs, 1977.

"Shoeless" Joe Jackson, 1889-1951, outfielder; 3rd highest career batting average (.356); one of the "Black Sox" banned for allegedly throwing 1919 World Series.

Jaromir Jagr, b 1972, (Czech.) hockey player; NHL MVP, 1999; Art Ross Trophy (leading scorer), 1995, 1998-2001.

LeBron James, b 1984, NBA forward; Rookie of the Year, 2004; member of 2008, '12 U.S. Olympic gold medal teams; NBA MVP, 2009, '10, '12, '13.

Ron Jaworski, b 1951, former NFL quarterback (1974-89); NFL analyst on ESPN.

Sally Jenkins, b 1960, sports journalist and writer for *Washington Post*.

Bruce Jenner, b 1949, Olympic decathlon gold medalist, 1976.

Lynn Jennings, b 1960, runner; 3-time World, 9-time U.S. cross country champ; bronze (10,000m), 1992 Olympics.

Derek Jeter, b 1974, shortstop; led NY Yankees to 5 World Series titles; World Series MVP, 2000; 1st Yankee to reach 3,000 hits, 2011.

Earvin "Magic" Johnson, b 1959, NBA MVP, 1987, '89, '90; playoff MVP, 1980, '82, '87; 4th in career assists.

Jack Johnson, 1878-1946, heavyweight champion, 1908-15.

Jimmie Johnson, b 1975, 5-time NASCAR Sprint Cup Series champ, 2006-10, '13; Daytona 500 winner, 2006.

Michael Johnson, b 1967, 4-time Olympic gold medalist (1992, '96, 2000); world and Olympic record, 400m and 4 × 400m.

Randy Johnson, b 1963, 5-time Cy Young winner; strikeout leader, 1992-95, 1999-2002, '04; 4,875 strikeouts (2nd all-time); pitched perfect game, 2004.

Walter Johnson, 1887-1946, Washington Senators pitcher; won 417 games; record 110 shutouts.

Bobby Jones, 1902-71, won golf's Grand Slam, 1930; U.S. amateur champ 5 times, U.S. Open champ 4 times.

Cobi Jones, b 1970, soccer player; most U.S. national team appearances with 164.

David "Deacon" Jones, 1938-2013, 5-time All-Pro with L.A. Rams (1965-69); "sack" specialist credited with inventing the term.

Marion Jones, b 1975, 2000 Olympic 100m, 200m, 1,600m relay gold medalist, bronze in long jump and 400m relay; stripped of medals in 2007 after admitting use of performance-enhancing drugs.

Roy Jones Jr., b 1969, light heavyweight champ, 1999-2004.

Michael Jordan, b 1963, guard; leading NBA scorer, 1987-93, '96-'98; MVP, 1988, '91-'92, '96, '98; playoff MVP, 1991-93, '96-'98; ESPN Athlete of the Century.

Dorothy Kamenshek, 1925-2010, led Rockford (IL) Peaches to 4 All-American Girls Baseball League titles in the 1940s.

Jackie Joyner-Kersee, b 1962, Olympic gold medalist in heptathlon (1988, '92), long jump (1988).

Clayton Kershaw, b 1988, pitcher; NL Cy Young Award (2011, '13).

Harmon Killebrew, 1936-2011, Minnesota Twins slugger; led AL in home runs 6 times; 573 lifetime.

Jean Claude Killy, b 1943, (Fr.) skier; 3 Olympic golds, 1968.

Kim Yu-Na, b 1990, (S. Kor.) figure skater; Olympic gold medal winner, 2010; world champion, 2009.

Ralph Kiner, 1922-2014, Pittsburgh Pirates slugger; led NL in home runs 7 consecutive years, 1946-52.

Billie Jean King, b 1943, U.S. singles champ 4 times; Wimbledon champ 6 times; beat Bobby Riggs, 1973.

Peter King, b 1957, senior writer for *Sports Illustrated*.

Bob Knight, b 1940, ESPN studio analyst, ret. basketball coach; led Indiana U. to NCAA title in 1976, '81, '87; winningest men's college basketball coach (902).

Olga Korbut, b 1955, (Belarus) gymnast; 3 Olympic golds, 1972.

Sandy Koufax, b 1935, 3-time Cy Young winner; lowest ERA in NL, 1962-66; pitched 4 no-hitters, 1 perfect game.

Jack Kramer, 1921-2009, world's number one tennis player, 1946-53; first at Wimbledon to compete in shorts.

Ingrid Kristiansen, b 1956, (Nor.) only runner to have held world records in 5,000m, 10,000m, and marathon.

Julie Krone, b 1963, winningest female jockey; first woman to ride a winner in a Triple Crown race (Belmont, 1993).

Petra Kvitová, b 1990, (Czech.) tennis player; won Wimbledon, 2011, '14.

Michelle Kwan, b 1980, figure skater; 9 U.S., 5 World titles; silver medalist at 1998 Olympics, bronze in 2002.

Guy Lafleur, b 1951, (Can.) 3-time NHL scoring leader; 1977-78 MVP.

Alexi Lalas, b 1970, soccer player; first modern-era American to play in Italian League Serie A.

Kenesaw Mountain Landis, 1866-1944, 1st commissioner of baseball (1920-44);

banned the 8 "Black Sox" involved in fixing 1919 World Series.

Tom Landry, 1924-2000, Dallas Cowboys head coach, 1960-88; won 2 Super Bowls (1972, '78); 3rd in career wins (270).

Dick "Night Train" Lane, 1928-2002, Hall of Fame defensive back; intercepted an NFL season record 14 passes (1952).

Don Larsen, b 1929, as NY Yankee, pitched only World Series perfect game, Oct. 8, 1956—2-0 win over Brooklyn.

Rod Laver, b 1938, (Austral.) won tennis Grand Slam, 1962, '69; Wimbledon champ 4 times.

Mario Lemieux, b 1965, (Can.) 6-time NHL leading scorer; MVP, 1988, '93, '96; playoff MVP, 1991-92.

Greg Lemond, b 1961, cyclist; 3-time Tour de France winner (1986, '89-'90); first American to win the event.

Ivan Lendl, b 1960, (Czech.) 8 Grand Slam tennis titles, including U.S. Open, 1985-87.

Sugar Ray Leonard, b 1956, boxer; held titles in 5 different weight classes.

Lisa Leslie, b 1972, L.A. Sparks center; 3-time WNBA MVP (2001, '04, '06).

Carl Lewis, b 1961, track-and-field star; won 9 Olympic gold medals in sprinting and long jump.

Lennox Lewis, b 1965, (Br.) heavyweight champ, 1994, 1997-2004; Olympic gold medalist, 1998.

Ray Lewis, b 1975, linebacker for the Baltimore Ravens; Super Bowl MVP, 2001.

Li Na, b 1982, (China) tennis player; won French Open, 2011, Austral. Open 2014.

Tim Lincecum, b 1984, S.F. Giants pitcher; NL Cy Young Award, 2008-09.

Tara Lipinski, b 1982, youngest figure skater to win U.S., world championships, 1997, and Winter Olympic gold, 1998.

Ryan Lochte, b 1984, swimmer; 11-time Olympic medalist, incl. 5 gold (2004, '08, '12).

Vince Lombardi, 1913-70, Green Bay Packers coach; led team to 5 NFL championships, 2 Super Bowl victories.

Nancy Lopez, b 1957, Hall of Fame golfer; 4-time LPGA Player of the Year, 3-time winner of the LPGA Championship.

Greg Louganis, b 1960, won Olympic gold medals in both springboard and platform diving, 1984, '88.

Joe Louis, 1914-81, heavyweight champion, 1937-49.

Sid Luckman, 1916-98, Chicago Bears quarterback; led team to 4 NFL championships; MVP, 1943.

Evan Lysacek, b 1985, figure skater; world champion, 2009; Olympic gold winner, 2010.

Connie Mack, 1862-1956, Philadelphia Athletics manager, 1901-50; won 9 pennants, 5 championships.

John Madden, b 1936, won Super Bowl as coach of Oakland Raiders (1977); former NFL TV analyst.

Greg Maddux, b 1966, NL pitcher; won 4 consecutive Cy Young awards, 1992-95; 355 career wins.

Karl Malone, b 1963, Utah Jazz, L.A. Lakers forward; MVP, 1997, '99; 14-time All-Star; 36,928 career points (2nd all-time).

Moses Malone, b 1955, NBA center; MVP, 1979, '82-'83.

Eli Manning, b 1981, NY Giants quarterback; Super Bowl MVP, 2008, '12.

Peyton Manning, b 1976, quarterback; most NFL MVP awards, 2003-04, '08-'09, '13; Super Bowl MVP, 2007; single-season passing yards record (5,477), 2013.

Mickey Mantle, 1931-95, NY Yankees outfielder; triple crown, 1956; 18 World Series home runs; MVP 3 times.

Diego Maradona, b 1960, (Arg.) soccer player; led Argentina to World Cup, 1986.

"Pistol" Pete Maravich, 1947-88, guard; scored NCAA record 44.2 ppg during collegiate career; led NBA in scoring, 1977.

Rocky Marciano, 1923-69, heavyweight champion, 1952-56; retired undefeated.

Dan Marino, b 1961, Miami quarterback; NFL record single-season yards passing (5,084), 1984.

Roger Maris, 1934-85, NY Yankees outfielder; hit AL record 61 home runs, 1961, record held 37 years; MVP, 1960-61.

Marta (Marta Vieira da Silva), b 1986, (Braz.) soccer forward; FIFA World Player of the Year, 2006-10.

Curtis Martin, b 1973, Jets running back; 5-time Pro-Bowler; 4th in all-time rushing yards with 14,101.

Eddie Mathews, 1931-2001, Milwaukee-Atlanta Braves 3rd baseman; hit 512 career home runs.

Christy Mathewson, 1880-1925, pitcher; won 373 games.

Bob Mathias, 1930-2006, decathlon gold, 1948, '52 Olympics.

Misty May-Treanor, b 1977, beach volleyball player; 3-time Olympic gold medalist with Kerri Walsh Jennings (2004, '08, '12).

Willie Mays, b 1931, NY-S.F. Giants center fielder; hit 660 home runs, led NL 4 times; had 3,283 hits; twice MVP.

Willie McCovey, b 1938, S.F. Giants slugger; hit 521 home runs, led NL 3 times; MVP, 1969.

John McEnroe, b 1959, U.S. Open tennis champ (1979-81, '84); Wimbledon champ (1981, '83-'84).

John McGraw, 1873-1934, NY Giants manager; led team to 10 pennants, 3 championships.

Mark McGwire, b 1963, hit then-record 70 home runs in 1998; 583 career home runs (10th); admitted career steroid use, 2010.

Rory McIlroy, b 1989, (N. Ire.) golfer; won U.S. Open, 2011; won PGA Championship, 2012, '14; British Open, 2014.

Tamara McKinney, b 1962, 1st U.S. skier to win overall Alpine World Cup championship (1983).

Andrea Mead Lawrence, 1932-2009, skier; first woman to win 2 gold medals in alpine skiing at one Olympics (1952).

Lionel Messi, b 1987, (Arg.) forward for FC Barcelona; FIFA World Player of the Year, 2009-10.

Mark Messier, b 1961, (Can.) center; NHL MVP, 1990, '92; Conn Smythe Trophy, 1994.

Debbie Meyer, b 1952, 1st swimmer to win 3 individual Olympic golds (1968).

Al Michaels, b 1944, *NBC Sunday Night Football* announcer; 5-time Outstanding Sports Personality Emmy winner.

Phil Mickelson, b 1970, golfer; 5 career major titles.

George Mikan, 1924-2005, Minn. Lakers center; considered the best basketball player of first half of 20th cent.

Stan Mikita, b 1940, (Czech.) Chicago Blackhawks center; led NHL in scoring 4 times; MVP twice.

Billy Mills, b 1938, runner; upset winner of the 1964 Olympic 10,000m; only American man ever to win the event.

Joe Montana, b 1956, S.F. 49ers quarterback; Super Bowl MVP, 1982, '85, '90.

Archie Moore, 1913-98, light-heavyweight champ, 1952-62.

Howie Morenz, 1902-37, (Can.) Montréal Canadiens forward; considered best hockey player of first half of 20th cent.

Edwin Moses, b 1955, undefeated in 122 consecutive 400m hurdles races, 1977-87; Olympic gold medalist, 1976, '84.

Shirley Muldowney, b 1940, 1st woman to race Natl. Hot Rod Assn. Top Fuel dragsters; 3-time NHRA points champ.

Eddie Murray, b 1956, 3rd player with both 3,000+ hits and 500+ home runs.

Stan Musial, 1920-2013, St. Louis Cardinals star; won 7 NL batting titles; MVP 3 times.

Rafael Nadal, b 1986, (Sp.) tennis player; won French Open (2005-08, '10-'14), Wimbledon (2008, '10), Australian Open (2009), U.S. Open (2010, '13); Olympic gold medal in men's singles (2008).

Bronko Nagurski, 1908-90, (Can.) Chicago Bears fullback and tackle; gained more than 4,000 yds rushing.

Joe Namath, b 1943, Jets quarterback; 1969 Super Bowl MVP.

Rosie Napravnik, b 1988, jockey.

Steve Nash, b 1974, (Can.) Phoenix Suns point guard; NBA MVP, 2005, '06.

Martina Navratilova, b 1956, (Czech.) Wimbledon champ 9 times; U.S. Open champ (1983-84, '86-'87); Austral. 3 times, French 2 times.

Byron Nelson, 1912-2006, won 11 consecutive golf tournaments in 1945; twice Masters and PGA titlist.

Ernie Nevers, 1903-76, Stanford football star; selected as best college fullback to play between 1919 and 1969.

Paula Newby-Fraser, b 1962, ([now] Zimbabwe) 8-time Ironman Triathlon world champ; holds women's course record.

John Newcombe, b 1944, (Austral.) twice U.S. Open tennis champ; Wimbledon champ 3 times.

Jack Nicklaus, b 1940, PGA Player of the Year, 1967, '72; leading money leader 8 times; won 18 majors (6 Masters).

Chuck Noll, 1932-2014, Pittsburgh Steelers coach; won 4 Super Bowls.

Dirk Nowitzki, b 1978, (Ger.) NBA forward; led Mavericks to NBA title, 2011; NBA MVP, 2007.

Paavo Nurmi, 1897-1973, (Fin.) distance runner; won 9 Olympic gold medals, 1920, '24, '28.

Lorena Ochoa, b 1981, (Mex.) LPGA Player of the Year, 2006-09, money leader 2006-08.

Al Oerter, 1936-2007, discus thrower; won gold medal at 4 consecutive Olympics, 1956, '60, '64, '68.

Apolo Ohno, b 1982, speed skater; most decorated American Winter Olympic athlete with 2 gold, 2 silver, 4 bronze (2002, '06, '10).

Hakeem Olajuwon, b 1963, (Nigeria) Houston center; NBA MVP, 1994, playoff MVP, 1994-95; career blocked shots leader (3,830).

Barney Oldfield, 1878-1946, pioneer auto racer; was first to drive a car 60 mph, 1903.

Shaquille O'Neal, b 1972, center; led L.A. Lakers to NBA titles, 2000-02, and Miami Heat to NBA title, 2006; Finals MVP 2000-02; NBA MVP 2000.

Bobby Orr, b 1948, (Can.) Boston Bruins defenseman; 8-time Norris Trophy winner; led NHL in scoring twice, assists 5 times.

Mel Ott, 1909-58, NY Giants right fielder; hit 511 home runs; led NL 6 times.

Jesse Owens, 1913-80, track and field; 4 1936 Olympic golds.

Terrell Owens, b 1973, wide receiver.

Satchel Paige, 1906-82, pitcher; starred in Negro leagues, 1924-48; entered major leagues at age 42.

Arnold Palmer, b 1929, golf's first $1 mil winner; won 4 Masters, 2 British Opens.

Jim Palmer, b 1945, Baltimore Orioles pitcher; won Cy Young award 3 times; 20-game winner 8 times.

Inbee Park, b 1988, (S. Kor.) golfer; U.S. Women's Open winner 2008, '13; 2nd player to win first 3 majors (2013).

Candace Parker, b 1986, L.A. Sparks forward; first woman to dunk in an NCAA tournament game; WNBA MVP (2008, '13) award, Rookie of the Year.

Joe Paterno, 1926-2012, Penn St. football coach; national title-winner, 1982, '86; most wins in NCAA Div. I coaching history until 111 wins (1998-2011) were vacated as penalty for child sex abuse scandal.

Danica Patrick, b 1982, race car driver; 4th woman to race at Indy 500, 1st to lead, 2005, 1st to win NASCAR Sprint Cup series pole, 2013.

Floyd Patterson, 1935-2006, 2-time heavyweight champion; first to ever regain the title after losing it.

Walter Payton, 1954-99, Chicago Bears running back; 2nd most rushing yards in NFL history; top NFC rusher, 1976-80.

Pelé (Edson Arantes do Nascimento), b 1940, (Braz.) soccer player; led Brazil to 3 World Cups (1958, '62, '70); scored 1,281 goals.

Bob Pettit, b 1932, first NBA player to score 20,000 points; twice NBA scoring leader.

Richard Petty, b 1937, NASCAR national champ 7 times; 7-time Daytona 500 winner.

Michael Phelps, b 1985, swimmer; holds record for most Olympic medals (22) and gold medals (18) won by single athlete; won 8 medals at 2004 Olympics; 8 gold in 2008; 6 medals in 2012.

Laffit Pincay Jr., b 1946, (Pan.) jockey; leading money-winner, 1970-74, '79, '85.

Oscar Pistorius, b 1986, (S. Afr.) sprinter, 1st double-leg amputee to compete in Olympics, 2012; charged with murder in the death of his girlfriend, 2013.

Jacques Plante, 1929-86, (Can.) NHL goaltender; 7 Vezina trophies; first goalie to wear mask in a game.

Gary Player, b 1935, (S. Afr.) golfer; won 3 Masters, 3 British Opens, 2 PGA Championships, and U.S. Open.

Mike Powell, b 1963, track and field athlete; holds world record for long jump (29 ft 4 in.).

Steve Prefontaine, 1951-75, runner; 1st to win 4 NCAA titles in same event (5,000m, 1970-73).

Kirby Puckett, 1960-2006, Minnesota Twins center fielder (1984-95); led team to World Series titles in 1987, '91.

Albert Pujols, b 1980, St. Louis first baseman; NL MVP, 2005, '08-'09.

Paula Radcliffe, b 1973, British runner; set marathon world record of 2:15:25 in London, 2003.

Kimi Räikkönen, b 1979, (Fin.) Formula One race car driver; 2007 Formula One World Drivers' Champion.

Manny Ramirez, b 1972, (Dom. Rep.) outfielder; 2004 World Series MVP; suspended for violating MLB performance-enhancing drug policy, 2009, '11.

Willis Reed, b 1942, NY Knicks center; MVP, 1970; playoff MVP, 1970, '73.

Mary Lou Retton, b 1968, gymnast; won all-around gold medal at 1984 Olympics; also won 2 silvers, 2 bronzes.

Claudio Reyna, b 1973, midfielder; U.S. National Team; named to the FIFA World Cup All-Star team, 2002.

Jerry Rice, b 1962, receiver; 1989 Super Bowl MVP; NFL record for career touchdowns (208), receptions (1,549).

Maurice Richard, 1921-2000, (Can.) Montréal Canadiens forward; scored 544 regular season goals, 82 playoff goals.

Branch Rickey, 1881-1965, MLB exec. helped break baseball's color barrier, 1947; initiated farm system, 1919.

Cal Ripken Jr., b 1960, Baltimore shortstop; AL MVP, 1983, '91; most consecutive games played (2,632).

Mariano Rivera, b 1969, (Pan.) relief pitcher; helped NY Yankees to 5 World Series titles; World Series MVP, 1999; all-time MLB leader in regular season and postseason saves.

Oscar Robertson, b 1938, NBA guard; averaged career 25.7 points per game; 5th in career assists (9,887); MVP, 1964.

Brooks Robinson, b 1937, Baltimore Orioles 3rd baseman; played in 4 World Series; MVP, 1964; 16 gold gloves.

Frank Robinson, b 1935, MVP in both NL and AL; triple crown, 1966; 586 career home runs; first black manager in majors.

Jackie Robinson, 1919-72, broke baseball's color barrier with Brooklyn Dodgers, 1947; NL MVP, 1949.

Sugar Ray Robinson, 1921-89, boxer; middleweight champion 5 times; welterweight champion, 1946-51.

Knute Rockne, 1888-1931, Notre Dame football coach, 1918-31; revolutionized game by stressing forward pass.

Aaron Rodgers, b 1983, Green Bay quarterback; led Packers to victory in Super Bowl XLV; Super Bowl MVP, 2011; NFL MVP, 2011, highest single-season passer rating (122.5), 2011.

Bill Rodgers, b 1947, runner; won Boston and New York City marathons 4 times each between 1975 and 1980.

Alex Rodriguez, b 1975, NY Yankees third baseman; AL MVP in 2003, '05, '07; 14-time All Star; youngest player to ever hit 500 HRs; admitted steroid use 2001-03; suspended 162 games for P.E.D. use, 2013-14.

Juan "Chi Chi" Rodriguez, b 1935, champion golfer; 8 PGA tour wins, 22 Champions tour wins.

Ben Roethlisberger, b 1982, Pittsburgh Steelers quarterback; youngest QB to win Super Bowl, 2005.

Ronaldinho, b 1980, (Braz.) soccer midfielder; led Brazil to World Cup finals in 2006; FIFA World Player of the Year, 2004, '05.

Ronaldo (Ronaldo Luiz Nazario de Lima), b 1976, (Braz.) soccer forward; led Brazil to 2002 World Cup title; 3-time FIFA world player of the year, 1996-97, 2002; most World Cup goals, 15.

Cristiano Ronaldo, b 1985, (Port.) soccer forward; FIFA player of the year, 2008.

Art Rooney, 1901-88, NFL owner; bought Pittsburgh Pirates in 1933, renamed Steelers, 1940.

Pete Rose, b 1941, won 3 NL batting titles; hit in 44 consecutive games, 1978; most career hits, 4,256; banned for gambling, 1989; admitted betting on his team, 2004.

Ken Rosewall, b 1934, (Austral.) tennis player; 2-time U.S. champ; 8 Grand Slam singles titles.

Patrick Roy, b 1965, (Can.) Montréal-Colorado goalie; only 3-time NHL playoffs MVP (Conn Smythe Trophy), 1986, '93, 2001.

Wilma Rudolph, 1940-94, sprinter; won 3 1960 Olympic golds.

Adolph Rupp, 1901-77, NCAA basketball coach; led Kentucky to 4 national titles, 1948-49, '51, '58.

Bill Russell, b 1934, Boston Celtics center; led team to 11 NBA titles; MVP 5 times; first black coach of major pro sports team.

Babe Ruth, 1895-1948, NY Yankees outfielder; hit 60 home runs, 1927, 714 lifetime (3rd all-time); led AL 12 times.

Johnny Rutherford, b 1938, auto racer; won 3 Indy 500s.

Nolan Ryan, b 1947, pitcher; holds season (383), career (5,714) strikeout records; won 324 games (7 no-hitters).

Pete Sampras, b 1971, tennis player; 1st man in Open era to win 7 Wimbledons; 2nd-most career Grand Slam wins (14).

Joan Benoit Samuelson, b 1957, won 1st Olympic women's marathon (1984), Boston Marathon (1979, '83).

Barry Sanders, b 1968, rushed for 2,053 yards in 1997; led NFL in rushing, 1990, '94, '96-'97.

Deion Sanders, b 1967, NFL cornerback (1989-2000, '04-'05) and MLB outfielder (1989-95, '97, 2005).

Gale Sayers, b 1943, Chicago running back; twice led NFL in rushing.

Mike Schmidt, b 1949, Phillies 3rd baseman; led NL in home runs 8 times; 548 lifetime; NL MVP, 1980-81, '86.

Michael Schumacher, b 1969, (Ger.) race-car driver; 7-time Formula 1 world champ (1994-95, 2000-04).

Tom Seaver, b 1944, pitcher; won NL Cy Young award 3 times; won 311 major league games.

Monica Seles, b 1973, (Yugo.) tennis player; won U.S. (1991-92), Austral. (1991-93, '96), French (1990-92) Opens; stabbed on court by spectator, 1993.

Maria Sharapova, b 1987, (Russ.) tennis star; won Wimbledon (2004), U.S. Open (2006), Australian Open (2008), French Open (2012, '14); Olympic silver, 2012.

Patty Sheehan, b 1956, Hall of Fame golfer; 3 LPGA Championships (1983-84, '93).

Willie Shoemaker, 1931-2003, jockey; rode 4 Kentucky Derby, 5 Belmont Stakes winners.

Frank Shorter, b 1947, runner; only American to win men's Olympic marathon (1972) since 1908; silver medalist (1976).

Don Shula, b 1930, all-time winningest NFL coach (347 games).

Bill Simmons, b 1969, columnist known as "The Sports Guy."

O. J. Simpson, b 1947, running back; rushed for 2,003 yds, 1973; AFC leading rusher 4 times; acquitted of murder, 1995; jailed after being found guilty of robbery and kidnapping, 2008.

Webb Simpson, b 1985, golfer; won U.S. Open, 2012.

Dean Smith, b 1931, retired basketball coach; winningest all-time; led North Carolina to 2 NCAA titles (1982, '93).

Emmitt Smith, b 1969, running back; NFL and Super Bowl MVP, 1993; rushed for career record 18,355 yds.

Conn Smythe, 1895-1980, (Can.) won 7 Stanley Cups as Toronto GM (1929-61); playoff MVP award named in his honor.

Sam Snead, 1912-2002, PGA and Masters champ 3 times each; record 82 PGA tournament victories.

Annika Sorenstam, b 1970, (Swed.) golfer; set LPGA 18-hole record of 59 (–13), 72-hole record of 27-under-par, 2001; won 10 LPGA majors, including career Grand Slam.

Sammy Sosa, b 1968, (Dom. Rep.) right fielder; 66 homers, NL MVP, 1998; 1st to hit 60+ homers 3 times (1998-99, 2001).

Warren Spahn, 1921-2003, pitcher; won 363 NL games; 20-game winner 13 times; Cy Young award, 1957.

Tris Speaker, 1888-1958, AL outfielder; batted .345 over 22 seasons; hit record 792 career doubles.

Mark Spitz, b 1950, swimmer; won 7 golds at 1972 Olympics.

Amos Alonzo Stagg, 1862-1965, football innovator; Univ. of Chicago football coach for 41 years, 5 undefeated seasons.

Bart Starr, b 1934, Green Bay Packers quarterback; led team to 5 NFL titles, 2 Super Bowl victories.

Roger Staubach, b 1942, Dallas Cowboys quarterback; leading NFC passer 5 times.

George Steinbrenner, 1930-2010, NY Yankees owner.

Casey Stengel, 1890-1975, managed Yankees to 10 pennants, 7 World Series wins between 1949 and 1960.

Jackie Stewart, b 1939, (Scot.) auto racer; 27 Grand Prix wins.

John Stockton, b 1962, Utah Jazz guard; NBA career leader in assists, steals; NBA assists leader, 1988-96.

Samantha Stosur, b 1984, (Austral.) tennis player; won U.S. Open, 2011; French Open, 2012.

Picabo Street, b 1971, skier; 2-time World Cup downhill champion (1995-96); Olympic super G gold medalist, 1998.

Louise Suggs, b 1923, golfer; U.S. Women's Open champ, 1949, '52; 11 major victories, ranks 3rd all-time.

John L. Sullivan, 1858-1918, last bare-knuckle champion, 1882-92.

Pat Summerall, 1930-2013, NFL kicker, radio and TV sportscaster who announced 26 Super Bowls.

Pat Summitt, b 1952, women's basketball coach; led Tennessee Lady Vols to 8 NCAA titles (1987, '89, '91, '96-'98, 2007-08); all-time winningest NCAA coach.

Ichiro Suzuki, b 1973, (Jpn.) center fielder; AL MVP, 2001; single-season hits record (262), 2004; 4,000th career (Japan/U.S.) hit (2013).

Sheryl Swoopes, b 1971, guard/forward; 1st player named WNBA MVP 3 times (2000, '02, '05).

Fran Tarkenton, b 1940, Minnesota, NY Giants quarterback; 4th in career TD passes (342); 1975 Player of the Year.

Diana Taurasi, b 1982, WNBA shooting guard, Phoenix Mercury; Olympic gold medalist, 2008, '12; WNBA MVP, 2009.

Lawrence Taylor, b 1959, linebacker; led NY Giants to 2 Super Bowl titles; played in 10 Pro Bowls.

Daley Thompson, b 1958, (Br.) decathlete; Olympic gold medalist in 1980, '84.

Jenny Thompson, b 1973, swimmer; most decorated U.S. female Olympian; 12 medals (8 gold) in 1992, '96, 2000, '04.

Bobby Thomson, 1923-2010, outfielder/3B; known for pennant-clinching "Shot Heard 'Round the World" for the NY Giants, 1951.

Jim Thorpe, 1888-1953, football All-American, 1911-12; won pentathlon and decathlon, 1912 Olympics.

Bill Tilden, 1893-1953, won 7 U.S. tennis titles, 3 Wimbledon.

Y. A. Tittle, b 1926, NY Giants quarterback; MVP, 1961, '63.

Alberto Tomba "La Bomba," b 1966, (It.) skier; 5 Olympic alpine medals (3 golds, 2 silver) in 1988, '92, '94.

LaDainian "L.T." Tomlinson, b 1979, running back; NFL records for single season touchdowns (31), rushing touchdowns (28), most points scored in a single season (186).

Joe Torre, b 1940, former MLB player; managed L.A. Dodgers, NY Yankees, St. Louis Cardinals, Atlanta Braves, and NY Mets.

Lee Trevino, b 1939, golfer; won U.S., British Open twice.

Bryan Trottier, b 1956, (Can.) Islanders, Penguins center for 6 Stanley Cup champs.

Gene Tunney, 1897-1978, heavyweight champion, 1926-28.

Mike Tyson, b 1966, undisputed heavyweight champ, 1987-90; at 20, youngest to win a heavyweight title (WBC, 1986).

Wyomia Tyus, b 1945, Olympic 100m gold medalist, 1964, '68.

Johnny Unitas, 1933-2002, Baltimore Colts quarterback; passed for more than 40,000 yds; MVP, 1957, '67.

Al Unser, b 1939, Indy 500 winner 4 times.

Bobby Unser, b 1934, Indy 500 winner 3 times.

Brian Urlacher, b 1978, Chicago Bears linebacker; Defensive Rookie of the Year, 2000; 7-time Pro Bowler.

Norm Van Brocklin, 1926-83, quarterback; passed for game record 554 yds, 1951; MVP, 1960.

Amy Van Dyken, b 1973, swimmer; first American woman to win 4 gold medals in one Olympics (1996).

Justin Verlander, b 1983, pitcher; won AL MVP and Cy Young, 2011.

Michael Vick, b 1980, quarterback; suspended and convicted (2007) of illegal dog fighting, gambling activities.

Lasse Viren, b 1949, (Fin.) runner; Olympic 5,000m and 10,000m gold medalist in 1972, '76.

Lindsey Vonn, b 1984; 1st U.S. woman to win the world super-G championship, gold medal in downhill, 2010 Olympics; 4 World Cup titles 2008-10, '12.

Joey Votto, b 1983, (Can.) Cincinnati Reds 1st baseman; NL MVP, 2010.

Dwyane Wade, b 1982, guard; led Miami Heat to NBA title, 2006, '12-'13; finals MVP, 2006; NBA scoring title, 2009.

Honus Wagner, 1874-1955, Pittsburgh Pirates shortstop; 8 NL batting titles.

Grete Waitz, 1953-2011, (Nor.) 9-time winner of the New York City Marathon (1978-80, '82-'86, '88).

"Jersey" Joe Walcott, 1914-94, boxer; became heavyweight champion at age 37, 1951-52.

Kerri Walsh Jennings, b 1978, beach volleyball player; 3-time Olympic gold medalist with Misty May-Treanor (2004, '08, '12).

Bill Walton, b 1952, center; led Portland Trail Blazers to 1977 NBA title; MVP, 1978; NBA TV commentator.

Abby Wambach, b 1980, soccer; 2 gold medals in Olympics (2004, '12); all-time intl.-competition scorer.

Kurt Warner, b 1971, Rams, Giants, Cardinals quarterback; NFL MVP, 1999, 2001; Super Bowl MVP, 2000.

Gerry "Bubba" Watson, b 1978, golfer; won Masters, 2012, '14.

Tom Watson, b 1949, golfer; 6-time PGA Player of the Year; won 5 British Opens, 2 Masters, U.S. Open.

Karrie Webb, b 1974, (Austral.) golfer; youngest woman (26 yrs., 6 mos.) to win career Grand Slam, 1999-2001.

Johnny Weissmuller, 1903-84, swimmer; won 52 national championships, 5 Olympic gold medals; set 67 world records.

Jerry West, b 1938, L.A. Lakers guard; had career average 27 pts. per game; first team all-star 10 times.

Dan Wheldon, 1978-2011, (Br.) race-car driver; 2-time Indy 500 winner (2005, '11).

Byron "Whizzer" White, 1917-2002, running back; led NCAA in scoring and rushing at Colorado, 1937; led NFL in rushing twice, 1938, '40; Supreme Court justice, 1962-93.

Shaun White, b 1986, snowboarder/skateboarder, Olympic gold medalist in half-pipe (2006, '10).

Kathy Whitworth, b 1939, 7-time LPGA Player of the Year (1966-69, '71-'73); 88 tour wins, most on LPGA or PGA tour.

Michelle Wie, b 1989, golfer; in 2002 became youngest-ever qualifier for LPGA event; turned pro at age 15.

Bradley Wiggins, b 1980, (Br.) cyclist; Tour de France winner, 2012; 4-time Olympic gold medalist (2004, '08, '12).

Michael Wilbon, b 1958, commentator/analyst for ESPN and ABC.

Lenny Wilkens, b 1937, 2nd winningest coach in NBA history; Hall of Fame player and coach.

Serena Williams, b 1981, tennis champ; won at Wimbledon (2002-03, '09-'10, '12), U.S. Open (1999, 2002, '08, '12-'14); Australian Open (2003, '05, '07, '09-'10); French Open (2002, '13); Olympic gold medals in singles (2012) and doubles (2000, '08, '12) with sister Venus.

Ted Williams, 1918-2002, Boston Red Sox outfielder; won 6 batting titles, 2 triple crowns; hit .406 in 1941.

Venus Williams, b 1980, tennis champ at Wimbledon (2000-01, '05, '07-'08), U.S. Open (2000-01); Olympic gold medals in singles (2000) and doubles with sister Serena (2000, '08, '12).

Helen Wills Moody, 1905-98, tennis star; won U.S. Open 7 times, Wimbledon 8 times.

Katarina Witt, b 1965, (Ger.) figure skater; won Olympic gold medal, 1984, '88; world champ, 1984-85, '87-'88.

John Wooden, 1910-2010, UCLA basketball coach; 10 NCAA titles.

Tiger Woods, b 1975, golfer; youngest to win career Grand Slam, at age 24 (1997-2000); 14 career major titles.

Mickey Wright, b 1935, golfer; won LPGA and U.S. Open championship 4 times; 82 career wins, including 13 majors.

Eric Wynalda, b 1969, soccer; scored 1st goal in major league soccer history (1996).

Kristi Yamaguchi, b 1971, figure skater; won national, world, Olympic titles, in 1992.

Yao Ming, b 1980, (China) center for Houston Rockets; 8-time NBA All-Star.

Carl Yastrzemski, b 1939, Boston Red Sox slugger; won 3 batting titles; triple crown, 1967.

Cy Young, 1867-1955, pitcher; won record 511 games.

Steve Young, b 1961, 49ers quarterback; led NFL in passing, 1991-94, '96-97; NFL MVP, 1992, '94; Super Bowl MVP, 1995.

Babe Didrikson Zaharias, 1911-56, all-around athlete; 3 track-and-field medals (2 golds), 1932 Olympics; won 10 golf majors; also played baseball; 6-time AP Female Athlete of the Year.

Emil Zátopek, 1922-2000, (Czech.) runner; won 3 gold medals at 1952 Olympics (5,000m, 10,000m, marathon).

Zinedine Zidane, b 1972, (Fr.) soccer midfielder; led France to 1998 World Cup title; named top player in 2006; 3-time FIFA world player of the year (1998, 2000, '03).

Writers of the Present

Name	Birthplace	Birthdate
Richard Adams	Newbury, England, UK	5/9/20
Chimamanda Ngozi Adichie	Enugu, Nigeria	9/15/77
Edward Albee	Washington, DC	3/12/28
Mitch Albom	Passaic, NJ.	5/23/58
Elizabeth Alexander	New York, NY	5/30/62
Isabel Allende	Lima, Peru	8/2/42
Dorothy Allison	Greenville, SC.	4/11/49
Martin Amis	Oxford, England, UK.	8/25/49
Piers Anthony	Oxford, England, UK	8/6/34
Jeffrey Archer	Somerset, England, UK	4/15/40
John Ashbery	Rochester, NY	7/28/27
Margaret Atwood	Ottawa, ON, Canada.	11/18/39
David Auburn	Chicago, IL	11/30/69
Jean Auel	Chicago, IL.	2/18/36
Paul Auster	Newark, NJ.	2/3/47
Alan Ayckbourn	Hampstead, England, UK.	4/12/39
Nicholson Baker	New York, NY	1/7/57
David Baldacci	Richmond, VA.	8/5/60
Russell Banks	Newton, MA	3/28/40
John Barth	Cambridge, MD	5/27/30
Ann Beattie	Washington, DC	9/8/47
Alan Bennett	Leeds, UK.	5/9/34
John Berendt	Syracuse, NY	12/5/39
Elizabeth Berg	St. Paul, MN	12/2/48
Thomas Berger	Cincinnati, OH	7/20/24
Judy Blume	Elizabeth, NJ	2/12/38
T. Coraghessan Boyle	Peekskill, NY.	12/2/48
Barbara Taylor Bradford	Leeds, England, UK	5/10/33
Christopher Bram	Buffalo, NY	2/22/52
Geraldine Brooks	Sydney, NSW, Australia	9/14/55
Dan Brown	Exeter, NH	6/22/64
Rita Mae Brown	Hanover, PA	11/28/44
Christopher Buckley	New York, NY	5/5/05
James Lee Burke	Houston, TX	12/5/36
Augusten Burroughs	Pittsburgh, PA.	10/23/65
Robert Olen Butler	Granite City, IL	1/20/45
A. S. Byatt	Sheffield, England, UK	8/24/36
Ethan Canin	Ann Arbor, MI	7/19/60
Peter Carey	Bacchus-Marsh, Victoria, Australia	5/7/43
Robert A. Caro	New York, NY	10/30/35
Caleb Carr	New York, NY	8/2/55
Michael Chabon	Washington, DC	5/24/63
Tracy Chevalier	Washington, DC	10/19/62
Sandra Cisneros	Chicago, IL	12/20/54
Mary Higgins Clark	Bronx, NY	12/24/27
Beverly Cleary	McMinnville, OR	4/12/16
Harlan Coben	Newark, NJ.	1/4/62
Paulo Coelho	Rio de Janeiro, Brazil	8/24/47
J(ohn) M(axwell) Coetzee	Capetown, South Africa	2/9/40
Billy Collins	New York, NY	3/22/41
Jackie Collins	London, England, UK	10/4/41
Suzanne Collins	Hartford, CT	8/10/62
Pat Conroy	Atlanta, GA	10/26/45
Robin Cook	New York, NY	5/4/40
Patricia Cornwell	Miami, FL	6/9/56
Michael Cunningham	Cincinnati, OH	11/6/52
Clive Cussler	Aurora, IL	7/15/31
Don DeLillo	Bronx, NY	11/20/36
Nelson DeMille	New York, NY	8/23/43
Junot Díaz	Santo Domingo, Dominican Republic	12/31/68
Joan Didion	Sacramento, CA	12/5/34
Annie Dillard	Pittsburgh, PA.	4/30/45
E. L. Doctorow	Bronx, NY.	1/6/31
Emma Donoghue	Dublin, Ireland.	10/24/69
Rita Dove	Akron, OH.	8/28/52
Roddy Doyle	Dublin, Ireland.	5/8/58
Carol Ann Duffy	Glasgow, Scotland, UK.	12/23/55
Umberto Eco	Alessandria, Italy	1/5/32
Jennifer Egan	Chicago, IL	9/7/62
Dave Eggers	Boston, MA	3/12/70
Bret Easton Ellis	Los Angeles, CA	3/7/64
James Ellroy	Los Angeles, CA.	3/4/48
Louise Erdrich	Little Falls, MN	6/7/54
Laura Esquivel	Mexico City, Mexico	9/30/50
Jeffrey Eugenides	Detroit, MI.	3/8/60
Janet Evanovich	South River, NJ.	4/22/43
Lawrence Ferlinghetti	Yonkers, NY	3/24/19
Helen Fielding	Morley, Yorkshire, England, UK	2/19/58
Fannie Flagg	Birmingham, AL	9/21/44
Gillian Flynn	Kansas City, MO.	2/24/71
Dario Fo	San Giano, Italy	3/26/26
Ken Follett	Cardiff, Wales, UK.	6/5/49
Richard Ford	Jackson, MS.	2/16/44
Frederick Forsyth	Ashford, England, UK.	8/25/38
Paula Fox	New York, NY.	4/22/23
Jonathan Franzen	Western Springs, IL	8/17/59
Michael Frayn	London, England, UK	9/8/33
Charles Frazier	Asheville, NC	11/4/50
Brian Friel	Killyclogher, N. Ireland, UK	1/9/29
Neil Gaiman	Portchester, England, UK	11/10/60
Ernest J. Gaines	Oscar, LA	1/15/33
Frank Gilroy	Bronx, NY	10/13/25
Malcolm Gladwell	Fareham, Hampshire, Eng., UK	9/3/63
Robert Goddard	Fareham, Hampshire, Eng., UK	11/13/54
Gail Godwin	Birmingham, AL	6/18/37
William Goldman	Highland Park, IL	8/12/31
Mary Gordon	Far Rockaway, NY.	12/8/49
Sue Grafton	Louisville, KY	4/24/40
Günter Grass	Danzig [now Gdansk], Poland	10/16/27
Shirley Ann Grau	New Orleans, LA	7/8/29
John Green	Indianapolis, IN.	8/24/77
John Grisham	Jonesboro, AR	2/8/55
John Guare	New York, NY	2/5/38
Pete Hamill	Brooklyn, NY.	6/24/35
David Handler	Los Angeles, CA.	9/14/52
Paul Harding	Wenham, MA	12/19/67
David Hare	St. Leonards, Sussex, England, UK	6/5/47
Jim Harrison	Grayling, MI	12/11/37
Robert Hass	San Francisco, CA	3/1/41
Mark Helprin	New York, NY	6/28/47
Carl Hiaasen	Plantation, FL	3/12/53
Laura Hillenbrand	Fairfax, VA.	5/15/67
S. E. Hinton	Tulsa, OK	7/22/48
Alice Hoffman	New York, NY	3/16/52
Alan Hollinghurst	Stroud, Gloucestershire, UK.	5/26/54
Khaled Hosseini	Kabul, Afghanistan	3/4/65
John Irving	Exeter, NH	3/2/42
Walter Isaacson	New Orleans, LA	5/20/52
Kazuo Ishiguro	Nagasaki, Japan.	11/8/54
John Jakes	Chicago, IL	3/31/32
E. L. James	London, England, UK.	1963
P. D. James	Oxford, England, UK.	8/3/20
Elfriede Jelinek	Müzzuschlag, Austria	10/20/46
Ha Jin	Liaoning, China.	2/21/56
Edward P. Jones	Washington, DC	10/5/50
Erica Jong	New York, NY	3/26/42
Sebastian Junger	Boston, MA.	1/17/62
Jan Karon	Lenoir, NC.	3/14/37
Garrison Keillor	Anoka, MN	8/7/42
Thomas Keneally	Sydney, NSW, Australia	10/7/35
William Kennedy	Albany, NY	1/16/28
Sue Monk Kidd	Sylvester, GA	8/12/48
Jamaica Kincaid	St. John's, Antigua and Barbuda	5/25/49
Stephen King	Portland, ME.	9/21/47
Barbara Kingsolver	Annapolis, MD	4/8/55
Maxine Hong Kingston	Stockton, CA.	10/27/40
Galway Kinnell	Providence, RI	2/1/27
Dean Koontz	Everett, PA	7/9/45
Ted Kooser	Ames, IA.	4/25/39
Jon Krakauer	Brookline, MA.	4/12/54
Judith Krantz	New York, NY	1/9/28
Milan Kundera	Brno, Czechoslovakia	4/1/29
Tony Kushner	New York, NY	7/16/56
Jhumpa Lahiri	London, England, UK	7/11/67
Erik Larson	Brooklyn, NY.	1/3/54
John Le Carré	Poole, England, UK	10/19/31
Jean Marie Gustave Le Clézio	Nice, France	4/13/40
Ursula K. Le Guin	Berkeley, CA.	10/21/29
David Leavitt	Pittsburgh, PA.	6/23/61
Harper Lee	Monroeville, AL	4/28/26
Jonathan Lethem	Brooklyn, NY.	2/19/64
David Lodge	South London, England, UK.	1/28/35
Alison Lurie	Chicago, IL.	9/3/26
Gregory Maguire	Albany, NY	6/9/54
David Malouf	Brisbane, Qld., Australia.	3/20/34
Thomas Mallon	Glen Cove, NY	11/2/51
David Mamet	Chicago, IL.	11/30/47
Hilary Mantel	Derbyshire, England, UK	7/6/52
Yann Martel	Salamanca, Spain	6/25/63
George R.R. Martin	Bayonne, NJ	9/20/48
Bobbie Ann Mason	nr. Mayfield, KY.	5/1/40
Armistead Maupin	Washington, DC	4/13/44
Cormac McCarthy	Providence, RI	7/20/33
Colleen McCullough	Wellington, NSW, Australia.	6/1/37
David McCullough	Pittsburgh, PA.	7/7/33
Alice McDermott	Brooklyn, NY.	6/27/53
Ian McEwan	Aldershot, England, UK.	6/21/48
Thomas McGuane	Wyandotte, MI.	12/11/39
Jay McInerney	Hartford, CT.	1/13/55
Terry McMillan	Port Huron, MI	10/18/51
Larry McMurtry	Wichita Falls, TX.	6/3/36
Terrence McNally	St. Petersburg, FL.	11/3/39
John McPhee	Princeton, NJ.	3/8/31

Name	Birthplace	Birthdate	Name	Birthplace	Birthdate
W(illiam) S(tanley) Merwin	New York, NY	9/30/27	J. K. Rowling	Chipping Sodbury, Eng., UK	7/31/65
Stephenie Meyer	Hartford, CT	12/24/73	Norman Rush	Oakland, CA	10/24/33
Steven Millhauser	New York, NY	8/3/43	Salman Rushdie	Bombay, India	6/19/47
Toni Morrison	Lorain, OH	2/18/31	Richard Russo	Johnstown, NY	7/15/49
Walter Mosley	Los Angeles, CA	1/12/52	Alice Sebold	Madison, WI	9/6/63
Andrew Motion	London, England, UK	10/26/52	David Sedaris	Johnson City, NY	12/26/56
Bharati Mukherjee	Calcutta, India	7/27/40	Vikram Seth	Calcutta, India	6/20/52
Herta Müller	Nitzkydorf, Banat, Romania	8/17/53	John Patrick Shanley	New York, NY	10/13/50
Alice Munro	Wingham, ON, Canada	7/10/31	Sam Shepard	Ft. Sheridan, IL	11/5/43
Haruki Murakami	Kyoto, Japan	1/12/49	Lionel Shriver	Gastonia, NC	5/18/57
V. S. Naipaul	Chaguanas, Trinidad and Tobago	8/17/32	Anne Rivers Siddons	Atlanta, GA	1/9/36
Joyce Carol Oates	Lockport, NY	6/16/38	Neil Simon	Bronx, NY	7/4/27
Edna O'Brien	Tuamgraney, Ireland	12/15/32	Jane Smiley	Los Angeles, CA	9/26/49
Tim O'Brien	Austin, MN	10/1/46	Wole Soyinka	Abeokuta, Nigeria	7/13/34
Kenzaburo Oe	Uchiko, Japan	1/31/35	Nicholas Sparks	Omaha, NE	12/31/65
Michael Ondaatje	Colombo, Sri Lanka	9/12/43	Danielle Steel	New York, NY	8/14/47
Cynthia Ozick	New York, NY	4/17/28	R(obert) L(awrence) Stine	Columbus, OH	10/8/43
Orhan Pamuk	Istanbul, Turkey	6/7/52	Kathryn Stockett	Jackson, MS	1969
Suzan-Lori Parks	Fort Knox, KY	5/10/63	Tom Stoppard	Zlin, Czechoslovakia	7/3/37
Ann Patchett	Los Angeles, CA	12/2/63	Mark Strand	Summerside, PE, Canada	4/11/34
James Patterson	Newburgh, NY	3/22/47	Elizabeth Strout	Portland, ME	1/6/56
Jodi Picoult	New York, NY	5/19/66	Amy Tan	Oakland, CA	2/19/52
Marge Piercy	Detroit, MI	3/31/36	Donna Tartt	Greenwood, MS	12/23/63
Robert Pinsky	Long Branch, NJ	10/20/40	Paul Theroux	Medford, MA	4/10/41
Michael Pollan	New York, NY	2/6/55	Calvin Trillin	Kansas City, MO	12/5/35
Richard Powers	Evanston, IL	6/18/57	Scott F. Turow	Chicago, IL	4/12/49
Terry Pratchett	Beaconsfield, Eng., UK	4/28/48	Anne Tyler	Minneapolis, MN	10/25/41
Richard Price	Bronx, NY	10/12/49	Mario Vargas Llosa	Arequipa, Peru	3/28/36
E. Annie Proulx	Norwich, CT	8/22/35	Paula Vogel	Washington, DC	11/16/51
Philip Pullman	Norwich, England, UK	10/19/46	Sarah Vowell	Muskogee, OK	12/27/69
Thomas Pynchon	Glen Cove, NY	5/8/37	Derek Walcott	Castries, Saint Lucia	1/23/30
David Rabe	Dubuque, IA	3/10/40	Alice Walker	Eatonton, GA	2/9/44
Ishmael Reed	Chattanooga, TN	2/22/38	Joseph Wambaugh	East Pittsburgh, PA	1/22/37
Ruth Rendell	London, England, UK	2/17/30	Edmund White	Cincinnati, OH	1/13/40
Anne Rice	New Orleans, LA	10/4/41	Elie Wiesel	Sighet, Romania	9/30/28
Mary Roach	Etna, NH	3/20/59	Tom Wolfe	Richmond, VA	3/2/31
Nora Roberts	Silver Spring, MD	10/10/50	Tobias Wolff	Birmingham, AL	6/19/45
Marilynne Robinson	Sandpoint, IL	11/26/43	Herman Wouk	New York, NY	5/27/15
Philip Roth	Newark, NJ	3/19/33	Yevgeny Yevtushenko	Zima, Russia	7/18/33

Writers of the Past

See also Journalists, and Greeks and Romans in Historical Figures chapter.

Chinua Achebe, 1930-2013, (Nigeria) novelist. *Things Fall Apart.*

Alice Adams, 1926-99, (U.S.) novelist, short-story writer. *Superior Woman.*

James Agee, 1909-55, (U.S.) novelist. *A Death in the Family.*

S(hmuel) Y(osef) Agnon, 1888-1970, (Isr.) Hebrew novelist. *Only Yesterday.*

Conrad Aiken, 1889-1973, (U.S.) poet, critic. *Ushant.*

Anna Akhmatova, 1889-1966, (Russ.) poet. *Requiem.*

Louisa May Alcott, 1832-88, (U.S.) novelist. *Little Women.*

Sholom Aleichem, 1859-1916, (Russ.) Yiddish writer. *Tevye's Daughters, The Old Country.*

Vicente Aleixandre, 1898-1984, (Sp.) poet. *La destrucción o el amor, Dialogos del conocimiento.*

Horatio Alger, 1832-99, (U.S.) "rags-to-riches" books.

Jorge Amado, 1912-2001, (Brazil) novelist. *Dona Flor and Her Two Husbands, The Violent Land.*

Eric Ambler, 1909-98, (Br.) suspense novelist. *A Coffin for Dimitrios.*

Kingsley Amis, 1922-95, (Br.) novelist, critic. *Lucky Jim.*

Hans Christian Andersen, 1805-75, (Den.) author of fairy tales. *The Ugly Duckling.*

Maxwell Anderson, 1888-1959, (U.S.) playwright. *What Price Glory?, High Tor, Winterset, Key Largo.*

Sherwood Anderson, 1876-1941, (U.S.) short-story writer. *"Death in the Woods," Winesburg, Ohio.*

Maya Angelou, 1928-2014, (U.S.) poet, memoirist. *I Know Why the Caged Bird Sings.*

Reinaldo Arenas, 1943-90, (Cuba) novelist, novelist. *Before Night Falls.*

Ludovico Ariosto, 1474-1533, (It.) poet. *Orlando Furioso.*

Matthew Arnold, 1822-88, (Br.) poet, critic. *"Thrysis," "Dover Beach," "Culture and Anarchy."*

Isaac Asimov, 1920-92, (U.S.) versatile writer, espec. of science fiction. *I Robot.*

Miguel Angel Asturias, 1899-1974, (Guat.) novelist. *El Señor Presidente.*

Louis Auchincloss, 1917-2010, (U.S.) novelist, memoirist, short-story writer. *The Rector of Justin.*

W(ystan) H(ugh) Auden, 1907-73, (Br.) poet, playwright, literary critic. *"The Age of Anxiety."*

Jane Austen, 1775-1817, (Br.) novelist. *Pride and Prejudice, Sense and Sensibility, Emma, Mansfield Park.*

Ba Jin (Li Yaotang), 1904-2005, (China) novelist of pre-revolutionary China.

Isaac Babel, 1894-1941, (Russ.) short-story writer, playwright. *Odessa Tales, Red Cavalry.*

James Baldwin, 1924-87, (U.S.) author, playwright. *The Fire Next Time, Blues for Mister Charlie.*

Honoré de Balzac, 1799-1850, (Fr.) novelist. *Le Père Goriot, Cousine Bette, Eugénie Grandet.*

James M. Barrie, 1860-1937, (Br.) playwright, novelist. *Peter Pan, Dear Brutus, What Every Woman Knows.*

Charles Baudelaire, 1821-67, (Fr.) poet. *Les Fleurs du Mal.*

L(yman) Frank Baum, 1856-1919, (U.S.) *Wizard of Oz* series.

Simone de Beauvoir, 1908-86, (Fr.) novelist, essayist. *The Second Sex, Memoirs of a Dutiful Daughter.*

Samuel Beckett, 1906-89, (Ire.) novelist, playwright. *Waiting for Godot, Endgame* (plays); *Murphy, Watt, Molloy* (novels).

Brendan Behan, 1923-64, (Ire.) playwright. *The Quare Fellow, The Hostage, Borstal Boy.*

Saul Bellow, 1915-2005, (U.S.) novelist. *The Adventures of Augie March, Humboldt's Gift.*

Robert Benchley, 1889-1945, (U.S.) humorist.

Stephen Vincent Benét, 1898-1943, (U.S.) poet, novelist. *John Brown's Body.*

Jan Berenstain, 1923-2012, and **Stan Berenstain**, 1923-2005, (both U.S.) co-writers and illustrators of Berenstain Bears series of children's books.

John Berryman, 1914-72, (U.S.) poet. *Homage to Mistress Bradstreet.*

Ambrose Bierce, 1842-1914, (U.S.) short-story writer, journalist. *In the Midst of Life, The Devil's Dictionary.*

Maeve Binchy, 1940-2012, (Ire.) novelist, short-story writer, *Circle of Friends, Tara Road.*

Elizabeth Bishop, 1911-79, (U.S.) poet. *North and South—A Cold Spring.*

William Blake, 1757-1827, (Br.) poet, artist. *Songs of Innocence, Songs of Experience.*

Aleksandr Blok, 1880-1921, (Russ.) poet. *"The Twelve," "The Scythians."*

Enid Blyton, 1897-1968, (Br.) children's writer. *Famous Five* series.

Giovanni Boccaccio, 1313-75, (It.) poet. *Decameron.*

Heinrich Böll, 1917-85, (Ger.) novelist, short-story writer. *Group Portrait With Lady.*

Jorge Luis Borges, 1900-86, (Arg.) short-story writer, poet. *Labyrinths.*

James Boswell, 1740-95, (Scot.) biographer. *The Life of Samuel Johnson.*

Pierre Boulle, 1913-94, (Fr.) novelist. *The Bridge Over the River Kwai, Planet of the Apes.*

Paul Bowles, 1910-99, (U.S.) novelist, short-story writer. *The Sheltering Sky.*

Ray Bradbury, 1920-2012, (U.S.) novelist, short-story writer. *Fahrenheit 451, The Martian Chronicles.*

Anne Bradstreet, c. 1612-72, (U.S.) poet. *The Tenth Muse Lately Sprung Up in America.*

Bertolt Brecht, 1898-1956, (Ger.) dramatist, poet. *The Threepenny Opera, Mother Courage and Her Children.*

Joseph Brodsky, 1940-96, (Russ.-U.S.) poet. *A Part of Speech, Less Than One, To Urania.*

Charlotte Brontë, 1816-55, (Br.) novelist. *Jane Eyre.*

Emily Brontë, 1818-48, (Br.) novelist. *Wuthering Heights.*

Sterling A. Brown, 1901-89, (U.S.) poet, literature professor. *Southern Road.*

William Wells Brown, 1815-84, (U.S.) writer, memoirist; first African American to publish a novel, *Clotel*, 1853.

Elizabeth Barrett Browning, 1806-61, (Br.) poet. *Sonnets From the Portuguese, Aurora Leigh.*

Robert Browning, 1812-89, (Br.) poet. "My Last Duchess," "Fra Lippo Lippi," *The Ring and the Book.*

Pearl S. Buck, 1892-1973, (U.S.) novelist. *The Good Earth.*

Charles Bukowski, 1920-94, (U.S.) novelist, poet. *Ham on Rye, Women.*

Mikhail Bulgakov, 1891-1940, (Russ.) novelist, playwright. *The Heart of a Dog, The Master and Margarita.*

John Bunyan, 1628-88, (Br.) writer. *Pilgrim's Progress.*

Anthony Burgess, 1917-93, (Br.) author. *A Clockwork Orange.*

Frances Hodgson Burnett, 1849-1924, (Br.-U.S.) novelist. *The Secret Garden.*

Robert Burns, 1759-96, (Scot.) poet. "Flow Gently, Sweet Afton," "My Heart's in the Highlands," "Auld Lang Syne."

Edgar Rice Burroughs, 1875-1950, (U.S.) writer; created Tarzan, John Carter.

William S. Burroughs, 1914-97, (U.S.) novelist. *Naked Lunch.*

George Gordon, Lord Byron, 1788-1824, (Br.) poet. *Don Juan, Childe Harold, Manfred, Cain.*

Pedro Calderon de la Barca, 1600-81, (Sp.) playwright. *Life Is a Dream.*

Hortense Calisher, 1911-2009, (U.S.) novelist, short-story writer. *False Entry.*

Italo Calvino, 1923-85, (It.) novelist, short-story writer. *If on a Winter's Night a Traveler.*

Luis Vaz de Camoes, 1524?-80 (Port.) poet. *The Lusiads.*

Albert Camus, 1913-60, (Fr.) writer. *The Stranger, The Fall.*

Elias Canetti, 1905-94, (Bulg.) novelist, essayist. *Auto-Da-Fe.*

Karel Capek, 1890-1938, (Czech.) playwright, novelist, essayist. *R.U.R. (Rossum's Universal Robots).*

Truman Capote, 1924-84, (U.S.) author. *Other Voices, Other Rooms; Breakfast at Tiffany's; In Cold Blood.*

Lewis Carroll (Charles Dodgson), 1832-98, (Br.) writer, mathematician. *Alice's Adventures in Wonderland.*

Barbara Cartland 1901-2000, (Br.) romance novelist.

Giacomo Casanova, 1725-98, (It.) adventurer, memoirist.

Willa Cather, 1873-1947, (U.S.) novelist. *O Pioneers!, My Antonia, Death Comes for the Archbishop.*

Constantine Cavafy, 1863-1933, (Gr.) poet. "Ithaka," "Sensual Pleasures."

Camilo Jose Cela, 1916-2001, (Sp.) novelist. *The Family of Pascual Duarte, The Hive.*

Miguel de Cervantes Saavedra, 1547-1616, (Sp.) novelist, dramatist, poet. *Don Quixote.*

Raymond Chandler, 1888-1959, (U.S.) writer of detective fiction. Philip Marlowe series.

Geoffrey Chaucer, c. 1340-1400, (Br.) poet. *The Canterbury Tales, Troilus and Criseyde.*

John Cheever, 1912-82, (U.S.) novelist, short-story writer. *The Wapshot Scandal,* "The Country Husband."

Anton Chekhov, 1860-1904, (Russ.) short-story writer, dramatist. *Uncle Vanya, The Cherry Orchard, The Three Sisters.*

Charles Waddell Chesnutt, 1858-1932, (U.S.) author known for his short stories. *The Conjure Woman.*

G(ilbert) K(eith) Chesterton, 1874-1936, (Br.) critic, novelist, relig. apologist. Father Brown series of mysteries.

Kate Chopin, 1851-1904, (U.S.) writer. *The Awakening.*

Agatha Christie, 1890-1976, (Br.) mystery writer; created Miss Marple, Hercule Poirot. *And Then There Were None, Murder on the Orient Express, Murder of Roger Ackroyd.*

Tom Clancy, 1947-2013, novelist. *The Hunt for Red October.*

Arthur C. Clarke, 1917-2008, (Br.) science-fiction writer. *2001: A Space Odyssey.*

James Clavell, 1924-94, (Br.-U.S.) novelist. *Shogun, King Rat.*

Jean Cocteau, 1889-1963, (Fr.) writer, visual artist, filmmaker. *The Beauty and the Beast, Les Enfants Terribles.*

Samuel Taylor Coleridge, 1772-1834, (Br.) poet, critic. "Kubla Khan," "The Rime of the Ancient Mariner."

(Sidonie) Colette, 1873-1954, (Fr.) novelist. *Claudine, Gigi.*

Wilkie Collins, 1824-89, (Br.) novelist. *The Moonstone.*

Evan S. Connell, 1924-2013, (Br.) novelist, short-story writer. *Mrs. Bridge.*

Joseph Conrad, 1857-1924, (Br.) novelist. *Lord Jim, Heart of Darkness, The Secret Agent.*

James Fenimore Cooper, 1789-1851, (U.S.) novelist. *Leatherstocking Tales, The Last of the Mohicans.*

Pierre Corneille, 1606-84, (Fr.) dramatist. *Medée, Le Cid.*

Hart Crane, 1899-1932, (U.S.) poet. "The Bridge."

Stephen Crane, 1871-1900, (U.S.) novelist, short-story writer. *The Red Badge of Courage,* "The Open Boat."

Harry Crews, 1935-2012, (U.S.) novelist. *A Feast of Snakes.*

Michael Crichton, 1942-2008, (U.S.) writer. *The Andromeda Strain, Jurassic Park.*

Countee Cullen, 1903-46, (U.S.) poet, prominent in the Harlem Renaissance of the 1920s. *The Black Christ.*

E. E. Cummings, 1894-1962, (U.S.) poet. *Tulips and Chimneys.*

Roald Dahl, 1916-90, (Br.-U.S.) writer. *Charlie and the Chocolate Factory, James and the Giant Peach.*

Gabriele D'Annunzio, 1863-1938, (It.) poet, novelist, dramatist. *The Child of Pleasure, The Intruder, The Victim.*

Dante Alighieri, 1265-1321, (It.) poet. *The Divine Comedy.*

Robertson Davies, 1913-95, (Can.) novelist, playwright, essayist. Salterton, Deptford, and Cornish trilogies.

Daniel Defoe, 1660-1731, (Br.) writer. *Robinson Crusoe, Moll Flanders, Journal of the Plague Year.*

Philip K. Dick, 1928-82, (U.S.) science-fiction writer. *Do Androids Dream of Electric Sheep?*

Charles Dickens, 1812-70, (Br.) novelist. *David Copperfield, Oliver Twist, Great Expectations, A Tale of Two Cities.*

James Dickey, 1923-97, (U.S.) poet, novelist. *Deliverance.*

Emily Dickinson, 1830-86, (U.S.) poet. "Because I could not stop for Death …," "Success is counted sweetest …"

Isak Dinesen (Karen Blixen), 1885-1962, (Den.) author. *Out of Africa, Seven Gothic Tales, Winter's Tales.*

John Donne, 1573-1631, (Br.) poet. *Songs and Sonnets.*

José Donoso, 1924-96, (Chile) surreal novelist and short-story writer. *The Obscene Bird of Night.*

John Dos Passos, 1896-1970, (U.S.) novelist. *U.S.A.*

Fyodor Dostoyevsky, 1821-81, (Russ.) novelist. *Crime and Punishment, The Brothers Karamazov, The Possessed.*

Arthur Conan Doyle, 1859-1930, (Br.) novelist. Sherlock Holmes mystery stories.

Theodore Dreiser, 1871-1945, (U.S.) novelist. *An American Tragedy, Sister Carrie.*

John Dryden, 1631-1700, (Br.) poet, dramatist, critic. *All for Love, Mac Flecknoe, Absalom and Achitophel.*

Alexandre Dumas (père), 1802-70, (Fr.) novelist, dramatist. *The Three Musketeers, The Count of Monte Cristo.*

Alexandre Dumas (fils), 1824-95, (Fr.) dramatist, novelist. *La Dame aux Camélias, Le Demi-Monde.*

Paul Laurence Dunbar, 1872-1906, (U.S.) poet, novelist. *Lyrics of Lowly Life.*

Lawrence Durrell, 1912-90, (Br.) novelist, poet. *Alexandria Quartet.*

Ilya G. Ehrenburg, 1891-1967, (Russ.) writer. *The Thaw.*

George Eliot (Mary Ann or Marian Evans), 1819-80, (Br.) novelist. *Silas Marner, Middlemarch.*

T(homas) S(tearns) Eliot, 1888-1965, (Br.) poet, critic. *The Waste Land,* "The Love Song of J. Alfred Prufrock."

Stanley Elkin, 1930-95, (U.S.) novelist, short-story writer. *George Mills.*

Ralph Ellison, 1914-94, (U.S.) writer. *Invisible Man.*

Ralph Waldo Emerson, 1803-82, (U.S.) poet, essayist. "Brahma," "Nature," "The Over-Soul," "Self-Reliance."

James T. Farrell, 1904-79, (U.S.) novelist. *Studs Lonigan.*

Howard Fast, 1914-2003, (U.S.) novelist. *Spartacus, The Immigrants.*

William Faulkner, 1897-1962, (U.S.) novelist. *Sanctuary; Light in August; The Sound and the Fury; Absalom, Absalom!*

Edna Ferber, 1887-1968, (U.S.) novelist, short-story writer, playwright. *So Big, Cimarron, Show Boat.*

Henry Fielding, 1707-54, (Br.) novelist. *Tom Jones.*

F(rancis) Scott Fitzgerald, 1896-1940, (U.S.) short-story writer, novelist. *The Great Gatsby, Tender Is the Night.*

Gustave Flaubert, 1821-80, (Fr.) novelist. *Madame Bovary.*

Ian Fleming, 1908-64, (Br.) novelist. James Bond spy thrillers: *Dr. No, Goldfinger.*

Horton Foote, 1916-2009, (U.S.) playwright, screenwriter. *The Trip to Bountiful.*

Ford Madox Ford, 1873-1939, (Br.) novelist, critic, poet. *The Good Soldier.*

C(ecil) S(cott) Forester, 1899-1966, (Br.) writer. Horatio Hornblower books.

E(dward) M(organ) Forster, 1879-1970, (Br.) novelist. *A Passage to India, Howards End.*

Anatole France, 1844-1924, (Fr.) writer. *Penguin Island, My Friend's Book, The Crime of Sylvestre Bonnard.*

Dick Francis, 1920-2010, (Br.) crime novelist.

Marilyn French, 1929-2009, (U.S.) novelist. *The Women's Room.*

Robert Frost, 1874-1963, (U.S.) poet. "Birches," "Fire and Ice," "Stopping by Woods on a Snowy Evening."

Carlos Fuentes, 1928-2012, (Pan.) novelist, essayist. *The Old Gringo.*

William Gaddis, 1922-98, (U.S.) novelist. *The Recognitions.*

John Galsworthy, 1867-1933, (Br.) novelist, dramatist. *The Forsyte Saga.*

Federico García Lorca, 1898-1936, (Sp.) poet, dramatist. *Blood Wedding.*

Gabriel García Márquez, 1927-2014, (Col.) novelist. *One Hundred Years of Solitude.*

Erle Stanley Gardner, 1889-1970, (U.S.) mystery writer; created Perry Mason.

Jean Genet, 1911-86, (Fr.) playwright, novelist. *The Maids.*

Kahlil Gibran, 1883-1931, (Leban.-U.S.) mystical novelist, essayist, poet. *The Prophet.*

André Gide, 1869-1951, (Fr.) writer. *The Immoralist*, *The Pastoral Symphony*, *Strait Is the Gate.*

Allen Ginsberg, 1926-97, (U.S.) Beat poet. "Howl."

Jean Giraudoux, 1882-1944, (Fr.) novelist, dramatist. *Electra*, *The Madwoman of Chaillot*, *Ondine*, *Tiger at the Gate.*

Johann Wolfgang von Goethe, 1749-1832, (Ger.) poet, dramatist, novelist. *Faust*, *Sorrows of Young Werther.*

Nikolai Gogol, 1809-52, (Russ.) short-story writer, dramatist, novelist. *Dead Souls*, *The Inspector General.*

William Golding, 1911-93, (Br.) novelist. *Lord of the Flies.*

Oliver Goldsmith, 1728-74, (Br.-Ire.) dramatist, novelist. *The Vicar of Wakefield*, *She Stoops to Conquer.*

Nadine Gordimer, 1923-2014, (S. Afr.) novelist. *Burger's Daughter.*

Maxim Gorky, 1868-1936, (Russ.) dramatist, novelist. *The Lower Depths.*

Robert Graves, 1895-1985, (Br.) poet, classical scholar, novelist. *I, Claudius*; *The White Goddess.*

Thomas Gray, 1716-71, (Br.) poet. "Elegy Written in a Country Churchyard," "The Progress of Poesy."

Julien Green, 1900-98, (U.S.-Fr.) expatriate American novelist. *Moira*, *Each Man in His Darkness.*

Graham Greene, 1904-91, (Br.) novelist. *The Power and the Glory*, *The Heart of the Matter*, *The Ministry of Fear.*

Zane Grey, 1872-1939, (U.S.) writer of Western stories.

Jakob Grimm, 1785-1863, philologist, folklorist; with brother **Wilhelm Grimm**, 1786-1859, (both Ger.) collected *Grimm's Fairy Tales.*

Alex Haley, 1921-92, (U.S.) author. *Roots.*

Dashiell Hammett, 1894-1961, (U.S.) detective-story writer; created Sam Spade. *The Maltese Falcon.*

Jupiter Hammon, c. 1720-1800, (U.S.) poet; first African American to have his works published, 1761.

Knut Hamsun, 1859-1952, (Nor.) novelist. *Hunger.*

Lorraine Hansberry, 1930-65, (U.S.) playwright. *A Raisin in the Sun.*

Thomas Hardy, 1840-1928, (Br.) novelist, poet. *The Return of the Native*, *Tess of the D'Urbervilles*, *Jude the Obscure.*

E. Lynn Harris, 1955-2009, (U.S.) novelist. *Invisible Life*, *Basketball Jones.*

Joel Chandler Harris, 1848-1908, (U.S.) writer. *Uncle Remus* stories.

Moss Hart, 1904-61, (U.S.) playwright. *Once in a Lifetime*, *You Can't Take It With You*, *The Man Who Came to Dinner.*

Bret Harte, 1836-1902, (U.S.) short-story writer, poet. *The Luck of Roaring Camp.*

Jaroslav Hasek, 1883-1923, (Czech.) writer, playwright. *The Good Soldier Schweik.*

Vaclav Havel, 1936-2011, (Czech.) essayist, poet, playwright. *The Power of the Powerless.*

John Hawkes, 1925-98, (U.S.) experimental fiction writer. *The Goose on the Grave*, *Blood Oranges.*

Nathaniel Hawthorne, 1804-64, (U.S.) novelist, short-story writer. *The Scarlet Letter*, "Young Goodman Brown."

Seamus Heaney, 1939-2013, (Ire.) poet. *Death of a Naturalist.*

Heinrich Heine, 1797-1856, (Ger.) poet. *Book of Songs.*

Robert Heinlein, 1907-88, (U.S.) science-fiction writer. *Stranger in a Strange Land.*

Joseph Heller, 1923-99, (U.S.) novelist. *Catch-22.*

Lillian Hellman, 1905-84, (U.S.) playwright, memoirist. *The Little Foxes*, *An Unfinished Woman*, *Pentimento.*

Ernest Hemingway, 1899-1961, (U.S.) novelist, short-story writer. *A Farewell to Arms*, *For Whom the Bell Tolls.*

O. Henry (W. S. Porter), 1862-1910, (U.S.) short-story writer. "The Gift of the Magi."

George Herbert, 1593-1633, (Br.) poet. "The Altar," "Easter Wings."

Zbigniew Herbert, 1924-98, (Pol.) poet. "Apollo and Marsyas."

Robert Herrick, 1591-1674, (Br.) poet. "To the Virgins to Make Much of Time."

John Hersey, 1914-93, (U.S.) novelist, journalist. *Hiroshima*, *A Bell for Adano.*

Hermann Hesse, 1877-1962, (Ger.) novelist, poet. *Death and the Lover*, *Steppenwolf*, *Siddhartha.*

Oscar Hijuelos, 1951-2013, (U.S.) novelist. *The Mambo Kings Play Songs of Love.*

Tony Hillerman, 1925-2008, (U.S.) novelist. *Dance Hall of the Dead.*

James Hilton, 1900-54, (Br.) novelist. *Lost Horizon.*

Chester Himes, 1909-84, (U.S.) novelist. *Cotton Comes to Harlem.*

Oliver Wendell Holmes, 1809-94, (U.S.) poet, novelist. *The Autocrat of the Breakfast-Table.*

Gerard Manley Hopkins, 1844-89, (Br.) poet. "Pied Beauty," "God's Grandeur."

A(lfred) E. Housman, 1859-1936, (Br.) poet. *A Shropshire Lad.*

William Dean Howells, 1837-1920, (U.S.) novelist, critic. *The Rise of Silas Lapham.*

Langston Hughes, 1902-67, (U.S.) poet, lyric writer, author; a major influence in 1920s Harlem Renaissance.

Ted Hughes, 1930-98, (Br.) British poet laureate, 1984-98. *Crow*, *The Hawk in the Rain.*

Victor Hugo, 1802-85, (Fr.) poet, dramatist, novelist. *Notre Dame de Paris*, *Les Misérables.*

Zora Neale Hurston, 1903-60, (U.S.) novelist, folklorist. *Their Eyes Were Watching God*, *Mules and Men.*

Aldous Huxley, 1894-1963, (Br.) writer. *Brave New World.*

Henrik Ibsen, 1828-1906, (Nor.) dramatist, poet. *A Doll's House*, *Ghosts*, *The Wild Duck*, *Hedda Gabler.*

William Inge, 1913-73, (U.S.) playwright. *Picnic*; *Come Back, Little Sheba*; *Bus Stop.*

Eugene Ionesco, 1910-94, (Fr.) surrealist dramatist. *The Bald Soprano*, *The Chairs.*

Washington Irving, 1783-1859, (U.S.) writer. "Rip Van Winkle," "The Legend of Sleepy Hollow."

Christopher Isherwood, 1904-86, (Br.) novelist, playwright. *The Berlin Stories.*

Shirley Jackson, 1919-65, (U.S.) short-story writer. "The Lottery."

Henry James, 1843-1916, (U.S.) novelist, short-story writer, critic. *The Portrait of a Lady*, *The Ambassadors*, *Daisy Miller.*

Robinson Jeffers, 1887-1962, (U.S.) poet, dramatist. *Tamar and Other Poems*, *Medea.*

James Weldon Johnson, 1871-1938, (U.S.) poet, novelist, diplomat; lyricist for *Lift Every Voice and Sing.*

Samuel Johnson, 1709-84, (Br.) author, scholar, critic. *Dictionary of the English Language*, *Vanity of Human Wishes.*

Ben Jonson, 1572-1637, (Br.) dramatist, poet. *Volpone.*

James Joyce, 1882-1941, (Ire.) writer. *Ulysses*, *Dubliners*, *A Portrait of the Artist as a Young Man*, *Finnegans Wake.*

Ernst Junger, 1895-1998, (Ger.) novelist, essayist. *The Peace*, *On the Marble Cliff.*

Franz Kafka, 1883-1924, (Austria-Hung./Czech.) novelist, short-story writer. *The Trial*, *The Castle*, "The Metamorphosis."

George S. Kaufman, 1889-1961, (U.S.) playwright. *The Man Who Came to Dinner*, *You Can't Take It With You.*

Yasunari Kawabata, 1899-1972, (Jpn.) novelist. *The Sound of the Mountains.*

Nikos Kazantzakis, 1883-1957, (Gr.) novelist. *Zorba the Greek*, *A Greek Passion.*

Alfred Kazin, 1915-98 (U.S.) author, critic, teacher. *On Native Grounds.*

John Keats, 1795-1821, (Br.) poet. "Ode on a Grecian Urn," "Ode to a Nightingale," "La Belle Dame Sans Merci."

Jack Kerouac, 1922-69, (U.S.) author, Beat poet. *On the Road*, *The Dharma Bums*, "Mexico City Blues."

Joyce Kilmer, 1886-1918, (U.S.) poet. "Trees."

Rudyard Kipling, 1865-1936, (Br.) author, poet. "The White Man's Burden," "Gunga Din," *The Jungle Book.*

Maxine Kumin, 1925-2014, (U.S.) poet, author. *Up Country: Poems of New England.*

Jean de la Fontaine, 1621-95, (Fr.) poet. *Fables choisies.*

Pär Lagerkvist, 1891-1974, (Swed.) poet, dramatist, novelist. *Barabbas*, *The Sybil.*

Selma Lagerlöf, 1858-1940, (Swed.) novelist. *Jerusalem*, *The Ring of the Lowenskolds.*

Alphonse de Lamartine, 1790-1869, (Fr.) poet, novelist, statesman. *Méditations poétiques.*

Charles Lamb, 1775-1834, (Br.) essayist. *Specimens of English Dramatic Poets*, *Essays of Elia.*

Louis L'Amour, 1908-88, (U.S.) Western author, screenwriter. *Hondo*, *The Cherokee Trail.*

Giuseppe di Lampedusa, 1896-1957, (It.) novelist. *The Leopard.*

William Langland, c. 1332-1400, (Br.) poet. *Piers Plowman.*

Ring Lardner, 1885-1933, (U.S.) short-story writer, humorist.

Steig Larsson, 1954-2004, (Swed.) novelist. *The Girl With the Dragon Tattoo.*

Arthur Laurents, 1917-2011, (U.S.) playwright and director. *West Side Story.*

D(avid) H(erbert) Lawrence, 1885-1930, (Br.) novelist. *Sons and Lovers*, *Women in Love*, *Lady Chatterley's Lover.*

Halldór Laxness, 1902-98, (Iceland) novelist. *Iceland's Bell.*

Madeleine L'Engle, 1918-2007, (U.S.) novelist of young adult fiction. *A Wrinkle in Time.*

Elmore Leonard, 1925-2013, (U.S.) novelist. *Get Shorty.*

Mikhail Lermontov, 1814-41, (Russ.) novelist, poet. "Demon," *Hero of Our Time.*

Alain-René Lesage, 1668-1747, (Fr.) novelist. *Gil Blas de Santillana.*

Doris Lessing, 1919-2013, (Br.) writer. *The Golden Notebook.*

Gotthold Lessing, 1729-81, (Ger.) dramatist, philosopher, critic. *Miss Sara Sampson*, *Minna von Barnhelm.*

Ira Levin, 1929-2007, (U.S.) novelist, playwright. *Deathtrap.*

C(live) S(taples) Lewis, 1898-1963, (Br.) critic, novelist, religious writer. *Allegory of Love*; *The Lion, the Witch and the Wardrobe*; *Out of the Silent Planet.*

Sinclair Lewis, 1885-1951, (U.S.) novelist. *Babbitt*, *Main Street*, *Arrowsmith*, *Dodsworth.*

Li Po, 701-762, (China) poet. "Song Before Drinking," "She Spins Silk."

Vachel Lindsay, 1879-1931, (U.S.) poet. *General William Booth Enters Into Heaven*, *The Congo.*

Hugh Lofting, 1886-1947, (Br.) writer. *Dr. Doolittle* series.

Jack London, 1876-1916, (U.S.) novelist, journalist. *Call of the Wild*, *The Sea-Wolf*, *White Fang.*

Henry Wadsworth Longfellow, 1807-82, (U.S.) poet. *Evangeline*, *The Song of Hiawatha.*

Lope de Vega, 1562-1635, (Sp.) playwright. *Noche de San Juan*, *Maestro de Danzar.*

H(oward) P(hillips) Lovecraft, 1890-1937, (U.S.) novelist, short-story writer. *"At the Mountains of Madness."*

Amy Lowell, 1874-1925, (U.S.) poet, critic. *"Lilacs."*

James Russell Lowell, 1819-91, (U.S.) poet, editor. *Poems, The Biglow Papers.*

Robert Lowell, 1917-77, (U.S.) poet. *"Lord Weary's Castle."*

Joaquim Maria Machado de Assis, 1839-1908, (Brazil) novelist, poet. *The Posthumous Memoirs of Bras Cubas.*

Archibald MacLeish, 1892-1982, (U.S.) poet. *Conquistador.*

Naguib Mahfouz, 1911-2006, (Egypt) novelist; first Arabic-language writer to win the Nobel Prize for Literature. *Cairo Trilogy.*

Norman Mailer, 1923-2007, (U.S.) novelist, essayist, journalist. *The Naked and the Dead.*

Bernard Malamud, 1914-86, (U.S.) short-story writer, novelist. *"The Magic Barrel," The Assistant, The Fixer.*

Stéphane Mallarmé, 1842-98, (Fr.) poet. *Poésies.*

Sir Thomas Malory, c. 1410-71, (Br.) writer. *Morte d'Arthur.*

Andre Malraux, 1901-76, (Fr.) novelist. *Man's Fate.*

Osip Mandelstam, 1891-1938, (Russ.) poet. *Stone, Tristia.*

Thomas Mann, 1875-1955, (Ger.) novelist, essayist. *Buddenbrooks, The Magic Mountain, "Death in Venice."*

Katherine Mansfield, 1888-1923, (Br.) short-story writer. *"Bliss."*

Christopher Marlowe, 1564-93, (Br.) dramatist, poet. *Tamburlaine the Great, Dr. Faustus, The Jew of Malta.*

Andrew Marvell, 1621-78, (Br.) poet. *"To His Coy Mistress."*

John Masefield, 1878-1967, (Br.) poet. *"Sea Fever," "Cargoes," Salt Water Ballads.*

Edgar Lee Masters, 1869-1950, (U.S.) poet, biographer. *Spoon River Anthology.*

Peter Matthiessen, 1927-2014, (U.S.) novelist. *The Snow Leopard.*

W(illiam) Somerset Maugham, 1874-1965, (Br.) author. *Of Human Bondage, The Moon and Sixpence.*

Guy de Maupassant, 1850-93, (Fr.) novelist, short-story writer. *"A Life," "Bel-Ami," "The Necklace."*

François Mauriac, 1885-1970, (Fr.) novelist, dramatist. *Viper's Tangle, The Kiss to the Leper.*

Vladimir Mayakovsky, 1893-1930, (Russ.) poet, dramatist. *The Cloud in Trousers.*

Mary McCarthy, 1912-89, (U.S.) critic, novelist, memoirist. *Memories of a Catholic Girlhood.*

Frank McCourt, 1930-2009, (U.S.) memoirist. *Angela's Ashes, 'Tis, Teacher Man.*

Carson McCullers, 1917-67, (U.S.) novelist. *The Heart Is a Lonely Hunter, Member of the Wedding.*

Herman Melville, 1819-91, (U.S.) novelist, poet. *Moby-Dick, Typee, Billy Budd, Omoo.*

George Meredith, 1828-1909, (Br.) novelist, poet. *The Ordeal of Richard Feverel, The Egoist.*

Prosper Mérimée, 1803-70, (Fr.) author. *Carmen.*

James Merrill, 1926-95, (U.S.) poet. *Divine Comedies.*

James Michener, 1907-97, (U.S.) novelist. *Tales of the South Pacific.*

Edna St. Vincent Millay, 1892-1950, (U.S.) poet. *The Harp Weaver and Other Poems.*

Arthur Miller, 1915-2005, (U.S.) playwright. *The Crucible, After the Fall, Death of a Salesman.*

Henry Miller, 1891-1980, (U.S.) erotic novelist. *Tropic of Cancer.*

A(lan) A(lexander) Milne, 1882-1956, (Br.) author. *Winnie-the-Pooh.*

Czeslaw Milosz, 1911-2004, (Pol.) essayist, poet. *"Esse," "Encounter."*

John Milton, 1608-74, (Br.) poet, writer. *Paradise Lost, Comus, Lycidas, Areopagitica.*

Mishima Yukio (Hiraoka Kimitake) 1925-70, (Jpn.) writer. *Confessions of a Mask.*

Gabriela Mistral, 1889-1957, (Chile) poet. *Sonnets of Death.*

Margaret Mitchell, 1900-49, (U.S.) novelist. *Gone With the Wind.*

Jean Baptiste Molière, 1622-73, (Fr.) dramatist. *Tartuffe, Le Misanthrope, Le Bourgeois Gentilhomme.*

Ferenc Molnár, 1878-1952, (Hung.) dramatist, novelist. *Liliom, The Guardsman, The Swan.*

Michel de Montaigne, 1533-92, (Fr.) essayist. *Essais.*

Eugenio Montale, 1896-1981, (It.) poet.

Brian Moore, 1921-99, (Ire.-U.S.) novelist. *The Lonely Passion of Judith Hearne.*

Clement C. Moore, 1779-1863, (U.S.) poet, educator. *"A Visit From Saint Nicholas."*

Marianne Moore, 1887-1972, (U.S.) poet.

Alberto Moravia, 1907-90, (It.) novelist, short-story writer. *The Time of Indifference.*

Sir Thomas More, 1478-1535, (Br.) writer, statesman, saint. *Utopia.*

Wright Morris, 1910-98, (U.S.) novelist. *My Uncle Dudley.*

Murasaki Shikibu, c. 978-1026, (Jpn.) novelist. *The Tale of Genji.*

Iris Murdoch, 1919-99, (Br.) novelist, philosopher. *The Sea, the Sea.*

Alfred de Musset, 1810-57, (Fr.) dramatist. *La Confession d'un Enfant du Siècle.*

Vladimir Nabokov, 1899-1977, (Russ.-U.S.) novelist. *Lolita, Pale Fire.*

R. K. Narayan, 1906-2001, (India) novelist. *The Guide.*

Ogden Nash, 1902-71, (U.S.) poet of light verse.

Irène Némirovsky, 1903-42, (Ukraine) novelist. *David Golder, Suite Française.*

Pablo Neruda, 1904-73, (Chile) poet. *Twenty Love Poems and One Song of Despair, Toward the Splendid City.*

Patrick O'Brian, 1914-2000, (Br.) historical novelist. *Master and Commander, Blue at the Mizzen.*

Sean O'Casey, 1884-1964, (Ire.) dramatist. *Juno and the Paycock, The Plough and the Stars.*

Flannery O'Connor, 1925-64, (U.S.) novelist, short-story writer. *Wise Blood, "A Good Man Is Hard to Find."*

Frank O'Connor (Michael Donovan), 1903-66, (Ire.) short-story writer. *"Guests of a Nation."*

Clifford Odets, 1906-63, (U.S.) playwright. *Waiting for Lefty, Awake and Sing, Golden Boy, The Country Girl.*

John O'Hara, 1905-70, (U.S.) novelist, short-story writer. *From the Terrace, Appointment in Samarra, Pal Joey.*

Omar Khayyam, c. 1028-1122, (Per.) poet. *Rubaiyat.*

Eugene O'Neill, 1888-1953, (U.S.) playwright. *Emperor Jones, Anna Christie, Long Day's Journey Into Night.*

George Orwell (Eric Arthur Blair), 1903-50, (Br.) novelist, essayist. *Animal Farm, Nineteen Eighty-Four.*

John Osborne, 1929-95, (Br.) dramatist, novelist. *Look Back in Anger, The Entertainer.*

Wilfred Owen, 1893-1918, (Br.) poet. *"Dulce et Décorum Est."*

Grace Paley, 1922-2007, (U.S.) short-story writer, poet. *The Little Disturbances of Man.*

Dorothy Parker, 1893-1967, (U.S.) poet, short-story writer. *Enough Rope, Laments for the Living.*

Robert B. Parker, 1932-2010, (U.S.) crime novelist. *"Spenser" novels.*

Boris Pasternak, 1890-1960, (Russ.) poet, novelist. *Doctor Zhivago.*

Alan Paton, 1903-88, (S. Africa) novelist. *Cry, the Beloved Country.*

Octavio Paz, 1914-98, (Mex.) poet, essayist. *The Labyrinth of Solitude, They Shall Not Pass!, The Sun Stone.*

Samuel Pepys, 1633-1703, (Br.) public official, diarist.

S(idney) J(oseph) Perelman, 1904-79, (U.S.) humorist. *The Road to Miltown, Under the Spreading Atrophy.*

Charles Perrault, 1628-1703, (Fr.) writer. *Tales From Mother Goose (Sleeping Beauty, Cinderella).*

Petrarch (Francesco Petrarca), 1304-74, (It.) poet. *Africa, Trionfi, Canzoniere.*

Harold Pinter, 1930-2008, (Br.) playwright. *The Birthday Party, The Caretaker, The Homecoming.*

Luigi Pirandello, 1867-1936, (It.) novelist, dramatist. *Six Characters in Search of an Author.*

Sylvia Plath, 1932-63, (U.S.) author, poet. *The Bell Jar.*

Edgar Allan Poe, 1809-49, (U.S.) poet, short-story writer, critic. *"Annabel Lee," "The Raven," "The Purloined Letter."*

Alexander Pope, 1688-1744, (Br.) poet. *The Rape of the Lock, The Dunciad, An Essay on Man.*

Katherine Anne Porter, 1890-1980, (U.S.) novelist, short-story writer. *Ship of Fools.*

Chaim Potok, 1929-2002, (U.S.) novelist. *The Chosen.*

Ezra Pound, 1885-1972, (U.S.) poet. *Cantos.*

Anthony Powell, 1905-2000, (Br.) novelist. *A Dance to the Music of Time series.*

Reynolds Price, 1933-2011, (U.S.) novelist, short-story writer, poet. *A Long and Happy Life.*

J(ohn) B(oynton) Priestley, 1894-1984, (Br.) novelist, dramatist. *The Good Companions.*

Marcel Proust, 1871-1922, (Fr.) novelist. *Remembrance of Things Past.*

Aleksandr Pushkin, 1799-1837, (Russ.) poet, novelist. *Boris Godunov, Eugene Onegin.*

Mario Puzo, 1920-99, (U.S.) novelist. *The Godfather.*

François Rabelais, 1495-1553, (Fr.) writer. *Gargantua.*

Jean Racine, 1639-99, (Fr.) dramatist. *Andromaque, Phèdre, Bérénice, Britannicus.*

David Rakoff, 1964-2012, (Can.-U.S.) essayist. *Fraud, Don't Get Too Comfortable.*

Ayn Rand, 1905-82, (Russ.-U.S.) novelist, moral theorist. *The Fountainhead, Atlas Shrugged.*

Terence Rattigan, 1911-77, (Br.) playwright. *Separate Tables, The Browning Version.*

Erich Maria Remarque, 1898-1970, (Ger.-U.S.) novelist. *All Quiet on the Western Front.*

Mary Renault, 1905-83, (Br.) novelist. *The Last of the Wine.*

Adrienne Rich, 1929-2012, (U.S.) poet. *Diving Into the Wreck: Poems, 1971-1972.*

Samuel Richardson, 1689-1761, (Br.) novelist. *Pamela; or Virtue Rewarded.*

Rainer Maria Rilke, 1875-1926, (Ger.) poet. *Life and Songs, Duino Elegies, Poems From the Book of Hours.*

Arthur Rimbaud, 1854-91, (Fr.) poet. *A Season in Hell.*

Harold Robbins, 1916-97, (U.S.) novelist. *The Carpetbaggers.*

Edwin Arlington Robinson, 1869-1935, (U.S.) poet. *"Richard Cory," "Miniver Cheevy," Merlin.*

Theodore Roethke, 1908-63, (U.S.) poet. *Open House, The Waking, The Far Field.*

Romain Rolland, 1866-1944, (Fr.) novelist, biographer. *Jean-Christophe.*

Pierre de Ronsard, 1524-85, (Fr.) poet. *Sonnets pour Hélène, La Franciade.*

Christina Rossetti, 1830-94, (Br.) poet. "When I Am Dead, My Dearest."

Dante Gabriel Rossetti, 1828-82, (Br.) poet, painter. "The Blessed Damozel."

Edmond Rostand, 1868-1918, (Fr.) dramatist. Cyrano de Bergerac.

Damon Runyon, 1880-1946, (U.S.) short-story writer, journalist. Guys and Dolls, Blue Plate Special.

John Ruskin, 1819-1900, (Br.) critic, social theorist. Modern Painters, The Seven Lamps of Architecture.

François Sagan (Françoise Quoirez), 1935-2004, (Fr.) novelist. Bonjour Tristesse.

Antoine de Saint-Exupéry, 1900-44, (Fr.) writer. Wind, Sand and Stars; The Little Prince.

Saki (or H[ector] H[ugh] Munro), 1870-1916, (Br.) writer. The Chronicles of Clovis.

J. D. Salinger, 1919-2010, (U.S.) novelist. The Catcher in the Rye.

George Sand (Amandine Lucie Aurore Dupin), 1804-76, (Fr.) novelist. Indiana, Consuelo.

Carl Sandburg, 1878-1967, (U.S.) poet. The People, Yes; Chicago Poems; Smoke and Steel; Harvest Poems.

Jose Saramago, 1922-2010, (Port.) novelist. Blindness.

William Saroyan, 1908-81, (U.S.) playwright, novelist. The Time of Your Life, The Human Comedy.

Nathalie Sarraute, 1900-99, (Fr.) Nouveau Roman novelist. Tropismes.

May Sarton, 1914-95, (Belg.-U.S.) poet, novelist. Encounter in April, Anger.

Dorothy L. Sayers, 1893-1957, (Br.) mystery writer; created Lord Peter Wimsey.

Richard Scarry, 1920-94, (U.S.) author of children's books. Richard Scarry's Best Story Book Ever.

Friedrich von Schiller, 1759-1805, (Ger.) dramatist, poet, historian. Don Carlos, Maria Stuart, Wilhelm Tell.

Sir Walter Scott, 1771-1832, (Scot.) novelist, poet. Ivanhoe.

Gil Scott-Heron, 1949-2011, (U.S.) poet. "The Revolution Will Not Be Televised."

Jaroslav Seifert, 1902-86, (Czech.) poet.

Maurice Sendak, 1928-2012, (U.S.) children's book author and illustrator. Where the Wild Things Are.

Dr. Seuss (Theodor Seuss Geisel), 1904-91, (U.S.) children's book author and illustrator. The Cat in the Hat.

William Shakespeare, 1564-1616, (Br.) dramatist, poet. Romeo and Juliet, Hamlet, King Lear, Julius Caesar, sonnets.

Karl Shapiro, 1913-2000, (U.S.) poet. "Elegy for a Dead Soldier."

George Bernard Shaw, 1856-1950, (Ire.-Br.) playwright, critic. St. Joan, Pygmalion, Major Barbara, Man and Superman.

Sidney Sheldon, 1917-2007, (U.S.) screenwriter, novelist. Rage of Angels, Memories of Midnight.

Mary Wollstonecraft Shelley, 1797-1851, (Br.) novelist, feminist. Frankenstein, The Last Man.

Percy Bysshe Shelley, 1792-1822, (Br.) poet. Prometheus Unbound, Adonais, "Ode to the West Wind," "To a Skylark."

Richard B. Sheridan, 1751-1816, (Br.) dramatist. The Rivals, School for Scandal.

Robert Sherwood, 1896-1955, (U.S.) playwright, biographer. The Petrified Forest, Abe Lincoln in Illinois.

Mikhail Sholokhov, 1906-84, (Russ.) writer. The Silent Don.

Shel Silverstein, 1932-99, (U.S.) poet, writer. The Giving Tree, Where the Sidewalk Ends.

Georges Simenon (Georges Sims), 1903-89, (Belg.-Fr.) mystery writer; created Inspector Maigret.

Upton Sinclair, 1878-1968, (U.S.) novelist. The Jungle.

Isaac Bashevis Singer, 1904-91, (Pol.-U.S.) novelist, short-story writer, in Yiddish. The Magician of Lublin.

C(harles) P(ercy) Snow, 1905-80, (Br.) novelist, scientist. Strangers and Brothers, Corridors of Power.

Aleksandr Solzhenitsyn, 1918-2008, (Russ.) novelist, dramatist. One Day in the Life of Ivan Denisovich.

Susan Sontag, 1933-2004, (U.S.) critic, essayist, novelist. Notes on Camp, The Volcano Lover, In America.

Stephen Spender, 1909-95, (Br.) poet, critic, novelist. Twenty Poems, "Elegy for Margaret."

Edmund Spenser, 1552-99, (Br.) poet. The Faerie Queen.

Mickey Spillane, 1918-2006, (U.S.) novelist; Mike Hammer detective novels. The Killing Man.

Johanna Spyri, 1827-1901, (Switz.) children's author. Heidi.

Christina Stead, 1903-83, (Austral.) novelist, short-story writer. The Man Who Loved Children.

Richard Steele, 1672-1729, (Br.) essayist, playwright; began the Tatler and Spectator. The Conscious Lovers.

Gertrude Stein, 1874-1946, (U.S.) writer. Three Lives.

John Steinbeck, 1902-68, (U.S.) novelist. The Grapes of Wrath, Of Mice and Men, The Winter of Our Discontent.

Stendhal (Marie Henri Beyle), 1783-1842, (Fr.) novelist. The Red and the Black, The Charterhouse of Parma.

Laurence Sterne, 1713-68, (Br.) novelist. Tristram Shandy.

Wallace Stevens, 1879-1955, (U.S.) poet. Harmonium, The Man With the Blue Guitar, Notes Toward a Supreme Fiction.

Robert Louis Stevenson, 1850-94, (Br.) novelist, poet, essayist. Treasure Island, A Child's Garden of Verses.

Mary Stewart, 1916-2014, (Br.) fantasy novelist. Merlin series.

Bram Stoker, 1847-1912, (Br.) writer. Dracula.

Rex Stout, 1886-1975, (U.S.) mystery writer; created Nero Wolfe.

Harriet Beecher Stowe, 1811-96, (U.S.) novelist. Uncle Tom's Cabin.

Lytton Strachey, 1880-1932, (Br.) biographer, critic. Eminent Victorians, Queen Victoria, Elizabeth and Essex.

August Strindberg, 1849-1912, (Swed.) dramatist, novelist. The Father, Miss Julie, The Creditors.

William Styron, 1925-2006, (U.S.) novelist, essayist. The Confessions of Nat Turner, Sophie's Choice, Darkness Visible: A Memoir of Madness.

Jonathan Swift, 1667-1745, (Br.) satirist, poet. Gulliver's Travels, "A Modest Proposal."

Algernon C. Swinburne, 1837-1909, (Br.) poet, dramatist. Atalanta in Calydon.

John M. Synge, 1871-1909, (Ire.) poet, dramatist. Riders to the Sea, The Playboy of the Western World.

Wislawa Szymborska, 1923-2012, (Pol.) poet. "Cat in an Empty Apartment."

Rabindranath Tagore, 1861-1941, (India) author, poet. Sadhana, The Realization of Life, Gitanjali.

Booth Tarkington, 1869-1946, (U.S.) novelist. The Magnificent Ambersons.

Peter Taylor, 1917-94, (U.S.) novelist. A Summons to Memphis.

Sara Teasdale, 1884-1933, (U.S.) poet. Helen of Troy and Other Poems, Rivers to the Sea.

Alfred, Lord Tennyson, 1809-92, (Br.) poet. Idylls of the King, In Memoriam, "The Charge of the Light Brigade."

William Makepeace Thackeray, 1811-63, (Br.) novelist. Vanity Fair, Henry Esmond, Pendennis.

Dylan Thomas, 1914-53, (Wales) poet. Under Milk Wood, A Child's Christmas in Wales.

Hunter S. Thompson, 1937-2005, (U.S.) author, journalist. Hell's Angels, Fear and Loathing in Las Vegas.

Henry David Thoreau, 1817-62, (U.S.) writer, philosopher, naturalist. Walden, "Civil Disobedience."

James Thurber, 1894-1961, (U.S.) humorist. "The Secret Life of Walter Mitty," My Life and Hard Times.

J(ohn) R(onald) R(euel) Tolkien, 1892-1973, (Br.) writer. The Hobbit, Lord of the Rings trilogy.

Leo Tolstoy, 1828-1910, (Russ.) novelist, short-story writer. War and Peace, Anna Karenina, "The Death of Ivan Ilyich."

Lionel Trilling, 1905-75, (U.S.) critic, author, teacher. The Liberal Imagination.

Anthony Trollope, 1815-82, (Br.) novelist. The Warden, Barchester Towers, the Palliser novels.

Ivan Turgenev, 1818-83, (Russ.) novelist, short-story writer. Fathers and Sons, First Love, A Month in the Country.

Amos Tutuola, 1920-97, (Nigeria) novelist. The Palm-Wine Drunkard, My Life in the Bush of Ghosts.

Mark Twain (Samuel Clemens), 1835-1910, (U.S.) writer, humorist. The Adventures of Huckleberry Finn.

Sigrid Undset, 1881-1949, (Nor.) novelist. Kristin Lavransdatter.

John Updike, 1932-2009, (U.S.) novelist, literary critic. Rabbit is Rich, The Witches of Eastwick.

Paul Valéry, 1871-1945, (Fr.) poet, critic. La Jeune Parque, The Graveyard by the Sea.

Paul Verlaine, 1844-96, (Fr.) Symbolist poet. Songs Without Words.

Jules Verne, 1828-1905, (Fr.) novelist. Twenty Thousand Leagues Under the Sea.

Gore Vidal, 1925-2012, (U.S.) novelist. The City and the Pillar.

François Villon, 1431-c. 1463, (Fr.) poet. The Lays, The Grand Testament.

Voltaire (F. M. Arouet), 1694-1778, (Fr.) writer of "philosophical romances"; philosopher, historian. Candide.

Kurt Vonnegut Jr., 1922-2007, (U.S.) novelist, essayist. Cat's Cradle, Slaughterhouse-Five, Breakfast of Champions.

David Foster Wallace, 1962-2008, (U.S.) novelist, essayist. Infinite Jest, A Supposedly Fun Thing I'll Never Do Again.

Robert Penn Warren, 1905-89, (U.S.) novelist, poet, critic. All the King's Men.

Wendy Wasserstein, 1950-2006, (U.S.) playwright. The Heidi Chronicles.

Evelyn Waugh, 1903-66, (Br.) novelist. The Loved One, Brideshead Revisited, A Handful of Dust.

H(erbert) G(eorge) Wells, 1866-1946, (Br.) novelist. The Time Machine, The Invisible Man, The War of the Worlds.

Eudora Welty, 1909-2001, (U.S.) Southern short-story writer, novelist. "Why I Live at the P.O.," "The Ponder Heart."

Rebecca West, 1893-1983, (Br.) novelist, critic, journalist. Black Lamb and Grey Falcon.

Edith Wharton, 1862-1937, (U.S.) novelist. The Age of Innocence, The House of Mirth, Ethan Frome.

Phillis Wheatley, c. 1753-84, (U.S.) poet; 2nd American woman and first black woman to be published, 1770.

E(lwyn) B(rooks) White, 1899-1985, (U.S.) essayist, novelist. Charlotte's Web, Stuart Little.

Patrick White, 1912-90, (Austral.) novelist. The Tree of Man.

T(erence) H(anbury) White, 1906-64, (Br.) author. The Once and Future King, A Book of Beasts.

Walt Whitman, 1819-92, (U.S.) poet. Leaves of Grass.

John Greenleaf Whittier, 1807-92, (U.S.) poet, journalist. Snow-Bound.

Oscar Wilde, 1854-1900, (Ire.) novelist, playwright. The Picture of Dorian Gray, The Importance of Being Earnest.

Laura Ingalls Wilder, 1867-1957, (U.S.) novelist. Little House on the Prairie series of children's books.

Thornton Wilder, 1897-1975, (U.S.) playwright. *Our Town*, *The Skin of Our Teeth*, *The Matchmaker*.

Tennessee Williams, 1911-83, (U.S.) playwright. *A Streetcar Named Desire*, *Cat on a Hot Tin Roof*, *The Glass Menagerie*.

William Carlos Williams, 1883-1963, (U.S.) poet, physician. *The Tempers*, *Al Que Quiere! Paterson*, "This Is Just to Say."

Edmund Wilson, 1895-1972, (U.S.) critic, novelist. *Axel's Castle*, *To the Finland Station*.

Lanford Wilson, 1937-2011, (U.S.) playwright. *Talley's Folly*, *Fifth of July*.

P(elham) G(renville) Wodehouse, 1881-1975, (Br.-U.S.) humorist. "Jeeves" novels, *Anything Goes*.

Thomas Wolfe, 1900-38, (U.S.) novelist. *Look Homeward, Angel*; *You Can't Go Home Again*.

Virginia Woolf, 1882-1941, (Br.) novelist, essayist. *Mrs. Dalloway*, *To the Lighthouse*, *A Room of One's Own*.

William Wordsworth, 1770-1850, (Br.) poet. "Tintern Abbey," "Ode: Intimations of Immortality," *The Prelude*.

Richard Wright, 1908-60, (U.S.) novelist, short-story writer. *Native Son*, *Black Boy*, *Uncle Tom's Children*.

Elinor Wylie, 1885-1928, (U.S.) poet. *Nets to Catch the Wind*.

William Butler Yeats, 1865-1939, (Ire.) poet, playwright. "The Second Coming," *The Wild Swans at Coole*.

Frank Yerby, 1916-91, (U.S.) first best-selling African American novelist. *The Foxes of Harrow*.

Émile Zola, 1840-1902, (Fr.) novelist. *Nana*, *Thérèse Raquin*.

Poets Laureate

There is no record of the origin of the office of Poet Laureate of England. Henry III (1216-72) reportedly had a Versificator Regis, or King's Poet, paid 100 shillings per year. Other poets said to have filled the role include Geoffrey Chaucer (d 1400), Edmund Spenser (d 1599), Ben Jonson (d 1637), and Sir William d'Avenant (d 1668). The first official English poet laureate was John Dryden, appointed 1668, for life (as was customary). Then came Thomas Shadwell, in 1689; Nahum Tate, 1692; Nicholas Rowe, 1715; Rev. Laurence Eusden, 1718; Colley Cibber, 1730; William Whitehead, 1757; Rev. Thomas Warton, 1785; Henry James Pye, 1790; Robert Southey, 1813; William Wordsworth, 1843; Alfred, Lord Tennyson, 1850; Alfred Austin, 1896; Robert Bridges, 1913; John Masefield, 1930; C. Day Lewis, 1968; Sir John Betjeman, 1972; Ted Hughes, 1984; Andrew Motion, 1999; and Carol Ann Duffy, 2009.

In the U.S., appointment is by the Librarian of Congress to a term of one year, which may be renewed: Robert Penn Warren, appointed 1986; Richard Wilbur, 1987; Howard Nemerov, 1988; Mark Strand, 1990; Joseph Brodsky, 1991; Mona Van Duyn, 1992; Rita Dove, 1993; Robert Hass, 1995; Robert Pinsky, 1997; Stanley Kunitz, 2000; Billy Collins, 2001; Louise Gluck, 2003; Ted Kooser, 2004; Donald Hall, 2006; Charles Simic, 2007; Kay Ryan, 2008; W. S. Merwin, 2010; Philip Levine, 2011; Natasha Trethewey, 2012; Charles Wright, 2014.

Composers of Classical and Avant Garde Music

John Adams, b 1947, (U.S.) *Nixon in China*, *The Death of Klinghoffer*.

Milton Babbitt, 1916-2011, (U.S.) serial and electronic music.

Carl Philipp Emanuel Bach, 1714-88, (Ger.) cantatas, passions, numerous keyboard and instrumental works.

Johann Christian Bach, 1735-82, (Ger.) concertos, operas, sonatas. Known as the "English" Bach.

Johann Sebastian Bach, 1685-1750, (Ger.) *St. Matthew Passion*, *The Well-Tempered Clavier*.

Samuel Barber, 1910-81, (U.S.) *Adagio for Strings*, *Vanessa*.

Béla Bartók, 1881-1945, (Hung.) *Concerto for Orchestra*, *The Miraculous Mandarin*.

Amy Beach (Mrs. H. H. A. Beach), 1867-1944, (U.S.) *The Year's at the Spring*, *Fireflies*, *The Chambered Nautilus*.

Ludwig van Beethoven, 1770-1827, (Ger.) concertos (*Emperor*), sonatas (*Moonlight*, *Pathétique*), 9 symphonies.

Vincenzo Bellini, 1801-35, (It.) *I Puritani*, *La Sonnambula*, *Norma*.

Alban Berg, 1885-1935, (Austria) *Wozzeck*, *Lulu*.

Hector Berlioz, 1803-69, (Fr.) *Damnation of Faust*, *Symphonie Fantastique*, *Requiem*.

Leonard Bernstein, 1918-90, (U.S.) *Chichester Psalms*, *Jeremiah Symphony*, *Mass*.

Georges Bizet, 1838-75, (Fr.) *Carmen*, *Pearl Fishers*.

Ernest Bloch, 1880-1959, (Switz.-U.S.) *Macbeth* (opera), *Schelomo*, *Voice in the Wilderness*.

Luigi Boccherini, 1743-1805, (It.) chamber music and guitar pieces.

Alexander Borodin, 1833-87, (Russ.) *Prince Igor*, *In the Steppes of Central Asia*, *Polovtzian Dances*.

Pierre Boulez, b 1925, (Fr.) *Le Visage nuptial*, *Edats/Multiple*, *Domaines*.

Johannes Brahms, 1833-97, (Ger.) Liebeslieder Waltzes, *Acad. Festival Overture*, chamber music, 4 symphonies.

Henry Brant, 1913-2008, (Can.) spatial music.

Benjamin Britten, 1913-76, (Br.) *Peter Grimes*, *Turn of the Screw*, *A Ceremony of Carols*, *War Requiem*.

Anton Bruckner, 1824-96, (Austria) 9 symphonies.

Dietrich Buxtehude, 1637-1707, (Den.) organ works, vocal music.

William Byrd, 1543-1623, (Br.) masses, motets.

John Cage, 1912-92, (U.S.) *Winter Music*, *Fontana Mix*.

Elliott Carter, 1908-2012, (U.S.) *Second String Quartet*, *Third String Quartet*.

Emmanuel Chabrier, 1841-94, (Fr.) *Le Roi Malgré Lui*, *España*.

Gustave Charpentier, 1860-1956, (Fr.) *Louise*.

Frédéric Chopin, 1810-49, (Pol.) mazurkas, waltzes, etudes, nocturnes, polonaises, sonatas.

Aaron Copland, 1900-90, (U.S.) *Appalachian Spring*, *Fanfare for the Common Man*, *Lincoln Portrait*.

John Corigliano, b 1938, (U.S.) *Symphony No. 2*.

Paul Creston, 1906-85, (U.S.) *Walt Whitman*.

Claude Debussy, 1862-1918, (Fr.) *Pelleas et Melisande*, *La Mer*, *Prelude to the Afternoon of a Faun*.

David Del Tredici, b 1937, (U.S.) *Child Alice*, *In Memory of a Summer Day*.

Gaetano Donizetti, 1797-1848, (It.) *Elixir of Love*, *Lucia di Lammermoor*, *Daughter of the Regiment*.

Paul Dukas, 1865-1935, (Fr.) *Sorcerer's Apprentice*.

Antonín Dvořák, 1841-1904, (Czech.) *Songs My Mother Taught Me*, *Symphony in E Minor (From the New World)*.

Edward Elgar, 1857-1934, (Br.) *Enigma Variations*, *Pomp and Circumstance*.

Manuel de Falla, 1876-1946, (Sp.) *El Amor Brujo*, *La Vida Breve*, *The Three-Cornered Hat*.

Gabriel Fauré, 1845-1924, (Fr.) *Requiem*, Elègie for Cello and Piano.

Cesar Franck, 1822-90, (Belg.) Symphony in D minor, Violin Sonata.

George Gershwin, 1898-1937, (U.S.) *Rhapsody in Blue*, *An American in Paris*, *Porgy and Bess*.

Philip Glass, b 1937, (U.S.) *Einstein on the Beach*, *The Voyage*.

Mikhail Glinka, 1804-57, (Russ.) *A Life for the Tsar*, *Ruslan and Ludmilla*.

Christoph W. Gluck, 1714-87, (Ger.) *Alceste*, *Iphigènie en Tauride*.

Henryk Gorecki, 1933-2010, (Pol.) Symphony no. 3 (*Symphony of Sorrowing Songs*).

Charles Gounod, 1818-93, (Fr.) *Faust*, *Romeo and Juliet*.

Percy Grainger, 1882-1961, (Austral.) *Country Gardens*.

Edvard Grieg, 1843-1907, (Nor.) *Peer Gynt Suite*, Concerto in A minor for piano.

George Frideric Handel, 1685-1759, (Ger.-Br.) *Messiah*, *Water Music*.

Howard Hanson, 1896-1981, (U.S.) Symphonies No. 1 (*Nordic*) and No. 2 (*Romantic*).

Roy Harris, 1898-1979, (U.S.) symphonies.

(Franz) Joseph Haydn, 1732-1809, (Austria) symphonies (*Clock*, *London*, *Toy*), chamber music, oratorios.

Hildegard von Bingen, 1098-1179, (Ger.) *Ordo virtutum*.

Paul Hindemith, 1895-1963, (U.S.) *Mathis der Maler*.

Gustav Holst, 1874-1934, (Br.) *The Planets*.

Arthur Honegger, 1892-1955, (Fr.) *Judith*, *Le Roi David*, *Pacific 231*.

Alan Hovhaness, 1911-2000, (U.S.) symphonies, *Magnificat*.

Engelbert Humperdinck, 1854-1921, (Ger.) *Hansel and Gretel*.

Charles Ives, 1874-1954, (U.S.) *Concord Sonata*, symphonies.

Aram Khachaturian, 1903-78, (Russ.) ballets, piano pieces, *Sabre Dance*.

Zoltán Kodály, 1882-1967, (Hung.) *Háry János*, *Psalmus Hungaricus*.

Fritz Kreisler, 1875-1962, (Austria) *Caprice Viennois*, *Tambourin Chinois*.

Edouard Lalo, 1823-92, (Fr.) *Symphonie Espagnole*.

David Lang, b 1957, (U.S.) *The Little Match Girl Passion*.

Morten Lauridsen, 1943 (U.S.) *Lux Aeterna*.

Ruggero Leoncavalo, 1857-1919, (It.) *Pagliacci*.

György Ligeti, 1923-2006, (Rom.) *Atmosphères*, *Requiem*.

Franz Liszt, 1811-86, (Hung.) 20 Hungarian rhapsodies, symphonic poems.

Edward MacDowell, 1861-1908, (U.S.) *To a Wild Rose*.

Gustav Mahler, 1860-1911, (Austria) *Das Lied von der Erde*; 9 complete symphonies.

Pietro Mascagni, 1863-1945, (It.) *Cavalleria Rusticana*.

Jules Massenet, 1842-1912, (Fr.) *Manon, Le Cid, Thaïs.*

Felix Mendelssohn, 1809-47, (Ger.) *A Midsummer Night's Dream, Songs Without Words,* violin concerto.

Gian Carlo Menotti, 1911-2007, (It.-U.S.) *The Medium, The Consul, Amahl and the Night Visitors.*

Olivier Messiaen, 1908-1992, (Fr.) *Apparition de l'Église Éternelle.*

Claudio Monteverdi, 1567-1643, (It.) opera, masses, madrigals.

Wolfgang Amadeus Mozart, 1756-91, (Austria) chamber music, concertos, operas (*Magic Flute, Marriage of Figaro*), 41 symphonies.

Modest Mussorgsky, 1839-81, (Russ.) *Boris Godunov, Pictures at an Exhibition.*

Carl Nielsen, 1865-1931, (Den.) *Saul og David.*

Jacques Offenbach, 1819-80, (Fr.) *Tales of Hoffmann.*

Carl Orff, 1895-1982, (Ger.) *Carmina Burana.*

Johann Pachelbel, 1653-1706, (Ger.) Canon and Fugue in D major.

Ignacy Paderewski, 1860-1941, (Pol.) Minuet in G.

Niccolò Paganini, 1782-1840, (It.) Caprices for violin solo.

Giovanni Palestrina, c. 1525-94, (It.) masses, madrigals.

Arvo Pärt, b 1935, (Eston.) sacred music. *Fratres, Cantus in memoriam Benjamin Britten, Tabula Rasa.*

Krzysztof Penderecki, b 1933, (Pol.) *Psalmus, Polymorphia, De natura sonoris.*

Francis Poulenc, 1899-1963, (Fr.) *Dialogues des Carmélites.*

Mel Powell, 1923-98, (U.S.) *Duplicates: A Concerto for Two Pianos and Orchestra, Cantilena Concertante.*

Sergei Prokofiev, 1891-1953, (Russ.) *Classical Symphony, Love for Three Oranges, Peter and the Wolf.*

Giacomo Puccini, 1858-1924, (It.) *La Boheme, Manon Lescaut, Tosca, Madama Butterfly.*

Henry Purcell, 1659-95, (Br.) *Dido and Aeneas.*

Sergei Rachmaninoff, 1873-1943, (Russ.) concertos, preludes (Prelude in C sharp minor), symphonies.

Maurice Ravel, 1875-1937, (Fr.) *Boléro, Daphnis et Chloè,* Piano Concerto in D for Left Hand Alone.

Steve Reich, b 1936, (U.S.) *Double Sextet, Three Tales.*

Nikolai Rimsky-Korsakov, 1844-1908, (Russ.) *Golden Cockerel, Scheherazade, Flight of the Bumblebee.*

Gioacchino Rossini, 1792-1868, (It.) *Barber of Seville, Otello, William Tell.*

John Rutter, b 1945, (Br.) *Magnificat, Requiem.*

Camille Saint-Saëns, 1835-1921, (Fr.) *Carnival of Animals (The Swan), Samson and Delilah, Danse Macabre.*

Alessandro Scarlatti, 1660-1725, (It.) cantatas, oratorios, operas.

Domenico Scarlatti, 1685-1757, (It.) harpsichord works.

Alfred Schnittke, 1934-98 (Russ.-Ger.) *Life With an Idiot.*

Arnold Schoenberg, 1874-1951, (Austria) *Pelleas and Melisande, Pierrot Lunaire, Verklärte Nacht.*

Franz Schubert, 1797-1828, (Austria) chamber music (*Trout Quintet*), lieder, symphonies ("Unfinished").

Robert Schumann, 1810-56, (Ger.) *Die Frauenliebe und Leben, Träumerei.*

Dmitri Shostakovich, 1906-75, (Russ.) symphonies, opera, *Lady Macbeth of the District Mzensk.*

Jean Sibelius, 1865-1957, (Fin.) *Finlandia.*

Bedrich Smetana, 1824-84, (Czech.) *The Bartered Bride.*

Karlheinz Stockhausen, 1928-2008, (Ger.) *Kontra-Punkte, Kontakte for Electronic Instruments.*

Richard Strauss, 1864-1949, (Ger.) *Salome, Elektra, Der Rosenkavalier, Thus Spake Zarathustra.*

Igor Stravinsky, 1882-1971, (Russ.) *Noah and the Flood, The Rake's Progress, The Rite of Spring.*

Toru Takemitsu, 1930-96, (Jpn.) *Requiem for Strings, Dorian Horizon.*

Thomas Tallis, c. 1505-85, (Br.) anthems, motets.

Peter I. Tchaikovsky, 1840-93, (Russ.) *Nutcracker, Swan Lake, The Sleeping Beauty.*

Georg Philipp Telemann, 1681-1767, (Ger.) church music, orchestral suites, chamber music.

Virgil Thomson, 1896-1989, (U.S.) opera, film music, *Four Saints in Three Acts.*

Dmitri Tiomkin, 1894-1979, (Russ.-U.S.) film scores, including *High Noon.*

Sir Michael Tippett, 1905-98, (Br.) *A Child of Our Time, The Midsummer Marriage, The Knot Garden.*

Michael Torke, b 1961, (U.S.) *Bright Blue Music, Ecstatic Orange.*

Eric Whitacre, b 1970, (U.S.) *Cloudburst.*

Ralph Vaughan Williams, 1872-1958, (Br.) *Fantasia on a Theme by Thomas Tallis,* symphonies, vocal music.

Giuseppe Verdi, 1813-1901, (It.) *Aida, Rigoletto, Don Carlo, Il Trovatore, La Traviata, Falstaff, Macbeth.*

Heitor Villa-Lobos, 1887-1959, (Braz.) *Bachianas Brasileiras.*

Antonio Vivaldi, 1678-1741, (It.) Concerto grossos (*The Four Seasons*).

Richard Wagner, 1813-83, (Ger.) *Rienzi, Tannhäuser, Lohengrin, Tristan and Isolde.*

William Walton, 1902-83, (Br.) *Façade, Belshazzar's Feast.*

Carl Maria von Weber, 1786-1826, (Ger.) *Der Freischutz.*

Composers of Operettas, Musicals, and Popular Music

Richard Adler, 1921-2012, (U.S.) *Pajama Game; Damn Yankees.*

Milton Ager, 1893-1979, (U.S.) "I Wonder What's Become of Sally"; "Hard-Hearted Hannah"; "Ain't She Sweet?"

Leroy Anderson, 1908-75, (U.S.) "Sleigh Ride"; "Blue Tango"; "Syncopated Clock."

Paul Anka, b 1941, (Can.) "My Way"; *Tonight Show* theme.

Harold Arlen, 1905-86, (U.S.) "Stormy Weather"; "Over the Rainbow"; "Blues in the Night"; "That Old Black Magic."

Burt Bacharach, b 1928, (U.S.) "Raindrops Keep Fallin' on My Head"; "Walk on By"; "What the World Needs Now Is Love."

Ernest Ball, 1878-1927, (U.S.) "Mother Machree"; "When Irish Eyes Are Smiling."

John Barry, 1933-2011, (U.S.) *Born Free; Lion in Winter;* Out of Africa.

Irving Berlin, 1888-1989, (U.S.) *Annie Get Your Gun; Call Me Madam;* "God Bless America"; "White Christmas."

Leonard Bernstein, 1918-90, (U.S.) *On the Town; Wonderful Town; Candide; West Side Story.*

Eubie Blake, 1883-1983, (U.S.) *Shuffle Along;* "I'm Just Wild About Harry."

Jerry Bock, 1928-2010, (U.S.) *Mr. Wonderful; Fiorello; Fiddler on the Roof; The Rothschilds.*

Carrie Jacobs Bond, 1862-1946, (U.S.) "I Love You Truly."

Nacio Herb Brown, 1896-1964, (U.S.) "Singing in the Rain"; "You Were Meant for Me"; "All I Do Is Dream of You."

Hoagy Carmichael, 1899-1981, (U.S.) "Stardust"; "Georgia on My Mind"; "Old Buttermilk Sky."

James Cleveland, 1931-91, (U.S.) composer, musician, singer; first black gospel artist to appear at Carnegie Hall.

George M. Cohan, 1878-1942, (U.S.) "Give My Regards to Broadway"; "You're a Grand Old Flag"; "Over There."

Cy Coleman, 1929-2004, (U.S.) *Sweet Charity;* "Witchcraft."

John Frederick Coots, 1895-1985, (U.S.) "Santa Claus Is Coming to Town"; "You Go to My Head"; "For All We Know."

Noël Coward, 1899-1973, (Br.) *Bitter Sweet;* "Mad Dogs and Englishmen"; "Mad About the Boy."

Neil Diamond, b 1941, (U.S.) "I'm a Believer"; "Sweet Caroline."

Walter Donaldson, 1893-1947, (U.S.) "My Buddy"; "Carolina in the Morning"; "Makin' Whoopee."

Vernon Duke, 1903-69, (U.S.) "April in Paris."

Bob Dylan, b 1941, (U.S.) "Blowin' in the Wind"; "Like a Rolling Stone."

Gus Edwards, 1879-1945, (U.S.) "School Days"; "By the Light of the Silvery Moon"; "In My Merry Oldsmobile."

Sherman Edwards, 1919-81, (U.S.) "See You in September"; "Wonderful! Wonderful!"

Duke Ellington, 1899-1974, (U.S.) "Sophisticated Lady"; "Satin Doll"; "It Don't Mean a Thing"; "Solitude."

Sammy Fain, 1902-89, (U.S.) "I'll Be Seeing You"; "Love Is a Many-Splendored Thing."

Fred Fisher, 1875-1942, (U.S.) "Peg O' My Heart"; "Chicago."

Stephen Collins Foster, 1826-64, (U.S.) "My Old Kentucky Home"; "Old Folks at Home"; "Beautiful Dreamer."

Rudolf Friml, 1879-1972, (Czech.-U.S.) *The Firefly; Rose Marie; Vagabond King; Bird of Paradise.*

John Gay, 1685-1732, (Br.) *The Beggar's Opera.*

George Gershwin, 1898-1937, (U.S.) "Someone to Watch Over Me"; "I've Got a Crush on You"; "Embraceable You."

Morton Gould, 1913-96, (U.S.) "Fall River Suite"; "Holocaust Suite"; "Spirituals for Orchestra"; "Stringmusic."

Ferde Grofe, 1892-1972, (U.S.) "Grand Canyon Suite."

Marvin Hamlisch, 1944-2012, (U.S.) "The Way We Were"; "Nobody Does It Better"; *A Chorus Line.*

Ray Henderson, 1896-1970, (U.S.) *George White's Scandals;* "That Old Gang of Mine"; "Five Foot Two, Eyes of Blue."

Victor Herbert, 1859-1924, (Ire.-U.S.) *Mlle. Modiste; Babes in Toyland; The Red Mill; Naughty Marietta; Sweethearts.*

Jerry Herman, b 1931, (U.S.) *Hello Dolly; Mame.*

Brian Holland, b 1941, **Lamont Dozier**, b 1941, **Eddie Holland**, b 1939, (all U.S.) "Heat Wave"; "Stop! In the Name of Love"; "Baby, I Need Your Loving."

Rupert Holmes, b 1947, (Br.-U.S.) *The Mystery of Edwin Drood; Curtains.*

Antonio Carlos Jobim, 1927-94, (Brazil) "The Girl From Ipanema"; "Desafinado"; "One Note Samba."

Billy Joel, b 1949, (U.S.) "Just the Way You Are"; "Honesty"; "Piano Man."

Elton John, b 1947, (Br.) *The Lion King;* "Candle in the Wind"; "Your Song."

Scott Joplin, 1868-1917, (U.S.) Maple Leaf Rag; *Treemonisha.*

John Kander, b 1927, (U.S.) *Cabaret; Chicago; Funny Lady.*

Jerome Kern, 1885-1945, (U.S.) *Sally; Sunny; Show Boat.*

Carole King, b 1942, (U.S.) "Will You Love Me Tomorrow?"; "Natural Woman"; "One Fine Day"; "Up on the Roof."

Burton Lane, 1912-97, (U.S.) *Finian's Rainbow.*

Jonathan Larson, 1960-96, (U.S.) *tick, tick... BOOM!; Rent.*

Franz Lehar, 1870-1948, (Hung.) *Merry Widow.*

Jerry Leiber, 1933-2011, and **Mike Stoller**, b 1933, (both U.S.) "Hound Dog"; "Searchin'"; "Yakety Yak"; "Love Me Tender."

Mitch Leigh, 1928-2014, (U.S.) *Man of La Mancha*.

John Lennon, 1940-80, and **Paul McCartney**, b 1942, (both Br.) "I Want to Hold Your Hand"; "She Loves You."

Jay Livingston, 1915-2001, (U.S.) "Mona Lisa"; "Que Sera, Sera."

Andrew Lloyd Webber, b 1948, (Br.) *Jesus Christ Superstar*; *Evita*; *Cats*; *The Phantom of the Opera*.

Frank Loesser, 1910-69, (U.S.) *Guys and Dolls*; *Where's Charley?*; *The Most Happy Fella*; *How to Succeed in Business....*

Frederick Loewe, 1901-88, (Austria-U.S.) *Brigadoon*; *Paint Your Wagon*; *My Fair Lady*; *Camelot*.

Robert Lopez, b 1975, (U.S.) *Avenue Q*; *The Book of Mormon*; *Frozen*.

Henry Mancini, 1924-94, (U.S.) "Moon River"; "Days of Wine and Roses"; "Pink Panther Theme."

Barry Mann, b 1939, and **Cynthia Weil**, b 1937, (both U.S.) "You've Lost That Loving Feeling."

Hugh Martin, 1914-2011, (U.S.) "Have Yourself a Merry Little Christmas"; "The Trolley Song."

Jimmy McHugh, 1894-1969, (U.S.) "Don't Blame Me"; "I'm in the Mood for Love"; "I Feel a Song Coming On."

Alan Menken, b 1949, (U.S.) *Little Shop of Horrors*; *Beauty and the Beast*.

Joseph Meyer, 1894-1987, (U.S.) "If You Knew Susie"; "California, Here I Come"; "Crazy Rhythm."

Chauncey Olcott, 1858-1932, (U.S.) "Mother Machree."

Jerome "Doc" Pomus, 1925-91, (U.S.) "Save the Last Dance for Me"; "A Teenager in Love."

Cole Porter, 1891-1964, (U.S.) *Anything Goes*; *Kiss Me Kate*; *Can Can*; *Silk Stockings*.

Smokey Robinson, b 1940, (U.S.) "Shop Around"; "My Guy"; "My Girl"; "Get Ready."

Richard Rodgers, 1902-79, (U.S.) *Oklahoma!*; *Carousel*; *South Pacific*; *The King and I*; *The Sound of Music*.

Sigmund Romberg, 1887-1951, (Hung.) *Maytime*; *The Student Prince*; *Desert Song*; *Blossom Time*.

Harold Rome, 1908-93, (U.S.) *Pins and Needles*; *Call Me Mister*; *Wish You Were Here*; *Fanny*; *Destry Rides Again*.

Vincent Rose, 1880-1944, (U.S.) "Avalon"; "Whispering"; "Blueberry Hill."

Harry Ruby, 1895-1974, (U.S.) "Three Little Words"; "Who's Sorry Now?"

Arthur Schwartz, 1900-84, (U.S.) *The Band Wagon*; "Dancing in the Dark"; "By Myself"; "That's Entertainment."

Steven Schwartz, b 1948, (U.S.) *Godspell*; *Pippin*; *Wicked*.

Neil Sedaka, b 1939, (U.S.) "Breaking Up Is Hard to Do."

Marc Shaiman, b 1959, (U.S.) *Hairspray*.

Paul Simon, b 1942, (U.S.) "Sounds of Silence"; "I Am a Rock"; "Mrs. Robinson"; "Bridge Over Troubled Waters."

Stephen Sondheim, b 1930, (U.S.) *A Little Night Music*; *Company*; *Sweeney Todd*; *Sunday in the Park With George*.

John Philip Sousa, 1854-1932, (U.S.) *El Capitan*; "Stars and Stripes Forever."

Oskar Straus, 1870-1954, (Austrian) *Chocolate Soldier*.

Johann Strauss, 1825-99, (Austrian) *Gypsy Baron*; *Die Fledermaus*; waltzes: Blue Danube; Artist's Life.

Charles Strouse, b 1928, (U.S.) *Bye Bye, Birdie*; *Annie*.

Jule Styne, 1905-94, (Br.-U.S.) *Gentlemen Prefer Blondes*; *Bells Are Ringing*; *Gypsy*; *Funny Girl*.

Arthur S. Sullivan, 1842-1900, (Br.) *H.M.S. Pinafore*; *Pirates of Penzance*; *The Mikado*.

Deems Taylor, 1885-1966, (U.S.) *Peter Ibbetson*.

Harry Tobias, 1905-94, (U.S.) *I'll Keep the Lovelight Burning*.

Egbert van Alstyne, 1882-1951, (U.S.) "In the Shade of the Old Apple Tree"; "Memories"; "Pretty Baby."

Jimmy Van Heusen, 1913-90, (U.S.) "Moonlight Becomes You"; "Swinging on a Star"; "All the Way"; "Love and Marriage."

Albert von Tilzer, 1878-1956, (U.S.) "I'll Be With You in Apple Blossom Time"; "Take Me Out to the Ball Game."

Harry von Tilzer, 1872-1946, (U.S.) "Only a Bird in a Gilded Cage"; "Wait 'til the Sun Shines, Nellie."

Fats Waller, 1904-43, (U.S.) "Honeysuckle Rose"; "Ain't Misbehavin."

Harry Warren, 1893-1981, (U.S.) "You're My Everything"; "We're in the Money"; "I Only Have Eyes for You."

Jimmy Webb, b 1946, (U.S.) "Up, Up and Away"; "By the Time I Get to Phoenix"; "Didn't We?"; "Wichita Lineman."

Kurt Weill, 1900-50, (Ger.-U.S.) *Threepenny Opera*; *Lady in the Dark*; *Knickerbocker Holiday*; *One Touch of Venus*.

Percy Wenrich, 1887-1952, (U.S.) "When You Wore a Tulip"; "Moonlight Bay"; "Put On Your Old Gray Bonnet."

Richard A. Whiting, 1891-1938, (U.S.) "Till We Meet Again"; "Sleepytime Gal"; "Beyond the Blue Horizon"; "My Ideal."

Fred Wildhorn, b 1959, (U.S.) *Jekyll and Hyde*; *Victor/Victoria*; *The Civil War*.

John Williams, b 1932, (U.S.) *Jaws*; *E.T.*; *Star Wars* series; *Raiders of the Lost Ark* series.

Meredith Willson, 1902-84, (U.S.) *The Music Man*.

Stevie Wonder, b 1950, (U.S.) "You Are the Sunshine of My Life"; "Signed, Sealed, Delivered, I'm Yours."

Vincent Youmans, 1898-1946, (U.S.) *Two Little Girls in Blue*; *Wildflower*; *No, No, Nanette*; *Hit the Deck*; *Rainbow*; *Smiles*.

Lyricists

Howard Ashman, 1950-91, (U.S.) *Little Shop of Horrors*; *The Little Mermaid*.

Johnny Burke, 1908-84, (U.S.) "Misty"; "Imagination."

Irving Caesar, 1895-1996, (U.S.) "Swanee"; "Tea for Two"; "Just a Gigolo."

Sammy Cahn, 1913-93, (U.S.) "High Hopes"; "Love and Marriage"; "The Second Time Around"; "It's Magic."

Leonard Cohen, b 1934, (Can.) "Suzanne"; "Stranger Song."

Betty Comden, 1917-2006, and **Adolph Green**, 1915-2002, (both U.S.) "The Party's Over"; "New York, New York."

Hal David, 1921-2012, (U.S.) "What the World Needs Now Is Love."

Buddy De Sylva, 1895-1950, (U.S.) "When Day Is Done"; "Look for the Silver Lining"; "April Showers."

Howard Dietz, 1896-1983, (U.S.) "Dancing in the Dark"; "That's Entertainment."

Al Dubin, 1891-1945, (U.S.) "Tiptoe Through the Tulips"; "Lullaby of Broadway."

Fred Ebb, 1936-2004, (U.S.) *Cabaret*; *Zorba*; *Woman of the Year*; *Chicago*.

Ray Evans, 1915-2007, (U.S.) "Mona Lisa"; "Que Sera, Sera."

Dorothy Fields, 1905-74, (U.S.) "On the Sunny Side of the Street"; "Don't Blame Me"; "The Way You Look Tonight."

Ira Gershwin, 1896-1983, (U.S.) "The Man I Love"; "S'Wonderful"; "Embraceable You."

William S. Gilbert, 1836-1911, (Br.) *H.M.S. Pinafore*; *Pirates of Penzance*.

Gerry Goffin, 1939-2014, (U.S.) "Will You Love Me Tomorrow"; "Take Good Care of My Baby"; "Up on the Roof."

Mack Gordon, 1905-59, (U.S.) "You'll Never Know"; "The More I See You"; "Chattanooga Choo-Choo."

Oscar Hammerstein II, 1895-1960, (U.S.) *Ol' Man River*; *Oklahoma!*; *Carousel*.

E. Y. (Yip) Harburg, 1898-1981, (U.S.) "Brother, Can You Spare a Dime"; "April in Paris"; "Over the Rainbow."

Sheldon Harnick, b 1924, (U.S.) *Fiddler on the Roof*; *She Loves Me*.

Lorenz Hart, 1895-1943, (U.S.) "Isn't It Romantic"; "Blue Moon"; "Lover"; "Manhattan"; "My Funny Valentine."

DuBose Heyward, 1885-1940, (U.S.) "Summertime."

Gus Kahn, 1886-1941, (U.S.) "Memories"; "Ain't We Got Fun."

Alan J. Lerner, 1918-86, (U.S.) *Brigadoon*; *My Fair Lady*; *Camelot*; *Gigi*; *On a Clear Day You Can See Forever*.

Johnny Mercer, 1909-76, (U.S.) "Blues in the Night"; "Come Rain or Come Shine"; "Laura"; "That Old Black Magic."

Bob Merrill, 1921-98, (U.S.) "People"; "(How Much Is That) Doggie in the Window."

Jack Norworth, 1879-1959, (U.S.) "Take Me Out to the Ball Game"; "Shine On Harvest Moon."

Mitchell Parish, 1901-93, (U.S.) "Stardust"; "Blue Moon"; "Stairway to the Stars."

Andy Razaf, 1895-1973, (U.S.) "Honeysuckle Rose"; "Ain't Misbehavin."

Leo Robin, 1900-84, (U.S.) "Thanks for the Memory"; "Diamonds Are a Girl's Best Friend."

Robert Sherman, 1925-2012, (U.S.) *Mary Poppins*; *The Jungle Book*.

Bernie Taupin, b 1947 (Br.) "Rocket Man"; "Your Song."

Paul Francis Webster, 1907-84, (U.S.) "Secret Love"; "The Shadow of Your Smile"; "Love Is a Many-Splendored Thing."

Jack Yellen, 1892-1991, (U.S.) "Ain't She Sweet"; "Happy Days Are Here Again."

Blues and Jazz Artists of the Past

Julian "Cannonball" Adderley, 1928-75, alto sax.

Nat Adderley, 1931-2000, cornet.

Henry "Red" Allen, 1908-67, trumpet.

Louis "Satchmo" Armstrong, 1901-71, trumpet, singer, bandleader.

Albert Ayler, 1936-70, tenor sax, alto sax.

Mildred Bailey, 1907-51, singer.

Chet Baker, 1929-88, trumpet, singer.

Ray Barretto, 1930-2006, conga drummer.

William "Count" Basie, 1904-84, bandleader, piano, composer.

Sidney Bechet, 1897-1959, soprano sax, clarinet.

Bix Beiderbecke, 1903-31, cornet, composer, piano.

Rowland "Bunny" Berigan, 1908-42, trumpet.

Barney Bigard, 1906-80, clarinet.

Eubie Blake, 1883-1983, composer, piano.

Art Blakey, 1919-90, drums, bandleader.

Jimmy Blanton, 1921-42, bass.

Charles "Buddy" Bolden, 1877-1931, cornet, pioneer bandleader.

Lester Bowie, 1941-99, trumpet, composer, bandleader.

Michael Brecker, 1949-2007, saxophone.

Big Bill Broonzy, 1893-1958, blues singer, guitar.

Clarence "Gatemouth" Brown, 1924-2005, guitar, singer.

Clifford Brown, 1930-56, trumpet.

Ray Brown, 1926-2002, bass.

Don Byas, 1912-72, tenor sax.

Charlie Byrd, 1925-99, guitar; popularized bossa nova.

Cab Calloway, 1907-94, bandleader, singer.

Harry Carney, 1910-74, baritone sax, clarinet.

Benny Carter, 1907-2003, alto sax.

Betty Carter, 1930-98, jazz singer.

Sidney "Big Sid" Catlett, 1910-51, drums.

Adolphus Anthony "Doc" Cheatham, 1905-97, trumpet.

Don Cherry, 1936-95, trumpet.

Charlie Christian, 1916-42, guitar.

Kenny "Klook" Clarke, 1914-85, drums.

Buck Clayton, 1911-91, trumpet.

Al Cohn, 1925-88, tenor sax.

Nat "King" Cole, 1919-65, piano, singer.

William "Cozy" Cole, 1909-81, drums.

Alice Coltrane, 1937-2007, piano, composer.

John Coltrane, 1926-67, tenor sax, soprano sax, composer.

Eddie Condon, 1905-73, guitar, bandleader.

Tadd Dameron, 1917-65, piano, composer.

Eddie "Lockjaw" Davis, 1921-86, tenor sax.

Miles Davis, 1926-91, trumpet, composer.

Wild Bill Davison, 1906-89, cornet.

Blossom Dearie, 1924-2009, singer.

Paul Desmond, 1924-77, alto sax.

Vic Dickenson, 1906-84, trombone.

Willie Dixon, 1915-92, composer, bass.

Johnny Dodds, 1892-1940, clarinet.

Warren "Baby" Dodds, 1898-1959, drums.

Eric Dolphy, 1928-64, alto sax, bass clarinet, flute.

Jimmy Dorsey, 1904-57, alto sax, bandleader.

Tommy Dorsey, 1905-56, trombone, bandleader.

Billy Eckstine, 1914-93, singer, bandleader.

Harry "Sweets" Edison, 1915-99, trumpet.

David "Honeyboy" Edwards, 1915-2011, guitar, singer.

Roy Eldridge, 1911-89, trumpet, singer.

Duke Ellington, 1899-1974, piano, bandleader, composer.

Bill Evans, 1929-80, piano.

Gil Evans, 1912-88, composer, arranger, piano.

Art Farmer, 1928-99, trumpet, flugelhorn.

Maynard Ferguson, 1926-2006, trumpet, bandleader.

Ella Fitzgerald, 1917-96, singer.

Tommy Flanagan, 1930-2001, piano.

Erroll Garner, 1921-77, piano, composer.

Stan Getz, 1927-91, tenor sax.

Dizzy Gillespie, 1917-93, trumpet, composer, singer.

Benny Goodman, 1909-86, clarinet, bandleader.

Dexter Gordon, 1923-90, tenor sax.

Stéphane Grappelli, 1908-97, violin.

Bobby Hackett, 1915-76, trumpet, cornet.

Lionel Hampton, 1908-2002, vibraphone, bandleader.

W. C. Handy, 1873-1958, composer.

Jimmy Harrison, 1900-31, trombone.

Coleman Hawkins, 1904-69, tenor sax.

Percy Heath, 1923-2005, bass.

Fletcher Henderson, 1898-1952, bandleader, arranger.

Woody Herman, 1913-87, clarinet, alto sax, bandleader.

Jay C. Higginbotham, 1906-73, trombone.

Ruiz Hilton, 1952-2006, piano, composer.

Earl "Fatha" Hines, 1903-83, piano.

Milt Hinton, 1910-2000, bass.

Al Hirt, 1922-99, trumpet.

Johnny Hodges, 1906-70, alto sax.

Billie Holiday, 1915-59, singer.

John Lee Hooker, 1917-2001, blues guitar, singer.

Sam "Lightnin'" Hopkins, 1912-82, blues singer, guitar.

Shirley Horn, 1934-2005, piano, singer.

Howlin' Wolf (Chester Burnett), 1910-76, blues singer, harmonica, guitar.

Alberta Hunter, 1895-1984, singer.

Mahalia Jackson, 1911-72, gospel singer.

Milt Jackson, 1923-99, vibraphone.

Elmore James, 1918-63, blues singer, guitar.

Etta James, 1938-2012, blues singer.

"Blind" Lemon Jefferson, 1897-1929, blues singer, guitar.

J. J. Johnson, 1924-2001, trombone.

James P. Johnson, 1891-1955, piano, composer.

Robert Johnson, 1912-38, blues singer, guitar.

William "Bunk" Johnson, 1879-1949, trumpet.

Elvin Jones, 1927-2004, drums.

Jo Jones, 1911-85, drums.

Philly Joe Jones, 1923-85, drums.

Thad Jones, 1923-86, cornet, bandleader, composer.

Scott Joplin, 1868-1917, ragtime composer.

Louis Jordan, 1908-75, singer, alto sax.

Stan Kenton, 1911-79, bandleader, composer, piano.

Barney Kessel, 1923-2004, guitar.

Albert King, 1923-92, blues guitar.

John Kirby, 1908-52, bandleader, bass.

Rahsaan Roland Kirk, 1936-77, saxophone, composer.

Gene Krupa, 1909-73, drums, bandleader.

Scott LaFaro, 1936-61, bass.

Lead Belly (Huddie Ledbetter), 1888-1949, folk and blues singer, guitar.

Peggy Lee, 1920-2002, singer.

John Lewis, 1920-2001, piano, Modern Jazz Quartet founder.

Mel Lewis, 1929-90, drums, bandleader.

Jimmie Lunceford, 1902-47, bandleader.

Machito (Frank Grillo), 1908-84, Latin percussion, singer, bandleader.

Shelly Manne, 1920-84, drums, bandleader.

Jackie McLean, 1931-2006, saxophone, composer.

Jimmy McPartland, 1907-91, trumpet.

Marian McPartland, 1918-2013, jazz pianist.

Carmen McRae, 1920-94, singer.

Glenn Miller, 1904-44, trombone, bandleader.

Charles Mingus, 1922-79, bass, composer, bandleader.

Thelonious Monk, 1917-82, piano, composer.

Wes Montgomery, 1925-68, guitar.

James Moody, 1925-2010, saxophone.

Ferdinand "Jelly Roll" Morton, 1885-1941, composer, piano.

Bennie Moten, 1894-1935, piano, bandleader.

Gerry Mulligan, 1927-96, baritone sax, composer.

Theodore "Fats" Navarro, 1923-50, trumpet.

Red Nichols, 1905-65, cornet, bandleader.

Red Norvo, 1908-99, vibraphone, xylophone, bandleader.

Anita O'Day, 1919-2006, singer.

Arturo "Chico" O'Farrill, 1921-2001, Latin composer, arranger.

King Oliver, 1885-1938, cornet, bandleader.

Sy Oliver, 1910-88, arranger, composer.

Edward "Kid" Ory, 1886-1973, trombone, bandleader.

Johnny Otis, 1921-2012, blues singer.

Oran "Hot Lips" Page, 1908-54, trumpet, singer.

Charlie "Bird" Parker, 1920-55, alto sax, composer.

Joe Pass, 1929-94, guitar.

Art Pepper, 1925-82, alto sax.

Pinetop Perkins, 1913-2011, piano.

Oscar Peterson, 1925-2007, piano.

Oscar Pettiford, 1922-60, bass.

Earl "Bud" Powell, 1924-66, piano.

Chano Pozo, 1915-48, Cuban percussion, singer.

Louis Prima, 1911-78, singer, bandleader.

Tito Puente, 1923-2000, Latin percussion, bandleader.

Gertrude "Ma" Rainey, 1886-1939, blues singer.

Lou Rawls, 1933-2006, singer.

Dewey Redman, 1931-2006, tenor sax.

Don Redman (Robert Rodney Chudnick), 1900-64, composer, arranger.

Django Reinhardt, 1910-53, guitar.

Buddy Rich, 1917-87, drums.

Max Roach, 1924-2007, drums, composer.

Red Rodney (Robert Chudnick), 1927-94, trumpet.

Jimmy Rowles, 1918-96, piano.

Jimmy Rushing, 1903-72, blues and jazz singer.

Charles "Pee Wee" Russell, 1906-69, clarinet.

Artie Shaw, 1910-2004, swing-era bandleader, clarinet.

George Shearing, 1919-2011, piano.

Nina Simone (Eunice Waymon), 1933-2003, singer.

John "Zoot" Sims, 1925-85, tenor sax.

Zutty Singleton, 1898-1975, drums.

Bessie Smith, 1894-1937, blues singer.

Clarence "Pinetop" Smith, 1904-29, piano, singer, boogie woogie pioneer.

Willie "The Lion" Smith, 1897-1973, piano, composer.

Francis "Muggsy" Spanier, 1906-67, cornet.

Edward "Sonny" Stitt, 1924-82, tenor sax, alto sax.

Billy Strayhorn, 1915-67, composer, piano, Duke Ellington collaborator.

Sun Ra (Herman Blount), 1915?-93, bandleader, piano, composer.

Art Tatum, 1910-56, piano.

Art Taylor, 1929-95, drums.

Billy Taylor, 1921-2010, piano.

Jack Teagarden, 1905-64, trombone, singer.

Mel Tormé, 1925-99, singer ("The Velvet Fog").

Dave Tough, 1908-48, drums.

Lennie Tristano, 1919-78, piano, composer.

Joe Turner, 1911-85, blues singer.

Sarah Vaughan, 1924-90, singer.

Joe Venuti, 1903-78, violin.

Aaron "T-Bone" Walker, 1910-75, blues guitar.

Thomas "Fats" Waller, 1904-43, piano, singer, composer.

Dinah Washington (Ruth Jones), 1924-63, singer.

Grover Washington Jr., 1943-99, pop-jazz sax, composer.

Ethel Waters, 1896-1977, jazz and blues singer.

Muddy Waters (McKinley Morganfield), 1915-83, blues singer, songwriter.

Julius Watkins, 1921-77, French horn.

William "Chick" Webb, 1902-39, bandleader, drums.

Ben Webster, 1909-73, tenor sax.

Junior Wells (Amos Blackmore), 1934-98, blues singer, harmonica.

Paul Whiteman, 1890-1967, bandleader.

Margaret Whiting, 1924-2011, singer.

Charles "Cootie" Williams, 1910-85, trumpet, bandleader.

Joe Williams, 1918-99, singer.

Mary Lou Williams, 1910-81, piano, composer.

Tony Williams, 1945-97, drums.

John Lee "Sonny Boy" Williamson, 1914-48, blues singer, harmonica.

Sonny Boy Williamson (Aleck "Rice" Miller), 1900?-65, blues singer, harmonica.

Teddy Wilson, 1912-86, piano.

Kai Winding, 1922-83, trombone.

Jimmy Yancey, 1894-1951, piano.

Lester "Pres" Young, 1909-59, tenor sax.

Country Music Artists of the Past and Present

Roy Acuff, 1903-92, fiddler, singer, songwriter; "Wabash Cannon Ball."

Alabama (Jeff Cook, b 1949; Teddy Gentry, b 1952; Mark Herndon, b 1955; Randy Owen, b 1949); "Feels So Right."

Jason Aldean, b 1977, singer; "Don't You Wanna Stay."

James "Whispering Bill" Anderson, b 1937, singer, songwriter; "Make Mine Night Time."

Eddy Arnold, 1918-2008, singer, guitarist, known as the "Tennessee Plowboy."

Chet Atkins, 1924-2001, guitarist, composer; helped create the "Nashville sound."

Gene Autry, 1907-98, first great singing movie cowboy; "Back in the Saddle Again."

Clint Black, b 1962, singer, songwriter; "Killin' Time."

Garth Brooks, b 1962, singer, songwriter; "Friends in Low Places."

Brooks & Dunn (Kix Brooks, b 1955; Ronnie Dunn, b 1953); "Hard Workin' Man."

Luke Bryan, b 1976, singer, songwriter; "Someone Else Calling You Baby."

Boudleaux, 1920-87, and **Felice Bryant**, 1925-2003, songwriting team; "Hey Joe."

Glen Campbell, b 1936, singer, guitarist; "Gentle on My Mind."

Mary Chapin Carpenter, b 1958, singer, songwriter; "I Feel Lucky."

Carter Family (original members A. P., 1891-1960; "Mother" Maybelle, 1909-78; Sara, 1898-1979); "Wildwood Flower."

Johnny Cash, 1932-2003, singer, songwriter; "I Walk the Line," "Ring of Fire," "Folsom Prison Blues."

Kenny Chesney, b 1968, guitarist, singer, songwriter; "You Had Me From Hello."

Roy Clark, b 1933, guitarist, banjoist, singer, co-host of *Hee Haw*; "Yesterday, When I Was Young."

Patsy Cline, 1932-63, singer; "Walkin' After Midnight," "Crazy," "Sweet Dreams."

Billy Ray Cyrus, b 1961, singer, songwriter; "Achy Breaky Heart."

Charlie Daniels, b 1936, guitarist, fiddler; "The Devil Went Down to Georgia."

Jimmy Dean, 1928-2010, singer; "Big Bad John."

John Denver, 1943-97, singer, songwriter; "Rocky Mountain High."

Dixie Chicks (Natalie Maines, b 1974; Emily Erwin Robison, b 1972; Martie Seidel, b 1969); "Wide Open Spaces."

Dale Evans, 1912-2001, singer, actress, married Roy Rogers.

Sara Evans, b 1971, singer, songwriter; "Born to Fly."

Flatt & Scruggs (Lester Flatt, 1914-79; Earl Scruggs, 1924-2012), guitar-banjo duo and soloists; "Foggy Mountain Breakdown."

Red Foley, 1910-68, singer; "Chattanoogie Shoe Shine Boy."

Tennessee Ernie Ford, 1919-91, singer, TV host; "Sixteen Tons."

William "Lefty" Frizzell, 1928-75, singer, guitarist; "Long Black Veil."

Vince Gill, b 1957, singer, songwriter; "When I Call Your Name."

Merle Haggard, b 1937, singer, songwriter; "Okie From Muskogee."

Emmylou Harris, b 1947, singer, songwriter, folk-country crossover artist; "If I Could Only Win Your Love."

Hunter Hayes, b 1991, singer; "Wanted."

Faith Hill, b 1967, singer, songwriter; "Breathe."

Alan Jackson, b 1958, singer, songwriter; "Where Were You (When the World Stopped Turning)."

Waylon Jennings, 1937-2002, singer, songwriter, "outlaw country" pioneer; "Luckenbach, Texas."

George Jones, 1931-2013, singer; "He Stopped Loving Her Today."

The Judds (Naomi, b 1946; Wynonna, b 1964), mother-daughter duo; Wynonna also a solo act.

Toby Keith, b 1961, singer, songwriter, guitarist; "Should've Been a Cowboy."

Alison Krauss, b 1971, bluegrass fiddler, singer, bandleader; "When You Say Nothing at All."

Kris Kristofferson, b 1936, singer, songwriter, actor; "Me and Bobby McGee."

Lady Antebellum (Dave Haywood, b 1982; Charles Kelley, b 1981; Hillary Scott, b 1984); "I Run to You."

Miranda Lambert, b 1983, singer, guitarist; "The House That Built Me."

Louvin Brothers (Charlie, 1927-2011; Ira, 1924-65), singers; "If I Could Only Win Your Love."

Patty Loveless, b 1957, singer, songwriter; "How Can I Help You Say Goodbye."

Lyle Lovett, b 1957, singer, songwriter, bandleader, actor; "Cowboy Man."

Loretta Lynn, b 1935?, singer; "Coal Miner's Daughter."

Barbara Mandrell, b 1948, singer; "I Was Country When Country Wasn't Cool."

Kathy Mattea, b 1959, singer, songwriter; "Eighteen Wheels and a Dozen Roses."

Martina McBride, b 1966, singer, songwriter; "Independence Day."

Reba McEntire, b 1955, singer, songwriter, actress; "Whoever's in New England."

Tim McGraw, b 1967, singer; "It's Your Love," "I Like It, I Love It."

Roger Miller, 1936-92, singer, songwriter; "King of the Road."

Ronnie Milsap, b 1944, singer, songwriter; "There's No Gettin' Over Me."

Bill Monroe, 1911-96, singer, songwriter, mandolin player, "father of bluegrass music"; "Mule Skinner Blues."

Anne Murray, b 1945, singer; "You Needed Me."

Willie Nelson, b 1933, singer, songwriter, actor; "On the Road Again."

Mark O'Connor, b 1961, fiddler, country-classical crossover composer.

Buck Owens, 1929-2006, singer, guitarist; "Act Naturally."

Brad Paisley, b 1972, singer, songwriter; "Whiskey Lullaby," "When I Get Where I'm Going."

Dolly Parton, b 1946, singer, songwriter, actress; "Here You Come Again," "9 to 5."

Johnny Paycheck, (Don Lytle), 1938-2003, singer, guitarist; "Take This Job and Shove It."

Minnie Pearl, 1912-96, comedienne, Grand Ole Opry star.

Kellie Pickler, b 1986, singer, songwriter.

Ray Price, b 1926, country singer, guitarist, songwriter; "Crazy Arms."

Charley Pride, b 1938, first African American country star; "Kiss an Angel Good Mornin'."

Eddie Rabbit, 1941-98, singer, songwriter; "I Love a Rainy Night."

Rascal Flatts (Jay DeMarcus, b 1971; Gary LeVox, b 1970; Joe Don Rooney, b 1975); "Life Is a Highway."

Jim Reeves, 1923-64, singer, songwriter; "Four Walls."

Charlie Rich, 1932-95, singer, songwriter called the "Silver Fox"; "The Most Beautiful Girl."

LeAnn Rimes, b 1982, singer; "Blue."

Tex Ritter, 1905-74, singer, songwriter; "Jingle, Jangle, Jingle."

Marty Robbins, 1925-82, singer, songwriter; "A White Sport Coat and a Pink Carnation."

Jimmie Rodgers, 1897-1933, singer, songwriter; "T for Texas."

Kenny Rogers, b 1938, singer, songwriter; "The Gambler."

Roy Rogers (Leonard Slye), 1911-98, singer, actor, "King of the Cowboys," sang with Sons of the Pioneers.

Fred Rose, 1898-1954, songwriter, singer, producer; "Blue Eyes Cryin' in the Rain."

Blake Shelton, b 1976, singer; "Home."

Ricky Skaggs, b 1954, singer, songwriter, bandleader; "Don't Cheat in Our Hometown."

Ralph Stanley, b 1927, singer, banjo player; "Man of Constant Sorrow."

George Strait, b 1952, singer, bandleader; "Ace in the Hole."

Sugarland (Kristian Bush, b 1970; Jennifer Nettles, b 1974); "Stay."

Taylor Swift, b 1989, singer, songwriter; "You Belong With Me."

Lonnie "Mel" Tillis, b 1932, singer, songwriter, bandleader; "I Ain't Never."

Merle Travis, 1917-83, singer, guitarist, songwriter; "Divorce Me C.O.D."

Randy Travis, b 1959, singer, songwriter; "Forever and Ever, Amen."

Ernest Tubb, 1914-84, singer, songwriter, guitarist; "Walking the Floor Over You."

Josh Turner, b 1977, singer; "Why Don't We Just Dance."

Shania Twain, b 1965, singer; "You're Still the One."

Conway Twitty, 1933-93, singer, songwriter; "Hello Darlin'."

Carrie Underwood, b 1983, singer, songwriter; *American Idol* winner.

Keith Urban, b 1967, guitarist, singer, songwriter; "It's a Love Thing."

Porter Wagoner, 1927-2007, singer, songwriter, guitarist; "I Will Always Love You."

Kitty Wells (Ellen Deason), 1919-2012, singer, songwriter; "It Wasn't God Who Made Honky-Tonk Angels."

Dottie West, 1932-91, singer, songwriter; "Here Comes My Baby."

Hank Williams Jr., b 1949, singer, songwriter; "Bocephus"; "All My Rowdy Friends (Have Settled Down)."

Hank Williams Sr., 1923-53, singer, songwriter; "Your Cheatin' Heart."

Bob Wills, 1905-75, Western Swing fiddler, singer, bandleader, songwriter; "New San Antonio Rose."

Lee Ann Womack, b 1966, singer, songwriter; "I Hope You Dance."

Tammy Wynette, 1942-98, singer; "Stand By Your Man."

Trisha Yearwood, b 1964, singer, songwriter; "How Do I Live."

Dwight Yoakam, b 1957, singer, songwriter, actor; "Ain't That Lonely Yet."

Zac Brown Band (Coy Bowles, b 1979; Zac Brown, b 1978; Clay Cook, Jimmy De Martini, Chris Fryar, b 1970; John Driskell Hopkins, b 1971); "Chicken Fried."

Dance Figures of the Past

Alvin Ailey, 1931-89, (U.S.) modern dancer, choreographer; melded modern dance and Afro-Caribbean techniques.

Frederick Ashton, 1904-88, (Br.) ballet choreographer; director of Great Britain's Royal Ballet, 1963-70.

Fred Astaire, 1899-1987, dancer, actor; teamed with dancer/actress **Ginger Rogers**, 1911-95, (both U.S.) in movie musicals.

George Balanchine, 1904-83, (Russ.-U.S.) ballet choreographer, teacher; most influential exponent of neoclassical style; founded, with Lincoln Kirstein, School of American Ballet and New York City Ballet.

Pina Bausch, 1940-2009, (Ger.) modern dance choreographer influencing the Tanztheater style of dance.

Carlo Blasis, 1795-1878, (It.) ballet dancer, choreographer, writer; his teaching methods are standards of classical dance.

August Bournonville, 1805-79, (Den.) ballet dancer, choreographer, teacher; exuberant, light style.

Fernando Bujones, 1955-2005, (Cuba-U.S.) ballet dancer.

Gisella Caccialanza, 1914-98, (U.S.) ballerina; charter member of Balanchine's American Ballet.

Irene, 1893-1969, (U.S.) and **Vernon Castle**, 1887-1918, (Br.) husband-and-wife ballroom dancers.

Enrico Cecchetti, 1850-1928, (It.) ballet dancer, leading dancer of Russia's Imperial Ballet; his technique was basis for Britain's Imperial Soc. of Teachers of Dancing.

Gower, 1921-80, dancer, choreographer, director; with wife **Marge Champion**, b 1923, (both U.S.) choreographed, danced in Broadway musicals and films.

John Cranko, 1927-73, (S. Afr.) choreographer; created narrative ballets based on literary works.

Merce Cunningham, 1919-2009, (U.S.) dancer, choreographer of avant-garde dance.

Alexandra Danilova, 1903-97, (Russ.) ballerina; noted teacher at the School of American Ballet.

Agnes de Mille, 1905-93, (U.S.) ballerina, choreographer; known for using American themes, she choreographed the ballet *Rodeo* and the musical *Oklahoma!*

Dame Ninette De Valois, 1898-2001, (Br.) choreographer, founding director of London's Royal Ballet; *The Rake's Progress*.

Sergei Diaghilev, 1872-1929, (Russ.) impresario; founded Les Ballet Russes; saw ballet as art unifying dance, drama, music, and decor.

Isadora Duncan, 1877-1927, (U.S.) expressive dancer who united free movement with serious music; one of the founders of modern dance.

Katherine Dunham, 1910-2006, (U.S.) dancer, choreographer; internationally known for African, Caribbean, and African American dance forms.

Fanny Elssler, 1810-84, (Austria) ballerina of the Romantic era; known for dramatic skill, sensual style.

Michel Fokine, 1880-1942, (Russ.) ballet dancer, choreographer, teacher; rejected strict classicism in favor of dramatically expressive style.

Margot Fonteyn, 1919-91, (Br.) prima ballerina, Royal Ballet of Great Britain; famed performance partner of Rudolf Nureyev.

Bob Fosse, 1927-87, (U.S.) jazz dancer, choreographer, director; Broadway musicals and film.

Serge Golovine, 1924-98, (Fr.) ballet dancer with Grand Ballet du Marquis de Cuevas, choreographer.

Martha Graham, 1894-1991, (U.S.) modern dancer, choreographer; created and codified her own dramatic technique.

Melissa Hayden, 1923-2006, (Can.) ballet dancer.

Martha Hill, 1900-95, (U.S.) educator; leading figure in modern dance. Founded American Dance Festival.

Gregory Hines, 1946-2003, (U.S.) tap-dance innovator; master of improvisation.

Doris Humphrey, 1895-1958, (U.S.) modern dancer, choreographer, writer, teacher.

Michael Jackson, 1958-2009, (U.S.) singer and dancer who perfected the "moonwalk."

Robert Joffrey, 1930-88, ballet dancer, choreographer; cofounded with **Gerald Arpino**, 1928-2008, (both U.S.) the Joffrey Ballet.

Kurt Jooss, 1901-79, (Ger.) choreographer, teacher; created expressionist works using modern and classical techniques.

Tamara Karsavina, 1885-1978, (Russ.) prima ballerina of Russia's Imperial Ballet and Diaghilev's Ballets Russes; partner of Nijinsky.

Nora Kaye, 1920-87, (U.S.) ballerina with Metropolitan Opera Ballet and Ballet Theater (now American Ballet Theatre).

Gene Kelly, 1912-96, (U.S.) dancer, actor in movie musicals.

Michael Kidd, 1915-2003, (U.S.) dancer, film and theater choreographer.

Lincoln Kirstein, 1907-96 (U.S.) brought ballet as an art form to U.S.; founded, with George Balanchine, School of American Ballet and New York City Ballet.

Serge Lifar, 1905-86, (Russ.-Fr.) prem. danseur, choreographer; director of dance at Paris Opera, 1930-45, 1947-58.

José Limón, 1908-72, (Mex.-U.S.) modern dancer, choreographer, teacher; developed technique based on Humphrey.

Catherine Littlefield, 1908-51, (U.S.) ballerina, choreographer, teacher; pioneer of American ballet.

Kenneth MacMillan, 1929-92, (Br.) dancer, choreographer; directed Royal Ballet of Great Britain, 1970-77.

Dame Alicia Markova, 1910-2004, (Br.) ballerina known for title role in *Giselle*; helped popularize ballet in U.S. and Britain.

Léonide Massine, 1896-1979, (Russ.-U.S.) ballet dancer, choreographer; known for his "symphonic ballet."

Fayard Nicholas, 1914-2006, tap dancer, choreographer, actor; together with brother **Harold Nicholas**, 1921-2000, (both U.S.) formed the "Nicholas Brothers."

Vaslav Nijinsky, 1890-50, (Russ.) prem. danseur, choreographer; leading member of Diaghilev's Ballets Russes. His ballets were revolutionary for their time.

Alwin Nikolais, 1910-93, (U.S.) modern choreographer; created dance theater utilizing mixed media effects.

Jean-George Noverre, 1727-1810, (Fr.) ballet choreographer, teacher, writer; "Shakespeare of the Dance."

Rudolf Nureyev, 1938-93, (Russ.) prem. danseur, choreographer; leading male dancer of his generation; director of dance at Paris Opera, 1983-89.

Ruth Page, 1899-1991, (U.S.) ballerina, choreographer; danced, directed ballet at Chicago Lyric Opera.

Anna Pavlova, 1881-1931, (Russ.) prima ballerina; toured with her own company to world acclaim.

Marius Petipa, 1818-1910, (Fr.) ballet dancer, choreographer; ballet master of the Imperial Ballet; established Russian classicism as leading style of late 19th cent.

Roland Petit, 1924-2011, (Fr.) dancer, choreographer; founder of Les Ballets de Paris.

Pearl Primus, 1919-95, (Trinidad-U.S.) modern dancer, choreographer, scholar; combined African, Caribbean, and African American styles.

Jerome Robbins, 1918-98, (U.S.) choreographer, director, dancer; *The King and I*, *West Side Story*, *Fiddler on the Roof*.

Bill "Bojangles" Robinson, 1878-1949, (U.S.) famed tap dancer; called "King of Tapology" on stage and screen.

Ruth St. Denis, 1877-1968, (U.S.) influential interpretive dancer, choreographer, teacher.

Ted Shawn, 1891-1972, (U.S.) modern dancer, choreographer; formed dance company and school with Ruth St. Denis; established Jacob's Pillow Dance Festival.

Marie Taglioni, 1804-84, (It.) ballerina, teacher; in title role of *La Sylphide* established image of the ethereal ballerina.

Maria Tallchief, 1925-2013, (U.S.) prima ballerina, 1st of Amer. Indian descent.

Glen Tetley, 1926-2007, (U.S.) dancer, choreographer, ballet director; fused elements of modern dance with ballet.

Antony Tudor, 1908-87, (Br.) choreographer, teacher; exponent of the "psychological ballet."

Galina Ulanova, 1910-98, (Russ.) revered ballerina with Bolshoi Ballet.

Agrippina Vaganova, 1879-1951, (Russ.) ballet teacher, director called "queen of variations"; codified Soviet ballet technique.

Mary Wigman, 1886-1973, (Ger.) modern dancer, choreographer, teacher; influenced European expressionist dance.

Opera Singers of the Past

Licia Albanese, 1909-2014, (It.) soprano.

Frances Alda, 1883?-1952, (N.Z.) soprano.

Pasquale Amato, 1878-1942, (It.) baritone.

Marian Anderson, 1897-1993, (U.S.) contralto.

Charles Anthony, 1929-2012, (U.S.) tenor.

Jussi Björling, 1911-60, (Swed.) tenor.

Lucrezia Bori, 1887-1960, (It.) soprano.

Maria Callas, 1923-77, (U.S.) soprano.

Emma Calvé, 1858-1942, (Fr.) soprano.

Enrico Caruso, 1873-1921, (It.) tenor.

Feodor Chaliapin, 1873-1938, (Russ.) bass.

Lili Chookasian, 1921-2012, (U.S.) contralto.

Boris Christoff, 1914-93, (Bulg.) bass.

Franco Corelli, 1921-2003, (It.) tenor.

Hughes Cuenod, 1902-2010, (Switz.) tenor.

Victoria De Los Angeles, 1923-2005, (Sp.) soprano.

Giuseppe De Luca, 1876-1950, (It.) baritone.

Fernando De Lucia, 1860-1925, (It.) tenor.

Edouard De Reszke, 1853-1917, (Pol.) bass.

Jean De Reszke, 1850-1925, (Pol.) tenor.

Emmy Destinn, 1878-1930, (Czech.) soprano.

Emma Eames, 1865-1952, (U.S.) soprano.

(Carlo Broschi) Farinelli, 1705-82, (It.) castrato.

Geraldine Farrar, 1882-1967, (U.S.) soprano.

Eileen Farrell, 1920-2002, (U.S.) soprano.

Kathleen Ferrier, 1912-53, (Eng.) contralto.

Dietrich Fischer-Dieskau, 1925-2012, (Ger.) baritone.

Kirsten Flagstad, 1895-1962, (Nor.) soprano.
Olive Fremstad, 1871-1951, (Swed.-U.S.) soprano.
Amelita Galli-Curci, 1882-1963, (It.) soprano.
Mary Garden, 1874-1967, (Br.) soprano.
Nicolai Ghiaurov, 1929-2004, (Bulg.) bass.
Beniamino Gigli, 1890-1957, (It.) tenor.
Tito Gobbi, 1913-84, (It.) baritone.
Giulia Grisi, 1811-69, (It.) soprano.
Frieda Hempel, 1885-1955, (Ger.) soprano.
Jerome Hines, 1921-2003, (U.S.) bass.
Hans Hotter, 1909-2003, (Ger.) bass-baritone.
Maria Jeritza, 1887-1982, (Czech.) soprano.
Sena Jurinac, 1921-2011, (Yugo.) soprano.
Alexander Kipnis, 1891-1978, (Russ.-U.S.) bass.
Dorothy Kirsten, 1910-92, (U.S.) soprano.
Alfredo Kraus, 1927-99, (Sp.) tenor.
Luigi Lablache, 1794-1858, (It.) bass.
Lilli Lehmann, 1848-1929, (Ger.) soprano.
Lotte Lehmann, 1888-1976, (Ger.-U.S.) soprano.
Jenny Lind, 1820-87, (Swed.) soprano.
Cornell MacNeil, 1922-2011, (U.S.) baritone.
Maria Malibran, 1808-36, (Sp.) mezzo-soprano.
Giovanni Martinelli, 1885-1969, (It.) tenor.
John McCormack, 1884-1945, (Ire.) tenor.

Nellie Melba, 1861-1931, (Austral.) soprano.
Lauritz Melchior, 1890-1973, (Den.) tenor.
Robert Merrill, 1919-2004, (U.S.) baritone.
Zinka Milanov, 1906-89, (Yugo.) soprano.
Patricia Neway, 1919-2012, (U.S.) soprano.
Birgit Nilsson, 1918-2005, (Swed.) soprano.
Lillian Nordica, 1857-1914, (U.S.) soprano.
Magda Olivero, 1910-2014, (It.) soprano.
Giuditta Pasta, 1797-1865, (It.) soprano.
Adelina Patti, 1843-1919, (It.) soprano.
Luciano Pavarotti, 1935-2007, (It.) tenor.
Peter Pears, 1910-86, (Eng.) tenor.
Jan Peerce, 1904-84, (U.S.) tenor.
Ezio Pinza, 1892-1957, (It.) bass.
Lily Pons, 1898-1976, (Fr.) soprano.
Rosa Ponselle, 1897-1981, (U.S.) soprano.
Hermann Prey, 1929-98, (Ger.) baritone.
Margaret Price, 1941-2011, (U.K.) soprano.
Regina Resnik, 1922-2013, (U.S.) soprano turned mezzo-soprano.
Elisabeth Rethberg, 1894-1976, (Ger.) soprano.
Giovanni Battista Rubini, 1794-1854, (It.) tenor.
Leonie Rysanek, 1926-98, (Austria) soprano.
Dorothy Sarnoff, 1914-2008, (U.S.) soprano.
Bidù Sayão, 1902-99, (Braz.) soprano.
Friedrich Schorr, 1888-1953, (Hung.) bass-baritone.
Elisabeth Schwarzkopf, 1915-2006, (Ger.) soprano.

Marcella Sembrich, 1858-1935, (Pol.) soprano.
Cesare Siepi, 1923-2010, (It.) bass.
Beverly Sills, 1929-2007, (U.S.) soprano.
Elisabeth Söderström, 1927-2009, (Swed.) soprano.
Eleanor Steber, 1914-90, (U.S.) soprano.
Risë Stevens, 1913-2013, (U.S.) mezzo-soprano.
Joan Sutherland, 1926-2010, (Austral.) soprano.
Ferruccio Tagliavini, 1913-95, (It.) tenor.
Renata Tebaldi, 1922-2004 (It.) soprano.
Luisa Tetrazzini, 1871-1940, (It.) soprano.
Lawrence Tibbett, 1896-1960, (U.S.) baritone.
Giorgio Tozzi, 1923-2011, (U.S.) bass-baritone.
Tatiana Troyanos, 1938-93, (U.S.) mezzo-soprano.
Richard Tucker, 1913-75, (U.S.) tenor.
Shirley Verrett, 1931-2010, (U.S.) mezzo-soprano.
Pauline Viardot, 1821-1910, (Fr.) mezzo-soprano.
William Warfield, 1920-2002, (U.S.) bass-baritone.
Leonard Warren, 1911-60, (U.S.) baritone.
Ljuba Welitsch, 1913-96, (Bulg.) soprano.
Camilla Williams, 1919-2012, (U.S.) soprano.
Wolfgang Windgassen, 1914-74, (Ger.) tenor.

Rock and Roll, Rhythm and Blues, and Rap Artists

Titles in quotation marks are singles; others are albums. * = Inducted into Rock and Roll Hall of Fame as performer between 1986 and 2014; year is in parentheses.

*ABBA (2010): "Dancing Queen"
Paula Abdul: "Straight Up"
*AC/DC (2003): "Back in Black"
Bryan Adams: "Cuts Like a Knife"
Adele: "Rolling in the Deep"
*Aerosmith (2001): "Sweet Emotion"
Christina Aguilera: "What a Girl Wants"
Alice in Chains: "Heaven Beside You"
*The Allman Brothers Band (1995): "Ramblin' Man"
*The Animals (1994): "House of the Rising Sun"
Paul Anka: "Lonely Boy"
Fiona Apple: "Criminal"
Frankie Avalon: "Venus"
The B-52s: "Love Shack"
Bachman Turner Overdrive: "Takin' Care of Business"
Backstreet Boys: "I Want That Way"
Bad Company: "Can't Get Enough"
Erykah Badu: "On and On"
*La Vern Baker (1991): "I Cried a Tear"
*Hank Ballard[1] and the Midnighters (1990): "Work With Me, Annie"
*The Band (1994): "The Weight"
Barenaked Ladies: "One Week"
*The Beach Boys (1988): "Good Vibrations"
*Beastie Boys (2012): "(You Gotta) Fight for Your Right to Party)"
*The Beatles (1988): *Sgt. Pepper's Lonely Hearts Club Band*
Beck: "Loser"
*Jeff Beck (2009): "Escape"
*The Bee Gees (1997): "Stayin' Alive"
Pat Benatar: "Hit Me With Your Best Shot"
*Chuck Berry (1986): "Johnny B. Goode"
Beyoncé: "Crazy in Love"
The Big Bopper: "Chantilly Lace"
Björk: "Human Behavior"
The Black Crowes: "Hard to Handle"
Black Eyed Peas: *Elephunk*
*Black Sabbath (2006): "Paranoid"
*Bobby "Blue" Bland (1992): "Turn On Your Love Light"
Mary J. Blige: *My Life*
Blind Faith: "Can't Find My Way Home"
Blink-182: "All the Small Things"
*Blondie (2006): "Heart of Glass"
Blood, Sweat, and Tears: "Spinning Wheel"
Blues Traveler: "Run-Around"
Gary "U.S." Bonds: "Quarter to Three"
Bon Jovi: "Livin' on a Prayer"
*Booker T. and the M.G.'s (1992): "Green Onions"
Boston: "More Than a Feeling"

*David Bowie (1996): "Space Oddity"
Boyz II Men: "I'll Make Love to You"
Toni Braxton: "Un-Break My Heart"
Chris Brown: "Kiss Kiss"
*James Brown (1986): "Papa's Got a Brand New Bag"
*Ruth Brown (1993): "Lucky Lips"
*Jackson Browne (2004): "Doctor My Eyes"
*Buffalo Springfield (1997): "For What It's Worth"
Jimmy Buffett: "Margaritaville"
*Solomon Burke (2001): "Over and Over (Huggin' and Lovin')"
*The Byrds (1991): "Turn! Turn! Turn!"
Mariah Carey: "Vision of Love"
The Carpenters: "(They Long to Be) Close to You"
The Cars: "Shake It Up"
*Johnny Cash (1992): "I Walk the Line"
*Ray Charles (1986): "Georgia on My Mind"
Cheap Trick: "Surrender"
Chubby Checker: "The Twist"
Chicago: "Saturday in the Park"
*Eric Clapton (2000): "Layla"
Kelly Clarkson: "Since U Been Gone"
*The Clash (2003): "Rock the Casbah"
*Jimmy Cliff (2010): "I Can See Clearly Now"
*The Coasters (1987): "Yakety Yak"
*Eddie Cochran (1987): "Summertime Blues"
Joe Cocker: "With a Little Help From My Friends"
*Leonard Cohen (2008): "Suzanne"
Coldplay: "Clocks"
Collective Soul: "The World I Know"
Phil Collins: "Against All Odds"
*Sam Cooke (1986): "You Send Me"
Coolio: "Gangsta's Paradise"
*Alice Cooper (2011): "School's Out"
Elvis Costello and the Attractions (2003): "Alison"
Counting Crows: "Mr. Jones"
*Cream (1993): "Sunshine of Your Love"
Creed: "Arms Wide Open"
*Creedence Clearwater Revival (1993): "Proud Mary"
Sheryl Crow: "All I Want to Do"
The Crystals: "Da Doo Ron Ron"
The Cure: "Boys Don't Cry"
Daft Punk: "Get Lucky"
Danny and the Juniors: "At the Hop"
*Bobby Darin (1990): "Splish Splash"
Daughtry: "It's Not Over"

*The Dave Clark Five (2008): "Glad All Over"
Dave Matthews Band: "Don't Drink the Water"
*Miles Davis (2006): *Bitches Brew*
Spencer Davis Group: "Gimme Some Lovin'"
Deep Purple: "Smoke on the Water"
Def Leppard: "Photograph"
*The Dells (2004): "Oh, What a Night"
Depeche Mode: "Strange Love"
Destiny's Child: "Survivor"
*Neil Diamond (2011): "Cracklin' Rosie"
*Bo Diddley (1987): "Who Do You Love?"
*Dion[1] and the Belmonts (1989): "A Teenager in Love"
Celine Dion: "Because You Loved Me"
Dire Straits: "Money for Nothing"
DMX: "What's My Name"
*Fats Domino (1986): "Blueberry Hill"
*Donovan (2012): "Mellow Yellow"
The Doobie Brothers: "What a Fool Believes"
*The Doors (1993): "Light My Fire"
Drake: "Over"
Dr. Dre: "Nothin' But a 'G' Thang"
*Dr. John (2011): "Right Place, Wrong Time"
*The Drifters (1988): "Save the Last Dance for Me"
Duran Duran: "Hungry Like the Wolf"
*Bob Dylan (1988): "Like a Rolling Stone"
*The Eagles (1998): "Hotel California"
*Earth, Wind, and Fire (2000): "Shining Star"
*Duane Eddy (1994): "Rebel-Rouser"
Missy Elliott: "Sock It 2 Me"
Eminem: "The Real Slim Shady"
En Vogue: "Hold On"
The Eurythmics: "Sweet Dreams (Are Made of This)"
Everclear: "Father Of Mine"
*The Everly Brothers (1986): "Wake Up, Little Susie"
50 Cent (Curtis Jackson): *Get Rich or Die Tryin'*
The Five Satins: "In the Still of the Night"
Roberta Flack: "The First Time Ever I Saw Your Face"
*The Flamingos (2001): "I Only Have Eyes for You"
*Fleetwood Mac (1998): *Rumours*
The Foo Fighters: "I'll Stick Around"
Foreigner: "Double Vision"
*The Four Seasons (1990): "Sherry"
*The Four Tops (1990): "I Can't Help Myself (Sugar Pie, Honey Bunch)"

*Aretha Franklin (1987): "Respect"
fun.: "We Are Young"
Nelly Furtado: "I'm Like a Bird"
*Peter Gabriel (2014): "Shock the Monkey"
*Gamble (Kenny) and Huff (Leon) (2008): "If You Don't Know Me By Now"
*Marvin Gaye (1987): "I Heard It Through the Grapevine"
*Genesis (2010): "No Reply at All"
Goo Goo Dolls: "Iris"
Grand Funk Railroad: "We're an American Band"
*Grandmaster Flash and the Furious Five (2007): "The Message"
*The Grateful Dead (1994): "Uncle John's Band"
*Al Green (1995): "Let's Stay Together"
Green Day: "Boulevard of Broken Dreams"
The Guess Who: "American Woman"
*Guns N' Roses (2012): "Sweet Child o' Mine"
*Buddy Guy (2005): A Man and His Blues
*Bill Haley[1] and His Comets (1987): "Rock Around the Clock"
*Hall and Oates (2014): "Kiss on My List"
*George Harrison (2004): "My Sweet Lord"
*Isaac Hayes (2002): "Theme From 'Shaft'"
*Heart (2013): "Barracuda"
*Jimi Hendrix (1992): "Purple Haze"
Lauryn Hill: "Doo-Wop (That Thing)"
*The Hollies (2010): "Long Cool Woman (In a Black Dress)"
*Buddy Holly (1986): "Peggy Sue"
*John Lee Hooker (1991): "Boogie Chillen"
Hootie and the Blowfish: Cracked Rear View
Whitney Houston: "I Will Always Love You"
*The Impressions (1991): "For Your Precious Love"
Indigo Girls: "Closer to Fine"
INXS: "Need You Tonight"
*The Isley Brothers (1992): "It's Your Thing"
Ja Rule: Venni, Vetti, Vecci
*The Jackson Five (1997): "ABC"
Janet Jackson: Rhythm Nation
*Michael Jackson (2001): Thriller
*Etta James (1993): "At Last"
Tommy James and the Shondells: "Crimson and Clover"
Jane's Addiction: "Jane Says"
Jay and the Americans: "This Magic Moment"
Jay Z: "99 Problems"
*Jefferson Airplane (1996): "White Rabbit"
Jethro Tull: Aqualung
Joan Jett: "I Love Rock 'n' Roll"
Jewel: "You Were Meant For Me"
*Billy Joel (1999): "Piano Man"
*Elton John (1994): "Candle in the Wind"
*Little Willie John (1996): "Sleep"
Norah Jones: Come Away With Me
*Janis Joplin (1995): "Me and Bobby McGee"
Journey: "Don't Stop Believin'"
K.C. and the Sunshine Band: "Get Down Tonight"
R. Kelly: "I Can't Sleep Baby (If I)"
Alicia Keys: "Fallin'"
Kid Rock: "Cowboy"
*B.B. King (1987): "The Thrill Is Gone"
Carole King: Tapestry
*The Kinks (1990): "You Really Got Me"
*Kiss (2014): "Rock 'n' Roll All Night"
*Gladys Knight and the Pips (1996): "Midnight Train to Georgia"
Korn: "Blind"
Lenny Kravitz: "Are You Gonna Go My Way?"
Lady Gaga: "Poker Face"
*Led Zeppelin (1995): "Stairway to Heaven"
*Brenda Lee (2002): "I'm Sorry"
John Legend: "Ordinary People"
*John Lennon (1994): "Imagine"
*Jerry Lee Lewis (1986): "Whole Lotta Shakin' Going On"
Lil' Kim: "No Matter What They Say"
Lil Wayne: The Block Is Hot.
Limp Bizkit: "Break Stuff"
Linkin Park: "One Step Closer"
*Little Anthony and the Imperials (2009): "Tears on My Pillow"
*Little Richard (1986): "Tutti Frutti"
*Little Walter (2008): "Juke"
LL Cool J: "Mama Said Knock You Out"
Jennifer Lopez: "Love Don't Cost a Thing"
*Darlene Love (2011): "He's a Rebel"

*The Lovin' Spoonful (2000): "Summer in the City"
Ludacris: "Money Maker"
*Frankie Lymon and the Teenagers (1993): "Why Do Fools Fall in Love?"
*Lynyrd Skynyrd (2006): "Free Bird"
*Madonna (2008): "Material Girl"
*The Mamas and the Papas (1998): "Monday, Monday"
Marilyn Manson: "Beautiful People"
*Bob Marley (1994): Exodus
Maroon 5: Songs About Jane
Bruno Mars: "Just the Way You Are"
*Martha and the Vandellas (1995): "Dancin' in the Streets"
The Marvelettes: "Please, Mr. Postman"
Matchbox 20: "Push"
John Mayer: "Daughters"
*Curtis Mayfield (1999): "Superfly"
*Paul McCartney (1999): "Band on the Run"
Don McLean: "American Pie"
*Clyde McPhatter (1987): "A Lover's Question"
Meat Loaf: "Paradise by the Dashboard Light"
*John (Cougar) Mellencamp (2008): "Jack and Diane"
Men at Work (2008): "Who Can It Be Now?"
*Metallica (2009): "Enter Sandman"
George Michael: "Faith"
Nicki Minaj: Pink Friday.
*Joni Mitchell (1997): "Both Sides Now"
Moby: "Bodyrock"
The Monkees: "I'm a Believer"
Moody Blues: "Nights in White Satin"
*The Moonglows (2000): "Blue Velvet"
Alanis Morissette: "Ironic"
*Van Morrison (1993): "Brown-Eyed Girl"
Mötley Crüe: "Live Wire"
Motörhead: "Ace of Spades"
Jason Mraz: "I'm Yours"
Mumford & Sons: "Little Lion Man"
Nelly: Country Grammar
*Ricky Nelson (1987): "Hello, Mary Lou"
Nine Inch Nails: "Closer"
*Nirvana (2014): Nevermind
No Doubt: Rock Steady
The Notorious B.I.G.: "Mo Money Mo Problems"
'N Sync: "Bye, Bye, Bye"
Ted Nugent: "Stranglehold"
*The O'Jays (2005): "Back Stabbers"
*Roy Orbison (1987): "Oh, Pretty Woman"
Ozzy Osbourne: "Crazy Train"
OutKast: Speakerboxxx/The Love Below
*Parliament/Funkadelic (1997): "One Nation Under a Groove"
Pearl Jam: "Jeremy"
*Carl Perkins (1987): "Blue Suede Shoes"
Katy Perry: "I Kissed a Girl"
Peter, Paul, and Mary: "Leaving on a Jet Plane"
*Tom Petty and the Heartbreakers (2002): "Refugee"
Liz Phair: Exile in Guyville
Phish: "Sample in a Jar"
*Wilson Pickett (1991): "Land of 1,000 Dances"
Pink: Missundaztood!
*Pink Floyd (1996): The Wall
*Gene Pitney (2002): "Only Love Can Break a Heart"
*The Platters (1990): "The Great Pretender"
The Pointer Sisters: "I'm So Excited"
*The Police (2003): "Every Breath You Take"
Iggy Pop: "Lust for Life"
*Elvis Presley (1986): "Love Me Tender"
*The Pretenders (2005): "Back on the Chain Gang"
*Lloyd Price (1998): "Stagger Lee"
*Prince (The Artist) (2004): "Purple Rain"
Public Enemy (2013): "Fight the Power"
Puff Daddy and the Family: No Way Out
*Queen (2001): "Bohemian Rhapsody"
Radiohead: OK Computer
Rage Against the Machine: "Bulls on Parade"
*Bonnie Raitt (2000): "Something to Talk About"
*The Ramones (2002): "I Wanna Be Sedated"
*Red Hot Chili Peppers (2012): "Under the Bridge"
*Otis Redding (1989): "(Sittin' on) The Dock of the Bay"
*Jimmy Reed (1991): "Ain't That Loving You, Baby?"

Lou Reed: "Walk on the Wild Side"
*R.E.M. (2007): "Losing My Religion"
REO Speedwagon: "Can't Fight This Feeling"
Busta Rhymes: "What's It Gonna Be?"
*The Righteous Brothers (2003): "You've Lost That Lovin' Feelin'"
Rihanna: "Rude Boy"
Johnny Rivers: "Poor Side of Town"
*Smokey Robinson[1] and the Miracles (1987): "Shop Around"
*The Rolling Stones (1989): "Satisfaction"
*The Ronettes (2007): "Be My Baby"
*Linda Ronstadt (2014): "You're No Good"
Diana Ross: "I'm Coming Out"
*Run-D.M.C. (2009): "Raisin' Hell"
*Rush (2013): "Tom Sawyer"
Sade: "Smooth Operator"
Salt-N-Pepa: "Shoop"
*Sam and Dave (1992): "Soul Man"
*Santana (1998): "Black Magic Woman"
Seal: "Kiss From a Rose"
Neil Sedaka: "Breaking Up Is Hard to Do"
*Bob Seger (2004): "Old Time Rock & Roll"
*Sex Pistols (2006): "Anarchy in the UK"
Shakira: "Whenever, Wherever"
Tupac Shakur: "How Do U Want It"
*Del Shannon (1999): "Runaway"
*The Shirelles (1996): "Soldier Boy"
Carly Simon: "You're So Vain"
*Paul Simon (2001): "50 Ways to Leave Your Lover"
*Simon and Garfunkel (1990): "Bridge Over Troubled Water"
*Percy Sledge (2005): "When a Man Loves a Woman"
*Sly and the Family Stone (1993): "Everyday People"
Smashing Pumpkins: "Today"
*Patti Smith (2007): "Because the Night"
Will Smith: "Gettin' Jiggy With It"
The Smiths: "This Charming Man"
Snoop Dogg (a.k.a. Snoop Lion, Snoopzilla): "Gin and Juice"
Sonic Youth: "Bull in the Heather"
Soundgarden: "Black Hole Sun"
Britney Spears: "Hit Me Baby One More Time"
Spice Girls: "Wannabe"
*Dusty Springfield (1999): "I Only Want to Be With You"
*Bruce Springsteen (1999): "Born to Run"
*Staple Singers (1999): "I'll Take You There"
*Steely Dan (2001): "Rikki Don't Lose That Number"
Gwen Stefani: "Hollaback Girl"
Steppenwolf: "Born to Be Wild"
*Cat Stevens (2014): "Wild World"
*Rod Stewart (1994): "Maggie Mae"
Sting: "If You Love Somebody, Set Them Free"
Stone Temple Pilots: "Plush"
*The Stooges (2010): "I Wanna Be Your Dog"
Styx: "Come Sail Away"
The Sugar Hill Gang: "Rapper's Delight"
*Donna Summer (2013): "Bad Girls"
*The Supremes (1988): "Stop! In the Name of Love"
*Talking Heads (2002): "Once in a Lifetime"
*James Taylor (2001): "You've Got a Friend"
*The Temptations (1989): "My Girl"
Robin Thicke: "Blurred Lines"
Three Dog Night: "Joy to the World"
Justin Timberlake: "SexyBack"
TLC: "Waterfalls"
*Traffic (2004): Traffic
*Big Joe Turner (1987): "Shake, Rattle & Roll"
*Ike and Tina Turner (1991): "Proud Mary"
*Tina Turner (1991): "What's Love Got to Do With It?"
The Turtles: "Happy Together"
*U2 (2005): "With or Without You"
Usher: "You Make Me Wanna"
*Ritchie Valens (2001): "La Bamba"
*Van Halen (2007): "Running With the Devil"
Stevie Ray Vaughan: "Crossfire"
*The Velvet Underground (1996): "Sweet Jane"
*The Ventures (2008): "Walk, Don't Run"
*Gene Vincent (1998): "Be-Bop-A-Lula"
*Tom Waits (2011): "Downtown Train"
The Wallflowers: "One Headlight"

Dionne Warwick: "I Say a Little Prayer"
*Muddy Waters (1987): "I Can't Be Satisfied"
Mary Wells: "My Guy"
Kanye West: "Gold Digger"
The White Stripes: "Seven Nation Army"
Whitesnake: "Here I Go Again"
*The Who (1990): Tommy

*Jackie Wilson (1987): "That's Why"
*Bobby Womack (2009): "Lookin' for a Love"
*Stevie Wonder (1989): "You Are the Sunshine of My Life"
Wu-Tang Clan: "Protect Ya Neck"
*The Yardbirds (1992): "For Your Love"

Yes: "Roundabout"
*Neil Young (1995): "Down by the River"
*The Young Rascals/The Rascals (1997): "Good Lovin' "
*Frank Zappa[1]/Mothers of Invention (1995): Hot Rats
*ZZ Top (2004): "Legs"

(1) Only individual performer is in Rock and Roll Hall of Fame.

Entertainment Personalities of the Present

Living actors, musicians, dancers, singers, producers, directors, and radio-TV performers.

Name	Birthplace	Birthdate
Abdul, Paula	San Fernando, CA	6/19/62
Abraham, F. Murray	Pittsburgh, PA	10/24/39
Abrams, J(effrey) J(acob)	New York, NY	6/27/66
Adams, Amy	Vicenza, Italy	8/20/74
Adams, Bryan	Kingston, ON, Canada	11/5/59
Adams, Yolanda	Houston, TX	8/27/61
Adele	London, England, UK	5/5/88
Adjani, Isabelle	Paris, France	6/27/55
Ad-Rock	South Orange, NJ	10/31/66
Affleck, Ben	Berkeley, CA	8/15/72
Affleck, Casey	Falmouth, MA	8/12/75
Aghdashloo, Shohreh	Tehran, Iran	5/11/52
Aguilera, Christina	Staten Island, NY	12/18/80
Aiello, Danny	New York, NY	6/20/33
Aiken, Clay	Raleigh, NC	11/30/78
Aimée, Anouk	Paris, France	4/27/32
Alba, Jessica	Pomona, CA	4/28/81
Alberghetti, Anna Maria	Pesaro, Italy	5/15/36
Albert, Marv	Brooklyn, NY	6/12/41
Alda, Alan	New York, NY	1/28/36
Alexander, Jane	Boston, MA	10/28/39
Alexander, Jason	Newark, NJ	9/23/59
Allen, Debbie	Houston, TX	1/16/50
Allen, Joan	Rochelle, IL	8/20/56
Allen, Karen	Carrollton, IL	10/5/51
Allen, Kris	Jacksonville, AR	6/21/85
Allen, Ted	Columbus, OH	5/20/65
Allen, Tim	Denver, CO	6/13/53
Allen, Woody	Bronx, NY	12/1/35
Alley, Kirstie	Wichita, KS	1/12/51
Allman, Gregg	Nashville, TN	12/8/47
Alonso, Maria Conchita	Cienfuegos, Cuba	6/29/57
Alpert, Herb	Los Angeles, CA	3/31/35
Almodóvar, Pedro	Calzada de Calatrava, Spain	9/24/49
Ambrose, Lauren	New Haven, CT	2/20/78
Ames, Ed	Malden, MA	7/9/27
Amos, John	Newark, NJ	12/27/39
Amos, Tori	Newton, NC	8/22/63
Anderson, Gillian	Chicago, IL	8/9/68
Anderson, Harry	Newport, RI	10/14/52
Anderson, Ian	Dunfermline, Scotland, UK	8/10/47
Anderson, Kevin	Gurnee, IL	1/13/60
Anderson, Loni	St. Paul, MN	8/5/46?
Anderson, Lynn	Grand Forks, ND	9/26/47
Anderson, Melissa Sue	Berkeley, CA	9/26/62
Anderson, Pamela	Ladysmith, BC, Canada	7/1/67
Anderson, Richard	Long Branch, NJ	8/8/26
Anderson, Richard Dean	Minneapolis, MN	1/23/50
Anderson, Wes	Houston, TX	5/1/69
Andersson, Bibi	Stockholm, Sweden	11/11/35
André 3000	Atlanta, GA	5/27/75
Andress, Ursula	Bern, Switzerland	3/19/36
Andrews, Julie	Walton-on-Thames, Surrey, England, UK	10/1/35
Andrews, Naveen	London, England, UK	1/17/69
Aniston, Jennifer	Sherman Oaks, CA	2/11/69
Anka, Paul	Ottawa, ON, Canada	7/30/41
Ann-Margret	Stockholm, Sweden	4/28/41
Ansari, Aziz	Columbia, SC	2/23/83
Anthony, Marc	New York, NY	9/16/68
Apatow, Judd	Syosset, NY	12/6/67
Apple, Fiona	New York, NY	9/13/77
Applegate, Christina	Los Angeles, CA	11/25/71
Archer, Anne	Los Angeles, CA	8/24/47
Arkin, Adam	Brooklyn, NY	8/19/56
Arkin, Alan	New York, NY	3/26/34
Armisen, Fred	Hattiesburg, MS	12/4/66
Arnaz, Desi, Jr.	Hollywood, CA	1/19/53
Arnaz, Lucie	Hollywood, CA	7/17/51
Arnett, Will	Toronto, ON, Canada	5/4/70
Arnold, Tom	Ottumwa, IA	3/6/59
Arquette, David	Winchester, VA	9/8/71
Arquette, Patricia	Chicago, IL	4/8/68
Arquette, Rosanna	New York, NY	8/10/59
Arroyo, Martina	New York, NY	2/2/37
Ashanti (Douglas)	Glen Cove, NY	10/13/80
Ashley, Elizabeth	Ocala, FL	8/30/39
Asner, Ed	Kansas City, KS	11/15/29
Assante, Armand	New York, NY	10/4/49
Astin, John	Baltimore, MD	3/30/30
Astin, Sean	Santa Monica, CA	2/25/71
Atkins, Eileen	London, England, UK	6/16/34
Atkins, Sharif	Pittsburgh, PA	1/29/75

Name	Birthplace	Birthdate
Atkinson, Rowan	Newcastle upon Tyne, Eng., UK	1/6/55
Auberjonois, Rene	New York, NY	6/1/40
Austin, Patti	New York, NY	8/10/48
Avalon, Frankie	Philadelphia, PA	9/18/40
Aykroyd, Dan	Ottawa, ON, Canada	7/1/52
Azaria, Hank	Forest Hills, Queens, NY	4/25/64
Aznavour, Charles	Paris, France	5/22/24
Babyface	Indianapolis, IN	4/10/59
Baccarin, Morena	Rio de Janeiro, Brazil	6/2/79
Bacon, Kevin	Philadelphia, PA	7/8/58
Badalucco, Michael	Brooklyn, NY	12/20/54
Bader, Diedrich	Alexandria, VA	12/24/66
Badu, Erykah	Dallas, TX	2/26/71
Baez, Joan	Staten Island, NY	1/9/41
Baio, Scott	Brooklyn, NY	9/22/60
Baker, Anita	Toledo, OH	1/26/58
Baker, Carroll	Johnstown, PA	5/28/31
Baker, Diane	Hollywood, CA	2/25/38
Baker, Joe Don	Groesbeck, TX	2/12/36
Baker, Kathy	Midland, TX	6/8/50
Baker, Simon	Launceston, Tas., Australia	7/30/69
Bakula, Scott	St. Louis, MO	10/9/54
Baldwin, Alec	Massapequa, NY	4/3/58
Baldwin, Daniel	Massapequa, NY	10/5/60
Baldwin, Stephen	Massapequa, NY	5/12/66
Baldwin, William	Massapequa, NY	2/21/63
Bale, Christian	Pembrokeshire, Wales, UK	1/30/74
Ballard, Kaye	Cleveland, OH	11/20/26
Ballas, Mark	Houston, TX	5/24/86
Bana, Eric	Melbourne, Vic., Australia	8/9/68
Banderas, Antonio	Málaga, Spain	8/10/60
Banks, Elizabeth	Pittsfield, MA	2/10/74
Banks, Jonathan	Washington, DC	1/31/47
Banks, Tyra	Los Angeles, CA	12/4/73
Baranski, Christine	Buffalo, NY	5/2/52
Barbeau, Adrienne	Sacramento, CA	6/11/45
Bardem, Javier	Las Palmas, Canary Islands, Spain	3/1/69
Bardot, Brigitte	Paris, France	9/28/34
Barker, Bob	Darrington, WA	12/12/23
Barkin, Ellen	Bronx, NY	4/16/55
Barrie, Barbara	Chicago, IL	5/23/31
Barrino, Fantasia	High Point, NC	6/30/84
Barrymore, Drew	Los Angeles, CA	2/22/75
Bartoli, Cecilia	Rome, Italy	6/4/66
Barton, Misha	London, England, UK	1/24/86
Baryshnikov, Mikhail	Riga, Latvia	1/28/48
Basinger, Kim	Athens, GA	12/8/53
Bass, Lance	Laurel, MS	5/4/79
Bassett, Angela	New York, NY	8/16/58
Bassey, Shirley	Cardiff, Wales, UK	1/8/37
Batali, Mario	Yakima, WA	9/9/60
Bateman, Jason	Rye, NY	1/14/69
Bateman, Justine	Rye, NY	2/19/66
Bates, Kathy	Memphis, TN	6/28/48
Batt, Bryan	New Orleans, LA	3/1/63
Battle, Kathleen	Portsmouth, OH	8/13/48
Baxter, Meredith	South Pasadena, CA	6/21/47
Bean, Orson	Burlington, VT	7/22/28
Bean, Sean	Sheffield, England, UK	4/17/59
Beatty, Ned	Louisville, KY	7/6/37
Beatty, Warren	Richmond, VA	3/30/37
Beauvais, Garcelle	St. Marc, Haiti	11/26/66
Beck	Los Angeles, CA	7/8/70
Beck, Jeff	Wallington, Surrey, Eng., UK	6/24/44
Beckham, Victoria	Hertfordshire, England, UK	4/17/74
Beckinsale, Kate	London, England, UK	7/26/73
Bedelia, Bonnie	New York, NY	3/25/48
Begley, Ed, Jr.	Los Angeles, CA	9/16/49
Behar, Joy	Brooklyn, NY	10/7/42
Belafonte, Harry	New York, NY	3/1/27
Bell, Art	Camp Lejeune, NC	6/17/45
Bell, Catherine	London, England, UK	8/14/68
Bell, Kristen	Huntington Woods, MI	7/18/80
Bello, Maria	Norristown, PA	4/18/67
Belmondo, Jean-Paul	Neuilly-sur-Seine, France	4/9/33
Belushi, Jim	Chicago, IL	6/15/54
Belzer, Richard	Bridgeport, CT	8/4/44
Benanti, Laura	Kinnelon, NJ	7/15/79
Benatar, Pat	Brooklyn, NY	1/10/53
Benedict, Dirk	Helena, MT	3/1/45
Benigni, Roberto	Misericordia, Italy	10/27/52
Bening, Annette	Topeka, KS	5/29/58

Name	Birthplace	Birthdate
Benjamin, Richard	New York, NY	5/22/38
Bennett, Alan	Leeds, England, UK	5/9/34
Bennett, Tony	Astoria, Queens, NY	8/3/26
Benson, George	Pittsburgh, PA	3/22/43
Benson, Robby	Dallas, TX	1/21/56
Berenger, Tom	Chicago, IL	5/31/50
Bergen, Candice	Beverly Hills, CA	5/9/46
Bergeron, Tom	Haverhill, MA	5/6/55
Berman, Shelley	Chicago, IL	2/3/25
Bernard, Crystal	Garland, TX	9/30/61
Bernhard, Sandra	Flint, MI	6/6/55
Bernsen, Corbin	North Hollywood, CA	9/7/54
Berry, Chuck	St. Louis, MO.	10/18/26
Berry, Halle	Cleveland, OH.	8/14/66
Berry, Ken	Moline, IL	11/3/33
Bertinelli, Valerie	Wilmington, DE	4/23/60
Bertolucci, Bernardo.	Parma, Italy	3/16/40
Best, Eve	London, England, UK	7/31/71
Bettany, Paul	London, England, UK	5/27/71
Bialik, Mayim	San Diego, CA.	12/12/75
Bichir, Demián	Mexico City, Mexico	8/1/63
Bieber, Justin	Stratford, ON, Canada	3/1/94
Biel, Jessica	Ely, MN	3/3/82
Big Boi	Savannah, GA	2/1/75
Bigelow, Kathryn	San Carlos, CA	11/27/51
Biggs, Jason	Pompton Plains, NJ	5/12/78
Bikel, Theodore	Vienna, Austria	5/2/24
Bilson, Rachel.	Los Angeles, CA	8/25/81
Binoche, Juliette	Paris, France	3/9/64
Birch, Thora	Beverly Hills, CA	3/11/82
Birney, David	Washington, DC	4/23/39
Bisset, Jacqueline.	Weybridge, England, UK	9/13/44
Bissett, Josie	Seattle, WA	10/5/70
Björk (Gudmundsdottir)	Reykjavik, Iceland	11/21/65
Black, Clint	Long Branch, NJ	2/4/62
Black, Jack	Santa Monica, CA	4/7/69
Black, Lewis	Washington, DC	8/30/48
Blades, Ruben	Panama City, Panama	7/16/48
Blair, Linda	St. Louis, MO.	1/22/59
Blake, Robert	Nutley, NJ	9/18/33
Blanchett, Cate	Melbourne, Vic., Australia	5/14/69
Bledsoe, Tempestt	Chicago, IL	8/1/73
Bleeth, Yasmine	New York, NY	6/14/68
Blethyn, Brenda	Ramsgate, Kent, Eng., UK	2/20/46
Blige, Mary J.	Bronx, NY	1/11/71
Bloom, Claire	London, England, UK	2/15/31
Bloom, Orlando	Canterbury, England, UK	1/13/77
Blyth, Ann	Mt. Kisco, NY	8/16/28
Bochco, Steven.	New York, NY	12/16/43
Bocelli, Andrea	Lajatico, Italy	9/22/58
Bogdanovich, Peter	Kingston, NY	7/30/39
Bogosian, Eric	Woburn, MA	4/24/53
Bologna, Joseph.	Brooklyn, NY	12/30/34?
Bolton, Michael.	New Haven, CT	2/26/53
Bomer, Matt	Spring, TX	10/11/77
Bon Jovi, Jon	Sayreville, NJ.	3/2/62
Bonet, Lisa	San Francisco, CA.	11/16/67
Bonham Carter, Helena	London, England, UK	5/26/66
Bonneville, Hugh.	London, England, UK	11/10/63
Bono	Dublin, Ireland	5/10/60
Boone, Debby	Hackensack, NJ.	9/22/56
Boone, Pat	Jacksonville, FL	6/1/34
Boreanaz, David	Buffalo, NY	5/16/69
Bosco, Philip	Jersey City, NJ.	9/26/30
Bostwick, Barry	San Mateo, CA	2/24/45
Bosworth, Kate	Los Angeles, CA	1/2/83
Bottoms, Timothy	Santa Barbara, CA.	8/30/51
Bourdain, Anthony	Leonia, NJ.	6/25/56
Bow Wow	Columbus, OH.	3/9/87
Bowen, Julie	Baltimore, MD	3/3/70
Bowie, David.	London, England, UK	1/8/47
Bowles, Peter	London, England, UK	10/16/36
Boxleitner, Bruce	Elgin, IL	5/12/50
Boy George	Bexleyheath, England, UK	6/14/61
Boyle, Danny	Manchester, England, UK	10/20/56
Boyle, Lara Flynn	Davenport, IA	3/24/70
Boyle, Susan.	Blackburn, Scotland, UK	4/1/61
Bracco, Lorraine	Brooklyn, NY	10/2/55
Brady, Wayne	Orlando, FL	6/2/72
Braff, Zach	South Orange, NJ	4/6/75
Branagh, Kenneth.	Belfast, N. Ireland, UK	12/10/60
Brand, Russell	Grays, Essex, UK	6/4/75
Brandauer, Klaus Maria	Steiermark, Austria	6/22/44
Brandy (Norwood)	McComb, MS.	2/11/79
Bratt, Benjamin	San Francisco, CA	12/16/63
Braugher, Andre	Chicago, IL	7/1/62
Braxton, Toni	Severn, MD	10/7/66
Bremner, Ewen	Edinburgh, Scotland, UK	1/23/72
Brendon, Nicholas	Los Angeles, CA	4/12/71
Brenneman, Amy	Glastonbury, CT.	6/22/64
Bridges, Beau	Los Angeles, CA	12/9/41
Bridges, Jeff	Los Angeles, CA	12/4/49
Brightman, Sarah	Berkhamsted, England, UK	8/14/60
Brimley, Wilford	Salt Lake City, UT	9/27/34
Brinkley, Christie	Monroe, MI	2/2/54
Britton, Connie	Boston, MA	3/6/67
Broadbent, Jim	Lincolnshire, England, UK	5/24/49
Broderick, Matthew	New York, NY	3/21/62
Brody, Adam	San Diego, CA.	12/15/79
Brody, Adrien	New York, NY	4/14/73
Brolin, James	Los Angeles, CA	7/18/40
Brolin, Josh.	Los Angeles, CA	2/12/68
Brooks, Albert	Beverly Hills, CA	7/22/47
Brooks, Garth	Tulsa, OK	2/7/62
Brooks, James L.	North Bergen, NJ.	5/9/40
Brooks, Mel.	Brooklyn, NY	6/28/26
Brosnan, Pierce	Navan, Co. Meath, Ireland	5/16/53
Brown, Blair	Washington, DC	4/23/46
Brown, Bobby	Roxbury, MA	2/5/69
Brown, Bryan	Panania, NSW, Australia	6/23/47
Brown, Chris	Tappahannock, VA.	5/5/89
Brown, Foxy	Brooklyn, NY.	9/6/79
Browne, Jackson	Heidelberg, Germany.	10/9/48
Bryson, Peabo	Greenville, SC	4/13/51
Bublé, Michael	Burnaby, BC, Canada	9/9/75
Buckley, Betty	Big Spring, TX	7/3/47
Buffett, Jimmy	Pascagoula, MS	12/25/46
Bujold, Genevieve	Montreal, QC, Canada.	7/1/42
Bullock, Sandra	Arlington, VA	7/26/64
Bumbry, Grace	St. Louis, MO.	1/4/37
Bündchen, Gisele	Horizontina, Brazil	7/20/80
Burghoff, Gary	Bristol, CT	5/24/43
Burke, Cheryl	San Francisco, CA.	5/3/84
Burke, Delta	Orlando, FL.	7/30/56
Burnett, Carol	San Antonio, TX.	4/26/33
Burns, Edward	Woodside, Queens, NY	1/29/68
Burrell, Ty	Grants Pass, OR	8/22/67
Burstyn, Ellen	Detroit, MI.	12/7/32
Burton, LeVar	Landstuhl, Germany	2/16/57
Burton, Tim	Burbank, CA	8/25/58
Buscemi, Steve	Brooklyn, NY	12/13/57
Busey, Gary	Goose Creek, TX.	6/29/44
Busfield, Timothy	Lansing, MI	6/12/57
Butler, Brett	Montgomery, AL	1/30/58
Butler, Dan	Fort Wayne, IN.	12/2/54
Butler, Gerard	Glasgow, Scot., UK	11/13/69
Butz, Norbert Leo	St. Louis, MO.	1/30/67
Buzzi, Ruth	Westerly, RI.	7/24/36
Bynes, Amanda	Thousand Oaks, CA	4/3/86
Byrne, David	Dumbarton, Scotland, UK	5/14/52
Byrne, Gabriel	Dublin, Ireland	5/12/50
Byrne, Rose	Sydney, NSW, Australia	7/24/79
Caan, James	Bronx, NY	3/26/40
Caballe, Montserrat	Barcelona, Spain	4/12/33
Cage, Nicolas	Long Beach, CA	1/7/64
Cain, Dean	Mt. Clemens, MI	7/31/66
Caine, Michael	London, England, UK	3/14/33
Caldwell, Zoe	Hawthorn, Vic., Australia	9/14/33
Callies, Sarah Wayne	LaGrange, IL	6/1/77
Callow, Simon	London, England, UK	6/15/49
Cameron, James	Kapuskasing, ON, Canada	8/16/54
Cameron, Kirk	Panorama City, CA	10/12/70
Campanella, Joseph	New York, NY	11/21/27
Campbell, Bruce	Royal Oak, MI	6/22/58
Campbell, Glen	Delight, AR	4/22/36
Campbell, Naomi	South London, Eng., UK	5/22/70
Campbell, Neve	Guelph, ON, Canada.	10/3/73
Campion, Jane	Waikanae, New Zealand	4/30/54
Cannavale, Bobby	Union City, NJ	5/3/71
Cannon, Dyan	Tacoma, WA	1/4/37
Cannon, Nick	San Diego, CA.	10/8/80
Caplan, Lizzy	Los Angeles, CA	6/30/82
Capshaw, Kate	Ft. Worth, TX.	11/3/53
Cara, Irene	New York, NY	3/18/59
Cardellini, Linda	Redwood City, CA	6/25/75
Cardinale, Claudia	Tunis, Tunisia	4/15/38
Carell, Steve	Concord, MA	8/16/62
Carey, Drew	Cleveland, OH.	5/23/58
Carey, Mariah	Huntington, NY	3/27/70
Cariou, Len	St. Boniface, MB, Canada	9/30/39
Carlton, Vanessa	Milford, PA.	8/16/80
Carlyle, Robert	Glasgow, Scotland, UK	4/14/61
Carmen, Eric	Cleveland, OH.	8/11/49
Caron, Leslie	Boulogne, France	7/1/31
Carpenter, John	Carthage, NY	1/16/48
Carpenter, Mary Chapin	Princeton, NJ.	2/21/58
Carr, Vikki	El Paso, TX.	7/19/41
Carreras, Jose	Barcelona, Spain.	12/5/46
Carrere, Tia	Honolulu, HI	1/2/67
Carrey, Jim	Newmarket, ON, Canada.	1/17/62
Carroll, Diahann	Bronx, NY	7/17/35
Carroll, Pat	Shreveport, LA	5/5/27
Carter, Jack	Brooklyn, NY	6/24/23
Carter, Jim	Harrogate, Yorkshire, England, UK	8/19/48
Carter, Lynda	Phoenix, AZ.	7/24/51
Carter, Nick	Jamestown, NY	1/28/80
Carter, Ron	Ferndale, MI	5/4/37
Cartwright, Nancy	Kettering, OH.	10/25/57
Caruso, David	Forest Hills, Queens, NY	1/17/56
Carvey, Dana	Missoula, MT.	6/2/55

Name	Birthplace	Birthdate
Case, Sharon	Detroit, MI	2/9/71
Cash, Rosanne	Memphis, TN	5/24/55
Cassidy, David	New York, NY	4/12/50
Castellaneta, Dan	Chicago, IL	10/29/57
Castle-Hughes, Keisha	Donnybrook, WA, Australia	3/24/90
Cates, Phoebe	New York, NY	7/16/63
Cattrall, Kim	Liverpool, England, UK	8/21/56
Cavanagh, Tom	Ottawa, ON, Canada	10/26/63
Cavett, Dick	Gibbon, NE	11/19/36
Caviezel, Jim	Mount Vernon, WA	9/26/68
Cavill, Henry	Jersey, Channel Islands, UK	5/5/83
Cedric the Entertainer	Jefferson City, MO	4/24/64
Cera, Michael	Brampton, ON, Canada	6/7/88
Chalke, Sarah	Ottawa, ON, Canada	8/27/76
Chamberlain, Richard	Beverly Hills, CA	3/31/34
Chambers, Justin	Springfield, OH	7/11/70
Chan, Jackie	Hong Kong	4/7/54
Chandler, Kyle	Buffalo, NY	9/17/65
Channing, Carol	Seattle, WA	1/31/21
Channing, Stockard	New York, NY	2/13/44
Chaplin, Geraldine	Santa Monica, CA	7/31/44
Chapman, Tracy	Cleveland, OH	3/30/64
Chappelle, Dave	Washington, DC	8/24/73
Charles, Josh	Baltimore, MD	9/15/71
Charo	Murcia, Spain	1/15/51?
Chase, Chevy	New York, NY	10/8/43
Chasez, J.C. (Joshua)	Washington, DC	8/8/76
Chastain, Jessica	Sacramento, CA	3/29/77
Cheadle, Don	Kansas City, MO	11/29/64
Checker, Chubby	Spring Gulley, SC	10/3/41
Chen, Julie	New York, NY	1/6/70
Chenoweth, Kristin	Broken Arrow, OK	7/24/68
Cher	El Centro, CA	5/20/46
Chesney, Kenny	Lutrelle, TN	3/26/68
Chianese, Dominic	Bronx, NY	2/24/31
Chiba, Sonny	Fukuoka, Kyushu, Japan	1/23/39
Chiklis, Michael	Lowell, MA	8/30/63
Chlumsky, Anna	Chicago, IL	12/3/80
Chmerkovskiy, Maksim	Odessa, Ukraine	1/17/80
Cho, Margaret	San Francisco, CA	12/5/68
Chong, Thomas	Edmonton, AB, Canada	5/24/38
Chow Yun-Fat	Lamma Island, Hong Kong	5/18/55
Christensen, Hayden	Vancouver, BC, Canada	4/19/81
Christie, Julie	Chukua, Assam, India	4/14/41
Christopher, William	Evanston, IL	10/20/32
Chuck D	Roosevelt, NY	8/1/60
Church, Charlotte	Llandaff, Cardiff, Wales, UK	2/21/86
Church, Thomas Haden	El Paso, TX	6/17/60
Clapp, Gordon	North Conway, NH	9/24/48
Clapton, Eric	Ripley, Surrey, England, UK	3/30/45
Clark, Petula	Epson, Surrey, England, UK	11/15/32
Clark, Roy	Meherrin, VA	4/15/33
Clarkson, Kelly	Burleson, TX	4/24/82
Clarkson, Patricia	New Orleans, LA	12/29/59
Clay, Andrew Dice	Brooklyn, NY	9/29/57
Cleese, John	Weston-super-Mare, Eng., UK	10/27/39
Clooney, George	Lexington, KY	5/6/61
Close, Glenn	Greenwich, CT	3/19/47
Cocker, Joe	Sheffield, England, UK	5/20/44
Coen, Ethan	St. Louis Park, MN	9/21/57
Coen, Joel	St. Louis Park, MN	11/29/54
Cohen, Leonard	Montreal, QC, Canada	9/21/34
Cohen, Sacha Baron	London, England, UK	10/13/71
Colbert, Stephen	Washington, DC	5/13/64
Cole, Gary	Park Ridge, IL	9/20/56
Cole, Natalie	Los Angeles, CA	2/6/50
Cole, Olivia	Memphis, TN	11/26/42
Coleman, Dabney	Austin, TX	1/3/32
Coleman, Ornette	Fort Worth, TX	3/19/30
Colfer, Chris	Fresno, CA	5/27/90
Collette, Toni	Blacktown, NSW, Australia	11/1/72
Collins, Joan	London, England, UK	5/23/33
Collins, Judy	Seattle, WA	5/1/39
Collins, Pauline	Exmouth, England, UK	9/3/40
Collins, Phil	London, England, UK	1/30/51
Collins, Stephen	Des Moines, IA	10/1/47
Columbus, Chris	Spangler, PA	9/10/58?
Colvin, Shawn	Vermillion, SD	1/10/56
Combs, Sean	New York, NY	11/4/69
Connelly, Jennifer	Round Top, NY	12/12/70
Connery, Sean	Edinburgh, Scotland, UK	8/25/30
Connick, Harry, Jr.	New Orleans, LA	9/11/67
Connolly, Kevin	Patchogue, NY	3/5/74
Connors, Mike	Fresno, CA	8/15/25
Conrad, Robert	Chicago, IL	3/1/35
Conroy, Frances	Monroe, GA	11/13/53
Constantine, Michael	Reading, PA	5/22/27
Conti, Tom	Paisley, Scotland, UK	11/22/41
Conway, Tim	Willoughby, OH	12/15/33
Cook, Barbara	Atlanta, GA	10/25/27
Cook, David	Houston, TX	12/20/82
Coolidge, Rita	Nashville, TN	5/1/45
Coolio	Compton, CA	8/1/63
Cooper, Alice	Detroit, MI	2/4/48
Cooper, Bradley	Philadelphia, PA	1/5/75
Cooper, Chris	Kansas City, MO	7/9/51

Name	Birthplace	Birthdate
Copperfield, David	Metuchen, NJ	9/16/56
Coppola, Francis Ford	Detroit, MI	4/7/39
Coppola, Sofia	New York, NY	5/14/71
Corbett, John	Wheeling, WV	5/9/61
Corbin, Barry	Lamesa, TX	10/16/40
Corea, Chick	Chelsea, MA	6/12/41
Corgan, Billy	Elk Grove, IL	3/17/67
Cornell, Chris	Seattle, WA	7/20/64
Corwin, Jeff	Norwell, MA	7/11/67
Cosby, Bill	Philadelphia, PA	7/12/37
Cosgrove, Miranda	Los Angeles, CA	5/14/93
Costas, Bob	Astoria, Queens, NY	3/22/52
Costello, Elvis	London, England, UK	8/25/54
Costner, Kevin	Compton, CA	1/18/55
Cotillard, Marion	Paris, France	9/30/75
Cowell, Simon	London, England, UK	10/7/59
Cox, Brian	Dundee, Scotland, UK	6/1/46
Cox, Courteney	Birmingham, AL	6/15/64
Cox, Ronny	Cloudcroft, NM	7/23/38
Coyote, Peter	New York, NY	10/10/41
Craig, Daniel	Chester, England, UK	3/2/68
Cranston, Bryan	San Fernando Valley, CA	3/7/56
Craven, Wes	Cleveland, OH	8/2/39
Crawford, Cindy	DeKalb, IL	2/20/66
Crawford, Michael	Salisbury, England, UK	1/19/42
Criss, Darren	San Francisco, CA	2/5/87
Cromwell, James	Los Angeles, CA	1/27/40
Crosby, David	Los Angeles, CA	8/14/41
Cross, Ben	London, England, UK	12/16/47
Cross, Marcia	Marlborough, MA	3/25/62
Crouse, Lindsay	New York, NY	5/12/48
Crow, Sheryl	Kennett, MO	2/11/62
Crowe, Cameron	Palm Springs, CA	7/13/57
Crowe, Russell	Wellington, New Zealand	4/7/64
Crudup, Billy	Manhasset, NY	7/8/48
Cruise, Tom	Syracuse, NY	7/3/62
Cruz, Penelope	Madrid, Spain	4/28/74
Cryer, Jon	New York, NY	4/16/65
Crystal, Billy	Long Beach, NY	3/14/48
Cuarón, Alfonso	Mexico City, Mexico	11/28/61
Culkin, Kieran	New York, NY	9/30/82
Culkin, Macaulay	New York, NY	8/26/80
Culkin, Rory	New York, NY	7/21/89
Cullum, John	Knoxville, TN	3/2/30
Cumberbatch, Benedict	London, England, UK	7/19/76
Cumming, Alan	Aberfeldy, Perthshire, Scotland, UK	1/27/65
Cuoco, Kaley	Camarillo, CA	11/30/85
Curry, Tim	Grappenhall, Cheshire, England, UK	4/19/46
Curtin, Jane	Cambridge, MA	9/6/47
Curtis, Jamie Lee	Los Angeles, CA	11/22/58
Cusack, Joan	New York, NY	10/11/62
Cusack, John	Evanston, IL	6/28/66
Cyrus, Billy Ray	Flatwoods, KY	8/25/61
Cyrus, Miley	Nashville, TN	11/23/92
Dafoe, Willem	Appleton, WI	7/22/55
Dahl, Arlene	Minneapolis, MN	8/11/25
Dale, Jim	Rothwell, England, UK	8/15/35
Dalton, Timothy	Colwyn Bay, Wales, UK	3/21/46
Daltrey, Roger	London, England, UK	3/1/44
Daly, Carson	Santa Monica, CA	6/22/73
Daly, Timothy	New York, NY	3/1/56
Daly, Tyne	Madison, WI	2/21/46
Damon, Matt	Cambridge, MA	10/8/70
Damone, Vic	Brooklyn, NY	6/12/28
Dane, Eric	San Francisco, CA	11/9/72
Danes, Claire	New York, NY	4/12/79
D'Angelo	Richmond, VA	2/11/74
D'Angelo, Beverly	Columbus, OH	11/15/54
Daniels, Anthony	Salisbury, England, UK	2/21/46
Daniels, Charlie	Wilmington, NC	10/28/36
Daniels, Jeff	Athens, GA	2/19/55
Daniels, William	Brooklyn, NY	3/31/27
Danner, Blythe	Rosemont, PA	2/3/43
Danson, Ted	San Diego, CA	12/29/47
Danza, Tony	Brooklyn, NY	4/21/51
Darby, Kim	Hollywood, CA	7/8/48
Daughtry, Chris	Roanoke Rapids, NC	12/26/79
David, Larry	Brooklyn, NY	7/2/47
Davidson, John	Pittsburgh, PA	12/13/41
Davis, Clifton	Chicago, IL	10/4/45
Davis, Geena	Wareham, MA	1/21/56
Davis, Hope	Englewood, NJ	3/23/64
Davis, Judy	Perth, WA, Australia	4/23/55
Davis, Kristin	Boulder, CO	2/24/65
Davis, Mac	Lubbock, TX	1/21/42
Davis, Viola	Saint Matthews, SC	8/11/65
Dawber, Pam	Farmington Hills, MI	10/18/51
Dawson, Rosario	New York, NY	5/9/79
Day, Doris	Cincinnati, OH	4/3/24
Day-Lewis, Daniel	London, England, UK	4/29/57
De Havilland, Olivia	Tokyo, Japan	7/1/16
De Mornay, Rebecca	Santa Rosa, CA	8/29/62
De Niro, Robert	New York, NY	8/17/43
De Rossi, Portia	Melbourne, Vic., Australia	1/31/73

Name	Birthplace	Birthdate
Deen, Paula	Albany, GA	1/19/47
DeFranco, Buddy	Camden, NJ	2/17/23
DeGeneres, Ellen	Metairie, LA	1/26/58
DeGraw, Gavin	Middletown, NY	2/4/77
DeHaven, Gloria	Los Angeles, CA	7/23/25
Del Toro, Benicio	Santurce, Puerto Rico	2/19/67
Delaney, Kim	Philadelphia, PA	11/29/61
Delany, Dana	New York, NY	3/13/56
Delon, Alain	Sceaux, France	11/8/35
Demme, Jonathan	Baldwin, NY	2/22/44
Dempsey, Patrick	Lewiston, ME	1/13/66
Dench, Judi	York, England, UK	12/9/34
Deneuve, Catherine	Paris, France	10/22/43
Dennehy, Brian	Bridgeport, CT	7/9/38
DePalma, Brian	Newark, NJ	9/11/40
Depardieu, Gerard	Chateauroux, France	12/27/48
Depp, Johnny	Owensboro, KY	6/9/63
Derek, Bo	Long Beach, CA	11/20/56
Dern, Bruce	Winnetka, IL	6/4/36
Dern, Laura	Santa Monica, CA	2/10/67
Deschanel, Zooey	Los Angeles, CA	1/17/80
Devine, Loretta	Houston, TX	8/21/49
DeVito, Danny	Neptune, NJ	11/17/44
DeWitt, Joyce	Wheeling, WV	4/23/49
Dey, Susan	Pekin, IL	12/10/52
Diamond, Neil	Brooklyn, NY	1/24/41
Diaz, Cameron	San Diego, CA	8/30/72
DiCaprio, Leonardo	Hollywood, CA	11/11/74
Dick, Andy	Charleston, SC	12/21/65
Dickinson, Angie	Kulm, ND	9/30/31
Diesel, Vin	New York, NY	7/18/67
Diggs, Taye	Newark, NJ	1/2/72
Dillahunt, Garret	Castro Valley, CA	11/24/64
Dillman, Bradford	San Francisco, CA	4/14/30
Dillon, Kevin	Mamaroneck, NY	8/19/65
Dillon, Matt	New Rochelle, NY	2/18/64
Dinklage, Peter	Morristown, NJ	6/11/69
DioGuardi, Kara	Scarsdale, NY	12/9/70
Dion, Celine	Charlemagne, QC, Canada	3/30/68
Djalili, Omid	London, England, UK	9/30/65
Dobrev, Nina	Sofia, Bulgaria	1/9/89
Dobson, Kevin	Jackson Heights, Queens, NY	3/18/43
Dockery, Michelle	Barking, Essex, England, UK	12/15/81
Doherty, Shannen	Memphis, TN	4/12/71
Dolenz, Mickey	Los Angeles, CA	3/8/45
Domingo, Placido	Madrid, Spain	1/21/41
Domino, Fats	New Orleans, LA	2/26/28
Donahue, Phil	Cleveland, OH	12/21/35
Donen, Stanley	Columbia, SC	4/13/24
D'Onofrio, Vincent	Brooklyn, NY	6/30/59
Donovan (Leitch)	Glasgow, Scotland, UK	5/10/46
Donovan, Tate	New York, NY	9/25/63
Dorn, Michael	Luling, TX	12/9/52
Dotrice, Roy	Guernsey, Channel Isls., UK	5/26/23
Douglas, Kirk	Amsterdam, NY	12/9/16
Douglas, Michael	New Brunswick, NJ	9/25/44
Dourdan, Gary	Philadelphia, PA	12/11/66
Dovolani, Tony	Pristina, Kosovo	7/17/73
Dow, Tony	Hollywood, CA	4/13/45
Down, Lesley-Anne	London, England, UK	3/17/54
Downey, Robert, Jr.	New York, NY	4/4/65
Downey, Roma	Derry, N. Ireland, UK	5/6/60
Downs, Hugh	Akron, OH	2/14/21
Drake	Toronto, ON, Canada	10/24/86
Drescher, Fran	Flushing, Queens, NY	9/30/57
Dreyfuss, Richard	Brooklyn, NY	10/29/47
Driver, Adam	San Bernardino, CA	11/19/83
Driver, Minnie	London, England, UK	1/31/70
Dryer, Fred	Hawthorne, CA	7/6/46
Duchovny, David	New York, NY	8/7/60
Duff, Haylie	Houston, TX	2/19/85
Duff, Hilary	Houston, TX	9/28/87
Duffy (Aimee Anne)	Bangor, Gwynedd, Wales, UK	6/23/84
Duffy, Julia	Minneapolis, MN	6/27/51
Duffy, Patrick	Townsend, MT	3/17/49
Duhamel, Josh	Minot, ND	11/14/72
Dujardin, Jean	Rueil-Malmaison, France	6/19/72
Dukakis, Olympia	Lowell, MA	6/20/31
Duke, Patty	Elmhurst, Queens, NY	12/14/46
Dullea, Keir	Cleveland, OH	5/30/36
Dunaway, Faye	Bascom, FL	1/14/41
Duncan, Lindsay	Edinburgh, Scotland, UK	11/7/50
Duncan, Sandy	Henderson, TX	2/20/46
Dunham, Lena	New York, NY	5/13/86
Dunne, Griffin	New York, NY	6/8/55
Dunst, Kirsten	Point Pleasant, NJ	4/30/82
Dussault, Nancy	Pensacola, FL	6/30/36
Dutton, Charles S.	Baltimore, MD	1/30/51
Duvall, Robert	San Diego, CA	1/5/31
Duvall, Shelley	Houston, TX	7/7/49
Dylan, Bob	Duluth, MN	5/24/41
Dylan, Jakob	New York, NY	12/9/69
Dysart, Richard	Brighton, MA	3/30/29
Dzundza, George	Rosenheim, Germany	7/19/45
Eads, George	Fort Worth, TX	3/1/67
Easton, Sheena	Bellshill, Scotland, UK	4/27/59

Name	Birthplace	Birthdate
Eastwood, Clint	San Francisco, CA	5/31/30
Ebersole, Christine	Chicago, IL	2/21/53
Eckhart, Aaron	Cupertino, CA	3/12/68
Eden, Barbara	Tucson, AZ	8/23/31
Edwards, Anthony	Santa Barbara, CA	7/19/62
Efron, Zac	San Luis Obispo, CA	10/18/87
Ehle, Jennifer	Winston-Salem, NC	12/29/69
Eikenberry, Jill	New Haven, CT	1/21/47
Eisenberg, Jesse	Bayside, NY	10/5/83
Ejiofor, Chiwetel	London, England, UK	7/10/74
Ekberg, Anita	Malmo, Sweden	9/29/31
Ekland, Britt	Stockholm, Sweden	10/6/42
Elba, Idris	London, England, UK	9/6/72
Electra, Carmen	Cincinnati, OH	4/20/72
Elfman, Jenna	Los Angeles, CA	9/30/71
Elizondo, Hector	New York, NY	12/22/36
Elliott, Bob	Boston, MA	3/26/23
Elliott, Chris	New York, NY	5/31/60
Elliott, Missy	Portsmouth, VA	7/1/71
Elliott, Sam	Sacramento, CA	8/9/44
Elvira	Manhattan, KS	9/17/51
Emerson, Michael	Cedar Rapids, IA	9/7/54
Eminem	St. Joseph, MO	10/17/72
Enberg, Dick	Mt. Clemens, MI	1/9/35
Englund, Robert	Glendale, CA	6/6/49
Enya	Gweedore, Ireland	5/17/61
Epps, Omar	Brooklyn, NY	7/23/73
Estefan, Gloria	Havana, Cuba	9/1/57
Estevez, Emilio	New York, NY	5/12/62
Estrada, Erik	New York, NY	3/16/49
Etheridge, Melissa	Leavenworth, KS	5/29/61
Evans, Chris	Framingham, MA	6/13/81
Evans, Linda	Hartford, CT	11/18/42
Evans, Robert	New York, NY	6/29/30
Everett, Rupert	Norfolk, England, UK	5/29/59
Everly, Don	Brownie, KY	2/1/37
Evigan, Greg	South Amboy, NJ	10/14/53
Fabares, Shelley	Santa Monica, CA	1/19/44
Fabian	Philadelphia, PA	2/6/43
Fabio (Lanzoni)	Milan, Italy	3/15/59
Fabolous	Brooklyn, NY	11/18/77
Facinelli, Peter	Queens, NY	11/26/73
Fairchild, Morgan	Dallas, TX	2/3/50
Faison, Donald	New York, NY	6/22/74
Falana, Lola	Philadelphia, PA	9/11/42
Falco, Edie	Brooklyn, NY	7/5/63
Fallon, Jimmy	Brooklyn, NY	9/19/74
Fanning, Dakota	Conyers, GA	2/23/94
Fargo, Donna	Mt. Airy, NC	11/10/49
Farmiga, Vera	Clifton, NJ	8/6/73
Farr, Jamie	Toledo, OH	7/1/34
Farrell, Colin	Dublin, Ireland	5/31/76
Farrell, Mike	St. Paul, MN	2/6/39
Farrell, Perry	Bayside, Queens, NY	3/29/59
Farrell, Suzanne	Cincinnati, OH	8/16/45?
Farrelly, Bobby	Cumberland, RI	6/17/58
Farrelly, Peter	Phoenixville, PA	12/17/56
Farrow, Mia	Los Angeles, CA	2/9/45
Fassbender, Michael	Heidelberg, Germany	4/2/77
Fatone, Joey	Brooklyn, NY	1/28/77
Feinstein, Michael	Columbus, OH	9/7/56
Feldon, Barbara	Bethel Park, PA	3/12/33
Feldshuh, Tovah	New York, NY	12/27/52
Feliciano, Jose	Lares, Puerto Rico	9/10/45
Fenn, Sherilyn	Detroit, MI	2/1/65
Fergie	Hacienda Heights, CA	3/27/75
Ferguson, Craig	Glasgow, Scotland, UK	5/17/62
Ferguson, Jesse Tyler	Missoula, MT	10/22/75
Ferrara, Jerry	Brooklyn, NY	11/29/79
Ferrell, Conchata	Charleston, WV	3/28/43
Ferrell, Will	Irvine, CA	7/16/67
Ferrera, America	Los Angeles, CA	4/18/84
Feuerstein, Mark	New York, NY	6/8/71
Fey, Tina	Upper Darby, PA	5/18/70
Field, Sally	Pasadena, CA	11/6/46
Fiennes, Joseph	Salisbury, England, UK	5/27/70
Fiennes, Ralph	Suffolk, England, UK	12/22/62
Fierstein, Harvey	Brooklyn, NY	6/6/54
50 Cent	Jamaica, Queens, NY	7/6/76
Fillion, Nathan	Edmonton, AB, Canada	3/27/71
Fincher, David	Denver, CO	8/28/62
Finney, Albert	Salford, England, UK	5/9/36
Fiorentino, Linda	Philadelphia, PA	3/9/60
Firth, Colin	Grayshott, England, UK	9/10/60
Firth, Peter	Bradford, Yorkshire, Eng., UK	10/27/53
Fischer, Jenna	Ft. Wayne, IN	3/7/74
Fishburne, Laurence	Augusta, GA	7/30/61
Fisher, Carrie	Beverly Hills, CA	10/21/56
Flack, Roberta	Black Mountain, NC	2/10/39
Flanagan, Fionnula	Dublin, Ireland	12/10/41
Flavor Flav	Roosevelt, NY	3/16/59
Fleetwood, Mick	Redruth, Cornwall, Eng., UK	6/24/42
Fleming, Rhonda	Hollywood, CA	8/10/23
Fletcher, Louise	Birmingham, AL	7/22/34
Flockhart, Calista	Freeport, IL	11/11/64
Florek, Dann	Flat Rock, MI	5/1/50

Name	Birthplace	Birthdate
Fogerty, John	Berkeley, CA	5/28/45
Foley, Dave	Etobicoke, ON, Canada	1/4/63
Fonda, Bridget	Los Angeles, CA	1/27/64
Fonda, Jane	New York, NY	12/21/37
Fonda, Peter	New York, NY	2/23/40
Ford, Faith	Alexandria, LA	9/14/64
Ford, Harrison	Chicago, IL	7/13/42
Forman, Milos	Caslav, Czechoslovakia	2/18/32
Forte, Will	Alameda Co., CA	6/17/70
Foster, Jodie	Los Angeles, CA	11/19/62
Foster, Sutton	Statesboro, GA	3/18/75
Fox, James	London, England, UK	5/19/39
Fox, Jorja	New York, NY	7/7/68
Fox, Matthew	Abington, PA	7/14/66
Fox, Megan	Rockwood, TN	5/16/86
Fox, Michael J.	Edmonton, AB, Canada	6/9/61
Fox, Vivica A.	South Bend, IN	7/30/64
Foxworth, Robert	Houston, TX	11/1/41
Foxworthy, Jeff	Atlanta, GA	9/6/58
Foxx, Jamie	Terrell, TX	12/13/67
Frampton, Peter	Kent, England, UK	4/22/50
Francis, Connie	Newark, NJ	12/12/38
Franco, James	Palo Alto, CA	4/19/78
Franken, Al	New York, NY	5/21/51
Franklin, Aretha	Memphis, TN	3/25/42
Franz, Dennis	Maywood, IL	10/28/44
Fraser, Brendan	Indianapolis, IN	12/3/68
Freeman, Martin	Aldershot, Hampshire, Eng., UK	9/8/71
Freeman, Morgan	Memphis, TN	6/1/37
French, Dawn	Holyhead, Wales, UK	10/11/57
Fricker, Brenda	Dublin, Ireland	2/17/45
Friedkin, William	Chicago, IL	8/29/39
Froggatt, Joanne	Littlebeck, North Yorkshire, England, UK	8/21/80
Fry, Stephen	London, England, UK	8/24/57
Fuentes, Daisy	Havana, Cuba	11/17/66
Fuller, Robert	Troy, NY	7/29/34
Furlong, Edward	Pasadena, CA	8/2/77
Furtado, Nelly	Victoria, BC, Canada	12/2/78
Gabor, Zsa Zsa	Budapest, Hungary	2/6/17
Gabriel, Peter	Surrey, England, UK	2/13/50
Gaines, Boyd	Atlanta, GA	5/11/53
Galecki, Johnny	Bree, Belgium	4/30/75
Galifianakis, Zach	Wilkesboro, NC	10/1/69
Gallagher, Peter	Armonk, NY	8/19/55
Gallo, Vincent	Buffalo, NY	4/11/61
Galway, James	Belfast, N. Ireland, UK	12/8/39
Garagiola, Joe	St. Louis, MO	2/12/26
Garber, Victor	London, ON, Canada	3/16/49
Garcia, Andy	Havana, Cuba	4/12/56
Garfield, Andrew	Los Angeles, CA	8/20/83
Garfunkel, Art	Forest Hills, Queens, NY	11/5/41
Garlin, Jeff	Chicago, IL	6/5/62
Garner, Jennifer	Houston, TX	4/17/72
Garofalo, Janeane	Newton, NJ	9/28/64
Garr, Teri	Lakewood, OH	12/11/44
Garrett, Brad	Woodland Hills, CA	4/14/60
Garth, Jennie	Urbana, IL	4/3/72
Gatlin, Larry	Seminole, TX	5/2/48
Gavin, John	Los Angeles, CA	4/8/31
Gayle, Crystal	Paintsville, KY	1/9/51
Gaynor, Mitzi	Chicago, IL	9/4/31
Geary, Anthony	Coalville, UT	5/29/47
Gedda, Nicolai	Stockholm, Sweden	7/11/25
Gellar, Sarah Michelle	New York, NY	4/14/77
Gere, Richard	Philadelphia, PA	8/31/49
Gervais, Ricky	Reading, England, UK	6/25/61
Giannini, Giancarlo	La Spezia, Italy	8/1/42
Gibb, Barry	Isle of Man, England, UK	9/1/46
Gibbons, Leeza	Hartsville, SC	3/26/57
Gibbs, Marla	Chicago, IL	6/14/31
Gibson, Debbie	Brooklyn, NY	8/31/70
Gibson, Mel	Peekskill, NY	1/3/56
Gibson, Thomas	Charleston, SC	7/3/62
Gifford, Frank	Santa Monica, CA	8/16/30
Gifford, Kathie Lee	Neuilly-sur-Seine, France	8/16/53
Gilbert, Melissa	Los Angeles, CA	5/8/64
Gilbert, Sara	Santa Monica, CA	1/29/75
Gilberto, Astrud	Salvador, Brazil	3/30/40
Gill, Vince	Norman, OK	4/12/57
Gillette, Anita	Baltimore, MD	8/16/36
Gilley, Mickey	Natchez, MS	3/9/36
Gilliam, Terry	Minneapolis, MN	11/22/40
Gilmour, David	Cambridge, England, UK	3/6/46
Gilpin, Peri	Waco, TX	5/27/61
Gilsig, Jessalyn	Montreal, QC, Canada	11/30/71
Givens, Robin	New York, NY	11/27/64
Glaser, Paul Michael	Cambridge, MA	3/25/43
Gleeson, Brendan	Belfast, N. Ireland, UK	11/29/55?
Glenn, Scott	Pittsburgh, PA	1/26/41
Gless, Sharon	Los Angeles, CA	5/31/43
Glover, Crispin	New York, NY	4/20/64
Glover, Danny	San Francisco, CA	7/22/47
Glover, John	Kingston, NY	8/7/44
Glover, Julian	London, England, UK	3/27/35

Name	Birthplace	Birthdate
Glover, Savion	Newark, NJ	11/19/73
Godard, Jean-Luc	Paris, France	12/3/30
Goldberg, Whoopi	New York, NY	11/13/55
Goldblum, Jeff	Pittsburgh, PA	10/22/52
Goldthwait, Bobcat	Syracuse, NY	5/26/62
Goldwyn, Tony	Los Angeles, CA	5/20/60
Gomez, Selena	Grand Prairie, TX	7/22/92
Gooding, Cuba, Jr.	Bronx, NY	1/2/68
Goodman, John	Affton, MO	6/20/52
Goodman, Len	London, England, UK	4/25/44
Gordon-Levitt, Joseph	Los Angeles, CA	2/17/81
Gosling, Ryan	London, ON, Canada	11/12/80
Gosselaar, Mark-Paul	Panorama City, CA	3/1/74
Gossett, Louis, Jr.	Brooklyn, NY	5/27/36
Gould, Elliott	Brooklyn, NY	8/29/38
Grace, Topher	New York, NY	7/12/78
Graham, Heather	Milwaukee, WI	1/29/70
Grammer, Kelsey	St. Thomas, U.S. Virgin Isls.	2/21/55
Grant, Amy	Augusta, GA	11/25/60
Grant, Hugh	London, England, UK	9/9/60
Grant, Lee	New York, NY	10/31/27?
Gray, Linda	Santa Monica, CA	9/12/40
Gray, Macy	Canton, OH	9/6/69
Green, Al	Forrest City, AR	4/13/46
Green, Cee Lo	Atlanta, GA	5/30/74
Green, Seth	Philadelphia, PA	2/8/74
Green, Tom	Pembroke, ON, Canada	7/30/71
Greene, Shecky	Chicago, IL	4/8/26
Greenfield, Max	Dobbs Ferry, NY	9/4/80
Greenwood, Bruce	Noranda, QC, Canada	8/12/56
Gregory, Cynthia	Los Angeles, CA	7/8/46
Gregory, Dick	St. Louis, MO	10/12/32
Grenier, Adrian	Santa Fe, NM	7/10/76
Grey, Jennifer	New York, NY	3/26/60
Grey, Joel	Cleveland, OH	4/11/32
Grier, David Alan	Detroit, MI	6/30/55
Grier, Pam	Winston-Salem, NC	5/26/49
Gries, Jon	Glendale, CA	6/17/57
Griffin, Kathy	Oak Park, IL	11/4/61
Griffith, Melanie	New York, NY	8/9/57
Griffiths, Rachel	Melbourne, Vic., Australia	12/18/68
Grimes, Tammy	Lynn, MA	1/30/34
Grint, Rupert	Walton-at-Stone, Hertfordshire, Eng., UK	8/24/88
Groban, Josh	Los Angeles, CA	2/27/81
Grodin, Charles	Pittsburgh, PA	4/21/35
Groff, Jonathan	Lancaster, PA	3/26/85
Grohl, David	Warren, OH	1/14/69
Gross, Michael	Chicago, IL	6/21/47
Guest, Christopher	New York, NY	2/5/48
Guillaume, Robert	St. Louis, MO	11/30/27
Gumbel, Greg	New Orleans, LA	5/3/46
Gunn, Anna	Santa Fe, NM	8/11/68
Gunn, Tim	Washington, DC	7/29/53
Guthrie, Arlo	Brooklyn, NY	7/10/47
Guttenberg, Steve	Brooklyn, NY	8/24/58
Guy, Buddy	Lettsworth, LA	7/30/36
Guy, Jasmine	Boston, MA	3/10/64
Gyllenhaal, Jake	Los Angeles, CA	12/19/80
Gyllenhaal, Maggie	New York, NY	11/16/77
Hackman, Gene	San Bernardino, CA	1/30/30
Hader, Bill	Tulsa, OK	6/7/78
Hagerty, Julie	Cincinnati, OH	6/15/55
Haggard, Merle	Bakersfield, CA	4/6/37
Haid, Charles	San Francisco, CA	6/2/43
Hale, Barbara	DeKalb, IL	4/18/22
Hale, Tony	West Point, NY	9/30/70
Hall, Anthony Michael	West Roxbury, MA	4/14/68
Hall, Arsenio	Cleveland, OH	2/12/55
Hall, Darryl	Pottstown, PA	10/11/46
Hall, Deidre	Milwaukee, WI	10/31/47
Hall, Michael C.	Raleigh, NC	2/1/71
Hall, Monty	Winnipeg, MB, Canada	8/25/21
Hall, Tom T.	Olive Hill, KY	5/25/36
Halliwell, Geri	Watford, England, UK	8/6/72
Hamill, Mark	Oakland, CA	9/25/51
Hamilton, George	Memphis, TN	8/12/39
Hamilton, Linda	Salisbury, MD	9/26/56
Hamlin, Harry	Pasadena, CA	10/30/51
Hamm, Jon	St. Louis, MO	3/10/71
Hammer, Armie	Los Angeles, CA	8/28/86
Hammer (M.C.)	Oakland, CA	3/30/63
Hammond, Darrell	Melbourne, FL	10/8/55
Hancock, Herbie	Chicago, IL	4/12/40
Handler, Chelsea	Livingston, NJ	2/25/75
Hanks, Colin	Sacramento, CA	11/24/77
Hanks, Tom	Concord, CA	7/9/56
Hannah, Daryl	Chicago, IL	12/3/60
Hannigan, Alyson	Washington, DC	3/24/74
Hanson, Curtis	Reno, NV	3/24/45
Hanson, Isaac	Tulsa, OK	11/17/80
Hanson, Taylor	Tulsa, OK	3/14/83
Hanson, Zac	Tulsa, OK	10/22/85
Harden, Marcia Gay	La Jolla, CA	8/14/59
Harewood, Dorian	Dayton, OH	8/6/50
Hargitay, Mariska	Los Angeles, CA	1/23/64

Name	Birthplace	Birthdate
Harmon, Angie	Highland Park, TX	8/10/72
Harmon, Mark	Burbank, CA	9/2/51
Harper, Ben	Claremont, CA	10/28/69
Harper, Tess	Mammoth Spring, AR	8/15/50
Harper, Valerie	Suffern, NY	8/22/39
Harrelson, Woody	Midland, TX	7/23/61
Harrington, Pat	New York, NY	8/13/29
Harris, Barbara	Evanston, IL	7/25/35
Harris, Ed	Tenafly, NJ	11/28/50
Harris, Emmylou	Birmingham, AL	4/2/47
Harris, Neil Patrick	Albuquerque, NM	6/15/73
Harris, Rosemary	Ashby, England, UK	9/19/27?
Harris, Steve	Chicago, IL	12/3/65
Harrison, Gregory	Avalon, CA	5/31/50
Harry, Deborah	Miami, FL	7/1/45
Hart, Mary	Madison, SD	11/8/50
Hart, Melissa Joan	Smithtown, NY	4/18/76
Hartley, Mariette	New York, NY	6/21/40
Hartman, David	Pawtucket, RI	5/19/35
Hartman Black, Lisa	Houston, TX	6/1/56
Hartnett, Josh	San Francisco, CA	7/21/78
Harvey, P. J.	Yeovil, Somerset, Eng., UK	10/9/69
Harvey, Steve	Welch, WV	11/23/56
Hasselbeck, Elisabeth	Cranston, RI	5/28/77
Hasselhoff, David	Baltimore, MD	7/17/52
Hatcher, Teri	Sunnyvale, CA	12/8/64
Hatfield, Juliana	Wiscasset, ME	7/27/67
Hathaway, Anne	Brooklyn, NY	11/12/82
Hauer, Rutger	Breukelen, Netherlands	1/23/44
Hawke, Ethan	Austin, TX	11/6/70
Hawn, Goldie	Washington, DC	11/21/45
Hayek, Salma	Coatzacoalcos, Mexico	9/2/66
Hayes, Sean	Glen Ellyn, IL	6/26/70
Haynes, Roy	Roxbury, MA	3/13/25
Hays, Robert	Bethesda, MD	7/24/47
Haysbert, Dennis	San Mateo, CA	6/2/55
Head, Anthony	Camden Town, Eng., UK	2/20/54
Heard, John	Washington, DC	3/7/45
Hearn, George	St. Louis, MO	6/18/34
Heaton, Patricia	Bay Village, OH	3/4/58
Heche, Anne	Aurora, OH	5/25/69
Heder, Jon	Fort Collins, CO	10/26/77
Hedren, Tippi	New Ulm, MN	1/19/30?
Heigl, Katherine	Washington, DC	11/24/78
Helberg, Simon	Los Angeles, CA	12/9/80
Helfgott, David	Melbourne, Vic., Australia	5/19/47
Helgenberger, Marg	Fremont, NE	11/16/58
Helmond, Katherine	Galveston, TX	7/5/28?
Helms, Ed	Atlanta, GA	1/24/74
Hemingway, Mariel	Mill Valley, CA	11/22/61
Hemsworth, Chris	Melbourne, Vic., Australia	8/11/83
Hemsworth, Liam	Melbourne, Vic., Australia	1/13/90
Henderson, Florence	Dale, IN	2/14/34
Hendricks, Christina	Knoxville, TN	5/3/75
Henley, Don	Gilmer, TX	7/22/47
Henner, Marilu	Chicago, IL	4/6/52
Hennessy, Jill	Edmonton, AB, Canada	11/25/68
Henry, Buck	New York, NY	12/9/30
Herman, Pee-Wee	Peekskill, NY	8/27/52
Herrmann, Edward	Washington, DC	7/21/43
Hershey, Barbara	Hollywood, CA	2/5/48
Hesseman, Howard	Lebanon, OR	2/27/40
Hetfield, James	Downey, CA	8/3/63
Hewitt, Jennifer Love	Waco, TX	2/21/79
Hicks, Catherine	Scottsdale, AZ	8/6/51
Higgins, John Michael	Boston, MA	2/12/63
Hightower, Chelsie	Las Vegas, NV	7/21/89
Hill, Dulé	Orange, NJ	5/3/75
Hill, Faith	Jackson, MS	9/21/67
Hill, Jonah	Los Angeles, CA	12/20/83
Hill, Lauryn	South Orange, NJ	5/26/75
Hill, Steven	Seattle, WA	2/24/22
Hillerman, John	Denison, TX	12/20/32
Hilton, Paris	New York, NY	2/17/81
Hines, Cheryl	Miami Beach, FL	9/21/65
Hirsch, Emile	Palms, CA	3/13/85
Hirsch, Judd	Bronx, NY	3/15/35
Hodgman, John	Cambridge, MA	6/3/71
Hoffman, Dustin	Los Angeles, CA	8/8/37
Hogan, Hulk	Augusta, GA	8/11/53
Hogan, Paul	Lightning Ridge, NSW, Australia	10/8/39
Holbrook, Hal	Cleveland, OH	2/17/25
Holliday, Polly	Jasper, AL	7/2/37
Holliman, Earl	Delhi, LA	9/11/28
Holloway, Josh	San Jose, CA	7/20/69
Holly, Lauren	Bristol, PA	10/28/63
Holm, Ian	Ilford, England, UK	9/12/31
Holmes, Katie	Toledo, OH	12/18/78
Hopkins, Anthony	Port Talbot, South Wales, UK	12/31/37
Hopkins, Bo	Greenville, SC	2/2/42
Hopkins, Telma	Louisville, KY	10/28/48
Horne, Marilyn	Bradford, PA	1/16/34
Hornsby, Bruce	Williamsburg, VA	11/23/54
Horsley, Lee	Muleshoe, TX	5/15/55
Hough, Derek	Salt Lake City, UT	5/17/85
Hough, Julianne	Salt Lake City, UT	7/20/88
Hounsou, Djimon	Cotonou, Benin	4/24/64
Howard, Clint	Burbank, CA	4/20/59
Howard, Ken	El Centro, CA	3/28/44
Howard, Ron	Duncan, OK	3/1/54
Howard, Terrence	Chicago, IL	3/11/69
Howell, C. Thomas	Van Nuys, CA	12/7/66
Howes, Sally Ann	St. John's Wood, London, England, UK	7/20/30
Hudgens, Vanessa	Salinas, CA	12/14/88
Hudson, Jennifer	Chicago, IL	9/12/81
Hudson, Kate	Los Angeles, CA	4/19/79
Huffman, Felicity	Bedford, NY	12/9/62
Hughley, D. L.	Los Angeles, CA	3/6/63
Hulce, Tom	Detroit, MI	12/6/53
Humperdinck, Engelbert	Madras, India	5/2/36
Humphries, Barry	Melbourne, Vic., Australia	2/17/34
Hunt, Bonnie	Chicago, IL	9/22/64
Hunt, Helen	Culver City, CA	6/15/63
Hunt, Linda	Morristown, NJ	4/2/45
Hunter, Holly	Conyers, GA	3/20/58
Hunter, Tab	New York, NY	7/11/31
Hurley, Elizabeth	Hampshire, England, UK	6/10/65
Hurt, John	Chesterfield, England, UK	1/22/40
Hurt, Mary Beth	Marshalltown, IA	9/26/48
Hurt, William	Washington, DC	3/20/50
Huston, Anjelica	Santa Monica, CA	7/8/51
Hutcherson, Josh	Union, KY	10/12/92
Hutton, Lauren	Charleston, SC	11/17/43
Hutton, Timothy	Malibu, CA	8/16/60
Hyman, Earle	Rocky Mount, NC	10/11/26
Ian, Janis	Bronx, NY	4/7/51
Ice Cube	Los Angeles, CA	6/15/69
Ice-T	Newark, NJ	2/16/58
Idle, Eric	S. Shields, England, UK	3/29/43
Idol, Billy	Middlesex, England, UK	11/30/55
Iglesias, Enrique	Madrid, Spain	5/8/75
Iglesias, Julio	Madrid, Spain	9/23/43
Iler, Robert	New York, NY	3/2/85
Iman	Mogadishu, Somalia	7/25/55
Imbruglia, Natalie	Sydney, NSW, Australia	2/4/75
Imperioli, Michael	Mount Vernon, NY	3/26/66
Imus, Don	Riverside, CA	7/23/40
Ingram, James	Akron, OH	2/16/52
Innes, Laura	Pontiac, MI	8/16/57?
Ireland, Kathy	Glendale, CA	3/20/63
Irons, Jeremy	Cowes, Isle of Wight, Eng., UK	9/19/48
Irving, Amy	Palo Alto, CA	9/10/53
Irving, George S.	Springfield, MA	11/1/22
Irwin, Bill	Santa Monica, CA	4/11/50
Ivanek, Zeljko	Ljubljana, Yugoslavia	8/15/57
Ivey, Judith	El Paso, TX	9/4/51
Ivory, James	Berkeley, CA	6/7/28
Izzard, Eddie	Aden, Yemen	2/7/62
Ja Rule	Hollis, Queens, NY	2/29/76
Jackée (Harry)	Winston-Salem, NC	8/14/56
Jackman, Hugh	Sydney, NSW, Australia	10/12/68
Jackson, Anne	Allegheny, PA	9/3/26
Jackson, Cheyenne	Newport, WA	7/12/75
Jackson, Glenda	Birkenhead, England, UK	5/9/36
Jackson, Janet	Gary, IN	5/16/66
Jackson, Jermaine	Gary, IN	12/11/54
Jackson, Jonathan	Orlando, FL	5/11/82
Jackson, Joshua	Vancouver, BC, Canada	6/11/78
Jackson, Kate	Birmingham, AL	10/29/48
Jackson, La Toya	Gary, IN	5/29/56
Jackson, Peter	Wellington, New Zealand	10/31/61
Jackson, Samuel L.	Washington, DC	12/21/48
Jacobi, Derek	London, England, UK	10/22/38
Jagger, Mick	Dartford, England, UK	7/26/43
James, Kevin	Mineola, NY	4/26/65
Jamison, Judith	Philadelphia, PA	5/10/43
Janis, Conrad	New York, NY	2/11/28
Janney, Allison	Dayton, OH	11/19/59
Janssen, Famke	Amsterdam, Netherlands	11/5/65
Jardine, Al	Lima, OH	9/3/42
Jarmusch, Jim	Akron, OH	1/22/53
Jarreau, Al	Milwaukee, WI	3/12/40
Jarrett, Keith	Allentown, PA	5/8/45
Jay Z	Brooklyn, NY	12/4/69
Jeffreys, Anne	Goldsboro, NC	1/26/23
Jenner, Kris	San Diego, CA	11/5/55
Jepsen, Carly Rae	Mission, BC, Canada	11/21/85
Jett, Joan	Philadelphia, PA	9/22/58
Jewel (Kilcher)	Payson, UT	5/23/74
Jewison, Norman	Toronto, ON, Canada	7/21/26
Jillette, Penn	Greenfield, MA	3/5/55
Jillian, Ann	Cambridge, MA	1/29/50
Joel, Billy	Bronx, NY	5/9/49
Johansson, Scarlett	New York, NY	11/22/84
John, Elton	Pinner, Middlesex, Eng., UK	3/25/47
Johns, Glynis	Durban, South Africa	10/5/23
Johnson, Arte	Benton Harbor, MI	1/20/29

Name	Birthplace	Birthdate
Johnson, Beverly	Buffalo, NY	10/13/52
Johnson, Don	Flatt Creek, MO	12/15/49
Johnson, Dwayne "The Rock"	Hayward, CA	5/2/72
Johnston, Bruce	Los Angeles, CA	6/24/42
Johnston, Kristen	Washington, DC	9/20/67
Jolie, Angelina	Los Angeles, CA	6/4/75
Jonas, Joe	Casa Grande, AZ	8/15/89
Jonas, Kevin	Teaneck, NJ	11/5/87
Jonas, Nick	Dallas, TX	9/16/92
Jones, Angus T.	Austin, TX	10/8/93
Jones, Bill T.	Bunnell, FL	2/15/52
Jones, Cherry	Paris, TN	11/21/56
Jones, Dean	Decatur, AL	1/25/31
Jones, Gemma	London, England, UK	12/4/42
Jones, Grace	Spanish Town, Jamaica	5/19/48
Jones, Jack	Hollywood, CA	1/14/38
Jones, James Earl	Arkabutla, MS	1/17/31
Jones, John Paul	Sidcup, England, UK	1/3/46
Jones, January	Sioux Falls, SD	1/5/78
Jones, Mick	London, England, UK	6/26/55
Jones, Norah	New York, NY	3/30/79
Jones, Quincy	Chicago, IL	3/14/33
Jones, Shirley	Charleroi, PA	3/31/34
Jones, Star	Badin, NC	3/24/62
Jones, Tom	Pontypridd, Wales, UK	6/7/40
Jones, Tommy Lee	San Saba, TX	9/15/46
Jonze, Spike	Rockville, MD	10/22/69
Jourdan, Louis	Marseilles, France	6/19/19
Jovovich, Milla	Kiev, Ukraine	12/17/75
Judd, Ashley	Granada Hills, CA	4/19/68
Judd, Naomi	Ashland, KY	1/11/46
Judd, Wynonna	Ashland, KY	5/30/64
Kaczmarek, Jane	Milwaukee, WI	12/21/55
Kaling, Mindy	Cambridge, MA	6/24/79
Kanaly, Steve	Burbank, CA	3/14/46
Kane, Carol	Cleveland, OH	6/18/52
Kaplan, Gabe	Brooklyn, NY	3/31/45
Kardashian, Khloe	Los Angeles, CA	6/27/84
Kardashian, Kim	Los Angeles, CA	10/21/80
Kardashian, Kourtney	Los Angeles, CA	4/18/79
Karlen, John	New York, NY	5/28/40
Karn, Richard	Seattle, WA	2/17/56
Kattan, Chris	Sherman Oaks, CA	10/19/70
Kavner, Julie	Burbank, CA	9/7/51
Kaye, Judy	Phoenix, AZ	12/11/48
Kazan, Lainie	New York, NY	5/15/40
Keach, Stacy	Savannah, GA	6/2/41
Keaton, Diane	Santa Ana, CA	1/5/46
Keaton, Michael	Coraopolis, PA	9/5/51
Keener, Catherine	Miami, FL	3/23/59
Keillor, Garrison	Anoka, MN	8/7/42
Keitel, Harvey	Brooklyn, NY	5/13/39
Keith, David	Knoxville, TN	5/8/54
Keith, Penelope	Sutton, Surrey, Eng., UK	4/2/40
Kellerman, Sally	Long Beach, CA	6/2/37
Kelly, Minka	Los Angeles, CA	6/24/80
Kelly, R(obert)	Chicago, IL	1/8/67
Kennedy, George	New York, NY	2/18/25
Kennedy, Jamie	Upper Darby, PA	5/25/70
Kennedy, Jayne	Washington, DC	10/27/51
Kenny G	Seattle, WA	6/5/56
Kent, Allegra	Santa Monica, CA	8/11/37
Keoghan, Phil	Christchurch, New Zealand	5/31/67
Kercheval, Ken	Wolcottville, IN	7/15/35
Kerns, Joanna	San Francisco, CA	2/12/53
Kesha	Los Angeles, CA	3/1/87
Keys, Alicia	New York, NY	1/25/81
Khan, Chaka	Great Lakes, IL	3/23/53
Kid Rock	Romeo, MI	1/17/71
Kidder, Margot	Yellowknife, NT, Canada	10/17/48
Kidman, Nicole	Honolulu, HI	6/20/67
Kiel, Richard	Detroit, MI	9/13/39
Kilborn, Craig	Kansas City, KS	8/24/62
Kilmer, Val	Los Angeles, CA	12/31/59
Kim, Daniel Dae	Pusan, South Korea	8/4/68
Kimmel, Jimmy	Brooklyn, NY	11/13/67
King, B.B.	Itta Bena, MS	9/16/25
King, Carole	Brooklyn, NY	2/9/42
King, Gayle	Chevy Chase, MD	12/28/54?
King, Larry	Brooklyn, NY	11/19/33
King, Perry	Alliance, OH	4/30/48
King, Regina	Los Angeles, CA	1/15/71
Kingsley, Ben	Scarborough, England, UK	12/31/43
Kingston, Alex	London, England, UK	3/11/63
Kinnear, Greg	Logansport, IN	6/17/63
Kinney, Kathy	Stevens Point, WI	11/3/54
Kinski, Nastassja	Berlin, W. Germany	1/24/60
Kirkland, Gelsey	Bethlehem, PA	12/29/52
Kirkpatrick, Chris	Clarion, PA	10/17/71
Kirshner, Mia	Toronto, ON, Canada	1/25/75
Kitsch, Taylor	Kelowna, BC, Canada	4/8/81
Klein, Robert	Bronx, NY	2/8/42
Kline, Kevin	St. Louis, MO	10/24/47
Klum, Heidi	Bergish-Gladbach, Germany	6/1/73
Knight, Gladys	Atlanta, GA	5/28/44
Knight, Shirley	Goessel, KS	7/5/36
Knight, T. R.	Minneapolis, MN	3/26/73
Knight, Wayne	New York, NY	8/7/55
Knightley, Keira	Teddington, England, UK	3/26/85
Knopfler, Mark	Glasgow, Scotland, UK	8/12/49
Knowles, Beyoncé	Houston, TX	9/4/81
Knoxville, Johnny	Knoxville, TN	3/11/71
Konitz, Lee	Chicago, IL	10/13/27
Kopell, Bernie	Brooklyn, NY	6/21/33
Kotto, Yaphet	New York, NY	11/15/37
Krakowski, Jane	Parsippany, NJ	10/11/68
Krasinski, John	Newton, MA	10/20/79
Krause, Peter	Alexandria, MN	8/12/65
Kressley, Carson	Allentown, PA	11/11/69
Kretschmann, Thomas	Dessau, E. Germany	9/8/62
Kristofferson, Kris	Brownsville, TX	6/22/36
Kudrow, Lisa	Encino, CA	7/30/63
Kunis, Mila	Kiev, Ukraine	8/14/83
Kuriyama, Chiaki	Tsuchiura, Ibaraki, Japan.	10/10/84
Kurtz, Swoosie	Omaha, NE	9/6/44
Kutcher, Ashton	Cedar Rapids, IA	2/7/78
Kwan, Nancy	Hong Kong	5/19/39
LaBelle, Patti	Philadelphia, PA	5/24/44
LaBeouf, Shia	Los Angeles, CA	6/11/86
Lachey, Nick	Harlan, KY	11/9/73
Ladd, Cheryl	Huron, SD	7/12/51
Ladd, Diane	Meridian, MS	11/29/32
Lady Gaga	New York, NY	3/28/86
Lagasse, Emeril	Fall River, MA	10/15/59
Lahti, Christine	Birmingham, MI	4/4/50
Laine, Cleo	Southall, England, UK	10/28/27
Lake, Ricki	Hastings-on-Hudson, NY.	9/21/68
Lamas, Lorenzo	Santa Monica, CA	1/20/58
Lambert, Adam	Indianapolis, IN	1/29/82
Lambert, Christopher	Great Neck, NY	3/29/57
Lambert, Miranda	Longview, TX.	11/10/83
Landau, Martin	Brooklyn, NY	6/20/28
Landis, John	Chicago, IL	8/3/50
Lane, Diane	New York, NY	1/22/65
Lane, Nathan	Jersey City, NJ	2/3/56
lang, k.d.	Consort, AB, Canada	11/2/61
Lang, Stephen	Jamaica Estates, Queens, NY	7/11/52
Lange, Jessica	Cloquet, MN	4/20/49
Langella, Frank	Bayonne, NJ	1/1/38
Lansbury, Angela	London, England, UK	10/16/25
LaPaglia, Anthony	Adelaide, SA, Australia	1/31/59
Larroquette, John	New Orleans, LA	11/25/47
LaSalle, Eriq	Hartford, CT	6/23/62
Lauper, Cyndi	Ozone Park, Queens, NY	6/22/53
Laurie, Hugh	Oxford, England, UK	6/11/59
Laurie, Piper	Detroit, MI	1/22/32
Lautner, Taylor	Grand Rapids, MI	2/11/92
Lavigne, Avril	Belleville, ON, Canada.	9/27/84
Lavin, Linda	Portland, ME	10/15/37
Law, Jude	London, England, UK	12/29/72
Lawless, Lucy	Mount Albert, New Zealand	3/29/68
Lawrence, Carol	Melrose Park, IL	9/5/34
Lawrence, Jennifer	Louisville, KY	8/15/90
Lawrence, Joey	Montgomery, PA	4/20/76
Lawrence, Martin	Frankfurt, Germany	4/16/65
Lawrence, Steve	Brooklyn, NY	7/8/35
Lawrence, Vicki	Inglewood, CA	3/26/49
Leach, Robin	London, England, UK	8/29/41
Leachman, Cloris	Des Moines, IA	4/30/26
Lear, Norman	New Haven, CT	7/27/22
Learned, Michael	Washington, DC	4/9/39
Leary, Denis	Worcester, MA.	8/18/57
LeBlanc, Matt	Newton, MA.	7/25/67
LeBon, Simon	Bushey, England, UK.	10/27/58
Lee, Ang	Pingtung, Taiwan	10/23/54
Lee, Brenda	Lithonia, GA	12/11/44
Lee, Christopher	London, England, UK	5/27/22
Lee, Jason	Huntington Beach, CA	4/25/70
Lee, Michele	Los Angeles, CA	6/24/42
Lee, Spike	Atlanta, GA	3/20/57
Leeves, Jane	Ilford, England, UK	4/18/61
Legrand, Michel	Paris, France	2/24/32
Leguizamo, John	Bogotá, Colombia	7/22/64
Lehmkuhl, Reichen	Cincinnati, OH	12/26/73
Leibman, Ron	New York, NY	10/11/37
Leigh, Jennifer Jason	Hollywood, CA.	2/5/62
Leighton, Laura	Iowa City, IA	7/24/68
Lennox, Annie	Aberdeen, Scotland, UK	12/25/54
Leno, Jay	New Rochelle, NY	4/28/50
Leo, Melissa	New York, NY	9/14/60
Leonard, Robert Sean	Westwood, NJ	2/28/69
Leoni, Tea	New York, NY	2/25/66
Leslie, Joan	Detroit, MI	1/26/25
Leto, Jared	Bossier City, LA.	12/26/71
Letterman, David	Indianapolis, IN	4/12/47
Levin, Harvey	Los Angeles, CA	9/2/60
Levine, Adam	Los Angeles, CA	3/18/79
Levine, James	Cincinnati, OH	6/23/43
Levine, Ted	Bellaire, OH.	5/29/57
Levinson, Barry	Baltimore, MD	4/6/42
Levy, Eugene	Hamilton, ON, Canada.	12/17/46

Name	Birthplace	Birthdate
Lewis, Damian	London, Eng., UK	2/11/71
Lewis, Huey	New York, NY	7/5/50
Lewis, Jason	Newport Beach, CA	6/25/71
Lewis, Jerry	Newark, NJ	3/16/26
Lewis, Jerry Lee	Ferriday, LA	9/29/35
Lewis, Juliette	Los Angeles, CA	6/21/73
Lewis, Leona	London, England, UK	4/3/85
Lewis, Richard	Brooklyn, NY	6/29/47
Li, Jet	Beijing, China	4/26/63
Light, Judith	Trenton, NJ	2/9/49
Lightfoot, Gordon	Orillia, ON, Canada	11/17/38
Lil' Kim	Brooklyn, NY	7/11/75
Lil' Romeo	New Orleans, LA	8/19/89
Lil Wayne	New Orleans, LA	9/27/82
Lilly, Evangeline	Fort Saskatchewan, AB, Can.	8/3/79
Lincoln, Andrew	London, England, UK	9/14/73
Linden, Hal	Bronx, NY	3/20/31
Ling, Lisa	Sacramento, CA	8/30/73
Linn-Baker, Mark	St. Louis, MO.	6/17/54
Linney, Laura	New York, NY	2/5/64
Liotta, Ray	Newark, NJ	12/18/54
Lithgow, John	Rochester, NY	10/19/45
Little, Rich	Ottawa, ON, Canada	11/26/38
Little Richard	Macon, GA	12/5/32
Littrell, Brian	Lexington, KY	2/20/75
Liu, Lucy	Jackson Heights, Queens, NY	12/2/68
Lively, Blake	Tarzana, CA	8/25/87
LL Cool J	St. Albans, Queens, NY	1/14/68
Lloyd, Christopher	Stamford, CT	10/22/38
Lloyd, Emily	North London, Eng., UK	9/29/70
Lloyd Webber, Andrew	London, England, UK	3/22/48
Locke, Sondra	Shelbyville, TN.	5/28/47
Lockhart, June	New York, NY	6/25/25
Locklear, Heather	Westwood, CA.	9/25/61
Loggia, Robert	Staten Island, NY.	1/3/30
Loggins, Kenny	Everett, WA	1/7/48
Lohan, Lindsay	New York, NY	7/2/86
Lollobrigida, Gina	Subiaco, Italy	7/4/27
Lonergan, Kenneth	New York, NY	10/16/62
Long, Nia	Brooklyn, NY	10/30/70
Long, Shelley	Ft. Wayne, IN.	8/23/49
Longoria, Eva	Corpus Christi, TX	3/15/75
Lopez, George	Mission Hills, CA	4/23/61
Lopez, Jennifer	Bronx, NY	7/24/69
Lopez, Mario	San Diego, CA	10/10/73
Lorde	Takapuna, New Zealand	11/7/96
Loren, Sophia	Rome, Italy	9/20/34
Loring, Gloria	New York, NY	12/10/46
Louis C.K.	Washington, DC	9/12/67
Louis-Dreyfus, Julia	New York, NY	1/13/61
Lovato, Demi	Dallas, TX	8/20/92
Love, Courtney	San Francisco, CA	7/9/64
Love, Mike	Baldwin Hills, CA.	3/15/41
Loveless, Patty	Pikeville, KY	1/4/57
Lovett, Lyle	Klein, TX	11/1/57
Lovitz, Jon	Tarzana, CA.	7/21/57
Lowe, Rob.	Charlottesville, VA	3/17/64
Lucas, George	Modesto, CA	5/14/44
Lucci, Susan.	Scarsdale, NY	12/23/46
Luckinbill, Laurence	Ft. Smith, AR	11/21/34
Ludacris	Champaign, IL.	9/11/77
Ludwig, Christa.	Berlin, Germany	3/16/24
Luhrmann, Baz	Sydney, NSW, Australia	9/17/62
LuPone, Patti	Northport, NY	4/21/49
Lynch, David	Missoula, MT.	1/20/46
Lynch, Jane	Dolton, IL.	7/14/60
Lynley, Carol	New York, NY	2/13/42
Lynn, Loretta	Butcher Hollow, KY	4/14/32
Lynn, Vera	London, England, UK	3/20/17
Lynne, Shelby	Quantico, VA	10/22/68
Ma, Yo-Yo.	Paris, France	10/7/55
Macchio, Ralph	Huntington, NY	11/4/61
MacDonald, Kelly	Glasgow, Scotland, UK	2/23/76
MacDowell, Andie	Gaffney, SC	4/21/58
MacFarlane, Seth	Kent, CT	10/26/73
MacGowan, Shane	Tunbridge, Kent, Eng., UK	12/25/57
MacGraw, Ali	Pound Ridge, NY	4/1/39
Macklemore	Seattle, WA	6/19/83
MacLachlan, Kyle	Yakima, WA.	2/22/59
MacLaine, Shirley	Richmond, VA	4/24/34
MacLeod, Gavin	Mt. Kisco, NY.	2/28/31
MacNee, Patrick	London, England, UK	2/6/22
MacNicol, Peter	Dallas, TX	4/10/54
MacPherson, Elle	Sydney, NSW, Australia	3/29/64
Macy, Bill.	Revere, MA	5/18/22
Macy, William H.	Miami, FL	3/13/50
Madden, John.	Austin, MN.	4/10/36
Madigan, Amy	Chicago, IL	9/11/50
Madonna (Ciccone)	Bay City, MI	8/16/58
Madsen, Michael	Chicago, IL	9/25/59
Maguire, Tobey	Santa Monica, CA	6/27/75
Maher, Bill	New York, NY	1/20/56
Mahoney, John	Blackpool, Lancashire, England, UK	6/20/40
Majors, Lee	Wyandotte, MI	4/23/39
Makarova, Natalia	Leningrad, Russia	11/21/40

Name	Birthplace	Birthdate
Malick, Terrence	Ottawa, IL	11/30/43
Malick, Wendie	Buffalo, NY	12/13/50
Malina, Joshua	New York, NY	1/17/66
Malkovich, John	Christopher, IL.	12/9/53
Malone, Dorothy	Chicago, IL	1/30/25
Mamet, David	Chicago, IL.	11/30/47
Manchester, Melissa	Bronx, NY	2/15/51
Mandel, Howie	Toronto, ON, Canada.	11/29/55
Mandrell, Barbara	Houston, TX	12/25/48
Mangione, Chuck	Rochester, NY	11/29/40
Manheim, Camryn	Caldwell, NJ	3/8/61
Manilow, Barry	Brooklyn, NY	6/17/43
Mann, Aimee.	Richmond, VA	8/9/60
Manoff, Dinah	New York, NY	1/25/58
Manson, Marilyn	Canton, OH	1/5/69
Mantegna, Joe	Chicago, IL.	11/13/47
Mantello, Joe	Rockford, IL.	12/27/62
Mara, Kate	Bedford, NY.	2/27/83
Mara, Rooney	Bedford, NY.	4/17/85
Marcil, Vanessa	Indio, CA	10/15/69
Margulies, Julianna	Spring Valley, NY	6/8/66
Marie, Constance	Hollywood, CA.	9/9/65
Marin, Cheech	Los Angeles, CA	7/13/46
Marinaro, Ed	New York, NY	3/31/50
Marriner, Neville	Lincoln, England, UK.	4/15/24
Mars, Bruno	Honolulu, HI	10/8/85
Marsalis, Branford	Breaux Bridge, LA	8/26/60
Marsalis, Wynton	New Orleans, LA.	10/18/61
Marsh, Jean	London, England, UK	7/1/34
Marshall, Garry	Bronx, NY	11/13/34
Marshall, Penny	Bronx, NY	10/15/42
Marshall, Peter	Huntington, WV	3/30/26
Martin, Chris	Devon, England, UK	3/2/77
Martin, Jesse L.	Rocky Mount, VA.	1/18/69
Martin, Kellie	Riverside, CA.	10/16/75
Martin, Ricky	San Juan, Puerto Rico.	12/24/71
Martin, Steve	Waco, TX.	8/14/45
Martindale, Margo	Jacksonville, TX.	7/18/51
Martins, Peter	Copenhagen, Denmark	10/27/46
Mason, Jackie	Sheboygan, WI	6/9/31
Mason, Marsha	St. Louis, MO.	4/3/42
Masterson, Christopher	Long Island, NY.	1/22/80
Masterson, Mary Stuart	New York, NY.	6/28/66
Mastrantonio, Mary Elizabeth	Lombard, IL.	11/17/58
Masur, Kurt	Brieg, Germany	7/18/27
Masur, Richard	New York, NY	11/20/48
Mathers, Jerry	Sioux City, IA.	6/2/48
Matheson, Tim	Glendale, CA.	12/31/47
Mathis, Johnny	Gilmer, TX.	9/30/35
Matlin, Marlee	Morton Grove, IL	8/24/65
Matthews, Dave	Johannesburg, South Africa	1/9/67
May, Elaine	Philadelphia, PA	4/21/32
Mayer, John	Bridgeport, CT.	10/16/77
Mays, Jayma	Bristol, TN	7/16/79
Mazar, Debi	Jamaica, Queens, NY	8/13/64
Mazursky, Paul	Brooklyn, NY	4/25/30
McAdams, Rachel	London, ON, Canada.	11/17/78
McArdle, Andrea	Abington, PA	11/5/63
McAvoy, James	Glasgow, Scotland, UK	4/21/79?
McBride, Patricia	Teaneck, NJ	8/23/42
McCallum, David	Glasgow, Scotland, UK	9/19/33
McCarthy, Andrew	Westfield, NJ.	11/29/62
McCarthy, Jenny	Chicago, IL.	11/1/72
McCarthy, Melissa	Plainfield, IL.	8/26/70
McCartney, Paul	Liverpool, England, UK	6/18/42
McCarver, Tim	Memphis, TN.	10/16/41
McConaughey, Matthew	Uvalde, TX.	11/4/69
McCoo, Marilyn	Jersey City, NJ.	9/30/43
McCormack, Eric	Toronto, ON, Canada.	4/18/63
McCormack, Mary	Plainsfield, NJ	2/8/69
McCrane, Paul	Philadelphia, PA	1/19/61
McCreery, Scotty	Garner, NC	10/9/93
McDaniel, James	Washington, DC	3/25/58
McDermott, Dylan.	Waterbury, CT	10/26/61
McDiarmid, Ian	Carnoustie, Tayside, Scot., UK	4/17/44?
McDonald, Audra	Berlin, Germany	7/3/70
McDonnell, Mary	Wilkes-Barre, PA	4/28/52
McDormand, Frances	Chicago, IL.	6/23/57
McDowell, Malcolm.	Leeds, England, UK.	6/13/43
McEntire, Reba	McAlester, OK	3/28/55
McFerrin, Bobby	New York, NY	3/11/50
McGillis, Kelly	Newport Beach, CA.	7/9/57
McGovern, Elizabeth	Evanston, IL	7/18/61
McGovern, Maureen	Youngstown, OH	7/27/49
McGraw, Tim	Delhi, LA	5/1/67
McGregor, Ewan	Crieff, Scotland, UK	3/31/71
McHale, Joel	Rome, Italy	11/20/71
McHale, Kevin	Plano, TX.	6/14/88
McKean, Michael	New York, NY	10/17/47
McKechnie, Donna	Pontiac, MI	11/16/42
McKellen, Ian	Burnley, England, UK.	5/25/39
McKenzie, Benjamin	Austin, TX	9/12/78
McKidd, Kevin	Elgin, Scotland, UK	8/9/73
McLachlan, Sarah	Halifax, NS, Canada	1/28/68
McLean, A. J.	West Palm Beach, FL	1/9/78

Name	Birthplace	Birthdate
McNichol, Kristy	Los Angeles, CA	9/11/62
McRaney, Gerald	Collins, MS	8/19/47
McQueen, Steve	London, England, UK	10/9/69
McQueen, Steven R.	Los Angeles, CA	7/13/88
McShane, Ian	Blackburn, England, UK.	9/29/42
Meadows, Jayne	Wu Chang, China	9/27/20
Meara, Anne	Brooklyn, NY	9/20/29
Meat Loaf	Dallas, TX	9/27/47
Meester, Leighton	Marco Island, FL	4/9/86
Mehta, Zubin	Bombay, India	4/29/36
Mellencamp, John	Seymour, IN	10/7/51
Meloni, Christopher	Washington, DC	4/2/61
Mendes, Sam	Redding, England, UK	8/1/65
Mendes, Sergio	Niteroi, Brazil	2/11/41
Menzel, Idina	Syosset, NY	5/30/71
Merchant, Natalie	Jamestown, NY	10/26/63
Merkerson, S. Epatha	Saginaw, MI	11/28/52
Merrill, Dina	New York, NY	12/9/25
Messing, Debra	Brooklyn, NY	8/15/68
Metcalf, Laurie	Carbondale, IL	6/16/55
Meyers, Seth	Bedford, NH.	12/28/73
Michael, George	London, England, UK	6/25/63
Michaels, Al	Brooklyn, NY	11/12/44
Michaels, Bret	Butler, PA	3/15/63
Michaels, Lorne	Toronto, ON, Canada.	11/17/44
Michele, Lea	Bronx, NY	8/29/86
Midler, Bette	Honolulu, HI	12/1/45
Midori (Goto).	Osaka, Japan	10/25/71
Mike D	Brooklyn, NY	11/20/65
Milano, Alyssa	Brooklyn, NY	12/19/72
Miles, Sarah	Ingatestone, England, UK	12/31/41
Miles, Vera	nr. Boise City, OK.	8/23/30
Miller, Dennis	Pittsburgh, PA	11/3/53
Miller, Jonny Lee	Kingston Upon Thames, England, UK	11/15/72
Miller, Penelope Ann.	Santa Monica, CA	1/13/64
Mills, Donna	Chicago, IL	12/11/43
Mills, Hayley	London, England, UK	4/18/46
Milner, Martin	Detroit, MI	12/28/31
Milnes, Sherrill	Downers Grove, IL.	1/10/35
Milsap, Ronnie	Robinsville, NC	1/16/44
Mimieux, Yvette.	Hollywood, CA.	1/8/42
Minaj, Nicki	St. James, Trinidad and Tobago	12/8/82
Ming-Na (Wen)	Coloane Island, Macao	11/20/63
Minnelli, Liza.	Los Angeles, CA	3/12/46
Minogue, Kylie	Melbourne, Vic., Australia	5/28/68
Mirren, Helen	London, England, UK	7/26/45
Mitchell, Brian Stokes	Seattle, WA	10/31/57
Mitchell, Elizabeth.	Los Angeles, CA	3/27/70
Mitchell, Jerry	Paw Paw, MI	1/15/60
Mitchell, Joni.	Fort McLeod, AB, Canada	11/7/43
Moby	New York, NY	9/11/65
Modine, Matthew	Loma Linda, CA.	3/22/59
Moffat, Donald	Plymouth, England, UK	12/26/30
Molina, Alfred	London, England, UK	5/24/53
Molinaro, Al	Kenosha, WI	6/24/19
Moll, Richard.	Pasadena, CA	1/13/43
Moloney, Janel	Woodland Hills, CA	10/3/69
Monaghan, Dominic	Berlin, Germany	12/8/76
Monica (Arnold)	College Park, GA.	10/24/80
Mo'Nique	Woodlawn, MD	12/11/67
Moody, Ron.	London, England, UK	1/8/24
Moore, Demi	Roswell, NM	11/11/62
Moore, Julianne	Fort Bragg, NC	12/3/60
Moore, Mandy.	Nashua, NH.	4/10/84
Moore, Mary Tyler	Brooklyn, NY	12/29/36
Moore, Melba	New York, NY	10/29/45
Moore, Michael	Flint, MI	4/23/54
Moore, Roger	London, England, UK	10/14/27
Moore, Terry	Los Angeles, CA	1/7/29
Morales, Esai	Brooklyn, NY	10/1/62
Moranis, Rick	Toronto, ON, Canada.	4/18/53
Moreau, Jeanne	Paris, France	1/23/28
Moreno, Rita	Humacao, Puerto Rico.	12/11/31
Morgan, Jeffrey Dean	Seattle, WA	4/22/66
Morgan, Piers	Guildford, Surrey, UK.	3/30/65
Morgan, Tracy	Bronx, NY	11/10/68
Moriarty, Michael	Detroit, MI	4/5/41
Morris, Garrett.	New Orleans, LA	2/1/37
Morissette, Alanis	Ottawa, ON, Canada	6/1/74
Morrison, Matthew	Fort Ord, CA	10/30/78
Morrison, Van	Belfast, N. Ireland, UK	8/31/45
Morrissey (Steven Patrick)	Manchester, England, UK	5/22/59
Morrow, Rob	New Rochelle, NY	9/21/62
Morse, David.	Beverly, MA	10/11/53
Morse, Robert.	Newton, MA.	5/18/31
Mortensen, Viggo	New York, NY	10/20/58
Mortimer, Emily.	London, England, UK	12/1/71
Morton, Joe.	New York, NY	10/18/47
Morton, Samantha	Nottingham, England, UK	5/13/77
Moses, William	Los Angeles, CA	11/17/59
Moss, Carrie-Anne	Vancouver, BC, Canada.	8/21/67
Moss, Elisabeth	Los Angeles, CA	7/24/82
Moss, Kate	Croydon, Surrey, Eng., UK.	1/16/74
Moyer, Stephen.	Brentwood, UK	10/11/69

Name	Birthplace	Birthdate
Moynahan, Bridget	Binghamton, NY	4/28/71
Mueller-Stahl, Armin	Tilsit, E. Prussia	12/17/30
Muldaur, Diana	Brooklyn, NY	8/19/38
Mulgrew, Kate	Dubuque, IA	4/29/55
Mull, Martin	Chicago, IL	8/18/43
Mullally, Megan	Los Angeles, CA	11/12/58
Mullan, Peter.	Peterhead, Scotland, UK	11/2/59
Mulroney, Dermot	Alexandria, VA	10/31/63
Muniz, Frankie	Wood-Ridge, NJ	12/5/85
Munsel, Patrice.	Spokane, WA.	5/14/25
Murphy, Ben	Jonesboro, AR.	3/6/42
Murphy, Donna	Corona, Queens, NY	3/7/58
Murphy, Eddie.	Brooklyn, NY	4/3/61
Murphy, Michael	Los Angeles, CA	5/5/38
Murray, Anne.	Springhill, NS, Canada	6/20/45
Murray, Bill	Wilmette, IL	9/21/50
Murray, Don	Hollywood, CA.	7/31/29
Musburger, Brent	Portland, OR.	5/26/39
Muti, Riccardo.	Naples, Italy.	7/28/41
Myers, Mike	Scarborough, ON, Canada	5/25/63
Nabors, Jim	Sylacauga, AL	6/12/30
Nagra, Parminder	Leicester, England, UK	10/5/75
Nash, Graham	Blackpool, England, UK.	2/2/42
Naughton, James	Middletown, CT	12/6/45
Navarro, Dave.	Santa Monica, CA	6/7/67
Nealon, Kevin	St. Louis, MO.	11/18/53
Neeson, Liam	Ballymena, N. Ireland, UK	6/7/52
Neff, Lucas	Chicago, IL	11/7/85
Neill, Sam	Ulster, N. Ireland, UK	9/14/47
Nelligan, Kate	London, ON, Canada.	3/16/51
Nelly	Austin, TX	11/2/74
Nelson, Craig T.	Spokane, WA.	4/4/44
Nelson, Judd.	Portland, ME	11/28/59
Nelson, Tracy	Santa Monica, CA	10/25/63
Nelson, Willie	Abbott, TX	4/30/33
Nero, Peter.	Brooklyn, NY	5/22/34
Nesmith, Mike.	Houston, TX	12/30/42
Neuwirth, Bebe	Newark, NJ	12/31/58
Neville, Aaron	New Orleans, LA	1/24/41
Newhart, Bob	Oak Park, IL	9/5/29
Newman, Randy.	New Orleans, LA	11/28/43
Newton, Wayne.	Norfolk, VA	4/3/42
Newton-John, Olivia	Cambridge, England, UK.	9/26/48
Nicholas, Denise.	Detroit, MI	7/12/44
Nichols, Mike	Berlin, Germany	11/6/31
Nicholson, Jack	Neptune, NJ	4/22/37
Nicks, Stevie	Phoenix, AZ.	5/26/48
Nighy, Bill	Caterham, Surrey, Eng., UK.	12/12/49
Nimoy, Leonard.	Boston, MA.	3/26/31
Nixon, Cynthia	New York, NY	4/9/66
Nolte, Nick	Omaha, NE.	2/8/41
Noone, Peter.	Manchester, England, UK	11/5/47
Norman, Jessye	Augusta, GA	9/15/45
Norris, Chuck	Ryan, OK.	3/10/40
Northam, Jeremy	Cambridge, England, UK	12/1/61
Norton, Edward.	Boston, MA	8/18/69
Noth, Christopher	Madison, WI	11/13/54
Novak, Kim	Chicago, IL.	2/13/33
Nuyen, France	Marseilles, France	7/31/39
Nyong'o, Lupita.	Mexico City, Mexico.	3/1/83
Oates, John	New York, NY	4/7/49
O'Brian, Hugh.	Rochester, NY	4/19/25
O'Brien, Conan	Brookline, MA	4/18/63
O'Brien, Margaret	San Diego, CA.	1/15/37
Ocean, Billy	Fyzabad, Trinidad and Tobago	1/21/50
Ocean, Frank	Long Beach, CA	10/28/87
O'Connor, Sinead	Glenageary, Ireland.	12/8/66
O'Donnell, Chris	Winnetka, IL	6/26/70
O'Donnell, Rosie.	Commack, NY	3/21/62
O'Grady, Gail	Detroit, MI	1/23/63
Oh, Sandra	Nepean, ON, Canada	7/20/71
O'Hara, Catherine.	Toronto, ON, Canada.	3/4/54
O'Hara, Maureen	Dublin, Ireland	8/17/20
O'Hare, Denis	Kansas City, MO	1/17/62
Oka, Masi	Tokyo, Japan.	12/27/74
Oldman, Gary	South London, Eng., UK	3/21/58
Olin, Ken	Chicago, IL	7/30/54
Olin, Lena	Stockholm, Sweden	3/22/55
Oliver, Jamie	Clavering, England, UK	5/27/75
Olmos, Edward James	E. Los Angeles, CA	2/24/47
Olsen, Ashley	Sherman Oaks, CA	6/13/86
Olsen, Mary-Kate	Sherman Oaks, CA	6/13/86
Olson, Nancy	Milwaukee, WI	7/14/28
Olyphant, Timothy	Honolulu, HI	5/20/68
O'Malley, Mike	Boston, MA.	10/31/66
O'Neal, Ryan	Los Angeles, CA	4/20/41
O'Neal, Tatum	Los Angeles, CA	11/5/63
O'Neill, Ed.	Youngstown, OH	4/12/46
Ontkean, Michael	Vancouver, BC, Canada.	1/24/46
O'Quinn, Terry	Newbury, MI	7/15/52
Orlando, Tony	New York, NY	4/3/44
Ormond, Julia	Epsom, England, UK.	1/4/65
Osbourne, Jack	London, England, UK	11/8/85
Osbourne, Kelly	London, England, UK	10/27/84
Osbourne, Ozzy	Birmingham, England, UK.	12/3/48
Osbourne, Sharon	London, England, UK	10/9/52

Name	Birthplace	Birthdate
Osment, Haley Joel	Los Angeles, CA	4/10/88
Osmond, Donny	Ogden, UT	12/9/57
Osmond, Marie	Ogden, UT	10/13/59
O'Toole, Annette	Houston, TX	4/1/51
Owen, Clive	Keresley, England, UK	10/3/64
Oz, Frank	Herford, England, UK	5/25/44
Ozawa, Seiji	Shenyang, China	9/1/35
Pacino, Al	New York, NY	4/25/40
Packer, Billy	Wellsville, NY	2/25/40
Page, Ellen	Halifax, NS, Canada	2/21/87
Page, Jimmy	Heston, England, UK	1/9/44
Paget, Debra	Denver, CO	8/19/33
Paige, Janis	Tacoma, WA	9/16/22
Paisley, Brad	Glen Dale, WV	10/28/72
Palin, Michael	Sheffield, England, UK	5/5/43
Palmer, Betsy	East Chicago, IN	11/1/26
Palmer, Geoffrey	London, England, UK	6/4/27
Palminteri, Chazz	Bronx, NY	5/15/51
Paltrow, Gwyneth	Los Angeles, CA	9/27/72
Panettiere, Hayden	Palisades, NY	8/21/89
Panjabi, Archie	Edgware, England, UK	5/31/72
Pantoliano, Joe	Hoboken, NJ	9/12/51
Papas, Irene	Chiliomodi, Greece	9/3/26
Paquin, Anna	Winnipeg, MB, Canada	7/24/82
Parker, Alan	Islington, England, UK	2/14/44
Parker, Jameson	Baltimore, MD	11/18/47
Parker, Mary-Louise	Fort Jackson, SC	8/2/64
Parker, Sarah Jessica	Nelsonville, OH	3/25/65
Parsons, Estelle	Marblehead, MA	11/20/27
Parsons, Jim	Houston, TX	3/24/73
Parton, Dolly	Sevierville, TN	1/19/46
Pasdar, Adrian	Pittsfield, MA	4/30/65
Patinkin, Mandy	Chicago, IL	11/30/52
Patric, Jason	Queens, NY	6/17/66
Pattinson, Robert	London, England, UK	5/13/86
Patton, Will	Charleston, SC	6/14/54
Paul, Aaron	Emmett, ID	8/27/79
Paul, Adrian	London, England, UK	5/29/59
Paulson, Sarah	Tampa, FL	12/17/75
Paxton, Bill	Fort Worth, TX	5/17/55
Pearce, Guy	Ely, England, UK	10/5/67
Peet, Amanda	New York, NY	1/11/72
Penn, Kal	Montclair, NJ	4/23/77
Penn, Sean	Burbank, CA	8/17/60
Pepper, Barry	Campbell River, BC, Can.	4/4/70
Perez, Rosie	Brooklyn, NY	9/6/64
Perkins, Elizabeth	Queens, NY	11/18/60
Perlman, Itzhak	Tel Aviv, Israel	8/31/45
Perlman, Rhea	Brooklyn, NY	3/31/48
Perlman, Ron	New York, NY	4/13/50
Perrine, Valerie	Galveston, TX	9/3/43
Perry, Katy	Santa Barbara, CA	10/25/84
Perry, Luke	Mansfield, OH	10/11/65
Perry, Matthew	Williamstown, MA	8/19/69
Perry, Tyler	New Orleans, LA	9/13/69
Persoff, Nehemiah	Jerusalem, Israel	8/2/19
Pesci, Joe	Newark, NJ	2/9/43
Peters, Bernadette	Ozone Park, Queens, NY	2/28/48
Peters, Roberta	Bronx, NY	5/4/30
Petersen, Wolfgang	Emden, Germany	3/14/41
Petty, Lori	Chattanooga, TN	10/23/63
Petty, Tom	Gainesville, FL	10/20/50
Pfeiffer, Michelle	Santa Ana, CA	4/29/58
Phair, Liz	New Haven, CT	4/17/67
Philbin, Regis	New York, NY	8/25/31
Phillippe, Ryan	New Castle, DE	9/10/74
Phillips, Lou Diamond	Subic Bay, Philippines	2/17/62
Phillips, Mackenzie	Alexandria, VA	11/10/59
Phillips, Michelle	Long Beach, CA	6/4/44
Phillips, Phillip	Leesburg, GA	9/20/90
Phillips, Sian	Bettws, Wales, UK	5/14/34
Phoenix, Joaquin	San Juan, Puerto Rico	10/28/74
Pierce, David Hyde	Albany, NY	4/3/59
Pinchot, Bronson	New York, NY	5/20/59
Pink	Doylestown, PA	9/8/79
Pinkett Smith, Jada	Baltimore, MD	9/18/71
Pirner, David	Green Bay, WI	4/16/64
Piscopo, Joe	Passaic, NJ	6/17/51
Pitt, Brad	Shawnee, OK	12/18/63
Piven, Jeremy	New York, NY	7/26/65
Plant, Robert	W. Bromwich, England, UK	8/20/48
Plimpton, Martha	New York ,NY	11/16/70
Plowright, Joan	Brigg, England, UK	10/28/29
Plummer, Amanda	New York, NY	3/23/57
Plummer, Christopher	Toronto, ON, Canada	12/13/27
Poehler, Amy	Newton, MA	9/16/71
Poitier, Sidney	Miami, FL	2/20/27
Polanski, Roman	Paris, France	8/18/33
Pompeo, Ellen	Everett, MA	11/10/69
Pop, Iggy	Muskegon, MI	4/21/47
Portman, Natalie	Jerusalem, Israel	6/9/81
Posey, Parker	Baltimore, MD	11/8/68
Post, Markie	Palo Alto, CA	11/4/50
Potente, Franka	Dulmen bei Munster, Germany	7/22/74
Potts, Annie	Nashville, TN	10/28/52
Povich, Maury	Washington, DC	1/17/39
Powell, Jane	Portland, OR	4/1/28
Powers, Stefanie	Hollywood, CA	11/2/42
Prentiss, Paula	San Antonio, TX	3/4/39
Prepon, Laura	Watchung, NJ	3/7/80
Presley, Priscilla	Brooklyn, NY	5/24/45
Pressly, Jaime	Kinston, NC	7/30/77
Previn, Andre	Berlin, Germany	4/6/29
Price, Leontyne	Laurel, MS	2/10/27
Price, Molly	North Plainfield, NJ	12/15/66
Pride, Charley	Sledge, MS	3/18/38
Priestley, Jason	Vancouver, BC, Canada	8/28/69
Prince (The Artist)	Minneapolis, MN	6/7/58
Prince, Faith	Augusta, GA	8/5/57
Principal, Victoria	Fukuoka, Japan	1/3/50
Probst, Jeff	Wichita, KS	11/4/62
Proctor, Emily	Raleigh, NC	10/8/68
Pryce, Jonathan	Holywell, N. Wales, UK	6/1/47
Puck, Wolfgang	St. Veit, Austria	1/8/49
Pulliam, Keshia Knight	Newark, NJ	4/9/79
Pullman, Bill	Hornell, NY	12/17/53
Purcell, Sarah	Richmond, IN	10/8/48
Purefoy, James	Taunton, England, UK	6/3/64
Quaid, Dennis	Houston, TX	4/9/54
Quaid, Randy	Houston, TX	10/1/50
Queen Latifah	Newark, NJ	3/18/70
Quinn, Aidan	Chicago, IL	3/8/59
Quinn, Colin	Brooklyn, NY	6/6/59
Quinn, Martha	Albany, NY	5/11/59
Quinto, Zachary	Pittsburgh, PA	6/2/77
Rachins, Alan	Cambridge, MA	10/3/42
Radcliffe, Daniel	London, England, UK	7/23/89
Radnor, Josh	Columbus, OH	7/29/74
Rae, Charlotte	Milwaukee, WI	4/22/26
Raffi (Cavoukian)	Cairo, Egypt	7/8/48
Rainer, Luise	Düsseldorf, Germany	1/12/1910
Raitt, Bonnie	Burbank, CA	11/8/49
Ramey, Samuel	Colby, KS	3/28/42
Ramirez, Efren	Los Angeles, CA	10/2/73
Ramirez, Sara	Mazatlan, Mexico	8/31/75
Rampling, Charlotte	Sturmer, MA	2/5/46
Rancic, Giuliana	Naples, Italy	8/17/75
Randolph, Joyce	Detroit, MI	10/21/24
Raphael, Sally Jessy	Easton, PA	2/25/35
Rashad, Phylicia	Houston, TX	6/19/48
Ratzenberger, John	Bridgeport, CT	4/6/47
Raver, Kim	New York, NY	3/15/69
Ray, Rachael	Glen Falls, NY	8/25/68
Reddy, Helen	Melbourne, Vic., Australia	10/25/41
Redford, Robert	Santa Monica, CA	8/18/36
Redgrave, Vanessa	London, England, UK	1/30/37
Reed, Rex	Ft. Worth, TX	10/2/38
Reese, Della	Detroit, MI	7/6/31
Reeves, Keanu	Beirut, Lebanon	9/2/64
Reeves, Martha	Eufaula, AL	7/18/41
Regalbuto, Joe	New York, NY	8/24/49
Reid, Tara	Wyckoff, NJ	11/8/75
Reid, Tim	Norfolk, VA	12/19/44
Reid, Vernon	London, England, UK	8/22/58
Reilly, John C.	Chicago, IL	5/24/65
Reiner, Carl	Bronx, NY	3/20/22
Reiner, Rob	Bronx, NY	3/6/47
Reinhold, Judge	Wilmington, DE	5/21/57
Reinking, Ann	Seattle, WA	11/10/49
Reiser, Paul	New York, NY	3/30/57
Reitman, Ivan	Komarno, Czechoslovakia	10/26/46
Remini, Leah	Brooklyn, NY	6/15/70
Renner, Jeremy	Modesto, CA	1/7/71
Reynolds, Burt	Waycross, GA	2/11/36
Reynolds, Debbie	El Paso, TX	4/1/32
Reynolds, Ryan	Vancouver, BC, Canada	10/23/76
Reznor, Trent	Mercer, PA	5/17/65
Rhames, Ving	New York, NY	5/12/59
Rhimes, Shonda	Chicago, IL	1/13/70
Rhymes, Busta	Brooklyn, NY	5/20/72
Rhys, Matthew	Cardiff, Wales, UK	11/4/74
Rhys Meyers, Jonathan	Dublin, Ireland	7/27/77
Ribisi, Giovanni	Los Angeles, CA	12/17/74
Ricci, Christina	Santa Monica, CA	2/12/80
Richards, Denise	Downers Grove, IL	2/17/71
Richards, Keith	Dartford, Kent, Eng., UK	12/18/43
Richards, Michael	Culver City, CA	7/24/49
Richardson, Kevin	Lexington, KY	10/3/71
Richardson, Miranda	Lancashire, England, UK	3/3/58
Richardson, Patricia	Bethesda, MD	2/23/51
Richie, Lionel	Tuskegee, AL	6/20/49
Richie, Nicole	Berkeley, CA	9/21/81
Richter, Andy	Grand Rapids, MI	10/28/66
Rickles, Don	Jackson Heights, Queens, NY	5/8/26
Rickman, Alan	Hammersmith, Eng., UK	2/21/46
Riegert, Peter	New York, NY	4/11/47
Rigg, Diana	Doncaster, England, UK	7/20/38
Rihanna	St. Michael, Barbados	2/20/88
Riley, Amber	Long Beach, CA	2/15/86
Rimes, LeAnn	Jackson, MS	8/28/82
Ringwald, Molly	Roseville, CA	2/18/68
Ripa, Kelly	Stratford, NJ	10/2/70

Name	Birthplace	Birthdate
Rivera, Chita	Washington, DC	1/23/33
Rivera, Geraldo	New York, NY	7/4/43
Robbins, Tim	W. Covina, CA	10/16/58
Roberts, Doris	St. Louis, MO.	11/4/25
Roberts, Eric	Biloxi, MS	4/18/56
Roberts, Julia	Smyrna, GA.	10/28/67
Roberts, Tony	New York, NY	10/22/39
Robinson, Smokey	Detroit, MI	2/19/40
Rock, Chris	Andrews, SC	2/7/65
Rodgers, Jimmy	Camas, WA	9/18/33
Rodriguez, Johnny	Sabinal, TX	12/10/51
Rodriguez, Michelle	Bexar County, TX.	7/12/78
Rogan, Joe	Newark, NJ	8/11/67
Rogen, Seth	Vancouver, BC, Canada.	4/15/82
Rogers, Kenny	Houston, TX	8/21/38
Rogers, Mimi	Coral Gables, FL	1/27/56
Rogers, Wayne	Birmingham, AL.	4/7/33
Rohm, Elisabeth	Dusseldorf, Germany.	4/28/73
Rollins, Henry	Washington, DC	2/13/61
Rollins, Sonny	New York, NY	9/7/30
Romano, Ray	Forest Hills, Queens, NY	12/21/57
Romijn, Rebecca	Berkeley, CA	11/6/72
Ronstadt, Linda	Tucson, AZ	7/15/46
Root, Stephen	Sarasota, FL	11/17/51
Rose, Axl	Lafayette, IN	2/6/62
Rose Marie	New York, NY	8/15/23
Roseanne	Salt Lake City, UT	11/3/52
Ross, Charlotte	Winnetka, IL	1/21/68
Ross, Diana	Detroit, MI	3/26/44
Ross, Katharine	Hollywood, CA.	1/29/40
Ross, Marion	Albert Lea, MN	10/25/28
Rossdale, Gavin	London, England, UK	10/30/65
Rossellini, Isabella	Rome, Italy	6/18/52
Rossum, Emmy	New York, NY	9/12/86
Roth, David Lee	Bloomington, IN.	10/10/55
Roth, Tim	London, England, UK	5/14/61
Rotten, Johnny	London, England, UK	1/31/56
Roundtree, Richard.	New Rochelle, NY	7/9/42
Rourke, Mickey	Schenectady, NY	9/16/52
Routh, Brandon	Des Moines, IA	10/9/79
Routledge, Patricia	Birkenhead, England, UK	2/17/29
Rowan, Kelly	Ottawa, ON, Canada	10/26/65
Rowlands, Gena	Cambria, WI	6/19/30
Rubinstein, John.	Beverly Hills, CA	12/8/46
Rudd, Paul	Passaic, NJ	4/6/1969
Rudner, Rita	Miami, FL	9/17/55?
Rudolph, Maya	Gainesville, FL	7/27/72
Ruehl, Mercedes	Jackson Heights, Queens, NY	2/28/48
Ruffalo, Mark.	Kenosha, WI	11/22/67
Rupp, Debra Jo.	Glendale, CA	2/24/51
Rush, Barbara	Denver, CO	1/4/27
Rush, Geoffrey	Toowoomba, Qld., Australia.	7/6/51
Russell, Keri	Fountain Valley, CA	3/23/76
Russell, Kurt.	Springfield, MA	3/17/51
Russell, Leon	Lawton, OK	4/2/41
Russell, Mark	Buffalo, NY	8/23/32
Russell, Theresa	San Diego, CA.	3/20/57
Russo, Rene	Burbank, CA	2/17/54
Ruttan, Susan	Oregon City, OR	9/16/50
Ryan, Meg	Fairfield, CT.	11/19/61
Ryan, Roz	Detroit, MI	7/7/51
Rydell, Bobby	Philadelphia, PA	4/26/42
Ryder, Winona	Winona, MN	10/29/71
Sabato, Antonio, Jr.	Rome, Italy	2/29/72
Sade (Adu)	Ibadan, Nigeria	1/16/59
Sagal, Katey	Hollywood, CA.	1/19/54
Saget, Bob	Philadelphia, PA	5/17/56
Sagnier, Ludivine	La Celle-St.-Cloud, France.	7/3/79
Sahl, Mort	Montreal, QC, Canada.	5/11/27
Saint, Eva Marie	Newark, NJ	7/4/24
St. James, Susan	Hollywood, CA.	8/14/46
St. John, Jill	Los Angeles, CA	8/19/40
St. Patrick, Mathew.	Philadelphia, PA	3/17/68
Sajak, Pat	Chicago, IL	10/26/46
Saks, Gene	New York, NY	11/8/21
Saldana, Zoë	Passaic, NJ	6/19/78
Salling, Mark.	Dallas, TX	8/17/82
Salonga, Lea	Manila, Philippines	2/22/71
Samberg, Andy	Berkeley, CA	8/18/78
Samms, Emma	London, England, UK	8/28/60
San Giacomo, Laura.	Hoboken, NJ	11/14/62
Sandler, Adam	Brooklyn, NY	9/9/66
Sands, Julian	West Yorkshire, Eng., UK.	1/15/58
Santana, Carlos	Autlan, Mexico.	7/20/47
Sara, Mia	Brooklyn, NY	6/19/67
Sarandon, Susan	New York, NY	10/4/46
Sartain, Gailard.	Tulsa, OK	9/18/46
Savage, Ben	Highland Park, IL.	9/13/80
Savage, Fred	Highland Park, IL.	7/9/76
Sawa, Devon.	Vancouver, BC, Canada.	9/7/78
Saxon, John	Brooklyn, NY	8/5/36
Sayles, John	Schenectady, NY.	9/28/50
Scacchi, Greta	Milan, Italy.	2/18/60
Scaggs, Boz	Canton, OH	6/8/44
Scales, Prunella	Sutton Abinger, Eng., UK.	6/22/32
Scalia, Jack	Brooklyn, NY	11/10/51

Name	Birthplace	Birthdate
Schallert, William	Los Angeles, CA	7/6/22
Schiff, Richard	Bethesda, MD	5/27/55
Schiffer, Claudia	Rheinbach, Germany.	8/25/70
Schneider, John	Mt. Kisco, NY.	4/8/60
Schneider, Rob	San Francisco, CA.	10/31/63
Schram, Bitty	New York, NY	7/17/68
Schreiber, Liev	San Francisco, CA.	10/4/67
Schroder, Rick	Staten Island, NY.	4/13/70
Schwarzenegger, Arnold.	Thal, Austria	7/30/47
Schwimmer, David	Astoria, Queens, NY	11/2/66
Sciorra, Annabella	Wethersfield, CT	3/24/64
Scolari, Peter	New Rochelle, NY	9/12/54
Scorsese, Martin.	Flushing, Queens, NY	11/17/42
Scott, Lizabeth	Scranton, PA	9/29/22
Scott, Ridley	South Shields, England, UK.	11/30/37
Scott, Seann William.	Cottage Grove, MN	10/3/76
Scott Thomas, Kristin	Redruth, England, UK	5/24/60
Scotto, Renata	Savona, Italy	2/24/34
Scully, Vin	Bronx, NY	11/29/27
Seacrest, Ryan	Atlanta, GA	12/24/74
Seagal, Steven	Lansing, MI	4/10/51
Secor, Kyle	Tacoma, WA	5/31/57
Sedaka, Neil	Brooklyn, NY	3/13/39
Sedgwick, Kyra	New York, NY	8/19/65
Segal, George	Great Neck, NY	2/13/34
Segel, Jason	Los Angeles, CA	1/18/80
Seidelman, Susan	Abington, PA	12/11/52
Seinfeld, Jerry.	Brooklyn, NY	4/29/54
Sellecca, Connie	Bronx, NY	5/25/55
Selleck, Tom.	Detroit, MI	1/29/45
Severinsen, Doc	Arlington, OR.	7/7/27
Sevigny, Chloë	Springfield, MA	11/18/74
Sewell, Rufus	Twickenham, Middlesex, England, UK	10/29/67
Seyfried, Amanda	Allentown, PA	12/3/85
Seymour, Jane	Hillingdon, England, UK.	2/15/51
Shackelford, Ted	Oklahoma City, OK	6/23/46
Shaffer, Paul	Thunder Bay, ON, Canada.	11/28/49
Shakira (Mebarak Ripoll)	Barranquilla, Colombia	2/2/77
Shalhoub, Tony	Green Bay, WI	10/9/53
Shandling, Garry.	Chicago, IL	11/29/49
Shannon, Molly	Shaker Heights, OH.	9/16/64
Sharif, Omar	Alexandria, Egypt	4/10/32
Shatner, William	Montreal, QC, Canada.	3/22/31
Shaughnessy, Charles.	London, England, UK	2/9/55
Shaver, Helen	St. Thomas, ON, Canada.	2/24/51
Shawkat, Alia	Riverside, CA.	4/18/89
Shea, John	North Conway, NH.	4/14/49
Shearer, Harry	Los Angeles, CA	12/23/43
Sheedy, Ally	New York, NY	6/13/62
Sheen, Charlie	Los Angeles, CA	9/3/65
Sheen, Martin.	Dayton, OH	8/3/40
Sheen, Michael.	Newport, Wales, UK	2/5/69
Sheindlin, Judy	Brooklyn, NY	10/21/42
Shelley, Carole	London, England, UK	8/16/39
Shelton, Blake	Ada, OK	6/18/76
Shepard, Sam.	Ft. Sheridan, IL	11/5/43
Shepherd, Cybill	Memphis, TN	2/18/50
Shepherd, Sherri	Chicago, IL	4/22/67
Sheridan, Nicollette.	Worthing, England, UK	11/21/63
Shields, Brooke.	New York, NY	5/31/65
Shire, Talia	Lake Success, NY.	4/25/46
Short, Martin.	Hamilton, ON., Canada.	3/26/50
Shortz, Will	Crawfordsville, IN.	8/26/52
Show, Grant	Detroit, MI.	2/27/62
Shue, Andrew	South Orange, NJ	2/20/67
Shue, Elisabeth	Wilmington, DE	10/6/63
Shyamalan, M. Night.	Pondicherry, India	8/6/70
Sidibe, Gabourey	Brooklyn, NY	5/6/83
Sigler, Jamie-Lynn	Jericho, NY	5/15/81
Sikking, James B.	Los Angeles, CA	3/5/34
Silverman, Jonathan.	Beverly Hills, CA	8/5/66
Silverman, Sarah	Bedford, NH.	12/1/70
Silverstone, Alicia	San Francisco, CA.	10/4/76
Simmons, Gene	Haifa, Israel	8/25/49
Simmons, Henry.	Stamford, CT.	7/1/70
Simmons, Richard	New Orleans, LA	7/12/48
Simon, Carly	New York, NY	6/25/45
Simon, Paul	Newark, NJ	10/13/41
Simpson, Ashlee	Waco, TX.	10/3/84
Simpson, Jessica	Abilene, TX	7/10/80
Sinatra, Nancy	Jersey City, NJ.	6/8/40
Sinbad	Benton Harbor, MI	11/10/56
Singleton, John.	Los Angeles, CA	1/6/68
Sinise, Gary	Blue Island, IL	3/17/55
Sirico, Tony	Brooklyn, NY	7/29/42
Sisto, Jeremy	Grass Valley, CA	10/6/74
Sizemore, Tom	Detroit, MI	9/29/61
Skerritt, Tom	Detroit, MI.	8/25/33
Slater, Christian	New York, NY	8/18/69
Slater, Helen.	Massapequa, NY.	12/15/63
Slattery, John	Boston, MA.	8/13/62
Sledge, Percy	Leighton, AL	11/25/40
Slezak, Erika	Hollywood, CA.	8/5/46
Slick, Grace	Evanston, IL	10/30/39

Name	Birthplace	Birthdate
Tyler, Steven	Yonkers, NY	3/26/48
Tyson, Cicely	New York, NY	12/19/33
Uecker, Bob	Milwaukee, WI	1/26/35
Uggams, Leslie	New York, NY	5/25/43
Ullman, Tracey	Slough, England, UK	12/30/59
Ullmann, Liv	Tokyo, Japan	12/16/38
Ulrich, Skeet	Lynchburg, VA	1/20/70
Underwood, Blair	Tacoma, WA	8/25/64
Underwood, Carrie	Muskogee, OK	3/10/83
Urban, Keith	Whangarei, North Island, New Zealand	10/26/67
Urie, Michael	Dallas, TX	8/8/80
Usher (Raymond IV)	Dallas, TX	10/14/78
Vaccaro, Brenda	Brooklyn, NY	11/18/39
Valley, Mark	Ogdensburg, NY	12/24/64
Valli, Frankie	Newark, NJ	5/3/34
Van Ark, Joan	New York, NY	6/16/43
Van Damme, Jean-Claude	Brussels, Belgium	10/18/60
Van Der Beek, James	Cheshire, CT	3/8/77
Van Doren, Mamie	Rowena, SD	2/6/31
Van Dyke, Dick	West Plains, MO	12/13/25
Van Dyke, Jerry	Danville, IL	7/27/31
Van Halen, Eddie	Nijmegen, Netherlands	1/26/55
Van Patten, Dick	Kew Gardens, Queens, NY	12/9/28
Van Peebles, Mario	Mexico City, Mexico	1/15/57
Van Sant, Gus	Louisville, KY	7/24/52
Van Zandt, Steven	Winthrop, MA	11/22/50
VanCamp, Emily	Port Perry, ON, Canada	5/12/86
Vance, Courtney B.	Detroit, MI	3/12/60
Vardalos, Nia	Winnipeg, MB, Canada	9/24/62
Vaughn, Robert	New York, NY	11/22/32
Vaughn, Vince	Minneapolis, MN	3/28/70
Vedder, Eddie	Evanston, IL	12/23/64
Vega, Alexa	Miami, FL	8/27/88
Ventimiglia, Milo	Anaheim, CA	7/8/77
Vereen, Ben	Miami, FL	10/10/46
Vergara, Sofia	Barranquilla, Colombia	7/10/72
Vickers, Jon	Prince Albert, SK, Canada	10/29/26
Vieira, Meredith	Providence, RI	12/30/53
Vigoda, Abe	New York, NY	2/24/21
Villella, Edward	Long Island, NY	10/1/36
Vincent, Jan-Michael	Denver, CO	7/15/44
Vinton, Bobby	Canonsburg, PA	4/16/35
Visnjic, Goran	Sibenik, Yugo. (Croatia)	9/9/72
Vitale, Dick	East Rutherford, NJ	6/9/39
Voight, Jon	Yonkers, NY	12/29/38
Von Stade, Frederica	Somerville, NJ	6/1/45
Von Sydow, Max	Lund, Sweden	4/10/29
Von Trier, Lars	Copenhagen, Denmark	4/30/56
Wagner, Jack	Washington, MO	10/3/59
Wagner, Lindsay	Los Angeles, CA	6/22/49
Wagner, Robert	Detroit, MI	2/10/30
Wahl, Ken	Chicago, IL	10/31/54
Wahlberg, Donnie	Dorchester, MA	8/17/69
Wahlberg, Mark	Dorchester, MA	6/5/71
Wain, Bea	Bronx, NY	4/30/17
Waits, Tom	Pomona, CA	12/7/49
Walden, Robert	New York, NY	9/25/43
Walken, Christopher	Astoria, Queens, NY	3/31/43
Walker, Clint	Hartford, IL	5/30/27
Wallis, Quvenzhané	Houma, LA	8/23/2008
Walsh, Kate	San Jose, CA	10/13/67
Walter, Jessica	Brooklyn, NY	1/31/41
Waltz, Christoph	Vienna, Austria	10/4/56
Warburton, Patrick	Paterson, NJ	11/14/64
Ward, Fred	San Diego, CA	12/30/42
Ward, Sela	Meridian, MS	7/11/56
Warfield, Marsha	Chicago, IL	3/5/54
Warner, Malcolm-Jamal	Jersey City, NJ	8/18/70
Warren, Lesley Ann	New York, NY	8/16/46
Warwick, Dionne	East Orange, NJ	12/12/40
Washington, Denzel	Mt. Vernon, NY	12/28/54
Washington, Isaiah	Houston, TX	8/3/63
Washington, Kerry	Bronx, NY	1/31/77
Wasikowska, Mia	Canberra, Australia	10/14/89
Watanabe, Ken	Koide, Niigata, Japan	10/21/59
Waters, John	Baltimore, MD	4/22/46
Waters, Roger	Great Bookham, Eng., UK	9/6/43
Waterston, Sam	Cambridge, MA	11/15/40
Watson, Emily	London, England, UK	1/14/67
Watson, Emma	Paris, France	4/15/90
Watts, Naomi	Shoreham, England, UK	9/28/68
Wayans, Damon	New York, NY	9/4/60
Wayans, Keenen Ivory	Brooklyn, NY	6/8/58
Wayans, Marlon	New York, NY	7/23/72
Wayans, Shawn	New York, NY	1/19/71
Weathers, Carl	New Orleans, LA	1/14/48
Weaver, Fritz	Pittsburgh, PA	1/19/26
Weaver, Sigourney	New York, NY	10/8/49
Weiland, Scott	Santa Cruz, CA	10/27/67
Weir, Peter	Sydney, NSW, Australia	8/21/44
Weisz, Rachel	London, England, UK	3/7/71
Weitz, Bruce	Norwalk, CT	5/27/43
Welch, Raquel	Chicago, IL	9/5/40
Weld, Tuesday	New York, NY	8/27/43

Name	Birthplace	Birthdate
Weller, Peter	Stevens Point, WI	6/24/47
Welling, Tom	Putnam Valley, NY	4/26/77
Wendt, George	Chicago, IL	10/17/48
Wentz, Pete	Wilmette, IL	6/5/79
West, Adam	Walla Walla, WA	9/19/28
West, Kanye	Atlanta, GA	6/8/77
West, Shane	Baton Rouge, LA	6/10/78
Wettig, Patricia	Cincinnati, OH	12/4/51
Whalley, Joanne	Manchester, England, UK	8/25/64
Wheaton, Wil	Burbank, CA	7/29/72
Whitaker, Forest	Longview, TX	7/15/61
White, Betty	Oak Park, IL	1/17/22
White, Jack	Detroit, MI	7/9/75
White, Jaleel	Pasadena, CA	11/27/76
White, Vanna	N. Myrtle Beach, SC	2/18/57
Whitford, Bradley	Madison, WI	10/10/59
Wiest, Dianne	Kansas City, MO	3/28/48
Wiig, Kristen	Canandaigua, NY	8/22/73
Wilde, Olivia	New York, NY	3/10/84
Wilder, Gene	Milwaukee, WI	6/11/33
Wilkinson, Tom	Leeds, England, UK	12/12/48
Williams, Armstrong	Marion, SC	2/5/59
Williams, Barry	Santa Monica, CA	9/30/54
Williams, Billy Dee	New York, NY	4/6/37
Williams, Cindy	Van Nuys, CA	8/22/47
Williams, Hal	Columbus, OH	12/14/38
Williams, Hank, Jr.	Shreveport, LA	5/26/49
Williams, JoBeth	Houston, TX	12/6/48
Williams, Kimberly	Rye, NY	9/14/71
Williams, Lucinda	Lake Charles, LA	1/26/53
Williams, Michelle	Kalispell, MT	9/9/80
Williams, Montel	Baltimore, MD	7/3/56
Williams, Paul	Omaha, NE	9/19/40
Williams, Pharrell	Virginia Beach, VA	4/5/73
Williams, Treat	Rowayton, CT	12/1/51
Williams, Vanessa	Millwood, NY	3/18/63
Williamson, Kevin	New Bern, NC	3/14/65
Willis, Bruce	Idar-Oberstein, W. Germany	3/19/55
Wilson, Brian	Inglewood, CA	6/20/42
Wilson, Cassandra	Jackson, MS	12/4/55
Wilson, Chandra	Houston, TX	8/27/69
Wilson, Demond	Valdosta, GA	10/13/46
Wilson, Elizabeth	Grand Rapids, MI	4/4/21
Wilson, Luke	Dallas, TX	9/21/71
Wilson, Nancy	Chillicothe, OH	2/20/37
Wilson, Owen	Dallas, TX	11/18/68
Wilson, Rainn	Seattle, WA	1/20/66
Wilson, Rebel	Sydney, NSW, Australia	2/3/86
Winfrey, Oprah	Kosciusko, MS	1/29/54
Winger, Debra	Cleveland, OH	5/16/55
Winkler, Henry	New York, NY	10/30/45
Winningham, Mare	Phoenix, AZ	5/16/59
Winokur, Marissa Jaret	New York, NY	2/2/73
Winslet, Kate	Reading, England, UK	10/5/75
Winwood, Steve	Birmingham, England, UK	5/12/48
Withers, Jane	Atlanta, GA	4/12/26
Witherspoon, Reese	New Orleans, LA	3/22/76
Witt, Alicia	Worcester, MA	8/21/75
Wolf, Scott	Boston, MA	6/4/68
Wonder, Stevie	Saginaw, MI	5/13/50
Wong, Faye	Beijing, China	8/8/69
Woo, John	Guangzhou, China	5/1/46
Wood, Elijah	Cedar Rapids, IA	1/28/81
Woodard, Alfre	Tulsa, OK	11/8/52
Woods, James	Vernal, UT	4/18/47
Woodward, Joanne	Thomasville, GA	2/27/30
Wopat, Tom	Lodi, WI	9/9/51
Worthington Sam	Godalming, Surrey, Eng., UK	8/2/76
Wright, Jeffrey	Washington, DC	12/7/65
Wright, Max	Detroit, MI	8/2/43
Wright, Robin	Dallas, TX	4/8/66
Wright, Steven	New York, NY	12/6/55
Wyle, Noah	Hollywood, CA	6/4/71
Wyman, Bill	London, England, UK	10/24/36
Yankovic, Weird Al	Lynwood, CA	10/23/59
Yanni (Chrysomallis)	Kalamata, Greece	11/14/54
Yarrow, Peter	New York, NY	5/31/38
Yearwood, Trisha	Monticello, GA	9/19/64
Yoakam, Dwight	Pikesville, KY	10/23/56
York, Michael	Fulmer, England, UK	3/27/42
Young, Alan	North Shields, England, UK	11/19/19
Young, Burt	New York, NY	4/30/40
Young, Neil	Toronto, ON, Canada	11/12/45
Young, Sean	Louisville, KY	11/20/59
Zane, Billy	Chicago, IL	2/24/66
Zeffirelli, Franco	Florence, Italy	2/12/23
Zellweger, Renée	Katy, TX	4/25/69
Zemeckis, Robert	Chicago, IL	5/14/52
Zerbe, Anthony	Long Beach, CA	5/20/36
Zeta-Jones, Catherine	Swansea, Wales, UK	9/25/69
Zimbalist, Stephanie	New York, NY	10/8/56
Zimmer, Kim	Grand Rapids, MI	2/2/55
Zhang, Ziyi	Beijing, China	2/9/79
Zukerman, Pinchas	Tel Aviv, Israel	7/16/48
Zuniga, Daphne	Berkeley, CA	10/28/62

Entertainment Personalities of the Past

See also other lists for some deceased entertainers not included here.

Name	Born	Died
Aaliyah (Haughton)	1979	2001
Abbado, Claudio	1933	2014
Abbott, Bud	1895	1974
Abbott, George	1887	1995
Acuff, Roy	1903	1992
Adams, Don	1923	2005
Adams, Edie	1927	2008
Adams, Joey	1911	1999
Adams, Maude	1872	1953
Adler, Jacob P.	1855	1926
Adoree, Renee	1898	1933
Agar, John	1921	2002
Aherne, Brian	1902	1986
Ailey, Alvin	1931	1989
Akins, Claude	1918	1994
Albert, Eddie	1906	2005
Albertson, Frank	1909	1964
Albertson, Jack	1907	1981
Alda, Robert	1914	1986
Allen, Fred	1894	1956
Allen, Gracie	1906	1964
Allen, Mel	1913	1996
Allen, Peter	1944	1992
Allen, Steve	1921	2000
Allgood, Sara	1883	1950
Allyson, June	1917	2006
Altman, Robert	1925	2006
Ameche, Don	1908	1993
Ames, Leon	1903	1993
Amsterdam, Morey	1908	1996
Anderson, G. M. "Bronco Billy"	1882	1971
Anderson, Judith	1897	1992
Anderson, Marian	1897	1993
Andre the Giant	1946	1993
Andrews, Dana	1909	1992
Andrews, Laverne	1913	1967
Andrews, Maxene	1916	1995
Andrews, Patty	1918	2013
Angeli, Pier	1932	1971
Antonioni, Michelangelo	1912	2007
Arbuckle, Fatty (Roscoe)	1887	1933
Archerd, Army	1922	2009
Arden, Eve	1908	1990
Arlen, Richard	1900	1976
Arliss, George	1868	1946
Armstrong, Louis	1901	1971
Arnaz, Desi	1917	1986
Arness, James	1923	2011
Arnold, Eddy	1918	2008
Arnold, Edward	1890	1956
Arquette, Cliff	1905	1974
Arthur, Beatrice	1922	2009
Arthur, Jean	1900	1991
Arzner, Dorothy	1897	1979
Ashcroft, Peggy	1907	1991
Astaire, Fred	1899	1987
Astor, Mary	1906	1987
Atkins, Chet	1924	2001
Attenborough, Richard	1923	2014
Atwill, Lionel	1885	1946
Auer, Mischa	1905	1967
Aumont, Jean-Pierre	1911	2001
Austin, Gene	1900	1972
Autry, Gene	1907	1998
Axton, Hoyt	1938	1999
Ayres, Lew	1908	1996
Bacall, Lauren	1924	2014
Backus, Jim	1913	1989
Bailey, Pearl	1918	1990
Bain, Conrad	1923	2013
Bainter, Fay	1892	1968
Baker, Josephine	1906	1975
Balanchine, George	1904	1983
Ball, Lucille	1911	1989
Balsam, Martin	1919	1996
Bancroft, Anne	1931	2005
Bankhead, Tallulah	1902	1968
Bara, Theda	1885?	1955
Barnett, Etta Moten	1902	2004
Barnum, Phineas T.	1810	1891
Barrett, Syd	1946	2006
Barry, Gene	1919	2009
Barrymore, Ethel	1879	1959
Barrymore, John	1882	1942
Barrymore, Lionel	1878	1954
Barrymore, Maurice	1848	1905
Barthelmess, Richard	1895	1963
Bartholomew, Freddie	1924	1992
Barty, Billy	1924	2000
Basehart, Richard	1914	1984
Basie, Count	1904	1984
Bates, Alan	1934	2003
Bavier, Frances	1902	1989
Baxter, Anne	1923	1985
Baxter, Warner	1889	1951
Beaumont, Hugh	1909	1982
Beavers, Louise	1902	1962
Beery, Noah, Jr.	1913	1994
Beery, Noah, Sr.	1884	1946
Beery, Wallace	1885	1949
Begley, Ed	1901	1970
Bel Geddes, Barbara	1922	2005
Bellamy, Ralph	1904	1991
Belushi, John	1949	1982
Benaderet, Bea	1906	1968
Bendix, William	1906	1964
Bennett, Constance	1904	1965
Bennett, Joan	1910	1990
Bennett, Michael	1943	1987
Benny, Jack	1894	1974
Berg, Gertrude	1899	1966
Bergen, Edgar	1903	1978
Bergen, Polly	1930	2014
Bergman, Ingmar	1918	2007
Bergman, Ingrid	1915	1982
Berkeley, Busby	1895	1976
Berle, Milton	1908	2002
Berlin, Irving	1888	1989
Bernardi, Herschel	1923	1986
Bernhardt, Sarah	1844	1923
Bernstein, Leonard	1918	1990
Berry, Jan	1941	2004
Bessell, Ted	1935	1996
Bickford, Charles	1889	1967
Big Bopper, The	1930	1959
Billingsley, Barbara	1915	2010
Bing, Rudolf	1902	1997
Bishop, Joey	1918	2007
Bitzer, Billy	1872	1944
Bixby, Bill	1934	1993
Black, Karen	1939	2013
Blackstone, Harry, Jr.	1934	1997
Blackstone, Harry, Sr.	1885	1965
Blaine, Vivian	1921	1995
Blake, Amanda	1931	1989
Blake, Eubie	1883	1983
Blanc, Mel	1908	1989
Blocker, Dan	1928	1972
Blondell, Joan	1909	1979
Blondin, Charles	1824	1897
Blore, Eric	1887	1959
Blue, Ben	1901	1975
Blyden, Larry	1925	1975
Bogarde, Dirk	1921	1999
Bogart, Humphrey	1899	1957
Boland, Mary	1880	1965
Boles, John	1895	1969
Bolger, Ray	1904	1987
Bond, Ward	1903	1960
Bondi, Beulah	1888	1981
Bono, Sonny	1935	1998
Boone, Richard	1917	1981
Booth, Edwin	1833	1893
Booth, John Wilkes	1838	1865
Booth, Junius Brutus	1796	1852
Booth, Shirley	1898	1992
Borge, Victor	1909	2000
Borgnine, Ernest	1917	2012
Borzage, Frank	1893	1962
Bosley, Tom	1927	2010
Bow, Clara	1905	1965
Bowes, Maj. Edward	1874	1946
Bowman, Lee	1914	1979
Boxcar Willie	1931	1999
Boyd, Stephen	1928	1977
Boyd, William	1898	1972
Boyer, Charles	1899	1978
Boyle, Peter	1935	2006
Bracken, Eddie	1915	2002
Brady, Alice	1892	1939
Brando, Marlon	1924	2004
Branigan, Laura	1957	2004
Brazzi, Rossano	1916	1994
Brennan, Eileen	1932	2013
Brennan, Walter	1894	1974
Brenner, David	1936	2014
Brent, George	1904	1979
Brett, Jeremy	1935	1995
Brewer, Teresa	1931	2007
Brice, Fanny	1891	1951
Bridges, Lloyd	1913	1998
Broderick, Helen	1891	1959
Bronson, Charles	1921	2003
Brooks, Foster	1912	2001
Brooks, Louise	1906	1985
Brown, Clarence	1890	1987
Brown, James	1933	2006
Brown, Joe E.	1892	1973
Brown, Les	1912	2001
Browne, Roscoe Lee	1925	2007
Browning, Tod	1882	1962
Brubeck, Dave	1920	2012
Bruce, Lenny	1925	1966
Bruce, Nigel	1895	1953
Bruce, Virginia	1910	1982
Brynner, Yul	1915	1985
Buchanan, Edgar	1903	1979
Buchholz, Horst	1933	2003
Buñuel, Luis	1900	1983
Buono, Victor	1938	1982
Burke, Billie	1885	1970
Burnette, Smiley	1911	1967
Burns, George	1896	1996
Burr, Raymond	1917	1993
Burton, Richard	1925	1984
Busch, Mae	1897	1946
Bushman, Francis X.	1883	1966
Buttons, Red	1919	2006
Byington, Spring	1893	1971
Cabot, Bruce	1904	1972
Cabot, Sebastian	1918	1977
Caesar, Sid	1922	2014
Cagney, James	1899	1986
Caldwell, Sarah	1924	2006
Calhern, Louis	1895	1956
Calhoun, Rory	1922	1999
Callas, Charlie	1927	2011
Callas, Maria	1923	1977
Calloway, Cab	1907	1994
Cambridge, Godfrey	1933	1976
Campbell, Mrs. Patrick	1865	1940
Candy, John	1950	1994
Cantinflas	1911	1993
Cantor, Eddie	1892	1964
Capra, Frank	1897	1991
Carey, Harry	1878	1947
Carey, Harry, Jr.	1921	2012
Carey, Macdonald	1913	1994
Carle, Frankie	1903	2001
Carlin, George	1937	2008
Carlisle Hart, Kitty	1910	2007
Carney, Art	1918	2003
Carpenter, Karen	1950	1983
Carradine, David	1936	2009
Carradine, John	1906	1988
Carrillo, Leo	1880	1961
Carroll, Leo G.	1892	1972
Carroll, Madeleine	1906	1987
Carson, Jack	1910	1963
Carson, Johnny	1925	2005
Carter, Benny	1907	2003
Carter, Dixie	1939	2010
Carter, Nell	1948	2003
Caruso, Enrico	1873	1921
Casals, Pablo	1876	1973
Cash, Johnny	1932	2003
Cash, June Carter	1929	2003
Cass, Peggy	1924	1999
Cassavetes, John	1929	1989
Cassidy, Jack	1927	1976
Castle, Irene	1893	1969
Castle, Vernon	1887	1918
Chaliapin, Feodor	1873	1938
Champion, Gower	1919	1980
Chandler, Jeff	1918	1961
Chaney, Lon	1883	1930
Chaney, Lon, Jr.	1905	1973
Chapin, Harry	1942	1981
Chaplin, Charles	1889	1977
Chapman, Graham	1941	1989
Charisse, Cyd	1921	2008
Charles, Ray	1930	2004
Chase, Ilka	1905	1978
Chatterton, Ruth	1893	1961
Cherrill, Virginia	1908	1996
Chevalier, Maurice	1888	1972
Child, Julia	1912	2004
Clair, René	1898	1981
Clark, Dick	1929	2012
Clayburgh, Jill	1944	2010
Clayton, Jan	1917	1983
Clemons, Clarence	1942	2011
Cliburn, Van	1934	2013
Clift, Montgomery	1920	1966
Cline, Patsy	1932	1963
Clooney, Rosemary	1928	2002
Clyde, Andy	1892	1967
Cobain, Kurt	1967	1994
Cobb, Lee J.	1911	1976
Coburn, Charles	1877	1961
Coburn, James	1928	2002
Coca, Imogene	1908	2001

Name	Born	Died	Name	Born	Died	Name	Born	Died
Coco, James	1930	1987	Dee, Ruby	1924	2014	Fassbinder, Rainer Werner	1946	1982
Cody, Buffalo Bill	1846	1917	Dee, Sandra	1942	2005	Fawcett, Farrah	1947	2009
Cody, Iron Eyes	1907	1999	Defore, Don	1917	1993	Faye, Alice	1915	1998
Cohan, George M.	1878	1942	Dekker, Albert	1905	1968	Fazenda, Louise	1895	1962
Cohen, Myron	1902	1986	Del Rio, Dolores	1905	1983	Feld, Fritz	1900	1993
Colbert, Claudette	1903	1996	DeLuise, Dom	1933	2009	Feldman, Marty	1933	1982
Cole, Nat "King"	1919	1965	Demarest, William	1892	1983	Fell, Norman	1924	1998
Coleman, Gary	1968	2010	Dennis, Sandy	1937	1992	Fellini, Federico	1920	1993
Collins, Gary	1938	2012	Denny, Reginald	1891	1967	Fenneman, George	1919	1997
Collins, Ray	1890	1965	Denver, Bob.	1935	2005	Ferrer, Jose	1912	1992
Colman, Ronald	1891	1958	Denver, John	1943	1997	Ferrer, Mel.	1917	2008
Columbo, Russ	1908	1934	Derek, John.	1926	1998	Fetchit, Stepin	1898	1985
Comden, Betty	1917	2006	DeSica, Vittorio	1901	1974	Fiedler, Arthur	1894	1979
Como, Perry	1912	2001	Devine, Andy	1905	1977	Fiedler, John	1925	2005
Conniff, Ray	1916	2002	Dewhurst, Colleen	1924	1991	Fields, Gracie	1898	1979
Connors, Chuck	1921	1992	Diamond, Selma	1920	1985	Fields, Totie	1930	1978
Conrad, William	1920	1994	Diddley, Bo	1928	2008	Fields, W. C.	1879	1946
Conried, Hans	1917	1982	Dietrich, Marlene	1901	1992	Finch, Peter.	1916	1977
Conte, Richard	1911	1975	Diller, Phyllis	1917	2012	Fine, Larry	1902	1975
Convy, Bert	1933	1991	Disney, Walt.	1901	1966	Fisher, Eddie	1928	2010
Conway, Tom	1904	1967	Dix, Richard.	1894	1949	Fiske, Minnie Maddern	1865	1932
Coogan, Jackie	1914	1984	Dmytryk, Edward	1908	1999	Fitzgerald, Barry	1888	1961
Cook, Elisha, Jr.	1904	1995	Donahue, Troy	1936	2001	Fitzgerald, Ella.	1917	1996
Cooke, Alistair	1908	2004	Donat, Robert	1905	1958	Fitzgerald, Geraldine	1913	2005
Cooke, Sam.	1931	1964	Donlevy, Brian	1901	1972	Fleischer, Richard	1916	2006
Cooper, Gary	1901	1961	Dors, Diana	1931	1984	Fleming, Art.	1924	1995
Cooper, Gladys	1888	1971	Dorsey, Jimmy	1904	1957	Fleming, Victor.	1889	1949
Cooper, Jackie.	1922	2011	Dorsey, Tommy	1905	1956	Flynn, Errol	1909	1959
Copland, Aaron	1900	1990	Douglas, Melvyn	1901	1981	Flynn, Joe	1925	1974
Corby, Ellen.	1913	1999	Douglas, Paul	1907	1959	Foch, Nina	1924	2008
Corelli, Franco	1921	2003	Dove, Billie	1900	1998	Fogelberg, Dan	1951	2007
Corey, Jeff	1914	2002	Downey, Morton, Jr.	1933	2001	Foley, Red	1910	1968
Corio, Ann	1914	1999	Doyle, David	1929	1997	Fonda, Henry	1905	1982
Corley, Pat.	1930	2006	Drake, Alfred	1914	1992	Fontaine, Frank	1920	1978
Cornelius, Don.	1936	2012	Draper, Ruth	1884	1956	Fontaine, Joan.	1917	2013
Cornell, Katharine	1893	1974	Dressler, Marie	1869	1934	Fontaine, Lynn	1887	1983
Correll, Charles	1890	1972	Drew, Ellen	1915	2003	Fonteyn, Margot	1919	1991
Costello, Dolores	1905	1979	Drew, Mrs. John.	1820	1897	Ford, Glenn	1916	2006
Costello, Lou	1906	1959	Dru, Joanne	1923	1996	Ford, John	1895	1973
Cotten, Joseph	1905	1994	Duchin, Eddy	1909	1951	Ford, Paul	1901	1976
Coward, Noel.	1899	1973	Duff, Howard	1917	1990	Ford, Tennessee Ernie.	1919	1991
Cox, Wally	1924	1973	Duggan, Andrew	1923	1988	Forrest, Helen	1917	1999
Crabbe, Buster	1908	1983	Dumbrille, Douglass	1890	1974	Forsythe, John.	1918	2010
Crain, Jeanne	1925	2003	Dumont, Margaret	1889	1965	Fosse, Bob	1927	1987
Crane, Bob	1928	1978	Duncan, Isadora	1878	1927	Foster, Phil	1914	1985
Crawford, Broderick	1911	1986	Duncan, Michael Clarke.	1957	2012	Foster, Preston	1901	1970
Crawford, Joan	1904	1977	Dunham, Katherine	1910	2006	Foxx, Redd	1922	1991
Crenna, Richard	1926	2003	Dunn, James	1905	1967	Foy, Eddie	1856	1928
Crews, Laura Hope	1880	1942	Dunne, Irene	1898	1990	Franchi, Sergio	1926	1990
Crisp, Donald.	1880	1974	Dunnock, Mildred.	1901	1991	Franciosa, Anthony	1928	2006
Crisp, Quentin	1908	1999	Durante, Jimmy	1893	1980	Francis, Anne	1930	2011
Croce, Jim	1942	1973	Durbin, Deanna	1921	2013	Francis, Arlene	1907	2001
Cronyn, Hume	1911	2003	Durning, Charles	1923	2012	Francis, Kay.	1905	1968
Crosby, Bing	1903	1977	Duryea, Dan	1907	1968	Franciscus, James.	1934	1991
Crothers, Scatman.	1910	1986	Duse, Eleanora	1858	1924	Frankenheimer, John	1930	2002
Cruz, Celia	1925	2003	Dvorak, Ann.	1912	1979	Franklin, Bonnie.	1944	2013
Cugat, Xavier	1900	1990	Eagels, Jeanne	1894	1929	Frann, Mary.	1943	1998
Cukor, George	1899	1983	Ebert, Roger	1942	2013	Frawley, William	1887	1966
Cullen, Bill.	1920	1990	Ebsen, Buddy	1908	2003	Frederick, Pauline	1885	1938
Culp, Robert	1930	2010	Eckstine, Billy	1914	1993	Freed, Alan	1921	1965
Cummings, Constance	1910	2005	Eddy, Nelson	1901	1967	Freeman, Al, Jr.	1934	2012
Cummings, Robert	1908	1990	Edelman, Herb	1933	1996	Freeman, Mona	1926	2014
Curtis, Ken	1916	1991	Edwards, Blake	1922	2010	French, Victor	1934	1989
Curtis, Tony	1925	2010	Edwards, Cliff	1895	1971	Friganza, Trixie	1870	1955
Curtiz, Michael	1888	1962	Edwards, Ralph	1913	2005	Froman, Jane	1907	1980
Cushing, Peter.	1913	1994	Edwards, Vince	1928	1996	Frost, David.	1939	2013
Da Silva, Howard	1909	1986	Egan, Richard	1923	1987	Funicello, Annette	1942	2013
Dailey, Dan	1915	1978	Eisenstein, Sergei	1898	1948	Funt, Allen	1914	1999
Dandridge, Dorothy	1923	1965	Elam, Jack.	1916	2003	Furness, Betty	1916	1994
Dangerfield, Rodney	1921	2004	Ellington, Duke	1899	1974	Gabin, Jean.	1904	1976
Daniell, Henry	1894	1963	Elliot, Cass	1941	1974	Gable, Clark	1901	1960
Daniels, Bebe	1901	1971	Elliott, Denholm	1922	1992	Gabor, Eva	1920	1995
Darin, Bobby	1936	1973	Ellis, Mary	1897	2003	Gandolfini, James	1961	2013
Darnell, Linda	1923	1965	Elman, Mischa	1891	1967	Garbo, Greta	1905	1990
Darwell, Jane.	1879	1967	Ephron, Nora	1941	2012	Garcia, Jerry	1942	1995
Davenport, Harry	1866	1949	Errol, Leon.	1881	1951	Gardenia, Vincent	1922	1992
Davies, Marion	1897	1961	Evans, Dale	1912	2001	Gardner, Ava	1922	1990
Davis, Ann B.	1926	2014	Evans, Edith	1888	1976	Garfield, John	1913	1952
Davis, Bette	1908	1989	Evans, Maurice	1901	1989	Garland, Beverly	1926	2008
Davis, Joan	1907	1961	Everett, Chad.	1936?	2012	Garland, Judy	1922	1969
Davis, Ossie	1917	2005	Everly, Phil.	1939	2014	Garner, James	1928	2014
Davis, Sammy, Jr.	1925	1990	Ewell, Tom.	1909	1994	Garrett, Betty	1919	2011
Dawson, Richard	1932	2012	Fadiman, Clifton.	1904	1999	Garson, Greer	1904	1996
Day, Dennis	1917	1988	Fairbanks, Douglas	1883	1939	Gassman, Vittorio	1922	2000
Day, Laraine	1920	2007	Fairbanks, Douglas, Jr.	1909	2000	Gaye, Marvin.	1939	1984
De Carlo, Yvonne	1922	2007	Falk, Peter.	1927	2011	Gaynor, Janet	1906	1984
De Laurentiis, Dino	1919	2010	Farentino, James.	1938	2012	Gazzara, Ben	1930	2012
de Mille, Agnes	1905	1993	Farina, Dennis	1944	2013	Gebel-Williams, Gunther	1934	2001
De Mille, Cecil B.	1881	1959	Farley, Chris	1964	1997	Geer, Will.	1902	1978
De Wilde, Brandon.	1942	1972	Farmer, Frances	1913	1970	George, Gladys	1904	1954
De Wolfe, Billy	1907	1974	Farnsworth, Richard	1920	2000	Gershwin, George	1898	1937
Dean, James	1931	1955	Farnum, Dustin	1874	1929	Getty, Estelle.	1923	2008
Dean, Jimmy	1928	2010	Farnum, William	1876	1953	Ghostley, Alice.	1926	2007
Dearie, Blossom	1924	2009	Farrar, Geraldine	1882	1967	Gibb, Andy.	1958	1988
De Carlo, Yvonne	1922	2007	Farrell, Charles	1901	1990	Gibb, Maurice	1949	2003
Dee, Frances	1907	2004	Farrell, Eileen	1920	2002	Gibb, Robin	1949	2012

Name	Born	Died
Gibson, Henry	1935	2009
Gibson, Hoot	1892	1962
Gielgud, John	1904	2000
Gilbert, Billy	1894	1971
Gilbert, John	1895	1936
Gilford, Jack	1907	1990
Gillespie, Dizzy	1917	1993
Gillette, William	1853	1937
Gingold, Hermione	1897	1987
Gish, Dorothy	1898	1968
Gish, Lillian	1893	1993
Giulini, Carlo Maria	1914	2005
Gleason, Jackie	1916	1987
Gleason, James	1886	1959
Gluck, Alma	1884	1938
Gobel, George	1919	1991
Goddard, Paulette	1905?	1990
Godfrey, Arthur	1903	1983
Godunov, Alexander	1949	1995
Goldwyn, Samuel	1882	1974
Goodman, Benny	1909	1986
Gorcey, Leo	1917	1969
Gordon, Gale	1906	1995
Gordon, Ruth	1896	1985
Gorme, Eydie	1932	2013
Gorshin, Frank	1934	2005
Gosden, Freeman	1899	1982
Gottschalk, Louis	1829	1869
Gould, Glenn	1932	1982
Gould, Harold	1923	2010
Gould, Morton	1913	1996
Goulet, Robert	1933	2007
Grable, Betty	1916	1973
Graham, Martha	1894	1991
Graham, Virginia	1912	1998
Grahame, Gloria	1925	1981
Granger, Farley	1925	2011
Granger, Stewart	1913	1993
Grant, Cary	1904	1986
Granville, Bonita	1923	1988
Grapewin, Charley	1869	1956
Graves, Peter	1926	2010
Gray, Dolores	1924	2002
Gray, Spalding	1941	2004
Grayson, Kathryn	1922	2010
Greco, Jose	1918	2000
Green, Adolph	1915	2002
Greene, Lorne	1915	1987
Greenstreet, Sydney	1879	1954
Greenwood, Charlotte	1890	1978
Gregory, James	1911	2002
Griffin, Merv	1925	2007
Griffith, Andy	1926	2012
Griffith, David Wark	1874	1948
Griffith, Hugh	1912	1980
Griffiths, Richard	1947	2013
Grizzard, George	1928	2007
Guardino, Harry	1925	1995
Guinness, Sir Alec	1914	2000
Guthrie, Woody	1912	1967
Gwenn, Edmund	1875	1959
Gwynne, Fred	1926	1993
Hackett, Buddy	1924	2003
Hackett, Joan	1934	1983
Hagen, Uta	1919	2004
Hagman, Larry	1931	2012
Haines, William	1900	1973
Hale, Alan, Jr.	1918	1990
Hale, Alan, Sr.	1892	1950
Haley, Bill	1925	1981
Haley, Jack	1899	1979
Hall, Huntz	1919	1999
Hall, Jon	1915	1979
Hamilton, Margaret	1902	1985
Hammerstein, Oscar	1847	1919
Hammerstein, Oscar, II	1895	1960
Hampton, Lionel	1908	2002
Hardwicke, Cedric	1893	1964
Hardy, Oliver	1892	1957
Harlow, Jean	1911	1937
Harris, Julie	1925	2013
Harris, Phil.	1904	1995
Harris, Richard	1930	2002
Harrison, George	1943	2001
Harrison, Rex	1908	1990
Hart, William S.	1864	1946
Hartman, Phil	1948	1998
Harvey, Laurence	1928	1973
Harvey, Paul	1918	2009
Harwell, Ernie	1918	2010
Hatfield, Bobby	1940	2003
Havens, Richie	1941	2013
Havoc, June	1912	2010
Hawkins, Jack	1910	1973
Hawkins, Screamin' Jay	1929	2000
Hawks, Howard	1896	1977
Hawthorne, Nigel	1929	2001
Hayakawa, Sessue	1890	1973
Hayden, Sterling	1916	1986
Hayes, Gabby	1885	1969
Hayes, Helen	1900	1993
Hayes, Isaac	1942	2008
Hayward, Leland	1902	1971
Hayward, Louis	1909	1985
Hayward, Susan	1917	1975
Hayworth, Rita	1918	1987
Head, Edith	1897	1981
Healy, Ted	1896	1937
Heckart, Eileen	1919	2001
Heflin, Van	1910	1971
Heifetz, Jascha	1901	1987
Held, Anna	1873	1918
Helm, Levon	1940	2012
Hemingway, Margaux	1955	1996
Hemmings, David	1941	2003
Hemsley, Sherman	1938	2012
Henderson, Skitch	1918	2005
Hendrix, Jimi	1942	1970
Henie, Sonja	1912	1969
Henreid, Paul	1908	1992
Henson, Jim	1936	1990
Hepburn, Audrey	1929	1993
Hepburn, Katharine	1907	2003
Hersholt, Jean	1886	1956
Heston, Charlton	1923	2008
Hewett, Christopher	1922	2001
Hickey, William	1928	1997
Hickson, Joan	1906	1998
Hildegarde	1906	2005
Hill, Arthur	1922	2006
Hill, Benny	1925	1992
Hill, George Roy	1921	2002
Hiller, Wendy	1912	2003
Hines, Gregory	1946	2003
Hines, Jerome	1921	2003
Hingle, Pat	1924	2009
Hirt, Al	1922	1999
Hitchcock, Alfred	1899	1980
Ho, Don	1930	2007
Hodiak, John	1914	1955
Hoffman, Philip Seymour	1967	2014
Holden, William	1918	1981
Holiday, Billie	1915	1959
Holliday, Judy	1921	1965
Holloway, Sterling	1905	1992
Holly, Buddy	1936	1959
Holm, Celeste	1919	2012
Holt, Jack	1888	1951
Holt, Tim	1918	1973
Homolka, Oscar	1898	1978
Hooker, John Lee	1917	2001
Hoon, Shannon	1967	1995
Hope, Bob	1903	2003
Hopkins, Miriam	1902	1972
Hopper, Dennis	1936	2010
Hopper, DeWolf	1858	1935
Hopper, Hedda	1885	1966
Hopper, William	1915	1970
Horowitz, Vladimir	1904	1989
Horne, Lena	1917	2010
Horton, Edward Everett	1886	1970
Hoskins, Bob	1942	2014
Houdini, Harry	1874	1926
Houseman, John	1902	1988
Houston, Whitney	1963	2012
Howard (Horwitz), Curly	1903	1952
Howard, Leslie	1890	1943
Howard (Horwitz), Moe	1897	1975
Howard (Horwitz), Shemp	1895	1955
Howard, Trevor	1916	1988
Hudson, Rock	1925	1985
Hughes, Bernard	1915	2006
Hughes, John	1950	2009
Hull, Henry	1890	1977
Hull, Josephine	1886	1969
Hunter, Jeffrey	1926	1969
Hunter, Kim	1922	2002
Hunter, Ross	1920	1996
Hussey, Ruth	1911	2005
Huston, John	1906	1987
Huston, Walter	1884	1950
Hutchence, Michael	1960	1997
Hutton, Betty	1921	2007
Hutton, Jim	1934	1979
Hyde-White, Wilfrid	1903	1991
Ingram, Rex	1895	1969
Ireland, Jill	1936	1990
Ireland, John	1915	1992
Irving, Henry	1838	1905
Ives, Burl	1909	1995
Irwin, Steve	1962	2006
Iturbi, Jose	1895	1980
Jack, Wolfman	1938	1995
Jackson, Joe	1875	1942
Jackson, Mahalia	1911	1972
Jackson, Michael	1958	2009
Jackson, Milt	1923	1999
Jaeckel, Richard	1926	1997
Jaffe, Sam	1891	1984
Jagger, Dean	1903	1991
Jam Master Jay	1965	2002
James, Dennis	1917	1997
James, Etta	1938	2012
James, Harry	1916	1983
James, Rick	1948	2004
Janis, Elsie	1889	1956
Jannings, Emil	1886	1950
Janssen, David	1930	1980
Jenkins, Allen	1900	1974
Jennings, Waylon	1937	2002
Jessel, George	1898	1981
Jeter, Michael	1952	2003
Johnson, Ben	1918	1996
Johnson, Celia	1908	1982
Johnson, Chic	1892	1962
Johnson, J.J.	1924	2001
Johnson, Robert	1911	1938
Johnson, Van	1916	2008
Jolson, Al	1886	1950
Jones, Brian	1942	1969
Jones, Buck	1889	1942
Jones, Carolyn	1933	1983
Jones, Charlie	1930	2008
Jones, Davy	1945	2012
Jones, Elvin	1927	2004
Jones, George	1931	2013
Jones, Henry	1912	1999
Jones, Jennifer	1919	2009
Jones, Spike	1911	1965
Joplin, Janis	1943	1970
Joplin, Scott	1868	1917
Jordan, Richard	1937	1993
Jory, Victor	1902	1982
Joslyn, Allyn	1905	1981
Julia, Raul	1940	1994
Jump, Gordon	1932	2003
Jurado, Katy	1924	2002
Jurgens, Curt	1915	1982
Kahn, Madeline	1942	1999
Kane, Helen	1904	1966
Kanin, Garson	1912	1999
Karloff, Boris	1887	1969
Karns, Roscoe	1893	1970
Karras, Alex	1935	2012
Kasem, Casey	1932	2014
Kaufman, Andy	1949	1984
Kaye, Danny	1913	1987
Kaye, Stubby	1918	1997
Kazan, Elia	1909	2003
Kean, Charles	1811	1868
Kean, Mrs. Charles	1806	1880
Kean, Edmund	1787	1833
Keaton, Buster	1895	1966
Keel, Howard	1919	2004
Keeler, Ruby	1910	1993
Keeshan, Bob (Captain Kangaroo)	1927	2004
Keith, Brian	1921	1997
Kellaway, Cecil	1893	1973
Kelley, DeForest	1920	1999
Kelly, Emmett	1898	1979
Kelly, Gene	1912	1996
Kelly, Grace	1929	1982
Kelly, Jack	1927	1992
Kelly, Patsy	1910	1981
Kennedy, Arthur	1914	1990
Kennedy, Edgar	1890	1948
Kerr, Deborah	1921	2007
Kibbee, Guy	1886	1956
Kilbride, Percy	1888	1964
Kiley, Richard	1922	1999
King, Alan	1927	2004
King, Henry	1896	1982
Kinski, Klaus	1926	1991
Kirby, Bruno	1949	2006
Kirby, George	1923	1995
Kirby, Durward	1912	2000
Kitt, Eartha	1927	2008
Klemperer, Werner	1920	2000
Klugman, Jack	1922	2012
Knight, Ted	1923	1986
Knotts, Don	1924	2006
Korman, Harvey	1927	2008
Kostelanetz, Andre	1901	1980
Kovacs, Ernie	1919	1962
Kramer, Stanley	1913	2001
Kruger, Otto	1885	1974
Kubrick, Stanley	1928	1999
Kulp, Nancy	1921	1991

Name	Born	Died	Name	Born	Died	Name	Born	Died
Kurosawa, Akira	1910	1998	MacLane, Barton	1902	1969	Mills, John	1889	1967
Kyser, Kay	1906	1985	MacMurray, Fred	1908	1991	Mills, Sir John	1908	2005
Ladd, Alan	1913	1964	MacRae, Gordon	1921	1986	Mineo, Sal	1939	1976
Lahr, Bert	1895	1967	Macready, George	1909	1973	Miner, Jan	1917	2004
Laine, Frankie	1913	2007	Madison, Guy	1922	1996	Minghella, Anthony	1954	2008
Lake, Arthur	1905	1987	Magnani, Anna	1908	1973	Mingus, Charles	1922	1979
Lake, Veronica	1919	1973	Mancini, Henry	1924	1994	Minnelli, Vincente	1903	1986
LaLanne, Jack	1914	2011	Main, Marjorie	1890	1975	Miranda, Carmen	1909	1955
Lamarr, Hedy	1913	2000	Malden, Karl	1912	2009	Mitchell, Thomas	1892	1962
Lamas, Fernando	1915	1982	Malle, Louis	1932	1995	Mitchum, Robert	1917	1997
Lamour, Dorothy	1914	1996	Mamoulian, Rouben	1897	1987	Mix, Tom	1880	1940
Lancaster, Burt	1913	1994	Mankiewicz, Joseph	1909	1993	Moffo, Anna	1932	2006
Lanchester, Elsa	1902	1986	Mann, Herbie	1930	2003	Monroe, Marilyn	1926	1962
Landis, Carole	1919	1948	Mansfield, Jayne	1932	1967	Monroe, Vaughn	1911	1973
Landon, Michael	1936	1991	Mantovani, Annunzio	1905	1980	Montalban, Ricardo	1920	2009
Lane, Priscilla	1917	1995	Marais, Jean	1913	1998	Montand, Yves	1921	1991
Lang, Fritz	1890	1976	March, Fredric	1897	1975	Monteith, Cory	1982	2013
Langdon, Harry	1884	1944	March, Hal	1920	1970	Montez, Maria	1917	1951
Lange, Hope	1931	2003	Marchand, Nancy	1928	2000	Montgomery, Elizabeth	1933	1995
Langford, Frances	1914	2005	Markova, Alicia	1910	2004	Montgomery, George	1916	2000
Langtry, Lillie	1853	1929	Marley, Bob	1945	1981	Montgomery, Robert	1904	1981
Lanza, Mario	1921	1959	Marshall, E.G.	1910	1998	Moore, Clayton	1914	1999
LaRue, Lash (Alfred)	1917	1996	Marshall, Herbert	1890	1966	Moore, Colleen	1900	1988
Lauder, Harry	1870	1950	Martin, Barney	1923	2005	Moore, Dudley	1935	2002
Laughton, Charles	1899	1962	Martin, Dean	1917	1995	Moore, Garry	1915	1993
Laurel, Stan	1890	1965	Martin, Dick	1922	2008	Moore, Grace	1898	1947
Lawford, Peter	1923	1984	Martin, Mary	1913	1990	Moorehead, Agnes	1906	1974
Lawrence, Florence	1886	1938	Martin, Ross	1920	1981	Moreland, Mantan	1902	1973
Lawrence, Gertrude	1898	1952	Martin, Tony	1913	2012	Morgan, Dennis	1910	1994
Lean, David	1908	1991	Marvin, Lee	1924	1987	Morgan, Frank	1890	1949
Ledger, Heath	1979	2008	Marx, Harpo (Arthur)	1888	1964	Morgan, Harry	1915	2011
Lee, Anna	1913	2004	Marx, Zeppo (Herbert)	1901	1979	Morgan, Helen	1900	1941
Lee, Bernard	1908	1981	Marx, Groucho (Julius)	1890	1977	Morgan, Henry	1915	1994
Lee, Bruce	1940	1973	Marx, Chico (Leonard)	1887	1961	Morita, Pat	1932	2005
Lee, Canada	1907	1952	Marx, Gummo (Milton)	1893	1977	Morley, Robert	1908	1992
Lee, Gypsy Rose	1914	1970	Mason, James	1909	1984	Morris, Chester	1901	1970
Lee, Peggy	1920	2002	Massey, Raymond	1896	1983	Morris, Greg	1934	1996
LeGallienne, Eva	1899	1991	Mastroianni, Marcello	1924	1996	Morris, Howard	1919	2005
Leigh, Janet	1927	2004	Matthau, Walter	1920	2000	Morris, Wayne	1914	1959
Leigh, Vivien	1913	1967	Mature, Victor	1913	1999	Morrison, Jim	1943	1971
Leighton, Margaret	1922	1976	Maxwell, Marilyn	1921	1972	Morrow, Vic	1929	1982
Lemmon, Jack	1925	2001	Mayer, Louis B.	1885	1957	Morton, Jelly Roll	1885	1941
Lennon, John	1940	1980	Mayfield, Curtis	1942	1999	Mostel, Zero	1915	1977
Lenya, Lotte	1898	1981	Mayo, Virginia	1920	2005	Mowbray, Alan	1897	1969
Leonard, Eddie	1870	1941	Mazurki, Mike	1909	1990	Mulhare, Edward	1923	1997
Leonard, Sheldon	1907	1997	MCA (Adam Yauch)	1964	2012	Mulligan, Gerry	1927	1996
Leone, Sergio	1929	1989	McCambridge, Mercedes	1916	2004	Mulligan, Richard	1932	2000
LeRoy, Mervyn	1900	1987	McCarey, Leo	1898	1969	Muni, Paul	1895	1967
Levant, Oscar	1906	1972	McCarthy, Kevin	1914	2010	Munshin, Jules	1915	1970
Levene, Sam	1905	1980	McCartney, Linda	1941	1998	Murnau, F. W.	1888	1931
Levenson, Sam	1911	1980	McClanahan, Rue	1934	2010	Murphy, Audie	1924	1971
Lewis, Al	1923	2006	McClure, Doug	1935	1995	Murphy, Brittany	1977	2009
Lewis, Joe E.	1902	1971	McCormack, John	1884	1945	Murphy, George	1902	1992
Lewis, Shari	1934	1998	McCrary, Tex	1910	2003	Murray, Arthur	1895	1991
Lewis, Ted	1892	1971	McCrea, Joel	1905	1990	Murray, Kathryn	1906	1999
Liberace	1919	1987	McDaniel, Hattie	1895	1952	Murray, Mae	1889	1965
Lillie, Beatrice	1894	1989	McDowall, Roddy	1928	1998	Nagel, Conrad	1897	1970
Lincoln, Elmo	1889	1952	McFarland, Spanky (George)	1928	1993	Naish, J. Carroll	1900	1973
Lind, Jenny	1820	1887	McGoohan, Patrick	1928	2009	Naldi, Nita	1898	1961
Lindfors, Viveca	1920	1995	McGuire, Al	1931	2001	Nance, Jack	1943	1996
Lindley, Audra	1918	1997	McGuire, Dorothy	1916	2001	Natwick, Mildred	1908	1994
Linkletter, Art	1912	2010	McHugh, Frank	1898	1981	Nazimova, Alla	1879	1945
Linville, Larry	1939	2000	McIntire, John	1907	1991	Neal, Patricia	1926	2010
Little, Cleavon	1939	1992	McLaglen, Victor	1886	1959	Negri, Pola	1897	1987
Llewelyn, Desmond	1914	1999	McMahon, Ed	1923	2009	Nelson, David	1936	2011
Lloyd, Harold	1893	1971	McNeill, Don	1907	1996	Nelson, Ed	1928	2014
Lloyd, Marie	1870	1922	McPartland, Marian	1918	2013	Nelson, Harriet (Hilliard)	1909	1994
Lockhart, Gene	1891	1957	McQueen, Butterfly	1911	1995	Nelson, Ozzie	1906	1975
Lom, Herbert	1917	2012	McQueen, Steve	1930	1980	Nelson, Rick	1940	1985
Lombard, Carole	1908	1942	Meader, Vaughn	1936	2004	Nesbit, Evelyn	1884	1967
Lombardo, Guy	1902	1977	Meadows, Audrey	1924	1996	Nettleton, Lois	1927	2008
Long, Richard	1927	1974	Meek, Donald	1880	1946	Newley, Anthony	1931	1999
Lopes, Lisa	1971	2002	Meeker, Ralph	1920	1988	Newman, Edwin	1919	2010
Lopez, Vincent	1895	1975	Melba, Nellie	1861	1931	Newman, Paul	1925	2008
Lord, Jack	1920	1998	Méliès, Georges	1861	1938	Nicholas, Fayard	1914	2006
Lorne, Marion	1888	1968	Menjou, Adolphe	1890	1963	Nicholas, Harold	1924	2000
Lorre, Peter	1904	1964	Menken, Helen	1902	1966	Nielsen, Leslie	1926	2010
Loudon, Dorothy	1933	2003	Menuhin, Yehudi	1916	1999	Nijinsky, Vaslav	1890	1950
Lowe, Edmund	1890	1971	Mercer, Marian	1935	2011	Nilsson, Anna Q.	1888	1974
Loy, Myrna	1905	1993	Mercouri, Melina	1925	1994	Niven, David	1910	1983
Lubitsch, Ernst	1892	1947	Mercury, Freddie	1946	1991	Nolan, Lloyd	1902	1985
Ludden, Allen	1918	1981	Meredith, Burgess	1909	1997	Normand, Mabel	1894	1930
Lugosi, Bela	1882	1956	Merman, Ethel	1908	1984	North, Sheree	1933	2005
Lukas, Paul	1894	1971	Merrick, David	1911	2000	Notorious B.I.G.	1972	1997
Lumet, Sidney	1924	2011	Merrill, Gary	1915	1990	Novarro, Ramon	1899	1968
Lunt, Alfred	1892	1977	Milestone, Lewis	1895	1980	Nureyev, Rudolf	1938	1993
Lupino, Ida	1918	1995	Mifune, Toshiro	1920	1997	Oakie, Jack	1903	1978
Lymon, Frankie	1942	1968	Milland, Ray	1905	1986	Oakley, Annie	1860	1926
Lynde, Paul	1926	1982	Miller, Ann	1923	2004	Oates, Warren	1928	1982
Maazel, Lorin	1930	2014	Miller, Glenn	1904	1944	Oberon, Merle	1911	1979
Mac, Bernie	1957	2008	Miller, Marilyn	1898	1936	O'Brien, Edmond	1915	1985
MacArthur, James	1937	2010	Miller, Mitch	1911	2010	O'Brien, Pat	1899	1983
MacCorkindale, Simon	1952	2010	Miller, Roger	1936	1992	O'Connell, Arthur	1908	1981
MacDonald, Jeanette	1903	1965	Mills, Donald	1915	1999	O'Connell, Helen	1921	1993
Mack, Ted	1904	1976	Mills, Harry	1913	1982	O'Connor, Carroll	1924	2001
MacKenzie, Gisele	1927	2003	Mills, Herbert	1912	1989	O'Connor, Donald	1925	2003

Name	Born	Died
O'Connor, Una	1880	1959
Odetta (Holmes)	1930	2008
O'Herlihy, Daniel	1919	2005
O'Keefe, Dennis	1908	1968
Oland, Warner	1880	1938
Olcott, Chauncey	1860	1932
Oliver, Edna May	1883	1942
Olivier, Laurence	1907	1989
Olsen, Merlin	1940	2010
Olsen, Ole	1892	1963
O'Neal, Ron	1937	2004
O'Neill, James	1849	1920
Ophüls, Max	1902	1957
Orbach, Jerry	1935	2004
Orbison, Roy	1936	1988
Ormandy, Eugene	1899	1985
O'Shea, Milo	1926	2013
O'Sullivan, Maureen	1911	1998
O'Toole, Peter	1932	2013
Ouspenskaya, Maria	1876	1949
Owen, Reginald	1887	1972
Owens, Buck	1929	2006
Paar, Jack	1918	2004
Paderewski, Ignace	1860	1941
Page, Bettie	1923	2008
Page, Geraldine	1924	1987
Page, Patti	1927	2013
Pakula, Alan	1928	1998
Palance, Jack	1919	2006
Pallette, Eugene	1889	1954
Palmer, Lilli	1914	1986
Palmer, Robert	1949	2003
Pangborn, Franklin	1894	1958
Pardo, Don	1918	2014
Parker, Eleanor	1922	2013
Parker, Fess	1925	2010
Parker, Jean	1915	2005
Parks, Bert	1914	1992
Parks, Larry	1914	1975
Pasternack, Josef A.	1881	1940
Pastor, Tony (vaudevillian)	1837	1908
Pastor, Tony (bandleader)	1907	1969
Patrick, Gail	1911	1980
Patti, Adelina	1843	1919
Patti, Carlotta	1840	1889
Paul, Les	1915	2009
Pavarotti, Luciano	1935	2007
Pavlova, Anna	1885	1931
Paycheck, Johnny	1938	2003
Payne, John	1912	1989
Pearl, Minnie	1912	1996
Peck, Gregory	1916	2003
Peckinpah, Sam	1925	1984
Peerce, Jan	1904	1984
Pendergrass, Teddy	1950	2010
Penn, Arthur	1922	2010
Penn, Chris	1965	2006
Penner, Joe	1905	1941
Peppard, George	1928	1994
Perkins, Anthony	1932	1992
Perkins, Carl	1932	1998
Perkins, Marlin	1905	1986
Peters, Brock	1927	2005
Peters, Jean	1926	2000
Peters, Susan	1921	1952
Peterson, Oscar	1925	2007
Phillips, John	1935	2001
Phoenix, River	1970	1993
Piaf, Edith	1915	1963
Pickens, Slim	1919	1983
Pickett, Wilson	1941	2006
Pickford, Mary	1893	1979
Picon, Molly	1898	1992
Pidgeon, Walter	1897	1984
Pinza, Ezio	1892	1957
Pitney, Gene	1941	2006
Pitts, Zasu	1898	1963
Plato, Dana	1964	1999
Pleasence, Donald	1919	1995
Pleshette, Suzanne	1937	2008
Pollack, Sydney	1934	2008
Pons, Lily	1904	1976
Ponselle, Rosa	1897	1981
Ponti, Carlo	1912	2007
Porter, Edwin S.	1870	1941
Postlethwaite, Pete	1946	2011
Poston, Tom	1921	2007
Powell, Dick	1904	1963
Powell, Eleanor	1912	1982
Powell, William	1892	1984
Power, Tyrone	1914	1958
Preminger, Otto	1905	1986
Presley, Elvis	1935	1977
Preston, Billy	1946	2006
Preston, Robert	1918	1987
Price, Ray	1926	2013
Price, Vincent	1911	1993
Prima, Louis	1911	1978
Prinze, Freddie	1954	1977
Prosky, Robert	1930	2008
Provine, Dorothy	1937	2010
Prowse, Juliet	1936	1996
Pryor, Richard	1940	2005
Puente, Tito	1923	2000
Pyle, Denver	1920	1997
Quayle, Anthony	1913	1989
Questel, Mae	1908	1998
Quinn, Anthony	1915	2001
Quintero, José	1924	1999
Rabb, Ellis	1930	1998
Rabbit, Eddie	1941	1998
Radner, Gilda	1946	1989
Rafferty, Gerry	1947	2011
Raft, George	1895	1980
Rains, Claude	1889	1967
Raitt, John	1917	2005
Ralston, Esther	1902	1994
Ramis, Harold	1944	2014
Ramone, Dee Dee	1952	2002
Ramone, Joey	1951	2001
Ramone, Johnny	1948	2004
Ramone, Tommy	1949	2014
Rampal, Jean-Pierre	1922	2000
Randall, Tony	1920	2004
Randolph, John	1915	2004
Rathbone, Basil	1892	1967
Ratoff, Gregory	1897	1960
Rawls, Lou	1933	2006
Ray, Aldo	1926	1991
Ray, Johnnie	1927	1990
Ray, Nicholas	1911	1979
Rayburn, Gene	1917	1999
Raye, Martha	1916	1994
Raymond, Gene	1908	1998
Reagan, Ronald	1911	2004
Redding, Otis	1941	1967
Redgrave, Corin	1939	2010
Redgrave, Lynn	1943	2010
Redgrave, Michael	1908	1985
Reed, Donna	1921	1986
Reed, Jerry	1937	2008
Reed, Lou	1942	2013
Reed, Oliver	1938	1999
Reed, Robert	1932	1992
Reeve, Christopher	1952	2004
Reeves, George	1914	1959
Reeves, Steve	1926	2000
Reid, Wallace	1891	1923
Reilly, Charles Nelson	1931	2007
Reinhardt, Max	1873	1943
Remick, Lee	1935	1991
Renaldo, Duncan	1904	1980
Rennie, Michael	1909	1971
Renoir, Jean	1894	1979
Rettig, Tommy	1941	1996
Reynolds, Marjorie	1921	1997
Rich, Charlie	1932	1995
Richardson, Ian	1934	2007
Richardson, Natasha	1963	2009
Richardson, Ralph	1902	1983
Riddle, Nelson	1921	1985
Riefenstahl, Leni	1902	2003
Ripperton, Minnie	1947	1979
Ritchard, Cyril	1898	1977
Ritter, John	1948	2003
Ritter, Tex	1905	1974
Ritter, Thelma	1905	1969
Ritz, Al	1901	1965
Ritz, Harry	1906	1986
Ritz, Jimmy	1903	1985
Rivers, Joan	1933	2014
Roach, Hall	1892	1992
Roach, Max	1924	2007
Robards, Jason	1922	2000
Robbins, Jerome	1918	1998
Robbins, Marty	1925	1982
Roberts, Pernell	1928	2010
Roberts, Rachel	1927	1980
Robertson, Cliff	1925	2011
Robertson, Dale	1923	2013
Robeson, Paul	1898	1976
Robinson, Bill	1878	1949
Robinson, Edward G.	1893	1973
Robson, Flora	1902	1984
Roche, Eugene	1928	2004
Rochester (Eddie Anderson)	1905	1977
Roddenberry, Gene	1921	1991
Rodgers, Jimmie	1897	1933
Rogers, Buddy	1904	1999
Rogers, Fred	1928	2003
Rogers, Ginger	1911	1995
Rogers, Roy	1911	1998
Rogers, Will	1879	1935
Rohmer, Eric	1920	2010
Roland, Gilbert	1905	1994
Rolle, Esther	1920?	1998
Rollins, Howard	1950	1996
Roman, Ruth	1924	1999
Romero, Cesar	1907	1994
Rooney, Mickey	1920	2014
Rose, Billy	1899	1966
Rossellini, Roberto	1906	1977
Rostropovich, Mstislav	1927	2007
Rowan, Dan	1922	1987
Rubinstein, Artur	1887	1982
Rubinstein, Zelda	1933	2010
Ruggles, Charles	1886	1970
Russell, Harold	1914	2002
Russell, Jane	1921	2011
Russell, Ken	1927	2011
Russell, Lillian	1861	1922
Russell, Nipsey	1923	2005
Russell, Rosalind	1911	1976
Rutherford, Ann	1917	2012
Rutherford, Margaret	1892	1972
Ryan, Irene	1903	1973
Ryan, Robert	1909	1973
Sabu (Dastagir)	1924	1963
St. Cyr, Lili	1917	1999
St. Denis, Ruth	1877	1968
Sakall, S. Z.	1883	1955
Sale (Chic), Charles	1885	1936
Sales, Soupy	1926	2009
Sanders, George	1906	1972
Sanford, Isabel	1917	2004
Sargent, Dick	1933	1994
Sarrazin, Michael	1940	2011
Savalas, Telly	1924	1994
Scheider, Roy	1935	2008
Schell, Maria	1926	2005
Schell, Maximilian	1930	2014
Schenkel, Chris	1923	2005
Schiavelli, Vincent	1948	2005
Schildkraut, Joseph	1896	1964
Schipa, Tito	1888	1965
Schlesinger, John	1926	2003
Schnabel, Artur	1882	1951
Schneider, Maria	1952	2011
Schneider, Romy	1938	1982
Schwartzkopf, Elizabeth	1915	2006
Scofield, Paul	1922	2008
Scott, George C.	1927	1999
Scott, Gordon	1926	2007
Scott, Hazel	1920	1981
Scott, Martha	1914	2003
Scott, Randolph	1898	1987
Scott, Zachary	1914	1965
Scott-Heron, Gil	1949	2011
Scott-Siddons, Mrs.	1843	1896
Seberg, Jean	1938	1979
Seeger, Pete	1919	2014
Seeley, Blossom	1892	1974
Segovia, Andres	1893	1987
Selena (Quintanilla)	1971	1995
Sellers, Peter	1925	1980
Selznick, David O.	1902	1965
Sennett, Mack	1880	1960
Señor Wences	1896	1999
Serling, Rod	1924	1975
Shakur, Tupac	1971	1996
Shankar, Ravi	1920	2012
Shaw, Artie	1910	2004
Shaw, Robert (actor)	1927	1978
Shaw, Robert (conductor)	1916	1999
Shawn, Ted	1891	1972
Shean, Al	1868	1949
Shearer, Moira	1926	2006
Shearer, Norma	1902	1983
Shearing, George	1919	2011
Sheppard, Bob	1910	2010
Sheridan, Ann	1915	1967
Shore, Dinah	1917	1994
Short, Bobby	1924	2005
Shubert, Lee	1875	1953
Shull, Richard B.	1929	1999
Siddons, Sarah	1755	1831
Sidney, Sylvia	1910	1999
Siegel, Don	1912	1991
Signoret, Simone	1921	1985
Sills, Beverly	1929	2007
Silver, Ron	1946	2009
Silverheels, Jay	1912	1980
Silvers, Phil	1912	1985
Sim, Alastair	1900	1976
Simmons, Jean	1929	2010
Simone, Nina	1933	2003
Sinatra, Frank	1915	1998
Sinclair, Madge	1938	1995

Name	Born	Died
Singleton, Penny	1908	2003
Sirk, Douglas	1900	1987
Siskel, Gene	1946	1999
Sjostrom, Victor	1879	1960
Skelton, Red	1913	1997
Skinner, Otis	1858	1942
Smith, Alexis	1921	1993
Smith, Bessie	1894?	1937
Smith, Buffalo Bob	1917	1998
Smith, C. Aubrey	1863	1948
Smith, Elliott	1969	2003
Smith, Kate	1907	1986
Snodgrass, Carrie	1946	2004
Snow, Hank	1914	1999
Snyder, Tom	1936	2007
Solti, George	1912	1997
Sondergaard, Gale	1899	1985
Sothern, Ann	1909	2001
Sousa, John Philip	1854	1932
Sparks, Ned	1884	1957
Spelling, Aaron	1923	2006
Spencer, John	1946	2005
Sperber, Wendy Jo	1958	2005
Springfield, Dusty	1939	1999
Stack, Robert	1919	2003
Stafford, Jo	1917	2008
Stander, Lionel	1908	1994
Stang, Arnold	1918	2009
Stanley, Kim	1925	2001
Stanwyck, Barbara	1907	1990
Stapleton, Jean	1923	2013
Stapleton, Maureen	1925	2006
Steiger, Rod	1925	2002
Sterling, Jan	1921	2004
Stern, Isaac	1920	2001
Stevens, Craig	1918	2000
Stevens, George	1904	1975
Stevens, Inger	1934	1970
Stevens, Mark	1916	1994
Stevens, Risë	1913	2013
Stevenson, McLean	1929	1996
Stewart, James	1908	1997
Stickney, Dorothy	1896	1998
Stokowski, Leopold	1882	1977
Stone, Fred	1873	1959
Stone, Lewis	1879	1953
Stone, Milburn	1904	1980
Storm, Gale	1922	2009
Straight, Beatrice	1918	2001
Strasberg, Lee	1901	1982
Strasberg, Susan	1938	1999
Stritch, Elaine	1925	2014
Strode, Woody	1914	1994
Strummer, Joe	1952	2002
Stuart, Gloria	1910	2010
Stuarti, Enzo	1919	2005
Sturges, Preston	1898	1959
Sullivan, Margaret	1911	1960
Sullivan, Barry	1912	1994
Sullivan, Ed	1902	1974
Sullivan, Francis L.	1903	1956
Sumac, Yma	1922	2008
Summer, Donna	1948	2012
Summerville, Slim	1892	1946
Sutherland, Joan	1926	2010
Swanson, Gloria	1899	1983
Swarthout, Gladys	1904	1969
Swayze, Patrick	1952	2009
Sweet, Blanche	1896	1986
Switzer, Carl "Alfalfa"	1927	1959
Talbot, Lyle	1902	1996
Tallchief, Maria	1925	2013
Talmadge, Constance	1900	1973
Talmadge, Norma	1893	1957
Tamiroff, Akim	1899	1972
Tandy, Jessica	1909	1994
Tanguay, Eva	1878	1947
Tati, Jacques	1908	1982
Taylor, Billy	1921	2010
Taylor, Deems	1885	1966
Taylor, Dub	1907	1994
Taylor, Elizabeth	1932	2011

Name	Born	Died
Taylor, Estelle	1899	1958
Taylor, Laurette	1887	1946
Taylor, Robert	1911	1969
Temple Black, Shirley	1928	2014
Terry, Ellen	1847	1928
Thalberg, Irving	1899	1936
Thaw, John	1942	2002
Thaxter, Phyllis	1919	2012
Thigpen, Lynne	1948	2003
Thomas, Danny	1912	1991
Thompson, Sada	1927	2011
Thorndike, Sybil	1882	1976
Thulin, Ingrid	1926	2004
Tierney, Gene	1920	1991
Tiny Tim	1932	1996
Todd, Michael	1909	1958
Todd, Richard	1919	2009
Tomlinson, David	1917	2000
Tone, Franchot	1905	1968
Torme, Mel	1925	1999
Toscanini, Arturo	1867	1957
Tracy, Lee	1898	1968
Tracy, Spencer	1900	1967
Travers, Henry	1874	1965
Travers, Mary	1936	2009
Treacher, Arthur	1894	1975
Tree, Herbert Beerbohm	1853	1917
Trevor, Claire	1909	2000
Truex, Ernest	1890	1973
Truffaut, Francois	1932	1984
Tucker, Forrest	1919	1986
Tucker, Richard	1913	1975
Tucker, Sophie	1884	1966
Turner, Big Joe	1911	1985
Turner, Ike	1931	2008
Turner, Lana	1920	1995
Turpin, Ben	1869	1940
Twitty, Conway	1933	1993
Urich, Robert	1946	2002
Ustinov, Peter	1921	2004
Valens, Ritchie	1941	1959
Valentino, Rudolph	1895	1926
Vallee, Rudy	1901	1986
Van, Bobby	1928	1980
Van Cleef, Lee	1925	1989
Van Fleet, Jo	1922	1996
Vance, Vivian	1912	1979
Vandross, Luther	1951	2005
Varney, Jim	1949	2000
Vaughan, Sarah	1924	1990
Veidt, Conrad	1893	1943
Velez, Lupe	1908	1944
Vera-Ellen (Rohe)	1926	1981
Verdon, Gwen	1925	2000
Verrett, Shirley	1931	2010
Vidor, King	1894	1982
Villechaize, Herve	1943	1993
Vincent, Gene	1935	1971
Vicious, Sid	1957	1979
Von Stroheim, Erich	1885	1957
Von Zell, Harry	1906	1981
Waite, Ralph	1928	2014
Walker, Junior	1942	1995
Walker, Nancy	1922	1992
Walker, Robert	1918	1951
Wallace, Marcia	1942	2013
Wallach, Eli	1915	2014
Wallenda, Karl	1905	1978
Walsh, J. T.	1943	1998
Walsh, Raoul	1887	1980
Walston, Ray	1914	2001
Walter, Bruno	1876	1962
Ward, Simon	1941	2012
Warden, Jack	1920	2006
Waring, Fred	1900	1984
Warner, H. B.	1876	1958
Warrick, Ruth	1915	2005
Washington, Dinah	1924	1963
Waters, Ethel	1896	1977
Waters, Muddy	1915	1983
Waxman, Al	1935	2001
Wayne, David	1914	1995

Name	Born	Died
Wayne, John	1907	1979
Weaver, Dennis	1924	2006
Webb, Clifton	1891	1966
Webb, Jack	1920	1982
Weems, Ted	1901	1963
Weissmuller, Johnny	1904	1984
Welk, Lawrence	1903	1992
Welles, Orson	1915	1985
Wellman, William	1896	1975
Wells, Kitty	1919	2012
Werner, Oskar	1922	1984
West, Mae	1893	1980
Weston, Jack	1924	1996
Whale, James	1889	1957
White, Barry	1944	2003
White, Jesse	1919	1997
White, Pearl	1889	1938
Whiteman, Paul	1891	1967
Whiting, Margaret	1924	2011
Whitmore, James	1921	2009
Whitty, May	1865	1948
Wickes, Mary	1910	1995
Widmark, Richard	1914	2008
Wilde, Cornel	1915	1989
Wilder, Billy	1906	2002
Wilding, Michael	1912	1979
Williams, Andy	1927	2012
Williams, Bert	1874	1922
Williams, Esther	1921	2013
Williams, Guy	1924	1989
Williams, Hank, Sr.	1923	1953
Williams, Robin	1951	2014
Williamson, Nicol	1936	2011
Wills, Bob	1905	1975
Wills, Chill	1902	1978
Wilson, Carl	1946	1998
Wilson, Dennis	1944	1983
Wilson, Dooley	1894	1953
Wilson, Flip	1933	1998
Wilson, Jackie	1934	1984
Wilson, Marie	1917	1972
Windom, William	1923	2012
Windsor, Marie	1919	2000
Winehouse, Amy	1983	2011
Winfield, Paul	1941	2004
Winter, Johnny	1944	2014
Winters, Jonathan	1925	2013
Winters, Shelley	1920	2006
Wise, Robert	1914	2005
Wiseman, Joseph	1918	2009
Wong, Anna May	1907	1961
Wood, Ed	1924	1978
Wood, Natalie	1938	1981
Wood, Peggy	1892	1978
Wood, Sam	1884	1949
Woodard, Edward	1930	2009
Wooley, Sheb	1921	2003
Woolley, Monty	1888	1963
Worth, Irene	1916	2002
Wray, Fay	1907	2004
Wright, Teresa	1918	2005
Wyatt, Jane	1910	2006
Wyler, William	1902	1981
Wyman, Jane	1914?	2007
Wynette, Tammy	1942	1998
Wynn, Ed	1886	1966
Wynn, Keenan	1916	1986
York, Dick	1928	1992
York, Susannah	1939	2011
Young, Clara Kimball	1890	1960
Young, Gig	1913	1978
Young, Loretta	1913	2000
Young, Robert	1907	1998
Young, Roland	1887	1953
Youngman, Henny	1906	1998
Zanuck, Darryl F.	1902	1979
Zappa, Frank	1940	1993
Zevon, Warren	1947	2003
Ziegfeld, Florenz	1869	1932
Zimbalist, Efrem, Jr.	1918	2014
Zinneman, Fred	1907	1997
Zukor, Adolph	1873	1976

Original Names of Selected Entertainers

Adele: Adele Laurie Blue Adkins
Ad-Rock: Adam Horovitz
Clay Aiken: Clayton Grissom
Alan Alda: Alphonso D'Abruzzo
Jason Alexander: Jay Greenspan
Woody Allen: Allen Konigsberg
André 3000: Andre Benjamin
Julie Andrews: Julia Wells
Criss Angel: Christopher Sarantakos
Beatrice Arthur: Bernice Frankel
Fred Astaire: Frederick Austerlitz

Babyface: Kenneth Edmonds
Lauren Bacall: Betty Joan Perske
Erykah Badu: Erica Wright
Eric Bana: Eric Banadinovich
Anne Bancroft: Anna Maria Italiano
Theda Bara: Theodosia Goodman
Beck: Bek David Campbell
Pat Benatar: Patricia Andrejewski
Tony Bennett: Anthony Benedetto
Jack Benny: Benjamin Kubelsky
Milton Berle: Mendel Berlinger

Irving Berlin: Israel Baline
Sarah Bernhardt: Henriette-Rosine Bernard
Jello Biafra: Eric Reed Boucher
Big Boi: Antwan Patton
The Big Bopper: Jiles Perry "J.P." Richardson
Robert Blake: Michael James Vijencio Gubitosi
Jon Bon Jovi: John Francis Bongiovi
Bono: Paul Hewson
David Bowie: David Robert Jones

Boy George: George Alan O'Dowd
Fanny Brice: Fanny Borach
Charles Bronson: Charles Buchinski
Albert Brooks: Albert Einstein
Mel Brooks: Melvin Kaminsky
Foxy Brown: Inga Marchand
George Burns: Nathan Birnbaum
Ellen Burstyn: Edna Gilhooley
Richard Burton: Richard Jenkins
Red Buttons: Aaron Chwatt
Nicolas Cage: Nicholas Coppola
Michael Caine: Maurice Micklewhite
Maria Callas: Maria Kalogeropoulos
Jackie Chan: Chan Kwong-Sung
Cyd Charisse: Tula Finklea
Ray Charles: Ray Charles Robinson
Charo: Maria Rosario Pilar Martinez Molina Baeza
Chubby Checker: Ernest Evans
Cher: Cherilyn Sarkisian
Chuck D: Carlton Ridenhour
Patsy Cline: Virginia Patterson Hensley
Claudette Colbert: Lily Chauchoin
Coolio: Artis Leon Ivey Jr.
Alice Cooper: Vincent Furnier
David Copperfield: David Kotkin
Howard Cosell: Howard Cohen
Elvis Costello: Declan McManus
Lou Costello: Louis Cristillo
Peter Coyote: Peter Cohon
Quentin Crisp: Denis Pratt
Tom Cruise: Thomas Cruise Mapother IV
Tony Curtis: Bernard Schwartz
Miley Cyrus: Destiny Hope Cyrus
D'Angelo: Michael D'Angelo Archer
Rodney Dangerfield: Jacob Cohen
Bobby Darin: Walden Robert Cassotto
Doris Day: Doris von Kappelhoff
Yvonne De Carlo: Peggy Middleton
Portia de Rossi: Amanda Lee Rogers
Sandra Dee: Alexandra Zuck
John Denver: Henry John Deutschendorf Jr.
Bo Derek: Mary Cathleen Collins
Danny DeVito: Daniel Michaeli
Angie Dickinson: Angeline Brown
Bo Diddley: Elias Bates
Vin Diesel: Mark Vincent
Phyllis Diller: Phyllis Driver
Divine: Harris Glenn Milstead
DMX: Earl Simmons
Troy Donahue: Merle Johnson Jr.
Kirk Douglas: Issur Danielovitch
Drake: Aubrey Drake Graham
Bob Dylan: Robert Zimmerman
Barbara Eden: Barbara Huffman
Elvira: Cassandra Peterson
Eminem: Marshall Mathers
Enya: Eithne Ni Bhraonian
Dale Evans: Frances Smith
Chad Everett: Raymon Cramton
Fabian: Fabian Anthony Forte
Fabolous: John Jackson
Douglas Fairbanks: Douglas Ullman
Morgan Fairchild: Patsy McClenny
Jamie Farr: Jameel Farah
Fergie: Stacy Ferguson
Stepin Fetchit: Lincoln Perry
W. C. Fields: William Claude Dukenfield
50 Cent: Curtis Jackson
Flavor Flav: William Drayton
Joan Fontaine: Joan de Havilland
Jodie Foster: Alicia Christian Foster
Jamie Foxx: Eric Bishop
Redd Foxx: John Sanford
Arlene Francis: Arlene Kazanjian
Connie Francis: Concetta Franconero
Greta Garbo: Greta Gustafsson
Judy Garland: Frances Gumm
James Garner: James Bumgarner
Crystal Gayle: Brenda Gail Webb
George Gershwin: Jacob Gershowitz
Kathie Lee Gifford: Kathie Epstein
Whoopi Goldberg: Caryn Johnson
Cary Grant: Archibald Leach
Lee Grant: Lyova Rosenthal
Robert Guillaume: Robert Williams
Buddy Hackett: Leonard Hacker
Hammer: Stanley Kirk Burrell
Jean Harlow: Harlean Carpenter
Helen Hayes: Helen Brown
Susan Hayward: Edythe Marrener
Rita Hayworth: Margarita Cansino

Pee-Wee Herman: Paul Reubenfeld
Charlton Heston: John Charles Carter
Perez Hilton: Mario Armando Lavandeira Jr.
Hulk Hogan: Terry Gene Bollea
Billie Holiday: Eleanora Fagan
Judy Holliday: Judith Tuvim
Bob Hope: Leslie Townes Hope
Harry Houdini: Erik Weisz
Howlin' Wolf: Chester Burnett
Rock Hudson: Roy Scherer Jr. (later Fitzgerald)
Engelbert Humperdinck: Arnold Dorsey
Kim Hunter: Janet Cole
Ice Cube: O'Shea Jackson
Ice-T: Tracy Morrow
Billy Idol: William Broad
Etta James: Jamesetta Hawkins
Ja Rule: Jeffrey Atkins
Jay-Z: Shawn Carter
Elton John: Reginald Dwight
Al Jolson: Asa Yoelson
Jennifer Jones: Phylis Isley
Tom Jones: Thomas Woodward
Spike Jonze: Adam Spiegel
Wynonna Judd: Christina Ciminella
Boris Karloff: William Henry Pratt
Diane Keaton: Diane Hall
Michael Keaton: Michael Douglas
Kesha: Kesha Rose Sebert
Alicia Keys: Alicia Augello Cook
Chaka Khan: Yvette Stevens
Kid Rock: Robert Ritchie
Carole King: Carole Klein
Larry King: Larry Zeiger
Ben Kingsley: Krishna Banji
Ted Knight: Tadewurz Wladziu Konopka
Cheryl Ladd: Cheryl Stoppelmoor
Lady Gaga: Stefani Germanotta
Veronica Lake: Constance Ockleman
Hedy Lamarr: Hedwig Kiesler
Dorothy Lamour: Mary Leta Dorothy Slaton
Michael Landon: Eugene Orowitz
Mario Lanza: Alfredo Cocozza
Queen Latifah: Dana Owens
Stan Laurel: Arthur Jefferson
Brenda Lee: Brenda Mae Tarpley
Gypsy Rose Lee: Rose Louise Hovick
Peggy Lee: Norma Egstrom
Janet Leigh: Jeanette Morrison
Vivien Leigh: Vivian Hartley
Huey Lewis: Hugh Cregg
Jerry Lewis: Joseph Levitch
Lil' Kim: Kimberly Denise Jones
Little Richard: Richard Penniman
LL Cool J: James Todd Smith
Carole Lombard: Jane Peters
Lorde: Ella Yelich-O'Connor
Sophia Loren: Sophia Scicolone
Peter Lorre: Laszlo Lowenstein
Louis C.K.: Louis Szekely
Myrna Loy: Myrna Williams
Bela Lugosi: Bela Ferenc Blasko
Moms Mabley: Loretta Mary Aiken
Macklemore: Ben Haggerty
Shirley MacLaine: Shirley Beaty
Elle Macpherson: Eleanor Gow
Madonna: Madonna Louise Veronica Ciccone
Lee Majors: Harvey Lee Yeary
Karl Malden: Mladen Sekulovich
Barry Manilow: Barry Alan Pincus
Jayne Mansfield: Vera Jane Palmer
Marilyn Manson: Brian Warner
Bruno Mars: Peter Gene Hernandez
Dean Martin: Dino Crocetti
Ricky Martin: Enrique Jose Martin Morales
MCA: Adam Yauch
Meat Loaf: Marvin Lee Aday
Freddie Mercury: Farrokh Bulsara
Ethel Merman: Ethel Zimmermann
George Michael: Georgios Panayiotou
Mike D: Michael Diamond
Nicki Minaj: Onika Tanya Maraj
Helen Mirren: Ilynea Lydia Mironoff
Joni Mitchell: Roberta Joan Anderson
Moby: Richard Melville Hall
Mo'Nique: Monique Imes
Marilyn Monroe: Norma Jean Mortenson (later Baker)
Yves Montand: Ivo Livi
Demi Moore: Demetria Guynes

Rita Moreno: Rosita Alverio
Harry Morgan: Harry Bratsburg
Morrissey: Steven Patrick Morrissey
Mr. T: Lawrence Tureaud
Paul Muni: Mehilem Weisenfreund
Nelly: Cornell Haynes Jr.
Mike Nichols: Michael Igor Peschowsky
Chuck Norris: Carlos Ray Norris
Notorious B.I.G.: Christopher Wallace
Hugh O'Brian: Hugh Krampke
Maureen O'Hara: Maureen FitzSimons
Jack Palance: Vladimir Palanuik
Minnie Pearl: Sarah Ophelia Cannon
Katy Perry: Kathryn Hudson
Bernadette Peters: Bernadette Lazzara
Joaquin Phoenix: Joaquin Bottom
Edith Piaf: Edith Gassion
Slim Pickens: Louis Lindley
Mary Pickford: Gladys Smith
Pink: Alecia Moore
Iggy Pop: James Newell Osterberg
Natalie Portman: Natalie Hershlag
Prince: Prince Rogers Nelson
Dee Dee Ramone: Douglas Colvin
Joey Ramone: Jeffrey Hyman
Johnny Ramone: John Cummings
Tommy Ramone: Tom Erdelyi
Tony Randall: Leonard Rosenberg
Della Reese: Delloreese Patricia Early
Busta Rhymes: Trevor Smith Jr.
Joan Rivers: Joan Sandra Molinsky
Edward G. Robinson: Emmanuel Goldenberg
The Rock: Dwayne Johnson
Ginger Rogers: Virginia McMath
Roy Rogers: Leonard Franklin Slye
Mickey Rooney: Joe Yule Jr.
Johnny Rotten: John Lydon
Lillian Russell: Helen Leonard
Meg Ryan: Margaret Hyra
Winona Ryder: Winona Horowitz
Sade: Helen Folsade Abu
Soupy Sales: Milton Supman
Susan Sarandon: Susan Tomaling
Seal: Seal Henry Olusegun Olumide Adeola Samuel
Jane Seymour: Joyce Frankenberg
Omar Sharif: Michael Shalhoub
Charlie Sheen: Carlos Irwin Estevez
Martin Sheen: Ramon Estevez
Talia Shire: Talia Coppola
Beverly Sills: Belle Silverman
Phil Silvers: Philip Silversmith
Gene Simmons: Chaim Witz
Sinbad: David Adkins
Anna Nicole Smith: Vickie Lynn Hogan
Snoop Dogg (a.k.a Snoop Lion, Snoopzilla): Calvin Broadus
Barbara Stanwyck: Ruby Stevens
Jean Stapleton: Jeanne Murray
Ringo Starr: Richard Starkey
Cat Stevens: Stephen Demetre Georgiou
Connie Stevens: Concetta Ingolia
Jon Stewart: Jonathan Stuart Leibowitz
Sting: Gordon Sumner
Joe Strummer: John Graham Mellor
Donna Summer: La Donna Gaines
Rip Taylor: Charles Elmer Taylor Jr.
Robert Taylor: Spangler Brugh
Danny Thomas: Muzyad Yakhoob (later Amos Jacobs)
Tiny Tim: Herbert Khaury
Rip Torn: Elmore Rual Torn Jr.
Randy Travis: Randy Traywick
Tina Turner: Annie Mae Bullock
Shania Twain: Eilleen Regina Edwards
Twiggy: Lesley Hornby
Conway Twitty: Harold Lloyd Jenkins
Steven Tyler: Stephen Tallarico
Rudolph Valentino: Rudolpho D'Antonguolla
Frankie Valli: Frank Castelluccio
Eddie Vedder: Edward Louis Seversen III
Sid Vicious: John Simon Ritchie
John Wayne: Marion Morrison
Raquel Welch: Raquel Tejada
Gene Wilder: Jerome Silberman
Shelley Winters: Shirley Schrift
Stevie Wonder: Stevland Morris
Jane Wyman: Sarah Jane Mayfield
Loretta Young: Gretchen Michaels Young
Buckwheat Zydeco: Stanley Dural Jr.

ARTS AND MEDIA

Some Notable Movies, Sept. 2013-Aug. 2014

Film (rating)	Stars	Director(s)
A Most Wanted Man (R)	Philip Seymour Hoffman, Rachel McAdams, Willem Dafoe	Anton Corbijn
A Touch of Sin (NR)	Zhangke Jia, Wu Jiang, Lanshan Luo	Zhangke Jia
All Is Lost (PG-13)	Robert Redford	J.C. Chandor
The Amazing Spider-Man 2 (PG-13)	Andrew Garfield, Emma Stone, Jamie Foxx	Marc Webb
American Hustle (R)	Christian Bale, Amy Adams, Bradley Cooper, Jennifer Lawrence, Jeremy Renner	David O. Russell
Anchorman 2: The Legend Continues (R)	Will Ferrell, Steve Carell, Paul Rudd, Christina Applegate	Adam McKay
August: Osage County (R)	Meryl Streep, Julia Roberts	John Wells
Bad Words (R)	Jason Bateman, Kathryn Hahn, Allison Janney	Jason Bateman
Belle (PG)	Gugu Mbatha-Raw, Miranda Richardson, Tom Wilkinson	Amma Asante
Blue Is the Warmest Color (NC-17)	Léa Seydoux, Adèle Exarchopoulos	Abdellatif Kechiche
The Book Thief (PG-13)	Sophie Nélisse, Geoffrey Rush, Emily Watson	Brian Percival
Boyhood (R)	Patricia Arquette, Ellar Coltrane, Lorelei Linklater, Ethan Hawke	Richard Linklater
Captain America: The Winter Soldier (PG-13)	Chris Evans, Scarlett Johansson, Samuel L. Jackson	Anthony Russo, Joe Russo
Captain Phillips (PG-13)	Tom Hanks, Barkhad Abdi, Catherine Keener	Paul Greengrass
Cesar Chavez (PG-13)	Michael Peña, America Ferrera, Rosario Dawson	Diego Luna
Cloudy With a Chance of Meatballs 2 (PG)	Animated, Bill Hader, Anna Faris, James Caan, Will Forte	Cody Cameron, Kris Pearn
Dallas Buyers Club (R)	Matthew McConaughey, Jennifer Garner, Jared Leto	Jean-Marc Vallée
Dawn of the Planet of the Apes (PG-13)	Andy Serkis, Jason Clarke, Gary Oldman, Keri Russell	Matt Reeves
Divergent (PG-13)	Shailene Woodley, Theo James, Ashley Judd, Kate Winslet	Neil Burger
Edge of Tomorrow (PG-13)	Tom Cruise, Emily Blunt, Bill Paxton	Doug Liman
Enough Said (PG-13)	Julia Louis-Dreyfus, James Gandolfini, Catherine Keener	Nicole Holofcener
The Expendables 3 (PG-13)	Sylvester Stallone, Jason Statham, Jet Li	Patrick Hughes
The Fault in Our Stars (PG-13)	Shailene Woodley, Ansel Elgort, Laura Dern, Willem Dafoe	Josh Boone
Frank (R)	Michael Fassbender, Maggie Gyllenhaal, Domhnall Gleeson	Lenny Abrahamson
Frozen (PG)	Animated, Kristen Bell, Idina Menzel, Jonathan Groff	Chris Buck, Jennifer Lee
The Giver (PG-13)	Jeff Bridges, Meryl Streep, Brenton Thwaites	Phillip Noyce
Godzilla (PG-13)	Aaron Taylor-Johnson, Ken Watanabe, Bryan Cranston	Gareth Edwards
The Grand Budapest Hotel (R)	Ralph Fiennes, Adrien Brody, Mathieu Amalric, F. Murray Abraham	Wes Anderson
Gravity (R)	Sandra Bullock, George Clooney	Alfonso Cuarón
The Great Beauty (La Grande Bellezza) (NR)	Toni Servillo, Carlo Verdone, Sabrina Ferilli, Carlo Buccirosso	Paolo Sorrentino
Guardians of the Galaxy (PG-13)	Chris Pratt, Zoe Saldana, Bradley Cooper, Vin Diesel	James Gunn
Her (R)	Joaquin Phoenix, Amy Adams, Scarlett Johansson	Spike Jonze
Hercules (PG-13)	Dwayne Johnson, Ian McShane, John Hurt	Brett Ratner
The Hobbit: The Desolation of Smaug (PG-13)	Ian McKellen, Martin Freeman, Richard Armitage	Peter Jackson
How to Train Your Dragon 2 (PG)	Animated, Jay Baruchel, Cate Blanchett, Gerard Butler	Dean DeBlois
The Hundred-Foot Journey (PG)	Helen Mirren, Om Puri, Manish Dayal, Charlotte Le Bon	Lasse Hallström
The Hunger Games: Catching Fire (PG-13)	Jennifer Lawrence, Josh Hutcherson, Liam Hemsworth	Francis Lawrence
Inside Llewyn Davis (R)	Oscar Isaac, Carey Mulligan, John Goodman	Ethan Coen, Joel Coen
Insidious: Chapter 2 (PG-13)	Patrick Wilson, Rose Byrne, Barbara Hershey	James Wan
Jersey Boys (R)	John Lloyd Young, Erich Bergen, Vincent Piazza	Clint Eastwood
Labor Day (PG-13)	Kate Winslet, Josh Brolin, Gattlin Griffith, Tobey Maguire	Jason Reitman
The LEGO Movie (PG)	Animated, Elizabeth Banks, Will Arnett, Chris Pratt, Will Ferrell	Phil Lord, Christopher Miller
Life Itself (R)	Documentary, Roger Ebert, Chaz Ebert, Gene Siskel	Steve James
Locke (R)	Tom Hardy	Steven Knight
Lone Survivor (R)	Mark Wahlberg, Taylor Kitsch, Emile Hirsch, Ben Foster	Peter Berg
Love Is Strange (R)	John Lithgow, Alfred Molina, Marisa Tomei, Cheyenne Jackson	Ira Sachs
Lucy (R)	Scarlett Johansson, Morgan Freeman, Min-sik Choi	Luc Besson
Magic in the Moonlight (PG-13)	Emma Stone, Colin Firth, Marcia Gay Harden, Eileen Atkins	Woody Allen
Maleficent (PG)	Angelina Jolie, Elle Fanning, Sharlto Copley	Robert Stromberg
Million Dollar Arm (PG)	Jon Hamm, Aasif Mandvi, Bill Paxton, Alan Arkin	Craig Gillespie
The Missing Picture (L'image manquante) (NR)	Documentary, Randal Douc, Jean-Baptiste Phou	Rithy Panh
Mr. Peabody & Sherman (PG)	Animated, Ty Burrell, Max Charles, Ariel Winter	Rob Minkoff
The Monuments Men (PG-13)	George Clooney, Matt Damon, Bill Murray, John Goodman	George Clooney
Muppets Most Wanted (PG)	Ricky Gervais, Tina Fey, Ty Burrell	James Bobin
Nebraska (R)	Bruce Dern, Will Forte, June Squibb	Alexander Payne
Neighbors (R)	Seth Rogen, Zac Efron, Rose Byrne, Dave Franco	Nicholas Stoller
Noah (PG-13)	Russell Crowe, Jennifer Connelly, Anthony Hopkins	Darren Aronofsky
Non-Stop (PG-13)	Liam Neeson, Julianne Moore, Michelle Dockery	Jaume Collet-Serra
Obvious Child (R)	Jenny Slate, Jake Lacy, Gaby Hoffmann, David Cross	Gillian Robespierre
Omar (NR)	Adam Bakri, Leem Lubany, Iyad Hoorani	Hany Abu-Assad
The Other Woman (PG-13)	Cameron Diaz, Leslie Mann, Kate Upton	Nick Cassavetes
Philomena (PG-13)	Judi Dench, Steve Coogan	Stephen Frears
Ride Along (PG-13)	Ice Cube, Kevin Hart	Tim Story
Rio 2 (G)	Animated, Jesse Eisenberg, Anne Hathaway, Will.i.am	Carlos Saldanha
Saving Mr. Banks (PG-13)	Emma Thompson, Tom Hanks, Jason Schwartzman	John Lee Hancock
The Secret Life of Walter Mitty (PG)	Ben Stiller, Kristen Wiig, Shirley MacLaine, Sean Penn	Ben Stiller
Snowpiercer (R)	Chris Evans, Jamie Bell, Tilda Swinton, Octavia Spencer	Bong Joon Ho
Tammy (R)	Melissa McCarthy, Susan Sarandon, Allison Janney	Ben Falcone
Teenage Mutant Ninja Turtles (PG-13)	Megan Fox, Will Arnett, William Fichtner	Jonathan Liebesman
Thor: The Dark World (PG-13)	Chris Hemsworth, Natalie Portman, Tom Hiddleston	Alan Taylor
300: Rise of an Empire (R)	Sullivan Stapleton, Eva Green, Lena Headey	Noam Murro
Transformers: Age of Extinction (PG-13)	Mark Wahlberg, Nicola Peltz, Jack Reynor	Michael Bay
The Trip to Italy (NR)	Steve Coogan, Rob Brydon	Michael Winterbottom
12 Years a Slave (R)	Chiwetel Ejiofor, Michael Fassbender, Lupita Nyong'o	Steve McQueen
22 Jump Street (R)	Channing Tatum, Jonah Hill, Ice Cube	Phil Lord, Christopher Miller
Tyler Perry's A Madea Christmas (PG-13)	Tyler Perry	Tyler Perry
Veronica Mars (PG-13)	Kristen Bell, Jason Dohring, Enrico Colantoni	Rob Thomas
The Wolf of Wall Street (R)	Leonardo DiCaprio, Jonah Hill	Martin Scorsese
X-Men: Days of Future Past (PG-13)	Hugh Jackman, James McAvoy, Michael Fassbender	Bryan Singer

50 Top-Grossing Movies, 2013

Source: Rentrak Corporation

Rank	Title	Gross (mil)	Rank	Title	Gross (mil)
1.	Iron Man 3	$409.0	26.	The Hangover 3	$112.2
2.	The Hunger Games: Catching Fire	400.1	27.	Epic	107.5
3.	Despicable Me 2	367.9	28.	Captain Phillips	104.7
4.	Man of Steel	291.0	29.	Pacific Rim	101.8
5.	Frozen	277.1	30.	This Is the End	101.5
6.	Monsters University	268.5	31.	Jackass Presents: Bad Grandpa	101.5
7.	Gravity	255.1	32.	Silver Linings Playbook	101.0
8.	Fast and Furious 6	238.7	33.	Olympus Has Fallen	98.9
9.	Oz the Great and Powerful	234.9	34.	Anchorman 2	98.1
10.	Star Trek Into Darkness	228.8	35.	42	95.0
11.	The Hobbit: The Desolation of Smaug	213.4	36.	Zero Dark Thirty	94.0
12.	Thor: The Dark World	203.0	37.	Elysium	93.1
13.	World War Z	202.4	38.	Planes	90.3
14.	The Croods	187.2	39.	The Lone Ranger	89.3
15.	The Heat	159.6	40.	Oblivion	89.1
16.	We're the Millers	150.4	41.	Insidious: Chapter 2	83.6
17.	The Great Gatsby	144.8	42.	Turbo	83.0
18.	The Conjuring	137.4	43.	Django Unchained	76.5
19.	Identity Thief	134.5	44.	2 Guns	75.6
20.	Grown Ups 2	133.7	45.	American Hustle	75.5
21.	The Wolverine	132.6	46.	White House Down	73.1
22.	G.I. Joe: Retaliation	122.5	47.	Mama	71.6
23.	Now You See Me	117.7	48.	Safe Haven	71.3
24.	Cloudy With a Chance of Meatballs 2	117.2	49.	Smurfs 2	71.0
25.	Lee Daniels' The Butler	116.2	50.	The Best Man Holiday	70.4

Note: Box-office grosses in the U.S. and Canada Jan. 4, 2013-Jan. 2, 2014; some films may have had 2012 release dates.

All-Time Top-Grossing American Movies

Source: Rentrak Corporation

Rank	Title (original release date)	Gross (mil)	Rank	Title (original release date)	Gross (mil)
1.	Avatar (2009)	$760.5	27.	Finding Nemo (2003)	$339.7
2.	The Avengers (2012)	623.4	28.	Spider-Man 3 (2007)	336.5
3.	Titanic (1997)	600.8	29.	Alice in Wonderland (2010)	334.2
4.	The Dark Knight (2008)	533.3	30.	Forrest Gump (1994)	329.7
5.	Star Wars: Episode I—The Phantom Menace (1999)	474.5	31.	Shrek the Third (2007)	322.7
6.	Star Wars (1977)	461.0	32.	Transformers (2007)	319.2
7.	The Dark Knight Rises (2012)	448.1	33.	Iron Man (2008)	318.6
8.	Shrek 2 (2004)	436.7	34.	Harry Potter and the Sorcerer's Stone (2001)	317.6
9.	E.T. the Extra-Terrestrial (1982)	435.0	35.	Indiana Jones and the Kingdom of the Crystal Skull (2008)	317.1
10.	The Hunger Games: Catching Fire (2013)	424.7	36.	The Lord of the Rings: The Fellowship of the Ring (2001)	314.2
11.	Pirates of the Caribbean: Dead Man's Chest (2006)	423.3	37.	The Lion King (1994)	312.9
12.	Toy Story 3 (2010)	415.0	38.	Iron Man 2 (2010)	312.4
13.	Iron Man 3 (2013)	409.0	39.	Star Wars: Episode II—Attack of the Clones (2002)	310.7
14.	The Hunger Games (2012)	408.0	40.	Pirates of the Caribbean: At World's End (2007)	309.4
15.	Spider-Man (2002)	403.7	41.	Star Wars: Episode VI—Return of the Jedi (1983)	309.2
16.	Transformers: Revenge of the Fallen (2009)	402.1	42.	Independence Day (1996)	306.2
17.	Frozen (2013)	400.7	43.	Pirates of the Caribbean: The Curse of the Black Pearl (2003)	305.4
18.	Harry Potter and the Deathly Hallows: Part 2 (2011)	381.0	44.	Skyfall (2012)	304.4
19.	Star Wars: Episode III—Revenge of the Sith (2005)	380.3	45.	The Hobbit: An Unexpected Journey (2012)	303.0
20.	The Lord of the Rings: The Return of the King (2003)	377.0	46.	Harry Potter and the Half-Blood Prince (2009)	302.0
21.	Spider-Man 2 (2004)	373.4	47.	The Twilight Saga: Eclipse (2010)	300.5
22.	The Passion of the Christ (2004)	370.3	48.	The Twilight Saga: New Moon (2009)	296.6
23.	Despicable Me 2 (2013)	368.1	49.	Harry Potter and the Deathly Hallows: Part I (2010)	296.0
24.	Jurassic Park (1993)	357.1	50.	The Sixth Sense (1999)	293.5
25.	Transformers: Dark of the Moon (2011)	352.4			
26.	The Lord of the Rings: The Two Towers (2002)	341.7			

Note: Box-office grosses in the U.S. and Canada through Aug. 30, 2014, in absolute dollars. Rising ticket prices favor newer films. Revenues from re-releases are included.

100 Best American Movies of All Time

Source: American Film Institute

First unveiled in 1998 based on ballots sent to 1,500 individuals, mostly from the film world, in 1997. Updated in 2007 (the version shown here) to include newly eligible films and reflect shifting cultural perspectives. Criteria for judging included historical significance, cultural impact, critical recognition and awards, and popularity. The year each film was first released is in parentheses.

1. Citizen Kane (1941)
2. The Godfather (1972)
3. Casablanca (1942)
4. Raging Bull (1980)
5. Singin' in the Rain (1952)
6. Gone With the Wind (1939)
7. Lawrence of Arabia (1962)
8. Schindler's List (1993)
9. Vertigo (1958)
10. The Wizard of Oz (1939)
11. City Lights (1931)
12. The Searchers (1956)
13. Star Wars (1977)
14. Psycho (1960)
15. 2001: A Space Odyssey (1968)
16. Sunset Boulevard (1950)
17. The Graduate (1967)
18. The General (1927)
19. On the Waterfront (1954)
20. It's a Wonderful Life (1946)
21. Chinatown (1974)
22. Some Like It Hot (1959)
23. The Grapes of Wrath (1940)
24. E.T. the Extra-Terrestrial (1982)
25. To Kill a Mockingbird (1962)
26. Mr. Smith Goes to Washington (1939)
27. High Noon (1952)
28. All About Eve (1950)
29. Double Indemnity (1944)
30. Apocalypse Now (1979)
31. The Maltese Falcon (1941)
32. The Godfather Part II (1974)
33. One Flew Over the Cuckoo's Nest (1975)
34. Snow White and the Seven Dwarfs (1937)
35. Annie Hall (1977)
36. The Bridge on the River Kwai (1957)
37. The Best Years of Our Lives (1946)

38. The Treasure of the Sierra Madre (1948)
39. Dr. Strangelove (1964)
40. The Sound of Music (1965)
41. King Kong (1933)
42. Bonnie and Clyde (1967)
43. Midnight Cowboy (1969)
44. The Philadelphia Story (1940)
45. Shane (1953)
46. It Happened One Night (1934)
47. A Streetcar Named Desire (1951)
48. Rear Window (1954)
49. Intolerance (1916)
50. The Lord of the Rings: The Fellowship of the Ring (2001)
51. West Side Story (1961)
52. Taxi Driver (1976)
53. The Deer Hunter (1978)
54. M*A*S*H (1970)
55. North by Northwest (1959)
56. Jaws (1975)
57. Rocky (1976)
58. The Gold Rush (1925)
59. Nashville (1975)
60. Duck Soup (1933)
61. Sullivan's Travels (1941)
62. American Graffiti (1973)
63. Cabaret (1972)
64. Network (1976)
65. The African Queen (1951)
66. Raiders of the Lost Ark (1981)
67. Who's Afraid of Virginia Woolf? (1966)
68. Unforgiven (1992)
69. Tootsie (1982)
70. A Clockwork Orange (1971)
71. Saving Private Ryan (1998)
72. The Shawshank Redemption (1994)
73. Butch Cassidy and the Sundance Kid (1969)
74. The Silence of the Lambs (1991)
75. In the Heat of the Night (1967)
76. Forrest Gump (1994)
77. All the President's Men (1976)
78. Modern Times (1936)
79. The Wild Bunch (1969)
80. The Apartment (1960)
81. Spartacus (1960)
82. Sunrise (1927)
83. Titanic (1997)
84. Easy Rider (1969)
85. A Night at the Opera (1935)
86. Platoon (1986)
87. 12 Angry Men (1957)
88. Bringing Up Baby (1938)
89. The Sixth Sense (1999)
90. Swing Time (1936)
91. Sophie's Choice (1982)
92. Goodfellas (1990)
93. The French Connection (1971)
94. Pulp Fiction (1994)
95. The Last Picture Show (1971)
96. Do the Right Thing (1989)
97. Blade Runner (1982)
98. Yankee Doodle Dandy (1942)
99. Toy Story (1995)
100. Ben-Hur (1959)

National Film Registry, 2013

Source: National Film Registry, Library of Congress

The National Film Registry adds 25 "culturally, historically, or aesthetically significant" American films annually.

Bless Their Little Hearts (1984)	Gilda (1946)	Martha Graham Early Dance films (1931-44)	The Quiet Man (1952)
Brandy in the Wilderness (1969)	The Hole (1962)	Mary Poppins (1964)	The Right Stuff (1983)
Cicero March (1966)	Judgment at Nuremberg (1961)	Men and Dust (1940)	Roger & Me (1989)
Daughter of Dawn (1920)	King of Jazz (1930)	Midnight (1939)	A Virtuous Vamp (1919)
Decasia (2002)	The Lunch Date (1989)	Notes on the Port of St. Francis (1951)	Who's Afraid of Virginia Woolf? (1966)
Ella Cinders (1926)	The Magnificent Seven (1960)	Pulp Fiction (1994)	Wild Boys of the Road (1933)
Forbidden Planet (1956)			

Movie Theaters, 1946-2013

Source: Motion Picture Association of America (MPAA); Rentrak Corporation

Year	Box office (mil)	Admissions (mil)	Admissions per week (mil)	Screens	Avg. ticket price	Films produced	Films released
1946	$1,692.0	4,067.3	78.2	NA	$0.42	NA	400
1950	1,379.0	3,017.5	58.0	NA	0.46	NA	483
1955	1,204.0	2,072.3	39.9	NA	0.58	NA	319
1960	984.4	1,304.5	25.1	NA	0.76	NA	248
1965	1,041.8	1,031.5	19.8	NA	1.01	NA	279
1970	1,429.2	920.6	17.7	NA	1.55	279	306
1975	2,114.8	1,032.8	19.9	15,030	2.05	258	233
1980	2,748.5	1,021.5	19.6	17,590	2.69	214	233
1985	3,749.4	1,056.1	20.3	21,147	3.55	264	470
1990	5,021.8	1,188.6	22.9	23,689	4.23	346	410
1995	5,269.0	1,211.0	23.3	27,805	4.35	631	411
2000	7,468.0	1,383.0	26.6	37,396	5.39	683	475
2001	8,125.0	1,438.0	27.7	36,764	5.66	611	454
2002	9,272.0	1,599.0	30.8	35,280	5.81	546	475
2003	9,165.0	1,521.0	29.3	35,786	6.03	593	455
2004	9,215.0	1,484.0	28.5	36,594	6.21	611	489
2005	8,832.0	1,376.0	26.5	38,852	6.41	920	507
2006	9,138.0	1,395.0	26.8	38,415	6.55	928	594
2007	9,629.0	1,400.0	26.9	38,974	6.88	789	611
2008	9,791.0	1,364.0	26.2	38,834	7.18	773	638
2009	10,543.6	1,415.0	27.2	39,233	7.50	751	558
2010	10,741.0	1,341.0	25.8	39,547	7.89	795	563
2011	10,186.1	1,285.0	24.7	39,641	7.93	818	609
2012	10,774.5	1,358.0	26.0	39,918	7.96	476[1]	677
2013	10,919.7	1,358.0	25.8	42,814	8.13	455[1]	659

NA = Not available. (1) Non-MPAA members with est. budget under $1 mil were not tracked in 2012 and 2013.

Top Film Websites, 2014

Source: comScore Media Metrix, Inc.; ranked by number of visitors

Rank	Website	Visitors[1]	Rank	Website	Visitors[1]
1.	IMDb	60,244	11.	CinemaBlend.com	4,808
2.	Fandango sites	30,032	12.	Regal Entertainment	4,655
3.	Yahoo Movies	17,189	13.	AMC Entertainment, Inc.	4,636
4.	Flixster	16,893	14.	MovieGoer Network	4,539
5.	Moviefone	13,326	15.	Megashare.info	4,242
6.	MSN Movies	10,923	16.	ComplexMovies	4,203
7.	Moviepilot.com	8,532	17.	Screenrant.com	4,031
8.	Disney Movies	5,237	18.	Paramount Online	2,976
9.	Viewster Media	5,165	19.	Cinemark.com	2,935
10.	Hollywood.com sites	4,977	20.	SnagFilms	2,823

NA = Not available. (1) Number of unique visitors, in thousands, who visited website at least once in June 2014.

Most Popular Movie DVDs, 2013
Source: Rentrak Corporation

Top Rentals, 2013

Rank	Movie	Rank	Movie
1.	Identity Thief	11.	Hansel and Gretel:
2.	World War Z		Witch Hunters
3.	Looper (2012)	12.	This Is 40 (2012)
4.	Flight (2012)	13.	Jack Reacher (2012)
5.	Here Comes the Boom	14.	Now You See Me
	(2012)	15.	Argo (2012)
6.	Taken 2 (2012)	16.	Hotel Transylvania (2012)
7.	Django Unchained	17.	The Heat
	(2012)	18.	Silver Linings Playbook
8.	Olympus Has Fallen		(2012)
9.	Ted (2012)	19.	Zero Dark Thirty (2012)
10.	Snitch	20.	Skyfall (2012)

Top-Selling DVDs, 2013

Rank	Movie	Rank	Movie
1.	Despicable Me 2	11.	Star Trek Into Darkness
2.	The Twilight Saga: Breaking	12.	The Little Mermaid
	Dawn Part 2 (2012)		(1989)
3.	The Hobbit: An Unexpected	13.	Hotel Transylvania (2012)
	Journey (2012)	14.	World War Z
4.	Monsters University	15.	Les Misérables (2012)
5.	The Croods	16.	The Heat
6.	Wreck-It Ralph (2012)	17.	Planes
7.	Fast and Furious 6	18.	Turbo
8.	Skyfall (2012)	19.	Rise of the Guardians
9.	Iron Man 3		(2012)
10.	Man of Steel	20.	Django Unchained (2012)

Note: Includes Blu-ray format titles. Top rentals exclude kiosk and online/by-mail channels. Top-selling DVDs exclude units sold into the rental channel, online, and in Canada. Movies released in 2013 unless otherwise noted.

Top-Selling Video Games, 2013
Source: The NPD Group/Retail Tracking Service; ranked by retail units sold

U.S. consumers spent $15.4 bil on video game content in 2013: $8.2 bil on physical software, $7.2 bil on content in digital formats, and $1.8 bil on other physical formats (including rental/used content). Spending decreased 8% on physical content, but digital content spending grew 15%.

Rank	Game (console)	Rank	Game (console)
1.	Grand Theft Auto V (360, PS3)*	6.	NBA 2K14 (360, PC, PS3, PS4, XBO)*
2.	Call of Duty: Ghosts (360, PC, PS3, PS4, Wii U, XBO)*	7.	Call of Duty: Black Ops II (360, PC, PS3, Wii U)*
3.	Madden NFL 25 (360, PS3, PS4, XBO)	8.	Just Dance 2014 (360, PS3, PS4, Wii, Wii U, XBO)*
4.	Battlefield 4 (360, PC, PS3, PS4, XBO)	9.	Minecraft (360)
5.	Assassin's Creed IV: Black Flag (360, PC, PS3, PS4, Wii U, XBO)*	10.	Disney Infinity (3DS, 360, PS3, Wii, Wii U)

* = Includes bundled, collector's, or game-of-the-year editions, except those bundled with hardware. 3DS = Nintendo 3DS; 360 = Microsoft Xbox 360; PC = personal computer; PS3 = PlayStation 3; PS4 = PlayStation 4; Wii/Wii U = Nintendo Wii or Wii U; XBO = Microsoft Xbox One.

Film and TV Content Ratings

The Motion Picture Association of America (MPAA) began rating movies in 1968. The system was revised in 1984 and in 1990. The MPAA, Natl. Cable Television Assn., and Natl. Assn. of Broadcasters developed the TV ratings system in 1997, in accordance with the Telecommunications Act of 1996; it was implemented in Oct. 1997.

Film Ratings

G: General Audience. All ages admitted. Does not contain themes, language, nudity, sex, or violence that the MPAA ratings board believes would offend parents whose younger children see the film. Does not necessarily denote a certificate of approval nor children's movie. No nudity, sex scenes, or drug use depicted.

PG: Parental Guidance Suggested. Some material may not be suited for children. The MPAA ratings board recommends that parents determine whether the content of the film is appropriate for their children. The film may contain more mature themes, some profanity, violence, or brief nudity. No drug use depicted.

PG-13: Parents Strongly Cautioned. Some material may be inappropriate for children under 13. The MPAA urges more strongly that parents vet the movie to see if its content is appropriate for their children. Any movie depicting drug use or more than brief nudity is automatically rated at least PG-13. Violence is permitted, though it is generally not both realistic or extreme and persistent violence. The single use of one sexually-derived expletive rates a PG-13; more than one use requires at least an R rating.

R: Restricted. Under 17 requires accompanying parent or adult guardian. Movies given R ratings contain some adult material, defined as adult themes or activity, hard language, intense or persistent violence, sexually-oriented nudity, or drug abuse.

NC-17: No One 17 and Under Admitted. The ratings board considers NC-17 films those that most parents would consider too adult for children under 17. An NC-17 rating does not mean the film is obscene or pornographic. The rating can be based on violence, sex, aberrational behavior, drug abuse, or any other element that most parents would consider too adult for children.

TV Ratings

TV-Y: All Children. Program designed to be acceptable for children of all ages. Its themes and elements are designed for a very young audience.

TV-Y7: Directed to Older Children. Program designed for children ages 7 and older, and more appropriate for those who have the skills to distinguish between make-believe and reality. May include mild fantasy/comedic violence. Programs with more than mild fantasy violence are denoted with FV.

TV-G: General Audience. Program not necessarily designed for children, but most parents would find it suitable for all ages. Little or no violence, no strong language, and little or no sexual dialogue or situations.

TV-PG: Parental Guidance Suggested. Program might contain material that parents would consider inappropriate for children, such as an adult theme or one or more of the following: suggestive dialogue (D), infrequent coarse language (L), some sexual situations (S), or moderate violence (V).

TV-14: Parents Strongly Cautioned. Program contains material that many parents would consider inappropriate for children under 14, such as one or more of the following: intensely suggestive dialogue (D), strong coarse language (L), intense sexual situations (S), or intense violence (V).

TV-MA: Mature Audience Only. Program specifically designed for adults and may be unsuitable for children under 17. Contains one or more of the following: crude indecent language (L), explicit sexual activity (S), or graphic violence (V).

Opera: Most Produced Works, 2013-14
Source: OPERA America

Work, composer	Productions	Work, composer	Productions	Work, composer	Productions
Carmen, Georges Bizet	12	The Magic Flute, Wolfgang Amadeus		La traviata, Giuseppe Verdi	7
The Barber of Seville, Gioachino		Mozart	9	The Elixir of Love, Gaetano	
Rossini	12	Tosca, Giacomo Puccini	9	Donizetti	6
La bohème, Giacomo Puccini	10	Madama Butterfly, Giacomo		Die Fledermaus, Johann Strauss Jr.	6
Falstaff, Giuseppe Verdi	9	Puccini	8		

Note: Scheduled productions of a given work (not individual performances) during the 2013-14 season (generally Oct.-Sept.) by members of OPERA America and Opera.ca.

Longest-Running Broadway Shows

Source: The Broadway League, New York, NY

Rank	Title (run)[1]	Performances[2]	Rank	Title (run)[1]	Performances[2]	Rank	Title (run)[1]	Performances[2]
1.	*The Phantom of the Opera (1988-)	10,951	16.	Fiddler on the Roof (1964-72)	3,242	34.	The Magic Show (1974-78)	1,920
2.	Cats (1982-2000)	7,485	17.	Life With Father (1939-47)	3,224	35.	Aida (2000-04)	1,852
3.	*Chicago (revival) (1996-)	7,277	18.	Tobacco Road (1933-41)	3,182	36.	Gemini (1977-81)	1,819
4.	*The Lion King (1997-)	6,870	19.	Hello, Dolly! (1964-70)	2,844	37.	Deathtrap (1978-82)	1,793
5.	Les Misérables (1987-2003)	6,680	20.	My Fair Lady (1956-62)	2,717	38.	Harvey (1944-49)	1,775
6.	A Chorus Line (1975-90)	6,137	21.	Hairspray (2002-09)	2,642	39.	Dancin' (1978-82)	1,774
7.	Oh! Calcutta! (revival) (1976-89)	5,959	22.	Mary Poppins (2006-13)	2,619	40.	La Cage aux Folles (1983-87)	1,761
8.	Beauty and the Beast (1994-2007)	5,461	23.	Avenue Q (2003-09)	2,534	41.	Hair (1968-72)	1,750
9.	*Mamma Mia! (2001-)	5,215	24.	The Producers (2001-07)	2,502	42.	The Wiz (1975-79)	1,672
10.	Rent (1996-2008)	5,123	25.	Cabaret (revival) (1998-2004)	2,377	43.	Born Yesterday (1946-49)	1,642
11.	*Wicked (2003-)	4,398	26.	Annie (1977-83)	2,377	44.	Crazy for You (1992-96)	1,622
12.	Miss Saigon (1991-2001)	4,092	27.	Man of La Mancha (1965-71)	2,328	45.	Ain't Misbehavin' (1978-82)	1,604
13.	*Jersey Boys (2005-)	3,540	28.	Abie's Irish Rose (1922-27)	2,327	46.	The Best Little Whorehouse in Texas (1978-82)	1,584
14.	42nd Street (1980-89)	3,486	29.	Oklahoma! (1943-48)	2,212	47.	Spamalot (2005-09)	1,575
15.	Grease (1972-80)	3,388	30.	*Rock of Ages (2009-)	2,056	48.	Mary, Mary (1961-64)	1,572
			31.	Smokey Joe's Cafe (1995-2000)	2,036	49.	Evita (1979-83)	1,567
			32.	Pippin (1972-77)	1,944	50.	The Voice of the Turtle (1943-48)	1,557
			33.	South Pacific (1949-54)	1,925			

* = Still running as of Sept. 1, 2014. (1) Unless noted, listings reflect a play's first run on Broadway. (2) Number of performances through May 25, 2014.

Broadway Season Statistics, 1959-2014

Source: The Broadway League, New York, NY

Season	Gross (mil $)	Attendance (mil)	Playing weeks	New productions	Season	Gross (mil $)	Attendance (mil)	Playing weeks	New productions
1959-1960	$46	7.9	1,156	58	2005-2006	$862	12.0	1,501	39
1964-1965	50	8.2	1,250	67	2006-2007	939	12.3	1,509	35
1969-1970	53	7.1	1,047	62	2007-2008	938	12.3	1,560	36
1974-1975	57	6.6	1,101	54	2008-2009	943	12.2	1,548	43
1979-1980	146	9.6	1,540	61	2009-2010	1,020	11.9	1,464	39
1984-1985	209	7.3	1,078	33	2010-2011	1,080	12.5	1,588	42
1989-1990	282	8.0	1,070	40	2011-2012	1,139	12.3	1,522	41
1994-1995	406	9.0	1,120	33	2012-2013	1,139	11.6	1,430	46
1999-2000	603	11.4	1,464	37	2013-2014	1,269	12.2	1,496	44*
2004-2005	769	11.5	1,494	39					

* = Includes one return engagement.

Notable U.S. Museums

This unofficial list of some of the largest museums in the U.S., by budget, was compiled with the assistance of the American Association of Museums, a national association representing the concerns of the museum community. Association members also include zoos, aquariums, arboretums, botanical gardens, and planetariums, but these are not included in *The World Almanac* listings.

Museum	City	State	Museum	City	State
American Museum of Natural History	New York	NY	Franklin Institute	Philadelphia	PA
Amon Carter Museum of Western Art	Ft. Worth	TX	The Frick Collection	New York	NY
The Art Institute of Chicago	Chicago	IL	J. Paul Getty Museum	Los Angeles	CA
Boston Children's Museum	Boston	MA	Solomon R. Guggenheim Museum of Art	New York	NY
Brooklyn Museum of Art	Brooklyn	NY	Harvard University Art Museums	Cambridge	MA
Busch-Reisinger Museum	Cambridge	MA	Henry F. DuPont Winterthur Museum	Winterthur	DE
California Academy of Sciences	San Francisco	CA	Henry Ford Museum/Greenfield Village	Dearborn	MI
California Science Center	Los Angeles	CA	High Museum of Art	Atlanta	GA
Carnegie Museums of Pittsburgh	Pittsburgh	PA	Houston Museum of Natural Science	Houston	TX
Children's Museum of Indianapolis	Indianapolis	IN	Jamestown-Yorktown Foundation	Williamsburg	VA
Cincinnati Art Museum	Cincinnati	OH	Jewish Museum	New York	NY
Cincinnati Museum Center	Cincinnati	OH	L.A. County Museum of Art	Los Angeles	CA
Cleveland Museum of Art	Cleveland	OH	Liberty Science Center, Liberty State Park	Jersey City	NJ
Colonial Williamsburg	Williamsburg	VA	Maryland Science Center	Baltimore	MD
Corning Museum of Glass	Corning	NY	Mashantucket Pequot Museum and Research Center	Mashantucket	CT
Crystal Bridges Museum of American Art	Bentonville	AR	Metropolitan Museum of Art	New York	NY
Dallas Museum of Art	Dallas	TX	Milwaukee Public Museum	Milwaukee	WI
Denver Art Museum	Denver	CO	Minneapolis Institute of Arts	Minneapolis	MN
Denver Museum of Nature and Science	Denver	CO	Museum of African American History	Detroit	MI
Detroit Institute of Arts	Detroit	MI	Museum of the American West	Los Angeles	CA
Exploratorium	San Francisco	CA	Museum of Contemporary Art	Los Angeles	CA
The Field Museum	Chicago	IL	Museum of Fine Arts	Boston	MA
Fine Arts Museums of San Francisco	San Francisco	CA			

Museum	City	State	Museum	City	State
Museum of Fine Arts	Houston	TX	New York State Museum	Albany	NY
Museum of Modern Art	New York	NY	Peabody Essex Museum	Salem	MA
Museum of New Mexico	Santa Fe	NM	Philadelphia Museum of Art	Philadelphia	PA
Museum of Science	Boston	MA	Rock and Roll Hall of Fame and		
Museum of Science and Industry	Chicago	IL	Museum, Inc.	Cleveland	OH
Musical Instrument Museum	Phoenix	AZ	St. Louis Science Center	St. Louis	MO
Mystic Seaport Museum	Mystic	CT	San Diego Museum of Art	San Diego	CA
National Air and Space Museum	Washington	DC	San Francisco Museum of Modern Art	San Francisco	CA
National Baseball Hall of Fame			Science Museum of Minnesota	St. Paul	MN
and Museum, Inc.	Cooperstown	NY	Toledo Museum of Art	Toledo	OH
National Constitution Center	Philadelphia	PA	U.S. Holocaust Memorial Museum	Washington	DC
National Gallery of Art	Washington	DC	Univ. of Pennsylvania Museum of		
National Museum of American History	Washington	DC	Archaeology and Anthropology	Philadelphia	PA
National Museum of the American Indian	Washington	DC	Virginia Museum of Fine Arts	Richmond	VA
National Museum of Natural History	Washington	DC	Wadsworth Atheneum	Hartford	CT
Nelson-Atkins Museum of Art	Kansas City	MO	Walker Art Center	Minneapolis	MN
New York Historical Society	New York	NY	Whitney Museum of American Art	New York	NY

Best-Selling U.S. Magazines, 2014

Source: Audit Bureau of Circulations (ABC)

General magazines, exclusive of comics; also excludes magazines that failed to file reports to ABC. Based on total average paid and verified circulation during the six months ending June 30, 2014; ranked by paid circulation size.

Publication	Paid circ.	Publication	Paid circ.	Publication	Paid circ.
1. AARP The Magazine	22,837,736	17. Taste of Home	2,501,098	34. Cooking Light	1,792,824
2. AARP Bulletin	22,183,316	18. O, The Oprah Magazine	2,385,199	35. InStyle	1,760,784
3. Better Homes and		19. Glamour	2,318,521	36. Entertainment Weekly	1,749,457
Gardens	7,639,661	20. Redbook	2,221,393	37. Money	1,737,129
4. Game Informer		21. American Rifleman	2,163,349	38. Every Day With Rachael	
Magazine	7,099,452	22. ESPN The Magazine	2,144,967	Ray	1,726,856
5. Good Housekeeping	4,315,330	23. FamilyFun Magazine	2,133,171	39. Golf Digest	1,662,611
6. Family Circle	4,015,728	24. American Legion		40. Shape	1,638,925
7. National Geographic	3,572,348	Magazine	2,129,891	41. Food Network Magazine	1,631,528
8. People	3,510,533	25. Parents	2,125,414	42. Country Living	1,614,883
9. Reader's Digest	3,393,573	26. Martha Stewart Living	2,067,293	43. All You	1,554,502
10. Woman's Day	3,288,335	27. Maxim	2,024,114	44. Women's Health	1,537,140
11. Time	3,286,467	28. Real Simple	2,022,267	45. Guideposts	1,528,741
12. Ladies' Home Journal	3,226,731	29. Seventeen	2,021,792	46. Fitness	1,520,501
13. Sports Illustrated	3,043,698	30. Smithsonian	2,005,512	47. Bon Appetit	1,518,622
14. Cosmopolitan	3,019,778	31. TV Guide Magazine	1,979,160	48. Self	1,515,880
15. Prevention	2,826,547	32. Us Weekly	1,961,530	49. Rolling Stone	1,470,183
16. Southern Living	2,804,454	33. Men's Health	1,839,433	50. Golf Magazine	1,415,842

Best-Selling Digital Replica U.S. Magazines, 2014

Source: Audit Bureau of Circulations (ABC)

General magazines, exclusive of comics; also excludes magazines that failed to file reports to ABC. Based on total average paid and verified circulation during the six months ending June 30, 2014; ranked by paid circulation size.

Publication	Paid circ.	Publication	Paid circ.	Publication	Paid circ.
1. Game Informer		17. Wired	106,466	35. Vogue	64,562
Magazine	2,894,248	18. Popular Science	103,775	36. Glamour	64,167
2. Shape	296,157	19. Women's Health	102,411	37. Black Enterprise	63,511
3. Star Magazine	237,333	20. O, The Oprah Magazine	99,312	38. SKI Magazine	62,794
4. OK! Weekly	196,248	21. Motor Trend	94,041	39. Backpacker	62,565
5. Working Mother	194,167	22. Us Weekly	93,740	40. Esquire	62,122
6. Maxim	186,863	23. GQ	92,013	41. Vanidades	61,307
7. National Geographic	164,408	24. Nylon	91,322	42. Fit Pregnancy	61,009
8. Taste of Home	160,198	25. The New Yorker	89,404	43. Time	60,911
9. Men's Fitness	156,600	26. HGTV Magazine	88,977	44. Runner's World	59,871
10. Cosmopolitan	154,278	27. Vanity Fair	81,610	45. Popular Photography	57,484
11. Men's Health	134,855	28. People	78,464	46. Fast Company	56,203
12. Reader's Digest	132,294	29. Prevention	72,262	47. Every Day With Rachael	
13. ESPN The Magazine	124,205	30. Real Simple	71,784	Ray	54,500
14. Competitor	123,435	31. Yoga Journal	69,107	48. Weight Watchers	54,479
15. Better Homes and		32. Martha Stewart Living	67,522	49. Out	54,312
Gardens	113,566	33. EatingWell	67,097	50. Automobile Magazine	53,957
16. Food Network Magazine	110,123	34. Popular Mechanics	64,718		

Most Challenged Books, 2013

Source: Office for Intellectual Freedom, American Library Association (ALA)

A challenge is a formal, written complaint filed with a library or school requesting that materials be removed because of content or appropriateness.

Rank	Title, author	Common reasons given for challenge
1.	*Captain Underpants* (series), Dav Pilkey	Offensive language, unsuited for age group
2.	*The Bluest Eye*, Toni Morrison	Offensive language, sexually explicit, unsuited to age group, violence
3.	*The Absolutely True Diary of a Part-Time Indian*, Sherman Alexie	Offensive language, racism, sexually explicit, unsuited for age group
4.	*Fifty Shades of Grey*, E. L. James	Offensive language, sexually explicit
5.	*The Hunger Games*, Suzanne Collins	Religious viewpoint, unsuited to age group
6.	*A Bad Boy Can Be Good for a Girl*, Tanya Lee Stone	Drugs/alcohol/smoking, nudity, offensive language, sexually explicit
7.	*Looking for Alaska*, John Green	Drugs/alcohol/smoking, sexually explicit, unsuited to age group
8.	*The Perks of Being a Wallflower*, Stephen Chbosky	Drugs/alcohol/smoking, homosexuality, sexually explicit, unsuited to age group
9.	*Bless Me Ultima*, Rudolfo Anaya	Occult/Satanism, offensive language, religious viewpoint, sexually explicit
10.	*Bone* (series), Jeff Smith	Political viewpoint, racism, violence

Some Notable New Books, 2014

Source: Reference and User Services Association, American Library Association (ALA)

Fiction

Americanah, Chimamanda Ngozi Adichie
Life After Life, Kate Atkinson
Claire of the Sea Light, Edwidge Danticat
Too Bright to Hear Too Loud to See, Juliann Garey
Enon, Paul Harding
Unchangeable Spots of Leopards, Kristopher Jansma
The Dinner, Herman Koch
Constellation of Vital Phenomena, Anthony Marra
The Woman Upstairs, Claire Messud
Tale for the Time Being, Ruth Ozeki
The Goldfinch, Donna Tartt

Poetry

The Ogre's Wife: Poems, Ron Koertge
Hum, Jamaal May

Nonfiction

Lawrence in Arabia: War, Deceit, Imperial Folly, and the Making of the Modern Middle East, Scott Anderson
Year Zero: A History of 1945, Ian Baruma

On Paper: The Everything of Its Two-Thousand Year History, Nicholas Basbanes
To the End of June: The Intimate Life of American Foster Care, Cris Beam
The Boys in the Boat: Nine Americans and Their Quest for Gold at the 1936 Berlin Olympics, Daniel James Brown
Five Days at Memorial: Life and Death in a Storm-Ravaged Hospital, Sheri Fink
The Riddle of the Labyrinth: The Quest to Crack an Ancient Code, Margalit Fox
On the Map: A Mind-Expanding Exploration of the Way the World Looks, Simon Garfield
Johnny Cash: The Life, Robert Hilburn
The Skies Belong to Us: Love and Terror in the Golden Age of Hijacking, Brendan I. Koerner
Animal Wise: The Thoughts and Emotions of Our Fellow Creatures, Virginia Morell
Command and Control: Nuclear Weapons, the Damascus Accident, and the Illusion of Safety, Eric Schlosser
Faraway Nearby, Rebecca Solnit

Some Notable New Books for Children, 2014

Source: Association for Library Service to Children, American Library Association (ALA)

Younger Readers

Alphablock, Christopher Franceschelli, Peskimo (illus.)
Ball, Mary Sullivan
The Bathing Costume, or, the Worst Vacation of My Life, Charlotte Moundlic, Olivier Tallec (illus.)
Benjamin Bear in "Bright Ideas!" Philippe Coudray
A Big Guy Took My Ball!, Mo Willems
Building Our House, Jonathan Bean
Bully, Laura Vaccaro Seeger
Count the Monkeys, Mac Barnett, Kevin Cornell (illus.)
The Dark, Lemony Snicket, Jon Klassen (illus.)
The Day the Crayons Quit, Drew Daywalt, Oliver Jeffers (illus.)
Deep in the Sahara, Kelly Cunnane, Hoda Hadadi (illus.)
Eat Like a Bear, April Pulley Sayre, Steve Jenkins (illus.)
Exclamation Mark, Amy Krouse Rosenthal, Tom Lichtenheld (illus.)
Flight of the Honey Bee, Raymond Huber, Brian Lovelock (illus.)
Flora and the Flamingo, Molly Schaar Idle
Fraidyzoo, Thyra Heder
Little Santa, Jon Agee
Locomotive, Brian Floca
Lulu and the Dog From the Sea, Hilary McKay, Priscilla Lamont (illus.)
Maria Had a Little Llama/María tenía una llamita pequeña, Angela Dominguez
Martin and Mahalia: His Words, Her Song, Andrea Davis Pinkney, Brian Pinkney (illus)
Mitchell Goes Bowling, Hallie Durand, Tony Fucile (illus.)
Mool, David LaRochelle, Mike Wohnoutka (illus.)
Mr. Tiger Goes Wild, Peter Brown
Mr. Wuffles!, David Wiesner
My Father's Arms Are a Boat, Stein Erik Lunde, Øyvind Torseter (illus.)
My Happy Life, Rose Lagercrantz, Eva Eriksson (illus.)

Nelson Mandela, Kadir Nelson
Niño Wrestles the World, Yuyi Morales
Old Mikamba Had a Farm, Rachel Isadora
On a Beam of Light: A Story of Albert Einstein, Jennifer Berne, Jennifer Vladimir Radunsky (illus.)
Parrots Over Puerto Rico, Susan L. Roth and Cindy Trumbore, Susan L. Roth (illus.)
Penny and Her Marble, Kevin Henkes
Robot, Go Bot!, Dana Meachen Rau, Wook Jin Jung (illus.)
Take Me Out to the Yakyu, Aaron Meshon
Ten Orange Pumpkins: A Counting Book, Stephen Savage
Tito Puente: Mambo King/Rey del Mambo, Monica Brown, Rafael López (illus.)
The Tortoise and the Hare, Jerry Pinkney
Warning: Do Not Open This Book!, Adam Lehrhaupt, Matthew Forsythe (illus.)
The Watermelon Seed, Greg Pizzoli
Xander's Panda Party, Linda Sue Park, Matt Phelan (illus.)
The Year of Billy Miller, Kevin Henkes

Middle Readers

The Animal Book: A Collection of the Fastest, Fiercest, Toughest, Cleverest, Shyest—and Most Surprising—Animals on Earth, Steve Jenkins
Barbed Wire Baseball, Marissa Moss, Yuko Shimizu (illus.)
Battle Bunny, Jon Scieszka and Mac Barnett, Matthew Myers (illus.)
Battling Boy, Paul Pope
Better Nate Than Ever, Tim Federle
Bluffton: My Summers With Buster, Matt Phelan
Bo at Ballard Creek, Kirkpatrick Hill, LeUyen Pham (illus.)
The Boy on the Wooden Box: How the Impossible Became Possible … on Schindler's List, Leon Leyson

The Boy Who Loved Math: The Improbable Life of Paul Erdős, Deborah Heiligman, LeUyen Pham (illus.)

Doll Bones, Holly Black, Eliza Wheeler (illus.)

Eruption! Volcanoes and the Science of Saving Lives, Elizabeth Rusch, Tom Uhlman (illus.)

Escape From Mr. Lemoncello's Library, Chris Grabenstein

Farmer Will Allen and the Growing Table, Jacqueline Briggs Martin, Eric-Shabazz Larkin (illus.)

Flora and Ulysses: The Illuminated Adventures, Kate DiCamillo, K. G. Campbell (illus.)

Gone Fishing: A Novel in Verse, Tamera Will Wissinger, Tamera Matthew Cordell (illus.)

The Great American Dust Bowl, Don Brown

How to Catch a Bogle, Catherine Jinks, Sarah Watts (illus.)

Knock Knock: My Dad's Dream for Me, Daniel Beaty, Bryan Collier (illus.)

The Lightning Dreamer: Cuba's Greatest Abolitionist, Margarita Engle

Lincoln's Grave Robbers, Steve Sheinkin

Look Up! Bird-Watching in Your Own Backyard, Annette LeBlanc Cate

The Mad Potter: George E. Ohr, Eccentric Genius, Jan Greenberg and Sandra Jordan

Mister Orange, Truus Matti, Jenni Desmond (illus.)

Monster on the Hill, Rob Harrell

Pancho Rabbit and the Coyote: A Migrant's Tale, Duncan Tonatiuh

P.S. Be Eleven, Rita Williams-Garcia

Rooftoppers, Katherine Rundell, Terry Fan (illus.)

Serafina's Promise: A Novel in Verse, Ann E. Burg

Soldier Dog, Sam Angus

A Splash of Red: The Life and Art of Horace Pippin, Jen Bryant, Melissa Sweet (illus.)

Sugar, Jewell Parker Rhodes

Treasury of Egyptian Mythology, Donna Jo Napoli, Christina Balit (illus.)

The True Blue Scouts of Sugar Man Swamp, Kathi Appelt

The War Within These Walls, Aline Sax, Caryl Strzelecki (illus.)

When the Beat Was Born: DJ Kool Herc and the Creation of Hip Hop, Laban Carrick Hill, Theodore Taylor III (illus.)

When Stravinsky Met Nijinsky: Two Artists, Their Ballet, and One Extraordinary Riot, Lauren Stringer

Words With Wings, Nikki Grimes

Older Readers

Becoming Ben Franklin: How a Candle-Maker's Son Helped Light the Flame of Liberty, Russell Freedman

Counting by 7s, Holly Goldberg Sloan

Courage Has No Color: The True Story of the Triple Nickles, America's First Black Paratroopers, Tanya Lee Stone

Darius and Twig, Walter Dean Myers

Diego Rivera: An Artist for the People, Susan Goldman Rubin

Emancipation Proclamation: Lincoln and the Dawn of Liberty, Tonya Bolden

Etiquette and Espionage, Gail Carriger

Far Far Away, Tom McNeal

Go: A Kidd's Guide to Graphic Design, Chip Kidd

The Living, Matt de la Peña

March: Book One, John Lewis and Andrew Aydin, Nate Powell (illus.)

Navigating Early, Clare Vanderpool

One Came Home, Amy Timberlake

Paperboy, Vince Vawter

Yaqui Delgado Wants to Kick Your Ass, Meg Medina

All Ages

Journey, Aaron Becker

Poems to Learn by Heart, Caroline Kennedy, Jon J. Muth (illus.)

Best-Selling Books, 2013
Source: Publishers Weekly

Hardcover Fiction

1. *Inferno*, Dan Brown
2. *Doctor Sleep*, Stephen King
3. *Sycamore Row*, John Grisham
4. *And the Mountains Echoed*, Khaled Hosseini
5. *Longest Ride*, Nicholas Sparks
6. *The First Call From Heaven*, Mitch Albom
7. *Takedown Twenty*, Janet Evanovich
8. *Cross My Heart*, James Patterson
9. *Command Authority*, Tom Clancy and Mark Greaney
10. *The Cuckoo's Calling*, Robert Galbraith

Hardcover Nonfiction

1. *Killing Jesus: A History*, Bill O'Reilly and Martin Dugard
2. *Happy, Happy, Happy: My Life and Legacy as the Duck Commander*, Phil Anderson
3. *Si-Cology 1: Tales and Wisdom From Duck Dynasty's Favorite Uncle*, Si Robertson
4. *Things That Matter: Three Decades of Passions, Pastimes and Politics*, Charles Krauthammer
5. *Lean In: Women, Work, and the Will to Lead*, Sheryl Sandberg
6. *David and Goliath: Underdogs, Misfits, and the Art of Battling Giants*, Malcolm Gladwell
7. *The Duck Commander Family: How Faith, Family, and Ducks Built a Dynasty*, Willie Robertson and Korie Robertson
8. *The Pioneer Woman Cooks: A Year of Holidays*, Ree Drummond
9. *I Am Malala: The Girl Who Stood Up for Education and Was Shot by the Taliban*, Malala Yousafzai
10. *George Washington's Secret Six: The Spy Ring That Saved the American Revolution*, Brian Kilmeade

Mass Market Fiction

1. *A Game of Thrones*, George R. R. Martin
2. *The Racketeer*, John Grisham
3. *To Kill a Mockingbird*, Harper Lee
4. *A Clash of Kings*, George R. R. Martin
5. *A Feast for Crows*, George R. R. Martin
6. *A Dance With Dragons*, George R. R. Martin.
7. *A Storm of Swords*, George R. R. Martin
8. *A Wanted Man*, Lee Child
9. *Notorious Nineteen*, Janet Evanovich
10. *The Best of Me*, Nicholas Sparks

Trade Paperback

1. *The Great Gatsby*, F. Scott Fitzgerald
2. *Proof of Heaven: A Neurosurgeon's Journey Into the Afterlife*, Alexander Eben
3. *Entwined With You*, Sylvia Day

4. *Fifty Shades of Grey*, E. L. James
5. *Dark Witch*, Nora Roberts
6. *The 5 Love Languages: The Secret to Love That Lasts*, Gary D. Chapman
7. *Miss Kay's Duck Commander Kitchen: Faith, Family, and Food—Bringing Our Home to Your Table*, Kay Robertson
8. *Fifty Shades Darker*, E. L. James
9. *Fifty Shades Freed*, E. L. James
10. *40 Days With Jesus: Celebrating His Presence*, Sarah Young

E-books

1. *Inferno*, Dan Brown
2. *Gone Girl*, Gillian Flynn
3. *Fifty Shades of Grey*, E. L. James
4. *Sycamore Row*, John Grisham
5. *Safe Haven*, Nicholas Sparks
6. *Entwined With You*, Sylvia Day
7. *Fifty Shades Darker*, E. L. James
8. *Fifty Shades Freed*, E. L. James
9. *The Husband's Secret*, Liane Moriarty
10. *The Cuckoo's Calling*, Robert Galbraith

Children's and Young Adult Hardcover

1. *Hard Luck (Diary of a Wimpy Kid #8)*, Jeff Kinney
2. *Allegiant (Divergent #3)*, Veronica Roth
3. *The House of Hades (Heroes of Olympus #4)*, Rick Riordan
4. *Rush Revere and the Brave Pilgrims*, Rush Limbaugh
5. *Tales From a Not-So-Happy Heartbreaker (Dork Diaries #6)*, Rachel Renée Russell
6. *Pete the Cat: The Wheels on the Bus*, James Dean
7. *OMG! All About My Diary (Dork Diaries)*, Rachel Renée Russell
8. *Emeraldalicious (Pinkalicious)*, Victoria Kann
9. *Clockwork Princess (The Infernal Devices #3)*, Cassandra Clare
10. *The Day the Crayons Quit*, Drew Daywalt, Oliver Jeffers (illus.)

Children's and Young Adult Paperback

1. *Catching Fire (The Hunger Games #2)*, Suzanne Collins
2. *Pete the Cat: Pete's Big Lunch*, James Dean
3. *Miss Peregrine's Home for Peculiar Children*, Ransom Riggs
4. *Pinkalicious and the Cupcake Calamity*, Victoria Kann
5. *Pete the Cat: Play Ball!*, James Dean
6. *Ender's Game*, Orson Scott Card
7. *Clockwork Princess (The Infernal Devices #3)*, Cassandra Clare
8. *Pink or Treat! (Pinkalicious)*, Victoria Kann
9. *Pete the Cat: Pete at the Beach*, James Dean
10. *The Care and Keeping of You 1: The Body Book for Younger Girls*, Valorie Schaefer, Josée Masse (illus.)

U.S. Daily Newspapers, 2014
Source: Alliance for Audited Media
(ranked by daily paid circulation for the six months ending Mar. 31, 2014)

Rank	Newspaper	Circulation	Rank	Newspaper	Circulation
1.	McLean (VA) *USA Today*	2,876,586	27.	San Diego (CA) *U-T*	222,541
2.	New York (NY) *Wall Street Journal*	2,273,767	28.	Cleveland (OH) *Plain Dealer*	214,300
3.	New York (NY) *Times*	1,897,890	29.	San Francisco (CA) *Chronicle*	212,179
4.	Los Angeles (CA) *Times*	671,797	30.	Kansas City (MO) *Star*	210,376
5.	New York (NY) *Post*	576,711	31.	Pittsburgh (PA) *Tribune-Review*	199,182
6.	San Jose (CA) *Mercury News*	571,804	32.	St. Paul (MN) *Pioneer Press*	197,727
7.	New York (NY) *Daily News*	467,110	33.	Detroit (MI) *Free Press*	196,955
8.	Chicago (IL) *Tribune*	453,568	34.	Milwaukee (WI) *Journal Sentinel*	194,321
9.	Long Island (NY) *Newsday*	437,457	35.	Sacramento (CA) *Bee*	190,579
10.	Washington (DC) *Post*	431,521	36.	Miami (FL) *Herald*	181,853
11.	Chicago (IL) *Sun-Times*	419,364	37.	Tampa (FL) *Tribune*	181,589
12.	Dallas (TX) *Morning News*	411,929	38.	Atlanta (GA) *Journal-Constitution*	174,610
13.	Los Angeles (CA) *Daily News*	410,068	39.	Fort Worth (TX) *Star-Telegram*	172,233
14.	Denver (CO) *Post*	403,039	40.	St. Louis (MO) *Post-Dispatch*	161,343
15.	Houston (TX) *Chronicle*	356,347	41.	Salt Lake City (UT) *Tribune*	161,108
16.	Orange County (CA) *Register*	330,246	42.	Baltimore (MD) *Sun*	155,352
17.	Philadelphia (PA) *Inquirer*	310,002	43.	Pittsburgh (PA) *Post-Gazette*	153,078
18.	Minneapolis (MN) *Star Tribune*	300,495	44.	Ft. Lauderdale (FL) *South Florida Sun-Sentinel*	151,413
19.	St. Petersburg (FL) *Times*	299,985	45.	Indianapolis (IN) *Star*	147,342
20.	Newark (NJ) *Star-Ledger*	285,249	46.	Little Rock (AR) *Democrat-Gazette*	146,292
21.	Honolulu (HI) *Star-Advertiser*	265,099	47.	Woodland Park (NJ) *Herald News*	144,897
22.	Boston (MA) *Globe*	253,373	48.	Buffalo (NY) *News*	142,509
23.	Phoenix (AZ) *Republic*	245,133	49.	Fresno (CA) *Bee*	142,385
24.	Seattle (WA) *Times*	241,320	50.	Orlando (FL) *Sentinel*	139,752
25.	Las Vegas (NV) *Review-Journal*	233,326			
26.	Portland (OR) *Oregonian*	225,868			

Note: Excludes newspapers for which no average M-F circulation number was available.

Paid U.S. Newspaper Circulation, 1940-2013
Source: *Editor & Publisher International Data Book*
(circulation figures in thousands)

Year	Number of daily newspapers			Circulation of daily newspapers			Sunday newspapers	
	Morning	Evening	Total	Morning	Evening	Total	Number	Circulation
1940	380	1,498	1,878	16,114	25,018	41,132	525	32,371
1950	322	1,450	1,772	21,266	32,563	53,829	549	46,582
1960	312	1,459	1,763	24,029	34,853	58,882	563	47,699
1970	334	1,429	1,748	25,934	36,174	62,108	586	49,217
1980	387	1,388	1,745	29,414	32,787	62,202	736	54,676
1990	559	1,084	1,611	41,311	21,017	62,328	863	62,635
2000	766	727	1,480	46,772	9,000	55,773	917	59,421
2005	817	645	1,452	46,122	7,222	53,345	914	55,270
2006	833	614	1,437	45,441	6,888	52,329	907	53,179
2007	867	565	1,422	44,548	6,194	50,742	907	51,246
2008	872	546	1,408	42,758	5,840	48,598	902	49,115
2009	869	528	1,397	40,796	5,482	46,278	919	46,850
2011	931	451	1,382	40,321	4,100	44,421	900	48,510
2012	985	442	1,427	38,723	4,709	43,432	981	48,821
2013	980	444	1,395	36,795	3,737	40,712	934	43,292

Newspaper Advertising Revenues, 1950-2013
Source: Research Dept., Newspaper Association of America

Year	National ad revenue (mil $)	Retail ad revenue (mil $)	Classified ad revenue (mil $)	Print advertising total revenue		Online advertising total revenue		Total advertising revenue	
				(mil $)	% change[1]	(mil $)	% change	(mil $)	% change
1950	$518	$1,175	$377	$2,070	—	—	—	—	—
1955	712	1,755	610	3,077	48.7%	—	—	—	—
1960	778	2,100	803	3,681	19.6	—	—	—	—
1965	783	2,429	1,214	4,426	20.2	—	—	—	—
1970	891	3,292	1,521	5,704	28.9	—	—	—	—
1975	1,109	4,966	2,159	8,234	44.4	—	—	—	—
1980	1,963	8,609	4,222	14,794	79.7	—	—	—	—
1985	3,352	13,443	8,375	25,170	70.1	—	—	—	—
1990	4,122	16,652	11,506	32,280	28.3	—	—	—	—
1995	4,251	18,099	13,742	36,092	11.8	—	—	—	—
2000	7,653	21,409	19,608	48,670	5.1	—	—	—	—
2005	7,910	22,187	17,312	47,408	1.5	$2,027	31.5%	$49,435	2.5%
2006	7,505	22,121	16,986	46,611	-1.7	2,664	31.4	49,275	-0.3
2007	7,005	21,018	14,186	42,209	-9.4	3,166	18.8	45,375	-7.9
2008	5,996	18,769	9,975	34,740	-17.7	3,109	-1.8	37,848	-16.6
2009	4,424	14,218	6,179	24,821	-28.6	2,743	-11.8	27,564	-27.2
2010	4,221	12,926	5,648	22,795	-8.2	3,042	10.9	25,838	-6.3
2011[2]	3,777	11,887	5,028	20,692	-9.2	3,249	6.8	23,941	-7.3
2012[2]	3,335	10,894	4,626	18,931	-8.5	3,370	3.7	22,314	-6.8
2013[2]	3,068	10,105	4,140	17,300	-8.6	3,420	1.5	20,720	-7.1

(1) Percent change for years 1950-2000 refers to the rate of change over the preceding five-year period; for 2005 and on, it represents the rate of change over the past year. (2) Revenue from niche publications, direct marketing, and non-daily publication advertising ($3.0 bil in 2011, $2.9 bil in 2012, and $2.85 bil in 2013) is excluded from total revenue.

Canadian Daily Newspapers, 2013

Source: *Editor & Publisher International Data Book*
(ranked by circulation as of Sept. 30, 2013)

Newspaper	Circulation	Newspaper	Circulation
1. Toronto (ON) *Globe and Mail*	360,658	6. Vancouver (BC) *Sun*	154,058
2. Montréal (QC) *La Presse*	267,603	7. Vancouver (BC) *Province*	137,061
3. Toronto (ON) *Star*	230,433	8. Toronto (ON) *Sun*	124,895
4. Montréal (QC) *Le Journal de Montréal*	194,266	9. Calgary (AB) *Herald*	114,919
5. Toronto (ON) *National Post*	159,483	10. Ottawa (ON) *The Ottawa Citizen*	111,272

Top Newspaper Websites, 2014

Source: comScore Media Metrix, Inc.; ranked by number of visitors.

Rank	Website	Visitors[1]	% change[2]	Rank	Website	Visitors[1]	% change[2]
1.	The New York Times Brand	49,287	82.2%	12.	Lee Enterprises, Inc.	11,792	65.7%
2.	Mail Online	39,975	139.9	13.	Independent.co.uk	9,240	185.2
3.	T365-Tribune Newspapers	38,885	64.1	14.	Mirror Online	9,184	NA
4.	WashingtonPost.com	32,357	106.1	15.	Cox Media Group-Newspaper	8,353	NA
5.	Hearst Newspapers	28,951	76.1	16.	Sun-Times Media/Chicago		
6.	The Guardian	21,651	70.4		Region-Wide Network (CRWN)	7,325	40.0
7.	McClatchy Corporation	20,519	79.2	17.	Philly.com sites	6,720	62.7
8.	MediaNews Group	17,610	60.4	18.	Michigan Media Solutions	6,358	NA
9.	Telegraph Media Group	15,556	161.8	19.	Boston.com	6,314	15.0
10.	NYPost Network	14,888	143.9	20.	A. H. Belo	6,255	NA
11.	Topix	11,817	77.0				

NA = Not available. (1) Number of unique visitors, in thousands, who visited website at least once in June 2014. (2) Percent change over June 2013.

Top News/Information Websites, 2014

Source: comScore Media Metrix, Inc.; ranked by number of visitors.

Rank	Website	Visitors[1]	% change[2]	Rank	Website	Visitors[1]	% change[2]
1.	Yahoo!-ABC News Network	128,990	54.6%	11.	New York Times Digital	49,459	61.6%
2.	HPMG News	118,707	96.8	12.	Fox News Digital Network	48,208	80.4
3.	CNN Network	114,040	86.1	13.	Mail Online	39,975	139.9
4.	The Weather Company	102,287	88.8	14.	T365-Tribune Newspapers	38,885	64.2
5.	Gannett sites	99,751	107.4	15.	AccuWeather sites	38,762	NA
6.	About.com	75,901	29.7	16.	Advance Digital	36,897	153.4
7.	Buzzfeed.com	74,767	NA	17.	The Washington Post Company	32,357	39.0
8.	NBC News Digital	74,140	41.8	18.	Hearst Newspapers	28,951	76.1
9.	CBS News	59,688	83.8	19.	Time.com sites	28,703	NA
10.	WorldNow sites	50,247	162.7	20.	Elite Daily	26,336	NA

NA = Not available. (1) Number of unique visitors, in thousands, who visited website at least once in June 2014. (2) Percent change over June 2013.

Top-Selling Albums of All-Time

Source: Recording Industry Assn. of America (RIAA)
(Sales figures represent RIAA multi-platinum certifications; albums ranked by latest sales certification. As of Aug. 24, 2014.)

Rank	Title, artist	Unit sales (mil)	Rank	Title, artist	Unit sales (mil)
1.	*Eagles/Their Greatest Hits 1971-1975*, Eagles	29.0	16.	*Hotel California*, Eagles	16.0
	Thriller, Michael Jackson	29.0		*Metallica*, Metallica	16.0
3.	*Led Zeppelin IV*, Led Zeppelin	23.0		*Cracked Rear View*, Hootie & the Blowfish	16.0
	The Wall, Pink Floyd	23.0		*Greatest Hits*, Elton John	16.0
	Greatest Hits Volume I & Volume II, Billy Joel	23.0		*Physical Graffiti*, Led Zeppelin	16.0
6.	*Back in Black*, AC/DC	22.0		*Jagged Little Pill*, Alanis Morissette	16.0
7.	*Double Live*, Garth Brooks	21.0	22.	*Supernatural*, Santana	15.0
8.	*Come on Over*, Shania Twain	20.0		*The Beatles 1962-1966*, The Beatles	15.0
9.	*The Beatles*, The Beatles	19.0		*Greatest Hits*, Journey	15.0
	Rumours, Fleetwood Mac	19.0		*Saturday Night Fever* (soundtrack), Bee Gees	15.0
11.	*Appetite for Destruction*, Guns N' Roses	18.0		*Born in the U.S.A.*, Bruce Springsteen	15.0
12.	*Boston*, Boston	17.0		*Dark Side of the Moon*, Pink Floyd	15.0
	The Bodyguard (soundtrack), Whitney Houston	17.0		*Legend*, Bob Marley and the Wailers	15.0
	No Fences, Garth Brooks	17.0			
	The Beatles 1967-1970, The Beatles	17.0			

Top-Selling Artists by Digital Sales

Source: Recording Industry Assn. of America (RIAA)
(Sales figures represent RIAA-confirmed digital units sold. As of Aug. 24, 2014.)

Artist	Unit sales (mil)	Artist	Unit sales (mil)	Artist	Unit sales (mil)	Artist	Unit sales (mil)
Katy Perry	72.0	The Black Eyed		Kenny Chesney	14.0	Linkin Park	11.0
Rihanna	52.0	Peas	22.0	Akon	13.5	Miranda Lambert	11.0
Taylor Swift	51.0	Adele	22.0	Lady Antebellum	13.0	Toby Keith	11.0
Lil Wayne	32.0	Jason Aldean	21.5	Macklemore and		Fun	11.0
Kanye West	31.5	Nicki Minaj	20.0	Ryan Lewis	13.0	The Fray	11.0
Eminem	31.0	Beyoncé	19.0	Tim McGraw	13.0	One Direction	11.0
Flo Rida	29.5	LMFAO	18.0	Train	12.5	One Republic	11.0
Lady Gaga	28.5	Luke Bryan	16.5	Blake Shelton	12.0	Justin Timberlake	11.0
Bruno Mars	28.0	Selena Gomez &		Florida Georgia Line	12.0	Wiz Khalifa	10.5
Justin Bieber	25.0	the Scene	15.0	Nelly	11.5	David Guetta	10.5
Drake	24.0	Maroon 5	15.0	Jason Mraz	11.5	Miley Cyrus	10.0
Carrie Underwood	22.5	Jason Derulo	14.5	Jay Z	11.0	Timbaland	10.0

U.S. Commercial Radio Stations by Format, 2004-14

Source: The Radio Book by Inside Radio © 2014
(as of June 2014; ranked by 2014 numbers)

Primary format	2014	2013	2012	2011	2010	2009	2008	2007	2006	2005	2004
1. Country..............	2,053	2,042	2,020	1,987	1,997	1,995	2,018	2,027	2,038	2,022	2,047
2. News/Talk.............	1,409	1,453	1,503	1,455	1,437	1,416	1,365	1,368	1,338	1,326	1,287
3. Spanish.................	844	835	816	818	806	803	799	786	706	696	665
4. Sports.................	788	740	692	670	665	634	595	564	535	508	472
5. Classic Hits............	754	678	657	657	637	582	524	477	429	271	237
6. Adult Contemporary.......	597	605	597	607	634	626	670	665	660	683	696
7. Top 40................	577	573	559	523	495	484	472	472	484	503	502
8. Classic Rock..........	486	486	477	477	481	477	474	456	456	461	451
9. Oldies................	476	566	597	628	637	649	708	709	725	762	811
10. Hot Adult Contemporary....	465	428	420	435	417	409	373	373	378	374	420
11. Religion (Teaching, Variety)	324	336	342	332	322	324	299	287	311	319	329
12. Rock.................	302	299	295	301	294	298	287	281	276	269	282
13. Adult Standards..........	221	227	240	251	265	327	358	369	368	404	458
14. Black Gospel...........	211	212	214	225	235	242	244	253	267	286	274
15. Southern Gospel..........	169	172	170	188	197	209	211	204	208	206	204
Stations off the air.........	216	237	264	261	253	223	135	92	88	72	81
Total operating stations...	**11,099**	**11,107**	**11,078**	**11,034**	**11,024**	**10,977**	**10,853**	**10,760**	**10,711**	**10,674**	**10,732**

Note: Totals include stations that are changing or did not report format, as well as formats not listed here.

Multi-Platinum and Platinum Awards for Recorded Music and Music Videos, 2013-14

Source: Recording Industry Assn. of America

To achieve platinum status, an **album** must reach minimum total sales of 1 mil units in LPs, CDs, and digital with a manufacturer's dollar volume of at least $2 mil based on one-third of the suggested retail list price for each record, CD, or digital copy sold. To achieve multi-platinum status, an album must reach minimum total sales of at least 2 mil units in LPs, CDs, and digital with a manufacturer's dollar volume of at least $4 mil based on one-third of the list price.

Singles must sell 1 mil units to achieve a platinum award and 2 mil to achieve a multi-platinum award. **Digital singles** are certified at the same levels; the digital sales award was first given in 2004. **Music videos** (longform) must sell 100,000 units to qualify for a platinum award and more than 200,000 units for a multi-platinum award.

Awards listed here are albums, digital singles, and music videos (released Sept. 2012-Aug. 2014) that were certified Sept. 2013-Aug. 2014. Number in parentheses represents millions sold. Alphabetized by artist name.

Albums, Multi-Platinum

Beyoncé, Beyoncé (2)
Crash My Party, Luke Bryan (2)
The Marshall Mathers LP 2, Eminem (2)
Here's to the Good Times, Florida Georgia Line (2)
Frozen soundtrack, various artists (3)
Night Visions, Imagine Dragons (2)
Magna Carta... Holy Grail, Jay Z (2)
Unorthodox Jukebox, Bruno Mars (2)
Truth About Love, Pink (2)
Formula Vol. 2, Romeo Santos (4)

Albums, Platinum

Blue-Eyed Soul, Garth Brooks
Melting Pot, Garth Brooks
Country Hits, Garth Brooks
Classic Rock, Garth Brooks
Wrapped in Red, Kelly Clarkson
Bangerz, Miley Cyrus
Random Access Memories, Daft Punk
Pure Heroine, Lorde
The Heist, Macklemore and Ryan Lewis
Midnight Memories, One Direction
Archivos de Mi Vida, Gerardo Ortiz
El Primer Ministro, Gerardo Ortiz
Pitch Perfect soundtrack, various artists
1969-Siempre, Jenni Rivera
Duck the Halls, The Robertsons
Soy El Mismo, Prince Royce
Number 1's, Prince Royce
Based on a True Story..., Blake Shelton
The 20/20 Experience 2 of 2, Justin Timberlake
Yeezus, Kanye West

Music Videos, Multi-Platinum

Minding the Monsters, Jeff Dunham (4)
Celebration Day, Led Zeppelin (3)
Time Machine, Rush (2)

Digital Singles, Platinum and Multi-Platinum

"Bugatti," Ace Hood
"Night Train," "The Only Way I Know," Jason Aldean

"Best Day of My Life" (2), American Authors
"F**kin' Problems" (2), A$AP Rocky
"Wake Me Up" (4), Avicii
"Fancy" (2), Iggy Azalea
"Harlem Shake" (2), Baauer
"Brave" (2), Sara Bareilles
"Pompeii" (3), Bastille
"Do You Want to Build a Snowman?", Kristen Bell
"Drunk in Love," Beyoncé
"The Man," Aloe Blacc
"Crash My Party" (2), "Drink a Beer," "Play It Again," "That's My Kind of Night" (2), Luke Bryan
"Safe and Sound" (2), Capital Cities
"Get Lucky" (4), Daft Punk
"Young and Beautiful," Lana Del Rey
"The Other Side," "Talk Dirty," Jason Derulo
"Latch," Disclosure
"Turn Down for What?" (3), DJ Snake & Lil Jon
"All Me," "Hold On, We're Going Home" (3), Drake
"My Songs Know What You Did in the Dark (Light Em Up)" (3), Fall Out Boy
"Redneck Crazy," Tyler Farr
"Round Here," "Stay," "This is How We Roll," Florida Georgia Line
"Animals," Martin Garrix
"Bottoms Up," Brantley Gilbert
"Come & Get It" (3), "Slow Down," Selena Gomez
"Problem" (2), Ariana Grande
"Say Something" (4), A Great Big World and Christina Aguilera
"I Need Your Love," "Summer," Calvin Harris
"Sweet Nothing" (2), Calvin Harris feat. Florence Welch
"Holy Grail" (3), Jay Z
"Cups" (3), Anna Kendrick
"Show Me," Kid Ink feat. Chris Brown
"All of Me" (5), John Legend
"Love Me" (2), "Rich As F**k," Lil Wayne

"Royals" (6), "Team" (2), Lorde
"Let It Go," "Neon Lights," Demi Lovato
"Same Love" (2), Macklemore and Ryan Lewis feat. Mary Lambert
"Rude," Magic!
"Treasure" (3), "When I Was Your Man" (4), Bruno Mars
"Let It Go" (3), Idina Menzel
"Classic," MKTO
"Merry Go 'Round," Kacey Musgraves
"Whatever She's Got," David Nail
"Drink to That All Night," Jerrod Neimann
"Best Song Ever," "Story of My Life" (2), One Direction
"Beachin'," Jake Owen
"Ain't It Fun," "Still Into You," Paramore
"Human," Christina Perri
"Dark Horse" (6), "Roar" (6), "Unconditionally," Katy Perry
"Wasting All These Tears," Cassadee Pope
"Darte Un Beso" (3), Prince Royce
"Gangnam Style" (5), Psy
"It Goes Like This," Thomas Rhett
"Diamonds" (4), "Stay" (4), Rihanna
"Wagon Wheel" (4), Darius Rucker
"Gas Pedal," Sage the Gemini
"Odio," Romeo Santos feat. Drake
"Boys 'Round Here" (2), Blake Shelton feat. Pistol Annies and friends
"Give It All We Got Tonight," George Strait
"Don't You Worry Child" (3), Swedish House Mafia
"I Knew You Were Trouble" (5), "22" (2), Taylor Swift
"Chillin' It," Cole Swindell
"Blurred Lines" (6), Robin Thicke
"Not A Bad Thing," Justin Timberlake
"Por Que Les Mientes," Tito El Bambino
"We Own It (Fast & Furious)," 2 Chainz
"Wicked Games," The Weeknd
"Clique" (2), Kanye West
"Happy" (4), Pharrell Williams
"My Hitta," YG
"Stay the Night," Zedd
"Replay," Zendaya

Top-Grossing North American Concert Tours, 1985-2013

Source: Pollstar

Rank Artist (year)	Total gross[1]	Cities/ shows	Rank Artist (year)	Total gross[1]	Cities/ shows
1. The Rolling Stones (2005)	$162.0	38/42	15. Bruce Springsteen & The E Street Band (2012)	$104.7	42/52
2. U2 (2011)	156.0	21/25	16. Pink Floyd (1994)	103.5	39/59
3. U2 (2005)	138.9	43/78	17. Paul McCartney (2002)	103.3	43/53
4. The Rolling Stones (2006)	138.5	35/39	18. The Rolling Stones (1989)	98.0	33/60
5. Madonna (2012)	133.7	31/45	19. Taylor Swift (2011)	97.7	59/80
6. The Police (2007)	133.2	41/54	20. Kenny Chesney and Tim McGraw (2012)	96.5	22/23
7. U2 (2009)	123.0	16/20	21. Bruce Springsteen & The E Street Band (2009)	94.5	44/58
8. The Rolling Stones (1994)	121.2	43/60	22. Céline Dion (2008)	94.0	31/47
9. Bruce Springsteen & The E Street Band (2003)	115.9	30/47	23. Barbra Streisand (2006)	92.5	16/20
10. Taylor Swift (2013)	112.7	47/66	24. Kenny Chesney (2013)	90.9	41/44
11. U2 (2001)	109.7	56/80	25. Roger Waters (2012)	90.2	38/42
12. Bon Jovi (2010)	108.2	38/51			
13. Bon Jovi (2013)	107.3	58/62			
14. Madonna (2008)	105.3	19/30			

(1) In millions. Not adjusted for inflation.

Sales of Recorded Music and Music Videos, by Units Shipped and Value, 2000-13

Source: Recording Industry Assn. of America
(in millions, net after returns)

	2000	2005	2007	2008	2009	2010	2011	2012	2013	% change, 2012-13
Physical units shipped	1,079.2	748.7	543.9	385.5	309.2	233.0	222.0	182.9	159.1	-13.0%
Dollar value	$14,323.7	11,195.0	7,985.8	5,758.5	4,555.9	3,438.7	3,170.9	2,584.3	2,267.7	-12.3
Compact discs (CDs)	942.5	705.4	511.1	368.4	292.9	253.0	240.8	198.2	172.2	-13.1
Dollar value	$13,214.5	10,520.2	7,452.3	5,471.4	4,274.1	3,389.4	3,100.7	2,485.6	2,123.5	-14.6
Cassettes	76.0	2.5	0.4	0.1	—	—	—	—	—	—
Dollar value	$626.0	13.1	3.0	0.9	—	—	—	—	—	—
LP/EP	2.2	1.0	1.3	2.9	3.2	4.2	5.5	6.9	9.4	35.2
Dollar value	$27.7	14.2	22.9	56.7	60.2	88.9	119.4	160.7	210.7	31.1
CD singles	34.2	2.8	2.6	0.7	0.9	1.0	1.3	1.1	0.6	-41.4
Dollar value	$142.7	10.9	12.2	3.5	3.1	2.9	3.5	3.2	2.4	-24.2
Vinyl singles	4.8	2.3	0.6	0.4	0.3	0.3	0.4	0.4	0.3	-18.8
Dollar value	$26.3	13.2	4.0	2.9	2.5	2.3	4.6	4.7	3.0	-37.2
Music videos[1]	18.2	33.8	27.5	12.8	11.8	9.1	7.7	6.0	4.7	-21.8
Dollar value	$281.9	602.2	484.9	218.9	212.0	177.6	151.0	116.6	104.7	-10.2
Digital formats[2]	—	383.1	868.4	1,128.6	1,236.8	1,283.4	1,454.7	1,521.4	1,459.0	-4.1
Dollar value	—	$503.6	1,257.5	1,711.5	2,030.7	2,232.9	2,628.3	2,852.9	2,825.4	-1.0
Download albums	—	13.6	42.5	63.6	76.4	85.8	103.9	116.7	118.0	1.1
Dollar value	—	$135.7	424.9	635.3	763.4	872.4	1,070.8	1,204.8	1,233.5	2.4
Download singles	—	366.9	809.9	1,042.7	1,138.3	1,177.4	1,332.3	1,392.2	1,328.9	-4.5
Dollar value	—	$363.3	801.6	1,032.2	1,220.3	1,317.4	1,522.4	1,623.6	1,569.0	-3.4
Music videos	—	1.9	14.2	20.8	20.4	18.4	16.3	10.5	8.4	-19.6
Dollar value	—	$3.7	28.2	41.3	40.6	36.6	32.4	20.8	16.8	-19.6
Mobile formats[3]	—	170.0	362.0	405.1	305.8	188.5	115.4	69.3	39.2	-43.4
Dollar value	—	$421.6	880.8	977.1	728.8	448.0	276.2	166.9	97.6	-41.5
Subscription formats[4]	—	1.3	1.8	1.6	1.2	1.5	1.8	3.4	6.1	81.3
Dollar value	—	$149.2	201.3	221.4	213.1	212.4	359.2	570.8	848.1	57.1
Digital performances & streaming[5]	—	27.4	47.0	100.0	155.5	249.2	292.0	462.0	590.4	27.8
Total units[6]	1,079.2	1,301.8	1,774.3	1,919.2	1,851.8	1,739.6	1,824.9	1,803.3	1,685.6	-6.5
Total value	$14,323.7	12,296.9	10,372.1	8,768.4	7,683.9	6,995.0	7,133.1	7,015.7	6,886.1	-1.8

— = Not available or not applicable. (1) Includes DVD videos. (2) Includes kiosk singles and albums. (3) Includes master ringtones, ringbacks, music videos, full-length downloads, and other mobile music. (4) Weighted annual average. (5) Estimated royalty payments in dollars to artists and copyright holders distributed by SoundExchange. (6) Includes albums and singles; excludes subscriptions and royalties.

Top Basic Cable TV Networks, 2013

Source: SNL Kagan

Rank	Network (year began)	Subscribers (mil)	Rank	Network (year began)	Subscribers (mil)
1.	The Weather Channel (1982)	99.7	11.	HGTV (1994)	98.5
2.	C-SPAN (1979)	99.4	12.	CNN (1980)	98.5
3.	TBS (1976)	99.1	13.	A&E (1984)	98.3
4.	Food Network (1993)	99.1	14.	History (1995)	98.2
5.	Discovery Channel (1985)	98.7	15.	AMC (1984)	98.2
6.	Nickelodeon/Nick At Nite (1979)	98.7	16.	HLN (1982)	98.0
7.	Lifetime Television (1984)	98.6	17.	Disney Channel (1983)	97.9
8.	USA Network (1980)	98.6	18.	TLC (1980)	97.9
9.	TNT (1988)	98.6	19.	Comedy Central (1991)	97.8
10.	Cartoon Network (1992)	98.5	20.	ESPN (1979)	97.8

U.S. Television Set Owners, 2014

Source: Nielsen Media Research, July 2014

Of the 115.8 mil U.S. households that owned at least one TV set in 2014:

84.2% had 2 or more TV sets	39.6% had a VCR	89.6% received basic cable
32.4% had 4 or more TV sets	80.9% had a DVD player	48.6% received premium cable
	48.5% had a DVR	

U.S. Households With Cable Television, 1980-2014
Source: Nielsen Media Research

Year[1]	Subscribers[2] (mil)	As % of households with TVs	Year[1]	Subscribers[2] (mil)	As % of households with TVs	Year[1]	Subscribers[2] (mil)	As % of households with TVs
1980	17.7	22.6%	1995	62.1	65.1%	2005	94.0	85.7%
1985	38.7	45.3	1996	63.6	66.3	2006	95.0	86.2
1986	40.9	47.4	1997	65.1	67.2	2007	94.5	83.8
1987	43.3	49.2	1998	65.9	67.2	2008	99.7	88.2
1988	46.3	52.0	1999	76.4	76.9	2009	103.0	89.7
1989	50.2	55.6	2000	78.6	77.9	2010	104.1	90.6
1990	53.9	58.6	2001	81.5	79.8	2011	104.8	90.4
1991	56.1	60.3	2002	87.8	83.8	2012	103.6	90.3
1992	56.2	61.1	2003	88.4	82.9	2013	103.3	90.5
1993	57.6	61.9	2004	92.4	85.3	2014	103.7	89.6
1994	59.7	63.4						

(1) After 1998, figures include wired-cable households as well as households that receive TV programming via alternate delivery systems (including satellite receivers, SMATV, MMDS). (2) Households that subscribe to basic cable service.

Selected Reality TV Show Winners, 2000-14
Numbers in parentheses represent the season, edition, or cycle of the show. As of Sept. 2014.

The Amazing Race. Debuted Aug. 2001 on CBS. Rob Frisbee & Brennan Swain (1); Chris Luca & Alex Boylan (2); Flo Pesenti & Zach Behr (3); Reichen Lehmkuhl & Chip Arndt (4); Chip & Kim McAllister (5); Freddy Holliday & Kendra Bentley (6); Uchenna & Joyce Agu (7); The Linz Family (8); B. J. Averell & Tyler MacNiven (9); Tyler Denk & James Branaman (10); All-Stars: Eric Sanchez & Danielle Turner (11); TK Erwin & Rachel Morales (12); Nick & Starr Spangler (13); Tammy & Victor Jih (14); Meghan Rickey & Cheyne Whitney (15); Dan & Jordan Pious (16); Natalie Strand & Katherine Chang (17); LaKisha & Jennifer Hoffman (18); Ernie Halvorsen & Cindy Chiang (19); Rachel Brown & Dave Brown Jr. (20); Josh Kilmer-Purcell & Brent Ridge (21); Bates & Anthony Battaglia (22); Jason Case & Amy Diaz (23).

American Idol. Debuted July 2002 on FOX. Kelly Clarkson (1); Ruben Studdard (2); Fantasia Barrino (3); Carrie Underwood (4); Taylor Hicks (5); Jordin Sparks (6); David Cook (7); Kris Allen (8); Lee DeWyze (9); Scotty McCreery (10); Phillip Phillips (11); Candice Glover (12); Caleb Johnson (13).

America's Got Talent. Debuted June 2006 on NBC. Bianca Ryan (1); Terry Fator (2); Neil E. Boyd (3); Kevin Skinner (4); Michael Grimm (5); Landau Eugene Murphy Jr. (6); Olate Dogs (7); Kenichi Ebina (8); Mat Franco (9).

America's Next Top Model. Debuted May 2003 on UPN. Adrianne Curry (1); Yoanna House (2); Naima Mora (4); Nicole Linkletter (5); Danielle Evans (6); CariDee English (7); Jaslene Gonzalez (8); Saleisha Stowers (9); Whitney Thompson (10); McKey Sullivan (11); Teyona Anderson (12); Nicole Fox (13); Krista White (14); Ann Ward (15); Brittani Kline (16); Lisa D'Amato (17); Sophie Sumner (18); Laura James (19); Jourdan Miller (20).

The Apprentice. Debuted Jan. 2004 on NBC. Bill Rancic (1); Kelly Perdew (2); Kendra Todd (3); Randal Pinkett (4); Sean Yazbeck (5); Stefani Schaeffer (6); Brandy Kuentzel (7). *Celebrity Apprentice:* Piers Morgan (1); Joan Rivers (2); Bret Michaels (3); John Rich (4); Arsenio Hall (5); Trace Adkins (6).

The Bachelor. Debuted Mar. 2002 on ABC. Alex Michel chose Amanda Marsh (1); Aaron Buerge chose Helene Eksterowicz (2); Andrew Firestone chose Jen Schefft (3); Bob Guiney chose Estella Gardinier (4); Jesse Palmer chose Jessica Bowlin (5); Byron Velvick chose Mary Delgado (6); Charlie O'Connell chose Sarah Brice (7); Travis Stork chose Sarah Stone (8); Lorenzo Borghese chose Jennifer Wilson (9); Andy Baldwin chose Tessa Horst (10); Brad Womack chose no one (11); Matt Grant chose Shayne Lamas (12); Jason Mesnick chose Melissa Rycroft (13); Jake Pavelka chose Vienna Girardi (14); Brad Womack chose Emily Maynard (15); Ben Flajnik chose Courtney Robertson (16); Sean Lowe chose Catherine Giudici (17); Juan Pablo Galavis chose Nikki Ferrell (18).

The Bachelorette. Debuted Jan. 2003 on ABC. Trista Rehn chose Ryan Sutter (1); Meredith Phillips chose Ian McKee (2); Jen Schefft chose Jerry Ferris (3); DeAnna Pappas chose Jesse Csincsak (4); Jillian Harris chose Ed Swiderski (5); Ali Fedotowsky chose Roberto Martinez (6); Ashley Hebert chose J. P. Rosenbaum (7); Emily Maynard chose Jef Holm (8); Desiree Hartsock chose Chris Siegfried (9); Andi Dorfman chose Josh Murray (10).

Big Brother. Debuted July 2000 on CBS. Eddie McGee (1); Will Kirby (2); Lisa Donahue (3); Jun Song (4); Drew Daniel (5); Maggie Ausburn (6); Mike Malinto (7); Dick Donato (8); Adam Jasinski (9); Dan Gheesling (10); Jordan Lloyd (11); Hayden Moss (12); Rachel Reilly (13); Ian Terry (14); Andy Herren (15); Derrick Levasseur (16).

The Biggest Loser. Debuted Oct. 2004 on NBC. Ryan Benson (1); Matt Hoover (2); Erik Chopin (3); Bill Germanakos (4); Ali Vincent (5); Michelle Aguilar (6); Helen Phillips (7); Danny Cahill (8); Michael Ventrella (9); Patrick House (10); Olivia Ward (11); John Rhode (12); Jeremy Britt (13); Danni Allen (14); Rachel Frederickson (15).

Dancing With the Stars. Debuted June 2005 on ABC. Kelly Monaco & Alex Mazo (1); Drew Lachey & Cheryl Burke (2); Emmitt Smith & Cheryl Burke (3); Apolo Anton Ohno & Julianne Hough (4); Helio Castroneves & Julianne Hough (5); Kristi Yamaguchi & Mark Ballas (6); Brooke Burke & Derek Hough (7); Shawn Johnson & Mark Ballas (8); Donny Osmond & Kym Johnson (9); Nicole Scherzinger & Derek Hough (10); Jennifer Grey & Derek Hough (11); Hines Ward & Kym Johnson (12); J.R. Martinez & Karina Smirnoff (13); Donald Driver & Peta Murgatroyd (14). All-Stars: Melissa Rycroft & Tony Dovolani (15); Kellie Pickler & Derek Hough (16); Amber Riley & Derek Hough (17); Meryl Davis & Maksim Chmerkovskiy (18).

Food Network Star. Debuted June 2005 on Food Network. Steve McDonagh & Dan Smith (1); Guy Fieri (2); Amy Finley (3); Aaron McCargo Jr. (4); Melissa d'Arabian (5); Aarti Sequeria (6); Jeff Mauro (7); Justin Warner (8); Damaris Phillips (9); Lenny McNab (10).

Hell's Kitchen. Debuted Mar. 2005 on FOX. Michael Wray (1); Heather West (2); Rock Harper (3); Christina Machamer (4); Danny Veltri (5); Dave Levey (6); Holli Ugalde (7); Nona Sivley (8); Paul Niedermann (9); Christina Wilson (10); Ja'Nel Witt (11); Scott Commings (12).

Project Runway. Debuted Dec. 2004 on Bravo. Jay McCarroll (1); Chloe Dao (2); Jeffrey Sebelia (3); Christian Siriano (4); Leanne Marshall (5); Irina Shabayeva (6); Seth Aaron Henderson (7); Gretchen Jones (8); Anya Ayoung-Chee (9); Dmitry Sholokhov (10); Michelle Lesniak Franklin (11); Dom Streater (12). All-Stars: Mondo Guerra (1); Anthony Ryan Auld (2); Seth Aaron Henderson (3).

So You Think You Can Dance. Debuted July 2005 on FOX. Nick Lazzarini (1); Benji Schwimmer (2); Sabra Johnson (3); Joshua Allen (4); Jeanine Mason (5); Russell Ferguson (6); Lauren Froderman (7); Melanie Moore (8); Eliana Girard & Chehon Wespi-Tschopp (9); DuShaunt "Fik-Shun" Stegall & Amy Yakima (10); Ricky Ubeda (11).

Survivor. Debuted May 2000 on CBS. Borneo: Richard Hatch (1); Outback: Tina Wesson (2); Africa: Ethan Zohn (3); Marquesas: Vecepia Towery (4); Thailand: Brian Heidik (5); The Amazon: Jenna Morasca (6); Pearl Islands: Sandra Diaz-Twine (7); All-Stars, Panama: Amber Brkich (8); Vanuatu: Chris Daugherty (9); Palau: Tom Westman (10); Guatemala: Danni Boatwright (11); Panama: Aras Baskauskas (12); Cook Islands: Yul Kwon (13); Fiji: Earl Cole (14); China: Todd Herzog (15); Micronesia: Parvati Shallow (16); Gabon: Robert Crowley (17); Tocantins: James "JT" Thomas (18); Samoa: Natalie White (19); Heroes vs. Villains: Sandra Diaz-Twine (20); Nicaragua: Jud Birza (21); Redemption Island: Rob Mariano (22); South Pacific: Sophie Clarke (23); One World: Kim Spradlin (24); Philippines: Denise Stapley (25); Caramoan—Fans vs. Favorites: John Cochran (26); Blood vs. Water: Tyson Apostol (27).

Top Chef. Debuted Mar. 2006 on Bravo. Harold Dieterle (1); Ilan Hall (2); Hung Huynh (3); Stephanie Izard (4); Hosea Rosenberg (5); Michael Voltaggio (6); Kevin Sbraga (7); Richard Blais (8); Paul Qui (9); Kristen Kish (10); Nicholas Elmi (11). *Top Chef Masters:* Rick Bayless (1); Marcus Samuelsson (2); Floyd Cardoz (3); Chris Cosentino (4); Douglas Keane (5).

The Voice. Debuted Apr. 2011 on NBC. Javier Colon (1); Jermaine Paul (2); Cassadee Pope (3); Danielle Bradbery (4); Tessanne Chin (5); Josh Kaufman (6).

Average U.S. Television Viewing Time, 2013-14

Source: Nielsen Media Research (hours:minutes per week)

Group	Age	Total per week	M-F 7-10 AM	M-F 10 AM-4 PM	M-Sun. 8-11 PM	M-F 11:30 PM-1 AM	Sat. 7 AM-1 PM	Sun. 1-7 PM
Men	18+	34:15	2:03	4:35	8:11	1:41	1:01	1:52
	18-24	20:50	0:59	3:03	4:25	1:15	0:32	1:05
	25-54	30:41	1:41	3:39	7:27	1:40	0:56	1:43
	55+	45:02	3:00	6:38	10:46	1:51	1:19	2:26
Women	18+	39:03	2:35	5:59	9:04	1:53	1:08	1:49
	18-24	23:24	1:13	3:45	5:05	1:19	0:36	1:03
	25-54	34:46	2:18	4:57	8:07	1:49	1:03	1:39
	55+	49:58	3:24	8:07	11:40	2:10	1:26	2:17
Children	2-11	24:30	1:44	4:01	4:53	0:48	1:08	1:17
Teens	12-17	20:45	0:56	2:24	4:51	1:02	0:41	1:05
All viewers		33:46	2:08	4:53	7:49	1:35	1:03	1:42

Note: For viewing period Sept. 23, 2013-Aug. 3, 2014. Includes DVR playback.

Highest-Rated Prime-Time Television Programs, 2013-14

Source: Nielsen Media Research

Data are for regularly scheduled network programs Sept. 23, 2013-Aug. 3, 2014. Ranked by average audience percentages, or ratings, which are estimates of the percentage of all TV-owning households watching a particular program live or on DVR within seven days of broadcast. Audience share percentages are estimates of the percentage of those watching TV at a certain time that are tuned in to a particular program.

Rank	Program, network	Avg. audience	Audience share	Rank	Program, network	Avg. audience	Audience share
1.	NCIS, CBS	11.2%	18%	27.	Hawaii Five-O, CBS	6.6%	11%
2.	The Big Bang Theory, CBS	10.8	19	28.	Intelligence, CBS	6.5	11
3.	Dancing With the Stars, ABC	10.0	15	29.	Chicago Fire, NBC	6.5	11
4.	Blacklist, NBC	9.5	16	30.	The Bachelor, ABC	6.4	10
5.	NCIS: Los Angeles, CBS	9.1	14	31.	Two and a Half Men, CBS	6.3	10
6.	The Voice, NBC	8.9	14	32.	The Millers, CBS	6.2	10
7.	The Voice-Tuesday, NBC	8.6	14	33.	The Crazy Ones, CBS	6.1	10
8.	Grey's Anatomy, ABC	8.6	14	34.	24: Live Another Day, FOX	5.9	9
9.	Castle, ABC	8.3	14	35.	Once Upon a Time, ABC	5.8	9
10.	Scandal, ABC	8.2	14	36.	Amazing Race, CBS	5.8	9
11.	Resurrection, ABC	8.1	12	37.	Revenge, ABC	5.8	9
12.	Person of Interest, CBS	7.9	13	38.	Unforgettable, CBS	5.8	10
13.	Blue Bloods, CBS	7.8	14	39.	Mike & Molly, CBS	5.6	9
14.	Under the Dome, CBS	7.8	13	40.	Law and Order: Special Victims Unit, NBC	5.6	9
15.	Extant, CBS	7.5	13				
16.	Criminal Minds, CBS	7.4	12	41.	Night Shift, NBC	5.5	10
17.	American Idol-Wednesday, FOX	7.4	12	42.	Bones, FOX	5.5	9
18.	60 Minutes, CBS	7.1	12	43.	Chicago P.D., NBC	5.5	9
19.	Survivor, CBS	7.0	11	44.	Marvel's Agents of S.H.I.E.L.D., ABC	5.3	8
20.	American Idol-Thursday, FOX	7.0	11				
21.	America's Got Talent-Tuesday, NBC	6.9	12	45.	2 Broke Girls, CBS	5.2	8
22.	CSI, CBS	6.9	12	46.	About a Boy, NBC	5.2	8
23.	The Good Wife, CBS	6.8	11	47.	Sleepy Hollow, FOX	5.2	8
24.	Modern Family, ABC	6.6	11	48.	60 Minutes Presents, CBS	5.2	8
25.	Elementary, CBS	6.6	11	49.	The Following, FOX	5.2	8
26.	How I Met Your Mother, CBS	6.6	10	50.	The Bachelorette, ABC	5.1	9

Highest-Rated Syndicated Programs, 2013-14

Source: Nielsen Media Research

Average audience percentages, or ratings, are estimates of the percentage of all TV-owning households watching a program live or on DVR within seven days of broadcast, Sept. 23, 2013-Aug. 3, 2014.

Rank	Program	Avg. audience	Rank	Program	Avg. audience
1.	Judge Judy	7.6%	13.	Entertainment Tonight	3.5%
2.	Litton's Weekend Adventure	6.9	14.	Law & Order: Special Victims Unit	3.5
3.	Wheel of Fortune	6.9	15.	Dr. Phil Show	3.2
4.	Jeopardy	6.5	16.	House	3.2
5.	The Big Bang Theory	6.2	17.	Family Guy (weekend)	3.2
6.	Family Feud	5.1	18.	Family Guy	3.0
7.	The Big Bang Theory (weekend B)	4.7	19.	Inside Edition	3.0
8.	Modern Family	4.5	20.	Live With Kelly & Michael	2.9
9.	Law & Order: Criminal Intent (weekend)	3.8	21.	Wheel of Fortune (weekend)	2.9
10.	Two and a Half Men	3.6	22.	The Ellen DeGeneres Show	2.7
11.	Modern Family (weekend)	3.6	23.	The Ellen DeGeneres Show (Olympics)	2.6
12.	Law & Order: Special Victims Unit (weekend)	3.6	24.	Criminal Minds	2.4
			25.	Castle	2.4

Highest-Rated Basic Cable Programs, 2013-14

Source: Nielsen Media Research

Data are for regularly scheduled basic cable programs Sept. 23, 2013-Aug. 3, 2014; excludes children's series, miniseries, movies, and news events. Average audience percentages, or ratings, are estimates of the percentage of all TV-owning households watching a program live or on DVR within seven days of broadcast. The highest-rated cable program for the period was Nickelodeon's special Kids' Choice Awards 2014 with a 2.1% average audience.

Rank	Program, channel	Avg. audience	Rank	Program, channel	Avg. audience
1.	Walking Dead, AMC	2.0%	16.	Rush, USA	0.7%
2.	The Last Ship, TNT	1.7	17.	Graceland, USA	0.7
3.	Rizzoli & Isles, TNT	1.7	18.	Falling Skies, TNT	0.7
4.	Major Crimes, TNT	1.7	19.	Dallas, TNT	0.7
5.	Murder in the First, TNT	1.2	20.	Teen Moms 2, MTV	0.7
6.	Perception, TNT	1.1	21.	Satisfaction, USA	0.6
7.	Teen Wolf, MTV	1.1	22.	Chrisley Knows Best, USA	0.6
8.	Suits, USA	0.9	23.	Cold Justice, TNT	0.6
9.	Royal Pains, USA	0.9	24.	Alaskan Women Looking for Love, TLC	0.6
10.	Covert Affairs, USA	0.8	25.	Sister Wives, TLC	0.6
11.	Mob City, TNT	0.8	26.	Secret Wedding, TLC	0.6
12.	White Collar, USA	0.7	27.	Pawn Stars, History	0.8
13.	Friday Night Tykes, USA	0.7	28.	Curse of Oak Island, History	0.8
14.	Total Divas, USA	0.7	29.	Mountain Men, History	0.8
15.	Psych, USA	0.7	30.	Pawnography, History	0.8

Highest-Rated Premium Cable Programs, 2013-14

Source: Nielsen Media Research

Average audience percentages, or ratings, are estimates of the percentage of all TV-owning households watching a program live or on DVR within seven days of broadcast, Sept. 23, 2013-Aug. 3, 2014.

	Highest-Rated Series			Highest-Rated Movies	
Rank	Program, channel	Avg. audience	Rank	Program, channel	Avg. audience
1.	Game of Thrones, HBO	5.2%	1.	Django Unchained, Showtime	1.1%
2.	True Blood, HBO	3.0	2.	Oblivion, HBO	0.8
3.	Boardwalk Empire, HBO	2.0	3.	The Twilight Saga: Breaking Dawn Part 2, Showtime	0.7
4.	Homeland, Showtime	1.9	4.	Silver Linings Playbook, Showtime	0.6
5.	True Detective, HBO	1.8	5.	The Internship, HBO	0.6
6.	The Leftovers, HBO	1.6	6.	Gravity, HBO	0.6
7.	Shameless, Showtime	1.6	7.	We're the Millers, HBO	0.6
8.	Silicon Valley, HBO	1.4	8.	Lincoln, Showtime	0.6
9.	Ray Donovan, Showtime	1.3	9.	Lee Daniels' The Butler, Showtime	0.5
10.	Masters of Sex (season 1), Showtime	1.2	10.	Alex Cross, Showtime	0.5
11.	Masters of Sex (season 2), Showtime	1.0	11.	Red 2, HBO	0.4
12.	Last Week Tonight With John Oliver, HBO	1.0	12.	The Wolverine, HBO	0.4
13.	Real Time With Bill Maher, HBO	1.0	13.	The Heat, HBO	0.4
14.	Penny Dreadful, Showtime	1.0	14.	Man of Steel, HBO	0.4
15.	The White Queen, Starz	1.0	15.	Fast and Furious 6, HBO	0.4

All-Time Most Watched Television Programs

Source: Nielsen Media Research, Jan. 1961-Aug. 2014

Estimates exclude unsponsored or joint network telecasts (e.g., presidential addresses) or programs under 30 minutes long. Ranked by number of TV-owning households tuned in to the program. (Rating is percentage of all TV-owning households tuned in.)

Rank	Program	Telecast date	Network	Rating	Avg. audience (thous.)
1.	Super Bowl XLVIII	2/2/2014	FOX	47.1%	54,585
2.	Super Bowl XLVI	2/5/2012	NBC	47.0	53,910
3.	Super Bowl XLV	2/6/2011	FOX	46.1	53,435
4.	Super Bowl XLVII	2/3/2013	CBS	46.7	53,363
5.	Super Bowl XLIV	2/7/2010	CBS	45.2	51,873
6.	Super Bowl XLVII Delay	2/3/2013	CBS	44.5	50,861
7.	M*A*S*H (last episode)	2/28/1983	CBS	60.2	50,150
8.	Super Bowl XLII	2/3/2008	FOX	43.2	48,721
9.	Super Bowl XLIII	2/1/2009	NBC	42.0	48,139
10.	Super Bowl XLI	2/4/2007	CBS	42.7	47,535
11.	Super Bowl XL	2/5/2006	ABC	41.6	45,869
12.	XVII Winter Olympics (Women's figure skating)	2/23/1994	CBS	48.5	45,690
13.	Super Bowl XXXIX	2/6/2005	FOX	41.1	45,080
14.	Super Bowl XXXVIII	2/1/2004	CBS	41.4	44,910
15.	Super Bowl XXX	1/28/1996	NBC	46.0	44,150
16.	Super Bowl XXXII	1/25/1998	NBC	44.5	43,630
17.	Super Bowl XXXIV	1/30/2000	ABC	43.3	43,620
18.	Super Bowl XXXVII	1/26/2003	ABC	40.7	43,430
19.	Super Bowl XXVIII	1/30/1994	NBC	45.5	42,860
20.	Super Bowl XXXVI	2/3/2002	FOX	40.4	42,660
21.	Cheers (last episode)	5/20/1993	NBC	45.5	42,360
22.	Super Bowl XXXI	1/26/1997	FOX	43.3	42,000
23.	Super Bowl XXVII	1/31/1993	NBC	45.1	41,990

Highest-Rated Television Programs by Season, 1950-2014

Source: Nielsen Media Research; regular series programs, Sept.-May season

Rating is percentage of all TV-owning households tuned in to the program. Data prior to 1988-89 exclude Alaska and Hawaii.

Season	Program	Rating	TV-owning households (thous.)	Season	Program	Rating	TV-owning households (thous.)
1950-51	Texaco Star Theatre	61.6%	10,320	1982-83	60 Minutes	25.5%	83,300
1951-52	Godfrey's Talent Scouts	53.8	15,300	1983-84	Dallas	25.7	83,800
1952-53	I Love Lucy	67.3	20,400	1984-85	Dynasty	25.0	84,900
1953-54	I Love Lucy	58.8	26,000	1985-86	Cosby Show	33.8	85,900
1954-55	I Love Lucy	49.3	30,700	1986-87	Cosby Show	34.9	87,400
1955-56	$64,000 Question	47.5	34,900	1987-88	Cosby Show	27.8	88,600
1956-57	I Love Lucy	43.7	38,900	1988-89	Roseanne	25.5	90,400
1957-58	Gunsmoke	43.1	41,920	1989-90	Roseanne	23.4	92,100
1958-59	Gunsmoke	39.6	43,950	1990-91	Cheers	21.6	93,100
1959-60	Gunsmoke	40.3	45,750	1991-92	60 Minutes	21.7	92,100
1960-61	Gunsmoke	37.3	47,200	1992-93	60 Minutes	21.6	93,100
1961-62	Wagon Train	32.1	48,555	1993-94	Home Improvement	21.9	94,200
1962-63	Beverly Hillbillies	36.0	50,300	1994-95	Seinfeld	20.5	95,400
1963-64	Beverly Hillbillies	39.1	51,600	1995-96	E.R.	22.0	95,900
1964-65	Bonanza	36.3	52,700	1996-97	E.R.	21.2	97,000
1965-66	Bonanza	31.8	53,850	1997-98	Seinfeld	22.0	98,000
1966-67	Bonanza	29.1	55,130	1998-99	E.R.	17.8	99,400
1967-68	Andy Griffith	27.6	56,670	1999-2000	Who Wants to Be a Millionaire	18.6	100,800
1968-69	Rowan & Martin's Laugh-In	31.8	58,250	2000-01	Survivor II	17.4	102,200
1969-70	Rowan & Martin's Laugh-In	26.3	58,500	2001-02	Friends	15.3	105,500
1970-71	Marcus Welby, M.D.	29.6	60,100	2002-03	CSI	16.1	106,700
1971-72	All in the Family	34.0	62,100	2003-04	CSI	15.9	108,400
1972-73	All in the Family	33.3	64,800	2004-05	CSI	16.3	106,900
1973-74	All in the Family	31.2	66,200	2005-06	American Idol-Tuesday	17.6	110,200
1974-75	All in the Family	30.2	68,500	2006-07	American Idol-Wednesday	17.3	112,800
1975-76	All in the Family	30.1	69,600	2007-08	American Idol-Tuesday	16.1	113,050
1976-77	Happy Days	31.5	71,200	2008-09	American Idol-Tuesday	15.1	114,900
1977-78	Laverne & Shirley	31.6	72,900	2009-10	American Idol-Tuesday	13.7	114,900
1978-79	Laverne & Shirley	30.5	74,500	2010-11	American Idol-Wednesday	14.5	115,900
1979-80	60 Minutes	28.2	76,300	2011-12	Dancing With the Stars	12.0	114,700
1980-81	Dallas	31.2	79,900	2012-13	NCIS	11.4	114,200
1981-82	Dallas	28.4	81,500	2013-14	NCIS	11.2	115,800

All-Time Highest-Rated Television Programs

Source: Nielsen Media Research, Jan. 1961-Aug. 2014

Estimates exclude unsponsored or joint network telecasts (e.g., presidential addresses) and programs under 30 minutes long. Ranked by rating (percentage of all TV-owning households tuned in to the program). Average audience is number of TV-owning households tuned in.

Rank	Program	Telecast date	Network	Rating	Avg. audience (thous.)
1.	M*A*S*H (last episode)	2/28/1983	CBS	60.2%	50,150
2.	Dallas ("Who Shot J.R.?" episode)	11/21/1980	CBS	53.3	41,470
3.	Roots-Pt. 8	1/30/1977	ABC	51.1	36,380
4.	Super Bowl XVI	1/24/1982	CBS	49.1	40,020
5.	Super Bowl XVII	1/30/1983	NBC	48.6	40,480
6.	XVII Winter Olympics (Women's figure skating)	2/23/1994	CBS	48.5	45,690
7.	Super Bowl XX	1/26/1986	NBC	48.3	41,490
8.	Gone With the Wind-Pt. 1	11/7/1976	NBC	47.7	33,960
9.	Gone With the Wind-Pt. 2	11/8/1976	NBC	47.4	33,750
10.	Super Bowl XII	1/15/1978	CBS	47.2	34,410
11.	Super Bowl XLVIII	2/2/2014	FOX	47.1	54,585
12.	Super Bowl XIII	1/21/1979	NBC	47.1	35,090
13.	Super Bowl XLVI	2/5/2012	NBC	47.0	53,910
14.	Super Bowl XLVII	2/3/2013	CBS	46.7	53,363
15.	Bob Hope Christmas Show	1/15/1970	NBC	46.6	27,260
16.	Super Bowl XIX	1/20/1985	ABC	46.4	39,390
17.	Super Bowl XVIII	1/22/1984	CBS	46.4	38,880
18.	Super Bowl XIV	1/20/1980	CBS	46.3	35,330
19.	Super Bowl XLV	2/6/2011	FOX	46.1	53,435
20.	Super Bowl XXX	1/28/1996	NBC	46.0	44,150
21.	ABC Sunday Night Movie ("The Day After")	11/20/1983	ABC	46.0	38,550
22.	Roots-Pt. 6	1/28/1977	ABC	45.9	32,680
23.	The Fugitive (last episode)	8/29/1967	ABC	45.9	25,700
24.	Super Bowl XXI	1/25/1987	CBS	45.8	40,030
25.	Roots-Pt. 5	1/27/1977	ABC	45.7	32,540
26.	Super Bowl XXVIII	1/30/1994	NBC	45.5	42,860
27.	Cheers (last episode)	5/20/1993	NBC	45.5	42,360
28.	The Ed Sullivan Show (First live U.S. TV appearance of The Beatles.)	2/9/1964	CBS	45.3	23,240

AWARDS — MEDALS — PRIZES

Alfred B. Nobel Prizes, 1901-2014

Alfred B. Nobel (1833-96) bequeathed $9 mil, the interest on which was to be distributed yearly to those judged to have most benefited humankind in chemistry, literature, promotion of peace, physics, and physiology or medicine. Prizes were first awarded in 1901. The prize in economics, funded by Sweden's central bank, was first awarded in 1969. Each prize is now worth 8 mil Swedish krona (about $1.1 mil). If year is omitted, no award was given. The Royal Swedish Academy selects prize winners for chemistry, economics, and physics; the Nobel Assembly at Karolinska Institutet, physiology or medicine; the Swedish Academy, literature; and the Norwegian Nobel Committee, the peace prize. The 2014 Nobel Prizes were announced Oct. 6-13. Winners sharing a prize are generally listed in alphabetical order, except when the awarding body has given a larger proportion of a shared prize to one or more recipients.

Nobel Prizes, 2014

Chemistry: Americans Eric Betzig and William E. Moerner and German Stefan W. Hell shared the prize "for the development of super-resolved fluorescence microscopy."

Economics: France's Jean Tirole was recognized for analysis of how large organizations should be regulated.

Literature: France's Patrick Modiano was awarded the prize for works investigating the nature of memory and identity.

Medicine: John O'Keefe, U.S.-UK, and Norwegians May-Britt Moser and Edvard I. Moser were recognized for discovering an "inner GPS" that allows humans to locate themselves in physical space.

Peace: Kailash Satyarthi, India, and Malala Yousafzai, Pakistan, were awarded the prize for advocating for the rights of young people. At 17 years old, girls' education advocate Yousafzai was the youngest-ever Nobel laureate. Satyarthi, who has worked to end child trafficking and forced child labor, is the second person from India to win the Nobel Peace Prize.

Physics: Isamu Akasaki and Hiroshi Amano of Japan and Shuji Nakamura, Japan-U.S., shared the prize for "invention of efficient blue light-emitting diodes, which has enabled bright and energy-saving white light sources."

Physics

1901 Wilhelm C. Röntgen, Ger.	1955 Polykarp Kusch, Willis E. Lamb, U.S.	1987 J. Georg Bednorz, Ger.;
1902 Hendrik A. Lorentz,	1956 John Bardeen, Walter H. Brattain,	K. Alex Müller, Switz.
Pieter Zeeman, Neth.	William Shockley, U.S.	1988 Leon M. Lederman, Melvin
1903 Antoine Henri Becquerel, Pierre	1957 Tsung-Dao Lee, Chen Ning Yang,	Schwartz, Jack Steinberger, U.S.
Curie, Fr.; Marie Curie, Pol.-Fr.	U.S.-China	1989 Norman F. Ramsey, U.S.;
1904 Lord Rayleigh (John W. Strutt), UK	1958 Pavel Cherenkov, Il'ja Frank,	Hans G. Dehmelt, Ger.-U.S.;
1905 Philipp E. A. von Lenard, Ger.	Igor Y. Tamm, USSR	Wolfgang Paul, Ger.
1906 Sir Joseph J. Thomson, UK	1959 Owen Chamberlain,	1990 Jerome I. Friedman, Henry W.
1907 Albert A. Michelson, U.S.	Emilio G. Segre, U.S.	Kendall, U.S.; Richard E. Taylor, Can.
1908 Gabriel Lippmann, Fr.	1960 Donald A. Glaser, U.S.	1991 Pierre-Gilles de Gennes, Fr.
1909 Carl F. Braun, Ger.;	1961 Robert Hofstadter, U.S.;	1992 Georges Charpak, Pol.-Fr.
Guglielmo Marconi, Ital.	Rudolf L. Mossbauer, Ger.	1993 Russell A. Hulse,
1910 Johannes D. van der Waals, Neth.	1962 Lev D. Landau, USSR	Joseph H. Taylor, U.S.
1911 Wilhelm Wien, Ger.	1963 Maria Goeppert-Mayer, Eugene P.	1994 Bertram N. Brockhouse, Can.;
1912 Nils G. Dalén, Swed.	Wigner, U.S.; J. Hans D. Jensen, Ger.	Clifford G. Shull, U.S.
1913 Heike Kamerlingh Onnes, Neth.	1964 Nicolay G. Basov,	1995 Martin Perl, Frederick Reines, U.S.
1914 Max von Laue, Ger.	Aleksandr M. Prokhorov, USSR;	1996 David M. Lee, Douglas D. Osheroff,
1915 Sir William H. Bragg,	Charles H. Townes, U.S.	Robert C. Richardson, U.S.
William L. Bragg, UK	1965 Richard P. Feynman,	1997 Steven Chu, William D. Phillips,
1917 Charles G. Barkla, UK	Julian S. Schwinger, U.S.;	U.S.; Claude Cohen-Tannoudji, Fr.
1918 Max K. E. L. Planck, Ger.	Sin-Itiro Tomonaga, Jpn.	1998 Robert B. Laughlin, U.S.;
1919 Johannes Stark, Ger.	1966 Alfred Kastler, Fr.	Horst L. Störmer, Ger.-U.S;
1920 Charles E. Guillaume, Fr.-Switz.	1967 Hans A. Bethe, U.S.	Daniel C. Tsui, China-U.S.
1921 Albert Einstein, Ger.-U.S.	1968 Luis W. Alvarez, U.S.	1999 Gerardus 't Hooft,
1922 Niels Bohr, Den.	1969 Murray Gell-Mann, U.S.	Martinus J. G. Veltman, Neth.
1923 Robert A. Millikan, U.S.	1970 Hannes Alfvén, Swed.;	2000 Jack S. Kilby, U.S.;
1924 Karl M. G. Siegbahn, Swed.	Louis Néel, Fr.	Herbert Kroemer, Ger.-U.S.;
1925 James Franck, Gustav Hertz, Ger.	1971 Dennis Gabor, UK	Zhores I. Alferov, Russ.
1926 Jean B. Perrin, Fr.	1972 John Bardeen, Leon N. Cooper,	2001 Eric A. Cornell, Carl E. Wieman,
1927 Arthur H. Compton, U.S.;	John R. Schrieffer, U.S.	U.S.; Wolfgang Ketterle, Ger.
Charles T. R. Wilson, UK	1973 Brian D. Josephson, UK	2002 Raymond Davis Jr.,
1928 Owen W. Richardson, UK	Leo Esaki, Jpn.; Ivar Giaever, U.S.	Riccardo Giacconi, U.S.;
1929 Prince Louis-Victor de Broglie, Fr.	1974 Antony Hewish, Sir Martin Ryle, UK	Masatoshi Koshiba, Jpn.
1930 Sir Chandrasekhara V. Raman,	1975 Aage Bohr, Den.;	2003 Alexei A. Abrikosov,
India	Ben Mottelson, U.S.-Den.;	Vitaly L. Ginzburg, Russ.;
1932 Werner Heisenberg, Ger.	Leo James Rainwater, U.S.	Anthony J. Leggett, UK
1933 Paul A. M. Dirac, UK;	1976 Burton Richter,	2004 David J. Gross, H. David Politzer,
Erwin Schrödinger, Austria	Samuel C. C. Ting, U.S.	Frank Wilczek, U.S.
1935 Sir James Chadwick, UK	1977 Philip W. Anderson,	2005 Roy J. Glauber, John L. Hall, U.S.;
1936 Carl D. Anderson, U.S.;	John H. van Vleck, U.S.;	Theodor W. Hänsch, Ger.
Victor F. Hess, Austria	Sir Nevill F. Mott, UK	2006 John C. Mather,
1937 Clinton J. Davisson, U.S.;	1978 Pyotr Kapitsa, USSR;	George F. Smoot, U.S.
Sir George P. Thomson, UK	Arno Penzias, Robert Wilson, U.S.	2007 Albert Fert, Fr.;
1938 Enrico Fermi, Ital.-U.S.	1979 Sheldon L. Glashow,	Peter Grünberg, Ger.
1939 Ernest O. Lawrence, U.S.	Steven Weinberg, U.S.;	2008 Yoichiro Nambu, U.S.;
1943 Otto Stern, U.S.	Abdus Salam, Pakistan	Makoto Kobayashi,
1944 Isidor Isaac Rabi, U.S.	1980 James W. Cronin, Val L. Fitch, U.S.	Toshihide Maskawa, Jpn.
1945 Wolfgang Pauli, U.S.-Austria	1981 Nicolaas Bloembergen,	2009 Charles K. Kao, U.S.-UK;
1946 Percy W. Bridgman, U.S.	Arthur Schawlow, U.S.;	Willard S. Boyle, U.S.-Can.;
1947 Sir Edward V. Appleton, UK	Kai M. Siegbahn, Swed.	George E. Smith, U.S.
1948 Patrick M. S. Blackett, UK	1982 Kenneth G. Wilson, U.S.	2010 Andre Geim, Russ.-Neth.;
1949 Hideki Yukawa, Jpn.	1983 Subramanyan Chandrasekhar,	Konstantin Novoselov, Russ.-UK
1950 Cecil F. Powell, UK	William A. Fowler, U.S.	2011 Saul Perlmutter, Adam G. Riess,
1951 Sir John D. Cockcroft, UK;	1984 Carlo Rubbia, Ital.;	U.S.; Brian P. Schmidt, Austral.-U.S.
Ernest T. S. Walton, Ire.	Simon van der Meer, Neth.	2012 Serge Haroche, Fr.;
1952 Felix Bloch, Edward M. Purcell, U.S.	1985 Klaus von Klitzing, Ger.	David J. Wineland, U.S.
1953 Frits Zernike, Neth.	1986 Ernest Ruska, Gerd Binnig, Ger.;	2013 François Englert, Belg.;
1954 Max Born, UK; Walter Bothe, Ger.	Heinrich Rohrer, Switz.	Peter W. Higgs, UK

Chemistry

1901 Jacobus H. van 't Hoff, Neth.
1902 Emil Fischer, Ger.
1903 Svante A. Arrhenius, Swed.
1904 Sir William Ramsay, UK
1905 Adolf von Baeyer, Ger.
1906 Henri Moissan, Fr.
1907 Eduard Buchner, Ger.
1908 Ernest Rutherford, UK
1909 Wilhelm Ostwald, Ger.
1910 Otto Wallach, Ger.
1911 Marie Curie, Pol.-Fr.
1912 Victor Grignard, Paul Sabatier, Fr.
1913 Alfred Werner, Switz.
1914 Theodore W. Richards, U.S.
1915 Richard M. Willstätter, Ger.
1918 Fritz Haber, Ger.
1920 Walther H. Nernst, Ger.
1921 Frederick Soddy, UK
1922 Francis W. Aston, UK
1923 Fritz Pregl, Austria
1925 Richard A. Zsigmondy, Ger.
1926 Theodor Svedberg, Swed.
1927 Heinrich O. Wieland, Ger.
1928 Adolf O. R. Windaus, Ger.
1929 Sir Arthur Harden, UK;
       Hans von Euler-Chelpin, Swed.
1930 Hans Fischer, Ger.
1931 Friedrich Bergius, Carl Bosch, Ger.
1932 Irving Langmuir, U.S.
1934 Harold C. Urey, U.S.
1935 Frédéric Joliot, Irene Joliot-Curie, Fr.
1936 Peter J. W. Debye, Neth.
1937 Walter N. Haworth, UK;
       Paul Karrer, Switz.
1938 Richard Kuhn, Ger.
1939 Adolf F. J. Butenandt, Ger.;
       Leopold Ruzicka, Switz.
1943 George de Hevesy, Hung.
1944 Otto Hahn, Ger.
1945 Artturi I. Virtanen, Fin.
1946 James B. Sumner, John H.
       Northrop, Wendell M. Stanley, U.S.
1947 Sir Robert Robinson, UK
1948 Arne W. K. Tiselius, Swed.
1949 William F. Giauque, U.S.
1950 Kurt Alder, Otto P. H. Diels, Ger.
1951 Edwin M. McMillan,
       Glenn T. Seaborg, U.S.
1952 Archer J. P. Martin,
       Richard L. M. Synge, UK

1953 Hermann Staudinger, Ger.
1954 Linus C. Pauling, U.S.
1955 Vincent du Vigneaud, U.S.
1956 Sir Cyril N. Hinshelwood, UK;
       Nikolay N. Semenov, USSR
1957 Lord (Alexander R.) Todd, UK
1958 Frederick Sanger, UK
1959 Jaroslav Heyrovsky, Czech.
1960 Willard F. Libby, U.S.
1961 Melvin Calvin, U.S.
1962 John C. Kendrew, Max F. Perutz, UK
1963 Giulio Natta, Ital.; Karl Ziegler, Ger.
1964 Dorothy C. Hodgkin, UK
1965 Robert B. Woodward, U.S.
1966 Robert S. Mulliken, U.S.
1967 Manfred Eigen, Ger.; Ronald G. W.
       Norrish, George Porter, UK
1968 Lars Onsager, U.S.
1969 Derek H. R. Barton, UK;
       Odd Hassel, Nor.
1970 Luis F. Leloir, Arg.
1971 Gerhard Herzberg, Can.
1972 Christian B. Anfinsen, Stanford
       Moore, William H. Stein, U.S.
1973 Ernst Otto Fischer, Ger.;
       Geoffrey Wilkinson, UK
1974 Paul J. Flory, U.S.
1975 John Cornforth, Austral.-UK;
       Vladimir Prelog, Bosnia-Switz.
1976 William N. Lipscomb, U.S.
1977 Ilya Prigogine, Belg.
1978 Peter Mitchell, UK
1979 Herbert C. Brown, U.S.;
       Georg Wittig, Ger.
1980 Paul Berg, Walter Gilbert, U.S.;
       Frederick Sanger, UK
1981 Kenichi Fukui, Jpn.;
       Roald Hoffmann, U.S.
1982 Aaron Klug, UK-Lith.
1983 Henry Taube, Can.
1984 Robert Bruce Merrifield, U.S.
1985 Herbert A. Hauptman,
       Jerome Karle, U.S.
1986 Dudley Herschbach, Yuan T. Lee,
       U.S.; John C. Polanyi, Can.
1987 Donald J. Cram,
       Charles J. Pedersen, U.S.;
       Jean-Marie Lehn, Fr.
1988 Johann Deisenhofer, Robert Huber,
       Hartmut Michel, Ger.

1989 Sidney Altman,
       Thomas R. Cech, U.S.
1990 Elias James Corey, U.S.
1991 Richard R. Ernst, Switz.
1992 Rudolph A. Marcus, Can.-U.S.
1993 Kary B. Mullis, U.S.;
       Michael Smith, UK-Can.
1994 George A. Olah, U.S.
1995 Paul Crutzen, Neth.;
       Mario Molina, Mex.-U.S.;
       Sherwood Rowland, U.S.
1996 Robert F. Curl Jr.,
       Richard E. Smalley, U.S.;
       Sir Harold W. Kroto, U.K.
1997 Paul D. Boyer, U.S.; John E. Walker,
       UK; Jens C. Skou, Den.
1998 Walter Kohn, U.S.;
       John A. Pople, UK
1999 Ahmed H. Zewail, U.S.
2000 Alan J. Heeger, U.S.;
       Alan G. MacDiarmid, N. Zea.-U.S.;
       Hideki Shirakawa, Jpn.
2001 K. Barry Sharpless,
       William S. Knowles, U.S.;
       Ryoji Noyori, Jpn.
2002 John B. Fenn, U.S.;
       Koichi Tanaka, Jpn.;
       Kurt Wüthrich, Switz.
2003 Peter Agre,
       Roderick MacKinnon, U.S.
2004 Aaron Ciechanover, Avram Hershko,
       Isr.; Irwin Rose, U.S.
2005 Yves Chauvin, Fr.; Robert H.
       Grubbs, Richard R. Schrock, U.S.
2006 Roger D. Kornberg, U.S.
2007 Gerhard Ertl, Ger.
2008 Martin Chalfie, Osamu Shimomura,
       Roger Y. Tsien, U.S.
2009 Venkatraman Ramakrishnan, UK;
       Thomas A. Steitz, U.S.;
       Ada E. Yonath, Isr.
2010 Richard F. Heck, U.S.; Ei-ichi
       Negishi, Jpn.-U.S.; Akira Suzuki,
       Jpn.
2011 Dan Shechtman, Isr.
2012 Brian K. Kobilka,
       Robert J. Lefkowitz, U.S.
2013 Martin Karplus, Austria-U.S.;
       Michael Levitt, S. Afr.-U.S.;
       Arieh Warshel, Isr.-U.S.

Physiology or Medicine

1901 Emil A. von Behring, Ger.
1902 Sir Ronald Ross, UK
1903 Niels R. Finsen, Den.
1904 Ivan P. Pavlov, Russ.
1905 Robert Koch, Ger.
1906 Camillo Golgi, Ital.;
       Santiago Ramón y Cajal, Spain
1907 Charles L. A. Laveran, Fr.
1908 Paul Ehrlich, Ger.;
       Ilya Mechnikov, Fr.
1909 Emil T. Kocher, Switz.
1910 Albrecht Kossel, Ger.
1911 Allvar Gullstrand, Swed.
1912 Alexis Carrel, Fr.
1913 Charles R. Richet, Fr.
1914 Robert Bárány, Austria
1919 Jules Bordet, Belg.
1920 Schack A. S. Krogh, Den.
1922 Archibald V. Hill, UK;
       Otto F. Meyerhof, Ger.
1923 Frederick G. Banting, Can.;
       John J. R. Macleod, UK
1924 Willem Einthoven, Neth.
1926 Johannes A. G. Fibiger, Den.
1927 Julius Wagner-Jauregg, Austria
1928 Charles J. H. Nicolle, Fr.
1929 Christiaan Eijkman, Neth.;
       Sir Frederick G. Hopkins, UK
1930 Karl Landsteiner, U.S.
1931 Otto H. Warburg, Ger.
1932 Edgar D. Adrian,
       Sir Charles S. Sherrington, UK
1933 Thomas H. Morgan, U.S.

1934 George R. Minot, William P. Murphy,
       G. H. Whipple, U.S.
1935 Hans Spemann, Ger.
1936 Sir Henry H. Dale, UK;
       Otto Loewi, U.S.
1937 Albert Szent-Gyorgyi, Hung.-U.S.
1938 Corneille J. F. Heymans, Belg.
1939 Gerhard Domagk, Ger.
1943 Henrik C. P. Dam, Den.;
       Edward A. Doisy, U.S.
1944 Joseph Erlanger,
       Herbert S. Gasser, U.S.
1945 Ernst B. Chain, Sir Alexander
       Fleming, Sir Howard W. Florey, UK
1946 Hermann J. Muller, U.S.
1947 Carl F. Cori, Gerty T. Cori, U.S.;
       Bernardo A. Houssay, Arg.
1948 Paul H. Müller, Switz.
1949 Walter R. Hess, Switz.;
       Antonio Egas Moniz, Port.
1950 Philip S. Hench, Edward C. Kendall,
       U.S.; Tadeus Reichstein, Switz.
1951 Max Theiler, U.S.
1952 Selman A. Waksman, U.S.
1953 Hans A. Krebs, UK;
       Fritz A. Lipmann, U.S.
1954 John F. Enders, Frederick C.
       Robbins, Thomas H. Weller, U.S.
1955 Alex H. T. Theorell, Swed.
1956 André F. Cournand,
       Dickinson W. Richards, U.S.;
       Werner Forssmann, Ger.
1957 Daniel Bovet, Ital.

1958 George W. Beadle, Edward L.
       Tatum, Joshua Lederberg, U.S.
1959 Arthur Kornberg,
       Severo Ochoa, U.S.
1960 Sir Frank Macfarlane Burnet,
       Austral.; Peter B. Medawar, UK
1961 Georg von Békésy, U.S.
1962 Francis H. C. Crick,
       Maurice H. F. Wilkins, UK;
       James D. Watson, U.S.
1963 Sir John C. Eccles, Austral.;
       Alan L. Hodgkin,
       Andrew F. Huxley, UK
1964 Konrad E. Bloch, U.S.;
       Feodor Lynen, Ger.
1965 François Jacob, André Lwoff,
       Jacques Monod, Fr.
1966 Charles B. Huggins,
       Peyton Rous, U.S.
1967 Ragnar Granit, Swed.;
       Haldan Keffer Hartline,
       George Wald, U.S.
1968 Robert W. Holley,
       H. Gobind Khorana,
       Marshall W. Nirenberg, U.S.
1969 Max Delbrück, Alfred D. Hershey,
       Salvador Luria, U.S.
1970 Julius Axelrod, U.S.;
       Sir Bernard Katz, UK;
       Ulf von Euler, Swed.
1971 Earl W. Sutherland Jr., U.S.
1972 Gerald M. Edelman, U.S.;
       Rodney R. Porter, UK

1973 Konrad Lorenz, Austria; Nikolaas Tinbergen, UK; Karl von Frisch, Ger.	**1985** Michael S. Brown, Joseph L. Goldstein, U.S.	**2001** Leland H. Hartwell, U.S.; R. Timothy (Tim) Hunt, Sir Paul M. Nurse, UK
1974 Albert Claude, Lux.-U.S.; Christian de Duve, Belg.; George Emil Palade, Rom.-U.S.	**1986** Stanley Cohen, U.S.; Rita Levi-Montalcini, Ital.-U.S. **1987** Susumu Tonegawa, Jpn.	**2002** Sydney Brenner, John E. Sulston, UK; H. Robert Horvitz, U.S.
1975 David Baltimore, Howard Temin, U.S.; Renato Dulbecco, Ital.-U.S.	**1988** Sir James W. Black, UK; Gertrude B. Elion, George H. Hitchings, U.S.	**2003** Paul C. Lauterbur, U.S.; Sir Peter Mansfield, UK **2004** Richard Axel, Linda B. Buck, U.S.
1976 Baruch S. Blumberg, Daniel Carleton Gajdusek, U.S.	**1989** J. Michael Bishop, Harold E. Varmus, U.S.	**2005** Barry J. Marshall, J. Robin Warren, Austral.
1977 Rosalyn S. Yalow, Roger C.L. Guillemin, Andrew V. Schally, U.S.	**1990** Joseph E. Murray, E. Donnall Thomas, U.S. **1991** Edwin Neher, Bert Sakmann, Ger.	**2006** Andrew Z. Fire, Craig C. Mello, U.S. **2007** Mario R. Capecchi,
1978 Werner Arber, Switz.; Daniel Nathans, Hamilton O. Smith, U.S.	**1992** Edmond H. Fisher, Edwin G. Krebs, U.S. **1993** Richard J. Roberts, UK;	Oliver Smithies, U.S.; Sir Martin J. Evans, UK **2008** Harald zur Hausen, Ger.;
1979 Allan M. Cormack, U.S.; Godfrey N. Hounsfield, UK	Phillip A. Sharp, U.S. **1994** Alfred G. Gilman,	Françoise Barré-Sinoussi, Luc Montagnier, Fr.
1980 Baruj Benacerraf, George Snell, U.S.; Jean Dausset, Fr.	Martin Rodbell, U.S. **1995** Edward B. Lewis,	**2009** Elizabeth H. Blackburn, Carol W. Greider,
1981 Roger W. Sperry, David H. Hubel, Torsten N. Wiesel, U.S.	Eric F. Wieschaus, U.S.; Christiane Nüsslein-Volhard, Ger.	Jack W. Szostak, U.S. **2010** Robert G. Edwards, UK
1982 Sune K. Bergström, Bengt I. Samuelsson, Swed.; John R. Vane, UK	**1996** Peter C. Doherty, Austral.; Rolf M. Zinkernagel, Switz. **1997** Stanley B. Prusiner, U.S.	**2011** Bruce A. Beutler, U.S.; Jules A. Hoffmann, Fr.; Ralph M. Steinman, Can.-U.S.
1983 Barbara McClintock, U.S.	**1998** Robert F. Furchgott, Louis J. Ignarro, Ferid Murad, U.S.	**2012** John B. Gurdon, UK; Shinya Yamanaka, Jpn.-U.S.
1984 Niels K. Jerne, UK-Den.; Georges J. F. Köhler, Ger.; César Milstein, UK-Arg.	**1999** Günter Blobel, U.S. **2000** Arvid Carlsson, Swed.; Paul Greengard, U.S.; Eric R. Kandel, Austria-U.S.	**2013** James E. Rothman, Randy W. Schekman, U.S.; Thomas C. Südhof, Ger.-U.S.

Literature

1901 Rene F. A. Sully Prudhomme, Fr.	**1939** Frans E. Sillanpää, Fin.	**1977** Vicente Aleixandre, Spain
1902 Theodor Mommsen, Ger.	**1944** Johannes V. Jensen, Den.	**1978** Isaac Bashevis Singer, U.S.
1903 Bjørnstjerne Bjørnson, Nor.	**1945** Gabriela Mistral, Chile	**1979** Odysseus Elytis, Greece
1904 José Echegaray y Eizaguirre, Spain; Fréderic Mistral, Fr.	**1946** Hermann Hesse, Ger.-Switz. **1947** André Gide, Fr.	**1980** Czeslaw Milosz, Pol.-U.S. **1981** Elias Canetti, Bulg.-UK
1905 Henryk Sienkiewicz, Pol.	**1948** T. S. Eliot, UK	**1982** Gabriel García Márquez, Colombia
1906 Giosuè Carducci, Ital.	**1949** William Faulkner, U.S.	**1983** William Golding, UK
1907 Rudyard Kipling, UK	**1950** Bertrand Russell, UK	**1984** Jaroslav Siefert, Czech.
1908 Rudolf C. Eucken, Ger.	**1951** Pär F. Lagerkvist, Swed.	**1985** Claude Simon, Fr.
1909 Selma Lagerlöf, Swed.	**1952** François Mauriac, Fr.	**1986** Wole Soyinka, Nigeria
1910 Paul J. L. Heyse, Ger.	**1953** Sir Winston Churchill, UK	**1987** Joseph Brodsky, USSR-U.S.
1911 Maurice Maeterlinck, Belg.	**1954** Ernest Hemingway, U.S.	**1988** Naguib Mahfouz, Egypt
1912 Gerhart Hauptmann, Ger.	**1955** Halldór K. Laxness, Ice.	**1989** Camilo José Cela, Spain
1913 Rabindranath Tagore, India	**1956** Juan Ramón Jiménez, Spain	**1990** Octavio Paz, Mex.
1915 Romain Rolland, Fr.	**1957** Albert Camus, Fr.	**1991** Nadine Gordimer, S. Afr.
1916 Verner von Heidenstam, Swed.	**1958** Boris L. Pasternak, USSR	**1992** Derek Walcott, St. Lucia
1917 Karl A. Gjellerup, Henrik Pontoppidan, Den.	(declined) **1959** Salvatore Quasimodo, Ital.	**1993** Toni Morrison, U.S. **1994** Kenzaburo Oe, Jpn.
1919 Carl F. G. Spitteler, Switz.	**1960** Saint-John Perse, Fr.	**1995** Seamus Heaney, Ire.
1920 Knut Hamsun, Nor.	**1961** Ivo Andric, Yugo.	**1996** Wislawa Szymborska, Pol.
1921 Anatole France, Fr.	**1962** John Steinbeck, U.S.	**1997** Dario Fo, Ital.
1922 Jacinto Benavente, Spain	**1963** Giorgos Seferis, Greece	**1998** Jose Saramago, Por.
1923 William Butler Yeats, Ire.	**1964** Jean-Paul Sartre, Fr. (declined)	**1999** Günter Grass, Ger.
1924 Wladyslaw S. Reymont, Pol.	**1965** Mikhail Sholokhov, USSR	**2000** Gao Xingjian, China-Fr.
1925 George Bernard Shaw, Ire.-UK	**1966** Shmuel Yosef Agnon, Isr.;	**2001** Sir V. S. Naipaul, UK
1926 Grazia Deledda, Ital.	Nelly Sachs, Swed.	**2002** Imre Kertész, Hung.
1927 Henri Bergson, Fr.	**1967** Miguel Angel Asturias, Guat.	**2003** J. M. Coetzee, S. Afr.
1928 Sigrid Undset, Nor.	**1968** Yasunari Kawabata, Jpn.	**2004** Elfriede Jelinek, Austria
1929 Thomas Mann, Ger.	**1969** Samuel Beckett, Ire.	**2005** Harold Pinter, UK
1930 Sinclair Lewis, U.S.	**1970** Aleksandr I. Solzhenitsyn, USSR	**2006** Orhan Pamuk, Turk.
1931 Erik A. Karlfeldt, Swed.	**1971** Pablo Neruda, Chile	**2007** Doris Lessing, UK
1932 John Galsworthy, UK	**1972** Heinrich Böll, Ger.	**2008** Jean-Marie Gustave Le Clézio, Fr.
1933 Ivan A. Bunin, USSR	**1973** Patrick White, Austral.	**2009** Herta Müller, Ger.
1934 Luigi Pirandello, Ital.	**1974** Eyvind Johnson,	**2010** Mario Vargas Llosa, Peru
1936 Eugene O'Neill, U.S.	Harry Edmund Martinson, Swed.	**2011** Tomas Tranströmer, Swed.
1937 Roger Martin du Gard, Fr.	**1975** Eugenio Montale, Ital.	**2012** Mo Yan, China
1938 Pearl S. Buck, U.S.	**1976** Saul Bellow, U.S.	**2013** Alice Munro, Can.

Peace

1901 Jean H. Dunant, Switz.; Frédéric Passy, Fr.	**1908** Klas P. Arnoldson, Swed.; Fredrik Bajer, Den.	**1920** Léon V. A. Bourgeois, Fr. **1921** Karl H. Branting, Swed.;
1902 Élie Ducommun, Charles A. Gobat, Switz.	**1909** Auguste M. F. Beernaert, Belg.; Paul H. B. B. d'Estournelles	Christian L. Lange, Nor. **1922** Fridtjof Nansen, Nor.
1903 Sir William R. Cremer, UK	de Constant, Fr.	**1925** Sir Austen Chamberlain, UK;
1904 Institute of International Law	**1910** Permanent Intl. Peace Bureau	Charles G. Dawes, U.S.
1905 Baroness Bertha von Suttner, Austria	**1911** Tobias M. C. Asser, Neth.; Alfred H. Fried, Austria	**1926** Aristide Briand, Fr.; Gustav Stresemann, Ger.
1906 Theodore Roosevelt, U.S.	**1912** Elihu Root, U.S.	**1927** Ferdinand E. Buisson, Fr.;
1907 Ernesto T. Moneta, Ital.; Louis Renault, Fr.	**1913** Henri La Fontaine, Belg. **1917** Intl. Committee of the Red Cross **1919** Woodrow Wilson, U.S.	Ludwig Quidde, Ger. **1929** Frank B. Kellogg, U.S. **1930** Nathan Söderblom, Swed.

1931 Jane Addams, Nicholas Murray Butler, U.S.	**1970** Norman E. Borlaug, U.S.	**1994** Yasser Arafat, Pal.; Shimon Peres, Yitzhak Rabin, Isr.
1933 Sir Norman Angell, UK	**1971** Willy Brandt, Ger.	**1995** Joseph Rotblat, Pol.-UK;
1934 Arthur Henderson, UK	**1973** Henry Kissinger, U.S.; Le Duc Tho, N. Viet. (Tho declined)	Pugwash Conferences
1935 Carl von Ossietzky, Ger.		**1996** Bishop Carlos Ximenes Belo,
1936 Carlos Saavedra Lamas, Arg.	**1974** Seán MacBride, Ire.; Eisaku Sato, Jpn.	José Ramos-Horta, Timor-Leste
1937 Lord Robert Cecil, UK	**1975** Andrei Sakharov, USSR	**1997** Jody Williams, U.S.;
1938 Nansen Intl. Office for Refugees	**1976** Mairead Corrigan, Betty Williams, N. Ire.	Intl. Campaign to Ban Landmines
1944 Intl. Committee of the Red Cross		**1998** John Hume, David Trimble, N. Ire.
1945 Cordell Hull, U.S.	**1977** Amnesty International	**1999** Doctors Without Borders
1946 Emily G. Balch, John R. Mott, U.S.	**1978** Anwar al-Sadat, Egypt; Menachem Begin, Isr.	(Médecins Sans Frontières), Fr.
1947 Friends Service Council, UK; Amer. Friends Service Committee, U.S.		**2000** Kim Dae Jung, S. Kor.
	1979 Mother Teresa of Calcutta, Alb.-India	**2001** UN; Kofi Annan, Ghana
1949 Lord John Boyd Orr of Brechin, UK		**2002** Jimmy Carter, U.S.
1950 Ralph J. Bunche, U.S.	**1980** Adolfo Pérez Esquivel, Arg.	**2003** Shirin Ebadi, Iran
1951 Léon Jouhaux, Fr.	**1981** Office of UN High Commissioner for Refugees	**2004** Wangari Maathai, Kenya
1952 Albert Schweitzer, Fr.		**2005** Mohamed ElBaradei, Egypt;
1953 George C. Marshall, U.S.	**1982** Alfonso García Robles, Mex.; Alva Myrdal, Swed.	Intl. Atomic Energy Agency, Austria
1954 Office of UN High Commissioner for Refugees		**2006** Muhammad Yunus,
	1983 Lech Walesa, Pol.	Grameen Bank, Bangl.
1957 Lester B. Pearson, Can.	**1984** Bishop Desmond Tutu, S. Afr.	**2007** Intergovernmental Panel on Climate Change, Switz.;
1958 Georges Pire, Belg.	**1985** Intl. Physicians for the Prevention of Nuclear War, U.S.	Albert Arnold Gore Jr., U.S.
1959 Philip J. Noel-Baker, UK		**2008** Martti Ahtisaari, Fin.
1960 Albert J. Lutuli, S. Afr.	**1986** Elie Wiesel, Rom.-U.S.	**2009** Barack H. Obama, U.S.
1961 Dag Hammarskjöld, Swed.	**1987** Oscar Arias Sánchez, Costa Rica	**2010** Liu Xiaobo, China
1962 Linus C. Pauling, U.S.	**1988** UN Peacekeeping Forces	**2011** Leymah Gbowee,
1963 Intl. Committee of the Red Cross, League of Red Cross Societies	**1989** Dalai Lama (Tenzin Gyatso), Tibet	Ellen Johnson Sirleaf, Liberia; Tawakkol Karman, Yemen
	1990 Mikhail S. Gorbachev, USSR	**2012** European Union
1964 Martin Luther King Jr., U.S.	**1991** Aung San Suu Kyi, Burma	**2013** Organization for the Prohibition of Chemical Weapons
1965 UN Children's Fund (UNICEF)	**1992** Rigoberta Menchú Tum, Guat.	
1968 René Cassin, Fr.	**1993** Frederik W. de Klerk, Nelson Mandela, S. Afr.	
1969 Intl. Labor Organization		

Nobel Memorial Prize in Economic Sciences

1969 Ragnar Frisch, Nor.; Jan Tinbergen, Neth.	**1987** Robert M. Solow, U.S.	**2002** Daniel Kahneman, U.S.-Isr.; Vernon L. Smith, U.S.
	1988 Maurice Allais, Fr.	
1970 Paul A. Samuelson, U.S.	**1989** Trygve Haavelmo, Nor.	**2003** Robert F. Engle, U.S.; Clive W. J. Granger, UK
1971 Simon Kuznets, U.S.	**1990** Harry M. Markowitz, Merton H. Miller, William F. Sharpe, U.S.	
1972 Kenneth J. Arrow, U.S.; John R. Hicks, UK		**2004** Finn E. Kydland, Nor.; Edward C. Prescott, U.S.
1973 Wassily Leontief, U.S.	**1991** Ronald H. Coase, UK-U.S.	**2005** Robert J. Aumann, Isr.-U.S.; Thomas C. Schelling, U.S.
1974 Gunnar Myrdal, Swed.; Friedrich A. von Hayek, Austria	**1992** Gary S. Becker, U.S.	
	1993 Robert W. Fogel, Douglass C. North, U.S.	**2006** Edmund S. Phelps, U.S.
1975 Leonid Kantorovich, USSR; Tjalling C. Koopmans, Neth.-U.S.		**2007** Leonid Hurwicz, Eric S. Maskin, Roger B. Myerson, U.S.
	1994 John C. Harsanyi, John F. Nash, U.S.; Reinhard Selten, Ger.	
1976 Milton Friedman, U.S.		**2008** Paul Krugman, U.S.
1977 James E. Meade, UK; Bertil Ohlin, Swed.	**1995** Robert E. Lucas Jr., U.S.	**2009** Elinor Ostrom, Oliver E. Williamson, U.S.
	1996 James A. Mirrlees, UK; William Vickrey, Can.-U.S.	
1978 Herbert A. Simon, U.S.		**2010** Peter A. Diamond, Dale T. Mortensen, U.S.; Christopher A. Pissarides, Cyprus-UK
1979 Sir Arthur Lewis, UK; Theodore W. Schultz, U.S.	**1997** Robert C. Merton, U.S.; Myron S. Scholes, Can.-U.S.	
1980 Lawrence R. Klein, U.S.	**1998** Amartya Sen, India	**2011** Thomas J. Sargent, Christopher A. Sims, U.S.
1981 James Tobin, U.S.	**1999** Robert A. Mundell, Can.	
1982 George J. Stigler, U.S.	**2000** James J. Heckman, Daniel L. McFadden, U.S.	**2012** Alvin E. Roth, Lloyd S. Shapley, U.S.
1983 Gerard Debreu, Fr.-U.S.		**2013** Eugene F. Fama, Lars Peter Hansen, Robert J. Shiller, U.S.
1984 Richard Stone, UK	**2001** George A. Akerlof, A. Michael Spence, Joseph E. Stiglitz, U.S.	
1985 Franco Modigliani, Ital.-U.S.		
1986 James M. Buchanan, U.S.		

Pulitzer Prizes in Journalism, Letters, and Music, 1917-2014

Endowed by Joseph Pulitzer (1847-1911), publisher of the *New York World*, in a bequest to Columbia Univ. and awarded annually, in years shown, for work published the previous year. Prizes are currently $10,000 in each category except Public Service (in Journalism), for which a gold medal is given. The prize board began considering submissions from online-only publications in 2009. For letters and music, prizes in past years are listed; if a year is omitted, no award was given that year.

Pulitzer Prizes in Journalism, 2014

Public Service: *Guardian US* and *Washington Post* for coverage of widespread, secret surveillance by the Natl. Security Agency.

Breaking News Reporting: *Boston Globe* staff, for coverage of the Boston Marathon bombings and ensuing manhunt.

Investigative Reporting: Chris Hamby, *Center for Public Integrity* (Washington, DC), for reports on how some doctors and lawyers conspired to deny benefits to coal miners with black lung disease.

Explanatory Reporting: Eli Saslow, *Washington Post*, for reporting on the prevalence of food stamps in post-recession America.

Local Reporting: Will Hobson, Michael LaForgia, *Tampa Bay Times* (FL), for investigating the squalid conditions in housing for the city's homeless population.

National Reporting: David Philipps, *The Gazette* (Colorado Springs, CO), for examining the mistreatment of wounded combat veterans.

International Reporting: Jason Szep, Andrew R.C. Marshall, Reuters, for reports on the persecution of Myanmar's Muslim-minority Rohingya, who often fall victim to predatory human trafficking networks.

Feature Writing: No award.

Commentary: Stephen Henderson, *Detroit Free Press*, for columns on Detroit's financial crisis.

Criticism: Inga Saffron, *The Philadelphia Inquirer*, for architecture criticism.

Editorial Writing: *The Oregonian* (Portland, OR) editorial staff, for lucid editorials explaining the issue of rising pension costs.

Editorial Cartooning: Kevin Siers, *Charlotte Observer* (NC), for thought-provoking cartoons drawn with a sharp wit and bold style.

Breaking News Photography: Tyler Hicks, *NY Times*, for compelling pictures of the unfolding terrorist attack at Westgate mall in Kenya.

Feature Photography: Josh Haner, *NY Times*, for essay on a Boston Marathon bombing victim who lost most of both legs.

Pulitzer Prizes in Letters, 1917-2014

Fiction

1918 Ernest Poole, *His Family*
1919 Booth Tarkington, *The Magnificent Ambersons*
1921 Edith Wharton, *The Age of Innocence*
1922 Booth Tarkington, *Alice Adams*
1923 Willa Cather, *One of Ours*
1924 Margaret Wilson, *The Able McLaughlins*
1925 Edna Ferber, *So Big*
1926 Sinclair Lewis, *Arrowsmith* (refused)
1927 Louis Bromfield, *Early Autumn*
1928 Thornton Wilder, *The Bridge of San Luis Rey*
1929 Julia Peterkin, *Scarlet Sister Mary*
1930 Oliver La Farge, *Laughing Boy*
1931 Margaret Ayer Barnes, *Years of Grace*
1932 Pearl S. Buck, *The Good Earth*
1933 T. S. Stribling, *The Store*
1934 Caroline Miller, *Lamb in His Bosom*
1935 Josephine W. Johnson, *Now in November*
1936 Harold L. Davis, *Honey in the Horn*
1937 Margaret Mitchell, *Gone With the Wind*
1938 John P. Marquand, *The Late George Apley*
1939 Marjorie Kinnan Rawlings, *The Yearling*
1940 John Steinbeck, *The Grapes of Wrath*
1942 Ellen Glasgow, *In This Our Life*
1943 Upton Sinclair, *Dragon's Teeth*
1944 Martin Flavin, *Journey in the Dark*
1945 John Hersey, *A Bell for Adano*
1947 Robert Penn Warren, *All the King's Men*
1948 James A. Michener, *Tales of the South Pacific*
1949 James Gould Cozzens, *Guard of Honor*
1950 A. B. Guthrie Jr., *The Way West*
1951 Conrad Richter, *The Town*
1952 Herman Wouk, *The Caine Mutiny*
1953 Ernest Hemingway, *The Old Man and the Sea*
1955 William Faulkner, *A Fable*
1956 MacKinlay Kantor, *Andersonville*
1958 James Agee, *A Death in the Family*
1959 Robert Lewis Taylor, *The Travels of Jaimie McPheeters*
1960 Allen Drury, *Advise and Consent*
1961 Harper Lee, *To Kill a Mockingbird*
1962 Edwin O'Connor, *The Edge of Sadness*
1963 William Faulkner, *The Reivers*
1965 Shirley Ann Grau, *The Keepers of the House*
1966 Katherine Anne Porter, *Collected Stories*
1967 Bernard Malamud, *The Fixer*
1968 William Styron, *The Confessions of Nat Turner*
1969 N. Scott Momaday, *House Made of Dawn*
1970 Jean Stafford, *Collected Stories*
1972 Wallace Stegner, *Angle of Repose*
1973 Eudora Welty, *The Optimist's Daughter*
1975 Michael Shaara, *The Killer Angels*
1976 Saul Bellow, *Humboldt's Gift*
1978 James Alan McPherson, *Elbow Room*
1979 John Cheever, *The Stories of John Cheever*
1980 Norman Mailer, *The Executioner's Song*
1981 John Kennedy Toole, *A Confederacy of Dunces*
1982 John Updike, *Rabbit Is Rich*
1983 Alice Walker, *The Color Purple*
1984 William Kennedy, *Ironweed*
1985 Alison Lurie, *Foreign Affairs*
1986 Larry McMurtry, *Lonesome Dove*
1987 Peter Taylor, *A Summons to Memphis*
1988 Toni Morrison, *Beloved*
1989 Anne Tyler, *Breathing Lessons*
1990 Oscar Hijuelos, *The Mambo Kings Play Songs of Love*
1991 John Updike, *Rabbit at Rest*
1992 Jane Smiley, *A Thousand Acres*
1993 Robert Olen Butler, *A Good Scent From a Strange Mountain*
1994 E. Annie Proulx, *The Shipping News*
1995 Carol Shields, *The Stone Diaries*
1996 Richard Ford, *Independence Day*
1997 Steven Millhauser, *Martin Dressler: The Tale of an American Dreamer*
1998 Philip Roth, *American Pastoral*
1999 Michael Cunningham, *The Hours*
2000 Jhumpa Lahiri, *Interpreter of Maladies*
2001 Michael Chabon, *The Amazing Adventures of Kavalier & Clay*
2002 Richard Russo, *Empire Falls*
2003 Jeffrey Eugenides, *Middlesex*
2004 Edward P. Jones, *The Known World*
2005 Marilynne Robinson, *Gilead*
2006 Geraldine Brooks, *March*
2007 Cormac McCarthy, *The Road*
2008 Junot Díaz, *The Brief Wondrous Life of Oscar Wao*
2009 Elizabeth Strout, *Olive Kitteridge*
2010 Paul Harding, *Tinkers*
2011 Jennifer Egan, *A Visit From the Goon Squad*
2013 Adam Johnson, *The Orphan Master's Son*
2014 Donna Tartt, *The Goldfinch*

Drama

1918 Jesse Lynch Williams, *Why Marry?*
1920 Eugene O'Neill, *Beyond the Horizon*
1921 Zona Gale, *Miss Lulu Bett*
1922 Eugene O'Neill, *Anna Christie*
1923 Owen Davis, *Icebound*
1924 Hatcher Hughes, *Hell-Bent Fer Heaven*
1925 Sidney Howard, *They Knew What They Wanted*
1926 George Kelly, *Craig's Wife*
1927 Paul Green, *In Abraham's Bosom*
1928 Eugene O'Neill, *Strange Interlude*
1929 Elmer Rice, *Street Scene*
1930 Marc Connelly, *The Green Pastures*
1931 Susan Glaspell, *Alison's House*
1932 George S. Kaufman, Morrie Ryskind, and Ira Gershwin, *Of Thee I Sing*
1933 Maxwell Anderson, *Both Your Houses*
1934 Sidney Kingsley, *Men in White*
1935 Zoe Akins, *The Old Maid*
1936 Robert E. Sherwood, *Idiot's Delight*
1937 George S. Kaufman and Moss Hart, *You Can't Take It With You*
1938 Thornton Wilder, *Our Town*
1939 Robert E. Sherwood, *Abe Lincoln in Illinois*
1940 William Saroyan, *The Time of Your Life*
1941 Robert E. Sherwood, *There Shall Be No Night*
1943 Thornton Wilder, *The Skin of Our Teeth*
1945 Mary Chase, *Harvey*
1946 Russel Crouse and Howard Lindsay, *State of the Union*
1948 Tennessee Williams, *A Streetcar Named Desire*
1949 Arthur Miller, *Death of a Salesman*
1950 Richard Rodgers, Oscar Hammerstein II, and Joshua Logan, *South Pacific*
1952 Joseph Kramm, *The Shrike*
1953 William Inge, *Picnic*
1954 John Patrick, *The Teahouse of the August Moon*
1955 Tennessee Williams, *Cat on a Hot Tin Roof*
1956 Frances Goodrich and Albert Hackett, *The Diary of Anne Frank*
1957 Eugene O'Neill, *Long Day's Journey Into Night*
1958 Ketti Frings, *Look Homeward, Angel*
1959 Archibald MacLeish, *J. B.*
1960 George Abbott, Jerome Weidman, Sheldon Harnick, and Jerry Bock, *Fiorello!*
1961 Tad Mosel, *All the Way Home*
1962 Frank Loesser and Abe Burrows, *How to Succeed in Business Without Really Trying*
1965 Frank D. Gilroy, *The Subject Was Roses*
1967 Edward Albee, *A Delicate Balance*
1969 Howard Sackler, *The Great White Hope*
1970 Charles Gordone, *No Place to Be Somebody*
1971 Paul Zindel, *The Effect of Gamma Rays on Man-in-the-Moon Marigolds*
1973 Jason Miller, *That Championship Season*
1975 Edward Albee, *Seascape*
1976 Michael Bennett, James Kirkwood, Nicholas Dante, Marvin Hamlisch, and Edward Kleban, *A Chorus Line*
1977 Michael Cristofer, *The Shadow Box*
1978 Donald L. Coburn, *The Gin Game*
1979 Sam Shepard, *Buried Child*
1980 Lanford Wilson, *Talley's Folly*
1981 Beth Henley, *Crimes of the Heart*
1982 Charles Fuller, *A Soldier's Play*
1983 Marsha Norman, *'night, Mother*
1984 David Mamet, *Glengarry Glen Ross*
1985 Stephen Sondheim and James Lapine, *Sunday in the Park With George*
1987 August Wilson, *Fences*
1988 Alfred Uhry, *Driving Miss Daisy*
1989 Wendy Wasserstein, *The Heidi Chronicles*
1990 August Wilson, *The Piano Lesson*
1991 Neil Simon, *Lost in Yonkers*
1992 Robert Schenkkan, *The Kentucky Cycle*
1993 Tony Kushner, *Angels in America: Millennium Approaches*
1994 Edward Albee, *Three Tall Women*
1995 Horton Foote, *The Young Man From Atlanta*
1996 Jonathan Larson, *Rent*

1998 Paula Vogel, *How I Learned to Drive*
1999 Margaret Edson, *Wit*
2000 Donald Margulies, *Dinner With Friends*
2001 David Auburn, *Proof*
2002 Suzan-Lori Parks, *Topdog/Underdog*
2003 Nilo Cruz, *Anna in the Tropics*
2004 Doug Wright, *I Am My Own Wife*
2005 John Patrick Shanley, *Doubt, a parable*
2007 David Lindsay-Abaire, *Rabbit Hole*
2008 Tracy Letts, *August: Osage County*
2009 Lynn Nottage, *Ruined*
2010 Tom Kitt and Brian Yorkey, *Next to Normal*
2011 Bruce Norris, *Clybourne Park*
2012 Quiara Alegría Hudes, *Water by the Spoonful*
2013 Ayad Akhtar, *Disgraced*
2014 Annie Baker, *The Flick*

History (U.S.)

1917 J. J. Jusserand, *With Americans of Past and Present Days*
1918 James Ford Rhodes, *History of the Civil War, 1861-1865*
1920 Justin H. Smith, *The War With Mexico*
1921 William Sowden Sims in collab. with Burton J. Hendrick, *The Victory at Sea*
1922 James Truslow Adams, *The Founding of New England*
1923 Charles Warren, *The Supreme Court in United States History*
1924 Charles Howard McIlwain, *The American Revolution: A Constitutional Interpretation*
1925 Frederick L. Paxton, *A History of the American Frontier*
1926 Edward Channing, *A History of the United States*
1927 Samuel Flagg Bemis, *Pinckney's Treaty*
1928 V. L. Parrington, *Main Currents in American Thought*
1929 Fred A. Shannon, *The Organization and Administration of the Union Army, 1861-1865*
1930 Claude H. Van Tyne, *The War of Independence*
1931 Bernadotte E. Schmitt, *The Coming of the War, 1914*
1932 John J. Pershing, *My Experiences in the World War*
1933 Frederick J. Turner, *The Significance of Sections in American History*
1934 Herbert Agar, *The People's Choice*
1935 Charles McLean Andrews, *The Colonial Period of American History*
1936 Andrew C. McLaughlin, *The Constitutional History of the United States*
1937 Van Wyck Brooks, *The Flowering of New England*
1938 Paul Herman Buck, *The Road to Reunion, 1865-1900*
1939 Frank Luther Mott, *A History of American Magazines*
1940 Carl Sandburg, *Abraham Lincoln: The War Years*
1941 Marcus Lee Hansen, *The Atlantic Migration, 1607-1860*
1942 Margaret Leech, *Reveille in Washington, 1860-1865*
1943 Esther Forbes, *Paul Revere and the World He Lived In*
1944 Merle Curti, *The Growth of American Thought*
1945 Stephen Bonsal, *Unfinished Business*
1946 Arthur M. Schlesinger Jr., *The Age of Jackson*
1947 James Phinney Baxter III, *Scientists Against Time*
1948 Bernard DeVoto, *Across the Wide Missouri*
1949 Roy F. Nichols, *The Disruption of American Democracy*
1950 Oliver W. Larkin, *Art and Life in America*
1951 R. Carlyle Buley, *The Old Northwest: Pioneer Period 1815-1840*
1952 Oscar Handlin, *The Uprooted*
1953 George Dangerfield, *The Era of Good Feelings*
1954 Bruce Catton, *A Stillness at Appomattox*
1955 Paul Horgan, *Great River: The Rio Grande in North American History*
1956 Richard Hofstadter, *The Age of Reform*
1957 George F. Kennan, *Russia Leaves the War*
1958 Bray Hammond, *Banks and Politics in America From the Revolution to the Civil War*
1959 Leonard D. White with Jean Schneider, *The Republican Era, 1869-1901*
1960 Margaret Leech, *In the Days of McKinley*
1961 Herbert Feis, *Between War and Peace: The Potsdam Conference*
1962 Lawrence H. Gipson, *The Triumphant Empire: Thunder-Clouds Gather in the West, 1763-1766*
1963 Constance McLaughlin Green, *Washington: Village and Capital, 1800-1878*
1964 Sumner Chilton Powell, *Puritan Village: The Formation of a New England Town*
1965 Irwin Unger, *The Greenback Era*
1966 Perry Miller, *The Life of the Mind in America*
1967 William H. Goetzmann, *Exploration and Empire*
1968 Bernard Bailyn, *The Ideological Origins of the American Revolution*
1969 Leonard W. Levy, *Origins of the Fifth Amendment*

1970 Dean Acheson, *Present at the Creation: My Years in the State Department*
1971 James MacGregor Burns, *Roosevelt: The Soldier of Freedom*
1972 Carl N. Degler, *Neither Black nor White*
1973 Michael Kammen, *People of Paradox: An Inquiry Concerning the Origins of American Civilization*
1974 Daniel J. Boorstin, *The Americans: The Democratic Experience*
1975 Dumas Malone, *Jefferson and His Time*
1976 Paul Horgan, *Lamy of Santa Fe*
1977 David M. Potter, *The Impending Crisis, 1841-1867*
1978 Alfred D. Chandler Jr., *The Visible Hand: The Managerial Revolution in American Business*
1979 Don E. Fehrenbacher, *The Dred Scott Case: Its Significance in American Law and Politics*
1980 Leon F. Litwack, *Been in the Storm So Long*
1981 Lawrence A. Cremin, *American Education: The National Experience, 1783-1876*
1982 C. Vann Woodward, ed., *Mary Chesnut's Civil War*
1983 Rhys L. Issac, *The Transformation of Virginia, 1740-1790*
1985 Thomas K. McCraw, *Prophets of Regulation*
1986 Walter A. McDougall, *The Heavens and the Earth*
1987 Bernard Bailyn, *Voyagers to the West*
1988 Robert V. Bruce, *The Launching of Modern American Science, 1846-1876*
1989 Taylor Branch, *Parting the Waters: America in the King Years, 1954-63*; James M. McPherson, *Battle Cry of Freedom: The Civil War Era*
1990 Stanley Karnow, *In Our Image: America's Empire in the Philippines*
1991 Laurel Thatcher Ulrich, *A Midwife's Tale: The Life of Martha Ballard, Based on Her Diary, 1785-1812*
1992 Mark E. Neely Jr., *The Fate of Liberty: Abraham Lincoln and Civil Liberties*
1993 Gordon S. Wood, *The Radicalism of the American Revolution*
1995 Doris Kearns Goodwin, *No Ordinary Time: Franklin and Eleanor Roosevelt: The Home Front in World War II*
1996 Alan Taylor, *William Cooper's Town: Power and Persuasion on the Frontier of the Early American Republic*
1997 Jack N. Rakove, *Original Meanings: Politics and Ideas in the Making of the Constitution*
1998 Edward J. Larson, *Summer for the Gods: The Scopes Trial and America's Continuing Debate Over Science and Religion*
1999 Edwin G. Burrows and Mike Wallace, *Gotham: A History of New York City to 1898*
2000 David M. Kennedy, *Freedom From Fear: The American People in Depression and War, 1929-1945*
2001 Joseph J. Ellis, *Founding Brothers: The Revolutionary Generation*
2002 Louis Menand, *The Metaphysical Club: A Story of Ideas in America*
2003 Rick Atkinson, *An Army at Dawn: The War in North Africa, 1942-1943*
2004 Steven Hahn, *A Nation Under Our Feet: Black Political Struggles in the Rural South From Slavery to the Great Migration*
2005 David Hackett Fischer, *Washington's Crossing*
2006 David M. Oshinsky, *Polio: An American Story*
2007 Gene Roberts and Hank Klibanoff, *The Race Beat: The Press, the Civil Rights Struggle, and the Awakening of a Nation*
2008 Daniel Walker Howe, *What Hath God Wrought: The Transformation of America, 1815-1848*
2009 Annette Gordon-Reed, *The Hemingses of Monticello: An American Family*
2010 Liaquat Ahamed, *Lords of Finance: The Bankers Who Broke the World*
2011 Eric Foner, *The Fiery Trial: Abraham Lincoln and American Slavery*
2012 Manning Marable, *Malcolm X: A Life of Reinvention*
2013 Fredrik Logevall, *Embers of War: The Fall of an Empire and the Making of America's Vietnam*
2014 Alan Taylor, *The Internal Enemy: Slavery and War in Virginia, 1772-1832*

Biography or Autobiography

1917 Laura E. Richards and Maude Howe Elliott, assisted by Florence Howe Hall, *Julia Ward Howe*
1918 William Cabell Bruce, *Benjamin Franklin, Self-Revealed*
1919 Henry Adams, *The Education of Henry Adams*
1920 Albert J. Beveridge, *The Life of John Marshall*
1921 Edward Bok, *The Americanization of Edward Bok*
1922 Hamlin Garland, *A Daughter of the Middle Border*
1923 Burton J. Hendrick, *The Life and Letters of Walter H. Page*

1924 Michael Pupin, *From Immigrant to Inventor*
1925 M. A. DeWolfe Howe, *Barrett Wendell and His Letters*
1926 Harvey Cushing, *The Life of Sir William Osler*
1927 Emory Holloway, *Whitman: An Interpretation in Narrative*
1928 Charles Edward Russell, *The American Orchestra and Theodore Thomas*
1929 Burton J. Hendrick, *The Training of an American: The Earlier Life and Letters of Walter H. Page*
1930 Marquis James, *The Raven* (Sam Houston)
1931 Henry James, *Charles W. Eliot*
1932 Henry F. Pringle, *Theodore Roosevelt*
1933 Allan Nevins, *Grover Cleveland*
1934 Tyler Dennett, *John Hay*
1935 Douglas Southall Freeman, *R. E. Lee*
1936 Ralph Barton Perry, *The Thought and Character of William James*
1937 Allan Nevins, *Hamilton Fish: The Inner History of the Grant Administration*
1938 Odell Shepard, *Pedlar's Progress*;
Marquis James, *Andrew Jackson, 2 vols.*
1939 Carl Van Doren, *Benjamin Franklin*
1940 Ray Stannard Baker, *Woodrow Wilson, Life and Letters*
1941 Ola Elizabeth Winslow, *Jonathan Edwards*
1942 Forrest Wilson, *Crusader in Crinoline* (Harriet Beecher Stowe)
1943 Samuel Eliot Morison, *Admiral of the Ocean Sea* (Christopher Columbus)
1944 Carleton Mabee, *The American Leonardo: The Life of Samuel F. B. Morse*
1945 Russell Blaine Nye, *George Bancroft: Brahmin Rebel*
1946 Linnie Marsh Wolfe, *Son of the Wilderness* (John Muir)
1947 William Allen White, *Autobiography of William Allen White*
1948 Margaret Clapp, *Forgotten First Citizen: John Bigelow*
1949 Robert E. Sherwood, *Roosevelt and Hopkins*
1950 Samuel Flagg Bemis, *John Quincy Adams and the Foundations of American Foreign Policy*
1951 Margaret Louise Coit, *John C. Calhoun: American Portrait*
1952 Merlo J. Pusey, *Charles Evans Hughes*
1953 David J. Mays, *Edmund Pendleton, 1721-1803*
1954 Charles A. Lindbergh, *The Spirit of St. Louis*
1955 William S. White, *The Taft Story*
1956 Talbot F. Hamlin, *Benjamin Henry Latrobe*
1957 John F. Kennedy, *Profiles in Courage*
1958 Douglas Southall Freeman, *George Washington, Vols. I-VI*
1959 Arthur Walworth, *Woodrow Wilson: American Prophet*
1960 Samuel Eliot Morison, *John Paul Jones*
1961 David Donald, *Charles Sumner and the Coming of the Civil War*
1963 Leon Edel, *Henry James: Vols. 2-3*
1964 Walter Jackson Bate, *John Keats*
1965 Ernest Samuels, *Henry Adams*
1966 Arthur M. Schlesinger Jr., *A Thousand Days* (JFK)
1967 Justin Kaplan, *Mr. Clemens and Mark Twain*
1968 George F. Kennan, *Memoirs (1925-1950)*
1969 Benjamin L. Reid, *The Man From New York: John Quinn and His Friends*
1970 T. Harry Williams, *Huey Long*
1971 Lawrence Thompson, *Robert Frost: The Years of Triumph, 1915-1938*
1972 Joseph P. Lash, *Eleanor and Franklin*
1973 W. A. Swanberg, *Luce and His Empire*
1974 Louis Sheaffer, *O'Neill, Son and Artist*
1975 Robert A. Caro, *The Power Broker: Robert Moses and the Fall of New York*
1976 R. W. B. Lewis, *Edith Wharton: A Biography*
1977 John E. Mack, *A Prince of Our Disorder: The Life of T. E. Lawrence*
1978 Walter Jackson Bate, *Samuel Johnson*
1979 Leonard Baker, *Days of Sorrow and Pain: Leo Baeck and the Berlin Jews*
1980 Edmund Morris, *The Rise of Theodore Roosevelt*
1981 Robert K. Massie, *Peter the Great: His Life and World*
1982 William S. McFeely, *Grant: A Biography*
1983 Russell Baker, *Growing Up*
1984 Louis R. Harlan, *Booker T. Washington*
1985 Kenneth Silverman, *The Life and Times of Cotton Mather*
1986 Elizabeth Frank, *Louise Bogan: A Portrait*
1987 David J. Garrow, *Bearing the Cross: Martin Luther King Jr. and the Southern Christian Leadership Conference*
1988 David Herbert Donald, *Look Homeward: A Life of Thomas Wolfe*
1989 Richard Ellmann, *Oscar Wilde*
1990 Sebastian de Grazia, *Machiavelli in Hell*

1991 Steven Naifeh and Gregory White Smith, *Jackson Pollock: An American Saga*
1992 Lewis B. Puller Jr., *Fortunate Son: The Healing of a Vietnam Vet*
1993 David McCullough, *Truman*
1994 David Levering Lewis, *W.E.B. Du Bois: Biography of a Race, 1868-1919*
1995 Joan D. Hedrick, *Harriet Beecher Stowe: A Life*
1996 Jack Miles, *God: A Biography*
1997 Frank McCourt, *Angela's Ashes: A Memoir*
1998 Katharine Graham, *Personal History*
1999 A. Scott Berg, *Lindbergh*
2000 Stacy Schiff, *Véra (Mrs. Vladimir Nabokov)*
2001 David Levering Lewis, *W.E.B. Du Bois: The Fight for Equality and the American Century, 1919-1963*
2002 David McCullough, *John Adams*
2003 Robert A. Caro, *The Years of Lyndon Johnson: Master of the Senate*
2004 William Taubman, *Khrushchev: The Man and His Era*
2005 Mark Stevens and Annalyn Swan, *de Kooning: An American Master*
2006 Kai Bird and Martin J. Sherwin, *American Prometheus: The Triumph and Tragedy of J. Robert Oppenheimer*
2007 Debby Applegate, *The Most Famous Man in America: The Biography of Henry Ward Beecher*
2008 John Matteson, *Eden's Outcasts: The Story of Louisa May Alcott and Her Father*
2009 Jon Meacham, *American Lion: Andrew Jackson in the White House*
2010 T. J. Stiles, *The First Tycoon: The Epic Life of Cornelius Vanderbilt*
2011 Ron Chernow, *Washington: A Life*
2012 John Lewis Gaddis, *George F. Kennan: An American Life*
2013 Tom Reiss, *The Black Count: Glory, Revolution, Betrayal, and the Real Count of Monte Cristo* (Alex Dumas)
2014 Megan Marshall, *Margaret Fuller: A New American Life*

Poetry

1922 Edwin Arlington Robinson, *Collected Poems*
1923 Edna St. Vincent Millay, *The Ballad of the Harp-Weaver; A Few Figs From Thistles;* and other works
1924 Robert Frost, *New Hampshire: A Poem With Notes and Grace Notes*
1925 Edwin Arlington Robinson, *The Man Who Died Twice*
1926 Amy Lowell, *What's O'Clock*
1927 Leonora Speyer, *Fiddler's Farewell*
1928 Edwin Arlington Robinson, *Tristram*
1929 Stephen Vincent Benet, *John Brown's Body*
1930 Conrad Aiken, *Selected Poems*
1931 Robert Frost, *Collected Poems*
1932 George Dillon, *The Flowering Stone*
1933 Archibald MacLeish, *Conquistador*
1934 Robert Hillyer, *Collected Verse*
1935 Audrey Wurdemann, *Bright Ambush*
1936 Robert P. Tristram Coffin, *Strange Holiness*
1937 Robert Frost, *A Further Range*
1938 Marya Zaturenska, *Cold Morning Sky*
1939 John Gould Fletcher, *Selected Poems*
1940 Mark Van Doren, *Collected Poems*
1941 Leonard Bacon, *Sunderland Capture*
1942 William Rose Benet, *The Dust Which Is God*
1943 Robert Frost, *A Witness Tree*
1944 Stephen Vincent Benet, *Western Star*
1945 Karl Shapiro, *V-Letter and Other Poems*
1947 Robert Lowell, *Lord Weary's Castle*
1948 W. H. Auden, *The Age of Anxiety*
1949 Peter Viereck, *Terror and Decorum*
1950 Gwendolyn Brooks, *Annie Allen*
1951 Carl Sandburg, *Complete Poems*
1952 Marianne Moore, *Collected Poems*
1953 Archibald MacLeish, *Collected Poems, 1917-1952*
1954 Theodore Roethke, *The Waking*
1955 Wallace Stevens, *Collected Poems*
1956 Elizabeth Bishop, *Poems: North and South*
1957 Richard Wilbur, *Things of This World*
1958 Robert Penn Warren, *Promises: Poems 1954-1956*
1959 Stanley Kunitz, *Selected Poems 1928-1958*
1960 W. D. Snodgrass, *Heart's Needle*
1961 Phyllis McGinley, *Times Three: Selected Verse From Three Decades*
1962 Alan Dugan, *Poems*
1963 William Carlos Williams, *Pictures From Brueghel*
1964 Louis Simpson, *At the End of the Open Road*
1965 John Berryman, *77 Dream Songs*

1966 Richard Eberhart, *Selected Poems*
1967 Anne Sexton, *Live or Die*
1968 Anthony Hecht, *The Hard Hours*
1969 George Oppen, *Of Being Numerous*
1970 Richard Howard, *Untitled Subjects*
1971 William S. Merwin, *The Carrier of Ladders*
1972 James Wright, *Collected Poems*
1973 Maxine Kumin, *Up Country*
1974 Robert Lowell, *The Dolphin*
1975 Gary Snyder, *Turtle Island*
1976 John Ashbery, *Self-Portrait in a Convex Mirror*
1977 James Merrill, *Divine Comedies*
1978 Howard Nemerov, *Collected Poems*
1979 Robert Penn Warren, *Now and Then: Poems 1976-1978*
1980 Donald Justice, *Selected Poems*
1981 James Schuyler, *The Morning of the Poem*
1982 Sylvia Plath, *The Collected Poems*
1983 Galway Kinnell, *Selected Poems*
1984 Mary Oliver, *American Primitive*
1985 Carolyn Kizer, *Yin*
1986 Henry Taylor, *The Flying Change*
1987 Rita Dove, *Thomas and Beulah*
1988 William Meredith, *Partial Accounts*
1989 Richard Wilbur, *New and Collected Poems*
1990 Charles Simic, *The World Doesn't End*
1991 Mona Van Duyn, *Near Changes*
1992 James Tate, *Selected Poems*
1993 Louise Glück, *The Wild Iris*
1994 Yusef Komunyakaa, *Neon Vernacular*
1995 Philip Levine, *The Simple Truth*
1996 Jorie Graham, *The Dream of the Unified Field*
1997 Lisel Mueller, *Alive Together: New and Selected Poems*
1998 Charles Wright, *Black Zodiac*
1999 Mark Strand, *Blizzard of One*
2000 C. K. Williams, *Repair*
2001 Stephen Dunn, *Different Hours*
2002 Carl Dennis, *Practical Gods*
2003 Paul Muldoon, *Moy Sand and Gravel*
2004 Franz Wright, *Walking to Martha's Vineyard*
2005 Ted Kooser, *Delights & Shadows*
2006 Claudia Emerson, *Late Wife*
2007 Natasha Trethewey, *Native Guard*
2008 Robert Hass, *Time and Materials*; Philip Schultz, *Failure*
2009 W. S. Merwin, *The Shadow of Sirius*
2010 Rae Armantrout, *Versed*
2011 Kay Ryan, *The Best of It: New and Selected Poems*
2012 Tracy K. Smith, *Life on Mars*
2013 Sharon Olds, *Stag's Leap*
2014 Vijay Seshadri, *3 Sections*

General Nonfiction

1962 Theodore H. White, *The Making of the President 1960*
1963 Barbara W. Tuchman, *The Guns of August*
1964 Richard Hofstadter, *Anti-Intellectualism in American Life*
1965 Howard Mumford Jones, *O Strange New World*
1966 Edwin Way Teale, *Wandering Through Winter*
1967 David Brion Davis, *The Problem of Slavery in Western Culture*
1968 Will and Ariel Durant, *Rousseau and Revolution*
1969 Norman Mailer, *The Armies of the Night*;
Rene Jules Dubos, *So Human an Animal: How We Are
Shaped by Surroundings and Events*
1970 Eric H. Erikson, *Gandhi's Truth*
1971 John Toland, *The Rising Sun*
1972 Barbara W. Tuchman, *Stilwell and the American
Experience in China, 1911-1945*
1973 Frances FitzGerald, *Fire in the Lake: The Vietnamese
and the Americans in Vietnam*;
Robert Coles, *Children of Crisis, Vols. II and III*
1974 Ernest Becker, *The Denial of Death*
1975 Annie Dillard, *Pilgrim at Tinker Creek*
1976 Robert N. Butler, *Why Survive? Being Old in America*
1977 William W. Warner, *Beautiful Swimmers*
1978 Carl Sagan, *The Dragons of Eden*

1979 Edward O. Wilson, *On Human Nature*
1980 Douglas R. Hofstadter, *Gödel, Escher, Bach:
An Eternal Golden Braid*
1981 Carl E. Schorske, *Fin-de-Siecle Vienna: Politics and Culture*
1982 Tracy Kidder, *The Soul of a New Machine*
1983 Susan Sheehan, *Is There No Place on Earth for Me?*
1984 Paul Starr, *Social Transformation of American Medicine*
1985 Studs Terkel, *The Good War*
1986 Joseph Lelyveld, *Move Your Shadow*;
J. Anthony Lukas, *Common Ground*
1987 David K. Shipler, *Arab and Jew: Wounded Spirits in a
Promised Land*
1988 Richard Rhodes, *The Making of the Atomic Bomb*
1989 Neil Sheehan, *A Bright Shining Lie: John Paul Vann
and America in Vietnam*
1990 Dale Maharidge and Michael Williamson,
And Their Children After Them
1991 Bert Holldobler and Edward O. Wilson, *The Ants*
1992 Daniel Yergin, *The Prize: The Epic Quest for Oil,
Money, and Power*
1993 Garry Wills, *Lincoln at Gettysburg*
1994 David Remnick, *Lenin's Tomb: The Last Days of the
Soviet Empire*
1995 Jonathan Weiner, *The Beak of the Finch: A Story of
Evolution in Our Time*
1996 Tina Rosenberg, *The Haunted Land: Facing Europe's
Ghosts After Communism*
1997 Richard Kluger, *Ashes to Ashes: America's Hundred-Year
Cigarette War, the Public Health, and the Unabashed
Triumph of Philip Morris*
1998 Jared Diamond, *Guns, Germs, and Steel: The Fates
of Human Societies*
1999 John McPhee, *Annals of the Former World*
2000 John W. Dower, *Embracing Defeat: Japan in the Wake of
World War II*
2001 Herbert P. Bix, *Hirohito and the Making of Modern Japan*
2002 Diane McWhorter, *Carry Me Home: Birmingham, Alabama,
the Climactic Battle of the Civil Rights Revolution*
2003 Samantha Power, *A Problem From Hell: America and the
Age of Genocide*
2004 Anne Applebaum, *Gulag: A History*
2005 David Coll, *Ghost Wars*
2006 Caroline Elkins, *Imperial Reckoning: The Untold Story of
Britain's Gulag in Kenya*
2007 Lawrence Wright, *The Looming Tower: Al-Qaeda and
the Road to 9/11*
2008 Saul Friedländer, *The Years of Extermination: Nazi
Germany and the Jews, 1939-1945*
2009 Douglas A. Blackmon, *Slavery by Another Name:
The Re-Enslavement of Black Americans From the
Civil War to World War II*
2010 David E. Hoffman, *The Dead Hand: The Untold Story of
the Cold War Arms Race and Its Dangerous Legacy*
2011 Siddhartha Mukherjee, *The Emperor of All Maladies:
A Biography of Cancer*
2012 Stephen Greenblatt, *The Swerve: How the World Became
Modern*
2013 Gilbert King, *Devil in the Grove: Thurgood Marshall,
the Groveland Boys, and the Dawn of a New America*
2014 Dan Fagin, *Toms River: A Story of Science and Salvation*

Special Citation in Letters

1944 Richard Rodgers and Oscar Hammerstein II, for *Oklahoma!*
1957 Kenneth Roberts, for his historical novels
1960 *The Armada*, by Garrett Mattingly
1961 *American Heritage Picture History of the Civil War*
1973 *George Washington*, Vols. I-IV, by James Thomas Flexner
1977 Alex Haley, for *Roots*
1978 E. B. White
1984 Theodor Seuss Geisel (Dr. Seuss)
1992 Art Spiegelman, for *Maus*
2006 Edmund S. Morgan
2007 Ray Bradbury

Pulitzer Prizes in Music, 1943-2014

1943 William Schuman, *Secular Cantata No. 2, A Free Song*
1944 Howard Hanson, *Symphony No. 4, Op. 34*
1945 Aaron Copland, *Appalachian Spring*
1946 Leo Sowerby, *The Canticle of the Sun*
1947 Charles Ives, *Symphony No. 3*
1948 Walter Piston, *Symphony No. 3*
1949 Virgil Thomson, *Louisiana Story*
1950 Gian-Carlo Menotti, *The Consul*

1951 Douglas Moore, *Giants in the Earth*
1952 Gail Kubik, *Symphony Concertante*
1954 Quincy Porter, *Concerto for Two Pianos and Orchestra*
1955 Gian-Carlo Menotti, *The Saint of Bleecker Street*
1956 Ernest Toch, *Symphony No. 3*
1957 Norman Dello Joio, *Meditations on Ecclesiastes*
1958 Samuel Barber, *Vanessa*
1959 John LaMontaine, *Concerto for Piano and Orchestra*

1960 Elliott Carter, *Second String Quartet*
1961 Walter Piston, *Symphony No. 7*
1962 Robert Ward, *The Crucible*
1963 Samuel Barber, *Piano Concerto No. 1*
1966 Leslie Bassett, *Variations for Orchestra*
1967 Leon Kirchner, *Quartet No. 3*
1968 George Crumb, *Echoes of Time and the River*
1969 Karel Husa, *String Quartet No. 3*
1970 Charles Wuorinen, *Time's Encomium*
1971 Mario Davidovsky, *Synchronisms No. 6*
1972 Jacob Druckman, *Windows*
1973 Elliott Carter, *String Quartet No. 3*
1974 Donald Martino, *Notturno*
1975 Dominick Argento, *From the Diary of Virginia Woolf*
1976 Ned Rorem, *Air Music*
1977 Richard Wernick, *Visions of Terror and Wonder*
1978 Michael Colgrass, *Deja Vu for Percussion and Orchestra*
1979 Joseph Schwantner, *Aftertones of Infinity*
1980 David Del Tredici, *In Memory of a Summer Day*
1982 Roger Sessions, *Concerto for Orchestra*
1983 Ellen Taaffe Zwilich, *Symphony No. 1*
1984 Bernard Rands, *Canti del Sole*
1985 Stephen Albert, *Symphony, RiverRun*
1986 George Perle, *Wind Quintet IV*
1987 John Harbison, *The Flight Into Egypt*
1988 William Bolcom, *12 New Etudes for Piano*
1989 Roger Reynolds, *Whispers Out of Time*
1990 Mel Powell, *Duplicates: A Concerto for Two Pianos and Orchestra*
1991 Shulamit Ran, *Symphony*
1992 Wayne Peterson, *The Face of the Night, The Heart of the Dark*
1993 Christopher Rouse, *Trombone Concerto*
1994 Gunther Schuller, *Of Reminiscences and Reflections*

1995 Morton Gould, *Stringmusic*
1996 George Walker, *Lilacs for Voice and Orchestra*
1997 Wynton Marsalis, *Blood on the Fields*
1998 Aaron Jay Kernis, *String Quartet No. 2 (musica instrumentalis)*
1999 Melinda Wagner, *Concerto for Flute, Strings, and Percussion*
2000 Lewis Spratlan, *Life is a Dream, Opera in Three Acts: Act II, Concert Version*
2001 John Corigliano, *Symphony No. 2 for String Orchestra*
2002 Henry Brant, *Ice Field*
2003 John Adams, *On the Transmigration of Souls*
2004 Paul Moravec, *Tempest Fantasy*
2005 Steven Stucky, *Second Concerto for Orchestra*
2006 Yehudi Wyner, *Piano Concerto: "Chiavi in Mano"*
2007 Ornette Coleman, *Sound Grammar*
2008 David Lang, *The Little Match Girl Passion*
2009 Steve Reich, *Double Sextet*
2010 Jennifer Higdon, *Violin Concerto*
2011 Zhou Long, *Madame White Snake*
2012 Kevin Puts, *Silent Night: Opera in Two Acts*
2013 Caroline Shaw, *Partita for 8 Voices*
2014 John Luther Adams, *Become Ocean*

Special Citation in Music

1974 Roger Sessions
1976 Scott Joplin
1982 Milton Babbitt
1985 William Schuman
1998 George Gershwin
1999 Edward Kennedy "Duke" Ellington
2006 Thelonious Monk
2007 John Coltrane
2008 Bob Dylan
2010 Hank Williams

Man Booker Prize for Fiction, 1969-2014

The Booker Prize for fiction, established in 1968 and renamed the Man Booker Prize in 2002, is £50,000, awarded annually to the author of the best new full-length novel written in English. Award-winning authors were required to be a citizen of the UK, the Commonwealth, or the Irish Republic until 2014, the first year in which all English-language novels published in Britain were considered.

Year Author, book

1969 P. H. Newby, *Something to Answer For*
1970 Bernice Rubens, *The Elected Member*
1971 V. S. Naipaul, *In a Free State*
1972 John Berger, *G*
1973 J. G. Farrell, *The Siege of Krishnapur*
1974 Nadine Gordimer, *The Conservationist*; Stanley Middleton, *Holiday*
1975 Ruth Prawer Jhabvala, *Heat and Dust*
1976 David Storey, *Saville*
1977 Paul Scott, *Staying On*
1978 Iris Murdoch, *The Sea, the Sea*
1979 Penelope Fitzgerald, *Offshore*
1980 William Golding, *Rites of Passage*
1981 Salman Rushdie, *Midnight's Children*[1]
1982 Thomas Keneally, *Schindler's Ark*
1983 J. M. Coetzee, *Life and Times of Michael K*
1984 Anita Brookner, *Hotel du Lac*
1985 Keri Hulme, *The Bone People*
1986 Kingsley Amis, *The Old Devils*
1987 Penelope Lively, *Moon Tiger*
1988 Peter Carey, *Oscar and Lucinda*
1989 Kazuo Ishiguro, *The Remains of the Day*
1990 A. S. Byatt, *Possession*
1991 Ben Okri, *The Famished Road*
1992 Michael Ondaatje, *The English Patient*; Barry Unsworth, *Sacred Hunger*

Year Author, book

1993 Roddy Doyle, *Paddy Clarke Ha Ha Ha*
1994 James Kelman, *How Late It Was, How Late*
1995 Pat Barker, *The Ghost Road*
1996 Graham Swift, *Last Orders*
1997 Arundhati Roy, *The God of Small Things*
1998 Ian McEwan, *Amsterdam*
1999 J. M. Coetzee, *Disgrace*
2000 Margaret Atwood, *The Blind Assassin*
2001 Peter Carey, *True History of the Kelly Gang*
2002 Yann Martel, *Life of Pi*
2003 DBC Pierre, *Vernon God Little*
2004 Alan Hollinghurst, *The Line of Beauty*
2005 John Banville, *The Sea*
2006 Kiran Desai, *The Inheritance of Loss*
2007 Anne Enright, *The Gathering*
2008 Aravind Adiga, *The White Tiger*
2009 Hilary Mantel, *Wolf Hall*
2010 Howard Jacobson, *The Finkler Question*
2011 Julian Barnes, *The Sense of an Ending*
2012 Hilary Mantel, *Bring up the Bodies*
2013 Eleanor Catton, *The Luminaries*
2014 Richard Flanagan, *The Narrow Road to the Deep North*

(1) Rushdie's *Midnight's Children* also won the Booker of Bookers prize in 1993 and the Best of the Booker prize in 2008.

Newbery Medal, 1922-2014

The Newbery Medal is awarded annually by the Association for Library Service to Children, a division of the American Library Association, to the most distinguished contribution to American children's literature published in the previous year.

Year Book, author

1922 *The Story of Mankind*, Hendrik Willem van Loon
1923 *The Voyages of Dr. Dolittle*, Hugh Lofting
1924 *The Dark Frigate*, Charles Boardman Hawes
1925 *Tales From Silver Lands*, Charles J. Finger
1926 *Shen of the Sea*, Arthur Bowie Chrisman
1927 *Smoky, the Cowhorse*, Will James
1928 *Gay-Neck: The Story of a Pigeon*, Dhan Gopal Mukerji
1929 *The Trumpeter of Krakow*, Eric P. Kelly
1930 *Hitty, Her First Hundred Years*, Rachel Field
1931 *The Cat Who Went to Heaven*, Elizabeth Coatsworth
1932 *Waterless Mountain*, Laura Adams Armer
1933 *Young Fu of the Upper Yangtze*, Elizabeth Foreman Lewis

Year Book, author

1934 *Invincible Louisa*, Cornelia Meigs
1935 *Dobry*, Monica Shannon
1936 *Caddie Woodlawn*, Carol Ryrie Brink
1937 *Roller Skates*, Ruth Sawyer
1938 *The White Stag*, Kate Seredy
1939 *Thimble Summer*, Elizabeth Enright
1940 *Daniel Boone*, James Daugherty
1941 *Call It Courage*, Armstrong Sperry
1942 *The Matchlock Gun*, Walter D. Edmonds
1943 *Adam of the Road*, Elizabeth Janet Gray
1944 *Johnny Tremain*, Esther Forbes
1945 *Rabbit Hill*, Robert Lawson

Year	Book, author
1946	*Strawberry Girl*, Lois Lenski
1947	*Miss Hickory*, Carolyn Sherwin Bailey
1948	*The Twenty-One Balloons*, William Pène du Bois
1949	*King of the Wind*, Marguerite Henry
1950	*The Door in the Wall*, Marguerite de Angeli
1951	*Amos Fortune, Free Man*, Elizabeth Yates
1952	*Ginger Pye*, Eleanor Estes
1953	*Secret of the Andes*, Ann Nolan Clark
1954	*...And Now Miguel*, Joseph Krumgold
1955	*The Wheel on the School*, Meindert DeJong
1956	*Carry On, Mr. Bowditch*, Jean Lee Latham
1957	*Miracles on Maple Hill*, Virginia Sorensen
1958	*Rifles for Watie*, Harold Keith
1959	*The Witch of Blackbird Pond*, Elizabeth George Speare
1960	*Onion John*, Joseph Krumgold
1961	*Island of the Blue Dolphins*, Scott O'Dell
1962	*The Bronze Bow*, Elizabeth George Speare
1963	*A Wrinkle in Time*, Madeleine L'Engle
1964	*It's Like This, Cat*, Emily Cheney Neville
1965	*Shadow of a Bull*, Maia Wojciechowska
1966	*I, Juan de Pareja*, Elizabeth Borton de Trevino
1967	*Up a Road Slowly*, Irene Hunt
1968	*From the Mixed-Up Files of Mrs. Basil E. Frankweiler*, E. L. Konigsburg
1969	*The High King*, Lloyd Alexander
1970	*Sounder*, William H. Armstrong
1971	*The Summer of the Swans*, Betsy Byars
1972	*Mrs. Frisby and the Rats of NIMH*, Robert C. O'Brien
1973	*Julie of the Wolves*, Jean Craighead George
1974	*The Slave Dancer*, Paula Fox
1975	*M. C. Higgins, the Great*, Virginia Hamilton
1976	*The Grey King*, Susan Cooper
1977	*Roll of Thunder, Hear My Cry*, Mildred D. Taylor
1978	*Bridge to Terabithia*, Katherine Paterson
1979	*The Westing Game*, Ellen Raskin
1980	*A Gathering of Days*, Joan Blos

Year	Book, author
1981	*Jacob Have I Loved*, Katherine Paterson
1982	*A Visit to William Blake's Inn: Poems for Innocent and Experienced Travelers*, Nancy Willard
1983	*Dicey's Song*, Cynthia Voigt
1984	*Dear Mr. Henshaw*, Beverly Cleary
1985	*The Hero and the Crown*, Robin McKinley
1986	*Sarah, Plain and Tall*, Patricia MacLachlan
1987	*The Whipping Boy*, Sid Fleischman
1988	*Lincoln: A Photobiography*, Russell Freedman
1989	*Joyful Noise: Poems for Two Voices*, Paul Fleischman
1990	*Number the Stars*, Lois Lowry
1991	*Maniac Magee*, Jerry Spinelli
1992	*Shiloh*, Phyllis Reynolds Naylor
1993	*Missing May*, Cynthia Rylant
1994	*The Giver*, Lois Lowry
1995	*Walk Two Moons*, Sharon Creech
1996	*The Midwife's Apprentice*, Karen Cushman
1997	*The View From Saturday*, E. L. Konigsburg
1998	*Out of the Dust*, Karen Hesse
1999	*Holes*, Louis Sachar
2000	*Bud, Not Buddy*, Christopher Paul Curtis
2001	*A Year Down Yonder*, Richard Peck
2002	*A Single Shard*, Linda Sue Park
2003	*Crispin: The Cross of Lead*, Avi
2004	*The Tale of Despereaux*, Kate DiCamillo
2005	*Kira-Kira*, Cynthia Kadohata
2006	*Criss Cross*, Lynne Rae Perkins
2007	*The Higher Power of Lucky*, Susan Patron
2008	*Good Masters! Sweet Ladies! Voices From a Medieval Village*, Laura Amy Schlitz
2009	*The Graveyard Book*, Neil Gaiman
2010	*When You Reach Me*, Rebecca Stead
2011	*Moon Over Manifest*, Clare Vanderpool
2012	*Dead End in Norvelt*, Jack Gantos
2013	*The One and Only Ivan*, Katherine Applegate
2014	*Flora & Ulysses: The Illuminated Adventures*, Kate DiCamillo

Caldecott Medal, 1938-2014

The Caldecott Medal is awarded annually by the Association for Library Service to Children, a division of the American Library Association, to the illustrator of the most distinguished American picture book for children.

Year	Book, illustrator
1938	*Animals of the Bible*, Dorothy P. Lathrop
1939	*Mei Li*, Thomas Handforth
1940	*Abraham Lincoln*, Ingri and Edgar Parin d'Aulaire
1941	*They Were Strong and Good*, Robert Lawson
1942	*Make Way for Ducklings*, Robert McCloskey
1943	*The Little House*, Virginia Lee Burton
1944	*Many Moons*, Louis Slobodkin
1945	*Prayer for a Child*, Elizabeth Orton Jones
1946	*The Rooster Crows*, Maude and Miska Petersham
1947	*The Little Island*, Leonard Weisgard
1948	*White Snow, Bright Snow*, Roger Duvoisin
1949	*The Big Snow*, Berta and Elmer Hader
1950	*Song of the Swallows*, Leo Politi
1951	*The Egg Tree*, Katherine Milhous
1952	*Finders Keepers*, Nicolas, pseud. (Nicholas Mordvinoff)
1953	*The Biggest Bear*, Lynd Ward
1954	*Madeline's Rescue*, Ludwig Bemelmans
1955	*Cinderella, or the Little Glass Slipper*, Marcia Brown
1956	*Frog Went A-Courtin'*, Feodor Rojankovsky
1957	*A Tree Is Nice*, Marc Simont
1958	*Time of Wonder*, Robert McCloskey
1959	*Chanticleer and the Fox*, Barbara Cooney
1960	*Nine Days to Christmas*, Marie Hall Ets
1961	*Baboushka and the Three Kings*, Nicolas Sidjakov
1962	*Once a Mouse*, Marcia Brown
1963	*The Snowy Day*, Ezra Jack Keats
1964	*Where the Wild Things Are*, Maurice Sendak
1965	*May I Bring a Friend?*, Beni Montresor
1966	*Always Room for One More*, Nonny Hogrogian
1967	*Sam, Bangs, and Moonshine*, Evaline Ness
1968	*Drummer Hoff*, Ed Emberley
1969	*The Fool of the World and the Flying Ship*, Uri Shulevitz
1970	*Sylvester and the Magic Pebble*, William Steig
1971	*A Story A Story*, Gail E. Haley
1972	*One Fine Day*, Nonny Hogrogian
1973	*The Funny Little Woman*, Blair Lent
1974	*Duffy and the Devil*, Margot Zemach
1975	*Arrow to the Sun*, Gerald McDermott
1976	*Why Mosquitoes Buzz in People's Ears*, Leo and Diane Dillon

Year	Book, illustrator
1977	*Ashanti to Zulu: African Traditions*, Leo and Diane Dillon
1978	*Noah's Ark*, Peter Spier
1979	*The Girl Who Loved Wild Horses*, Paul Goble
1980	*Ox-Cart Man*, Barbara Cooney
1981	*Fables*, Arnold Lobel
1982	*Jumanji*, Chris Van Allsburg
1983	*Shadow*, Marcia Brown
1984	*The Glorious Flight: Across the Channel With Louis Bleriot*, Alice and Martin Provensen
1985	*Saint George and the Dragon*, Trina Schart Hyman
1986	*The Polar Express*, Chris Van Allsburg
1987	*Hey, Al*, Richard Egielski
1988	*Owl Moon*, John Schoenherr
1989	*Song and Dance Man*, Stephen Gammell
1990	*Lon Po Po: A Red-Riding Hood Story From China*, Ed Young
1991	*Black and White*, David Macaulay
1992	*Tuesday*, David Wiesner
1993	*Mirette on the High Wire*, Emily Arnold McCully
1994	*Grandfather's Journey*, Allen Say
1995	*Smoky Night*, David Diaz
1996	*Officer Buckle and Gloria*, Peggy Rathmann
1997	*Golem*, David Wisniewski
1998	*Rapunzel*, Paul O. Zelinsky
1999	*Snowflake Bentley*, Mary Azarian
2000	*Joseph Had a Little Overcoat*, Simms Taback
2001	*So You Want to be President?*, David Small
2002	*The Three Pigs*, David Wiesner
2003	*My Friend Rabbit*, Eric Rohmann
2004	*The Man Who Walked Between the Towers*, Mordicai Gerstein
2005	*Kitten's First Full Moon*, Kevin Henkes
2006	*The Hello, Goodbye Window*, Chris Raschka
2007	*Flotsam*, David Wiesner
2008	*The Invention of Hugo Cabret*, Brian Selznick
2009	*The House in the Night*, Beth Krommes
2010	*The Lion & the Mouse*, Jerry Pinkney
2011	*A Sick Day for Amos McGee*, Erin E. Stead
2012	*A Ball for Daisy*, Chris Raschka
2013	*This Is Not My Hat*, Jon Klassen
2014	*Locomotive*, Brian Floca

National Book Awards, 1950-2013

The National Book Awards (known as American Book Awards 1980-86) are administered by the National Book Foundation and have been given annually since 1950. The prizes, each valued at $10,000, are awarded to U.S. citizens for works published in the U.S. In some years, multiple awards were given for nonfiction in various categories; in such cases, the history and biography (if any) or biography winner is listed. Selected additional awards in nonfiction are listed in footnotes.

Other National Book Awards, 2013: Poetry: Mary Szybist, *Incarnadine: Poems*. Young People's Literature: Cynthia Kadohata, *The Thing About Luck*. Distinguished Contribution to American Letters: E. L. Doctorow. Literarian Award: Maya Angelou.

Fiction

Year	Author, book	Year	Author, book
1950	Nelson Algren, *The Man With the Golden Arm*	1982	John Updike, *Rabbit Is Rich*
1951	William Faulkner, *The Collected Stories*	1983	Alice Walker, *The Color Purple*
1952	James Jones, *From Here to Eternity*	1984	Ellen Gilchrist, *Victory Over Japan*
1953	Ralph Ellison, *Invisible Man*	1985	Don DeLillo, *White Noise*
1954	Saul Bellow, *The Adventures of Augie March*	1986	E. L. Doctorow, *World's Fair*
1955	William Faulkner, *A Fable*	1987	Larry Heinemann, *Paco's Story*
1956	John O'Hara, *Ten North Frederick*	1988	Pete Dexter, *Paris Trout*
1957	Wright Morris, *The Field of Vision*	1989	John Casey, *Spartina*
1958	John Cheever, *The Wapshot Chronicle*	1990	Charles Johnson, *Middle Passage*
1959	Bernard Malamud, *The Magic Barrel*	1991	Norman Rush, *Mating*
1960	Philip Roth, *Goodbye, Columbus*	1992	Cormac McCarthy, *All the Pretty Horses*
1961	Conrad Richter, *The Waters of Kronos*	1993	E. Annie Proulx, *The Shipping News*
1962	Walker Percy, *The Moviegoer*	1994	William Gaddis, *A Frolic of His Own*
1963	J. F. Powers, *Morte d'Urban*	1995	Philip Roth, *Sabbath's Theater*
1964	John Updike, *The Centaur*	1996	Andrea Barrett, *Ship Fever and Other Stories*
1965	Saul Bellow, *Herzog*	1997	Charles Frazier, *Cold Mountain*
1966	Katherine Anne Porter, *The Collected Stories*	1998	Alice McDermott, *Charming Billy*
1967	Bernard Malamud, *The Fixer*	1999	Ha Jin, *Waiting*
1968	Thornton Wilder, *The Eighth Day*	2000	Susan Sontag, *In America*
1969	Jerzy Kosinski, *Steps*	2001	Jonathan Franzen, *The Corrections*
1970	Joyce Carol Oates, *Them*	2002	Julia Glass, *Three Junes*
1971	Saul Bellow, *Mr. Sammler's Planet*	2003	Shirley Hazzard, *The Great Fire*
1972	Flannery O'Connor, *The Complete Stories*	2004	Lily Tuck, *The News From Paraguay*
1973	John Barth, *Chimera*	2005	William T. Vollmann, *Europe Central*
1974	Thomas Pynchon, *Gravity's Rainbow*	2006	Richard Powers, *The Echo Maker*
1974	Isaac Bashevis Singer, *A Crown of Feathers*	2007	Denis Johnson, *Tree of Smoke*
1975	Robert Stone, *Dog Soldiers*	2008	Peter Matthiessen, *Shadow Country*
1976	William Gaddis, *JR*	2009	Colum McCann, *Let the Great World Spin*
1977	Wallace Stegner, *The Spectator Bird*	2010	Jaimy Gordon, *Lord of Misrule*
1978	Mary Lee Settle, *Blood Ties*	2011	Jesmyn Ward, *Salvage the Bones*
1979	Tim O'Brien, *Going After Cacciato*	2012	Louise Erdrich, *The Round House*
1980	William Styron, *Sophie's Choice*	2013	James McBride, *The Good Lord Bird*
1981	Wright Morris, *Plains Song*		

Nonfiction

Year	Author, book	Year	Author, book
1950	Ralph L. Rusk, *Ralph Waldo Emerson*	1975	Richard B. Sewall, *The Life of Emily Dickinson*[6]
1951	Newton Arvin, *Herman Melville*	1976	David Brion Davis, *The Problem of Slavery in the Age of Revolution, 1770-1823*
1952	Rachel Carson, *The Sea Around Us*		
1953	Bernard A. De Voto, *The Course of an Empire*	1977	W. A. Swanberg, *Norman Thomas: The Last Idealist*[7]
1954	Bruce Catton, *A Stillness at Appomattox*	1978	W. Jackson Bate, *Samuel Johnson*
1955	Joseph Wood Krutch, *The Measure of Man*	1979	Arthur M. Schlesinger Jr., *Robert Kennedy and His Times*
1956	Herbert Kubly, *An American in Italy*	1980	Tom Wolfe, *The Right Stuff*
1957	George F. Kennan, *Russia Leaves the War*	1981	Maxine Hong Kingston, *China Men*
1958	Catherine Drinker Bowen, *The Lion and the Throne*	1982	Tracy Kidder, *The Soul of a New Machine*
1959	J. Christopher Herold, *Mistress to an Age: A Life of Madame De Stael*	1983	Fox Butterfield, *China: Alive in the Bitter Sea*
1960	Richard Ellman, *James Joyce*	1984	Robert V. Remini, *Andrew Jackson and the Course of American Democracy, 1833-1845*
1961	William L. Shirer, *The Rise and Fall of the Third Reich*		
1962	Lewis Mumford, *The City in History: Its Origins, Its Transformations, and Its Prospects*	1985	J. Anthony Lukas, *Common Ground: A Turbulent Decade in the Lives of Three American Families*
1963	Leon Edel, *Henry James, Vol. II: The Conquest of London and Vol. III: The Middle Years*	1986	Barry Lopez, *Arctic Dreams*
		1987	Richard Rhodes, *The Making of the Atom Bomb*
1964	William H. McNeill, *The Rise of the West: A History of the Human Community*	1988	Neil Sheehan, *A Bright Shining Lie: John Paul Vann and America in Vietnam*
1965	Louis Fisher, *The Life of Lenin*	1989	Thomas L. Friedman, *From Beirut to Jerusalem*
1966	Arthur M. Schlesinger Jr., *A Thousand Days: John F. Kennedy in the White House*	1990	Ron Chernow, *The House of Morgan: An American Banking Dynasty and the Rise of Modern Finance*
1967	Peter Gay, *The Enlightenment, An Interpretation, Vol I: The Rise of Modern Paganism*	1991	Orlando Patterson, *Freedom*
1968	George F. Kennan, *Memoirs: 1925-1950*[1]	1992	Paul Monette, *Becoming a Man: Half a Life Story*
1969	Winthrop D. Jordan, *White Over Black: American Attitudes Toward the Negro, 1550-1812*[2]	1993	Gore Vidal, *United States: Essays 1952-1992*
		1994	Sherwin B. Nuland, *How We Die: Reflections on Life's Final Chapter*
1970	T. Harry Williams, *Huey Long*[3]		
1971	James MacGregor Burns, *Roosevelt: The Soldier of Freedom*	1995	Tina Rosenberg, *The Haunted Land: Facing Europe's Ghosts After Communism*
1972	Joseph P. Lash, *Eleanor and Franklin: The Story of Their Relationship, Based on Eleanor Roosevelt's Private Papers*	1996	James Carroll, *An American Requiem: God, My Father, and the War That Came Between Us*
		1997	Joseph J. Ellis, *American Sphinx: The Character of Thomas Jefferson*
1973	James Thomas Flexner, *George Washington, Vol. IV: Anguish and Farewell, 1793-1799*[4]	1998	Edward Ball, *Slaves in the Family*
1974	John Clive, *Macaulay, The Shaping of the Historian;* Douglas Day, *Malcolm Lowry: A Biography*[5]	1999	John W. Dower, *Embracing Defeat: Japan in the Wake of World War II*
		2000	Nathaniel Philbrick, *In the Heart of the Sea: The Tragedy of the Whaleship Essex*

Year	Author, book
2001	Andrew Solomon, *The Noonday Demon: An Atlas of Depression*
2002	Robert A. Caro, *Master of the Senate: The Years of Lyndon Johnson*
2003	Carlos Eire, *Waiting for Snow in Havana: Confessions of a Cuban Boy*
2004	Kevin Boyle, *Arc of Justice: A Saga of Race, Civil Rights, and Murder in the Jazz Age*
2005	Joan Didion, *The Year of Magical Thinking*
2006	Timothy Egan, *The Worst Hard Time: The Untold Story of Those Who Survived the Great American Dust Bowl*
2007	Tim Weiner, *Legacy of Ashes: The History of the CIA*
2008	Annette Gordon-Reed, *The Hemingses of Monticello: An American Family*
2009	T. J. Stiles, *The First Tycoon: The Epic Life of Cornelius Vanderbilt*
2010	Patti Smith, *Just Kids*
2011	Stephen Greenblatt, *The Swerve: How the World Became Modern*
2012	Katherine Boo, *Behind the Beautiful Forevers: Life, Death, and Hope in a Mumbai Undercity*
2013	George Packer, *The Unwinding: An Inner History of the New America*

(1) Science, Philosophy, & Religion: Jonathan Kozol, *Death at an Early Age*. (2) Arts & Letters: Norman Mailer, *The Armies of the Night: History as a Novel, the Novel as History*. (3) Arts & Letters: Lillian Hellman, *An Unfinished Woman: A Memoir*. (4) Contemp. Affairs: Frances FitzGerald, *Fire in the Lake: The Vietnamese and the Americans in Vietnam*. (5) Arts & Letters: Pauline Kael, *Deeper Into the Movies*. (6) Arts & Letters: Roger Shattuck, *Marcel Proust*; Lewis Thomas, *The Lives of a Cell: Notes of a Biology Watcher*. (7) Contemp. Thought: Bruno Bettelheim, *The Uses of Enchantment: The Meaning and Importance of Fairy Tales*.

Journalism Awards, 2014

National Magazine Awards, by American Society of Magazine Editors and Columbia Journalism School. Magazine of the Year: *Fast Company*. General Excellence: Active Interest, *Field & Stream*; General Interest, *New York*; Literature/Science/Politics, *Poetry*; Service/Lifestyle, *Sunset*; Special-Interest, *Inc.*; Style/Design, *Bon Appétit*. Columns and Commentary: *The New Yorker*. Design: *New York*. Essays and Criticism: *The New Yorker*. Feature Photography: *W*. Feature Writing: *The New Yorker*. Fiction: *The New Yorker*. Leisure Interests: *O, The Oprah Magazine*. Magazine Section: *Modern Farmer*. Multimedia: *National Geographic*. Personal Service: *Cosmopolitan*. Photography: *Bon Appétit*. Public Interest: *Time*. Reporting: *The New York Times Magazine*. Single-Topic Issue: *Bloomberg Businessweek*. Tablet Magazine: *National Geographic*. Video: *Glamour*. Website: *New York*.

George Foster Peabody Awards, by Univ. of Georgia, awarded to the best in electronic media. Tom Brokaw. *Scandal*, ABC. "Haiti in a Time of Cholera," "Made in Bangladesh," *Fault Lines*, Al Jazeera America. *Breaking Bad*, AMC. *Broadchurch*, *Orphan Black*, BBC America. *Inside Syria's War*, BBC World News. *One-on-One With Assad*, CBS. *Anthony Bourdain: Parts Unknown*, CNN. *Key & Peele*, Comedy Central. *Borgen*, DR1 (Denmark). "NFL at a Crossroads: Investigating a Health Crisis," *Outside the Lines*, ESPN. *The Bridge*, FX. *Burka Avenger*, Geo Tez (Pakistan). *Coverage of Supertyphoon Yolanda (Haiyan)*, GMA Network Inc. (Philippines). *Life According to Sam*, *Mea Maxima Culpa: Silence in the House of God*, *Six by Sondheim*, HBO. *Hollow*, www.hollowdocumentary.com. *Hanford's Dirty Secrets*, KING-TV, Seattle. *In Plain Sight: Poverty in America*, NBC. *House of Cards*, *Orange Is the New Black*, Netflix. *A Short History of the Highrise*, www.nytimes.com. *The Race Card Project*, NPR's *Morning Edition*. *The African Americans: Many Rivers to Cross with Henry Louis Gates Jr.*; *Best Kept Secret*; *The Central Park Five*; *A Chef's Life*; "League of Denial: The NFL's Concussion Crisis," *Frontline*; "Broadway Musicals: A Jewish Legacy," *Great Performances*; "How to Survive a Plague," "The House I Live In," "The Invisible War," *Independent Lens*; *Latino Americans*; *The Law in These Parts*; *180 Days: A Year Inside an American High School*; PBS. *Reveal: The VA's Opiate Overload*, Public Radio Exchange. *The Returned*, Sundance Channel. *The Story of Film*, TCM. "Harper High School," *This American Life*, WBEZ Chicago. *Coverage of Boston Marathon Bombings*, WBZ-TV, Boston, and WBZ Newsradio 1030. *NewsChannel 5 Investigates: Questions of Influence*, WTVF-TV, Nashville. *Louisiana Purchased*, WVUE-TV and NOLA.com, New Orleans. *A Needed Response*, YouTube/Samantha Stendal.

Scripps Howard Awards, by Scripps Howard Foundation. Breaking News: *Arizona Republic*. Business/Economics Reporting: Intl. Consortium of Investigative Journalists, Center for Public Integrity. Commentary: Danny Westneat, *Seattle Times*. Community Journalism: *Portland Press Herald* (Maine) and *Maine Sunday Telegram*. Distinguished Service to the First Amendment: Better Government Assn. (Chicago). Editorial Writing: Tony Messenger and Kevin Horrigan, *St. Louis Post-Dispatch*. Environmental Reporting: Craig Welch and Steve Ringman, *Seattle Times*. Human Interest Storytelling: Andrea Elliott, *NY Times*. Investigative Reporting: *Milwaukee Journal Sentinel*. Digital Innovation: NPR's *Planet Money*. Photojournalism: John Tlumacki, *Boston Globe*. Public Service Reporting: *The Guardian US*. Radio In-Depth Coverage: *This American Life*. TV/Cable In-Depth Local Coverage: KARE-TV (Minneapolis-St. Paul, MN). TV/Cable In-Depth Natl. and Intl. Coverage: Associated Producers Ltd. and HBO Documentary Films.

Miscellaneous Book Awards, 2014

Bollingen Prize for American Poetry, by the Yale Univ. Library, $150,000 (biennial, 2013): Charles Wright.

Coretta Scott King Awards, by American Library Assn., for African American authors and illustrators of outstanding books for children and young adults. Author: Rita Williams-Garcia, *P.S. Be Eleven*. Illustrator: Bryan Collier, *Knock Knock: My Dad's Dream for Me*.

Costa Book Awards. Book of the Year (formerly Whitbread Award): *The Shock of the Fall*, Nathan Filer. Short Story: Angela Readman, "The Keeper of the Jackalopes."

Edgar Awards, by the Mystery Writers of America. Novel: *Ordinary Grace*, William Kent Krueger. First Novel: *Red Sparrow*, Jason Matthews. Paperback Original: *The Wicked Girls*, Alex Marwood. Fact Crime: *The Hour of Peril: The Secret Plot to Murder Lincoln Before the Civil War*, Daniel Stashower. Critical/Biographical: *America Is Elsewhere: The Noir Tradition in the Age of Consumer Culture*, Erik Dussere. Short Story: "The Caxton Private Lending Library & Book Depository," John Connolly, *Bibliomysteries*. Juvenile: *One Came Home*, Amy Timberlake. Young Adult: *Ketchup Clouds*, Annabel Pitcher. TV Episode: "Episode 1," *The Fall*, Netflix. Grand Master: Robert Crais, Carolyn Hart. Raven Award: Aunt Agatha's Bookstore, Ann Arbor, MI.

Golden Kite Awards, by the Society of Children's Book Writers and Illustrators. Fiction: *Better Nate Than Ever*, Tim Federle. Nonfiction: *Call of the Klondike*, David Meissner. Picture Book Text: *Sophie's Squash*, Pat Zietlow Miller. Picture Book Illustration: *Mr. Tiger Goes Wild*, Peter Brown.

Hugo Awards, by the World Science Fiction Society (WSFS). Novel: *Ancillary Justice*, Ann Leckie. Novella: "Equoid," Charles Stross. Novelette: "The Lady Astronaut of Mars," Mary Robinette Kowal. Short Story: "The Water That Falls on You From Nowhere," John Chu. Related Work: "We Have Always Fought: Challenging the Women, Cattle, and Slaves Narrative," Kameron Hurley. Graphic Story: "Time," Randall Munroe. Dramatic Presentation, long form: *Gravity*. Dramatic Presentation, short form: "The Rains of Castamere," *Game of Thrones*, HBO.

Lincoln Prize, by Gettysburg College and the Gilder Lehrman Inst. of American History, $50,000: Allen C. Guelzo, *Gettysburg: The Last Invasion*, and Martin P. Johnson, *Writing the Gettysburg Address*.

National Book Critics Circle Awards. Fiction: Chimamanda Ngozi Adichie, *Americanah*. Nonfiction: Sheri Fink, *Five Days at Memorial: Life and Death in a Storm-Ravaged Hospital*. Autobiography: Amy Wilentz, *Farewell, Fred Voodoo: A Letter From Haiti*. Biography: Leo Damrosch, *Jonathan Swift: His Life and His World*. Criticism: Franco Moretti, *Distant Reading*. Poetry: Frank Bidart, *Metaphysical Dog*. John Leonard Prize: Anthony Marra, *A Constellation of Vital Phenomena*. Ivan Sandrof Lifetime Achievement Award: Rolando Hinojosa-Smith. Nona Balakian Citation for Excellence in Reviewing: Katherine A. Powers.

Nebula Awards, by the Science Fiction and Fantasy Writers of America. Novel: *Ancillary Justice*, Ann Leckie. Novella: "The Weight of the Sunrise," Vylar Kaftan. Novelette: "The Waiting Stars," Aliette de Bodard. Short Story: "If You Were a Dinosaur, My Love," Rachel Swirsky. Ray Bradbury Award: *Gravity*. Andre Norton Award: *Sister Mine*, Nalo Hopkinson. Damon Knight Grand Master Award: Samuel R. Delany. Special Honoree: Frank M. Robinson.

PEN/Faulkner Award, for fiction, $15,000: Karen Joy Fowler, *We Are All Completely Beside Ourselves*.

Spingarn Medal, 1915-2013

The Spingarn Medal has been awarded annually since 1915 (except in 1938 and 2012) by the National Assn. for the Advancement of Colored People for outstanding achievement by an African American.

1915 Ernest E. Just	1941 Richard Wright	1965 Leontyne Price	1990 L. Douglas Wilder
1916 Charles Young	1942 A. Philip Randolph	1966 John H. Johnson	1991 Gen. Colin L. Powell
1917 Harry T. Burleigh	1943 William H. Hastie	1967 Edward W. Brooke	1992 Barbara Jordan
1918 William S. Braithwaite	1944 Charles Drew	1968 Sammy Davis Jr.	1993 Dorothy I. Height
1919 Archibald H. Grimké	1945 Paul Robeson	1969 Clarence M. Mitchell Jr.	1994 Maya Angelou
1920 W. E. B. Du Bois	1946 Thurgood Marshall	1970 Jacob Lawrence	1995 John Hope Franklin
1921 Charles S. Gilpin	1947 Dr. Percy L. Julian	1971 Leon H. Sullivan	1996 A. Leon Higginbotham
1922 Mary B. Talbert	1948 Channing H. Tobias	1972 Gordon Parks	1997 Carl T. Rowan
1923 George W. Carver	1949 Ralph J. Bunche	1973 Wilson C. Riles	1998 Myrlie Evers-Williams
1924 Roland Hayes	1950 Charles H. Houston	1974 Damon Keith	1999 Earl G. Graves Sr.
1925 James W. Johnson	1951 Mabel K. Staupers	1975 Henry (Hank) Aaron	2000 Oprah Winfrey
1926 Carter G. Woodson	1952 Harry T. Moore	1976 Alvin Ailey	2001 Vernon E. Jordan Jr.
1927 Anthony Overton	1953 Paul R. Williams	1977 Alex Haley	2002 John Lewis
1928 Charles W. Chesnutt	1954 Theodore K. Lawless	1978 Andrew Young	2003 Constance Baker Motley
1929 Mordecai W. Johnson	1955 Carl Murphy	1979 Rosa L. Parks	2004 Robert L. Carter
1930 Henry A. Hunt	1956 Jack R. Robinson	1980 Dr. Rayford W. Logan	2005 Oliver W. Hill
1931 Richard B. Harrison	1957 Martin Luther King Jr.	1981 Coleman Young	2006 Dr. Benjamin S. Carson
1932 Robert R. Moton	1958 Daisy Bates and the Little Rock Nine	1982 Dr. Benjamin E. Mays	2007 John Conyers Jr.
1933 Max Yergan		1983 Lena Horne	2008 Ruby Dee
1934 William T. B. Williams	1959 Duke Ellington	1984 Thomas Bradley	2009 Julian Bond
1935 Mary McLeod Bethune	1960 Langston Hughes	1985 Bill Cosby	2010 Cicely Tyson
1936 John Hope	1961 Kenneth B. Clark	1986 Dr. Benjamin L. Hooks	2011 Frankie Muse Freeman
1937 Walter White	1962 Robert C. Weaver	1987 Percy E. Sutton	2012 Harry Belafonte
1939 Marian Anderson	1963 Medgar W. Evers	1988 Frederick D. Patterson	2013 Jessye Norman
1940 Louis T. Wright	1964 Roy Wilkins	1989 Jesse Jackson	

Miss America Winners, 1921-2015

Year	Winner, hometown	Year	Winner, hometown
1921	Margaret Gorman, Washington, DC	1973	Terry Anne Meeuwsen, DePere, Wisconsin
1922-23	Mary Campbell, Columbus, Ohio	1974	Rebecca Ann King, Denver, Colorado
1924	Ruth Malcolmson, Philadelphia, Pennsylvania	1975	Shirley Cothran, Denton, Texas
1925	Fay Lamphier, Oakland, California	1976	Tawney Elaine Godin, Saratoga Springs, New York
1926	Norma Smallwood, Tulsa, Oklahoma	1977	Dorothy Kathleen Benham, Edina, Minnesota
1927	Lois Delander, Joliet, Illinois	1978	Susan Perkins, Columbus, Ohio
1933	Marion Bergeron, West Haven, Connecticut	1979	Kylene Barker, Roanoke, Virginia
1935	Henrietta Leaver, Pittsburgh, Pennsylvania	1980	Cheryl Prewitt, Ackerman, Mississippi
1936	Rose Coyle, Philadelphia, Pennsylvania	1981	Susan Powell, Elk City, Oklahoma
1937	Bette Cooper, Bertrand Island, New Jersey	1982	Elizabeth Ward, Russellville, Arkansas
1938	Marilyn Meseke, Marion, Ohio	1983	Debra Maffett, Anaheim, California
1939	Patricia Donnelly, Detroit, Michigan	1984[1]	Suzette Charles, Mays Landing, New Jersey
1940	Frances Marie Burke, Philadelphia, Pennsylvania	1985	Sharlene Wells, Salt Lake City, Utah
1941	Rosemary LaPlanche, Los Angeles, California	1986	Susan Akin, Meridian, Mississippi
1942	Jo-Caroll Dennison, Tyler, Texas	1987	Kellye Cash, Memphis, Tennessee
1943	Jean Bartel, Los Angeles, California	1988	Kaye Lani Rae Rafko, Monroe, Michigan
1944	Venus Ramey, Washington, DC	1989	Gretchen Carlson, Anoka, Minnesota
1945	Bess Myerson, New York, New York	1990	Debbye Turner, Columbia, Missouri
1946	Marilyn Buferd, Los Angeles, California	1991	Marjorie Vincent, Oak Park, Illinois
1947	Barbara Walker, Memphis, Tennessee	1992	Carolyn Suzanne Sapp, Honolulu, Hawaii
1948	BeBe Shopp, Hopkins, Minnesota	1993	Leanza Cornett, Jacksonville, Florida
1949	Jacque Mercer, Litchfield, Arizona	1994	Kimberly Aiken, Columbia, South Carolina
1951	Yolande Betbeze, Mobile, Alabama	1995	Heather Whitestone, Birmingham, Alabama
1952	Coleen Kay Hutchins, Salt Lake City, Utah	1996	Shawntel Smith, Muldrow, Oklahoma
1953	Neva Jane Langley, Macon, Georgia	1997	Tara Dawn Holland, Overland Park, Kansas
1954	Evelyn Margaret Ay, Ephrata, Pennsylvania	1998	Kate Shindle, Evanston, Illinois
1955	Lee Meriwether, San Francisco, California	1999	Nicole Johnson, Roanoke, Virginia
1956	Sharon Ritchie, Denver, Colorado	2000	Heather Renee French, Maysville, Kentucky
1957	Marian McKnight, Manning, South Carolina	2001	Angela Perez Baraquio, Honolulu, Hawaii
1958	Marilyn Van Derbur, Denver, Colorado	2002	Katie Harman, Gresham, Oregon
1959	Mary Ann Mobley, Brandon, Mississippi	2003	Erika Harold, Urbana, Illinois
1960	Lynda Lee Mead, Natchez, Mississippi	2004	Ericka Dunlap, Orlando, Florida
1961	Nancy Fleming, Montague, Michigan	2005	Deidre Downs, Birmingham, Alabama
1962	Maria Fletcher, Asheville, North Carolina	2006	Jennifer Berry, Tulsa, Oklahoma
1963	Jacquelyn Mayer, Sandusky, Ohio	2007	Lauren Nelson, Lawton, Oklahoma
1964	Donna Axum, El Dorado, Arkansas	2008	Kirsten Haglund, Farmington Hills, Michigan
1965	Vonda Kay Van Dyke, Phoenix, Arizona	2009	Katie Stam, Seymour, Indiana
1966	Deborah Irene Bryant, Overland Park, Kansas	2010	Caressa Cameron, Fredricksburg, Virginia
1967	Jane Anne Jayroe, Laverne, Oklahoma	2011	Teresa Scanlan, Gering, Nebraska
1968	Debra Dene Barnes, Moran, Kansas	2012	Laura Kaeppeler, Kenosha, Wisconsin
1969	Judith Anne Ford, Belvidere, Illinois	2013	Mallory Hytes Hagen, Brooklyn, New York
1970	Pamela Anne Eldred, Birmingham, Michigan	2014	Nina Davuluri, Syracuse, New York
1971	Phyllis Ann George, Denton, Texas	2015	Kira Kazantsev, New York, New York
1972	Laurie Lea Schaefer, Bexley, Ohio		

Note: Since the 1950 pageant, winners have been crowned Miss America of the following year (e.g., Miss America 1951 competed in 1950). (1) Miss New York, Vanessa Williams, resigned July 23, 1984.

Entertainment Awards
Selected Tony (Antoinette Perry) Awards, 2014

Play: *All the Way*, Robert Schenkkan
Musical: *A Gentleman's Guide to Love & Murder*
Book of a musical: *A Gentleman's Guide to Love & Murder*, Robert L. Freedman
Original score: *The Bridges of Madison County*, Jason Robert Brown
Play revival: *A Raisin in the Sun*
Musical revival: *Hedwig and the Angry Inch*
Actor, play: Bryan Cranston, *All the Way*
Actress, play: Audra McDonald, *Lady Day at Emerson's Bar & Grill*
Actor, musical: Neil Patrick Harris, *Hedwig and the Angry Inch*
Actress, musical: Jessie Mueller, *Beautiful—The Carole King Musical*
Featured actor, play: Mark Rylance, *Twelfth Night*
Featured actress, play: Sophie Okonedo, *A Raisin in the Sun*
Featured actor, musical: James Monroe Iglehart, *Aladdin*

Featured actress, musical: Lena Hall, *Hedwig and the Angry Inch*
Director, play: Kenny Leon, *A Raisin in the Sun*
Director, musical: Darko Tresnjak, *A Gentleman's Guide to Love & Murder*
Choreography: Warren Carlyle, *After Midnight*
Orchestrations: Jason Robert Brown, *The Bridges of Madison County*
Scenic design, play: Beowulf Boritt, *Act One*
Scenic design, musical: Christopher Barreca, *Rocky*
Costume design, play: Jenny Tiramani, *Twelfth Night*
Costume design, musical: Linda Cho, *A Gentleman's Guide to Love & Murder*
Regional theater: Signature Theatre, New York City
Special Tony Award, lifetime achievement: Jane Greenwood
Isabelle Stevenson Award: Rosie O'Donnell
Tony Honors for Excellence in the Theatre: Joseph P. Benincasa, Joan Marcus, Charlotte Wilcox

Tony Awards, 1948–2014

Year	Play	Musical	Year	Play	Musical
1948	*Mister Roberts*	No award	1983	*Torch Song Trilogy*	*Cats*
1949	*Death of a Salesman*	*Kiss Me Kate*	1984	*The Real Thing*	*La Cage aux Folles*
1950	*The Cocktail Party*	*South Pacific*	1985	*Biloxi Blues*	*Big River*
1951	*The Rose Tattoo*	*Guys and Dolls*	1986	*I'm Not Rappaport*	*The Mystery of Edwin Drood*
1952	*The Fourposter*	*The King and I*	1987	*Fences*	*Les Miserables*
1953	*The Crucible*	*Wonderful Town*	1988	*M. Butterfly*	*Phantom of the Opera*
1954	*The Teahouse of the August Moon*	*Kismet*	1989	*The Heidi Chronicles*	*Jerome Robbins' Broadway*
1955	*The Desperate Hours*	*The Pajama Game*	1990	*The Grapes of Wrath*	*City of Angels*
1956	*The Diary of Anne Frank*	*Damn Yankees*	1991	*Lost in Yonkers*	*The Will Rogers Follies*
1957	*Long Day's Journey Into Night*	*My Fair Lady*	1992	*Dancing at Lughnasa*	*Crazy for You*
1958	*Sunrise at Campobello*	*The Music Man*	1993	*Angels in America: Millennium Approaches*	*Kiss of the Spider Woman*
1959	*J.B.*	*Redhead*	1994	*Angels in America: Perestroika*	*Passion*
1960	*The Miracle Worker*	*Fiorello!* and *The Sound of Music*	1995	*Love! Valour! Compassion!*	*Sunset Boulevard*
1961	*Becket*	*Bye, Bye Birdie*	1996	*Master Class*	*Rent*
1962	*A Man for All Seasons*	*How to Succeed in Business Without Really Trying*	1997	*The Last Night of Ballyhoo*	*Titanic*
1963	*Who's Afraid of Virginia Woolf?*	*A Funny Thing Happened on the Way to the Forum*	1998	*Art*	*The Lion King*
1964	*Luther*	*Hello, Dolly!*	1999	*Side Man*	*Fosse*
1965	*The Subject Was Roses*	*Fiddler on the Roof*	2000	*Copenhagen*	*Contact*
1966	*Marat/Sade*	*Man of La Mancha*	2001	*Proof*	*The Producers*
1967	*The Homecoming*	*Cabaret*	2002	*Edward Albee's The Goat or Who Is Sylvia?*	*Thoroughly Modern Millie*
1968	*Rosencrantz and Guildenstern Are Dead*	*Hallelujah, Baby!*	2003	*Take Me Out*	*Hairspray*
1969	*The Great White Hope*	*1776*	2004	*I Am My Own Wife*	*Avenue Q*
1970	*Borstal Boy*	*Applause*	2005	*Doubt*	*Monty Python's Spamalot*
1971	*Sleuth*	*Company*	2006	*The History Boys*	*Jersey Boys*
1972	*Sticks and Bones*	*Two Gentlemen of Verona*	2007	*The Coast of Utopia*	*Spring Awakening*
1973	*That Championship Season*	*A Little Night Music*	2008	*August: Osage County*	*In the Heights*
1974	*The River Niger*	*Raisin*	2009	*God of Carnage*	*Billy Elliot, The Musical*
1975	*Equus*	*The Wiz*	2010	*Red*	*Memphis*
1976	*Travesties*	*A Chorus Line*	2011	*War Horse*	*The Book of Mormon*
1977	*The Shadow Box*	*Annie*	2012	*Clybourne Park*	*Once*
1978	*Da*	*Ain't Misbehavin'*	2013	*Vanya and Sonia and Masha and Spike*	*Kinky Boots*
1979	*The Elephant Man*	*Sweeney Todd*	2014	*All the Way*	*A Gentleman's Guide to Love & Murder*
1980	*Children of a Lesser God*	*Evita*			
1981	*Amadeus*	*42nd Street*			
1982	*The Life and Adventures of Nicholas Nickelby*	*Nine*			

Selected Daytime Emmy Awards, 2014

Drama: *The Young and the Restless*, CBS
Game show: *Jeopardy!*, synd.
Culinary show: *The Mind of a Chef*, PBS
Entertainment news show: *Entertainment Tonight*, CBS, and *Extra*, synd.
Legal/courtroom show: *The People's Court*, synd.
Morning show: *Good Morning America*, ABC
Talk show, entertainment: *The Ellen DeGeneres Show*, synd.

Talk show, informative: Steve Harvey, synd.
Lead actress: Eileen Davidson, *Days of Our Lives*, NBC
Lead actor: Billy Miller, *The Young and the Restless*, CBS
Culinary host: Bobby Flay, *Bobby Flay's Barbecue Addiction*, Food Network
Game show host: Steve Harvey, *Family Feud*, synd.
Talk show host: Mehmet Oz, *The Dr. Oz Show*, synd., and Katie Couric, *Katie*, ABC

Selected Prime-Time Emmy Awards, 2014

Drama series: *Breaking Bad*, AMC
Comedy series: *Modern Family*, ABC
Miniseries or movie: *Fargo*, FX
Variety series: *The Colbert Report*, Comedy Central
Lead actor, drama: Bryan Cranston, *Breaking Bad*, AMC
Lead actress, drama: Julianna Margulies, *The Good Wife*, CBS
Lead actor, comedy: Jim Parsons, *The Big Bang Theory*, CBS
Lead actress, comedy: Julia Louis-Dreyfus, *Veep*, HBO
Lead actor, miniseries/movie: Benedict Cumberbatch, *Sherlock: His Last Vow*, PBS
Lead actress, miniseries/movie: Jessica Lange, *American Horror Story: Coven*, FX

Sup. actor, drama: Aaron Paul, *Breaking Bad*, AMC
Sup. actress, drama: Anna Gunn, *Breaking Bad*, AMC
Sup. actor, comedy: Ty Burrell, *Modern Family*, ABC
Sup. actress, comedy: Allison Janney, *Mom*, CBS
Sup. actor, miniseries/movie: Martin Freeman, *Sherlock: His Last Vow*, PBS
Sup. actress, miniseries/movie: Kathy Bates, *American Horror Story: Coven*, FX
Animated program: *Bob's Burgers*, FOX
Reality-competition program: *The Amazing Race*, CBS
Host, reality/reality-competition program: Jane Lynch, *Hollywood Game Night*, NBC

Prime-Time Emmy Awards, 1952-2014

The Academy of Television Arts and Sciences presented the first Emmy Awards in 1949. Through the years, award categories have changed, but since 1952, the Academy has given out an outstanding comedy and drama award annually.

Year	Comedy	Drama	Year	Comedy	Drama
1952	Red Skelton Show, NBC	Studio One, CBS	1980	Taxi, ABC	Lou Grant, CBS
1953	I Love Lucy, CBS	Robert Montgomery Presents, NBC	1981	Taxi, ABC	Hill Street Blues, NBC
			1982	Barney Miller, ABC	Hill Street Blues, NBC
1954	I Love Lucy, CBS	The U.S. Steel Hour, ABC	1983	Cheers, NBC	Hill Street Blues, NBC
1955	Make Room for Daddy, ABC	The U.S. Steel Hour, ABC	1984	Cheers, NBC	Hill Street Blues, NBC
1956	Phil Silvers Show, CBS	Producers' Showcase, NBC	1985	The Cosby Show, NBC	Cagney & Lacey, CBS
1957	Phil Silvers Show, CBS	"Requiem for a Heavyweight," CBS[1]	1986	Golden Girls, NBC	Cagney & Lacey, CBS
			1987	Golden Girls, NBC	L.A. Law, NBC
1958	Phil Silvers Show, CBS	Gunsmoke, CBS	1988	The Wonder Years, ABC	thirtysomething, ABC
1959[2]	Jack Benny Show, CBS	(3)	1989	Cheers, NBC	L.A. Law, NBC
1960	Art Carney Special, NBC	Playhouse 90, CBS	1990	Murphy Brown, CBS	L.A. Law, NBC
1961	Jack Benny Show, CBS	Hallmark Hall of Fame: Macbeth, NBC	1991	Cheers, NBC	L.A. Law, NBC
			1992	Murphy Brown, CBS	Northern Exposure, CBS
1962	Bob Newhart Show, CBS	The Defenders, CBS	1993	Seinfeld, NBC	Picket Fences, CBS
1963	Dick Van Dyke Show, CBS	The Defenders, CBS	1994	Frasier, NBC	Picket Fences, CBS
1964	Dick Van Dyke Show, CBS	The Defenders, CBS	1995	Frasier, NBC	NYPD Blue, ABC
1965	Dick Van Dyke Show, CBS	Hallmark Hall of Fame: The Magnificent Yankee, NBC	1996	Frasier, NBC	ER, NBC
			1997	Frasier, NBC	Law & Order, NBC
1966	Dick Van Dyke Show, CBS	The Fugitive, ABC	1998	Frasier, NBC	The Practice, ABC
1967	The Monkees, NBC	Mission: Impossible, CBS	1999	Ally McBeal, FOX	The Practice, ABC
1968	Get Smart, NBC	Mission: Impossible, CBS	2000	Will & Grace, NBC	The West Wing, NBC
1969	Get Smart, NBC	NET Playhouse, NET	2001	Sex and the City, HBO	The West Wing, NBC
1970	My World and Welcome to It, NBC	Marcus Welby, M.D., ABC	2002	Friends, NBC	The West Wing, NBC
			2003	Everybody Loves Raymond, CBS	The West Wing, NBC
1971	All in the Family, CBS	The Bold Ones: The Senator, NBC	2004	Arrested Development, FOX	The Sopranos, HBO
1972	All in the Family, CBS	Masterpiece Theatre: Elizabeth R, PBS	2005	Everybody Loves Raymond, CBS	Lost, ABC
1973	All in the Family, CBS	The Waltons, CBS	2006	The Office, NBC	24, FOX
1974	M*A*S*H, CBS	Masterpiece Theatre: Upstairs, Downstairs; PBS	2007	30 Rock, NBC	The Sopranos, HBO
1975	Mary Tyler Moore Show, CBS	Masterpiece Theatre: Upstairs, Downstairs; PBS	2008	30 Rock, NBC	Mad Men, AMC
			2009	30 Rock, NBC	Mad Men, AMC
1976	Mary Tyler Moore Show, CBS	Police Story, NBC	2010	Modern Family, ABC	Mad Men, AMC
1977	Mary Tyler Moore Show, CBS	Masterpiece Theatre: Upstairs, Downstairs; PBS	2011	Modern Family, ABC	Mad Men, AMC
			2012	Modern Family, ABC	Homeland, Showtime
1978	All in the Family, CBS	The Rockford Files, NBC	2013	Modern Family, ABC	Breaking Bad, AMC
1979	Taxi, ABC	Lou Grant, CBS	2014	Modern Family, ABC	Breaking Bad, AMC

(1) Best single program of the year; shown on Playhouse 90, which was named best new series. (2) Beginning in 1959, Emmys were awarded for work in the season encompassing the previous and current year. (3) Playhouse 90 (CBS) was best dramatic series of one hour or longer, Alcoa-Goodyear Theatre (NBC) of less than one hour.

Golden Globe Awards, 2014

The Hollywood Foreign Press Association (then the Hollywood Foreign Correspondents Association) presented its first awards for achievement in film in 1944; television was considered for the first time in 1955.

Film

Drama: 12 Years a Slave
Comedy/musical: American Hustle
Actress, drama: Cate Blanchett, Blue Jasmine
Actor, drama: Matthew McConaughey, Dallas Buyers Club
Actress, comedy/musical: Amy Adams, American Hustle
Actor, comedy/musical: Leonardo DiCaprio, The Wolf of Wall Street
Supporting actress: Jennifer Lawrence, American Hustle
Supporting actor: Jared Leto, Dallas Buyers Club
Director: Alfonso Cuarón, Gravity
Screenplay: Spike Jonze, Her
Animated film: Frozen
Foreign-language film: The Great Beauty, Italy
Original score: Alex Ebert, All Is Lost
Original song: "Ordinary Love," Mandela: Long Walk to Freedom, words and music by U2
Cecil B. DeMille Award: Woody Allen

Television

Series, drama: Breaking Bad, AMC
Series, comedy/musical: Brooklyn Nine-Nine, FOX
Actress, drama: Robin Wright, House of Cards, Netflix
Actor, drama: Bryan Cranston, Breaking Bad, AMC
Actress, comedy/musical: Amy Poehler, Parks and Recreation, NBC
Actor, comedy/musical: Andy Samberg, Brooklyn Nine-Nine, FOX
Miniseries/TV movie: Behind the Candelabra, HBO
Actress, miniseries/TV movie: Elisabeth Moss, Top of the Lake, Sundance Channel
Actor, miniseries/TV movie: Michael Douglas, Behind the Candelabra, HBO
Supporting actress: Jacqueline Bisset, Dancing on the Edge, BBC
Supporting actor: Jon Voight, Ray Donovan, Showtime

Selected People's Choice Awards, 2014

The first People's Choice Awards were presented in 1975. Sponsored by Procter & Gamble, the nominees and awards were initially selected by a Gallup Poll. Since 2005, winners have been selected by Internet voting.

Film

Movie: Iron Man 3
Actor: Johnny Depp
Actress: Sandra Bullock
Duo: Sandra Bullock and George Clooney, Gravity
Comedy: The Heat
Comedic actor: Adam Sandler
Comedic actress: Sandra Bullock
Drama: Gravity
Dramatic actor: Leonardo DiCaprio
Dramatic actress: Sandra Bullock

Music

Album: The 20/20 Experience, Justin Timberlake
Song: "Roar," Katy Perry
Male artist: Justin Timberlake
Female artist: Demi Lovato
Band: One Direction

Television

Network comedy: The Big Bang Theory
Network drama: The Good Wife
Cable comedy: Psych
Cable drama: The Walking Dead
Movie/miniseries: American Horror Story
New comedy: Super Fun Night
New drama: Reign
Premium cable show: Homeland
Series we miss most: Breaking Bad
Streaming series: Orange Is the New Black
Comedic actor: Chris Colfer, Glee
Comedic actress: Kaley Cuoco, The Big Bang Theory
Dramatic actor: Josh Charles, The Good Wife
Dramatic actress: Stana Katic, Castle
Daytime host: Ellen DeGeneres
Late-night talk show host: Stephen Colbert

Academy Awards (Oscars), 1927-2013

Year Picture	Actor	Actress	Supporting actor[1]	Supporting actress[1]	Director
1927 *Wings* -28	Emil Jannings *The Way of All Flesh*	Janet Gaynor *Seventh Heaven*	NA	NA	Frank Borzage *Seventh Heaven*; Lewis Milestone *Two Arabian Knights*
1928 *Broadway* -29 *Melody*	Warner Baxter *In Old Arizona*	Mary Pickford *Coquette*	NA	NA	Frank Lloyd *The Divine Lady*
1929 *All Quiet on the* -30 *Western Front*	George Arliss *Disraeli*	Norma Shearer *The Divorcee*	NA	NA	Lewis Milestone *All Quiet on the Western Front*
1930 *Cimarron* -31	Lionel Barrymore *Free Soul*	Marie Dressler *Min and Bill*	NA	NA	Norman Taurog *Skippy*
1931 *Grand Hotel* -32	Fredric March *Dr. Jekyll and Mr. Hyde*; Wallace Beery *The Champ*	Helen Hayes *The Sin of Madelon Claudet*	NA	NA	Frank Borzage *Bad Girl*
1932 *Cavalcade* -33	Charles Laughton *The Private Life of Henry VIII*	Katharine Hepburn *Morning Glory*	NA		Frank Lloyd *Cavalcade*
1934 *It Happened One Night*	Clark Gable *It Happened One Night*	Claudette Colbert *It Happened One Night*	NA	NA	Frank Capra *It Happened One Night*
1935 *Mutiny on the Bounty*	Victor McLaglen *The Informer*	Bette Davis *Dangerous*	NA	NA	John Ford *The Informer*
1936 *The Great Ziegfeld*	Paul Muni *Story of Louis Pasteur*	Luise Rainer *The Great Ziegfeld*	Walter Brennan *Come and Get It*	Gale Sondergaard *Anthony Adverse*	Frank Capra *Mr. Deeds Goes to Town*
1937 *Life of Emile Zola*	Spencer Tracy *Captains Courageous*	Luise Rainer *The Good Earth*	Joseph Schildkraut *Life of Emile Zola*	Alice Brady *In Old Chicago*	Leo McCarey *The Awful Truth*
1938 *You Can't Take It With You*	Spencer Tracy *Boys Town*	Bette Davis *Jezebel*	Walter Brennan *Kentucky*	Fay Bainter *Jezebel*	Frank Capra *You Can't Take It With You*
1939 *Gone With the Wind*	Robert Donat *Goodbye, Mr. Chips*	Vivien Leigh *Gone With the Wind*	Thomas Mitchell *Stage Coach*	Hattie McDaniel *Gone With the Wind*	Victor Fleming *Gone With the Wind*
1940 *Rebecca*	James Stewart *The Philadelphia Story*	Ginger Rogers *Kitty Foyle*	Walter Brennan *The Westerner*	Jane Darwell *The Grapes of Wrath*	John Ford *The Grapes of Wrath*
1941 *How Green Was My Valley*	Gary Cooper *Sergeant York*	Joan Fontaine *Suspicion*	Donald Crisp *How Green Was My Valley*	Mary Astor *The Great Lie*	John Ford *How Green Was My Valley*
1942 *Mrs. Miniver*	James Cagney *Yankee Doodle Dandy*	Greer Garson *Mrs. Miniver*	Van Heflin *Johnny Eager*	Teresa Wright *Mrs. Miniver*	William Wyler *Mrs. Miniver*
1943 *Casablanca*	Paul Lukas *Watch on the Rhine*	Jennifer Jones *The Song of Bernadette*	Charles Coburn *The More the Merrier*	Katina Paxinou *For Whom the Bell Tolls*	Michael Curtiz *Casablanca*
1944 *Going My Way*	Bing Crosby *Going My Way*	Ingrid Bergman *Gaslight*	Barry Fitzgerald *Going My Way*	Ethel Barrymore *None But the Lonely Heart*	Leo McCarey *Going My Way*
1945 *The Lost Weekend*	Ray Milland *The Lost Weekend*	Joan Crawford *Mildred Pierce*	James Dunn *A Tree Grows in Brooklyn*	Anne Revere *National Velvet*	Billy Wilder *The Lost Weekend*
1946 *The Best Years of Our Lives*	Fredric March *The Best Years of Our Lives*	Olivia de Havilland *To Each His Own*	Harold Russell *The Best Years of Our Lives*	Anne Baxter *The Razor's Edge*	William Wyler *The Best Years of Our Lives*
1947 *Gentleman's Agreement*	Ronald Colman *A Double Life*	Loretta Young *The Farmer's Daughter*	Edmund Gwenn *Miracle on 34th Street*	Celeste Holm *Gentleman's Agreement*	Elia Kazan *Gentleman's Agreement*
1948 *Hamlet*	Laurence Olivier *Hamlet*	Jane Wyman *Johnny Belinda*	Walter Huston *Treasure of Sierra Madre*	Claire Trevor *Key Largo*	John Huston *Treasure of Sierra Madre*
1949 *All the King's Men*	Broderick Crawford *All the King's Men*	Olivia de Havilland *The Heiress*	Dean Jagger *Twelve O'Clock High*	Mercedes McCambridge *All the King's Men*	Joseph L. Mankiewicz *Letter to Three Wives*
1950 *All About Eve*	Jose Ferrer *Cyrano de Bergerac*	Judy Holliday *Born Yesterday*	George Sanders *All About Eve*	Josephine Hull *Harvey*	Joseph L. Mankiewicz *All About Eve*
1951 *An American in Paris*	Humphrey Bogart *The African Queen*	Vivien Leigh *A Streetcar Named Desire*	Karl Malden *A Streetcar Named Desire*	Kim Hunter *A Streetcar Named Desire*	George Stevens *A Place in the Sun*
1952 *The Greatest Show on Earth*	Gary Cooper *High Noon*	Shirley Booth *Come Back Little Sheba*	Anthony Quinn *Viva Zapata!*	Gloria Grahame *The Bad and the Beautiful*	John Ford *The Quiet Man*
1953 *From Here to Eternity*	William Holden *Stalag 17*	Audrey Hepburn *Roman Holiday*	Frank Sinatra *From Here to Eternity*	Donna Reed *From Here to Eternity*	Fred Zinnemann *From Here to Eternity*

Year Picture	Actor	Actress	Supporting actor[1]	Supporting actress[1]	Director
1954 On the Waterfront	Marlon Brando On the Waterfront	Grace Kelly The Country Girl	Edmond O'Brien The Barefoot Contessa	Eva Marie Saint On the Waterfront	Elia Kazan On the Waterfront
1955 Marty	Ernest Borgnine Marty	Anna Magnani The Rose Tattoo	Jack Lemmon Mister Roberts	Jo Van Fleet East of Eden	Delbert Mann Marty
1956 Around the World in 80 Days	Yul Brynner The King and I	Ingrid Bergman Anastasia	Anthony Quinn Lust for Life	Dorothy Malone Written on the Wind	George Stevens Giant
1957 The Bridge on the River Kwai	Alec Guinness The Bridge on the River Kwai	Joanne Woodward The Three Faces of Eve	Red Buttons Sayonara	Miyoshi Umeki Sayonara	David Lean The Bridge on the River Kwai
1958 Gigi	David Niven Separate Tables	Susan Hayward I Want to Live	Burl Ives The Big Country	Wendy Hiller Separate Tables	Vincente Minnelli Gigi
1959 Ben-Hur	Charlton Heston Ben-Hur	Simone Signoret Room at the Top	Hugh Griffith Ben-Hur	Shelley Winters Diary of Anne Frank	William Wyler Ben-Hur
1960 The Apartment	Burt Lancaster Elmer Gantry	Elizabeth Taylor Butterfield 8	Peter Ustinov Spartacus	Shirley Jones Elmer Gantry	Billy Wilder The Apartment
1961 West Side Story	Maximilian Schell Judgment at Nuremberg	Sophia Loren Two Women	George Chakiris West Side Story	Rita Moreno West Side Story	Jerome Robbins and Robert Wise West Side Story
1962 Lawrence of Arabia	Gregory Peck To Kill a Mockingbird	Anne Bancroft The Miracle Worker	Ed Begley Sweet Bird of Youth	Patty Duke The Miracle Worker	David Lean Lawrence of Arabia
1963 Tom Jones	Sidney Poitier Lilies of the Field	Patricia Neal Hud	Melvyn Douglas Hud	Margaret Rutherford The V.I.P.s	Tony Richardson Tom Jones
1964 My Fair Lady	Rex Harrison My Fair Lady	Julie Andrews Mary Poppins	Peter Ustinov Topkapi	Lila Kedrova Zorba the Greek	George Cukor My Fair Lady
1965 The Sound of Music	Lee Marvin Cat Ballou	Julie Christie Darling	Martin Balsam A Thousand Clowns	Shelley Winters A Patch of Blue	Robert Wise The Sound of Music
1966 A Man for All Seasons	Paul Scofield A Man for All Seasons	Elizabeth Taylor Who's Afraid of Virginia Woolf?	Walter Matthau The Fortune Cookie	Sandy Dennis Who's Afraid of Virginia Woolf?	Fred Zinnemann A Man for All Seasons
1967 In the Heat of the Night	Rod Steiger In the Heat of the Night	Katharine Hepburn Guess Who's Coming to Dinner	George Kennedy Cool Hand Luke	Estelle Parsons Bonnie and Clyde	Mike Nichols The Graduate
1968 Oliver!	Cliff Robertson Charly	Katharine Hepburn The Lion in Winter; Barbra Streisand Funny Girl	Jack Albertson The Subject Was Roses	Ruth Gordon Rosemary's Baby	Sir Carol Reed Oliver!
1969 Midnight Cowboy	John Wayne True Grit	Maggie Smith The Prime of Miss Jean Brodie	Gig Young They Shoot Horses Don't They?	Goldie Hawn Cactus Flower	John Schlesinger Midnight Cowboy
1970 Patton	George C. Scott Patton (refused)	Glenda Jackson Women in Love	John Mills Ryan's Daughter	Helen Hayes Airport	Franklin Schaffner Patton
1971 The French Connection	Gene Hackman The French Connection	Jane Fonda Klute	Ben Johnson The Last Picture Show	Cloris Leachman The Last Picture Show	William Friedkin The French Connection
1972 The Godfather	Marlon Brando The Godfather (refused)	Liza Minnelli Cabaret	Joel Grey Cabaret	Eileen Heckart Butterflies Are Free	Bob Fosse Cabaret
1973 The Sting	Jack Lemmon Save the Tiger	Glenda Jackson A Touch of Class	John Houseman The Paper Chase	Tatum O'Neal Paper Moon	George Roy Hill The Sting
1974 The Godfather Part II	Art Carney Harry and Tonto	Ellen Burstyn Alice Doesn't Live Here Anymore	Robert DeNiro The Godfather Part II	Ingrid Bergman Murder on the Orient Express	Francis Ford Coppola The Godfather Part II
1975 One Flew Over the Cuckoo's Nest	Jack Nicholson One Flew Over the Cuckoo's Nest	Louise Fletcher One Flew Over the Cuckoo's Nest	George Burns The Sunshine Boys	Lee Grant Shampoo	Milos Forman One Flew Over the Cuckoo's Nest
1976 Rocky	Peter Finch Network	Faye Dunaway Network	Jason Robards All the President's Men	Beatrice Straight Network	John G. Avildsen Rocky
1977 Annie Hall	Richard Dreyfuss The Goodbye Girl	Diane Keaton Annie Hall	Jason Robards Julia	Vanessa Redgrave Julia	Woody Allen Annie Hall
1978 The Deer Hunter	Jon Voight Coming Home	Jane Fonda Coming Home	Christopher Walken The Deer Hunter	Maggie Smith California Suite	Michael Cimino The Deer Hunter
1979 Kramer vs. Kramer	Dustin Hoffman Kramer vs. Kramer	Sally Field Norma Rae	Melvyn Douglas Being There	Meryl Streep Kramer vs. Kramer	Robert Benton Kramer vs. Kramer
1980 Ordinary People	Robert DeNiro Raging Bull	Sissy Spacek Coal Miner's Daughter	Timothy Hutton Ordinary People	Mary Steenburgen Melvin and Howard	Robert Redford Ordinary People
1981 Chariots of Fire	Henry Fonda On Golden Pond	Katharine Hepburn On Golden Pond	John Gielgud Arthur	Maureen Stapleton Reds	Warren Beatty Reds
1982 Gandhi	Ben Kingsley Gandhi	Meryl Streep Sophie's Choice	Louis Gossett Jr. An Officer and a Gentleman	Jessica Lange Tootsie	Richard Attenborough Gandhi
1983 Terms of Endearment	Robert Duvall Tender Mercies	Shirley MacLaine Terms of Endearment	Jack Nicholson Terms of Endearment	Linda Hunt The Year of Living Dangerously	James L. Brooks Terms of Endearment

Year	Picture	Actor	Actress	Supporting actor[1]	Supporting actress[1]	Director
1984	Amadeus	F. Murray Abraham, Amadeus	Sally Field, Places in the Heart	Haing S. Ngor, The Killing Fields	Peggy Ashcroft, A Passage to India	Milos Forman, Amadeus
1985	Out of Africa	William Hurt, Kiss of the Spider Woman	Geraldine Page, The Trip to Bountiful	Don Ameche, Cocoon	Anjelica Huston, Prizzi's Honor	Sydney Pollack, Out of Africa
1986	Platoon	Paul Newman, The Color of Money	Marlee Matlin, Children of a Lesser God	Michael Caine, Hannah and Her Sisters	Dianne Wiest, Hannah and Her Sisters	Oliver Stone, Platoon
1987	The Last Emperor	Michael Douglas, Wall Street	Cher, Moonstruck	Sean Connery, The Untouchables	Olympia Dukakis, Moonstruck	Bernardo Bertolucci, The Last Emperor
1988	Rain Man	Dustin Hoffman, Rain Man	Jodie Foster, The Accused	Kevin Kline, A Fish Called Wanda	Geena Davis, The Accidental Tourist	Barry Levinson, Rain Man
1989	Driving Miss Daisy	Daniel Day-Lewis, My Left Foot	Jessica Tandy, Driving Miss Daisy	Denzel Washington, Glory	Brenda Fricker, My Left Foot	Oliver Stone, Born on the Fourth of July
1990	Dances With Wolves	Jeremy Irons, Reversal of Fortune	Kathy Bates, Misery	Joe Pesci, Goodfellas	Whoopi Goldberg, Ghost	Kevin Costner, Dances With Wolves
1991	The Silence of the Lambs	Anthony Hopkins, The Silence of the Lambs	Jodie Foster, The Silence of the Lambs	Jack Palance, City Slickers	Mercedes Ruehl, The Fisher King	Jonathan Demme, The Silence of the Lambs
1992	Unforgiven	Al Pacino, Scent of a Woman	Emma Thompson, Howards End	Gene Hackman, Unforgiven	Marisa Tomei, My Cousin Vinny	Clint Eastwood, Unforgiven
1993	Schindler's List	Tom Hanks, Philadelphia	Holly Hunter, The Piano	Tommy Lee Jones, The Fugitive	Anna Paquin, The Piano	Steven Spielberg, Schindler's List
1994	Forrest Gump	Tom Hanks, Forrest Gump	Jessica Lange, Blue Sky	Martin Landau, Ed Wood	Dianne Wiest, Bullets Over Broadway	Robert Zemeckis, Forrest Gump
1995	Braveheart	Nicolas Cage, Leaving Las Vegas	Susan Sarandon, Dead Man Walking	Kevin Spacey, The Usual Suspects	Mira Sorvino, Mighty Aphrodite	Mel Gibson, Braveheart
1996	The English Patient	Geoffrey Rush, Shine	Frances McDormand, Fargo	Cuba Gooding Jr., Jerry Maguire	Juliette Binoche, The English Patient	Anthony Minghella, The English Patient
1997	Titanic	Jack Nicholson, As Good As It Gets	Helen Hunt, As Good As It Gets	Robin Williams, Good Will Hunting	Kim Basinger, L.A. Confidential	James Cameron, Titanic
1998	Shakespeare in Love	Roberto Benigni, Life Is Beautiful	Gwyneth Paltrow, Shakespeare in Love	James Coburn, Affliction	Judi Dench, Shakespeare in Love	Steven Spielberg, Saving Private Ryan
1999	American Beauty	Kevin Spacey, American Beauty	Hilary Swank, Boys Don't Cry	Michael Caine, The Cider House Rules	Angelina Jolie, Girl, Interrupted	Sam Mendes, American Beauty
2000	Gladiator	Russell Crowe, Gladiator	Julia Roberts, Erin Brockovich	Benicio Del Toro, Traffic	Marcia Gay Harden, Pollock	Steven Soderbergh, Traffic
2001	A Beautiful Mind	Denzel Washington, Training Day	Halle Berry, Monster's Ball	Jim Broadbent, Iris	Jennifer Connelly, A Beautiful Mind	Ron Howard, A Beautiful Mind
2002	Chicago	Adrien Brody, The Pianist	Nicole Kidman, The Hours	Chris Cooper, Adaptation	Catherine Zeta-Jones, Chicago	Roman Polanski, The Pianist
2003	The Lord of the Rings: The Return of the King	Sean Penn, Mystic River	Charlize Theron, Monster	Tim Robbins, Mystic River	Renée Zellweger, Cold Mountain	Peter Jackson, The Lord of the Rings: The Return of the King
2004	Million Dollar Baby	Jamie Foxx, Ray	Hilary Swank, Million Dollar Baby	Morgan Freeman, Million Dollar Baby	Cate Blanchett, The Aviator	Clint Eastwood, Million Dollar Baby
2005	Crash	Philip Seymour Hoffman, Capote	Reese Witherspoon, Walk the Line	George Clooney, Syriana	Rachel Weisz, The Constant Gardener	Ang Lee, Brokeback Mountain
2006	The Departed	Forest Whitaker, The Last King of Scotland	Helen Mirren, The Queen	Alan Arkin, Little Miss Sunshine	Jennifer Hudson, Dreamgirls	Martin Scorsese, The Departed
2007	No Country for Old Men	Daniel Day-Lewis, There Will Be Blood	Marion Cotillard, La Vie en Rose	Javier Bardem, No Country for Old Men	Tilda Swinton, Michael Clayton	Joel Coen and Ethan Coen, No Country for Old Men
2008	Slumdog Millionaire	Sean Penn, Milk	Kate Winslet, The Reader	Heath Ledger, The Dark Knight	Penelope Cruz, Vicky Cristina Barcelona	Danny Boyle, Slumdog Millionaire
2009	The Hurt Locker	Jeff Bridges, Crazy Heart	Sandra Bullock, The Blind Side	Christoph Waltz, Inglourious Basterds	Mo'Nique, Precious	Kathryn Bigelow, The Hurt Locker
2010	The King's Speech	Colin Firth, The King's Speech	Natalie Portman, Black Swan	Christian Bale, The Fighter	Melissa Leo, The Fighter	Tom Hooper, The King's Speech
2011	The Artist	Jean Dujardin, The Artist	Meryl Streep, The Iron Lady	Christopher Plummer, Beginners	Octavia Spencer, The Help	Michel Hazanavicius, The Artist
2012	Argo	Daniel Day-Lewis, Lincoln	Jennifer Lawrence, Silver Linings Playbook	Christoph Waltz, Django Unchained	Anne Hathaway, Les Misérables	Ang Lee, Life of Pi
2013	12 Years a Slave	Matthew McConaughey, Dallas Buyers Club	Cate Blanchett, Blue Jasmine	Jared Leto, Dallas Buyers Club	Lupita Nyong'o, 12 Years a Slave	Alfonso Cuarón, Gravity

(1) Award not given until 1936.

Other Academy Award Winners, 2013

Animated feature film: Frozen
Cinematography: Gravity
Costume design: The Great Gatsby
Documentary feature: 20 Feet From Stardom
Film editing: Gravity
Foreign language film: The Great Beauty, Italy

Original score: Gravity, Steven Price
Original song: "Let It Go," Frozen, Kristen Anderson-Lopez and Robert Lopez
Production design: The Great Gatsby
Screenplay, adapted: 12 Years a Slave, John Ridley
Screenplay, original: Her, Spike Jonze

Other Film Awards, 2014
(Awarded in 2013, unless otherwise noted.)

British Academy of Film and Television Awards (BAFTAs)

Awarded in 2014 to films released in the UK in 2013.
Best film: *12 Years a Slave*
British film: *Gravity*
Director: Alfonso Cuarón, *Gravity*
Original screenplay: Eric Warren Singer and David O. Russell, *American Hustle*
Adapted screenplay: Steve Coogan and Jeff Pope, *Philomena*
Foreign language film: *La grande bellezza* [*The Great Beauty*], Italy
Animated film: *Frozen*
Actor: Chiwetel Ejiofor, *12 Years a Slave*
Actress: Cate Blanchett, *Blue Jasmine*
Supporting actor: Barkhad Abdi, *Captain Phillips*
Supporting actress: Jennifer Lawrence, *American Hustle*

Canadian Screen Awards

Motion picture: *Gabrielle*
Actor: Gabriel Arcand, *Le Démantèlement* [*The Auction*]
Actress: Gabrielle Marion-Rivard, *Gabrielle*
Supporting actor: Gordon Pinsent, *The Grand Seduction*
Supporting actress: Sarah Gadon, *Enemy*
Director: Denis Villeneuve, *Enemy*

Cannes International Film Festival Awards

Palme d'Or: *Winter Sleep*, Turkey/France/Germany
Grand Prix: *Le Meraviglie* [*The Wonders*], Italy/Switzerland/Germany
Best Director: Bennett Miller, *Foxcatcher*, U.S.
Best Screenplay: Andrey Zvyagintsev and Oleg Negin, *Leviathan*, Russia
Best Actress: Julianne Moore, *Maps to the Stars*, Canada/Germany
Best Actor: Timothy Spall, *Mr. Turner*, UK
Jury Prize: *Mommy*, Canada, and *Adieu au langage* [*Goodbye to Language*], France
Palme d'Or, short film: *Leidi*, Colombia

Director's Guild of America Awards

Feature film: Alfonso Cuarón, *Gravity*
Documentary: Jehane Noujaim, *The Square*
TV movie/miniseries: Steven Soderbergh, *Behind the Candelabra*
TV series (drama): Vince Gilligan, *Breaking Bad*, "Felina"
TV series (comedy): Beth McCarthy-Miller, *30 Rock*, "Hogcock/Last Lunch"

Sundance Film Festival Awards

Grand Jury Prize: *Whiplash* (drama); *Rich Hill* (doc.)
World Cinema Jury Prize: *To Kill a Man*, Chile/France (drama); *Return to Homs*, Syria/Germany (doc.)
Audience Award: *Whiplash* (drama); *Alive Inside: A Story of Music and Memory* (doc.)
World Cinema Audience Award: *Difret*, Ethiopia (drama); *The Green Prince*, Germany/Israel/UK (doc.)
Best of Next Audience Award: *Imperial Dreams*
Directing: Cutter Hodierne, *Fishing Without Nets* (drama); Ben Cotner and Ryan White, *The Case Against 8* (doc.)
World Cinema Directing Award: Sophie Hyde, *52 Tuesdays*, Australia (drama); Iain Forsyth and Jane Pollard, *20,000 Days on Earth*, UK (doc.)
Waldo Salt Screenwriting Award: Craig Johnson and Mark Heyman, *The Skeleton Twins*
World Cinema Screenwriting Award: Eskil Vogt, *Blind*, Norway/Netherlands

Toronto International Film Festival

People's Choice Award: *The Imitation Game*
People's Choice Documentary Award: *Beats of the Antonov*
People's Choice Midnight Madness Award: *What We Do in the Shadows*
Canadian Feature Film: *Felix and Meira*
Canadian Short Film: *The Weatherman and the Shadowboxer*
Canadian First Feature Film: *Bang Bang Baby*
Prize of the International Critics (FIPRESCI Prize) for Discovery: *May Allah Bless France!*
FIPRESCI Prize for Special Presentations: *Time out of Mind*
NETPAC Award: *Margarita, With a Straw*

Academy of Country Music Awards, 2014

Entertainer of the year: George Strait
Male vocalist: Jason Aldean
Female vocalist: Miranda Lambert
Vocal duo: Florida Georgia Line
Vocal group: The Band Perry
New artist: Justin Moore

Album: *Same Trailer Different Park*, Kacey Musgraves
Record (single): "Mama's Broken Heart," Miranda Lambert
Song: "I Drive Your Truck," Lee Brice
Vocal event: "We Were Us," Keith Urban and Miranda Lambert
Video: "Highway Don't Care," Tim McGraw feat. Taylor Swift and Keith Urban

Selected Grammy Awards, 2013
Source: National Academy of Recording Arts and Sciences
For albums released Oct. 1, 2012-Sept. 30, 2013, awarded in Jan. 2014.

Record of the year (single): "Get Lucky," Daft Punk feat. Pharrell Williams and Nile Rodgers
Album of the year: *Random Access Memories*, Daft Punk
Song of the year: "Royals," Lorde
New artist: Macklemore & Ryan Lewis
Pop perf., solo: "Royals," Lorde
Pop perf., duo/group: "Get Lucky," Daft Punk feat. Pharrell Williams and Nile Rodgers
Pop album, instrumental: *Steppin' Out*, Herb Alpert
Pop album, traditional vocal: *To Be Loved*, Michael Bublé
Pop album, vocal: *Unorthodox Jukebox*, Bruno Mars
Dance recording: "Clarity," Zedd feat. Foxes
Dance/electronica album: *Random Access Memories*, Daft Punk
Rock perf.: "Radioactive," Imagine Dragons
Metal perf.: "God Is Dead?" Black Sabbath
Rock song: "Cut Me Some Slack," Paul McCartney, Dave Grohl, Krist Novoselic, Pat Smear
Rock album: *Celebration Day*, Led Zeppelin
Alternative album: *Modern Vampires of the City*, Vampire Weekend
R&B perf.: "Something," Snarky Puppy With Lalah Hathaway
R&B perf., traditional: "Please Come Home," Gary Clark Jr.
R&B song: "Pusher Love Girl," Justin Timberlake
R&B album: *Girl on Fire*, Alicia Keys

Urban contemporary album: *Unapologetic*, Rihanna
Rap perf.: "Thrift Shop," Macklemore & Ryan Lewis feat. Wanz
Rap/sung collaboration: "Holy Grail," Jay Z feat. Justin Timberlake
Rap song: "Thrift Shop," Macklemore & Ryan Lewis feat. Wanz
Rap album: *The Heist*, Macklemore & Ryan Lewis
Country perf., solo: "Wagon Wheel," Darius Rucker
Country perf., duo/group: "From This Valley," The Civil Wars
Country song: "Merry Go 'Round," Kacey Musgraves
Country album: *Same Trailer Different Park*, Kacey Musgraves
Bluegrass album: *The Streets of Baltimore*, Del McCoury Band
Jazz album, instrumental: *Money Jungle: Provocative in Blue*, Terri Lyne Carrington
Jazz album, vocal: *Liquid Spirit*, Gregory Porter
New age album: *Love's River*, Laura Sullivan
Comedy album: *Calm Down Gurrl*, Kathy Griffin
Spoken word album: *America Again: Re-becoming the Greatness We Never Weren't*, Stephen Colbert
Soundtrack album, compilation: *Sound City: Real to Reel*, Butch Vig, producer, various artists
Soundtrack album, score: *Skyfall*, Thomas Newman
Song, visual media: "Skyfall," *Skyfall*, Adele
Music video: "Suit & Tie," Justin Timberlake feat. Jay Z
Music film: *Live Kisses*, Paul McCartney

Grammy Awards, 1958-2013

Record of the Year (single)	Year	Album of the Year
Domenico Modugno, "Nel Blu Dipinto Di Blu (Volare)"	1958	Henry Mancini, *The Music From Peter Gunn*
Bobby Darin, "Mack the Knife"	1959	Frank Sinatra, *Come Dance With Me*
Percy Faith, "Theme From a Summer Place"	1960	Bob Newhart, *Button Down Mind*
Henry Mancini, "Moon River"	1961	Judy Garland, *Judy at Carnegie Hall*
Tony Bennett, "I Left My Heart in San Francisco"	1962	Vaughn Meader, *The First Family*
Henry Mancini, "The Days of Wine and Roses"	1963	Barbra Streisand, *The Barbra Streisand Album*
Stan Getz and Astrud Gilberto, "The Girl From Ipanema"	1964	Stan Getz and João Gilberto, *Getz/Gilberto*
Herb Alpert, "A Taste of Honey"	1965	Frank Sinatra, *September of My Years*
Frank Sinatra, "Strangers in the Night"	1966	Frank Sinatra, *A Man and His Music*
5th Dimension, "Up, Up and Away"	1967	The Beatles, *Sgt. Pepper's Lonely Hearts Club Band*
Simon and Garfunkel, "Mrs. Robinson"	1968	Glen Campbell, *By the Time I Get to Phoenix*
5th Dimension, "Aquarius/Let the Sunshine In"	1969	Blood, Sweat & Tears, *Blood, Sweat & Tears*
Simon and Garfunkel, "Bridge Over Troubled Water"	1970	Simon and Garfunkel, *Bridge Over Troubled Water*
Carole King, "It's Too Late"	1971	Carole King, *Tapestry*
Roberta Flack, "The First Time Ever I Saw Your Face"	1972	George Harrison and Friends, *The Concert for Bangla Desh*
Roberta Flack, "Killing Me Softly With His Song"	1973	Stevie Wonder, *Innervisions*
Olivia Newton-John, "I Honestly Love You"	1974	Stevie Wonder, *Fulfillingness' First Finale*
Captain & Tennille, "Love Will Keep Us Together"	1975	Paul Simon, *Still Crazy After All These Years*
George Benson, "This Masquerade"	1976	Stevie Wonder, *Songs in the Key of Life*
Eagles, "Hotel California"	1977	Fleetwood Mac, *Rumours*
Billy Joel, "Just the Way You Are"	1978	Bee Gees, *Saturday Night Fever*
The Doobie Brothers, "What a Fool Believes"	1979	Billy Joel, *52nd Street*
Christopher Cross, "Sailing"	1980	Christopher Cross, *Christopher Cross*
Kim Carnes, "Bette Davis Eyes"	1981	John Lennon and Yoko Ono, *Double Fantasy*
Toto, "Rosanna"	1982	Toto, *Toto IV*
Michael Jackson, "Beat It"	1983	Michael Jackson, *Thriller*
Tina Turner, "What's Love Got to Do With It"	1984	Lionel Richie, *Can't Slow Down*
USA for Africa, "We Are the World"	1985	Phil Collins, *No Jacket Required*
Steve Winwood, "Higher Love"	1986	Paul Simon, *Graceland*
Paul Simon, "Graceland"	1987	U2, *The Joshua Tree*
Bobby McFerrin, "Don't Worry, Be Happy"	1988	George Michael, *Faith*
Bette Midler, "Wind Beneath My Wings"	1989	Bonnie Raitt, *Nick of Time*
Phil Collins, "Another Day in Paradise"	1990	Quincy Jones, *Back on the Block*
Natalie Cole, with Nat "King" Cole, "Unforgettable"	1991	Natalie Cole, with Nat "King" Cole, *Unforgettable*
Eric Clapton, "Tears in Heaven"	1992	Eric Clapton, *Unplugged*
Whitney Houston, "I Will Always Love You"	1993	Whitney Houston, *The Bodyguard*
Sheryl Crow, "All I Wanna Do"	1994	Tony Bennett, *MTV Unplugged*
Seal, "Kiss From a Rose"	1995	Alanis Morissette, *Jagged Little Pill*
Eric Clapton, "Change the World"	1996	Celine Dion, *Falling Into You*
Shawn Colvin, "Sunny Came Home"	1997	Bob Dylan, *Time Out of Mind*
Celine Dion, "My Heart Will Go On"	1998	Lauryn Hill, *The Miseducation of Lauryn Hill*
Santana feat. Rob Thomas, "Smooth"	1999	Santana, *Supernatural*
U2, "Beautiful Day"	2000	Steely Dan, *Two Against Nature*
U2, "Walk On"	2001	Various artists, *O Brother, Where Art Thou?*
Norah Jones, "Don't Know Why"	2002	Norah Jones, *Come Away With Me*
Coldplay, "Clocks"	2003	OutKast, *Speakerboxxx/The Love Below*
Ray Charles and Norah Jones, "Here We Go Again"	2004	Ray Charles and various artists, *Genius Loves Company*
Green Day, "Boulevard of Broken Dreams"	2005	U2, *How to Dismantle an Atomic Bomb*
Dixie Chicks, "Not Ready to Make Nice"	2006	Dixie Chicks, *Taking the Long Way*
Amy Winehouse, "Rehab"	2007	Herbie Hancock, *River: The Joni Letters*
Robert Plant and Alison Krauss, "Please Read the Letter"	2008	Robert Plant and Alison Krauss, *Raising Sand*
Kings of Leon, "Use Somebody"	2009	Taylor Swift, *Fearless*
Lady Antebellum, "Need You Now"	2010	Arcade Fire, *The Suburbs*
Adele, "Rolling in the Deep"	2011	Adele, *21*
Gotye, "Somebody That I Used to Know"	2012	Mumford & Sons, *Babel*
Daft Punk feat. Pharrell Williams and Nile Rodgers, "Get Lucky"	2013	Daft Punk, *Random Access Memories*

MTV Video Music Awards, 2014

Video of the year: "Wrecking Ball," Miley Cyrus
Artist to watch: "Miss Movin On," Fifth Harmony
Female video: "Dark Horse," Katy Perry feat. Juicy J
Male video: "Sing," Ed Sheeran
Clubland award: "Stay the Night," Zedd feat. Hayley Williams
Video with a social message: "Pretty Hurts," Beyoncé
Hip-hop video: "Hold On (We're Going Home)," Drake feat. Majid Jordan
Pop video: "Problem," Ariana Grande feat. Iggy Azalea

Rock video: "Royals," Lorde
Collaboration: "Drunk in Love," Beyoncé feat. Jay Z
Art direction: "Reflektor," Arcade Fire
Choreography: "Chandelier," Sia
Cinematography: "Pretty Hurts," Beyoncé
Direction: "Turn Down for What," DJ Snake and Lil Jon
Editing: "Rap God," Eminem
Lyric video: "Don't Stop," 5 Seconds of Summer
Visual effects: "The Writing's on the Wall," OK Go

SCIENCE AND TECHNOLOGY

Science and Technology News, 2014

The following were some of the more newsworthy developments in science and technology in the past year.

Gigantic Virus

A primarily French team of scientists discovered the largest virus ever recorded in a sample of deeply buried permafrost soil from Siberia that was more than 30,000 years old. Named Pithovirus sibericum, the virus is bigger than some bacteria. Most known viruses are so tiny they can be seen only with an electron microscope. In recent years, scientists have discovered a few supersized viruses big enough to be seen through an ordinary light microscope. Pithovirus sibericum is the biggest yet found. Shaped like an elongated oval, it measures about 0.00006 in. long and 0.00002 in. wide and is roughly 30% bigger than Pandoravirus, the largest known contemporary virus. Although Pithovirus sibericum spent millennia in a deep freeze, it was found to still be able to infect single-celled organisms. Despite being bigger than Pandoravirus, Pithovirus has a much smaller genome. Furthermore, "60% of its gene content doesn't resemble anything on Earth," according to Chantal Abergel, who, with her husband, led the team that discovered the virus. The paper appeared in the Mar. 18, 2014, issue of Proceedings of the National Academy of Sciences.

Supersized Dinosaurs

A new analysis of dinosaur body weights in May 2014 came up with new answers to the question of which dinosaur was the largest. Such figures, based on fossil finds that often comprise just a few bones, are necessarily estimates. The May analysis, contained in a study by a multinational group of scientists in PLOS Biology, applied a consistent methodology to hundreds of different known dinosaurs. The top heavyweight, at about 100 U.S. tons, was Argentinosaurus, which lived more than 90 mil years ago in present-day Argentina. A member of the long-necked plant-eating group called sauropods, it was about 6 mil times heavier than the smallest dinosaur in the data set, Qiliania graffini, which weighed about half an ounce and inhabited what is now China about 120 mil years ago.

New contenders for the heavyweight crown continued to emerge in Argentina. In May, researchers reported finding huge bones from a sauropod that may have even surpassed Argentinosaurus. A thighbone, at 7.9 ft, was believed to be the longest ever recorded. The creature was expected to receive a formal name once the fossil bones were analyzed. A study published in Scientific Reports Sept. 4, 2014, described another sauropod, Dreadnoughtus schrani, that lived 70-80 mil years ago. Researchers estimated the specimen's weight at 65 U.S. tons and its length at 85 ft, while noting that it was young and still growing when it died.

New Family of Recyclable Plastics

Countless products today contain the moldable substances known as plastics, typically composed of polymers (large molecules consisting of repetitions of small molecular units). A report in the May 16, 2014, issue of Science described a completely new class of such polymers, the first to be discovered in decades. Jeannette Garcia, an IBM chemist, made the discovery by accident when a solution in a flask unexpectedly turned into a solid mass that was extremely hard and strong but lightweight. She had neglected to add a key component for the reaction she'd planned to study. Identifying the processes involved in the new substance's creation took a combination of laboratory work and computational chemistry, using IBM's powerful computer resources.

The research gave rise to two types of lightweight polymer materials: one strong and rigid, one gel-like. Both are "thermosets," which take on a fixed shape when heated or cured. It is difficult or impossible to recycle or rework previously known thermoset plastics, because they cannot be remolded; they decompose if heated to a high temperature. The two new polymers are fully recyclable and can be readily reduced to their constituent small-molecular units. The gel-like polymer is "self healing"; if cut apart and placed so the pieces touch, they will rebond within seconds. The new plastics might eventually find application in electronics, planes, cars, paints, and adhesives, and their recyclability could help reduce waste in landfills.

Water From a Stone

Scientists have long theorized that water is trapped in minerals deep inside the Earth in seeking to explain the origin of oceans and plate tectonics. One such mineral, a form of olivine called ringwoodite, had been heretofore found only in meteorites and in laboratory creations. In the Mar. 13, 2014, issue of Nature, an international team of scientists announced the discovery of a diamond that contained a bit of ringwoodite that was about 1.5% water by weight. The diamond was found to have originated in the "transition zone" of the Earth's mantle, roughly 250-400 mi below the surface, and was the first direct evidence of ringwoodite at such depths.

U.S. geologists reported in the June 13 issue of Science that seismic waves indicate the presence of magma about 400 mi below North America, which suggests the presence of a form of water. If seismic studies throughout other parts of the world yield similar results, the zone may contain as much as three times the amount of water as the Earth's oceans, bound up in minerals.

Early Humans Interbred

Tens of thousands of years ago at least three different lineages of humans were living on Earth: Neanderthals, Denisovans, and the direct ancestors of today's Homo sapiens. Comparisons of the genetic code of modern humans with DNA from fossil remains have suggested that interbreeding took place between the three lineages. Two separate reports by multinational teams addressed this possibility in 2014. One paper, published in the Aug. 14 issue of Nature, focused on Tibetans' ability—linked to a particular pattern of genetic mutations—to cope with the thin air and reduced oxygen levels at high altitudes. A search for the genetic pattern in a number of other modern human populations, along with Neanderthals and the Denisovans, found it in the Denisovan genome.

The second paper, published in the July 22 issue of Proceedings of the National Academy of Sciences, illustrated the complexity of studying peoples of the distant past. It focused on a 100,000-year-old human skull unearthed in China. The researchers discovered that the inner ear structure known as the temporal labyrinth was of a type previously seen only in Neanderthals, and which had even been used to identify their remains. The skull's unusual temporal labyrinth could conceivably be a result of interbreeding between Neanderthals and the ancestors of today's humans, or it might indicate that scientists have been mistaken in regarding this structure type as distinctively Neanderthal.

Probing the Genetics of Schizophrenia

Schizophrenia, a potentially crippling mental illness that produces such symptoms as delusions, hallucinations, confused thinking, and paranoia, affects millions. A tendency to develop it can be inherited, but progress in unraveling the genetics has been slow. But a new study published in the July 24, 2014, issue of Nature documented the largest and most far-reaching genomic investigation ever made of a psychiatric disorder. The study, carried out by over 300 members of the Schizophrenia Working Group of the multinational Psychiatric Genomics Consortium, examined the DNA of more than 30,000 individuals who have schizophrenia, along with the DNA of more than 100,000 who do not. Researchers identified more than 100 loci in the human genome where a variation in a single DNA building block can be linked to the disorder. Only about a quarter of these had previously been known.

The findings may eventually lead to the development of the first new forms of treatment since the 1950s. The study also lent support to a long-held theory that schizophrenia is linked to the body's immune response. Several of the loci identified were associated with the workings of the immune system.

Science Glossary

This glossary covers some concepts that come up frequently in the news, in biology, chemistry, geology, and physics.

Biology

Amino acid: one of about 20 similar small molecules that are the building blocks of proteins.

Antibiotic: a substance produced by or derived from a bacterium, fungus, or other organism that battles infections and diseases caused by microorganisms, especially bacteria; it works by killing the microorganism or halting its growth.

Archaeon (plural, archaea): one of a group of single-celled microorganisms; archaea are prokaryotes, like bacteria, but they share some similarities with eukaryotes.

Autoimmunity: a condition in which an individual's immune system reacts against his or her own tissues; leads to diseases such as lupus, some types of diabetes, inflammatory bowel disease, and rheumatoid arthritis.

Bacterium (plural, bacteria): one of a large, varied class of microscopic and simple, single-celled organisms; bacteria live almost everywhere—some forms cause disease, while others are useful in digestion and other natural processes.

Biodiversity: richness of variety of life-forms—both plant and animal—in a given environment.

Cell: the smallest unit of life capable of living independently, or with other cells; usually bounded by a membrane. May include a nucleus and other specialized parts.

Cholesterol: a fatty substance in animal tissues. It is produced by the liver in humans; is found in foods such as butter, eggs, and meat; and is an essential body constituent.

Chromosome: one of the rod-like structures in cell nuclei that carry genetic material (DNA).

Cloning: the process of copying a particular piece of DNA to allow it to be sequenced, studied, or used in some other way; can also refer to producing a genetic copy of an organism.

DNA (deoxyribonucleic acid): the usually double-stranded chemical substance that carries genetic information, which determines the form and functioning of all living things.

Ecosystem: an interdependent community of living organisms and their climatic and geographical habitat.

Enzyme: a protein that promotes a particular chemical reaction in the body.

Estrogen: one of a group of hormones that promote development of female secondary sex characteristics and the growth and health of the female reproductive system; males also produce small amounts of estrogen.

Eukaryote: any of the group of single- or multi-celled organisms whose cells have distinct nuclei.

Evolution: the process of gradual change that can occur as a species adapts to its environment; natural selection is the process by which evolution occurs.

Gene: a portion of a DNA molecule that provides the blueprint for the assembly of a protein.

Gene pool: the collection and total diversity of genes in an interbreeding population.

Gene therapy: a treatment in which scientists try to implant functioning genes into a person's cells so the genes can produce proteins that the person lacks or that help the person fight disease.

Genetic sequencing: the process of finding the order of subunits in a gene or the order of all an organism's genes.

Genome: the complete set of an organism's genetic material.

Hormone: a substance secreted in one part of an organism that regulates the functioning of other tissues or organs.

Meiosis: the process of cell division that results in gametes (sperm or egg cells), all of which contain half the number of chromosomes as their precursor.

Metabolism: the sum total of the body's chemical processes providing energy for vital functions and enabling new material to be synthesized.

Mitosis: the process by which a cell divides its nucleus and other cell materials into two duplicate daughter cells with the same DNA.

Neuron or **nerve cell:** any of the cells in the nervous system that send electrical and chemical messages to other cells.

Nucleus (plural, nuclei): the center of an atom; or the portion of a eukaryotic cell that contains most of the cell's genetic material and regulates growth and metabolism.

Organism: a living entity, capable of growth, metabolism, and usually reproduction.

Phenotype: the observable properties and characteristics of an organism arising at least in part from its genetic makeup.

Pheromone: a chemical secreted by an animal or plant to influence the behavior of other members of its species.

Placebo effect: a phenomenon in which patients show improvements even though they have taken a medically inactive substance, called a placebo.

Prokaryote: a single-celled organism that does not have a distinct nucleus, such as a bacterium or archaeon.

Protein: a complex molecule made up of one or more chains of amino acids; essential to the structure and function of all cells.

RNA (ribonucleic acid): a complex molecule similar to the genetic material DNA but usually single-stranded; several forms of RNA translate the genetic code of DNA and use that code to assemble proteins for structural and biological functions in the body. RNA also serves as the genetic material of some viruses.

Species: a population of organisms that breed with each other in nature and produce fertile offspring; other definitions of species exist to accommodate the diversity of life on Earth.

Stem cell: a cell that can give rise to other types of cells; for instance, bone marrow stem cells may divide and produce different types of blood cells.

Steroid: a type of chemical substance with a certain molecular structure. Some steroids are hormones that can suppress immune response or influence stress reaction, blood pressure, or sexual development.

Testosterone: a steroid hormone that stimulates the development and maintenance of male sexual characteristics and the production of sperm; women also produce small amounts of testosterone.

Virus: a microscopic, often disease-causing, "organism" made of genetic material surrounded by a protein shell; can only reproduce inside a living cell.

Chemistry

Acid: a class of compound that contrasts with bases. Acids taste sour, turn litmus red/pink, and often produce hydrogen gas in contact with some metals. Acids donate protons (hydrogen atoms minus the electron) in chemical reactions.

Base: a substance that yields hydroxyl ions (OH-) when dissolved in water; any of a class of compounds whose aqueous solutions taste bitter, feel slippery, turn litmus blue, and react with acids to form salts; also known as **alkaline**.

Carbon fiber: an extremely strong, thin fiber made by pyrolyzing (decomposing by heat) synthetic fibers, such as rayon, until charred; used to make high-strength composites.

Chlorofluorocarbon (CFC): one of a group of industrial chemicals that contain chlorine, fluorine, and carbon and can damage Earth's ozone layer.

Element: a substance that cannot be chemically decomposed into simpler substances; all the atoms of an element have the same number of protons and electrons.

Isotope: an atom of a chemical element with the same number of protons in its nucleus as other atoms of that element, but with a different number of neutrons.

Molecule: the basic unit of a chemical compound, composed of two or more atoms bound together.

Noble gases or **inert gases:** a group of gases including helium, neon, argon, krypton, xenon, and radon that are not reactive except in rare and limited instances.

Osmosis: the transfer of a fluid across a semipermeable membrane, usually from an area of higher concentration to one of lower concentration.

Phase: any of the possible states of matter—solid, liquid, gas, or plasma—that change according to temperature and pressure.

Polymer: a huge molecule containing hundreds or thousands of smaller molecules arranged in repeating units.

Salt: a neutral compound produced by the reaction of an acid and a base.

Geology

Fault, tectonic: a crack or break in Earth's crust, often due to the slippage of tectonic plates past or over one another; usually geologically unstable.

Igneous: a type of rock formed by solidification from a molten state, especially from molten magma.

Magma: hot liquid rock material under Earth's surface, from which igneous rock is formed by cooling.

Metamorphic: in geology, the name given to rocks or minerals that have recrystallized under the influence of heat and pressure since their original formation.

Pangaea: a single supercontinent that scientists believe began to break apart at least 200 mil years ago to form the current continents.

Plate tectonics: theory that Earth's lithosphere—the uppermost layer that includes the crust—is made up of many separate rigid plates of rock that float on top of hot semi-liquid rock.

Sedimentary: a type of rock formed by the buildup of material at the bottoms of bodies of water.

Physics

Absolute zero: the theoretical temperature at which all motion within a molecule stops, corresponding to −273.15°C (−459.67°F).

Antimatter: matter that consists of antiparticles, such as antiprotons, that have an opposite charge from normal particles; when matter meets antimatter, both are destroyed, and their combined mass is converted to energy. Antimatter is created in certain radioactive decay processes but appears to be present in only small amounts in the universe.

Atom: the basic unit of a chemical element.

Atomic mass: the total mass of an atom of a given element; atoms of the same element with different atomic masses (different numbers of neutrons, not protons) are called **isotopes**.

Atomic number: the number of protons in an atom of a given element of the periodic table; the characteristic that sets atoms of different elements apart.

Axion: a hypothetical subatomic particle with low mass and energy that is thought to exist because of the properties of the strong nuclear force.

Bose-Einstein condensate (BEC): a "super-atom" comprising thousands of atoms super-cooled to within a few hundred millionths of a degree of absolute zero and thus condensed into the lowest energy state. Atoms bound in the BEC behave synchronously, giving the BEC wavelike properties.

Boson: one of the two primary categories of particles in the Standard Model; bosons include the Higgs boson and force-carrying particles such as photons, gluons, and the W and Z particles.

Dark energy: a mysterious, undefined energy leading to a repulsive force pervading all of space-time; proposed by cosmologists as counteracting gravity and accelerating the expansion of the universe; predicted to make up 68.3% of the universe's composition.

Dark matter: hypothetical, invisible matter that some scientists believe makes up 26.8% of the universe (dark matter and ordinary matter together make up 31.7% of the universe). Its existence was proposed to account for otherwise inexplicable gravitational forces observed in space.

Doppler effect: a change in the frequency of sound, light, or radio waves caused by the motion of the source emitting the waves or the motion of the person or instrument perceiving the waves.

Electron: negatively charged particle that is the least massive electrically charged fundamental particle.

Energy: capacity to perform work. Energy can take various forms, such as potential energy, kinetic energy, and chemical energy.

Entropy: a measure of disorder in a system.

Fermion: any one of a number of matter particles including electrons, protons, neutrons, neutrinos, and quarks; one of the two primary categories of particles in the Standard Model, the other being bosons.

Field: the existence of physical effects such as forces (gravitational, electric, etc.) is visualized and described mathematically by physicists in terms of fields, which show the strength and direction of a force at a given position.

Fission: a nuclear reaction that occurs when the nuclei of large, unstable atoms break apart, releasing large amounts of energy.

Fluorescence: luminescence that is caused by the absorption of radiation at one wavelength followed by an almost immediate re-radiation, usually at a different wavelength, that stops almost immediately when the radiation stops.

Force: in classical physics, something that causes acceleration in a body; can be thought of as a push or pull.

Fusion: a nuclear reaction occurring when atomic nuclei collide at high temperatures and combine to form one heavier atomic nucleus, releasing enormous energy in the process.

Gravity: an attractive force between any two objects or particles, proportional to the mass (or energy) of the objects; strength of the force decreases with greater distance; the only fundamental force still unaccounted for by the Standard Model.

Half-life: the time it takes for half of a given amount of a radioactive element to decay.

Hertz (Hz): a measure of frequency, or how many times a given event occurs per second; applied to sound waves, electrical current, and microchip clock speeds.

Higgs boson: a boson associated with a field accounting for the existence of mass in many particles.

Laser: light consisting of a cascade of photons all having the same wavelength; stands for Light Amplification by Stimulated Emission of Radiation.

Light-emitting diode (LED): a semiconductor that emits light when an electrical current is passed through it. The color of the light depends on the material used in making the diode.

Neutrino: a tiny fundamental particle with no electrical charge and very small mass that moves very quickly through the universe; comes in three varieties, or flavors, called electron, muon, and tau.

Neutron: a neutral particle found in the nuclei of atoms.

Particle accelerator: a large machine with a circular or long, straight tunnel in which charged particles are accelerated to extremely high speeds.

Phosphorescence: luminescence that is caused by the absorption of radiation at one wavelength followed by a delayed re-radiation, usually at a different wavelength, that continues for at least a hundredth of a second after the radiation stops.

Photon: the elementary unit, or quantum, of electromagnetic radiation, such as light. It has no mass or electrical charge and is one of the fundamental force-carrying particles described by the Standard Model.

Plasma: a high-energy state of matter different from solid, liquid, or gas in which atomic nuclei and the electrons orbiting them separate from each other.

Proton: a positively charged subatomic particle found in the nuclei of atoms.

Quantum: a natural unit of some physically measurable property, such as energy or electrical charge.

Quark: a fermion and a fundamental matter particle that makes up neutrons and protons, forming atomic nuclei; there are six different varieties, or flavors, of quarks grouped in pairs: up and down, charm and strange, top and bottom.

Radiation: energy emitted as rays or particles. Radiation includes heat, light, ultraviolet rays, gamma rays, X-rays, cosmic rays, alpha particles, and beta particles.

Relativity, general theory of: a theory of space-time proposed by Albert Einstein in 1915; it links gravity to the curvature of space-time.

Relativity, special theory of: Einstein's theory of space and time: all laws of physics are valid in all uniformly moving frames of reference, and the speed of light in a vacuum is always the same, so long as the source and the observer are moving uniformly (not accelerating).

Standard Model: prevailing theory of the interaction of subatomic particles. Particles are either fermions, such as electrons, neutrinos, and quarks, or bosons, such as Higgs bosons, gluons, W or Z bosons, and photons; successfully explains three of the four elementary forces acting on particles (strong, weak, electromagnetic) but thus far has not incorporated gravity.

String theory: a theory that seeks to unify quantum mechanics and general relativity, positing that the basic constituents of matter can best be understood not as point objects but as tiny oscillating "strings."

Subatomic particle: one of the small particles, such as electrons, neutrons, and protons, which make up an atom.

Superconductivity: the property of certain materials, usually metals and chemically complex ceramics, to conduct electricity without resistance, generally at very cold temperatures.

Thermodynamics: the branch of physics that describes how energy, heat, and temperature flow in physical systems.

Ultraviolet radiation: a form of light, invisible to the human eye, that has a shorter wavelength and greater energy than visible light but a longer wavelength and less energy than X-rays.

Virtual particle: subatomic particles that rapidly pop into and out of existence and can exert real forces; usually occur in particle-antiparticle pairs and are rapidly annihilated.

Mohs Scale of Hardness

Hardness is the ability of a solid substance to resist abrasion or deformation on its surface. Soft minerals scratch more easily than hard ones. For example, a diamond will scratch graphite because graphite is softer. In 1812, German mineralogist Frederich Mohs (1773-1839) created the arbitrary scale shown below to measure relative hardness using 10 minerals that were readily available at that time. The numbers in the Mohs scale are arranged in order of increasing hardness. An item's hardness is obtained by determining which mineral in the Mohs scale can scratch it.

Mohs scale		Selected items and their relative hardness	
1 . . . . Talc	6 . . . . . Orthoclase feldspar	2.5 . . . . . . Fingernail	5.5 . . . . . Knife blade
2 . . . . Gypsum	7 . . . . . Quartz	2.5-3 . . . . Gold, silver	6-7 . . . . . Glass
3 . . . . Calcite	8 . . . . . Topaz	3 . . . . Copper penny	6.5 . . . . . Iron pyrite
4 . . . . Fluorite	9 . . . . . Corundum	4-4.5 . . . . Platinum	7+. . . . . . Hardened steel file
5 . . . . Apatite	10 . . . . . Diamond	4-5 . . . . . . Iron	

Chemical Elements, Atomic Numbers, Year Discovered

See Periodic Table of the Elements on the following page for atomic weights.

Element	Symbol	Atomic number	Year discov.	Element	Symbol	Atomic number	Year discov.	Element	Symbol	Atomic number	Year discov.
Actinium	Ac	89	1899	Gold	Au	79	BCE	Protactinium	Pa	91	1917
Aluminum	Al	13	1825	Hafnium	Hf	72	1923	Radium	Ra	88	1898
Americium	Am	95	1944	Hassium	Hs	108	1984	Radon	Rn	86	1900
Antimony	Sb	51	1450	Helium	He	2	1868	Rhenium	Re	75	1925
Argon	Ar	18	1894	Holmium	Ho	67	1878	Rhodium	Rh	45	1803
Arsenic	As	33	13th cent.	Hydrogen	H	1	1766	Roentgenium	Rg	111	1995
Astatine	At	85	1940	Indium	In	49	1863	Rubidium	Rb	37	1861
Barium	Ba	56	1808	Iodine	I	53	1811	Ruthenium	Ru	44	1845
Berkelium	Bk	97	1949	Iridium	Ir	77	1804	Rutherfordium	Rf	104	1969
Beryllium	Be	4	1798	Iron	Fe	26	BCE	Samarium	Sm	62	1879
Bismuth	Bi	83	15th cent.	Krypton	Kr	36	1898	Scandium	Sc	21	1879
Bohrium	Bh	107	1981	Lanthanum	La	57	1839	Seaborgium	Sg	106	1974
Boron	B	5	1808	Lawrencium	Lr	103	1961	Selenium	Se	34	1817
Bromine	Br	35	1826	Lead	Pb	82	BCE	Silicon	Si	14	1823
Cadmium	Cd	48	1817	Lithium	Li	3	1817	Silver	Ag	47	BCE
Calcium	Ca	20	1808	Livermorium	Lv	116	2000	Sodium	Na	11	1807
Californium	Cf	98	1950	Lutetium	Lu	71	1907	Strontium	Sr	38	1790
Carbon	C	6	BCE	Magnesium	Mg	12	1829	Sulfur	S	16	BCE
Cerium	Ce	58	1803	Manganese	Mn	25	1774	Tantalum	Ta	73	1802
Cesium	Cs	55	1860	Meitnerium	Mt	109	1982	Technetium	Tc	43	1937
Chlorine	Cl	17	1774	Mendelevium	Md	101	1955	Tellurium	Te	52	1782
Chromium	Cr	24	1797	Mercury	Hg	80	BCE	Terbium	Tb	65	1843
Cobalt	Co	27	1735	Molybdenum	Mo	42	1782	Thallium	Tl	81	1861
Copernicium	Cn	112	1996	Neodymium	Nd	60	1885	Thorium	Th	90	1828
Copper	Cu	29	BCE	Neon	Ne	10	1898	Thulium	Tm	69	1879
Curium	Cm	96	1944	Neptunium	Np	93	1940	Tin	Sn	50	BCE
Darmstadtium	Ds	110	1995	Nickel	Ni	28	1751	Titanium	Ti	22	1791
Dubnium (Hahnium)[1]	Db (Ha)	105	1970	Niobium[2]	Nb	41	1801	Tungsten (Wolfram)	W	74	1783
Dysprosium	Dy	66	1886	Nitrogen	N	7	1772	*Ununoctium	Uuo	118	2006
Einsteinium	Es	99	1952	Nobelium	No	102	1958	*Ununpentium	Uup	115	2004
Erbium	Er	68	1843	Osmium	Os	76	1804	*Ununseptium	Uus	117	2010
Europium	Eu	63	1901	Oxygen	O	8	1774	*Ununtrium	Uut	113	2004
Fermium	Fm	100	1953	Palladium	Pd	46	1803	Uranium	U	92	1789
Flerovium	Fl	114	1999	Phosphorus	P	15	1669	Vanadium	V	23	1830
Fluorine	F	9	1771	Platinum	Pt	78	1735	Xenon	Xe	54	1898
Francium	Fr	87	1939	Plutonium	Pu	94	1941	Ytterbium	Yb	70	1878
Gadolinium	Gd	64	1886	Polonium	Po	84	1898	Yttrium	Y	39	1794
Gallium	Ga	31	1875	Potassium	K	19	1807	Zinc	Zn	30	BCE
Germanium	Ge	32	1886	Praseodymium	Pr	59	1885	Zirconium	Zr	40	1789
				Promethium	Pm	61	1945				

Note: 118 elements are listed here. Of those, 4 have not yet been accepted by the IUPAC and are indicated by an asterisk (*). Between 2004 and 2010, observations of isotopes of these four elements—113, 115, 117, and 118—were reported in refereed journals. Their numbers are shown in italics in the periodic table. (1) The name Dubnium (Db) has been approved by IUPAC for element 105, but the name Hahnium (Ha) was used in most of the scientific literature before 1998 and is still sometimes used in the U.S. (2) Formerly Columbium.

Periodic Table of the Elements

Source: Los Alamos National Laboratory Chemistry Division; International Union of Pure and Applied Chemistry (IUPAC)

Key:
- atomic number: 14
- name: Silicon
- symbol: Si
- atomic weight[1]: 28.09

alkali metals

Z	Symbol	Atomic weight[1]	Name
1	H	1.007-1.009	Hydrogen
3	Li	6.938-6.997	Lithium
11	Na	22.99	Sodium
19	K	39.10	Potassium
37	Rb	85.47	Rubidium
55	Cs	132.9	Cesium
87	Fr	[223]	Francium

alkaline earth metals

Z	Symbol	Atomic weight[1]	Name
4	Be	9.012	Beryllium
12	Mg	24.30-24.31	Magnesium
20	Ca	40.08	Calcium
38	Sr	87.62	Strontium
56	Ba	137.3	Barium
88	Ra	[226]	Radium

transitional metals

Z	Symbol	Atomic weight[1]	Name
21	Sc	44.96	Scandium
22	Ti	47.87	Titanium
23	V	50.94	Vanadium
24	Cr	52.00	Chromium
25	Mn	54.94	Manganese
26	Fe	55.85	Iron
27	Co	58.93	Cobalt
28	Ni	58.69	Nickel
29	Cu	63.55	Copper
30	Zn	65.38	Zinc
39	Y	88.91	Yttrium
40	Zr	91.22	Zirconium
41	Nb	92.91	Niobium
42	Mo	95.96	Molybdenum
43	Tc	[98]	Technetium
44	Ru	101.1	Ruthenium
45	Rh	102.9	Rhodium
46	Pd	106.4	Palladium
47	Ag	107.9	Silver
48	Cd	112.4	Cadmium
57-71	Lanthanoids		Lanthanoids
72	Hf	178.5	Hafnium
73	Ta	180.9	Tantalum
74	W	183.8	Tungsten
75	Re	186.2	Rhenium
76	Os	190.2	Osmium
77	Ir	192.2	Iridium
78	Pt	195.1	Platinum
79	Au	197.0	Gold
80	Hg	200.6	Mercury
89-103	Actinoids		Actinoids
104	Rf	[265]	Rutherfordium
105	Db	[268]	Dubnium
106	Sg	[271]	Seaborgium
107	Bh	[270]	Bohrium
108	Hs	[277]	Hassium
109	Mt	[276]	Meitnerium
110	Ds	[281]	Darmstadtium
111	Rg	[280]	Roentgenium
112	Cn	[285]	Copernicium

other metals / nonmetals

Z	Symbol	Atomic weight[1]	Name
5	B	10.80-10.83	Boron
6	C	12.00-12.02	Carbon
7	N	14.00-14.01	Nitrogen
8	O	15.99-16.00	Oxygen
9	F	19.00	Fluorine
13	Al	26.98	Aluminum
14	Si	28.08-28.09	Silicon
15	P	30.97	Phosphorus
16	S	32.05-32.08	Sulfur
17	Cl	35.44-35.46	Chlorine
31	Ga	69.72	Gallium
32	Ge	72.63	Germanium
33	As	74.92	Arsenic
34	Se	78.96	Selenium
35	Br	79.90-79.91	Bromine
49	In	114.8	Indium
50	Sn	118.7	Tin
51	Sb	121.8	Antimony
52	Te	127.6	Tellurium
53	I	126.9	Iodine
81	Tl	204.3-204.4	Thallium
82	Pb	207.2	Lead
83	Bi	209.0	Bismuth
84	Po	[209]	Polonium
85	At	[210]	Astatine
113	113	[284]	
114	Fl	[289]	Flerovium
115	115	[288]	
116	Lv	[293]	Livermorium
117	117	[294]	
118	118	[294]	

noble gases

Z	Symbol	Atomic weight[1]	Name
2	He	4.003	Helium
10	Ne	20.18	Neon
18	Ar	39.95	Argon
36	Kr	83.80	Krypton
54	Xe	131.3	Xenon
86	Rn	[222]	Radon

Lanthanide series

Z	Symbol	Atomic weight[1]	Name
57	La	138.9	Lanthanum
58	Ce	140.1	Cerium
59	Pr	140.9	Praseodymium
60	Nd	144.2	Neodymium
61	Pm	[145]	Promethium
62	Sm	150.4	Samarium
63	Eu	152.0	Europium
64	Gd	157.3	Gadolinium
65	Tb	158.9	Terbium
66	Dy	162.5	Dysprosium
67	Ho	164.9	Holmium
68	Er	167.3	Erbium
69	Tm	168.9	Thulium
70	Yb	173.1	Ytterbium
71	Lu	175.0	Lutetium

Actinide series

Z	Symbol	Atomic weight[1]	Name
89	Ac	[227]	Actinium
90	Th	232.0	Thorium
91	Pa	231.0	Protactinium
92	U	238.0	Uranium
93	Np	[237]	Neptunium
94	Pu	[244]	Plutonium
95	Am	[243]	Americium
96	Cm	[247]	Curium
97	Bk	[247]	Berkelium
98	Cf	[251]	Californium
99	Es	[252]	Einsteinium
100	Fm	[257]	Fermium
101	Md	[258]	Mendelevium
102	No	[259]	Nobelium
103	Lr	[262]	Lawrencium

[1]Element has no characteristic terrestrial nuclides. The value enclosed in brackets, e.g. [209], indicates the mass number of the longest-lived isotope of the element. However, three such elements (Th, Pa, and U) do have a characteristic terrestrial isotopic composition, and for these an atomic weight is tabulated. (1) For elements whose atomic weight varies, a range is shown.

Basic Laws of Physics

Newton's Laws of Motion

1. An object in motion moves at a constant velocity in a straight line unless acted upon by a force. Likewise, an object at rest will stay at rest. These two properties are known as inertia.

2. The acceleration of an object is proportional to the force acting on it and inversely proportional to the mass of an object. Force (F) equals mass (m) times acceleration (a):

$$F = ma$$

3. For every action, there is an equal and opposite reaction. For example, if a force of one ton pushes down on an object, the object pushes up with an equal force. As per the second law, the amount of movement (acceleration) produced in the object will depend on the object's mass.

Law of Gravity

In common usage, gravity refers to the gravitational force between planets and objects on or near them. But in scientific parlance, gravitation represents one of four basic forces controlling the interactions of matter. The others are the strong and weak nuclear forces and electromagnetic force. The gravitational force (F) between objects is proportional to the product of their masses (m_1 and m_2) and inversely proportional to the square of the distance (d) between them. G represents the gravitational constant in Newton's law of gravity, a fixed ratio of approximately 6.67384×10^{-11} newton m²/kg². The basic law of gravity is:

$$F = G\,\frac{m_1 m_2}{d^2}$$

Near Earth's surface, Earth's gravitational force pulls objects downward at a constant acceleration of 9.8 m/s² (g). This allows calculation of the vertical velocity (v) of an object with an initial vertical velocity of v_0 in free fall at a given point in time (t) and calculation of the distance (d) of an object from Earth at any given time with a given initial velocity (v_0) and a known initial height (a) via the following equations (here, the effects of air resistance are ignored, and downward velocities and directions are negative):

$$v = v_0 - g\,t$$
$$d = -\tfrac{1}{2}g(t^2) + v_0 t + a$$

Assuming that height is measured in feet and speeds in feet per second, the maximum height (H) reached by an object with a positive (upward) initial velocity is expressed as:

$$H = a + \frac{v_0^2}{64}$$

For motion not near Earth's surface, more complicated equations are required. Also, if the object's upward velocity is very great, the object may escape Earth's gravity. Even near Earth's surface, there are slight complications. Gravity is lessened by the centrifugal force of the Earth's rotation. At the poles, where centrifugal force is absent, acceleration due to gravity is greater.

Gravity is weaker on a mountaintop than at sea level because the mountaintop is farther from Earth's center.

Conservation Laws

In physics, laws of conservation state that in a closed system, where neither mass nor energy is added or subtracted, certain measurable quantities remain constant.

Conservation of Mass: Mass is neither created nor destroyed within a closed system except when converted to energy.

Conservation of Momentum: All moving objects have momentum, and in a closed system, total momentum is always conserved. Linear momentum is the product of the mass of an object and its velocity. In the following equation, M and V represent the initial total mass and velocity of objects within a closed system. After a collision between those objects, the mass and velocity of individual objects may change (for example, one object breaks into smaller pieces, each traveling at a different velocity), but the product of the total mass and velocity in the system after the collision (mv) will remain the same.

$$MV = mv$$

Any object moving in a circle has another kind of momentum—angular momentum. This is because circular motion requires acceleration toward the center of the circle. The amount of acceleration depends on the speed of the object and the square of the radius of the circle. (Angular momentum is the product of this speed, the mass of the object, and the square of the radius.)

Conservation of Energy: The total amount of energy in a closed system will not change except when converted to mass.

Conservation of Mass-Energy: Although mass and energy can be converted into one another, the total amount of mass and energy together must be conserved. This is reflected in Einstein's famous equation, where m is mass, E is energy, and c is the speed of light in a vacuum (which is constant):

$$E = mc^2$$

Relativistic mass can describe how mass increases with velocity. The following equation—where m is the mass of a moving object, m_0 is the object's mass when not moving, v is the object's velocity in relation to a stationary observer, and c is the speed of light—shows the relationship:

$$m = \frac{m_0}{\sqrt{1 - \dfrac{v^2}{c^2}}}$$

The theory that no object can travel faster than the speed of light is based in this equation. As an object approaches c, so much energy is converted to mass that it no longer accelerates.

Laws of Thermodynamics

1. Heat is a form of energy. Within a closed system energy must be conserved except in nuclear reactions or other extreme conditions. It is neither created nor destroyed.

2. Within a self-sustaining system, heat can never go from an area of low temperature to an area of high temperature, for this would require added energy. Without added energy, disorder, or entropy, can only increase.

3. Absolute zero cannot be attained by any procedure in a finite number of steps. Although it can be approached asymptotically, it can never be reached.

Laws of Current Electricity

Electric current generally represents the flow of electrons through a conductor. The rate at which electrons flow can be measured in amperes, defined as the number of electrons (measured in a unit called the coulomb, equal to about 6.24 quintillion or 6.24×10^{18} electrons) moving past a particular point every second. One ampere is equal to 1 coulomb of charge passing each second. Like water, electrons tend to move from areas of high pressure to low pressure. The difference between these two pressures, known as potential difference, is measured in volts.

Certain substances, such as copper and carbon, allow electric currents to pass more readily than others—that is, they have greater conductivity. Resistance to conductivity is measured in ohms.

Ohm's Law: Electric current is directly proportional to the potential difference and inversely proportional to the total resistance of the circuit. I is electric current (measured in amperes), V is the potential difference (measured in volts), and R is resistance (measured in ohms):

$$I = \frac{V}{R}$$

Law of Electric Power: Electric power (P), measured in watts, represents the rate at which electricity is converted into some other form of energy (such as light, in the case of a lightbulb). For a direct-current circuit, P is the product of current and potential difference:

$$P = IV$$

Two Basic Laws of Quantum Physics

1. Heisenberg's uncertainty principle: Certain pairs of observable quantities like energy and time or position and momentum cannot be measured with complete accuracy simultaneously. Also known as the indeterminacy principle.

2. Pauli's exclusion principle: Two electrons in an atom cannot simultaneously occupy the same quantum or energy state. This has since been shown to be true for many subatomic particles.

Breaking the Sound Barrier; Speed of Sound

The prefix **Mach** is used to describe supersonic speed. It was named for Ernst Mach (1838-1916), a Czech-born Austrian physicist. Mach may be defined as the ratio of the velocity of an object to the velocity of sound in a particular medium. A plane moving at the speed of sound moves at Mach 1. At twice the speed of sound, it moves at Mach 2.

When a plane passes the sound barrier—that is, flies faster than the speed at which sound travels—people in the area, though not the people on the plane, hear what seem to be thunderclaps. These sounds are sometimes called sonic booms.

Sound is produced by vibrations of an object. It is transmitted by the alternating increase and decrease in pressure that radiates outward from a source through a material medium of molecules, like waves spreading out on a pond after a rock has been tossed in.

The **frequency of sound** is determined by the number of times the vibrating waves undulate per second. It is measured in cycles per second. The slower the cycle of waves, the lower the frequency. As the frequency increases, the sound becomes higher in pitch. The human ear is sensitive to frequencies between 20 and 20,000 vibrations per second, although this range varies among individuals.

Intensity, or loudness, is the strength of the pressure of these radiating waves and is measured in decibels.

The **speed of sound** varies depending on temperature and altitude. It moves faster in water than in air, for example. At sea level and a temperature of 59°F (15°C), the speed of sound is approximately 761 mph, or 1,100 ft per sec.

Light; Colors of the Spectrum

Light, a form of electromagnetic radiation similar to radiant heat, radio waves, and X-rays, is emitted from a source in straight lines and spreads in area as it travels. For emission from a point source, light per unit area diminishes in proportion to the square of the distance.

The English mathematician and physicist Isaac Newton (1642-1727) described light as an **emission of particles**; the Dutch astronomer, mathematician, and physicist Christiaan Huygens (1629-95) and others developed the theory that light travels in a **wave motion**. It is now believed that these two theories are essentially complementary. The development of quantum theory has led to results where light acts like a series of particles in some experiments and like a wave in others.

The first relatively accurate measurement of the **speed of light** was made by French physicist Armand Hippolyte Louis Fizeau (1819-96). Today the speed of light is known precisely as 299,792.458 km per sec (or 186,282.397 mi/sec) in a vacuum. In water the speed of light is about 25% less, and in glass, 33% less.

Color sensations are produced through the excitation of the retina of the eye by light vibrating at different frequencies. The different colors of the visible spectrum may be seen by viewing light refracted by passage through a prism, which separates light into its component wavelengths.

Customarily, the basic colors are taken to be the six monochromatic (single) colors that occupy relatively large areas of the spectrum: red, orange, yellow, green, blue, and violet. So-called primary colors can be combined to produce the sensation of other colors. However, scientists disagree about how many and what primary colors to recognize. The color sensation of **black** is due to complete lack of stimulation of the retina, that of **white** to complete stimulation.

Infrared and **ultraviolet rays**, which are below the red (long) end and above the violet (short) end of the visible spectrum, respectively, are invisible to the naked eye. Heat is the principal effect of infrared rays, and chemical action that of ultraviolet rays.

Discoveries and Innovations: Biology, Chemistry, Medicine, Physics

Discovery	Date	Discoverer(s)	Nationality
Acetylene gas	1862	Berthelot	French
ACTH	1927	Evans, Long	U.S.
Adrenaline	1901	Takamine	Japanese
Aluminum, electrolytic process	1886	Hall	U.S.
Aluminum, isolated	1825	Oersted	Danish
Anesthesia, ether	1842	Long	U.S.
Anesthesia, local	1885	Koller	Austrian
Anesthesia, spinal	1898	Bier	German
Aniline dye	1856	Perkin	English
Anti-rabies	1885	Pasteur	French
Antiseptic surgery	1867	Lister	English
Antitoxin, diphtheria	1891	Von Behring	German
Argyrol	1897	Bayer	German
Arsphenamine	1910	Ehrlich	German
Aspirin	1853	Gerhardt	French
Atabrine	1932	Mietzsch, et al.	German
Atomic numbers	1913	Moseley	English
Atomic theory	1803	Dalton	English
Atomic time clock	1948	Lyons	U.S.
Atom-smashing theory	1919	Rutherford	English
Bacitracin	1943	Johnson, Meleneyl	U.S.
Bacteria, description	1676	Leeuwenhoek	Dutch
Bleaching powder	1798	Tennant	English
Blood, circulation	1628	Harvey	English
Bordeaux mixture	1885	Millardet	French
Bromine from the sea	1826	Balard	French
Calcium carbide	1888	Wilson	U.S.
Calculus	1670	Newton	English
Camphor synthetic	1896	Haller	French
Canning (food)	1804	Appert	French
Carbon oxides	1925	Fisher	German
Chemotherapy	1909	Ehrlich	German
Chloramphenicol	1947	Burkholder	U.S.
Chlorine	1774	Scheele	Swedish
Chloroform	1831	Guthrie	U.S.
Chlortetracycline	1948	Duggen	U.S.
Classification of plants and animals	1735	Linnaeus	Swedish
Cloning, DNA	1973	Boyer, Cohen	U.S.
Cloning, mammal	1996	Wilmut, et al.	Scottish
Cocaine	1860	Niermann	German
Combustion explained	1777	Lavoisier	French
Conditioned reflex	1914	Pavlov	Russian
Cortisone	1936	Kendall	U.S.
Cortisone, synthesis	1946	Sarett	U.S.
Cosmic rays	1910	Gockel	Swiss
Cyclotron	1930	Lawrence	U.S.
DDT (not applied as insecticide until 1939)	1874	Zeidler	German
Denisovan humans (DNA analysis)	2010	Krause, et al.	German
		Pääbo	Swedish
Deuterium	1932	Urey, Brickwedde, Murphy	U.S.
DNA (structure)	1953	Crick, Wilkins	English
		Watson	U.S.
Electric resistance, law of	1827	Ohm	German
Electric waves	1888	Hertz	German
Electrolysis	1852	Faraday	English
Electromagnetism	1819	Oersted	Danish
Electron	1897	Thomson, J.	English
Electron diffraction	1936	Thomson, G.	English
		Davisson	U.S.
Electroshock treatment	1938	Cerletti, Bini	Italian
Erythromycin	1952	McGuire	U.S.
Evolution, natural selection	1858	Darwin	English
Falling bodies, law of	1590	Galileo	Italian
Gases, law of combining volumes	1808	Gay-Lussac	French
Geometry, analytic	1619	Descartes	French
Gold, cyanide process for extraction	1887	MacArthur, R.Forrest, W. Forrest	British
Gravitation, law of	1687	Newton	English
HIV (human immuno-deficiency virus)	1984	Montagnier	French
		Gallo	U.S.
Higgs boson	2012	CERN	International
Holograph	1948	Gabor	British
Homo floresiensis ("hobbit" humans)	2003	Morwood, et al.	New Zea.
Human heart transplant	1967	Barnard	S. African
Indigo, synthesis of	1880	Baeyer	German
Induction, electric	1830	Henry	U.S.
Insulin	1922	Banting, Best, Macleod	Canadian / Scottish

Discovery	Date	Discoverer(s)	Nationality
Intelligence testing	1905	Binet, Simon	French
In vitro fertilization	1978	Steptoe, Edwards	English
Isotopes, theory	1912	Soddy	English
Laser	1957	Gould	U.S.
Light, velocity	1675	Roemer	Danish
Light, wave theory	1690	Huygens	Dutch
Lithography	1796	Senefelder	Bohemian
Logarithms	1614	Napier	Scottish
LSD-25	1943	Hoffman	Swiss
Mendelian laws	1866	Mendel	Austrian
Mercator projection (map)	1568	Mercator (Kremer)	Flemish
Methanol	1661	Boyle	Irish
Milk condensation	1853	Borden	U.S.
Molecular hypothesis	1811	Avogadro	Italian
Motion, laws of	1687	Newton	English
Neomycin	1949	Waksman, Lechevalier	U.S.
Neutrino	1956	Reines, Cowan	U.S.
Neutron	1932	Chadwick	English
Nitric acid	1648	Glauber	German
Nitric oxide	1772	Priestley	English
Nitroglycerin	1846	Sobrero	Italian
Oil cracking process	1891	Dewar	U.S.
Oxygen	1774	Priestley	English
Oxytetracycline	1950	Finlay, et al.	U.S.
Ozone	1840	Schonbein	German
Paper, sulfite process	1867	Tilghman	U.S.
Paper, wood pulp, sulfate process	1884	Dahl	German
Penicillin	1928	Fleming	Scottish
Penicillin, practical use	1941	Florey, Chain	English
Periodic law and table of elements	1869	Mendeleyev	Russian
Physostigmine synthesis	1935	Julian	U.S.
Pill, birth-control	1954	Pincus, Rock	U.S.
Planetary motion, laws	1609	Kepler	German
Plutonium fission	1940	Kennedy, Wahl, Seaborg, Segre	U.S.
Polymyxin	1947	Ainsworth	English
Positron	1932	Anderson	U.S.
Proton	1919	Rutherford	New Zeal.
Psychoanalysis	1900	Freud	Austrian
Pulsars	1967	Bell	English
Quantum theory	1900	Planck	German
Quasars	1963	Matthews, Sandage	U.S.
Quinine synthetic	1946	Woodward, Doering	U.S.
Radioactivity	1896	Becquerel	French
Radiocarbon dating	1947	Libby	U.S.
Radium	1898	Curie, Pierre; Curie, Marie	French; Pol.-Fr.
Relativity theory	1905	Einstein	German
Reserpine	1949	Jal Vakil	Indian
Schick test	1913	Schick	U.S.
Silicon	1823	Berzelius	Swedish
Smallpox eradication	1979	World Health Org.	UN
Streptomycin	1944	Waksman, et al.	U.S.
Sulfanilamide	1935	Bovet, Trefouel	French
Sulfanilamide theory	1908	Gelmo	German
Sulfapyridine	1938	Ewins, Phelps	English
Sulfathiazole	1939	Fosbinder, Walter	U.S.
Sulfuric acid	1831	Phillips	English
Sulfuric acid, lead	1746	Roebuck	English
Superconductivity	1911	Onnes	Dutch
Superconductivity theory	1957	Bardeen, Cooper, Schreiffer	U.S.
Superconductors, high-temp.	1986	Bednorz, Muller	Ger., Swiss
Syphilis test	1906	Wassermann	German
Transplant, heart	1967	Barnard	S. African
Tuberculin	1890	Koch	German
Uranium fission, atomic reactor	1942	Fermi, Szilard	U.S.
Uranium fission theory	1939	Hahn, Meitner, Strassmann	German
		Bohr	Danish
		Fermi	Italian
		Einstein, Pegram, Wheeler	U.S.
Vaccine, measles	1963	Enders	U.S.
Vaccine, measles-mumps-rubella	1971	Hilleman	U.S.
Vaccine, meningitis (first conjugate)	1987	Gordon, et al., Connaught Labs	U.S.
Vaccine, polio	1954	Salk	U.S.
Vaccine, polio, oral	1960	Sabin	U.S.
Vaccine, rabies	1885	Pasteur	French
Vaccine, smallpox	1796	Jenner	English
Vaccine, typhus	1909	Nicolle	French
Vaccine, varicella	1974	Takahashi	Japanese
Van Allen belts, radiation	1958	Van Allen	U.S.
Vitamin A	1913	McCollum, Davis	U.S.
Vitamin B	1916	McCollum	U.S.
Vitamin C	1928	Szent-Gyorgyi, King	Hungarian
Vitamin D	1922	McCollum	U.S.
Vitamin K	1935	Dam, Doisy	U.S.
Xerography	1938	Carlson	U.S.
X-ray	1895	Roentgen	German

Inventions

Invention	Date	Inventor(s)	Nationality
Adding machine	1642	Pascal	French
Adding machine	1885	Burroughs	U.S.
Aerosol spray	1926	Rotheim	Norwegian
Air brake	1868	Westinghouse	U.S.
Air conditioning	1902	Carrier	U.S.
Air pump	1654	Guericke	German
Airbag	1952	Hetrick	U.S.
Airplane, automatic pilot	1912	Sperry	U.S.
Airplane, experimental	1896	Langley	U.S.
Airplane, hydro	1911	Curtiss	U.S.
Airplane jet engine	1939	Ohain	German
Airplane with motor	1903	Wright Bros.	U.S.
Airship	1852	Giffard	French
Aqua-Lung	1943	Cousteau, Gagnan	French
Arc welder	1919	Thomson	U.S.
Aspartame	1965	Schlatter	U.S.
Autogyro	1920	de la Cierva	Spanish
Automobile, differential gear	1885	Benz	German
Automobile, electric	1892	Morrison	U.S.
Automobile, exp'mtl	1864	Marcus	Austrian
Automobile, gasoline	1889	Daimler	German
Automobile, gasoline	1892	Duryea	U.S.
Automobile magneto	1897	Bosch	German
Automobile muffler	1904	Pope	U.S.
Automobile self-starter	1911	Kettering	U.S.
Bakelite	1907	Baekeland	Belg., U.S.
Bar code	1952	Woodland, Silver	U.S.
Barometer	1643	Torricelli	Italian
Bicycle, modern	1885	Starley	English
Bifocal lens	1780	Franklin	U.S.
Bottle machine	1895	Owens	U.S.
Braille printing	1829	Braille	French
Brassiere, modern	1913	Jacob	U.S.
Bubble gum	1928	Diemer	U.S.
Burner, gas	1855	Bunsen	German
Calculating machine	1833	Babbage	English
Calculator, electronic pocket	1972	Merryman, Van Tassel	U.S.
Camera, digital	1977	Lloyd, Sasson	U.S.
Camera, Kodak	1888	Eastman, Walker	U.S.
Camera, Polaroid Land	1948	Land	U.S.
Can, pop-top	1959	Fraze	U.S.
Car coupler	1873	Janney	U.S.
Carburetor, gasoline	1893	Maybach	German
Carding machine	1797	Whittemore	U.S.
Carpet sweeper	1876	Bissell	U.S.
Cash register	1879	Ritty	U.S.
Cassette, audio	1963	Philips Co.	Dutch
Cassette, videotape	1969	Sony	Japanese
CAT, or CT, scan	1973	Hounsfield	English
Cathode-ray tube	1897	Braun	German
Cellophane	1908	Brandenberger	Swiss
Celluloid	1870	Hyatt	U.S.
Cement, Portland	1824	Aspdin	English
Chronometer	1735	Harrison	English
Circuit breaker	1925	Hilliard	U.S.
Circuit, integrated	1959	Kilby, Noyce, Texas Instr.	U.S.
Clock, pendulum	1657	Huygens	Dutch
Coaxial cable system	1929	Affel, Espensched	U.S.
Coca-Cola	1885	Pemberton	U.S.
Coffeemaker, automatic drip	1963	Bunn Corp.	U.S.
Compressed air rock drill	1871	Ingersoll	U.S.
Comptometer	1887	Felt	U.S.
Computer, automatic sequence	1944	Aiken, et al.	U.S.
Computer, electronic	1942	Atanasoff, Berry	U.S.
Computer, laptop	1987	Sinclair	English
Computer, mini	1960	Digital Corp.	U.S.
Condenser microphone (telephone)	1916	Wente	U.S.
Contact lens, corneal	1948	Tuohy	U.S.
Contraceptive, oral	1954	Pincus, Rock	U.S.
Corn, hybrid	1917	Jones	U.S.
Cotton gin	1793	Whitney	U.S.
Cream separator	1878	DeLaval	Swedish

Invention	Date	Inventor(s)	Nationality
Cultivator, disc	1878	Mallon	U.S.
Cyclotron	1931	Lawrence	U.S.
Cystoscope	1878	Nitze	German
Diapers, disposable	1950	Donovan	U.S.
Diesel engine	1895	Diesel	German
Disc, compact	1972	RCA	U.S.
Disc player, compact	1979	Sony, Philips Co.	Japanese, Dutch
Dishwasher	1893	Cochrane	U.S.
Disk, floppy	1970	IBM	U.S.
Disk, video	1972	Philips Co.	Dutch
Dynamite	1866	Nobel	Swedish
Dynamo, contin. current	1871	Gramme	Belgian
Electric battery	1800	Volta	Italian
Electric fan	1882	Wheeler	U.S.
Electrocardiograph	1903	Einthoven	Dutch
Electroencephalograph	1929	Berger	German
Electromagnet	1824	Sturgeon	English
Electron microscope	1931	Ruska, Knoll	German
Electron spectrometer	1944	Deutsch, Elliott, Evans	U.S.
Electron tube multigrid	1913	Langmuir	U.S.
Electronic paper (e-ink)	1974	Sheridon	U.S.
Electroplating	1805	Brugnatelli	Italian
Electrostatic generator	1929	Van de Graaff	U.S.
Elevator brake	1852	Otis	U.S.
Elevator, push button	1922	Larson	U.S.
Engine, automatic transmission	1910	Fottinger	German
Engine, coal-gas 4-cycle	1876	Otto	German
Engine, compression ignition	1883	Daimler	German
Engine, electric ignition	1883	Benz	German
Engine, gas, compound	1926	Eickemeyer	U.S.
Engine, gasoline	1872	Brayton	U.S.
Engine, gasoline	1889	Daimler	German
Engine, jet	1930	Whittle	English
Engine, steam, piston	1705	Newcomen	English
Engine, steam, piston	1769	Watt	Scottish
Engraving, half-tone	1852	Talbot	U.S.
Ferris wheel	1893	Ferris	U.S.
Fiber optic wire	1970	Keck, Maurer, Schultz	U.S.
Fiber optics	1955	Kapany	English
Fiberglass	1938	Owens-Corning	U.S.
Filament, tungsten	1913	Coolidge	U.S.
Flanged rail	1831	Stevens	U.S.
Flatiron, electric	1882	Seely	U.S.
Food, frozen	1923	Birdseye	U.S.
Freon	1930	Midgley, et al.	U.S.
Furnace (for steel)	1858	Siemens	German
Galvanometer	1820	Sweigger	German
Garbage bag, polyethylene	1950	Wasylyk	Canadian
Gas discharge tube	1922	Hull	U.S.
Gas lighting	1792	Murdoch	Scottish
Gas mantle	1885	Welsbach	Austrian
Gasoline, cracked	1913	Burton	U.S.
Gasoline, high octane	1930	Ipatieff	Russian
Gasoline (lead ethyl)	1922	Midgley	U.S.
Geiger counter	1913	Geiger	German
Geodesic dome	1948	Fuller	U.S.
Glass, laminated safety	1909	Benedictus	French
Glider	1853	Cayley	English
Google search software	1996	Brin, Page	U.S.
Gun, breechloader	1811	Thornton	U.S.
Gun, Browning	1897	Browning	U.S.
Gun, magazine	1875	Hotchkiss	U.S.
Gun, silencer	1908	Maxim, H. P.	U.S.
Guncotton	1847	Schoenbein	German
Gyrocompass	1911	Sperry	U.S.
Gyroscope	1852	Foucault	French
Hard drive, computer	1955	Johnson	U.S.
Harvester-thresher	1818	Lane	U.S.
Heart, artificial	1982	Jarvik	U.S.
Helicopter	1939	Sikorsky	U.S.
Hovercraft	1955	Cockerell	English
Hydrometer	1768	Baume	French
Ice resurfacing machine	1949	Zamboni	U.S.
Iron lung	1928	Drinker, Slaw	U.S.
Jet Ski	1973	Jacobsen	U.S.
Kaleidoscope	1817	Brewster	Scottish
Kevlar	1965	Kwolek, Blades	U.S.
Kidney dialysis machine	1941	Kolff	Dutch
Kinetoscope	1889	Edison	U.S.
Lamp, arc	1847	Staite	English
Lamp, fluorescent	1938	General Electric, Westinghouse	U.S.
Lamp, incandescent	1879	Edison	U.S.
Lamp, incand., gas	1913	Langmuir	U.S.
Lamp, klieg	1911	Kliegl, A. and J.	U.S.
Lamp, mercury vapor	1912	Hewitt	U.S.
Lamp, miner's safety	1816	Davy	English
Lamp, neon	1909	Claude	French
Lathe, turret	1845	Fitch	U.S.
Launderette	1934	Cantrell	U.S.
Lens, achromatic	1758	Dollond	English
Lens, fused bifocal	1908	Borsch	U.S.
Leyden jar (condenser)	1745	von Kleist	German
Lightning rod	1752	Franklin	U.S.
Linoleum	1860	Walton	English
Linotype	1884	Mergenthaler	U.S.
Linux	1991	Torvalds	Finnish
Liquid Paper	c.1951	Graham	U.S.
Lock, cylinder	1851	Yale	U.S.
Locomotive, electric	1851	Vail	U.S.
Locomotive, exp'mtl	1802	Trevithick	English
Locomotive, exp'mtl	1812	Fenton, et al.	English
Locomotive, exp'mtl	1814	Stephenson	English
Locomotive, 1st U.S.	1830	Cooper	U.S.
Locomotive, practical	1829	Stephenson	English
Loom, power	1785	Cartwright	English
Loudspeaker, dynamic	1924	Rice, Kellogg	U.S.
Machine gun	1862	Gatling	U.S.
Machine gun, improved	1872	Hotchkiss	U.S.
Machine gun (Maxim)	1883	Maxim, H. S.	U.S.-Eng.
Magnet, electro	1828	Henry	U.S.
Magnetic Resonance Imaging (MRI)	1971	Damadian	U.S.
Maser	1953	Townes	U.S.
Mason jar	1858	Mason	U.S.
Match, friction	1827	Walker	English
Mercerized textiles	1843	Mercer	English
Meter, induction	1888	Shallenberger	U.S.
Metronome	1816	Malezel	German
Microcomputer	1973	Truong, et al.	French
Micrometer	1636	Gascoigne	English
Microphone	1877	Berliner	U.S.
Microprocessor	1971	Intel Corp.	U.S.
Microscope, compound	1590	Janssen	Dutch
Microscope, electronic	1931	Knoll, Ruska	German
Microscope, field ion	1951	Mueller	German
Microwave oven	1947	Spencer	U.S.
Monitor, warship	1861	Ericsson	U.S.
Monotype	1887	Lanston	U.S.
Motor, AC	1892	Tesla	U.S.
Motor, DC	1837	Davenport	U.S.
Motor, induction	1887	Tesla	U.S.
Motorcycle	1885	Daimler	German
Mouse, computer	1968	Engelbart	U.S.
Movie machine	1894	Jenkins	U.S.
Movie, panoramic	1952	Waller	U.S.
Movie, talking	1927	Warner Bros.	U.S.
Mower, lawn	1831	Budding, Ferrabee	English
Mowing machine	1822	Bailey	U.S.
Neoprene	1930	Carothers	U.S.
Nylon	1937	Carothers, DuPont.	U.S.
Oil cracking furnace	1891	Gavrilov	Russian
Oil filled power cable	1921	Emanueli	Italian
Oleomargarine	1869	Mege-Mouries	French
Ophthalmoscope	1851	Helmholtz	German
Pacemaker	1952	Zoll	U.S.
Pacemaker, implantable cardiac	1958	Greatbatch	U.S.
Paper	105	Ts'ai	Chinese
Paper clip	1900	Waaler	Norwegian
Paper machine	1809	Dickinson	U.S.
Parachute	1785	Blanchard	French
Pen, ballpoint	1888	Loud	U.S.
Pen, fountain	1884	Waterman	U.S.
Pen, steel	1780	Harrison	English
Pendulum	1583	Galileo	Italian
Percussion cap	1807	Forsythe	Scottish
Phonograph	1877	Edison	U.S.
Photo, color	1892	Ives	U.S.
Photo film, celluloid	1893	Reichenbach	U.S.
Photo film, transparent	1884	Eastman, Goodwin	U.S.
Photocopier	1938	Carlson	U.S.
Photoelectric cell	1895	Elster	German
Photographic paper	1835	Talbot	English
Photography	1816	Niepce	French
Photography	1835	Talbot	English
Photography	1835	Daguerre	French

Invention	Date	Inventor(s)	Nationality
Photophone	1880	Bell	U.S.-Scot.
Phototelegraphy	1925	Bell Labs.	U.S.
Piano	1709	Cristofori	Italian
Piano, player	1863	Fourneaux	French
Pin, safety	1849	Hunt	U.S.
Pistol (revolver)	1836	Colt	U.S.
Plow, cast iron	1785	Ransome	English
Plow, disc	1896	Hardy	U.S.
Pneumatic hammer	1890	King	U.S.
Post-it note	1980	Fry, Silver	U.S.
Potato chip	1853	Crum	U.S.
Powder, smokeless	1884	Vieille	French
Printing press, rotary	1845	Hoe	U.S.
Printing press, web	1865	Bullock	U.S.
Propeller, screw	1804	Stevens	U.S.
Propeller, screw	1837	Ericsson	Swedish
Punch card accounting	1889	Hollerith	U.S.
Radar	1940	Watson-Watt	Scottish
Radio amplifier	1906	De Forest	U.S.
Radio beacon	1928	Donovan	U.S.
Radio crystal oscillator	1918	Nicolson	U.S.
Radio FM, 2-path	1933	Armstrong	U.S.
Radio, magnetic detector	1902	Marconi	Italian
Radio receiver, cascade tuning	1913	Alexanderson	U.S.
Radio receiver, heterodyne	1913	Fessenden	Canadian
Radio, signals	1895	Marconi	Italian
Radio transmitter triode modulation	1914	Alexanderson	U.S.
Radio tube diode	1904	Fleming	English
Radio tube oscillator	1915	De Forest	U.S.
Radio tube triode	1906	De Forest	U.S.
Rayon (acetate)	1895	Cross	English
Rayon (cuprammonium)	1890	Despeissis	French
Rayon (nitrocellulose)	1884	Chardonnet	French
Razor, electric	1917	Schick	U.S.
Razor, safety	1895	Gillette	U.S.
Reaper	1834	McCormick	U.S.
Record, cylinder	1887	Bell, Tainter	U.S.
Record, disc	1887	Berliner	U.S.
Record, long playing	1947	Goldmark	U.S.
Record, wax cylinder	1888	Edison	U.S.
Refrigerator car	1868	David	U.S.
Remote control	1898	Tesla	U.S.
Resin, synthetic	1931	Hill	English
Richter scale	1935	Richter	U.S.
Rifle, repeating	1860	Henry	U.S.
Rocket, liquid fuel	1926	Goddard	U.S.
Rollerblades	1980	Olson	U.S.
Rubber, vulcanized	1839	Goodyear	U.S.
Saccharin	1879	Remsen, Fahlberg	U.S.
Saw, circular	1777	Miller	English
Scotch tape	1930	Drew	U.S.
Seat belt	1959	Volvo	Swedish
Segway human transporter	2001	Kamen	U.S.
Seismograph	1880	Milne, Ewing, Gray	Eng.-Scot.
Sewing machine	1846	Howe	U.S.
Shoe-lasting machine	1883	Matzeliger	U.S.
Shoe-sewing machine	1860	McKay	U.S.
Shrapnel shell	1784	Shrapnel	English
Shuttle, flying	1733	Kay	English
Skates, in-line	1759	Merlin	Belgian
Sleeping-car	1865	Pullman	U.S.
Slide rule	1620	Oughtred	English
Slinky	1943	James	U.S.
Smoke detector	1969	Smith, House	U.S.
Soap, hardwater	1928	Bertsch	German
Spectroscope	1859	Kirchoff, Bunsen	German
Spectroscope (mass)	1918	Dempster	U.S.
Spinning jenny	c.1764	Hargreaves	English
Spinning mule	1779	Crompton	English
Steam car	1770	Cugnot	French
Steam turbine	1884	Parsons	English
Steamboat, exp'mtl.	1778	Jouffroy	French
Steamboat, exp'mtl.	1785	Fitch	U.S.
Steamboat, exp'mtl.	1787	Rumsey	U.S.
Steamboat, exp'mtl.	1803	Fulton	U.S.
Steamboat, exp'mtl.	1804	Stevens	U.S.
Steamboat, practical	1802	Symington	Scottish
Steamboat, practical	1807	Fulton	U.S.

Invention	Date	Inventor(s)	Nationality
Steel (converter)	1856	Bessemer	English
Steel alloy, high-speed	1901	Taylor, White	U.S.
Steel, manganese	1884	Hadfield	English
Steel, stainless	1916	Brearley	English
Stereoscope	1838	Wheatstone	English
Stethoscope	1819	Laennec	French
Stethoscope, binaural	1840	Cammann	U.S.
Stock ticker	1870	Edison	U.S.
Storage battery, rechargeable	1859	Plante	French
Stove, electric	1896	Hadaway	U.S.
Submarine	1891	Holland	U.S.
Submarine, even keel	1894	Lake	U.S.
Submarine, torpedo	1776	Bushnell	U.S.
Synthesizer	1964	Moog	U.S.
Tank, military	1914	Swinton	English
Tape recorder, magnetic	1899	Poulsen	Danish
Taser	1974	Cover	U.S.
Teflon	1938	Du Pont	U.S.
Telegraph, magnetic	1837	Morse	U.S.
Telegraph, quadruplex	1864	Edison	U.S.
Telegraph, railroad	1887	Woods	U.S.
Telegraph, wireless high frequency	1895	Marconi	Italian
Telephone[1]	1871	Meucci	U.S.-Italian
Telephone[1]	1876	Bell	U.S.-Scot.
Telephone amplifier	1912	De Forest	U.S.
Telephone answering machine (1st practical)	1954	Hashimoto	Japanese
Telephone, automatic	1891	Strowger	U.S.
Telephone, cellular	1947	Bell Labs	U.S.
Telephone, cordless[2]	1950	Gross	U.S.
Telephone, radio	1900	Poulsen	Danish
		Fessenden	Canadian
Telephone, radio	1906	De Forest	U.S.
Telephone, radio, long dist.	1915	AT&T	U.S.
Telephone, recording	1898	Poulsen	Danish
Telescope	1608	Lippershey	Dutch
Telescope	1609	Galileo	Italian
Telescope, astronomical	1611	Kepler	German
Telescope, reflecting	1668	Newton	English
Teletype	1928	Morkrum, Kleinschmidt	U.S.
Television, color	1928	Baird	Scottish
Television, electronic	1927	Farnsworth	U.S.
Television, iconoscope	1923	Zworykin	U.S.
Television, mech. scanner	1923	Baird	Scottish
Tesla Coil	1891	Tesla	U.S.
Thermometer	1593	Galileo	Italian
Thermometer	1730	Reaumur	French
Thermometer, mercury	1714	Fahrenheit	German
3D printing (stereolithography)	1984	Hull	U.S.
Time recorder	1890	Bundy	U.S.
Tire, double-tube	1845	Thomson	Scottish
Tire, pneumatic	1888	Dunlop	Scottish
Toaster, automatic	1918	Strite	U.S.
Toilet, flush	1589	Harington	English
Torpedo, marine	1804	Fulton	U.S.
Tractor, crawler	1904	Holt	U.S.
Transformer, AC	1885	Stanley	U.S.
Transistor	1947	Shockley, Brattain, Bardeen	U.S.
Trolley car, electric	1884-87	Van DePoele, Sprague	U.S.
Tungsten, ductile	1912	Coolidge	U.S.
Tupperware®	1945	Tupper	U.S.
Turbine, gas	1849	Bourdin	French
Turbine, hydraulic	1849	Francis	U.S.
Turbine, steam	1884	Parsons	English
Type, movable	1447	Gutenberg	German
Typewriter	1867	Sholes, Soule, Glidden	U.S.
Universal Serial Bus (USB)	1994	Bhatt, et al.	U.S.
Vacuum cleaner, electric	1907	Spangler	U.S.
Vacuum evaporating pan	1846	Rillieux	U.S.
Velcro	1948	de Mestral	Swiss
Video game ("Pong")	1972	Bushnell	U.S.

Invention	Date	Inventor(s)	Nationality
Video home system (VHS)	1975	Matsushita, JVC	Japanese
Vinyl	1926	Semon	U.S.
Washer, electric	1901	Fisher	U.S.
Welding, atomic hydrogen	1924	Langmuir, Palmer	U.S.
Welding, electric	1877	Thomson	U.S.
Wheelchair, multiterrain	1986	Twitchell	U.S.
Wheelchair, stair-climbing	1962	Blanco	U.S.

Invention	Date	Inventor(s)	Nationality
Wiki software	1995	Cunningham	U.S.
Wind tunnel	1912	Eiffel	French
Windshield wiper	1903	Anderson	U.S.
Wire, barbed	1874	Glidden	U.S.
World Wide Web	1989	Berners-Lee	English
Wrench, double-acting	1913	Owen	U.S.
X-ray tube	1913	Coolidge	U.S.
Zeppelin	1900	Zeppelin	German
Zipper, early model	1893	Judson	U.S.
Zipper, improved	1913	Sundback	Canadian

(1) While Alexander Graham Bell has traditionally been credited with invention of the telephone, which he patented, Antonio Meucci developed a working model before Bell. (2) Al Gross held a number of important early patents in the field of wireless communication; other people were also involved in the development of practical cordless telephones.

U.S. Patent-Receiving Corporations, 2013

Source: U.S. Patent and Trademark Office, U.S. Dept. of Commerce

(ranked by number of "utility patents," or patents for inventions, granted)

Rank	Company	No. of patents	Rank	Company	No. of patents
1.	International Business Machines Corp.	6,788	11.	Fujitsu Limited	1,802
2.	Samsung Electronics Co., Ltd.	4,652	12.	Apple, Inc.	1,775
3.	Canon Kabushiki Kaisha	3,820	13.	General Electric Co.	1,737
4.	Sony Corp.	3,073	14.	GM Global Technology Operations LLC.	1,621
5.	Microsoft Corp.	2,659	15.	Seiko Epson Corp.	1,488
6.	Panasonic Corp.	2,582	16.	Ricoh Co., Ltd.	1,469
7.	Toshiba Corp.	2,365	17.	Intel Corp.	1,454
8.	Qualcomm, Inc.	2,103	18.	Hewlett-Packard Development Co., L.P.	1,358
9.	LG Electronics Inc.	1,945	19.	Samsung Display Co., Ltd.	1,259
10.	Google, Inc.	1,851	20.	Toyota Jidosha K.K.	1,171

Note: Reflects patent ownership at time of patent granting. Changes may occur after patent is granted. Where more than one assignee exists, patents are attributed to first-named assignee.

U.S. Patents by Country, 2013

Source: U.S. Patent and Trademark Office, U.S. Dept. of Commerce

Rank	Country	Patents	% change, 2012-13	% share of total issued	Rank	Country	Patents	% change, 2012-13	% share of total issued
1.	Japan	51,919	2.5%	18.7%	7.	China	5,928	27.8%	2.1%
2.	Germany	15,498	12.0	5.6	8.	UK.	5,806	11.4	2.1
3.	South Korea	14,548	9.9	5.2	9.	Israel	3,012	21.7	1.1
4.	Taiwan	11,071	4.0	4.0	10.	Italy	2,499	17.9	0.9
5.	Canada	6,547	13.4	2.4		United States	133,593	10.4	48.1
6.	France	6,083	12.9	2.2		All countries	277,835	9.7	100.0

Note: Country of origin is determined by residence of first-named inventor in patent.

U.S. Patents by Category, Pre–1993-2013

Source: U.S. Patent and Trademark Office, U.S. Dept. of Commerce

(ranked by number of patents issued in 2013)

Rank	Category	Pre-1993	1993	2002	2012	2013	% change, 1993-2013
1.	Multiplex communications	4,189	526	2,241	8,401	9,289	1,666.0%
2.	Active solid-state devices (e.g., transistors, solid-state diodes)	7,940	1,006	3,583	6,885	8,528	747.7
3.	Telecommunications	3,402	413	1,773	7,615	8,259	1,899.8
4.	Drug, bio-affecting and body treating compositions (class 514)	28,724	2,581	4,289	5,367	6,328	145.2
5.	Data processing: financial, business practice, management, or cost/price determination	911	163	458	4,862	5,904	3,522.1
6.	Computer graphics processing and selective visual display systems	3,897	533	1,867	4,854	5,858	999.1
7.	Semiconductor device manufacturing: process	7,169	1,140	5,480	5,176	5,572	388.8
8.	Electrical computers and digital processing systems: multicomputer data transferring	441	113	1,246	5,313	5,380	4,661.1
9.	Image analysis	2,874	429	1,243	5,145	5,149	1,100.2
10.	Data processing: database and file management or data structures	416	143	1,253	4,973	5,086	3,456.6
11.	Drug, bio-affecting and body treating compositions	10,107	1,280	3,255	3,847	4,667	264.6
12.	Pulse or digital communications	3,877	519	1,462	4,369	4,501	767.2
13.	Television	8,804	839	1,053	4,330	4,281	410.3
14.	Data processing: vehicles, navigation, and relative location	2,709	294	1,268	3,222	4,175	1,320.1
15.	Chemistry: molecular biology and microbiology	9,551	1,503	3,527	3,707	3,911	160.2
16.	Surgery (class 600)	7,676	942	1,939	2,942	3,534	275.2
17.	Recording, communication, or information retrieval equipment	6,508	872	1,423	2,626	3,364	285.8
18.	Surgery (class 606)	4,388	666	1,245	2,895	3,321	398.6
19.	Facsimile and static presentation processing	3,545	525	717	2,536	3,152	500.4
20.	Information security	76	15	140	2,246	3,095	20,533.3

Geologic Time Scale

Our understanding of Earth's ancient history is largely a result of geoscientists' study of climate, rock strata, ice samples, mineral deposits, and fossils from around the world; clues to the planet's origin have also been found through the study of extraterrestrial bodies. Geologists divide Earth's history into the following units (MYA = million years ago):

PRECAMBRIAN TIME (4,600-541 MYA)

HADEAN EON (4,600-4,000 MYA) Earth has no continents, oceans, or life; surface conditions are defined by intense volcanic activity and widespread meteorite impact. Oldest known minerals and rocks, many of meteoric origin, date to this era.

ARCHEAN EON (4,000-2,500 MYA) Earth's surface cools and water vapor in atmosphere condenses to form early oceans, which define small protocontinents; the first single-celled organisms, bacteria and archaea, appear in these oceans.

PROTEROZOIC EON (2,500-541 MYA) Protocontinents merge into larger landmasses as Earth's crust continues to shift. Atmospheric oxygen levels increase, and first known multicellular life appears. Later, soft-bodied marine animals emerge.

PHANEROZOIC EON (541 MYA-present)

Paleozoic Era (541-252 MYA)

Cambrian Period (541-485 MYA) The supercontinent known as Gondwana, or Gondwanaland, dominates the Southern Hemisphere. Seas experience an explosion of invertebrate animal life, including thousands of species of trilobites; the first known vertebrates appear. There is no life on land.

Ordovician Period (485-443 MYA) Gondwanaland extends from South Pole to tropic regions; Northern Hemisphere is mostly open ocean. Average global temperatures are warmer than in the current era. First primitive land plants, early ancestors of starfish and mollusks, and first armored, jawless fishes appear. The period ends in extinction of a majority of species, possibly a result of a global drop in sea level due to glaciation.

Silurian Period (443-419 MYA) South Pole remains covered by supercontinent, but precursors of present-day N America, Europe, and Asia coalesce around the equator and middle latitudes. Appearance of first known vascular land plants, first freshwater fish, first jawed fish, first coral reefs, and first air-breathing animals (certain eurypterids, a scorpion-like creature).

Devonian Period (419-359 MYA) Collisions between Gondwanaland and ancestral landmasses of N America and Eurasia produce mountains visible today as northern Appalachians. Newly-formed ozone layer offers protection from sun's rays, allowing first air-breathing spiders and mites to appear on dry land. Fish with fins and scales and first amphibians emerge.

Carboniferous Period (359-299 MYA) Precursors of modern N America and Northern Europe lie in tropical latitudes north of the equator; warm and humid conditions there facilitate spread of lush forests and peat swamps that later form most of the world's coal and limestone. Later period sees emergence of first true conifers, Lepidodendrales ("scale trees") as tall as 100 ft, and first true reptiles.

Permian Period (299-252 MYA) All major landmasses collide to form the supercontinent Pangaea, surrounded by the world ocean Panthalassa. Gradual warming through much of the Permian allows for initial flourishing of species—including dinosaur precursors (up to 10 ft in length) and marine species in shallow inland seas. The period ended with a mass extinction of as much as 95% of all marine species and most land species.

Mesozoic Era (252-66 MYA)

Triassic Period (252-201 MYA) Pangaea separates into supercontinents of Laurasia and Gondwana; subtropical conditions extend as far north as present-day Wyoming and New England. Emergence of icthyosaurs and plesiosaurs (large marine reptiles), several species of dinosaurs (up to 15 ft long), first true mammals, and first insects to undergo metamorphosis from larva to pupa to adult.

Jurassic Period (201-145 MYA) N American continent drifts westward, opening Gulf of Mexico; rift forms between S America and Africa. Warm, moist climate contributes to flourishing of coral reefs and temperate and subtropical forests. Appearance of first angiosperms (flowering plants), pterosaurs (winged reptiles), the earliest known birds, and huge dinosaurs such as the carnivorous *Allosaurus* and herbivorous *Apatosaurus*.

Cretaceous Period (145-66 MYA) African continental plate drifts north, creating roots of European Alps; gap between S America and Africa broadens; western movement of N America drives formation of Sierra Nevada and Rocky Mountains, turning the western interior of continent into a vast swamp. Later, sea levels rise and cover about one-third of Earth's present land area. The global climate is warm and mild. The period ends in a mass extinction of plant and animal species (including dinosaurs), likely caused by the impact of one or more asteroids or comet fragments.

Cenozoic Era (66 MYA-present)

Paleogene Period (66-23 MYA)

• Paleocene Epoch (66-56 MYA) Australia begins to separate from Antarctica; N America and Greenland begin to spread apart. Mammalian life predominates, including early marsupials, insectivores, creodonts (carnivorous relatives of cats and dogs), and primitive hoofed mammals.

• Eocene Epoch (56-33.9 MYA) Australia drifts farther from Antarctica; the Indian subcontinent becomes welded to Asia, and tectonic forces drive the upheaval of the Alpine-Himalayan system. Climate in N America and Europe is subtropical and moist, with temperate forests as far north as Greenland and Siberia. Ancestors of modern horses, elephants, rhinoceroses, camels, bats, primates, and squirrel-like rodents emerge; earliest known marine mammals appear in later Eocene.

• Oligocene Epoch (33.9-23 MYA) San Andreas fault develops between N American and Pacific plates. Mammalian species continue to diversify, producing modern horse and multiple rodent, camel, and rhinoceros-like species, as well as first known species of great ape. Long-term cooling trend begins that would later cause Pleistocene ice ages.

Neogene Period (23 MYA-2.6 MYA)

• Miocene Epoch (23-5.3 MYA) Crustal plate collisions continue to drive uplift of Alps, Himalayas, and Cordilleran Ranges in Americas; eroded sediment is deposited in shallow marine basins, forming reservoirs for oil fields of California, Romania, and Caspian Sea. Ocean currents prevent Antarctica from receiving warmer waters, fostering growth of Antarctic ice sheet. Northern forests become grassy prairies. Large apes related to the orangutan live in Asia and southern Europe. Oldest hominid fossils from Africa date to this epoch.

• Pliocene Epoch (5.3-2.6 MYA) Alps continue to rise in Europe, and subduction of the Pacific tectonic plate elevates the Sierra Nevada and volcanic Cascade Range. Climate becomes cooler and drier, driving formation of permanent Arctic ice cap. Rapid primate evolution produces *Australopithecus*, earliest direct ancestor of *Homo sapiens*.

Quaternary Period (2.6 MYA-present)

• Pleistocene Epoch (2.6 MYA-11,700 years ago) Glacier ice covers as much as 25% or more of Earth's land surface, carving numerous present-day features including the Great Lakes; increased rainfall in lower latitudes allows plant and animal life to flourish in northern and eastern Africa. Late Pleistocene brings worldwide extinction of many large mammals, including the mastodon, saber-toothed tiger, and ground sloth. Evidence of Neanderthals and Denisovans dates from the latter part of the Pleistocene.

• Holocene Epoch (11,700 years ago-present) Melting ice caused sea levels to rise 100 ft or more in early Holocene, covering large areas of land and extending continental shelf of N America. Humans proliferate, and civilization begins.

Biological Classification

Source: *Funk & Wagnalls New Encyclopedia*

In biology, classification is the identification, naming, and grouping of organisms into a formal system. The two fields that are most directly concerned with classification are taxonomy and systematics. Although they overlap, taxonomy is more concerned with nomenclature (naming) and with constructing hierarchical systems, and systematics with uncovering evolutionary relationships. Two kingdoms of living forms, Plantae and Animalia, have been recognized since Aristotle established the first taxonomy in the 4th century BCE. Plants and animals are examples of eukaryotes; their cells have nuclei bound by membranes. Two other kingdoms of eukaryotes that have been identified are Protista (one-celled organisms) and Fungi. The single-celled bacteria and archaea lack such nuclei. They are referred to as prokaryotes (or procaryotes) and are commonly placed in separate kingdoms. The seven basic categories of classification (from most general to most specific) are kingdom, phylum (or division), class, order, family, genus, and species. (In addition, many scientists group all eukaryotes together in a single "domain." The bacteria and archaea are also often treated as separate domains.) Below are two examples of classification:

ZOOLOGICAL HIERARCHY

Kingdom	Phylum	Class	Order	Family	Genus	Species name	Common name
Animalia	Chordata	Mammalia	Primates	Hominidae	*Homo*	*Homo sapiens*	Human

BOTANICAL HIERARCHY

Kingdom	Division*	Class	Order	Family	Genus	Species name	Common name
Plantae	Magnoliophyta	Magnoliopsida	Magnoliales	Magnoliaceae	*Magnolia*	*M. virginiana*	Sweet bay

*In botany, the division is generally used in place of the phylum.

Gestation, Longevity, and Incubation of Selected Animals

Information reviewed by Ronald M. Nowak, author of *Walker's Mammals of the World* (6th ed., Johns Hopkins University Press, 1999). Average longevity figures supplied by Ronald T. Reuther. These apply to animals in captivity; the potential life span of animals is rarely attained in nature. Figures on gestation and incubation are averages based on estimates.

Animal	Gestation (days)	Average longevity (yrs.)	Maximum longevity (yrs.-mos.)	Animal	Gestation (days)	Average longevity (yrs.)	Maximum longevity (yrs.-mos.)
Ass	365	12	47	Leopard	98	12	23
Baboon	187	20	45	Lion	100	15	30
Bear (black)	219	18	36-10	Monkey (rhesus)	166	15	37
Bear (grizzly)	225	25	50	Moose	240	12	27
Bear (polar)	240	20	45	Mouse (domestic white)	19	3	6
Beaver	105	5	50	Mouse (meadow)	21	3	4
Bison	285	15	40	Opossum (American)	13	1	5
Camel	406	12	50	Pig (domestic)	112	10	27
Cat (domestic)	63	12	38	Puma	90	12	20
Chimpanzee	230	20	60	Rabbit (domestic)	31	5	18-10
Chipmunk	31	6	10	Rhinoceros (black)	450	15	45-10
Cow	284	15	30	Rhinoceros (white)	480	20	50
Deer (white-tailed)	201	8	20	Sea lion (California)	350	12	34
Dog (domestic)	61	12	21	Sheep (domestic)	154	12	23
Elephant (African)	660	35	70	Squirrel (gray)	44	10	23-6
Elephant (Asian)	645	40	77	Tiger	105	16	26-3
Elk	250	15	26-8	Wolf (maned)	63	5	15-8
Fox (red)	52	7	14	Zebra (Grant's)	365	15	50
Giraffe	457	10	36-2				
Goat (domestic)	151	8	18				
Gorilla	258	20	54				
Guinea pig	68	4	8				
Hippopotamus	238	41	61				
Horse	330	20	50				
Kangaroo (gray)	36	7	24				

Animal	Incubation time (days)
Chicken	21
Duck	30
Goose	30
Pigeon	18
Turkey	26

Major Venomous Animals

Snakes

Asian pit viper—2 to 5 ft long; throughout Asia; reactions and mortality vary, but most bites cause tissue damage; mortality generally low.

Australian brown snake—4 ft to 7 ft long; very slow onset of cardiac or respiratory distress; moderate mortality, but because death can be sudden and unexpected, it is the most dangerous of the Australian snakes; antivenom.

Barba amarilla or fer-de-lance—up to 7 ft long; from tropical Mexico to Brazil; severe tissue damage common; moderate mortality; antivenom.

Black mamba—up to 14 ft long; southern and central Africa; rapid onset of dizziness, difficulty breathing, erratic heartbeat; mortality high, nears 100% without antivenom.

Boomslang—less than 6 ft long; African savannahs; rapid onset of nausea and dizziness, often followed by slight recovery and then sudden death from internal hemorrhaging; bites rare, mortality high; antivenom.

Bushmaster—up to 12 ft long; tropical forests of Central and S America; few bites occur, but mortality high.

Common, or Asian, cobra—4 ft to 8 ft long; throughout S Asia; considerable tissue damage, sometimes paralysis; mortality probably not more than 10%; antivenom.

Copperhead—less than 4 ft long; New England to Texas; pain and swelling; very seldom fatal; antivenom seldom needed.

Coral snake—2 ft to 5 ft long; in Americas south of Canada; bite may be painless; slow onset of paralysis, impaired breathing; mortalities rare but high without antivenom and mechanical respiration.

Cottonmouth water moccasin—up to 5 ft long; wetlands of southern U.S. from Virginia to Texas; rapid onset of severe pain, swelling, tissue destruction can be extensive; mortality low; antivenom.

Death adder—less than 3 ft long; Australia; rapid onset of faintness, cardiac and respiratory distress; at least 50% mortality without antivenom.

Desert horned viper—up to 2 ft long; dry areas of Africa and western Asia; swelling and tissue damage; mortality low; antivenom.

European viper—1 ft to 3 ft long; throughout Europe; bleeding and tissue damage; mortality low; antivenom.

Gaboon viper—more than 6 ft long; S of the Sahara; massive tissue damage, internal bleeding; few recorded bites.

King cobra—up to 16 ft long; throughout S Asia; rapid swelling, dizziness, loss of consciousness, difficulty breathing, erratic heartbeat; mortality varies with amount of venom involved, but most bites involve nonfatal amounts; antivenom.

Krait—up to 5 ft long; SE Asia; rapid onset of sleepiness, numbness; up to 50% mortality even with use of antivenom.

Puff adder—up to 5 ft long, fat; S of the Sahara, throughout the Middle East; rapid large swelling, great pain, dizziness; moderate mortality, often from internal bleeding; antivenom.

Rattlesnakes—2 ft to 6 ft long; throughout Western Hemisphere; rapid onset of severe pain, swelling; mortality low, but amputation of affected digits is sometimes necessary; antivenom. Mojave rattler may produce temporary paralysis.

Ringhals, or spitting, cobra—5 ft to 7 ft long; southern Africa; squirts venom through holes in front of fangs as a defense; venom severely irritating and can cause blindness.

Russell's viper or tic-polonga—more than 5 ft long; throughout Asia; internal bleeding; bite reports common; moderate mortality rate; antivenom.

Saw-scaled, or carpet, viper—up to 2 ft long; dry areas from India to Africa; severe bleeding, fever; high mortality, causes more human fatalities than any other snake; antivenom.

Sea snakes—3 ft to 10 ft long; throughout Pacific, Indian Oceans except NE Pacific; almost painless bite; variety of muscle pain, paralysis; mortality low, many bites not envenomed; some antivenoms.

Sharp-nosed pit viper or hundred-pace snake—up to 5 ft long; S Vietnam, Taiwan, and China; the most toxic of Asian pit vipers; very rapid onset of swelling and tissue damage, internal bleeding; moderate mortality; antivenom.

Taipan—up to 11 ft long; Australia and New Guinea; rapid paralysis with severe breathing difficulty; mortality nears 100% without antivenom.

Tiger snake—2 ft to 6 ft long; southern Australia; pain, numbness, mental disturbances with rapid paralysis; may be deadliest of all land snakes, but antivenom is quite effective.

Yellow, or cape, cobra—7 ft long; southern Africa; most toxic venom of any cobra; rapid onset of swelling, breathing and cardiac difficulties; mortality is high without treatment; antivenom.

Note: Not all bites by venomous snakes are actually envenomed. Any animal bite, however, carries the danger of tetanus, and anyone suffering a venomous snake bite should seek medical attention. Antivenoms do not cure; they are only an aid in the treatment of bites. Mortality rates above are for envenomed bites: low mortality, c. 2% or less; moderate, 2%-5%; high, 5%-15%.

Lizards

Gila monster—up to 24 in. long, with heavy body and tail; high desert in SW U.S. and northern Mexico; immediate severe pain, transient low blood pressure; no recent mortality.

Mexican beaded lizard—similar to Gila monster; W coast of Mexico; reaction and mortality similar to Gila monster.

Insects

Ants, bees, hornets, wasps—global distribution; usual reaction is piercing pain in area of sting, though many people suffer allergic reactions (swelling, rashes); not directly fatal, except in cases of massive multiple stings, and a few may die within minutes from severe sensitivity to the venom (anaphylactic shock).

Spiders, scorpions

Black widow—small, round-bodied with red hourglass marking; the widow and its relatives are found in tropical and temperate zones; severe musculoskeletal pain, weakness, breathing difficulty, convulsions, which may be more serious in small children; low mortality; antivenom. The **redback** spider of Australia has the hourglass marking on its back, rather than on its front, but is otherwise identical to the black widow.

Brown recluse, or fiddleback, spider—small, oblong body; throughout U.S.; pain with later ulceration, which may last months, at place of bite; fever, nausea, and stomach cramps in severe cases; very low mortality.

Funnel web spider—several varieties, often large; Australia; slow onset of breathing, circulation difficulties; low mortality; antivenom.

Scorpions—crablike body with stinger in tail, various sizes; many varieties throughout tropical and subtropical areas; severe pain spreading from the wound, numbness, severe agitation, cramps, and even respiratory failure; low mortality, usually in children; antivenoms.

Tarantula—large, hairy spider; worldwide; the American tarantula, and probably all other tarantulas, are harmless to humans, though their bite may cause some pain and swelling.

Sea life

Cone-shell—mollusk in small shell; S Pacific and Indian Oceans; shoots barbs into victims; paralysis; low mortality.

Octopus—global distribution, usually in warm waters; rapid onset of paralysis with breathing difficulty; all varieties produce venom, but only a few can cause death.

Portuguese man-of-war—jellyfish-like, with tentacles up to 100 ft long; in most warm water areas; immediate severe pain; not directly fatal, though shock may cause death in rare cases.

Sea wasp—jellyfish, with tentacles up to 30 ft long; S Pacific; very rapid onset of circulatory problems; high mortality because of speed of toxic reaction; antivenom.

Stingray—several varieties of differing sizes; tropical and temperate seas and some freshwater; severe pain, rapid onset of nausea, vomiting, breathing difficulties; wound area may ulcerate, gangrene may occur; seldom fatal.

Stonefish—brownish fish that lies motionless on bottom of shallow waters; throughout S Pacific and Indian Oceans; extraordinary pain, rapid paralysis; low mortality; antivenom, warm water relieves pain.

Speeds of Selected Animals

Source: *Natural History* magazine. © American Museum of Natural History

Animal	Speed (mph)	Animal	Speed (mph)	Animal	Speed (mph)
Cheetah	70	Mongolian wild ass	40	Human	27.89
Pronghorn antelope	61	Greyhound	39.35	Elephant	25
Wildebeest	50	Whippet	35.50	Black mamba snake	20
Lion	50	Rabbit (domestic)	35	Six-lined race runner (lizard)	18
Thomson's gazelle	50	Mule deer	35	Wild turkey	15
Quarterhorse	47.5	Jackal	35	Squirrel	12
Elk	45	Reindeer	32	Pig (domestic)	11
Cape hunting dog	45	Giraffe	32	Chicken	9
Coyote	43	White-tailed deer	30	Spider (*Tegenaria atrica*)	1.17
Gray fox	42	Warthog	30	Giant tortoise	0.17
Hyena	40	Grizzly bear	30	Three-toed sloth	0.15
Zebra	40	Cat (domestic)	30	Garden snail	0.03

Note: Most of these measurements are for maximum speeds over approximate quarter-mile distances. Exceptions are the lion and elephant, whose speeds were clocked in the act of charging; the whippet, which was timed over a 200-yd course; the cheetah, timed over a 100-yd distance; a human, timed over a 15-yd segment of a 100-yd run; and the black mamba, six-lined race runner, spider, giant tortoise, three-toed sloth, and garden snail, which were measured over various small distances.

Top American Kennel Club Breed Registrations, 2003-13
Source: American Kennel Club (AKC)

Breed	Rank				Breed	Rank			
	2013	2012	2008	2003		2013	2012	2008	2003
Labrador Retrievers	1	1	1	1	Havanese	25	28	36	55
German Shepherd Dogs	2	2	3	4	Mastiffs	26	26	28	33
Golden Retrievers	3	3	4	2	Maltese	27	25	20	20
Beagles	4	4	5	3	English Springer Spaniels	28	29	27	28
Bulldogs	5	5	8	16	Cocker Spaniels	29	27	21	14
Yorkshire Terriers	6	6	2	6	Brittanys	30	31	30	30
Boxers	7	7	6	7	Pugs	31	30	15	12
Poodles	8	8	9	8	Bernese Mountain Dogs	32	33	40	47
Rottweilers	9	9	14	15	Weimaraners	33	32	31	29
Dachshunds	10	10	7	5	Vizslas	34	34	44	45
French Bulldogs	11	14	26	54	Collies	35	35	38	32
Doberman Pinschers	12	12	18	22	West Highland White Terriers	36	36	34	31
German Shorthaired Pointers	13	15	16	21	Newfoundlands	37	42	46	46
Siberian Huskies	14	16	23	23	Papillons	38	37	37	36
Shih Tzu	15	11	10	9	Rhodesian Ridgebacks	39	41	50	53
Great Danes	16	17	22	27	Bichons Frises	40	38	35	26
Miniature Schnauzers	17	13	11	11	Basset Hounds	41	40	33	25
Cavalier King Charles Spaniels	18	20	25	35	Bullmastiffs	42	39	39	48
Pomeranians	19	19	13	13	Chesapeake Bay Retrievers	43	46	48	41
Australian Shepherds	20	22	29	34	Border Collies	44	44	53	65
Shetland Sheepdogs	21	21	19	17	Akitas	45	45	52	44
Chihuahuas	22	18	12	10	Shiba Inu	46	50	65	62
Boston Terriers	23	23	17	18	Saint Bernards	47	49	45	39
Pembroke Welsh Corgis	24	24	24	24	Bloodhounds	48	48	43	49
					Portuguese Water Dogs	49	55	64	71
					Cane Corso	50	60	NA	NA

NA = Not available.

Dog Breeds by Type
Source: American Kennel Club (AKC)

As of Sept. 2014, the AKC recognized 180 breeds and used the following seven groups to classify breeds, according to functions and other distinctive traits.

Herding Group: Australian Cattle Dog, Australian Shepherd, Bearded Collie, Beauceron, Belgian Malinois, Belgian Sheepdog, Belgian Tervuren, Border Collie, Bouvier des Flandres, Briard, Canaan Dog, Cardigan Welsh Corgi, Collie, Entlebucher Mountain Dog, Finnish Lapphund, German Shepherd Dog, Icelandic Sheepdog, Norwegian Buhund, Old English Sheepdog, Pembroke Welsh Corgi, Polish Lowland Sheepdog, Puli, Pyrenean Shepherd, Shetland Sheepdog, Swedish Vallhund.

Hound Group: Afghan Hound, American English Coonhound, American Foxhound, Basenji, Basset Hound, Beagle, Black and Tan Coonhound, Bloodhound, Bluetick Coonhound, Borzoi, Dachshund, English Foxhound, Greyhound, Harrier, Ibizan Hound, Irish Wolfhound, Norwegian Elkhound, Otterhound, Petit Basset Griffon Vendéen, Pharaoh Hound, Plott, Portuguese Podengo Pequeno, Redbone Coonhound, Rhodesian Ridgeback, Saluki, Scottish Deerhound, Treeing Walker Coonhound, Whippet.

Non-Sporting Group: American Eskimo Dog, Bichon Frise, Boston Terrier, Bulldog, Chinese Shar-Pei, Chow Chow, Coton de Tulear, Dalmatian, Finnish Spitz, French Bulldog, Keeshond, Lhasa Apso, Löwchen, Norwegian Lundehund, Poodle (standard and miniature), Schipperke, Shiba Inu, Tibetan Spaniel, Tibetan Terrier, Xoloitzcuintli.

Sporting Group: American Water Spaniel, Boykin Spaniel, Brittany, Chesapeake Bay Retriever, Clumber Spaniel, Cocker Spaniel, Curly-Coated Retriever, English Cocker Spaniel, English Setter, English Springer Spaniel, Field Spaniel, Flat-Coated Retriever, German Shorthaired Pointer, German Wirehaired Pointer, Golden Retriever, Gordon Setter, Irish Red and White Setter, Irish Setter, Irish Water Spaniel, Labrador Retriever, Nova Scotia Duck Tolling Retriever, Pointer, Spinone Italiano, Sussex Spaniel, Vizsla, Weimaraner, Welsh Springer Spaniel, Wirehaired Pointing Griffon, Wirehaired Vizsla.

Terrier Group: Airedale Terrier, American Staffordshire Terrier, Australian Terrier, Bedlington Terrier, Border Terrier, Bull Terrier, Cairn Terrier, Cesky Terrier, Dandie Dinmont Terrier, Glen of Imaal Terrier, Irish Terrier, Kerry Blue Terrier, Lakeland Terrier, Manchester Terrier, Miniature Bull Terrier, Miniature Schnauzer, Norfolk Terrier, Norwich Terrier, Parson Russell Terrier, Rat Terrier, Russell Terrier, Scottish Terrier, Sealyham Terrier, Skye Terrier, Smooth Fox Terrier, Soft Coated Wheaten Terrier, Staffordshire Bull Terrier, Welsh Terrier, West Highland White Terrier, Wire Fox Terrier.

Toy Group: Affenpinscher, Brussels Griffon, Cavalier King Charles Spaniel, Chihuahua, Chinese Crested, English Toy Spaniel, Havanese, Italian Greyhound, Japanese Chin, Maltese, Manchester Terrier (toy), Miniature Pinscher, Papillon, Pekingese, Pomeranian, Poodle (toy), Pug, Shih Tzu, Silky Terrier, Toy Fox Terrier, Yorkshire Terrier.

Working Group: Akita, Alaskan Malamute, Anatolian Shepherd Dog, Bernese Mountain Dog, Black Russian Terrier, Boxer, Bullmastiff, Cane Corso, Chinook, Doberman Pinscher, Dogue de Bordeaux, German Pinscher, Giant Schnauzer, Great Dane, Great Pyrenees, Greater Swiss Mountain Dog, Komondor, Kuvasz, Leonberger, Mastiff, Neapolitan Mastiff, Newfoundland, Portuguese Water Dog, Rottweiler, Saint Bernard, Samoyed, Siberian Husky, Standard Schnauzer, Tibetan Mastiff.

Registrations for Pedigreed Cats, 2013
Source: The Cat Fanciers' Association
(ranked by total registrations)

Rank	Breed	Rank	Breed	Rank	Breed	Rank	Breed	Rank	Breed
1.	Persian	6.	Abyssinian	11.	Norwegian Forest Cat	16.	Burmese	22.	Japanese Bobtail
2.	Exotic	7.	American Shorthair	12.	Oriental	17.	Tonkinese	23.	Turkish Angora
3.	Maine Coon Cat	8.	Sphynx	13.	Scottish Fold	18.	Siberian	24.	Manx
4.	Ragdoll	9.	Siamese	14.	Cornish Rex	19.	Russian Blue	25.	Singapura
5.	British Shorthair	10.	Devon Rex	15.	Birman	20.	Egyptian Mau		
						21.	Ocicat		

COMPUTERS AND TELECOMMUNICATIONS

Computer Milestones

1623: German mathematician Wilhelm Schickard developed the first mechanical calculator, capable of adding, subtracting, multiplying, and dividing.

1642: French mathematician Blaise Pascal built the first of more than four dozen copies of an adding and subtracting machine that he invented.

1801: French inventor Joseph Marie Jacquard demonstrated a new control system for looms. He "programmed" the loom, communicating desired weaving operations to the machine via patterns of holes in paper cards.

1833-71: British mathematician and scientist Charles Babbage used the Jacquard punch-card system in his design for a sophisticated, programmable "Analytical Engine" that foreshadowed basic features of today's computers. Babbage's concept was beyond the capabilities of the technology of his time, and the machine remained unfinished at his death in 1871.

1889: American engineer Herman Hollerith patented an electromechanical punch-card tabulating system that facilitated the handling of large amounts of statistical data and quickly found use in censuses in the U.S. and other countries.

1911: Hollerith's Tabulating Machine Company merged with two other enterprises to form the Computing-Tabulating-Recording Company, which was renamed the International Business Machines Corporation (IBM) in 1924.

1941: German engineer Konrad Züse completed the Z3, the first fully functional digital computer to be controlled by a program; the Z3 was not electronic—it was based on electrical switches called relays.

1942: Iowa State Coll. physicist John Vincent Atanasoff and his assistant Clifford Berry completed a working model of the first fully electronic computer using vacuum tubes, which could operate much more quickly than relays; the rudimentary machine was not programmable.

1943: IBM and Harvard professor Howard Aiken completed the first large-scale automatic digital computer, the Mark I, a relay-based machine 55 ft long and 8 ft high. British scientists built the Colossus, an electronic computer for breaking German codes during World War II.

1946: ENIAC (Electronic Numerical Integrator and Computer), a 30-ton room-sized electronic computer with more than 18,000 vacuum tubes, was completed by physicist John Mauchly and engineer J. Presper Eckert at the Univ. of Pennsylvania for the U.S. Army. ENIAC could be programmed to do different tasks, but cables had to be plugged in, and switches had to be set by hand.

1951: Eckert and Mauchly's UNIVAC (Universal Automatic Computer) became the first commercially available computer in the U.S. The first customer was the Census Bureau. CBS-TV used a UNIVAC in 1952 to predict presidential election results.

1959: COBOL, a computer programming language designed for business use, first appeared, based on programming language innovations of Grace Hopper.

1967: Computer pioneer Doug Engelbart applied for a patent on the mouse.

1969-71: The powerful Unix operating system was developed at Bell Laboratories; later versions became widely used on large computers and formed the basis for the Macintosh OS X operating system.

1971: Intel released the 4004, the first commercial microprocessor (an entire computer processing unit on a chip).

1973: The Alto computer, developed at Xerox's Palo Alto Research Center, became operational, implementing many features of modern commercial personal computers, including a graphical user interface (GUI) featuring windows, icons, and pointers that could be manipulated by a mouse.

1975: The first widely marketed personal computer (PC), the MITS Altair 8800, was introduced in kit form, with no keyboard, video display, or printer, for under $400. Microsoft was founded by Bill Gates and Paul Allen.

1976: The first word-processing program for personal computers, Electric Pencil, was written. Apple Computer Company was founded by Steven Jobs and Stephen Wozniak.

1977: Apple introduced the Apple II; capable of displaying text and graphics in color, the machine enjoyed phenomenal success.

1981: IBM unveiled its Personal Computer (IBM 5150), which used an operating system from Microsoft known as MS-DOS (Disk Operating System).

1984: Apple introduced the first Macintosh. The easy-to-use Macintosh came with a proprietary operating system and was the first popular computer to have a GUI and a mouse.

1990: Microsoft released Windows 3.0, the first workable version of its own GUI.

1991: The Unix-like Linux operating system was invented by Helsinki Univ. student Linus Torvalds and made available for free.

1996: The Palm Pilot, the first widely successful handheld computer and personal information manager, arrived.

1997: The IBM computer Deep Blue beat world chess champion Garry Kasparov in a 6-game match, 2-1, with 3 draws.

2000: Microsoft was found guilty of antitrust violations by a federal district judge. Microsoft settled in 2001 by accepting certain restrictions on its competitive practices.

2001: Apple introduced the Unix-based operating system OS X for the Macintosh.

2002: The total number of personal computers, including desktop and laptop machines of all types, shipped by manufacturers since 1975 reached 1 bil.

2006: Apple began using Intel microprocessors instead of the IBM PowerPC in its Macintosh computers.

2007: Amazon launched the Kindle, a hardware/software system for displaying books electronically; the product line later included tablet computers.

2008: Google released the Linux-based Android operating system for mobile devices.

2010: Apple released the iPad tablet computer and sold more than 3 mil devices in the first 80 days.

2012: Microsoft released Windows 8, featuring enhanced support for touchscreens and an interface with a grid of tiles displaying actively updated content and apps.

Nations With the Most Personal Computers in Use, 2013

Source: Computer Industry Almanac at www.c-i-a.com for year-end 2013

Rank	Nations	PCs in use (mil)	% of world total	Rank	Nations	PCs in use (mil)	% of world total
1.	U.S.	340.6	17.79%	10.	Italy	50.3	2.63%
2.	China	269.5	14.08	11.	South Korea	44.8	2.34
3.	Japan	106.3	5.55	12.	Mexico	34.2	1.79
4.	India	82.8	4.32	13.	Canada	33.8	1.76
5.	Germany	77.6	4.05	14.	Spain	29.5	1.54
6.	Russia	67.8	3.54	15.	Australia	21.2	1.10
7.	UK	59.5	3.11	**Top 15 countries**		**1,335**	**69.72**
8.	France	59.3	3.10				
9.	Brazil	57.8	3.02	**World**		**1,915**	**100.00**

World's Fastest Supercomputers, 2014

Source: Top500.org, as of midyear 2014

Rank	Name	Location	Manufacturer/ vendor	Processors (cores)	Top speed[1]
1.	Tianhe-2 (Milky Way-2)	National Supercomputing Center, Guangzhou, China	NUDT[2]	3,120,000	33.86
2.	Titan	Oak Ridge National Laboratory, TN, U.S.	Cray	560,640	17.59
3.	Sequoia	Lawrence Livermore National Laboratory, CA, U.S.	IBM	1,572,864	17.17
4.	K Computer	RIKEN Advanced Institute for Computational Science, Japan	Fujitsu	705,024	10.51
5.	Mira	Argonne National Laboratory, IL, U.S.	IBM	786,432	8.59
6.	Piz Daint	Swiss National Supercomputing Centre, Switzerland	Cray	115,984	6.27
7.	Stampede	Texas Advanced Computing Center/Univ. of Texas, TX, U.S.	Dell	462,462	5.17
8.	JUQUEEN	Forschungszentrum Juelich, Germany	IBM	458,752	5.01
9.	Vulcan	Lawrence Livermore National Laboratory, CA, U.S.	IBM	393,216	4.29
10.	(undisclosed)	Undisclosed government site, U.S.	Cray	225,984	3.14

Note: The 10 fastest supercomputers, and almost all of the 500 fastest supercomputers, use a version of the Linux operating system. (1) Top speed, in petaflops, achieved as measured according to the Linpack Benchmark. 1 petaflop = 1 quadrillion floating-point operations per sec. (2) NUDT = National University of Defense Technology.

U.S. Sales of Selected Hardware, 2010-13

Source: Consumer Electronics Association
(factory sales to dealers in thousands of units and millions of dollars)

Hardware	2010 Units	2010 Sales	2012 Units	2012 Sales	2013 Units	2013 Sales
Desktop computers[1]	10,739	$7,390	10,527	$6,997	10,359	$6,876
Tablets	NA	NA	60,102	23,139	87,084	27,312
Mobile PCs[2]	NA	NA	25,095	16,331	26,025	17,181
Smartphones	54,136	17,594	111,037	33,228	126,582	37,880
Electronic gaming hardware[3]	NA	5,809	NA	2,752	NA	2,702
Digital video recorders (DVRs)	16,891	2,618	16,669	2,745	13,545	2,249
Digital cameras	36,545	6,778	23,702	6,470	15,395	4,563
Digital camcorders	7,246	1,150	2,663	237	1,670	137
Portable media/MP3 players[4]	39,686	7,030	26,472	3,929	20,402	2,959

NA = Not available. (1) Includes all-in-one computers. (2) Includes notebooks, netbooks, ultrabooks. (3) Does not include systems or software for direct use with personal computer. (4) Includes flash media and drive-based portable MP3 players.

U.S. Sales and Household Penetration of Selected Products, 1985-2012

Source: Consumer Electronics Association

Product	1985 Sales (mil)	1985 % of all households	1990 Sales (mil)	1990 % of all households	1995 Sales (mil)	1995 % of all households	2000 Sales (mil)	2000 % of all households	2005 Sales (mil)	2005 % of all households	2012 Sales (mil)	2012 % of all households
Cordless telephones	$280	11%	$842	28%	$1,141	55%	$1,307	80%	$943	88%	$701	NA
Pagers	NA	NA	118	1	300	11	750	23	525	11	7	NA
Modems/fax modems	10	0	191	2.7	770	16	1,564	55	1,525	70	1,372	70%
Telephone answering devices	325	7	827	35	1,077	57	984	75	1,279	76	577	63
Cellular phones[1]	116	0.1	1,098	5	2,574	29	8,995	60	14,265	NA	39,473	91

NA = Not available. (1) For 2005 and 2012, also includes other wireless communication devices such as PDAs and smartphones. Smartphones were 27% of sales in 2005 and 85% of sales in 2012.

About the Internet

The Internet is not owned or funded by any one institution, organization, or government. It has no CEO and is not a commercial service. Its development is guided by the Internet Society (ISOC), which is composed of volunteers. The ISOC appoints the Internet Architecture Board (IAB), which oversees issues of standards and network resources, among others.

Major Historical Highlights

1969: ARPANET, an experimental four-computer network, was established by the Advanced Research Projects Agency (ARPA) of the U.S. Defense Dept. Two years later, ARPANET linked about 23 computers ("hosts") at 15 sites, including MIT and Harvard.

1978: The first spam, or junk email, was sent over ARPANET.

1983: The set of communications rules (protocol) known as TCP/IP became the main networking protocol of ARPANET. Its adoption was tantamount to the birth of the Internet. The military portion of ARPANET was moved onto MILNET.

1986: The U.S. National Science Foundation (NSF) launched NSFNET, the first large-scale network using Internet technology.

1988: Internet Relay Chat (IRC) was developed by Finnish student Jarkko Oikarinen, enabling people to communicate via the Internet in "real time."

1988: A "worm" crafted by Cornell Univ. computer science graduate student Robert Morris Jr. infected thousands of computers, shutting many down and causing millions of

dollars of damage—the first known case of large-scale damage caused by a computer virus spread via the Internet.

1989: The World—the first commercial Internet service provider supplying dial-up access—debuted.

1989-90: Tim Berners-Lee invented the World Wide Web. Created as an environment in which scientists at the European Center for Nuclear Research in Switzerland could share information, it gradually evolved into a medium with text, graphics, audio, animation, and video.

1990: ARPANET was disbanded.

1991: NSFNET was opened to commercial traffic. Berners-Lee introduced the first browser, or software for accessing the Web.

1993: The National Center for Supercomputing Applications released versions of Mosaic, the first Web browser able to present both text and images on a single page.

1994: Netscape Communications released the Netscape Navigator browser.

1995: Microsoft released its Internet Explorer browser. It initially failed to make a dent in Netscape's dominance of the browser market but surpassed it by 1999.

1996: A group of universities launched Internet2, an advanced, high-performance network for the research community and a test bed for development of new capabilities that might find use in the commercial Internet.

1998: Under a contract with the U.S. Dept. of Commerce, the nonprofit Internet Corporation for Assigned Numbers and Names (ICANN) took over the management of assigning domain names and Internet Protocol (IP) addresses.

1999: Release of the free Napster file-sharing service enabled users to easily exchange files containing music or other content without regard to copyright restrictions.

2003: Niue, a self-governing Pacific island associated with New Zealand, became the first country to offer free nationwide wireless access to the Internet, using Wi-Fi technology.

2004: The Mozilla Foundation released the first official version of the open-source browser Mozilla Firefox.

2008: Google introduced its Chrome browser. By 2012, Chrome ranked as the most widely used browser in the world, according to StatCounter.com.

2011: ICANN decided to allow generic top-level domains to be almost any word in any alphabet.

Safety and Security on the Internet

Common sense dictates some basic security rules:

- Pick passwords that are difficult to guess, preferably consisting of letters, numbers, and symbols, if permitted. Avoid using the same password for multiple websites. A password manager can generate passwords and then save them.
- Do not give out your phone number, address, credit card number, or other personal information unless needed for a transaction at a site you trust.
- If you feel someone is being threatening or dangerous, inform your Internet service provider.
- Use protective "firewall," antivirus, and antispyware software to guard your system against attacks by hackers.
- Be careful about opening email and file attachments from unknown correspondents.
- To avoid falling victim to the scam known as **phishing**—which uses a forged email message, purportedly from a respectable organization, to elicit personal data—do not click on hyperlinks in emails from companies with which you do business. Phishing emails typically contain a link leading to a fabricated website resembling the site of the ostensible sender. If you want to visit a company's website, open your browser and manually enter the site's address.
- Users of so-called **peer-to-peer** (P2P) file-sharing networks or protocols should open up only part of their computer system to sharing, not the entire hard drive.
- When manufacturers provide **patches** to solve security flaws or other problems with operating systems, Web browsers, or other software, it is usually advisable to install these fixes. If a fix is not available for a serious security problem, consider switching to an alternative program.

Internet Addresses

The fundamental part of an address on the Internet is called the domain. The final part of a domain name, known as the **top-level domain (TLD)**, is its most basic part. For example, .com is the top-level domain of *The World Almanac*'s web address (www.worldalmanac.com).

So-called generic top-level domains (gTLDs), consisting of three or more letters, include the following:

Domain	What it is (usually)
.aero	an organization in the air-transport industry
.asia	an entity or individual associated with the Pan-Asia and Asia-Pacific region
.biz	a business
.cat	a site associated with Catalan language and culture
.com	generally a commercial organization, business, or company
.coop	a nonprofit business cooperative, such as a rural electric co-op
.edu	an educational institution
.gov	a nonmilitary governmental entity in the U.S.
.info	an informational site for an individual or organization
.int	an international organization
.jobs	information about employment
.mil	a U.S. military organization
.mobi	a site providing content for mobile devices
.museum	a museum
.name	an individual
.net	suggested for a network administration but actually used by a wide variety of sites
.org	suggested for a nonprofit organization but actually used by a wide variety of sites
.post	postal services
.pro	a professional, such as an accountant, lawyer, or physician
.tel	contact data for a group or individual
.travel	information about travel
.xxx	adult entertainment community

Domain names with two letters are generally for countries or regions. Country-code TLDs (ccTLDs) are usually managed by an organization within a certain country.

Nations With Highest Percentage of Population Using the Internet, 2000-13
Source: © International Telecommunication Union; ranked by 2013 figures

Rank	Nation	2000	2005	2007	2008	2009	2010	2011	2012	2013
1.	Iceland	44.47%	87.00%	90.60%	91.00%	93.00%	93.39%	94.82%	96.21%	96.55%
2.	Norway	52.00	81.99	86.93	90.57	92.08	93.39	93.49	94.65	95.05
3.	Sweden	45.69	84.83	82.01	90.00	91.00	90.00	92.77	93.18	94.78
4.	Denmark	39.17	82.74	85.03	85.02	86.84	88.72	89.81	92.26	94.63
5.	Andorra	10.54	37.61	70.87	70.04	78.53	81.00	81.00	86.43	94.00
6.	Netherlands	43.98	81.00	85.82	87.42	89.63	90.72	91.42	92.86	93.96
7.	Liechtenstein	36.52	63.37	65.08	70.00	75.00	80.00	85.00	89.41	93.80
8.	Luxembourg	22.89	70.00	78.92	82.23	87.31	90.62	90.03	91.95	93.78
9.	Finland	37.25	74.48	80.78	83.67	82.49	86.89	88.71	89.88	91.51
10.	Monaco	42.18	55.46	64.38	67.25	70.10	75.00	80.30	87.00	90.70
11.	Bahrain	6.15	21.30	32.91	51.95	53.00	55.00	77.00	88.00	90.00
12.	United Kingdom	26.82	70.00	75.09	78.39	83.56	85.00	85.38	87.48	89.84
13.	United Arab Emirates	23.63	40.00	61.00	63.00	64.00	68.00	78.00	85.00	88.00
14.	Switzerland	47.10	70.10	77.20	79.20	81.30	83.90	85.19	85.20	86.70
15.	Japan	29.99	66.92	74.30	75.40	78.00	78.21	79.05	86.25	86.25
16.	Canada	51.30	71.66	73.20	76.70	80.30	80.30	83.00	83.00	85.80
17.	Qatar	4.86	24.73	37.00	44.30	53.10	69.00	69.00	69.30	85.30
18.	South Korea	44.70	73.50	78.80	81.00	81.60	83.70	83.76	84.07	84.77
19.	United States	43.08	67.97	75.00	74.00	71.00	71.69	69.73	79.30	84.20
20.	Germany	30.22	68.71	75.16	78.00	79.00	82.00	81.27	82.35	83.96

Nations With the Most Internet Users, 2013

Source: Computer Industry Almanac at www.c-i-a.com for year-end 2013

Rank	Nation	Internet users (mil)	% of worldwide users	Rank	Nation	Internet users (mil)	% of worldwide users
1.	China	537.3	19.96%	10.	France	51.8	1.92%
2.	U.S.	277.0	10.29	11.	Italy	48.0	1.78
3.	India	218.2	8.11	12.	South Korea	42.0	1.56
4.	Japan	109.5	4.07	13.	Mexico	39.2	1.45
5.	Brazil	90.3	3.36	14.	Spain	35.5	1.32
6.	Germany	68.8	2.55	15.	Turkey	33.9	1.26
7.	Russia	68.2	2.53	**Top 15 countries**		**1,735**	**64.45**
8.	Indonesia	62.7	2.33	**World**		**2,692**	**100.00**
9.	United Kingdom	52.7	1.96				

Most-Visited World Websites, 2014

Source: comScore Media Metrix

Some websites represent an aggregation of commonly owned domain names; examples of popular domains within a group added in parentheses by World Almanac editors.

Rank	Website	Visitors[1]	Rank	Website	Visitors[1]
1.	Google sites (YouTube, Blogger)	1,227,322	12.	SINA Corp.	277,179
2.	Microsoft sites (Bing, Xbox Live)	884,956	13.	Youku & Tudou	273,315
3.	Facebook	835,439	14.	Apple Inc. (iTunes)	269,196
4.	Yahoo sites (Yahoo! Voices, Flickr)	665,979	15.	CBS Interactive (CNET, ZDNet)	268,590
5.	Baidu.com Inc.	445,035	16.	MODE Media [formerly Glam Media] (Glam, Brash)	254,856
6.	Wikimedia Foundation sites (Wikipedia)	431,791	17.	Ask Network	240,563
7.	Alibaba.com Corp.	424,535	18.	NetEase.com Inc.	238,044
8.	Sohu.com Inc.	417,912	19.	BitTorrent Network	237,687
9.	Tencent Inc. (QQ)	411,775	20.	eBay (PayPal, Half.com, StubHub)	228,176
10.	Qihoo.com sites	392,478			
11.	Amazon sites (Zappos, Audible, IMDb)	364,439			

(1) Number of persons age 15 or older, in thousands, who visited a website from any location, using a desktop computer, at least once in June 2014.

Top Web Browsers Worldwide, 2009-14

Source: StatCounter Global Stats, gs.statcounter.com

Browser	% of browser market				
	2009	2010	2012	2013	2014
Chrome	3.01%	9.88%	33.81%	43.12%	45.28%
Internet Explorer	60.11	52.68	32.04	24.53	21.38
Firefox	30.50	30.69	23.73	20.09	17.52
Safari	3.02	4.09	7.12	8.59	10.60
Opera	2.64	1.91	1.72	1.10	1.39

Note: Percent of World Wide Web users accessing the Web via a particular browser, for July of year shown.

Top Operating Systems Worldwide, 2009-14

Source: StatCounter Global Stats, gs.statcounter.com

Operating system	% of OS market				
	2009	2010	2012	2013	2014
Windows 7	0.97%	17.34%	45.50%	43.83%	36.39%
Android	0.02	0.23	3.29	7.62	16.38
Apple iOS	0.36	0.88	5.16	7.72	11.62
Windows XP	69.21	54.70	25.89	17.09	9.96
Mac OSX	4.07	5.38	6.16	6.14	5.65
Windows 8	—	—	0.17	5.52	4.94
Windows 8.1	—	—	—	0.01	4.90
Windows Vista	22.47	17.93	7.22	4.37	2.32

— = Not available. **Note:** Percent of World Wide Web users accessing Web with a particular operating system (OS), for July of year shown. Includes mobile devices' operating systems.

U.S. Broadband and Dial-Up Adoption, 2000-13

Source: Pew Research Center

(% of American adults who access the Internet via broadband or dial-up)

Note: Based on annual survey of adults (persons age 18 and older), which takes place Mar.-June of each year.

U.S. Internet Use by Selected Characteristics, 2012-14

Source: Pew Research Center

	% who are users		Race/ethnicity	% who are users			% who are users	
	2012	2014		2012	2014		2012	2014
All adults	81%	87%	White	84%	85%	Annual household income		
Gender			Black	73	81	Less than $30,000	67%	77%
Male	80	87	Hispanic	74	83	$30,000-$49,999	86	85
Female	82	86	**Education**			$50,000-$74,999	90	93
Age			No high school diploma	51	—	$75,000 or more	98	99
18-29	94	97	High school graduate	74	76[1]	**Geography**		
30-49	89	93	Some college	89	91	Urban	81	88
50-64	77	88	College graduate	95	97	Suburban	83	87
65+	54	57				Rural	77	83

Note: Percent of U.S. adults, age 18 and over, who use the Internet, email, or access the Internet via a mobile device. Surveys conducted Nov. 14-Dec. 9, 2012, and Jan. 9-26, 2014. (1) The 2014 survey described this group as "high school grad. or less."

Most-Visited U.S. Websites, 2014

Source: comScore Media Metrix; comScore qSearch

Some websites represent an aggregation of commonly owned domain names; examples of popular domains within a group as of June 2014 added in parentheses by World Almanac editors.

All U.S. Sites

Rank	Website	Visitors[1]
1.	Google sites (YouTube, Blogger)	235,672
2.	Yahoo! Sites (Flickr, Rivals.com, Tumblr)	221,142
3.	Facebook (Instagram)	203,027
4.	Microsoft sites (Bing, Xbox Live)	202,570
5.	AOL, Inc. (Moviefone, Patch, Huffington Post)	174,551
6.	Amazon sites (Zappos, Audible, IMDb)	159,570
7.	Apple Inc. (iTunes)	133,620
8.	Turner Digital (CNN, SI, NBA, NCAA, PGA)	127,219
9.	MODE Media [formerly Glam Media] (Glam, Brash)	122,255
10.	Twitter	117,006

Blog Sites

Rank	Website	Visitors[1]
1.	Blogger	61,664
2.	Gawker Media (Gizmodo, Lifehacker)	51,958
3.	Wordpress.com	49,342
4.	Federated Media Publishing	37,242
5.	Reddit	14,904

Email

Rank	Website	Visitors[1]
1.	Google Gmail	116,418
2.	Yahoo! Mail	79,330
3.	Outlook	37,974
4.	AOL Email	18,795

Social Networking Sites

Rank	Website	Visitors[1]
1.	Facebook	200,441
2.	Twitter	117,006
3.	LinkedIn	72,382
4.	Pinterest	57,924
5.	Tumblr	42,927

Search and Navigation

Rank	Website	Searches (mil)	% of searches
1.	Google sites	12,304	67.7%
2.	Microsoft sites (Bing)	3,528	19.4
3.	Yahoo! sites	1,747	9.6
4.	Ask Network	378	2.1
5.	AOL Inc.	231	1.3

Video Sites

Rank	Website[2]	Visitors[1]
1.	Google sites (YouTube)	153,328
2.	Facebook	91,477
3.	AOL, Inc.	67,024
4.	Yahoo! sites (Flickr)	53,194
5.	Vevo	41,689
6.	NDN (News Distribution Network)	38,893
7.	Maker Studios Inc.	37,437
8.	Vimeo	37,151
9.	Microsoft sites (Xbox Live)	33,646
10.	Fullscreen	32,901

(1) Number of persons age 2 and older in any U.S. location, in thousands, who visited the website at least once in June 2014. (2) Ad videos excluded.

Internet Connections in the U.S. by Speed, 2010-13

Source: Federal Communications Commission
(Internet connections in millions, as of June of given year)

	2010		2011		2012		2013	
Speeds, upstream/downstream	Fixed	Mobile	Fixed	Mobile	Fixed	Mobile	Fixed	Mobile
Greater than 6 Mbps/1.5 Mbps	23.4	1.7	29.6	4.3	36.8	18.7	48.2	52.3
Between 3 Mbps/768 kbps and 6 Mbps/1.5 Mbps	18.0	2.5	19.0	11.9	20.5	24.3	22.3	40.9
Less than 3 Mbps/768 kbps[1]	40.4	71.1	38.0	103.3	32.7	110.4	23.8	88.1

Note: Includes residential and business connections. Upstream speed is the speed of transmission from the user to the Internet. Downstream speed is the reverse. Mbps = megabits per second; kbps = kilobits per second. (1) Includes only connections greater than 200 kbps in at least one direction.

U.S. Broadband Residential Internet Connections by Technology, 2009-13

Source: Federal Communications Commission
(Internet connections in thousands, as of June of given year)

Connection type	2009	2010	2011	2012	2013
DSL	4,897	5,559	7,913	11,575	14,366
Cable modem	23,025	29,398	32,321	36,583	43,061
Fiber optic (FTTP)	3,177	3,982	4,894	5,632	6,512
Total nonmobile[1]	31,161	39,037	45,263	53,070	65,041
Mobile wireless	196	3,206	6,520	25,539	72,014
Total[1,2]	31,356	42,243	51,783	78,609	137,056

Note: Includes connections with transmission speeds of at least 3 megabits per second downstream (Internet to user) and 768 kilobits per second upstream (user to Internet). (1) Includes categories not listed individually. (2) Numbers may not add up to totals due to rounding.

Internet Use in the U.S., 2000-12

Source: The 2013 Digital Future Report, USC Annenberg School Center for the Digital Future

	2000	2001	2002	2003	2005	2006	2007	2008	2009	2010	2012
% of Americans accessing Internet ...	67%	72%	71%	76%	79%	78%	79%	80%	82%	82%	86%
% of households with broadband connection....................	10	13	22	36	48	51	76	79	82	84	83
% of Internet users who make purchases online................	45	51	40	43	46	51	67	65	65	68	78
Weekly time online[1]	9.4	9.8	11.1	12.5	13.3	14.0	15.3	17.3	19.0	18.3	20.4
Weekly time online, at home[1]........	3.3	5.9	6.8	6.9	7.8	8.9	10.0	10.1	10.6	12.3	14.1
Weekly time online, at work[2]	NA	4.6	5.5	4.9	5.6	7.8	7.4	8.3	9.0	9.2	9.2

NA = Not available. (1) Average number of active-use hours per week among Internet users. (2) Average number of hours per week among Internet users who access the Internet at work.

U.S. Internet Use by Race and Ethnicity, 2000-12

Source: Current Population Survey, U.S. Census Bureau, U.S. Dept. of Commerce

Year	White, non-Hispanic Households (thous.)	% with Internet use	Black Households (thous.)	% with Internet use	Asian Households (thous.)	% with Internet use	Hispanic[1] Households (thous.)	% with Internet use
2000	78,719	46.1%	13,171	23.6%	3,457	56.2%	9,565	23.6%
2001	80,734	55.2	13,304	31.1	4,081	67.5	10,476	32.2
2003	81,857	59.9	13,746	36.0	4,009	66.7	12,023	36.0
2007	83,294	66.9	14,730	45.3	4,576	75.2	13,619	43.4
2009	83,810	73.3	15,254	54.5	4,625	80.5	13,799	52.8
2010	83,613	74.9	15,357	58.1	4,744	82.6	14,142	59.1
2011	83,148	76.2	15,369	56.9	4,795	82.7	14,222	58.3
2012	83,512	78.6	15,843	61.9	5,384	85.0	15,632	64.3

Note: Numbers by race/ethnicity of householder. (1) Hispanic persons may be of any race.

U.S. Internet Use by Educational Attainment, 2000-12

Source: Current Population Survey, U.S. Census Bureau, U.S. Dept. of Commerce

Year	Less than high school Households (thous.)	% with Internet use	High school degree[1] Households (thous.)	% with Internet use	Some college Households (thous.)	% with Internet use	Bachelor's degree or more Households (thous.)	% with Internet use
2000	17,402	11.7%	32,278	29.9%	27,883	49.0%	27,684	66.0%
2001	17,463	18.0	33,469	39.7	29,410	57.7	28,765	75.2
2003	16,972	20.2	34,377	43.1	30,320	62.6	31,457	78.3
2007	13,978	24.0	33,099	49.5	30,434	68.9	33,302	84.0
2009	13,711	32.2	32,990	57.5	31,050	74.7	34,910	88.5
2010	13,257	35.5	33,008	60.4	31,549	77.2	35,156	89.2
2011	13,183	36.9	33,060	61.2	31,586	77.3	35,301	89.9
2012	12,951	39.3	32,687	64.8	32,517	79.5	37,239	91.7

Note: Numbers by educational attainment of householders 25 years and older. (1) Includes householders with GEDs.

Popular U.S. Online Purchases, 2002-12

Source: The 2013 Digital Future Report, USC Annenberg School Center for the Digital Future
(percent of Internet users who buy item(s) online)

Item	2002	2006	2008	2010	2012	Item	2002	2006	2008	2010	2012
Books	29%	34%	60%	63%	66%	Videos/DVDs	6%	13%	48%	47%	42%
Clothes	39	42	61	59	66	Computers/peripherals	10	11	43	44	40
Travel	16	17	57	57	66	Software/games	12	11	43	44	37
Gifts	10	12	61	63	60	CDs................	15	17	42	41	35
Electronic goods/ appliances..........	14	11	47	50	51	Products for hobbies...	5	2	40	41	34

Frequency of Selected Internet Activities in the U.S., 2012

Source: The 2013 Digital Future Report, USC Annenberg School Center for the Digital Future
(as % of all Internet users age 12 and older)

Online activity	Several times a day	Daily	Weekly	Monthly	Less than monthly	Never
Check email	55%	32%	8%	2%	1%	2%
Browse (surf)	29	30	19	7	7	9
Look for news..............................	15	33	18	8	13	13
Instant message	9	11	11	6	17	46
Find or check a fact	8	21	32	16	14	9
Play games	8	14	14	7	16	42
Listen/download music......................	7	10	16	16	17	34
Watch/download videos	6	10	19	10	18	37
Listen to online radio.......................	6	8	14	8	18	48
Look up a definition	5	10	28	21	23	15
Online banking	3	17	38	16	4	22

Telecommunications Milestones

1753: Scottish surgeon Charles Morrison proposed using 26 electric lines, one for each letter of the alphabet, to make an electric telegraph. A letter would be indicated by charging the corresponding line, causing movement of a light object at the receiving end. Swiss scientist Georges-Louis Lesage built such a 26-line "electrostatic" system in 1774.

1837: In England, Charles Wheatstone and William Fothergill Cooke patented an electromagnetic telegraph. To indicate letters, their system used the magnetic field generated by a current to deflect compass needles. In 1839, they built the first commercial electric telegraph along a 13-mi (21-km) route.

1837: American inventor Samuel Morse filed a provisional patent application for a different type of electric telegraph that indicated letters by making marks of various lengths on paper. In 1844, he completed a 30-mi telegraph line from Washington, DC, to Baltimore, MD.

1866: The first successful transatlantic telegraph cable was laid.

1876: Alexander Graham Bell applied for a U.S. patent on the telephone. In his first successful experiment, on Mar. 10, he used the device to call his assistant.

1901: Italian inventor Guglielmo Marconi successfully transmitted the first transatlantic radio signal—from Cornwall, England, to Newfoundland, Canada.

1927: Commercial transatlantic telephone service (via radio) began between New York and London.

1946: The first commercial mobile phone service was launched, in St. Louis, MO.

1947: U.S. scientists invented the transistor, thereby giving birth to a revolution in telecommunications and electronics.

1948: U.S. mathematician/engineer Claude Shannon's epochal paper "A Mathematical Theory of Communication" laid the foundation for modern information theory. Its treatment of such crucial concepts as data compression and error detection and correction opened the way to digital communication.

1951: The mayors of Englewood, NJ, and Alameda, CA, made the first customer-dialed long-distance telephone call, facilitated by the introduction of area codes.

1956: The first transoceanic telephone cable went into service.

1962: NASA launched the world's first active communications satellite, AT&T's *Telstar 1*.

1978: Trials were conducted in Chicago and Newark, NJ, on a cellular approach to mobile telephony. This divided a region into a multitude of small overlapping areas, or cells, and made possible a significant increase in quality of calls and quantity of callers. Callers could be switched from one cell to another as they moved about.

1983: The first commercial cellular system in the U.S. went into operation in Chicago. A similar system was also launched in the Baltimore, MD-Washington, DC, area.

1984: As a result of a 1982 antitrust settlement with the U.S. government, AT&T, which handled most telephone service in the U.S., was broken up into several separate entities.

1994: The first smartphone, IBM's Simon Personal Communicator, went on the market. A bricklike touchscreen device, it combined a cellular phone with such features as an address book, calendar, calculator, email and faxing capability, and games.

2007: Apple released the iPhone, inaugurating a new era in multifunctional smartphones.

2012: By late in the year more than 1 bil smartphones of all types were in use worldwide.

Global Communications Technology Developments, 2001-14

Source: ITU World Telecommunication/Information and Communication Technology (ICT) Indicators Database
(per 100 inhabitants; 2014 data is estimated)

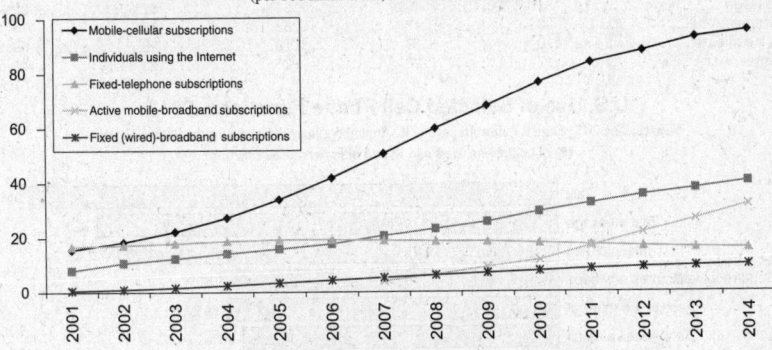

Nations With the Most Cell Phone Use, 2013

Source: © International Telecommunication Union, estimated; ranked by countries with most cell phone subscriptions

Rank	Country	Subscriptions (thous.)	Per 100 pop.	Rank	Country	Subscriptions (thous.)	Per 100 pop.
1.	China	1,229,113	88.71	14.	Egypt	99,705	121.51
2.	India	886,304	70.78	15.	Germany	98,470	119.03
3.	United States	305,743	95.53	16.	Italy	96,904	158.88
4.	Indonesia	303,695	121.54	17.	Thailand	92,463	137.98
5.	Brazil	271,100	135.31	18.	United Kingdom	78,144	123.77
6.	Russia	218,300	152.84	19.	South Africa	77,826	147.46
7.	Japan	146,455	115.19	20.	Turkey	69,661	92.96
8.	Pakistan	127,737	70.13	21.	Argentina	65,910	159.03
9.	Nigeria	127,246	73.29	22.	Iran	65,246	84.25
10.	Vietnam	120,000	130.89	23.	France	63,324	98.50
11.	Bangladesh	105,051	67.08	24.	Ukraine	62,459	138.06
12.	Mexico	105,006	85.84	25.	Poland	57,332	150.02
13.	Philippines	102,824	104.50		World	6,661,978	93.08

U.S. Wireless Industry, 1985-2013

Source: CTIA Semi-Annual Industry Survey, used with permission of CTIA. As of Dec. of year shown.

Year	Est. total subscribers	Total service revenues (thous.)	Cell phone antennas	Avg. monthly revenue per subscriber unit	Avg. local call length (min.)
1985	340,213	$482,428	913	NA	NA
1987	1,230,855	1,151,519	2,305	NA	2.33
1989	3,508,944	3,340,595	4,169	NA	2.48
1991	7,557,148	5,708,522	7,847	NA	2.38
1993	16,009,461	10,892,175	12,824	$76.55	2.41
1995	33,785,661	19,081,239	22,663	59.43	2.15
1997	55,312,293	27,485,633	51,600	49.39	2.31
1998	69,209,321	33,133,175	65,887	47.23	2.39
1999	86,047,003	40,018,489	81,698	46.39	2.38
2000	109,478,031	52,466,020	104,288	48.55	2.56
2001	128,374,512	65,316,235	127,540	49.79	2.74
2002	140,766,842	76,508,187	139,338	51.00	2.73
2003	158,721,981	87,624,093	162,986	51.55	3.07
2004	182,140,362	102,121,210	175,725	52.54	3.05
2005	207,896,198	113,538,221	183,689	50.65	3.00
2006	233,040,781	125,456,825	195,613	49.07	3.03
2007	255,395,599	138,869,304	213,299	49.26	NA
2008	270,333,881	148,084,170	242,130	48.87	2.27
2009	285,646,191	152,551,854	247,081	47.97	1.81
2010	296,285,629	159,929,648	253,086	47.53	1.79
2011	315,963,848	169,767,314	283,385	46.11	1.78
2012	326,475,248	185,013,936	301,779	48.99	1.80
2013	335,652,171	189,192,812	304,360	48.79	NA

NA = Not available.

U.S. Use of Selected Cell Phone Functions, 2007-12

Source: The 2013 Digital Future Report, USC Annenberg School Center for the Digital Future
(as % of cell phone users age 12 and older)

Function	2007	2008	2009	2010	2012
Text message	31%	45%	54%	62%	82%
Take pictures	33	47	52	60	79
Access the Internet	8	13	18	23	59
Play games	17	22	20	23	43

U.S. Use of Selected Cell Phone Functions, 2012

Source: The 2013 Digital Future Report, USC Annenberg School Center for the Digital Future
(% of cell phone users age 12 and older who used function)

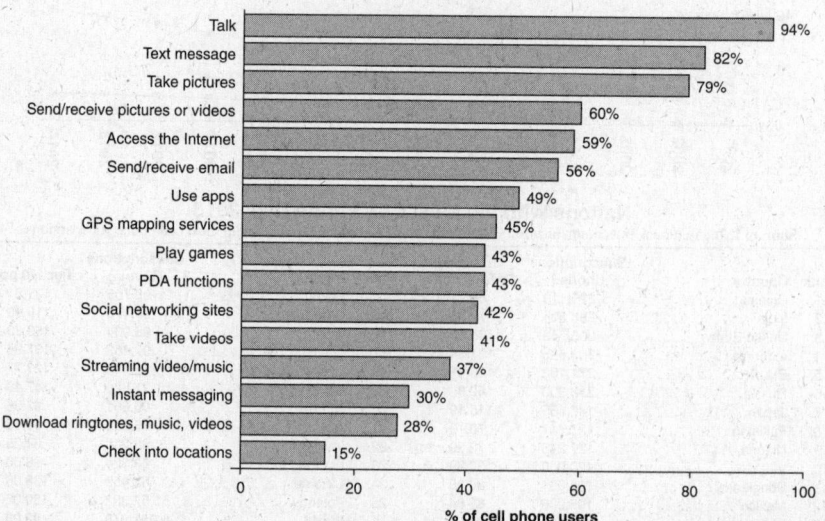

Function	% of cell phone users
Talk	94%
Text message	82%
Take pictures	79%
Send/receive pictures or videos	60%
Access the Internet	59%
Send/receive email	56%
Use apps	49%
GPS mapping services	45%
Play games	43%
PDA functions	43%
Social networking sites	42%
Take videos	41%
Streaming video/music	37%
Instant messaging	30%
Download ringtones, music, videos	28%
Check into locations	15%

% of cell phone users

ENVIRONMENT

U.S. Greenhouse Gas Emissions From Human Activities, 1990-2012

Source: U.S. Environmental Protection Agency

Gas and major source(s)	1990	2005	2008	2009	2010	2011	2012	% change, 1990-2012
Carbon dioxide (CO_2)	5,108.7	6,112.2	5,936.9	5,506.1	5,722.3	5,592.2	5,383.2	5.4%
Fossil fuel combustion	4,745.1	5,752.9	5,593.4	5,225.7	5,404.9	5,271.1	5,072.3	6.9
Methane (CH_4)	635.7	585.7	606.0	596.5	585.5	578.3	567.3	-10.8
Landfills	147.8	112.1	114.3	115.3	109.9	107.4	102.8	-30.4
Enteric fermentation[1]	137.9	142.5	147.0	146.1	144.9	143.0	141.0	2.2
Natural gas systems	156.4	152.0	151.6	142.9	134.7	133.2	129.9	-16.9
Coal mining	81.1	53.6	63.5	67.1	69.2	59.8	55.8	-31.2
Nitrous oxide (N_2O)	398.6	415.8	423.3	412.2	409.3	417.2	410.1	2.9
Agricultural soil management	282.1	297.3	319.0	316.4	310.1	307.8	306.6	8.7
Hydrofluorocarbons, etc.	36.9	119.8	136.0	135.1	144.0	148.6	151.2	309.8
Total U.S. emissions	6,233.2	7,253.8	7,118.1	6,662.9	6,874.7	6,753.0	6,525.6	4.7
Net U.S. emissions[2]	5,402.1	6,223.1	6,137.1	5,701.2	5,906.7	5,772.7	5,546.3	2.7

Note: Emissions given in terms of equivalent emissions of carbon dioxide (CO_2), using units of teragrams of carbon dioxide equivalents (Tg CO_2 eq.). (1) Digestive process of ruminant animals, such as cattle and sheep, producing methane as a by-product. (2) Total emissions minus carbon dioxide absorbed by forests or other means.

U.S. Greenhouse Gas Emissions, 2012
Source: U.S. Environmental Protection Agency

World Carbon Dioxide Emissions From the Use of Fossil Fuels, 2011
Source: U.S. Energy Information Administration

U.S. Greenhouse Gas Emissions, 2012:
- HFCs, PFCs, and sulfur hexafluoride, 2.5%
- Methane, 8.7%
- Nitrous oxide, 6.3%
- Carbon dioxide, 82.5%

World Carbon Dioxide Emissions From the Use of Fossil Fuels, 2011:
- N America, 20.0% (U.S., 16.9%)
- Central and S America, 4.1%
- Europe, 13.2%
- Eurasia, 8.1%
- Middle East, 6.0%
- Africa, 3.5%
- Asia and Oceania, 45.1%

HFC = hydrofluorocarbon; PFC = perfluorocarbon. **Note:** Emissions sources are independently rounded; percentages may not add up to 100.

Top 20 Nations Producing Carbon Dioxide Emissions, 1980-2011

Source: U.S. Dept. of Energy

(in million metric tons of carbon dioxide emitted from the consumption of energy; ranked by 2011 totals)

Country	1980	1990	1995	2000	2005	2010	2011	% change, 1980-2011	% change, 1990-2011
China	1,448.5	2,177.7	2,722.7	3,271.8	5,463.7	7,997.0	8,715.3	502%	300%
United States	4,775.8	5,040.4	5,319.1	5,863.3	5,999.2	5,636.7	5,490.6	15	9
Russia[1]	3,081.9	3,820.9	1,603.1	1,498.8	1,587.5	1,642.3	1,788.1	NA	NA
India	291.2	578.6	870.2	991.0	1,181.4	1,601.2	1,725.8	493	198
Japan	947.0	1,047.0	1,116.2	1,201.4	1,241.3	1,179.8	1,180.6	25	13
Germany[2]	759.3	698.1	890.8	854.7	847.4	793.3	748.5	NA	NA
Iran	116.8	202.1	262.3	321.5	451.1	564.6	624.9	435	209
Korea, South	131.7	242.1	381.4	438.7	493.8	581.1	611.0	364	152
Canada	457.4	470.6	508.7	573.3	623.8	546.7	552.6	21	17
Saudi Arabia	176.9	208.0	235.3	290.5	401.9	468.7	513.5	190	147
United Kingdom	613.6	601.8	560.1	560.3	583.1	528.9	496.8	-19	-17
Brazil	185.7	237.3	289.1	344.4	370.9	451.0	475.4	156	100
Mexico	240.3	302.2	321.4	382.9	397.8	432.2	462.3	92	53
South Africa	235.0	298.0	347.5	386.0	432.4	473.2	461.6	96	55
Indonesia	85.8	156.0	214.8	266.2	330.8	414.5	426.8	397	174
Italy	371.8	415.4	431.4	447.7	471.9	416.8	400.9	8	-3
Australia	198.8	267.6	289.1	356.3	412.6	423.7	392.3	97	47
France	488.9	367.7	372.5	401.7	414.0	388.7	374.3	-23	2
Spain	195.0	224.1	243.4	315.6	379.4	312.4	318.6	63	42
Poland	428.9	333.8	308.2	292.6	287.6	304.7	307.9	-28	-8
World total[3]	18,433.2	21,523.2	22,009.8	24,149.9	28,261.8	31,502.4	32,578.6	77	51

NA = Not applicable. (1) Numbers for 1980-90 are for the former Soviet Union. (2) Numbers for 1980-90 are for former West Germany. (3) Includes nations not listed.

Atmospheric Concentration of Carbon Dioxide, 1744-2013

Source: Carbon Dioxide Information Analysis Center, U.S. Dept. of Energy; Earth System Research Laboratory, Natl. Oceanic and Atmospheric Admin., U.S. Dept. of Commerce

Year[1]	CO_2 in ppm	Year[1]	CO_2 in ppm	Year[1]	CO_2 in ppm	Year[1]	CO_2 in ppm	Year[1]	CO_2 in ppm
1744	277	1878	290	1960	317	2005	380	2010	390
1791	280	1903	295	1970	326	2006	382	2011	392
1816	284	1915	301	1980	339	2007	384	2012	394
1843	287	1927	306	1990	354	2008	386	2013	396
1869	289	1943	308	2000	369	2009	387		

ppm = Parts per million. (1) Measurements for the years 1744-1943 were derived from a 200-m-deep ice core sample drilled near Siple Station in Antarctica in 1983-84. Measurements from 1960-2013 were taken directly from the atmosphere at Mauna Loa Observatory in Hawaii.

Emissions of Principal Air Pollutants in the U.S., 1970-2013

Source: Office of Air Quality Planning and Standards, U.S. Environmental Protection Agency; in est. million tons

Pollutant	1970	1975	1980	1985	1990	1995	2000	2005	2010	2013
Carbon monoxide	204.0	188.4	185.4	176.8	154.2	126.8	114.5	88.5	74.7	73.4
Nitrogen oxides[1]	26.9	26.4	27.1	25.8	25.5	25.0	22.6	20.4	15.0	13.1
Particulate matter[2]										
PM10	13.0	7.6	7.0	41.3	27.8	25.8	23.7	21.3	20.9	20.9
PM2.5	NA	NA	NA	NA	7.6	6.9	7.3	5.6	6.0	6.3
Sulfur dioxide	31.2	28.0	25.9	23.3	23.1	18.6	16.3	14.5	7.8	5.2
Volatile org. compounds[1]	34.7	30.8	31.1	27.4	24.1	22.0	17.5	17.8	17.9	17.7
Ammonia	NA	NA	NA	NA	4.3	4.7	4.9	3.9	4.3	4.3
Total[3]	309.8	281.2	276.5	294.6	266.6	229.8	206.8	172.0	146.6	140.9

NA = Not available. (1) Ozone, a major air pollutant and the primary constituent of smog, is not emitted directly to the air but is formed by sunlight acting on emissions of nitrogen oxides and volatile organic compounds. (2) PM10 = particulates 10 microns or smaller in diameter. PM2.5 = particulates 2.5 microns or smaller in diameter. (3) Totals are rounded, as are components of totals.

Sources of Air Pollutants in the U.S., 1970-2013

Source: Office of Air Quality Planning and Standards, U.S. Environmental Protection Agency; in thousand tons

Carbon monoxide sources	1970	1975	1980	1985	1990	1995	2000	2005	2010	2013
Fuel combustion, elec. util.	237	276	322	291	363	372	484	643	767	784
Industrial processes[1]	10,610	8,304	7,700	5,894	5,572	5,631	3,628	3,074	2,794	2,882
Transportation[2]	174,602	167,884	160,512	153,216	131,702	107,755	92,239	64,729	43,980	39,441
Total carbon dioxide[3]	204,042	188,398	185,408	176,845	154,188	126,778	114,467	88,546	74,653	73,433
Nitrogen oxide sources										
Fuel combustion, elec. util.	4,900	5,694	7,024	6,127	6,663	6,384	5,330	3,792	2,458	1,825
Industrial processes[1]	5,100	4,546	4,110	4,009	3,831	3,909	3,518	2,783	2,436	2,461
Transportation[2]	15,276	15,029	14,846	14,508	13,373	12,989	12,560	12,612	9,094	7,736
Total nitrogen oxide[3]	26,882	26,378	27,080	25,757	25,527	24,955	22,598	20,355	14,974	13,119
Sulfur dioxide sources										
Fuel combustion, elec. util.	17,398	18,268	17,469	16,272	15,909	12,080	11,396	10,404	5,696	3,257
Industrial processes[1]	11,661	7,993	6,725	5,597	5,402	4,945	3,516	2,721	1,501	1,336
Transportation[2]	551	635	717	809	874	741	697	682	163	107
Total sulfur dioxide[3]	31,218	28,044	25,926	23,307	23,077	18,619	16,347	14,546	7,805	5,170

(1) Industrial fuel combustion, chemical and allied manufacturing, metals processing, and petroleum and other industrial sectors. (2) Highway and off-highway vehicles. (3) Numbers may not add up to totals because not all categories are listed.

Average Global Temperature and Atmospheric Carbon Dioxide, 1880-2013

Source: *Climate Change Impacts in the United States*, U.S. Global Change Research Program

Air Pollution in Selected World Cities

Source: *World Development Indicators 2014*, The World Bank

Particulate matter in the following table refers to smoke, soot, dust, and liquid droplets from combustion that are in the air—specifically, to particulates less than 10 microns in diameter (PM10) capable of reaching deep into the respiratory tract. The level of particulates, an important indicator of air quality, is significantly affected by the state of technology and pollution controls. Particulate pollution causes an estimated 500,000 premature deaths each year. **Sulfur dioxide** is a pollutant formed when fossil fuels containing sulfur are burned. **Nitrogen dioxide** is a poisonous, pungent gas formed when nitric oxide combines with hydrocarbons and sunlight, producing a photochemical reaction. Nitrogen oxides are emitted by bacteria, nitrogenous fertilizers, aerobic decomposition of organic matter, biomass combustion, and, especially, burning fuel for vehicles and industrial activities. Emissions of sulfur dioxide and nitrogen oxides lead to acid rain.

Data in the table represent the annual average of outdoor particulates, in micrograms per cubic meter (mpcm), that a resident of a city is exposed to. They are based on reports from urban monitoring sites. The figures give a general indication of air quality, but results should be interpreted with caution. World Health Organization standards for acceptable air quality are annual mean concentrations of 20 mpcm for particulate matter less than 10 microns in diameter and 40 mpcm for nitrogen dioxide and daily mean concentrations of 20 mpcm for sulfur dioxide.

City, country	Particulate matter[1]	Sulfur dioxide[2]	Nitrogen dioxide[2]
Accra, Ghana	83	NA	NA
Amsterdam, Netherlands	24	10	58
Athens, Greece	36	34	64
Bangkok, Thailand	46	11	23
Barcelona, Spain	34	11	43
Beijing, China	118	90	122
Berlin, Germany	27	18	26
Cairo, Egypt	134	69	NA
Cape Town, South Africa	24	21	72
Caracas, Venezuela	35	33	57
Chicago, IL, U.S.	21	14	57
Delhi, India	154	24	41
Jakarta, Indonesia	50	NA	NA
Kolkata, India	127	49	34
London, England, UK	22	25	77
Los Angeles, CA, U.S.	27	9	74
Manila, Philippines	44	33	NA
Mexico City, Mexico	54	74	130
Milan, Italy	42	31	248
Montréal, QC, Canada	17	10	42
Moscow, Russia	29	109	NA
Mumbai, India	87	33	39
Nairobi, Kenya	72	NA	NA
New York, NY, U.S.	16	26	79
Oslo, Norway	26	8	43
Paris, France	25	14	57
Prague, Czech Republic	30	14	33
Quito, Ecuador	41	22	NA
Rio de Janeiro, Brazil	60	129	NA
Rome, Italy	34	NA	NA
São Paulo, Brazil	40	43	83
Seoul, South Korea	48	44	60
Shanghai, China	74	53	73
Sofia, Bulgaria	46	39	122
Tokyo, Japan	23	18	68
Toronto, ON, Canada	14	17	43
Warsaw, Poland	33	16	32

NA = Not available. (1) Urban-population weighted PM10 data as of 2011. (2) As of 2001.

Air Quality of Selected U.S. Urban Areas, 2000-13

Source: Office of Air Quality Planning and Standards, U.S. Environmental Protection Agency

Data indicate the number of days metropolitan statistical areas or corresponding core-based statistical areas failed to meet acceptable air-quality standards.

Urban area	2000	2005	2008	2009	2010	2011	2012	2013
Atlanta-Sandy Springs-Marietta, GA	26	5	4	0	2	0	3	1
Bakersfield, CA	62	33	40	23	14	10	17	21
Baltimore-Towson, MD	7	6	4	1	6	5	2	0
Baton Rouge, LA	19	9	0	0	3	1	0	0
Boston-Cambridge-Quincy, MA-NH	1	3	0	0	0	0	1	0
Chicago-Naperville-Joliet, IL-IN-WI	1	6	0	1	0	1	10	1
Cincinnati-Middletown, OH-KY-IN	3	5	0	0	0	3	4	0
Cleveland-Elyria-Mentor, OH	2	6	0	0	1	0	5	0
Dallas-Fort Worth-Arlington, TX	17	16	1	3	0	6	4	1
Denver-Aurora, CO	0	0	0	0	0	1	3	0
Detroit-Warren-Livonia, MI	1	7	1	0	0	0	3	0
Fresno, CA	69	19	17	10	11	22	16	15
Houston-Sugar Land-Baytown, TX	30	19	3	6	1	7	4	1
Indianapolis-Carmel, IN	6	1	0	0	1	0	2	0
Kansas City, MO-KS	6	4	0	0	0	2	4	1
Las Vegas-Paradise, NV	1	3	0	0	0	0	2	1
Los Angeles-Long Beach-Santa Ana, CA	36	29	31	18	4	11	10	4
Memphis, TN-MS-AR	6	4	1	0	0	0	1	0
Miami-Fort Lauderdale-Pompano Beach, FL	0	1	0	0	0	1	0	0
Minneapolis-St. Paul-Bloomington, MN-WI	1	2	0	0	0	0	1	0
Nashville-Davidson–Murfreesboro–Franklin, TN	5	1	0	0	0	0	1	0
New Orleans-Metairie-Kenner, LA	5	0	0	0	16	26	7	3
New York-Northern New Jersey-Long Island, NY-NJ-PA	7	12	2	0	1	3	0	0
Philadelphia-Camden-Wilmington, PA-NJ-DE-MD	9	9	4	0	3	3	2	0
Phoenix-Mesa-Scottsdale, AZ	2	1	84	17	3	45	16	27
Pittsburgh, PA	7	13	2	3	10	3	4	1
Riverside-San Bernardino-Ontario, CA	65	50	57	47	31	35	34	28
Sacramento-Arden-Arcade–Roseville, CA	22	22	19	8	4	3	6	4
Salt Lake City, UT	9	2	1	4	5	1	0	9
San Francisco-Oakland-Fremont, CA	1	0	1	0	1	0	0	0
Seattle-Tacoma-Bellevue, WA	1	0	0	1	0	0	1	0
Tucson, AZ	0	0	0	1	0	0	0	3
Washington-Arlington-Alexandria, DC-VA-MD-WV	5	4	3	0	3	2	0	0
Winston-Salem, NC	4	0	0	1	0	0	0	0

Toxics Release Inventory in the U.S., 2011-12

Source: U.S. Environmental Protection Agency

Releases of toxic chemicals into the environment, by manner of release and industry sector; pollutant transfers by destination of transfer. Numbers may not add up to totals because of rounding.

	2011	2012		2011	2012
Pollutant releases	mil lbs	mil lbs	**Top industries, total releases**	%	%
Air releases	804	762	Metal mining	45%	40%
Surface water discharges	213	206	Chemicals	12	14
Underground injection	196	203	Electric utilities	15	14
On-site land releases	2,121	1,664	Primary metals	10	10
Off-site releases	414	411	Paper	4	5
Total on- and off-site releases	4,090	3,608	All others	14	17
Pollutant transfers	mil lbs	mil lbs	**Top carcinogens, air/water/land**		
To recycling	2,287	2,394	releases	mil lbs	mil lbs
To energy recovery	355	390	Lead compounds	764	602
To treatment	289	363	Arsenic compounds	341	124
To publicly owned treatment works	240	246	Chromium compounds	39	47
Other transfers	<1	<1	Nickel compounds	23	27
Off-site to disposal	446	445	Styrene	26	27
Total	3,617	3,839	Formaldehyde	19	20

Note: This information does not indicate whether or to what degree the public has been exposed to toxic chemicals.

States With Most Toxics Releases, 2012

Source: U.S. Environmental Protection Agency

State	Pounds	State	Pounds	State	Pounds	State	Pounds
Alaska	876,182,435	Tennessee	69,672,432	Pennsylvania	50,687,763	Iowa	32,170,544
Nevada	279,326,611	Alabama	69,455,938	Mississippi	50,665,611	North Dakota	31,107,748
Texas	201,575,407	Illinois	69,343,479	N. Carolina	47,104,348	Arkansas	30,320,489
Utah	190,130,191	Missouri	68,607,229	Michigan	39,823,184	West Virginia	29,934,001
Louisiana	132,975,409	Kentucky	67,345,116	Idaho	37,856,524	California	26,326,745
Ohio	88,573,538	Oklahoma	63,755,257	S. Carolina	36,186,441	New Mexico	24,345,584
Indiana	88,571,073	Georgia	62,365,214	Virginia	35,532,639	U.S. total	3,196,819,244
Arizona	84,396,701	Florida	60,174,167	Montana	32,957,278		

Note: Total includes states not shown, DC, Puerto Rico, American Samoa, Guam, Northern Mariana Isls., and U.S. Virgin Isls.

Hazardous Waste Sites in the U.S., 2014

Source: *National Priorities List*, U.S. Environmental Protection Agency; as of May 2014

State/territory	Proposed Gen.	Proposed Fed.	Final Gen.	Final Fed.	Total	State/territory	Proposed Gen.	Proposed Fed.	Final Gen.	Final Fed.	Total
Alabama	1	0	11	3	15	Nebraska	0	0	14	1	15
Alaska	0	0	1	5	6	Nevada	0	0	1	0	1
Arizona	0	0	7	2	9	New Hampshire	1	0	20	1	22
Arkansas	0	0	10	0	10	New Jersey	2	0	108	6	116
California	1	0	73	24	98	New Mexico	0	0	14	1	15
Colorado	3	0	15	3	21	New York	1	0	82	4	87
Connecticut	1	0	13	1	15	North Carolina	0	0	37	2	39
Delaware	1	0	12	1	14	North Dakota	0	0	0	0	0
District of Columbia	0	0	0	1	1	Ohio	4	2	34	3	43
Florida	1	0	49	6	56	Oklahoma	1	0	6	1	8
Georgia	1	0	14	2	17	Oregon	1	0	12	2	15
Guam	0	0	1	1	2	Pennsylvania	3	0	89	6	98
Hawaii	0	0	1	2	3	Puerto Rico	0	0	15	1	16
Idaho	3	0	4	2	9	Rhode Island	0	0	10	2	12
Illinois	3	1	40	4	48	South Carolina	0	0	23	2	25
Indiana	1	0	36	0	37	South Dakota	0	0	1	1	2
Iowa	1	0	10	1	12	Tennessee	0	0	14	3	17
Kansas	1	0	11	1	13	Texas	1	0	46	4	51
Kentucky	0	0	13	1	14	Utah	3	0	11	5	19
Louisiana	4	0	8	1	13	Vermont	1	0	11	0	12
Maine	0	0	11	3	14	Virgin Islands	0	0	1	0	1
Maryland	1	0	10	10	21	Virginia	0	0	20	11	31
Massachusetts	1	0	25	6	32	Washington	0	0	37	13	50
Michigan	1	1	65	0	67	West Virginia	0	0	7	2	9
Minnesota	0	0	23	2	25	Wisconsin	1	0	38	0	39
Mississippi	1	0	8	0	9	Wyoming	0	0	1	1	2
Missouri	0	0	30	3	33	Total	47	4	1,169	157	1,326
Montana	2	0	16	0	18						

Note: Fed. = Hazardous waste produced by federal agency; Gen. = Non-fed. sites. Sites that have been proposed for federal Superfund financing are listed under Proposed; sites that have qualified for Superfund financing are under Final.

Renewable Water Resources, 2012

Source: Food and Agriculture Organization (FAO), United Nations

Globally, water supplies are abundant, but they are unevenly distributed among and within countries. In some areas, water withdrawals are so high, relative to supply, that surface water supplies are shrinking, and groundwater reserves are being depleted faster than they can be replenished by precipitation. According to the FAO, the U.S. (including Alaska and Hawaii) has 8,924 cubic meters per capita and 2,818 cubic kilometers of internal renewable water resources total.

The tables below take into account only countries for which data are available, draw upon studies done over a number of years, and use 2012 population data. Numbers represent each country's internal resources. Countries ranked by per capita figures.

Countries With Greatest Internal Water Resources

Country	Cubic m per capita	Total cubic km
Iceland	518,293	170.0
Guyana	317,942	241.0
Suriname	164,794	88.0
Papua New Guinea	111,715	801.0
Gabon	104,859	164.0
Bhutan	104,000	78.0
Canada	82,192	2,850.0
Solomon Islands	78,975	44.7
Norway	77,016	382.0
New Zealand	73,302	327.0

Countries With Lowest Internal Water Resources

Country	Cubic m per capita	Total cubic km
Kuwait	0.0	0.0
Bahrain	2.943	0.004
United Arab Emirates	18.50	0.15
Egypt	21.44	1.8
Qatar	28.88	0.056
Bahamas, The	56.98	0.02
Yemen	82.13	2.1
Saudi Arabia	83.61	2.4
Maldives	92.59	0.03
Israel	97.47	0.75

Top Countries by Forest Area, 1990-2012

Source: Food and Agriculture Organization, United Nations
(in square kilometers; ranked by 2012 area)

Country	Forest area, 1990	Forest area, 2012	% change, 1990-2012	% of land area covered by forest in 2012	Country	Forest area, 1990	Forest area, 2012	% change, 1990-2012	% of land area covered by forest in 2012
Russia	8,089,500	8,092,100	0.0%	49.4%	Papua New Guinea	315,230	284,416	−9.8%	69.6%
Brazil	5,748,390	5,151,332	−10.4	68.8	Sweden	272,810	282,030	3.4	67.0
Canada	3,101,340	3,101,340	0.0	34.1	Japan	249,500	249,966	0.2	68.4
United States	2,963,350	3,047,876	2.9	32.4	Central African Rep.	232,030	225,450	−2.8	37.2
China	1,571,410	2,123,873	35.2	16.7	Congo Rep.	227,260	223,870	−1.5	66.5
Congo, Dem. Rep. of	1,603,630	1,535,122	−4.3	70.7	Finland	218,890	221,570	1.2	72.0
Australia	1,545,000	1,474,520	−4.6	20.1	Gabon	220,000	220,000	0.0	85.4
Indonesia	1,185,450	930,620	−21.5	65.4	Malaysia	223,760	202,824	−9.4	68.1
India	639,390	687,240	7.5	21.5	Cameroon	243,160	194,760	−19.9	51.4
Peru	701,560	676,920	−3.5	54.8	Thailand	195,490	190,016	−2.8	38.3
Mexico	702,910	644,916	−8.3	36.2	Spain	138,180	185,253	34.1	27.7
Colombia	625,190	602,970	−3.6	56.3	Paraguay	211,570	172,248	−18.6	53.3
Angola	609,760	582,304	−4.5	48.9	Chile	152,630	163,062	6.8	20.5
Bolivia	627,950	565,808	−9.9	58.0	France	145,370	160,500	10.4	26.5
Zambia	528,000	491,348	−6.9	71.0	Laos	173,140	155,946	−9.9	75.0
Venezuela	520,260	456,998	−12.2	59.0	Guyana	152,050	152,050	0.0	77.2
Mozambique	433,780	385,992	−11.0	55.2	Zimbabwe	221,640	149,700	−32.5	57.3
Tanzania	414,950	326,212	−21.4	46.8	Suriname	147,760	147,508	−0.2	94.7
Myanmar	392,180	311,538	−20.6	60.0	Vietnam	93,630	140,850	50.4	30.2
Argentina	347,930	289,204	−16.9	12.7	Madagascar	136,920	124,390	−9.2	23.5
					World	40,330,620	40,219,108	−0.3	31.0

NA = Not available.

Trees of the U.S.

Source: American Forests

More than 870 native and naturalized species of trees grow in the U.S. The trunk of the world's largest known living tree, the General Sherman giant sequoia in California, weighs almost 1,400 tons—about as much as 15 adult blue whales. To determine the country's largest trees (or "national champions"), American Forests uses a point system whereby trunk circumference, or girth (in inches) + height (in feet) + ¼ average crown spread (in feet) = total points. As of June 2, 2014.

10 Largest National Champion Trees

Tree type	Girth at 4.5 ft (in.)	Height (ft)	Crown spread (ft)	Total points	Location
Giant sequoia (Gen. Sherman tree)	1,020	274	107	1,321	Sequoia National Park, CA
Coast redwood	950	321	75	1,290	Jedediah Smith Redwoods State Park, CA
Coast redwood	895	307	83	1,223	Jedediah Smith Redwoods State Park, CA
Coast redwood	845	349	89	1,216	Redwood National Park, CA
Coast redwood	867	299	101	1,191	Prairie Creek Redwoods State Park, CA
Western redcedar	761	159	45	931	Olympic National Park, WA
Sitka spruce	668	191	96	883	Olympic National Park, WA
Coast Douglas-fir	505	281	71	804	Olympic National Forest, WA
Port-Orford-cedar	522	242	35	773	Coos, OR
Common baldcypress	647	96	74	762	Cat Island, LA

Selected Endangered Animal Species

Source: Fish and Wildlife Service, U.S. Dept. of the Interior

Common name	Scientific name	Range
Albatross, Amsterdam	Diomedia amsterdamensis	Amsterdam Island, Indian Ocean
Antelope, giant sable	Hippotragus niger variani	Angola
Armadillo, giant	Priodontes maximus	Venezuela, Guyana to Argentina
Bandicoot, desert	Perameles eremiana	Australia
Bat, gray	Myotis grisescens	Central, southeastern U.S.
Bear, Mexican grizzly	Ursus arctos	Mexico
Bobcat, Mexican	Lynx rufus escuinapae	Central Mexico
Camel, Bactrian	Camelus bactrianus	Mongolia, China
Caribou, woodland	Rangifer tarandus caribou	Canada, northern U.S.
Cheetah	Acinonyx jubatus	Africa to India
Chimpanzee, pygmy	Pan paniscus	Dem. Rep. of the Congo
Condor, California	Gymnogyps californianus	U.S. (AZ, CA, OR), Mexico (Baja California)
Crane, whooping	Grus americana	Canada, Mexico, U.S. (Rocky Mts. to Carolinas)
Crocodile, American	Crocodylus acutus	U.S. (FL), Mexico, Caribbean Sea, Central and South America
Deer, Columbian white-tailed	Odocoileus virginianus leucurus	U.S. (OR, WA)
Dolphin, Chinese river	Lipotes vexillifer	China
Elephant, Asian	Elephas maximus	South-central and southeastern Asia
Fox, northern swift	Vulpes velox hebes	U.S. (northern Great Plains), Canada
Frog, mountain yellow-legged	Rana muscosa	U.S. (CA, NV)
Gorilla	Gorilla gorilla	Central and West Africa
Hawk, Hawaiian	Buteo solitarius	U.S. (HI)
Hyena, brown	Parahyaena brunnea	Southern Africa
Impala, black-faced	Aepyceros melampus petersi	Angola, Namibia
Kangaroo, Tasmanian forester	Macropus giganteus tasmaniensis	Australia (Tasmania)
Leopard	Panthera pardus	Africa, Asia
Lion, Asiatic	Panthera leo persica	Turkey to India
Manatee, West Indian	Trichechus manatus	Southeastern U.S., Caribbean Sea, Mexico
Monkey, spider	Ateles geoffroyi frontatus	Costa Rica, Nicaragua
Ocelot	Leopardus pardalis	U.S. (AZ, TX) to Central and S America
Orangutan	Pongo pygmaeus	Borneo, Sumatra
Ostrich, West African	Struthio camelus spatzi	Western Sahara
Otter, marine	Lontra felina	Peru south to Straits of Magellan
Panda, giant	Ailuropoda melanoleuca	China
Panther, Florida	Puma concolor coryi	U.S. (LA, AR to SC, FL)
Parakeet, golden	Aratinga guarouba	Brazil
Parrot, imperial	Amazona imperialis	West Indies (Dominica)
Penguin, Galapagos	Spheniscus mendiculus	Ecuador (Galapagos Islands)
Puma, eastern	Puma concolor couguar	Eastern N America (presumed extinct in wild)
Rhinoceros, black	Diceros bicornis	Sub-Saharan Africa
Salamander, Chinese giant	Andrias davidianus	Western China
Sea-lion, Steller	Eumetopias jubatus	U.S. (AK, CA, OR, WA), Russia, Canada, N Pacific Ocean
Squirrel, Carolina northern flying	Glaucomys sabrinus coloratus	U.S. (NC, TN)
Tiger	Panthera tigris	Asia
Tortoise, Galapagos	Geochelone nigra	Ecuador (Galapagos Islands)
Whale, gray	Eschrichtius robustus	N Pacific Ocean, Bering Sea
Whale, humpback	Megaptera novaeangliae	All major oceans
Wolf, red	Canis rufus	Southeastern U.S.
Woodpecker, ivory-billed	Campephilus principalis	South-central and southeastern U.S., Cuba
Yak, wild	Bos mutus	China (Tibet), India
Zebra, mountain	Equus zebra zebra	South Africa

Status of Endangered and Threatened Species, 2014

Source: Fish and Wildlife Service, U.S. Dept. of the Interior; as of June 2014

Group	Endangered		Threatened		Total species[1]	U.S. species with recovery plans
	U.S.	Foreign	U.S.	Foreign		
Mammals	70	256	20	20	366	62
Birds	80	212	17	16	325	86
Reptiles	14	70	21	20	125	36
Amphibians	20	8	14	1	43	17
Fishes	83	11	71	1	166	103
Clams	75	2	13	0	90	71
Snails	34	1	12	0	47	29
Insects	60	4	10	0	74	40
Arachnids	12	0	0	0	12	12
Crustaceans	22	0	3	0	25	18
Corals	0	0	2	0	2	0
Animal subtotal	**470**	**564**	**183**	**58**	**1,275**	**474**
Flowering plants	688	1	152	0	841	641
Conifers and cycads	2	0	1	2	5	3
Ferns and allies	28	0	2	0	30	26
Lichens	2	0	0	0	2	2
Plant subtotal	**720**	**1**	**155**	**2**	**878**	**672**
Grand total	**1,190**	**565**	**338**	**60**	**2,153**	**1,146**

(1) 19 animal species are counted more than once in the above table, primarily because these animals have distinct population segments, each with its own individual listing status. The dual status species, all tallied as endangered, are (U.S.) California tiger salamander, chinook salmon, chum salmon, coho salmon, green sea turtle, loggerhead sea turtle, mountain yellow-legged frog, piping plover, roseate tern, sockeye salmon, steelhead, Steller sea-lion; (foreign) argali, broad-snouted caiman, chimpanzee, dugong, leopard, loggerhead sea turtle, saltwater crocodile.

METEOROLOGY

National Weather Service Watches and Warnings

Source: National Weather Service, National Oceanic and Atmospheric Admin. (NOAA), U.S. Dept. of Commerce; *Glossary of Meteorology*, American Meteorological Society

The National Weather Service issues watches, warnings, and advisories for specific geographic areas to alert people to the possibility or imminent arrival of severe weather or of flooding. Often the weather hazard is a convective storm (a storm involving upward and downward movement of heat and moisture). A severe thunderstorm or tornado watch is issued when a severe convective storm, covering a relatively small geographic area or moving in a narrow path, is sufficiently intense to threaten life and property. Excessive localized convective rains are not classified as severe storms but are often the product of severe local storms. Such rainfall may result in phenomena, such as flash floods, that threaten life and property. Lightning occurs with all thunderstorms and, along with flash floods, is a leading cause of storm deaths and injuries.

Cyclone: Atmospheric circulation of winds rotating counterclockwise in the Northern Hemisphere and clockwise in the Southern Hemisphere. Tornadoes, hurricanes/typhoons, and the lows shown on weather maps are all examples of cyclones. Cyclones are usually accompanied by precipitation or stormy weather.

Severe thunderstorm: Thunderstorm (any local atmospheric disturbance) that produces a tornado, winds of at least 50 knots (58 mph), and/or hail at least 1 in. in diameter. A severe thunderstorm watch indicates conditions are favorable for the development of a severe thunderstorm within 4 to 8 hours. A severe thunderstorm warning indicates a severe thunderstorm has been sighted by radar or reported by a spotter.

Tornado: Violently rotating column of air that extends from the base of a thunderstorm to the ground. On a local scale, it is the most destructive of all atmospheric phenomena. Tornado paths range from a few feet to more than 100 mi long (average 5 mi) and from a few feet to more than 1 mi in diameter (avg. 220 yds). The average forward speed is 30 mph, and wind speeds can reach to more than 200 mph. A rotating column of air over water, whether or not linked to a thunderstorm, is called a **waterspout.**

Tropical storm: Cyclone that develops over tropical or subtropical waters with 1-min. sustained surface winds between 34 and 63 knots (39-73 mph). A tropical storm watch is issued when tropical storm conditions pose a threat to specified coastal areas within 48 hours. A tropical storm warning is issued when such conditions are expected in a specified coastal area within 36 hours.

Hurricane: Tropical cyclone having 1-min. sustained surface winds of 64 knots (74 mph) or more. (In the western North Pacific Ocean, west of the International Date Line, such storms are known as **typhoons.**) The hurricane-force winds form a circle or oval, sometimes as wide as 300 mi in diameter. In the lower latitudes, hurricanes usually move W or NW at 10-15 mph. When the center approaches 25° to 30° N, the direction of motion often changes to the NE, with increased forward speed. In the Atlantic, hurricane season is June 1-Nov. 30.

Hurricane season is May 15-Nov. 30 in the eastern Pacific. A hurricane warning is issued when a hurricane is forecast for an area within 36 hours.

Winter storm and **blizzard:** A winter storm watch is issued when there is a potential for heavy snow or significant ice accumulations, usually at least 24-36 hours in advance. A winter storm warning is issued when a winter storm is producing or is forecast to produce heavy snow or significant ice accumulations. A blizzard warning is issued for winter storm conditions where winds are 35 mph or more, there is sufficient falling and/or blowing snow that frequently reduces visibility to less than ¼ mi, and the conditions are expected to prevail for at least 3 hours.

River flooding: Occurs when rains, sometimes coupled with melting snow, quickly fill river basins with an excess of water. Torrential rains from decaying hurricanes or tropical systems are also a major cause. **Coastal flooding:** Tropical storm and hurricane winds or intense offshore low-pressure systems can drive ocean water inland. Coastal floods can also be produced by sea waves called **tsunamis,** produced by earthquakes or underwater volcanic eruptions or landslides. **Flash flooding:** Usually due to copious amounts of rain falling in a short time. Ice can also cause flash flooding. When ice accumulates at natural or artificial obstructions, it can stop the flow of water. The resulting buildup of water can lead to flooding upstream. If the jam suddenly gives way, a flash flood can happen downstream. Flash flooding typically occurs within 6 hours of the causative event.

Flash floods account for the majority of flood deaths in the U.S. and are the leading cause of deaths associated with thunderstorms. Urbanization significantly increases runoff because less rain is absorbed by the terrain, making flash flooding in urban areas extremely dangerous. Streets can become swift-moving rivers, and basements can fill with water.

A (flash) flood watch indicates flooding or flash flooding is possible within a designated area. A (flash) flood warning indicates flooding is in progress, imminent, or highly likely.

National Weather Service Marine Warnings and Advisories

Primary sources of dissemination are commercial radio, TV, U.S. Coast Guard radio stations, and NOAA VHF radio broadcasts. The NOAA Weather Radio All Hazards (NWR) network broadcasts on seven frequencies between 162.40 and 162.55 MHz. These broadcasts can usually be received within about 40 mi of the transmission site using a special radio receiver. The following are examples of the warnings and advisories that may be addressed to mariners.

Small craft advisory: Alerts mariners to sustained weather and/or sea conditions, present or forecast, potentially hazardous to small boats, including winds 20-33 knots (23-38 mph) and/or dangerous wave conditions. The advisory is also issued when sea or lake ice exists that could be hazardous to small boats. Criteria vary depending on region and type of marine environment.

Special marine warning: Indicates potentially hazardous weather conditions not covered by existing marine warnings.

The conditions are usually of short duration (2 hours or less) and involve wind speeds of 34 knots (39 mph) or more, and/or hail at least ¾ in. in diameter or waterspouts.

Gale warning: Indicates winds of 34-47 knots (39-54 mph) not directly associated with a tropical storm are forecast for the area.

Storm warning: Indicates winds 48-63 knots (55-73 mph) not directly associated with a tropical storm are forecast for the area.

Hurricane and Tornado Classifications

Source: National Weather Service, NOAA, U.S. Dept. of Commerce

The Saffir-Simpson Hurricane Wind Scale, created by Herbert Saffir and expanded upon by Robert Simpson, rates a hurricane's intensity from 1 to 5. The scale, updated in 2012, provides examples of the type of damage and impacts associated with winds of the indicated intensity. The Fujita (or F) Scale was created by T. Theodore Fujita in 1971 to classify tornadoes. The Enhanced Fujita Scale, an update, was implemented in the U.S. in 2007. It uses 3-sec. gusts estimated at the point of damage based on a judgment of eight levels of damage to 28 indicators.

Saffir-Simpson Wind Scale (Hurricanes)			Enhanced Fujita Scale (Tornadoes)	
Category	Wind speed[1]	Summary of damage	Rank	3-sec. gust
1	74-95 mph	Very dangerous winds will produce some damage.	EF-0	65-85 mph
2	96-110 mph	Extremely dangerous winds will cause extensive damage.	EF-1	86-110 mph
3	111-129 mph	Devastating damage will occur.	EF-2	111-135 mph
4	130-156 mph	Catastrophic damage will occur.	EF-3	136-165 mph
5	Over 156 mph	Catastrophic damage will occur.	EF-4	166-200 mph
			EF-5	Over 200 mph

(1) 1-min. sustained winds.

Monthly Normal Mean Temperatures, Precipitation in U.S. Cities

Source: National Climatic Data Center, NESDIS, NOAA, U.S. Dept. of Commerce

Normals are averages covering a 30-year period. The temperature and precipitation normals given here are based on records for 1981-2010. Temperatures listed below represent means of the normal daily maximum and normal daily minimum temperatures for each month. For stations that did not have continuous records from the same site for the entire 30 years, the means have been adjusted to the record at the present site. (*) = city station. Other figures are for airport stations. T = Temperature in Fahrenheit; P = Precipitation in inches.

	Jan.		Feb.		Mar.		Apr.		May		June		July		Aug.		Sept.		Oct.		Nov.		Dec.	
Station	T	P	T	P	T	P	T	P	T	P	T	P	T	P	T	P	T	P	T	P	T	P	T	P
Albany, NY	23	2.6	26	2.2	35	3.2	48	3.2	58	3.6	67	3.8	72	4.1	70	3.5	62	3.3	50	3.7	40	3.3	29	2.9
Albuquerque, NM	36	0.4	41	0.5	48	0.5	56	0.6	66	0.5	75	0.7	78	1.5	76	1.6	69	1.1	58	1.0	45	0.6	36	0.5
Anchorage, AK	17	0.7	20	0.7	27	0.6	37	0.5	48	0.7	55	1.0	59	1.8	57	3.3	49	3.0	35	2.0	22	1.2	19	1.1
Asheville, NC	37	3.7	40	3.8	47	3.8	55	3.3	63	3.7	71	4.7	74	4.3	73	4.4	66	3.8	56	2.9	47	3.7	39	3.6
Atlanta, GA	43	4.2	47	4.7	54	4.8	62	3.4	70	3.7	77	4.0	80	5.3	79	3.9	74	4.5	63	3.4	54	4.1	45	3.9
Atlantic City, NJ	33	3.2	35	2.9	42	4.2	52	3.6	61	3.4	71	3.1	76	3.7	74	4.1	67	3.2	56	3.4	47	3.3	37	3.7
Baltimore, MD	33	3.1	36	2.9	44	3.9	54	3.2	54	4.0	72	3.5	77	4.1	75	3.3	68	4.0	56	3.3	47	3.3	37	3.4
Barrow, AK	–13	0.1	–14	0.1	–13	0.1	2	0.2	21	0.2	36	0.3	41	1.0	39	1.1	32	0.1	17	0.4	–2	0.2	–8	0.1
Birmingham, AL	44	4.8	48	4.5	55	5.2	63	4.4	71	5.0	78	4.4	81	4.8	81	3.9	75	3.9	64	3.4	54	4.9	46	4.5
Bismarck, ND	13	0.4	18	0.5	30	0.9	44	1.3	56	2.4	65	3.2	71	2.9	70	2.3	59	1.6	45	1.3	29	0.7	16	0.5
Boise, ID	31	1.2	37	1.0	45	1.4	51	1.2	59	1.4	68	0.7	76	0.3	75	0.2	65	0.6	53	0.8	40	1.4	31	1.6
Boston, MA	29	3.4	32	3.3	38	4.3	48	3.7	58	3.7	67	3.7	73	3.4	72	3.4	65	3.4	54	3.9	45	4.0	35	3.8
Buffalo, NY	25	3.2	26	2.5	34	2.9	46	3.0	57	3.5	66	3.7	71	3.2	70	3.3	63	3.9	52	3.5	41	4.0	30	3.9
Burlington, VT	19	2.1	22	1.8	31	2.2	45	2.8	57	3.5	66	3.7	71	4.2	69	3.9	61	3.6	48	3.6	38	3.1	26	2.4
Caribou, ME	10	2.7	14	2.2	25	2.5	39	2.7	52	3.3	61	3.5	66	4.1	64	3.8	55	3.3	43	3.5	32	3.6	18	3.3
Charleston, SC	48	3.7	52	3.0	58	3.7	65	2.9	73	3.0	79	5.7	82	6.5	81	7.2	76	6.1	67	3.8	59	2.4	51	3.1
Charleston, WV	34	3.0	38	3.2	46	3.9	56	3.2	64	4.3	72	4.3	75	4.9	74	3.7	67	3.3	57	2.7	47	3.7	37	3.3
Chicago, IL	24	1.7	28	1.8	38	2.5	49	3.4	59	3.7	69	3.5	74	4.0	72	4.9	65	3.2	53	3.2	40	3.2	28	2.3
Cleveland, OH	28	2.7	31	2.3	38	2.9	50	3.5	60	3.7	69	3.5	74	3.5	72	3.5	65	3.8	54	3.1	44	3.6	32	3.1
Columbus, OH	30	2.7	33	2.3	42	3.0	53	3.4	63	4.2	72	4.0	75	4.8	73	4.3	67	2.8	55	2.6	44	3.2	34	3.0
Dallas-Ft. Worth, TX	46	2.1	50	2.7	58	3.5	66	3.1	74	4.9	81	3.8	85	2.2	86	1.9	78	2.6	68	4.2	57	2.7	47	2.6
Denver, CO	31	0.4	33	0.3	40	0.9	47	1.7	57	2.2	67	2.0	74	1.9	73	1.6	63	1.0	51	1.0	38	0.6	30	0.3
Des Moines, IA	23	1.0	27	1.3	39	2.3	52	3.9	62	4.7	72	4.5	76	4.4	74	4.1	66	3.1	53	2.6	39	2.2	26	1.4
Detroit, MI	26	2.0	28	2.0	37	2.3	49	2.9	60	3.4	69	3.5	74	3.4	72	3.0	64	3.3	52	2.5	42	2.8	30	2.4
Dodge City, KS	32	0.6	36	0.7	44	1.6	54	1.8	64	2.9	74	3.2	80	2.8	78	2.8	69	1.7	57	1.7	43	0.8	33	0.8
Duluth, MN	10	1.0	15	0.8	26	1.5	40	2.4	51	3.2	60	4.2	66	3.9	64	3.7	56	4.1	43	2.9	29	2.1	15	1.2
Fairbanks, AK	–8	0.6	–1	0.4	11	0.3	33	0.3	49	0.6	60	1.4	63	2.2	56	1.9	45	1.1	24	0.8	3	0.7	–4	0.6
Fresno, CA	47	2.2	52	2.0	57	2.0	62	1.0	70	0.4	77	0.2	83	0.0	82	0.0	76	0.2	66	0.6	54	1.1	47	1.8
Galveston, TX*	53	3.7	55	3.0	61	2.9	68	2.2	76	3.0	82	4.8	84	3.9	84	3.4	80	5.4	73	4.2	64	3.4	56	3.4
Grand Rapids, MI	24	2.1	27	1.8	36	2.4	48	3.4	59	4.0	68	3.8	73	3.6	71	3.6	63	4.3	51	3.3	40	3.5	29	2.5
Helena, MT	23	0.4	28	0.3	36	0.6	45	1.0	54	1.9	62	2.1	70	1.2	68	1.2	58	1.1	46	0.7	33	0.5	22	0.4
Honolulu, HI	73	2.3	73	2.0	75	2.0	76	0.6	78	0.6	80	0.3	81	0.5	82	0.7	80	1.8	78	2.4	75	3.2	73	3.2
Houston, TX	53	3.4	56	3.2	63	3.4	70	3.3	77	5.1	82	5.9	84	3.8	85	3.8	80	4.1	72	5.7	62	4.3	54	3.7
Huron, SD	17	0.5	22	0.6	33	1.5	47	2.3	58	3.1	68	3.9	74	2.8	72	2.4	62	2.5	48	1.8	33	0.9	19	0.5
Indianapolis, IN	28	2.7	32	2.3	42	3.6	53	3.8	63	5.1	72	4.3	75	4.6	74	3.1	67	3.1	55	3.1	44	3.7	32	3.2
Jackson, MS	46	5.0	50	4.8	57	5.0	64	5.0	72	4.4	79	4.1	82	4.8	81	4.2	76	3.6	65	3.9	56	4.8	48	5.2
Jacksonville, FL	53	3.3	56	3.2	62	4.0	67	2.6	74	2.5	80	6.5	82	6.6	82	6.8	78	8.2	70	3.9	62	2.1	55	2.8
Juneau, AK	28	5.4	30	4.1	34	3.8	41	2.9	49	3.4	55	3.2	57	4.6	56	5.7	50	8.6	42	8.6	33	6.0	30	5.8
Kansas City, MO	29	1.1	34	1.5	44	2.4	55	3.7	65	5.2	74	5.2	78	4.5	77	3.9	68	4.6	56	3.4	44	2.2	32	1.5
Knoxville, TN	38	4.3	42	4.3	50	4.3	59	4.0	67	4.5	75	3.8	78	5.1	78	3.3	71	3.2	60	2.5	50	4.0	41	4.5
Lander, WY	22	0.4	25	0.6	36	1.2	44	1.9	53	2.2	63	1.3	71	0.8	70	0.6	59	1.1	46	1.3	31	0.9	21	0.6
Lexington, KY	33	3.2	37	3.2	46	4.1	55	3.6	64	5.3	73	4.4	77	4.7	75	3.3	68	2.9	57	3.1	46	3.5	36	3.9
Little Rock, AR	41	3.6	45	3.7	53	4.7	62	5.1	71	4.9	79	3.7	83	3.3	83	2.6	75	3.2	64	4.9	53	5.3	43	5.0
Los Angeles, CA*	58	3.1	59	3.8	61	2.4	63	0.9	66	0.3	69	0.1	73	0.0	74	0.0	73	0.2	69	0.7	62	1.0	58	2.3
Louisville, KY	35	3.2	39	3.2	48	4.2	58	4.0	67	5.3	76	3.8	79	4.2	78	3.3	71	3.1	60	3.2	49	3.6	38	3.8
Marquette, MI*	19	1.8	21	1.3	29	2.0	40	2.5	51	2.5	60	2.7	67	2.8	67	2.6	59	3.2	47	3.1	35	2.6	24	2.0
Memphis, TN	41	4.0	46	4.4	54	5.2	63	5.5	72	5.3	80	3.6	83	4.6	82	2.9	75	3.1	64	4.0	53	5.5	44	5.7
Miami, FL	68	1.6	70	2.3	73	3.0	76	3.1	80	5.3	83	9.7	84	6.5	84	8.9	83	9.9	80	6.3	75	3.3	71	2.0
Milwaukee, WI	22	1.8	26	1.7	35	2.3	46	3.6	56	3.4	66	3.9	72	3.7	71	4.0	63	3.2	51	2.7	39	2.7	27	2.0
Minneapolis, MN	16	0.9	21	0.8	33	1.9	48	2.7	59	3.4	69	4.2	74	4.0	71	4.3	62	3.1	49	2.4	34	1.8	20	1.2
Mobile, AL	50	5.7	54	5.1	60	6.1	66	4.8	74	5.1	80	6.1	82	7.2	82	7.0	78	5.1	68	3.7	60	5.1	52	5.1
Moline, IL	23	1.5	27	1.6	39	2.9	51	3.6	62	4.3	72	4.5	75	4.3	74	4.5	65	3.1	53	3.0	40	2.6	27	2.2
Nashua, NH	24	3.7	27	3.2	35	4.3	46	4.0	57	3.9	66	4.3	71	3.7	70	4.5	62	3.4	50	4.7	40	4.1	30	3.7
Nashville, TN	38	3.8	42	3.9	50	4.1	59	4.0	68	5.5	76	4.1	79	3.6	79	3.2	72	3.4	60	3.0	50	4.3	40	4.2
New Orleans, LA	53	5.2	57	5.3	63	4.6	69	4.6	77	4.6	82	8.1	83	5.9	83	6.0	80	5.1	71	3.6	63	4.3	56	5.3
New York, NY*	33	3.7	35	3.1	43	4.4	53	4.5	62	4.2	71	4.4	77	4.6	76	4.4	68	4.3	57	4.4	48	4.0	38	4.0
Newark, NJ	32	3.5	35	2.9	43	4.3	53	4.2	63	4.1	72	4.0	77	4.8	76	3.7	68	4.3	57	3.6	47	3.7	37	3.8
Norfolk, VA	40	3.4	43	3.1	49	3.7	58	3.4	67	3.4	75	4.3	80	5.1	78	5.5	72	4.8	62	3.4	53	3.2	44	3.3
Oklahoma City, OK	39	1.4	44	1.6	52	3.1	61	3.1	70	4.7	78	4.9	83	2.9	83	2.6	74	4.1	63	3.7	51	2.0	41	1.9
Omaha, NE	24	0.7	28	0.9	40	2.0	52	3.0	62	4.8	72	4.2	77	3.8	75	3.6	66	2.7	53	2.2	39	1.6	26	1.0
Philadelphia, PA	33	3.0	36	2.7	44	3.8	54	3.6	64	3.7	73	3.4	78	4.4	77	3.5	69	3.8	58	3.2	48	3.0	38	3.6
Phoenix, AZ	56	0.9	60	0.9	65	1.0	73	0.3	82	0.1	91	0.0	95	1.0	94	1.0	88	0.6	77	0.6	64	0.7	55	0.9
Pittsburgh, PA	29	2.7	32	2.7	40	3.1	52	3.2	61	4.2	69	4.0	73	3.9	71	3.5	65	3.3	53	2.5	43	3.4	33	2.9
Portland, ME	22	3.4	26	3.3	34	4.2	44	4.3	54	4.0	63	3.8	69	3.3	68	3.1	60	3.7	49	4.9	39	4.9	29	4.0
Portland, OR	41	4.9	44	3.7	48	3.7	52	2.7	58	2.5	64	1.7	69	0.7	70	0.7	65	1.5	55	3.0	47	5.6	40	5.5
Providence, RI	29	3.9	32	3.3	39	5.0	49	4.4	59	3.6	68	3.6	74	3.2	73	3.9	65	3.9	54	4.5	45	4.5	34	4.2
Raleigh, NC	41	3.5	45	3.2	52	4.1	60	2.9	68	3.3	76	3.5	80	4.7	79	4.3	72	4.4	61	3.3	52	3.1	44	3.1
Rapid City, SD	25	0.3	27	0.4	35	0.9	45	1.8	55	3.2	65	2.5	73	2.1	72	1.6	61	1.3	48	1.4	35	0.5	25	0.4
Reno, NV	36	1.0	40	1.0	46	0.8	51	0.5	60	0.5	68	0.5	73	0.2	73	0.2	65	0.4	54	0.5	43	0.5	35	1.0
Richmond, VA	38	3.0	41	2.8	49	4.0	58	3.3	67	4.7	74	4.5	78	4.7	76	4.1	70	3.9	58	3.3	50	3.2	41	3.3
St. Louis, MO	32	2.4	36	2.2	46	3.3	57	3.7	67	4.7	76	4.3	81	3.9	79	3.0	70	3.1	59	3.3	47	3.3	35	2.8
Salt Lake City, UT	30	1.3	34	1.3	44	1.8	51	2.0	60	2.0	70	1.0	79	0.6	77	0.7	66	1.2	53	1.5	40	1.5	30	1.4
San Antonio, TX	52	1.8	56	1.8	62	2.3	69	2.1	77	4.0	82	4.1	85	2.0	85	2.6	80	3.0	71	4.1	61	2.3	53	1.9
San Diego, CA	57	2.0	58	2.3	59	1.8	62	0.8	64	0.1	66	0.1	70	0.0	72	0.0	71	0.2	67	0.6	62	1.0	56	2.4
San Francisco, CA	50	4.2	53	4.1	55	3.0	57	1.3	60	0.5	62	0.1	64	0.0	65	0.0	65	0.2	62	1.0	56	2.4	51	4.0
San Juan, PR	78	3.8	78	2.4	79	2.0	80	4.7	82	5.9	83	4.4	83	5.1	84	5.5	84	5.8	83	5.6	81	6.4	79	5.0
Santa Fe, NM	32	0.6	36	0.5	43	0.8	50	0.7	60	0.9	69	1.1	73	1.8	71	2.6	64	1.6	53	1.4	40	0.7	31	0.8
Savannah, GA	50	3.7	53	2.8	59	3.7	66	3.1	73	3.0	80	6.0	82	6.6	77	4.6	68	3.7	59	2.4	52	2.7	31	0.8
Seattle, WA	42	5.6	43	3.5	47	3.7	52	2.7	56	1.9	61	1.6	66	0.7	66	0.9	61	1.5	53	3.5	46	6.6	41	5.4
Spokane, WA	30	1.8	33	1.3	40	1.6	47	1.3	55	1.6	62	1.3	70	0.6	69	0.7	60	0.7	48	1.2	36	2.3	27	2.3
Springfield, MO	33	2.5	37	2.5	46	3.6	56	4.3	65	5.1	73	4.9	78	3.7	76	3.8	69	4.6	58	3.6	46	4.2	35	3.0
Tampa, FL	61	2.6	63	2.8	67	3.0	72	2.0	78	2.1	82	6.7	83	7.1	83	7.8	82	6.5	75	2.9	69	1.6	63	2.5
Washington, DC	36	2.8	39	2.6	47	3.5	57	3.1	66	4.0	75	3.8	80	3.7	78	2.9	71	3.7	60	3.4	50	3.2	40	3.1
Wilmington, DE	32	3.0	35	2.7	43	3.9	53	3.5	63	4.0	72	3.8	78	4.6	75	3.7	68	3.7	56	3.4	47	3.1	37	3.5
Windsor Locks, CT	26	3.2	30	2.9	38	3.6	49	3.7	60	4.4	69	4.4	74	4.2	72	3.9	64	3.9	52	4.4	42	3.9	32	3.4

Normal High and Low Temperatures, Precipitation in U.S. Cities

Source: National Climatic Data Center, NESDIS, NOAA, U.S. Dept. of Commerce

The normal temperatures and precipitation data given here are based on records for the period 1981-2010. The extreme temperatures are based on records from the time of each station's installation. (*) = city station. Other figures are for airport stations.

State	Station	NORMAL TEMPERATURE (°F) January Max.	January Min.	July Max.	July Min.	EXTREME TEMPERATURE (°F) Highest	Lowest	AVG. ANNUAL PRECIPITATION (in.)
Alabama	Mobile	61	40	91	73	105	3	66.15
Alaska	Anchorage	23	11	65	52	85	−34	16.58
Alaska	Barrow	−7	−20	47	35	79	−56	4.53
Alaska	Juneau	33	24	64	50	90	−22	62.27
Arizona	Phoenix	67	46	106	78	122	17	8.03
Arkansas	North Little Rock	50	33	92	73	111	−6	50.03
California	Los Angeles	65	49	74	64	110	23	12.82
California	San Francisco	56	44	72	55	106	20	20.65
Colorado	Denver	44	17	89	59	105	−19	14.92
Connecticut	Windsor Locks	35	18	85	63	102	−26	45.85
Delaware	Wilmington	40	25	86	68	103	11	43.08
District of Columbia	Washington–Reagan	43	29	88	71	105	−5	39.74
Florida	Jacksonville	65	41	92	73	105	7	52.39
Florida	Miami	76	60	91	77	98	30	61.90
Georgia	Atlanta	52	34	89	71	105	−8	49.71
Georgia	Savannah	60	39	92	73	105	3	47.96
Hawaii	Honolulu	80	66	88	75	95	53	17.10
Idaho	Boise	38	25	91	60	111	−25	11.73
Illinois	Chicago	31	17	84	64	104	−27	36.89
Indiana	Indianapolis	36	21	85	66	104	−27	42.44
Iowa	Des Moines	31	14	86	67	108	−26	36.01
Kansas	Dodge City	44	20	93	66	110	−21	21.60
Kentucky	Lexington	41	25	86	66	103	−21	45.17
Kentucky	Louisville	43	27	89	70	106	−22	44.91
Louisiana	New Orleans	62	45	91	75	102	11	62.66
Maine	Caribou	20	1	76	55	96	−41	38.49
Maine	Portland	31	13	79	59	103	−39	47.25
Maryland	Baltimore	41	24	87	67	105	−7	41.88
Massachusetts	Boston	36	22	81	65	102	−12	43.77
Michigan	Detroit	32	19	83	64	104	−21	33.47
Michigan	Grand Rapids	31	18	83	62	100	−22	38.27
Michigan	Sault Ste. Marie	23	8	76	54	98	−36	32.95
Minnesota	Duluth	19	2	76	55	97	−39	30.96
Minnesota	Minneapolis	24	8	83	64	105	−34	30.61
Mississippi	Jackson	56	35	92	72	107	2	54.14
Missouri	Kansas City	38	20	88	68	109	−23	38.86
Missouri	St. Louis	40	24	89	71	107	−18	40.96
Montana	Helena	33	13	86	54	105	−42	11.22
Nebraska	Omaha	33	14	87	66	114	−23	30.62
Nevada	Reno	46	25	92	58	108	−16	7.40
New Hampshire	Concord	31	10	82	58	102	−37	40.61
New Jersey	Atlantic City	42	25	86	67	106	−11	41.75
New Mexico	Albuquerque	47	26	90	66	107	−17	9.45
New York	Albany	31	15	82	61	100	−28	39.35
New York	Buffalo	31	19	80	62	99	−20	40.48
New York	New York–Central Park*	38	27	84	69	106	−15	49.94
North Carolina	Raleigh	51	31	90	70	105	−9	43.34
North Dakota	Bismarck	23	2	85	57	112	−44	17.85
Ohio	Cleveland	34	22	83	64	104	−20	39.14
Ohio	Columbus	37	23	85	66	102	−22	39.31
Oklahoma	Oklahoma City	50	29	94	72	110	−8	36.52
Oregon	Portland	47	36	81	58	107	−3	36.03
Pennsylvania	Philadelphia	40	26	87	69	104	−7	41.53
Pennsylvania	Pittsburgh	36	21	83	63	103	−22	38.19
Puerto Rico	San Juan	83	72	89	78	98	60	56.35
Rhode Island	Providence	37	21	83	64	104	−13	47.18
South Carolina	Charleston	59	38	91	73	105	6	51.03
South Dakota	Huron	27	7	86	61	112	−41	22.90
South Dakota	Rapid City	37	13	87	58	111	−31	16.29
Tennessee	Memphis	50	33	92	74	108	−13	53.68
Tennessee	Nashville	47	28	89	68	107	−17	47.25
Texas	Dallas-Fort Worth	56	36	96	75	113	−1	36.14
Texas	Houston	63	43	94	75	109	7	49.77
Utah	Salt Lake City	37	22	93	65	107	−30	16.10
Vermont	Burlington	27	10	81	60	101	−30	36.82
Virginia	Norfolk	48	33	87	72	105	−3	46.53
Virginia	Richmond	47	28	90	69	105	−12	43.60
Washington	Seattle-Tacoma	47	37	76	56	103	0	37.49
Washington	Spokane	34	25	83	56	108	−25	16.56
West Virginia	Charleston	43	26	85	66	104	−16	44.03
Wisconsin	Milwaukee	29	16	80	64	103	−26	34.76
Wyoming	Lander	33	10	87	56	101	−37	12.66

Mean annual snowfall (in.), selected cities: Based on climate normals 1981-2010: Albany, NY, 59.1; Anchorage, AK, 74.5; Boston, MA, 43.8; Burlington, VT, 81.2; Lander, WY, 91.4; Sault Ste. Marie, MI, 123.4.

Wettest spot: Mt. Waialeale in Kauai, HI, may be the rainiest place in the U.S. It has a recorded average annual rainfall of 422 in.

Temperature extremes: The highest temperature ever recorded under standard conditions in the U.S. was 134°F in Death Valley, CA, on July 10, 1913. The record low in the U.S. was −80°F at Prospect Creek, AK, Jan. 23, 1971.

Annual Climatological Data for U.S. Cities, 2013

Source: National Climatic Data Center, NESDIS, NOAA, U.S. Dept. of Commerce

Station	Elev. (ft)	TEMPERATURE (°F) Highest	Date	Lowest	Date	PRECIPITATION Total (in.)	Greatest in 24 hrs. (in.)	Date	Snowfall[1] Total snowfall (in.)	Greatest in 24 hrs. (in.)	Date	FASTEST WIND[2] MPH	Date	NO. OF DAYS Prec. 0.01 in. or more	Snow, sleet 1 in. or more
Albany, NY	281	96	7/19	-5	12/17	43.83	2.46	5/21-22	60.1	6.5	12/14	39	6/17	132	16
Albuquerque, NM	5,308	105	6/27	8	1/13	9.32	1.49	9/14-15	7.9	3.7	12/5	64	7/26	55	2
Anchorage, AK	222	81	6/18+	-11	12/17	24.83	1.27	9/10-11	103.4	8.5	12/14	35	3/12	131	30
Asheville, NC	2,174	90	6/12	18	12/25	75.22	3.50	5/4-5	0.7	0.3	3/20	37	11/27	145	0
Atlanta, GA	974	92	8/29	22	11/28	66.02	4.14	6/5	0.4	0.4	11/27	43	6/13	128	0
Atlantic City, NJ	117	97	7/19	9	1/26+	46.12	2.86	6/7-8	15.3	2.3	2/1	40	3/6	127	7
Baltimore, MD	196	97	7/18	11	1/25	42.93	4.10	10/10-11	9.5	3.2	3/25	36	11/18	119	4
Barrow, AK	38	66	6/13	-39	2/7	8.41	0.57	7/27-28	60.8	3.9	12/9	49	1/13	145	11
Birmingham, AL	630	95	8/31	18	11/28	67.87	3.57	6/5	2.1	2.1	1/17	39	3/18	125	1
Bismarck, ND	1,654	102	8/20	-31	12/23	26.75	2.43	10/4-5	52.2	17.3	4/14	44	8/29	118	11
Boise, ID	2,861	110	7/1	-7	12/9	9.55	0.72	10/28	20.4	2.5	1/28	47	8/22	69	9
Boston, MA	180	99	7/19	4	1/24	40.36	3.58	6/7-8	71.3	24.8	2/8	48	1/31	129	12
Buffalo, NY	717	92	7/16	.1	1/25	46.02	2.79	9/21	75.3	7.8	2/2	46	11/1	174	21
Burlington, VT	348	98	7/19	-12	1/24	44.99	2.53	5/23-24	70.1	9.6	2/8	37	4/7	175	20
Caribou, ME	626	94	7/15	-21	1/18	50.16	3.81	7/1	133.3	15.5	12/15	38	2/17	173	34
Charleston, SC	48	97	8/12	27	3/4	58.11	3.41	3/23-24	T	T	2/16	40	2/26	109	0
Chicago, IL	658	96	8/30+	-6	12/10	42.09	5.42	4/17-18	44.3	9.2	3/5	43	11/17	144	12
Cleveland, OH	805	96	9/10	6	1/3	41.85	2.43	12/21-22	58.4	5.5	12/14	46	11/17	159	17
Columbus, OH	812	95	9/10	7	1/22	41.55	2.32	10/6-7	42.9	5.1	12/6	51	7/10	141	13
Dallas-Ft. Worth, TX	562	105	8/31+	19	12/10	29.40	3.26	1/8-9	2.4	2.0	12/6	45	8/9	73	1
Denver, CO	5,382	100	7/11	-15	12/5	17.60	2.39	9/14-15	74.1	9.1	2/24	53	9/22	82	20
Des Moines, IA	971	104	8/30	-14	12/24	31.99	3.57	4/17-18	54.7	6.1	1/30	49	5/27	106	15
Detroit, MI	631	95	7/19	-1	1/22	39.90	2.46	8/12	53.4	7.7	12/14	46	11/17	144	18
Duluth, MN	1,429	91	8/25	-22	2/1	30.44	2.03	6/20-21	149.8	11.2	4/18	44	6/21	145	33
Fairbanks, AK	464	92	6/26+	-48	1/27	10.65	0.82	8/19-20	72.0	4.8	12/22	41	11/14	107	29
Fresno, CA	375	110	8/19	27	12/9	3.01	0.52	11/20-21	0.0	0.0	—	31	9/21	23	0
Grand Rapids, MI	788	96	7/19	-2	1/22	45.48	4.25	4/17-18	95.4	5.9	2/2	46	11/17	164	33
Helena, MT	3,867	100	7/2	-17	12/7	10.58	0.98	8/1-2	20.3	4.8	1/10	44	8/1	88	7
Honolulu, HI	18	90	9/15+	59	1/16	16.18	2.06	12/15	—	—	—	35	2/17	83	—
Houston, TX	107	107	6/29	29	1/17	38.84	3.47	9/20	T	T	8/16	43	8/16	90	0
Huron, SD	1,284	100	8/29	-25	12/23	25.19	3.03	10/14-15	61.4	9.0	2/10	69	6/21	113	18
Indianapolis, IN	797	96	9/10	2	12/12	45.92	2.95	12/20-21	28.4	6.2	3/24	49	11/17	124	11
Jackson, MS	296	99	8/8+	22	3/3	64.25	4.93	9/20-21	—	—	—	39	2/25	111	—
Jacksonville, FL	34	96	6/13+	24	2/18	45.22	3.20	2/25	—	—	—	41	8/31	119	—
Kansas City, MO	1,008	100	9/8	-2	12/24	34.48	2.58	9/19	33.8	9.2	2/21	38	11/17	98	10
Knoxville, TN	982	93	7/17	19	2/17	69.35	3.03	7/6-7	4.6	1.4	1/17	37	10/31	142	1
Lander, WY	5,560	94	7/22	-19	12/5	15.54	1.60	4/8-9	138.0	12.6	4/8	54	9/7	67	29
Lexington, KY	984	95	7/17	5	2/1	59.53	2.90	6/26-27	11.1	2.1	2/2	47	12/21	139	3
Los Angeles, CA	326	92	8/30	38	1/15+	3.65	0.79	1/23-24	—	—	—	36	4/8	23	—
Louisville, KY	484	96	8/28	9	2/1	53.60	6.97	10/5-6	12.9	3.5	12/6	43	7/10	131	5
Marquette, MI	1,415	92	8/25	-20	2/4	39.94	2.17	11/13	230.6	14.4	3/11	—	—	199	58
Memphis, TN	286	98	9/8	21	11/28	59.43	4.18	5/21	T	T	12/30+	43	1/29	114	0
Miami, FL	29	94	7/24	45	3/4	70.42	5.64	10/2-3	—	—	—	28	9/15	146	—
Milwaukee, WI	680	95	9/10	-5	12/30	40.02	2.61	4/17-18	59.4	8.0	12/22	48	4/11	126	18
Minneapolis, MN	874	98	5/14	-13	12/24	32.77	2.79	7/13	68.9	6.4	4/18	45	6/21	129	18
Mobile, AL	212	95	8/7+	25	11/28	69.28	4.48	5/1-2	0.0	0.0	—	44	4/3	121	0
Moline, IL	607	99	9/9	-13	12/24	39.24	4.46	6/24	44.0	6.1	2/26	49	6/24	110	13
Nashville, TN	574	97	7/17	16	11/28	54.88	3.62	12/5-6	2.4	0.5	11/25	45	1/30	139	0
New Orleans, LA	28	101	7/18	11	1/24+	42.94	3.72	6/6-7	30.4	6.6	3/8	45	1/30	113	7
New York, NY	7	97	8/7	32	11/29	66.37	3.75	5/10-11	—	—	—	44	4/24	126	—
Newark, NJ	161	98	7/18	11	1/23	46.32	4.60	6/7-8	29.6	6.3	2/8	30	3/6	118	8
Norfolk, VA	69	96	6/13	23	12/26+	45.65	3.27	7/22	1.8	1.8	1/25	45	1/31	121	1
North Little Rock, AR	565	99	9/8	18	12/7	51.30	4.90	12/20-21	1.7	1.0	12/6	29	1/30	120	1
Oklahoma City, OK	1,284	103	8/31	5	12/7	52.78	5.64	5/31	10.4	3.5	2/12	56	5/31	86	3
Philadelphia, PA	62	98	7/18	12	1/23	55.89	8.27	7/28-29	19.1	8.6	12/8	41	7/20	119	6
Phoenix, AZ	1,106	119	6/29	29	1/15	8.42	1.79	11/21-22	—	—	—	47	8/26	27	—
Pittsburgh, PA	1,175	91	7/19+	4	1/23	36.65	2.66	7/9-10	67.3	5.0	3/6	41	11/17	165	28
Portland, ME	72	95	7/19	-6	12/17	43.87	2.79	9/12-13	97.0	16.6	2/9	43	2/9	131	16
Portland, OR	223	97	6/30	12	12/8	26.72	1.98	9/28-29	—	—	—	33	12/6	136	—
Providence, RI	53	98	7/19	4	1/24	45.46	4.08	6/7-8	42.8	10.6	2/8	46	2/8	130	12
Raleigh-Durham, NC	430	96	7/24	18	11/25	50.70	5.43	6/6-7	1.7	0.7	2/16	47	4/19	119	0
Rapid City, SD	3,153	101	8/27	-15	12/23+	21.70	2.66	10/3-4	100.5	20.0	4/9	55	10/11	97	20
Reno, NV	4,407	105	7/21+	-2	12/9	4.02	1.03	8/8	6.1	2.6	12/3	47	7/1	35	2
Richmond, VA	167	96	7/17+	14	1/23	53.68	2.74	10/9-10	8.6	3.8	3/24	41	1/31	123	4
St. Louis, MO	710	103	8/31	7	12/24	42.68	2.48	4/18	31.4	12.4	3/24	48	11/17	115	5
Salt Lake City, UT	4,224	105	6/29+	-2	1/14	11.62	0.91	12/18-19	64.0	9.3	1/27	37	8/23	89	18
San Antonio, TX	821	108	6/29	29	12/7	32.00	12.17	5/24-25	T	T	4/2	40	6/11	77	0
San Diego, CA	81	89	8/30	39	1/14	5.57	1.38	11/21-22	—	—	—	26	2/20	28	—
San Francisco, CA	89	89	5/2	34	12/9	3.38	0.91	11/19-20	—	—	—	48	5/21	25	—
San Juan, PR	10	96	9/29	69	12/5	85.13	9.42	7/17-18	0.0	0.0	—	35	5/27	240	0
Sault Ste. Marie, MI	727	92	7/16	-15	12/30+	48.78	3.60	9/9-10	162.9	9.5	2/19	35	11/18	182	54
Savannah, GA	143	97	8/12	26	2/18	54.07	3.86	2/12-13	0.0	0.0	—	41	6/10	115	0
Scottsbluff, NE	3,949	102	9/6	-17	12/5	13.37	1.09	9/22-23	55.2	7.4	4/9	56	8/6	92	16
Seattle, WA	434	93	9/11	19	12/7	32.56	1.93	1/8-9	1.1	1.1	12/20	43	11/2	152	1
Spokane, WA	2,384	99	7/1	-2	12/8	11.36	1.12	6/20	26.3	6.9	1/7	43	9/15	101	9
Springfield, MO	1,280	96	8/31	1	12/10	51.84	2.64	7/29-30	25.0	4.3	12/9	38	5/30	114	9
Tampa, FL	40	95	8/12	38	11/28	42.48	3.57	6/1-2	T	T	7/10	33	6/6	116	0
Washington, DC	3	97	7/17	15	1/23	44.24	2.86	6/28	4.4	1.4	3/25	46	6/28	118	1
Wilmington, DE	77	97	7/17	9	1/23	48.35	3.42	6/6-7	16.7	8.5	12/8	37	3/6	125	4
Windsor Locks, CT	165	97	7/19	-4	2/10	51.71	3.79	8/9	53.8	13.4	2/8	36	1/31	130	12

(+) = Indicates value for extreme also occurred on an earlier date(s). (T) = Trace amount. — = Data not available or unreported. (1) Comprises all forms of frozen precipitation, including hail and sleet. (2) Sustained for at least 2 min., not peak gust.

Record Temperatures by State

Source: National Climatic Data Center, NESDIS, NOAA, U.S. Dept. of Commerce
(as of May 2, 2014)

State	°F	LOWEST TEMPERATURE Latest date	Station	Approx. elevation (ft)	°F	HIGHEST TEMPERATURE Latest date	Station	Approx. elevation (ft)
Alabama	−27	Jan. 30, 1966	New Market	732	112	Sept. 6, 1925	Centerville	220
Alaska	−80	Jan. 23, 1971	Prospect Creek Camp	955	100	June 27, 1915	Fort Yukon	445
Arizona	−40	Jan. 7, 1971	Hawley Lake	8,180	128	June 29, 1994	Lake Havasu City	505
Arkansas	−29	Feb. 13, 1905	Gravette	1,260	120	Aug. 10, 1936	Ozark	390
California	−45	Jan. 20, 1937	Boca	5,575	134	July 10, 1913	Greenland Ranch	−194
Colorado	−61	Feb. 1, 1985	Maybell	5,944	114	July 11, 1954[1]	Sedgwick	3,584
Connecticut	−32	Jan. 22, 1961[1]	Coventry	480	106	July 15, 1995[1]	Danbury	405
Delaware	−17	Jan. 17, 1893	Millsboro	20	110	July 21, 1930	Millsboro	20
Florida	−2	Feb. 13, 1899	Tallahassee	192	109	June 29, 1931	Monticello	98
Georgia	−17	Jan. 27, 1940	CCC Fire Camp F-16	1,000	112	Aug. 20, 1983[1]	Greenville	960
Hawaii	12	May 17, 1979	Mauna Kea Observ.	13,773	100	Apr. 27, 1931	Pahala	840
Idaho	−60	Jan. 18, 1943	Island Park	6,290	118	July 28, 1934	Orofino	1,320
Illinois	−36	Jan. 5, 1999	Congerville	635	117	July 14, 1954	East St. Louis	410
Indiana	−36	Jan. 19, 1994	New Whiteland	785	116	July 14, 1936	Collegeville	650
Iowa	−47	Feb. 3, 1996[1]	Elkader	788	118	July 20, 1934	Keokuk	651
Kansas	−40	Feb. 13, 1905	Lebanon	1,874	121	July 24, 1936[1]	Alton	1,591
Kentucky	−37	Jan. 19, 1994	Shelbyville	730	114	July 28, 1930	Greensburg	590
Louisiana	−16	Feb. 13, 1899	Minden	200	114	Aug. 10, 1936	Plain Dealing	290
Maine	−50	Jan. 16, 2009	Big Black River	885	105	July 10, 1911[1]	North Bridgton	449
Maryland	−40	Jan. 13, 1912	Oakland	2,420	109	July 10, 1936[1]	Cumberland Frederick	899 380
Massachusetts	−35	Jan. 12, 1981[1]	Chester	640	107	Aug. 2, 1975	Chester New Bedford	640 70
Michigan	−51	Feb. 9, 1934	Vanderbilt	905	112	July 13, 1936	Mio Stanwood	960 830
Minnesota	−60	Feb. 2, 1996	Tower	1,485	115	July 29, 1917	Beardsley	1,089
Mississippi	−19	Jan. 30, 1966	Corinth	420	115	July 29, 1930	Holly Springs	502
Missouri	−40	Feb. 13, 1905	Warsaw	705	118	July 14, 1954	Warsaw Union	705 540
Montana	−70	Jan. 20, 1954	Rogers Pass	5,545	117	July 5, 1937[1]	Medicine Lake	1,942
Nebraska	−47	Dec. 22, 1989[1]	Oshkosh	3,390	118	July 24, 1936[1]	Minden	2,160
Nevada	−50	Jan. 8, 1937	San Jacinto	5,203	125	June 29, 1994	Laughlin	605
New Hampshire	−50	Jan. 22, 1885	Mt. Washington	6,267	106	July 4, 1911	Nashua	140
New Jersey	−34	Jan. 5, 1904	River Vale	70	110	July 10, 1936	Runyon	20
New Mexico	−50	Feb. 1, 1951	Gavilan	7,425	122	June 27, 1994	Waste Isolat. Pilot Plant	3,411
New York	−52	Feb. 18, 1979	Old Forge	1,748	108	July 22, 1926	Troy	35
North Carolina	−34	Jan. 21, 1985	Mt. Mitchell	6,240	110	Aug. 21, 1983	Fayetteville	186
North Dakota	−60	Feb. 15, 1936	Parshall	1,952	121	July 6, 1936	Steele	1,885
Ohio	−39	Feb. 10, 1899	Milligan	875	113	July 21, 1934	Gallipolis	669
Oklahoma	−31	Feb. 10, 2011	Nowata	NA	120	Aug. 12, 1936[1]	Altus Irrigation Res. Sta.	1,380
Oregon	−54	Feb. 10, 1933[1]	Seneca	4,660	119	Aug. 10, 1898[1]	Pendleton	1,040
Pennsylvania	−42	Jan. 5, 1904	Smethport	1,469	111	July 10, 1936[1]	Phoenixville	105
Rhode Island	−28	Jan. 11, 1942	Wood River Junction	49	104	Aug. 2, 1975	Providence	60
South Carolina	−19	Jan. 21, 1985	Caesars Head	3,200	113	June 29, 2012	Columbia	242
South Dakota	−58	Feb. 17, 1936	McIntosh	2,175	120	July 15, 2006[1]	Fort Pierre	1,590
Tennessee	−32	Dec. 30, 1917	Mountain City	2,503	113	Aug. 9, 1930[1]	Perryville	371
Texas	−23	Feb. 8, 1933	Seminole	3,336	120	June 28, 1994[1]	Monahans	2,547
Utah	−50	Jan. 5, 1913	East Portal	7,615	117	July 5, 1985	Saint George	2,770
Vermont	−50	Dec. 30, 1933	Bloomfield	1,040	107	July 7, 1912	Vernon	226
Virginia	−30	Jan. 21, 1985	Mountain Lake Bio. Station	3,870	110	July 15, 1954[1]	Balcony Falls	732
Washington	−48	Dec. 30, 1968	Mazama Winthrop	2,106 1,749	118	Aug. 5, 1961[1]	Ice Harbor Dam	368
West Virginia	−37	Dec. 30, 1917	Lewisburg	2,251	112	July 10, 1936[1]	Martinsburg	534
Wisconsin	−55	Feb. 4, 1996[1]	Couderay	1,300	114	July 13, 1936	Wisconsin Dells	835
Wyoming	−66	Feb. 9, 1933	Riverside Ranger Sta.	6,500	115	July 15, 1988[1]	Diversion Dam	5,575

NA = Not available. (1) Also on earlier dates at the same or other places.

Tropical Cyclone Names in 2015

Source: National Weather Service, NOAA, U.S. Dept. of Commerce

Atlantic: Ana, Bill, Claudette, Danny, Erika, Fred, Grace, Henri, Ida, Joaquin, Kate, Larry, Mindy, Nicholas, Odette, Peter, Rose, Sam, Teresa, Victor, Wanda. If there are more than 21 named Atlantic storms in one season, remaining storms take names from the Greek alphabet, starting with Alpha. (To date, this has only occurred in 2005.)

Eastern North Pacific: Andres, Blanca, Carlos, Dolores, Enrique, Felicia, Guillermo, Hilda, Ignacio, Jimena, Kevin, Linda, Marty, Nora, Olaf, Patricia, Rick, Sandra, Terry, Vivian, Waldo, Xina, York, Zelda.

World Temperature and Precipitation

Source: World Meteorological Organization (WMO)

Average daily maximum and minimum temperatures and annual precipitation based on records for the period 1961-90. Records of extreme temperatures include all available years of data for a given location and are usually for a longer period. Surface elevations are supplied by the WMO and may differ from figures in other sections of The World Almanac.

Station	Surface elevation (ft)	Temperature (°F)						Avg. annual precipitation (in.)
		AVERAGE DAILY				EXTREME		
		January		July				
		Max.	Min.	Max.	Min.	Max.	Min.	
Algiers, Algeria	82	61.7	42.6	87.1	65.3	NA	NA	27.0
Athens, Greece	49	56.1	44.6	88.9	73.0	NA	NA	14.6
Auckland, New Zealand	20	74.8	61.2	58.5	46.4	NA	NA	49.4
Bangkok, Thailand	66	89.6	69.8	90.9	77.0	104	51	59.0
Beijing, China	177	34.9	15.1	87.4	70.9	105	−17	22.7
Berlin, Germany	190	35.2	26.8	73.6	55.2	107	−4	23.3
Bogotá, Colombia	8,357	67.3	41.7	64.6	45.5	75	21	32.4
Bucharest, Romania	298	34.7	22.1	83.8	60.1	105	−18	23.4
Budapest, Hungary	456	34.2	24.8	79.7	59.7	103	−10	20.3
Buenos Aires, Argentina	82	85.8	67.3	59.7	45.7	104	22	45.2
Cairo, Egypt	243	65.8	48.2	93.9	71.1	118	34	1.0
Cape Town, South Africa	138	79.0	60.3	63.3	44.6	105	28	20.5
Caracas, Venezuela	2,739	79.9	60.8	81.3	66.0	96	45	36.1
Casablanca, Morocco	203	62.8	47.1	77.7	66.7	NA	NA	16.8
Copenhagen, Denmark	16	35.6	28.4	68.9	55.0	NA	NA	NA
Damascus, Syria	2,004	54.3	32.9	97.2	61.9	NA	NA	5.6
Dubai, United Arab Emirates[1]	16	75.2	56.7	105.1	84.0	117	45	3.7
Dublin, Ireland	279	45.7	36.5	66.0	52.5	86	8	28.8
Geneva, Switzerland	1,364	38.3	27.9	76.3	53.2	101	−3	35.6
Havana, Cuba	164	78.4	65.5	88.3	74.8	NA	NA	46.9
Hong Kong, China	203	65.5	56.5	88.7	79.9	97	32	87.2
Istanbul, Turkey	108	47.8	37.2	82.8	65.3	105	7	27.4
Jerusalem, Israel	2,483	53.4	39.4	83.8	63.0	107	26	23.2
Karachi, Pakistan	69	78.4	50.7	91.6	81.3	117	34	8.6
Lagos, Nigeria	125	90.0	72.3	82.8	72.1	NA	NA	59.3
Lima, Peru	43	79.0	66.9	66.4	59.4	NA	NA	0.2
London, England	203	44.1	32.7	71.1	52.3	99	2	29.7
Manila, Philippines	79	85.8	74.8	89.1	76.8	NA	NA	49.6
Mexico City, Mexico	7,570	70.3	43.7	73.8	53.2	NA	NA	33.4
Montreal, Canada	118	21.6	5.2	79.2	59.7	100	−36	37.0
Mumbai (Bombay), India	36	85.3	66.7	86.2	77.5	110	46	85.4
Nairobi, Kenya	5,897	77.9	50.9	71.6	48.6	NA	NA	41.9
New Delhi, India[2]	709	69.8	45.7	94.5	80.2	113	34	31.3
Paris, France	213	42.8	33.6	75.2	55.2	105	−1	25.6
Prague, Czech Republic	1,197	32.7	22.5	73.9	53.2	98	−16	20.7
Reykjavik, Iceland	200	35.4	26.6	55.9	46.9	76	−3	31.5
Riyadh, Saudi Arabia	2,034	68.4	46.8	109.0	81.3	120	28	NA
Rome, Italy	79	53.8	35.4	88.2	62.1	NA	NA	33.0
San Salvador, El Salvador	2,037	86.5	61.3	86.2	66.4	105	45	68.3
São Paulo, Brazil	2,598	81.1	65.7	71.2	53.1	NA	NA	57.4
Seoul, South Korea	285	33.4	19.2	83.3	70.9	NA	NA	NA
Shanghai, China	23	45.9	32.9	88.9	76.6	104	10	43.8
Singapore	52	85.8	73.6	87.4	75.6	NA	NA	84.6
Stockholm, Sweden	171	30.7	23.0	71.4	56.1	97	−26	21.2
Sydney, Australia	10	79.5	65.5	62.4	43.9	114	32	46.4
Tehran, Iran	3,906	45.0	30.0	98.2	75.2	109	−5	9.1
Tokyo, Japan	118	49.1	34.2	83.8	72.1	NA	NA	55.4
Toronto, Canada	567	27.5	12.0	80.2	57.6	105	−26	30.8

NA = Not available. (1) Records are for 1974-91. (2) Records are for 1971-90.

Speed of Winds in the U.S.

Source: National Climatic Data Center, NESDIS, NOAA, U.S. Dept. of Commerce

Based on available records through 2013. Maximum speeds are highest 3-sec. wind speeds.

Station	Avg. mph	Max. mph	Station	Avg. mph	Max. mph	Station	Avg. mph	Max. mph
Albuquerque, NM	8.3	89	Helena, MT	6.9	64	Oklahoma City, OK	11.4	76
Anchorage, AK	7.0	71	Honolulu, HI	10.4	48	Omaha, NE	10.0	92
Atlanta, GA	8.4	71	Houston, TX	7.5	70	Philadelphia, PA	9.3	75
Baltimore, MD	7.4	72	Indianapolis, IN	9.5	85	Phoenix, AZ	6.1	77
Birmingham, AL	6.2	72	Jackson, MS	6.1	72	Pittsburgh, PA	7.9	62
Bismarck, ND	9.4	78	Jacksonville, FL	6.7	77	Portland, ME	8.0	72
Boise, ID	7.7	68	Little Rock, AR	7.0	87	Portland, OR	7.5	59
Boston, MA	11.6	76	Los Angeles, CA	7.5	53	Providence, RI	9.3	64
Buffalo, NY	10.3	75	Louisville, KY	7.8	75	Richmond, VA	7.7	72
Burlington, VT	8.3	63	Miami, FL	8.5	104	St. Louis, MO	9.1	70
Charleston, SC	7.9	67	Milwaukee, WI	10.2	70	Salt Lake City, UT	8.5	75
Chicago, IL	9.9	70	Minneapolis, MN	9.7	71	San Francisco, CA	10.6	71
Cleveland, OH	9.6	68	Mobile, AL	7.6	83	San Juan, PR	7.8	93
Dallas-Ft. Worth, TX	10.5	78	Mount Washington, NH	35.1	231	Seattle, WA	7.9	69
Denver, CO	10.0	72	Nashville, TN	7.2	67	Sioux Falls, SD	10.2	77
Des Moines, IA	9.9	77	New Orleans, LA	8.0	77	Washington, DC	9.0	74
Detroit, MI	9.6	78	New York, NY	6.7	62	Wichita, KS	11.5	101
Fairbanks, AK	4.5	59	Newark, NJ	9.9	78	Wilmington, DE	8.5	76

Wind Chill Temperature

Source: National Weather Service, NOAA, U.S. Dept. of Commerce

Temperature and wind combine to cause heat loss from body surfaces. For example, a temperature of 5°F, plus a 10-mph wind, causes body heat loss equal to that which would occur in −10°F with no wind. In other words, a 10-mph wind makes 5°F feel like −10°F. Wind speeds greater than 45 mph have little additional chilling effect. Direct sunlight can increase the wind chill temperature 10° to 15°F. When the wind chill temperature falls within the shaded area, frostbite can occur in 30 min. or less.

Wind speed (mph) / Calm	Air temperature (°F)																	
	40	35	30	25	20	15	10	5	0	−5	−10	−15	−20	−25	−30	−35	−40	−45
	Wind chill temperature (°F)																	
5	36	31	25	19	13	7	1	−5	−11	−16	−22	−28	−34	−40	−46	−52	−57	−63
10	34	27	21	15	9	3	−4	−10	−16	−22	−28	−35	−41	−47	−53	−59	−66	−72
15	32	25	19	13	6	0	−7	−13	−19	−26	−32	−39	−45	−51	−58	−64	−71	−77
20	30	24	17	11	4	−2	−9	−15	−22	−29	−35	−42	−48	−55	−61	−68	−74	−81
25	29	23	16	9	3	−4	−11	−17	−24	−31	−37	−44	−51	−58	−64	−71	−78	−84
30	28	22	15	8	1	−5	−12	−19	−26	−33	−39	−46	−53	−60	−67	−73	−80	−87
35	28	21	14	7	0	−7	−14	−21	−27	−34	−41	−48	−55	−62	−69	−76	−82	−89
40	27	20	13	6	−1	−8	−15	−22	−29	−36	−43	−50	−57	−64	−71	−78	−84	−91
45	26	19	12	5	−2	−9	−16	−23	−30	−37	−44	−51	−58	−65	−72	−79	−86	−93

Heat Index

Source: National Weather Service, NOAA, U.S. Dept. of Commerce

The heat index, or apparent temperature, is a measure of how hot it feels when the relative humidity is factored in with the actual air temperature. For example, when air temperature is 100°F, and relative humidity is 50%, it feels as if it's 118°F with no humidity. Full sunlight can make one feel even hotter. On the chart, the shaded area above 103°-105°F apparent temperature corresponds to a level that may cause increasingly severe heat disorders with continued exposure and/or physical activity.

Relative humidity (%)	Air temperature (°F)															
	80	82	84	86	88	90	92	94	96	98	100	102	104	106	108	110
	Apparent temperature (°F)															
40	80	81	83	85	88	91	94	97	101	105	109	114	119	124	130	136
45	80	82	84	87	89	93	96	100	104	109	114	119	124	130	137	
50	81	83	85	88	91	95	99	103	108	113	118	124	131	137		
55	81	84	86	89	93	97	101	106	112	117	124	130	137			
60	82	84	88	91	95	100	105	110	116	123	129	137				
65	82	85	89	93	98	103	108	114	121	128	136					
70	83	86	90	95	100	105	112	119	126	134						
75	84	88	92	97	103	109	116	124	132							
80	84	89	94	100	106	113	121	129								
85	85	90	96	102	110	117	126	135								
90	86	91	98	105	113	122	131									
95	86	93	100	108	117	127										
100	87	95	103	112	121	132										

☐ Caution   ▨ Extreme caution   ▦ Danger   ▧ Extreme danger

Ultraviolet (UV) Index Forecast

Source: National Weather Service (NWS), NOAA, U.S. Dept. of Commerce; U.S. Environmental Protection Agency (EPA); U.S. Food and Drug Administration, U.S. Dept. of Health and Human Services

The NWS and EPA developed and began offering a UV index in 1994 in response to increasing incidences of skin cancer, cataracts, and other effects from exposure to the sun's harmful rays. In 2004, they adapted their index to the Global Solar UV Index sponsored by the World Health Organization. The UV index is now a regular element of NWS atmospheric forecasts.

The UV index, ranging from 0 to 11+, is an indication of the expected intensity of UV radiation reaching the Earth's surface during the solar noon hour (the time of day when the sun appears to have reached its highest point in the sky; it depends on location and time of year). The lower the UV index value, the less the radiation. The UV index forecast is produced daily for 58 cities by the NWS Climate Prediction Center and uses the following scale.

UV index	Exposure	Minimum precautions
0-2	Low	Sunscreen with an SPF of at least 15
3-5	Moderate	Sunscreen, covering up
6-7	High	Sunscreen, hat, UV-blocking sunglasses, avoid sun 10 AM-4 PM
8-10	Very high	Same as above
11+	Extreme	Same as above

UV levels are influenced by:

Ozone. Ozone, a form of oxygen, the molecules of which consist of three atoms rather than two, absorbs UV radiation. The more ozone, the lower the UV radiation at the surface.

Sun height. The higher the sun is in the sky, the higher the UV radiation level.

Cloudiness. UV radiation levels are highest under cloudless skies. Even with cloud cover, UV radiation levels can be high due to the scattering of UV radiation by water molecules and fine particles in the atmosphere.

Reflectivity. Reflective surfaces intensify UV exposure. White sand reflects about 15% of UV radiation that reaches it; sea foam, 25%; snow, as much as 80%; water, up to 100% depending on reflection angle.

Altitude. At higher altitudes, UV radiation travels a shorter distance to reach Earth's surface so there is less atmosphere to absorb the rays. For every 1,000 m (3,281 ft) one travels above sea level, UV levels increase by 10%-12%. Snow and lack of pollutants intensify UV exposure at higher altitudes.

Latitude. The closer a location is to the equator, the higher the UV radiation level.

Further information. For precautions to take after learning the UV index value, call the EPA's Stratospheric Ozone Protection Hotline at (800) 296-1996. For questions on scientific aspects, visit the NWS Climate Prediction Center online at www.cpc.ncep.noaa.gov.

Lightning

Source: National Weather Service, NOAA, U.S. Dept. of Commerce

Lightning is a powerful electric discharge, or spark, that can occur in the atmosphere when an imbalance of positive and negative charges develops. It can travel within a cloud, between clouds, between a cloud and clear sky, or between a cloud and the ground. Lightning generally accompanies rainstorms but it can also be seen with snowstorms, volcano eruption clouds, and violent forest fires. In a common form of cloud-to-ground lightning, a negatively charged area in a thunderstorm sends charges down toward positively charged objects. Lightning can travel miles away from the area of a storm.

The transfer of charges in lightning generates a huge amount of heat, sending the temperature in the channel to 50,000°F or more and causing the air within it to expand rapidly. The sound of that expansion is thunder. Sound travels more slowly than light, so lightning is usually observed before thunder is heard.

An estimated 25 mil cloud-to-ground lightning bolts happen in the U.S. each year. They killed an annual average of 51 people in 1984-2013. This is a small number compared to U.S. deaths from fire (about 3,000 a year) and motor vehicle crashes (more than 30,000 annually in recent years), but it is still significant. In comparison, tornadoes caused an average of 75 deaths a year and hurricanes an average of 47 over the same 30-year time period. According to preliminary figures from the National Weather Service, 23 people were struck and killed by lightning in 2013; 145 more were injured.

Most lightning deaths and injuries occur in summer when people are outdoors. If outdoors, one should run to a safe building or vehicle when thunder is first heard, lightning is seen, or dark threatening clouds are observed developing overhead. Even while indoors, one is advised to stay away from windows and doors and to avoid contact with anything conducting electricity, including corded phones, computers and other electrical equipment, and tubs, showers, and other plumbing. One should stay inside until 30 min. after the last occurrence of lightning or thunder.

More information about lightning can be found online at www.lightningsafety.noaa.gov.

Global Temperature Extremes and Precipitation Records

Source: World Weather/Climate Extremes Archive, World Meteorological Organization (WMO) Commission for Climatology
(records in each category ranked from most to least extreme)

Highest Temperature Extremes

Continent	Highest temp. (°F)	Place	Elevation (ft)	Date
North America	134	Death Valley, CA, U.S. (Greenland Ranch/Furnace Creek)	-179	July 10, 1913
Africa	131[1]	Kebili, Tunisia	125	July 7, 1931
Asia	129.2	Tirat Tsvi, Israel	-722	June 21, 1942
Australia	123	Oodnadatta, South Australia	367	Jan. 2, 1960
South America	120	Rivadavia, Argentina	2,192	Dec. 11, 1905
Europe	118.4	Athens, Greece (and Elefsina, Greece)	774	July 10, 1977
Oceania	108	Tuguegarao, Philippines	676	Apr. 29, 1912
Antarctica	59	Vanda Station (New Zealand), Wright Valley	49	May 1, 1974

(1) Previous record of 136.4°F set on Sept. 13, 1922, in El Azizia, Libya, was invalidated in Sept. 2012 after the WMO determined that an error had been made in recording the temperature.

Lowest Temperature Extremes

Continent	Lowest temp. (°F)	Place	Elevation (ft)	Date
Antarctica	-128.6	Vostok Station (Soviet Union/Russia)	11,220	July 21, 1983
Asia	-90	Verkhoyansk, Russia	350	Feb. 5 and 7, 1892
	-90	Oimekon, Russia	2,625	Feb. 6, 1933
North America	-81.4	Snag, Yukon, Canada	2,120	Feb. 3, 1947
Europe	-72.6	Ust'-Shchugor, Russia	279	Dec. 31, 1978
South America	-27	Sarmiento, Argentina	879	June 1, 1907
Africa	-11	Ifrane, Morocco	5,364	Feb. 11, 1935
Australia	-9.4	Charlotte Pass, New South Wales	5,758	June 29, 1994

Highest Measured Average Annual Precipitation Extremes

Continent	Highest avg. (in.)[1]	Place	Elevation (ft)	Years in averaging period
Asia	467.4	Mawsynram, India	4,695	38
Oceania	460	Mt. Waialeale, Kauai, HI, U.S.	5,148	30
Africa	405	Debundscha, Cameroon	30	32
South America	354	Quibdo, Colombia	230	29
Australia	316.3	Bellenden Ker, Queensland	5,102	34
North America	276	Henderson Lake, British Columbia, Canada	12	15
Europe	183	Crkvica, Bosnia-Herzegovina	4,298	22
Antarctica	>31.5[2]	Along coast of E and W and over the Antarctic Peninsula		3[3]

(1) Official greatest average annual precipitation. The frequently cited record of 523.6 in. in Lloro, Colombia (14 mi SE and at a higher elevation than Quibdo) is an estimate. (2) Water equivalent. (3) July 1996-June 1999.

Lowest Measured Average Annual Precipitation Extremes

Continent	Lowest avg. (in.)	Place	Elevation (ft)	Years in averaging period
South America	0.03	Arica, Chile	213	59
Antarctica	0.08	Amundsen-Scott South Pole Station (U.S.)	9,301	10
Africa	<0.1	Wadi Halfa, Sudan	590	39
North America	1.2	Bataques, Mexico	69	14
Asia	1.8	Aden, Yemen	63	50
Australia	4.05	Troudaninna, South Australia	46	42
Europe	6.4	Astrakhan, Russia	78	25
Oceania	7.41	Mauna Kea Observatory, HI, U.S.	13,780	11[1]

(1) 1972-82.

OCEANOGRAPHY

Tides and Their Causes

Source: National Ocean Service, NOAA, U.S. Dept. of Commerce

The tides are natural phenomena involving the movement of waves in the Earth's large fluid bodies as a result of the gravitational attraction of the sun and moon. These two variable influences combined produce the complex recurrent cycle of the tides. Tides may occur in both oceans and seas; to a limited extent in large lakes and in the atmosphere; and, to a very minute degree, in the Earth itself. The length of time between succeeding tides can vary.

The tide-generating force represents the difference between (1) the centrifugal force produced by Earth's revolution around the common center-of-gravity of the Earth-moon system and (2) the gravitational attraction of the moon acting upon the Earth's overlying waters. The moon is about 390 times closer to Earth than is the sun. So despite its smaller mass, the moon's tide-raising force is two times greater.

The tide-generating forces of the moon and sun acting tangentially to the Earth's surface tend to cause a maximum accumulation of waters at two diametrically opposite points on the Earth's surface and to withdraw compensating amounts of water from all points 90° removed from these tidal bulges. As the Earth rotates beneath the maxima and minima of these tide-generating forces, a sequence of two high tides, separated by two low tides, is produced each lunar day (24 hrs. and 50 min., the time it takes for a specific site on the Earth to rotate from an exact point under the moon to the same point under the moon) in what is called a **semidiurnal tide**. Each ocean basin reacts differently to tidal forces.

Twice each month, when the sun, moon, and Earth are directly aligned—the moon between the Earth and sun (at new moon) or on the opposite side of Earth from the sun (at full moon)—the sun and moon exert gravitational forces in a mutual or additive fashion. The highest high tides and lowest low tides, called **spring tides**, are produced at these times. At two positions 90° in between, the moon and sun's gravitational forces—imposed at right angles—counteract each other to the greatest extent, and the range between high and low tides is reduced, resulting in **neap tides**.

The inclination of the moon's monthly orbit and of the sun to the equator during Earth's yearly passage through its orbit produce a difference in the height of succeeding high and low tides, known as the diurnal inequality. In most cases, this produces a so-called **mixed tide**. In extreme cases, these phenomena may result in a **diurnal tide**, with only one high tide and one low tide each day. There are other monthly and yearly variations in the tides because of the elliptical shape of the orbits.

The range of tides in the open ocean is generally less than in the coastal regions, where the incoming tide can be augmented by the continental shelves, as well as by bays and estuaries. The largest tidal ranges in the world occur in the Bay of Fundy, Canada, where the range of tide reaches 53.5 ft. In New Orleans, the periodic rise and fall of the diurnal tide is affected by the seasonal stages of the Mississippi River, being about 10 in. at low stage and 0 at high.

In every case, actual high or low tide can vary considerably from the average as a result of weather conditions such as strong winds, abrupt barometric pressure changes, or prolonged periods of extreme high or low pressure.

Mean Ranges of Tide

Place	Ft	In.	Place	Ft	In.	Place	Ft	In.
Baltimore, MD	1	2	Key West, FL	1	3	Provincetown, MA	9	3
Biloxi, MS	1	7	Los Angeles, CA	3	10	St. Petersburg, FL	1	7
Boston, MA	9	6	Miami Beach, FL	2	6	San Diego, CA	4	1
Charleston, SC	5	3	New London, CT	2	7	San Francisco, CA	4	1
Eastport, ME	18	4	New York, NY	4	6	San Juan, PR	1	1
Ft. Pulaski, GA	6	11	Newport, RI	3	6	Sandy Hook, NJ	4	8
Galveston, TX	1	0	Philadelphia, PA	6	1	Seattle, WA	7	8
Honolulu, HI	1	3	Portland, ME	9	1	Washington, DC	2	9

Note: Mean range is the difference in height between mean high water and mean low water.

El Niño and La Niña

Source: National Weather Service, NOAA, U.S. Dept. of Commerce

El Niño is a climatically significant disruption of the ocean-atmosphere system characterized by large-scale weakening of trade winds and warming of surface layer waters in the central and eastern equatorial Pacific. The term *El Niño*, Spanish for "the little boy" or "the Christ Child," was originally used by fishing crews to refer to a warm ocean current that appeared around Christmas off the west coast of Ecuador and Peru lasting several months. The term has come to be reserved for exceptionally strong, warm currents that bring heavy rains.

El Niño events generally occur at irregular intervals of two to seven years, at an average of once every three to four years. They typically last 12 to 18 months. The intensity of El Niño events varies depending on the area encompassed by the abnormally warm ocean temperatures. Some are strong, such as in 1982-83 and 1997-98. Others are considerably weaker, such as the 2009-10 event. The eastward extent of warmer-than-normal water varies from episode to episode.

El Niño influences weather around the globe, and its impacts are most clearly seen in the winter. During El Niño years, winter temperatures in the continental U.S. tend to be warmer than normal in the northern states and on the West Coast and cooler than normal in the Southeast. Conditions tend to be wetter than normal over central and southern California, the Southwest and across much of the South, and drier than normal over the northern portions of the Rocky Mountains and in the Ohio Valley. Globally, El Niño brings wetter than normal conditions to Peru and Chile and dry conditions to Australia and Indonesia. It should be noted that El Niño is only one of a number of factors influencing seasonal variations of climate.

La Niña ("the little girl") is characterized by colder than normal sea surface temperatures in the equatorial Pacific. La Niña typically brings wetter, cooler conditions to the Pacific Northwest and drier, warmer conditions to much of the southern U.S. El Niño and La Niña are opposite phases of the El Niño-Southern Oscillation (ENSO) cycle, which involves a shift in tropical sea-level pressure between the Eastern and Western Hemispheres.

NOAA and other agencies monitor these events using satellites, weather balloons, and buoys in the Pacific Ocean. Numerical computer models of the ocean and atmosphere use these data to predict the onset and evolution of El Niño and La Niña. In Sept. 2014, NOAA put the chance of an El Niño occurrence during the Northern Hemisphere fall and winter at 60%-65%.

DISASTERS

Some Notable Aircraft Disasters Since 1937

Source: National Transportation Safety Board; World Almanac research.

Particularly notable disasters are in bold. Asterisk (*) indicates number of deaths includes people on ground. As of Aug. 2014.

Date	Aircraft	Site of accident	Deaths
1937, May 6	**German zeppelin Hindenburg**	**Burned at mooring, Lakehurst, NJ**	**36***
1944, Aug. 23	U.S. Air Force B-24 Liberator bomber	Hit school, Freckleton, England, UK.	61*
1945, July 28	U.S. Army B-25.	Hit Empire State Building after getting lost in fog, New York, NY.	14*
1952, Dec. 20	U.S. Air Force C-124	Crashed at Moses Lake, WA	87
1953, Mar. 3	**Canadian Pacific DH-106 Comet**	**Crashed on takeoff from Karachi, Pakistan; world's first fatal commercial passenger jet crash**	**11**
1953, June 18	U.S. Air Force C-124	Crashed, burned near Tokyo, Japan.	129
1955, Oct. 6	United Airlines DC-4.	Crashed in Medicine Bow Peak, WY	66
1955, Nov. 1	United Airlines DC-6.	Bomb on board exploded near Longmont, CO.	44[1]
1956, June 20	Venezuelan Super Constellation	Crashed into Atlantic off Asbury Park, NJ	74
1956, June 30	TWA Super Const., United DC-7	Collided over Grand Canyon, AZ	128
1960, Dec. 16	United DC-8, TWA Super Const.	Collided over New York, NY, killing all 128 on planes, 6 on ground.	134*
1962, Mar. 16	Flying Tiger Super Constellation	Vanished in W Pacific en route to Philippines from Guam	107
1962, June 3	Air France Boeing 707	Crashed on takeoff from Paris, France.	130
1962, June 22	Air France Boeing 707	Crashed in storm, Guadeloupe, French W Indies	113
1963, Feb. 1	Lebanese Middle East Airlines Vickers Viscount 754, Turkish Mil. Douglas C-47	Collided over Ankara, Turkey, killing all 17 on planes, 87 on ground	104*
1963, Nov. 29	Trans-Canada Air Lines DC-8	Crashed after takeoff from Montreal, QC, Canada.	118
1965, May 20	Pakistani Boeing 720	Crashed at airport in Cairo, Egypt	121
1966, Jan. 24	Air India Boeing 707	Crashed on Mont Blanc, France-Italy.	117
1966, Feb. 4	All-Nippon Boeing 727	Plunged into Tokyo Bay, Japan.	133
1966, Mar. 5	BOAC Boeing 707	Crashed into Mt. Fuji, Japan, after encountering severe turbulence	124
1966, Dec. 24	U.S. military-chartered CL-44	Crashed into village in S Vietnam.	129*
1967, Apr. 20	Globe Air Bristol Britannia	Crashed on approach to airport, Nicosia, Cyprus.	126
1967, July 19	Piedmont Boeing 727, Cessna 310	Collided over Hendersonville, NC.	82
1968, Apr. 20	S. African Airways Boeing 707	Crashed on takeoff from Windhoek, Namibia.	122
1968, May 3	Braniff International Electra	Crashed in storm near Dawson, TX	85
1968, May 12	U.S. Air Force Lockheed C-130B	Hit by enemy mortar while evacuating Kham Duc Camp, S Vietnam	155
1969, Mar. 16	Venezuelan DC-9.	Crashed after takeoff from Maracaibo, Venezuela.	155[2]
1970, July 3	British-chartered DH-106 Comet	Crashed near Barcelona, Spain.	112
1970, July 5	Air Canada DC-8	Crashed near Toronto Intl. Airport, ON, Canada.	108
1970, Nov. 14	Southern Airways DC-9	Crashed into mountains near Huntington, WV.	75[3]
1971, July 30	All-Nippon Boeing 727, Japan Air Force F-86 fighter.	Collided over Morioka, Japan.	162[4]
1971, Sept. 4	Alaska Airlines Boeing 727.	Crashed into mountain near Juneau, AK.	111
1972, May 18	Aeroflot Antonov 10A	Wings separated from fuselage; crashed on approach to Kharkov, USSR.	122
1972, June 18	British European Airways Trident-1C	Crashed near A30 motorway after takeoff from London, Eng., UK.	118
1972, Aug. 14	East German Ilyushin 62	Crashed on takeoff from East Berlin, E Germany	156
1972, Aug. 31	Aeroflot Ilyushin 18V.	Crashed in field near Magnitogorsk, USSR.	101
1972, Oct. 1	Aeroflot Ilyushin 18V.	Crashed into Black Sea, USSR	109
1972, Oct. 13	Aeroflot Ilyushin 62.	Crashed near Moscow, USSR.	174
1972, Dec. 3	Spanish-chartered Convair CV-990	Crashed on takeoff from Canary Islands, Spain.	155
1972, Dec. 29	Eastern Airlines Lockheed Tristar	Crashed on approach to Miami Intl. Airport, FL.	99
1973, Jan. 22	Nigerian-chartered Boeing 707.	Burst into flames upon landing at Kano Airport, Nigeria.	176
1973, Feb. 21	**Libyan Arab Boeing 727**	**Flew off course, shot down by Israeli fighter planes over Sinai Desert**	**108**
1973, Apr. 10	Invicta Airways Vickers Vanguard	Crashed during snowstorm on approach to Basel, Switzerland.	108
1973, June 3	Soviet Supersonic Tu-144	Crashed near Goussainville, France	14[5]
1973, July 11	Varig Airlines (Brazil) Boeing 707.	Crashed on approach to Orly Airport, Paris, France	123
1973, July 31	Delta Airlines DC-9.	Crashed while attempting landing in fog, Logan Airport, Boston, MA	89
1973, Sept. 30	Aeroflot Tupolev 104B	Crashed after takeoff from Sverdlovsk, USSR.	108
1973, Oct. 13	Aeroflot Tupolev 104B	Crashed on approach to Moscow, USSR.	122
1973, Dec. 22	Royal Air Maroc SE 210 Caravelle VIN	Flew into side of a mountain near Tangier, Morocco	106
1974, Mar. 3	Turkish DC-10	Crashed in Ermenonville, near Paris, France.	346
1974, Apr. 22	Pan American Boeing 707	Crashed in Bali, Indonesia.	107
1974, Apr. 27	Aeroflot Ilyushin 18V.	Crashed after takeoff from Leningrad, USSR.	109
1974, Dec. 1	TWA Boeing 727	Crashed on approach in storm, Upperville, VA.	92
1974, Dec. 4	Dutch-chartered DC-8	Crashed in storm near Colombo, Sri Lanka	191
1975, Apr. 4	U.S. Air Force Galaxy C-5A	First mission of Operation Babylift, bringing Vietnamese orphans to U.S., crashed on takeoff near Saigon.	155
1975, Apr. 4	Air Force Galaxy C-5A	Crashed on takeoff nr. Saigon, S Vietnam; carried orphans	172
1975, June 24	Eastern Airlines 727.	Crashed in storm, JFK Airport, New York, NY	113
1975, Aug. 3	Alia Royal Jordanian Boeing 707	Hit mountainside in heavy fog near Agadir, Morocco.	188
1975, Aug. 20	Czechoslovakian Air Ilyushin 62.	Crashed on approach to Damascus, Syria.	126
1976, Mar. 6	Aeroflot Ilyushin 18E.	Crashed between Moscow, USSR, and Yerevan, Armenia.	111
1976, Sept. 10	British Airways Trident, Yugoslavian DC-9	Collided near Zagreb, Yugoslavia.	176
1976, Sept. 19	Turkish Boeing 727.	Hit mountain in southern Turkey.	154
1976, Oct. 13	Lloyd Aero Boliviano Boeing 707	Crashed into soccer field after takeoff from Santa Cruz, Bolivia.	91[6]
1977, Mar. 27	**KLM 747, Pan American 747**	**Collided on runway, Tenerife, Canary Islands, Spain; world's worst airline disaster**	**583**
1977, Nov. 19	TAP Portugal Boeing 727.	Crashed in Madeira, Portugal.	131
1977, Dec. 4	Malaysian Airlines Boeing 737.	Hijacked and forced to fly to Singapore, crashed near Johor Strait.	100
1978, Jan. 1	Air India 747.	Crashed into sea after takeoff from Bombay, India.	213
1978, Sept. 25	Pacific SW Air Boeing 727, Cessna 172.	Collided over San Diego, CA.	144*
1978, Nov. 15	Indonesian-chartered DC-8	Crashed on approach to airport, Colombo, Sri Lanka.	183
1979, May 25	**American Airlines DC-10**	**Crashed after takeoff from O'Hare Airport, Chicago, IL; highest death toll in U.S. aviation history**	**275***
1979, Aug. 11	Aeroflot/Moldova Tu-134, Aeroflot Tu-134	Collided over Ukraine.	178
1979, Nov. 26	Pakistani Boeing 707	Crashed near Jidda, Saudi Arabia	156
1979, Nov. 28	Air New Zealand DC-10	Crashed into mountain after takeoff from Antarctica	257

Date	Aircraft	Site of accident	Deaths
1980, Mar. 14	PLL LOT Ilyushin 62	Crashed making emergency landing, Warsaw, Poland	87[7]
1980, Apr. 25	Dan-Air Services Boeing 727	Crashed into mountain, Tenerife, Canary Islands, Spain	146
1980, July 8	Aeroflot Tupolev 154B	Crashed after takeoff from Alma-Ata, USSR	166
1980, Aug. 19	Saudi Arabian Tristar	Burned after emergency landing in Riyadh, Saudi Arabia	301
1981, Dec. 1	Inex Adria (Yugoslavia) DC-9	Crashed into mountain on island of Corsica, France	180
1982, Jan. 13	Air Florida Boeing 737	Crashed into Potomac R. after takeoff from Washington, DC	78
1982, June 8	VASP (Brazil) Boeing 727	Crashed into mountain near Fortaleza, Brazil	137
1982, June 28	Aeroflot Yokovlev 42	Crashed near Mozyr, USSR	132
1982, July 9	Pan Am Boeing 727	Crashed after takeoff from Kenner, LA, near New Orleans	153*
1983, July 11	Ecuadorean Boeing 737	Inexperienced pilot crashed into hill near Cuenca, Ecuador	119
1983, Sept. 1	**S. Korean Boeing 747**	**Shot down after violating Soviet airspace near Sakhalin; plane apparently misidentified**	**269**
1983, Sept. 23	Gulf Air Boeing 737	Bomb exploded in cargo hold over Mina Jebel Ali, UAE	112
1983, Nov. 27	Avianca Boeing 747	Crashed near Barajas Airport, Madrid, Spain	181
1984, Oct. 11	Aeroflot/East Siberia Tu-154	Crashed into vehicles on runway while landing in poor weather, Omsk, Russia	178*
1985, Feb. 19	Spanish Boeing 727	Crashed into Mt. Oiz, Spain	148
1985, June 23	Air India Boeing 747	Crashed into Atlantic off Ireland after bomb detonated on board	329
1985, July 10	Aeroflot Tupolev 154B	Crashed after takeoff from Uzbekistan, USSR	200
1985, Aug. 2	Delta Air Lines L-1011	Crashed at Dallas-Ft. Worth Airport, TX	135
1985, Aug. 12	**Japan Air Lines Boeing 747**	**Crashed into Mt. Ogura, Japan; world's worst single-plane disaster**	**520**
1985, Dec. 12	Arrow Air DC-8	Crashed after takeoff from Gander, NL, Canada	256[8]
1986, Mar. 31	Mexican Boeing 727	Crashed NW of Mexico City, Mexico	167
1986, Aug. 31	Aeromexico DC-9, Piper PA-28	Collided over Cerritos, CA	82*
1987, May 9	Polish IL-62M	Crashed after takeoff from Warsaw, Poland	183
1987, Aug. 16	Northwest Airlines MD-82	Crashed after takeoff from Romulus, MI	156
1987, Nov. 28	S. African Boeing 747	Crashed into Indian Ocean near Mauritius	159
1987, Nov. 29	Korean Air Boeing 707	Bomb planted by 2 N. Korean agents exploded while plane over Andaman Sea off Burma	115
1988, Mar. 17	Colombian Boeing 707	Crashed into mountainside near Venezuela border	143
1988, July 3	**Iran Air Airbus A300**	**Misidentified as hostile aircraft, shot down by U.S. Navy warship Vincennes over Persian Gulf**	**290**
1988, Oct. 19	Indian Airlines Boeing 737	Exploded after striking trees near runway, Ahmedabad, India	131
1988, Dec. 21	**Pan Am Boeing 747**	**Libyan agent planted bomb on board; exploded over Lockerbie, Scotland**	**270[9]**
1989, Feb. 8	U.S.-chartered Boeing 707	Crashed into mountain on Azores Isls., off Portugal	144
1989, June 7	Suriname DC-8	Crashed near Paramaribo Airport, Suriname	176
1989, July 19	United Airlines DC-10	Crashed on landing in Sioux City, IA	111
1989, Sept. 3	Cubana Aviacion Ilyushin 62M	Crashed on takeoff from Havana, Cuba	171*
1989, Sept. 19	**UTA DC-10**	**Bomb exploded on board flight from Chad to France while over desert in Niger**	**170**
1989, Oct. 21	Honduran Boeing 727	Crashed into mountain near Tegucigalpa, Honduras	131
1989, Nov. 27	Avianca Boeing 727	Bomb exploded on flight from Bogotá, Colombia	107
1990, Jan. 25	Avianca Air Boeing 707	Crashed on landing at JFK Airport, New York, NY	73
1990, Oct. 2	Xiamen Airlines Boeing 737	Hijacked after takeoff from Xiamen; collided with China Southern Airlines 757 on runway, Guangzhou, China	128
1991, May 26	Lauda-Air (Austria) Boeing 767-300	Exploded over rural Thailand	223
1991, July 11	Nigerian DC-8	Crashed on landing at Jidda, Saudi Arabia	261
1991, Oct. 5	U.S. Air Force Lockheed C-130 Hercules	Crashed after takeoff from Jakarta, Indonesia	135*
1992, July 31	Thai Airbus A300-310	Crashed into mountain N of Kathmandu, Nepal	113
1992, Sept. 26	Nigerian Air Force Lockheed C-130 Hercules	Transport full of military officers crashed near Lagos, Nigeria	158
1992, Sept. 28	Pakistan Intl. Air Airbus A300	Crashed into mountain near Kathmandu, Nepal	167
1992, Oct. 4	**El Al Boeing 747-200F**	**Crashed into 2 apartment bldgs., Amsterdam, Netherlands**	**120***
1992, Nov. 24	China Southern Airlines Boeing 737	Crashed on approach to Giulin, China	141
1992, Dec. 22	Libyan Arab Air Boeing 727	Collided with Libyan Air Force MiG-23 on approach to Tripoli, Libya	159
1993, Feb. 8	Iran Air Tu-154, Iranian Air Force jet	Collided after military jet took off from Tehran, Iran	131
1993, May 19	SAM Colombia Boeing 727	Crashed into mountain near Medellin, Colombia	132
1993, Nov. 20	Macedonian Yakovlev 42D	Crashed into mountain near Skopje, Macedonia	116
1994, Jan. 3	Aeroflot Tu-154	Crashed and exploded after takeoff from Irkutsk, Russia	125*
1994, Apr. 26	China Airlines Airbus A300	Crashed on approach to Nagoya Airport, Japan	264
1994, June 6	China Northwest Airlines Tu-154	Crashed near Xian, China	160
1994, Sept. 8	USAir Boeing 737-300	Crashed near Pittsburgh Intl. Airport, Aliquippa, PA.	132
1994, Oct. 31	American Eagle ATR-72-210	Crashed in field near Roselawn, IN	68
1995, Dec. 18	Zairean Lockheed L-188C Electra	Overloaded charter crashed in Lunda Norte, Angola	141
1995, Dec. 20	American Airlines Boeing 757	Crashed into mountain N of Cali, Colombia	159
1996, Jan. 8	African Air Antonov-32 cargo plane	Crashed into a market in Kinshasa, Zaire; all deaths on ground	237*
1996, Feb. 6	Dominican Boeing 757	Crashed into Atlantic off Dominican Republic	189
1996, Feb. 29	Peruvian Boeing 737	Crashed into hillside near Arequipa, Peru	123
1996, Apr. 3	U.S. Air Force Boeing T-43A	Crashed into mountain near Dubrovnik, Croatia	35[10]
1996, May 11	ValuJet DC-9	Crashed into Florida Everglades after takeoff	110
1996, July 17	Trans World Airlines Boeing 747	Exploded and crashed into Atlantic off Long Island, NY.	230
1996, Aug. 29	Vnukovo Airlines (Russia) Tu-154	Crashed into mountain on Arctic island of Spitsbergen	141
1996, Nov. 7	Nigerian Boeing 727	Crashed into lagoon SE of Lagos, Nigeria	144
1996, Nov. 12	**Saudi Arabian Boeing 747, Kazakh Ilyushin 76 cargo plane**	**Collided near New Delhi, India; world's worst midair collision**	**349**
1996, Nov. 23	Ethiopian Airlines Boeing 767	Hijacked, then crashed into Indian Ocean off the Comoros	127
1997, Aug. 6	Korean Air Boeing 747-300	Crashed into jungle on Guam on approach to airport.	228
1997, Sept. 26	Indonesian Airbus A300	Crashed near airport, Medan, Indonesia	234
1998, Feb. 16	China Airlines Airbus A300	Crashed on approach to airport in Taipei, Taiwan	203*
1998, Sept. 2	Swissair MD-11	Crashed into Atlantic off Nova Scotia, Canada	229
1999, Oct. 31	EgyptAir Boeing 767	Crashed off Nantucket, MA; result of deliberate actions by copilot, motives unknown	217
2000, Jan. 30	Kenya Airways Airbus A310	Crashed into Atlantic after takeoff from Abidjan, Côte d'Ivoire	169

Date	Aircraft	Site of accident	Deaths
2000, Jan. 31	Alaska Airlines MD-83	Crashed into Pacific off coast of Southern CA	88
2000, Apr. 19	Air Philippines Boeing 737-200	Crashed on approach to airport, Davao, Philippines	131
2000, July 25	**Air France Concorde**	**Crashed into hotel after takeoff from Paris; world's first Concorde crash**	**113***
2000, Aug. 23	Gulf Air Airbus A320	Crashed into Persian Gulf on approach to airport in Bahrain	143
2001, July 3	Vladivostokavia Tu-154	Crashed on approach to airport, Irkutsk, Russia	145
2001, Sept. 11	**2 Boeing 767s, 2 Boeing 757s**	**September 11 terrorist attacks**	**265¹¹**
2001, Oct. 8	Cessna 525A Citation, Scandinavian Airlines System (SAS) MD-87	Collided in heavy fog on takeoff from Milan, Italy	118*
2001, Nov. 12	**American Airlines Airbus A300**	**Crashed after takeoff from JFK Airport, New York, NY**	**265***
2002, Feb. 12	Iran Air Tours Tu-154	Crashed in Khorramabad, Iran	119
2002, Apr. 15	Air China Boeing 767	Crashed into mountainside in rain and fog on approach to airport, Pusan, S. Korea	129
2002, May 4	EAS Airlines BAC 1-11	Crashed shortly after takeoff from Kano, Nigeria	149
2002, May 7	China Northern Airlines MD-82	Plunged into sea, apparently after a passenger started fire in cabin, NE China	112
2002, May 25	China Airlines Boeing 747	Broke apart in midair, plunged into Taiwan Strait en route to Hong Kong airport	225
2002, July 27	**Ukraine Air Force Sukhoi Su-27**	**Crashed while performing, Lviv, Ukraine; world's worst air-show crash**	**77¹²**
2002, Aug. 19	Russian Mi-26 transport helicopter	Hit by Chechen missile near Grozny, Chechnya	127
2003, Jan. 8	Turkish Airlines British Aerospace RJ-100	Crashed on approach to airport in Diyarbakir, Turkey	75
2003, Feb. 19	Iranian Revolutionary Guard Ilyushin 76	Crashed into mountain near Kerman, Iran; passengers were Revolutionary Guard members.	275
2003, May 26	Ukrain.-Medit. Airlines Yak-42	Crashed into mountain in fog approaching Trabzon, Turkey; passengers incl. Spanish peacekeepers returning from Afghan.	75
2003, July 8	Sudan Airways Boeing 737-200	Mechanical problems reported shortly after takeoff; crashed upon return to Port Sudan Airport	115
2003, Dec. 25	Union Transp. Africains Boeing 727	Overloading caused crash on takeoff from Cotonou, Benin	141
2004, Jan. 3	Flash Airlines Boeing 737-300	Crashed into Red Sea after takeoff from Sharm el-Sheik, Egypt	148
2004, Aug. 24	Volga-Aviaexpress Tu-134, Sibir Airlines Tu-154	2 planes that took off from Moscow crashed within minutes of each other; brought down by Chechen suicide bombers	90
2005, Aug. 14	Helios Airways Boeing 737-300	Crashed after air pressure failure on board, near Athens, Greece.	121
2005, Aug. 16	West Caribbean Airways MD-82	Crashed after engine failure, near Machiques, Venezuela.	160
2005, Sept. 5	Mandala Airlines Boeing 737-200.	Crashed shortly after takeoff from Medan, Sumatra, Indonesia.	145*
2005, Oct. 22	Bellview Airlines Boeing 737-200	Crashed during heavy electrical storm near Lagos, Nigeria.	117
2005, Dec. 6	Islamic Rep. of Iran Air Force Lockheed C-130	Crashed into apartment building after reportedly attempting emergency landing back at airport, Tehran, Iran	116*
2005, Dec. 10	Sosoliso Airlines DC-9-30.	Crashed during storm on approach to Port Harcourt, Nigeria	107
2006, May 3	Armavia Airbus A320	Crashed into Black Sea on approach to airport, Sochi, Russia	113
2006, July 9	S7 Airlines Airbus A310	Skidded off runway, crashed into concrete barrier after landing, Irkutsk, Russia	125
2006, Aug. 22	Pulkovo Aviation Tu-154.	Crashed after encountering storm, near Donetsk, Ukraine	170
2006, Sept. 29	Gol Airlines Boeing 737	Crashed into Amazon jungle after midair collision with Embraer Legacy jet, Brazil	154
2007, May 5	Kenya Airways Boeing 737-800	Crashed shortly after takeoff from Douala, Cameroon.	114
2007, July 17	TAM Airlines Airbus 320.	Crashed into cargo depot, gas station after skidding off airport runway, São Paulo, Brazil	199*
2008, Aug. 20	Spanair Boeing-MD-82.	Swerved off runway, caught fire on takeoff attempt, Madrid, Spain.	154
2009, Feb. 12	Colgan Air Bombardier Dash 8 Q400.	Crashed into house near airport, Buffalo, NY	50*
2009, June 1	**Air France Airbus A330**	**Plunged into Atlantic Ocean en route from Rio de Janeiro, Brazil, to Paris, France**	**228**
2009, June 29	Yemenia Airbus A310-300	Fell into Indian Ocean on approach to Moroni, Comoros.	152
2009, July 15	Caspian Airlines Tupolev 154.	Crashed after takeoff from Tehran, Iran	168
2010, Apr. 10	Polish Air Force Tupolev 154M	Crashed on approach to Smolensk Air Base, killing Polish Pres. Lech Kaczynski, his wife, and several members of parliament.	96
2010, May 12	Afriqiyah Airways Airbus A330-200	Crashed short of runway in Tripoli, Libya	103
2010, May 22	Air India Express Boeing 737-800	Overran runway on landing at Mangalore, India.	158
2010, July 28	Airblue Airbus 321-231	Crashed into Margalla Hills near Islamabad, Pakistan.	152
2012, Apr. 20	Bhoja Airlines Boeing 737-236.	Crashed on approach to airport in Islamabad, Pakistan.	127
2012, June 3	Dana Air MD-83	Crashed into residential area of Lagos, Nigeria	163*
2014, Mar. 8	Malaysia Airlines Boeing 777	All communication ceased shortly after takeoff from Kuala Lumpur.	239
2014, July 17	Malaysia Airlines Boeing 777	Shot down in missile attack in Russian-occupied Donetsk, Ukraine	298
2014, July 24	Air Algérie Boeing-MD-83.	Crashed in desert near Gossi, Mali	116

(1) Bomb was planted by Jack G. Graham in insurance plot to kill his mother, Daisie E. King, a passenger. (2) 84 on plane, 71 on ground killed. (3) Incl. 43 Marshall Univ. (WV) football players and coaches. (4) Fighter pilot parachuted to safety. (5) First supersonic plane crash; killed 8 on ground. (6) Crew of 3, 88 on ground killed. (7) Incl. 22 members of U.S. amateur boxing team. (8) Incl. 248 members of U.S. 101st Airborne Division. (9) Incl. 11 on ground. (10) Incl. U.S. Sec. of Commerce Ron Brown. (11) 4 planes were hijacked and crashed, with all on board killed (265, incl. 19 hijackers). American Airlines Flight 11, a Boeing 767-200, with 81 passengers, 11 crew, crashed into Tower 1 of World Trade Center (WTC); United Airlines Flight 175, a Boeing 767-200, with 56 passengers, 9 crew, crashed into Tower 2 of WTC; American Airlines Flight 77, a Boeing 757-200, with 58 passengers, 6 crew, crashed into Pentagon outside Washington, DC; United Airlines Flight 93, a Boeing 757-200, with 37 passengers, 7 crew, crashed near Shanksville, PA. The official death toll of 2,977 includes all those who perished on the ground at the Pentagon and the WTC, as well as those who died as many as 10 years later from pulmonary sarcoidosis, a lung disease caused by exposure to toxic dust created by the disaster. (12) The two pilots ejected to safety. All spectator deaths.

World Natural Disaster Trends

If you seem to be noticing more natural disasters than ever before, it's because statistically speaking, you are. A 2012 report by the insurance giant Munich Re found that the number of "weather-related loss events" rose on every continent by at least 150% between 1980 and 2011. The increase was steepest in North America, which saw the number of catastrophes nearly quintuple, in part because it is vulnerable to "every type of hazardous weather peril: tropical cyclone, thunderstorm, winter storm, tornado, wildfire, drought, and flood," not to mention volcanic eruptions and earthquakes. The report, "Severe Weather in North America," cites climate change as a major reason for the increase in the number and intensity of natural catastrophes.

Some Notable Shipwrecks Since 1854

Does not include most wartime disasters.

Date—vessel(s)	Incident	Est. deaths
1854, Mar. 1—City of Glasgow	British steamer left Liverpool for Philadelphia, never heard from again	480
1854, Sept. 27—Arctic and Vesta	U.S. Collins Line steamer sunk in collision with French steamer nr. Cape Race, Canada	285-351
1856, Jan. 23—Pacific	U.S. Collins Line steamer went missing in N Atlantic	186-286
1857, Sept. 12—Central America	U.S. mail steamship sank off Florida coast with $1.5 mil in gold	427
1858, Sept. 23—Austria	German steamer destroyed by fire in N Atlantic	471
1863, Apr. 27—Anglo-Saxon	British steamer wrecked at Cape Race, Canada	238
1865, Apr. 27—Sultana	Mississippi R. steamer carrying 2,300 released Civil War prisoners exploded nr. Memphis, TN. Worst maritime disaster in U.S. history	1,700+
1869, Feb. 20—Radetzky	Austrian steam frigate exploded in Adriatic Sea	345
1869, Oct. 27—Stonewall	U.S. steamer burned, Mississippi R. below Cairo, IL	200
1872, Nov. 7—Mary Celeste	U.S. half-brig sailing from New York to Genoa, Italy, found abandoned	Unknown
1873, Jan. 22—Northfleet	British steamer rammed by Spanish steamer Murillo off Dungeness, England, UK	300
1873, Apr. 1—Atlantic	British White Star steamer off Halifax, Nova Scotia, Canada	585
1873, Nov. 23—Ville du Havre and Loch Earn	French steamer sank after collision with British sailing ship	226
1874, Nov. 17—Cospatrick	Burned off Auckland, New Zealand	468
1875, May 7—Schiller	German steamer off Isles of Scilly, UK	312
1875, Nov. 4—Pacific	U.S. steamer sank off collision off Cape Flattery, WA	236
1878, Mar. 24—Eurydice	British frigate sank off Isle of Wight, England, UK	398
1878, Sept. 3—Princess Alice	British steamer sank after collision with Bywell Castle in Thames R.	700
1878, Dec. 18—Byzantin and Rinaldo	French and British steamers collided in Dardanelles, off Turkey	210
1883, Jan. 19—Cimbria and Sultan	German steamer sank in collision with British steamer in North Sea	389
1887, Nov. 15—Wah Yeung	Chinese steamer burned in Canton R., Hong Kong	400
1890, Feb. 17—Duburg	British steamer wrecked, China Sea.	400
1890, Sept. 19—Ertogrul	Turkish frigate off Japan	540
1891, Mar. 17—Utopia and Anson	British steamer sank in collision with British ironclad off Gibraltar	562
1893, June 22—Victoria	British battleship sank after collision with warship Camperdown, off Syrian coast	358
1895, Jan. 30—Elbe and Craithie	German steamer sank in collision with British steamer in North Sea	332
1895, Mar. 11—Reina Regenta	Spanish cruiser foundered nr. Gibraltar	400
1898, Feb. 15—USS Maine	Explosion caused battleship to sink in Havana Harbor, Cuba	260
1898, July 4—La Bourgogne and Cromartyshire	French steamer sank in collision with British sailing ship off Nova Scotia, Canada	549
1904, May 15—Yoshino	Japanese cruiser sank after collision with cruiser Kasuga in fog off Liao-Tung Peninsula, China	329
1904, June 15—General Slocum	Excursion steamer burned off N. Brother Isl., New York, NY.	1,021
1904, June 28—Norge	Danish steamer wrecked on Rockall Isl., Scotland, UK	620
1906, Aug. 4—Sirio	Italian steamer wrecked off Cape Palos, Spain.	350
1907, Feb. 11—Larchmont	U.S. steamer sank after collision with U.S. schooner Harry Knowlton nr. Block Island, RI	131
1908, Mar. 23—Mutsu Maru	Japanese steamer sank in collision with another steamer nr. Hakodate, Japan	300
1909, Aug. 1—Waratah	British steamer vanished en route from Sydney to London	300
1911, Sept. 25—Liberté	French battleship exploded at Toulon	285
1912, Apr. 14-15—Titanic	British White Star steamer hit iceberg in N Atlantic.	1,503
1912, Sept. 28—Kichemaru	Japanese steamer sank off Japan coast	1,000
1914, May 29—Empress of Ireland	Canadian Pacific steamer collided with Norwegian coal transporter Storstad in St. Lawrence R., Canada	1,014
1914, Nov. 26—Bulwark	British battleship exploded in Sheerness Harbor, England, UK	788
1915, May 7—Lusitania	British Cunard Line steamer torpedoed and sunk by German submarine off Ireland	1,198
1915, July 24—Eastland	Steamer capsized, Chicago R., IL	844
1916, Feb. 26—Provence	French cruiser sank in Mediterranean; then-worst disaster in maritime history	3,100
1916, Mar. 5—Principe de Asturias	Spanish steamer wrecked nr. Santos, Brazil.	558
1917, Dec. 6—Mont Blanc and Imo	French ammunition ship and Belgian steamer collided in Halifax Harbor, Canada	1,600
1918, Apr. 25—Kiang-Kwan	Chinese steamer sank after collision with Chinese gunboat Chutai off Hankow, China.	500
1918, July 12—Kawachi	Japanese battleship blew up in Tokayama Bay	500
1918, Oct. 25—Princess Sophia	Canadian-Pacific steamer sank off Vanderbilt Reef, Alaska	398
1919, Jan. 17—Chaonia	French steamer lost in Straits of Messina, Italy	460
1919, Sept. 9—Valbanera	Spanish steamer lost off FL coast	500
1920, Jan. 11—Afrique	French liner sank nr. La Rochelle, France.	553
1921, Mar. 18—Hong Kong	Chinese steamer wrecked, S China Sea	1,000
1922, Aug. 26—Niitaka	Japanese cruiser sank in storm off Kamchatka, USSR	300
1927, Sept. 20—Gentoku Maru	Japanese steamer capsized in Tsingtao Bay, China	278
1927, Oct. 25—Principessa Mafalda	Italian steamer blew up, sank off Porto Seguro, Brazil	314
1934, Sept. 8—Morro Castle	U.S. steamer en route from Havana to New York, burned off Asbury Park, NJ	134
1940, June 17—Lancastria	Nazi forces sank Cunard liner evacuating British troops from France	2,500-6,000
1940, July 24—Meknes	French liner torpedoed by Nazis in English Channel	350
1942, Feb. 18—USS Truxtun and USS Pollux	Destroyer and cargo ship ran aground, sank off Newfoundland, Canada	204
1942, Oct. 2—Curacao and Queen Mary	British cruiser sank off inland after collision with liner carrying U.S. troops	338
1944, Dec. 17-18—Spence, Monaghan, Hull	3 U.S. destroyers sank during typhoon, Philippine Sea	790
1945, Jan. 30—Wilhelm Gustloff	Liner with German refugees, soldiers sunk by Soviet submarine in Baltic	5,000-9,000
1945, Apr. 16—Goya	Cargo ship carrying German refugees, soldiers sunk by Soviet submarine in Baltic	6,000-7,000
1945, May 3—Cap Arcona and Thielbeck	German liners carrying concentration camp inmates sunk by British warplanes in Lubeck Bay, Germany	7,000-8,000

Captain's Not Courageous

Date: Apr. 16, 2014. **Location:** Near Jindo, South Korea. **Fatalities:** 304.

A 479-ft-long South Korean ferry to the resort island of Jeju carrying 476 people, at least 325 of them high school students on a field trip, capsized in calm waters off the country's southwest coast Apr. 16, 2014. The vessel was believed to have been severely overloaded, with improperly stored cargo of more than three times the legal weight limit. The ship's captain and 14 other crew members went on trial June 10 for abandoning the ship, failing to deploy the vessel's lifeboats, and telling passengers to stay on board even as the ship sank. The CEO and other officials of Cheonghaejin Marine Co., which operated the ferry, were also arrested.

Date—vessel(s)	Incident	Est. deaths
1947, Jan. 19—Himera	Greek steamer hit mine off Athens, Greece	392
1947, Apr. 16—Grandcamp	Ammonium nitrate explosion aboard French freighter caused fires throughout port, Texas City, TX	576+
1948, Dec. 3—Kiangya	Chinese refugee ship wrecked in explosion S of Shanghai	1,100+
1954, Sept. 26—Toya Maru	Japanese ferry sank, Tsugaru Strait, Japan	1,172
1956, July 26—Andrea Doria and Stockholm	Italian liner and Swedish liner collided off Nantucket Isl., MA	51
1957, July 14—Eshghabad	Soviet fishing boat ran aground in Caspian Sea	270
1961, Apr. 8—Dara	British liner exploded in Persian Gulf	236
1961, July 8—Save	Portuguese ship ran aground off Mozambique	259
1965, Nov. 13—Yarmouth Castle	Cruise ship burned and sank off Nassau, The Bahamas	89
1970, Dec. 15—Namyong-Ho	S. Korean ferry sank in Korea Strait	308
1975, Nov. 10—Edmund Fitzgerald	U.S. cargo ship sank during storm on Lake Superior	29
1980, Apr. 22—Don Juan	Sank off Mindoro Isl., Philippines, after colliding with barge	1,000+
1981, Jan. 27—Tamponas II	Indonesian car ferry caught fire and sank in Java Sea	580
1983, May 25—10th of Ramadan	Nile steamer caught fire and sank in Lake Nasser, Egypt	357
1986, May 25—Shamia	Ferry capsized in storm, Meghna R., Bangladesh	500+
1986, Sept. 1—Admiral Nakhimov and Pyotr Vasev	Soviet cruise ship collided with Soviet freighter in Black Sea	425
1987, Dec. 20—Doña Paz and Victor	Philippine ferry and oil tanker collided in Tablas Strait, Philippines	4,341
1988, Aug. 6	Indian ferry capsized on Ganges R.	400+
1988, Oct. 24—Doña Marilyn	Philippine ferry sank by typhoon near Leyte Isl.	350+
1991, Dec. 14—Salem Express	Ferry rammed coral reef nr. Safaga, Egypt	462
1993, Feb. 17—Neptune	Ferry capsized off Port-au-Prince, Haiti	500+
1993, Oct. 10—Seohae	S. Korean ferry capsized in Yellow Sea during storm	292
1994, Sept. 28—Estonia	Ferry sank in Baltic Sea off Finland	850+
1996, May 21—Bukoba	Overcrowded Tanzanian ferry sank in Lake Victoria	500+
1997, Sept. 8—Pride of la Gonâve	Haitian ferry sank off Montrouis, Haiti	200+
1999, Feb. 6—Harta Rimba	Cargo ship sank off Indonesia	280+
1999, May 1—Miss Majestic	"Duck" boat on tour sank, Lake Hamilton, AR	13
1999, Nov. 24—Dashun	Passenger ferry capsized nr. Yantai, China	280
2000, June 29—Cahaya Bahari	Overloaded ferry carrying refugees from religious strife capsized in storm off Sulawesi Isl., Indonesia	500+
2001, Oct. 19	Fishing boat overloaded with refugees, mainly from Middle East, sank off Indonesia	350+
2002, May 4—Salahuddin-2	Overloaded Bangladesh ferry sank in Meghna R.	300+
2002, Sept. 26—Joola	Overloaded Senegalese ferry capsized in ocean off The Gambia	1,863
2003, July 8—MV-Nasrin 1	Overcrowded ferry sank nr. Chandpur in Bangladesh R.	400
2003, Oct. 15—Andrew J. Barberi	NYC ferry crashed into dock on approach to Staten Island	11
2006, Feb. 3—Al-Salam Boccaccio 98	Ferry caught fire, sank in Red Sea off Egypt	1,000+
2006, Dec. 30—Senopati Nusantara	High waves capsized ferry en route to Java, Indonesia	400+
2007, Nov. 23—Explorer	Canadian cruise ship hit Antarctic iceberg; first commercial passenger ship to sink in region	0
2008, June 23—Princess of the Stars	Philippine ferry capsized during Typhoon Fengshen nr. Manila	800
2011, Sept. 10—MV Spice Islander	Overloaded ferry sank off coast of Tanzania	240+
2012, Jan 17—Costa Concordia	Cruise ship ran aground off Italian coast; captain abandoned ship before passengers	32
2013, Oct. 3	Boat carrying migrants fleeing Eritrea sank near Lampedusa Isl., Italy	366
2014, Apr. 16—Sewol	Ferry carrying 476 people sank off Korea's SW coast	304

Some Notable Railroad Disasters Since 1925

Date	Location	Deaths	Date	Location	Deaths
1925, June 16	Hackettstown, NJ	50	1952, Oct. 8	Harrow, England, UK	112
1933, Dec. 23	Lagny-Pomponne, France	230	1953, Dec. 24	Tangiwai, New Zealand	151
1937, July 16	Near Patna, India	107	1953, Dec. 24	Sakvice, Czechoslovakia	103
1938, Dec. 25	Near Kishinev, Romania	150	1955, Apr. 3	Guadalajara, Mexico	300
1939, Dec. 22	Near Magdeburg, Germany	132	1957, Sept. 1	Kendal, Jamaica	178
1943, Sept. 6	Frankford Junction, Philadelphia, PA	79	1957, Sept. 29	Montgomery, W Pakistan	300
1943, Dec. 16	Between Rennert and Buie, NC	72	1957, Dec. 4	London, England, UK	90
1944, Jan. 16	León Province, Spain	500	1958, May 8	Rio de Janeiro, Brazil	128
1944, Mar. 2	Salerno, Italy	521	1960, Nov. 14	Pardubice, Czechoslovakia	117
1944, Dec. 31	Bagley, UT	50	1962, May 3	Tokyo, Japan	163
1945, July 16	Munich, Germany	102	1963, Nov. 9	Yokohama, Japan	162
1946, Mar. 20	Aracaju, Mexico	185	1965, Feb. 27	Near Port Sudan, Sudan	124
1949, Oct. 22	Near Dwor, Poland	200+	1970, Feb. 1	Buenos Aires, Argentina	236
1950, Nov. 22	Richmond Hill, NY	79	1972, June 16	Near Soissons, France	108
1951, Feb. 6	Woodbridge, NJ	84	1972, Oct. 6	Near Saltillo, Mexico	204
1952, Mar. 4	Near Rio de Janeiro, Brazil	119	1974, Aug. 30	Zagreb, Yugoslavia	153
1952, July 9	Rzepin, Poland	160	1981, June 6	Near Mansi, India	268

Date	Location	Deaths	Date	Location	Deaths
1982, Jan. 27	El Asnam, Algeria	120	1995, Jan. 13	Dinajpur, Bangladesh	150
1982, July 11	Tepic, Mexico	120	1995, Aug. 20	Firozabad, India	350
1983, Feb. 19	Empalme, Mexico	100	1995, Nov. 28	Baku, Azerbaijan	337
1985, Jan. 13	Awash, Ethiopia	392	1997, Mar. 3	Punjab Province, Pakistan	128
1985, Sept. 12	Viseu, Portugal	118	1997, May 4	Kisangani, Zaire	100+
1986, Aug. 6	Bihar, India	202	1998, Feb. 19	Yaounde, Cameroon	120
1987, July 2	Kasumbalesha Shaba, Zaire	125	1998, June 3	Eschede, Germany	102
1987, Aug. 7	Between Moscow and Rostov, USSR.	106	1998, Nov. 26	Khanna, India	108
1987, Oct. 19	Jakarta, Indonesia	153	1999, Aug. 2	Gauhati, India	285
1988, June 4	Arzamas, USSR	100	2002, Feb. 20	S of Cairo, Egypt.	377
1988, July 8	Kerala, India	108	2002, May 25	Muamba, Mozambique	195
1989, Jan. 15	Maizdi Khan, Bangladesh.	135	2002, June 24	Igandu, Tanzania	281
1989, June 4	Ufa, USSR	645	2002, Sept. 10	Bihar, India	112
1989, Aug. 11	Sinaloa, Mexico	112	2004, Feb. 18	Neyshabur, NE Iran	300
1990, Jan. 4	Sindh Province, Pakistan	307	2004, Apr. 22	Ryongchon, North Korea	161
1991, Mar. 5	Nacala, Mozambique	109	2005, Apr. 25	Near Amagasaki, Japan	107
1991, June 8	Ghotki, Pakistan	100	2005, July 13	Ghotki, Pakistan	132
1991, Sept. 5	Pointe-Noire, Congo Republic.	110	2005, Oct. 29	Andra Pradesh, India	110
1993, Jan. 30	Rural Kenya	340	2007, Aug. 2	Nr. Benaleka, Dem. Rep. of Congo.	100
1993, Apr. 25	Near Karachi, Pakistan.	150	2010, May 28	W. Bengal, India	148
1994, Sept. 22	Lubango, Angola.	300	2011, July 23	Wenzhou, China.	140
1994, Dec. 30	Near Namkham, Myanmar	102			

Principal U.S. Mine Disasters Since 1900

Source: Bureau of Mines, U.S. Dept. of the Interior; Mine Safety and Health Admin., U.S. Dept. of Labor; World Almanac research
All are bituminous coal mines unless otherwise noted.

Date	Location	Deaths	Date	Location	Deaths	Date	Location	Deaths
1900, May 1	Scofield, UT	200	1913, Oct. 22	Dawson, NM	263	1940, Mar. 16	St. Clairesville, OH	72
1902, May 19	Coal Creek, TN	184	1914, Apr. 28	Eccles, WV	181	1942, Mar. 26	Allentown, PA[4]	31
1902, July 10	Johnstown, PA	112	1915, Mar. 2	Layland, WV	115	1943, Feb. 27	Washoe, MT	74
1903, June 30	Hanna, WY	169	1917, Apr. 27	Hastings, CO	121	1947, Mar. 25	Centralia, IL	111
1904, Jan. 25	Cheswick, PA	179	1917, June 8	Butte, MT[1]	163	1951, Dec. 21	West Frankfort, IL.	119
1905, Feb. 20	Virginia City, AL	112	1919, June 5	Wilkes-Barre, PA[2]	92	1968, Mar. 6	Belle Isle, LA[5]	21
1907, Jan. 29	Stuart, WV	84	1922, Nov. 6	Spangler, PA	79	1968, Nov. 20	Farmington, WV	78
1907, Dec. 6	Monongah, WV	362	1922, Nov. 22	Dolomite, AL	90	1970, Dec. 30	Hyden, KY	38
1907, Dec. 19	Jacobs Creek, PA	239	1923, Feb. 8	Dawson, NM	120	1972, May 2	Kellogg, ID[6]	91
1908, Nov. 28	Marianna, PA	154	1923, Aug. 14	Kemmerer, WY	99	1976, Mar. 9	Oven Fork, KY	15
1909, Nov. 13	Cherry, IL	259	1924, Mar. 8	Castle Gate, UT	172	1981, Apr. 15	Redstone, CO	15
1910, Jan. 31	Primero, CO	75	1924, Apr. 28	Benwood, WV	119	1981, Dec. 8	Whitwell, TN	13
1910, May 5	Palos, AL	84	1926, Jan. 13	Wilburton, OK	91	1984, Dec. 19	Orangeville, UT.	27
1910, Nov. 8	Delagua, CO	79	1926, Nov. 3	Ishpeming, MI[3]	51	1989, Sept. 13	Wheatcroft, KY	10
1911, Apr. 8	Littleton, AL	128	1927, Apr. 30	Everettville, WV	97	2001, Sept. 23	Brookwood, AL	13
1911, Dec. 9	Briceville, TN	84	1928, May 19	Mather, PA	195	2006, Jan. 2	Buckhannon, WV	12
1912, Mar. 26	Jed, WV	81	1930, Nov. 5	Millfield, OH	82	2010, Apr. 5	Montcoal, WV	29
1913, Apr. 23	Finleyville, PA	98	1940, Jan. 10	Bartley, WV	91			

Note: The world's worst mine disaster killed 1,549 workers in Manchuria, China, Apr. 25, 1942. (1) Copper mine. (2) Anthracite mine. (3) Iron mine. (4) Limestone mine. (5) Salt mine. (6) Silver mine.

Some Notable U.S. Tornadoes Since 1925

Date	Location	Deaths	Date	Location	Deaths
1925, Mar. 18	MO, IL, IN.	747	1973, May 26-27	South, Midwest.	47
1927, Apr. 12	Rocksprings, TX.	74	1974, Apr. 3-4	AL; GA; KY; Xenia, OH; other states	315
1927, May 9	AR; Poplar Bluff, MO	92	1977, Apr. 4	AL, MS, GA	22
1927, Sept. 29	St. Louis, MO	90	1979, Apr. 10	TX, OK.	60
1930, May 6	Hill, Navarro, Ellis Cos., TX	41	1984, Mar. 28	NC, SC	57
1932, Mar. 21	Alabama	268	1985, May 31	NY; PA; OH; Ontario, Can.	75
1936, Apr. 5-6	Tupelo, MS; Gainesville, GA	454	1987, May 22	Saragosa, TX.	30
1938, Sept. 29	Charleston, SC	32	1989, Nov. 15	Huntsville, AL.	18
1942, Mar. 16	Central to NE Mississippi	75	1990, Aug. 28	Northern IL.	25
1942, Apr. 27	Rogers and Mayes Cos., OK	52	1991, Apr. 26	KS, OK	23
1944, June 23	OH, PA, WV, MD	150	1992, Nov. 21-23	South, Midwest.	26
1945, Apr. 12	OK, AR	102	1994, Mar. 27-28	AL, TN, GA, NC, SC	52
1947, Apr. 9	TX; Woodward, OK; KS	181	1995, May 6-7	Southern Oklahoma, northern Texas	23
1948, Mar. 19	Bunker Hill and Gillespie, IL.	33	1997, Mar. 1	Central AR	26
1949, Jan. 3	LA, AR	58	1997, May 27	Jarrell, TX	27
1952, Mar. 21-22	AR, MO, TN	208	1998, Feb. 22-23	Central FL	42
1953, May 11	Waco, TX	114	1998, Apr. 8	AL, GA, MS	39
1953, June 8	Flint-Beecher, MI; OH	142	1999, May 3	OK, KS	54
1953, June 9	Worcester and vicinity, MA	90	2000, Feb. 14	SW Georgia	22+
1953, Dec. 5	Vicksburg, MS	38	2002, Nov. 10-11	AL, MS, TN, IN, OH, PA	36
1955, May 25	Udall, KS; MO; Blackwell, OK; TX	115	2003, May 4-11	TN, MO, KS, IL, OK, WV, AL.	48
1957, May 20	KS, MO.	48	2005, Nov. 6	KY, IN	22
1958, June, 4	NW Wisconsin	30	2007, Mar. 1	AL, GA, MO, Midwest	20
1959, Feb. 10	St. Louis, MO	21	2008, Feb. 25	"Super Tuesday"—TN, AR, KY, AL, MO.	57
1960, May 5-6	Southeastern OK, AR	30			
1962, Mar. 31	Milton, FL	17	2008, May 10	MS, OK, GA.	23
1965, Apr. 11	IA, IN, IL, OH, MI, WI	271	2011, Apr. 14-16	Southeast, Midwest, OK to VA	38
1966, Mar. 3	Jackson, MS; AL	57	2011, Apr. 25-28	305 funnels from TX to NY	321
1967, Apr. 21	IL, MO, IA, MI.	33	2011, May 22	Joplin, MO	161
1968, May 15	Midwest	71	2012, Mar. 2-3	IL, IN, KY, OH, AL	42
1969, Jan. 23	Mississippi	32	2013, May 20	Moore, OK	24
1970, May 11	Lubbock, TX.	23	2013, May 31	El Reno, OK.	21
1971, Feb. 21	Mississippi Delta: MS, LA, AR, TN	110			

Some Notable Hurricanes, Typhoons, Blizzards, Other Storms

C. = cyclone; H. = hurricane; TS. = tropical storm; T. = typhoon[1].

Date	Location	Est. deaths	Date	Location	Est. deaths
1881, Aug. 24-29	H., GA, SC	700	1991, Apr. 30	C., Bangladesh	139,000
1888, Mar. 11-14	Blizzard, Eastern U.S.	400	1991, Nov. 5	TS. Thelma, flash floods,	
1893, Aug. 15-Sept. 2	H., GA, SC	1,000+		central Philippines	7,000+
1893, Oct. 1	H., LA	1,100+	1992, Aug. 24-26	H. Andrew, Southern FL, LA.	65
1900, Sept. 8	H., Galveston, TX	8,000+	1993, Mar. 12-14	Blizzard, Eastern U.S.	270+
1906, Sept. 18	T., Hong Kong	10,000+	1993, June	Monsoon, Bangladesh	2,000
1906, Sept. 19-24	H., LA, MS	350	1994, Nov. 8-18	TS. Gordon, Caribbean, FL	830
1909, Sept. 20	H., LA	350+	1995, Oct. 2-4	H. Opal, S Mexico, FL, AL	59
1915, Aug. 16	H., Galveston, TX	275	1995, Nov. 2-3	T. Angela, Philippines	600+
1915, Sept. 29	H., LA	275	1996, Jan. 7-8	Blizzard, NE U.S.	100
1919, Sept. 6-14	H., Carib., FL Keys, Gulf, TX	600+[2]	1996, Aug. 22	Blizzard, Himalayas, N India.	239
1922, July 27	T., Swatow, China	100,000	1996, Aug. 29-Sept. 6	H. Fran, Carib., NC, VA, WV	30
1926, Sept. 11-22	H., FL, AL, MS	370+	1996, Sept. 9	T. Sally, S China	114
1926, Oct. 20	H., Cuba	600	1996, Nov. 6	C., Andhra Pradesh, India	1,000+
1928, Sept. 6-20	H., southern FL	2,500+	1996, Dec. 25	TS. Greg, eastern Malaysia	100+
1930, Sept. 3	H., Dominican Republic	2,000	1997, May 19	C., Bangladesh	108
1935, Aug. 29-	H., "Labor Day Hurricane,"		1997, Aug. 18-21	T. Winnie, Taiwan, E China	140+
Sept. 10	Caribbean, SE U.S.	400+	1997, Oct. 8-10	H. Pauline, SW Mexico	230
1937, Sept. 2	T., "The Great Typhoon,"		1998, June 9	C., Gujarat, India	1,320
	Hong Kong	10,000+	1998, Aug.	Monsoon, Bangladesh	326
1938, Sept. 21	H., "Long Isl. Express," NY,		1998, Sept. 21-23	H. Georges, Carib., FL, U.S. Gulf	600+
	New England	682	1998, Oct. 27-29	H. Mitch, Honduras, Nicaragua,	
1940, Nov. 11-12	"Armistice Day Blizzard,"			Guatemala, El Salvador	14,600
	NE, Midwest U.S.	154	1999, Sept. 4-17	H. Floyd, The Bahamas,	
1942, Oct.	T., W. Sundarbans, Bangladesh	61,000		E seaboard U.S.	56
1942, Oct. 15-16	H., Bengal, India	40,000	1999, Oct. 29	C., E India	9,392
1947, Dec. 26	Blizzard, NYC, N Atl. states	55	1999, Dec. 26-29	Gales, France, Switz., Germany	120
1952, Oct. 22	T., Philippines	440	2000, Dec. 27	Winter storm, TX, OK, AR	40+
1954, Aug. 30	H. Carol, NE U.S.	68	2001, July 30	T. Toraji, Taiwan	200
1954, Sept. 5-18	H. Hazel, E Canada, U.S., Haiti	347	2001, Nov. 6-12	T. Lingling, S Philip., Vietnam.	220+
1955, Aug. 7-21	H. Diane, Eastern U.S.	400	2002, Aug.-Sept.	T. Rusa, N. and S. Korea	115+
1955, Sept. 19	H. Hilda, Mexico	200	2003, Feb. 16-17	Blizzard, E seaboard U.S.	59
1956, Feb. 1-29	Blizzard, W Europe	1,000	2003, Sept. 7-19	H. Isabel, NC, VA, E seaboard	40+
1957, June 25-30	H. Audrey, TX to AL	390	2003, Sept. 12	T. Maemi, S. Korea	130
1958, Feb. 15-16	Blizzard, NE U.S.	171	2004, Mar. 7-19	C. Gafilo, Madagascar	198
1959, Sept. 17-19	T. Sarah, Japan, S. Korea	2,000	2004, May 19	C., Myanmar	220
1959, Sept. 26-27	T. Vera, Honshu, Japan	4,466	2004, Aug. 12-15	T. Rananim, eastern China	164
1960, Sept. 4-12	H. Donna, Caribbean, E U.S.	148	2004, Aug. 13-14	H. Charley, FL, SC	36
1961, Oct. 31	H. Hattie, Brit. Honduras	400	2004, Sept. 5-6	H. Frances, The Bahamas, FL	35
1962, Sept. 1	T. Wanda, Hong Kong	130-200	2004, Sept. 7-16	H. Ivan, Barbados, Grenada,	
1963, May 28-29	Windstorm, Bangladesh	22,000		U.S. Gulf Coast	115
1963, Oct. 4-8	H. Flora, Caribbean	6,000	2004, Sept. 16-26	H. Jeanne, Dom. Rep., Haiti, FL	1,500+
1964, June 30	T. Winnie, N Philippines	107	2005, July 7-11	H. Dennis, Jamaica, Haiti,	
1964, Sept. 5	T. Ruby, Hong Kong, China	735		Cuba, FL	50
1965, May 11-12	Windstorm, Bangladesh	17,000	2005, Aug. 25-29	H. Katrina, LA, MS, FL, AL, GA	1,833+[3]
1965, June 1-2	Windstorm, Bangladesh	30,000	2005, Aug. 31-Sept. 1	T. Talim, Taiwan, E China	129+
1965, Sept. 7-12	H. Betsy, FL, MS, LA	74	2005, Sept. 21-24	H. Rita, TX, LA	62[4]
1965, Dec. 15	Windstorm, Bangladesh	10,000	2005, Sept. 21-28	T. Damrey, SE Asia; Philippines;	
1966, June 4-10	H. Alma, Honduras, SE U.S.	51		Hainan, China	145
1966, Sept. 24-30	H. Inez, Carib., FL, Mexico	293	2005, Oct. 4	H. Stan, Central Amer., Mex.	1,000+[5]
1967, July 9	T. Billie, SW Japan	347	2006, Jul. 14	TS. Bilis, SE China	612
1967, Sept. 5-23	H. Beulah, Carib., Mex., TX	54	2006, Aug. 10	T. Saomai, SE China	295
1967, Dec. 12-20	Blizzard, SW U.S.	51	2006, Nov. 30	T. Durian, Philippines	450-1,000+
1969, Aug. 17-18	H. Camille, MS, LA	256	2007, June 6-7	C. Gonu, Oman, Iran	54[6]
1970, Sept. 15	T. Pitang (Georgia), Philippines	300	2007, Nov. 15	C. Sidr, southern Bangladesh.	3,363
1970, Oct. 14	T. Sening (Joan), Philippines	583	2008, May 2-3	C. Nargis, Southern Myanmar	138,366
1970, Oct. 15	T. Titang (Kate), Philippines	526	2008, June 20-25	T. Fengshen, Philippines, China	233
1970, Nov. 13	C., Bay of Bengal, Bangladesh	300,000	2008, Aug. 26-Sept. 1	H. Gustav, Haiti, Dom. Rep., U.S.	138
1971, Aug. 1	T. Rose, Hong Kong	130	2008, Sept. 1-4	TS. Hanna, Haiti	529
1972, June 19-29	H. Agnes, FL to NY	118	2008, Sept. 7-13	H. Ike, Haiti; Cuba; Galveston, TX	164
1972, Dec. 3	T. Theresa, Philippines	169	2009, May 23-26	C. Alia, Bangladesh	260
1973, June-Aug.	Monsoon rains, India	1,217	2009, Aug. 7-9	T. Morakot, mudslides, Taiwan	700+
1974, July 11	T. Gilda, Japan, S. Korea	108	2009, Sept. 23-30	T. Ketsana, Philippines, Vietnam,	
1974, Sept. 19-20	H. Fifi, Honduras	2,000		Cambodia, Laos	498+
1975, Sept. 13-27	H. Eloise, Caribbean, NE U.S.	71	2009, Oct. 3-10	T. Parma, Philippines	375
1976, May 20	T. Olga, floods, Philippines	215	2009, Oct. 30-Nov. 3	T. Mirinae, Philippines, Vietnam	159+
1976, Sept. 25-Oct. 2	H. Liza, western Mexico	630	2010, May 29	TS. Agatha, Guatemala,	
1978, Oct. 27	T. Rita, Philippines	400		El Salvador, Honduras	184
1979, Aug. 30-Sept. 7	H. David, Caribbean, E U.S.	1,100	2010, July 13-17	T. Conson, Luzon Isl.,	
1980, Aug. 4-11	H. Allen, Caribbean, TX	272		Philippines	105+
1981, Nov. 25	T. Irma, Luzon Isl., Philippines	176	2011, Dec. 16	TS. Washi, Philippines	1,257
1983, June	Monsoon, India	900	2012, Jan. 24-Feb. 14	Blizzard/cold snap, E Europe	650+
1984, Sept. 2	T. Ike, southern Philippines	1,363	2012, Oct. 22-31	H. Sandy, Cuba, Haiti, Jamaica,	
1985, May 25	C., Bangladesh	15,000		Eastern U.S.	245[7]
1985, Oct. 26-Nov. 6	H. Juan, SE U.S.	97	2012, Dec. 4	T. Bopha, Philippines	1,146
1987, Nov. 25	T. Nina, Philippines	650	2013, Nov. 8	T. Haiyan, Philippines	6,000+
1988, Sept. 10-17	H. Gilbert, Carib., Gulf of Mex.	260	2013, Nov. 10	C., Puntland, Somalia	162
1989, Sept. 16-22	H. Hugo, Caribbean, SE U.S.	86	2014, July 15	T. Rammasun, Philippines,	
1990, May 6-10	C. (mult.), SE India	450		China	139

(1) What hurricanes are called W of Intl. Date Line and N of equator. (2) Incl. about 500 lost on ships at sea. (3) Official toll as of Aug. 2006 was 1,577 in LA, 238 in MS, 14 in FL, and 2 each in AL and GA. (4) Incl. 55 indirect deaths, among them 20 people, mostly elderly evacuees from a nursing home, whose bus exploded and caught fire outside Dallas. (5) Incl. deaths from floods and landslides generated by heavy rainstorms. (6) First documented super cyclone in Arabian Sea. (7) Includes 87 indirect deaths in the U.S.

Some Notable Floods, Tidal Waves

Source: EM-DAT: The OFDA/CRED Intl. Disaster Database, Université catholique de Louvain, Brussels, Belgium, www.emdat.be; World Almanac research

Date	Location	Est. deaths	Date	Location	Est. deaths
1703	Awa, Japan	100,000+	1981, Apr.	N China	550
1889, May 31	Johnstown, PA	2,200+	1981, July	Sichuan, Hubei Prov.,	
1903, June 15	Heppner, OR	325		China	1,300
1911	Chang Jiang R., China	100,000	1982, Jan. 23	Near Lima, Peru	600
1913, Mar. 25-27	OH, IN	732	1982, May 12	Guangdong, China	430
1915, Aug. 17	Galveston, TX	275	1982, Sept. 17-21	El Salvador, Guatemala	1,300+
1927, Jan.-July	Mississippi Valley	246+	1984, Aug.-Sept.	South Korea	200+
1927, Nov. 1	Mostagenem, Algeria	3,000	1987, July 22	Bangladesh	2,055
1928, Mar. 13	Dam collapse, Saugus,		1987, Aug.-Sept.	Northern Bangladesh	1,000+
	CA	450	1988, June-Sept.	Bangladesh	2,379
1928, Sept. 16	Lake Okeechobee, FL	1,770+	1988, Sept.	N India	1,000+
1931, Aug.	Huang He R., China	3,700,000	1989, July 14	China	2,000
1933	Shandong, China	18,000	1994, May-Oct.	Assam, India	2,001
1937, Jan. 22	OH, MS valleys	250	1995, July	NE China	1,200
1939, July	Hunan province, China	500,000	1995, Sept. 1-20	India	1,479
1946, Apr. 1	HI, AK	159	1996, June-July	Guizhou, Hebei, China	2,775
1947, Sept. 20	Honshu Isl., Japan	2,000	1997, Oct.-Nov.	Somalia	2,311
1949, July	China	57,000	1998, July 17	Papua New Guinea	3,000
1949, Oct.	Guatemala	40,000	1998, July-Aug.	Hunan, Sichuan, China	3,656
1950	Pakistan	2,900	1998, July-Sept.	Bangladesh	1,441
1951, Aug. 28	Manchuria	4,800	1998, Aug.	India	1,811
1953, Jan. 31	Storm surge, Zuiderzee,		1999, Oct.-Dec.	Central Vietnam	700+
	Netherlands	2,000	1999, Dec. 15-20	NW Venezuela	30,000
1953, June 23	Japan	2,566	2000, Feb.-Mar.	Mozambique	700
1954, Aug.	China	30,000	2000, Sept. 19-30	India, Bangladesh	1,000+
1954, Aug. 17	Farahzad, Iran	2,000	2001, Aug. 1-6	Taiwan	100+
1955, Oct. 7-12	India, Pakistan	1,700	2001, Nov. 9-10	Northern Algeria	711+
1959, Nov. 1	Western Mexico	2,000	2002, Apr.-Aug.	China	800+
1959, Dec. 2	Frejus, France	412	2002, July-Aug.	India, Nepal, Bangladesh	1,100+
1959-61	China	2,000,000	2004, May 23-Jun. 1	Dom. Republic, Haiti	2,665
1960, Oct. 10	Bangladesh	6,000	2004, June-Sept.	Bangladesh, India,	
1960, Oct. 31	Bangladesh	4,000		Myanmar, Nepal	2,000+
1961, July	N India	2,000	2004, June-Sept.	China	500
1962, Sept. 27	Barcelona, Spain	445	2004, Nov.-Dec.	Philippines	1,060+
1963, Oct. 9	Dam collapse, Vaiont, Italy	1,800	2004, Dec. 26	Indian Ocean nations	227,898
1967, Jan. 18-24	Eastern Brazil	894	2005, July 26-Aug. 5	Western Maharashtra state,	
1967, Mar. 19	Rio de Janeiro, Brazil	436		India	1,200
1967, Nov. 26	Lisbon, Portugal	464	2006, Feb. 17	Leyte Isl., Philippines	1,000
1968, July	Rajasthan, Gujarat states,		2006, July 17	S of Java, Indonesia	530+
	India	4,892	2007, July 21-Aug. 3	Bangladesh	1,110
1968, Oct. 7	NE India	780	2007, July-Sept.	India	1,103
1969, Jan. 18-26	Southern CA	100	2008, June-July	India	1,063
1969, Aug. 20-22	Western VA	189	2009, July-Sept.	India	992
1969, Oct. 1-8	Tunisia	500	2010, May-Aug.	China	1,691
1970, July 22	Himalayas, India	500	2010, June 13-24	Cenxi, China	377+
1972, Feb. 26	Buffalo Creek, WV	118	2010, July-Aug.	Pakistan	1,985
1972, June 9	Rapid City, SD	238	2010, Aug. 1-4	Zhouqu County, China	1,500+
1972, Aug. 7	Luzon Isl., Philippines	454	2011, Jan. 11-12	SE Brazil	900
1972, Aug. 19-31	Pakistan	1,500	2011, Mar. 11	NE Japan	20,896
1974, Mar. 29	Tubaro, Brazil	1,000	2011, Apr.-May	Northern Colombia	425+
1974, July	Bangladesh	28,700	2011, July-Dec.	Thailand	708+
1974, Aug. 12	Monty-Long, Bangladesh	2,500	2011, July-Dec.	Philippines, Cambodia,	
1976, July 31	Big Thompson Canyon, CO	140		Myanmar	2,000+
1978, July	N, NE India	3,800	2012, July-Oct.	Nigeria	363
1979, July 17	Lomblem Isl., Indonesia	539	2012, Aug.-Oct.	Pakistan	480
1979, Aug. 11	Morvi, India	15,000	2012, Sept.-Oct.	Nigeria	431
1980, June	Sichuan, China	6,200	2013, June	Uttarakhand, India	5,700+

Swept Away

Date: Mar. 23, 2014. **Location:** Oso, WA. **Fatalities:** 43

A hillside above the north fork of Washington state's Stillaguamish River collapsed from heavy rains, causing a massive mudslide that swallowed up everything within its approximately one-mi-wide path, including state highway 530. After months of combing through the rubble, state officials confirmed 43 people were dead. The clear-cut hillside, located 60 miles northeast of Seattle, had witnessed so many previous mudslides (in 1949, 1951, 1967, 1998, and 2006) that it was known locally as "Slide Hill." A 1999 Army Corps of Engineers report warned of a "potential for a large catastrophic failure," and a 2010 report commissioned by Snohomish County ranked the area as among the most at risk for destructive landslides. Yet seven homes affected by the latest slide were built in 2006 or later.

Some Major Earthquakes

Source: Global Volcanism Network, Smithsonian Institution; U.S. Geological Survey, U.S. Dept. of the Interior; World Almanac research
Magnitude of earthquakes (mag.) is a relative measurement of an earthquake's energy.

Date	Location	Deaths	Mag.	Date	Location	Deaths	Mag.
526, May 20	Antioch, Syria	250,000	NA	1949, July 10	Khait, Tajikistan	12,000	7.5
856	Corinth, Greece	45,000	NA	1949, Aug. 5	Pelileo, Ecuador	5,050	6.8
856, Dec. 22	Damghan, Iran	200,000	NA	1950, Aug. 15	Assam, India	1,526	8.6
893, Mar. 23	Ardabil, Iran	150,000	NA	1954, Sept. 9	Orleansville, Algeria	1,250	6.8
1057	Chihli, China	25,000	NA	1956, June 10-17	Northern Afghanistan	2,000	7.7
1138, Aug. 9	Aleppo, Syria	230,000	NA	1957, July 2	Northern Iran	1,200	7.1
1169, Feb. 11	Nr. Mt. Etna, Sicily	15,000	NA[1]	1960, Feb. 29	Agadir, Morocco	12,000	5.7
1268	Silicia, Asia Minor	60,000	NA	1960, May 21-30	Southern Chile	1,655	9.5[5]
1290, Sept. 27	Chihli, China	100,000	NA	1962, Sept. 1	NW Iran	12,255	7.1
1293, May 20	Kamakura, Japan	30,000	NA	1964, Mar. 27	Prince Wm. Sound, AK	131	9.2[6]
1531, Jan. 26	Lisbon, Portugal	30,000	NA	1966, Aug. 19	Eastern Turkey	2,529	6.8
1556, Jan. 24	Shaanxi, China	830,000	NA	1968, Aug. 31	NE Iran	12,000	7.3
1667, Nov.	Shemakha, Caucasia			1969, July 25	Guangdong, China	3,000	5.9
	(now Azerbaijan)	80,000	NA	1970, Jan. 5	Yunnan Prov., China	10,000	7.5
1693, Jan. 11	Catania, Italy	60,000	NA	1970, May 31	Chimbote, Peru	70,000	7.9
1737, Oct. 11	India, Calcutta	300,000	NA	1971, Feb. 9	San Fernando Valley, CA	65	6.6
1755, June 7	N Persia (current-day Iran)	40,000	NA	1972, Apr. 10	Southern Iran	5,054	7.1
1755, Nov. 1	Lisbon, Portugal	60,000	8.75[2]	1972, Dec. 23	Managua, Nicaragua	5,000	6.2
1783, Feb. 4	Calabria, Italy	30,000	NA	1974, May 10	China	20,000	6.8
1797, Feb. 4	Quito, Ecuador	41,000	NA	1974, Dec. 28	Northern Pakistan	5,300	6.2
1822, Sept. 5	Asia Minor, Aleppo	22,000	NA	1975, Feb. 4	Haicheng, China	2,000	7.0
1828, Dec. 28	Echigo, Japan	30,000	NA	1975, Sept. 6	Eastern Turkey	2,300	6.7
1868, Aug. 13-15	Peru, Ecuador	40,000	NA	1976, Feb. 4	Guatemala	23,000	7.5
1875, May 16	Venezuela, Colombia	16,000	NA	1976, May 6	NE Italy	1,000	6.5
1886, Aug. 31	Charleston, SC	60	6.6	1976, June 25	Irian Jaya, New Guinea	422	7.1
1896, June 15	Sanriku, Japan (tsunami)	27,120	8.5	1976, July 28	Tangshan, China	242,769	7.5
1902, Apr. 19	Quezaltenango and San			1976, Aug. 16	Mindanao, Philippines	8,000	7.9
	Marcos, Guatemala	2,000	7.5	1976, Nov. 24	NW Iran-Turkey border	5,000	7.3
1902, Dec. 16	Uzbekistan, Russia	4,700	6.4	1977, Mar. 4	Romania	1,500	7.2
1903, Apr. 28	Malazgirt, Turkey	3,500	7.0	1978, Sept. 16	NE Iran	15,000	7.8
1905, Apr. 4	Kangra, India	19,000	7.5	1980, Oct. 10	NW Algeria	5,000	7.7
1906, Jan. 31	Off coast of Esmeraldas,			1980, Nov. 23	Southern Italy	2,735	6.5
	Ecuador	1,000	8.8	1981, June 11	Southern Iran	3,000	6.9
1906, Mar. 16	Chia-i, Taiwan	1,250	6.8	1981, July 28	Southern Iran	1,500	7.3
1906, Apr. 18-19	San Francisco, CA	3,000+	7.7[3]	1982, Dec. 13	W Arabian Peninsula	2,800	6.0
1906, Aug. 17	Valparaiso, Chile	3,882	8.6	1983, Oct. 30	Eastern Turkey	1,342	6.9
1907, Oct. 21	Central Asia	12,000	8.1	1985, Sept. 19	Michoacan, Mexico	9,500	8.0
1908, Dec. 28	Messina, Italy	72,000	7.2	1986, Oct. 10	El Salvador	1,000+	5.5
1909, Jan. 23	Silakhor, Iran	5,000-		1987, Mar. 6	Colombia-Ecuador	1,000	7.0
		6,000	7.3	1988, Aug. 20	India-Nepal border	1,000	6.8
1912, Aug. 9	Murefte, Turkey	2,800	7.4	1988, Dec. 7	Spitak, Armenia	25,000	6.8
1914, Oct. 3	Burdur, Turkey	4,000	7.0	1989, Oct. 17	San Francisco Bay area, CA	63	6.9
1915, Jan. 13	Avezzano, Italy	32,610	7.0	1990, June 20	Western Iran	40,000+	7.4
1917, July 30	Yunnan prov., China	1,800	7.5	1990, July 16	Luzon, Philippines	1,621	7.7
1920, Dec. 16	Gansu, China	200,000	7.8[4]	1991, Feb. 1	Pakistan-Afgh. border	1,200	6.8
1923, Mar. 24	Sichuan, China	3,500	7.3	1991, Oct. 19	Northern India	2,000	7.0
1923, Mar. 25	Torbat-e Heydariyeh, Iran	2,200	5.7	1992, Dec. 12	Flores Isl., Indonesia	2,500	7.5
1923, Sept. 1	Yokohama, Japan	142,800	7.9	1993, Sept. 30	Maharashtra, S India	9,748	6.2
1925, Mar. 16	Yunnan prov., China	5,800	7.0	1994, Jan. 17	Northridge, CA	61	6.8
1927, Mar. 7	Tango, Japan	3,020	7.6	1994, June 6	Cauca, SW Colombia	1,000	6.8
1927, May 22	Gansu, China	40,900	7.6	1995, Jan. 16	Kobe, Japan	5,502	6.9
1929, May 1	Koppeh Dagh, Iran	3,800	7.2	1995, May 27	Sakhalin Isl., Russia	1,989	7.5
1930, May 6	Salmas, Iran	2,500	7.2	1997, Feb. 28	NW Iran	1,000+	6.1
1930, July 23	Irpinia, Italy	1,404	6.5	1997, May 10	Northern Iran	1,567	7.3
1931, Mar. 31	Managua, Nicaragua	2,500	6.0	1998, Feb. 4, 8	Hindu Kush, Afghanistan	2,323	5.9
1931, Apr. 27	Armenia-Azerbaijan border	2,800	5.7	1998, May 30	Afghanistan-Tajikistan		
1931, Aug. 10	Xinjiang, China	10,000	8.0		border	4,000+	6.6
1933, Mar. 2	Sanriku, Japan (tsunami)	2,990	8.4	1998, July 17	Papua New Guinea	2,183	7.0
1933, Mar. 10	Long Beach, CA	115	6.2	1999, Jan. 25	Armenia, Colombia	1,185+	6.1
1933, Aug. 25	Sichuan, China	9,300	7.5	1999, Aug. 17	Izmit, western Turkey	17,118+	7.6
1934, Jan. 15	Bihar, India-Nepal	10,700	8.1	1999, Sept. 20	Taichung, Taiwan	2,400	7.6
1935, Apr. 21	Miao-li, Taiwan	3,270	7.1	2001, Jan. 26	Gujarat, India	20,085	7.6
1935, May 30	Quetta, Pakistan	30,000	7.6	2002, Mar. 25-26	Hindu Kush, Afghanistan	1,000+	6.1
1939, Jan. 25	Chillan, Chile	28,000	7.8	2003, May 21	Northern Algeria	2,266	6.8
1939, Dec. 26	Erzincan, Turkey	32,700	7.8	2003, Dec. 26	Bam, SE Iran	31,000	6.6
1943, Sept. 10	Tottori, Japan	1,190	7.4	2004, Dec. 26	Sumatra-Andaman Isls.,		
1943, Nov. 26	Ladik, Turkey	4,000	7.6		Indonesia	227,898	9.1[7]
1944, Jan. 15	San Juan, Argentina	8,000	7.4	2005, Mar. 28	N Sumatra, Indonesia	1,313	8.6
1944, Feb. 1	Gerede, Turkey	2,790	7.4	2005, Oct. 8	Kashmir, Pakistan, India	86,000	7.6
1945, Jan. 12	Mikawa, Japan	1,961	7.1	2006, May 26	Java, Indonesia	5,749	6.3
1945, Nov. 27	Makran Coast, Pakistan	4,000	8.0	2008, May 12	E Sichuan Prov., China	87,857	7.9
1946, May 31	Ustukran, Turkey	1,300	5.9	2009, Sept. 30	Sumatra, Indonesia	1,117	7.5
1946, Nov. 10	Ancash, Peru	1,400	7.3	2010, Jan. 12	Haiti	316,000	7.0
1946, Dec. 20	Honshu, Japan	1,362	8.1	2010, Feb. 27	Chile	800	8.8
1948, June 28	Fukui, Japan	3,769	7.3	2010, Apr. 13	Southern Qinghai, China	2,698+	6.9
1948, Oct. 5	Ashgabat, Turkmenistan	110,000	7.3	2011, Mar. 11	NE Japan	20,896	9.0[8]

NA = Not available. (1) Once thought to have been a volcanic eruption; evidence indicates a destructive earthquake and tsunami occurred on this date. (2) This earthquake caused the most deadly tsunami to date in the Atlantic Ocean. (3) Incl. deaths from resulting fires; revised estimates of magnitude range from 7.7 to 7.9. (4) Commonly referred to as the Gansu Quake; actually located within the Ningxia autonomous region. (5) The largest recorded earthquake; caused a deadly tsunami that spread across the Pacific Ocean as far as Japan. (6) The "Good Friday" earthquake sent a tsunami that hit British Columbia, Canada, and the U.S. Pacific coast. (7) This undersea earthquake triggered devastating Indian Ocean tsunamis. (8) The most powerful earthquake in Japan's history set off a tsunami that inundated much of the coast and caused a partial meltdown of the Fukushima nuclear power plant.

Some Notable Fires Since 1918

See also Some Notable Explosions Since 1920.

Date	Location	Deaths	Date	Location	Deaths
1918, Oct. 12	Cloquet-Moose Lake, MN	453	1983, Feb. 16	"Ash Wednesday" bushfires, S Australia	75
1922, Oct. 4-5	Wind-blown fire, Haileybury, ON, Canada	43	1983, Dec. 17	Discotheque, Madrid, Spain	83
1929, May 10	Forest fire, Xochilapa, Mexico	60	1984, May 11	Great Adventure Amusement Park, Jackson Twp., NJ	8
1930, Apr. 21	Penitentiary, Columbus, OH	320	1985, Apr. 21	Movie theaters, Tabaco, Philippines	44
1931, July 24	Home for aged, Pittsburgh, PA	48	1985, Apr. 26	Hospital, Buenos Aires, Argentina	79
1934, Dec. 11	Hotel Kerns, Lansing, MI	34	1985, May 11	Soccer stadium, Bradford, Eng., UK	53
1938, May 16	Terminal Hotel, Atlanta, GA	35	1985, May 13	MOVE headquarters, row houses, Philadelphia, PA	11
1940, Apr. 23	Nightclub, Natchez, MS	198	1986, Dec. 31	Dupont Plaza Hotel, Puerto Rico	96
1942, Nov. 28	Cocoanut Grove Nightclub, Boston, MA	492	1987, May 6-June 2	Forest fire, Mohe, China	191
1942, Dec. 12	Hostel, St. John's, NL, Canada	100	1987, Nov. 17	Subway, London, England	30
1943, Sept. 7	Gulf Hotel, Houston, TX	55	1988, Mar. 20	About 2,000 buildings, Lashio, Myan.	134
1944, July 6	Ringling Circus, Hartford, CT	168	1990, Mar. 25	Social club, Bronx, NY	87
1946, June 5	LaSalle Hotel, Chicago, IL	61	1991, Mar. 3	Munitions dump, Addis Ababa, Ethiopia	260+
1946, Dec. 7	Winecoff Hotel, Atlanta, GA	119	1991, Aug-Oct.	Wildfires, Sumatra, Borneo, Indonesia	57
1946, Dec. 12	Ice plant, tenement, New York, NY	37	1991, Sept. 3	Processing plant, Hamlet, NC	25
1949, Apr. 5	Hospital, Effingham, IL	77	1991, Oct. 20-21	Wildfire, Oakland, Berkeley, CA	24
1949, Aug.	Forest fire, Landes, France	80	1992, Mar.	Forest fire, Terai, Nepal	56
1950, Jan. 7	Mercy Hospital, Davenport, IA	41	1993, Apr. 19	Cult compound, Waco, TX	72
1953, Mar. 29	Nursing home, Largo, FL	35	1994, May 10	Toy factory, Bangkok, Thailand	213
1953, Apr. 16	Metalworking plant, Chicago, IL	35	1994, July 4-10	South Canyon fire, Glenwood Springs, CO	14
1957, Feb. 17	Home for aged, Warrenton, MO	72	1994, Nov. 2	Burning fuel flood, Durunka, Egypt	500
1958, Mar. 19	Loft building, New York, NY	24	1994, Dec. 10	Theater, Karamay, China	300
1958, Dec. 1	Parochial school, Chicago, IL	95	1995, Oct. 28	Subway train, Baku, Azerbaijan	300
1958, Dec. 16	Store, Bogotá, Colombia	83	1995, Dec. 23	School, Mandi Dabwali, India	500+
1960, Mar. 12	Chemical plant, Pusan, Korea	68	1996, Mar. 19	Nightclub, Quezon City, Philippines	150+
1960, July 14	Mental hospital, Guatemala City	225	1996, Mar. 28	Shopping mall, Bogor, Indonesia	78
1960, Nov. 13	Movie theater, Amude, Syria	152	1996, Nov. 20	Garley Building, Hong Kong	39
1960, Dec. 19	USS *Constellation*, Brooklyn, NY	49	1997, Feb. 23	Worship site, Baripada, India	164
1961, Jan. 6	Thomas Hotel, San Francisco, CA	20	1997, Apr. 15	Encampment, Mina, Saudi Arabia	343
1961, Dec. 17	Circus, Niteroi, Brazil	323	1997, June 7	Temple, Thanjavur, India	60+
1963, May 4	Theater, Diourbel, Senegal	64	1997, June 13	Movie theater, New Delhi, India	60
1963, Nov. 18	Surfside Hotel, Atlantic City, NJ	25	1997, July 11	Hotel, Pattaya, Thailand	90
1963, Nov. 23	Nursing home, Fitchville, OH	63	1997, Sept.-Nov.	Drought-fueled fire, Sumatra, Indonesia	240
1963, Dec. 29	Roosevelt Hotel, Jacksonville, FL	22	1998, Apr.-June	Wildfire, Oaxaca, Mexico	50
1964, Dec. 18	Nursing home, Fountaintown, IN	20	1998, Dec. 3	Orphanage, Manila, Philippines	28
1965, Aug. 11-16	Watts riot fires, Los Angeles, CA	30+	1999, Mar. 24	Mt. Blanc Tunnel, France, Italy	40
1966, Dec. 7	Barracks, Erzurum, Turkey	68	1999, Oct. 30	Karaoke salon, Inchon, S. Korea	55+
1967, Feb. 7	Restaurant, Montgomery, AL	25	2000, Mar. 17	Church, Kanungu, Uganda	530
1967, Feb. 7	Scrub fire, Hobart, Tasmania, Australia	62	2000, Nov. 11	Cable car, Kaprun, Austria	155
1967, May 22	Dept. store, Brussels, Belgium	322	2000, Dec. 25	Shopping center, Luoyang, China	309
1967, July 16	State prison, Jay, FL	37	2001, Mar. 26	School, Machakos, Kenya	64
1967, July 29	USS *Forrestal*, off N Vietnam	134	2001, Aug. 18	Hotel, Quezon City, Philippines	73
1968, May 11	Wedding hall, Vijayawada, India	58	2001, Sept. 1	Nightclub, Tokyo, Japan	44
1969, Dec. 2	Nursing home, Notre Dame, QC, Canada	54	2001, Dec. 29	Fireworks accident, Lima, Peru	291
1970, Jan. 9	Nursing home, Marietta, OH	27	2003, Feb. 18	Subway train, Taegu, S. Korea	198
1970, Nov. 1	Dance hall, Grenoble, France	145	2003, Feb. 20	Pyrotechnics in nightclub, Warwick, RI	100
1970, Dec. 20	Hotel, Tucson, AZ	28	2003, Sept. 15	Prison, Riyadh, Saudi Arabia	94
1971, Dec. 25	Hotel, Seoul, S. Korea	162	2003, Nov. 24	Students' hostel, Moscow, Russia	36
1972, May 13	Nightclub, Osaka, Japan	116	2004, May 17	Prison, San Pedro Sula, Honduras	104
1972, July 5	Hospital, Sherborne, England, UK	30	2004, July 16	Pvt. school, Kumbakonam, India	80+
1973, June 24	Bar, New Orleans, LA	32	2004, Aug. 1	Market, Asunción, Paraguay	400+
1973, Aug. 3	Amusement park, Isle of Man, UK	51	2004, Dec. 30	Club, Buenos Aires, Argentina	194
1973, Nov. 29	Dept. store, Kumamoto, Japan	107	2005, Feb. 14	Mosque, Tehran, Iran	59
1973, Dec. 2	Theater, Seoul, S. Korea	50	2005, Mar. 7	Prison, Higuey, Dom. Republic	159
1974, Feb. 1	Bank building, São Paulo, Brazil	189	2005, Apr. 15	Hotel, Paris, France	22
1974, June 30	Discotheque, Port Chester, NY	24	2005, Sept. 5	Theater, Beni Suef, Egypt	32
1974, Nov. 3	Hotel, disco, Seoul, S. Korea	88	2006, Dec. 9	Drug treatment center, Moscow, Russ.	45
1975, Dec. 12	Tent city, Mina, Saudi Arabia	138	2007, Mar. 20	Nursing home Kamyshevatskaya, Russia	62
1976, Oct. 24	Social club, Bronx, NY	25	2007, Aug. 24-Sept. 2	Wildfires (arson), Greece	67
1977, Feb. 25	Rossiya Hotel, Moscow, Russia	45	2008, Apr. 26	Factory fire, Casablanca, Morocco	55
1977, May 28	Nightclub, Southgate, KY	164	2008, Sept.	Wildfires, Mozambique, S. Africa, Swaziland	89
1977, June 9	Nightclub, Abidjan, Ivory Coast	41	2009, Jan. 1	Nightclub fire, Bangkok, Thailand	67
1977, June 26	Jail, Columbia, TN	42	2009, Jan.-Feb.	Wildfires (arson), Victoria, Australia	173
1977, Nov. 14	Hotel, Manila, Philippines	47	2010, July	Bushfires, Nizhiny Novgorod, Russia	53
1978, Aug. 19	Movie theater, Abadan, Iran	425+	2010, Dec. 5	Grassland fire, Israel	44
1979, July 14	Hotel, Saragossa, Spain	80	2012, Feb. 14	Prison fire, Comayagua, Honduras	360+
1979, Dec. 31	Social club, Chapais, QC, Can.	42	2013, Jan. 27	Pyrotechnics in nightclub, Santa Maria, Brazil	241
1980, May 20	Nursing home, Kingston, Jamaica	157	2013, June 30	Wildfire, Prescott, AZ	19
1980, Nov. 21	MGM Grand Hotel, Las Vegas, NV	84	2014, May 2	Trade union building, Odessa, Ukraine	40+
1980, Dec. 4	Stouffer Inn, Harrison, NY	26			
1981, Jan. 9	Boarding home, Keansburg, NJ	30			
1981, Feb. 14	Discotheque, Dublin, Ireland	44			
1982, Nov. 8	County jail, Biloxi, MS	29			
1983, Feb. 13	Movie theater, Turin, Italy	64			

Some Notable Explosions Since 1920

See also Principal U.S. Mine Disasters Since 1900. Some bombings related to political conflicts and terrorism are not included.

Date	Location	Deaths	Date	Location	Deaths
1920, Sept. 16	Wall Street, New York, NY	30	1998, Feb. 14	2 oil tankers, Yaounde, Cameroon	120
1921, Sept. 21	Chem. storage facility, Oppau, Ger.	561	1998, Feb. 14	17 bombs, Coimbatore, India	50
1924, Jan. 3	Food plant, Pekin, IL.	42	1998, Apr. 4	Coal mine, Donetsk, Ukraine	63
1927, May 18	School bombing, Bath, MI	45	1998, Aug. 7	Bomb, U.S. emb., Nairobi, Kenya.	213
1928, Apr. 13	Dance hall, West Plains, MO	40	1998, Aug. 7	Bomb, U.S. emb., Dar-es-Salaam,	
1937, Mar. 18	School, New London, TX	311		Tanzania	11
1940, Sept. 12	Hercules Powder factory, Kenvil, NJ	55	1998, Sept. 8	2 buses, São Paulo, Brazil	59
1942, June 5	Ordnance plant, Elwood, IL	49	1998, Oct. 17	Oil pipeline, Jesse, Nigeria	700+
1944, Apr. 14	Harbor, Bombay, India	700	1999, May 16	Fuel truck, Punjab Prov., Pakistan	75
1944, July 17	Munitions ships, depot, Port Chicago,		1999, Sept. 10	Apartment building, Moscow, Russia	94
	CA	322	1999, Sept. 13	Apartment building, Moscow, Russia	118
1944, Oct. 20	Liquid natural gas tanks, Cleveland, OH	130	1999, Sept. 16	Apartment building, Moscow, Russia	18
1947, Apr. 16	Freighter, chemical co. plant,		1999, Sept. 26	Fireworks factory, Celaya, Mexico	56
	Texas City, TX.	576	2000, Feb. 25	Bombs on 2 buses, Ozamis, Philippines	41
1948, July 28	Farben works, Ludwigshafen, Ger.	184	2000, Mar. 11	Coal mine, Krasnodon, Ukraine	80
1950, May 19	Munitions barges, S. Amboy, NJ	30	2000, Apr. 16	Airport hangar, Dem. Rep. of Congo	100+
1954, May 26	USS Bennington, off RI	103	2000, July 16	Oil pipeline, Warri, Nigeria	30
1956, Aug. 7	Dynamite trucks, Cali, Colombia	1,100	2000, Sept. 9	Truck explosion, Urumqi, China	60
1958, Apr. 18	Sunken munitions ship, Okinawa, Japan	40	2000, Oct. 12	U.S. destroyer, Yemen	17
1959, Apr. 10	WWII bomb, Philippines	38	2001, Mar. 6	School, Jianxi Prov., China.	41
1959, June 28	Rail tank cars, Meldrim, GA	25	2001, Apr. 21	Coal mine, Shaanxi, China	51
1959, Nov. 2	Explosives, Jamuri Bazar, India	46	2001, June 1	Dance club, Tel Aviv, Israel	21
1959, Dec. 13	2 apt. bldgs., Dortmund, Ger.	26	2001, July 17	Coal mine, Guanxi, China.	76+
1960, Mar. 4	Belgian munitions ship, Havana, Cuba.	100	2001, Aug. 19	Coal mine, Donetsk region, Ukraine.	52
1962, Oct. 3	New York Telephone Co. office,		2001, Sept. 21	Chem. plant, Toulouse, France	29
	New York, NY	23	2002, Jan. 21	Volcanic lava caused gas station blast,	
1963, Jan. 2	Packing plant, Terre Haute, IN	17		Goma, Dem. Rep. of Congo	50+
1963, Mar. 9	Dynamite plant, S. Africa	45	2002, Jan. 27	Munitions dump, Lagos, Nigeria	1,000+
1963, Aug. 13	Explosives dump, Gauhaiti, India	32	2002, May 9	Land mine at parade, Kaspiisk,	
1963, Oct. 31	State Fair Coliseum, Indianapolis, IN	73		Russia	34+
1964, July 23	Harbor munitions, Bone, Algeria	100	2002, June 14	Car bomb outside U.S. consulate,	
1965, Aug. 9	Missile silo, Searcy, AR	53		Karachi, Pakistan	12
1965, Oct. 21	Bridge, Tila Bund, Pakistan	80	2002, June 18	Bomb on bus, Jerusalem, Israel	20
1965, Nov. 24	Armory, Keokuk, IA.	20	2002, July 5	Bomb in market, Larba, Algeria	35+
1967, Dec. 25	Apartment bldg., Moscow, USSR.	20	2002, Aug. 9	Explosion, Jalalabad, Afghanistan	25+
1968, Apr. 6	Sports store, Richmond, IN	43	2002, Sept. 5	Car bomb, Kabul, Afghanistan	30
1969, Mar. 31	Coal mine, nr. Barroteran, Mexico	180	2002, Oct. 12	Nightclub bombings, Bali, Indonesia	202
1970, Apr. 8	Subway construction, Osaka, Japan	73	2003, Aug. 25	Bombs in 2 taxis, Mumbai, India.	52
1971, June 24	Tunnel under construction, Sylmar, CA	17	2003, Dec. 5	Bomb on train, Yessentuki, Russia.	45
1973, Feb., 10	Liquid gas tank, Staten Island, NY	40	2003, Dec. 23	Gas well explosion, Chongqing, China.	233
1975, Dec. 27	Coal mine, Chasnala, India	431	2004, Jan. 19	Natural gas facility, Skikda, Algeria	27
1976, Apr. 13	Munitions works, Lapua, Finland	40	2004, Feb. 6	Bomb on subway car, Moscow, Russia	39
1977, Nov. 11	Freight train, Iri, S. Korea	57	2004, Mar. 11	Bombs on commuter trains, Madrid,	
1977, Dec. 22	Grain elevator, Westwego, LA	35		Spain.	191
1978, July 11	Propylene tank truck, Tarragona, Spain	150	2005, Feb. 14	Coal mine, NE China	214
1980, Oct. 23	School, Ortuella, Spain.	64	2005, Mar. 23	Oil refinery, Texas City, TX.	15
1982, Apr. 25	Antiques exhibition, Todi, Italy	33	2005, May 2	Arms cache, Baghlan Prov., Afghan.	34
1982, Nov. 2	Salang Tunnel, Afghanistan	1,000+	2005, July 7	Bombs in mass transit, London, Eng., UK	56
1984, Feb. 25	Oil pipeline, Cubatao, Brazil	508	2005, Oct. 1	Bombings of restaurants, Bali, Indonesia	26
1984, June 21	Naval supply depot, Severomorsk,		2005, Nov. 27	Coal mine, NE China	161+
	USSR	200+	2006, May 12	Oil pipeline, nr. Lagos, Nigeria	200
1984, Nov. 19	Gas storage area, NE Mexico City	334	2006, July 1	Bombings of trains, station, Mumbai,	
1984, Dec. 3	Chemical plant, Bhopal, India.	3,849		India	207
1984, Dec. 5	Coal mine, Taipei, Taiwan	94	2007, Mar. 19	Coal mine, Siberia, Russia	108
1985, June 25	Fireworks factory, Hallett, OK.	21	2007, Mar. 22	Natl. weapons depot, Maputo,	
1988, Apr. 10	Army ammunitions dump nr. Rawalpindi			Mozambique	117
	and Islamabad, Pakistan	100	2007, June 9	Oil pipeline, Pyongan Prov., N. Korea	110
1988, July 6	Oil rig, North Sea off NE Scotland, UK.	167	2007, Nov. 18	Methane gas buildup in coal mine,	
1989, June 3	Gas pipeline, between Ufa, Asha, USSR	650+		E Ukraine	90
1992, Mar. 3	Coal mine, Kozlu, Turkey.	270+	2008, May 15	Pipeline explosion in Lagos, Nigeria.	100+
1992, Apr. 22	Gas leak in sewers, Guadalajara,		2008, Sept. 20	Truck bomb outside hotel, Islamabad,	
	Mexico.	200+		Pakistan	40+
1992, May 9	Coal mine, Plymouth, Nova Scotia, Can.	26	2009, Feb. 22	Coal mine, N China	74
1993, Feb. 26	World Trade Center, New York, NY.	6	2010, Apr. 5	Coal mine, Montcoal, WV	29
1994, July 18	Jewish comm. center,		2010, May 8-9	Coal mine, Siberia, Russia	91
	Buenos Aires, Arg.	100	2010, June 17	Coal mine, Amaga, Colombia.	73
1995, Apr. 19	Fed. office building, Oklahoma City, OK	168	2010, Nov. 19	Coal mine, Ataru, New Zealand	29
1995, Apr. 29	Subway construction, S. Korea	110	2011, Mar. 28	Munitions factory, Abyan, Yemen.	150+
1996, Jan. 31	Bank, Colombo, Sri Lanka	53	2011, July 13	Bombs in three locations in Mumbai,	
1996, Mar. 3-4	Jerusalem and Tel Aviv, Israel	33		India	27
1996, June 25	U.S. military housing complex,		2012, Mar. 4	Arms depot, Brazzaville, Congo Rep.	250+
	nr. Dhahran, Saudi Arabia	19	2013, Apr. 17	Fire at fertilizer plant, West, TX.	14
1996, July 24	Train, Colombo, Sri Lanka	86	2013, June 3	Poultry plant, Mishzai, China	119+
1996, Nov. 16	Military apt., Dagestan region, Russia	68	2013, June 30	Fuel tanker, Kampala, Uganda	30+
1996, Nov. 21	Propane gas leak in bldg., San Juan,		2013, July 6	Derailed oil train, Lac-Megantic,	
	Puerto Rico.	33		QC, Canada	47
1996, Nov. 27	Coal mine, Shanxi Prov., China	91+	2013, Aug. 1	Weapons cache, Homs, Syria	40
1996, Dec. 30	Train, Assam, India.	59+	2014, May 13	Coal mine, Soma, Turkey.	301
1997, Dec. 2	Coal mine, Novokuznetsk, Russia	68	2014, May 19	Bus fire nr. Barranquilla, Colombia.	32

Notable Nuclear Accidents

Oct. 7, 1957: Fire in the Windscale plutonium production reactor N of Liverpool, England, UK, released radioactive material; later blamed for 39 cancer deaths.

Jan. 3, 1961: Reactor explosion at a federal installation near Idaho Falls, ID, killed 3 workers. Radiation contained.

Oct. 5, 1966: Sodium cooling system malfunction caused a partial core meltdown at the Enrico Fermi demonstration breeder reactor, near Detroit, MI. Radiation contained.

Jan. 21, 1969: Coolant malfunction from an experimental underground reactor at Lucens Vad, Switzerland, released radiation into a cavern, which was then sealed.

Mar. 22, 1975: Fire at the Brown's Ferry reactor in Decatur, AL, caused dangerous lowering of cooling water levels.

Mar. 28, 1979: Worst commercial nuclear accident in the U.S. occurred as equipment failures and human mistakes led to a loss of coolant and a partial core meltdown at the Three Mile Island reactor in Middletown, PA.

Feb. 11, 1981: Eight workers were contaminated when 100,000 gallons of radioactive coolant leaked into the containment building of TVA's Sequoyah 1 plant near Chattanooga, TN.

Apr. 25, 1981: Some 100 workers were exposed to radiation during repairs of a nuclear plant at Tsuruga, Japan.

Jan. 6, 1986: Cylinder of nuclear material burst after being improperly heated at a Kerr-McGee plant in Gore, OK. One worker died; 100 were hospitalized.

Apr. 26, 1986: Fires and resulting explosions at the Chernobyl nuclear power plant near Kiev, USSR (now in Ukraine), left at least 31 dead in the immediate aftermath and spread radioactive material over much of Europe. An estimated 135,000 people were evacuated. Tens of thousands of excess cancer deaths (as well as increased birth defects) were expected.

Sept. 1987: Cesium chloride from an improperly discarded hospital irradiation machine contaminated more than 200 people and killed at least 4 in Goiânia, Brazil. The event focused international attention on improving security and safety standards for radioactive waste.

Mar. 11, 2011: A 9.0-magnitude earthquake caused a devastating tsunami that inundated the Fukushima Daiichi nuclear power plant on Japan's NE coast. Three of the plant's reactors suffered partial meltdowns, and more than 12,000 tons of radioactive water was released into the sea. More than two years later, the plant's owners reported that 300 tons of radioactive water was still leaking into the ocean every day.

Record Oil Spills

The exact number of barrels in a ton varies with the type of oil, but a good approximation is 7 barrels per ton. Each barrel contains 42 gallons.

Name, location	Date	Cause	Est. tons
BP *Deepwater Horizon* rig, Gulf of Mexico, U.S.	Apr. 20-July 15, 2010	Explosion	700,000[1]
Ixtoc I oil well, S Gulf of Mexico	June 3, 1979	Blowout	600,000
Nowruz oil field, Persian Gulf	Feb. 1983	Blowout	600,000
Atlantic Empress and *Aegean Captain*, off Trinidad and Tobago	July 19, 1979	Collision	300,000
ABT Summer, off Angola	May 28, 1991	Explosion	260,000
Castillo de Bellver, off Cape Town, South Africa	Aug. 6, 1983	Fire	250,000
Amoco Cadiz, near Portsall, France	Mar. 16, 1978	Grounding	223,000
Torrey Canyon, off Land's End, England, UK.	Mar. 18, 1967	Grounding	119,000
Sea Star, Gulf of Oman	Dec. 19, 1972	Collision	115,000
Urquiola, La Coruna, Spain	May 12, 1976	Grounding	100,000

(1) The Dept. of Energy estimated the spill at 4.9 mil barrels, or more than 200 mil gallons.

Other Notable Oil Spills

Name, location	Date	Cause	Gallons
Persian Gulf	Jan. 21, 1991	Intentional spillage by Iraq	130,000,000[1]
Braer, off Shetland Islands, UK	Jan. 5, 1993	Grounding	26,000,000
Prestige, off N Spain	Nov. 13-19, 2002	Ship broke in half	22,600,000
Aegean Sea, off N Spain	Dec. 3, 1992	Grounding	21,500,000
Sea Empress, off SW Wales, UK.	Feb. 15, 1996	Grounding	18,000,000
Newtown Creek, Greenpoint, Brooklyn, NY	Oct. 5, 1950-present	Industrial explosion[2]	17,000,000
World Glory, off South Africa	June 13, 1968	Hull failure	13,524,000
Exxon Valdez, Prince William Sound, AK.	Mar. 24, 1989	Grounding	10,080,000
Ashland Oil facility, Floreffe, PA; Monongahela R.	Jan. 2, 1988	Storage tank collapse	3,850,000

(1) Est. by Saudi Arabia. Some estimates as low as 25 mil gal. (2) Preceded by leaks in 1940s-50s.

Notable Droughts

Source: EM-DAT: The OFDA/CRED Intl. Disaster Database, Université catholique de Louvain, Brussels, Belgium, www.emdat.be; World Almanac research

Date	Location	Est. deaths	Date	Location	Est. deaths
1900	Bengal, India.	1,250,000	1974-76	Somalia.	19,000
1900	Cape Verde islands.	11,000	1981-85	Mozambique.	100,000
1910-14	Zinder Dept., Niger.	85,000	1981-85	Chad.	3,000
1920	China.	500,000	1983	Swaziland.	500
1920	Cape Verde islands.	24,000	1983-84	Eritrea, Ethiopia.	300,000
1921	S Ukraine, Volga, USSR.	1,200,000	1983-85	N Sudan.	150,000
1928-30	Shaanxi, Henan, Gansu, China.	3,000,000	1987	Somalia, Eritrea, Ethiopia.	967
1940-44	Cape Verde islands.	20,000	1987	NW India.	300
1942	Calcutta, Bengal, India.	1,500,000	1988	Central China.	1,400
1943	Bangladesh.	1,900,000	1991	Jiangxi, Hunan Provinces, China.	2,000
1946	Cape Verde islands.	30,000	1997	Irian Jaya, Indonesia.	672
1965	Ethiopia.	2,000	1999-2003	Pakistan.	143
1965-67	India.	1,500,000	2002	Malawi.	500
1966	Lombok, Indonesia.	8,000	2005-06	Burundi.	120
1973-78	Ethiopia.	100,000	2006	SW China.	134

Some Notable Miscellaneous Disasters Since 1950

Date	Event	Location	Details	Est. deaths
1952, Dec.	Pollution	London, England, UK	Heavy smog blanketed city; impeded breathing	4,000
1980, summer	Heat wave.	United States	June through Sept.	1,265
1984, Dec. 3	Industrial accident.	Bhopal, India.	Toxic gas leaked from a Union Carbide factory.	16,000
1986, Aug. 21	Gas.	Nr. Lake Nyos, Cameroon	Volcanic lake released cloud of carbon dioxide gas	1,700
1990, July 2	Stampede.	Mecca, Saudi Arabia	Pilgrims panicked in tunnel leading to the holy city	1,426
2003, summer	Heat wave.	Europe	Abnormally high temperatures from Russia to Britain; France suffered most, with 14,800 dead	35,000
2013, Apr. 24	Building collapse.	Savar, Bangladesh	Garment factory found to have substandard foundation collapsed	1,100+

AEROSPACE

Notable Human Spaceflight Missions

Source: National Aeronautics and Space Administration (NASA); Congressional Research Service; World Almanac research

The spaceflights listed are a selection of notable U.S. missions by NASA, unless otherwise noted, plus non-U.S. missions (shown with an asterisk). The non-U.S missions were sponsored by the USSR—later, the Commonwealth of Independent States (CIS) and, from 1997, Russia—or by China. Launch dates are Eastern standard time. **EVA** = extravehicular activity. **ASTP** = Apollo-Soyuz Test Project. **STS** = Space Transportation System, NASA's name for the overall shuttle program.

For shuttle flights, mission name is in parentheses following name of orbiter. Duration of flight is listed in hours:minutes for 1961-Apr. 1970; days (d.), hours (hr.), and minutes (min.) for June 1970-Apr. 1981; days only thereafter. Number of total flights taken by each crew member is given in parentheses when flight listed is not the person's first.

4/12/1961: *Vostok 1*; 1:48; Yuri A. Gagarin. **1st human orbital flight.**

5/5/1961: *Mercury-Redstone 3*; 0:15; Alan B. Shepard Jr. **1st American in space.**

7/21/1961: *Mercury-Redstone 4*; 0:15; Virgil I. Grissom. Flight successful but spacecraft sank shortly after splashdown; Grissom rescued.

8/6/1961: *Vostok 2*; 25:18; Gherman S. Titov. 1st spaceflight of more than 24 hours.

2/20/1962: *Mercury-Atlas 6*; 4:55; John H. Glenn Jr. **1st American in orbit;** three orbits.

5/24/1962: *Mercury-Atlas 7*; 4:56; M. Scott Carpenter. Manual retrofire error caused 250-mi landing overshoot.

8/11/1962: *Vostok 3*; 94:22; Andrian G. Nikolayev. *Vostok 3* and *4* made 1st group flight.

8/12/1962: *Vostok 4*; 70:57; Pavel R. Popovich. On 1st orbit, it came within 3 mi of *Vostok 3*.

10/3/1962: *Mercury-Atlas 8*; 9:13; Walter M. Schirra Jr. Landed 5 mi from target; six orbits.

5/15/1963: *Mercury-Atlas 9*; 34:19; L. Gordon Cooper. 1st U.S. evaluation of effects of one day in space on a person; 22 orbits.

6/14/1963: *Vostok 5*; 119:06; Valery F. Bykovsky. *Vostok 5* and *6* made 2nd group flight.

6/16/1963: *Vostok 6*; 70:50; Valentina V. Tereshkova. **1st woman in space;** passed within 3 mi of *Vostok 5*.

10/12/1964: *Voskhod 1*; 24:17; Vladimir M. Komarov, Konstantin P. Feoktistov, Boris B. Yegorov. 1st three-person orbital flight; 1st without space suits.

3/18/1965: *Voskhod 2*; 26:02; Pavel I. Belyayev, Aleksei A. Leonov. Leonov made **1st spacewalk** (10 min.).

3/23/1965: *Gemini-Titan 3*; 4:53; Virgil I. Grissom (2), John W. Young. 1st piloted spacecraft to change its orbital path.

6/3/1965: *Gemini-Titan 4*; 97:56; James A. McDivitt, Edward H. White II. White was **1st American to "walk in space"** (36 min.).

8/21/1965: *Gemini-Titan 5*; 190:55; L. Gordon Cooper (2), Charles Conrad Jr. Longest-duration human flight to date.

12/4/1965: *Gemini-Titan 7*; 330:35; Frank Borman, James A. Lovell Jr. Longest-duration *Gemini* flight.

12/15/1965: *Gemini-Titan 6A*; 25:51; Walter M. Schirra Jr. (2), Thomas P. Stafford. Completed 1st U.S. space rendezvous, with *Gemini 7*.

3/16/1966: *Gemini-Titan 8*; 10:41; Neil A. Armstrong, David R. Scott. **1st docking of one space vehicle with another;** mission aborted, control malfunction; 1st Pacific landing.

6/3/1966: *Gemini-Titan 9A*; 72:21; Thomas P. Stafford (2), Eugene A. Cernan. Performed simulation of lunar module rendezvous.

7/18/1966: *Gemini-Titan 10*; 70:47; John W. Young (2), Michael Collins. 1st use of Agena target vehicle's propulsion systems; 1st orbital docking.

9/12/1966: *Gemini-Titan 11*; 71:17; Charles Conrad Jr. (2), Richard F. Gordon Jr. 1st tethered flight; highest Earth-orbit altitude (850 mi).

11/11/1966: *Gemini-Titan 12*; 94:34; James A. Lovell Jr. (2), Edwin E. "Buzz" Aldrin Jr. Final *Gemini* mission; 5-hr. EVA.

1/27/1967: *Apollo 1*; Virgil I. Grissom, Edward H. White II, and Roger B. Chaffee died in a fire on the ground at Cape Canaveral, FL.

4/23/1967: *Soyuz 1*; 26:40; Vladimir M. Komarov (2). Crashed on reentry, killing Komarov; **1st space fatality.**

10/11/1968: *Apollo-Saturn 7*; 260:09; Walter M. Schirra Jr. (3), Donn F. Eisele, R. Walter Cunningham. **1st piloted flight of Apollo** spacecraft command-service module only; live TV footage of crew.

12/21/1968: *Apollo-Saturn 8*; 147:00; Frank Borman (2), James A. Lovell Jr. (3), William A. Anders. **1st lunar orbit** and piloted lunar return reentry (command-service module only); views of lunar surface televised to Earth.

1/14/1969: *Soyuz 4*; 71:21; Vladimir A. Shatalov. Docked with *Soyuz 5.*

1/15/1969: *Soyuz 5*; 72:54; Boris V. Volyanov, Aleksei S. Yeliseyev, Yevgeny V. Khrunov. Docked with *Soyuz 4*; Yeliseyev and Khrunov transferred to *Soyuz 4* via a spacewalk.

3/3/1969: *Apollo-Saturn 9*; 241:00; James A. McDivitt (2), David R. Scott (2), Russell L. Schweickart. 1st piloted flight of lunar module.

5/18/1969: *Apollo-Saturn 10*; 192:03; Thomas P. Stafford (3), John W. Young (3), Eugene A. Cernan (2). 1st lunar module orbit of Moon, 50,000 ft from Moon's surface.

7/16/1969: *Apollo-Saturn 11*; 195:18; Neil A. Armstrong (2), Michael Collins (2), Edwin E. "Buzz" Aldrin Jr. (2). **1st Moon landing** made by Armstrong and Aldrin (7/20); collected 48.5 lbs of soil, rock samples; lunar stay time 21:36.

10/11/1969: *Soyuz 6*; 118:43; Georgi S. Shonin, Valery N. Kubasov. 1st welding of metals in space.

10/12/1969: *Soyuz 7*; 118:40; Anatoly V. Flipchenko, Vladislav N. Volkov, Viktor V. Gorbatko. Space lab construction test made; *Soyuz 6, 7,* and *8:* 1st time three spacecraft, seven crew members orbited the Earth at once.

10/13/1969: *Soyuz 8*; 118:51; Vladimir A. Shatalov (2), Aleksei S. Yeliseyev (2). Part of space lab construction team.

11/14/1969: *Apollo-Saturn 12*; 244:36; Charles Conrad Jr. (3), Richard F. Gordon Jr. (2), Alan L. Bean. Conrad and Bean made **2nd Moon landing** (11/18); collected 74.7 lbs of samples; lunar stay time 31:31.

4/11/1970: *Apollo-Saturn 13*; 142:54; James A. Lovell Jr. (4), Fred W. Haise Jr., John L. Swigert Jr. Aborted after service module oxygen tank ruptured; crew returned in lunar module.

6/1/1970: *Soyuz 9*; 17 d., 16 hr., 59 min.; Andrian G. Niko-layev (2), Vitaly I. Sevastyanov. Longest human spaceflight to date.

1/31/1971: *Apollo-Saturn 14*; 9 d., 2 min.; Alan B. Shepard Jr. (2), Stuart A. Roosa, Edgar D. Mitchell. Shepard and Mitchell made **3rd Moon landing** (2/3); collected 96 lbs of lunar sam-ples; lunar stay 33:31.

4/19/1971: *Salyut 1*; launched without crew. **1st space station.**

4/22/1971: *Soyuz 10*; 1 d., 23 hr., 46 min.; Vladimir A. Shatalov (3), Aleksei S. Yeliseyev (3), Nikolay N. Rukavishnikov. **1st successful docking with a space station;** failed to enter space station.

6/6/1971: *Soyuz 11*; 23 d., 28 hr., 22 min.; Georgi T. Dobrovol-skiy, Vladislav N. Volkov (2), Viktor I. Patsayev. Docked and entered *Salyut 1* space station; **crew died** during reentry from loss of pressurization.

7/26/1971: *Apollo-Saturn 15*; 12 d., 17 hr., 12 min.; David R. Scott (3), James B. Irwin, Alfred M. Worden. Scott and Irwin made **4th Moon landing** (7/30). 1st lunar rover use; 1st deep spacewalk; 170 lbs of samples; 66:55 stay.

4/16/1972: *Apollo-Saturn 16*; 11 d., 1 hr., 51 min.; John W. Young (4), Charles M. Duke Jr., Thomas K. Mattingly II.

Young and Duke made **5th Moon landing** (4/20); collected 213 lbs of lunar samples; lunar stay 71:02.

12/7/1972: *Apollo-Saturn 17*; 12 d., 13 hr., 52 min.; Eugene A. Cernan (3), Ronald E. Evans, Harrison H. Schmitt. Cernan and Schmitt made 6th and **last crewed lunar landing** (12/11); collected 243 lbs of samples; record lunar stay over 75 hr.

5/14/1973: *Skylab 1*; launched without crew. **1st U.S. space station**; fell out of orbit 7/11/1979.

5/25/1973: *Skylab 2*; 28 d., 49 min.; Charles Conrad Jr. (4), Joseph P. Kerwin, Paul J. Weitz. 1st U.S.-piloted orbiting space station; crew repaired damage caused in boost.

7/28/1973: *Skylab 3*; 59 d., 11 hr., 1 min.; Alan L. Bean (2), Owen K. Garriott, Jack R. Lousma. Crew systems and operational tests; scientific activities; three EVAs, 13:44.

11/16/1973: *Skylab 4*; 84 d., 1 hr., 16 min.; Gerald P. Carr, Edward G. Gibson, William R. Pogue. Final *Skylab* mission.

7/15/1975: *Soyuz 19 (ASTP)*; 6 d., 11 hr., 31 min.; Aleksei A. Leonov (2), Valery N. Kubasov (2). U.S.-USSR joint flight; crews linked up in space (7/17), conducted experiments, shared meals, held a joint news conference.

7/15/1975: *Apollo (ASTP)*; 9 d., 7 hr., 28 min.; Vance D. Brand, Thomas P. Stafford (4), Donald K. Slayton. Joint flight with *Soyuz 19*.

12/10/1977: *Soyuz 26*; 96 d., 10 hr.; Yuri V. Romanenko, Georgiy M. Grechko (2). 1st multiple docking at a space station (*Soyuz 26* and 27 docked at *Salyut 6*).

1/10/1978: *Soyuz 27*; 5 d., 22 hr., 59 min.; Vladimir A. Dzhanibekov. See *Soyuz 26*.

3/2/1978: *Soyuz 28*; 7 d., 22 hr., 16 min.; Aleksei A. Gubarev (2), Vladimir Remek. 1st international crew launch; Remek was 1st Czech in space.

4/12/1981: *Columbia (STS-1)*; 2 d., 6 hr., 21 min.; John W. Young (5), Robert L. Crippen. **1st reusable space shuttle** to fly into Earth's orbit.

11/12/1981: *Columbia (STS-2)*; 3 days; Joe H. Engle, Richard H. Truly. 1st scientific payload; 1st reuse of space shuttle.

11/11/1982: *Columbia (STS-5)*; 6 days; Vance D. Brand (2), Robert F. Overmyer, Joseph P. Allen, William B. Lenoir. 1st four-person crew.

6/18/1983: *Challenger (STS-7)*; 7 days; Robert L. Crippen (3), Frederick H. Hauck, John M. Fabian, Sally K. Ride, Norman E. Thagard. Ride was **1st U.S. woman in space**; 1st 5-person crew.

6/27/1983: *Soyuz T-9*; 150 days; Vladimir A. Lyakhov (2), Aleksandr Pavlovich. Docked at *Salyut 7*. 1st construction in space.

8/30/1983: *Challenger (STS-8)*; 7 days; Richard H. Truly (2), Daniel C. Brandenstein, Dale A. Gardner, Guion S. Bluford Jr., William E. Thornton. Bluford was **1st African American in space**; **1st night launch**.

11/28/1983: *Columbia (STS-9)*; 11 days; John W. Young (6), Brewster H. Shaw Jr., Owen K. Garriott (2), Robert A.R. Parker, Byron K. Lichtenberg, Ulf Merbold. 1st six-person crew; 1st Spacelab mission.

2/3/1984: *Challenger (41-B)*; 8 days; Vance Brand (3), Robert L. Gibson, Ronald E. McNair, Bruce McCandless II, Robert L. Stewart. 1st untethered EVA.

2/8/1984: *Soyuz T-10B*; 63 days; Leonid Kizim, Vladimir Solovyov, Oleg Atkov. Docked with *Salyut 7*; crew set space duration record of 237 days.

4/3/1984: *Soyuz T-11*; 182 days; Yury Malyshev (2), Gennady Strekalov (3), Rakesh Sharma. Docked with *Salyut 7*; Sharma was 1st Indian in space.

4/6/1984: *Challenger (41-C)*; 7 days; Robert L. Crippen (3), Francis R. Scobee, George D. Nelson, Terry J. Hart, James D. van Hoften. 1st in-orbit satellite repair.

7/17/1984: *Soyuz T-12*; 12 days; Vladimir A. Dzhanibekov (4), Svetlana Y. Savitskaya (2), Igor P. Volk. Docked at *Salyut 7*; Savitskaya was 1st woman to perform EVA.

8/30/1984: *Discovery (41-D)*; 7 days; Henry W. Hartsfield Jr. (2), Michael L. Coats, Richard M. Mullane, Steven A. Hawley,

Judith A. Resnik, Charles D. Walker. 1st flight of non-astronaut (payload specialist Walker).

10/5/1984: *Challenger (41-G)*; 9 days; Robert L. Crippen (4), Jon A. McBride, Kathryn D. Sullivan, Sally K. Ride (2), David C. Leestma, Marc Garneau, Paul D. Scully-Power. 1st seven-person crew.

11/8/1984: *Discovery (51-A)*; 8 days; Frederick H. Hauck (2), David M. Walker, Anna L. Fisher, Dale A. Gardner, Joseph P. Allen (2). 1st satellite retrieval/repair.

4/12/1985: *Discovery (51-D)*; 7 days; Karol J. Bobko, Donald E. Williams, Charles D. Walker (2), M. Rhea Seddon, Jeffrey A. Hoffman, S. David Griggs, E. Jake Garn. Garn (R, UT) was **1st U.S. senator in space**.

6/17/1985: *Discovery (51-G)*; 8 days; Daniel C. Brandenstein (2), John O. Creighton, Shannon W. Lucid, John M. Fabian (2), Steven R. Nagel, Prince Sultan Salman al-Saud, Patrick Baudry. Launched three satellites; Salman al-Saud was 1st Arab in space; Baudry was 1st French person on U.S. mission.

10/3/1985: *Atlantis (51-J)*; 5 days; Karol J. Bobko (3), Ronald J. Grabe, David C. Hilmers, Robert L. Stewart (2), William A. Pailes. 1st *Atlantis* flight.

10/30/1985: *Challenger (61-A)*; 8 days; Henry W. Hartsfield Jr. (3), Steven R. Nagel (2), James F. Buchli (2), Guion S. Bluford (2), Bonnie J. Dunbar, Wubbo J. Ockels, Richard Furrer, Ernst Messerschmid. 1st eight-person crew; 1st German Spacelab mission.

1/12/1986: *Columbia (61-C)*; 7 days; Robert L. Gibson (2), Charles F. Bolden Jr., Franklin R. Chang Díaz, Steven A. Hawley (2), George D. Nelson (2), Robert J. Cenker, Bill Nelson. B. Nelson (D, FL) was **1st U.S. representative in space**.

1/28/1986: *Challenger (51-L)*; 73 seconds; Francis R. Scobee (2), Michael J. Smith, Judith A. Resnik (2), Ellison S. Onizuka (2), Ronald E. McNair, Gregory B. Jarvis, Christa McAuliffe. **Exploded 73 seconds after liftoff; all aboard were killed**, including McAuliffe, a New Hampshire schoolteacher who had won a national competition to become 1st private citizen in space.

2/20/1986: *Mir[1]*; launched without crew. **Space station** with six docking ports launched.

3/13/1986: *Soyuz T-15*; 125 days; Leonid Kizim (3), Vladimir Solovyov (2). Ferry between stations; docked at *Mir*.

2/5/1987: *Soyuz TM-2*; 327 days; Yuri V. Romanenko (3), Aleksandr I. Laveikin. Romanenko set then-endurance record.

7/22/1987: *Soyuz TM-3*; 161 days; Aleksandr Viktorenko, Aleksandr Pavlovich Aleksandrov (2), Mohammed Faris. Docked with *Mir*; Faris was 1st Syrian in space.

9/29/1988: *Discovery (STS-26)*; 4 days; Frederick H. Hauck (3), Richard O. Covey (2), George D. Nelson (3), John M. Lounge (2), David C. Hilmers (2). **1st shuttle flight since Challenger explosion** 1/28/1986.

5/4/1989: *Atlantis (STS-30)*; 4 days; David M. Walker (2), Ronald J. Grabe (2), Norman E. Thagard (3), Mary L. Cleave (2), Mark C. Lee. Launched Venus orbiter *Magellan*.

10/18/1989: *Atlantis (STS-34)*; 5 days; Donald E. Williams (2), Michael J. McCulley, Shannon W. Lucid (2), Franklin R. Chang Díaz (2), Ellen S. Baker. Launched Jupiter probe and orbiter *Galileo*.

4/24/1990: *Discovery (STS-31)*; 6 days; Loren J. Shriver (2), Charles F. Bolden Jr. (2), Steven A. Hawley (3), Bruce McCandless (2), Kathryn D. Sullivan (2). **Launched Hubble Space Telescope**.

10/6/1990: *Discovery (STS-41)*; 5 days; Richard N. Richards (2), Robert D. Cabana, Bruce E. Melnick, William M. Shepherd (2), Thomas D. Akers. Launched *Ulysses* spacecraft to investigate interstellar space and the Sun.

5/18/1991: *Soyuz TM-12*; 145 days; Anatoly Artsebarsky, Sergei Krikalev (2) (to *Mir*), Helen Sharman. Docked with *Mir*; Sharman was 1st Briton in space.

3/17/1992: *Soyuz TM-14*; 146 days; Aleksandr Viktorenko (3) (to *Mir*), Alexandr Kaleri (to *Mir*), Klaus-Dietrich Flade, Aleksandr Volkov (3) (from *Mir*), Sergei Krikalev (3) (from *Mir*). 1st human CIS space mission; docked with *Mir* 3/19; Krikalev was in space 313 days.

5/7/1992: *Endeavour (STS-49)*; 9 days; Daniel C. Brandenstein (4), Kevin P. Chilton, Pierre J. Thuot (2), Kathryn Thornton (2), Richard J. Hieb (2), Thomas D. Akers (2), Bruce E. Melnick (2). 1st 3-person EVA; satellite recovery and redeployment.

9/12/1992: *Endeavour (STS-47)*; 8 days; Robert L. Gibson (4), Curtis L. Brown Jr., Mark C. Lee (2), N. Jan Davis, Jay Apt (2), Mae Carol Jemison, Mamoru Mohri. Jemison was **1st black woman in space**; Lee and Davis were **1st married couple to travel together in space**; 1st Japanese Spacelab.

6/21/1993: *Endeavour (STS-57)*; 10 days; Ronald J. Grabe (4), Brian J. Duffy (2), G. David Low (3), Nancy J. Sherlock, Janice E. Voss, Peter J. K. Wisoff. Carried Spacelab commercial payload module.

12/2/1993: *Endeavour (STS-61)*; 11 days; Richard O. Covey (3), Kenneth D. Bowersox (2), F. Story Musgrave (5), Kathryn Thornton (3), Claude Nicollier (2), Jeffrey A. Hoffman (4), Thomas D. Akers (4). Hubble Space Telescope repaired; Akers set new U.S. EVA duration record (29 hr., 40 min.).

2/3/1994: *Discovery (STS-60)*; 9 days; Charles F. Bolden Jr. (3), Kenneth S. Reightler Jr. (2), N. Jan Davis (2), Franklin R. Chang Díaz (3), Ronald M. Sega, Sergei Krikalev (3). Krikalev was 1st Russian on U.S. shuttle.

7/1/1994: *Soyuz TM-19*; 126 days; Yuri I. Malenchenko, Talgat A. Musabayev, Ulf Merbold (2) (from *Mir*). Docked with *Mir*.

9/9/1994: *Discovery (STS-64)*; 11 days; Richard N. Richards (4), L. Blaine Hammond Jr. (2), Jerry M. Linenger, Susan J. Helms (2), Carl J. Meade (3), Mark C. Lee (3). Performed atmospheric research; 1st untethered EVA in more than 10 years.

2/3/1995: *Discovery (STS-63)*; 9 days; James D. Wetherbee (3), Eileen M. Collins, Bernard A. Harris (2), C. Michael Foale (3), Janice E. Voss (2), Vladimir Titov (4). *Discovery* and Russian space station rendezvous.

3/2/1995: *Endeavour (STS-67)*; 17 days; Stephen S. Oswald (3), William G. Gregory, Tamara E. Jernigan (3), John M. Grunsfeld, Wendy B. Lawrence, Ronald Parise (2), Samuel T. Durrance (2). Shuttle data made available on the Internet.

3/14/1995: *Soyuz TM-21*; 112 days; Norman E. Thagard (5), Vladimir Dezhurov, Gennady Strekalov (3). Docked with *Mir* 3/16. Thagard was 1st American onboard Russian spacecraft; Valery Polyakov returned to Earth, 3/22/1995, after record stay in space (439 days).

6/27/1995: *Atlantis (STS-71)*; 10 days; Robert L. Gibson (5), Charles J. Precourt (2), Ellen S. Baker (3), Bonnie J. Dunbar (4), Gregory J. Harbaugh (3), Anatoly Solovyev (4) (to *Mir*), Nikolai M. Budarin (to *Mir*), Norman E. Thagard (5) (from *Mir*), Gennady Strekalov (from *Mir*), Vladimir Dezhurov (from *Mir*). **1st shuttle-*Mir* docking**; exchanged crew members with *Mir*.

11/12/1995: *Atlantis (STS-74)*; 9 days; Kenneth D. Cameron (3), James D. Halsell Jr. (2), Jerry L. Ross (5), William S. McArthur Jr. (2), Chris A. Hadfield. 2nd shuttle-*Mir* docking (11/15-11/18); erected a 15-ft permanent docking tunnel to *Mir* for future use by U.S. orbiters.

2/22/1996: *Columbia (STS-75)*; 16 days; Andrew M. Allen (3), Scott J. Horowitz, Franklin R. Chang Díaz (5), Umberto Guidoni, Jeffrey A. Hoffman (5), Maurizio Cheli, Claude Nicollier (3). Lost an Italian satellite when its tether was severed; microgravity experiments performed; singe marks found on two O-rings.

3/22/1996: *Atlantis (STS-76)*; 10 days; Kevin P. Chilton (3), Richard A. Searfoss (2), Shannon W. Lucid (5) (to *Mir*), Linda M. Godwin (3), Michael R. Clifford (3), Ronald M. Sega (2). 3rd shuttle-*Mir* docking (5 days); two-person EVA.

9/16/1996: *Atlantis (STS-79)*; 11 days; William F. Readdy (3), Terry W. Wilcutt (2), Thomas D. Akers (4), John E. Blaha (5) (to *Mir*), Jay Apt (4), Carl E. Walz (3), Shannon W. Lucid (5)

(from *Mir*). Docked with *Mir* 9/18; exchanged crew members; Lucid set **U.S. and women's duration in space record** (188 days).

11/19/1996: *Columbia (STS-80)*; 18 days; Kenneth D. Cockrell (3), Kent V. Rominger (2), Tamara E. Jernigan (4), Thomas D. Jones (3), F. Story Musgrave (6). Longest-duration shuttle flight; Musgrave, 61, oldest thus far to fly in space; two science satellites deployed, retrieved.

1/12/1997: *Atlantis (STS-81)*; 11 days; Michael A. Baker (4), Brent W. Jett (2), John M. Grunsfeld (2), Marsha S. Ivins (4), Peter J. K. Wisoff (3), Jerry M. Linenger (2) (to *Mir*), John E. Blaha (5) (from *Mir*). Docked with *Mir* 1/14-1/19; Blaha spent 128 days in space.

2/11/1997: *Discovery (STS-82)*; 10 days; Kenneth D. Bowersox (4), Scott J. Horowitz (2), Mark C. Lee (4), Steven A. Hawley (4), Gregory J. Harbaugh (4), Steven L. Smith (2), Joseph R. Tanner (2). Increased capabilities of Hubble Space Telescope; five EVAs conducted to service it.

5/15/1997: *Atlantis (STS-84)*; 10 days; Charles J. Precourt (3), Eileen M. Collins (2), C. Michael Foale (4) (to *Mir*), Carlos I. Noriega, Edward T. Lu, Jean-François Clervoy (2), Elena Kondakova, Jerry M. Linenger (2) (from *Mir*). Docked with *Mir* 5/16-5/21. Foale's stay on *Mir* marked by major collision with cargo ship 6/25/1997.

8/5/1997: *Soyuz TM-26*; 198 days; Anatoly Solovyev (5), Pavel Vinogradov. Docked with *Mir* 8/7; repaired damaged space station.

8/7/1997: *Discovery (STS-85)*; 12 days; Curtis L. Brown Jr. (4), Kent V. Rominger (3), N. Jan Davis (3), Robert L. Curbeam Jr., Stephen K. Robinson, Bjarni V. Tryggvason. Deployed and retrieved satellite designed to study Earth's middle atmosphere; demonstrated robotic arm.

9/25/1997: *Atlantis (STS-86)*; 11 days; James D. Wetherbee (4), Michael J. Bloomfield, Vladimir Titov (5), Scott E. Parazynski (2), Jean-Loup J. Chrétien (3), Wendy B. Lawrence (2), David A. Wolf (2) (to *Mir*), C. Michael Foale (4) (from *Mir*). Docked with *Mir* 9/27-10/3; delivered new computer to *Mir*.

4/17/1998: *Columbia (STS-90)*; 16 days; Richard A. Searfoss (3), Scott D. Altman, Richard M. Linnehan (2), Dave R. Williams, Kathryn P. Hire, Jay C. Buckey, James A. Pawelczyk. Studied effects of microgravity on the nervous systems of the crew and more than 2,000 live animals; 1st surgery in space on animals meant to survive.

6/2/1998: *Discovery (STS-91)*; 10 days; Charles J. Precourt (4), Dominic L. Gorie, Wendy B. Lawrence (3), Franklin R. Chang Díaz (6), Janet L. Kavandi, Valery V. Ryumin (4), Andrew S. W. Thomas (2) (from *Mir*). Final docking mission with *Mir*; Thomas from *Mir*, 141 days in space.

10/29/1998: *Discovery (STS-95)*; 10 days; Curtis L. Brown Jr. (5), Steven W. Lindsey (2), Scott E. Parazynski (3), Stephen K. Robinson (2), Pedro Duque, Chiaki Mukai (2), John H. Glenn Jr. (2). The 77-year-old Glenn, one of the original Mercury astronauts, and at that point a senator (D, OH), became **oldest person to fly in space**; Duque was 1st Spaniard in space; experiments to study aging performed on Glenn.

12/4/1998: *Endeavour (STS-88)*; 12 days; Robert D. Cabana (4), Frederick W. Sturckow, Nancy J. Currie (3), Jerry L. Ross (6), James H. Newman (3), Sergei K. Krikalev (4). **1st assembly of International Space Station (ISS)**; attached U.S.-built *Unity* connecting module to Russian-built *Zarya* control module; 1st crew to enter ISS.

7/23/1999: *Columbia (STS-93)*; 5 days; Eileen M. Collins (3), Jeffrey S. Ashby, Steven A. Hawley (5), Catherine G. Coleman (2), Michel Tognini (2). Collins was **1st woman space shuttle commander**; deployed Chandra X-ray Observatory telescope.

2/11/2000: *Endeavour (STS-99)*; 12 days; Kevin R. Kregel (4), Dominic L. Gorie (2), Janet L. Kavandi (2), Janice E. Voss (5), Mamoru Mohri (2), Gerhard P.J. Thiele (2). Used radar to make most complete topographic map of Earth's surface ever produced.

9/8/2000: *Atlantis (STS-106)*; 12 days; Terry W. Wilcutt (4), Scott D. Altman (2), Edward T. Lu (2), Richard A. Mastracchio, Daniel C. Burbank, Yuri I. Malenchenko (2), Boris V. Morukov. Prepared ISS for 1st permanent crew; one EVA by all seven crew members.

10/31/2000: **Soyuz TM-31*; William M. Shepherd (4), Yuri Gidzenko (2), Sergei Krikalev (5). Established **1st permanent manning of ISS** with three-person crew for a 4-month stay.

3/8/2001: *Discovery (STS-102)*; 13 days; James D. Wetherbee (5), James M. Kelly, Andrew S.W. Thomas (2), Paul Richards, Susan J. Helms (2) (to ISS), James S. Voss (5) (to ISS), Yuri V. Usachev (4) (to ISS), William M. Shepherd (4) (from ISS), Sergei K. Krikalev (5) (from ISS), Yuri P. Gidzenko (2) (from ISS). Transported 2nd permanent crew to ISS and returned 1st crew to Earth; two EVAs.

7/12/2001: *Atlantis (STS-104)*; 13 days; Steven W. Lindsey (3), Charles O. Hobaugh, Michael L. Gernhardt (4), Janet L. Kavandi (3), James F. Reilly II (2). Installed the Joint Airlock, with nitrogen and oxygen tanks to permit future spacewalks from the ISS; three EVAs.

3/1/2002: *Columbia (STS-109)*; 11 days; Scott D. Altman (3), Duane G. Carey, John M. Grunsfeld (4), Nancy J. Currie (4), Richard M. Linnehan (3), James H. Newman (4), Michael J. Massimino. Installed powerful new camera and upgraded other equipment on Hubble Space Telescope; five EVAs.

4/8/2002: *Atlantis (STS-110)*; 11 days; Michael J. Bloomfield (3), Stephen N. Frick, Jerry L. Ross (7), Steven L. Smith (4) Ellen Ochoa (4), Lee M.E. Morin, Rex J. Walheim. Installed S0 Truss, backbone for expansion of ISS; Ross set records with 7th spaceflight, 9th spacewalk.

10/30/2002: **Soyuz TMA-1*[2]; Sergei Zalyotin (2), Frank De Winne, Yuri Lonchakov (2). 1st launch of *Soyuz TMA* (crew returned 11/10/2002 on *Soyuz TM-34* already docked at ISS).

1/16/2003: *Columbia (STS 107)*; 16 days; Rick D. Husband (2), William C. McCool, Michael P. Anderson (2), David M. Brown, Kalpana Chawla (2), Laurel B. Clark, Ilan Ramon. Entire crew lost when *Columbia* burned during reentry, 2/1; Ramon was 1st Israeli astronaut.

10/15/2003: **Shenzhou 5*; 21 hr.; Yang Liwei. **1st Chinese manned spacecraft.**

6/21/2004: *SpaceShipOne*[3]; 90 min.; Mike Melvill. **1st privately funded manned spaceflight.**

7/26/2005: *Discovery (STS-114)*; 14 days; Eileen M. Collins (4), James M. Kelly (2), Charles J. Camarda, Wendy B. Lawrence (4), Soichi Noguchi, Stephen K. Robinson (3), Andrew S.W. Thomas (3). **1st space shuttle flight since *Columbia* disaster**; tested new safety modifications to craft.

7/4/2006: *Discovery (STS-121)*; 13 days; Steven W. Lindsey (4), Mark E. Kelly, Michael E. Fossum, Piers J. Sellers (2), Lisa M. Nowak, Thomas Reiter (to ISS), Stephanie D. Wilson. 1st shuttle to launch on Independence Day; conducted more safety tests to craft; brought supplies and performed maintenance on ISS.

4/7/2007: **Soyuz TMA-10*[2]; Oleg Kotov (to ISS), Sheikh Muszaphar Shukor (from ISS), Charles Simonyi (U.S.), Fyodor Yurchikhin (to ISS). Kotov and Yurchikhin joined ISS expedition 15; Simonyi became **5th space tourist** (returned on *TMA-9*); Shukor was 1st Malaysian in space (arrived on *TMA-11*).

6/8/2007: *Atlantis (STS-117)*; 14 days; Frederick W. Sturckow (3), Lee J. Archambault, Patrick G. Forrester (2), John "Danny" Olivas, James F. Reilly (3), Steven R. Swanson, Clayton C. Anderson (to ISS), Sunita L. Williams (from ISS). Delivered

truss segments and solar arrays to ISS; Williams set record for **longest spaceflight by a woman**.

8/8/2007: *Endeavour (STS-118)*; 13 days; Scott J. Kelly (2), Charles O. Hobaugh (2), Alvin B. Drew, Barbara R. Morgan, Tracy Caldwell Dyson, Rick A. Mastracchio (2), Dave R. Williams (2). Brought **Teacher in Space** project participant Morgan to ISS; attached new truss segment; repaired faulty gyroscope.

10/10/2007: **Soyuz TMA-11*[2]; Yuri I. Malenchenko (3), Sheikh Muszaphar Shukor (to ISS), Peggy A. Whitson (2) (from ISS), Yi So-yeon (from ISS). Delivered and installed components of ISS; malfunctioned on return to Earth, landing short of its touchdown area but causing no fatalities.

10/23/2007: *Discovery (STS-120)*; 16 days; Pamela A. Melroy (3), George D. Zamka, Scott E. Parazynski (5), Douglas H. Wheelock, Stephanie D. Wilson (2), Paolo Nespoli, Daniel M. Tani (2) (to ISS), Clayton C. Anderson (from ISS). Installed living space (Harmony Node 2) on ISS.

2/7/2008: *Atlantis (STS-122)*; 13 days; Stephen N. Frick (2), Stanley G. Love, Leland D. Melvin, Alan G. Poindexter, Hans Schlegel (2), Léopold Eyharts (to ISS), Daniel M. Tani (from ISS), Rex J. Walheim (2). Installed European Space Agency's Columbus laboratory on the ISS; minor damage to a thermal plate caused concern about the shuttle's safety during reentry, but *Atlantis* landed safely.

3/11/2008: *Endeavour (STS-123)*; 16 days; Dominic L. Gorie (4), Gregory H. Johnson, Richard M. Linnehan (4), Robert L. Behnken, Michael J. Foreman, Takao Doi (2), Garrett Reisman (to ISS), Léopold Eyharts (from ISS). Delivered and installed components of the Japanese Kibo science laboratory.

4/8/2008: **Soyuz TMA-12*[2]; Oleg Kononenko, Sergei Volkov, Yi So-yeon (to ISS), Richard Garriott (from ISS). Yi became 1st S. Korean in space.

5/31/2008: *Discovery (STS-124)*; 14 days; Mark E. Kelly (3), Kenneth T. Ham, Karen J. Nyberg, Ronald J. Garan Jr., Michael E. Fossum (2), Akihiko Hoshide, Gregory E. Chamitoff (to ISS), Garrett E. Reisman (from ISS). Delivered and installed pressurized and experimental modules of Kibo.

9/25/2008: **Shenzhou 7*; 68 hr.; Jing Haipeng, Liu Boming, Zhai Zhigang. Zhai completed 1st Chinese spacewalk.

10/12/2008: **Soyuz TMA-13*[2]; Richard Garriott (to ISS), Yuri V. Lonchakov (3), Michael Fincke. Garriott became 6th space tourist.

3/15/2009: *Discovery (STS-119)*; 13 days; Lee J. Archambault (2), Dominic A. Antonelli, Joseph M. Acaba, John L. Phillips, Steven R. Swanson (2), Richard R. Arnold, Koichi Wakata (to ISS), Sandra H. Magnus (from ISS). Delivered final solar panels and last U.S.-made truss segment.

5/11/2009: *Atlantis (STS-125)*; 13 days; Scott D. Altman (4), Gregory C. Johnson, Andrew J. Feustel, Michael T. Good, John M. Grunsfeld (5), Michael J. Massimino (2), K. Megan McArthur. Final Hubble Space Telescope servicing mission.

11/16/2009: *Atlantis (STS-129)*; 11 days; Charles O. Hobaugh (3), Barry E. Wilmore, Leland D. Melvin (2), Michael J. Foreman (2), Randolph J. Bresnik, Robert L. Satcher Jr., Nicole P. Stott (from ISS). Final space shuttle crew rotation flight.

6/15/2010: **Soyuz TMA-19*[2]; Fyodor Yurchikhin (3), Shannon Walker, Douglas H. Wheelock (2). 100th mission since launching of the International Space Station.

7/8/2011: *Atlantis (STS-135)*; 13 days; Christopher Ferguson (3), Doug Hurley (2), Sandy H. Magnus (3), Rex J. Walheim (3). **Final Space Shuttle mission.**

Note: Four Soviet cosmonauts have died during spaceflight: one person was killed on *Soyuz 1* (1967) when parachute lines tangled during descent; the three-person *Soyuz 11* crew (1971) was asphyxiated. Three Americans died in the *Apollo 1* (1967) fire on the ground at Cape Canaveral, FL; seven Americans died in the *Challenger* (1986) explosion; and six Americans and an Israeli astronaut died aboard *Columbia* (2003). (1) Space stations, such as the *Salyuts* and *Mir*, were used to house crews starting in 1971. (2) *Soyuz* crew often return from the ISS on spacecraft that launched and were docked at the station before their arrival. (3) Date of first successful flight; later, *SpaceShipOne* flew at least 100 km (62 mi) into space, 9/29/2004, piloted by Mike Melvill, and 10/4/2004, piloted by Brian Binnie, winning the $10-mil Ansari Prize for first private venture to accomplish this feat twice within two weeks.

U.S. Manned Space Program

Source: National Aeronautics and Space Administration (NASA)

After 50 years of sending men and women into space, the United States ended its manned space program with the safe landing of the *Atlantis* space shuttle on July 21, 2011, at Florida's Kennedy Space Center. In the short-term, all U.S. astronauts will have to rent space on Russian rockets. In Oct. 2012, Hawthorne, CA-based SpaceX became the first private company to resupply cargo to the International Space Station. Under a $1.6-bil deal with NASA, SpaceX will send a total of 12 such flights to the space station, with the hope of eventually carrying passengers into space.

The surviving space shuttles are now on display at museums around the country. *Discovery* was placed at the Smithsonian National Air and Space Museum's Udvar-Hazy Center in Chantilly, VA. It replaced *Enterprise*, which performed test runs but never went into space. *Enterprise* was moved to New York City's Intrepid Air, Sea, and Space Museum. *Endeavour* took up residence at the California Science Center in Los Angeles. *Atlantis* remained on permanent display at the Kennedy Space Center.

International Space Station

Source: National Aeronautics and Space Administration (NASA)

The International Space Station (ISS) is considered the largest cooperative scientific project in history. Construction began in 1998 and was completed in 2011. It has been inhabited by more than 200 international crew members since 2000.

15 cooperating nations: Belgium, Canada, Denmark, France, Germany, Italy, Japan, Netherlands, Norway, Russia, Spain, Sweden, Switzerland, United Kingdom, and the U.S.

About the ISS
- It has a mass of 924,739 lbs and is about as long as a football field at 357.5 ft.
- It is entirely powered by an acre of solar panels.
- It requires three people to keep it running but has room for up to 10 people to live aboard.
- Astronauts typically spend 4-6 months aboard the Space Station.

ISS Research
- Studying the effects of long-term exposure to reduced gravity on plants, crystals, plant and animal cells, and pathogens
- Studying the effects on humans of long-term exposure to reduced gravity
- Recording large-scale long-term changes in Earth's environment by observing the planet from orbit
- Testing recycling technologies for human life support

Summary of Worldwide Successful Launches, 1957-2014

Source: National Aeronautics and Space Administration (NASA); Space Launch Report

Year	1957-59	1960-69	1970-79	1980-89	1990-99	2000-09	2010-14[1]	Total[1]
Russia[2]	6	399	1,028	1,132	542	246	137	3,490
U.S.	18	614	247	191	300	206	72	1,648
China	—	—	8	16	33	52	67	176
ESA[3]	—	2	5	14	55	63	27	166
Ukraine	—	—	—	—	59	57	18	134
Japan	—	—	18	26	23	18	12	97
India	—	—	1	9	11	13	12	46
France	—	4	14	5	16	0	(3)	39
UK	—	1	6	4	7	0	(3)	18
Germany	—	—	3	7	6	0	(3)	16
Canada	—	—	4	5	4	0	0	13
Israel	—	—	—	—	—	3	2	5
Iran	—	—	—	—	—	1	2	3
S. Korea	—	—	—	—	—	1	0	1
N. Korea	—	—	—	—	—	—	1	1
Total	24	1,020	1,334	1,409	1056	660	350	5,853

— = Not applicable. (1) As of July 23, 2014. (2) Data for 1957-91 apply to the Soviet Union, for 1992-96 to the Commonwealth of Independent States, after 1996 to Russia. (3) European Space Agency. Member states are Austria, Belgium, Denmark, Finland, France, Germany, Greece, Ireland, Italy, Luxembourg, the Netherlands, Norway, Portugal, Spain, Sweden, Switzerland, and the United Kingdom. Canada, Czech Republic, and Hungary also participate in some projects under cooperation agreements.

Notable U.S. Lunar and Planetary Science Missions

Source: National Aeronautics and Space Administration (NASA)

Spacecraft	Launch date[1]	Mission	Remarks
Mariner 2	Aug. 27, 1962	Venus	Passed within 22,000 mi of Venus 12/14/1962; confirmed high surface temperature on planet; contact lost 1/3/1963 at 54 mil mi.
Ranger 7	July 28, 1964	Moon	Yielded over 4,000 photos of lunar surface.
Mariner 4	Nov. 28, 1964	Mars	1st probe to fly by Mars; passed behind planet 7/14/1965.
Ranger 8	Feb. 17, 1965	Moon	Yielded over 7,000 photos of lunar surface.
Venera 3	Nov. 16, 1965	Venus	Soviet probe; 1st artificial probe to impact on the surface of another planet, 3/1/1966; probe failed to send back data.
Surveyor 3	Apr. 17, 1967	Moon	Scooped and tested lunar soil.
Mariner 5	June 14, 1967	Venus	In solar orbit; closest Venus flyby 10/19/1967; allowed scientists to obtain accurate readings on the composition of the Venusian atmosphere.
Mariner 6	Feb. 24, 1969	Mars	Came within 2,000 mi of Mars 7/31/1969; collected data, photos.
Mariner 7	Mar. 27, 1969	Mars	Came within 2,000 mi of Mars 8/5/1969.
Venera 7	Aug. 17, 1970	Venus	Soviet probe; 1st probe to land safely on the surface of another planet.
Mariner 9	May 30, 1971	Mars	1st craft to orbit Mars 11/13/1971; sent back over 7,000 photos.
Pioneer 10	Mar. 2, 1972	Jupiter	Passed Jupiter 12/4/1973; took readings on Jupiter's composition and found that the planet is composed mostly of hydrogen. Exited the planetary system 6/13/1983; transmission ended 3/31/1997 at 6.39 bil mi.
Pioneer 11	Apr. 5, 1973	Jupiter, Saturn	Passed Jupiter 12/3/1974, Saturn 9/1/1979; discovered an additional ring and 2 moons around Saturn. Transmission ended 9/30/1995.
Mariner 10	Nov. 3, 1973	Venus, Mercury	Passed Venus 2/5/1974, arrived at Mercury 3/29/1974. 1st time gravity of 1 planet (Venus) used to whip spacecraft toward another (Mercury); 1st probe to visit 2 planets; took cloud and wind pattern readings in Venusian atmosphere.
Viking 1	Aug. 20, 1975	Mars	Landed on Mars 7/20/1976; 1st probe to land safely on Mars; performed chemical analysis of soil; functioned 6 years.
Viking 2	Sept. 9, 1975	Mars	Sister probe of *Viking 1*; landed on Mars 9/3/1976; functioned 3 years.

Spacecraft	Launch date[1]	Mission	Remarks
Voyager 2	Aug. 20, 1977	Jupiter, Saturn, Uranus, Neptune	Encountered Jupiter 7/9/1979, Saturn 8/25/1981, Uranus 1/24/1986, Neptune 8/25/1989. Confirmed existence of rings around Neptune. Entered boundary of solar system 10/2007. As of 6/2014, it was 9.8 bil mi (15.7 bil km) from Sun and still returning data to Earth.
Voyager 1	Sept. 5, 1977	Jupiter, Saturn	Encountered Jupiter 3/5/1979; provided evidence of rings around Jupiter; passed near Saturn 11/12/1980; passed *Pioneer 10* to become most distant human-made object 2/17/1998. As of 6/2014, it was 11.9 bil mi (19.2 bil km) from Sun and still returning data to Earth.
Pioneer Venus 1	May 20, 1978	Venus	Entered Venus orbit 12/4/1978; studied atmosphere, magnetic field, weather, and surface; fuel ran out; probe was destroyed in atmospheric entry, 8/1992.
Pioneer Venus 2 (multiprobe)	Aug. 8, 1978	Venus	Consisted of a "bus" carrying 1 large and 3 small atmospheric probes. All 4 probes entered the Venus atmosphere 12/9/1978, followed by the bus; took readings of atmosphere; probes impacted surface.
Magellan	May 4, 1989	Venus	Landed on Venus 8/10/1990; monitored geological activity; mapped more than 99% of planet surface, observed more than 1,600 volcanoes and volcanic features, enabling creation of a 3-D map; showed that about 85% of the surface is covered by volcanic flows; ceased operating 10/11/1994.
Galileo	Oct. 18, 1989	Jupiter	Used Earth's gravity to propel itself towards Jupiter; encountered Venus 2/1990, Jupiter 12/7/1995; encountered moons. Released probe into Jovian atmosphere; intentionally flown into Jupiter 9/21/2003 to prevent accidental contamination of Jupiter's moon Europa.
Mars Global Surveyor	Nov. 7, 1996	Mars	Began orbiting Mars 9/11/1997; began mapping entire surface 3/9/1999; discovered a weak magnetic field on planet; observed Martian moon Phobos; found evidence of liquid water in past 6/22/2000.
Mars Pathfinder	Dec. 4, 1996	Mars	Landed on Mars 7/4/1997; rover *Sojourner* made measurements of climate and soil composition, sending thousands of surface images; ceased operating 9/27/1997.
Cassini-Huygens	Oct. 15, 1997	Saturn	Began orbiting Saturn 6/30/2004; 4-year mission to study planet's atmosphere, rings, and moons; spotted evidence of a subterranean ocean and 300-mi-wide hot spots region on moon Titan; detected an atmosphere on moon Enceladus. *Huygens* probe landed on Titan 1/14/2005; found a muddy surface, possible deposits of water ice, channels carved by liquid methane springs.
Lunar Prospector	Jan. 6, 1998	Moon	Began orbiting Moon 1/11/1998; mapped abundance of 11 elements on Moon's surface; discovered evidence of water ice at both lunar poles; crashed into crater near Moon's south pole 7/31/1999 to end mission.
Deep Space 1	Oct. 24, 1998	Comet Borrelly	Flew within 1,500 mi of comet; sent back photos showing 6-mi-long nucleus.
Stardust	Feb. 7, 1999	Comet Wild 2	Reached comet 1/2/2004; gathered dust samples, capsule returned to Earth 1/15/2006. Spacecraft, on new mission Stardust-NExT (follow up for Deep Impact), reached comet Tempel 1, 2/14/2011.
2001 Mars Odyssey	Apr. 7, 2001	Mars	Reached Mars 10/24/2001; detected evidence of water ice near south pole; primary mission to study climate and geologic history completed 8/2004; began extended mission, aiming to identify minerals on Mars.
Genesis	Aug. 8, 2001	Sun	Orbited Sun, collected particles from solar wind; capsule containing specimens crashed to Earth 9/8/2004; some samples survived.
Mars Express/ Beagle 2 lander	June 3, 2003	Mars	1st European Space Agency probe to another planet; arrived at Mars 12/2003; performed remote sensing including photography in search of subsurface water; *Beagle 2* lander was deployed 12/19/2003, but contact was lost.
Mars Exploration Rovers	June 7 and July 10, 2003	Mars	Rovers *Spirit* and *Opportunity* landed on Mars 1/2004; found further evidence that water existed on surface; *Spirit* took 1st photo of a Martian meteor; survived severe dust storms in 2007. *Opportunity* explored massive Victoria Crater 2007-08, set record for most distance driven off-Earth (25 mi) 7/2014.
MESSENGER	Mar. 2, 2004	Mercury	Began returning images of Mercury during initial flyby 1/14/2008; entered orbit 3/17/2011; delivered 100,000th image 5/3/2012.
Deep Impact	Jan. 12, 2005	Comet Tempel 1	Reached Tempel 1; deployed impact probe that slammed into comet 7/4/2005 with force roughly equivalent to 5 tons of TNT. Flyby spacecraft, on supplemental mission EPOXI, reached comet Hartley 2, 11/4/2010.
Mars Reconnaissance Orbiter	Aug. 12, 2005	Mars	Reached Mars 3/10/2006 and began taking detailed images of Martian surface; in 3/2008, found salt deposits suggesting ancient water supplies; in 6/2008, found largest known crater in solar system.
New Horizons (Pluto)	Jan. 19, 2006	Pluto, Charon	Flew by Jupiter 7/2007. Due to reach Pluto and Charon in 7/2015; may examine other Kuiper Belt Objects.
Phoenix Mars Lander	Aug. 4, 2007	Mars	Landed on Mars 5/25/2008; examined northern polar region; monitored weather and analyzed minerals; evidence of water ice verified 7/31/2008; lost contact 11/2/2008.
Dawn	Sept. 27, 2007	Asteroid Belt (bet. Jupiter and Mars)	Will compare the evolution of dwarf planet Ceres with Vesta, an asteroid, in an effort to shed light on formation of the solar system. Departed Vesta 8/2012; expected to arrive at Ceres 2/2015.
Kepler	Mar. 9, 2009	Extrasolar planets	Detect potentially habitable Earth-size planets around other Milky Way stars.
Lunar Crater Observation and Sensing Satellite (LCROSS)	June 18, 2009	Moon	Impacted the Cabeus crater; detected presence of water ice in Moon's surface on 10/9/2009; subsequent analysis found methane, ammonia, hydrogen gas, and large amounts of sodium and mercury. Lunar Reconnaissance Orbiter (LRO), launched with LCROSS, mapped Moon's surface.
Mars Science Laboratory	Nov. 26, 2011	Mars	*Curiosity* rover landed 8/6/2012 and began assessing Mars's past and present ability to support life and other habitability factors.
Lunar Atmosphere and Dust Environment Explorer (LADEE)	Sept. 6, 2013	Moon	Studied fragile lunar atmosphere from orbit; completed mission with planned impact of lunar surface 4/17/2014.
Mars Atmosphere and Volatile Evolution (MAVEN)	Nov. 18, 2013	Mars	Entered Mars orbit 9/21/2014; will explore upper atmosphere to determine how loss of volatile organic compounds has affected the climate.
InSight	Mar. 2016	Mars	Lander will drill below Mars's surface and investigate its interior to discover how planets are formed.
Transiting Exoplanet Survey Satellite (TESS)	Aug. 2017	Solar neighborhood	Two-year survey will monitor more than 500,000 stars for temporary changes in brightness caused by planetary transits.
Mars 2020	2020	Mars	Rover to investigate potential for human habitation.
Europa Clipper	TBD	Jupiter	Proposed spacecraft would determine whether Jupiter's moon Europa is suitable for life.

TBD = To be determined. (1) In Coordinated Universal Time.

General Aviation and Air Taxi Active Aircraft, 2012

Source: Federal Aviation Administration; aircraft not associated with major airlines or the military

Aircraft	Total active	Personal	Busi- ness	Cor- porate	Instruc- tional	Aerial apps.	Aerial obser- vation	Other work	Sight- seeing	Air medical	Other	On-demand operations
Fixed Wing	165,257	109,870	16,556	9,070	10,559	2,957	2,934	690	371	173	4,695	6,875
Piston	143,160	106,885	13,885	1,148	10,394	1,378	2,515	524	369	123	3,649	2,074
Turboprop	10,304	1,852	1,617	2,026	139	1,579	393	153	2	27	369	1,872
Turbojet	11,793	1,133	1,054	5,896	27	0	26	13	0	23	678	2,929
Rotorcraft	10,055	1,216	377	245	1,273	537	2,134	81	148	110	880	2,397
Piston	3,292	941	246	25	1,110	241	213	10	111	0	269	93
Turbine	6,763	276	131	221	162	296	1,921	71	37	110	611	2,305
Other Aircraft	5,006	3,874	109	0	297	17	0	91	545	0	37	36
Gliders	1,820	1,510	12	0	240	0	0	0	50	0	9	0
Lighter-than-air	3,186	2,364	98	0	57	17	0	91	495	0	28	36
Experimental	26,715	24,764	443	76	424	96	206	46	29	14	527	76
Amateur	18,843	17,963	307	2	261	0	86	4	2	0	217	0
Exhibition	1,923	1,734	19	2	25	0	2	6	0	0	135	0
Experimental Light-sport	4,631	4,360	12	0	104	0	74	10	16	0	55	0
Other	1,317	707	105	72	35	96	44	26	12	14	120	76
Special Light-sport	2,001	1,592	57	0	285	0	20	2	4	0	41	0
TOTAL ALL AIRCRAFT	209,034	141,317	17,542	9,392	12,838	3,606	5,294	910	1,097	296	6,180	9,385

Note: Columns may not add to totals due to rounding. **Personal**—Flying for personal reasons; **Business**—Individual or group use for business transportation without a paid, professional crew; **Corporate**—Individual or group business transportation with a paid, professional crew (includes fractional ownership); **Instructional**—Flying under the supervision of a flight instructor; **Aerial applications**—Includes agriculture, forestry, public health, fire fighting, and other applications; **Aerial observation**—Includes aerial mapping/photography, patrol, search and rescue, hunting, traffic advisory, ranching, surveillance, oil and mineral exploration, etc.; **Other work use**—Construction work, parachuting, aerial advertising, towing gliders, etc.; **Sight-seeing**—Commercial sight-seeing; **Air medical services**—Air ambulance services, rescue, human organ transportation, emergency medical services; **Other**—Positioning flights, proficiency flights, training, ferrying, sales demos; **On-demand operations**—On-demand air taxi, air tours, commuter, and air medical services.

Estimated Active Airmen Certificates Held, 2013

Source: Federal Aviation Administration, U.S. Dept. of Transportation

Category	Certificates	Category	Certificates	Category	Certificates
Pilot total	599,086	Rotorcraft (helicopters)		Repairmen	39,952
Student	120,285	(only)	15,114	Parachute Rigger	8,491
Recreational (only)	238	Glider (only)	20,381	Ground Instructor	72,493
Sport (only)	4,824	**Flight Instructor**		Dispatcher	22,401
Airplane[1]		Certificates	98,842	Flight Navigator	126
Private	180,214	Instrument Ratings	307,120	Flight Attendant	179,531
Commercial	108,206	Nonpilot total	707,155	Flight Engineer	45,317
Airline Transport	149,824	Mechanic	338,844		

Note: The term airmen includes men and women certified as pilots, mechanics, or other aviation technicians. (1) Includes pilots with an airplane-only certificate as well as those with an airplane and a helicopter and/or glider certificate.

Aircraft Operating Statistics

Source: Airbus S.A.S.; The Boeing Company; Embraer S.A.; as of July 30, 2014

Manufacturer and model	Max. # of seats	Typical # of seats	Fuel capacity (gal)	Typical cruising speed (mph)[1]	Max. range (naut. mi)	Max. thrust (thous. lbs)	Manufacturer and model	Max. # of seats	Typical # of seats	Fuel capacity (gal)	Typical cruising speed (mph)[1]	Max. range (naut. mi)	Max. thrust (thous. lbs)
Airbus							757-300*	280	243	11,466	614	3,395	43.5
A318	132	107	6,400	630	3,200	24.0	767-200ER	255	181	23,980	614	6,385	62.1
A319	156	124	6,400	630	3,700	27.0	767-300ER	350	218	23,980	614	5,990	63.3
A320	180	150	6,400	630	3,300	27.0	767-400ER	375	245	23,980	614	5,625	63.5
A321	220	185	6,350	630	6,200	33.0	777-200	440	305	31,000	645	5,420	77.0
A330-200	380	253	36,750	660	7,250	72.0	777-200ER	440	301	45,220	645	7,725	93.7
A330-300	440	295	26,765	660	5,850	72.0	777-200LR	314	301	47,890	645	9,395	115.3
A340-200	440	295	37,150	660	7,400	34.0	777-300	550	368	45,220	645	6,005	98.0
A340-500	375	313	56,870	660	9,000	56.0	777-300ER	386	386	47,890	645	7,390	115.3
A340-600	475	380	51,750	660	7,900	60.0	**787-8**						
A380	853	525	84,600	684	8,300	70.0	Dreamliner	242	210	NA	652	8,200	NA
Boeing							**787-9**						
727-200*	189	148	9,806	605	2,500	17.4	Dreamliner	280	250	NA	652	8,500	NA
737-600	132	110	6,875	602	3,225	22.7	**Embraer**						
737-700	149	126	6,875	602	3,440	26.3	190	114	98	NA	630	2,400	20.0
737-700C	140	126	6,875	599	3,285	27.3	195	122	108	NA	630	2,200	20.0
737-800	189	162	6,875	602	3,115	27.3	**McDonnell- Douglas**						
737-900	215	180	7,837	599	3,265	27.3	DC-10 series*	380	250	36,650	600	6,220	24.0
747-100*	452	366	48,445	645	6,100	50.1	MD-11*	410	285	NA	NA	7,360	NA
747-200/300*	452	366	52,410	645	7,900	54.8	MD-80 series*	172	155	5,840	584	2,504	21.0
747-400	524	416	57,285	653	7,260	63.3	MD-90 series*	172	153	7,620	584	3,205	28.0
747-8	467	467	64,055	653	8,000	66.5							
757-200*	228	200	11,489	614	3,900	43.5							

* = Aircraft no longer in production. NA = Not available. **Note:** Figures are for most commonly flown passenger models. When models within a series vary, maximums are shown. McDonnell-Douglas merged with Boeing in 1997. (1) Figures shown are converted from Mach speed (speed of sound), which varies depending on altitude and temperature. For comparison purposes, this table uses 768 mph as equivalent to Mach 1.

Milestones in Aviation History

Source: National Aeronautics and Space Administration (NASA); Smithsonian National Air and Space Museum; Air Transport Association of America; National Museum of the U.S. Air Force (USAF); National Park Service, U.S. Dept. of the Interior

1903, Dec. 17: Brothers Wilbur and Orville Wright (U.S.) made the first human-carrying, powered flight near Kitty Hawk, NC. Each brother made two flights; the longest, about 852 ft, lasted 59 sec.

1908, May 14: Charles Furnas (U.S.), worker for Wright brothers, became first American airplane passenger.

1911, Feb.: The Burgess Company and Curtiss, Inc. receive authorization to build Wright planes, becoming the first licensed airplane manufacturer in the U.S.

1911, Sept. 23: First transportation of mail by airplane officially approved by the U.S. Postal Service.

1914, Jan. 1: First scheduled passenger airline service began. A seaplane that landed on water operated between St. Petersburg and Tampa, FL.

1914, June 18: Lawrence Burst Sperry (U.S.) released the controls and stood in his airborne plane, successfully demonstrating his gyrostabilizer, the first autopilot system.

1918, Mar. 6: The Curtiss-Sperry "Flying Bomb" (U.S.) made its first successful flight. The first radio-controlled plane led to the development of cruise missiles.

1918, May 14: First scheduled airmail service began, between New York and Washington, DC, with intermediate stop in Philadelphia. In 1921, scheduled transcontinental airmail service began between New York City and San Francisco.

1919, June 14-15: Capt. John Alcock (UK) and Lt. Arthur W. Brown (U.S.) completed the first nonstop flight across the Atlantic Ocean. They traveled from Newfoundland, Canada, to Ireland in 16 hr., 12 min.

1923, Aug.: Rotating beacons enabled the first U.S. night flights.

1924, Apr. 6-Sept. 28: Two U.S. Army planes landed in Seattle, completing the first circumnavigation of the globe. They completed the 26,000-mi journey in 371 hours of flying time.

1926, May 12-13: Roald Amundsen (Norway), Umberto Nobile (Italy), Lincoln Ellsworth (U.S.), and Oscar Wisting (Norway) made the first flight over the North Pole, in a dirigible that flew between Spitsbergen, Norway, and Teller, AK. Two weeks earlier, Adm. Richard E. Byrd and Floyd Bennett (both U.S.) claimed to have made the first flight over the Pole (May 9, 1926) in a Fokker F-VII. But when Byrd's diary was released to the public in 1996, some historians began to question whether his plane had reached the Pole.

1927, May 20-21: Charles Lindbergh (U.S.) completed the first solo transatlantic flight in the *Spirit of St. Louis*. "Lucky Lindy" traveled 3,610 mi from New York to Paris in 33 hr., 29 min., 30 sec.

1929, Aug. 8-29: Hugo Eckener (Germany) piloted the *Graf Zeppelin* around the world in record time: 20,373 mi in 21 days, 5 hr., 31 min.

1929, Nov. 28: Adm. Richard E. Byrd (U.S.) and Bernt Balchen (Norway) became the first to fly to the South Pole and back, in 18 hr., 41 min.

1930, May 15: Ellen Church (U.S.) became first flight attendant.

1931, June 23-July 1: Wiley Post and Harold Gatty (both U.S.) broke the speed record for around-the-world flight. They traveled 15,474 mi in 8 days, 15 hr., 51 min., in the monoplane *Winnie Mae*.

1931, Oct. 3-5: Clyde Pangborn and Hugh Herndon (both U.S.) completed the first nonstop transpacific flight. They traveled 4,558 mi from Misawa, Japan, to East Wenatchee, WA, in 41 hr., 34 min.

1932, May 20-21: Amelia Earhart (U.S.) completed first solo transoceanic flight by a woman. She completed the 2,026-mi journey from Newfoundland, Canada, to Ireland in 14 hr., 56 min.

1933, July 15-22: Wiley Post (U.S.) completed the first solo circumnavigation of the globe. His 15,596-mi trip took 7 days, 18 hr., 49 min.

1936, June 25: American Airlines began scheduled passenger service of the first Douglas DC-3 aircraft. The DC-3 was the first aircraft with a kitchen onboard and hence offered the first in-flight hot meal service.

1937, May 6: German *Hindenburg* zeppelin exploded in Lakehurst, NJ, killing 35 of the 97 people aboard (and one on the ground). The airship had made 34 transatlantic flights in 1936.

1938, July 10-13: Howard Hughes (U.S.) and four assistants established a new speed record for circumnavigating the globe: 14,824 mi in 3 days, 9 hr., 17 min.

1939, Aug. 27: The German-made Heinkel He 178 made the first successful flight powered by a jet engine.

1947, June 17-30: Pan American Airways began the first scheduled around-the-world passenger flights, from New York or San Francisco.

1947, Oct. 14: Chuck Yeager (U.S.) broke the sound barrier, reaching Mach 1 speed in a Bell X-1 rocket-powered aircraft.

1947, Nov. 2: Howard Hughes (U.S.) piloted the *Spruce Goose* on its maiden and only flight. The largest airplane ever built, it could carry 750 troops or two Sherman tanks.

1949, Mar. 2: James Gallagher (U.S.) piloted the first round-the-world flight to be refueled in midair. The *Lucky Lady* USAF B-50 covered 23,452 mi in 94 hr., 1 min. and was refueled four times.

1950, Sept. 22: Col. David Schilling (USAF) made the first nonstop transatlantic jet flight, covering 3,300 mi in 10 hr., 1 min.

1952, Aug. 26: The UK bomber Canberra made the first round-trip transatlantic crossing on the same day, from Northern Ireland to Newfoundland, Canada, and back in 7 hr., 59 min.

1953, May 18: Jacqueline Cochran (U.S.) became the first woman to fly faster than the speed of sound.

1956, Mar. 10: Britain's Fairey FD-2 aircraft set a world speed record of 1,132 mph.

1956, Nov. 11: Convair B-58 (USAF), the first supersonic bomber, was introduced.

1957, Jan. 15-18: Three USAF B-52 Stratofortresses made the first nonstop global flight by jet planes. They were refueled in flight by KC-97 aerial tankers.

1958, Oct. 24: A Mirage III-A achieved Mach 2 (twice the speed of sound) in level flight, the first European plane to reach that speed.

1962, Nov. 29: Britain and France signed an agreement to jointly develop the Concorde, a supersonic plane that could fly twice as fast as most U.S. jets.

1969, June 5: The Soviet Tupolev Tu-144 became the first passenger airliner to reach Mach 2.

1970, May 26: The Tupolev Tu-144 reached a top speed of about 1,335 mph at 53,475 ft.

1976, Aug. 23: The Concorde began the first scheduled supersonic commercial service.

1977, Aug. 23: The *Gossamer Condor*, built by aeronautical engineer Paul MacCready (U.S.), successfully demonstrated human-powered flight through pedalling, completing a figure-8 course of 1.15 mi.

1979, June 12: MacCready's human-powered *Gossamer Albatross* crossed the English Channel in 2 hr., 49 min.

1981, July 7: The MacCready-developed *Solar Challenger* became the first solar-powered airplane to cross the English Channel.

1995, Aug. 15-16: The Concorde set a new around-the-world speed record of 31 hr., 27 min., 49 sec.

1999, Mar. 1-21: Bertrand Piccard (Switz.) and Brian Jones (UK) completed the first around-the-world flight in a hot-air balloon. Their 29,055-mi journey began in Chateau-d'Oex, Switzerland, and ended 19 days, 21 hr., 55 min. later in the Egyptian desert.

2001, Aug. 13: Solar-powered, propeller-driven plane *Helios* (NASA) reached 96,863 ft, breaking altitude record for non-rocket-powered aircraft.

2002, June 19-July 4: Steve Fossett (U.S.) completed the first nonstop solo circumnavigation of globe in a balloon.

2003, Nov. 26: The Concorde flew its final flight.

2005, Mar. 1-3: Steve Fossett (U.S.) achieved the first nonstop solo circumnavigation in an airplane without refueling.

2006, Feb. 8-11: Steve Fossett (U.S.) flew the longest nonstop, non-refueled solo flight (25,766 mi).

2009, Dec. 15: Boeing's 787 Dreamliner, the company's most fuel-efficient plane and the first to be constructed primarily from composite materials, made its maiden voyage.

2011, Feb. 4: Northrop Grumman and the U.S. Navy reported the first successful flight for the unmanned X-47B fighter jet.

2013, July 6: *Solar Impulse* became the first solar-powered airplane to fly across the U.S. without fuel. Flying during both day and night, it traveled from San Francisco to New York, NY, with stops in Phoenix, Dallas, St. Louis, and Washington, DC, in 62 days.

ASTRONOMY

Edited by Michael J. Kaufman, Dept. of Physics and Astronomy, San Jose State University

Celestial Events Summary, 2015

There are four eclipses in 2015: two total lunar eclipses, one total solar eclipse, and one partial solar eclipse. The lunar eclipses will be visible across wide areas of the Earth: the Apr. eclipse from East Asia and western North America and the Sept. eclipse will be visible to observers in Europe, Africa, and the Americas. The total solar eclipse occurs almost entirely over water, passing land only at the Faroe Islands and Svalbard, though observers in Africa, Europe, and Asia will be able to see the Sun partially eclipsed. The Sept. partial solar eclipse begins over southern Africa and then proceeds to the Antarctic.

The best meteor shower viewing will be the Lyrids in Apr., the Perseids in Aug., the Leonids in Nov., and the Geminids in Dec. All four of these showers occur during favorable dark skies, with little moonlight, in 2015. At the start of the year, Jupiter is in the East at sunset and up much of the night. Venus is low in the West at sunset at the start of the year, where it can be seen through July; by late Aug., it is visible in the early morning sky, where it remains for the rest of the year. Mars is an early evening object from Jan.-Apr., setting soon after the Sun; by early fall, it rises before sunrise and can be seen low in the eastern pre-dawn sky. Saturn is high in the East before sunrise through Apr., moves to the evening sky in May, then returns to the morning sky in late Nov. The best opportunities for seeing Mercury in the morning sky occur in late Feb., late June, and mid-Oct.; the planet is visible in the evening sky in mid-Jan., early May, and early Sept.

The crescent Moon, with its subdued light, regularly pairs with the two brightest planets, Venus and Jupiter. Waxing crescent pairings are visible in the early evening soon after sunset, while waning crescent pairings are visible in the early morning before sunrise. The waxing crescent Moon pairs with Venus in each of the months from Jan. through July, while the waning crescent pairs with Venus in the early morning sky each month from Sept. through Dec. The waxing crescent Moon pairs with Jupiter in the evening in June and July and the waning crescent pairs with Jupiter in Oct. and Nov. Jupiter and Venus are close neighbors throughout the month of July. The waxing crescent Moon joins Mars and Venus after sunset on Feb. 20. The waning crescent Moon joins Mars, Venus, and Jupiter in the morning Sept. 10-11, Oct. 8-9, and Nov. 7-8.

On July 14, 2015, NASA's *New Horizons* spacecraft will fly by Pluto on the way to the Kuiper Belt, a debris field of icy solar system remnants. A spacecraft has never approached Pluto so closely, and the mission should provide unprecedented imaging, measurements of Pluto's surface, atmospheric compositions, and other never-before-seen details. After passing Pluto, the spacecraft's mission into the Kuiper Belt is expected to extend at least five more years.

Astronomical Positions and Constants

Two celestial bodies are in **conjunction** when they are due north and south of each other, either in **right ascension** (with respect to the north celestial pole) or in **celestial longitude** (with respect to the north ecliptic pole). Celestial bodies in conjunction will rise and set at nearly the same time. For the inner planets—Mercury and Venus—**inferior conjunction** occurs when either planet passes between Earth and the Sun, while **superior conjunction** occurs when either Mercury or Venus is on the far side of the Sun. Celestial bodies are in **opposition** when their right ascensions differ by exactly 12 hours, or when their celestial longitudes differ by 180°. In this case one of the two objects in opposition will rise while the other is setting. **Quadrature** refers to the arrangement where the coordinates of two bodies differ by exactly 90°. These terms may refer to the relative positions of any two bodies as seen from Earth, but one of the bodies is so frequently the Sun that mention of the Sun is omitted in that case.

When objects are in conjunction, the alignment is not perfect, and one is usually passing above or below the other. The geocentric angular separation between the Sun and an object is termed **elongation**. Elongation is limited only for Mercury and Venus; the greatest elongation for each of these bodies is approximately the time for longest observation. **Perihelion** is the point in an object's orbit when it is nearest to the Sun, and **aphelion** is the point when it is farthest from the Sun. **Perigee** is the point in an orbit where an object is nearest Earth, and **apogee** the point when it is farthest from Earth. An **occultation** of a planet or a star is an eclipse of it by some other body, usually the Moon. A **transit** of the Sun occurs when Mercury or Venus passes directly between Earth and the Sun, appearing to cross the Sun's disk.

The following were adopted as part of the International Astronomical Union System of Astronomical Constants (1976): **Speed of light**, 299,792.458 km per sec., or about 186,282 statute mi per sec.; **solar parallax**, 8".794148; **astronomical unit** (AU, mean distance between the Earth and Sun), 149,597,870 km, or 92,955,807 mi; **constant of nutation**, 9".2025; and **constant of aberration**, 20".49552.

Celestial Events Highlights, 2015

(In Coordinated Universal Time, or UTC, the standard time of the prime meridian.)

January

Mercury is visible low in the SW after sunset in the middle of the month.

Venus is visible low in the SW after sunset from mid-month on.

Mars is in the SW after sunset all month.

Jupiter rises in the E mid-evening and low in the W at sunrise.

Saturn rises in the middle of the night and is high in the SE at sunrise.

Uranus and **Neptune** are in the SW after sunset and set several hours later.

Jan. 1: Sun, Mercury, and Venus in Sagittarius; Mars in Capricorn; Jupiter in Leo; Saturn in Libra; Uranus in Pisces all year; Neptune in Aquarius all year.
Jan. 2: Aldebaran 1.38° South of Moon
Jan. 3: Venus enters Capricorn, Quadrantid meteor shower
Jan. 4: Earth at perihelion

Jan. 5: Full Moon, Mercury enters Capricorn
Jan. 6: Pollux 11.78° North of Moon
Jan. 8: Jupiter 5.06° North of Moon, Mars enters Capricorn
Jan. 9: Moon at apogee, Regulus 4.12° North of Moon
Jan. 13: Spica 3.09° South of Moon, Last Quarter Moon
Jan. 14: Mercury at greatest elongation 18.9° East of Sun
Jan. 16: Saturn 1.85° South of Moon, Antares 8.81° South of Moon
Jan. 18: Saturn enters Scorpius
Jan. 19: Neptune 0.23° North of Mars
Jan. 20: New Moon, Sun enters Capricorn
Jan. 21: Moon at perigee, Mercury 2.97° South of Moon
Jan. 22: Venus 5.63° South of Moon, Mercury enters Aquarius
Jan. 23: Neptune 3.92° South of Moon, Mars 3.93° South of Moon
Jan. 25: Uranus 0.62° South of Moon, Venus enters Aquarius
Jan. 27: First Quarter Moon
Jan. 29: Aldebaran 1.18° South of Moon
Jan. 30: Mercury in inferior conjunction 3.46° North of Sun

February

Mercury is visible low in the SE before sunrise by the second half of the month.
Venus and **Mars** are visible in the SW after sunset all month.
Jupiter is low in the E at sunset and is up all night.
Saturn rises after midnight and is low in the S at sunrise.
Uranus sets several hours after the Sun.
Neptune begins the month setting just after the Sun and is lost in the Sun's glare by the end of the month.

Feb. 1: Neptune 0.84° North of Venus, Mercury enters Capricorn
Feb. 2: Pollux 11.80° North of Moon
Feb. 3: Full Moon, Jupiter enters Cancer
Feb. 4: Jupiter 5.21° North of Moon
Feb. 5: Regulus 3.99° North of Moon
Feb. 6: Moon at apogee, Jupiter at opposition
Feb. 9: Spica 3.34° South of Moon
Feb. 11: Mars enters Pisces
Feb. 12: Last Quarter Moon
Feb. 13: Saturn 2.13° South of Moon, Antares 9.03° South of Moon
Feb. 16: Sun enters Aquarius, Venus enters Pisces
Feb. 17: Mercury 3.50° South of Moon
Feb. 19: Moon at perigee, Neptune 3.76° South of Moon
Feb. 19: New Moon
Feb. 21: Venus 2.04° South of Moon, Mars 1.53° South of Moon, Mars 0.46° North of Venus, Uranus 0.31° South of Moon
Feb. 24: Mercury at greatest elongation 26.7° West of Sun
Feb. 25: Aldebaran 0.98° South of Moon, First Quarter Moon
Feb. 26: Neptune 0.73° South of Sun, Venus enters Cetus
Feb. 27: Venus enters Pisces

March

Mercury is low in the SE before sunrise all month.
Venus is visible in the SW after sunset all month.
Mars is visible low in the SW after sunset all month.
Jupiter is high in the E at sunset and sets after midnight.
Saturn rises before midnight and is high in the SW at sunrise.
Uranus is low in the SW at sunset at the start of the month and is lost in the Sun's glare by late in the month.
Neptune is visible low in the SE before sunrise.

Mar. 1: Pollux 11.91° North of Moon, Mars enters Cetus
Mar. 2: Mars enters Pisces
Mar. 3: Jupiter 5.45° North of Moon
Mar. 4: Regulus 3.99° North of Moon, Uranus 0.10° South of Venus
Mar. 5: Moon at apogee, Full Moon
Mar. 8: Spica 3.47° South of Moon
Mar. 11: Uranus 0.29° South of Mars, Mercury enters Aquarius
Mar. 12: Saturn 2.24° South of Moon, Antares 9.18° South of Moon, Sun enters Pisces
Mar. 13: Last Quarter Moon
Mar. 16: Venus enters Aries
Mar. 18: Neptune 1.60° North of Mercury
Mar. 19: Moon at perigee, Neptune 3.70° South of Moon, Mercury 5.18° South of Moon
Mar. 20: Vernal Equinox, New Moon, Total Solar Eclipse
Mar. 21: Uranus 0.11° South of Moon, Mars 0.97° North of Moon
Mar. 22: Venus 2.84° North of Moon
Mar. 25: Aldebaran 0.88° South of Moon
Mar. 27: First Quarter Moon
Mar. 28: Pollux 11.98° North of Moon
Mar. 29: Mercury enters Pisces, Mars enters Aries
Mar. 30: Jupiter 5.58° North of Moon
Mar. 31: Regulus 4.03° North of Moon

April

Mercury is lost in the Sun's glare most of the month, but reemerges low in the W after sunset by the end of the month.
Venus is in the W after sunset all month.
Mars is low in the W at sunset at the beginning of the month.
Jupiter is high overhead at sunset and sets after midnight.
Saturn rises mid-evening and is visible the rest of the night.
Uranus and **Neptune** are low in the SE at sunrise by the end of the month.

Apr. 1: Moon at apogee
Apr. 4: Full Moon, Mercury enters Cetus, Total Lunar Eclipse
Apr. 5: Spica 3.47° South of Moon
Apr. 6: Uranus 0.62° South of Sun, Mercury enters Pisces
Apr. 7: Venus enters Taurus
Apr. 8: Uranus 0.52° North of Mercury, Saturn 2.17° South of Moon, Antares 9.03° South of Moon
Apr. 10: Mercury in superior conjunction 0.84° South of Sun
Apr. 12: Last Quarter Moon
Apr. 15: Neptune 3.63° South of Moon, Mercury enters Aries
Apr. 17: Moon at perigee
Apr. 18: Uranus 0.04° North of Moon, New Moon
Apr. 19: Mercury 3.47° North of Moon, Mars 3.11° North of Moon, Sun enters Aries
Apr. 21: Aldebaran 7.50° South of Venus, Aldebaran 0.91° South of Moon, Venus 6.64° North of Moon
Apr. 22: Lyrid meteor shower
Apr. 23: Mars 1.39° South of Mercury
Apr. 25: Pollux 11.93° North of Moon
Apr. 26: Jupiter 5.47° North of Moon, First Quarter Moon
Apr. 28: Regulus 3.98° North of Moon, Mercury enters Taurus
Apr. 29: Moon at apogee

May

Mercury is visible low in the W after sunset early in the month.
Venus is high in the W after sunset all month.
Mars is lost in the Sun's glare all month.
Jupiter is high overhead at sunset and sets after midnight.
Saturn rises after sunset and is up most of the night.
Uranus and **Neptune** rise a few hours before the Sun.

May 2: Spica 3.48° South of Moon, Mars enters Taurus
May 4: Full Moon
May 5: Saturn 1.99° South of Moon, Eta Aquarid meteor shower
May 6: Antares 9.13° South of Moon
May 7: Mercury at greatest elongation 21.2° East of Sun
May 8: Venus enters Gemini
May 11: Last Quarter Moon
May 12: Aldebaran 7.83° South of Mercury, Neptune 3.48° South of Moon, Saturn enters Libra
May 14: Sun enters Taurus
May 15: Moon at perigee, Uranus 0.22° North of Moon
May 18: Mars 4.65° North of Moon, New Moon
May 19: Aldebaran 0.98° South of Moon, Mercury 5.70° North of Moon
May 21: Venus 7.89° North of Moon
May 22: Pollux 11.77° North of Moon
May 23: Saturn at opposition
May 24: Jupiter 5.13° North of Moon
May 25: Regulus 3.80° North of Moon, First Quarter Moon
May 26: Moon at apogee
May 27: Aldebaran 5.99° South of Mars, Mars 1.69° North of Mercury, Aldebaran 4.28° South of Mercury
May 29: Spica 3.58° South of Moon
May 30: Pollux 4.08° North of Venus, Mercury in inferior conjunction 2.08° South of Sun

June

Mercury is visible low in the E before sunrise by the very end of the month.
Venus is high in the W after sunset all month.
Mars is lost in the Sun's glare all month.
Jupiter is high the W at sunset and sets around midnight.

Saturn is in the SE at sunset and sets in the early morning hours.

Uranus and **Neptune** rise in the middle of the night and are high overhead at sunrise.

June 1: Saturn 1.89° South of Moon

June 2: Antares 9.09° South of Moon, Full Moon

June 3: Venus enters Cancer

June 6: Venus at greatest elongation 45.4° East of Sun

June 9: Neptune 3.26° South of Moon, Last Quarter Moon, Jupiter enters Leo

June 10: Moon at perigee

June 11: Uranus 0.49° North of Moon

June 14: Mars 0.62° North of Sun

June 15: Mercury 0.04° North of Moon, Aldebaran 0.98° South of Moon

June 16: Mars 5.54° North of Moon, New Moon

June 18: Pollux 11.61° North of Moon

June 20: Venus 5.79° North of Moon

June 21: Northern Solstice, Jupiter 4.65° North of Moon, Regulus 3.56° North of Moon, Sun enters Gemini

June 23: Moon at apogee

June 24: Mercury at greatest elongation 22.5° West of Sun, Aldebaran 2.05° South of Mercury, Mars enters Gemini, First Quarter Moon

June 25: Venus enters Leo

June 26: Spica 3.80° South of Moon

June 29: Saturn 1.97° South of Moon, Antares 9.16° South of Moon

July

Mercury is low in the NE at sunrise early in the month.

Venus is visible low in the W after sunset all month.

Mars is low in the NE at sunrise late in the month.

Jupiter is visible low in the W after sunset all month.

Saturn is high in the SE at sunset and sets after midnight.

Uranus and **Neptune** rise in the middle of the night and are high overhead at sunrise.

July 1: Jupiter 0.40° North of Venus

July 2: Full Moon

July 5: Moon at perigee

July 6: Earth at aphelion, Neptune 3.05° South of Moon

July 7: Mercury enters Orion

July 8: Last Quarter Moon, Mercury enters Gemini

July 9: Uranus 0.78° North of Moon

July 12: Aldebaran 0.87° South of Moon

July 14: *New Horizons* closest approach to Pluto

July 15: Mercury 5.56° North of Moon, Mars 5.83° North of Moon

July 16: Mars 0.14° North of Mercury, Pollux 11.55° North of Moon, New Moon

July 18: Jupiter 4.13° North of Moon

July 19: Venus 0.41° North of Moon, Regulus 3.37° North of Moon

July 20: Pollux 5.42° North of Mercury

July 21: Moon at apogee, Sun enters Cancer

July 22: Mercury enters Cancer

July 23: Spica 4.06° South of Moon, Mercury in superior conjunction 1.61° North of Sun

July 24: First Quarter Moon

July 26: Saturn 2.23° South of Moon

July 27: Antares 9.33° South of Moon

July 31: Pollux 5.82° North of Mars, Jupiter 6.43° North of Venus, Full Moon, Mercury enters Leo

August

Mercury is visible low in W after sunset late in the month.

Venus is visible low in the W at sunset early in the month.

Mars is in the E at sunrise all month.

Jupiter is visible low in the W at sunset early in the month.

Saturn is high in the SW at sunset and sets around midnight.

Uranus and **Neptune** rise in the late evening and in the W at sunrise.

Aug. 2: Moon at perigee, Neptune 2.94° South of Moon

Aug. 3: Venus enters Sextans

Aug. 5: Uranus 1.01° North of Moon, Venus 8.18° South of Mercury, Mercury 8.18° North of Venus, Mars enters Cancer

Aug. 7: Jupiter 0.58° South of Mercury, Regulus 0.96° South of Mercury, Last Quarter Moon

Aug. 9: Aldebaran 0.69° South of Moon

Aug. 10: Regulus 0.42° South of Jupiter, Venus enters Hydra

Aug. 11: Sun enters Leo

Aug. 12: Pollux 11.59° North of Moon, Perseid meteor shower

Aug. 13: Mars 5.55° North of Moon

Aug. 14: Venus 4.66° South of Moon, New Moon, Venus enters Leo

Aug. 15: Regulus 3.29° North of Moon, Jupiter 3.64° North of Moon, Venus in inferior conjunction 7.84° South of Sun

Aug. 16: Mercury 1.97° North of Moon

Aug. 18: Moon at apogee, Venus enters Cancer

Aug. 19: Spica 4.24° South of Moon

Aug. 22: Saturn 2.54° South of Moon, First Quarter Moon

Aug. 23: Antares 9.51° South of Moon, Mercury enters Virgo

Aug. 26: Jupiter 0.87° North of Sun

Aug. 29: Mars 9.42° North of Venus, Venus 9.42° South of Mars, Full Moon

Aug. 30: Moon at perigee, Neptune 2.96° South of Moon

September

Mercury is low in the W after sunset early in the month.

Venus and **Mars** are visible in the E before sunrise all month.

Jupiter is low in the E at sunrise by the end of the month.

Saturn is in the SW at sunset and sets several hours later.

Uranus and **Neptune** rise around sunset and set near sunrise.

Sept. 1: Neptune at opposition, Uranus 1.09° North of Moon

Sept. 4: Mercury at greatest elongation 27.1° East of Sun

Sept. 5: Aldebaran 0.55° South of Moon, Last Quarter Moon

Sept. 6: Mars enters Leo

Sept. 8: Pollux 11.68° North of Moon

Sept. 10: Venus 2.66° South of Moon, Mars 4.72° North of Moon

Sept. 11: Regulus 3.31° North of Moon

Sept. 12: Jupiter 3.18° North of Moon

Sept. 13: New Moon, Partial Solar Eclipse

Sept. 14: Moon at apogee

Sept. 15: Mercury 5.34° South of Moon

Sept. 16: Spica 4.31° South of Moon

Sept. 17: Sun enters Virgo

Sept. 19: Saturn 2.79° South of Moon, Antares 9.59° South of Moon

Sept. 21: First Quarter Moon

Sept. 23: Equinox, Venus enters Leo

Sept. 24: Regulus 0.84° South of Mars

Sept. 26: Neptune 3.04° South of Moon

Sept. 28: Moon at perigee, Full Moon, Total Lunar Eclipse

Sept. 29: Uranus 1.01° North of Moon

Sept. 30: Mercury in inferior conjunction 2.46° South of Sun

October

Mercury is visible low in the E just before sunrise mid-month.

Venus, **Mars**, and **Jupiter** are in the SE at sunrise all month.

Saturn is visible low in the SW after sunset and sets soon afterwards.

Uranus and **Neptune** are high in the SE at sunset and set in the early morning.

Oct. 2: Aldebaran 0.52° South of Moon

Oct. 4: Last Quarter Moon

Oct. 6: Pollux 11.69° North of Moon

Oct. 8: Venus 0.69° North of Moon, Regulus 3.31° North of Moon

Oct. 9: Mars 3.43° North of Moon, Regulus 2.55° North of Venus

Oct. 10: Jupiter 2.73° North of Moon
Oct. 11: Moon at apogee, Mercury 0.95° North of Moon
Oct. 12: Uranus at opposition
Oct. 13: Spica 4.29° South of Moon, New Moon
Oct. 16: Mercury at greatest elongation 18.1° West of Sun, Saturn 2.94° South of Moon, Saturn enters Scorpius
Oct. 17: Antares 9.54° South of Moon, Jupiter 0.41° South of Mars
Oct. 20: First Quarter Moon
Oct. 23: Neptune 3.03° South of Moon
Oct. 26: Venus at greatest elongation 46.4° West of Sun, Moon at perigee, Jupiter 1.07° North of Venus, Uranus 0.92° North of Moon
Oct. 27: Full Moon
Oct. 28: Spica 4.15° South of Mercury
Oct. 29: Aldebaran 0.60° South of Moon
Oct. 31: Sun enters Libra

November

Mercury is lost in the Sun's glare.
Venus, **Mars**, and **Jupiter** are high in the SE before sunrise all month.
Saturn is visible low in the SE before sunrise late in the month.
Uranus and **Neptune** are high overhead at sunset and set after midnight.

Nov. 1: Mars enters Virgo
Nov. 2: Pollux 11.57° North of Moon, Venus enters Virgo
Nov. 3: Mars 0.70° North of Venus, Last Quarter Moon
Nov. 5: Regulus 3.20° North of Moon
Nov. 6: Jupiter 2.26° North of Moon, Mercury enters Libra
Nov. 7: Moon at apogee, Mars 1.82° North of Moon, Venus 1.24° North of Moon
Nov. 9: Spica 4.31° South of Moon
Nov. 11: Mercury 3.23° South of Moon, New Moon
Nov. 13: Saturn 3.03° South of Moon, Antares 9.44° South of Moon
Nov. 17: Mercury in superior conjunction 0.25° South of Sun, Leonid meteor shower
Nov. 19: First Quarter Moon
Nov. 20: Neptune 2.86° South of Moon, Mercury enters Scorpius
Nov. 22: Uranus 0.94° North of Moon

Nov. 23: Moon at perigee, Sun enters Scorpius
Nov. 25: Saturn 2.76° North of Mercury, Full Moon, Mercury enters Ophiuchus
Nov. 26: Aldebaran 0.68° South of Moon, Antares 3.40° South of Mercury
Nov. 28: Spica 4.47° South of Venus
Nov. 29: Pollux 11.37° North of Moon
Nov. 30: Saturn 1.64° North of Sun, Sun enters Ophiuchus, Saturn enters Ophiuchus

December

Mercury is low in the SW after sunset late in the month.
Venus and **Mars** are in the SE at sunrise all month.
Jupiter rises around midnight and is high in the S at sunrise.
Saturn is visible in the SE before sunrise all month.
Uranus and **Neptune** are overhead at sunset and in the late evening.

Dec. 2: Regulus 2.96° North of Moon
Dec. 3: Last Quarter Moon
Dec. 4: Jupiter 1.79° North of Moon
Dec. 5: Moon at apogee
Dec. 6: Mars 0.10° North of Moon, Spica 4.47° South of Moon
Dec. 7: Venus 0.66° South of Moon, Mercury enters Sagittarius
Dec. 10: Saturn 3.14° South of Moon, Antares 9.42° South of Moon
Dec. 11: New Moon, Venus enters Libra
Dec. 12: Mercury 7.20° South of Moon
Dec. 13: Antares 6.27° South of Saturn, Geminid meteor shower
Dec. 17: Neptune 2.56° South of Moon
Dec. 18: First Quarter Moon, Sun enters Sagittarius
Dec. 20: Uranus 1.16° North of Moon
Dec. 21: Moon at perigee, Spica 3.82° South of Mars
Dec. 22: Solstice
Dec. 23: Aldebaran 0.65° South of Moon
Dec. 25: Full Moon
Dec. 27: Pollux 11.21° North of Moon
Dec. 29: Mercury at greatest elongation 19.7° East of Sun, Regulus 2.69° North of Moon
Dec. 31: Jupiter 1.46° North of Moon

Meteorites and Meteor Showers

When a chunk of material, ice or rock, plunges into Earth's atmosphere and burns up in a fiery display, the event is a **meteor**. While the chunk of material is still in space, it is a **meteoroid**. If a portion of the material survives passage through the atmosphere and reaches the ground, the remnant on the ground is a **meteorite**.

Meteorites found on Earth are classified into types, depending on their composition: **irons**, those composed chiefly of iron, a small percentage of nickel, and traces of other metals such as cobalt; **stones**, stony meteors consisting of silicates; and **stony irons**, containing varying proportions of both iron and stone.

Serious study of meteorites as non-Earth objects began in the 20th century. Scientists use sophisticated chemical analysis, X-rays, and mass spectrography in determining their origin and composition. Although most meteorites are now believed to be fragments of asteroids or comets, geochemical studies have shown that a few Antarctic stones came from the Moon or from Mars, presumably ejected by the explosive impact of asteroids.

The largest known meteorite, estimated to weigh about 55 metric tons, is the Hoba meteorite near Grootfontein, Namibia. The Manicouagan impact crater in Quebec, Canada, with an estimated diameter of 60 mi, is one of the largest crater structures still visible on the surface of the Earth. Not obvious to the eye because of erosion, larger impact craters identified include the Vredefort crater in South Africa at 185 mi across and the Sudbury crater in Ontario, Canada, estimated at 125 mi across. The Bedout impact site off the NW coast of Australia gained attention in 2004 when scientists identified further evidence in support of the idea that it may be linked to the Permian extinction event 250 mil years ago.

Meteor showers vary in strength, but usually the three most visible meteor showers of the year are the **Perseids**, around Aug. 13, the **Orionids**, around Oct. 21, and the **Geminids**, around Dec. 14. These showers feature meteors at the rate of about 60 per hour. Best observing conditions occur in the absence of moonlight, usually when the Moon's phase is between waning crescent and waxing quarter. Bright Moons can adversely affect viewing of some of the best showers of the year.

For most meteor showers the cometary debris is relatively uniformly scattered along the comet's orbit. However, in the case of the **Leonid** meteor shower, which occurs every year around Nov. 17-18, the debris from Comet Temple-Tuttle seems to be bunched up in one stretch. Hence, the meteor shower produced in most years is relatively weak. However, about every 33 years, Earth encounters the bunched-up debris when it crosses the comet's orbit. Sometimes the expected shower is a disappointment, as in 1899 and 1933; at other times, the dense debris provides a spectacular show, as in 1833 and 1866. The Leonids stormed again more recently, producing rates of 1,000-3,000 meteors per hour in 2001.

Rising and Setting of Planets, 2015

(In Coordinated Universal Time, or UTC, the standard time of the prime meridian. 0 in the *h* column designates 12 AM.)

Venus, 2015

Date	20° N Latitude Rise h m	Set h m	30° N Latitude Rise h m	Set h m	40° N Latitude Rise h m	Set h m	50° N Latitude Rise h m	Set h m	60° N Latitude Rise h m	Set h m
Jan. 1	7 47	18 45	8 07	18 25	8 31	18 00	9 06	17 25	10 07	16 25
11	7 55	19 02	8 12	18 45	8 33	18 24	9 03	17 55	9 51	17 06
21	8 00	19 19	8 13	19 05	8 30	18 49	8 53	18 26	9 29	17 50
31	8 01	19 34	8 11	19 24	8 23	19 13	8 38	18 58	9 03	18 34
Feb. 10	8 01	19 48	8 06	19 43	8 12	19 37	8 21	19 29	8 34	19 16
20	7 59	20 01	8 00	20 00	8 01	20 00	8 02	19 59	8 03	19 58
Mar. 2	7 56	20 14	7 53	20 17	7 48	20 22	7 42	20 29	7 32	20 39
12	7 54	20 26	7 46	20 35	7 36	20 45	7 22	20 59	7 01	21 21
22	7 53	20 40	7 40	20 52	7 25	21 08	7 04	21 30	6 30	22 05
Apr. 1	7 53	20 54	7 37	21 10	7 16	21 31	6 48	22 00	6 00	22 49
11	7 56	21 08	7 36	21 28	7 11	21 53	6 35	22 30	5 33	23 33
21	8 01	21 22	7 39	21 45	7 10	22 14	6 28	22 56	5 11	0 11
May 1	8 09	21 35	7 44	22 00	7 13	22 31	6 27	23 17	4 58	0 44
11	8 18	21 46	7 53	22 10	7 21	22 42	6 34	23 29	5 00	1 02
21	8 27	21 52	8 03	22 16	7 32	22 47	6 47	23 32	5 19	1 00
31	8 35	21 54	8 13	22 17	7 45	22 45	7 03	23 25	5 48	0 42
June 10	8 41	21 51	8 21	22 11	7 56	22 35	7 20	23 10	6 18	0 15
20	8 42	21 42	8 25	21 58	8 04	22 19	7 35	22 48	6 45	23 36
30	8 37	21 26	8 23	21 39	8 06	21 56	7 43	22 19	7 05	22 56
July 10	8 24	21 02	8 13	21 12	8 00	21 25	7 42	21 43	7 13	22 11
20	7 59	20 28	7 51	20 36	7 41	20 45	7 28	20 59	7 07	21 19
30	7 20	19 42	7 14	19 48	7 06	19 55	6 56	20 06	6 40	20 22
Aug. 9	6 24	18 44	6 19	18 50	6 12	18 56	6 03	19 06	5 48	19 20
19	5 20	17 42	5 14	17 48	5 06	17 56	4 56	18 07	4 39	18 23
29	4 20	16 48	4 12	16 55	4 03	17 05	3 50	17 18	3 30	17 38
Sept. 8	3 35	16 08	3 26	16 17	3 15	16 28	3 00	16 43	2 36	17 07
18	3 06	15 41	2 56	15 51	2 44	16 03	2 28	16 19	2 02	16 45
28	2 49	15 25	2 39	15 34	2 28	15 46	2 11	16 02	1 46	16 27
Oct. 8	2 41	15 14	2 33	15 22	2 22	15 33	2 07	15 47	1 45	16 10
18	2 39	15 06	2 33	15 13	2 24	15 21	2 12	15 33	1 54	15 51
28	2 42	15 01	2 37	15 05	2 32	15 10	2 24	15 18	2 12	15 29
Nov. 7	2 47	14 56	2 45	14 58	2 43	14 59	2 41	15 02	2 36	15 06
17	2 54	14 52	2 56	14 51	2 58	14 49	3 00	14 46	3 04	14 42
27	3 03	14 50	3 08	14 45	3 14	14 38	3 23	14 30	3 35	14 17
Dec. 7	3 14	14 49	3 22	14 40	3 33	14 29	3 47	14 15	4 09	13 53
17	3 26	14 50	3 38	14 38	3 53	14 23	4 13	14 02	4 45	13 30
27	3 40	14 53	3 55	14 38	4 14	14 19	4 39	13 53	5 21	13 11

Mars, 2015

Date	20° N Latitude Rise h m	Set h m	30° N Latitude Rise h m	Set h m	40° N Latitude Rise h m	Set h m	50° N Latitude Rise h m	Set h m	60° N Latitude Rise h m	Set h m
Jan. 1	9 14	20 33	9 28	20 19	9 44	20 03	10 07	19 41	10 43	19 05
11	9 01	20 28	9 12	20 17	9 25	20 04	9 43	19 46	10 11	19 18
21	8 47	20 22	8 55	20 14	9 05	20 04	9 18	19 51	9 39	19 30
31	8 32	20 16	8 37	20 11	8 44	20 04	8 53	19 56	9 07	19 42
Feb. 10	8 16	20 10	8 19	20 07	8 22	20 04	8 27	20 00	8 34	19 53
20	8 00	20 04	8 01	20 03	8 01	20 04	8 01	20 04	8 01	20 04
Mar. 2	7 44	19 57	7 42	19 59	7 39	20 03	7 34	20 07	7 27	20 14
12	7 28	19 50	7 23	19 55	7 17	20 01	7 08	20 10	6 54	20 25
22	7 12	19 42	7 05	19 50	6 55	20 00	6 42	20 14	6 21	20 35
Apr. 1	6 57	19 35	6 47	19 46	6 34	19 59	6 16	20 16	5 49	20 44
11	6 42	19 28	6 29	19 41	6 13	19 57	5 52	20 19	5 17	20 54
21	6 27	19 21	6 12	19 36	5 54	19 55	5 28	20 21	4 46	21 03
May 1	6 13	19 14	5 56	19 31	5 35	19 52	5 06	20 22	4 16	21 12
11	6 00	19 07	5 41	19 26	5 18	19 49	4 45	20 23	3 48	21 20
21	5 48	18 59	5 28	19 20	5 02	19 45	4 26	20 22	3 22	21 26
31	5 36	18 52	5 15	19 13	4 48	19 40	4 09	20 19	2 59	21 29
June 10	5 25	18 43	5 03	19 05	4 35	19 34	3 54	20 14	2 39	21 29
20	5 15	18 34	4 52	18 57	4 23	19 26	3 42	20 07	2 24	21 25
30	5 05	18 24	4 42	18 47	4 13	19 16	3 31	19 58	2 13	21 16
July 10	4 55	18 14	4 33	18 36	4 04	19 04	3 23	19 45	2 07	21 01
20	4 45	18 02	4 24	18 23	3 56	18 51	3 16	19 30	2 04	20 42
30	4 36	17 49	4 15	18 10	3 49	18 36	3 11	19 13	2 04	20 19
Aug. 9	4 26	17 35	4 06	17 54	3 42	18 19	3 07	18 53	2 06	19 54
19	4 16	17 20	3 58	17 38	3 35	18 00	3 03	18 32	2 09	19 25
29	4 05	17 04	3 49	17 20	3 28	17 40	3 00	18 09	2 12	18 56
Sept. 8	3 54	16 47	3 40	17 01	3 22	17 19	2 56	17 44	2 15	18 25
18	3 43	16 29	3 30	16 41	3 14	16 57	2 53	17 18	2 18	17 53
28	3 31	16 10	3 20	16 21	3 07	16 34	2 49	16 52	2 20	17 20
Oct. 8	3 19	15 51	3 10	16 00	2 59	16 10	2 45	16 25	2 21	16 47
18	3 06	15 31	2 59	15 38	2 51	15 46	2 40	15 57	2 22	16 14
28	2 53	15 11	2 48	15 16	2 42	15 21	2 35	15 29	2 23	15 41
Nov. 7	2 39	14 51	2 37	14 53	2 34	14 56	2 29	15 00	2 22	15 07
17	2 25	14 30	2 25	14 30	2 24	14 31	2 23	14 32	2 21	14 33
27	2 11	14 09	2 13	14 07	2 14	14 06	2 17	14 03	2 20	14 00
Dec. 7	1 57	13 48	2 00	13 45	2 04	13 40	2 10	13 35	2 18	13 26
17	1 42	13 27	1 48	13 22	1 54	13 15	2 03	13 06	2 16	12 53
27	1 27	13 06	1 34	12 59	1 43	12 50	1 55	12 38	2 13	12 20

Jupiter, 2015

Date	20° N Latitude Rise h m	20° N Latitude Set h m	30° N Latitude Rise h m	30° N Latitude Set h m	40° N Latitude Rise h m	40° N Latitude Set h m	50° N Latitude Rise h m	50° N Latitude Set h m	60° N Latitude Rise h m	60° N Latitude Set h m
Jan. 1	20 28	9 20	20 14	9 33	19 57	9 50	19 34	10 13	18 56	10 51
11	19 44	8 38	19 31	8 51	19 13	9 08	18 50	9 32	18 11	10 11
21	19 00	7 55	18 46	8 09	18 28	8 26	18 04	8 51	17 24	9 31
31	18 15	7 11	18 01	7 25	17 43	7 44	17 17	8 09	16 36	8 50
Feb. 10	17 30	6 27	17 15	6 42	16 56	7 01	16 30	7 27	15 48	8 09
20	16 45	5 43	16 30	5 59	16 10	6 18	15 44	6 45	15 00	7 29
Mar. 2	16 01	5 00	15 45	5 16	15 25	5 35	14 58	6 03	14 13	6 48
12	15 17	4 17	15 01	4 33	14 41	4 53	14 13	5 21	13 27	6 07
22	14 35	3 35	14 19	3 52	13 58	4 12	13 30	4 40	12 43	5 27
Apr. 1	13 54	2 55	13 37	3 11	13 17	3 31	12 49	4 00	12 01	4 47
11	13 14	2 15	12 58	2 31	12 37	2 52	12 09	3 20	11 22	4 07
21	12 36	1 37	12 20	1 53	11 59	2 13	11 31	2 41	10 44	3 28
May 1	11 59	0 59	11 43	1 15	11 23	1 35	10 55	2 03	10 08	2 50
11	11 23	0 23	11 07	0 38	10 48	0 58	10 20	1 26	9 35	2 11
21	10 49	23 43	10 33	0 02	10 14	0 22	9 47	0 49	9 03	1 33
				23 59						
31	10 15	23 09	10 00	23 24	9 41	23 42	9 15	0 12	8 32	0 55
June 10	9 42	22 34	9 28	22 49	9 09	23 07	8 44	23 32	8 02	0 18
20	9 10	22 01	8 56	22 15	8 39	22 32	8 14	22 57	7 34	23 36
30	8 39	21 27	8 25	21 41	8 08	21 58	7 45	22 21	7 07	22 59
July 10	8 08	20 55	7 55	21 08	7 39	21 24	7 16	21 46	6 40	22 22
20	7 37	20 22	7 25	20 34	7 10	20 50	6 48	21 11	6 14	21 45
30	7 07	19 50	6 55	20 01	6 41	20 16	6 21	20 36	5 49	21 08
Aug. 9	6 37	19 17	6 26	19 28	6 12	19 42	5 53	20 01	5 23	20 31
19	6 07	18 45	5 57	18 55	5 44	19 08	5 26	19 26	4 58	19 54
29	5 37	18 13	5 28	18 22	5 16	18 34	4 59	18 51	4 33	19 17
Sept. 8	5 07	17 40	4 58	17 49	4 47	18 00	4 32	18 16	4 08	18 40
18	4 37	17 08	4 29	17 16	4 19	17 26	4 05	17 40	3 43	18 02
28	4 07	16 35	3 59	16 43	3 50	16 52	3 37	17 05	3 17	17 25
Oct. 8	3 36	16 02	3 29	16 09	3 21	16 18	3 09	16 30	2 51	16 48
18	3 05	15 29	2 59	15 36	2 51	15 43	2 41	15 54	2 24	16 11
28	2 34	14 56	2 28	15 01	2 21	15 08	2 11	15 18	1 56	15 33
Nov. 7	2 02	14 22	1 57	14 27	1 50	14 33	1 41	14 42	1 28	14 56
17	1 29	13 47	1 24	13 52	1 18	13 58	1 10	14 06	0 58	14 18
27	0 55	13 12	0 51	13 16	0 46	13 22	0 38	13 29	0 27	13 40
Dec. 7	0 20	12 36	0 16	12 40	0 12	12 45	0 05	12 52	23 51	13 02
17	23 41	11 59	23 37	12 03	23 33	12 08	23 26	12 14	23 17	12 24
27	23 04	11 22	23 00	11 25	22 56	11 30	22 50	11 36	22 40	11 45

Saturn, 2015

Date	20° N Latitude Rise h m	20° N Latitude Set h m	30° N Latitude Rise h m	30° N Latitude Set h m	40° N Latitude Rise h m	40° N Latitude Set h m	50° N Latitude Rise h m	50° N Latitude Set h m	60° N Latitude Rise h m	60° N Latitude Set h m
Jan. 1	3 40	14 48	3 56	14 32	4 16	14 11	4 44	13 44	5 30	12 58
11	3 05	14 12	3 21	13 56	3 42	13 35	4 10	13 07	4 56	12 21
21	2 29	13 36	2 46	13 20	3 07	12 59	3 35	12 31	4 22	11 44
31	1 53	13 00	2 10	12 43	2 31	12 22	2 59	11 54	3 47	11 06
Feb. 10	1 17	12 23	1 34	12 06	1 54	11 45	2 23	11 16	3 11	10 29
20	0 39	11 45	0 56	11 28	1 17	11 07	1 46	10 39	2 34	9 51
Mar. 2	0 01	11 07	0 18	10 50	0 39	10 29	1 08	10 00	1 56	9 12
	23 58									
12	23 19	10 28	23 36	10 11	0 00	9 50	0 29	9 22	1 17	8 34
					23 56					
22	22 39	9 49	22 56	9 32	23 17	9 11	23 46	8 42	0 37	7 55
Apr. 1	21 59	9 09	22 16	8 52	22 36	8 31	23 05	8 02	23 52	7 15
11	21 18	8 28	21 34	8 11	21 55	7 51	22 24	7 22	23 11	6 35
21	20 36	7 47	20 53	7 30	21 13	7 10	21 42	6 41	22 28	5 55
May 1	19 54	7 05	20 11	6 49	20 31	6 28	20 59	6 00	21 45	5 14
11	19 12	6 23	19 28	6 07	19 48	5 47	20 16	5 19	21 02	4 33
21	18 29	5 41	18 45	5 25	19 05	5 05	19 33	4 37	20 18	3 52
31	17 47	4 59	18 03	4 43	18 22	4 23	18 50	3 56	19 35	3 11
June 10	17 04	4 17	17 20	4 01	17 40	3 41	18 07	3 14	18 51	2 30
20	16 22	3 35	16 38	3 19	16 57	3 00	17 24	2 33	18 08	1 49
30	15 40	2 54	15 56	2 38	16 15	2 19	16 42	1 52	17 26	1 08
July 10	14 59	2 13	15 15	1 57	15 34	1 38	16 01	1 11	16 44	0 27
20	14 19	1 32	14 34	1 17	14 54	0 57	15 20	0 31	16 04	23 43
30	13 39	0 52	13 55	0 37	14 14	0 17	14 41	23 47	15 24	23 03
Aug. 9	13 00	0 13	13 15	23 53	13 35	23 34	14 02	23 07	14 45	22 24
19	12 21	23 30	12 37	23 15	12 57	22 55	13 24	22 28	14 07	21 44
29	11 44	22 52	11 59	22 37	12 19	22 17	12 46	21 50	13 31	21 05
Sept. 8	11 07	22 15	11 23	21 59	11 42	21 39	12 10	21 12	12 55	20 27
18	10 30	21 38	10 46	21 22	11 06	21 02	11 34	20 34	12 19	19 49
28	9 54	21 01	10 11	20 45	10 31	20 25	10 59	19 57	11 45	19 11
Oct. 8	9 19	20 25	9 35	20 09	9 56	19 48	10 24	19 20	11 11	18 33
18	8 44	19 50	9 01	19 33	9 21	19 12	9 50	18 43	10 38	17 56
28	8 09	19 14	8 26	18 57	8 47	18 36	9 17	18 07	10 05	17 18
Nov. 7	7 35	18 39	7 52	18 22	8 13	18 01	8 43	17 31	9 32	16 42
17	7 01	18 04	7 18	17 47	7 40	17 25	8 10	16 55	9 00	16 05
27	6 27	17 30	6 44	17 12	7 06	16 50	7 37	16 20	8 28	15 29
Dec. 7	5 53	16 55	6 10	16 37	6 33	16 15	7 04	15 44	7 55	14 52
17	5 18	16 20	5 36	16 02	5 59	15 40	6 30	15 09	7 23	14 16
27	4 44	15 45	5 02	15 27	5 25	15 05	5 57	14 33	6 50	13 40

Morning and Evening "Stars," 2015

(In Coordinated Universal Time, or UTC, the standard time of the prime meridian.)

	Morning	Evening		Morning	Evening
Jan.	Jupiter Saturn	Mercury Venus Mars Uranus Neptune	**July**	Mercury to July 23 Mars Uranus Neptune	Mercury from July 24 Venus Jupiter Saturn
Feb.	Mercury Jupiter to Feb. 6 Saturn	Venus Mars Jupiter from Feb. 7 Uranus Neptune	**Aug.**	Venus from Aug. 16 Mars Jupiter from Aug. 27 Uranus Neptune	Mercury Saturn Venus to Aug. 15 Jupiter to Aug. 26
Mar.	Mercury Saturn Neptune	Venus Mars Jupiter Uranus	**Sept.**	Venus Mars Jupiter Uranus	Mercury Saturn Neptune
Apr.	Mercury to Apr. 10 Saturn Uranus from Apr. 6 Neptune	Mercury from Apr. 11 Venus Mars Jupiter Uranus to Apr. 5	**Oct.**	Mercury Venus Mars Jupiter Uranus to Oct. 12	Saturn Uranus from Oct. 13 Neptune
May	Saturn to May 23 Uranus Neptune	Mercury Venus Mars Jupiter Saturn from May 24	**Nov.**	Mercury to Nov. 17 Venus Mars Jupiter	Mercury from Nov. 18 Saturn Uranus Neptune
June	Mercury Mars from June 17 Uranus Neptune	Venus Mars to June 16 Jupiter Saturn	**Dec.**	Venus Mars Jupiter Saturn	Mercury Uranus Neptune

Greenwich Sidereal Time for 0h UTC, 2015

UTC = Coordinated Universal Time. Add 12 hours to obtain right ascension of mean sun.

Date	d	h	m	Date	d	h	m	Date	d	h	m	Date	d	h	m
Jan.	1	6	41.3	**Apr.**	1	12	36.2	**July**	10	19	10.4	**Oct.**	8	1	5.2
	11	7	20.7		11	13	15.6		20	19	49.8		18	1	44.7
	21	8	0.2		21	13	55.0		30	20	29.3		28	2	24.1
	31	8	39.6	**May**	1	14	34.4	**Aug.**	9	21	8.7	**Nov.**	7	3	3.5
Feb.	10	9	19.0		11	15	13.9		19	21	48.1		17	3	42.9
	20	9	58.4		21	15	53.3		29	22	27.5		27	4	22.4
Mar.	2	10	37.9		31	16	32.7	**Sept.**	8	23	7.0	**Dec.**	7	5	1.8
	12	11	17.3	**June**	10	17	12.1		18	23	46.4		17	5	41.2
	22	11	56.7		20	17	51.6		28	0	25.8		27	6	20.7
					30	18	31.0								

Largest Telescopes

Astronomers indicate the size of telescopes not by length or magnification but by the diameter of the primary light-gathering component of the system, such as the lens or mirror. This measurement is a direct indication of the telescope's light-gathering power. The larger the diameter of the mirror or lens, the fainter the objects that can be detected. In principle, larger telescopes have better resolving power—the ability to discern small details—than smaller telescopes. However, the Earth's atmosphere limits the details that can be seen using ground-based telescopes. That is why the Hubble Space Telescope, which orbits the Earth outside of its atmosphere, can achieve higher resolution with its 2.4-m (7.9-ft) mirror than much larger telescopes on Earth. Adaptive optics systems, which help compensate for the blurring effects of the Earth's atmosphere, allow ground-based telescopes to achieve similar levels of detail as space-based telescopes. Telescopes to detect ultraviolet, X-ray, and gamma radiation must be placed in space or high-altitude balloons because the Earth's atmosphere absorbs most of these types of radiation; as a result, telescopes to detect such radiation are generally much smaller than optical, infrared, and radio telescopes.

Refracting (lens) telescopes are currently not made with lens diameters of more than 40 in. Because **reflecting telescopes** can be made less expensively and with more precision than refracting telescopes, all modern large optical telescopes are made with mirrors. **Radio telescopes** view at wavelengths not visible to optical telescopes or to the human eye. Radio telescopes are larger than optical telescopes because larger diameters are required to obtain equivalent resolution at longer wavelengths. Arrays of telescopes are used to achieve even better resolution through a technique called interferometry. Originally developed for radio telescopes, the technique is now also used with optical and infrared telescopes.

Largest refracting (lens) optical telescope: Yerkes Observatory, 1 m (40 in.), at Williams Bay, WI

Largest reflecting (mirror) optical/infrared telescope: Gran Telescopio Canarias, 10.4 m (34 ft), on La Palma, Canary Islands (segmented mirror)

Largest infrared interferometer: Four 8.2-m (27-ft) telescopes of the Very Large Telescope Interferometer (VLTI) with a 200-m (656-ft) baseline on Cerro Paranal in Chile

Largest fully steerable radio dish: Robert Byrd Green Bank Telescope (GBT), 100 m x 110 m (328 ft x 360 ft), in Green Bank, WV

Largest single radio dish: Arecibo Observatory, 305 m (1,000 ft), in Puerto Rico

Largest baseline radio interferometer: 10 25-m (82-ft) diameter telescopes of the Very Long Baseline Array (VLBA), dispersed from Hawaii to the Virgin Islands with a resolution equal to a radio dish of 8,600 km (5,000 mi), making it the highest resolution telescope in the solar system

Largest submillimeter interferometer: 54 12-m (39-ft) and 12 7-m (23-ft) antennas of the Atacama Large Millimeter Array (ALMA), located at a site above 5,000-m (16,400-ft) in the Atacama Desert in Chile. The antennas can be spread out over a 16-km (10-mi) distance to increase the resolving power of the array.

Largest airborne telescope: Stratospheric Observatory for Infrared Astronomy (SOFIA), 2.5-m (8.2-ft) infrared telescope aboard a NASA 747

Constellations

Culturally, constellations are imagined patterns among the stars that, in some cases, have been recognized through millennia. Knowledge of constellations was once necessary in order to function as an astronomer. For today's astronomers, constellations are simply areas of the sky in which objects await observation and interpretation.

Because Western culture has dominated much of modern scientific discourse, constellations and celestial traditions of other cultures are not well known outside their regions of origin. Even the patterns with which we are most familiar today have undergone considerable change over the centuries.

Today, **88 constellations** are officially recognized. Although many have ancient origins, some are modern, devised out of unclaimed stars by astronomers a few centuries ago. Unclaimed stars were those too faint or inconveniently placed to be included in the more prominent constellations. Stars in a constellation are not necessarily near each other; they are just located in the same direction on the celestial sphere.

When Western astronomers began to travel to South Africa in the 16th and 17th centuries, they found an unfamiliar sky that showed numerous brilliant stars. Thus, constellations in the Southern Hemisphere are named after technological marvels of the time, as well as some arguably traditional forms, such as Musca, the fly.

Many of the commonly recognized constellations have their origins in ancient Asia Minor. These were adopted by the Greeks and Romans, who translated their names and stories into their own languages, modifying some details in the process. After the decline of those cultures, most such knowledge entered oral tradition or remained hidden in monastic libraries. In the 8th century, Muslims began to spread through the Mediterranean world. Wherever possible, everything was translated into Arabic to be taught in the universities the Muslims established throughout their newfound world.

In the 13th century, King Alfonso X of Castile, an avid student of astronomy, had Ptolemy's astronomical treatise *Almagest* translated into Latin. It thus became widely available to European scholars. In the process, the constellation names were translated, but the star names were retained in their Arabic forms. Thus the names of many stars—Altair, Alnitak, and Mirfak, among others—have Arabic roots, although linguistic adaptation and the inaccuracies of transliteration have wrought changes.

Until the 1920s, astronomers used curved boundaries for the constellation areas. As these were rather arbitrary, the International Astronomical Union adopted new constellation boundaries that run due N-S and E-W. These boundaries divide the sky into the 88 constellations, much as the contiguous U.S. is made up of the lower 48 states.

Common names of stars often referred to parts of the traditional figures they represented: Deneb, the tail of the swan, and Betelgeuse, the armpit of the giant. Astronomers may avoid traditional names by labeling stars with Greek letters, generally to denote order of brightness. Thus, the "alpha star" would typically be the brightest star in a constellation. The "of" implies possession, so the genitive (possessive) form of the constellation name is used as in Alpha Orionis, the first star of Orion (Betelgeuse). Astronomers usually use a three-letter abbreviation for the constellation name, as indicated below.

Asterisms are widely recognized patterns of stars. The so-called Big Dipper is a small part of the constellation Ursa Major, the big bear; the Sickle is the traditional head and mane of Leo, the lion; the three stars of the Summer Triangle are each in a different constellation, with Vega in Lyra the lyre, Deneb in Cygnus the swan, and Altair in Aquila the eagle. The northeast star of the asterism Great Square of Pegasus is Alpha Andromedae.

Name	Genitive case	Abbr.	Meaning	Name	Genitive case	Abbr.	Meaning
Andromeda	Andromedae	And	Chained Maiden	Lacerta	Lacertae	Lac	Lizard
Antlia	Antliae	Ant	Air Pump	Leo	Leonis	Leo	Lion
Apus	Apodis	Aps	Bird of Paradise	Leo Minor	Leonis Minoris	LMi	Littler Lion
Aquarius	Aquarii	Aqr	Water Bearer	Lepus	Leporis	Lep	Hare
Aquila	Aquilae	Aql	Eagle	Libra	Librae	Lib	Balance
Ara	Arae	Ara	Altar	Lupus	Lupi	Lup	Wolf
Aries	Arietis	Ari	Ram	Lynx	Lyncis	Lyn	Lynx
Auriga	Aurigae	Aur	Charioteer	Lyra	Lyrae	Lyr	Lyre
Boötes	Boötis	Boo	Herder	Mensa	Mensae	Men	Table Mountain
Caelum	Caeli	Cae	Chisel	Microscopium	Microscopii	Mic	Microscope
Camelopardalis	Camelopardalis	Cam	Giraffe	Monoceros	Monocerotis	Mon	Unicorn
Cancer	Cancri	Cnc	Crab	Musca	Muscae	Mus	Fly
Canes Venatici	Canum Venaticorum	CVn	Hunting Dogs	Norma	Normae	Nor	Square (rule)
				Octans	Octantis	Oct	Octant
Canis Major	Canis Majoris	CMa	Greater Dog	Ophiuchus	Ophiuchi	Oph	Serpent Bearer
Canis Minor	Canis Minoris	CMi	Littler Dog	Orion	Orionis	Ori	Hunter
Capricornus	Capricorni	Cap	Sea-Goat	Pavo	Pavonis	Pav	Peacock
Carina	Carinae	Car	Keel	Pegasus	Pegasi	Peg	Flying Horse
Cassiopeia	Cassiopeiae	Cas	Queen	Perseus	Persei	Per	Hero
Centaurus	Centauri	Cen	Centaur	Phoenix	Phoenicis	Phe	Phoenix
Cepheus	Cephei	Cep	King	Pictor	Pictoris	Pic	Painter
Cetus	Ceti	Cet	Whale	Pisces	Piscium	Psc	Fishes
Chamaeleon	Chamaeleontis	Cha	Chameleon	Piscis Austrinus	Piscis Austrini	PsA	Southern Fish
Circinus	Circini	Cir	Compass (drawing)	Puppis	Puppis	Pup	Stern (deck)
Columba	Columbae	Col	Dove	Pyxis	Pyxidis	Pyx	Compass (sea)
Coma Berenices	Comae Berenices	Com	Berenice's Hair	Reticulum	Reticuli	Ret	Reticle
Corona Australis	Coronae Australis	CrA	Southern Crown	Sagitta	Sagittae	Sge	Arrow
Corona Borealis	Coronae Borealis	CrB	Northern Crown	Sagittarius	Sagittarii	Sgr	Archer
Corvus	Corvi	Crv	Crow	Scorpius	Scorpii	Sco	Scorpion
Crater	Crateris	Crt	Cup	Sculptor	Sculptoris	Scl	Sculptor
Crux	Crucis	Cru	Cross (southern)	Scutum	Scuti	Sct	Shield
Cygnus	Cygni	Cyg	Swan	Serpens	Serpentis	Ser	Serpent
Delphinus	Delphini	Del	Dolphin	Sextans	Sextantis	Sex	Sextant
Dorado	Doradus	Dor	Dolphinfish	Taurus	Tauri	Tau	Bull
Draco	Draconis	Dra	Dragon	Telescopium	Telescopii	Tel	Telescope
Equuleus	Equulei	Equ	Little Horse	Triangulum	Trianguli	Tri	Triangle
Eridanus	Eridani	Eri	River	Triangulum Australe	Trianguli Australis	TrA	Southern Triangle
Fornax	Fornacis	For	Furnace	Tucana	Tucanae	Tuc	Toucan
Gemini	Geminorum	Gem	Twins	Ursa Major	Ursae Majoris	UMa	Greater Bear
Grus	Gruis	Gru	Crane (bird)	Ursa Minor	Ursae Minoris	UMi	Littler Bear
Hercules	Herculis	Her	Hercules	Vela	Velorum	Vel	Sail
Horologium	Horologii	Hor	Clock	Virgo	Virginis	Vir	Maiden
Hydra	Hydrae	Hya	Water Snake (female)	Volans	Volantis	Vol	Flying Fish
Hydrus	Hydri	Hyi	Water Snake (male)	Vulpecula	Vulpeculae	Vul	Fox
Indus	Indi	Ind	Indian				

Eclipses, 2015

(In Coordinated Universal Time, or UTC, the standard time of the prime meridian.)

There will be four eclipses in 2015: a total solar eclipse, two total lunar eclipses, and a partial solar eclipse. The total solar eclipse path extends from the North Atlantic to the Arctic Ocean, only crossing land at the Faroe Islands and Svalbard, but the partial phase will be visible across wide areas of West Africa, Europe, and Asia. The first lunar eclipse is in the total phase for less than 5 min., though a wide region extending across the western U.S. to East Asia will be able to see all or most of the eclipse. The partial solar eclipse will be visible in southern Africa, Madagascar, and Antarctica. The second lunar eclipse will be visible across the Americas, much of Africa, and Europe.

During an annular eclipse of the Sun, the Moon's angular diameter is not large enough to block the entire disk of the Sun, and the Sun appears as a bright ring about the dark disk of the Moon. During a partial solar eclipse, the Moon blocks some of the Sun's disk. The tables below give the times in UTC of when the Moon or Sun reaches certain phases of eclipse. In the case of the lunar eclipses, the times are relevant for any observer who can see the Moon. In the case of solar eclipses, the tabulated times refer to when the given event begins or ends from specific points along the eclipse path; as the Moon's shadow sweeps quickly across the Earth, the observed duration and degree of eclipse depends on the observer's precise location.

I. Total Eclipse of the Sun: Mar. 20

This total eclipse will only be visible from two populated locations: the Faroe Islands and Svalbard. Observers in a wide area from West Africa to Europe and Eastern Russia will see a partially eclipsed Sun. Totality lasts just under 4 min.

Event	Date	h	m
Partial eclipse begins	Mar. 20	7	40.9
Total eclipse begins	20	9	9.5
Greatest eclipse	20	9	45.6
Total eclipse ends	20	10	21.4
Partial eclipse ends	20	11	50.2

II. Total Eclipse of the Moon: Apr. 4

The entirety of this eclipse will only be visible from eastern Australia and parts of Asia and the Pacific, though large portions will be visible throughout Asia and the western U.S. Totality lasts less than 5 min.—very short for a lunar eclipse—but the Moon will be partially eclipsed for 3.5 hr.

Event	Date	h	m
Penumbral eclipse begins	Apr. 4	9	1.5
Partial eclipse begins	4	10	15.8
Total eclipse begins	4	11	57.9
Greatest eclipse	4	12	0.2
Total eclipse ends	4	12	2.6
Partial eclipse ends	4	13	44.8
Penumbral eclipse ends	4	14	58.9

III. Partial Eclipse of the Sun: Sept. 13

The partial eclipse path extends from southern Africa to the Antarctic.

Event	Date	h	m
Partial eclipse begins	Sept. 13	4	41.7
Greatest eclipse	13	6	54.2
Penumbral eclipse ends	13	9	6.4

IV. Total Eclipse of the Moon: Sept. 27-28

This total lunar eclipse will be visible over a wide area including the Americas, Europe, Africa, and the Middle East. In contrast to the lunar eclipse in Apr., the Moon will be totally eclipsed for nearly 75 min. The eclipse occurs in the early AM hours of Sept. 28 in Africa and Asia, and on the night of Sept. 27 from the Americas.

Event	Date	h	m
Penumbral eclipse begins	Sept. 28	8	15.6
Partial eclipse begins	28	9	14.8
Total eclipse begins	28	10	25.2
Greatest eclipse	28	10	55.7
Total eclipse ends	28	11	24.0
Partial eclipse ends	28	12	34.3
Penumbral eclipse ends	28	13	33.7

Total Solar Eclipses, 2015-35

Total solar eclipses actually take place nearly as often as total lunar eclipses. Total lunar eclipses are visible over at least half of the Earth, while total solar eclipses can be seen only along a very narrow path up to a few hundred miles wide and a few thousand miles long. Observing a total solar eclipse is thus a rarity for most people.

Solar eclipses can be dangerous to observe. This is not because the Sun emits more potent rays, but because the Sun is always dangerous to observe directly, and people are particularly likely to stare at it during a solar eclipse.

Date	Duration[1] m	s	Width (mi)	Path of totality
2015, Mar. 20	2	47	304	N Atlantic Ocean, Arctic Ocean
2016, Mar. 9	4	10	96	Indonesia, Pacific Ocean
2017, Aug. 21	2	40	71	Pacific Ocean, U.S., Atlantic Ocean
2019, July 2	4	33	125	S Pacific Ocean, S America
2020, Dec. 14	2	10	56	S Pacific Ocean, S America, S Atlantic Ocean
2021, Dec. 4	1	54	260	Antarctica
2024, Apr. 8	4	27	123	Mexico, midwestern U.S., E Canada
2026, Aug. 12	2	18	183	Greenland, Iceland, Spain
2027, Aug. 2	6	24	160	Spain, N Africa, Arabian peninsula
2028, July 22	5	10	140	Indian Ocean, Australia, New Zealand
2030, Nov. 25	3	45	105	Namibia, Botswana, South Africa, Indian Ocean, E Australia
2033, Mar. 30	2	37	485	Alaska, E Russia, Arctic
2034, Mar. 20	4	9	100	Central and NE Africa, Arabian Peninsula, Central and E Asia
2035, Sept. 2	2	54	72	China, Korea, Japan, Pacific Ocean

(1) Length of time at optimal viewing area.

Total Solar Eclipses in the U.S. in the 21st Century

During the 21st century there will be eight total solar eclipses visible somewhere in the continental U.S. The first comes after a long gap. The last total solar eclipse was on Feb. 26, 1979, in the northwestern U.S.

Date	Path of totality	Date	Path of totality
Aug. 21, 2017	Oregon to South Carolina	Mar. 30, 2052	Florida to Georgia
Apr. 8, 2024	Mexico to Texas and N through Maine	May 11, 2078	Louisiana to North Carolina
Aug. 23, 2044	Montana to North Dakota	May 1, 2079	New Jersey to the lower edge of New England
Aug. 12, 2045	Northern California to Florida	Sept. 14, 2099	North Dakota to Virginia

Beginnings of the Universe

One of the dominating astronomical discoveries of the 20th century was that the galaxies of the universe all seem to be moving away from Earth. Doppler redshifts were observed for spiral nebulae around 1920 even though they were not yet known to be galaxies. By the early 1930s, Edwin Hubble and M. L. Humason had established that the more distant a galaxy, the faster it was receding. It turned out that they were moving away not just from the Earth but from one another—that is, the **universe is expanding**. Scientists conclude that the universe must once, very long ago, have been extremely compact and dense, until an explosion or a similar event caused the matter to spread out. The explosion that gave birth to the universe is called the **Big Bang**.

On the subatomic level, according to this theory, there were vast changes of energy and matter and the way physical laws operated during the first few minutes. After those early minutes the percentages of the basic matter of the universe— hydrogen, helium, and lithium—were set. Everything was so compact and hot that radiation dominated the early universe and there were no stable, un-ionized atoms. The universe was opaque, in the sense that any energy emitted was quickly absorbed and then re-emitted. As the universe expanded, density and temperature continued to drop. A few hundred thousand years after the Big Bang, the temperature dropped far enough that electrons and nuclei could combine to form stable atoms as the universe became transparent. Once that occurred, the radiation that had been trapped was free to escape.

In the 1940s, George Gamov and others predicted remnants of this escaped radiation should be observable. They had started to search for this background radiation when physicists Arno Penzias and Robert Wilson, using a radio telescope, inadvertently found it.

In 2003, NASA's Wilkinson Microwave Anisotropy Probe made measurements of the temperature of this **cosmic microwave background radiation** to within millionths of a degree. From these measurements, scientists were able to deduce that our universe is 13.7 bil years old and that first-generation stars began to form a mere 200 mil years after the Big Bang.

In 2014, scientists operating a telescope in Antarctica claimed to have found direct evidence for cosmic inflation, the rapid expansion of the Universe during the first 10^{-32} seconds after the Big Bang that helps explain why variations of the cosmic background radiation are so small. However, further study will be needed to confirm these findings.

A related mystery is evidence suggesting hidden matter and hidden energy that cannot be directly observed. This **dark matter** may be composed of gas; large numbers of cool, small objects; or even subatomic particles. The presence of dark matter is indicated by the rotation curves of galaxies and the dynamics of clusters of galaxies. Evidence for **dark energy** is derived from studies of distant Type Ia supernovae indicating that the expansion of the universe is accelerating rather than slowing. Dark energy seems to work on the very fabric of the universe, spreading it apart. Visible matter seems to constitute only about 4% of the total mass of the universe while the rest of the universe's mass is in the form of dark matter (27%) and dark energy (68%).

Galaxies

The 20th century might be called the century of the galaxy. By the start of the century, more than 10,000 **nebulae**— cloud-like luminous objects in the sky—had been discovered. Some were correctly identified as star clusters and others as clouds of gas and dust. Those nebulae which were spiral or elliptical in shape were found in regions of the sky far from the glowing band that is our own Milky Way galaxy. Immanuel Kant had written in 1775 that some of these fuzzy objects might be **"island universes"** apart from our own. But the idea remained speculative until 1923-24, when Edwin Hubble discovered the existence of variable stars in some of these nebulae. This provided conclusive evidence that these systems were outside our own island universe, the Milky Way galaxy.

Galaxies range in size from small dwarf elliptical ones, with perhaps 1 mil stars, to spiral galaxies containing 300 bil stars, to giant elliptical galaxies that may be home to more than 10 tril stars. The diameters of galaxies range from 3,000 light-years in dwarf elliptical galaxies to over 500,000 light-years in giant elliptical galaxies. It is estimated that the Milky Way galaxy is about 100,000 light-years in diameter with about 400 bil stars.

Galaxies also congregate into **clusters**. The smallest are poor clusters of only a few dozen galaxies, while the largest rich clusters may contain thousands. The Milky Way is part of a poor cluster of about three dozen galaxies called the **Local Group**. The largest galaxy of the Local Group is Andromeda, a spiral galaxy visible to the unaided eye in the constellation of Andromeda on a very dark night. The Milky Way is the second largest galaxy in this group; most of the others are small.

The Solar System

The major planets of the solar system, in order of mean distance from the Sun, are **Mercury, Venus, Earth, Mars, Jupiter, Saturn, Uranus,** and **Neptune**. The dwarf planets in order of average distance from the Sun are **Ceres** (located between Mars and Jupiter), **Pluto, Haumea, Makemake,** and **Eris**. All planets orbit counterclockwise around the Sun as viewed from above the Earth's North Pole.

Because Mercury and Venus are nearer to the Sun than is Earth, their motions about the Sun appear from Earth as wide swings first to one side of the Sun then to the other, though both planets move around the Sun in almost circular orbits. When their passage takes them between Earth and the Sun or beyond the Sun in relation to Earth, they cannot be seen.

The planets that lie farther from the Sun than does Earth may be seen for longer periods. They are invisible only when so located in the sky that they rise and set at about the same time as the Sun and are thus overwhelmed by the Sun's light.

Mercury and Venus, because they are between Earth and the Sun, show phases much as the Moon does. The planets farther from the Sun are always seen as full, although Mars does occasionally present a slightly gibbous phase, like the Moon when it is not quite full.

The planets appear to move rapidly among the stars because they are relatively closer to Earth. The stars are also in motion, some at tremendous speeds, but they are so far away that their motion does not change their apparent positions in the heavens enough to be perceived. The nearest star is about 9,000 times farther away than Neptune. The count for identified **moons** in the solar system orbiting planets and dwarf planets stood at 181 as of July 2014. Several dwarf planet candidates are also known to have moons.

Planet Superlatives			
Largest, most massive planet	Jupiter	Smallest, least massive planet	Mercury
Fastest orbiting planet	Mercury	Slowest orbiting planet	Neptune
Fastest sidereal rotation	Jupiter	Slowest sidereal rotation	Venus
Longest (synodic) day	Mercury	Shortest (synodic) day	Jupiter
Rotational pole closest to ecliptic	Uranus	Hottest planet	Venus
Most moons	Jupiter	No moons	Mercury, Venus
Planet with largest moon	Jupiter	Planet with moon with most eccentric orbit	Neptune
Greatest average density	Earth	Lowest average density	Saturn
Tallest mountain	Mars	Deepest oceans	Jupiter
Strongest magnetic fields	Jupiter	Greatest amount of liquid, surface water	Earth
Most circular orbit	Venus		

Selected Characteristics of the Sun and Planets

Object	Radius— at unit distance[1] "	at mean least distance[2] "	in mi mean radius	Volume[3]	Mass[3]	Density[3]	Sidereal period d	h	m	s	Gravity at surface[3]	Reflecting power[4]	Daytime surface temp. (°F)
Sun	959.50	976.0	432,500	1,304,000	333,000	0.26	25	9	7		28.00	—	9,941
Mercury	3.36	6.5	1,516	0.0562	0.0553	0.98	58	15	36		0.38	0.11	845
Venus	8.34	33.0	3,760	0.857	0.815	0.95	243		30R		0.91	0.65	867
Earth	8.78	—	3,959	1.000	1.000	1.00		23	56	4.2	1.00	0.37	59
Moon	2.40	986.2	1,079	0.0203	0.0123	0.61	27	7	43	40	0.16	0.12	260
Mars	4.67	12.8	2,106	0.151	0.107	0.71		24	37	22	0.38	0.15	-24
Jupiter	96.40	24.5	43,441	1,321	317.8	0.24		9	55	30	2.53	0.52	-162
Saturn	80.29	10.05	36,184	764	95.16	0.12		10	39	20	1.06	0.47	-218
Uranus	34.97	2.05	15,759	63.1	14.54	0.23		17	14	20R	0.90	0.51	-323
Neptune	33.95	1.2	15,301	57.7	17.15	0.30		16	6	40	1.14	0.41	-330

R = Retrograde rotation. (1) Angular radius, in seconds of arc, if object were seen at a distance of 1 astronomical unit. (2) Angular radius, in seconds of arc, when object is closest to Earth. (3) Earth = 1. (4) A value of 1 would indicate a perfect reflector.

Planets: Motion, Distance, and Brightness

Planet	Mean daily motion[1]	Orbital velocity (mi per sec.)[2]	Sidereal revolution days[3]	Synodic revolution days[4]	Distance from Sun (mil of mi) Max.	Min.	Distance from Earth (mil of mi) Max.	Min.	Light at[5]— perihelion	aphelion
Mercury	14,732	29.75	87.97	115.9	43.4	28.6	137.9	48	10.56	4.59
Venus	5,768	21.76	224.7	583.9	67.7	66.8	162.2	23.7	1.94	1.89
Earth	3,548	18.50	365.256	—	94.5	91.4	—	—	1.03	0.97
Mars	1,887	15.00	686.98	779.9	154.9	128.4	249.4	33.9	0.52	0.36
Jupiter	299	8.12	4,332.6	398.9	507.4	460.1	602	366	0.041	0.034
Saturn	120	6.02	10,759.2	378.1	941.1	840.4	1,031	743	0.012	0.0098
Uranus	42	4.23	30,685.4	369.7	1,866.4	1,703.4	1,962	1,605	0.0030	0.0025
Neptune	22	3.37	60,189.0	367.5	2,824.5	2,761.7	2,913	2,676	0.0011	0.0011

(1) Average angular motion measured in seconds of arc per day. (2) Speed of revolution around Sun. (3) Number of Earth days to orbit Sun with respect to background stars. (4) Number of Earth days to get back to the same position in its orbit around Sun, relative to Earth. (5) Solar illumination measured in units of mean illumination at Earth.

Planets of the Solar System

The International Astronomical Union (IAU) on Aug. 24, 2006, at their General Assembly in Prague, Czech Republic, agreed on a new definition for planet, and in the process effectively removed Pluto's planet status. The ruling came after years of debate as to whether Pluto, discovered in 1930, should still be considered the ninth planet in our solar system because of its size, orbit, and other characteristics. New discoveries of other Pluto-like objects in the solar system, such as the 2003 discovery of Eris, a **Kuiper Belt object** (KBO) bigger than Pluto, also contributed to the debate.

Under the IAU's new definition, Mercury, Venus, Earth, Mars, Jupiter, Saturn, Uranus, and Neptune are regarded as "classical" planets. A **planet** is now defined as a celestial body that (a) is in orbit around the Sun, (b) has sufficient mass for its self-gravity to overcome rigid body forces so that it assumes a hydrostatic equilibrium (nearly round) shape, and (c) has cleared the neighborhood around its orbit.

Pluto, Eris, Ceres, Makemake, and Haumea are regarded as dwarf planets, with the status of Pluto's largest moon, Charon, still to be determined. A **dwarf planet** is a celestial body that (a) is in orbit around the Sun, (b) has sufficient mass for its self-gravity to overcome rigid body forces so that it assumes a hydrostatic equilibrium (nearly round) shape, (c) has not cleared the neighborhood around its orbit, and (d) is not a satellite.

The IAU also created a new category, **small solar system bodies**, for all other objects orbiting the Sun, including comets, asteroids, KBOs, and other small objects. It has not yet established a process by which other solar system objects will be classified.

Note: AU = astronomical unit (92.96 mil mi, mean distance of Earth from the Sun); **d** = 1 Earth synodic (solar) day (24 hours); **synodic day** = rotation period of a planet measured with respect to the Sun (the "true" day, i.e., the time from midday to midday, or from sunrise to sunrise); **sidereal day** = rotation period of a planet with respect to the stars.

Mercury

Distance from the Sun
Perihelion . . . . .28.6 mil mi
Semi-major axis (mean distance) . . 36 mil mi (0.387 AU)
Aphelion . . . . .43.4 mil mi
Period of revolution around Sun . . . . .87.97 d
Orbital eccentricity 0.2056
Orbital inclination . . . . .7.00°
Synodic day (midday to midday) . . . . .175.94 d
Sidereal day . . . . .58.65 d
Rotational inclination . . . . .0.01°
Mass (Earth = 1) 0.0553
Mean radius . . . . 1,516 mi
Mean density (Earth = 1) 0.984
Natural satellites 0
Average surface temperature . . . . 333°F

Mercury, named for the Roman gods' messenger, is the closest planet to the Sun and the smallest in the solar system. Mercury is too much in line with the Sun to be observed against a dark sky; therefore it is always seen during morning or evening twilight. In 2008, the *MESSENGER* spacecraft made the first fly-bys of Mercury since the 1970s. *Messenger* went into orbit about Mercury in Mar. 2011 for a reconnaissance mission; the original one-year science program was extended in 2012. The goals of the mission included mapping, imaging, and measuring the surface composition of Mercury, as well as probing the planet's interior structure and interactions with the Sun.

Among the discoveries were that at least part of Mercury's metallic core is liquid, that there may be water ice in shadowed craters near the poles, and that the planet's magnetic field is offset from the planet's center.

Orbit and rotation. Mercury moves with great speed around the Sun, averaging about 30 mi per second to complete its orbit, which takes about 88 Earth days. Mercury takes nearly 59 days to rotate on its axis. Because its orbital period is only about 50% longer than its sidereal rotation, the time from one sunrise to the next on Mercury is about 176 days—twice as long as a Mercurial year. Oddly, Mercury has a magnetic field, albeit a very weak one. It has been held that both a fluid core and rapid rotation—neither of which Mercury was believed to have—are necessary for the generation of a planetary magnetic field. Mercury may demonstrate the contrary.

Atmosphere. Mercury's atmosphere is almost nonexistent. What very little it has is composed of 42% oxygen, 29% sodium, 22% hydrogen, 6% helium, 0.5% potassium, and 0.5% other particles. Because of Mercury's lack of atmosphere, the surface during the day may reach a temperature of about 845°F, while the temperature at night may fall as low as −300°F. Earth-based observation has provided evidence of water ice near the poles.

Surface and composition. Mercury's surface is rocky and cratered similar to that of the Earth's moon. The most imposing feature on Mercury, the Caloris Basin, is a huge impact crater more than 800 mi in diameter. Mercury has a huge iron core that takes up about 75% of the planet's radius; it has a higher percentage of iron than any other planet in the solar system.

Venus

Distance from the Sun	
Perihelion	.66.8 mil mi
Semi-major axis (mean distance). . .	.67.2 mil mi (0.723 AU)
Aphelion	.67.7 mil mi
Period of revolution around Sun	224.7 d
Orbital eccentricity	0.0067
Orbital inclination	3.39°
Synodic day (midday to midday)	116.75 d (retrograde)
Sidereal day	243.02 d (retrograde)
Rotational inclination	177.4°
Mass (Earth = 1)	0.815
Mean radius	3,760 mi
Mean density (Earth = 1)	0.951
Natural satellites	0
Average surface temperature	867°F

Venus, named for the Roman goddess of love, is the second planet out from the Sun. Because Venus is almost the same size as Earth, it is believed that the two planets were formed at the same time by the same general process and from the same mixture of chemical elements. Venus can easily be seen from Earth with the naked eye; it is the third-brightest object in the sky, exceeded only by the Sun and the Moon.

Orbit and rotation. It takes Venus 225 Earth days to complete its orbit around the Sun. Its synodic revolution—the amount of time it takes for Venus to return to the same position relative to Earth and the Sun, which is a result of the combination of its own motion with that of Earth—is 584 days. Because of this, every 19 months Venus is closer to Earth than to any other planet. The rotation period of Venus appears to be 243 days clockwise. In other words, its rotation is contrary to the rotation of the other planets and contrary to its own motion around the Sun. This rate and sense of rotation makes for a solar day (sunrise to sunrise) on Venus of 116.8 Earth days. Night lasts 58 days, and day lasts 58 days. Venus has no detectable magnetic field.

Atmosphere. The Venusian atmosphere is very thick and toxic. It is composed primarily of 96.5% carbon dioxide, 3.5% nitrogen, and trace concentrations of sulfur dioxide, argon, water, carbon monoxide, helium, and neon. In addition, it exerts an atmospheric pressure at the surface more than 90 times Earth's normal sea-level pressure. The planet is covered with a dense, white, cloudy atmosphere that conceals whatever is below. These clouds are believed to contain sulfuric acid, meaning that it rains sulfuric acid on Venus. Due to the thickness of the atmosphere and resulting extreme greenhouse effect, the temperature is essentially the same day and night; the planet has an average surface temperature of about 867°F, making it the hottest planet in the solar system. Winds of about 200 mph in the clouds may account for the transfer of heat into the night side despite the low rotation speed of the planet. However, at the surface, the winds are very slow.

Surface and composition. Radar-produced maps of the planet show large craters, continent-sized highlands, and extensive dry lowlands. No tectonic activity has been found similar to Earth's moving tectonic plates, but a system of global rift zones and numerous broad, low, dome-like structures, called coronae, may have been produced by the upwelling and subsidence of magma from the mantle. Volcanic surface features, such as vast lava plains, fields of small lava domes, and large shield volcanoes, are common. About 1,600 volcanoes and volcanic features appear on the Venusian surface; more than 85% of the surface is covered by volcanic flows. Theia Mons, a huge shield volcano, has a diameter of over 600 mi and a height of over 3.5 mi. (The largest Hawaiian volcano is only about 125 mi in diameter but rises nearly 5.5 mi from the ocean floor.) Aside from volcanoes, there are highly deformed mountain belts across Venus along with a few meteor-impact craters more than 20 mi wide. Erosion is a very slow process on Venus due to the lack of water. There are indications of some wind movement of dust and sand. The few impact craters on Venus suggest that the surface is generally geologically young—less than 800 mil years old. Despite the fact that probes have landed on Venus, there are very few pictures because the probes couldn't survive the high temperature and atmospheric pressure.

Mars

Distance from the Sun	
Perihelion	128.4 mil mi
Semi-major axis (mean distance).	.141.6 mil mi (1.524 AU)
Aphelion	154.9 mil mi
Period of revolution around Sun	686.98 d (1.88 y)
Orbital eccentricity	0.0935
Orbital inclination	1.85°
Synodic day (midday to midday)	24h 39m 35s
Sidereal day	24h 37m 22s
Rotational inclination	25.19°
Mass (Earth = 1)	0.107
Mean radius	2,106 mi
Mean density (Earth = 1)	0.713
Natural satellites	2
Average surface temperature	−81°F

Named for the Roman god of war, the Red Planet has some features much like Earth. Mars has climate, seasons, volcanoes, and possibly once had liquid water flowing across its surface. Mars can easily be seen with the naked eye on most clear nights, which is why it was one of the first planets to be studied by ancient astronomers. Later, when telescopes came into use, many observers claimed that canals made by Martians existed on the planet's surface, which led to speculation as to whether there was intelligent life there. Unmanned probes have since put all those theories to rest; the canals turned out to be topographic patterns and dust storms.

Mars is currently being explored by a number of robotic craft, both on the surface and in orbit. The *Curiosity*/Mars Science Laboratory, an SUV-sized robot, landed on the surface in Aug. 2012. Its mission was to understand the history of the Martian geology and climate, search for the presence of organic matter, and to assess the planet's past suitability for life.

Orbit and rotation. Although Mars's orbital path is nearly circular, it is somewhat more eccentric than that of most other planets. Mars is more than 26 mil mi farther from the Sun at its most distant point compared to its closest approach. Its orbit and speed in relation to Earth's bring it fairly close to Earth about every two years. Every 15-17 years the close approaches are especially favorable for observation.

Mars rotates in 24 hours and 37 minutes, almost the same period of time as Earth. Mars's mean distance from the Sun is 142 mil mi. Because Mars's axis of rotation is inclined by about 25° from the vertical to the plane of its solar orbit about the Sun, the planet has seasons.

Unlike Earth's global magnetic field, the Martian magnetic field is small, weak, and localized and may be the remnant of a stronger field from the planet's past.

Atmosphere. The Martian atmosphere is composed primarily of 95.32% carbon dioxide, 2.7% nitrogen, 1.6% argon, 0.13% oxygen, 0.08% carbon monoxide, and in very minor quantities, water, hydrogen oxide, and neon. The atmosphere on Mars is very thin. It has an atmospheric pressure between 1% and 2% of Earth's (if Earth's atmosphere were that thin, there would not be enough oxygen to breathe). Because the Martian atmosphere is so thin and because of the planet's weak magnetic field, its surface is bombarded by cosmic radiation about 100 times as intense as on Earth.

Martian weather systems consist mainly of huge dust storms. On the poles, white caps (believed to be both water ice and carbon dioxide ice) grow in winter and shrink in summer. It is mainly the carbon dioxide that comes and goes with the seasons. The water ice is apparently in many layers with dust between them, indicating climatic cycles.

Surface and composition. Mars is an alien world with rust-red sand and pink skies. In the planet's beginning stages when it was much hotter, Mars's surface melted to a sufficient extent to separate into dense and lighter layers. Mars later cooled enough to allow liquid water to possibly flow across its surface. Today, Mars is very dry.

Natural satellites. Mars has two satellites called Phobos and Deimos, each discovered in 1877 by Asaph Hall. (Phobos measures about 11 by 17 mi and Deimos about 7 by 9 mi.) Deimos, the outer satellite, revolves around the planet in about 31 hours. Phobos, the inner satellite, whips around Mars in a little more than 7 hours, making three trips each Martian day. Since it orbits Mars faster than the planet rotates, Phobos rises in the west and sets in the east, opposite to what other bodies appear to do in the Martian sky. Both moons are irregularly shaped and pitted with numerous craters. Their origins are not known; however, some astronomers consider them to be asteroid-like objects that were captured by Mars very early in its history.

Jupiter

Distance from the Sun	
Perihelion	460.1 mil mi
Semi-major axis (mean distance)	483.8 mil mi (5.204 AU)
Aphelion	507.4 mil mi
Period of revolution around Sun	11.862 y
Orbital eccentricity	0.0489
Orbital inclination	1.304°
Synodic day (midday to midday)	9h 55m 33s
Sidereal day	9h 55m 30s
Rotational inclination	3.13°
Mass (Earth = 1)	317.8
Mean radius	43,441 mi
Mean density (Earth = 1)	0.24
Natural satellites	67
Average temperature*	−162°F

*i.e., temperature where atmospheric pressure equals 1 Earth atmosphere.

Jupiter, named for the Roman ruler of the gods, is the largest planet in the solar system (11 times the diameter of Earth). Its mass is more than twice the mass of all the other planets, moons, and asteroids put together. Visible to the naked eye and known to the ancients, it was a focus of the Italian scientist Galileo Galilei, who viewed the planet and its four largest moons through a homemade telescope.

Orbit and rotation. Jupiter is at an average distance of 484 mil mi from the Sun and takes almost 12 Earth years to make a complete revolution. The largest of the planets, Jupiter has an equatorial diameter of 88,846 mi; its polar diameter is more than 5,700 mi shorter. This noticeable oblateness is a result of the liquidity of the planet and its extremely rapid rotation rate—a Jupiter day is less than 10 Earth hours long. A point on Jupiter's equator moves at a speed of 22,000 mph, as compared with 1,000 mph for a point on Earth's equator. Jupiter's magnetic field is by far the strongest of any planet. Electrical activity caused by this field is so strong that it discharges billions of watts into Earth's magnetic field daily.

Atmosphere. Jupiter's atmosphere is primarily composed of 90% molecular hydrogen and 10% helium. Minor constituents include methane, ammonia, hydrogen deuteride, ethane, and water. Jupiter has a turbulent atmosphere characterized by thick clouds, high winds, and huge lightning storms many times larger than those on Earth. The atmospheric temperature varies, but the temperature at the tops of clouds may be about −280°F. The Great Red Spot seen prominently on Jupiter is a huge hurricane-like storm that is three times the diameter of Earth. In 2006, the Hubble Space Telescope detected the appearance of a second, smaller red spot.

Surface and composition. Gas giant planets like Jupiter, Saturn, and Neptune do not have a surface like Earth or any of the other rocky planets. The gases become denser with depth, until they may turn into a slush or slurry. Jupiter has a liquid hydrogen ocean more than 35,000 mi deep. It likely has a rocky core about the size of Earth, but 13 times more massive. There is no sharp interface between the gaseous atmosphere and the hydrogen ocean that accounts for most of Jupiter's volume. At lower depths, under enormous pressure, the liquid hydrogen takes on the properties of a metal. It is likely that this liquid metallic hydrogen is the source for both Jupiter's persistent radio noise and for its improbably strong magnetic field.

Natural satellites. Jupiter has 67 known satellites. Four of the moons (in order of distance from Jupiter), Io, Europa, Ganymede, and Callisto—all discovered by Galileo in 1610—are large and bright and are close in diameter to Earth's moon and Mercury. Because they move so rapidly around Jupiter, their change in position from night to night can be seen from Earth using binoculars.

Io is one of the most volcanically active bodies in the solar system. A gaseous, doughnut-shaped ring, or torus, enveloping Io's orbit around Jupiter may have been formed by material ejected from Io's active volcanoes. (This is not to be confused with Jupiter's rings.) These volcanoes, hotter than Earth's volcanoes, erupt mainly molten sulfur.

Europa may have a 30-mi-deep salty, liquid ocean beneath its icy crust, perhaps a small metallic core, and a very tenuous atmosphere. Ganymede is the biggest moon in the solar system. With a diameter of 3,120 mi, it is bigger than both Mercury and Pluto. Ganymede also has it own magnetic field produced by a molten core perhaps of iron sulfide. Callisto has the oldest, most heavily cratered surface in the solar system, a very thin atmosphere of carbon dioxide, and possibly a subsurface liquid ocean.

The other satellites are much smaller, with four closer to Jupiter than Io, five between Ganymede and Callisto, and the rest farther out. Most of Jupiter's moons revolve around Jupiter clockwise as seen from the north, contrary to the motions of most satellites in the solar system and to the direction of revolution of planets around the Sun. These moons may be captured asteroids.

Rings. Jupiter has a set of rings that cannot be seen from Earth without powerful telescopes. They are composed of small dust grains possibly blasted off the four innermost moons by meteoroid impacts.

Saturn

Distance from the Sun	
Perihelion	840.44 mil mi
Semi-major axis (mean distance)	890.8 mil mi (9.582 AU)
Aphelion	941.07 mil mi
Period of revolution around Sun	29.458 y
Orbital eccentricity	0.0565
Orbital inclination	2.485°
Synodic day (midday to midday)	10h 39m 23s
Sidereal day	10h 39m 22s
Rotational inclination	26.73°
Mass (Earth = 1)	95.159
Mean radius	36,184 mi
Mean density (Earth = 1)	0.125
Natural satellites	62
Average temperature*	−218°F

*i.e., temperature where atmospheric pressure equals 1 Earth atmosphere.

Saturn, named for the Roman ruler of the Titans, is the sixth planet from the Sun and most distant of the planets visible to the unaided eye. Saturn is second in size to Jupiter, but its mass is much smaller. Saturn is the only planet less dense than water, meaning that Saturn would float if there were a pool of water gigantic enough to hold it.

Orbit and rotation. Saturn's diameter is almost 74,900 mi at the equator, while its polar diameter is more than 7,300 mi shorter. Like Jupiter, its noticeable oblateness is a result of the liquidity of the planet and its extremely rapid rate of rotation; a day is little more than 10 Earth hours long.

Atmosphere. Saturn's atmosphere is composed primarily of 96.3% hydrogen, 3.3% helium, and traces of methane, ammonia, hydrogen deuteride, ethane, and water. Saturn's atmosphere is much like that of Jupiter, except that the temperature at the top of its cloud layer is at least 50°F colder.

Surface and composition. Saturn's atmosphere resembles Jupiter's; it likely has a small dense center surrounded by a deep ocean of hydrogen.

Natural satellites. Saturn has 62 known natural satellites, most of which were not discovered until space probes reached the planet. Saturn's moon Mimas has an impact crater 81 mi across (the moon itself is only 249 mi across). Enceladus has an atmosphere and shows evidence of geysers that spit water ice and vapor. Two tiny moons orbit within the rings, plowing through and making gaps in the rings along their orbits. Pan, the innermost satellite, creates the Encke Gap of Saturn's A-ring. Daphnis creates the Keeler Gap. The most intriguing Saturnian moon is Titan. The second-biggest moon in the solar system, Titan is bigger than Mercury. Its atmosphere is similar to Earth's atmosphere of long ago; it is made up of approximately 95% nitrogen with traces of methane. Titan's atmosphere extends about 360 mi into space whereas Earth's atmosphere extends about 37 mi. Photographs from its surface show a muddy terrain, with possible deposits of water ice, channels carved by liquid methane springs, and an interesting boundary between light and dark material on the surface. In 2006, scientists found sand dunes on Titan's surface. The "sand" is believed to be tiny water ice crystals or organic compounds. Surface phenomena such as sand dunes are signs of erosion and wind. Unlike winds on Earth or Mars, Titan's winds are not the result of uneven solar heating on the moon's surface but rather Saturn's gravitational pull (similar to how the Moon acts on the Earth's oceans).

Rings. Saturn's ring system is the planet's most recognizable feature. It begins about 4,000 mi above the visible disk of Saturn lying above its equator and extends about 260,000 mi into space. The diameter of the ring system visible from Earth is about 170,000 mi; the rings are estimated to be about 700 ft thick. The rings are composed of rock and ice and range in size from tiny particles to large chunks of material the size of a bus. There are several divisions in the rings. The 2,920-mi Cassini division, the gap between the A and B rings, is the largest division.

Uranus

Distance from the Sun	
Perihelion	1,703.4 mil mi
Semi-major axis (mean distance)	1,784.8 mil mi (19.201 AU)
Aphelion	1,866.4 mil mi
Period of revolution around Sun	84.01 y
Orbital eccentricity	0.0457
Orbital inclination	0.772°
Synodic day (midday to midday)	17h 14m 23s (retrograde)
Sidereal day	17h 14m 24s (retrograde)
Rotational inclination	97.77°
Mass (Earth = 1)	14.536
Mean radius	15,759 mi
Mean density (Earth = 1)	0.23
Natural satellites	27
Average temperature*	−323°F

*i.e., temperature where atmospheric pressure equals 1 Earth atmosphere.

Uranus, discovered by Sir William Herschel in 1781, was the first planet discovered using a telescope. It was named for the father of the Titans in Roman mythology.

Orbit and rotation. Uranus has a diameter of over 31,000 mi and spins once in approximately 17.23 hours, according to flyby magnetic data. One of the most fascinating features of Uranus is how far over it is tipped. Its north pole lies 98° from its orbital plane. Thus, its seasons are extreme. Over its 84-year orbit, when the Sun rises at the north pole, it shines there for about 42 Earth years; then it sets, and the north pole is in darkness for 42 Earth years. In addition to its rotational tilt, Uranus's magnetic field axis is tipped 58.6° from its rotational axis and is displaced about 30% of its radius away from the planet's center.

Atmosphere. The atmosphere is composed primarily of 82.5% hydrogen, 15.2% helium, and 2.3% methane, with small amounts of hydrogen deuteride, ammonia ice, water ice, ammonia hydrosulfide, and methane ice.

Surface and composition. Uranus has no solid surface, and likely no rocky core but rather a mixture of rocks and assorted ices with about 15% hydrogen and some helium.

Natural satellites. Uranus has 27 known moons, which have orbits lying in the plane of the planet's equator. Five moons are relatively large, while 22 are very small and were only discovered with the *Voyager 2* mission or in later observations. Miranda has grooved markings, reminiscent of Jupiter's Ganymede, but often arranged in a chevron pattern. Rifts and channels on Ariel provide evidence of liquid flowing over its surface in the past. Umbriel is extremely dark, prompting some observers to regard its surface as among the oldest in the system. Titania has rifts and fractures, but not the evidence of flow found on Ariel. Oberon's main feature is its surface saturated with craters, unrelieved by other formations.

Rings. In the equatorial plane there is also a complex of 11 rings, 9 of which were discovered in 1978 by observers watching Uranus pass before a star.

Neptune

Distance from the Sun	
Perihelion	2,761.7 mil mi
Semi-major axis (mean distance)	2,793.1 mil mi (30.047 AU)
Aphelion	2,824.5 mil mi
Period of revolution around Sun	164.79 y
Orbital eccentricity	0.0113
Orbital inclination	1.769°
Synodic day (midday to midday)	16h 6m 37s
Sidereal day	16h 6m 36s
Rotational inclination	28.32°
Mass (Earth = 1)	17.147
Mean radius	15,301 mi
Mean density (Earth = 1)	0.297
Natural satellites	14
Average temperature*	−330°F

*i.e., temperature where atmospheric pressure equals 1 Earth atmosphere.

Named for the Roman god of the sea, Neptune was the first planet discovered through mathematical calculations and not observation. Its approximate orbit and position were first calculated independently by British astronomer John Couch Adams and French astronomer Urbain Le Verrier in 1845. In 1846, German astronomer Johann Galle first observed Neptune through a telescope.

Orbit and rotation. Neptune orbits the Sun in 164.8 Earth years in a nearly circular orbit. Its magnetic field is considerably asymmetric to the planet's structure, similar to, but not so extreme as, Uranus's magnetic field. Neptune's magnetic field axis is tipped 46.9° from its rotational axis and is displaced more than 55% of its radius away from the planet's center.

Atmosphere. The Neptunian atmosphere is composed primarily of 80% hydrogen, 19% helium, 1.5% methane, and small amounts of hydrogen deuteride, ethane, ammonia ice, water ice, ammonia hydrosulfide, and methane ice. Neptune's atmosphere is quite blue, with quickly changing white clouds often suspended high above an apparent surface. A Great Dark Spot, reminiscent of Jupiter's Great Red Spot, was discovered in 1989 when *Voyager 2* visited the planet. Observations with the Hubble Space Telescope have shown that the Great Dark Spot originally seen by *Voyager* has apparently dissipated, but a new dark spot has since appeared. Lightning and auroras have been found on other giant planets, but only the aurora phenomenon has been seen on Neptune. As with the other giant planets, Neptune emits more energy than it receives from the Sun. The excess has been found to be 2.7 times the solar contribution.

Surface and composition. As with the other giant planets, Neptune may have no solid surface or exact diameter. However, a mean value of 30,600 mi may be assigned to a diameter between atmosphere levels where the pressure is about the same as sea level on Earth.

Natural satellites. Largest of Neptune's 14 satellites is Triton. It is the only large moon in a retrograde orbit, which suggests that it was captured rather than having been there from the beginning. Triton's large size, sufficient to raise significant tides on the planet, may one day, billions of years from now, bring Triton close enough to Neptune for Triton to be torn apart. Triton has a tenuous atmosphere of nitrogen with a trace of hydrocarbons and evidence of active geysers injecting material into it. Triton is the coldest object yet measured in the solar system with a surface temperature of −391°F. Only about half of Triton has been observed, but its terrain shows cratering and a strange regional feature described as resembling the skin of a cantaloupe. Nereid has the highest orbital eccentricity (0.75) of any moon. Its long looping orbit suggests that it was captured. In 2003, two more moons, which orbit farther from their parent planet than any other moons in the solar system, were discovered. In July 2013, Hubble Space Telescope observations confirmed the existence of a 14th natural satellite of Neptune. At less than 20 km diameter, it is the smallest of Neptune's known moons. The *Voyager 2* probe in 1989 confirmed the existence of six rings around Neptune composed of very fine particles. There may be some clumps in the rings' structure. It is not known whether Neptune's satellites influence the formation or maintenance of the rings.

Dwarf Planets

Ceres

Distance from the Sun	
Perihelion	237 mil mi (2.55 AU)
Semi-major axis (mean distance)	257 mil mi (2.77 AU)
Period of revolution around Sun	4.6 y
Orbital eccentricity	0.0789
Orbital inclination	10.58°
Sidereal day	9.075 h
Mass (Earth = 1)	0.00016
Mean radius	300 mi

Ceres was the first asteroid discovered; it was found by Italian astronomer Guiseppe Piazzi on Jan. 1, 1801. In the 1800s, it was considered a planet but lost that designation. In Aug. 2006, it was designated a dwarf planet by the Intl. Astronomical Union (IAU).

No probe has ever visited Ceres. NASA's *Dawn* space probe, launched in 2007, may become the first. The probe's mission is to Vesta and Ceres, the solar system's two largest asteroids. When *Dawn* arrives at Ceres in Feb. 2015, it will be the first mission to study a dwarf planet.

Orbit and rotation. Ceres orbits the Sun in the asteroid belt region between Mars and Jupiter.

Surface and composition. Ceres is in a class of stony meteorites known as carbonaceous chondrites. These are considered to be the oldest materials in the solar system, with a composition reflecting that of the primitive solar nebula. Extremely dark in color, probably because of their hydrocarbon content, they show evidence of having absorbed water of hydration. Thus, unlike the Earth and the Moon, they have never melted nor been reheated since they first formed.

Pluto

Distance from the Sun	
Perihelion	2,756.9 mil mi
Semi-major axis (mean distance)	3,647.2 mil mi
	(39.482 AU)
Aphelion	4,583.2 mil mi
Period of revolution around Sun	247.68 y
Orbital eccentricity	0.2488
Orbital inclination	17.16°
Synodic day (midday to midday)	6d 9h 17m (retrograde)
Sidereal day	6d 9h 18m (retrograde)
Rotational inclination	122.53°
Mass (Earth = 1)	0.0021
Mean radius	742.5 mi
Mean density (Earth = 1)	0.317
Natural satellites	5
Average surface temperature	−369°F

Pluto, named for the Roman god of the underworld, is the second-largest known Kuiper Belt object (KBO) in the solar system. It was first discovered in 1930 by American astronomer Clyde Tombaugh and classified as a planet until 2006, when the IAU changed its designation to dwarf planet. The *New Horizons* spacecraft was launched on a voyage to Pluto and beyond in 2006; the spacecraft will make its closest approach to Pluto in July 2015. In 2008, Pluto was designated by the IAU as the prototype for a class of objects called **plutoids**, bodies that (a) have an average distance from the Sun greater than Neptune's; (b) are large enough that gravity determines their shape; and (c) have not cleared their orbit of other objects. Haumea, Makemake, and Eris are also plutoids. More than 40 other plutoid candidates have been identified through mid-2014.

Orbit and rotation. Pluto's orbit and rotation are highly irregular. Although on average it stays about 3.6 bil mi from the Sun, it may get as close as 2.76 bil mi. And for about 20 years of its orbit, it is closer to the Sun than Neptune. Currently, it is beyond Neptune's orbit.

Atmosphere and surface. Because no probes have visited Pluto, it is difficult for astronomers to accurately take readings of the dwarf planet's atmospheric composition. It is believed that an atmosphere of methane, nitrogen, and carbon monoxide exists when the dwarf planet is closer to the Sun. When Pluto is farther away from the Sun, the atmosphere freezes and becomes part of the surface. Large regions of Pluto are dark, others light; Pluto has spots and perhaps polar caps. There is also evidence of temperature fluctuations on the dwarf planet that may indicate primitive weather. Its core may be rocky with a mantle of water ice surrounding it.

Natural satellites. Pluto has five known natural satellites. Charon, the biggest, has a diameter of 737 mi—about half of Pluto's diameter of 1,485 mi. No other planet in the solar system has a moon so close to its size. Discovered in 1978, Charon orbits Pluto at a distance of 12,200 mi and takes 6.39 days to move around the dwarf planet. In this same length of time, Pluto and Charon both rotate once on their axes, meaning that the Pluto-Charon system appears to rotate as virtually a rigid body. Both worlds are roughly spherical and have comparable densities. Because of these similarities and their peculiar relationship, there is debate as to whether Charon should one day be designated a dwarf planet.

Two other moons, discovered in 2005 and 2006, were officially named Nix and Hydra. Two moons, discovered in 2011 and 2012, were officially named Kerberos and Styx by the IAU in 2013. Astronomers expect to discover more moons when the *New Horizons* spacecraft flies by in July 2015.

Haumea

Distance from the Sun	
Semi-major axis (mean distance)	43.335 AU
Period of revolution around Sun	285 y
Orbital eccentricity	0.189
Orbital inclination	28.19°
Mass (Earth = 1)	0.0007
Mean radius	420 mi
Natural satellites	2

Haumea was discovered in 2004 and was accepted as a dwarf planet by the IAU in 2008.
Orbit and rotation. Haumea has a moderately eccentric orbit and takes about 285 years to go around the Sun.
Surface and composition. Spectra of Haumea indicate the presence of almost pure crystalline water ice. The surface reflects about 60% of the sunlight that reaches it. Haumea has a very oblong shape, about as long as it is wide.
Natural satellites. Haumea has two natural satellites.

Makemake

Distance from the Sun	
Semi-major axis (mean distance)	45.791 AU
Period of revolution around Sun	310 y
Orbital eccentricity	0.159
Orbital inclination	28.96°
Mass (Earth = 1)	0.0007
Mean radius	450 mi

Makemake was discovered in 2005 and was accepted as a dwarf planet by the IAU in 2008.
Orbit and rotation. Makemake has a moderately eccentric orbit and takes about 310 years to go around the Sun.
Surface and composition. Spectra of Makemake indicate the presence of frozen methane, as well as several organic compounds. The surface is highly reflective and appears similar to that of Pluto.

Eris

Distance from the Sun	
Semi-major axis (mean distance)	67.6681 AU
Period of revolution around Sun	560 y
Orbital eccentricity	0.44177
Orbital inclination	44.177°
Mass (Earth = 1)	0.0027
Mean radius	925 mi
Natural satellites	1

Eris is the largest known dwarf planet. Discovered in 2003 by astronomers at the California Institute of Technology, it is the most distant object ever seen in orbit around the Sun.
Orbit and rotation. Eris has a highly elliptical orbit and takes about 560 years to go around the Sun—more than twice the time it takes Pluto. Its inclination is steep, tilted at 44° to the planetary plane. It also has an extremely eccentric orbit. It will be at its closest to the Sun, actually coming inside part of Pluto's orbit, in about 280 years.
Surface and composition. Eris, with a surface covered in frozen methane, may be similar to Pluto and the Neptunian moon Triton. Observations made by the Hubble Space Telescope show that Eris's surface is almost white and uniform, reflecting 86% of the light that hits it. This makes it the most reflective body in the solar system. The dwarf planet's interior is likely a mixture of rock and ice.
Natural satellites. Eris has one moon, Dysnomia.

Small Solar System Bodies: Asteroids, Comets, Kuiper Belt, and the Oort Cloud

Asteroids

Besides planets and moons, many smaller objects orbit the Sun. In 2006, the International Astronomical Union (IAU) officially designated these objects "small solar system bodies." Asteroids or minor planets are found mainly in a belt between the orbits of Mars and Jupiter. Within this belt there may be millions of asteroids of varying sizes. Most asteroids are very small. Ceres, which can be classified both as an asteroid and a dwarf planet, is 588 mi in diameter, about one-quarter the diameter of our Moon.

Some of these objects, or asteroids, are gravitationally locked with Jupiter and the Sun so that they have roughly the same orbit as Jupiter but are either 60° ahead or behind the planet. These are the **Trojan asteroids**. Many of the smaller moons of the solar system, especially those in retrograde orbits, may be captured asteroids. Asteroids whose orbits either cross or come close to the Earth's orbit are labeled **Near Earth asteroids** or NEAs. A handful of asteroids have actually been imaged by the Arecibo and Goldstone radio telescopes and by the NEAR Shoemaker space probe. The *Galileo* spacecraft imaged the asteroids Gaspra and Ida (including its moon Dactyl) on its way to Jupiter.

Comets

Comets are small icy bodies that orbit the Sun. When one approaches the Sun, the energy from the Sun boils off material from the comet's icy nucleus, producing an enlarged head (or **coma**), and in many cases an extended tail. Because of that, comets are brighter when near the Sun. For large comets, the head may be 100,000 mi across and the tail more than a million mi long, though both are mainly empty space.

Comets have been known since ancient times. British astronomer Edmund Halley (1656-1742) ultimately realized that a group of historical reports were just repeated visits of the same object. Comets are the only astronomical objects named after

their discoverers. In 1986, the European spacecraft *Giotto* took the first close-up images of a comet's nucleus, specifically of Comet Halley, showing it had a peanut-shaped nucleus and whose longest dimension was about 10 mi.

In 1995, U.S. observers Alan Hale (1958-) and Thomas Bopp (1949-) independently discovered a comet that was then beyond the orbit of Jupiter. It is one of the brightest comets of all time. It also holds the record for length of time visible to the naked eye—19 months—and is the most photographed comet in history. In July 2009, an amateur astronomer discovered a large impact scar in the upper atmosphere of Jupiter, likely the result of another cometary impact.

Kuiper Belt

The Kuiper Belt is a doughnut-shaped region that extends to about 50 AU (astronomical units) from the Sun and is thought to be the source of short-period comets such as Comets Halley or Swift-Tuttle. It is filled with icy bodies that are in solar orbit. The more than 1,000 objects found in this region in recent years are called Kuiper Belt objects (KBOs). It is estimated that there are more than 70,000 objects 60 mi in diameter or larger within the Kuiper Belt. Dwarf planets Pluto and Eris are considered KBO. There are at least six KBOs larger than 300 mi in diameter.

Oort Cloud

The Oort Cloud is a vast spherical shell hypothesized to exist around the Sun. Dutch astronomer Jan Oort (1900-92) proposed its existence as the origin for long-period comets that enter the inner part of the solar system where the planets orbit. Current technology is not sufficient to detect any members of the Oort Cloud other than observed comets whose orbits may reach out as far as 50,000 AU. Recent examples of such long-period comets are Comets Hale-Bopp and Hyakutake.

The Sun

Distance from Earth, mean	92.96 mil mi (1 AU)
Sidereal day (rotation period)	25.38 d
Mass (Earth=1)	332,900
Mean radius	432,200 mi
Mean density (Earth=1)	0.255
Average surface temperature	9,941°F

The Sun is the Earth's primary source of light and heat and its closest star. The biggest object in the solar system, the Sun is 332,900 times more massive than Earth and contains 99.86% of the mass of the entire solar system. On the whole, the Sun is made up of about 92.1% hydrogen and 7.8% helium, with trace amounts of other elements. It has a mass and luminosity greater than that of 90% of the stars in the Milky Way galaxy. Although most of the stars that can be easily seen on a clear night are bigger and brighter than the Sun, its proximity to Earth makes it appear tremendously large and bright. The Sun is 400,000 times as bright as the full moon, and it gives Earth 6 mil times as much light as do all the other stars put together. Because of the great distance between the Sun and Earth, it takes about 499 seconds, or slightly more than 8 minutes, for light from the Sun to reach Earth.

Composition. The Sun has six regions. The first three from the inside out are the core, the radiative zone, and the convective zone. Together they form the interior. The others, which comprise the visible surface, are the photosphere, the chromosphere, and the outermost region, the corona.

The Sun's heat and energy are produced in its core. Through a series of nuclear fusion reactions, hydrogen nuclei are converted to helium nuclei. Temperatures in the core are theorized to be 28 mil °F. From the core, photons transport the energy outward through the radiative zone. It can take photons several million years to pass through this area. In the convective zone, gases move energy outward at a faster rate. Like a boiling pot, bubbles of gas bring energy to the surface.

The photosphere is the visible surface of the Sun, that is, the light that we see as sunlight. When sunlight is analyzed with a spectroscope, it is found to consist of a continuous spectrum composed of all the colors of the rainbow, crossed by many dark lines. The dark "absorption lines" are produced by gaseous materials in the outer layers of the Sun. More than 60 of the natural terrestrial elements have been identified in the Sun, all in gaseous form because of the Sun's intense heat.

Just above the photosphere is the chromosphere, which is visible to the naked eye only in total solar eclipses, during which it appears to be a pinkish-violet layer with occasional great prominences projecting above its general level. With proper instruments, the chromosphere can be seen or photographed whenever the Sun is visible. Above the chromosphere is the corona, also visible to the naked eye only at times of total eclipse or with instruments that permit the brighter portions of the corona to be seen. The light of the corona surges millions of miles from the Sun; its atoms are all in a state of extreme attenuation and high ionization that indicates temperatures nearly 2 mil °F.

Sunspots. These dark, irregularly shaped regions may reach diameters of thousands of miles. There is an intimate connection between sunspots and the corona. At times of low sunspot activity, the fine streamers of the corona are longer above the Sun's equator than over the polar regions of the Sun; during periods of high sunspot activity, the corona extends fairly evenly outward from all regions of the Sun but to a much greater distance in space. The average life of a sunspot group is two months, but some have lasted for more than a year. Sunspots reach a low point, on average, every 11.3 years, with a peak of activity occurring irregularly between two successive periods of minimal activity. Currently, the number of sunspots is declining. Solar minimum occurred late in 2006.

Solar wind and magnetic field. Magnetic arches, called prominences, may extend tens of thousands of miles into the corona and may release enormous amounts of energy heating the corona. Coronal mass ejections are enormous releases of solar energy. Coronal holes are regions where the corona appears dark in X-rays, and are associated with open magnetic field lines, where the magnetic field lines project out into space instead of back toward the Sun. It is in these regions where the high-speed solar wind originates.

The solar wind carries the Sun's magnetic field, which extends beyond the planets. This is called the interplanetary magnetic field (IMF). Far past Pluto and the Kuiper Belt, the solar wind and the IMF lose their influence. The boundary between them and interstellar space is called the heliopause. In 2013, NASA announced that the *Voyager 1* spacecraft, launched in 1977, seemed at last to have reached the heliopause, at a distance 18 bil km (11 bil mi) from the Sun.

Searching for Extrasolar Planets

The Sun is a typical star in many respects and—with over 400 bil stars in the Milky Way—it is plausible that many other stars might have planets. During the last 10 years of the 20th century, astronomers began to note evidence of planets orbiting stars other than the Sun. Astronomers have not directly observed most of these objects but merely inferred their existence from observations of their parent stars. As of mid-2014, astronomers had found more than 1,500 planets orbiting some 1,100 stars. Of those, more than 1,200 were at least as massive as Jupiter. Planets with masses less than Jupiter are now regularly discovered.

Astronomers have used two main techniques to detect planets. The first, called the radial-velocity method, uses the Doppler effect to detect periodic changes in the motion of a star caused by the gravitational tug of an unseen planet. The magnitude of the star's motion and the time it takes to repeat can be used to infer the planet's mass and distance from its host star. This technique is most sensitive to high-mass planets orbiting close to their stars because that situation produces more noticeable changes in a star's motion. The first planets discovered using this technique were as massive as the planet Jupiter and orbiting stars at distances closer than Mercury orbits the Sun.

The second technique, the transit method, relies on the dimming of a star's light as an unseen planet repeatedly passes in front of it. Astronomers are able to infer the diameter of the planet and the distance at which the planet orbits the star. When combined with the mass determined from the radial-velocity method, astronomers can determine the density of the unseen planet and begin to infer its similarity to planets in our solar system.

Astronomers have also used optical gravitational lensing to detect extrasolar planets. This technique, which detects the observed brightening of a distant background star as a planet passes in front of it, has allowed Southern Hemisphere astronomers to find the most distant planet yet detected, about halfway to the center of our own Milky Way galaxy.

In 2005, astronomers obtained the first direct image of an extrasolar planet around a normal star called GQ Lupi, which is like our Sun but younger. The planet is about 100 AU (astronomical units) away from the star and estimated to be about twice as massive as Jupiter.

In 2006, astronomers discovered what they call a "super Earth" orbiting a red dwarf 9,000 light-years away. The planet appears to have about 13 times Earth's mass and may be composed of rock and ice, but it is believed not to have liquid on its surface. In 2007, astronomers detected water in the atmosphere of an extrasolar planet for the first time.

In 2009, NASA launched Kepler, the first telescope sensitive enough to detect Earth-sized planets around other stars. Kepler's first released data in 2010 indicated that small planets are more common. Kepler has now detected a large number of planets with diameters similar to that of Earth. Some of the planets are known to orbit within the host star's habitable zone, meaning that the conditions are such that liquid water could exist on the planetary surface. As of June 2014, the Kepler mission alone had identified nearly 1,000 planets along with more than 3,000 additional planet candidates. Kepler 186f is the first Earth-size planet to be confirmed in the habitable zone.

NASA approved the Transiting Exoplanet Survey Satellite (TESS) mission in 2013. The mission, scheduled for 2017, would conduct an all-sky survey of extrasolar planets.

Earth: Size, Computation of Time, Seasons

Distance from the Sun	
Perihelion	91.4 mil mi
Semi-major axis (mean distance)	93 mil mi (1.0000 AU)
Aphelion	94.5 mil mi
Period of revolution	365.256 d
Orbital eccentricity	0.0167
Orbital inclination	0°
Synodic day (midday to midday)	24h 0m 0s
Sidereal day (rotation period)	23h 56m 4.2s
Rotational inclination	23.45°
Mass (Earth = 1)	1
Mean radius	3,958.8 mi
Mean density (Earth = 1)	1
Natural satellites	1
Average surface temperature	59°F

Earth is the fifth-largest planet and the third from the Sun. Its mass is 5.9736×10^{24} kg. Earth's equatorial diameter is 7,926 mi while its polar diameter is only 7,900 mi.

Size and dimensions. Earth is considered a solid mass, yet it has a large, liquid iron, **magnetic core** with a radius of about 2,160 mi. Surprisingly, it has a solid **inner core** that may be a large iron crystal, with a radius of 760 mi. Around the core is a thick shell, or **mantle**, of dense rock. This mantle is composed of materials rich in iron and magnesium. It is somewhat plastic-like, and under slow steady pressure, it can flow like a liquid. The mantle, in turn, is covered by a thin **crust** forming the solid granite and basalt base of the continents and ocean basins. Over broad areas of Earth's surface, the crust has a thin cover of sedimentary rock such as sandstone, shale, and limestone formed by weathering and by deposits of sands, clays, and plant and animal remains.

The temperature inside the Earth increases about 1°F with every 100 to 200 ft in depth, in the upper 100 km of Earth. It reaches nearly 8,000°F–9,000°F at the center. The heat is believed to come from radioactivity in rocks, pressures within Earth, and the original heat of formation.

Atmosphere. Earth's atmosphere is a blanket composed of 78% nitrogen, 21% oxygen, and 1% argon. Present in minute quantities are carbon dioxide, hydrogen, neon, helium, krypton, and xenon. Water vapor displaces other gases and varies from nearly zero to about 4% by volume. The atmosphere rests on Earth's surface with a weight equivalent to a layer of water 34 ft deep. For about 300,000 ft upward, the gases

remain in the proportions stated. Gravity holds the gases to Earth. The weight of the air compresses it at the bottom so that the greatest density is at Earth's surface. Pressure and density decrease as height increases.

The lowest layer of the atmosphere extending up from the Earth's surface about 7.5 mi is the **troposphere**, which contains 90% of the air. This is also where most weather phenomena occur. The temperature drops with increasing height through this layer. The **stratosphere** extends about 23 mi above the troposphere; the temperature generally increases with height within this layer. The stratosphere contains **ozone**, which prevents ultraviolet rays from reaching Earth's surface. Since there is very little convection in the stratosphere, jets regularly cruise in the lower parts to provide a smoother ride for passengers.

Above the stratosphere is the **mesosphere**, where the temperature again decreases with height for another 19 mi. Extending above the mesosphere to the outer fringes of the atmosphere is the **thermosphere**, a region where temperature once more increases with height to a value measured in thousands of degrees Fahrenheit. The lower portion of this region, extending from 50 to about 400 mi in altitude, is characterized by high ion density and is thus called the **ionosphere**. Most meteors are in the lower thermosphere or the mesosphere at the time they are observed.

Longitude and latitude. Position on the globe is measured by meridians and parallels. Meridians, which are imaginary lines drawn around Earth through the poles, determine **longitude**. The meridian running through Greenwich, England, is the **prime meridian** of longitude; all others are either E or W. Parallels, which are imaginary circles parallel with the equator, determine **latitude**. The length of a degree of longitude varies as the cosine of the latitude. At the equator a degree of longitude is 69.171 statute mi; this is gradually reduced toward the poles. Value of a longitude degree at the poles is zero.

Latitude is reckoned by the number of degrees N or S of the **equator**, an imaginary circle on Earth's surface everywhere equidistant between the two poles. According to the International Astronomical Union, the length of a degree of latitude is 68.708 statute mi at the equator and varies slightly N and S because of the oblate form of the globe. At the poles, it is 69.403 statute mi.

Definitions of time. Earth rotates on its axis and follows an elliptical orbit around the Sun. The rotation makes the Sun appear to move across the sky from E to W. This rotation determines day and night, and the complete rotation, in relation to the Sun, is called the **apparent or true solar day**. A sundial thus measures **apparent solar time**. This length of time varies, but an average determines a mean solar day of 24 hours.

The mean solar day and **mean solar time** are in universal use for civil purposes. Mean solar time may be obtained from apparent solar time by correcting observations of the Sun for the **equation of time**. Mean solar time may be up to 16 minutes different from apparent solar time.

Sidereal time is the measure of time defined by the diurnal motion of the vernal equinox and is determined from observation of the meridian transits of stars. One complete rotation of Earth relative to the equinox is called the **sidereal day**. The **mean sidereal day** is 23 hours, 56 minutes, 4.2 seconds of mean solar time.

The interval required for Earth to make one absolute revolution around the Sun is a **sidereal year**; it consisted of 365 days, 6 hours, 9 minutes, and 9.5 seconds of mean solar time (approximately 24 hours per day) in 1900 and has been increasing at the rate of 0.0001 second annually.

The **tropical year**, upon which our calendar is based, is the interval between two consecutive returns of the Sun to the vernal equinox. The tropical year consisted of 365 days, 5 hours, 48 minutes, and 46 seconds in 1900. It has been decreasing at the rate of 0.53 second per century. The **calendar year** begins at midnight precisely, local clock time, on the night of Dec. 31-Jan. 1. The day and the calendar month also begin at midnight by the clock.

On Jan. 1, 1972, the Bureau International des Poids et Mesures in Paris introduced **International Atomic Time** (TAI) as the most precisely determined time scale for astronomical usage. The fundamental unit of TAI in the international system of units is the second, defined as the duration of 9,192,631,770 periods of the radiation corresponding to the transition between two hyperfine levels of the ground state of the cesium-133 atom. **Coordinated Universal Time** (UTC), which serves as the basis for civil timekeeping and is the standard time of the prime meridian, is officially defined by a formula which relates UTC to mean sidereal time in Greenwich, England. (UTC replaced Greenwich Mean Time as the basis for standard time for the world.)

Zones and seasons. The five zones of Earth's surface are the Torrid, lying between the Tropics of Cancer and Capricorn; the N Temperate, between Cancer and the Arctic Circle; the S Temperate, between Capricorn and the Antarctic Circle; and the two Frigid Zones, between the Polar Circles and the Poles.

The inclination, or tilt, of Earth's axis, 23°45′ away from a perpendicular to Earth's orbit of the Sun, determines the seasons. These are commonly marked in the N Temperate Zone, where spring begins at the vernal equinox, summer at the summer solstice, autumn at the autumnal equinox, and winter at the winter solstice. In the S Temperate Zone, the seasons are reversed. Spring begins at the autumnal equinox, summer at the winter solstice and so on.

The points at which the Sun crosses the equator are the **equinoxes**, when day and night are most nearly equal. The points at which the Sun is at a maximum distance from the equator are the **solstices**. Days and nights are then most unequal. However, at the equator, day and night are equal throughout the year.

In June, the North Pole is tilted 23°27′ toward the Sun, and the days in the Northern Hemisphere are longer than the nights, while the days in the Southern Hemisphere are shorter than the nights. In Dec., the North Pole is tilted 23°27′ away from the Sun, and the situation is reversed.

Seasons in 2015. In 2015, the four seasons begin in the Northern Hemisphere as shown. (Add 1 hour to Eastern Standard Time for Atlantic Time; subtract 1 hour for Central, 2 for Mountain, 3 for Pacific, 4 for Alaska, 5 for Hawaii-Aleutian. Also shown is Coordinated Universal Time.)

Season	Date	UTC	EST/EDT
Vernal Equinox (spring)	Mar. 20	22:45	18:45 EDT
Northern Solstice (summer)	June 21	16:38	12:38 EDT
Autumnal Equinox (fall)	Sept. 23	08:21	04:21 EDT
Southern Solstice (winter)	Dec. 21	04:48	23:48 EST Dec. 20

Poles. The geographic (rotation) poles, or points where Earth's axis of rotation cuts the surface, are not absolutely fixed in the body of Earth. The pole of rotation describes an irregular curve about its mean position.

Two periods have been detected in this motion: (1) an annual period due to seasonal changes in barometric pressure, to load of ice and snow on the surface, and to other seasonal phenomena; (2) a period of about 14 months due to the shape and constitution of Earth. In addition, there are small but as yet unpredictable irregularities. The whole motion is so small that the actual pole at any time remains within a circle of 30 or 40 ft in radius centered at the mean position of the pole.

The pole of rotation for the time being is of course the pole having a latitude of 90° and an indeterminate longitude.

Magnetic poles. Although Earth's magnetic field resembles that of an ordinary bar magnet, this magnetic field is probably produced by electric currents in the liquid currents of the Earth's outer core. The **north magnetic pole** of Earth is that region where the magnetic force is downward, and the **south magnetic pole** is that region where the magnetic force is upward. A compass placed at the magnetic poles experiences no directive force in azimuth (i.e., direction).

There are slow changes in the distribution of Earth's magnetic field. This slow temporal change is referred to as the secular change of the main magnetic field, and the magnetic poles shift due to this. The location of the N magnetic pole was first measured in 1831 at Cape Adelaide on the W coast of Boothia Peninsula in Canada's Northwest Territories (about latitude 70° N and longitude 96° W). Since then it has moved over 500 mi. It is now estimated to be at 82.7° N and 114.4° W, NW of Ellef Ringnes Island in northern Canada. Measurement for several decades by Canadian scientists indicates the motion of the pole has accelerated, now averaging about 25 mi per year.

The direction of the horizontal components of the magnetic field at any point is known as magnetic N at that point, and the angle by which it deviates E or W of true N is known as the magnetic declination.

A compass without error points in the direction of magnetic north. (In general, this is not the direction of the true rotational north pole.) If you follow the direction indicated by the N end of the compass, you will go along an irregular curve that eventually reaches the north magnetic pole (though not usually by a great-circle route). However, the action of the compass should not be thought of as due to any influence of the distant pole, but simply as an indication of the distribution of Earth's magnetism at the place of observation.

Rotation. The speed of Earth's rotation about its axis is slightly variable. The variations may be classified as:

(A) **Secular.** Tidal friction acts as a brake on the rotation and causes a slow secular increase in the length of the day, about 1 millisecond per century.

(B) **Irregular.** The speed of rotation may increase for a number of years (about 5 to 10) and then start decreasing. The maximum difference from the mean in the length of the day during a century is about 5 milliseconds. The accumulated difference in time has amounted to approximately 44 seconds since 1900. The cause is probably motion in the interior of Earth.

(C) **Periodic.** Seasonal variations exist with periods of 1 year and 6 months. The cumulative effect is such that each year, Earth is late about 30 milliseconds near June 1 and is ahead about 30 milliseconds near Oct. 1. The maximum seasonal variation in the length of the day is about 0.5 millisecond. It is believed that the principal cause of the annual variation is the seasonal change in the wind patterns of the Northern and Southern Hemispheres. The semiannual variation is due chiefly to tidal action of the Sun, which distorts the shape of Earth slightly.

The Moon

Distance from Earth	
Perigee	225,744 mi
Semi-major axis (mean distance)	238,855 mi
Apogee	251,966 mi
Period of revolution	27.322 d
Orbital eccentricity	0.0549
Orbital inclination	5.145°
Synodic orbital period (period of phases)	29.53 d
Sidereal day (rotation period)	27.322 d
Rotational inclination	6.68°
Mass (Earth = 1)	0.0123
Mean radius	1,079 mi
Mean density (Earth = 1)	0.607
Average surface temperature	−100°F

The Moon is the second-brightest object in the sky (the Sun is the first). Earth's only natural satellite, the Moon is the force behind the rising and falling of tides, and it helps to regulate Earth's orbit around the Sun. Many probes have been sent to the Moon, and between 1969 and 1972, 12 U.S. astronauts walked on its surface. The Moon is the subject of renewed international interest. In 2007, Japan and China orbited satellites around the Moon, India orbited a spacecraft in fall 2008, and the U.S. sent an orbiter and impactor in 2009. In Sept. 2009, American scientists announced the discovery of a thin layer of water ice near the lunar poles. The *LCROSS* impactor mission impacted the lunar south polar region in Oct. 2009. The plume of material thrown up in the impact included water plus a variety of other chemical species, indicating that the lunar regolith harbors a rich and active chemistry. In Sept. 2013, NASA launched *LADEE*, a mission to study the ephemeral lunar atmosphere and lunar dust from a low orbit. In Dec. 2013, China became the third nation to land a spacecraft on the Moon when *Chang'e 3* set down on Mare Imbrium. *Chang'e 3* released the *Yutu* rover to study the lunar surface.

Orbit and rotation. The Moon completes a circuit around Earth in a period that averages 27 days, 7 hours, 43.2 minutes. This is the Moon's sidereal period. Because of the motion of the Moon in common with Earth around the Sun, the mean duration of the lunar month—the period from one new moon to the next new moon—is 29 days, 12 hours, 44.05 minutes. This is the Moon's synodic period.

The mean distance of the Moon from Earth is 238,855 mi, but its orbit about Earth is elliptical, and thus the actual distance varies considerably. The maximum distance from Earth that the Moon may reach is 251,966 mi and the least distance is 225,744 mi.

The Moon rotates on its axis in a period of time that is exactly equal to its sidereal revolution about Earth—27.322 days. Thus the backside, or farside, of the Moon always faces away from Earth. But this does not mean that the backside is always dark. The farside of the Moon gets as much direct sunlight as the nearside; at new moon phase, the farside of the Moon is fully lit but not visible from Earth.

The Moon's revolution about Earth is irregular because of its elliptical orbit. The Moon's rotation, however, is regular, and this, together with the irregular revolution, produces what is called libration in longitude, which permits an observer on Earth to see first farther around the eastern side and then farther around the western side of the Moon. The Moon's variation north or south of the ecliptic permits one to see farther over first one pole of the Moon and then the other; this is called libration in latitude. These two libration effects permit observers on Earth to see a total of about 60% of the Moon's surface over a period of time.

Atmosphere and surface. The Moon, like the planet Mercury, has no real atmosphere to speak of. What little exists is variable and tenuous. With its long day and night, the daytime temperature can reach 260°F. The coldest nighttime temperature is −280°F. This day-to-night contrast is exceeded only by that on Mercury. The lunar surface has not changed much since humans began observing it. The side visible from Earth has large craters and vast dark areas called *maria* that were once lava. The farside has almost no maria but is pockmarked with craters; it was first photographed in 1959 by the Soviet space probe *Lunik III*.

Recent findings show that up to 300 mil metric tons of water ice may exist in craters at the lunar poles. In its interior, the Moon may have a small core, which supports the idea that most of the Moon's mass was ripped away from the early Earth when a Mars-size object collided with Earth.

Harvest moon and hunter's moon. The harvest moon, the full moon nearest the autumnal equinox, ushers in a period of several days when the Moon rises soon after sunset. This phenomenon gives farmers in temperate latitudes extra hours of light in which to harvest their crops. The 2015 harvest moon falls on Sept. 28. Harvest moon in the Southern Hemisphere temperate latitudes falls on Apr. 4.

The next full moon after harvest moon is called the hunter's moon; it is accompanied by a similar but less marked phenomenon. In 2015, the hunter's moon occurs on Oct. 27 in the Northern Hemisphere and on May 4 in the Southern Hemisphere.

Moon's Perigee and Apogee, 2015

Perigee is the point in the Moon's orbit where it is closest to the Earth. Apogee is the point where it is farthest.

(In Coordinated Universal Time, or UTC, the standard time of the prime meridian.)

Perigee						Apogee					
Month	Day	Hour	Month	Day	Hour	Month	Day	Hour	Month	Day	Hour
Jan.	21	20	Aug.	2	10	Jan.	9	18	July	21	11
Feb.	19	8	Aug.	30	15	Feb.	6	6	Aug.	18	3
Mar.	19	20	Sept.	28	2	Mar.	5	8	Sept.	14	11
Apr.	17	4	Oct.	26	13	Apr.	1	13	Oct.	11	13
May	15	0	Nov.	23	20	Apr.	29	4	Nov.	7	22
June	10	5	Dec.	21	9	May	26	22	Dec.	5	15
July	5	19				June	23	17			

Moon Phases, 2015

(In Coordinated Universal Time, or UTC, the standard time of the prime meridian.)

New Moon			Waxing Quarter			Full Moon			Waning Quarter		
Month	d	h	m	Month	d	h	m	Month	d	h	m	Month	d	h	m

New Moon				Waxing Quarter				Full Moon				Waning Quarter			
Month	d	h	m	Month	d	h	m	Month	d	h	m	Month	d	h	m
Jan.	20	13	14	Jan.	27	4	48	Jan.	5	4	53	Jan.	13	9	46
Feb.	18	23	47	Feb.	25	17	14	Feb.	3	23	9	Feb.	12	3	50
Mar.	20	9	36	Mar.	27	7	43	Mar.	5	18	5	Mar.	13	17	48
Apr.	18	18	57	Apr.	25	23	55	Apr.	4	12	6	Apr.	12	3	44
May	18	4	13	May	25	17	19	May	4	3	42	May	11	10	36
June	16	14	5	June	24	11	3	June	2	16	19	June	9	15	42
July	16	1	24	July	24	4	4	July	2	2	20	July	8	20	24
Aug.	14	14	53	Aug.	22	19	31	July	31	10	43	Aug.	7	2	3
Sept.	13	6	41	Sept.	21	8	59	Aug.	29	18	35	Sept.	5	9	54
Oct.	13	0	6	Oct.	20	20	31	Sept.	28	2	51	Oct.	4	21	6
Nov.	11	17	47	Nov.	19	6	27	Oct.	27	12	5	Nov.	3	12	24
Dec.	11	10	29	Dec.	18	15	14	Nov.	25	22	44	Dec.	3	7	40
								Dec.	25	11	11				

Western Calendars

The **Julian calendar**, under which all Western nations measured time until 1582 CE, was authorized by Julius Caesar in 46 BCE. It called for a year of 365¼ days, starting in Jan., with every fourth year being a **leap year** of 366 days. St. Bede, an Anglo-Saxon monk also known as the Venerable Bede, announced in 730 CE that the Julian year was 11 min., 14 sec. too long, a cumulative error of about a day every 128 years, but nothing was done about this for centuries.

By 1582 the accumulated error was estimated at 10 days. In that year, Pope Gregory XIII decreed that the day following Oct. 4, 1582, should be called Oct. 15, thus dropping 10 days and initiating the **Gregorian calendar**.

The Gregorian calendar perpetuated a chronological system devised by the monk Dionysius Exiguus (fl. 6th cent.). His chronology started with the first year following the birth of Jesus Christ, which he inaccurately took to be year 753 in the Roman calendar. Leap years were continued but, to prevent further displacements, centesimal years (years ending in 00) were made common years, not leap years, unless divisible by 400. Under this plan, 1600 and 2000 were leap years; 1700, 1800, and 1900 were not.

The Gregorian calendar was adopted at once by France, Italy, Spain, Portugal, and Luxembourg. Within two years, most German Catholic states, Belgium, and parts of Switzerland and the Netherlands were brought under the new calendar, and Hungary followed in 1587. The rest of the Netherlands, along with Denmark and the German Protestant states, made the change in 1699-1700.

The British government adopted the Gregorian calendar and imposed it on all its possessions, including the American colonies, in 1752, decreeing that the day following Sept. 2, 1752, should be called Sept. 14, a loss of 11 days. All dates preceding were marked OS, for Old Style. In addition, New Year's Day was moved to Jan. 1 from Mar. 25. (Under the old reckoning, for example, Mar. 24, 1700, was followed by Mar. 25, 1701.) Thus George Washington's birth date, which was Feb. 11, 1731, OS, became Feb. 22, 1732, NS (New Style). In 1753, Sweden also went Gregorian.

In 1793, the French revolutionary government adopted a calendar of 12 months of 30 days each with five extra days in Sept. of each common year and six extra days every fourth year. Napoleon reinstated the Gregorian calendar in 1806.

The Gregorian system later spread to non-European regions, replacing traditional calendars at least for official purposes. Japan in 1873, Egypt in 1875, China in 1912, and Turkey in 1925 made the change, usually in conjunction with political upheaval. In China, the republican government began reckoning years from its 1911 founding. After 1949, the People's Republic adopted the Common, or Christian Era, year count, even for the traditional lunar calendar, which it retained. In 1918, the Soviet Union decreed that the day after Jan. 31, 1918, OS, would be Feb. 14, 1918, NS. Greece changed over in 1923. For the first time in history, all major nations had one calendar. The Russian Orthodox church and some other Christian sects retained the Julian calendar.

To convert from the Julian to the Gregorian calendar, add 10 days to dates Oct. 5, 1582, through Feb. 28, 1700; after that date, add 11 days through Feb. 28, 1800; 12 days through Feb. 28, 1900; and 13 days through Feb. 28, 2100.

A **century** consists of 100 consecutive years. The 1st century CE may be said to have run from the years 1 through 100. The 20th century by this reckoning consisted of the years 1901 through 2000 and ended Dec. 31, 2000, as did the 2nd millennium CE. The 21st century thus technically began on Jan. 1, 2001.

For a **perpetual calendar**, see pages 366-67.

Gregorian Calendar

Choose the desired year from the table below or from the perpetual calendar (for years 1803 to 2080). The number after each year designates which calendar to use for that year, as shown in the perpetual calendar. (The Gregorian calendar was inaugurated Oct. 15, 1582. From that date through Dec. 31, 1582, use calendar 6.)

1583-1802

1583 7	1603 4	1623 1	1643 5	1663 2	1683 6	1703 2	1723 6	1743 3	1763 7	1783 4
1584 8	1604 12	1624 9	1644 13	1664 10	1684 14	1704 10	1724 14	1744 11	1764 8	1784 12
1585 3	1605 7	1625 4	1645 1	1665 5	1685 2	1705 5	1725 2	1745 6	1765 3	1785 7
1586 4	1606 1	1626 5	1646 2	1666 6	1686 3	1706 6	1726 3	1746 7	1766 4	1786 1
1587 5	1607 2	1627 6	1647 3	1667 7	1687 4	1707 7	1727 4	1747 1	1767 5	1787 2
1588 13	1608 10	1628 14	1648 11	1668 8	1688 12	1708 8	1728 12	1748 9	1768 13	1788 10
1589 1	1609 5	1629 2	1649 6	1669 3	1689 7	1709 3	1729 7	1749 4	1769 1	1789 5
1590 2	1610 6	1630 3	1650 7	1670 4	1690 1	1710 4	1730 1	1750 5	1770 2	1790 6
1591 3	1611 7	1631 4	1651 1	1671 5	1691 2	1711 5	1731 2	1751 6	1771 3	1791 7
1592 11	1612 8	1632 12	1652 9	1672 13	1692 10	1712 13	1732 10	1752 14	1772 11	1792 8
1593 6	1613 3	1633 7	1653 4	1673 1	1693 5	1713 1	1733 5	1753 2	1773 6	1793 3
1594 7	1614 4	1634 1	1654 5	1674 2	1694 6	1714 2	1734 6	1754 3	1774 7	1794 4
1595 1	1615 5	1635 2	1655 6	1675 3	1695 7	1715 3	1735 7	1755 4	1775 1	1795 5
1596 9	1616 13	1636 10	1656 14	1676 11	1696 8	1716 11	1736 8	1756 12	1776 9	1796 13
1597 4	1617 1	1637 5	1657 2	1677 6	1697 3	1717 6	1737 3	1757 7	1777 4	1797 1
1598 5	1618 2	1638 6	1658 3	1678 7	1698 4	1718 7	1738 4	1758 1	1778 5	1798 2
1599 6	1619 3	1639 7	1659 4	1679 1	1699 5	1719 1	1739 5	1759 2	1779 6	1799 3
1600 14	1620 11	1640 8	1660 12	1680 9	1700 6	1720 9	1740 13	1760 10	1780 14	1800 4
1601 2	1621 6	1641 3	1661 7	1681 4	1701 7	1721 4	1741 1	1761 5	1781 2	1801 5
1602 3	1622 7	1642 4	1662 1	1682 5	1702 1	1722 5	1742 2	1762 6	1782 3	1802 6

The Julian Period

How many days have you lived? To determine this, multiply your age by 365, add the number of days since your last birthday, and account for all leap years. Chances are your calculations will go wrong somewhere. Astronomers, however, find it convenient to express dates and time intervals in days rather than in years, months, and days. This is done by placing events within the Julian period.

The Julian period was devised in 1582 by the French classical scholar Joseph Scaliger (1540-1609), who named it after his father, Julius Caesar Scaliger, not after the Julian calendar as might be supposed.

Scaliger began with a zero hour, or starting time, of noon on Jan. 1, 4713 BCE (on the Julian calendar). This was the most recent time that three major chronological cycles began on the same day: (1) the 28-year solar cycle, after which dates in the Julian calendar (e.g., Feb. 11) return to the same days of the week (e.g., Monday); (2) the 19-year lunar cycle, after which the phases of the moon return to the same dates of the year; and (3) the 15-year indiction cycle, used in ancient Rome to regulate taxes.

It will take 7,980 years to complete the period, the product of the numbers 28, 19, and 15.

Noon (Universal Time) of Jan. 1, 2015, will be Julian date (JD) 2,457,024; that many days will have passed since the start of the Julian period. The JD at noon of any date in 2015 may be found by adding to that number the day of the year for that date and subtracting one.

Julian Calendar

To find which of the 14 calendars of the perpetual calendar (pages 366-67) applies to any year under the Julian system, find the century for the desired year in the three leftmost columns below. Locate the desired year from among the four top rows. The number at the intersection of that row and column is the calendar designation for that year. For some years and countries, the Julian new year did not start Jan. 1; to find the correct perpetual calendar for Britain and its possessions, you can generally add one year for dates from Jan. 1 to Mar. 24. For example, to look up Feb. 2, 1705, Old Style, use the year 1706.

Year (last 2 digits of desired year)

		01	02	03	04	05	06	07	08	09	10	11	12	13	14	15	16	17	18	19	20	21	22	23	24	25	26	27	28
		29	30	31	32	33	34	35	36	37	38	39	40	41	42	43	44	45	46	47	48	49	50	51	52	53	54	55	56
		57	58	59	60	61	62	63	64	65	66	67	68	69	70	71	72	73	74	75	76	77	78	79	80	81	82	83	84
Century		00	85	86	87	88	89	90	91	92	93	94	95	96	97	98	99												
0	700 1400	12	7	1	2	10	5	6	7	8	3	4	5	13	1	2	3	11	6	7	1	9	4	5	6	14	2	3	4	12
100	800 1500	11	6	7	1	9	4	5	6	14	2	3	4	12	7	1	2	10	5	6	7	8	3	4	5	13	1	2	3	11
200	900 1600	10	5	6	7	8	3	4	5	13	1	2	3	11	6	7	1	9	4	5	6	14	2	3	4	12	7	1	2	10
300	1000 1700	9	4	5	6	14	2	3	4	12	7	1	2	10	5	6	7	8	3	4	5	13	1	2	3	11	6	7	1	9
400	1100 1800	8	3	4	5	13	1	2	3	11	6	7	1	9	4	5	6	14	2	3	4	12	7	1	2	10	5	6	7	8
500	1200 1900	14	2	3	4	12	7	1	2	10	5	6	7	8	3	4	5	13	1	2	3	11	6	7	1	9	4	5	6	14
600	1300 2000	13	1	2	3	11	6	7	1	9	4	5	6	14	2	3	4	12	7	1	2	10	5	6	7	8	3	4	5	13

Signs of the Zodiac

The zodiac is the apparent yearly path of the sun among the stars as viewed from Earth and was divided by the ancients into 12 equal sections or signs, each named for the constellation situated within its limits in ancient times. Astrologers claim that the temperament and destiny of each individual depend on the zodiac sign under which the person was born and the relationships between the planets at that time and throughout the person's life.

Below are the 12 traditional signs and the traditional range of dates pertaining to each:

♈ **Aries** (Ram), March 21-April 19

♉ **Taurus** (Bull), April 20-May 20

♊ **Gemini** (Twins), May 21-June 21

♋ **Cancer** (Crab), June 22-July 22

♌ **Leo** (Lion), July 23-August 22

♍ **Virgo** (Virgin), August 23-September 22

♎ **Libra** (Scales), September 23-October 23

♏ **Scorpio** (Scorpion), October 24-November 21

♐ **Sagittarius** (Archer), November 22-December 21

♑ **Capricorn** (Goat), December 22-January 19

♒ **Aquarius** (Water Bearer), January 20-February 18

♓ **Pisces** (Fishes), February 19-March 20

Chinese Calendar and Asian Festivals

The Chinese calendar, like the Jewish and Islamic calendars (see the Religion chapter), is a lunar calendar. It is divided into 12 months of 29 or 30 days (compensating for the lunar month's mean duration of 29 days, 12 hr., 44.05 min.). This calendar is synchronized with the solar year by the addition of extra months at fixed intervals.

The Chinese calendar runs on a 60-year cycle. The cycles 1876-1935 and 1936-95, along with the first 36 years of the current cycle, are shown below grouped by their association with 1 of 12 animals in the Chinese zodiac. This cycle began in 1996 and will last until 2055. Feb. 19, 2015, marks the beginning of the year 4713 in the Chinese calendar and is designated the Year of the Sheep. (Note: The first 3-7 weeks of each Western year belong to the previous Chinese year.)

Both the Western (Gregorian) and traditional lunar calendars are used publicly in China and in North and South Korea, and two New Year's celebrations are held. In Taiwan, overseas Chinese communities, and Vietnam, the lunar calendar is used only to set the dates for traditional festivals, with the Gregorian system in general use.

The 4-day Chinese New Year; the 3-day Vietnamese New Year festival, Tet; and the 3-to-4-day Korean festival, Suhl, begin at the second new moon after the winter solstice. The new moon in East Asia, which is west of the International Date Line, may be a day later than the new moon in the U.S. The festivals may start, therefore, anywhere between Jan. 21 and Feb. 19 of the Gregorian calendar.

Rat	Ox	Tiger	Hare (Rabbit)	Dragon	Snake	Horse	Sheep (Goat)	Monkey	Rooster	Dog	Pig (Boar)
1876	1877	1878	1879	1880	1881	1882	1883	1884	1885	1886	1887
1888	1889	1890	1891	1892	1893	1894	1895	1896	1897	1898	1899
1900	1901	1902	1903	1904	1905	1906	1907	1908	1909	1910	1911
1912	1913	1914	1915	1916	1917	1918	1919	1920	1921	1922	1923
1924	1925	1926	1927	1928	1929	1930	1931	1932	1933	1934	1935
1936	1937	1938	1939	1940	1941	1942	1943	1944	1945	1946	1947
1948	1949	1950	1951	1952	1953	1954	1955	1956	1957	1958	1959
1960	1961	1962	1963	1964	1965	1966	1967	1968	1969	1970	1971
1972	1973	1974	1975	1976	1977	1978	1979	1980	1981	1982	1983
1984	1985	1986	1987	1988	1989	1990	1991	1992	1993	1994	1995
1996	1997	1998	1999	2000	2001	2002	2003	2004	2005	2006	2007
2008	2009	2010	2011	2012	2013	2014	2015	2016	2017	2018	2019
2020	2021	2022	2023	2024	2025	2026	2027	2028	2029	2030	2031

Calendar for the Year 2015

January

S	M	T	W	T	F	S
				1	2	3
4	5	6	7	8	9	10
11	12	13	14	15	16	17
18	19	20	21	22	23	24
25	26	27	28	29	30	31

February

S	M	T	W	T	F	S
1	2	3	4	5	6	7
8	9	10	11	12	13	14
15	16	17	18	19	20	21
22	23	24	25	26	27	28

March

S	M	T	W	T	F	S
1	2	3	4	5	6	7
8	9	10	11	12	13	14
15	16	17	18	19	20	21
22	23	24	25	26	27	28
29	30	31				

April

S	M	T	W	T	F	S
			1	2	3	4
5	6	7	8	9	10	11
12	13	14	15	16	17	18
19	20	21	22	23	24	25
26	27	28	29	30		

May

S	M	T	W	T	F	S
					1	2
3	4	5	6	7	8	9
10	11	12	13	14	15	16
17	18	19	20	21	22	23
24	25	26	27	28	29	30
31						

June

S	M	T	W	T	F	S
	1	2	3	4	5	6
7	8	9	10	11	12	13
14	15	16	17	18	19	20
21	22	23	24	25	26	27
28	29	30				

July

S	M	T	W	T	F	S
			1	2	3	4
5	6	7	8	9	10	11
12	13	14	15	16	17	18
19	20	21	22	23	24	25
26	27	28	29	30	31	

August

S	M	T	W	T	F	S
						1
2	3	4	5	6	7	8
9	10	11	12	13	14	15
16	17	18	19	20	21	22
23	24	25	26	27	28	29
30	31					

September

S	M	T	W	T	F	S
		1	2	3	4	5
6	7	8	9	10	11	12
13	14	15	16	17	18	19
20	21	22	23	24	25	26
27	28	29	30			

October

S	M	T	W	T	F	S
				1	2	3
4	5	6	7	8	9	10
11	12	13	14	15	16	17
18	19	20	21	22	23	24
25	26	27	28	29	30	31

November

S	M	T	W	T	F	S
1	2	3	4	5	6	7
8	9	10	11	12	13	14
15	16	17	18	19	20	21
22	23	24	25	26	27	28
29	30					

December

S	M	T	W	T	F	S
		1	2	3	4	5
6	7	8	9	10	11	12
13	14	15	16	17	18	19
20	21	22	23	24	25	26
27	28	29	30	31		

Federal Holidays and Other Notable Dates, 2015

Some dates may be subject to change.

The dates in bold in the calendar above and named below in italics are U.S. federal holidays, designated by the president or Congress and applicable to federal employees and in the District of Columbia. Most U.S. states also observe these holidays, and many states observe others; practices vary by state. In most states the secretary of state's office can provide details.

January

- **1** *New Year's Day*; Sugar Bowl; Rose Bowl (BCS playoff game); Cotton Bowl (BCS playoff game)
- **12** BCS Football Championship Game (Arlington, TX)
- **19** *Martin Luther King Jr. Day*
- **19-Feb. 1** Australian Open tennis tournament
- **25** NFL Pro Bowl (Glendale, AZ)
- **26** Australia Day

February

- **1** Super Bowl XLIX (Glendale, AZ)
- **2** Groundhog Day
- **12** Lincoln's Birthday
- **13-18** Carnival, Brazil
- **14** Valentine's Day
- **15** NBA All-Star Game (New York, NY)
- **16** *Washington's Birthday* (observed); President's Day, or Washington-Lincoln Day (3rd Mon. in Feb.)
- **16-17** Westminster Dog Show
- **17** Mardi Gras
- **18** Ash Wednesday
- **22** Academy Awards; Daytona 500

March

- **5** Purim (Feast of Lots) begins previous night
- **7** Iditarod Trail Sled Dog Race begins
- **8** Daylight-saving time begins in U.S.
- **17** St. Patrick's Day
- **20** First day of spring (Northern Hemisphere)
- **21** Benito Juárez's Birthday, Mexico

April

- **1** April Fools' Day
- **3** Good Friday
- **4** Passover, first full day
- **4, 6** NCAA Men's Basketball Final Four (Indianapolis, IN)
- **5** Easter
- **5, 7** NCAA Women's Basketball Final Four (Tampa Bay, FL)
- **6-12** Masters golf tournament
- **12** Easter (Orthodox)
- **15** Tax Day (income-tax filing deadline)
- **20** Patriot's Day; Boston Marathon (3rd Mon. in April)
- **22** Earth Day
- **23** Take Our Daughters and Sons to Work Day
- **24** Arbor Day

May

- **1** May Day (International Workers' Day)
- **2** Kentucky Derby
- **5** Cinco de Mayo (Battle of Puebla Day), Mexico
- **10** Mother's Day
- **16** Armed Forces Day; Preakness Stakes
- **18** Victoria Day, Canada
- **24-June 7** French Open tennis tournament
- **25** *Memorial Day*, or Decoration Day (last Mon. in May); Buddha's Birthday, Korea, Hong Kong

June

- **6** Belmont Stakes
- **14** Flag Day
- **18** Ramadan (Islamic month of fasting), first full day
- **18-21** U.S. Open golf tournament (University Place, WA)
- **20** Dragon Boat Festival, China
- **21** Father's Day; first day of summer (Northern Hemisphere)
- **29-July 12** Wimbledon tennis tournament

July

- **1** Canada Day, Canada
- **3** *Independence Day* (federal holiday observed)
- **4** *Independence Day*
- **6-14** Running of the Bulls (Pamplona, Spain)
- **9-12** U.S. Women's Open golf tournament (Lancaster, PA)
- **14** Bastille Day, France
- **16-19** British Open golf tournament (Fife, Scotland, UK)

August

- **10-16** PGA Championship (Kohler, WI)

September

- **7** *Labor Day*, U.S., Canada (first Mon. in Sept.)
- **13** Grandparents' Day, U.S.
- **14** Rosh Hashanah (New Year), first full day
- **16** Independence Day, Mexico
- **17** Constitution and Citizenship Day, U.S.
- **23** First day of autumn (Northern Hemisphere); Yom Kippur (Day of Atonement) begins previous night

October

- **3** German Unity Day, Germany
- **5** U.S. Supreme Court session begins
- **12** *Columbus Day* (2nd Mon. in Oct.); Día de la Raza, Spain, Mexico; Thanksgiving Day, Canada
- **14** Islamic New Year (Muharram 1) begins previous night
- **31** Halloween

November

- **1** All Saints' Day; daylight-saving time ends in U.S.; New York City Marathon
- **3** Election Day (1st Tues. after 1st Mon. in Nov.)
- **5** Guy Fawkes Day
- **8** Remembrance Sunday, UK
- **11** *Veterans' Day*; Remembrance Day, Canada
- **26** *Thanksgiving Day* (4th Thurs. in Nov.)

December

- **7-14** Hanukkah (Festival of Lights) begins previous night
- **10** Nobel Prizes awarded (winners announced in Oct.)
- **12** Día de la Virgen de Guadalupe, Mexico
- **21** First day of winter (Northern Hemisphere)
- **25** *Christmas Day*
- **26** Boxing Day, Australia, Canada, New Zealand, UK
- **26-Jan. 1** Kwanzaa
- **31** Orange Bowl; Cotton Bowl; Chick-fil-A Peach Bowl

Perpetual Calendar

The number shown for each year indicates which Gregorian calendar to use. For 1583–1802, see "Gregorian Calendar" on page 363. For 1803–20, use numbers for 1983–2000, respectively. The years in the calendar labels are the last and next occurrences of each calendar.

Year	No.	Year	No.	Year	No.	Year	No.	Year	No.
1821	2	1847	6	1873	3	1899	1	1925	5
1822	3	1848	14	1874	4	1900	2	1926	6
1823	4	1849	2	1875	5	1901	3	1927	7
1824	12	1850	3	1876	13	1902	4	1928	8
1825	7	1851	4	1877	1	1903	5	1929	3
1826	1	1852	12	1878	2	1904	13	1930	4
1827	2	1853	7	1879	3	1905	1	1931	5
1828	10	1854	1	1880	11	1906	2	1932	13
1829	5	1855	2	1881	6	1907	3	1933	1
1830	6	1856	10	1882	7	1908	11	1934	2
1831	7	1857	5	1883	1	1909	6	1935	3
1832	8	1858	6	1884	9	1910	7	1936	11
1833	3	1859	7	1885	4	1911	1	1937	6
1834	4	1860	8	1886	5	1912	9	1938	7
1835	5	1861	3	1887	6	1913	4	1939	1
1836	13	1862	4	1888	14	1914	5	1940	9
1837	1	1863	5	1889	2	1915	6	1941	4
1838	2	1864	13	1890	3	1916	14	1942	5
1839	3	1865	1	1891	4	1917	2	1943	6
1840	11	1866	2	1892	12	1918	3	1944	14
1841	6	1867	3	1893	7	1919	4	1945	2
1842	7	1868	11	1894	1	1920	12	1946	3
1843	1	1869	6	1895	2	1921	7	1947	4
1844	9	1870	7	1896	10	1922	1	1948	12
1845	4	1871	1	1897	5	1923	2	1949	7
1846	5	1872	9	1898	6	1924	10	1950	1

Year	No.	Year	No.	Year	No.	Year	No.	Year	No.
1951	2	1977	7	2003	4	2029	2	2055	6
1952	10	1978	1	2004	12	2030	3	2056	14
1953	5	1979	2	2005	7	2031	4	2057	2
1954	6	1980	10	2006	1	2032	12	2058	3
1955	7	1981	5	2007	2	2033	7	2059	4
1956	8	1982	6	2008	10	2034	1	2060	12
1957	3	1983	7	2009	5	2035	2	2061	7
1958	4	1984	8	2010	6	2036	10	2062	1
1959	5	1985	3	2011	7	2037	5	2063	2
1960	13	1986	4	2012	8	2038	6	2064	10
1961	1	1987	5	2013	3	2039	7	2065	5
1962	2	1988	13	2014	4	2040	8	2066	6
1963	3	1989	1	2015	5	2041	3	2067	7
1964	11	1990	2	2016	13	2042	4	2068	8
1965	6	1991	3	2017	1	2043	5	2069	3
1966	7	1992	11	2018	2	2044	13	2070	4
1967	1	1993	6	2019	3	2045	1	2071	5
1968	9	1994	7	2020	11	2046	2	2072	13
1969	4	1995	1	2021	6	2047	3	2073	1
1970	5	1996	9	2022	7	2048	11	2074	2
1971	6	1997	4	2023	1	2049	6	2075	3
1972	14	1998	5	2024	9	2050	7	2076	11
1973	2	1999	6	2025	4	2051	1	2077	6
1974	3	2000	14	2026	5	2052	9	2078	7
1975	4	2001	2	2027	6	2053	4	2079	1
1976	12	2002	3	2028	14	2054	5	2080	9

Calendar 1 — 2006/2017
Months: January, February, March, April, May, June, July, August, September, October, November, December (S M T W T F S)

Calendar 2 — 2007/2018
Months: January, February, March, April, May, June, July, August, September, October, November, December (S M T W T F S)

Calendar 3 — 2013/2019
Months: January, February, March, April, May, June, July, August, September, October, November, December (S M T W T F S)

Calendar 4 — 2014/2025
Months: January, February, March, April, May, June, July, August, September, October, November, December (S M T W T F S)

Calendar 5 — 2009/2015
Months: January, February, March, April, May, June, July, August, September, October, November, December (S M T W T F S)

Calendar 6 — 2010/2021
Months: January, February, March, April, May, June, July, August, September, October, November, December (S M T W T F S)

2008/2036 — 10

JANUARY · FEBRUARY · MARCH · APRIL · MAY · JUNE · JULY · AUGUST · SEPTEMBER · OCTOBER · NOVEMBER · DECEMBER

2000/2028 — 14

JANUARY · FEBRUARY · MARCH · APRIL · MAY · JUNE · JULY · AUGUST · SEPTEMBER · OCTOBER · NOVEMBER · DECEMBER

1996/2024 — 9

JANUARY · FEBRUARY · MARCH · APRIL · MAY · JUNE · JULY · AUGUST · SEPTEMBER · OCTOBER · NOVEMBER · DECEMBER

1988/2016 — 13

JANUARY · FEBRUARY · MARCH · APRIL · MAY · JUNE · JULY · AUGUST · SEPTEMBER · OCTOBER · NOVEMBER · DECEMBER

2012/2040 — 8

JANUARY · FEBRUARY · MARCH · APRIL · MAY · JUNE · JULY · AUGUST · SEPTEMBER · OCTOBER · NOVEMBER · DECEMBER

2004/2032 — 12

JANUARY · FEBRUARY · MARCH · APRIL · MAY · JUNE · JULY · AUGUST · SEPTEMBER · OCTOBER · NOVEMBER · DECEMBER

2011/2022 — 7

JANUARY · FEBRUARY · MARCH · APRIL · MAY · JUNE · JULY · AUGUST · SEPTEMBER · OCTOBER · NOVEMBER · DECEMBER

1992/2020 — 11

JANUARY · FEBRUARY · MARCH · APRIL · MAY · JUNE · JULY · AUGUST · SEPTEMBER · OCTOBER · NOVEMBER · DECEMBER

Other Calendars: Year and New Year's Day, 2015

Era	Year	Begins in 2015	Era	Year	Begins in 2015
Byzantine	7524	Sept. 14	Islamic/Muslim (Hijra)	1437	Oct. 14[1]
Chinese (Year of the Sheep)	4713	Feb. 19	Japanese (starts at 0 with new emperor)	27	Jan. 1
Diocletian	1732	Sept. 12	Jewish	5776	Sept. 14[1]
Grecian (Seleucidae)	2327	Sept. 14 or Oct. 14	Nabonassar (Babylonian)	2764	Apr. 20
Indian (Saka)	1937	Mar. 22	Roman (Ab Urbe Condita)	2768	Jan. 14

(1) Year begins the previous night.

Chronological Cycles, 2015

Dominical Letter	D	Roman Indiction	8	Solar Cycle	8
Golden Number (Lunar Cycle)	II	Epact	10	Julian Period (year of)	6728

Special Months

There are many thousands of special months, days, and weeks because of anniversaries, official proclamations, and promotional events, both trivial and serious. Here are a few of the special months:

January: Jump Out of Bed Month, National Mentoring Month, National Poverty in America Awareness Month

February: African American History Month, American Heart Month, Library Lovers Month, Youth Leadership Month, Return Shopping Carts to the Supermarket Month

March: Irish-American Heritage Month, National Women's History Month, Red Cross Month, National Frozen Food Month, National Talk With Your Teen About Sex Month, National Colorectal Cancer Awareness Month

April: National Child Abuse Prevention Month, National Humor Month, Stress Awareness Month, Grange Month

May: Clean Air Month, Get Caught Reading Month, National Barbecue Month, Asian American and Pacific Islander Heritage Month, National Inventors Month, National Mental Health Awareness Month

June: National Candy Month; Lesbian, Gay, Bisexual, and Transgender Pride Month; National Potty Training Awareness Month; National Safety Month

July: Cell Phone Courtesy Month, National HIV Awareness Month, National Hot Dog Month, Women's Motorcycle Month

August: National Black Business Month, Happiness Happens Month, National Immunization Awareness Month, National Toddler Month

September: Library Card Sign-Up Month, National Hispanic Heritage Month (Sept. 15-Oct. 15), National Biscuit Month

October: National Domestic Violence Awareness Month, National Breast Cancer Awareness Month, Diversity Awareness Month, National Popcorn Poppin' Month

November: National American Indian Heritage Month, National Adoption Month, American Diabetes Month, National Peanut Butter Lovers' Month

December: Universal Human Rights Month, National Impaired Driving Prevention Month, National Tie Month

Standard Time Differences: World Cities

The time indicated in the table is fixed by law and is called the legal time or, more generally, standard time. Use of daylight-saving time varies widely. An asterisk (*) indicates morning of the following day. At 12:00 noon, Eastern Standard Time, the standard time (in 24-hour time) in selected cities is as shown.

City			City			City			City		
Addis Ababa	20	00	Denver	10	00	London	17	00	Santiago	13	00
Amsterdam	18	00	Dhaka	23	00	Los Angeles	9	00	São Paulo	14	00
Ankara	19	00	Dublin	17	00	Madrid	18	00	Sarajevo	18	00
Athens	19	00	Edinburgh	17	00	Manila	1	00*	Seoul	2	00*
Auckland	5	00*	Geneva	18	00	Mecca	20	00	Shanghai	1	00*
Baghdad	20	00	Helsinki	19	00	Melbourne	3	00*	Singapore	1	00*
Bangkok	0	00*	Ho Chi Minh City	0	00*	Montevideo	14	00	Stockholm	18	00
Beijing	1	00*	Hong Kong	1	00*	Moscow	21	00	Sydney	3	00*
Belfast	17	00	Houston	11	00	Mumbai (Bombay)	22	30	Taipei	1	00*
Belgrade	18	00	Islamabad	22	00	Munich	18	00	Tashkent	22	00
Berlin	18	00	Istanbul	19	00	Nagasaki	2	00*	Tehran	20	30
Bogotá	12	00	Jakarta	0	00*	Nairobi	20	00	Tel Aviv	19	00
Brussels	18	00	Jerusalem	19	00	New Delhi	22	30	Tokyo	2	00*
Bucharest	19	00	Johannesburg	19	00	New York	12	00	Toronto	12	00
Budapest	18	00	Kabul	21	50	Oslo	18	00	Vancouver	9	00
Buenos Aires	14	00	Karachi	22	00	Paris	18	00	Vienna	18	00
Cairo	19	00	Kathmandu	22	45	Prague	18	00	Vladivostok	4	00*
Cape Town	19	00	Kiev	19	00	Quito	12	00	Warsaw	18	00
Caracas	12	30	Kolkata (Calcutta)	22	30	Rio de Janeiro	14	00	Wellington	5	00*
Casablanca	17	00	Lagos	18	00	Riyadh	20	00	Yangon (Rangoon)	23	30
Chicago	11	00	Lima	12	00	Rome	18	00	Yokohama	2	00*
Copenhagen	18	00	Lisbon	17	00	St. Petersburg	21	00	Zurich	18	00

Wedding Anniversary Gifts

The traditional names for wedding anniversaries go back many years in social usage and have been used to suggest types of appropriate anniversary gifts. Traditional products for gifts are listed here in capital letters, with allowable revisions in parentheses, followed by common modern gifts in each category.

1st	PAPER, clocks	9th	POTTERY (CHINA), leather goods	25th	SILVER, sterling silver
2nd	COTTON, china	10th	TIN, ALUMINUM, diamond	30th	PEARL, diamond
3rd	LEATHER, crystal, glass	11th	STEEL, fashion jewelry	35th	CORAL (JADE), jade
4th	LINEN (SILK), appliances	12th	SILK, pearls, colored gems	40th	RUBY, ruby
5th	WOOD, silverware	13th	LACE, textiles, furs	45th	SAPPHIRE, sapphire
6th	IRON, wood objects	14th	IVORY, gold jewelry	50th	GOLD, gold
7th	WOOL (COPPER), desk sets	15th	CRYSTAL, watches	55th	EMERALD, emerald
8th	BRONZE, linens, lace	20th	CHINA, platinum	60th	DIAMOND, diamond

Birthstones

Source: Jewelry Industry Council

Birth month	Ancient birthstone	Modern birthstone	Birth month	Ancient birthstone	Modern birthstone
January	Garnet	Garnet	July	Onyx	Ruby
February	Amethyst	Amethyst	August	Carnelian	Sardonyx or Peridot
March	Jasper	Bloodstone or Aquamarine	September	Chrysolite	Sapphire
April	Sapphire	Diamond	October	Aquamarine	Opal or Tourmaline
May	Agate	Emerald	November	Topaz	Topaz
June	Emerald	Pearl, Moonstone, or Alexandrite	December	Ruby	Turquoise or Zircon

Standard Time and Daylight Saving Time

Source: National Institute of Standards and Technology, U.S. Dept. of Commerce
See also Time Zone map, page 460.

Standard Time

Standard Time is reckoned from the prime meridian of longitude in Greenwich, England. The world is divided into 24 zones, each 15 deg of arc, or one hour in time apart. The Greenwich meridian (0 deg) extends through the center of the initial zone. Zones to the east are numbered from 1 to 12, with the prefix "minus" indicating the number of hours to be subtracted to obtain Greenwich Time. Each zone extends 7.5 deg on either side of its central meridian.

Westward zones are similarly numbered, but prefixed "plus," showing the number of hours that must be added to get Greenwich Time. Although these zones apply generally to ocean areas, the standard time maintained in many countries does not coincide with zone time.

The U.S. and possessions are divided into nine standard time zones. All places in each zone use, instead of their local time, the time counted from the transit of the "mean sun" across the standard time meridian that passes near the middle of that zone. These time zones are designated as Atlantic, Eastern, Central, Mountain, Pacific, Alaska, Hawaii-Aleutian, Samoa, and Chamorro (Guam and Northern Mariana Isls.); the time in these zones is reckoned from the 60th, 75th, 90th, 105th, 120th, 135th, 150th, and 165th meridians west of Greenwich and the 150th meridian east of Greenwich. The time zone line wanders to conform to local geography. The time in the various zones in the U.S. and U.S. territories west of Greenwich is earlier than Greenwich Time by 4, 5, 6, 7, 8, 9, 10, and 11 hours, respectively. However, Chamorro crosses the International Date Line and is 10 hours later than Greenwich Time.

24-Hour Time

With the 24-hour system, the day begins at midnight, and times are designated 00:00 through 23:59. Twenty-four-hour time is widely used in scientific work throughout the world. In the U.S., it is also used in operations of the armed forces. In Europe, it is frequently used by the transportation networks in preference to the 12-hour AM and PM system.

International Date Line

The Date Line, approximately coinciding with the 180th meridian, separates the calendar dates. The date must be advanced one day when crossing in a westerly direction and set back one day when crossing in an easterly direction. The Date Line frequently deviates from the 180th meridian because of decisions made by individual nations affected. The line is deflected eastward through the Bering Strait and westward of the Aleutians to prevent separating these areas by date. The line is deflected eastward of the Tonga and New Zealand islands in the South Pacific. In 1995, Kiribati announced that all of its islands east of the Date Line would observe the same date as islands to the west, though most maps and atlases do not depict this as a deviation in the Date Line. The line is established by international custom; there is no international authority prescribing its exact course.

Daylight-Saving Time

Daylight-saving time is achieved by advancing the clock one hour. Since 2007, daylight-saving time has begun at 2 AM on the 2nd Sunday in Mar. and has ended at 2 AM on the first Sunday in Nov. **In 2015, daylight-saving time begins at 2 AM on Mar. 8 and ends at 2 AM on Nov. 1.** Prior to 2007, daylight-saving time traditionally ran from the first Sunday in Apr. to the last Sunday in Oct.

Daylight-saving time was first observed in the U.S. during World War I, and then again during World War II. In the intervening years, some states and communities observed daylight-saving time, using whatever beginning and ending dates they chose. In 1966, Congress passed the Uniform Time Act, which provided that any state or territory choosing to observe daylight-saving time must begin and end on the federal dates. Any state could, by law, exempt itself; a 1972 amendment to the act authorized states in more than one time zone to exempt the entire state or one time zone only. Currently, most of Arizona, Hawaii, Puerto Rico, the U.S. Virgin Islands, Guam, American Samoa, and Northern Mariana Isls. do not observe daylight-saving time. On Apr. 2, 2006, all of Indiana observed daylight-saving time for the first time. (The state is divided between two time zones.)

Congress and the secretary of transportation both have authority to change time zone boundaries, which they have done on a number of occasions since 1966. In addition, efforts to conserve energy have prompted various changes in the times that daylight-saving time is observed.

Daylight-Saving Time: International Usage

Adjusting clock time so as to gain daylight on summer evenings is common throughout the world.

Canada, which extends over six time zones, generally observes daylight-saving time during the same period as the U.S. Most provincial governments observe the four-week extension to daylight-saving time that went into effect in 2007. Most of Saskatchewan remains on standard time year-round. Communities elsewhere in Canada also may exempt themselves from daylight-saving time. Except for the state of Sonora, which shares a border with Arizona, most of Mexico observes daylight-saving time.

Member nations of the European Union observe a "summer-time period," a version of daylight-saving time, from the last Sunday of Mar. until the last Sunday in Oct.

Russia, which extends geographically over 11 time zones and uses 9, historically has maintained its standard time one hour ahead of its zone designation. Additionally, Russian observation of daylight-saving time ended in 2011. Though an hour of time was added in Mar. 2011, clocks were not set back an hour in the fall, meaning that standard time in most of Russia is effectively 2 hours ahead of the zone designation.

China, which extends across five time zones, has decreed that the entire country be placed on Greenwich time plus 8 hours. Daylight-saving time is not observed. Japan, which lies within one time zone, also does not modify its legal time during the summer months.

Many countries in the Southern Hemisphere maintain daylight-saving time generally from Oct. to Mar. However, most countries near the equator do not deviate from standard time.

WEIGHTS AND MEASURES

Source: National Institute of Standards and Technology (NIST), U.S. Dept. of Commerce

International System of Units (SI)

Two systems of weights and measures coexist in the U.S. today: the **U.S. Customary System** and the **International System of Units** (SI, for Système International d'Unités). The SI is a more complete, coherent version of the **metric system**. Throughout U.S. history, the Customary System—parts of which were inherited but are now different from the British Imperial System—has been generally used. Federal and state legislation gave it, through implication, standing as the primary weights and measures system. The metric system, however, is the only system that Congress has ever specifically sanctioned, dating back to an 1866 law. The U.S. was one of the original 17 countries to sign the International Metric Convention (or Treaty of the Meter) May 20, 1875, which established several intergovernmental organizations to oversee and refine the SI. The U.S. is represented at these organizations by the Natl. Institute of Standards and Technology (NIST).

Since that time, use of the metric system in the U.S. has slowly increased, particularly in the scientific community, the pharmaceutical industry, and the manufacturing sector—the last motivated by the predominant use of the metric system in international commerce.

On Dec. 23, 1975, Pres. Gerald R. Ford signed the Metric Conversion Act of 1975. It defined the "metric system of measurement" as the SI, as established in 1960 by the General Conference on Weights and Measures and interpreted in the U.S. by the secretary of commerce, who delegated that authority to the director of the NIST. The Trade and Competitiveness Act of 1988 declared the metric system the preferred system of weights and measures for U.S. trade and commerce, but explicitly permitted "the continued use of traditional systems of weights and measures in nonbusiness activities." The Code of Federal Regulations made the use of metric units mandatory for federal agencies in 1991. However, the metric system has still not become the system of choice for most Americans' daily use.

The following are the seven base SI units: **length**—meter; **mass**—kilogram; **time**—second; **electric current**—ampere; **thermodynamic temperature**—kelvin; **amount of substance**—mole; and **luminous intensity**—candela.

Frequently Used Conversions

Boldface indicates exact values. For greater accuracy, use the "multiply by" number in parentheses. For weights, avoirdupois (avdp) weight is the system applied to all goods except medicines, precious metals, and precious stones.

U.S. Customary to Metric

	If you have:	Multiply by:		To get:
Length	inches	**25.4**		millimeters
	inches	**2.54**		centimeters
	inches	**0.0254**		meters
	feet	0.3	**(0.3048)**	meters
	yards	0.9	**(0.9144)**	meters
	miles[1]	1.6	**(1.609344)**	kilometers
Area	sq inches	6.5	**(6.4516)**	sq cm
	sq feet	0.09	**(0.09290304)**	sq meters
	sq yards	0.84	**(0.83612736)**	sq meters
	acres	0.4	(0.4046873)	hectares
	sq miles[1]	2.6	(2.58998811)	sq kilometers
Weight	ounces (avdp)	28	(28.34952)	grams
	pounds (avdp)	454	(453.59237)	grams
	pounds (avdp)	0.45	**(0.45359237)**	kilograms
	short tons[2]	0.91	**(0.90718474)**	metric tons
	long tons[3]	1	(1.016047)	metric tons
Liquid	ounces	0.03	(0.02957353)	liters
	cups	0.24	(0.23658824)	liters
	pints	0.47	(0.473176473)	liters
	quarts	0.95	(0.946352946)	liters
	gallons	3.79	(3.785412)	liters

Metric to U.S. Customary

	If you have:	Multiply by:		To get:
Length	millimeters	0.04	(0.03937)	inches
	centimeters	0.4	(0.3937)	inches
	meters	.39	(39.37)	inches
	meters	3.3	(3.280840)	feet
	meters	1.1	(1.093613)	yards
	kilometers	0.6	(0.621371)	miles[1]
Area	sq cm	0.16	(0.15500)	sq inches
	sq meters	10.8	(10.76391)	sq feet
	sq meters	1.2	(1.195990)	sq yards
	hectares	2.5	(2.471044)	acres
	sq kilometers	0.39	(0.386102)	sq miles[1]
Weight	grams	0.035	(0.03527396)	ounces (avdp)
	grams	0.002	(0.00220462)	pounds (avdp)
	kilograms	2.2	(2.204623)	pounds (avdp)
	metric tons	1.1	(1.102311)	short tons[2]
	metric tons	0.98	(0.9842065)	long tons[3]
Liquid	liters	33.8	(33.81402)	ounces
	liters	4.2	(4.226752)	cups
	liters	2.1	(2.113376)	pints
	liters	1.1	(1.056688)	quarts
	liters	0.26	(0.264172)	gallons

(1) Survey mile. (2) A short ton is 2,000 pounds. (3) A long ton is 2,240 pounds.

Temperature Conversions

The left-hand column below gives a temperature according to the **Celsius** scale, and the right-hand gives the same temperature according to the **Fahrenheit** scale. The lowest number on each scale is equivalent to absolute zero, the theoretical temperature at which all molecular motion would stop.

For temperatures not shown: To convert Fahrenheit to Celsius, subtract 32 degrees and divide by 1.8; to convert Celsius to Fahrenheit, multiply by 1.8 and add 32 degrees.

Celsius	Fahrenheit	Celsius	Fahrenheit	Celsius	Fahrenheit	Celsius	Fahrenheit	Celsius	Fahrenheit
−273.15	−459.67	−45.6	−50	−1.1	30	30	86	65.6	150
−250	−418	**−40**	**−40**	**0**	**32**	32.2	90	70	158
−200	−328	−34.4	−30	4.4	40	35	95	80	176
−184.4	−300	−30	−22	10	50	**37**	**98.6**	90	194
−156.7	−250	−28.9	−20	15.6	60	37.8	100	93.3	200
−150	−238	−23.3	−10	**20**	**68**	40	104	**100**	**212**
−128.9	−200	−20	−4	21.1	70	43.3	110	121.1	250
−101.1	−150	−17.8	0	23.9	75	48.9	120	148.9	300
−100	−148	−12.2	10	25	77	50	122	150	302
−73.3	−100	−10	14	26.7	80	54.4	130	200	392
−50	−58	−6.7	20	29.4	85	60	140	300	572

Note: Although the term *centigrade* is still frequently used, the International Committee on Weights and Measures and the National Institute of Standards and Technology have recommended since 1948 that this scale be called *Celsius*.

Boiling and Freezing Points

Water boils at 212°F (100°C) at sea level. For every 550 feet above sea level, the boiling point of water is lower by about 1°F. Methyl alcohol boils at 148.5°F. Average human oral temperature is 98.6°F. **Water freezes** at 32°F (0°C).

Mathematical Formulas

The value of π (the Greek letter pi) is approximately 3.14159265 (equal to the ratio of the circumference of a circle to its diameter). The equivalence is typically rounded further to 3.1416 or 3.14.

Calculating Circumference

Circle: Multiply the diameter by π.

Calculating Area

Circle: Multiply the square of the radius (equal to ½ the diameter) by π.
Rectangle: Multiply the length of the base by the height.
Sphere (surface): Multiply the square of the radius by π and multiply by 4.
Square: Square the length of one side.
Trapezoid: Add the 2 parallel sides, multiply by the height, and divide by 2.
Triangle: Multiply the base by the height and divide by 2.

Calculating Volume

Cone: Multiply the square of the radius of the base by π, multiply by the height, and divide by 3.
Cube: Cube the length of one edge.
Cylinder: Multiply the square of the radius of the base by π and multiply by the height.
Pyramid: Multiply the area of the base by the height and divide by 3.
Rectangular prism: Multiply the length by the width by the height.
Sphere: Multiply the cube of the radius by π, multiply by 4, and divide by 3.

Playing Cards and Dice Chances

5-Card Poker Hands

Hand	Number possible	Odds against
Royal flush	4	649,739 to 1
Other straight flush	36	72,192 to 1
Four of a kind	624	4,164 to 1
Full house	3,744	693 to 1
Flush	5,108	508 to 1
Straight	10,200	254 to 1
Three of a kind	54,912	46 to 1
Two pairs	123,552	20 to 1
One pair	1,098,240	4 to 3 (1.37 to 1)
Nothing	1,302,540	1 to 1
Total	**2,598,960**	

Bridge

The odds—against suit distribution in a hand of 4-4-3-2 are about 4 to 1; against 5-4-2-2 about 8 to 1; against 6-4-2-1 about 20 to 1; against 7-4-1-1 about 254 to 1; against 8-4-1-0 about 2,211 to 1; and against 13-0-0-0 about 158,753,389,899 to 1.

Dice
(probabilities on 2 dice)

Total	Odds against (single toss)	Total	Odds against (single toss)
2	35 to 1	8	31 to 5
3	17 to 1	9	8 to 1
4	11 to 1	10	11 to 1
5	8 to 1	11	17 to 1
6	31 to 5	12	35 to 1
7	5 to 1		

Large Numbers

No. of zeros	U.S.	British[1], French, German	No. of zeros	U.S.	British[1], French, German
6	million	million	42	tredecillion	septillion
9	billion	milliard	45	quattuordecillion	1,000 septillion
12	trillion	billion	48	quindecillion	octillion
15	quadrillion	1,000 billion	51	sexdecillion	1,000 octillion
18	quintillion	trillion	54	septendecillion	nonillion
21	sextillion	1,000 trillion	57	octodecillion	1,000 nonillion
24	septillion	quadrillion	60	novemdecillion	decillion
27	octillion	1,000 quadrillion	63	vigintillion	1,000 decillion
30	nonillion	quintillion	100	googol	googol
33	decillion	1,000 quintillion	303	centillion	NA
36	undecillion	sextillion	600	NA	centillion
39	duodecillion	1,000 sextillion	googol	googolplex	googolplex

NA = Not available. (1) In recent years, it has become more common in Britain to use U.S. terminology for large numbers.

Prime Numbers to 1,009

A prime number is any positive integer greater than 1 that is divisible only by two positive integers—1 and itself.

	2	3	5	7	11	13	17	19	23
29	31	37	41	43	47	53	59	61	67
71	73	79	83	89	97	101	103	107	109
113	127	131	137	139	149	151	157	163	167
173	179	181	191	193	197	199	211	223	227
229	233	239	241	251	257	263	269	271	277
281	283	293	307	311	313	317	331	337	347
349	353	359	367	373	379	383	389	397	401
409	419	421	431	433	439	443	449	457	461
463	467	479	487	491	499	503	509	521	523
541	547	557	563	569	571	577	587	593	599
601	607	613	617	619	631	641	643	647	653
659	661	673	677	683	691	701	709	719	727
733	739	743	751	757	761	769	773	787	797
809	811	821	823	827	829	839	853	857	859
863	877	881	883	887	907	911	919	929	937
941	947	953	967	971	977	983	991	997	1,009

Common Fractions Converted to Decimals

8ths	16ths	32nds	64ths	=
			1	= 0.015625
		1	2	= 0.03125
			3	= 0.046875
	1	2	4	= 0.0625
			5	= 0.078125
	3	6		= 0.09375
			7	= 0.109375
1	2	4	8	= 0.125
			9	= 0.140625
	5	10		= 0.15625
			11	= 0.171875
	3	6	12	= 0.1875
			13	= 0.203125
	7	14		= 0.21875
			15	= 0.234375
2	4	8	16	= 0.25

8ths	16ths	32nds	64ths	=
			17	= 0.265625
	9	18		= 0.28125
			19	= 0.296875
	5	10	20	= 0.3125
			21	= 0.328125
	11	22		= 0.34375
			23	= 0.359375
3	6	12	24	= 0.375
			25	= 0.390625
	13	26		= 0.40625
			27	= 0.421875
	7	14	28	= 0.4375
			29	= 0.453125
	15	30		= 0.46875
			31	= 0.484375
4	8	16	32	= 0.5

8ths	16ths	32nds	64ths	=
			33	= 0.515625
	17	34		= 0.53125
			35	= 0.546875
	9	18	36	= 0.5625
			37	= 0.578125
	19	38		= 0.59375
			39	= 0.609375
5	10	20	40	= 0.625
			41	= 0.640625
	21	42		= 0.65625
			43	= 0.671875
	11	22	44	= 0.6875
			45	= 0.703125
	23	46		= 0.71875
			47	= 0.734375
6	12	24	48	= 0.75

8ths	16ths	32nds	64ths	=
			49	= 0.765625
	25	50		= 0.78125
			51	= 0.796875
	13	26	52	= 0.8125
			53	= 0.828125
	27	54		= 0.84375
			55	= 0.859375
7	14	28	56	= 0.875
			57	= 0.890625
	29	58		= 0.90625
			59	= 0.921875
	15	30	60	= 0.9375
			61	= 0.953125
	31	62		= 0.96875
			63	= 0.984375
8	16	32	64	= 1.0

Roman Numerals

I — 1	IV — 4	VII — 7	X — 10	XX — 20	L — 50	C — 100	D — 500
II — 2	V — 5	VIII — 8	XI — 11	XXX — 30	LX — 60	CC — 200	CM — 900
III — 3	VI — 6	IX — 9	XIX — 19	XL — 40	XC — 90	CD — 400	M — 1,000

Note: The numerals V, X, L, C, D, or M shown with a horizontal line on top denote 1,000 times the original value.

Ancient Measures

Biblical
Cubit . . . . = 21.8 inches
Omer . . . . = 0.45 peck
= 3.964 liters
Ephah . . . . = 10 omers
Shekel . . . . = 0.497 ounce
= 14.1 grams

Greek
Cubit . . . . = 18.3 inches
Stadion . . . . = 607.2 or 622 feet
Obolos . . . . = 715.38 milligrams
Drachma . . . . = 4.2923 grams
Mina . . . . = 0.9463 pound
Talent . . . . = 60 mina

Roman
Cubit . . . . = 17.5 inches
Stadium . . . . = 202 yards
As, libra,
pondus . . . . = 325.971 grams
= 0.71864 pound

Metric System Prefixes

The following prefixes, in combination with the basic unit names, provide the multiples and submultiples in the metric system. For example, the unit name *meter*, with the prefix *kilo* added, produces *kilometer*, meaning "1,000 meters."

Prefix	Symbol	Multiples	Equivalent	Prefix	Symbol	Multiples	Equivalent
yotta	Y	10^{24}	septillionfold	deci	d	10^{-1}	tenth part
zetta	Z	10^{21}	sextillionfold	centi	c	10^{-2}	hundredth part
exa	E	10^{18}	quintillionfold	milli	m	10^{-3}	thousandth part
peta	P	10^{15}	quadrillionfold	micro	µ	10^{-6}	millionth part
tera	T	10^{12}	trillionfold	nano	n	10^{-9}	billionth part
giga	G	10^{9}	billionfold	pico	p	10^{-12}	trillionth part
mega	M	10^{6}	millionfold	femto	f	10^{-15}	quadrillionth part
kilo	k	10^{3}	thousandfold	atto	a	10^{-18}	quintillionth part
hecto	h	10^{2}	hundredfold	zepto	z	10^{-21}	sextillionth part
deka	da	10^{1}	tenfold	yocto	y	10^{-24}	septillionth part

Weight and Measurement Equivalents

In this table, there is a distinction between the international foot and the survey foot. The international foot, defined in 1959 as exactly equal to 0.3048 meter, is shorter than the survey foot by exactly 2 parts in 1 million. This means that an international mile is about ⅛ inch shorter than the survey mile. The survey foot is still used in the publication of some geodetic surveys within the U.S. In this table, the survey foot is indicated with capital letters, as FEET.

When the name of a unit is enclosed in brackets, either (1) the unit is not in general current use in the U.S. or (2) the unit is believed to be based on custom and usage rather than on formal definition.

Equivalents involving decimals are, in most instances, rounded to the third decimal place; exact equivalents are so designated.

Lengths

1 angstrom (Å) . . . . = 0.1 nanometer (exactly)
= 0.0001 micrometer (exactly)
= 0.0000001 millimeter (exactly)
= 0.000000004 inch
1 cable's length . . . . = 120 fathoms (exactly)
= 720 FEET (exactly)
= 219 meters
1 centimeter (cm) . . . . = 0.3937 inch
1 chain (ch) (engineer's) . . . . . . = 30.48 meters (exactly)
= 100 feet
1 chain (Gunter's
or surveyor's) . . . . = 66 FEET (exactly)
= 20.1168 meters
1 decimeter (dm) . . . . = 3.937 inches
1 degree (geographical) . . . . . . = 364,566.929 feet
= 69.047 miles (avg.)
= 111.123 kilometers (avg.)
of latitude . . . . = 68.708 miles at equator
= 69.403 miles at poles
of longitude . . . . = 69.171 miles at equator

1 dekameter (dam) . . . . = 32.808 feet
1 fathom (fath) . . . . = 6 FEET (exactly)
= 1.8288 meters
1 foot (ft) . . . . = 12 inches (exactly)
= 0.3048 meters (exactly)
= 0.015 chains (surveyor's)
1 furlong (fur) . . . . = 660 FEET (exactly)
= ⅛ survey mile (exactly)
= 201.168 meters
[1 hand (height measure for
horses, from ground to top
of their shoulders)] . . . . = 4 inches
1 inch (in.) . . . . = 2.54 centimeters (exactly)
1 kilometer (km) . . . . = 0.621371 mile
= 3,280.8 feet
1 league (land) . . . . = 3 survey miles (exactly)
= 4.828 kilometers
1 link (engineer's) . . . . = 1 foot
= 0.305 meter
1 link (Gunter's or surveyor's) . . = 7.92 inches (exactly)
= 0.201 meter

1 meter (m). . . . . = 39.37 inches
= 1.09361 yards
1 micrometer (µm) . . . . = 0.001 millimeter (exactly)
= 0.00003937 inch
1 mil . . . . = 0.001 inch (exactly)
= 0.0254 millimeter (exactly)
1 mile (mi) (statute or land). . . = 5,280 FEET (exactly)
= 1.609344 kilometers (exactly)
1 mile (nmi) (international
nautical) . . . . = 1.852 kilometers (exactly)
= 1.151 miles
= 6,076.1 feet
1 millimeter (mm) . . . . = 0.03937 inch
1 nanometer (nm) . . . . = 0.001 micrometer (exactly)
= 0.00000003937 inch
1 pica (typography) . . . . = 12 points
1 point (pt) (typography) . . . . . . = 0.013837 inch (exactly)
= 0.351 millimeter
1 rod (rd), pole, or perch. . . . . . = 16½ FEET (exactly)
= 5.029 meters
1 yard (yd) . . . . = 3 feet (exactly)
= 0.9144 meter (exactly)

Areas or Surfaces

1 acre (A) . . . . = 43,560 square FEET (exactly)
= 4,840 square yards
= 0.405 hectare
1 are (a) . . . . = 119.599 square yards
= 0.025 acre
1 bolt (cloth measure):
length . . . . = 100 yards
width . . . . = 45 or 60 inches
1 hectare (ha). . . . . = 2.471 acres
[1 square (building)] . . . . = 100 square feet
1 square centimeter (cm²) . . . . = 0.155 square inch
1 square decimeter (dm²) . . . . . = 15.500 square inches
1 square foot (ft²) . . . . = 929.030 square centimeters
1 square inch (in.²) . . . . = 6.4516 square centimeters
(exactly)
1 square kilometer (km²) . . . . . = 247.104 acres
= 0.386102 square mile
1 square meter (m²) . . . . = 1.196 square yards
= 10.764 square feet
1 square mile (mi²) . . . . = 640 acres (exactly)
= 258.999 hectares
1 square millimeter (mm²) . . . . = 0.002 square inch
1 square rod (rd²), square
pole, or square perch . . . . . . = 25.293 square meters
1 square yard (yd²) . . . . = 0.836127 square meter

Capacities or Volumes

1 barrel (bbl), liquid . . . . = 31 to 42 gallons*
*There are a variety of "barrels" established by law or usage. For
example, federal taxes on fermented liquors are based on a
barrel of 31 gallons. Many state laws fix the "barrel for liquids" as
31½ gallons; one state fixes a 36-gallon barrel for cistern
measurement. Federal law recognizes a 40-gallon barrel for
"proof spirits." By custom, 42 gallons constitute a barrel of
crude oil or petroleum products for statistical purposes, and this
equivalent is recognized "for liquids" by some states.

1 barrel (bbl), standard for
fruits, vegetables, and other
dry commodities except dry
cranberries . . . . = 7,056 cubic inches
= 105 dry quarts
= 3.281 bushels, struck measure
1 barrel, standard, cranberry . . = 86⁴⁵/₆₄ dry quarts
= 2.709 bushels, struck measure
= 5,826 cubic inches
1 board foot (lumber measure) = a foot-square board 1 inch
thick
1 bushel (U.S.) (struck
measure) . . . . = 2,150.42 cu in. (exactly)
= 35.239 liters
[1 bushel, heaped (U.S.)] . . . . . = 2,747.715 cubic inches
= 1.278 bushels,
struck measure**
**Frequently recognized as 1¼ bushels, struck measure.
[1 bushel (bu) (British Imperial)
(struck measure)] . . . . = 1.032 U.S. bushels,
struck measure
= 2,219.36 cubic inches
1 cord (cd) (firewood) . . . . = 128 cubic feet (exactly)

1 cubic centimeter (cm³) . . . . . = 0.061 cubic inch
1 cubic decimeter (dm³). . . . . . = 61.024 cubic inches
1 cubic inch (in³) . . . . = 0.554 fluid ounce
= 4.433 fluid drams
= 16.387 cubic centimeters
1 cubic foot (ft³) . . . . = 7.481 gallons
= 28.317 cubic decimeters
1 cubic meter (m³) . . . . = 1.308 cubic yards
1 cubic yard (yd³). . . . . = 0.765 cubic meter
1 cup, measuring . . . . = 8 fluid ounces (exactly)
= ½ liquid pint (exactly)
1 dekaliter (daL) . . . . = 2.642 gallons
= 1.135 pecks
[1 dram, fluid (fl dr) (British)] . . . = 0.961 U.S. fluid dram
= 0.217 cubic inch
= 3.552 milliliters
1 gallon (gal) (U.S.) . . . . = 4 quarts, liquid (exactly)
= 231 cubic inches (exactly)
= 3.785 liters
= 0.833 British gallon
= 128 U.S. fluid ounces (exactly)
[1 gallon (British Imperial)]. . . . = 277.42 cubic inches
= 1.201 U.S. gallons
= 4.546 liters
= 160 British fluid ounces
(exactly)
1 gill (gi) . . . . = 7.219 cubic inches
= 4 fluid ounces (exactly)
= 0.118 liter
1 hectoliter (hL) . . . . = 26.418 gallons
= 2.838 bushels
1 liter (L) (1 cubic decimeter
exactly). . . . . = 1.057 liquid quarts
= 0.908 dry quart
= 61.024 cubic inches
1 milliliter (mL) (1 cu cm
exactly). . . . . = 0.271 fluid dram
= 16.231 minims
= 0.061 cubic inch
1 ounce, liquid (U.S.) . . . . = 1.805 cubic inches
= 29.574 milliliters
= 1.041 British fluid ounces
[1 ounce, fluid (fl oz) (British)] = 0.961 U.S. fluid ounce
= 1.734 cubic inches
= 28.412 milliliters
1 peck (pk) . . . . = 8.810 liters
1 pint (pt), dry . . . . = 33.600 cubic inches
= 0.551 liter
1 pint, liquid . . . . = 28.875 cubic inches (exactly)
= 0.473 liter
1 quart (qt), dry (U.S.) . . . . = 67.201 cubic inches
= 1.101 liters
= 0.969 British quart
1 quart, liquid (U.S.). . . . . = 2 pints, liquid (exactly)
= 4 cups (exactly)
= 57.75 cubic inches (exactly)
= 0.946 liter
= 0.833 British quart
[1 quart (British)] . . . . = 69.354 cubic inches
= 1.032 U.S. dry quarts
= 1.201 U.S. liquid quarts
1 tablespoon (T., Tbs, tbsp.) . . = 3 teaspoons (exactly)
= 4 fluid drams
= ½ fluid ounce (exactly)
1 teaspoon (t., tsp.) . . . . = ⅓ tablespoon (exactly)
= 1⅓ fluid drams***
***The equivalent "1 teaspoon = 1⅓ fluid drams" has been found
to correspond more closely with the actual capacities of
teaspoons in use than the equivalent "1 teaspoon = 1 fluid dram"
given by many dictionaries.

Weights or Masses

1 assay ton* (AT) . . . . = 29.167 grams
*Used in assaying. The assay ton bears the same relation to the
milligram that a ton of 2,000 pounds avoirdupois bears to the
ounce troy; hence, the weight in milligrams of precious metal
obtained from one assay ton of ore gives directly the number of
troy ounces to the net ton.

1 carat (c). . . . . = 200 milligrams (exactly)
= 3.086 grains
1 dram avoirdupois (dr avdp). . = 27¹¹/₃₂ (= 27.344) grains
= 1.772 grams
1 gamma (γ) . . . . = 1 microgram (exactly)
1 grain (gr) . . . . = 64.79891 milligrams (exactly)

1 gram (g)	= 15.432 grains
	= 0.035 ounce, avoirdupois
1 hundredweight, gross or long**	= 112 pounds (exactly)
	= 50.802 kilograms

**The gross, or long, ton and hundredweight are used commercially in the U.S. to only a limited extent, usually in restricted industrial fields. These units are the same as the British ton and hundredweight.

1 hundredweight, gross or short (cwt or net cwt)	= 100 pounds (exactly)
	= 45.359 kilograms
1 kilogram (kg)	= 2.20462 pounds
1 microgram (µg)	= 0.000001 gram (exactly)
1 milligram (mg)	= 0.015 grain
1 ounce, avoirdupois (oz avdp)	= 437.5 grains (exactly)
	= 0.911 troy ounce
	= 28.3495 grams
1 ounce, troy (oz t)	= 480 grains (exactly)
	= 1.097 avoirdupois ounces
	= 31.103 grams

1 pennyweight (dwt)	= 1.555 grams
1 pound, avoirdupois (lb avdp)	= 7,000 grains (exactly)
	= 1.215 troy pounds
	= 453.59237 grams (exactly)
1 pound, troy (lb t)	= 5,760 grains (exactly)
	= 0.823 avoirdupois pound
	= 373.242 grams
1 stone (st)	= 14 pounds avdp (exactly)
	= 6.350 kilograms
1 ton, gross or long	= 2,240 pounds (exactly)
	= 1.12 net tons (exactly)
	= 1.016 metric tons
1 ton, metric (t)	= 2,204.623 pounds
	= 0.984 gross ton
	= 1.102 net tons
1 ton, net or short (tn)	= 2,000 pounds (exactly)
	= 0.893 gross ton
	= 0.907 metric ton

Electrical Units

The **watt** (W) is the unit of power (electrical, mechanical, thermal). Electrical power is given by the product of the voltage and the current.

Energy is sold by the **joule** (J), but in common practice the billing of electrical energy is expressed in terms of the **kilowatt-hour** (kWh), which is 3,600,000 joules, or 3.6 megajoules.

The **horsepower** (hp) is a nonmetric unit sometimes used in mechanics. It is equal to 746 watts.

The **ohm** (Ω) is the unit of electrical resistance and represents the physical property of a conductor that offers a resistance to the flow of electricity, permitting just 1 ampere to flow at 1 volt of pressure.

Measures of Force and Pressure

Dyne (dyn) = force necessary to accelerate a 1-gram mass 1 centimeter per second squared = 0.000072 poundal

Poundal (pdl) = force necessary to accelerate a 1-pound mass 1 foot per second squared = 13,825.5 dynes = 0.138255 newton

Newton (N) = force needed to accelerate a 1-kilogram mass 1 meter per second squared = 100,000 dynes (exactly)

Pascal (pressure) (Pa) = 1 newton per square meter = 0.020885 pound per square foot

Atmosphere (air pressure at sea level) (atm) = 2,116.217 pounds per square foot = 14.6959 pounds per square inch = 1.0332 kilograms per square centimeter = 101,325 newtons per square meter

Measures of Alcohol

Pony	= 1.0 fluid ounce
Shot	= varies, usu. 1.0-1.5 fluid ounces
Jigger	= 1.5 fluid ounces
Pint (pt)	= 16 fluid ounces
	= 0.625 fifth
Fifth	= 25.6 fluid ounces
	= 1.6 pints
	= 0.8 quart
	= 0.757 liter

Quart (qt)	= 32 fluid ounces
	= 1.25 fifths
Wine bottle (standard)	= 0.75 liter
	= 25.4 fluid ounces
Magnum	= 1.5 liters

For champagne and brandy:

Jeroboam	= 2 magnums
	= 3 liters
	= 101 fluid ounces

For champagne:

Rehoboam	= 3 magnums
Methuselah	= 4 magnums
Salmanazar	= 6 magnums
Balthazar	= 8 magnums
Nebuchadnezzar	= 10 magnums

Miscellaneous Measures

Caliber (cal)—the diameter of a gun bore. In the U.S., caliber is traditionally expressed in hundredths of inches, e.g., .22. In Britain, caliber is often expressed in thousandths of inches, e.g., .270. Now it is commonly expressed in millimeters, e.g., the 5.56 mm M16 rifle. The caliber of heavier weapons has long been expressed in millimeters, e.g., the 155 mm howitzer. Naval guns' caliber refers to the barrel length as a multiple of the bore diameter. A 5-inch, 50-caliber naval gun has a 5-inch bore and a barrel length of 250 inches.

Decibel (dB)—a measure of the relative intensity of sound. The threshold of hearing is given as 0 decibels. A 20-decibel sound is 10 times more intense than a 10-decibel sound; 30 decibels is 100 times more intense. (A 10-decibel increase corresponds generally to the perception of a sound being twice as loud.) One decibel is the smallest difference between sounds detectable by the human ear. A 125-decibel sound is painful.

10 decibels	breathing
20	rustling leaves
30	whisper
40	refrigerator humming
50	quiet conversation
60	conversation, laughter
70	vacuum cleaner
80	city traffic
90	subway, lawn mower
100	chainsaw

Em—a printer's measure designating the square width of any given type size. For example, an em of 10-point type is 10 points. An en is half an em.

Gauge (ga)—the diameter of a shotgun bore. Gauge numbers originally referred to the number of lead balls—of equal diameter as the gun barrel—required to make a pound. Thus, a 16-gauge shotgun's bore was smaller than a 12-gauge shotgun's. Today, an international agreement assigns millimeter measures to each gauge.

Gauge	Bore diameter (mm)	Gauge	Bore diameter (mm)
6	23.34	14	17.60
10	19.67	16	16.81
12	18.52	20	15.90

Horsepower (hp)—the power needed to lift 550 pounds 1 foot in 1 second or to lift 33,000 pounds 1 foot in 1 minute. Equivalent to 746 watts or 2,546 British thermal units per hour.

Karat or carat (k or c)—a measure of fineness for gold equal to $\frac{1}{24}$ part of pure gold in an alloy. Thus 24-karat gold is pure; 18-karat gold is ¼ alloy. The carat is also used as a unit of weight for precious stones; it is equal to 200 milligrams or 3.086 grains.

Knot (kn or kt)—a measure of the speed of ships. A knot equals 1 nautical mile per hour.

Quire (qr)—25 sheets of paper of the same size and quality.

Ream (rm)—500 sheets of paper of the same size and quality.

POSTAL INFORMATION

Administration of the U.S. Postal Service

The Postal Reorganization Act, creating a government-owned postal service under the executive branch and replacing the old Post Office Department, was signed into law by Pres. Richard Nixon, Aug. 12, 1970. The service officially came into being on July 1, 1971. The U.S. Postal Service is governed by an 11-person board of governors. Nine of the members are appointed by the president, with Senate approval. These nine choose a postmaster general. The board and the postmaster general choose the 11th member, who serves as deputy postmaster general.

Congress passed the Postal Accountability and Enhancement Act, which overhauled postal service operations for the first time since 1971, on Dec. 8, 2006. New operating provisions included the ability to adjust rates annually, negotiate for contracts, and invest profits in internal improvements. (The Postal Service last received a public service subsidy, i.e., taxpayer dollars, in 1982.)

Historical Postage Rates, 1851-2014

Postage cost for a prepaid, 1-oz. letter (the first-class standard after July 1, 1885).

Effective date	Rate	2014 dollars	Effective date	Rate	2014 dollars	Effective date	Rate	2014 dollars
July 1, 1851	$0.06[1]	NA	May 16, 1971	$0.08	$0.47	Jan. 10, 1999	$0.33	$0.47
July 1, 1863	0.06	NA	Mar. 2, 1974	0.10	0.48	Jan. 7, 2001	0.34	0.46
Oct. 1, 1883	0.04	NA	Dec. 31, 1975	0.13	0.58	June 30, 2002	0.37	0.49
July 1, 1885	0.02	NA	May 29, 1978	0.15	0.55	Jan. 8, 2006	0.39	0.46
Nov. 2, 1917	0.03[2]	$0.56	Mar. 22, 1981	0.18	0.47	May 14, 2007	0.41	0.47
July 1, 1919	0.02[2]	0.28	Nov. 1, 1981	0.20	0.52	May 12, 2008	0.42	0.46
July 6, 1932	0.03	0.52	Feb. 17, 1985	0.22	0.49	May 11, 2009	0.44	0.49
Aug. 1, 1958	0.04	0.33	Apr. 3, 1988	0.25	0.50	Jan. 22, 2012	0.45	0.47
Jan. 7, 1963	0.05	0.39	Feb. 3, 1991	0.29	0.51	Jan. 27, 2013	0.46	0.47
Jan. 7, 1968	0.06	0.41	Jan. 1, 1995	0.32	0.50	Jan. 26, 2014	0.49[3]	0.49

(1) For prepaid domestic letters traveling under 3,000 miles. (2) The price increased one cent during World War I; Congress restored its prewar rate in 1919. (3) The Postal Regulatory Commission approved a 6% total price increase: a 1.7% increase for inflation and an additional 4.3% temporary increase to compensate for USPS losses during the 2008-09 recession.

Status of the U.S. Postal Service, 2001-13

Source: *Postal Facts 2014*, U.S. Postal Service

	2001	2005	2007	2008	2009	2010	2011	2012	2013	% change, 2001-13
Total mail items (bil)	207.5	211.7	212.2	202.7	177.0	170.9	168.3	159.9	158.4	-23.7%
First-class mail items (bil)	103.7	98.1	95.9	91.7	83.8	77.6	72.5	68.7	65.8	-36.5
Stamped mail items (bil)	53.6	45.9	42.3	35.4	31.6	28.9	25.8	23.2	22.6	-57.8
Advertising mail items (bil)	89.9	100.9	103.5	99.1	82.7	81.8	84.0	79.5	80.9	-10.0
Annual revenue (bil)	$65.8	$69.9	$74.7	$74.9	$68.0	$67.1	$65.7	$65.2	$67.3	2.3
Total retail revenue (bil)	$14.8	$17.3	$18.5	$18.7	$17.7	$17.5	$16.9	$17.5	$18.3	23.6
Total customer visits (bil)	1.4	1.3	1.2	1.2	1.1	1.1	1.0	1.0	1.0	-27.3
Delivery points (mil)	137.7	144.3	148.0	149.2	150.0	150.9	151.5	152.1	152.9	11.0
Total delivery routes	242,600	243,000	246,500	244,800	232,900	230,600	228,160	227,000	225,152	-7.2
Total retail offices	38,123	37,142	36,451	36,723	36,496	36,222	35,756	35,369	35,074	-8.0
Career employees	775,903	704,716	684,762	663,238	623,128	583,908	551,570	522,144	489,727	-36.9

U.S. Domestic Mail Rates

Source: *Price List (Notice 123)*, U.S. Postal Service. Effective Jan. 26, 2014. Rates are for domestic retail customers unless otherwise noted. Domestic rates apply to the U.S., its territories and possessions, APOs, FPOs, and Freely Associated States.

First-Class Mail

Includes written matter such as letters, postcards, bills, account statements, and any matter sealed or closed against inspection up to 13 oz. In most cases, **delivery is within 2-3 business days**.

Letters measuring up to 6⅛ by 11½ in. cost **49¢** for the first oz., 21¢ for each additional oz. or fraction thereof, up to 3.5 oz. Postcard postage is **34¢**. Large envelopes up to 12 by 15 in. (or letters over 3.5 oz.) cost **98¢** for the first ounce and 21¢ for each additional ounce or fraction thereof. Presort- and automation-compatible mail can qualify for lower rates if certain piece minimums, mailing permits, and other requirements are met.

Forever Stamps. The USPS introduced the "Forever" stamp Apr. 12, 2007, at an initial cost of 41¢. The Forever stamp can be purchased at the current First-Class standard rate and will always be valid as First-Class postage on standard envelopes weighing 1 oz. or less, even after rates increase.

Priority Mail

Due to expeditious handling and transportation, Priority Mail is **delivered within 1-3 business days** in most cases. Can be any mailable article up to 70 lbs and not over 108 in. in length and girth combined.

Priority Mail Flat Rate: $5.60, $5.75, or $5.95, regardless of weight, if matter fits into designated USPS flat-rate envelope. **$5.80, $12.35, or $17.45** if matter fits into flat-rate box.

Priority Mail Forever Prepaid Flat Rate packaging can be purchased online at the current priority mail flat rate and remains valid for use after future price increases.

Priority Mail Rates

Weight not over	Zone							
	1-2	3	4	5	6	7	8	9
1 lb	$5.60	$5.70	$5.85	$6.00	$6.20	$6.45	$6.95	$8.35
2	5.80	6.15	6.85	8.75	9.50	10.25	11.25	13.50
3	6.50	7.50	8.60	10.50	11.90	12.75	15.10	18.10
4	7.35	8.75	9.90	13.90	15.25	16.30	18.15	21.80
5	8.70	10.05	11.35	15.80	17.35	18.70	21.00	25.20
6	9.60	11.10	12.70	17.55	19.50	21.00	23.70	28.45
7	10.20	12.00	13.70	19.55	21.60	23.60	26.65	32.00
8	10.95	13.10	15.30	21.25	23.70	26.05	29.85	35.80
9	11.65	14.15	16.60	23.00	25.80	28.15	33.20	39.85
10	12.45	15.15	18.05	24.95	27.85	31.00	36.15	43.40

Priority Mail Express

Provides guaranteed expedited service for any mailable article up to 70 lbs and not over 108 in. in combined length and girth. Offers **next-day delivery** to most destinations; $12.50 additional charge for Sunday or holiday delivery. Prices start at $16.95 for items weighing up to 8 oz., dependent on distance. Includes insurance up to $100, mailing receipt, proof of delivery signature record, and tracking.

Priority Mail Express Flat Rate: $19.99, regardless of weight, if matter fits into designated USPS flat-rate envelope. **$44.95**, regardless of weight, if matter fits into designated flat-rate box.

Priority Mail Express Rates

Wt. not over	Zone							
	1-2	3	4	5	6	7	8	9
0.5 lb	$16.95	$21.25	$23.70	$25.75	$27.55	$29.25	$31.20	$38.05
1	17.95	23.95	28.85	32.30	33.45	35.50	36.60	44.65
2	19.15	25.55	31.45	35.20	36.65	38.80	40.15	49.00
3	20.05	26.75	35.35	40.50	42.25	44.75	46.00	56.10
4	21.35	28.50	37.70	45.80	47.60	50.40	51.75	63.15
5	24.00	32.00	40.20	49.00	53.50	56.05	57.55	70.20
6	27.45	36.65	46.60	55.70	58.60	61.60	63.50	77.45
7	30.10	40.15	53.40	60.90	63.65	67.30	69.70	85.05
8	33.05	44.05	57.85	65.50	69.10	73.05	75.05	91.55
9	34.35	45.80	60.00	70.05	74.45	78.70	80.80	98.60
10	36.15	47.75	62.30	73.20	78.30	82.75	84.85	103.50

Standard Post

Applies to nonurgent shipping and oversized packages not mailed as Priority Mail, Priority Mail Express, Media Mail, or Library Mail. (Parcel Select, a separate commercial service, is used by medium- and large-sized shippers.) **Delivery takes 2-8 business days** depending on distance.

Standard Post packages must not exceed 70 lbs or 130 in. in combined length and girth. Packages more than 84 in. and up to 108 in. in combined length and girth weighing under 20 lbs use the 20-lb (balloon) price. Packages exceeding 108 in. use the oversized price. Shipping costs to zones 1-4 are only available for the mailing of hazardous materials, live animals, or other items requiring ground transport.

Standard Post Rates

Weight not over	Zone						
	1-2	3	4	5	6	7	8-9
1 lb	$5.60	$5.70	$5.85	$5.87	$6.16	$6.45	$6.73
2	5.80	6.15	6.85	6.99	7.87	8.76	9.64
3	6.50	7.50	8.60	8.62	10.01	11.39	12.78
4	7.35	8.75	9.90	9.92	11.07	12.23	13.38
5	8.70	10.05	11.35	11.37	12.36	13.34	14.33
6	9.60	11.10	12.70	12.72	13.84	14.96	16.08
7	10.20	12.00	13.70	13.72	15.07	16.41	17.76
8	10.95	13.10	15.30	15.32	17.02	18.72	20.43
9	11.65	14.15	16.60	16.62	18.67	20.71	22.76
10	12.45	15.15	18.05	18.07	20.30	22.53	24.77
Balloon	19.60	24.60	30.00	30.02	32.75	35.48	38.21
Oversized	63.04	67.99	72.94	77.90	96.03	114.16	132.29

Library Mail

Applies to books, printed music, bound academic theses, periodicals, sound recordings, and certain other materials mailed between schools, public libraries, museums, and nonprofit religious, educational, scientific, labor, veterans, and fraternal organizations (or to or from such organizations). Advertising restrictions apply. **Delivery is in 2-8 business days.** Packages may not exceed 108 in. in combined length and girth. Rates are calculated by weight of a single piece: **$2.56,** up to 1 lb; $0.46 for each additional pound or fraction thereof up to 7 lbs; additional pounds thereafter, $0.44.

Media Mail

Applies to books of at least eight printed pages; 16-mm or narrower-width films; printed music; printed test materials; sound recordings; playscripts and book manuscripts; printed educational charts; loose-leaf pages and binders consisting of medical information; and computer-readable media. Advertising restrictions apply. **Delivery is in 2-8 business days.** Packages may not exceed 108 in. in combined length and girth. Maximum weight is 70 lbs.

Rates are calculated by weight of a single piece: **$2.69,** up to 1 lb; $0.48, each additional pound or fraction thereof up to 7 lbs; additional pounds thereafter, $0.46.

Standard Mail

(Commercial only) Limited to items less than 16 oz. such as solicitations, newsletters, flyers, advertising, and catalogs. May not be used for personal correspondence. There is a minimum volume of 200 pieces or 50 lbs per mailing. Specific bulk mail preparation and sortation requirements apply.

A minimum rate per piece applies to letters 3.3 oz. or less. Discounts for automation, presorted, carrier route, and destination entry, among others. Separate rates available for authorized nonprofit organizations.

Any mailer who uses standard mail is required to pay an annual fee of $220. Additional standards apply to mailings of nonidentical-weight pieces.

Periodicals

(Commercial only) Includes newspapers, magazines, and other printed matter published in a serial format (e.g., educational institution's course catalog).

Bound Printed Matter

(Commercial only) Applies to advertising, promotional, directory, or editorial material bound by permanent fastening (e.g., staples, glue, stitching) and consisting of sheets of which at least 90% are imprinted by any process other than handwriting or typewriting. Does not include stationery, such as pads of blank forms, or personal correspondence. **Delivery is in 2-8 business days.** Maximum weight is 15 lbs.

Domestic Mail Services and Fees

Adult signature required: $5.20 per piece; person 21 years of age or older must sign for shipment.

Adult signature restricted delivery: $5.45 per piece; specific addressee or agent 21 years of age or older must sign for shipment.

Certificate of mailing: $1.30 per piece.

Domestic money order: $1.25 for money orders $0.01 to $500; $1.65 for $500.01 to $1,000.

Pickup on demand: $20.00 per pickup; available for Priority Mail, Priority Mail Express, and Standard Post.

Restricted delivery: $5.05 per item. Item is delivered to addressee only or to an agent authorized to receive mail on behalf of addressee.

Return receipt: $2.70 for a receipt by mail if requested at time of mailing, $1.35 for email receipt. Fee is $5.25 if request is submitted after mailing.

Signature confirmation: $2.35 online, $2.90 at post office.

Tracking

Formerly known as Delivery Confirmation, tracking can be used with First-Class Mail parcels, Priority Mail, Standard Post, Standard Mail parcels, and Package Services (Bound Printed Matter, Media Mail, and Library Mail). Available for purchase at time of mailing only. Provides mailer with date and time of delivery or attempted deliveries. Electronic confirmation available for bar-coded matter.

Fee: First-Class Mail retail, $1.05; electronic, free. Priority Mail or Standard Post, free. Standard Mail electronic, $0.23. Package Services retail, $1.05; electronic, $0.23.

Change of Address

The USPS will forward mail to another address provided a Change of Address (COA) form has been filed in person (free) or online at www.usps.com ($1.05 fee). The form, which can be picked up at any post office, printed off the Internet, or requested by phone at (800) ASK-USPS, can also be dropped in any mailbox for free filing.

Special Handling

Provides preferential handling (for items such as live poultry and bees), but not preferential delivery, to a practical extent. Available for Priority Mail, First-Class Mail, Standard Post, and Media Mail for the following surcharge: up to 10 lb, $9.90; over 10 lb, $13.00.

Registered Mail

The most secure service provided by the USPS. USPS maintains a delivery record and provides sender with a mailing receipt. May be used with First-Class Mail or Priority Mail. Full value of item must be declared at time of registration and mailing. Insurance is included in fee for articles with a declared value of $0.01 up to $25,000. Fee: $11.95 for a declared value of $0, up to $31.80 for articles with a declared value of $10,000.01 to $11,000.00. For each additional $1,000.00 or fraction thereof above $11,000.00, add $1.55.

Collect on Delivery (COD)

Charge determined by amount to be collected or amount of insurance coverage desired, whichever is higher. Fee: $6.95 for amounts up to $50; $8.60 for $50.01-$100.00; $1.70 for each additional $100. Items must be sent as bona fide orders or be in conformity with agreements between senders and addressees. Maximum amount collectible is $1,000.

Certified Mail

Available on First-Class Mail or Priority Mail. A receipt is furnished at time of mailing, and evidence of delivery is obtained. Insurance coverage not provided. Fee: $3.30 in addition to regular postage. Can be combined with Return Receipt and Restricted Delivery with additional payment.

Insurance

Available with First-Class Mail, Priority Mail Express, Priority Mail, Standard Post, and Media Mail. Maximum liability $5,000. Matter for sale addressed to prospective purchasers who have not ordered it or authorized its sending cannot be insured. **Note:** Fees shown do not apply to Priority Mail Express items, which include $100 of insurance. Additional insurance on Priority Mail Express shipments can be purchased: $1.00 for a declared value of $100.01-$200.00; $2.60 for $200.01-$500.00; and $1.65 for each additional $500.

Declared value	Fee
$0.01 to $50.00	$2.10
$50.01 to $100.00	2.60
$100.01 to $200.00	3.30
$200.01 to $300.00	5.50
Each additional $100 or fraction thereof	1.25

International Mail Rates

Source: *Price List (Notice 123)*, U.S. Postal Service. Effective Jan. 26, 2014. Refer to www.usps.com for USPS price groups not shown here and weight limits by country.

First-Class Mail International

Letter-post items weighing up to 1 oz. and single postcards can be sent airmail for **$1.15** to all countries.

First-Class Package International

Weight not over	Price group 1 Canada	Price group 2 Mexico	Price group 3-5	Price group 6-9
2 oz.	$6.55	$6.55	$6.55	$6.55
4	7.65	8.85	9.45	9.15
8	8.80	11.55	12.75	12.15
12	9.55	13.50	14.90	14.30
16	10.95	15.05	16.75	16.25
20	12.35	16.60	18.60	18.20
24	13.75	18.15	20.45	20.15
28	15.15	19.70	22.30	22.10
32	16.55	21.25	24.15	24.05
36	17.95	22.80	26.00	26.00

Global Express Guaranteed

Provides international expedited delivery, in partnership with FedEx, to certain countries. Item to be mailed must not weigh more than 70 lbs nor measure more than 108 in. in combined length and girth. Rate: From $51.50 to countries in price group 1 up to $88.75 to countries in price group 8, for items not over 0.5 lb in weight.

Priority Mail Express International

Priority Mail Express International Flat Rate: $35.95 to Canada, **$46.50** to all other countries if matter fits into designated USPS legal flat-rate envelope (max. weight 4 lbs). **$66.95** to Canada, **$84.95** to all other countries if matter fits into flat-rate envelope or box (max. weight 20 lbs).

Priority Mail International

Delivery is in 6-10 business days in many markets. Items must not be more than 108 in. in length and girth combined; max. weight is 70 lbs, though the limit varies by country.
Priority Mail International Flat Rate: $20.55 to Canada, **$24.75** to all other countries if matter fits into designated USPS flat-rate envelope. **$20.55** (Canada)/**$24.75** (all other countries), **$42.25/$61.75**, or **$55.75/$80.50** if matter fits into USPS flat-rate box.

International Mail Services and Fees

Customs clearance and delivery: $6.00 per piece.
Insurance: Available to many countries for loss of or damage to items. Consult USPS for each country's indemnity limits.
International registered mail: Available for letter-post items only to most countries. Fee: $13.65.
International return receipt: Shows to whom and when item is delivered. Fee: $3.75 per piece (must be purchased at time of mailing).

International business reply: Provides foreign addressee with prepaid means of response to U.S. sender. Fee: $1.35 per card; $1.85 per envelope (up to 2 oz.).
International postal money order: $4.50 per money order; maximum amount for a single money order is $700. Only accepted in certain countries.

U.S. Postal Abbreviations

The abbreviations below are approved by the U.S. Postal Service for use in addresses.

Alabama	AL	Illinois	IL	Missouri	MO	Pennsylvania	PA
Alaska	AK	Indiana	IN	Montana	MT	Puerto Rico	PR
American Samoa	AS	Iowa	IA	Nebraska	NE	Rhode Island	RI
Arizona	AZ	Kansas	KS	Nevada	NV	South Carolina	SC
Arkansas	AR	Kentucky	KY	New Hampshire	NH	South Dakota	SD
California	CA	Louisiana	LA	New Jersey	NJ	Tennessee	TN
Colorado	CO	Maine	ME	New Mexico	NM	Texas	TX
Connecticut	CT	Marshall Islands[1]	MH	New York	NY	Utah	UT
Delaware	DE	Maryland	MD	North Carolina	NC	Vermont	VT
District of Columbia	DC	Massachusetts	MA	North Dakota	ND	Virgin Islands	VI
Florida	FL	Michigan	MI	Northern Mariana Isls.	MP	Virginia	VA
Georgia	GA	Micronesia,		Ohio	OH	Washington	WA
Guam	GU	Federated States of[1]	FM	Oklahoma	OK	West Virginia	WV
Hawaii	HI	Minnesota	MN	Oregon	OR	Wisconsin	WI
Idaho	ID	Mississippi	MS	Palau[1]	PW	Wyoming	WY

(1) Although an independent nation, this country is subject to domestic rates and fees.

Canadian Province and Territory Postal Abbreviations

Source: Canada Post

Alberta	AB	Nunavut	NU	Quebec	QC
British Columbia	BC	Ontario	ON	Saskatchewan	SK
Manitoba	MB	Prince Edward Island	PE	Yukon	YT
New Brunswick	NB				
		Newfoundland and Labrador	NL		
		Northwest Territories	NT		
		Nova Scotia	NS		

SOCIAL SECURITY AND WELFARE
Social Security Coverage

Source: Social Security Administration; World Almanac research; provisions shown are as under current law, Aug. 2014

Social Security Benefits

Social Security's **Old-Age, Survivors, and Disability Insurance (OASDI)** program benefits are based on a worker's **primary insurance amount (PIA)**, which is related by law to the average indexed monthly earnings (AIME) on which Social Security contributions have been paid. The full PIA is payable to a worker who retires at full retirement age (FRA), which is 65-67 depending on birth year, and to an entitled disabled worker at any age. Spouses and children of retired or disabled workers and survivors of deceased workers receive set proportions of the PIA subject to a family maximum amount.

The PIA is calculated by applying varying percentages to succeeding parts of the AIME. The formula is adjusted annually to reflect changes in average annual wages.

Increases in Social Security benefits are initiated for Dec. of each year, assuming the Consumer Price Index (CPI) for the third calendar quarter of the year increased relative to the base quarter, which is the third calendar quarter of the year in which an increase last took effect. The size of the benefit increase is determined by the percentage rise of the CPI between the quarters measured.

The **average monthly benefit** payable to all retired workers amounted to $1,294 in Dec. 2013. The average benefit for disabled workers in that month was $1,146.

Maximum Monthly Retired-Worker Benefits Payable for Individuals who Retired at Age 65[1]

Year attaining age 65	Maximum benefit—Payable at retirement	Payable effective Dec. 2013
1990	$975	$1,819
1995	1,199	1,885
1998	1,342	1,958
1999	1,373	1,977
2000	1,435	2,016
2001	1,538	2,087
2002	1,660	2,196
2003	1,721	2,246
2004	1,784	2,281
2005	1,874	2,332
2006	1,961	2,345
2007	1,998	2,313
2008	2,030	2,297
2009	2,172	2,323
2010	2,191	2,343
2011	2,249	2,405
2012	2,310	2,384
2013	2,414	2,450
2014	2,431	2,431

(1) Assumes retirement at beginning of year.

Amount of Work Required

To qualify for benefits, the worker generally must have worked a certain length of time in covered employment. Just how long depends on when the worker reaches age 62 or, if earlier, when he or she dies or becomes disabled. A person born after 1929 who dies, becomes disabled, or reaches 62 after 1991 must generally have had at least 10 years of work credit to qualify for benefits.

Contribution and Benefit Base

Calendar year	OASDI[1]	Calendar year	OASDI[1]	Calendar year	OASDI[1]
1994	$60,600	2001	$80,400	2008	$102,000
1995	61,200	2002	84,900	2009	106,800
1996	62,700	2003	87,000	2010	106,800
1997	65,400	2004	87,900	2011	106,800
1998	68,400	2005	90,000	2012	110,100
1999	72,600	2006	94,200	2013	113,700
2000	76,200	2007	97,500	2014	117,000

(1) Old-Age, Survivors, and Disability Insurance.

A person is **fully insured** when he or she has one quarter of coverage for every year after age 21 is reached (or 1950, if later) up to but not including the year the worker reaches 62, dies, or becomes disabled. In 2014, a person earns one quarter of coverage for each $1,200 of annual earnings in covered employment, up to four quarters per year.

To receive **disability benefits**, the worker, in addition to being fully insured, must generally have credit for 20 quarters of coverage out of the 40 calendar quarters before he or she became disabled. A disabled blind worker need meet only the fully insured requirement. Persons disabled before age 31 can qualify with a briefer period of coverage. Certain survivor benefits are payable if the deceased worker had 6 quarters of coverage in the 13 quarters preceding death.

Tax Rate Schedule
(percentage of covered earnings)

Year	Total (for employees and employers, each)	OASDI[1]	HI[2]
1979-80	6.13%	5.08%	1.05%
1981	6.65.	5.35.	1.30
1982-83	6.70.	5.40.	1.30
1984	7.00.	5.70.	1.30
1985	7.05.	5.70.	1.35
1986-87	7.15.	5.70.	1.45
1988-89	7.51.	6.06.	1.45
1990 and after[3]	7.65.	6.20.	1.45

Year	(for self-employed)		
1979-80	8.10%	7.05%	1.05%
1981	9.30.	8.00.	1.30
1982-83	9.35.	8.05.	1.30
1984	14.00.	11.40.	2.60
1985	14.10.	11.40.	2.70
1986-87	14.30.	11.40.	2.90
1988-89	15.02.	12.12.	2.90
1990 and after[3]	15.30.	12.40.	2.90

(1) Old-Age, Survivors, and Disability Ins. (2) Hospital Ins. (Medicare). (3) Public Law 111-147 exempted most employers from paying the employer share of OASDI payroll tax on wages paid Mar. 19-Dec. 31, 2010, to certain qualified individuals hired after Feb. 8, 2010. PL 111-312 reduced the OASDI payroll tax rate for 2011 by 2 percentage points for employees and for self-employed workers. PL 112-96 extended the 2011 rate reduction through 2012. The laws require that the general fund of the Treasury reimburses the OASI and DI Trust Funds for these temporary reductions.

What Aged Workers Receive

A person may receive monthly old-age benefits when he or she has enough work in covered employment and has reached retirement age—age 62 for reduced benefits or the age below for full benefits.

Full Retirement Age (FRA) by Birth Year

Year of birth	FRA	Year of birth	FRA
1937 or earlier	65	1955	66 and 2 mos.
1938	65 and 2 mos.	1956	66 and 4 mos.
1939	65 and 4 mos.	1957	66 and 6 mos.
1940	65 and 6 mos.	1958	66 and 8 mos.
1941	65 and 8 mos.	1959	66 and 10 mos.
1942	65 and 10 mos.	1960 or later	67
1943-54	66		

Note: If born on Jan. 1, refer to the previous birth year.

In 2000, the retirement earnings test was eliminated beginning with the month when the beneficiary reaches **full retirement age (FRA)**. A person at or above FRA no longer receives reduced benefits because of earnings. However, a person's benefits are reduced $1 for every $3 of earnings above the limit allowed by law ($41,400 for 2014) if he or she retires in the same calendar year but months prior to FRA. For retirees who have not yet attained FRA, the reduction is $1 for every $2 of earnings over the exempt amount ($15,480 for 2014).

For workers who reached age 65 between 1982 and 1989, Social Security benefits are raised by 3% for each year in which the worker did not receive benefits between FRA and 70 (72 before 1984), whether because of earnings from work, because the worker did not apply for benefits, or because the worker declined benefits after entitlement. The **delayed retirement credit** is 1% per year for workers who reached age 65 before 1982. The rate for workers who reached age 65 in 1998-99 is 5.5%; 2000-01, 6.0%; 2002-03, 6.5%; 2004-05, 7.0%. For 2006-07, it is 7.5%. The delayed retirement credit rose to 8% per year for 2008 and years after.

For workers retiring early, benefits are permanently reduced 5/9 of 1% for each month before the FRA, up to 36 months. If the number of months exceeds 36, then the benefit is further reduced 5/12 of 1% per month.

For example, when FRA reaches 67, for workers who retire at exactly age 62, there are a total of 60 months of reduction. The reduction for the first 36 months is 5/9 of 36%, or 20%. The reduction for the remaining 24 months is 5/12 of 24%, or 10%. Thus, when the FRA reaches 67, the amount of reduction at age 62 will be 30%. The nearer to FRA a person is when he or she begins collecting a benefit, the larger the monthly benefit will be.

Benefits for Worker's Spouse

The spouse of a worker who is getting Social Security retirement or disability payments may become entitled to an insurance benefit of **one-half of the worker's PIA** if claiming benefits at full retirement age. Reduced spouse's benefits are available at age 62 and are permanently reduced $25/36$ of 1% for each month before FRA, up to 36 months. If the number of months exceeds 36, then the benefit is further reduced $5/12$ of 1% per month. Benefits are also payable to the aged divorced spouse of an insured worker if he or she was married to the worker for at least 10 years. To qualify for divorced spouse benefits, the insured worker does not have to be receiving benefits if the divorce occurred at least two years earlier. Benefits received as a spouse are reduced by the amount of one's PIA.

Benefits for Children of Workers

If a retired or disabled worker has a child under age 18, the child will usually get a benefit equal to **one-half of the worker's unreduced benefit**. So will the worker's spouse, regardless of age, if he or she is caring for an entitled child of the worker, and the child is under 16 or became disabled before age 22. However, total benefits paid on a worker's earnings record are subject to a family maximum. Total monthly benefits paid to the family of a worker who retired in 2014 at age 66 and always had the maximum earnings creditable under Social Security cannot exceed $4,647.

Entitled children generally stop receiving benefits at age 18, though they can continue receiving benefits until age 19 if they attend elementary or secondary school full-time. A child disabled before age 22 may get a benefit as long as the disability meets the definition in the law.

Benefits may also be paid to a grandchild or step-grandchild of a worker or of his or her spouse, in special circumstances.

OASDI Beneficiaries				
Beneficiaries	May 2005	May 2010	May 2012	May 2014
Total (in thous.)[1]	48,068	53,349	56,158	58,586
Age 65 and over, total..	33,811	36,914	38,905	41,390
Retired workers.....	27,413	30,734	32,714	35,256
Disabled workers ...	112	339	453	457
Survivors/ dependents......	6,286	5,841	5,738	5,677
Under age 65, total...	14,257	16,435	17,253	17,196
Retired workers.....	2,809	3,314	3,407	3,184
Disabled workers	6,239	7,628	8,254	8,491
Survivors/ dependents......	5,209	5,492	5,592	5,521
Total monthly benefits (in mil)	$42,074	$56,966	$63,243	$69,518

OASDI = Old-Age, Survivors, and Disability Ins. (1) Numbers may not add up to totals due to rounding or incomplete enumeration.

What Disabled Workers Receive

A worker who becomes unable to work may be eligible for a monthly disability benefit. Benefits continue until it is determined that the individual is no longer disabled. When a disabled-worker beneficiary reaches FRA (66 years for workers born 1943-54), the disability benefit becomes a retired-worker benefit.

Benefits—like those for dependents of retired-worker beneficiaries generally—may be paid to dependents of disabled beneficiaries. However, the maximum family benefit in disability cases is generally lower than in retirement cases.

Survivor Benefits

If an insured worker should die, one or more types of benefits may be payable to survivors, again subject to a maximum family benefit described above.

1. If claiming benefits at FRA, the **surviving spouse** will receive a benefit equal to 100% of the deceased worker's benefit. Benefits claimed before FRA are reduced, with a maximum reduction of 28.5% at age 60. However, if the deceased worker claimed benefits before FRA, the surviving spouse's benefits are limited to the reduced amount the worker would be getting if alive, but not less than 82.5% of the worker's PIA. Remarriage after the worker's death ends the surviving spouse's benefit rights. However, if the widow(er) marries, and the marriage later ends, he or she regains benefit rights.

(A marriage after age 60, age 50 if disabled, is deemed not to have occurred for benefit purposes.) Survivor benefits may also be paid to a divorced spouse if the marriage lasted for at least 10 years.

Disabled widows and widowers may under certain circumstances qualify for benefits after attaining age 50 at the rate of 71.5% of the deceased worker's PIA. The widow or widower must have become totally disabled before or within seven years after the spouse's death or the last month in which he or she received mother's or father's insurance benefits.

2. There is a benefit for each **child under age 18**. The monthly benefit for a child of a deceased worker is $3/4$ of the PIA, subject to the family maximum. A child who became disabled before age 22 may also receive benefits. Also, a child can receive benefits until age 19 if he or she is in full-time attendance at an elementary or secondary school.

3. There is a **mother's or father's benefit** for the widow(er) if children of the worker who are under age 16 are in his or her care. The benefit is 75% of the PIA (subject to the family maximum), and it continues until the youngest child reaches age 16, at which time payments stop even if the child's benefit continues. Benefits may continue if the widow(er) has a disabled child beneficiary age 16 or over in his or her care.

4. Dependent parents may be eligible for benefits if they have been receiving at least half their support from the worker before his or her death, have reached age 62, and (except in certain circumstances) have not remarried since the worker's death. Each parent gets 75% of the worker's PIA; if only one parent survives, the benefit is 82% (could be reduced for the family maximum).

5. A lump sum cash payment of **$255** is made if the worker was living with a spouse or has a child who is eligible for immediate monthly survivor benefits.

Self-Employed Workers

A self-employed person who has **net earnings of $400 or more** in a year must report such earnings for Social Security tax and credit purposes. Income from real estate, savings, dividends, loans, pensions, or insurance policies are not included unless it is part of a person's business.

A self-employed person receives one quarter of coverage for each $1,200 for 2014, up to a maximum of four quarters per year.

The nonfarm self-employed have the option of reporting their earnings as $2/3$ of their gross income from self-employment. This option can be used only if actual net earnings from self-employment income are less than $1,600 and less than $2/3$ of their gross income. The option may be used only five times. Also, the self-employed person must have actual net earnings of $400 or more in two of the three taxable years immediately preceding the year in which he or she uses the option.

When a person has both taxable wages and earnings from self-employment, wages are credited for Social Security purposes first; only as much self-employment income as brings total earnings up to the current taxable maximum becomes subject to the self-employment tax.

Farm Owners and Workers

Self-employed farmers whose gross annual earnings from farming are from **$600 to $2,400** may report $2/3$ of their gross earnings instead of net earnings for Social Security purposes. (Farmers whose gross annual earnings are under $600 cannot use the optional method.) Farmers whose gross income is over $2,400 and whose net earnings are less than $1,600 can report $1,600. Cash or crop shares received from a tenant or share farmer count if the owner participated materially in production or management. The self-employed farmer pays contributions at the same rate as other self-employed persons.

Agricultural employees. A worker's earnings from farm work count toward benefits if (1) the employer pays the worker $150 or more in cash during the year or (2) the employer spends $2,500 or more in the year for agricultural labor. Under these rules, a person gets credit for one calendar quarter for each $1,200 in cash pay in 2014.

Foreign farm workers admitted to the U.S. on a temporary basis are not covered.

Household Workers

If an employer pays a household worker (e.g., maid, cook, laundry worker, nurse, babysitter, chauffeur, gardener) who is age 18 or older $1,900 or more in wages in 2014, the wages are covered under Social Security. This includes transportation costs paid for in cash. The job need not be regular or full-time.

The employee should get a Social Security card at the Social Security office and show it to the employer. The employer deducts the amount of the employee's Social Security tax from the worker's pay, adds an identical amount as the employer's Social Security tax, and sends the total amount to the federal government.

Medicare Coverage

Source: Centers for Medicare & Medicaid Services, U.S. Dept. of Health and Human Services

The Medicare health insurance program provides acute-care coverage for Social Security and Railroad Retirement beneficiaries age 65 and over; workers and spouses age 65 and over with sufficient Medicare-only coverage in federal, state, or local government employment; certain persons entitled to receive Social Security or Railroad Retirement disability benefits; certain disabled persons with Medicare-only coverage through government employment; certain persons with end-stage kidney disease; and certain persons in the vicinity of Libby, MT, with asbestos-related conditions. What follows is a basic description that may not cover all circumstances.

The **basic Medicare plan**, available nationwide, is a fee-for-service arrangement where the beneficiary may use any provider accepting Medicare. Some services are not covered, and there are some out-of-pocket costs.

Hospital insurance (Part A). The basic hospital insurance program pays covered services for hospital and post-hospital care, including:

- All necessary inpatient hospital care for the first 60 days of each benefit period, except for a deductible ($1,216 in 2014). For days 61-90, Medicare pays for services over and above the coinsurance ($304 per day in 2014). After 90 days, the beneficiary has 60 lifetime reserve days for which Medicare helps pay. The coinsurance amount for reserve days was $608 in 2014.
- Up to 100 days of care in a skilled-nursing facility in each benefit period. Hospital insurance pays for all covered services for the first 20 days; for days 21-100, the beneficiary pays coinsurance ($152 per day in 2014).
- Part-time home health care provided by nurses or other health workers.
- Limited coverage of hospice care for terminally ill.

There is a premium for this insurance in certain—but not most—cases.

Medical insurance (Part B). Eligible elderly and disabled persons can receive benefits under this supplementary program only if they sign up and agree to a monthly premium. As of 2007, the monthly premium is tied to annual income. Individuals with an income of $85,000 or less and couples with an income of $170,000 or less pay $104.90 per person if they sign up upon becoming eligible in 2014. Part B covers certain medical services and supplies, including:

- Physicians' and surgeons' services, as well as some services furnished by other medical professionals.
- Services in an emergency room, outpatient clinic, or ambulatory surgical center.
- Home health care not covered under Part A.
- Laboratory tests, X-rays, and other diagnostic radiology services.
- Certain preventative care services and screening tests.
- Most physical and occupational therapy and speech pathology services.
- Comprehensive outpatient rehabilitation facility services and mental health care in a partial hospitalization psychiatric program, if inpatient care would otherwise be required.
- Radiation therapy, renal (kidney) dialysis and transplants, heart, lung, heart-lung, liver, pancreas, bone marrow, and intestinal transplants.
- Approved durable medical equipment for home use.
- Drugs that are not usually self-administered. Certain services for diabetes.
- Ambulance services when other transportation methods are contraindicated.
- Rural health clinic and health center services, including some telemedicine.

Part B services are generally subject to a deductible ($147 in 2014), coinsurance (generally 20% of the remaining allowed charges with certain exceptions), a deductible for blood, and amounts above the allowed charge if a doctor or supplier does not accept the Medicare-approved rate as payment in full. For outpatient hospital services, coinsurance varies by service, usually falling between 20% and 50% of allowed charges. There are no deductibles or coinsurance for certain services, such as clinical lab tests, home health agency services (except some durable medical equipment, which is subject to 20% coinsurance), and some preventative care services. Payments for certain physical, speech, and occupational therapy services are subject to certain limits. Dental care, hearing aids, and routine eye care are generally not covered under the basic plan.

To get medical insurance (Part B), persons approaching age 65 may enroll during the seven-month initial enrollment period, which includes the month of their 65th birthday as well as the three months before and after. Persons desiring coverage to begin in the month they reach age 65 must enroll in the three months before their birthday. Persons who enroll after their initial enrollment period may be subject to late-enrollment premiums.

The monthly premium is deducted from the cash benefit for persons receiving Social Security, Railroad Retirement, or Civil Service Retirement benefits. Income from the medical premiums and the federal matching payments are put in a Supplementary Medical Insurance Trust Fund, from which benefits and administrative expenses are paid.

Medicare Advantage (Part C) (formerly Medicare+Choice). Persons eligible for Medicare may have the option of getting services through a Medicare-certified local coordinated care plan, such as a health maintenance organization (HMO), local preferred provider organization (PPO), provider-sponsored organization (PSO), other local Medicare-certified **managed care** plan, regional preferred provider organization (RPPO), a private fee-for-service plan, or in certain cases through a special-needs plan. Any such plan must provide at least the same benefits as Parts A and B, except for hospice services. They may provide added benefits (such as vision or hearing coverage) or reduce cost sharing or premiums. Enrollees may be required to use the plan's network of participating providers or pay higher out-of-pocket costs to go outside the network. Also available as options in some areas are Medicare-approved private fee-for-service plans and, for certain beneficiaries, special needs plans.

Prescription Drug Coverage (Part D). Effective Jan. 1, 2006, a Medicare prescription drug plan provides insurance coverage for prescription drugs. Medicare recipients pay a monthly premium (averaging about $31 in 2014, depending on the provider) and a portion of drug costs. Enrollment is scheduled to take place Oct. 15-Dec. 7 and is optional. Coverage varies depending on the drug plan selected.

Further details are available on the Internet at www.medicare.gov or by calling 1-800-MEDICARE (1-800-633-4227).

Medicare card. Persons qualifying for hospital insurance under Social Security receive a health insurance card. The card indicates whether the individual has taken out medical insurance protection. It is to be shown to the hospital, skilled-nursing facility, home health agency, doctor, or whoever provides the covered services.

Payments are generally made only in the 50 states, Puerto Rico, U.S. Virgin Isls., Guam, American Samoa, and Northern Mariana Isls.

Social Security Financing

Social Security is paid for by a tax on certain earnings (for 2014, on earnings up to $117,000) for **Old-Age, Survivors, and Disability Insurance (OASDI)** and on all earnings (no upper limit) for hospital insurance with the **Medicare** program; the taxable earnings base for OASDI is adjusted annually to reflect changes in average wages. The employed worker and his or her employer share Social Security taxes equally.

Employers remit amounts withheld from employee wages for Social Security and income taxes to the Internal Revenue Service; employer Social Security taxes are also payable at the same time. (Self-employed workers pay Social Security taxes when filing their regular income tax forms.) The Social Security taxes (along with revenues arising from partial taxation of the Social Security benefits of certain high-income people) are transferred to the Social Security Trust Funds; they can be used only to pay benefits, the cost of rehabilitation services, and administrative expenses. By law, money not immediately needed for those purposes is invested in obligations of the federal government, which must pay interest on the money borrowed and must repay the principal when the obligations are redeemed or mature.

On Jan. 1, 1974, the **Supplemental Security Income (SSI)** program, established by the Social Security Amendments of 1972, replaced federal grants to states for aid to the needy aged, blind, and disabled in the 50 states and the District of Columbia. The program provides for federal payments, based on uniform national standards and eligibility requirements, and for state supplementary payments, which vary by state. The Social Security Administration administers the federal payments—financed by general funds of the Treasury—as well as the state supplement for those states that choose to have it federally administered. States may supplement the federal payment of all recipients and must supplement it for persons otherwise adversely affected by the transition from the former public assistance programs. In May 2014, the number of persons receiving federally administered SSI payments was 8,383,570; the payments totaled about $4.7 bil.

The **maximum monthly federal SSI payment** for individuals without an eligible spouse and with no other countable income, living in their own household, was $721 in 2014. For couples where both members were eligible, the maximum payment was $1,082.

For further information, contact the Social Security Administration toll-free at 1-800-772-1213 or visit its website at www.socialsecurity.gov.

Examples of Monthly Social Security Benefits Available, 2014

Benefit or beneficiary	For low earnings ($20,308)[1]	For med. earnings ($45,128)[1]	For max. earnings ($108,570)[1,2]
Primary insurance amount (worker retiring at 66 years, 0 months) ..	$1,002.00	$1,650.30	$2,642.60
Maximum family benefit (worker retiring at 66 years, 0 months).....	1,502.90	3,013.90	4,624.60
Maximum family disability benefit (worker disabled at 55)	1,433.90	2,508.90	4,005.10
Disabled worker (worker disabled at 55):			
Worker alone	1,013.10	1,672.60	2,670.10
Worker, spouse, and 1 child	1,433.90	2,508.80	4,005.10
Retired worker claiming benefits at age 62:			
Worker alone[3]	753.60	1,240.80	1,981.90
Worker with spouse claiming benefits at—			
NRA or over................................	1,256.00	2,068.00	3,303.10
Age 62[3]	1,105.20	1,819.80	2,906.70
Widow or widower claiming benefits at—			
Age 66 or over[4]............................	1,002.00	1,650.30	2,642.60
Age 60[4]	720.30	1,186.40	1,899.90
Disabled widow or widower claiming benefits at age 50-59[5]	716.40	1,179.90	1,889.40
1 surviving child[4]	751.50	1,237.70	1,981.90
Widow or widower at NRA or over and 1 child[4]	1,502.90	2,888.00	4,624.50
Widowed mother or father and 1 child[4]...................	1,503.00	2,475.40	3,963.90
Widowed mother or father and 2 children[4]	1,502.70	3,013.80	4,624.50

NRA = Normal retirement age. **Note:** Effective Jan. 2014. (1) Career average earnings: an average of lifetime earnings indexed to the year prior to entitlement (2013 in this case). (2) Assumes work beginning at age 22. (3) Assumes maximum reduction. (4) Assumes worker lived and worked until NRA without receiving reduced benefits. (5) Effective Jan. 1984, disabled widow or widower claiming a benefit at age 50-59 receives a benefit equal to 71.5% of the primary insurance amount.

Social Security Recipients by Age, Sex, Race, and Hispanic Origin, 2013

Source: Social Security Administration

Characteristic/benefit	Total[2]	White	Black	American Indian, Alaska Native	Asian	Native Hawaiian/ other Pacific Isl.	Hispanic
Social Security beneficiaries (thous.)[1]	47,818	41,166	4,960	727	1,407	63	3,483
Sex							
Male..................................	21,283	18,499	2,054	331	594	22	1,562
Female	26,535	22,666	2,906	396	813	41	1,921
Age							
15-54 years............................	5,097	3,936	978	181	128	15	581
55-64 years............................	6,365	5,311	862	112	152	6	542
65-74 years............................	19,686	17,122	1,797	267	651	24	1,353
75 years or older........................	16,669	14,796	1,323	167	477	18	1,006
Supplemental Security Income recipients (thous.)[1] ..	5,999	3,989	1,618	224	305	12	987
Sex							
Male..................................	2,549	1,710	669	95	137	2	369
Female	3,450	2,280	949	129	167	9	618
Age							
15-54 years............................	3,405	2,261	1,013	141	84	8	500
55-64 years............................	1,440	994	380	51	48	1	235
65-74 years............................	674	446	139	17	78	2	140
75 years or older........................	480	287	87	14	95	1	111
Average annual benefit in 2012 (dollars)							
Social Security	$13,695	$13,903	$12,241	$12,779	$12,823	NA	$11,492
Supplemental Security Income.................	7,601	7,802	7,179	6,856	7,627	NA	6,815

NA = Not available. **Note:** Race categories include people who reported being of that race, alone or in combination with another race. Persons of Hispanic origin may be of any race. The sum of the individual categories may not add up to totals because of rounding and because the totals include persons who reported being of more than one race. (1) Persons 15 or older receiving Social Security benefits or Supplemental Security Income in Mar. 2012.

OASDI Recipients and Monthly Payments, 1940-2013

Source: Social Security Administration

Year	Total recipients	Monthly benefits Total (thous.)	Avg.[1]	Avg. (2013 dollars)[2]	Year	Total recipients	Monthly benefits Total (thous.)	Avg.[1]	Avg. (2013 dollars)[2]
1940	222,488	$4,070	$18.29	$297.30	1995	43,387,259	$28,148,078	$648.76	$992.92
1945	1,288,107	23,801	18.48	234.13	2000	45,414,794	34,848,920	767.35	1,041.37
1950	3,477,243	126,857	36.48	345.64	2005	48,434,445	44,351,772	915.71	1,099.01
1955	7,960,616	411,613	51.71	439.79	2006	49,122,831	46,938,176	955.53	1,110.95
1960	14,844,589	936,321	63.07	485.91	2007	49,864,982	49,218,232	987.03	1,116.30
1965	20,866,767	1,516,802	72.69	525.44	2008	50,898,396	53,666,202	1,054.38	1,145.66
1970	26,228,629	2,628,326	100.21	588.57	2009	52,522,819	55,905,731	1,064.41	1,164.41
1975	32,085,372	5,727,903	178.52	755.86	2010	54,032,097	58,048,364	1,074.33	1,151.44
1980	35,618,840	10,694,022	300.23	829.82	2011	55,404,480	62,213,382	1,122.89	1,162.16
1985	37,058,353	15,901,643	429.10	919.90	2012	56,758,185	65,430,104	1,152.79	1,168.56
1990	39,832,125	21,686,763	544.45	967.05	2013	57,978,610	68,544,382	1,182.24	1,182.24

OASDI = Old-Age, Survivors, and Disability Insurance. **Note:** Disability insurance payments began in 1957. (1) Avg. monthly benefit does not necessarily reflect individual payments to OASDI recipients. (2) Adjusted for inflation.

Social Security Trust Funds

Source: Social Security Administration

Old-Age and Survivors Insurance Trust Fund, 1940-2013

(in millions)

Fiscal year[1]	INCOME Total	Net payroll tax contribs.	Income from taxing benefits	General fund reimburse-ments[2]	Net interest[3]	DISBURSEMENTS Total	Benefit pymts.[4]	Admin. expenses	Transfers to Railroad Retirement program	Net increase in fund[5]	Year-end balance
1940	$592	$550	—	—	$42	$28	$16	$12	—	$564	$1,745
1950	2,367	2,106	—	$4	257	784	727	57	—	1,583	12,893
1960	10,360	9,843	—	—	517	11,073	10,270	202	$600	−713	20,829
1970	31,746	29,955	—	442	1,350	27,321	26,268	474	579	4,425	32,616
1980	100,051	97,608	—	557	1,886	103,228	100,626	1,160	1,442	−3,177	24,566
1990	278,607	260,069	$2,924	1,471	14,143	223,481	218,048	1,564	2,969	55,126	203,445
2000	484,228	418,219	12,476	1	53,532	353,396	347,868	1,990	3,538	130,832	893,003
2005	599,992	502,998	15,332	—	81,662	436,919	430,439	2,900	3,579	163,073	1,615,623
2006	632,157	530,006	15,176	−350	87,324	455,560	449,191	2,911	3,458	176,597	1,792,220
2007	663,376	553,414	16,661	—	93,300	488,557	481,828	3,151	3,575	174,822	1,967,042
2008	692,873	573,750	16,396	—	102,727	509,864	502,973	3,259	3,632	183,009	2,150,052
2009	697,326	571,228	18,967	—	107,131	551,542	544,484	3,369	3,690	145,784	2,295,835
2010	682,448	552,037	21,068	737	108,606	579,907	572,515	3,462	3,930	102,541	2,398,375
2011	692,510	495,031	21,174	68,886	107,419	599,232	591,477	3,645	4,110	93,278	2,491,654
2012	728,981	500,661	27,150	95,927	105,243	634,700	627,208	3,352	4,139	94,281	2,585,936
2013	739,668	589,976	23,144	26,433	100,115	670,554	663,195	3,410	3,949	69,114	2,655,049

Note: Numbers may not add up to totals due to rounding. (1) Fiscal years 1977 and later consist of the 12 months ending on Sept. 30 of each year. Fiscal years prior to 1977 consisted of the 12 months ending on June 30 of each year. (2) Includes reimbursements from the general fund of the Treasury to the OASI Trust Fund for certain legislated measures since 1957. (3) Includes net profits or losses on marketable investments. Beginning in 1967, the trust fund paid administrative expenses on an estimated basis, with a final adjustment including interest made in the following fiscal year. Net interest includes these interest adjustments. Beginning in Oct. 1973, figures include relatively small gifts to the fund. (4) Beginning in 1967, includes payments for vocational rehabilitation services furnished to disabled persons receiving benefits because of their disabilities; beginning in 1983, includes reimbursements paid from the general fund to the trust fund for unnegotiated benefit checks. (5) Net change in assets during fiscal year, including amounts borrowed or repaid by other funds.

Disability Insurance Trust Fund, 1960-2013

(in millions)

Fiscal year[1]	INCOME Total	Net payroll tax contribs.	Income from taxing benefits	General fund reimburse-ments[2]	Net interest[3]	DISBURSEMENTS Total	Benefit pymts.[4]	Admin. expenses	Transfers to Railroad Retirement program	Net increase in fund[5]	Year-end balance
1960	$1,034	$987	—	—	$47	$533	$528	$32	−$27	$501	$2,167
1970	4,380	4,141	—	$16	223	2,954	2,795	149	10	1,426	5,104
1980	17,376	16,805	—	118	453	15,320	14,998	334	−12	2,056	7,680
1990	28,215	27,154	$158	138	766	25,124	24,327	717	80	3,091	11,455
2000	77,023	70,001	756	—	6,266	56,008	54,244	1,608	159	21,014	113,752
2005	96,765	85,418	1,164	—	10,183	86,360	83,721	2,301	338	10,405	193,298
2006	101,571	90,001	1,174	—	10,396	92,932	90,064	2,480	388	8,640	201,938
2007	108,396	93,973	1,351	—	13,072	96,758	93,955	2,357	445	11,638	213,577
2008	109,816	97,432	1,373	8	11,003	107,153	104,222	2,513	418	2,663	216,239
2009	109,681	97,008	1,841	—	10,832	118,144	115,073	2,623	448	−8,462	207,777
2010	105,513	93,739	1,745	125	9,904	126,334	122,935	2,947	462	−20,831	186,946
2011	106,225	84,031	1,878	11,745	8,571	131,489	127,990	3,034	465	−25,264	161,682
2012	108,845	85,072	383	16,234	7,156	138,546	135,114	2,920	512	−29,701	131,981
2013	111,262	100,169	1,051	4,504	5,538	142,757	139,446	2,760	551	−31,494	100,486

Note: Numbers may not add up to totals due to rounding. (1) Fiscal years 1977 and later consist of the 12 months ending on Sept. 30 of each year. Fiscal years prior to 1977 consisted of the 12 months ending on June 30 of each year. (2) Includes reimbursements from the general fund of the Treasury to the DI Trust Fund for certain legislated measures since 1957. (3) Includes net profits or losses on marketable investments. Beginning in 1967, the trust fund paid administrative expenses on an estimated basis, with a final adjustment including interest made in the following fiscal year. Net interest includes these interest adjustments. The 1970 report describes the accounting for administrative expenses for years prior to 1967. Beginning in July 1974, figures include relatively small gifts to the fund. (4) Beginning in 1967, includes payments for vocational rehabilitation services furnished to persons receiving benefits because of a disability; beginning in 1983, includes reimbursements paid from the general fund to the trust fund for unnegotiated benefit checks. (5) Net change in assets during fiscal year, including amounts borrowed or repaid by other funds.

Supplementary Medical Insurance Trust Fund (Medicare SMI), 1975-2013

Source: Centers for Medicare & Medicaid Services, U.S. Dept. of Health and Human Services

(in millions)

Fiscal year[1]	Total	INCOME Premium from participants[2]	Govt. contribs.[3]	Transfers from states[4]	Interest and other income[5,6]	DISBURSEMENTS Total	Benefit pymts.[6,7,8]	Admin. expenses	Net change	Year-end balance[9]
1975	$4,322	$1,887	$2,330	—	$106	$4,170	$3,765	$404	$152	$1,424
1980	10,275	2,928	6,932	—	416	10,737	10,144	593	−462	4,532
1990	46,138[10]	11,494[10]	33,210	—	1,434[10]	43,022[10]	41,498	1,524[10]	3,115[10]	14,527[10]
2000	89,239	20,515	65,561	—	3,164	88,992	87,212[11]	1,780	247	45,896
2005	152,505	35,939	115,200	—	1,366	152,735	149,820[12]	2,914	−230	16,885
2006	211,951	44,241[13]	162,601	$3,630	1,478	195,557	192,083[12,13]	3,474	16,394	33,279
2007	237,890	49,666[13]	179,181	6,977	2,065	232,022	228,596[12,13]	3,426	5,867	39,146
2008	244,872	54,158[13]	180,434	7,042	3,238	224,869	221,445[13,14]	3,423	20,003	59,149
2009	262,573	57,709[13]	194,267	7,504	3,093	260,257	256,938[13]	3,318	2,317	61,466
2010	282,734	61,364[13]	213,709	4,493	3,168	272,224	268,710[13]	3,514	10,510	71,976
2011	301,523	64,502[13]	225,178	6,536	5,307	300,672	296,842[13]	3,830	851	72,827
2012	290,850	66,053[13]	210,508	8,324	5,965	291,893	287,763[13]	4,130	−1,043	71,783
2013	310,556	71,299[13]	227,208	8,666	3,384	315,122	311,365[13]	3,756	−4,565	67,218

Note: Numbers may not add up to totals because of rounding. (1) Fiscal year 1975 consists of the 12 months ending on June 30, 1975; fiscal years 1980 and later consist of the 12 months ending on Sept. 30 of each year. (2) For Part D, premiums include both amounts withheld from Social Security benefit checks (and certain other federal benefit payments) and amounts paid directly to Part D plans (estimated). (3) For Part B, includes matching payments from the general fund, plus certain interest-adjustment items. For Part D, includes all federal govt. transfers. (4) As of 2006, Medicaid is no longer the primary payer for full-benefit dual eligibles; states pay 90% of estimated costs. (5) Other income includes recoveries of amounts reimbursed from the trust fund that are not trust fund obligations and other miscellaneous income. In 2008, includes an adjustment of $812 mil for interest inadvertently unearned as a result of HI hospice costs misallocated to, and paid from, the Part B account of the SMI trust fund May 2005-Sept. 2007. (6) Values after 2005 include additional premiums for Medicare Advantage (MA) plans that are deducted from beneficiaries' Social Security checks, transferred to Hospital Insurance (HI) and SMI trust funds, and then transferred to the plans. (7) Includes costs of Peer Review Organizations in 1983-2001 and costs of Quality Review Organizations beginning in 2002. (8) For Part D, includes payments to plans, subsidies to employer-sponsored retiree drug plans, payments to states for low-income eligibility determinations, and Part D drug premiums (the amount collected from beneficiaries and transferred to plans and an estimated amount for premiums paid directly by enrollees to plans). Includes amounts for transitional assistance benefits in 2004-06. (9) The financial status of SMI depends on the trust fund's assets and liabilities. (10) Includes the impact of the Medicare Catastrophic Coverage Act of 1988. (11) Benefit payments less monies transferred from the HI trust fund for home health agency costs. (12) Certain HI hospice costs were misallocated to, and paid from, the Part B account of the SMI trust fund. See also footnote 14. (13) Includes an estimated $1.804 bil (2006), $2.295 bil (2007), $2.970 bil (2008), $3.699 bil (2009), $4.221 bil (2010), $4.843 bil (2011), $5.209 bil (2012), and $6.304 bil (2013) for premiums paid directly to Part D plans. (14) Benefit payments were $229.9 bil; amount shown does not include transfer of $8.5 bil from the general fund of the Treasury for HI hospice costs that were misallocated to, and paid from, the Part B account of the SMI trust fund from May 2005 to Sept. 2007. (The HI trust fund, in turn, transferred $8.5 bil to the general fund.)

Hospital Insurance Trust Fund (Medicare HI), 1975-2013

Source: Centers for Medicare & Medicaid Services, U.S. Dept. of Health and Human Services

(in millions)

Fiscal year[1]	Total	INCOME Payroll taxes	Taxation of benefits	Transfers from Railroad Retirement acct.	Reimb. for uninsured persons	Premiums from voluntary enrollees	Pymts. for military wage credits	Interest and other income[2,3]	DISBURSEMENTS Total	Benefit pymts.[3,4]	Admin. expenses[5]	Net change	Year-end balance
1975	$12,568	$11,291	—	$132	$481	$6	$48	$609	$10,612	$10,353	$259	$1,956	$9,870
1980	25,415	23,244	—	244	697	17	141	1,072	24,288	23,790	497	1,127	14,490
1990	79,563	70,655	—	367	413	113	107	7,908	66,687	65,912	774	12,876	95,631
2000	159,681	137,738	$8,787	465	470	1,392	2	10,827	130,284	127,934[6]	2,350	29,397	168,084
2005	196,921	168,954	8,765	445	286	2,303	0	16,168	184,142	181,292[7]	2,850	12,779	277,723
2006	210,309	180,392	10,319	471	408	2,632	0	16,086	184,901	181,815[7]	3,086	25,408	303,130
2007	219,207	187,992	10,593	483	468	2,761	0	16,910	202,827	200,191[7]	2,636	16,380	319,510
2008	229,729	197,195	11,733	526	506	2,913	0	16,856	230,240	227,008[8]	3,231	−511	319,000
2009	228,915	194,102	12,376	524	614	2,817	968[9]	17,514	238,001	234,659	3,343	−9,086	309,914
2010	218,004	183,603	13,760	535	−142	3,314	0	16,933	248,978	245,650	3,328	−30,975	278,939
2011	226,486	192,063	15,143	477	275	3,273	0	15,255	259,628	255,717	3,911	−33,142	245,797
2012	241,730	204,752	18,643	511	262	3,400	0	14,162	258,155	254,459	3,696	−16,425	229,372
2013	243,560	212,901	14,310	577	0	3,397	0	12,375	266,546	262,411	4,135	−22,986	206,386

Note: Numbers may not add up to totals because of rounding. (1) Fiscal year 1975 consists of the 12 months ending on June 30, 1975; fiscal years 1980 and later consist of the 12 months ending on Sept. 30 of each year. (2) Other income includes recoveries of amounts reimbursed from the trust fund that are not trust fund obligations, receipts from the fraud and abuse control program, and other small amounts of miscellaneous income. In 2008, includes an adjustment of −$853 mil for interest inadvertently earned as a result of HI hospice costs that were misallocated to, and paid from, the Part B account of the Supplementary Medical Insurance (SMI) trust fund from May 2005 to Sept. 2007. (3) Values after 2005 include additional premiums for Medicare Advantage (MA) plans that are deducted from beneficiaries' Social Security checks, transferred to the HI and SMI trust funds, and then transferred to the plans. (4) Includes costs of Peer Review Organizations from 1983 through 2001 (beginning with implementation of the Prospective Payment System on Oct. 1, 1983), and costs of Quality Improvement Organizations beginning in 2002. (5) Includes costs of experiments and demonstration projects. Beginning in 1997, includes fraud and abuse control expenses. (6) Includes monies transferred to the SMI trust fund for home health agency costs. (7) Certain HI hospice costs were misallocated to, and paid from, the Part B account of the SMI trust fund. (8) Benefit payments were $218.5 bil. Amount shown includes transfer of $8.484 bil to the general fund of the Treasury for HI hospice costs that were misallocated to, and paid from, the Part B account of the SMI trust fund from May 2005 to Sept. 2007. (The general fund, in turn, transferred $8.484 bil to the Part B account of the SMI trust fund.) (9) Includes the lump-sum general revenue adjustment of −$968 mil.

Temporary Assistance for Needy Families (TANF), 2012

Source: Office of Family Assistance, Admin. for Children and Families, U.S. Dept. of Health and Human Services

State/territory	Total federal and state TANF expenditures, 2012[1]	2012 average monthly expenditure per— Family	Recipient	2012 average monthly number of— Families	Recipients	Children
Alabama	$168,394	$650.12	$269.49	21,585	52,072	38,327
Alaska	71,922	1,588.21	586.64	3,774	10,217	6,907
Arizona	325,894	1,558.16	681.88	17,429	39,828	28,274
Arkansas	174,595	1,914.00	844.68	7,602	17,225	12,282
California	6,115,367	882.67	364.76	577,357	1,397,103	1,101,633
Colorado	306,473	1,840.04	711.75	13,880	35,883	26,181
Connecticut	466,988	2,534.93	1,295.07	15,352	30,049	21,214
Delaware	88,067	1,379.77	486.36	5,319	15,090	9,309
Dist. of Columbia	170,408	2,322.39	934.69	6,115	15,193	11,703
Florida	813,782	1,291.08	740.56	52,526	91,573	75,820
Georgia	522,679	2,317.61	1,203.38	18,794	36,195	31,940
Guam	NA	NA	NA	1,348	3,271	2,450
Hawaii	242,120	2,078.00	702.52	9,710	28,721	18,991
Idaho	33,894	1,497.66	982.31	1,886	2,875	2,669
Illinois	1,184,512	2,927.79	992.37	33,715	99,468	80,053
Indiana	222,319	1,048.64	478.60	17,667	38,710	32,319
Iowa	190,824	836.38	326.69	19,013	48,676	33,596
Kansas	159,102	1,171.77	462.98	11,315	28,637	19,878
Kentucky	259,632	710.47	351.97	30,453	61,472	48,790
Louisiana	244,652	2,201.42	964.17	9,261	21,145	17,973
Maine	114,999	520.56	217.73	18,410	44,014	27,311
Maryland	546,728	1,888.00	775.74	24,132	58,732	42,534
Massachusetts	1,029,478	1,342.09	609.17	63,923	140,830	93,264
Michigan	1,506,418	2,820.14	1,184.53	44,514	105,978	76,014
Minnesota	438,367	1,506.91	681.37	24,242	53,613	40,518
Mississippi	80,535	589.91	277.56	11,377	24,180	17,499
Missouri	368,341	810.56	336.33	37,869	91,264	62,015
Montana	45,127	1,164.49	466.38	3,229	8,063	5,799
Nebraska	93,397	1,076.61	444.90	7,229	17,494	14,009
Nevada	98,196	773.50	302.39	10,579	27,061	20,233
New Hampshire	73,935	900.65	377.22	6,841	16,333	11,212
New Jersey	1,036,994	2,524.30	1,037.66	34,234	83,280	57,905
New Mexico	182,230	834.35	330.43	18,201	45,958	33,262
New York	4,841,951	2,568.13	1,019.09	157,117	395,938	284,983
North Carolina	530,538	2,038.69	1,055.00	21,686	41,907	35,305
North Dakota	37,339	1,885.22	744.90	1,651	4,177	3,194
Ohio	1,040,358	737.89	301.80	117,492	287,266	207,364
Oklahoma	148,559	1,448.68	645.88	8,546	19,168	15,713
Oregon	344,750	739.08	306.61	38,871	93,700	66,307
Pennsylvania	904,981	967.21	383.25	77,972	196,773	139,471
Puerto Rico	NA	NA	NA	14,811	39,693	26,182
Rhode Island	142,202	1,807.16	752.14	6,557	15,755	10,751
South Carolina	148,538	857.30	372.58	14,439	33,223	25,520
South Dakota	27,332	700.53	338.31	3,251	6,733	5,724
Tennessee	340,342	490.99	196.96	57,765	143,995	104,116
Texas	880,911	1,602.94	704.41	45,797	104,214	90,071
Utah	96,423	1,566.22	624.25	5,130	12,872	9,215
Vermont	68,070	1,609.67	694.75	3,524	8,165	5,623
Virgin Islands	NA	NA	NA	426	1,220	873
Virginia	272,735	671.52	310.63	33,846	73,167	52,550
Washington	977,742	1,545.88	658.66	52,707	123,704	84,130
West Virginia	133,594	1,177.76	527.51	9,453	21,105	15,336
Wisconsin	525,043	1,670.10	695.62	26,198	62,899	47,165
Wyoming	29,523	7,917.18	4,092.48	311	601	494
Totals by year						
2012 totals........	28,867,300	1,472.32	645.32	1,876,426	4,476,476	3,351,971
2011 totals........	30,624,118	1,546.36	673.70	1,921,243	4,599,846	3,435,218
2010 totals........	33,255,476	1,500.30	634.69	1,847,152	4,364,979	3,280,150
2009 totals........	30,577,765	1,475.65	630.53	1,726,799	4,041,292	3,084,413
2008 totals........	28,129,745	1,438.71	620.06	1,629,344	3,780,543	2,911,078
2007 totals........	26,921,973	1,321.70	566.92	1,697,432	3,957,330	3,047,043
2006 totals........	25,593,809	1,191.88	510.33	1,789,460	4,179,295	3,207,216
2005 totals........	25,580,110	1,120.87	474.21	1,901,810	4,495,175	3,428,885
2004 totals........	25,821,230	1,094.51	455.63	1,965,960	4,722,588	3,581,448
2003 totals........	26,339,994	1,092.22	447.88	2,009,666	4,900,889	3,693,056
2002 totals........	25,414,383	1,039.00	417.89	2,038,373	5,067,963	3,791,560
2001 totals........	25,667,381	1,024.57	400.86	2,087,646	5,335,891	3,968,499
2000 totals........	24,780,711	926.32	353.72	2,229,315	5,838,043	4,303,943
1997 totals........	19,010,190	144.87	144.87	3,936,610	10,935,125	NA

NA = Not available. **Note:** Under 1996 legislation, the Aid to Families with Dependent Children (AFDC) program was converted to this state block-grant program. Covers period from previous Oct. to Sept. of fiscal years shown. (1) In thousands.

Adults Receiving TANF Funds by Employment Status, 2012

Source: Office of Family Assistance, Admin. for Children and Families, U.S. Dept. of Health and Human Services

State/terr.	Adults	Employed	State/terr.	Adults	Employed	State/terr.	Adults	Employed	State/terr.	Adults	Employed
AL......	14,038	36.0%	IL........	19,593	20.8%	NE......	2,266	40.5%	SC......	8,603	24.4%
AK......	3,308	30.6	IN........	6,001	26.6	NV......	6,860	34.2	SD......	1,020	17.9
AZ......	10,324	73.4	IA........	12,300	41.7	NH......	2,455	26.5	TN......	38,894	29.1
AR......	4,996	28.0	KS........	8,748	34.6	NJ......	24,791	11.8	TX......	13,968	27.5
CA......	313,337	23.1	KY........	12,646	25.7	NM......	13,045	22.3	UT......	2,279	25.6
CO......	9,306	35.8	LA........	3,171	22.0	NY......	71,125	30.5	VT......	1,817	19.4
CT......	8,997	28.2	ME........	7,469	18.1	NC......	6,736	16.9	Virgin Isls.	347	2.2
DE......	2,202	26.8	MD........	14,683	16.4	ND......	983	41.0	VA......	18,818	26.4
DC......	3,489	10.9	MA........	32,013	8.0	OH......	42,510	18.8	WA......	39,564	12.5
FL......	15,928	13.6	MI........	30,329	28.6	OK......	3,457	6.6	WV......	4,630	21.8
GA......	4,312	11.9	MN........	11,553	31.0	OR......	21,470	3.7	WI......	15,293	21.4
Guam	829	2.5	MS........	6,793	19.3	PA......	55,277	21.5	WY......	107	6.7
HA......	9,516	39.5	MO........	26,039	14.4	Puerto Rico	13,635	1.5	U.S. 1,009,349		22.8
ID......	206	6.0	MT........	2,269	28.0	RI......	5,003	14.5			

NA = Not available; TANF = Temporary Assistance for Needy Families state block-grant program. **Note:** For fiscal year 2012; covers period from Oct. 2011 to Sept. 2012.

TAXES

Federal Personal Income Tax Return Facts, 2014

Source: George W. Smith III, CPA, Managing Partner, George W. Smith & Company, P.C.

Deadlines. The deadline for filing a 2014 U.S. individual income tax return (1040, 1040A, or 1040EZ) is Apr. 15, 2015.

Extensions. Individuals who cannot file a 2014 individual income tax return by Apr. 15, 2015, may apply for a six-month extension to Oct. 15, 2015. To qualify for an extension, Form 4868 must be filed no later than Apr. 15, 2015. Approximately 9 mil extensions were filed in 2014. The IRS projected that up to 5 mil taxpayers will amend their 2013 returns by filing Form 1040X during 2014.

E-Filing. On June 10, 2011, the IRS announced that 1 bil individual tax returns had been processed since the electronic filing program began as a pilot program in 1986. By May 16, 2014, 117.8 mil returns had been e-filed with the IRS, compared to 114.4 mil by mid-May in 2013.

Penalties. The IRS can levy two potential penalties after the filing due date when there is a balance owed. One penalty is for failing to file a timely tax return; the other is for failure to pay the tax when due. In addition, interest can be charged on any unpaid tax balance.

Refunds. The average refund was $2,689 for 2014 filing season returns, up from $2,652 in the previous tax year. The IRS refunded $274.7 bil through May 16, 2014.

Statute of Limitations. Taxpayers who have not yet filed their 2011 federal tax return have until Apr. 15, 2015, to file and claim their refund. After that date, any refunds for 2011 income tax or withholding tax, including the earned income tax credit, will be lost.

Individual Federal Income Tax Rates and Brackets, 2014

Tax rate	Single	Married filing jointly or qualifying widow(er)	Married filing separately	Head of household other than surviving spouses
10%	$1 to $9,075	$1 to $18,150	$1 to $9,075	$1 to $12,950
15%	$9,076 to $36,900	$18,151 to $73,800	$9,076 to $36,900	$12,951 to $49,400
25%	$36,901 to $89,350	$73,801 to $148,850	$36,901 to $74,425	$49,401 to $127,550
28%	$89,351 to $186,350	$148,851 to $226,850	$74,426 to $113,425	$127,551 to $206,600
33%	$186,351 to $405,100	$226,851 to $405,100	$113,426 to $202,550	$206,601 to $405,100
35%	$405,101 to $406,750	$405,101 to $457,600	$202,951 to $228,800	$405,101 to $432,200
39.6%	More than $406,750	More than $457,600	More than $228,800	More than $432,200

Standard Deduction, 2014

The standard deduction is a flat amount subtracted from the adjusted gross income of taxpayers who do not itemize deductions.

Single	$6,200
Married filing jointly or qualifying widow(er)	$12,400
Married filing separately	$6,200
Head of household	$9,100

Dependents. An individual reported as a dependent on another person's tax return generally may claim the greater of (1) $1,000 or (2) the sum of $350 plus the individual's earned income, not to exceed the standard deduction.

Personal exemption. Unless another person can claim the individual as a dependent in 2014, the personal exemption is $3,950 (phased out at higher income levels).

Additional Standard Deduction, 2014

Taxpayers in 2014 who do not itemize, are 65 or older, and/or blind may claim an additional standard deduction.

Single or head of household, 65 or older OR blind	$1,550
Single or head of household, 65 or older AND blind	$3,100
Married filing jointly or qualifying widow(er), 65 or older OR blind (per person)	$1,200
Married filing jointly or qualifying widow(er), 65 or older AND blind (per person)	$2,400
Married filing separately, 65 or older OR blind	$1,200
Married filing separately, 65 or older AND blind	$2,400

IRS Rulings on Deductions and Other Tax Matters

Auto Damage. Damage to a person's car may be a deductible casualty loss unless it was caused by the person's willful conduct, such as drunken driving.

Charitable Giving. Charitable donations of real estate and securities that result in long-term capital gains are deductible at fair market value. Donations also include tangible personal property such as furniture, books, jewelry, paintings, and cars.

Combat Pay. For enlisted personnel or warrant officers serving in a combat zone for any part of a month, all pay received for military service that month is not taxable. For officers, tax-free income is capped at the highest enlisted pay level plus any hostile-fire or imminent-danger pay.

Community Property. In community property states (Arizona, California, Idaho, Louisiana, Nevada, New Mexico, Texas, Washington, Wisconsin), each spouse or registered domestic partner is (usually) considered to own half the community property.

Counseling. Parent(s) of a child with psychological problems may deduct as a medical expense that part of a private school fee directly related to psychological aid given to the child.

Day Camp. The cost of day camps for children may qualify for the child care credit. The child must be under the age of 13, and the expenses must be incurred so the parent(s) can work.

Estate Taxes. In general, after the death of an individual, federal estate tax returns may only need to be filed for 2014 when a decedent's gross estate, plus adjusted taxable gifts and specific exemptions, is more than $5.34 mil.

First Jobs. Graduates may not deduct expenses for seeking their first job. First job expenses include auto rental, plane travel, lodging costs, and meals.

Frivolous Claims. Taxpayers may have to pay a penalty if they file an erroneous claim for refund or credit. The penalty for filing a frivolous individual income tax return is $5,000.

Garage Sales. Revenues received from a garage sale usually do not result in taxable income. In most cases, the items that were sold cost more than the revenue received. These losses are considered personal and, therefore, not deductible.

Investment Expenses. Investors may take a miscellaneous deduction for financial newspapers, reports, and other expenses incurred in managing their investment portfolio. However, investors cannot deduct expenses for attending a convention, seminar, or similar meeting.

IRA Contributions for Dependents. Dependent children can open IRAs and Roth IRAs as long as they have earned income from a job up to a maximum of $5,500.

Mileage, Business. Beginning Jan. 1, 2014, the standard mileage rate for the use of a car, van, pickup, or panel truck is 56 cents per mile for business-miles driven. The business portion of parking fees and tolls may be deducted in addition to the mileage.

Mileage, Personal. The 2014 IRS mileage allowance deduction for moving and medical expenses is 23.5 cents per mile. The rate for volunteer work or charitable activities is 14 cents per mile. Charitable rates are set by Congress, not the IRS.

Penalties. Penalties and fines paid to a governmental agency or department are not deductible. This includes parking and speeding tickets as well as penalties for late filing of a tax return.

Refunds. Not all taxpayers expecting a refund will necessarily receive one. If an individual owes taxes to the federal government, has failed to pay child support, or has unpaid education loans, the IRS can take the individual's refund to satisfy the debt.

Sale of Residence. Married couples filing jointly who have lived in their principal residence for at least two years out of the last five can exclude up to $500,000 of the gain on its sale. Single taxpayers can exclude up to $250,000.

Same-Sex Marriage. All legally married same-sex couples may file a joint federal tax return, even if they reside in a state that does not perform or recognize same-sex marriages. Married same-sex couples can file amended qualified returns for all open tax years.

Smoking. The cost of participation in a smoking-cessation program or prescription drugs to alleviate nicotine withdrawal are deductible, but over-the-counter products such as nicotine patches and chewing gum are nondeductible.

Full-Time Students. Taxpayers in 2014 may not claim a dependency exemption for an individual who qualifies as a full-time student and is over age 23 at the end of the year, unless the student's gross income is less than $3,950.

Student Loans. For the 2014 tax year, the income phase-out range for the $2,500 maximum deduction for interest paid on qualified education loans for single taxpayers is $65,000-$80,000 and $130,000-$160,000 for married taxpayers filing jointly.

Transportation Fringe Benefits. For 2014, the monthly tax exclusion for transit passes or for transportation in a commuter highway vehicle is $130. The monthly parking exclusion amount is $250.

Weight Loss. The IRS allows a medical deduction for costs of certain weight-loss programs. Participation must be for treatment of a physician-diagnosed disease, including obesity.

Working Abroad. Many Americans who live and work abroad are eligible to exclude a certain amount of their pay from U.S. income taxes. The amount of earned income excludable for 2014 is $99,200.

Retirement Savings Plans

401(k) Plan. The maximum amount that an individual can contribute to a 401(k) plan for 2014 is $17,500. Individuals born before 1965 can put away an additional $5,500, for a total of $23,000.

IRAs. The 2014 limits for IRAs and Roth IRAs remain $5,500. Anyone who was born before 1965 can contribute an extra $1,000. Funds may be deposited into a traditional IRA for 2014 until Apr. 15, 2015. Contributions after Apr. 15 will automatically be considered funds deposited for 2015.

Roth IRA. Contributions paid into a Roth IRA are not tax deductible. Distributions of funds including investment earnings held in the account for five years or longer and distributed after age 59½ are both free of income tax and the 10% early-withdrawal penalty. Withdrawals from the account in less than five years can be subject to tax and a 10% withdrawal penalty regardless of age. There are income limitations on contributions.

Distributions. There is a 10% penalty for IRA distributions before age 59½. Distributions paid to a beneficiary due to disability/death of the owner are not subject to this penalty,

nor are payments used for certain unreimbursed medical expenses, higher-education expenses, or first-time homebuyer acquisition costs (up to $10,000).

The owner of a traditional IRA (or a SIMPLE plan, pension, or profit-sharing plan account) must begin receiving distributions by Apr. 1 of the calendar year following the year in which he or she reaches age 70½. Any employee who works beyond 70½ and is not a 5% or more owner of the business can continue to defer profit-sharing and pension plan distributions.

Itemized Deductions

If the total amount of itemized deductions is more than the standard deduction, taxpayers generally should itemize deductions on Schedule A, Form 1040. The following examples are just a few of the many deductions that may be itemized. Some are subject to income limitations.

Business Expenses. Deductible miscellaneous expenses include unreimbursed employee business expenses such as travel, automobile, telephone, and gifts. However, only 50% of the cost of customer meals and entertainment is deductible.

Charitable Contributions. Individuals may not deduct the value of volunteer work they personally perform for charities.

Gambling. Lottery, slots, poker, craps, bingo, or other gambling expenses are deductible if the taxpayer itemizes on Schedule A. However, expenses are limited to gambling winnings reported on Form 1040. If there are no reported winnings, the taxpayer cannot deduct expenses.

Interest. Mortgage interest paid on a primary residence or a second home is deductible. However, there are limitations on mortgages in excess of $1 mil. Interest on home equity loans also is deductible but only for the first $100,000 of equity debt. Personal credit card interest is not deductible.

Lamaze Classes. A mother-to-be may deduct, as a medical expense, the cost of classes taken for Lamaze breathing and relaxation techniques, stages of labor, and delivery procedures.

Long-Term Care Insurance. Based on various annual limits, long-term care insurance premiums are deductible as medical expenses. For 2014, taxpayers age 71 and older can claim as much as $4,660 per person; ages 61-70, up to $3,720; ages 51-60, up to $1,400; ages 41-50, up to $700; and ages 40 and younger, limited to $370.

Medical Expenses. Cosmetic surgery for a congenital abnormality including personal injury from an accident, trauma, or for a disfiguring disease, may qualify as a medical deduction.

Medical Traveling. Taxpayers may deduct part of the travel expense, including auto expenses and airfare, to seek health care.

Moving Expenses. Taxpayers who change jobs or are transferred usually can deduct part of their moving expenses, including travel and the cost of moving household goods.

Personal Losses. Casualty and theft losses are deductible subject to a $100 reduction and further reduced 10% for each occurrence. Separate rules apply for federally declared disasters. Unreimbursed automobile accident damage may be a deductible casualty loss.

Taxes. State and local income taxes including real estate taxes are deductible. An auto license fee based on weight, model, year, or horsepower is not deductible. A tax based on the car's value qualifies as a personal property tax deduction.

Tax Credits

A tax deduction reduces a taxpayer's taxable income whereas tax credits reduce the amount of tax owed.

Adoption Credit. The adoption credit in 2014 for qualified expenses is $13,190. The credit limit is per person, not per year, and is adjusted annually for inflation. The credit is not refundable and phases out for taxpayers at higher income levels.

American Opportunity Tax Credit. This education credit provides up to $2,500 per student per year in the first four years of a student's postsecondary education.

Child and Dependent Care Credit. This credit is for expenses for the care of taxpayers' qualifying children under age 13 or for a disabled spouse or dependent, while the taxpayer works or looks for work.

Common Income Tax Errors

Periodically, the IRS issues a list of the most commonly made income tax errors.

1. Incorrect or missing Social Security numbers.
2. Incorrect tax entered based on taxable income and filing status.
3. Computation errors in figuring the taxable income, withholding and estimated tax payments, Earned Income Credit, standard deduction for those age 65 or over or blindness, taxable amount of Social Security benefits, and child and dependent care credit. Also, missing or incorrect identification numbers for child care providers.
4. Withholding and estimated tax payments entered on the wrong line.
5. Math errors, both addition and subtraction.

Child Tax Credit. The maximum child tax credit is $1,000 for each qualifying child.

Earned Income Credit. Lower-income workers who maintain a household may be eligible for an Earned Income Credit. This credit is based on total earned income such as wages, commissions, and tips. Military personnel can include tax-free combat pay in income to compute the credit.

Energy Credits. There are many energy-related credits—from the purchase of an alternative fuel vehicle and the installation of solar/fuel cell property in a residence, to the production of biodiesel or ethanol.

Alternative Minimum Tax

The Alternative Minimum Tax (AMT) was established in 1969 to prevent individuals with very high incomes from using special tax breaks to pay little or no tax. The AMT exemption for a single taxpayer is $52,800 and $82,100 for married filing jointly.

Estate and Gift Taxes

Estate Tax. The Tax Relief Act of 2010 reinstated the estate tax with a 35% flat rate and increased the exemptions to $5 mil in 2011 and $5.12 mil in 2012.The rate was increased to 40% for 2013 and 2014, and the exemption was set at $5.34 mil.

Gifting. U.S. citizens, residents, and nonresident aliens have an annual gift tax exclusion of up to $14,000 per individual to as many individuals as he or she chooses. For married couples the exclusion is $28,000, even if only one spouse does all the gifting.

International Property. All property owned worldwide by American citizens is subject to U.S. estate tax rules and regulations.

Resident Aliens. Aliens residing in the U.S. are subject to the same rules as American citizens

Tax Rates for Estates and Trusts

If taxable income is—	The tax is—
Not over $2,500	15% of the taxable income
Over $2,500 but not over $5,800	$375 plus 25% of the excess over $5,800
Over $5,800 but not over $8,900	$1,200 plus 28% of the excess over $8,900
Over $8,900 but not over $12,150	$2,068 plus 33% of the excess over $8,900
Over $12,150	$3,140 plus 39.6% of the excess over $12,150

Taxable Social Security Benefits

Earnings Limitations. Social Security recipients who have not reached the full retirement age of 66 in 2014 will lose $1 of their benefits for every $2 of earned income over $15,480. Recipients who reached full retirement age in 2014 will not lose any benefits if they earned $41,400 or less. Recipients will have to pay back some benefits if their income exceeded that amount.

Taxable Benefits. Up to 50% of Social Security benefits may be taxable if the person's total income is more than $25,000 but less than $34,000 for a single individual, head of household, qualifying widow(er), or a married person who is filing separately if spouses lived apart all year; or more than $32,000 but less than $44,000 for married individuals filing jointly. For higher incomes, 85% of Social Security benefits may become taxable.

If the only income received during the year was Social Security, these benefits are not taxable, and the recipient probably does not have to file a tax return.

Retention of Income Tax Records

Federal tax returns generally can be audited for up to three years after filing or six years if the IRS suspects underreported income, so it's wise to keep copies of an income tax return and records for at least seven years after filing a return.

Tax Audits

Audit Odds. The IRS audit rate for fiscal year 2013 was 0.96%. The odds of an audit increase with higher taxpayer income, especially certain types of income. For taxpayers with incomes of $200,000 or higher, the audit rate was 3.26%. For taxpayers with gross income of $1 mil or more, the rate is 10.6%. If income is lower than $200,000, the audit rate drops to one in 100. Most taxpayers have no reason to be concerned about being audited.

The audit selection process is not random. It is based on a set of formulas that are designed to spot questionable returns. If the IRS concludes that the taxpayer owes more tax and he or she disagrees with the findings, the taxpayer can meet with a supervisor.

If the taxpayer still does not agree, he or she can appeal to a separate Appeals Office, or take it to the U.S. Tax Court, Federal District Court, or the U.S. Court of Federal Claims.

Tax Court. The U.S. Tax Court is a federal court where taxpayers can dispute tax deficiencies as determined by the Commissioner of Internal Revenue before payment of the disputed amounts. The Tax Court is composed of presidentially appointed members. Many taxpayers choose the Tax Court because they are not required to pay the contested tax up front.

Appeals. For more information about audits, call the IRS at (800) TAX-FORM (829-3676) for its free Publication 556, *Examination of Returns, Appeal Rights, and Claims for Refund* or visit www.irs.gov.

IRS Contact Information

Website: www.irs.gov
Tax questions: (800) 829-1040
Forms/publications: (800) TAX-FORM (829-3676)
Spanish forms/publications: Taxpayers can view and download tax forms and publications in Spanish directly from www.irs.gov/Spanish/.
Hearing impaired: (800) 829-4059 (TTY/TDD)
Additional services: Request Publication 910, *IRS Guide to Free Tax Services*. This guide contains a list of free tax publications and other information including tax education and assistance programs.
Report wrongdoing: Report misconduct, waste, fraud, or abuse by an IRS employee to the Treasury Inspector General for Tax Administration at (800) 366-4484.

Working With a Tax Preparer

The following are some suggestions when using a tax preparer:

- **Choose** wisely. Regulations require all paid tax return preparers including attorneys, certified public accountants, and IRS-enrolled agents to have a Preparer Tax Identification Number. Check the preparer's qualifications and history. Ask about service fees in advance.
- **Review** last year's tax return. Make note of any changes since then such as marriage, divorce, number of dependents, retirement, job changes, additional income, or new deductions.
- **Organize** your records with income items first, followed by itemized deductions (medical, taxes, interest, and charitable and other miscellaneous deductions), followed by gains, losses, rentals, or other items.
- **Time** spent with your preparer may affect your bill. If you provide disorganized records and deductions, there may be an additional cost to have your tax preparer organize your information.
- **Prepare** a list of questions in advance. Ask about any invoices or bills that you are not sure apply.
- **Alert** your preparer if you're waiting to receive additional information. He or she can begin preparing your tax return and include the missing data later to finalize your return. Amending a return after it is completed may incur additional fees.
- **Review** your tax return before signing it. Ask questions about any item you don't understand. Even though your preparer is required to sign the return, you are responsible for its contents.

Total U.S. Tax Collections by Type of Tax, 1960-2013

Source: *Internal Revenue Service Data Book, 2013*, Internal Revenue Service, U.S. Dept. of the Treasury
(as percent of total gross collection or total income taxes)

Fiscal year	Total IRS collections (bil)[1]	Income taxes				Employment taxes[4]	Estate taxes	Gift taxes	Excise taxes[5]
		Total	Business[2]	Individual[3]	Estate and trust[3]				
1960	$92	73.1%	24.2%	49.0%	—	12.2%	1.6%	0.20%	12.9%
1965	114	69.7	22.8	46.9	—	14.9	2.1	0.25	12.9
1970	196	70.9	17.9	53.0	—	19.1	1.7	0.22	8.1
1975	294	68.8	15.6	53.2	—	23.9	1.5	0.13	5.7
1980	519	69.3	13.9	55.4	—	24.7	1.2	0.04	4.7
1985	743	63.8	10.4	53.4	—	30.3	0.8	0.04	5.0
1990	1,056	61.6	10.4	51.1	—	34.8	0.9	0.20	2.6
1995	1,376	61.8	12.7	49.1	—	33.8	1.0	0.13	3.3
2000	2,097	65.5	11.2	54.2	—	30.5	1.2	0.20	2.6
2005	2,269	62.3	13.5	48.8	—	34.0	1.0	0.09	2.5
2010	2,345	62.0	11.9	49.6	0.5%	35.1	0.7	0.12	2.0
2011	2,415	65.8	10.1	55.1	0.6	31.8	0.1	0.27	2.0
2012	2,524	66.1	11.1	54.1	0.7	31.1	0.5	0.08	2.2
2013	2,855	65.7	10.9	53.9	0.9	31.4	0.5	0.20	2.1

Note: Numbers may not add up to totals because of rounding. (1) Credits to taxpayer accounts excluded beginning with fiscal year 2009. (2) Incl. taxes on corporation income and unrelated business income from tax-exempt organizations. (3) Income tax reported for estates and trusts is included in individual income tax in FY1960-2007. Estate and trust income tax is reported separately from FY2008 on. (4) Incl. taxes for Old-Age, Survivors, Disability, and Hospital Insurance; federal unemployment insurance; and Railroad Retirement. (5) Excl. excise taxes collected by the U.S. Customs and Border Protection and the Alcohol and Tobacco Tax and Trade Bureau. The IRS collected taxes on alcohol and tobacco until FY1988 and taxes on firearms until FY1991.

Taxes Collected by State Governments, 2013

Source: Annual Survey of State Government Tax Collections, U.S. Census Bureau, U.S. Dept. of Commerce
(as percent of total taxes collected or total sales and gross receipts)

State	Total taxes collected in dollars (mil)[1]	Property taxes	Sales and gross receipts taxes			License taxes[3]	Individual income taxes	Corporation net income taxes	Other taxes[4]
			Total	General	Selective[2]				
Alabama	$9,266	3.5%	50.8%	49.5%	50.5%	5.3%	34.6%	4.1%	1.7%
Alaska	5,133	1.9	4.9	—	100.0	2.6	—	12.3	78.3
Arizona	13,472	5.7	60.9	78.9	21.1	3.1	25.2	4.9	0.2
Arkansas	8,586	11.9	46.8	70.6	29.4	4.2	30.9	4.7	1.6
California	133,184	1.5	36.1	70.5	29.5	6.6	50.2	5.6	0.1
Colorado	11,246	—	38.1	56.5	43.5	5.7	49.2	5.8	1.3
Connecticut	16,137	—	41.8	57.1	42.9	2.8	48.4	3.5	3.4
Delaware	3,346	—	14.6	—	100.0	37.6	33.8	9.3	4.8
Florida	34,588	<0.1	82.5	72.9	27.1	5.8	—	6.0	5.8
Georgia	17,794	0.3	41.6	71.2	28.8	4.2	49.3	4.5	0.1
Hawaii	6,093	—	64.5	74.9	25.1	3.8	28.5	2.0	1.2
Idaho	3,579	—	49.5	74.7	25.3	8.6	36.1	5.6	0.2
Illinois	38,715	0.2	38.0	55.5	44.5	6.7	42.7	11.5	0.9
Indiana	16,931	<0.1	60.8	66.0	34.0	4.1	29.4	4.6	1.0
Iowa	8,374	—	43.1	69.8	30.2	9.5	41.0	5.1	1.2
Kansas	7,620	1.0	49.1	77.4	22.6	5.0	38.8	5.0	1.0
Kentucky	10,816	5.2	47.3	59.1	40.9	4.3	34.4	6.0	2.9
Louisiana	9,224	0.6	53.9	56.8	43.2	4.0	29.7	2.7	9.0
Maine	3,884	1.0	45.8	60.2	39.8	6.7	39.4	4.4	2.6
Maryland	18,118	4.1	40.6	56.0	44.0	4.4	42.5	5.3	3.1
Massachusetts	23,901	<0.1	31.2	69.5	30.5	4.0	53.9	7.9	3.1
Michigan	25,083	7.8	48.9	68.7	31.3	5.8	32.8	3.6	1.1
Minnesota	21,032	3.9	39.4	60.4	39.6	5.6	42.6	6.5	2.0
Mississippi	7,403	0.3	61.8	69.8	30.2	7.2	23.7	5.6	1.4
Missouri	11,141	0.3	43.0	65.8	34.2	4.9	48.3	3.4	0.1
Montana	2,645	9.9	21.1	—	100.0	12.1	39.5	6.5	10.8
Nebraska	4,719	<0.1	46.6	76.0	24.0	2.8	44.5	5.8	0.3
Nevada	7,027	3.3	77.8	66.5	33.5	8.4	—	—	10.5
New Hampshire	2,370	16.9	39.9	—	100.0	11.5	4.2	23.3	4.2
New Jersey	29,077	<0.1	42.0	69.3	30.7	5.2	41.6	7.8	3.3
New Mexico	5,202	1.4	51.0	74.2	25.8	4.9	23.9	5.1	13.7
New York	73,667	—	31.5	52.2	47.8	2.7	54.6	6.7	4.5
North Carolina	23,769	—	40.9	57.6	42.4	6.5	46.6	5.4	0.7
North Dakota	5,299	0.1	33.3	71.9	28.1	3.9	12.1	4.3	46.4
Ohio	27,331	—	49.9	63.3	36.7	12.6	36.1	1.0	0.4
Oklahoma	8,893	—	43.3	65.4	34.6	11.4	32.8	6.6	6.0
Oregon	9,161	0.2	14.9	—	100.0	10.1	68.3	5.0	1.4
Pennsylvania	33,966	0.2	50.4	54.0	46.0	7.6	31.7	6.5	3.6
Rhode Island	2,940	0.1	51.6	58.1	41.9	4.7	37.0	4.9	1.7
South Carolina	8,721	0.1	51.3	71.5	28.5	5.0	38.5	4.4	0.6
South Dakota	1,534	—	80.1	69.5	30.5	16.8	—	2.4	0.7
Tennessee	12,367	—	73.8	72.6	27.4	11.5	2.1	10.2	2.4
Texas	51,714	—	76.0	66.5	33.5	15.1	—	—	9.0
Utah	6,329	—	43.3	68.8	31.2	4.6	45.1	5.2	1.8
Vermont	2,879	33.8	34.2	35.3	64.7	3.7	23.0	3.7	1.7
Virginia	19,187	0.2	32.3	59.9	40.1	4.2	56.8	4.0	2.5
Washington	18,667	10.4	78.5	75.9	24.1	7.3	—	—	3.9
West Virginia	5,378	0.1	48.0	48.7	51.3	2.6	33.4	4.5	11.5
Wisconsin	16,523	0.9	42.9	62.2	37.8	6.3	43.7	5.8	0.4
Wyoming	2,186	15.2	37.8	85.0	15.0	7.1	—	—	39.9
U.S. total	846,215	1.6	46.4	64.9	35.1	6.6	36.6	5.3	3.6

— = Tax not collected by state. **Note:** For fiscal year 2013 (July 1, 2012-June 30, 2013) for all states except Alabama and Michigan (ends Sept. 30), New York (Mar. 31), and Texas (Aug. 31). (1) Incl. taxes not shown separately. (2) Incl. taxes on sale of alcoholic beverages, insurance premiums, motor fuels, public utilities, and tobacco products. (3) Incl. taxes on licenses for motor vehicles and corporations among others. (4) Incl. death and gift taxes and severance taxes (on extraction or harvest of natural resources).

State Government Personal Income Tax Rates, 2014

Source: Reproduced with permission from *CCH State Tax Guide*, published and copyrighted by CCH Inc., a Wolters Kluwer business. Alaska, Florida, Nevada, South Dakota, Texas, Washington, and Wyoming did not have state income taxes and are thus not listed. Tax rates apply in stages—for example, a single person in Arizona making $60,000 in taxable income would pay 2.59% on the first $10,000 of income, 2.88% on the next $15,000, and so on. For further details, see notes at end of table.

Alabama

Single, Head of household, or Married filing separately
- $0 to $500. . . . . .2%
- $501 to $3,000 . . . . .4%
- $3,001 and over 5%

Married filing jointly
- $0 to $1,000 . . . . .2%
- $1,001 to $6,000. . . . . .4%
- $6,001 and over 5%

Arizona[1]

Single or Married filing separately
- $0 to $10,000 . . . . 2.59%
- $10,001 to $25,000. . . . . 2.88%
- $25,001 to $50,000. . . . . 3.36%
- $50,001 to $150,000. . . . 4.24%
- $150,001 and over 4.54%

Married filing jointly or Head of household
- $0 to $20,000 . . . . 2.59%
- $20,001 to $50,000. . . . . 2.88%
- $50,001 to $100,000. . . . 3.36%
- $100,001 to $300,000. . . 4.24%
- $300,001 and over 4.54%

Arkansas[2,3]

Single, Head of household, Married filing jointly, or Married filing separately
- $0 to $4,199 . . . . .1%
- $4,200 to $8,299. . . . . 2.5%
- $8,300 to $12,399. . . . . . . 3.5%
- $12,400 to $20,699. . . . . . 4.5%
- $20,700 to $34,599. . . . . . . 6%
- $34,600 and over 7%

California[1,2]

Single, Married filing separately, or Registered domestic partner filing separately
- $0 to $7,749 . . . . .1%
- $7,750 to $18,371. . . . . 2%
- $18,372 to $28,995. . . . . . . 4%
- $28,996 to $40,250. . . . . . . 6%
- $40,251 to $50,869. . . . . . . 8%
- $50,870 to $259,844. . . . . 9.3%
- $259,845 to $311,812. . . 10.3%
- $311,813 to $519,687. . . 11.3%
- $519,688 and over 12.3%

Head of household
- $0 to $15,508 . . . . .1%
- $15,509 to $36,743. . . . . . . 2%
- $36,744 to $47,366. . . . . . .4%
- $47,367 to $58,621. . . . . . . 6%
- $58,622 to $69,242. . . . . . .8%
- $69,243 to $353,387. . . . . 9.3%
- $353,388 to $424,065. . . 10.3%
- $424,066 to $706,774. . . 11.3%
- $706,775 and over 12.3%

Married filing jointly, Registered domestic partner filing jointly, or Qualifying widow(er)
- $0 to $15,498 . . . . .1%
- $15,499 to $36,742. . . . . . . 2%
- $36,743 to $57,990. . . . . . . 4%
- $57,991 to $80,500. . . . . . . 6%
- $80,501 to $101,738. . . . . . 8%
- $101,739 to $519,688. . . . 9.3%
- $519,689 to $623,624. . . 10.3%
- $623,625 to $1,039,374   11.3%
- $1,039,375 and over. . . . 12.3%

Colorado

4.63% of federal taxable income

Connecticut

Single or Married filing separately
- $0 to $10,000 . . . . .3%
- $10,001 to $50,000. . . . . . . 5%
- $50,001 to $100,000. . . . . 5.5%
- $100,001 to $200,000. . . . . 6%
- $200,001 to $250,000. . . . 6.5%
- $250,001 and over 6.7%

Head of household
- $0 to $16,000. . . . . .3%
- $16,001 to $80,000. . . . . . .5%
- $80,001 to $160,000. . . . 5.5%
- $160,001 to $320,000. . . . .6%
- $320,001 to $400,000. . . 6.5%
- $400,001 and over 6.7%

Married filing jointly or Qualifying widow(er)
- $0 to $20,000. . . . . 3%
- $20,001 to $100,000. . . . . . 5%
- $100,001 to $200,000. . . .5.5%
- $200,001 to $400,000. . . . . 6%
- $400,001 to $500,000. . . . 6.5%
- $500,001 and over 6.7%

Delaware

Single, Head of household, Married filing jointly, or Married filing separately
- $0 to $2,000 . . . . 0%
- $2,001 to $5,000. . . . . .2.2%
- $5,001 to $10,000. . . . . . . 3.9%
- $10,001 to $20,000. . . . . . . 4.8%
- $20,001 to $25,000. . . . . . 5.2%
- $25,001 to $60,000. . . . . 5.55%
- $60,001 and over 6.6%

District of Columbia

- $0 to $10,000 . . . . 4%
- $10,001 to $40,000. . . . . . . 6%
- $40,001 to $350,000. . . . . 8.5%
- $350,001 and over 8.95%

Georgia

Single
- $0 to $750. . . . . 1%
- $751 to $2,250 . . . . 2%
- $2,251 to $3,750 . . . . 3%
- $3,751 to $5,250. . . . . 4%
- $5,251 to $7,000. . . . . 5%
- $7,001 and over 6%

Head of household, Married filing jointly, or Qualifying widow(er)
- $0 to $1,000 . . . . 1%
- $1,001 to $3,000. . . . . 2%
- $3,001 to $5,000. . . . . 3%
- $5,001 to $7,000. . . . . 4%
- $7,001 to $10,000. . . . . 5%
- $10,001 and over 6%

Married filing separately
- $0 to $500. . . . . 1%
- $501 to $1,500 . . . . 2%
- $1,501 to $2,500. . . . . 3%
- $2,501 to $3,500. . . . . 4%
- $3,501 to $5,000. . . . . 5%
- $5,001 and over 6%

Hawaii

Single or Married filing separately
- $0 to $2,400 . . . . .1.4%
- $2,401 to $4,800. . . . . .3.2%
- $4,801 to $9,600. . . . . 5.5%
- $9,601 to $14,400. . . . . . .6.4%
- $14,401 to $19,200. . . . . . 6.8%
- $19,201 to $24,000. . . . . . 7.2%
- $24,001 to $36,000. . . . . . 7.6%
- $36,001 to $48,000. . . . . . 7.9%
- $48,001 to $150,000. . . . 8.25%
- $150,001 to $175,000. . . . . 9%
- $175,001 to $200,000. . . . 10%
- $200,001 and over 11%

Head of household
- $0 to $3,600 . . . . .1.4%
- $3,601 to $7,200. . . . . .3.2%
- $7,201 to $14,400. . . . . . . 5.5%
- $14,401 to $21,600. . . . . . 6.4%
- $21,601 to $28,800. . . . . . 6.8%
- $28,801 to $36,000. . . . . . 7.2%
- $36,001 to $54,000. . . . . . 7.6%
- $54,001 to $72,000. . . . . . 7.9%
- $72,001 to $225,000. . . . 8.25%
- $225,001 to $262,500 . . . . 9%
- $262,501 to $300,000. . . . 10%
- $300,001 and over 11%

Married filing jointly or Surviving spouse

- $0 to $4,800 . . . . .1.4%
- $4,801 to $9,600. . . . . .3.2%
- $9,601 to $19,200. . . . . . . 5.5%
- $19,201 to $28,800. . . . . . 6.4%
- $28,801 to $38,400. . . . . . 6.8%
- $38,401 to $48,000. . . . . . 7.2%
- $48,001 to $72,000. . . . . . 7.6%
- $72,001 to $96,000. . . . . . 7.9%
- $96,001 to $300,000. . . . 8.25%
- $300,001 to $350,000. . . . . 9%
- $350,001 to $400,000. . . . 10%
- $400,001 and over 11%

Idaho[1,2]

Single or Married filing separately
- $0 to $1,428 . . . . .1.6%
- $1,429 to $2,857. . . . . 3.6%
- $2,858 to $4,286. . . . . 4.1%
- $4,287 to $5,715. . . . . 5.1%
- $5,716 to $7,144. . . . . 6.1%
- $7,145 to $10,717. . . . . . . 7.1%
- $10,718 and over 7.4%

Head of household, Married filing jointly, or Surviving spouse
- $0 to $2,857 . . . . .1.6%
- $2,858 to $5,715. . . . . 3.6%
- $5,716 to $8,573. . . . . 4.1%
- $8,574 to $11,431. . . . . . . 5.1%
- $11,432 to $14,289. . . . . . 6.1%
- $14,290 to $21,435. . . . . . 7.1%
- $21,436 and over 7.4%

Illinois

5% of federal AGI with modifications

Indiana

3.4% of AGI

Iowa[2]

- $0 to $1,515 . . . . 0.36%
- $1,516 to $3,030. . . . . . . 0.72%
- $3,031 to $6,060. . . . . . . 2.43%
- $6,061 to $13,635. . . . . . . 4.5%
- $13,636 to $22,725. . . . . 6.12%
- $22,726 to $30,300. . . . . 6.48%
- $30,301 to $45,450. . . . . . 6.8%
- $45,451 to $68,175. . . . . 7.92%
- $68,176 and over 8.98%

Kansas

Single, Head of household, or Married filing separately
- $0 to $15,000 . . . . 2.7%
- $15,001 and over 4.8%

Married filing jointly
- $0 to $30,000 . . . . 2.7%
- $30,001 and over 4.8%

Kentucky

Single, Head of household, Married filing jointly, or Married filing separately
- $0 to $3,000. . . . . 2%
- $3,001 to $4,000. . . . . 3%
- $4,001 to $5,000. . . . . 4%
- $5,001 to $8,000. . . . . 5%
- $8,001 to $75,000. . . . . . . 5.8%
- $75,001 and over 6%

Louisiana[1]

Single, Head of household, or Married filing separately
- $0 to $12,500 . . . . 2%
- $12,501 to $50,000. . . . . . . 4%
- $50,001 and over 6%

Married filing jointly
- $0 to $25,000 . . . . 2%
- $25,001 to $100,000. . . . . . 4%
- $100,001 and over 6%

Maine[2]

Single or Married filing separately
- $0 to $5,199 . . . . 0%
- $5,200 to $20,899. . . . . . . 6.5%
- $20,900 and over 7.95%

Head of household

- $0 to $7,849 . . . . 0%
- $7,850 to $31,349. . . . . . . 6.5%
- $31,350 and over 7.95%

Married filing jointly or Qualifying widow(er)
- $0 to $10,449 . . . . 0%
- $10,450 to $41,849. . . . . . 6.5%
- $41,850 and over 7.95%

Maryland

Single, Married filing separately, or Dependent taxpayers
- $0 to $1,000 . . . . 2%
- $1,001 to $2,000. . . . . 3%
- $2,001 to $3,000. . . . . 4%
- $3,001 to $100,000. . . . . 4.75%
- $100,001 to $125,000. . . . . 5%
- $125,001 to $150,000. . . . 5.25%
- $150,001 to $250,000. . . . 5.5%
- $250,001 and over 5.75%

Head of household, Married filing jointly, or Qualifying widow(er)
- $0 to $1,000 . . . . 2%
- $1,001 to $2,000. . . . . 3%
- $2,001 to $3,000. . . . . 4%
- $3,001 to $150,000. . . . . 4.75%
- $150,001 to $175,000. . . . . 5%
- $175,001 to $225,000. . . . 5.25%
- $225,001 to $300,000. . . . 5.5%
- $300,001 and over 5.75%

Massachusetts

Part A income (short-term capital gains)   12%
Part A income (interest and dividends). . 5.2%
Part B income. 5.2%
Part C income. 5.2%

Michigan

4.25% of taxable income

Minnesota[2]

Single
- $0 to $24,680 . . . . 5.35%
- $24,681 to $81,080. . . . . 7.05%
- $81,081 to $152,540. . . . 7.85%
- $152,541 and over 9.85%

Head of household
- $0 to $30,390 . . . . 5.35%
- $30,391 to $122,110. . . . 7.05%
- $122,111 to $203,390. . . 7.85%
- $203,391 and over 9.85%

Married filing jointly
- $0 to $36,080 . . . . 5.35%
- $36,081 to $143,350. . . . 7.05%
- $143,351 to $254,240. . . 7.85%
- $254,241 and over 9.85%

Married filing separately
- $0 to $18,040 . . . . 5.35%
- $18,041 to $71,680. . . . . 7.05%
- $71,681 to $127,120. . . . 7.85%
- $127,121 and over 9.85%

Mississippi

- $0 to $5,000 . . . . 3%
- $5,001 to $10,000. . . . . 4%
- $10,001 and over 5%

Missouri

- $0 to $1,000 . . . . .1.5%
- $1,001 to $2,000. . . . . 2%
- $2,001 to $3,000. . . . . 2.5%
- $3,001 to $4,000. . . . . 3%
- $4,001 to $5,000. . . . . 3.5%
- $5,001 to $6,000. . . . . 4%
- $6,001 to $7,000. . . . . 4.5%
- $7,001 to $8,000. . . . . 5%
- $8,001 to $9,000. . . . . 5.5%
- $9,001 and over 6%

Montana[2,3]

- $0 to $2,800 . . . . 1%
- $2,801 to $5,000. . . . . 2%
- $5,001 to $7,600. . . . . 3%

$7,601 to $10,300. . . . . 4%
$10,301 to $13,300 . . . . . . 5%
$13,301 to $17,100. . . . . . 6%
$17,101 and over 6.9%

Nebraska

Single
$0 to $3,000 . . . . 2.46%
$3,001 to $18,000. . . . . . . 3.51%
$18,001 to $29,000. . . . . . 5.01%
$29,001 and over 6.84%

Head of household
$0 to $5,600 . . . . 2.46%
$5,601 to $28,800. . . . . . . 3.51%
$28,801 to $43,000. . . . . . 5.01%
$43,001 and over 6.84%

Married filing jointly or Surviving spouse
$0 to $6,000 . . . . 2.46%
$6,001 to $36,000. . . . . . . 3.51%
$36,001 to $58,000. . . . . . 5.01%
$58,001 and over 6.84%

Married filing separately
$0 to $3,000 . . . . 2.46%
$3,001 to $18,000. . . . . . . 3.51%
$18,001 to $29,000. . . . . . 5.01%
$29,001 and over 6.84%

New Hampshire

5% on interest and dividends only

New Jersey

Single or Married/civil-union partner filing separately
$0 to $20,000 . . . . 1.4%
$20,001 to $35,000. . . . . . 1.75%
$35,001 to $40,000. . . . . . 3.5%
$40,001 to $75,000. . . . 5.525%
$75,001 to $500,000. . . . 6.37%
$500,001 and over 8.97%

Head of household, Married/civil-union couple filing jointly, or Qualifying widow(er)/Surviving civil-union partner
$0 to $20,000 . . . . 1.4%
$20,001 to $50,000. . . . . . 1.75%
$50,001 to $70,000. . . . . . 2.45%
$70,001 to $80,000. . . . . . 3.5%
$80,001 to $150,000. . . . 5.525%
$150,001 to $500,000. . . . 6.37%
$500,001 and over 8.97%

New Mexico[1]

Single
$0 to $5,500 . . . . 1.7%
$5,501 to $11,000. . . . . . . 3.2%
$11,001 to $16,000. . . . . . 4.7%
$16,001 and over 4.9%

Head of household
$0 to $8,000 . . . . 1.7%
$8,001 to $16,000. . . . . . . 3.2%
$16,001 to $24,000. . . . . . 4.7%
$24,001 and over 4.9%

Married filing jointly or Qualifying widow(er)
$0 to $8,000 . . . . 1.7%
$8,001 to $16,000. . . . . . . 3.2%
$16,001 to $24,000. . . . . . 4.7%
$24,001 and over 4.9%

Married filing separately
$0 to $4,000 . . . . 1.7%
$4,001 to $8,000. . . . . 3.2%
$8,001 to $12,000. . . . . . . 4.7%
$12,001 and over 4.9%

New York[2]

Single or Married filing separately
$0 to $8,300. . . . . 4%
$8,301 to $11,450. . . . . . . 4.5%
$11,451 to $13,550. . . . . . 5.25%
$13,551 to $20,850. . . . . . 5.9%
$20,851 to $78,400. . . . . . 6.45%
$78,401 to $209,250. . . . . 6.65%
$209,251 to $1,046,350 6.85%
$1,046,351 and over. . . . 8.82%

Head of household
$0 to $12,550 . . . . 4%
$12,551 to $17,200. . . . . . 4.5%
$17,201 to $20,350. . . . . . 5.25%
$20,351 to $31,350. . . . . . 5.9%
$31,351 to $104,600. . . . . 6.45%
$104,601 to $261,550. . . . 6.65%
$261,551 to $1,569,550 6.85%
$1,569,551 and over. . . . 8.82%

Married filing jointly or Qualifying widow(er)
$0 to $16,700 . . . . 4%
$16,701 to $22,950. . . . . . 4.5%
$22,951 to $27,150. . . . . . 5.25%
$27,151 to $41,800. . . . . . 5.9%
$41,801 to $156,900. . . . . 6.45%
$156,901 to $313,850. . . . 6.65%
$313,851 to $2,092,800 6.85%
$2,092,801 and over. . . . 8.82%

North Carolina

5.8% on state taxable income

North Dakota[2]

Single
$0 to $36,900 . . . . 1.22%
$36,901 to $89,350. . . . . . 2.27%
$89,351 to $186,350. . . . . 2.52%
$186,351 to $405,100. . . . 2.93%
$405,101 and over 3.22%

Head of household
$0 to $49,400 . . . . 1.22%
$49,401 to $127,550. . . . . 2.27%
$127,551 to $206,600. . . . 2.52%
$206,601 to $405,100. . . . 2.93%
$405,101 and over 3.22%

Married filing jointly or Surviving spouse
$0 to $61,700 . . . . 1.22%
$61,701 to $148,850. . . . . 2.27%
$148,851 to $226,850. . . . 2.52%
$226,851 to $405,100. . . . 2.93%
$405,101 and over 3.22%

Married filing separately
$0 to $30,850 . . . . 1.22%
$30,851 to $74,425. . . . . . 2.27%
$74,426 to $113,425. . . . . 2.52%
$113,426 to $202,550. . . . 2.93%
$202,551 and over 3.22%

Ohio[2]

$0 to $5,000 . . . . 0.528%
$5,001 to $10,000. . . . . . 1.057%
$10,001 to $15,000. . . . . 2.113%
$15,001 to $20,000. . . . . 2.642%
$20,001 to $40,000. . . . . 3.169%

Oklahoma

Single or Married filing separately
$0 to $1,000 . . . . 0.5%
$1,001 to $2,500. . . . . 1%
$2,501 to $3,750. . . . . 2%
$3,751 to $4,900. . . . . 3%
$4,901 to $7,200. . . . . 4%
$7,201 to $8,700. . . . . 5%
$8,701 and over 5.25%

Head of household, Married filing jointly, or Qualifying widow(er)
$0 to $2,000 . . . . 0.5%
$2,001 to $5,000. . . . . 1%
$5,001 to $7,500. . . . . 2%
$7,501 to $9,800. . . . . 3%
$9,801 to $12,200. . . . . 4%
$12,201 to $15,000. . . . . . . 5%
$15,001 and over 5.25%

Oregon[2]

Single or Married filing separately
$0 to $3,300 . . . . 5%
$3,301 to $8,250. . . . . 7%
$8,251 to $125,000. . . . . . . 9%
$125,001 and over 9.9%

Married filing jointly, Head of household, or Qualifying widow(er)
$0 to $6,600 . . . . 5%
$6,601 to $16,500. . . . . 7%
$16,501 to $250,000. . . . . . 9%
$250,001 and over 9.9%

Pennsylvania

3.07% of taxable compensation, net profits, net gains from the sale or property, rent, royalties, patents or copyrights, income from estates or trusts, dividends, interest, and winnings

Rhode Island[2]

Single, Head of household, Married filing jointly, Qualifying widow(er), or Married filing separately
$0 to $59,600 . . . . 3.75%
$59,601 to $135,500. . . . 4.75%
$135,501 and over 5.99%

South Carolina[2]

$0 to $2,880 . . . . 0%
$2,881 to $5,760. . . . . 3%
$5,761 to $8,640. . . . . 4%
$8,641 to $11,520. . . . . 5%
$11,521 to $14,400. . . . . . . 6%
$14,401 and over 7%

Tennessee

6% on interest and dividend income

Utah

5% on state taxable income

Vermont[2]

Single
$0 to $36,900 . . . . 3.55%
$36,901 to $89,350. . . . . 6.8%

$40,001 to $80,000. . . . 3.698%
$80,001 to $100,000. . . . 4.226%
$100,001 to $200,000. . . 4.906%
$200,001 and over 5.333%

Virginia

Single, Head of household, Married filing jointly, or Married filing separately
$0 to $3,000 . . . . 2%
$3,001 to $5,000. . . . . 3%
$5,001 to $17,000. . . . . 5%
$17,001 and over 5.75%

West Virginia

Single, Head of household, Married filing jointly, or Widower with dependent child
$0 to $10,000 . . . . 3%
$10,001 to $25,000. . . . . . . 4%
$25,001 to $40,000. . . . . . 4.5%
$40,001 to $60,000. . . . . . . 6%
$60,001 and over 6.5%

Married filing separately
$0 to $5,000 . . . . 3%
$5,001 to $12,500. . . . . 4%
$12,501 to $20,000. . . . . . 4.5%
$20,001 to $30,000. . . . . . . 6%
$30,001 and over 6.5%

Wisconsin[1,2]

Single or Head of household
$0 to $10,910 . . . . 4%
$10,911 to $21,820. . . . . 5.84%
$21,821 to $240,190. . . . 6.27%
$240,191 and over. 7.65%

Married filing jointly
$0 to $14,540. . . . . 4%
$14,541 to $29,090. . . . . 5.84%
$29,091 to $320,250. . . . 6.27%
$320,251 and over. 7.65%

Married filing separately
$0 to $7,270. . . . . 4%
$7,271 to $14,540. . . . . . 5.84%
$14,541 to $160,130. . . . 6.27%
$160,131 and over. 7.65%

(Second column, repeated header area)

Married filing separately
$0 to $4,000 . . . . 1.7%
$4,001 to $8,000. . . . . . . 3.2%
$8,001 to $12,000. . . . . . 4.7%
$12,001 and over 4.9%

$89,351 to $186,350. . . . 7.8%
$186,351 to $405,100. . . . 8.8%
$405,101 and over . . . 8.95%

Head of household
$0 to $49,400 . . . . 3.55%
$49,401 to $127,550. . . . 6.8%
$127,551 to $206,600. . . . 7.8%
$206,601 to $405,100. . . . 8.8%
$405,101 and over . . . 8.95%

Married or Civil union filing jointly
$0 to $61,600 . . . . 3.55%
$61,601 to $148,850. . . . 6.8%
$148,851 to $226,850. . . . 7.8%
$226,851 to $405,100. . . . 8.8%
$405,101 and over . . . 8.95%

Married or Civil union filing separately
$0 to $30,800 . . . . 3.55%
$30,801 to $74,425. . . . . 6.8%
$74,426 to $113,425. . . . 7.8%
$113,426 to $202,550. . . . 8.8%
$202,551 and over . . . 8.95%

AGI = Adjusted gross income; AMT = Alternative minimum tax. (1) Community property state in which, in general, one-half of the community income is taxable to each spouse. (2) Brackets indexed for inflation annually. (3) 2014 adjusted brackets were not available. Bracketed rates listed are for 2013. **Arizona:** Brackets will be indexed for inflation for 2015 tax year. **Arkansas:** Tax rates are reduced to 0.9% to 1% for tax years beginning after 2014, except that the 0.9% rate is applicable to tax years beginning after 2013. **California:** An additional 1% tax is imposed on taxable income in excess of $1 mil. **Colorado:** Individual taxpayers are subject to an AMT equal to the amount by which 3.47% of their Colorado alternative minimum taxable income exceeds their Colorado normal tax. **Connecticut:** Resident estates and trusts are subject to a 6.7% tax rate on all income. **Indiana:** Counties may impose an AGI tax on residents or on nonresidents, or a county option income tax. **Iowa:** An AMT of 6.7% of alternative minimum income is imposed if the minimum tax exceeds the taxpayer's regular income tax liability. **Maine:** Inflation adjustment suspended for 2014 and 2015 tax years. **Massachusetts:** Part A income represents either interest and dividends or short-term capital gains, long-term capital gains from collectibles, and long-term capital gains from pre-1996 installment sales. Part B income represents wages, salaries, tips, pensions, business income, rents, etc. Part C income represents gains from the sale of capital assets held for more than one year. 5.85% optional rate may be elected for Part A interest and dividend income, Part B income after exemptions, and Part C income. **Minnesota:** A 6.75% AMT is imposed. **Montana:** Minimum tax, $1. **Nebraska:** There is an additional tax on taxpayers with federal AGI of more than a certain amount, which is $305,050 for married filing jointly ($152,525 for married filing separately) in 2014. **New Mexico:** Qualified nonresident taxpayers may pay an alternative tax of 0.75% of gross receipts from sales in New Mexico. **New York:** A supplemental tax is imposed to recapture the tax table benefit. **Vermont:** The tax amount is increased by 24% for certain items.

EDUCATION

U.S. Public Schools: Students, Staff, Spending, 1899-2012
Source: National Center for Education Statistics, U.S. Dept. of Education

	1899-1900	1919-20	1939-40	1959-60	1969-70	1979-80	1989-90	1999-2000	2011-12[1]
Population (thous.)									
Total U.S. population[2]	75,995	104,514	131,028	177,830	201,385	225,055	246,819	279,040	311,588
Population 5-17 years of age	21,573	27,571	30,151	43,881	52,386	48,043	44,947	52,811	53,783
Percentage 5-17 years of age	28.4%	26.4%	23.0%	24.7%	26.0%	21.3%	18.2%	18.9%	17.3%
Enrollment (thous.)									
Elementary and secondary[3]	15,503	21,578	25,434	36,087	45,550	41,651	40,543	46,857	49,522
Pre-kindergarten and grades 1-8	14,984	19,378	18,833	27,602	32,513	28,034	29,152	33,486	34,773
Grades 9-12	519	2,200	6,601	8,485	13,037	13,616	11,390	13,371	14,749
Percentage pop. ages 5-17 enrolled	71.9%	78.3%	84.4%	82.2%	87.0%	86.7%	90.2%	88.7%	92.1%
Percentage high school of all enrolled	3.3%	10.2%	26.0%	23.5%	28.6%	32.7%	28.1%	28.5%	29.8%
High school graduates	62	231	1,143	1,627	2,589	2,748	2,320	2,554	3,148
Instructional staff (thous.)									
Total instructional staff	*	678	912	1,457	2,286	2,406	2,986	3,819	4,134
Teachers, librarians, and other nonsupervisory instructional staff	423	657	875	1,393	2,195	2,300	2,860	3,682	3,967
Revenue and expenditures (mil)									
Total revenue	$220	$970	$2,261	$14,747	$40,267	$96,881	$208,548	$372,944	$604,293
Total expenditures	215	1,036	2,344	15,613	40,683	95,962	212,770	381,838	604,215
Current expenditures[4,5]	180	861	1,942	12,329	34,218	86,984	188,229	323,889	527,166
Capital outlay	35	154	258	2,662	4,659	6,506	17,781	43,357	50,928
Interest on school debt	*	18	131	490	1,171	1,874	3,776	9,135	17,934
Others	*	3	14	133	636	598	2,983	5,457	8,187
Salaries and pupil cost									
Avg. annual salary of instruct. staff[6]	$325	$871	$1,441	$4,995	$8,626	$15,970	$31,367	$41,807	$55,418
Expenditure per capita total pop.	2.83	9.91	17.89	88	202	426	862	1,368	1,939
Current expenditure per pupil ADA[5,7]	16.67	53.32	88.09	375	816	2,272	4,980	7,394	10,658

* = Data not collected. **Note:** Because of rounding, details may not add up to totals. Prior to 1959-60, data do not include Alaska and Hawaii. (1) Revenues and expenditures are fiscal year 2011 (2010-11 school year) provisional data. (2) Data for 1899-1900 are based on total population from the decennial census. From 1919-20 to 1959-60, total population includes armed forces overseas, as of July 1 preceding the school year. Data for later years are for resident population excluding armed forces overseas. (3) Data for 1899-1960 are school year enrollment; data for later years are fall enrollment. (4) In 1899-1900, includes interest on school debt. (5) Because of changes in the definition of "current expenditures," data for 1959-60 and later years are not entirely comparable with prior years. (6) Data prior to 1959-60 include supervisors, principals, teachers, and nonsupervisory instructional staff. (7) ADA = average daily attendance.

U.S. Public High School Graduation Rates, 2011-12
Source: National Center for Education Statistics, U.S. Dept. of Education

State	Rate	Rank	State	Rate	Rank	State	Rate	Rank	State	Rate	Rank
Alabama	75%	43	Illinois	82%	22	Montana	86%	12	Rhode Island	76%	42
Alaska	79	30	Indiana	80	27	Nebraska	93	1	South Carolina	72	46
Arizona	77	39	Iowa	89	5	Nevada	60	51	South Dakota	83	20
Arkansas	78	34	Kansas	89	5	New Hampshire	87	9	Tennessee	83	20
California	82	22	Kentucky	82	22	New Jersey	87	9	Texas	82	22
Colorado	82	22	Louisiana	72	46	New Mexico	74	45	Utah	78	34
Connecticut	86	12	Maine	87	9	New York	78	34	Vermont	93	1
Delaware	77	39	Maryland	84	16	North Carolina	79	30	Virginia	84	16
Dist. of Columbia	71	48	Massachusetts	86	12	North Dakota	91	4	Washington	79	30
Florida	75	43	Michigan	77	39	Ohio	84	16	West Virginia	80	27
Georgia	70	49	Minnesota	88	7	Oklahoma	79	30	Wisconsin	92	3
Hawaii	78	34	Mississippi	68	50	Oregon	78	34	Wyoming	80	27
Idaho	84	16	Missouri	86	12	Pennsylvania	88	7	**Total U.S.**	81	

Note: The averaged freshman graduation rate provides an estimate of the percentage of high school students who graduate within 4 years of first starting 9th grade. The rate uses aggregate student enrollment data to estimate the size of an incoming freshman class and counts of the comparable to diplomas awarded 4 years later. (1) Data are imputed. Texas did not report any graduate data.

High School Dropouts by Sex, Race, and Ethnicity, 1960-2012
Source: Current Population Survey, U.S. Census Bureau, U.S. Dept. of Commerce

(data for Oct. of year shown unless otherwise noted)

Year[1]	Total dropout rate				Male dropout rate				Female dropout rate			
	All races[2]	White	Black	Hispanic	All races[2]	White	Black	Hispanic	All races[2]	White	Black	Hispanic
1960[3]	27.2%	NA	NA	NA	27.8%	NA	NA	NA	26.7%	NA	NA	NA
1970[4]	15.0	13.2%	27.9%	NA	14.2	12.2%	29.4%	NA	15.7	14.1%	26.6%	NA
1980	14.1	11.4	19.1	35.2%	15.1	12.3	20.8	37.2%	13.1	10.5	17.7	33.2%
1990	12.1	9.0	13.2	32.4	12.3	9.3	11.9	34.3	11.8	8.7	14.4	30.3
1995	12.0	8.6	12.1	30.0	12.2	9.0	11.1	30.0	11.7	8.2	12.9	30.0
2000	10.9	6.9	13.1	27.8	12.0	7.0	15.3	31.8	9.9	6.9	11.1	23.5
2001	10.7	7.3	10.9	27.0	12.2	7.9	13.0	31.6	9.3	6.7	9.0	22.1
2002	10.5	6.5	11.3	25.7	11.8	6.7	12.8	29.6	9.2	6.3	9.9	21.2
2003[5]	9.9	6.3	10.9	23.5	11.3	7.1	12.5	26.7	8.4	5.6	9.5	20.1
2004[5]	10.3	6.8	11.8	23.8	11.6	7.1	13.5	28.5	9.0	6.4	10.2	18.5
2005[5]	9.4	6.0	10.4	22.4	10.8	6.6	12.0	26.4	8.0	5.3	9.0	18.1
2006[5]	9.3	5.8	10.7	22.1	10.3	6.4	9.7	25.7	8.3	5.3	11.7	18.1
2007[5]	8.7	5.3	8.4	21.4	9.8	6.0	8.0	24.7	7.7	4.5	8.8	18.0
2008[5]	8.0	4.8	9.9	18.3	8.5	5.4	8.7	19.9	7.5	4.2	11.1	16.7
2009[5]	8.1	5.2	9.3	17.6	9.1	6.3	10.6	19.0	7.0	4.1	8.1	16.1
2010[5]	7.4	5.1	8.0	15.1	8.5	5.9	9.5	17.3	6.3	4.2	6.7	12.8
2011[5]	7.1	5.0	7.3	13.6	7.7	5.4	8.3	14.6	6.5	4.6	6.4	12.4
2012[5]	6.6	4.3	7.5	12.7	7.3	4.8	8.1	13.9	5.9	3.8	7.0	11.3

NA = Not available. **Note:** Table shows "status" dropouts, defined as 16- to 24-year-olds who are not enrolled in school and who have not completed a high school program, regardless of when they left school. People who have received GED credentials are not shown. Excludes persons in prison or in the military, and other persons not living in households. Race categories exclude persons of Hispanic ethnicity unless otherwise noted. (1) Because of changes in data collection procedures, data for years prior to 1992 may not be comparable to later years. (2) Includes other racial/ethnic categories not separately shown. (3) Based on the Apr. 1960 decennial census. (4) White and black data include persons of Hispanic ethnicity. (5) White and black data exclude persons identifying themselves as being of two or more races.

Overview of U.S. Public Schools, 2012-13

Source: National Center for Education Statistics, U.S. Dept. of Education; National Education Association (NEA)

State	Local school districts	Elementary schools[1,2]	Secondary schools[2,3]	Classroom teachers	Total enrollment	Pupils per teacher	Teachers' avg. pay	Expend. per pupil
Alabama	134	712	415	46,300	735,605	15.9	$47,949	$8,811
Alaska	54	201	82	9,618	127,937	13.3	65,468	18,192
Arizona	627*	1,323	744	60,986*	1,069,802*	17.5*	49,885*	6,949*
Arkansas	255	716	384	31,333	471,532	15.0	46,631	9,384
California	1,042*	6,925	2,624	248,699*	6,184,927*	24.9*	69,324*	9,060*
Colorado	178*	1,295	393	49,240*	868,619*	17.6*	49,844*	10,884*
Connecticut	196*	817	279	41,739*	550,429	13.2*	69,397	16,403*
Delaware	37*	158	39	9,197*	131,065*	14.3*	59,679*	14,890*
Dist. of Columbia	41*	170	37	6,156*	76,017*	12.3*	70,906*	14,406*
Florida	67*	2,756	683	169,376	2,680,778	15.8	46,598	8,539
Georgia	198	1,797	470	108,778	1,702,758	15.7	52,880	9,426*
Hawaii	1	206	52	11,198	177,441	15.8	54,300	11,799
Idaho	137*	448	230	16,111*	294,077*	18.3*	49,734*	8,528*
Illinois	865*	3,170	989	130,733*	2,083,995*	15.9*	59,113*	12,927*
Indiana	369	1,372	454	55,381	1,031,103	18.6	50,065	8,064
Iowa	348	980	387	34,916	500,601	14.3	50,946	9,609
Kansas	286*	949	365	35,088*	486,281*	13.9*	47,464*	9,689*
Kentucky	174*	995	441	41,738	658,708	15.8	50,203	10,033
Louisiana	126*	978	288	51,209*	708,272*	13.8*	51,381*	10,310*
Maine	195	448	148	14,898	185,033	12.4	48,430	10,476
Maryland	24	1,129	258	58,544	859,638	14.7	64,248	15,229*
Massachusetts	403	1,414	370	68,425	953,787	13.9	72,334	15,881
Michigan	855	2,269	958	84,092	1,543,573	18.4	61,560	13,686*
Minnesota	519*	1,263	849	52,889*	843,318*	15.9*	56,268*	11,632*
Mississippi	151*	625	324	32,354	492,847	15.2	41,814	8,466*
Missouri	524*	1,581	646	68,722*	906,811*	13.2*	47,517*	10,093*
Montana	410	479	347	10,692*	142,908	13.4*	48,855	10,341*
Nebraska	249	718	317	30,929	303,242	9.8	48,997	9,621*
Nevada	17*	479	129	26,408*	477,881*	18.1*	55,957*	8,501*
New Hampshire	161*	373	104	15,620*	188,799*	12.1*	55,599*	15,394*
New Jersey	590	1,946	544	113,431*	1,357,728*	12.0*	68,797*	19,291*
New Mexico	89	604	239	22,229	334,138	15.0	45,453	11,019
New York	695*	3,279	1,105	215,678*	2,589,670*	12.0*	75,279*	19,523*
North Carolina	115	1,887	536	98,349	1,488,150	15.1	45,737	8,363
North Dakota	179	297	184	8,116	99,192	12.2	47,344*	8,549
Ohio	1,016*	2,544	1,004	107,379	1,867,582*	17.4*	56,307	9,941*
Oklahoma	520	1,213	554	41,832	673,190	16.1	44,373	7,912
Oregon	196	890	294	25,862	563,714	21.8	57,612	10,251
Pennsylvania	499*	2,252	824	119,219	1,738,700*	14.6*	62,994	14,467*
Rhode Island	49*	227	76	10,042*	134,242*	13.4*	63,474*	17,666*
South Carolina	85	907	277	47,898	682,820	14.3	48,375	9,795
South Dakota	151	434	246	9,158	126,798	13.8	39,018	9,347*
Tennessee	136	1,295	349	65,144	979,806*	15.0*	47,563	8,647*
Texas	1,228	5,918	2,113	327,516	5,058,939	15.4	48,819	8,275
Utah	125	630	301	27,820*	600,595	21.6*	49,393*	7,223*
Vermont	286*	235	69	8,981*	82,346*	9.2*	52,526*	19,752*
Virginia	132	1,503	399	102,669*	1,266,128*	12.3*	48,670*	10,695*
Washington	295	1,517	631	53,565	1,053,061	19.7	52,234	9,908*
West Virginia	55*	571	127	19,737	282,309	14.3	45,453	12,112*
Wisconsin	424	1,553	583	56,425	872,436	15.5	53,797	11,395*
Wyoming	48	241	96	7,331	90,993	12.4	56,775	15,943
Total U.S.	**15,556***	**66,689**	**24,357**	**3,109,751***	**49,380,319***	**15.9***	**56,103***	**10,938***

* = NEA estimate. (1) Includes primary and middle schools (schools with no grade higher than 8th). (2) 2011-12 estimates. (3) Includes schools with no grade lower than 7th.

Programs for the Disabled, 1995-2013

Source: Office of Special Education and Rehabilitative Services, U.S. Dept. of Education

Number of children and young adults 3-21 years old served annually in federally funded educational programs for the disabled.
(in thousands)

Type of disability	1995 -96	2000 -01	2003 -04	2004 -05	2005 -06	2006 -07	2007 -08	2008 -09	2009 -10	2010 -11	2011 -12	2012 -13
Learning disabilities	2,578	2,868	2,831	2,798	2,735	2,665	2,577	2,537	2,498	2,423	2,364	2,347
Speech impairments	1,022	1,409	1,441	1,463	1,468	1,475	1,458	1,451	1,449	1,429	1,413	1,397
Intellectual disabilities[1]	571	624	593	578	556	534	500	488	473	457	443	439
Emotional disturbance	437	481	489	489	477	464	442	421	409	391	375	364
Multiple disabilities	93	133	140	140	141	142	138	132	132	131	133	135
Hearing impairments	67	78	79	79	79	80	79	79	79	79	79	78
Orthopedic impairments	63	83	77	73	71	69	67	70	66	63	62	60
Other health impairments[2]	133	303	464	521	570	611	641	666	698	724	755	792
Visual impairments	25	29	28	29	29	29	29	29	29	29	29	29
Autism	28	94	163	191	223	258	296	338	380	419	458	502
Deaf-blindness	1	1	2	2	2	2	2	2	2	2	2	2
Traumatic brain injury	9	16	23	24	24	25	25	26	25	26	26	26
Developmental delay	—	178	305	332	339	333	358	354	368	381	393	403
All disabilities	**5,572**	**6,296**	**6,634**	**6,719**	**6,713**	**6,686**	**6,613**	**6,593**	**6,608**	**6,553**	**6,531**	**6,574**

— = Not available or not reliable data. **Note:** Counts based on reports from states and District of Columbia. Details may not add up to totals because of rounding and/or incomplete enumeration. (1) Referred to in some prior years as "mental retardation." (2) Includes limited strength, vitality, or alertness due to chronic or acute health problems such as a heart condition, tuberculosis, rheumatic fever, nephritis, asthma, sickle cell anemia, hemophilia, epilepsy, lead poisoning, leukemia, or diabetes.

Revenues for Public Elementary and Secondary Schools by State, 2010-11

Source: National Center for Education Statistics, U.S. Dept. of Education; amounts in thousands

State/territory	Total	Federal Amount	Federal % of tot. rev.	State Amount	State % of tot. rev.	Local and intermediate Amount	Local and intermediate % of tot. rev.
Alabama	$7,386,471	$1,250,581	16.9%	$3,827,907	51.8%	$2,307,983	31.2%
Alaska	2,470,274	424,422	17.2	1,524,083	61.7	521,768	21.1
American Samoa	82,921	72,007	86.8	10,689	12.9[2]	225	0.3
Arizona	9,764,472	1,639,892	16.8	3,924,369	40.2	4,200,211	43.0
Arkansas	5,273,728	859,309	16.3	2,703,033	51.3	1,711,386	32.5
California	67,864,062	9,248,710	13.6	38,411,425	56.6	20,203,927	29.8
Colorado	8,820,783	991,623	11.2	3,540,865	40.1	4,288,294	48.6
Connecticut	9,989,986	827,618	8.3	3,422,642	34.3	5,739,726	57.5
Delaware	1,748,658	207,823	11.9	1,024,557	58.6	516,279	29.5
District of Columbia[1]	1,925,824	227,198	11.8	0	0.0	1,698,626	88.2
Florida	26,358,355	4,796,329	18.2	9,069,113	34.4	12,492,913	47.4
Georgia	18,047,879	2,312,872	12.8	7,526,257	41.7	8,208,751	45.5
Guam	333,235	142,766	42.8	0	0.0	190,469	57.2
Hawaii[1]	2,470,432	347,361	14.1	2,059,791	83.4	63,280	2.6
Idaho	2,183,491	305,826	14.0	1,382,052	63.3	495,614	22.7
Illinois	28,895,633	2,900,110	10.0	9,304,471	32.2	16,691,051	57.8
Indiana	11,761,793	1,046,267	8.9	6,534,419	55.6	4,181,108	35.5
Iowa	5,906,171	613,528	10.4	2,550,546	43.2	2,742,097	46.4
Kansas	5,670,547	662,971	11.7	2,979,230	52.5	2,028,345	35.8
Kentucky	6,993,349	1,149,658	16.4	3,622,461	51.8	2,221,230	31.8
Louisiana	8,246,484	1,533,440	18.6	3,479,231	42.2	3,233,813	39.2
Maine	2,597,927	289,249	11.1	1,052,058	40.5	1,256,620	48.4
Maryland	13,437,322	1,256,210	9.3	5,508,344	41.0	6,672,768	49.7
Massachusetts	15,357,042	1,271,995	8.3	5,797,874	37.8	8,287,173	54.0
Michigan	19,466,487	2,705,858	13.9	10,717,834	55.1	6,042,795	31.0
Minnesota	10,938,581	905,392	8.3	6,397,541	58.5	3,635,648	33.2
Mississippi	4,483,191	1,006,453	22.4	2,071,471	46.2	1,405,267	31.3
Missouri	10,169,473	1,381,908	13.6	3,008,369	29.6	5,779,196	56.8
Montana	1,654,729	298,964	18.1	723,125	43.7	632,641	38.2
Nebraska	3,911,430	634,411	16.2	1,186,279	30.3	2,090,741	53.5
Nevada	4,212,793	463,653	11.0	1,388,359	33.0	2,360,780	56.0
New Hampshire	2,844,769	205,572	7.2	1,041,561	36.6	1,597,636	56.2
New Jersey	25,217,564	1,336,982	5.3	9,403,391	37.3	14,477,191	57.4
New Mexico	3,744,076	721,936	19.3	2,423,599	64.7	598,541	16.0
New York	57,538,128	5,368,090	9.3	23,097,859	40.1	29,072,179	50.5
North Carolina	13,228,999	2,139,214	16.2	7,688,360	58.1	3,401,425	25.7
North Dakota	1,258,921	186,727	14.8	629,843	50.0	442,351	35.1
Northern Mariana Islands	87,377	57,619	65.9	29,758	34.1[2]	0	0.0
Ohio	22,973,368	2,702,863	11.8	9,921,997	43.2	10,348,507	45.0
Oklahoma	5,874,001	994,189	16.9	2,754,252	46.9	2,125,560	36.2
Oregon	6,120,056	864,118	14.1	2,792,707	45.6	2,463,231	40.2
Pennsylvania	27,174,139	3,318,881	12.2	9,378,294	34.5	14,476,964	53.3
Puerto Rico	3,711,167	1,382,157	37.2	2,328,968	62.8[2]	43	0.0
Rhode Island	2,278,564	250,194	11.0	830,217	36.4	1,198,154	52.6
South Carolina	7,873,340	1,085,533	13.8	3,414,705	43.4	3,373,102	42.8
South Dakota	1,307,520	265,922	20.3	380,410	29.1	661,188	50.6
Tennessee	8,915,680	1,312,271	14.7	3,995,291	44.8	3,608,119	40.5
Texas	50,874,695	7,968,095	15.7	20,430,187	40.2	22,476,413	44.2
Utah	4,597,983	577,903	12.6	2,340,850	50.9	1,679,229	36.5
Vermont	1,641,955	175,721	10.7	1,340,743	81.7	125,491	7.6
Virgin Islands (U.S.)	243,250	44,858	18.4	0	0.0	198,392	81.6
Virginia	14,444,511	1,427,295	9.9	5,349,193	37.0	7,668,024	53.1
Washington	11,801,402	1,365,968	11.6	6,757,950	57.3	3,677,484	31.2
West Virginia	3,499,055	513,739	14.7	1,951,616	55.8	1,033,700	29.5
Wisconsin	11,429,211	1,045,227	9.1	5,246,795	45.9	5,137,189	44.9
Wyoming	1,647,905	155,403	9.4	878,878	53.3	613,623	37.2

NA = Not applicable. **Note:** Included as revenue receipts are all appropriations from general funds of federal, state, county, and local governments; receipts from taxes levied for school purposes; income from permanent school funds and endowments; and income from leases of school lands and miscellaneous sources (interest on bank deposits, tuition, gifts, school lunch charges, etc.). (1) Both DC and Hawaii have only one school district each; therefore, neither is comparable to other states. Local revenues in Hawaii consist almost entirely of student fees and charges for services, such as food services, summer school, and student activities. (2) Reported state revenue data are revenues received from the central government of the jurisdiction.

Fighting, Bullying, and Safety Concerns of High School Students, 2013

Source: *Youth Risk Behavior Surveillance–United States, 2013*, Centers for Disease Control and Prevention

	In a physical fight on school property[1]			Bullied on school property[2]			Electronically bullied[2,3]			Did not go to school because of safety concerns[4]		
	Female	Male	Total	Female	Male	Total	Female	Male	Total	Female	Male	Total
Race/ethnicity[5]												
White......	3.8%	8.9%	6.4%	27.3%	16.2%	21.8%	25.2%	8.7%	16.9%	7.4%	3.8%	5.6%
Black......	11.2	14.5	12.8	15.1	10.2	12.7	10.5	6.9	8.7	8.0	7.8	7.9
Hispanic ...	6.7	12.1	9.4	20.7	14.8	17.8	17.1	8.3	12.8	12.6	6.9	9.8
Grade												
9	8.6	13.0	10.9	29.2	20.8	25.0	22.8	9.4	16.1	9.9	5.5	7.7
10	6.3	10.2	8.3	28.8	15.8	22.2	21.9	7.2	14.5	10.7	5.3	8.0
11	4.1	10.9	7.5	20.3	13.1	16.8	20.6	8.9	14.9	8.1	5.8	7.0
12	2.6	7.3	4.9	15.5	11.2	13.3	18.3	8.6	13.5	5.9	5.0	5.5
Total	5.6	10.7	8.1	23.7	15.6	19.6	21.0	8.5	14.8	8.7	5.4	7.1

(1) One or more times during the 12 months before the survey. (2) During the 12 months before the survey. (3) Including being bullied through email, chat rooms, instant messaging, websites, or texting. (4) On at least one day during the 30 days before the survey. (5) Race categories include non-Hispanics only. Hispanics may be of any race.

Program for International Student Assessment (PISA) Scores, 2003-12

Source: National Center for Education Statistics, U.S. Dept. of Education

Education system	Mathematics			Science			Education system	Mathematics			Science		
	2003	2012	% change, 2003-12	2006	2012	% change, 2006-12		2003	2012	% change, 2003-12	2006	2012	% change, 2006-12
Albania	—	394	—	—	397	—	Macao.	527	538	2.06%	511	521	1.90%
Argentina . . .	—	388	—	391	406	3.68%	Malaysia	—	421	—	—	420	—
Australia* . . .	524	504	−3.84%	527	521	−1.02	Mexico*	385	413	7.28	410	415	1.29
Austria*	506	506	−0.01	511	506	−0.99	Montenegro[1]	—	410	—	412	410	−0.41
Belgium*	529	515	−2.75	510	505	−0.96	Netherlands*	538	523	−2.76	525	522	−0.53
Brazil.	356	391	9.96	390	405	3.68	New Zealand*	523	500	−4.53	530	516	−2.78
Bulgaria	—	439	—	434	446	2.85	Norway*	495	489	−1.17	487	495	1.64
Canada*	532	518	−2.71	534	525	−1.69	Peru	—	368	—	—	373	—
Chile*	—	423	—	438	445	1.54	Poland*	490	518	5.56	498	526	5.63
Colombia . . .	—	376	—	388	399	2.74	Portugal*	466	487	4.52	474	489	3.16
Costa Rica . .	—	407	—	—	429	—	Qatar.	—	376	—	349	384	9.83
Croatia	—	471	—	493	491	−0.37	Romania	—	445	—	418	439	4.87
Cyprus	—	440	—	—	438	—	Russia.	468	482	2.94	479	486	1.42
Czech Rep.*	516	499	−3.39	513	508	−0.89	Serbia[1]	—	449	—	436	445	2.10
Denmark* . . .	514	500	−2.77	496	498	0.52	Shanghai,						
Estonia*	—	521	—	531	541	1.88	China.	—	613	—	—	580	—
Finland*	544	519	−4.69	563	545	−3.17	Singapore . . .	—	573	—	—	551	—
France*	511	495	−3.10	495	499	0.76	Slovakia*	498	482	−3.32	488	471	−3.53
Germany* . . .	503	514	2.10	516	524	1.64	Slovenia*	—	501	—	519	514	−0.90
Greece*	445	453	1.81	473	467	−1.41	Spain*	485	484	−0.16	488	496	1.64
Hong Kong . .	550	561	1.97	542	555	2.35	Sweden*	509	478	−6.05	503	485	−3.68
Hungary*	490	477	−2.65	504	494	−1.91	Switzerland*	527	531	0.83	512	515	0.74
Iceland*	515	493	−4.33	491	478	−2.58	Taiwan	—	560	—	532	523	−1.72
Indonesia . . .	360	375	4.15	393	382	−2.94	Thailand	417	427	2.34	421	444	5.46
Ireland*	503	501	−0.27	508	522	2.69	Tunisia	359	388	8.11	386	398	3.25
Israel*	—	466	—	454	470	3.56	Turkey*	423	448	5.80	424	463	9.34
Italy*	466	485	4.22	475	494	3.82	United Arab						
Japan*	534	536	0.43	531	547	2.89	Emirates . .	—	434	—	—	448	—
Jordan.	—	386	—	422	409	−2.99	UK*	—	494	—	515	514	−0.13
Kazakhstan. .	—	432	—	—	425	—	U.S.*	483	481	−0.31	489	497	1.74
Korea, South*	542	554	2.13	522	538	3.00	Uruguay	422	409	−3.06	428	416	−2.87
Latvia	483	491	1.49	490	502	2.58	Vietnam	—	511	—	—	528	—
Liechtenstein	536	535	−0.15	522	525	0.49	OECD trend						
Lithuania	—	479	—	488	496	1.59	score[2]	500	496	−0.68	498	501	0.57
Luxembourg*	493	490	−0.68	486	491	1.01							

— = Not available. * = Organization for Economic Cooperation and Development (OECD) nation. **Note:** Scores are given for the earliest year available for each category and are reported on a scale from 0 to 1,000. The PISA test is administered to 15-year-old students. (1) Montenegro and Serbia were a united country under the 2003 assessment. (2) The OECD trend scores are based on the averages of OECD countries with each country weighted equally.

Mathematics, Reading, and Science Achievement of U.S. Students, 1998-2013

Source: National Assessment of Educational Progress, National Center for Education Statistics, U.S. Dept. of Education

Percent of public school students in a grade who scored at or above basic levels in national tests. Basic level denotes a partial mastery of prerequisite knowledge and skills fundamental for proficient work at each grade.

State	4th grade				8th grade						State	4th grade				8th grade					
	Math		Reading		Math		Reading		Science			Math		Reading		Math		Reading		Science	
	2000	2013	1998	2013	2000	2013	1998	2013	2000	2011		2000	2013	1998	2013	2000	2013	1998	2013	2000	2011
AL	55	75	56	65	52	60	67	68	53	54	MT	72	86	72	70	80	80	83	84	79	80
AK	NA	77	NA	58	NA	72	NA	71	NA	68	NE	65	84	NA	71	74	76	NA	81	52	72
AZ	57	82	51	60	62	69	72	72	55	57	NV	60	80	51	61	58	68	70	72	NA	58
AR	55	83	54	66	52	69	68	73	53	62	NH	NA	93	75	80	NA	84	NA	84	NA	79
CA	50	74	48	58	52	65	63	72	38	52	NJ	NA	87	NA	75	NA	82	NA	85	NA	69
CO	NA	87	69	74	NA	77	77	81	NA	74	NM	50	74	51	52	50	63	71	67	48	58
CT	76	83	76	76	72	74	81	83	64	69	NY	66	82	62	70	68	72	76	76	NA	62
DE	NA	86	53	73	NA	71	64	77	NA	63	NC	73	87	58	69	70	75	74	76	54	61
DC	24	66	27	50	23	54	44	57	NA	24	ND	73	89	NA	73	77	82	NA	81	72	82
FL	NA	84	53	75	NA	70	67	77	NA	62	OH	73	86	NA	71	75	79	NA	79	72	73
GA	57	81	54	67	55	68	68	75	52	63	OK	67	83	66	65	64	68	80	75	60	63
HI	55	83	45	62	52	72	59	71	40	55	OR	65	81	58	66	71	73	78	79	68	71
ID	68	83	NA	68	71	78	NA	82	71	75	PA	NA	85	NA	73	NA	78	NA	81	NA	66
IL	63	79	NA	64	68	74	NA	77	59	60	RI	65	83	64	70	64	74	76	77	58	63
IN	77	90	NA	73	76	77	NA	79	66	68	SC	59	79	53	60	55	69	66	73	48	61
IA	75	87	67	72	NA	76	NA	81	NA	73	SD	NA	84	NA	66	NA	79	NA	81	NA	79
KS	76	89	70	71	77	79	81	78	NA	70	TN	59	80	57	67	53	69	71	77	55	64
KY	59	84	62	71	63	71	74	80	60	71	TX	76	84	59	63	68	80	74	76	52	67
LA	57	75	44	56	48	64	63	68	44	56	UT	69	83	62	71	68	75	77	81	67	77
ME	73	88	72	71	76	78	83	79	72	78	VT	73	87	NA	75	75	84	NA	84	71	80
MD	60	82	58	77	65	74	70	82	57	64	VA	71	88	62	74	67	77	78	78	61	73
MA	77	90	70	79	76	86	79	84	70	76	WA	NA	86	64	72	NA	79	76	81	NA	73
MI	71	77	62	64	70	70	NA	77	68	72	WV	65	81	60	62	62	65	75	70	57	64
MN	76	90	69	74	80	83	78	82	72	76	WI	NA	85	72	68	NA	78	78	NA	NA	75
MS	45	74	47	53	41	61	62	64	41	47	WY	71	90	64	75	70	81	76	84	69	77
MO	71	83	61	70	67	74	75	78	66	72	U.S.	64	83	58	68	65	74	71	78	57	65

NA = Not administered.

Enrollment in U.S. Public and Private Schools, 1899-2024

Source: National Center for Education Statistics, U.S. Dept. of Education

Of all students enrolled in private schools in 2011-12, 70% attended religious schools, and 30% attended nonsectarian schools.

School year[1]	Public school[2]	Private school[2]	% private[3]	School year[1]	Public school[2]	Private school[2]	% private[3]
1899-1900	15,503	1,352	8.0%	1979-80	41,651	5,000[4]	10.7%
1909-10	17,814	1,558	8.0	1989-90	40,543	5,599	12.1
1919-20	21,578	1,699	7.3	1999-2000	46,857	6,018	11.4
1929-30	25,678	2,651	9.4	2009-10	49,373	5,488	10.0
1939-40	25,434	2,611	9.3	2011-12	49,522	5,268	9.6
1949-50	25,111	3,380	11.9	2021-22[4]	51,485	4,857	8.6
1959-60	35,182	5,675	13.9	2022-23[4]	51,804	4,880	8.6
1969-70	45,550	5,500[4]	10.8	2023-24[4]	52,113	4,910	8.6

Note: "Private" includes all nonpublic schools. (1) Fall enrollment. (2) In thousands. Data from fall 1980 onward covers an expanded universe of private schools; comparisons with earlier years should be avoided. (3) Percent of U.S. students enrolled in private schools. (4) Projected.

Characteristics of Public Charter Schools and Students, 1999-2012

Source: National Center for Education Statistics, U.S. Dept. of Education

	1999-2000	2001-02	2003-04	2005-06	2007-08	2009-10	2011-12
Number of charter school students	339,678	571,029	789,479	1,012,906	1,276,731	1,610,285	2,057,599
			Percentage of charter school students who were—				
Sex							
Male	51.0%	50.8%	50.3%	49.9%	49.5%	49.5%	49.6%
Female	49.0	49.2	49.7	50.1	50.5	50.5	50.4
Race/ethnicity							
White	42.5	42.6	41.8	40.5	38.8	37.3	35.6
Black	33.5	32.5	31.9	32.1	31.8	30.3	28.7
Asian/Pacific Islander	2.8	3.1	3.2	3.6	3.8	3.9	4.0
American Indian/Alaska Native	1.5	1.7	1.5	1.4	1.2	1.0	0.9
Two or more races	NA	NA	NA	NA	NA	1.4	2.8
Hispanic	19.6	20.1	21.5	22.4	24.5	26.0	28.0
Number of charter schools	1,524	2,348	2,977	3,780	4,388	4,952	5,696
			Percentage of charter schools that were—				
School level							
Elementary	54.6%	50.6%	52.0%	52.1%	53.3%	54.1%	54.9%
Secondary	25.9	24.2	26.2	28.0	27.8	26.8	24.9
Combined	18.6	21.6	21.0	18.6	18.3	18.8	19.5
Enrollment size							
Under 300	77.1	73.6	71.1	69.6	65.6	61.5	55.8
300-499	12.0	13.6	15.6	16.5	19.3	20.8	23.1
500-999	8.6	9.9	10.1	10.9	12.0	14.0	17.0
1,000 or more	2.4	2.8	3.2	3.0	3.1	3.7	4.2
Locale							
City	NA	NA	52.7	52.5	54.3	54.8	55.4
Suburban	NA	NA	22.0	22.2	22.0	21.1	21.2
Town	NA	NA	9.6	9.4	8.5	8.0	7.4
Rural	NA	NA	15.8	16.0	15.2	16.1	16.0

NA = Not available. **Note:** Race categories exclude persons of Hispanic ethnicity, who may be of any race.

Homeschooled Students, 2011-12

Source: National Center for Education Statistics, U.S. Dept. of Education

A total of 1,770,000 U.S. students in grades K-12 were homeschooled in 2011-12, up from 1.5 mil in 2007 and 850,000 in 1999. In a 2012 U.S. Dept. of Education survey of parents who homeschool their children, the reasons they gave as most important in their decision to homeschool included concern over the school environment, including such factors as safety, drugs, or negative peer pressure (25%); dissatisfaction with academic instruction in schools (19%); desire to provide religious instruction (16%); desire to provide moral instruction (5%); desire to provide a nontraditional approach to education (5%); and the child having a physical or mental health problem (5%). In all, 91% cited concern over school environment as one of their reasons, 77% cited moral instruction, 74% cited dissatisfaction with academic instruction, and 64% cited religious instruction.

Characteristic	No. of students (thous.)	% distrib.	Home-schooling rate[1]	Characteristic	No. of students (thous.)	% distrib.	Home-schooling rate[1]
Total	1,770	NA	3.4%	**Grade equivalent**			
Household locale				Kindergarten-2nd grade	415	23%	3.1%
City	489	28%	3.2	3rd-5th grade	416	23	3.4
Suburban	601	34	3.1	6th-8th grade	425	24	3.5
Town	132	7	2.7	9th-12th grade	514	29	3.7
Rural	548	31	4.5				
Race/ethnicity[2]				**Parents' education**			
White	1,201	68	4.5	Less than high school	203	11	3.4
Black	139	8	1.9	High school	355	20	3.4
Asian/Pacific Islander	73	4	2.6	Vocational/technical			
Other race(s)	90	5	3.2	or some college	525	30	3.4
Hispanic (any race)	267	15	2.3	Bachelor's degree	436	25	3.7
Poverty status				Graduate/professional			
Poor	348	20	3.5	school	252	14	3.4
Nonpoor	1,422	80	3.4				

NA = Not applicable. **Note:** Numbers may not add up to totals because of rounding. Homeschooled students are school-age children in a grade equivalent to K-12 who receive instruction at home all or most of the time. Excludes students enrolled in public or private school more than 25 hours per week or homeschooled because of temporary illness only. (1) Percentage of total group or subgroup within general homeschooled pop. (2) Race categories exclude persons of Hispanic ethnicity, who may be of any race.

Common Core State Standards
Source: Common Core State Standards Initiative

In 2009, members of the Council of Chief State School Officers and the National Governors Association Center for Best Practices met to develop the Common Core State Standards, a set of college- and career-readiness standards for kindergarten through 12th grade in English language arts/literacy and mathematics. The Common Core State Standards were released in June 2010. As of Aug. 2014, 43 states; Washington, DC; American Samoa; Guam; Northern Mariana Islands; and the U.S. Virgin Islands had adopted and were working to implement the standards, which are designed to ensure that students graduating from high school are prepared to take credit-bearing introductory courses in two- or four-year college programs or to enter the workforce.

Assessment is expected to take place starting in the 2014-15 school year. Most states will use tests developed by the Partnership for Assessment of Readiness for College and Careers (PARCC) or the Smarter Balanced Assessment Consortium.

The Common Core standards have received both support and criticism. Proponents claim that the Common Core standards would better prepare students for college or the workforce and make them more competitive in the world. Critics claim that teachers and parents did not have enough input in developing the standards, that the federal government would be too involved in education (in spite of the state-level adoption of Common Core), and that implementing the standards would be too costly.

Top 50 Libraries in U.S. by Volumes Held, 2010
Source: ALA Library Fact Sheet Number 22, American Library Association (ALA)

Rank	Institution	Volumes held	Rank	Institution	Volumes held
1.	Library of Congress	34,528,818	26.	Univ. of Pennsylvania	6,438,305
2.	Boston Public Library[1]	19,090,261	27.	Duke Univ.	6,174,814
3.	Harvard Univ.	16,832,952	28.	Ohio State Univ.	6,161,657
4.	New York Public Library[1]	16,342,365	29.	Univ. of Pittsburgh	6,148,036
5.	Univ. of Illinois–Urbana-Champaign	13,158,748	30.	Univ. of Arizona	5,998,148
6.	Yale Univ.	12,787,962	31.	Chicago Public Library	5,790,289
7.	Univ. of California–Berkeley	11,545,418	32.	Univ. of Oklahoma	5,662,666
8.	Columbia Univ.	11,189,036	33.	Michigan State Univ.	5,609,761
9.	Univ. of Michigan	10,778,736	34.	Univ. of Virginia	5,607,915
10.	Univ. of Texas–Austin	9,990,941	35.	San Diego Public Library	5,535,415
11.	Univ. of Chicago	9,837,021	36.	Univ. of Iowa	5,490,825
12.	Univ. of California–Los Angeles	9,151,964	37.	Pennsylvania State Univ.	5,441,121
13.	Public Library of Cincinnati and Hamilton County (OH)	8,819,759	38.	New York Univ.	5,382,424
14.	Indiana Univ.	8,677,974	39.	Northwestern Univ.	5,047,970
15.	Stanford Univ.	8,500,000	40.	Free Library of Philadelphia	5,043,943
16.	Univ. of Wisconsin–Madison	8,421,198	41.	Dallas Public Library	4,972,494
17.	Cornell Univ.	8,173,778	42.	Hennepin County Library (MN)	4,961,514
18.	Princeton Univ.	7,226,744	43.	Univ. of Georgia	4,810,192
19.	Univ. of Washington	7,203,156	44.	Rutgers Univ.	4,722,407
20.	Univ. of Minnesota	7,111,311	45.	Univ. of Colorado	4,681,261
21.	Detroit Public Library	7,070,433	46.	Texas A&M Univ.	4,577,498
22.	Univ. of North Carolina–Chapel Hill	7,012,787	47.	Arizona State Univ.	4,497,114
23.	County of Los Angeles Public Library	6,795,552	48.	Univ. of Florida	4,414,450
24.	Queens Borough Public Library (NY)	6,544,609	49.	Univ. of Cincinnati	4,379,445
25.	Los Angeles Public Library	6,459,552	50.	North Carolina State Univ.	4,332,899

Note: For academic libraries, a volume is a single physical unit of any printed, typewritten, handwritten, mimeographed, or processed work, distinguished from other units by a separate binding, encasement, portfolio, or other clear distinction, which has been cataloged, classified, and made ready for use, and which is typically the unit used to charge circulation transactions. For public libraries, holdings are the number of cataloged items plus paperbacks and videocassettes even if uncataloged. (1) Includes both public library and research library collection numbers.

Number of Public Libraries and Operating Revenue by State, 2011
Source: Public Libraries Survey, Institute of Museum and Library Services

State	No.[1]	Revenue[2] (thous.)	State	No.[1]	Revenue[2] (thous.)	State	No.[1]	Revenue[2] (thous.)	State	No.[1]	Revenue[2] (thous.)
AL	212	$94,743	IL	621	$762,248	MT	81	$24,556	RI	48	$46,889
AK	72	32,973	IN	238	313,552	NE	216	50,689	SC	42	120,217
AZ	90	176,830	IA	531	111,863	NV	22	96,675	SD	103	22,364
AR	55	67,861	KS	311	111,529	NH	221	53,537	TN	185	107,722
CA	182	1,279,915	KY	118	169,709	NJ	281	477,239	TX	553	455,914
CO	114	264,038	LA	68	196,875	NM	82	43,957	UT	72	91,080
CT	183	183,237	ME	214	40,013	NY	756	1,200,933	VT	159	19,903
DE	21	25,538	MD	24	254,505	NC	77	199,574	VA	91	260,594
DC	1	37,515	MA	359	259,396	ND	76	15,764	WA	61	380,651
FL	77	519,635	MI	389	417,495	OH	251	774,641	WV	97	36,197
GA	61	190,390	MN	138	206,542	OK	117	106,565	WI	382	225,867
HI	1	31,759	MS	50	49,299	OR	126	185,674	WY	23	29,480
ID	101	47,034	MO	147	225,320	PA	634	324,787	Total U.S.	8,956	11,421,285

(1) Includes central libraries only. (2) Some totals may be estimated because of nonresponse.

Population With Upper Secondary Education in Selected Countries, 2012
Source: Organization for Economic Cooperation and Development

Ranked by percentage of the population ages 25-64 that have received at least an upper secondary (senior high school) education.

Country	%	Country	%	Country	%	Country	%	Country	%
Czech Republic	92%	Germany	86%	South Korea	82%	New Zealand	74%	Chile[1]	57%
Slovak Republic	92	Switzerland	86	Norway	82	France	73	Italy	57
Estonia	90	Finland	85	Denmark	78	Netherlands	73	Spain	55
Poland	90	Israel	85	Luxembourg	78	Belgium	72	Portugal	38
Canada	89	Slovenia	85	United Kingdom	78	Iceland	71	Mexico	37
United States	89	Austria	83	Australia	76	Greece	68	Turkey	34
Sweden	88	Hungary	82	Ireland	75				

(1) 2011 data.

Financial Aid to U.S. Undergraduate Students, 2000-12

Source: National Center for Education Statistics, U.S. Dept. of Education

Control and level of institution/ year	Number enrolled	Number receiving financial aid	Percent receiving aid	Percent of enrolled students in student aid programs				Average award[1]			
				Federal grants	State/ local grants	Institu- tional grants	Student loans[2]	Federal grants	State/ local grants	Institu- tional grants	Student loans[2]
All institutions											
2000-01	1,976,600	1,390,527	70.3%	31.6%	31.2%	31.1%	40.1%	$3,285	$2,694	$6,263	$4,974
2011-12	2,571,801	2,140,298	83.2	47.6	30.8	37.9	51.2	4,493	2,959	8,908	6,765
Public											
2000-01	1,333,236	872,109	65.4	30.0	33.5	22.7	30.7	3,181	2,255	3,005	4,030
2011-12	1,766,681	1,417,798	80.3	46.7	35.6	29.6	42.5	4,468	2,816	4,503	6,034
4-year											
2000-01	804,793	573,430	71.3	26.6	36.5	29.6	40.7	3,395	2,732	3,457	4,244
2011-12	1,059,832	878,851	82.9	39.1	37.1	42.1	52.6	4,540	3,584	4,965	6,454
2-year											
2000-01	528,443	298,679	56.5	35.2	28.8	12.1	15.3	2,936	1,334	1,326	3,166
2011-12	706,849	538,947	76.2	58.1	33.4	10.9	27.4	4,396	1,534	1,819	4,826
Private nonprofit											
2000-01	439,369	363,044	82.6	28.4	31.8	68.1	57.7	3,804	3,961	9,735	5,311
2011-12	512,814	457,300	89.2	35.0	27.0	79.3	63.5	4,724	3,593	15,314	7,598
4-year											
2000-01	419,499	347,638	82.9	27.4	32.2	70.1	58.1	3,872	3,966	9,854	5,285
2011-12	499,961	445,217	89.1	33.9	27.1	80.5	63.4	4,751	3,610	15,428	7,610
2-year											
2000-01	19,870	15,406	77.5	49.2	23.9	25.7	49.5	2,999	3,821	2,864	5,958
2011-12	12,853	12,083	94.0	76.3	24.3	31.8	65.5	4,250	2,877	4,143	7,130
Private for-profit											
2000-01	203,995	155,374	76.2	49.3	15.2	6.2	63.5	3,055	3,295	2,034	7,290
2011-12	292,306	265,200	90.7	75.4	8.4	15.2	82.3	4,396	3,043	2,155	7,918
4-year											
2000-01	81,075	51,739	63.8	36.1	11.9	8.3	57.7	3,033	3,817	2,135	7,596
2011-12	112,917	102,422	90.7	75.7	10.8	22.3	82.8	4,764	3,050	2,945	8,360
2-year											
2000-01	122,920	103,635	84.3	58.0	17.3	4.8	67.3	3,064	3,057	1,919	7,117
2011-12	179,389	162,778	90.7	75.2	6.9	10.8	82.0	4,162	3,036	1,126	7,638

Note: Data for full-time, first-time, degree-seeking undergraduate students. (1) Average amounts for students participating in indicated programs, in constant 2012-13 dollars. (2) Includes only loans made directly to students. Does not include Parent Loans for Undergraduate Students (PLUS) and other loans made directly to parents.

College Enrollment by Selected Characteristics, 1947-2012

Source: National Center for Education Statistics, U.S. Dept. of Education

Year	Total enrollment[1]	Attendance status			Sex of student		Control of institution			
		Full-time	Part-time	% part- time	Male	Female	Public	Total	Private Nonprofit	For-profit
1947[2]	2,338,226	NA	NA	NA	1,659,249	678,977	1,152,377	1,185,849	NA	NA
1950[2]	2,281,298	NA	NA	NA	1,560,392	720,906	1,139,699	1,141,599	NA	NA
1955[2]	2,653,034	NA	NA	NA	1,733,184	919,850	1,476,282	1,176,752	NA	NA
1965	5,920,864	4,095,728	1,825,136[3]	30.8%	3,630,020	2,290,844	3,969,596	1,951,268	NA	NA
1970	8,580,887	5,816,290	2,764,597	32.2	5,043,642	3,537,245	6,428,134	2,152,753	2,134,420	18,333
1975	11,184,859	6,841,334	4,343,525	38.8	6,148,997	5,035,862	8,834,508	2,350,351	2,311,448	38,903
1980	12,096,895	7,097,958	4,998,937	41.3	5,874,374	6,222,521	9,457,394	2,639,501	2,527,787	111,714[4]
1985	12,247,055	7,075,221	5,171,834	42.2	5,818,450	6,428,605	9,479,273	2,767,782	2,571,791	195,991
1990	13,818,637	7,820,985	5,997,652	43.4	6,283,909	7,534,728	10,844,717	2,973,920	2,760,227	213,693
1995	14,261,781	8,128,802	6,132,979	43.0	6,342,539	7,919,242	11,092,374	3,169,407	2,929,044	240,363
2000	15,312,289	9,009,600	6,302,689	41.2	6,721,769	8,590,520	11,752,786	3,559,503	3,109,419	450,084
2001	15,927,987	9,447,502	6,480,485	40.7	6,960,815	8,967,172	12,233,156	3,694,831	3,167,330	527,501
2002	16,611,711	9,946,359	6,665,352	40.1	7,202,116	9,409,595	12,751,993	3,859,718	3,265,476	594,242
2003	16,911,481	10,326,133	6,585,348	38.9	7,260,264	9,651,217	12,858,694	4,052,783	3,341,048	711,735
2004	17,272,044	10,610,177	6,661,867	38.6	7,387,262	9,884,782	12,980,112	4,291,932	3,411,685	880,247
2005	17,487,475	10,797,011	6,690,464	38.3	7,455,925	10,031,550	13,021,834	4,465,641	3,454,692	1,010,949
2006	17,758,870	10,957,305	6,801,565	38.3	7,574,815	10,184,055	13,180,133	4,578,737	3,512,866	1,065,871
2007	18,248,128	11,269,892	6,978,236	38.2	7,815,914	10,432,214	13,490,780	4,757,348	3,571,150	1,186,198
2008	19,102,814	11,747,743	7,355,071	38.5	8,188,895	10,913,919	13,972,153	5,130,661	3,661,519	1,469,142
2009	20,427,711	12,722,782	7,704,929	37.7	8,769,504	11,658,207	14,810,642	5,617,069	3,765,083	1,851,986
2010	21,016,126	13,082,267	7,933,859	37.8	9,044,811	11,971,315	15,142,809	5,873,317	3,854,920	2,018,397
2011	20,994,113	13,001,457	7,992,656	38.1	9,026,499	11,967,614	15,110,196	5,883,917	3,927,186	1,956,513
2012	20,642,819	12,737,013	7,905,806	38.3	8,919,087	11,723,732	14,880,343	5,762,476	3,953,578	1,808,898

NA = Not available. Note: Data for 1947-95 are for institutions of higher education, while later data are for degree-granting institutions. Degree-granting institutions grant associate's or higher degrees and participate in Title IV federal financial aid programs. The degree-granting classification is very similar to the earlier higher education classification, but it includes more two-year colleges and excludes a few higher education institutions that do not grant degrees. (1) Fall enrollment. (2) Degree-credit enrollment only. (3) Includes part-time resident students and all extension students (students attending courses at sites separate from the primary reporting campus). In later years, part-time student enrollment was collected as a distinct category. (4) Large increases is due to the addition of schools accredited by the Accrediting Commission of Career Schools and Colleges of Technology.

Charges at U.S. Institutions of Higher Education, 1969-2013

Source: National Center for Education Statistics, U.S. Dept. of Education

Data are for the entire academic year and are average charges for full-time students at degree-granting postsecondary institutions. Room and board based on full-time students. For 1989-90 on, board is based on 20 meals per week.

Public (in-state)	Tuition and fees			Board rates			Dormitory charges		
	All institutions	2-yr	4-yr	All institutions	2-yr	4-yr	All institutions	2-yr	4-yr
1969-70	$323	$178	$358	$508	$465	$510	$366	$308	$369
1979-80	583	355	738	867	893	865	715	574	725
1989-90	1,356	756	1,780	1,635	1,581	1,638	1,513	962	1,557
1999-2000	2,504	1,348	3,349	2,364	1,834	2,406	2,440	1,549	2,519
2001-02	2,700	1,380	3,735	2,598	2,036	2,645	2,723	1,722	2,816
2002-03	2,903	1,483	4,046	2,669	2,164	2,712	2,930	1,954	3,029
2003-04	3,319	1,702	4,587	2,822	2,221	2,876	3,106	2,089	3,212
2004-05	3,629	1,849	5,027	2,931	2,353	2,981	3,304	2,174	3,418
2005-06	3,874	1,935	5,351	3,035	2,306	3,093	3,545	2,251	3,664
2006-07	4,102	2,018	5,666	3,191	2,390	3,253	3,757	2,407	3,878
2007-08	4,291	2,061	5,943	3,331	2,409	3,404	3,952	2,506	4,082
2008-09	4,512	2,136	6,312	3,554	2,769	3,619	4,190	2,664	4,331
2009-10	4,751	2,285	6,695	3,653	2,574	3,754	4,399	2,845	4,565
2010-11	5,076	2,439	7,136	3,848	2,685	3,958	4,640	2,960	4,824
2011-12	5,559	2,652	7,703	3,955	2,831	4,055	4,862	3,090	5,046
2012-13	5,899	2,792	8,070	4,061	2,889	4,163	5,062	3,247	5,241
Private (nonprofit and for-profit)									
1969-70	$1,533	$1,034	$1,562	$560	$546	$561	$434	$413	$436
1979-80	3,130	2,062	3,225	955	923	957	827	766	831
1989-90	8,147	5,196	8,396	1,948	1,811	1,953	1,923	1,663	1,935
1999-2000	14,100	8,225	14,616	2,877	2,753	2,879	3,236	3,067	3,242
2001-02	15,742	10,076	16,211	3,104	2,633	3,109	3,567	3,116	3,576
2002-03	16,383	10,651	16,826	3,206	3,870	3,197	3,752	3,232	3,764
2003-04	17,315	11,545	17,763	3,364	4,432	3,354	3,945	3,581	3,952
2004-05	18,154	12,122	18,604	3,485	3,700	3,483	4,178	4,475	4,173
2005-06	18,862	12,450	19,292	3,645	4,781	3,637	4,400	4,173	4,404
2006-07	20,048	12,708	20,517	3,785	3,429	3,788	4,606	4,147	4,613
2007-08	20,972	13,126	21,427	3,992	4,074	3,991	4,804	4,484	4,808
2008-09	21,570	13,562	22,036	4,209	4,627	4,206	5,025	4,537	5,032
2009-10	21,444	14,876	21,908	4,331	4,390	4,331	5,249	5,217	5,249
2010-11	22,186	14,467	22,771	4,434	4,475	4,433	5,406	4,928	5,413
2011-12	22,850	14,003	23,460	4,584	4,483	4,584	5,624	5,168	5,629
2012-13	23,943	14,129	24,525	4,709	3,977	4,712	5,831	5,222	5,837

Endowment Assets of Colleges and Universities, 2013

Source: *2013 NACUBO-Commonfund Study of Endowments*, National Association of College and University Business Officers (NACUBO)

Rank	College/university	Endowment assets[1]	% change, 2012-13	Rank	College/university	Endowment assets[1]	% change, 2012-13
1.	Harvard University	$32,334,293	6.2%	22.	Dartmouth College	$3,733,596	7.1%
2.	Yale University	20,780,000	7.4	23.	Vanderbilt University	3,673,434	8.1
3.	University of Texas System	20,448,313	12.0	24.	Ohio State University	3,149,169	33.1
4.	Stanford University	18,688,868	9.7	25.	Johns Hopkins University	2,987,298	11.5
5.	Princeton University	18,200,433	7.4	26.	University of Pittsburgh	2,975,896	13.7
6.	Massachusetts Institute of Technology	11,005,932	6.8	27.	Pennsylvania State University	2,956,803	66.1
7.	Texas A&M University System and Foundations	8,732,010	14.3	28.	New York University	2,949,000	7.0
				29.	University of Minnesota and Foundations	2,757,476	10.6
8.	University of Michigan	8,382,311	9.0	30.	Brown University	2,669,948	8.4
9.	Columbia University	8,197,880	7.1	31.	University of North Carolina at Chapel Hill and Foundations	2,381,151	9.3
10.	Northwestern University	7,883,323	10.7				
11.	University of Pennsylvania	7,741,396	14.6	32.	University of Washington	2,346,693	11.1
12.	University of Notre Dame	6,856,301	8.3	33.	Purdue University	2,182,171	13.8
13.	University of Chicago	6,668,974	1.5	34.	University of Richmond	2,023,357	8.3
14.	University of California	6,377,379	7.0	35.	University of Wisconsin Foundation	2,020,019	11.5
15.	Duke University	6,040,973	8.7				
16.	Emory University	5,816,046	6.5	36.	Williams College	1,996,681	11.0
17.	Washington University in St. Louis	5,651,860	8.1	37.	University of Illinois and Foundation	1,925,949	16.8
18.	Cornell University	5,272,228	6.6	38.	California Institute of Technology	1,849,880	5.9
19.	University of Virginia	5,166,660	7.9				
20.	Rice University	4,836,728	9.5	39.	Amherst College	1,823,748	11.2
21.	University of Southern California	3,868,355	10.9	40.	Pomona College	1,823,441	8.6

Note: Market value of endowment assets in the fiscal year. (1) In thousands.

U.S. Higher Education Trends: Bachelor's Degrees Conferred, 1899-2024

Source: National Center for Education Statistics, U.S. Dept. of Education
(*) figures are projected.

Financial Aid for College and Other Postsecondary Education

As of Aug. 2014. Reviewed by National Association of Student Financial Aid Administrators.

The cost of postsecondary education in the U.S. continues to increase, but financial aid—in the form of **grants** (no repayment needed), **loans**, and/or **work-study** programs—is widely available to help families meet these expenses. Most federal aid is limited to families that demonstrate financial need as determined by standard formulas and is designed to help students attend the college of their choice regardless of their ability to pay. Financial aid personnel at each school can provide information about all aid programs (federal, state, institutional, and private) available to students, how to apply, and deadlines.

All applicants for federal aid must file a Free Application for Federal Student Aid (**FAFSA**), generally as soon as possible after Jan. 1 for the academic year starting the following Aug. or Sept. Figures provided should match federal income tax forms filed for the previous year. This is made easier by the availability of the IRS Data Retrieval Tool, which allows online applicants to access and transfer IRS tax return information directly into their FAFSA. Many other sources of aid—state governments, employers and unions, civic organizations, and the institutions themselves—also use the FAFSA to determine eligibility for aid. There are also federal programs that pay for postsecondary education in return for service: AmeriCorps (1-800-942-2677), Reserve Officers' Training Corps (1-800-USA-ROTC), the G.I. Bill (1-888-GIBILL-1), and the National Health Service Corps (1-800-221-9393). A student must reapply for aid annually.

A **federal formula**, based on information provided in the FAFSA, takes into account such factors as family income in the preceding calendar year, parental and student assets (excluding the parents' home, farm, or certain small businesses), length of time to parents' retirement, and unusual expenses (such as very high medical expenses). Outside scholarships are also taken into account in determining eligibility for federal, institutional, and state financial aid programs.

The formula determines a family's **expected family contribution** (EFC), which is divided among the number of family members—excluding parents—in college. The EFC is subtracted from the total cost of attending college for each person. The difference determines financial need and the maximum federal aid for which the family may be eligible. (Some institutions use a separate formula for need-based institutional aid.) Some schools guarantee to meet the full financial need of each admitted student; most do their best to cover a student's financial need using various forms of financial aid but may not be able to because of a lack of funds.

The **aid package** offered by each school may include one or more of the following resources: Federal Pell Grants, for those who demonstrate sufficient financial need; Federal Supplemental Educational Opportunity Grants, for those who still have significant need after receiving Pell Grants; grants from the school; Federal Work-Study or other work programs; low-interest Federal Perkins loans; and federal Direct Subsidized and Unsubsidized loans (often referred to as Stafford loans). Parents of undergraduates and students in graduate or professional school may apply for a PLUS loan. Unsubsidized Direct Loans and PLUS loans are available regardless of financial need, but students and parents must still complete the FAFSA to get these loans.

Loans have varying interest rates and other requirements. Repayment of Federal Perkins Loans, Direct Subsidized Loans, and Direct Unsubsidized Loans does not begin until after graduation; deferments, income-based repayment plans, and loan forgiveness are available on federal loans for students who meet certain requirements. For PLUS loans, parents and graduate-level students must pass a credit check and may need to begin repayment of both principal and interest while the student is still in school.

Terms may vary, but federal student loans must be repaid, even if financial circumstances change, education is incomplete or not as expected, or post-graduation income is less than expected. The loan servicer or lender is required to provide a loan repayment schedule that states the first payment due date, the number and frequency of payments, and the amount due. Some loans have a grace period, a set period of time (in most cases six months) after graduation before repayment begins. Some loan servicers have a number of repayment plan options—including graduated repayments, extended repayment, income-based repayment—or offer loan consolidation.

Certain federal income **tax credits and refunds** are also available to families who meet requirements; see the chapter on taxes.

Rules for financial aid are complex and changeable. *Funding Your Education: The Guide to Federal Student Aid*, a comprehensive resource on financial aid from the U.S. Dept. of Education, is available online in English and Spanish at studentaid.ed.gov/resources/.

Further information and FAFSA forms are available from schools or from the Federal Student Aid Information Center: 1-800-4-FED-AID, Mon.-Fri., 8 AM-10 PM EST; www.fafsa.ed.gov.

Average Salaries of U.S. College Professors, 2013-14

Source: American Association of University Professors

		Men			Women		
Teaching level		Public institution	Private/ independent institution	Religiously affiliated institution	Public institution	Private/ independent institution	Religiously affiliated institution
Doctoral level	Professor	$130,229	$177,289	$142,981	$116,951	$162,733	$130,310
	Associate	89,066	110,919	97,112	82,966	103,572	91,608
	Assistant	78,627	97,677	83,918	71,964	88,743	76,390
Master's level	Professor	92,056	109,795	97,414	87,596	101,864	89,386
	Associate	74,289	82,657	76,182	71,191	78,824	71,757
	Assistant	63,972	70,246	63,632	61,455	66,672	60,982
Baccalaureate level	Professor	88,648	108,653	81,963	84,684	103,121	78,586
	Associate	72,428	79,897	65,269	68,767	78,116	63,866
	Assistant	60,524	65,185	55,444	59,208	63,485	54,813
2-year	Professor	77,892	NA	NA	77,426	NA	NA
	Associate	63,222	NA	NA	61,487	NA	NA
	Assistant	54,068	NA	NA	53,517	NA	NA

NA = Not available. **Note:** Salaries are for full-time faculty members only.

Average ACT Scores and Characteristics of College-Bound Students, 1990-2014

Source: ACT, Inc. (formerly American College Testing)

SCORES	Unit	1990	1995	2000	2005	2008	2009	2010	2011	2012	2013	2014
Composite score	Points	20.6	20.8	21.0	20.9	21.1	21.1	21.0	21.1	21.1	20.9	21.0
Male	Points	21.0	21.0	21.2	21.1	21.2	21.3	21.2	21.2	21.2	20.9	21.1
Female	Points	20.3	20.7	20.9	20.9	21.0	20.9	20.9	21.0	21.0	20.9	20.9
English score	Points	20.5	20.2	20.5	20.4	20.6	20.6	20.5	20.6	20.5	20.2	20.3
Male	Points	20.1	19.8	20.0	20.0	20.1	20.2	20.1	20.2	20.0	19.8	20.0
Female	Points	20.9	20.6	20.9	20.8	21.0	20.9	20.8	20.9	20.9	20.6	20.7
Math score	Points	19.9	20.2	20.7	20.7	21.0	21.0	21.0	21.1	21.1	20.9	20.9
Male	Points	20.7	20.9	21.4	21.3	21.6	21.6	21.6	21.6	21.7	21.4	21.4
Female	Points	19.3	19.7	20.2	20.2	20.4	20.4	20.5	20.6	20.6	20.5	20.5
PARTICIPANTS												
Total number	(Thous.)	817	945	1,065	1,186	1,422	1,480	1,569	1,623	1,666	1,799	1,846
Male	Percent	46%	44%	43%	44%	44%	45%	45%	46%	46%	46%	46%
White	Percent	79	80	72	66	63	64	62	60	59	58	56
Black	Percent	9	9	10	12	13	13	14	14	13	13	13
Hispanic[1]	Percent	4	5	5	7	8	9	10	12	14	14	15
Composite score												
27 or above	Percent	12	13	14	14	9[2]	12	16	17	17	13	17
18 or below	Percent	35	34	32	34	33	34	35	34	34	36	36

Note: Minimum score, 1; maximum score, 36. Test scores and characteristics of college-bound students are based on the performance of all ACT-tested students who graduated in the spring of a given school year and took the ACT assessment during junior or senior year of high school. (1) Persons of Hispanic origin may be of any race. (2) Composite score of 28 or above.

Average ACT Composite Scores by State, 2014

Source: ACT, Inc. (formerly American College Testing)

State	Avg. comp. score	% grads taking ACT	State	Avg. comp. score	% grads taking ACT	State	Avg. comp. score	% grads taking ACT
Alabama	20.6	80%	Louisiana	19.2	100%	Ohio	22.0	72%
Alaska	21.0	37	Maine	23.6	9	Oklahoma	20.7	75
Arizona	19.7	55	Maryland	22.6	22	Oregon	21.4	36
Arkansas	20.4	93	Massachusetts	24.3	23	Pennsylvania	22.7	19
California	22.3	29	Michigan	20.1	100	Rhode Island	22.9	16
Colorado	20.6	100	Minnesota	22.9	76	South Carolina	20.4	58
Connecticut	24.2	29	Mississippi	19.0	100	South Dakota	21.9	78
Delaware	23.2	18	Missouri	21.8	76	Tennessee	19.8	100
District of Columbia	21.6	37	Montana	20.5	100	Texas	20.9	40
Florida	19.6	81	Nebraska	21.7	86	Utah	20.8	100
Georgia	20.8	53	Nevada	21.2	36	Vermont	23.2	29
Hawaii	18.2	90	New Hampshire	24.2	20	Virginia	22.8	28
Idaho	22.4	45	New Jersey	23.1	25	Washington	23.0	22
Illinois	20.7	100	New Mexico	19.9	69	West Virginia	20.6	65
Indiana	21.9	40	New York	23.4	27	Wisconsin	22.2	73
Iowa	22.0	68	North Carolina	18.9	100	Wyoming	20.1	100
Kansas	22.0	75	North Dakota	20.6	100	**U.S. average**	**21.0**	**57**
Kentucky	19.9	100						

Mean SAT Scores of College-Bound Seniors, 1975-2013

Source: The College Board

(recentered scale; for school year ending in year shown)

	1975	1980	1985	1990	1995	2000	2004	2005	2006	2007	2008	2009	2010	2011	2012	2013
Critical reading score[1]	512	502	509	500	504	505	508	508	503	501	500	499	500	497	496	496
Male	515	506	514	505	505	507	512	513	505	503	502	502	502	500	498	499
Female	509	498	503	496	502	504	504	505	502	500	499	497	498	495	493	494
Math score	498	492	500	501	506	514	518	520	518	515	514	514	515	514	514	514
Male	518	515	522	521	525	533	537	538	536	532	533	533	533	531	532	531
Female	479	473	480	483	490	498	501	504	502	499	499	498	499	500	499	499
Writing score	NA	NA	NA	NA	NA	NA	NA	NA	497	493	493	492	491	489	488	488
Male	NA	NA	NA	NA	NA	NA	NA	NA	491	487	486	485	485	482	481	482
Female	NA	NA	NA	NA	NA	NA	NA	NA	502	499	499	498	497	496	494	493

NA = Not applicable. **Note:** In 1995, the College Board recentered the scoring scale for the SAT by reestablishing the original mean score of 500 on the 200-800 scale. Earlier scores have been adjusted to account for this recentering. The writing test was first given in Mar. 2005; only the scores of the first graduating class to take the revised test are given. (1) Pre-2006 scores are for the Verbal section.

Mean SAT Scores by State, 1990-2013

Source: The College Board

(for school year ending in year shown; V = Verbal, M = Math, CR = Critical reading, W = Writing)

State	1990 V	1990 M	2000 V	2000 M	2010 CR	2010 M	2010 W	2012 CR	2012 M	2012 W	2013 CR	2013 M	2013 W	% grads taking SAT[1]
Alabama	545	534	559	555	556	550	544	538	531	527	544	534	530	8%
Alaska	514	501	519	515	518	515	491	512	507	485	508	505	482	54
Arizona	521	520	521	523	519	525	500	517	525	499	521	528	502	27
Arkansas	545	532	563	554	566	566	552	565	566	549	572	570	555	4
California	494	508	497	518	501	516	500	495	512	496	498	512	495	55
Colorado	533	534	534	537	568	572	555	575	581	562	578	581	562	17
Connecticut	506	496	508	509	509	514	513	506	512	510	508	512	512	88
Delaware	510	496	502	496	493	495	481	456	462	444	451	457	443	100
District of Columbia	483	467	494	486	474	464	466	466	460	456	473	466	461	83
Florida	495	493	498	500	496	498	479	492	492	476	492	490	475	66
Georgia	478	473	488	486	488	490	475	488	489	475	490	487	475	81
Hawaii	480	505	488	519	483	505	470	478	500	467	481	504	468	66
Idaho	542	524	540	541	543	541	517	547	541	525	454	459	451	20
Illinois	542	547	568	586	585	600	577	596	615	587	600	617	590	5
Indiana	486	486	498	501	494	505	477	493	501	476	493	500	477	69
Iowa	584	588	589	600	603	613	582	603	606	580	592	601	570	3
Kansas	566	563	574	580	590	595	567	584	594	561	589	595	568	6
Kentucky	548	541	548	550	575	575	563	579	575	566	585	584	572	6
Louisiana	551	537	562	558	555	550	547	542	536	529	556	553	546	9
Maine	501	490	504	500	468	467	454	470	472	452	467	451	453	93
Maryland	506	502	507	509	501	506	495	497	502	488	497	500	486	74
Massachusetts	503	498	511	513	512	526	509	513	530	508	515	529	509	89
Michigan	529	534	557	569	585	605	576	586	603	574	590	610	582	4
Minnesota	552	558	581	594	594	607	580	592	606	573	595	608	577	7
Mississippi	552	538	562	549	566	548	552	561	544	551	568	547	558	4
Missouri	548	541	572	577	593	595	580	589	592	575	596	595	582	5
Montana	540	542	543	546	538	538	517	536	536	511	539	540	516	28
Nebraska	559	562	560	571	585	593	568	576	585	562	584	583	567	5
Nevada	511	511	510	517	496	501	473	491	493	466	492	494	468	49
New Hampshire	518	510	520	519	520	524	510	521	525	510	524	528	515	75
New Jersey	495	498	498	513	495	514	497	495	517	499	499	522	500	78
New Mexico	554	546	549	543	553	549	534	550	546	529	550	545	531	13
New York	489	496	494	506	484	499	478	483	500	475	485	501	477	90
North Carolina	478	470	492	496	497	511	477	491	506	472	495	506	478	68
North Dakota	579	578	588	609	580	594	559	588	610	568	609	609	581	3
Ohio	526	522	533	539	538	548	522	543	552	525	548	556	531	19
Oklahoma	553	542	563	560	569	568	547	568	566	546	571	569	549	5
Oregon	515	509	527	527	523	524	499	521	523	498	520	520	499	57
Pennsylvania	497	490	498	497	492	501	480	491	501	480	494	504	482	74
Rhode Island	498	488	505	500	494	495	488	490	491	485	491	490	487	69
South Carolina	475	467	484	482	484	495	468	481	488	462	484	487	465	73
South Dakota	580	570	587	588	592	603	571	589	610	570	592	601	567	3
Tennessee	558	544	563	553	576	571	565	576	570	566	574	569	566	10
Texas	490	489	493	500	484	505	473	474	499	461	477	499	461	62
Utah	566	555	570	569	568	559	547	568	566	548	569	566	549	6
Vermont	507	493	513	508	519	521	506	519	523	505	516	519	505	69
Virginia	501	496	509	500	512	512	497	510	512	495	516	514	498	72
Washington	513	511	526	528	524	532	508	519	530	503	515	523	499	58
West Virginia	520	514	526	511	515	507	500	516	502	497	514	501	498	17
Wisconsin	552	559	584	597	595	604	579	594	605	577	591	604	576	4
Wyoming	534	538	545	545	570	567	546	567	579	549	581	588	558	5
National average	500	501	505	514	501	516	492	496	514	488	496	514	488	

Note: In 1995, the College Board recentered the scoring scale for the SAT by reestablishing the original mean score of 500 on the 200-800 scale. In 2005, the SAT was changed. The Verbal portion became Critical reading, and a writing test was added. The 2006 graduating class was the first to take the new test. (1) Based on number of high school graduates in 2012, as projected by the Western Interstate Commission for Higher Education, and number of students in the class of 2012 who took the SAT.

Four-Year Colleges and Universities

Source: Peterson's College Database © 2014 Peterson's Nelnet, LLC. All rights reserved.

Note: These listings **include only accredited degree-granting institutions** in the U.S. and U.S. territories with a total enrollment of 1,000 or more. Only four-year colleges and universities (which award a bachelor's degree as their highest undergraduate degree) are included. Data reported **only for institutions that provided updated information** on Peterson's Annual Survey of Undergraduate Institutions for the 2013-14 academic year, with some exceptions.

All institutions are coeducational except those where the ZIP code is followed directly by a number in parentheses: (1) = men only, (2) = primarily men, (3) = women only, (4) = primarily women.

The **Tuition & fees** column shows the annual tuition and required fees for full-time students or, where indicated, the tuition and standard fees per unit for part-time students. Where tuition varies according to residence, the figure is given for the most local resident and is coded as follows: (A) = area residents, (S) = state residents; all other figures apply to all students regardless of residence. Where annual expenses are expressed as a lump sum (including full-time tuition, mandatory fees, and room and board), the figure is entered under Tuition & fees and coded (C) = comprehensive fee. **Room & board** is the average cost for one academic year.

Control: 1 = independent (nonprofit), 2 = independent-religious, 3 = proprietary (profit-making), 4 = federal, 5 = state, 6 = commonwealth (Puerto Rico), 7 = territory (U.S. territories), 8 = county, 9 = district, 10 = city, 11 = state and local, 12 = state-related, 13 = private (unspecified). **Degree** means the highest degree offered: B = bachelor's, M = master's, D = doctorate.

Enrollment is the total number of matriculated undergraduate and (if applicable) graduate students.

Faculty is the total number of faculty members teaching undergraduate courses and (if available) graduate courses.

Grad. rate is the percentage of full-time, first-time bachelor's (or equivalent) degree-seeking undergraduate students entering school in 2007 who obtained their degrees within six years.

NA indicates category is inapplicable, or data is not available from a consistent source.

Name, address	Year founded	Tuition & fees	Room & board	Control, degree	Enrollment	Faculty	Grad. rate
Abilene Christian Univ., Abilene, TX 79699-9100	1906	$28,350	$8,800	2-D	4,461	379	57%
Abraham Baldwin Agr. Coll., Tifton, GA 31793	1933	$3,920(S)	$4,630	5-B	3,327	162	NA
Academy of Art Univ., San Francisco, CA 94105-3410	1929	$24,600	$14,160	3-M	16,002	1,496	33
Adams State Univ., Alamosa, CO 81101	1921	$7,449(S)	$7,700	5-D	3,207	237	25
Adelphi Univ., Garden City, NY 11530-0701	1896	$30,800	$12,330	1-D	7,645	1,011	63
Adrian Coll., Adrian, MI 49221-2575	1859	$32,660	$9,740	2-M	1,656	195	54
Adventist Univ. of Health Sciences, Orlando, FL 32803	1913	$12,430	$4,000	1-M	2,293	221	NA
AIB Coll. of Bus, Des Moines, IA 50321-1799	1921	$15,600	$3,612	1-B	1,019	72	NA
Alabama Agr. & Mech. Univ., Huntsville, AL 35811	1875	NA	NA	5-D	5,814	290	100
Alabama State Univ., Montgomery, AL 36101-0271	1867	$8,720(S)	$5,422	5-D	6,075	NA	26
Albany Coll. of Pharm. and Health Sciences, Albany, NY 12208	1881	$28,900	$10,000	1-D	1,633	124	72
Albany State Univ., Albany, GA 31705-2717	1903	$5,912(S)	$7,388	5-M	4,663	270	90
Albertus Magnus Coll., New Haven, CT 06511-1189	1925	$28,378	$12,342	2-M	1,582	76	57
Albion Coll., Albion, MI 49224-1831	1835	$35,866	$10,144	1-B	1,307	142	74
Albright Coll., Reading, PA 19612-5234	1856	$36,660	$10,000	2-M	1,751	168	54
Alcorn State Univ., Alcorn State, MS 39096-7500	1871	$5,724(S)	$7,999	5-M	3,848	219	35
Alderson Broaddus Univ., Philippi, WV 26416	1871	$22,740	$7,236	2-M	1,117	100	46
Alfred Univ., Alfred, NY 14802-1205	1836	$28,774	$11,618	1-D	2,362	190	64
Allegheny Coll., Meadville, PA 16335	1815	$40,660	$10,320	1-B	2,161	202	79
Alliant Intl. Univ., San Diego, CA 92131-1799	1952	$15,812	$11,268	1-D	3,523	626	NA
Alma Coll., Alma, MI 48801-1599	1886	$33,135	$9,265	2-B	1,419	166	61
Alvernia Univ., Reading, PA 19607-1799	1958	$30,080	$10,450	2-D	2,871	318	51
Alverno Coll., Milwaukee, WI 53234-3922	1887	$23,231	$7,252	2-M	2,536	266	39
Amberton Univ., Garland, TX 75041-5595	1971	$5,640	NA	2-M	1,461	40	NA
Amer. InterContinental Univ. Online, Schaumburg, IL 60173	1970	NA	NA	3-M	22,424	396	NA
Amer. Intl. Coll., Springfield, MA 01109-3189	1885	$30,040	$12,150	1-D	3,401	323	34
Amer. Public Univ. System, Charles Town, WV 25414	1991	$6,400	NA	3-M	55,422	2,154	NA
Amer. Univ., Washington, DC 20016-8001	1893	$41,833	$14,408	2-D	12,819	1,382	80
Amer. Univ. of Puerto Rico, Bayamón, PR 00960-2037	1963	$5,347	NA	1-M	2,468	162	NA
Amherst Coll., Amherst, MA 01002-5000	1821	$46,574	$12,170	1-B	1,785	263	96
Anderson Univ., Anderson, IN 46012-3495	1917	$26,200	$9,110	2-D	2,442	274	57
Anderson Univ., Anderson, SC 29621-4035	1911	$22,840	$8,354	2-D	2,922	259	41
Andrews Univ., Berrien Springs, MI 49104	1874	$25,676	$7,968	2-D	3,516	323	60
Angelo State Univ., San Angelo, TX 76909	1928	$7,493(S)	$8,098	5-D	6,536	351	31
Anna Maria Coll., Paxton, MA 01612	1946	$30,456	$11,450	2-M	1,554	NA	47
Antioch Univ., Seattle, Seattle, WA 98121-1814	1975	$20,595	NA	1-D	1,080	NA	NA
Appalachian State Univ., Boone, NC 28608	1899	$6,553(S)	$7,675	5-D	17,838	1,261	68
Aquinas Coll., Grand Rapids, MI 49506-1799	1886	$27,726	$8,350	2-M	1,981	246	58
Arcadia Univ., Glenside, PA 19038-3295	1853	$36,810	$12,560	2-D	3,905	465	61
Arkansas State Univ., State University, AR 72467	1909	$7,510(S)	$7,470	5-D	13,552	689	36
Arizona State Univ. at the Downtown Phoenix campus, Phoenix, AZ 85004	2006	$10,002(S)	$11,466	5-D	10,400	NA	47
Arizona State Univ. at the Polytechnic campus, Mesa, AZ 85212	1995	$9,054(S)	$10,242	5-D	3,701	NA	55
Arizona State Univ. at the Tempe campus, Tempe, AZ 85287	1885	$10,002(S)	$9,782	5-D	48,739	NA	60
Arizona State Univ. at the West campus, Glendale, AZ 85306	1984	$9,054(S)	$9,378	5-D	3,662	NA	55
Arkansas Tech. Univ., Russellville, AR 72801	1909	$6,918(S)	$6,246	5-M	11,389	551	42
Armstrong State Univ., Savannah, GA 31419-1997	1935	$6,010(S)	$10,266	5-D	7,101	408	34
Art Ctr. Coll. of Design, Pasadena, CA 91103	1930	$37,830	NA	1-M	1,985	NA	64
Asbury Univ., Wilmore, KY 40390-1198	1890	$26,868	$6,132	2-M	1,782	214	63
Ashford Univ., Clinton, IA 52733-2967	1918	NA	NA	3-M	10,568	748	NA
Ashland Univ., Ashland, OH 44805-3702	1878	$19,852	$9,502	2-D	6,491	591	59
Ashworth Coll., Norcross, GA 30092	1987	NA	NA	3-M	57,650	NA	NA
Aspen Univ., Denver, CO 80246-1930	1987	$750/course	NA	1-D	2,000	NA	NA
Assumption Coll., Worcester, MA 01609-1296	1904	$34,975	$6,777	2-M	2,524	215	73
Athens State Univ., Athens, AL 35611	1822	$5,760(S)	NA	5-B	3,162	207	NA
Atlantic Univ. Coll., Guaynabo, PR 00997	1983	NA	NA	1-M	1,236	NA	NA
Auburn Univ., Auburn University, AL 36849	1856	$9,852(S)	$11,552	5-D	24,864	1,363	68
Auburn Univ. at Montgomery, Montgomery, AL 36124-4023	1967	$8,750(S)	$7,860	5-D	5,096	335	33
Augsburg Coll., Minneapolis, MN 55454-1351	1869	$34,431	$9,104	2-D	3,554	355	66
Augustana Coll., Rock Island, IL 61201-2296	1860	$37,236	$9,435	2-B	2,524	239	78
Augustana Coll., Sioux Falls, SD 57197	1860	$28,630	$6,920	2-M	1,765	191	66
Aurora Univ., Aurora, IL 60506-4892	1893	$21,340	$9,542	1-D	4,946	405	52
Austin Coll., Sherman, TX 75090-4400	1849	$34,840	$11,503	2-M	1,224	136	72
Austin Peay State Univ., Clarksville, TN 37044	1927	$6,876(S)	$7,774	5-M	10,399	627	38
Avila Univ., Kansas City, MO 64145-1698	1916	$25,700	$7,500	2-M	1,971	209	48
Azusa Pacific Univ., Azusa, CA 91702-7000	1899	$32,256	$5,188	2-D	10,755	1,004	65
Babson Coll., Babson Park, MA 02457-0310	1919	$45,120	$14,494	1-M	3,343	257	91
Baker Coll. of Allen Park, Allen Park, MI 48101 (4)	2003	$8,280	NA	1-B	3,719	88	NA
Baker Coll. of Auburn Hills, Auburn Hills, MI 48326-1586	1911	$8,280	NA	1-B	3,102	155	NA
Baker Coll. of Cadillac, Cadillac, MI 49601	1986	$8,280	NA	1-B	1,550	105	NA

Name, address	Year founded	Tuition & fees	Room & board	Control, degree	Enroll- ment	Faculty	Grad. rate
Baker Coll. of Clinton Township, Clinton Township, MI 48035-4701	1990	$8,280	NA	1-B	4,380	208	NA
Baker Coll. of Flint, Flint, MI 48507-5508	1911	$8,280	$3,000	1-B	4,944	315	NA
Baker Coll. of Jackson, Jackson, MI 49202	1994	$8,280	NA	1-B	2,254	85	NA
Baker Coll. of Muskegon, Muskegon, MI 49442-3497	1888	$8,280	$3,000	1-B	4,011	177	NA
Baker Coll. of Owosso, Owosso, MI 48867-4400	1984	$8,280	$3,000	1-B	2,749	144	NA
Baker Coll. of Port Huron, Port Huron, MI 48060-2597	1990	$8,280	NA	1-B	1,037	126	NA
Baldwin Wallace Univ., Berea, OH 44017-2088	1845	$27,840	$7,740	2-M	4,053	421	71%
Ball State Univ., Muncie, IN 47306-1099	1918	$9,344(S)	$9,126	5-D	20,503	1,172	60
Baptist Bible Coll. of Pennsylvania, Clarks Summit, PA 18411-1297	1932	$19,710	$7,180	2-D	1,001	47	36
Baptist Coll. of Health Sciences, Memphis, TN 38104 (4)	1994	$11,870	$2,200	2-B	1,043	107	60
Bard Coll., Annandale-on-Hudson, NY 12504	1860	$46,370	$13,502	1-D	2,278	271	74
Barnard Coll., New York, NY 10027-6598 (3)	1889	$44,790	$14,210	1-B	2,489	322	90
Barry Univ., Miami Shores, FL 33161-6695	1940	$28,160	$10,200	2-D	9,030	NA	37
Barton Coll., Wilson, NC 27893-7000	1902	$26,664	$8,906	2-M	1,065	110	48
Baruch Coll. of the City Univ. of New York, New York, NY 10010-5585	1919	$6,030(S)	NA	11-M	17,505	1,116	67
Bastyr Univ., Kenmore, WA 98028-4966	1978	$22,812	$6,975	1-D	1,115	294	NA
Bates Coll., Lewiston, ME 04240-6028	1855	$60,720(C)	NA	1-B	1,791	204	93
Bayamón Central Univ., Bayamón, PR 00960-1725	1970	$8,200	NA	2-M	1,202	153	NA
Baylor Univ., Waco, TX 76798	1845	$38,120	$12,209	2-D	15,616	1,153	75
Bay Path Coll., Longmeadow, MA 01106-2292	1897	$29,959	$12,000	1-M	2,359	277	61
Becker Coll., Worcester, MA 01609	1784	$32,870	$12,000	1-B	1,902	199	24
Belhaven Univ., Jackson, MS 39202-1789	1883	$20,780	$7,700	2-M	2,987	288	40
Bellarmine Univ., Louisville, KY 40205-0671	1950	$36,290	$11,076	2-D	3,419	390	66
Bellevue Univ., Bellevue, NE 68005-3098	1965	$7,700	NA	1-D	10,304	411	37
Belmont Abbey Coll., Belmont, NC 28012-1802	1876	$18,500	$10,094	2-B	1,647	129	38
Belmont Univ., Nashville, TN 37212-3757	1951	$27,380	$10,000	2-D	6,915	735	68
Beloit Coll., Beloit, WI 53511-5596	1846	$42,500	$7,470	1-B	1,306	137	78
Bemidji State Univ., Bemidji, MN 56601-2699	1919	$8,124(S)	$7,256	5-M	4,952	174	48
Benedict Coll., Columbia, SC 29204	1870	$18,286	$8,104	2-B	2,641	NA	NA
Benedictine Coll., Atchison, KS 66002-1499	1859	$24,285	$8,605	2-M	2,177	211	59
Benedictine Univ., Lisle, IL 60532-0900	1887	$26,950	$8,280	2-D	5,368	577	52
Bentley Univ., Waltham, MA 02452-4705	1917	$41,110	$13,445	1-D	5,658	459	87
Berea Coll., Berea, KY 40404	1855	$870	$6,322	1-B	1,623	168	62
Berkeley Coll., Woodland Park, NJ 07424-3353	1931	NA	NA	3-B	3,709	NA	NA
Berkeley Coll.–New York City campus, New York, NY 10017-4604	1936	NA	NA	3-B	4,430	NA	NA
Berklee Coll. of Music, Boston, MA 02215-3693	1945	$36,490	$16,950	1-M	4,521	569	52
Berry Coll., Mount Berry, GA 30149-0159	1902	$29,090	$10,164	2-M	2,223	216	60
Bethel Coll., Mishawaka, IN 46545-5591	1947	$25,830	$7,780	2-M	1,804	191	62
Bethel Univ., McKenzie, TN 38201	1842	$14,520	$8,364	2-M	5,553	420	34
Bethel Univ., St. Paul, MN 55112-6999	1871	$31,760	$9,200	2-D	5,331	302	71
Beth Medrash Govoha, Lakewood, NJ 08701-2797 (1)	1943	NA	NA	2-M	5,639	NA	NA
Bethune-Cookman Univ., Daytona Beach, FL 32114-3099	1904	$14,410	$8,548	2-M	3,787	260	55
Binghamton Univ., State Univ. of New York, Vestal, NY 13850	1946	$8,144(S)	$12,688	5-D	16,077	908	81
Biola Univ., La Mirada, CA 90639-0001	1908	$32,142	$9,316	2-D	6,323	516	69
Birmingham-Southern Coll., Birmingham, AL 35254	1856	$30,765	$10,700	2-B	1,231	114	65
Black Hills State Univ., Spearfish, SD 57799	1883	$11,685(S)	$5,945	5-M	4,464	235	30
Bloomfield Coll., Bloomfield, NJ 07003-9981	1868	$26,750	$11,100	2-M	1,977	217	37
Bloomsburg Univ. of Pennsylvania, Bloomsburg, PA 17815-1301	1839	$8,582(S)	$7,848	5-D	10,127	510	62
Bluefield State Coll., Bluefield, WV 24701-2198	1895	$233/cr. hr.(S)	NA	5-B	1,747	149	22
Bluffton Univ., Bluffton, OH 45817	1899	$28,504	$9,360	2-M	1,146	95	60
Bob Jones Univ., Greenville, SC 29614	1927	$641/cr. hr.	NA	2-D	3,364	238	61
Boise State Univ., Boise, ID 83725-0399	1932	$6,640(S)	NA	5-D	21,981	1,175	38
Boricua Coll., New York, NY 10032-1560	1974	$11,750	NA	1-M	1,058	133	49
Boston Coll., Chestnut Hill, MA 02467-3800	1863	$45,622	$12,884	2-D	13,525	1,508	92
Boston Univ., Boston, MA 02215	1839	$44,910	$13,620	1-D	32,411	2,630	84
Bowdoin Coll., Brunswick, ME 04011	1794	$45,446	$12,388	1-B	1,795	230	93
Bowie State Univ., Bowie, MD 20715-9465	1865	$6,971(S)	$10,048	5-D	5,561	408	40
Bowling Green State Univ., Bowling Green, OH 43403	1910	$10,726(S)	$8,244	5-D	16,958	1,058	54
Bradley Univ., Peoria, IL 61625-0002	1897	$29,664	$9,050	1-D	5,459	595	78
Brandeis Univ., Waltham, MA 02454-9110	1948	$46,106	$12,714	1-D	5,825	498	90
Briarcliffe Coll., Bethpage, NY 11714	1966	NA	NA	3-B	1,779	NA	NA
Briar Cliff Univ., Sioux City, IA 51104-0100	1930	$27,212	$7,888	2-M	1,174	93	46
Bridgewater Coll., Bridgewater, VA 22812-1599	1880	$30,380	$11,070	2-B	1,848	140	60
Bridgewater State Univ., Bridgewater, MA 02325-0001	1840	$8,052(S)	$11,100	5-M	11,267	784	58
Brigham Young Univ., Provo, UT 84602-1001	1875	$5,000	$7,330	2-D	31,123	1,734	77
Brigham Young Univ.–Hawaii, Laie, HI 96762-1294	1955	$4,630	$5,048	2-B	2,555	228	52
Brigham Young Univ.–Idaho, Rexburg, ID 83460	1888	$3,650	$4,000	2-B	14,944	NA	NA
Brookline Coll., Phoenix, AZ 85021	1979	NA	NA	3-B	1,072	43	NA
Brooklyn Coll. of the City Univ. of New York, Brooklyn, NY 11210-2889	1930	$5,884(S)	NA	11-D	17,094	1,401	43
Brooks Inst., Santa Barbara, CA 93101	1945	NA	NA	3-M	1,240	NA	NA
Brown Univ., Providence, RI 02912	1764	$47,434	$11,994	1-D	8,943	NA	94
Bryan Coll., Dayton, TN 37321	1930	$22,200	$6,550	2-M	1,704	113	63
Bryant & Stratton Coll.–Wauwatosa campus, Wauwatosa, WI 53226	1854	NA	NA	3-B	1,264	NA	NA
Bryant Univ., Smithfield, RI 02917	1863	$38,574	$14,102	1-M	3,454	298	82
Bryn Mawr Coll., Bryn Mawr, PA 19010-2899	1885	$45,540	$14,350	1-D	1,738	213	84
Bucknell Univ., Lewisburg, PA 17837	1846	$48,498	$11,642	1-M	3,608	421	91
Buffalo State Coll., State Univ. of New York, Buffalo, NY 14222-1095	1867	$8,175(S)	$6,724	5-M	11,091	841	48
Butler Univ., Indianapolis, IN 46208-3485	1855	$34,368	$11,530	1-D	4,902	512	74
Cabrini Coll., Radnor, PA 19087-3698	1957	$29,842	$12,026	2-M	2,448	274	46
Cairn Univ., Langhorne, PA 19047-2990	1913	$23,320	$9,085	2-M	1,095	108	67
Caldwell Coll., Caldwell, NJ 07006-6195	1939	$29,000	$11,000	2-D	2,182	210	55
California Baptist Univ., Riverside, CA 92504-3206	1950	$28,122	$9,220	2-M	7,144	565	58
California Coll., San Diego, CA 92111	1978	NA	NA	3-B	1,299	NA	NA
California Coll. of the Arts, San Francisco, CA 94107	1907	$40,334	$8,000	1-M	1,949	477	61
California Inst. of Integral Studies, San Francisco, CA 94103	1968	$24,231	NA	1-D	1,271	158	NA
California Inst. of Tech., Pasadena, CA 91125-0001	1891	$41,538	$12,507	1-D	2,181	339	93
California Inst. of the Arts, Valencia, CA 91355-2340	1961	NA	NA	1-D	1,454	314	60
California Lutheran Univ., Thousand Oaks, CA 91360-2787	1959	$35,720	$11,920	2-D	4,282	410	70
California Polytechnic State Univ., San Luis Obispo, San Luis Obispo, CA 93407	1901	$8,724(S)	$11,123	5-M	19,703	1,307	72
California State Polytechnic Univ., Pomona, Pomona, CA 91768-2557	1938	$6,350(S)	$12,111	5-D	22,501	1,058	53
California State Univ., Bakersfield, Bakersfield, CA 93311	1970	NA	$10,926	5-M	8,371	NA	NA
California State Univ., Channel Islands, Camarillo, CA 93012	2002	NA	NA	5-D	3,599	294	NA
California State Univ., Chico, Chico, CA 95929-0722	1887	$8,472(S)	$10,480	5-M	16,356	901	57
California State Univ., Dominguez Hills, Carson, CA 90747-0001	1960	NA	NA	5-M	14,670	751	28
California State Univ., East Bay, Hayward, CA 94542-3000	1957	NA	NA	5-M	14,526	761	38
California State Univ., Fresno, Fresno, CA 93740-8027	1911	NA	$10,604	5-D	23,060	1,259	49

Name, address	Year founded	Tuition & fees	Room & board	Control, degree	Enrollment	Faculty	Grad. rate
California State Univ., Fullerton, Fullerton, CA 92834-9480.	1957	$6,186(S)	$12,816	5-D	38,325	1,910	53%
California State Univ., Long Beach, Long Beach, CA 90840	1949	$6,240(S)	$11,300	5-D	35,586	1,990	60
California State Univ., Los Angeles, Los Angeles, CA 90032-8530	1947	$6,335(S)	$9,728	5-D	23,258	1,020	36
California State Univ., Monterey Bay, Seaside, CA 93955-8001	1994	$5,963(S)	$9,748	5-M	5,732	358	38
California State Univ., Northridge, Northridge, CA 91330	1958	$6,544(S)	$10,980	5-M	38,310	1,972	46
California State Univ., Sacramento, Sacramento, CA 95819	1947	$6,602(S)	$6,538	5-D	28,811	1,401	42
California State Univ., San Bernardino, San Bernardino, CA 92407-2397	1965	NA	$9,966	5-D	18,398	938	43
California State Univ., San Marcos, San Marcos, CA 92096-0001	1990	$7,064(S)	NA	5-M	11,023	645	48
California State Univ., Stanislaus, Turlock, CA 95382	1957	$6,584(S)	$9,056	5-D	8,917	483	53
California Univ. of Pennsylvania, California, PA 15419-1394	1852	$9,239(S)	$10,680	5-M	8,243	375	54
Calumet Coll. of St. Joseph, Whiting, IN 46394-2195	1951	$15,620	NA	2-M	1,149	127	29
Calvin Coll., Grand Rapids, MI 49546-4388	1876	$28,250	$9,335	2-M	4,034	367	73
Cambridge Coll., Cambridge, MA 02138-5304.	1971	NA	NA	1-D	3,757	453	NA
Cameron Univ., Lawton, OK 73505-6377.	1908	$5,055(S)	$4,212	5-M	5,901	310	20
Campbellsville Univ., Campbellsville, KY 42718-2799	1906	$22,842	$7,550	2-M	3,557	304	41
Campbell Univ., Buies Creek, NC 27506	1887	$26,240	$9,300	2-D	4,743	305	52
Canisius Coll., Buffalo, NY 14208-1098.	1870	$33,332	$12,270	2-M	4,537	459	68
Capella Univ., Minneapolis, MN 55402	1993	NA	NA	3-D	36,375	NA	NA
Capital Univ., Columbus, OH 43209-2394	1830	$31,990	$8,710	2-D	3,628	395	58
Cardinal Stritch Univ., Milwaukee, WI 53217-3985	1937	$24,330	$7,030	2-D	4,641	431	NA
Caribbean Univ., Bayamón, PR 00960-0493	1969	$4,970	NA	1-M	4,835	452	27
Carleton Coll., Northfield, MN 55057-4001.	1866	$46,167	$11,982	1-B	2,045	247	92
Carlow Univ., Pittsburgh, PA 15213-3165 (4).	1929	$25,416	$10,014	2-D	3,027	263	62
Carnegie Mellon Univ., Pittsburgh, PA 15213-3891	1900	$49,022	$12,400	1-D	12,991	1,017	88
Carroll Coll., Helena, MT 59625-0002	1909	$27,914	$8,304	2-B	1,431	164	67
Carroll Univ., Waukesha, WI 53186-5593	1846	$27,724	$8,299	2-D	3,385	330	57
Carson-Newman Univ., Jefferson City, TN 37760	1851	$24,440	$7,060	2-M	2,045	210	50
Carthage Coll., Kenosha, WI 53140	1847	$34,850	$9,500	2-M	2,778	NA	54
Case Western Reserve Univ., Cleveland, OH 44106	1826	$41,800	$12,898	1-D	10,325	955	80
Castleton State Coll., Castleton, VT 05735	1787	$10,772(S)	$9,414	5-M	2,175	232	51
Catawba Coll., Salisbury, NC 28144-2488	1851	$27,360	$9,745	2-M	1,310	142	52
Catholic Univ. of America, Washington, DC 20064	1887	$38,525	$14,326	2-D	6,725	825	69
Cazenovia Coll., Cazenovia, NY 13035-1084	1824	$29,410	$12,420	1-B	1,077	129	44
Cedar Crest Coll., Allentown, PA 18104-6196 (4)	1867	$33,000	$10,171	2-M	1,486	170	60
Cedarville Univ., Cedarville, OH 45314-0601.	1887	$26,420	$6,460	2-D	3,462	352	73
Centenary Coll., Hackettstown, NJ 07840-2100.	1867	$30,540	$10,320	2-M	2,400	226	57
Central Coll., Pella, IA 50219	1853	$32,124	$9,980	2-B	1,386	127	65
Central Connecticut State Univ., New Britain, CT 06050-4010	1849	$10,127(S)	$10,506	5-D	11,865	916	52
Central Methodist Univ., Fayette, MO 65248-1198	1854	$21,830	$7,130	2-M	1,107	111	43
Central Michigan Univ., Mount Pleasant, MI 48859	1892	$11,220(S)	$8,544	5-D	26,902	1,066	59
Central Penn Coll., Summerdale, PA 17093-0309	1881	$16,167	$6,960	3-M	1,297	141	31
Central State Univ., Wilberforce, OH 45384	1887	$6,058(S)	$9,046	5-M	2,068	227	25
Central Washington Univ., Ellensburg, WA 98926	1891	$8,976(S)	$9,795	5-M	11,287	683	51
Centre Coll., Danville, KY 40422-1394	1819	$37,100	$9,340	2-B	1,381	142	82
Chadron State Coll., Chadron, NE 69337	1911	NA	NA	5-M	2,649	NA	NA
Chamberlain Coll. of Nursing, Addison, IL 60101-6106	2005	$16,960	NA	3-B	9,871	449	NA
Chaminade Univ. of Honolulu, Honolulu, HI 96816-1578.	1955	$665/credit	NA	2-M	2,062	154	36
Champlain Coll., Burlington, VT 05402-0670	1878	$31,350	$13,500	1-M	3,317	411	58
Chapman Univ., Orange, CA 92866	1861	$45,393	$12,954	2-D	7,892	841	76
Charleston Southern Univ., Charleston, SC 29423-8087.	1964	$22,090	$8,650	2-M	3,269	259	38
Charter Oak State Coll., New Britain, CT 06053-2142.	1973	$8,100(S)	NA	5-B	1,581	159	NA
Chatham Univ., Pittsburgh, PA 15232-2826.	1869	$33,429	$10,410	1-D	2,170	325	50
Chestnut Hill Coll., Philadelphia, PA 19118-2693	1924	$32,500	$10,000	2-D	2,179	354	47
Cheyney Univ. of Pennsylvania, Cheyney, PA 19319	1837	$8,806(S)	$11,270	5-M	1,212	84	25
Chicago State Univ., Chicago, IL 60628	1867	$9,427(S)	$8,470	5-D	5,701	420	21
Chowan Univ., Murfreesboro, NC 27855	1848	$23,050	$8,230	2-M	1,367	105	25
Christian Brothers Univ., Memphis, TN 38104-5581	1871	$27,620	NA	2-M	1,581	166	54
Christopher Newport Univ., Newport News, VA 23606-3072	1960	$11,092(S)	$9,958	5-M	5,232	416	66
The Citadel, The Military Coll. of South Carolina, Charleston, SC 29409 (2).	1842	$12,237(S)	$6,265	5-M	3,499	266	70
City Coll. of the City Univ. of New York, New York, NY 10031-9198	1847	$6,440(S)	$13,848	11-D	15,464	1,806	42
City Univ. of Seattle, Bellevue, WA 98005	1973	$14,880	NA	1-D	2,065	332	28
Claflin Univ., Orangeburg, SC 29115	1869	$15,010	$8,420	2-M	1,886	162	44
Claremont McKenna Coll., Claremont, CA 91711	1946	$45,625	$14,385	1-M	1,328	159	93
Clarion Univ. of Pennsylvania, Clarion, PA 16214	1867	$9,404(S)	$9,326	5-M	6,080	303	53
Clark Atlanta Univ., Atlanta, GA 30314	1865	$21,100	$8,956	2-D	3,458	294	39
Clarke Univ., Dubuque, IA 52001-3198	1843	$28,900	$8,700	2-D	1,225	155	70
Clarkson Univ., Potsdam, NY 13699	1896	$42,530	$13,440	1-D	3,726	271	75
Clark Univ., Worcester, MA 01610-1477	1887	$40,730	$7,800	1-D	3,551	284	81
Clayton State Univ., Morrow, GA 30260-0285	1969	$6,066(S)	$9,577	5-M	7,260	375	28
Clemson Univ., Clemson, SC 29634	1889	$13,054(S)	$8,142	5-D	21,303	1,199	83
Cleveland State Univ., Cleveland, OH 44115.	1964	$9,499(S)	$11,870	5-D	17,741	1,070	34
Coastal Carolina Univ., Conway, SC 29528-6054	1954	$9,760(S)	$7,860	5-M	9,478	671	46
Coe Coll., Cedar Rapids, IA 52402-5092	1851	$35,730	$7,860	2-B	1,420	167	67
Coker Coll., Hartsville, SC 29550	1908	$24,576	$7,610	1-M	1,207	130	43
Colby Coll., Waterville, ME 04901-8840.	1813	$45,760	$11,750	1-B	1,820	215	93
Colby-Sawyer Coll., New London, NH 03257.	1837	$38,040	$12,750	1-B	1,409	131	54
Colegio Universitario de San Juan, San Juan, PR 00918	1971	NA	NA	10-B	1,785	NA	NA
Colgate Univ., Hamilton, NY 13346-1386.	1819	$46,380	$11,510	1-M	2,898	344	91
Coll. at Brockport, State Univ. of New York, Brockport, NY 14420-2997	1867	$7,544(S)	$11,448	5-M	8,128	591	67
Coll. for Creative Studies, Detroit, MI 48202-4034	1926	$37,090	$8,510	1-M	1,423	275	56
Coll. of Charleston, Charleston, SC 29424-0001	1770	$10,670(S)	$11,043	5-M	11,619	949	65
Coll. of Coastal Georgia, Brunswick, GA 31520	1961	$4,238(S)	$8,382	5-B	2,987	181	NA
Coll. of Idaho, Caldwell, ID 83605.	1891	$23,725	$8,551	1-M	1,059	113	64
Coll. of Mount St. Vincent, Riverdale, NY 10471-1093.	1911	$30,290	$12,060	1-M	1,918	NA	52
Coll. of New Jersey, Ewing, NJ 08628	1855	$14,730(S)	$11,343	5-M	7,420	821	85
Coll. of New Rochelle, New Rochelle, NY 10805-2308 (4)	1904	$31,260	$11,690	1-M	1,549	183	35
Coll. of St. Benedict, Saint Joseph, MN 56374 (3).	1887	$37,926	$9,644	2-B	2,051	181	82
Coll. of St. Elizabeth, Morristown, NJ 07960-6989 (4)	1899	$31,095	$12,744	2-D	1,512	193	56
Coll. of St. Rose, Albany, NY 12203-1419	1920	$29,016	$11,532	1-M	4,542	419	66
Coll. of St. Scholastica, Duluth, MN 55811-4199	1912	$32,842	$8,598	2-D	4,240	370	68
Coll. of Staten Island of the City Univ. of New York, Staten Island, NY 10314-6600.	1955	$6,158(S)	$10,620	11-D	14,439	1,406	50
Coll. of the Holy Cross, Worcester, MA 01610-2395	1843	$45,692	$12,350	2-B	2,912	323	91
Coll. of the Ozarks, Point Lookout, MO 65726	1906	$430	$6,200	2-B	1,531	135	66
Coll. of William & Mary, Williamsburg, VA 23187-8795	1693	$15,463(S)	$9,622	5-D	8,376	NA	90
Coll. of Wooster, Wooster, OH 44691-2363.	1866	$41,680	$9,920	2-B	2,116	217	75
Colorado Christian Univ., Lakewood, CO 80226	1914	$25,046	$9,640	2-M	2,511	NA	NA

Name, address	Year founded	Tuition & fees	Room & board	Control, degree	Enrollment	Faculty	Grad. rate
Colorado Coll., Colorado Springs, CO 80903-3294	1874	$46,410	$10,752	1-M	2,060	200	87%
Colorado Mesa Univ., Grand Junction, CO 81501-3122	1925	$5,922(S)	$8,386	5-D	9,676	607	33
Colorado Mountain Coll., Glenwood Springs, CO 81601	1965	$1,860(A)	$8,164	9-B	2,465	NA	NA
Colorado Mountain Coll., Alpine campus, Steamboat Springs, CO 80487	1965	$1,860(A)	$8,164	9-B	1,550	NA	NA
Colorado Mountain Coll., Timberline campus, Leadville, CO 80461	1965	$1,860(A)	$8,164	9-B	1,209	NA	NA
Colorado Sch. of Mines, Golden, CO 80401-1887	1874	$16,485(S)	$10,103	5-D	5,608	489	70
Colorado State Univ., Fort Collins, CO 80523-0015	1870	$9,313(S)	$10,776	5-D	31,256	1,009	65
Colorado State Univ.–Pueblo, Pueblo, CO 81001-4901	1933	$7,327(S)	$8,856	5-M	6,805	405	34
Colorado Tech. Univ. Colorado Springs, Colorado Springs, CO 80907-3896	1965	NA	NA	3-D	2,359	343	NA
Colorado Tech. Univ. Online, Colorado Springs, CO 80907	NA	NA	NA	3-M	25,797	613	NA
Columbia Centro Universitario, Caguas, PR 00726	1966	$9,435	NA	3-M	1,788	136	27
Columbia Coll., Columbia, MO 65216-0002	1851	$20,963	$8,240	2-M	1,199	121	41
Columbia Coll., Columbia, SC 29203-5998	1854	$27,350	$7,200	2-D	3,013	132	46
Columbia Coll. Chicago, Chicago, IL 60605-1996	1890	$22,682	$12,375	1-M	10,142	1,525	41
Columbia Intl. Univ., Columbia, SC 29230-3122	1923	$19,480	$7,310	2-D	1,156	81	65
Columbia Southern Univ., Orange Beach, AL 36561	1993	$4,895	NA	3-D	19,970	559	NA
Columbia Univ., New York, NY 10027	1754	$49,138	$11,978	1-D	6,068	1,965	98
Columbia Univ., Sch. of General Studies, New York, NY 10027-6939	1754	$47,781	$10,450	1-B	1,763	NA	NA
Columbus Coll. of Art and Design, Columbus, OH 43215-1758	1879	$29,892	$7,740	1-M	1,364	202	55
Columbus State Univ., Columbus, GA 31907-5645	1958	$6,592(S)	$8,542	5-D	8,164	500	31
Concord Univ., Athens, WV 24712-1000	1872	$5,716(S)	$7,386	5-M	2,809	218	35
Concordia Coll., Moorhead, MN 56562	1891	$32,814	$7,160	2-M	2,558	283	71
Concordia Univ. Chicago, River Forest, IL 60305-1499	1864	$28,908	$8,992	2-D	5,286	430	53
Concordia Univ. Irvine, Irvine, CA 92612-3299	1972	$30,640	$9,270	2-D	4,046	373	63
Concordia Univ. Nebraska, Seward, NE 68434-1556	1894	$25,950	$7,080	2-M	2,206	195	64
Concordia Univ. Portland, OR 97211-6099	1905	$27,420	$8,030	2-M	3,111	259	45
Concordia Univ. St. Paul, St. Paul, MN 55104-5494	1893	$20,252	$8,000	2-M	3,632	376	46
Concordia Univ. Texas, Austin, TX 78726	1926	$25,880	$9,090	2-M	2,565	342	37
Concordia Univ. Wisconsin, Mequon, WI 53097-2402	1881	$24,950	$9,320	2-D	7,943	494	56
Connecticut Coll., New London, CT 06320-4196	1911	$46,085	$12,695	1-M	1,922	250	84
Converse Coll., Spartanburg, SC 29302-0006	1889	$16,500	$9,500	1-M	1,335	84	62
Coppin State Univ., Baltimore, MD 21216-3698	1900	NA	NA	5-M	3,800	312	15
Corban Univ., Salem, OR 97301-9392	1935	$27,485	$8,550	2-D	1,089	111	54
Cornell Coll., Mount Vernon, IA 52314-1098	1853	$37,500	$8,500	2-B	1,125	124	68
Cornell Univ., Ithaca, NY 14853-0001	1865	$45,358	$13,678	1-D	21,593	1,842	93
Cornerstone Univ., Grand Rapids, MI 49525-5897	1941	$24,168	$7,910	2-M	2,809	121	43
Covenant Coll., Lookout Mountain, GA 30750	1955	$29,100	$8,530	2-M	1,173	97	58
Creighton Univ., Omaha, NE 68178-0001	1878	$34,330	$9,728	2-D	8,019	782	76
Crown Coll., St. Bonifacius, MN 55375-9001	1916	$22,430	$7,480	2-M	1,269	160	50
Culinary Inst. of America, Hyde Park, NY 12538-1499	1946	$28,240	$9,652	1-B	2,814	196	NA
Cumberland Univ., Lebanon, TN 37087	1842	$20,200	$7,400	1-M	1,375	122	31
Curry Coll., Milton, MA 02186-9984	1879	$34,415	$13,130	1-M	3,074	391	45
Daemen Coll., Amherst, NY 14226-3592	1947	$24,090	$11,300	1-D	2,888	270	49
Dakota State Univ., Madison, SD 57042-1799	1881	$8,286(S)	$5,525	5-D	3,129	124	49
Dallas Baptist Univ., Dallas, TX 75211-9299	1965	$22,350	$6,768	2-D	5,422	600	55
Dalton State Coll., Dalton, GA 30720	1963	$3,326(S)	$6,320	5-B	5,047	215	15
Dartmouth Coll., Hanover, NH 03755	1769	$48,108	$13,819	1-D	6,342	705	95
Davenport Univ., Grand Rapids, MI 49512	1866	$13,966	$8,692	1-M	10,221	892	NA
Davidson Coll., Davidson, NC 28035	1837	$42,849	$11,834	2-B	1,788	186	95
Delaware State Univ., Dover, DE 19901-2277	1891	$6,481(S)	$9,386	5-D	4,336	NA	88
Delaware Valley Coll., Doylestown, PA 18901-2697	1896	$32,890	$11,977	1-M	2,253	195	55
Delta State Univ., Cleveland, MS 38733-0001	1924	$6,388(S)	$7,350	5-D	4,785	283	44
Denison Univ., Granville, OH 43023	1831	$45,670	$11,180	1-B	2,274	252	82
DePaul Univ., Chicago, IL 60604-2287	1898	$33,990	$12,103	2-D	24,414	1,944	70
DePauw Univ., Greencastle, IN 46135	1837	$40,640	$10,700	2-B	2,304	253	74
DeSales Univ., Center Valley, PA 18034-9568	1964	$31,250	$11,420	2-D	3,266	317	67
DeVry Coll. of New York, New York, NY 10016-5267	1998	$16,156	NA	3-M	1,646	96	NA
DeVry Univ., Chicago, IL 60618-5994	1931	$16,156	NA	3-M	1,446	145	NA
DeVry Univ., Columbus, OH 43209-2705	1952	$16,156	NA	3-M	2,068	100	NA
DeVry Univ., Decatur, GA 30030-2556	1969	$16,156	NA	3-M	2,193	153	NA
DeVry Univ., North Brunswick, NJ 08902-3362	1969	$16,156	NA	3-M	1,211	141	NA
DeVry Univ., Orlando, FL 32839	2000	$16,156	NA	3-M	1,344	55	NA
DeVry Univ., Phoenix, AZ 85021-2995	1967	$16,156	NA	3-M	1,089	109	NA
DeVry Univ., Pomona, CA 91768-2642	1983	$16,156	NA	3-M	2,077	102	NA
DeVry Univ. Online, Addison, IL 60101-6106	2000	$16,156	NA	3-M	24,623	2,809	NA
Dickinson Coll., Carlisle, PA 17013-2896	1773	$46,094	$11,568	1-B	2,396	257	85
Dickinson State Univ., Dickinson, ND 58601-4896	1918	$4,704(S)	$5,582	5-B	1,449	161	27
DigiPen Inst. of Tech., Redmond, WA 98052	1988	$36,480	NA	3-M	1,007	101	NA
Dillard Univ., New Orleans, LA 70122-3097	1869	$16,094	$9,314	2-B	1,183	137	46
Dixie State Univ., St. George, UT 84770-3876	1911	$4,291(S)	$5,048	5-B	8,350	458	18
Doane Coll., Crete, NE 68333-2430	1872	$26,180	$7,550	2-M	1,113	121	61
Dominican Coll., Orangeburg, NY 10962-1210	1952	$24,790	$11,650	1-D	1,998	236	36
Dominican Univ., River Forest, IL 60305-1099	1901	$29,770	$9,100	2-D	3,470	396	63
Dominican Univ. of California, San Rafael, CA 94901-2298	1890	$41,730	$13,380	2-M	2,148	347	54
Dordt Coll., Sioux Center, IA 51250-1697	1955	$26,540	$7,620	2-M	1,405	105	62
Dowling Coll., Oakdale, NY 11769-1999	1955	$27,124	$10,590	1-D	4,416	431	36
Drake Univ., Des Moines, IA 50311-4516	1881	$32,246	$9,270	1-D	5,139	437	73
Drew Univ., Madison, NJ 07940-1493	1867	$44,068	$11,944	2-D	2,291	196	69
Drexel Univ., Philadelphia, PA 19104-2875	1891	$37,505	$14,415	1-D	25,500	2,014	65
Drury Univ., Springfield, MO 65802	1873	$23,885	$8,200	1-M	1,993	179	64
Duke Univ., Durham, NC 27708-0586	1838	$44,020	$12,902	2-D	15,386	1,335	94
Duquesne Univ., Pittsburgh, PA 15282-0001	1878	$31,385	$10,632	2-D	9,904	993	76
D'Youville Coll., Buffalo, NY 14201-1084	1908	$23,462	$10,800	1-D	3,150	317	41
Earlham Coll., Richmond, IN 47374-4095	1847	$41,450	$8,260	2-M	1,164	119	71
East Carolina Univ., Greenville, NC 27858-4353	1907	$6,143(S)	$8,488	5-D	26,887	1,530	57
East Central Univ., Ada, OK 74820-6899	1909	$5,241(S)	$4,982	5-M	4,587	279	34
East Stroudsburg Univ. of Pennsylvania, East Stroudsburg, PA 18301-2999	1893	$8,315(S)	$9,176	5-M	6,778	316	56
East Tennessee State Univ., Johnson City, TN 37614	1911	$7,543(S)	$7,600	5-D	14,691	845	41
East Texas Baptist Univ., Marshall, TX 75670-1498	1912	$23,280	$8,297	2-M	1,247	117	33
Eastern Connecticut State Univ., Willimantic, CT 06226-2295	1889	$9,376(S)	$11,168	5-M	5,368	487	51
Eastern Illinois Univ., Charleston, IL 61920-3099	1895	$11,144(S)	$9,358	5-M	9,775	711	60
Eastern Kentucky Univ., Richmond, KY 40475-3102	1906	$7,536(S)	$7,724	5-D	16,062	1,114	38
Eastern Mennonite Univ., Harrisonburg, VA 22802-2462	1917	$30,800	$9,860	2-M	1,640	204	63
Eastern Michigan Univ., Ypsilanti, MI 48197	1849	$9,364(S)	$8,597	5-D	23,317	1,390	38
Eastern Nazarene Coll., Quincy, MA 02170	1918	$27,922	$8,700	2-M	1,036	122	52
Eastern New Mexico Univ., Portales, NM 88130	1934	$4,558(S)	$6,268	5-M	5,847	361	29
Eastern Oregon Univ., La Grande, OR 97850-2899	1929	$7,530(S)	$8,805	5-M	4,157	139	32

Name, address	Year founded	Tuition & fees	Room & board	Control, degree	Enroll-ment	Faculty	Grad. rate
Eastern Univ., St. Davids, PA 19087-3696.	1952	$29,550	$9,940	2-D	4,004	149	55%
Eastern Washington Univ., Cheney, WA 99004-2431	1882	$8,437(S)	$9,633	5-D	12,791	687	45
Eckerd Coll., St. Petersburg, FL 33711	1958	$37,362	$10,144	2-B	1,821	169	66
ECPI Univ., Virginia Beach, VA 23462	1966	NA	NA	3-B	13,717	1,371	NA
Edgewood Coll., Madison, WI 53711-1997	1927	$25,590	$8,973	2-D	2,894	322	57
Edinboro Univ. of Pennsylvania, Edinboro, PA 16444	1857	$8,849(S)	$8,973	2-D	2,894	322	57
EDP Univ. of Puerto Rico, Hato Rey, PR 00918	1968	$5,940	$10,976	5-D	7,098	371	46
Elizabeth City State Univ., Elizabeth City, NC 27909-7806	1891	$4,428(S)	NA	3-M	1,347	144	27
Elizabethtown Coll., Elizabethtown, PA 17022-2298	1899	$39,920	$7,213	5-M	2,421	211	NA
Elmhurst Coll., Elmhurst, IL 60126-3296	1871	$34,100	$9,820	2-M	1,892	221	77
Elmira Coll., Elmira, NY 14901	1855	$38,150	$9,386	2-M	3,210	357	74
Elms Coll., Chicopee, MA 01013-2839.	1928	$31,281	$11,800	1-M	1,542	185	63
Elon Univ., Elon, NC 27244-2010.	1889	$30,149	$10,930	2-D	1,678	189	68
Embry-Riddle Aeron Univ.–Daytona, Daytona Beach, FL 32114-3900	1926	$31,948	$9,897	2-D	6,305	562	82
Embry-Riddle Aeron Univ.–Prescott, Prescott, AZ 86301-3720.	1978	$31,648	$9,850	1-D	5,279	414	56
Embry-Riddle Aeron Univ.–Worldwide, Daytona Beach, FL 32114-3900	1970	$8,040	$9,510	1-M	1,855	128	59
Emerson Coll., Boston, MA 02116-4624	1880	$35,730	NA	1-D	15,411	2,809	NA
Emmanuel Coll., Boston, MA 02115.	1919	$34,670	$14,516	1-D	4,540	443	81
Emory Univ., Atlanta, GA 30322-1100	1836	$45,008	$13,315	2-M	2,436	217	58
Emporia State Univ., Emporia, KS 66801-5415	1863	$5,614(S)	$12,760	2-D	14,513	1,442	91
Endicott Coll., Beverly, MA 01915-2096.	1939	$28,926	$7,284	5-D	6,033	273	41
Eugene Lang Coll., New Sch. for Liberal Arts, New York, NY 10011-8601	1978	$38,570	$13,464	1-D	5,232	393	70
Evangel Univ., Springfield, MO 65802	1955	$20,040	$17,300	1-B	1,487	147	57
Everest Univ., Pompano Beach, FL 33062	1940	NA	$6,910	2-M	2,274	NA	45
Everest Univ., Tampa, FL 33614-5899.	1890	NA	NA	3-M	1,633	NA	NA
Everglades Univ., Boca Raton, FL 33431	1989	NA	NA	3-M	3,430	61	NA
Evergreen State Coll., Olympia, WA 98505	1967	$8,497(S)	NA	1-M	1,039	NA	NA
Excelsior Coll., Albany, NY 12203-5159.	1970	$425/cr. hr.	$9,492	5-M	4,398	232	57
Fairfield Univ., Fairfield, CT 06824-5195	1942	$43,770	NA	1-M	37,491	NA	NA
Fairleigh Dickinson Univ., Coll. at Florham, Madison, NJ 07940-1099	1942	$37,344	$13,190	2-D	4,919	590	82
Fairleigh Dickinson Univ., Metropolitan campus, Teaneck, NJ 07666-1914	1942	$34,878	$12,294	1-D	3,029	442	54
Fairmont State Univ., Fairmont, WV 26554	1865	$5,804(S)	$12,742	1-D	8,546	831	47
Farmingdale State Coll., Farmingdale, NY 11735	1912	$7,483(S)	$7,686	5-M	4,232	299	34
Fashion Inst. of Tech., New York, NY 10001-5992 (4)	1944	$5,105(S)	$12,190	5-B	8,162	632	43
Faulkner Univ., Montgomery, AL 36109-3398	1942	$17,380	$12,818	11-M	9,755	943	NA
Fayetteville State Univ., Fayetteville, NC 28301-4298	1867	$4,955(S)	$6,650	2-D	3,327	349	32
Felician Coll., Lodi, NJ 07644-2117	1942	$30,605	$7,631	5-D	6,179	337	32
Ferris State Univ., Big Rapids, MI 49307	1884	$10,950(S)	$11,650	2-D	1,933	223	46
Ferrum Coll., Ferrum, VA 24088	1913	$27,425	$8,910	5-D	14,707	961	54
Fisher Coll., Boston, MA 02116-1500.	1903	$28,260	$9,130	2-B	1,512	114	32
Fitchburg State Univ., Fitchburg, MA 01420-2697.	1894	$8,985(S)	$14,714	1-B	1,930	189	35
Flagler Coll., St. Augustine, FL 32085-1027.	1968	$16,180	$8,602	5-M	6,583	288	50
Florida Agr. & Mech. Univ., Tallahassee, FL 32307-3200	1887	$5,785(S)	$8,780	1-B	2,839	222	63
Florida Atlantic Univ., Boca Raton, FL 33431-0991	1961	$5,986(S)	$9,356	5-D	10,743	733	40
Florida Gulf Coast Univ., Fort Myers, FL 33965-6565	1991	$4,895(S)	$11,556	5-D	30,803	1,145	41
Florida Inst. of Tech., Melbourne, FL 32901-6975	1958	$36,020	NA	5-D	14,098	654	44
Florida Intl. Univ., Miami, FL 33199	1965	$6,417(S)	$12,470	1-D	5,644	484	54
Florida Memorial Univ., Miami-Dade, FL 33054.	1879	NA	$11,330	5-D	47,736	2,152	52
Florida Natl. Univ., Hialeah, FL 33012	1982	$13,230	NA	1-M	1,750	173	33
Florida Southern Coll., Lakeland, FL 33801-5698	1885	$29,990	NA	3-M	2,438	130	NA
Florida State Univ., Tallahassee, FL 32306	1851	$6,507(S)	$10,000	2-D	2,395	233	58
Fontbonne Univ., St. Louis, MO 63105-3098.	1917	$22,324	$9,912	5-D	41,509	1,670	75
Fordham Univ., New York, NY 10458	1841	$43,577	$9,630	2-M	1,997	271	41
Fort Hays State Univ., Hays, KS 67601-4099	1902	$3,314(S)	$15,835	2-D	15,170	NA	NA
Fort Lewis Coll., Durango, CO 81301-3999	1911	$7,252(S)	$7,130	5-M	13,441	522	44
Fort Valley State Univ., Fort Valley, GA 31030	1895	$6,288(S)	$10,346	5-M	4,065	228	37
Framingham State Univ., Framingham, MA 01701-9101	1839	$8,080(S)	$7,520	5-M	3,180	187	28
Francis Marion Univ., Florence, SC 29502-0547	1970	$9,386(S)	$9,540	5-M	6,429	318	51
Franciscan Univ. of Steubenville, Steubenville, OH 43952-1763	1946	$23,160	$7,032	5-M	4,058	293	41
Franklin & Marshall Coll., Lancaster, PA 17604-3003	1787	$46,285	$7,700	2-M	2,823	223	70
Franklin Coll., Franklin, IN 46131	1834	$28,185	$12,010	1-B	2,365	288	83
Franklin Pierce Univ., Rindge, NH 03461-0060	1962	$31,000	$8,400	2-B	1,014	103	73
Franklin Univ., Columbus, OH 43215-5399	1902	$13,320	$11,598	1-D	2,216	322	44
Freed-Hardeman Univ., Henderson, TN 38340-2399	1869	$20,468	NA	1-M	6,274	793	15
Fresno Pacific Univ., Fresno, CA 93702-4709	1944	$25,716	$7,390	2-D	1,811	150	54
Friends Univ., Wichita, KS 67213.	1898	$24,630	$7,288	2-M	3,483	427	54
Frostburg State Univ., Frostburg, MD 21532-1099	1898	$7,728(S)	$7,040	2-M	2,178	588	33
Full Sail Univ., Winter Park, FL 32792-7437 (2)	1979	NA	$7,990	5-D	5,474	392	47
Furman Univ., Greenville, SC 29613	1826	$43,164	NA	3-M	8,921	702	NA
Gallaudet Univ., Washington, DC 20002-3625.	1864	$15,274	$10,844	1-D	2,953	266	84
Gannon Univ., Erie, PA 16541-0001	1925	$27,546	$12,370	1-D	1,561	184	48
Gardner-Webb Univ., Boiling Springs, NC 28017	1905	$25,830	$10,940	2-D	4,211	356	64
Geneva Coll., Beaver Falls, PA 15010-3599	1848	$25,220	$8,330	2-D	4,636	300	56
George Fox Univ., Newberg, OR 97132-2697	1891	$31,100	$9,250	2-M	1,646	187	67
George Washington Univ., Washington, DC 20052	1821	$48,850	$9,630	2-D	3,712	415	62
Georgetown Coll., Georgetown, KY 40324-1696.	1829	$32,310	$11,700	5-D	33,917	2,461	67
Georgetown Univ., Washington, DC 20057	1789	$44,805	$8,230	2-M	25,264	NA	80
Georgia Coll. and State Univ., Milledgeville, GA 31061	1889	$8,790(S)	$13,620	2-D	1,399	152	57
Georgia Gwinnett Coll., Lawrenceville, GA 30043	2006	$5,246(S)	$9,426	5-D	17,849	1,562	93
Georgia Inst. of Tech., Atlanta, GA 30332-0001	1885	$10,650(S)	$10,770	5-D	6,551	425	61
Georgia Southern Univ., Statesboro, GA 30460	1906	$7,066(S)	$9,814	5-D	9,719	544	NA
Georgia Southwestern State Univ., Americus, GA 31709-4693	1906	$5,924(S)	$9,348	5-D	21,471	1,160	82
Georgia State Univ., Atlanta, GA 30302-3083	1913	$9,928(S)	$7,834	5-M	20,517	884	50
Georgian Court Univ., Lakewood, NJ 08701-2697 (4)	1908	$29,606	$13,028	5-D	2,806	159	36
Gettysburg Coll., Gettysburg, PA 17325-1483.	1832	$47,480	$10,120	2-M	32,168	1,684	53
Glenville State Coll., Glenville, WV 26351-1200	1872	$6,384(S)	$11,340	2-B	2,533	293	84
Global Univ., Springfield, MO 65804	1948	$3,870	$8,810	5-B	1,850	111	30
Golden Gate Univ., San Francisco, CA 94105-2968	1901	NA	NA	5-D	4,551	633	NA
Goldey-Beacom Coll., Wilmington, DE 19808-1999.	1886	$22,140	NA	1-D	3,528	489	NA
Gonzaga Univ., Spokane, WA 99258.	1887	$36,535	$5,353	1-M	1,352	56	49
Gordon Coll., Wenham, MA 01984-1899	1889	$34,390	$9,906	2-D	7,605	738	82
Goucher Coll., Baltimore, MD 21204-2794.	1885	$39,084	$9,930	2-M	2,109	185	72
Governors State Univ., Univ. Park, IL 60484	1969	$9,386(S)	$11,168	1-M	2,111	202	67
Grace Coll., Winona Lake, IN 46590-1294.	1948	$23,290	$14,715	5-D	5,568	455	NA
Graceland Univ., Lamoni, IA 50140	1895	$24,920	$7,454	2-D	1,616	85	55
			$8,060	2-D	2,283	202	47

Name, address	Year founded	Tuition & fees	Room & board	Control, degree	Enroll-ment	Faculty	Grad. rate
Grambling State Univ., Grambling, LA 71245	1901	$5,950(S)	$10,018	5-D	5,071	218	31%
Grand Valley State Univ., Allendale, MI 49401-9403	1960	$10,454(S)	$8,080	5-D	24,477	1,658	66
Grand View Univ., Des Moines, IA 50316-1599	1896	$23,516	$7,554	2-M	2,129	232	48
Granite State Coll., Concord, NH 03301	1972	$7,065(S)	NA	11-M	2,053	190	59
Grantham Univ., Lenexa, KS 66219	1951	$6,480	NA	3-M	9,463	10	NA
Greensboro Coll., Greensboro, NC 27401-1875	1838	$26,206	$4,700	2-M	1,264	96	43
Greenville Coll., Greenville, IL 62246-0159	1892	$24,324	$8,044	2-M	1,368	190	50
Grinnell Coll., Grinnell, IA 50112-1690	1846	$43,656	$9,998	1-B	1,721	205	86
Grove City Coll., Grove City, PA 16127-2104	1876	$14,880	$8,108	2-B	2,491	211	82
Guilford Coll., Greensboro, NC 27410-4173	1837	$32,470	$8,800	2-B	2,302	187	57
Gustavus Adolphus Coll., St. Peter, MN 56082-1498	1862	$40,080	$9,250	2-B	2,455	252	83
Gwynedd Mercy Univ., Gwynedd Valley, PA 19437-0901	1948	$30,460	$11,040	2-D	2,371	319	67
Hamilton Coll., Clinton, NY 13323-1296	1812	$46,080	$11,710	1-B	1,926	228	93
Hamline Univ., St. Paul, MN 55104-1284	1854	$36,270	$9,952	2-D	4,581	387	66
Hampden-Sydney Coll., Hampden-Sydney, VA 23943 (1).	1776	$37,352	$11,726	2-B	1,070	107	62
Hampshire Coll., Amherst, MA 01002	1965	$48,265	$12,450	1-B	1,492	159	66
Hampton Univ., Hampton, VA 23668	1868	$20,724	$9,230	1-D	4,622	385	68
Hannibal-LaGrange Univ., Hannibal, MO 63401-1999	1858	$19,380	$7,110	2-M	1,230	120	48
Hanover Coll., Hanover, IN 47243-0108	1827	$31,760	$9,690	2-B	1,163	105	72
Harding Univ., Searcy, AR 72149-0001	1924	$17,040	$6,516	2-D	6,238	499	64
Hardin-Simmons Univ., Abilene, TX 79698-0001	1891	$22,350	$6,962	2-D	2,224	205	51
Harrison Coll., Indianapolis, IN 46204	1902	NA	NA	3-B	3,756	290	33
Harris-Stowe State Univ., St. Louis, MO 63103-2136	1857	$5,220(S)	$8,900	5-B	1,298	163	10
Hartwick Coll., Oneonta, NY 13820-4020	1797	$38,930	$10,485	1-B	1,615	201	58
Harvard Univ., Cambridge, MA 02138	1636	$42,292	$14,115	1-D	10,693	1,131	97
Hastings Coll., Hastings, NE 68901-7696	1882	$25,520	$7,270	2-M	1,138	123	62
Haverford Coll., Haverford, PA 19041-1392	1833	$47,214	$14,350	1-B	1,187	148	93
Hawai'i Pacific Univ., Honolulu, HI 96813	1965	$19,980	$13,230	1-M	6,736	550	41
Heidelberg Univ., Tiffin, OH 44883-2462	1850	$27,480	$9,226	2-M	1,422	145	51
Henderson State Univ., Arkadelphia, AR 71999-0001	1890	$7,284(S)	$5,566	5-M	3,583	240	29
Hendrix Coll., Conway, AR 72032-3080	1876	$39,290	$10,912	2-M	1,432	152	68
Heritage Univ., Toppenish, WA 98948-9599	1982	$17,864	NA	1-M	1,115	NA	NA
High Point Univ., High Point, NC 27262-3598	1924	$31,480	$11,480	2-D	4,199	353	62
Hilbert Coll., Hamburg, NY 14075-1597	1957	$20,500	$8,650	1-M	1,075	122	50
Hillsdale Coll., Hillsdale, MI 49242-1298	1844	$880/credit	NA	1-D	1,511	166	81
Hiram Coll., Hiram, OH 44234-0067	1850	$30,290	$10,010	1-M	1,324	146	62
Hobart & William Smith Colls., Geneva, NY 14456-3397	1822	$46,165	$11,685	1-M	2,372	238	79
Hodges Univ., Naples, FL 34119	1990	$12,740	NA	2-M	2,081	151	NA
Hofstra Univ., Hempstead, NY 11549	1935	$37,400	$13,050	1-D	10,928	1,123	62
Holy Family Univ., Philadelphia, PA 19114	1954	$27,100	$12,930	2-D	2,956	327	55
Holy Names Univ., Oakland, CA 94619-1699 (4).	1868	$33,020	$10,648	2-M	1,343	207	35
Hood Coll., Frederick, MD 21701-8575	1893	$34,120	$11,610	1-M	2,393	257	66
Hope Coll., Holland, MI 49422-9000	1866	$29,560	$9,090	2-B	3,388	349	78
Hope Intl. Univ., Fullerton, CA 92831-3138	1928	$27,000	$8,750	2-M	1,449	243	44
Houghton Coll., Houghton, NY 14744	1883	$28,556	$8,252	2-M	1,100	128	73
Houston Baptist Univ., Houston, TX 77074-3298	1960	$28,750	$3,725	2-M	2,910	238	43
Howard Payne Univ., Brownwood, TX 76801-2715	1889	$24,600	$7,166	2-M	1,170	144	42
Howard Univ., Washington, DC 20059-0002	1867	$22,783	$7,327	1-D	10,297	1,520	61
Humboldt State Univ., Arcata, CA 95521-8299	1913	$372/cr. hr.(S)	$11,440	5-M	8,293	553	NA
Hunter Coll. of the City Univ. of New York, New York, NY 10065-5085	1870	$6,129(S)	$6,500	11-D	23,019	1,988	50
Huntingdon Coll., Montgomery, AL 36106-2148	1854	$23,500	$8,350	2-B	1,110	120	43
Huntington Univ., Huntington, IN 46750-1299	1897	$24,771	$8,306	2-M	1,134	106	62
Husson Univ., Bangor, ME 04401-2999	1898	$15,590	$8,604	1-D	3,052	317	44
Idaho State Univ., Pocatello, ID 83209	1901	$6,344(S)	$5,963	5-D	14,209	787	27
Illinois Coll., Jacksonville, IL 62650-2299	1829	$27,800	$8,840	2-M	1,028	103	64
Illinois Inst. of Tech., Chicago, IL 60616-3793	1890	$41,645	$10,900	1-D	7,850	784	63
Illinois State Univ., Normal, IL 61790-2200	1857	$13,010(S)	$9,624	5-D	20,272	1,208	72
Illinois Wesleyan Univ., Bloomington, IL 61702-2900	1850	$40,844	$9,446	1-B	2,009	227	78
Immaculata Univ., Immaculata, PA 19345	1920	$32,000	$12,880	2-D	3,675	444	48
Indiana State Univ., Terre Haute, IN 47809	1865	$8,256(S)	$9,010	5-D	12,448	703	43
Indiana Tech., Fort Wayne, IN 46803-1297	1930	$24,860	$9,380	1-D	6,355	510	35
Indiana Univ. Bloomington, Bloomington, IN 47405-7000	1820	$10,388(S)	NA	5-D	46,817	2,381	77
Indiana Univ. East, Richmond, IN 47374-1289	1971	$6,787(S)	NA	5-M	4,456	288	24
Indiana Univ. Kokomo, Kokomo, IN 46904-9003	1945	$6,810(S)	NA	5-M	4,178	213	28
Indiana Univ. Northwest, Gary, IN 46408-1197	1959	$6,853(S)	NA	5-M	6,387	401	24
Indiana Univ. of Pennsylvania, Indiana, PA 15705-1087	1875	$9,080(S)	$11,100	5-D	14,728	723	50
Indiana Univ.–Purdue Univ. Fort Wayne, Fort Wayne, IN 46805-1499	1917	$7,013(S)	$7,632	5-M	13,459	819	22
Indiana Univ.–Purdue Univ. Indianapolis, Indianapolis, IN 46202-2896.	1969	$8,909(S)	NA	5-D	30,488	3,280	42
Indiana Univ. South Bend, South Bend, IN 46634-7111	1922	$6,905(S)	NA	5-M	8,073	519	26
Indiana Univ. Southeast, New Albany, IN 47150-6405	1941	$6,827(S)	NA	5-M	6,733	503	30
Indiana Wesleyan Univ., Marion, IN 46953-4974	1920	$24,102	$3,797	2-D	3,018	290	71
Indian River State Coll., Fort Pierce, FL 34981-5596	1960	NA	NA	5-B	17,248	743	NA
Inter Amer. Univ. of Puerto Rico, Aguadilla campus, Aguadilla, PR 00605	1957	$5,534	NA	1-M	4,595	252	27
Inter Amer. Univ. of Puerto Rico, Arecibo campus, Arecibo, PR 00614-4050.	1957	$4,660	NA	1-M	4,878	298	NA
Inter Amer. Univ. of Puerto Rico, Barranquitas campus, Barranquitas, PR 00794	1957	$4,660	NA	1-M	2,418	135	NA
Inter Amer. Univ. of Puerto Rico, Bayamón campus, Bayamón, PR 00957	1912	$5,860	NA	1-M	4,845	306	23
Inter Amer. Univ. of Puerto Rico, Fajardo campus, Fajardo, PR 00738-7003.	1965	$170/credit	NA	1-M	2,199	120	NA
Inter Amer. Univ. of Puerto Rico, Guayama campus, Guayama, PR 00785.	1958	$5,962	NA	1-M	2,169	196	28
Inter Amer. Univ. of Puerto Rico, Metropolitan campus, San Juan, PR 00919-1293.	1960	$6,723	NA	1-D	NA	590	28
Inter Amer. Univ. of Puerto Rico, Ponce campus, Ponce, PR 00715-1602.	1962	$4,826	NA	1-M	5,821	292	31
Inter Amer. Univ. of Puerto Rico, San Germán campus, San Germán, PR 00683-5008.	1912	$5,860	$2,700	1-D	5,147	292	36
Iona Coll., New Rochelle, NY 10801-1890	1940	$34,030	$13,570	2-M	4,241	360	63
Iowa State Univ. of Sci. and Tech., Ames, IA 50011	1858	$7,726(S)	$7,721	5-D	32,955	1,777	68
Ithaca Coll., Ithaca, NY 14850	1892	$38,400	$13,900	1-D	6,723	785	76
Jackson State Univ., Jackson, MS 39217	1877	$6,348(S)	$7,164	5-D	8,783	525	36
Jacksonville State Univ., Jacksonville, AL 36265-1602	1883	$8,790(S)	$6,985	5-D	9,161	497	29
Jacksonville Univ., Jacksonville, FL 32211	1934	$29,900	$10,390	1-D	4,157	332	38
James Madison Univ., Harrisonburg, VA 22807	1908	$9,662(S)	$8,828	5-D	20,181	1,487	NA
Jefferson Coll. of Health Sciences, Roanoke, VA 24031-3186	1982	NA	NA	1-M	1,039	140	29
John Brown Univ., Siloam Springs, AR 72761-2121	1919	$23,588	$8,468	2-M	2,317	159	65
John Carroll Univ., University Heights, OH 44118-4581	1886	$35,800	$10,500	2-M	3,723	392	75
John F. Kennedy Univ., Pleasant Hill, CA 94523-4817 (4).	1964	NA	NA	1-D	1,580	237	NA
John Hancock Univ., Oakbrook Terrace, IL 60181	NA	NA	NA	3-M	1,950	NA	NA
John Jay Coll. of Criminal Justice of the City Univ. of New York, New York, NY 10019-1093.	1964	$6,059(S)	NA	11-M	15,008	NA	43

Name, address	Year founded	Tuition & fees	Room & board	Control, degree	Enroll-ment	Faculty	Grad. rate
Johns Hopkins Univ., Baltimore, MD 21218-2699	1876	$45,470	$13,832	1-D	7,216	665	93%
Johnson & Wales Univ., Charlotte, NC 28202	2004	NA	NA	1-B	2,587	110	62
Johnson & Wales Univ., Denver, CO 80220	1993	NA	NA	1-B	1,532	87	53
Johnson & Wales Univ., North Miami, FL 33181	1992	NA	NA	1-B	2,098	90	51
Johnson & Wales Univ., Providence, RI 02903-3703	1914	$27,156	$12,000	1-D	10,974	519	56
Johnson C. Smith Univ., Charlotte, NC 28216-5398	1867	$18,236	$7,100	1-B	1,387	156	44
Johnson State Coll., Johnson, VT 05656	1828	$10,286(S)	$9,138	5-M	1,744	137	35
Johnson Univ., Knoxville, TN 37998-1001	1893	$12,050	$5,550	2-D	1,031	85	54
Jones Intl. Univ., Centennial, CO 80112	1995	$12,720	NA	3-D	2,739	110	NA
Judson Univ., Elgin, IL 60123-1498	1963	$27,530	$9,080	2-D	1,170	173	50
Juilliard Sch., New York, NY 10023-6588	1905	$33,630	$12,770	1-D	1,009	307	93
Juniata Coll., Huntingdon, PA 16652-2119	1876	$38,630	$10,710	2-M	1,635	149	75
Kalamazoo Coll., Kalamazoo, MI 49006-3295	1833	$39,351	$8,475	2-B	1,458	126	77
Kansas State Univ., Manhattan, KS 66506	1863	$8,585(S)	$7,710	5-D	24,581	1,265	60
Kean Univ., Union, NJ 07083	1855	$10,918(S)	$11,142	5-D	14,404	1,340	46
Keene State Coll., Keene, NH 03435	1909	$12,776(S)	$9,558	5-M	4,923	436	63
Keiser Univ., Fort Lauderdale, FL 33309	1977	$15,064	NA	1-D	17,129	1,597	68
Kendall Coll., Chicago, IL 60201-2899	1934	NA	NA	3-B	2,545	209	37
Kennesaw State Univ., Kennesaw, GA 30144-5591	1963	$6,807(S)	$6,199	5-D	24,629	1,400	43
Kent State Univ., Kent, OH 44242-0001	1910	$9,816(S)	$9,536	5-D	28,998	1,756	52
Kent State Univ. at Geauga, Burton, OH 44021-9500	1964	$5,554(S)	NA	5-B	2,653	148	26
Kent State Univ. at Stark, Canton, OH 44720-7599	1967	$5,554(S)	NA	5-M	4,886	262	30
Kentucky State Univ., Frankfort, KY 40601	1886	$7,061(S)	$6,690	12-M	2,533	155	18
Kenyon Coll., Gambier, OH 43022-9623	1824	$47,330	$11,560	1-B	1,705	208	89
Kettering Univ., Flint, MI 48504	1919	$35,600	$6,980	1-M	1,991	133	61
Keuka Coll., Keuka Park, NY 14478-0098	1890	$27,340	$10,590	2-M	2,033	147	48
Keystone Coll., La Plume, PA 18440	1868	$21,200	$9,800	1-B	1,595	244	39
King's Coll., Wilkes-Barre, PA 18711-0801	1946	$30,310	$11,368	2-M	2,391	231	66
King Univ., Bristol, TN 37620-2699	1867	$24,960	$8,180	2-M	2,587	311	47
Knox Coll., Galesburg, IL 61401	1837	$40,497	$8,724	1-B	1,424	154	79
Kutztown Univ. of Pennsylvania, Kutztown, PA 19530-0730	1866	$8,524(S)	$8,350	5-M	9,513	448	55
La Roche Coll., Pittsburgh, PA 15237-5898	1963	$24,778	$10,024	2-M	1,481	187	45
La Salle Univ., Philadelphia, PA 19141-1199	1863	$38,200	$13,420	2-D	6,448	453	65
La Sierra Univ., Riverside, CA 92515	1922	$29,103	$7,500	2-D	2,440	263	59
Lafayette Coll., Easton, PA 18042-1798	1826	$45,635	$13,520	2-B	2,486	266	88
Lake Erie Coll., Painesville, OH 44077-3389	1856	$28,355	$8,586	1-M	1,089	106	46
Lake Forest Coll., Lake Forest, IL 60045	1857	$39,842	$9,292	1-M	1,622	178	64
Lake Superior State Univ., Sault Sainte Marie, MI 49783	1946	$422/cr. hr.(S)	NA	5-M	2,438	175	40
Lakeland Coll., Sheboygan, WI 53082-0359	1862	$22,950	$7,700	2-M	3,749	71	42
Lamar Univ., Beaumont, TX 77710	1923	$9,361(S)	$7,966	5-D	14,035	563	34
Lander Univ., Greenwood, SC 29649-2099	1872	$10,100(S)	$9,152	5-M	3,049	249	40
Lane Coll., Jackson, TN 38301-4598	1882	$9,180	$6,520	2-B	1,512	91	38
Langston Univ., Langston, OK 73050	1897	$3,815(S)	$8,690	5-M	2,567	229	44
Lasell Coll., Newton, MA 02466-2709	1851	$30,000	$12,500	1-M	2,081	252	53
Lawrence Tech. Univ., Southfield, MI 48075-1058	1932	$28,948	$8,682	1-D	4,002	392	48
Lawrence Univ., Appleton, WI 54911	1847	$41,226	$8,496	1-B	1,555	195	82
Lebanon Valley Coll., Annville, PA 17003-1400	1866	$35,700	$9,530	2-D	2,022	233	73
Lee Univ., Cleveland, TN 37320-3450	1918	$14,280	$6,865	2-M	4,922	405	52
Lehigh Univ., Bethlehem, PA 18015-3094	1865	$43,520	$11,560	1-D	7,096	691	86
Lehman Coll. of the City Univ. of New York, Bronx, NY 10468-1589	1931	$6,108(S)	$8,085	11-M	12,220	912	36
Le Moyne Coll., Syracuse, NY 13214	1946	$31,340	$12,130	2-M	3,319	349	74
LeMoyne-Owen Coll., Memphis, TN 38126-6595	1862	$10,680	$4,852	2-B	1,023	88	22
Lenoir-Rhyne Univ., Hickory, NC 28601	1891	$29,310	$10,040	2-M	1,780	200	49
Lesley Univ., Cambridge, MA 02138-2790 (4)	1909	$24,810	$14,400	1-D	4,707	254	46
LeTourneau Univ., Longview, TX 75607-7001	1946	$26,910	$9,300	2-M	2,733	215	61
Lewis & Clark Coll., Portland, OR 97219-7899	1867	$41,928	$10,636	1-D	3,545	417	74
Lewis-Clark State Coll., Lewiston, ID 83501-2698	1893	$5,784(S)	$6,510	5-B	4,304	NA	29
Lewis Univ., Romeoville, IL 60446	1932	$27,830	$9,750	2-D	6,525	682	63
Liberty Univ., Lynchburg, VA 24515	1971	$21,850	$8,200	2-D	12,928	713	50
Life Univ., Marietta, GA 30060-2903	1974	$10,621	$12,480	1-D	2,776	177	17
LIM Coll., New York, NY 10022-5268 (4)	1939	$24,225	$19,850	3-M	1,647	167	46
Limestone Coll., Gaffney, SC 29340-3799	1845	$23,000	$7,800	1-M	1,121	101	37
Lincoln Memorial Univ., Harrogate, TN 37752-1901	1897	$19,460	$6,740	1-D	3,952	290	48
Lincoln Univ., Jefferson City, MO 65101	1866	$6,838(S)	$5,531	5-M	3,043	204	22
Lincoln Univ., Lincoln Univ., PA 19352	1854	$7,018(S)	$8,554	12-M	1,963	177	40
Lindenwood Univ., St. Charles, MO 63301-1695	1827	$15,580	$7,880	2-D	12,213	942	45
Lindsey Wilson Coll., Columbia, KY 42728	1903	$22,550	$8,670	2-D	2,644	248	29
Linfield Coll., McMinnville, OR 97128-6894	1849	$36,240	$9,926	2-B	1,671	184	67
Lipscomb Univ., Nashville, TN 37204-3951	1891	$26,094	$9,628	2-D	4,580	531	64
Livingstone Coll., Salisbury, NC 28144-5298	1879	$13,404	NA	2-B	1,175	73	NA
Lock Haven Univ. of Pennsylvania, Lock Haven, PA 17745-2390	1870	$8,899(S)	$8,352	5-M	5,260	245	49
Loma Linda Univ., Loma Linda, CA 92350	1905	NA	NA	2-D	4,270	840	NA
Long Island Univ.–LIU Brooklyn, Brooklyn, NY 11201-8423	1926	$34,120	$12,064	1-D	8,483	960	25
Long Island Univ.–LIU Post, Brookville, NY 11548-1300	1954	$34,070	$12,534	1-D	10,599	986	39
Longwood Univ., Farmville, VA 23909	1839	$11,580(S)	$9,948	5-M	4,960	288	63
Loras Coll., Dubuque, IA 52004-0178	1839	$29,741	$8,293	2-M	1,621	161	61
Louisiana Coll., Pineville, LA 71359-0001	1906	$13,780	$4,448	2-M	1,557	115	46
Louisiana State Univ. and Agr. and Mech. Coll., Baton Rouge, LA 70803	1860	$7,873(S)	$10,804	5-D	30,225	1,399	67
Louisiana State Univ. at Alexandria, Alexandria, LA 71302-9121	1960	$4,768(S)	$6,240	5-B	2,430	139	NA
Louisiana State Univ. Health Sciences Ctr., New Orleans, LA 70112-2223	1931	$5,036(S)	$3,708	5-D	2,644	893	NA
Louisiana State Univ. in Shreveport, Shreveport, LA 71115-2399	1965	$5,607(S)	NA	5-M	4,114	176	33
Louisiana Tech. Univ., Ruston, LA 71272	1894	$7,302(S)	$5,430	5-D	11,015	433	50
Lourdes Univ., Sylvania, OH 43560-2898	1958	$17,530	$8,400	2-M	2,187	277	20
Loyola Marymount Univ., Los Angeles, CA 90045-2659	1911	$40,040	$14,295	2-D	9,661	1,133	74
Loyola Univ. Chicago, Chicago, IL 60660	1870	$37,413	$13,110	2-D	15,957	1,551	71
Loyola Univ. Maryland, Baltimore, MD 21210-2699	1852	$43,250	$12,300	2-D	5,977	577	84
Loyola Univ. New Orleans, New Orleans, LA 70118-6195	1912	$36,610	$12,660	2-D	4,686	441	55
Lubbock Christian Univ., Lubbock, TX 79407-2099	1957	$18,740	$6,778	2-M	2,002	186	41
Luther Coll., Decorah, IA 52101	1861	$38,370	$7,350	2-B	2,466	257	76
Luther Rice Univ., Lithonia, GA 30038-2454	1962	$5,352	NA	2-M	1,650	NA	NA
Lycoming Coll., Williamsport, PA 17701-5192	1812	$33,746	$9,890	2-B	1,307	118	64
Lynchburg Coll., Lynchburg, VA 24501-3199	1903	$33,565	$9,080	2-D	2,713	281	56
Lyndon State Coll., Lyndonville, VT 05851-0919	1911	$10,286(S)	$9,138	5-M	1,436	160	39
Lynn Univ., Boca Raton, FL 33431-5598	1962	$34,550	$10,900	1-D	2,297	180	41
Macalester Coll., St. Paul, MN 55105-1899	1874	$1,668/cr. hr.	NA	2-M	2,039	238	87
Madonna Univ., Livonia, MI 48150-1173	1947	$16,340	$8,200	2-D	4,427	335	56
Maharishi Univ. of Mgmt., Fairfield, IA 52557	1971	$26,430	$7,400	1-D	1,132	94	NA

Name, address	Year founded	Tuition & fees	Room & board	Control, degree	Enrollment	Faculty	Grad. rate
Maine Maritime Academy, Castine, ME 04420 (2)	1941	$11,525(S)	$9,548	5-M	1,013	90	NA
Malone Univ., Canton, OH 44709	1892	$26,416	$8,948	2-M	2,096	203	59%
Manchester Univ., North Manchester, IN 46962-1225	1889	$29,040	$9,300	2-D	1,349	103	57
Manhattan Coll., Riverdale, NY 10471	1853	$37,188	$13,740	2-M	3,883	424	74
Manhattanville Coll., Purchase, NY 10577-2132	1841	$36,220	$14,520	1-D	2,800	320	58
Mansfield Univ. of Pennsylvania, Mansfield, PA 16933	1857	$9,192(S)	$10,276	5-M	2,970	181	50
Maranatha Baptist Univ., Watertown, WI 53094	1968	$13,120	$6,480	2-M	1,033	74	57
Marian Univ., Fond du Lac, WI 54935-4699	1936	$24,720	$6,330	2-D	2,188	268	49
Marian Univ., Indianapolis, IN 46222-1997	1851	$29,400	$9,140	2-D	2,715	286	53
Marietta Coll., Marietta, OH 45750-4000	1835	$33,142	$10,394	1-M	1,542	178	55
Marist Coll., Poughkeepsie, NY 12601-1387	1929	$31,200	$13,100	1-M	6,365	595	80
Marquette Univ., Milwaukee, WI 53201-1881	1881	$35,930	NA	2-D	11,782	1,173	78
Mars Hill Univ., Mars Hill, NC 28754	1856	$25,636	$9,188	2-M	1,440	157	38
Marshall Univ., Huntington, WV 25755	1837	$6,216(S)	$9,256	5-D	13,407	740	45
Martin Univ., Indianapolis, IN 46218-3867	1977	NA	NA	1-M	1,236	43	13
Mary Baldwin Coll., Staunton, VA 24401-3610 (4)	1842	$28,720	$8,400	1-M	1,707	129	48
Marygrove Coll., Detroit, MI 48221-2599 (4)	1905	NA	NA	2-M	2,953	64	34
Maryland Inst. Coll. of Art, Baltimore, MD 21217	1826	$40,890	$11,260	1-M	2,155	342	73
Marylhurst Univ., Marylhurst, OR 97036-0261 (4)	1893	$19,665	NA	2-M	1,722	263	NA
Marymount California Univ., Rancho Palos Verdes, CA 90275-6299	1932	$31,890	$13,005	2-M	1,038	125	NA
Marymount Manhattan Coll., New York, NY 10021-4597	1936	$26,640	$14,600	1-B	1,833	303	44
Marymount Univ., Arlington, VA 22207-4299	1950	$26,430	$11,550	2-D	3,486	358	58
Maryville Coll., Maryville, TN 37804-5907	1819	$31,754	$10,088	2-B	1,168	111	56
Maryville Univ. of St. Louis, St. Louis, MO 63141-7299	1872	$25,002	$9,918	1-D	5,033	493	67
Marywood Univ., Scranton, PA 18509-1598	1915	$31,695	$13,900	2-D	3,175	432	65
Massachusetts Coll. of Art and Design, Boston, MA 02115-5882	1873	$10,400(S)	$12,600	5-M	2,264	279	74
Massachusetts Coll. of Liberal Arts, North Adams, MA 01247-4100	1894	$8,525(S)	$9,322	5-M	1,716	167	57
Massachusetts Inst. of Tech., Cambridge, MA 02139-4307	1861	$43,498	$12,744	1-D	11,301	1,506	93
Massachusetts Maritime Academy, Buzzards Bay, MA 02532-1803 (2)	1891	$7,265(S)	$10,590	5-M	1,476	107	71
Master's Coll. and Seminary, Santa Clarita, CA 91321-1200	1927	$1,235/cr. hr.	NA	2-D	1,485	199	56
Mayville State Univ., Mayville, ND 58257-1299	1889	$6,353(S)	$5,048	5-B	1,036	79	36
McDaniel Coll., Westminster, MD 21157-4390	1867	$36,960	$8,640	1-M	3,256	373	72
McKendree Univ., Lebanon, IL 62254-1299	1828	$26,900	$8,920	2-D	3,027	295	48
McMurry Univ., Abilene, TX 79697	1923	$24,121	$7,538	2-M	1,216	120	38
McNeese State Univ., Lake Charles, LA 70609	1939	$5,120(S)	$7,468	5-M	8,349	415	38
MCPHS Univ., Boston, MA 02115-5896	1823	$28,470	$14,240	1-D	6,548	NA	71
Medaille Coll., Buffalo, NY 14214-2695	1875	$23,812	$11,300	1-D	2,391	294	50
Medgar Evers Coll. of the City Univ. of New York, Brooklyn, NY 11225-2298	1969	$6,032(S)	NA	11-B	6,491	501	NA
Med. Univ. of South Carolina, Charleston, SC 29425	1824	$15,438(S)	NA	5-D	2,775	223	NA
Mercer Univ., Macon, GA 31207-0003	1833	$33,120	$11,081	2-D	6,470	736	61
Mercy Coll., Dobbs Ferry, NY 10522-1189	1951	$17,766	$12,690	1-D	11,648	1,042	35
Mercy Coll. of Ohio, Toledo, OH 43604 (4)	1993	$11,370	NA	2-B	1,195	163	59
Mercyhurst Univ., Erie, PA 16546	1926	$30,300	$10,400	2-M	3,011	260	61
Meredith Coll., Raleigh, NC 27607-5298	1891	$30,642	$8,766	1-M	1,980	207	59
Merrimack Coll., North Andover, MA 01845-5800	1947	$35,085	$12,150	2-M	3,032	321	59
Messiah Coll., Mechanicsburg, PA 17055	1909	$31,340	$9,350	2-M	3,084	316	76
Methodist Univ., Fayetteville, NC 28311-1498	1956	$27,930	$10,414	2-M	2,416	213	44
Metropolitan Coll. of New York, New York, NY 10013	1964	$17,270	NA	1-M	1,255	248	19
Metropolitan State Univ., St. Paul, MN 55106-5000	1971	$6,642(S)	NA	5-D	8,475	NA	NA
Metropolitan State Univ. of Denver, Denver, CO 80217-3362	1963	$5,744(S)	NA	5-M	23,381	1,494	25
Miami Univ., Oxford, OH 45056	1809	$13,799(S)	$10,900	12-D	17,901	1,112	81
Miami Univ. Hamilton, Hamilton, OH 45011-3399	1968	$13,846(S)	$10,900	5-M	4,194	224	NA
Michigan State Univ., East Lansing, MI 48824	1855	$12,863(S)	$8,806	5-D	49,343	2,756	79
Michigan Tech. Univ., Houghton, MI 49931	1885	$13,728(S)	$9,175	5-D	6,979	454	66
MidAmerica Nazarene Univ., Olathe, KS 66062-1899	1966	$22,290	$7,250	2-M	1,862	82	55
Middle Georgia State Coll., Cochran, GA 31014-1599	1884	$3,028(S)	$7,736	5-B	3,614	170	NA
Middle Tennessee State Univ., Murfreesboro, TN 37132	1911	$7,546(S)	$8,000	5-D	23,881	1,285	NA
Middlebury Coll., Middlebury, VT 05753-6002	1800	$46,044	$13,116	1-D	2,495	329	94
Midland Univ., Midland, TX 79705-6329	1969	$2,160(S)	$4,650	11-B	5,530	271	NA
Midway Univ., Midway, KY 40347-1120 (4)	1847	$22,000	$8,000	2-D	1,600	118	38
Midwestern State Univ., Wichita Falls, TX 76308	1922	$7,238(S)	$6,350	5-M	5,870	335	44
Miles Coll., Fairfield, AL 35064	1905	$12,276	$6,896	2-B	1,738	147	NA
Millersville Univ. of Pennsylvania, Millersville, PA 17551-0302	1855	$8,866(S)	$9,632	5-M	8,368	442	65
Milligan Coll., Milligan College, TN 37682	1866	$27,915	$6,000	2-M	1,198	134	52
Millikin Univ., Decatur, IL 62522-2084	1901	$28,644	$9,210	2-D	2,262	288	60
Mills Coll., Oakland, CA 94613-1000	1852	$41,494	$12,625	1-D	1,595	211	62
Milwaukee Sch. of Engineering, Milwaukee, WI 53202-3109 (2)	1903	$35,520	$8,520	1-M	2,658	249	56
Minnesota State Univ. Mankato, Mankato, MN 56001	1868	$8,396(S)	$7,053	5-D	15,195	762	55
Minnesota State Univ. Moorhead, Moorhead, MN 56563-0002	1885	$7,818(S)	$7,132	5-M	6,624	452	46
Minot State Univ., Minot, ND 58707-0002	1913	$6,086(S)	$5,550	5-M	3,533	261	37
Misericordia Univ., Dallas, PA 18612-1098	1924	$29,010	$12,050	2-D	3,111	330	69
Mississippi Coll., Clinton, MS 39058	1826	$14,868	$7,200	2-D	5,070	461	62
Mississippi State Univ., Mississippi State, MS 39762	1878	$6,772(S)	$8,647	5-D	20,365	1,008	60
Mississippi Univ. for Women, Columbus, MS 39701-9998	1884	$5,640(S)	$6,183	5-D	2,629	215	39
Mississippi Valley State Univ., Itta Bena, MS 38941-1400	1946	$6,066(S)	$6,836	5-M	2,203	147	26
Missouri Baptist Univ., St. Louis, MO 63141-8660	1964	$21,670	$8,640	2-D	5,345	300	44
Missouri Southern State Univ., Joplin, MO 64801-1595	1937	$5,376(S)	$6,265	5-M	5,616	310	34
Missouri State Univ., Springfield, MO 65897	1905	$7,696(S)	$7,450	5-D	21,271	1,112	53
Missouri Univ. of Sci. and Tech., Rolla, MO 65409	1870	$9,537(S)	$9,540	5-D	8,130	513	63
Missouri Valley Coll., Marshall, MO 65340-3197	1889	$18,800	$4,600	2-B	1,639	90	23
Missouri Western State Univ., St. Joseph, MO 64507-2294	1915	$6,498(S)	$7,128	5-M	5,795	387	33
Molloy Coll., Rockville Centre, NY 11571-5002	1955	$25,710	$13,240	1-D	4,455	714	66
Monmouth Coll., Monmouth, IL 61462-1998	1853	$31,500	$7,600	2-B	1,256	125	59
Monmouth Univ., West Long Branch, NJ 07764-1898	1933	$32,310	NA	1-D	6,316	597	61
Monroe Coll., Bronx, NY 10468-5407	1933	$13,740	$9,200	3-M	7,215	251	71
Montana State Univ., Bozeman, MT 59717	1893	$6,821(S)	$8,220	5-D	15,294	924	50
Montana State Univ. Billings, Billings, MT 59101-0298	1927	$5,745(S)	$6,680	5-M	4,969	326	33
Montana State Univ.–Northern, Havre, MT 59501-7751	1929	$5,070(S)	$6,275	5-M	1,273	96	30
Montana Tech. of the Univ. of Montana, Butte, MT 59701-8997	1895	$6,722(S)	$7,928	5-M	2,923	216	48
Montclair State Univ., Montclair, NJ 07043-1624	1908	$11,318(S)	$13,910	5-D	19,465	1,689	63
Moody Bible Inst., Chicago, IL 60610-3284	1886	NA	NA	2-M	3,349	211	NA
Moravian Coll., Bethlehem, PA 18018-6650	1742	$35,518	$10,644	2-M	1,841	163	74
Morehead State Univ., Morehead, KY 40351	1922	$7,498(S)	$7,580	5-D	11,358	486	43
Morehouse Coll., Atlanta, GA 30314 (1)	1867	$25,460	$13,180	1-B	2,170	214	54
Morgan State Univ., Baltimore, MD 21251	1867	$7,218(S)	NA	5-D	7,005	558	100
Morningside Coll., Sioux City, IA 51106	1894	$25,990	$7,930	2-M	2,542	222	58
Morrisville State Coll., Morrisville, NY 13408-0901	1908	$8,092(S)	$11,260	5-B	3,028	256	NA

Name, address	Year founded	Tuition & fees	Room & board	Control, degree	Enrollment	Faculty	Grad. rate
Mount Aloysius Coll., Cresson, PA 16630-1999	1939	$19,798	$8,830	2-M	1,835	NA	NA
Mount Carmel Coll. of Nursing, Columbus, OH 43222 (4)	1903	$11,675	$5,000	1-M	1,121	103	55%
Mount Holyoke Coll., South Hadley, MA 01075 (3)	1837	$41,456	$12,140	1-M	2,251	263	82
Mount Ida Coll., Newton, MA 02459-3310	1899	$29,377	$12,500	1-M	1,481	189	38
Mount Marty Coll., Yankton, SD 57078-3724	1936	$22,892	$6,646	2-M	1,225	64	52
Mount Mary Univ., Milwaukee, WI 53222-4597	1913	$25,098	$7,738	2-D	1,481	200	41
Mount Mercy Univ., Cedar Rapids, IA 52402-4797	1928	$26,310	$8,075	2-M	1,761	150	73
Mount St. Joseph Univ., Cincinnati, OH 45233-1670	1920	$26,850	$8,710	2-D	2,326	230	57
Mount St. Mary Coll., Newburgh, NY 12550-3494	1960	$26,250	$13,290	1-M	2,556	258	52
Mount St. Mary's Coll., Los Angeles, CA 90049-1599 (4)	1925	$34,826	$10,793	2-D	3,281	433	61
Mount St. Mary's Univ., Emmitsburg, MD 21727-7799	1808	$34,644	$11,514	2-M	2,240	201	66
Mount Vernon Nazarene Univ., Mount Vernon, OH 43050-9500	1964	$24,650	$7,260	2-M	2,229	230	60
Muhlenberg Coll., Allentown, PA 18104-5586	1848	$42,755	$10,080	2-B	2,448	274	86
Murray State Univ., Murray, KY 42071	1922	$7,044(S)	$7,900	5-D	10,943	655	53
Musians Inst., Hollywood, CA 90028	1976	$30,420	NA	3-B	1,337	204	NA
Muskingum Univ., New Concord, OH 43762	1837	$24,036	$7,818	2-M	2,099	NA	NA
Natl. Louis Univ., Chicago, IL 60603	1886	NA	NA	1-D	5,737	521	20
Natl. Paralegal Coll., Phoenix, AZ 85014	2002	NA	NA	3-M	1,150	33	NA
Natl. Univ., La Jolla, CA 92037-1011	1971	$14,670	NA	1-M	18,207	2,911	38
Natl. Univ., Coll., Bayamón, PR 00960	1983	NA	NA	13-B	2,703	NA	NA
Nazareth Coll. of Rochester, Rochester, NY 14618-3790	1924	$29,426	$12,100	1-D	2,823	434	68
Nebraska Wesleyan Univ., Lincoln, NE 68504-2796	1887	$27,240	$7,550	2-M	2,071	156	65
Neumann Univ., Aston, PA 19014-1298	1965	$24,948	$11,512	2-D	2,956	310	50
Nevada State Coll. at Henderson, Henderson, NV 89015	2002	NA	NA	5-B	2,988	94	17
New England Coll., Henniker, NH 03242-3293	1946	$33,000	$12,930	1-D	2,401	223	40
New England Inst. of Tech., East Greenwich, RI 02818	1940	$22,230	NA	1-A	2,933	321	NA
New Jersey City Univ., Jersey City, NJ 07305-1597	1927	$10,652(S)	$10,406	5-M	8,443	769	32
New Jersey Inst. of Tech., Newark, NJ 07102	1881	$15,218(S)	$12,500	5-D	10,130	693	58
New Mexico Highlands Univ., Las Vegas, NM 87701	1893	$4,000(S)	$5,720	5-M	3,690	285	18
New Mexico Inst. of Mining and Tech., Socorro, NM 87801	1889	$5,714(S)	$6,520	5-D	2,134	171	44
New Mexico State Univ., Las Cruces, NM 88003-8001	1888	$6,220(S)	$7,292	5-D	16,765	1,116	46
New Orleans Baptist Theol. Seminary, New Orleans, LA 70126-4858 (2)	1917	NA	NA	2-D	2,036	NA	NA
New Sch. for Public Engagement, New York, NY 10011-8603	1919	NA	NA	1-D	2,014	447	NA
New York City Coll. of Tech. of the City Univ. of New York, Brooklyn, NY 11201-2983	1946	$6,069(S)	NA	11-B	16,860	1,350	24
New York Inst. of Tech., Old Westbury, NY 11568-8000	1955	$30,780	$12,230	1-D	7,506	808	47
New York Univ., New York, NY 10012-1019	1831	$44,848	$16,622	1-D	44,599	6,461	84
Newberry Coll., Newberry, SC 29108-2197	1856	$23,800	$10,965	2-B	1,039	120	44
Newman Univ., Wichita, KS 67213-2097	1933	$23,650	$6,780	2-M	3,736	267	50
Niagara Univ., Niagara Univ., NY 14109	1856	$28,200	$11,600	2-D	4,054	412	65
Nicholls State Univ., Thibodaux, LA 70310	1948	$5,679(S)	$8,560	5-M	6,540	309	42
Nichols Coll., Dudley, MA 01571-5000	1815	$31,740	$10,700	1-M	1,547	80	38
Norfolk State Univ., Norfolk, VA 23504	1935	$6,860(S)	$8,130	5-D	6,728	NA	100
North Carolina Agr. & Tech. State Univ., Greensboro, NC 27411	1891	$6,798(S)	$6,309	5-D	10,561	710	43
North Carolina Central Univ., Durham, NC 27707-3129	1910	$5,525(S)	$8,165	5-D	8,093	573	40
North Carolina State Univ., Raleigh, NC 27695	1887	$8,206(S)	$9,434	5-D	34,009	2,068	71
North Carolina Wesleyan Coll., Rocky Mount, NC 27804-8677	1956	$26,982	$8,680	2-B	1,522	213	24
North Central Coll., Naperville, IL 60566-7063	1861	$34,230	$9,795	2-M	3,048	273	64
North Central Univ., Minneapolis, MN 55404-1322	1930	$19,066	$5,886	2-B	1,125	102	37
North Dakota State Univ., Fargo, ND 58108	1890	$7,540(S)	$7,102	5-D	14,629	851	53
North Greenville Univ., Tigerville, SC 29688-1892	1892	$15,510	$9,180	2-D	2,467	184	54
North Park Univ., Chicago, IL 60625-4895	1891	$24,600	$8,220	2-D	3,138	305	56
Northcentral Univ., Prescott Valley, AZ 86314	1996	$10,000	NA	3-D	13,091	494	NA
Northeastern Illinois Univ., Chicago, IL 60625-4699	1961	$9,926(S)	NA	5-M	10,813	631	20
Northeastern State Univ., Tahlequah, OK 74464-2399	1846	$5,192(S)	$5,600	5-D	8,559	540	30
Northeastern Univ., Boston, MA 02115-5096	1898	$41,686	$14,100	1-D	24,745	1,686	83
Northern Arizona Univ., Flagstaff, AZ 86011	1899	$9,742(S)	$9,078	5-D	26,606	1,589	49
Northern Illinois Univ., DeKalb, IL 60115-2854	1895	$11,733(S)	$10,990	5-D	21,138	1,168	51
Northern Kentucky Univ., Highland Heights, KY 41099	1968	$8,376(S)	$6,900	5-D	15,263	1,054	38
Northern Michigan Univ., Marquette, MI 49855-5301	1899	$9,037(S)	$8,696	5-M	8,879	481	49
Northern State Univ., Aberdeen, SD 57401-7198	1901	$7,563(S)	$6,457	5-M	3,278	151	NA
Northwest Missouri State Univ., Maryville, MO 64468-6001	1905	$7,988(S)	$8,896	5-M	6,485	294	52
Northwest Nazarene Univ., Nampa, ID 83686-5897	1913	$26,550	$6,400	2-D	2,232	107	55
Northwest Univ., Kirkland, WA 98033	1934	$26,968	$7,620	2-D	1,634	235	43
Northwestern Coll., Orange City, IA 51041-1996	1882	$27,930	$8,410	2-B	1,233	140	63
Northwestern Oklahoma State Univ., Alva, OK 73717-2799	1897	$5,483(S)	$3,960	5-M	2,307	179	28
Northwestern State Univ. of Louisiana, Natchitoches, LA 71497	1884	$6,246(S)	$8,122	5-D	8,944	492	42
Northwestern Univ., Evanston, IL 60208	1851	$45,519	$13,862	1-D	20,439	1,535	93
Northwood Univ., Michigan campus, Midland, MI 48640-2398	1959	$22,130	$9,040	1-M	1,698	130	53
Norwich Univ., Northfield, VT 05663	1819	$33,373	$11,524	1-M	3,111	328	57
Notre Dame Coll., South Euclid, OH 44121-4293	1922	$25,694	$8,598	2-M	1,393	118	NA
Notre Dame de Namur Univ., Belmont, CA 94002-1908	1851	$31,822	$12,494	2-D	2,030	248	48
Notre Dame of Maryland Univ., Baltimore, MD 21210-2476 (4)	1873	$33,010	$10,716	2-D	2,877	134	53
Nova Southeastern Univ., Fort Lauderdale, FL 33314-7796	1964	$25,430	$10,130	1-D	25,670	1,734	41
Nyack Coll., Nyack, NY 10960-3698	1882	$23,800	$8,800	2-D	3,082	288	42
Oakland City Univ., Oakland City, IN 47660-1099	1885	$19,800	$8,700	2-D	2,418	97	52
Oakland Univ., Rochester, MI 48309-4401	1957	$10,613(S)	$8,452	5-D	20,169	1,072	43
Oakwood Univ., Huntsville, AL 35896	1896	$16,232	$9,312	2-M	1,824	171	46
Oberlin Coll., Oberlin, OH 44074	1833	$48,682	$13,106	1-M	2,911	218	88
Occidental Coll., Los Angeles, CA 90041-3314	1887	$46,270	$12,940	1-M	2,128	274	88
Oglala Lakota Coll., Kyle, SD 57752-0490	1970	NA	NA	11-M	1,000	NA	NA
Oglethorpe Univ., Atlanta, GA 30319-2797	1835	$31,280	$11,300	1-M	1,082	125	62
Ohio Dominican Univ., Columbus, OH 43219-2099	1911	$28,932	$9,970	2-M	2,573	188	42
Ohio Northern Univ., Ada, OH 45810-1599	1871	$36,720	$10,520	2-D	3,557	305	67
Ohio State Univ., Columbus, OH 43210	1870	$10,037(S)	$10,370	5-D	57,466	5,108	83
Ohio State Univ.–Lima, Lima, OH 45804	1960	$7,140(S)	NA	5-M	1,077	89	38
Ohio State Univ.–Marion, Marion, OH 43302-5695	1958	$7,140(S)	NA	5-M	1,259	102	44
Ohio State Univ.–Mansfield campus, Mansfield, OH 44906-1599	1958	$7,140(S)	$6,020	5-M	1,204	88	42
Ohio State Univ.–Newark campus, Newark, OH 43055-1797	1957	$7,140(S)	$10,370	5-M	2,315	146	37
Ohio Univ., Athens, OH 45701-2979	1804	$10,446(S)	$10,230	5-D	28,722	1,326	67
Ohio Univ.–Chillicothe, Chillicothe, OH 45601	1946	$4,908(S)	NA	5-M	2,200	NA	NA
Ohio Univ.–Lancaster, Lancaster, OH 43130-1097	1968	$4,908(S)	NA	5-M	1,728	NA	NA
Ohio Univ.–Southern campus, Ironton, OH 45638-2214	1956	NA	NA	5-M	1,836	NA	NA
Ohio Univ.–Zanesville, Zanesville, OH 43701-2695	1946	$4,908(S)	NA	5-B	2,042	130	NA
Ohio Wesleyan Univ., Delaware, OH 43015	1842	$41,920	$11,210	2-B	1,830	221	69
Oklahoma Baptist Univ., Shawnee, OK 74804	1910	$22,800	$6,520	2-M	2,097	201	55
Oklahoma Christian Univ., Oklahoma City, OK 73136-1100	1950	$19,120	$6,670	2-M	2,415	210	46

Name, address	Year founded	Tuition & fees	Room & board	Control, degree	Enroll-ment	Faculty	Grad. rate
Oklahoma City Univ., Oklahoma City, OK 73106-1402	1904	$29,426	$9,310	2-D	NA	407	NA
Oklahoma Panhandle State Univ., Goodwell, OK 73939-0430	1909	$6,677(S)	$3,906	5-B	1,387	91	38%
Oklahoma State Univ., Stillwater, OK 74078	1890	$7,442(S)	$7,010	5-D	25,939	1,331	62
Oklahoma Wesleyan Univ., Bartlesville, OK 74006-6299	1909	$22,252	$7,344	2-M	1,355	164	57
Old Dominion Univ., Norfolk, VA 23529	1930	$8,820(S)	$9,582	5-D	24,828	1,341	51
Olivet Coll., Olivet, MI 49076-9701	1844	$23,021	NA	2-M	1,206	90	43
Olivet Nazarene Univ., Bourbonnais, IL 60914	1907	$31,390	$7,900	2-M	4,579	228	57
Oral Roberts Univ., Tulsa, OK 74171	1963	$22,438	$9,296	2-D	3,414	271	51
Oregon Health and Sci. Univ., Portland, OR 97239-3098	1974	NA	NA	12-D	2,838	101	NA
Oregon Inst. of Tech., Klamath Falls, OR 97601-8801	1947	NA	NA	5-M	3,911	257	45
Oregon State Univ., Corvallis, OR 97331	1868	$8,250(S)	$10,695	5-D	27,925	1,416	62
Otis Coll. of Art and Design, Los Angeles, CA 90045-9785	1918	$38,330	$8,576	1-M	1,086	481	57
Otterbein Univ., Westerville, OH 43081	1847	$31,424	$9,405	2-D	2,984	333	60
Ouachita Baptist Univ., Arkadelphia, AR 71998-0001	1886	$23,320	$6,900	2-B	1,543	149	60
Our Lady of Holy Cross Coll., New Orleans, LA 70131-7399	1916	$9,950	NA	2-M	1,298	NA	NA
Our Lady of the Lake Coll., Baton Rouge, LA 70808	1990	$11,150	NA	2-M	1,704	164	29
Our Lady of the Lake Univ. of San Antonio, San Antonio, TX 78207-4689	1895	$23,400	NA	2-D	2,927	269	34
Pace Univ., New York, NY 10038	1906	$38,069	$13,120	1-D	12,624	1,326	54
Pacific Lutheran Univ., Tacoma, WA 98447	1890	$36,530	$10,230	2-M	3,462	277	70
Pacific Oaks Coll., Pasadena, CA 91103 (4)	1945	NA	NA	1-M	1,028	125	NA
Pacific Union Coll., Angwin, CA 94508-9707	1882	$28,131	$7,485	2-M	1,647	146	45
Pacific Univ., Forest Grove, OR 97116-1797	1849	$38,510	$11,116	1-D	3,582	NA	62
Palm Beach Atlantic Univ., West Palm Beach, FL 33416-4708	1968	$25,532	$8,350	2-D	3,764	355	48
Palm Beach State Coll., Lake Worth, FL 33461-4796	1933	$2,378(S)	NA	5-B	29,174	1,185	NA
Palmer Coll. of Chiropractic, Davenport, IA 52803-5287	1897	NA	NA	1-D	2,310	15	NA
Park Univ., Parkville, MO 64152-3795	1875	$9,900	$7,151	1-M	2,458	174	39
Parsons the New Sch. for Design, New York, NY 10011-8878	1896	$40,140	$15,100	1-M	5,134	1,083	69
Patten Univ., Oakland, CA 94601-2699	1944	$3,432	NA	2-M	1,050	125	37
Peirce Coll., Philadelphia, PA 19102-4699 (4)	1865	$17,040	NA	1-M	1,792	NA	56
Penn Foster Coll., Scottsdale, AZ 85260	1890	$75/credit	NA	3-B	28,900	164	NA
Penn State Abington, Abington, PA 19001	1950	$13,356(S)	NA	12-B	3,694	244	49
Penn State Altoona, Altoona, PA 16601-3760	1939	$13,900(S)	$9,690	12-B	3,861	294	71
Penn State Berks, Reading, PA 19610-6009	1924	$13,900(S)	$10,560	12-B	2,732	212	57
Penn State Erie, the Behrend Coll., Erie, PA 16563-0001	1948	$13,900(S)	$9,690	12-M	4,057	300	69
Penn State Harrisburg, Middletown, PA 17057-4898	1966	$13,900(S)	$11,000	12-D	4,441	344	61
Penn State Univ. Park, Univ. Park, PA 16802	1855	$16,992(S)	$10,090	12-D	46,615	2,942	85
Pennsylvania Coll. of Tech., Williamsport, PA 17701-5778	1965	$14,940(S)	$10,713	12-B	5,678	482	NA
Pepperdine Univ., Malibu, CA 90263	1937	$44,902	$12,890	2-D	7,315	706	80
Peru State Coll., Peru, NE 68421	1867	$5,746(S)	$6,382	5-M	2,358	109	NA
Pfeiffer Univ., Misenheimer, NC 28109-0960	1885	$24,150	$9,230	2-M	2,019	150	59
Philadelphia Univ., Philadelphia, PA 19144	1884	$33,300	$10,540	1-D	3,539	529	58
Piedmont Coll., Demorest, GA 30535-0010	1897	$21,350	$8,786	2-M	2,368	250	46
Pittsburg State Univ., Pittsburg, KS 66762	1903	$5,906(S)	$6,954	5-M	7,400	415	43
Pitzer Coll., Claremont, CA 91711-6101	1963	$46,992	$14,758	1-B	1,081	115	81
Plymouth State Univ., Plymouth, NH 03264-1595	1871	$12,610(S)	$10,218	5-D	5,237	490	56
Point Loma Nazarene Univ., San Diego, CA 92106-2899	1902	$30,360	$9,810	2-M	3,359	340	72
Point Park Univ., Pittsburgh, PA 15222-1984	1960	$27,190	$10,320	1-M	3,841	454	50
Point Univ., West Point, GA 31833	1937	$17,650	$6,650	2-B	1,439	140	49
Polk State Coll., Winter Haven, FL 33881-4299	1964	$3,367(S)	NA	5-B	11,085	649	NA
Polytechnic Univ. of Puerto Rico, Hato Rey, PR 00919	1966	$7,548	NA	1-M	4,646	248	15
Pomona Coll., Claremont, CA 91711	1887	$43,580	$14,100	1-B	1,612	232	96
Pontifical Catholic Univ. of Puerto Rico, Ponce, PR 00717-0777	1948	$5,560	$1,369	2-D	7,682	385	39
Portland State Univ., Portland, OR 97207-0751	1946	$7,878(S)	$11,349	5-D	28,731	1,734	40
Prairie View A&M Univ., Prairie View, TX 77446-0519	1878	$8,098(S)	$7,467	5-D	8,250	542	83
Pratt Inst., Brooklyn, NY 11205-3899	1887	$44,804	$11,152	1-M	4,627	1,041	65
Presbyterian Coll., Clinton, SC 29325	1880	$33,650	$9,028	2-D	1,433	131	68
Princeton Univ., Princeton, NJ 08544-1019	1746	$40,715	$13,080	1-D	8,014	1,100	97
Providence Coll., Providence, RI 02918	1917	$43,245	$12,750	2-M	4,396	410	85
Purchase Coll., State Univ. of New York, Purchase, NY 10577-1400	1967	$7,573(S)	$12,708	5-M	4,379	425	60
Purdue Univ., West Lafayette, IN 47907	1869	$9,992(S)	NA	5-D	38,788	2,376	68
Purdue Univ. Calumet, Hammond, IN 46323-2094	1951	$7,132(S)	$7,915	5-M	9,422	478	30
Purdue Univ. North Central, Westville, IN 46391-9542	1967	$7,186(S)	NA	5-M	6,102	281	22
Queens Coll. of the City Univ. of New York, Flushing, NY 11367-1597	1937	$6,030(S)	NA	11-M	18,974	1,467	55
Queens Univ. of Charlotte, Charlotte, NC 28274-0002	1857	$29,250	$10,642	2-M	2,386	254	59
Quincy Univ., Quincy, IL 62301-2699	1860	$25,834	$9,880	2-M	1,455	NA	50
Quinnipiac Univ., Hamden, CT 06518-1940	1929	$40,670	$14,250	1-D	8,803	1,021	76
Radford Univ., Radford, VA 24142	1910	$8,976(S)	$8,156	5-D	9,928	697	59
Ramapo Coll. of New Jersey, Mahwah, NJ 07430-1680	1969	$13,388(S)	$11,550	5-M	5,852	482	73
Randolph-Macon Coll., Ashland, VA 23005-5505	1830	$34,850	$10,550	2-B	1,315	149	61
Rasmussen Coll. Ocala, Ocala, FL 34471	1984	$12,114	NA	3-B	1,192	NA	NA
Reed Coll., Portland, OR 97202-8199	1908	$46,010	$11,770	1-M	1,411	161	82
Regent Univ., Virginia Beach, VA 23464-9800	1977	$16,008	$8,430	2-D	5,953	533	47
Regis Coll., Weston, MA 02493	1927	$34,380	$13,185	2-D	2,069	186	49
Regis Univ., Denver, CO 80221-1099	1877	$33,060	$9,500	2-D	9,722	869	58
Reinhardt Univ., Waleska, GA 30183-2981	1883	$18,670	$7,064	2-M	1,154	157	39
Rensselaer Polytechnic Inst., Troy, NY 12180-3590	1824	$47,908	$13,620	1-D	6,995	505	85
Rhode Island Coll., Providence, RI 02908-1991	1854	$7,602(S)	$9,811	5-D	8,700	767	43
Rhode Island Sch. of Design, Providence, RI 02903-2784	1877	$42,932	$12,272	1-M	2,420	546	87
Rhodes Coll., Memphis, TN 38112-1690	1848	$41,572	$10,328	1-M	2,040	217	78
Rice Univ., Houston, TX 77251-1892	1912	$40,665	$13,400	1-D	6,628	791	91
Richard Stockton Coll. of New Jersey, Galloway, NJ 08205-9441	1969	$12,322(S)	$10,952	5-D	8,458	662	65
Rider Univ., Lawrenceville, NJ 08648-3001	1865	$35,270	$12,900	1-M	5,410	594	65
Ringling Coll. of Art and Design, Sarasota, FL 34234-5895	1931	$38,540	$12,670	1-B	1,253	156	65
Rivier Univ., Nashua, NH 03060	1933	$27,855	$10,570	2-D	2,346	208	58
Roanoke Coll., Salem, VA 24153-3794	1842	$38,052	$11,924	2-B	2,029	216	64
Robert Morris Univ., Moon Township, PA 15108-1189	1921	$25,114	$11,585	1-D	5,481	487	56
Robert Morris Univ. Illinois, Chicago, IL 60605	1913	$23,700	$10,800	1-M	3,233	227	80
Roberts Wesleyan Coll., Rochester, NY 14624-1997	1866	$27,364	$9,630	2-M	1,885	251	59
Rochester Inst. of Tech., Rochester, NY 14623-5603	1829	$34,424	$11,178	1-D	16,362	1,481	66
Rockford Univ., Rockford, IL 61108-2393	1847	$27,530	$7,710	1-M	1,241	152	50
Rockhurst Univ., Kansas City, MO 64110-2561	1910	$31,290	$8,420	2-D	2,920	274	69
Rocky Mountain Coll., Billings, MT 59102-1796	1878	$24,530	$7,712	2-M	1,068	122	40
Roger Williams Univ., Bristol, RI 02809	1956	$31,718	$14,620	1-D	5,152	471	61
Rogers State Univ., Claremore, OK 74017-3252	1909	$177/cr. hr.(S)	NA	5-B	4,289	281	20
Rollins Coll., Winter Park, FL 32789-4499	1885	$41,460	$12,960	1-D	2,422	211	68
Roosevelt Univ., Chicago, IL 60605	1945	$26,900	$12,532	1-D	6,145	733	42
Rose-Hulman Inst. of Tech., Terre Haute, IN 47803-3999 (2)	1874	$40,254	$11,484	1-M	2,302	185	78

Name, address	Year founded	Tuition & fees	Room & board	Control, degree	Enroll- ment	Faculty	Grad. rate
Rowan Univ., Glassboro, NJ 08028-1701	1923	$12,380(S)	$11,190	5-D	13,349	1,407	72%
Rush Univ., Chicago, IL 60612-3832	1969	NA	NA	1-D	1,566	796	NA
Rutgers, the State Univ. of New Jersey, Camden, Camden, NJ 08102-1401	1927	$13,348(S)	$10,906	5-D	6,264	610	55
Rutgers, the State Univ. of New Jersey, Newark, Newark, NJ 07102	1892	$12,998(S)	$12,379	5-D	11,212	1,025	67
Rutgers, the State Univ. of New Jersey, New Brunswick, Piscataway, NJ 08854-8097	1766	$13,499(S)	$11,578	5-D	48,036	4,865	79
Sacred Heart Univ., Fairfield, CT 06825-1000	1963	$35,750	$13,514	2-D	6,983	664	70
Sage Colls., Troy, NY 12180	1916	NA	NA	1-D	2,832	267	58
Saginaw Valley State Univ., Univ. Center, MI 48710	1963	$8,423(S)	$8,190	5-D	10,245	746	42
St. Ambrose Univ., Davenport, IA 52803-2898	1882	$26,740	$9,016	2-D	3,671	425	63
St. Anselm Coll., Manchester, NH 03102-1310	1889	$36,336	$13,040	2-B	1,923	215	75
St. Augustine Coll., Chicago, IL 60640-3501	1980	$9,120	NA	1-B	1,430	154	NA
St. Augustine's Univ., Raleigh, NC 27610-2298.	1867	$17,890	$7,942	2-B	1,299	160	NA
St. Bonaventure Univ., St. Bonaventure, NY 14778-2284	1858	$29,589	$10,715	2-M	2,244	240	67
St. Catherine Univ., St. Paul, MN 55105	1905	$34,844	$8,568	2-D	5,017	514	61
St. Cloud State Univ., St. Cloud, MN 56301-4498	1869	$6,153(S)	$7,236	5-D	16,245	880	47
St. Edward's Univ., Austin, TX 78704.	1885	$36,550	$11,234	2-M	4,861	495	69
St. Francis Coll., Brooklyn Heights, NY 11201-4398	1884	$20,700	NA	2-M	2,819	273	52
St. Francis Univ., Loretto, PA 15940-0600.	1847	$31,077	$10,760	2-D	2,345	215	70
St. John Fisher Coll., Rochester, NY 14618-3597	1948	$28,430	$10,940	2-D	3,987	429	72
St. John's Univ., Collegeville, MN 56321	1857	$37,162	$8,984	2-M	1,978	166	80
St. John's Univ., Queens, NY 11439	1870	$37,260	$15,880	2-D	20,729	1,467	55
St. Joseph's Coll., Rensselaer, IN 47978	1889	$27,350	$8,440	2-M	1,170	123	45
St. Joseph's Coll., Long Island campus, Patchogue, NY 11772-2399	1916	$21,880	NA	1-M	3,893	407	72
St. Joseph's Coll., New York, Brooklyn, NY 11205-3688	1916	$21,870	NA	1-M	1,461	169	72
St. Joseph's Coll. of Maine, Standish, ME 04084.	1912	$30,990	$11,900	2-M	3,355	126	50
St. Joseph's Univ., Philadelphia, PA 19131-1395	1851	$39,040	$13,232	2-D	8,954	745	79
St. Lawrence Univ., Canton, NY 13617-1455.	1856	$47,686	$12,286	1-M	2,506	207	80
St. Leo Univ., Saint Leo, FL 33574-6665.	1889	$20,110	$9,920	2-D	5,869	207	46
St. Louis Coll. of Pharm., St. Louis, MO 63110-1088.	1864	$28,200	$9,780	1-D	1,350	186	65
St. Louis Univ., St. Louis, MO 63103-2097	1818	$36,726	$9,868	2-D	13,505	1,324	70
St. Martin's Univ., Lacey, WA 98503	1895	$29,834	$9,660	2-M	1,771	215	48
St. Mary's Coll., Notre Dame, IN 46556 (3)	1844	$34,600	$10,560	2-B	1,479	198	71
St. Mary's Coll. of California, Moraga, CA 94575.	1863	$41,380	$14,400	2-D	4,257	525	60
St. Mary's Coll. of Maryland, St. Mary's City, MD 20686-3001.	1840	$14,865(S)	$11,635	5-M	1,858	214	79
St. Mary's Univ., San Antonio, TX 78228-8507	1852	$25,188	$8,666	2-D	3,868	359	53
St. Mary's Univ. of Minnesota, Winona, MN 55987-1399.	1912	$29,315	$7,700	2-D	5,528	560	55
St. Michael's Coll., Colchester, VT 05439	1904	$39,375	$10,600	2-M	2,378	216	75
St. Norbert Coll., De Pere, WI 54115-2099	1898	$33,023	$8,455	2-M	2,222	204	74
St. Olaf Coll., Northfield, MN 55057-1098	1874	$40,700	$9,260	2-B	3,125	333	87
St. Petersburg Coll., St. Petersburg, FL 33733-3489.	1927	$2,634(S)	NA	11-B	31,793	1,731	28
St. Peter's Univ., Jersey City, NJ 07306-5997	1872	$32,230	$13,458	2-D	3,194	271	53
St. Thomas Aquinas Coll., Sparkill, NY 10976	1952	$28,130	$11,680	1-M	1,972	157	52
St. Thomas Univ., Miami Gardens, FL 33054-6459.	1961	$26,370	$7,500	2-D	2,315	222	38
St. Vincent Coll., Latrobe, PA 15650-2690.	1846	$30,350	$9,894	2-D	1,813	207	70
St. Xavier Univ., Chicago, IL 60655-3105	1847	$28,110	$9,490	2-M	4,709	431	52
Salem State Univ., Salem, MA 01970-5353.	1854	$8,130(S)	NA	5-M	9,301	NA	46
Salisbury Univ., Salisbury, MD 21801-6837.	1925	$8,128(S)	$10,240	5-D	8,643	662	67
Salve Regina Univ., Newport, RI 02840-4192	1934	$34,950	$12,300	2-D	2,603	317	64
Sam Houston State Univ., Huntsville, TX 77341	1879	$8,594(S)	$8,324	5-D	19,210	879	51
Samford Univ., Birmingham, AL 35229	1841	$27,324	$9,736	2-D	4,833	471	69
Samuel Merritt Univ., Oakland, CA 94609-3108 (4)	1909	$39,456	NA	1-D	1,530	271	NA
San Diego State Univ., San Diego, CA 92182	1897	$6,766(S)	$13,812	5-D	32,759	1,607	67
San Diego State Univ.–Imperial Valley campus, Calexico, CA 92231	1959	NA	NA	5-M	1,003	NA	NA
San Francisco State Univ., San Francisco, CA 94132-1722	1899	$6,450(S)	$7,556	5-D	29,905	1,679	46
San Jose State Univ., San Jose, CA 95192-0001	1857	$7,303(S)	$11,733	5-M	31,278	1,663	48
Sanford-Brown Coll., Chicago, IL 60602.	1977	NA	NA	3-B	1,832	113	15
Santa Clara Univ., Santa Clara, CA 95053	1851	$42,156	$12,546	2-D	8,770	874	84
Santa Fe Coll., Gainesville, FL 32606	1966	$3,164(S)	NA	11-B	15,745	829	NA
Sarah Lawrence Coll., Bronxville, NY 10708-5999	1926	$48,696	$14,026	1-M	1,782	309	69
Savannah Coll. of Art and Design, Savannah, GA 31402-3146.	1978	$33,450	$13,374	1-M	11,618	678	68
Savannah State Univ., Savannah, GA 31404	1890	$6,340(S)	$7,262	5-M	4,080	200	35
Sch. of the Art Inst. of Chicago, Chicago, IL 60603-3103	1866	$40,585	$12,200	1-M	3,403	744	60
Sch. of Visual Arts, New York, NY 10010-3994	1947	$33,560	$16,800	3-M	4,214	929	69
Schreiner Univ., Kerrville, TX 78028-5697	1923	$22,484	$10,250	2-M	1,136	118	41
Scripps Coll., Claremont, CA 91711-3948 (3)	1926	$45,564	$14,006	1-B	1,009	114	84
Seattle Pacific Univ., Seattle, WA 98119-1997	1891	$33,813	$9,867	2-D	4,270	378	69
Seattle Univ., Seattle, WA 98122-1090	1891	$36,465	$10,545	2-D	7,422	750	77
Seton Hall Univ., South Orange, NJ 07079-2697.	1856	$36,926	$13,692	2-D	9,903	952	64
Seton Hill Univ., Greensburg, PA 15601	1883	$30,300	$10,100	2-M	2,044	193	62
Sewanee: The Univ. of the South, Sewanee, TN 37383-1000.	1857	$37,100	$10,600	2-D	1,701	186	78
Shawnee State Univ., Portsmouth, OH 45662-4344	1986	$7,177(S)	$9,368	5-M	4,341	312	24
Shaw Univ., Raleigh, NC 27601-2399	1865	$16,480	$8,158	2-M	2,062	173	30
Shenandoah Univ., Winchester, VA 22601-5195.	1875	$29,704	$9,564	2-D	4,003	427	45
Shepherd Univ., Shepherdstown, WV 25443.	1871	$6,125(S)	$8,612	5-M	4,221	377	38
Shippensburg Univ. of Pennsylvania, Shippensburg, PA 17257-2299.	1871	$9,448(S)	$10,514	5-M	7,548	404	55
Shorter Univ., Rome, GA 30165.	1873	$19,670	$10,200	2-M	1,696	186	43
Siena Coll., Loudonville, NY 12211-1462.	1937	$32,293	$13,060	2-M	3,216	347	80
Siena Heights Univ., Adrian, MI 49221-1796	1919	$21,890	$8,710	2-M	2,684	NA	43
Simmons Coll., Boston, MA 02115.	1899	$36,230	$13,736	1-D	4,655	637	71
Simpson Coll., Indianola, IA 50125-1297.	1860	$30,999	$7,963	2-M	1,773	207	65
Simpson Univ., Redding, CA 96003-8606	1921	$24,300	$7,900	2-M	1,255	198	49
Skidmore Coll., Saratoga Springs, NY 12866	1903	$45,724	$12,202	1-M	2,702	345	86
Slippery Rock Univ. of Pennsylvania, Slippery Rock, PA 16057-1383.	1889	$9,027(S)	$9,598	5-D	8,347	409	63
Smith Coll., Northampton, MA 01063.	1871	$44,724	$14,950	1-D	3,033	299	86
Sojourner-Douglass Coll., Baltimore, MD 21205-1814 (4)	1980	$8,850	NA	1-M	1,268	240	22
Sonoma State Univ., Rohnert Park, CA 94928-3609.	1960	$8,996(S)	$11,545	5-M	9,120	524	54
South Carolina State Univ., Orangeburg, SC 29117-0001.	1896	$9,776(S)	$9,286	5-D	3,463	265	34
South Dakota Sch. of Mines and Tech., Rapid City, SD 57701-3995	1885	$10,040(S)	$6,130	5-D	2,641	173	45
South Dakota State Univ., Brookings, SD 57007	1881	$7,713(S)	$5,849	5-D	12,554	NA	57
Southeast Missouri State Univ., Cape Girardeau, MO 63701-4799.	1873	$6,863(S)	$8,120	5-M	11,917	573	49
Southeastern Baptist Theol. Seminary, Wake Forest, NC 27588-1889.	1950	NA	NA	2-M	2,332	85	NA
Southeastern Louisiana Univ., Hammond, LA 70402.	1925	$5,705(S)	$6,714	5-D	14,949	606	34
Southeastern Oklahoma State Univ., Durant, OK 74701-0609	1909	$5,315(S)	$4,970	5-M	3,840	259	31
Southeastern Univ., Lakeland, FL 33801-6099	1935	$19,986	$8,648	2-M	2,703	169	42
Southern Adventist Univ., Collegedale, TN 37315-0370	1892	$19,790	$5,900	2-M	3,053	269	48
Southern Arkansas Univ.–Magnolia, Magnolia, AR 71753.	1909	$7,466(S)	$5,022	5-M	3,404	247	31

Name, address	Year founded	Tuition & fees	Room & board	Control, degree	Enrollment	Faculty	Grad. rate
Southern Baptist Theol. Seminary, Louisville, KY 40280-0004	1858	NA	NA	2-D	3,190	NA	NA
Southern Connecticut State Univ., New Haven, CT 06515-1355	1893	$8,981(S)	$10,960	5-D	10,804	1,063	49%
Southern Illinois Univ. Carbondale, Carbondale, IL 62901-4701	1869	$12,093(S)	$9,527	5-D	17,964	939	44
Southern Illinois Univ. Edwardsville, Edwardsville, IL 62026-0001	1957	$9,666(S)	$8,531	5-M	13,850	906	50
Southern Methodist Univ., Dallas, TX 75275	1911	$45,940	$14,645	2-D	10,929	1,156	79
Southern Nazarene Univ., Bethany, OK 73008	1899	$22,680	$7,970	2-M	2,177	226	46
Southern New Hampshire Univ., Manchester, NH 03106-1045	1932	$29,604	$11,462	1-D	28,143	1,767	55
Southern Oregon Univ., Ashland, OR 97520	1926	$7,521(S)	$9,918	5-M	5,864	331	38
Southern Polytechnic State Univ., Marietta, GA 30060-2896	1948	$6,678(S)	$7,280	5-M	6,202	309	37
Southern Univ. and Agr. & Mech. Coll., Baton Rouge, LA 70813	1880	$6,534(S)	NA	5-D	7,699	546	30
Southern Univ. at New Orleans, New Orleans, LA 70126-1009 (4)	1959	NA	NA	5-M	3,141	102	5
Southern Utah Univ., Cedar City, UT 84720-2498	1897	$5,924(S)	$3,078	5-M	7,745	415	41
Southern Wesleyan Univ., Central, SC 29630-1020	1906	NA	NA	2-M	1,883	193	39
Southwest Baptist Univ., Bolivar, MO 65613-2597	1878	$20,040	$6,800	2-D	3,812	280	54
Southwest Florida Coll., Fort Myers, FL 33907	1940	NA	NA	1-B	1,263	NA	NA
Southwest Minnesota State Univ., Marshall, MN 56258	1963	$8,074(S)	$7,208	5-M	6,588	180	39
Southwestern Assemblies of God Univ., Waxahachie, TX 75165-5735	1927	$16,630	$6,784	2-M	2,012	161	39
Southwestern Coll., Winfield, KS 67156-2499	1885	$24,835	$6,846	2-D	1,661	162	53
Southwestern Oklahoma State Univ., Weatherford, OK 73096-3098	1901	$5,460(S)	$4,800	5-D	4,942	282	30
Southwestern Univ., Georgetown, TX 78626	1840	$36,120	$11,760	2-B	1,535	170	70
Spalding Univ., Louisville, KY 40203-2188	1814	$22,200	$10,400	2-D	2,365	NA	40
Spelman Coll., Atlanta, GA 30314-4399 (3)	1881	$24,634	$11,945	1-B	2,129	250	73
Spring Arbor Univ., Spring Arbor, MI 49283-9799	1873	$23,400	$8,170	2-M	3,961	135	57
Springfield Coll., Springfield, MA 01109-3797	1885	$32,560	$10,920	1-D	3,286	353	69
Spring Hill Coll., Mobile, AL 36608-1791	1830	$30,924	$11,296	2-M	1,449	130	56
Stanford Univ., Stanford, CA 94305-9991	1891	$42,690	$13,166	1-D	18,136	1,510	95
State Coll. of Florida Manatee-Sarasota, Bradenton, FL 34206-7046	1957	$2,460(S)	NA	5-B	10,533	468	NA
State Univ. of New York at Fredonia, Fredonia, NY 14063-1136	1826	$7,400(S)	$11,620	5-M	5,405	480	64
State Univ. of New York at New Paltz, New Paltz, NY 12561	1828	$7,083(S)	$10,520	5-M	7,578	649	70
State Univ. of New York at Oswego, Oswego, NY 13126	1861	$7,181(S)	$12,610	5-M	8,117	573	58
State Univ. of New York at Plattsburgh, Plattsburgh, NY 12901-2681	1889	$7,145(S)	$10,526	5-M	6,051	496	60
State Univ. of New York Coll. at Cortland, Cortland, NY 13045	1868	$7,327(S)	$11,790	5-M	7,110	620	70
State Univ. of New York Coll. at Geneseo, Geneseo, NY 14454-1401	1871	$7,430(S)	$11,242	5-M	5,644	355	78
State Univ. of New York Coll. at Old Westbury, Old Westbury, NY 11568-0210	1965	$6,924(S)	$10,120	5-M	4,364	325	36
State Univ. of New York Coll. at Oneonta, Oneonta, NY 13820-4015	1889	$7,220(S)	$11,066	5-M	6,023	483	67
State Univ. of New York Coll. at Potsdam, Potsdam, NY 13676	1816	$7,174(S)	$10,580	5-M	4,042	384	51
State Univ. of New York Coll. of Agr. & Tech. at Cobleskill, Cobleskill, NY 12043	1916	$7,149(S)	$11,720	5-B	2,470	186	44
State Univ. of New York Coll. of Env. Sci. & Forestry, Syracuse, NY 13210-2779	1911	$7,303(S)	$14,630	5-D	2,373	186	71
State Univ. of New York Coll. of Tech. at Canton, Canton, NY 13617	1906	$7,451(S)	$10,800	5-B	3,550	247	29
State Univ. of New York Coll. of Tech. at Delhi, Delhi, NY 13753	1913	$7,200(S)	$10,660	5-B	3,441	220	35
State Univ. of New York Downstate Med. Ctr., Brooklyn, NY 11203-2098	1858	NA	NA	5-D	1,694	981	NA
State Univ. of New York Empire State Coll., Saratoga Springs, NY 12866-4391	1971	$245/cr. hr.(A)	NA	5-M	11,849	1,307	NA
State Univ. of New York Inst. of Tech., Utica, NY 13504-3050	1966	$7,090(S)	$10,810	5-M	2,483	187	NA
State Univ. of New York Maritime Coll., Throggs Neck, NY 10465-4198	1874	$6,170(S)	NA	5-M	1,755	147	50
State Univ. of New York Upstate Med. Univ., Syracuse, NY 13210-2334	1950	$6,600(S)	$10,500	5-D	1,787	54	NA
Stephen F. Austin State Univ., Nacogdoches, TX 75962	1923	$8,412(S)	$8,609	5-D	12,772	675	43
Stetson Univ., DeLand, FL 32723	1883	$38,330	$11,172	1-D	4,044	420	64
Stevens Inst. of Tech., Hoboken, NJ 07030	1870	$41,942	$13,800	1-D	5,541	406	79
Stevenson Univ., Stevenson, MD 21153	1952	$27,082	$12,490	1-M	4,290	523	NA
Stillman Coll., Tuscaloosa, AL 35403-9990	1876	$15,865	$7,056	2-B	1,072	61	34
Stonehill Coll., Easton, MA 02357	1948	$37,426	$14,190	2-B	2,481	275	85
Stony Brook Univ., State Univ. of New York, Stony Brook, NY 11794	1957	$8,000(S)	$11,364	5-D	24,259	1,467	66
Suffolk Univ., Boston, MA 02108-2770	1906	$32,660	$14,638	1-D	8,796	775	55
Sullivan Univ., Louisville, KY 40205	1864	NA	NA	3-D	5,019	319	NA
Sul Ross State Univ., Alpine, TX 79832	1920	$3,618(S)	NA	5-M	1,901	112	30
Susquehanna Univ., Selinsgrove, PA 17870	1858	$38,780	$10,390	2-B	2,179	251	75
Swarthmore Coll., Swarthmore, PA 19081-1397	1864	$44,718	$13,152	1-B	1,534	206	92
Syracuse Univ., Syracuse, NY 13244	1870	$40,458	$14,054	1-D	21,267	1,609	81
Tarleton State Univ., Stephenville, TX 76402	1899	$6,659(S)	$9,042	5-D	10,937	594	43
Taylor Univ., Upland, IN 46989-1001	1846	$28,753	$7,989	2-M	2,245	200	74
Temple Univ., Philadelphia, PA 19122-6096	1884	$14,096(S)	$10,296	12-D	37,270	2,941	66
Tennessee State Univ., Nashville, TN 37209-1561	1912	$6,498(S)	$4,795	5-M	8,816	617	34
Tennessee Tech. Univ., Cookeville, TN 38505	1915	$6,519(S)	$7,936	5-D	11,118	680	51
Tennessee Wesleyan Coll., Athens, TN 37303	1857	$22,300	$7,100	2-M	1,081	126	44
Texas A&M Intl. Univ., Laredo, TX 78041-1900	1969	$7,142(S)	$7,606	5-D	7,431	328	44
Texas A&M Univ., College Station, TX 77843	1876	$8,506(S)	$8,450	5-D	55,378	2,695	81
Texas A&M Univ. at Galveston, Galveston, TX 77553-1675	1962	$8,282(S)	$8,032	5-D	2,177	147	53
Texas A&M Univ.–Commerce, Commerce, TX 75429-3011	1889	$8,376(S)	$7,150	5-D	11,068	637	45
Texas A&M Univ.–Corpus Christi, Corpus Christi, TX 78412-5503	1947	$7,778(S)	$9,965	5-D	10,913	539	35
Texas A&M Univ.–Kingsville, Kingsville, TX 78363	1925	$6,940(S)	$7,484	5-D	7,730	412	34
Texas A&M Univ.–Texarkana, Texarkana, TX 75505-5518	1971	$5,794(S)	$5,910	5-M	1,653	NA	NA
Texas Christian Univ., Fort Worth, TX 76129-0002	1873	$36,590	$10,980	2-D	9,925	931	76
Texas Lutheran Univ., Seguin, TX 78155-5999	1891	$25,890	$8,180	2-M	1,341	129	52
Texas Southern Univ., Houston, TX 77004-4584	1947	$7,946(S)	$10,566	5-D	8,703	573	16
Texas State Univ., San Marcos, TX 78666	1899	$9,151(S)	$7,344	5-D	35,546	1,711	57
Texas Tech. Univ., Lubbock, TX 79409	1923	$8,942(S)	$8,275	5-D	33,111	1,646	59
Texas Wesleyan Univ., Fort Worth, TX 76105-1536	1890	$22,040	$7,846	2-D	2,614	215	42
Texas Woman's Univ., Denton, TX 76201 (4)	1901	$7,290(S)	$6,780	5-D	15,129	689	42
Thiel Coll., Greenville, PA 16125-2181	1866	$27,202	$10,476	2-B	1,109	105	39
Thomas Edison State Coll., Trenton, NJ 08608-1176	1972	$5,700(S)	NA	5-M	20,606	NA	NA
Thomas Jefferson Univ., Philadelphia, PA 19107	1824	NA	NA	1-D	3,326	NA	NA
Thomas More Coll., Crestview Hills, KY 41017-3495	1921	$27,220	$7,540	2-M	1,600	174	57
Thomas Univ., Thomasville, GA 31792-7499	1950	$14,740	$4,800	1-M	1,124	53	NA
Tiffin Univ., Tiffin, OH 44883-2161	1888	$21,510	$9,870	1-M	4,954	373	43
Touro Coll., New York, NY 10010	1971	$15,520	$10,600	1-D	17,544	NA	NA
Towson Univ., Towson, MD 21252-0001	1866	$8,342(S)	$10,662	5-D	22,499	1,654	65
Transylvania Univ., Lexington, KY 40508-1797	1780	$33,360	$9,300	2-B	1,081	117	72
Trevecca Nazarene Univ., Nashville, TN 37210-2877	1901	$22,330	$7,788	2-D	2,406	214	47
Trine Univ., Angola, IN 46703-1764	1884	$29,600	$9,800	1-M	1,876	145	51
Trinity Christian Coll., Palos Heights, IL 60463-0929	1959	$24,210	$8,730	2-M	1,380	157	58
Trinity Coll., Hartford, CT 06106-3100	1823	$47,510	$12,300	1-M	2,387	250	83
Trinity Intl. Univ., Deerfield, IL 60015-1284	1897	NA	NA	2-D	2,671	82	52
Trinity Univ., San Antonio, TX 78212-7200	1869	$35,262	$10,968	2-M	2,442	309	82

Name, address	Year founded	Tuition & fees	Room & board	Control, degree	Enrollment	Faculty	Grad. rate
Trinity Washington Univ., Washington, DC 20017-1094 (3)	1897	$21,330	$9,658	2-M	1,630	NA	NA
Troy Univ., Troy, AL 36082	1887	$9,416(S)	$7,144	5-D	20,574	1,157	35%
Truett-McConnell Coll., Cleveland, GA 30528	1946	$16,510	$7,000	2-B	1,606	125	28
Truman State Univ., Kirksville, MO 63501-4221	1867	$7,368(S)	$7,720	5-M	6,209	362	72
Tufts Univ., Medford, MA 02155	1852	$48,488	$12,612	1-D	10,883	1,049	92
Tulane Univ., New Orleans, LA 70118-5669	1834	$46,930	$12,012	1-D	13,462	1,140	76
Tusculum Coll., Greeneville, TN 37743-9997	1794	$22,250	$8,500	2-M	2,199	224	48
Tuskegee Univ., Tuskegee, AL 36088	1881	$18,900	$8,450	1-D	3,118	269	46
Union Coll., Barbourville, KY 40906-1499	1879	$23,055	$6,900	2-M	1,164	106	34
Union Coll., Schenectady, NY 12308-2311	1795	$46,785	$11,463	1-B	2,246	236	88
Union Inst. and Univ., Cincinnati, OH 45206-1925	1969	$11,904	NA	1-D	1,767	319	NA
Union Univ., Jackson, TN 38305-3697	1823	$26,880	$8,430	2-D	3,996	244	64
United States Air Force Academy, USAF Academy, CO 80840-5025	1954	$0(C)	NA	4-B	3,993	514	85
United States Merchant Marine Academy, Kings Point, NY 11024-1699	1943	$1,032	NA	4-B	1,034	145	76
United States Military Academy, West Point, NY 10996 (2)	1802	$0(C)	$0	4-M	4,591	614	84
United States Naval Academy, Annapolis, MD 21402-5000	1845	$0(C)	NA	4-B	4,526	534	88
United Talmudical Seminary, Brooklyn, NY 11211 (1)	1949	NA	NA	2-M	1,500	NA	NA
Universidad Adventista de las Antillas, Mayagüez, PR 00681-0118	1957	$5,550	$2,900	2-M	1,322	95	30
Universidad del Este, Carolina, PR 00984	1949	$5,434	NA	1-M	13,317	NA	NA
Universidad del Turabo, Gurabo, PR 00778-3030	1972	$19,512	$8,600	1-D	17,287	1,317	16
Universidad de Puerto Rico en Aguadilla, Aguadilla, PR 00604	1972	$1,662(S)	NA	6-B	3,076	NA	NA
Universidad de Puerto Rico en Cayey, Cayey, PR 00736	1967	NA	NA	6-B	3,830	164	41
Universidad Metropolitana, San Juan, PR 00928-1150	1980	$5,434	NA	1-D	13,631	1,093	23
Univ. at Albany, State Univ. of New York, Albany, NY 12222-0001	1844	$8,040(S)	$11,634	5-D	17,338	1,286	66
Univ. at Buffalo, the State Univ. of New York, Buffalo, NY 14260	1846	$8,426(S)	$11,857	5-D	29,850	1,771	72
Univ. of Advancing Tech., Tempe, AZ 85283-1042 (2)	1983	NA	NA	3-M	1,073	60	NA
Univ. of Akron, Akron, OH 44325	1870	$10,054(S)	$10,382	5-D	24,928	1,675	40
Univ. of Alabama, Tuscaloosa, AL 35487	1831	$9,450(S)	$8,756	5-D	34,752	1,731	67
Univ. of Alabama at Birmingham, Birmingham, AL 35294	1969	$8,904(S)	$5,955	5-D	18,568	931	54
Univ. of Alabama in Huntsville, Huntsville, AL 35899	1950	$9,192(S)	$8,433	5-D	7,376	464	48
Univ. of Alaska Anchorage, Anchorage, AK 99508	1954	$6,079(S)	$10,143	5-D	18,107	1,390	26
Univ. of Alaska Fairbanks, Fairbanks, AK 99775-7520	1917	$6,752(S)	$7,450	5-D	9,256	1,019	38
Univ. of Alaska Southeast, Juneau, AK 99801	1972	$4,944(S)	$6,150	5-M	3,458	229	31
Univ. of Arizona, Tucson, AZ 85721	1885	$10,391(S)	$9,714	5-D	40,621	1,808	61
Univ. of Arkansas, Fayetteville, AR 72701-1201	1871	$7,818(S)	$9,042	5-D	25,341	1,263	60
Univ. of Arkansas at Little Rock, Little Rock, AR 72204-1099	1927	$7,094(S)	$9,701	5-D	12,377	766	24
Univ. of Arkansas at Monticello, Monticello, AR 71656	1909	$5,700(S)	$4,880	5-M	3,920	240	24
Univ. of Arkansas at Pine Bluff, Pine Bluff, AR 71601-2799	1873	$5,754(S)	$7,250	5-M	3,428	234	24
Univ. of Arkansas for Med. Sciences, Little Rock, AR 72205-7199	1879	$7,896(S)	$5,535	5-D	2,809	1,271	NA
Univ. of Arkansas–Fort Smith, Fort Smith, AR 72913-3649	1928	$5,625(S)	$8,512	11-B	7,170	440	24
Univ. of Baltimore, Baltimore, MD 21201-5779	1925	$6,915(S)	NA	5-D	3,526	405	NA
Univ. of Bridgeport, Bridgeport, CT 06604	1927	$29,090	$12,400	1-D	4,842	478	28
Univ. of California, Berkeley, Berkeley, CA 94720-1500	1868	$12,864(S)	$15,180	5-D	25,951	NA	91
Univ. of California, Davis, Davis, CA 95616	1905	$13,896(S)	$13,961	5-D	33,307	1,789	81
Univ. of California, Irvine, Irvine, CA 92697	1965	$14,688(S)	$12,073	5-D	28,895	1,413	86
Univ. of California, Los Angeles, Los Angeles, CA 90095	1919	$12,697(S)	$12,895	5-D	42,190	2,681	90
Univ. of California, Merced, Merced, CA 95343	2005	NA	$14,272	5-D	5,760	306	58
Univ. of California, Riverside, Riverside, CA 92521-0102	1954	$12,972(S)	$13,500	5-D	21,297	915	69
Univ. of California, San Diego, La Jolla, CA 92093	1959	$13,234(S)	$11,924	5-D	28,294	1,213	86
Univ. of California, Santa Barbara, Santa Barbara, CA 93106-2014	1909	$13,746(S)	$13,805	5-D	22,225	1,054	81
Univ. of California, Santa Cruz, Santa Cruz, CA 95064	1965	$13,416(S)	$14,409	5-D	17,203	804	72
Univ. of Central Arkansas, Conway, AR 72035-0001	1907	$7,358(S)	$5,280	5-D	11,534	723	42
Univ. of Central Florida, Orlando, FL 32816	1963	$6,317(S)	$9,394	5-D	59,740	1,849	67
Univ. of Central Missouri, Warrensburg, MO 64093	1871	$5,812(S)	$7,734	5-M	12,513	640	53
Univ. of Central Oklahoma, Edmond, OK 73034-5209	1890	$5,437(S)	$6,856	5-M	17,217	953	36
Univ. of Charleston, Charleston, WV 25304-1099	1888	$20,700	$9,000	1-M	1,935	191	46
Univ. of Chicago, Chicago, IL 60637-1513	1891	$46,386	$13,653	1-D	12,289	1,727	93
Univ. of Cincinnati, Cincinnati, OH 45221	1819	$10,784(S)	$10,290	5-D	34,379	1,183	64
Univ. of Colorado Boulder, Boulder, CO 80309	1876	$10,240(S)	$12,258	5-D	31,702	1,938	70
Univ. of Colorado Colorado Springs, Colorado Springs, CO 80933-7150	1965	$8,658(S)	$8,800	5-D	11,018	825	46
Univ. of Colorado Denver, Denver, CO 80217-3364	1912	$9,625(S)	$10,790	5-D	22,206	3,544	41
Univ. of Connecticut, Storrs, CT 06269	1881	$12,700(S)	$12,006	5-D	25,911	1,520	83
Univ. of Dallas, Irving, TX 75062-4736	1955	$34,430	$11,070	2-D	2,597	259	66
Univ. of Dayton, Dayton, OH 45469-1300	1850	$35,800	$11,490	2-D	10,834	929	77
Univ. of Delaware, Newark, DE 19716	1743	$12,112(S)	$11,200	12-D	21,308	1,490	82
Univ. of Denver, Denver, CO 80208	1864	$42,090	$11,307	1-D	11,778	1,365	78
Univ. of Detroit Mercy, Detroit, MI 48221	1877	$35,920	$10,070	2-D	5,725	NA	NA
Univ. of Dubuque, Dubuque, IA 52001-5099	1852	$25,520	$8,160	2-D	2,003	166	41
Univ. of Evansville, Evansville, IN 47722	1854	$30,596	$10,460	2-D	2,630	231	63
Univ. of Findlay, Findlay, OH 45840-3653	1882	$30,640	$9,350	2-D	4,880	279	56
Univ. of Florida, Gainesville, FL 32611	1853	$6,263(S)	$9,520	5-D	49,878	NA	85.1
Univ. of Georgia, Athens, GA 30602	1785	$10,262(S)	$9,246	5-D	34,536	2,228	83
Univ. of Great Falls, Great Falls, MT 59405	1932	$20,960	$6,800	2-M	1,142	116	30
Univ. of Guam, Mangilao, GU 96923	1952	$5,098(S)	$1,910	7-M	3,836	250	28
Univ. of Hartford, West Hartford, CT 06117-1599	1877	$35,444	$11,518	1-D	6,820	839	60
Univ. of Hawaii at Hilo, Hilo, HI 96720-4091	1970	$7,036(S)	$7,662	5-M	4,043	360	36
Univ. of Hawaii at Manoa, Honolulu, HI 96822	1907	$10,622(S)	$10,218	5-D	20,006	1,271	57
Univ. of Hawaii–West Oahu, Pearl City, HI 96782-3366	1976	$5,592(S)	NA	5-B	1,997	101	NA
Univ. of Houston, Houston, TX 77204	1927	$10,272(S)	$8,912	5-D	39,540	1,987	48
Univ. of Houston–Clear Lake, Houston, TX 77058-1002	1971	$6,810(S)	$8,538	5-D	8,164	490	NA
Univ. of Houston–Downtown, Houston, TX 77002	1974	$6,267(S)	NA	5-B	13,757	662	14
Univ. of Houston–Victoria, Victoria, TX 77901-4450	1973	$6,397(S)	$7,216	5-M	4,491	219	NA
Univ. of Idaho, Moscow, ID 83844-2282	1889	$6,524(S)	$8,034	5-D	11,884	714	54
Univ. of Illinois at Chicago, Chicago, IL 60607-7128	1946	$13,354(S)	$10,882	5-D	27,589	1,672	58
Univ. of Illinois at Springfield, Springfield, IL 62703-5407	1969	$11,132(S)	$10,350	5-D	5,137	385	43
Univ. of Illinois at Urbana-Champaign, Champaign, IL 61820	1867	$15,602(S)	$10,848	5-D	44,942	1,893	84
Univ. of Indianapolis, Indianapolis, IN 46227-3697	1902	$25,394	$9,010	2-D	5,444	535	54
Univ. of Iowa, Iowa City, IA 52242-1316	1847	$8,079(S)	$9,614	5-D	31,065	1,624	70
Univ. of Kansas, Lawrence, KS 66045	1866	$9,278(S)	$7,702	5-D	26,968	1,760	62
Univ. of Kentucky, Lexington, KY 40506-0032	1865	$9,966(S)	$10,328	5-D	28,434	1,719	60
Univ. of La Verne, La Verne, CA 91750-4443	1891	$36,744	$12,200	1-D	5,111	509	59
Univ. of Louisiana at Lafayette, Lafayette, LA 70504	1898	$6,192(S)	$8,594	5-D	16,687	754	44
Univ. of Louisiana at Monroe, Monroe, LA 71209-0001	1931	$5,443(S)	$6,486	5-D	8,645	NA	NA
Univ. of Louisville, Louisville, KY 40292-0001	1798	$9,750(S)	$7,710	5-D	21,447	1,277	54

Name, address	Year founded	Tuition & fees	Room & board	Control, degree	Enroll-ment	Faculty	Grad. rate
Univ. of Maine, Orono, ME 04469	1865	$10,600(S)	$9,112	5-D	11,247	793	56%
Univ. of Maine at Augusta, Augusta, ME 04330-9410	1965	$7,448(S)	NA	5-B	4,770	279	12
Univ. of Maine at Farmington, Farmington, ME 04938-1990	1863	$9,137(S)	$8,454	5-M	2,180	171	57
Univ. of Maine at Fort Kent, Fort Kent, ME 04743-1292	1878	$7,575(S)	$7,720	5-B	1,209	98	44
Univ. of Maine at Presque Isle, Presque Isle, ME 04769-2888	1903	$7,435(S)	$7,576	5-B	1,263	100	30
Univ. of Mary, Bismarck, ND 58504-9652	1959	$14,730	$5,736	2-D	3,135	257	52
Univ. of Mary Hardin-Baylor, Belton, TX 76513	1845	$23,940	$7,020	2-D	3,492	295	47
Univ. of Maryland, Baltimore County, Baltimore, MD 21250	1963	$10,068(S)	$10,366	5-D	13,908	769	61
Univ. of Maryland, College Park, College Park, MD 20742	1856	$9,162(S)	$10,280	5-D	37,272	2,409	84
Univ. of Maryland Eastern Shore, Princess Anne, MD 21853-1299	1886	$9,368(S)	$8,656	5-D	4,454	345	32
Univ. of Maryland Univ. Coll., Adelphi, MD 20783	1947	$6,552(S)	NA	5-D	39,557	2,608	NA
Univ. of Mary Washington, Fredericksburg, VA 22401-5358	1908	$9,660(S)	$10,548	5-M	4,831	386	74
Univ. of Massachusetts Amherst, Amherst, MA 01003	1863	$1,714(S)	$11,166	5-D	28,518	1,378	73
Univ. of Massachusetts Boston, Boston, MA 02125-3393	1964	$11,966(S)	NA	5-D	16,277	1,173	44
Univ. of Massachusetts Dartmouth, North Dartmouth, MA 02747-2300	1895	$11,681(S)	$10,908	5-D	9,053	623	49
Univ. of Massachusetts Lowell, Lowell, MA 01854-2881	1894	$12,097(S)	$10,793	5-D	16,932	1,003	54
Univ. of Memphis, Memphis, TN 38152	1912	$8,666(S)	$8,716	5-D	21,480	1,468	44
Univ. of Miami, Coral Gables, FL 33124	1925	$42,852	$12,314	1-D	16,935	1,500	82
Univ. of Michigan, Ann Arbor, MI 48109	1817	$13,977(S)	$9,996	5-D	43,710	3,235	90
Univ. of Michigan–Dearborn, Dearborn, MI 48128-1491	1959	$10,854(S)	NA	5-D	8,789	571	52
Univ. of Michigan–Flint, Flint, MI 48502-1950	1956	$9,844(S)	$7,703	5-D	8,555	563	38
Univ. of Minnesota, Crookston, Crookston, MN 56716-5001	1966	$11,448(S)	$6,502	5-B	2,839	90	44
Univ. of Minnesota, Duluth, Duluth, MN 55812-2496	1947	$12,815(S)	$6,956	5-D	11,241	628	60
Univ. of Minnesota, Morris, Morris, MN 56267-2134	1959	$12,584(S)	$7,482	5-B	1,946	165	63
Univ. of Minnesota, Twin Cities campus, Minneapolis, MN 55455-0213	1851	$13,618(S)	$8,532	5-D	51,526	2,877	75
Univ. of Mississippi, University, MS 38677	1844	$6,660(S)	$9,566	5-D	19,431	988	58
Univ. of Mississippi Med. Ctr., Jackson, MS 39216-4505	1955	NA	NA	5-D	2,092	836	NA
Univ. of Missouri, Columbia, MO 65211	1839	$9,415(S)	$9,286	5-D	34,658	1,505	70
Univ. of Missouri–Kansas City, Kansas City, MO 64110-2499	1929	$9,456(S)	$11,500	5-D	15,746	1,203	57
Univ. of Missouri–St. Louis, St. Louis, MO 63121	1963	$9,474(S)	$8,960	5-D	16,814	1,011	46
Univ. of Mobile, Mobile, AL 36613	1961	$18,540	$9,330	2-M	1,610	179	49
Univ. of Montana, Missoula, MT 59812-0002	1893	$6,276(S)	$8,109	5-D	14,946	885	48
Univ. of Montana Western, Dillon, MT 59725-3598	1893	$5,860(S)	$6,536	5-B	1,511	91	46
Univ. of Montevallo, Montevallo, AL 35115	1896	$10,000(S)	$6,062	5-M	3,066	219	45
Univ. of Mount Olive, Mount Olive, NC 28365	1951	NA	NA	2-B	3,855	183	44
Univ. of Mount Union, Alliance, OH 44601-3993	1846	$27,380	$8,780	2-M	2,187	248	63
Univ. of Nebraska at Kearney, Kearney, NE 68849-0001	1903	$6,521(S)	$8,434	5-M	7,052	442	53
Univ. of Nebraska at Omaha, Omaha, NE 68182	1908	$6,550(S)	$8,090	5-D	15,227	1,044	42
Univ. of Nebraska–Lincoln, Lincoln, NE 68588	1869	$7,975(S)	$9,532	5-D	24,445	1,091	67
Univ. of Nebraska Med. Ctr., Omaha, NE 68198	1869	NA	NA	5-D	3,625	1,232	NA
Univ. of Nevada, Las Vegas, Las Vegas, NV 89154	1957	$6,550(S)	$10,524	5-D	27,858	NA	43
Univ. of Nevada, Reno, Reno, NV 89557	1874	$6,645(S)	$9,769	5-D	18,776	1,029	53
Univ. of New England, Biddeford, ME 04005-9526	1831	$33,145	$13,000	1-D	6,032	501	58
Univ. of New Hampshire, Durham, NH 03824	1866	$16,496(S)	$10,056	5-D	14,942	1,002	80
Univ. of New Haven, West Haven, CT 06516-1916	1920	$33,740	$13,900	1-D	6,555	620	55
Univ. of New Mexico, Albuquerque, NM 87131-2039	1889	$5,727(S)	$8,312	5-D	27,337	1,427	48
Univ. of New Orleans, New Orleans, LA 70148	1958	$6,668(S)	$8,946	5-D	9,323	412	32
Univ. of North Alabama, Florence, AL 35632-0001	1830	$8,662(S)	$6,055	5-M	6,931	335	32
Univ. of North Carolina at Asheville, Asheville, NC 28804-3299	1927	$6,241(S)	$7,984	5-M	3,784	277	60
Univ. of North Carolina at Chapel Hill, Chapel Hill, NC 27599	1789	$8,340(S)	$10,008	5-D	29,127	2,012	90
Univ. of North Carolina at Charlotte, Charlotte, NC 28223-0001	1946	$6,107(S)	$8,600	5-D	26,571	1,474	54
Univ. of North Carolina at Greensboro, Greensboro, NC 27412-5001	1891	$6,439(S)	$7,688	5-D	17,707	1,004	55
Univ. of North Carolina at Pembroke, Pembroke, NC 28372-1510	1887	$5,144(S)	$7,318	5-M	6,269	402	76
Univ. of North Carolina Wilmington, Wilmington, NC 28403-3297	1947	$6,343(S)	$8,624	5-D	13,937	1,009	71
Univ. of North Dakota, Grand Forks, ND 58202	1883	$7,508(S)	$6,586	5-D	15,143	731	54
Univ. of Northern Colorado, Greeley, CO 80639	1890	$6,514(S)	$10,040	5-D	12,084	764	46
Univ. of Northern Iowa, Cedar Falls, IA 50614	1876	$7,685(S)	$7,820	5-D	12,159	801	67
Univ. of North Florida, Jacksonville, FL 32224	1965	$6,353(S)	$8,662	5-D	16,083	816	50
Univ. of North Georgia, Dahlonega, GA 30597	1873	$6,692(S)	$8,896	5-D	15,455	770	52
Univ. of North Texas, Denton, TX 76203	1890	$9,105(S)	$7,355	5-D	36,168	1,450	46
Univ. of Northwestern Ohio, Lima, OH 45805-1498	1920	NA	NA	1-B	3,848	127	NA
Univ. of Northwestern–St. Paul, St. Paul, MN 55113-1598	1902	$28,120	$8,510	2-M	3,267	159	68
Univ. of Notre Dame, Notre Dame, IN 46556	1842	$44,605	$12,512	2-D	12,124	1,221	95
Univ. of Oklahoma, Norman, OK 73019-0390	1890	$7,341(S)	$8,718	5-D	27,292	1,407	66
Univ. of Oklahoma Health Sciences Ctr., Oklahoma City, OK 73190	1890	$6,066(S)	NA	5-D	3,315	454	NA
Univ. of Oregon, Eugene, OR 97403	1876	$9,703(S)	$11,109	5-D	24,473	1,473	67
Univ. of Pennsylvania, Philadelphia, PA 19104	1740	$45,890	$12,922	1-D	21,358	2,248	96
Univ. of Phoenix–Online campus, Phoenix, AZ 85034-7209	1989	NA	NA	3-D	292,797	11,477	NA
Univ. of Pikeville, Pikeville, KY 41501	1889	$17,750	$7,000	2-D	2,204	127	28
Univ. of Pittsburgh, Pittsburgh, PA 15260	1787	$17,100(S)	$10,700	12-D	28,649	2,156	80
Univ. of Pittsburgh at Bradford, Bradford, PA 16701-2812	1963	$13,078(S)	$8,238	12-B	1,481	157	54
Univ. of Pittsburgh at Greensburg, Greensburg, PA 15601-5860	1963	$13,068(S)	$9,260	12-B	1,677	100	53
Univ. of Pittsburgh at Johnstown, Johnstown, PA 15904-2990	1927	$13,130(S)	$8,322	12-B	2,957	NA	60
Univ. of Portland, Portland, OR 97203-5798	1901	$36,870	$11,004	2-D	4,036	332	76
Univ. of Puerto Rico in Arecibo, Arecibo, PR 00613	1967	$1,662(S)	NA	6-B	4,352	NA	NA
Univ. of Puerto Rico in Bayamón, Bayamón, PR 00959	1971	$2,212(S)	NA	6-B	5,075	258	45
Univ. of Puerto Rico in Carolina, Carolina, PR 00984-4800	1974	$1,662(S)	NA	6-B	4,321	NA	NA
Univ. of Puerto Rico in Humacao, Humacao, PR 00791	1962	$2,019(S)	$8,280	6-B	3,774	257	45
Univ. of Puerto Rico in Ponce, Ponce, PR 00732-7186	1970	$2,019(S)	$8,280	6-B	3,089	193	38
Univ. of Puerto Rico in Utuado, Utuado, PR 00641-2500	1979	$1,662(S)	NA	6-B	1,623	107	NA
Univ. of Puerto Rico, Mayagüez campus, Mayagüez, PR 00681-9000	1911	$1,662(S)	NA	6-D	13,852	NA	NA
Univ. of Puerto Rico, Med. Sciences campus, San Juan, PR 00936-5067 (4)	1950	NA	NA	6-D	2,381	NA	NA
Univ. of Puerto Rico, Río Piedras campus, San Juan, PR 00931-3300	1903	$1,662(S)	NA	6-D	18,966	1,084	47
Univ. of Puget Sound, Tacoma, WA 98416	1888	$41,868	$10,780	1-D	2,814	276	78
Univ. of Redlands, Redlands, CA 92373-0999	1907	$41,290	$12,314	1-D	5,147	524	73
Univ. of Rhode Island, Kingston, RI 02881	1892	$12,360(S)	$7,150	5-D	16,561	1,189	60
Univ. of Richmond, University of Richmond, VA 23173	1830	$46,680	$10,790	1-D	3,531	428	85
Univ. of Rio Grande, Rio Grande, OH 45674	1876	$20,960	$9,000	1-M	2,278	182	NA
Univ. of Rochester, Rochester, NY 14627	1850	$45,372	$13,128	1-D	11,020	779	85
Univ. of St. Francis, Joliet, IL 60435-6169	1920	$27,970	$8,520	2-D	2,398	276	57
Univ. of St. Francis, Fort Wayne, IN 46808-3994	1890	$25,180	$8,312	2-M	2,464	249	NA
Univ. of St. Joseph, West Hartford, CT 06117-2700 (4)	1932	$33,417	$14,006	2-D	2,640	312	52
Univ. of St. Mary, Leavenworth, KS 66048-5082	1923	$22,170	$8,000	2-D	1,325	216	53

Name, address	Year founded	Tuition & fees	Room & board	Control, degree	Enroll- ment	Faculty	Grad. rate
Univ. of St. Thomas, St. Paul, MN 55105-1096	1885	$36,682	$5,770	2-D	10,219	NA	75%
Univ. of St. Thomas, Houston, TX 77006-4696	1947	$28,240	$8,250	2-D	3,589	351	51
Univ. of San Diego, San Diego, CA 92110-2492	1949	$42,908	$11,910	2-D	8,321	910	75
Univ. of San Francisco, San Francisco, CA 94117-1080	1855	$41,450	$13,320	2-D	10,130	NA	69
Univ. of Scranton, Scranton, PA 18510	1888	$38,754	$13,186	2-D	5,633	518	82
Univ. of Sioux Falls, Sioux Falls, SD 57105-1699	1883	$25,480	$6,900	2-M	1,564	140	49
Univ. of South Alabama, Mobile, AL 36688-0002	1963	$8,310(S)	$6,860	5-D	15,065	966	33
Univ. of South Carolina, Columbia, SC 29208	1801	$10,816(S)	$8,909	5-D	31,964	NA	73
Univ. of South Carolina Aiken, Aiken, SC 29801-6309	1961	$9,308(S)	$6,970	5-M	3,291	254	42
Univ. of South Carolina Beaufort, Bluffton, SC 29909	1959	$8,972(S)	$7,200	5-B	1,874	141	20
Univ. of South Carolina Upstate, Spartanburg, SC 29303-4999	1967	$10,198(S)	$7,475	5-M	5,358	416	39
Univ. of South Dakota, Vermillion, SD 57069-2390	1862	$8,022(S)	$7,089	5-D	10,235	573	56
Univ. of Southern California, Los Angeles, CA 90089	1880	$46,298	$12,902	1-D	41,368	3,277	91
Univ. of Southern Indiana, Evansville, IN 47712-3590	1965	$6,977(S)	$7,680	5-D	9,902	682	37
Univ. of Southern Maine, Portland, ME 04104-9300	1878	$8,920(S)	$9,820	5-D	8,923	659	32
Univ. of Southern Mississippi, Hattiesburg, MS 39406-0001	1910	$6,744(S)	$7,206	5-D	15,249	923	45
Univ. of South Florida, Tampa, FL 33620-9951	1956	$6,410(S)	$9,250	5-D	41,428	1,652	57
Univ. of South Florida–St. Petersburg campus, St. Petersburg, FL 33701	1965	$5,199(S)	$7,570	5-M	4,391	255	29
Univ. of South Florida Sarasota-Manatee, Sarasota, FL 34243	1956	$5,587(S)	NA	5-M	1,889	139	NA
Univ. of Tampa, Tampa, FL 33606-1490	1931	$25,772	$9,388	1-M	7,260	646	61
Univ. of Tennessee, Knoxville, TN 37996	1794	$11,194(S)	$9,170	5-D	30,030	2,074	68
Univ. of Tennessee at Chattanooga, Chattanooga, TN 37403-2598	1886	$6,064(S)	$7,847	5-D	11,674	759	37
Univ. of Tennessee at Martin, Martin, TN 38238-1000	1900	$7,507(S)	$5,710	5-M	7,423	561	46
Univ. of Texas at Arlington, Arlington, TX 76019	1895	$8,878(S)	$7,864	5-D	33,329	1,385	44
Univ. of Texas at Austin, Austin, TX 78712-1111	1883	$9,790(S)	$11,362	5-D	52,059	3,035	79
Univ. of Texas at Brownsville, Brownsville, TX 78520-4991	1973	$5,011(S)	$6,706	5-D	8,612	NA	26
Univ. of Texas at Dallas, Richardson, TX 75080	1969	$11,806(S)	$9,240	5-D	21,193	1,040	63
Univ. of Texas at El Paso, El Paso, TX 79968-0001	1913	$7,255(S)	$9,180	5-D	23,003	1,189	39
Univ. of Texas at San Antonio, San Antonio, TX 78249-0617	1969	$8,737(S)	$8,229	5-D	28,623	1,313	30
Univ. of Texas at Tyler, Tyler, TX 75799-0001	1971	$7,222(S)	$11,334	5-D	7,476	453	44
Univ. of Texas Health Sci. Ctr. at Houston, Houston, TX 77225-0036	1972	$6,357(S)	NA	5-D	4,615	132	NA
Univ. of Texas Health Sci. Ctr. at San Antonio, San Antonio, TX 78229-3900	1976	NA	NA	5-D	3,093	NA	NA
Univ. of Texas Med. Branch, Galveston, TX 77555	1891	NA	NA	5-D	2,430	NA	NA
Univ. of Texas of the Permian Basin, Odessa, TX 79762-0001	1969	$6,457(S)	$7,989	5-M	5,131	212	27
Univ. of Texas–Pan Amer., Edinburg, TX 78539	1927	$5,969(S)	$5,720	5-D	20,053	816	39
Univ. of the Arts, Philadelphia, PA 19102-4944	1870	$36,582	$13,335	1-M	2,063	499	64
Univ. of the Cumberlands, Williamsburg, KY 40769-1372	1889	$20,000	$8,000	2-D	4,924	238	43
Univ. of the District of Columbia, Washington, DC 20008-1175	1976	$7,255(S)	$6,600	9-D	5,011	NA	21
Univ. of the Incarnate Word, San Antonio, TX 78209-6397	1881	$26,490	$10,826	2-D	8,685	531	40
Univ. of the Pacific, Stockton, CA 95211-0197	1851	$39,810	$12,336	1-D	6,421	807	63
Univ. of the Sacred Heart, San Juan, PR 00914-0383	1935	$5,660	$2,900	2-M	5,666	367	35
Univ. of the Sciences, Philadelphia, PA 19104-4495	1821	$36,096	$14,108	1-D	2,799	325	72
Univ. of the Virgin Islands, Saint Thomas, VI 00802-9990	1962	$4,794(S)	$9,900	7-M	2,321	242	26
Univ. of Toledo, Toledo, OH 43606-3390	1872	$9,275(S)	$9,876	5-D	20,782	1,043	46
Univ. of Tulsa, Tulsa, OK 74104-3189	1894	$35,370	$10,476	1-D	4,597	435	69
Univ. of Utah, Salt Lake City, UT 84112-1107	1850	$7,935(S)	$8,528	5-D	32,077	1,916	60
Univ. of Vermont, Burlington, VT 05405	1791	$16,196(S)	$10,810	5-D	12,723	755	76
Univ. of Virginia, Charlottesville, VA 22903	1819	$12,458(S)	$9,717	5-D	23,464	1,327	93
Univ. of Virginia's Coll. at Wise, Wise, VA 24293	1954	$8,509(S)	$9,440	5-B	2,291	168	42
Univ. of Washington, Seattle, WA 98195	1861	$12,394(S)	$10,833	5-D	43,762	6,054	82
Univ. of Washington, Bothell, Bothell, WA 98011-8246	1990	NA	NA	5-M	4,159	219	64
Univ. of Washington, Tacoma, Tacoma, WA 98402-3100	1990	$11,902(S)	NA	5-D	3,906	232	NA
Univ. of West Alabama, Livingston, AL 35470	1835	$7,660(S)	$6,052	5-M	4,427	247	31
Univ. of West Florida, Pensacola, FL 32514-5750	1963	$8,394(S)	$9,323	5-D	12,588	578	42
Univ. of West Georgia, Carrollton, GA 30118	1933	$6,832(S)	$8,020	5-D	11,929	626	42
Univ. of Wisconsin–Eau Claire, Eau Claire, WI 54702-4004	1916	$8,710(S)	$6,720	5-D	10,902	556	68
Univ. of Wisconsin–Green Bay, Green Bay, WI 54311-7001	1968	$7,676(S)	$7,224	5-M	6,667	356	46
Univ. of Wisconsin–La Crosse, La Crosse, WI 54601-3742	1909	$8,769(S)	$5,950	5-D	10,427	595	69
Univ. of Wisconsin–Madison, Madison, WI 53706-1380	1848	$10,403(S)	$8,354	5-D	43,275	2,899	84
Univ. of Wisconsin–Milwaukee, Milwaukee, WI 53201-0413	1956	$9,300(S)	$8,796	5-D	27,784	1,648	41
Univ. of Wisconsin–Oshkosh, Oshkosh, WI 54901	1871	$7,360(S)	$6,926	5-D	13,413	651	52
Univ. of Wisconsin–Parkside, Kenosha, WI 53141-2000	1968	$7,316(S)	$6,572	5-M	4,617	256	31
Univ. of Wisconsin–Platteville, Platteville, WI 53818-3099	1866	$7,484(S)	$6,790	5-M	8,505	432	52
Univ. of Wisconsin–River Falls, River Falls, WI 54022	1874	$7,721(S)	$7,304	5-M	6,173	389	54
Univ. of Wisconsin–Stevens Point, Stevens Point, WI 54481-3897	1894	$7,505(S)	$6,538	5-D	9,677	481	59
Univ. of Wisconsin–Stout, Menomonie, WI 54751	1891	$8,968(S)	$6,234	5-D	9,286	493	NA
Univ. of Wisconsin–Superior, Superior, WI 54880-4500	1893	$7,946(S)	$5,780	5-M	2,656	221	41
Univ. of Wisconsin–Whitewater, Whitewater, WI 53190-1790	1868	$7,578(S)	$6,000	5-M	11,629	529	56
Univ. of Wyoming, Laramie, WY 82071	1886	$4,404(S)	$9,451	5-D	12,778	838	54
Upper Iowa Univ., Fayette, IA 52142-1857	1857	$24,400	$7,510	1-M	5,304	611	40
Urbana Univ., Urbana, OH 43078-2091	1850	$20,896	NA	1-M	1,551	120	NA
Ursinus Coll., Collegeville, PA 19426-1000	1869	$46,075	$11,500	1-B	1,596	173	79
Ursuline Coll., Pepper Pike, OH 44124-4398 (4)	1871	$26,760	$8,900	2-D	1,357	213	50
Utah State Univ., Logan, UT 84322	1888	$6,183(S)	$5,620	5-D	27,812	1,079	51
Utah Valley Univ., Orem, UT 84058-5999	1941	$5,086(S)	NA	5-M	30,564	1,555	22
Utica Coll., Utica, NY 13502-4892	1946	$32,800	$11,934	1-D	4,028	346	47
Valdosta State Univ., Valdosta, GA 31698	1906	$5,889(S)	$7,544	5-D	11,885	675	40
Valencia Coll., Orlando, FL 32802-3028	1967	$2,377(S)	NA	5-B	42,915	1,602	41
Valley City State Univ., Valley City, ND 58072	1890	$6,506(S)	$5,510	5-M	1,366	111	46
Valley Forge Christian Coll., Phoenixville, PA 19460	1938	$20,424	$8,116	2-M	1,007	85	42
Valparaiso Univ., Valparaiso, IN 46383	1859	$33,480	$9,560	2-D	4,508	401	70
Vanderbilt Univ., Nashville, TN 37240-1001	1873	$42,978	$14,094	1-D	12,757	1,174	93
Vanguard Univ. of Southern California, Costa Mesa, CA 92626-9601	1920	$30,050	$9,420	2-M	2,415	251	52
Vassar Coll., Poughkeepsie, NY 12604	1861	$47,890	$11,180	1-M	2,436	327	94
Vaughn Coll. of Aeronautics and Tech., Flushing, NY 11369 (2)	1932	$20,650	$12,780	1-M	1,742	216	56
Vermont Tech. Coll., Randolph Center, VT 05061-0500	1866	$13,200(S)	$9,414	5-B	1,545	200	NA
Villanova Univ., Villanova, PA 19085-1699	1842	$44,430	$11,856	2-D	10,697	967	90
Virginia Coll. in Birmingham, Birmingham, AL 35209	1989	NA	NA	3-M	3,826	NA	NA
Virginia Commonwealth Univ., Richmond, VA 23284-9005	1838	$12,002(S)	$9,082	5-D	31,288	3,313	57
Virginia Military Inst., Lexington, VA 24450 (2)	1839	$14,400(S)	$8,088	5-B	1,675	185	71
Virginia Polytechnic Inst. and State Univ., Blacksburg, VA 24061	1872	$11,455(S)	$7,598	5-D	31,205	1,665	82
Virginia State Univ., Petersburg, VA 23806-0001	1882	$7,784(S)	$10,008	5-D	6,208	426	40
Virginia Union Univ., Richmond, VA 23220-1170	1865	$14,930	$8,074	2-D	1,718	125	31
Virginia Wesleyan Coll., Norfolk, VA 23502-5599	1961	$33,286	$8,594	2-B	1,459	131	44
Viterbo Univ., La Crosse, WI 54601-4797	1890	$23,790	$7,010	2-M	2,762	320	46

Name, address	Year founded	Tuition & fees	Room & board	Control, degree	Enroll-ment	Faculty	Grad. rate
Wagner Coll., Staten Island, NY 10301-4495.	1883	$39,220	$11,660	1-M	2,241	248	62%
Wake Forest Univ., Winston-Salem, NC 27109	1834	$46,200	$12,638	1-D	7,602	728	87
Walden Univ., Minneapolis, MN 55401	1970	$13,830	NA	3-D	51,016	2,988	NA
Waldorf Coll., Forest City, IA 50436-1713	1903	$20,316	$6,856	2-B	1,150	46	42
Walla Walla Univ., College Place, WA 99324-1198	1892	$25,377	$5,970	2-M	1,940	202	53
Walsh Coll. of Accountancy and Business Admin., Troy, MI 48007-7006	1922	NA	NA	1-M	3,106	178	NA
Walsh Univ., North Canton, OH 44720-3396	1958	$25,840	$9,260	2-D	2,963	268	64
Wartburg Coll., Waverly, IA 50677-0903	1852	$36,120	$8,920	2-B	1,714	171	63
Washburn Univ., Topeka, KS 66621	1865	$5,774(S)	$6,391	10-D	6,973	555	37
Washington Adventist Univ., Takoma Park, MD 20912	1904	$21,020	$7,900	2-M	1,493	134	26
Washington & Jefferson Coll., Washington, PA 15301	1781	$39,710	$10,490	1-B	1,328	154	77
Washington & Lee Univ., Lexington, VA 24450-0303	1749	$44,507	$10,250	1-D	2,277	348	90
Washington Coll., Chestertown, MD 21620-1197	1782	$41,120	$9,442	1-M	1,512	181	68
Washington State Univ., Pullman, WA 99164	1890	$12,327(S)	$10,868	5-D	27,642	1,735	65
Washington State Univ. Tri-Cities, Richland, WA 99352-1671.	1989	NA	NA	5-D	1,347	NA	NA
Washington State Univ. Vancouver, Vancouver, WA 98686	1989	NA	NA	5-M	3,096	NA	NA
Washington Univ. in St. Louis, St. Louis, MO 63130-4899.	1853	$46,467	$14,377	1-D	14,032	1,219	94
Wayland Baptist Univ., Plainview, TX 79072-6998	1908	$15,430	$5,586	2-M	6,222	563	33
Waynesburg Univ., Waynesburg, PA 15370-1222	1849	$20,540	$8,560	2-D	2,190	265	54
Wayne State Coll., Wayne, NE 68787	1910	$5,574(S)	$6,190	5-M	3,506	208	53
Wayne State Univ., Detroit, MI 48202	1868	$325/cr. hr.(S)	$8,504	5-D	27,897	1,840	32
Weber State Univ., Ogden, UT 84408-1001,	1889	$4,991(S)	$8,000	5-M	25,155	1,211	45
Webster Univ., St. Louis, MO 63119-3194.	1915	$23,700	$10,290	1-D	4,946	812	59
Wellesley Coll., Wellesley, MA 02481 (3).	1870	$45,078	$13,960	1-B	2,474	351	86
Wentworth Inst. of Tech., Boston, MA 02115-5998	1904	$27,950	$12,526	1-M	4,111	362	61
Wesleyan Univ., Middletown, CT 06459.	1831	$46,944	$12,940	1-D	3,205	385	92
Wesley Coll., Dover, DE 19901-3875.	1873	$23,590	$10,440	2-M	1,770	170	22
West Chester Univ. of Pennsylvania, West Chester, PA 19383.	1871	$8,850(S)	$7,986	5-D	15,845	NA	69
West Coast Univ., North Hollywood, CA 91606	1909	NA	NA	3-B	1,792	NA	NA
West Liberty Univ., West Liberty, WV 26074	1837	$6,916(S)	$8,370	5-M	2,776	233	41
West Texas A&M Univ., Canyon, TX 79016-0001	1909	$9,270(S)	$6,864	5-D	8,381	407	40
West Virginia State Univ., Institute, WV 25112-1000	1891	$5,932(S)	$7,282	5-M	2,677	207	18
West Virginia Univ., Morgantown, WV 26506.	1867	$6,456(S)	$9,318	5-D	29,707	1,632	56
West Virginia Univ. Inst. of Tech., Montgomery, WV 25136.	1895	$5,808(S)	$8,794	5-B	1,222	114	30
West Virginia Wesleyan Coll., Buckhannon, WV 26201.	1890	$26,794	$7,740	2-M	1,469	135	60
Western Carolina Univ., Cullowhee, NC 28723	1889	$6,531(S)	$8,016	5-D	10,107	651	51
Western Connecticut State Univ., Danbury, CT 06810-6885.	1903	$9,077(S)	$11,106	5-D	6,025	586	44
Western Governors Univ., Salt Lake City, UT 84107	1998	NA	NA	1-M	46,733	1,328	NA
Western Illinois Univ., Macomb, IL 61455-1390.	1899	$10,939(S)	$9,190	5-D	11,707	720	56
Western Intl. Univ., Phoenix, AZ 85021-2718	1978	NA	NA	3-M	2,993	369	NA
Western Kentucky Univ., Bowling Green, KY 42101	1906	$8,722(S)	$7,016	5-D	20,448	1,219	50
Western Michigan Univ., Kalamazoo, MI 49008.	1903	$10,355(S)	$8,687	5-D	24,294	1,471	55
Western New England Univ., Springfield, MA 01119.	1919	$33,020	$12,570	1-D	3,800	358	59
Western New Mexico Univ., Silver City, NM 88062-0680	1893	$4,723(S)	NA	5-M	2,697	259	NA
Western Oregon Univ., Monmouth, OR 97361-1394	1856	$8,634(S)	$9,264	5-M	6,177	377	44
Western State Colorado Univ., Gunnison, CO 81231	1901	$7,343(S)	$8,792	5-M	2,404	140	42
Western Washington Univ., Bellingham, WA 98225-5996	1893	$8,862(S)	$9,656	5-M	14,950	858	69
Westfield State Univ., Westfield, MA 01086.	1838	$8,694(S)	$9,795	5-M	6,370	501	59
Westminster Coll., Fulton, MO 65251-1299	1851	$22,560	$9,160	2-B	1,044	93	62
Westminster Coll., New Wilmington, PA 16172-0001	1852	$32,445	$9,860	2-M	1,608	163	74
Westminster Coll., Salt Lake City, UT 84105-3697	1875	$29,500	$8,208	1-M	3,108	401	60
Westmont Coll., Santa Barbara, CA 93108-1099.	1937	$38,510	$12,160	2-B	1,378	151	77
Westwood Coll.–Anaheim, Anaheim, CA 92806	NA	NA	NA	3-B	1,206	82	NA
Westwood Coll.–Inland Empire, Upland, CA 91786.	NA	NA	NA	3-B	1,140	94	NA
Westwood Coll.–Online campus, Broomfield, CO 80021.	NA	NA	NA	3-M	7,584	281	NA
Wheaton Coll., Wheaton, IL 60187-5593	1860	$30,880	$8,770	2-D	2,993	293	87
Wheaton Coll., Norton, MA 02766	1834	$45,074	$11,500	1-B	1,656	181	76
Wheeling Jesuit Univ., Wheeling, WV 26003-6295	1954	$27,830	$5,140	2-D	1,563	156	58
Wheelock Coll., Boston, MA 02215-4176 (4)	1888	$30,955	$12,800	1-M	1,378	91	58
Whitman Coll., Walla Walla, WA 99362-2083	1859	$44,800	$11,228	1-B	1,541	209	88
Whittier Coll., Whittier, CA 90608-0634	1887	$40,096	$11,494	1-D	2,373	167	66
Whitworth Univ., Spokane, WA 99251-0001	1890	$36,012	$9,814	2-M	2,568	324	74
Wichita State Univ., Wichita, KS 67260	1895	$6,927(S)	$6,689	5-D	14,550	788	46
Widener Univ., Chester, PA 19013-5792	1821	$38,028	$12,340	1-D	6,311	656	56
Wilkes Univ., Wilkes-Barre, PA 18766-0002	1933	$30,350	$12,436	1-D	4,665	378	58
Willamette Univ., Salem, OR 97301-3931	1842	$42,305	$10,380	2-D	3,024	302	78
William Carey Univ., Hattiesburg, MS 39401-5499	1906	$10,800	$4,050	2-M	3,248	NA	NA
William Jessup Univ., Rocklin, CA 95765.	1939	$24,990	$10,000	2-M	1,096	164	56
William Jewell Coll., Liberty, MO 64068-1843	1849	$31,620	$8,410	1-M	1,043	143	59
William Paterson Univ. of New Jersey, Wayne, NJ 07470-8420	1855	$11,918(S)	$10,600	5-D	11,414	1,118	49
William Peace Univ., Raleigh, NC 27604-1194	1857	$23,900	$9,000	2-B	1,076	125	41
William Penn Univ., Oskaloosa, IA 52577-1799.	1873	$23,480	$6,298	2-M	1,875	95	34
Williams Coll., Williamstown, MA 01267.	1793	$46,600	$12,300	1-M	2,131	337	95
William Woods Univ., Fulton, MO 65251-1098.	1870	$20,650	$8,400	2-M	2,020	357	50
Wilmington Coll., Wilmington, OH 45177	1870	$27,720	$9,216	2-M	1,458	119	52
Wilmington Univ., New Castle, DE 19720-6491.	1967	$7,970	NA	1-D	13,959	1,273	35
Wingate Univ., Wingate, NC 28174-0159.	1896	$26,300	$10,400	2-D	3,002	275	53
Winona State Univ., Winona, MN 55987	1858	$6,860(S)	$7,800	5-D	8,755	618	56
Winston-Salem State Univ., Winston-Salem, NC 27110-0003.	1892	$6,844(S)	$7,700	5-M	6,427	336	37
Winthrop Univ., Rock Hill, SC 29733	1886	$13,430(S)	$7,690	5-M	6,130	574	56
Wisconsin Lutheran Coll., Milwaukee, WI 53226-9942	1973	$25,960	$8,900	2-M	1,178	151	64
Wittenberg Univ., Springfield, OH 45501-0720	1845	$38,030	$9,932	2-M	1,979	196	63
Wofford Coll., Spartanburg, SC 29303-3663	1854	$37,120	NA	2-B	1,584	162	82
Woodbury Univ., Burbank, CA 91504-1099.	1884	$33,150	$10,048	1-M	1,607	271	47
Worcester Polytechnic Inst., Worcester, MA 01609-2280	1865	$42,778	$13,082	1-D	6,296	478	81
Worcester State Univ., Worcester, MA 01602-2597.	1874	$8,157(S)	$10,877	5-M	6,447	405	49
Wright State Univ., Dayton, OH 45435.	1964	$8,542(S)	$8,797	5-D	16,656	654	41
Xavier Univ., Cincinnati, OH 45207	1831	$33,960	$11,020	2-D	6,671	710	76
Xavier Univ. of Louisiana, New Orleans, LA 70125-1098	1925	$19,100	$8,000	2-D	3,121	250	46
Yale Univ., New Haven, CT 06520.	1701	$44,000	$13,500	1-D	12,109	1,684	98
Yeshiva Univ., New York, NY 10033-3201.	1886	$37,600	$11,150	1-D	6,744	1,473	92
York Coll. of Pennsylvania, York, PA 17405-7199.	1787	$17,630	$9,870	1-D	5,268	532	58
York Coll. of the City Univ. of New York, Jamaica, NY 11451-0001	1967	$6,096(S)	NA	11-M	8,305	546	24
Young Harris Coll., Young Harris, GA 30582	1886	$25,280	$9,660	2-B	1,034	105	NA
Youngstown State Univ., Youngstown, OH 44555-0001	1908	$8,129(S)	$8,475	5-D	13,374	1,113	35

Associations and Organizations

Source: World Almanac research

Selected list, generally by category and first distinctive key word in each title. Listed by acronym when that is the official name. Year established is in parentheses. Entries for religious organizations include addresses and leadership information for 2013.

Academic and Educational

Academies, Natl. (1863): (202) 334-2000; www.nationalacademies.org

African American Life and History, Assn. for the Study of (1915): (202) 238-5910; www.asalh.org

Alpha Delta Kappa (1947): (816) 363-5525; www.alphadeltakappa.org

AMIDEAST (America-Mideast Educational and Training Services, Inc.) (1951): (202) 776-9600; www.amideast.org

Anthropological Assn., American (1902): (703) 528-1902; www.aaanet.org

Archaeological Institute of America (1879): (617) 353-9361; www.archaeological.org

Arts, Americans for the (1960): (202) 371-2830; www.artsusa.org

Arts and Sciences, American Academy of (1780): (617) 576-5000; www.amacad.org

Beta Gamma Sigma Honor Society (1913): (314) 432-5650; www.betagamma sigma.org

Beta Sigma Phi Intl. (1931): (816) 444-6800; www.betasigmaphi.org

Biological Sciences, American Institute of (1947): (703) 674-2500; www.aibs.org

Classical Studies, Society for (formerly American Philological Assn.) (1869): (215) 898-4975; www.apaclassics.org

College Board (1900): (212) 713-8000; www.collegeboard.org

Colleges and Universities, Assn. of American (1915): (202) 387-3760; www.aacu.org

Community Colleges, American Assn. of (1920): (202) 728-0200; www.aacc.nche.edu

Consumer Interests, American Council on (1953): (727) 493-2131; www.consumer interests.org

Delta Kappa Gamma Society Intl. (1929): (512) 478-5748; www.dkg.org

Education, American Council on (1918): (202) 939-9300; www.acenet.edu

Education, Council for Advancement and Support of (1974): (202) 328-2273; www.case.org

Education of Young Children, Natl. Assn. for the (1926): (202) 232-8777; www.naeyc.org

Educators for World Peace, Intl. Assn. of (1973): (256) 534-5501; www.iaewp.org

English-Speaking Union of the U.S. (1920): (212) 818-1200; www.esuus.org

Entomological Society of America (1889): (301) 731-4535; www.entsoc.org

Family Relations, Natl. Council on (1938): (888) 781-9331; www.ncfr.org

Foreign Study, American Institute for (1964): (866) 906-2437; www.aifs.com

Freedom of Information Coalition, Natl. (1958): (573) 882-3075; www.nfoic.org

French Institute/Alliance Française (1971): (212) 355-6100; www.fiaf.org

Genealogical Society, Natl. (1903): (703) 525-0050; www.ngsgenealogy.org

Genetic Assn., American (1914): (541) 867-0334; www.theaga.org

Geological Society of America (1888): (303) 357-1000; www.geosociety.org

Hemispheric Affairs, Council on (1975): (202) 223-4975; www.coha.org

Industrial and Applied Mathematics, Society for (1952): (215) 382-9800; www.siam.org

Intl. Education, Institute of (1919): (212) 883-8200; www.iie.org

Intl. Educational Exchange, Council on (1947): (207) 553-4000; www.ciee.org

Intl. Law, American Society of (1906): (202) 939-6000; www.asil.org

Irish American Cultural Inst. (1962): (973) 605-1991; www.iaci-usa.org

IRTS Foundation (formerly Intl. Radio and TV Society Foundation) (1939): (312) 867-6650; www.irts.org

Law Libraries, American Assn. of (1906): (312) 939-4764; www.aallnet.org

Learned Societies, American Council of (1919): (212) 697-1505; www.acls.org

Libraries Assn., Special (1909): (703) 647-4900; www.sla.org

Linguistic Society of America (1924): (202) 835-1714; www.lsadc.org

Mathematical Society, American (1888): (401) 455-4000; www.ams.org

Mensa, Ltd., American (1960): (817) 607-0060; www.us.mensa.org

Meteorological Society, American (1919): (617) 227-2425; www.ametsoc.org

Metric Assn., Inc., U.S. (1916): (310) 832-3763; www.metric.org

Microbiology, American Society for (1899): (202) 737-3600; www.asm.org

Modern Language Assn. of America (1883): (646) 576-5000; www.mla.org

Museums, American Alliance of (1906): (202) 289-1818; www.aam-us.org

Music Education, Natl. Assn. for (formerly Music Educators Natl. Conference) (1907): (703) 860-4000; musiced.nafme.org

Musicological Society, American (1934): (207) 798-4243; www.ams-net.org

Negro College Fund, United (1944): (800) 331-2244; www.uncf.org

Oriental Society, American (1842): (734) 647-4760; www.umich.edu/~aos/

ORT America (1922): (212) 505-7700; www.ortamerica.org

PEN American Center (1922): (212) 334-1660; www.pen.org

Phi Beta Kappa Society (1776): (202) 265-3808; www.pbk.org

Phi Theta Kappa Honor Society (1918): (800) 946-9995; www.ptk.org

Philosophical Assn., American (1900): (302) 831-1112; www.apaonline.org

Physics, American Inst. of (1931): (301) 209-3100; www.aip.org

Physiological Society, American (1887): (301) 634-7164; www.the-aps.org

Poetry Society of America (1910): (212) 254-9628; www.poetrysociety.org

Poets, Academy of American (1934): (212) 274-0343; www.poets.org

Political Science, Academy of (1880): (212) 870-2500; www.psqonline.org

Reading Assn., Intl. (1956): (302) 731-1600; www.reading.org

Religion, American Academy of (1909): (404) 727-3049; www.aarweb.org

Science, American Assn. for the Advancement of (1848): (202) 326-6400; www.aaas.org

Science Fiction Society, World (1939): www.wsfs.org

Sciences, Natl. Academy of (1863): (202) 334-2000; www.nasonline.org

Sigma Beta Delta (1994): (314) 516-4723; www.sigmabetadelta.org

Sociological Assn., American (1905): (202) 383-9005; www.asanet.org

Tau Beta Pi Assn. (1885): (865) 546-4578; www.tbp.org

Teach For America (1990): (212) 279-2080; www.teachforamerica.org

Theological Schools in the U.S. and Canada, Assn. of (1918): (412) 788-6505; www.ats.edu

Theosophical Society in America (1875): (630) 668-1571; www.theosophical.org

Universities, Assn. of American (1900): (202) 408-7500; www.aau.edu

World Learning (1932): (802) 257-7751; www.worldlearning.org

Animal Welfare and Environment

Animal Welfare Institute (1951): (202) 337-2332; www.awionline.org

Animals, American Society for the Prevention of Cruelty to (ASPCA) (1866): (212) 876-7700; www.aspca.org

Animals, People for the Ethical Treatment of (PETA) (1980): (757) 622-7382; www.peta.org

Appalachian Trail Conservancy (1925): (304) 535-6331; www.appalachiantrail.org

Audubon Society, Natl. (1905): (212) 979-3000; www.audubon.org

Cat Fanciers' Assn., Inc., The (1906): (330) 680-4070; www.cfa.org

Conservation Intl. (1987): (703) 341-2400; www.conservation.org

Defenders of Wildlife (1947): (800) 385-9712; www.defenders.org

Ducks Unlimited (1937): (901) 758-3825; www.ducks.org

Forest History Society (1946): (919) 682-9319; www.foresthistory.org

Foresters, Society of American (1900): (301) 897-8720; www.safnet.org

Friends of the Earth (1969): (202) 783-7400; www.foe.org

Garden Club of America (1913): (212) 753-8287; www.gcamerica.org

Garden Clubs, Inc., Natl. (1929): (314) 776-7574; www.gardenclub.org

Geographic Society, Natl. (1888): (813) 979-6845; www.nationalgeographic.com

Green Mountain Club (1910): (802) 244-7037; www.greenmountainclub.org

Greenpeace (1971): (202) 462-1177; www.greenpeaceusa.org

Hiking Society, American (1976): (301) 565-6704; www.americanhiking.org

Horse Council, American (1969): (202) 296-4031; www.horsecouncil.org

Humane Society of the U.S., The (1954): (202) 452-1100; www.humanesociety.org

Natural Resources Defense Council (1970): (212) 727-2700; www.nrdc.org

Nature Conservancy, The (1951): (703) 841-5300; www.nature.org

Ocean Conservancy (1972): (202) 429-5609; www.oceanconservancy.org

Ornithologists' Union, American (1883): (254) 399-9636; www.aou.org

Recreation and Park Assn., Natl. (1965): (800) 626-6772; www.nrpa.org

Recycling Coalition, Inc., Natl. (1978): (202) 618-2107; www.nrcrecycles.org

Rose Society, American (1892): (318) 938-5402; www.ars.org

Save the Redwoods League (1918): (415) 362-2352; www.savetheredwoods.org

Sierra Club (1892): (415) 977-5500; www.sierraclub.org

Water Environment Federation (1928): (800) 666-0206; www.wef.org

Wildflower Center, Lady Bird Johnson (1982): (512) 232-0100; www.wildflower.org

Wildlife Federation, Natl. (1936): (800) 822-9919; www.nwf.org

World Wildlife Fund (1961): (202) 293-4800; www.worldwildlife.org

Children and Social Services

Big Brothers Big Sisters of America (1904): (469) 351-3100; www.bbbs.org

Boy Scouts of America (1910): (972) 580-2000; www.scouting.org

Boys & Girls Clubs of America (1906): (404) 487-5700; www.bgca.org

Camp Fire (formerly Camp Fire Boys & Girls) (1910): (816) 285-2010; www.camp fireusa.org

Child Welfare League of America (1920): (202) 688-4200; www.cwla.org

Children's Aid Society (1913): (205) 251-7148; www.childrensaid.org

Children's Book Council, The (1945): (212) 966-1990; www.cbcbooks.org

Feeding America (formerly America's Second Harvest) (1976): (800) 771-2303; feedingamerica.org

4-H Council, Natl. (1914): (301) 961-2800; www.4-h.org

Future Business Leaders of America-Phi Beta Lambda, Inc. (1942): (800) 325-2946; www.fbla-pbl.org

Future Farmers of America Org., Natl. (1928): (317) 802-6060; www.ffa.org

Gifted Children, Natl. Assn. for (1954): (202) 785-4268; www.nagc.org

Girl Scouts of the USA (1912): (212) 852-8000; www.girlscouts.org

Honor Society, Natl. (1921): (703) 860-0200; www.nhs.us

Junior Achievement, Inc. (1919): (719) 540-8000; www.ja.org

Junior Auxiliaries, Inc., Natl. Assn. of (1941): (662) 332-3000; www.najanet.org

Junior Chamber, U.S. (1914): (636) 681-1857; www.usjaycees.org

Junior Honor Society, Natl. (1929): (703) 860-0200; www.njhs.us

Missing and Exploited Children, Natl. Center for (1984): (703) 224-2150; www.missingkids.org

Pilot Intl. (1921): (478) 477-1208; www.pilotinternational.org

Student Councils, Natl. Assn. of (1931): (703) 860-0200; www.nasc.us

Fraternal

Eagles, Fraternal Order of (1898): (614) 883-2200; www.foe.com

Eastern Star, General Grand Chapter, Order of the (1876): (202) 667-4737; www.easternstar.org

Elks of the USA, Benevolent and Protective Order of (1868): (773) 755-4700; www.elks.org

Freemasonry, Scottish Rite, Supreme Council, 33°, Northern Masonic Jurisdiction (1813): (781) 862-4410; www.scottishritenmj.org

Freemasonry, Scottish Rite, Supreme Council, 33°, Southern Jurisdiction (1802): (202) 232-3579; www.srmason-sj.org

Kiwanis Intl. (1915): (317) 875-8755; www.kiwanis.org

Knights of Columbus (1882): (203) 752-4000; www.kofc.org

Knights of Pythias, Order of (1864): (781) 341-2422; www.pythias.org

Lions Clubs Intl. (1917): (630) 571-5466; www.lionsclubs.org

Men, Natl. Coalition for (1977): (888) 223-1280; www.ncfm.org

Moose Intl., Inc. (1888): (630) 859-2000; www.mooseintl.org

Odd Fellows, Independent Order of (1819): (336) 725-5955; www.ioof.org

Rotary Intl. (1905): (847) 866-3000; www.rotary.org

Shriners Intl. (1872): (813) 281-0300; www.shrinersinternational.org

Sons of Italy in America, Order (1905): (202) 547-2900; www.osia.org

Sons of Norway (1895): (612) 827-3611; www.sofn.com

Woodmen of America, Modern (1883): (800) 447-9811; www.modern-woodmen.org

Historical

Civil War Trust (1987): (202) 367-1861; www.civilwar.org

Colonial Dames XVII Century, Natl. Soc. (1915): (202) 293-1700; www.colonialdames17c.org

Daughters of the American Revolution (1890): (202) 628-1776; www.dar.org

Daughters of the Confederacy, United (1894): (804) 355-1636; www.hqudc.org

Historic Preservation, Natl. Trust for (1949): (202) 588-6000; www.preservationnation.org

Historical Assn., American (1884): (202) 544-2422; www.historians.org

Lewis and Clark Trail Heritage Foundation (1969): (406) 454-1234; lewisandclark.org

Mayflower Descendants, General Soc. of (1897): (508) 746-3188; www.themayflowersociety.com

Pilgrims, Natl. Soc. Sons and Daughters of the (1908): www.nssdp.com

Railway Historical Society, Natl. (1935): (215) 557-6606; www.nrhs.com

Sons of the American Revolution, Natl. Soc. (1889): (502) 589-1776; www.sar.org

Sons of Confederate Veterans (1896): (800) 380-1896; www.scv.org

State and Local History, American Assn. for (1940): (615) 320-3203; www.aaslh.org

Supreme Court Historical Society (1974): (202) 543-0400; www.supremecourthistory.org

Theodore Roosevelt Assn. (1920): (516) 921-6319; www.theodoreroosevelt.org

Thoreau Society (1941): (978) 369-5310; www.thoreausociety.org

Titanic Historical Society, Inc. (1963): (413) 543-4770; www.titanichistoricalsociety.org

Victorian Society in America (1966): (215) 636-9872; www.victoriansociety.org

Industrial and Trade

Aerospace Industries Assn. (1919): (703) 358-1000; www.aia-aerospace.org

Better Business Bureaus, Council of (1912): (703) 276-0100; www.bbb.org

Chamber of Commerce of the U.S.A. (1912): (202) 659-6000; www.uschamber.com

Chemistry Council, American (1872): (202) 249-7000; www.americanchemistry.com

Construction Specifications Institute (1948): (800) 689-2900; www.csinet.org

CropLife America (1933): (202) 296-1585; www.croplifeamerica.org

Electrical Manufacturers Assn., Natl. (1926): (703) 841-3200; www.nema.org

Fire Protection Assn., Natl. (NFPA) (1896): (617) 770-3000; www.nfpa.org

Fisheries Soc., American (1870): (301) 897-8616; www.fisheries.org

Foreign Trade Council, Natl. (1914): (202) 887-0278; www.nftc.org

Funeral Consumers Alliance (1963): (802) 865-8300; www.funerals.org

Hotel & Lodging Assn., American (1910): (202) 289-3100; www.ahla.com

Insurance Assn., American (1866): (202) 828-7100; www.aiadc.org

Magazine Media, Assn. of (1919): (212) 872-3700; www.magazine.org

Manufacturers, Natl. Assn. of (1895): (202) 637-3000; www.nam.org

Newspaper Assn. of America (1992): (571) 366-1000; www.naa.org

Nuclear Society, American (1954): (708) 352-6611; www.ans.org

Orchestras, League of American (1942): (212) 262-5161; www.symphony.org

Petroleum Institute, American (1919): (202) 682-8000; www.api.org

Printing Industries of America, Inc. (1887): (412) 741-6860; www.printing.org

Publishers, Assn. of American (1970): (202) 347-3375; www.publishers.org

Retail Federation, Natl. (1908): (202) 783-7971; www.nrf.com

Safety Council, Natl. (1913): (630) 285-1121; www.nsc.org

Shipbuilders Council of America (1920): (202) 772-5577; www.shipbuilders.org

Small Business Assn., Natl. (1937): (800) 345-6728; www.nsba.biz

Software & Information Industry Assn. (1999): (202) 289-7442; www.siia.net

Tall Buildings and Urban Habitat, Council on (1969): (312) 567-3487; www.ctbuh.org

Toy Industry Assn., Inc. (1916): (212) 675-1141; www.toyassociation.org

Water Works Assn., American (1881): (303) 794-7711; www.awwa.org

Zoos & Aquariums, Assn. of (1924): (301) 562-0777; www.aza.org

Lifestyle and Travel

AAA (American Automobile Assn.) (1902): (407) 444-7000; www.aaa.com

AARP (formerly American Assn. of Retired Persons) (1958): (888) 687-2277; www.aarp.org

AFS Intercultural Programs USA (1947): (800) 237-4636; www.afsusa.org

Aircraft Owners and Pilots Assn. (1939): (800) 872-2672; www.aopa.org

Appalachian Mountain Club (1876): (617) 523-0636; www.outdoors.org

Boat Owners Assn. of the U.S. (1966): (800) 395-2628; www.boatus.com

Camp Assn., American (1910): (765) 342-8456; www.acacamps.org

Consumer Federation of America (1968): (202) 387-6121; www.consumerfed.org

Consumers Union (1936): (914) 378-2000; www.consumersunion.org

Green America (formerly Co-op America) (1982): (800) 584-7336; www.greenamerica.org

Helicopter Society Intl., American (1943): (703) 684-6777; www.vtol.org

Hostelling Intl. USA (1934): (240) 650-2100; www.hiusa.org

Jewish Community Centers Assn. of North America (1917): (212) 532-4949; www.jcca.org

Motorcyclist Assn., American (1924): (614) 856-1900; www.americanmotorcyclist.com

Parents Without Partners, Inc. (1957): (800) 637-7974; www.parentswithoutpartners.org

Planetary Society (1980): (626) 793-5100; www.planetary.org

SCRABBLE® Players Assn., N. American (2009): www.scrabbleplayers.org

Sports Car Club of America (1944): (785) 357-7222; www.scca.org

Toastmasters Intl. (1924): (949) 858-8255; www.toastmasters.org

YMCA (Young Men's Christian Assn.) of the USA (1851): (800) 872-9622; www.ymca.net

YWCA (Young Women's Christian Assn.) USA (1858): (202) 467-0801; www.ywca.org

Military and Veterans

Air Force Assn. (1946): (703) 247-5800; www.afa.org

American Legion (1919): (317) 630-1200; www.legion.org

American Legion Auxiliary (1919): (317) 569-4500; www.alaforveterans.org

AMVETS (American Veterans) (1944): (877) 726-8387; www.amvets.org

Army, Assn. of the United States (1950): (703) 841-4300; www.ausa.org

Blinded Veterans Assn. (1958): (202) 371-8880; www.bva.org

Civil Air Patrol (1941): (877) 227-9142; www.gocivilairpatrol.com

Coast Guard Combat Veterans Assn. (1985): (610) 539-1000; www.coastguardcombatvets.com

Disabled American Veterans (1920): (859) 441-7300; www.dav.org

82nd Airborne Division Assn. (1946): (910) 223-1182; www.82ndassociation.org

Ex-Prisoners of War, American (1942): (817) 649-2979; www.axpow.org

Fleet Reserve Assn. (1924): (703) 683-1400; www.fra.org

Iraq and Afghanistan Veterans of America (2004): (212) 982-9699; www.iava.org

Jewish War Veterans of the U.S.A. (1896): (202) 265-6280; www.jwv.org

Legion of Valor Museum (1991): (559) 498-0510; www.fresnovetmuseum.com

Marine Corps League (1937): (703) 207-9588; www.mcleague.org

Military Officers Assn. of America (1929): (703) 549-2311; www.moaa.org

Military Order of the World Wars (1919): (703) 683-4911; www.moww.org

National Guard Assn. of the U.S. (1878): (202) 789-0031; www.ngaus.org

Naval Institute, U.S. (1873): (410) 268-6110; www.usni.org

Navy League of the United States (1902): (703) 528-1775; www.navyleague.org

Ninety-Nines, Inc. (Intl. Org. of Women Pilots) (1929): (405) 685-7969; www.ninety-nines.org

Non-Commissioned Officers Assn. (1960): (210) 653-6161; www.ncoausa.org

Paralyzed Veterans of America (1946): (800) 424-8200; www.pva.org

POW/MIA Families, Natl. League of (1970): (703) 465-7432; www.pow-miafamilies.org

Purple Heart, Military Order of the (1932): (703) 354-2140; www.purpleheart.org

Reserve Officers Assn. of the U.S. (1922): (202) 479-2200; www.roa.org

Sons of the American Legion (1932): (317) 630-1200; www.legion.org/sons

Tin Can Sailors (Natl. Assn. of Destroyer Veterans) (1976): (800) 223-5535; www.destroyers.org

Uniformed Services, Natl. Assn. for (1968): (800) 842-3451; www.naus.org

USO, Inc. (United Service Org.) (1941): (888) 484-3876; www.uso.org

USS Los Angeles CA-135 Assn. (1977): www.uss-la-ca135.org/2la-assoc.htm

USS Missouri Memorial Assn., Inc. (1998): (808) 455-1600; www.ussmissouri.org

Veterans of Foreign Wars (1899): (816) 756-3390; www.vfw.org

Veterans of Foreign Wars, Ladies Auxiliary to the (1914): (816) 561-8655; www.ladiesauxvfw.org

Vietnam Veterans of America (1978): (301) 585-4000; www.vva.org

Women's Army Corps Veterans' Assn. (1946): (256) 820-6824; www.armywomen.org

Wounded Warrior Project (2002): (877) 832-6997; www.woundedwarriorproject.org

Political

Abortion Federation, Natl. (1977): (202) 667-5881; www.prochoice.org

Action Network, American (2010): (202) 559-6420; americanactionnetwork.org

Advancement and Support of Education, Council for (1974): (202) 328-2273; www.case.org

American Indians, Natl. Congress of (1944): (202) 466-7767; www.ncai.org

American-Islamic Relations, Council on (1994): (202) 488-8787; www.cair.com

Brady Campaign to Prevent Gun Violence (1974): (202) 370-8100; www.brady campaign.org

Center for Responsive Politics (1983): (202) 857-0044; www.opensecrets.org

Cities, Natl. League of (1924): (202) 626-3100; www.nlc.org

Civil Liberties Union, American (ACLU) (1920): (212) 549-2500; www.aclu.org

Coffee Party USA (2010): (301) 259-1869; www.coffeepartyusa.com

Common Cause (1970): (202) 833-1200; www.commoncause.org

Concerned Women for America (1979): (202) 488-7000; www.cwfa.org

Congress of Racial Equality (CORE) (1942): (212) 598-4000; www.core-online.org

Conservation Voters, League of (1969): (202) 785-8683; www.lcv.org

Constitution Party (1992): (717) 390-1993; www.constitutionparty.com

Crime and Delinquency, Natl. Council on (1907): (800) 306-6223; www.nccdglobal.org

Crossroads GPS (Grassroots Political Strategies) (2010): (202) 706-7051; www.crossroadsgps.org

Democratic Natl. Committee (1848): (202) 863-8000; www.democrats.org

Feminists for Life of America (1972): (703) 836-3354; www.feministsforlife.org

Future Fund, Amer. (2007): (515) 661-4233; www.americanfuturefund.org

Gay & Lesbian Alliance Against Defamation (GLAAD) (1985): (212) 629-3322; www.glaad.org

Gay and Lesbian Task Force, Natl. (1973): (202) 393-5177; www.thetaskforce.org

Governors Assn., Natl. (1908): (202) 624-5300; www.nga.org

Grange of the Order of Patrons of Husbandry, Natl. (1867): (202) 628-3507; www.nationalgrange.org

Gray Panthers (1970): (202) 737-6637; www.graypanthers.org

Greens/Green Party of the USA (1984): (202) 319-7191; www.gp.org

Homeless, Natl. Coalition for the (1984): (202) 462-4822; www.nationalhomeless.org

Human Rights Campaign (1980): (202) 628-4160; www.hrc.org

Immigration Equality (1994): (202) 347-0002; immigrationequality.org

Immigration Reform, Federation for American (FAIR) (1979): (202) 328-7004; www.fairus.org

Japanese American Citizens League (1929): (415) 921-5225; www.jacl.org

Jewish Committee, American (1906): (212) 751-4000; www.ajc.org

John Birch Society (1958): (920) 749-3780; www.jbs.org

Libertarian Party (1971): (202) 333-0008; www.lp.org

Marriage, Natl. Org. for (2007): (888) 894-3604; www.nationformarriage.org

Marry, Freedom to (2003): (212) 851-8418; www.freedomtomarry.org

Mayors, U.S. Conference of (1932): (202) 293-7330; www.usmayors.org

NAACP (Natl. Assn. for the Advancement of Colored People) (1909): (410) 580-5777; www.naacp.org

NRA (National Rifle Assn.) (1871): (800) 672-3888; www.nra.org

Parliamentarians, Natl. Assn. of (1930): (816) 833-3892; www.parliamentarians.org

Patriot Majority (2005): www.patriot majority.org

Progress, Center for American (2003): (202) 682-1611; www.americanprogress.org

Reform Party Natl. Committee (1995): (972) 275-9297; www.reformparty.org

Republican Natl. Committee (1856): (202) 863-8500; www.rnc.org

Southern Christian Leadership Conference (1957): (404) 522-1420; sclcnational.org

Southern Poverty Law Center (1971): (334) 956-8200; www.splcenter.org

State Governments, Council of (1933): (859) 244-8000; www.csg.org

Tax Foundation (1937): (202) 464-6200; www.taxfoundation.org

Tax Reform, Americans for (1985): (202) 785-0266; www.atr.org

Taxpayers Union, Natl. (1969): (703) 683-5700; www.ntu.org

Tea Party Federation, Natl. (2010): www.thenationalteapartyfederation.com

Tea Party Patriots (2009): www.teaparty patriots.org

Term Limits, U.S. (1992): (561) 578-8636; www.termlimits.org

Urban League, Natl. (1910): (212) 558-5300; www.nul.org

Women, Natl. Organization for (NOW) (1966): (202) 628-8669; www.now.org

Women and Families, Natl. Partnership for (1971): (202) 986-2600; www.national partnership.org

Women Voters of the U.S., League of (1920): (202) 429-1965; www.lwv.org

Women's Christian Temperance Union (1874): (847) 864-1397; www.wctu.org

Zionist Organization of America (1897): (212) 481-1500; www.zoa.org

Religious

African Methodist Episcopal Church (1787): 500 8th Ave. S., Nashville, TN 37203; (615) 254-0911; www.ame-church.com; Gen. Sec., Dr. Jeffery Cooper

African Methodist Episcopal Zion Church (1796): 3225 West Sugar Creek Rd., Charlotte, NC 28269; (704) 599-4630; www.amez.org; Senior Bishop, George E. Battle Jr.

American Baptist Churches USA (1907): P.O. Box 851, Valley Forge, PA 19482; (610) 768-2000; www.abc-usa.org; Gen. Sec., A. Roy Medley

Antiochian Orthodox Christian Archdiocese of North America (1895): P.O. Box 5238, Englewood, NJ 07631; (201) 871-1355; www.antiochian.org; Primate, Archbishop Metropolitan Joseph

Armenian Apostolic Church of America: *Eastern Prelacy* (1958): 138 E. 39th St., New York, NY 10016; (212) 689-7810; www.armenianprelacy.org; Prelate, Archbishop Oshagan Choloyan; *Western Prelacy* (1973): 6252 Honolulu Ave., La Crescenta, CA 91214; (818) 248-7737; www.westernprelacy.org; Prelate, Archbishop Moushegh Mardirossian

Assemblies of God USA (1914): 1445 N. Boonville Ave., Springfield, MO 65802; (417) 862-2781; www.ag.org; Gen. Supt., George O. Wood

Atheists, American (1963): P.O. Box 158, Cranford, NJ 07016; (908) 276-7300; www.atheists.org; Pres., David P. Silverman

Bahá'ís of the U.S., Natl. Spiritual Assembly of the (1909): 1233 Central St., Evanston, IL 60201; (847) 733-3400; www.bahai.us; Sec., Kenneth E. Bowers

Baptist Bible Fellowship Intl. (1950): 720 E. Kearney St., Springfield, MO 65803;

(417) 862-5001; www.bbfi.org; Pres., Linzy Slayden

Baptist Convention, Southern (1845): 901 Commerce St., Nashville, TN 37203; (615) 244-2355; www.sbc.net; Pres., Frank S. Page

Baptist Convention, USA, Inc., Natl. (1886): 1700 Baptist World Center Dr., Nashville, TN 37207; (615) 228-6292; www.nationalbaptist.com; Pres., Dr. Julius R. Scruggs

Baptist Convention of America Intl., Inc., Natl. (1880): 777 S.R.L. Thornton Freeway, Ste. 210, Dallas, TX 75203; (214) 942-3311; www.nbcainc.com; Pres., Rev. Stephen J. Thurston

Baptist Conventional of America, Natl. Missionary (1880): 6925 Wofford Dr., Dallas, TX 75227; (877) 886-6222; www.nmbca.com; Pres., Dr. Nehemiah Davis

Bible Society, American (1816): 1865 Broadway, New York, NY 10023; (212) 408-1200; www.americanbible.org; Pres., Dr. Roy L. Peterson

Biblical Literature, Society of (1880): 825 Houston Mill Rd., Atlanta, GA 30329; (404) 727-3100; www.sbl-site.org; Exec. Dir., Dr. John F. Kutsko

B'nai B'rith Intl. (1843): 1120 20th St. NW, Ste. 300 N, Washington, DC 20036; (202) 857-6600; www.bnaibrith.org; Pres., Allan J. Jacobs

Brethren in Christ Church (c. 1778): 431 Grantham Rd., Mechanicsburg, PA 17055; (717) 697-2634; www.bic-church.org; Natl. Dir., Dr. Alan Robinson

Buddhist Churches of America (1899): 1710 Octavia St., San Francisco, CA 94109; (415) 776-5600; www.buddhist churchesofamerica.com; Pres., Kent Matsuda

Catholic Bishops, U.S. Conference of (2001): 3211 4th St. NE, Washington, DC 20017; (202) 541-3000; www.usccb.org; Gen. Sec., Msgr. Ronny E. Jenkins

Christian Church (Disciples of Christ) (1832): Disciples Center, 130 E. Washington St., Indianapolis, IN 46204; (317) 635-3100; www.disciples.org; Gen. Min. and Pres., Rev. Dr. Sharon E. Watkins

Christian Methodist Episcopal Church (1870): 4466 Elvis Presley Blvd., Memphis, TN 38116; (901) 345-0580; www.c-m-e.org; Senior Bishop, Paul A. G. Stewart Sr.

Church of the Brethren (1708): General Offices, 1451 Dundee Ave., Elgin, IL 60120; (847) 742-5100; www.brethren.org; Gen. Sec., Stanley J. Noffsinger

Church of Christ (1830): P.O. Box 472, Independence, MO 64051; (816) 206-0147; www.churchofchrist-tl.org; Sec., Council of Apostles, Duane L. Ely

Church of God (Anderson, IN) (1881): Box 2420, Anderson, IN 46018; (765) 642-0256; www.jesusisthesubject.org; Gen. Dir., Jim Lyon

Church of God (Cleveland, TN) (1886): 2490 Keith St. NW, Cleveland, TN 37320; (423) 472-3361; www.churchofgod.org; Gen. Overseer, Dr. Mark Williams

Church of God in Christ (1897): Mason Temple, 930 Mason St., Memphis, TN 38126; (901) 947-9300; www.cogic.org; Presiding Bishop, Bishop Charles E. Blake Sr.

Church of Jesus Christ (1862): World Operations Ctr., 110 Walton Tea Room Rd., Greensburg, PA 15601; (412) 771-1686; www.thechurchofjesuschrist.org; Pres., Paul A. Palmieri

Church of Jesus Christ of Latter-day Saints, The (Mormons) (1830): 50 W. North Temple St., Salt Lake City, UT 84150; (801) 240-2640; www.lds.org; Pres., Thomas S. Monson

Church of the Nazarene (1908): Global Ministry Center, 17001 Prairie Star Pkwy., Lenexa, KS 66220; (913) 577-0500; www.nazarene.org; Gen. Sec., David P. Wilson

Community of Christ (reorganized Church of Jesus Christ of Latter-Day Saints) (1830): Intl. Headquarters, 1001 W. Walnut, Independence, MO 64050; (816) 833-1000; www.cofchrist.org; Pres., Stephen M. Veazey

Community Churches, International Council of (1950): 21116 Washington

Pkwy., Frankfort, IL 60423; (815) 464-5690; www.icccusa.com; Interim Exec. Dir., Don Ashmall

Conservative Judaism, United Synagogue of (1913): 820 Second Ave., New York, NY 10017; (212) 533-7800; www.uscj.org; Pres., Richard Skolnik

Converge Worldwide (formerly Baptist General Conference) (1852): 2002 S. Arlington Heights Rd., Arlington Heights, IL 60005; (800) 323-4215; www.convergeworldwide.org; Pres. and CEO, Jerry Sheveland

Cumberland Presbyterian Church (1810): 8207 Traditional Pl., Cordova, TN 38016; (901) 276-4572; www.cumberland.org; Moderator, Forest Prosser

Episcopal Church (1789): 815 Second Ave., New York, NY 10017; (212) 716-6000; www.episcopalchurch.org; Presiding Bishop and Primate, Most Rev. Katharine Jefferts Schori

Evangelical Lutheran Church in America (1988): 8765 W. Higgins Rd., Chicago, IL 60631; (773) 380-2700; www.elca.org; Presiding Bishop, Rev. Elizabeth A. Eaton

First Church of Christ, Scientist, The (1879): 210 Massachusetts Ave., Boston, MA 02115; (617) 450-2000; www.christianscience.com; Pres., Linda Kohler

Free Methodist Church USA (1860): 770 N. High School Rd., Indianapolis, IN 46214; (317) 244-3660; www.fmcusa.org; Chief Operating Officer, Larry Roberts

Freedom From Religion Foundation (1978): PO Box 750, Madison, WI 53701; (608) 256-8900; www.ffrf.org

Friends General Conference (1900): 1216 Arch St., #2B, Philadelphia, PA 19107; (215) 561-1700; www.fgcquaker.org; Gen. Sec., Barry Crossno

Gideons Intl. (1899): P.O. Box 140800, Nashville, TN 37214; (615) 564-5000; www.gideons.org

Greek Orthodox Archdiocese of America (1922): 8 E. 79th St., New York, NY 10075; (212) 570-3500; www.goarch.org; Primate, Archbishop Demetrios

Hadassah, the Women's Zionist Organization of America, Inc. (1912): 50 W. 58th St., New York, NY 10019; (888)

303-3640; www.hadassah.org; Exec. Dir. and CEO, Janice Weinman

Interfaith Alliance (1994): 1250 24th St. NW, Ste. 300, Washington, DC 20037; (202) 466-0567; www.interfaithalliance.org; Pres., Rev. Dr. C. Welton Gaddy

Islamic Society of North America: 6555 S. County Rd. 750 East, Plainfield, IN 46168; (317) 839-8157; www.isna.net; Pres., Mohamed Hagmagid Ali

Jehovah's Witnesses (1931): 25 Columbia Heights, Brooklyn, NY 11201; (718) 560-5000; www.jw.org

Jewish Congress, American (1918): 260 Madison Ave., 2nd Fl., New York, NY 10016; (212) 879-4500; www.ajcongress.org; Pres., Jack Rosen

Jewish Reconstructionist Communities (2012): 1299 Church Rd., Wyncote, PA 19095; (215) 576-0800; www.jewishrecon.org; Pres., Rabbi Deborah Waxman

Jewish Women, Natl. Council of (1893): 475 Riverside Dr., Ste. 1901, New York, NY 10115; (212) 645-4048; www.ncjw.org; Pres., Debbie Hoffmann

Lutheran Church—Missouri Synod (1847): 1333 S. Kirkwood Rd., St. Louis, MO 63122; (800) 248-1930; www.lcms.org; Pres., Rev. Dr. Matthew C. Harrison

Mennonite Church USA (2001): 718 N. Main St., Newton, KS 67114; (316) 283-5100; www.mennoniteusa.org; Exec. Dir., Ervin Stutzman

Moravian Church in North America (1735): www.moravian.org; *Northern Prov.:* 1021 Center St., P.O. Box 1245, Bethlehem, PA 18016; (610) 867-7566; Pres., Betsy Miller; *Southern Prov.:* 459 S. Church St., Winston-Salem, NC 27101; (336) 725-5811; Pres., Rt. Rev. David Guthrie

North American Shia Ithnasheri Muslim Communities, Org. of (1986): P.O. Box 29691, Minneapolis, MN 55429; (905) 763-7512; www.nasimco.info; Pres., Gulamabbas Najafi

Orthodox Union (1898): 11 Broadway, New York, NY 10004; (212) 563-4000; www.ou.org; Exec. Vice Pres., Allen Fagin

Pentecostal Assemblies of the World, Inc. (1906): 3939 N. Meadows Dr.,

Indianapolis, IN 46205; (317) 547-9541; www.pawinc.org; Presiding Bishop, Charles H. Ellis, III

Presbyterian Church (U.S.A.) (1983): 100 Witherspoon St., Louisville, KY 40202; (800) 728-7228; www.pcusa.org; Exec. Dir., Linda Valentine

Progressive Natl. Baptist Convention, Inc. (1961): 601 50th St. NE, Washington, DC 20019; (202) 396-0558; www.pnbc.org; Pres., Dr. Carroll A. Baltimore Sr.

Rabbis, Central Conference of American (1889): 355 Lexington Ave., New York, NY 10017; (212) 972-3636; www.ccarnet.org; Pres., Richard A. Block

Reform Judaism, Union for (1873): 633 3rd Ave., New York, NY 10017; (212) 650-4000; www.urj.org; Pres., Rabbi Rick Jacobs

Secular Humanism, Council for (1980): P.O. Box 664, Amherst, NY 14226; (716) 636-7571; www.secularhumanism.org; Pres. and CEO, Ronald A. Lindsay

Separation of Church and State, Americans United for (1947): 1301 K St. NW, Ste. 850E, Washington, DC 20005; (202) 466-3234; www.au.org; Exec. Dir., Rev. Barry W. Lynn

Seventh-day Adventist Church (1863): 12501 Old Columbia Pike, Silver Spring, MD 20904; (301) 680-6000; www.adventist.org; Pres., Ted N. C. Wilson

Unitarian Universalist Assn. of Congregations (1961): 24 Farnsworth St., Boston, MA 02210; (617) 742-2100; www.uua.org; Pres., Rev. Peter Morales

United Church of Christ (1957): 700 Prospect Ave., Cleveland, OH 44115; (216) 736-2100; www.ucc.org; Pres., Rev. Geoffrey A. Black

United Methodist Church (1968): 100 Maryland Ave. NE, Washington, DC 20002; (202) 488-5600; www.umc.org

United Pentecostal Church Intl. (1945): 8855 Dunn Rd., Hazelwood, MO 63042; (314) 837-7300; www.upci.org; Gen. Supt., David K. Bernard

Wesleyan Church (1843): 13300 Olio Rd., Fishers, IN 46037; (317) 774-7900; www.wesleyan.org; Gen. Supt., Dr. Jo Anne Lyon

Businesses and Corporations

Source: World Almanac research

Listed below are major corporations offering products and services to U.S. consumers, as of June 2013. Alphabetization is by first key word or founder last name. Listings generally include examples of products offered.

Company name (NYSE/Nasdaq symbol, if traded on those markets): Address; Telephone number; Website; Top executive; Business, products, or services.

A&P: see Great Atlantic & Pacific Tea Co., Inc.

Abbott Laboratories (ABT): 100 Abbott Park Rd., Abbott Park, IL 60064; (847) 937-6100; www.abbott.com; Miles D. White; develops, mfr. pharmaceutical, nutritional, diagnostic prods. Spun off indep. pharm. co. Abbvie, 1/1/2013. Announced plans to acquire CFR Pharmaceuticals, 5/16/2014.

ABC: see Walt Disney Co.

adidas Group: Adi-Dassler-Strasse 1, D-91074 Herzogenaurach, Germany; +49 (0) 9132-84-0; www.adidas-group.com; Herbert Hainer; apparel and accessories mfr. (Reebok, Rockport, Taylor Golf).

Advance Publications, Inc.: 950 W. Fingerboard Rd., Staten Island, NY, 10305; (718) 981-1234; www.advance.net; Steven Newhouse; communications, newspaper and magazine publisher (Parade; Condé Nast subsids.: *New Yorker, Vanity Fair, Vogue*).

Aetna, Inc. (AET): 151 Farmington Ave., Hartford, CT 06156; (860) 273-0123; www.aetna.com; Mark T. Bertolini; health care, employee benefits.

Aflac, Inc. (AFL): 1932 Wynnton Rd., Columbus, GA 31999; (706) 596-3493; www.aflac.com; Daniel P. Amos; supplemental health and life insurance.

Alaska Air Group, Inc. (ALK): 19300 International Blvd., Seattle, WA 98188; (206) 433-3200; www.alaskaair.com; Bradley D. Tilden; airline carriers (Alaska Airlines, Horizon Air).

Alcatel-Lucent (ALU): 148/152 route de la Reine, Boulogne-Billancourt 92100,

France; +33 (0) 15514-1010; www.alcatel-lucent.com; Michel Combes; telecom. equip., broadband networks.

Alcoa Inc. (AA): 201 Isabella St., Pittsburgh, PA 15212; (412) 553-4545; www.alcoa.com; Klaus Kleinfeld; prod., mfr. of aluminum, aluminum prods. (aerospace, automotive, industrial materials and components).

Allegheny Technologies Inc. (ATI): 1000 Six PPG Pl., Pittsburgh, PA 15222; (412) 394-2800; www.atimetals.com; Richard J. Harshman; specialty metals mfr. (titanium, alloys).

Allstate Corp. (ALL): 2775 Sanders Rd., Northbrook, IL 60062; (847) 402-5000; www.allstate.com; Thomas J. Wilson; personal property and casualty insurance; financial services.

Altria Group, Inc. (MO): 6601 W. Broad St., Richmond, VA 23230; (804) 484-8897; www.altria.com; Martin J. Barrington; tobacco co. (Marlboro, Merit, Parliament, Virginia Slims). (Altria spun off Philip Morris's intl. operations in 2008 but owns Philip Morris brands in U.S.)

Amazon.com, Inc. (AMZN): 440 Terry Ave. N., Seattle, WA 98109; (206) 266-1000; www.amazon.com; Jeffrey P. Bezos; online retailer of books, music, other consumer and household prods.

American Airlines Group, Inc. (AAL): 4333 Amon Carter Blvd., Ft. Worth, TX 76155; (817) 963-1234; www.aa.com; Doug Parker; airlines (American Airlines, American Eagle, US Airways). Formed

from merger of American Airlines and US Airways, 12/9/2013.

American Electric Power Co., Inc. (AEP): 1 Riverside Plz., Columbus, OH 43215; (614) 716-1000; www.aep.com; Nicholas K. Akins; public utilities.

American Express Co. (AXP): World Financial Ctr., 200 Vesey St., NY, NY 10285; (212) 640-2000; www.americanexpress.com; Kenneth I. Chenault; charge and credit cards, travel-related services.

American Greetings Corp.: 1 American Rd., Cleveland, OH 44144; (216) 252-7300; www.americangreetings.com; Morry Weiss; greeting cards, stationery, party goods, gift items. Acquired by Weiss Family, 8/7/2013.

American Intl. Group, Inc. (AIG): 180 Maiden Ln., NY, NY 10038; (212) 770-7000; www.aigcorporate.com; Robert H. Benmosche; insurance, financial services. AIG received $182 bil in govt. bailouts, 2008.

AmerisourceBergen (ABC): 1300 Morris Dr., Chesterbrook, PA, 19087; (610) 727-7000; www.amerisourcebergen.com; Steven H. Collis; distrib. of generic and brand-name pharmaceuticals.

Anheuser-Busch InBev (BUD): Brouwerijplein 1, 3000 Leuven, Belgium; +32 (16) 276111; www.ab-inbev.com; Carlos Brito; world's largest brewer (Budweiser, Bud Light, Michelob, Busch), soft drinks.

Apple Inc. (AAPL): 1 Infinite Loop, Cupertino, CA 95014; (408) 996-1010;

www.apple.com; Tim Cook; mfr. of computers (Mac), digital media devices (iPod, iPhone, iPad) and distrib. (iTunes store). Announced plans to acquire Beats Music, 5/28/2014.

ARAMARK Corp. (ARMK): 1101 Market St., Philadelphia, PA 19107; (215) 238-3000; www.aramark.com; Eric J. Foss; food/support services to institutions and facilities, uniforms and career apparel. IPO, 12/12/2013.

ArcelorMittal USA, Inc.: 1 South Dearborn, Chicago, IL 60603; (312) 899-3400; www.arcelormittal.com; Michael G. Rippey; U.S. subsidiary of Arcelor Mittal, world's largest steel co., based in Luxembourg.

Archer Daniels Midland Co. (ADM): 4666 Faries Pkwy., Decatur, IL 62526; (217) 424-5200; www.adm.com; Patricia A. Woertz; agricultural commodities and prods.

Armstrong World Industries, Inc. (AWI): 2500 Columbia Ave., P.O. Box 3001, Lancaster, PA 17604; (717) 397-0611; www.armstrong.com; Matthew J. Espe; mfr. of flooring, ceiling prods., cabinets.

ArvinMeritor, Inc.: see Meritor, Inc.

Ashland Inc. (ASH): 50 E. RiverCenter Blvd., P.O. Box 391, Covington, KY 41012; (859) 815-3333; www.ashland.com; James J. O'Brien; petroleum producer and refiner (Valvoline, plastics), chemicals, road construction.

AT&T Inc. (T): 208 S. Akard St., Dallas, TX 75202; (210) 821-4105; www.att.com; Randall L. Stephenson; telecommunications, global information management. Announced plans to acquire DirecTV, 5/18/2014.

AutoNation, Inc. (AN): 200 SW 1st Ave., Ste. 1600, Ft. Lauderdale, FL 33301; (954) 769-6000; www.autonation.com; Mike Jackson; auto retailer; new and used vehicles; auto parts, maintenance, and repair; auto finance and insurance.

Avon Products, Inc. (AVP): 777 Third Ave., NY, NY 10017; (212) 282-7000; www.avon.com; Sheri S. McCoy; cosmetics, fragrances, skin and personal care items; fashion.

Bank of America Corp. (BAC): 100 N. Tryon St., Charlotte, NC 28255; (704) 386-5681; www.bankofamerica.com; Brian T. Moynihan; banking and nonbanking financial services.

Barnes & Noble (BKS): 122 Fifth Ave., NY, NY 10011; (212) 633-3300; www.barnesandnoblieinc.com; Leonard S. Riggio; leading U.S. bookseller (retail and college), publisher (Sterling Pub. Co.).

Baxter International Inc. (BAX): 1 Baxter Pkwy., Deerfield, IL 60015; (224) 948-2000; www.baxter.com; Robert L. Parkinson Jr.; mfr. of health care prods. Announced plan to spin off pharmaceutical business into separate co., 3/27/2014.

Beam Suntory: 510 Lake Cook Rd., Deerfield, IL 60015; (847) 948-8888; www.beamsuntory.com; Matt Shattock; spirits (Jim Beam, Maker's Mark, Courvoisier, Sauza). Beam Inc. acquired by Suntory Holdings, Ltd., renamed Beam Suntory, 4/30/2014.

Bear Stearns Cos. Inc.: see JPMorgan Chase & Co.

Becton, Dickinson & Co. (BDX): 1 Becton Dr., Franklin Lakes, NJ 07417; (201) 847-6800; www.bd.com; Vincent A. Forlenza; medical, laboratory, diagnostic prods. Acquired med. tech. firm Alverix, Inc., 1/7/2014.

Berkshire Hathaway Inc. (BRK.A): 3555 Farnam St., Ste. 1440, Omaha, NE 68131; (402) 346-1400; www.berkshirehathaway.com; Warren E. Buffett; diversified holdings incl. insurance (GEICO), building materials (Benjamin Moore & Co., Shaw), apparel (Fruit of the Loom), food (Dairy Queen). Energy subsidiary acquired utility NV Energy, 12/19/2013.

Bertelsmann AG: Carl-Bertelsmann-Str. 270, 33311 Gütersloh, Germany; +49 (0) 5241-80-62321; www.bertelsmann.de; Thomas Rabe; intl. media corp., trade book publisher (Random House: Knopf, Doubleday). Formed Penguin Random House with Pearson, 7/1/2013.

Best Buy Co., Inc. (BBY): 7601 Penn Ave. S., Richfield, MN 55423; (612) 291-1000; www.bestbuy.com; Hubert Joly; retailer of software, appliances, cellular phones, largest U.S. retailer of consumer electronics.

Blackstone Group LP, The (BX): 345 Park Ave., NY, NY 10154; (212) 583-5000; www.blackstone.com; Stephen A. Schwarzman; asset mgmt., financial services.

Blockbuster LLC: see DISH Network.

Boeing Co. (BA): 100 N. Riverside, Chicago, IL 60606; (312) 544-2000; www.boeing.com; W. James McNerney Jr.; world's leading aerospace co., mfr. of commercial jet and military aircraft; one of the largest U.S. defense contractors.

Brink's Co., The (BCO): 1801 Bayberry Ct., P.O. Box 18100, Richmond, VA 23226; (469) 549-6000; www.brinkscompany.com; Thomas C. Schievelbein; security (armored transport, money processing, trans. of valuables).

Bristol-Myers Squibb Co. (BMY): 345 Park Ave., NY, NY 10154; (212) 546-4000; www.bms.com; Lamberto Andreotti; development, mfr., and sale of pharmaceuticals (Plavix, Abilify, Atripla).

Brown-Forman Corp. (BFB): 850 Dixie Hwy., Louisville, KY 40210; (502) 585-1100; www.brown-forman.com; Paul C. Varga; distilled spirits (Jack Daniel's, Southern Comfort, Finlandia), wine and champagne (Sonoma-Cutrer, Korbel).

Brown Shoe Co., Inc. (BWS): 8300 Maryland Ave., St. Louis, MO 63105; (314) 854-4000; www.brownshoe.com; Diane M. Sullivan; shoe mfr. (Buster Brown, Naturalizer, Dr. Scholl's, AVIA) and retailer (Famous Footwear, shoes.com). Acquired American Sporting Goods Corp., 2/17/2011.

Brunswick Corp. (BC): 1 N. Field Ct., Lake Forest, IL 60045; (847) 735-4700; www.brunswick.com; Dustan E. McCoy; leisure and recreation prods., incl. marine engines and boats; billiards, bowling, and fitness equip. bowling centers.

Burger King (BKW): 5505 Blue Lagoon Dr., Miami, FL 33126; (305) 378-3000; www.bk.com; Daniel Schwartz; fast food restaurants.

Cablevision Systems Corp. (CVC): 1111 Stewart Ave., Bethpage, NY 11714; (516) 803-2300; www.cablevision.com; James L. Dolan; cable and Internet services provider (Optimum); local media and programming; movie theaters (Clearview). Sold Optimum West to Charter, 7/1/2013.

Caesars Entertainment Corp. (CZR): One Caesars Palace Dr., Las Vegas, NV 89109; (702) 407-6000; www.caesars.com; Gary W. Loveman; casinos; gambling services (Caesars, Harrah's, Horseshoe, World Series of Poker).

Campbell Soup Co. (CPB): One Campbell Pl., Camden, NJ 08103; (856) 342-4800; www.campbellsoupcompany.com; Denise Morrison; world's largest soup mfr.; sauces (Pace, Prego), V8 juice, Pepperidge Farm prods.

Cardinal Health, Inc. (CAH): 7000 Cardinal Pl., Dublin, OH 43017; (614) 757-5000; www.cardinalhealth.com; George S. Barrett; pharmaceutical and med. equip. dist. co. Acquired med. device mfr. AccessClosure, 5/12/2014.

Carlyle Group, The (CG): 1001 Pennsylvania Ave. NW, Washington, DC 20004; (202) 729-5399; www.carlyle.com; William E. Conway Jr.; private equity group.

Caterpillar Inc. (CAT): 100 NE Adams St., Peoria, IL 61629; (309) 675-1000; www.caterpillar.com; Douglas R. Oberhelman; world's largest mfr. of construction and mining equip. Acquired Berg Propulsion, 9/6/2013.

CBS Corp. (CBS): 51 W. 52nd St., NY, NY 10019; (212) 975-4321; www.cbscorporation.com; Leslie Moonves; TV networks (CBS, Showtime); TV distribution; radio stations; book publishing (Simon & Schuster).

CenturyLink, Inc. (CTL): 100 CenturyLink Dr., Monroe, LA 71203; (318) 388-9000; www.centurylink.com; Glen F. Post III; telecommunications provider.

Charter Communications, Inc. (CHTR): 400 Atlantic St., Stamford, CT 06901; (203) 905-7801; www.charter.com; Tom Rutledge; cable TV provider.

Chevron Corp. (CVX): 6001 Bollinger Canyon Rd., San Ramon, CA 94583; (925) 842-1000; www.chevron.com; John S. Watson; one of the world's largest integrated-energy cos.

Chiquita Brands Intl., Inc. (CQB): 550 S. Caldwell St., Charlotte, NC 28202; (980) 636-5000; www.chiquita.com; Edward F. Lonergan; bananas and other fruits and vegetables.

CHS, Inc. (CHSCP): 5500 Cenex Dr., Inver Grove Heights, MN 55077; (651) 355-6000; www.chsinc.com; Carl Casale; grain marketing, oil refining, and pipeline operations.

Church & Dwight Co., Inc. (CHD): Princeton South Corporate Center, 500 Charles Ewing Blvd., Ewing, NJ 08628; (800) 524-1328; www.churchdwight.com; James R. Craigie; top world producer of sodium bicarbonate (ARM & HAMMER baking soda); household (OxiClean) and personal care prods. (Arrid, Trojan, First Response).

Cigna Corp. (CI): 900 Cottage Grove Rd., Bloomfield, CT 06002; (860) 226-6000; www.cigna.com; David M. Cordani; health-care, life, and accident insurance provider.

Cintas Corp. (CTAS): 6800 Cintas Blvd., Cincinnati, OH 45262; (513) 459-1200; www.cintas.com; Scott D. Farmer; largest uniform supplier in U.S.

Circuit City Stores, Inc.: see Systemax Inc.

Cisco Systems, Inc. (CSCO): 170 W. Tasman Dr., San Jose, CA 95134; (408) 526-4000; www.cisco.com; John T. Chambers; networking and communication prods.

Citigroup, Inc. (C): 399 Park Ave., NY, NY 10022; (212) 559-1000; www.citigroup.com; Michael L. Corbat; diversified financial services.

Clear Channel Communications, Inc.: 200 E. Basse Rd., San Antonio, TX 78209; (210) 822-2828; www.clearchannel.com; Robert Pittman; radio stations (850+ stations); outdoor advertising (billboards, mass transit ads).

Clorox Co. (CLX): 1221 Broadway, Oakland, CA 94612; (510) 271-7000; www.clorox.com; Donald R. Knauss; consumer prods. (Clorox, Formula 409, Pine-Sol, S.O.S., Tilex; Scoop Away, Fresh Step cat litters; Kingsford charcoal; Hidden Valley dressing; Glad plastic bags; Brita water systems; Burt's Bees personal care prods.).

Coca-Cola Co. (KO): 1 Coca-Cola Plz., Atlanta, GA 30313; (404) 676-2121; www.coca-cola.com; Muhtar Kent; world's largest beverage co. (Coca-Cola, Sprite, DASANI water), juice prods. (Minute Maid).

Colgate-Palmolive Co. (CL): 300 Park Ave., NY, NY 10022; (212) 310-2000; www.colgate.com; Ian M. Cook; soap (Irish Spring), detergent (Palmolive), household cleansers (Ajax), toothpaste (Colgate, Tom's of Maine), pet food (Hill's Science Diet).

Comcast Corp. (CMCSA): 1701 JFK Blvd., Philadelphia, PA 19103; (215) 286-1700; www.comcast.com; Brian L. Roberts; largest U.S. cable provider; broadband media services; programming (E!, NBC, Bravo, USA, Telemundo). Agreed to acquire Time Warner Cable, 2/13/2014.

Computer Sciences Corp. (CSC): 3170 Fairview Park Dr., Falls Church, VA 22042; (703) 876-1000; www.csc.com; Mike Lawrie; technology services.

ConAgra Foods, Inc. (CAG): 1 ConAgra Dr., Omaha, NE 68102; (402) 240-4000; www.conagrafoods.com; Gary M. Rodkin; food processor (Chef Boyardee, Healthy Choice frozen dinners, Egg Beaters, Reddi-wip); food service supplier. Acquired Ralcorp Holdings, 1/29/2013.

ConocoPhillips Co. (COP): 600 N. Dairy Ashford, P.O. Box 2197, Houston, TX 77079; (281) 293-1000; www.conocophillips.com; Ryan M. Lance; oil and gas exploration and prod. co. Spun off refining and marketing segment, 5/1/2012, as Phillips 66.

Consolidated Edison, Inc. (ED): 4 Irving Pl., NY, NY 10003; (212) 460-4600; www.conedison.com; John McAvoy; electric, natural gas utilities.

Continental Airlines, Inc.: see United Continental Holdings, Inc.

Corning Inc. (GLW): 1 Riverfront Plz., Corning, NY 14831; (607) 974-9000; www.corning.com; Wendell P. Weeks; mfr. of telecommunications, specialty equip. fiber optics.

Costco Wholesale Corp. (COST): 999 Lake Dr., Issaquah, WA 98027; (425) 313-8100; www.costco.com; W. Craig Jelinek; largest U.S. chain of wholesale warehouse stores.

Countrywide Financial: see Bank of America Corp.

Crane Co. (CR): 100 First Stamford Pl., Stamford, CT 06902; (203) 363-7300; www.craneco.com; Max H. Mitchell; mfr. of fluid control devices, vending machines, aircraft components.

Crown Holdings, Inc. (CCK): 1 Crown Way, Philadelphia, PA 19154; (215) 698-5100; www.crowncork.com; John W. Conway; leading producer of packaging prods. Acquired Mivisa Envases, 4/23/2014.

CSX Corp. (CSX): 500 Water St., 15th Fl., Jacksonville, FL 32202; (904) 359-3200; www.csx.com; Michael J. Ward; rail freight transport.

CVS Caremark Corp. (CVS): 1 CVS Dr., Woonsocket, RI 02895; (401) 765-1500; www.cvs.com; Larry J. Merlo; retail drugstores.

Dana Holding Corp. (DAN): 3939 Technology Dr., Maumee, OH 43537; (419) 887-3000; www.dana.com; Roger J. Wood; truck and auto parts, supplies.

Darden Restaurants, Inc. (DRI): 1000 Darden Center Dr., Orlando, FL 32837; (407) 245-4000; www.darden.com; Clarence Otis Jr.; casual dining restaurants (Olive Garden, LongHorn Steakhouse). Agreed to sell Red Lobster to Golden Gate Capital, 5/16/2014.

Dean Foods Co. (DF): 2711 N. Haskell Ave., Ste. 3400, Dallas, TX 75204; (214) 303-3400; www.deanfoods.com; Greg A. Tanner; milk and specialty dairy prods. (Land O' Lakes, Horizon Organic, Silk soy milk, International Delight coffee creamers). Spun off WhiteWave Foods Co., 5/23/2013.

Deere & Co. (DE): One John Deere Pl., Moline, IL 61265; (309) 765-8000; www.deere.com; Samuel R. Allen; mfr. of farm equip., industrial equip., lawn and garden tractors.

Dell Inc.: 1 Dell Way, Round Rock, TX 78682; (512) 338-4400; www.dell.com; Michael S. Dell; laptop and desktop computers, network accessories, peripherals, tablets, smartphones. Acquired by founder Michael Dell and Silver Lake Partners, 10/29/2013. Bought data mining co. StatSoft, 3/24/2014.

Delta Air Lines, Inc. (DAL): 1030 Delta Blvd., Atlanta, GA 30354; (404) 715-2600; www.delta.com; Richard H. Anderson; air transportation.

Diebold, Inc. (DBD): 5995 Mayfair Rd., North Canton, OH 44720; (330) 490-4000; www.diebold.com; Andy W. Mattes; mfr. ATMs, security systems and prods.

Dillard's, Inc. (DDS): 1600 Cantrell Rd., Little Rock, AR 72201; (501) 376-5200; www.dillards.com; William Dillard II; dept. store chain.

Dish Network Corp. (DISH): 9601 S. Meridian Blvd., Englewood, CO 80112; (303) 723-1000; www.dish.com; Joseph P. Clayton; satellite media services. Acquired Blockbuster, Inc., 4/6/2011.

Walt Disney Co., The (DIS): 500 S. Buena Vista St., Burbank, CA 91521; (818) 560-1000; disney.go.com; Robert A. Iger; one of the world's largest media conglomerates; motion pictures (Lucasfilm, Touchstone, Pixar); TV (ABC, ESPN) and radio; publishing; theme parks (Walt Disney World, Disneyland) and resorts. Agreed to acquire Maker Studios, 3/24/2014.

Doctor's Associates Inc.: 325 Bic Dr., Milford, CT 06461; (203) 877-4281; www.subway.com; Frederick A. DeLuca; restaurants (Subway).

Dole Food Co., Inc.: One Dole Dr., Westlake Village, CA 91362; (818) 879-6600; www.dole.com; David Murdock; food prods., fresh fruits, vegetables.

R. R. Donnelley & Sons Co. (RRD): 111 S. Wacker Dr., Chicago, IL 60606; (312) 326-8000; www.rrdonnelley.com; Thomas J. Quinlan III; commercial printing; photos/graphics, translation; printer of *The World Almanac*.

Dow Chemical Co. (DOW): 2030 Dow Ctr., Midland, MI 48674; (989) 636-1000; www.dow.com; Andrew N. Liveris; chemicals, plastics.

Dow Jones & Co., Inc.: see News Corp.

Dr Pepper Snapple Group, Inc. (DPS): 5301 Legacy Dr., Plano, TX 75024; (972) 673-7000; www.drpeppersnapplegroup.com; Larry D. Young; bottler and distrib. of nonalcoholic beverages (Dr Pepper, Hawaiian Punch, 7UP, Snapple, Mott's).

Duke Energy Corp. (DUK): 550 S. Tryon St., Charlotte, NC 28202; (704) 594-6200; www.duke-energy.com; Lynn J. Good; utilities, fiber optic networks.

Dun & Bradstreet Corp. (DNB): 103 JFK Pkwy., Short Hills, NJ 07078; (973) 921-5500; www.dnb.com; Bob Carrigan; business information, research.

Dupont (E. I. du Pont de Nemours & Co.) (DD): 1007 Market St., Wilmington, DE 19898; (302) 774-1000; www.dupont.com; Ellen J. Kullman; 2nd-largest U.S. chemical co.; petroleum, consumer prods.

Eastman Kodak Co. (KODK): 343 State St., Rochester, NY 14650; (585) 724-4000; www.kodak.com; Jeffrey J. Clarke; imaging technology and services. Emerged from Chap. 11 reorganization, 9/3/2013; relisted on NYSE, 11/1/2013.

Eaton Corp. (ETN): Eaton Ctr., 1111 Superior Ave., Cleveland, OH 44114; (216) 523-5000; www.eaton.com; Alexander M. Cutler; mfr. vehicle components, controls.

eBay Inc. (EBAY): 2065 Hamilton Ave., San Jose, CA 95125; (408) 376-7400; www.ebay.com; John Donahoe; e-commerce (PayPal, StubHub).

Edison Intl. (EIX): 2244 Walnut Grove Ave., Rosemead, CA 91770; (626) 302-2222; www.edison.com; Theodore F. Craver Jr.; electric utilities.

Electronic Arts Inc. (EA): 209 Redwood Shores Pkwy., Redwood City, CA 94065; (650) 628-1500; www.ea.com; Andrew Wilson; leading U.S. video game publisher (Madden NFL, Battlefield, The Sims, UFC).

Electronic Data Systems: see Hewlett-Packard Co.

Eli Lilly and Co. (LLY): Lilly Corporate Center, Indianapolis, IN 46285; (317) 276-2000; www.lilly.com; John C. Lechleiter; pharmaceutical research, development, and manufacturing (Prozac, Strattera, Cialis).

EMC Corp. (EMC): 176 South St., Hopkinton, MA 01748; (508) 435-1000; www.emc.com; Joseph M. Tucci; data storage/protection.

Emerson Electric Co. (EMR): 8000 W. Florissant Ave., St. Louis, MO 63136; (314) 553-2000; www.emerson.com; David N. Farr; electrical, electronics prods. and systems.

Energizer Holdings, Inc. (ENR): 533 Maryville Univ. Dr., St. Louis, MO 63141; (314) 985-2000; www.energizer.com; Ward M. Klein; batteries, flashlights, personal care prods.

Enterprise Products Partners L.P. (EPD): 1100 Louisiana St., Houston, TX 77002; (713) 381-6500; www.enterpriseproducts.com; Michael A. Creel; oil processing/transport and waterborne freight.

Estée Lauder Cos. Inc. (EL): 767 Fifth Ave., NY, NY 10153; (212) 572-4200; www.elcompanies.com; Fabrizio Freda; cosmetics (Clinique, Bobbi Brown), fragrance, skin care prods.

Exelon Corp. (EXC): 10 S. Dearborn St., 48th Fl., Chicago, IL 60680; (800) 483-3220; www.exeloncorp.com; Christopher M. Crane; electricity generation/distrib.;

natural gas. Agreed to acquire Pepco Holdings, 4/30/2014.

Express Scripts Holding Co. (ESRX): 1 Express Way, St. Louis, MO 63121; (314)-996-0900; www.express-scripts.com; George Paz; U.S. pharmacy benefits mgmt. co.

ExxonMobil Corp. (XOM): 5959 Las Colinas Blvd., Irving, TX 75039; (972) 444-1000; www.exxonmobil.com; Rex W. Tillerson; world's largest integrated oil co.

Facebook, Inc. (FB): 1601 Willow Rd., Menlo Park, CA 94025; (650) 308-7300; www.facebook.com; Mark Zuckerberg; social networking services. Acquired Instagram, 9/6/2012; Little Eye Labs, 1/7/2014; WhatsApp, 2/19/2014; Oculus VR, 7/21/2014.

Federal Home Loan Mortgage Corp. (Freddie Mac): 8200 Jones Branch Dr., McLean, VA 22102; (703) 903-2000; www.freddiemac.com; Donald H. Layton; residential mortgage provider. Under U.S. govt. mgmt. since 9/7/2008.

Federal Natl. Mortgage Assn. (Fannie Mae): 3900 Wisconsin Ave. NW, Washington, DC 20016; (202) 752-7000; www.fanniemae.com; Timothy J. Mayopoulos; provider of residential mortgage funds. Under U.S. govt. mgmt. since 9/7/2008.

FedEx Corp. (FDX): 942 S. Shady Grove Rd., Memphis, TN 38120; (901) 818-7500; www.fedex.com; Frederick W. Smith; delivery services.

Fifth & Pacific Cos., Inc.: see Kate Spade & Co.

First Data Corp.: 5565 Glenridge Connector NE, Ste. 2000, Atlanta, GA 30342; (404) 890-2000; www.firstdata.com; Frank Bisignano; financial transaction processing.

FirstEnergy Corp. (FE): 76 S. Main St., Akron, OH 44308; (800) 736-3402; www.firstenergycorp.com; Anthony J. Alexander; public electricity supplier.

Fluor Corp. (FLR): 6700 Las Colinas Blvd., Irving, TX 75039; (469) 398-7000; www.fluor.com; David T. Seaton; international engineering and construction co.

Foot Locker, Inc. (FL): 112 W. 34th St., NY, NY 10120; (212) 720-3700; www.footlocker-inc.com; Ken C. Hicks; retail athletic stores (Footaction, Foot Locker, Champs Sports). Acquired Runners Point Group, 7/10/2013.

Ford Motor Co. (F): 1 American Rd., Dearborn, MI 48126; (313) 322-3000; www.ford.com; William C. Ford Jr.; auto mfr.; motor vehicle sales (Ford, Lincoln); auto financing (Ford Motor Credit).

Fortune Brands Home and Security, Inc. (FBHS): 520 Lake Cook Rd., Deerfield, IL 60015; (847) 484-4400; www.fbhs.com; Christopher Klein; cabinetry, plumbing (Moen), windows and doors, security and storage (Master Lock).

Fox: see News Corp.

Gannett Co., Inc. (GCI): 7950 Jones Branch Dr., McLean, VA 22107; (703) 854-6000; www.gannett.com; Gracia Martore; newspaper publisher (*USA Today*); network and cable TV; employment website (CareerBuilder). Acquired Belo Corp., 12/23/2013.

Gap Inc. (GPS): 2 Folsom St., San Francisco, CA 94105; (650) 952-4400; www.gapinc.com; Glenn K. Murphy; casual apparel retailer (Gap, Banana Republic, Old Navy).

General Dynamics Corp. (GD): 2941 Fairview Park Dr., Ste. 100, Falls Church, VA 22042; (703) 876-3000; www.general dynamics.com; Phebe N. Novakovic; defense contractor: aerospace, combat systems, marine systems, computing devices.

General Electric Co. (GE): 3135 Easton Tpke., Fairfield, CT 06828; (203) 373-2211; www.ge.com; Jeffrey Immelt; electrical, electronic equip., financial services, radio and TV broadcasting, aircraft engines, power generation, appliances.

General Mills, Inc. (GIS): One General Mills Blvd., Minneapolis, MN 55426; (763) 764-7600; www.generalmills.com; Kendall J. Powell; food mfr. (Betty Crocker, Bisquick, Cheerios, Chex, Green Giant, Häagen-Dazs, Pillsbury, Progresso, Total, Wheaties, Yoplait).

General Motors Co. (GM): 300 Renaissance Ctr., Detroit, MI 48265; (313) 556-5000; www.gm.com; Mary T. Barra; world's largest auto mfr. (Chevrolet, Cadillac, Buick, GMC); auto financing (GM Financial); vehicle security (OnStar). General Motors Corp. filed for Chap. 11 reorganization, 6/1/2009; sold profitable components to a new, smaller co. called General Motors Co., 7/10/2009.

Genuine Parts Co. (GPC): 2999 Circle 75 Pkwy., Atlanta, GA 30339; (770) 953-1700; www.genpt.com; Thomas C. Gallagher; distrib. of auto (NAPA), industrial replacement parts.

Goldman Sachs Group, Inc. (GS): 200 West St., 29th Fl., NY, NY 10282; (212) 902-1000; www.goldmansachs.com; Lloyd C. Blankfein; investment banking, asset mgmt., securities services.

Goodyear Tire & Rubber Co. (GT): 200 Innovation Way, Akron, OH 44316; (330) 796-2121; www.goodyear.com; Richard J. Kramer; tires and other auto prods.

Google, Inc. (GOOG): 1600 Amphitheatre Pkwy., Mountain View, CA 94043; (650) 253-0000; www.google.com; Larry Page; Internet-related prods. and services (leading search engine, ad sales; YouTube). Acquired robot mfr. Boston Dynamics, 12/16/2013. Announced plan to acquire Nest Labs, Inc., 1/13/2014; agreed to sell Motorola Mobility to Lenovo, 1/29/2014.

W. R. Grace & Co. (GRA): 7500 Grace Dr., Columbia, MD 21044; (410) 531-4000; www.grace.com; Fred E. Festa; chemicals, construction prods. Emerged from Chap. 11 reorganization, 2/3/2014.

Graham Holdings Co. (GHC): 1150 15th St. NW, Washington, DC 20071; (202) 334-6000; www.ghco.com; Donald E. Graham; media (newspapers, Slate.com, TV), education (Kaplan), and home healthcare. Formerly Washington Post Co.; renamed 11/29/2013 after sale of Washington Post newspaper to Amazon.com CEO Jeff Bezos, 10/1/2013.

Great Atlantic & Pacific Tea Co., Inc.: 2 Paragon Dr., Montvale, NJ 07645; (201) 573-9700; www.aptea.com; Paul Hertz; supermarkets (A&P, Food Basics, Food Emporium, Super Fresh, Waldbaum's, Pathmark).

Halliburton Co. (HAL): 3000 N. Sam Houston Pkwy. E., Houston, TX 77032; (281) 871-4000; www.halliburton.com; David J. Lesar; oil field mgmt., energy services.

Hanesbrands Inc. (HBI): 1000 E. Hanes Mill Rd., Winston-Salem, NC 27105; (336) 519-8080; www.hanesbrands.com; Richard A. Noll; apparel mfr. (Hanes, barely there, Bali, Champion, Flexees, Glamorise, Gear for Sports, Just My Size, L'eggs, Lilyette, Playtex, Wonderbra). Acquired Maidenform Brands, Inc., 10/7/2013.

Harley-Davidson, Inc. (HOG): 3700 W. Juneau Ave., Milwaukee, WI 53208; (414) 342-4680; www.harley-davidson.com; Keith E. Wandell; mfr. motorcycles, parts, and accessories.

Hartford Financial Services Group, Inc. (HIG): One Hartford Plz., Hartford, CT 06155; (860) 547-5000; www.thehartford.com; Liam E. McGee; insurance, financial services.

Hasbro, Inc. (HAS): 1027 Newport Ave., Pawtucket, RI 02862; (401) 431-8697; www.hasbro.com; Brian Goldner; toy and game mfr. (Milton Bradley, Playskool, G.I. Joe, Parker Bros., Nerf, Play-Doh).

HCA Holdings, Inc. (HCA): 1 Park Plz., Nashville, TN 37203; (615) 344-9551; www.hcahealthcare.com; R. Milton Johnson; owns and operates hospitals; other diagnostic, surgical, health treatment centers.

H. J. Heinz Co.: 1 PPG Pl., Ste. 3100, Pittsburgh, PA 15222; (412) 456-5700; www.heinz.com; Bernardo Hees; food mfr. (Ore-Ida, 57 Varieties ketchup, Weight Watchers foods). Acquired by Berkshire Hathaway and 3G Capital, 6/7/2013.

Henkel Corp.: 19001 N. Scottsdale Rd., Scottsdale, AZ 85255; (480) 754-3425; www.henkelna.com; Jeffrey C. Piccolomini;

consumer prods. (Dial soap, Purex detergent, Right Guard antiperspirant, Renuzit air fresheners); U.S. subsidiary of Germany's Henkel co.

Hershey Co., The (HSY): 100 Crystal A Dr., Hershey, PA 17033; (717) 534-4200; www.thehersheycompany.com; John P. Bilbrey; largest North American producer of chocolate prods. (Reese's, Kit Kat, Mounds, Almond Joy, Jolly Rancher, Twizzlers, Milk Duds, Good & Plenty, York, Krackel).

Hertz Global Holdings, Inc. (HTZ): 225 Brae Blvd., Park Ridge, NJ 07656; (201) 307-2000; www.hertz.com; Mark P. Frissora; car rentals.

Hess Corp. (HES): 1185 Ave. of the Americas, 40th Fl., NY, NY 10036; (212) 997-8500; www.hess.com; John B. Hess; integrated oil and gas co.

Hewlett-Packard Co. (HPQ): 3000 Hanover St., Palo Alto, CA 94304; (650) 857-1501; www.hp.com; Meg Whitman; computers, electronic prods. and systems.

Hillenbrand, Inc. (HI): One Batesville Blvd., Batesville, IN 47006; (812) 934-7000; www.hillenbrandinc.com; Joe Raver; holder of Batesville Caskets, coffin mfr.

Hill-Rom Holdings, Inc. (HRC): 1069 State Rte. 46 E., Batesville, IN 47006; (812) 934-7777; www.hill-rom.com; John J. Greisch; mfr. hospital beds, other hospital equip. Acquired Trumpf Medical Systems, 8/1/2014.

Hillshire Brands Co. (HSH): 400 S. Jefferson St., Chicago, IL 60607; (312) 614-6000; www.hillshirebrands.com; Sean Connolly; food processor. Acquired Van's Natural Foods, 6/15/2014; announced plans to merge with Tyson Foods, 7/2/2014.

Hilton Worldwide (HLT): 7930 Jones Branch Dr., Ste. 1100, McLean, VA 22102; (703) 883-1000; www.hiltonworldwide.com; Christopher J. Nassetta; hotels and resorts (Doubletree, Embassy, Hampton).

Home Depot, Inc. (HD): 2455 Paces Ferry Rd. NW, Atlanta, GA 30339; (770) 433-8211; www.homedepot.com; Francis S. Blake; home improvement warehouse stores. Acquired Blinds.com, 1/23/2014.

Honeywell Intl. Inc. (HON): 101 Columbia Rd., Morristown, NJ 07962; (973) 455-2000; www.honeywell.com; David Cote; industrial and home control systems, aerospace guidance systems.

Hormel Foods Corp. (HRL): 1 Hormel Pl., Austin, MN 55912; (507) 437-5611; www.hormelfoods.com; Jeffrey M. Ettinger; food processor, primarily meat (SPAM, Dinty Moore, Jennie-O, Skippy). Agreed to acquire Muscle Milk, 6/30/2014.

Hostess Brands LLC: 1 E Armour Blvd., Kansas City, MO 64111; (816) 701-4600; www.hostessbrands.com; William Toler; baked goods wholesaler, distrib.

Houghton Mifflin Harcourt Co. (HMHC): 222 Berkeley St., Boston, MA 02116; (617) 351-5000; www.hmhco.com; Linda K. Zecher; publisher of textbooks and other educational prods. (Holt McDougal Clarion), trade and reference books. Emerged from Chap. 11 reorganization, 6/22/2012. Acquired online educational co. Tribal Nova, 4/11/2013.

H&R Block, Inc. (HRB): 1 H&R Block Way, Kansas City, MO 64105; (816) 854-3000; www.hrblock.com; William C. Cobb; tax return preparation; business and consulting services.

Humana Inc. (HUM): 500 W. Main St., Louisville, KY 40202; (502) 580-1000; www.humana.com; Bruce D. Broussard; managed health care service provider, related specialty prods. Agreed to buy American Eldercare, 7/24/2013.

IAC/InterActiveCorp (IACI): 555 W. 18th St., NY, NY 10011; (212) 314-7300; www.iac.com; Barry Diller; Internet conglomerate (Ask.com, Match.com, Citysearch, Urbanspoon, Vimeo).

Illinois Tool Works Inc. (ITW): 3600 W. Lake Ave., Glenview, IL 60026; (847) 724-7500; www.itw.com; E. Scott Santi; consumer, industrial tools; food equip. (Hobart), packaging (Zip-Pak).

Ingersoll-Rand plc (IR): 170/175 Lakeview Dr., Airside Business Park, Swords, Dublin, Ireland; 353-1-870-7400; company.ingersollrand.com; Michael W. Lamach; locks and security systems (Schlage, Kryptonite); refrigeration equip. (Thermo King, Hussmann); industrial equip.; air conditioning systems (Trane). Spun off security prods. business as Allegion, 12/2/2013.

Ingram Micro Inc. (IM): 1600 E. St. Andrew Pl., Santa Ana, CA 92705; (714) 566-1000; www.ingrammicro.com; Alain Monié; IT equip. wholesaler and distrib. in over 160 countries.

Intel Corp. (INTC): 2200 Mission College Blvd., Santa Clara, CA 95054; (408) 765-8080; www.intel.com; Andy D. Bryant; mfr. Semiconductors, microprocessors (Core, Centrino).

International Business Machines Corp. (IBM): One New Orchard Rd., Armonk, NY 10504; (914) 499-1900; www.ibm.com; Virginia M. Rometty; advanced information processing technology equip., services.

International Paper Co. (IP): 6400 Poplar Ave., Memphis, TN 38197; (901) 419-7000; www.internationalpaper.com; John V. Faraci Jr.; world's largest paper/forest prods. co. Spun off distr. business xpedx, which merged with Unisource to form Veritiv Corp., 7/1/2014.

International Textile Group, Inc.: 804 Green Valley, Greensboro, NC 27408; (336) 379-6220; www.itg-global.com; Joseph L. Gorga; apparel and home textiles/fabrics.

INTL FCStone Inc. (INTL): 708 Third Ave., 15th Fl., NY, NY 10017; (212) 485-3500; www.intlfcstone.com; Sean O'Connor; securities and commodities advising.

J.C. Penney Co., Inc. (JCP): 6501 Legacy Dr., Plano, TX 75024; (972) 431-1000; www.jcpenney.net; Mike Ullman; dept. store retailer, general merchandise catalog sales.

J.Crew Group, Inc.: 770 Broadway, NY, NY 10003; (212) 209-2500; www.jcrew.com; Millard S. Drexler; retail and mail order apparel and accessories.

JetBlue Airways Corp. (JBLU): 27-01 Queens Plz. N., Long Island City, NY 11101; (718) 286-7900; www.jetblue.com; David Barger; air transportation.

Jo-Ann Stores, Inc.: 5555 Darrow Rd., Hudson, OH 44236; (330) 656-2600; www.joann.com; Travis Smith; nation's largest specialty fabric and craft stores.

Johnson Controls, Inc. (JCI): 5757 N. Green Bay Ave., Milwaukee, WI 53209; (414) 524-1200; www.johnsoncontrols.com; Alex A. Molinaroli; equip. and controls for heating, ventilating, AC, refrigeration, and building security; auto interiors, batteries. Acquired Air Distribution Technologies, 6/16/2014.

Johnson & Johnson (JNJ): 1 Johnson & Johnson Plz., New Brunswick, NJ 08933; (732) 524-0400; www.jnj.com; Alex Gorsky; health care prods. (Band-Aid, Neosporin), pharmaceuticals (Tylenol, Motrin, Sudafed), toiletries (Neutrogena, Aveeno). Agreed to sell Ortho-Clinical Diagnostics, Inc. to The Carlyle Group, 3/31/2014.

S. C. Johnson & Son, Inc.: 1525 Howe St., Racine, WI 53403; (262) 260-2000; www.scjohnson.com; H. Fisk Johnson; cleaning and other household prods. (Johnson's Wax, Windex, Pledge, Fantastik, Raid, OFF!, Shout, Glade, Scrubbing Bubbles, Ziploc bags).

Jones Group, Inc.: 1411 Broadway, NY, NY 10018; (212) 642-3860; www.jny.com; Wesley R. Card; apparel (Jones New York, Gloria Vanderbilt), shoes (Nine West, Anne Klein); retail and outlet stores. Acquired by Sycamore Partners, 4/8/2014.

JPMorgan Chase & Co. (JPM): 270 Park Ave., Fl. 12, NY, NY 10017; (212) 270-6000; www.jpmorganchase.com; James Dimon; financial services.

Kate Spade & Co. (KATE): 2 Park Ave., NY, NY 10016; (212) 354-4900; katespade.com; Craig. A. Leavitt; women's apparel.

KBR, Inc. (KBR): 601 Jefferson St., Ste. 3400, Houston, TX 77002; (713) 753-2000; www.kbr.com; Stuart Bradie; engineering; construction mgmt. services.

Kellogg Co. (K): One Kellogg Sq., Battle Creek, MI 49016; (269) 961-2000; www. kelloggcompany.com; John A. Bryant; mfr. of ready-to-eat cereals, other food prods. (Frosted Flakes, Rice Krispies, Pop-Tarts, Nutri-Grain, Keebler, Eggo, Pringles).

Kelly Services, Inc. (KELYA): 999 W. Big Beaver Rd., Troy, MI 48084; (248) 362-4444; www.kellyservices.com; Carl T. Camden; temporary staffing services.

Kimberly-Clark Corp. (KMB): 351 Phelps Dr., Irving, TX 75038; (972) 281-1200; www.kimberly-clark.com; Thomas J. Falk; personal care prods. (Kleenex, Scott, Cottonelle, Huggies, Kotex).

Kinder Morgan, Inc. (KMI): 1001 Louisiana St., Ste. 1000, Houston, TX 77002; (713) 369-9000; www.kindermorgan.com; Richard D. Kinder; energy trans. and storage.

Kmart Corp.: see Sears Holdings Corp.

Koch Industries, Inc.: P.O. Box 2256, Wichita, KS 67201; (316) 828-5500; www. kochind.com; Charles G. Koch; forest prod. mfr.; oil refineries/pipeline; chemicals; pollution-control equip.; ranching.

Kraft Foods Group Inc. (KRFT): Three Lakes Dr., Northfield, IL 60093; (847) 646-2000; www.kraftfoodsgroup.com; W. Anthony Vernon; global packaged food co. (Maxwell House, Oscar Mayer, Planters, Velveeta, Capri Sun, Jell-O, Lunchables). Kraft Foods split into two public cos., Mondelēz International and Kraft Foods Group Inc., 10/1/2012.

Kroger Co. (KR): 1014 Vine St., Cincinnati, OH 45202; (513) 762-4000; www. thekrogerco.com; W. Rodney McMullen; grocery, convenience, and mall jewelry stores.

L Brands, Inc. (formerly Limited Brands) (LB): 3 Limited Pkwy., Columbus, OH 43230; (614) 415-7000; www.lb.com; Sharen Jester Turney; apparel stores (La Senza, Victoria's Secret, PINK, Henri Bendel), home decor, personal care (Bath & Body Works).

La-Z-Boy Inc. (LZB): 1284 N. Telegraph Rd., Monroe, MI 48162; (734) 242-1444; www.la-z-boy.com; Kurt L. Darrow; reclining chairs, other furniture.

Leggett & Platt, Inc. (LEG): No. 1 Leggett Rd., Carthage, MO 64836; (417) 358-8131; www.leggett.com; David S. Haffner; furniture and its components, industrial materials, automotive seating suspension, control and power train cable systems.

Levi Strauss & Co.: 1155 Battery St., San Francisco, CA 94111; (415) 501-6000; www.levistrauss.com; Charles Bergh; blue jeans, casual sportswear (Dockers).

Lexmark Intl., Inc. (LXK): 740 W. New Circle Rd., Lexington, KY 40550; (859) 232-2000; www.lexmark.com; Paul Rooke; computer printers and peripherals.

Liberty Mutual Holding Co. Inc.: 175 Berkeley St., Boston, MA 02116; (617) 357-9500; www.libertymutual.com; David H. Long; insurance and services.

LinkedIn Corp. (LNKD): 2029 Stierlin Ct. Ste. 200, Mountain View, CA 94043; (650) 687-3600; Jeff Weiner; social networking services.

Liz Claiborne, Inc.: see J.C. Penney Co., Inc.

L.L.Bean, Inc.: 15 Casco St., Freeport, ME 04033; (207) 552-2000; www.llbean.com; Christopher J. McCormick; catalog and retail outdoor apparel, footwear, gear.

Lockheed Martin Corp. (LMT): 6801 Rockledge Dr., Bethesda, MD 20817; (301) 897-6000; www.lockheedmartin. com; Marillyn A. Hewlson; leading U.S. defense contractor; commercial and military aircraft, electronics, missiles, information tech., and communications. Announced plans to acquire Zeta Associates, 6/30/2014.

Loews Corp. (L): 667 Madison Ave., NY, NY 10065; (212) 521-2000; www.loews.com; James S. Tisch; hotels, insurance (CNA Financial), offshore drilling (Diamond).

Longs Drug Stores: see CVS Caremark Corp.

Lorillard, Inc. (LO): 714 Green Valley Rd., Greensboro, NC 27408; (336) 335-7000; www.lorillard.com; Murray S. Kessler; cigarette mfr. (Newport, Kent, True). Announced plans to merge with Reynolds American, 7/15/2014.

Lowe's Cos., Inc. (LOW): 1000 Lowe's Blvd., Mooresville, NC 28117; (704) 758-1000; www.lowes.com; Robert A. Niblock; building material and home improvement superstores.

Macy's, Inc. (M): 7 W. 7th St., Cincinnati, OH 45202; (513) 579-7000; www. macysinc.com; Terry J. Lundgren; dept. stores (Macy's, Bloomingdale's).

ManpowerGroup (MAN): 100 Manpower Pl., Milwaukee, WI 53212; (414) 961-1000; www.manpowergroup.com; Jonas Prising; employment services.

Marathon Oil Corp. (MRO): 5555 San Felipe St., Houston, TX 77056; (713) 629-6600; www.marathonoil.com; Lee M. Tillman; integrated oil co. Announced plans to acquire Hess Corp.'s gas station business, 5/22/2014.

Marriott International, Inc. (MAR): 10400 Fernwood Rd., Bethesda, MD 20817; (301) 380-3000; www.marriott.com; Arne M. Sorenson; hotels (Renaissance, Courtyard, Fairfield Inn, Ritz-Carlton). Acquired Protea Hospitality Group, 4/1/2014.

Mars, Inc.: 6885 Elm St., McLean, VA 22101; (703) 821-4900; www.mars.com; Paul S. Michaels; food mfr., including of chocolate (M&M's, Snickers, Dove), food (Uncle Ben's), pet food (Pedigree, Whiskas, Iams, Eukanuba, Natura).

Masco Corp. (MAS): 21001 Van Born Rd., Taylor, MI 48180; (313) 274-7400; www. masco.com; Keith J. Allman; mfr. kitchen, bathroom prods. (Delta, Peerless faucets; Merillat cabinets); paints (Behr).

Massachusetts Mutual Life Insurance Co. (MassMutual Financial Group): 1295 State St., Springfield, MA 01111; (413) 744-1000; www.massmutual.com; Roger W. Crandall; financial planning and investment, life insurance.

Mattel, Inc. (MAT): 333 Continental Blvd., El Segundo, CA 90245; (310) 252-2000; www.mattel.com; Bryan Stockton; world's largest toymaker (Barbie, Fisher-Price, Hot Wheels, Matchbox, American Girls). Acquired MEGA Brands, 4/30/2014.

McClatchy Co. (MNI): 2100 Q St., Sacramento, CA 95816; (916) 321-1855; www. mcclatchy.com; Patrick J. Talamantes; newspaper publisher.

McDonald's Corp. (MCD): 2111 McDonald's Dr., Oak Brook, IL 60523; (630) 623-3000; www.mcdonalds.com; Don Thompson; world's largest fast food co.

McGraw-Hill Financial (MHFI): 1221 Ave. of the Americas, NY, NY 10020; (212) 512-2000; www.mcgraw-hill.com; Douglas L. Peterson; information and financial services (Standard & Poor's).

McKesson Corp. (MCK): 1 Post St., San Francisco, CA 94104; (415) 983-8300; www.mckesson.com; John H. Hammergren; distrib. of drugs and toiletries; provides mgmt. software and services.

MeadWestvaco Corp. (MWV): 501 S. 5th St., Richmond, VA 23219; (804) 444-1000; www. meadwestvaco.com; John A. Luke Jr.; packaging, shipping containers, chemicals. Spun off consumer and office prods., 5/1/2012.

Medco Health Solutions, Inc.: see Express Scripts Holding Co.

Medtronic, Inc. (MDT): 710 Medtronic Pkwy., Minneapolis, MN 55432; (763) 514-4000; www.medtronic.com; Omar Ishrak; mfr. of implantable biomedical devices. Agreed to acquire medical tech. co. Covidien, 6/15/2014.

Merck & Co., Inc. (MRK): 1 Merck Dr., Whitehouse Station, NJ 08889; (908) 423-1000; www.merck.com; Kenneth C. Frazier; pharmaceuticals (Gardasil, Propecia, Singulair, Vytorin, Zocor); consumer health prods. (Claritin, Coppertone, Dr. Scholl's, MiraLAX). Announced plans to acquire Idenix Pharmaceuticals, 6/9/2014.

Meredith Corp. (MDP): 1716 Locust St., Des Moines, IA 50309; (515) 284-3000; www.meredith.com; Stephen M. Lacy; magazine publishing (Better Homes and Gardens, Ladies' Home Journal, Parents, Family Circle, Every Day With Rachael Ray, FamilyFun), book publishing, broadcasting, online media (allrecipes.com).

Meritor, Inc. (MTOR): 2135 W. Maple Rd., Troy, MI 48084; (248) 435-1000; www. meritor.com; Ivor J. Evans; commercial vehicles systems and components.

Merrill Lynch & Co., Inc.: see Bank of America Corp.

MetLife, Inc. (MET): 200 Park Ave., NY, NY 10166; (212) 578-2211; www.metlife.com; Steven A. Kandarian; insurance, financial services.

MGM Resorts Intl. (MGM): 3600 Las Vegas Blvd. S., Las Vegas, NV 89109; (702) 693-7120; www.mgmresorts.com; James J. Murren; hotel-casino operator (Mirage, New York-New York, Luxor, Bellagio, Circus Circus, Monte Carlo). Announced formation of joint venture hotel co. MGM Hakkasan Hospitality, 4/15/2014.

Microsoft Corp. (MSFT): One Microsoft Way, Redmond, WA 98052; (425) 882-8080; www.microsoft.com; Satya Nadella; world's largest consumer software maker (Windows, Word, Excel); video game consoles (Xbox). Acquired Nokia's devices and services businesses, 4/25/2014.

Miller Brewing Co.: see SABMiller plc.

Molson Coors Brewing Co. (TAP): 1225 17th St., Ste. 3200, Denver, CO 80202; (303) 927-2337; www.molsoncoors.com; Peter Swinburn; brewer (Coors, Killian's, Molson, Heineken, Miller).

Mondelēz International, Inc. (MDLZ): 3 Pkwy N., Northfield, IL 60093; (847) 646-2000; www.mondelezinternational. com; Irene B. Rosenfeld; global snack food co., including Nabisco (Oreo), Cadbury, Tang, Trident. Spun off from Kraft Foods, 10/1/2012.

Morgan Stanley (MS): 1585 Broadway, NY, NY 10036; (212) 761-4000; www.morgan stanley.com; James P. Gorman; diversified financial services. Agreed to sell controlling stake in petroleum distrib. co. TransMontaigne to NGL Energy Partners, 6/9/2014.

Motorola Solutions, Inc. (MSI): 1303 E. Algonquin Rd., Schaumburg, IL 60196; (847) 576-5000; www.motorolasolutions. com; Rick Osterloh; electronic equip. and components; communication devices. Spun off from Motorola, Inc., 1/4/2011.

Murphy Oil Corp. (MUR): 200 Peach St., El Dorado, AR 71730; (870) 862-6411; www. murphyoilcorp.com; Roger W. Jenkins; oil and gas exploration and production.

Nationwide Mutual Insurance Co.: One Nationwide Plz., Columbus, OH 43215; (614) 249-7111; www.nationwide.com; Stephen S. Rasmussen; property/casualty, life insurance; financial services.

Navistar Intl. Corp. (NAV): 2701 Navistar Dr., Lisle, IL 60532; (331) 332-5000; www. navistar.com; Troy Clarke; mfr. heavy-duty trucks, parts, school buses.

NBC Universal: 30 Rockefeller Plaza, NY, NY 10112; (212) 664-4444; www. nbcuni.com; Stephen B. Burke; news/ entertainment producer and developer; TV and CATV stations (NBC, Bravo, USA, Telemundo); film production. Owned by Comcast and General Electric.

NCR Corp. (NCR): 3097 Satellite Blvd., Duluth, GA 30096; (937) 445-1936; www. ncr.com; William R. Nuti; mfr. ATMs, retail technology, hardware and software; computer services and supplies.

Nestlé USA, Inc.: 800 N. Brand Blvd., Glendale, CA 91203; (818) 549-6000; www. nestleusa.com; Paul Grimwood; candy (Baby Ruth, Raisinets), beverages (Nestea, Juicy Juice), food (Buitoni, Coffee-Mate), frozen foods (Stouffer's, Häagen-Dazs, Lean Cuisine), pet foods (Purina, Alpo, Friskies). Subsidiary of Nestlé SA in Switzerland, world's largest food co.

Netflix, Inc. (NFLX): 100 Winchester Cir., Los Gatos, CA 95032; (408) 540-3700;

www.netflix.com; Reed Hastings; online DVD rentals; streaming video.

New York Life Insurance Co.: 51 Madison Ave., NY, NY 10010; (212) 576-7000; www.newyorklife.com; Theodore A. Mathas; life insurance, annuities, mutual funds.

New York Times Co. (NYT): 620 8th Ave., NY, NY 10018; (212) 556-1234; www.nytco.com; Arthur O. Sulzberger Jr.; newspapers. Sold New England Media Group (incl. *Boston Globe*), 10/24/2013.

Newell Rubbermaid Inc. (NWL): 3 Glenlake Pkwy., Atlanta, GA 30328; (770) 418-7000; www.newellrubbermaid.com; Michael B. Polk; housewares (Rubbermaid, Levolor, Calphalon); hair accessories (Goody); writing utensils (Parker, Sharpie, Paper Mate); hardware and tools (Irwin, Amerock); juvenile prods. (Graco).

News Corp. (NWS): 1211 Ave. of the Americas, NY, NY 10036; (212) 416-3400; www.newscorp.com; K. Rupert Murdoch; global newspaper, magazine, book publishing (HarperCollins; *Wall Street Journal*); TV and CATV stations (FOX, Fox News Channel, FX); film production; websites (Hulu). Split into 2 cos., publishing and entertainment, 6/28/2013. Agreed to acquire Harlequin Enterprises from Torstar Corp., 5/2/2014.

NIKE, Inc. (NKE): 1 Bowerman Dr., Beaverton, OR 97005; (503) 671-6453; nikeinc.com; Mark G. Parker; world's largest mfr. athletic footwear and apparel.

Nordstrom, Inc. (JWN): 1617 6th Ave., Seattle, WA 98101; (206) 628-2111; www.nordstrom.com; Blake W. Nordstrom; upscale dept. store chain.

Norfolk Southern Corp. (NSC): Three Commercial Pl., Norfolk, VA 23510; (855) 667-3655; www.nscorp.com; Charles W. Moorman; railway operator; freight carrier.

Northrop Grumman Corp. (NOC): 2980 Fairview Park Dr., Falls Church, VA 22042; (703) 280-2900; www.northropgrumman.com; Wes Bush; defense contractor: aircraft, electronics, data systems, information systems, missiles.

Northwest Airlines Corp.: see Delta Air Lines, Inc.

Northwestern Mutual Life Insurance Co.: 720 E. Wisconsin Ave., Milwaukee, WI 53202; (414) 271-1444; www.northwesternmutual.com; John E. Schlifske; life insurance, investment prods. and services, annuities. Agreed to sell Russell Investments to London Stock Exchange Group, 6/26/2014.

Occidental Petroleum Corp. (OXY): 10889 Wilshire Blvd., Los Angeles, CA 90024; (310) 208-8800; www.oxy.com; Stephen I. Chazen; oil, natural gas, chemicals, plastics. Announced plans to spin off California assets into separate co., 2/14/2014.

Office Depot, Inc. (ODP): 6600 N. Military Trl., Boca Raton, FL 33496; (561) 438-4800; www.officedepot.com; Roland C. Smith; office supply retail stores.

Omnicom Group Inc. (OMC): 437 Madison Ave., NY, NY 10022; (212) 415-3600; www.omnicomgroup.com; John D. Wren; advertising, marketing, interactive/digital media.

Oracle Corp. (ORCL): 500 Oracle Pkwy., Redwood City, CA 94065; (650) 506-7000; www.oracle.com; Lawrence J. Ellison; database and file mgmt. software. Agreed to acquire MICROS Systems, 6/23/2014.

Owens Corning (OC): 1 Owens Corning Pkwy., Toledo, OH 43659; (419) 248-8000; www.owenscorning.com; Michael H. Thaman; world leader in insulation, advanced glass, composite materials. Acquired Thermafiber, Inc., 6/3/2013.

Owens-Illinois, Inc. (OI): 1 Michael Owens Way, Perrysburg, OH 43551; (567) 336-5000; Albert P. L. Stroucken; www.o-i.com; mfr. of glass containers.

Payless ShoeSource, Inc.: 3231 SE 6th Ave., Topeka, KS 66607; (785) 233-5171; www.collectivebrands.com; W. Paul Jones; shoe mfr./retailer.

PepsiCo, Inc. (PEP): 700 Anderson Hill Rd., Purchase, NY 10577; (914) 253-2000; www.pepsico.com; Indra K. Nooyi; soft drinks and other beverages (Pepsi-Cola, Mountain Dew, Gatorade, Tropicana), snacks and cereals (Fritos, Lay's, Ruffles, Quaker).

Pfizer, Inc. (PFE): 235 E. 42nd St., NY, NY 10017; (212) 733-2323; www.pfizer.com; Ian Read; biopharmaceuticals (Celebrex, Lipitor, Viagra, Zoloft); human and animal health care prods.

PG&E Corp. (PCG): 77 Beale St., 24th Fl., San Francisco, CA 94105; (415) 973-8200; www.pgecorp.com; Anthony F. Earley Jr.; operates Pacific Gas and Electric public utility.

Philip Morris Intl. Inc. (PM): 120 Park Ave., NY, NY 10017; (917) 663-2000; www.pmi.com; André Calantzopoulos; intl. mfr. and distrib. of tobacco. (Altria spun off intl. Philip Morris operations in 2008 but owns Philip Morris brands in U.S.) Acquired Nicocigs, Ltd., 6/26/2014.

Phillips 66 Co. (PSX): P.O. Box 4428, Houston, TX 77210; (281) 293-6600; www.phillips66.com; Greg C. Garland; oil, gas co. Formed when refining and marketing segment of ConocoPhillips was spun off, 5/1/2012.

Pitney Bowes Inc. (PBI): 1 Elmcroft Rd., Stamford, CT 06926; (203) 356-5000; www.pb.com; Marc B. Lautenbach; postage meters and mailing equip.

Plains All American Pipeline, L.P. (PAA): 333 Clay St., Ste. 1600, Houston, TX 77002; (713) 646-4100; www.paalp.com; Greg L. Armstrong; oil and natural gas transportation, storage.

Post Holdings, Inc. (POST): 2503 S. Hanley Rd., St. Louis, MO 63144; (314) 644-7600; www.postfoods.com; William Stiritz; ready-to-eat cereals. Spun off from Ralcorp Holdings, 2/6/2012.

PPG Industries, Inc. (PPG): 1 PPG Pl., Pittsburgh, PA 15272; (412) 434-3131; www.ppg.com; Charles E. Bunch; glass prods., silicas, fiberglass, chemicals, sealants. Agreed to acquire Comex, 6/30/2014; acquired Masterwork Paint Co., 7/1/2014.

Procter & Gamble Co. (PG): 1 Procter & Gamble Plz., Cincinnati, OH 45202; (513) 983-1100; www.pg.com; Alan G. Lafley; soaps and detergents (Ivory, Cheer, Tide, Mr. Clean); toiletries (Crest, Scope, Head & Shoulders, Old Spice); pharmaceuticals (Pepto-Bismol, Vicks cough medicines); paper prods. (Charmin toilet tissues, Bounty towels), Tampax tampons; disposable diapers (Pampers, Luvs); CoverGirl and Max Factor cosmetics, Clairol hair care; Gillette razors.

Prudential Financial, Inc. (PRU): 751 Broad St., Newark, NJ 07102; (973) 802-6000; www.prudential.com; John R. Strangfeld Jr.; insurance, financial services.

Publix Super Markets Inc. (PUSH): 3300 Publix Corporate Pkwy., Lakeland, FL 33811; (863) 688-1188; www.publix.com; William Crenshaw; supermarket chain.

PVH Corp. (PVH): 200 Madison Ave., NY, NY 10016; (212) 381-3500; www.pvh.com; Emanuel Chirico; mfr. of apparel, including licensed brands (Calvin Klein, IZOD, Geoffrey Beene, Kenneth Cole, Tommy Hilfiger, Sean John).

Quest Diagnostics Inc. (DGX): 3 Giralda Farms, Madison, NJ 07940; (800) 222-0446; www.questdiagnostics.com; Stephen H. Rusckowski; leading clinical laboratory. Acquired Summit Health, 4/21/2014.

RadioShack Corp. (RSH): 300 RadioShack Cir., Fort Worth, TX 76102; (817) 415-3011; www.radioshack.com; Joseph C. Magnacca; consumer electronics retailer.

Ralcorp Holdings, Inc.: see ConAgra Foods, Inc.

Ralph Lauren Corp. (RL): 650 Madison Ave., NY, NY 10022; (212) 318-7000; www.ralphlauren.com; Ralph Lauren; men's and women's apparel, home furnishings, fragrances.

Raytheon Co. (RTN): 870 Winter St., Waltham, MA 02451; (781) 522-3000; www.raytheon.com; Thomas A. Kennedy; defense, communications systems.

Reader's Digest Assn., Inc.: 750 Third Ave., NY, NY 10017; (914) 238-1000; www.rda.com; Bonnie Kintzer; magazine publisher; marketer of books, music, video prods. Emerged from second Chap. 11 reorganization since 2010, 7/31/2013.

Republic Services, Inc. (RSG): 18500 N. Allied Way, Phoenix, AZ 85054; (480) 627-2700; www.republicservices.com; Donald W. Slager; waste mgmt. co.

Revlon, Inc. (REV): 237 Park Ave., NY, NY 10017; (212) 527-4000; www.revlon.com; Lorenzo Delpani; cosmetics, skin care. Acquired The Colomer Group (TCG), 10/9/2013.

Reynolds American Inc. (RAI): 401 N. Main St., Winston-Salem, NC 27101; (336) 741-2000; www.reynoldsamerican.com; Susan M. Cameron; 2nd-largest U.S. producer of cigarettes (Winston, Camel, Pall Mall, Kool, Doral). Announced plans to acquire Lorillard, 7/15/2014.

Rite Aid Corp. (RAD): 30 Hunter Ln., Camp Hill, PA 17011; (717) 761-2633; www.riteaid.com; John T. Standley; retail drugstores.

Rock-Tenn Co. (RKT): 504 Thrasher St., Norcross, GA 30071; (770) 448-2193; www.rocktenn.com; J. Powell Brown; corrugated and consumer packaging. Acquired Tacoma Mill, 5/16/2014.

Rockwell Automation, Inc. (ROK): 1201 S. 2nd St., Milwaukee, WI 53204; (414) 382-2000; www.rockwellautomation.com; Keith D. Nosbusch; industrial automation co.

Rohm and Haas Co.: see Dow Chemical Co.

Ryder System, Inc. (R): 11690 NW 105th St., Miami, FL 33178; (305) 500-3726; www.ryder.com; Robert E. Sanchez; truck-leasing service.

SABMiller plc: 1 Stanhope Gate, London, W1K 1AF, United Kingdom; + 44 1483 264000; www.sabmiller.com; Alan Clark; brewing company (Miller, Peroni, Grolsch). Acquired Foster's Group Ltd., 12/16/2011.

Safeway Inc. (SWY): 5918 Stoneridge Mall Rd., Pleasanton, CA 94588; (925) 467-3000; www.safeway.com; Robert Edwards; supermarkets. Announced plans to merge with Albertsons, 3/6/2014.

Sara Lee Corp.: see Hillshire Brands Co.

Schering-Plough Corp.: see Merck & Co., Inc.

Sears Holdings Corp. (SHLD): 3333 Beverly Rd., Hoffman Estates, IL 60179; (847) 286-2500; www.searsholdings.com; Edward S. Lampert; U.S. retailer. Spun off Land's End, Inc., 4/4/2014.

Shell Oil Co.: 910 Louisiana St., Houston, TX 77002; (713) 241-6161; www.shell.us; Ben van Beurden; integrated oil co.; subsidiary of Royal Dutch Shell, world's 2nd-largest oil co.

Sherwin-Williams Co. (SHW): 101 W. Prospect Ave., Cleveland, OH 44115; (216) 566-2000; www.sherwin-williams.com; Christopher M. Connor; paint and varnish producer (Dutch Boy, Krylon, Minwax).

Smithfield Foods, Inc.: 200 Commerce St., Smithfield, VA 23430; (757) 365-3000; www.smithfieldfoods.com; C. Larry Pope; largest U.S. producer and processor of pork. Subsidiary of China-based WH Group since 9/26/2013.

J. M. Smucker Co. (SJM): One Strawberry Ln., Orrville, OH 44667; (330) 682-3000; www.smuckers.com; Timothy P. Smucker; leading producer of fruit spreads, peanut butter (Jif), oils (Crisco), coffee (Folgers), baking prods. (Pillsbury).

Smurfit-Stone Container Corp.: see Rock-Tenn Co.

Sony Corp. of America: 550 Madison Ave., NY, NY 10022; (212) 833-6800; www.sony.com; Michael Lynton; U.S. subsidiary of Japan-based Sony Corp.; electronics, movies, music.

Southwest Airlines Co. (LUV): 2702 Love Field Dr., Dallas, TX 75235; (214) 792-4000; www.southwest.com; Gary C. Kelly; air transportation. Acquired AirTran Holdings, Inc., 5/2/2011.

Sprint Nextel Corp. (S): 6200 Sprint Pkwy., Overland Park, KS 66251; (703) 433-4000; www.sprint.com; Dan Hesse; wireless and long-distance telecommunications. Sold 72% of co. shares to SoftBank Corp., 7/5/2013.

Stanley Black & Decker, Inc. (SWK): 1000 Stanley Dr., New Britain, CT 06053; (860) 225-5111; www.stanleyblackanddecker.com; John F. Lundgren; one of the top U.S. mfrs. of hand and power prods. (DeWalt, Bostitch), household prods. (Kwikset, Baldwin).

Staples, Inc. (SPLS): 500 Staples Dr., Framingham, MA 01702; (508) 253-5000; www.staples.com; Ronald L. Sargent; office-supply retailer. Acquired online retail software co. Runa, 10/2/2013; acquired PNI Digital Media, 7/11/2014.

Starbucks Corp. (SBUX): 2401 Utah Ave. S., Seattle, WA 98134; (206) 447-1575; www.starbucks.com; Howard D. Schultz; coffee producer; world's leading specialty coffee retailer.

Starwood Hotels & Resorts Worldwide, Inc. (HOT): 1 StarPoint, Stamford, CT 06902; (203) 964-6000; www.starwoodhotels.com; Frits van Paasschen; hotel and resort co. (Westin, Sheraton, W Hotels).

State Farm Mutual Automobile Ins. Co.: 1 State Farm Plz., Bloomington, IL 61710; (309) 766-2311; www.statefarm.com; Edward B. Rust Jr.; largest U.S. provider of auto/homeowners insurance. Agreed to sell Canadian operations to Desjardins Group, 1/15/2014.

Sun Microsystems, Inc.: see Oracle Corp.

SUPERVALU Inc. (SVU): East View Innovation Ctr., 7075 Flying Cloud Dr., Eden Prairie, MN 55344; (952) 828-4000; www.supervalu.com; Sam Duncan; food retailer, wholesale distrib. (Acme, Albertsons, Shoppers).

SYSCO Corp. (SYY): 1390 Enclave Pkwy., Houston, TX 77077; (281) 584-1390; www.sysco.com; William J. DeLaney; food-service distrib. Agreed to acquire U.S. Foods, 12/9/2013.

Systemax Inc. (SYX): 11 Harbor Park Dr., Port Washington, NY 11050; (516) 608-7000; www.systemax.com; Richard Leeds; computers, electronics, industrial prod. retailer.

Target Corp. (TGT): 1000 Nicollet Mall, Minneapolis, MN 55403; (612) 304-6073; www.target.com; Brian Cornell; 2nd-largest U.S. discount retailer.

Tenneco Inc. (TEN): 500 N. Field Dr., Lake Forest, IL 60045; (847) 482-5000; www.tenneco.com; Gregg M. Sherrill; automotive parts (Monroe, Walker).

Texas Instruments Inc. (TXN): 12500 TI Blvd., Dallas, TX 75266; (972) 995-2011; www.ti.com; Richard K. Templeton; processors, semiconductors, software, handheld calculators.

Textron Inc. (TXT): 40 Westminster St., Providence, RI 02903; (401) 421-2800; www.textron.com; Scott C. Donnelly; aircraft (Cessna, Bell, Beechcraft), industrial, automotive prods.; financial services.

3M Co. (MMM): 3M Center, St. Paul, MN 55144; (651) 733-1110; www.3m.com; Inge G. Thulin; abrasives, adhesives, electrical, health care, cleaning (Scotch-Brite, O-Cel-O sponges, Scotchgard), printing, consumer prods. (Scotch Tape, Post-it).

TIAA-CREF: 730 Third Ave., NY, NY 10017; (212) 490-9000; www.tiaa-cref.org; Roger W. Ferguson Jr.; financial services provider. Agreed to buy Nuveen Investments, 4/14/2014.

Time Inc. (TIME): 1271 Ave. of the Americas, NY, NY 10020; (212) 522-1212; Joseph A. Ripp; magazine publishing (*Time, Sports Illustrated, People, Fortune*). Spun off from Time Warner, 6/9/2014.

Time Warner Inc. (TWX): One Time Warner Ctr., NY, NY 10019; (212) 484-8000; www.timewarner.com; Jeffrey L. Bewkes; TV and CATV (Cartoon Network, HBO, CNN, TBS, TNT), motion pictures (Warner Bros.), recordings. AOL and Time Warner completed the largest corporate merger in history in 2001; Time Warner spun off AOL, 12/9/2009. Spun off magazine holdings as Time Inc., 6/9/2014.

TJX Cos., Inc. (TJX): 770 Cochituate Rd., Framingham, MA 01701; (508) 390-1000; www.tjx.com; Carol Meyrowitz; off-price apparel retailer (T.J. Maxx, Marshalls); home furnishing retailer (HomeGoods).

Toro Co. (TTC): 8111 Lyndale Ave. S, Bloomington, MN 55420; (952) 888-8801; www.thetorocompany.com; Michael J. Hoffman; lawn and turf maintenance prods. (Lawn-Boy), snow removal equip.; irrigation systems.

Toys "R" Us, Inc.: 1 Geoffrey Way, Wayne, NJ 07470; (973) 617-3500; www.toysrus.com; Antonio Urcelay; children's specialty retailer.

Tribune Co.: 435 N. Michigan Ave., Chicago, IL 60611; (312) 222-9100; www.tribune.com; Peter Liguori; broadcasting (incl. WGN and 23 other television and radio stations). Emerged from Chap. 11 reorganization, 12/31/2012. Spun off newspaper holdings (*L.A. Times, Chicago Tribune*) as Tribune Publishing Co., 8/4/2014.

Trinity Industries, Inc. (TRN): 2525 Stemmons Fwy., Dallas, TX 75207; (214) 631-4420; www.trin.net; Timothy R. Wallace; mfr. metal prods., rail and freight equip. Agreed to acquire Thomas & Betts' Utility Steel Structures Division, 6/27/2014.

Twitter, Inc. (TWTR): 1355 Market St., San Francisco, CA, 94103; (415) 222-9670; twitter.com; Dick Costolo; microblogging/social networking services.

Tyco Intl. Ltd. (TYC): 9 Roszel Rd., Princeton, NJ 08540; (609) 720-4200; www.tyco.com; George R. Oliver; security and fire safety prods. Acquired Exacq Technologies, 7/29/2013. Bought fire protection services co. Westfire, 11/14/2013.

Tyson Foods, Inc. (TSN): 2200 W. Don Tyson Pkwy., Springdale, AR 72762; (479) 290-4000; www.tysonfoods.com; Donnie Smith; fresh and processed poultry; beef and pork prods. Announced plans to acquire Hillshire Brands Co., 7/2/2014.

UBS Financial Services Inc.: 1285 Ave. of the Americas, NY, NY 10019; (212) 713-2000; www.ubs.com; Sergio P. Ermotti; financial services; subsidiary of Switzerland's UBS AG.

Unilever USA (UN/UL): 800 Sylvan Ave., Englewood Cliffs, NJ 07632; (201) 894-4000; www.unilever.com; Paul Polman; food (Hellmann's mayonnaise, Knorr soups, Wish-Bone salad dressing, Lipton, Slim-Fast), hygiene prods. (Dove, Q-tips, Vaseline). Subsidiary of Unilever NV (Neth.) and Unilever plc (UK).

Union Pacific Corp. (UNP): 1400 Douglas St., Omaha, NE, 68179; (402) 544-5000; www.up.com; John J. Koraleski; one of the largest railroad freight cos. in U.S.

Unisys Corp. (UIS): 801 Lakeview Dr., Ste. 100, Blue Bell, PA 19422; (215) 986-4011; www.unisys.com; J. Edward Coleman; designs, manuf. computer information systems; IT consulting.

United Continental Holdings, Inc. (UAL): 77 W. Wacker Dr., Chicago IL 60601; (312) 997-8000; www.unitedcontinentalholdings.com; Jeffery A. Smisek; air transportation (United Airlines, Continental Airlines).

United Parcel Service, Inc. (UPS): 55 Glenlake Pkwy. NE, Atlanta, GA 30328; (404) 828-6000; www.ups.com; D. Scott Davis; shipping, logistics. Acquired UK-based pharmaceutical logistics firm Polar Speed, 2/11/2014.

United States Steel Corp. (X): 600 Grant St., Pittsburgh, PA 15219; (412) 433-1121; www.ussteel.com; Mario Longhi; steel, tin prods., resource mgmt.

United Technologies Corp. (UTX): One Financial Plz., Hartford, CT 06103; (860) 728-7000; www.utc.com; Louis R. Chênevert; aerospace, industrial prods. and services (Carrier, Otis, Pratt & Whitney, Sikorsky).

UnitedHealth Group Inc. (UNH): UHG Center, 9900 Bren Rd. E., Minnetonka, MN 55343; (952) 936-1300; www.unitedhealthgroup.com; Stephen J. Hemsley; health insurer.

Valero Energy Corp. (VLO): One Valero Way, San Antonio, TX 78249; (210) 345-2000; www.valero.com; Joe Gorder; fuel mfg. and marketing. Spun off CST Brands, 5/1/2013.

Verizon Communications Inc. (VZ): 140 West St., NY, NY 10007; (212) 395-1000; www.verizon.com; Lowell C. McAdam; broadband, wireless, wireline services provider. Acquired Vodafone's 45% stake in Verizon Wireless, giving it full ownership, 2/21/2014.

VF Corp. (VFC): 105 Corporate Center Blvd., Greensboro, NC 27408; (336) 424-6000; www.vfc.com; Eric C. Wiseman; apparel (Lee, Wrangler, North Face, Timberland). Acquired Timberland 9/13/2011.

Viacom Inc. (VIA): 1515 Broadway, NY, NY 10036; (212) 258-6000; www.viacom.com; Philippe P. Dauman; media networks (BET, Comedy Central, MTV, VH1, Nickelodeon); movies (Paramount).

Visteon Corp. (VC): One Village Center Dr., Van Buren Twp., MI 48111; (734) 710-5000; www.visteon.com; Timothy D. Leuliette; automotive parts mfr. Acquired Johnson Controls' automotive electronics business, 7/1/2014.

Walgreen Co. (Walgreens) (WAG): 200 Wilmot Rd., Deerfield, IL 60015; (847) 940-2500; www.walgreens.com; Gregory D. Wasson; retail drugstores.

Wal-Mart Stores, Inc. (WMT): 702 SW 8th St., Bentonville, AR 72716; (479) 273-4000; www.walmartstores.com; Doug McMillon; world's largest retailer; discount stores, discount warehouse clubs (Sam's Club).

Washington Post Co.: see Graham Holdings.

Waste Management, Inc. (WM): 1001 Fannin St., Ste. 4000, Houston, TX 77002; (713) 512-6200; www.wm.com; David P. Steiner; North America's largest waste co., recycler.

WellPoint, Inc. (WLP): 120 Monument Cir., Indianapolis, IN 46204; (317) 488-6000; www.wellpoint.com; Joseph R. Swedish; U.S. health benefits co.; HMOs and PPOs, an independent licensee of the Blue Cross Blue Shield Assn.

Wells Fargo & Co. (WFC): 420 Montgomery St., San Francisco, CA 94163; (866) 249-3302; www.wellsfargo.com; John G. Stumpf; financial services.

Wendy's Co. (WEN): 1 Dave Thomas Blvd., Dublin, OH 43017; (614) 764-3100; www.aboutwendys.com; Emil J. Brolick; fast food restaurants.

Western Union Co. (WU): 12500 E. Belford Ave., Englewood, CO 80112; (720) 332-1000; www.westernunion.com; Hikmet Ersek; money transfers, payment services.

Weyerhaeuser Co. (WY): 33663 Weyerhaeuser Way S., Federal Way, WA 98001; (253) 924-2345; www.weyerhaeuser.com; Doyle R. Simons; produces, distributes wood prods.; real estate development. Announced plan to spin off real estate business, 5/12/2014.

Whirlpool Corp. (WHR): 2000 N. M-63, Benton Harbor, MI 49022; (269) 923-5000; www.whirlpoolcorp.com; Jeff M. Fettig; mfr. of major home appliances (KitchenAid, Amana, Maytag).

Whole Foods Market, Inc. (WFM): 550 Bowie St., Austin, TX 78703; (512) 477-4455; www.wholefoodsmarket.com; John P. Mackey/Walter Robb; grocery stores specializing in natural/organic foods.

Winnebago Industries, Inc. (WGO): 605 W. Crystal Lake Rd., Forest City, IA 50436; (641) 585-3535; www.winnebagoind.com; Randy J. Potts; mfr. of motor homes, recreational vehicles (RVs).

Wm. Wrigley Jr. Co.: see Mars, Inc.

World Fuel Services Corp. (INT): 9800 NW 41st St., Ste. 400, Miami, FL 33178; (305) 428-8000; www.wfscorp.com; Michael J. Kasbar; marketer and financer of fuel to large-scale aviation and marine-related firms. Acquired Watson Petroleum Ltd., 3/10/2014.

Xerox Corp. (XRX): 45 Glover Ave., P.O. Box 4505, Norwalk, CT 06856; (203) 968-3000; www.xerox.com; Ursula M. Burns; printers, multifunction devices, document publishing technology and support.

Yahoo! Inc. (YHOO): 701 First Ave., Sunnyvale, CA 94089; (408) 349-3300; www.yahoo.com; Marissa Mayer; Internet media

co. Acquired blogging platform and social networking site Tumblr, 6/20/2013.

Yum! Brands, Inc. (YUM): 1441 Gardiner Ln., Louisville, KY 40213; (502) 874-8300; www.yum.com; David C. Novak; fast food restaurants (Pizza Hut, KFC, Taco Bell). Sold Long John Silver's, 12/5/2011; sold A&W, 12/19/2011.

Labor Unions and Professional Organizations

Source: Bureau of Labor Statistics, U.S. Dept. of Labor; AFL-CIO; World Almanac research

= Member of Change to Win Federation, formed in 2005 by unions disaffiliated from AFL-CIO. * = Independent union or one not otherwise affiliated with Change to Win or AFL-CIO. All other unions listed are affiliated with AFL-CIO as of 2014. Year established is in parentheses.

Labor Unions

Air Line Pilots Assn. (ALPA) (1931): 48,500+ members, 31 U.S. and Canadian airlines; (703) 689-2270; www.alpa.org

American Federation of Labor and Congress of Industrial Organizations (AFL-CIO) (1955): federation of 56 unions, 11.6 mil+ members; (202) 637-5000; www.aflcio.org

Automobile, Aerospace & Agricultural Implement Workers of America, International Union, United (UAW) (1935): 391,000+ members, 750+ locals; (313) 926-5000; www.uaw.org

Bakery, Confectionery, Tobacco Workers, and Grain Millers International Union (BCTGM) (1886): nearly 74,000+ members, 147 locals; (301) 933-8600; www.bctgm.org

Bricklayers and Allied Craftworkers, International Union of (BAC) (1865): 76,000+ members, 50 locals; (202) 783-3788; www.bacweb.org

***Carpenters and Joiners of America, United Brotherhood of (UBC)** (1881): 500,000 members, 600+ locals; (202) 546-6206; www.carpenters.org

#Change to Win Federation (2005): 4 unions, ex-affiliates of AFL-CIO, 4.2 mil+ members; (202) 721-0660; www.changetowin.org

Communications Workers of America (CWA) (1938): 475,000+ members, 1,200 locals; (202) 434-1100; www.cwa-union.org

***Education Assn., Natl. (NEA)** (1857): 3 mil+ members, 14,000+ affiliates; (202) 833-4000; www.nea.org

Electrical Workers, International Brotherhood of (IBEW) (1891): nearly 660,000 members, 900 locals; (202) 833-7000; www.ibew.org

Engineers, International Union of Operating (IUOE) (1896): nearly 380,000 members, 123 locals; (202) 429-9100; www.iuoe.org

#Farm Workers of America, United (UFW) (1962): 10,000+ members; (661) 823-6151; www.ufw.org

***Federal Employees, Natl. Federation of (NFFE;** affiliated with IAMAW (1917): 110,000 members, nearly 200 locals; (202) 216-4420; www.nffe.org

Fire Fighters, International Assn. of (IAFF) (1918): nearly 295,000 members, 3,200+ locals; (202) 737-8484; www.iaff.org

Flight Attendants, Assn. of (AFA-CWA) (1945): 39,500+ members, 19 airlines; merged with Communications Workers of America in 2004; (202) 434-1300; www.afanet.org

#Food and Commercial Workers International Union, United (UFCW) (1979): nearly 1.3 mil members, 400+ locals; (202) 223-3111; www.ufcw.org

Glass, Molders, Pottery, Plastics and Allied Workers Intl. Union (GMP) (1842): nearly 28,000 members, 250+ locals; (610) 565-5051; www.gmpiu.org

Government Employees, American Federation of (AFGE) (1932): 301,000+ members, 1,100 locals; (202) 737-8700; www.afge.org

#Graphic Communications Conference (GCC/IBT) (1983): 70,000+ members; merged with Teamsters in 2005; (202) 462-1400; www.gciu.org

Iron Workers, Intl. Assn. of Bridge, Structural, Ornamental, and Reinforcing (1896): 120,000 members, 200+ locals; (202) 383-4800; www.ironworkers.org

Laborers' International Union of North America (LiUNA) (1903): nearly 558,000 members, 400 locals; (202) 737-8320; www.liuna.org

Letter Carriers, Natl. Assn. of (NALC) (1889): nearly 300,000 members, 2,300 locals; (202) 393-4695; www.nalc.org

#Locomotive Engineers and Trainmen, Brotherhood of (BLET) (1863): 52,000+ members, 500+ locals; (216) 241-2630; www.ble-t.org

Longshoremen's Assn., Intl. (ILA) (1892): 43,500 members, approx. 200 locals; (212) 425-1200; www.ilaunion.org

Machinists and Aerospace Workers, International Assn. of (IAM) (1888): 570,000+ members; affiliated with TCU in 2005; (301) 967-4500; www.goiam.org

#Maintenance of Way Employes, Division of the Intl. Brotherhood of Teamsters; Brotherhood of (BMWED) (1887): nearly 36,000 members, 770 locals; merged with Teamsters in 2004; (248) 662-2660; www.bmwed.org (Note: In honor of tradition, the union maintains the variant spelling of "employes" in its logo.)

Mine Workers of America, United (UMWA) (1890): 73,000+ members, 600 locals; (703) 291-2400; www.umwa.org

Musicians of the United States and Canada, American Federation of (AFM) (1896): 79,000+ members, 240+ locals; (212) 869-1330; www.afm.org

Newspaper Guild—Communications Workers of America, The (TNG) (CWA) (1933): 34,000+ members, 90 locals; (202) 434-7177; www.newsguild.org

***Nurses Assn., American (ANA)** (1911): 146,000 members, 54 constituent state and territorial assns.; (301) 628-5000; www.nursingworld.org

Office and Professional Employees Intl. Union (OPEIU) (1945): 113,000+ members, 200 locals; (800) 346-7348; www.opeiu.org

Painters and Allied Trades, International Union of (IUPAT) (1887): nearly 104,000 members, 425 locals; (410) 564-5900; www.iupat.org

Plumbing and Pipe Fitting Industry of the U.S. and Canada, United Assn. of Journeymen and Apprentices of the (UA) (1889): 370,000+ members, 300+ locals; (410) 269-2000; www.ua.org

***Police, Fraternal Order of** (1915): 325,000+ members, 2,100+ affiliates; (615) 399-0900; www.grandlodgefop.org

Police Assns., International Union of (IUPA) (1979): 80,000 members; (941) 487-2560; www.iupa.org

Postal Workers Union, American (APWU) (1971): 238,000+ members, 1,000+ locals; (202) 842-4200; www.apwu.org

Roofers, Waterproofers and Allied Workers, United Union of (1906): 22,000 members; (202) 463-7663; www.unionroofers.com

***Rural Letter Carriers' Assn., Natl.** (1903): 100,000+ members, 50 state org.; (703) 684-5545; www.nrlca.org

***Security, Police, Fire Professionals of America, Intl. Union, (SPFPA)** (1948): 24,500+ members, 200 locals; (586) 772-7250; www.spfpa.org

#Service Employees International Union (SEIU) (1921): nearly 1.9 mil members, 150+ locals; (202) 730-7000; www.seiu.org

Sheet Metal, Air, Rail, and Transportation Workers, Int. Assn. of (SMART) (2008, from merger of Sheet Metal Workers' Intl. Assn. and United Transportation Union): 216,000 members, 700 locals; (202) 662-0800; www.smart-union.org

State, County, and Municipal Employees, American Federation of (AFSCME) (1932): nearly 1.4 mil members, 3,400 locals; (202) 429-1000; www.afscme.org

Steel, Paper and Forestry, Rubber, Manufacturing, Energy, Allied Industrial and Service Workers International Union, United (USW) (2005): 599,000+ members, 1,800+ locals; formed from merger of the unions United Steelworkers of America (USWA) (1936) and Paper, Allied-Industrial, Chemical and Energy Workers (PACE) (1999); (412) 562-2400; www.usw.org

Teachers, American Federation of (AFT) (1916): 1.5 mil+ members, 3,000+ locals; (202) 879-4400; www.aft.org

#Teamsters, International Brotherhood of (IBT) (1903): 1.2 mil+ members, 475 locals; (202) 624-6800; www.teamster.org

Theatrical Stage Employees, Moving Picture Technicians, Artists and Allied Crafts of the U.S., Its Territories, and Canada, Intl. Alliance of (IATSE) (1893): 116,000+ members, 375+ locals; (212) 730-1770; www.iatse-intl.org

Transit Union, Amalgamated (ATU) (1892): 192,000+ members, 270 locals; (202) 537-1645; www.atu.org

Transport Workers Union of America (TWU) (1934): 115,000+ members, 114 locals; (212) 719-3900; www.twu.org

Transportation Communications Intl. Union (TCU) (1899): affiliated with IAM in 2005; see Machinists and Aerospace Workers.

***Treasury Employees Union, Natl. (NTEU)** (1938): 82,000+ members, 270+ chapters; (202) 572-5500; www.nteu.org

UNITE HERE (UNITE, 1900; **HERE,** 1891; merged 2004): 251,000+ members; (212) 265-7000; www.unitehere.org

#Workers United (affiliated with SEIU) (2009): 83,796 members

***Writers Guild of America, West** (1933): nearly 12,000 members; (323) 951-4000; www.wga.org

Professional Organizations and Societies

Accountants, American Institute of Certified Public (1887): 394,000+ members; (888) 777-7077; www.aicpa.org

ACMP—The Chamber Music Network (1947): 5,400 members; (212) 645-7424; www.acmp.net

Actuaries, Soc. of (1949): 22,000+ members; (847) 706-3500; www.soa.org

Administrative Professionals, Intl. Assn. of (1942): 24,000 members; (816) 891-6600; www.iaap-hq.org

Aerospace Medical Assn. (1929): 2,600+ members; (703) 739-2240; www.asma.org

Agricultural and Biological Engineers, American Soc. of (1907): 8,000 members; (269) 429-0300; www.asabe.org

AIGA (formerly American Institute of Graphic Arts) (1914): 25,000+ members; (212) 807-1990; www.aiga.org

Air & Waste Management Assn. (1907): 5,000+ members; (412) 232-3444; www.awma.org

AMSUS—The Society of the Federal Health Professionals (1891): nearly 8,000 members; (301) 897-8800; www.amsus.org

APICS—The Assn. for Operations Management (1957): 37,000+ members; (773) 867-1777; www.apics.org

Architects, American Institute of (1857): 81,000+ members; (202) 626-7300; www.aia.org

ASIS Intl. (formerly Amer. Soc. for Industrial Security) (1955): 38,000+ members; (703) 519-6200; www.asisonline.org

Astrologers, Inc., American Federation of (1938): 4,000 members; (480) 838-1751; www.astrologers.com

Astronautical Society, American (1954): 1,400 members; (703) 866-0020; www.astronautical.org

Astronomical Society, American (1899): 7,000 members; (202) 328-2010; www.aas.org

Authors Guild, The (1912): 9,000+ members; (212) 563-5904; www.authorsguild.org

Bankers of America, Independent Community (1930): nearly 5,000 members; (202) 659-8111; www.icba.org

Bar Assn., American (1878): nearly 400,000 members; (312) 988-5000; www.abanet.org

Bar Assn., Federal (1920): 16,000+ members; (571) 481-9100; www.fedbar.org

Biochemistry and Molecular Biology, American Society for (1906): 12,000+ members; (240) 283-6600; www.asbmb.org

Broadcasters, Natl. Assn. of (1923): 8,300 members; (202) 429-5300; www.nab.org

Business Women's Assn., American (1949): 40,000 members; (800) 228-0007; www.abwa.org

Cartoonists Society, Natl. (1946): 500+ members; (407) 647-8839; www.reuben.org

Ceramic Society, American (1898): 9,500+ members; (240) 646-7054; www.ceramics.org

Chemical Society, American (1876): 164,000+ members; (202) 872-4600; www.chemistry.org

Chiefs of Police, Intl. Assn. of (1893): 20,000+ members; (703) 836-6767; www.theiacp.org

Chiropractic Assn., American (1963): 15,000 members; (703) 276-8800; www.acatoday.org

Civil Engineers, American Soc. of (1852): 145,000+ members; (703) 295-6300; www.asce.org

College Admission Counseling, Natl. Assn. for (1937): 13,000+ members; (703) 836-2222; www.nacacnet.org

Commercial Law League of America (1895): nearly 3,000 members; (312) 240-1400; www.clla.org

Communication Assn., Natl. (1914): 8,000+ members; (202) 464-4622; www.natcom.org

Composers, Authors & Publishers, American Soc. of (ASCAP) (1914): 500,000+ members; (212) 621-6000; www.ascap.com

Computing Machinery, Assn. for (1947): 100,000+ members; (212) 626-0500; www.acm.org

Computing Professionals, Institute for the Certification of (1973): nearly 55,000 members; (847) 299-4227; www.iccp.org

Construction Inspectors, Assn. of (1974): 1,000 members; (760) 327-5284; www.aci-assoc.org

Counseling Assn., American (1952): 50,000+ members; (800) 347-6647; www.counseling.org

Country Music Assn. (1958): 7,100+ members; (615) 244-2840; www.cmaworld.com

Customs Brokers and Forwarders Assn. of America, Inc., Natl. (1897): nearly 940 cos.; (202) 466-0222; www.ncbfaa.org

Dental Assn., American (1859): 158,000+ members; (312) 440-2500; www.ada.org

Directors Guild of America (1936): 15,000+ members; (310) 289-2000; www.dga.org

Electrical and Electronics Engineers, Institute of (1963): 430,000+ members; (732) 981-0060; www.ieee.org

Electronics Technicians, Intl. Soc. of Certified (1980): 50,000+ members; (817) 921-9101; www.iscet.org

Energy Engineers, Assn. of (1977): 16,000+ members; (770) 447-5083; www.aeecenter.org

Engineers, Natl. Society of Professional (1934): 35,000 members; (703) 684-2800; www.nspe.org

Environmental Assessment Assn. (1972): 3,500 members; (877) 743-6806; www.eaa-assoc.org

Environmental Health Assn., Natl. (1937): 4,500+ members; (303) 756-9090; www.neha.org

Family Physicians, American Academy of (1947): 115,900+ members; (913) 906-6000; www.aafp.org

Farm Bureau Federation, American (1919): 6.2 mil+ members; (202) 406-3600; www.fb.org

Farmers Union, Natl. (1902): 250,000 families; (202) 554-1600; www.nfu.org

Financial Professionals, Assn. for (1979): 16,000+ members; (301) 907-2862; www.afponline.org

Financial Service Professionals, Soc. of (1928): 15,000 members; (610) 526-2500; www.financialpro.org

Fire Chiefs, Intl. Assn. of (1873): 10,000+ members; (703) 273-0911; www.iafc.org

Fire Protection Engineers, Soc. of (1950): 4,500+ members; (301) 718-2910; www.sfpe.org

Food Technologists, Institute of (1939): 22,000 members; (312) 782-8424; www.ift.org

Forensic Sciences, American Academy of (1948): 6,260 members; (719) 636-1100; www.aafs.org

Funeral Directors Assn., Natl. (1882): 19,000 members; (262) 789-1880; www.nfda.org

General Contractors of America, Associated (1918): 30,000+ cos.; (703) 548-3118; www.agc.org

Geographers, Assn. of American (1904): 10,000 members; (202) 234-1450; www.aag.org

Ground Water Assn., Natl. (1948): 12,000+ members; (614) 898-7791; www.ngwa.org

Heating, Refrigerating and Air-Conditioning Engineers, Inc., American Soc. of (1894): 54,000+ members; (404) 636-8400; www.ashrae.org

Home Builders, Natl. Assn. of (1942): 140,000+ members; (202) 266-8200; www.nahb.org

Human Resource Management, Soc. for (SHRM) (1948): 250,000+ members; (703) 548-3440; www.shrm.org

Illustrators, Society of (1901): 1,000 members; (212) 838-2560; www.societyillustrators.org

Industrial Designers Society of America (1965): 3,200+ members; (703) 707-6000; www.idsa.org

Intelligence Officers, Assn. of Former (1975): 18 chap., 5,000+ members; (703) 790-0320; www.afio.com

Interior Designers, American Soc. of (1975): 24,000+ members; (202) 546-3480; www.asid.org

Investigative Pathology, American Soc. for (1900): 1,718 members; (301) 634-7130; www.asip.org

Jail Assn., American (1981): 4,000+ members; (301) 790-3930; www.aja.org

Journalists, Society of Professional (1909): 9,000 members; (317) 927-8000; www.spj.org

Journalists and Authors, American Soc. of (1948): 1,200+ members; (212) 997-0947; www.asja.org

Judicature Society, American (1913): 6,000 members; (615) 873-4675; www.ajs.org

Landscape Architects, American Society of (1899): 15,000+ members; (202) 898-2444; www.asla.org

Legal Administrators, Assn. of (1971): 10,000+ members; (847) 267-1252; www.alanet.org

Library Assn., American (1876): 58,000 members; (800) 545-2433; www.ala.org

Lifesaving Assn., U.S. (1964): 11,000 members; (866) 367-8752; www.usla.org

Logistics, Intl. Society of (SOLE) (1966): 3,000+ members; (301) 459-8446; www.sole.org

Magicians, Intl. Brotherhood of (1922): 13,000 members; (636) 724-2400; www.magician.org

Management Accountants, Inst. of (1919): 65,000+ members; (201) 573-9000; www.imanet.org

Management Assn., American (1923): 4,100 cos., 38,000 ind.; (212) 903-7976; www.amanet.org

Marketing Assn., American (1937): 30,000+ members; (312) 542-9000; www.marketingpower.com

Master Brewers Assn. of the Americas (1887): 2,700+ members; (651) 454-7250; www.mbaa.com

Material and Process Engineering, Soc. for the Advancement of (1944): 4,500 members; (626) 331-0616; www.sampe.org

Mechanical Engineers, American Soc. of (1880): 130,000+ members; (973) 882-1170; www.asme.org

Medical Assn., American (1847): 250,000 members; (800) 621-8335; www.ama-assn.org

Medical Library Assn. (1898): 4,000+ members; (312) 419-9094; www.mlanet.org

Motion Picture Arts & Sciences, Academy of (1927): 6,000+ members; (310) 247-3000; www.oscars.org

Motion Picture and Television Engineers, Soc. of (1916): 6,000+ members; (914) 761-1100; www.smpte.org

Mystery Writers of America (1945): 3,000+ members; (212) 888-8171; www.mysterywriters.org

NALS...the association for legal professionals (formerly the Natl. Assn. of Legal Secretaries) (1929): 6,000 members; (918) 582-5188; www.nals.org

Notaries, American Society of (1965): approx. 20,000 members; (850) 671-5164; www.notaries.org

Nursing, Natl. League for (1893): 33,000 members, 1,200 institutions; (800) 669-1656; www.nln.org

Operations Management, Assn. for (APICS) (1957): 37,000+ members, 250+ intl. partners; (773) 867-1777; www.apics.org

Optometric Assn., American (1898): 36,000 members; (800) 365-2219; www.aoa.org

Organists, American Guild of (1896): 20,000 members; (212) 870-2310; www.agohq.org

Pen Women, Natl. League of American (1897): 2,600+ members; (202) 785-1997; www.nlapw.org

Pharmacists Assn., American (1852): 62,000+ members; (202) 628-4410; www.pharmacist.com

Physical Therapy Assn., American (1921): 88,000+ members; (703) 684-2782; www.apta.org

Plastics Engineers, Society of (1942): 15,000+ members; (203) 775-0471; www.4spe.org

Police Assn.—United States Section, Intl. (1962): 10,000 members; (855) 241-9998; www.ipa-usa.org

Population Assn. of America (1930): 3,000 members; (301) 565-6710; www.populationassociation.org

Postmasters of the U.S., Natl. Assn. of (1898): 42,000+ members, 95 clubs; (703) 683-9027; www.napus.org

Press Club, Natl. (1908): 3,500+ members; (202) 662-7500; www.press.org

Professional Ball Players of America, Assn. of (1924): 11,000 members; (714) 528-2012; www.apbpa.org

Professional Beauty Assn. (1904): 12,000+ members; (480) 281-0424; www.probeauty.org

Psychiatric Assn., American (1844): 35,000+ members; (703) 907-7300; www.psychiatry.org

Psychological Assn., American (1892): nearly 130,000 members; (202) 336-5500; www.apa.org

Public Administration, American Soc. for (1939): 8,000 members; (202) 393-7878; www.aspanet.org

Public Health Assn., American (1872): 25,000+ members; (202) 777-2742; www.apha.org

Public Relations Soc. of America (1947): 21,000+ members; (212) 460-1400; www.prsa.org

Range Management, Society for (1948): 4,000+ members; (303) 986-3309; www.rangelands.org

Real Estate Appraisers, Natl. Assn. of (1966): 10,000+ members; (877) 743-6806; www.narea-assoc.org

Rehabilitation Assn., Natl. (1923): 5,600 members; (703) 836-0850; www.nationalrehab.org

Road & Transportation Builders Assn., American (1902): 6,000+ members; (202) 289-4434; www.artba.org

Safety Engineers, American Soc. of (1911): 35,000+ members; (847) 699-2929; www.asse.org

School Administrators, American Assn. of (1865): 13,000+ members; (703) 528-0700; www.aasa.org

Science Teachers Assn., Natl. (1944): 55,000 members; (703) 243-7100; www.nsta.org

Science Writers, Natl. Assn. of (1955): 2,100+ members; (510) 647-9500; www.nasw.org

Screen Actors Guild—American Federation of Television and Radio Artists (2012): 165,000+ members; (855) 724-2387; www.sagaftra.org

Songwriters Guild of America (1931): 5,000+ members; (615) 742-9945; www.songwritersguild.com

Sportscasters Assn., American (1980): 500+ members; (212) 227-8080; www.americansportscastersonline.com

Surgeons, American College of (1913): 80,000 members; (312) 202-5000; www.facs.org

Tax Administrators, Federation of (1937): (202) 624-5890; www.taxadmin.org

Teachers of English, Natl. Council of (1911): 35,000+ members; (217) 328-3870; www.ncte.org

Teachers of English to Speakers of Other Languages, Inc. (1966): 13,040 members; (703) 836-0774; www.tesol.org

Teachers of French, American Assn. of (1927): nearly 10,000 members; (618) 453-5731; www.frenchteachers.org

Teachers of German, American Assn. of (1926): 4,000+ members; (856) 795-5553; www.aatg.org

Teachers of Mathematics, Natl. Council of (1920): 80,000 members; (703) 620-9840; www.nctm.org

Teachers of Spanish and Portuguese, American Assn. of (1917): 11,000+ members; (248) 960-2180; www.aatsp.org

Television Arts and Sciences, Natl. Academy of (1955): (212) 586-8424; www.emmyonline.org

Theological Library Assn., American (1946): 800+ members; (312) 454-5100; www.atla.com

Transportation Engineers, Inst. of (1930): nearly 17,000 members; (202) 785-0060; www.ite.org

Travel Agents, American Soc. of (1931): 12,000 members; (703) 739-2782; www.asta.org

Underwriters, Soc. of Chartered Property Casualty (1944): 22,000+ members; (800) 932-2728; www.cpcusociety.org

University Women, American Assn. of (1881): 100,000+ members; (202) 785-7700; www.aauw.org

Veterinary Medical Assn., American (1863): 85,000+ members; (800) 248-2862; www.avma.org

Women in Communications, The Assn. for (1909): 2,000+ members; (703) 370-7436; www.womcom.org

Women Engineers, Society of (1950): 17,000 members; (877) 793-4636; societyofwomenengineers.swe.org

Women in Media, Alliance for (1951): nearly 10,000 members; (703) 506-3290; www.allwomeninmedia.org

Professional Sports Organizations

Source: World Almanac research

Major League Baseball

Office of the Commissioner, 245 Park Ave., 31st Fl., New York, NY 10167; (212) 931-7800; www.mlb.com

American League

Baltimore Orioles (1953): 333 W. Camden St., Baltimore, MD 21201; (410) 685-9800; www.orioles.com

Boston Red Sox (1901): 4 Yawkey Way, Boston, MA 02215; (617) 267-9440; www.redsox.com

Chicago White Sox (1900, as Chicago White Stockings): 333 W. 35th St., Chicago, IL 60616; (312) 674-1000; www.whitesox.com

Cleveland Indians (1901, as Cleveland Blues): 2401 Ontario St., Cleveland, OH 44115; (216) 420-4200; www.indians.com

Detroit Tigers (1901): 2100 Woodward Ave., Detroit, MI 48201; (313) 471-2000; www.tigers.com

Houston Astros (1962, as Houston Colt .45s): 501 Crawford St., Houston, TX 77002; (713) 259-8000; www.astros.com. (The Astros were a National League team, 1962-2012; the franchise joined the AL West beginning with the 2013 season.)

Kansas City Royals (1969): One Royal Way, Kansas City, MO 64129; (816) 921-8000; www.royals.com

Los Angeles Angels of Anaheim (1961): 2000 Gene Autry Way, Anaheim, CA 92806; (714) 940-2000; www.angelsbaseball.com

Minnesota Twins (1960): 1 Twins Way, Minneapolis, MN 55403; (612) 659-3400; www.twinsbaseball.com

New York Yankees (1903): One E. 161st St., Bronx, NY 10451; (718) 293-4300; www.yankees.com

Oakland Athletics (1901, as Philadelphia Athletics): 7000 Coliseum Way, Oakland, CA 94621; (510) 638-4900; oakland.athletics.mlb.com

Seattle Mariners (1977): P.O. Box 4100, Seattle, WA 98194; (206) 346-4000; www.mariners.com

Tampa Bay Rays (1995, as Tampa Bay Devil Rays): One Tropicana Dr., St. Petersburg, FL 33705; (727) 825-3137; www.raysbaseball.com

Texas Rangers (1960, as Washington Senators): 1000 Ballpark Way, Arlington, TX 76011; (817) 273-5222; www.texasrangers.com

Toronto Blue Jays (1976): One Blue Jays Way, Ste. 3200, Toronto, ON M5V 1J1, Canada; (416) 341-1000; www.bluejays.com

National League

Arizona Diamondbacks (1998): 401 E. Jefferson St., Phoenix, AZ 85004; (602) 462-6500; www.dbacks.com

Atlanta Braves (1876, as Boston Red Stockings): 755 Hank Aaron Dr., Atlanta, GA 30315; (404) 522-7630; www.braves.com

Chicago Cubs (1876, as Chicago White Stockings): 1060 W. Addison, Chicago, IL 60613; (773) 404-2827; www.cubs.com

Cincinnati Reds (1869, as Cincinnati Red Stockings): 100 Main St., Cincinnati, OH 45202; (513) 765-7000; www.reds.com

Colorado Rockies (1991): 2001 Blake St., Denver, CO 80205; (303) 292-0200; www.coloradorockies.com

Houston Astros: see American League.

Los Angeles Dodgers (1890): 1000 Elysian Park Ave., Los Angeles, CA 90012; (323) 224-1500; www.dodgers.com

Miami Marlins (1991, as Florida Marlins): 501 Marlins Way, Miami, FL 33125; (305) 480-1300; www.marlins.com

Milwaukee Brewers (1970): One Brewers Way, Milwaukee, WI 53214; (414) 902-4400; www.brewers.com

New York Mets (1961): Citi Field, Flushing, NY 11368; (718) 507-6387; www.mets.com

Philadelphia Phillies (1883): One Citizens Bank Way, Philadelphia, PA 19148; (215) 463-6000; www.phillies.com

Pittsburgh Pirates (1887, as Pittsburgh Alleghenies): 115 Federal St., Pittsburgh, PA 15212; (412) 323-5000; www.pirates.com

St. Louis Cardinals (1892, as St. Louis Browns): 700 Clark St., St. Louis, MO 63102; (314) 345-9600; www.cardinals.com

San Diego Padres (1969): 100 Park Blvd., San Diego, CA 92101; (619) 795-5000; www.padres.com

San Francisco Giants (1883, as New York Gothams): 24 Willie Mays Plz., San Francisco, CA 94107; (415) 972-2000; www.sfgiants.com

Washington Nationals (1969, as Montréal Expos): 1500 South Capitol St., SE, Washington, DC 20003; (202) 675-6287; www.nationals.com

National Basketball Association

League Office, 645 Fifth Ave., New York, NY 10022; (212) 407-8000; www.nba.com

Atlanta Hawks (1949, as Tri-Cities Blackhawks): 101 Marietta St. NW, Ste. 1900, Atlanta, GA 30303; (866) 715-1500; www.nba.com/hawks/

Boston Celtics (1946): 226 Causeway St., 4th Fl., Boston, MA 02114; (866) 423-5849; www.nba.com/celtics/

Brooklyn Nets (1967, as New Jersey Americans): 15 MetroTech Ctr., 11th Fl., Brooklyn, NY 11201; (718) 933-3000; www.nba.com/nets/

Charlotte Hornets (2004, as Charlotte Bobcats): 333 E. Trade St., Charlotte, NC 28202; (704) 688-8600; www.nba.com/hornets/

Chicago Bulls (1966): 1901 W. Madison St., Chicago, IL 60612; (312) 455-4000; www.nba.com/bulls/

Cleveland Cavaliers (1970): One Center Ct., Cleveland, OH 44115; (216) 420-2000; www.nba.com/cavaliers/

Dallas Mavericks (1980): 2909 Taylor St., Dallas, TX 75226; (214) 747-6287; www.nba.com/mavericks/

Denver Nuggets (1967, as Denver Rockets): 1000 Chopper Cir., Denver, CO 80204; (303) 405-1100; www.nba.com/nuggets/

Detroit Pistons (1957): Six Championship Dr., Auburn Hills, MI 48326; (248) 377-0100; www.nba.com/pistons/

Golden State Warriors (1946, as Philadelphia Warriors): 1011 Broadway, Oakland, CA 94605; (510) 986-2200; www.nba.com/warriors/

Houston Rockets (1967, as San Diego Rockets): 1510 Polk St., Houston, TX 77002; (713) 627-3865; www.nba.com/rockets/

Indiana Pacers (1967): 125 S. Pennsylvania St., Indianapolis, IN 46204; (317) 917-2500; www.nba.com/pacers/

Los Angeles Clippers (1970, as Buffalo Braves): 1111 S. Figueroa St., Ste. 1100, Los Angeles, CA 90015; (213) 742-7500; www.nba.com/clippers/

Los Angeles Lakers (1947, as Minneapolis Lakers): 555 N. Nash St., El Segundo, CA 90245; (310) 426-6000; www.nba.com/lakers/

Memphis Grizzlies (1995, as Vancouver Grizzlies): 191 Beale St., Memphis, TN 38103; (901) 888-4667; www.nba.com/grizzlies/

Miami Heat (1988): 601 Biscayne Blvd., Miami, FL 33132; (786) 777-1000; www.nba.com/heat/

Milwaukee Bucks (1968): 1001 N. 4th St., Milwaukee, WI 53203; (414) 227-0500; www.nba.com/bucks/

Minnesota Timberwolves (1989): 600 1st Ave. North, Minneapolis, MN 55403; (612) 673-1600; www.nba.com/timberwolves/

New Orleans Pelicans (1988, as Charlotte Hornets): 5800 Airline Dr., Metairie, LA 70003; (504) 593-4700; www.nba.com/pelicans/

New York Knickerbockers (1946): Two Pennsylvania Plz., New York, NY 10121; (212) 465-6471; www.nba.com/knicks/

Oklahoma City Thunder (1967, as Seattle SuperSonics): 2 Leadership Square, 211 N. Robinson Ave., Ste. 300; Oklahoma City, OK 73102; (405) 208-4800; www.nba.com/thunder/

Orlando Magic (1989): 8701 Maitland Summit Blvd., Orlando, FL 32810; (407) 916-2400; www.nba.com/magic/

Philadelphia 76ers (1937, as Syracuse Nationals): 3601 S. Broad St., Philadelphia, PA 19148; (215) 339-7676; www.nba.com/sixers/

Phoenix Suns (1968): 201 E. Jefferson St., Phoenix, AZ 85004; (602) 379-7900; www.nba.com/suns/

Portland Trail Blazers (1970): One Center Ct., Ste. 200, Portland, OR 97227; (503) 234-9291; www.nba.com/blazers/

Sacramento Kings (1945, as Rochester Royals): One Sports Pkwy., Sacramento, CA 95834; (916) 928-0000; www.nba.com/kings/

San Antonio Spurs (1967, as Dallas Chaparrals): One AT&T Center, San Antonio, TX 78219; (210) 444-5000; www.nba.com/spurs/

Toronto Raptors (1995): 40 Bay St., Toronto, ON M5J 2X2, Canada; (416) 366-3865; www.nba.com/raptors/

Utah Jazz (1974, as New Orleans Jazz): 301 W. South Temple, Salt Lake City, UT 84101; (801) 325-2500; www.nba.com/jazz/

Washington Wizards (1961, as Chicago Packers): 601 F St. NW, Washington, DC 20004; (202) 661-5000; www.nba.com/wizards/

National Hockey League

NHL Headquarters, 1185 Ave. of the Americas, 15th Fl., New York, NY 10036; (212) 789-2000; www.nhl.com

Anaheim Ducks (1993): 2695 E. Katella Ave., Anaheim, CA 92806; (877) 945-3946; ducks.nhl.com

Boston Bruins (1924): 100 Legends Way, Boston, MA 02114; (617) 624-1900; bruins.nhl.com

Buffalo Sabres (1970): One Seymour H. Knox III Plz., Buffalo, NY 14203; (716) 855-4100; sabres.nhl.com

Calgary Flames (1980): P.O. Box 1540, Station M, Calgary, AB T2P 3B9, Canada; (403) 777-2177; flames.nhl.com

Carolina Hurricanes (1972, as New England Whalers): 1400 Edwards Mill Rd., Raleigh, NC 27607; (919) 467-7825; hurricanes.nhl.com

Chicago Blackhawks (1926): 1901 W. Madison St., Chicago, IL 60612; (312) 455-7000; blackhawks.nhl.com

Colorado Avalanche (1972, as Quebec Nordiques): 1000 Chopper Cir., Denver, CO 80204; (303) 405-1100; avalanche.nhl.com

Columbus Blue Jackets (2000): 200 W. Nationwide Blvd., Suite Level, Columbus, OH 43215; (614) 246-4625; bluejackets.nhl.com

Dallas Stars (1967, as Minnesota North Stars): 2601 Ave. of the Stars, Frisco, TX 75034; (214) 387-5500; stars.nhl.com

Detroit Red Wings (1926, as Detroit Cougars): 600 Civic Center Dr., Detroit, MI 48226; (313) 471-6606; redwings.nhl.com

Edmonton Oilers (1972, as Alberta Oilers): 11230 - 110 St., Edmonton, AB T5G 3H7, Canada; (780) 414-4000; oilers.nhl.com

Florida Panthers (1993): One Panther Pkwy., Sunrise, FL 33323; (954) 835-7000; panthers.nhl.com

Los Angeles Kings (1967): 1111 S. Figueroa St., Ste. 3100, Los Angeles, CA 90015; (213) 742-7100; kings.nhl.com

Minnesota Wild (2000): 317 Washington St., St. Paul, MN 55102; (651) 602-6000; wild.nhl.com

Montréal Canadiens (1917): 1909, avenue des Canadiens-de-Montréal, Montréal, QC H3C 5L2, Canada; (514) 932-2582; canadiens.nhl.com

Nashville Predators (1998): 501 Broadway, Nashville, TN 37203; (615) 770-2355; predators.nhl.com

New Jersey Devils (1974, as Kansas City Scouts): Prudential Center, 25 Lafayette St., Newark, NJ 07102; (973) 757-6100; devils.nhl.com

New York Islanders (1972): 1255 Hempstead Tpke., Uniondale, NY 11553; (516) 501-6700; islanders.nhl.com

New York Rangers (1926): Two Pennsylvania Plz., New York, NY 10121; (212) 465-6000; rangers.nhl.com

Ottawa Senators (1992): 1000 Palladium Dr., Ottawa, ON K2V 1A5, Canada; (613) 599-0250; senators.nhl.com

Philadelphia Flyers (1967): 3601 S. Broad St., Philadelphia, PA 19148; (215) 336-3600; flyers.nhl.com

Phoenix Coyotes (1979, as Winnipeg Jets): 9300 W. Maryland Ave., Glendale, AZ 85305; (623) 772-3200; coyotes.nhl.com

Pittsburgh Penguins (1967): 1001 5th Ave., Pittsburgh, PA 15219; (412) 642-1800; penguins.nhl.com

St. Louis Blues (1967): 1401 Clark Ave. at Brett Hull Way, St. Louis, MO 63103; (314) 622-2500; blues.nhl.com

San Jose Sharks (1991): 525 W. Santa Clara St., San Jose, CA 95113; (408) 287-7070; sharks.nhl.com

Tampa Bay Lightning (1992): 401 Channelside Dr., Tampa, FL 33602; (813) 301-6500; lightning.nhl.com

Toronto Maple Leafs (1919, as Toronto St. Pats): 40 Bay St., Ste. 400, Toronto, ON M5J 2X2, Canada; (416) 815-5700; mapleleafs.nhl.com

Vancouver Canucks (1946, joined NHL in 1970): 800 Griffiths Way, Vancouver, BC V6B 6G1, Canada; (604) 899-7400; canucks.nhl.com

Washington Capitals (1974): 627 N. Glebe Rd., Ste. 850, Arlington, VA 22203; (202) 266-2200; capitals.nhl.com

Winnipeg Jets (1999, as Atlanta Thrashers): 345 Graham Ave., Winnipeg, MB R3C 5S6, Canada; (204) 987-7825; jets.nhl.com

National Football League

League Office, 345 Park Ave., New York, NY 10154; (212) 450-2000; www.nfl.com

Arizona Cardinals (1898, as Morgan Athletic Club): P.O. Box 888, Phoenix, AZ 85001; (602) 379-0101; www.azcardinals.com

Atlanta Falcons (1966): 4400 Falcon Pkwy., Flowery Branch, GA 30542; (770) 965-3115; www.atlantafalcons.com

Baltimore Ravens (1996): 1101 Russell St., Baltimore, MD 21230; (410) 261-7283; www.baltimoreravens.com

Buffalo Bills (1960): One Bills Dr., Orchard Park, NY 14127; (716) 648-1800; www.buffalobills.com

Carolina Panthers (1995): 800 S. Mint St., Charlotte, NC 28202; (704) 358-7000; www.panthers.com

Chicago Bears (1920, as Decatur Staleys): 1000 Football Dr., Lake Forest, IL 60045; (847) 615-2327; www.chicagobears.com

Cincinnati Bengals (1968): One Paul Brown Stadium, Cincinnati, OH 45202; (513) 621-3550; www.bengals.com

Cleveland Browns (1946): 76 Lou Groza Blvd., Berea, OH 44017; (440) 824-3434; www.clevelandbrowns.com

Dallas Cowboys (1960): One AT&T Way, Arlington, TX 76011; (817) 892-4000; www.dallascowboys.com

Denver Broncos (1960): 13655 Broncos Pkwy., Englewood, CO 80112; (303) 649-9000; www.denverbroncos.com

Detroit Lions (1930, as Portsmouth Spartans): 222 Republic Dr., Allen Park, MI 48101; (313) 262-2000; www.detroitlions.com

Green Bay Packers (1919): 1265 Lombardi Ave., Green Bay, WI 54304; (920) 569-7500; www.packers.com

Houston Texans (2002): Two NRG Park, Houston, TX 77054; (832) 667-2002; www.houstontexans.com

Indianapolis Colts (1953, as Baltimore Colts): 7001 W. 56th St., Indianapolis, IN 46254; (317) 297-2658; www.colts.com

Jacksonville Jaguars (1995): One Ever-Bank Field Dr., Jacksonville, FL 32202; (904) 633-2000; www.jaguars.com

Kansas City Chiefs (1960, as Dallas Texans): One Arrowhead Dr., Kansas City, MO 64129; (816) 920-9300; www.kcchiefs.com

Miami Dolphins (1966): 347 Don Shula Dr., Miami Gardens, FL 33056; (305) 943-8000; www.miamidolphins.com

Minnesota Vikings (1961): 9520 Viking Dr., Eden Prairie, MN 55344; (952) 828-6500; www.vikings.com

New England Patriots (1960): One Patriot Pl., Foxboro, MA 02035; (508) 543-8200; www.patriots.com

New Orleans Saints (1967): 5800 Airline Dr., Metairie, LA 70003; (504) 733-0255; www.neworleanssaints.com

New York Giants (1925): MetLife Stadium, E. Rutherford, NJ 07073; (201) 935-8111; www.giants.com

New York Jets (1960, as New York Titans): One Jets Dr., Florham Park, NJ 07932; (800) 469-5387; www.newyorkjets.com

Oakland Raiders (1960): 1220 Harbor Bay Pkwy., Alameda, CA 94502; (510) 864-5000; www.raiders.com

Philadelphia Eagles (1933): One NovaCare Way, Philadelphia, PA 19145; (215) 463-2500; www.philadelphiaeagles.com

Pittsburgh Steelers (1933): 3400 S. Water St., Pittsburgh, PA 15203; (412) 432-7800; www.steelers.com

St. Louis Rams (1937, as Cleveland Rams): One Rams Way, St. Louis, MO 63045; (314) 982-7267; www.stlouisrams.com

San Diego Chargers (1960, as Los Angeles Chargers): P.O. Box 609609, San Diego, CA 92160; (858) 874-4500; www.chargers.com

San Francisco 49ers (1946): 4949 Centennial Blvd., Santa Clara, CA 95054; (408) 562-4949; www.49ers.com

Seattle Seahawks (1976): 12 Seahawks Way, Renton, WA 98056; (888) 635-4295; www.seahawks.com

Tampa Bay Buccaneers (1976): One Buccaneer Pl., Tampa, FL 33607; (813) 870-2700; www.buccaneers.com

Tennessee Titans (1960, as Houston Oilers): 460 Great Circle Rd., Nashville, TN 37228; (615) 565-4000; www.titansonline.com

Washington Redskins (1932, as Boston Braves): 21300 Redskin Park Dr., Ashburn, VA 20147; (703) 726-7000; www.redskins.com

Health Organizations

Source: World Almanac research

Entries are roughly alphabetized by the basic condition addressed or organization name. Year established is in parentheses. Always check with a physician before embarking on any new health-related undertaking.

Al-Anon Family Groups (1951): (757) 563-1600; www.al-anon.alateen.org

Alcoholics Anonymous (1935): (212) 870-3400; www.aa.org

Alcoholism and Drug Dependence, Inc., Natl. Council on (1944): (212) 269-7797; www.ncadd.org

Aging, Natl. Institute on (1974): (301) 496-1752; www.nia.nih.gov

Aging's Eldercare Locator, Admin. on (1991): (800) 677-1116; www.eldercare.gov

AIDSinfo: (800) 448-0440; www.aidsinfo.nih.gov

Allergy, Asthma, and Immunology, American Academy of (1943): (414) 272-6071; www.aaaai.org

ALS Assn. [Lou Gehrig's disease] (1985): (202) 407-8580; www.alsa.org

Alzheimer's Assn. (1979): (312) 335-8700; www.alz.org

Anorexia Nervosa and Associated Disorders, Natl. Assn. of (1976): (630) 577-1333; www.anad.org

Arc of the United States, The (1950): (800) 433-5255; www.thearc.org

Arthritis Foundation (1948): (800) 283-7800; www.arthritis.org

Arthritis and Musculoskeletal and Skin Diseases, Natl. Institute of (1986): (877) 226-4267; www.niams.nih.gov

Asthma and Allergy Foundation of America (1953): (800) 727-8462; www.aafa.org

Autism Society (1965): (800) 328-8476; www.autism-society.org

Blind, American Council of the (1961): (202) 467-5081; (800) 424-8666; www.acb.org

Blind, Natl. Federation of the (1940): (410) 659-9314; www.nfb.org

Blindness, Foundation Fighting (1971): (800) 683-5555; www.blindness.org

Blindness America, Prevent (1908): (800) 331-2020; www.preventblindness.org

Brain Tumor Society, Natl. (2008): (617) 924-9997; www.braintumor.org

Breast Cancer Diagnosis, After (ABCD) (1999): (414) 977-1780; (800) 977-4121; www.abcdbreastcancersupport.org

Cancer Institute's Cancer Information Service, Natl. (1975): (800) 422-6237; www.cancer.gov/aboutnci/cis/

Cancer Society, American (1913): (800) 227-2345; www.cancer.org

Centers for Disease Control and Prevention (CDC) (1946): (800) 232-4636; www.cdc.gov

Cerebral Palsy, United (1949): (202) 776-0406; (800) 872-5827; www.ucp.org

Child Abuse and Family Violence, Natl. Council on (1984): (202) 429-6695; www.nccafv.org

Childhelp Natl. Child Abuse Hotline (1959): (800) 422-4453; www.childhelp.org

Children, Natl. Center for Missing and Exploited (1984): (703) 224-2150; www.missingkids.com

Children's Tumor Foundation (1978): (212) 344-6633; www.ctf.org

Chronic Pain Assn., American (1980): (800) 533-3231; www.theacpa.org

Continence, Natl. Assn. for (1982): (843) 352-2559; (800) 252-3777; www.nafc.org

Cooley's Anemia Foundation (1954): (800) 522-7222; www.thalassemia.org

Crohn's and Colitis Foundation of America (1967): (800) 932-2423; www.ccfa.org

Cystic Fibrosis Foundation (1955): (800) 344-4823 or (301) 951-4422; www.cff.org

Deaf, Natl. Assn. of the (1880): (301) 587-1788, TTY (301) 587-1789; www.nad.org

Depression and Bipolar Support Alliance (1985): (800) 826-3632; www.dbsalliance.org

Diabetes Assn., American (1940): (800) 342-2383; www.diabetes.org

Diabetes and Digestive and Kidney Diseases, Natl. Institute of (1950): (800) 891-5390; www.kidney.niddk.nih.gov

Dial-A-Hearing Screening Test: (800) 222-EARS (222-3277)

Domestic Violence Hotline, Natl. (1996): (800) 799-7233; TTY (800) 787-3224; www.thehotline.org

Down Syndrome Congress, Natl. (1973): (800) 232-6372; www.ndsccenter.org

Down Syndrome Assn., Natl. (1979): (800) 221-4602; www.ndss.org

Dyslexia Assn., Intl. (1949): (410) 296-0232; www.interdys.org

Easter Seals [special needs] (1919): (800) 221-6827; www.easterseals.com

Endometriosis Assn. (1980): (414) 355-2200; www.endometriosisassn.org

Epilepsy Foundation (1967): (800) 332-1000; www.epilepsyfoundation.org

Fat Acceptance, Natl. Assn. to Advance (1969): (916) 558-6880; www.naafa.org

First Candle [sudden infant death syndrome] (1987): (800) 221-7437; www.sidsalliance.org

FoodSafety.gov—Gateway to Federal Food Safety Information: Food: (888) 723-3366; Meat, poultry, eggs: (888) 674-6854; Illness or food poisoning: (800) 232-4636 (CDC)

Gamblers Anonymous (1957): (626) 960-3500; www.gamblersanonymous.org

Geriatrics Society, American (1942): (212) 308-1414; www.americangeriatrics.org

Headache Foundation, Natl. (1970): (888) 643-5552; www.headaches.org

HealthyWomen (1988): (877) 986-9472; www.healthywomen.org

Hearing Society, Intl. (1951): (734) 522-7200; www.ihsinfo.org

Heart Assn., American (1924): (800) 242-8721; www.heart.org

Hearts, Inc., Mended (1951): (888) 432-7899; www.mendedhearts.org

Hospice Education Institute (1985): (800) 331-1620; www.hospiceworld.org

Hospice Intl., Children's (1983): (703) 684-0330; www.chionline.org

Hospital Assn., American (1899): (312) 422-3000; (800) 424-4301; www.aha.org

Huntington's Disease Society of America (1967): (800) 345-4372; www.hdsa.org

JDRF (formerly Juvenile Diabetes Research Foundation) (1970): (800) 533-2873; www.jdrf.org

Kidney Foundation, Natl. (1950): (800) 622-9010; www.kidney.org

Kidney Fund, American (1971): (800) 638-8299; www.kidneyfund.org

La Leche League Intl. [breastfeeding] (1957): (800) 525-3243; www.llli.org

Leukemia and Lymphoma Society (1949): (800) 955-4572; www.lls.org

Liver Foundation, American (1976): (800) 465-4837; www.liverfoundation.org

Living Bank [organ donation] (1968): (800) 528-2971; www.livingbank.org

Lung Assn., American (1904): (800) 586-4872; www.lungusa.org

Lung Line (1983): (800) 222-5864; www.nationaljewish.org/about/contact/lung-line/

Lupus Foundation of America, Inc. (1977): (800) 558-0121; www.lupus.org

March of Dimes [babies' health] (1938): (914) 997-4488; www.marchofdimes.com

Marfan Foundation, Natl. (1981): (800) 8-MARFAN (862-7326); www.marfan.org

Mayo Clinic (1889): (507) 284-2511; www.mayoclinic.com

ME/CFS Initiative, Solve [myalgic encephalomyelitis/chronic fatigue syndrome] (1987): (704) 365-2343; solvecfs.org

Mental Health, Natl. Institute of (1946): (866) 615-6464; www.nimh.nih.gov

Mental Health America (1909): (800) 969-6642; www.nmha.org

Mental Illness, Natl. Alliance on (1979): (888) 950-6264; www.nami.org

Multiple Sclerosis Society, Natl. (1946): (800) 344-4867; www.nationalmssociety.org

Muscular Dystrophy Assn. (1950): (800) 572-1717; www.mdausa.org

Myeloma Foundation, Intl. (1990): (800) 452-2873; www.myeloma.org

Narcotics Anonymous (1953): (818) 773-9999; www.na.org

Natl. Health Council (1920): (202) 785-3910; www.nationalhealthcouncil.org

Natl. Health Information Center (1979): (240) 453-8280; www.health.gov/NHIC/

Natl. Institutes of Health (NIH) (1887): (301) 496-4000; www.nih.gov

Neurological Disorders and Stroke, Natl. Institute of (1950): (800) 352-9424; www.ninds.nih.gov

Organ Sharing, United Network for (1984): (804) 782-4800; www.unos.org

Osteoporosis Foundation, Natl. (1984): (800) 231-4222; www.nof.org

Overeaters Anonymous (1960): (505) 891-2664; www.oa.org

Parkinson Foundation, Natl. (1957): (800) 473-4636; www.parkinson.org

Parkinson's Disease Foundation (1957): (800) 457-6676; www.pdf.org

Pediatrics, American Academy of (1930): (800) 433-9016; www.aap.org

Phoenix House [substance abuse] (1967): (800) 378-4435; www.phoenixhouse.org

Planned Parenthood Federation of America, Inc. (1916): (800) 230-7526; www.plannedparenthood.org

Plastic Surgeons, American Society of (1931): (800) 514-5058; www.plasticsurgery.org

Post-Polio Health Intl. (1960): (314) 534-0475; www.post-polio.org

Psoriasis Foundation, Natl. (1966): (800) 723-9166; www.psoriasis.org

Rare Disorders, Natl. Org. for (1983): (203) 744-0100; www.rarediseases.org

Rehabilitation Information Center, Natl. (1977): (800) 346-2742; TTY (301) 459-5984; www.naric.com

Reye's Syndrome Foundation, Natl. (1974): (800) 233-7393; www.reyessyndrome.org

Runaway Safeline, Natl. (1971): (800) 786-2929; www.1800runaway.org

Scleroderma Foundation (1989): (800) 722-4673; www.scleroderma.org

Sexual Health Assn., American (1914): (919) 361-8400; www.ashastd.org

Sickle Cell Disease Assn. of America (1971): (800) 421-8453; www.sicklecelldisease.org

Sjögren's Syndrome Foundation (1983): (800) 475-6473; www.sjogrens.org

Speech-Language-Hearing Assn., American (1925): (800) 638-8255, TTY (301) 296-5650; www.asha.org

Spinal Cord Injury Assn., Natl. (1948): (718) 803-3782; www.spinalcord.org

Stroke Assn., Natl. (1984): (800) 787-6537; www.stroke.org

Stuttering Assn., Natl. (1977): (212) 944-4050; (800) 937-8888; www.nsastutter.org

Stuttering Foundation of America (1947): (800) 992-9392; www.stutteringhelp.org

Substance Abuse and Mental Health Services Admin.: (877) 726-4727; www.samhsa.gov

Sudden Infant Death Syndrome Institute, Amer. (1983): (239) 431-5425; www.sids.org

Suicide Prevention Lifeline, Natl. (2004): (800) 273-TALK (8255); www.suicidepreventionlifeline.org

Therapy Dogs Intl. (1976): (973) 252-9800; www.tdi-dog.org

Tourette Syndrome Assn. (1972): (718) 224-2999; tsa-usa.org

Tuberous Sclerosis Alliance (1974): (800) 225-6872; www.tsalliance.org

Urological Assn., American (1902): (866) 746-4282; www.auanet.org

Visual Impairments, Natl. Assn. for Parents of Children with (1980): www.napvi.org

Women's Health Network, Natl. (1975): (202) 682-2640; www.nwhn.org

UNITED STATES FACTS

Superlative U.S. Statistics

Source: U.S. Geological Survey, U.S. Dept. of the Interior; U.S. Census Bureau, U.S. Dept. of Commerce; World Almanac research

Superlative Statistics for the 50 States

Total area for 50 states and Washington, DC		3,796,742 sq mi
Land area for 50 states and Washington, DC		3,531,905 sq mi
Water area for 50 states and Washington, DC		264,837 sq mi
Largest state	Alaska	665,384 sq mi
Smallest state	Rhode Island	1,545 sq mi
Largest county (excluding Alaska)	San Bernardino County, CA	20,105 sq mi
Smallest county	Arlington County, VA[1]	26 sq mi
Largest incorporated city (by area, pop. 1,000+)	Sitka, AK	4,811 sq mi
Northernmost city	Barrow, AK	71°17′ N
Northernmost point	Point Barrow, AK	71°23′ N
Southernmost city	Hilo, HI	19°43′ N
Southernmost settlement	Naalehu, HI	19°03′ N
Southernmost point	Ka Lae (South Cape), island of Hawaii	18°55′ N (155°41′ W)
Easternmost city	Eastport, ME	66°59′24′′ W
Easternmost settlement[2]	Attu Station, AK	173°11′ E
Easternmost point[2]	Pochnoi Point, Semisopochnoi Island, AK	179°52′ E
Westernmost city	Adak Station, AK	173°11′ E
Westernmost settlement	Adak Station, AK	173°11′ E
Westernmost point	Amatignak Island, AK	179°09′ W
Highest settlement	Tordal Estates, CO	10,653 ft
Lowest settlement	Bombay Beach, CA	−223 ft
Highest point on Atlantic coast	Cadillac Mountain, Mount Desert Island, ME	1,530 ft
Oldest national park	Yellowstone National Park (1872), WY-MT-ID	2,219,791 acres
Largest national park	Wrangell-St. Elias, AK	8,323,147 acres
Highest waterfall	Yosemite Falls—total in three sections	2,425 ft
	(Upper Yosemite Fall, 1,430 ft; Cascades, 675 ft; Lower Yosemite Fall, 320 ft)	
Longest river system	Mississippi-Missouri-Red Rock	3,710 mi
Highest mountain	Mount McKinley (Denali), AK	20,320 ft
Lowest point	Death Valley, CA	−282 ft
Deepest lake	Crater Lake, OR	1,958 ft
Rainiest spot	Mount Waialeale, Kauai, HI	annual avg. rainfall 422 in.
Largest gorge	Grand Canyon, Colorado River, AZ	277 mi long, 600 ft to 18 mi wide, 1 mi deep
Deepest gorge	Hells Canyon, Snake River, OR-ID	7,900 ft
Largest dam	New Cornelia Tailings, Ten Mile Wash, AZ[3]	274,026,000 cu yds material used
Tallest building	One World Trade Center, New York, NY	1,776 ft
Largest building	Boeing Manufacturing Plant, Everett, WA	472,000,000 cu ft; covers 98 acres
Largest office building	Pentagon, Arlington, VA	77,015,000 cu ft; covers 29 acres
Tallest supported structure	KVLY-TV Tower, Blanchard, ND	2,063 ft
Tallest freestanding tower	Stratosphere Tower, Las Vegas, NV	1,149 ft
Longest bridge span	Verrazano-Narrows Bridge, New York, NY	4,260 ft
Highest bridge	Royal Gorge Bridge, Cañon City, CO	1,053 ft above water
Deepest well	Bertha Rogers gas well (inactive), Washita County, OK	31,441 ft

Superlative Statistics for the 48 Contiguous States

Total area for 48 states and Washington, DC		3,129,611 sq mi
Land area for 48 states and Washington, DC		2,958,868 sq mi
Water area for 48 states and Washington, DC		170,743 sq mi
Largest state	Texas	268,596 sq mi
Northernmost city	Bellingham, WA	48°46′ N
Northernmost settlement	Angle Inlet, MN	49°20′ N
Northernmost point	Northwest Angle, MN	49°21′ N
Southernmost city	Key West, FL	24°33′ N
Southernmost mainland city	Florida City, FL	25°27′ N
Southernmost point	Ballast Key, FL	24°31′ N
Easternmost settlement	Lubec, ME	66°58′49′′ W
Easternmost point	West Quoddy Head, ME	66°57′ W
Westernmost town	La Push, WA	124°38′ W
Westernmost point	Bodelteh Islands, WA	124°46′ W
Highest mountain	Mount Whitney, CA	14,505 ft

(1) Smallest county by land area is Kalawao County, Hawaii, at 12 sq mi; its total area (including water) is 53 sq mi. Superlative shown is for smallest total area. (2) Alaska's Aleutian Islands extend into the Eastern Hemisphere (across 180° longitude) and thus technically contain the easternmost point and settlement in the U.S. (3) Privately owned industrial dam composed of tailings, remnants of a mining process.

Highest and Lowest Elevations in U.S. States and Territories

Source: U.S. Geological Survey, U.S. Dept. of the Interior
(negative sign indicates below sea level)

State/territory	Highest point Name	County	Elev. (ft)	Lowest point Name	County	Elev. (ft)
Alabama	Cheaha Mountain	Cleburne	2,407	Gulf of Mexico		Sea level
Alaska	Mount McKinley/Denali	Denali	20,237	Pacific Ocean		Sea level
American Samoa	Lata Mountain	Tau Island	3,160	Pacific Ocean		Sea level
Arizona	Humphreys Peak	Coconino	12,637	Colorado R.	Yuma	70
Arkansas	Magazine Mountain	Logan	2,753	Ouachita R.	Ashley-Union	55
California	Mount Whitney	Inyo-Tulare	14,505	Death Valley	Inyo	−282
Colorado	Mount Elbert	Lake	14,440	Arikaree R.	Yuma	3,315
Connecticut	S. slope of Mt. Frissell	Litchfield	2,380	Long Island Sound		Sea level
Delaware	Ebright Azimuth	New Castle	448	Atlantic Ocean		Sea level
Dist. of Columbia	Tenleytown	NW quadrant	410	Potomac R.		1
Florida	Britton Hill	Walton	345	Atlantic Ocean		Sea level
Georgia	Brasstown Bald	Towns-Union	4,784	Atlantic Ocean		Sea level
Guam	Mount Lamlam	Agat District	1,332	Pacific Ocean		Sea level
Hawaii	Pu'u Wekiu, Mauna Kea	Hawaii	13,796	Pacific Ocean		Sea level
Idaho	Borah Peak	Custer	12,661	Snake R.	Nez Perce	710
Illinois	Charles Mound	Jo Daviess	1,235	Mississippi R.	Alexander	279
Indiana	Hoosier Hill	Wayne	1,257	Ohio R.	Posey	320
Iowa	Hawkeye Point	Osceola	1,670	Mississippi R.	Lee	480
Kansas	Mount Sunflower	Wallace	4,039	Verdigris R.	Montgomery	679
Kentucky	Black Mountain	Harlan	4,145	Mississippi R.	Fulton	257
Louisiana	Driskill Mountain	Bienville	535	New Orleans	Orleans	−8
Maine	Mount Katahdin	Piscataquis	5,268	Atlantic Ocean		Sea level
Maryland	Hoye Crest	Garrett	3,360	Atlantic Ocean		Sea level
Massachusetts	Mount Greylock	Berkshire	3,491	Atlantic Ocean		Sea level
Michigan	Mount Arvon	Baraga	1,979	Lake Erie		571
Minnesota	Eagle Mountain	Cook	2,301	Lake Superior		601
Mississippi	Woodall Mountain	Tishomingo	806	Gulf of Mexico		Sea level
Missouri	Taum Sauk Mountain	Iron	1,772	St. Francis R.	Dunklin	230
Montana	Granite Peak	Park	12,804	Kootenai R.	Lincoln	1,800
Nebraska	Panorama Point	Kimball	5,424	Missouri R.	Richardson	840
Nevada	Boundary Peak	Esmeralda	13,146	Colorado R.	Clark	479
New Hampshire	Mount Washington	Coos	6,288	Atlantic Ocean		Sea level
New Jersey	High Point	Sussex	1,803	Atlantic Ocean		Sea level
New Mexico	Wheeler Peak	Taos	13,166	Red Bluff Reservoir	Eddy	2,842
New York	Mount Marcy	Essex	5,344	Atlantic Ocean		Sea level
North Carolina	Mount Mitchell	Yancey	6,684	Atlantic Ocean		Sea level
North Dakota	White Butte	Slope	3,506	Red R. of the North	Pembina	750
Ohio	Campbell Hill	Logan	1,550	Ohio R.	Hamilton	455
Oklahoma	Black Mesa	Cimarron	4,973	Little R.	McCurtain	289
Oregon	Mount Hood	Clackamas-Hood R.	11,240	Pacific Ocean		Sea level
Pennsylvania	Mount Davis	Somerset	3,213	Delaware R.	Delaware	Sea level
Puerto Rico	Cerro de Punta	Ponce District	4,390	Atlantic Ocean		Sea level
Rhode Island	Jerimoth Hill	Providence	812	Atlantic Ocean		Sea level
South Carolina	Sassafras Mountain	Pickens	3,560	Atlantic Ocean		Sea level
South Dakota	Harney Peak	Pennington	7,242	Big Stone Lake	Roberts	966
Tennessee	Clingmans Dome	Sevier	6,643	Mississippi R.	Shelby	178
Texas	Guadalupe Peak	Culberson	8,749	Gulf of Mexico		Sea level
Utah	Kings Peak	Duchesne	13,534	Beaver Dam Wash	Washington	2,000
Vermont	Mount Mansfield	Chittenden	4,393	Lake Champlain		95
Virginia	Mount Rogers	Grayson-Smyth	5,729	Atlantic Ocean		Sea level
Virgin Islands	Crown Mountain	St. Thomas Island	1,556	Atlantic Ocean		Sea level
Washington	Mount Rainier	Pierce	14,416	Pacific Ocean		Sea level
West Virginia	Spruce Knob	Pendleton	4,863	Potomac R.	Jefferson	240
Wisconsin	Timms Hill	Price	1,951	Lake Michigan		579
Wyoming	Gannett Peak	Fremont	13,810	Belle Fourche R.	Crook	3,099

U.S. Coastline by State

Source: National Oceanic and Atmospheric Administration, U.S. Dept. of Commerce
(in statute miles; only states with coastline or shoreline are shown)

	Coastline[1]	Shoreline[2]		Coastline[1]	Shoreline[2]
Atlantic Coast	2,069	28,673	**Gulf Coast**	1,631	17,141
Connecticut	0	618	Alabama	53	607
Delaware	28	381	Florida	770	5,095
Florida	580	3,331	Louisiana	397	7,721
Georgia	100	2,344	Mississippi	44	359
Maine	228	3,478	Texas	367	3,359
Maryland	31	3,190			
Massachusetts	192	1,519	**Pacific Coast**	7,623	40,298
New Hampshire	13	131	Alaska	5,580	31,383
New Jersey	130	1,792	California	840	3,427
New York	127	1,850	Hawaii	750	1,052
North Carolina	301	3,375	Oregon	296	1,410
Pennsylvania	0	89	Washington	157	3,026
Rhode Island	40	384			
South Carolina	187	2,876	**Arctic Coast**	1,060	2,521
Virginia	112	3,315	**United States**	12,383	88,633

(1) Length of general outline of seacoast. Measurements were made in 1948 with a unit measure of 30 minutes of latitude on charts as near the scale of 1:1,200,000 as possible. Includes coastlines of large sounds and bays. (2) Shoreline of outer coast, offshore islands, sounds, bays, rivers, and creeks to the head of tidewater or to a point where tidal waters narrow to a width of 100 ft. Figures obtained in 1939-40 with a recording instrument on the largest-scale charts and maps then available.

States: Capitals, Key Dates, Geographic Data

Source: *Statistical Abstract of the United States*, U.S. Census Bureau, U.S. Dept. of Commerce

The 13 colonies that declared independence from Great Britain and fought the War of Independence (American Revolution) became the 13 original states. They were, in the order in which they ratified the Constitution: Delaware, Pennsylvania, New Jersey, Georgia, Connecticut, Massachusetts, Maryland, South Carolina, New Hampshire, Virginia, New York, North Carolina, and Rhode Island.

State	Settled[1]	Capital	Entered Union Date	Order	Extent (mi) Length (approx. mean)	Width	Area (sq mi) Land	Water	Total	Rank by tot. area
AL	1702	Montgomery	Dec. 14, 1819	22	330	190	50,645	1,775	52,420	30
AK	1784	Juneau	Jan. 3, 1959	49	1,480[2]	810	570,641	94,743	665,384	1
AZ	1776	Phoenix	Feb. 14, 1912	48	400	310	113,594	396	113,990	6
AR	1686	Little Rock	June 15, 1836	25	260	240	52,035	1,143	53,179	29
CA	1769	Sacramento	Sept. 9, 1850	31	770	250	155,779	7,916	163,695	3
CO	1858	Denver	Aug. 1, 1876	38	380	280	103,642	452	104,094	8
CT	1634	Hartford	Jan. 9, 1788	5	110	70	4,842	701	5,543	48
DE	1638	Dover	Dec. 7, 1787	1	96	30	1,949	540	2,489	49
DC	NA	NA	NA	NA	NA	NA	61	7	68	51
FL	1565	Tallahassee	Mar. 3, 1845	27	447	361	53,625	12,133	65,758	22
GA	1733	Atlanta	Jan. 2, 1788	4	300	230	57,513	1,912	59,425	24
HI	1820	Honolulu	Aug. 21, 1959	50	NA	NA	6,423	4,509	10,932	43
ID	1842	Boise	July 3, 1890	43	570	300	82,643	926	83,569	14
IL	1720	Springfield	Dec. 3, 1818	21	390	210	55,519	2,395	57,914	25
IN	1733	Indianapolis	Dec. 11, 1816	19	270	140	35,826	593	36,420	38
IA	1788	Des Moines	Dec. 28, 1846	29	310	200	55,857	416	56,273	26
KS	1727	Topeka	Jan. 29, 1861	34	400	210	81,759	520	82,278	15
KY	1774	Frankfort	June 1, 1792	15	380	140	39,486	921	40,408	37
LA	1699	Baton Rouge	Apr. 30, 1812	18	380	130	43,204	9,174	52,378	31
ME	1624	Augusta	Mar. 15, 1820	23	320	190	30,843	4,537	35,380	39
MD	1634	Annapolis	Apr. 28, 1788	7	250	90	9,707	2,699	12,406	42
MA	1620	Boston	Feb. 6, 1788	6	190	50	7,800	2,754	10,554	44
MI	1668	Lansing	Jan. 26, 1837	26	490	240	56,539	40,175	96,714	11
MN	1805	St. Paul	May 11, 1858	32	400	250	79,627	7,309	86,936	12
MS	1699	Jackson	Dec. 10, 1817	20	340	170	46,923	1,509	48,432	32
MO	1735	Jefferson City	Aug. 10, 1821	24	300	240	68,742	965	69,707	21
MT	1809	Helena	Nov. 8, 1889	41	630	280	145,546	1,494	147,040	4
NE	1823	Lincoln	Mar. 1, 1867	37	430	210	76,824	524	77,348	16
NV	1849	Carson City	Oct. 31, 1864	36	490	320	109,781	791	110,572	7
NH	1623	Concord	June 21, 1788	9	190	70	8,953	397	9,349	46
NJ	1660	Trenton	Dec. 18, 1787	3	150	70	7,354	1,368	8,723	47
NM	1610	Santa Fe	Jan. 6, 1912	47	370	343	121,298	292	121,590	5
NY	1614	Albany	July 26, 1788	11	330	283	47,126	7,429	54,555	27
NC	1660	Raleigh	Nov. 21, 1789	12	500	150	48,618	5,201	53,819	28
ND	1812	Bismarck	Nov. 2, 1889	39	340	211	69,001	1,698	70,698	19
OH	1788	Columbus	Mar. 1, 1803	17	220	220	40,861	3,965	44,826	34
OK	1889	Oklahoma City	Nov. 16, 1907	46	400	220	68,595	1,304	69,899	20
OR	1811	Salem	Feb. 14, 1859	33	360	261	95,988	2,391	98,379	9
PA	1682	Harrisburg	Dec. 12, 1787	2	283	160	44,743	1,312	46,054	33
RI	1636	Providence	May 29, 1790	13	40	30	1,034	511	1,545	50
SC	1670	Columbia	May 23, 1788	8	260	200	30,061	1,960	32,020	40
SD	1859	Pierre	Nov. 2, 1889	40	380	210	75,811	1,305	77,116	17
TN	1769	Nashville	June 1, 1796	16	440	120	41,235	909	42,144	36
TX	1682	Austin	Dec. 29, 1845	28	790	660	261,232	7,365	268,596	2
UT	1847	Salt Lake City	Jan. 4, 1896	45	350	270	82,170	2,727	84,897	13
VT	1724	Montpelier	Mar. 4, 1791	14	160	80	9,217	400	9,616	45
VA	1607	Richmond	June 25, 1788	10	430	200	39,490	3,285	42,775	35
WA	1811	Olympia	Nov. 11, 1889	42	360	240	66,456	4,842	71,298	18
WV	1727	Charleston	June 20, 1863	35	240	130	24,038	192	24,230	41
WI	1766	Madison	May 29, 1848	30	310	260	54,158	11,339	65,496	23
WY	1834	Cheyenne	July 10, 1890	44	360	280	97,093	720	97,813	10

NA = Not applicable. **Note:** Land and water areas may not add up to totals because of rounding. (1) First permanent settlement by Europeans. (2) Does not include Aleutian Islands or Alexander Archipelago.

Continental Divide of the U.S.

The Continental Divide of the U.S., also known as the Great Divide, is located at the watershed created by the mountain ranges, or tablelands, of the Rocky Mountains. This watershed separates the waters that ultimately drain into the Atlantic Ocean and its marginal seas from those waters that drain into the Pacific Ocean. The majority of water flowing E in the U.S. drains into the Gulf of Mexico and then the Atlantic. The majority of water flowing W drains through the Columbia River or Colorado River, which flows into the Gulf of California before reaching the Pacific.

The location and route of the Continental Divide across the U.S. can be described as follows:

Beginning at the U.S.-Mexico border, near longitude 108°45′ W, the Divide, in a northerly direction, crosses New Mexico along the western edge of the Rio Grande drainage basin, entering Colorado near longitude 106°41′ W. From there by an irregular route N across Colorado along the western summits of the Rio Grande and Arkansas, South Platte, and North Platte river basins, and across Rocky Mountain National Park, entering Wyoming near longitude 106°52′ W.

From there in a northwesterly direction, forming the western rims of the North Platte, Big Horn, and Yellowstone river basins, crossing the SW portion of Yellowstone National Park. From there in a westerly and then northerly direction forming the boundary between Idaho and Montana, to a point on the boundary near longitude 114°00′ W. From there northeasterly and northwesterly through Montana and Glacier National Park, entering Canada near longitude 114°04′ W.

Depending on how a "divide" is defined, the U.S. can also be characterized as having a Northern (or Laurentian) Divide, Eastern Divide, and St. Lawrence Seaway Divide. Some of the waters at the Northern Divide drain into Hudson Bay and the Arctic Ocean. The Appalachian Mountains mark the Eastern Divide, with waters joining the Atlantic or Gulf of Mexico. The waters at the St. Lawrence Seaway Divide, near Chicago, flow into the Gulf of St. Lawrence or Gulf of Mexico.

Chronological List of Territories, With State Admissions to Union

Source: U.S. National Archives and Records Administration

Territory	Date of act creating territory	When act took effect	Date of admission as state	Years as terr.
Northwest Territory[1]	July 13, 1787	No fixed date	Mar. 1, 1803[2]	16
Territory southwest of Ohio River	May 26, 1790	No fixed date	June 1, 1796[3]	6
Mississippi	Apr. 7, 1798	When president acted	Dec. 10, 1817	19
Indiana	May 7, 1800	July 4, 1800	Dec. 11, 1816	16
Orleans	Mar. 26, 1804	Oct. 1, 1804	Apr. 30, 1812[4]	7
Michigan	Jan. 11, 1805	June 30, 1805	Jan. 26, 1837	31
Louisiana-Missouri[5]	Mar. 3, 1805	July 4, 1805	Aug. 10, 1821	16
Illinois	Feb. 3, 1809	Mar. 1, 1809	Dec. 3, 1818	9
Alabama	Mar. 3, 1817	When MS formed state govt.	Dec. 14, 1819	2
Arkansas	Mar. 2, 1819	July 4, 1819	June 15, 1836	17
Florida	Mar. 30, 1822	No fixed date	Mar. 3, 1845	23
Wisconsin	Apr. 20, 1836	July 3, 1836	May 29, 1848	12
Iowa	June 12, 1838	July 3, 1838	Dec. 28, 1846	8
Oregon	Aug. 14, 1848	Date of act	Feb. 14, 1859	10
Minnesota	Mar. 3, 1849	Date of act	May 11, 1858	9
New Mexico	Sept. 9, 1850	On president's proclamation	Jan. 6, 1912	61
Utah	Sept. 9, 1850	Date of act	Jan. 4, 1896	46
Washington	Mar. 2, 1853	Date of act	Nov. 11, 1889	36
Nebraska	May 30, 1854	Date of act	Mar. 1, 1867	12
Kansas	May 30, 1854	Date of act	Jan. 29, 1861	6
Colorado	Feb. 28, 1861	Date of act	Aug. 1, 1876	15
Nevada	Mar. 2, 1861	Date of act	Oct. 31, 1864	3
Dakota	Mar. 2, 1861	Date of act	Nov. 2, 1889	28
Arizona	Feb. 24, 1863	Date of act	Feb. 14, 1912	49
Idaho	Mar. 3, 1863	Date of act	July 3, 1890	27
Montana	May 26, 1864	Date of act	Nov. 8, 1889	25
Wyoming	July 25, 1868	When officers were qualified	July 10, 1890	22
Alaska	May 17, 1884[6]	No fixed date	Jan. 3, 1959	75
Oklahoma	May 2, 1890	Date of act	Nov. 16, 1907	17
Hawaii	Apr. 30, 1900	June 14, 1900	Aug. 21, 1959	59

(1) Included what is now Ohio, Indiana, Illinois, Michigan, Wisconsin, and E Minnesota. (2) Date of admission for Ohio, the first state created out of NW territory. (3) Admitted as the state of Tennessee. (4) Admitted as the state of Louisiana. (5) The act renaming Louisiana Territory as Missouri Territory (June 4, 1812) became effective Dec. 7, 1812. (6) Act constituted Alaska as a district, though it was often referred to and administered as a territory. The Territory of Alaska was formally organized by an act of Aug. 24, 1912.

U.S. Geographic Centers

Source: U.S. Geological Survey, U.S. Dept. of the Interior

There is no generally accepted definition of a geographic center and no uniform method for determining it. Geographic center is defined here as the center of gravity of the surface of an area, or that point on which an area would balance if it were a plane of uniform thickness.

No government agency has officially established any points marking the geographic center of the U.S., the conterminous U.S. (48 states), or the North American continent. Private citizens erected a monument in Lebanon, KS, marking it as the geographic center of the conterminous U.S.; a cairn in Rugby, ND, asserts that location as the center of the North American continent.

The geographic centers in the following list are approximate. They are indicated by county then city unless otherwise noted.

U.S., including Alaska and Hawaii: W of Castle Rock, Butte County, South Dakota; 44°58′ N, 103°46′ W
Conterminous U.S. (48 states): near Lebanon, Smith County, Kansas; 39°50′ N, 98°35′ W
North American continent: 6 mi W of Balta, Pierce County, North Dakota; 48°10′ N, 100°10′ W
Alabama: Chilton, 12 mi SW of Clanton
Alaska: approx. 60 mi NW of Mt. McKinley (Denali); 63°50′ N, 152° W
Arizona: Yavapai, 55 mi E-SE of Prescott
Arkansas: Pulaski, 12 mi NW of Little Rock
California: Madera, 38 mi E of Madera
Colorado: Park, 30 mi NW of Pikes Peak
Connecticut: Hartford, at East Berlin
Delaware: Kent, 11 mi S of Dover
District of Columbia: near 4th and L Sts. NW
Florida: Hernando, 12 mi N-NW of Brooksville
Georgia: Twiggs, 18 mi SE of Macon
Hawaii: off Maui; 20°15′ N, 156°20′ W
Idaho: Custer, SW of Challis
Illinois: Logan, 28 mi NE of Springfield
Indiana: Boone, 14 mi N-NW of Indianapolis
Iowa: Story, 5 mi NE of Ames
Kansas: Barton, 15 mi NE of Great Bend
Kentucky: Marion, 3 mi N-NW of Lebanon
Louisiana: Avoyelles, 3 mi SE of Marksville
Maine: Piscataquis, 18 mi N of Dover
Maryland: Prince George's, 4.5 mi NW of Davidsonville
Massachusetts: Worcester, N part of city of Worcester
Michigan: Wexford, 5 mi N-NW of Cadillac
Minnesota: Crow Wing, 10 mi SW of Brainerd
Mississippi: Leake, 9 mi W-NW of Carthage
Missouri: Miller, 20 mi SW of Jefferson City
Montana: Fergus, 11 mi W of Lewistown
Nebraska: Custer, 10 mi NW of Broken Bow
Nevada: Lander, 26 mi SE of Austin
New Hampshire: Belknap, 3 mi E of Ashland
New Jersey: Mercer, 5 mi SE of Trenton
New Mexico: Torrance, 12 mi S-SW of Willard
New York: Madison, 12 mi S of Oneida and 26 mi SW of Utica
North Carolina: Chatham, 10 mi NW of Sanford
North Dakota: Sheridan, 5 mi SW of McClusky
Ohio: Delaware, 25 mi N-NE of Columbus
Oklahoma: Oklahoma, 8 mi N of Oklahoma City
Oregon: Crook, 25 mi S-SE of Prineville
Pennsylvania: Centre, 2.5 mi SW of Bellefonte
Rhode Island: Kent, 1 mi S-SW of Crompton
South Carolina: Richland, 13 mi SE of Columbia
South Dakota: Hughes, 8 mi NE of Pierre
Tennessee: Rutherford, 5 mi NE of Murfreesboro
Texas: McCulloch, 15 mi NE of Brady
Utah: Sanpete, 3 mi N of Manti
Vermont: Washington, 3 mi E of Roxbury
Virginia: Buckingham, 5 mi SW of Buckingham
Washington: Chelan, 10 mi W-SW of Wenatchee
West Virginia: Braxton, 4 mi E of Sutton
Wisconsin: Wood, 9 mi SE of Marshfield
Wyoming: Fremont, 58 mi E-NE of Lander

Lengths of U.S. Boundaries

The length of the N boundary of the conterminous U.S.—the U.S.-Canadian border excluding Alaska—is 3,987 mi according to the U.S. Geological Survey. The length of the Alaskan-Canadian border is 1,538 mi. The U.S.-Mexican border, from the Gulf of Mexico to the Pacific Ocean, is about 1,933 mi per a 1963 boundary agreement.

Origins of the Names of U.S. States

Source: State officials; Smithsonian Institution; Topographic Division, U.S. Geological Survey, U.S. Dept. of the Interior

Alabama: Choctaw word for a Chickasaw tribe. First noted in accounts of Hernando de Soto expedition.

Alaska: Russian version of Aleutian (Eskimo) word *alakshak* for "peninsula," "great lands," or "land that is not an island."

Arizona: Spanish version of Pima Indian word for "little spring place" or Aztec *arizuma*, meaning "silver-bearing."

Arkansas: Algonquin name for Quapaw Indians, meaning "south wind."

California: Bestowed by Spanish conquistadors (possibly Hernán Cortés). It was the name of an imaginary island in the 1510 Spanish novel *Las Sergas de Esplandián*, by Garci Rodríguez de Montalvo. The Spanish first visited *Baja* (Lower) *California* in 1533. The present-day U.S. state was called *Alta* (Upper) *California*.

Colorado: From Spanish for "red," first applied to Colorado River.

Connecticut: From Mohican and other Algonquin words meaning "long river place."

Delaware: Named for Lord De La Warr, early governor of Virginia; first applied to river, then to Indian tribe (Lenni-Lenape).

District of Columbia: For Christopher Columbus, 1791.

Florida: Named by Juan Ponce de León *Pascua Florida*, "Flowery Easter," on Easter Sunday, 1513.

Georgia: Named by colonial administrator James Oglethorpe for King George II of England in 1732.

Hawaii: Possibly derived from *Hawaiki* or *Owhyhee*, Polynesian word for "homeland."

Idaho: Said to be a coined name with the invented meaning "gem of the mountains"; suggested for the Pikes Peak mining territory (Colorado), then applied to the new mining territory of the Pacific Northwest. Another theory suggests *Idaho* may be a Kiowa Apache term for the Comanche.

Illinois: French for *Illini* or "land of *Illini*," Algonquin word meaning "men" or "warriors."

Indiana: Means "land of the Indians."

Iowa: Indian word variously translated as "here I rest" or "beautiful land." Named for the Iowa River, which was named for the Iowa Indians.

Kansas: Sioux word for "south wind people."

Kentucky: Indian word variously translated as "dark and bloody ground," "meadowland," and "land of tomorrow."

Louisiana: Part of territory called Louisiana by René-Robert Cavelier Sieur de La Salle for French King Louis XIV.

Maine: From Maine, ancient French province. Also descriptive, referring to the mainland as distinct from coastal islands.

Maryland: For Queen Henrietta Maria, wife of Charles I of England.

Massachusetts: From Indian tribe whose name meant "at or about the Great Hill" in Blue Hills region south of Boston.

Michigan: From Chippewa *mici gama*, meaning "great water," after lake of the same name.

Minnesota: From Dakota Sioux word meaning "cloudy water" or "sky-tinted water" of the Minnesota River.

Mississippi: Probably Chippewa *mici zibi*, meaning "great river" or "gathering-in of all the waters." Also Algonquin word *messipi*.

Missouri: Algonquin Indian term meaning "river of the big canoes."

Montana: Latin or Spanish for "mountainous."

Nebraska: From Omaha or Otos Indian word meaning "broad water" or "flat river," describing the Platte River.

Nevada: Spanish, meaning "snow-clad."

New Hampshire: Named by Capt. John Mason of Plymouth Council, in 1629, for his home county in England.

New Jersey: The Duke of York, in 1664, gave a patent to Lord John Berkeley and Sir George Carteret for *Nova Caesaria*, or New Jersey, after England's Isle of Jersey.

New Mexico: Spaniards in Mexico applied term to land north and west of Rio Grande in the 16th century.

New York: For James, Duke of York and Albany, who received patent for New Netherland from his brother Charles II and sent an expedition to capture it, 1664.

North Carolina: In 1619, Charles I gave patent to Sir Robert Heath for Province of Carolana, from *Carolus*, Latin name for Charles. Charles II granted a new patent to Earl of Clarendon and others. Divided into North and South Carolina, 1710.

North Dakota: Sioux word *Dakota*, meaning "friend" or "ally."

Ohio: Iroquois word for "fine or good river."

Oklahoma: Choctaw word meaning "red man," proposed by Rev. Allen Wright, Choctaw-speaking Indian.

Oregon: Origin unknown. One theory is that the name derives from *wauregan*, meaning "beautiful," term used by Indians in New England.

Pennsylvania: William Penn, Quaker who was made full proprietor of area by King Charles II in 1681, suggested "Sylvania," or "woodland," for his tract. The king's government owed 16,000 pounds to Penn's father, Adm. William Penn, and the land was granted as partial settlement. Charles II added "Penn" to "Sylvania," against the modest proprietor's desires, in honor of the admiral.

Puerto Rico: Spanish for "rich port."

Rhode Island: Origin unknown. One theory notes that Giovanni de Verrazano recorded observing an island about the size of the Greek island of Rhodes in 1524. Another theory is that Dutch explorer Adriaen Block named the state *Roode Eylandt* for its red clay.

South Carolina: See North Carolina.

South Dakota: See North Dakota.

Tennessee: *Tanasi* was the name of Cherokee villages on the Little Tennessee River. From 1784 to 1788, this was the State of Franklin, or Frankland.

Texas: Variant of word used by Caddo and other Indians meaning "friends" or "allies" and applied to them by the Spanish in eastern Texas. Also written *Texias*, *Tejas*, *Teysas*.

Utah: From a Navajo word meaning "upper," or "higher up," as applied to Shoshone tribe called Ute. Proposed name *Deseret*, "land of honeybees," from Book of Mormon, was rejected by Congress.

Vermont: From French words *vert* (green) and *mont* (mountain). The Green Mountains were said to have been named by Samuel de Champlain. When the state was formed in 1777, Dr. Thomas Young suggested combining *vert* and *mont*.

Virginia: Named by Sir Walter Raleigh, who outfitted an expedition in 1584, in honor of England's Queen Elizabeth, the Virgin Queen.

Washington: Named after George Washington. When the bill creating the Territory of Columbia was introduced in the 32nd Congress, its name was changed to Washington because of the existence of the District of Columbia.

West Virginia: So named when western counties of Virginia refused to secede from the U.S. in 1863.

Wisconsin: Indian name, spelled *Ouisconsin* or *Mesconsing* by early chroniclers, believed to mean "grassy place" in Chippewa. Congress made it *Wisconsin*.

Wyoming: From Algonquin words for "large prairie place," "at the big plains," or "on the great plain."

Territorial Sea of the U.S.

According to a Dec. 27, 1988, proclamation by Pres. Ronald Reagan, "The territorial sea of the United States henceforth extends to 12 nautical miles from the baselines of the United States determined in accordance with international law. In accordance with international law, as reflected in the applicable provisions of the 1982 United Nations Convention on the Law of the Sea, within the territorial sea of the United States, the ships of all countries enjoy the right of innocent passage and the ships and aircraft of all countries enjoy the right of transit passage through international straits."

Major Accessions of Territory by the U.S.

Source: U.S. Dept. of the Interior; U.S. Census Bureau, U.S. Dept. of Commerce

Not including territories such as the Panama Canal Zone and the Philippines, which are no longer under U.S. jurisdiction.

Accession	Date	Area (sq mi)	Accession	Date	Area (sq mi)	Accession	Date	Area (sq mi)
Territory in 1790[1]	NA	888,685	Mexican Cession	1848	529,017	Guam[3]	1899	212
Louisiana Purchase	1803	827,192	Gadsden Purchase	1853	29,640	American Samoa[4]	1900	76
Treaty of Florida	1819	72,003	Alaska	1867	586,412	U.S. Virgin Islands	1917	133
Texas	1845	390,143	Hawaii	1898	6,450	Northern Marianas[5]	1986	179
Oregon Territory	1846	285,680	Puerto Rico[2]	1899	3,435			

NA = Not applicable. (1) Includes that part of a drainage basin of Red River of the North, south of 49th parallel, sometimes considered part of Louisiana Purchase. (2) Ceded by Spain in 1898, ratified in 1899, and became the Commonwealth of Puerto Rico by Act of Congress on July 25, 1952. (3) Acquired in 1898; ratified 1899. (4) Acquired in 1899; ratified 1900. (5) Part of the UN Trust Territory of the Pacific Islands, which U.S. began administering in 1947; became U.S. commonwealth Nov. 3, 1986.

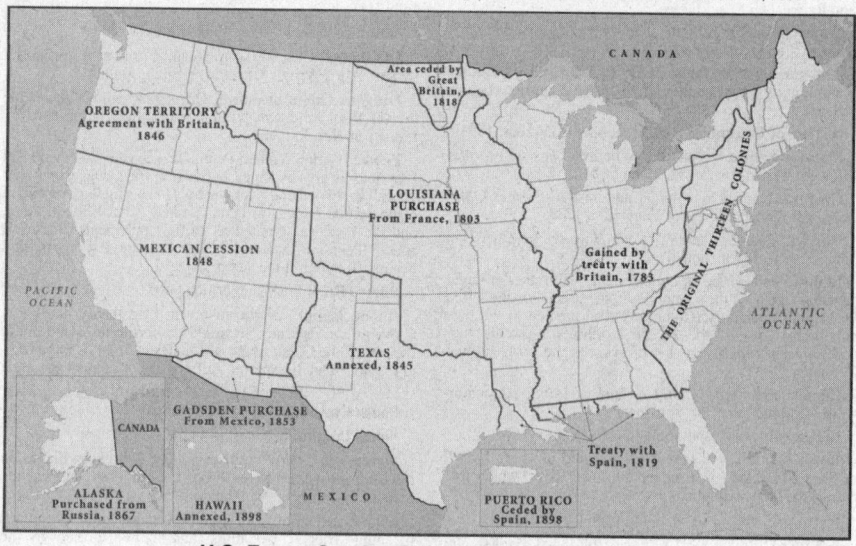

U.S. Forest Service Special Designated Areas

Source: U.S. Forest Service, U.S. Dept. of Agriculture; as of Sept. 30, 2013

These areas within the National Forest System have been specially designated by presidential proclamation or act of Congress. Size of an area does not include acreage within National Forest boundaries that is not federally owned or administered by the Forest Service.

NM = Natl. Monument; NRA = Natl. Recreation Area; NS(A) = Natl. Scenic (Area); NVM = Natl. Volcanic Monument; SRA = Scenic Recreation Act

Area	Location	Estab.	Acreage	Area	Location	Estab.	Acreage
Admiralty Island NM	AK	1980	985,567	Moosalamoo NRA	VT	2006	15,913
Allegheny NRA	PA	1984	23,790	Mount Baker NRA	WA	1984	8,789
Arapaho NRA	CO	1978	32,124	Mount Hood NRA	OR	2009	34,465
Bear Creek NSA	VA	2009	5,122	Mount Pleasant NSA	VA	1994	6,864
Beech Creek NS and Botanic Area	OK	1988	8,042	Mount Rogers NRA	VA	1966	114,242
Cascade Head NS Research Area	OR	1974	6,948	Mount St. Helens NVM	WA	1989	112,864
Chimney Rock NM	CO	2012	4,725	Newberry NVM	OR	1990	56,483
Columbia River Gorge NSA	OR-WA	1986	82,625	North Cascades NSA	WA	1984	88,178
Coosa Bald NSA	GA	1991	7,043	Opal Creek SRA	OR	1996	13,011
Ed Jenkins NRA	GA	1991	23,550	Oregon Dunes NRA	OR	1972	28,310
Flaming Gorge NRA	UT-WY	1968	187,410	Pine Ridge NRA	NE	1986	6,636
Giant Sequoia NM	CA	2000	328,374	Rattlesnake NRA	MT	1980	60,081
Grand Island NRA	MI	1990	13,334	Robert T. Stafford White Rocks NRA	VT	1984	36,563
Grey Towers Natl. Historic Landmark	PA	1963	95	Santa Rosa/San Jacinto Mtns. NM	CA	2000	69,434
Hells Canyon NRA	OR-ID	1975	634,168	Sawtooth NRA	ID	1972	730,861
Indian Nations NS Wildlife Area	OK	1988	44,518	Seng Mountain NSA	VA	2009	5,195
Jemez NRA	NM	1993	48,844	Smith River NRA	CA	1990	321,025
Jewel Cave NM	SD	1908	2,531	Spring Mountains NRA	NV	1993	316,561
Land Between the Lakes NRA	KY-TN	1998	171,251	Spruce Knob-Seneca Rocks NRA	WV	1965	57,499
Misty Fiords NM	AK	1980	2,292,664	Whiskeytown-Shasta-Trinity NRA	CA	1965	175,181
Mono Basin NSA	CA	1984	51,353	Winding Stair Mountain NRA	OK	1988	26,617

Most-Visited Sites in the National Park System, 2013
Source: National Park Service (NPS), U.S. Dept. of the Interior

Attendance at 377 of 401 NPS sites totaled 273,630,895 recreation visits in 2013. (Not all units report public use statistics.) Most sites were closed for 16 days in Oct. 2013 because of a federal government shutdown.

Rank	Site (location)	Recreation visits	Rank	Site (location)	Recreation visits
1.	Golden Gate Natl. Recreation Area (CA)....	14,289,121	11.	Gulf Islands Natl. Seashore (FL-MS).......	4,837,965
2.	Blue Ridge Parkway (NC-VA)	12,877,368	12.	Grand Canyon Natl. Park (AZ)...........	4,564,840
3.	Great Smoky Mountains Natl. Park (NC-TN)	9,354,695	13.	Cape Cod Natl. Seashore (MA)	4,501,898
4.	George Washington Memorial Parkway (VA-MD-DC)........................	7,360,392	14.	San Francisco Maritime Natl. Historical Park (CA)	4,154,455
5.	Lincoln Memorial (DC)	6,546,518	15.	Vietnam Veterans Memorial (DC)	4,142,721
6.	Lake Mead Natl. Recreation Area (AZ-NV) ..	6,344,714	16.	World War II Memorial (DC)	3,934,166
7.	Gateway Natl. Recreation Area (NJ-NY)	6,191,246	17.	Yosemite Natl. Park (CA)...............	3,691,191
8.	Natchez Trace Parkway (MS-AL-TN).......	6,012,740	18.	Independence Natl. Historical Park (PA)	3,553,070
9.	Chesapeake & Ohio Canal Natl. Historical Park (DC-MD-WV)	4,941,367	19.	Korean War Veterans Memorial (DC)	3,209,279
10.	Delaware Water Gap Natl. Recreation Area (NJ-PA)	4,843,350	20.	Martin Luther King Jr. Memorial (DC)	3,205,654

National Parks and Other Areas Administered by National Park Service

As of Dec. 31, 2013, the National Park Service (NPS) administered about 84,479,316 acres of federal and non-federal land across 401 sites. Date when area was authorized or established by Congress or by presidential proclamation is given in parentheses; any date that follows indicates when a site received its current designation or was transferred to the NPS. Figure after the date is gross area in acres as of Dec. 31, 2013. Refer to the National Trails System table for National Park Service trails.

National Parks

Acadia, ME (1916/1929): 48,877. Incl. Mount Desert Isl., half of Isle au Haut, Schoodic Peninsula on mainland. Highest elevation on Eastern seaboard.

American Samoa, AS (1988): 8,257. Paleotropical rain forest, coral reef.

Arches, UT (1929/1971): 76,679. Contains giant red sandstone arches and other products of erosion.

Badlands, SD (1929/1978): 242,756. Reformations and native prairie; animal fossils 23-37 mil years old.

Big Bend, TX (1935): 801,163. Rio Grande, Chisos Mts.

Biscayne, FL (1968/1980): 172,971. Aquatic park encompassing chain of islands south of Miami.

Black Canyon of the Gunnison, CO (1933/1999): 30,750. Has canyon 2,900 ft deep and 40 ft wide at narrowest part.

Bryce Canyon, UT (1923/1928): 35,835. Colorful display of erosion effects.

Canyonlands, UT (1964): 337,598. At junction of Colorado and Green Rivers; extensive evidence of prehistoric peoples.

Capitol Reef, UT (1937/1971): 241,904. 70-mi uplift of sandstone cliffs dissected by high-walled gorges.

Carlsbad Caverns, NM (1923/1930): 46,766. More than 110 limestone caves, incl. Carlsbad Cavern; Chihuahuan Desert.

Channel Islands, CA (1938/1980): 249,561. Sea lion breeding place, nesting seabirds, unique plants.

Congaree, SC (1976/2003): 26,276. Largest intact tract of old-growth bottomland hardwood forest in U.S.

Crater Lake, OR (1902): 183,224. Deepest U.S. lake, in crater of Mt. Mazama, volcano that erupted about 7,700 years ago.

Cuyahoga Valley, OH (1974/2000): 32,831. Along Ohio and Erie Canal system between Akron and Cleveland.

Death Valley, CA-NV (1933/1994): 3,373,063. Large desert. Incl. lowest point in Western Hemisphere and Scotty's Castle.

Denali, AK (1917/1980): 4,740,911. Formerly known as Mt. McKinley; highest mountain in U.S.

Dry Tortugas, FL (1935/1992): 64,701. Ft. Jefferson and seven coral reef and sand islands near Key West.

Everglades, FL (1934): 1,508,974. Largest remaining subtropical wilderness in continental U.S.

Gates of the Arctic, AK (1978/1984): 7,523,897. Vast wilderness in north central region. Limited federal facilities.

Glacier, MT (1910): 1,013,322. Rocky Mt. scenery, numerous glaciers and glacial lakes. Part of Waterton-Glacier Intl. Peace Park established by U.S. and Canada in 1932.

Glacier Bay, AK (1925/1986): 3,223,383. Tidewater glaciers that move down mountainsides and break up into seas.

Grand Canyon, AZ (1893/1919): 1,217,191. Carved by Colorado River.

Grand Teton, WY (1929): 310,044. Most impressive part of Teton Mts.; winter feeding ground of largest American elk herd.

Great Basin, NV (1922/1986): 77,180. Incl. Wheeler Peak, Lexington Arch, Lehman Caves.

Great Sand Dunes, CO (1932/2000): 94,688. North America's tallest dunes.

Great Smoky Mountains, NC-TN (1926/1934): 522,427. Largest Eastern U.S. mountain range; magnificent forests.

Guadalupe Mountains, TX (1966): 86,367. Extensive Permian limestone fossil reef; tremendous earth fault.

Haleakalā, HI (1916/1960): 33,265. Dormant volcano on island of Maui with large craters.

Hawai'i Volcanoes, HI (1916/1961): 323,431. Contains Kilauea and Mauna Loa, active volcanoes.

Hot Springs, AR (1832/1921): 5,549. Waters from park's 47 hot springs used for bathing and drinking.

Isle Royale, MI (1931): 571,790. Largest island in Lake Superior.

Joshua Tree, CA (1936/1994): 790,636. Desert region incl. Joshua trees, other plant and animal life.

Katmai, AK (1918/1980): 3,674,368. "Valley of Ten Thousand Smokes," scene of 1912 volcanic eruption.

Kenai Fjords, AK (1978/1980): 669,984. Marine mammals, birdlife; Harding Icefield, one of four major icecaps in U.S.

Kings Canyon, CA (1890/1940): 461,901. Mountain wilderness, dominated by Kings River Canyons and High Sierra; giant sequoias.

Kobuk Valley, AK (1978/1980): 1,750,716. Contains geological and recreational sites. Limited federal facilities.

Lake Clark, AK (1978/1980): 2,619,713. Across Cook Inlet from Anchorage; scenic wilderness, fish and wildlife. Limited federal facilities.

Lassen Volcanic, CA (1907/1916): 106,452. Contains Lassen Peak, recently active volcano; other volcanic phenomena.

Mammoth Cave, KY (1926/1941): 52,830. Longest known cave system in world (more than 390 mi currently surveyed), river 300 ft below surface.

Mesa Verde, CO (1906): 52,485. Most notable and best preserved prehistoric cliff dwellings in U.S.

Mount Rainier, WA (1899): 236,381. Most glaciated peak in contiguous U.S.

North Cascades, WA (1968): 504,781. Mountainous region with many glaciers, lakes.

Olympic, WA (1909/1938): 922,650. Mountain wilderness containing remnant of Pacific Northwest rain forest, active glaciers, shoreline, rare elk.

Petrified Forest, AZ (1906/1962): 221,415. Extensive petrified wood and Indian artifacts. Contains part of Painted Desert.

Pinnacles, CA (1908/2013): 26,606. A release site for captive-bred California condors; talus caves.

Redwood, CA (1968): 138,885. 40 mi of Pacific coastline, groves of ancient redwoods and world's tallest trees.

Rocky Mountain, CO (1915): 265,795. On Continental Divide; incl. peaks over 14,000 ft.

Saguaro, AZ (1933/1994): 91,442. Part of Sonoran Desert; incl. giant saguaro cacti, unique to region.

Sequoia, CA (1890): 404,063. Giant sequoia groves; world's largest tree (by volume). Mt. Whitney, highest mountain in conterminous U.S.

Shenandoah, VA (1926): 199,117. Portion of Blue Ridge Mts.; overlooks Shenandoah Valley; Skyline Drive.

Theodore Roosevelt, ND (1947/1978): 70,447. Contains part of Roosevelt's ranch and scenic badlands.

Virgin Islands, VI (1956): 14,945. Covers 75% of St. John Isl. and Hassel Isl.; beaches, Carib Indian petroglyphs, evidence of colonial Danes.

Voyageurs, MN (1971): 218,200. Abundant lakes, forests, wildlife.

Wind Cave, SD (1903): 33,847. Limestone caverns in Black Hills; extensive wildlife incl. bison herd.

Wrangell-St. Elias, AK (1978/1980): 8,323,147. Largest area in park system; most peaks over 16,000 ft. No federal facilities.

Yellowstone, ID-MT-WY (1872): 2,219,791. World's first national park. World's greatest geyser area with about 10,000 geysers, hot springs; falls and canyons of Yellowstone River; grizzly bear, moose, bison.

Yosemite, CA (1890): 761,268. Yosemite Valley, country's highest waterfall, grove of sequoias, mountains.

Zion, UT (1909/1919): 147,237. Unusual shapes, landscapes resulting from erosion and faulting; evidence of past volcanic activity; contains 2,394-ft monolith "Great White Throne."

National Historical Parks

Abraham Lincoln Birthplace, Hodgenville, KY (1916/1959): 345. Memorial building, sinking spring.

Adams, Quincy, MA (1946/1998): 24. Home of Pres. John Adams, John Quincy Adams, and descendants.

Appomattox Court House, VA (1930/1954): 1,774. Where Confederate Gen. Lee surrendered to Gen. Grant, signaling Civil War's end.

Boston, MA (1974): 44. Incl. Faneuil Hall, Old North Church, Bunker Hill, Paul Revere House.

Cane River Creole, LA (1994): 206. Preserves Creole culture as it developed along the Cane River.

Cedar Creek & Belle Grove, VA (2002): 3,712. Civil War battle site and an antebellum plantation in Shenandoah Valley.

Chaco Culture, NM (1907/1980): 33,960. Ruins of pueblos built by prehistoric peoples incl. Pueblo, Hopi, and Navajo.

Chesapeake & Ohio Canal, MD-DC-WV (1938/1971): 19,612. 184-mi historic canal; DC to Cumberland, MD.

Colonial, VA (1930/1936): 8,677. Incl. most of Jamestown Isl., site of first successful English colony; Yorktown, site of Cornwallis's surrender to George Washington; Colonial Parkway.

Cumberland Gap, KY-TN-VA (1940): 24,547. Mountain pass of Wilderness Road, which carried first great migration of pioneers into America's interior.

Dayton Aviation Heritage, OH (1992): 111. Commemorates area's involvement in aviation.

George Rogers Clark, Vincennes, IN (1966): 26. Commemorates American defeat of British in West during Revolution.

Harpers Ferry, MD-VA-WV (1944/1963): 3,670. At confluence of Shenandoah and Potomac Rivers, the site of John Brown's 1859 raid on the Army arsenal.

Hopewell Culture, OH (1923/1992): 1,765. Remains of ceremonial mounds built in the Ohio River Valley, 200 BCE-500 CE.

Independence, Philadelphia, PA (1948): 45. Several properties associated with American Revolution and founding of U.S., incl. Independence Hall, Liberty Bell Center.

Jean Lafitte (and Preserve), LA (1907/1978): 22,421. Incl. Chalmette, site of 1815 Battle of New Orleans; French Quarter.

Kalaupapa, HI (1980): 10,779. Former colony on Molokai Isl. for those with Hansen's disease (leprosy).

Kaloko-Honokohau, HI (1978): 1,163. Preserves native culture of Hawaii.

Keweenaw, MI (1992): 1,869. Site of first significant copper mine in U.S.

Klondike Gold Rush, AK-WA (1976): 12,996. Preserves Chilkoot Trail used in 1898 Gold Rush. Museum in Seattle.

Lewis and Clark, OR-WA (1958/2004): 3,410. Lewis and Clark encampment, 1805-06. Incorporates former Fort Clatsop Natl. Mem. Park and OR-WA state parks.

Lowell, MA (1978): 141. Textile mills, canal, 19th-cent. structures; park shows planned city of Industrial Revolution.

Lyndon B. Johnson, TX (1969/1980): 1,570. President's birthplace, boyhood home, ranch.

Marsh-Billings-Rockefeller, VT (1992): 643. Boyhood home of conservationist George Perkins Marsh.

Minute Man, MA (1959): 1,027. Where Minute Men battled British, Apr. 19, 1775. Also contains Nathaniel Hawthorne's home.

Morristown, NJ (1933): 1,711. Site of important military encampments during the American Revolution; Washington's headquarters, 1779-80.

Natchez, MS (1988): 108. Mansions, townhouses, and villas related to history of Natchez.

New Bedford Whaling, MA (1996): 34. Preserves structures and relics associated with the city's 19th-cent. whaling industry.

New Orleans Jazz, LA (1994): 5. Preserves, educates, and interprets jazz as it has evolved in New Orleans.

Nez Perce, ID-MT-OR-WA (1965): 4,565. Illustrates history and culture of Nez Perce, or Nimiipuu, homeland (38 separate sites).

Palo Alto Battlefield, TX (1978): 3,442. Scene of first battle of the Mexican War.

Paterson Great Falls, NJ (2011): 36. Falls helped make city one of U.S.'s earliest industrial centers.

Pecos, NM (1965/1990): 6,703. Ruins of ancient Pueblo of Pecos, archaeological sites, and two associated Spanish colonial missions from 17th and 18th centuries.

Pu'uhonua o Hōnaunau, HI (1955/1978): 420. Until 1819, a sanctuary for Hawaiians vanquished in battle and for those guilty of crimes or breaking taboos.

Rosie the Riveter/WWII Home Front, Richmond, CA (2000): 145. Site of shipyard that employed thousands of women during WWII; commemorates women who worked in wartime industries.

Salt River Bay (and Ecological Preserve), St. Croix, VI (1992): 986. Only known site where, in 1493, members of a Columbus party landed on what is now U.S. territory.

San Antonio Missions, TX (1978): 825. Four Spanish missions, 18th-cent. irrigation system.

San Francisco Maritime, CA (1988): 50. Artifacts, photographs, and historic vessels related to development of the Pacific Coast.

San Juan Island, WA (1966): 2,146. Commemorates peaceful relations between U.S., Canada, and Great Britain since the 1872 boundary disputes.

Saratoga, NY (1938): 3,415. Scene of a major 1777 battle that became a turning point in the American Revolution.

Sitka, AK (1910/1972): 116. Scene of last major resistance of Tlingit to the Russians, 1804.

Thomas Edison, West Orange, NJ (1955/1962): 21. Inventor's home and laboratory.

Tumacacori, AZ (1908/1990): 360. Historic Spanish mission building near site first visited by Father Kino in 1691.

Valley Forge, PA (1976): 3,468. Continental Army campsite in 1777-78 winter.

War in the Pacific, GU (1978): 2,037. Seven distinct units illustrating the Pacific theater of WWII. Limited federal facilities.

Women's Rights, NY (1980): 7. Seneca Falls site where Lucretia Mott, Elizabeth Cady Stanton organized movement in 1848.

National Battlefields/Parks/Sites

Antietam, MD (1890/1978): 3,230. Battle here ended first Confederate invasion of North, Sept. 17, 1862.

Big Hole, MT (1910/1963): 1,011. Site of major battle with Nez Perce Indians, Aug. 9-10, 1877.

Brices Cross Roads, Baldwyn, MS (1929): 1. Site of Confederate victory, June 10, 1864.

Cowpens, SC (1929/1972): 842. American Revolution battlefield, Jan. 17, 1781.

Fort Donelson, TN-KY (1928/1985): 1,025. Site of first major Union victory, Feb. 14-16, 1862.

Fort Necessity, PA (1931/1961): 903. Site of first battle of French and Indian War, July 3, 1754.

Kennesaw Mountain, GA (1917/1935): 2,853. Site of major battle of Atlanta campaign in Civil War.

Manassas, VA (1940): 5,073. Scene of two Civil War battles.

Monocacy, MD (1934/1976): 1,647. Civil War battle in defense of Washington, DC, fought here, July 9, 1864.

Moores Creek, Currie, NC (1926/1980): 88. Commemorates Feb. 27, 1776, battle between Patriots and Loyalists.

Petersburg, VA (1926/1962): 2,740. Scene of Union campaigns, 1864-65.

Richmond, VA (1936): 6,956. Site of battles defending Confederate capital.

River Raisin, Monroe, MI (2010): 42. Site of major battles of War of 1812.

Stones River, TN (1927/1960): 709. Scene of battle that began federal offensive to trisect Confederacy, Dec. 31, 1862-Jan. 2, 1863.

Tupelo, MS (1929/1961): 1. Site of crucial battle over Union Gen. Sherman's supply line, July 14-15, 1865.

Wilson's Creek, MO (1960/1970): 2,369. Scene of Civil War battle for control of Missouri, Aug. 10, 1861.

National Military Parks

Chickamauga and Chattanooga, GA-TN (1890): 9,036. Where Gen. Sherman and Union armies gained control of TN, 1863.

Fredericksburg and Spotsylvania, VA (1927/1933): 8,382. Sites of several major Civil War battles and campaigns.

Gettysburg, PA (1895/1933): 5,988. Site of decisive Confederate defeat in North, July 1863, and of Gettysburg Address.

Guilford Courthouse, NC (1917/1933): 250. American Revolution battle site.

Horseshoe Bend, AL (1956): 2,040. On Tallapoosa River, where Gen. Andrew Jackson broke power of Upper Creek Indian Confederacy on Mar. 27, 1814.

Kings Mountain, SC (1931/1933): 3,945. Site of American Revolution battle, fought on Oct. 7, 1780.

Pea Ridge, AR (1956): 4,300. Civil War battle, Mar. 7-8, 1862.

Shiloh, TN-MS (1894/1933): 5,978. Major Civil War battle site; incl. Indian burial mounds.

Vicksburg, MS-LA (1899/1933): 1,802. Union victory gave North control of Mississippi and split Confederate forces.

National Memorials

Arkansas Post, AR (1960): 758. First permanent French settlement in lower Mississippi River valley.

Arlington House, The Robert E. Lee Memorial, VA (1925/1972): 28. Lee's home overlooking the Potomac River.

Chamizal, El Paso, TX (1966/1974): 55. Commemorates 1963 settlement of 99-year border dispute with Mexico.

Coronado, AZ (1941/1952): 4,830. Commemorates first European exploration of the Southwest.

De Soto, Bradenton, FL (1948): 30. Commemorates 16th-cent. Spanish explorations.

Federal Hall, New York, NY (1939/1955): 0.45. First seat of U.S. government under the Constitution.

Flight 93, Shanksville, PA (2002): 2,320. Commemorates passengers and crew of Flight 93, who died thwarting an attack on Sept. 11, 2001. First instance of memorial completed and dedicated in 2011.

Fort Caroline, Jacksonville, FL (1950): 138. On St. Johns River, site of first attempt by France, in 16th cent., at permanent North American settlement.

Franklin Delano Roosevelt Memorial, DC (1982): 8. Statues of Pres. Roosevelt and Eleanor Roosevelt; waterfalls and gardens.

General Grant, New York, NY (1958): 0.76. Tomb of Ulysses Grant and wife; largest mausoleum in U.S.

Hamilton Grange, New York, NY (1962): 1. Home of Alexander Hamilton.

Jefferson National Expansion, St. Louis, MO (1935): 193. Commemorates 19th cent. westward expansion; incl. Gateway Arch.

Johnstown Flood, PA (1964): 178. Commemorates 1889 flood.

Korean War Veterans Memorial, DC (1986): 2. Honors those who served in the Korean War.

Lincoln Boyhood, Lincoln City, IN (1962): 200. Site of Abraham Lincoln's boyhood home and grave site of his mother.

Lincoln Memorial, DC (1911/1933): 7. Marble statue of 16th president.

Lyndon Baines Johnson Memorial Grove on the Potomac, DC (1973): 17. Overlooks Potomac River; vista of the Capitol.

Martin Luther King Jr., DC (1996): 3. Granite statue of Dr. King close to where he delivered "I Have a Dream" speech.

Mount Rushmore, SD (1925): 1,278. World-famous sculpture of presidents Washington, Jefferson, Lincoln, T. Roosevelt.

Perry's Victory and International Peace Memorial, Put-in-Bay, OH (1936/1972): 25. World's most massive Doric column promotes pursuit of peace through arbitration and disarmament.

Port Chicago Naval Magazine, Danville, CA (2009): 5. Where 1944 munitions ship explosion killed 320 men.

Roger Williams, Providence, RI (1965): 5. Memorial to founder of Rhode Island.

Thaddeus Kosciuszko, Philadelphia, PA (1972): 0.02. Memorial to Polish hero of American Revolution.

Theodore Roosevelt Island, DC (1932/1933): 89. Statue of Roosevelt in wooded island sanctuary.

Thomas Jefferson Memorial, DC (1934): 18. Statue of Jefferson in an inscribed circular, colonnaded structure.

Vietnam Veterans Memorial, DC (1980): 2. Black granite wall with names of those missing or killed in action in Vietnam War.

Washington Monument, DC (1848/1933): 106. Obelisk honoring the first U.S. president.

World War II Memorial, DC (1994/2004): 8. Oval plaza with central pool commemorating those who fought and died.

Wright Brothers, Kill Devil Hills, NC (1927/1953): 428. Site of first powered flight.

National Historic Sites

Allegheny Portage Railroad, PA (1964): 1,284. Linked Pennsylvania Canal system and the West.

Andersonville, GA (1970): 515. Noted Civil War POW camp.

Andrew Johnson, Greeneville, TN (1935/1963): 17. Two homes and the tailor shop of 17th U.S. president.

Bent's Old Fort, CO (1960): 799. Replica of fort on Sante Fe Trail.

Boston African-American, MA (1980): 0.59. Pre-Civil War black-owned structures.

Brown v. Board of Education, Topeka, KS (1992): 2. Commemorates landmark 1954 U.S. Supreme Court decision, which ended legal segregation in schools.

Carl Sandburg Home, Flat Rock, NC (1968): 264. Home of Pulitzer Prize-winning poet and biographer.

Carter G. Woodson Home, DC (1976/2006): 0.15. Home of "Father of Black History."

Charles Pinckney, Mt. Pleasant, SC (1988): 28. Farm of a principal author and signer of the Constitution.

Christiansted, St. Croix, VI (1952/1961): 27. Commemorates Danish colony.

Clara Barton, Glen Echo, MD (1974): 9. Home of American Red Cross founder.

Edgar Allan Poe, Philadelphia, PA (1978/1980): 0.52. Writer's home.

Eisenhower, Gettysburg, PA (1967): 690. Home of 34th president.

Eleanor Roosevelt, Hyde Park, NY (1977): 181. Former first lady's personal retreat.

Eugene O'Neill, Danville, CA (1976): 13. Home where playwright wrote his final plays, incl. The Iceman Cometh.

First Ladies, Canton, OH (2000): 0.46. Home of first lady Ida Sexton McKinley. Library now devoted to America's first ladies.

Ford's Theatre, DC (1866/1970): 0.30. Incl. theater where Lincoln was assassinated, house where he died, and Lincoln Museum.

Fort Bowie, AZ (1964): 999. Focal point of operations against Geronimo and Apaches.

Fort Davis, TX (1961): 523. Frontier outpost in West Texas; established to guard the San Antonio-El Paso Road.

Fort Laramie, WY (1938/1960): 867. Military post on Oregon Trail.

Fort Larned, KS (1964/1966): 718. Military post on Santa Fe Trail.

Fort Point, CA (1970): 29. West Coast fortification; protected San Francisco during and after Civil War.

Fort Raleigh, NC (1941): 513. First attempted English settlement in North America.

Fort Scott, KS (1965/1978): 17. Commemorates U.S. frontier. Focal point of black troop activity, training during Civil War.

Fort Smith, AR-OK (1961): 75. One of the earliest U.S. posts in Missouri Territory, active 1817-90.

Fort Union Trading Post, MT-ND (1966): 440. Principal fur-trading post on upper Missouri, 1829-67.

Fort Vancouver, WA-OR (1948/1961): 207. Headquarters for Hudson's Bay Company.

Frederick Douglass, DC (1962/1988): 9. Home of black abolitionist, writer, orator.

Frederick Law Olmsted, Brookline, MA (1979): 7. Home of city planner, famous for designing Central Park in NYC.

Friendship Hill, PA (1978): 675. Home of Albert Gallatin, Jefferson's and Madison's secretary of treasury.

Golden Spike, UT (1957): 2,735. Commemorates completion of first transcontinental railroad in 1869.

Grant-Kohrs Ranch, MT (1972): 1,618. Ranch house owned by John Grant, 19th-cent. range-cattle industry pioneer.

Hampton, Towson, MD (1948): 62. 18th-cent. Georgian mansion, which in 1790 was largest house in U.S.

Harry S. Truman, MO (1983): 13. House of 33rd president from 1919 on and farm where he worked as young man.

Herbert Hoover, West Branch, IA (1965): 187. Birthplace and boyhood home of 31st president.

Home of Franklin D. Roosevelt, Hyde Park, NY (1944): 850. FDR's birthplace, home, and "summer White House."

Hopewell Furnace, PA (1938/1985): 848. 19th-cent. iron-making village.

Hubbell Trading Post, AZ (1965): 160. Oldest continuously operating trading post in SW; founded in 1878 on Navajo Nation.

James A. Garfield, Mentor, OH (1980): 8. Home of 20th president; site of his front-porch campaign.

Jimmy Carter, Plains, GA (1987): 72. Birthplace and home of 39th president.

John Fitzgerald Kennedy, Brookline, MA (1967): 0.09. Birthplace and childhood home of 35th president.

John Muir, Martinez, CA (1964): 344. Home of Sierra Club co-founder and "Father of the National Park Service."

Knife River Indian Villages, ND (1974): 1,749. Remnants of villages last occupied by Hidatsa and Mandan Indians.

Lincoln Home, Springfield, IL (1971): 12. Lincoln's residence when he was elected 16th president, 1860.

Little Rock Central High School, AR (1998): 27. Commemorates 1957 desegregation during which federal troops were called in to protect nine black students.

Longfellow House–Washington's Headquarters, Cambridge, MA (1972): 2. Poet's home, 1837-82; Washington's headquarters during Boston siege, 1775-76.

Maggie L. Walker, Richmond, VA (1978): 1. Home of black leader and first female bank president, daughter of former slave.

Manzanar, Lone Pine, CA (1992): 814. Manzanar War Relocation Ctr., a WWII Japanese-American internment camp.

Martin Luther King Jr., Atlanta, GA (1980): 39. Birthplace, grave, church of the civil rights leader.

Martin Van Buren, Kinderhook, NY (1974): 285. Lindenwald, home of 8th president.

Mary McLeod Bethune Council House, DC (1982/1991): 0.07. Commemorates Bethune's leadership in the black women's movement.

Minidoka, ID (2008): 396. WWII Japanese internment center.

Minuteman Missile, SD (1999): 44. Missile launch facilities dating back to Cold War era.

Nicodemus, KS (1996): 5. Only remaining Western town established by African Americans during Reconstruction.

Ninety Six, SC (1976): 1,022. Colonial trading village and site of Gen. Nathanael Greene's siege on Loyalist-held fort in 1781.

Pennsylvania Avenue, DC (1965): 19. Incl. area between Capitol and White House, encompassing U.S. Navy Memorial, Freedom Plaza, Old Post Office Pavilion, and other sites.

President William Jefferson Clinton Birthplace Home, Hope, AR (2010): 1. Birthplace and early home of 42nd president.

Pu'ukoholā Heiau, Kawaihae, HI (1972): 86. Ruins of temple built by King Kamehameha, first king of united Hawaiian islands.

Sagamore Hill, Oyster Bay, NY (1962): 83. Home of Pres. Theodore Roosevelt from 1885 until his death in 1919.

Saint-Gaudens, Cornish, NH (1964): 191. Home, studio, and gardens of American sculptor Augustus Saint-Gaudens.

Saint Paul's Church, New York, NY (1943): 6. Site associated with John Peter Zenger's "freedom of the press" trial.

Salem Maritime, MA (1938): 9. Major fishing and whaling port famous for 1692 witchcraft trials.

Sand Creek Massacre, CO (2000): 12,583. Site where more than 160 Cheyenne and Arapaho Indians were killed by U.S. soldiers in 1864.

San Juan, PR (1949): 75. 16th-cent. Spanish fortifications.

Saugus Iron Works, MA (1974): 9. Reconstructed 17th-cent. colonial ironworks.

Springfield Armory, MA (1974): 55. Small-arms manufacturing center for nearly 200 years.

Steamtown, Scranton, PA (1986): 62. Rail yard, roadhouse, repair shops of former Delaware, Lackawanna & Western Railroad.

Theodore Roosevelt Birthplace, New York, NY (1962): 0.11. Reconstructed brownstone where 26th president was born.

Theodore Roosevelt Inaugural, Buffalo, NY (1966): 1. Wilcox House, where 26th president took oath of office, 1901.

Thomas Stone, Port Tobacco, MD (1978): 328. Home of signer of Declaration of Independence.

Tuskegee Airmen, AL (1998): 90. Airfield where pilots of all-black WWII air corps unit received flight training.

Tuskegee Institute, AL (1974): 58. College founded by Booker T. Washington in 1881 for blacks.

Ulysses S. Grant, St. Louis, MO (1989): 10. Home of Grant during pre-Civil War years.

Vanderbilt Mansion, Hyde Park, NY (1940): 212. Mansion of 19th-cent. financier.

Washita Battlefield, OK (1996): 315. Scene of Nov. 27, 1868, battle between Plains tribes and U.S. army.

Weir Farm, Wilton, CT (1990): 74. Home and studio of American impressionist painter J. Alden Weir.

Whitman Mission, Walla Walla, WA (1936/1963): 139. Site of Protestant missionaries to Cayuse Indians beginning in 1830s.

William Howard Taft, Cincinnati, OH (1969): 4. Birthplace and early home of 27th president.

Name	Location	Year[1]	Acreage
National Lakeshores			
Apostle Islands	WI	1970	69,372
Indiana Dunes	IN	1966	15,314
Pictured Rocks	MI	1966	73,236
Sleeping Bear Dunes	MI	1970	71,213
National Monuments			
African Burial Ground	NY	2006	0.35
Agate Fossil Beds	NE	1965	3,058
Alibates Flint Quarries	TX	1965	1,371
Aniakchak[2]	AK	1978	137,176
Aztec Ruins	NM	1923	318
Bandelier	NM	1916	33,677
Booker T. Washington	VA	1956	239
Buck Island Reef	VI	1961	19,015
Cabrillo	CA	1913	160
Canyon de Chelly	AZ	1931	83,840
Cape Krusenstern	AK	1978	649,125
Capulin Volcano	NM	1916	793
Casa Grande Ruins	AZ	1889	473
Castillo de San Marcos	FL	1924	19
Castle Clinton	NY	1946	1
Cedar Breaks	UT	1933	6,155
César E. Chávez	CA	2012	117
Charles Young Buffalo Soldiers	OH	2013	60
Chiricahua	AZ	1924	11,985
Colorado	CO	1911	20,536
Craters of the Moon	ID	1924	53,571
Devils Postpile	CA	1911	798
Devils Tower	WY	1906	1,347
Dinosaur	CO-UT	1915	210,283
Effigy Mounds	IA	1949	2,526
El Malpais	NM	1987	114,314
El Morro	NM	1906	1,279
First State	DE-PA	2013	1,151
Florissant Fossil Beds	CO	1969	5,998
Fort Frederica	GA	1936	284
Fort Matanzas	FL	1924	300
Fort McHenry (and Historic Shrine)	MD	1925	43
Fort Monroe	VA	2011	325
Fort Pulaski	GA	1924	5,623
Fort Stanwix	NY	1935	16
Fort Sumter	SC	1948	235
Fort Union	NM	1954	721
Fossil Butte	WY	1972	8,198
George Washington Birthplace	VA	1930	662
George Washington Carver	MO	1943	210
Gila Cliff Dwellings	NM	1907	533
Governors Island	NY	2001	23
Grand Portage	MN	1951	710
Hagerman Fossil Beds	ID	1988	4,351
Harriet Tubman Underground Railroad	MD	2013	480
Hohokam Pima[3]	AZ	1972	1,690
Homestead NM of America	NE	1936	211
Hovenweep	CO-UT	1923	785
Jewel Cave	SD	1908	1,274
John Day Fossil Beds	OR	1974	14,062
Lava Beds	CA	1925	46,692
Little Bighorn Battlefield	MT	1879	765
Montezuma Castle	AZ	1906	1,016
Muir Woods	CA	1908	554
Natural Bridges	UT	1908	7,636
Navajo	AZ	1909	360
Ocmulgee	GA	1934	702
Oregon Caves	OR	1909	488
Organ Pipe Cactus	AZ	1937	330,689
Petroglyph	NM	1990	7,209
Pipe Spring	AZ	1923	40
Pipestone	MN	1937	282
Poverty Point[2]	LA	1988	911
Rainbow Bridge	UT	1910	160
Russell Cave	AL	1961	310
Salinas Pueblo Missions	NM	1909	1,071
Scotts Bluff	NE	1919	3,005
Statue of Liberty	NJ-NY	1924	61
Sunset Crater Volcano	AZ	1930	3,040
Timpanogos Cave	UT	1922	250
Tonto	AZ	1907	1,120
Tuzigoot	AZ	1939	812
Virgin Islands Coral Reef	VI	2001	12,708
Walnut Canyon	AZ	1915	3,529
White Sands	NM	1933	143,733
World War II Valor in the Pacific	HI-CA	2008	59
Wupatki	AZ	1924	35,422
Yucca House[2]	CO	1919	34

Name	Location	Year[1]	Acreage
National Parkways			
Blue Ridge	NC-VA	1933	95,928
George Washington Memorial	MD-DC-VA	1930	7,035
John D. Rockefeller Jr. Memorial	WY	1972	23,777
Natchez Trace	MS-TN-AL	1938	52,302
National Preserves			
Aniakchak[2]	AK	1980	464,118
Bering Land Bridge	AK	1980	2,697,391
Big Cypress	FL	1974	720,564
Big Thicket	TX	1974	109,086
Craters of the Moon	ID	2002	410,733
Denali	AK	1917	1,334,118
Gates of the Arctic	AK	1978	948,608
Glacier Bay	AK	1925	58,406
Great Sand Dunes	CO	2000	41,686
Katmai	AK	1918	418,699
Lake Clark	AK	1978	1,410,294
Little River Canyon	AL	1992	15,288
Mojave	CA	1994	1,540,653
Noatak	AK	1978	6,587,071
Tallgrass Prairie	KS	1996	10,894
Timucuan Ecological and Historic	FL	1988	46,301
Wrangell-St. Elias	AK	1978	4,852,653
Yukon-Charley Rivers	AK	1978	2,526,512
National Recreation Areas			
Amistad	TX	1965	58,500
Bighorn Canyon	MT-WY	1966	120,296
Boston Harbor Islands	MA	1996	1,482
Chattahoochee River	GA	1978	9,792
Chickasaw	OK	1902	9,899
Curecanti	CO	1965	43,095
Delaware Water Gap	NJ-PA	1965	66,741
Gateway	NJ-NY	1972	26,607
Gauley River	WV	1988	11,565
Glen Canyon	AZ-UT	1958	1,254,117
Golden Gate	CA	1972	79,959
Lake Chelan	WA	1968	61,949
Lake Mead	AZ-NV	1936	1,495,806
Lake Meredith	TX	1965	44,978
Lake Roosevelt (formerly Coulee Dam)	WA	1946	100,390
Ross Lake	WA	1968	117,575
Santa Monica Mountains	CA	1978	156,670
Whiskeytown-Shasta-Trinity[4]	CA	1965	42,503
National Reserves			
City of Rocks	ID	1988	14,407
Ebey's Landing Historical	WA	1978	19,333
National Rivers			
Big South Fork (and Rec. Area)	KY-TN	1976	125,310
Buffalo	AR	1972	94,293
Mississippi (and Rec. Area)	MN	1988	53,775
New River Gorge	WV	1978	72,186
Ozark Scenic Riverways	MO	1964	80,785
National Seashores			
Assateague Island[5]	MD-VA	1965	41,320
Canaveral	FL	1975	57,662
Cape Cod	MA	1961	43,607
Cape Hatteras	NC	1937	30,351
Cape Lookout	NC	1966	28,243
Cumberland Island	GA	1972	36,347
Fire Island	NY	1964	19,580
Gulf Islands	FL-MS	1971	137,989
Padre Island	TX	1962	130,434
Point Reyes	CA	1962	71,055
International Historic Site			
Saint Croix Island	ME	1949	7
Other Designations			
Catoctin Mountain Park	MD	1954	5,891
Constitution Gardens	DC	1974	39
Fort Washington Park	MD	1930	341
Greenbelt Park	MD	1950	1,175
National Capital Parks	DC-MD	1933	6,841
National Mall	DC	1933	156
Piscataway Park	MD	1961	4,626
Prince William Forest Park	VA	1948	16,063
Rock Creek Park	DC	1890	1,755
White House	DC	1933	18
Wolf Trap National Park for the Performing Arts	VA	1966	130

National Wild and Scenic Rivers

Rivers in this system are designated by Congress or the Secretary of the Interior. As of Sept. 2012, the system included 12,602 miles of 203 rivers in 39 states and Puerto Rico. Not all of the rivers that the NPS administers are official units of the park system. Only NPS units are listed here.

Name	Location	Year[1]	Acreage
Alagnak Wild[2]	AK	1980	30,665
Bluestone Scenic	WV	1978	4,310

Name	Location	Year[1]	Acreage	Name	Location	Year[1]	Acreage
Delaware Scenic............	NJ-PA	1978	1,973	Gloria Dei (Old Swedes')			
Great Egg Harbor Scenic				Church NHS.............	PA	1942	4
and Rec.................	NJ	1992	43,311	Green Springs Natl. Historic			
Missouri Recreational........	NE-SD	1991	34,099	Landmark District	VA	1974	14,004
Niobrara Scenic	NE	1991	29,101	Historic Camden Revolutionary			
Obed	TN	1976	5,073	War Site	SC	1982	107
Rio Grande	TX	1978	9,600	Ice Age Natl. Scientific Reserve	WI	1964	32,500
Saint Croix Scenic Riverway....	MN-WI	1968	92,746	International Peace Garden ...	ND-MB	1949	2,339
Upper Delaware Scenic and Rec.	NY-PA	1978	75,000	Iñupiat Heritage Center	AK	1999	NA
				Jamestown NHS...........	VA	1940	23
Affiliated Areas				Kate Mullany NHS	NY	2004	0.06
Affiliated areas are administered in connection with the NPS				Lower East Side Tenement			
but are not owned by that agency.				NHS....................	NY	1998	NA
Aleutian World War II				New Jersey Coastal Heritage			
Natl. Historic Site (NHS)	AK	1996	81	Trail Route..............	NJ	1988	NA
American Memorial Park	MP	1978	133	Oklahoma City Natl. Memorial	OK	2004	3
Benjamin Franklin Natl.				Pinelands Natl. Reserve......	NJ	1978	1,100,000
Memorial................	PA	1972	NA	Red Hill Patrick Henry Natl.			
Chicago Portage NHS	IL	1952	91	Memorial................	VA	1986	117
Chimney Rock NHS	NE	1956	83	Roosevelt Campobello Intl.			
Fallen Timbers Battlefield				Park....................	NB	1964	2,861
and Fort Miamis NHS......	OH	1999	185	Sewall-Belmont House NHS...	DC	1974	0.35
Father Marquette Natl.				Thomas Cole NHS	NY	1999	3
Memorial................	MI	1975	52	Touro Synagogue NHS	RI	1946	0.23

NA = Not available. (1) Year current designation received. (2) No federal facilities. (3) Located on Gila River Indian Reservation; not open to the public. (4) Shasta and Trinity units are administered by the Forest Service. Figure given is NPS acreage only. (5) Figure given includes acreage administered by Fish and Wildlife Service.

National Trails System

Source: National Park Service (NPS) and Bureau of Land Management (BLM), U.S. Dept. of the Interior; U.S. Forest Service, U.S. Dept. of Agriculture

As of Dec. 31, 2013, the National Trails System included 11 national scenic trails, 19 national historic trails, more than 1,200 national recreation trails, and 6 connecting and side trails. National scenic trails and national historic trails are established by Congress and administered by the NPS, Forest Service, or BLM. Official NPS units are indicated by an asterisk.

Name	Location	Year[1]	Length (mi)[2]	Name	Location	Year[1]	Length (mi)[2]
National Scenic Trails				El Camino Real de los Tejas....	TX, LA	2004	2,580
*Appalachian	ME to GA	1968	2,185	El Camino Real de Tierra Adentro	NM, TX	2000	404
Arizona	AZ	2009	819	Iditarod	AK	1978	2,300
Continental Divide	MT, ID, WY,			Juan Bautista de Anza	AZ, CA	1990	1,200
	CO, NM	1978	3,100	Lewis and Clark	IL to Pacific	1978	3,700
Florida	FL	1983	1,300	Mormon Pioneer............	IL to UT	1978	1,300
Ice Age	WI	1980	1,200	Nez Perce (Nee-Me-Poo)	OR to MT	1986	1,182
*Natchez Trace.............	MS-AL-TN	1983	150	Old Spanish	NM to CA	2002	2,700
New England	MA, CT	2009	215	Oregon	MO to OR	1978	2,130
North Country	NY to ND	1980	4,500	Overmountain Victory........	NC, SC,		
Pacific Crest...............	CA, OR, WA	1968	2,650		TN, VA	1980	330
Pacific Northwest	MT, ID, WA	2009	1,206	Pony Express	MO to CA	1992	2,005
*Potomac Heritage	VA to PA	1983	836	Santa Fe.................	MO, KS, OK,		
					CO, NM	1987	1,203
National Historic Trails[3]				Selma to Montgomery	AL	1996	54
Ala Kahakai	HI	2000	175	Star-Spangled Banner	VA, DC, MD	2008	560
California	MO, NE to			Trail of Tears	GA, AL, TN		
	CA, OR	1992	5,839		to OK	1987	5,043
Captain John Smith Chesapeake	VA, DC,			Washington-Rochambeau			
	MD, DE	2006	3,000	Revolutionary Route	MA to VA	2009	680

(1) Year designation was received. (2) Authorized length; some trails are not yet complete. (3) Trails may include both overland and water routes.

National Heritage Areas

Source: National Park Service (NPS), U.S. Dept. of the Interior; Alliance of National Heritage Areas

National Heritage Areas (NHAs) are designated by Congress for their national importance. NHAs are not units of the National Park system, though the NPS advises and provides limited financial assistance.

Name	Location	Year[1]	Size (sq mi)	Name	Location	Year[1]	Size (sq mi)
Abraham Lincoln............	IL	2008	25,975	Gullah Geechee Cultural	NC, SC,		
Arabia Mountain............	GA	2006	64	Heritage Corridor	GA, FL	2006	12,818
Atchafalaya	LA	2006	10,400	Hudson River Valley[2]	NY	1996	154
Augusta Canal	GA	1996	3+	Illinois & Michigan Canal NHC	IL	1984	862
Baltimore	MD	2009	18	John H. Chafee Blackstone			
Blue Ridge	NC	2003	11,000	River Valley NHC..........	MA, RI	1986	550
Cache La Poudre River[2]......	CO	1996	45	Journey Through Hallowed	PA, MD,		
Cane River	LA	1994	181	Ground[2].................	WV, VA	2008	180
Champlain Valley Natl.				Kenai Mountains-Turnagain Arm	AK	2009	NA
Heritage Partnership.......	NY, VT	2006	(3)	Lackawanna River Heritage Trail[2]	PA	2000	70
Crossroads of the American				Mississippi Delta...........	MS	2009	10,976
Revolutions.............	NJ	2006	2,155	Mississippi Gulf Coast	MS	2004	4,289
Delaware & Lehigh Natl.				Mississippi Hills	MS	2009	(4)
Heritage Corridor (NHC)[2] ...	PA	1988	165	Mormon Pioneer...........	UT	2006	16,070
Erie Canalway NHC	NY	2000	4,834	MotorCities	MI	1998	10,000
Essex	MA	1996	500	Muscle Shoals	AL	2009	3,913
Freedom's Frontier	KS, MO	2006	31,021	National Aviation Heritage Area	OH	2004	(5)
Freedom's Way	MA, NH	2009	994	National Coal Heritage Area...	WV	1996	5,300
Great Basin Natl. Heritage				Niagara Falls[2].............	NY	2008	13
Route	NV, UT	2006	15,704	Northern Plains.............	ND	2009	800

Name	Location	Year[1]	Size (sq mi)	Name	Location	Year[1]	Size (sq mi)
Northern Rio Grande	NM	2006	10,000	Shenandoah Valley Battlefields			
Ohio & Erie Canalway[2]	OH	1996	110	Natl. Historic District	VA	1996	3,939
Oil Region.	PA	2004	708	Silos and Smokestacks.	IA	1996	20,000+
Path of Progress Natl.				South Carolina NHC[2]	SC	1996	240
Heritage Tour Route[2]	PA	1988	500	South Park	CO	2009	1,800
Quinebaug and Shetucket				Tennessee Civil War[6]	TN	1996	42,144
Rivers Valley NHC.	CT, MA	1994	1,086	Upper Housatonic Valley.	MA, CT	2006	964
Rivers of Steel	PA	1996	5,000+	Wheeling.	WV	2000	12
Sangre de Cristo.	CO	2009	3,000+	Yuma Crossing	AZ	2000	21
Schuylkill River Valley	PA	2000	1,750				

NA = Not available. (1) Year designation was received. (2) Figure given is length of area. (3) Covers 11 counties in both states. (4) Parts of 30 counties. (5) 8 counties. (6) Spans entire state of Tennessee.

Attractions in and Around Washington, DC

Most attractions are free. All times are subject to change. For more details call the Washington, DC, Convention and Visitors Association at 1-800-422-8644, or visit www.washington.org.

Arlington National Cemetery

Arlington National Cemetery, on the former Custis-Lee estate in Arlington, VA, is the site of the **Tomb of the Unknowns** and the final resting place of Pres. W. H. Taft and Pres. John F. Kennedy and his wife, Jacqueline Bouvier Kennedy Onassis. An eternal flame burns over the site of Kennedy's grave. Other famous Americans are buried at Arlington, as well as more than 400,000 U.S. military personnel, from every major war.

A number of monuments and memorials are located throughout the cemetery. The **Women in Military Service for America Memorial**, near the cemetery's Ceremonial Entrance, was dedicated Oct. 18, 1997. It honors the 2.5 mil women who have served in the U.S. military since the American Revolution.

Open daily, 8 AM-5 PM (8 AM-7 PM, Apr.-Sept.). Arlington, VA; (877) 907-8585. **Website:** www.arlingtoncemetery.mil

The **U.S. Marine Corps War Memorial**, also known as Iwo Jima, stands just north of Arlington National Cemetery. A bronze statue depicts the raising of the U.S. flag on Mt. Suribachi, Feb. 23, 1945, during World War II. It was executed by Felix de Weldon from a photograph by Joe Rosenthal. The grounds of the memorial are open daily 6 AM-midnight. (703) 289-2553.

Bureau of Engraving and Printing

The Bureau of Engraving and Printing of the U.S. Treasury Dept. is the headquarters for the making of U.S. paper money. Public tours are offered Mon.-Fri., 9 AM-2 PM (6 PM in spring and summer), except on federal holidays and during the week between Christmas and New Year's Day. 14th and C Sts. SW; (866) 874-2330. **Website:** www.moneyfactory.gov

Capitol

The United States Capitol was originally designed by Dr. William Thornton, an amateur architect, who submitted a plan in 1793 that won him $500 and a city lot. Three other architects designed or supervised the construction of the Capitol before its completion.

The present cast iron dome at its greatest exterior height measures 135 ft, 5 in. and is topped by the bronze Statue of Freedom, which stands 19½ ft and weighs 14,985 lbs. On its base are the words *E Pluribus Unum* (out of many, one).

The Capitol is open to the public Mon.-Sat., 8:30 AM-4:30 PM. It is closed Jan. 1, Inauguration Day, Thanksgiving Day, and Dec. 25. Tours available 8:50 AM to 3:20 PM.

To observe Congress while it is in session, those living in the U.S. may obtain tickets from their U.S. representative or senators. Visitors from other countries may obtain passes at the Capitol. Between Constitution and Independence Aves., bounded by First St.; (202) 226-8000. **Website:** www.visitthecapital.com

Federal Bureau of Investigation

The Federal Bureau of Investigation does not currently offer tours of its headquarters. Visitors to the city may learn about the FBI through exhibits at the Newseum, the National Museum of Crime and Punishment, and the International Spy Museum. J. Edgar Hoover Bldg., Pennsylvania Ave., between 9th and 10th Sts. NW; (202) 324-3000. **Website:** www.fbi.gov

Folger Shakespeare Library

The Folger Shakespeare Library, on Capitol Hill, is a research institution with the largest collection of Shakespearean materials in the world and other rare books and manuscripts of the

Renaissance period. Open to the public Mon.-Sat., 10 AM-5 PM, and Sun., 12 PM-5 PM, except on federal holidays. Building and garden tours are available. 201 E. Capitol St. SE; (202) 544-4600. **Website:** www.folger.edu

Holocaust Memorial Museum

The U.S. Holocaust Memorial Museum opened Apr. 21, 1993. The museum documents the events of the Holocaust through displays, interactive videos, and lectures. The permanent exhibition is recommended for visitors age 11 and up.

The museum is open daily, 10 AM-5:20 PM, except Yom Kippur and Dec. 25, with extended hours in spring. Admission is free though entry into the permanent exhibition is timed, Mar. through Aug. Timed passes are available at the door each day on a first-come, first-served basis; advance passes may be ordered online for a fee. 100 Raoul Wallenberg Pl. SW; (202) 488-0400. **Website:** www.ushmm.org

Jefferson Memorial

Dedicated Apr. 13, 1943, the Thomas Jefferson Memorial stands on the south shore of the Tidal Basin in West Potomac Park. It is a circular stone structure that combines architectural elements of the dome of the Pantheon in Rome and the rotunda designed by Jefferson for the Univ. of Virginia.

The memorial is open 24 hrs. a day and staffed 9:30 AM-11:30 PM. Ohio and E. Basin Drs. SW; (202) 426-6841. **Website:** www.nps.gov/thje/

John F. Kennedy Center

The John F. Kennedy Center for the Performing Arts opened Sept. 8, 1971. Designed by Edward Durell Stone, it includes an opera house, a concert hall, several theaters, restaurants, and a library. Free tours are available Mon.-Fri., 10 AM-5 PM and Sat.-Sun., 10 AM-1 PM. 2700 F St. NW; (800) 444-1324. **Website:** www.kennedy-center.org

Martin Luther King Jr. Memorial

Officially dedicated Aug. 28, 2011, the MLK Jr. Memorial features a 30-ft figure of Dr. King emerging from a block of granite, the "Stone of Hope." Designed by sculptor Lei Yixin, the memorial is located on the Tidal Basin between the Lincoln and Jefferson Memorials.

The memorial is open 24 hrs. a day and staffed 9:30 AM-11:30 PM. Independence Ave. SW and West Basin Dr. SW; (202) 426-6841. **Website:** www.nps.gov/mlkm/

Korean War Veterans Memorial

Dedicated on July 27, 1995, the Korean War Veterans Memorial honors Americans who served in the war. Situated at the west end of the Mall, the triangular-shaped stone and steel memorial features a multiservice formation of 19 combat-ready soldiers clad in ponchos with the wind at their backs. A granite wall, with images of men and women who served, juts into the Pool of Remembrance.

The memorial is open 24 hrs. a day and staffed 9:30 AM-11:30 PM. Independence Ave. SW and French Dr. SW; (202) 426-6841. **Website:** www.nps.gov/kowa/

Library of Congress

Established by and for Congress in 1800, the Library of Congress extends its services to other government agencies and libraries, scholars, and the public. It contains more than 158 mil items in some 470 languages, making it the world's largest library.

The Thomas Jefferson Building (Main Reading Room and exhibition galleries) is open Mon.-Sat., 8:30 AM-4:30 PM. The James Madison Memorial and John Adams Buildings have longer hours. A few areas are open on most federal holidays; all buildings are closed Jan. 1, Thanksgiving, and Dec. 25. 101 Independence Ave. SE; (202) 707-8000. **Website:** www.loc.gov

Lincoln Memorial

Designed by Henry Bacon, the Lincoln Memorial in West Potomac Park is a large marble hall enclosing a statue of Abraham Lincoln seated on an armchair. The memorial was dedicated May 30, 1922. The statue was designed by Daniel Chester French and sculpted by French and the six Piccirilli brothers. The text of the Gettysburg Address is in the south chamber; that of Lincoln's second inaugural speech is in the north chamber. Each is engraved on a stone tablet.

The memorial is open 24 hrs. a day and staffed 9:30 AM-11:30 PM, and is wheelchair-accessible. Independence Ave. and French Dr. SW; (202) 426-6841. **Website:** www.nps.gov/linc/

Mount Vernon

Mount Vernon, George Washington's estate, is on the south bank of the Potomac R., 16 mi from Washington, DC, in northern Virginia. The present house is believed to be an enlargement of one built by Augustine Washington in 1735. His son Lawrence renamed the estate after British Adm. Edward Vernon. George Washington, Lawrence's half brother, inherited it in 1761. The estate has been restored to its 18th-cent. appearance and includes many original furnishings. Washington and his wife, Martha, are buried on the grounds.

Open year-round, Apr.-Aug. 8 AM-5 PM; Mar., Sept., and Oct. 9 AM-5 PM; Nov.-Feb. 9 AM-4 PM; (703) 780-2000 or (800) 429-1520. Admission: adults $17, seniors (62+) $16, children (6-11) $8, ages 5 and under free. **Website:** www.mountvernon.org

National Archives and Records

Original copies of the Declaration of Independence, the Constitution, and the Bill of Rights are on display at the National Archives Museum. The National Archives also holds other U.S. government records, historic maps, photographs, and manuscripts. Research rooms are open to the public for genealogical study.

The museum is open daily 10 AM-5:30 PM, except Thanksgiving and Dec. 25. Constitution Ave. bet. 7th and 9th Sts. NW; (866) 272-6272. **Website:** www.archives.gov

National Gallery of Art

The National Gallery of Art was established by Congress, Mar. 24, 1937, and opened Mar. 17, 1941. The original West Building was designed by John Russell Pope. The East Building, opened in 1978, was designed by I. M. Pei. Galleries are open Mon.-Sat., 10 AM-5 PM, and Sun., 11 AM-6 PM. The Sculpture Garden has extended hours in summer. Closed Jan. 1 and Dec. 25. 4th St. and Constitution Ave NW; (202) 737-4215. **Website:** www.nga.gov

The Pentagon

The Pentagon, headquarters of the Dept. of Defense, is the largest office building in the U.S. It houses some 23,000 employees in offices occupying 3,705,793 sq ft. The building was severely damaged when struck by a plane Sept. 11, 2001.

Tours are available by reservation only, which must be made online 14 to 90 days in advance. Non-U.S. citizens must be able to present a foreign passport or permanent resident card to enter the Pentagon. Arlington, VA; (703) 697-1776. **Website:** pentagontours.osd.mil

Franklin Delano Roosevelt Memorial

Opened May 2, 1997, the FDR Memorial features four spaces with bronze statues and panels depicting FDR through his four terms of office. This 8-acre memorial is located on the Potomac River Tidal Basin.

Open daily, with staff on grounds 9:30 AM-11:30 PM. Ohio and W. Basin Drs. SW; (202) 426-6841. **Website:** www.nps.gov/fdrm/

Smithsonian Institution

The Smithsonian Institution, established in 1846, is the world's largest museum and research complex. It holds some 137 mil

artifacts and specimens in its trust. Seventeen of its 19 museums and the National Zoo are in the DC area. The **Smithsonian Institution Building** (or The Castle) houses the Smithsonian Information Center. Also on the National Mall are the **National Museum of American History**, the **National Museum of Natural History**, the **National Air and Space Museum**, the **National Museum of the American Indian**, the **Hirshhorn Museum and Sculpture Garden**, the **Arthur M. Sackler Gallery**, the **Freer Gallery of Art**, the **National Museum of African Art**, and the **Arts and Industries Building** (currently closed for renovation). Located nearby are the **National Postal Museum**, the **National Museum of American Art**, the **National Portrait Gallery**, and the **Renwick Gallery** (closed for renovation). The **Anacostia Community Museum** is in SE DC. The Air and Space Museum's **Udvar-Hazy Center** is near Dulles Airport in Virginia. The **National Museum of African American History and Culture** is expected to open on the Mall in 2016.

Most museums are open daily except Dec. 25, 10 AM-5:30 PM (later in summer); (202) 633-1000. **Website:** www.si.edu

Vietnam Veterans Memorial

Originally dedicated Nov. 13, 1982, the Vietnam Veterans Memorial recognizes the men and women who served in the armed forces in the Vietnam War. The names of more than 58,000 Americans who lost their lives or remain missing are inscribed on polished black-granite walls arranged to form a V, designed by Maya Ying Lin.

Since its opening, two additions have been made to the Memorial. The first, dedicated on Nov. 11, 1984, is the Frederick Hart sculpture *Three Servicemen*. On Nov. 11, 1993, the Vietnam Women's Memorial, designed by Glenna Goodacre, was dedicated, honoring the more than 11,500 women who served in Vietnam.

The memorial is open 24 hrs. a day. Constitution Ave. and Bacon Dr. NW; (202) 426-6841. **Website:** www.nps.gov/vive/

Washington Monument

The Washington Monument, dedicated in 1885, is a tapering shaft, or obelisk, of white marble, 555 ft, 5⅛ in. in height and 55 ft, 1½ in. square at base. Eight small windows, two on each side, are located on the observation deck at the 500-ft level.

Open daily, 9 AM-5 PM (10 PM in summer), except July 4 and Dec. 25. Free timed passes are available same day; advance passes can be obtained for a small fee. 15th St. and Constitution Ave. NW; (202) 426-6841. **Website:** www.nps.gov/wamo/

White House

The White House, the president's residence, stands on 18 acres on the south side of Pennsylvania Ave., between the Treasury and the old Executive Office Building. The walls are of sandstone, quarried at Aquia Creek, VA. The building was first made white with lime-based whitewash in 1798, but the name did not become official until 1901.

Free self-guided tours of the residence's public areas are available Tues.-Thurs., 7:30-11 AM; Fri. and Sat., 7:30 AM-1:30 PM, except for federal holidays. Tour requests must be made at least 21 days in advance through one's member of Congress. They are scheduled on a first-come, first-served basis. 1600 Pennsylvania Ave. The White House Visitor Center at 1450 Pennsylvania Ave. is open daily 7:30 AM-4 PM; (202) 456-7041. **Website:** www.whitehouse.gov

National World War II Memorial

The National WWII Memorial is dedicated to the approx. 16 mil veterans who served and the more than 400,000 who died in the war. The 8.25-acre site is at the east end of the Lincoln Memorial Reflecting Pool. The memorial opened on Apr. 29, 2004, and was dedicated on May 29.

At the north and south entrances are 43-ft archways, representing the Atlantic and Pacific theaters. Inside the grounds is a large, oval plaza with a wall of 4,000 gold stars; each represents 100 American deaths. Fifty-six pillars ringing the center represent the states, territories, and District of Columbia. There is also a garden enclosed by a stone wall, the Circle of Remembrance.

The memorial is open 24 hrs. a day and staffed 9:30 AM-11:30 PM. 17th St. and Independence Ave. SW; (202) 426-6841. **Website:** www.nps.gov/nwwm/

UNITED STATES HISTORY

Chronology of Events

1492 Christopher Columbus and crew sighted land Oct. 12 in what is now the Bahamas.

1513 Juan Ponce de León explored Florida coast.

1524 Giovanni da Verrazano led French expedition along coast from Carolina north to Nova Scotia; entered New York Harbor.

1526 San Miguel de Guadalupe, **first European settlement** in what became U.S. territory, was established in the summer off South Carolina coast; abandoned in Oct.

1539 Hernando de Soto landed in Florida May 28; crossed Mississippi River, 1541.

1540 Francisco Vásquez de Coronado explored Southwest north of Rio Grande. **Hernando de Alarcón** reached Colorado River; **García López de Cárdenas** reached Grand Canyon. Others explored California coast.

1562 First French colony in what became U.S. territory founded on Parris Island off South Carolina coast; abandoned, 1564.

1565 St. Augustine, FL, oldest continuously occupied European settlement in U.S., founded Sept. 8 by Pedro Menéndez de Avilés. Spain ceded settlement to U.S. in 1821.

1579 Sir Francis Drake entered San Francisco Bay and claimed region for Britain.

1585 First English colony in America, sponsored by Sir Walter Raleigh, founded on **Roanoke Island**, off North Carolina coast; colony failed.

1587 Second colony attempted on Roanoke Island. Virginia Dare of colony became **first English infant born** in the New World. Settlers of second colony found to have vanished, 1590.

1607 Capt. **John Smith** and 105 cavaliers in three ships landed on Virginia coast and started Jamestown, **first permanent English settlement** in New World.

1609 Henry Hudson, English explorer of Northwest Passage, employed by Dutch, sailed into New York Harbor in Sept. and up Hudson to Albany. **Samuel de Champlain** explored Lake Champlain, to the north. Spaniards settled **Santa Fe, NM**.

1619 House of Burgesses, **first representative assembly** in New World, elected July 30 at Jamestown, VA. **First black laborers**—indentured servants—in English North American colonies, brought by Dutch to Jamestown in Aug. Chattel slavery legally recognized, 1650.

1620 Pilgrims, Puritan separatists, left Plymouth, England, Sept. 16 on *Mayflower*; reached Cape Cod Nov. 19; 103 passengers landed at Plymouth, Dec. 26. **Mayflower Compact**, signed Nov. 11, was agreement to form a self-government. Half of colony died during harsh winter.

1624 Dutch settled in Albany and along Hudson River, establishing the colony of **New Netherland** in May.

1626 Peter Minuit bought **Manhattan** for Dutch West India Co. from Manahatta Indians during summer for goods valued at $24; named island **New Amsterdam**.

1630 Settlement of **Boston** established by Massachusetts colonists led by John Winthrop; Winthrop began *The History of New England*. **William Bradford**, a governor of Plymouth Colony, began his chronicle *History of Plymouth Plantation (1620-1647)*, first published in entirety in 1856.

1634 Maryland founded as Catholic colony under charter to Lord Baltimore. Act of Toleration passed 1649 provided for religious tolerance.

1635 Boston Latin School, **oldest public school** in continuous existence in U.S., founded Apr. 23.

1636 Roger Williams founded **Providence, RI**, in June, as a democratically ruled colony with separation of church and state. Charter granted, 1644. **Harvard College** founded; oldest institution of higher learning in U.S.

1640 First book printed in America, the so-called *Bay Psalm Book*.

1647 Liberal constitution drafted in Rhode Island. First law in America providing for **free compulsory basic education** enacted in Massachusetts.

1660 British Parliament passed first **Navigation Act** Dec. 1, regulating colonial commerce to suit English needs.

1661 Missionary John Eliot's translation of the New Testament into Algonquian became the **first Bible printed** in North America.

1664 British troops Sept. 8 seized New Netherland from Dutch. Charles II granted New Netherland and city of New Amsterdam to brother, Duke of York; both renamed **New York**. Dutch recaptured colony 1673 but ceded it to Britain Nov. 10, 1674.

1670 Charles Town, SC, founded by English colonists in Apr.

1673 Regular mail service on horseback instituted Jan. 1 between New York and Boston. **Jacques Marquette** and **Louis Jolliet** reached the upper Mississippi and traveled down it.

1674 Future **Salem witch trial** judge Samuel Sewall began renowned diary covering events through 1729.

1676 Bloody **Indian war** in New England ended Aug. 12. King Philip, Wampanoag chief, and Narragansett Indians killed. **Nathaniel Bacon** led planters against autocratic British Gov. Sir William Berkeley, burned Jamestown, VA, Sept. 19. Rebellion collapsed when Bacon died; 23 followers executed.

1678 A book of poetry by **Anne Bradstreet** (first published in Britain) revised and expanded for posthumous publication in Massachusetts. Considered first female poet in American colonies.

1679 Fire destroyed 150 houses in Boston. City imported **first fire engines** from England.

1681 John Bunyan's *The Pilgrim's Progress* published in America; became best seller.

1682 René-Robert Cavelier, Sieur de La Salle, claimed lower Mississippi River country for France and called it Louisiana Apr. 9. Had French outposts built in Illinois and Texas, 1684. Killed during mutiny, 1687. Spanish colonists became the **first Europeans to settle Texas**, at site of present-day El Paso.

1683 William Penn signed treaty with Delaware Indians Apr. 23 and made payment for **Pennsylvania** lands. The **first German colonists** in America settled near Philadelphia.

1689 New York's English colonial governor, **Sir Edmund Andros**, resigned after armed uprising in Boston on Apr. 18.

1690 First colonial newspaper, *Publick Occurrences*, published by Benjamin Harris but promptly shut down for lack of official permission. Harris also published *New England Primer* for use as elementary school textbook. Large-scale **whaling** operations began in Nantucket, MA.

1626: Peter Minuit buys the island of Manhattan from Native Americans for goods valued at $24 (according to a 19th-cent. estimate).

1692 Hysteria over **witchcraft** began in Salem Village (now Danvers), MA; 19 women and 1 man were executed by special court.

1697 *The Essays* of **Sir Francis Bacon**, first published in England in 1597, was published in America; it became a best seller.

1699 Former privateer Capt. **William Kidd** arrested and sent to England; hanged for piracy, 1701. French settlements made in Mississippi, Louisiana.

1702 Legislation enacted making **Church of England** the established church in Maryland.

1704 Indians attacked **Deerfield**, MA, Feb. 28-29; killed 40, carried off 100. *Boston News Letter*, **first regular newspaper**, started by postmaster John Campbell.

1710 British-colonial troops captured French fort, Port Royal, Nova Scotia, in **Queen Anne's War**, 1702-13. France yielded Nova Scotia by treaty, 1713.

1712 Slaves revolted in New York City Apr. 6; 21 were executed. Second uprising, 1741; 13 slaves hanged, 13 burned, 71 deported.

1716 First theater in colonies opened in Williamsburg, VA.

1726 Great Awakening, general revival of evangelical religion, began in colonies.

1731 America's **first circulating library** founded in Philadelphia by Benjamin Franklin.

1732 Benjamin Franklin published the **first** *Poor Richard's Almanack*; published annually until 1757. Georgia, last of 13 colonies, chartered.

1733 Influenza epidemic swept through New York City and Philadelphia.

1735 Editor **John Peter Zenger** was acquitted of libel Aug. 5 in New York City after criticizing the British governor's conduct in office.

1739 A series of **slave uprisings** put down in South Carolina.

1741 Famous sermon "Sinners in the Hands of an Angry God," delivered July 8 at Enfield, MA, by Jonathan Edwards, one of the most important preachers in the **Great Awakening** religious revival. Danish navigator **Vitus Bering**, commanding Russian expedition, reached Alaska.

1744 King George's War pitted British and colonials versus French. Colonials captured Louisbourg, Cape Breton Isl., Nova Scotia, June 17, 1745. Returned to France 1748 by Treaty of Aix-la-Chapelle.

1752 According to legend, **Benjamin Franklin**, flying kite in thunderstorm, proved lightning is electricity, June 15; invented lightning rod. **Liberty Bell**, cast in England, was delivered to Pennsylvania.

1754 French and Indian War began with Ft. Necessity campaign in Pennsylvania. Skirmish May 28, battle at fort July 3-4. British moved Acadian French from Nova Scotia to Louisiana Oct. 8, 1755. British captured Québec Sept. 18, 1759, in battles in which French Gen. Joseph de Montcalm and British Gen. James Wolfe were killed. Peace pact signed Feb. 10, 1763. French lost Canada and Midwest. Delegates from seven colonies to New York for **Albany Congress**, July 19, approved plan of union by Benjamin Franklin; plan rejected by the colonies.

1757 First streetlights appeared in Philadelphia.

1764 Sugar Act, Apr. 5, placed duties on lumber, foodstuffs in colonies. First law passed by Parliament to specifically raise revenue from colonies, alleviate French and Indian War debts. British enforced this act, unlike with **Molasses Act** of 1733.

1765 Stamp Act, enacted by Parliament Mar. 22, required revenue stamps to help fund royal troops. Nine colonies, at Stamp Act Congress in New York Oct. 7-25, adopted Declaration of Rights. Stamp Act repealed Mar. 17, 1766. **Quartering Act**, requiring colonists to house British troops, went into effect Mar. 24.

1767 Townshend Acts levied taxes on glass, lead, paper, paint, and tea. In 1770 all duties except on tea were repealed.

1770 British troops fired Mar. 5 into Boston mob, killed five including **Crispus Attucks**, a black man, reportedly leader of group; later called **Boston Massacre**.

1773 East India Co. tea ships turned back at Boston, New York, and Philadelphia in May. Cargo ship burned at Annapolis, Oct. 14; cargo thrown overboard at **Boston Tea Party**, Dec. 16, to protest the tea tax. **First museum** in the colonies was officially established in Charleston, SC; later named the Charleston Museum.

1774 "Intolerable Acts" of Parliament curtailed Massachusetts self-rule; barred use of Boston Harbor until dumped tea was paid for. **First Continental Congress** held in Philadelphia Sept. 5-Oct. 26; called for civil disobedience against British. Rhode Island **abolished slavery**.

1775 Patrick Henry addressed Virginia convention, Mar. 23, said, "Give me liberty or give me death!" **Paul Revere, William Dawes**, and Dr. **Samuel Prescott**, Apr. 18, rode to alert patriots that British were on their way to Concord, MA, to destroy arms. At **Lexington**, MA, Apr. 19, Minutemen lost eight. On return from Concord, British suffered 273 casualties. Col. Ethan Allen (joined by Col. Benedict Arnold) captured **Ft. Ticonderoga** in New York, May 10, also Crown Point. Colonials headed for **Bunker Hill** and fortified nearby Breed's Hill, Charlestown, MA. Repulsed British under Gen. William Howe twice before retreating, June 17. Continental Congress June 15 named **George Washington** commander in chief; established a postal system, July 26. Benjamin Franklin became the **first postmaster general**.

1776 Thomas Paine's *Common Sense*, famous pro-independence pamphlet, published Jan. 10; quickly sold some 100,000 copies. France and Spain agreed May 2 to provide arms to U.S. In Continental Congress June 7, Richard Henry Lee (VA) moved "that these united colonies are, and of right ought to be, free and independent states." Resolution adopted July 2. **Declaration of Independence** approved July 4, signed Aug. 2. Col. William Moultrie's batteries at **Charleston, SC**, repulsed British sea attack June 28. Washington lost **Battle of Long Island** Aug. 27; evacuated New York. **Nathan Hale** executed as spy by British Sept. 22. Brig. Gen. Arnold's Lake Champlain fleet was defeated in **Battle of Valcour Island** Oct. 11, but British returned to Canada. Howe failed to destroy Washington's army at White Plains, NY, Oct. 28. Hessians captured Ft. Washington, Manhattan, and 3,000 men, Nov. 16; captured Ft. Lee, NJ, Nov. 20. Washington, in Pennsylvania, recrossed **Delaware River** Dec. 25-26, defeated Hessians at **Battle of Trenton**, NJ, Dec. 26.

1777 Washington defeated Lord Charles Cornwallis at **Princeton**, NJ, Jan. 3. Continental Congress, June 14, authorized an **American flag**, the Stars and Stripes. Maj. Gen. John Burgoyne's force of 8,000 from Canada captured **Ft. Ticonderoga**, NY, July 6. Americans beat back Burgoyne at Bemis Heights, Oct. 7, cut off British escape route.

1765: Ten years before his renowned "Give me liberty or give me death!" speech, Patrick Henry speaks against the Stamp Act before the Virginia House of Burgesses.

Burgoyne surrendered 5,000 men at Saratoga, NY, Oct. 17. **Articles of Confederation** adopted by Continental Congress, Nov. 15; took effect Mar. 1, 1781.
1778 France signed treaty of aid with U.S. Feb. 6; sent fleet. British evacuated Philadelphia, June 18.
1779 George Rogers Clark took Ft. Vincennes in what is now Indiana in Feb. **John Paul Jones** on the *Bonhomme Richard* defeated *Serapis* in British North Sea waters, Sept. 23.
1780 Charleston, SC, fell to the British May 12, but Loyalists were defeated in battle of **Kings Mountain**, NC, Oct. 7 in what Thomas Jefferson called "the turn of the tide of success." **Benedict Arnold** found to be a traitor Sept. 23. Arnold escaped, made brigadier general in British army.
1781 Bank of North America, **first commercial bank**, incorporated May 26. Cornwallis retired to **Yorktown, VA**. Adm. Francois Joseph de Grasse landed 3,000 French and stopped British fleet in **Hampton Roads**, VA. Washington and Jean Baptiste de Rochambeau joined forces, arrived near Williamsburg, Sept. 26. Siege of Cornwallis began, Oct. 6; **Cornwallis surrendered** Oct. 19.
1782 New British cabinet agreed in Mar. to **recognize U.S. independence.** Preliminary agreement signed in Paris, Nov. 30. Use of **scarlet letter A**, sewn on clothing or branded on skin of adulterers, discontinued in New England.
1783 Massachusetts Supreme Court decision in final Quock Walker trial **declared slavery illegal.** Newspapers typically published weekly; **first regular daily newspaper,** *Pennsylvania Evening Post*, went on sale in Philadelphia, May 30. Britain, U.S. signed **Paris peace treaty**, Sept. 3, recognizing American independence; Congress ratified it Jan. 14, 1784. Washington ordered army disbanded Nov. 3, bade farewell to his officers at Fraunces Tavern, New York City, Dec. 4.
1784 Thomas Jefferson's proposal to **ban slavery in new territories** after 1802 was narrowly defeated, Mar. 1.
1785 Regular **stagecoach routes** established between Albany, NY; New York City; and Philadelphia.
1786 Delegates from five states at Annapolis, MD, Sept. 11-14 asked Congress to call a **constitutional convention.**
1787 Shays's Rebellion of debt-ridden farmers in Massachusetts failed, Jan. 25. **Constitutional convention** opened in Philadelphia, May 25, with Washington presiding. Constitution accepted by delegates, Sept. 17. Delaware was first state to ratify it, Dec. 7; Pennsylvania and New Jersey followed. **Northwest Ordinance** adopted July 13 by Continental Congress for Northwest Territory, north of Ohio River, west of New York; made rules for statehood and guaranteed freedom of religion, support for schools, no slavery. *Federalist Papers* first appeared in *NY Independent Journal.*
1788 A large fire in **New Orleans**, then a Spanish territory, destroyed much of the city, Mar. 21. **Constitution adopted** June 21 after being ratified by the requisite ninth state (New Hampshire); also ratified by Georgia, Connecticut, Massachusetts, Maryland, South Carolina, Virginia, and New York throughout the year. **First U.S. senators elected** Sept. 30, from Pennsylvania.
1789 George Washington chosen president by all electors voting (73 eligible, 69 voting, 4 absent); **John Adams,** vice president, got 34 votes. **First Congress** met at Federal Hall, New York City, and declared Constitution in effect, Mar. 4; Washington inaugurated Apr. 30; **first inaugural ball** held May 7. U.S. **State Dept.** established by Congress July 27. (Thomas Jefferson installed as first secretary of state Feb. 1790.) **War Dept.** created Aug. 7, with Henry Knox as secretary; **Treasury Dept.** created Sept. 2, with Alexander Hamilton as secretary. **Supreme Court** created by Federal Judiciary Act, Sept. 24; **John Jay** confirmed by Congress as first Supreme Court chief justice, Sept. 26.
1790 First Supreme Court session held Feb. 2 in New York City. Congress, Mar. 1, authorized decennial **U.S. census.** Collection of data took 18 months. **Naturalization Act** (two-year residency) passed Mar. 26. John Carroll consecrated as **first American Catholic bishop**, Aug. 15. Congress met in **Philadelphia**, new temporary capital, Dec. 6.
1791 Bill of Rights, submitted to states, Sept. 25, 1789, went into effect Dec. 15. First Bank of the United States, **first bank chartered by federal government**, established in Philadelphia.
1792 Coinage Act established **U.S. Mint** in Philadelphia, Apr. 2. Gen. **"Mad" Anthony Wayne** made commander in

1789: George Washington is inaugurated as the first U.S. president, nine days after Vice Pres. John Adams took office.

Ohio-Indiana area, trained American Legion, established string of forts. Routed Indians at Fallen Timbers on Maumee River, Aug. 20, 1794; checked British at Fort Miami, OH, same year. **White House** cornerstone laid Oct. 13.
1793 Washington inaugurated for second term, Mar. 4, having received 132 electoral votes; **John Adams** again became vice president, having received second highest total, 77. Washington declared **U.S. neutrality**, Apr. 22, in war between Britain and France. Eli Whitney invented **cotton gin**, reviving Southern slavery.
1794 Whiskey Rebellion, western Pennsylvania farmers protesting liquor tax of 1791, suppressed by federal militia in Sept. **Jay's Treaty**, controversial treaty with Britain negotiated by John Jay, signed Nov. 19, ratified June 24, 1795. This treaty intended to settle long-standing differences between U.S. and Britain.
1795 U.S. bought peace from **Algerian pirates** by paying $1 mil ransom for 115 seamen Sept. 5, followed by annual tributes. Gen. Wayne signed **Treaty of Greenville** with Indians, opening Northwest Territory to settlers. Univ. of North Carolina became **first operating state university**.
1796 Washington's farewell address as president delivered Sept. 17. Warned against permanent alliances with foreign powers, big public debt, large military establishment, and devices of "small, artful, enterprising minority."
1797 John Adams inaugurated as second president Mar. 4, having received 71 electoral votes; **Thomas Jefferson** became vice president, having received 68. U.S. frigate *United States* launched at Philadelphia, July 10; *Constellation* at Baltimore, Sept. 7; *Constitution* (Old Ironsides) at Boston, Sept. 20.
1798 Alien and Sedition Acts passed by Federalists June-July; intended to silence political opposition. **War with France threatened** over French raids on U.S. shipping and rejection of U.S. diplomats. Navy (45 ships) and 365 privateers captured 84 French ships. USS *Constellation* took French warship *Insurgente*, 1799. Napoleon stopped French raids after becoming first consul.
1800 Federal government moved to **Washington, DC**.
1801 John Marshall named Supreme Court chief justice, Jan. 20. **Thomas Jefferson**, who had received same number of electoral votes as Aaron Burr in 1800 election, won out over Burr in House vote Feb. 17; Burr named vice president. **Tripoli declared war** June 10 against U.S., which refused added tribute to commerce-raiding Arab corsairs. Land and naval campaigns forced Tripoli to negotiate peace, June 4, 1805. **Oldest U.S. art institution**, Pennsylvania Academy of Fine Arts, founded in Philadelphia.
1802 Congress established U.S. Military Academy at **West Point**, NY.
1803 Supreme Court, in *Marbury v. Madison*, overturned U.S. law for first time, Feb. 24. Napoleon sold all of Louisiana, stretching to Canadian border, to U.S. for $11.25 mil in

bonds, plus $3.75 mil indemnities to American citizens with claims against France. U.S. took title Dec. 20. **Louisiana Purchase** doubled U.S. area.

1804 **Meriwether Lewis** and **William Clark** expedition ordered by Pres. Thomas Jefferson to explore what is now Northwest U.S. Started from St. Louis May 14; ended Sept. 23, 1806, back in St. Louis. Vice Pres. **Aaron Burr** shot Alexander Hamilton in duel July 11 in Weehawken, NJ; Hamilton died next day.

1805 U.S. Marines aided by Arab mercenaries, Apr. 27, captured Tripolitan port of Derna. Major victory in war against **Barbary pirates**; inspiration for "to the shores of Tripoli" in Marines Corps hymn.

1807 Robert Fulton made **first practical steamboat trip**; left New York City Aug. 17 and reached Albany, NY, 150 mi away, in 32 hr. **Embargo Act** banned all trade with foreign countries, forbidding ships to set sail for foreign ports Dec. 22.

1808 Slave importation outlawed. Some 250,000 slaves were illegally imported 1808-60.

1810 **Third U.S. Census** found population of 7,239,814. The slave population was put at 1,191,364 and the population of all other non-white free persons at 186,446.

1811 Indiana Territory governor William Henry Harrison defeated Indians led by Tenskwatawa, called the Prophet, in **Battle of Tippecanoe**, Nov. 7. Construction began on **Cumberland Road** in Cumberland, MD; road became important route to West. About 400 **slaves revolted** in Louisiana, killing the son of a plantation owner and marching on New Orleans. The insurrection was suppressed; some 75 slaves killed.

1812 **War of 1812** had three main causes: Britain seized U.S. ships trading with France; Britain had seized 4,000 naturalized U.S. sailors by 1810; Britain armed Indians, who raided Western border. U.S. stopped trade with Europe 1807 and 1809. Trade with Britain only was stopped 1810. Unaware that Britain had raised blockade against France two days before, **Congress declared war** June 18. British took **Detroit** Aug. 16.

1813 Oliver H. Perry defeated British fleet at **Battle of Lake Erie**, Sept. 10. U.S. won **Battle of the Thames**, Ontario, Oct. 5, but failed in Canadian invasion attempts. York (Toronto) and Buffalo, NY, were burned.

1814 Troops under Andrew Jackson defeated Creek Indians led by Chief Weatherford at Battle of Horseshoe Bend in Alabama, Mar. 29, ending **Creek Indian War**, begun a year earlier. British landed in Maryland in Aug., defeated U.S. force Aug. 24, **burned Capitol and White House**. Maryland

1808: Laws outlawing slave importation go into effect, but an estimated 250,000 slaves are illegally imported, 1808-60.

militia stopped British advance, Sept. 12. British bombardment of Ft. McHenry, Baltimore, for 25 hr., Sept. 13-14, failed, inspiring **Francis Scott Key** to write the words to **"The Star-Spangled Banner."** U.S. won naval **Battle of Lake Champlain** Sept. 11. Peace treaty with Great Britain signed at Ghent, Belgium, Dec. 24.

1815 Some 5,300 British, unaware of peace treaty, attacked U.S. entrenchments near **New Orleans**, Jan. 8. British had more than 2,000 casualties; Americans lost 70. U.S. flotilla finally ended attacks by **pirates** from Ottoman states of Algiers, Tunis, Tripoli.

1816 **Second Bank of the U.S.** chartered Apr. 10. The **American Colonization Society**, which sought to address slavery issue by transporting freed blacks to Africa, formed in Washington, DC, Dec. 1816-Jan. 1817.

1817 Thomas Hopkins Gallaudet established the **first free public school for the deaf** in Hartford, CT.

1818 Connecticut expanded **suffrage** among white male voters. Massachusetts followed suit in 1820, and New York in 1821, reducing or eliminating property qualifications.

1819 Spain ceded **Florida** to U.S. Feb. 22. American steamship *Savannah* made first part-steam-powered, part-sail-powered **crossing of Atlantic**, traveling from Savannah, GA, to Liverpool, England, in 29 days. **Washington Irving's** *Sketch Book* became best seller.

1820 **First organized immigration of blacks to Africa** from U.S. began with 86 free blacks sailing to Sierra Leone in Feb. Henry Clay's **Missouri Compromise** bill passed by Congress, Mar. 3. Slavery was allowed in Missouri but not west of the Mississippi River, north of 36° 30' (the southern line of Missouri). Compromise repealed 1854.

1821 Emma Willard founded Troy Female Seminary, **first U.S. women's college**. Stephen Austin established **first American community in Texas**, San Felipe de Austin. James Fenimore Cooper's *The Spy*, novel set during American Revolution, published and became a best seller.

1822 Tension between sports and academics surfaced when Yale College Pres. Timothy Dwight banned a **primitive form of football**, setting fines for violators.

1823 **Monroe Doctrine**, opposing European intervention in the Americas, enunciated by Pres. James Monroe Dec. 2. The **Hudson River School**, painters who focused on the beauties of nature, began to receive public attention.

1824 Pawtucket, RI, **weavers strike**, first such action by women workers. **Slavery abolished** in state of Illinois Aug. 2.

1825 After a deadlocked election, **John Quincy Adams** was elected president by the House, Feb. 9. **Erie Canal** opened; first boat left Buffalo, NY, Oct. 26, reached New York City Nov. 4. John Stevens, of Hoboken, NJ, built and operated **first experimental steam locomotive** in U.S.

1826 **Thomas Jefferson** and **John Adams** both died July 4. **James Fenimore Cooper's** *The Last of the Mohicans* published.

1827 Massachusetts became first state to pass a law providing for tax-supported **public high schools**.

1828 Baltimore & Ohio, the **first U.S. passenger railroad**, began operations July 4. South Carolina Dec. 19 declared right of **state nullification of federal laws**, opposing the "Tariff of Abominations." **Noah Webster** published his *American Dictionary of the English Language*.

1829 **Andrew Jackson** inaugurated as president, Mar. 4.

1830 Famous debate Jan. 27 between Sen. **Daniel Webster** (MA) and Robert Hayne (SC), on state right to nullify federal law. **Mormon church** organized by Joseph Smith in Fayette, NY, Apr. 6. Pres. Jackson, May 28, signed **Indian Removal Act**, granting president authority to negotiate treaties whereby Indians living east of Mississippi R. give up lands in exchange for lands in West.

1831 William Lloyd Garrison began **abolitionist newspaper** *The Liberator* Jan. 1. **Nat Turner**, black slave in Virginia, led local slave rebellion, starting Aug. 21; 57 whites killed. Troops called in, 100 slaves killed. Turner captured, tried, and hanged Nov. 11.

1832 **Black Hawk War** in Illinois and Wisconsin Apr.-Sept. pushed Sauk and Fox Indians west across Mississippi.

1833 **American Anti-Slavery Society** founded in Philadelphia, Dec. 4. **Oberlin College** became first to adopt coeducation in U.S.

1835 According to tradition, the **Liberty Bell** cracked July 8 while tolling death of Chief Justice John Marshall. **Seminole Indians** in Florida under Osceola began attacks Nov. 1, protesting forced removal. The unpopular war ended Aug. 14, 1842; most of the Indians sent to Oklahoma. **Texas** proclaimed right to secede from Mexico; **Sam Houston** put in command of Texas army, Nov. 2-4. **Gold** discovered on Cherokee land in Georgia. Indians forced to cede lands, Dec. 20, and to cross Mississippi.

1836 Texans besieged at **Alamo** in San Antonio by Mexicans under Antonio López de Santa Anna, Feb. 23-Mar. 6; entire garrison killed. Texas independence had been declared, Mar. 2. At San Jacinto Apr. 21, Sam Houston and Texans defeated Mexicans. Ralph Waldo Emerson published his first work, *Nature*, espousing his philosophy of **transcendentalism**. Marcus Whitman, H. H. Spaulding, and wives reached Fort Walla Walla on Columbia River, OR, **first white women to cross the Continental Divide**, in the Rocky Mountains.

1838 Cherokee Indians forced to walk **"Trail of Tears"** from southeast U.S. to area in present-day Oklahoma. At least 4,000—nearly one-fifth of Cherokee population—are estimated to have died.

1841 **First emigrant wagon train bound for California**, 47 people, left Independence, MO, May 1; reached California Nov. 4. Edgar Allan Poe published one of the **first American detective stories**, *The Murders in the Rue Morgue.*

1842 **Webster-Ashburton Treaty** signed Aug. 9, fixing U.S.-Canada border in Maine and Minnesota. **First use of anesthetic** (sulfuric ether gas) in an operation performed by Georgia doctor Crawford Long.

1843 More than 1,000 settlers left Independence, MO, for Oregon May 22, arriving in Oct. via **Oregon Trail.**

1844 **First message over first telegraph line** sent May 24 by inventor Samuel F. B. Morse from Washington to Baltimore: "What hath God wrought?"

1845 Congress **overrode a presidential veto for the first time,** Mar. 3, after Pres. John Tyler vetoed a tariff bill. Congress of **Texas** voted for annexation by U.S., July 4; Texas admitted to Union, Dec. 29. **Edgar Allan Poe**'s poem "The Raven" published.

1846 **Mexican War** began after Pres. James K. Polk ordered Gen. Zachary Taylor to seize disputed Texan land settled by Mexicans. After border clash, U.S. declared war May 13; Mexico declared war May 23. About 12,000 U.S. troops took Vera Cruz Mar. 27, 1847, and Mexico City Sept. 14, 1847. Treaty signed Feb. 2, 1848, ended war, and Mexico ceded claims to Texas, California, and other territory. Bear flag of **Republic of California** raised by American settlers at Sonoma, June 14. Treaty with Britain June 15 set **Oregon territory** boundary at 49th parallel (extension of existing line). Expansionists had used slogan "54°40′ or fight." The term **"manifest destiny,"** coined by journalist in 1845, also came into play. **Mormons,** after violent clashes with settlers over polygamy, left Nauvoo, IL, for West under Brigham Young. They settled July 1847 at Salt Lake City, UT. Elias Howe invented **sewing machine.**

1847 **First adhesive U.S. postage stamps**—Benjamin Franklin 5¢, Washington 10¢—sold July 1. Henry Wadsworth Longfellow's *Evangeline* published.

1838: Cherokee Indians are marched from their homes in southeast U.S. to present-day Oklahoma on the "Trail of Tears."

1848 **Gold** discovered Jan. 24 in California; 80,000 prospectors emigrated in 1849. Lucretia Mott and Elizabeth Cady Stanton led Seneca Falls, NY, **Women's Rights Convention** July 19-20.

1850 Sen. Henry Clay's **Compromise of 1850** admitted California as 31st state Sept. 9, with slavery forbidden; made Utah and New Mexico territories; made **Fugitive Slave Law** harsher; and ended District of Columbia slave trade. **Nathaniel Hawthorne**'s *The Scarlet Letter* published.

1851 **Herman Melville**'s *Moby-Dick* published.

1852 **Harriet Beecher Stowe**'s *Uncle Tom's Cabin* published.

1853 Japan receives Comm. Matthew C. Perry, July 14. He negotiated treaty to **open Japan** to U.S. ships. New York City hosted **first World's Fair** in the U.S., beginning July 14. **Stephen Foster** published "My Old Kentucky Home."

1854 **Republican Party** formed at Ripon, WI, Feb. 28. Opposed Kansas-Nebraska Act, which left issue of slavery to vote of settlers. Act became law May 30. Treaty ratified with Mexico Apr. 25, providing for **Gadsden Purchase** of a strip of land. Henry David Thoreau's *Walden* published.

1855 **First railroad train crossed Mississippi River** on river's first bridge, between Rock Island, IL, and Davenport, IA, Apr. 21. **Walt Whitman**'s *Leaves of Grass* published.

1856 Proslavery group sacked **Lawrence, KS,** May 21; abolitionist John Brown led antislavery contingent against Missourians at Osawatomie, KS, Aug. 30. Antislavery Republican Party's **first presidential nominee,** John C. Frémont, defeated by James Buchanan. Abraham Lincoln made 50 speeches for Frémont. **First U.S. kindergarten** opened in Watertown, WI.

1857 In **Dred Scott** case, which involved determination of constitutionality of already-repealed Missouri Compromise, Supreme Court decided Mar. 6 that slaves did not become free in a free state, and blacks were not and could not be citizens. **Currier & Ives,** firm of American lithographers, issued their first print.

1858 **First Atlantic cable** completed by Cyrus W. Field Aug. 5. **Lincoln-Douglas debates** in Illinois, Aug. 21-Oct. 15.

1859 Edwin L. Drake drilled the **first commercially productive oil well** near Titusville, PA, Aug. 27. Abolitionist John Brown, with 21 men, seized U.S. armory at **Harpers Ferry,** WV, Oct. 16. U.S. Marines captured raiders, killing several. Brown was hanged for treason Dec. 2.

1860 Shoeworkers in Lynn, MA, went on strike Feb. 22. Within a week, strike spread to include 20,000 shoeworkers throughout New England in country's **largest strike to date.** **First Pony Express** between Sacramento, CA, and St. Joseph, MO, started Apr. 3. Republican **Abraham Lincoln** elected president Nov. 6 in four-way race.

1861 Seven southern states set up **Confederate States of America** Feb. 8, with **Jefferson Davis** as president. **Civil War** began as Confederates fired on **Ft. Sumter** in Charleston, SC, Apr. 12; they captured it Apr. 14. Pres. Lincoln called for 75,000 volunteers Apr. 15. Lincoln blockaded Southern ports Apr. 19, cutting off vital exports and aid. By May, 11 states had seceded. Confederates repelled Union forces at first **Battle of Bull Run,** July 21. **First transcontinental telegraph line** put in operation.

1862 Union forces were victorious in Western campaigns, took New Orleans May 1. Battles in East were largely inconclusive despite heavy casualties. The **Battle of Antietam,** in western Maryland Sept. 17, was bloodiest one-day battle of war; each side lost more than 2,000 men. **Homestead Act,** which granted free farms to settlers, approved May 20. **Land Grant Act,** which provided for public land sale to benefit agricultural education, approved July 7. It eventually led to establishment of state university systems.

1863 Pres. Lincoln issued **Emancipation Proclamation** Jan. 1, freeing "all slaves in areas still in rebellion." Union forces won major victory at Gettysburg, PA, July 1-3. Confederate forces under siege surrendered **Vicksburg, MS,** to Union forces under Gen. Ulysses S. Grant, July 4; control of Mississippi River in Union hands. About 1,000 were killed or wounded in **draft riots** in New York City; some blacks were hanged by mobs July 13-16. Pres. Lincoln gave his **Gettysburg Address** Nov. 19. Lincoln declared **Thanksgiving** a national holiday.

1864 Gen. **William Tecumseh Sherman** marched through Georgia, taking Atlanta Sept. 1 and Savannah Dec. 22. **Sand**

Creek massacre of Cheyenne and Arapaho Indians Nov. 29. Soldiers drove Indians out of village; about 150 killed.

1865 Gen. **Robert E. Lee surrendered** 27,800 Confederate troops to Gen. Grant at Appomattox Court House in VA, Apr. 9. J. E. Johnston surrendered 31,200 to Sherman at Durham Station, NC, Apr. 18. Last rebel troops surrendered May 26. Pres. Lincoln shot Apr. 14 by **John Wilkes Booth** in Ford's Theater, Washington, DC; died the following morning. Vice Pres. **Andrew Johnson** was sworn in as president. Booth was hunted down and fatally wounded, perhaps by his own hand, Apr. 26. Four co-conspirators were hanged July 7. **13th Amendment**, abolishing slavery, ratified Dec. 6.

1866 Congress took control of Southern Reconstruction, backed freedmen's rights in legislation vetoed by Pres. Johnson; veto overridden by Congress, Apr. 9. **Ku Klux Klan** formed secretly in South to terrorize blacks who voted. Disbanded 1869-71.

1867 Alaska sold to U.S. by Russia for $7.2 mil Mar. 30, through efforts of Sec. of State William H. Seward. Fraternal society the **Grange** was organized Dec. 4 to protect farmer interests. **Horatio Alger**'s *Ragged Dick* published.

1868 Pres. Johnson dismissed Sec. of War Edwin M. Stanton without Senate approval. **Johnson impeached** by the House Feb. 24 for violation of Tenure of Office Act, though charges were actually made in response to his opposition to congressional Reconstruction. He was acquitted by the Senate Mar.-May. **14th Amendment**, providing for citizenship of all persons born or naturalized in U.S. and subject to the jurisdiction thereof, ratified July 9. **Louisa May Alcott**'s *Little Women* published. *The World Almanac*, a publication of the *New York World* newspaper, appeared for first time.

1869 Transcontinental railroad completed; golden spike driven at Promontory Summit, UT, May 10, marking junction of Central Pacific and Union Pacific lines. Attempt to "corner" gold led to financial **"Black Friday"** in New York Sept. 24. **Woman suffrage law** passed in Wyoming Territory Dec. 10. **Knights of Labor** labor union formed in Philadelphia. By 1886, it had 700,000 members nationally.

1870 **15th Amendment**, making race no bar to voting rights, ratified Feb. 8. **First U.S. boardwalk** completed, in Atlantic City, NJ. **U.S. Weather Bureau** founded.

1871 Great Chicago fire destroyed city Oct. 8-11. **National Rifle Association (NRA)** founded.

1872 **Amnesty Act** May 22 restored civil rights to citizens of the South, except for 500 Confederate leaders. Congress established Yellowstone, **first national park**. James McNeill Whistler painted famous portrait known informally as **"Whistler's Mother."**

1873 **First U.S. postal card** issued May 1. **Jesse James** and his gang robbed their first passenger train July 21. Banks failed, panic began in Sept. **Depression** lasted five years. **"Boss" William Tweed** of New York City was convicted Nov. 19 of stealing public funds; he died in jail in 1878. New York's Bellevue Hospital started **first nursing school**.

1874 **Women's Christian Temperance Union** established in Cleveland. **First public zoo** in U.S. established in Philadelphia.

1865: Confederate Gen. Robert E. Lee surrenders to Union Gen. Ulysses S. Grant at Appomattox Court House, VA.

1875 Congress passed **Civil Rights Act** Mar. 1, giving equal rights to blacks in public accommodations and jury duty. Supreme Court invalidated act in 1883. First **Kentucky Derby** held May 17. First **Jim Crow segregation law** enacted, in Tennessee.

1876 **Alexander Graham Bell** patented the telephone Mar. 7. Col. **George A. Custer** and 264 soldiers of the 7th Cavalry were killed June 25 in "last stand," **Battle of the Little Bighorn**, MT, in Sioux Indian War. Democrat **Samuel J. Tilden** received majority of popular votes for president over Republican **Rutherford B. Hayes**, Nov. 7, but 22 electoral votes were in dispute. Congress agreed to certify Hayes as winner in Feb. 1877 after Republicans agreed to end federal Reconstruction of South.

1877 **Molly Maguires**—Irish terrorist society in mining areas of Scranton, PA—was broken up by hanging, June 21, of 11 leaders for murders of mine officials and police. Pres. Rutherford B. Hayes sent federal troops to control violent national **railroad strike**, which began in July.

1878 **First commercial telephone exchange** opened, New Haven, CT, Jan. 28. **Thomas A. Edison** founded Edison Electric Light Co. on Oct. 15.

1879 **F. W. Woolworth** opened his first five-and-ten store, in Utica, NY, Feb. 22. French actress **Sarah Bernhardt** made her U.S. debut Nov. 8 at New York City's Booth Theater. Economist and social philosopher **Henry George** published *Progress & Poverty*, advocating single tax on land.

1881 **Clara Barton** founded **American Red Cross** May 21. Pres. **James A. Garfield** shot in Washington, DC, July 2; died Sept. 19. Famous gun battle between the Earp brothers and outlaw rustlers Oct. 26 near the **OK Corral**, Tombstone, AZ. **Booker T. Washington** founded Tuskegee Institute for blacks. **Helen Hunt Jackson**'s *A Century of Dishonor*, about mistreatment of Indians, published.

1882 **Chinese Exclusion Act**, barring immigration of Chinese laborers for 10 years, later made permanent, passed by Congress May 6; prohibited naturalization of Chinese resident aliens.

1883 Civil Service Act, or **Pendleton Act**, passed Jan. 16, created foundations of American civil service system. The **Brooklyn Bridge** opened May 24 as world's longest suspension bridge. Transcontinental **Northern Pacific Railroad** was completed Sept. 8. Buffalo Bill Cody's Wild West Show began its 30-year touring run.

1884 **First long-distance telephone call** completed, Mar. 27, between Boston and New York. Switchback Railway—**first U.S. roller coaster** built as amusement park ride—opened at Coney Island in New York City. **Mark Twain**'s *The Adventures of Huckleberry Finn* published.

1885 **Washington Monument** dedicated Feb. 21.

1886 **Haymarket riot** and bombing, May 4, followed labor battles for 8-hr. work day in Chicago; seven police and four workers died. Eight anarchists found guilty Aug. 20; four hanged Nov. 11. **Coca-Cola** first sold, May 8, at Jacob's Pharmacy in Atlanta. Apache Indian **Geronimo** surrendered Sept. 4, ending last major Indian war. **Statue of Liberty** dedicated Oct. 28. **American Federation of Labor** (AFL) formed Dec. 8 by 25 craft unions.

1887 **Interstate Commerce Act** enacted Feb. 4, created interstate Commerce Commission.

1888 **Great blizzard** struck Eastern U.S. Mar. 11-14, causing about 400 deaths. Ernest Thayer's poem **"Casey at the Bat"** recited for first time in public at New York City theater.

1889 U.S. opened 2-mil acre **Oklahoma District** to settlement Apr. 22, initiating land run; "sooner" settlers illegally entered the territory before that date to stake favorable claims. More than 2,200 lives lost in **Johnstown flood** (PA) May 31. **Electric lights** installed at White House.

1890 **Sherman Antitrust Act** passed July 2, began federal effort to curb monopolies. Massacre at **Wounded Knee**, SD, Dec. 29, the last major conflict between Indians and U.S. troops; about 200 Indian men, women, and children and 29 soldiers were killed. **Jacob Riis**'s *How the Other Half Lives*, about city slums, published, instigating reform legislation in New York City. **Emily Dickinson**'s poems published, four years after her death.

1891 **Forest Reserve Act**, Mar. 3, let president close public forest land to settlement for establishment of national parks. **Carnegie Hall**, in New York City, opened May 5.

1892 Ellis Island, in New York Bay, opened Jan. 1 to receive immigrants; closed 1954. **Homestead strike** (PA) at Carnegie steel mills; 7 guards and 11 strikers and spectators shot to death July 6. James J. Corbett defeated John L. Sullivan Sept. 7 to become **first world heavyweight champion** under Marquess of Queensbury rules.

1893 Columbian Exposition world's fair held May-Oct. in Chicago. Financial panic led to four-year **depression. Mormon Temple** dedicated in Salt Lake City, UT.

1894 Thomas A. Edison's **kinetoscope**, for motion pictures (invented 1887), given first public showing Apr. 14. **Jacob S. Coxey** led army of unemployed from the Midwest, reaching Washington, DC, Apr. 30. Coxey arrested May 1 for trespassing on Capitol grounds; his army disbanded. **Pullman strike** began May 11 at railroad car plant in Chicago. Milton Hershey started **Hershey Chocolate Company.**

1895 "**America, the Beautiful**" appeared for first time, in church publication, July 4. Stephen Crane's *The Red Badge of Courage* published.

1896 Supreme Court, in *Plessy v. Ferguson*, May 18, approved racial segregation under the "**separate but equal**" doctrine. **William Jennings Bryan** delivered "Cross of Gold" speech July 9; won Democratic Party nomination. **John Philip Sousa** composed "Stars and Stripes Forever" on Dec. 25.

1897 Olney-Pauncefote Treaty with Britain, Jan. 11, gave wide scope to arbitration in settling disputes; never ratified by U.S. John J. McDermott won **first Boston Marathon** Apr. 19. First Klondike gold arrived in San Francisco July 14, helping set off **Klondike gold rush. First subway service** in country opens to public in Boston, Sept. 1.

1898 U.S. battleship *Maine* blown up Feb. 15 in Havana, Cuba; 260 killed. U.S. blockaded Cuba Apr. 22 in aid of independence forces. U.S. declared **war on Spain** Apr. 24; destroyed Spanish fleet in Philippines May 1; took Guam June 20. U.S. took **Puerto Rico** July 25-Aug. 12. Spain agreed Dec. 10 to cede Philippines, Puerto Rico, and Guam, and approved independence for Cuba. Annexation of **Hawaii** signed by Pres. William McKinley, July 7.

1899 Filipino insurgents, unable to get recognition of independence from U.S., started guerrilla war Feb. 4. Their leader, Emilio Aguinaldo, captured May 23, 1901. **Philippine insurrection** ended 1902. Killed were 20,000 Filipino troops and some 200,000 civilians, mostly from disease and starvation. Pres. McKinley signed treaty officially ending **Spanish-American War**, Feb. 10. U.S. declared **Open Door Policy** Sept. 6, to make China an open international market. Philosopher **John Dewey**'s *School and Society*, advocating progressive education ("learn by doing"), published. Pianist Scott Joplin's "Maple Leaf Rag" published, popularizing **ragtime music.**

1900 International Ladies' Garment Workers Union founded in New York City June 3. Fought sweatshop working conditions. **Carry Nation**, Kansas temperance leader, began raiding saloons with a hatchet. U.S. helped suppress **Boxer Rebellion** in Beijing, China. Eastman Kodak Co. introduced the **Brownie camera**, popularizing picture-taking.

1901 Texas had first significant oil strike at **Spindletop** well near Beaumont, Jan. 10. U.S. withdrew troops from **Cuba** May 20, and Cuba became independent. Pres. **McKinley** shot Sept. 6 in Buffalo, NY, by anarchist Leon Czolgosz; died Sept. 14. Vice Pres. **Theodore Roosevelt** sworn in as youngest-ever president, at age 42 years, 11 months. **Booker T. Washington**'s *Up From Slavery* published.

1902 Permanent **Bureau of the Census** established Mar. 6. Helen Keller autobiography appeared in serial form.

1903 Treaty between U.S. and Colombia to have U.S. dig **Panama Canal** signed Jan. 22, but rejected by Colombia's Congress; Panama declared independence from Colombia with U.S. support Nov. 3; recognized by Pres. Roosevelt Nov. 6. U.S., Panama signed canal treaty Nov. 18. Wisconsin set first **direct primary voting system**, May 23. **Henry Ford** founded Ford Motor Co., June 16. Boston defeated Pittsburgh, 5 games to 3, Oct. 13 in **first modern World Series. First successful flight** in heavier-than-air mechanically propelled airplane by Orville Wright Dec. 17 near Kitty Hawk, NC, 120 ft in 12 sec. Later flight same day by Wilbur Wright, 852 ft in 59 sec. Improved plane patented, 1906. **Iroquois Theater fire** in Chicago killed about 600 out of 1,900 in

audience, Dec. 30. Pioneering film *Great Train Robbery* produced.

1904 St. Louis hosted **first Olympics in U.S.**, July 1-Nov. 23. First section of **New York subway** system opened, Oct. 27. **Ida Tarbell** published muckraking *The History of the Standard Oil Company.* **Henry James**'s last major novel, *The Golden Bowl*, published.

1905 Industrial Workers of the World, which advocated Marxian theory of class struggle between workers and capitalists, founded in Chicago, June 27. **Rotary**, oldest service club organization in U.S., founded in Chicago.

1906 San Francisco earthquake and fire, Apr. 18-19, caused more than 3,000 deaths and $400 mil in damages. **Upton Sinclair**'s *The Jungle*, which exposed working conditions in meat-packing industry, published. Helped spur passage of the **Pure Food and Drug Act** and **Meat Inspection Act** June 30.

1907 Financial panic and **depression** started Mar. 13. Pres. Roosevelt sent "**Great White Fleet**" of 16 U.S. battleships around the world in show of power.

1908 Springfield, IL, torn by **anti-black rioting**, Aug. 14-15. Henry Ford introduced **Model T** car, priced at $850, Oct. 1.

1909 Adm. Robert E. Peary claimed to have reached **North Pole** Apr. 6 on sixth attempt, accompanied by black explorer Matthew Henson and four Inuit; may have fallen short. National Conference on the Negro convened May 30, leading to founding of **National Association for the Advancement of Colored People** (NAACP).

1910 Boy Scouts of America founded Feb. 8. Former Pres. Roosevelt called for "**new nationalism**" in famous speech in Kansas, Aug. 10.

1911 Building with New York City's **Triangle Shirtwaist Co.** factory caught fire Mar. 25; 146 died. Supreme Court ruled May 15 that **Standard Oil Co.** must be dissolved because it unreasonably restrained trade. **First transcontinental airplane flight** (with numerous stops) by C. P. Rodgers, from New York to Pasadena, CA, Sept. 17-Nov. 5; time in air 82 hr., 4 min.

1912 American Girl Guides founded Mar. 12; name changed in 1913 to **Girl Scouts.** U.S. Marines, Aug. 14, sent to **Nicaragua**, which was in default of loans to U.S. and Europe.

1913 16th Amendment, authorizing federal income tax, ratified Feb. 3. The **Armory Show** in New York City brought modern art to U.S. for first time, Feb. 17. **17th Amendment**, providing for direct popular election of U.S. senators, ratified Apr. 8. **Federal Reserve System** authorized Dec. 23, in major reform of U.S. banking and finance.

1914 Ford Motor Co. raised basic wage rates from $2.40 for 9-hr. day to $5 for 8-hr. day, Jan. 5, increasing stability in labor force. When U.S. sailors were arrested in Tampico, Mexico, Apr. 9, Atlantic fleet was sent to **Veracruz**, occupied city. Pres. Woodrow Wilson proclaimed **U.S. neutrality** in the European war, Aug. 4. The **Panama Canal** officially opened Aug. 15. The **Clayton Antitrust Act** passed Oct. 15, strengthening federal antimonopoly powers.

1915 First transcontinental telephone call, New York to San Francisco, completed Jan. 25 by Alexander Graham Bell and Thomas A. Watson. British ship *Lusitania* sunk May 7

1915: A German submarine sinks the British liner *Lusitania* with 128 Americans aboard; Germany's attacks on civilian ships are a component of the U.S. decision to join the conflict two years later.

by German submarine; 1,198 passengers died, including 128 Americans. (In notice in morning newspapers the day *Lusitania* set sail, Germany had warned Americans against taking passage on British vessels.) As result of U.S. campaign, Germany issued apology and promise of payments, Oct. 5. U.S. troops landed in **Haiti**, July 28. Haiti became virtual U.S. protectorate under Sept. 16 treaty. Pres. Wilson asked for a military fund increase, Dec. 7. D. W. Griffith's film *The Birth of a Nation* released. William J. Simmons partly inspired by film to revive **Ku Klux Klan**, which peaks in 1920s.

1916 Gen. **John J. Pershing** entered Mexico in Mar. to pursue **Francisco (Pancho) Villa**, who had raided U.S. border areas. Forces withdrew Feb. 5, 1917. **Rural Credits Acts** passed July 17, followed by **Warehouse Act** Aug. 11; both provided financial aid to farmers. Bomb exploded during **San Francisco Preparedness Day parade** July 22, killed 10. Thomas J. Mooney, labor organizer, and Warren K. Billings, shoeworker, convicted 1917; both later pardoned. U.S. bought **Virgin Islands** from Denmark Aug. 4. U.S. established military government in the **Dominican Republic** Nov. 29. Jeannette Rankin (R, MT) elected to House of Representatives, **first female member of Congress**.

1917 Germany, suffering from British blockade, declared almost unrestricted **submarine warfare** Jan. 31. U.S. cut diplomatic ties with Germany Feb. 3 and formally **declared war** Apr. 6. Jones Act, passed Mar. 2, made **Puerto Rico** a U.S. territory, its inhabitants U.S. citizens. **Conscription law** passed May 18. First U.S. troops arrived in Europe June 26.

1918 Pres. Wilson set out his **14 Points** as basis for peace, Jan. 8. More than 1 mil American troops were in Europe by July. Allied counteroffensive launched at Château-Thierry July 18. War ended with signing of **armistice**, Nov. 11. **Influenza epidemic** killed an estimated 20 mil worldwide, 548,000 in U.S.

1919 18th Amendment, providing for prohibition of manufacture, sale, or transportation of alcoholic beverages, ratified Jan. 16, to take effect on Jan. 16, 1920. **First transatlantic flight**, by U.S. Navy seaplane, left Rockaway, NY, May 8; stopped at Newfoundland, Azores, Lisbon May 27. **Boston police strike** Sept. 9, earliest strike conducted by government employees. About 250 **foreign-born radicals** deported Dec. 21 to Soviet Union.

1920 In national **Red Scare**, some 2,700 Communists, anarchists, and other radicals were arrested Jan.-May. **League of Women Voters** founded Feb. 14. Senate refused Mar. 19 to ratify **League of Nations Covenant**. Nicola **Sacco** and **Bartolomeo Vanzetti** accused of killing two men in Massachusetts payroll holdup Apr. 15; found guilty 1921. A seven-year campaign for their release failed; both executed Aug. 23, 1927. Verdict repudiated 1977 by proclamation of Massachusetts Gov. Michael Dukakis. **19th Amendment** ratified Aug. 18, giving women the vote. **First regular licensed radio broadcasting** began Aug. 20. **Wall St. bombing** in New York City killed 30, injured 100, did $2 mil damage, Sept. 16. **Sinclair Lewis's** *Main Street* published.

1921 Congress sharply curbed immigration, set **national quota system** May 19. Joint congressional resolution declaring **peace with Germany, Austria, and Hungary** signed July 2 by Pres. Warren G. Harding; treaties were signed in Aug. In so-called **Black Sox scandal**, eight Chicago White Sox players were banned from baseball Aug. 4 for conspiring with gamblers to throw the 1919 World Series. Limitation of Armaments Conference met in Washington, DC, Nov. 12-Feb. 6, 1922. Major powers agreed to curtail naval construction, outlaw poison gas, restrict submarine attacks on merchant vessels, and respect China's integrity.

1922 During nationwide coal strike, union miners killed some 21 strikebreakers at Herrin, IL, June 21-22, in incident referred to as the **Herrin Massacre**. **T. S. Eliot's** *The Waste Land* published.

1923 First **sound-on-film motion picture**, *Phonofilm*, shown at Rivoli Theater, New York City, beginning in Apr. Pres. Calvin Coolidge addressed Congress, Dec. 6; **first radio broadcast of president's annual speech**.

1924 Law approved by Congress June 15 made all **Native Americans U.S. citizens**. Nellie Tayloe Ross elected governor of Wyoming, and **Miriam (Ma) Ferguson** elected governor of Texas Nov. 9. Ross inaugurated as nation's **first female**

1920: The ratification of the 19th Amendment gives all women the right to vote.

governor Jan. 5, 1925. Ferguson installed Jan. 20, 1925. **George Gershwin** wrote "Rhapsody in Blue."

1925 In so-called "Monkey Trial," John T. Scopes found guilty of having taught **evolution** in Dayton, TN, high school and fined, July 24. **F. Scott Fitzgerald's** *The Great Gatsby* published.

1926 Dr. Robert H. Goddard, Mar. 16, demonstrated **first liquid-fuel rocket**. Congress established **Army Air Corps** July 2. **Air Commerce Act** passed Nov. 2, established government agencies for development of airports, radio navigation, and other services. **Ernest Hemingway's** *The Sun Also Rises* published.

1927 Capt. **Charles A. Lindbergh** left Roosevelt Field, NY, May 20 alone in *Spirit of St. Louis* on first New York-Paris nonstop flight. Reached Le Bourget airfield May 21, 3,610 mi in 33½ hr. *The Jazz Singer*, **first feature-length film in which spoken dialogue was part of narrative action**, released Oct. 6. The musical *Show Boat* opened in New York City Dec. 27.

1928 Amelia Earhart became first woman to fly across the Atlantic, June 17. **Herbert Hoover** elected president Nov. 6, defeating New York Gov. Alfred E. Smith, a Catholic.

1929 Gangsters killed seven rivals in Chicago **St. Valentine's Day massacre** Feb. 14, which won Al Capone control of Chicago's underworld. Stock market crash Oct. 29 marked end of past prosperity as stock prices plummeted. Stock losses for 1929-31 estimated at $50 bil; beginning of **Great Depression**. Albert B. Fall, former interior sec., was convicted of accepting $10,000 bribe in leasing of the **Elk Hills (Teapot Dome)** naval oil reserve; sentenced Nov. 1 to a year in prison and fined. **William Faulkner's** *The Sound and the Fury* published.

1930 London **Naval Reduction Treaty** signed by U.S., Britain, Italy, France, and Japan Apr. 22; in effect Jan. 1, 1931; expired Dec. 31, 1936. **Hawley-Smoot Tariff** signed; rate hikes slash world trade. **Sinclair Lewis** became first American to win a Nobel Prize in literature. **Dashiell Hammett's** *The Maltese Falcon* published.

1931 Empire State Building opened in New York City May 1, displacing NYC's Chrysler Building as world's tallest. **Al Capone** convicted of tax evasion Oct. 17. **Pearl Buck's** *The Good Earth* published. **Charlie Chaplin** film *City Lights* released.

1932 Reconstruction Finance Corp. established Jan. 22 to stimulate banking and business. Unemployment at 12 mil. Twenty-month-old **Charles Lindbergh Jr.** kidnapped Mar. 1; found dead May 12. Bruno Hauptmann found guilty Feb. 1935; executed Apr. 3, 1936. Unemployed World War I veterans demanding Congress pay promised bonus early launched **Bonus March** on Washington, DC, May 29. **Franklin D. Roosevelt** elected president for first time in Democratic landslide, Nov. 8. Chicago Bears won **first NFL title game** Dec. 18, defeating the Portsmouth (OH) Spartans, 9-0.

1933 Pres. Roosevelt named **Frances Perkins** U.S. sec. of labor; **first woman in U.S. cabinet**. Pres. Roosevelt ordered

all U.S. banks closed Mar. 6. In a "100 days" special session, Mar. 9-June 16, Congress passed **New Deal**, including measures to regulate banks, distribute funds to the jobless, create jobs, raise agricultural prices, and set wage and production standards for industry. **Gold standard** dropped by U.S. in favor of "modified gold bullion standard"; announced by Pres. Roosevelt Apr. 19, ratified by Congress June 5. **Tennessee Valley Authority (TVA)** created by act of Congress, May 18. **Prohibition** ended in the U.S. as 36th state ratified **21st Amendment** Dec. 5. Pres. Roosevelt foreswore armed intervention in **Western Hemisphere** nations, Dec. 26.

1934 Pres. Roosevelt signed law creating **Securities and Exchange Commission**, June 6. U.S. troops pulled out of **Haiti**, Aug. 6.

1935 Works Progress Administration (WPA) instituted May 6. Rural Electrification Administration created May 11. National Industrial Recovery Act struck down by Supreme Court May 27. **Boulder Dam** (later renamed **Hoover Dam**) completed, May 29. **Social Security Act** passed by Congress Aug. 8-9. Comedian **Will Rogers** and aviator Wiley Post killed Aug. 15 in Alaska plane crash. **Huey Long**, Louisiana senator and national political leader, shot Sept. 8; died Sept. 10. George Gershwin's jazz opera **Porgy and Bess** opened Oct. 10 in New York. **Committee for Industrial Organization** (later Congress of Industrial Organizations) formed to expand industrial unionism Nov. 9.

1936 Jesse Owens won four gold medals at the **Berlin Olympics** in Aug. **Baseball Hall of Fame** founded in Cooperstown, NY. **Margaret Mitchell**'s *Gone With the Wind* published.

1937 Airship **Hindenburg** caught fire May 6 as it was landing in Lakehurst, NJ; 36 killed. **Golden Gate Bridge** in San Francisco opened May 27. **Joe Louis** knocked out James J. Braddock to become world heavyweight champ June 22. Aviator **Amelia Earhart** and copilot Fred Noonan disappeared July 2 near Howland Isl., in the Pacific. Pres. Roosevelt proposed judicial reforms that would allow him to appoint additional Supreme Court justices; his **"court-packing" plan** defeated. **Auto, steel labor unions** won first big contracts.

1938 National minimum wage enacted June 25. Orson Welles's radio dramatization of H. G. Wells's *War of the Worlds*, Oct. 30, caused Martian invasion scare among some who had missed the introduction. **Seabiscuit** beat War Admiral in match race of the century, at Pimlico track, MD, Nov. 1. Artist Anna Mary Robertson, **"Grandma Moses,"** discovered. **Thornton Wilder**'s *Our Town* produced on Broadway.

1939 Opera singer **Marian Anderson** performed for integrated crowd of 75,000 at Lincoln Memorial Apr. 9 after Daughters of the American Revolution refused to let Anderson sing in DC's Constitution Hall. **New York World's Fair**—theme: "The World of Tomorrow"—opened Apr. 30, closed Oct. 31. Reopened for second season May 11-Oct. 27, 1940. **Lou Gehrig**, seriously ill with disease that would come to bear his name, said farewell to fans at Yankee Stadium, July 4. Albert Einstein alerted Pres. Roosevelt to **A-bomb possibilities** in Aug. 2 letter. **U.S. declared its neutrality** in European war Sept. 5. Pres. Roosevelt proclaimed limited **national emergency** Sept. 8, unlimited emergency May 27, 1941. Both ended by Pres. Harry Truman, Apr. 28, 1952.

Pocket Books, **first paperback publisher** in U.S., established. **John Steinbeck**'s *The Grapes of Wrath* published. *The Wizard of Oz* and *Gone With the Wind* released, the latter to become highest-grossing film of all time (inflation-adjusted).

1940 U.S. OK'd sale of **surplus war material** to Britain June 3; announced transfer of 50 overaged destroyers Sept. 3. **First peacetime military draft** in U.S. history approved, Sept. 14. **Forty-hour work week** went into effect, Oct. 24. Pres. Roosevelt elected Nov. 5 to third presidential term. **Richard Wright**'s *Native Son* published.

1941 Four Freedoms—freedom of speech and religion, freedom from want and fear—termed essential by Pres. Roosevelt in speech to Congress Jan. 6. **Lend-Lease Act** signed Mar. 11 provided $7 bil in military credits for Britain. Lend-lease for USSR approved in Nov. Pres. Roosevelt signed executive order June 25 barring federal government and war contractors from **racial discrimination**. Order also established Fair Employment Practice Committee. The **Atlantic Charter**, 8-point declaration of principles, issued by Pres. Roosevelt and British Prime Min. Winston Churchill, Aug. 14. Japan attacked **Pearl Harbor**, Hawaii, 7:55 AM Hawaiian time, Dec. 7; 19 ships sunk or damaged, 2,403 dead. Pres. Roosevelt called it "a date which will live in infamy." U.S. declared war on Japan Dec. 8. Germany and Italy declared war on U.S. Dec. 11. U.S. responded with declaration of war later on same day. Japanese invaded **Philippines**, Dec. 22; Wake Island fell, Dec. 23. *Citizen Kane*, directed by Orson Welles, released.

1942 Pres. Roosevelt issued executive order Feb. 19 authorizing relocation of Japanese-Americans. Federal government began forcibly moving 110,000 Japanese-Americans from West Coast to **detention camps**; exclusion lasted three years. Japanese troops took **Bataan** peninsula Apr. 8 and **Corregidor** May 6. **Battle of Midway** June 4-7 was Japan's first major defeat. Marines landed on **Guadalcanal** Aug. 7; last Japanese not expelled until Feb. 9, 1943. U.S., Britain invaded **North Africa** Nov. 8. **First nuclear chain reaction** (fission of uranium isotope U-235) produced at Univ. of Chicago under physicists Arthur Compton, Enrico Fermi, others, Dec. 2. The movie *Casablanca*, starring Humphrey Bogart and Ingrid Bergman, released.

1943 *Oklahoma!* opened Mar. 31 on Broadway. Pres. Roosevelt signed June 10 pay-as-you-go income tax bill. Starting July 1, wage and salary earners were subject to **paycheck withholding tax**. **Detroit race riot** June 21 left 34 dead, 700 injured. Six killed in riot in New York City's **Harlem** section Aug. 2. U.S., Britain invaded **Sicily** July 9, Italian **mainland** Sept. 3. Marines in Nov. recaptured the **Gilbert Islands**, captured by Japan in 1941 and 1942.

1944 U.S., Allied forces invaded Europe at Normandy, France, on **"D Day,"** June 6, in greatest amphibious landing in history. **GI Bill of Rights**, providing benefits to veterans, signed by Pres. Roosevelt June 22. Representatives of the U.S. and other major powers met at **Dumbarton Oaks**, Washington, DC, Aug. 21-Oct. 7, to work out formation of postwar world organization that would become the **United Nations**. U.S. forces landed on **Leyte**, Philippines, Oct. 20. Pres. **Roosevelt** elected to fourth term as president Nov. 7. **Battle of the Bulge**, failed Nazi counteroffensive, waged Dec. 16 to Jan. 28, 1945.

1945 Yalta Conference met in the Crimea, USSR, Feb. 4-11. Pres. Roosevelt, Prime Min. Churchill, and Soviet leader Joseph Stalin agreed that their countries, plus France, would occupy Germany and that the Soviet Union would enter war against Japan. Marines landed on **Iwo Jima** Feb. 19, won control Mar. 16 after heavy casualties. U.S. forces invaded **Okinawa** Apr. 1, captured it June 21. Pres. **Roosevelt** died in Warm Springs, GA, Apr. 12; Vice Pres. **Harry S. Truman** became president. Germany surrendered May 7; May 8 proclaimed **V-E Day**. **First atomic bomb**, produced at Los Alamos, NM, exploded at Alamogordo, NM, July 16. Bomb dropped on **Hiroshima**, Japan, Aug. 6, killing about 75,000; bomb dropped on **Nagasaki**, Japan, Aug. 9, killing about 40,000. Japan agreed to surrender Aug. 14; formally

1941: Japan's attack on the U.S. at Pearl Harbor attempts to devastate the U.S. Pacific fleet and kills 2,403.

1944: More than 160,000 Allied troops storm a heavily fortified stretch of French coastline on D-Day (June 6).

surrendered Sept. 2. At **Potsdam Conference**, July 17-Aug. 2, leaders of U.S., USSR, and Britain agreed on disarmament of Germany, occupation zones, war crimes trials. **Empire State Building** struck accidentally by Army B-25 bomber, July 28, killing 14. U.S. forces entered **Korea** south of 38th parallel to displace Japanese Sept. 8. Gen. **Douglas MacArthur** took over supervision of Japan Sept. 9.

1946 Steel strike by 750,000 started Jan. 21, settled in four weeks. Strike by 400,000 **mine workers** began Apr. 1 (settled May 29); other industries (including rail, maritime) followed. Former Prime Min. Winston Churchill employed the phrase **"Iron Curtain"** in Mar. 5 speech at Westminster College in Fulton, MO. Atomic bomb tested off **Bikini Atoll** in Pacific, July 1. In all, U.S. conducted 23 nuclear tests between 1946 and 1958. **Philippines** given independence by U.S. July 4. Mother Frances Xavier Cabrini **first American to be canonized**, July 7. Dr. Benjamin Spock's *Baby and Child Care* published as **baby boom** began.

1947 Pres. Truman asked Congress for financial and military aid for Greece and Turkey to help combat Communist subversion, Mar. 12; **Truman Doctrine** approved May 15. UN Security Council voted Apr. 2 to place under U.S. trusteeship the **Pacific islands** formerly mandated to Japan. **Jackie Robinson** joined Brooklyn Dodgers Apr. 11, breaking color barrier in major league baseball. The **Marshall Plan** for U.S. aid to European countries proposed by Sec. of State George C. Marshall June 5. Congress authorized some $12 bil in next four years. **Taft-Hartley Labor Act** restricting labor union power vetoed by Pres. Truman June 20; Congress overrode veto. Air Force Capt. **Chuck Yeager** broke sound barrier, Oct. 14, in X-1 rocket plane.

1948 Organization of American States (OAS) founded Apr. 30 by 21 countries. USSR halted all surface traffic into **West Berlin** June 24; in response, U.S. and British troops launched an **airlift**. Soviet blockade halted May 12, 1949; airlift ended Sept. 30. Pres. **Truman** elected Nov. 2, defeating NY Gov. Thomas E. Dewey in historic upset. **Alger Hiss** indicted Dec. 15 for perjury, after denying he had passed secret documents to Whittaker Chambers to go to a Communist spy ring; convicted Jan. 21, 1950. **Kinsey Report** on sexuality in the human male published.

1949 North Atlantic Treaty Organization **(NATO)** established Aug. 24 by U.S., Canada, and 10 Western European nations, agreeing that an armed attack against one would be considered an attack against all. Eleven leaders of US **Communist Party** convicted Oct. 14 of advocating violent overthrow of U.S. government; sentenced to prison. Supreme Court upheld convictions, 1951. Pres. Truman, Oct. 26, signed legislation raising **federal minimum wage** from 40¢ an hour to 75¢. **Arthur Miller**'s *Death of a Salesman* opened on Broadway.

1950 Masked bandits robbed **Brink's, Inc.**, Boston express office, Jan. 17, of $2.8 mil. Case solved 1956; eight sentenced to life. Pres. Truman authorized production of **H-bomb** Jan. 31. Special Senate committee to investigate organized crime established May 3, chaired by Sen. **Estes Kefauver** (D, TN).

North Korean forces **invaded South Korea** June 25. UN asked for troops to restore peace. Pres. Truman ordered Air Force and Navy to Korea June 27. Truman approved ground forces, air strikes against North Korea June 30. U.S. sent 35 military advisers to **South Vietnam** June 27 and agreed to aid anti-Communist government. U.S. forces landed at **Inchon**, South Korea, Sept. 15. UN forces took Pyongyang Oct. 20, reached China border Nov. 20. China sent troops across border Nov. 26. U.S. banned shipments Dec. 8 to **Communist China** and to Asiatic ports trading with it.

Army **seized all railroads** Aug. 27 on Truman's order to prevent general strike; returned to owners in 1952. Two members of **Puerto Rican nationalist movement** tried to kill Pres. Truman Nov. 1.

Peanuts comic strip appeared in newspapers. Variety show *Your Show of Shows* debuted on TV. David Riesman's *The Lonely Crowd* published.

1951 22nd Amendment, limiting presidential term of office, ratified Feb. 27. **Julius Rosenberg**; his wife, **Ethel Rosenberg**; and **Morton Sobell** found guilty Mar. 29 of conspiracy to commit wartime espionage. Rosenbergs received death penalty. Sobell sentenced to 30 years; released 1969.

Pres. Truman removed Gen. **Douglas MacArthur** from Korea command Apr. 11 for unauthorized policy statements. **Korea cease-fire** talks began in July; lasted two years. Fighting ended July 27, 1953.

Transcontinental TV began Sept. 4 with Pres. Truman's address at Japanese Peace Treaty Conference in San Francisco. **Japanese peace treaty** signed in San Francisco Sept. 8 by U.S., Japan, and 47 other nations. **J. D. Salinger**'s *Catcher in the Rye* published. *I Love Lucy* sitcom premiered on TV.

1952 Pres. Truman ordered seizure of nation's **steel mills** Apr. 8 to avert strike; ruled illegal by Supreme Court June 2. **Peace contract** between West Germany, U.S., Great Britain, and France signed May 26. Last racial and ethnic barriers to naturalization removed, June 26-27, with passage of **Immigration and Naturalization Act** of 1952. **Puerto Rico** proclaimed commonwealth July 25, after referendum Mar. 3. Richard Nixon, as vice-pres. candidate, gave **"Checkers" speech**, so called because of sentimental reference to his dog Checkers, Sept. 23. **First hydrogen device explosion** Nov. 1 in Pacific. **Ralph Ellison**'s *Invisible Man* published.

1953 Federal jury in New York convicted 13 **Communist** leaders on conspiracy charges, Jan. 20. **Julius and Ethel Rosenberg** executed in electric chair, June 19, for relaying nuclear secrets to Soviet Union. **Korean War** armistice signed July 27. California Gov. **Earl Warren** sworn in Oct. 5 as 14th chief justice of U.S. Supreme Court.

1954 *Nautilus*, **first atomic-powered submarine**, launched at Groton, CT, Jan. 21. Five members of Congress were wounded in the House Mar. 1 by four **Puerto Rican independence supporters** who fired at random from a spectators' gallery.

At televised hearings, Apr. 22-June 17, before a Senate subcommittee, Army officials accused Sen. **Joseph McCarthy** (R, WI) of seeking preferential treatment for a draftee, and McCarthy accused Army of hindering probe of Communist infiltration. McCarthy was cleared in the hearings, but the Senate later voted to condemn him, 67-22, for abuse of the Senate during hearings and debates.

Supreme Court ruled unanimously May 17 that racial segregation in public schools was unconstitutional, in *Brown v. Board of Education* of Topeka. **Ernest Hemingway** won Nobel Prize in literature for *The Old Man and the Sea*.

1955 U.S. agreed Feb. 12 to help train **South Vietnamese army**. Supreme Court ordered "all deliberate speed" in **integration** of public schools, May 31. A summit meeting of leaders of **Big 4**—U.S., Britain, France, and USSR—took place July 18-23 in Geneva, Switzerland.

Rosa Parks refused Dec. 1 to give her seat to white man on bus in Montgomery, AL. Her arrest, detention, and conviction sparked boycott of bus system, organized by Rev. **Martin Luther King Jr.**, by Montgomery's black community, Dec. 5. Bus segregation ordinance declared unconstitutional by federal court in 1956. Boycott ended Dec. 23 of that year.

America's two largest labor organizations merged Dec. 5, creating **AFL-CIO**. Russian-born U.S. citizen **Vladimir Nabokov**'s *Lolita* published.

1956 Massive resistance to Supreme Court **desegregation rulings** was called for Mar. 12 by 101 Southern congressmen. U.S. Supreme Court, Apr. 23, unanimously ruled against **racial segregation** on intrastate buses.

Federal-Aid Highway Act signed June 29, creating **interstate highway system**. **First transatlantic telephone cable** activated Sept. 25. On Oct. 8, in Game 5, Yankee right-hander Don Larsen pitched **only perfect World Series game**. **Eugene O'Neill**'s *Long Day's Journey Into Night* opened Nov. 7 on Broadway.

1957 Congress approved **Civil Rights Act of 1957**, Apr. 29, first such bill since Reconstruction to protect voting rights. Pres. Eisenhower signed act into law Sept. 9; provided for creation of Civil Rights Commission. The U.S. surgeon general July 12 said studies showed "direct link" between cigarette **smoking and lung cancer**.

Arkansas Gov. Orval Faubus (D) called National Guardsmen Sept. 4 to bar nine black students from entering all-white high school in **Little Rock**. Faubus complied Sept. 21 with federal court order to remove Guardsmen, but local authorities ordered black students to withdraw. Pres. Eisenhower sent troops Sept. 24 to enforce court order.

Jack Kerouac's *On the Road* published.

1958 Army launched **first U.S. Earth-orbiting satellite**, *Explorer I*, Jan. 31 from Cape Canaveral, FL; discovered Van Allen radiation belt. U.S. Marines sent to **Lebanon** to protect elected government from threatened overthrow July-Oct. Nuclear sub *Nautilus* made **first undersea crossing of North Pole** Aug. 5. Presidential aide **Sherman Adams** resigned Sept. 22 over scandal involving alleged improper gifts. **First domestic jet airline passenger service** in U.S. opened by National Airlines Dec. 10 between New York and Miami.

1959 Alaska admitted as 49th state, Jan. 3; **Hawaii** admitted as 50th, Aug. 21. **St. Lawrence Seaway** opened to traffic, Apr. 25.

Vice Pres. Richard Nixon, on tour of USSR, held **"kitchen debate,"** July 24, with Soviet Prem. Nikita Khrushchev at U.S. exhibit in Moscow. Prem. **Khrushchev** paid unprecedented visit to U.S. Sept. 15-27; made transcontinental tour.

Pres. Eisenhower issued injunction Oct. 12, upheld and made effective by Supreme Court Nov. 7, ending record **116-day steel strike**. In quiz show scandal, Columbia Univ. Prof. Charles Van Doren admitted to U.S. House subcommittee Nov. 2 that he had been coached before appearances on NBC-TV's *21* in 1956; he had won $129,000. William Wyler's *Ben-Hur* released; the movie won a record 11 Academy Awards the following year.

1960 Sit-ins began Feb. 1 when four black college students in Greensboro, NC, refused to move from a Woolworth lunch counter after being denied service. By Sept. 1961, more than 70,000 students, whites and blacks, had participated in sit-ins. Pres. Eisenhower signed **Civil Rights Act** May 6.

A U.S. **U-2 reconnaissance plane** was shot down in the Soviet Union May 1; pilot Gary Powers captured. The incident led to cancellation of Paris summit conference;

Powers traded for Soviet spy, 1962. A **birth control pill** approved as safe for first time by Food and Drug Administration May 9. Vice Pres. **Richard Nixon** and Sen. **John F. Kennedy** faced each other Sept. 26 in first in series of televised debates. Kennedy defeated Nixon to win presidency, Nov. 8. U.S. announced Dec. 15 its backing of rightist group in **Laos**, which took power the next day.

Alfred Hitchcock film *Psycho* released.

1961 U.S. severed diplomatic and consular relations with Cuba Jan. 3, after disputes over nationalizations of U.S. firms, U.S. military presence at Guantánamo base. U.S.-directed invasion of Cuba's **Bay of Pigs** Apr. 17 by Cuban exiles unsuccessfully attempted to overthrow the regime of Prem. Fidel Castro.

Peace Corps created by executive order, Mar. 1. **23rd Amendment**, giving DC citizens the right to vote in presidential elections, ratified Mar. 29. Comm. Alan B. Shepard Jr. rocketed from Cape Canaveral, FL, in a Mercury capsule May 5, in **first U.S.-crewed suborbital space flight**.

"Freedom Rides" from Washington, DC, across Deep South were launched May 20 to protest segregation in interstate transportation.

Joseph Heller's *Catch-22* published.

1962 Pres. Kennedy said Feb. 14 that U.S. military advisers in **Vietnam** would fire if fired upon. Lt. Col. John H. Glenn Jr. became **first American in orbit** Feb. 20 when he circled the Earth three times in the Mercury capsule *Friendship 7*.

In *Baker v. Carr*, Mar. 26, Supreme Court ruled that constitutional challenges to unequal distribution of voters among legislative districts could be resolved by federal courts. **James Meredith** became first black student at Univ. of Mississippi Oct. 1 after 3,000 troops put down riots.

A Soviet **offensive missile buildup** in Cuba was revealed Oct. 22 by Pres. Kennedy, who ordered naval and air quarantine on shipment of offensive military equipment to the island. He and Soviet Prem. Khrushchev agreed Oct. 28 on formula to end crisis. Kennedy announced Nov. 2 that missile bases in Cuba were being dismantled. **Rachel Carson**'s *Silent Spring* launched environmentalist movement.

1963 In *Gideon v. Wainwright*, Mar. 18, Supreme Court ruled that all criminal defendants must have counsel.

March for civil rights began May 2 in Birmingham, AL; led to desegregation accord, which in turn sparked rioting and violence. Univ. of Alabama **desegregated** after Gov. George Wallace stepped aside when confronted by federally deployed National Guard troops June 11. Civil rights leader **Medgar Evers** assassinated June 12. On Aug. 28, 200,000 joined in **March on Washington** in support of black demands for equal rights led by Rev. **Martin Luther King Jr.**; highlight was King's **"I Have a Dream" speech**.

Supreme Court ruled June 17 that laws requiring **recitation of Lord's Prayer or Bible verses** in public schools were unconstitutional. Pres. Kennedy, on Europe trip, addressed huge crowd in **West Berlin**, June 23. **Limited nuclear test-ban treaty** agreed upon July 25 by the U.S., the Soviet Union, and Britain. Four black girls killed in bombing of **16th St. Baptist Church** in Birmingham, AL, Sept. 15.

South Vietnam leader **Ngo Dinh Diem** assassinated Nov. 2; U.S. had earlier withdrawn support. Pres. **Kennedy** shot and fatally wounded Nov. 22 as he rode in motorcade through downtown Dallas, TX. Vice Pres. **Lyndon B. Johnson** sworn in as president. **Lee Harvey Oswald** arrested and charged with murder but was himself shot and fatally wounded Nov. 24. Nightclub owner **Jack Ruby** convicted of Oswald's murder; Ruby died in 1967 while awaiting retrial following reversal of his conviction. **Betty Friedan**'s feminist work *The Feminine Mystique* published.

1964 Panama suspended relations with U.S. Jan. 9 after riots. U.S. offered Dec. 18 to negotiate new canal treaty. **The Beatles** appeared Feb. 9 on *The Ed Sullivan Show*. Supreme Court ruled Feb. 17 that **congressional districts** as near as practicable be equal in population. U.S. reported May 27 it was sending military planes to **Laos**.

Three **civil rights workers** reported missing in Mississippi June 22; bodies found Aug. 4. Eighteen white men tried. On Oct. 20, 1967, an all-white federal jury convicted seven of conspiracy in the slayings. Omnibus **civil rights bill** signed by Pres. Johnson July 2, banning discrimination in voting, jobs, public accommodations.

1957: Federal troops enforce a court order to enroll the "Little Rock Nine" and integrate Central High School.

AFGHANISTAN	ALBANIA	ALGERIA	ANDORRA	ANGOLA
ANTIGUA AND BARBUDA	ARGENTINA	ARMENIA	AUSTRALIA	AUSTRIA
AZERBAIJAN	THE BAHAMAS	BAHRAIN	BANGLADESH	BARBADOS
BELARUS	BELGIUM	BELIZE	BENIN	BHUTAN
BOLIVIA	BOSNIA AND HERZEGOVINA	BOTSWANA	BRAZIL	BRUNEI
BULGARIA	BURKINA FASO	BURUNDI	CABO VERDE	CAMBODIA
CAMEROON	CANADA	CENTRAL AFRICAN REPUBLIC	CHAD	CHILE
CHINA	COLOMBIA	COMOROS	CONGO, DEM. REP. OF THE	CONGO REPUBLIC
COSTA RICA	CÔTE D'IVOIRE	CROATIA	CUBA	CYPRUS
CZECH REPUBLIC	DENMARK	DJIBOUTI	DOMINICA	DOMINICAN REPUBLIC
ECUADOR	EGYPT	EL SALVADOR	EQUATORIAL GUINEA	ERITREA

Note: Flag proportions have been standardized to fit page.

ESTONIA	ETHIOPIA	FIJI	FINLAND	FRANCE
GABON	THE GAMBIA	GEORGIA	GERMANY	GHANA
GREECE	GRENADA	GUATEMALA	GUINEA	GUINEA-BISSAU
GUYANA	HAITI	HONDURAS	HUNGARY	ICELAND
INDIA	INDONESIA	IRAN	IRAQ	IRELAND
ISRAEL	ITALY	JAMAICA	JAPAN	JORDAN
KAZAKHSTAN	KENYA	KIRIBATI	NORTH KOREA	SOUTH KOREA
KOSOVO	KUWAIT	KYRGYZSTAN	LAOS	LATVIA
LEBANON	LESOTHO	LIBERIA	LIBYA	LIECHTENSTEIN
LITHUANIA	LUXEMBOURG	MACEDONIA	MADAGASCAR	MALAWI
MALAYSIA	MALDIVES	MALI	MALTA	MARSHALL ISLANDS

Note: Flag proportions have been standardized to fit page.

MAURITANIA	MAURITIUS	MEXICO	MICRONESIA	MOLDOVA
MONACO	MONGOLIA	MONTENEGRO	MOROCCO	MOZAMBIQUE
MYANMAR (BURMA)	NAMIBIA	NAURU	NEPAL	NETHERLANDS
NEW ZEALAND	NICARAGUA	NIGER	NIGERIA	NORWAY
OMAN	PAKISTAN	PALAU	PANAMA	PAPUA NEW GUINEA
PARAGUAY	PERU	PHILIPPINES	POLAND	PORTUGAL
QATAR	ROMANIA	RUSSIA	RWANDA	ST. KITTS AND NEVIS
ST. LUCIA	ST. VINCENT AND THE GRENADINES	SAMOA	SAN MARINO	SÃO TOMÉ AND PRÍNCIPE
SAUDI ARABIA	SENEGAL	SERBIA	SEYCHELLES	SIERRA LEONE
SINGAPORE	SLOVAKIA	SLOVENIA	SOLOMON ISLANDS	SOMALIA
SOUTH AFRICA	SOUTH SUDAN	SPAIN	SRI LANKA	SUDAN

Note: Flag proportions have been standardized to fit page.

SURINAME

SWAZILAND

SWEDEN

SWITZERLAND

SYRIA

TAIWAN

TAJIKISTAN

TANZANIA

THAILAND

TIMOR-LESTE (EAST TIMOR)

TOGO

TONGA

TRINIDAD AND TOBAGO

TUNISIA

TURKEY

TURKMENISTAN

TUVALU

UGANDA

UKRAINE

UNITED ARAB EMIRATES

UNITED KINGDOM

UNITED STATES

URUGUAY

UZBEKISTAN

VANUATU

VATICAN CITY

VENEZUELA

VIETNAM

YEMEN

ZAMBIA

ZIMBABWE

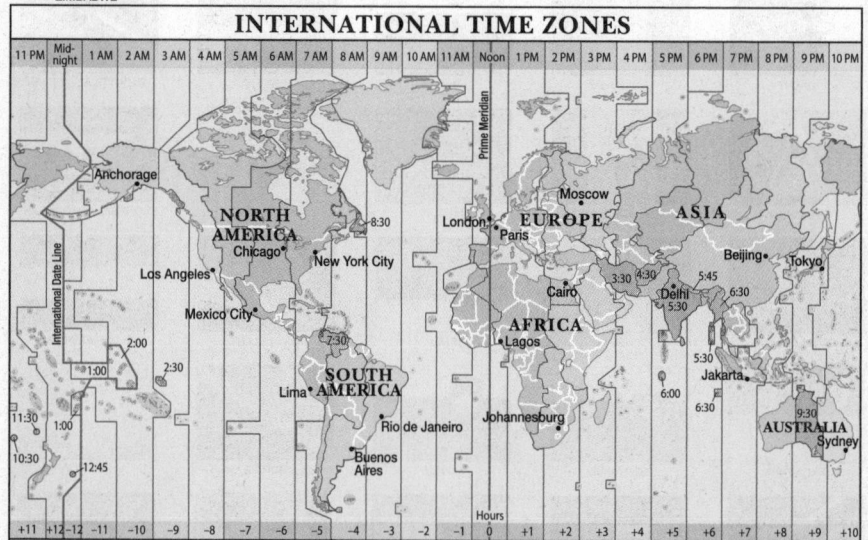

INTERNATIONAL TIME ZONES

The world is divided into 24 time zones, each 15° longitude wide. The longitudinal meridian passing through Greenwich, England, is the starting point, and is called the *prime meridian*. The 12th zone is divided by the 180th meridian (International Date Line). When the line is crossed going west, the date is advanced one day; when crossed going east, the date becomes a day earlier.

UNITED STATES

RUSSIA

ASIA

NORWAY

Oslo

EUROPE

GREAT BRITAIN

ICELAND

Reykjavik

Svalbard (Nor.)

Greenland Sea

Denmark Strait

Arctic Circle

Tasiilaq

Cape Farewell

Nuuk

GREENLAND (KALAALLIT NUNAAT) (Den.)

Ittoqqortoormiit (Scoresbysund)

Labrador Sea

Newfoundland and Labrador

St. Anthony

Newfoundland

St. John's

Corner Brook

St. Pierre and Miquelon Is. (Fr.)

Sydney

Anticosti I.

New P.E.I.

Happy Valley-Goose Bay

Labrador

Labrador City

Quebec

Schefferville

Sept-Îles

Hebron

Chibougamau

CANADIAN SHIELD

Nord

Cape Morris Jesup

ARCTIC OCEAN

+ North Pole

Baffin Bay

Davis Strait

Quaanaaq (Thule)

Grise Fiord

Alert

Cape Columbia

Ellesmere I.

Devon I.

Pond Inlet

Pangnirtung

Iqaluit

UNGAVA PENINSULA

Puvirnituq

Hudson Strait

Belcher Is.

James Bay

Moosonee

Queen Elizabeth Islands

Resolute

Arctic Bay

Baffin Island

Repulse Bay

Southampton I.

Hudson Bay

Melville I.

Cambridge Bay

Chukchi Sea

Point Hope

Beaufort Sea

Banks I.

Sachs Harbour

Victoria I.

Kugluktuk

Carmacks

Nunavut

Rankin Inlet

Arviat

Churchill

Lake Winnipeg

Manitoba

Thompson

Flin Flon

Saskatchewan

La Ronge

Prince Albert

Saskatoon

Point Barrow

Barrow

Bering Strait

Nome

SEWARD PENINSULA

Kotzebue

BROOKS RANGE

Inuvik

Fort McPherson

Mackenzie

Great Bear Lake

Deline

Fort Simpson

Hay River

Great Slave Lake

Northwest Territories

Yellowknife

Fort Smith

Uranium City

Lake Athabasca

La Loche

Alaska

Fairbanks

Fort Yukon

Yukon

Dawson

YUKON PLATEAU

Watson Lake

Whitehorse

British Columbia

Dawson Creek

Peace River

Grande Prairie

Alberta

Fort McMurray

Athabasca

Edmonton

Prince Albert

ALASKA RANGE

Highest point in North America Mt. McKinley 6194 m (20,320 ft)

Anchorage

Valdez

Kenai

Seward

Mt. Logan 5959 m (19,551 ft)

Skagway

Juneau

Sitka

COAST MOUNTAINS

Prince George

Williams Lake

Jasper

ROCKY MOUNTAINS

Calgary

Mt. Katmai 2047 m 6,715 ft.

Bethel

Kodiak I.

Kodiak

Gulf of Alaska

Alexander Archipelago

Ketchikan

Prince Rupert

Queen Charlotte Is.

Kitimat

Port Hardy

Vancouver I.

Mt. Waddington 3994 m (13,104 ft)

Vancouver

Victoria

Arctic Circle

NORTH AMERICA
AND THE CARIBBEAN

ATLANTIC OCEAN

PACIFIC OCEAN

Caribbean Sea

CENTRAL AMERICA

HONDURAS
San Salvador • Tegucigalpa
EL SALVADOR
San José • Managua
COSTA RICA • NICARAGUA

PANAMA
Panama City • Panama

Galápagos Islands (Ecuador)

COLOMBIA
Bogotá • Medellín • Cali • Cúcuta • Bucaramanga • Manizales • Pereira • Armenia • Ibagué • Neiva • Popayán • Pasto • Tunja • Villavicencio
Barranquilla • Cartagena • Santa Marta • Montería • Sincelejo
Buenaventura • Tumaco • Florencia
Nevada del Huila 5364 m (17,598 ft)

VENEZUELA
Caracas • Maracaibo • Valencia • Barquisimeto • Maracay • Barcelona • Ciudad Bolívar • Cumaná • Ciudad Guayana
Maracaibo • Coro • Cabimas • Valera • Mérida • San Cristóbal
Puerto Ayacucho • San Fernando de Apure • El Tigre
Pico Cristóbal Colón 5775 m (18,947 ft)

Margarita I.
Aruba (Neth.) • Bonaire (Neth.) • Curaçao (Neth.)
TRINIDAD AND TOBAGO • Port-of-Spain

GUYANA • Georgetown • New Amsterdam
SURINAME • Paramaribo
French Guiana (Fr.) • Cayenne • Kourou

GUIANA HIGHLANDS
Pico do Neblina 2994 m (9,823 ft)

ECUADOR
Quito • Guayaquil • Cuenca • Ambato • Riobamba • Loja • Machala • Portoviejo • Manta • Esmeraldas
Cotopaxi 5911 m (19,393 ft)
Chimborazo 6310 m (20,702 ft)
Aguja Point

PERU
Lima • Callao • Trujillo • Chiclayo • Piura • Iquitos • Cuzco • Arequipa • Huancayo • Ica • Chimbote • Sullana • Talara • Tumbes • Pucallpa • Cajamarca • Cerro de Pasco • Huánuco • Ayacucho • Huaraz • Yurimaguas
Nev. Huascarán 6768 m (22,205 ft)
Nev. Yerupajá 6634 m (21,765 ft)
LA MONTAÑA
ANDES
LLANOS

BRAZIL
Natal • João Pessoa • Recife • Maceió • Aracaju • Salvador • Fortaleza • Teresina • São Luís • Belém • Macapá • Santarém • Manaus • Brasília • Goiânia • Belo Horizonte • Vitória • Niterói • Rio de Janeiro • São Paulo • Campinas • Londrina • Bauru • Santos • Curitiba • Porto Alegre
Campina Grande • Mossoró • Juazeiro do Norte • Caruaru • Caxias • Imperatriz • Marabá • Araguaína • Altamira • Itaituba
Feira de Santana • Ilhéus • Jequié • Itabuna • Vitória da Conquista • Teófilo Otoni • Governador Valadares • Montes Claros • Uberlândia • Uberaba • Ribeirão Preto • São José do Rio Preto • Presidente Prudente • Volta Redonda • Juiz de Fora • Jundiaí • Anápolis • Campo Grande • Corumbá • Cuiabá • Rondonópolis • Jataí • Petrolina • Juazeiro • Floriano • Barreiras • Gurupi • Porto Velho • Ji-Paraná • Guajará-Mirim
Pico da Bandeira 2890 m (9,482 ft)
MATO GROSSO PLATEAU
BRAZILIAN HIGHLANDS
AMAZON BASIN
SELVAS
São Francisco • Tocantins • Xingu • Tapajós • Madeira • Negro • Purus • Juruá • Paraná • Paraguay

BOLIVIA
La Paz • Santa Cruz • Cochabamba • Sucre • Potosí • Oruro • Trinidad • Tarija • Camiri • Riberalta • Cobija • Puerto Maldonado
ALTIPLANO

Iquique • Antofagasta • Tocopilla • Arica • Calama
ATACAMA DESERT

CHACO

PARAGUAY
Concepción • Dourados

Letícia • Benjamin Constant • Orizona do Sul

San Salvador

Equator

EUROPE

GREENLAND
(KALAALLIT NUNAAT)
(Denmark)

Ísafjördur

ICELAND
Akureyri
Keflavík
Reykjavík
Seydhisfjördhur

Norwegian Sea

Torshavn
Faroe Islands
(Den.)

NORWAY   SWEDE

Namsos

Trondheim
Molde
Ålesund

Shetland
Islands
(U.K.)

Bergen

Østen

Sunds

Bode

ATLANTIC
OCEAN

Orkney
Islands
Thurso

Haugesund
Stavanger
Drammen
Oslo
Skien
Karlstad
Kristiansand

Borl
Uppsa
Örebro

Hebrides

Inverness

Scotland   Aberdeen
Dundee

Göteborg
Vänern
Vättern

Norrköping
Jönköping
Link

Glasgow
Edinburgh
Ayr

*North
Sea*

Ålborg
Jutland   Halmstad   Växjö
Århus   Helsingborg
Copenhagen   Malmö
DENMARK   Odense
Esbjerg   Bornho
(Den.)
Gd

Londonderry
Northern
Ireland
Belfast

UNITED
KINGDOM
Newcastle

Galway
IRELAND   Dublin
Limerick
Cork   Waterford

Liverpool   Leeds
Manchester   Kingston upon Hull
Sheffield
Birmingham
Wales   Coventry
Swansea   Norwich
Cardiff   England
Bristol   London
Plymouth   Thames
Portsmouth   Dover
Land's End   English Channel

Kiel
Lübeck   Rostock
Hamburg   NORTHER
Groningen   Bremen   Szczecin
NETHERLANDS   Hannover   Berlin   Bydgos
Amsterdam   Bielefeld   Elbe   POLA
The Hague   Essen   Magdeburg   Oder   Po
Rotterdam   GERMANY   Leipzig   Wró
Antwerp   Cologne   Kassel   Dresden
BELGIUM   Bonn   Erfurt   Liberec   Ostr
Brussels   Wiesbaden   Chemnitz   Pilzen   CZECH REP.   Bri
Lille   Liège   Frankfurt   Prague
LUXEMBOURG   Mannheim   Nürnberg   Regensburg
Luxembourg   Saarbrücken   Stuttgart   Linz
Nancy   Augsburg   Munich   Vienna
Strasbourg   SWITZERLAND   Salzburg   AUSTRIA   G
Basel   Zürich   LIECHTENSTEIN   Innsbruck   H
Bern   Klagenfurt   Graz
Dijon   ALPS   SLOVENIA
Geneva   Mt. Blanc   Bergamo   Udine   Ljubljana   Zagre
Lyon   4807 m (15,771 ft)   Matterhorn   Trieste   CROATI
Clermont-Ferrand   4478 m (14,692 ft)   Milan   Verona   Rijeka
Saint-Étienne   Grenoble   Torino   Venice   BO
Bordeaux   Parma   Bologna   Adriatic   Se
Avignon   Genoa   APENNINES
Montpellier   Pisa   SAN   MARINO
Marseille   Nice   Florence   Ancona   Split   Sera
Toulon   MONACO   Perugia
Corsica   Elba   VATICAN CITY   Rome   ITALY   Dubrov
(Fr.)   Foggia
Ajaccio   Naples   Tara
Sardinia   Vesuvius   Salerno
(It.)   1277 m (4,190 ft)

Channel Is.
(U.K.)
Le Havre
Brest   Caen   Rouen
Rennes   Paris
Le Mans
Nantes   Orleans
Seine
Tours
Loire
FRANCE
Limoges

Bay
of
Biscay

A Coruña
Vigo
Porto
Braga

Gijón
Santander
Bilbao
Donostia-
San Sebastián
Pamplona
PYRENEES

Toulouse

Leon
Vitoria-Gasteiz
Valladolid
Duero
Salamanca
Pico de Aneto
3404 m
(11,169 ft)
Zaragoza
ANDORRA

Barcelona
Tarragona

IBERIAN

PORTUGAL
Lisbon
Setubal
Badajoz

Coimbra

Madrid
Toledo
Tagus
SPAIN

PENINSULA
Cordoba

Castellon de la Plana
Valencia

Cape
St. Vincent
Cádiz
Seville
Málaga   Granada
Strait of   Almería
Gibraltar   GIBRALTAR
(U.K.)

Alicante
Murcia
Cartagena

Majorca   Minorca
Palma de
Mallorca
Balearic
(Sp.)

Rabat

ALGIERS

Sassari

Cagliari

Palermo
Sicily
(It.)

Messina
Etna
3369 m (11,053 ft)
Reggio di
Calabria
Catania

*Tyrrhenian
Sea*

AFRICA

250   500 Miles

250   500   750 Kilometers

Mediterranean

Algiers

Tunis

TUNISIA   MALTA   Valletta   Se

MOROCCO   ALGERIA

Arctic Circle

Brahm
60°
30°
70°
20°   10°   0°   10°

30°

50°

20°

40°

10°   0°   10°

ASIA

Chukchi
Sea
Bering Strait
Providentya
Wrangel I.
East
Siberian
Sea
New Siberian
Islands
Laptev
Sea
Anadyr
Bering
Sea

KOLYMA MOUNTAINS
Cherskiy
Zyryanka
Susuman
Magadan
Shiveluch
3283 m (10,771 ft)
Klyuchevskaya
4835 m (15,863 ft)
Karymsky
1536 m (5,039 ft)
Petropavlovsk-Kamchatskiy

KAMCHATKA PEN.

Tiksi
Verkhoyansk
Vilyuysk
Yakutsk
Okhotsk
Okhotnyy
Sea of
Okhotsk
Alaid
2339 m
(7,674 ft)
Sarycheva
1496 m
(4,908 ft)
Kuril
Is.
(Russia)

VERKHOYANSK RA.
Aldan

Lensk
STANOVOY
RANGE
Tynda
Komsomol'sk-
na-Amure
Svobodnyy
Blagoveshchensk
Khabarovsk
Sakhalin
Okha
Yuzhno-
Sakhalinsk
Tiatia
1819 m
(3,968 ft)
Hokkaido
Sapporo

Berkakit
Aldan
Ust'-Kut
Bodaybo
Tynda
Chita

YABLONOVYY RANGE
GREATER KHINGAN RANGE

Lake
Baykal
Ulan-
Ude
Irkutsk
Choybalsan
Ulaanbaatar

ONGOLIA
MONGOLIAN
PLATEAU

GOBI DESERT

Haila'er
Yichun
Qiqihar
Jixi
Ussuriysk
Vladivostok
Chongjin
Hamhung
Pyongyang
N. KOREA
Seoul
Incheon
Sejong
City
Daejeon
Daegu
S. KOREA
Busan
Fukuoka

Harbin
Jilin
Changchun
Fushun
Shenyang
Anshan
Dalian
Hohhot
Beijing
Tianjin

Moron
nhongor

Daman
Moron
Ulan-
Ude

Hakodate
Akita
Sendai
Honshu
Niigata
Tokyo
Yokohama
JAPAN
Mt. Fuji 3776 m (12,388 ft)
Kyoto
Nagoya
Kobe
Osaka
Hiroshima
Shikoku
Kitakyushu
Nagasaki
Kagoshima
Kyushu

Yinchuan
Baotou
Shijiazhuang
Taiyuan
Jinan
Xuzhou
Zhengzhou
Handan
Huainan
Hefei
Nanjing
Shanghai
Hangzhou

Xining
Lanzhou
Xi'an
Luoyang

CHINA
Wuhan
Nanchang
Changsha
Chengdu
Chongqing
Zigong
Shaoyang
Ganzhou
Jingdezhen
Wenzhou
Fuzhou
East China
Sea

Yellow
Sea

Ryukyu Is.
(Japan)
Okinawa
Naha

Tropic of Cancer

PACIFIC
OCEAN

Northern
Mariana
Islands
(U.S.)

Kunming
Myitkyina
Guiyang
Guilin
Liuzhou
Guangzhou
Xiamen
Taipei
TAIWAN
Kaohsiung

Nanning
Macao
Hong Kong
Zhanjiang

Phongsali
Haiphong
Hanoi
Louangphabang
Vinh
LAOS
Hainan
(China)
Haikou
Laoag
Luzon
Baguio
PHILIPPINES
Quezon City
Manila
Naga
Samar
Tacloban
Leyte
Philippine
Sea

PALAU

andalay
Mandalay
Taunggyi
Nay Pyi Taw
Chiang Mai
Hue
Da Nang
Mindoro
Panay
Iloilo
Cebu
Butuan

Yangon
(Rangoon)
Mawlamyine
khon Sawan
Nakhon
Ratchasima
THAILAND
VIETNAM
South
China
Sea
Puerto
Princesa
Palawan
Negros
Mindanao
Davao
Zamboanga

Jawei
Bangkok
Battambang
Nha Trang
CAMBODIA
Phnom Penh
Ho Chi Minh City
Kompong Som
Can Tho
Sulu
Sea

sthmus
of Kra
Phuket
Gulf of
Thailand
Hat Yai
Kota Kinabalu
Sandakan
Halmahera
Ternate
Jayapura
PAPUA
NEW GUINEA
Port Moresby

Andaman
Sea
George
Town
MALAYSIA
Bandar Seri Begawan
BRUNEI
Tarakan
New
Guinea

Banda Aceh
Medan
Kuala
Lumpur
Kelang
Natuna Is.
Kuching
Manado
Gorontalo
Ceram
Ambon
Celebes
Sea

Sibolga
Pekanbaru
Putrajaya
Singapore
SINGAPORE
Pontianak
Samainda
Balikpapan
Borneo
Celebes
Palopo
Baubau
Banda
Sea
Molluccas
Arafura
Sea

Padang
Jambi
Palembang
Sampit
Banjarmasin
Parepare
Makassar

Bengkulu
Sumatra
Bandar Lampung
Jakarta
Semarang
Surabaya
Mataram
Ende
Timor-Leste
Dili
Timor
Timor
Sea

Bandung
Yogyakarta
Java
Malang
Bali
Sumba
Kupang
AUSTRALIA

INDONESIA

500   1,000 Miles

500   1,000   1,500 Kilometers

AFRICA

SEYCHELLES

INDIAN OCEAN

SOMALIA
Mogadishu
Marka

Kismaayo

UGANDA
KENYA
Marsabit
Meru
Eldoret
Nairobi
Machacos
Mt. Kenya 5199 m (17,057 ft)
HIGHLANDS
Mombasa

Kampala
Jinja
Kisumu
Nakuru
Lake Victoria
SERENGETI PLAIN
Mt. Meru 4565 m (14,977 ft)
Kilimanjaro 5895 m (19,341 ft)
(Highest point in Africa)

RWANDA
Kigali
BURUNDI
Bujumbura
Goma
Bukavu
Kindu

Beni

Margherita Pk. 5109 m (16,763 ft)

Butembo

DEMOCRATIC REPUBLIC OF THE CONGO

CONGO BASIN

Bumba
Buta
Bondo

Mbandaka
Kisangani
Boyoma Falls

Ilebo
Kikwit
Tshikapa
Kananga
Mbuji-Mayi
Kabinda
Kamina

Kasai

Kinshasa
Bandundu
Kwango

Matadi
Mbanza-Ngungu
Boma

REPUBLIC OF THE CONGO
Brazzaville
Franceville
Loubomo
Pointe-Noire
Cabinda (Angola)

GABON
Libreville
Lambaréné
Port-Gentil

EQUATORIAL GUINEA
Bioko
Malabo

SÃO TOMÉ AND PRÍNCIPE
Príncipe
São Tomé
Annobón (Eq. Guinea)

Gulf of Guinea

ATLANTIC OCEAN

Ascension (U.K.)

Equator

COMOROS
Moroni
Mayotte (Fr.)

Antsiranana
Antalaha
Mahajanga
Toamasina
Antananarivo
Antsirabe
Fianarantsoa
Toliara
Tolanaro

MADAGASCAR

Mozambique Channel

TANZANIA
Mwanza
Tabora
Kigoma
Dodoma
Morogoro
Iringa
Mbeya
Songea

Tanga
Zanzibar I.
Dar es Salaam
Pemba I.
Zanzibar
Mtwara
Nacala

Lake Tanganyika
RIFT VALLEY

Mbala
Kasama

Lake Mweru

KATANGA

Lubumbashi
Likasi
Kolwezi

ZAMBIA
PLATEAU
Chingola
Kitwe
Ndola
Kabwe
Lusaka
Livingstone

Lake Nyasa

MALAWI
Lilongwe
Blantyre

MOZAMBIQUE
Nampula
Quelimane
Chimoio
Beira
Tete

Harare
Mutare
ZIMBABWE
Gweru
Bulawayo
Francistown
Masvingo

Victoria Falls
Zambezi

Mbeya

Thohoyandou
Musina
Xai-Xai
Maputo
SWAZILAND
Mbabane
Manzini
Maseru

BOTSWANA
KALAHARI DESERT
Serowe
Palapye
Gaborone
Mahalapye
Francistown

ANGOLA
Malanje
Luena
Menongue
Lobito
Benguela
Luanda
Huambo
Lubango
Namibe

NAMIBIA
NAMIB DESERT
Windhoek
Tsumeb
Grootfontein
Ruacana Falls
Keetmanshoop
Walvis Bay
Lüderitz

Augrabies Falls

Springbok
Upington
Mmabatho
Klerksdorp
Vereeniging
Johannesburg
Pretoria (Tshwane)
Kimberley
Welkom
Bloemfontein
LESOTHO
Newcastle
Pietermaritzburg
Durban
Umtata
Bisho
East London
Port Elizabeth

SOUTH AFRICA
Worcester
Cape Town
Cape of Good Hope
Cape Agulhas
Middelburg
Orange

Tropic of Capricorn

472

AUSTRALIA AND THE PACIFIC

Congress Aug. 7 passed **Tonkin Gulf Resolution**, authorizing presidential action in Vietnam, after North Vietnamese boats reportedly attacked U.S. destroyers Aug. 2. Congress approved War on Poverty bill Aug. 11, providing for a domestic Peace Corps (**VISTA**), **Job Corps**, and antipoverty funding. The **Warren Commission** released a report Sept. 27 concluding that Lee Harvey Oswald was solely responsible for the Kennedy assassination. Pres. **Johnson** elected to full term, Nov. 3, defeating Sen. **Barry Goldwater** (R, AZ) in landslide. **Verrazano-Narrows Bridge** opened in New York City, Nov. 21, with world's then-longest suspension span.

1965 In State of the Union address Jan. 4, Pres. Johnson outlined plans for "**Great Society,**" program of civil rights, antipoverty, and health-care legislation. Johnson in Feb. ordered continuous bombing of **North Vietnam** below 20th parallel.

Malcolm X assassinated Feb. 21 at New York City rally. March from **Selma to Montgomery**, AL, Mar. 21-25, by Rev. Martin Luther King Jr. to demand federal protection of blacks' voting rights. Some 14,000 U.S. troops sent to **Dominican Republic** during civil war Apr. 28. All troops withdrawn by next year. Bill establishing **Medicare**, government health insurance program for elderly, signed by Pres. Johnson July 30.

New **Voting Rights Act**, which banned literacy tests and other voter qualification tests, signed Aug. 6. Arrest of black motorist by white police officers precipitated **Watts riot** in predominantly-black Los Angeles neighborhood Aug. 11-16. Riots resulted in 34 deaths and $200 mil in property damage.

National **immigration quota system** abolished Oct. 3. **Electric power failure** blacked out most of northeastern U.S., parts of two Canadian provinces the night of Nov. 9-10.

1966 U.S. forces began firing into **Cambodia** May 1. Bombing of **Hanoi** area of North Vietnam by U.S. planes began June 29. By Dec. 31, 385,300 U.S. troops were stationed in South Vietnam, plus 60,000 offshore and 33,000 in Thailand.

Supreme Court ruled June 13, in *Miranda v. Arizona*, that suspects must be read their rights before police questioning. **Medicare** began July 1. In **Univ. of Texas shooting** rampage, 25-year-old student Charles Whitman killed 15 and wounded 31 from tower observation deck on Austin campus, Aug. 1; shot dead by police.

Dept. of Transportation created, Oct. 15. Edward Brooke (R, MA) elected Nov. 8 as first black U.S. senator in 85 years. Robert C. Weaver named secretary of newly created Dept. of Housing and Urban Development, becoming **first black cabinet member**.

1967 Green Bay Packers beat Kansas City Chiefs, 35-10, in **first Super Bowl**, Jan. 15, in Los Angeles. Three astronauts died Jan. 27 in *Apollo 1* fire on ground at Cape Canaveral, FL. **25th Amendment**, providing for presidential succession, ratified Feb. 10. Pres. Johnson and Soviet Prem. **Aleksei Kosygin** met June 23 and 25 at Glassboro State College in New Jersey; agreed not to let any crisis push them into war.

Riots erupted among residents of predominantly black **Newark**, NJ, July 12-17; 26 killed, 1,500 injured, more than 1,000 arrested. In **Detroit**, MI, July 23-30, 43 died, 2,000 injured; 5,000 left homeless by rioting, looting, and burning in city's black neighborhoods. **Thurgood Marshall** sworn in Oct. 2 as first black U.S. Supreme Court justice. **Antiwar march** on Washington, DC, Oct. 21-22, drew at least 70,000 participants. Carl B. Stokes (D, Cleveland) and Richard G. Hatcher (D, Gary, IN) elected **first black mayors** of major U.S. cities Nov. 7.

1968 In "**Tet offensive,**" Communist troops attacked several provincial capitals and other major cities, including Saigon, Jan. 30, but suffered heavy casualties. Pres. Johnson **curbed bombing** of North Vietnam Mar. 31. Peace talks began in Paris May 10. All bombing of North halted Oct. 31.

Rev. **Martin Luther King Jr.** assassinated Apr. 4 in Memphis, TN. **James Earl Ray**, an escaped convict, pleaded guilty to slaying, was sentenced to 99 years. Students at **Columbia Univ.**, Apr. 23-24, seized school buildings in protest against school's involvement in military research, among other issues. Sen. **Robert F. Kennedy** (D, NY) shot June 5 in Los Angeles after celebrating presidential primary victories, died June 6.

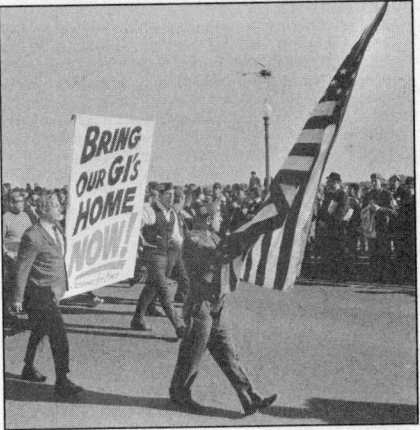

1967: A major anti-Vietnam War demonstration, a march on the Pentagon, draws more than 70,000 protesters.

Sirhan Sirhan convicted of murder, 1969; death sentence commuted to life in prison, 1972.

Vice Pres. Hubert Humphrey nominated for president at **Democratic National Convention** in Chicago, marked by clash between police and antiwar protesters, Aug. 26-29. Republican nominee **Richard Nixon** won presidency, defeating Humphrey in close race Nov. 5.

Apollo 8 **orbited moon** in five-day mission, Dec. 21-27. North Korea released 82-man crew of the USS *Pueblo* Dec. 22, 11 months after seizing the ship in Sea of Japan; one crew member had been killed in battle.

1969 Expanded four-party **Vietnam peace talks** began Jan. 18. U.S. force peaked at 543,400 in Apr.; withdrawal started July 8. Pres. Nixon set Vietnamization policy Nov. 3. Earl Warren retired upon swearing in **Warren Burger**, June 23, as Supreme Court chief justice. In incident that marked birth of **gay rights** movement, police clashed with patrons of gay bar, the **Stonewall Inn**, in New York City June 27.

U.S. astronaut **Neil Armstrong**, commander of the *Apollo 11* mission, became the **first person to set foot on the moon**, July 20, followed by astronaut **Edwin "Buzz" Aldrin**. Astronaut **Michael Collins** remained aboard command module.

Woodstock rock music festival near Bethel, NY, drew 300,000-500,000 people, Aug. 15-18. **Anti-Vietnam War demonstrations** held in cities across the U.S., marking Vietnam Moratorium day, Oct. 15; on Nov. 15, some 250,000 marched in Washington, DC. Massacre of hundreds of civilians by U.S. troops at **My Lai**, South Vietnam, in 1968 reported Nov. 16. **Kurt Vonnegut**'s *Slaughterhouse Five* published. *Sesame Street* launched on public TV.

1970 A federal jury Feb. 18 found the "**Chicago 7**" antiwar activists not guilty of conspiring to incite riots during 1968 Democratic National Convention. However, five were convicted of crossing state lines with intent to incite riots.

Three astronauts safely returned to Earth Apr. 17 after oxygen tank on *Apollo 13* ruptured. Lunar landing was canceled. Millions of Americans participated in antipollution demonstrations Apr. 22 to mark **first Earth Day**.

U.S. and South Vietnamese forces crossed **Cambodian** borders Apr. 30 to get at enemy bases. Four students killed May 4 at **Kent State Univ.** in Ohio by National Guardsmen during war protest. In protest at **Jackson State Univ.** in Mississippi, two killed when police fired on protesters.

First female U.S. generals appointed June 11. **Postal reform** measure signed Aug. 12 created an independent U.S. Postal Service. Pres. Nixon, Dec. 31, signed **clean air bill** calling for development of cleaner auto engine and national air quality standards for 10 major pollutants. Garry Trudeau's *Doonesbury* comic strip launched in 30 papers.

1971 Charles Manson and three of his cult followers found guilty Jan. 25 of first-degree murder in 1969 slaying of actress Sharon Tate and six others. A court-martial jury Mar. 29 convicted Lt. **William Calley** in murder of 22 South Vietnamese at **My Lai** on Mar. 16, 1968. He was sentenced to life in prison Mar. 31, later reduced to 20 years.

Pres. Nixon, Apr. 14, relaxed 20-year **trade embargo with China.** *New York Times* began publishing June 13 classified **Pentagon Papers**, secret Pentagon study on U.S. involvement in Vietnam leaked by Daniel Ellsberg, military analyst consulting for government. Supreme Court June 30 upheld, 6-3, right to publish the documents. **26th Amendment**, lowering the minimum voting age to 18, ratified June 30. Pres. Nixon, Aug. 15, instituted 90-day **wage and price freeze.**

U.S. bombers initiated massive five-day strike Dec. 26 in North Vietnam in retaliation for alleged violations of agreements reached prior to 1968 bombing halt.

1972 Pres. Nixon arrived in **Beijing** Feb. 21 for eight-day visit to China, in "journey for peace." Joint communiqué released Feb. 27 called for increased Sino-U.S. contacts. Senate, Mar. 22, approved **Equal Rights Amendment** banning discrimination on basis of sex; sent measure to states for ratification.

North Vietnamese forces launched biggest attacks in four years across the demilitarized zone Mar. 30. The U.S. responded Apr. 15 with **resumption of bombing** of Hanoi and Haiphong. Pres. Nixon announced May 8 the mining of North Vietnam ports.

Gov. **George C. Wallace** (D, AL), campaigning for president at Laurel, MD, shopping center May 15, shot and seriously wounded. **Arthur Bremer** convicted Aug. 4, sentenced to 63 years for shooting Wallace and three others. In **first visit of U.S. president to Moscow**, Pres. Nixon arrived May 22 for summit talks with Kremlin leaders that culminated in landmark strategic arms pact (**SALT I**). Five men arrested June 17 for breaking into Democratic National Committee offices in **Watergate** office complex in Washington, DC. Supreme Court in *Furman v. Georgia* June 29 ruled **capital punishment** as currently practiced was unconstitutional.

Mark Spitz won seven gold medals in world record times at the Munich Olympics in Aug.-Sept.

Last **U.S. combat troops** left Vietnam Aug. 11. Pres. **Nixon** reelected Nov. 7 in landslide, carrying 49 states to defeat Sen. George McGovern (D, SD). Three astronauts, part of *Apollo 17*, made 6th and last lunar landing on Dec. 11. Full-scale **bombing of North Vietnam** resumed after Paris peace negotiations reached impasse Dec. 18.

The Godfather, directed by Francis Ford Coppola, is released.

1973 In *Roe v. Wade*, Supreme Court ruled, 7-2, Jan. 22, fetus not a person with constitutional rights and the right to privacy protected woman's decision to have abortion; states may not ban abortions during first three months of pregnancy but may regulate, not ban, abortions during second trimester.

Four-party **Vietnam peace pacts** signed in Paris Jan. 27. **End of military draft** announced on same day. Last U.S. troops left Vietnam Mar. 29. North Vietnam released some 590 U.S. prisoners by Apr. 1. Pres. Nixon announced, Apr. 30, resignation of top Nixon aides H. R. Haldeman and John Ehrlichman and firing of White House Counsel **John Dean** as a consequence of the widening **Watergate** scandal. Dean told Senate hearings June 25 that Nixon, his aides, and Justice Dept. had conspired to cover up Watergate facts. The U.S. officially ceased bombing in **Cambodia** at midnight Aug. 14 in accord with June congressional action.

Vice Pres. **Spiro Agnew**, Oct. 10, resigned and pleaded no contest to charge of tax evasion while Maryland governor. **Gerald R. Ford**, Oct. 12, became **first appointed vice president** under 25th Amendment; sworn in Dec. 6. The **"Saturday Night Massacre"** occurred Oct. 20, when Pres. Nixon ordered Atty. Gen. Elliot Richardson to fire Watergate special prosecutor **Archibald Cox**, who had sought handover of Nixon's subpoenaed **White House tapes**. Richardson refused to comply and resigned;

1974: Pres. Richard Nixon resigns from office and departs the White House.

Dep. Atty. Gen. William Ruckelshaus refused and was fired. Solicitor Gen. Robert Bork, as acting atty. gen., then fired Cox. Nixon administration named **Leon Jaworski**, Nov. 1, to succeed Cox.

Skylab, **first U.S. space station**, launched May 14. **Secretariat** became first Triple Crown winner since *Citation* in 1948 by winning Belmont Stakes June 9 in record time. **Billie Jean King** defeated Bobby Riggs in three straight sets in tennis's nationally televised "Battle of the Sexes," Sept. 20. Total **ban on oil exports** to U.S. imposed by Arab oil-producing nations Oct. 19-21 after outbreak of an Arab-Israeli war; lifted Mar. 1974. Congress overrode Nov. 7 Pres. Nixon's veto of **war powers bill** curbing president's power to commit forces to hostilities abroad without congressional approval.

1974 On Apr. 8, **Hank Aaron** of the Atlanta Braves hit his 715th career home run to break Babe Ruth's record.

House Judiciary Committee opened **impeachment** hearings May 9 against Pres. Nixon. John Ehrlichman and three **White House "plumbers"** found guilty July 12 of conspiring to violate the civil rights of the psychiatrist of **Pentagon Papers** leaker Daniel Ellsberg by breaking into psychiatrist's office. Supreme Court ruled, 8-0, July 24 that Pres. Nixon had to turn over 64 **audio tapes of White House conversations**. House Judiciary Committee, in televised hearings July 24-30, recommended **articles of impeachment** against Pres. Nixon, involving conspiracy to obstruct justice in Watergate cover-up, abuses of power, and defiance of committee subpoenas.

Pres. **Nixon** announced his **resignation**, Aug. 8, and stepped down the next day. His support in Congress had begun to collapse Aug. 5 after release of tapes appearing to implicate him in Watergate cover-up. Vice Pres. **Ford** sworn in Aug. 9 as 38th U.S. president. Pres. Ford, Aug. 20, nominated **Nelson Rockefeller** to be vice president; Rockefeller sworn in Dec. 10. Citing need to move on, Pres. Ford, Sept. 8, issued **pardon to Nixon** for any federal crimes he committed while president.

New York Times published article Dec. 22 on CIA engagement in illegal domestic surveillance. Reports of other apparently illegal CIA activities, recorded in **"family jewels"** file kept by the CIA, leaked out over the years.

1975 Former Atty. Gen. John Mitchell and ex-presidential advisers H. R. Haldeman and John Ehrlichman found guilty Jan. 1 of **Watergate cover-up** charges. Mitchell released 1979, last of 25 jailed over scandal to leave prison.

U.S. launched **evacuation from Saigon** of Americans and some South Vietnamese Apr. 29 as Communist forces completed takeover of South Vietnam; **South Vietnamese** government officially surrendered Apr. 30. U.S. merchant ship *Mayaguez* and its crew of 39 seized by Cambodian forces in Gulf of Siam May 12. In rescue operation, U.S. Marines attacked Tang Island, planes bombed air base; Cambodia surrendered ship and crew. Congress voted $405 mil for .**South Vietnam refugees** May 16; 140,000 flown to U.S.

Publishing heiress **Patricia (Patty) Hearst**, kidnapped Feb. 5, 1974, by Symbionese Liberation Army (SLA), captured in San Francisco Sept. 18 with other militants. She was convicted Mar. 20, 1976, of bank robbery.

1976 In **right-to-die** case, New Jersey Supreme Court, Mar. 31, allowed comatose Karen Ann Quinlan to be removed from respirator; she survived until 1985. U.S. Supreme Court reinstated **death penalty**, July 2, subject to conditions.

U.S. celebrated **200th anniversary of independence** July 4 with festivals, parades, and New York City's Operation Sail, gathering of tall ships from around the world. "**Legionnaire's disease**" killed 29 people who attended American Legion convention July 21-24 in Philadelphia.

Viking I made successful landing on Mars, July 20. Two U.S. officers on routine mission near DMZ slain by **North Korean soldiers** Aug. 18; North Korea stated "regret."

1977 Convicted murderer Gary Gilmore executed by Utah firing squad Jan. 17; **first use of capital punishment** in U.S. since 1967. Pres. Jimmy Carter Jan. 21 pardoned most Vietnam War **draft evaders**.

Natural gas shortage caused by severe winter weather led Congress Feb. 2 to approve emergency gas bill temporarily authorizing reallocation from surplus areas. Pres. Carter signed act Aug. 4 creating new cabinet-level **Energy Dept.** FBI Dec. 7 released 40,000 pages of previously secret files relating to **Kennedy assassination**.

George Lucas's first *Star Wars* film released.

1978 Senate voted Apr. 18 to turn over **Panama Canal** to Panama on Dec. 31, 1999; Mar. 16 vote had given approval to treaty guaranteeing area's neutrality after the year 2000. Californians, June 6, approved **Proposition 13**, state constitutional amendment slashing property taxes.

Supreme Court, June 28, ruled that while race could be a factor in admission to institutions of higher education, **numerical quotas** could not be used.

Egyptian Pres. Anwar al-Sadat and Israeli Prem. **Menachem Begin** reached accord on "framework for peace," Sept. 17, after Pres. Carter-mediated talks at **Camp David.** New York's Chemical Bank Dec. 20 initiated industry-wide move to raise **lending rate** to near-record 11.75%.

1979 Partial meltdown released radioactive material Mar. 28 at nuclear reactor on **Three Mile Island** near Middletown, PA. American Airlines DC-10 **jetliner crashed** May 25 after takeoff from Chicago, killing 275 people.

In speech July 15, Pres. Carter spoke of national "crisis of confidence" and outlined proposed 10-year $140 bil program to reduce **dependence on foreign oil**. Militant followers of **Ayatollah Khomeini** took hostage some 90 people, including 66 Americans, Nov. 4 at **American embassy in Tehran**, Iran. Khomeini demanded return of ailing former Shah Muhammad Reza Pahlavi to stand trial.

1980 Pres. Carter announced, Jan. 4, economic sanctions against USSR in retaliation for Soviet invasion of Afghanistan. At Carter's request, U.S. Olympic Committee voted, Apr. 12, against U.S. participation in **Moscow Summer Olympics**. At **Winter Olympics** in Lake Placid, NY, U.S. hockey team defeated Russian team Feb. 22 en route to gold medal in "miracle on ice."

Eight Americans were killed, Apr. 24, in ill-fated attempt to rescue hostages held by Iranian militants. **Mt. St. Helens**, in Washington state, erupted May 18. The blast, with others May 25 and June 12, left 57 dead. In sweeping victory, Nov. 4, **Ronald Reagan** (R) was elected 40th president, defeating incumbent Pres. Carter. Republicans gained control of Senate. Former Beatle **John Lennon** was shot and killed by Mark David Chapman, Dec. 8, in New York City.

1981 Minutes after Reagan's inauguration Jan. 20, 52 **American hostages in Iran** were freed after being held for 444 days. Pres. **Reagan** was shot and seriously wounded, Mar. 30, in Washington, DC; also seriously wounded were a Secret Service agent, a policeman, and Press Sec. **James Brady. John W. Hinckley Jr.** arrested, found not guilty by reason of insanity in 1982, and committed to mental institution.

World's **first reusable spacecraft**, space shuttle *Columbia*, sent into space, Apr. 12. U.S. Centers for Disease Control, June 5, reported first cases of what became known as **AIDS**.

Air controllers went on **strike** Aug. 3; most were fired by Pres. Reagan after defying back-to-work order. Reagan signed into law Aug. 13 **tax-cut legislation**, expected to save taxpayers $750 bil over five years, largest tax cut to date. The Senate confirmed, Sept. 21, appointment of **Sandra Day O'Connor** as **first female Supreme Court justice.**

1982 The 13-year-old Justice Dept. lawsuit against AT&T was settled Jan. 8. AT&T agreed to give up 22 Bell System companies and was allowed to expand. **Equal Rights Amendment**, sent to states in 1972, defeated when deadline for ratification passed June 30 with support from only 35 of the 38 states needed. The economy showed signs of recovery from a **recession** that began in mid-1981, as Dow Jones Industrial Average hit 1,016.93 Oct. 13, its highest level in 18 months.

NFL strike ended Nov. 16 after 57 days when players and team owners settled with $1.6-bil pact. Singer **Michael Jackson**'s album *Thriller*, released Nov. 30, became monumental best-seller. Retired dentist Dr. Barney B. Clark became **first permanent artificial heart recipient**, Dec. 2; he died Mar. 23, 1983. The House, Dec. 16, cited EPA administrator Anne Gorsuch for contempt after she refused to release records relating to enforcement of **Superfund** law.

1983 Pres. Reagan, Jan. 3, declared Times Beach, MO, a federal disaster area because of toxic **dioxin** in soil, prompting evacuation of residents and town's closure. Harold Washington (D) elected Apr. 12 as **first black mayor of Chicago**. On Apr. 20, Pres. Reagan signed compromise bipartisan bill designed to save **Social Security** from bankruptcy.

Sally Ride became **first American woman to travel in space**, June 18, when space shuttle *Challenger* launched from Cape Canaveral, FL. On Sept. 1, **South Korean passenger jet** in Soviet air space and apparently misidentified was shot down; 269 people, including 61 Americans, killed.

On Oct. 23, 241 U.S. Marines and sailors were killed when TNT-laden **suicide truck bomb** blew up Marine barracks at Beirut International Airport in **Lebanon**. U.S. troops, with small force from six Caribbean nations, invaded **Grenada** Oct. 25; deposed Marxist regime.

1984 Seven regional companies took over **local telephone service** from AT&T, Jan. 1. On space shuttle *Challenger*'s fourth trip, launched Feb. 3, two astronauts became **first humans to fly free of a spacecraft**. On May 7, Vietnam War veterans reached out-of-court settlement with chemical

1984: The Democratic presidential ticket of former Vice Pres. Walter Mondale and Rep. Geraldine Ferraro (NY) makes history with the first female major-party nominee, but Pres. Ronald Reagan scores a landslide victory.

companies in class-action suit over the herbicide **Agent Orange**.

Former Vice Pres. **Walter Mondale** won Democratic presidential nomination, June 6. He chose Rep. **Geraldine Ferraro** (D, NY) as vice presidential candidate, first woman to be nominated for position by major political party. Pres. Reagan signed bill July 17 cutting federal transportation aid to states that keep their **drinking age** under 21. Pres. **Reagan** reelected Nov. 6 in Republican landslide, carrying 49 states for record 525 electoral votes. **Bernhard Goetz** shot and wounded four allegedly menacing teenage boys on NYC subway train, Dec. 22; later acquitted of major charges but was successfully sued.

1985 Visiting Germany, Pres. Reagan, May 5, laid wreath at Bergen-Belsen Nazi concentration camp site and at military cemetery at **Bitburg**, where some Nazis were buried. Philadelphia police bombed a rowhouse occupied by **MOVE radical group**, May 13; 11 killed, and fire damaged two blocks of houses. On June 14, **terrorists seized TWA jet** after takeoff from Athens, Greece, with 153 passengers and crew. Thirty-nine Americans held hostage for 17 days; one U.S. service member killed.

Reversing an Apr. 23 decision to market "new" Coke, the **Coca-Cola Co.** said, July 10, it would resume marketing soda made under its original "Classic" formula. **Live Aid** rock concert broadcast around the world July 13, raised $70 mil for famine relief in Ethiopia.

On Oct. 7, four **Palestinian hijackers** seized Italian cruise ship *Achille Lauro* in the Mediterranean for two days. One American, Leon Klinghoffer, killed. For first time in six years U.S. and Soviet leaders met at **summit in Geneva**, Nov. 19-20. **General Electric** agreed Dec. 11 to buy RCA Corp.

1986 The U.S. officially observed **Martin Luther King Jr. Day** for first time Jan. 20. Space shuttle *Challenger* exploded 73 seconds after liftoff, Jan. 28, killing six astronauts and Teacher in Space Project participant Christa McAuliffe. In four-day extravaganza in July, the U.S. celebrated 100th birthday of the **Statue of Liberty**.

The Senate confirmed, Sept. 17, Reagan's nomination of **William Rehnquist** as chief justice and **Antonin Scalia** as associate justice of Supreme Court. Congress completed action Oct. 2 overriding a veto to place economic sanctions on **South Africa**. Lebanese newspaper first broke news of **Iran-Contra scandal** Nov. 3, involving secret U.S. sale of arms to Iran and diversion of some of the proceeds to support the Contras, a right-wing, anti-Communist insurgent movement in Nicaragua.

Financier **Ivan Boesky** agreed Nov. 14 to pay $100 mil in fines and illicit profits for **insider trading**. Robert Penn Warren named America's **first poet laureate**.

1987 Pres. Reagan produced nation's **first trillion-dollar budget**, Jan. 5. FDA approved, Mar. 20, AZT—first drug shown to be effective in fight against **AIDS**. Nearly 1.4 mil **illegal aliens** met May 4 deadline for applying for amnesty under immigration measure passed in 1986.

Joint public hearings by Senate and House committees investigating **Iran-Contra affair** opened May 5. Lt. Col. **Oliver North**, former National Security Council staff member, said he had believed all his activities were authorized by his superiors. Hearings ended Aug. 3. Pres. Reagan, Aug. 12, denied knowing of diversion of funds to Contras.

An **Iraqi missile** killed 37 sailors on the USS *Stark* in the Persian Gulf, May 17. Iraq called it an accident. The 200th anniversary of **U.S. Constitution** signing was observed, Sept. 17, in Philadelphia and around the U.S. **Stock market crashed**, Oct. 19, with the Dow Jones plummeting a then-record 508 points to 1,738, ending bull market that began mid-1982. Pres. Reagan and Soviet leader Mikhail Gorbachev Dec. 8, signed **pact to dismantle** all 1,752 U.S. and 859 Soviet missiles with 300- to 3,400-mi range.

1988 *Phantom of the Opera* opened Jan. 26; it would go on to be longest running Broadway play ever. In report issued May 16, Surgeon Gen. C. Everett Koop declared **cigarettes** addictive. Congress approved, in June, expansion of **Medicare** benefits to protect against "catastrophic" medical costs; act was repealed in Nov. 1989.

A missile, fired from U.S. Navy warship *Vincennes* in the Persian Gulf, mistakenly struck a commercial **Iranian airliner**, July 3, killing all 290 aboard. **George H. W. Bush** (R)

elected 41st U.S. president, Nov. 8, decisively defeating Massachusetts Gov. **Michael Dukakis** (D). **Pan Am Flight 103** exploded and crashed, due to terrorist bomb, into town of Lockerbie, Scotland, Dec. 21, killing all 259 people aboard and 11 on the ground. **Drexel Burnham Lambert** agreed, Dec. 21, to plead guilty to insider trading and other violations, and pay penalties of $650 mil. U.S. suffered widespread **drought** conditions, the worst in over 50 years.

1989 Major oil spill occurred when *Exxon Valdez* struck Bligh Reef in Alaska's Prince William Sound, Mar. 24. Oliver North convicted, May 4, on charges related to **Iran-Contra scandal**. Conviction thrown out on appeal in 1991 because of his immunized testimony. TV comedy series *Seinfeld* premiered July 5 on NBC.

A measure to rescue **savings and loan industry** signed into law, Aug. 9, by Pres. Bush, launching largest federal rescue to date. Army Gen. **Colin Powell** became **first black chairman of Joint Chiefs of Staff** after being nominated Aug. 10 by Pres. Bush.

Baseball legend **Pete Rose** banned from game for life Aug. 24 for involvement with gamblers. **Hurricane Hugo** swept through the Carolinas Sept. 22, causing at least 86 deaths and $7 bil damage. An **earthquake** struck the San Francisco Bay area just before a World Series game, Oct. 17, causing 63 deaths.

L. Douglas Wilder (D) declared governor of Virginia Nov. 27, **first elected black governor** in U.S. history. U.S. troops invaded Panama, Dec. 20, overthrowing the government of **Manuel Noriega**. Noriega, wanted by U.S. authorities on drug charges, surrendered Jan. 3, 1990.

1990 Junk bond financier **Michael Milken** pleaded guilty to fraud-related charges, Apr. 14; agreed to pay $500 mil in restitution and sentenced Nov. 21 to 10 years in prison. Pres. Bush signed **Americans With Disabilities Act** barring discrimination against and requiring accommodations for the disabled, July 26.

Operation Desert Shield forces left for Saudi Arabia Aug. 7 to defend that country following invasion of **Kuwait** by Iraq, Aug. 2. David Souter confirmed Sept. 27 to serve on Supreme Court, replacing retiring Justice **William Brennan**. Pres. Bush Nov. 15 signed new **Clean Air Act**, focused on urban pollution, cancer-causing emissions from industrial sources.

1991 The U.S. and its allies defeated Iraq in **Persian Gulf War** and liberated Kuwait, which Iraq had invaded. On Jan. 17, the allies launched devastating air attacks, followed by rapid ground war starting Feb. 24. Pres. Bush ordered cease-fire Feb. 27.

An 8-month **recession** showed signs of having ended in Mar. The **Dow Jones** Industrial Average closed above 3,000 for first time, Apr. 17. Justice **Thurgood Marshall** announced, June 17, plans to retire. Senate, voting 52-48 on Oct. 15, confirmed nomination of **Clarence Thomas** to replace Marshall, after contentious hearings marked by allegations that Thomas had sexually harassed former aide Anita Hill. House Speaker Tom Foley announced Oct. 3 closure of **House Bank** by end of year after revelations that House members had written numerous bad checks.

1989: The *Exxon Valdez* oil spill causes environmental devastation in Alaska's Prince William Sound.

1992 Retail giant **R.H. Macy & Co.** filed for bankruptcy, Jan. 27. Major U.S. carrier Trans World Airlines (**TWA**) filed for bankruptcy, Jan. 31. **Riots** swept South Central Los Angeles Apr. 29 after jury acquitted four white police officers on all but one count in 1991 videotaped beating of black motorist **Rodney King**. Death toll in L.A. violence was put at 53. **27th Amendment**, regarding congressional pay raises, ratified May 7.

Hurricane Andrew ravaged South Florida and Louisiana Aug. 24-26, causing 65 deaths. White supremacist and fugitive Randall Weaver surrendered Aug. 31 after 11-day **FBI siege** at his **Ruby Ridge**, ID, cabin, during which his wife, son, and a deputy sheriff were killed.

Bill Clinton (D) elected 42nd president, Nov. 3, defeating Pres. Bush (R) and independent Ross Perot. A UN-sanctioned military force, led by U.S. troops, arrived in **Somalia** Dec. 9. Presidents of U.S., Canada, and Mexico Dec. 17 signed North American Free Trade Agreement (**NAFTA**), which took effect Jan. 1, 1994.

1993 A bomb exploded in a parking garage beneath the **World Trade Center** in New York City, Feb. 26, killing six. Four men found guilty, Mar. 4, 1994. Four federal agents killed, Feb. 28, during unsuccessful raid on **Branch Davidian** compound near **Waco**, TX. A 51-day siege by agents ended Apr. 19 when the compound burned down, leaving more than 70 cult members dead. Eleven cult members acquitted Feb. 26, 1994, of deaths of federal agents.

Janet Reno became **first female attorney general** Mar. 12. Federal jury, Apr. 17, found two Los Angeles police officers guilty and two not guilty of violating civil rights of motorist **Rodney King** in 1991 videotaped beating.

In a May 14 plebiscite, voters in **Puerto Rico** supported continuing commonwealth status with U.S. **"Motor-voter"** bill signed by Pres. Clinton, May 20, easing voting procedures. **"Great Flood of 1993"** inundated parts of nine Midwestern states in summer, leaving about 50 dead and $15 bil in damages.

Pres. Clinton, July 2, approved recommendations that 33 major U.S. military bases be closed. On July 19 he announced **"don't ask, don't tell, don't pursue"** policy for homosexuals in the military. **Ruth Bader Ginsburg** sworn in, Aug. 10, as 107th Supreme Court justice, replacing retiring Justice **Byron White**. Pres. Clinton, Aug. 10, signed measure designed to **cut federal budget deficits** by $496 bil over five years, through spending cuts and new taxes. **Brady Bill**, a major gun-control measure, signed into law by Pres. Clinton Nov. 30.

1994 A predawn **earthquake** in the Los Angeles area, Jan. 17, claimed 61 lives. Pres. Clinton Feb. 3 lifted 19-year ban on U.S. trade with **Vietnam**. Byron De La Beckwith convicted Feb. 5 of 1963 murder of civil rights leader **Medgar Evers**. Longtime CIA officer **Aldrich Ames** and his wife charged, Feb. 21, with spying for Russians. Under plea bargain, he received life in prison, while she drew 63 months.

U.S. troops, Mar. 25, officially ended peacekeeping and humanitarian aid mission in **Somalia**, begun in 1992. Congressional committees, late July, began **Whitewater hearings**. Kenneth Starr named Aug. 5 as independent counsel to probe Whitewater affair. Major league **baseball players** went on strike following Aug. 11 games. World Series canceled; strike ended Apr. 25, 1995. Senate Majority Leader George Mitchell (D, ME), Sept. 26, dropped efforts to pass Pres. Clinton's **health-care reform** package.

Republicans gained control of both House and Senate in Nov. 8 elections after many years of Democratic control. House speaker **Tom Foley** (MA) was among the defeated Democrats.

1995 Newt Gingrich (R, GA) elected U.S. House speaker. A bill to end Congress's exemption from federal labor laws, first in series of measures in Republicans' **"Contract With America,"** cleared Congress Jan. 17; signed into law Jan. 23. Pres. Clinton, Jan. 31, authorized $20 bil loan to **Mexico**. Last UN peacekeeping troops withdrew from **Somalia** Feb. 28-Mar. 3, with aid of U.S. Marines. In **Haiti**, peacekeeping responsibilities were transferred from U.S. to UN forces Mar. 31, with U.S. providing 2,400 soldiers.

Truck **bomb exploded outside Oklahoma City federal office** building Apr. 19, killing 168 people; Timothy McVeigh

arrested as key suspect, Apr. 21. U.S. space shuttle *Atlantis* made first in series of dockings with Russian space station *Mir*, June 29-July 4. The U.S. announced July 11 it was reestablishing **relations with Vietnam**.

Ten Muslim militants convicted, Oct. 1, in failed **plot to blow up UN Headquarters**, other buildings and assassinate political leaders. Former football star **O. J. Simpson** found not guilty Oct. 3 of June 1994 murders of former wife, Nicole Brown Simpson, and a friend of hers. Hundreds of thousands of black men participated in **Million Man March** and rally in Washington, DC, Oct. 16, organized by Rev. Louis Farrakhan.

Five Americans among seven killed, Nov. 13, in **bombing** of U.S. military post in **Riyadh, Saudi Arabia**. Budget impasse between Congress and Pres. Clinton led to partial **government shutdown** Nov. 14; operations resumed Nov. 20 under continuing resolutions. After talks outside Dayton, OH, warring parties in **Bosnia and Herzegovina** reached agreement Nov. 21 to end their conflict; treaty signed Dec. 14, and U.S. peacekeeping troops arrived. A 1973 federal law imposing **55-mph speed limit** repealed Nov. 28.

1996 Senate, Jan. 26, approved, 87-4, Second Strategic Arms Reduction Treaty (**START II**). Congress, Mar. 27-28, approved **line item veto**; struck down by Supreme Court, June 1998.

James and Susan McDougal convicted May 28 of fraud and conspiracy in **Whitewater** case; Arkansas Gov. Jim Guy Tucker (D) convicted on similar charges. The antitax **Freemen** surrendered to federal authorities June 13 after 81-day standoff near Jordan, MT; four were convicted, July 1998, of conspiring to defraud banks.

Bomb exploded at **Khobar Towers** military complex near Dhahran, Saudi Arabia, June 25, killing 19 American service personnel. Homemade pipe bomb exploded July 27 in **Atlanta**, GA, park during **Summer Olympics**; one person killed. Extremist Eric Robert Rudolph, arrested in May 2003, pleaded guilty to this and other bombings.

Major **welfare reform bill** signed into law, Aug. 22. Defense of Marriage Act (**DOMA**), passed by wide margins

1995: The Murrah Federal Building in Oklahoma City is targeted in the deadliest act of domestic terrorism in U.S. history.

and signed Sept. 21, barred federal recognition of same-sex marriages and permitted states to disregard same-sex marriages from other states. U.S. signed **Comprehensive Test Ban Treaty**, Sept. 24, which banned all nuclear weapons tests and explosions; Senate failed to ratify treaty. Pres. **Clinton reelected**, Nov. 5.

1997 Madeleine Albright sworn in as sec. of state Jan. 23, becoming first female State Dept. head. Former CIA official Harold Nicholson pleaded guilty, Mar. 3, to **spying for Russia**. Thirty-nine members of **Heaven's Gate** religious cult found dead in Rancho Santa Fe, CA, house Mar. 26, in apparent mass suicide.

Timothy McVeigh convicted of conspiracy and murder, June 2, in 1995 **Oklahoma City** bombing; executed June 2001. Terry Nichols convicted Dec. 23 on related charges. Two Islamic militants convicted, Nov. 12, of key roles in 1993 bombing of **World Trade Center**. The film *Titanic*, released Dec. 14, went on to win 11 Oscars and gross over $600 mil.

1998 Media outlets reported Jan. 21 on evidence of sexual relationship between Pres. Clinton and former White House intern **Monica Lewinsky**. Clinton initially denied affair, but in grand jury testimony and address to the nation, Aug. 17, acknowledged relationship that was "not appropriate." On Sept. 9, independent counsel **Kenneth Starr** sent findings to House of Representatives; Judiciary Committee, Oct. 5, voted 21-16 to recommend full inquiry. House, Dec. 19, approved two articles of **impeachment** charging Pres. Clinton with grand jury perjury and obstruction of justice in cover-up.

"Unabomber" Theodore Kaczynski, arrested in Montana in 1993, pleaded guilty Jan. 22 to California and New Jersey bombings that killed three people; sentenced in May to four life terms plus 30 years. Texas, Feb. 3, executed its first female convict in 135 years.

Bombs at U.S. embassies in Nairobi, Kenya, and Dar-es-Salaam, Tanzania, killed at least 257, Aug. 7; U.S. launched retaliatory strikes, Aug. 20, against targets in Afghanistan and Sudan. On Sept. 30, Pres. Clinton announced federal **budget surplus** of $70 bil for fiscal 1998, first since 1969.

Pres. Clinton, Nov. 13, settled suit by agreeing to pay $850,000 to **Paula Jones**, who alleged he had made an unwanted sexual advance in 1991. Biggest U.S. **tobacco companies**, in settlement Nov. 23, agreed to pay states and territories $206 bil over 25 years to cover public health costs.

1999 *The Sopranos* TV drama debuted, Jan. 10. Pres. **Clinton** was acquitted, Feb. 12, at end of Senate impeachment trial. Perjury article failed with 45 votes; obstruction of justice article drew 50-50 vote, with two-thirds vote needed for conviction.

Dr. **Jack Kevorkian** convicted of second-degree murder Mar. 26 in death of terminally ill man. One man pleaded guilty Apr. 5, another convicted Nov. 4, in 1998 kidnapping and beating death of **Matthew Shepard**, an openly gay student at the Univ. of Wyoming.

Eric Harris, 18, and Dylan Klebold, 17, killed 12 fellow students and a teacher Apr. 20 at **Columbine High School** in Littleton, CO, then fatally shot themselves. **John F. Kennedy Jr.** killed in crash of private plane July 16.

2000 Across U.S., midnight celebrations marked changeover to year 2000 on Jan. 1; feared **Y2K** computer glitch caused only minor problems. In the first such state law, Vermont Gov. Howard Dean (D) signed legislation Apr. 26 allowing same-sex couples to gain legal rights by forming **civil unions**. Scientists from U.S. and Britain announced jointly, June 26, that they had determined structure of the **human genome**.

Six-year-old **Elián González** was returned to father in Cuba June 28, seven months after rescue from boat wreck in which his mother and other refugees drowned. **Tiger Woods** became youngest player, at age 24, to win all four of golf's majors, with record score in British Open, July 23.

Food and Drug Administration announced, Sept. 28, approval of **RU-486**, a pill that induces abortions. Seventeen U.S. sailors died Oct. 12 in terrorist bombing of USS *Cole*, which was refueling in Aden, Yemen.

On election night, Nov. 7, the winner of **Florida's electoral votes** remained uncertain, leaving national result in doubt.

2001: The attacks of Sept. 11 kill more than 2,750 people in New York.

Florida Supreme Court, Dec. 8, ordered manual recount of certain ballots; on Dec. 12, U.S. Supreme Court reversed that decision, and Vice Pres. **Al Gore** (D), next day, conceded to Texas Gov. **George W. Bush** (R).

2001 AOL-Time Warner merger completed Jan. 11. FBI agent **Robert Hanssen** arrested Feb. 20, charged with spying for Soviet Union and Russia over 20-year period; under plea bargain, sentenced in 2002 to life in prison. **U.S. Navy spy plane** collided with Chinese fighter plane over South China Sea Apr. 1, killing fighter pilot; 24 U.S. crew members detained in Hainan until U.S. apology, Apr. 12.

Sen. **James Jeffords** (R, VT) May 24 left his party, giving Democrats control of Senate. Pres. George W. Bush signed, June 7, $1.35-tril tax-cut package. Bush announced Aug. 9 he would allow federal funding of limited research on existing **stem-cell** lines from human embryos.

On morning of **Sept. 11**, two hijacked commercial airliners struck **World Trade Center twin towers** in New York City in **worst-ever terrorist attack** on American soil. A third hijacked plane destroyed a portion of the **Pentagon**; a fourth crashed in a field near Shanksville, PA. Some 3,000 people were killed, including about 2,750 at World Trade Center. Five people died and became ill from exposure to **anthrax** through U.S. postal system, Oct. 4-Nov. 21.

U.S. and Britain, Oct. 7, launched air-strike campaign against Afghan-based terrorist organization **al-Qaeda** and Afghanistan's ruling **Taliban** militia. Pres. Bush created **Office of Homeland Security**, Oct. 8, and on Oct. 26 signed USA **Patriot Act**, with wide-ranging provisions aimed at preventing terrorism. **Taliban** surrendered Kabul, Nov. 13, and fled from Kandahar, their stronghold, Dec. 7. U.S. government, Dec. 11, indicted al-Qaeda member **Zacarias Moussaoui** as Sept. 11 co-conspirator; he pleaded guilty, sentenced in May 2006 to life in prison. Operation in Afghanistan's **Tora Bora** cave complex, Dec. 12-17, failed to capture al-Qaeda leader **Osama bin Laden**.

Leading energy-trading company **Enron** filed for bankruptcy, Dec. 2. Pres. Bush announced, Dec. 13, U.S. withdrawal from **1972 Antiballistic Missile Treaty**.

2002 Taliban and al-Qaeda fighters captured in Afghanistan flown to U.S. naval base at **Guantánamo Bay** in Cuba, starting Jan. 11. Congress, Jan. 24, began hearings into **Enron bankruptcy**.

In State of the Union address, Jan. 29, Pres. Bush called Iran, Iraq, and North Korea part of **"axis of evil."** By Mar. 6, 1,200 U.S. troops were involved in **Operation Anaconda** against al-Qaeda and Taliban forces in Afghanistan.

Independent prosecutor's report, Mar. 20, found insufficient evidence that Pres. Clinton or Hillary Clinton committed any crime in connection with **Whitewater**. Pres. Bush, Mar. 27, signed into law McCain-Feingold **campaign-finance reform bill** banning unregulated, unrestricted "soft money" donations; part of bill struck down by Supreme Court, June 2007.

Ceremonial last girder removed May 30 from **World Trade Center** site, signaling end of massive clean-up and recovery operation. **WorldCom** filed for bankruptcy, July 21.

"Shoe-Bomber" Richard Reid pleaded guilty Oct. 4 to all charges stemming from incident aboard plane in Dec. 2001; sentenced Jan. 2003 to life in prison. On Oct. 10-11 the House, 296-133, and Senate, 77-23, gave Bush backing to use military force against **Iraq**. Bush administration revealed Oct. 16 that **North Korea** had acknowledged developing nuclear arms. Bush signed measure, Nov. 25, creating cabinet **Dept. of Homeland Security**.

U.S. Roman Catholic bishops, Nov. 13, approved revised, Vatican-vetted policies dealing with priests who sexually abuse minors. Cardinal **Bernard Law**, Dec. 13, resigned as archbishop of Boston; he had been accused of covering up sexual abuse by priests. **Trent Lott** (R, MS) bowed out as new Senate majority leader Dec. 20 after remarks apparently supporting segregation.

2003 On Jan. 10-11, Gov. George Ryan (R) pardoned or **commuted death sentences** of all 171 Illinois death row convicts.

Space shuttle *Columbia* broke apart Feb. 1 during descent toward planned landing; all seven crew members killed. Report issued Aug. 26 blamed damage sustained during liftoff; also cited "broken safety culture" at NASA. Senate, Mar. 6, approved the **Strategic Offensive Reductions Treaty** (Moscow Treaty) for reducing nuclear stockpiles signed in 2002 by U.S. and Russian leaders.

U.S.-led military offensive aimed at ousting **Saddam Hussein** got underway Mar. 19, when 40 Tomahawk cruise missiles hit targets in Baghdad. U.S. forces Mar. 21 seized oil fields near Basra. By Apr. 9, U.S. forces reported control over much of Baghdad. Pres. Bush, speaking from aircraft carrier May 1, declared **end of major combat operations in Iraq**; insurgents continued to mount attacks.

Pres. Bush signed bill May 28 providing $330 bil in **tax cuts** over several years. A power failure caused **blackouts** affecting some 50 mil people in Ohio, Michigan, and the Northeast, as well as eastern Canada, on Aug. 14.

The Roman Catholic archdiocese of Boston agreed to pay up to $85 mil in **sex abuse settlement** announced Sept. 9. Californians, Oct. 7, voted to recall Gov. Gray Davis (D) and replace him with actor-turned-politician **Arnold Schwarzenegger** (R). Rev. V. Gene Robinson consecrated Nov. 2 as Episcopal Church's **first openly gay bishop**. Massachusetts court decided, Nov. 18, that gay couples had **right to marry**.

Senate, Nov. 3, approved $87.5 bil for **U.S. military forces in Iraq** and help rebuilding the country. Virginia jury, Nov. 17, found **John Muhammad** guilty in 2002 Washington, DC, area **sniper attacks** that killed 10; sentenced to death. Another Virginia jury found accomplice **Lee Malvo** guilty of murder in the attacks, Dec. 18; sentenced to life in prison without parole.

Pres. Bush signed bill Dec. 8 to overhaul **Medicare**, adding prescription drug benefit and expanding role of private insurance companies. **Saddam Hussein captured** by U.S. forces Dec. 13, in underground hideout southeast of Tikrit.

2004 *The Lord of the Rings: The Return of the King* won 11 Oscars, Feb. 29.

Photos showing abuse of **Abu Ghraib prison** inmates in Iraq by American soldiers emerged Apr. 3. **National World War II Memorial** in Washington, DC, opened Apr. 29. On May 17, as a result of a 2003 court decision, Massachusetts became the first state in which **same-sex marriage** was legal.

U.S.-led coalition transferred power to interim Iraqi government, June 28. **9/11 Commission Report**, released July 22, called for restructuring U.S. intelligence operations.

Boston Red Sox won World Series Oct. 27, for first time since 1918.

Pres. **Bush reelected** Nov. 2, with 286 electoral votes, defeating Sen. John Kerry (D, MA), with 251. Republicans increased majorities in Senate and House. Nov. 14. Pres. Bush signed intelligence reform bill Dec. 17, creating a director of national intelligence.

2005 Two U.S. soldiers found guilty, Jan. 14, in **Abu Ghraib** prisoner abuses in Iraq and sentenced to prison terms.

Condoleezza Rice became first black woman sec. of state, Jan. 26. **Alberto Gonzales** became first Hispanic U.S.

atty. gen., Feb. 3. **Terri Schiavo**, in a persistent vegetative state since 1990, died Mar. 31, 13 days after feeding tube was removed following legal battle.

Vanity Fair article revealed May 31 that former FBI official W. Mark Felt was **"Deep Throat"**—key source for *Washington Post* reporters Bob Woodward and Carl Bernstein probing 1972 Watergate break-in.

Hurricane Katrina hit Gulf coast, Aug. 29, causing devastation in Louisiana, Mississippi, and Alabama. Breach in a levee on Lake Pontchartrain, Aug. 30, flooded New Orleans. Relief efforts widely criticized as insufficient.

Chief Justice **William H. Rehnquist** died Sept. 3. Bush Sept. 5 nominated as successor **John G. Roberts Jr.**; on Sept. 29 he was confirmed by Senate, 78-22, and sworn in as 17th chief justice. On Oct. 31 Bush nominated **Samuel A. Alito Jr.** to replace retiring Justice Sandra Day O'Connor; confirmed Jan. 31, 2006.

House Majority Leader **Tom DeLay** (R, TX) indicted in Texas Sept. 28 on money laundering charges; stepped down from leadership and later convicted.

New York Times, Dec. 16, reported that Pres. Bush in 2002 had secretly authorized National Security Agency to **eavesdrop without court warrant** on people in U.S. suspected of terrorist activities. Congress passed and Bush, Dec. 30, signed **anti-torture legislation**.

2006 Former top Republican lobbyist **Jack Abramoff** pleaded guilty Jan. 3 to bribery and other charges; in plea agreement, promised to cooperate with investigation into his dealings with members of Congress.

U.S. Supreme Court ruled June 29 that Pres. Bush's system for trying terrorism detainees at **Guantánamo** Bay was unauthorized under federal law and Geneva Conventions. Bush, July 19, issued his **first veto**, on bill to end funding constraints on human embryonic **stem cell research**.

British authorities announced Aug. 10 they had foiled terrorist plot to use **liquid explosives** on flights between Britain and U.S. In speech Sept. 6 Bush confirmed existence of **secret overseas prisons** for terrorism suspects run by CIA.

Pres. Bush signed bill Oct. 26 authorizing construction of 700-mi fence along **U.S.-Mexico border**; broader immigration bill failed in Congress.

Democrats won control of House and Senate in **midterm congressional elections** Nov. 7. Pres. Bush announced Nov. 8 that Defense Sec. **Donald Rumsfeld**, a focus of criticism over Iraq war, had resigned.

2007 Rep. Nancy Pelosi (D, CA) chosen Jan. 4 as **first woman Speaker of the House**. On Jan. 10, Pres. Bush announced troop **"surge"** in Iraq, backed by Lt. Gen. **David Petraeus**, new top U.S. commander there.

Reports of substandard conditions at **Walter Reed Army Medical Center** in Washington, DC, resulted in dismissals of military officials, Mar. 1-2. I. Lewis **"Scooter" Libby**, former chief of staff for Vice Pres. Cheney, found guilty Mar. 6 of perjury and obstructing justice in the investigation into a leak exposing undercover CIA agent; Bush commuted his prison sentence.

2005: Hurricane Katrina and subsequent failure of levees cause unprecedented destruction in New Orleans and along the Gulf Coast.

A senior at **Virginia Tech** killed 27 students and five faculty members on Apr. 16 before killing himself. On Apr. 18, Supreme Court upheld, 5-4, a 2003 federal law that banned so-called **partial birth abortions**.

U.S. Senate and House May 24 approved Iraq and Afghanistan **war-funding bill** with benchmarks for withdrawal of U.S. troops from Iraq; Congress also raised **minimum wage** from $5.15 to $7.25 per hour over two years.

Dow Jones closed over 14,000 July 19, just 59 trading days after passing 13,000. Pres. Bush issued an executive order July 20 banning any "cruel, inhuman, or degrading" treatment of **imprisoned terror suspects**. *Harry Potter and the Deathly Hallows,* final novel in J. K. Rowling's series, released July 21, earning record U.S. sales.

A **Minneapolis highway bridge** collapsed Aug. 1, causing the deaths of 13 people. Congress, Aug. 4, cleared measure allowing **National Security Agency** to monitor communications without court warrants if believed related to terrorism. Barry Bonds tied Hank Aaron's all-time career **home-run record** at 755 on Aug. 4 in San Diego; hit No. 756 on Aug. 7.

José Padilla convicted of conspiracy in terrorism case, Aug. 16; sentenced to 17 years, 4 months. Atty. Gen. **Alberto Gonzales**, blamed for alleged firing of U.S. attorneys, announced resignation Aug. 27.

Report by former U.S. Sen. George J. Mitchell, released Dec. 13, presented evidence of **performance-enhancing drug use** by 86 Major League Baseball players.

Under law signed Dec. 17, New Jersey became the first state to **repeal the death penalty** since Supreme Court reinstated it in 1976. An energy bill mandating an increase in automobile **fuel-economy standards** to 35 mi per gallon by 2030 signed by Pres. Bush Dec. 19.

2008 Sen. **John McCain** (AZ) won New Hampshire primary, Jan. 8; clinched 2008 Republican presidential nomination by early Mar. Among Democrats, Sen. **Barack Obama** (IL) moved ahead of closest rival Sen. **Hillary Clinton** (NY) to clinch nomination in early June.

The Federal Reserve cut key interest rates, Jan. 22 and 30, to aid U.S. economy; $168-bil **economic stimulus** package, signed Feb. 13 by Pres. Bush, provided tax rebates.

In Mar. 18 speech, Sen. Obama discussed America's racial divide and condemned inflammatory rhetoric used by Rev. **Jeremiah Wright**, his former pastor.

U.S. Supreme Court ruled June 12 that foreign prisoners at **Guantánamo Bay** could challenge detention by filing writs of **habeas corpus**. **Oil prices** spiked above $140 per barrel in June; national average price for gallon of regular gas topped $4.

Sec. of State Condoleezza Rice signed agreements in Czech Republic, July 8, and Poland, Aug. 20, to place components of a U.S. **missile defense system** there (agreements rescinded by Obama administration, Sept. 17, 2009). Measure signed July 10 by Pres. Bush expanded government power to spy on suspected terrorists. U.S., Sept. 1, gave Iraqi forces security responsibilities in Anbar province, formerly center of a Sunni insurgency. U.S. air strike in **Afghanistan** village of Aziz-

abad, Aug. 22, killed up to 90 civilians, according to Afghan sources.

Meeting Aug. 25-28, Democrats nominated **Obama** for president and Sen. **Joe Biden** (DE) for vice president. Meeting Sept. 1-4, Republicans nominated **McCain** for president and Alaska Gov. **Sarah Palin** for vice president.

With financial system in crisis, federal government Sept. 7 took control of mortgage finance companies **Fannie Mae** and **Freddie Mac**. On Wall Street a week later, investment titan **Merrill Lynch** agreed to sell itself to Bank of America for $50 bil, and **Lehman Brothers** declared bankruptcy, after finding no buyer. The Fed Sept. 16 took control of insurance giant **AIG**, giving it a credit line that expanded to $144 bil by Oct. 31.

On Sept. 20, a Treasury Dept. plan was introduced to purchase up to $700 bil of "**toxic**" **mortgage-backed securities** to restore confidence. Legislation to implement Troubled Assets Relief Program (**TARP**) failed in the House, Sept. 29, sending Dow Jones down 778 points. Revised **bailout plan** passed Senate Oct. 1, 74-25, and House Oct. 3, 263-171; gave Treasury immediate access to half of $700 bil in TARP funds, with broad discretion in their use. On Oct. 21 Fed pledged $540 bil as a backup to protect money market funds.

Barack Obama elected, Nov. 4, as **first African-American president** in U.S. history, earning 53% of popular vote and 365 of 538 electoral votes. Democrats also increased majorities in House and Senate. California voters approved **Proposition 8**, banning same-sex marriages in the state.

U.S. government Nov. 23 announced plan to provide $20 bil in cash and up to $306 bil more as backup to protect ailing **Citigroup** from potential mortgage losses. Pres.-elect Obama Nov. 24 named **Timothy Geithner** to be treasury sec.; he was confirmed Jan. 26, 2009. Dow Jones dropped 7.7% Dec. 1 after reports that manufacturing had hit 26-year low and that U.S. economy fell into **recession** in Dec. 2007.

Pres.-elect Obama named former rival **Hillary Clinton**, Dec. 1, to be sec. of state (confirmed Jan. 2009). Illinois Gov. **Rod Blagojevich** (D) arrested Dec. 9, accused of seeking to sell Senate seat being vacated by Obama. Convicted in a state senate trial, he was removed from office, Jan. 2009. **Bernard Madoff** arrested Dec. 11 for **Ponzi scheme**; sentenced to 150 years in jail in guilty plea, June 2009. Fed Dec. 16, cut benchmark interest rate to near zero. On Dec. 19, Pres. Bush announced that $17 bil in **TARP funds** would be used to help keep **General Motors** and **Chrysler** afloat.

2009 Treasury Dept., Jan. 15, gained access to remaining $350 bil in TARP funds; provided funds to prop up **Bank of America**.

Barack Obama inaugurated Jan. 20 as 44th U.S. president. He issued executive orders Jan. 22 restricting CIA interrogation practices and calling for closing of U.S. military prison at **Guantánamo Bay**, Cuba, within a year (closing blocked by Congress). Treasury Sec. Geithner, Feb. 10, outlined $2 tril program to stabilize banking and ease credit markets with "**stress tests**" that led to greater capital requirements for some banks. Pres. Obama signed **economic stimulus** bill Feb. 17, providing for $212 bil in tax cuts and $575 bil in new spending; introduced $275-bil program Feb. 18 to aid homeowners.

Pres. Obama announced, Feb. 17, that U.S. would send 17,000 more troops to **Afghanistan** and said, Feb. 27, that most U.S. troops would be out of Iraq by Aug. 2010. **California** legislators, ending 15-week deadlock, closed $42 bil budget gap, Feb. 19; revised plan passed July 24.

Treasury Sec. Geithner, Mar. 23, introduced Public-Private Investment Program (PPIP), offering incentives to encourage purchases of "**toxic assets**."

The Vermont state legislature, Apr. 7, enacted a law allowing **same-sex marriage**, becoming first to do so without prior judicial mandate. Obama administration Apr. 13 eased restrictions on family travel and remittances to **Cuba**.

Justice Dept. Apr. 16 released memos offering legal rationale for CIA interrogation methods, including **waterboarding**. On Aug. 24, Atty. Gen. Eric Holder appointed special prosecutor to investigate **possible detainee abuse**.

2007: Pres. George W. Bush sends a "surge" of additional U.S. troops to Iraq.

After outbreak of influenza A (H1N1), or **swine flu**, in Mexico and then in U.S., U.S. officials declared public health emergency Apr. 26.

Chrysler LLC filed for bankruptcy protection Apr. 30; auto workers' union retirement health-care fund given 55% stake in reorganized company. Pres. Obama, May 19, tightened **fuel efficiency** standards for vehicles. **General Motors** filed for bankruptcy June 1, under plan providing new federal funds. On June 9, 10 financial firms got permission from U.S. Treasury to return some $68 bil in **TARP funds**.

George Tiller, Kansas doctor who performed **late-term abortions**, murdered May 31; anti-abortion activist was convicted Jan. 2010 and sentenced Mar. 2010 to life in prison.

Speaking June 4 in Egypt, Pres. Obama called for "new beginning" in relations with **Muslim world**. U.S. military completed **withdrawal from Iraq's cities** and towns June 30.

Pres. Obama, June 22, signed measure to regulate content and marketing of tobacco products. Obama and Russian Pres. Dmitri Medvedev, in Russia July 6, agreed on reducing **nuclear arsenals** and allowing U.S. flights to Afghanistan through Russian airspace.

Short-term federal **"cash for clunkers"** program, for trading in old gas-guzzling vehicles, began July 24; ultimately funded at $3 bil.

Judge **Sonia Sotomayor** confirmed Aug. 6 for Supreme Court vacancy left by retirement of **David Souter**; sworn in Aug. 8, she became first Hispanic to join the court.

Airport shuttle driver Najibullah Zazi charged, Sept. 24, with plot to produce bombs for **terror attacks** in the New York City subway system; he later pleaded guilty.

Government reported Oct. 29 that real GDP grew at 3.5% annual rate in July-Sept., signaling end of **recession**. However, **unemployment** in Oct. passed 10%. Pres. Obama Nov. 6 signed measure extending unemployment benefits and $8,000 tax credit for first-time homebuyers.

Pres. Obama announced Oct. 30 end to U.S. travel and immigration restrictions on people with **AIDS** virus. On Nov. 5, 12 soldiers and a civilian were killed in mass shooting at **Ft. Hood**, TX; Army psychiatrist Maj. Nidal Malik Hasan, shot and captured by police SWAT team, was charged.

Pres. Obama Dec. 1 announced a **surge** of 30,000 additional troops to **Afghanistan** so as to peak at 100,000. He received **Nobel Peace Prize** Dec. 10 in Oslo, Norway.

Obama brokered **greenhouse-gas accord**, Dec. 18 in Copenhagen, establishing nonbinding reduction goals.

Detroit-bound airline passengers, Dec. 25, thwarted attempt by Nigerian man to ignite **explosives hidden in his underwear**. On Dec. 30, a Jordanian CIA informant acting as a double agent set off bomb at CIA meeting site near Afghan-Pakistan border, killing himself and eight others.

2010 On Jan. 19 in Massachusetts, state sen. **Scott Brown** (R) won U.S. Senate seat held by Sen. Edward Kennedy (D, MA); result cost Democrats filibuster-proof majority. U.S. Supreme Court Jan. 21 held that corporations and unions had right to spend unlimited funds on advertising to influence election outcomes.

U.S. and other coalition troops launched offensive in **Helmand Province**, Afghanistan, Feb. 13, targeting Taliban. Pres. Obama, Mar. 18, signed $18-bil **job-stimulus** measure providing tax cuts and other employer incentives.

Long effort by Democrats to enact **health care reform** legislation succeeded on Mar. 21 when the House voted, 219-212, with no Republican support, to approve bill as passed by Senate in Dec. 2009. The wide-ranging, controversial measure, signed by Pres. Obama on Mar. 23, aimed in part at extending health insurance to millions of uninsured.

Meeting Apr. 8 in Prague, Pres. Obama and Russian Pres. Dmitri Medvedev signed New Strategic Arms Reduction Treaty, or **New START** (ratified by Senate Dec. 2010; in force Feb. 2011). On Apr. 15, Pres. Obama outlined plans for **NASA** to send manned missions to an asteroid by 2025 and to Mars by the mid-2030s; defended decision to terminate Bush administration program to return astronauts to the moon by 2020.

On Apr. 20, a gas explosion and fire engulfed *Deepwater Horizon* drilling platform off Louisiana, killing 11 people on board and damaging the ecology and state economy.

Arizona Gov. Jan Brewer (R), Apr. 23, signed controversial **immigration measure**. (Key provisions struck down by U.S. Supreme Court, June 2012.) New York City police May 1 dismantled **car bomb in Times Square**; suspect pleaded guilty to terrorism charges.

Pres. Obama May 10 nominated **Elena Kagan** to the U.S. Supreme Court to replace retiring Justice **John Paul Stevens**; confirmed by Senate, Aug. 5.

Obama June 23 named Gen. **David Petraeus** as commander of troops in Afghanistan, replacing Gen. Stanley McChrystal, forced to resign after publication of disparaging comments about Obama administration. Ten **Russian agents** were arrested June 27 on spy charges; later exchanged for four Americans held by Russia as alleged spies.

Goldman Sachs agreed July 15 to pay $550 mil to settle case brought by the SEC, alleging it had duped investors. Obama signed major **financial reform measure**, July 21.

More than 75,000 Afghanistan documents, many of them classified, were published July 25 on website run by **WikiLeaks** and in some news outlets. U.S. had filed charges, July 6, against Pfc. Bradley Manning, arrested May 26 in connection with earlier WikiLeaks releases.

Last U.S. combat unit left Iraq Aug. 19 and Pres. Obama, Aug. 31, declared **U.S. combat mission in Iraq ended**; however, 50,000 troops remained in noncombat units.

Congress passed measures to **aid small businesses** with loans and tax breaks; signed into law Sept. 27. **TARP program** reached two-year mark Oct. 3, the day its authority to make new commitments expired. Treasury Dept. estimated net cost at $51 bil or less, though this figure was disputed.

WikiLeaks released documents covering Iraq conflict Oct. 22. Authorities in the UK and UAE Oct. 29 confiscated packages with bombs concealed in printer cartridges, bound for Chicago area.

In Nov. 2 elections **Republicans gained control** of the U.S. House but fell short in the Senate. The Fed Nov. 3 announced plan to buy $600 bil worth of Treasury securities over eight months as means of stimulating the sluggish economy.

Bipartisan presidential commission chaired by former Clinton chief of staff **Erskine Bowles** and former Sen. **Alan Simpson** (R, WY), released report, Dec. 1, calling for deep cuts in government spending and entitlements and for lowering taxes while closing loopholes, so as to stabilize national debt. Obama, Dec. 17, signed $858-bil compromise measure that extended **Bush-era tax cuts** for two years, while also extending **unemployment** insurance benefits for 13 months and reducing Social Security payroll tax rate for one year. **"Don't ask, don't tell"** policy for gays in the military was repealed, Dec. 22.

2011 The 112th Congress convened Jan. 5; **John Boehner** (R, OH) elected House Speaker. Gunman in Tucson, AZ, Jan. 8, killed six people and injured 13 others, including Rep. **Gabrielle Giffords** (D, AZ); shooter Jared Loughner sentenced, Nov. 2012, to seven life terms plus 140 years.

Atty. Gen. Eric Holder disclosed Feb. 23 that the Obama administration would no longer defend in court the 1996 **Defense of Marriage Act**.

2011: The deadliest single tornado since 1947 devastates Joplin, MO, with 161 dead and more than 1,000 injured.

A measure to limit **collective bargaining** by most public sector employees, championed by Wisconsin Gov. **Scott Walker** (R), passed state legislature Mar. 9-10 despite mass demonstrations and a walkout by Senate Democrats.

With federal government shutdown looming, congressional leaders reached agreement Apr. 9 on omnibus appropriations bill. Pres. Obama outlined plan, Apr. 13, to cut $4 tril from projected deficits over 12 years by cutting spending and raising taxes on the wealthy. Two days later, House approved budget resolution based on plan by Rep. Paul Ryan (R, WI). **Ryan plan** would cut both spending and taxes, replace Medicaid with block grants to states, and change Medicare into subsidized private insurance for new recipients. House plan defeated in Senate, May 25.

Former baseball slugger **Barry Bonds** was convicted Apr. 13 of obstructing justice in 2003 for evasive answers to a grand jury investigating banned **performance-enhancing drugs**. Pres. Obama Apr. 27 denounced rumors by so-called birthers; released copies of **birth certificate**.

On May 2, in Abbottabad, Pakistan, a CIA-led squadron of U.S. Navy SEALs breached hideout of al-Qaeda leader **Osama bin Laden**, responsible for Sept. 11, 2001, attacks on U.S., and killed him; he was buried at sea the same day.

The single **deadliest U.S. tornado** in more than a half-century hit Joplin, MO, May 22, claiming about 160 lives. Congress cleared and Obama, May 26, signed measure extending key provisions of USA **Patriot Act**.

House rejected measure to raise federal **debt ceiling** from $14.3 tril to $16.7 tril without compensating deficit reductions May 31; talks between Obama and House Speaker Boehner on possible "grand bargain" collapsed July 22. Budget control act shaped by Vice Pres. Biden and Senate minority leader Mitch McConnell (R, KY) passed by bipartisan votes in Congress, Aug. 1-2. It called for rise in the debt ceiling and some $900 bil in spending cuts, with an additional $1.5 tril in cuts to be worked out by supercommittee. Standard & Poor's, Aug. 5, downgraded nation's **credit rating**.

U.S. stepped up **drone attacks** against jihadists in Yemen after Pres. Ali Abdullah Saleh and others were wounded June 3 in a rocket attack. Obama administration June 22 announced a drawing down of troops in **Afghanistan**, with all combat troops to be out by the end of 2014.

After jury failed to reach a verdict on most counts in Aug. 2010, former Gov. **Rod Blagojevich** (D, IL) was convicted in a retrial on 17 felony corruption charges June 27; sentenced Dec. 7 to 14 years in prison. **Bank of America**, June 29, agreed to pay $8.5 bil to cover investor losses on mortgage-backed securities issued by its Countrywide unit.

Gen. **David Petraeus** confirmed June 30 to replace **Leon Panetta** as CIA director; Panetta confirmed July 1 to replace retiring Defense Sec. **Robert Gates**.

NASA's **space shuttle** program ended with landing of the *Atlantis*, July 21, at Florida's Kennedy Space Center.

Taliban insurgents in **Afghanistan** shot down U.S. transport helicopter Aug. 6, killing 38 people, including 17 Navy SEAL commandos.

Atty. Gen. Eric Holder announced Aug. 30 the departure of two senior Justice Dept. officials who had overseen **Operation Fast and Furious**, a failed gun-trafficking sting operation. Obama, Sept. 8, proposed $447-bil economic **stimulus plan**, to be paid for by limiting tax breaks and raising taxes on high incomes.

A left-wing movement that began Sept. 17 as **Occupy Wall Street** in New York City expanded to demonstrations across the U.S. and overseas. **Anwar al-Awlaki**, a U.S. citizen and Muslim cleric linked to terrorist attacks in U.S., was killed Sept. 30 in U.S. drone attack in Yemen.

Formalities Dec. 12-15 marked the end of the U.S. military mission in **Iraq**. Last U.S. troop convoy crossed into Kuwait, Dec. 18. Since 2003 U.S.-led invasion, nearly 4,500 U.S. service members had been killed and 32,000 wounded.

Averting new government shutdown, Congress Dec. 16-17 passed $915-bil omnibus measure to fund agencies through 2012 fiscal year. Congress Dec. 23 also approved temporary extension of a **payroll tax** break and benefits for long-term unemployed.

2012 Pres. Obama Feb. 10 announced a compromise **health insurance** mandate that avoided requiring religiously affiliated employers to directly provide contraceptive coverage. Congress voted Feb. 17 to extend **payroll tax cut** through 2012, continue unemployment benefits, and halt cut in Medicare reimbursement rates.

In a settlement reached Mar. 2 between oil-and-gas giant BP and victims of 2010 *Deepwater Horizon* explosion in Gulf of Mexico, BP agreed to cover medical expenses and accept court administration of a $20-bil escrow fund. BP also pleaded guilty Nov. 15 to criminal charges related to the explosion and agreed to pay $4.5 bil in fines and penalties.

Former Gov. **Mitt Romney** (R, MA), winner of Jan. 10 New Hampshire primary, took six of 10 primary contests on "Super Tuesday" Mar. 6. By May 29, he had clinched nomination as GOP presidential candidate.

Obama became first sitting president to endorse same-sex marriage, in May 9 TV interview. Social networking giant **Facebook**'s initial public offering raised $16 bil May 18, but its stock lost value in following days.

Wisconsin Gov. **Scott Walker** (R) easily survived a June 5 recall election. Obama June 15 announced executive action ending deportation of qualified **undocumented immigrants** under age 30.

Jerry Sandusky, former assistant football coach at Penn State Univ., was convicted June 22 in sexual abuse of 10 boys. An investigation concluded that head coach Joe Paterno had covered up Sandusky's actions, and Penn State was penalized by NCAA, July 23.

Key provisions of **"Obamacare"** health insurance law were upheld June 28 by U.S. Supreme Court, including the individual mandate that would penalize those who declined to obtain health insurance.

The House, June 28, found Atty. Gen. **Eric Holder** in contempt of Congress for rebuffing a subpoena for Justice Dept. documents related to the failed Operation Fast and Furious. An inspector general's report, Sept. 19, cited serious flaws in that operation.

Twelve people were killed July 20, in a **movie-theater shooting** in Aurora, CO; James Holmes, arrested outside theater, was charged. A gunman opened fire Aug. 5 at a **Sikh temple** in Oak Creek, WI, leaving six dead; he killed himself after being wounded in shootout with police.

NASA rover *Curiosity* landed on Mars Aug. 6.

Romney and running mate Rep. **Paul Ryan** (WI) were nominated at Republican convention Aug. 27-30. Meeting Sept. 4-6, Democrats nominated the **Obama-Biden** ticket. Leftist magazine *Mother Jones* Sept. 17 posted a video, covertly recorded at a May 2012 fundraising dinner, in which Romney appeared to write off 47% of Americans as dependent on government handouts.

On the night of Sept. 11-12, U.S. facility in **Benghazi**, Libya, was attacked by terrorists, who killed ambassador **J. Christopher Stevens** and three other Americans; report released Dec. 18 blamed State Dept. for "grossly inadequate" security.

The **Fed** announced Sept. 13 it would begin buying mortgage-backed securities at a rate of $40 bil per month until job market significantly improved, unless inflation spiraled.

On Oct. 22, **Lance Armstrong**, accused in doping scandal, was banned from cycling and stripped of seven Tour de France wins.

Hurricane Sandy made landfall in the U.S. as a tropical storm Oct. 29, causing devastation in coastal areas of New Jersey and New York and leaving over 200 dead.

Obama was reelected Nov. 6, with 51% of the popular vote, earning 332 electoral votes. Democrats slightly increased their Senate majority, and Republicans held onto the House. Voters in Maine, Maryland, and Washington approved ballot measures to legalize **same-sex marriage**, becoming the first states to do so by popular vote. Colorado and Washington became the first states to legalize recreational use of **marijuana**.

Retired Army Gen. **David Petraeus** resigned as CIA director Nov. 9 after an FBI cybercrime investigation uncovered his involvement in an extramarital affair. Adam Lanza entered **Sandy Hook** Elementary School in Newtown, CT, Dec. 14, and shot to death 20 small children and six adults before killing himself.

With **"fiscal cliff"** of automatic budget cuts (**sequestration**) and expiring tax breaks looming as of Jan. 1, 2013, Vice Pres. Biden and Senate Minority Leader Mitch McConnell (R, KY) negotiated compromise, Dec. 30-31, to make **Bush-era tax cuts** permanent up to certain ceilings, while deferring possible sequestration to Mar. 1, 2013.

2013 The House (257-167) and Senate (89-8) passed compromise measure to temporarily avert **fiscal cliff** Jan. 1; signed by Pres. Obama the next day. **Obama** was sworn in for a **second term** in private ceremony Sun., Jan. 20, and public ceremony Jan. 21.

In hearings before Congress Jan. 23, outgoing Sec. of State **Hillary Clinton** defended the administration response to the Sept. 11 **Benghazi** terror attack, while accepting responsibility for security lapses. Defense Sec. **Leon Panetta**, Jan. 24, reversed Pentagon policy barring women from combat missions. Sen. **John Kerry** (D, MA) easily confirmed as secretary of state, Jan. 29. The Senate Feb. 26 voted 58-41 to confirm nomination of former Sen. **Chuck Hagel** (R, NE) to succeed Panetta as defense secretary. Because Congress failed to pass a negotiated budget deal, **sequestration** went into effect Mar. 1, triggering $1.2 tril in cuts to defense and domestic programs over 10 years.

Bomb blasts at the **Boston Marathon**, Apr. 15, killed three spectators and injured 264 people, many of whom lost limbs. Surveillance video was used to identify bombers as Dzhokhar and Tamerlan **Tsarnaev**, Chechen brothers who emigrated to U.S. in 2002. In shootout Apr. 18 with police, after they allegedly killed an MIT security officer and hijacked his car, Tamerlan, 26, was killed; Dzhokhar, 19, fled wounded and was captured Apr. 19.

Lois Lerner, director of **IRS** division handling tax-exempt organizations, apologized May 10 for the singling out of groups with "Tea Party" or "patriot" in their names but denied political motivation. Acting IRS commissioner Steven Miller resigned May 15. Lerner was suspended May 23 after invoking Fifth Amendment and refusing to answer questions by a House Oversight Committee; she later resigned.

Three missing women, two of them abducted as teenagers, were found May 6 when one escaped from the Cleveland, OH, home where they had been held for up to 11 years. Captor **Ariel Castro** pleaded guilty to charges that included kidnapping and rape; sentenced to life in prison, he was found dead Sept. 3 in an apparent suicide. Researchers in Oregon announced in a paper published May 13 that they had extracted **stem cells** from a human embryo produced via cloning for therapeutic purposes. **Boy Scouts** of America leadership voted May 23 to let openly **gay youths** join troops but left standing a ban on gay troop leaders

U.S. Justice Dept. notified the Associated Press May 10 that it had confiscated phone records of more than 20 reporters following AP's May 7 leak of a secret CIA operation that broke up a Yemen-based terrorist plot. The *Guardian* newspaper, June 5, disclosed details of a highly classified U.S. **Natl. Security Agency surveillance** program involving monitoring of customers' phone records and tracking of emails and Internet activities. **Edward Snowden**, a private contractor working for the CIA, claimed responsibility after having fled to a secret location in Hong Kong. U.S. officials claimed the controversial program, code-named PRISM, was legal under the Patriot Act. Snowden, charged June 14 with espionage, fled and was granted asylum in Moscow, Aug. 1. Obama outlined proposals to improve oversight of the NSA Aug. 9.

The U.S. Supreme Court, 5-4, June 25 struck down a provision of the 1965 **Voting Rights Act** that had required places with a history of discriminatory voting practices to obtain federal permission before changing voting procedures. In two 5-4 decisions, June 26, the court struck down provision in the 1996 Defense of Marriage Act (**DOMA**) that denied federal benefits to same-sex couples, and let stand a lower court

2013: Bombs explode near the Boston Marathon finish line, killing three and injuring more than 260.

ruling throwing out California's **Proposition 8**, which had barred same-sex marriage in the state.

A jury found **George Zimmerman** not guilty July 13 in the 2012 killing of **Trayvon Martin**, an unarmed black teenager, in a gated community in Sanford, FL. Zimmerman, a neighborhood watch volunteer, claimed to have shot Martin in self-defense as the two fought; protests broke out after the verdict. **Detroit** became the largest U.S. city to file for bankruptcy protection July 18.

Once-fugitive mobster **James "Whitey" Bulger** was found guilty of murder and other charges Aug. 12 in Boston and sentenced Nov. 14 to life in prison. A military judge sentenced Pfc. **Chelsea Manning** Aug. 21 to 30 years in prison. Manning (then known as Bradley) had been found guilty of numerous counts of **espionage** in leaking over 700,000 U.S. military and diplomatic documents to the WikiLeaks website, though not guilty of willfully aiding the enemy. Staff Sgt. Robert Bales, who pleaded guilty to having killed 16 Afghan civilians, was sentenced to life without parole Aug. 23. Maj. **Nidal Malik Hasan**, accused of killing 13 people at **Ft. Hood** (TX) Army base in 2009, was convicted by a military jury, Aug. 23, and sentenced to death Aug. 28. A man with symptoms of mental illness shot and killed 12 people at the **Navy Yard** in Washington, DC, Sept. 16; he was killed by responding police.

After wrangling in Congress failed to produce a budget agreement, the U.S. **government partially shut down** Oct. 1, leaving some 800,000 federal workers on furlough or working without pay. With the public widely opposed to the shutdown, and Democrats in control of Senate and White House, House Republicans could not get traction on a move to **defund Obamacare** as a condition for continued government funding or for raising the debt ceiling by an Oct. 17 deadline. On Oct. 16, the Senate (81-18) approved a compromise measure and the House went along (285-144). It funded the government through Jan. 15, 2014, and raised the debt limit until Feb. 7.

Federal and state health insurance exchanges opened Oct. 1, in a rollout of a signature Obamacare feature, but the federal website was plagued by serious design flaws and technical glitches that took weeks to resolve. Health and Human Services Sec. **Kathleen Sebelius** apologized for the unreadiness in congressional hearings Oct. 30.

In elections Nov. 5, **Terry McAuliffe** (D) won Virginia governorship, and Gov. **Chris Christie** (R) was reelected in New Jersey; **Bill de Blasio** (D) was elected mayor of New York City. JPMorgan Chase agreed, Nov. 19, to $13-bil settlement of charges of deceptive practices in sales of troubled mortgages. Voting 52-48, the Senate Nov. 21 approved a procedural change for most presidential nominations, allowing them to advance by a simple majority vote.

Two federal appeals courts issued conflicting rulings, Dec. 16 and 27, on constitutionality of **NSA's** collection of telephone metadata. White House panel, Dec. 18, issued sweeping recommendations aimed at limiting NSA surveillance powers and increasing oversight. **Dow Jones** closed 2013 up 26.5%, its biggest yearly gain since 1995.

Patrick Henry's Speech to the Virginia Convention

The following is an excerpt from Patrick Henry's speech to the Virginia Convention, which met at St. John's Church in Richmond, on Mar. 23, 1775, to react to British oppression.

Gentlemen may cry, peace, peace—but there is no peace. The war is actually begun! The next gale that sweeps from the north will bring to our ears the clash of resounding arms! Our brethren are already in the field! Why stand we here idle? What is it that gentlemen wish? What would they have? Is life so dear, or peace so sweet, as to be purchased at the price of chains and slavery? Forbid it, Almighty God! I know not what course others may take; but as for me, give me liberty, or give me death!

Adoption of the Declaration of Independence

On June 7, 1776, Richard Henry Lee, who had issued the first call for a congress of the colonies, introduced in the Continental Congress at Philadelphia a resolution declaring "that these United Colonies are, and of right ought to be, free and independent states, that they are absolved from all allegiance to the British Crown, and that all political connection between them and the state of Great Britain is, and ought to be, totally dissolved."

The resolution, seconded by John Adams on behalf of the Massachusetts delegation, came up again June 11 when a committee of five chaired by Thomas Jefferson (VA) was appointed to express the purpose of the resolution in a declaration of independence. The other four were John Adams, Benjamin Franklin (PA), Robert R. Livingston (NY), and Roger Sherman (CT).

Drafting the Declaration was assigned to Jefferson, who worked on a portable desk of his own construction in a room at Market and 7th St. The committee reported the result on June 28, 1776. The members of the Congress suggested a number of changes, which Jefferson called "deplorable." They did not approve Jefferson's arraignment of the British people and King George III for encouraging and fostering the slave trade, which Jefferson called "an execrable commerce." They eliminated 630 words and added 146, leaving 1,322 words in the final draft. In its final form, capitalization was erratic. Jefferson had written that men were endowed with "inalienable" rights; in the final copy it came out as "unalienable" and has been thus ever since.

The Lee-Adams resolution of independence was adopted by 12 yeas on July 2—the actual date of the act of independence. The Declaration, which explains the act, was adopted July 4.

After the Declaration was adopted, July 4, 1776, it was turned over to printer John Dunlap to be printed on broadsides. The original copy was lost and one of his broadsides was attached to a page in the journal of the Congress. It was read aloud July 8 in Philadelphia; Easton, PA; and Trenton, NJ. On July 9, it was read by order of Gen. George Washington to the troops assembled on the Common in New York City (now City Hall Park).

The Continental Congress of July 19, 1776, adopted the following resolution:

"Resolved, That the Declaration passed on the 4th, be fairly engrossed on parchment with the title and stile of 'The Unanimous Declaration of the thirteen United States of America' and that the same, when engrossed, be signed by every member of Congress." (Engrossing meant clearly writing out an official document.)

Not all delegates who signed the engrossed Declaration had been present on July 4. Among them were Robert Morris (PA), William Williams (CT), and Samuel Chase (MD), who signed on Aug. 2. Oliver Wolcott (CT), George Wythe (VA), Richard Henry Lee (VA), and Elbridge Gerry (MA) signed in Aug. and Sept.; Matthew Thornton (NH) joined the Congress Nov. 4 and signed later. Thomas McKean (DE) rejoined Washington's army before signing and said later that he signed in 1781.

Charles Carroll of Carrollton was appointed a delegate by Maryland on July 4, 1776, presented his credentials July 18, and signed the engrossed Declaration on Aug. 2. Born Sept. 19, 1737, he was 95 years old and the last surviving signer when he died Nov. 14, 1832.

Two Pennsylvania delegates who did not support the Declaration July 4, 1776, were replaced. The four New York delegates did not have authority from their state to vote on July 4. On July 9, the New York state convention authorized its delegates to approve the Declaration, and the Congress was so notified on July 15, 1776. The four signed the Declaration on Aug. 2.

Declaration of Independence

The Declaration of Independence was adopted by the Continental Congress in Philadelphia on July 4, 1776. John Hancock was president of the Congress, and Charles Thomson was secretary. A copy of the Declaration, engrossed (i.e., written in a clear hand) on parchment, was signed by members of Congress on and after Aug. 2, 1776. On Jan. 18, 1777, Congress ordered that "an authenticated copy, with the names of the members of Congress subscribing the same, be sent to each of the United States, and that they be desired to have the same put on record." Authenticated copies were printed in broadside form in Baltimore, where the Continental Congress was then in session. The following text is that of the original printed by John Dunlap in Philadelphia for the Continental Congress. The original is on display at the National Archives in Washington, DC.

In CONGRESS, July 4, 1776.
A DECLARATION
By the REPRESENTATIVES of the
UNITED STATES OF AMERICA,
In GENERAL CONGRESS assembled.

When in the Course of human Events, it becomes necessary for one People to dissolve the Political Bands which have connected them with another, and to assume among the Powers of the Earth, the separate and equal Station to which the Laws of Nature and of Nature's God entitle them, a decent Respect to the Opinions of Mankind requires that they should declare the causes which impel them to the Separation.

We hold these Truths to be self-evident, that all Men are created equal, that they are endowed by their Creator with certain unalienable Rights, that among these are Life, Liberty, and the Pursuit of Happiness—That to secure these Rights, Governments are instituted among Men, deriving their just Powers from the Consent of the Governed, that whenever any Form of Government becomes destructive of these Ends, it is the Right of the People to alter or to abolish it, and to institute new Government, laying its Foundation on such Principles, and organizing its Powers in such Form, as to them shall seem most likely to effect their Safety and Happiness. Prudence, indeed, will dictate that Governments long established should not be changed for light and transient Causes; and accordingly all Experience hath shewn, that Mankind are more disposed to suffer, while Evils are sufferable, than to right themselves by abolishing the Forms to which they are accustomed. But when a long Train of Abuses and Usurpations, pursuing invariably the same Object, evinces a Design to reduce them under absolute Despotism, it is their Right, it is their Duty, to throw off such Government, and to provide new Guards for their future Security. Such has been the patient Sufferance of these Colonies; and such is now the Necessity which constrains them to alter their former Systems of Government. The History of the present King of Great Britain is a History of repeated Injuries and Usurpations, all having in direct Object the Establishment of an absolute Tyranny over these States. To prove this, let Facts be submitted to a candid World.

He has refused his Assent to Laws, the most wholesome and necessary for the public Good.

He has forbidden his Governors to pass Laws of immediate and pressing Importance, unless suspended in their Operation till his Assent should be obtained; and when so suspended, he has utterly neglected to attend to them.

He has refused to pass other Laws for the Accommodation of large Districts of People, unless those People would relinquish the Right of Representation in the Legislature, a Right inestimable to them, and formidable to Tyrants only.

He has called together Legislative Bodies at Places unusual, uncomfortable, and distant from the Depository of their Public Records, for the sole Purpose of fatiguing them into Compliance with his Measures.

He has dissolved Representative Houses repeatedly, for opposing with manly Firmness his Invasions on the Rights of the People.

He has refused for a long Time, after such Dissolutions, to cause others to be elected; whereby the Legislative Powers, incapable of Annihilation, have returned to the People at large for their exercise; the State remaining in the mean time exposed to all the Dangers of Invasion from without, and Convulsions within.

He has endeavoured to prevent the Population of these States; for that Purpose obstructing the Laws for Naturalization of Foreigners; refusing to pass others to encourage their Migrations hither, and raising the Conditions of new Appropriations of Lands.

He has obstructed the Administration of Justice, by refusing his Assent to Laws for establishing Judiciary Powers.

He has made Judges dependent on his Will alone, for the Tenure of their Offices, and the Amount and payment of their Salaries.

He has erected a Multitude of new Offices, and sent hither Swarms of Officers to harrass our People, and eat out their Substance.

He has kept among us, in Times of Peace, Standing Armies, without the consent of our Legislatures.

He has affected to render the Military independent of, and superior to the Civil Power.

He has combined with others to subject us to a Jurisdiction foreign to our Constitution, and unacknowledged by our Laws; giving his Assent to their Acts of pretended Legislation:

For Quartering large bodies of armed troops among us:

For protecting them, by a mock Trial, from Punishment for any Murders which they should commit on the Inhabitants of these States:

For cutting off our Trade with all Parts of the World:

For imposing Taxes on us without our Consent:

For depriving us, in many Cases, of the Benefits of Trial by Jury:

For transporting us beyond Seas to be tried for pretended Offences:

For abolishing the free System of English Laws in a neighbouring Province, establishing therein an arbitrary Government, and enlarging its Boundaries, so as to render it at once an Example and fit Instrument for introducing the same absolute Rule into these Colonies:

For taking away our Charters, abolishing our most valuable Laws, and altering fundamentally the Forms of our Governments:

For suspending our own Legislatures, and declaring themselves invested with Power to legislate for us in all Cases whatsoever.

He has abdicated Government here, by declaring us out of his Protection and waging War against us.

He has plundered our Seas, ravaged our Coasts, burnt our towns, and destroyed the Lives of our People.

He is, at this Time, transporting large Armies of foreign Mercenaries to complete the works of Death, Desolation, and Tyranny, already begun with circumstances of Cruelty

and Perfidy, scarcely paralleled in the most barbarous Ages, and totally unworthy the Head of a civilized Nation.

He has constrained our fellow Citizens taken Captive on the high Seas to bear Arms against their Country, to become the Executioners of their Friends and Brethren, or to fall themselves by their Hands.

He has excited domestic Insurrections amongst us, and has endeavoured to bring on the Inhabitants of our Frontiers, the merciless Indian Savages, whose known Rule of Warfare, is an undistinguished Destruction, of all Ages, Sexes and Conditions.

In every stage of these Oppressions we have Petitioned for Redress in the most humble Terms: Our repeated Petitions have been answered only by repeated Injury. A Prince, whose Character is thus marked by every act which may define a Tyrant, is unfit to be the Ruler of a free People.

Nor have we been wanting in Attentions to our British Brethren. We have warned them from Time to Time of Attempts by their Legislature to extend an unwarrantable Jurisdiction over us. We have reminded them of the Circumstances of our Emigration and Settlement here. We have appealed to their native Justice and Magnanimity, and we have conjured them by the Ties of our common Kindred to disavow these Usurpations, which, would inevitably interrupt our Connections and Correspondence. They too have been deaf to the Voice of Justice and of Consanguinity. We must, therefore, acquiesce in the Necessity, which denounces our Separation, and hold them, as we hold the rest of Mankind, Enemies in War, in Peace, Friends.

We, therefore, the Representatives of the UNITED STATES OF AMERICA, in General Congress, Assembled, appealing to the Supreme Judge of the World for the Rectitude of our Intentions, do, in the Name, and by Authority of the good People of these Colonies, solemnly Publish and Declare, That these United Colonies are, and of Right ought to be, Free and Independent States; that they are absolved from all Allegiance to the British Crown, and that all political Connection between them and the State of Great Britain, is and ought to be totally dissolved; and that as Free and Independent States, they have full Power to levy War, conclude Peace, contract Alliances, establish Commerce, and to do all other Acts and Things which Independent States may of right do. And for the support of this declaration, with a firm Reliance on the Protection of Divine Providence, we mutually pledge to each other our lives, our Fortunes, and our sacred Honor.

JOHN HANCOCK, President.

Attest.

CHARLES THOMSON, Secretary.

Signers of the Declaration of Independence

Delegate (state)	Occupation	Birthplace	Born	Died
Adams, John (MA)	Lawyer	Braintree (Quincy), MA	Oct. 30, 1735	July 4, 1826
Adams, Samuel (MA)	Political leader	Boston, MA	Sept. 27, 1722	Oct. 2, 1803
Bartlett, Josiah (NH)	Physician, judge	Amesbury, MA	Nov. 21, 1729	May 19, 1795
Braxton, Carter (VA)	Farmer	Newington Plantation, VA	Sept. 10, 1736	Oct. 10, 1797
Carroll, Charles, of Carrollton (MD)	Merchant	Annapolis, MD	Sept. 19, 1737	Nov. 14, 1832
Chase, Samuel (MD)	Judge	Princess Anne, MD	Apr. 17, 1741	June 19, 1811
Clark, Abraham (NJ)	Surveyor	Elizabethtown, NJ	Feb. 15, 1726	Sept. 15, 1794
Clymer, George (PA)	Merchant	Philadelphia, PA	Mar. 16, 1739	Jan. 23, 1813
Ellery, William (RI)	Lawyer	Newport, RI	Dec. 22, 1727	Feb. 15, 1820
Floyd, William (NY)	Soldier	Brookhaven, NY	Dec. 17, 1734	Aug. 4, 1821
Franklin, Benjamin (PA)	Printer, publisher	Boston, MA	Jan. 17, 1706	Apr. 17, 1790
Gerry, Elbridge (MA)	Merchant	Marblehead, MA	July 17, 1744	Nov. 23, 1814
Gwinnett, Button (GA)	Merchant	Gloucester, England	c. 1735	May 19, 1777
Hall, Lyman (GA)	Physician	Wallingford, CT	Apr. 12, 1724	Oct. 19, 1790
Hancock, John (MA)	Merchant	Braintree (Quincy), MA	Jan. 12, 1737	Oct. 8, 1793
Harrison, Benjamin (VA)	Farmer	Charles City County, VA	Apr. 5, 1726	Apr. 24, 1791
Hart, John (NJ)	Farmer	Stonington, CT	c. 1711	May 11, 1779
Hewes, Joseph (NC)	Merchant	Kingston, NJ	Jan. 23, 1730	Nov. 10, 1779
Heyward, Thomas, Jr. (SC)	Lawyer, farmer	St. Luke's Parish, SC	July 28, 1746	Mar. 6, 1809
Hooper, William (NC)	Lawyer	Boston, MA	June 17, 1742	Oct. 14, 1790
Hopkins, Stephen (RI)	Judge, educator	Providence, RI	Mar. 7, 1707	July 13, 1785
Hopkinson, Francis (NJ)	Judge, author	Philadelphia, PA	Oct. 2, 1737	May 9, 1791
Huntington, Samuel (CT)	Judge	Windham, CT	July 3, 1731	Jan. 5, 1796
Jefferson, Thomas (VA)	Lawyer	Shadwell, VA	Apr. 13, 1743	July 4, 1826
Lee, Francis Lightfoot (VA)	Farmer	Westmoreland County, VA	Oct. 14, 1734	Jan. 11, 1797
Lee, Richard Henry (VA)	Farmer	Westmoreland County, VA	Jan. 20, 1732	June 19, 1794
Lewis, Francis (NY)	Merchant	Llandaff, Wales	Mar. 21, 1713	Dec. 31, 1802
Livingston, Philip (NY)	Merchant	Albany, NY	Jan. 15, 1716	June 12, 1778
Lynch, Thomas, Jr. (SC)	Farmer	Winyah, SC	Aug. 5, 1749	(at sea) 1779
McKean, Thomas (DE)	Lawyer	New London, PA	Mar. 19, 1734	June 24, 1817
Middleton, Arthur (SC)	Farmer	Charleston, SC	June 26, 1742	Jan. 1, 1787
Morris, Lewis (NY)	Farmer	Morrisania (Bronx County), NY	Apr. 8, 1726	Jan. 22, 1798
Morris, Robert (PA)	Merchant	Liverpool, England	Jan. 31, 1734	May 8, 1806
Morton, John (PA)	Judge	Ridley, PA	c. 1724	Apr. 1777
Nelson, Thomas, Jr. (VA)	Farmer	Yorktown, VA	Dec. 26, 1738	Jan. 4, 1789
Paca, William (MD)	Judge	Abingdon, MD	Oct. 31, 1740	Oct. 23, 1799
Paine, Robert Treat (MA)	Judge	Boston, MA	Mar. 11, 1731	May 12, 1814
Penn, John (NC)	Lawyer	Caroline County, VA	May 17, 1741	Sept. 14, 1788
Read, George (DE)	Judge	Cecil County, MD	Sept. 18, 1733	Sept. 21, 1798
Rodney, Caesar (DE)	Judge	Dover, DE	Oct. 7, 1728	June 29, 1784
Ross, George (PA)	Judge	New Castle, DE	May 10, 1730	July 14, 1779
Rush, Benjamin (PA)	Physician	Byberry (Philadelphia), PA	Jan. 4, 1746	Apr. 19, 1813
Rutledge, Edward (SC)	Lawyer	Charleston, SC	Nov. 23, 1749	Jan. 23, 1800
Sherman, Roger (CT)	Lawyer	Newton, MA	Apr. 19, 1721	July 23, 1793
Smith, James (PA)	Lawyer	Northern Ireland	c. 1719	July 11, 1806
Stockton, Richard (NJ)	Lawyer	Princeton, NJ	Oct. 1, 1730	Feb. 28, 1781
Stone, Thomas (MD)	Lawyer	Charles County, MD	c. 1743	Oct. 5, 1787
Taylor, George (PA)	Ironmaster	Ireland	c. 1716	Feb. 23, 1781
Thornton, Matthew (NH)	Physician	Ireland	c. 1714	June 24, 1803
Walton, George (GA)	Judge	Cumberland County, VA	c. 1741	Feb. 2, 1804
Whipple, William (NH)	Merchant, judge	Kittery, ME	Jan. 14, 1730	Nov. 28, 1785
Williams, William (CT)	Merchant	Lebanon, CT	Apr. 8, 1731	Aug. 2, 1811
Wilson, James (PA)	Judge	Carskerdo, Scotland	Sept. 14, 1742	Aug. 21, 1798
Witherspoon, John (NJ)	Clergyman, educator	Gifford, Scotland	Feb. 5, 1723	Nov. 15, 1794
Wolcott, Oliver (CT)	Judge	Windsor, CT	Nov. 20, 1726	Dec. 1, 1797
Wythe, George (VA)	Lawyer	Elizabeth City County, VA	c. 1726	June 8, 1806

Origin of the Constitution

The War of Independence was conducted by delegates from the original 13 states, who composed the Congress of the United States of America, known as the Continental Congress. In 1777 the Congress submitted to the legislatures of the states the Articles of Confederation and Perpetual Union, which were ratified by New Hampshire, Massachusetts, Rhode Island, Connecticut, New York, New Jersey, Pennsylvania, Delaware, Virginia, North Carolina, South Carolina, Georgia, and finally, in 1781, Maryland.

The first article read: "The stile of this confederacy shall be the United States of America." This did not signify a sovereign nation, because the states delegated only those powers they could not handle individually, such as to wage war, make treaties, and contract debts for general expenses (e.g., paying the army). Taxes for payment of such debts were levied by the individual states. The president signed himself "President of the United States in Congress assembled," but here the United States were considered in the plural, a cooperating group.

When the war was over, it became evident that a stronger federal union was needed. The Congress left the initiative to the legislatures. Virginia in Jan. 1786 appointed commissioners to meet with representatives of other states; delegates from Virginia, Delaware, New York, New Jersey, and Pennsylvania met at Annapolis. Alexander Hamilton prepared their call asking delegates from all states to meet in Philadelphia in May 1787 "to render the Constitution of the federal government adequate to the exigencies of the union." Congress endorsed the plan on Feb. 21, 1787. Delegates were appointed by all states except Rhode Island.

The convention was called for May 14, 1787, but a quorum was not present until May 25. George Washington was chosen president (presiding officer). The states certified 65 delegates, but 10 did not attend. The work was done by 55, not all of whom were present at all sessions. Of the 55 attending delegates, 39 signed Sept. 17, 1787, some with reservations, and 16 failed to sign. Some historians have said 74 delegates (nine more than the 65 actually certified) were named, and 19 failed to attend. These additional persons refused the appointment, were never delegates, and were never counted as absentees. Washington sent the Constitution to Congress, and that body, Sept. 28, 1787, ordered it sent to the legislatures, "in order to be submitted to a convention of delegates chosen in each state by the people thereof."

The Constitution was ratified by votes of state conventions as follows: Delaware, Dec. 7, 1787, unanimous; Pennsylvania, Dec. 12, 1787, 46 to 23; New Jersey, Dec. 18, 1787, unanimous; Georgia, Jan. 2, 1788, unanimous; Connecticut, Jan. 9, 1788, 128 to 40; Massachusetts, Feb. 6, 1788, 187 to 168; Maryland, Apr. 28, 1788, 63 to 11; South Carolina, May 23, 1788, 149 to 73; New Hampshire, June 21, 1788, 57 to 46; Virginia, June 25, 1788, 89 to 79; New York, July 26, 1788, 30 to 27. Nine states were needed to establish the operation of the Constitution "between the states so ratifying the same," and New Hampshire was the ninth state. The government did not declare the Constitution in effect until the first Wednesday in Mar. 1789, which was Mar. 4. After that, North Carolina ratified it on Nov. 21, 1789, 194 to 77; and Rhode Island, May 29, 1790, 34 to 32. Vermont in convention ratified it on Jan. 10, 1791, and by act of Congress approved on Feb. 18, 1791, was admitted into the Union as the 14th state, Mar. 4, 1791.

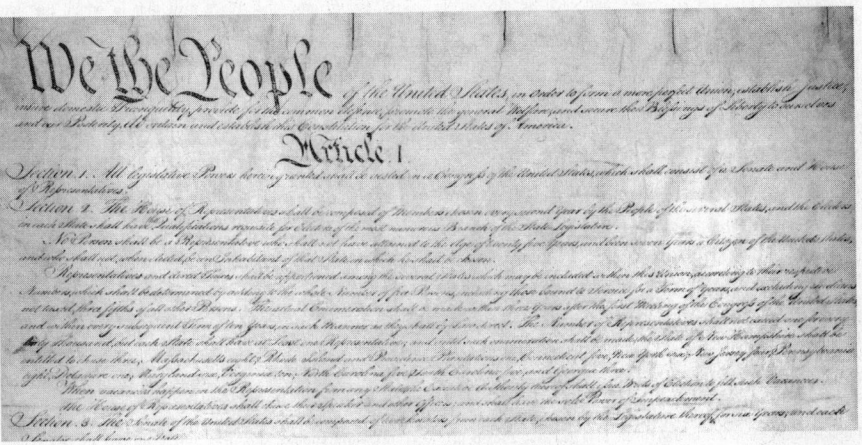

Constitution of the United States

The text of the Constitution given here (except for Amendment XXVII) is from the pocket-size edition of the Constitution published by the U.S. Government Printing Office as a result of a congressional resolution to print the Constitution in its original form as amended through July 5, 1971. *Text in brackets* indicates that an item has been superseded or amended, or provides background information. **Boldface text** preceding an article, section, or amendment is a brief summary, added by *The World Almanac*.

The Original Seven Articles

PREAMBLE

We, the People of the United States, in Order to form a more perfect Union, establish Justice, insure domestic Tranquility, provide for the common defence, promote the general Welfare, and secure the Blessings of Liberty to ourselves and our Posterity, do ordain and establish this Constitution for the United States of America.

ARTICLE I.

Section 1—Legislative powers; in whom vested.

All legislative Powers herein granted shall be vested in a Congress of the United States, which shall consist of a Senate and House of Representatives.

Section 2—House of Representatives, how and by whom chosen. Qualifications of a Representative. Representatives and direct taxes, how apportioned. Enumeration. Vacancies to be filled. Power of choosing officers, and of impeachment.

The House of Representatives shall be composed of Members chosen every second Year by the People of the several States, and the Electors in each State shall have the Qualifications requisite for Electors of the most numerous Branch of the State Legislature.

No Person shall be a Representative who shall not have attained to the Age of twenty five Years, and been seven Years a Citizen of the United States, and who shall not, when elected, be an Inhabitant of that State in which he shall be chosen.

[*Representatives and direct taxes shall be apportioned among the several States which may be included within this Union, according to their respective Numbers, which shall be determined by adding to the whole Number of free Persons, including those bound to Service for a Term of Years, and excluding Indians not taxed, three-fifths of all other persons.*] [*The previous sentence was superseded by Amendment XIV, section 2.*] The actual Enumeration shall be made within three Years after the first Meeting of the Congress of the United States, and within every subsequent Term of ten Years, in such Manner as they shall by Law direct. The Number of Representatives shall not exceed one for every thirty Thousand, but each State shall have at Least one Representative; and until such enumeration shall be made, the State of New Hampshire shall be entitled to chuse three, Massachusetts eight, Rhode-Island and Providence Plantations one, Connecticut five, New-York six, New Jersey four, Pennsylvania eight, Delaware one, Maryland six, Virginia ten, North Carolina five, South Carolina five, and Georgia three.

When vacancies happen in the Representation from any State, the Executive Authority thereof shall issue Writs of Election to fill such Vacancies.

The House of Representatives shall chuse their Speaker and other Officers; and shall have the sole Power of Impeachment.

Section 3—Senators, how and by whom chosen. How classified. Qualifications of a Senator. President of the Senate, his right to vote. President pro tem., and other officers of the Senate, how chosen. Power to try impeachments. When President is tried, Chief Justice to preside. Sentence.

The Senate of the United States shall be composed of two Senators from each State, *[chosen by the Legislature thereof] [The preceding five words were superseded by Amendment XVII.]* for six Years; and each Senator shall have one Vote.

Immediately after they shall be assembled in Consequence of the first Election, they shall be divided as equally as may be into three Classes. The Seats of the Senators of the first Class shall be vacated at the Expiration of the second Year, of the second Class at the Expiration of the fourth Year, and of the third Class at the Expiration of the Sixth year, so that one-third may be chosen every second Year; *[and if Vacancies happen by Resignation, or otherwise, during the Recess of the Legislature of any State, the Executive thereof may make temporary Appointments until the next Meeting of the Legislature, which shall then fill such Vacancies.] [The words in brackets were superseded by Amendment XVII.]*

No Person shall be a Senator who shall not have attained to the Age of thirty Years, and been nine Years a Citizen of the United States, and who shall not, when elected, be an Inhabitant of that State for which he shall be chosen.

The Vice President of the United States shall be President of the Senate, but shall have no Vote, unless they be equally divided.

The Senate shall chuse their other Officers, and also a President pro tempore, in the absence of the Vice President, or when he shall exercise the Office of President of the United States.

The Senate shall have the sole Power to try all Impeachments. When sitting for that Purpose, they shall be on Oath or Affirmation. When the President of the United States is tried, the Chief Justice shall preside: And no Person shall be convicted without the Concurrence of two thirds of the Members present.

Judgment in Cases of Impeachment shall not extend further than to removal from Office, and disqualification to hold and enjoy any Office of honor, Trust or Profit under the United States: but the Party convicted shall nevertheless be liable and subject to Indictment, Trial, Judgment and Punishment, according to Law.

Section 4—Times, etc., of holding elections, how prescribed. One session each year.

The Times, Places and Manner of holding Elections for Senators and Representatives, shall be prescribed in each State by the Legislature thereof; but the Congress may at any time by Law make or alter such Regulations, except as to the Places of Chusing Senators.

The Congress shall assemble at least once in every Year, and such Meeting shall be *[on the first Monday in December,] [The words in brackets were superseded by Amendment XX, section 2.]* unless they shall by Law appoint a different Day.

Section 5—Membership, quorum, adjournments, rules. Power to punish or expel. Journal. Time of adjournments, how limited, etc.

Each House shall be the Judge of the Elections, Returns and Qualifications of its own Members, and a Majority of each shall constitute a Quorum to do Business; but a smaller number may adjourn from day to day, and may be authorized to compel the Attendance of absent Members, in such manner, and under such Penalties as each House may provide.

Each House may determine the Rules of its Proceedings, punish its members for disorderly Behavior, and, with the Concurrence of two thirds, expel a Member.

Each House shall keep a Journal of its Proceedings, and from time to time publish the same, excepting such Parts as may in their Judgment require Secrecy; and the Yeas and Nays of the Members of either House on any question shall, at the Desire of one fifth of those Present, be entered on the Journal.

Neither House, during the Session of Congress, shall, without the Consent of the other, adjourn for more than three days, nor to any other Place than that in which the two Houses shall be sitting.

Section 6—Compensation, privileges, disqualifications in certain cases.

The Senators and Representatives shall receive a Compensation for their Services, to be ascertained by Law, and paid out of the Treasury of the United States. They shall in all Cases, except Treason, Felony and Breach of the Peace, be privileged from Arrest during their Attendance at the Session of their respective Houses, and in going to and returning from the same; and for any Speech or Debate in either House, they shall not be questioned in any other Place.

No Senator or Representative shall, during the Time for which he was elected, be appointed to any civil Office under the Authority of the United States, which shall have been created, or the Emoluments whereof shall have been encreased during such time; and no Person holding any Office under the United States, shall be a Member of either House during his Continuance in Office.

Section 7—House to originate all revenue bills. Veto. Bill may be passed by two-thirds of each House, notwithstanding, etc. Bill, not returned in ten days, to become a law. Provisions as to orders, concurrent resolutions, etc.

All bills for raising Revenue shall originate in the House of Representatives; but the Senate may propose or concur with Amendments as on other Bills.

Every Bill which shall have passed the House of Representatives and the Senate, shall, before it become a Law, be presented to the President of the United States; If he approve he shall sign it, but if not he shall return it, with his Objections to that House in which it shall have originated, who shall enter the Objections at large on their Journal, and proceed to reconsider it. If after such Reconsideration two thirds of that House shall agree to pass the Bill, it shall be sent, together with the Objections, to the other House, by which it shall likewise be reconsidered, and if approved by two thirds of that House, it shall become a Law. But in all such Cases the Votes of both Houses shall be determined by Yeas and Nays, and the Names of the Persons voting for and against the Bill shall be entered on the Journal of each House respectively. If any Bill shall not be returned by the President within ten Days (Sundays excepted) after it shall have been presented to him, the Same shall be a Law, in like Manner as if he had signed it, unless the Congress by their Adjournment prevent its Return, in which Case it shall not be a Law.

Every order, Resolution, or Vote to which the Concurrence of the Senate and House of Representatives may be necessary (except on a question of Adjournment) shall be presented to the President of the United States; and before the Same shall take Effect, shall be approved by him, or being disapproved by him, shall be repassed by two thirds of the Senate and House of Representatives, according to the Rules and Limitations prescribed in the Case of a Bill.

Section 8—Powers of Congress.

The Congress shall have Power To lay and collect Taxes, Duties, Imposts and Excises, to pay the Debts and provide for the common Defence and general Welfare of the United States; but all Duties, Imposts and Excises shall be uniform throughout the United States;

To borrow money on the credit of the United States;

To regulate Commerce with foreign Nations, and among the several States, and with the Indian Tribes;

To establish an uniform Rule of Naturalization, and uniform Laws on the subject of Bankruptcies throughout the United States;

To coin Money, regulate the Value thereof, and of foreign Coin, and fix the Standard of Weights and Measures;

To provide for the Punishment of counterfeiting the Securities and current Coin of the United States;

To establish Post Offices and post Roads;

To promote the Progress of Science and useful Arts, by securing for limited Times to Authors and Inventors the exclusive Right to their respective Writings and Discoveries;

To constitute Tribunals inferior to the supreme Court;

To define and punish Piracies and Felonies committed on the high Seas, and Offenses against the Law of Nations;

To declare War, grant Letters of Marque and Reprisal, and make Rules concerning Captures on Land and Water;

To raise and support Armies, but no Appropriation of Money to that Use shall be for a longer Term than two Years;

To provide and maintain a Navy;

To make Rules for the Government and Regulation of the land and naval Forces;

To provide for calling forth the Militia to execute the Laws of the Union, suppress Insurrections and repel Invasions;

To provide for organizing, arming, and disciplining the Militia, and for governing such Part of them as may be employed in the Service of the United States, reserving to the States respectively, the Appointment of the Officers, and the Authority of training the Militia according to the discipline prescribed by Congress;

To exercise exclusive Legislation in all Cases whatsoever, over such District (not exceeding ten Miles square) as may, by Cession of particular States, and the acceptance of Congress, become the Seat of the Government of the United States, and to exercise like Authority over all Places purchased by the Consent of the Legislature of the State in which the Same shall be, for the Erection of Forts, Magazines, Arsenals, dock-Yards, and other needful Buildings;—And

To make all Laws which shall be necessary and proper for carrying into Execution the foregoing Powers, and all other Powers vested by this Constitution in the Government of the United States, or in any Department or Officer thereof.

Section 9—Provision as to migration or importation of certain persons. Habeas corpus, bills of attainder, etc. Taxes, how apportioned. No export duty. No commercial preference. Money, how drawn from Treasury, etc. No titular nobility. Officers not to receive presents, etc.

The Migration or Importation of such Persons as any of the States now existing shall think proper to admit, shall not be prohibited by the Congress prior to the Year one thousand eight hundred and eight, but a tax or duty may be imposed on such Importation, not exceeding ten dollars for each Person.

The privilege of the Writ of Habeas Corpus shall not be suspended, unless when in Cases of Rebellion or Invasion the public Safety may require it.

No Bill of Attainder or ex post facto Law shall be passed.

[No capitation, or other direct, Tax shall be laid, unless in Proportion to the Census or Enumeration herein before directed to be taken.] [Words in brackets modified by Amendment XVI.]

No Tax or Duty shall be laid on Articles exported from any State.

No Preference shall be given by any Regulation of Commerce or Revenue to the Ports of one State over those of another: nor shall Vessels bound to, or from, one State, be obliged to enter, clear, or pay Duties in another.

No Money shall be drawn from the Treasury, but in Consequence of Appropriations made by Law; and a regular Statement and Account of the Receipts and Expenditures of all public Money shall be published from time to time.

No Title of Nobility shall be granted by the United States: and no Person holding any Office of Profit or Trust under them, shall, without the Consent of the Congress, accept of any present, Emolument, Office, or Title, of any kind whatever, from any King, Prince, or foreign State.

Section 10—States prohibited from the exercise of certain powers.

No State shall enter into any Treaty, Alliance, or Confederation; grant Letters of Marque and Reprisal; coin Money; emit Bills of Credit; make any Thing but gold and silver Coin a Tender in Payment of Debts; pass any Bill of Attainder, ex post facto Law, or Law impairing the Obligation of Contracts, or grant any Title of Nobility.

No State shall, without the Consent of the Congress, lay any Imposts or Duties on Imports or Exports, except what may be absolutely necessary for executing its inspection Laws: and the net Produce of all Duties and Imposts, laid by any State on Imports or Exports, shall be for the Use of the Treasury of the United States; and all such Laws shall be subject to the Revision and Control of the Congress.

No State shall, without the Consent of Congress, lay any duty of Tonnage, keep Troops, or Ships of War in time of Peace, enter into any Agreement or Compact with another State, or with a foreign Power, or engage in War, unless actually invaded, or in such imminent Danger as will not admit of delay.

ARTICLE II.

Section 1—President: his term of office. Electors of President; number and how appointed. Electors to vote on same day. Qualification of President. On whom his duties devolve in case of his removal, death, etc. President's compensation. His oath of office.

The executive Power shall be vested in a President of the United States of America. He shall hold his Office during the Term of four Years, and, together with the Vice President, chosen for the same Term, be elected, as follows.

Each State shall appoint, in such Manner as the Legislature thereof may direct, a Number of Electors, equal to the whole Number of Senators and Representatives to which the State may be entitled in the Congress: but no Senator or Representative, or Person holding an Office of Trust or Profit under the United States, shall be appointed an Elector.

[The Electors shall meet in their respective States, and vote by Ballot for two persons, of whom at least one shall not be an Inhabitant of the same State with themselves. And they shall make a List of all the Persons voted for, and of the Number of Votes for each; which List they shall sign and certify, and transmit sealed to the Seat of the Government of the United States, directed to the President of the Senate. The President of the Senate shall, in the Presence of the Senate and House of Representatives, open all the Certificates, and the Votes shall then be counted. The Person having the greatest Number of Votes shall be the President, if such Number be a Majority of the whole Number of Electors appointed; and if there be more than one who have such Majority, and have an equal Number of Votes, then the House of Representatives shall immediately chuse by Ballot one of them for President; and if no Person have a Majority, then from the five highest on the List the said House shall in like Manner chuse the President. But in chusing the President,

the Votes shall be taken by States, the Representation from each State having one Vote; a quorum for this Purpose shall consist of a Member or Members from two thirds of the States, and a Majority of all the States shall be necessary to a Choice. In every Case, after the Choice of the President, the Person having the greatest Number of Votes of the Electors shall be the Vice President. But if there should remain two or more who have equal Votes, the Senate shall chuse from them by Ballot the Vice-President.] [This clause was superseded by Amendment XII.]

The Congress may determine the Time of chusing the Electors, and the Day on which they shall give their Votes; which Day shall be the same throughout the United States.

No person except a natural born Citizen, or a Citizen of the United States, at the time of the Adoption of this Constitution, shall be eligible to the Office of President; neither shall any Person be eligible to that Office who shall not have attained to the Age of thirty-five Years, and been fourteen Years a Resident within the United States. [For qualification of the Vice President, see Amendment XII.]

[In Case of the Removal of the President from Office, or of his Death, Resignation, or Inability to discharge the Powers and Duties of the said Office, the same shall devolve on the Vice President, and the Congress may by Law, provide for the Case of Removal, Death, Resignation or Inability, both of the President and Vice President, declaring what Officer shall then act as President, and such Officer shall act accordingly, until the Disability be removed, or a President shall be elected.] [This clause was superseded by Amendment XXV.]

The President shall, at stated Times, receive for his Services, a Compensation, which shall neither be encreased nor diminished during the Period for which he shall have been elected, and he shall not receive within that Period any other Emolument from the United States, or any of them.

Before he enter on the Execution of his Office, he shall take the following Oath or Affirmation:–"I do solemnly swear (or affirm) that I will faithfully execute the Office of President of the United States, and will to the best of my Ability, preserve, protect and defend the Constitution of the United States."

Section 2—President to be Commander-in-Chief. He may require opinions of cabinet officers, etc., may pardon. Treaty-making power. Nomination of certain officers. When President may fill vacancies.

The President shall be Commander in Chief of the Army and Navy of the United States, and of the Militia of the several States, when called into the actual Service of the United States; he may require the Opinion in writing, of the principal Officer in each of the executive Departments, upon any subject relating to the Duties of their respective Offices, and he shall have Power to Grant Reprieves and Pardons for Offenses against the United States, except in Cases of Impeachment.

He shall have Power, by and with the Advice and Consent of the Senate, to make Treaties, provided two-thirds of the Senators present concur; and he shall nominate, and by and with the Advice and Consent of the Senate, shall appoint Ambassadors, other public Ministers and Consuls, Judges of the supreme Court, and all other Officers of the United States, whose Appointments are not herein otherwise provided for, and which shall be established by Law: but the Congress may by Law vest the Appointment of such inferior Officers, as they think proper, in the President alone, in the Courts of Law, or in the Heads of Departments.

The President shall have Power to fill up all Vacancies that may happen during the Recess of the Senate, by granting Commissions which shall expire at the End of their next Session.

Section 3—President shall communicate to Congress. He may convene and adjourn Congress, in case of disagreement, etc. Shall receive ambassadors, execute laws, and commission officers.

He shall from time to time give to the Congress Information of the State of the Union, and recommend to their Consideration such Measures as he shall judge necessary and expedient; he may, on extraordinary Occasions, convene both Houses, or either of them, and in Case of Disagreement between them, with Respect to the Time of Adjournment, he may adjourn them to such Time as he shall think proper; he shall receive Ambassadors and other public Ministers; he shall take Care that the Laws be faithfully executed, and shall Commission all the Officers of the United States.

Section 4—All civil offices forfeited for certain crimes.

The President, Vice President and all civil Officers of the United States, shall be removed from Office on Impeachment for, and Conviction of, Treason, Bribery, or other high Crimes and Misdemeanors.

ARTICLE III.

Section 1—Judicial powers, tenure. Compensation.

The judicial Power of the United States, shall be vested in one supreme Court, and in such inferior Courts as the Congress may from time to time ordain and establish. The Judges, both of the supreme and inferior Courts, shall hold their Offices during good Behaviour, and shall, at stated Times, receive for their Services, a Compensation, which shall not be diminished during their Continuance in Office.

Section 2—Judicial power; to what cases it extends. Original jurisdiction of Supreme Court; appellate jurisdiction. Trial by jury, etc. Trial, where.

The judicial Power shall extend to all Cases, in Law and Equity, arising under this Constitution, the Laws of the United States, and Treaties made, or which shall be made, under their Authority;–to all Cases affecting Ambassadors, other public Ministers and Consuls;–to all Cases of admiralty and maritime Jurisdiction;–to Controversies to which the United States shall be a Party;–to Controversies between two or more States; [–between a State and Citizens of another State;–] between Citizens of different States; –between Citizens of the same State claiming Lands under Grants of different States, [and between a State, or the Citizens thereof, and foreign States, Citizens or Subjects.] [This section is modified by Amendment XI.]

In all Cases affecting Ambassadors, other public Ministers and Consuls, and those in which a State shall be Party, the supreme Court shall have original Jurisdiction. In all the other Cases before mentioned, the supreme Court shall have appellate Jurisdiction, both as to Law and Fact, with such Exceptions, and under such Regulations as the Congress shall make.

The trial of all Crimes, except in Cases of Impeachment, shall be by Jury; and such Trial shall be held in the State where the said Crimes shall have been committed; but when not committed within any State, the Trial shall be at such Place or Places as the Congress may by Law have directed.

Section 3—Treason Defined. Proof of. Punishment of.

Treason against the United States, shall consist only in levying War against them, or in adhering to their Enemies, giving them Aid and Comfort. No Person shall be convicted of Treason unless on the Testimony of two Witnesses to the same overt Act, or on Confession in open Court.

The Congress shall have Power to declare the Punishment of Treason, but no Attainder of Treason shall work Corruption of Blood, or Forfeiture except during the Life of the Person attainted.

ARTICLE IV.

Section 1—Each State to give credit to the public acts, etc., of every other State.

Full Faith and Credit shall be given in each State to the public Acts, Records, and judicial Proceedings of every other State. And the Congress may by general Laws prescribe the Manner in which such Acts, Records and Proceedings shall be proved, and the Effect thereof.

Section 2—Privileges of citizens of each State. Fugitives from justice to be delivered up. Persons held to service having escaped, to be delivered up.

The Citizens of each State shall be entitled to all Privileges and Immunities of Citizens in the several States.

A Person charged in any State with Treason, Felony, or other Crime, who shall flee from Justice, and be found in another State, shall on demand of the executive Authority of the State from which he fled, be delivered up, to be removed to the State having Jurisdiction of the Crime.

[No Person held to Service or Labour in one State, under the Laws thereof, escaping into another, shall, in Consequence of any Law or Regulation therein, be discharged from such Service or Labour, but shall be delivered up on Claim of the Party to whom such Service or Labour may be due.] [This clause was superseded by Amendment XIII.]

Section 3—Admission of new States. Power of Congress over territory and other property.

New States may be admitted by the Congress into this Union; but no new State shall be formed or erected within the Jurisdiction of any other State; nor any State be formed by the Junction of two or more States, or parts of States, without the Consent of the Legislatures of the States concerned as well as of the Congress.

The Congress shall have Power to dispose of and make all needful Rules and Regulations respecting the Territory or other Property belonging to the United States; and nothing in this Constitution shall be so construed as to Prejudice any Claims of the United States, or of any particular State.

Section 4—Republican form of government guaranteed. Each State to be protected.

The United States shall guarantee to every State in this Union a Republican Form of Government, and shall protect each of them against Invasion; and on Application of the Legislature, or of the Executive (when the Legislature cannot be convened) against domestic Violence.

ARTICLE V.

Constitution: how amended; proviso.

The Congress, whenever two-thirds of both Houses shall deem it necessary, shall propose Amendments to this Constitution, or, on the Application of the Legislatures of two-thirds of the several States, shall call a Convention for proposing Amendments, which, in either Case, shall be valid to all Intents and Purposes, as part of this Constitution, when ratified by the Legislatures of three-fourths of the several States, or by Conventions in three-fourths thereof, as the one or the other Mode of Ratification may be proposed by the Congress: Provided that no Amendment which may be made prior to the Year One thousand eight hundred and eight shall in any Manner affect the first and fourth Clauses in the Ninth Section of the first Article; and that no State, without its Consent, shall be deprived of its equal Suffrage in the Senate.

ARTICLE VI.

Certain debts, etc., declared valid. Supremacy of Constitution, treaties, and laws of the United States. Oath to support Constitution, by whom taken. No religious test.

All Debts contracted and Engagements entered into, before the Adoption of this Constitution, shall be as valid against the United States under this Constitution, as under the Confederation.

This Constitution, and the Laws of the United States which shall be made in Pursuance thereof; and all Treaties made, or which shall be made, under the Authority of the United States, shall be the supreme Law of the Land; and the Judges in every State shall be bound thereby, any Thing in the Constitution or Laws of any State to the Contrary notwithstanding.

The Senators and Representatives before mentioned, and the Members of the several State Legislatures, and all executive and judicial Officers, both of the United States and of the several States, shall be bound by Oath or Affirmation, to support this Constitution; but no religious Test shall ever be required as a Qualification to any Office or public Trust under the United States.

ARTICLE VII.

What ratification shall establish Constitution.

The Ratification of the Conventions of nine States shall be sufficient for the Establishment of this Constitution between the States so ratifying the Same.

Done in Convention by the Unanimous Consent of the States present the Seventeenth Day of September in the Year of our Lord one thousand seven hundred and Eighty seven and of the Independence of the United States of America the Twelfth.

In Witness whereof We have hereunto subscribed our Names.

G°. Washington, Presidt and deputy from Virginia

New Hampshire—John Langdon, Nicholas Gilman

Massachusetts—Nathaniel Gorham, Rufus King

Connecticut—Wm. Saml. Johnson, Roger Sherman

New York—Alexander Hamilton

New Jersey—Wil: Livingston, David Brearley, Wm. Paterson, Jona: Dayton

Pennsylvania—B Franklin, Thomas Mifflin, Robt. Morris, Geo. Clymer, Thos. FitzSimons, Jared Ingersoll, James Wilson, Gouv Morris

Delaware—Geo: Read, Gunning Bedford jun, John Dickinson, Richard Bassett, Jaco: Broom

Maryland—James McHenry, Dan of St Thos. Jenifer, Danl Carroll

Virginia—John Blair, James Madison Jr.

North Carolina—Wm. Blount, Rich'd Dobbs Spaight, Hu Williamson

South Carolina—J. Rutledge, Charles Cotesworth Pinckney, Charles Pinckney, Pierce Butler

Georgia—William Few, Abr Baldwin

Attest: William Jackson, Secretary.

The Bill of Rights
In force Dec. 15, 1791

[Congress, at its first session in New York, NY, submitted to the states 12 amendments Sept. 25, 1789, to clarify certain individual and state rights not named in the Constitution. They are generally called the Bill of Rights.]

[Influential in framing these amendments was the Declaration of Rights of Virginia, written by George Mason (1725-92) in 1776. Mason, a Virginia delegate to the Constitutional Convention, did not sign the Constitution and opposed its ratification on the ground that it did not sufficiently oppose slavery or safeguard individual rights.]

[In the preamble to the resolution offering the proposed amendments, Congress said: "The conventions of a number of the States having at the time of their adopting the Constitution, expressed a desire, in order to prevent misconstruction or abuse of its powers, that further declaratory and restrictive clauses should be added, and as extending the ground of public confidence in the government will best insure the beneficent ends of its institution, be it resolved," etc.]

[Ten of these amendments, now commonly known as one to 10 inclusive, but originally three to 12 inclusive, were ratified by the states as follows: New Jersey, Nov. 20, 1789; Maryland, Dec. 19, 1789; North Carolina, Dec. 22, 1789; South Carolina, Jan. 19, 1790; New Hampshire, Jan. 25, 1790; Delaware, Jan. 28, 1790; New York, Feb. 27, 1790; Pennsylvania, Mar. 10, 1790; Rhode Island, June 7, 1790; Vermont, Nov. 3, 1791; Virginia, Dec. 15, 1791; Massachusetts, Mar. 2, 1939; Georgia, Mar. 18, 1939; Connecticut, Apr. 19, 1939. These original 10 ratified amendments follow as Amendments I to X inclusive.]

[Of the two original proposed amendments that were not ratified promptly by the necessary number of states, the first related to apportionment of Representatives; the second, relating to compensation of members of Congress, was ratified in 1992 and became Amendment XXVII.]

AMENDMENT I.

Religious establishment prohibited. Freedom of speech, of press, right to assemble and to petition.

Congress shall make no law respecting an establishment of religion, or prohibiting the free exercise thereof; or abridging the freedom of speech, or of the press; or the right of the people peaceably to assemble, and to petition the Government for a redress of grievances.

AMENDMENT II.

Right to keep and bear arms.

A well regulated Militia, being necessary to the security of a free State, the right of the people to keep and bear Arms, shall not be infringed.

AMENDMENT III.

Conditions for quarters for soldiers.

No Soldier shall, in time of peace be quartered in any house, without the consent of the Owner, nor in time of war, but in a manner to be prescribed by law.

AMENDMENT IV.

Protection from unreasonable search and seizure.

The right of the people to be secure in their persons, houses, papers, and effects, against unreasonable searches and seizures, shall not be violated, and no Warrants shall issue, but upon probable cause, supported by Oath or affirmation, and particularly describing the place to be searched, and the persons or things to be seized.

AMENDMENT V.

Provisions concerning prosecution and due process of law. Double jeopardy restriction. Private property not to be taken without compensation.

No person shall be held to answer for a capital, or otherwise infamous crime, unless on a presentment or indictment of a Grand Jury, except in cases arising in the land or naval forces, or in the Militia, when in actual service in time of War or public danger; nor shall any person be subject for the same offence to be twice put in jeopardy of life or limb; nor

shall be compelled in any criminal case to be a witness against himself, nor be deprived of life, liberty, or property, without due process of law; nor shall private property be taken for public use, without just compensation.

AMENDMENT VI.

Right to speedy trial, witnesses, etc.

In all criminal prosecutions, the accused shall enjoy the right to a speedy and public trial, by an impartial jury of the State and district wherein the crime shall have been committed, which district shall have been previously ascertained by law, and to be informed of the nature and cause of the accusation; to be confronted with the witnesses against him; to have compulsory process for obtaining witnesses in his favor, and to have the Assistance of Counsel for his defence.

AMENDMENT VII.

Right of trial by jury.

In suits at common law, where the value in controversy shall exceed twenty dollars, the right of trial by jury shall be preserved, and no fact tried by a jury, shall be otherwise reexamined in any Court of the United States, than according to the rules of the common law.

AMENDMENT VIII.

Excessive bail or fines; cruel and unusual punishment.

Excessive bail shall not be required, nor excessive fines imposed, nor cruel and unusual punishments inflicted.

AMENDMENT IX.

Rule of construction of Constitution.

The enumeration in the Constitution, of certain rights, shall not be construed to deny or disparage others retained by the people.

AMENDMENT X.

Rights of States under Constitution.

The powers not delegated to the United States by the Constitution, nor prohibited by it to the States, are reserved to the States respectively, or to the people.

Amendments Since the Bill of Rights

AMENDMENT XI.

Judicial powers construed.

The Judicial power of the United States shall not be construed to extend to any suit in law or equity, commenced or prosecuted against one of the United States by Citizens of another State, or by Citizens or Subjects of any Foreign State.

[This amendment was proposed to the Legislatures of the several States by the Third Congress on Mar. 4, 1794, and was declared to have been ratified in a message from the President to Congress, dated Jan. 8, 1798.]

[It was on Jan. 5, 1798, that Secretary of State Pickering received from 12 of the States authenticated ratifications, and informed President John Adams of that fact.]

[As a result of later research in the Department of State, it is now established that Amendment XI became part of the Constitution on Feb. 7, 1795, for on that date it had been ratified by 12 States as follows.]

[1. New York, Mar. 27, 1794. 2. Rhode Island, Mar. 31, 1794. 3. Connecticut, May 8, 1794. 4. New Hampshire, June 16, 1794. 5. Massachusetts, June 26, 1794. 6. Vermont, between Oct. 9, 1794, and Nov. 9, 1794. 7. Virginia, Nov. 18, 1794. 8. Georgia, Nov. 29, 1794. 9. Kentucky, Dec. 7, 1794. 10. Maryland, Dec. 26, 1794. 11. Delaware, Jan. 23, 1795. 12. North Carolina, Feb. 7, 1795]

[On June 1, 1796, more than a year after Amendment XI had become a part of the Constitution—but before anyone was officially aware of this—Tennessee had been admitted as a State; but not until Oct. 16, 1797, was a certified copy of the resolution of Congress proposing the amendment sent to the Governor of Tennessee, John Sevier, by Secretary of State Pickering, whose office was then at Trenton, New Jersey, because of the epidemic of yellow fever at Philadelphia; it seems, however, that the Legislature of Tennessee took no action on Amendment XI, owing doubtless to the fact that public announcement of its adoption was made soon thereafter.]

[Besides the necessary 12 States, one other, South Carolina, ratified Amendment XI, but this action was not taken until Dec. 4, 1797; the two remaining States, New Jersey and Pennsylvania, failed to ratify.]

AMENDMENT XII.

Manner of choosing President and Vice-President.

[Proposed by Congress Dec. 9, 1803; ratified June 15, 1804.]

The Electors shall meet in their respective states and vote by ballot for President and Vice-President, one of whom, at least, shall not be an inhabitant of the same state with themselves; they shall name in their ballots the person voted for as President, and in distinct ballots the person voted for as Vice-President, and they shall make distinct lists of all persons voted for as President, and of all persons voted for as Vice-President, and of the number of votes for each, which lists they shall sign and certify, and transmit sealed to the seat of the government of the United States, directed to the President of the Senate;—the President of the Senate shall, in presence of the Senate and House of Representatives, open all the certificates and the votes shall then be counted;—The person having the greatest number of votes for President, shall be the President, if such number be a majority of the whole number of Electors appointed; and if no person have such majority, then from the persons having the highest numbers not exceeding three on the list of those voted for as President, the House of Representatives shall choose immediately, by ballot, the President. But in choosing the President, the votes shall be taken by states, the representation from each state having one vote; a quorum for this purpose shall consist of a member or members from two-thirds of the states, and a majority of all the states shall be necessary to a choice. *[And if the House of Representatives shall not choose a President whenever the right of choice shall devolve upon them, before the fourth day of March next following, then the Vice-President shall act as President, as in the case of the death or other constitutional disability of the President.]* *[The words in brackets were superseded by Amendment XX, section 3.]* The person having the greatest number of votes as Vice-President, shall be the Vice-President, if such number be a majority of the whole number of Electors appointed, and if no person have a majority, then from the two highest numbers on the list, the Senate shall choose the Vice-President; a quorum for the purpose shall consist of two-thirds of the whole number of Senators, and a majority of the whole number shall be necessary to a choice. But no person constitutionally ineligible to the office of President shall be eligible to that of Vice-President of the United States.

THE RECONSTRUCTION AMENDMENTS

[Amendments XIII, XIV, and XV are commonly known as the Reconstruction Amendments, inasmuch as they followed the Civil War, and were drafted by Republicans who were bent on imposing their own policy of reconstruction on the South. Postbellum legislatures there—Mississippi, South Carolina, Georgia, for example—had set up laws which, it was charged, were contrived to perpetuate Negro slavery under other names.]

AMENDMENT XIII.

Slavery abolished.

[Proposed by Congress Jan. 31, 1865; ratified Dec. 6, 1865. The amendment, when first proposed by a resolution in Congress, was passed by the Senate, 38 to 6, on Apr. 8, 1864, but was defeated in the House, 95 to 66 on June 15, 1864. On reconsideration by the House, on Jan. 31, 1865, the resolution passed, 119 to 56. It was approved by President Lincoln on Feb. 1, 1865, although the Supreme Court had decided in 1798 that the President has nothing to do with the proposing of amendments to the Constitution, or their adoption.]

1. Neither slavery nor involuntary servitude, except as a punishment for crime whereof the party shall have been duly convicted, shall exist within the United States, or any place subject to their jurisdiction.

2. Congress shall have power to enforce this article by appropriate legislation.

AMENDMENT XIV.

Citizenship rights not to be abridged.

[The following amendment was proposed to the Legislatures of the several states by the 39th Congress, June 13, 1866, ratified July 9, 1868, and declared to have been ratified in a proclamation by the Secretary of State, July 28, 1868.]

[The 14th Amendment was adopted only by virtue of ratification subsequent to earlier rejections. Newly constituted legislatures in both North Carolina and South Carolina (respectively July 4 and 9, 1868), ratified the proposed amendment, although earlier legislatures had rejected the proposal. The Secretary of State issued a proclamation, which, though doubtful as to the effect of attempted withdrawals by Ohio and New Jersey, entertained no doubt as to the validity of the ratification by North and South Carolina. The following day (July 21, 1868), Congress passed a resolution which declared the 14th Amendment to be a part of the Constitution and directed the Secretary of State so to promulgate it. The Secretary waited, however, until the newly constituted Legislature of Georgia had ratified the amendment, subsequent to an earlier rejection, before the promulgation of the ratification of the new amendment.]

1. All persons born or naturalized in the United States, and subject to the jurisdiction thereof, are citizens of the United States and of the State wherein they reside. No State shall make or enforce any law which shall abridge the privileges or immunities of citizens of the United States; nor shall any State deprive any person of life, liberty, or property, without due process of law; nor deny to any person within its jurisdiction the equal protection of the laws.

2. Representatives shall be apportioned among the several States according to their respective numbers, counting the whole number of persons in each State, excluding Indians not taxed. But when the right to vote at any election for the choice of electors for President and Vice-President of the United States, Representatives in Congress, the Executive and Judicial officers of a State, or the members of the Legislature thereof, is denied to any of the male inhabitants of such State, being *[twenty-one]* *[The words in brackets were changed by Amendment XXVI.]* years of age, and citizens of the United States, or in any way abridged, except

for participation in rebellion, or other crime, the basis of representation therein shall be reduced in the proportion which the number of such male citizens shall bear to the whole number of male citizens twenty-one years of age in such State.

3. No person shall be a Senator or Representative in Congress, or elector of President and Vice-President, or hold any office, civil or military, under the United States, or under any State, who, having previously taken an oath, as a member of Congress, or as an officer of the United States, or as a member of any State legislature, or as an executive or judicial officer of any State, to support the Constitution of the United States, shall have engaged in insurrection or rebellion against the same, or given aid or comfort to the enemies thereof. But Congress may by a vote of two-thirds of each House, remove such disability.

4. The validity of the public debt of the United States, authorized by law, including debts incurred for payment of pensions and bounties for services in suppressing insurrection or rebellion, shall not be questioned. But neither the United States nor any State shall assume or pay any debt or obligation incurred in aid of insurrection or rebellion against the United States, or any claim for the loss or emancipation of any slave; but all such debts, obligations and claims shall be held illegal and void.

5. The Congress shall have power to enforce, by appropriate legislation, the provisions of this article.

AMENDMENT XV.

Race no bar to voting rights.

[The following amendment was proposed to the legislatures of the several States by the 40th Congress, Feb. 26, 1869, and ratified Feb. 3, 1870.]

1. The right of citizens of the United States to vote shall not be denied or abridged by the United States or by any State on account of race, color, or previous condition of servitude–

2. The Congress shall have power to enforce this article by appropriate legislation.

AMENDMENT XVI.

Income taxes authorized.

[Proposed by Congress July 12, 1909; ratified Feb. 3, 1913.]

The Congress shall have power to lay and collect taxes on incomes, from whatever source derived, without apportionment among the several States, and without regard to any census or enumeration.

AMENDMENT XVII.

United States Senators to be elected by direct popular vote.

[Proposed by Congress May 13, 1912; ratified Apr. 8, 1913.]

The Senate of the United States shall be composed of two Senators from each State, elected by the people thereof, for six years; and each Senator shall have one vote. The electors in each State shall have the qualifications requisite for electors of the most numerous branch of the State legislatures.

When vacancies happen in the representation of any State in the Senate, the executive authority of such State shall issue writs of election to fill such vacancies: *Provided,* That the legislature of any State may empower the executive thereof to make temporary appointments until the people fill the vacancies by election as the legislature may direct.

This amendment shall not be so construed as to affect the election or term of any Senator chosen before it becomes valid as part of the Constitution.

AMENDMENT XVIII.

Liquor prohibition amendment.

[Proposed by Congress Dec. 18, 1917; ratified Jan. 16, 1919. Repealed by Amendment XXI, effective Dec. 5, 1933.]

1. After one year from the ratification of this article the manufacture, sale, or transportation of intoxicating liquors within, the importation thereof into, or the exportation thereof from the United States and all territory subject to the jurisdiction thereof for beverage purposes is hereby prohibited.

2. The Congress and the several States shall have concurrent power to enforce this article by appropriate legislation.

3. This article shall be inoperative unless it shall have been ratified as an amendment to the Constitution by the legislatures of the several States as provided in the Constitution, within seven years from the date of the submission hereof to the States by the Congress.

[The total vote in the Senates of the various States was 1,310 for, 237 against—84.6% dry. In the lower houses of the States the vote was 3,782 for, 1,035 against—78.5% dry.

[The amendment ultimately was adopted by all the States except Rhode Island.]

AMENDMENT XIX.

Giving nationwide suffrage to women.

[Proposed by Congress June 4, 1919; ratified Aug. 18, 1920.]

The right of citizens of the United States to vote shall not be denied or abridged by the United States or by any State on account of sex.

Congress shall have power to enforce this Article by appropriate legislation.

AMENDMENT XX.

Terms of President and Vice President to begin on Jan. 20; those of Senators, Representatives, Jan. 3.

[Proposed by Congress Mar. 2, 1932; ratified Jan. 23, 1933.]

1. The terms of the President and Vice President shall end at noon on the 20th day of January, and the terms of Senators and Representatives at noon on the 3d day of January, of the years in which such terms would have ended if this article had not been ratified; and the terms of their successors shall then begin.

2. The Congress shall assemble at least once in every year, and such meeting shall begin at noon on the 3d day of January, unless they shall by law appoint a different day.

3. If, at the time fixed for the beginning of the term of the President, the President elect shall have died, the Vice President elect shall become President. If a President shall not have been chosen before the time fixed for the beginning of his term, or if the President elect shall have failed to qualify, then the Vice President elect shall act as President until a President shall have qualified; and the Congress may by law provide for the case wherein neither a President elect nor a Vice President elect shall have qualified, declaring who shall then act as President, or the manner in which one who is to act shall be selected, and such person shall act accordingly until a President or Vice President shall have qualified.

4. The Congress may by law provide for the case of the death of any of the persons from whom the House of Representatives may choose a President whenever the right of choice shall have devolved upon them, and for the case of the death of any of the persons from whom the Senate may choose a Vice President whenever the right of choice shall have devolved upon them.

5. Sections 1 and 2 shall take effect on the 15th day of October following the ratification of this article. *[Oct. 1933]*

6. This article shall be inoperative unless it shall have been ratified as an amendment to the Constitution by the legislatures of three-fourths of the several States within seven years from the date of its submission.

AMENDMENT XXI.

Repeal of Amendment XVIII.

[Proposed by Congress Feb. 20, 1933; ratified Dec. 5, 1933.]

1. The eighteenth article of amendment to the Constitution of the United States is hereby repealed.

2. The transportation or importation into any State, Territory, or possession of the United States for delivery or use therein of intoxicating liquors, in violation of the laws thereof, is hereby prohibited.

3. This article shall be inoperative unless it shall have been ratified as an amendment to the Constitution by conventions in the several States, as provided in the Constitution, within seven years from the date of the submission hereof to the States by the Congress.

AMENDMENT XXII.

Limiting Presidential terms of office.

[Proposed by Congress Mar. 24, 1947; ratified Feb. 27, 1951.]

1. No person shall be elected to the office of the President more than twice, and no person who has held the office of President, or acted as President, for more than two years of a term to which some other person was elected President shall be elected to the office of the President more than once. But this Article shall not apply to any person holding the office of President when this Article was proposed by the Congress, and shall not prevent any person who may be holding the office of President, or acting as President, during the term within which this Article becomes operative from holding the office of President or acting as President during the remainder of such term.

2. This article shall be inoperative unless it shall have been ratified as an amendment to the Constitution by the legislatures of three-fourths of the several States within seven years from the date of its submission to the States by the Congress.

AMENDMENT XXIII.

Presidential vote for District of Columbia.

[Proposed by Congress June 16, 1960; ratified Mar. 29, 1961.]

1. The District constituting the seat of Government of the United States shall appoint in such manner as the Congress may direct:

A number of electors of President and Vice President equal to the whole number of Senators and Representatives in Congress to which the District would be entitled if it were a State, but in no event more than the least populous State; they shall be in addition to those appointed by the States, but they shall be considered, for the purposes of the election of President and Vice President, to be electors appointed by a State; and they shall meet in the District and perform such duties as provided by the twelfth article of amendment.

2. The Congress shall have power to enforce this article by appropriate legislation.

AMENDMENT XXIV.

Barring poll tax in federal elections.

[Proposed by Congress Sept. 14, 1962; ratified Jan. 23, 1964.]

1. The right of citizens of the United States to vote in any primary or other election for President or Vice President, for electors for President or Vice President, or for Senator or Representative in Congress, shall not be denied or abridged by the United States or any State by reason of failure to pay any poll tax or other tax.

2. The Congress shall have power to enforce this article by appropriate legislation.

AMENDMENT XXV.

Presidential disability and succession.

[Proposed by Congress July 6, 1965; ratified Feb. 10, 1967.]

1. In case of the removal of the President from office or of his death or resignation, the Vice President shall become President.

2. Whenever there is a vacancy in the office of the Vice President, the President shall nominate a Vice President who shall take office upon confirmation by a majority vote of both houses of Congress.

3. Whenever the President transmits to the President pro tempore of the Senate and the Speaker of the House of Representatives his written declaration that he is unable to discharge the powers and duties of his office, and until he transmits to them a written declaration to the contrary, such powers and duties shall be discharged by the Vice President as Acting President.

4. Whenever the Vice President and a majority of either the principal officers of the executive departments or of such other body as Congress may by law provide, transmit to the President pro tempore of the Senate and the Speaker of the House of Representatives their written declaration that the President is unable to discharge the powers and duties of his office, the Vice President shall immediately assume the powers and duties of the office as Acting President.

Thereafter, when the President transmits to the President pro tempore of the Senate and the Speaker of the House of Representatives his written declaration that no inability exists, he shall resume the powers and duties of his office unless the Vice President and a majority of either the principal officers of the executive department or of such other body as Congress may by law provide, transmit within four days to the President pro tempore of the Senate and the Speaker of the House of Representatives their written declaration that the President is unable to discharge the powers and duties of his office. Thereupon Congress shall decide the issue, assembling within forty-eight hours for that purpose if not in session. If the Congress, within twenty-one days after receipt of the latter written declaration, or, if Congress is not in session, within twenty-one days after Congress is required to assemble, determines by two-thirds vote of both Houses that the President is unable to discharge the powers and duties of his office, the Vice President shall continue to discharge the same as Acting President; otherwise, the President shall resume the powers and duties of his office.

AMENDMENT XXVI.

Lowering voting age to 18 years.

[Proposed by Congress Mar. 23, 1971; ratified July 1, 1971.]

1. The right of citizens of the United States, who are eighteen years of age or older, to vote shall not be denied or abridged by the United States or by any State on account of age.

2. The Congress shall have the power to enforce this article by appropriate legislation.

AMENDMENT XXVII.

Congressional pay.

[Proposed by Congress Sept. 25, 1789; ratified May 7, 1992.]

No law, varying the compensation for the services of the Senators and Representatives, shall take effect, until an election of Representatives shall have intervened.

How a Bill Becomes a Law

A senator or representative introduces a bill in Congress by sending it to the clerk of the Senate or the House, who assigns it a number and title. This procedure is termed the first reading. The clerk then refers the bill to the appropriate committee of the Senate or House.

If the committee does not wish to consider the bill, it will table it. Otherwise, the committee holds hearings to listen to opinions and facts offered by members and other interested parties. The committee then debates the bill and may offer amendments. A vote is taken, and if favorable, the bill is sent back to the clerk of the Senate or House.

The clerk reads the bill to the house—the second reading. Members may then debate the bill and suggest amendments.

After debate and any amendments, the bill is given a third reading, simply of the title, and put to a voice or roll-call vote.

If the bill passes, it goes to the other house, where it may be defeated or passed, with or without amendments. If defeated, the bill dies. If passed with amendments, a conference committee made up of members of both houses works out the differences between the two bills and arrives at a compromise.

After passage of the final version by both houses, the bill is sent to the president. If the president signs it, the bill becomes a law. The president may instead veto the bill by refusing to sign it and sending it back to the house where it originated, with reasons for the veto.

The president's objections are then read and debated, and a roll-call vote is taken. If the bill receives less than a two-thirds majority, it is defeated. If it receives at least two-thirds, it is sent to the other house. If that house also passes it by at least a two-thirds majority, the president's veto is overridden, and the bill becomes a law.

If the president neither signs nor vetoes the bill within 10 days—not including Sundays—it automatically becomes a law even without the president's signature. However, if Congress adjourns within those 10 days, the bill is automatically killed; this indirect rejection is termed a pocket veto.

Note: Under the Line Item Veto Act, effective Jan. 1, 1997, the president was authorized, under certain circumstances, to veto a bill in part. The legislation was found unconstitutional by the Supreme Court, June 25, 1998.

Confederate States and Secession

The American Civil War (1861-65) grew out of sectional disputes over the continued existence of slavery in the South. Southern legislators contended that the states retained many rights, including the right to own slaves and the right to secede.

The war was not fought by state against state but by one federal regime against another. A Confederate government in Richmond assumed control over the economic, political, and military life of the seceding states, under protest from Georgia and South Carolina.

South Carolina voted unanimously in convention to secede from the Union, repealing its 1788 ratification of the U.S. Constitution on Dec. 20, 1860, to take effect on Dec. 24. Other states seceded in 1861. Their votes in conventions were: Mississippi, Jan. 9, 84-15; Florida, Jan. 10, 62-7; Alabama, Jan. 11, 61-39; Georgia, Jan. 19, 208-89; Louisiana, Jan. 26, 113-17; Texas, Feb. 1, 166-7, ratified by popular vote (34,794 to 11,325) Feb. 23; Virginia, Apr. 17, 88-55, ratified by popular vote (128,884 to 32,134) May 23; Arkansas, May 6,

69-1; Tennessee, May 7, ratified by popular vote (104,019 to 47,238) June 8; North Carolina, unanimous, May 20.

Missouri Unionists stopped secession in conventions Feb. 28 and Mar. 9, 1861. The legislature condemned secession Mar. 7. Under the protection of Confederate troops, secessionist members of the legislature adopted a resolution of secession at Neosho, Oct. 31. The Confederate Congress seated the secessionists' representatives.

Kentucky did not secede, and its government remained Unionist. In a part of the state occupied by Confederate troops, Kentuckians approved secession, and the Confederate Congress admitted their representatives.

The Maryland legislature voted against secession Apr. 27, 1861, 53-13. Delaware did not secede. Western Virginia held conventions at Wheeling, named a pro-Union governor on June 11, 1861, and was admitted to the Union as West Virginia on June 20, 1863. Its constitution provided for gradual abolition of slavery.

Confederate Government

Forty-two delegates from South Carolina, Georgia, Alabama, Mississippi, Louisiana, and Florida met in convention at Montgomery, AL, on Feb. 4, 1861. They adopted a provisional constitution of the Confederate States of America and elected Jefferson Davis (MS) as provisional president and Alexander H. Stephens (GA) as provisional vice president.

A permanent constitution was adopted Mar. 11. It banned African slave trade, but it did not bar interstate commerce in

slaves. On July 20 the Congress moved to Richmond, VA. Davis was elected president in Nov. 1861 and was inaugurated Feb. 22, 1862.

The Congress adopted a flag consisting of a red field with a white stripe, and a blue jack with a circle of white stars. Later, the more popular flag was the red field with blue diagonal crossbars that held 13 white stars, for the 11 states in the Confederacy plus Kentucky and Missouri.

The Gettysburg Address

Delivered by Pres. Abraham Lincoln at Gettysburg, PA, on Nov. 19, 1863. Five handwritten copies of the Gettysburg Address as made by Lincoln are known to exist. The text differs slightly between copies. The text of the Bliss version, considered the standard, is reproduced here.

Four score and seven years ago our fathers brought forth on this continent, a new nation, conceived in Liberty, and dedicated to the proposition that all men are created equal.

Now we are engaged in a great civil war, testing whether that nation, or any nation so conceived and so dedicated, can long endure. We are met on a great battle-field of that war. We have come to dedicate a portion of that field, as a final resting place for those who here gave their lives that that nation might live. It is altogether fitting and proper that we should do this.

But, in a larger sense, we can not dedicate—we can not consecrate—we can not hallow—this ground. The brave men, living and dead, who struggled here, have consecrated

it, far above our poor power to add or detract. The world will little note, nor long remember what we say here, but it can never forget what they did here.

It is for us the living, rather, to be dedicated here to the unfinished work which they who fought here have thus far so nobly advanced. It is rather for us to be here dedicated to the great task remaining before us—that from these honored dead we take increased devotion to that cause for which they gave the last full measure of devotion—that we here highly resolve that these dead shall not have died in vain—that this nation, under God, shall have a new birth of freedom—and that government of the people, by the people, for the people, shall not perish from the earth.

Presidential Oath of Office

The Constitution (Article II) directs that the president-elect shall take the following oath or affirmation to be inaugurated as president: "I do solemnly swear [affirm] that I will faithfully execute the office of President of the United States, and will, to the best of my ability, preserve, protect, and defend the Constitution of the United States."

Custom decrees the addition of the words "So help me God" at the end of the oath when taken by the president-elect, with the left hand on the Bible for the duration of the oath, and the right hand slightly raised.

Presidential Succession

If, by reason of death, resignation, removal from office, inability, or failure to qualify, there is neither a president nor vice president to discharge the powers and duties of the office of president, then the speaker of the House of Representatives shall upon his resignation as speaker and as representative, act as president. The same rule shall apply in the case of the death, resignation, removal from office, or inability of an individual acting as president.

If, at the time when a speaker is to begin the discharge of the powers and duties of the office of president, there is no speaker, or the speaker fails to qualify as acting president, then the president pro tempore of the Senate, upon his resignation as president pro tempore and as senator, shall act as president.

An individual acting as president shall continue to act until the expiration of the then current presidential term, except that (1) if his discharge of the powers and duties of the office is founded in whole or in part in the failure of both the president-elect and the vice president-elect to qualify, then

he shall act only until a president or vice president qualifies, and (2) if his discharge of the powers and duties of the office is founded in whole or in part on the inability of the president or vice president, then he shall act only until the removal of the disability of one of such individuals.

If, by reason of death, resignation, removal from office, or failure to qualify, there is no president pro tempore to act as president, then the officer of the United States who is highest on the following list, and who is not under any disability to discharge the powers and duties of president shall act as president: the secretaries of state, treasury, defense, attorney general, secretaries of interior, agriculture, commerce, labor, health and human services, housing and urban development, transportation, energy, education, veterans affairs, homeland security.

Legislation approved July 18, 1947; amended Sept. 9, 1965, Oct. 15, 1966, Aug. 4, 1977, Sept. 27, 1979, and Mar. 9, 2006. See also Constitutional Amendment XXV.

Origin of the United States National Motto

In God We Trust, designated as the U.S. National Motto by Congress in 1956, originated during the Civil War as an inscription for U.S. coins, although it was used by Francis Scott Key in a slightly different form when he wrote "The Star-Spangled Banner" in 1814. On Nov. 13, 1861, when Union morale had been shaken by battlefield defeats, the Rev. M. R. Watkinson, of Ridleyville, PA, wrote to Sec. of the Treasury Salmon P. Chase. "From my heart I have felt our national shame in disowning God as not the least of our present national disasters," the minister wrote,

suggesting "recognition of the Almighty God in some form on our coins." Sec. Chase ordered designs prepared with the inscription *In God We Trust* and backed coinage legislation that authorized use of this slogan. The motto first appeared on some U.S. coins in 1864, and it appeared sporadically on coins until 1938, after which all U.S. coins bear the inscription. A joint resolution passed by the 84th Congress and signed by Pres. Dwight D. Eisenhower July 30, 1956, declared *In God We Trust* the national motto of the United States.

The Great Seal of the U.S.

On July 4, 1776, the Continental Congress appointed a committee consisting of Benjamin Franklin, John Adams, and Thomas Jefferson "to bring in a device for a seal of the United States of America." The designs submitted by this and a subsequent committee were

considered unacceptable. After many delays, a third committee, appointed early in 1782, presented a design prepared by lawyer William Barton. Charles Thomson, the secretary of Congress, suggested certain changes, and Congress finally approved the design on June 20, 1782. The obverse side of the seal shows an American bald eagle. In its mouth is a ribbon bearing the motto *E Pluribus Unum* (out of many, one). In the eagle's talons are 13 arrows of war and an olive branch of peace. The reverse side shows an unfinished pyramid with an eye (Eye of Providence) above it.

The Flag of the U.S.—The Stars and Stripes

The 50-star flag of the United States was raised for the first time officially at 12:01 AM on July 4, 1960, at Ft. McHenry National Monument in Baltimore, MD. The 50th star had been added for Hawaii; a year earlier the 49th, for Alaska. Before that, no star had been added since 1912, when New Mexico and Arizona were admitted to the Union.

The true history of the Stars and Stripes has become so cluttered by myth and tradition that the facts are difficult, and in some cases impossible, to establish. For example, it is not certain who designed the Stars and Stripes, who made the first such flag, or even whether it ever flew during any battle of the American Revolution.

All agree, however, that the Stars and Stripes originated as the result of a resolution offered by the Marine Committee of the Second Continental Congress at Philadelphia and adopted on June 14, 1777. It read:

"Resolved: that the flag of the United States be thirteen stripes, alternate red and white; that the union be thirteen stars, white in a blue field, representing a new constellation."

Congress gave no hint as to the designer of the flag, no instructions as to the arrangement of the stars, and no information on its appropriate uses. Historians have been unable to find the original flag details.

The resolution establishing the flag was not even published until Sept. 2, 1777. Despite repeated requests, Washington did not get the flags until 1783, after the American Revolution was over. And there is no certainty that they were the Stars and Stripes.

Early Flags

Many historians consider the first flag of the U.S. to have been the Grand Union (sometimes called Great Union) flag, although the Continental Congress never officially adopted it. This flag was a modification of the British Meteor flag, which had the red cross of St. George and the white cross of St. Andrew combined in the blue canton. For the Grand Union flag, six horizontal stripes were imposed on the red field, dividing it into 13 alternating red and white stripes. On

Jan. 1, 1776, when the Continental Army came into formal existence, this flag was unfurled on Prospect Hill, Somerville, MA. Washington wrote that "we hoisted the Union Flag in compliment to the United Colonies."

One of several flags about which controversy has raged for years is in Easton, PA. Containing the devices of the national flag in reversed order, this flag has been in the public library at Easton for more than 150 years. Some contend that this flag was actually the first Stars and Stripes, first displayed on July 8, 1776. This flag has 13 red and white stripes in the canton, 13 white stars centered in a blue field.

A flag was hastily improvised from garments by the defenders of Ft. Schuyler at Rome, NY, Aug. 3-22, 1777. Historians believe it was the Grand Union Flag.

The Sons of Liberty had a flag of nine red and white stripes, to signify nine colonies, when they met in New York in 1765 to oppose the Stamp Tax. By 1775, the flag had grown to 13 red and white stripes, with a rattlesnake on it.

At Concord, Apr. 19, 1775, the minutemen from Bedford, MA, are said to have carried a flag having a silver arm with sword on a red field. At Cambridge, MA, the Sons of Liberty used a plain red flag with a green pine tree on it.

In June 1775, Washington went from Philadelphia to Boston to take command of the army, escorted to New York by the Philadelphia Light Horse Troop. It carried a yellow flag that had an elaborate coat of arms—the shield charged with 13 knots, the motto "For These We Strive"—and a canton of 13 blue and silver stripes.

In Feb. 1776, Col. Christopher Gadsden, a member of the Continental Congress, gave the South Carolina Provincial Congress a flag "such as is to be used by the commander-in-chief of the American Navy." It had a yellow field, with a rattlesnake about to strike and the words "Don't Tread on Me."

At the Battle of Bennington, Aug. 16, 1777, patriots used a flag of seven white and six red stripes with a blue canton extending down nine stripes and showing an arch of 11 white stars over the figure 76 and a star in each of the upper corners. The stars are seven-pointed. This flag is preserved in the historical museum in Bennington, VT.

At the Battle of Cowpens, Jan. 17, 1781, the 3rd Maryland Regiment is said to have carried a flag of 13 red and white stripes, with a blue canton containing 12 stars in a circle around one star.

Who Designed the Flag? No one knows for certain. Francis Hopkinson, designer of a naval flag, declared he had designed the flag and in 1781 asked Congress to reimburse him for his services. Congress did not do so. Dumas Malone of Columbia Univ. wrote, "This talented man . . . designed the American flag."

Who Called the Flag "Old Glory"? The flag is said to have been named Old Glory by William Driver, a sea captain of Salem, MA. One legend has it that when he raised the flag on his brig, the *Charles Doggett*, in 1824, he said: "I name thee Old Glory." But his daughter, who presented the flag to the Smithsonian Institution, said he named it at his 21st birthday celebration on Mar. 17, 1824, when his mother presented the homemade flag to him.

The Betsy Ross Legend. The widely publicized legend that Betsy Ross made the first Stars and Stripes in June 1776, at the request of a committee composed of George Washington, Robert Morris, and George Ross, an uncle, was first made public in 1870, by a grandson of Ross. Historians have been unable to find a historical record of such a meeting or committee.

Adding New Stars

The flag of 1777 was used until 1795. Then, on the admission of Vermont and Kentucky to the Union, Congress passed and Pres. Washington signed an act that after May 1, 1795, the flag should have 15 stripes, alternating red and white, and 15 white stars on a blue field.

When new states were admitted, it became evident that the flag would become burdened with stripes. Congress thereupon ordered that after July 4, 1818, the flag should have 13 stripes, symbolizing the 13 original states; that the union have 20 stars, and that whenever a new state was admitted a new star should be added on the July 4 following admission.

No law designates the permanent arrangement of the stars. However, since 1912, when a new state has been admitted, the new design has been announced by executive order. No star is specifically identified with any state.

Code of Etiquette for Display and Use of the U.S. Flag
Reviewed by National Flag Foundation

Although the Stars and Stripes originated in 1777, it was not until 146 years later that there was a serious attempt to establish a uniform code of etiquette for the U.S. flag. On Feb. 15, 1923, the War Department issued a circular on the rules of flag usage. These rules were adopted almost in their entirety June 14, 1923, by a conference of 68 patriotic organizations in Washington, DC. A joint resolution of Congress June 22, 1942, amended by Public Law 94-344, July 7, 1976, codified "existing rules and customs pertaining to the display and use of the flag." Military branches have their own codes of etiquette regarding the flag; this guide is for civilian purposes.

When to Display the Flag. The flag should be displayed on all days, especially on legal holidays and other special occasions, on official buildings when in use, in or near polling places on election days, and in or near schools when in session. Citizens may fly the flag at any time. It is customary to display it only from sunrise to sunset on buildings and on stationary flagstaffs in the open. It may be displayed at night, however, on special occasions, preferably lighted. The flag

now flies over the White House both day and night. It flies over the Senate wing of the Capitol when the Senate is in session and over the House wing when that body is in session. It flies day and night over the east and west fronts of the Capitol, without floodlights at night but receiving illumination from the Capitol Dome. It flies 24 hours a day at several other places, including the Ft. McHenry National Monument in Baltimore, where it inspired Francis Scott Key to write "The Star Spangled Banner." The flag also flies 24 hours a day, properly illuminated, at U.S. Customs ports of entry.

Flying the Flag at Half-Staff. Flying the flag at half-staff, that is, halfway up the staff, is a signal of mourning. The flag should be hoisted to the top of the staff for an instant before being lowered to half-staff. It should be hoisted to the peak again before being lowered for the day.

As provided by presidential proclamation, the flag should fly at half-staff for 30 days from the day of death of a president or former president; for 10 days from the day of death of a vice president, chief justice or retired chief justice of the U.S., or speaker of the House of Representatives; from day of death until burial of an associate justice of the Supreme Court, cabinet member, former vice president, Senate president pro tempore, or majority or minority Senate or House leader; for a U.S. senator, representative, territorial delegate, or the resident commissioner of Puerto Rico, on day of death and the following day within the metropolitan area of the District of Columbia and from day of death until burial within the decedent's state, congressional district, territory or commonwealth; and for the death of the governor of a state, territory, or possession of the U.S., from day of death until burial.

On Memorial Day, the flag should fly at half-staff until noon and then be raised to the peak. The flag should also fly at half-staff on Korean War Veterans Armistice Day (July 27), National Pearl Harbor Remembrance Day (Dec. 7), and Peace Officers Memorial Day (May 15).

How to Fly the Flag. The flag should be hoisted briskly and lowered ceremoniously and should never be allowed to touch the ground or the floor. When the flag is hung over a sidewalk from a rope extending from a building to a pole, the union (the blue field with white stars) should be away from the building. When the flag is hung over the center of a street the union should be to the north in an east-west street and to the east in a north-south street. No other flag may be flown above or, if on the same level, to the right of the U.S. flag, except that at the United Nations Headquarters, the UN flag may be placed above flags of all member nations and other national flags may be flown with equal prominence or honor with the flag of the U.S.

When two flags are placed against a wall with crossed staffs, the U.S. flag should be at right—its own right, and its staff should be in front of the staff of the other flag; when a number of flags are grouped and displayed from staffs, it should be at the center and highest point of the group.

Church and Platform Use. In an auditorium, the flag may be displayed flat, above and behind the speaker. When displayed from a staff in a church or in a public auditorium, the flag should hold the position of superior prominence, in advance of the audience, and in the position of honor at the speaker's right as she or he faces the audience. Any other flag so displayed should be placed on the left of the speaker or to the right of the audience.

When the flag is displayed horizontally or vertically against a wall, the stars should be uppermost and at the observer's left.

When used to cover a casket, the flag should be placed so that the union is at the head and over the left shoulder. It should not be lowered into the grave nor touch the ground.

How to Dispose of Worn Flags. When the flag is in such condition that it is no longer a fitting emblem for display, it should be destroyed in a dignified way, preferably by burning.

When to Salute the Flag. All persons present should face the flag, stand at attention, and salute on the following occasions: (1) when the flag is passing in a parade or in a review, (2) during the ceremony of hoisting or lowering, (3) when the national anthem is played, and (4) during the Pledge of Allegiance. Those present in uniform should render the military salute. Those not in uniform should place the right hand over the heart. A man wearing a hat should remove it with his right hand and hold it to his left shoulder during the salute.

Prohibited Uses of the Flag. The flag should not be dipped to any person or thing. (An exception—customarily, ships salute by dipping their colors.) It should never be displayed with the union down save as a distress signal. It should never be carried flat or horizontally, but always aloft and free.

It should not be displayed on a float, an automobile, or a boat except from a staff. It should never be used as a covering for a ceiling, nor have placed on it any word, design, or drawing. It should never be used as a receptacle for carrying anything. It should not be used to cover a statue or a monument.

The flag should never be used for advertising purposes, nor be embroidered on such articles as cushions or handkerchiefs, printed or otherwise impressed on boxes or anything that is designed for temporary use and discard; or used as a costume or athletic uniform. Advertising signs should not be fastened to its staff or halyard.

The flag should never be used as drapery of any sort, never festooned, drawn back, nor up, in folds, but always allowed to fall free. Bunting of blue, white, and red, always arranged with the blue above and the white in the middle, should be used for covering a speaker's desk, draping the front of a platform, and for decoration in general.

An act of Congress approved on Feb. 8, 1917, provided certain penalties for the desecration, mutilation, or improper use of the flag within the District of Columbia. A 1968 federal law provided penalties of as much as a year's imprisonment or a $1,000 fine or both for publicly burning or otherwise desecrating any U.S. flag. In addition, many states have laws against flag desecration. In 1989, the Supreme Court ruled that no laws could prohibit political protesters from burning the flag. The decision had the effect of declaring unconstitutional the flag desecration laws of 48 states, as well as a similar federal statute, in cases of peaceful political expression.

The Supreme Court, in June 1990, declared that a new federal law making it a crime to burn or deface the American flag violated the free-speech guarantee of the First Amendment. The 5-4 Court decision led to renewed calls in Congress for a constitutional amendment to make it possible to prosecute flag burners. In 2005, the House passed a flag desecration amendment with the requisite two-thirds majority, but the measure failed by one vote to achieve two-thirds majority in the Senate in 2006.

Pledge of Allegiance to the Flag

I pledge allegiance to the flag of the United States of America and to the republic for which it stands, one nation under God, indivisible, with liberty and justice for all.

This, the current official version of the Pledge of Allegiance, developed from the original pledge, which was first published in the Sept. 8, 1892, issue of *Youth's Companion*, a weekly magazine. The original pledge contained the phrase "my flag," which was changed more than 30 years later to "flag of the United States of America." A 1954 act of Congress added the words "under God." (In 2002, the 9th Circuit U.S. Court of Appeals ruled that recitation of the pledge in public schools could not include that phrase. In 2004, however, the U.S. Supreme Court voted to decline to decide the case on a technicality. The lower court's decision was thus overturned.)

The authorship of the pledge was in dispute for many years. *Youth's Companion* stated in 1917 that the original draft was written by James B. Upham, an executive of the magazine who died in 1910. A leaflet circulated by the magazine later named Upham as the originator of the draft "afterwards condensed and perfected by him and his associates of the Companion force."

Francis Bellamy, a former member of *Youth's Companion* editorial staff, publicly claimed authorship of the pledge in 1923. In 1939, the United States Flag Association, acting on the advice of a committee named to study the controversy, upheld the claim of Bellamy, who had died eight years earlier. In 1957 the Library of Congress issued a report attributing the authorship to Bellamy.

History of the U.S. National Anthem

"The Star-Spangled Banner" was ordered played by the military and naval services by Pres. Woodrow Wilson in 1916. It was designated the national anthem by Act of Congress, Mar. 3, 1931. The words were written by Francis Scott Key, of Georgetown, MD, during the bombardment of Ft. McHenry in Baltimore MD, Sept. 13-14, 1814. Key was a lawyer, a graduate of St. John's College, Annapolis, MD, and a volunteer in a light artillery company. When a friend, Dr. Beanes, a Maryland physician, was taken aboard Adm. Cockburn's British squadron for interfering with ground troops, Key and J. S. Skinner, carrying a note from Pres. Madison, went to the fleet under a flag of truce on a cartel ship to ask Beanes's release. Cockburn consented, but as the fleet was about to sail up the Patapsco to bombard Ft. McHenry, he detained them, first on HMS *Surprise* and then on a supply ship.

Key witnessed the bombardment from his own vessel. It began at 7 AM, Sept. 13, 1814, and lasted 25 hours. The British fired more than 1,500 shells, each weighing as much as 220 lbs. They were unable to approach closely because the U.S. had sunk 22 vessels. Only four Americans were killed and 24 wounded. A British bomb-ship was disabled.

During the event, Key wrote a stanza on the back of an envelope. The next day at Indian Queen Inn in Baltimore, he wrote out the poem and gave it to his brother-in-law, Judge J. H. Nicholson. Nicholson suggested use of the tune, "Anacreon in Heaven" (attributed to a British composer named John Stafford Smith), and had the poem printed on broadsides, of which two survive. On Sept. 20 it appeared in the *Baltimore American*. Later Key made three copies; one is in the Library of Congress, and one in the Pennsylvania Historical Society. The copy Key wrote on Sept. 14 remained in the Nicholson family for 93 years. In 1907, it was sold to Henry Walters of Baltimore. In 1934, it was bought by Walters Art Gallery in Baltimore for $26,400. In 1953, it was sold to the Maryland Historical Society for the same price.

The flag that Key saw during the bombardment is preserved in the Smithsonian Institution, Washington, DC. It measures 30 by 42 ft and has 15 alternating red and white stripes and 15 stars, for the original 13 states plus Kentucky and Vermont. It was made by Mary Pickersgill. The Star-Spangled Banner Flag House, a museum, occupies her premises, which were restored in 1953.

The Star-Spangled Banner

I

Oh, say can you see by the dawn's early light
What so proudly we hailed at the twilight's last gleaming?
Whose broad stripes and bright stars thru the perilous fight,
O'er the ramparts we watched were so gallantly streaming?
And the rocket's red glare, the bombs bursting in air,
Gave proof through the night that our flag was still there.
Oh, say does that star-spangled banner yet wave
O'er the land of the free and the home of the brave?

II

On the shore, dimly seen through the mists of the deep,
Where the foe's haughty host in dread silence reposes,
What is that which the breeze, o'er the towering steep,
As it fitfully blows, half conceals, half discloses?
Now it catches the gleam of the morning's first beam,
In full glory reflected now shines in the stream:
'Tis the star-spangled banner! Oh long may it wave
O'er the land of the free and the home of the brave!

III

And where is that band who so vauntingly swore
That the havoc of war and the battle's confusion,
A home and a country should leave us no more!
Their blood has washed out their foul footsteps' pollution.
No refuge could save the hireling and slave
From the terror of flight, or the gloom of the grave:
And the star-spangled banner in triumph doth wave
O'er the land of the free and the home of the brave!

IV

Oh! thus be it ever, when freemen shall stand
Between their loved home and the war's desolation!
Blest with victory and peace, may the heav'n rescued land
Praise the Power that hath made and preserved us a nation.
Then conquer we must, when our cause it is just,
And this be our motto: "In God is our trust."
And the star-spangled banner in triumph shall wave
O'er the land of the free and the home of the brave!

History of the Liberty Bell

The Liberty Bell is housed in the Liberty Bell Center, located in Philadelphia's Independence National Historical Park.

The original bell was ordered by Isaac Norris, Assembly Speaker and Chairman of the State House Superintendents, from Thomas Lester of Whitechapel Foundry in London. It reached Philadelphia at the end of Aug. 1752. It bore an inscription from Leviticus 25:10: "Proclaim LIBERTY throughout all the land unto all the inhabitants thereof."

The bell was cracked by a stroke of its clapper in Sept. 1752 while it hung on a truss in the State House yard for testing. Pass & Stow, Philadelphia founders, recast the bell, adding 1½ ounces of copper to a pound of the original Whitechapel metal to reduce its high tone and brittleness. That proved to be too much copper, injuring its tone, so Pass & Stow recast it once more.

In June 1753, the bell was hung in the old wooden steeple of the State House. It rang out in defiance of British tax and trade restrictions while the Continental Congress was in session in the State House. It proclaimed the Boston Tea Party as well as the first public reading of the Declaration of Independence, on July 8, 1776.

On Sept. 18, 1777, when the British Army was about to occupy Philadelphia, the Liberty Bell was moved in a baggage train to Allentown, PA, where it was hidden until June 27, 1778. The bell was moved back to Philadelphia after the British left the city.

In 1781, the wooden steeple became insecure and had to be taken down. The bell was lowered into the brick section of the tower, where it remained until 1828. Between 1828 and 1844, the old State House bell continued to ring on special occasions. According to tradition, it cracked in 1835 as it tolled the death of U.S. Supreme Court Chief Justice John Marshall. It rang for the last time on Feb. 23, 1846, in honor of George Washington's birthday. In 1852 it was placed on exhibition in the Declaration Chamber of Independence Hall.

In 1876, when thousands of Americans visited Philadelphia for the Centennial Exposition, the bell was placed in its old wooden support in the tower hallway. In 1877, it was hung from the ceiling of the tower by a chain of 13 links. In 1896, it was placed within a glass case to prevent souvenir hunters and vandals from taking some of the metal. In 1915, the case was removed so that the public might touch the bell. To mark the opening of the Bicentennial Year, the bell was moved just after midnight on Jan. 1, 1976, to a new glass and steel pavilion behind Independence Hall for easier viewing.

On Oct. 9, 2003, the bell was transferred to its present location, where exhibits and displays explain the history of the bell.

Measurements of the bell: circumference around the lip, 12 ft ½ in.; circumference around the crown, 6 ft 11¼ in.; lip to the crown, 3 ft; height over the crown, 2 ft 3 in.; thickness at lip, 3 in.; thickness at crown, 1¼ in.; weight, 2,080 lbs; length of clapper, 3 ft 2 in.

Statue of Liberty National Monument

Since 1886, the Statue of Liberty, formally known as "Liberty Enlightening the World," has stood as a symbol of freedom in New York harbor. It also commemorates French-American friendship because it was given by the people of France to the people of the U.S. It was designed by French sculptor Frédéric Auguste Bartholdi (1834-1904).

On Washington's Birthday, Feb. 22, 1877, Congress approved the use of a site on Bedloe's Island suggested by Bartholdi. This island of 12 acres had been owned in the 17th cent. by a Walloon colonist named Isaac Bedloe. On Aug. 3, 1956, Pres. Dwight Eisenhower approved a measure changing the name to Liberty Island.

The statue was finished on May 21, 1884, and presented to the U.S. minister to France, Levi Parsons Morton, July 4, 1884, by Ferdinand de Lesseps, head of the Franco-American Union, promoter of the Panama Canal, and builder of the Suez Canal.

On Aug. 5, 1884, the cornerstone for the pedestal was laid on the foundations of Fort Wood, erected by the government in 1811. The American Committee for the Statue of Liberty had raised an inadequate $125,000, and *New York World* newspaper owner Joseph Pulitzer appealed Mar. 16, 1885, for general donations. By Aug. 11, 1885, he had raised $100,000. The statue itself arrived dismantled, in 214 packing cases, from Rouen, France, in June 1885. The last rivet of the statue was driven on Oct. 28, 1886, when Pres. Grover Cleveland dedicated the monument.

The Statue of Liberty National Monument was designated as such in 1924. It is administered by the National Park Service. A $2.5-mil building housing the American Museum of Immigration was opened by Pres. Richard Nixon on Sept. 26, 1972, at the base of the statue. It houses a permanent exhibition tracing the history of American immigration.

Four years of restoration work funded and led by the Statue of Liberty-Ellis Island Foundation were completed before the statue's 1986 centennial. The $87-mil project included the replacement of the 1,600 wrought iron bands that hold the statue's copper skin to its frame, replacement of the torch, and installation of an elevator. A four-day Liberty Weekend extravaganza of concerts, tall ships, ethnic festivals, and fireworks, July 3-6, 1986, celebrated the 100th anniversary. U.S. Supreme Court Chief Justice Warren E. Burger swore in 5,000 new citizens on Ellis Island, while 20,000 others across the country were sworn in through a satellite telecast. Other ceremonies followed on Oct. 28, 1986, the statue's exact 100th birthday.

After the Sept. 11, 2001, terrorist attacks, Liberty Island was closed to visitors. On Dec. 20, 2001, the secretary of the interior reopened the island after installing airport-type screening facilities at passenger embarkation areas at Battery Park in Manhattan and Liberty State Park in New Jersey.

To open the statue, the federal government needed to increase security throughout the park. In addition to federally funded security upgrades, significant safety improvements were made to meet building codes. Access to the statue was restored on Aug. 3, 2004.

Following the 125th anniversary celebration Oct. 28, 2011, the statue was closed. A $30-mil renovation brought the statue up to contemporary safety standards and allowed for increased visitor access. The island remained open to visitors, and views of the statue were largely unobstructed, but visitors could not go inside. The statue interior reopened Oct. 28, 2012, but damages caused by Hurricane Sandy the next week forced all of Liberty Island to close again.

The island and the statue officially reopened for visitors July 4, 2013. Advance reservations are required to visit the museum, statue pedestal, or crown. Reservations are available by visiting www.statuecruises.com or by calling 1-877-LADY-TIX. Visitors to the statue's interior must follow a number of guidelines including ones on height requirements and locker rentals, for which there is a $2 fee. (Inside the statue, visitors may carry only a camera, a ferry ticket with crown reservation, and necessary medication.) For more information, visit www.nps.gov/stli/ and www.statueofliberty.org.

Statue Statistics

The statue weighs 450,000 lbs, or 225 tons. The copper sheeting weighs 200,000 lbs. There are 377 steps from the main lobby to the crown platform. There are 146 steps from the top of the pedestal (the statue's feet) to the crown platform.

	Ft	In.
Height from base to torch tip	151	1
Foundation of pedestal to torch tip	305	1
Heel to top of head	111	1
Hand, length	16	5
Index finger, length	8	0
Fingernail size		13x10
Head from chin to cranium	17	3
Head thickness, ear to ear	10	0
Nose, length	4	6
Right arm, length	42	0
Right arm, max. thickness	12	0
Waist, thickness	35	0
Mouth, width	3	0
Tablet, length	23	7
Tablet, width	13	7

Ellis Island

Ellis Island was the gateway to America for over 12 mil immigrants between 1892 and 1924. In the late 18th cent., Samuel Ellis, a New York City merchant, purchased the island and gave it his name. From Ellis, it passed to New York state, and the U.S. government bought it in 1808. On Jan. 1, 1892, the government opened the first federal immigration center in the U.S. there. The 27.5-acre site eventually supported more than 35 buildings, including the Main Building with its Great Hall, in which as many as 5,000 people a day were processed.

Closed as an immigration station in 1954, Ellis Island was proclaimed part of the Statue of Liberty National Monument in 1965 by Pres. Lyndon B. Johnson. After a six-year, $170 mil restoration project funded by the Statue of Liberty-Ellis Island Foundation, Ellis Island was reopened as a museum in 1990. Artifacts, historic photographs and documents, oral histories, and ethnic music depicting 400 years of American immigration are housed in the museum.

In 1998, the U.S. Supreme Court ruled that nearly 90% of the island (the 24.2 acres that are landfill) lies in New Jersey, while the original 3.3 acres, on which the museum is located, are in New York.

The American Family Immigration History Center opened in Apr. 2001. It contains an electronic database of ship passenger arrival information through the Port of New York and Ellis Island from 1892 to 1924. Data on over 22 mil individuals are available, as well multimedia presentations on various immigration groups and patterns, reproductions of original ships' passenger manifests, and pictures of over 800 immigrant ships (www.ellisisland.org).

Damages caused by storm surges of Hurricane Sandy in late Oct. 2012 forced Ellis Island to close for repairs. As of Sept. 2014, the island had reopened but parts of the Main Building and Museum remained closed.

PRESIDENTS OF THE UNITED STATES

U.S. Presidents

	Name	Politics	Born	Birthplace	Inaug.	Age at inaug.	Died	Age at death
1.	George Washington	Fed.	1732, Feb. 22	VA	1789	57	1799, Dec. 14	67
2.	John Adams	Fed.	1735, Oct. 30	MA	1797	61	1826, July 4	90
3.	Thomas Jefferson	Dem.-Rep.	1743, Apr. 13	VA	1801	57	1826, July 4	83
4.	James Madison	Dem.-Rep.	1751, Mar. 16	VA	1809	57	1836, June 28	85
5.	James Monroe	Dem.-Rep.	1758, Apr. 28	VA	1817	58	1831, July 4	73
6.	John Quincy Adams	Dem.-Rep.	1767, July 11	MA	1825	57	1848, Feb. 23	80
7.	Andrew Jackson	Dem.	1767, Mar. 15	SC	1829	61	1845, June 8	78
8.	Martin Van Buren	Dem.	1782, Dec. 5	NY	1837	54	1862, July 24	79
9.	William Henry Harrison	Whig	1773, Feb. 9	VA	1841	68	1841, Apr. 4	68
10.	John Tyler	Whig	1790, Mar. 29	VA	1841	51	1862, Jan. 18	71
11.	James Knox Polk	Dem.	1795, Nov. 2	NC	1845	49	1849, June 15	53
12.	Zachary Taylor	Whig	1784, Nov. 24	VA	1849	64	1850, July 9	65
13.	Millard Fillmore	Whig	1800, Jan. 7	NY	1850	50	1874, Mar. 8	74
14.	Franklin Pierce	Dem.	1804, Nov. 23	NH	1853	48	1869, Oct. 8	64
15.	James Buchanan	Dem.	1791, Apr. 23	PA	1857	65	1868, June 1	77
16.	Abraham Lincoln	Rep.	1809, Feb. 12	KY	1861	52	1865, Apr. 15	56
17.	Andrew Johnson	(1)	1808, Dec. 29	NC	1865	56	1875, July 31	66
18.	Ulysses S. Grant	Rep.	1822, Apr. 27	OH	1869	46	1885, July 23	63
19.	Rutherford Birchard Hayes	Rep.	1822, Oct. 4	OH	1877	54	1893, Jan. 17	70
20.	James Abram Garfield	Rep.	1831, Nov. 19	OH	1881	49	1881, Sept. 19	49
21.	Chester Alan Arthur	Rep.	1829, Oct. 5	VT	1881	51	1886, Nov. 18	57
22.	Grover Cleveland	Dem.	1837, Mar. 18	NJ	1885	47	1908, June 24	71
23.	Benjamin Harrison	Rep.	1833, Aug. 20	OH	1889	55	1901, Mar. 13	67
24.	Grover Cleveland	Dem.	1837, Mar. 18	NJ	1893	55	1908, June 24	71
25.	William McKinley	Rep.	1843, Jan. 29	OH	1897	54	1901, Sept. 14	58
26.	Theodore Roosevelt	Rep.	1858, Oct. 27	NY	1901	42	1919, Jan. 6	60
27.	William Howard Taft	Rep.	1857, Sept. 15	OH	1909	51	1930, Mar. 8	72
28.	(Thomas) Woodrow Wilson	Dem.	1856, Dec. 28	VA	1913	56	1924, Feb. 3	67
29.	Warren Gamaliel Harding	Rep.	1865, Nov. 2	OH	1921	55	1923, Aug. 2	57
30.	(John) Calvin Coolidge	Rep.	1872, July 4	VT	1923	51	1933, Jan. 5	60
31.	Herbert Clark Hoover	Rep.	1874, Aug. 10	IA	1929	54	1964, Oct. 20	90
32.	Franklin Delano Roosevelt	Dem.	1882, Jan. 30	NY	1933	51	1945, Apr. 12	63
33.	Harry S. Truman	Dem.	1884, May 8	MO	1945	60	1972, Dec. 26	88
34.	Dwight David Eisenhower	Rep.	1890, Oct. 14	TX	1953	62	1969, Mar. 28	78
35.	John Fitzgerald Kennedy	Dem.	1917, May 29	MA	1961	43	1963, Nov. 22	46
36.	Lyndon Baines Johnson	Dem.	1908, Aug. 27	TX	1963	55	1973, Jan. 22	64
37.	Richard Milhous Nixon[2]	Rep.	1913, Jan. 9	CA	1969	56	1994, Apr. 22	81
38.	Gerald Rudolph Ford	Rep.	1913, July 14	NE	1974	61	2006, Dec. 26	93
39.	James Earl (Jimmy) Carter	Dem.	1924, Oct. 1	GA	1977	52		
40.	Ronald Wilson Reagan	Rep.	1911, Feb. 6	IL	1981	69	2004, June 5	93
41.	George Herbert Walker Bush	Rep.	1924, June 12	MA	1989	64		
42.	Wm. Jefferson (Bill) Clinton	Dem.	1946, Aug. 19	AR	1993	46		
43.	George Walker Bush	Rep.	1946, July 6	CT	2001	54		
44.	Barack Hussein Obama	Dem.	1961, Aug. 4	HI	2009	47		

(1) Andrew Johnson, a Democrat, had been nominated vice president by Republicans and elected with Lincoln on National Union ticket. (2) Resigned Aug. 9, 1974.

U.S. Presidents, Vice Presidents, Congresses

	President	Service		Vice President	Congresses
1.	George Washington	Apr. 30, 1789-Mar. 3, 1797	1.	John Adams	1, 2, 3, 4
2.	John Adams	Mar. 4, 1797-Mar. 3, 1801	2.	Thomas Jefferson	5, 6
3.	Thomas Jefferson	Mar. 4, 1801-Mar. 3, 1805	3.	Aaron Burr	7, 8
		Mar. 4, 1805-Mar. 3, 1809	4.	George Clinton	9, 10
4.	James Madison	Mar. 4, 1809-Mar. 3, 1813		George Clinton[1]	11, 12
		Mar. 4, 1813-Mar. 3, 1817	5.	Elbridge Gerry[2]	13, 14
5.	James Monroe	Mar. 4, 1817-Mar. 3, 1825	6.	Daniel D. Tompkins	15, 16, 17, 18
6.	John Quincy Adams	Mar. 4, 1825-Mar. 3, 1829	7.	John C. Calhoun	19, 20
7.	Andrew Jackson	Mar. 4, 1829-Mar. 3, 1833		John C. Calhoun[3]	21, 22
		Mar. 4, 1833-Mar. 3, 1837	8.	Martin Van Buren	23, 24
8.	Martin Van Buren	Mar. 4, 1837-Mar. 3, 1841	9.	Richard M. Johnson	25, 26
9.	William Henry Harrison[4]	Mar. 4, 1841-Apr. 4, 1841	10.	John Tyler	27
10.	John Tyler	Apr. 6, 1841-Mar. 3, 1845		(None)	27, 28
11.	James K. Polk	Mar. 4, 1845-Mar. 3, 1849	11.	George M. Dallas	29, 30
12.	Zachary Taylor[4]	Mar. 5, 1849-July 9, 1850	12.	Millard Fillmore	31
13.	Millard Fillmore	July 10, 1850-Mar. 3, 1853		(None)	31, 32
14.	Franklin Pierce	Mar. 4, 1853-Mar. 3, 1857	13.	William R. King[5]	33, 34
15.	James Buchanan	Mar. 4, 1857-Mar. 3, 1861	14.	John C. Breckinridge	35, 36
16.	Abraham Lincoln	Mar. 4, 1861-Mar. 3, 1865	15.	Hannibal Hamlin	37, 38
	(4)	Mar. 4, 1865-Apr. 15, 1865	16.	Andrew Johnson	39
17.	Andrew Johnson	Apr. 15, 1865-Mar. 3, 1869		(None)	39, 40
18.	Ulysses S. Grant	Mar. 4, 1869-Mar. 3, 1873	17.	Schuyler Colfax	41, 42
		Mar. 4, 1873-Mar. 3, 1877	18.	Henry Wilson[6]	43, 44
19.	Rutherford B. Hayes	Mar. 4, 1877-Mar. 3, 1881	19.	William A. Wheeler	45, 46
20.	James A. Garfield[4]	Mar. 4, 1881-Sept. 19, 1881	20.	Chester A. Arthur	47
21.	Chester A. Arthur	Sept. 20, 1881-Mar. 3, 1885		(None)	47, 48
22.	Grover Cleveland[7]	Mar. 4, 1885-Mar. 3, 1889	21.	Thomas A. Hendricks[8]	49, 50
23.	Benjamin Harrison	Mar. 4, 1889-Mar. 3, 1893	22.	Levi P. Morton	51, 52
24.	Grover Cleveland[7]	Mar. 4, 1893-Mar. 3, 1897	23.	Adlai E. Stevenson	53, 54
25.	William McKinley	Mar. 4, 1897-Mar. 3, 1901	24.	Garret A. Hobart[9]	55, 56
	(4)	Mar. 4, 1901-Sept. 14, 1901	25.	Theodore Roosevelt	57
26.	Theodore Roosevelt	Sept. 14, 1901-Mar. 3, 1905		(None)	57, 58
		Mar. 4, 1905-Mar. 3, 1909	26.	Charles W. Fairbanks	59, 60
27.	William H. Taft	Mar. 4, 1909-Mar. 3, 1913	27.	James S. Sherman[10]	61, 62

President	Service	Vice President	Congresses
28. Woodrow Wilson	Mar. 4, 1913-Mar. 3, 1921	28. Thomas R. Marshall	63, 64, 65, 66
29. Warren G. Harding[4]	Mar. 4, 1921-Aug. 2, 1923	29. Calvin Coolidge	67
30. Calvin Coolidge	Aug. 3, 1923-Mar. 3, 1925	(None)	68
	Mar. 4, 1925-Mar. 3, 1929	30. Charles G. Dawes	69, 70
31. Herbert C. Hoover	Mar. 4, 1929-Mar. 3, 1933	31. Charles Curtis	71, 72
32. Franklin D. Roosevelt[11]	Mar. 4, 1933-Jan. 20, 1941	32. John N. Garner	73, 74, 75, 76, 77
	Jan. 20, 1941-Jan. 20, 1945	33. Henry A. Wallace	77, 78, 79
(4)	Jan. 20, 1945-Apr. 12, 1945	34. Harry S. Truman	79
33. Harry S. Truman	Apr. 12, 1945-Jan. 20, 1949	(None)	79, 80, 81
	Jan. 20, 1949-Jan. 20, 1953	35. Alben W. Barkley	81, 82, 83
34. Dwight D. Eisenhower	Jan. 20, 1953-Jan. 20, 1961	36. Richard M. Nixon	83, 84, 85, 86, 87
35. John F. Kennedy[4]	Jan. 20, 1961-Nov. 22, 1963	37. Lyndon B. Johnson	87, 88
36. Lyndon B. Johnson	Nov. 22, 1963-Jan. 20, 1965	(None)	88, 89
	Jan. 20, 1965-Jan. 20, 1969	38. Hubert H. Humphrey	89, 90, 91
37. Richard M. Nixon	Jan. 20, 1969-Jan. 20, 1973	39. Spiro T. Agnew[12]	91, 92, 93
(13)	Jan. 20, 1973-Aug. 9, 1974	40. Gerald R. Ford[14]	93
38. Gerald R. Ford[15]	Aug. 9, 1974-Jan. 20, 1977	41. Nelson A. Rockefeller[16]	93, 94, 95
39. Jimmy Carter	Jan. 20, 1977-Jan. 20, 1981	42. Walter F. Mondale	95, 96, 97
40. Ronald W. Reagan	Jan. 20, 1981-Jan. 20, 1989	43. George H. W. Bush	97, 98, 99, 100, 101
41. George H. W. Bush	Jan. 20, 1989-Jan. 20, 1993	44. Dan Quayle	101, 102, 103
42. Bill Clinton	Jan. 20, 1993-Jan. 20, 2001	45. Al Gore	103, 104, 105, 106, 107
43. George W. Bush	Jan. 20, 2001-Jan. 20, 2009	46. Dick Cheney	107, 108, 109, 110, 111
44. Barack H. Obama	Jan. 20, 2009-	47. Joe Biden	111, 112, 113

(1) Died Apr. 20, 1812. (2) Died Nov. 23, 1814. (3) Resigned Dec. 28, 1832, to become U.S. senator. (4) Died in office. (5) Died Apr. 18, 1853. (6) Died Nov. 22, 1875. (7) Terms not consecutive. (8) Died Nov. 25, 1885. (9) Died Nov. 21, 1899. (10) Died Oct. 30, 1912. (11) First president to be inaugurated under 20th Amendment, Jan. 20, 1937. (12) Resigned Oct. 10, 1973, after pleading no contest to a charge of tax evasion. (13) Resigned Aug. 9, 1974. (14) First nonelected vice president, chosen under 25th Amendment procedure. (15) First president never elected president or vice president. (16) Second nonelected vice president, chosen under 25th Amendment. Confirmed Dec. 19, 1974.

Vice Presidents of the U.S.

The numerals given vice presidents do not coincide with those given presidents because some presidents (Tyler, Fillmore, A. Johnson, Arthur) had none, and some had more than one.

Name	Birthplace	Year of birth	Home	Inaug.	Politics	Place of death	Year of death	Age at death
1. John Adams	Quincy, MA	1735	MA	1789	Fed.	Quincy, MA	1826	90
2. Thomas Jefferson	Shadwell, VA	1743	VA	1797	Dem.-Rep.	Monticello, VA	1826	83
3. Aaron Burr	Newark, NJ	1756	NY	1801	Dem.-Rep.	Staten Island, NY	1836	80
4. George Clinton	Little Britain, NY	1739	NY	1805	Dem.-Rep.	Washington, DC	1812	73
5. Elbridge Gerry	Marblehead, MA	1744	MA	1813	Dem.-Rep.	Washington, DC	1814	70
6. Daniel D. Tompkins	Scarsdale, NY	1774	NY	1817	Dem.-Rep.	Staten Island, NY	1825	51
7. John C. Calhoun[1]	Abbeville, SC	1782	SC	1825	Dem.-Rep.	Washington, DC	1850	68
8. Martin Van Buren	Kinderhook, NY	1782	NY	1833	Dem.	Kinderhook, NY	1862	79
9. Richard M. Johnson[2]	Louisville, KY	1780	KY	1837	Dem.	Frankfort, KY	1850	70
10. John Tyler	Greenway, VA	1790	VA	1841	Whig	Richmond, VA	1862	71
11. George M. Dallas	Philadelphia, PA	1792	PA	1845	Dem.	Philadelphia, PA	1864	72
12. Millard Fillmore	Cayuga Co., NY	1800	NY	1849	Whig	Buffalo, NY	1874	74
13. William R. King	Sampson Co., NC	1786	AL	1853	Dem.	Cahaba, AL	1853	67
14. John C. Breckinridge	Lexington, KY	1821	KY	1857	Dem.	Lexington, KY	1875	54
15. Hannibal Hamlin	Paris, ME	1809	ME	1861	Rep.	Bangor, ME	1891	81
16. Andrew Johnson	Raleigh, NC	1808	TN	1865	(3)	Carter Co., TN	1875	66
17. Schuyler Colfax	New York, NY	1823	IN	1869	Rep.	Mankato, MN	1885	62
18. Henry Wilson	Farmington, NH	1812	MA	1873	Rep.	Washington, DC	1875	63
19. William A. Wheeler	Malone, NY	1819	NY	1877	Rep.	Malone, NY	1887	68
20. Chester A. Arthur	Fairfield, VT	1829	NY	1881	Rep.	New York, NY	1886	57
21. Thomas A. Hendricks	Zanesville, OH	1819	IN	1885	Dem.	Indianapolis, IN	1885	66
22. Levi P. Morton	Shoreham, VT	1824	NY	1889	Rep.	Rhinebeck, NY	1920	96
23. Adlai E. Stevenson[4]	Christian Co., KY	1835	IL	1893	Dem.	Chicago, IL	1914	78
24. Garret A. Hobart	Long Branch, NJ	1844	NJ	1897	Rep.	Paterson, NJ	1899	55
25. Theodore Roosevelt	New York, NY	1858	NY	1901	Rep.	Oyster Bay, NY	1919	60
26. Charles W. Fairbanks	Unionville Centre, OH	1852	IN	1905	Rep.	Indianapolis, IN	1918	66
27. James S. Sherman	Utica, NY	1855	NY	1909	Rep.	Utica, NY	1912	57
28. Thomas R. Marshall	N. Manchester, IN	1854	IN	1913	Dem.	Washington, DC	1925	71
29. Calvin Coolidge	Plymouth Notch, VT	1872	MA	1921	Rep.	Northampton, MA	1933	60
30. Charles G. Dawes	Marietta, OH	1865	IL	1925	Rep.	Evanston, IL	1951	85
31. Charles Curtis	Topeka, KS	1860	KS	1929	Rep.	Washington, DC	1936	76
32. John Nance Garner	Red River Co., TX	1868	TX	1933	Dem.	Uvalde, TX	1967	98
33. Henry A. Wallace	Adair County, IA	1888	IA	1941	Dem.	Danbury, CT	1965	77
34. Harry S. Truman	Lamar, MO	1884	MO	1945	Dem.	Kansas City, MO	1972	88
35. Alben W. Barkley	Graves County, KY	1877	KY	1949	Dem.	Lexington, VA	1956	78
36. Richard M. Nixon	Yorba Linda, CA	1913	CA	1953	Rep.	New York, NY	1994	81
37. Lyndon B. Johnson	Stonewall, TX	1908	TX	1961	Dem.	San Antonio, TX	1973	64
38. Hubert H. Humphrey	Wallace, SD	1911	MN	1965	Dem.	Waverly, MN	1978	66
39. Spiro T. Agnew[5]	Baltimore, MD	1918	MD	1969	Rep.	Berlin, MD	1996	77
40. Gerald R. Ford[6]	Omaha, NE	1913	MI	1973	Rep.	Rancho Mirage, CA	2006	93
41. Nelson A. Rockefeller[7]	Bar Harbor, ME	1908	NY	1974	Rep.	New York, NY	1979	70
42. Walter F. Mondale	Ceylon, MN	1928	MN	1977	Dem.			
43. George H. W. Bush	Milton, MA	1924	TX	1981	Rep.			
44. James Danforth (Dan) Quayle Jr.	Indianapolis, IN	1947	IN	1989	Rep.			
45. Albert A. Gore	Washington, DC	1948	TN	1993	Dem.			
46. Richard B. Cheney	Lincoln, NE	1941	WY	2001	Rep.			
47. Joseph R. Biden Jr.	Scranton, PA	1942	DE	2009	Dem.			

(1) Resigned Dec. 28, 1832, having been elected to the Senate to fill a vacancy. (2) Richard M. Johnson was the only vice president to be chosen by the Senate because of a tied vote in the Electoral College. (3) Democrat Andrew Johnson was nominated vice president by Republicans and elected with Lincoln on the National Union Ticket. (4) Grandfather of Democratic candidate for president in 1952 and 1956. (5) Resigned Oct. 10, 1973, after pleading no contest to a charge of tax evasion. (6) First nonelected vice president, chosen under 25th Amendment procedure. (7) Second nonelected vice president, chosen under 25th Amendment.

Biographies of the Presidents

George Washington (1789-97), first president, Federalist, was born on Feb. 22, 1732, in Wakefield on Pope's Creek, Westmoreland Co., VA, the son of Augustine and Mary Ball Washington. He spent his early childhood on a farm near Fredericksburg. His father died when Washington was 11. He studied mathematics and surveying, and at 16, he went to live with his elder half brother, Lawrence, who built and named Mount Vernon in Virginia. Washington surveyed the lands of Thomas Fairfax in the Shenandoah Valley. He accompanied Lawrence to Barbados, West Indies, where he contracted smallpox and was deeply scarred. Lawrence died in 1752, and Washington inherited his property. He valued land, and when he died, he owned 70,000 acres in Virginia and 40,000 acres in what is now West Virginia.

Washington's military service began in 1753, when Lt. Gov. Robert Dinwiddie of Virginia sent him on missions deep into Ohio country. He clashed with the French and had to surrender Fort Necessity on July 3, 1754. He was an aide to the British general Edward Braddock and was at his side when the army was ambushed and defeated (July 9, 1755) on a march to Fort Duquesne. He helped take Fort Duquesne from the French in 1758.

After Washington's marriage to Martha Dandridge Custis, a widow, in 1759, he managed his family estate at Mount Vernon. Although not at first for independence, he opposed the repressive measures of the British crown and took charge of the Virginia troops before war broke out. He was made commander of the newly created Continental Army by the Continental Congress on June 15, 1775.

The American victory was due largely to Washington's leadership. He was resourceful, a disciplinarian, and the one dependable force for unity. Washington favored a federal government. He became chairman of the Constitutional Convention of 1787 and helped get the Constitution ratified. Unanimously elected president by the Electoral College he was inaugurated Apr. 30, 1789, on the balcony of New York's Federal Hall. He was reelected in 1792. Washington made an effort to avoid partisan politics as president.

Refusing to consider a third term, Washington retired to Mount Vernon in Mar. 1797. A ride in snow and rain around his estate led to what present-day doctors believe to have been an attack of acute epiglottitis. Doctors were unsuccessful in treating the inflammation in his throat, and Washington died Dec. 14, 1799.

John Adams (1797-1801), second president, Federalist, was born on Oct. 30, 1735, in Braintree (now Quincy), MA, the son of John and Susanna Boylston Adams. He was a great-grandson of Henry Adams, who came from England in 1636. He graduated from Harvard in 1755, then taught school and studied law. He married Abigail Smith in 1764. In 1765 he argued against taxation without representation before the royal governor. In 1770, he successfully defended in court the British soldiers who fired on civilians in the Boston Massacre. He was a delegate to the Continental Congress and a signer of the Declaration of Independence. In 1778, Congress sent Adams and John Jay to join Benjamin Franklin as diplomatic representatives in Europe. Because he ran second to Washington in Electoral College balloting in Feb. 1789, Adams became the nation's first vice president, a post he characterized as highly insignificant; he was reelected in 1792.

In 1796 Adams was chosen president by the electors. His administration was marked by growing conflict with fellow Federalist Alexander Hamilton and with others in his own cabinet who supported Hamilton's strongly anti-French position. Adams avoided full-scale war with France but became unpopular, especially after securing passage of the Alien and Sedition Acts in 1798. His foreign policy contributed significantly to the election of Thomas Jefferson in 1800.

Adams lived for a quarter century after he left office, during which time he wrote extensively. He died July 4, 1826, on the same day as his rival Thomas Jefferson (the 50th anniversary of the Declaration of Independence).

Thomas Jefferson (1801-09), third president, Democratic-Republican, was born on Apr. 13, 1743, in Shadwell in Goochland (now Albemarle) Co., VA, the son of Peter and Jane Randolph Jefferson. His father died when Jefferson was 14, leaving him 2,750 acres and his slaves. Jefferson attended (1760-62) the College of William and Mary, read Greek and Latin classics, and played the violin. In 1769 he was elected to the Virginia House of Burgesses. In 1770 he began building his home, Monticello, and in 1772 he married Martha Wayles Skelton, a wealthy widow. Jefferson helped establish the Virginia Committee of Correspondence. As a member of the Second Continental Congress he drafted the Declaration of Independence. He also was a member of the Virginia House of Delegates (1776-79) and was elected governor of Virginia in 1779. Reelected in 1780, he resigned the next year after British troops invaded Virginia. During his term he wrote the statute on religious freedom. After his wife's death in 1782, Jefferson again became a delegate to the Congress, and in 1784 he drafted the report that was the basis for the Ordinances of 1784, 1785, and 1787. He was minister to France from 1785 to 1789, when George Washington appointed him secretary of state.

Jefferson's strong faith in the consent of the governed conflicted with the emphasis on executive control, favored by Sec. of the Treasury Alexander Hamilton, and Jefferson resigned on Dec. 31, 1793. In the 1796 election Jefferson was the Democratic-Republican candidate for president; John Adams won the election, and Jefferson became vice president. In 1800, Jefferson and Aaron Burr received equal Electoral College votes; the House of Representatives elected Jefferson president. Jefferson was a strong advocate of westward expansion; major events of his first term were the Louisiana Purchase (1803) and the Lewis and Clark expedition. An important development during his second term was passage of the Embargo Act, barring U.S. ships from setting sail to foreign ports. Jefferson established the Univ. of Virginia and designed its buildings. He died July 4, 1826, on the same day as John Adams (the 50th anniversary of the Declaration of Independence).

Analysis of contemporary accounts, plantation records, and DNA taken from descendants of Jefferson and of Sally Hemings, one of his slaves, has caused many historians to conclude Jefferson fathered one or more of her six children.

James Madison (1809-17), fourth president, Democratic-Republican, was born on Mar. 16, 1751, in Port Conway, King George Co., VA, the son of James and Eleanor Rose Conway Madison. Madison graduated from the College of New Jersey in 1771. He served in the Virginia Constitutional Convention (1776), and, in 1780, became a delegate to the Second Continental Congress. He was chief recorder at the Constitutional Convention in 1787 and supported ratification in the *Federalist Papers*, written with Alexander Hamilton and John Jay. In 1789, Madison was elected to the House of Representatives, where he helped frame the Bill of Rights and fought against passage of the Alien and Sedition Acts. In the 1790s, he helped found the Democratic-Republican Party, which ultimately became the Democratic Party. He became Jefferson's secretary of state in 1801.

Madison was elected president in 1808. His first term was marked by tensions with Great Britain, and his conduct of foreign policy was criticized by the Federalists and by his own party. Nevertheless, he was reelected in 1812, the year war was declared on Great Britain. The war that many considered a second American revolution ended with a treaty that did not settle any of the issues. Madison's most important action after the war was demilitarizing the U.S.-Canadian border.

In 1817, Madison retired to his estate, Montpelier, where he served as an elder statesman. He edited his famous papers on the Constitutional Convention and helped found the Univ. of Virginia, of which he became rector in 1826. He died June 28, 1836.

James Monroe (1817-25), fifth president, Democratic-Republican, was born on Apr. 28, 1758, in Westmoreland Co., VA, the son of Spence and Elizabeth Jones Monroe. He entered the College of William and Mary in 1774 but left to serve in the Third Virginia Regiment during the American Revolution. After the war, he studied law with Thomas Jefferson. In 1782 he was elected to the Virginia House of Delegates, and he served (1783-86) as a delegate to the Continental Congress. He opposed ratification of the Constitution because it lacked a bill of rights. Monroe was elected to the U.S. Senate in 1790. In 1794, Pres. Washington appointed Monroe minister to France. He served twice as governor of Virginia (1799-1802, 1811). Pres. Jefferson also sent him to France as minister (1803), and from 1803 to 1807, he served as minister to Great Britain.

In 1816 Monroe was elected president; he was reelected in 1820 with all but one Electoral College vote. His administration became known as the Era of Good Feeling. He obtained Florida from Spain, settled boundary disputes with Britain over Canada, and eliminated border forts. He supported the antislavery position that led to the Missouri Compromise. His most significant contribution was the Monroe Doctrine, which opposed European intervention in the Western Hemisphere and became a cornerstone of U.S. foreign policy.

Although Monroe retired to Oak Hill, VA, financial problems forced him to sell his property and move to New York City. He died there on July 4, 1831.

John Quincy Adams (1825-29), sixth president, independent Federalist, later Democratic-Republican, was born on July 11, 1767, in Braintree (now Quincy), MA, the son of John and Abigail Adams. His father was the second president. He studied abroad and at Harvard College, from which he graduated in 1787. In 1803, he was elected to the U.S. Senate. President Monroe chose him as his secretary of state in 1817. In this capacity he negotiated the cession of Florida from Spain, supported exclusion of slavery in the Missouri Compromise, and helped formulate the Monroe Doctrine.

After no candidate won an Electoral College majority in 1824, the presidential election was thrown into the House of Representatives; Adams won with support from rival Henry Clay, whom he named secretary of state, fueling accusations of a "corrupt bargain." His expansion of executive powers was strongly opposed, and in the 1828 election he lost to Andrew Jackson. In 1831 he entered the House of Representatives and served 17 years with distinction. He opposed slavery, the annexation of Texas, and the Mexican War. He helped establish the Smithsonian Institution.

Adams suffered a stroke in the House and died in the Speaker's Room on Feb. 23, 1848.

Andrew Jackson (1829-37), seventh president, Democratic-Republican, later a Democrat, was born on Mar. 15, 1767, in the Waxhaw district, on the border of North and South Carolina, the son of Andrew and Elizabeth Hutchinson Jackson. At the age of 13, he joined the militia to fight in the American Revolution and was captured. Orphaned at age 14, Jackson was brought up by a well-to-do uncle. By age 20, he was practicing law, and he later served as prosecuting attorney in Nashville, TN. In 1796 he helped draft the constitution of Tennessee, and for a year he occupied its one seat in the House of Representatives. The next year he served in the U.S. Senate.

In the War of 1812, Jackson crushed the Creek Indians at Horseshoe Bend, AL (1814), and, with a greatly outnumbered army consisting chiefly of backwoods militia members and volunteers, defeated Gen. Edward Pakenham's British troops at the Battle of New Orleans (1815). Nicknamed "Old Hickory" for his toughness, he emerged a national hero.

In 1818 Jackson briefly invaded Spanish Florida to quell Seminoles and outlaws who harassed frontier settlements. He ran for president against John Quincy Adams in 1824, but, although he won the most popular and electoral votes, he did not have a majority. The House of Representatives decided the election and chose Adams. In the 1828 election, however, Jackson defeated Adams, carrying the West and the South.

As president, Jackson introduced what became known as the spoils system—rewarding party members with government posts. A self-professed champion of the common man, he also viewed the Second Bank of the U.S. as a bastion of privilege and made it a major issue in the election of 1832, the first where candidates were chosen at national conventions rather than in congressional caucuses. Defeating Henry Clay, Jackson increasingly diverted funds from the national bank into so-called pet banks run by members of his own party. When South Carolina refused to collect imports under a federal tariff, which it declared null and void, Jackson won passage of legislation confirming his right to use military force to obtain compliance; eventually the tariff rate was reduced and the nullifiers backed down. After leaving office in 1837, he retired to the Hermitage, his estate outside Nashville, where he died on June 8, 1845.

Martin Van Buren (1837-41), eighth president, Democrat, was born on Dec. 5, 1782, in Kinderhook, NY, the son of Abraham and Maria Hoes Van Buren. After attending local schools, he studied law and became a lawyer at the age of 20. A consummate politician, Van Buren began his career in the New York state senate and then served as state attorney general (1816-19). He was elected to the U.S. Senate in 1821. He helped swing Eastern support to Andrew Jackson in the 1828 election and then served as Jackson's secretary of state from 1829 to 1831. In 1832 he was elected vice president. Known as the "Little Magician," Van Buren was extremely influential in Jackson's administration.

In 1836, Van Buren defeated William Henry Harrison for president and took office as the financial panic of 1837 initiated a nationwide depression. Although he instituted the independent treasury system, his refusal to spend land revenues led to his defeat by William Henry Harrison in 1840. In 1844 he lost the Democratic nomination to James K. Polk. In 1848 he again ran for president on the Free Soil ticket but lost. He died in Kinderhook on July 24, 1862.

William Henry Harrison (1841), ninth president, Whig, who served only 31 days, was born on Feb. 9, 1773, in Berkeley, Charles City Co., VA, the son of Benjamin Harrison—a signer of the Declaration of Independence—and of Elizabeth Bassett Harrison. He attended Hampden-Sydney College. Harrison served as secretary of the Northwest Territory in 1798 and was its delegate to the House of Representatives in 1799. He was the first governor of Indiana Territory and served as superintendent of Indian affairs. With 900 men he put down a Shawnee uprising at Tippecanoe, IN, on Nov. 7, 1811. A generation later, in 1840, he waged a rousing presidential campaign, using the slogan "Tippecanoe and Tyler Too." The Tyler of the slogan was his running mate, John Tyler.

Although born to one of the wealthiest, most prestigious, and most influential families in Virginia, Harrison was elected president with the slogan, "Log Cabin and Hard Cider." He caught pneumonia during his inauguration and died Apr. 4, 1841, after only one month in office.

John Tyler (1841-45), 10th president, independent Whig, was born on Mar. 29, 1790, in Greenway, Charles City Co., VA, the son of John and Mary Armistead Tyler. His father was governor of Virginia (1808-11). Tyler graduated from the College of William and Mary in 1807 and in 1811 was elected to the Virginia legislature. In 1816 he was chosen for the U.S. House of Representatives. He served in the Virginia legislature again from 1823 to 1825, when he was elected governor of Virginia. After a stint in the U.S. Senate (1827-36), he was elected vice president (1840).

When William Henry Harrison died only a month after taking office, Tyler succeeded him. Because he was the first person to occupy the presidency without having been elected to that office, he was referred to as "His Accidency." He gained passage of the Preemption Act of 1841, which gave squatters on government land the right to buy 160 acres at the minimum auction price. His last act as president was to sign a resolution annexing Texas. Tyler accepted renomination in 1844 from some Democrats but withdrew in favor of the official party candidate, James K. Polk. A strong advocate of states' rights, he served briefly in the Confederate House of Representatives before he died in Richmond, VA, on Jan. 18, 1862.

James Knox Polk (1845-49), 11th president, Democrat, was born on Nov. 2, 1795, in Mecklenburg Co., NC, the son of Samuel and Jane Knox Polk. He graduated from the Univ. of North Carolina in 1818 and served in the Tennessee state legislature from 1823 to 1825. He served in the U.S. House of Representatives from 1825 to 1839, the last four years as Speaker. He was governor of Tennessee from 1839 to 1841. In 1844, after the Democratic National Convention became deadlocked, it nominated Polk, who became the first "dark horse" candidate for president. He was nominated primarily because he favored annexation of Texas.

As president, Polk reestablished the independent treasury system originated by Van Buren. He was so intent on acquiring California from Mexico that he sent troops to the Mexican border and, when Mexicans attacked, declared that a state of war existed. The Mexican War ended with the annexation of California and much of the Southwest as part of America's "manifest destiny." Polk compromised on the Oregon boundary ("54-40 or fight!") by accepting the 49th parallel and yielding Vancouver Island to the British. Polk died in Nashville, TN, on June 15, 1849, a few months after leaving office.

Zachary Taylor (1849-50), 12th president, Whig, who served only 16 months, was born on Nov. 24, 1784, in Orange Co., VA, the son of Richard and Sarah Strother Taylor. He grew up on his father's plantation near Louisville, KY, where he was educated by private tutors. In 1808 Taylor joined the regular army and was commissioned first lieutenant. He fought in the War of 1812, the Black Hawk War (1832), and the second Seminole War (beginning in 1837). He was called "Old Rough and Ready." In 1846 Pres. Polk sent him with an army to the Rio Grande. When the Mexicans attacked him, Polk declared war. Outnumbered four to one, Taylor defeated Antonio López de Santa Anna at Buena Vista (1847).

A national hero, Taylor received the Whig nomination in 1848 and was elected president, even though he had never bothered to vote. He resumed the spoils system and, though a slaveholder, worked to admit California as a free state. He fell ill, likely from a case of acute gastroenteritis, and died in office on July 9, 1850.

Millard Fillmore (1850-53), 13th president, Whig, was born on Jan. 7, 1800, in Cayuga Co., NY, the son of Nathaniel and Phoebe Millard Fillmore. Although he had little schooling, he became a law clerk at the age of 22 and a year later was admitted to the bar. He was elected to the New York state assembly in 1828 and served until 1831. From 1833 until 1835 and again from 1837 to 1843, he represented his district in the U.S. House of Representatives. He opposed the entrance of Texas as a slave state and voted for a protective tariff. In 1844 he was defeated for governor of New York.

In 1848, he was elected vice president, and he succeeded as president after Taylor's death. Fillmore favored the Compromise of 1850 and signed the Fugitive Slave Law. His policies pleased neither expansionists nor slaveholders, and he was not renominated in 1852. In 1856 he was nominated by the American (Know-Nothing) Party, but despite the support of the Whigs, he was defeated by James Buchanan. He died in Buffalo, NY, on Mar. 8, 1874.

Franklin Pierce (1853-57), 14th president, Democrat, was born on Nov. 23, 1804, in Hillsboro, NH, the son of Benjamin Pierce, Revolutionary War general and governor of New Hampshire, and Anna Kendrick. He graduated from Bowdoin College in 1824 and was admitted to the bar in 1827. He was elected to the New Hampshire state legislature in 1829 and was chosen Speaker in 1831. He went to the U.S. House in 1833 and was elected a U.S. senator in 1837. He enlisted in the Mexican War and became brigadier general under Gen. Winfield Scott.

In 1852 Pierce was nominated as the Democratic presidential candidate on the 49th ballot. He decisively defeated Gen. Scott, his Whig opponent, in the election. Although he was against slavery, Pierce was influenced by proslavery Southerners. He supported the controversial Kansas-Nebraska Act, which left the question of slavery in the new territories of Kansas and Nebraska to popular vote. Pierce signed a reciprocity treaty with Canada and approved the Gadsden Purchase of a border area on a proposed railroad route, from Mexico. Denied renomination, he spent most of his remaining years in Concord, NH, where he died on Oct. 8, 1869.

James Buchanan (1857-61), 15th president, Federalist, later Democrat, was born on Apr. 23, 1791, near Mercersburg, PA, the son of James and Elizabeth Speer Buchanan. He graduated from Dickinson College in 1809 and was admitted to the bar in 1812. He fought in the War of 1812 as a volunteer. He was twice elected to the Pennsylvania general assembly, and in 1821 he entered the U.S. House of Representatives. After briefly serving (1832-33) as minister to Russia, he was elected U.S. senator from Pennsylvania. As Polk's secretary of state (1845-49), he ended the Oregon dispute with Britain and supported the Mexican War and annexation of Texas. As minister to Great Britain, he signed the Ostend Manifesto (1854), declaring a U.S. right to take Cuba by force should efforts to purchase it fail.

Nominated by Democrats, Buchanan was elected president in 1856. On slavery he favored popular sovereignty and choice by state constitutions but did not consistently uphold this position. He denied the right of states to secede but opposed coercion and attempted to keep peace by not provoking secessionists. Buchanan left office having failed to deal decisively with the situation. He died at Wheatland, his estate, near Lancaster, PA, on June 1, 1868.

Abraham Lincoln (1861-65), 16th president, Whig, then Republican, was born on Feb. 12, 1809, in a log cabin on a farm in Hardin (now Larue) Co., KY, the son of Thomas and Nancy Hanks Lincoln. The Lincolns moved to Spencer Co., IN, near Gentryville, when Lincoln was 7. After Lincoln's mother died, his father married Mrs. Sarah Bush Johnston in 1819. In 1830 the family moved to Macon Co., IL.

Defeated in 1832 in a race for the state legislature, Lincoln was elected on the Whig ticket two years later and served in the lower house from 1834 to 1842. In 1837 Lincoln was admitted to the bar and became partner in a Springfield, IL, law office. In 1846, he was elected to Congress, where he attracted attention during a single term for his opposition to the Mexican War and his position on slavery. In 1856 he campaigned for the newly founded Republican Party, and in 1858 he became its senatorial candidate against Stephen A. Douglas. Although he lost the election, Lincoln gained national recognition from his debates with Douglas.

In 1860, Lincoln was nominated for president by the Republican Party on a platform of restricting slavery. He ran against Douglas, a northern Democrat; John C. Breckinridge, a Southern proslavery Democrat; and John Bell, of the Constitutional Union Party. In response to Lincoln's victory, South Carolina seceded from the Union on Dec. 20, 1860, soon followed by six other Southern states.

The Civil War erupted when Fort Sumter, which Lincoln decided to resupply, was attacked by Confederate forces on Apr. 12, 1861. Lincoln called successfully for recruits from the North, and four more Southern states seceded. Hundreds of thousands of Union and Confederate soldiers were killed or wounded in four years of battle that followed. On Sept. 22, 1862, five days after the Battle of Antietam, Lincoln announced that slaves in territory then in rebellion would be free Jan. 1, 1863, under his Emancipation Proclamation. His speeches, including his Gettysburg and inaugural addresses, are remembered for their eloquence.

Lincoln was reelected, in 1864, over Gen. George B. McClellan, a Democrat. Confederate Gen. Robert E. Lee surrendered on Apr. 9, 1865. On Apr. 14, Lincoln was shot by actor

John Wilkes Booth in Ford's Theater, in Washington, DC. He died the next day.

Andrew Johnson (1865-69), 17th president, Democrat, was born on Dec. 29, 1808, in Raleigh, NC, the son of Jacob and Mary McDonough Johnson. He was apprenticed to a tailor as a youth but ran away after two years and eventually settled in Greeneville, TN, where he was elected councilman and later mayor. In 1835 he was sent to the state general assembly. In 1843 he was elected to the U.S. House of Representatives, where he served for 10 years. Johnson was also governor of Tennessee from 1853 to 1857, when he was elected to the U.S. Senate. Although Johnson had held slaves, he opposed secession and tried to prevent Tennessee from seceding. In Mar. 1862, Lincoln appointed him military governor of occupied Tennessee.

In 1864, in order to balance Lincoln's ticket with a Southern Democrat, the Republicans nominated Johnson for vice president. He was elected vice president with Lincoln and then succeeded to the presidency upon Lincoln's death. Soon afterward, in a controversy with Congress over the president's power over the South, he proclaimed an amnesty to all Confederates, except certain leaders, if they would ratify the 13th Amendment abolishing slavery. States doing so added anti-Negro provisions that enraged Congress, which restored military control over the South. When Johnson removed Sec. of War Edwin M. Stanton without notifying the Senate, the House impeached him in Feb. 1868. Charging him with thereby having violated the Tenure of Office Act, the House was actually responding to his opposition to harsh congressional Reconstruction, expressed in repeated vetoes. He was acquitted in the Senate by one-vote margins on each of two counts.

Johnson was denied renomination but remained politically active. He was reelected to the Senate in 1874. Johnson died July 31, 1875, at Carter Station, TN.

Ulysses S. Grant (1869-77), 18th president, Republican, was born on Apr. 27, 1822, in Point Pleasant, OH, the son of Jesse R. and Hannah Simpson Grant. The next year the family moved to Georgetown, OH. Grant was named Hiram Ulysses. Upon entering West Point in 1839, he found his name had been put down as Ulysses S. Grant, with his middle name first and his mother's maiden name as his middle name. He eventually adopted it as his true name but maintained the "S" did not stand for anything. Grant graduated in 1843. During the Mexican War, Grant served under both Gen. Zachary Taylor and Gen. Winfield Scott. In 1854, he resigned his commission because of loneliness and drinking problems, and in the following years he engaged in generally unsuccessful farming and business ventures. With the start of the Civil War, he was named colonel and then brigadier general of the Illinois Volunteers. He took Forts Henry and Donelson and fought at Shiloh. His brilliant campaign against Vicksburg and his victory at Chattanooga made him so prominent that Lincoln placed him in command of all Union armies. Grant accepted Confederate Gen. Robert E. Lee's surrender at Appomattox Court House on Apr. 9, 1865.

Grant was nominated for president by the Republicans in 1868 and elected over Democrat Horatio Seymour. The 15th Amendment, the amnesty bill, and peaceful settlement of disputes with Great Britain were events of his administration. The Liberal Republicans and Democrats opposed him with Horace Greeley in the 1872 election, but Grant was reelected. His second administration was marked by scandals, including the Crédit Mobilier affair, the Whiskey Ring, in which high-ranked officials conspired to defraud the government of taxes, and the impeachment of his secretary of war. An attempt by the Stalwarts (Old Guard Republicans) to nominate him in 1880 failed. Left penniless by the 1884 collapse of an investment firm in which he was a partner, he wrote his well-regarded memoirs to provide income for his family while he was suffering from cancer. He died at Mt. McGregor, NY, on July 23, 1885.

Rutherford Birchard Hayes (1877-81), 19th president, Republican, was born on Oct. 4, 1822, in Delaware, OH, the son of Rutherford and Sophia Birchard Hayes. He was reared by his uncle, Sardis Birchard. Hayes graduated from Kenyon College in 1842 and from Harvard Law School in 1845. He practiced law in Lower Sandusky (now Fremont), OH, and was city solicitor of Cincinnati from 1858 to 1861. During the Civil War, he was major of the 23rd Ohio Volunteers. He was wounded several times, and by the end of the war he had risen to the rank of brevet major general. While serving (1865-67) in the U.S. House of Representatives, Hayes supported Reconstruction and Johnson's impeachment. He was twice elected governor of Ohio (1867, 1869). After losing a race for the U.S. House in 1872, he was reelected governor of Ohio in 1875.

In 1876, Hayes was nominated for president and believed he had lost the election to Democrat Samuel J. Tilden. But a few Southern states submitted two sets of electoral votes, and the result was in dispute. An electoral commission, consisting of 8 Republicans and 7 Democrats, awarded all disputed votes to Hayes, allowing him to become president by one electoral vote. Hayes, keeping a promise to Southerners, withdrew troops from areas still occupied in the South, ending the era of Reconstruction. He proposed civil service reforms, alienating those favoring the spoils system, and advocated repeal of the Tenure of Office Act restricting presidential power to dismiss officials. He supported sound money and specie payments.

Hayes died in Fremont, OH, on Jan. 17, 1893.

James Abram Garfield (1881), 20th president, Republican, was born on Nov. 19, 1831, in Orange, Cuyahoga Co., OH, the son of Abram and Eliza Ballou Garfield. His father died in 1833, and he was reared in poverty by his mother. He worked as a canal bargeman, a farmer, and a carpenter. He attended Western Reserve Eclectic Institute and graduated from Williams College in 1856. He returned to Western Reserve to teach and in 1857, at age 25, he became the school's president. In 1859 he was elected to the Ohio legislature. Antislavery and antisecession, he volunteered for military service in the Civil War, becoming colonel of the 42nd Ohio Infantry and brigadier in 1862. He fought at Shiloh, TN, as chief of staff for Gen. William Starke Rosecrans, and was made major general for gallantry at Chickamauga, GA. He entered Congress as a radical Republican in 1863, calling for execution or exile of Confederate leaders, but he moderated his views after the Civil War. On the electoral commission in 1877 he voted for Hayes against Tilden on strict party lines.

Garfield was a senator-elect in 1880 when he became the Republican nominee for president. He was chosen as a compromise over Gen. Grant, James G. Blaine, and John Sherman, and won election despite some bitterness among Grant's supporters. For much of his brief tenure as president, Garfield was concerned with a fight with New York Sen. Roscoe Conkling, who opposed two major appointments made by Garfield. On July 2, 1881, Garfield was shot and seriously wounded by a mentally disturbed office seeker, Charles J. Guiteau, while entering a railroad station in Washington, DC. He died on Sept. 19, 1881, in Elberon, NJ.

Chester Alan Arthur (1881-85), 21st president, Republican, was born on Oct. 5, 1829, in Fairfield, VT, to William and Malvina Stone Arthur. He graduated from Union College in 1848, taught school in Vermont, then studied law and practiced in New York City. In 1853, he argued in a fugitive slave case that slaves transported through New York State were thereby freed. In 1871, he was appointed collector of the Port of New York. Pres. Hayes, an opponent of the spoils system, forced him to resign in 1878. This made the New York machine enemies of Hayes. Arthur and the Stalwarts (Old Guard Republicans) tried to nominate Grant for a third term as president in 1880. When Garfield was nominated, Arthur was nominated for vice president in the interests of harmony.

Upon Garfield's assassination, Arthur became president. Despite his past connections, he signed major civil service reform legislation. Arthur tried to dissuade Congress from enacting the high protective tariff of 1883. He was defeated for renomination in 1884 by James G. Blaine. He died in New York City on Nov. 18, 1886.

Grover Cleveland (1885-89; 1893-97) *(According to a State Dept. ruling, Grover Cleveland should be counted as both the 22nd and the 24th president because his two terms were not consecutive)*, Democrat, was born Stephen Grover Cleveland on Mar. 18, 1837, in Caldwell, NJ, the son of Richard F. and Ann Neal Cleveland. When he was a small boy, his family moved to New York. Prevented by his father's death from attending college, he studied by himself and was admitted to the bar in Buffalo, NY, in 1859. In succession he became assistant district attorney (1863), sheriff (1871), mayor (1881), and governor of New York (1882). He was an independent, honest administrator who hated corruption. Cleveland was nominated for president over Tammany Hall opposition in 1884 and defeated Republican James G. Blaine.

As president, he enlarged the civil service and vetoed many pension raids on the Treasury. In the 1888 election he was defeated by Benjamin Harrison, although his popular vote was larger. Reelected over Harrison in 1892, he faced a money crisis brought about by a lowered gold reserve, circulation of paper, and exorbitant silver purchases under the Sherman Silver Purchase Act. He obtained a repeal of the Sherman Act but was unable to secure effective tariff reform. A severe economic depression and labor troubles racked his administration, but he refused to interfere in business matters and rejected Jacob Coxey's demand for unemployment relief. In 1894, he broke the Pullman strike. Cleveland was not renominated in 1896. He died in Princeton, NJ, on June 24, 1908.

Benjamin Harrison (1889-93), 23rd president, Republican, was born on Aug. 20, 1833, in North Bend, OH, the son of John Scott and Elizabeth Irwin Harrison. His great-grandfather, Benjamin Harrison, was a signer of the Declaration of Independence; his grandfather, William Henry Harrison, was the ninth president; his father was a member of Congress. He attended school on his father's farm and graduated from Miami Univ. in Oxford, OH, in 1852. He was admitted to the bar in 1854 and practiced in Indianapolis, IN. During the Civil War, he rose to the rank of brevet brigadier general and fought at Kennesaw Mountain, Peachtree Creek, Nashville, and in the Atlanta campaign. He lost the 1876 gubernatorial election in Indiana but succeeded in becoming a U.S. senator in 1881.

In 1888 he defeated Cleveland for president despite receiving fewer popular votes. As president, he expanded the pension list and signed the McKinley high tariff bill, the Sherman Antitrust Act, and the Sherman Silver Purchase Act. During his administration, six states were admitted to the Union. He was defeated for reelection in 1892. He died in Indianapolis, IN, on Mar. 13, 1901.

William McKinley (1897-1901), 25th president, Republican, was born on Jan. 29, 1843, in Niles, OH, the son of William and Nancy Allison McKinley. McKinley briefly attended Allegheny College. When the Civil War broke out in 1861, he enlisted and served for the duration. He rose to captain and in 1865 was made brevet major. After studying law in Albany, NY, he opened a law office in Canton, OH (1867). He served twice in the U.S. House (1877-83; 1885-91) and led the fight there for the McKinley Tariff, passed in 1890; he was not reelected to the House as a result. He served two terms (1892-96) as governor of Ohio.

In 1896 he was elected president as a proponent of a protective tariff and sound money (gold standard) over William Jennings Bryan, the Democrat and a proponent of free silver. McKinley was reluctant to intervene in Cuba, but the loss of the battleship *Maine* at Havana crystallized opinion. He demanded Spain's withdrawal from Cuba; Spain made some concessions, but Congress announced a state of war as of Apr. 21, 1898. He was reelected in the 1900 campaign, defeating Bryan's anti-imperialist arguments with the promise of a "full dinner pail." He was known for a conservative stance on business issues. On Sept. 6, 1901, at the Pan-American Exposition, in Buffalo, NY, he was shot by Leon Czolgosz, an anarchist. He died Sept. 14.

Theodore Roosevelt (1901-09), 26th president, Republican, was born on Oct. 27, 1858, in New York City, the son of Theodore and Martha Bulloch Roosevelt. He was a 5th cousin of Franklin D. Roosevelt and an uncle of Eleanor Roosevelt. Roosevelt graduated from Harvard Univ. in 1880. He attended Columbia Law School briefly but abandoned law to enter politics. He was elected to the New York State Assembly in 1881 and served until 1884. He spent the next two years ranching and hunting in the Dakota Territory. In 1886, he ran unsuccessfully for mayor of New York City. He was civil service commissioner in Washington, DC, from 1889 to 1895. From 1895 to 1897, he served as New York City's police commissioner. He was assistant secretary of the Navy under McKinley. The Spanish-American War made him nationally known. He organized the First U.S. Volunteer Cavalry (Rough Riders) and, as lieutenant colonel, led the charge up Kettle Hill in San Juan. Elected New York governor in 1898, he fought the spoils system and achieved taxation of corporation franchises.

Nominated for vice president in 1900, Roosevelt became the nation's youngest president when McKinley was assassinated. He was reelected in 1904. As president he fought corruption of politics by big business, dissolved the Northern Securities Co. and others for violating antitrust laws, intervened in the 1902 coal strike on behalf of the public, obtained the Elkins Law (1903) forbidding rebates to favored corporations, and helped pass the Hepburn Railway Rate Act of 1906 (extending jurisdiction of the Interstate Commerce Commission). He helped obtain passage of the Pure Food and Drug Act (1906) and of employers' liability laws. Roosevelt vigorously organized conservation efforts. He mediated the peace between Japan and Russia in 1905, for which he won the Nobel Peace Prize. He abetted the 1903 revolution in Panama that led to U.S. acquisition of territory for the Panama Canal.

In 1908 Roosevelt obtained the nomination of William H. Taft, who was elected. Feeling that Taft had abandoned his policies, he unsuccessfully sought the nomination in 1912. He then ran on the Progressive "Bull Moose" ticket against Taft and Woodrow Wilson, splitting the Republicans and ensuring Wilson's election. During the campaign he was shot by a mentally deranged man but was not seriously wounded. In 1916, after unsuccessfully seeking the presidential nomination, he supported the Republican candidate, Charles E. Hughes. He strongly promoted U.S. intervention in World War I.

Roosevelt was a voracious reader and wrote some 40 books, including *The Winning of the West*. He died Jan. 6, 1919, at Sagamore Hill, his home in Oyster Bay, NY.

William Howard Taft (1909-13), 27th president, Republican, and 10th chief justice of the U.S., was born on Sept. 15, 1857, in Cincinnati, OH, the son of Alphonso and Louisa Maria Torrey Taft. His father was secretary of war and attorney general in Grant's cabinet and minister to Austria and Russia under Arthur. Taft graduated from Yale in 1878 and from Cincinnati Law School in 1880. After working as a law reporter for Cincinnati newspapers, he served as assistant prosecuting attorney (1881-82), assistant county solicitor (1885), superior court judge (1887), U.S. solicitor-general (1890), and federal circuit judge (1892). In 1900 he became head of the U.S. Philippines Commission and was the first civil governor of the Philippines (1901-04). In 1904 he served as secretary of war, and in 1906 he was sent to Cuba to help avert a threatened revolution.

Taft was groomed for the presidency by Theodore Roosevelt and elected over William Jennings Bryan in 1908. Taft vigorously continued Roosevelt's trust-busting, instituted the Dept. of Labor, and drafted amendments calling for direct election of senators and an income tax. However, his tariff and conservation policies angered progressives. Although renominated in 1912, he was opposed by Roosevelt, who ran on the Progressive Party ticket; the result was Wilson's election.

Taft, with reservations, supported the League of Nations. After leaving office, he was professor of constitutional law at Yale (1913-21) and chief justice of the U.S. (1921-30). Taft was the only person to have been both president and chief justice. He died in Washington, DC, on Mar. 8, 1930.

(Thomas) Woodrow Wilson (1913-21), 28th president, Democrat, was born on Dec. 28, 1856, in Staunton, VA, the son of Joseph Ruggles and Janet (Jessie) Woodrow Wilson. He grew up in Georgia and South Carolina. He attended Davidson College in North Carolina before graduating from Princeton Univ. in 1879. He studied law at the Univ. of Virginia and political science at Johns Hopkins Univ., where he received his PhD in 1886. He taught at Bryn Mawr (1885-88) and at Wesleyan (1888-90) before joining the faculty at Princeton. He was president of Princeton from 1902 until 1910, when he was elected governor of New Jersey. In 1912 he was nominated for president with the aid of William Jennings Bryan, who sought to block James "Champ" Clark and Tammany Hall. Wilson won because Theodore Roosevelt, running as a "Bull Moose" Progressive, siphoned votes away from Republican candidate Taft.

As president, Wilson protected American interests in revolutionary Mexico and fought for American rights on the high seas. He oversaw the creation of the Federal Reserve system, cut the tariff, and developed a reputation as a reformer. His sharp warnings to Germany led to the resignation of his secretary of state, Bryan, a pacifist. In 1916 he was reelected by a slim margin with the slogan, "He kept us out of war," although his attempts to mediate in the war failed. After several American ships were sunk by the Germans, he secured a declaration of war against Germany on Apr. 6, 1917.

Wilson outlined his peace program on Jan. 8, 1918, in the Fourteen Points, a state paper that enunciated a doctrine of self-determination for the settlement of territorial disputes. The Germans accepted his terms and an armistice on Nov. 11, 1918. Wilson went to Paris to help negotiate the peace treaty, the crux of which he considered the League of Nations. The Senate demanded reservations that would not make the U.S. subordinate to the votes of other nations in case of war. Wilson refused and toured the country to get support. After he suffered a severe stroke in Oct. 1919, his wife, Edith Wilson, concealed the extent of his infirmity, controlled access to him, and in effect largely acted in his place.

Wilson was awarded the 1919 Nobel Peace Prize, but the treaty embodying the League of Nations was ultimately rejected by the Senate in 1920. He left the White House in Mar. 1921. He died in Washington, DC, on Feb. 3, 1924.

Warren Gamaliel Harding (1921-23), 29th president, Republican, was born on Nov. 2, 1865, near Corsica (now Blooming Grove), OH, the son of George Tyron and Phoebe Elizabeth Dickerson Harding. He attended Ohio Central College, studied law, and became editor and publisher of a county newspaper. He entered the political arena as state senator (1901-04) and then served as lieutenant governor (1904-06). In 1910 he ran unsuccessfully for governor of Ohio; in 1914 he was elected to the U.S. Senate. In the Senate he voted for antistrike legislation, women's suffrage, and the Volstead Prohibition Enforcement Act over Pres. Wilson's veto. He opposed the League of Nations.

In 1920 he was nominated for president and defeated James M. Cox in the election. The Republicans capitalized on war weariness and fear that Wilson's League of Nations would curtail U.S. sovereignty. Harding stressed a return to "normalcy" and worked for tariff revision and the repeal of excess profits law and high income taxes. In what became known as the Teapot Dome scandal, his secretary of the interior, Albert B. Fall, resigned and was later convicted of accepting bribes in the leasing of government-owned oil reserves to private companies.

As rumors began to circulate about the corruption in his administration, Harding fell ill after a trip to Alaska, and he died

suddenly in San Francisco on Aug. 2, 1923. Harding's letters to a longtime mistress were made public by the Library of Congress in 2014.

(John) Calvin Coolidge (1923-29), 30th president, Republican, was born on July 4, 1872, in Plymouth Notch, VT, the son of John Calvin and Victoria J. Moor Coolidge. Coolidge graduated from Amherst College in 1895. He entered Republican state politics and served as mayor of Northampton, MA, as state senator, as lieutenant governor, and, in 1919, as governor. In Sept. 1919, Coolidge attained national prominence by calling out the state guard in the Boston police strike. He declared, "There is no right to strike against the public safety by anybody, anywhere, anytime." This brought his name before the Republican convention of 1920, where he was nominated for vice president.

Coolidge succeeded to the presidency on Harding's death. As president, he opposed the League of Nations and the soldiers' bonus bill, which was passed over his veto. In 1924 he was elected to the presidency by a huge majority. He substantially reduced the national debt. He twice vetoed legislation to aid financially hard-pressed farmers.

With Republicans eager to renominate him, Coolidge simply announced on Aug. 2, 1927, "I do not choose to run for president in 1928." He died in Northampton, MA, on Jan. 5, 1933.

Herbert Clark Hoover (1929-33), 31st president, Republican, was born on Aug. 10, 1874, in West Branch, IA, the son of Jesse Clark and Hulda Randall Minthorn Hoover. Hoover grew up in Indian Territory (now Oklahoma) and Oregon and graduated from Stanford Univ. with a degree in geology in 1895. He worked briefly with the U.S. Geological Survey and then managed mines in Australia, Asia, Europe, and Africa. While chief engineer of imperial mines in China, he directed food relief for victims of the Boxer Rebellion. He gained a reputation not only as an engineer but as a humanitarian as he directed the American Relief Committee, London (1914-15) and the U.S. Commission for Relief in Belgium (1915-19). He was U.S. Food Administrator (1917-19), American Relief Administrator (1918-21), and in charge of Russian Relief (1918-23). He served as secretary of commerce under both Harding and Coolidge. Some historians believe that he was the most effective secretary of commerce ever to hold that office.

In 1928 Hoover was elected president over Alfred E. Smith. In 1929 the stock market crashed, and the economy collapsed. During the Great Depression, Hoover inaugurated some government assistance programs, but he was opposed to administration of aid through a federal bureaucracy. As the effects of the depression continued, he was defeated in the 1932 election by Franklin D. Roosevelt. Hoover remained active after leaving office. President Truman named him coordinator of the European Food Program (1946) and chairman of the Commission on Organization of the Executive Branch (1947-49); he was later appointed by President Eisenhower to serve in the same role (1953-55).

Hoover died in New York City on Oct. 20, 1964.

Franklin Delano Roosevelt (1933-45), 32nd president, Democrat, was born on Jan. 30, 1882, in Hyde Park, NY, the son of James and Sara Delano Roosevelt. He graduated from Harvard Univ. in 1903. He attended Columbia University Law School without taking a degree and was admitted to the New York State bar in 1907. His political career began when he was elected to the New York State senate in 1910. In 1913 Pres. Wilson appointed him assistant secretary of the navy, a post he held during World War I.

In 1920 Roosevelt ran for vice president with James Cox and was defeated. From 1921 to 1928 he worked in his New York law office and was also vice president of a bank. In Aug. 1921, he was stricken with poliomyelitis, which left his legs paralyzed. As a result of therapy he was able to stand, or walk a few steps, with the aid of leg braces.

Roosevelt served two terms as governor of New York (1929-33). In 1932, Democratic convention delegate W. G. McAdoo, pledged to nominee John N. Garner, threw his votes to Roosevelt, who was nominated for president. The Depression and the promise to repeal Prohibition ensured his election. He asked for emergency powers, proclaimed the New Deal, and put into effect a vast number of administrative changes. Foremost was the use of public funds for relief and public works, resulting in deficit financing. He greatly expanded the federal government's regulation of business and by an excess profits tax and progressive income taxes produced a redistribution of earnings on an unprecedented scale. He also promoted legislation establishing the Social Security system. He was the last president inaugurated on Mar. 4 (1933) and the first inaugurated on Jan. 20 (1937).

Roosevelt was the first president to use radio for "fireside chats." When the Supreme Court nullified some New Deal laws, he sought power to "pack" the Court with additional justices, but Congress refused to give him the authority. He was the first president to break the "no third term" tradition (1940) and was elected to a fourth term in 1944, despite failing health.

Roosevelt was openly hostile to fascist governments before World War II and launched a lend-lease program on behalf of the Allies. With British Prime Min. Winston Churchill he wrote a declaration of principles to be followed after Nazi defeat (the Atlantic Charter of Aug. 14, 1941) and urged the Four Freedoms (freedom of speech, of worship, from want, from fear) Jan. 6, 1941. After Japan attacked Pearl Harbor on Dec. 7, 1941, the U.S. entered the war. Roosevelt guided the nation through the war and conferred with allied heads of state but did not live to see the end of the war. He died of a cerebral hemorrhage in Warm Springs, GA, on Apr. 12, 1945.

Harry S. Truman (1945-53), 33rd president, Democrat, was born on May 8, 1884, in Lamar, MO, the son of John Anderson and Martha Ellen Young Truman. A family disagreement over whether his middle name should be Shipp or Solomon, after his two grandfathers, resulted in his using only the middle initial S. After graduating from high school (1901) in Independence, MO, he worked in the mailroom of the *Kansas City Star*, as a railroad timekeeper, and as a clerk in Kansas City banks until about 1905. He ran his family's farm from 1906 to 1917, then served in France during World War I. After the war he opened a haberdashery, was a judge on the Jackson Co. Court (1922-24), and attended Kansas City School of Law (1923-25).

Truman was elected to the U.S. Senate in 1934 and reelected in 1940. In 1944, with Roosevelt's backing, he was nominated for vice president and elected. On Roosevelt's death in 1945, Truman became president. In 1948, in a famous upset victory, he defeated Republican Thomas E. Dewey to win a new term.

Truman authorized the first uses of the atomic bomb (Hiroshima and Nagasaki, Aug. 6 and 9, 1945), bringing World War II to a rapid end. He was responsible for what came to be called the Truman Doctrine to aid nations such as Greece and Turkey, threatened by Communist takeover, and his strong commitment to NATO and the Marshall Plan helped bring the two about. In 1948-49, he broke a Soviet blockade of West Berlin with a massive airlift. When Communist North Korea invaded South Korea (June 1950), he won UN approval for a "police action" and, without prior congressional consent, sent in forces under Gen. Douglas MacArthur. When MacArthur opposed his policy of limited objectives, Truman removed him.

He died in Kansas City, MO, on Dec. 26, 1972.

Dwight David Eisenhower (1953-61), 34th president, Republican, was born on Oct. 14, 1890, in Denison, TX, the son of David Jacob and Ida Elizabeth Stover Eisenhower, as David Dwight Eisenhower. He grew up on a small farm in Abilene, KS, and graduated from West Point in 1915. He was on the staff of Gen. Douglas MacArthur in the Philippines from 1935 to 1939. In 1942, he was made commander of Allied forces landing in North Africa; the next year he was made full general. He became supreme Allied commander in Europe that same year and led the Normandy invasion (June 6, 1944). He was subsequently given the rank of general of the Army.

On May 7, 1945, Eisenhower received the surrender of Germany at Rheims, France. He returned to the U.S. to serve as chief of staff (1945-48). His memoir, *Crusade in Europe* (1948), was a best-seller. In 1948 he became president of Columbia Univ.; in 1950 he became commander of NATO forces.

Eisenhower was nominated for president by the Republicans in 1952. He defeated Illinois Gov. Adlai E. Stevenson in the 1952 election and defeated Stevenson in 1956 to win reelection. Eisenhower called himself a moderate, favored the "free market system" versus government price and wage controls, kept government out of labor disputes, reorganized the defense establishment, and promoted missile programs. He continued foreign aid, helped negotiate a cease fire truce in the Korean War, endorsed Taiwan and SE Asia defense treaties, backed the UN in condemning the Anglo-French raid on Egypt, and advocated the "open skies" policy of mutual inspection with the USSR. He sent U.S. troops into Little Rock, AR, in Sept. 1957, to enforce school integration.

Eisenhower died on Mar. 28, 1969, in Washington, DC.

John Fitzgerald Kennedy (1961-63), 35th president, Democrat, was born on May 29, 1917, in Brookline, MA, the son of Joseph P. and Rose Fitzgerald Kennedy. He graduated from Harvard Univ. in 1940. While serving in the Navy (1941-45), he commanded a PT (patrol torpedo) boat in the Solomons and won the Navy and Marine Corps Medal. In 1956, while recovering from spinal surgery, he wrote *Profiles in Courage*, which won a Pulitzer Prize in 1957. He served in the House of Representatives from 1947 to 1953 and was elected to the Senate in 1952 and 1958. In 1960, he won the Democratic nomination for president and narrowly defeated Republican Vice Pres. Richard M. Nixon. Kennedy was the youngest president ever elected to the office and the first Catholic.

Despite the image of youth and vigor he conveyed to the public, Kennedy suffered from serious medical problems, including Addison's disease and severe chronic back pain that required him to wear a back brace. The public was not aware of the extent of these problems, or of his frequent sexual liaisons.

In Apr. 1961, the new Kennedy administration suffered a severe setback when an invasion force of anti-Castro Cubans, trained and directed by the CIA, failed to establish a beachhead at the Bay of Pigs in Cuba. But he weathered a major foreign crisis with his successful demand on Oct. 22, 1962, that the Soviet Union dismantle its missile bases in Cuba. Kennedy also defied Soviet attempts to force the Allies out of Berlin. He established the Peace Corps, spurred space exploration, and won passage of other "New Frontier" legislation. But Congress balked at initiatives such as medical coverage for the aged and aid to education. After some delay he introduced major civil rights legislation, but death intervened before it could be passed.

On Nov. 22, 1963, Kennedy was assassinated while riding in a motorcade in Dallas, TX. A commission chaired by Chief Justice Earl Warren concluded in Sept. 1964 that the sole assassin had been Lee Harvey Oswald, a former U.S. Marine and an ardent Marxist. Oswald was captured a short time after the assassination and charged, but two days later, he was shot dead by nightclub owner Jack Ruby while being moved to a county jail.

Lyndon Baines Johnson (1963-69), 36th president, Democrat, was born on Aug. 27, 1908, near Stonewall, TX, the son of Sam Ealy and Rebekah Baines Johnson. He graduated from Southwest Texas State Teachers College in 1930 and attended Georgetown University Law School. He taught public speaking in Houston (1930-31) and then served as secretary to Rep. R. M. Kleberg (1931-35). In 1937 Johnson won an election to fill the vacancy caused by the death of a U.S. representative. In 1938 he was elected to the first of five full terms. During 1941 and 1942 he also served in the Navy in the Pacific, earning a Silver Star for bravery. He was elected U.S. senator in 1948 and reelected in 1954. He became Democratic leader of the Senate in 1953. Johnson had strong support for the Democratic presidential nomination at the 1960 convention and was elected vice president on the ticket led by the successful Democratic nominee, John F. Kennedy.

Johnson became president when Kennedy was assassinated. He was elected to a full term in 1964. Johnson's domestic program was of considerable importance. He won passage of major civil rights, anti-poverty, aid to education, and healthcare (Medicare, Medicaid) legislation—the "Great Society" program. However, his escalation of the war in Vietnam came to overshadow the achievements of his administration. In the face of increasing division in the nation and in his own party over his handling of the war, Johnson declined to seek another term.

Johnson died on Jan. 22, 1973, in San Antonio, TX.

Richard Milhous Nixon (1969-74), 37th president, Republican, was born on Jan. 9, 1913, in Yorba Linda, CA, the son of Francis Anthony and Hannah Milhous Nixon. He graduated from Whittier College in 1934 and from Duke University Law School in 1937. After practicing law in Whittier, CA, and serving briefly in the Office of Price Administration in 1942, he entered the Navy and served in the South Pacific. Nixon was elected to the House of Representatives in 1946 and 1948. He achieved prominence as the House Un-American Activities Committee member who forced the showdown leading to the Alger Hiss perjury conviction. In 1950 he was elected to the Senate.

Nixon was elected vice president in the Eisenhower landslides of 1952 and 1956. He won the Republican nomination for president in 1960 but was narrowly defeated by John F. Kennedy. He ran unsuccessfully for governor of California in 1962. In 1968 he again won the GOP presidential nomination, then defeated Hubert Humphrey for the presidency.

As president, Nixon appointed four Supreme Court justices, including the chief justice, moving the court to the right. As a "new federalist," he sought to shift greater responsibility to state and local governments. At the same time, he championed important federal initiatives, including creation of the Office of Management and Budget and the Environmental Protection Agency. The economy suffered periods of high unemployment and inflation, and he imposed wage and price controls in 1971.

In foreign affairs, Nixon dramatically altered relations with China, which he visited in 1972—the first U.S. president to do so. With adviser Henry Kissinger, he pursued détente with the Soviet Union, signing major arms limitation and other treaties and increasing trade. He began a gradual withdrawal from Vietnam, but U.S. troops remained there through his first term. He ordered an incursion into Cambodia (1970) and the bombing of Hanoi and mining of Haiphong Harbor (1972). Reelected by a large majority in Nov. 1972, he secured a Vietnam cease-fire in Jan. 1973.

Nixon's second term was cut short by scandal, after disclosures relating to a June 1972 burglary of Democratic Party headquarters in the Watergate office complex in DC. The courts and Congress sought tapes of Nixon's office conversations; Nixon claimed executive privilege, but the Supreme Court ruled against him. In July 1974, the House Judiciary Committee recommended adoption of three impeachment articles charging him with obstruction of justice, abuse of power, and contempt of Congress. On Aug. 5, he released transcripts of conversations that linked him to cover-up activities. He resigned on Aug. 9, becoming the first president ever to do so.

In later years, Nixon emerged as an elder statesman. He died Apr. 22, 1994, in New York City.

Gerald Rudolph Ford (1974-77), 38th president, Republican, was born on July 14, 1913, in Omaha, NE, the son of Leslie and Dorothy Gardner King, and was named Leslie Lynch King Jr. When he was two, his parents divorced, and he and his mother moved to Grand Rapids, MI. There she married Gerald R. Ford, who formally adopted him and gave him his name. Ford graduated from the Univ. of Michigan in 1935 and from Yale Law School in 1941. He began practicing law in Grand Rapids, but in 1942, he joined the Navy and served in the Pacific, leaving the service in 1946 as a lieutenant commander. He entered the House of Representatives in 1949 and spent 25 years in the House, eight of them as Republican leader.

On Oct. 12, 1973, after Vice Pres. Spiro T. Agnew resigned, Pres. Nixon nominated Ford to replace him. It was the first use of the procedures set out in the 25th Amendment. When Nixon resigned, Aug. 9, 1974, because of the Watergate scandal, Ford became president; he was the only president who was never elected either to the presidency or to the vice presidency.

Ford was widely credited with having contributed to rebuilding morale after the Nixon presidency. But he was also criticized by many when he pardoned Nixon for any federal crimes he might have committed as president. Ford vetoed 48 bills in his first 21 months in office, mostly in the interest of fighting high inflation; he was less successful in curbing high unemployment. In foreign policy, Ford continued to pursue détente.

Ford was narrowly defeated in the 1976 election. He died Dec. 26, 2006, at home in Rancho Mirage, CA.

James Earl (Jimmy) Carter (1977-81), 39th president, Democrat, was the first president from the Deep South since before the Civil War. He was born on Oct. 1, 1924, in Plains, GA, the son of James and Lillian Gordy Carter. Carter graduated from the U.S. Naval Academy in 1946 and in 1952 entered the Navy's nuclear submarine program as an aide to Capt. (later Adm.) Hyman Rickover. He studied nuclear physics at Union College. Carter's father died in 1953, and he left the Navy to take over the family peanut farming businesses. He served in the Georgia state senate (1963-67) and as governor of Georgia (1971-75). In 1976, Carter won the Democratic nomination and defeated Pres. Gerald R. Ford.

On his first full day in office, Carter pardoned all Vietnam draft evaders. He played a major role in the negotiations leading to the 1979 peace treaty between Israel and Egypt, and he won passage of new treaties with Panama providing for U.S. control of the Panama Canal to end in 2000. Carter was widely criticized, however, for the poor state of the economy and was viewed by some as weak in his handling of foreign policy. In Nov. 1979, Iranian student militants attacked the U.S. embassy in Tehran and held members of the embassy staff hostage. Efforts to obtain release of the hostages were a major preoccupation during the rest of his term. He reacted to the Soviet invasion of Afghanistan by imposing a grain embargo and boycotting the Moscow Olympic Games.

Carter was defeated by Ronald Reagan in the 1980 election. The 52 American hostages in Iran were finally released on inauguration day, 1981, just after Reagan officially became president. After leaving office, Carter played an active role in diplomatic and humanitarian efforts around the world, especially through the Carter Center, which he founded with his wife in 1982. He was awarded the Nobel Peace Prize in 2002.

Ronald Wilson Reagan (1981-89), 40th president, Republican, was born on Feb. 6, 1911, in Tampico, IL, the son of John Edward and Nellie Wilson Reagan. Reagan graduated from Eureka College in 1932, after which he worked as a sports announcer in Des Moines, IA. He began a successful career as a movie actor in 1937. During World War II Reagan served in the Army Air Force, making training films. He was president of the Screen Actors Guild in 1947-52 and in 1959-60. Reagan was elected governor of California in 1966 and reelected in 1970.

In 1980, Reagan gained the Republican presidential nomination and won a landslide victory over Jimmy Carter. He was easily reelected in 1984. Reagan forged a bipartisan coalition in Congress, which led to enactment of his program of large-scale tax cuts, cutbacks in many government programs, and a major defense buildup. He signed a Social Security reform bill designed to provide for the long-term solvency of the system. In 1986, he signed into law a major tax-reform bill. He was shot and seriously wounded in 1981 by John Hinckley, who was tried and found not guilty by reason of insanity.

In 1982, the U.S. joined France and Italy in maintaining a peacekeeping force in Beirut, Lebanon, and the next year Reagan sent a task force to invade Grenada after two Marxist coups on the island. Reagan's opposition to international terrorism led to the U.S. bombing of Libyan military installations in 1986. He strongly supported El Salvador, the Nicaraguan contras, and other anticommunist governments and forces throughout the world. He also held four summit meetings with Soviet leader Mikhail Gorbachev and signed a treaty in 1987 eliminating short- and medium-range missiles from Europe.

In 1986, it was revealed that the U.S. had sold weapons through Israeli brokers to Iran in exchange for the release of U.S. hostages being held in Lebanon and that subsequently some of the money had been illegally diverted to the Nicaraguan contras. The scandal led to the resignation of leading White House aides, but no proof of Reagan's involvement was discovered. As Reagan left office in Jan. 1989, the nation was experiencing its sixth consecutive year of economic prosperity, while also piling up large budget deficits.

In 1994, Reagan revealed that he was suffering from Alzheimer's disease. He died on June 5, 2004, in Los Angeles, CA, from complications of the disease.

George Herbert Walker Bush (1989-93),
41st president, Republican, was born on June 12, 1924, in Milton, MA, the son of Prescott and Dorothy Walker Bush. He served as a U.S. Navy pilot in World War II. After graduating from Yale Univ. in 1948, he settled in Texas, where, in 1953, he helped found an oil company. After losing a bid for a U.S. Senate seat in 1964, he was elected to the House of Representatives in 1966 and 1968. He lost a second U.S. Senate race in 1970. Subsequently he served as U.S. ambassador to the United Nations (1971-73), headed the U.S. Liaison Office in Beijing (1974-75), and was director of the CIA (1976-77). Following an unsuccessful bid for the 1980 Republican presidential nomination, Bush became Ronald Reagan's running mate, and served as vice president from 1981 to 1989.

In 1988, Bush gained the GOP presidential nomination and defeated Gov. Michael Dukakis (D, MA) to win the presidency. Bush took office faced with U.S. budget and trade deficits, and insolvent U.S. savings and loan institutions. He faced a severe budget deficit annually, struggled with military cutbacks, and vetoed abortion-rights legislation. In 1990 he agreed to a budget deficit-reduction plan that included tax hikes, despite a campaign promise to the contrary, angering many conservatives.

Bush supported Soviet reforms, Eastern Europe democratization, and good relations with Beijing. In Dec. 1989, he sent troops to Panama; they overthrew the government and captured military dictator Gen. Manuel Noriega. Bush reacted to Iraq's Aug. 1990 invasion of Kuwait by sending U.S. forces to the Persian Gulf area and assembling a UN-backed coalition, including NATO and Arab League members. After a month-long air war, in Feb. 1991, Allied forces retook Kuwait in a four-day ground assault. The quick victory, with extremely light casualties on the U.S. side, gave Bush at that time one of the highest presidential approval ratings in history. His popularity plummeted by the end of 1991, however, as the economy slipped into recession. He was defeated by Bill Clinton in the 1992 election.

Bush saw his son George W. inaugurated as the 43rd president in 2001. In 2005 the elder Bush teamed with former Pres. Clinton to raise money for natural disaster victims.

William Jefferson (Bill) Clinton (1993-2001),
42nd president, Democrat, was born Aug. 19, 1946, in Hope, AR, son of William Blythe and Virginia Cassidy Blythe, and was named William Jefferson Blythe IV. Blythe died in an auto accident before his son was born. His widow married Roger Clinton, whose last name Bill Clinton then took. Clinton earned his undergraduate degree from Georgetown Univ. in 1968. While attending Oxford Univ. as a Rhodes scholar, he legally avoided the draft and possible service in Vietnam, according to some critics by misleading his draft board. Clinton worked on George McGovern's 1972 presidential campaign and earned a degree from Yale Law School in 1973. He taught at the Univ. of Arkansas law school until 1976, when he was elected state attorney general. In 1978 he was elected governor, becoming the nation's youngest at the time. Though defeated for reelection in 1980, he was returned to office several times thereafter. He married law school classmate Hillary Rodham in 1975.

Clinton won most of the 1992 presidential primaries, moving his party toward the center as he tried to broaden his appeal; as the Democratic nominee he defeated Pres. George H. W. Bush and independent candidate H. Ross Perot in the Nov. election. In 1993, Clinton won passage of deficit reduction measure and won congressional approval of the North American Free Trade Agreement. However, his administration's plan for major health care reform legislation died in Congress. After 1994 midterm elections, Clinton faced Republican majorities in both houses of Congress. He followed a centrist course at home, sent troops to Bosnia to help implement a peace settlement, and cultivated relations with Russia and China.

Though accused of improprieties in his involvement in the Whitewater Development Corp., an Arkansas land-development venture, Clinton won reelection with 49% of the vote in 1996. Independent prosecutor Kenneth Starr did not find wrongdoing related to Whitewater, but did report evidence of an affair between Clinton and White House intern Monica Lewinsky. In 1998, Clinton became only the second U.S. president to be impeached by the House of Representatives. He was charged with perjury and obstruction of justice in an attempted cover-up of the affair but was acquitted by the Senate.

In 1999 the United States joined other NATO nations in an aerial bombing campaign that induced Serbia to withdraw troops from Kosovo, where they had been terrorizing ethnic Albanians. On Clinton's last full day in office, the Whitewater investigation ended in a deal; Clinton admitted having given false testimony and agreed to penalties. He remained active in politics, and campaigned for his wife, who became a U.S. senator (D, NY), ran unsuccessfully for the 2008 Democratic presidential nomination, then served as Pres. Obama's secretary of state. He took a leadership role in various humanitarian programs and founded an institute to promote practical solutions to global problems.

George Walker Bush (2001-09),
43rd president, Republican, was born on July 6, 1946, in New Haven, CT. He was the oldest of six children born to the 41st president, George Herbert Walker Bush, and the former Barbara Pierce. He became the first son of a former president to occupy the White House since John Quincy Adams took office in 1825.

Bush grew up in Midland and Houston, TX. He attended Phillips Academy in Andover, MA, and then Yale Univ., graduating in 1968. Eligible for the draft, he fulfilled his military service requirement with the Texas Air National Guard. After earning a master's degree from Harvard Business School, he returned to Midland in 1975 and went into the oil business. Two years later he married Laura Welch, a librarian; they had twin daughters, Barbara and Jenna, in 1981. After aiding his father's winning 1988 presidential campaign, he became managing partner of the Texas Rangers baseball team. He was elected governor of Texas in 1994 and reelected in 1998.

In 2000, Bush won the Republican presidential nomination and, with running mate Dick Cheney, defeated the Democratic ticket led by Vice Pres. Al Gore, in one of the closest-ever U.S. presidential elections. The result was not settled until a mid-Dec. ruling by the U.S. Supreme Court left Florida's crucial electoral votes in Bush's column.

In May 2001, Bush won passage of a tax cut package projected at $1.35 tril over 10 years. After the Sept. 11, 2001, terrorist attacks on the U.S., he rallied support for a "war against terrorism." By Dec. 2001, the U.S. military, aided by forces from other nations, had deposed Afghanistan's Taliban regime, which was sheltering al-Qaeda terrorists. In Mar. 2003, the U.S., aided mainly by UK forces, launched an air and ground war against Iraq and deposed its autocratic leader, Saddam Hussein. No evidence was found that his regime had developed weapons of mass destruction, the key rationale for the war. A sovereign government was formed in June 2004, but insurgent violence and U.S. troop casualties continued.

Bush was reelected in Nov. 2004 with 51% of the popular vote, but his push for Social Security and immigration reforms in his second term failed in Congress, and his administration drew criticism for its response to Hurricane Katrina in Aug.-Sept. 2005. The Senate confirmed Bush's nominations of a new chief justice and associate justice of the Supreme Court. In 2006, Bush exercised his first veto to maintain restrictions on federal funding for stem cell research.

After Democrats won majorities in House and Senate 2006 midterm elections, Bush accepted the resignation of Defense Sec. Donald Rumsfeld, a target of widespread criticism over the Iraq war. Two months later, he announced a "surge" in U.S. troop strength in Iraq. A sharp drop in casualties ensued, aided also by a shift in alliances, and in late 2008 the administration reached an agreement with Iraq allowing U.S. troops to remain there through but not beyond 2011. But the Taliban was gaining strength in Afghanistan and Pakistan, and the Bush administration was damaged by revelations of prisoner abuse and extreme interrogation methods.

The U.S. economy fell into recession in Dec. 2007; Bush and congressional leaders responded with a $168-bil stimulus plan. Problems in home finance and credit markets triggered a deep economic crisis in Sept. and the Treasury Dept. announced a bailout of mortgage finance firms Fannie Mae and Freddie Mac. Lehman Bros. filed for bankruptcy, and the Federal Reserve rescued insurance giant AIG with a line of credit reaching $144 bil. A Bush administration-backed plan to buy up to

$700 bil in devalued mortgage-related assets cleared Congress Oct. 3, after a severe stock market plunge bolstered support. The crisis added to Bush's unpopularity and contributed to the 2008 defeat of GOP presidential candidate Sen. John McCain (AZ).

In early 2010 Bush and former Pres. Clinton established a nonprofit organization to raise funds for earthquake relief in Haiti. In Nov. 2010, Bush published a memoir entitled *Decision Points*. He later wrote a biography of his father, scheduled for publication in Nov. 2014.

Barack Hussein Obama (2009-), 44th president, Democrat, was born Aug. 4, 1961, in Honolulu, HI. His father, Barack Obama Sr., was a black Kenyan, and his mother, Stanley Ann Dunham, a white American. They divorced, and, after his mother married an Indonesian man, the family moved to Indonesia. Obama lived with his maternal grandparents in Hawaii while attending high school. He graduated from Columbia Univ. (1983) and, after working as a community organizer in Chicago, earned a law degree from Harvard Univ. (1991), where he was president of the law review. Obama later practiced civil rights law in Chicago and taught at the Univ. of Chicago Law School. In 1992, he married attorney Michelle Robinson (1964-). They have two daughters, Malia (1998-) and Natasha (Sasha) (2001-).

Obama served eight years (1997-2004) in the Illinois state senate. He lost the Democratic nomination for a U.S. House seat in 2000, but was nominated to a U.S. Senate seat in a Mar. 2004 primary. Already somewhat known for his 1995 memoir, *Dreams From My Father*, he gained national attention with his keynote address at the Democratic National Convention in July 2004 and was easily elected in Nov. His second book, *The Audacity of Hope* (2006), was an immediate best-seller.

Stressing his opposition to the Iraq war and aim to bring change to Washington, Obama won the 2008 Democratic presidential nomination in a tight race against expected front-runner Sen. Hillary Clinton (NY). As a major recession deepened, Obama and running mate Sen. Joe Biden (DE) defeated the Republican ticket, headed by Sen. John McCain (R, AZ). He became the nation's first African-American president. Sen. Clinton served as secretary of state in Obama's first term.

Obama sounded a cooperative and conciliatory note in foreign relations; on that basis he was awarded the 2009 Nobel Peace Prize. He gradually ended U.S. military involvement in Iraq, and after implementing a temporary troop surge in Afghanistan, he began troop reductions and set a deadline for withdrawal there. He greatly stepped up drone strikes against militants and other targets in Afghanistan and Pakistan, and ordered an operation by Navy SEALs in May 2011 that killed al-Qaeda leader Osama bin Laden.

Obama called for the resignation of Egypt's repressive leader Hosni Mubarak, a longtime U.S. ally, in the face of 2011 Arab Spring protests. He did not intervene there, but in Libya, citing the need to prevent massacres of civilians, he authorized U.S. participation in NATO air strikes, leading to the Oct. 2011 overthrow of longtime ruler Muammar al-Qaddafi. The U.S. ambassador and three other Americans were killed in an attack on the U.S. consulate in Benghazi, Libya, in Sept. 2012. Inadequate security was blamed, and several congressional investigations found no evidence of deliberate wrongdoing on the part of the administration.

On the domestic front, the administration, early in 2009, won passage of a $787-bil economic stimulus package, and the U.S. pulled out of recession, but economic growth was slow and unemployment remained high. Obama's approval rating, close to 70% when he took office, fell by 2010 to the mid-40s. In Mar. 2010, Obama won passage of his top priority, a controversial health care reform bill aimed in part at extending coverage to uninsured Americans. The Affordable Care Act (ACA), known as "Obamacare," survived a major obstacle in 2012 when most components of the legislation were upheld by the Supreme Court. The administration also won passage of a financial reform bill, and the Senate confirmed two Obama Supreme Court nominees.

Democrats lost their U.S. House majority in Nov. 2010 elections. Obama then reached a compromise with Republicans on an $858-bil spending plan that kept all G.W. Bush-era tax cuts for two years while extending unemployment benefits and temporarily reducing payroll taxes. With the federal government set to reach its debt limit in Aug. 2011, congressional Republicans insisted that the ceiling not be raised without compensating cost

savings. A last-minute compromise called for cuts to be worked out by a bipartisan congressional committee; when no agreement was reached, large automatic cuts ("sequester") in domestic spending and defense were slated to take effect in 2013. In May 2012, Obama became the first sitting president to publicly support same-sex marriage. In June 2012, Obama signed an executive order ending deportations for most young undocumented immigrants who came to the U.S. as children.

Obama and Biden were reelected in Nov. 2012, defeating a ticket headed by former Gov. Mitt Romney (R, MA). A compromise reached in Congress averted a year-end fiscal cliff by making expiring Bush tax cuts permanent for most people, while postponing the sequester; further negotiations failed, and the sequester took effect, Mar. 1, 2013.

In early 2013, it was reported that the Internal Revenue Service had singled out Tea Party organizations for scrutiny; however, no link to the White House was found. In June 2013, Edward Snowden, a Natl. Security Agency (NSA) contractor, leaked classified information about the wide scope of U.S. surveillance programs; Obama defended the NSA program while pledging limited reform. The Boston Marathon bombing, which killed three in Apr. 2013, was a reminder that the U.S. homeland remained vulnerable to terrorist attacks.

The acquittal in July 2013 of a neighborhood watch volunteer in the shooting death of an unarmed black teenager in Florida led Obama to draw attention to fears and concerns specific to the black community. The following summer he called for calm after the shooting death of another unarmed black youth by a police officer led to protests and riots in Ferguson, MO.

The federal government partially shut down in Oct. 2013, with Republicans seeking concessions on spending and to defund or postpone implementation of Obamacare. Blamed for the unpopular shutdown, Republicans backed down after 16 days. But the administration was widely criticized in late 2013 for a botched rollout of health insurance exchanges meant to enroll people in Obamacare. In 2014, revelations of mismanagement at the Dept. of Veterans Affairs that jeopardized care of veterans led to resignation of the VA secretary. Controversy over illegal immigration heightened as increasing numbers of unaccompanied children fleeing violence and poverty in Central America flooded into the U.S. Obama indicated he would use executive actions to address broad immigration issues after the Nov. 2014 elections.

Economic recovery continued slowly, with unemployment slowly moving down toward 6%. With the public sharply divided on many issues, such as immigration policy and gun control, and a polarized Congress often failing to take action, Obama accused Republicans of intransigence, and Republicans blamed him for failing to work with them.

Serious instability continued to escalate abroad, notably in Eastern Europe and the Middle East. In Ukraine, Russian forces annexed the Crimean region in Mar. 2014 and pro-Russian separatists, reportedly bolstered by Russian troops and tanks, expanded their control in areas of eastern Ukraine. Obama joined Europe in limited economic sanctions against Russia in response. In the Middle East, the administration revived Arab-Israeli peace talks in mid-2013, but they broke down; new violence climaxed in a major Israeli operation launched July 2014 in Gaza, with heavy civilian casualties, following rocket attacks on Israel by the militant Islamic group Hamas. In return for reduced economic sanctions, Iran in early 2014 accepted a temporary nuclear freeze and talks with the West, but progress toward an anti-nuclear agreement appeared stalled by midyear.

Obama called for an end to the repressive regime of Syria's Bashar al-Assad, pitted against many different rebel factions in a bloody civil war since 2011. When the regime in Aug. 2013 appeared to cross what Obama had called a "red line" in launching a chemical weapons attack on civilians, Obama held back from punitive action, agreeing to a Russian-brokered pact with the regime. Meanwhile, the Sunni extremist group Islamic State in Iraq and Syria (ISIS) emerged as a key force and, aided by foreign recruits, took over large areas of both countries, proclaiming a Sunni Islamic caliphate in June 2014 and driving out or massacring religious minorities and others. Obama authorized sending U.S. military advisers to Iraq, and in early Aug. authorized limited air strikes in Iraq to protect minorities and U.S. interests. After ISIS disclosed its executions of abducted American journalists, Obama announced a controversial plan Sept. 10, 2014, for a long-lasting intervention against ISIS, with expected cooperation from other nations, involving extended U.S. air strikes in Iraq and Syria and ground operations by Iraqi troops and moderate Syrian rebels armed by the U.S.

Presidential Facts

Oldest president: Ronald Reagan, who was 77 when he left office

Youngest president: Theodore Roosevelt, who was 42 when sworn in after McKinley's death

Youngest person elected president: John F. Kennedy, who was 43 when elected in 1960

Tallest president: Abraham Lincoln, who was 6 feet, 4 inches

Shortest president: James Madison, who was 5 feet, 4 inches

Heaviest president: William Howard Taft, who was 332 pounds in 1911

First president to live in the White House: John Adams, who moved there in 1800

First president inaugurated in Washington, DC: Thomas Jefferson, in 1801

First president whose parents were immigrants: Andrew Jackson; his parents emigrated from Ireland in 1765

First president born a U.S. citizen: Martin Van Buren, in Kinderhook, NY, 1782

First president born outside the original colonies: Abraham Lincoln, in Kentucky, 1809

First president born west of the Mississippi: Herbert Hoover, in West Branch, IA, 1874

Most common presidential home state: Virginia, with 8 presidents

First president born in a hospital: Jimmy Carter, in Plains, GA, 1924

First president to have a telephone in the White House: Rutherford B. Hayes, in 1879

First president to travel outside U.S. while in office: Theodore Roosevelt visited Panama Canal site, 1906

First president to address the nation on radio: Warren G. Harding, in 1922

First president to appear on TV: Franklin D. Roosevelt, at opening ceremonies for the 1939 World's Fair

First president to give a live, televised news conference: John F. Kennedy, in 1961

First president to hold an Internet chat: Bill Clinton, in 1999

Presidents who lost the popular vote while winning election: John Quincy Adams, in 1824 (elected by the House after general election failed to produce a majority); Rutherford B. Hayes, in 1876; Benjamin Harrison, in 1888; George W. Bush, in 2000 (Popular vote totals before 1824 are unknown.)

Only presidents chosen by the House of Representatives: Thomas Jefferson (1st term) and John Quincy Adams

Only president never elected either president or vice president: Gerald Ford; named vice president when Spiro Agnew resigned (1973), became president when Nixon resigned (1974)

Only left-handed presidents: James Garfield, Herbert Hoover, Harry Truman, Gerald Ford, Ronald Reagan, George H. W. Bush, Bill Clinton, and Barack Obama

Only Catholic president: John F. Kennedy; the most common religious affiliations have been Episcopalian (11) and Presbyterian (7)

Only bachelor presidents: James Buchanan, who never married, and Grover Cleveland, who married Frances Folsom in the White House in 1886

Only divorced president: Ronald Reagan; divorced from Jane Wyman in 1948, married Nancy Davis in 1952

Presidents who died on July 4: John Adams and Thomas Jefferson (both 1826) and James Monroe (1831)

Only president buried in Washington, DC: Woodrow Wilson, interred at Washington National Cathedral

Presidential Libraries

Presidential libraries are coordinated by the National Archives and Records Administration (www.archives.gov/presidential-libraries/). Materials for presidents before Herbert Hoover are held by private institutions. Under the Presidential Records Act, presidential records are available to the public through Freedom of Information Act requests starting five years after the president has left office. Records of Pres. George W. Bush became available Jan. 20, 2014.

Herbert Hoover Library and Museum
210 Parkside Dr.
West Branch, IA 52358
Phone: (319) 643-5301
Email: hoover.library@nara.gov
Website: hoover.archives.gov

Franklin D. Roosevelt Library and Museum
4079 Albany Post Rd.
Hyde Park, NY 12538-1990
Phone: (800) FDR-VISIT
Email: roosevelt.library@nara.gov
Website: www.fdrlibrary.marist.edu

Harry S. Truman Library and Museum
500 West U.S. Hwy. 24
Independence, MO 64050-2481
Phone: (800) 833-1225
Email: truman.library@nara.gov
Website: www.trumanlibrary.org

Dwight D. Eisenhower Library
200 SE 4th St.
Abilene, KS 67410-2900
Phone: (877) RING-IKE
Email: eisenhower.library@nara.gov
Website: eisenhower.archives.gov

John F. Kennedy Library and Museum
Columbia Pt.
Boston, MA 02125-3312
Phone: (866) JFK-1960

Email: kennedy.library@nara.gov
Website: www.jfklibrary.org

Lyndon Baines Johnson Library and Museum
2313 Red River St.
Austin, TX 78705-5737
Phone: (512) 721-0200
Email: johnson.library@nara.gov
Website: www.lbjlibrary.org

Richard Nixon Library and Museum
18001 Yorba Linda Blvd.
Yorba Linda, CA 92886-3903
Phone: (714) 983-9120
Email: nixon@nara.gov
Website: www.nixonlibrary.gov
MD office: Natl. Archives at College Park
8601 Adelphi Rd.
College Park, MD 20740-6001
Phone: (301) 837-3290

Gerald R. Ford Library and Museum
Library: 1000 Beal Ave.
Ann Arbor, MI 48109-2109
Phone: (734) 205-0555
Museum: 303 Pearl St. NW
Grand Rapids, MI 49504-5353
Phone: (616) 254-0400
Email: ford.library@nara.gov
Website: www.fordlibrarymuseum.gov

Jimmy Carter Library and Museum
441 Freedom Pkwy.

Atlanta, GA 30307-1498
Phone: (404) 865-7100
Email: carter.library@nara.gov
Website: www.jimmycarterlibrary.gov

Ronald Reagan Library and Museum
40 Presidential Dr.
Simi Valley, CA 93065-0600
Phone: (800) 410-8354
Email: reagan.library@nara.gov
Website: www.reagan.utexas.edu

George Bush Library and Museum
1000 George Bush Dr. West
College Station, TX 77845
Phone: (979) 691-4000
Email: library.bush@nara.gov
Website: bushlibrary.tamu.edu

William J. Clinton Library and Museum
1200 President Clinton Ave.
Little Rock, AR 72201
Phone: (501) 374-4242
Email: clinton.library@nara.gov
Website: www.clintonlibrary.gov

George W. Bush Library and Museum
2943 SMU Blvd.
Dallas, TX 75205
Phone: (214) 346-1650
Email: gwbush.library@nara.gov
Website: www.georgewbushlibrary.smu.edu

Presidential Impeachment in U.S. History

The U.S. Constitution provides for impeachment and removal from office of federal officials on grounds of "Treason, Bribery, or other high Crimes and Misdemeanors" (Article II, Sect. 4). Impeachment is the bringing of charges by the House of Representatives. It is followed by a Senate trial; a two-thirds majority vote of Senators present is needed for conviction and removal from office.

In 1868, **Andrew Johnson** became the first president impeached by the House, for his removal of Sec. of War Edwin M. Stanton without first notifying the Senate. He was tried but not convicted. In 1974, impeachment articles against Pres. **Richard Nixon**, in connection with the Watergate scandal, were adopted by the House Judiciary Committee. He resigned Aug. 9, and the House accepted the committee report without taking further action. In 1998, Pres. **Bill Clinton** was impeached by the House in connection with covering up a sexual relationship with former White House intern Monica Lewinsky. He was tried in the Senate in 1999 and acquitted.

Wives and Children of the Presidents

Name (born-died; married)	State	Sons/ daughters	Name (born-died; married)	State	Sons/ daughters
Martha Dandridge Custis Washington (1731-1759; 1759)	VA	None	Mary Scott Lord Dimmick Harrison (1858-1948; 1896)	PA	0/1
Abigail Smith Adams (1744-1818; 1764)	MA	3/2	Ida Saxton McKinley (1847-1907; 1871)	OH	0/2
Martha Wayles Skelton Jefferson (1748-82; 1772)	VA	1/5	Alice Hathaway Lee Roosevelt (1861-84; 1880)	MA	0/1
Dolley Payne Todd Madison (1768-1849; 1794)	NC	None	Edith Kermit Carow Roosevelt (1861-1948; 1886)	CT	4/1
Elizabeth Kortright Monroe (1768-1830; 1786)	NY	1/2	Helen Herron Taft (1861-1943; 1886)	OH	2/1
Louisa Catherine Johnson Adams (1775-1852; 1797)	MD[1]	3/1	Ellen Louise Axson Wilson (1860-1914; 1885)	GA	0/3
Rachel Donelson Robards Jackson (1767-1828; 1791)	VA	1/0[2]	Edith Bolling Galt Wilson (1872-1961; 1915)	VA	None
Hannah Hoes Van Buren (1783-1819; 1807)	NY	4/0	Florence Kling De Wolfe Harding (1860-1924; 1891)	OH	None
Anna Tuthill Symmes Harrison (1775-1864; 1795)	NJ	6/4	Grace Anna Goodhue Coolidge (1879-1957; 1905)	VT	2/0
Letitia Christian Tyler (1790-1842; 1813)	VA	3/5	Lou Henry Hoover (1875-1944; 1899)	IA	2/0
Julia Gardiner Tyler (1820-89; 1844)	NY	5/2	Anna Eleanor Roosevelt (1884-1962; 1905)	NY	5/1
Sarah Childress Polk (1803-91; 1824)	TN	None	Elizabeth Virginia (Bess) Wallace Truman (1885-1982; 1919)	MO	0/1
Margaret (Peggy) Mackall Smith Taylor (1788-1852; 1810)	MD	1/5	Mamie Geneva Doud Eisenhower (1896-1979; 1916)	IA	2/0
Abigail Powers Fillmore (1798-1853; 1826)	NY	1/1	Jacqueline Lee Bouvier Kennedy (1929-94; 1953)	NY	2/1
Caroline Carmichael McIntosh Fillmore (1813-81; 1858)	NJ	None	Claudia (Lady Bird) Alta Taylor Johnson (1912-2007; 1934)	TX	0/2
Jane Means Appleton Pierce (1806-63; 1834)	NH	3/0	Thelma Catherine Patricia Ryan Nixon (1912-93; 1940)	NV	0/2
Mary Todd Lincoln (1818-82; 1842)	KY	4/0	Elizabeth (Betty) Bloomer Warren Ford (1918-2011; 1948)	IL	3/1
Eliza McCardle Johnson (1810-76; 1827)	TN	3/2	Eleanor Rosalynn Smith Carter (1927- ; 1946)	GA	3/1
Julia Boggs Dent Grant (1826-1902; 1848)	MO	3/1	Anne Frances (Nancy) Robbins Davis Reagan (1921- ; 1952)	NY	1/1[3]
Lucy Ware Webb Hayes (1831-89; 1852)	OH	7/1	Barbara Pierce Bush (1925- ; 1945)	NY	4/2
Lucretia Rudolph Garfield (1832-1918; 1858)	OH	5/2	Hillary Diane Rodham Clinton (1947- ; 1975)	IL	0/1
Ellen Lewis Herndon Arthur (1837-80; 1859)	VA	2/1	Laura Lane Welch Bush (1946- ; 1977)	TX	0/2
Frances Folsom Cleveland (1864-1947; 1886)	NY	2/3	Michelle LaVaughn Robinson Obama (1964- ; 1992)	IL	0/2
Caroline Lavinia Scott Harrison (1832-92; 1853)	OH	1/1			

Note: Pres. Buchanan was unmarried. (1) Born in London, father a MD citizen. (2) Adopted son. (3) Pres. Reagan's first wife, whom he later divorced, was Jane Wyman. They had a daughter who died in infancy, a daughter who lived past infancy, and an adopted son.

First Lady Michelle Obama

Michelle Robinson Obama was born in Chicago, IL, Jan. 17, 1964. She graduated from Princeton Univ., 1985, earned a law degree from Harvard Univ., 1988, and joined Chicago law firm Sidley & Austin. She served as assistant commissioner of planning and development for the city of Chicago, then as founding executive director of the Chicago chapter of Public Allies, an AmeriCorps program. She began working for the Univ. of Chicago in 1996, first as associate dean of student services, then as the Univ. of Chicago Medical Center's vice president of community and external affairs. Michelle and Barack Obama were married in 1992; in 1998, their daughter Malia was born, followed by Natasha (Sasha) in 2001.

As First Lady, Michelle Obama has focused on supporting military families, helping women balance career and family, encouraging national service, and promoting the arts and arts education. She has also launched a major campaign to deal with the problem of childhood obesity in the U.S.

Burial Places of the Presidents

President	Burial place	President	Burial place	President	Burial place
Washington	Mt. Vernon, VA	Pierce	Concord, NH	Wilson	Wash. Natl. Cathedral, DC
J. Adams	Quincy, MA	Buchanan	Lancaster, PA	Harding	Marion, OH
Jefferson	Charlottesville, VA	Lincoln	Springfield, IL	Coolidge	Plymouth Notch, VT
Madison	Montpelier Station, VA	A. Johnson	Greeneville, TN	Hoover	West Branch, IA
Monroe	Richmond, VA	Grant	New York, NY	F. Roosevelt	Hyde Park, NY
J. Q. Adams	Quincy, MA	Hayes	Fremont, OH	Truman	Independence, MO
Jackson	Nashville, TN	Garfield	Cleveland, OH	Eisenhower	Abilene, KS
Van Buren	Kinderhook, NY	Arthur	Albany, NY	Kennedy	Arlington Natl. Cem., VA
W. H. Harrison	North Bend, OH	Cleveland	Princeton, NJ	L. B. Johnson	Stonewall, TX
Tyler	Richmond, VA	B. Harrison	Indianapolis, IN	Nixon	Yorba Linda, CA
Polk	Nashville, TN	McKinley	Canton, OH	Ford	Grand Rapids, MI
Taylor	Louisville, KY	T. Roosevelt	Oyster Bay, NY	Reagan	Simi Valley, CA
Fillmore	Buffalo, NY	Taft	Arlington Natl. Cem., VA		

PRESIDENTIAL ELECTIONS

Electoral and Popular Vote, 2008 and 2012

Source: Federal Election Commission

| | 2012 | | | | | 2008 | | | | | |
State	Electoral vote Obama	Romney	Popular vote Obama	Romney	Johnson	Electoral vote Obama	McCain	Popular vote Obama	McCain	Nader	State
AL	0	9	795,696	1,255,925	12,328	0	9	813,479	1,266,546	6,788	AL
AK	0	3	122,640	164,676	7,392	0	3	123,594	193,841	3,783	AK
AZ	0	11	1,025,232	1,233,654	32,100	0	10	1,034,707	1,230,111	11,301	AZ
AR	0	6	394,409	647,744	16,276	0	6	422,310	638,017	12,882	AR
CA	55	0	7,854,285	4,839,958	143,221	55	0	8,274,473	5,011,781	108,381	CA
CO	9	0	1,323,102	1,185,243	35,545	9	0	1,288,633	1,073,629	13,352	CO
CT	7	0	905,083	634,892	12,580	7	0	997,772	629,428	19,162	CT
DE	3	0	242,584	165,484	3,882	3	0	255,459	152,374	2,401	DE
DC	3	0	267,070	21,381	2,083	3	0	245,800	17,367	958	DC
FL	29	0	4,237,756	4,163,447	44,726	27	0	4,282,074	4,045,624	28,124	FL
GA	0	16	1,773,827	2,078,688	45,324	0	15	1,844,123	2,048,759	1,158	GA
HI	4	0	306,658	121,015	3,840	4	0	325,871	120,566	3,825	HI
ID	0	4	212,787	420,911	9,453	0	4	236,440	403,012	7,175	ID
IL	20	0	3,019,512	2,135,216	56,229	21	0	3,419,348	2,031,179	30,948	IL
IN	0	11	1,152,887	1,420,543	50,111	11	0	1,374,039	1,345,648	909	IN
IA	6	0	822,544	730,617	12,926	7	0	828,940	682,379	8,014	IA
KS	0	6	440,726	692,634	20,456	0	6	514,765	699,655	10,527	KS
KY	0	8	679,370	1,087,190	17,063	0	8	751,985	1,048,462	15,378	KY
LA	0	8	809,141	1,152,262	18,157	0	9	782,989	1,148,275	6,997	LA
ME	4	0	401,306	292,276	9,352	4	0	421,923	295,273	10,636	ME
MD	10	0	1,677,844	971,869	30,195	10	0	1,629,467	959,862	14,713	MD
MA	11	0	1,921,290	1,188,314	30,920	12	0	1,904,097	1,108,854	28,841	MA
MI	16	0	2,564,569	2,115,256	7,774	17	0	2,872,579	2,048,639	33,085	MI
MN	10	0	1,546,167	1,320,225	35,098	10	0	1,573,354	1,275,409	30,152	MN
MS	0	6	562,949	710,746	6,676	0	6	554,662	724,597	4,011	MS
MO	0	10	1,223,796	1,482,440	43,151	0	11	1,441,911	1,445,814	17,813	MO
MT	0	3	201,839	267,928	14,165	0	3	231,667	242,763	3,686	MT
NE[1]	0	5	302,081	475,064	11,109	1	4	333,319	452,979	5,406	NE[1]
NV	6	0	531,373	463,567	10,968	5	0	533,736	412,827	6,150	NV
NH	4	0	369,561	329,918	8,212	4	0	384,826	316,534	3,503	NH
NJ	14	0	2,125,101	1,477,568	21,045	15	0	2,215,422	1,613,207	21,298	NJ
NM	5	0	415,335	335,788	27,788	5	0	472,422	346,832	5,327	NM
NY	29	0	4,485,741	2,490,431	47,256	31	0	4,804,945	2,752,771	41,249	NY
NC	0	15	2,178,391	2,270,395	44,515	15	0	2,142,651	2,128,474	1,448	NC
ND	0	3	124,827	188,163	5,231	0	3	141,278	168,601	4,189	ND
OH	18	0	2,827,709	2,661,437	49,493	20	0	2,940,044	2,677,820	42,337	OH
OK	0	7	443,547	891,325	—	0	7	502,496	960,165	—	OK
OR	7	0	970,488	754,175	24,089	7	0	1,037,291	738,475	18,614	OR
PA	20	0	2,990,274	2,680,434	49,991	21	0	3,276,363	2,655,885	42,977	PA
RI	4	0	279,677	157,204	4,388	4	0	296,571	165,391	4,829	RI
SC	0	9	865,941	1,071,645	16,321	0	8	862,449	1,034,896	5,053	SC
SD	0	3	145,039	210,610	5,795	0	3	170,924	203,054	4,267	SD
TN	0	11	960,709	1,462,330	18,623	0	11	1,087,437	1,479,178	11,560	TN
TX	0	38	3,308,124	4,569,843	88,580	0	34	3,528,633	4,479,328	5,751	TX
UT	0	6	251,813	740,600	12,572	0	5	327,670	596,030	8,416	UT
VT	3	0	199,239	92,698	3,487	3	0	219,262	98,974	3,339	VT
VA	13	0	1,971,820	1,822,522	31,216	13	0	1,959,532	1,725,005	11,483	VA
WA	12	0	1,755,396	1,290,670	42,202	11	0	1,750,848	1,229,216	29,489	WA
WV	0	5	238,269	417,655	6,302	0	5	303,857	397,466	7,219	WV
WI	10	0	1,620,985	1,410,966	20,439	10	0	1,677,211	1,262,393	17,605	WI
WY	0	3	69,286	170,962	5,326	0	3	82,868	164,958	2,525	WY
Total	332	206	65,915,796	60,933,500	1,275,971	365	173	69,498,516	59,948,323	739,034	Total

— = Not listed on state's ballot. (1) Nebraska is one of two states (the other is Maine) that allows electoral votes to be split between candidates.

Presidential Popular Vote, 2012

Candidate (party)	Vote total	Percent of vote
Barack Obama (Democrat)	65,915,796	51.06%
Mitt Romney (Republican)	60,933,500	47.20
Gary Johnson (Libertarian)	1,275,971	0.99
Jill Stein (Green)	469,628	0.36
Virgil Goode (Constitution/U.S. Taxpayers)	122,388	0.09
Roseanne Barr (Peace and Freedom)	67,326	0.05
Ross C. "Rocky" Anderson (Justice/Natural Law)	43,018	0.03
Tom Hoefling (American Independent, America's Party)	40,628	0.03
Randall Terry (Independent/no party affiliation)	13,105	0.01
Richard Duncan (Independent)	12,557	0.01
Peta Lindsay (Socialism and Liberation)	7,791	0.01
Chuck Baldwin (Reform)	5,017	<0.01
Will Christensen (Constitution)	4,453	<0.01
Stewart Alexander (Socialist)	4,405	<0.01
James Harris (Socialist Workers)	4,117	<0.01
Thomas Robert Stevens (Objectivist)	4,091	<0.01%
Jim Carlson (Grassroots)	3,149	<0.01
Jill Reed (Unaffiliated)	2,875	<0.01
Merlin Miller (American Third Position)	2,701	<0.01
Sheila "Samm" Tittle (We the People)	2,572	<0.01
Gloria La Riva (Socialism and Liberation)	1,608	<0.01
Jerry White (Socialist Equality)	1,279	<0.01
Dean Morstad (Constitutional Govt.)	1,094	<0.01
Jerry Litzel (nominated by petition)	1,027	<0.01
Barbara Dale Washer (Reform)	1,016	<0.01
Jeff Boss (NSA Did 911)	1,007	<0.01
Andre Barnett (Reform)	956	<0.01
Jack Fellure (Prohibition)	518	<0.01
Write-in votes (other/miscellaneous)	136,040	0.11
None of these candidates (Nevada)	5,770	<0.01
Total	129,085,403	

Voting age population, Nov. 2012 235,248,000
Percentage casting vote for president 54.87%

Note: Party designations vary from one state to another; party label listed may not necessarily represent a political party organization. Vote totals for the candidates listed above include any write-in votes they received.

The Electoral College

The president and the vice president are the only elective federal officials not chosen by direct vote of the people. They are elected by the members of the Electoral College, an institution provided for in the U.S. Constitution.

On presidential election day, the first Tuesday after the first Monday in Nov. of every fourth year, each state chooses as many electors as it has senators and representatives in Congress. In 1964, for the first time, as provided by the 23rd Amendment to the Constitution, the District of Columbia voted for three electors. Thus, with 100 senators and 435 representatives, there are 538 members of the Electoral College, with a majority of 270 electoral votes needed to elect the president and vice president.

Although political parties were not part of the original plan created by the Founding Fathers, today political parties customarily nominate their lists of electors at their respective state conventions. Some states print names of the candidates for president and vice president at the top of the Nov. ballot; others list only the electors' names. In either case, the electors of the party receiving the highest vote are elected. Two states, Maine and Nebraska, allow for proportional allocation.

The electors meet on the first Monday after the second Wednesday in Dec. in their respective state capitals or in some other place prescribed by state legislatures. By long-established custom, they vote for their party nominees, although this is not required by federal law; some states do require it.

The Constitution requires electors to cast a ballot for at least one person who is not an inhabitant of that elector's home state. This ensures that presidential and vice presidential candidates from the same party will not be from the same state. (In 2000, Republican vice presidential nominee Dick Cheney changed his voter registration to Wyoming, where he grew up and which he'd once represented in Congress, from George W. Bush's home state of Texas.) Also, an elector cannot be a member of Congress or hold federal office.

Certified and sealed lists of the votes of the electors in each state are sent to the president of the U.S. Senate, who then opens them in the presence of the members of the Senate and House of Representatives in a joint session held in early Jan., and the electoral votes of all the states are then officially counted.

If no candidate for president has a majority, the House of Representatives chooses a president from the top three candidates, with all representatives from each state combining to cast one vote for that state. The House decided the outcome of the 1800 and 1824 presidential elections. If no candidate for vice president has a majority, the Senate chooses from the top two, with the senators voting as individuals. The Senate chose the vice president following the 1836 election.

Under the electoral college system, a candidate who fails to be the top vote getter in the popular vote still may win a majority of electoral votes. This happened in the elections of 1876, 1888, and 2000.

Electoral Votes for President, 2012

Electoral votes based on the 2010 Census were in force beginning with the 2012 elections.

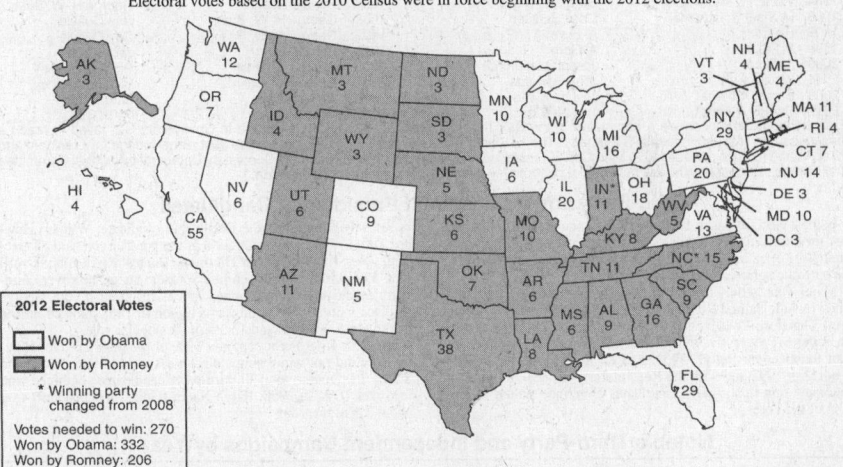

2012 Electoral Votes
☐ Won by Obama
■ Won by Romney
* Winning party changed from 2008
Votes needed to win: 270
Won by Obama: 332
Won by Romney: 206

Voter Turnout in Presidential Elections, 1932-2012

Source: Federal Election Commission; Center for the Study of the American Electorate, American Univ.; *Congressional Quarterly*

Year	Candidates	Voter participation (% of voting-age population)	Year	Candidates	Voter participation (% of voting-age population)
1932	F. D. Roosevelt-Hoover	52.4%	1976	Carter-Ford	53.5%
1936	F. D. Roosevelt-Landon	56.0	1980	Reagan-Carter	54.0
1940	F. D. Roosevelt-Willkie	58.9	1984	Reagan-Mondale	53.1
1944	F. D. Roosevelt-Dewey	56.0	1988	G. H. W. Bush-Dukakis	50.2
1948	Truman-Dewey	51.1	1992	Clinton-G. H. W. Bush-Perot	55.9
1952	Eisenhower-Stevenson	61.6	1996	Clinton-Dole-Perot	49.0
1956	Eisenhower-Stevenson	59.3	2000	G. W. Bush-Gore	51.3
1960	Kennedy-Nixon	62.8	2004	G. W. Bush-Kerry	60.7
1964	L. B. Johnson-Goldwater	61.9	2008	Obama-McCain	58.2
1968	Nixon-Humphrey	60.9	2012	Obama-Romney	54.9
1972	Nixon-McGovern	55.2[1]			

(1) The drop in voter participation followed the expansion of eligibility with the enfranchisement of 18- to 20-year-olds.

Major-Party Nominees for President and Vice President, 1856-2012

Asterisk (*) denotes winning ticket.

	Democratic			Republican	
Year	President	Vice President	Year	President	Vice President
1856	James Buchanan*	John Breckinridge	1856	John Frémont	William Dayton
1860	Stephen A. Douglas[1]	Herschel V. Johnson	1860	Abraham Lincoln*	Hannibal Hamlin
1864	George McClellan	G. H. Pendleton	1864	Abraham Lincoln*	Andrew Johnson
1868	Horatio Seymour	Francis Blair	1868	Ulysses S. Grant*	Schuyler Colfax
1872	Horace Greeley	B. Gratz Brown	1872	Ulysses S. Grant*	Henry Wilson
1876	Samuel J. Tilden	Thomas Hendricks	1876	Rutherford B. Hayes*	William Wheeler
1880	Winfield Hancock	William English	1880	James A. Garfield*	Chester A. Arthur
1884	Grover Cleveland*	Thomas Hendricks	1884	James G. Blaine	John Logan
1888	Grover Cleveland	A. G. Thurman	1888	Benjamin Harrison*	Levi Morton
1892	Grover Cleveland*	Adlai Stevenson	1892	Benjamin Harrison	Whitelaw Reid
1896	William J. Bryan	Arthur Sewall	1896	William McKinley*	Garret Hobart
1900	William J. Bryan	Adlai Stevenson	1900	William McKinley*	Theodore Roosevelt
1904	Alton Parker	Henry Davis	1904	Theodore Roosevelt*	Charles Fairbanks
1908	William J. Bryan	John Kern	1908	William H. Taft*	James Sherman
1912	Woodrow Wilson*	Thomas Marshall	1912	William H. Taft	James Sherman[2]
1916	Woodrow Wilson*	Thomas Marshall	1916	Charles E. Hughes	Charles Fairbanks
1920	James M. Cox	Franklin D. Roosevelt	1920	Warren G. Harding*	Calvin Coolidge
1924	John W. Davis	Charles W. Bryan	1924	Calvin Coolidge*	Charles G. Dawes
1928	Alfred E. Smith	Joseph T. Robinson	1928	Herbert Hoover*	Charles Curtis
1932	Franklin D. Roosevelt*	John N. Garner	1932	Herbert Hoover	Charles Curtis
1936	Franklin D. Roosevelt*	John N. Garner	1936	Alfred M. Landon	Frank Knox
1940	Franklin D. Roosevelt*	Henry A. Wallace	1940	Wendell L. Willkie	Charles McNary
1944	Franklin D. Roosevelt*	Harry S. Truman	1944	Thomas E. Dewey	John W. Bricker
1948	Harry S. Truman*	Alben W. Barkley	1948	Thomas E. Dewey	Earl Warren
1952	Adlai E. Stevenson	John J. Sparkman	1952	Dwight D. Eisenhower*	Richard M. Nixon
1956	Adlai E. Stevenson	Estes Kefauver	1956	Dwight D. Eisenhower*	Richard M. Nixon
1960	John F. Kennedy*	Lyndon B. Johnson	1960	Richard M. Nixon	Henry Cabot Lodge
1964	Lyndon B. Johnson*	Hubert H. Humphrey	1964	Barry M. Goldwater	William E. Miller
1968	Hubert H. Humphrey	Edmund S. Muskie	1968	Richard M. Nixon*	Spiro T. Agnew
1972	George S. McGovern	R. Sargent Shriver Jr.[3]	1972	Richard M. Nixon*	Spiro T. Agnew
1976	Jimmy Carter*	Walter F. Mondale	1976	Gerald R. Ford	Bob Dole
1980	Jimmy Carter	Walter F. Mondale	1980	Ronald Reagan*	George H. W. Bush
1984	Walter F. Mondale	Geraldine Ferraro	1984	Ronald Reagan*	George H. W. Bush
1988	Michael S. Dukakis	Lloyd Bentsen	1988	George H. W. Bush*	Dan Quayle
1992	Bill Clinton*	Al Gore	1992	George H. W. Bush	Dan Quayle
1996	Bill Clinton*	Al Gore	1996	Bob Dole	Jack Kemp
2000	Al Gore	Joseph Lieberman	2000	George W. Bush*	Richard Cheney
2004	John Kerry	John Edwards	2004	George W. Bush*	Richard Cheney
2008	Barack Obama*	Joseph Biden	2008	John McCain	Sarah Palin
2012	Barack Obama*	Joseph Biden	2012	Mitt Romney	Paul Ryan

(1) Douglas and Johnson were nominated at the Baltimore convention. An earlier convention in Charleston, SC, failed to reach a consensus and resulted in a split in the party. The Southern faction of the Democrats nominated John Breckinridge for president and Joseph Lane for vice president. (2) Died Oct. 30; replaced on ballot by Nicholas Butler. (3) Chosen by Democratic National Committee after Thomas Eagleton withdrew because of controversy over past treatments for depression.

Third-Party and Independent Presidential Candidates

In most elections since 1860, fewer than one vote in 20 has been cast for a third-party candidate. Still, independent and third-party candidates often bring attention to prominent issues and can affect the outcome between major-party candidates.

Major vote getters among third-party and independent candidates include James B. Weaver (People's Party), 1892; former Pres. Theodore Roosevelt (Progressive Party), 1912; Robert M. La Follette (Progressive Party), 1924; George C. Wallace (American Independent Party), 1968; and H. Ross Perot, as an independent in 1992 and with the Reform Party in 1996. In these six elections, non-major-party candidates combined polled at least 10% of the vote.

Roosevelt outpolled the Republican candidate, William Howard Taft, in 1912, capturing 28% of the popular vote and 88 electoral votes. In 1948, Strom Thurmond (States' Rights [Dixiecrat]) won 39 electoral votes from five Southern states; however, third-party candidates received only 5.75% of the popular vote. George Wallace's popularity in the same region in 1968 allowed him to get 46 electoral votes and 13.5% of the popular vote.

In 1992, Ross Perot captured 19% of the popular vote. However, he did not win a single electoral vote. In 1996, Perot won 8% of the popular vote; all third-party candidates combined won just over 10%. In 2000, Ralph Nader (Green, independent) won about 3% of the vote.

Notable Third-Party and Independent Campaigns by Year

Party	Presidential nominee	Year	Issues	Strength in
Anti-Masonic	William Wirt	1832	Against secret societies and oaths	PA, VT
Liberty	James G. Birney	1844	Anti-slavery	North
Free Soil	Martin Van Buren	1848	Anti-slavery	NY, OH
American (Know-Nothing)	Millard Fillmore	1856	Anti-immigrant	Northeast, South
Greenback	Peter Cooper	1876	For "cheap money," labor rights	National
Greenback	James B. Weaver	1880	For "cheap money," labor rights	National
Prohibition	John P. St. John	1884	Anti-liquor	National
People's (Populist)	James B. Weaver	1892	For "cheap money," end of national banks	South, West
Socialist	Eugene V. Debs	1900-12; 1920	For public ownership	National
Progressive (Bull Moose)	Theodore Roosevelt	1912	Against high tariffs	Midwest, West
Progressive	Robert M. La Follette	1924	For farmer and labor rights	Midwest, West
Socialist	Norman Thomas	1928-48	For liberal reforms	National
Union	William Lemke	1936	Anti-New Deal	National
States' Rights (Dixiecrat)	Strom Thurmond	1948	For states' rights	South
Progressive	Henry A. Wallace	1948	Anti-Cold War	NY, CA
American Independent	George C. Wallace	1968	For states' rights	South
American	John G. Schmitz	1972	For "law and order"	West, OH, LA
None (independent)	John B. Anderson	1980	A third choice	National
None (independent)	H. Ross Perot	1992	Federal budget deficit	National
Reform	H. Ross Perot	1996	Deficit, campaign finance	National
Green, independent	Ralph Nader	2000-08	Corporate power, domestic priorities	National
Libertarian	Gary Johnson	2012	Public debt, civil liberties	National

Popular and Electoral Vote for President, 1789-2012

(D) Democrat; (DR) Democratic Republican; (F) Federalist; (LB) Libertarian; (LR) Liberal Republican; (NR) National Republican; (P) People's; (PR) Progressive; (R) Republican; (W) Whig; * = See notes below table.

Year	President elected	Popular	Elec.	Major losing candidate(s)	Popular	Elec.
1789	George Washington	Unknown	69	No major opposition	—	—
1792	George Washington	Unknown	132	No major opposition	—	—
1796	John Adams (F)	Unknown	71	Thomas Jefferson (DR)	Unknown	68
1800*	Thomas Jefferson (DR)	Unknown	73	Aaron Burr (DR)	Unknown	73
1804	Thomas Jefferson (DR)	Unknown	162	Charles Pinckney (F)	Unknown	14
1808	James Madison (DR)	Unknown	122	Charles Pinckney (F)	Unknown	47
1812	James Madison (DR)	Unknown	128	DeWitt Clinton (F)	Unknown	89
1816	James Monroe (DR)	Unknown	183	Rufus King (F)	Unknown	34
1820	James Monroe (DR)	Unknown	231	John Quincy Adams (DR)	Unknown	1
1824*	John Quincy Adams (DR)	113,122	84	Andrew Jackson (DR)	151,271	99
				Henry Clay (DR)	46,587	37
				William H. Crawford (DR)	44,282	41
1828	Andrew Jackson (D)	642,553	178	John Quincy Adams (NR)	500,897	83
1832	Andrew Jackson (D)	701,780	219	Henry Clay (NR)	484,205	49
1836	Martin Van Buren (D)	764,176	170	William H. Harrison (W)	550,816	73
1840	William H. Harrison (W)	1,275,390	234	Martin Van Buren (D)	1,128,854	60
1844	James K. Polk (D)	1,339,494	170	Henry Clay (W)	1,300,004	105
1848	Zachary Taylor (W)	1,361,393	163	Lewis Cass (D)	1,223,460	127
				Martin Van Buren (Free Soil)	291,501	—
1852	Franklin Pierce (D)	1,607,510	254	Winfield Scott (W)	1,386,942	42
1856	James Buchanan (D)	1,836,072	174	John C. Fremont (R)	1,342,345	114
				Millard Fillmore (W-American)	873,053	8
1860	Abraham Lincoln (R)	1,865,908	180	Stephen A. Douglas (D)	848,019	12
				John C. Breckinridge (D)	845,763	72
				John Bell (Constitutional Union)	589,581	39
1864	Abraham Lincoln (R)	2,218,388	212	George McClellan (D)	1,812,807	21
1868	Ulysses S. Grant (R)	3,013,650	214	Horatio Seymour (D)	2,708,744	80
1872*	Ulysses S. Grant (R)	3,598,235	286	Horace Greeley (D-LR)	2,834,671	—
1876*	Rutherford B. Hayes (R)	4,034,311	185	Samuel J. Tilden (D)	4,288,546	184
1880	James A. Garfield (R)	4,446,158	214	Winfield S. Hancock (D)	4,444,260	155
1884	Grover Cleveland (D)	4,874,621	219	James G. Blaine (R)	4,848,936	182
1888	Benjamin Harrison (R)	5,443,892	233	Grover Cleveland (D)	5,534,488	168
1892	Grover Cleveland (D)	5,551,883	277	Benjamin Harrison (R)	5,179,244	145
				James Weaver (P)	1,027,329	22
1896	William McKinley (R)	7,108,480	271	William J. Bryan (D-P)	6,511,495	176
1900	William McKinley (R)	7,218,039	292	William J. Bryan (D)	6,358,345	155
1904	Theodore Roosevelt (R)	7,626,593	336	Alton B. Parker (D)	5,082,898	140
1908	William H. Taft (R)	7,676,258	321	William J. Bryan (D)	6,406,801	162
1912	Woodrow Wilson (D)	6,293,152	435	Theodore Roosevelt (PR)	4,119,207	88
				William H. Taft (R)	3,483,922	8
1916	Woodrow Wilson (D)	9,126,300	277	Charles E. Hughes (R)	8,546,789	254
1920	Warren G. Harding (R)	16,153,115	404	James M. Cox (D)	9,133,092	127
1924	Calvin Coolidge (R)	15,719,921	382	John W. Davis (D)	8,386,704	136
				Robert M. La Follette (PR)	4,822,856	13
1928	Herbert Hoover (R)	21,437,277	444	Alfred E. Smith (D)	15,007,698	87
1932	Franklin D. Roosevelt (D)	22,829,501	472	Herbert Hoover (R)	15,760,684	59
1936	Franklin D. Roosevelt (D)	27,757,333	523	Alfred Landon (R)	16,684,231	8
1940	Franklin D. Roosevelt (D)	27,313,041	449	Wendell Willkie (R)	22,348,480	82
1944	Franklin D. Roosevelt (D)	25,612,610	432	Thomas E. Dewey (R)	22,117,617	99
1948	Harry S. Truman (D)	24,179,345	303	Thomas E. Dewey (R)	21,991,291	189
				Strom Thurmond (States' Rights)	1,169,021	39
				Henry A. Wallace (PR)	1,157,172	—
1952	Dwight D. Eisenhower (R)	33,936,234	442	Adlai E. Stevenson (D)	27,314,992	89
1956*	Dwight D. Eisenhower (R)	35,590,472	457	Adlai E. Stevenson (D)	26,022,752	73
1960*	John F. Kennedy (D)	34,226,731	303	Richard M. Nixon (R)	34,108,157	219
1964	Lyndon B. Johnson (D)	43,129,566	486	Barry M. Goldwater (R)	27,178,188	52
1968	Richard M. Nixon (R)	31,785,480	301	Hubert H. Humphrey (D)	31,275,166	191
				George C. Wallace (Amer. Indep.)	9,906,473	46
1972*	Richard M. Nixon (R)	47,169,911	520	George S. McGovern (D)	29,170,383	17
1976*	Jimmy Carter (D)	40,830,763	297	Gerald R. Ford (R)	39,147,793	240
1980	Ronald Reagan (R)	43,904,153	489	Jimmy Carter (D)	35,483,883	49
				John B. Anderson (independent)	5,719,437	—
1984	Ronald Reagan (R)	54,455,075	525	Walter F. Mondale (D)	37,577,185	13
1988*	George H. W. Bush (R)	48,886,097	426	Michael S. Dukakis (D)	41,809,074	111
1992	Bill Clinton (D)	44,908,254	370	George H. W. Bush (R)	39,102,343	168
				H. Ross Perot (independent)	19,741,065	—
1996	Bill Clinton (D)	45,590,703	379	Bob Dole (R)	37,816,307	159
				H. Ross Perot (Reform)	7,866,284	—
2000*	George W. Bush (R)	50,459,211	271	Al Gore (D)	51,003,894	266
				Ralph Nader (Green)	2,834,410	—
2004*	George W. Bush (R)	62,040,610	286	John Kerry (D)	59,028,444	251
2008	Barack H. Obama (D)	69,498,516	365	John McCain (R)	59,948,283	173
2012	Barack H. Obama (D)	65,915,796	332	Mitt Romney (R)	60,933,500	206

*1800—Elected by House of Representatives because of tied electoral vote. 1824—Elected by House of Representatives because no candidate polled a majority. By 1824, the Democratic Republicans had become a loose coalition of competing political groups. By 1828, the supporters of Jackson were known as Democrats and John Q. Adams and Henry Clay supporters as National Republicans. 1872—Greeley died Nov. 29, 1872. His electoral votes were split among four individuals. 1876—FL, LA, OR, and SC election returns were disputed. Congress in joint session (Mar. 2, 1877) declared Hayes and Wheeler elected president and vice president. 1956—Democrats elected 74 electors, but one from AL refused to vote for Stevenson. 1960—Sen. Harry F. Byrd (D, VA) received 15 electoral votes. 1972—John Hospers of CA received a vote from an elector of VA. 1976—Ronald Reagan of CA received a vote from an elector of WA. 1988—Sen. Lloyd Bentsen (D, TX) received a vote from an elector of WV. 2000—One Gore elector from Washington, DC, abstained. Nader was listed as "independent" on the ballot in some states; he was not on the ballot in all states. 2004—One MN elector voted for VP candidate John Edwards for both president and vice president.

Presidential Election Results by State, 1960-2012

Source: Federal Election Commission; local secretaries of state; state elections offices. State election results may vary slightly from those provided by the FEC.

Alabama

County	2012		2008	
	Obama (D)	Romney (R)	Obama (D)	McCain (R)
Autauga	6,363	17,379	6,093	17,403
Baldwin	18,424	66,016	19,386	61,271
Barbour	5,912	5,550	5,697	5,866
Bibb	2,202	6,132	2,299	6,262
Blount	2,970	20,757	3,522	20,389
Bullock	4,061	1,251	4,011	1,391
Butler	4,374	5,087	4,188	5,485
Calhoun	15,511	30,278	16,334	32,348
Chambers	6,871	7,626	6,799	8,067
Cherokee	2,132	7,506	2,306	7,298
Chilton	3,397	13,932	3,674	13,960
Choctaw	3,786	4,152	3,636	4,223
Clarke	6,334	7,470	5,914	7,466
Clay	1,777	4,817	1,760	4,984
Cleburne	971	5,272	1,168	5,216
Coffee	4,925	14,666	5,079	14,919
Colbert	9,166	13,936	9,703	14,739
Conecuh	3,555	3,439	3,429	3,470
Coosa	2,191	3,049	2,273	3,248
Covington	3,158	12,153	3,240	12,444
Crenshaw	2,050	4,331	1,938	4,319
Cullman	5,052	28,999	5,864	28,896
Dale	5,286	13,108	5,270	13,886
Dallas	14,612	6,288	13,986	6,798
De Kalb	5,239	18,331	5,658	17,957
Elmore	8,954	26,253	8,301	25,777
Escambia	5,489	9,287	5,188	9,375
Etowah	12,803	29,130	13,497	30,595
Fayette	1,817	6,054	1,994	5,883
Franklin	3,171	7,567	3,469	8,048
Geneva	2,039	9,175	2,134	9,417
Greene	4,521	804	4,408	876
Hale	5,411	3,210	4,982	3,200
Henry	3,083	5,628	3,018	5,585
Houston	12,367	29,270	12,225	29,254
Jackson	5,822	14,439	6,374	14,083
Jefferson	159,876	141,683	166,121	149,921
Lamar	1,646	5,457	1,614	5,419
Lauderdale	12,511	23,911	13,329	24,068
Lawrence	5,069	8,874	5,164	9,277
Lee	21,381	32,194	21,498	32,230
Limestone	9,829	25,295	9,536	23,598
Lowndes	5,747	1,756	5,449	1,809
Macon	9,045	1,331	9,450	1,396
Madison	62,015	90,884	64,117	86,965
Marengo	6,167	5,336	5,926	5,516
Marion	2,249	9,697	2,600	9,536
Marshall	6,299	25,867	7,038	25,727
Mobile	78,760	94,893	82,181	98,049
Monroe	4,914	5,741	5,025	6,175
Montgomery	63,085	38,332	62,166	42,031
Morgan	13,439	35,391	13,895	36,014
Perry	4,568	1,506	4,457	1,679
Pickens	4,455	5,124	4,594	5,434
Pike	6,035	7,963	5,879	8,004
Randolph	3,078	7,224	3,064	7,175
Russell	10,500	8,278	10,085	8,705
St. Clair	5,801	29,031	6,091	27,649
Shelby	20,051	71,436	20,625	69,060
Sumter	5,421	1,586	5,264	1,731
Talladega	13,905	19,246	13,779	20,112
Tallapoosa	6,319	12,396	6,063	13,116
Tuscaloosa	32,048	45,748	32,796	45,405
Walker	6,557	21,651	7,420	20,722
Washington	2,976	5,761	3,067	5,654
Wilcox	4,868	1,679	4,612	1,868
Winston	1,286	8,312	1,757	8,103
Totals	**795,696**	**1,255,925**	**813,479**	**1,266,546**

Alabama Vote Since 1960

2012: Romney, R., 1,255,925; Obama, D., 795,696; Johnson, Ind., 12,328; Stein, Ind., 3,397; Goode, Ind., 2,981.
2008: McCain, R., 1,266,546; Obama, D., 813,479; Nader, Ind., 6,788; Barr, Ind., 4,991; Baldwin, Ind., 4,310.
2004: Bush, R., 1,176,394; Kerry, D., 693,933; Nader, Ind., 6,701; Badnarik, Ind., 3,529; Peroutka, Ind., 1,994.
2000: Bush, R., 941,173; Gore, D., 692,611; Nader, Ind., 18,323; Buchanan, Ind., 6,351; Browne, Ind., 5,893; Phillips, Ind., 775; Hagelin, Ind., 447.

1996: Dole, R., 769,044; Clinton, D., 662,165; Perot, RF., 92,149; Browne, LB., 5,290; Phillips, Ind., 2,365; Hagelin, Natural Law, 1,697; Harris, Ind., 516.
1992: Bush, R., 804,283; Clinton, D., 690,080; Perot, Ind., 183,109; Marrou, LB., 5,737; Fulani, New Alliance, 2,161.
1988: Bush, R., 815,576; Dukakis, D., 549,506; Paul, LB., 8,460; Fulani, Ind., 3,311.
1984: Reagan, R., 872,849; Mondale, D., 551,899; Bergland, LB., 9,504.
1980: Reagan, R., 654,192; Carter, D., 636,730; Anderson, Ind., 16,481; Rarick, Amer. Ind., 15,010; Clark, LB., 13,318; Bubar, Statesman, 1,743; Hall, Comm., 1,629; DeBerry, Soc. Workers, 1,303; McReynolds, Soc., 1,006; Commoner, Citizens, 517.
1976: Carter, D., 659,170; Ford, R., 504,070; Maddox, Amer. Ind., 9,198; Bubar, Prohib., 6,669; Hall, Comm., 1,954; MacBride, LB., 1,481.
1972: Nixon, R., 728,701; McGovern, D., 219,108 plus 37,815 Natl. Dem. Party of AL; Schmitz, Conservative, 11,918; Munn, Prohib., 8,551.
1968: Wallace, 3rd party, 691,425; Humphrey, D., 196,579; Nixon, R., 146,923; Munn, Prohib., 4,022.
1964: Goldwater, R., 479,085; D. (electors unpledged), 209,848; scattered, 105.
1960: Kennedy, D., 324,050; Nixon, R., 237,981; Faubus, States' Rights, 4,367; Decker, Prohib., 2,106; King, Afro-Americans, 1,485; scattered, 236.

Alaska

	2012		2008	
	Obama (D)	Romney (R)	Obama (D)	McCain (R)
Totals	122,640	164,676	123,594	193,841

Alaska Vote Since 1960

2012: Romney, R., 164,676; Obama, D., 122,640; Johnson, LB., 7,392; Stein, Green, 2,917.
2008: McCain, R., 193,841; Obama, D., 123,594; Nader, Ind., 3,783; Baldwin, AK Ind., 1,660; Barr, LB., 1,589.
2004: Bush, R., 190,889; Kerry, D., 111,025; Nader, Populist, 5,069; Peroutka, AK Ind., 2,092; Badnarik, LB., 1,675; Cobb, Green, 1,058.
2000: Bush, R., 167,398; Gore, D., 79,004; Nader, Green, 28,747; Buchanan, RF., 5,192; Browne, LB., 2,636; Hagelin, Natural Law, 919; Phillips, Const., 596.
1996: Dole, R., 122,746; Clinton, D., 80,380; Perot, RF., 26,333; Nader, Green, 7,597; Browne, LB., 2,276; Phillips, U.S. Taxpayers, 925; Hagelin, Natural Law, 729.
1992: Bush, R., 102,000; Clinton, D., 78,294; Perot, Ind., 73,481; Gritz, Populist/America First, 1,379; Marrou, LB., 1,378.
1988: Bush, R., 119,251; Dukakis, D., 72,584; Paul, LB., 5,484; Fulani, New Alliance, 1,024.
1984: Reagan, R., 138,377; Mondale, D., 62,007; Bergland, LB., 6,378.
1980: Reagan, R., 86,112; Carter, D., 41,842; Clark, LB., 18,479; Anderson, Ind., 11,155; write-in, 857.
1976: Ford, R., 71,555; Carter, D., 44,058; MacBride, LB., 6,785.
1972: Nixon, R., 55,349; McGovern, D., 32,967; Schmitz, Amer., 6,903.
1968: Nixon, R., 37,600; Humphrey, D., 35,411; Wallace, 3rd party, 10,024.
1964: Johnson, D., 44,329; Goldwater, R., 22,930.
1960: Nixon, R., 30,953; Kennedy, D., 29,809.

Arizona

County	2012		2008	
	Obama (D)	Romney (R)	Obama (D)	McCain (R)
Apache	17,147	8,250	15,390	8,551
Cochise	18,546	29,497	18,943	29,026
Coconino	29,257	21,220	31,433	22,186
Gila	7,697	13,455	7,884	14,095
Graham	3,609	8,076	3,487	8,376
Greenlee	1,310	1,592	1,165	1,712
La Paz	1,880	3,714	1,929	3,509
Maricopa	602,288	749,885	602,166	746,448
Mohave	19,533	49,168	22,092	44,333
Navajo	16,945	19,884	15,579	19,761
Pima	201,251	174,779	206,254	182,406
Pinal	44,306	62,079	44,254	59,421
Santa Cruz	9,486	4,235	8,683	4,518
Yavapai	33,918	64,468	36,889	61,192
Yuma	18,059	23,352	18,559	24,577
Totals	**1,025,232**	**1,233,654**	**1,034,707**	**1,230,111**

Arizona Vote Since 1960

2012: Romney, R., 1,233,654; Obama, D., 1,025,232; Johnson, LB., 32,100; Stein, Green, 7,816.
2008: McCain, R., 1,230,111; Obama, D., 1,034,707; Barr, LB., 12,555; Nader, New Prog., 11,301; McKinney, Green, 3,406.
2004: Bush, R., 1,104,294; Kerry, D., 893,524; Badnarik, LB., 11,856.
2000: Bush, R., 781,652; Gore, D., 685,341; Nader, Green, 45,645; Buchanan, RF., 12,373; Smith, LB., 5,775; Hagelin, Natural Law, 1,120.
1996: Clinton, D., 653,288; Dole, R., 622,073; Perot, RF., 112,072; Browne, LB., 14,358.
1992: Bush, R., 572,086; Clinton, D., 543,050; Perot, Ind., 353,741; Gritz, Populist/America First, 8,141; Marrou, LB., 6,759; Hagelin, Natural Law, 2,267.
1988: Bush, R., 702,541; Dukakis, D., 454,029; Paul, LB., 13,351; Fulani, New Alliance, 1,662.
1984: Reagan, R., 681,416; Mondale, D., 333,854; Bergland, LB., 10,585.
1980: Reagan, R., 529,688; Carter, D., 246,843; Anderson, Ind., 76,952; Clark, LB., 18,784; DeBerry, Soc. Workers, 1,100; Commoner, Citizens, 551; Hall, Comm., 25; Griswold, Workers World, 2.
1976: Ford, R., 418,642; Carter, D., 295,602; McCarthy, Ind., 19,229; MacBride, LB., 7,647; Camejo, Soc. Workers, 928; Anderson, Amer., 564; Maddox, Amer. Ind., 85.
1972: Nixon, R., 402,812; McGovern, D., 198,540; Jenness, Soc. Workers, 30,945; Schmitz, Amer. Ind., 21,208.
1968: Nixon, R., 266,721; Humphrey, D., 170,514; Wallace, 3rd party, 46,573; McCarthy, New Party, 2,751; Cleaver, Peace/Freedom, 217; Halstead, Soc. Workers, 85; Blomen, Soc. Labor, 75.
1964: Goldwater, R., 242,535; Johnson, D., 237,753; Hass, Soc. Labor, 482.
1960: Nixon, R., 221,241; Kennedy, D., 176,781; Hass, Soc. Labor, 469.

Arkansas

County	2012 Obama (D)	Romney (R)	2008 Obama (D)	McCain (R)
Arkansas	2,455	3,897	2,619	4,185
Ashley	2,859	4,867	2,976	5,406
Baxter	5,172	13,688	6,539	12,852
Benton	22,636	54,646	23,331	51,124
Boone	3,772	11,159	4,435	10,575
Bradley	1,449	2,134	1,680	2,262
Calhoun	660	1,458	691	1,462
Carroll	3,696	6,125	4,172	6,083
Chicot	2,649	1,670	3,043	2,119
Clark	3,811	4,343	4,267	4,608
Clay	1,738	3,225	2,244	3,032
Cleburne	2,620	8,693	2,951	7,962
Cleveland	845	2,313	911	2,451
Columbia	3,557	5,790	3,554	5,861
Conway	3,005	4,514	3,149	4,691
Craighead	10,527	20,350	11,294	18,881
Crawford	4,881	15,145	5,238	14,688
Crittenden	9,487	6,998	10,330	7,650
Cross	2,279	4,269	2,580	4,393
Dallas	1,337	1,665	1,471	1,757
Desha	2,443	1,896	2,569	1,999
Drew	2,630	3,887	2,598	3,860
Faulkner	13,621	26,722	14,955	25,362
Franklin	1,726	4,631	1,869	4,411
Fulton	1,452	2,949	1,819	2,702
Garland	13,804	26,014	15,899	26,825
Grant	1,468	4,829	1,562	5,023
Greene	4,000	9,071	4,541	8,578
Hempstead	2,468	4,284	2,869	4,273
Hot Spring	3,830	7,097	4,288	7,209
Howard	1,471	2,892	1,746	2,957
Independence	3,281	8,728	3,688	8,255
Izard	1,524	3,575	1,792	3,193
Jackson	2,095	3,072	2,207	3,118
Jefferson	17,470	9,520	18,465	10,655
Johnson	2,799	5,064	3,034	4,922
Lafayette	1,173	1,713	1,133	1,685
Lawrence	1,788	3,536	2,138	3,357
Lee	2,107	1,280	2,263	1,454
Lincoln	1,425	2,199	1,710	2,513
Little River	1,552	3,385	1,753	3,247
Logan	2,009	5,079	2,286	5,350
Lonoke	5,625	17,880	5,968	17,242
Madison	2,099	4,263	2,144	3,972
Marion	2,037	4,774	2,384	4,524
Miller	4,518	10,622	4,869	9,913
Mississippi	6,467	6,603	6,667	6,976
Monroe	1,583	1,585	1,615	1,754
Montgomery	920	2,369	1,092	2,365
Nevada	1,314	1,996	1,474	2,062

County	2012 Obama (D)	Romney (R)	2008 Obama (D)	McCain (R)
Newton	993	2,508	1,182	2,588
Ouachita	4,633	5,521	4,346	5,427
Perry	1,187	2,581	1,352	2,743
Phillips	5,202	2,598	5,695	3,097
Pike	851	2,847	1,089	2,727
Poinsett	2,390	4,974	2,742	4,903
Polk	1,556	5,955	1,957	5,473
Pope	5,126	14,763	6,002	15,568
Prairie	880	2,153	1,048	2,223
Pulaski	87,248	68,984	88,854	70,212
Randolph	2,046	3,701	2,469	3,615
St. Francis	4,910	3,368	5,486	3,917
Saline	12,869	32,963	12,695	30,981
Scott	897	2,631	1,053	2,791
Searcy	814	2,699	961	2,726
Sebastian	13,092	29,169	13,673	28,637
Sevier	1,042	3,136	1,291	3,125
Sharp	2,092	4,921	2,436	4,535
Stone	1,356	3,776	1,598	3,534
Union	6,196	10,699	6,190	10,677
Van Buren	1,832	4,365	2,151	4,274
Washington	28,236	39,688	29,021	37,963
White	5,765	20,011	6,732	19,467
Woodruff	1,340	1,227	1,412	1,206
Yell	1,722	4,042	2,003	3,808
Totals	**394,409**	**647,744**	**422,310**	**638,017**

Arkansas Vote Since 1960

2012: Romney, R., 647,744; Obama, D., 394,409; Johnson, LB., 16,276; Stein, Green, 9,305; Lindsay, Socialism/Liberation, 1,734.
2008: McCain, R., 638,017; Obama, D., 422,310; Nader, Ind., 12,882; Barr, LB., 4,776; Baldwin, Const., 4,023; McKinney, Green, 3,470; La Riva, Socialism/Liberation, 1,139.
2004: Bush, R., 572,898; Kerry, D., 469,953; Nader, Populist, 6,171; Badnarik, LB., 2,352; Peroutka, Const., 2,083; Cobb, Green, 1,488.
2000: Bush, R., 472,940; Gore, D., 422,768; Nader, Green, 13,421; Buchanan, RF., 7,358; Browne, LB., 2,781; Phillips, Const., 1,415; Hagelin, Natural Law, 1,098.
1996: Clinton, D., 475,171; Dole, R., 325,416; Perot, RF., 69,884; Nader, Ind., 3,649; Browne, Ind., 3,076; Phillips, Ind., 2,065; Forbes, Ind., 932; Collins, Ind., 823; Masters, Ind., 749; Moorehead, Ind., 747; Hagelin, Ind., 729; Hollis, Ind., 538; Dodge, Ind., 483.
1992: Clinton, D., 505,823; Bush, R., 337,324; Perot, Ind., 99,132; Phillips, U.S. Taxpayers, 1,437; Marrou, LB., 1,261; Fulani, New Alliance, 1,022.
1988: Bush, R., 466,578; Dukakis, D., 349,237; Duke, Populist, 5,146; Paul, LB., 3,297.
1984: Reagan, R., 534,774; Mondale, D., 338,646; Bergland, LB., 2,220.
1980: Reagan, R., 403,164; Carter, D., 398,041; Anderson, Ind., 22,468; Clark, LB., 8,970; Commoner, Citizens, 2,345; Bubar, Statesman, 1,350; Hall, Comm., 1,244.
1976: Carter, D., 498,604; Ford, R., 267,903; McCarthy, Ind., 639; Anderson, Amer. Ind., 389.
1972: Nixon, R., 445,751; McGovern, D., 198,899; Schmitz, Amer. Ind., 3,016.
1968: Wallace, 3rd party, 235,627; Nixon, R., 189,062; Humphrey, D., 184,901.
1964: Johnson, D., 314,197; Goldwater, R., 243,264; Kasper, Natl. States' Rights, 2,965.
1960: Kennedy, D., 215,049; Nixon, R., 184,508; Faubus, Natl. States' Rights, 28,952.

California

County	2012 Obama (D)	Romney (R)	2008 Obama (D)	McCain (R)
Alameda	469,684	108,182	489,106	119,555
Alpine	389	236	422	252
Amador	6,830	10,281	7,813	10,561
Butte	42,669	44,479	49,013	46,706
Calaveras	8,670	12,365	9,813	12,835
Colusa	2,314	3,601	2,569	3,733
Contra Costa	290,824	136,517	306,983	136,436
Del Norte	3,791	4,614	4,323	4,967
El Dorado	35,166	50,973	40,529	50,314
Fresno	129,129	124,490	136,706	131,015
Glenn	3,301	5,632	3,734	5,910
Humboldt	34,457	18,825	39,692	21,713
Imperial	25,136	12,777	24,162	14,008
Inyo	3,422	4,340	3,743	4,523
Kern	89,495	126,618	93,457	134,793
Kings	12,979	17,671	14,747	19,710
Lake	13,163	9,200	14,854	9,935
Lassen	3,053	7,296	3,586	7,483
Los Angeles	2,216,903	885,333	2,295,853	956,425

County	2012 Obama (D)	Romney (R)	2008 Obama (D)	McCain (R)
Madera	16,018	22,852	17,952	23,583
Marin	99,896	30,880	109,320	28,384
Mariposa	3,498	5,140	4,100	5,298
Mendocino	23,193	9,658	27,843	10,721
Merced	33,005	27,581	34,031	28,704
Modoc	1,111	2,777	1,313	2,981
Mono	2,733	2,285	3,093	2,354
Monterey	82,920	37,390	88,453	38,797
Napa	35,870	19,526	38,849	19,484
Nevada	24,663	24,986	28,617	25,663
Orange	512,440	582,302	549,558	579,064
Placer	66,818	99,921	75,112	94,647
Plumas	4,026	5,721	4,715	6,035
Riverside	329,063	318,127	325,017	310,041
Sacramento	300,503	202,514	316,506	213,583
San Benito	11,276	7,343	11,917	7,425
San Bernardino	305,109	262,358	315,720	277,408
San Diego	626,957	536,726	666,581	541,032
San Francisco	301,723	47,076	322,220	52,292
San Joaquin	114,121	86,071	113,974	91,607
San Luis Obispo	61,258	59,967	68,176	61,055
San Mateo	206,085	72,756	222,826	75,057
Santa Barbara	94,129	64,606	105,614	65,585
Santa Clara	450,818	174,843	462,241	190,039
Santa Cruz	90,805	24,047	98,745	25,244
Shasta	25,819	48,067	28,867	49,588
Sierra	653	1,056	743	1,158
Siskiyou	8,046	11,077	9,292	11,520
Solano	96,783	52,092	102,095	56,035
Sonoma	153,942	54,784	168,888	55,127
Stanislaus	77,724	73,459	80,279	77,497
Sutter	12,192	18,122	13,412	18,911
Tehama	7,934	14,235	8,945	14,843
Trinity	2,674	2,716	3,233	2,940
Tulare	41,752	56,956	43,634	59,765
Tuolumne	9,998	13,880	11,532	14,988
Ventura	170,929	147,958	187,601	145,853
Yolo	48,715	23,368	53,488	24,592
Yuba	7,711	11,275	·8,866	12,007
Totals	**7,854,285**	**4,839,958**	**8,274,473**	**5,011,781**

California Vote Since 1960

2012: Obama, D., 7,854,285; Romney, R., 4,839,958; Johnson, LB., 143,221; Stein, Green, 85,638; Barr, Peace/Freedom, 53,824; Hoefling, Amer. Ind., 38,372.

2008: Obama, D., 8,274,473; McCain, R., 5,011,781; Nader, Peace/Freedom, 108,381; Barr, LB., 67,582; Alan Keyes, Amer. Ind., 40,673; McKinney, Green, 38,774.

2004: Kerry, D., 6,745,485; Bush, R., 5,509,826; Badnarik, LB., 50,165; Cobb, Green, 40,771; Peltier, Peace/Freedom, 27,607; Peroutka, Amer. Ind., 26,645.

2000: Gore, D., 5,861,203; Bush, R., 4,567,429; Nader, Green, 418,707; Browne, LB., 45,520; Buchanan, RF., 44,987; Phillips, Amer. Ind., 17,042; Hagelin, Natural Law, 10,934.

1996: Clinton, D., 5,119,835; Dole, R., 3,828,380; Perot, RF., 697,847; Nader, Green, 237,016; Browne, LB., 73,600; Feinland, Peace/Freedom, 25,332; Phillips, Amer. Ind., 21,202; Hagelin, Natural Law, 15,403.

1992: Clinton, D., 5,121,325; Bush, R., 3,630,575; Perot, Ind., 2,296,006; Marrou, LB., 48,139; Daniels, Ind., 18,597; Phillips, U.S. Taxpayers, 12,711.

1988: Bush, R., 5,054,917; Dukakis, D., 4,702,233; Paul, LB., 70,105; Fulani, Ind., 31,181.

1984: Reagan, R., 5,305,410; Mondale, D., 3,815,947; Bergland, LB., 48,400.

1980: Reagan, R., 4,524,858; Carter, D., 3,083,661; Anderson, Ind., 739,833; Clark, LB., 148,434; Commoner, Ind., 61,063; Smith, Peace/Freedom, 18,116; Rarick, Amer. Ind., 9,856.

1976: Ford, R., 3,882,244; Carter, D., 3,742,284; McCarthy, write-in, 58,412; MacBride, LB., 56,388; Maddox, Amer. Ind., 51,098; Wright, People's, 41,731; Camejo, Soc. Workers, 17,259; Hall, Comm., 12,766; write-in, 4,935.

1972: Nixon, R., 4,602,096; McGovern, D., 3,475,847; Schmitz, Amer. Ind., 232,554; Spock, Peace/Freedom, 55,167; Hospers, LB., 980; Jenness, Soc. Workers, 574; Hall, Comm., 373; Fisher, Soc. Labor, 197; Munn, Prohib., 53; Green, Universal, 21.

1968: Nixon, R., 3,467,664; Humphrey, D., 3,244,318; Wallace, 3rd party, 487,270; Peace/Freedom, 27,707; McCarthy, Alternative, 20,721; Gregory, write-in, 3,230; Blomen, Soc. Labor, 341; Mitchell, Comm., 260; Munn, Prohib., 59; Soeters, Defense, 17.

1964: Johnson, D., 4,171,877; Goldwater, R., 2,879,108; Hass, Soc. Labor, 489; DeBerry, Soc. Workers, 378; Munn, Prohib., 305; Hensley, Universal, 19.

1960: Nixon, R., 3,259,722; Kennedy, D., 3,224,099; Decker, Prohib., 21,706; Hass, Soc. Labor, 1,051.

Colorado

County	2012 Obama (D)	Romney (R)	2008 Obama (D)	McCain (R)
Adams	100,649	70,972	93,443	63,976
Alamosa	3,811	2,705	3,521	2,635
Arapahoe	153,905	125,588	148,218	113,866
Archuleta	2,679	3,872	2,836	3,638
Baca	467	1,559	536	1,572
Bent	815	1,075	799	1,077
Boulder	125,091	49,981	124,159	44,904
Broomfield	16,966	15,008	16,168	12,757
Chaffee	5,086	5,070	4,861	4,873
Cheyenne	172	889	198	890
Clear Creek	3,119	2,430	3,332	2,300
Conejos	2,213	1,835	2,154	1,653
Costilla	1,340	446	1,245	415
Crowley	535	924	552	976
Custer	868	1,788	912	1,672
Delta	4,622	10,915	5,084	10,067
Denver	222,018	73,111	204,882	62,567
Dolores	334	859	369	818
Douglas	61,094	104,397	61,960	88,108
Eagle	12,792	9,411	13,187	8,179
El Paso	111,819	170,952	108,899	160,318
Elbert	3,603	10,266	3,819	9,108
Fremont	6,704	13,174	6,844	12,668
Garfield	11,305	12,535	11,357	11,359
Gilpin	1,892	1,346	1,954	1,253
Grand	3,684	4,253	4,037	4,128
Gunnison	5,044	3,341	5,556	3,131
Hinsdale	229	353	240	344
Huerfano	1,953	1,646	1,989	1,580
Jackson	216	600	277	624
Jefferson	159,296	144,197	158,153	131,627
Kiowa	118	677	178	650
Kit Carson	838	2,785	912	2,455
La Plata	15,489	12,794	16,057	11,503
Lake	1,839	1,098	1,859	1,078
Larimer	92,747	82,376	89,822	73,641
Las Animas	3,445	3,263	3,562	3,086
Lincoln	552	1,687	546	1,717
Logan	2,712	6,179	2,846	6,002
Mesa	23,846	47,472	24,008	44,578
Mineral	291	344	270	334
Moffat	1,330	4,695	1,582	4,135
Montezuma	4,542	7,401	4,661	6,961
Montrose	6,138	13,552	6,495	12,199
Morgan	3,912	6,602	3,813	6,272
Otero	3,647	4,382	3,546	4,393
Ouray	1,646	1,481	1,636	1,367
Park	3,862	5,236	4,250	4,896
Phillips	588	1,637	622	1,612
Pitkin	6,849	3,024	7,349	2,484
Prowers	1,519	3,230	1,487	3,043
Pueblo	42,551	31,894	41,097	30,257
Rio Blanco	568	2,724	655	2,437
Rio Grande	2,478	2,918	2,448	2,930
Routt	7,547	5,469	8,270	4,725
Saguache	1,865	964	1,730	953
San Juan	266	212	264	218
San Miguel	2,992	1,154	3,349	933
Sedgwick	419	881	468	857
Summit	9,347	5,571	9,802	4,883
Teller	4,333	8,702	4,513	8,146
Washington	468	2,076	529	1,949
Weld	49,050	63,775	47,292	56,526
Yuma	987	3,490	1,117	3,286
Totals	**1,323,102**	**1,185,243**	**1,288,633**	**1,073,629**

Colorado Vote Since 1960

2012: Obama, D., 1,323,102; Romney, R., 1,185,243; Johnson, LB., 35,545; Stein, Green, 7,508; Goode, Const., 6,234; Barr, Peace/Freedom, 5,059; Reed, unaff., 2,589; Anderson, Justice, 1,260; Tittle, We the People, 792; Hoefling, Amer. Ind., 679; La Riva, Socialism/Liberation, 317; Alexander, Soc. USA, 308; Miller, A3P, 266; Stevens, Objectivist, 235; Harris, Soc. Workers, 192; White, Soc. Equality, 189.

2008: Obama, D., 1,288,633; McCain, R., 1,073,629; Nader, Unaff., 13,352; Barr, LB., 10,898; Baldwin, Const., 6,233; Alan Keyes, Amer. Ind., 3,051; McKinney, Green, 2,822; McEnulty, unaff., 829; Jay, Boston Tea, 589; Allen, HeartQuake '08, 348; Stevens, Objectivist, 336; Moore, Soc. USA, 226; La Riva, Socialism/Liberation, 158; Harris, Soc. Workers, 154; Lyttle, U.S. Pacifist, 110; Amondson, Prohib., 85.

2004: Bush, R., 1,101,255; Kerry, D., 1,001,732; Nader, RF., 12,718; Badnarik, LB., 7,664; Peroutka, Amer. Const., 2,562; Cobb, Green, 1,591; Andress, Ind., 804; Amondson, Concerns of People, 378; Van Auken, Soc. Equal., 329; Harris, Soc. Workers, 241; Brown, Soc., 216; Dodge, Prohib., 140.

2000: Bush, R., 883,748; Gore, D., 738,227; Nader, Green, 91,434; Browne, LB., 12,799; Buchanan, RF., 10,465; Hagelin,

RF., 2,240; Phillips, Amer. Const., 1,319; McReynolds, Soc., 712; Harris, Soc. Workers, 216; Dodge, Prohib., 208.
1996: Dole, R., 691,848; Clinton, D., 671,152; Perot, RF., 99,629; Nader, Green, 25,070; Browne, LB., 12,392; Phillips, Amer. Const., 2,813; Collins, Ind., 2,809; Hagelin, Natural Law, 2,547; Hollis, Soc., 669; Moorehead, Workers World, 599; Templin, Amer., 557; Dodge, Prohib., 375; Harris, Soc. Workers, 244.
1992: Clinton, D., 629,681; Bush, R., 562,850; Perot, Ind., 366,010; Marrou, LB., 8,669; Fulani, New Alliance, 1,608.
1988: Bush, R., 728,177; Dukakis, D., 621,453; Paul, LB., 15,482; Dodge, Prohib., 4,604.
1984: Reagan, R., 821,817; Mondale, D., 454,975; Bergland, LB., 11,257.
1980: Reagan, R., 652,264; Carter, D., 367,973; Anderson, Ind., 130,633; Clark, LB., 25,744; Commoner, Citizens, 5,614; Bubar, Statesman, 1,180; Pulley, Soc., 520; Hall, Comm., 487.
1976: Ford, R., 584,367; Carter, D., 460,353; McCarthy, Ind., 26,107; MacBride, LB., 5,330; Bubar, Prohib., 2,882.
1972: Nixon, R., 597,189; McGovern, D., 329,980; Schmitz, Amer., 17,269; Fisher, Soc. Labor, 4,361; Spock, People's, 2,403; Hospers, LB., 1,111; Jenness, Soc. Workers, 555; Munn, Prohib., 467; Hall, Comm., 432.
1968: Nixon, R., 409,345; Humphrey, D., 335,174; Wallace, 3rd party, 60,813; Blomen, Soc. Labor, 3,016; Gregory, New Party, 1,393; Munn, Prohib., 275; Halstead, Soc. Workers, 235.
1964: Johnson, D., 476,024; Goldwater, R., 296,767; DeBerry, Soc. Workers, 2,537; Munn, Prohib., 1,356; Hass, Soc. Labor, 302.
1960: Nixon, R., 402,242; Kennedy, D., 330,629; Hass, Soc. Labor, 2,803; Dobbs, Soc. Workers, 572.

Connecticut

City	2012 Obama (D)	Romney (R)	2008 Obama (D)	McCain (R)
Bridgeport	32,135	5,168	33,976	6,507
Bristol	14,146	10,004	15,966	10,203
Danbury	15,290	10,590	16,028	10,732
East Hartford	14,149	4,556	14,811	5,195
Fairfield	15,283	14,357	17,236	13,071
Greenwich	13,079	16,456	16,233	13,937
Hamden	19,181	7,482	19,960	8,531
Hartford	31,735	2,138	31,741	2,686
Manchester	15,565	7,961	17,782	8,457
Meriden	14,886	6,880	15,913	7,363
Middletown	13,834	6,105	15,143	5,907
Milford	13,668	11,462	14,873	11,772
New Britain	16,052	4,783	16,742	5,442
New Haven	39,865	4,430	39,112	5,098
Norwalk	22,369	12,773	24,489	12,651
Shelton	8,362	10,327	9,655	10,428
Southington	10,727	10,452	12,066	9,845
Stamford	29,623	17,473	31,733	17,510
Stratford	13,483	9,324	14,626	10,199
Wallingford	11,560	9,259	12,833	9,372
Waterbury	20,931	11,043	22,599	12,821
West Hartford	21,069	10,511	23,576	10,021
West Haven	14,286	5,789	14,186	7,005
Other	483,805	425,569	546,493	414,675
Totals	**905,083**	**634,892**	**997,772**	**629,428**

Connecticut Vote Since 1960

2012: Obama, D., 905,083; Romney, R., 634,892; Johnson, LB., 12,580; Anderson, Ind., 5,487.
2008: Obama, D., 997,772; McCain, R., 629,428; Nader, Ind., 19,162.
2004: Kerry, D., 857,488; Bush, R., 693,826; Nader, petitioning cand., 12,969; Cobb, Green, 9,564; Badnarik, LB., 3,367; Peroutka, Concerned Citizens, 1,543.
2000: Gore, D., 816,015; Bush, R., 561,094; Nader, Green, 64,452; Phillips, Concerned Citizens, 9,695; Buchanan, RF., 4,731; Browne, LB., 3,484.
1996: Clinton, D., 735,740; Dole, R., 483,109; Perot, RF., 139,523; Nader, Green, 24,321; Browne, LB., 5,788; Phillips, Concerned Citizens, 2,425; Hagelin, Natural Law, 1,703.
1992: Clinton, D., 682,318; Bush, R., 578,313; Perot, Ind., 348,771; Marrou, LB., 5,391; Fulani, New Alliance, 1,363.
1988: Bush, R., 750,241; Dukakis, D., 676,584; Paul, LB., 14,071; Fulani, New Alliance, 2,491.
1984: Reagan, R., 890,877; Mondale, D., 569,597.
1980: Reagan, R., 677,210; Carter, D., 541,732; Anderson, Ind., 171,807; Clark, LB., 8,570; Commoner, Citizens, 6,130; scattered, 836.
1976: Ford, R., 719,261; Carter, D., 647,895; Maddox, George Wallace Party, 7,101; LaRouche, U.S. Labor, 1,789.
1972: Nixon, R., 810,763; McGovern, D., 555,498; Schmitz, Amer., 17,239; scattered, 777.
1968: Humphrey, D., 621,561; Nixon, R., 556,721; Wallace, 3rd party, 76,650; scattered, 1,300.
1964: Johnson, D., 826,269; Goldwater, R., 390,996; scattered, 1,313.
1960: Kennedy, D., 657,055; Nixon, R., 565,813.

Delaware

County	2012 Obama (D)	Romney (R)	2008 Obama (D)	McCain (R)
Kent	35,527	32,135	36,392	29,827
New Castle	167,082	81,230	178,768	74,608
Sussex	39,975	52,119	40,299	47,939
Totals	**242,584**	**165,484**	**255,459**	**152,374**

Delaware Vote Since 1960

2012: Obama, D., 242,584; Romney, R., 165,484; Johnson, LB., 3,882; Stein, Green, 1,940.
2008: Obama, D., 255,459; McCain, R., 152,374; Nader, Ind. (DE), 2,401; Barr, LB., 1,109; Baldwin, Const., 626; McKinney, Green, 385; Calero, Soc. Workers, 58.
2004: Kerry, D., 200,152; Bush, R., 171,660; Nader, Ind., 2,153; Badnarik, LB., 586; Peroutka, Const., 289; Cobb, Green, 250; Brown, Natural Law, 100.
2000: Gore, D., 180,068; Bush, R., 137,288; Nader, Green, 8,307; Buchanan, RF., 777; Browne, LB., 774; Phillips, Const., 208; Hagelin, Natural Law, 107.
1996: Clinton, D., 140,355; Dole, R., 99,062; Perot, RF., 28,719; Browne, LB., 2,052; Phillips, U.S. Taxpayers, 348; Hagelin, Natural Law, 274.
1992: Clinton, D., 126,054; Bush, R., 102,313; Perot, Ind., 59,213; Fulani, New Alliance, 1,105.
1988: Bush, R., 139,639; Dukakis, D., 108,647; Paul, LB., 1,162; Fulani, New Alliance, 443.
1984: Reagan, R., 152,190; Mondale, D., 101,656; Bergland, LB., 268.
1980: Reagan, R., 111,252; Carter, D., 105,754; Anderson, Ind., 16,288; Clark, LB., 1,974; Greaves, Amer., 400.
1976: Carter, D., 122,596; Ford, R., 109,831; McCarthy, nonpartisan, 2,437; Anderson, Amer., 645; LaRouche, U.S. Labor, 136; Bubar, Prohib., 103; Levin, Soc. Labor, 86.
1972: Nixon, R., 140,357; McGovern, D., 92,283; Schmitz, Amer., 2,638; Munn, Prohib., 238.
1968: Nixon, R., 96,714; Humphrey, D., 89,194; Wallace, 3rd party, 28,459.
1964: Johnson, D., 122,704; Goldwater, R., 78,078; Munn, Prohib., 425; Hass, Soc. Labor, 113.
1960: Kennedy, D., 99,590; Nixon, R., 96,373; Faubus, States' Rights, 354; Decker, Prohib., 284; Hass, Soc. Labor, 82.

District of Columbia

	2012 Obama (D)	Romney (R)	2008 Obama (D)	McCain (R)
Totals	267,070	21,381	245,800	17,367

District of Columbia Vote Since 1964

2012: Obama, D., 267,070; Romney, R., 21,381; Stein, DC Statehood Green, 2,458; Johnson, LB., 2,083.
2008: Obama, D., 245,800; McCain, R., 17,367; Nader, Ind., 958; McKinney, Green, 590.
2004: Kerry, D., 202,970; Bush, R., 21,256; Nader, Ind., 1,485; Cobb, DC Statehood Green, 737; Badnarik, LB., 502; Harris, Soc. Workers, 130.
2000: Gore, D., 171,923; Bush, R., 18,073; Nader, Green, 10,576; Browne, LB., 669; Harris, Soc. Workers, 114.
1996: Clinton, D., 158,220; Dole, R., 17,339; Nader, Green, 4,780; Perot, RF., 3,611; Browne, LB., 588; Hagelin, Natural Law, 283; Harris, Soc. Workers, 257.
1992: Clinton, D., 192,619; Bush, R., 20,698; Perot, Ind., 9,681; Fulani, New Alliance, 1,459; Daniels, Ind., 1,186.
1988: Dukakis, D., 159,407; Bush, R., 27,590; Fulani, New Alliance, 2,901; Paul, LB., 554.
1984: Mondale, D., 180,408; Reagan, R., 29,009; Bergland, LB., 279.
1980: Carter, D., 130,231; Reagan, R., 23,313; Anderson, Ind., 16,131; Commoner, Citizens, 1,826; Clark, LB., 1,104; Hall, Comm., 369; DeBerry, Soc. Workers, 173; Griswold, Workers World, 52; write-in, 690.
1976: Carter, D., 137,818; Ford, R., 27,873; Camejo, Soc. Workers, 545; MacBride, LB., 274; Hall, Comm., 219; LaRouche, U.S. Labor, 157.
1972: McGovern, D., 127,627; Nixon, R., 35,226; Reed, Soc. Workers, 316; Hall, Comm., 252.
1968: Humphrey, D., 139,566; Nixon, R., 31,012.
1964: Johnson, D., 169,796; Goldwater, R., 28,801.

Florida

County	2012 Obama (D)	Romney (R)	2008 Obama (D)	McCain (R)
Alachua	69,699	48,797	75,565	48,513
Baker	2,311	8,975	2,327	8,672
Bay	22,051	56,876	23,653	56,683
Bradford	3,325	8,219	3,430	8,136
Brevard	122,993	159,300	127,620	157,589
Broward	508,312	244,101	492,640	237,729
Calhoun	1,664	4,366	1,821	4,345

County	2012 Obama (D)	Romney (R)	2008 Obama (D)	McCain (R)
Charlotte	35,906	47,996	39,031	45,205
Citrus	28,460	44,662	31,460	43,706
Clay	25,759	70,022	26,697	67,203
Collier	51,698	96,520	54,450	86,379
Columbia	8,462	18,429	9,171	18,670
De Soto	4,174	5,587	4,383	5,632
Dixie	1,798	5,052	1,925	5,194
Duval	196,737	211,615	202,618	210,537
Escambia	58,185	88,711	61,572	91,411
Flagler	23,207	26,969	24,726	23,951
Franklin	1,845	3,570	2,134	3,818
Gadsden	15,770	6,630	15,582	6,811
Gilchrist	1,885	5,917	1,996	5,656
Glades	1,603	2,344	1,381	1,938
Gulf	2,014	4,995	2,149	4,980
Hamilton	2,228	3,138	2,364	3,179
Hardee	2,463	4,696	2,568	4,763
Hendry	4,751	5,355	4,998	5,780
Hernando	37,830	44,938	41,886	45,021
Highlands	16,148	25,915	18,135	26,221
Hillsborough	286,467	250,186	272,963	236,355
Holmes	1,264	6,919	1,446	7,033
Indian River	27,492	43,450	29,710	40,176
Jackson	7,342	13,418	7,671	13,717
Jefferson	3,945	3,808	4,088	3,797
Lafayette	687	2,668	642	2,679
Lake	61,799	87,643	62,948	82,802
Lee	110,151	154,163	119,701	147,608
Leon	90,881	55,805	91,747	55,705
Levy	6,119	12,054	6,711	11,754
Liberty	942	2,301	895	2,339
Madison	4,176	4,474	4,270	4,544
Manatee	66,503	85,627	70,034	80,721
Marion	66,831	93,043	70,839	89,628
Martin	30,107	48,183	33,508	44,143
Miami-Dade	541,440	332,981	499,831	360,551
Monroe	19,404	19,234	20,907	18,933
Nassau	10,251	29,929	10,618	27,403
Okaloosa	23,421	70,168	25,872	68,789
Okeechobee	4,856	7,328	5,108	7,561
Orange	273,665	188,589	273,009	186,832
Osceola	67,239	40,592	59,962	40,086
Palm Beach	349,651	247,398	361,271	226,037
Pasco	98,263	112,427	102,417	110,104
Pinellas	239,104	213,258	248,299	210,066
Polk	114,622	131,577	113,865	128,878
Putnam	11,667	19,326	13,236	19,637
St. Johns	35,190	78,513	35,791	69,222
St. Lucie	65,869	56,202	67,125	52,512
Santa Rosa	17,768	58,186	19,470	55,972
Sarasota	95,119	110,504	102,686	102,897
Seminole	96,445	109,943	99,335	105,070
Sumter	19,524	40,646	17,655	30,866
Suwannee	4,751	12,672	4,916	12,534
Taylor	2,764	6,249	2,803	6,457
Union	1,339	3,980	1,300	3,940
Volusia	114,748	117,490	127,795	113,938
Wakulla	5,175	9,290	5,311	8,877
Walton	6,671	21,490	7,174	19,561
Washington	2,820	8,038	2,863	8,178
Totals	**4,237,756**	**4,163,447**	**4,282,074**	**4,045,624**

Florida Vote Since 1960

2012: Obama, D., 4,237,756; Romney, R., 4,163,447; Johnson, LB., 44,726; Stein, Green, 8,947; Barr, Peace/Freedom, 8,154; Stevens, Objectivist, 3,856; Goode, Const., 2,607; Anderson, Justice, 1,754; Hoefling, Amer. Ind.. 946; Barnett, RF., 820; Alexander, Soc., 799; Lindsay, Socialism/Liberation, 322.
2008: Obama, D., 4,282,074; McCain, R., 4,045,624; Nader, Ecology (FL), 28,124; Barr, LB., 17,218; Baldwin, Const., 7,915; McKinney, Green, 2,887; Keyes, Amer. Ind., 2,550; La Riva, Socialism/Liberation, 1,516; Jay, Boston Tea, 795; Harris, Soc. Workers, 533; Stevens, Objectivist, 419; Moore, Soc. USA, 405; Amondson, Prohib., 293.
2004: Bush, R., 3,964,522; Kerry, D., 3,583,544; Nader, RF., 32,971; Badnarik, LB., 11,996; Peroutka, Const., 6,626; Cobb, Green, 3,917; Brown, Soc., 3,502; Harris, Soc. Workers, 2,732.
2000: Bush, R., 2,912,790; Gore, D., 2,912,253; Nader, Green, 97,488; Buchanan, RF., 17,484; Browne, LB., 16,415; Hagelin, Natural Law, 2,281; Moorehead, Workers World, 1,804; Phillips, Const., 1,371; McReynolds, Soc., 622; Harris, Soc. Workers, 562.
1996: Clinton, D., 2,545,968; Dole, R., 2,243,324; Perot, Ind., 483,776; Browne, LB., 23,312.
1992: Bush, R., 2,171,781; Clinton, D., 2,071,651; Perot, Ind., 1,052,481; Marrou, LB., 15,068.
1988: Bush, R., 2,618,597; Dukakis, D., 1,655,851; Paul, LB., 19,796; Fulani, New Alliance, 6,655.
1984: Reagan, R., 2,728,775; Mondale, D., 1,448,344.
1980: Reagan, R., 2,046,951; Carter, D., 1,419,475; Anderson, Ind., 189,692; Clark, LB., 30,524; write-in, 285.

1976: Carter, D., 1,636,000; Ford, R., 1,469,531; McCarthy, Ind., 23,643; Anderson, Amer., 21,325.
1972: Nixon, R., 1,857,759; McGovern, D., 718,117; scattered, 7,407.
1968: Nixon, R., 886,804; Humphrey, D., 676,794; Wallace, 3rd party, 624,207.
1964: Johnson, D., 948,540; Goldwater, R., 905,941.
1960: Nixon, R., 795,476; Kennedy, D., 748,700.

Georgia

County	2012 Obama (D)	Romney (R)	2008 Obama (D)	McCain (R)
Appling	1,758	5,233	1,846	5,085
Atkinson	930	1,938	938	1,941
Bacon	791	3,093	817	3,089
Baker	794	785	846	828
Baldwin	8,483	7,589	8,587	7,823
Banks	786	5,354	1,027	5,120
Barrow	6,028	18,725	6,657	17,625
Bartow	8,396	26,876	9,662	25,976
Ben Hill	2,512	3,396	2,590	3,417
Berrien	1,273	4,843	1,471	4,901
Bibb	38,585	25,623	38,987	27,037
Bleckley	1,269	3,587	1,380	3,657
Brantley	939	4,964	1,119	5,080
Brooks	3,138	3,554	2,669	3,507
Bryan	3,707	9,560	3,636	9,112
Bulloch	9,593	14,174	9,586	14,174
Burke	5,405	4,301	5,233	4,344
Butts	2,968	6,306	3,065	5,947
Calhoun	1,298	883	1,342	862
Camden	6,377	11,343	6,482	10,502
Candler	1,157	2,344	1,209	2,286
Carroll	12,688	28,280	14,334	28,661
Catoosa	5,365	17,858	6,025	18,218
Charlton	1,197	2,527	1,197	2,466
Chatham	60,246	47,204	62,755	46,829
Chattahoochee	729	735	830	811
Chattooga	2,232	5,452	2,596	5,572
Cherokee	19,841	76,514	22,350	70,279
Clarke	25,431	13,815	29,591	15,333
Clay	862	537	879	558
Clayton	81,479	14,164	82,527	16,506
Clinch	852	1,598	989	1,678
Cobb	133,124	171,722	141,216	170,957
Coffee	5,057	9,248	4,811	8,872
Colquitt	3,973	9,243	4,139	9,185
Columbia	16,451	41,765	15,703	39,322
Cook	2,042	3,935	2,075	3,782
Coweta	15,168	39,653	15,521	37,571
Crawford	1,706	3,368	1,832	3,358
Crisp	3,167	4,182	3,085	4,424
Dade	1,411	4,471	1,612	4,703
Dawson	1,241	8,847	1,632	8,242
Decatur	4,591	5,824	4,424	5,890
DeKalb	238,224	64,392	254,594	65,581
Dodge	2,442	5,214	2,595	5,543
Dooly	2,285	1,985	2,138	1,991
Dougherty	26,295	11,449	26,135	12,547
Douglas	28,441	26,241	27,825	26,812
Early	2,765	2,557	2,603	2,711
Echols	173	917	201	981
Effingham	4,947	15,596	4,936	15,230
Elbert	3,181	4,859	3,366	4,868
Emanuel	2,927	5,100	3,068	5,110
Evans	1,268	2,268	1,374	2,462
Fannin	2,028	7,857	2,611	7,807
Fayette	19,736	38,075	20,313	38,501
Floyd	9,640	22,733	10,691	23,132
Forsyth	14,571	65,908	15,406	59,166
Franklin	1,499	6,114	1,914	6,069
Fulton	255,470	137,124	272,000	130,136
Gilmer	1,958	8,926	2,614	8,408
Glascock	176	1,135	210	1,202
Glynn	11,950	20,893	12,676	20,479
Gordon	3,440	13,197	4,268	13,113
Grady	3,419	5,924	3,539	5,775
Greene	3,201	5,071	3,339	4,532
Gwinnett	132,509	159,855	129,025	158,746
Habersham	2,301	12,166	2,900	11,766
Hall	12,999	47,481	14,457	44,962
Hancock	3,308	769	3,535	795
Haralson	1,789	8,446	2,248	8,658
Harris	4,145	11,197	4,184	10,648
Hart	2,870	6,517	3,365	6,537
Heard	948	3,160	1,042	3,133
Henry	43,761	46,774	40,567	47,157
Houston	22,702	34,662	22,094	33,392
Irwin	1,141	2,538	1,197	2,605
Jackson	4,238	19,135	4,950	17,776
Jasper	1,845	4,136	1,935	3,916

County	2012 Obama (D)	Romney (R)	2008 Obama (D)	McCain (R)
Jeff Davis	1,275	3,996	1,356	3,867
Jefferson	4,261	2,999	4,149	3,061
Jenkins	1,488	1,887	1,482	1,936
Johnson	1,305	2,440	1,198	2,426
Jones	4,274	7,744	4,572	7,782
Lamar	2,602	4,899	2,752	4,873
Lanier	1,114	1,820	1,062	1,787
Laurens	7,513	11,950	7,769	12,052
Lee	3,196	10,314	3,100	9,925
Liberty	10,457	5,565	10,474	5,828
Lincoln	1,586	2,807	1,650	2,731
Long	1,442	2,306	1,288	2,119
Lowndes	17,470	21,327	17,597	21,269
Lumpkin	2,055	8,647	2,586	8,326
Macon	3,211	1,545	3,251	1,712
Madison	2,494	8,443	2,965	8,226
Marion	1,412	1,733	1,381	1,772
McDuffie	4,044	5,475	3,989	5,400
McIntosh	2,864	3,409	2,905	3,282
Meriwether	4,331	4,856	4,465	4,982
Miller	852	1,905	818	1,899
Mitchell	4,081	4,155	3,872	4,201
Monroe	3,785	8,361	4,106	7,933
Montgomery	1,135	2,662	1,045	2,521
Morgan	2,753	6,186	3,091	5,987
Murray	2,542	8,443	3,026	8,180
Muscogee	42,573	27,510	44,158	29,568
Newton	21,851	20,982	20,827	20,337
Oconee	4,421	13,098	4,825	12,120
Oglethorpe	1,914	4,251	2,232	4,144
Paulding	15,825	40,846	17,229	39,192
Peach	6,148	5,287	5,927	5,173
Pickens	1,975	10,547	2,595	10,004
Pierce	1,124	5,667	1,253	5,500
Pike	1,356	6,668	1,575	6,547
Polk	3,615	9,811	4,052	9,850
Pulaski	1,219	2,444	1,377	2,553
Putnam	2,926	6,215	3,102	5,966
Quitman	612	510	597	509
Rabun	1,559	5,754	2,001	5,487
Randolph	1,770	1,271	1,833	1,370
Richmond	52,560	25,845	52,100	26,842
Rockdale	22,023	15,716	20,526	16,921
Schley	448	1,286	479	1,252
Screven	2,774	3,287	3,024	3,423
Seminole	1,478	2,245	1,660	2,315
Spalding	9,898	14,911	10,141	14,885
Stephens	2,131	7,221	2,705	7,689
Stewart	1,323	745	1,305	783
Sumter	6,375	5,378	6,454	5,717
Talbot	2,265	1,202	2,369	1,301
Taliaferro	636	323	643	339
Tattnall	1,897	4,706	1,932	4,730
Taylor	1,572	1,948	1,536	2,021
Telfair	1,805	2,480	1,862	2,486
Terrell	2,544	1,834	2,501	1,890
Thomas	7,653	11,156	7,720	10,642
Tift	4,660	9,185	4,749	9,431
Toombs	2,746	6,524	2,964	6,658
Towns	1,273	4,876	1,391	4,292
Treutlen	1,074	1,652	1,112	1,826
Troup	10,547	15,179	10,455	15,391
Turner	1,510	2,028	1,427	2,096
Twiggs	2,270	1,907	2,402	2,087
Union	2,139	8,773	2,486	8,013
Upson	3,959	7,230	4,061	7,291
Walker	5,274	16,247	6,095	17,110
Walton	8,148	29,036	8,469	27,253
Ware	3,900	7,941	4,034	8,311
Warren	1,529	990	1,554	1,087
Washington	4,714	4,035	4,607	4,216
Wayne	2,596	7,557	2,858	7,601
Webster	582	601	515	588
Wheeler	772	1,366	794	1,408
White	1,671	8,651	2,174	8,467
Whitfield	7,210	19,305	8,167	19,230
Wilcox	1,060	2,053	978	2,159
Wilkes	2,087	2,635	2,315	2,705
Wilkinson	2,181	2,246	2,298	2,349
Worth	2,487	5,869	2,542	5,780
Totals	**1,773,827**	**2,078,688**	**1,844,123**	**2,048,759**

Georgia Vote Since 1960

2012: Romney, R., 2,078,688; Obama, D., 1,773,827; Johnson, LB., 45,324.
2008: McCain, R., 2,048,759; Obama, D., 1,844,123; Barr, LB., 28,731.
2004: Bush, R., 1,914,254; Kerry, D., 1,366,149; Badnarik, LB., 18,387.

2000: Bush, R., 1,419,720; Gore, D., 1,116,230; Browne, LB., 36,332; Buchanan, Ind., 10,926.
1996: Dole, R., 1,080,843; Clinton, D., 1,053,849; Perot, RF., 146,337; Browne, LB., 17,870.
1992: Clinton, D., 1,008,966; Bush, R., 995,252; Perot, Ind., 309,657; Marrou, LB., 7,110.
1988: Bush, R., 1,081,331; Dukakis, D., 714,792; Paul, LB., 8,435; Fulani, New Alliance, 5,099.
1984: Reagan, R., 1,068,722; Mondale, D., 706,628.
1980: Carter, D., 890,955; Reagan, R., 654,168; Anderson, Ind., 36,055; Clark, LB., 15,627.
1976: Carter, D., 979,409; Ford, R., 483,743; write-in, 4,306.
1972: Nixon, R., 881,496; McGovern, D., 289,529; Schmitz, Amer., 812; scattered, 2,935.
1968: Wallace, 3rd party, 535,550; Nixon, R., 380,111; Humphrey, D., 334,440; write-in, 162.
1964: Goldwater, R., 616,600; Johnson, D., 522,557.
1960: Kennedy, D., 458,638; Nixon, R., 274,472; write-in, 239.

Hawaii

County	2012 Obama (D)	Romney (R)	2008 Obama (D)	McCain (R)
Hawaii	47,224	14,753	50,819	14,866
Honolulu	204,349	88,461	214,909	88,301
Kauai	18,641	6,121	20,416	6,245
Maui	36,052	11,602	39,727	11,154
Overseas	392	78	NA	NA
Totals	**306,658**	**121,015**	**325,871**	**120,566**

Hawaii Vote Since 1960

2012: Obama, D., 306,658; Romney, R., 121,015; Johnson, LB., 3,840; Stein, Green, 3,184.
2008: Obama, D., 325,871; McCain, R., 120,566; Nader, Ind. (HI), 3,825; Barr, LB., 1,314; Baldwin, Const., 1,013; McKinney, Green, 979.
2004: Kerry, D., 231,708; Bush, R., 194,191; Cobb, Green, 1,737; Badnarik, LB., 1,377.
2000: Gore, D., 205,286; Bush, R., 137,845; Nader, Green, 21,623; Browne, LB., 1,477; Buchanan, RF., 1,071; Phillips, Const., 343; Hagelin, Natural Law, 306.
1996: Clinton, D., 205,012; Dole, R., 113,943; Perot, RF., 27,358; Nader, Green, 10,386; Browne, LB., 2,493; Hagelin, Natural Law, 570; Phillips, Taxpayers, 358.
1992: Clinton, D., 179,310; Bush, R., 136,822; Perot, Ind., 53,003; Gritz, Populist/America First, 1,452; Marrou, LB., 1,119.
1988: Dukakis, D., 192,364; Bush, R., 158,625; Paul, LB., 1,999; Fulani, New Alliance, 1,003.
1984: Reagan, R., 184,934; Mondale, D., 147,098; Bergland, LB., 2,167.
1980: Carter, D., 135,879; Reagan, R., 130,112; Anderson, Ind., 32,021; Clark, LB., 3,269; Commoner, Citizens, 1,548; Hall, Comm., 458.
1976: Carter, D., 147,375; Ford, R., 140,003; MacBride, LB., 3,923.
1972: Nixon, R., 168,865; McGovern, D., 101,409.
1968: Humphrey, D., 141,324; Nixon, R., 91,425; Wallace, 3rd party, 3,469.
1964: Johnson, D., 163,249; Goldwater, R., 44,022.
1960: Kennedy, D., 92,410; Nixon, R., 92,295.

Idaho

County	2012 Obama (D)	Romney (R)	2008 Obama (D)	McCain (R)
Ada	77,137	97,554	82,236	93,328
Adams	577	1,413	728	1,517
Bannock	13,214	21,010	14,792	19,356
Bear Lake	302	2,489	502	2,377
Benewah	1,164	2,596	1,407	2,646
Bingham	3,822	13,440	4,424	12,230
Blaine	5,992	3,939	6,947	3,439
Boise	1,053	2,284	1,240	2,433
Bonner	6,500	11,367	7,840	11,145
Bonneville	9,903	32,276	11,417	29,334
Boundary	1,225	3,138	1,484	3,078
Butte	258	1,001	318	1,056
Camas	159	402	187	422
Canyon	19,866	44,369	20,147	42,752
Caribou	386	2,608	553	2,656
Cassia	1,098	7,154	1,332	6,309
Clark	66	235	64	305
Clearwater	1,032	2,541	1,211	2,569
Custer	530	1,744	611	1,694
Elmore	2,513	5,227	2,591	5,665
Franklin	325	5,195	600	4,246
Fremont	810	4,907	1,065	4,700
Gem	1,957	5,311	2,166	5,585
Gooding	1,287	3,696	1,489	3,765
Idaho	1,708	5,921	2,017	5,895

County	2012		2008	
	Obama (D)	Romney (R)	Obama (D)	McCain (R)
Jefferson	1,303	9,895	1,641	8,540
Jerome	1,699	4,804	1,794	4,897
Kootenai	18,851	39,381	22,120	38,387
Latah	8,306	7,589	9,195	7,988
Lemhi	960	3,029	1,061	2,938
Lewis	396	1,173	479	1,275
Lincoln	469	1,141	545	1,232
Madison	832	13,445	1,627	11,131
Minidoka	1,390	5,442	1,630	5,087
Nez Perce	6,451	9,967	7,123	10,357
Oneida	217	1,838	381	1,724
Owyhee	833	2,794	944	3,024
Payette	2,271	6,004	2,415	5,988
Power	982	1,870	1,027	1,754
Shoshone	2,277	2,699	2,521	2,953
Teton	1,926	2,458	2,302	2,263
Twin Falls	7,541	19,773	8,621	19,032
Valley	2,095	2,664	2,405	2,772
Washington	1,104	3,128	1,241	3,168
Totals	**212,787**	**420,911**	**236,440**	**403,012**

Idaho Vote Since 1960

2012: Romney, R., 420,911; Obama, D., 212,787; Johnson, LB., 9,453; Stein, Ind., 4,402; Anderson, Ind., 2,499; Goode, Const., 2,222.

2008: McCain, R., 403,012; Obama, D., 236,440; Nader, Ind., 7,175; Baldwin, Const., 4,747; Barr, LB., 3,658.

2004: Bush, R., 409,235; Kerry, D., 181,098; Badnarik, LB., 3,844; Peroutka, Const., 3,084.

2000: Bush, R., 336,937; Gore, D., 138,637; Buchanan, RF., 7,615; Browne, LB., 3,488; Phillips, Const., 1,469; Hagelin, Natural Law, 1,177.

1996: Dole, R., 256,595; Clinton, D., 165,443; Perot, RF., 62,518; Browne, LB., 3,325; Phillips, U.S. Taxpayers, 2,230; Hagelin, Natural Law, 1,600.

1992: Bush, R., 202,645; Clinton, D., 137,013; Perot, Ind., 130,395; Gritz, Populist/America First, 10,281; Marrou, LB., 1,167.

1988: Bush, R., 253,881; Dukakis, D., 147,272; Paul, LB., 5,313; Fulani, Ind., 2,502.

1984: Reagan, R., 297,523; Mondale, D., 108,510; Bergland, LB., 2,823.

1980: Reagan, R., 290,699; Carter, D., 110,192; Anderson, Ind., 27,058; Clark, LB., 8,425; Rarick, Amer., 1,057.

1976: Ford, R., 204,151; Carter, D., 126,549; Maddox, Amer., 5,935; MacBride, LB., 3,558; LaRouche, U.S. Labor, 739.

1972: Nixon, R., 199,384; McGovern, D., 80,826; Schmitz, Amer., 28,869; Spock, People's, 903.

1968: Nixon, R., 165,369; Humphrey, D., 89,273; Wallace, 3rd party, 36,541.

1964: Johnson, D., 148,920; Goldwater, R., 143,557.

1960: Nixon, R., 161,597; Kennedy, D., 138,853.

Illinois

County	2012		2008	
	Obama (D)	Romney (R)	Obama (D)	McCain (R)
Adams	9,648	20,416	11,794	18,711
Alexander	1,965	1,487	2,189	1,692
Bond	3,020	4,095	3,843	3,947
Boone	9,883	11,096	11,333	10,403
Brown	787	1,513	986	1,544
Bureau	8,134	8,164	8,889	7,911
Calhoun	1,080	1,440	1,423	1,221
Carroll	3,665	3,555	3,965	3,596
Cass	2,053	2,707	2,690	2,617
Champaign	40,831	35,312	48,597	33,871
Christian	5,494	8,885	6,918	7,872
Clark	2,591	5,144	3,742	4,409
Clay	1,584	4,190	2,425	3,926
Clinton	5,596	10,524	7,657	9,357
Coles	9,262	11,631	11,716	10,978
Cook	1,488,537	495,542	1,629,024	487,736
Crawford	2,858	5,585	3,883	5,070
Cumberland	1,641	3,509	2,055	3,156
DeKalb	21,207	18,934	25,784	18,266
DeWitt	2,601	4,579	3,308	4,348
Douglas	2,430	5,334	3,228	5,005
DuPage	199,460	195,046	228,698	183,626
Edgar	2,565	5,132	3,743	4,398
Edwards	754	2,405	1,140	2,137
Effingham	3,861	12,501	5,262	11,323
Fayette	2,853	5,951	3,967	5,499
Ford	1,656	4,229	2,227	4,079
Franklin	7,254	10,267	8,880	9,404
Fulton	8,328	6,632	9,732	6,251
Gallatin	1,029	1,492	1,587	1,212
Greene	2,023	3,451	2,619	3,053

County	2012		2008	
	Obama (D)	Romney (R)	Obama (D)	McCain (R)
Grundy	9,451	11,343	11,063	10,687
Hamilton	1,269	2,566	1,796	2,353
Hancock	3,650	5,271	4,141	5,161
Hardin	742	1,535	892	1,330
Henderson	1,978	1,541	2,215	1,541
Henry	12,332	11,583	13,181	11,263
Iroquois	3,413	9,120	4,643	8,695
Jackson	13,319	9,864	15,248	9,687
Jasper	1,436	3,514	2,063	2,964
Jefferson	6,089	9,811	7,462	9,302
Jersey	3,667	6,039	5,042	5,329
Jo Daviess	5,667	5,534	6,403	5,170
Johnson	1,572	3,963	1,871	3,912
Kane	90,332	88,335	106,756	83,963
Kankakee	21,595	23,136	24,750	22,527
Kendall	22,471	24,047	24,742	21,380
Knox	13,451	9,408	14,191	9,419
Lake	153,757	129,764	177,242	118,545
LaSalle	23,073	23,256	27,443	21,872
Lawrence	2,011	3,857	3,016	3,403
Lee	6,937	8,059	7,765	8,258
Livingston	5,020	9,753	6,189	9,191
Logan	3,978	7,844	5,250	7,429
Macon	22,780	25,309	25,487	24,948
Macoupin	9,464	10,946	12,090	9,891
Madison	58,922	60,608	68,979	57,177
Marion	6,225	9,248	8,345	8,691
Marshall	2,455	3,290	3,081	3,145
Mason	2,867	3,265	3,542	3,141
Massac	2,092	4,278	2,693	4,371
McDonough	5,967	6,147	6,783	6,055
McHenry	59,797	71,598	72,288	64,845
McLean	31,883	39,947	37,689	36,767
Menard	2,100	3,948	2,706	3,672
Mercer	4,507	3,876	4,887	3,833
Monroe	6,215	10,888	7,953	9,881
Montgomery	5,058	6,776	6,491	6,150
Morgan	5,806	7,972	7,467	7,591
Moultrie	2,144	3,784	2,668	3,471
Ogle	9,514	13,422	11,253	13,144
Peoria	40,209	36,774	45,906	34,579
Perry	3,819	5,507	4,701	5,086
Piatt	3,090	5,413	3,859	4,991
Pike	2,278	4,860	3,024	4,457
Pope	650	1,512	845	1,343
Pulaski	1,389	1,564	1,638	1,593
Putnam	1,559	1,502	1,900	1,378
Randolph	5,759	8,290	7,395	7,538
Richland	2,362	4,756	3,181	4,329
Rock Island	39,157	24,934	42,210	25,364
St. Clair	67,285	50,125	76,160	47,958
Saline	3,701	6,806	5,083	6,099
Sangamon	42,107	50,225	51,300	46,945
Schuyler	1,727	2,069	1,900	1,833
Scott	903	1,587	1,090	1,455
Shelby	3,342	6,843	4,245	6,396
Stark	1,095	1,528	1,357	1,513
Stephenson	10,165	10,512	11,349	9,909
Tazewell	24,438	35,335	29,384	33,247
Union	3,137	4,957	3,918	5,003
Vermilion	12,878	16,892	16,246	16,054
Wabash	1,590	3,478	2,462	3,254
Warren	4,044	3,618	4,286	3,637
Washington	2,450	4,792	3,342	4,473
Wayne	1,514	5,988	2,547	5,390
White	2,188	4,731	3,315	3,987
Whiteside	14,833	10,448	15,607	10,883
Will	144,229	128,969	160,406	122,597
Williamson	10,647	17,909	12,914	17,387
Winnebago	61,732	55,138	70,034	53,886
Woodford	5,572	12,961	6,999	12,191
Totals	**3,019,512**	**2,135,216**	**3,419,348**	**2,031,179**

Illinois Vote Since 1960

2012: Obama, D., 3,019,512; Romney, R., 2,135,216; Johnson, LB., 56,229; Stein, Green, 30,222.

2008: Obama, D., 3,419,348; McCain, R., 2,031,179; Nader, Ind., 30,948; Barr, LB., 19,642; McKinney, Green, 11,838; Baldwin, Const., 8,256; Polachek, New Party, 1,149.

2004: Kerry, D., 2,891,550; Bush, R., 2,345,946; Badnarik, LB., 32,442.

2000: Gore, D., 2,589,026; Bush, R., 2,019,421; Nader, Green, 103,759; Buchanan, Ind., 16,106; Browne, LB., 11,623; Hagelin, RF., 2,127.

1996: Clinton, D., 2,341,744; Dole, R., 1,587,021; Perot, RF., 346,408; Browne, LB., 22,548; Phillips, U.S. Taxpayers, 7,606; Hagelin, Natural Law, 4,606.

1992: Clinton, D., 2,453,350; Bush, R., 1,734,096; Perot, Ind., 840,515; Marrou, LB., 9,218; Fulani, New Alliance, 5,267; Gritz, Populist/America First, 3,577; Hagelin, Natural Law, 2,751; Warren, Soc. Workers, 1,361.
1988: Bush, R., 2,310,939; Dukakis, D., 2,215,940; Paul, LB., 14,944; Fulani, Solidarity, 10,276.
1984: Reagan, R., 2,707,103; Mondale, D., 2,086,499; Bergland, LB., 10,086.
1980: Reagan, R., 2,358,049; Carter, D., 1,981,413; Anderson, Ind., 346,754; Clark, LB., 38,939; Commoner, Citizens, 10,692; Hall, Comm., 9,711; Griswold, Workers World, 2,257; DeBerry, Soc. Workers, 1,302; write-in, 604.
1976: Ford, R., 2,364,269; Carter, D., 2,271,295; McCarthy, Ind., 55,939; Hall, Comm., 9,250; MacBride, LB., 8,057; Camejo, Soc. Workers, 3,615; Levin, Soc. Labor, 2,422; LaRouche, U.S. Labor, 2,018; write-in, 1,968.
1972: Nixon, R., 2,788,179; McGovern, D., 1,913,472; Fisher, Soc. Labor, 12,344; Hall, Comm., 4,541; Schmitz, Amer., 2,471; others, 2,229.
1968: Nixon, R., 2,174,774; Humphrey, D., 2,039,814; Wallace, 3rd party, 390,958; Blomen, Soc. Labor, 13,878; write-in, 325.
1964: Johnson, D., 2,796,833; Goldwater, R., 1,905,946; write-in, 62.
1960: Kennedy, D., 2,377,846; Nixon, R., 2,368,988; Hass, Soc. Labor, 10,560; write-in, 15.

Indiana

County	2012		2008	
	Obama (D)	Romney (R)	Obama (D)	McCain (R)
Adams	3,806	8,937	4,928	8,404
Allen	60,036	84,613	71,263	77,793
Bartholomew	10,625	18,083	13,567	17,067
Benton	1,159	2,329	1,563	2,183
Blackford	1,927	2,711	2,677	2,690
Boone	8,328	18,808	9,752	16,622
Brown	3,060	4,332	3,854	4,060
Carroll	2,635	4,999	3,736	4,858
Cass	5,371	8,443	7,011	8,346
Clark	20,807	25,450	21,953	25,326
Clay	3,460	7,096	4,954	6,267
Clinton	3,308	6,338	5,307	6,919
Crawford	2,041	2,421	2,286	2,393
Daviess	2,437	7,638	3,370	7,098
Dearborn	6,528	15,394	7,123	14,886
Decatur	2,941	7,119	3,892	6,449
DeKalb	5,419	10,587	7,175	9,780
Delaware	22,654	21,251	28,384	20,916
Dubois	6,522	11,654	8,748	9,526
Elkhart	24,399	42,378	31,398	39,396
Fayette	3,555	5,045	4,389	4,917
Floyd	14,812	19,878	16,263	19,957
Fountain	2,237	4,664	3,094	4,158
Franklin	2,909	7,424	3,404	7,018
Fulton	2,621	5,317	3,702	5,147
Gibson	4,928	9,487	6,455	8,449
Grant	9,589	15,151	11,293	14,734
Greene	4,350	8,457	5,709	7,691
Hamilton	43,796	90,747	49,704	78,401
Hancock	9,319	22,796	11,874	22,008
Harrison	6,607	10,640	7,288	10,551
Hendricks	21,112	44,312	24,548	39,728
Henry	7,613	10,838	10,059	10,896
Howard	15,135	20,327	17,871	20,248
Huntington	4,596	10,862	5,843	10,291
Jackson	5,838	10,419	7,354	9,726
Jasper	4,672	7,955	5,044	7,669
Jay	3,063	4,645	3,748	4,401
Jefferson	5,728	7,096	6,255	7,053
Jennings	3,821	6,120	5,312	6,261
Johnson	17,260	39,513	21,553	36,487
Knox	5,228	9,612	7,569	8,639
Kosciusko	6,862	22,558	9,236	20,488
LaGrange	2,898	6,231	3,663	5,702
Lake	130,897	68,431	139,301	67,742
LaPorte	24,107	18,615	28,258	17,918
Lawrence	5,779	11,622	7,208	11,018
Madison	24,407	26,769	30,152	26,403
Marion	216,336	136,509	241,987	134,313
Marshall	6,137	11,260	7,889	10,406
Martin	1,351	3,262	1,706	3,122
Miami	4,222	8,174	5,564	8,312
Monroe	33,436	22,481	41,450	21,118
Montgomery	4,271	9,824	6,013	9,060
Morgan	7,969	19,591	10,330	18,129
Newton	2,212	3,291	2,625	3,301
Noble	5,229	10,680	7,064	9,673
Ohio	994	1,759	1,158	1,713
Orange	2,939	4,617	3,390	4,536
Owen	2,823	5,062	3,570	4,415
Parke	2,110	4,234	2,924	3,909
Perry	4,316	3,403	5,141	3,202
Pike	2,125	3,627	2,700	3,221
Porter	37,252	34,406	39,178	33,857
Posey	4,533	7,430	5,828	6,804
Pulaski	1,899	3,366	2,466	3,388
Putnam	4,507	9,005	6,334	8,086
Randolph	3,769	6,218	4,839	5,788
Ripley	3,241	7,484	4,187	7,794
Rush	2,221	4,633	3,229	4,271
St. Joseph	56,460	52,578	68,710	48,510
Scott	3,998	4,539	4,271	4,445
Shelby	5,359	10,978	6,987	10,333
Spencer	4,026	5,515	5,039	5,001
Starke	3,809	4,738	4,778	4,473
Steuben	4,853	8,547	6,284	7,674
Sullivan	3,191	4,902	4,284	4,343
Switzerland	1,437	1,872	1,638	1,940
Tippecanoe	26,711	28,757	37,781	29,822
Tipton	2,432	4,773	3,250	4,452
Union	1,018	2,022	1,224	2,061
Vanderburgh	31,725	39,389	39,423	37,512
Vermillion	2,979	3,426	4,003	3,010
Vigo	19,712	19,369	25,040	18,121
Wabash	3,973	8,644	5,456	8,238
Warren	1,324	2,377	1,755	2,166
Warrick	8,793	15,351	12,329	16,013
Washington	3,909	6,533	4,562	6,519
Wayne	10,591	14,321	13,459	14,558
Wells	3,436	9,256	4,403	8,504
White	3,637	5,970	4,839	5,731
Whitley	4,420	10,258	5,862	9,124
Totals	**1,152,887**	**1,420,543**	**1,374,039**	**1,345,648**

Indiana Vote Since 1960

2012: Romney, R., 1,420,543; Obama, D., 1,152,887; Johnson, LB., 50,111.
2008: Obama, D., 1,374,039; McCain, R., 1,345,648; Barr, LB., 29,257.
2004: Bush, R., 1,479,438; Kerry, D., 969,011; Badnarik, LB., 18,058.
2000: Bush, R., 1,245,836; Gore, D., 901,980; Buchanan, Ind., 16,959; Browne, LB., 15,530.
1996: Dole, R., 1,006,693; Clinton, D., 887,424; Perot, RF., 224,299; Browne, LB., 15,632.
1992: Bush, R., 989,375; Clinton, D., 848,420; Perot, Ind., 455,934; Marrou, LB., 7,936; Fulani, New Alliance, 2,583.
1988: Bush, R., 1,297,763; Dukakis, D., 860,643; Fulani, New Alliance, 10,215.
1984: Reagan, R., 1,377,230; Mondale, D., 841,481; Bergland, LB., 6,741.
1980: Reagan, R., 1,255,656; Carter, D., 844,197; Anderson, Ind.,111,639; Clark, LB., 19,627; Commoner, Citizens, 4,852; Greaves, Amer., 4,750; Hall, Comm., 702; DeBerry, Soc., 610.
1976: Ford, R., 1,185,958; Carter, D., 1,014,714; Anderson, Amer., 14,048; Camejo, Soc. Workers, 5,695; LaRouche, U.S. Labor, 1,947.
1972: Nixon, R., 1,405,154; McGovern, D., 708,568; Reed, Soc. Workers, 5,575; Spock, Peace/Freedom, 4,544; Fisher, Soc. Labor, 1,688.
1968: Nixon, R., 1,067,885; Humphrey, D., 806,659; Wallace, 3rd party, 243,108; Munn, Prohib., 4,616; Halstead, Soc. Workers, 1,293; Gregory, write-in, 36.
1964: Johnson, D., 1,170,848; Goldwater, R., 911,118; Munn, Prohib., 8,266; Hass, Soc. Labor, 1,374.
1960: Nixon, R., 1,175,120; Kennedy, D., 952,358; Decker, Prohib., 6,746; Hass, Soc. Labor, 1,136.

Iowa

County	2012		2008	
	Obama (D)	Romney (R)	Obama (D)	McCain (R)
Adair	1,790	2,114	1,924	2,060
Adams	1,028	1,108	1,118	1,046
Allamakee	3,553	3,264	3,971	2,965
Appanoose	2,951	3,161	2,970	3,086
Audubon	1,611	1,802	1,739	1,634
Benton	6,862	6,940	7,058	6,447
Black Hawk	39,821	26,235	39,184	24,662
Boone	7,512	6,556	7,356	6,293
Bremer	6,763	6,405	6,940	5,741
Buchanan	5,911	4,450	6,050	4,139
Buena Vista	3,700	4,554	4,075	4,223
Butler	3,329	4,106	3,364	3,700
Calhoun	2,238	2,891	2,341	2,741
Carroll	4,947	5,601	5,302	4,922

County	2012 Obama (D)	Romney (R)	2008 Obama (D)	McCain (R)
Cass	2,858	4,217	3,211	4,006
Cedar	4,972	4,529	5,221	4,289
Cerro Gordo	13,316	10,128	14,405	9,375
Cherokee	2,634	3,662	2,890	3,372
Chickasaw	3,554	2,836	3,923	2,557
Clarke	2,189	2,124	2,218	2,118
Clay	3,385	4,951	3,925	4,355
Clayton	4,806	4,164	5,195	3,651
Clinton	15,141	9,432	15,018	9,324
Crawford	3,066	3,595	3,715	3,345
Dallas	16,576	20,988	15,149	16,954
Davis	1,520	2,138	1,680	2,029
Decatur	1,791	1,947	1,986	2,020
Delaware	4,616	4,636	4,649	4,113
Des Moines	11,888	8,136	12,462	7,721
Dickinson	4,095	5,912	4,625	5,162
Dubuque	28,768	21,280	28,611	18,651
Emmet	2,099	2,507	2,570	2,373
Fayette	5,732	4,492	5,908	4,205
Floyd	4,680	3,472	4,822	3,051
Franklin	2,266	2,823	2,575	2,501
Fremont	1,637	1,972	1,848	1,989
Greene	2,375	2,380	2,371	2,349
Grundy	2,635	4,215	2,790	3,945
Guthrie	2,569	3,171	2,625	3,074
Hamilton	3,782	3,991	4,018	3,913
Hancock	2,521	3,317	2,805	3,016
Hardin	4,075	4,670	4,393	4,315
Harrison	3,136	4,065	3,555	3,909
Henry	4,460	5,035	4,349	4,822
Howard	2,768	1,795	2,941	1,722
Humboldt	1,972	3,099	2,160	2,895
Ida	1,321	2,286	1,454	2,036
Iowa	4,144	4,569	4,202	4,188
Jackson	5,907	4,177	6,102	3,673
Jasper	10,257	8,877	10,250	8,794
Jefferson	4,798	3,436	5,070	3,324
Johnson	50,666	23,698	51,027	20,732
Jones	5,534	4,721	5,446	4,405
Keokuk	2,303	2,843	2,518	2,712
Kossuth	3,850	4,937	4,625	4,329
Lee	10,714	7,785	9,821	7,062
Linn	68,581	47,622	68,037	43,626
Louisa	2,452	2,420	2,523	2,314
Lucas	1,987	2,254	2,029	2,330
Lyon	1,423	4,978	1,675	4,471
Madison	3,630	4,638	3,733	4,579
Mahaska	4,213	6,448	4,464	6,271
Marion	7,507	9,828	7,421	9,256
Marshall	10,257	8,472	10,023	8,278
Mills	2,848	4,216	2,976	4,183
Mitchell	2,831	2,643	3,179	2,469
Monona	2,101	2,557	2,295	2,411
Monroe	1,731	2,026	1,798	2,000
Montgomery	1,922	3,001	2,326	2,887
Muscatine	11,323	8,168	10,920	7,929
O'Brien	1,969	5,266	2,338	4,894
Osceola	912	2,230	1,037	2,027
Page	2,613	4,348	2,900	4,351
Palo Alto	2,139	2,660	2,428	2,294
Plymouth	4,164	8,597	4,629	7,765
Pocahontas	1,523	2,396	1,800	2,138
Polk	128,465	96,096	120,984	89,668
Pottawattamie	19,644	21,860	20,436	21,237
Poweshiek	5,357	4,424	5,519	4,340
Ringgold	1,186	1,368	1,236	1,401
Sac	2,122	3,094	2,256	2,705
Scott	50,652	38,251	48,927	36,365
Shelby	2,469	3,911	2,863	3,488
Sioux	2,700	14,407	3,030	13,490
Story	26,192	19,668	26,548	18,995
Tama	4,768	4,098	4,899	3,820
Taylor	1,262	1,683	1,347	1,607
Union	3,043	2,813	3,000	2,781
Van Buren	1,402	2,064	1,546	1,986
Wapello	8,663	6,789	8,820	6,663
Warren	12,551	13,052	12,299	12,144
Washington	5,115	5,562	5,170	5,247
Wayne	1,251	1,583	1,357	1,565
Webster	9,537	8,469	9,917	8,337
Winnebago	2,903	2,906	3,254	2,730
Winneshiek	6,256	4,622	6,829	4,273
Woodbury	22,302	21,841	21,983	22,219
Worth	2,350	1,744	2,567	1,612
Wright	2,836	3,349	3,102	3,198
Totals	**822,544**	**730,617**	**828,940**	**682,379**

Iowa Vote Since 1960

2012: Obama, D., 822,544; Romney, R., 730,617; Johnson, LB., 12,926; Stein, Green, 3,769; Goode, Const., 3,038; Litzel, Ind., 1,027; Harris, Soc. Workers, 445; La Riva, Socialism/Liberation, 372.

2008: Obama, D., 828,940; McCain, R., 682,379; Nader, Peace/Freedom, 8,014; Barr, LB., 4,590; Baldwin, Const., 4,445; McKinney, Green, 1,423; Harris, Soc. Workers, 292; Moore, Soc. USA, 182; La Riva, Socialism/Liberation, 121.

2004: Bush, R., 751,957; Kerry, D., 741,898; Nader, petitioning cand., 5,973; Badnarik, LB., 2,992; Peroutka, Const., 1,304; Cobb, Green, 1,141; Harris, Soc. Workers, 373; Van Auken, petitioning cand., 176.

2000: Gore, D., 638,517; Bush, R., 634,373; Nader, Green, 29,374; Buchanan, RF., 5,731; Browne, LB., 3,209; Hagelin, Ind., 2,281; Phillips, Const., 613; Harris, Soc. Workers, 190; McReynolds, Soc., 107.

1996: Clinton, D., 620,258; Dole, R., 492,644; Perot, RF., 105,159; Nader, Green, 6,550; Hagelin, Natural Law, 3,349; Browne, LB., 2,315; Phillips, Taxpayers, 2,229; Harris, Soc. Workers, 331.

1992: Clinton, D., 586,353; Bush, R., 504,891; Perot, Ind., 253,468; Hagelin, Natural Law, 3,079; Gritz, Populist/America First, 1,177; Marrou, LB., 1,076.

1988: Dukakis, D., 670,557; Bush, R., 545,355; LaRouche, Ind., 3,526; Paul, LB., 2,494.

1984: Reagan, R., 703,088; Mondale, D., 605,620; Bergland, LB., 1,844.

1980: Reagan, R., 676,026; Carter, D., 508,672; Anderson, Ind., 115,633; Clark, LB., 13,123; Commoner, Citizens, 2,273; McReynolds, Soc., 534; Hall, Comm., 298; DeBerry, Soc. Workers, 244; Greaves, Amer., 189; Bubar, Statesman, 150; scattered, 519.

1976: Ford, R., 632,863; Carter, D., 619,931; McCarthy, Ind., 20,051; Anderson, Amer., 3,040; MacBride, LB., 1,452.

1972: Nixon, R., 706,207; McGovern, D., 496,206; Schmitz, Amer., 22,056; Jenness, Soc. Workers, 488; Hall, Comm., 272; Green, Universal, 199; Fisher, Soc. Labor, 195; scattered, 321.

1968: Nixon, R., 619,106; Humphrey, D., 476,699; Wallace, 3rd party, 66,422; Halstead, Soc. Workers, 3,377; Cleaver, Peace/Freedom, 1,332; Munn, Prohib., 362; Blomen, Soc. Labor, 241.

1964: Johnson, D., 733,030; Goldwater, R., 449,148; Munn, Prohib., 1,902; Hass, Soc. Labor, 182; DeBerry, Soc. Workers, 159.

1960: Nixon, R., 722,381; Kennedy, D., 550,565; Hass, Soc. Labor, 230; write-in, 634.

Kansas

County	2012 Obama (D)	Romney (R)	2008 Obama (D)	McCain (R)
Allen	1,869	3,316	2,189	3,552
Anderson	944	2,276	1,175	2,362
Atchison	2,567	3,917	3,241	3,791
Barber	482	1,772	598	1,833
Barton	2,297	7,874	3,027	7,802
Bourbon	1,996	4,102	2,394	4,240
Brown	1,076	2,829	1,317	2,985
Butler	7,282	18,157	9,159	18,155
Chase	358	875	383	976
Chautauqua	280	1,304	401	1,418
Cherokee	2,930	5,456	3,594	5,886
Cheyenne	233	1,159	323	1,148
Clark	174	805	245	897
Clay	834	2,788	1,009	2,998
Cloud	974	2,954	1,233	3,121
Coffey	898	2,903	1,121	3,054
Comanche	143	767	194	765
Cowley	4,319	8,081	5,012	8,492
Crawford	6,826	7,708	7,957	7,735
Decatur	266	1,218	343	1,189
Dickinson	2,020	5,832	2,422	6,081
Doniphan	902	2,414	1,115	2,372
Douglas	29,267	17,401	34,398	17,929
Edwards	298	1,059	333	995
Elk	281	1,049	363	1,042
Ellis	3,057	8,399	4,010	8,021
Ellsworth	702	1,930	851	2,017
Finney	2,682	6,219	3,275	6,926
Ford	2,600	5,602	2,991	5,730
Franklin	3,694	6,984	4,433	7,079
Geary	3,332	4,372	3,491	4,492
Gove	176	1,168	261	1,136
Graham	256	1,056	325	1,060
Grant	456	1,811	635	1,995
Gray	324	1,603	436	1,643
Greeley	113	543	151	591
Greenwood	478	1,590	622	1,619
Hamilton	163	693	233	844
Harper	550	1,759	736	1,999
Harvey	5,373	8,588	6,318	9,006

County	2012 Obama (D)	Romney (R)	2008 Obama (D)	McCain (R)
Haskell	215	1,159	278	1,277
Hodgeman	179	868	211	865
Jackson	1,901	3,527	2,308	3,811
Jefferson	2,977	4,827	3,542	5,220
Jewell	229	1,235	313	1,231
Johnson	110,526	158,401	127,091	152,627
Kearny	268	1,097	309	1,159
Kingman	733	2,397	963	2,603
Kiowa	163	976	200	912
Labette	3,117	4,742	3,839	5,001
Lane	172	739	193	814
Leavenworth	11,357	17,059	13,255	16,791
Lincoln	289	1,165	347	1,204
Linn	1,170	3,177	1,425	3,086
Logan	197	1,126	225	1,187
Lyon	5,111	6,470	5,924	6,698
Marion	1,385	3,889	1,801	4,159
Marshall	1,469	3,195	1,784	3,157
McPherson	3,449	8,545	4,218	8,937
Meade	258	1,428	357	1,540
Miami	4,712	9,858	5,742	9,382
Mitchell	584	2,327	701	2,440
Montgomery	3,501	8,630	4,338	9,309
Morris	718	1,773	907	1,875
Morton	189	1,072	229	1,153
Nemaha	1,000	3,930	1,432	3,817
Neosho	2,050	4,272	2,563	4,473
Ness	218	1,209	289	1,207
Norton	398	1,878	497	1,878
Osage	2,268	4,427	2,534	4,820
Osborne	324	1,479	403	1,490
Ottawa	558	2,295	704	2,323
Pawnee	718	1,836	882	1,946
Phillips	382	2,135	525	2,105
Pottawatomie	2,335	6,804	2,599	6,929
Pratt	980	2,771	1,294	2,822
Rawlins	190	1,223	273	1,247
Reno	8,085	15,718	9,916	16,112
Republic	477	2,134	640	1,978
Rice	911	2,676	1,163	2,780
Riley	8,977	11,507	10,495	12,111
Rooks	361	2,038	468	2,068
Rush	367	1,166	504	1,225
Russell	593	2,553	736	2,509
Saline	7,040	13,840	8,186	14,165
Scott	277	1,728	321	1,823
Sedgwick	71,977	106,506	82,337	106,849
Seward	1,490	3,617	1,493	3,791
Shawnee	36,975	37,782	41,235	41,476
Sheridan	168	1,154	254	1,108
Sherman	577	1,976	688	1,959
Smith	358	1,624	446	1,719
Stafford	404	1,385	542	1,495
Stanton	143	605	188	628
Stevens	252	1,749	283	1,815
Sumner	2,658	6,260	3,353	6,737
Thomas	598	2,788	787	2,837
Trego	291	1,261	420	1,225
Wabaunsee	918	2,256	1,036	2,395
Wallace	68	719	96	690
Washington	524	2,316	659	2,248
Wichita	157	821	163	840
Wilson	1,636	5,650	1,170	2,850
Woodson	380	1,035	512	1,055
Wyandotte	34,302	15,496	39,865	16,506
Totals	**440,726**	**692,634**	**514,765**	**699,655**

Kansas Vote Since 1960

2012: Romney, R., 692,634; Obama, D., 440,726; Johnson, LB., 20,456; Baldwin, RF., 5,017.
2008: McCain, R., 699,655; Obama, D., 514,765; Nader, Ind., 10,527; Barr, LB., 6,706; Baldwin, RF., 4,148.
2004: Bush, R., 736,456; Kerry, D., 434,993; Nader, RF., 9,348; Badnarik, LB., 4,013; Peroutka, Ind., 2,899.
2000: Bush, R., 622,332; Gore, D., 399,276; Nader, Ind., 36,086; Buchanan, RF., 7,370; Browne, LB., 4,525; Hagelin, Ind., 1,373; Phillips, Const., 1,254.
1996: Dole, R., 583,245; Clinton, D., 387,659; Perot, RF., 92,639; Browne, LB., 4,557; Phillips, Ind., 3,519; Hagelin, Ind., 1,655.
1992: Bush, R., 449,951; Clinton, D., 390,434; Perot, Ind., 312,358; Marrou, LB., 4,314.
1988: Bush, R., 554,049; Dukakis, D., 422,636; Paul, Ind., 12,553; Fulani, Ind., 3,806.
1984: Reagan, R., 674,646; Mondale, D., 332,471; Bergland, LB., 3,585.
1980: Reagan, R., 566,812; Carter, D., 326,150; Anderson, Ind., 68,231; Clark, LB., 14,470; Shelton, Amer., 1,555; Hall, Comm., 967; Bubar, Statesman, 821; Rarick, Conservative, 789.

1976: Ford, R., 502,752; Carter, D., 430,421; McCarthy, Ind., 13,185; Anderson, Amer., 4,724; MacBride, LB., 3,242; Maddox, Conservative, 2,118; Bubar, Prohib., 1,403.
1972: Nixon, R., 619,812; McGovern, D., 270,287; Schmitz, Conservative, 21,808; Munn, Prohib., 4,188.
1968: Nixon, R., 478,674; Humphrey, D., 302,996; Wallace, 3rd party, 88,921; Munn, Prohib., 2,192.
1964: Johnson, D., 464,028; Goldwater, R., 386,579; Munn, Prohib., 5,393; Hass, Soc. Labor, 1,901.
1960: Nixon, R., 561,474; Kennedy, D., 363,213; Decker, Prohib., 4,138.

Kentucky

County	2012 Obama (D)	Romney (R)	2008 Obama (D)	McCain (R)
Adair	1,660	5,841	1,668	5,512
Allen	1,808	5,184	2,024	5,258
Anderson	3,315	6,822	3,462	6,885
Ballard	1,189	2,647	1,427	2,537
Barren	5,400	10,922	5,434	11,133
Bath	1,770	2,275	2,210	2,234
Bell	2,224	7,127	2,782	6,681
Boone	15,629	35,922	16,292	33,812
Bourbon	3,075	4,692	3,385	4,820
Boyd	7,776	10,884	8,886	11,430
Boyle	4,471	7,703	4,769	7,701
Bracken	1,147	2,029	1,241	2,066
Breathitt	1,562	3,318	2,205	2,671
Breckinridge	2,825	5,025	3,110	5,281
Bullitt	9,971	21,306	10,177	20,102
Butler	1,293	3,716	1,555	3,696
Caldwell	1,852	3,904	2,212	3,866
Calloway	5,317	9,440	6,165	8,991
Campbell	15,080	24,240	15,622	24,046
Carlisle	750	1,835	879	1,699
Carroll	1,629	1,999	1,716	2,032
Carter	3,383	5,279	4,316	5,252
Casey	1,086	4,904	1,219	4,679
Christian	8,252	13,475	8,880	13,699
Clark	5,228	9,931	5,749	9,664
Clay	1,111	6,176	1,552	5,710
Clinton	752	3,569	761	3,366
Crittenden	960	2,839	1,254	2,604
Cumberland	599	2,216	697	2,056
Daviess	16,208	25,092	19,282	23,692
Edmonson	1,374	3,232	1,652	3,562
Elliott	1,186	1,126	1,535	902
Estill	1,356	3,749	1,555	3,685
Fayette	62,080	60,795	66,042	59,884
Fleming	1,911	3,780	2,279	3,432
Floyd	4,733	9,784	7,530	7,741
Franklin	11,535	11,345	11,767	11,911
Fulton	1,022	1,425	1,238	1,530
Gallatin	1,238	1,758	1,278	1,840
Garrard	1,661	5,310	2,012	5,118
Grant	2,810	5,664	3,112	5,510
Graves	4,547	10,699	5,843	10,056
Grayson	2,744	6,404	3,154	6,605
Green	1,165	3,634	1,204	3,785
Greenup	6,027	8,855	6,621	8,849
Hancock	1,833	2,212	2,135	1,928
Hardin	15,214	23,357	15,650	23,896
Harlan	1,830	8,652	2,586	7,165
Harrison	2,471	4,556	2,916	4,520
Hart	2,283	4,257	2,290	4,397
Henderson	8,091	10,296	10,049	9,523
Henry	2,530	3,940	2,725	4,081
Hickman	686	1,431	812	1,406
Hopkins	5,789	13,681	7,104	11,916
Jackson	612	4,365	743	4,407
Jefferson	186,181	148,423	196,435	153,957
Jessamine	6,001	14,233	6,236	13,711
Johnson	1,723	7,095	2,407	5,948
Kenton	24,920	41,389	26,480	40,714
Knott	1,420	4,130	2,612	3,070
Knox	2,484	8,467	3,074	8,150
LaRue	1,733	3,911	1,913	4,153
Laurel	3,905	18,151	4,618	17,660
Lawrence	1,520	3,995	2,036	3,503
Lee	595	1,977	752	1,978
Leslie	433	4,439	766	3,574
Letcher	1,702	6,811	2,623	5,367
Lewis	1,342	3,326	1,510	3,213
Lincoln	2,582	6,416	2,752	6,273
Livingston	1,346	3,089	1,622	2,890
Logan	3,469	6,899	3,811	6,925
Lyon	1,373	2,412	1,577	2,220
Madison	11,512	21,128	12,392	19,694
Magoffin	1,433	3,391	2,105	2,434
Marion	3,418	3,800	3,596	3,842
Marshall	5,022	10,402	5,683	9,512
Martin	574	3,180	808	2,824

County	2012 Obama (D)	Romney (R)	2008 Obama (D)	McCain (R)
Mason	2,592	4,197	2,891	4,102
McCracken	10,062	19,979	11,285	19,043
McCreary	1,069	4,564	1,258	4,078
McLean	1,432	2,705	1,963	2,386
Meade	4,122	6,606	4,343	6,691
Menifee	1,048	1,484	1,276	1,155
Mercer	2,966	6,820	3,159	6,781
Metcalfe	1,425	2,676	1,350	2,734
Monroe	936	3,762	1,067	3,537
Montgomery	3,701	6,398	4,234	5,947
Morgan	1,369	3,021	1,879	2,396
Muhlenberg	4,771	7,762	6,221	6,447
Nelson	7,611	10,673	7,654	10,139
Nicholas	948	1,583	1,272	1,634
Ohio	2,987	6,470	4,059	5,687
Oldham	9,240	20,179	10,000	18,997
Owen	1,501	2,971	1,694	2,969
Owsley	283	1,279	381	1,279
Pendleton	1,859	3,556	2,027	3,676
Perry	2,047	8,040	3,444	6,762
Pike	5,646	17,590	9,525	12,655
Powell	1,620	2,766	2,065	2,837
Pulaski	4,976	20,714	5,590	19,862
Robertson	340	579	451	533
Rockcastle	1,097	5,028	1,410	4,757
Rowan	3,438	4,035	4,074	3,907
Russell	1,445	6,346	1,569	5,779
Scott	7,532	12,679	7,712	11,782
Shelby	6,634	11,790	6,871	11,451
Simpson	2,650	4,355	2,775	4,437
Spencer	2,549	5,726	2,519	5,378
Taylor	3,285	7,551	3,165	7,568
Todd	1,403	3,247	1,543	3,336
Trigg	2,115	4,520	2,246	4,189
Trimble	1,355	2,133	1,484	2,239
Union	1,942	3,955	2,804	3,120
Warren	16,805	26,384	17,669	25,993
Washington	1,669	3,495	1,890	3,305
Wayne	1,855	5,289	2,201	4,868
Webster	1,765	3,607	2,390	3,037
Whitley	2,683	10,232	3,484	10,015
Wolfe	976	1,542	1,493	1,408
Woodford	4,883	7,219	5,027	7,130
Totals	**679,370**	**1,087,190**	**751,985**	**1,048,462**

Kentucky Vote Since 1960

2012: Romney, R., 1,087,190; Obama, D., 679,370; Johnson, LB., 17,063; Terry, Ind., 6,872; Stein, Green, 6,337.
2008: McCain, R., 1,048,462; Obama, D., 751,985; Nader, Ind., 15,378; Barr, LB., 5,989; Baldwin, Const., 4,694.
2004: Bush, R., 1,069,439; Kerry, D., 712,733; Nader, Ind., 8,856; Badnarik, LB., 2,619; Peroutka, Const., 2,213.
2000: Bush, R., 872,520; Gore, D., 638,923; Nader, Green, 23,118; Buchanan, RF., 4,152; Browne, LB., 2,885; Hagelin, Natural Law, 1,513; Phillips, Const., 915.
1996: Clinton, D., 636,614; Dole, R., 623,283; Perot, RF., 120,396; Browne, LB., 4,009; Phillips, U.S. Taxpayers, 2,204; Hagelin, Natural Law, 1,493.
1992: Clinton, D., 665,104; Bush, R., 617,178; Perot, Ind., 203,944; Marrou, LB., 4,513.
1988: Bush, R., 734,281; Dukakis, D., 580,368; Duke, Populist, 4,494; Paul, LB., 2,118.
1984: Reagan, R., 815,345; Mondale, D., 536,756.
1980: Reagan, R., 635,274; Carter, D., 616,417; Anderson, Ind., 31,127; Clark, LB., 5,531; McCormack, Respect for Life, 4,233; Commoner, Citizens, 1,304; Pulley, Soc., 393; Hall, Comm., 348.
1976: Carter, D., 615,717; Ford, R., 531,852; Anderson, Amer., 8,308; McCarthy, Ind., 6,837; Maddox, Amer. Ind., 2,328; MacBride, LB., 814.
1972: Nixon, R., 676,446; McGovern, D., 371,159; Schmitz, Amer., 17,627; Spock, People's, 1,118; Jenness, Soc. Workers, 685; Hall, Comm., 464.
1968: Nixon, R., 462,411; Humphrey, D., 397,547; Wallace, 3rd party, 193,098; Halstead, Soc. Workers, 2,843.
1964: Johnson, D., 669,659; Goldwater, R., 372,977; Kasper, Natl. States' Rights, 3,469.
1960: Nixon, R., 602,607; Kennedy, D., 521,855.

Louisiana

Parish	2012 Obama (D)	Romney (R)	2008 Obama (D)	McCain (R)
Acadia	6,560	19,931	7,028	19,229
Allen	2,617	6,495	2,891	6,333
Ascension	16,349	33,856	14,625	31,239
Assumption	4,754	6,083	4,756	5,981
Avoyelles	6,077	10,670	6,327	10,236
Beauregard	2,828	11,112	3,071	10,718
Bienville	3,490	3,641	3,589	3,776

Parish	2012 Obama (D)	Romney (R)	2008 Obama (D)	McCain (R)
Bossier	12,956	34,988	12,703	32,713
Caddo	58,042	52,459	55,536	52,228
Calcasieu	28,359	51,850	30,244	50,449
Caldwell	1,016	3,640	1,118	3,696
Cameron	408	3,260	613	3,089
Catahoula	1,408	2,744	1,659	3,486
Claiborne	3,014	3,649	3,025	3,750
Concordia	3,833	5,450	3,766	5,668
DeSoto	5,553	7,353	5,242	6,883
East Baton Rouge	102,656	92,292	99,652	95,390
East Carroll	2,478	1,508	2,267	1,254
East Feliciana	4,648	5,397	4,383	5,432
Evangeline	5,330	10,181	5,853	9,793
Franklin	2,921	6,294	2,961	6,278
Grant	1,422	7,082	1,474	6,907
Iberia	12,132	20,892	12,492	20,127
Iberville	9,548	7,271	9,023	7,185
Jackson	2,305	5,132	2,456	5,190
Jefferson	70,384	102,536	65,096	113,191
Jefferson Davis	3,484	10,014	3,923	9,278
Lafayette	31,768	64,992	32,145	62,055
Lafourche	9,623	28,592	9,662	27,089
LaSalle	764	5,726	860	5,602
Lincoln	7,956	10,739	8,292	10,680
Livingston	7,451	45,513	6,681	43,269
Madison	3,154	2,000	3,100	2,152
Morehouse	5,888	6,591	5,792	7,258
Natchitoches	7,942	9,077	7,801	9,054
Orleans	126,722	28,003	117,102	28,130
Ouachita	26,645	40,948	24,813	41,741
Plaquemines	3,599	6,471	3,380	6,894
Pointe Coupee	5,436	6,548	5,516	6,702
Rapides	20,045	37,193	20,127	36,611
Red River	2,253	2,483	2,080	2,484
Richland	3,387	5,846	3,311	5,751
Sabine	2,194	7,738	2,245	7,226
St. Bernard	5,059	8,501	3,491	9,643
St. Charles	8,896	15,937	8,522	16,457
St. Helena	3,780	2,529	3,567	2,522
St. James	7,059	5,209	6,994	5,432
St. John the Baptist	13,179	7,620	12,424	8,912
St. Landry	19,668	21,475	20,268	21,650
St. Martin	9,422	15,653	9,419	14,443
St. Mary	9,450	13,885	9,345	13,183
St. Tammany	25,728	84,723	24,596	83,078
Tangipahoa	17,722	31,590	16,438	31,434
Tensas	1,564	1,230	1,646	1,367
Terrebonne	12,074	29,503	11,581	28,210
Union	3,075	7,561	3,103	7,619
Vermilion	5,720	18,910	6,266	18,069
Vernon	3,173	12,150	3,534	11,946
Washington	6,466	11,798	6,122	12,215
Webster	6,802	11,400	6,610	11,417
West Baton Rouge	5,692	6,922	5,043	6,654
West Carroll	853	3,628	878	4,045
West Feliciana	2,441	3,257	2,415	3,150
Winn	1,919	4,541	2,047	4,632
Totals	**809,141**	**1,152,262**	**782,989**	**1,148,275**

Louisiana Vote Since 1960

2012: Romney, R., 1,152,262; Obama, D., 809,141; Johnson, LB., 18,157; Stein, Green, 6,978; Goode, Const., 2,508; Title, We the People, 1,767; Anderson, Justice, 1,368; Lindsay, Socialism/Liberation, 622; Fellure, Prohib., 518; Harris, Soc. Workers, 389; White, Soc. Equality, 355.
2008: McCain, R., 1,148,275; Obama, D., 782,989; Paul, LA Taxpayers, 9,368; McKinney, Green, 9,187; Nader, Ind., 6,997; Baldwin, Const., 2,581; Harris, Soc. Workers, 735; La Riva, Socialism/Liberation, 354; Amondson, Prohib., 275.
2004: Bush, R., 1,102,169; Kerry, D., 820,299; Nader, Better Life, 7,032; Peroutka, Const., 5,203; Badnarik, LB., 2,781; Brown, Protect Working Families, 1,795; Amondson, Prohib., 1,566; Cobb, Green, 1,276; Harris, Soc. Workers, 985.
2000: Bush, R., 927,871; Gore, D., 792,344; Nader, Green, 20,473; Buchanan, RF., 14,356; Phillips, Const., 5,483; Browne, LB., 2,951; Harris, Soc. Workers, 1,103; Hagelin, Natural Law, 1,075.
1996: Clinton, D., 927,837; Dole, R., 712,586; Perot, RF., 123,293; Browne, LB., 7,499; Nader, Liberty, Ecology, Community, 4,719; Phillips, U.S. Taxpayers, 3,366; Hagelin, Natural Law, 2,981; Moorehead, Workers World, 1,678.
1992: Clinton, D., 815,971; Bush, R., 733,386; Perot, Ind., 211,478; Gritz, Populist/America First, 18,545; Marrou, LB., 3,155; Daniels, Ind., 1,663; Phillips, U.S. Taxpayers, 1,552; Fulani, New Alliance, 1,434; LaRouche, Ind., 1,136.

1988: Bush, R., 883,702; Dukakis, D., 717,460; Duke, Populist, 18,612; Paul, LB., 4,115.
1984: Reagan, R., 1,037,299; Mondale, D., 651,586; Bergland, LB., 1,876.
1980: Reagan, R., 792,853; Carter, D., 708,453; Anderson, Ind., 26,345; Rarick, Amer. Ind., 10,333; Clark, LB., 8,240; Commoner, Citizens, 1,584; DeBerry, Soc. Workers, 783.
1976: Carter, D., 661,365; Ford, R., 587,446; Maddox, Amer., 10,058; Hall, Comm., 7,417; McCarthy, Ind., 6,588; MacBride, LB., 3,325.
1972: Nixon, R., 686,852; McGovern, D., 298,142; Schmitz, Amer., 52,099; Jenness, Soc. Workers, 14,398.
1968: Wallace, 3rd party, 530,300; Humphrey, D., 309,615; Nixon, R., 257,535.
1964: Goldwater, R., 509,225; Johnson, D., 387,068.
1960: Kennedy, D., 407,339; Nixon, R., 230,890; States' Rights (unpledged), 169,572.

Maine

County	2012		2008	
	Obama (D)	Romney (R)	Obama (D)	McCain (R)
Androscoggin	28,989	22,232	31,017	22,671
Aroostook	17,777	15,196	19,345	15,898
Cumberland	101,950	57,821	105,218	56,186
Franklin	9,367	6,369	10,113	6,627
Hancock	17,569	12,324	18,895	12,686
Kennebec	35,068	26,519	37,238	27,482
Knox	13,223	8,248	13,728	8,816
Lincoln	11,315	8,899	11,886	9,287
Oxford	16,330	11,996	17,940	12,863
Penobscot	38,811	36,547	41,614	37,495
Piscataquis	4,149	4,530	4,430	4,785
Sagadahoc	11,821	8,429	12,152	8,721
Somerset	12,216	11,800	13,335	11,867
Waldo	11,296	9,058	11,967	9,423
Washington	7,803	7,550	8,246	8,077
York	61,551	43,900	64,799	42,389
Outside U.S.	2,071	858	NA	NA
Totals	**401,306**	**292,276**	**421,923**	**295,273**

Maine Vote Since 1960

2012: Obama, D., 401,306; Romney, R., 292,276; Johnson, LB., 9,352; Stein, Green, 8,119.
2008: Obama, D., 421,923; McCain, R., 295,273; Nader, Ind., 10,636; McKinney, Green, 2,900.
2004: Kerry, D., 396,842; Bush, R., 330,201; Nader, Better Life, 8,069; Cobb, Green, 2,936; Badnarik, LB., 1,965; Peroutka, Const., 735.
2000: Gore, D., 319,951; Bush, R., 286,616; Nader, Green, 37,127; Buchanan, RF., 4,443; Browne, LB., 3,074; Phillips, Const., 579.
1996: Clinton, D., 312,788; Dole, R., 186,378; Perot, RF., 85,970; Nader, Green, 15,279; Browne, LB., 2,996; Phillips, Taxpayers, 1,517; Hagelin, Natural Law, 825.
1992: Clinton, D., 263,420; Perot, Ind., 206,820; Bush, R., 206,504; Marrou, LB., 1,681.
1988: Bush, R., 307,131; Dukakis, D., 243,569; Paul, LB., 2,700; Fulani, New Alliance, 1,405.
1984: Reagan, R., 336,500; Mondale, D., 214,515.
1980: Reagan, R., 238,522; Carter, D., 220,974; Anderson, Ind., 53,327; Clark, LB., 5,119; Commoner, Citizens, 4,394; Hall, Comm., 591; write-in, 84.
1976: Ford, R., 236,320; Carter, D., 232,279; McCarthy, Ind., 10,874; Bubar, Prohib., 3,495.
1972: Nixon, R., 256,458; McGovern, D., 160,584; scattered, 229.
1968: Humphrey, D., 217,312; Nixon, R., 169,254; Wallace, 3rd party, 6,370.
1964: Johnson, D., 262,264; Goldwater, R., 118,701.
1960: Nixon, R., 240,608; Kennedy, D., 181,159.

Maryland

County	2012		2008	
	Obama (D)	Romney (R)	Obama (D)	McCain (R)
Allegany	9,805	19,230	10,693	18,405
Anne Arundel	126,635	126,832	125,015	129,682
Baltimore	220,322	154,908	214,151	158,714
Calvert	20,529	23,952	20,299	23,095
Caroline	4,970	8,098	4,971	8,015
Carroll	27,939	56,761	28,060	54,503
Cecil	16,557	24,806	17,665	23,855
Charles	48,774	25,178	43,635	25,732
Dorchester	7,257	7,976	6,912	8,168
Frederick	55,146	58,798	54,013	55,170
Garrett	3,124	9,743	3,736	8,903
Harford	49,729	72,911	48,552	71,751
Howard	91,393	57,758	87,120	55,393
Kent	4,842	4,870	4,953	4,905
Montgomery	323,400	123,353	314,444	118,608

County	2012		2008	
	Obama (D)	Romney (R)	Obama (D)	McCain (R)
Prince				
George's	347,938	35,734	332,396	38,833
Queen Anne's	8,556	15,823	8,575	15,087
St. Mary's	19,711	26,797	19,023	24,705
Somerset	5,240	5,042	4,779	5,037
Talbot	8,808	11,339	9,035	10,995
Washington	25,042	36,074	26,245	34,169
Wicomico	19,635	21,764	19,436	21,849
Worcester	11,014	15,951	11,374	15,607
City				
Baltimore	221,478	28,171	214,385	28,681
Totals	**1,677,844**	**971,869**	**1,629,467**	**959,862**

Maryland Vote Since 1960

2012: Obama, D., 1,677,844; Romney, R., 971,869; Johnson, LB., 30,195; Stein, Green, 17,110.
2008: Obama, D., 1,629,467; McCain, R., 959,862; Nader, MD Ind., 14,713; Barr, LB., 9,842; McKinney, Green, 4,747; Baldwin, RF., 3,760.
2004: Kerry, D., 1,334,493; Bush, R., 1,024,703; Nader, Populist, 11,854; Badnarik, LB., 6,094; Cobb, Green, 3,632; Peroutka, Const., 3,421.
2000: Gore, D., 1,144,008; Bush, R., 813,827; Nader, Green, 53,768; Browne, LB., 5,310; Buchanan, RF., 4,248; Phillips, Const., 918.
1996: Clinton, D., 966,207; Dole, R., 681,530; Perot, RF., 115,812; Browne, LB., 8,765; Phillips, Taxpayers, 3,402; Hagelin, Natural Law, 2,517.
1992: Clinton, D., 988,571; Bush, R., 707,094; Perot, Ind., 281,414; Marrou, LB., 4,715; Fulani, New Alliance, 2,786.
1988: Bush, R., 876,167; Dukakis, D., 826,304; Paul, LB., 6,748; Fulani, New Alliance, 5,115.
1984: Reagan, R., 879,918; Mondale, D., 787,935; Bergland, LB., 5,721.
1980: Carter, D., 726,161; Reagan, R., 680,606; Anderson, Ind., 119,537; Clark, LB., 14,192.
1976: Carter, D., 759,612; Ford, R., 672,661.
1972: Nixon, R., 829,305; McGovern, D., 505,781; Schmitz, Amer., 18,726.
1968: Humphrey, D., 538,310; Nixon, R., 517,995; Wallace, 3rd party, 178,734.
1964: Johnson, D., 730,912; Goldwater, R., 385,495; write-in, 50.
1960: Kennedy, D., 565,800; Nixon, R., 489,538.

Massachusetts

County	2012		2008	
	Obama (D)	Romney (R)	Obama (D)	McCain (R)
Barnstable	70,822	60,446	74,264	55,694
Berkshire	48,843	14,252	49,558	14,876
Bristol	142,962	93,752	146,861	90,531
Dukes	7,978	2,792	7,913	2,442
Essex	210,302	150,480	208,976	137,129
Franklin	27,072	9,344	27,919	9,545
Hampden	123,619	73,392	121,454	71,350
Hampshire	57,359	21,480	56,869	20,618
Middlesex	471,804	267,321	464,484	245,766
Nantucket	3,830	2,187	4,073	1,863
Norfolk	202,714	148,393	200,675	136,841
Plymouth	131,845	121,086	131,817	112,904
Suffolk	223,896	59,999	207,127	57,194
Worcester	198,244	163,390	202,107	152,101
Totals	**1,921,290**	**1,188,314**	**1,904,097**	**1,108,854**

Massachusetts Vote Since 1960

2012: Obama, D., 1,921,290; Romney, R., 1,188,314; Johnson, LB., 30,920; Stein, Green, 20,691.
2008: Obama, D., 1,904,097; McCain, R., 1,108,854; Nader, Ind., 28,841; Barr, LB., 13,189; McKinney, Green, 6,550; Baldwin, RF., 4,971.
2004: Kerry, D., 1,803,800; Bush, R., 1,071,109; Badnarik, LB., 15,022; Cobb, Green, 10,623.
2000: Gore, D., 1,616,487; Bush, R., 878,502; Nader, Green, 173,564; Browne, LB., 16,366; Buchanan, RF., 11,149; Hagelin, Natural Law, 2,884.
1996: Clinton, D., 1,571,509; Dole, R., 718,058; Perot, RF., 227,206; Browne, LB., 20,424; Hagelin, Natural Law, 5,183; Moorehead, Workers World, 3,276.
1992: Clinton, D., 1,318,639; Bush, R., 805,039; Perot, Ind., 630,731; Marrou, LB., 9,021; Fulani, New Alliance, 3,172; Phillips, U.S. Taxpayers, 2,218; Hagelin, Natural Law, 1,812; LaRouche, Ind., 1,027.
1988: Dukakis, D., 1,401,415; Bush, R., 1,194,635; Paul, LB., 24,251; Fulani, New Alliance, 9,561.
1984: Reagan, R., 1,310,936; Mondale, D., 1,239,606.
1980: Reagan, R., 1,057,631; Carter, D., 1,053,802; Anderson, Ind., 382,539; Clark, LB., 22,038; DeBerry, Soc. Workers, 3,735; Commoner, Citizens, 2,056; McReynolds, Soc., 62; Bubar, Statesman, 34; Griswold, Workers World, 19; scattered, 2,382.

1976: Carter, D., 1,429,475; Ford, R., 1,030,276; McCarthy, Ind., 65,637; Camejo, Soc. Workers, 8,138; Anderson, Amer., 7,555; LaRouche, U.S. Labor, 4,922; MacBride, LB., 135.
1972: McGovern, D., 1,332,540; Nixon, R., 1,112,078; Jenness, Soc. Workers, 10,600; Schmitz, Amer., 2,877; Fisher, Soc. Labor, 129; Spock, People's, 101; Hall, Comm., 46; Hospers, LB., 43; scattered, 342.
1968: Humphrey, D., 1,469,218; Nixon, R., 766,844; Wallace, 3rd party, 87,088; Blomen, Soc. Labor, 6,180; Munn, Prohib., 2,369; scattered, 53; blank, 25,394.
1964: Johnson, D., 1,786,422; Goldwater, R., 549,727; Hass, Soc. Labor, 4,755; Munn, Prohib., 3,735; scattered, 159; blank, 48,104.
1960: Kennedy, D., 1,487,174; Nixon, R., 976,750; Hass, Soc. Labor, 3,892; Decker, Prohib., 1,633; others, 31; blank and void, 26,024.

Michigan

County	2012 Obama (D)	Romney (R)	2008 Obama (D)	McCain (R)
Alcona	2,472	3,571	2,896	3,404
Alger	2,212	2,330	2,472	2,188
Allegan	20,806	31,123	24,165	30,061
Alpena	6,549	7,298	7,705	7,125
Antrim	5,107	7,917	6,079	7,506
Arenac	3,669	4,057	4,155	3,807
Baraga	1,574	1,866	1,725	1,846
Barry	11,491	16,655	13,449	16,431
Bay	27,877	24,911	32,589	23,795
Benzie	4,685	5,075	5,451	4,687
Berrien	33,465	38,209	40,381	36,130
Branch	6,913	10,035	8,413	9,534
Calhoun	29,267	28,333	34,561	28,553
Cass	9,591	12,659	12,083	11,114
Charlevoix	5,939	8,000	6,817	7,306
Cheboygan	5,831	7,286	6,720	6,920
Chippewa	7,100	8,278	8,184	8,267
Clare	6,338	6,988	7,496	6,793
Clinton	18,191	20,650	20,005	19,726
Crawford	2,994	3,744	3,441	3,561
Delta	8,330	9,534	9,974	8,763
Dickinson	4,952	7,688	5,995	7,049
Eaton	27,913	26,197	30,742	25,900
Emmet	7,225	10,253	8,515	9,314
Genesee	128,978	71,808	143,927	72,451
Gladwin	5,760	6,661	6,590	6,391
Gogebic	4,058	3,444	4,757	3,330
Grand Traverse	20,875	26,534	23,258	24,716
Gratiot	7,610	8,241	9,105	8,322
Hillsdale	7,106	11,727	8,765	11,221
Houghton	6,801	8,196	7,476	8,101
Huron	6,518	8,806	8,367	8,434
Ingham	80,847	45,306	93,994	46,483
Ionia	11,018	14,315	12,565	14,156
Iosco	6,242	6,909	7,309	6,583
Iron	2,687	3,224	3,080	2,947
Isabella	13,038	10,800	16,679	11,220
Jackson	32,301	36,298	37,480	35,692
Kalamazoo	69,051	52,662	77,051	51,554
Kalkaska	3,272	4,901	3,780	4,527
Kent	133,408	155,925	149,909	148,336
Keweenaw	582	774	610	756
Lake	2,752	2,487	2,919	2,269
Lapeer	18,796	23,734	21,457	22,831
Leelanau	6,576	7,483	7,355	6,938
Lenawee	21,776	22,351	24,640	22,225
Livingston	37,216	60,083	42,349	55,592
Luce	991	1,580	1,191	1,490
Mackinac	2,652	3,397	3,027	3,268
Macomb	208,016	191,913	223,784	187,663
Manistee	6,473	5,737	7,235	5,510
Marquette	18,115	13,606	19,635	12,906
Mason	6,856	7,580	7,817	7,147
Mecosta	7,515	9,176	9,101	9,238
Menominee	5,242	5,564	5,981	4,855
Midland	17,450	23,919	20,701	22,263
Missaukee	2,274	4,665	2,898	4,469
Monroe	36,310	35,593	39,180	35,858
Montcalm	11,430	13,621	13,208	13,291
Montmorency	2,049	2,928	2,403	2,841
Muskegon	44,436	30,884	53,821	29,145
Newaygo	8,728	12,457	10,790	11,862
Oakland	349,002	296,514	372,566	276,956
Oceana	5,063	6,239	6,405	5,860
Ogemaw	4,791	5,437	5,391	5,133
Ontonagon	1,586	1,906	1,966	1,823
Osceola	3,981	6,141	4,855	5,973
Oscoda	1,657	2,308	1,887	2,320
Otsego	4,681	7,011	5,634	6,752
Ottawa	42,737	88,166	50,828	83,330
Presque Isle	3,192	3,794	3,722	3,606

County	2012 Obama (D)	Romney (R)	2008 Obama (D)	McCain (R)
Roscommon	6,198	6,701	7,082	6,727
Saginaw	54,381	42,720	60,276	42,225
St. Clair	33,983	39,271	40,677	38,536
St. Joseph	10,112	12,978	12,322	12,886
Sanilac	7,212	10,963	9,047	10,679
Schoolcraft	1,865	2,142	2,184	2,058
Shiawassee	17,197	15,962	19,397	16,268
Tuscola	11,425	14,240	13,503	13,740
Van Buren	16,290	16,141	18,588	15,534
Washtenaw	120,890	56,412	130,578	53,946
Wayne	595,846	213,814	660,085	219,582
Wexford	6,184	8,450	7,379	8,044
Totals	**2,564,569**	**2,115,256**	**2,872,579**	**2,048,639**

Michigan Vote Since 1960

2012: Obama, D., 2,564,569; Romney, R., 2,115,256; Stein, Green, 21,897; Goode, U.S. Taxpayers, 16,119; Johnson, Ind., 7,774, Anderson, Natural Law, 5,147;
2008: Obama, D., 2,872,579; McCain, R., 2,048,639; Nader, Natural Law, 33,085; Barr, LB., 23,716; Baldwin, U.S. Taxpayers, 14,685; McKinney, Green, 8,892.
2004: Kerry, D., 2,479,183; Bush, R., 2,313,746; Nader, Ind., 24,035; Badnarik, LB., 10,552; Cobb, Green, 5,325; Peroutka, U.S. Taxpayers, 4,980; Brown, Natural Law, 1,431.
2000: Gore, D., 2,170,418; Bush, R., 1,953,139; Nader, Green, 84,165; Browne, LB., 16,711; Phillips, U.S. Taxpayers, 3,791; Hagelin, Natural Law, 2,426.
1996: Clinton, D., 1,989,653; Dole, R., 1,481,212; Perot, RF., 336,670; Browne, LB., 27,670; Hagelin, Natural Law, 4,254; Moorehead, Workers World, 3,153; White, Soc. Equality, 1,554.
1992: Clinton, D., 1,871,182; Bush, R., 1,554,940; Perot, Ind., 824,813; Marrou, LB., 10,175; Phillips, U.S. Taxpayers, 8,263; Hagelin, Natural Law, 2,954.
1988: Bush, R., 1,965,486; Dukakis, D., 1,675,783; Paul, LB., 18,336; Fulani, Ind., 2,513.
1984: Reagan, R., 2,251,571; Mondale, D., 1,529,638; Bergland, LB., 10,055.
1980: Reagan, R., 1,915,225; Carter, D., 1,661,532; Anderson, Ind., 275,223; Clark, LB., 41,597; Commoner, Citizens, 11,930; Hall, Comm., 3,262; Griswold, Workers World, 30; Greaves, Amer., 21; Bubar, Statesman, 9.
1976: Ford, R., 1,893,742; Carter, D., 1,696,714; McCarthy, Ind., 47,905; MacBride, LB., 5,406; Wright, People's, 3,504; Camejo, Soc. Workers, 1,804; LaRouche, U.S. Labor, 1,366; Levin, Soc. Labor, 1,148; scattered, 2,160.
1972: Nixon, R., 1,961,721; McGovern, D., 1,459,435; Schmitz, Amer., 63,321; Fisher, Soc. Labor, 2,437; Jenness, Soc. Workers, 1,603; Hall, Comm., 1,210.
1968: Humphrey, D., 1,593,082; Nixon, R., 1,370,665; Wallace, 3rd party, 331,968; Halstead, Soc. Workers, 4,099; Blomen, Soc. Labor, 1,762; Cleaver, New Politics, 4,585; Munn, Prohib., 60; scattered, 29.
1964: Johnson, D., 2,136,615; Goldwater, R., 1,060,152; DeBerry, Soc. Workers, 3,817; Hass, Soc. Labor, 1,704; Prohib. (no candidate listed), 699; scattered, 145.
1960: Kennedy, D., 1,687,269; Nixon, R., 1,620,428; Dobbs, Soc. Workers, 4,347; Decker, Prohib., 2,029; Daly, Tax Cut, 1,767; Hass, Soc. Labor, 1,718; Ind. Amer. (unpledged), 539.

Minnesota

County	2012 Obama (D)	Romney (R)	2008 Obama (D)	McCain (R)
Aitkin	4,412	4,533	4,595	4,589
Anoka	88,614	93,430	86,976	91,357
Becker	6,829	9,204	7,687	8,851
Beltrami	11,818	9,637	12,019	9,762
Benton	8,173	10,849	8,454	10,338
Big Stone	1,345	1,385	1,552	1,362
Blue Earth	18,164	14,916	19,325	14,782
Brown	5,630	7,938	5,809	7,456
Carlton	11,389	6,586	11,501	6,549
Carver	20,745	31,155	20,654	28,156
Cass	6,858	8,957	7,276	8,660
Chippewa	3,083	2,967	3,280	2,907
Chisago	12,524	16,227	12,783	15,789
Clay	15,208	12,920	16,666	11,978
Clearwater	1,753	2,359	1,877	2,291
Cook	1,993	1,221	2,019	1,240
Cottonwood	2,433	3,316	2,759	3,157
Crow Wing	14,760	19,415	15,859	18,567
Dakota	116,255	109,516	116,778	104,364
Dodge	4,487	5,522	4,463	5,468
Douglas	8,653	11,884	9,256	11,241
Faribault	3,407	4,104	3,736	4,196
Fillmore	5,713	4,913	5,921	4,993
Freeborn	9,326	6,969	9,915	6,955
Goodhue	12,212	12,986	12,420	12,775
Grant	1,647	1,748	1,850	1,646

County	2012		2008	
	Obama (D)	Romney (R)	Obama (D)	McCain (R)
Hennepin	423,982	240,073	420,958	231,054
Houston	5,281	4,951	5,906	4,743
Hubbard	4,676	6,622	4,872	6,558
Isanti	8,024	11,675	8,248	11,324
Itasca	12,852	10,501	13,460	10,309
Jackson	2,268	3,044	2,618	2,858
Kanabec	3,593	4,328	3,743	4,479
Kandiyohi	9,805	11,240	10,125	11,319
Kittson	1,241	1,095	1,492	1,016
Koochiching	3,451	2,841	3,649	2,962
Lac Qui Parle	1,974	1,938	2,160	1,912
Lake	4,043	2,610	4,174	2,636
Lake of the Woods	859	1,306	971	1,278
Le Sueur	6,753	7,715	6,994	7,636
Lincoln	1,429	1,595	1,517	1,491
Lyon	5,465	6,594	6,110	6,315
Mahnomen	1,276	871	1,436	843
Marshall	1,998	2,569	2,311	2,285
Martin	4,054	6,657	4,413	6,053
McLeod	6,968	11,069	7,505	10,993
Meeker	4,969	6,913	5,380	6,737
Mille Lacs	5,829	6,951	6,072	7,049
Morrison	6,153	10,159	6,547	9,735
Mower	11,129	6,938	11,605	7,075
Murray	2,160	2,504	2,345	2,320
Nicollet	9,652	8,214	9,887	7,968
Nobles	3,793	4,581	4,244	4,368
Norman	1,730	1,384	2,129	1,204
Olmsted	39,338	36,832	38,711	36,202
Otter Tail	12,165	18,860	13,856	18,077
Pennington	3,024	3,305	3,394	3,248
Pine	6,750	6,845	7,084	6,862
Pipestone	1,725	2,826	2,023	2,652
Polk	6,773	7,615	7,850	7,148
Pope	2,981	3,142	3,317	3,069
Ramsey	184,938	86,800	182,974	88,942
Red Lake	928	978	1,120	983
Redwood	3,008	4,570	3,250	4,308
Renville	3,394	4,149	3,904	3,956
Rice	17,054	14,384	17,381	13,723
Rock	1,946	2,810	2,079	2,775
Roseau	2,772	4,409	3,097	4,438
St. Louis	73,378	39,131	77,351	38,742
Scott	29,712	40,323	29,208	36,724
Sherburne	17,597	27,848	17,957	26,140
Sibley	2,916	4,693	2,998	4,492
Stearns	33,551	43,015	35,690	41,194
Steele	8,706	9,903	9,016	10,068
Stevens	2,742	2,766	2,781	2,710
Swift	2,751	2,248	2,907	2,184
Todd	4,819	6,719	5,277	6,637
Traverse	943	861	1,043	933
Wabasha	5,415	6,049	5,646	5,935
Wadena	2,492	4,143	2,882	4,128
Waseca	4,370	5,116	4,401	5,211
Washington	70,203	69,137	70,277	64,334
Watonwan	2,494	2,517	2,562	2,526
Wilkin	1,258	1,884	1,550	1,786
Winona	14,980	11,480	16,308	10,975
Wright	25,741	40,466	26,343	37,779
Yellow Medicine	2,465	2,806	2,816	2,579
Totals	**1,546,167**	**1,320,225**	**1,573,354**	**1,275,409**

Minnesota Vote Since 1960

2012: Obama, D., 1,546,167; Romney, R., 1,320,225; Johnson, LB., 35,098; Stein, Green, 13,023; Goode, Const., 3,722; Carlson, Grassroots, 3,149; Anderson, Justice, 1,996; Morstad, Constitutional, 1,092; Harris, Soc. Workers, 1,051; Lindsay, Socialism/Liberation, 397.

2008: Obama, D., 1,573,354; McCain, R., 1,275,409; Nader, Ind., 30,152; Barr, LB., 9,174; Baldwin, Const., 6,787; McKinney, Green, 5,174; Calero, Soc. Workers, 790.

2004: Kerry, D., 1,445,014; Bush, R., 1,346,695; Nader, Better Life, 18,683; Badnarik, LB., 4,639; Cobb, Green, 4,408; Peroutka, Const., 3,074; Harens, other, 2,387; Van Auken, Soc. Equal., 539; Calero, Soc. Workers, 416.

2000: Gore, D., 1,168,266; Bush, R., 1,109,659; Nader, Green, 126,696; Buchanan, RF. MN, 22,166; Browne, LB., 5,282; Phillips, Const., 3,272; Hagelin, RF., 2,294; Harris, Soc. Workers, 1,022.

1996: Clinton, D., 1,120,438; Dole, R., 766,476; Perot, RF., 257,704; Nader, Green, 24,908; Browne, LB., 8,271; Peron, Grass Roots, 4,898; Phillips, U.S. Taxpayers, 3,416; Hagelin, Natural Law, 1,808; Birrenbach, Ind. Grass Roots, 787; Harris, Soc. Workers, 684; White, Soc. Equality, 347.

1992: Clinton, D., 1,020,997; Bush, R., 747,841; Perot, Ind., 562,506; Marrou, LB., 3,373; Gritz, Populist/America First, 3,363; Hagelin, Natural Law, 1,406.

1988: Dukakis, D., 1,109,471; Bush, R., 962,337; McCarthy, Minn. Prog., 5,403; Paul, LB., 5,109.

1984: Mondale, D., 1,036,364; Reagan, R., 1,032,603; Bergland, LB., 2,996.

1980: Carter, D., 954,173; Reagan, R., 873,268; Anderson, Ind., 174,997; Clark, LB., 31,593; Commoner, Citizens, 8,406; Hall, Comm., 1,117; DeBerry, Soc. Workers, 711; Griswold, Workers World, 698; McReynolds, Soc., 536; write-in, 281.

1976: Carter, D., 1,070,440; Ford, R., 819,395; McCarthy, Ind., 35,490; Anderson, Amer., 13,592; Camejo, Soc. Workers, 4,149; MacBride, LB., 3,529; Hall, Comm., 1,092.

1972: Nixon, R., 898,269; McGovern, D., 802,346; Schmitz, Amer., 31,407; Fisher, Soc. Labor, 4,261; Spock, People's, 2,805; Jenness, Soc. Workers, 940; Hall, Comm., 662; scattered, 962.

1968: Humphrey, D., 857,738; Nixon, R., 658,643; Wallace, 3rd party, 68,931; Cleaver, Peace/Freedom, 935; Halstead, Soc. Workers, 808; McCarthy, write-in, 585; Mitchell, Comm., 415; Blomen, Industrial Govt., 285; scattered, 2,613.

1964: Johnson, D., 991,117; Goldwater, R., 559,624; Hass, Industrial Govt., 2,544; DeBerry, Soc. Workers, 1,177.

1960: Kennedy, D., 779,933; Nixon, R., 757,915; Dobbs, Soc. Workers, 3,077; Hass, Industrial Govt., 962.

Mississippi

County	2012		2008	
	Obama (D)	Romney (R)	Obama (D)	McCain (R)
Adams	9,061	6,293	9,021	6,566
Alcorn	3,511	11,111	4,130	10,805
Amite	3,242	4,414	3,348	4,245
Attala	3,927	5,126	3,849	5,273
Benton	2,051	2,041	2,227	2,329
Bolivar	10,582	4,701	10,334	4,891
Calhoun	2,586	4,412	2,522	4,467
Carroll	2,007	3,960	2,037	3,902
Chickasaw	4,378	3,994	4,588	4,395
Choctaw	1,428	2,812	1,459	2,624
Claiborne	4,838	625	4,682	748
Clarke	3,111	5,049	3,121	5,229
Clay	6,712	4,291	6,558	4,466
Coahoma	7,792	2,712	7,597	2,917
Copiah	7,749	6,282	7,710	6,701
Covington	3,878	5,405	3,852	5,523
DeSoto	21,575	43,559	19,627	44,222
Forrest	13,272	16,574	11,622	15,296
Franklin	1,726	2,735	1,733	2,909
George	1,359	8,376	1,532	7,700
Greene	1,325	4,531	1,366	4,361
Grenada	5,288	5,986	5,029	6,234
Hancock	3,917	12,964	3,768	13,020
Harrison	23,119	39,470	22,673	38,757
Hinds	76,112	29,664	75,401	32,949
Holmes	7,812	1,435	7,765	1,714
Humphreys	3,903	1,293	3,634	1,462
Issaquena	479	302	579	364
Itawamba	1,706	7,393	2,084	7,663
Jackson	17,299	35,747	17,781	35,993
Jasper	5,097	4,193	5,025	4,135
Jefferson	3,951	468	3,883	551
Jefferson Davis	4,267	2,507	4,454	2,871
Jones	9,211	20,687	8,846	20,157
Kemper	3,239	1,789	3,256	1,935
Lafayette	8,091	11,075	7,997	10,278
Lamar	5,494	19,101	5,159	18,497
Lauderdale	13,814	18,700	13,332	19,582
Lawrence	2,468	4,192	2,587	4,369
Leake	4,079	4,863	4,151	5,148
Lee	12,563	22,415	12,021	22,694
Leflore	9,119	3,587	8,914	4,105
Lincoln	5,471	10,839	5,505	10,781
Lowndes	13,388	13,518	13,209	13,994
Madison	20,722	28,507	19,831	27,203
Marion	4,393	8,237	4,422	8,513
Marshall	9,650	6,473	9,685	6,683
Monroe	7,056	9,723	7,169	10,184
Montgomery	2,675	2,947	2,609	3,071
Neshoba	3,089	7,837	3,114	8,209
Newton	3,319	6,394	3,218	6,579
Noxubee	4,920	1,325	5,030	1,525
Oktibbeha	9,095	8,761	9,326	9,320
Panola	9,079	7,629	8,690	7,620
Pearl River	4,366	17,549	4,320	17,881
Perry	1,527	4,137	1,533	4,067
Pike	9,650	8,181	9,276	8,651
Pontotoc	2,804	9,448	2,982	9,727
Prentiss	2,817	7,075	3,020	7,703
Quitman	2,837	1,116	2,803	1,334

County	2012 Obama (D)	Romney (R)	2008 Obama (D)	McCain (R)
Rankin	14,988	48,444	14,372	48,140
Scott	5,031	6,089	5,025	6,584
Sharkey	1,782	737	1,907	873
Simpson	4,723	7,424	4,817	7,641
Smith	1,979	6,049	1,968	6,265
Stone	2,003	5,420	1,996	5,149
Sunflower	8,199	2,929	7,838	3,245
Tallahatchie	3,959	2,499	4,105	2,786
Tate	4,933	7,332	5,003	7,678
Tippah	2,317	6,717	2,623	6,937
Tishomingo	1,643	6,133	1,962	6,249
Tunica	3,475	883	3,279	1,017
Union	2,742	8,498	2,985	9,072
Walthall	3,422	4,051	3,456	4,253
Warren	10,786	10,457	10,489	11,152
Washington	13,981	5,651	13,148	6,347
Wayne	4,148	6,111	3,890	6,070
Webster	1,190	3,992	1,349	4,072
Wilkinson	3,412	1,415	3,534	1,560
Winston	4,607	5,168	4,653	5,497
Yalobusha	3,030	3,276	3,151	3,628
Yazoo	6,603	4,941	6,116	5,290
Totals	**562,949**	**710,746**	**554,662**	**724,597**

Mississippi Vote Since 1960

2012: Romney, R., 710,746; Obama, D., 562,949; Johnson, LB., 6,676; Goode, Const., 2,609; Stein, Green, 1,588; Washer, RF., 1,016.

2008: McCain, R., 724,597; Obama, D., 554,662; Nader, Ind., 4,011; Baldwin, Const., 2,551; Barr, LB., 2,529; McKinney, Green, 1,034; Weill, RF., 481.

2004: Bush, R., 684,981; Kerry, D., 458,094; Nader, RF., 3,177; Badnarik, LB., 1,793; Peroutka, Const., 1,759; Harris, Ind., 1,268; Cobb, Green, 1,073.

2000: Bush, R., 572,844; Gore, D., 404,614; Nader, Ind., 8,122; Phillips, Const., 3,267; Buchanan, RF., 2,265; Browne, LB., 2,009; Harris, Ind., 613; Hagelin, Natural Law, 450.

1996: Dole, R., 439,838; Clinton, D., 394,022; Perot, RF., 52,222; Browne, LB., 2,809; Phillips, U.S. Taxpayers, 2,314; Hagelin, Natural Law, 1,447; Collins, Ind., 1,205.

1992: Bush, R., 487,793; Clinton, D., 400,258; Perot, Ind., 85,626; Fulani, New Alliance, 2,625; Marrou, LB., 2,154; Phillips, U.S. Taxpayers, 1,652; Hagelin, Natural Law, 1,140.

1988: Bush, R., 557,890; Dukakis, D., 363,921; Duke, Ind., 4,232; Paul, LB., 3,329.

1984: Reagan, R., 582,377; Mondale, D., 352,192; Bergland, LB., 2,336.

1980: Reagan, R., 441,089; Carter, D., 429,281; Anderson, Ind., 12,036; Clark, LB., 5,465; Griswold, Workers World, 2,402; Pulley, Soc. Workers, 2,347.

1976: Carter, D., 381,309; Ford, R., 366,846; Anderson, Amer., 6,678; McCarthy, Ind., 4,074; Maddox, Ind., 4,049; Camejo, Soc. Workers, 2,805; MacBride, LB., 2,609.

1972: Nixon, R., 505,125; McGovern, D., 126,782; Schmitz, Amer., 11,598; Jenness, Soc. Workers, 2,458.

1968: Wallace, 3rd party, 415,349; Humphrey, D., 150,644; Nixon, R., 88,516.

1964: Goldwater, R., 356,528; Johnson, D., 52,618.

1960: D. (electors unpledged), 116,248; Kennedy, D., 108,362; Nixon, R., 73,561. *Mississippi's victorious slate of 8 unpledged Democratic electors cast their votes for Sen. Harry F. Byrd (D, VA).

Missouri

County	2012 Obama (D)	Romney (R)	2008 Obama (D)	McCain (R)
Adair	4,219	5,651	5,735	5,891
Andrew	2,649	5,457	3,345	5,279
Atchison	756	1,902	1,000	1,936
Audrain	3,539	6,186	4,434	6,167
Barry	3,667	9,832	4,630	9,758
Barton	1,230	4,418	1,455	4,414
Bates	2,557	5,020	3,271	4,833
Benton	2,925	6,069	3,629	5,759
Bollinger	1,213	4,095	1,690	3,972
Boone	39,847	37,404	47,062	36,849
Buchanan	15,594	18,660	19,164	19,110
Butler	4,363	12,248	5,316	11,805
Caldwell	1,312	2,721	1,814	2,654
Callaway	6,071	11,745	7,580	11,389
Camden	6,458	15,092	7,773	14,074
Cape Girardeau	9,728	25,370	12,208	24,768
Carroll	1,154	3,072	1,535	2,955
Carter	754	1,978	984	1,840
Cass	17,044	30,912	19,844	29,695
Cedar	1,537	4,376	2,060	4,194
Chariton	1,339	2,402	1,799	2,339
Christian	9,813	27,473	11,883	25,382
Clark	1,398	1,730	1,572	1,782
Clay	47,310	56,191	53,761	54,516
Clinton	3,688	5,931	4,545	5,709
Cole	12,005	24,490	13,959	24,385
Cooper	2,474	4,887	2,996	4,902
Crawford	2,951	6,434	3,911	6,007
Dade	939	2,895	1,184	2,864
Dallas	2,122	4,992	2,656	4,895
Daviess	1,125	2,290	1,400	2,263
DeKalb	1,194	3,056	1,692	2,889
Dent	1,585	4,883	2,056	4,655
Douglas	1,710	4,649	2,140	4,405
Dunklin	3,636	6,850	4,540	7,044
Franklin	16,347	29,396	21,256	27,355
Gasconade	2,099	4,895	2,899	4,763
Gentry	937	1,988	1,235	1,964
Greene	46,219	76,900	56,181	77,683
Grundy	1,212	3,030	1,580	3,006
Harrison	984	2,624	1,287	2,512
Henry	3,606	6,229	4,869	6,095
Hickory	1,733	2,835	2,171	2,850
Holt	551	1,725	802	1,794
Howard	1,723	3,017	2,036	2,708
Howell	4,395	11,544	5,736	10,982
Iron	1,669	2,252	2,213	2,090
Jackson	78,283	93,199	90,722	92,833
Jasper	12,809	31,349	15,730	31,667
Jefferson	41,564	53,978	53,467	50,804
Johnson	7,667	12,763	9,480	12,183
Knox	698	1,205	759	1,212
Laclede	4,093	10,934	5,218	10,875
Lafayette	5,655	9,803	6,902	9,442
Lawrence	4,017	11,421	5,097	11,263
Lewis	1,508	2,677	1,837	2,594
Lincoln	7,734	14,332	10,234	12,924
Linn	2,041	3,344	2,638	3,140
Livingston	1,906	4,006	2,435	3,993
Macon	2,309	4,701	2,784	4,586
Madison	1,588	3,227	2,042	2,897
Maries	1,299	3,165	1,599	2,853
Marion	4,031	7,923	4,703	7,705
McDonald	1,920	5,694	2,454	5,499
Mercer	353	1,255	519	1,169
Miller	2,651	8,099	3,553	7,797
Mississippi	1,858	2,997	2,247	3,034
Moniteau	1,608	4,704	2,084	4,467
Monroe	1,398	2,564	1,703	2,533
Montgomery	1,740	3,490	2,347	3,428
Morgan	2,773	5,733	3,565	5,451
New Madrid	2,814	4,284	3,370	4,593
Newton	6,425	18,181	7,450	17,637
Nodaway	3,172	5,593	4,493	5,568
Oregon	1,419	2,886	1,811	2,652
Osage	1,473	5,329	1,907	5,062
Ozark	1,261	3,080	1,661	2,918
Pemiscot	2,671	3,598	3,029	3,954
Perry	2,184	5,669	3,005	5,527
Pettis	5,904	10,842	6,932	11,018
Phelps	5,798	11,895	7,394	11,706
Pike	2,582	4,577	3,487	4,268
Platte	19,175	25,618	21,459	24,460
Polk	3,580	9,252	4,553	8,956
Pulaski	4,199	9,092	5,249	9,552
Putnam	587	1,673	695	1,591
Ralls	1,736	3,231	2,041	2,987
Randolph	3,031	6,667	3,984	6,457
Ray	4,275	5,815	5,241	5,593
Reynolds	1,157	1,931	1,418	1,782
Ripley	1,396	3,743	1,795	3,407
St. Charles	71,838	110,784	84,183	102,550
St. Clair	1,460	3,019	1,886	2,981
St. Francois	8,829	13,248	11,540	12,660
St. Louis Co.	297,097	224,742	333,123	221,705
Ste. Genevieve	3,813	4,055	4,979	3,732
Saline	3,790	5,104	4,712	4,962
Schuyler	697	1,174	775	1,139
Scotland	643	1,246	793	1,249
Scott	5,122	11,623	6,258	11,563
Shannon	1,302	2,262	1,637	2,075
Shelby	966	2,188	1,114	2,166
Stoddard	3,153	9,496	3,899	9,172
Stone	3,923	11,787	5,029	11,147
Sullivan	908	1,610	1,173	1,607
Taney	5,479	15,746	6,683	14,736

County	2012 Obama (D)	Romney (R)	2008 Obama (D)	McCain (R)
Texas	2,871	7,618	3,410	7,215
Vernon	2,580	5,758	3,381	5,334
Warren	5,219	9,150	6,705	8,675
Washington	3,417	5,071	4,711	4,706
Wayne	1,813	3,790	2,243	3,784
Webster	4,409	10,708	5,685	10,431
Worth	341	664	427	707
Wright	1,953	5,830	2,557	5,784
City				
Kansas City	105,670	29,509	120,102	31,854
St. Louis	118,780	22,943	132,925	24,662
Totals	**1,223,796**	**1,482,440**	**1,441,911**	**1,445,814**

Missouri Vote Since 1960

2012: Romney, R., 1,482,440; Obama, D., 1,223,796; Johnson, LB., 43,151; Goode, Const., 7,936.
2008: McCain, R., 1,445,814; Obama, D., 1,441,911; Nader, Ind., 17,813; Barr, LB., 11,386; Baldwin, Const., 8,201.
2004: Bush, R., 1,455,713; Kerry, D., 1,259,171; Badnarik, LB., 9,831; Peroutka, Const., 5,355.
2000: Bush, R., 1,189,924; Gore, D., 1,111,138; Nader, Green, 38,515; Buchanan, RF., 9,818; Browne, LB., 7,436; Phillips, Const., 1,957; Hagelin, Natural Law, 1,104.
1996: Clinton, D., 1,025,935; Dole, R., 890,016; Perot, RF., 217,188; Phillips, U.S. Taxpayers, 11,521; Browne, LB., 10,522; Hagelin, Natural Law, 2,287.
1992: Clinton, D., 1,053,873; Bush, R., 811,159; Perot, Ind., 518,741; Marrou, LB., 7,497.
1988: Bush, R., 1,084,953; Dukakis, D., 1,001,619; Fulani, New Alliance, 6,656; Paul, write-in, 434.
1984: Reagan, R., 1,274,188; Mondale, D., 848,583.
1980: Reagan, R., 1,074,181; Carter, D., 931,182; Anderson, Ind., 77,920; Clark, LB., 14,422; DeBerry, Soc. Workers, 1,515; Commoner, Citizens, 573; write-in, 31.
1976: Carter, D., 999,163; Ford, R., 928,808; McCarthy, Ind., 24,329.
1972: Nixon, R., 1,154,058; McGovern, D., 698,531.
1968: Nixon, R., 811,932; Humphrey, D., 791,444; Wallace, 3rd party, 206,126.
1964: Johnson, D., 1,164,344; Goldwater, R., 653,535.
1960: Kennedy, D., 972,201; Nixon, R., 962,221.

Montana

County	2012 Obama (D)	Romney (R)	2008 Obama (D)	McCain (R)
Beaverhead	1,371	3,289	1,617	3,008
Big Horn	2,882	1,667	3,516	1,628
Blaine	1,616	1,178	1,702	1,139
Broadwater	764	2,152	857	1,875
Carbon	2,146	3,533	2,443	3,108
Carter	96	678	111	573
Cascade	15,232	18,345	17,664	16,857
Chouteau	978	1,758	1,122	1,634
Custer	1,833	3,373	2,267	3,047
Daniels	237	740	343	694
Dawson	1,219	3,029	1,593	2,639
Deer Lodge	2,860	1,448	3,402	1,502
Fallon	237	1,128	318	1,064
Fergus	1,640	4,257	1,933	4,108
Flathead	13,892	28,309	16,138	25,559
Gallatin	21,961	24,358	24,205	22,578
Garfield	66	622	110	598
Glacier	2,924	1,415	3,423	1,451
Golden Valley	110	351	124	343
Granite	533	1,107	601	1,013
Hill	3,403	3,164	3,596	2,787
Jefferson	2,272	4,055	2,582	3,538
Judith Basin	337	854	397	801
Lake	5,805	7,135	6,766	6,498
Lewis and Clark	15,620	16,803	17,114	14,966
Liberty	257	702	367	594
Lincoln	2,552	6,057	3,025	5,704
Madison	1,289	3,130	1,607	2,822
McCone	223	745	321	726
Meagher	269	670	298	624
Mineral	700	1,216	845	1,053
Missoula	32,824	22,652	36,531	20,743
Musselshell	492	1,833	636	1,581
Park	3,783	4,709	4,173	4,376
Petroleum	49	240	68	227
Phillips	471	1,688	638	1,423
Pondera	975	1,673	1,223	1,588
Powder River	170	833	208	802
Powell	888	1,806	1,021	1,683
Prairie	167	520	211	503
Ravalli	7,285	14,307	8,400	13,002

County	2012 Obama (D)	Romney (R)	2008 Obama (D)	McCain (R)
Richland	1,002	3,510	1,203	3,184
Roosevelt	2,086	1,514	2,564	1,473
Rosebud	1,422	2,004	1,919	1,768
Sanders	1,720	3,980	1,970	3,563
Sheridan	665	1,207	953	987
Silver Bow	10,857	5,430	11,676	4,818
Stillwater	1,248	3,337	1,512	2,991
Sweet Grass	475	1,594	541	1,494
Teton	1,082	2,113	1,294	1,874
Toole	582	1,440	737	1,317
Treasure	114	319	156	314
Valley	1,385	2,337	1,645	2,121
Wheatland	272	693	289	657
Wibaux	98	421	146	379
Yellowstone	26,403	40,500	32,038	36,483
Totals	**201,839**	**267,928**	**231,667**	**242,763**

Montana Vote Since 1960

2012: Romney, R., 267,928; Obama, D., 201,839; Johnson, LB., 14,165.
2008: McCain, R., 242,763; Obama, D., 231,667; Paul, Const., 10,638; Nader, Ind., 3,686; Barr, LB., 1,355.
2004: Bush, R., 266,063; Kerry, D., 173,710; Nader, Ind., 6,168; Peroutka, Const., 1,764; Badnarik, LB., 1,733; Cobb, Green, 996.
2000: Bush, R., 240,178; Gore, D., 137,126; Nader, Green, 24,437; Buchanan, RF., 5,697; Browne, LB., 1,718; Phillips, Const., 1,155; Hagelin, Natural Law, 675.
1996: Dole, R., 179,652; Clinton, D., 167,922; Perot, RF., 55,229; Browne, LB., 2,526; Hagelin, Natural Law, 1,754.
1992: Clinton, D., 154,507; Bush, R., 144,207; Perot, Ind., 107,225; Gritz, Populist/America First, 3,658.
1988: Bush, R., 190,412; Dukakis, D., 168,936; Paul, LB., 5,047; Fulani, New Alliance, 1,279.
1984: Reagan, R., 232,450; Mondale, D., 146,742; Bergland, LB., 5,185.
1980: Reagan, R., 206,814; Carter, D., 118,032; Anderson, Ind., 29,281; Clark, LB., 9,825.
1976: Ford, R., 173,703; Carter, D., 149,259; Anderson, Amer., 5,772.
1972: Nixon, R., 183,976; McGovern, D., 120,197; Schmitz, Amer., 13,430.
1968: Nixon, R., 138,835; Humphrey, D., 114,117; Wallace, 3rd party, 20,015; Munn, Prohib., 510; Caton, New RF., 470; Halstead, Soc. Workers, 457.
1964: Johnson, D., 164,246; Goldwater, R., 113,032; Kasper, Natl. States' Rights, 519; Munn, Prohib., 499; DeBerry, Soc. Workers, 332.
1960: Nixon, R., 141,841; Kennedy, D., 134,891; Decker, Prohib., 456; Dobbs, Soc. Workers, 391.

Nebraska

County	2012 Obama (D)	Romney (R)	2008 Obama (D)	McCain (R)
Adams	4,062	8,316	4,685	8,252
Antelope	571	2,596	757	2,383
Arthur	30	227	39	217
Banner	55	346	62	348
Blaine	29	268	43	266
Boone	615	2,138	742	2,042
Box Butte	1,692	2,869	1,886	2,932
Boyd	188	873	250	839
Brown	224	1,302	311	1,208
Buffalo	5,365	13,570	5,867	13,097
Burt	1,291	2,029	1,413	1,907
Butler	1,045	2,738	1,190	2,557
Cass	4,367	7,556	4,753	7,120
Cedar	958	3,278	1,190	2,912
Chase	254	1,584	341	1,477
Cherry	436	2,557	599	2,360
Cheyenne	1,084	3,449	1,173	3,572
Clay	667	2,232	780	2,177
Colfax	969	2,051	1,125	2,018
Cuming	1,031	2,876	1,274	2,732
Custer	1,083	4,296	1,192	4,301
Dakota	2,922	3,094	2,994	3,292
Dawes	1,132	2,478	1,285	2,376
Dawson	2,199	5,460	2,399	5,460
Deuel	215	763	243	732
Dixon	870	1,745	946	1,785
Dodge	5,673	8,995	6,689	8,557
Douglas	106,456	113,220	116,810	106,291
Dundy	176	792	218	783
Fillmore	807	2,007	962	1,913
Franklin	384	1,112	442	1,079
Frontier	271	1,007	349	1,034
Furnas	423	1,782	556	1,725
Gage	3,903	5,513	4,473	5,435
Garden	242	829	283	844

County	2012 Obama (D)	Romney (R)	2008 Obama (D)	McCain (R)
Garfield	149	769	212	800
Gosper	230	734	260	776
Grant	30	322	41	318
Greeley	340	820	458	715
Hall	7,161	12,646	7,855	12,977
Hamilton	1,146	3,600	1,332	3,389
Harlan	354	1,395	402	1,329
Hayes	51	476	85	461
Hitchcock	274	1,178	346	1,001
Holt	882	3,922	1,089	3,746
Hooker	59	330	75	355
Howard	914	1,890	1,083	1,847
Jefferson	1,195	2,166	1,520	2,103
Johnson	790	1,225	914	1,142
Kearney	773	2,349	876	2,224
Keith	928	3,044	974	2,942
Keya Paha	80	393	115	409
Kimball	395	1,235	439	1,346
Knox	1,059	2,885	1,255	2,728
Lancaster	62,015	62,434	65,734	59,398
Lincoln	4,450	10,728	5,046	10,817
Logan	68	356	81	327
Loup	62	290	86	302
Madison	3,485	10,062	4,142	9,655
McPherson	41	237	45	240
Merrick	925	2,490	986	2,375
Morrill	455	1,681	557	1,725
Nance	481	1,106	549	1,116
Nemaha	1,128	2,012	1,240	2,134
Nuckolls	568	1,574	657	1,498
Otoe	2,561	4,258	2,915	4,033
Pawnee	400	899	483	859
Perkins	238	1,135	310	1,092
Phelps	880	3,400	1,050	3,360
Pierce	637	2,707	783	2,385
Platte	3,148	10,061	3,796	9,373
Polk	528	1,890	668	1,822
Red Willow	952	3,891	1,216	3,735
Richardson	1,191	2,443	1,513	2,342
Rock	103	672	139	640
Saline	2,289	2,557	2,674	2,434
Sarpy	26,671	43,213	28,010	38,816
Saunders	3,307	6,770	3,767	6,188
Scotts Bluff	4,327	9,648	4,745	9,708
Seward	2,386	5,003	2,703	4,647
Sheridan	390	2,021	454	1,941
Sherman	552	927	585	950
Sioux	101	624	117	603
Stanton	614	1,949	664	1,781
Thayer	728	1,874	860	1,749
Thomas	42	360	51	331
Thurston	1,247	939	1,120	972
Valley	498	1,657	706	1,657
Washington	3,132	6,899	3,711	6,425
Wayne	1,074	2,493	1,249	2,503
Webster	442	1,258	552	1,233
Wheeler	93	345	96	334
York	1,373	4,874	1,607	4,848
Totals	**302,081**	**475,064**	**333,319**	**452,979**

Nebraska Vote Since 1960

2012: Romney, R., 475,064; Obama, D., 302,081; Johnson, LB., 11,109; Terry, petitioning cand., 2,408.
2008: McCain, R., 452,979; Obama, D., 333,319; Nader, petitioning cand., 5,406; Baldwin, Nebraska, 2,972; Barr, LB., 2,740; McKinney, Green, 1,028.
2004: Bush, R., 512,814; Kerry, D., 254,328; Nader, petitioning cand., 5,698; Badnarik, LB., 2,041; Peroutka, Nebraska, 1,314; Cobb, Green, 978; Calero, petitioning cand., 82.
2000: Bush, R., 433,862; Gore, D., 231,780; Nader, Green, 24,540; Buchanan, Ind., 3,646; Browne, LB., 2,245; Hagelin, Natural Law, 478; Phillips, Ind., 468.
1996: Dole, R., 363,467; Clinton, D., 236,761; Perot, RF., 71,278; Browne, LB., 2,792; Phillips, Ind., 1,928; Hagelin, Natural Law, 1,189.
1992: Bush, R., 343,678; Clinton, D., 216,864; Perot, Ind., 174,104; Marrou, LB., 1,340.
1988: Bush, R., 397,956; Dukakis, D., 259,235; Paul, LB., 2,534; Fulani, New Alliance, 1,740.
1984: Reagan, R., 459,135; Mondale, D., 187,475; Bergland, LB., 2,075.
1980: Reagan, R., 419,214; Carter, D., 166,424; Anderson, Ind., 44,854; Clark, LB., 9,041.
1976: Ford, R., 359,219; Carter, D., 233,287; McCarthy, Ind., 9,383; Maddox, Amer. Ind., 3,378; MacBride, LB., 1,476.
1972: Nixon, R., 406,298; McGovern, D., 169,991; scattered, 817.
1968: Nixon, R., 321,163; Humphrey, D., 170,784; Wallace, 3rd party, 44,904.

1964: Johnson, D., 307,307; Goldwater, R., 276,847.
1960: Nixon, R., 380,553; Kennedy, D., 232,542.

Nevada

County	2012 Obama (D)	Romney (R)	2008 Obama (D)	McCain (R)
Churchill	2,961	7,061	3,494	6,832
Clark	389,936	289,053	380,765	257,078
Douglas	9,297	16,276	10,672	14,648
Elko	3,511	12,014	4,541	10,969
Esmeralda	92	317	104	303
Eureka	107	663	144	564
Humboldt	1,737	3,810	1,909	3,586
Lander	534	1,580	577	1,466
Lincoln	400	1,691	518	1,498
Lyon	7,380	13,520	8,405	12,154
Mineral	863	1,080	1,082	1,131
Nye	6,320	10,566	7,226	9,537
Pershing	632	1,167	673	1,075
Storey	920	1,321	1,102	1,247
Washoe	95,409	88,453	99,671	76,880
White Pine	983	2,601	1,230	2,440
City				
Carson City	10,291	12,394	11,623	11,419
Totals	**531,373**	**463,567**	**533,736**	**412,827**

Nevada Vote Since 1960

2012: Obama, D., 531,373; Romney, R., 463,567; Johnson, LB., 10,968; None of These Candidates, 5,770; Goode, Ind. Amer., 3,240.
2008: Obama, D., 533,736; McCain, R., 412,827; None of These Candidates, 6,267; Nader, Ind., 6,150; Barr, LB., 4,263; Baldwin, Const., 3,194; McKinney, Green, 1,411.
2004: Bush, R., 418,690; Kerry, D., 397,190; Nader, Ind., 4,838; None of These Candidates, 3,688; Badnarik, LB., 3,176; Peroutka, Ind. Amer., 1,152; Cobb, Green, 853.
2000: Bush, R., 301,575; Gore, D., 279,978; Nader, Green, 15,008; Buchanan, Citizens First, 4,747; None of These Candidates, 3,315; Browne, LB., 3,311; Phillips, Ind. Amer., 621; Hagelin, Natural Law, 415.
1996: Clinton, D., 203,974; Dole, R., 199,244; Perot, RF., 43,986; None of These Candidates, 5,608; Nader, Green, 4,730; Browne, LB., 4,460; Phillips, Ind. Amer., 1,732; Hagelin, Natural Law, 545.
1992: Clinton, D., 189,148; Bush, R., 175,828; Perot, Ind., 132,580; Gritz, Populist/America First, 2,892; Marrou, LB., 1,835.
1988: Bush, R., 206,040; Dukakis, D., 132,738; Paul, LB., 3,520; Fulani, New Alliance, 835.
1984: Reagan, R., 188,770; Mondale, D., 91,655; Bergland, LB., 2,292.
1980: Reagan, R., 155,017; Carter, D., 66,666; Anderson, Ind., 17,651; Clark, LB., 4,358.
1976: Ford, R., 101,273; Carter, D., 92,479; MacBride, LB., 1,519; Maddox, Amer. Ind., 1,497; scattered, 5,108.
1972: Nixon, R., 115,750; McGovern, D., 66,016.
1968: Nixon, R., 73,188; Humphrey, D., 60,598; Wallace, 3rd party, 20,432.
1964: Johnson, D., 79,339; Goldwater, R., 56,094.
1960: Kennedy, D., 54,880; Nixon, R., 52,387.

New Hampshire

County	2012 Obama (D)	Romney (R)	2008 Obama (D)	McCain (R)
Belknap	15,890	17,571	16,796	16,402
Carroll	13,977	14,207	15,221	13,387
Cheshire	25,380	15,156	26,971	15,205
Coos	9,095	6,342	9,532	6,558
Grafton	29,826	18,208	31,446	17,687
Hillsborough	102,303	99,991	104,820	97,178
Merrimack	44,756	34,524	45,078	34,010
Rockingham	80,142	87,921	83,723	81,917
Strafford	36,026	26,729	37,990	25,021
Sullivan	12,166	9,269	13,249	9,169
Totals	**369,561**	**329,918**	**384,826**	**316,534**

New Hampshire Vote Since 1960

2012: Obama, D., 369,561; Romney, R., 329,918; Johnson, LB., 8,212; Goode, Const., 708.
2008: Obama, D., 384,826; McCain, R., 316,534; Nader, Ind., 3,503; Barr, LB., 2,217; Phillies, LB., 531.
2004: Kerry, D., 340,511; Bush, R., 331,237; Nader, Ind., 4,479.
2000: Bush, R., 273,559; Gore, D., 266,348; Nader, Green, 22,198; Browne, LB., 2,757; Buchanan, Independence, 2,615; Phillips, Const., 328.
1996: Clinton, D., 246,166; Dole, R., 196,486; Perot, RF., 48,387; Browne, LB., 4,214; Phillips, Taxpayers, 1,344.

1992: Clinton, D., 209,040; Bush, R., 202,484; Perot, Ind., 121,337; Marrou, LB., 3,548.
1988: Bush, R., 281,537; Dukakis, D., 163,696; Paul, LB., 4,502; Fulani, New Alliance, 790.
1984: Reagan, R., 267,051; Mondale, D., 120,377; Bergland, LB., 735.
1980: Reagan, R., 221,705; Carter, D., 108,864; Anderson, Ind., 49,693; Clark, LB., 2,067; Commoner, Citizens, 1,325; Hall, Comm., 129; Griswold, Workers World, 76; DeBerry, Soc. Workers, 72; scattered, 68.
1976: Ford, R., 185,935; Carter, D., 147,645; McCarthy, Ind., 4,095; MacBride, LB., 936; Reagan, write-in, 388; LaRouche, U.S. Labor, 186; Camejo, Soc. Workers, 161; Levin, Soc. Labor, 66; scattered, 215.
1972: Nixon, R., 213,724; McGovern, D., 116,435; Schmitz, Amer., 3,386; Jenness, Soc. Workers, 368; scattered, 142.
1968: Nixon, R., 154,903; Humphrey, D., 130,589; Wallace, 3rd party, 11,173; New Party, 421; Halstead, Soc. Workers, 104.
1964: Johnson, D., 182,065; Goldwater, R., 104,029.
1960: Nixon, R., 157,989; Kennedy, D., 137,772.

New Jersey

County	2012		2008	
	Obama (D)	Romney (R)	Obama (D)	McCain (R)
Atlantic	65,600	46,522	67,830	49,902
Bergen	212,754	169,070	225,367	186,118
Burlington	126,377	87,401	131,219	89,626
Camden	153,682	69,476	159,259	73,819
Cape May	21,657	25,781	22,893	27,288
Cumberland	34,055	20,658	34,919	22,360
Essex	236,618	64,406	240,306	74,063
Gloucester	74,013	59,456	77,267	60,315
Hudson	153,108	42,369	154,140	55,360
Hunterdon	26,876	38,687	29,776	39,092
Mercer	104,377	47,355	107,926	50,223
Middlesex	190,555	107,310	193,812	123,695
Monmouth	133,145	147,513	148,737	160,433
Morris	100,146	124,947	112,275	132,331
Ocean	102,300	146,474	110,189	160,677
Passaic	115,926	64,523	113,257	72,552
Salem	14,719	14,334	16,044	14,816
Somerset	74,592	66,603	79,321	70,085
Sussex	26,104	40,625	28,840	44,184
Union	139,752	68,314	141,417	78,768
Warren	18,745	25,744	20,628	27,500
Totals	**2,125,101**	**1,477,568**	**2,215,422**	**1,613,207**

New Jersey Vote Since 1960

2012: Obama, D., 2,125,101; Romney, R., 1,477,568; Johnson, LB., 21,045; Stein, Green, 9,888; Goode, Const., 2,064; Anderson, Justice, 1,724; Boss, Ind., 1,007; Harris, Soc. Workers, 710; Miller, A3P, 664; Lindsay, Socialism/Liberation, 521.
2008: Obama, D., 2,215,422; McCain, R., 1,613,207; Nader, Ind., 21,298; Barr, Ind., 8,441; Baldwin, Ind., 3,956; McKinney, Ind., 3,636; Moore, Ind., 699; Boss, Ind., 639; Calero, Ind., 523; La Riva, Ind., 416.
2004: Kerry, D., 1,911,430; Bush, R., 1,670,003; Nader, Ind., 19,418; Badnarik, Ind., 4,514; Peroutka, Ind., 2,750; Cobb, Ind., 1,807; Brown, Ind., 664; Van Auken, Ind., 575; Calero, Ind., 530.
2000: Gore, D., 1,788,850; Bush, R., 1,284,173; Nader, Ind., 94,554; Buchanan, Ind., 6,989; Browne, Ind., 6,312; Hagelin, Ind., 2,215; McReynolds, Ind., 1,880; Phillips, Ind., 1,409; Harris, Ind., 844.
1996: Clinton, D., 1,652,361; Dole, R., 1,103,099; Perot, RF., 262,134; Nader, Green, 32,465; Browne, LB., 14,763; Hagelin, Natural Law, 3,887; Phillips, U.S. Taxpayers, 3,440; Harris, Soc. Workers, 1,837; Moorehead, Workers World, 1,337; White, Soc. Equality, 537.
1992: Clinton, D., 1,436,206; Bush, R., 1,356,865; Perot, Ind., 521,829; Marrou, LB., 6,822; Fulani, New Alliance, 3,513; Phillips, U.S. Taxpayers, 2,670; LaRouche, Ind., 2,095; Warren, Soc. Workers, 2,011; Daniels, Ind., 1,996; Gritz, Populist/America First, 1,867; Hagelin, Natural Law, 1,353.
1988: Bush, R., 1,740,604; Dukakis, D., 1,317,541; Lewin, Peace/Freedom, 9,953; Paul, LB., 8,421.
1984: Reagan, R., 1,933,630; Mondale, D., 1,261,323; Bergland, LB., 6,416.
1980: Reagan, R., 1,546,557; Carter, D., 1,147,364; Anderson, Ind., 234,632; Clark, LB., 20,652; Commoner, Citizens, 8,203; McCormack, Right to Life, 3,927; Lynen, Middle Class, 3,694; Hall, Comm., 2,555; Pulley, Soc. Workers, 2,198; McReynolds, Soc., 1,973; Gahres, Down With Lawyers, 1,718; Griswold, Workers World, 1,288; Wendelken, Ind., 923.
1976: Ford, R., 1,509,688; Carter, D., 1,444,653; McCarthy, Ind., 32,717; MacBride, LB., 9,449; Maddox, Amer., 7,716; Levin, Soc. Labor, 3,686; Hall, Comm., 1,662; LaRouche, U.S. Labor,

1,650; Camejo, Soc. Workers, 1,184; Wright, People's, 1,044; Bubar, Prohib., 554; Zeidler, Soc., 469.
1972: Nixon, R., 1,845,502; McGovern, D., 1,102,211; Schmitz, Amer., 34,378; Spock, People's, 5,355; Fisher, Soc. Labor, 4,544; Jenness, Soc. Workers, 2,233; Mahalchik, Amer. First, 1,743; Hall, Comm., 1,263.
1968: Nixon, R., 1,325,467; Humphrey, D., 1,264,206; Wallace, 3rd party 262,187; Halstead, Soc. Workers, 8,667; Gregory, Peace/Freedom, 8,084; Blomen, Soc. Labor, 6,784.
1964: Johnson, D., 1,867,671; Goldwater, R., 963,843; DeBerry, Soc. Workers, 8,181; Hass, Soc. Labor, 7,075.
1960: Kennedy, D., 1,385,415; Nixon, R., 1,363,324; Dobbs, Soc. Workers, 11,402; Lee, Conservative, 8,708; Hass, Soc. Labor, 4,262.

New Mexico

County	2012		2008	
	Obama (D)	Romney (R)	Obama (D)	McCain (R)
Bernalillo	150,739	106,408	171,556	110,521
Catron	560	1,494	664	1,398
Chaves	6,604	13,088	8,197	13,651
Cibola	4,961	2,998	5,827	3,131
Colfax	2,828	2,699	3,490	2,805
Curry	4,022	9,251	4,670	9,599
De Baca	287	586	359	676
Doña Ana	37,139	27,322	40,282	28,068
Eddy	6,142	12,583	7,351	12,500
Grant	7,090	5,358	8,142	5,406
Guadalupe	1,488	557	1,557	620
Harding	260	327	260	358
Hidalgo	995	899	993	936
Lea	4,080	12,548	5,108	13,347
Lincoln	2,942	5,961	3,535	6,001
Los Alamos	5,191	4,796	5,824	5,064
Luna	3,583	3,670	4,311	3,870
McKinley	15,841	5,546	16,572	6,382
Mora	1,955	595	2,168	569
Otero	6,829	12,451	8,610	12,806
Quay	1,383	2,202	1,547	2,367
Rio Arriba	11,465	3,397	12,703	4,086
Roosevelt	1,727	4,043	2,303	4,311
San Juan	15,855	28,849	18,028	27,869
San Miguel	8,850	2,303	10,320	2,478
Sandoval	27,236	24,387	32,669	25,193
Santa Fe	50,872	15,500	55,567	15,807
Sierra	1,964	2,928	2,352	3,017
Socorro	4,058	2,722	4,696	3,032
Taos	11,978	2,730	13,816	2,866
Torrance	2,428	3,529	3,087	3,735
Union	472	1,236	492	1,227
Valencia	13,511	12,825	15,366	13,136
Totals	**415,335**	**335,788**	**472,422**	**346,832**

New Mexico Vote Since 1960

2012: Obama, D., 415,335; Romney, R., 335,788; Johnson, LB., 27,788; Stein, Green, 2,691; Anderson, Ind., 1,174; Goode, Const., 982.
2008: Obama, D., 472,422; McCain, R., 346,832; Nader, Ind., 5,327; Barr, LB., 2,428; Baldwin, Const., 1,597; McKinney, Green, 1,552.
2004: Bush, R., 376,930; Kerry, D., 370,942; Nader, Ind., 4,053; Badnarik, LB., 2,382; Cobb, Green, 1,226; Peroutka, Const., 771.
2000: Gore, D., 286,783; Bush, R., 286,417; Nader, Green, 21,251; Browne, LB., 2,058; Buchanan, RF., 1,392; Hagelin, Natural Law, 361; Phillips, Const., 343.
1996: Clinton, D., 273,495; Dole, R., 232,751; Perot, RF., 32,257; Nader, Green, 13,218; Browne, LB., 2,996; Phillips, Taxpayers, 713; Hagelin, Natural Law, 644.
1992: Clinton, D., 261,617; Bush, R., 212,824; Perot, Ind., 91,895; Marrou, LB., 1,615.
1988: Bush, R., 270,341; Dukakis, D., 244,497; Paul, LB., 3,268; Fulani, New Alliance, 2,237.
1984: Reagan, R., 307,101; Mondale, D., 201,769; Bergland, LB., 4,459.
1980: Reagan, R., 250,779; Carter, D., 167,826; Anderson, Ind., 29,459; Clark, LB., 4,365; Commoner, Citizens, 2,202; Bubar, Statesman, 1,281; Pulley, Soc. Workers, 325.
1976: Ford, R., 211,419; Carter, D., 201,148; Camejo, Soc. Workers, 2,462; MacBride, LB., 1,110; Zeidler, Soc., 240; Bubar, Prohib., 211.
1972: Nixon, R., 235,606; McGovern, D., 141,084; Schmitz, Amer., 8,767; Jenness, Soc. Workers, 474.
1968: Nixon, R., 169,692; Humphrey, D., 130,081; Wallace, 3rd party, 25,737; Chavez, 1,519; Halstead, Soc. Workers, 252.
1964: Johnson, D., 194,017; Goldwater, R., 131,838; Hass, Soc. Labor, 1,217; Munn, Prohib., 543.
1960: Kennedy, D., 156,027; Nixon, R., 153,733; Decker, Prohib., 777; Hass, Soc. Labor, 570.

New York

County	2012 Obama (D)	Romney (R)	2008 Obama (D)	McCain (R)
Albany	87,556	45,064	93,937	50,586
Allegany	6,139	10,390	7,016	11,013
Bronx[1]	339,211	29,967	338,261	41,683
Broome	41,970	37,641	47,204	40,077
Cattaraugus	12,649	16,569	14,307	17,770
Cayuga	17,007	13,454	18,128	15,243
Chautauqua	23,812	27,971	29,129	28,579
Chemung	16,797	17,612	18,888	19,364
Chenango	9,116	9,713	10,100	10,337
Clinton	18,961	11,115	20,216	12,579
Columbia	16,221	12,225	17,556	13,337
Cortland	10,482	8,695	11,861	9,678
Delaware	8,304	9,938	9,462	10,524
Dutchess	65,312	56,025	71,060	59,628
Erie	237,356	169,675	256,299	178,815
Essex	9,784	6,647	10,390	7,913
Franklin	9,894	5,740	10,571	6,676
Fulton	8,607	10,814	9,695	11,709
Genesee	9,601	14,607	10,762	15,705
Greene	9,030	11,174	9,850	12,059
Hamilton	1,128	1,932	1,225	2,141
Herkimer	11,273	13,282	12,094	14,619
Jefferson	17,099	18,122	18,166	20,220
Kings (Brooklyn)[1]	604,443	124,551	603,525	151,872
Lewis	4,724	5,651	4,986	5,969
Livingston	11,705	14,448	13,655	16,030
Madison	13,871	13,622	14,692	14,434
Monroe	193,501	133,362	207,371	144,262
Montgomery	8,493	9,394	9,080	10,711
Nassau	302,695	259,308	342,185	288,776
New York (Manhattan)[1]	502,674	89,559	572,126	89,906
Niagara	43,986	43,240	47,303	46,348
Oneida	40,468	44,530	43,506	49,256
Onondaga	122,254	78,831	129,317	84,972
Ontario	23,087	23,820	25,103	25,171
Orange	73,315	65,367	78,326	72,042
Orleans	5,787	8,594	6,614	9,708
Oswego	23,515	19,980	24,777	23,571
Otsego	12,117	11,461	13,570	12,026
Putnam	19,512	24,083	21,613	25,145
Queens[1]	470,732	118,589	480,692	155,221
Rensselaer	37,408	29,113	39,753	32,840
Richmond (Staten Island)[1]	78,181	74,223	79,311	86,062
Rockland	65,657	57,363	69,543	61,752
Saratoga	52,957	50,382	23,706	16,956
Schenectady	36,844	26,568	56,645	52,855
Schoharie	5,427	7,467	38,611	29,758
Schuyler	3,674	4,281	6,009	8,071
Seneca	7,094	5,889	3,933	4,542
St. Lawrence	21,353	15,138	7,422	7,038
Steuben	15,787	21,954	17,148	24,203
Suffolk	304,079	282,131	346,549	307,021
Sullivan	15,268	12,705	16,850	13,900
Tioga	8,930	12,117	10,172	12,536
Tompkins	27,244	11,107	29,826	11,927
Ulster	47,752	29,759	54,320	33,300
Warren	14,806	14,119	16,281	15,429
Washington	11,523	11,085	12,741	12,533
Wayne	16,635	20,060	18,184	22,239
Westchester	240,785	143,122	261,810	147,824
Wyoming	5,661	10,348	6,379	10,998
Yates	4,488	4,798	4,890	5,269
Totals	**4,485,741**	**2,490,431**	**4,804,945**	**2,752,771**

(1) Borough of New York City.

New York Vote Since 1960

2012: Obama, D., 4,485,741; Romney, R., 2,490,431; Johnson, LB., 47,256; Stein, Green, 39,982; Goode, Const., 6,274; Lindsay, Socialism/Liberation, 2,050.

2008: Obama, D., 4,804,945; McCain, R., 2,752,771; Nader, Populist, 41,249; Barr, LB., 19,596; McKinney, Green, 12,801; Calero, Soc. Workers, 3,615; La Riva, Socialism/Liberation, 1,639.

2004: Kerry, D., 4,314,280; Bush, R., 2,962,567; Nader, Ind., 99,873; Badnarik, LB., 11,607; Calero, Soc. Workers, 2,405.

2000: Gore, D., 4,112,965; Bush, R., 2,405,570; Nader, Green, 244,360; Buchanan, RF., 31,554; Hagelin, Independence, 24,369; Browne, LB., 7,664; Harris, Soc. Workers, 1,790; Phillips, Const., 1,503.

1996: Clinton, D., 3,756,177; Dole, R., 1,933,492; Perot, RF., 503,458; Nader, Green, 75,956; Phillips, Right to Life, 23,580;

Browne, LB., 12,220; Hagelin, Natural Law, 5,011; Moorehead, Workers World, 3,473; Harris, Soc. Workers, 2,762.

1992: Clinton, D., 3,444,450; Bush, R., 2,346,649; Perot, Ind., 1,090,721; Warren, Soc. Workers, 15,472; Marrou, LB., 13,451; Fulani, New Alliance, 11,318; Hagelin, Natural Law, 4,420.

1988: Dukakis, D., 3,347,882; Bush, R., 3,081,871; Marra, Right to Life, 20,497; Fulani, New Alliance, 15,845.

1984: Reagan, R., 3,664,763; Mondale, D., 3,119,609; Bergland, LB., 11,949.

1980: Reagan, R., 2,893,831; Carter, D., 2,728,372; Anderson, Liberal, 467,801; Clark, LB., 52,648; McCormack, Right to Life, 24,159; Commoner, Citizens, 23,186; Hall, Comm., 7,414; DeBerry, Soc. Workers, 2,068; Griswold, Workers World, 1,416; scattered, 1,064.

1976: Carter, D., 3,389,558; Ford, R., 3,100,791; MacBride, LB., 12,197; Hall, Comm., 10,270; Camejo, Soc. Workers, 6,996; LaRouche, U.S. Labor, 5,413; blank, void, and scattered, 143,037.

1972: Nixon, R., 3,824,642; McGovern, D., 2,767,956 and Liberal, 183,128 (total, 2,951,084); Reed, Soc. Workers, 7,797; Fisher, Soc. Labor, 4,530; Hall, Comm., 5,641; blank, void, and scattered, 161,641.

1968: Humphrey, D., 3,378,470; Nixon, R., 3,007,932; Wallace, 3rd party, 358,864; Gregory, Peace/Freedom, 24,517; Halstead, Soc. Workers, 11,851; Blomen, Soc. Labor, 8,432; blank, void, and scattered, 171,624.

1964: Johnson, D., 4,913,156; Goldwater, R., 2,243,559; Hass, Soc. Labor, 6,085; DeBerry, Soc. Workers, 3,215; scattered, 188; blank and void, 151,383.

1960: Kennedy, D., 3,423,909 and Liberal, 406,176 (total, 3,830,085); Nixon, R., 3,446,419; Dobbs, Soc. Workers, 14,319; scattered, 256; blank and void, 88,896.

North Carolina

County	2012 Obama (D)	Romney (R)	2008 Obama (D)	McCain (R)
Alamance	28,875	38,170	28,918	34,859
Alexander	4,611	12,253	5,167	11,790
Alleghany	1,583	3,390	2,021	3,124
Anson	7,019	4,166	6,456	4,207
Ashe	4,116	8,242	4,872	7,916
Avery	1,882	5,766	2,178	5,681
Beaufort	9,435	13,977	9,454	13,460
Bertie	6,695	3,387	6,365	3,376
Bladen	8,062	7,748	7,853	7,532
Brunswick	22,038	34,743	21,331	30,753
Buncombe	70,625	54,701	69,716	52,494
Burke	13,701	22,267	14,901	22,102
Cabarrus	32,849	49,557	31,546	45,924
Caldwell	10,898	23,229	12,081	22,526
Camden	1,508	3,109	1,597	3,140
Carteret	10,301	24,775	11,130	23,131
Caswell	5,348	5,594	5,545	5,208
Catawba	24,069	44,538	25,656	42,993
Chatham	18,361	16,665	17,862	14,668
Cherokee	3,378	9,278	3,785	8,643
Chowan	3,556	3,891	3,688	3,773
Clay	1,579	3,973	1,734	3,707
Cleveland	17,062	25,793	17,363	26,078
Columbus	11,050	12,941	11,076	12,994
Craven	18,763	26,928	19,352	24,901
Cumberland	75,792	50,666	74,693	52,151
Currituck	3,562	7,496	3,737	7,234
Dare	7,393	10,248	8,074	9,745
Davidson	20,624	49,383	22,433	45,419
Davie	5,134	14,687	6,178	13,981
Duplin	9,033	11,416	8,958	10,834
Durham	111,224	33,769	103,456	32,353
Edgecombe	18,310	8,546	17,403	8,445
Forsyth	92,323	79,768	91,085	73,674
Franklin	13,436	14,603	13,085	13,273
Gaston	33,171	56,138	31,384	52,507
Gates	2,786	2,564	2,830	2,547
Graham	1,119	2,750	1,265	2,824
Granville	13,598	12,405	13,074	11,447
Greene	3,778	4,411	3,796	4,272
Guilford	146,365	104,789	142,101	97,718
Halifax	17,176	8,763	16,047	8,961
Harnett	17,331	25,565	16,785	23,579
Haywood	11,833	15,633	12,730	14,910
Henderson	18,642	32,994	20,082	30,930
Hertford	7,843	3,007	7,513	3,089
Hoke	10,076	6,819	9,227	6,293
Hyde	1,163	1,193	1,241	1,212
Iredell	26,076	49,299	27,318	45,148
Jackson	8,095	8,254	8,766	7,854
Johnston	27,290	48,427	26,795	43,622
Jones	2,352	2,837	2,378	2,817
Lee	10,801	13,158	10,784	12,775
Lenoir	13,948	13,980	13,378	13,401
Lincoln	11,024	25,267	11,713	23,631

County	2012		2008	
	Obama (D)	Romney (R)	Obama (D)	McCain (R)
Macon	5,712	10,835	6,620	10,317
Madison	4,484	5,404	5,026	5,192
Martin	6,583	5,995	6,539	5,957
McDowell	6,031	11,775	6,571	11,534
Mecklenburg	272,262	171,668	253,958	153,848
Mitchell	1,838	5,806	2,238	5,499
Montgomery	4,706	6,404	4,926	6,155
Moore	16,505	29,495	17,624	27,314
Nash	24,313	23,842	23,099	23,728
New Hanover	48,668	53,385	49,145	50,544
Northampton	7,232	3,483	6,903	3,671
Onslow	18,490	32,243	19,499	30,278
Orange	53,901	21,539	53,806	20,266
Pamlico	2,647	4,051	2,838	3,823
Pasquotank	10,282	7,633	10,272	7,778
Pender	9,632	14,617	9,907	13,618
Perquimans	2,759	3,822	2,772	3,678
Person	8,418	10,496	8,446	10,030
Pitt	41,843	36,214	40,501	33,927
Polk	4,013	6,236	4,396	5,990
Randolph	14,773	45,160	16,414	40,998
Richmond	9,904	9,332	9,713	9,424
Robeson	24,988	17,510	23,058	17,433
Rockingham	16,351	25,227	17,255	23,899
Rowan	22,650	38,775	23,391	37,451
Rutherford	9,374	18,954	9,641	18,769
Sampson	11,556	14,422	11,836	14,038
Scotland	8,215	5,831	8,151	6,005
Stanly	8,431	19,904	8,878	19,329
Stokes	6,018	15,237	6,875	14,488
Surry	9,112	19,923	10,475	18,730
Swain	2,618	2,976	2,806	2,900
Transylvania	6,826	9,634	7,275	9,401
Tyrrell	837	930	933	960
Union	32,473	61,107	31,189	54,123
Vance	13,323	7,429	13,166	7,606
Wake	267,262	211,596	250,891	187,001
Warren	6,978	3,140	7,086	3,063
Washington	3,833	2,622	3,748	2,670
Watauga	13,002	13,861	14,558	13,344
Wayne	23,314	27,641	22,671	25,804
Wilkes	8,148	20,515	8,934	20,288
Wilson	20,875	17,954	19,652	17,375
Yadkin	3,957	12,578	4,527	12,409
Yancey	3,981	5,278	4,486	5,045
Totals	**2,178,391**	**2,270,395**	**2,142,651**	**2,128,474**

North Carolina Vote Since 1960

2012: Romney, R., 2,270,395; Obama, D., 2,178,391; Johnson, LB., 44,515.

2008: Obama, D., 2,142,651; McCain, R., 2,128,474; Barr, LB., 25,722.

2004: Bush, R., 1,961,166; Kerry, D., 1,525,849; Badnarik, LB., 11,731.

2000: Bush, R., 1,631,163; Gore, D., 1,257,692; Browne, LB., 13,891; Buchanan, RF., 8,874.

1996: Dole, R., 1,225,938; Clinton, D., 1,107,849; Perot, RF., 168,059; Browne, LB., 8,740; Hagelin, Natural Law, 2,771.

1992: Bush, R., 1,134,661; Clinton, D., 1,114,042; Perot, Ind., 357,864; Marrou, LB., 5,171.

1988: Bush, R., 1,237,258; Dukakis, D., 890,167; Fulani, New Alliance, 5,682; Paul, write-in, 1,263.

1984: Reagan, R., 1,346,481; Mondale, D., 824,287; Bergland, LB., 3,794.

1980: Reagan, R., 915,018; Carter, D., 875,635; Anderson, Ind., 52,800; Clark, LB., 9,677; Commoner, Citizens, 2,287; DeBerry, Soc. Workers, 416.

1976: Carter, D., 927,365; Ford, R., 741,960; Anderson, Amer., 5,607; MacBride, LB., 2,219; LaRouche, U.S. Labor, 755.

1972: Nixon, R., 1,054,889; McGovern, D., 438,705; Schmitz, Amer., 25,018.

1968: Nixon, R., 627,192; Wallace, 3rd party, 496,188; Humphrey, D., 464,113.

1964: Johnson, D., 800,139; Goldwater, R., 624,844.

1960: Kennedy, D., 713,136; Nixon, R., 655,420.

North Dakota

County	2012		2008	
	Obama (D)	Romney (R)	Obama (D)	McCain (R)
Adams	328	918	435	788
Barnes	2,394	2,964	2,741	2,826
Benson	1,235	868	1,569	773
Billings	89	472	114	375
Bottineau	1,183	2,280	1,387	2,059
Bowman	414	1,280	478	1,107
Burke	230	769	286	640
Burleigh	14,122	27,951	15,600	25,443

County	2012		2008	
	Obama (D)	Romney (R)	Obama (D)	McCain (R)
Cass	34,712	36,855	37,622	32,566
Cavalier	818	1,195	930	1,128
Dickey	853	1,610	1,044	1,525
Divide	385	733	464	630
Dunn	508	1,506	527	1,080
Eddy	486	634	583	548
Emmons	383	1,435	546	1,230
Foster	607	1,030	687	914
Golden Valley	162	742	210	642
Grand Forks	14,032	15,060	16,104	14,520
Grant	334	1,025	280	587
Griggs	536	771	598	682
Hettinger	313	1,000	406	893
Kidder	393	870	422	752
LaMoure	740	1,377	868	1,310
Logan	232	810	299	726
McHenry	943	1,678	981	1,374
McIntosh	459	1,035	579	916
McKenzie	927	2,458	933	1,740
McLean	1,670	3,141	1,867	2,767
Mercer	1,166	3,152	1,476	2,789
Morton	4,469	8,680	5,079	7,869
Mountrail	1,403	1,962	1,477	1,406
Nelson	767	865	907	800
Oliver	281	693	332	682
Pembina	1,253	1,899	1,494	1,722
Pierce	660	1,465	792	1,301
Ramsey	2,164	2,665	2,314	2,361
Ransom	1,343	1,009	1,371	998
Renville	398	851	505	799
Richland	3,198	4,229	3,513	3,900
Rolette	3,353	1,092	3,403	1,045
Sargent	1,075	879	1,115	778
Sheridan	163	642	229	555
Sioux	900	225	1,145	215
Slope	83	341	106	297
Stark	2,812	8,521	3,802	7,024
Steele	518	498	614	404
Stutsman	3,585	5,685	4,056	5,499
Towner	516	623	621	536
Traill	1,811	1,996	2,136	1,845
Walsh	1,985	2,656	2,325	2,415
Ward	8,441	16,230	10,144	15,061
Wells	673	1,654	841	1,468
Williams	2,322	7,184	2,921	6,291
Totals	**124,827**	**188,163**	**141,278**	**168,601**

North Dakota Vote Since 1960

2012: Romney, R., 188,163; Obama, D., 124,827; Johnson, LB., 5,231; Stein, Green, 1,361; Goode, Const., 1,185.

2008: McCain, R., 168,601; Obama, D., 141,278; Nader, Ind., 4,189; Barr, LB., 1,354; Baldwin, Const., 1,199.

2004: Bush, R., 196,651; Kerry, D., 111,052; Nader, Ind., 3,756; Badnarik, LB., 851; Peroutka, Const., 514.

2000: Bush, R., 174,852; Gore, D., 95,284; Nader, Ind., 9,486; Buchanan, RF., 7,288; Browne, Ind., 660; Phillips, Const., 373; Hagelin, Ind., 313.

1996: Dole, R., 125,050; Clinton, D., 106,905; Perot, RF., 32,515; Browne, LB., 847; Phillips, Ind., 745; Hagelin, Natural Law, 349.

1992: Bush, R., 136,244; Clinton, D., 99,168; Perot, Ind., 71,084.

1988: Bush, R., 166,559; Dukakis, D., 127,739; Paul, LB., 1,315; LaRouche, Natl. Econ. Recovery, 905.

1984: Reagan, R., 200,336; Mondale, D., 104,429; Bergland, LB., 703.

1980: Reagan, R., 193,695; Carter, D., 79,189; Anderson, Ind., 23,640; Clark, LB., 3,743; Commoner, Ind., 429; McLain, Natl. People's League, 296; Greaves, Amer., 235; Hall, Comm., 93; DeBerry, Soc. Workers, 89; McReynolds, Soc., 82; Bubar, Statesman, 54.

1976: Ford, R., 153,470; Carter, D., 136,078; Anderson, Amer., 3,698; McCarthy, Ind., 2,952; Maddox, Amer. Ind., 269; Mac-Bride, LB., 256; scattered, 371.

1972: Nixon, R., 174,109; McGovern, D., 100,384; Schmitz, Amer., 5,646; Jenness, Soc. Workers, 288; Hall, Comm., 87.

1968: Nixon, R., 138,669; Humphrey, D., 94,769; Wallace, 3rd party, 14,244; Halstead, Soc. Workers, 128; Munn, Prohib., 38; Troxell, Ind., 34.

1964: Johnson, D., 149,784; Goldwater, R., 108,207; DeBerry, Soc. Workers, 224; Munn, Prohib., 174.

1960: Nixon, R., 154,310; Kennedy, D., 123,963; Dobbs, Soc. Workers, 158.

Ohio

County	2012		2008	
	Obama (D)	Romney (R)	Obama (D)	McCain (R)
Adams	3,976	6,865	4,170	6,914
Allen	17,914	29,502	19,521	29,941
Ashland	8,281	15,519	9,300	15,158

County	2012 Obama (D)	Romney (R)	2008 Obama (D)	McCain (R)
Ashtabula	23,803	18,298	25,027	18,949
Athens	18,307	8,543	20,722	9,742
Auglaize	5,831	17,169	6,727	16,395
Belmont	14,156	16,758	16,302	15,422
Brown	7,107	11,916	7,503	12,192
Butler	62,388	105,176	66,030	105,340
Carroll	5,543	7,315	6,423	7,097
Champaign	7,044	11,045	7,385	11,141
Clark	31,297	31,820	31,958	33,634
Clermont	30,458	64,208	31,611	62,559
Clinton	5,791	12,009	6,558	12,410
Columbiana	19,821	25,251	21,882	25,585
Coshocton	6,940	8,390	7,689	8,675
Crawford	7,507	11,852	8,288	12,316
Cuyahoga	447,273	190,660	458,204	199,864
Darke	6,826	18,108	7,964	17,290
Defiance	7,732	10,176	8,399	10,407
Delaware	37,292	60,194	36,653	54,778
Erie	21,793	16,952	23,148	17,432
Fairfield	29,890	41,034	29,250	41,580
Fayette	4,249	6,620	4,401	7,102
Franklin	346,373	215,997	334,684	218,478
Fulton	9,073	11,738	9,900	11,689
Gallia	4,557	7,750	4,777	8,247
Geauga	19,659	30,589	21,250	29,096
Greene	32,256	49,819	33,540	48,936
Guernsey	7,450	8,993	7,625	9,197
Hamilton	219,927	193,326	224,644	195,107
Hancock	12,564	22,443	13,870	22,420
Hardin	4,619	7,489	5,013	7,749
Harrison	2,950	4,019	3,683	3,872
Henry	5,658	8,257	6,320	8,239
Highland	6,054	11,413	6,857	11,908
Hocking	6,157	6,285	6,231	6,326
Holmes	2,608	8,702	3,141	7,720
Huron	11,006	13,060	12,076	12,884
Jackson	5,166	7,904	5,397	8,219
Jefferson	15,385	17,034	17,635	17,559
Knox	10,470	17,266	11,014	16,640
Lake	57,680	58,744	60,155	59,142
Lawrence	10,744	14,651	11,262	15,415
Licking	34,201	45,503	33,896	46,886
Logan	7,062	13,633	7,936	13,848
Lorain	81,464	59,405	85,276	59,068
Lucas	136,616	69,940	142,852	73,706
Madison	6,845	10,342	6,532	10,603
Mahoning	77,059	42,641	79,173	45,319
Marion	12,504	14,265	12,870	15,454
Medina	38,785	50,418	40,924	48,189
Meigs	4,027	5,895	4,094	6,015
Mercer	4,745	16,561	5,853	15,100
Miami	16,383	34,606	18,372	33,417
Monroe	3,035	3,548	3,705	3,066
Montgomery	137,139	124,841	145,997	128,679
Morgan	2,814	3,179	2,966	3,440
Morrow	5,933	9,865	6,177	10,067
Muskingum	17,002	19,264	17,730	20,549
Noble	2,131	3,563	2,474	3,450
Ottawa	11,503	10,538	12,049	10,618
Paulding	3,538	5,354	4,165	5,317
Perry	7,033	7,627	7,261	7,721
Pickaway	9,684	14,037	9,077	14,228
Pike	5,684	5,685	6,033	6,162
Portage	39,453	35,242	41,856	34,822
Preble	6,211	13,535	6,999	13,562
Putnam	4,318	13,721	5,281	13,072
Richland	22,687	33,867	25,727	34,034
Ross	14,569	15,008	14,445	16,759
Sandusky	14,541	13,755	15,601	14,190
Scioto	15,077	15,492	14,926	16,994
Seneca	11,353	13,243	13,087	13,823
Shelby	6,343	17,142	7,317	15,924
Stark	89,432	88,581	96,990	86,743
Summit	153,041	111,001	155,105	110,499
Trumbull	61,672	38,279	64,145	40,164
Tuscarawas	18,407	22,242	21,498	20,454
Union	8,805	16,289	8,761	15,744
Van Wert	4,029	9,585	5,178	9,168
Vinton	2,436	2,856	2,463	3,021
Warren	32,909	76,564	33,398	71,691
Washington	11,651	17,284	12,368	17,019
Wayne	19,808	30,251	21,712	29,342
Williams	7,266	10,047	8,174	9,880
Wood	32,802	29,704	34,285	29,648
Wyandot	4,137	6,180	4,461	6,270
Totals	2,827,709	2,661,437	2,940,044	2,677,820

Ohio Vote Since 1960

2012: Obama, D., 2,827,709; Romney, R., 2,661,437; Johnson, LB., 49,493; Stein, Green, 18,573; Duncan, Ind., 12,502; Goode, Const., 8,152; Alexander, Soc., 2,944.
2008: Obama, D., 2,940,044; McCain, R., 2,677,820; Nader, Ind., 42,337; Barr, LB., 19,917; Baldwin, Const., 12,565; McKinney, Green, 8,518; Duncan, Ind., 3,905; Moore, Soc., 2,735.
2004: Bush, R., 2,859,768; Kerry, D., 2,741,167; Badnarik, non-partisan, 14,676; Peroutka, nonpartisan, 939.
2000: Bush, R., 2,351,209; Gore, D., 2,186,190; Nader, Ind., 117,857; Buchanan, Ind., 26,724; Browne, LB., 13,475; Hagelin, Natural Law, 6,169; Phillips, Ind., 3,823.
1996: Clinton, D., 2,148,222; Dole, R., 1,859,883; Perot, RF., 483,207; Browne, Ind., 12,851; Moorehead, Ind., 10,813; Hagelin, Natural Law, 9,120; Phillips, Ind., 7,361.
1992: Clinton, D., 1,984,942; Bush, R., 1,894,310; Perot, Ind., 1,036,426; Marrou, LB., 7,252; Fulani, New Alliance, 6,413; Gritz, Populist/America First, 4,699; Hagelin, Natural Law, 3,437; LaRouche, Ind., 2,446.
1988: Bush, R., 2,416,549; Dukakis, D., 1,939,629; Fulani, Ind., 12,017; Paul, Ind., 11,926.
1984: Reagan, R., 2,678,559; Mondale, D., 1,825,440; Bergland, LB., 5,886.
1980: Reagan, R., 2,206,545; Carter, D., 1,752,414; Anderson, Ind., 254,472; Clark, LB., 49,033; Commoner, Citizens, 8,564; Hall, Comm., 4,729; Congress, Ind., 4,029; Griswold, Workers World, 3,790; Bubar, Statesman, 27.
1976: Carter, D., 2,011,621; Ford, R., 2,000,505; McCarthy, Ind., 58,258; Maddox, Amer. Ind., 15,529; MacBride, LB., 8,961; Hall, Comm., 7,817; Camejo, Soc. Workers, 4,717; LaRouche, U.S. Labor, 4,335; scattered, 130.
1972: Nixon, R., 2,441,827; McGovern, D., 1,558,889; Schmitz, Amer., 80,067; Fisher, Soc. Labor, 7,107; Hall, Comm., 6,437; Wallace, Ind., 460.
1968: Nixon, R., 1,791,014; Humphrey, D., 1,700,586; Wallace, 3rd party, 467,495; Gregory, 372; Blomen, Soc. Labor, 120; Halstead, Soc. Workers, 69; Mitchell, Comm., 23; Munn, Prohib., 19.
1964: Johnson, D., 2,498,331; Goldwater, R., 1,470,865.
1960: Nixon, R., 2,217,611; Kennedy, D., 1,944,248.

Oklahoma

County	2012 Obama (D)	Romney (R)	2008 Obama (D)	McCain (R)
Adair	2,127	4,381	2,052	4,638
Alfalfa	322	1,761	411	2,023
Atoka	1,243	3,538	1,370	3,511
Beaver	244	2,062	265	2,199
Beckham	1,417	5,508	1,625	5,772
Blaine	992	2,824	1,011	3,101
Bryan	3,681	9,520	4,426	9,307
Caddo	3,164	5,687	3,404	6,413
Canadian	10,537	35,625	11,426	36,428
Carter	4,908	12,214	5,603	13,241
Cherokee	6,144	8,162	7,194	9,186
Choctaw	1,494	3,572	1,860	3,730
Cimarron	115	1,082	152	1,119
Cleveland	34,771	59,116	39,681	64,749
Coal	649	1,710	600	1,672
Comanche	12,521	17,664	14,120	20,127
Cotton	657	1,796	690	1,793
Craig	1,747	3,559	2,073	3,858
Creek	7,128	18,986	8,318	20,187
Custer	2,359	7,446	2,660	7,842
Delaware	4,196	10,080	5,085	10,277
Dewey	301	1,792	346	1,857
Ellis	226	1,575	282	1,627
Garfield	4,733	15,177	5,545	17,067
Garvin	2,559	6,925	3,028	7,710
Grady	4,786	14,833	5,520	15,195
Grant	393	1,675	514	1,836
Greer	488	1,344	566	1,548
Harmon	264	659	333	757
Harper	173	1,261	221	1,342
Haskell	1,175	3,069	1,474	3,207
Hughes	1,370	2,838	1,709	3,134
Jackson	1,954	5,965	2,264	6,719
Jefferson	605	1,634	805	1,652
Johnston	1,137	2,649	1,249	2,708
Kay	4,627	11,499	5,463	13,230
Kingfisher	898	4,870	1,009	5,372
Kiowa	1,106	2,316	1,226	2,537
Latimer	1,170	2,628	1,313	2,860
Le Flore	4,662	11,177	5,136	11,605
Lincoln	3,273	9,553	3,504	10,470
Logan	4,724	12,314	5,717	12,556
Love	1,034	2,436	1,257	2,589
Major	446	2,700	515	2,956
Marshall	1,396	3,744	1,643	3,730
Mayes	4,823	9,637	5,749	10,234
McClain	3,194	11,112	3,551	11,193

County	2012 Obama (D)	Romney (R)	2008 Obama (D)	McCain (R)
McCurtain	2,440	7,635	2,794	7,745
McIntosh	2,779	4,509	3,320	4,903
Murray	1,540	3,606	1,592	3,746
Muskogee	9,952	13,404	11,294	15,289
Noble	1,143	3,488	1,174	3,881
Nowata	1,244	2,832	1,411	3,031
Okfuskee	1,256	2,335	1,480	2,643
Oklahoma	106,982	149,728	116,182	163,172
Okmulgee	5,432	7,731	6,191	8,727
Osage	6,704	11,242	7,498	12,160
Ottawa	3,509	6,466	4,268	6,905
Pawnee	1,813	4,232	2,063	4,533
Payne	9,198	16,481	10,601	18,435
Pittsburg	4,831	10,841	5,457	11,752
Pontotoc	3,947	8,945	4,512	9,750
Pottawatomie	7,188	16,250	7,910	17,753
Pushmataha	1,043	3,087	1,265	3,208
Roger Mills	272	1,402	287	1,502
Rogers	9,148	27,553	10,772	27,743
Seminole	2,600	4,856	2,977	5,600
Sequoyah	4,193	9,578	4,454	9,466
Stephens	3,939	12,908	4,538	14,394
Texas	862	4,930	923	5,336
Tillman	906	1,815	1,042	2,195
Tulsa	82,744	145,062	96,133	158,363
Wagoner	7,791	20,900	8,810	21,441
Washington	5,532	15,668	6,308	16,457
Washita	822	3,494	1,052	3,724
Woods	671	2,727	873	3,043
Woodward	1,133	5,945	1,350	6,404
Totals	443,547	891,325	502,496	960,165

Oklahoma Vote Since 1960

2012: Romney, R., 891,325; Obama, D., 443,547.
2008: McCain, R., 960,165; Obama, D., 502,496.
2004: Bush, R., 959,792; Kerry, D., 503,966.
2000: Bush, R., 744,337; Gore, D., 474,276; Buchanan, RF., 9,014; Browne, LB., 6,602.
1996: Dole, R., 582,315; Clinton, D., 488,105; Perot, RF., 130,788; Browne, LB., 5,505.
1992: Bush, R., 592,929; Clinton, D., 473,066; Perot, Ind., 319,878; Marrou, LB., 4,486.
1988: Bush, R., 678,367; Dukakis, D., 483,423; Paul, LB., 6,261; Fulani, New Alliance, 2,985.
1984: Reagan, R., 861,530; Mondale, D., 385,080; Bergland, LB., 9,066.
1980: Reagan, R., 695,570; Carter, D., 402,026; Anderson, Ind., 38,284; Clark, LB., 13,828.
1976: Ford, R., 545,708; Carter, D., 532,442; McCarthy, Ind., 14,101.
1972: Nixon, R., 759,025; McGovern, D., 247,147; Schmitz, Amer., 23,728.
1968: Nixon, R., 449,697; Humphrey, D., 301,658; Wallace, 3rd party, 191,731.
1964: Johnson, D., 519,834; Goldwater, R., 412,665.
1960: Nixon, R., 533,039; Kennedy, D., 370,111.

Oregon

County	2012 Obama (D)	Romney (R)	2008 Obama (D)	McCain (R)
Baker	2,369	5,702	2,805	5,650
Benton	27,776	14,991	29,901	15,264
Clackamas	95,493	88,592	103,476	83,595
Clatsop	9,861	7,249	10,701	7,192
Columbia	12,004	10,772	13,390	10,413
Coos	12,845	14,673	14,401	15,354
Crook	3,104	6,790	3,632	6,371
Curry	4,625	6,598	5,230	6,646
Deschutes	36,961	42,463	38,819	39,064
Douglas	17,145	30,776	20,298	30,919
Gilliam	371	639	430	648
Grant	853	2,926	1,006	2,785
Harney	832	2,607	950	2,595
Hood River	6,058	3,429	6,302	3,265
Jackson	44,468	49,020	49,090	49,043
Jefferson	3,301	4,642	3,682	4,402
Josephine	14,953	23,673	17,412	22,973
Klamath	8,302	18,898	9,370	19,113
Lake	770	2,808	957	2,638
Lane	102,652	62,509	114,037	63,835
Lincoln	13,401	8,686	14,258	8,791
Linn	20,378	28,944	22,163	28,071
Malheur	2,759	6,851	2,949	7,157
Marion	56,376	60,190	61,816	59,059
Morrow	1,202	2,532	1,410	2,509
Multnomah	274,887	75,302	279,696	75,171
Polk	16,292	17,819	17,536	17,714
Sherman	319	678	385	634
Tillamook	6,293	5,684	7,072	5,757
Umatilla	8,584	15,499	9,484	15,254
Union	3,973	7,636	4,613	7,581
Wallowa	1,253	2,804	1,492	2,836
Wasco	5,211	5,229	5,906	5,103
Washington	135,291	93,974	141,544	89,185
Wheeler	266	545	281	498
Yamhill	19,260	22,045	20,797	21,390
Totals	970,488	754,175	1,037,291	738,475

Oregon Vote Since 1960

2012: Obama, D., 970,488; Romney, R., 754,175; Johnson, LB., 24,089; Stein, Pacific Green, 19,427; Christensen, Const., 4,432; Anderson, OR Prog., 3,384.
2008: Obama, D., 1,037,291; McCain, R., 738,475; Nader, Peace Party of OR, 18,614; Baldwin, Const., 7,693; Barr, LB., 7,635; McKinney, Pacific Green, 4,543.
2004: Kerry, D., 943,163; Bush, R., 866,831; Badnarik, LB., 7,260; Cobb, Pacific Green, 5,315; Peroutka, Const., 5,257.
2000: Gore, D., 720,342; Bush, R., 713,577; Nader, Green, 77,357; Browne, LB., 7,447; Buchanan, Ind., 7,063; Hagelin, RF., 2,574; Phillips, Const., 2,189.
1996: Clinton, D., 649,641; Dole, R., 538,152; Perot, RF., 121,221; Nader, Pacific, 49,415; Browne, LB., 8,903; Phillips, Taxpayers, 3,379; Hagelin, Natural Law, 2,798; Hollis, Soc., 1,922.
1992: Clinton, D., 621,314; Bush, R., 475,757; Perot, Ind., 354,091; Marrou, LB., 4,277; Fulani, New Alliance, 3,030.
1988: Dukakis, D., 616,206; Bush, R., 560,126; Paul, LB., 14,811; Fulani, Ind., 6,487.
1984: Reagan, R., 658,700; Mondale, D., 536,479.
1980: Reagan, R., 571,044; Carter, D., 456,890; Anderson, Ind., 112,389; Clark, LB., 25,838; Commoner, Citizens, 13,642; scattered, 1,713.
1976: Ford, R., 492,120; Carter, D., 490,407; McCarthy, Ind., 40,207; write-in, 7,142.
1972: Nixon, R., 486,686; McGovern, D., 392,760; Schmitz, Amer., 46,211; write-in, 2,289.
1968: Nixon, R., 408,433; Humphrey, D., 358,866; Wallace, 3rd party, 49,683; write-ins: McCarthy, 1,496; N. Rockefeller, 69; others, 1,075.
1964: Johnson, D., 501,017; Goldwater, R., 282,779; write-in, 2,509.
1960: Nixon, R., 408,060; Kennedy, D., 367,402.

Pennsylvania

County	2012 Obama (D)	Romney (R)	2008 Obama (D)	McCain (R)
Adams	15,091	26,767	17,633	26,349
Allegheny	352,687	262,039	373,153	272,347
Armstrong	9,045	20,142	11,138	18,542
Beaver	37,055	42,344	40,499	42,895
Bedford	4,788	16,702	6,059	16,124
Berks	83,011	54,702	97,047	80,513
Blair	16,276	33,319	19,813	32,708
Bradford	8,624	14,410	10,306	15,057
Bucks	160,521	156,579	179,031	150,248
Butler	28,550	59,761	32,260	57,074
Cambria	24,249	35,163	32,451	31,995
Cameron	724	1,359	879	1,323
Carbon	11,580	13,504	13,464	12,957
Centre	34,176	34,001	41,950	32,992
Chester	124,311	124,840	137,833	114,421
Clarion	5,056	10,828	6,756	10,737
Clearfield	11,121	20,347	14,555	18,662
Clinton	5,734	7,303	7,097	7,504
Columbia	10,937	14,236	13,230	14,477
Crawford	13,883	20,901	16,780	20,750
Cumberland	44,367	64,809	48,306	63,739
Dauphin	64,965	57,450	69,975	58,238
Delaware	171,792	110,853	178,870	115,273
Elk	5,463	7,579	7,290	6,676
Erie	68,036	49,025	75,775	50,351
Fayette	21,971	26,018	25,866	26,081
Forest	896	1,383	1,038	1,366
Franklin	18,995	43,260	21,169	41,906
Fulton	1,310	4,814	1,576	4,642
Greene	5,852	8,428	7,829	7,889
Huntingdon	5,409	11,979	6,621	11,745
Indiana	14,473	21,257	17,065	19,727
Jefferson	4,787	13,048	6,447	12,057
Juniata	2,547	6,862	3,068	6,484
Lackawanna	61,838	35,085	67,520	39,488
Lancaster	88,481	130,669	99,586	126,568
Lawrence	17,513	21,047	19,711	21,851
Lebanon	19,900	35,872	23,310	34,314
Lehigh	78,283	66,874	87,089	63,382
Luzerne	64,307	58,325	72,492	61,127

County	2012 Obama (D)	Romney (R)	2008 Obama (D)	McCain (R)
Lycoming	15,203	30,658	18,381	30,280
McKean	5,297	9,545	6,465	9,224
Mercer	24,232	25,925	26,411	26,565
Mifflin	4,273	11,939	5,375	10,929
Monroe	35,221	26,867	39,453	28,293
Montgomery	233,356	174,381	253,393	165,552
Montour	3,053	4,652	3,364	4,574
Northampton	67,606	61,446	75,255	58,551
Northumberland	13,072	19,518	14,329	19,018
Perry	5,685	13,120	6,396	13,058
Philadelphia	588,806	96,467	595,980	117,221
Pike	10,210	12,786	11,493	12,518
Potter	1,897	5,231	2,300	5,109
Schuylkill	24,546	32,278	28,300	33,767
Snyder	4,687	10,073	5,382	9,900
Somerset	9,436	23,984	12,878	21,686
Sullivan	1,034	1,868	1,233	1,841
Susquehanna	6,935	10,800	8,381	10,633
Tioga	5,357	11,342	6,390	11,326
Union	6,109	9,896	7,333	9,859
Venango	7,945	13,815	9,238	13,718
Warren	6,995	10,010	8,537	9,685
Washington	40,345	53,230	46,122	50,752
Wayne	8,396	12,896	9,892	12,702
Westmoreland	63,722	103,932	72,721	102,294
Wyoming	5,061	6,587	5,985	6,983
York	73,191	113,304	82,839	109,268
Totals	2,990,274	2,680,434	3,276,363	2,655,885

Pennsylvania Vote Since 1960

2012: Obama, D., 2,990,274; Romney, R., 2,680,434; Johnson, LB., 49,991; Stein, Green, 21,341.
2008: Obama, D., 3,276,363; McCain, R., 2,655,885; Nader, Ind., 42,977; Barr, LB., 19,912.
2004: Kerry, D., 2,938,095; Bush, R., 2,793,847; Badnarik, LB., 21,185; Cobb, Green, 6,319; Peroutka, Const., 6,318.
2000: Gore, D., 2,485,967; Bush, R., 2,281,127; Nader, Green, 103,392; Buchanan, RF., 16,023; Phillips, Const., 14,428; Browne, LB., 11,248.
1996: Clinton, D., 2,215,819; Dole, R., 1,801,169; Perot, RF., 430,984; Browne, LB., 28,000; Phillips, Const., 19,552; Hagelin, Natural Law, 5,783.
1992: Clinton, D., 2,239,164; Bush, R., 1,791,841; Perot, Ind., 902,667; Marrou, LB., 21,477; Fulani, New Alliance, 4,661.
1988: Bush, R., 2,300,087; Dukakis, D., 2,194,944; McCarthy, Consumer, 19,158; Paul, LB., 12,051.
1984: Reagan, R., 2,584,323; Mondale, D., 2,228,131; Bergland, LB., 6,982.
1980: Reagan, R., 2,261,872; Carter, D., 1,937,540; Anderson, Ind., 292,921; Clark, LB., 33,263; DeBerry, Soc. Workers, 20,291; Commoner, Consumer, 10,430; Hall, Comm., 5,184.
1976: Carter, D., 2,328,677; Ford, R., 2,205,604; McCarthy, Ind., 50,584; Maddox, Const., 25,344; Camejo, Soc. Workers, 3,009; LaRouche, U.S. Labor, 2,744; Hall, Comm., 1,891; others, 2,934.
1972: Nixon, R., 2,714,521; McGovern, D., 1,796,951; Schmitz, Amer., 70,593; Jenness, Soc. Workers, 4,639; Hall, Comm., 2,686; others, 2,715.
1968: Humphrey, D., 2,259,405; Nixon, R., 2,090,017; Wallace, 3rd party, 378,582; Gregory, Peace/Freedom, 7,821; Blomen, Soc. Labor, 4,977; Halstead, Soc. Workers, 4,862; others, 2,264.
1964: Johnson, D., 3,130,954; Goldwater, R., 1,673,657; DeBerry, Soc. Workers, 10,456; Hass, Soc. Labor, 5,092; scattered, 2,531.
1960: Kennedy, D., 2,556,282; Nixon, R., 2,439,956; Hass, Soc. Labor, 7,185; Dobbs, Soc. Workers, 2,678; scattered, 440.

Rhode Island

City	2012 Obama (D)	Romney (R)	2008 Obama (D)	McCain (R)
Bristol	6,359	3,707	6,833	3,834
Coventry	9,122	6,969	9,622	7,367
Cranston	21,388	13,008	22,520	13,981
Cumberland	9,291	7,106	9,707	6,941
East Providence	14,095	5,752	15,380	6,216
Johnston	7,503	5,417	7,763	6,066
Lincoln	6,028	4,866	6,264	4,831
Newport	6,174	2,959	6,989	3,215
North Kingstown	7,847	6,451	8,562	6,285
North Providence	9,613	5,404	9,954	5,933
Pawtucket	18,155	5,228	18,486	6,098

City	2012 Obama (D)	Romney (R)	2008 Obama (D)	McCain (R)
Providence	43,617	7,282	46,276	8,548
Smithfield	5,293	4,681	5,464	4,660
South Kingstown	8,611	4,720	9,336	4,689
Warwick	24,448	15,027	25,802	16,541
West Warwick	6,956	4,332	7,475	4,735
Westerly	6,071	4,382	6,490	4,710
Woonsocket	7,985	4,114	8,678	4,398
Other	60,853	45,746	64,970	46,343
Totals	279,677	157,204	296,571	165,391

Rhode Island Vote Since 1960

2012: Obama, D., 279,677; Romney, R., 157,204; Johnson, LB., 4,388; Stein, Green, 2,421; Goode, Const., 430; Anderson, Justice, 416; Lindsay, Socialism/Liberation, 132.
2008: Obama, D., 296,571; McCain, R., 165,391; Nader, Ind., 4,829; Barr, LB., 1,382; McKinney, Green, 797; Baldwin, Const., 675; La Riva, Socialism/Liberation, 122.
2004: Kerry, D., 259,765; Bush, R., 169,046; Nader, RF., 4,651; Cobb, Green, 1,333; Badnarik, LB., 907; Peroutka, Const., 339; Parker, Workers World, 253.
2000: Gore, D., 249,508; Bush, R., 130,555; Nader, Ind., 25,052; Buchanan, RF., 2,273; Browne, Ind., 742; Hagelin, Ind., 271; Moorehead, Ind., 199; Phillips, Ind., 97; McReynolds, Ind., 52; Harris, Ind., 34.
1996: Clinton, D., 233,050; Dole, R., 104,683; Perot, RF., 43,723; Nader, Green, 6,040; Browne, Ind., 1,109; Phillips, U.S. Taxpayers, 1,021; Hagelin, Natural Law, 435; Moorehead, Workers World, 186.
1992: Clinton, D., 213,299; Bush, R., 131,601; Perot, Ind., 105,045; Fulani, New Alliance, 1,878.
1988: Dukakis, D., 225,123; Bush, R., 177,761; Paul, LB., 825; Fulani, New Alliance, 280.
1984: Reagan, R., 212,080; Mondale, D., 197,106; Bergland, LB., 277.
1980: Carter, D., 198,342; Reagan, R., 154,793; Anderson, Ind., 59,819; Clark, LB., 2,458; Hall, Comm., 218; McReynolds, Soc., 170; DeBerry, Soc. Workers, 90; Griswold, Workers World, 77.
1976: Carter, D., 227,636; Ford, R., 181,249; MacBride, LB., 715; Camejo, Soc. Workers, 462; Hall, Comm., 334; Levin, Soc. Labor, 188.
1972: Nixon, R., 220,383; McGovern, D., 194,645; Jenness, Soc. Workers, 729.
1968: Humphrey, D., 246,518; Nixon, R., 122,359; Wallace, 3rd party, 15,678; Halstead, Soc. Workers, 383.
1964: Johnson, D., 315,463; Goldwater, R., 74,615.
1960: Kennedy, D., 258,032; Nixon, R., 147,502.

South Carolina

County	2012 Obama (D)	Romney (R)	2008 Obama (D)	McCain (R)
Abbeville	4,543	5,981	4,593	6,264
Aiken	25,322	44,042	26,101	42,849
Allendale	3,297	838	3,029	947
Anderson	22,405	48,709	24,132	48,690
Bamberg	4,624	2,194	4,426	2,309
Barnwell	5,188	4,659	4,931	4,769
Beaufort	29,848	42,687	30,396	37,821
Berkeley	28,542	38,475	27,755	36,205
Calhoun	4,045	3,707	3,970	3,695
Charleston	81,487	77,629	82,698	69,822
Cherokee	7,231	13,314	7,215	13,305
Chester	7,891	6,367	7,478	6,318
Chesterfield	7,958	8,490	7,842	8,325
Clarendon	9,091	7,071	8,673	6,758
Colleton	8,475	8,443	8,616	8,525
Darlington	15,457	14,434	14,505	14,544
Dillon	7,523	5,427	7,408	5,874
Dorchester	23,445	32,531	21,806	29,929
Edgefield	4,967	6,512	5,075	6,334
Fairfield	7,777	3,999	7,591	3,912
Florence	28,614	28,961	28,012	29,861
Georgetown	14,163	16,526	14,199	15,790
Greenville	68,070	121,685	70,886	116,363
Greenwood	11,972	16,348	12,348	16,995
Hampton	5,834	3,312	5,816	3,439
Horry	38,885	72,127	38,879	64,609
Jasper	5,757	4,169	5,389	3,365
Kershaw	11,259	16,324	11,226	16,466
Lancaster	13,419	19,333	12,139	16,441
Laurens	10,318	14,746	10,578	15,334
Lee	5,977	2,832	5,960	3,074
Lexington	34,148	76,662	33,303	74,960
Marion	9,688	5,164	9,608	5,416
Marlboro	6,100	3,676	6,794	3,996
McCormick	2,653	2,467	2,755	2,437

County	2012		2008	
	Obama (D)	Romney (R)	Obama (D)	McCain (R)
Newberry	6,913	9,260	6,708	9,616
Oconee	8,550	21,611	9,481	21,164
Orangeburg	30,720	12,022	27,263	12,115
Pickens	11,156	33,474	11,691	32,552
Richland	103,989	53,105	105,656	57,941
Saluda	3,328	5,135	3,323	5,191
Spartanburg	41,461	66,969	41,632	65,042
Sumter	27,589	19,274	25,431	18,581
Union	5,796	6,584	5,935	7,449
Williamsburg	11,335	4,824	11,279	5,004
York	39,131	59,546	37,918	54,500
Totals	**865,941**	**1,071,645**	**862,449**	**1,034,896**

South Carolina Vote Since 1960

2012: Romney, R., 1,071,645; Obama, D., 865,941; Johnson, LB., 16,321; Stein, Green, 5,446; Goode, Const., 4,765.
2008: McCain, R., 1,034,896; Obama, D., 862,449; Barr, LB., 7,283; Baldwin, Const., 6,827; Nader, petitioning cand., 5,053; McKinney, Green, 4,461.
2004: Bush, R., 937,974; Kerry, D., 661,699; Nader, Ind., 5,520; Peroutka, Const., 5,317; Badnarik, LB., 3,608; Brown, United Citizens, 2,124; Cobb, Green, 1,488.
2000: Bush, R., 786,892; Gore, D., 566,039; Nader, United Citizens, 20,279; Browne, LB., 4,898; Buchanan, RF., 3,309; Phillips, Const., 1,682; Hagelin, Natural Law, 943.
1996: Dole, R., 573,458; Clinton, D., 506,283; Perot, RF./Patriot, 64,386; Browne, LB., 4,271; Phillips, U.S. Taxpayers, 2,043; Hagelin, Natural Law, 1,248.
1992: Bush, R., 577,507; Clinton, D., 479,514; Perot, Ind., 138,872; Marrou, LB., 2,719; Phillips, U.S. Taxpayers, 2,680; Fulani, New Alliance, 1,235.
1988: Bush, R., 606,443; Dukakis, D., 370,554; Paul, LB., 4,935; Fulani, United Citizens, 4,077.
1984: Reagan, R., 615,539; Mondale, D., 344,459; Bergland, LB., 4,359.
1980: Reagan, R., 439,277; Carter, D., 428,220; Anderson, Ind., 13,868; Clark, LB., 4,807; Rarick, Amer. Ind., 2,086.
1976: Carter, D., 450,807; Ford, R., 346,149; Anderson, Amer., 2,996; Maddox, Amer. Ind., 1,950; write-in, 681.
1972: Nixon, R., 477,044; McGovern, D., 184,559, and United Citizens, 2,265 (total, 186,824); Schmitz, Amer., 10,075; write-in, 77.
1968: Nixon, R., 254,062; Wallace, 3rd party, 215,430; Humphrey, D., 197,486.
1964: Goldwater, R., 309,048; Johnson, D., 215,700; write-ins: Wallace, 5; Nixon, 1; Powell, 1; Thurmond, 1.
1960: Kennedy, D., 198,129; Nixon, R., 188,558; write-in, 1.

South Dakota

County	2012		2008	
	Obama (D)	Romney (R)	Obama (D)	McCain (R)
Aurora	556	804	655	794
Beadle	2,881	4,230	3,493	4,054
Bennett	548	626	557	614
Bon Homme	1,167	1,830	1,367	1,712
Brookings	5,827	6,220	7,207	6,431
Brown	7,250	8,321	9,041	8,067
Brule	824	1,499	965	1,407
Buffalo	472	166	454	156
Butte	1,002	3,073	1,306	2,821
Campbell	153	616	243	591
Charles Mix	1,483	2,230	1,807	2,109
Clark	713	1,067	830	1,065
Clay	2,955	2,147	3,808	2,296
Codington	4,588	6,696	5,595	6,374
Corson	648	515	837	535
Custer	1,335	3,062	1,475	2,909
Davison	3,042	4,757	3,554	4,731
Day	1,497	1,320	1,785	1,372
Deuel	941	1,175	1,054	1,088
Dewey	1,207	663	1,328	659
Douglas	332	1,334	424	1,293
Edmunds	622	1,264	819	1,213
Fall River	1,140	2,258	1,338	2,348
Faulk	331	765	426	739
Grant	1,493	2,034	1,786	1,951
Gregory	599	1,507	771	1,423
Haakon	138	940	187	939
Hamlin	921	1,803	1,043	1,661
Hand	575	1,242	718	1,247
Hanson	760	1,627	961	1,426
Harding	82	638	135	575
Hughes	2,786	5,219	3,037	5,298
Hutchinson	923	2,451	1,242	2,285
Hyde	189	531	226	547
Jackson	426	661	435	668
Jerauld	452	538	542	546
Jones	108	490	147	463

County	2012		2008	
	Obama (D)	Romney (R)	Obama (D)	McCain (R)
Kingsbury	1,092	1,451	1,277	1,435
Lake	2,724	3,419	3,033	2,993
Lawrence	3,973	7,025	4,932	6,787
Lincoln	7,982	13,611	8,642	11,803
Lyman	605	933	710	894
Marshall	1,061	889	1,261	900
McCook	905	1,655	1,219	1,646
McPherson	272	921	441	915
Meade	2,928	7,566	3,751	7,515
Mellette	375	381	373	445
Miner	479	636	605	577
Minnehaha	34,674	40,342	39,838	39,251
Moody	1,429	1,535	1,663	1,508
Pennington	15,125	28,232	17,802	27,603
Perkins	319	1,205	499	1,102
Potter	339	1,029	482	937
Roberts	2,302	1,883	2,672	1,781
Sanborn	389	688	500	669
Shannon	2,937	188	2,971	331
Spink	1,300	1,670	1,550	1,660
Stanley	435	1,063	510	1,017
Sully	186	613	233	581
Todd	1,976	498	2,208	571
Tripp	737	1,905	914	1,859
Turner	1,411	2,715	1,681	2,538
Union	2,782	4,698	3,244	4,310
Walworth	671	1,731	923	1,668
Yankton	4,226	5,495	4,838	5,039
Ziebach	439	314	554	312
Totals	**145,039**	**210,610**	**170,924**	**203,054**

South Dakota Vote Since 1960

2012: Romney, R., 210,610; Obama, D., 145,039; Johnson, LB., 5,795; Goode, Const., 2,371.
2008: McCain, R., 203,054; Obama, D., 170,924; Nader, Ind., 4,267; Baldwin, Const., 1,895; Barr, Ind., 1,835.
2004: Bush, R., 232,584; Kerry, D., 149,244; Nader, Ind., 4,320; Peroutka, Const., 1,103; Badnarik, LB., 964.
2000: Bush, R., 190,700; Gore, D., 118,804; Buchanan, RF., 3,322; Phillips, Ind., 1,781; Browne, LB., 1,662.
1996: Dole, R., 150,543; Clinton, D., 139,333; Perot, RF., 31,250; Browne, LB., 1,472; Phillips, Taxpayers, 912; Hagelin, Natural Law, 316.
1992: Bush, R., 136,718; Clinton, D., 124,888; Perot, Ind., 73,295.
1988: Bush, R., 165,415; Dukakis, D., 145,560; Paul, LB., 1,060; Fulani, New Alliance, 730.
1984: Reagan, R., 200,267; Mondale, D., 116,113.
1980: Reagan, R., 198,343; Carter, D., 103,855; Anderson, Ind., 21,431; Clark, LB., 3,824; Pulley, Soc. Workers, 250.
1976: Ford, R., 151,505; Carter, D., 147,068; MacBride, LB., 1,619; Hall, Comm., 318; Camejo, Soc. Workers, 168.
1972: Nixon, R., 166,476; McGovern, D., 139,945; Jenness, Soc. Workers, 994.
1968: Nixon, R., 149,841; Humphrey, D., 118,023; Wallace, 3rd party, 13,400.
1964: Johnson, D., 163,010; Goldwater, R., 130,108.
1960: Nixon, R., 178,417; Kennedy, D., 128,070.

Tennessee

County	2012		2008	
	Obama (D)	Romney (R)	Obama (D)	McCain (R)
Anderson	10,122	18,968	11,396	19,675
Bedford	4,211	10,034	5,027	10,217
Benton	2,258	3,850	2,645	3,696
Bledsoe	1,267	3,022	1,517	3,166
Blount	12,934	35,441	15,253	35,571
Bradley	8,037	27,422	9,357	28,333
Campbell	3,328	8,604	3,867	8,535
Cannon	1,564	3,309	2,011	3,322
Carroll	3,475	7,225	3,980	7,455
Carter	4,789	15,503	5,587	15,852
Cheatham	4,659	10,268	5,498	10,702
Chester	1,624	4,684	1,797	4,587
Claiborne	2,433	7,617	3,078	7,175
Clay	1,037	1,747	1,248	1,676
Cocke	2,804	8,459	3,340	8,945
Coffee	5,870	13,023	7,132	13,250
Crockett	1,669	3,783	1,967	3,994
Cumberland	6,261	18,653	7,889	17,436
Davidson	143,120	97,622	158,423	102,915
Decatur	1,303	2,874	1,566	3,101
DeKalb	2,174	4,143	2,832	4,085
Dickson	6,233	11,296	7,506	11,677
Dyer	3,757	9,921	4,411	9,859
Fayette	6,688	12,689	6,892	12,173
Fentress	1,561	5,243	1,831	4,789

County	2012 Obama (D)	Romney (R)	2008 Obama (D)	McCain (R)
Franklin	5,603	10,262	6,613	10,539
Gibson	6,564	12,883	7,406	13,516
Giles	3,760	6,915	4,614	6,902
Grainger	1,668	5,470	2,066	5,297
Greene	6,225	17,245	7,110	17,151
Grundy	1,643	2,516	1,971	2,563
Hamblen	5,234	14,522	6,807	15,508
Hamilton	58,836	79,933	64,246	81,702
Hancock	475	1,527	604	1,588
Hardeman	5,482	4,865	5,919	5,225
Hardin	2,467	7,886	2,794	7,077
Hawkins	5,088	14,382	5,930	14,756
Haywood	4,569	2,960	4,893	3,165
Henderson	2,517	7,421	3,021	7,669
Henry	4,339	8,193	5,153	8,182
Hickman	2,698	4,758	3,563	4,784
Houston	1,400	1,579	1,678	1,608
Humphreys	2,905	3,833	3,600	3,818
Jackson	1,739	2,383	2,224	2,185
Jefferson	4,232	13,038	5,178	13,092
Johnson	1,483	4,611	1,837	4,621
Knox	59,399	109,707	70,215	113,015
Lake	884	1,163	1,024	1,175
Lauderdale	4,011	4,616	4,322	4,933
Lawrence	4,237	10,770	5,161	10,566
Lewis	1,447	3,117	1,804	2,951
Lincoln	3,290	9,803	3,695	9,231
Loudon	5,058	16,707	6,058	15,815
Macon	1,552	5,260	2,060	5,145
Madison	18,367	21,993	20,209	23,290
Marion	3,953	6,272	4,506	6,746
Marshall	3,725	6,832	4,320	6,755
Maury	11,825	20,708	13,058	20,288
McMinn	4,609	12,967	5,541	12,989
McNairy	2,645	7,015	3,131	7,135
Meigs	1,163	2,734	1,372	2,797
Monroe	4,372	11,731	5,053	11,484
Montgomery	24,499	30,245	25,716	30,175
Moore	705	2,053	881	2,010
Morgan	1,725	4,669	1,969	4,717
Obion	3,321	8,814	4,308	8,873
Overton	2,805	4,775	3,419	4,497
Perry	992	1,578	1,329	1,596
Pickett	712	1,712	854	1,786
Polk	1,856	4,108	2,124	4,267
Putnam	7,802	17,254	9,739	17,101
Rhea	2,628	7,802	2,907	8,042
Roane	6,018	14,724	7,224	15,658
Robertson	8,290	17,643	9,318	17,903
Rutherford	36,414	60,846	40,460	59,892
Scott	1,452	5,117	1,720	4,931
Sequatchie	1,489	3,541	1,717	3,610
Sevier	7,418	25,984	8,604	24,922
Shelby	232,443	135,649	256,297	145,458
Smith	2,470	4,495	2,992	4,563
Stewart	2,069	2,963	2,470	2,950
Sullivan	15,321	43,562	18,354	44,808
Sumner	18,579	46,003	21,487	44,949
Tipton	7,133	16,672	7,931	17,165
Trousdale	1,240	1,612	1,475	1,688
Unicoi	1,913	5,032	2,107	5,011
Union	1,478	4,282	1,829	4,467
Van Buren	875	1,386	849	1,294
Warren	4,752	8,010	5,515	8,562
Washington	14,325	32,808	15,941	32,341
Wayne	1,163	4,253	1,355	4,076
Weakley	3,548	8,605	4,596	8,855
White	2,795	6,197	3,372	6,103
Williamson	25,142	69,850	27,886	64,858
Wilson	14,695	36,109	15,886	34,595
Totals	**960,709**	**1,462,330**	**1,087,437**	**1,479,178**

Tennessee Vote Since 1960

2012: Romney, R., 1,462,330; Obama, D., 960,709; Johnson, Ind., 18,623; Stein, Green, 6,515; Goode, Const., 6,022; Anderson, Ind., 2,639, Miller, Ind., 1,739.

2008: McCain, R., 1,479,178; Obama, D., 1,087,437; Nader, Ind., 11,560; Barr, Ind., 8,547; Baldwin, Ind., 8,191; McKinney, Ind., 2,499; Moore, Ind., 1,326; Jay, Ind., 1,011.

2004: Bush, R., 1,384,375; Kerry, D., 1,036,477; Nader, Ind., 8,992; Badnarik, Ind., 4,866; Peroutka, Ind., 2,570.

2000: Bush, R., 1,061,949; Gore, D., 981,720; Nader, Green, 19,781; Browne, LB., 4,284; Buchanan, RF., 4,250; Brown, Ind., 1,606; Phillips, Ind., 1,015; Hagelin, RF., 613; Venson, Ind., 535.

1996: Clinton, D., 909,146; Dole, R., 863,530; Perot, RF., 105,918; Nader, Ind., 6,427; Browne, Ind., 5,020; Phillips, Ind., 1,818; Collins, Ind., 688; Hagelin, Ind., 636; Michael, Ind., 408; Dodge, Ind., 324.

1992: Clinton, D., 933,521; Bush, R., 841,300; Perot, Ind., 199,968; Marrou, LB., 1,847.

1988: Bush, R., 947,233; Dukakis, D., 679,794; Paul, Ind., 2,041; Duke, Ind., 1,807.

1984: Reagan, R., 990,212; Mondale, D., 711,714; Bergland, LB., 3,072.

1980: Reagan, R., 787,761; Carter, D., 783,051; Anderson, Ind., 35,991; Clark, LB., 7,116; Commoner, Citizens, 1,112; Bubar, Statesman, 521; McReynolds, Soc., 519; Hall, Comm., 503; DeBerry, Soc. Workers, 490; Griswold, Workers World, 400; write-in, 152.

1976: Carter, D., 825,879; Ford, R., 633,969; Anderson, Amer., 5,769; McCarthy, Ind., 5,004; Maddox, Amer. Ind., 2,303; MacBride, LB., 1,375; Hall, Comm., 547; LaRouche, U.S. Labor, 512; Bubar, Prohib., 442; Miller, Ind., 316; write-in, 230.

1972: Nixon, R., 813,147; McGovern, D., 357,293; Schmitz, Amer., 30,373; write-in, 369.

1968: Nixon, R., 472,592; Wallace, 3rd party, 424,792; Humphrey, D., 351,233.

1964: Johnson, D., 635,047; Goldwater, R., 508,965; write-in, 34.

1960: Nixon, R., 556,577; Kennedy, D., 481,453; Faubus, States' Rights, 11,304; Decker, Prohib., 2,458.

Texas

County	2012 Obama (D)	Romney (R)	2008 Obama (D)	McCain (R)
Anderson	3,813	12,262	4,630	11,884
Andrews	795	3,639	790	3,816
Angelina	7,834	20,303	9,379	19,569
Aransas	2,704	6,830	3,006	6,693
Archer	525	3,600	740	3,595
Armstrong	98	828	128	856
Atascosa	5,133	7,461	4,415	5,462
Austin	2,252	9,265	2,821	8,786
Bailey	466	1,339	682	1,618
Bandera	1,864	7,426	2,250	6,935
Bastrop	9,864	14,033	11,687	13,817
Baylor	267	1,297	366	1,262
Bee	3,452	4,356	3,645	4,471
Bell	35,512	49,574	40,413	49,242
Bexar	264,856	241,617	275,527	246,275
Blanco	1,220	3,638	1,467	3,418
Borden	32	324	40	316
Bosque	1,367	5,885	1,797	5,762
Bowie	10,196	24,869	10,815	24,162
Brazoria	34,421	70,802	36,480	67,515
Brazos	17,477	37,209	20,502	37,465
Brewster	1,765	1,976	1,970	1,855
Briscoe	117	578	205	617
Brooks	1,886	507	1,747	556
Brown	1,904	11,895	2,822	12,052
Burleson	1,705	4,671	2,053	4,547
Burnet	3,674	12,843	4,608	12,059
Caldwell	4,791	6,021	5,403	6,107
Calhoun	2,410	4,144	2,729	4,106
Callahan	751	4,378	1,063	4,589
Cameron	49,975	26,099	48,480	26,671
Camp	1,428	2,881	1,734	2,798
Carson	292	2,451	406	2,548
Cass	2,924	8,763	3,490	8,279
Castro	630	1,470	719	1,562
Chambers	2,790	11,787	3,188	9,988
Cherokee	3,875	12,094	4,610	11,695
Childress	320	1,665	497	1,782
Clay	740	4,266	1,085	4,213
Cochran	256	649	284	758
Coke	179	1,218	299	1,252
Coleman	442	3,012	643	3,011
Collin	101,415	196,888	109,047	184,897
Collingsworth	177	962	234	943
Colorado	2,029	6,026	2,508	5,795
Comal	11,450	39,318	12,384	35,233
Comanche	890	3,944	1,334	3,813
Concho	194	793	257	807
Cooke	2,246	11,951	3,051	11,871
Coryell	5,158	11,220	6,619	11,550
Cottle	180	555	187	509
Crane	275	985	319	1,119
Crockett	480	957	512	1,026
Crosby	639	1,132	684	1,221
Culberson	568	295	492	257
Dallam	253	1,248	302	1,269
Dallas	405,571	295,813	422,989	310,000
Dawson	1,019	2,591	1,152	2,906
Deaf Smith	1,239	3,042	1,247	3,466
Delta	454	1,524	589	1,580
Denton	80,978	157,579	91,160	149,935
DeWitt	1,467	5,122	1,716	4,888
Dickens	216	793	234	730
Dimmit	2,141	762	2,692	874

County	2012 Obama (D)	Romney (R)	2008 Obama (D)	McCain (R)	County	2012 Obama (D)	Romney (R)	2008 Obama (D)	McCain (R)
Donley	226	1,287	291	1,374	Marion	1,495	2,733	1,644	2,567
Duval	3,331	980	3,298	1,076	Martin	248	1,368	314	1,389
Eastland	970	5,444	1,271	5,165	Mason	380	1,565	546	1,544
Ector	8,118	24,010	9,123	26,199	Matagorda	3,980	8,040	4,440	7,835
Edwards	232	642	346	673	Maverick	8,303	2,171	8,554	2,316
El Paso	112,952	57,150	122,021	61,783	McCulloch	537	2,419	728	2,263
Ellis	13,881	39,574	15,333	38,078	McLennan	25,694	47,903	29,998	49,044
Erath	1,965	10,329	3,128	10,768	McMullen	67	431	132	400
Falls	2,033	3,356	2,225	3,328	Medina	4,784	11,079	5,147	10,480
Fannin	2,486	8,161	3,464	8,092	Menard	171	665	295	712
Fayette	2,315	8,106	3,014	7,582	Midland	8,286	35,689	9,691	36,155
Fisher	512	1,094	687	1,083	Milam	2,636	5,481	3,044	5,217
Floyd	551	1,523	730	1,784	Mills	279	1,882	398	1,753
Foard	140	348	198	327	Mitchell	538	1,756	586	1,815
Fort Bend	101,144	116,126	98,368	103,206	Montague	1,116	6,549	1,597	6,245
Franklin	751	3,446	1,036	3,392	Montgomery	32,920	137,969	36,703	119,884
Freestone	1,850	5,646	2,034	5,205	Moore	964	3,968	1,123	4,282
Frio	2,376	1,559	2,405	1,644	Morris	1,858	3,232	2,055	3,158
Gaines	535	3,484	650	3,385	Motley	55	538	67	522
Galveston	39,511	69,059	41,805	62,258	Nacogdoches	6,465	13,925	8,393	14,828
Garza	279	1,263	375	1,356	Navarro	4,350	10,847	5,400	10,810
Gillespie	2,055	10,306	2,576	9,563	Newton	1,677	4,112	1,751	3,446
Glasscock	44	526	52	502	Nolan	1,216	3,282	1,521	3,485
Goliad	1,127	2,294	1,329	2,298	Nueces	45,772	48,966	47,912	52,391
Gonzales	1,777	4,216	2,167	4,076	Ochiltree	253	2,719	243	2,851
Gray	886	6,443	1,153	6,924	Oldham	71	790	102	813
Grayson	10,670	30,936	13,900	31,136	Orange	6,800	23,366	7,646	21,509
Gregg	12,398	28,742	13,166	29,203	Palo Pinto	1,811	7,393	2,499	7,264
Grimes	2,339	6,141	2,704	5,562	Panola	2,211	7,950	2,586	7,582
Guadalupe	15,744	33,117	16,156	30,869	Parker	7,853	39,243	10,502	36,974
Hale	2,243	6,490	2,708	7,171	Parmer	529	2,011	719	2,969
Hall	265	832	324	930	Pecos	1,591	2,512	1,476	2,480
Hamilton	591	2,918	863	2,876	Polk	4,859	14,071	6,230	13,771
Hansford	159	1,788	240	1,847	Potter	7,126	18,918	8,939	20,761
Hardeman	302	1,176	373	1,199	Presidio	1,282	504	1,252	489
Hardin	3,359	17,746	3,939	16,603	Rains	761	3,279	1,048	3,146
Harris	587,044	586,073	590,982	571,883	Randall	7,574	41,447	9,468	41,948
Harrison	8,456	17,512	8,887	17,103	Reagan	158	676	197	795
Hartley	184	1,708	250	1,711	Real	277	1,236	375	1,238
Haskell	553	1,424	699	1,388	Red River	1,482	3,549	1,539	3,461
Hays	25,537	31,661	28,431	29,638	Reeves	1,655	1,188	1,606	1,445
Hemphill	192	1,298	216	1,345	Refugio	998	1,663	1,382	1,855
Henderson	6,106	21,231	7,913	20,857	Roberts	33	468	41	477
Hidalgo	97,969	39,865	90,261	39,668	Robertson	2,798	4,419	2,675	3,980
Hill	2,752	9,132	3,811	9,264	Rockwall	8,120	27,113	8,492	23,300
Hockley	1,486	5,546	1,797	5,795	Runnels	519	3,104	720	3,118
Hood	3,843	18,409	5,087	17,299	Rusk	4,451	13,924	4,983	13,646
Hopkins	2,777	9,836	3,530	9,299	Sabine	807	3,727	1,077	3,749
Houston	2,265	5,880	2,656	5,872	San Augustine	1,193	2,469	1,328	2,342
Howard	2,110	6,453	2,545	7,029	San Jacinto	2,410	7,107	2,721	6,151
Hudspeth	379	471	430	458	San Patricio	7,856	12,005	8,854	12,404
Hunt	6,671	21,011	8,594	20,573	San Saba	323	1,905	487	1,941
Hutchinson	1,045	6,804	1,322	7,361	Schleicher	221	787	324	970
Irion	112	668	164	644	Scurry	838	4,124	1,088	4,414
Jack	303	2,580	470	2,528	Shackelford	131	1,218	208	1,284
Jackson	1,070	3,906	1,301	3,723	Shelby	2,322	6,879	2,548	6,630
Jasper	3,423	9,957	3,658	9,022	Sherman	121	908	107	884
Jeff Davis	440	719	468	749	Smith	21,456	57,331	23,726	55,187
Jefferson	44,668	43,242	44,888	42,905	Somervell	613	2,871	799	2,677
Jim Hogg	1,301	356	1,336	472	Starr	10,260	1,547	8,274	1,492
Jim Wells	6,492	4,598	6,706	4,841	Stephens	475	2,892	626	2,869
Johnson	10,496	37,661	12,912	36,685	Sterling	31	459	97	520
Jones	1,226	4,262	1,528	4,203	Stonewall	160	507	206	524
Karnes	1,325	2,825	1,760	2,736	Sutton	369	1,110	381	1,189
Kaufman	9,472	24,846	11,161	23,735	Swisher	579	1,655	813	1,683
Kendall	3,043	14,508	3,599	12,971	Tarrant	253,071	348,920	274,880	348,420
Kenedy	82	84	108	94	Taylor	9,750	32,904	12,690	34,317
Kent	66	335	99	342	Terrell	184	358	186	323
Kerr	4,338	17,274	5,570	16,752	Terry	1,059	2,602	1,379	2,879
Kimble	217	1,667	342	1,487	Throckmorton	109	700	166	671
King	5	139	8	151	Titus	2,648	6,084	3,145	6,028
Kinney	522	880	633	907	Tom Green	9,294	26,878	11,158	27,362
Kleberg	4,754	4,058	5,256	4,540	Travis	232,788	140,152	254,017	136,981
Knox	332	1,160	367	986	Trinity	1,614	4,537	1,925	4,095
La Salle	965	669	1,052	714	Tyler	1,668	5,910	2,166	5,644
Lamar	4,181	12,826	5,243	12,952	Upshur	2,971	12,015	3,790	11,222
Lamb	998	3,058	1,156	3,344	Upton	333	953	288	898
Lampasas	1,479	5,621	1,903	5,651	Uvalde	3,825	4,529	4,126	4,590
Lavaca	1,428	6,796	1,869	6,293	Val Verde	6,285	5,635	6,982	5,752
Lee	1,632	4,507	2,000	4,312	Van Zandt	3,084	15,794	4,505	15,734
Leon	1,062	5,814	1,418	5,566	Victoria	8,802	19,692	9,832	19,878
Liberty	5,202	17,323	5,991	15,448	Walker	6,252	12,140	7,334	11,623
Limestone	2,208	5,288	2,516	5,079	Waller	6,514	9,244	7,153	8,265
Lipscomb	119	1,044	155	1,093	Ward	841	2,366	899	2,667
Live Oak	919	3,154	1,048	3,095	Washington	3,381	10,847	4,034	10,176
Llano	1,822	7,610	2,250	7,281	Webb	37,597	11,078	33,452	13,119
Loving	9	54	12	67	Wharton	4,235	9,750	4,937	9,431
Lubbock	26,271	63,469	30,486	66,304	Wheeler	232	1,878	314	1,918
Lynn	506	1,439	627	1,473	Wichita	10,525	29,812	13,868	31,731
Madison	967	3,028	1,146	2,891	Wilbarger	971	2,956	1,196	3,283

County	2012		2008	
	Obama (D)	Romney (R)	Obama (D)	McCain (R)
Willacy	3,600	1,416	3,409	1,456
Williamson	61,875	97,006	67,691	88,323
Wilson	4,821	12,218	5,362	10,904
Winkler	398	1,311	477	1,529
Wise	3,221	17,207	4,471	15,973
Wood	3,056	14,351	4,010	13,658
Yoakum	409	1,698	450	1,989
Young	992	6,225	1,303	5,942
Zapata	2,527	997	1,939	919
Zavala	3,042	574	3,263	596
Totals	3,308,124	4,569,843	3,528,633	4,479,328

Texas Vote Since 1960

2012: Romney, R., 4,569,843; Obama, D., 3,308,124; Johnson, LB., 88,580; Stein, Green, 24,657.
2008: McCain, R., 4,479,328; Obama, D., 3,528,633 Barr, LB., 56,116.
2004: Bush, R., 4,526,917; Kerry, D., 2,832,704; Badnarik, LB., 38,787.
2000: Bush, R., 3,799,639; Gore, D., 2,433,746; Nader, Green, 137,994; Browne, LB., 23,160; Buchanan, Ind., 12,394.
1996: Dole, R., 2,736,167; Clinton, D., 2,459,683; Perot, RF., 378,537; Browne, LB., 20,256; Phillips, U.S. Taxpayers, 7,472; Hagelin, Natural Law, 4,422.
1992: Bush, R., 2,496,071; Clinton, D., 2,281,815; Perot, Ind., 1,354,781; Marrou, LB., 19,699.
1988: Bush, R., 3,036,829; Dukakis, D., 2,352,748; Paul, LB., 30,355; Fulani, New Alliance, 7,208.
1984: Reagan, R., 3,433,428; Mondale, D., 1,949,276.
1980: Reagan, R., 2,510,705; Carter, D., 1,881,147; Anderson, Ind., 111,613; Clark, LB., 37,643; write-in, 528.
1976: Carter, D., 2,082,319; Ford, R., 1,953,300; McCarthy, Ind., 20,118; Anderson, Amer., 11,442; Camejo, Soc. Workers, 1,723; write-in, 2,982.
1972: Nixon, R., 2,298,896; McGovern, D., 1,154,289; Jenness, Soc. Workers, 8,664; Schmitz, Amer., 6,039; others, 3,393.
1968: Humphrey, D., 1,266,804; Nixon, R., 1,227,844; Wallace, 3rd party, 584,269; write-in, 489.
1964: Johnson, D., 1,663,185; Goldwater, R., 958,566; Lightburn, Const., 5,060.
1960: Kennedy, D., 1,167,932; Nixon, R., 1,121,699; Sullivan, Const., 18,169; Decker, Prohib., 3,870; write-in, 15.

Utah

County	2012		2008	
	Obama (D)	Romney (R)	Obama (D)	McCain (R)
Beaver	346	2,174	542	1,902
Box Elder	1,984	17,101	3,311	15,228
Cache	6,244	35,039	10,294	29,127
Carbon	2,275	5,090	3,468	4,091
Daggett	94	406	131	297
Davis	21,889	96,861	30,477	77,341
Duchesne	581	5,698	911	4,689
Emery	569	3,777	973	3,358
Garfield	308	1,832	405	1,710
Grand	1,727	1,996	2,067	1,871
Iron	2,148	14,200	3,258	12,518
Juab	451	3,448	741	2,683
Kane	744	2,522	856	2,212
Millard	431	4,478	758	3,653
Morgan	403	4,114	689	3,311
Piute	74	697	141	635
Rich	83	915	154	831
Salt Lake	146,147	223,811	176,988	176,692
San Juan	2,139	3,074	2,406	2,638
Sanpete	980	8,406	1,631	6,664
Sevier	738	7,207	1,359	6,394
Summit	8,072	8,884	9,532	6,956
Tooele	4,524	14,268	5,830	10,998
Uintah	997	10,421	1,462	8,441
Utah	17,281	156,950	29,567	122,224
Wasatch	2,191	7,220	2,892	5,430
Washington	8,337	44,698	10,826	37,311
Wayne	215	1,089	335	940
Weber	19,841	54,224	25,666	45,885
Totals	251,813	740,600	327,670	596,030

Utah Vote Since 1960

2012: Romney, R., 740,600; Obama, D., 251,813; Johnson, LB., 12,572; Anderson, Justice, 5,335; Stein, Green, 3,817; Goode, Const., 2,871; La Riva, unaff., 393.
2008: McCain, R., 596,030; Obama, D., 327,670; Baldwin, Const., 12,012; Nader, unaff., 8,416; Barr, LB., 6,966; McKinney, unaff., 982; La Riva, unaff., 262.
2004: Bush, R., 663,742; Kerry, D., 241,199; Nader, Ind., 11,305; Peroutka, Const., 6,841; Badnarik, LB., 3,375; Jay, Pers. Choice, 946; Harris, Soc. Workers, 393.

2000: Bush, R., 515,096; Gore, D., 203,053; Nader, Green, 35,850; Buchanan, RF., 9,319; Browne, LB., 3,616; Phillips, Ind. Amer., 2,709; Hagelin, Natural Law, 763; Harris, Soc. Workers, 186; Youngkeit, Ind., 161.
1996: Dole, R., 361,911; Clinton, D., 221,633; Perot, RF., 66,461; Nader, Green, 4,615; Browne, LB., 4,129; Phillips, Taxpayers, 2,601; Templin, Ind. Amer., 1,290; Crane, Ind., 1,101; Hagelin, Natural Law, 1,085; Moorehead, Workers World, 298; Harris, Soc. Workers, 235; Dodge, Prohib., 111.
1992: Bush, R., 322,632; Perot, Ind., 203,400; Clinton, D., 183,429; Gritz, Populist/America First, 28,602; Marrou, LB., 1,900; Hagelin, Natural Law, 1,319; LaRouche, Ind., 1,089.
1988: Bush, R., 428,442; Dukakis, D., 207,352; Paul, LB., 7,473; Dennis, Amer., 2,158.
1984: Reagan, R., 469,105; Mondale, D., 155,369; Bergland, LB., 2,447.
1980: Reagan, R., 439,687; Carter, D., 124,266; Anderson, Ind., 30,284; Clark, LB., 7,226; Commoner, Citizens, 1,009; Greaves, Amer., 965; Rarick, Amer. Ind., 522; Hall, Comm., 139; DeBerry, Soc. Workers, 124.
1976: Ford, R., 337,908; Carter, D., 182,110; Anderson, Amer., 13,304; McCarthy, Ind., 3,907; MacBride, LB., 2,438; Maddox, Amer. Ind., 1,162; Camejo, Soc. Workers, 268; Hall, Comm., 121.
1972: Nixon, R., 323,643; McGovern, D., 126,284; Schmitz, Amer., 28,549.
1968: Nixon, R., 238,728; Humphrey, D., 156,665; Wallace, 3rd party, 26,906; Peace/Freedom, 180; Halstead, Soc. Workers, 89.
1964: Johnson, D., 219,628; Goldwater, R., 181,785.
1960: Nixon, R., 205,361; Kennedy, D., 169,248; Dobbs, Soc. Workers, 100.

Vermont

County	2012		2008	
	Obama (D)	Romney (R)	Obama (D)	McCain (R)
Addison	12,257	5,203	13,202	5,667
Bennington	11,514	5,687	12,524	6,133
Caledonia	8,192	5,088	8,900	5,472
Chittenden	53,626	21,571	59,611	22,237
Essex	1,539	1,164	1,733	1,284
Franklin	12,057	7,405	13,179	7,853
Grand Isle	2,531	1,471	2,694	1,490
Lamoille	8,371	3,342	8,914	3,515
Orange	9,076	4,588	9,799	5,047
Orleans	7,117	4,306	7,998	4,482
Rutland	17,088	10,835	19,355	11,584
Washington	20,351	8,093	22,324	9,129
Windham	16,026	5,347	17,585	5,997
Windsor	19,494	8,598	21,444	9,068
Totals	199,239	92,698	219,262	98,974

Vermont Vote Since 1960

2012: Obama, D., 199,239; Romney, R., 92,698; Johnson, LB., 3,487; Anderson, Justice, 1,128; Lindsay, Socialism/Liberation, 695.
2008: Obama, D., 219,262; McCain, R., 98,974; Nader, Ind., 3,339; Barr, LB., 1,067; Baldwin, Const., 500; Calero, Soc. Workers, 150; La Riva, Socialism/Liberation, 149; Moore, Liberty Union, 141.
2004: Kerry, D., 184,067; Bush, R., 121,180; Nader, Ind., 4,494; Badnarik, LB., 1,102; Parker, Liberty Union, 265; Calero, Soc. Workers, 244.
2000: Gore, D., 149,022; Bush, R., 119,775; Nader, Green, 20,374; Buchanan, RF., 2,192; Lane, Grass Roots, 1,044; Browne, LB., 784; Hagelin, Natural Law, 219; McReynolds, Liberty Union, 161; Phillips, Const., 153; Harris, Soc. Workers, 70.
1996: Clinton, D., 137,894; Dole, R., 80,352; Perot, RF., 31,024; Nader, Green, 5,585; Browne, LB., 1,183; Hagelin, Natural Law, 498; Peron, Grass Roots, 480; Phillips, Taxpayers, 382; Hollis, Liberty Union, 292; Harris, Soc. Workers, 199.
1992: Clinton, D., 133,590; Bush, R., 88,122; Perot, Ind., 65,985.
1988: Bush, R., 124,331; Dukakis, D., 115,775; Paul, LB., 1,000; LaRouche, Ind., 275.
1984: Reagan, R., 135,865; Mondale, D., 95,730; Bergland, LB., 1,002.
1980: Reagan, R., 94,598; Carter, D., 81,891; Anderson, Ind., 31,760; Commoner, Citizens, 2,316; Clark, LB., 1,900; McReynolds, Liberty Union, 136; Hall, Comm., 118; DeBerry, Soc. Workers, 75; scattered, 413.
1976: Ford, R., 100,387; Carter, D., 77,798 and Ind. Vermonters, 991 (total, 79,789); McCarthy, Ind., 4,001; Camejo, Soc. Workers, 430; LaRouche, U.S. Labor, 196; scattered, 99.
1972: Nixon, R., 117,149; McGovern, D., 68,174; Spock, Liberty Union, 1,010; Jenness, Soc. Workers, 296; scattered, 318.
1968: Nixon, R., 85,142; Humphrey, D., 70,255; Wallace, 3rd party, 5,104; Gregory, New Party, 579; Halstead, Soc. Workers, 295.
1964: Johnson, D., 107,674; Goldwater, R., 54,868.
1960: Nixon, R., 98,131; Kennedy, D., 69,186.

Virginia

County	2012 Obama (D)	Romney (R)	2008 Obama (D)	McCain (R)
Accomack	7,655	8,213	7,607	7,833
Albemarle	29,757	23,297	29,792	20,576
Alleghany	3,403	3,595	3,553	3,715
Amelia	2,490	4,331	2,488	3,970
Amherst	5,900	8,876	6,094	8,470
Appomattox	2,453	5,340	2,641	4,903
Arlington	81,269	34,474	78,994	29,876
Augusta	9,451	23,624	9,825	23,120
Bath	894	1,274	1,043	1,349
Bedford	10,209	26,679	11,017	24,420
Bland	735	2,144	864	2,031
Botetourt	5,452	12,479	5,693	11,471
Brunswick	4,994	2,968	4,973	2,877
Buchanan	3,094	6,436	4,063	4,541
Buckingham	3,750	3,569	3,489	3,428
Campbell	7,595	17,695	8,091	17,444
Caroline	7,276	6,151	7,163	5,617
Carroll	3,685	8,736	4,109	8,187
Charles City	2,772	1,396	2,838	1,288
Charlotte	2,503	3,311	2,705	3,372
Chesterfield	77,694	90,934	74,310	86,413
Clarke	3,239	4,296	3,457	3,840
Craig	830	1,757	877	1,695
Culpeper	8,285	11,580	8,802	10,711
Cumberland	2,422	2,538	2,255	2,418
Dickenson	2,473	4,274	3,278	3,324
Dinwiddie	6,550	6,875	6,246	6,526
Essex	3,016	2,602	2,934	2,379
Fairfax	315,273	206,773	310,359	200,994
Fauquier	13,965	21,034	14,616	19,227
Floyd	2,732	4,673	2,937	4,441
Fluvanna	5,893	6,678	6,185	6,420
Franklin	9,090	16,718	9,618	15,414
Frederick	12,690	22,858	12,961	20,149
Giles	2,730	4,660	3,192	4,462
Gloucester	6,764	12,137	6,916	12,089
Goochland	4,676	8,448	4,813	7,643
Grayson	2,068	4,801	2,480	4,540
Greene	3,290	5,569	3,174	4,980
Greensville	3,135	1,766	3,122	1,729
Halifax	7,766	8,489	8,126	8,600
Hanover	18,294	39,940	18,447	37,344
Henrico	89,594	70,449	86,323	67,381
Henry	10,317	13,984	11,118	13,758
Highland	459	924	590	930
Isle of Wight	8,761	11,802	8,573	11,258
James City	17,879	22,843	17,352	20,912
King and Queen	1,745	1,865	1,918	1,763
King George	4,477	6,604	4,473	5,888
King William	3,344	5,466	3,344	4,966
Lancaster	3,149	3,753	3,235	3,647
Lee	2,583	6,847	3,219	5,825
Loudoun	82,479	75,292	74,845	63,336
Louisa	6,953	9,215	6,978	8,182
Lunenburg	2,684	2,969	2,703	2,900
Madison	2,639	3,869	2,862	3,758
Mathews	1,807	3,488	1,934	3,456
Mecklenburg	6,921	7,973	7,127	7,817
Middlesex	2,370	3,619	2,391	3,545
Montgomery	19,903	20,006	21,031	19,028
Nelson	4,171	3,947	4,391	3,647
New Kent	3,555	7,246	3,493	6,385
Northampton	3,741	2,676	3,800	2,713
Northumberland	3,191	4,310	3,312	4,041
Nottoway	3,344	3,409	3,413	3,499
Orange	6,870	9,244	7,107	8,506
Page	3,724	6,344	4,235	6,041
Patrick	2,417	5,622	2,879	5,491
Pittsylvania	10,858	19,263	11,415	18,730
Powhatan	4,088	11,200	4,237	10,088
Prince Edward	5,132	3,952	5,101	4,174
Prince George	6,991	8,879	7,130	8,752
Prince William	103,331	74,458	93,435	67,621
Pulaski	5,292	8,920	5,918	8,857
Rappahannock	1,980	2,311	2,105	2,227
Richmond	1,574	2,160	1,618	2,092
Roanoke	18,711	31,624	19,812	30,571
Rockbridge	4,088	5,898	4,347	5,732
Rockingham	10,065	24,186	10,453	22,468
Russell	3,718	8,180	4,932	6,389
Scott	2,395	7,439	2,725	6,903
Shenandoah	6,469	12,538	6,912	12,005
Smyth	4,171	8,379	4,239	7,817
Southampton	4,437	4,733	4,402	4,583
Spotsylvania	25,165	31,844	24,897	28,610
Stafford	27,182	32,480	25,716	29,221
Surry	2,576	1,671	2,626	1,663
Sussex	3,358	2,021	3,301	2,026
Tazewell	3,661	13,843	5,596	11,221
Warren	6,452	9,869	6,997	8,879
Washington	7,076	18,141	8,063	16,077
Westmoreland	4,295	3,731	4,577	3,719
Wise	3,760	11,076	4,995	8,914
Wythe	3,783	8,324	4,107	8,207
York	13,183	20,204	13,700	19,833
City				
Alexandria	52,199	20,249	50,473	19,181
Bedford	1,225	1,527	1,208	1,497
Bristol	2,492	4,780	2,665	4,579
Buena Vista	919	1,564	1,108	1,282
Charlottesville	16,510	4,844	15,705	4,078
Chesapeake	55,052	53,900	53,994	52,625
Colonial Heights	2,544	5,941	2,562	6,161
Covington	1,319	975	1,304	1,020
Danville	12,218	7,763	12,352	8,361
Emporia	1,793	886	1,702	897
Fairfax	6,651	4,775	6,575	4,691
Falls Church	5,015	2,147	4,695	1,970
Franklin	2,833	1,496	2,819	1,576
Fredericksburg	7,131	4,060	6,155	3,413
Galax	900	1,332	1,052	1,317
Hampton	46,966	18,640	46,917	20,476
Harrisonburg	8,654	6,565	8,444	6,048
Hopewell	5,179	3,739	5,285	4,149
Lexington	1,486	1,146	1,543	914
Lynchburg	15,948	19,806	16,269	17,638
Manassas	8,478	6,463	7,518	5,975
Manassas Park	2,879	1,699	2,463	1,634
Martinsville	3,855	2,312	4,139	2,311
Newport News	51,100	27,230	51,972	28,667
Norfolk	62,687	23,147	62,819	24,814
Norton	566	895	743	744
Petersburg	14,283	1,527	13,774	1,583
Poquoson	1,679	5,312	1,748	5,229
Portsmouth	32,501	12,858	32,327	13,984
Radford	2,732	2,520	2,930	2,418
Richmond	75,921	20,050	73,623	18,649
Roanoke	24,134	14,991	24,934	15,394
Salem	4,760	7,299	5,164	7,088
Staunton	5,728	5,272	5,569	5,330
Suffolk	27,247	17,820	22,446	17,165
Virginia Beach	94,299	99,291	98,885	100,319
Waynesboro	3,840	4,790	3,906	4,815
Williamsburg	4,903	2,682	4,328	2,353
Winchester	5,094	4,946	5,268	4,725
Totals	**1,971,820**	**1,822,522**	**1,959,532**	**1,725,005**

Virginia Vote Since 1960

2012: Obama, D., 1,971,820; Romney, R., 1,822,522; Johnson, LB., 31,216; Goode, Const., 13,058; Stein, Green, 8,627.
2008: Obama, D., 1,959,532; McCain, R., 1,725,005; Nader, Ind., 11,483; Barr, LB., 11,067; Baldwin, Ind. Green, 7,474; McKinney, Green, 2,344.
2004: Bush, R., 1,716,959; Kerry, D., 1,454,742; Badnarik, LB., 11,032; Peroutka, Const., 10,161.
2000: Bush, R., 1,437,490; Gore, D., 1,217,290; Nader, Green, 59,398; Browne, LB., 15,198; Buchanan, RF., 5,455; Phillips, Const., 1,809.
1996: Dole, R., 1,138,350; Clinton, D., 1,091,060; Perot, RF., 159,861; Phillips, Taxpayers, 13,687; Browne, LB., 9,174; Hagelin, Natural Law, 4,510.
1992: Bush, R., 1,150,517; Clinton, D., 1,038,650; Perot, Ind., 348,639; LaRouche, Ind., 11,937; Marrou, LB., 5,730; Fulani, New Alliance, 3,192.
1988: Bush, R., 1,309,162; Dukakis, D., 859,799; Fulani, Ind., 14,312; Paul, LB., 8,336.
1984: Reagan, R., 1,337,078; Mondale, D., 796,250.
1980: Reagan, R., 989,609; Carter, D., 752,174; Anderson, Ind., 95,418; Commoner, Citizens, 14,024; Clark, LB., 12,821; DeBerry, Soc. Workers, 1,986.
1976: Ford, R., 836,554; Carter, D., 813,896; Camejo, Soc. Workers, 17,802; Anderson, Amer., 16,686; LaRouche, U.S. Labor, 7,508; MacBride, LB., 4,648.
1972: Nixon, R., 988,493; McGovern, D., 438,887; Schmitz, Amer., 19,721; Fisher, Soc. Labor, 9,918.
1968: Nixon, R., 590,319; Humphrey, D., 442,387; Wallace, 3rd party, 320,272; Blomen, Soc. Labor, 4,671; Gregory, Peace/Freedom, 1,680; Munn, Prohib., 601. *10,561 votes for Wallace were omitted in the count.
1964: Johnson, D., 558,038; Goldwater, R., 481,334; Hass, Soc. Labor, 2,895.
1960: Nixon, R., 404,521; Kennedy, D., 362,327; Coiner, Conservative, 4,204; Hass, Soc. Labor, 397.

Washington

County	2012		2008	
	Obama (D)	Romney (R)	Obama (D)	McCain (R)
Adams	1,540	3,171	1,552	3,222
Asotin	4,003	5,654	4,139	5,451
Benton	28,145	49,461	26,288	45,345
Chelan	13,112	18,402	13,781	17,605
Clallam	18,580	18,437	19,470	18,199
Clark	93,382	92,951	95,356	84,212
Columbia	645	1,568	686	1,499
Cowlitz	22,726	20,746	24,597	19,554
Douglas	5,166	9,425	5,848	9,098
Ferry	1,294	1,995	1,467	1,916
Franklin	8,398	13,748	7,361	12,037
Garfield	336	913	385	968
Grant	8,950	17,852	9,601	17,153
Gray's Harbor	15,960	11,914	16,354	12,104
Island	21,478	19,605	22,058	19,426
Jefferson	12,739	6,405	13,252	6,330
King	668,004	275,700	648,230	259,716
Kitsap	67,277	52,846	68,624	53,297
Kittitas	7,949	9,782	8,030	9,471
Klickitat	4,598	5,316	4,965	4,944
Lewis	12,664	20,452	13,624	20,278
Lincoln	1,673	4,063	2,032	3,803
Mason	14,764	12,761	15,050	12,600
Okanogan	7,108	9,221	7,613	8,798
Pacific	5,711	4,499	6,094	4,555
Pend Oreille	2,508	3,952	2,562	3,717
Pierce	186,430	148,467	181,824	141,673
San Juan	7,125	3,111	7,374	2,958
Skagit	28,688	25,071	30,053	24,687
Skamania	2,628	2,687	2,817	2,524
Snohomish	188,516	133,016	187,294	126,722
Spokane	102,295	115,285	105,786	108,314
Stevens	7,762	13,691	8,499	13,132
Thurston	74,037	49,287	75,882	48,366
Wahkiakum	1,094	1,119	1,121	1,105
Walla Walla	9,768	14,648	10,081	14,182
Whatcom	57,089	42,703	58,236	40,205
Whitman	8,037	8,507	9,070	8,104
Yakima	33,217	42,239	33,792	41,946
Totals	1,755,396	1,290,670	1,750,848	1,229,216

Washington Vote Since 1960

2012: Obama, D., 1,755,396; Romney, R., 1,290,670; Johnson, LB., 42,202; Stein, Green, 20,928; Goode, Const., 8,851; Anderson, Justice, 4,946; Lindsay, Socialism/Liberation, 1,318; Harris, Soc. Workers, 1,205.

2008: Obama, D., 1,750,848; McCain, R., 1,229,216; Nader, Ind., 29,489; Barr, LB., 12,728; Baldwin, Const., 9,432; McKinney, Green, 3,819; La Riva, Socialism/Liberation, 705; Harris, Soc. Workers, 641.

2004: Kerry, D., 1,510,201; Bush, R., 1,304,894; Nader, Ind., 23,283; Badnarik, LB., 11,955; Peroutka, Const., 3,922; Cobb, Green, 2,974; Parker, Workers World, 1,077; Harris, Soc. Workers, 547; Van Auken, Soc. Equality, 231.

2000: Gore, D., 1,247,652; Bush, R., 1,108,864; Nader, Green, 103,002; Browne, LB., 13,135; Buchanan, Freedom, 7,171; Hagelin, Natural Law, 2,927; Phillips, Const., 1,989; Moorehead, Workers World, 1,729; McReynolds, Soc., 660; Harris, Soc. Workers, 304.

1996: Clinton, D., 1,123,323; Dole, R., 840,712; Perot, RF., 201,003; Nader, Ind., 60,322; Browne, LB., 12,522; Hagelin, Natural Law, 6,076; Phillips, U.S. Taxpayers, 4,578; Collins, Ind., 2,374; Moorehead, Workers World, 2,189; Harris, Soc. Workers, 738.

1992: Clinton, D., 993,037; Bush, R., 731,234; Perot, Ind., 541,780; Marrou, LB., 7,533; Gritz, Populist/America First, 4,854; Hagelin, Natural Law, 2,456; Phillips, U.S. Taxpayers, 2,354; Fulani, New Alliance, 1,776; Daniels, Ind., 1,171.

1988: Dukakis, D., 933,516; Bush, R., 903,835; Paul, LB., 17,240; LaRouche, Ind., 4,412.

1984: Reagan, R., 1,051,670; Mondale, D., 798,352; Bergland, LB., 8,844.

1980: Reagan, R., 865,244; Carter, D., 650,193; Anderson, Ind., 185,073; Clark, LB., 29,213; Commoner, Citizens, 9,403; DeBerry, Soc. Workers, 1,137; McReynolds, Soc., 956; Hall, Comm., 834; Griswold, Workers World, 341.

1976: Ford, R., 777,732; Carter, D., 717,323; McCarthy, Ind., 36,986; Maddox, Amer. Ind., 8,585; Anderson, Amer., 5,046; MacBride, LB., 5,042; Wright, People's, 1,124; Camejo, Soc. Workers, 905; LaRouche, U.S. Labor, 903; Hall, Comm., 817; Levin, Soc. Labor, 713; Zeidler, Soc., 358.

1972: Nixon, R., 837,135; McGovern, D., 568,334; Schmitz, Amer., 58,906; Spock, Ind., 2,644; Hospers, LB., 1,537; Fisher, Soc. Labor, 1,102; Jenness, Soc. Workers 623; Hall, Comm., 566.

1968: Humphrey, D., 616,037; Nixon, R., 588,510; Wallace, 3rd party, 96,990; Cleaver, Peace/Freedom, 1,609; Blomen, Soc. Labor, 488; Mitchell, Free Ballot, 377; Halstead, Soc. Workers, 270.

1964: Johnson, D., 779,699; Goldwater, R., 470,366; Hass, Ind. Labor, 7,772; DeBerry, Freedom Soc., 537.

1960: Nixon, R., 629,273; Kennedy, D., 599,298; Hass, Soc. Labor, 10,895; Curtis, Const., 1,401; Dobbs, Soc. Workers, 705.

West Virginia

County	2012		2008	
	Obama (D)	Romney (R)	Obama (D)	McCain (R)
Barbour	1,768	3,824	2,419	3,685
Berkeley	14,275	22,156	15,994	20,841
Boone	2,790	5,467	4,529	3,632
Braxton	1,998	2,725	2,704	2,629
Brooke	4,005	5,060	4,717	4,961
Cabell	13,568	17,985	15,292	18,793
Calhoun	818	1,319	993	1,366
Clay	931	1,971	1,421	1,755
Doddridge	575	2,130	735	2,218
Fayette	5,419	8,350	7,242	7,658
Gilmer	840	1,595	1,004	1,445
Grant	718	3,783	997	3,166
Greenbrier	4,710	7,930	5,881	7,567
Hampshire	2,299	5,523	2,983	5,222
Hancock	4,627	7,226	5,504	7,518
Hardy	1,482	3,536	1,901	3,376
Harrison	9,732	15,876	13,582	17,824
Jackson	3,854	7,408	4,861	7,148
Jefferson	10,398	11,258	11,687	10,600
Kanawha	32,480	41,364	40,594	40,952
Lewis	1,736	4,375	2,109	4,335
Lincoln	2,227	4,383	3,029	3,637
Logan	3,469	8,222	5,873	7,326
Marion	8,959	12,054	11,618	11,501
Marshall	4,484	8,135	5,996	7,759
Mason	3,778	5,741	4,484	5,853
McDowell	2,109	3,959	3,430	2,882
Mercer	5,432	15,450	7,450	13,246
Mineral	2,885	7,833	3,750	7,616
Mingo	2,428	6,191	3,582	4,587
Monongalia	13,826	16,831	17,060	15,775
Monroe	1,455	3,616	2,014	3,397
Morgan	2,363	4,513	2,721	4,428
Nicholas	2,664	5,898	4,357	4,804
Ohio	6,786	10,768	8,593	10,694
Pendleton	1,074	2,095	1,310	2,035
Pleasants	955	1,825	1,142	1,772
Pocahontas	1,303	2,182	1,548	2,011
Preston	2,931	7,889	4,205	7,325
Putnam	7,256	16,032	9,334	15,162
Raleigh	7,739	20,614	10,237	17,548
Randolph	3,342	6,160	4,539	6,060
Ritchie	768	2,921	998	2,781
Roane	1,939	2,982	2,511	2,943
Summers	1,621	2,981	2,290	2,891
Taylor	1,941	3,840	2,462	3,605
Tucker	880	2,176	1,288	2,123
Tyler	890	2,314	1,241	2,415
Upshur	2,158	5,939	2,925	5,911
Wayne	4,931	8,688	6,137	8,947
Webster	947	1,710	1,552	1,386
Wetzel	2,217	3,473	2,942	3,342
Wirt	676	1,427	782	1,496
Wood	11,230	22,183	12,573	22,896
Wyoming	1,583	5,769	2,735	4,621
Totals	238,269	417,655	303,857	397,466

West Virginia Vote Since 1960

2012: Romney, R., 417,655; Obama, D., 238,269; Johnson, LB., 6,302; Stein, Mountain, 4,406; Terry, NPA, 3,806.

2008: McCain, R., 397,466; Obama, D., 303,857; Nader, unaff., 7,219; Baldwin, Const., 2,465; McKinney, Mountain, 2,355.

2004: Bush, R., 423,778; Kerry, D., 326,541; Nader, Ind., 4,063; Badnarik, LB., 1,405.

2000: Bush, R., 336,475; Gore, D., 295,497; Nader, Green, 10,680; Buchanan, RF., 3,169; Browne, LB., 1,912; Hagelin, Natural Law, 367.

1996: Clinton, D., 327,812; Dole, R., 233,946; Perot, RF., 71,639; Browne, LB., 3,062.

1992: Clinton, D., 331,001; Bush, R., 241,974; Perot, Ind., 108,829; Marrou, LB., 1,873.

1988: Dukakis, D., 341,016; Bush, R., 310,065; Fulani, New Alliance, 2,230.

1984: Reagan, R., 405,483; Mondale, D., 328,125.

1980: Carter, D., 367,462; Reagan, R., 334,206; Anderson, Ind., 31,691; Clark, LB., 4,356.

1976: Carter, D., 435,864; Ford, R., 314,726.

1972: Nixon, R., 484,964; McGovern, D., 277,435.

1968: Humphrey, D., 374,091; Nixon, R., 307,555; Wallace, 3rd party, 72,560.

1964: Johnson, D., 538,087; Goldwater, R., 253,953.

1960: Kennedy, D., 441,786; Nixon, R., 395,995.

Wisconsin

County	2012 Obama (D)	Romney (R)	2008 Obama (D)	McCain (R)
Adams	5,542	4,644	5,806	3,974
Ashland	5,399	2,820	5,818	2,634
Barron	10,890	11,443	12,078	10,457
Bayfield	6,033	3,603	5,972	3,365
Brown	62,526	64,836	67,269	55,854
Buffalo	3,570	3,364	3,949	2,923
Burnett	3,986	4,550	4,337	4,200
Calumet	11,489	14,539	13,295	12,722
Chippewa	15,237	15,322	16,239	13,492
Clark	6,172	7,412	7,454	6,383
Columbia	17,175	13,026	16,661	12,193
Crawford	4,629	3,067	4,987	2,830
Dane	216,071	83,644	205,984	73,065
Dodge	18,762	25,211	19,183	23,015
Door	9,357	8,121	10,142	7,112
Douglas	14,863	7,705	15,830	7,835
Dunn	11,316	10,224	13,002	9,566
Eau Claire	30,666	23,256	33,146	20,959
Florence	953	1,645	1,134	1,512
Fond du Lac	22,339	30,355	23,463	28,164
Forest	2,425	2,172	2,673	1,963
Grant	13,594	10,255	14,875	9,068
Green	11,206	7,857	11,502	6,730
Green Lake	3,793	5,782	4,000	5,393
Iowa	8,105	4,287	7,987	3,829
Iron	1,784	1,790	1,914	1,464
Jackson	5,298	3,900	5,572	3,552
Jefferson	20,158	23,517	21,448	21,096
Juneau	6,242	5,411	6,186	5,148
Kenosha	44,867	34,977	45,836	31,609
Kewaunee	5,153	5,747	5,902	4,711
La Crosse	36,693	25,751	38,524	23,701
Lafayette	4,536	3,314	4,732	2,984
Langlade	4,573	5,816	5,182	5,081
Lincoln	7,563	7,455	8,424	6,519
Manitowoc	20,403	21,604	22,428	19,234
Marathon	32,363	36,617	36,367	30,345
Marinette	9,882	10,619	11,195	9,726
Marquette	4,014	3,992	4,068	3,654
Menominee	1,191	179	1,257	185
Milwaukee	332,438	154,924	319,819	149,445
Monroe	9,515	9,675	10,198	8,666
Oconto	8,865	10,741	9,927	8,755
Oneida	10,452	10,917	11,907	9,630
Outagamie	45,659	47,372	50,294	39,677
Ozaukee	19,159	36,077	20,579	32,172
Pepin	1,876	1,794	2,102	1,616
Pierce	10,235	10,397	11,803	9,812
Polk	10,073	12,094	10,876	11,282
Portage	22,075	16,615	24,817	13,810
Price	3,887	3,884	4,559	3,461
Racine	53,008	49,347	53,408	45,954
Richland	4,969	3,573	5,041	3,298
Rock	49,219	30,517	50,529	27,364
Rusk	3,397	3,676	3,855	3,253
St. Croix	19,910	25,503	21,177	22,837
Sauk	18,736	12,838	18,617	11,562
Sawyer	4,486	4,442	4,765	4,199
Shawano	9,000	11,022	10,259	9,538
Sheboygan	27,918	34,072	30,395	30,801
Taylor	3,763	5,601	4,563	4,586
Trempealeau	7,605	5,707	8,321	4,808
Vernon	8,044	5,942	8,463	5,367
Vilas	5,951	7,749	6,491	7,055
Walworth	22,552	29,006	24,177	25,485
Washburn	4,447	4,699	4,693	4,303
Washington	23,166	54,765	25,719	47,729
Waukesha	78,779	162,798	85,339	145,152
Waupaca	11,578	14,002	12,952	12,232
Waushara	5,335	6,562	5,868	5,770
Winnebago	45,449	42,122	48,167	37,946
Wood	18,581	19,704	21,710	16,581
Totals	**1,620,985**	**1,407,966**	**1,677,211**	**1,262,393**

Wisconsin Vote Since 1960

2012: Obama, D., 1,620,985; Romney, R., 1,407,966; Johnson, LB., 20,439; Stein, Green, 7,665; White, Soc. Equality, 553; La Riva, Socialism/Liberation, 526.

2008: Obama, D., 1,677,211; McCain, R., 1,262,393; Nader, Ind., 17,605; Barr, LB., 8,858; Baldwin, Ind., 5,072; McKinney, Green, 4,216; Wamboldt, Ind., 764; Moore, Ind., 540; La Riva, Ind., 237.

2004: Kerry, D., 1,489,504; Bush, R., 1,478,120; Nader, Ind., 16,390; Badnarik, LB., 6,464; Cobb, Green, 2,661; Brown, Ind., 471; Harris, Ind., 411.

2000: Gore, D., 1,242,987; Bush, R., 1,237,279; Nader, Green, 94,070; Buchanan, RF., 11,446; Browne, LB., 6,640; Phillips, Const., 2,042; Moorehead, Workers World, 1,063; Hagelin, RF., 878; Harris, Soc. Workers, 306.

1996: Clinton, D., 1,071,971; Dole, R., 845,029; Perot, RF., 227,339; Nader, Green, 28,723; Phillips, U.S. Taxpayers, 8,811; Browne, LB., 7,929; Hagelin, Natural Law, 1,379; Moorehead, Workers World, 1,333; Hollis, Soc., 848; Harris, Soc. Workers, 483.

1992: Clinton, D., 1,041,066; Bush, R., 930,855; Perot, Ind., 544,479; Marrou, LB., 2,877; Gritz, Populist/America First, 2,311; Daniels, Ind., 1,883; Phillips, U.S. Taxpayers, 1,772; Hagelin, Natural Law, 1,070.

1988: Dukakis, D., 1,126,794; Bush, R., 1,047,499; Paul, LB., 5,157; Duke, Populist, 3,056.

1984: Reagan, R., 1,198,584; Mondale, D., 995,740; Bergland, LB., 4,883.

1980: Reagan, R., 1,088,845; Carter, D., 981,584; Anderson, Ind., 160,657; Clark, LB., 29,135; Commoner, Citizens, 7,767; Rarick, Const., 1,519; McReynolds, Soc., 808; Hall, Comm., 772; Griswold, Workers World, 414; DeBerry, Soc. Workers, 383; scattered, 1,337.

1976: Carter, D., 1,040,232; Ford, R., 1,004,987; McCarthy, Ind., 34,943; Maddox, Amer. Ind., 8,552; Zeidler, Soc., 4,298; MacBride, LB., 3,814; Camejo, Soc. Workers, 1,691; Wright, People's, 943; Hall, Comm., 749; LaRouche, U.S. Labor, 738; Levin, Soc. Labor, 389; scattered, 2,839.

1972: Nixon, R., 989,430; McGovern, D., 810,174; Schmitz, Amer., 47,525; Spock, Ind., 2,701; Fisher, Soc. Labor, 998; Hall, Comm., 663; Reed, Ind., 506; scattered, 893.

1968: Nixon, R., 809,997; Humphrey, D., 748,804; Wallace, 3rd party, 127,835; Blomen, Soc. Labor, 1,338; Halstead, Soc. Workers, 1,222; scattered, 2,342.

1964: Johnson, D., 1,050,424; Goldwater, R., 638,495; DeBerry, Soc. Workers, 1,692; Hass, Soc. Labor, 1,204.

1960: Nixon, R., 895,175; Kennedy, D., 830,805; Dobbs, Soc. Workers, 1,792; Hass, Soc. Labor, 1,310.

Wyoming

County	2012 Obama (D)	Romney (R)	2008 Obama (D)	McCain (R)
Albany	7,458	7,866	8,644	7,936
Big Horn	868	4,285	1,108	4,045
Campbell	2,163	14,953	2,990	13,011
Carbon	2,110	4,148	2,336	4,331
Converse	1,089	5,043	1,380	4,922
Crook	426	3,109	612	2,967
Fremont	5,333	11,075	6,016	11,083
Goshen	1,458	4,178	1,832	3,942
Hot Springs	523	1,895	619	1,834
Johnson	749	3,363	908	3,334
Laramie	14,295	23,904	16,072	24,549
Lincoln	1,287	7,144	1,823	6,485
Natrona	8,961	22,132	10,475	21,906
Niobrara	200	1,022	244	1,017
Park	2,927	11,234	3,757	10,839
Platte	1,223	3,136	1,407	3,002
Sheridan	3,618	10,267	4,458	10,177
Sublette	767	3,472	936	3,316
Sweetwater	4,774	11,428	5,762	10,360
Teton	6,213	4,858	7,472	4,565
Uinta	1,628	6,615	2,317	5,763
Washakie	794	3,014	1,042	2,956
Weston	422	2,821	658	2,618
Totals	**69,286**	**170,962**	**82,868**	**164,958**

Wyoming Vote Since 1960

2012: Romney, R., 170,962; Obama, D., 69,286; Johnson, LB., 5,326; Goode, Const., 1,452.

2008: McCain, R., 164,958; Obama, D., 82,868; Nader, Ind., 2,525; Barr, LB., 1,594; Baldwin, Ind., 1,192.

2004: Bush, R., 167,629; Kerry, D., 70,776; Nader, Ind., 2,741; Badnarik, LB., 1,171; Peroutka, Ind., 631.

2000: Bush, R., 147,947; Gore, D., 60,481; Buchanan, RF., 2,724; Browne, LB., 1,443; Phillips, Ind., 720; Hagelin, Natural Law, 411.

1996: Dole, R., 105,388; Clinton, D., 77,934; Perot, RF., 25,928; Browne, LB., 1,739; Hagelin, Natural Law, 582.

1992: Bush, R., 79,347; Clinton, D., 68,160; Perot, Ind., 51,263.

1988: Bush, R., 106,867; Dukakis, D., 67,113; Paul, LB., 2,026; Fulani, New Alliance, 545.

1984: Reagan, R., 133,241; Mondale, D., 53,370; Bergland, LB., 2,357.

1980: Reagan, R., 110,700; Carter, D., 49,427; Anderson, Ind., 12,072; Clark, LB., 4,514.

1976: Ford, R., 92,717; Carter, D., 62,239; McCarthy, Ind., 624; Reagan, Ind., 307; Anderson, Amer., 290; MacBride, LB., 89; Brown, Ind., 47; Maddox, Amer. Ind., 30.

1972: Nixon, R., 100,464; McGovern, D., 44,358; Schmitz, Amer., 748.

1968: Nixon, R., 70,927; Humphrey, D., 45,173; Wallace, 3rd party, 11,105.

1964: Johnson, D., 80,718; Goldwater, R., 61,998.

1960: Nixon, R., 77,451; Kennedy, D., 63,331.

UNITED STATES GOVERNMENT

EXECUTIVE BRANCH	LEGISLATIVE BRANCH	JUDICIAL BRANCH
President **Vice President** **Executive Office of the President** Council of Economic Advisers Council on Environmental Quality Executive Residence National Security Council Office of Administration Office of Management and Budget Office of National Drug Control Policy Office of Science and Technology Policy Office of the U.S. Trade Representative Office of the Vice President White House Office*	**CONGRESS** **Senate/House of Representatives** Architect of the Capitol U.S. Botanic Garden Government Accountability Office Government Printing Office Library of Congress Congressional Budget Office Medicare Payment Advisory Commission Stennis Center for Public Service	**Supreme Court of the United States** Courts of Appeals District Courts Territorial Courts Court of International Trade Bankruptcy Courts Court of Federal Claims Tax Court Court of Appeals for the Armed Forces Court of Appeals for Veterans Claims Administrative Office of the Courts Federal Judicial Center Sentencing Commission Judicial Panel on Multidistrict Litigation

*Includes Domestic Policy Council, National Security Advisor, National Economic Council, Office of Cabinet Affairs, Office of the Chief of Staff, Office of Communications, Office of Digital Strategy, Office of the First Lady, Office of Legislative Affairs, Office of Management and Administration, Oval Office Operations, Office of Presidential Personnel, Office of Public Engagement and Intergovernmental Affairs, Office of Scheduling and Advance, Office of the Staff Secretary, and Office of the White House Counsel.

The Obama Administration

As of Aug. 2014; mailing addresses are for Washington, DC, except where otherwise noted.
Terms of office of the president and vice president: Jan. 20, 2013, to Jan. 20, 2017.

President: By law, Pres. Barack H. Obama received an annual salary of $400,000 (taxable) and an annual expense allowance of $50,000 (nontaxable) for costs resulting from official duties. This does not include amounts available for expenditures within the Executive Office of the President, including $3,850,000 for necessary expenses for the White House, up to $100,000 a year for travel expenses, and up to $19,000 for official entertainment.
Website: www.whitehouse.gov/administration/president-obama

Vice President: By law, Vice Pres. Joseph R. Biden received an annual salary of $233,000 (taxable) and an annual expense allowance of $20,000 for costs resulting from official duties, plus $90,000 for official entertainment expenses (nontaxable).
Website: www.whitehouse.gov/administration/vice-president-biden

Cabinet Department Heads

(Salary: $201,700 per year)

Secretary of State: John Kerry
Secretary of the Treasury: Jack Lew
Secretary of Defense: Chuck Hagel
Attorney General (Dept. of Justice): Eric H. Holder Jr.
Secretary of the Interior: Sally Jewell
Secretary of Agriculture: Thomas J. Vilsack
Secretary of Commerce: Penny Pritzker
Secretary of Labor: Thomas E. Perez
Secretary of Health and Human Services: Sylvia Mathews Burwell
Secretary of Housing and Urban Development: Julián Castro
Secretary of Transportation: Anthony Foxx
Secretary of Energy: Ernest Moniz
Secretary of Education: Arne Duncan
Secretary of Veterans Affairs: Robert A. McDonald
Secretary of Homeland Security: Jeh Johnson

Executive Agencies

Council of Economic Advisers: Jason Furman, chair; www.whitehouse.gov/administration/eop/cea/
Council on Environmental Quality: Mike Boots, act. chair; www.whitehouse.gov/administration/eop/ceq/
Office of Administration: Beth Jones, dir.; www.whitehouse.gov/administration/eop/oa/
Office of Management and Budget: Shaun L. S. Donovan, dir.; www.whitehouse.gov/omb/
Office of Natl. Drug Control Policy: Michael Botticelli, act. dir.; www.whitehouse.gov/ondcp/
Office of Science and Technology Policy: John Holdren, dir.; www.whitehouse.gov/administration/eop/ostp/
Office of the U.S. Trade Representative: Amb. Michael Froman; www.ustr.gov

White House Staff

1600 Pennsylvania Ave. NW, 20500;
www.whitehouse.gov

Counselor to the President: John D. Podesta
Physician to the President: Ronny Jackson
Director, National Intelligence: James R. Clapper
Assistants to the President:
Chief of Staff: Denis McDonough
Deputy Chief of Staff for Implementation: Kristie A. Canegallo
Deputy Chief of Staff for Operations: Anita J. Breckenridge
Deputy Chief of Staff for Policy: Robert L. Nabors II
Cabinet Secretary: Broderick D. Johnson
Counsel to the President: Warren N. Eggleston
White House Press Secretary: Joshua R. Earnest
National Security Advisor: Susan Rice
Deputy National Security Advisors: Antony J. Blinken, Benjamin J. Rhodes
Director of Communications: Jennifer M. Palmieri
Director of the Domestic Policy Council: Cecilia Muñoz
Economic Policy and Director of the National Economic Council: Jeffrey D. Zients
Homeland Security and Counterterrorism: Lisa O. Monaco
Director of Legislative Affairs: Katherine B. Fallon
Director of Political Strategy and Outreach: David M. Simas
Director of Speechwriting: Cody S. Keenan
Director of Scheduling and Advance: Danielle M. White
Management and Administration: Katy A. Kale
Senior Advisors: Valerie B. Jarrett, Dan Pfeiffer
Chief of Staff to the Vice President: Steve Ricchetti
White House Social Secretary: Jeremy M. Bernard
Chief of Staff to the First Lady: Christina M. Tchen
Senior Adviser to the First Lady: Melissa E. Winter

The U.S. Cabinet

The heads of major executive departments of the federal government constitute the Cabinet. This institution, not provided for in the U.S. Constitution, developed as an advisory body out of the desire of presidents to consult on policy matters. Aside from its advisory role, the Cabinet as a body has no formal function and wields no executive authority. Individual members exercise authority as heads of their departments, reporting to the president. The Cabinet meets at times set by the president. In addition, the Cabinet commonly includes other officials designated by the president as being of Cabinet rank.

The officials so designated by Pres. Barack Obama include Vice Pres. Joseph R. Biden, White House Chief of Staff Denis McDonough, Environmental Protection Agency Administrator Gina McCarthy, Office of Management and Budget Director Shaun L. S. Donovan, U.S. Trade Representative Ambassador Michael Froman, U.S. Ambassador to the United Nations Samantha Power, Council of Economic Advisers Chair Jason Furman, and Small Business Administration Administrator Maria Contreras-Sweet.

Department of State

2201 C St. NW, 20520; www.state.gov

The Dept. of Foreign Affairs was created by act of Congress on July 27, 1789, and the name changed to Dept. of State on Sept. 15, 1789. Conducts U.S. foreign policy. The Foreign Service protects American citizens and interests through embassies in some 180 countries under eight geographic bureaus. Maintains contact with foreign governments, negotiates agreements and treaties, and supports U.S. foreign trade. Promotes democracy, international security, human rights—including issues related to AIDS, human trafficking, war crimes, and migration—and arms and narcotics control. Represents the nation in international organizations. Issues passports to U.S. citizens and visas to foreigners. **Budget:** $26.9 bil (2012); $25.9 bil (2013); $27.8 bil (est. 2014). Budget for other intl. programs: $20.0 bil (2012); $19.7 bil (2013); $20.4 bil (est. 2014).

- Intl. Boundary and Water Commission (4171 North Mesa, Ste. C-100, El Paso, TX 79902); www.ibwc.gov
- Intl. Information Programs (2201 C St. NW, SA-5, Rm. 5B17, 20520); www.state.gov/r/iip/
- Intl. Narcotics and Law Enforcement Affairs (2201 C St. NW, Rm. 7826 HST, 20520); www.state.gov/j/inl/
- Intl. Organization Affairs (2201 C St. NW, Rm. 6323, 20520); www.state.gov/p/io/
- Population, Refugees, and Migration (2201 C St. NW, Rm. 6825 HST, 20520); www.state.gov/j/prm/
- U.S. Global AIDS Coordinator (2201 C St. NW, SA-29, Ste. 200, 20520); www.state.gov/s/gac/

Secretaries of State

President	Secretary	Home	Sworn in
Washington	Thomas Jefferson	VA	1789
	Edmund J. Randolph	VA	1794
	Timothy Pickering	PA	1795
Adams, J.	Timothy Pickering	PA	1797
	John Marshall	VA	1800
Jefferson	James Madison	VA	1801
Madison	Robert Smith	MD	1809
	James Monroe	VA	1811
Monroe	John Quincy Adams	MA	1817
Adams, J. Q.	Henry Clay	KY	1825
Jackson	Martin Van Buren	NY	1829
	Edward Livingston	LA	1831
	Louis McLane	DE	1833
	John Forsyth	GA	1834
Van Buren	John Forsyth	GA	1837
Harrison, W. H.	Daniel Webster	MA	1841
Tyler	Daniel Webster	MA	1841
	Abel P. Upshur	VA	1843
	John C. Calhoun	SC	1844
Polk	John C. Calhoun	SC	1845
	James Buchanan	PA	1845
Taylor	James Buchanan	PA	1849
	John M. Clayton	DE	1849
Fillmore	John M. Clayton	DE	1850
	Daniel Webster	MA	1850
	Edward Everett	MA	1852
Pierce	William L. Marcy	NY	1853
Buchanan	William L. Marcy	NY	1857
	Lewis Cass	MI	1857
	Jeremiah S. Black	PA	1860
Lincoln	Jeremiah S. Black	PA	1861
	William H. Seward	NY	1861
Johnson, A.	William H. Seward	NY	1865
Grant	Elihu B. Washburne	IL	1869
	Hamilton Fish	NY	1869
Hayes	Hamilton Fish	NY	1877
	William M. Evarts	NY	1877
Garfield	William M. Evarts	NY	1881
	James G. Blaine	ME	1881
Arthur	James G. Blaine	ME	1881
	F. T. Frelinghuysen	NJ	1881
Cleveland	F. T. Frelinghuysen	NJ	1885
	Thomas F. Bayard	DE	1885
Harrison, B.	Thomas F. Bayard	DE	1889
	James G. Blaine	ME	1889
	John W. Foster	IN	1892
Cleveland	Walter Q. Gresham	IN	1893
	Richard Olney	MA	1895
McKinley	Richard Olney	MA	1897
	John Sherman	OH	1897
	William R. Day	OH	1898
	John M. Hay	DC	1898

President	Secretary	Home	Sworn in
Roosevelt, T.	John M. Hay	DC	1901
	Elihu Root	NY	1905
	Robert Bacon	NY	1909
Taft	Robert Bacon	NY	1909
	Philander C. Knox	PA	1909
Wilson	Philander C. Knox	PA	1913
	William J. Bryan	NE	1913
	Robert Lansing	NY	1915
	Bainbridge Colby	NY	1920
Harding	Charles E. Hughes	NY	1921
Coolidge	Charles E. Hughes	NY	1923
	Frank B. Kellogg	MN	1925
Hoover	Frank B. Kellogg	MN	1929
	Henry L. Stimson	NY	1929
Roosevelt, F. D.	Cordell Hull	TN	1933
	Edward R. Stettinius Jr.	VA	1944
Truman	Edward R. Stettinius Jr.	VA	1945
	James F. Byrnes	SC	1945
	George C. Marshall	PA	1947
	Dean G. Acheson	CT	1949
Eisenhower	John Foster Dulles	NY	1953
	Christian A. Herter	MA	1959
Kennedy	D. Dean Rusk	NY	1961
Johnson, L. B.	D. Dean Rusk	NY	1963
Nixon	William P. Rogers	NY	1969
	Henry A. Kissinger	DC	1973
Ford	Henry A. Kissinger	DC	1974
Carter	Cyrus R. Vance	NY	1977
	Edmund S. Muskie	ME	1980
Reagan	Alexander M. Haig Jr.	CT	1981
	George P. Shultz	CA	1982
Bush, G. H. W.	James A. Baker III	TX	1989
	Lawrence S. Eagleburger	MI	1992
Clinton	Warren M. Christopher	CA	1993
	Madeleine K. Albright	DC	1997
Bush, G. W.	Colin L. Powell	NY	2001
	Condoleezza Rice	AL	2005
Obama	Hillary Rodham Clinton	NY	2009
	John Kerry	MA	2013

Department of the Treasury

1500 Pennsylvania Ave. NW, 20220; www.treasury.gov

Organized by act of Congress on Sept. 2, 1789. Responsible for the fiscal affairs of the U.S. Serves as the government's financial agent; collects, borrows, and disburses funds for the federal government. Monitors the nation's financial infrastructure and economic development; recommends domestic and international financial, monetary, economic, trade, and tax policies. Manufactures currency and coins. Carries out monetary and tax law enforcement activities, sanctions, embargoes, and fights illicit finance—counterfeiting, money laundering, narcotics trafficking, terrorist financing. **Budget** (including interest on the public debt): $464.7 bil (2012); $399.1 bil (2013); $469.2 bil (est. 2014).

- Alcohol and Tobacco Tax and Trade Bureau (1310 G St. NW, Box 12, 20005); www.ttb.gov
- Bureau of Engraving and Printing (14th and C Sts. SW, 20228); www.moneyfactory.gov
- Bureau of the Fiscal Service (401 14th St. SW, 20227); www.fiscal.treasury.gov
- Financial Crimes Enforcement Network (P.O. Box 39, Vienna, VA 22183); www.fincen.gov
- Internal Revenue Service (1111 Constitution Ave. NW, 20224); www.irs.gov
- U.S. Mint (801 9th St. NW, 20220); www.usmint.gov

Secretaries of the Treasury

President	Secretary	Home	Sworn in
Washington	Alexander Hamilton	NY	1789
	Oliver Wolcott Jr.	CT	1795
Adams, J.	Oliver Wolcott Jr.	CT	1797
	Samuel Dexter	MA	1801
Jefferson	Samuel Dexter	MA	1801
	Albert Gallatin	PA	1801
Madison	Albert Gallatin	PA	1809
	George W. Campbell	TN	1814
	Alexander J. Dallas	PA	1814
	William H. Crawford	GA	1816
Monroe	William H. Crawford	GA	1817
Adams, J. Q.	Richard Rush	PA	1825

President	Secretary	Home	Sworn in
Jackson	Samuel D. Ingham	PA	1829
	Louis McLane	DE	1831
	William J. Duane	PA	1833
	Roger B. Taney	MD	1833
	Levi Woodbury	NH	1834
Van Buren	Levi Woodbury	NH	1837
Harrison, W. H.	Thomas Ewing	OH	1841
Tyler	Thomas Ewing	OH	1841
	Walter Forward	PA	1841
	John C. Spencer	NY	1843
	George M. Bibb	KY	1844
Polk	Robert J. Walker	MS	1845
Taylor	William M. Meredith	PA	1849
Fillmore	Thomas Corwin	OH	1850
Pierce	James Guthrie	KY	1853
Buchanan	Howell Cobb	GA	1857
	Phillip F. Thomas	MD	1860
	John A. Dix	NY	1861
Lincoln	Salmon P. Chase	OH	1861
	William P. Fessenden	ME	1864
	Hugh McCulloch	IN	1865
Johnson, A.	Hugh McCulloch	IN	1865
Grant	George S. Boutwell	MA	1869
	William A. Richardson	MA	1873
	Benjamin H. Bristow	KY	1874
	Lot M. Morrill	ME	1876
Hayes	John Sherman	OH	1877
Garfield	William Windom	MN	1881
Arthur	Charles J. Folger	NY	1881
	Walter Q. Gresham	IN	1884
	Hugh McCulloch	IN	1884
Cleveland	Daniel Manning	NY	1885
	Charles S. Fairchild	NY	1887
Harrison, B.	William Windom	MN	1889
	Charles Foster	OH	1891
Cleveland	John G. Carlisle	KY	1893
McKinley	Lyman J. Gage	IL	1897
Roosevelt, T.	Lyman J. Gage	IL	1901
	Leslie M. Shaw	IA	1902
	George B. Cortelyou	NY	1907
Taft	Franklin MacVeagh	IL	1909
Wilson	William G. McAdoo	NY	1913
	Carter Glass	VA	1918
	David F. Houston	MO	1920
Harding	Andrew W. Mellon	PA	1921
Coolidge	Andrew W. Mellon	PA	1923
Hoover	Andrew W. Mellon	PA	1929
	Ogden L. Mills	NY	1932
Roosevelt, F. D.	William H. Woodin	NY	1933
	Henry Morgenthau Jr.	NY	1934
Truman	Fred M. Vinson	KY	1945
	John W. Snyder	MO	1946
Eisenhower	George M. Humphrey	OH	1953
	Robert B. Anderson	CT	1957
Kennedy	C. Douglas Dillon	NJ	1961
Johnson, L. B.	C. Douglas Dillon	NJ	1963
	Henry H. Fowler	VA	1965
	Joseph W. Barr	IN	1968
Nixon	David M. Kennedy	IL	1969
	John B. Connally	TX	1971
	George P. Shultz	IL	1972
	William E. Simon	NJ	1974
Ford	William E. Simon	NJ	1974
Carter	W. Michael Blumenthal	MI	1977
	G. William Miller	RI	1979
Reagan	Donald T. Regan	CA	1981
	James A. Baker III	TX	1985
	Nicholas F. Brady	NJ	1988
Bush, G. H. W.	Nicholas F. Brady	NJ	1989
Clinton	Lloyd M. Bentsen	TX	1993
	Robert E. Rubin	NY	1995
	Lawrence H. Summers	CT	1999
Bush, G. W.	Paul H. O'Neill	MO	2001
	John W. Snow	OH	2003
	Henry M. Paulson Jr.	FL	2006
Obama	Timothy F. Geithner	NY	2009
	Jack Lew	NY	2013

Department of Defense

1400 Defense Pentagon, 20301; www.defense.gov

The Dept. of Defense, originally designated the National Military Establishment, was created on Sept. 18, 1947. Directs and controls the armed forces and assists the president in protecting the nation's security. Military departments of the Army, Navy, and Air Force are each separately organized under its own secretary but all function under the command of the secretary of defense. They conduct military operations as unified commands. The chairman of the Joint Chiefs of Staff is the principal military adviser to the president. Undersecretaries supervise acquisition, technology, and logistics; intelligence; personnel and readiness; and policy. **Budget** for military programs: $650.9 bil (2012); $607.8 bil (2013); $593.3 bil (est. 2014). **Budget** for civil programs: $85.1 bil (2012); $63.1 bil (2013); $65.0 bil (est. 2014).

- Def. Advanced Research Projects Agency (675 N. Randolph St., Arlington, VA 22203); www.darpa.mil
- Def. Intelligence Agency (200 MacDill Blvd., 20340); www.dia.mil
- Def. Security Cooperation Agency (2800 Defense Pentagon, 20301); www.dsca.mil
- Missile Def. Agency (5700 18th St., Bldg. 245, Fort Belvoir, VA 22060-5573); www.mda.mil
- Natl. Geospatial-Intelligence Agency (7500 GEOINT Dr., Springfield, VA 22150); www.nga.mil
- Natl. Security Agency/Central Security Service (9800 Savage Rd., Ft. Meade, MD 20755); www.nsa.gov

Secretaries of Defense

President	Secretary	Home	Sworn in
Truman	James V. Forrestal	NY	1947
	Louis A. Johnson	WV	1949
	George C. Marshall	PA	1950
	Robert A. Lovett	NY	1951
Eisenhower	Charles E. Wilson	MI	1953
	Neil H. McElroy	OH	1957
	Thomas S. Gates Jr.	PA	1959
Kennedy	Robert S. McNamara	MI	1961
Johnson, L. B.	Robert S. McNamara	MI	1963
	Clark M. Clifford	MD	1968
Nixon	Melvin R. Laird	WI	1969
	Elliot L. Richardson	MA	1973
	James R. Schlesinger	VA	1973
Ford	James R. Schlesinger	VA	1974
	Donald H. Rumsfeld	IL	1975
Carter	Harold Brown	CA	1977
Reagan	Caspar W. Weinberger	CA	1981
	Frank C. Carlucci	PA	1987
Bush, G. H. W.	Richard B. Cheney	WY	1989
Clinton	Les Aspin	WI	1993
	William J. Perry	CA	1994
	William S. Cohen	ME	1997
Bush, G. W.	Donald H. Rumsfeld	IL	2001
	Robert M. Gates	TX	2006
Obama	Robert M. Gates	TX	2009
	Leon E. Panetta	CA	2011
	Chuck Hagel	NE	2013

Secretaries of War

The War Dept. (which included jurisdiction over the Navy until 1798) was created by act of Congress on Aug. 7, 1789.

President	Secretary	Home	Sworn in
Washington	Henry Knox	MA	1789
	Timothy Pickering	PA	1795
	James McHenry	MD	1796
Adams, J.	James McHenry	MD	1797
	Samuel Dexter	MA	1800
Jefferson	Henry Dearborn	MA	1801
Madison	William Eustis	MA	1809
	John Armstrong	NY	1813
	James Monroe	VA	1814
	William H. Crawford	GA	1815
Monroe	John C. Calhoun	SC	1817
Adams, J. Q.	James Barbour	VA	1825
	Peter B. Porter	NY	1828
Jackson	John H. Eaton	TN	1829
	Lewis Cass	MI	1831
	Benjamin F. Butler	NY	1837
Van Buren	Joel R. Poinsett	SC	1837
Harrison, W. H.	John Bell	TN	1841
Tyler	John Bell	TN	1841
	John C. Spencer	NY	1841
	James M. Porter	PA	1843
	William Wilkins	PA	1844
Polk	William L. Marcy	NY	1845
Taylor	George W. Crawford	GA	1849
Fillmore	Charles M. Conrad	LA	1850
Pierce	Jefferson Davis	MS	1853

President	Secretary	Home	Sworn in
Buchanan	John B. Floyd	VA	1857
	Joseph Holt	KY	1861
Lincoln	Simon Cameron	PA	1861
	Edwin M. Stanton	PA	1862
Johnson, A.	Edwin M. Stanton	PA	1865
	John M. Schofield	IL	1868
Grant	John A. Rawlins	IL	1869
	William T. Sherman	OH	1869
	William W. Belknap	IA	1869
	Alphonso Taft	OH	1876
	James D. Cameron	PA	1876
Hayes	George W. McCrary	IA	1877
	Alexander Ramsey	MN	1879
Garfield	Robert T. Lincoln	IL	1881
Arthur	Robert T. Lincoln	IL	1881
Cleveland	William C. Endicott	MA	1885
Harrison, B.	Redfield Proctor	VT	1889
	Stephen B. Elkins	WV	1891
Cleveland	Daniel S. Lamont	NY	1893
McKinley	Russell A. Alger	MI	1897
	Elihu Root	NY	1899
Roosevelt, T.	Elihu Root	NY	1901
	William H. Taft	OH	1904
	Luke E. Wright	TN	1908
Taft	Jacob M. Dickinson	TN	1909
	Henry L. Stimson	NY	1911
Wilson	Lindley M. Garrison	NJ	1913
	Newton D. Baker	OH	1916
Harding	John W. Weeks	MA	1921
Coolidge	John W. Weeks	MA	1923
	Dwight F. Davis	MO	1925
Hoover	James W. Good	IL	1929
	Patrick J. Hurley	OK	1929
Roosevelt, F. D.	George H. Dern	UT	1933
	Harry H. Woodring	KS	1937
	Henry L. Stimson	NY	1940
Truman	Robert P. Patterson	NY	1945
	Kenneth C. Royall[1]	NC	1947

(1) Last member of Cabinet with this title. The War Dept. became the Dept. of the Army with the creation of the Defense Dept. in 1947, though the Army secretary maintained Cabinet-level status until 1949.

Secretaries of the Navy

The Navy Dept. was created by act of Congress on Apr. 30, 1798. The Marine Corps is part of this department.

President	Secretary	Home	Sworn in
Adams, J.	Benjamin Stoddert	MD	1798
Jefferson	Benjamin Stoddert	MD	1801
	Robert Smith	MD	1801
Madison	Paul Hamilton	SC	1809
	William Jones	PA	1813
	Benjamin W. Crowninshield	MA	1814
Monroe	Benjamin W. Crowninshield	MA	1817
	Smith Thompson	NY	1818
	Samuel L. Southard	NJ	1823
Adams, J. Q.	Samuel L. Southard	NJ	1825
Jackson	John Branch	NC	1829
	Levi Woodbury	NH	1831
	Mahlon Dickerson	NJ	1834
Van Buren	Mahlon Dickerson	NJ	1837
	James K. Paulding	NY	1838
Harrison, W. H.	George E. Badger	NC	1841
Tyler	George E. Badger	NC	1841
	Abel P. Upshur	VA	1841
	David Henshaw	MA	1843
	Thomas W. Gilmer	VA	1844
	John Y. Mason	VA	1844
Polk	George Bancroft	MA	1845
	John Y. Mason	VA	1846
Taylor	William B. Preston	VA	1849
Fillmore	William A. Graham	NC	1850
	John P. Kennedy	MD	1852
Pierce	James C. Dobbin	NC	1853
Buchanan	Isaac Toucey	CT	1857
Lincoln	Gideon Welles	CT	1861
Johnson, A.	Gideon Welles	CT	1865
Grant	Adolph E. Borie	PA	1869
	George M. Robeson	NJ	1869

President	Secretary	Home	Sworn in
Hayes	Richard W. Thompson	IN	1877
	Nathan Goff Jr.	WV	1881
Garfield	William H. Hunt	LA	1881
Arthur	William E. Chandler	NH	1882
Cleveland	William C. Whitney	NY	1885
Harrison, B.	Benjamin F. Tracy	NY	1889
Cleveland	Hilary A. Herbert	AL	1893
McKinley	John D. Long	MA	1897
Roosevelt, T.	John D. Long	MA	1901
	William H. Moody	MA	1902
	Paul Morton	IL	1904
	Charles J. Bonaparte	MD	1905
	Victor H. Metcalf	CA	1906
	Truman H. Newberry	MI	1908
Taft	George von L. Meyer	MA	1909
Wilson	Josephus Daniels	NC	1913
Harding	Edwin Denby	MI	1921
Coolidge	Edwin Denby	MI	1923
	Curtis D. Wilbur	CA	1924
Hoover	Charles Francis Adams	MA	1929
Roosevelt, F. D.	Claude A. Swanson	VA	1933
	Charles Edison	NJ	1940
	Frank Knox	IL	1940
	James V. Forrestal	NY	1944
Truman	James V. Forrestal[1]	NY	1945

(1) Last member of Cabinet with this title. The Navy Dept. became a branch of the Dept. of Defense when the latter was created in 1947, though the Navy secretary maintained Cabinet-level status until 1949.

Department of Justice

950 Pennsylvania Ave. NW, 20530; www.justice.gov

The Office of Attorney General was established by act of Congress on Sept. 24, 1789. It officially reached Cabinet rank in Mar. 1792, when the first attorney general, Edmund Randolph, attended his initial Cabinet meeting. The Dept. of Justice, headed by the attorney general, was created June 22, 1870. Provides for the enforcement of federal laws and investigation of violations; furnishes legal counsel in cases involving the federal government and interprets laws relating to the activities of other federal departments; supervises federal penal institutions. The attorney general and Office of Legal Counsel render legal advice, upon request, to the president and department heads. The solicitor general conducts all suits brought before the U.S. Supreme Court in which the federal government is concerned. The Civil Division represents the U.S. government in many civil or criminal matters. The 94 U.S. attorneys are the principal litigators in the U.S. and its territories. **Budget:** $31.2 bil (2012); $29.7 bil (2013); $28.7 bil (est. 2014).

- Bureau of Alcohol, Tobacco, Firearms, and Explosives (99 New York Ave. NE, Rm. 5S 144, 20226); www.atf.gov
- Bureau of Prisons (320 First St. NW, 20534); www.bop.gov
- Drug Enforcement Admin. (8701 Morrissette Dr., Springfield, VA 22152); www.justice.gov/dea
- Executive Office for Immigration Review (5107 Leesburg Pike, Falls Church, VA 20530); www.justice.gov/eoir/
- Federal Bureau of Investigation (935 Pennsylvania Ave. NW, 20535); www.fbi.gov
- INTERPOL Washington (U.S. Natl. Central Bureau) (20530); www.justice.gov/interpol-washington/
- U.S. Marshals Service (2604 Jefferson Davis Hwy., Alexandria, VA 22301-1025); www.usmarshals.gov
- U.S. Parole Commission (90 K St. NE, 3rd Fl., 20530); www.justice.gov/uspc/

Attorneys General

President	Attorney General	Home	Sworn in
Washington	Edmund J. Randolph	VA	1789
	William Bradford	PA	1794
	Charles Lee	VA	1795
Adams, J.	Charles Lee	VA	1797
Jefferson	Levi Lincoln	MA	1801
	John Breckenridge	KY	1805
	Caesar A. Rodney	DE	1807
Madison	Caesar A. Rodney	DE	1807
	William Pinkney	MD	1811
	Richard Rush	PA	1814
Monroe	Richard Rush	PA	1817
	William Wirt	VA	1817
Adams, J. Q.	William Wirt	VA	1825

President	Attorney General	Home	Sworn in
Jackson	John M. Berrien	GA	1829
	Roger B. Taney	MD	1831
	Benjamin F. Butler	NY	1833
Van Buren	Benjamin F. Butler	NY	1837
	Felix Grundy	TN	1838
	Henry D. Gilpin	PA	1840
Harrison, W. H.	John J. Crittenden	KY	1841
Tyler	John J. Crittenden	KY	1841
	Hugh S. Legaré	SC	1841
	John Nelson	MD	1843
Polk	John Y. Mason	VA	1845
	Nathan Clifford	ME	1846
	Isaac Toucey	CT	1848
Taylor	Reverdy Johnson	MD	1849
Fillmore	John J. Crittenden	KY	1850
Pierce	Caleb Cushing	MA	1853
Buchanan	Jeremiah S. Black	PA	1857
	Edwin M. Stanton	PA	1860
Lincoln	Edward Bates	MO	1861
	James Speed	KY	1864
Johnson, A.	James Speed	KY	1865
	Henry Stanbery	OH	1866
	William M. Evarts	NY	1868
Grant	Ebenezer R. Hoar	MA	1869
	Amos T. Akerman	GA	1870
	George H. Williams	OR	1871
	Edwards Pierrepont	NY	1875
	Alphonso Taft	OH	1876
Hayes	Charles Devens	MA	1877
Garfield	I. Wayne MacVeagh	PA	1881
Arthur	Benjamin H. Brewster	PA	1882
Cleveland	Augustus H. Garland	AR	1885
Harrison, B.	William H. H. Miller	IN	1889
Cleveland	Richard Olney	MA	1893
	Judson Harmon	OH	1895
McKinley	Joseph McKenna	CA	1897
	John W. Griggs	NJ	1898
	Philander C. Knox	PA	1901
Roosevelt, T.	Philander C. Knox	PA	1901
	William H. Moody	MA	1904
	Charles J. Bonaparte	MD	1906
Taft	George W. Wickersham	NY	1909
Wilson	James C. McReynolds	TN	1913
	Thomas W. Gregory	TX	1914
	A. Mitchell Palmer	PA	1919
Harding	Harry M. Daugherty	OH	1921
Coolidge	Harry M. Daugherty	OH	1923
	Harlan F. Stone	NY	1924
	John G. Sargent	VT	1925
Hoover	William D. Mitchell	MN	1929
Roosevelt, F. D.	Homer S. Cummings	CT	1933
	Frank Murphy	MI	1939
	Robert H. Jackson	NY	1940
	Francis Biddle	PA	1941
Truman	Thomas C. Clark	TX	1945
	J. Howard McGrath	RI	1949
	James P. McGranery	PA	1952
Eisenhower	Herbert Brownell Jr.	NY	1953
	William P. Rogers	MD	1957
Kennedy	Robert F. Kennedy	MA	1961
Johnson, L. B.	Robert F. Kennedy	MA	1963
	Nicholas Katzenbach	IL	1964
	W. Ramsey Clark	TX	1967
Nixon	John N. Mitchell	NY	1969
	Richard G. Kleindienst	AZ	1972
	Elliot L. Richardson	MA	1973
	William B. Saxbe	OH	1974
Ford	William B. Saxbe	OH	1974
	Edward H. Levi	IL	1975
Carter	Griffin B. Bell	GA	1977
	Benjamin R. Civiletti	MD	1979
Reagan	William French Smith	CA	1981
	Edwin Meese III	CA	1985
	Richard L. Thornburgh	PA	1988
Bush, G. H. W.	Richard L. Thornburgh	PA	1989
	William P. Barr	NY	1991
Clinton	Janet Reno	FL	1993
Bush, G. W.	John Ashcroft	MO	2001
	Alberto R. Gonzales	TX	2005
	Michael B. Mukasey	NY	2007
Obama	Eric H. Holder Jr.	DC	2009

Department of the Interior

1849 C St. NW, 20240; www.doi.gov

Created by act of Congress on Mar. 3, 1849. Custodian of natural resources. Has the responsibility of protecting and conserving the country's land, water, minerals, fish, and wildlife; of promoting the wise use of all these natural resources; of maintaining national parks and recreation areas; and of preserving historic places. It also provides for the welfare of American Indian reservation communities and of inhabitants of island territories under U.S. administration. **Budget:** $12.9 bil (2012); $9.6 bil (2013); $12.8 bil (est. 2014).

- Bureau of Indian Affairs (MS-3658-MIB, 1849 C St. NW, 20240); www.bia.gov
- Bureau of Land Management (1849 C St. NW, 20240); www.blm.gov
- Bureau of Ocean Energy Management (1849 C St. NW, 20240); www.boem.gov
- Bureau of Reclamation (1849 C St. NW, 20240); www.usbr.gov
- Bureau of Safety and Environmental Enforcement (1849 C St. NW, 20240); www.bsee.gov
- National Park Service (1849 C St. NW, 20240); www.nps.gov
- Office of Surface Mining Reclamation and Enforcement (1951 Constitution Ave. NW, 20240); www.osmre.gov
- U.S. Fish and Wildlife Service (1849 C St. NW, 20240); www.fws.gov
- U.S. Geological Survey (12201 Sunrise Valley Dr., Reston, VA 20192); www.usgs.gov

Secretaries of the Interior

President	Secretary	Home	Sworn in
Taylor	Thomas Ewing	OH	1849
Fillmore	Thomas M. T. McKennan	PA	1850
	Alex H. H. Stuart	VA	1850
Pierce	Robert McClelland	MI	1853
Buchanan	Jacob Thompson	MS	1857
Lincoln	Caleb B. Smith	IN	1861
	John P. Usher	IN	1863
Johnson, A.	John P. Usher	IN	1865
	James Harlan	IA	1865
	Orville H. Browning	IL	1866
Grant	Jacob D. Cox	OH	1869
	Columbus Delano	OH	1870
	Zachariah Chandler	MI	1875
Hayes	Carl Schurz	MO	1877
Garfield	Samuel J. Kirkwood	IA	1881
Arthur	Henry M. Teller	CO	1882
Cleveland	Lucius Q. C. Lamar	MS	1885
	William F. Vilas	WI	1888
Harrison, B.	John W. Noble	MO	1889
Cleveland	M. Hoke Smith	GA	1893
	David R. Francis	MO	1896
McKinley	Cornelius N. Bliss	NY	1897
	Ethan A. Hitchcock	MO	1898
Roosevelt, T.	Ethan A. Hitchcock	MO	1901
	James R. Garfield	OH	1907
Taft	Richard A. Ballinger	WA	1909
	Walter L. Fisher	IL	1911
Wilson	Franklin K. Lane	CA	1913
	John B. Payne	IL	1920
Harding	Albert B. Fall	NM	1921
	Hubert Work	CO	1923
Coolidge	Hubert Work	CO	1923
	Roy O. West	IL	1929
Hoover	Ray Lyman Wilbur	CA	1929
Roosevelt, F. D.	Harold L. Ickes	IL	1933
Truman	Harold L. Ickes	IL	1945
	Julius A. Krug	WI	1946
	Oscar L. Chapman	CO	1949
Eisenhower	Douglas McKay	OR	1953
	Fred A. Seaton	NE	1956
Kennedy	Stewart L. Udall	AZ	1961
Johnson, L. B.	Stewart L. Udall	AZ	1963
Nixon	Walter J. Hickel	AK	1969
	Rogers C. B. Morton	MD	1971
Ford	Rogers C. B. Morton	MD	1971
	Stanley K. Hathaway	WY	1975
	Thomas S. Kleppe	ND	1975
Carter	Cecil D. Andrus	ID	1977
Reagan	James G. Watt	CO	1981
	William P. Clark	CA	1983
	Donald P. Hodel	OR	1985
Bush, G. H. W.	Manuel Lujan	NM	1989
Clinton	Bruce Babbitt	AZ	1993
Bush, G. W.	Gale Norton	CO	2001
	Dirk Kempthorne	ID	2006
Obama	Kenneth L. Salazar	CO	2009
	Sally Jewell	WA	2013

Department of Agriculture

1400 Independence Ave. SW, 20250; www.usda.gov

Created by act of Congress on May 15, 1862. On Feb. 8, 1889, s commissioner was renamed secretary of agriculture and became a member of the Cabinet. Provides leadership on food, agriculture, and natural resources; supports scientific research and education for agriculture, nutrition, and food safety. Develops nutrition assistance programs, promotes healthy eating, supplies food stamps, grades and inspects the commercial safety of food. Responsible for the health of the land through sustainable management and conservation, manages public lands in national forests and grasslands; safeguards against invasive pests and diseases; ensures the health and care of animals and plants. Oversees assistance and conservation programs for farmers and ranchers and programs to improve the rural economy and quality of life. Facilitates domestic and international marketing of U.S. agricultural products. **Budget:** $139.7 bil (2012); $155.9 bil 2013); $149.2 bil (est. 2014).

- Agricultural Research Service (1400 Independence Ave. SW, 20250); www.ars.usda.gov
- Economic Research Service (1400 Independence Ave. SW, Mail Stop 1800, 20250); www.ers.usda.gov
- Food and Nutrition Service (3101 Park Center Dr., Alexandria, VA 22302); www.fns.usda.gov
- Food Safety and Inspection Service (1400 Independence Ave. SW, 20250); www.fsis.usda.gov
- Foreign Agricultural Service (1400 Independence Ave. SW, Mail Stop 1001, 20250); www.fas.usda.gov
- Forest Service (1400 Independence Ave. SW, 20250); www.fs.fed.us
- Natl. Agricultural Statistics Service (1400 Independence Ave. SW, 20250); www.nass.usda.gov
- Natural Resources Conservation Service (1400 Independence Ave. SW, 20250); www.nrcs.usda.gov

Secretaries of Agriculture

President	Secretary	Home	Sworn in
Cleveland	Norman J. Colman	MO	1889
Harrison, B.	Jeremiah M. Rusk	WI	1889
Cleveland	J. Sterling Morton	NE	1893
McKinley	James Wilson	IA	1897
Roosevelt, T.	James Wilson	IA	1901
Taft	James Wilson	IA	1909
Wilson	David F. Houston	MO	1913
	Edwin T. Meredith	IA	1920
Harding	Henry C. Wallace	IA	1921
Coolidge	Henry C. Wallace	IA	1923
	Howard M. Gore	WV	1924
	William M. Jardine	KS	1925
Hoover	Arthur M. Hyde	MO	1929
Roosevelt, F. D.	Henry A. Wallace	IA	1933
	Claude R. Wickard	IN	1940
Truman	Clinton P. Anderson	NM	1945
	Charles F. Brannan	CO	1948
Eisenhower	Ezra Taft Benson	UT	1953
Kennedy	Orville L. Freeman	MN	1961
Johnson, L. B.	Orville L. Freeman	MN	1963
Nixon	Clifford M. Hardin	IN	1969
	Earl L. Butz	IN	1971
Ford	Earl L. Butz	IN	1974
	John A. Knebel	VA	1976
Carter	Bob Bergland	MN	1977
Reagan	John R. Block	IL	1981
	Richard E. Lyng	CA	1986
Bush, G. H. W.	Clayton K. Yeutter	NE	1989
	Edward Madigan	IL	1991
Clinton	Mike Espy	MS	1993
	Dan Glickman	KS	1995
Bush, G. W.	Ann M. Veneman	CA	2001
	Mike Johanns	NE	2005
	Ed Schafer	ND	2008
Obama	Thomas J. Vilsack	IA	2009

Department of Commerce

1401 Constitution Ave. NW, 20230; www.commerce.gov

The Dept. of Commerce was formed by Congress Mar. 4, 1913, when it divided the Dept. of Commerce and Labor into two departments. Fosters, serves, and promotes the nation's economic development and technological advancement; supports the comprehension and use of the environment and its oceanic life; assists states, communities, and individuals with economic progress; promotes trade abroad and ensures an effective export control and treaty compliance system. Issues trademarks and patents, maintains measurement standards, and manages the federal telecommunications spectrum. Collects, analyzes, and distributes statistics regarding the nation and the economy through the Bureaus of the Census and of Economic Analysis. NOAA explores, monitors, and conserves oceans and coasts, tracks weather and other environmental data. **Budget:** $10.3 bil (2012); $9.1 bil (2013); $8.2 bil (est. 2014).

- Bureau of the Census (4600 Silver Hill Rd., 20233); www.census.gov
- Bureau of Economic Analysis (1441 L St. NW, 20230); www.bea.gov
- Minority Business Development Agency (1401 Constitution Ave. NW, 20230); www.mbda.gov
- Natl. Institute of Standards and Technology (100 Bureau Dr., Stop 1070, Gaithersburg, MD 20899); www.nist.gov
- Natl. Oceanic and Atmospheric Admin. (1401 Constitution Ave. NW, Rm. 5128, 20230); www.noaa.gov
- Natl. Technical Information Service (5301 Shawnee Rd., Alexandria, VA 22312); www.ntis.gov
- Natl. Telecommunications and Information Admin. (1401 Constitution Ave. NW, 20230); www.ntia.doc.gov

Secretaries of Commerce

President	Secretary	Home	Sworn in
Wilson	William C. Redfield	NY	1913
	Joshua W. Alexander	MO	1919
Harding	Herbert C. Hoover	CA	1921
Coolidge	Herbert C. Hoover	CA	1923
	William F. Whiting	MA	1928
Hoover	Robert P. Lamont	IL	1929
	Roy D. Chapin	MI	1932
Roosevelt, F. D.	Daniel C. Roper	SC	1933
	Harry L. Hopkins	NY	1939
	Jesse H. Jones	TX	1940
	Henry A. Wallace	IA	1945
Truman	Henry A. Wallace	IA	1945
	W. Averell Harriman	NY	1947
	Charles W. Sawyer	OH	1948
Eisenhower	Sinclair Weeks	MA	1953
	Lewis L. Strauss	NY	1958
	Frederick H. Mueller	MI	1959
Kennedy	Luther H. Hodges	NC	1961
Johnson, L. B.	Luther H. Hodges	NC	1963
	John T. Connor	NJ	1965
	Alex B. Trowbridge	NJ	1967
	Cyrus R. Smith	NY	1968
Nixon	Maurice H. Stans	MN	1969
	Peter G. Peterson	IL	1972
	Frederick B. Dent	SC	1973
Ford	Frederick B. Dent	SC	1974
	Rogers C. B. Morton	MD	1975
	Elliot L. Richardson	MA	1975
Carter	Juanita M. Kreps	NC	1977
	Philip M. Klutznick	IL	1979
Reagan	Malcolm Baldrige	CT	1981
	C. William Verity Jr.	OH	1987
Bush, G. H. W.	Robert A. Mosbacher	TX	1989
	Barbara H. Franklin	PA	1992
Clinton	Ronald H. Brown	DC	1993
	Mickey Kantor	CA	1996
	William M. Daley	IL	1997
	Norman Y. Mineta	CA	2000
Bush, G. W.	Donald L. Evans	TX	2001
	Carlos M. Gutierrez	MI	2005
Obama	Gary F. Locke	WA	2009
	John Bryson	CA	2011
	Penny Pritzker	IL	2013

Secretaries of Commerce and Labor

The Dept. of Commerce and Labor was created by Congress on Feb. 14, 1903.

President	Secretary	Home	Sworn in
Roosevelt, T.	George B. Cortelyou	NY	1903
	Victor H. Metcalf	CA	1904
	Oscar S. Straus	NY	1906
Taft	Charles Nagel	MO	1909

Department of Labor

200 Constitution Ave. NW, 20210; www.dol.gov

The Dept. of Labor was formed by Congress Mar. 4, 1913, when it divided the Dept. of Commerce and Labor into two departments. Administers federal labor laws to foster, promote, and develop the welfare of job seekers, wage earners, and retirees of the U.S.; to improve working conditions; and to advance opportunities for profitable employment. Administers standards for wages and overtime pay, safety and health conditions, workers' compensation. Tracks changes in employment, prices, and other national economic measurements. Regulates pension and welfare benefit plans, the hiring and employment of migrant and seasonal workers, and requirements pertaining to the mining, construction, and transportation industries. Monitors labor unions and their funds. **Budget:** $104.6 bil (2012); $80.3 bil (2013); $76.5 bil (est. 2014).

- Bureau of Labor Statistics (2 Massachusetts Ave. NE, 20212); www.bls.gov
- Employment and Training Admin. (200 Constitution Ave. NW, 20210); www.doleta.gov
- Mine Safety and Health Admin. (1100 Wilson Blvd., 21st Fl., Arlington, VA 22209); www.msha.gov
- Occupational Safety and Health Admin. (200 Constitution Ave. NW, 20210); www.osha.gov
- Office of Federal Contract Compliance Programs (200 Constitution Ave. NW, 20210); www.dol.gov/ofccp/
- Office of Labor-Management Standards (200 Constitution Ave. NW, 20210); www.dol.gov/olms/
- Office of Workers' Compensation Programs (200 Constitution Ave. NW, 20210); www.dol.gov/owcp/
- Wage and Hour Div. (200 Constitution Ave. NW, 20210); www.dol.gov/whd/

Secretaries of Labor

President	Secretary	Home	Sworn in
Wilson	William B. Wilson	PA	1913
Harding	James J. Davis	PA	1921
Coolidge	James J. Davis	PA	1923
Hoover	James J. Davis	PA	1929
	William N. Doak	VA	1930
Roosevelt, F. D.	Frances Perkins	NY	1933
Truman	L. B. Schwellenbach	WA	1945
	Maurice J. Tobin	MA	1949
Eisenhower	Martin P. Durkin	IL	1953
	James P. Mitchell	NJ	1953
Kennedy	Arthur J. Goldberg	IL	1961
	W. Willard Wirtz	IL	1962
Johnson, L. B.	W. Willard Wirtz	IL	1963
Nixon	George P. Shultz	IL	1969
	James D. Hodgson	CA	1970
	Peter J. Brennan	NY	1973
Ford	Peter J. Brennan	NY	1974
	John T. Dunlop	CA	1975
	W. J. Usery Jr.	GA	1976
Carter	F. Ray Marshall	TX	1977
Reagan	Raymond J. Donovan	NJ	1981
	William E. Brock	TN	1985
	Ann D. McLaughlin	DC	1987
Bush, G. H. W.	Elizabeth H. Dole	NC	1989
	Lynn Martin	IL	1991
Clinton	Robert B. Reich	MA	1993
	Alexis M. Herman	AL	1997
Bush, G. W.	Elaine L. Chao	KY	2001
Obama	Hilda L. Solis	CA	2009
	Thomas E. Perez	MD	2013

Department of Housing and Urban Development

451 7th St. SW, 20410; www.hud.gov

Created by act of Congress on Sept. 9, 1965. Responsible for housing needs and the improvement and development of urban areas. Supports affordable housing, provides grants for community development and redevelopment. Enforces fair and safe housing standards. Provides funds to assist homeless individuals and families with emergency and transitional shelters. The FHA provides mortgage insurance on loans made by approved lenders. **Budget:** $49.6 bil (2012); $56.6 bil (2013); $42.1 bil (est. 2014).

- Fannie Mae (Federal Natl. Mortgage Association) (3900 Wisconsin Ave. NW, 20016); www.fanniemae.com
- Federal Housing Admin. (451 7th St. SW, 20410); www.fha.gov
- Freddie Mac (Federal Home Loan Mortgage Corporation) (8200 Jones Branch Dr., McLean, VA 22102); www.freddiemac.com
- Ginnie Mae (Government Natl. Mortgage Association) (451 7th St. SW, Rm. B-133, 20410); www.ginniemae.gov

Note: Fannie Mae and Freddie Mac are government-sponsored enterprises (GSEs).

Secretaries of Housing and Urban Development

President	Secretary	Home	Sworn in
Johnson, L. B.	Robert C. Weaver	WA	1966
	Robert C. Wood	MA	1969
Nixon	George W. Romney	MI	1969
	James T. Lynn	OH	1973
Ford	James T. Lynn	OH	1974
	Carla Anderson Hills	CA	1975
Carter	Patricia Roberts Harris	DC	1977
	Moon Landrieu	LA	1979
Reagan	Samuel R. Pierce Jr.	NY	1981
Bush, G. H. W.	Jack F. Kemp	NY	1989
Clinton	Henry G. Cisneros	TX	1993
	Andrew M. Cuomo	NY	1997
Bush, G. W.	Mel Martinez	FL	2001
	Alphonso Jackson	TX	2004
	Steve Preston	VA	2008
Obama	Shaun L. S. Donovan	NY	2009
	Julián Castro	TX	2014

Department of Transportation

1200 New Jersey Ave. SE, 20590; www.dot.gov

Created by act of Congress on Oct. 15, 1966. Promotes and develops rapid, safe, efficient, and convenient transportation in the U.S.; monitors and administers assistance to transportation industries; negotiates and implements international transportation agreements. Manages airspace, commercial space transportation, and the movement of hazardous materials. Resolves railroad rate and service disputes and reviews proposed railroad mergers. Analyzes and shares research and statistics to develop and improve transportation through RITA. Develops and enforces regulations on the nation's pipeline transportation system. The Maritime Administration maintains a fleet of cargo ships in reserve for war or national emergencies and commissions officers of the merchant marines. Operates the U.S. portion of the St. Lawrence Seaway between Montréal and Lake Erie. **Budget:** $75.1 bil (2012); $76.3 bil (2013); $80.5 bil (est. 2014).

- Federal Aviation Admin. (800 Independence Ave. SW, 20591); www.faa.gov
- Federal Highway Admin. (1200 New Jersey Ave. SE, 20590); www.fhwa.dot.gov
- Federal Railroad Admin. (1200 New Jersey Ave. SE, 20590); www.fra.dot.gov
- Federal Transit Admin. (East Bldg., 1200 New Jersey Ave. SE, 20590); www.fta.dot.gov
- Maritime Admin. (1200 New Jersey Ave. SE, 20590); www.marad.dot.gov
- Natl. Highway Traffic Safety Admin. (West Bldg., 1200 New Jersey Ave. SE, 20590); www.nhtsa.gov
- Research and Innovative Technology Admin. (1200 New Jersey Ave. SE, 20590); www.rita.dot.gov

Secretaries of Transportation

President	Secretary	Home	Sworn in
Johnson, L. B.	Alan S. Boyd	FL	1966
Nixon	John A. Volpe	MA	1969
	Claude S. Brinegar	CA	1973
Ford	Claude S. Brinegar	CA	1974
	William T. Coleman Jr.	PA	1975
Carter	Brock Adams	WA	1977
	Neil E. Goldschmidt	OR	1979
Reagan	Andrew L. Lewis Jr.	PA	1981
	Elizabeth H. Dole	NC	1983
	James H. Burnley	NC	1987
Bush, G. H. W.	Samuel K. Skinner	IL	1989
	Andrew H. Card Jr.	MA	1992
Clinton	Federico F. Peña	CO	1993
	Rodney E. Slater	AR	1997
Bush, G. W.	Norman Y. Mineta	CA	2001
	Mary E. Peters	AZ	2006
Obama	Raymond L. LaHood	IL	2009
	Anthony Foxx	NC	2013

Department of Energy

1000 Independence Ave. SW, 20585; energy.gov

Created by federal law on Aug. 4, 1977. Secures the nation's energy and promotes scientific and technological innovation. Oversees the national energy supply and electric grid. Investigates and promotes clean and reliable energy. Manages and cleans up nuclear and other radioactive material, including nuclear weapons. The OSTI supports much of America's scientific research through program offices, education initiatives, national laboratories, and technology centers. Four power administrations sell hydroelectric power across the West and Southeast. **Budget:** $32.5 bil (2012); $24.7 bil (2013); $27.8 bil (est. 2014).

- Energy Information Admin. (1000 Independence Ave. SW, 20585); www.eia.gov
- Federal Energy Regulatory Commission (independent regulatory agency) (888 1st St. NE, 20426); www.ferc.gov
- Natl. Nuclear Security Admin. (1000 Independence Ave. SW, 20585); www.nnsa.energy.gov
- Office of Scientific and Technical Information (P.O. Box 62, Oak Ridge, TN 37831); www.osti.gov

Secretaries of Energy

President	Secretary	Home	Sworn in
Carter	James R. Schlesinger	VA	1977
	Charles W. Duncan Jr.	WY	1979
Reagan	James B. Edwards	SC	1981
	Donald P. Hodel	OR	1982
	John S. Herrington	CA	1985
Bush, G. H. W.	James D. Watkins	CA	1989
Clinton	Hazel R. O'Leary	MN	1993
	Federico F. Peña	CO	1997
	Bill Richardson	NM	1998
Bush, G. W.	Spencer Abraham	MI	2001
	Samuel W. Bodman	MA	2005
Obama	Steven Chu	CA	2009
	Ernest Moniz	MA	2013

Department of Health and Human Services

200 Independence Ave. SW, 20201; www.hhs.gov
The Dept. of Health, Education, and Welfare was created by Congress on Apr. 11, 1953. On Sept. 27, 1979, Congress approved creation of a separate Dept. of Education. The existing department was renamed the Dept. of Health and Human Services. Administers a wide range of programs in the fields of health care and social services that affect nearly all Americans. Medicare and Medicaid provide health care insurance for one in four Americans. The HRSA improves health care services for people who are uninsured, isolated, or medically vulnerable; also oversees organ, tissue, and blood cell donations. The FDA assures the safety of food, drugs, cosmetics, biological products, and medical devices. The CDC monitors and safeguards against disease outbreaks. The NIH supports research projects nationwide and 27 health institutes and centers. The surgeon general is the nation's chief health educator and leads the U.S. Public Health Service Commissioned Corps. **Budget:** $848.1 bil (2012); $886.3 bil (2013); $958.0 bil (est. 2014).

- Agency for Healthcare Research and Quality (540 Gaither Rd., Rockville, MD 20850); www.ahrq.gov
- Centers for Disease Control and Prevention (1600 Clifton Rd., Atlanta, GA 30333); www.cdc.gov
- Centers for Medicare and Medicaid Services (7500 Security Blvd., Baltimore, MD 21244); www.cms.gov
- Food and Drug Admin. (10903 New Hampshire Ave., Silver Spring, MD 20993); www.fda.gov
- Health Resources and Services Admin. (5600 Fishers Ln., Rockville, MD 20857); www.hrsa.gov
- Natl. Institutes of Health (9000 Rockville Pike, Bethesda, MD 20892); www.nih.gov
- Office of the Surgeon General (Tower Bldg., Plaza Level 1, Rm. 100, 1101 Wootton Pkwy., Rockville, MD 20852); www.surgeongeneral.gov

Secretaries of Health and Human Services

President	Secretary	Home	Sworn in
Carter	Patricia Roberts Harris	DC	1979
Reagan	Richard S. Schweiker	PA	1981
	Margaret M. Heckler	MA	1983
Reagan	Otis R. Bowen	IN	1985
Bush, G. H. W.	Louis W. Sullivan	GA	1989
Clinton	Donna E. Shalala	WI	1993
Bush, G. W.	Tommy Thompson	WI	2001
	Michael O. Leavitt	UT	2005
Obama	Kathleen Sebelius	KS	2009
	Sylvia Mathews Burwell	WV	2014

Secretaries of Health, Education, and Welfare

President	Secretary	Home	Sworn in
Eisenhower	Oveta Culp Hobby	TX	1953
	Marion B. Folsom	NY	1955
	Arthur S. Flemming	OH	1958
Kennedy	Abraham A. Ribicoff	CT	1961
	Anthony J. Celebrezze	OH	1962
Johnson, L. B.	Anthony J. Celebrezze	OH	1963
	John W. Gardner	NY	1965
	Wilbur J. Cohen	MI	1968
Nixon	Robert H. Finch	CA	1969
	Elliot L. Richardson	MA	1970
	Caspar W. Weinberger	CA	1973
Ford	Caspar W. Weinberger	CA	1974
	Forrest D. Mathews	AL	1975
Carter	Joseph A. Califano Jr.	DC	1977
	Patricia Roberts Harris	DC	1979

Department of Education

400 Maryland Ave. SW, 20202; www.ed.gov
The Dept. of Health, Education, and Welfare was created by Congress on Apr. 11, 1953. On Sept. 27, 1979, Congress approved creation of a separate Dept. of Education. Works with state agencies and local systems to ensure equal access to all levels of education and seeks to improve the quality of that education through federal support, research programs, and information sharing. Oversees a variety of financial aid distributed through competition, need-based requests, or a set formula. Sets policy goals and initiatives like No Child Left Behind. Conducts research and gathers educational information to disseminate to educators and the general public. **Budget:** $57.2 bil (2012); $40.9 bil (2013); $65.6 bil (est. 2014).

Secretaries of Education

President	Secretary	Home	Sworn in
Carter	Shirley Hufstedler	CA	1979
Reagan	Terrel H. Bell	UT	1981
	William J. Bennett	NY	1985
	Lauro F. Cavazos	TX	1988
Bush, G. H. W.	Lauro F. Cavazos	TX	1989
	Lamar Alexander	TN	1991
Clinton	Richard W. Riley	SC	1993
Bush, G. W.	Roderick R. Paige	TX	2001
	Margaret Spellings	TX	2005
Obama	Arne Duncan	IL	2009

Department of Veterans Affairs

810 Vermont Ave. NW, 20420; www.va.gov
Pres. Ronald Reagan signed a bill in 1988 granting Cabinet-level status to the Veterans Administration. The agency became the Dept. of Veterans Affairs on Mar. 15, 1989. Supports veterans and their families with nationwide programs for health care, financial assistance, and burial benefits. Compensates for disabilities incurred during wartime. Provides pensions for veterans with low incomes, education assistance, loan guaranty, and life insurance. Manages America's largest medical education and health professions training program which includes hospitals, clinics, nursing homes, veterans centers, rehabilitation treatment, readjustment counseling, and home-care programs. Also funds medical research pertaining to veterans issues. Manages 131 national cemeteries; provides headstones and markers. **Budget:** $124.1 bil (2012); $138.5 bil (2013); $150.7 bil (est. 2014).

Secretaries of Veterans Affairs

President	Secretary	Home	Sworn in
Bush, G. H. W.	Edward J. Derwinski	IL	1989
Clinton	Jesse Brown	IL	1993
	Togo D. West Jr.	NC	1998
Bush, G. W.	Anthony J. Principi	CA	2001
	R. James Nicholson	CO	2005
	James B. Peake	MO	2007
Obama	Eric K. Shinseki	VA	2009
	Robert A. McDonald	OH	2014

Department of Homeland Security

20528 (requires no street address); www.dhs.gov
Created by act of Congress on Nov. 25, 2002. Provides a unified core for the national network of organizations and institutions involved in efforts to secure the U.S., its borders, infrastructure, and major events. Provides funding, intelligence, and

training for law enforcement and disaster relief. Leads and coordinates response teams to natural and manmade emergencies. Identifies threats, administers the Natl. Terrorism Advisory System. **Budget:** $47.4 bil (2012); $57.2 bil (2013); $51.6 bil (est. 2014).

- Fed. Emergency Management Agency (500 C St. SW, 20472); www.fema.gov
- Immigration and Customs Enforcement (500 12th St. SW, 20536); www.ice.gov
- Transportation Security Admin. (601 S. 12th St., Arlington, VA 20598); www.tsa.gov
- U.S. Citizenship and Immigration Services (20 Massachusetts Ave. NW, 20529); www.uscis.gov
- U.S. Coast Guard (2100 2nd St. SW, 20593); www.uscg.mil

- U.S. Customs and Border Protection (1300 Pennsylvania Ave. NW, 20229); www.cbp.gov
- U.S. Fire Admin. (16825 S. Seton Ave., Emmitsburg, MD 21727); www.usfa.dhs.gov
- U.S. Secret Service (245 Murray Dr., Bldg. 410, 20223); www.secretservice.gov

Secretaries of Homeland Security

President	Secretary	Home	Sworn in
Bush, G. W.	Thomas Ridge	PA	2003
	Michael Chertoff	NJ	2005
Obama	Janet A. Napolitano	AZ	2009
	Jeh Johnson	NY	2014

Other Notable U.S. Government Agencies

Source: *The U.S. Government Manual*; National Archives and Records Administration; World Almanac research

All addresses are Washington, DC, unless otherwise noted; as of Aug. 2014.

Administrative Conference of the U.S.: Paul R. Verkuil, chair (1120 20th St. NW, Ste. 706S, 20036); www.acus.gov
African Development Foundation: Shari Berenbach, pres. and CEO (1400 I St. NW, Ste. 1000, 20005); www.adf.gov
AMTRAK: Joseph H. Boardman, pres. and CEO (60 Mass. Ave. NE, 20002); www.amtrak.com
Broadcasting Board of Governors: Jeffrey Shell, chair (330 Independence Ave. SW, 20237); www.bbg.gov
Central Intelligence Agency: John O. Brennan, dir. (20505); www.cia.gov
Commodity Futures Trading Commission: Timothy G. Massad, chair (1155 21st St. NW, 20581); www.cftc.gov
Consumer Financial Protection Bureau: Rich Cordray, dir. (P.O. Box 4503, Iowa City, IA 52244); www.consumerfinance.gov
Consumer Product Safety Commission: Elliot F. Kaye, chair (4330 East West Hwy., Bethesda, MD 20814); www.cpsc.gov
Corp. for Natl. and Community Service: Wendy Spencer, CEO (1201 New York Ave. NW, 20525); www.nationalservice.gov
Court Services and Offender Supervision Agency for DC: Nancy M. Ware, dir. (633 Indiana Ave. NW, 20004); www.csosa.gov
Defense Nuclear Facilities Safety Board: Peter S. Winokur, chair (625 Indiana Ave. NW, Ste. 700, 20004); www.dnfsb.gov
Election Assistance Commission: chair vacant (1335 East West Hwy., Ste. 4300, Silver Spring, MD 20910); www.eac.gov
Environmental Protection Agency: Gina McCarthy, admin. (Cabinet rank) (1200 Pennsylvania Ave. NW, 20460); www.epa.gov
Equal Employment Opportunity Commission: Jacqueline A. Berrien, chair (131 M St. NE, 20507); www.eeoc.gov
Export-Import Bank of the U.S.: Fred P. Hochberg, pres. and chair (811 Vermont Ave. NW, 20571); www.exim.gov
Farm Credit Admin.: Jill Long Thompson, chair and CEO (1501 Farm Credit Dr., McLean, VA 22102); www.fca.gov
Federal Communications Commission: Tom Wheeler, chair (445 12th St. SW, 20554); www.fcc.gov
Federal Deposit Insurance Corp.: Martin J. Gruenberg, chair (550 17th St. NW, 20429); www.fdic.gov
Federal Election Commission: Lee E. Goodman, chair (999 E St. NW, 20463); www.fec.gov
Federal Housing Finance Agency: Melvin L. Watt, dir. (400 7th St. SW, 20024); www.fhfa.gov
Federal Labor Relations Authority: Carol Waller Pope, chair (1400 K St. NW, 20424); www.flra.gov
Federal Maritime Commission: Mario Cordero, chair (800 N. Capitol St. NW, 20573); www.fmc.gov
Federal Mediation and Conciliation Service: Scot L. Beckenbaugh, act. dir. (2100 K St. NW, 20427); www.fmcs.gov
Federal Mine Safety and Health Review Commission: Mary Lu Jordan, chair (1331 Pennsylvania Ave. NW, Ste. 520N, 20004); www.fmshrc.gov
Federal Reserve System: Janet L. Yellen, chair (20th St. and Constitution Ave. NW, 20551); www.federalreserve.gov
Federal Retirement Thrift Investment Board: Michael D. Kennedy, chair (77 K St. NE, 20002); www.frtib.gov
Federal Trade Commission: Edith Ramirez, chair (600 Pennsylvania Ave. NW, 20580); www.ftc.gov
General Services Admin.: Daniel M. Tangherlini, admin. (1800 F St. NW, 20405); www.gsa.gov
Institute of Museum and Library Services: Susan Hildreth, dir. (1800 M St. NW, 9th Fl., 20036); www.imls.gov
Inter-American Foundation: Robert N. Kaplan, pres. (1331 Pennsylvania Ave. NW, Ste. 1200N, 20004); www.iaf.gov
Merit Systems Protection Board: Susan Tsui Grundmann, chair (1615 M St. NW, 20419); www.mspb.gov
Natl. Aeronautics and Space Admin.: Charles F. Bolden Jr., admin. (Suite 2R40, 20546); www.nasa.gov

Natl. Archives and Records Admin.: David S. Ferriero, archivist (8601 Adelphi Rd., College Park, MD 20740); www.archives.gov
Natl. Capital Planning Commission: L. Preston Bryant Jr., chair (401 9th St. NW, N. Lobby, Ste. 500, 20004); www.ncpc.gov
Natl. Council on Disability: Jeff Rosen, chair (1331 F St. NW, Ste. 850, 20004); www.ncd.gov
Natl. Credit Union Admin.: Debbie Matz, chair (1775 Duke St., Alexandria, VA 22314); www.ncua.gov
Natl. Endowment for the Arts: Jane Chu, chair (400 7th St. SW, 20506); www.arts.gov
Natl. Endowment for the Humanities: William Adams, chair (400 7th St. SW, 20506); www.neh.gov
Natl. Indian Gaming Commission: Jonodev Osceola Chaudhuri, act. chair (1441 L St. NW, Ste. 9100, 20005); www.nigc.gov
Natl. Labor Relations Board: Mark G. Pearce, chair (1099 14th St. NW, 20570); www.nlrb.gov
Natl. Mediation Board: Harry Hoglander, chair (1301 K St. NW, Ste. 250 East, 20005); www.nmb.gov
Natl. Science Foundation: France A. Córdova, dir. (4201 Wilson Blvd., Arlington, VA 22230); www.nsf.gov
Natl. Transportation Safety Board: Christopher A. Hart, act. chair (490 L'Enfant Plaza SW, 20594); www.ntsb.gov
Nuclear Regulatory Commission: Allison M. Macfarlane, chair (20555); www.nrc.gov
Nuclear Waste Technical Review Board: Rodney C. Ewing, chair (2300 Clarendon Blvd., Ste. 1300, Arlington, VA 22201); www.nwtrb.gov
Occupational Safety and Health Review Commission: Thomasina V. Rogers, chair (1120 20th St. NW, 9th Fl., 20036); www.oshrc.gov
Office of the Dir. of Natl. Intelligence: James R. Clapper, dir. (20511); www.dni.gov
Office of Government Ethics: Walter M. Shaub Jr., dir. (1201 New York Ave. NW, Ste. 500, 20005); www.oge.gov
Office of Personnel Management: Katherine Archuleta, dir. (1900 E St. NW, 20415); www.opm.gov
Office of Special Counsel: Carolyn Lerner, spec. counsel (1730 M St. NW, Ste. 218, 20036); www.osc.gov
Overseas Private Investment Corp.: Elizabeth L. Littlefield, pres. and CEO (1100 New York Ave. NW, 20527); www.opic.gov
Peace Corps: Carrie Hessler-Radelet, dir. (1111 20th St. NW, 20526); www.peacecorps.gov
Pension Benefit Guaranty Corp.: Josh Gotbaum, dir. (1200 K St. NW, 20005); www.pbgc.gov
Postal Regulatory Commission: Ruth Y. Goldway, chair (901 New York Ave. NW, Ste. 200, 20268); www.prc.gov
Railroad Retirement Board: Michael S. Schwartz, chair (844 N. Rush St., Chicago, IL 60611); www.rrb.gov
Securities and Exchange Commission: Mary Jo White, chair (100 F St. NE, 20549); www.sec.gov
Selective Service System: Lawrence G. Romo, dir. (Natl. Headquarters, Arlington, VA 22209); www.sss.gov
Small Business Admin.: Maria Contreras-Sweet, admin. (Cabinet rank) (409 3rd St. SW, 20416); www.sba.gov
Social Security Admin.: Carolyn W. Colvin, act. comm. (6401 Security Blvd., Baltimore, MD 21235); www.ssa.gov
Tennessee Valley Authority: Bill Johnson, CEO and pres. (400 W. Summit Hill Dr., Knoxville, TN 37902); www.tva.gov
U.S. Agency for Intl. Development: Rajiv Shah, admin. (1300 Pennsylvania Ave. NW, 20523); www.usaid.gov
U.S. Commission on Civil Rights: Martin R. Castro, chair (1331 Pennsylvania Ave. NW, Ste. 1150, 20425); www.usccr.gov
U.S. Intl. Trade Commission: Meredith Broadbent, chair (500 E St. SW, 20436); www.usitc.gov
U.S. Postal Service: Patrick R. Donahoe, postmaster general and CEO (475 L'Enfant Plaza SW, 20260); www.usps.com
U.S. Trade and Development Agency: Leocadia I. Zak, dir. (1000 Wilson Blvd., Ste. 1600, Arlington, VA 22209); www.ustda.gov

CONGRESS

Floor Leaders in the U.S. Senate, 1920-2014

Majority leaders				Minority leaders			
Name	Party	State	Tenure	Name	Party	State	Tenure
Charles Curtis[1]	Rep.	KS	1925-1929	Oscar W. Underwood[2]	Dem.	AL	1920-1923
James E. Watson	Rep.	IN	1929-1933	Joseph T. Robinson	Dem.	AR	1923-1933
Joseph T. Robinson	Dem.	AR	1933-1937	Charles L. McNary	Rep.	OR	1933-1944
Alben W. Barkley	Dem.	KY	1937-1947	Wallace H. White	Rep.	ME	1944-1947
Wallace H. White	Rep.	ME	1947-1949	Alben W. Barkley	Dem.	KY	1947-1949
Scott W. Lucas	Dem.	IL	1949-1951	Kenneth S. Wherry	Rep.	NE	1949-1951
Ernest W. McFarland	Dem.	AZ	1951-1953	Henry Styles Bridges	Rep.	NH	1952-1953
Robert A. Taft	Rep.	OH	1953	Lyndon B. Johnson	Dem.	TX	1953-1955
William F. Knowland	Rep.	CA	1953-1955	William F. Knowland	Rep.	CA	1955-1959
Lyndon B. Johnson	Dem.	TX	1955-1961	Everett M. Dirksen	Rep.	IL	1959-1969
Mike Mansfield	Dem.	MT	1961-1977	Hugh D. Scott	Rep.	PA	1969-1977
Robert C. Byrd	Dem.	WV	1977-1981	Howard H. Baker Jr.	Rep.	TN	1977-1981
Howard H. Baker Jr.	Rep.	TN	1981-1985	Robert C. Byrd	Dem.	WV	1981-1987
Robert J. Dole	Rep.	KS	1985-1987	Robert J. Dole	Rep.	KS	1987-1995
Robert C. Byrd	Dem.	WV	1987-1989	Thomas A. Daschle	Dem.	SD	1995-2001[3]
George J. Mitchell	Dem.	ME	1989-1995	Trent Lott	Rep.	MS	2001-2002[3,4]
Robert J. Dole	Rep.	KS	1995-1996	Thomas A. Daschle	Dem.	SD	2003-2005
Trent Lott	Rep.	MS	1996-2001[3]	Harry M. Reid	Dem.	NV	2005-2007
Thomas A. Daschle	Dem.	SD	2001-2003[3]	Mitch McConnell	Rep.	KY	2007-
William Frist	Rep.	TN	2003-2007[4]				
Harry M. Reid	Dem.	NV	2007-				

Note: The offices of party (majority and minority) leaders in the Senate did not evolve until the 20th century. (1) First Republican to be formally designated floor leader. Henry Cabot Lodge (MA) served as unofficial party leader prior to Curtis's election. (2) First Democrat to be designated floor leader. (3) Democrats held the majority Jan. 3, 2001, until Dick Cheney (R) was installed as vice pres., Jan. 20. Republicans subsequently lost the majority when Jim Jeffords (VT) switched from Republican to Independent, June 6, 2001. (4) Trent Lott resigned from Republican leadership Dec. 20, 2002. William Frist was elected Republican leader Dec. 23, 2002, and began service Jan. 7, 2003, as majority leader.

Speakers of the U.S. House of Representatives, 1789-2014

Name	Party	State	Tenure	Name	Party	State	Tenure
Frederick A. C. Muhlenberg	Federalist	PA	1789-1791	Michael C. Kerr	Dem.	IN	1875-1876
Jonathan Trumbull	Federalist	CT	1791-1793	Samuel J. Randall	Dem.	PA	1876-1881
Frederick A. C. Muhlenberg	Federalist	PA	1793-1795	J. Warren Keifer	Rep.	OH	1881-1883
Jonathan Dayton	Federalist	NJ	1795-1799	John G. Carlisle	Dem.	KY	1883-1889
Theodore Sedgwick	Federalist	MA	1799-1801	Thomas B. Reed	Rep.	ME	1889-1891
Nathaniel Macon	Dem.-Rep.	NC	1801-1807	Charles F. Crisp	Dem.	GA	1891-1895
Joseph B. Varnum	Dem.-Rep.	MA	1807-1811	Thomas B. Reed	Rep.	ME	1895-1899
Henry Clay	Dem.-Rep.	KY	1811-1814	David B. Henderson	Rep.	IA	1899-1903
Langdon Cheves	Dem.-Rep.	SC	1814-1815	Joseph G. Cannon	Rep.	IL	1903-1911
Henry Clay	Dem.-Rep.	KY	1815-1820	Champ Clark	Dem.	MO	1911-1919
John W. Taylor	Dem.-Rep.	NY	1820-1821	Frederick H. Gillett	Rep.	MA	1919-1925
Philip P. Barbour	Dem.-Rep.	VA	1821-1823	Nicholas Longworth	Rep.	OH	1925-1931
Henry Clay	Dem.-Rep.	KY	1823-1825	John N. Garner	Dem.	TX	1931-1933
John W. Taylor	Dem.	NY	1825-1827	Henry T. Rainey	Dem.	IL	1933-1934
Andrew Stevenson	Dem.	VA	1827-1834	Joseph W. Byrns	Dem.	TN	1935-1936
John Bell	Dem.	TN	1834-1835	William B. Bankhead	Dem.	AL	1936-1940
James K. Polk	Dem.	TN	1835-1839	Sam Rayburn	Dem.	TX	1940-1947
Robert M. T. Hunter	Dem.	VA	1839-1841	Joseph W. Martin Jr.	Rep.	MA	1947-1949
John White	Whig	KY	1841-1843	Sam Rayburn	Dem.	TX	1949-1953
John W. Jones	Dem.	VA	1843-1845	Joseph W. Martin Jr.	Rep.	MA	1953-1955
John W. Davis	Dem.	IN	1845-1847	Sam Rayburn	Dem.	TX	1955-1961
Robert C. Winthrop	Whig	MA	1847-1849	John W. McCormack	Dem.	MA	1962-1971
Howell Cobb	Dem.	GA	1849-1851	Carl B. Albert	Dem.	OK	1971-1977
Linn Boyd	Dem.	KY	1851-1855	Thomas P. O'Neill Jr.	Dem.	MA	1977-1987
Nathaniel P. Banks	American	MA	1856-1857	James C. Wright Jr.	Dem.	TX	1987-1989
James L. Orr	Dem.	SC	1857-1859	Thomas S. Foley	Dem.	WA	1989-1995
William Pennington	Rep.	NJ	1860-1861	Newt Gingrich	Rep.	GA	1995-1999
Galusha A. Grow	Rep.	PA	1861-1863	J. Dennis Hastert	Rep.	IL	1999-2007
Schuyler Colfax	Rep.	IN	1863-1869	Nancy Pelosi	Dem.	CA	2007-2011
Theodore M. Pomeroy	Rep.	NY	1869	John Boehner	Rep.	OH	2011-
James G. Blaine	Rep.	ME	1869-1875				

Political Divisions of Congress, 1901-2014

Source: Office of the Clerk, U.S. House of Representatives; Congressional Research Service, Library of Congress

All figures reflect post-election party breakdown except where noted; **boldface** denotes party in majority immediately after election.

Congress	Years	SENATE					HOUSE OF REPRESENTATIVES				
		Total members	Dem.	Rep.	Other parties	Vacant	Total members	Dem.	Rep.	Other parties	Vacant
57th	1901-1903	90	32	**56**	2		357	151	**200**	6	
58th	1903-1905	90	33	**57**			386	176	**207**	3	
59th	1905-1907	90	32	**58**			386	135	**251**		
60th	1907-1909	92	31	**61**			391	167	**223**	1	
61st	1909-1911	92	32	**60**			391	172	**219**		
62nd	1911-1913	96	44	**52**			394	**230**	162	2	
63rd	1913-1915	96	**51**	44	1		435	**291**	134	10	
64th	1915-1917	96	**56**	40			435	**230**	196	9	
65th	1917-1919	96	**54**	42			435	214[1]	**215**	6	
66th	1919-1921	96	47	**49**			435	192	**240**	2	1
67th	1921-1923	96	37	**59**			435	131	**302**	2	
68th	1923-1925	96	42	**53**	1		435	207	**225**	3	
69th	1925-1927	96	41	**54**	1		435	183	**247**	5	

Congress	Years	SENATE Total members	Dem.	Rep.	Other parties	Vacant	HOUSE OF REPRESENTATIVES Total members	Dem.	Rep.	Other parties	Vacant
70th	1927-1929	96	46	**48**	1	1	435	194	**238**	3	
71st	1929-1931	96	39	**56**	1		435	164	**270**	1	
72nd	1931-1933	96	47	**48**	1		435	**216²**	218	1	
73rd	1933-1935	96	**59**	36	1		435	**313**	117	5	
74th	1935-1937	96	**69**	25	2		435	**322**	103	10	
75th	1937-1939	96	**76**	16	4		435	**334**	88	13	
76th	1939-1941	96	**69**	23	4		435	**262**	169	4	
77th	1941-1943	96	**66**	28	2		435	**267**	162	6	
78th	1943-1945	96	**57**	38	1		435	**222**	209	4	
79th	1945-1947	96	**57**	38	1		435	**242**	191	2	
80th	1947-1949	96	45	**51**			435	188	**246**	1	
81st	1949-1951	96	**54**	42			435	**263**	171	1	
82nd	1951-1953	96	**49**	47			435	**235**	199	1	
83rd	1953-1955	96	47	**48**	1		435	213	**221**	1	
84th	1955-1957	96	**48**	47	1		435	**232**	203		
85th	1957-1959	96	**49**	47			435	**234**	201		
86th	1959-1961	100	**65**	35			437³	**283**	153	1	
87th	1961-1963	100	**64**	36			437	**263**	174		
88th	1963-1965	100	**66**	34			435	**259**	176		
89th	1965-1967	100	**68**	32			435	**295**	140		
90th	1967-1969	100	**64**	36			435	**247**	187		1
91st	1969-1971	100	**57**	43			435	**243**	192		
92nd	1971-1973	100	**54**	44	2		435	**255**	180		
93rd	1973-1975	100	**56**	42	2		435	**242**	192	1	
94th	1975-1977	100	**60**	38	2		435	**291**	144		
95th	1977-1979	100	**61**	38	1		435	**292**	143		
96th	1979-1981	100	**58**	41	1		435	**277**	158		
97th	1981-1983	100	46	**53**	1		435	**242**	192	1	
98th	1983-1985	100	46	**54**			435	**269**	166		
99th	1985-1987	100	47	**53**			435	**253**	182		
100th	1987-1989	100	**55**	45			435	**258**	177		
101st	1989-1991	100	**55**	45			435	**260**	175		
102nd	1991-1993	100	**56**	44			435	**267**	167	1	
103rd	1993-1995	100	**57**	43			435	**258**	176	1	
104th	1995-1997	100	48	**52**			435	204	**230**	1	
105th	1997-1999	100	45	**55**			435	206	**228**	1	
106th	1999-2001	100	45	**55**			435	211	**223**	1	
107th	2001-2003	100	50	**50⁴**			435	212	**221**	2	
108th	2003-2005	100	48	**51**	1		435	204	**229**	1	1
109th	2005-2007	100	44	**55**	1		435	202	**232**	1	
110th	2007-2009	100	49	49	2⁵		435	**233**	202		
111th	2009-2011	100	**57**	41	2⁵		435	**257**	178		
112th	2011-2013	100	**51**	47	2⁵		435	193	**242**		
113th	2013-	100	**53**	45	2⁵		435	201	**234**		

(1) Democrats organized the House with help of other parties. (2) Democrats organized the House because of Republican deaths. (3) Number of House seats was increased temporarily when proclamations were issued declaring Alaska (Jan. 3, 1959) and Hawaii (Aug. 21, 1959) new states. (4) While the Senate was split 50-50, control was held by whichever party had an incumbent vice president. Republican Sen. Jim Jeffords (VT) changed his party designation to Independent on June 6, 2001, switching control of the Senate to Democrats. (5) Both Independent senators chose to caucus with the Democrats.

Congressional Bills Vetoed, 1789-2014

Source: Virtual Reference Desk, U.S. Senate

President	Regular vetoes	Pocket vetoes	Total vetoes	Vetoes overridden	President	Regular vetoes	Pocket vetoes	Total vetoes	Vetoes overridden
Washington	2	—	2	—	B. Harrison	19	25	44	1
J. Adams	—	—	—	—	Cleveland²	42	128	170	5
Jefferson	—	—	—	—	McKinley	6	36	42	—
Madison	5	2	7	—	T. Roosevelt	42	40	82	1
Monroe	1	—	1	—	Taft	30	9	39	1
J. Q. Adams	—	—	—	—	Wilson	33	11	44	6
Jackson	5	7	12	—	Harding	5	1	6	—
Van Buren	—	1	1	—	Coolidge	20	30	50	4
W. H. Harrison	—	—	—	—	Hoover	21	16	37	3
Tyler	6	4	10	1	F. D. Roosevelt	372	263	635	9
Polk	2	1	3	—	Truman	180	70	250	12
Taylor	—	—	—	—	Eisenhower	73	108	181	2
Fillmore	—	—	—	—	Kennedy	12	9	21	—
Pierce	9	—	9	5	L. Johnson	16	14	30	—
Buchanan	4	3	7	—	Nixon	26	17	43	7
Lincoln	2	5	7	—	Ford	48	18	66	12
A. Johnson	21	8	29	15	Carter	13	18	31	2
Grant	45	48	93	4	Reagan	39	39	78	9
Hayes	12	1	13	1	G. H. W. Bush³	29	15	44	1
Garfield	—	—	—	—	Clinton⁴	36	1	37	2
Arthur	4	8	12	1	G. W. Bush	12	—	12	4
Cleveland¹	304	110	414	2	Obama	2	—	2	—
					Total³,⁴	**1,498**	**1,066**	**2,564**	**110**

— = 0. (1) First term only. (2) Second term only. (3) Excluded from the figures are two bills that Pres. George H. W. Bush claimed to be vetoed but Congress considered enacted into law because the president failed to return them to Congress during a recess period. (4) Does not include line-item vetoes, which were ruled unconstitutional by the U.S. Supreme Court on June 25, 1998.

U.S. SUPREME COURT

Justices of the U.S. Supreme Court

The Supreme Court comprises the chief justice of the U.S. and eight associate justices, all appointed for life by the president with advice and consent of the U.S. Senate. Names of chief justices are in **boldface**. Terms of service begin with the year each justice took the judicial oath. Service years are the number of complete years served by a justice. Current salaries: chief justice, $255,500; associate justice, $244,400. The U.S. Supreme Court Building is at 1 First St. NE, Washington, DC 20543.

Website: www.supremecourt.gov.

Current membership. Chief justice: John G. Roberts Jr.; associate justices in seniority order: Antonin Scalia, Anthony M. Kennedy, Clarence Thomas, Ruth Bader Ginsburg, Stephen G. Breyer, Samuel A. Alito Jr., Sonia Sotomayor, Elena Kagan.

Name, appointed from	Service Term	Yrs.	Born	Died
John Jay, NY	1789-1795	5	1745	1829
John Rutledge, SC[1]	1790-1791	1	1739	1800
William Cushing, MA	1790-1810*	20	1732	1810
James Wilson, PA	1789-1798	8	1742	1798
John Blair, VA	1790-1795*	5	1732	1800
James Iredell, NC	1790-1799	9	1751	1799
Thomas Johnson, MD	1792-1793	<1	1732	1819
William Paterson, NJ	1793-1806	13	1745	1806
John Rutledge, SC[2,3]	1795	<1	1739	1800
Samuel Chase, MD	1796-1811	15	1741	1811
Oliver Ellsworth, CT	1796-1800	4	1745	1807
Bushrod Washington, VA	1799-1829*	30	1762	1829
Alfred Moore, NC	1800-1804	3	1755	1810
John Marshall, VA	1801-1835	34	1755	1835
William Johnson, SC	1804-1834	30	1771	1834
Henry B. Livingston, NY	1807-1823	16	1757	1823
Thomas Todd, KY	1807-1826	18	1765	1826
Gabriel Duvall, MD	1811-1835	23	1752	1844
Joseph Story, MA	1812-1845*	33	1779	1845
Smith Thompson, NY	1823-1843	20	1768	1843
Robert Trimble, KY	1826-1828	2	1777	1828
John McLean, OH	1830-1861*	31	1785	1861
Henry Baldwin, PA	1830-1844	14	1780	1844
James M. Wayne, GA	1835-1867	32	1790	1867
Roger B. Taney, MD	1836-1864	28	1777	1864
Philip P. Barbour, VA	1836-1841	4	1783	1841
John Catron, TN	1837-1865	28	1786	1865
John McKinley, AL	1838-1852*	14	1780	1852
Peter V. Daniel, VA	1842-1860*	18	1784	1860
Samuel Nelson, NY	1845-1872	27	1792	1873
Levi Woodbury, NH	1845-1851	5	1789	1851
Robert C. Grier, PA	1846-1870	23	1794	1870
Benjamin R. Curtis, MA	1851-1857	5	1809	1874
John A. Campbell, AL	1853-1861*	8	1811	1889
Nathan Clifford, ME	1858-1881	23	1803	1881
Noah H. Swayne, OH	1862-1881	18	1804	1884
Samuel F. Miller, IA	1862-1890	28	1816	1890
David Davis, IL	1862-1877	14	1815	1886
Stephen J. Field, CA	1863-1897	33	1816	1899
Salmon P. Chase, OH	1864-1873	8	1808	1873
William Strong, PA	1870-1880	10	1808	1895
Joseph P. Bradley, NJ	1870-1892	21	1813	1892
Ward Hunt, NY	1873-1882	9	1810	1886
Morrison R. Waite, OH	1874-1888	14	1816	1888
John M. Harlan, KY	1877-1911	33	1833	1911
William B. Woods, GA	1881-1887	6	1824	1887
Stanley Matthews, OH	1881-1889	7	1824	1889
Horace Gray, MA	1882-1902	20	1828	1902
Samuel Blatchford, NY	1882-1893	11	1820	1893
Lucius Q.C. Lamar, MS	1888-1893	5	1825	1893
Melville W. Fuller, IL	1888-1910	21	1833	1910
David J. Brewer, KS	1890-1910	20	1837	1910
Henry B. Brown, MI	1891-1906	15	1836	1913
George Shiras Jr., PA	1892-1903	10	1832	1924
Howell E. Jackson, TN	1893-1895	2	1832	1895
Edward D. White, LA[1]	1894-1910	16	1845	1921
Rufus W. Peckham, NY	1896-1909	13	1838	1909
Joseph McKenna, CA	1898-1925	26	1843	1926
Oliver W. Holmes, MA	1902-1932	29	1841	1935
William R. Day, OH	1903-1922	19	1849	1923
William H. Moody, MA	1906-1910	3	1853	1917
Horace H. Lurton, TN	1910-1914	4	1844	1914
Charles E. Hughes, NY[1]	1910-1916	5	1862	1948
Willis Van Devanter, WY	1911-1937	26	1859	1941
Joseph R. Lamar, GA	1911-1916	5	1857	1916
Edward D. White, LA[2]	1910-1921	10	1845	1921
Mahlon Pitney, NJ	1912-1922	10	1858	1924
James C. McReynolds, TN	1914-1941	26	1862	1946
Louis D. Brandeis, MA	1916-1939	22	1856	1941
John H. Clarke, OH	1916-1922	5	1857	1945
William H. Taft, CT	1921-1930	8	1857	1930
George Sutherland, UT	1922-1938	15	1862	1942
Pierce Butler, MN	1923-1939	16	1866	1939
Edward T. Sanford, TN	1923-1930	7	1865	1930
Harlan F. Stone, NY[1]	1925-1941	16	1872	1946
Charles E. Hughes, NY[2]	1930-1941	11	1862	1948
Owen J. Roberts, PA	1930-1945	15	1875	1955
Benjamin N. Cardozo, NY	1932-1938	6	1870	1938
Hugo L. Black, AL	1937-1971	34	1886	1971
Stanley F. Reed, KY	1938-1957	19	1884	1980
Felix Frankfurter, MA	1939-1962	23	1882	1965
William O. Douglas, CT	1939-1975	36[4]	1898	1980
Frank Murphy, MI	1940-1949	9	1890	1949
Harlan F. Stone, NY[2]	1941-1946	4	1872	1946
James F. Byrnes, SC	1941-1942	1	1879	1972
Robert H. Jackson, NY	1941-1954	13	1892	1954
Wiley B. Rutledge, IA	1943-1949	6	1894	1949
Harold H. Burton, OH	1945-1958	13	1888	1964
Fred M. Vinson, KY	1946-1953	7	1890	1953
Tom C. Clark, TX	1949-1967	17	1899	1977
Sherman Minton, IN	1949-1956	7	1890	1965
Earl Warren, CA	1953-1969	15	1891	1974
John Marshall Harlan, NY	1955-1971	16	1899	1971
William J. Brennan Jr., NJ	1956-1990	33	1906	1997
Charles E. Whittaker, MO	1957-1962	5	1901	1973
Potter Stewart, OH	1958-1981	22	1915	1985
Byron R. White, CO	1962-1993	31	1917	2002
Arthur J. Goldberg, IL	1962-1965	2	1908	1990
Abe Fortas, TN	1965-1969	3	1910	1982
Thurgood Marshall, NY	1967-1991	24	1908	1993
Warren E. Burger, VA	1969-1986	17	1907	1995
Harry A. Blackmun, MN	1970-1994	24	1908	1999
Lewis F. Powell Jr., VA	1972-1987	15	1907	1998
William H. Rehnquist, AZ[1]	1972-1986	14	1924	2005
John Paul Stevens, IL	1975-2010	34	1920	
Sandra Day O'Connor, AZ	1981-2006	24	1930	
William H. Rehnquist, VA[2]	1986-2005	18	1924	2005
Antonin Scalia, VA	1986-		1936	
Anthony M. Kennedy, CA	1988-		1936	
David H. Souter, NH	1990-2009	18	1939	
Clarence Thomas, GA	1991-		1948	
Ruth Bader Ginsburg, NY	1993-		1933	
Stephen G. Breyer, MA	1994-		1938	
John G. Roberts Jr., MD	2005-		1955	
Samuel A. Alito Jr., NJ	2006-		1950	
Sonia Sotomayor, NY	2009-		1954	
Elena Kagan, MA	2010-		1960	

*Because of inadequate government record keeping, date of oath is estimated. (1) Later, chief justice, as listed. (2) Formerly associate justice. (3) Named acting chief justice; confirmation rejected by the Senate. (4) Longest term of service.

Supreme Court History and Notable Firsts

The U.S. Supreme Court first convened Feb. 1, 1790, in New York, NY. Acting on the authority of Congress as outlined in the Judiciary Act of 1789, the Court consisted of Chief Justice John Jay and five associate justices who held sessions for a few weeks in Feb. and Aug. The justices also served twice a year in each of the nation's then-13 judicial districts, a requirement known as riding circuit.

The Court's first major legal decision, *Chisholm v. Georgia* (1793), ruled that federal courts held jurisdiction over disputes between individual states and citizens of other states. (The 11th Amendment, which the states ratified in 1795, removed that jurisdiction.)

Since it was established, 112 justices have served on the Court for an average of 16 years. Of 160 nominations to the Court (including chief justice nominations), just 12 have been rejected by the Senate, most recently Robert Bork in 1987. (George W. Bush nominee Harriet Miers withdrew her nomination, before the Senate considered it, in 2005.) Justices may be removed from the Court by impeachment. In 1805, the House of Representatives impeached Samuel Chase; he was later acquitted by the Senate. No other justice has ever been impeached.

The Court over time has expanded its impact on the nation's affairs. Since 1803 it has declared unconstitutional 170 acts of Congress and more than 1,070 state and territorial laws and municipal statutes. Operating on an est. $85-mil budget, the Court receives approximately 10,000 petitions annually and hears oral arguments in about 75-80 cases per term.

The Court begins its term the first Monday in October and recesses in late June or early July.

First fully vested justice: James Wilson took the Constitutional Oath of the Court Oct. 5, 1789
First Jewish justice: Louis D. Brandeis (1916-39)
First and only person to serve as both U.S. president and chief justice: William Howard Taft (president, 1909-13; chief justice, 1921-30)

First justice to take an oath at the White House: Frank Murphy, Jan. 18, 1940
First African-American justice: Thurgood Marshall (1967-91)
First woman justice: Sandra Day O'Connor (1981-2006)
First Hispanic justice: Sonia Sotomayor (2009-)

U.S. Supreme Court Decisions by Issue and Leadership Era, 1946-2014

Source: The Supreme Court Database, supremecourtdatabase.org

Decisions through the end of the 2013-14 term. Figures are the number of cases decided in each issue category (number of 5-4 decisions in parentheses).

Issue	Number of decisions under Chief Justice—				
	Vinson (1946-53)	Warren (1953-69)	Burger (1969-86)	Rehnquist (1986-2005)	Roberts (2005-)
Attorneys[1]	2 (0)	12 (1)	37 (5)	31 (7)	15 (2)
Civil rights	74 (7)	316 (27)	555 (78)	323 (69)	119 (24)
Criminal procedure	123 (29)	462 (70)	627 (109)	509 (136)	213 (53)
Due process	47 (6)	40 (5)	144 (18)	86 (23)	17 (4)
Economic activity	225 (37)	493 (48)	450 (52)	346 (40)	143 (15)
Federal taxation	49 (2)	118 (5)	75 (7)	56 (3)	11 (2)
Federalism	30 (1)	94 (3)	108 (6)	123 (26)	38 (8)
First amendment	44 (8)	206 (44)	236 (56)	140 (36)	36 (12)
Interstate relations	12 (2)	14 (0)	40 (0)	23 (1)	5 (1)
Judicial power	134 (18)	300 (20)	365 (33)	286 (28)	92 (20)
Miscellaneous[2]	1 (0)	13 (0)	13 (0)	22 (0)	4 (1)
Privacy	4 (0)	2 (0)	48 (9)	42 (6)	16 (1)
Private action[3]	0 (0)	0 (0)	0 (0)	0 (0)	2 (1)
Unions	41 (4)	131 (8)	109 (24)	54 (11)	15 (4)
Total	**786 (114)**	**2,201 (231)**	**2,807 (397)**	**2,041 (386)**	**726 (148)**

Note: Decision types include orally argued judgments, per curiams, and opinions; per curiams without oral arguments; equally divided votes; and decrees. (1) Includes cases on commercial fees, attorneys' fees, admission to state or federal bar, attorney discipline, and disbarment. (2) Includes cases that could not be classified. (3) Includes cases on civil procedures, commercial transactions, contracts, evidence, personal and real property, torts, and wills and trusts.

Selected Landmark Decisions of the U.S. Supreme Court, 1803-2013

1803: *Marbury v. Madison.* The Court ruled that Congress exceeded its power in the Judiciary Act of 1789. The Court thus established its power to review acts of Congress and to declare invalid those it found to be in conflict with the Constitution.

1819: *Trustees of Dartmouth College v. Woodward.* The Court ruled that a state could not arbitrarily alter the terms of a college's contract. The Court later used a similar principle to limit the states' ability to interfere with business contracts.

1819: *McCulloch v. Maryland.* The Court ruled that Congress had the authority to charter a national bank, under the Constitution's granting of power to enact all laws "necessary and proper" to responsibilities of government.

1824: *Gibbons v. Ogden.* The Court ruled that New York state had overstepped its authority in granting a monopoly to two steamboat operators. According to the ruling, Congress's power to regulate interstate commerce included transportation.

1857: *Dred Scott v. Sandford.* The Court declared unconstitutional the already-repealed Missouri Compromise of 1820 because it deprived a person of property—a slave—without due process of law. The Court also ruled that slaves were not citizens of any state nor of the U.S. The latter part of the decision was overturned by ratification of the 14th Amendment in 1868.

1880: *Strauder v. West Virginia.* The Court struck down a state law mandating that jurors must be white, ruling it a violation of the right to equal protection under the 14th Amendment.

1896: *Plessy v. Ferguson.* The Court ruled that a state law requiring federal railroad trains to provide separate but equal facilities for black and white passengers neither infringed upon federal authority to regulate interstate commerce nor violated the 13th and 14th Amendments. The "separate but equal" doctrine remained effective until the 1954 ***Brown v. Board of Education*** decision.

1904: *Northern Securities Co. v. U.S.* The Court ruled that a holding company formed solely to eliminate competition between two railroad lines was a combination in restraint of trade, violating the 1890 federal Sherman Antitrust Act.

1908: *Muller v. Oregon.* The Court upheld a state law limiting the working hours of women. (Louis D. Brandeis, counsel for the state, cited evidence from social workers, physicians, and factory inspectors that the number of hours women worked affected their health and morals.)

1911: *Standard Oil Co. of New Jersey v. U.S.* The Court ruled that the Standard Oil Trust must be dissolved because of its unreasonable restraint of trade.

1919: *Schenck v. U.S.* The Court sustained the Espionage Act of 1917, maintaining that freedom of speech and press could be constrained if "the words used ... create a clear and present danger."

1925: *Gitlow v. New York.* The Court ruled that the 1st Amendment prohibition against government abridgment of the freedom of speech applied to the states as well as to the federal government. The decision was the first of a number of rulings holding that the 14th Amendment extended the guarantees of the Bill of Rights to state action.

1935: Schechter Poultry Corp. v. U.S. The Court ruled that Congress exceeded its authority to delegate legislative powers and to regulate interstate commerce when it enacted the National Industrial Recovery Act (1933), which afforded the U.S. president too much discretionary power.

1944: Korematsu v. U.S. The Court upheld the constitutionality of an order barring all persons of Japanese ancestry, including U.S. citizens, from much of the West Coast, forcing them into internment camps, ruling that the need to prevent espionage outweighed the petitioner's civil rights. The ruling, never officially overturned, followed **Hirabayashi v. U.S.** (1943), in which the Court upheld the imposition of curfews on minority populations perceived to be a potential wartime threat.

1951: Dennis v. U.S. The Court upheld convictions under the Smith Act of 1940 for invoking Communist theory advocating the forcible overthrow of the government. In **Yates v. U.S.** (1957), the Court moderated this ruling by allowing such advocacy in the abstract, if not connected to action to achieve the goal.

1952: Youngstown Sheet & Tube Co. v. Sawyer. The Court ruled that the president had exceeded his wartime power in ordering the seizure of private steel mills during a nationwide steelworkers' strike. The Court held that neither the Constitution nor his role as commander-in-chief gave the president the authority to interfere in labor issues.

1954: Brown v. Board of Education of Topeka. The Court ruled that separate public schools for black and white students were inherently unequal, so state-sanctioned segregation in public schools violated the equal protection guarantee of the 14th Amendment. And in **Bolling v. Sharpe** the same year, the Court ruled that the congressionally mandated segregated public school system in the District of Columbia violated the 5th Amendment's due process guarantee of personal liberty. The Brown ruling also led to abolition of state-sponsored segregation in other public facilities.

1957: Roth v. U.S.; Alberts v. California. The Court ruled obscene material—defined as appealing primarily to "prurient interest" in the view of "the average person, applying contemporary community standards"—was not protected by 1st Amendment guarantees of freedom of speech and press, being "utterly without redeeming social importance." This definition was modified in later decisions, including **Miller v. California** (1973).

1958: Cooper v. Aaron. The Court held that Arkansas could not nullify **Brown v. Board of Education** by arguing mandatory school desegregation was unconstitutional. The opinion of the Court affirmed its reading of the Constitution as the "supreme law of the land."

1961: Mapp v. Ohio. The Court ruled that evidence obtained in violation of the 4th Amendment guarantee against unreasonable search and seizure must be excluded from use in state as well as federal trials.

1962: Baker v. Carr. The Court held that constitutional challenges to the unequal distribution of voters among legislative districts could be resolved by federal courts.

1962: Engel v. Vitale. The Court held that government bodies could not encourage the recitation of a state-composed prayer in public schools, even if nondenominational, because that would be an unconstitutional attempt to establish religion.

1963: Gideon v. Wainwright. The Court ruled that defendants in state cases must have access to an attorney even if they could not afford one.

1964: New York Times Co. v. Sullivan. The Court ruled that the 1st Amendment protected the press from libel suits for defamatory reports about public officials unless an injured party could prove that a defamatory report was made out of "actual malice," with "reckless disregard" for the truth.

1964: Heart of Atlanta Motel v. U.S. The Court upheld the constitutionality of Title II of the 1964 Civil Rights Act banning racial discrimination in motels/hotels engaged in interstate commerce (by accommodating travelers from other states). The Court in **Katzenbach v. McClung** (1964) held that Title II also applied to restaurants and businesses that purchased a substantial percentage of food or goods from other states.

1965: Griswold v. Connecticut. The Court ruled that a state unconstitutionally interfered with privacy in a marriage when it prohibited all persons, including married couples, from using contraceptives.

1966: Miranda v. Arizona. The Court ruled that, under the guarantee of due process, suspects in custody, before being questioned, must be informed that they have the right to remain silent, that anything they say may be used against them, and that they have the right to counsel.

1968: Terry v. Ohio. The Court ruled that a "stop and frisk" performed without a warrant or probable cause was not a violation of 4th Amendment rights, provided that the law enforcement officer had a reasonable suspicion that the subject was armed and dangerous, or had committed or was about to commit a crime.

1973: Roe v. Wade; Doe v. Bolton. The Court ruled that the fetus was not a "person" with constitutional rights and that a right to privacy inherent in the 14th Amendment's due process guarantee of personal liberty protected a woman's decision to have an abortion. During the first trimester of pregnancy, the Court maintained, the decision should be left entirely to a woman and her physician. Some regulation of abortion procedures was allowed in the second trimester and some restriction of abortion in the third.

1974: U.S. v. Nixon. The Court ruled that neither the separation of powers nor the need to preserve the confidentiality of presidential communications could alone justify an absolute executive privilege of immunity from judicial demands for evidence to be used in a criminal trial.

1976: Gregg v. Georgia; Proffitt v. Florida; Jurek v. Texas. The Court held that death, as a punishment for persons convicted of first-degree murder, was not in and of itself cruel and unusual punishment in violation of the 8th Amendment. But the Court ruled that the sentencing judge and jury must consider the character of the offender and the circumstances of the particular crime.

1978: Regents of the Univ. of Calif. v. Bakke. The Court ruled that an admissions program for a state medical school, under which a set number of places were reserved for minorities, violated the 1964 Civil Rights Act, which forbids the exclusion of anyone from a federally funded program based on race. However, the Court ruled that race could be considered as one of a complex of factors.

1985: New Jersey v. T.L.O. The Court ruled that officials who carry out searches on school grounds do not violate students' 4th Amendment rights because students' privacy rights can be outweighed by schools' need to maintain learning environments. The ruling put in place less stringent standards of required "reasonableness" for such searches.

1986: Bowers v. Hardwick. The Court refused to extend any right of privacy to homosexual activity, upholding a Georgia antisodomy law that in effect made such activity a crime. Georgia's supreme court struck down the law in 1998, and in **Lawrence v. Texas** (2003), the U.S. Supreme Court struck down all state antisodomy laws as violations of liberty prohibited in the 14th Amendment's due process clause. In **Romer v. Evans** (1996), the Court struck down a Colorado constitutional provision that barred homosexuals from recognition as a protected class, ruling that it violated the 14th Amendment's Equal Protection clause.

1989: Texas v. Johnson. The Court held that the actions of a political activist who burned an American flag outside of the 1984 Republican National Convention were expressive and therefore protected by the 1st Amendment. The ruling invalidated laws in 48 states prohibiting flag desecration.

1990: Cruzan v. Missouri. The Court ruled that while a person had the right to refuse life-sustaining medical treatment, a state could require evidence that a comatose patient would not have wanted to live before withholding treatment. In two 1997 rulings, **Washington v. Glucksberg** and **Vacco v. Quill**, the Court ruled that states could ban doctor-assisted suicide.

1995: U.S. Term Limits, Inc. v. Thornton. The Court ruled that neither states nor Congress could limit terms of members of Congress because the Constitution reserves to the people the right to choose federal lawmakers.

1995: Adarand Constructors, Inc. v. Peña. The Court held that federal programs that classify people by race, unless "narrowly tailored" to further a "compelling governmental interest," may violate the right to equal protection and are thus subject to strict scrutiny.

1997: *Clinton v. Jones.* Rejecting an appeal by Pres. Clinton in a sexual harassment suit, the Court ruled that a sitting president did not have temporary immunity from a lawsuit for actions outside the realm of official duties.

1997: *City of Boerne v. Flores.* The Court overturned the portion of a 1993 law banning enforcement of state laws that "substantially burden" religious practice unless there is a "compelling governmental interest" to do so. The Court held that the act was an unwarranted intrusion by Congress on states' prerogatives and an infringement of the judiciary's role.

1997: *Reno v. ACLU.* Citing the right to free expression, the Court overturned a provision making it a crime to display or distribute "obscene or indecent" or "patently offensive" material on the Internet. The Court ruled, however, in *NEA v. Finley* (1998) that "general standards of decency" may be used as a criterion in federal arts funding.

1998: *Clinton v. City of New York.* The Court struck down the Line-Item Veto Act (1996), holding that it unconstitutionally gave the president "the unilateral power to change the text of duly enacted statutes."

1998: *Faragher v. City of Boca Raton; Burlington Industries, Inc. v. Ellerth.* The Court issued new guidelines for workplace sexual harassment suits, holding employers responsible for misconduct by supervisory employees. And in *Oncale v. Sundowner Offshore Services, Inc.*, the Court ruled that the law against discrimination based on sex applies regardless of whether the harasser and harassed are the same sex.

1999: *Dept. of Commerce v. U.S. House of Representatives.* Upholding a challenge to plans for the 2000 census, the Court prohibited statistical sampling, favored by Democrats, in apportioning seats in the U.S. House. The Court maintained that an actual head count was required.

1999: *Alden v. Maine; Florida Prepaid v. College Savings Bank; College Savings Bank v. Florida Prepaid.* In a series of rulings, the Court applied the principle of sovereign immunity to shield states in large part from being sued under federal law.

2000: *Boy Scouts of America v. Dale.* The Court ruled that the Boy Scouts could dismiss a troop leader after learning he was gay, holding that the right to freedom of association outweighed a New Jersey antidiscrimination statute.

2000: *Bush v. Gore.* The Court ruled that manual recounts in Florida of ballots cast in the 2000 presidential election could not proceed because inconsistent evaluation standards violated the equal protection clause. In effect, the ruling meant the existing official results would stand, making George W. Bush the narrow winner of the election.

2001: *Good News Club v. Milford Central School.* The justices found that a private religious organization could not be denied equal access to a public school facility for after-school meetings because that would be a violation of the group's free speech rights.

2002: *Federal Maritime Commission v. South Carolina State Ports Authority.* The Court ruled that the 11th Amendment gave states immunity from private lawsuits involving federal agencies.

2002: *Atkins v. Virginia.* The Court ruled that the execution of mentally retarded felons violated the 8th Amendment ban on cruel and unusual punishment. The Court ruled in *Roper v. Simmons* (2005) that executions of convicts who committed their crimes before age 18 were also prohibited on the same grounds.

2002: *Zelman v. Simmons-Harris.* The Court ruled that publicly funded tuition vouchers could be used at religious schools without violating the separation of church and state.

2003: *Grutter v. Bollinger; Gratz v. Bollinger.* The Court upheld the use of race as a factor in the Univ. of Michigan Law School's admissions policies because of the school's interest in a diverse student body. In a second decision, however, the Court ruled against a strict point system based on racial and ethnic backgrounds as used in the university's undergraduate admissions process.

2004: *Tennessee v. Lane.* The Court ruled that disabled individuals could sue states under the Americans With Disabilities Act (1990) for failing to provide adequate access to state courthouses, despite states' usual immunity from private lawsuits in federal court under the 11th Amendment, which the Court ruled on in *Federal Maritime Commission v. South Carolina State Ports Authority* (2002).

2004: *Locke v. Davey.* The justices decided that a scholarship program provided by the state of Washington did not violate the right to free exercise of religion in denying aid to students preparing for the clergy.

2004: *Ashcroft v. ACLU.* The Court struck down federal legislation passed in 1998 to restrict online access to pornography by minors, on the basis that the law violated the 1st Amendment right of free speech.

2005: *Kelo v. City of New London.* The Court ruled that local governments could force property owners to sell their land in order to facilitate private development projects deemed to be economically beneficial to the community.

2006: *Garcetti v. Ceballos.* The Court ruled that the 1st Amendment guarantee of free speech did not protect statements made by public employees in the course of their official duties.

2006: *Hamdan v. Rumsfeld.* The Court ruled that Pres. George W. Bush's system for trying terrorism detainees at the U.S. military base in Guantánamo Bay, Cuba, was unauthorized under federal law and the international Geneva Conventions. The Court furthermore ruled in *Boumediene v. Bush* (2008) that detainees had a right to challenge their detention in federal court by applying for a writ of habeas corpus.

2007: *Gonzales v. Carhart; Gonzales v. Planned Parenthood Federation of America.* The Court upheld a 2003 federal law prohibiting the abortion procedure known as intact dilation and extraction, or "partial-birth" abortion.

2007: *Parents Involved in Community Schools v. Seattle School District No. 1; Meredith v. Jefferson County Board of Education.* The Court ruled that two school districts could not, to encourage diversity, use "racial classifications in making school assignments."

2008: *Crawford v. Marion County Election Board.* The Court upheld the constitutionality of an Indiana law requiring voters to present valid government photo identification.

2008: *District of Columbia v. Heller.* The Court overturned DC's handgun ban, ruling that the 2nd Amendment protected an individual's right to own guns for personal use.

2010: *Citizens United v. Federal Election Commission.* The Court ruled that a federal law barring corporations from using general funds to finance campaign advertisements was unconstitutional. The decision cast doubt on many laws restricting political spending by corporations and unions.

2011: *Snyder v. Phelps.* The justices found that an antigay church whose members protested at the funeral of a Marine could not be held liable for intrusion or the emotional distress of the father of the deceased because the protests were protected by the 1st Amendment.

2012: *U.S. v. Jones.* The Court ruled that attaching a GPS tracking device to a suspect's car and monitoring its movements requires a search warrant, as the 4th Amendment prohibition against unreasonable search and seizure applies.

2012: *Miller v. Alabama.* The Court ruled that mandatory life sentences without the possibility of parole violate juvenile offenders' 8th Amendment right to freedom from cruel and unusual punishment. The decision extended *Graham v. Florida*, a 2010 case in which the Court held that juveniles may not receive life sentences for crimes that do not result in homicides.

2012: *Natl. Federation of Independent Business v. Sebelius.* The Court ruled Congress acted within its powers of taxation in enacting the individual-mandate provision of the Patient Protection and Affordable Care Act, which required Americans without government- or employer-provided health insurance to purchase it or pay a fine. The Court ruled unconstitutional the provision of the act's Medicaid expansion that threatened noncompliant states with loss of funding.

2013: *Shelby County v. Holder.* The justices ruled that a key provision of the 1965 Voting Rights Act, meant to prevent discriminatory voting regulations from being enacted, was unconstitutional because it relied on outdated information to identify areas for additional scrutiny.

2013: *U.S. v. Windsor.* The Court struck down the central provision of the 1996 federal Defense of Marriage Act (DOMA), which prohibited federal recognition of same-sex marriages. A separate decision, in *Hollingsworth v. Perry*, had the effect of legalizing same-sex marriage in California.

See also Year in Review: Notable Supreme Court Decisions, 2013-14.

STATES AND OTHER AREAS OF THE U.S.

Sources: Population: Decennial Censuses and Population Estimates Program, U.S. Census Bureau, U.S. Dept. of Commerce; population as of July 1, 2013, unless otherwise noted. Pop. density is for land area only. **Racial distribution** categories are abbreviated; their full forms are white, black or African American, Asian, American Indian and Alaska Native, Native Hawaiian and Other Pacific Islander, two or more races. Categories may not add up to 100% due to rounding. **Hispanic** or Latino persons may be of any race. **Area:** Geography Division, U.S. Census Bureau, U.S. Dept. of Commerce. **Acres forested:** U.S. Forest Service, U.S. Dept. of Agriculture; source year may vary. **Chief airports:** Federal Aviation Admin., U.S. Dept. of Transportation. Chief airports had 500,000+ boardings in 2013. All **Economy** data as of 2013 unless otherwise noted. **Chief manuf. goods:** Manufacturing and Construction Division, U.S. Census Bureau, U.S. Dept. of Commerce. **Chief crops** and **Livestock:** Agriculture Dept., Natl. Agricultural Statistics Service, U.S. Dept. of Agriculture. Chicken/broilers as of Dec./Nov. 2013; cattle/calves and sheep/lambs as of Jan. 2014; hogs/pigs as of June 2014. Many states do not disclose broiler or hog/pig data. **Nonfuel minerals:** Office of Mineral Information, U.S. Dept. of Interior; preliminary data. Some states exclude small amounts to avoid disclosing proprietary data. **Commercial fishing:** Natl. Marine Fisheries Service, U.S. Dept. of Commerce. **Gross state product** and **Per cap. pers. income:** Bureau of Economic Analysis, U.S. Dept. of Commerce; as of Dec. 2013. **Sales tax:** Federation of Tax Administrators; as of Jan. 1, 2014. **Employment distrib.** and **Unemployment:** Bureau of Labor Statistics, U.S. Dept. of Labor; distribution is for non-farm jobs as of May 2014. **New private housing:** Manufacturing and Construction Division, U.S. Census Bureau, U.S. Dept. of Commerce. Figures are building permits issued and est. value of the construction. **Broadband Internet:** Industry Analysis and Tech. Division, Fed. Communications Commission. Broadband connections have minimum speeds of at least 768 kilobytes per second (Kbps) downstream and 200 Kbps upstream; figure given is broadband as a percentage of total Internet connections. **Commercial banks** and **Savings institutions:** Federal Deposit Insurance Corp., as of June 30, 2013; FDIC-insured institutions only. **Lottery:** North American Assn. of State and Provincial Lotteries. Data may be unaudited and in some cases were gathered by third party. Some states report round sums; others report exact figures. **Federal employees:** Office of Personnel Mgmt., U.S. Dept. of Labor; as of Mar. 2014. **Higher education:** Natl. Ctr. for Education Statistics; as of 2012-13 school year. Data for private 4-yr. institutions does not include for-profit colleges/universities. **Energy:** Energy Information Admin., U.S. Dept. of Energy; average per capita monthly electricity consumption and cost for residential customers in 2012. **Tourism:** U.S. Travel Assn.; tourist spending in 2012. Other information from sources in individual states. NA = Not available.

Famous persons lists may include non-natives associated with the state as well as persons born there. **Websites** are subject to change and are not endorsed by *The World Almanac.*

Alabama (AL)
Heart of Dixie, Camellia State

People. Population: 4,833,722; rank: 23. **Pop. change** (2010-13): 1.1%. **Pop. density:** 95.4 per sq mi. **Racial distribution:** 69.8% white; 26.6% black; 1.3% Asian; 0.7% Amer. Ind.; 0.1% Hawaiian/Pacific Islander; 2 or more races, 1.5%. **Hispanic pop.:** 4.1%.

Geography. Total area: 52,420 sq mi; rank: 30. **Land area:** 50,645 sq mi; rank: 28. **Acres forested:** 22.9 mil. **Location:** East South Central state extending N-S from Tennessee to the Gulf of Mexico; E of the Mississippi R. **Climate:** long, hot summers; mild winters; generally abundant rain. **Topography:** coastal plains, including Prairie Black Belt, give way to hills, broken terrain; highest elevation 2,407 ft. **Capital:** Montgomery. **Chief airports:** Birmingham, Huntsville.

Economy. Chief industries: chemicals, electronics, apparel, primary metals, lumber and wood products, food processing, fabricated metals, automotive tires, oil and gas exploration. **Chief manuf. goods:** poultry processing, paper and paperboard, iron and steel, petroleum, automotive tires, aerospace, aluminum, auto body and parts. **Chief crops:** cotton, greenhouse and nursery, hay, peanuts, corn, soybeans. **Livestock:** 15.61 mil chickens (excl. broilers), 1.05 bil broilers, 1.24 mil cattle/calves. **Nonfuel minerals:** $990 mil; cement (portland), stone (crushed), lime, sand and gravel (construction), cement (masonry). **Commercial fishing:** $46.5 mil. **Chief port:** Mobile. **Gross state product:** $193.6 bil. **Sales tax:** 4.0%. **Employment distrib.:** 19.7% govt.; 19.1% trade/trans./util.; 13.1% mfg.; 11.7% ed./health; 11.6% prof./bus. serv.; 9.8% leisure/hosp.; 4.9% finance; 4.8% constr./mining/log.; 1.2% info.; 4.1% other serv. **Unemployment:** 6.5%. **Per cap. pers. income:** $36,501. **New private housing:** 11,763 units/$2.1 bil. **Broadband Internet:** 81.8%. **Commercial banks:** 160; deposits: $85 bil. **Savings institutions:** 11; deposits: $1.1 bil.

Federal govt. civ. employees: 39,865; **avg. salary:** $79,209. **Notable fed. facilities:** Redstone Arsenal; Ft. Rucker; Marshall Space Flight Ctr.; Anniston Army Depot; Maxwell AFB and Gunter Annex; Army Corps of Engineers, Mobile District.

Higher education. 4-year public coll./univ.: 14; **2-yr. public:** 25; **4-yr. private:** 19.

Energy. Electricity use/cost: 1,187 kWh, $135.26.

State data. Motto: Audemus Jura Nostra Defendere (We dare defend our rights). **Flower:** Camellia. **Bird:** Northern flicker (yellowhammer is local nickname). **Tree:** Southern longleaf pine. **Song:** "Alabama." **Entered union:** Dec. 14, 1819; rank: 22nd.

Tourism. Tourist spending: $8.4 bil. **Attractions:** First White House of the Confederacy, Civil Rights Memorial, Alabama Shakespeare Festival, in Montgomery; Ivy Green (Helen Keller birthplace), Tuscumbia; Barber Vintage Motorsports Museum, Civil Rights Institute, Vulcan Park and Museum (world's largest cast iron statue), in Birmingham; G. W. Carver Interpretive Museum, Tuskegee; W. C. Handy Home, Museum, and Library, Frank Lloyd Wright's Rosenbaum House, in Florence; U.S. Space & Rocket Ctr., Huntsville; Moundville Archaeological Park; USS *Alabama* Memorial Park, Mobile; Gulf State Park, Gulf Shores. **Information:** Alabama Tourism Dept., 401 Adams Ave., Ste. 126, P.O. Box 4927, Montgomery, AL 36103; 1-800-ALABAMA, (334) 242-4169; www.alabama.travel

History. Alabama was inhabited by the Creek, Cherokee, Chickasaw, Alabama, and Choctaw peoples when Spanish explorers arrived in the early 1500s. The French made the first permanent settlement at Ft. Louis, 1702, and founded Mobile, 1711. France later gave up the entire region to England under the Treaty of Paris, 1763. Spanish forces took control of the Mobile Bay area, 1780, and it remained under Spanish control until seized by U.S. troops, 1813. Most of present-day Alabama was held by the Creeks until Gen. Andrew Jackson broke their power, 1814. When Alabama became a state, 1819, black slaves made up about one-third of the population. The Indian Removal Act of 1830 forced most remaining Creeks west. The state seceded, 1861, and the Confederate states were organized Feb. 4, at Montgomery, the first capital. The state was readmitted, 1868. Birmingham, founded 1871, became a center for iron- and steelmaking. The Montgomery bus boycott, 1955, sparked by Rosa Parks, helped launch the civil rights movement. Other confrontations occurred at Birmingham, 1963, and Selma, 1965. The leading political figure from the 1960s through the '80s, four-term gov. George Wallace, started as a segregationist but later won with black support. Growth in the auto industry boosted the state economy as the 21st cent. began. A string of tornadoes in western Alabama in Apr. 2011 killed at least 248. Jefferson County, which includes the city of Birmingham, filed for the then-most expensive municipal bankruptcy in history in Nov. 2011 due to more than $3.1 bil in sewer-system debt.

Famous Alabamians. Hank Aaron, Tallulah Bankhead, Charles Barkley, Hugo L. Black, Paul "Bear" Bryant, George Washington Carver, Nat King Cole, Courteney Cox, William Christopher "W. C." Handy, Polly Holliday, Bo Jackson, Helen Keller, Coretta Scott King, Harper Lee, Joe Louis, Willie Mays, Jim Nabors, Jesse Owens, Terrell Owens, Rosa Parks, Condoleezza Rice, Lionel Richie, Octavia Spencer, Channing Tatum, George C. Wallace, Booker T. Washington, Hank Williams.

Website. www.alabama.gov

Alaska (AK)
The Last Frontier (unofficial)

People. Population: 735,132; rank: 47. **Pop. change** (2010-13): 3.5%. **Pop. density:** 1.3 per sq mi. **Racial distribution:** 67.3% white; 3.9% black; 5.8% Asian; 14.7% Amer. Ind.; 1.2% Hawaiian/Pacific Islander; 2 or more races, 7.1%. **Hispanic pop.:** 6.6%.

Geography. Total area: 665,384 sq mi; rank: 1. **Land area:** 570,641 sq mi; rank: 1. **Acres forested:** 15.2 mil. **Location:** NW corner of North America, bordered on E by Canada.

Climate: SE, SW, and central regions, moist and mild; far N extremely dry. Extended summer days, winter nights throughout. **Topography:** includes Pacific and Arctic mountain systems, central plateau, and Arctic slope. Mt. McKinley, 20,320 ft, is the highest point in N. America. **Capital:** Juneau. **Chief airport:** Anchorage.

Economy. Chief industries: petroleum, tourism, fishing, mining, forestry, transportation, aerospace. **Chief manuf. goods:** petroleum, seafood. **Chief crops:** greenhouse products, barley, oats, hay, potatoes, carrots. **Livestock:** 10,000 cattle/calves. **Nonfuel minerals:** $3.4 bil; gold, zinc, lead, silver, sand and gravel (construction). **Commercial fishing:** $1.7 bil. **Chief ports:** Anchorage, Dutch Harbor, Kodiak, Juneau, Sitka, Valdez. **Gross state product:** $59.4 bil. **Sales tax:** none. **Employment distrib.:** 24.6% govt.; 20.1% trade/trans./util.; 3.8% mfg.; 13.9% ed./health; 8.9% prof./bus. serv.; 9.8% leisure/hosp.; 3.5% finance; 10.2% constr./mining/log.; 1.8% info.; 3.4% other serv. **Unemployment:** 6.5%. **Per cap. pers. income:** $50,032. **New private housing:** 1,079 units/$257.5 mil. **Broadband Internet:** 83.2%. **Commercial banks:** 6; deposits $9.7 bil. **Savings institutions:** 2; deposits: $412 mil.

Federal govt. Fed. civ. employees: 11,758; **avg. salary:** $76,596. **Notable fed. facilities:** Joint Base Elmendorf-Richardson; Ft. Wainwright; Eielson AFB; Ft. Greely.

Higher education. 4-year public coll./univ.: 3; **2-yr. public:** 2; **4-yr. private:** 2.

Energy. Electricity use/cost: 654 kWh, $116.89.

State data. Motto: North to the future. **Flower:** Forget-me-not. **Bird:** Willow ptarmigan. **Tree:** Sitka spruce. **Song:** "Alaska's Flag." **Entered union:** Jan. 3, 1959; rank: 49th.

Tourism. Tourist spending: $2.4 bil. **Attractions:** Portage Glacier, in Chugach Natl. Forest; Mendenhall Glacier, in Tongass Natl. Forest; Totem Heritage Ctr., Ketchikan; Glacier Bay Natl. Park and Preserve; Mt. McKinley (or Denali, N. America's highest peak), in Denali Natl. Park and Preserve; Mt. Roberts Tramway, Juneau; Alaska Maritime Natl. Wildlife Refuge; St. Michael's Cathedral, Alaska Raptor Ctr., in Sitka; White Pass & Yukon Route railroad, Skagway; Katmai Natl. Park and Preserve; Univ. of Alaska Museum of the North, Fairbanks. **Information:** Alaska Travel Industry Association, 2600 Cordova St., Ste. 201, Anchorage, AK 99503; 1-800-327-9372; www.travelalaska.com

History. Early inhabitants included the Tlingit-Haida and Athabascan peoples. Ancestors of the Aleut and Inuit (Eskimo) probably arrived from Siberia between 10,000 and 6,000 years ago. Vitus Bering, a Dane sailing for Russia, was the first European to land in Alaska, 1741. Russians, pursuing the fur trade, established a permanent settlement on Kodiak Island, 1784. Sec. of State William H. Seward bought Alaska from Russia for $7.2 mil in 1867, a deal some called "Seward's Folly." Discovery of gold in the Klondike region of Canada's Yukon Territory, 1896, triggered an Alaskan gold rush. Alaska became a territory, 1912, and a state, 1959. A huge oil find at Prudhoe Bay, 1968, led to construction of the Trans-Alaska Pipeline, 1974-77. The *Exxon Valdez* supertanker ran aground, 1989, spilling about 11 mil gallons of crude oil; the cleanup cost more than $2.2 bil. Repeated attempts by Congress members to allow oil and gas drilling in the Arctic National Wildlife Refuge have failed.

Famous Alaskans. Tom Bodett, Susan Butcher, Ernest Gruening, Jewel (Kilcher), Tony Knowles, Sydney Laurence, Sarah Palin, Libby Riddles, Curt Schilling, Jefferson "Soapy" Smith.

Website. www.alaska.gov

Arizona (AZ)
Grand Canyon State

People. Population: 6,626,624; rank: 15. **Pop. change** (2010-13): 3.7%. **Pop. density:** 58.3 per sq mi. **Racial distribution:** 84.0% white; 4.6% black; 3.2% Asian; 5.3% Amer. Ind.; 0.3% Hawaiian/Pacific Islander; 2 or more races, 2.6%. **Hispanic pop.:** 30.3%.

Geography. Total area: 113,990 sq mi; rank: 6. **Land area:** 113,594 sq mi; rank: 6. **Acres forested:** 18.6 mil. **Location:** southwestern U.S. **Climate:** clear and dry in southern regions and northern plateau; high central areas have heavy winter snows. **Topography:** Colorado Plateau in the N, containing the Grand Canyon; Mexican Highlands run NW to SE; Sonoran Desert in the SW. **Capital:** Phoenix. **Chief airports:** Mesa, Phoenix, Tucson.

Economy. Chief industries: manufacturing, construction, tourism, mining, agriculture. **Chief manuf. goods:** aerospace,

semiconductors, navigational instruments, cement, plastics, structural metals, dairy, printing, furniture. **Chief crops:** cotton, grapes, apples, lettuce, hay, potatoes, sorghum, barley, corn, wheat. **Livestock:** 920,000 cattle/calves, 150,000 sheep/lambs. **Nonfuel minerals:** $7.5 bil; Copper, molybdenum concentrates, sand and gravel (construction), cement (portland), stone (crushed). **Gross state product:** $279.0 bil. **Sales tax:** 5.6%. **Employment distrib.:** 15.9% govt.; 19.0% trade/trans./util.; 6.1% mfg.; 15.2% ed./health; 14.7% prof./bus. serv.; 11.3% leisure/hosp.; 7.5% finance; 5.3% constr./mining/log.; 1.6% info.; 3.5% other serv. **Unemployment:** 8.0%. **Per cap. pers. income:** $36,823. **New private housing:** 25,209 units/$5.4 bil. **Broadband Internet:** 81.4%. **Commercial banks:** 63; deposits: $88 bil. **Savings institutions:** 8; deposits: $3.8 bil. **Lottery:** total sales: $692.9 mil; profit: $176.5 mil.

Federal govt. Fed. civ. employees: 40,688; **avg. salary:** $67,907. **Notable fed. facilities:** Luke AFB; Davis-Monthan AFB; Ft. Huachuca; Yuma Proving Ground.

Higher education. 4-year public coll./univ.: 4; **2-yr. public:** 20; **4-yr. private:** 11.

Energy. Electricity use/cost: 1,061 kWh, $119.84.

State data. Motto: Ditat Deus (God enriches). **Flower:** Blossom of the saguaro cactus. **Bird:** Cactus wren. **Tree:** Paloverde. **Song:** "Arizona." **Entered union:** Feb. 14, 1912; rank: 48th.

Tourism. Tourist spending: $16.2 bil. **Attractions:** Grand Canyon; Painted Desert, in Grand Canyon and Petrified Forest Natl. Parks; Glen Canyon Natl. Recreation Area; Canyon de Chelly Natl. Monument; Meteor Crater, near Winslow; London Bridge, Lake Havasu City; Biosphere 2, Oracle; Navajo Natl. Monument; Tombstone historic mining town; Tempe Town Lake. **Information:** Arizona Office of Tourism, 1110 W. Washington St., Ste. 155, Phoenix, AZ 85007; 1-866-275-5816; www.arizonaguide.com

History. Paleo-Indians hunted large game in the area at least 12,000 years ago. Anasazi, Mogollon, and Hohokam civilizations lived there c. 300 BCE-1300 CE; Navajo and Apache came c. 15th cent. Marcos de Niza, a Franciscan, and Estevanico, a black former slave, explored, 1539; Spanish explorer Francisco Vásquez de Coronado visited, 1540. Eusebio Francisco Kino, a Jesuit missionary, taught Indians, 1692-1711, and left missions. Tubac, a Spanish fort, became the first European settlement, 1752. Spain ceded Arizona to Mexico, 1821, The U.S. took over, 1848, after the Mexican War. The area below the Gila R. came from Mexico in the Gadsden Purchase, 1853. Arizona became a territory, 1863. Apache wars ended with Geronimo's surrender, 1886. Arizona became a state, 1912, and grew rapidly after 1960 with a fourfold rise in population over the next four decades. Barry Goldwater was a leading conservative voice in the U.S. Senate (1953-65, 1969-87). The border with Mexico is a major gateway for illegal immigration to the U.S. In 2012, the U.S. Supreme Court struck down most provisions of a 2010 state immigration law that allowed police to make warrantless arrests of those reasonably suspected of having immigrated illegally, but left a provision requiring police to check the immigration status of those stopped or arrested for any other reason.

Famous Arizonans. Bruce Babbitt, Cochise, Alice Cooper, Geronimo, Gabrielle Giffords, Barry Goldwater, Zane Grey, Carl Hayden, George W. P. Hunt, Helen Hull Jacobs, Bil Keane, Percival Lowell, John McCain, John J. Rhodes, Linda Ronstadt, Emma Stone, Morris K. Udall, Stewart L. Udall, Frank Lloyd Wright.

Website. www.az.gov

Arkansas (AR)
Natural State, Razorback State

People. Population: 2,959,373; rank: 32. **Pop. change** (2010-13): 1.5%. **Pop. density:** 56.9 per sq mi. **Racial distribution:** 79.9% white; 15.6% black; 1.5% Asian; 1.0% Amer. Ind.; 0.3% Hawaiian/Pacific Islander; 2 or more races, 1.9%. **Hispanic pop.:** 6.9%.

Geography. Total area: 55,179 sq mi; rank: 29. **Land area:** 52,035 sq mi; rank: 27. **Acres forested:** 19.0 mil. **Location:** West South Central state. **Climate:** long, hot summers, mild winters; generally abundant rainfall. **Topography:** eastern delta and prairie, southern lowland forests, and the northwestern highlands, which include the Ozark Plateaus. **Capital:** Little Rock. **Chief airports:** Bentonville, Little Rock.

Economy. Chief industries: manufacturing, agriculture, tourism, forestry. **Chief manuf. goods:** poultry processing, motor vehicles and parts; iron and steel, paper and paperboard, plastics, preserved fruits and vegetables, aerospace, rubber. **Chief crops:** rice, soybeans, cotton, hay, wheat, corn, sorghum, tomatoes, peaches, watermelons, pecans, blueberries, grapes. **Livestock:** 20.62 mil chickens (excl. broilers), 996.4 mil broilers, 1.66 mil cattle/calves. **Nonfuel minerals:** $1 bil; cement (portland), bromine, stone (crushed), sand and gravel (industrial), sand and gravel (construction). **Chief port:** Helena. **Gross state product:** $124.2 bil. **Sales tax:** 6.5%. **Employment distrib.:** 18.3% govt.; 20.4% trade/trans./util.; 12.9% mfg.; 14.6% ed./health; 10.8% prof./bus. serv.; 9.3% leisure/hosp.; 4.1% finance; 4.8% constr./mining/log.; 1.2% info.; 3.7% other serv. **Unemployment:** 7.5%. **Per cap. pers. income:** $36,086. **New private housing:** 7,481 units/$1.2 bil. **Broadband Internet:** 86.8%. **Commercial banks:** 140; deposits: $52.3 bil. **Savings institutions:** 6; deposits: $844 mil. **Lottery:** total sales $439.5 mil; profit: $90.3 mil.

Federal govt. Fed. civ. employees: 14,085; **avg. salary:** $65,422. **Notable fed. facilities:** Little Rock AFB; Pine Bluff Arsenal; Natl. Ctr. for Toxicological Research, Jefferson.

Higher education. 4-year public coll./univ.: 11; **2-yr. public:** 22; **4-yr. private:** 12.

Energy. Electricity use/cost: 1,120 kWh, $104.14.

State data. Motto: Regnat Populus (The people rule). **Flower:** Apple blossom. **Bird:** Mockingbird. **Tree:** Pine. **Song:** "Arkansas." **Entered union:** June 15, 1836; rank: 25th.

Tourism. Tourist spending: $6.2 bil. **Attractions:** Eureka Springs; Ozark Folk Ctr. State Park, Mountain View; Blanchard Springs Caverns, in Ozark Natl. Forest; Crater of Diamonds State Park, Murfreesboro; Toltec Mounds Archeological State Park, Scott; Buffalo Natl. River; Hot Springs Natl. Park; Pea Ridge Natl. Military Park; William J. Clinton Presidential Library and Museum, Little Rock Central High School Natl. Historic Site, in Little Rock; Crystal Bridges Museum of American Art, Bentonville. **Information:** Arkansas Dept. of Parks & Tourism, 1 Capitol Mall, Little Rock, AR 72201; 1-800-NATURAL; www.arkansas.com

History. Quapaw, Caddo, Osage, Cherokee, and Choctaw peoples lived in the area at the time of European contact. The first European explorers were Hernando de Soto, 1541; Jacques Marquette and Louis Jolliet, 1673; and René-Robert Cavelier, sieur de La Salle, 1682. French fur trader Henri de Tonty founded the first settlement, 1686, at Arkansas Post. In 1762, the area was ceded by France to Spain, then given back, 1800, and was part of the Louisiana Purchase, 1803. It was made a territory, 1819, and entered the Union as a slave state, 1836. Arkansas seceded in 1861, after the Civil War began; it was readmitted, 1868. Pres. Eisenhower sent federal troops, 1957, to keep Gov. Orval Faubus from blocking racial integration at Central High School in Little Rock. Wal-Mart, now the world's leading retailer, opened its first store in Rogers, 1962. Elected five times as governor, Bill Clinton later served two terms as president (1993-2001). His presidential library opened, 2004, in Little Rock.

Famous Arkansans. Daisy Bates, Dee Brown, Paul "Bear" Bryant, Glen Campbell, Hattie Wyatt Caraway, Johnny Cash, Wesley Clark, Bill Clinton, Jay Hanna "Dizzy" Dean, Orval Faubus, James William Fulbright, Al Green, John Grisham, Levon Helm, John H. Johnson, Douglas MacArthur, John Little McClellan, James S. McDonnell, Scottie Pippen, Dick Powell, Brooks Robinson, Winthrop Rockefeller, Mary Steenburgen, Edward Durell Stone, Billy Bob Thornton, Sam Walton, Archibald Yell.

Website. www.arkansas.gov

California (CA)
Golden State

People. Population: 38,332,521; rank: 1. **Pop. change (2010-13):** 2.9%. **Pop. density:** 246.1 per sq mi. **Racial distribution:** 73.5% white; 6.6% black; 14.1% Asian; 1.7% Amer. Ind.; 0.5% Hawaiian/Pacific Islander; 2 or more races, 3.7%. **Hispanic pop.:** 38.4%.

Geography. Total area: 163,695 sq mi; rank: 3. **Land area:** 155,779 sq mi; rank: 3. **Acres forested:** 32.5 mil. **Location:** western coast of U.S. **Climate:** moderate temperatures and rainfall along the coast; extremes in the interior. **Topography:** long mountainous coastline; central valley; Sierra Nevada on the E; desert basins in southern interior; rugged mountains in N. **Capital:** Sacramento. **Chief airports:** Burbank, Fresno, Long Beach, Los Angeles, Oakland, Ontario, Palm Springs, Sacramento, San Diego, San Francisco, San Jose, Santa Ana.

Economy. Chief industries: agriculture, tourism, apparel, electronics, telecommunications, entertainment. **Chief manuf. goods:** petroleum, aerospace, precision instruments, semiconductors, telecom. and broadcasting equip., pharmaceutical, wineries, plastics, medical equip., preserved fruits and vegetables, printing, dairy, cut and sew apparel, motor vehicles. **Chief crops:** grapes, nursery products, almonds, lettuce, hay, strawberries, floriculture, tomatoes, cotton, oranges, pistachios, walnuts, broccoli, carrots, rice, peaches, lemons. **Livestock:** 20.75 mil chickens (excl. broilers), 5.25 mil cattle/calves, 550,000 sheep/lambs. **Nonfuel minerals:** $3.1 bil; boron minerals, cement (portland), sand and gravel (construction), stone (crushed), gold. **Commercial fishing:** $244.0 mil. **Chief ports:** Long Beach, Los Angeles, San Diego, San Francisco, Richmond, Oakland, San Francisco, Stockton. **Gross state product:** $2.2 tril. **Sales tax:** 7.5%. **Employment distrib.:** 15.7% govt.; 18.2% trade/trans./util.; 8.0% mfg.; 15.4% ed./health; 15.6% prof./bus. serv.; 11.1% leisure/hosp.; 5.0% finance; 4.5% constr./mining/log.; 3.0% info.; 3.4% other serv. **Unemployment:** 8.9%. **Per cap. pers. income:** $47,401. **New private housing:** 80,742 units/$18.3 bil. **Broadband Internet:** 86.8%. **Commercial banks:** 251; deposits: $983 bil. **Savings institutions:** 24; deposits: $32.1 bil. **Lottery:** total sales: $4.4 bil; profit: $1.3 bil.

Federal govt. Fed. civ. employees: 163,016; **avg. salary:** $79,597. **Notable fed. facilities:** USMC Camp Pendleton; Naval Base Coronado; Marine Corps Air Ground Combat Ctr., 29 Palms; Marine Corps Air Station Miramar; Travis AFB; Naval Research Lab, Monterey; Lawrence Livermore Natl. Lab; Lawrence Berkeley Natl. Lab; NASA Jet Propulsion Lab; Edwards AFB (NASA Dryden Flight Research Ctr., AF Flight Test Ctr.); San Francisco Mint.

Higher education. 4-year public coll./univ.: 35; **2-yr. public:** 114; **4-yr. private:** 135.

Energy. Electricity use/cost: 573 kWh, $87.91.

State data. Motto: Eureka (I have found it). **Flower:** Golden poppy. **Bird:** California valley quail. **Tree:** California redwood. **Song:** "I Love You, California." **Entered union:** Sept. 9, 1850; rank: 31st.

Tourism. Tourist spending: $110.8 bil. **Attractions:** *Queen Mary*, Aquarium of the Pacific, in Long Beach; Palomar Observatory, Palomar Mountain; Disneyland Resort, Anaheim; Getty Center, Universal Studios Hollywood, Griffith Observatory, in Los Angeles; Tournament of Roses and Rose Bowl, Pasadena; The California Museum, California State Railroad Museum, in Sacramento; San Diego Zoo, USS *Midway* Museum, in San Diego; Yosemite Valley; Lassen Volcanic, Sequoia, and Kings Canyon Natl. Parks; Mojave and Sonoran Deserts; Death Valley; Golden Gate Park, Alcatraz Island, in San Francisco; Napa Valley wine region; Monterey Bay Aquarium, Monterey Peninsula; Ancient Bristlecone Pine Forest (oldest known living trees on Earth), in Inyo Natl. Forest; Redwood Natl. and State Parks; Muir Woods Natl. Monument, Mill Valley. **Information:** California Tourism, P.O. Box 1499, Sacramento, CA 95812-1499; 1-877-225-4367; www.visitcalifornia.com

History. Early inhabitants included more than 100 different Native American tribes with multiple dialects. The first European explorers were Juan Rodríguez Cabrillo, 1542, and Sir Francis Drake, 1579. The first settlement was the Spanish Alta California mission at San Diego, 1769, first in a string founded by Franciscan Father Junípero Serra. California became a province of independent Mexico, 1821. U.S. traders and settlers arrived in the 19th cent. and staged the Bear Flag revolt, 1846, in protest against Mexican rule; later that year U.S. forces occupied California. At the end of the Mexican War, Mexico ceded the territory to the U.S., 1848; that same year gold was discovered, and the famed gold rush began. California became a state, 1850. An economic downturn in the 1870s spurred riots against Chinese immigrants, who had come as laborers in the boom years. An earthquake and related fires devastated San Francisco, 1906. During World War II, Japanese Americans, many of them U.S. citizens, were held in detention camps, 1942-45. Ronald Reagan, a former movie actor, became state governor (1967-75) and U.S. president (1981-89). A budget crisis, 2003, resulted in the recall of Gov. Gray Davis and the election of another actor, Arnold Schwarzenegger. Led by Hollywood in entertainment and Silicon Valley in technology, the state's economy dwarfs that of most nations. Still, billion-dollar budget deficits have been a perennial problem. The U.S. Supreme Court in 2013 effectively upheld the right of same-sex couples to marry in the state. After much of the state experienced its driest year in recorded history, Gov. Jerry Brown declared a drought state of emergency in Jan. 2014; continued parched conditions contributed to widespread forest fires that prompted a second state of emergency in Aug.

Famous Californians. Tom Brady, Edmund G. (Pat) Brown, Jerry Brown, Luther Burbank, Julia Child, Ted Danson, Cameron Diaz, Leonardo DiCaprio, Joe DiMaggio, Landon Donovan, Clint Eastwood, Dianne Feinstein, John C. Fremont, Tom Hanks, Bret Harte, William Randolph Hearst, Helen Hunt, Steve Jobs, Jimmie Johnson, Angelina Jolie, Jack Kemp, Jason Kidd, Lisa Leslie, Monica Lewinsky, Jack London, George Lucas, Phil Mickelson, Marilyn Monroe, John Muir, Richard M. Nixon, Gwyneth Paltrow, George S. Patton Jr., Gregory Peck, Nancy Pelosi, Ronald Reagan, Sally K. Ride, William Saroyan, Arnold Schwarzenegger, Father Junípero Serra, O. J. Simpson, Kevin Spacey, Leland Stanford, Gwen Stefani, John Steinbeck, Shirley Temple, Earl Warren, Serena Williams, Ted Williams, Venus Williams, Tiger Woods.

Website. www.ca.gov

Colorado (CO)
Centennial State

People. Population: 5,268,367; rank: 22. **Pop. change** (2010-13): 4.8%. **Pop. density:** 50.8 per sq mi. **Racial distribution:** 88.0% white; 4.4% black; 3.0% Asian; 1.6% Amer. Ind.; 0.2% Hawaiian/Pacific Islander; 2 or more races, 2.8%. **Hispanic pop.:** 21.0%.

Geography. Total area: 104,094 sq mi; rank: 8. **Land area:** 103,642 sq mi; rank: 8. **Acres forested:** 22.9 mil. **Location:** W central U.S. **Climate:** low relative humidity, abundant sunshine, wide daily/seasonal temperature ranges; alpine conditions in the high mountains. **Topography:** eastern dry high plains; hilly to mountainous central plateau; western Rocky Mts. of high ranges with broad valleys, deep, narrow canyons. **Capital:** Denver. **Chief airports:** Colorado Springs, Denver.

Economy. Chief industries: manufacturing, construction, government, tourism, agriculture, aerospace, electronics equip. **Chief manuf. goods:** animal slaughtering, beer, petroleum, pharmaceuticals, aerospace, medical equip., precision instruments, printing, semiconductors. **Chief crops:** hay, corn, potatoes, wheat, onions, dry edible beans, sunflowers, sugar beets, barley, proso millet, cabbage, peaches, lettuce, apples, cantaloupes. **Livestock.** 5.99 mil chickens (excl. broilers), 2.48 mil cattle/calves, 365,000 sheep/lambs, 160,000 hogs/pigs. **Non-fuel minerals:** $2.1 bil; molybdenum concentrates, gold, sand and gravel (construction), cement (portland), stone (crushed). **Gross state product:** $294.4 bil. **Sales tax:** 2.9%. **Employment distrib.:** 17.2% govt.; 17.3% trade/trans./util.; 5.6% mfg.; 12.3% ed./health; 15.8% prof./bus. serv.; 12.0% leisure/hosp.; 6.1% finance; 6.9% constr./mining/log.; 2.8% info.; 4.0% other serv. **Unemployment:** 6.8%. **Per cap. pers. income:** $46,610. **New private housing:** 27,517 units/$5.9 bil. **Broadband Internet:** 87.8%. **Commercial banks:** 138; deposits: $102.9 bil. **Savings institutions:** 14; deposits: $2.8 bil. **Lottery:** total sales: $566.3 mil; profit: $135.6 mil.

Federal govt. Fed. civ. employees: 38,979; **avg. salary:** $78,129. **Notable fed. facilities:** U.S. Air Force Academy; Peterson AFB; Denver Mint; Ft. Carson; Natl. Renewable Energy Lab; Transportation Tech. Ctr.; NORAD and USNORTHCOM Alt. Command Ctr., Cheyenne Mtn. Complex; Denver Federal Ctr.; Natl. Ctr. for Atmospheric Research; Natl. Inst. of Standards & Tech., Boulder; Natl. Wildlife Research Ctr.; NOAA Earth Systems Research Environmental Lab.

Higher education. 4-year public coll./univ.: 14; **2-yr. public:** 14; **4-yr. private:** 11.

Energy. Electricity use/cost: 706 kWh, $80.94.

State data. Motto: Nil Sine Numine (Nothing without Providence). **Flower:** Rocky Mountain columbine. **Bird:** Lark bunting. **Tree:** Colorado blue spruce. **Songs:** "Where the Columbines Grow"; "Rocky Mountain High." **Entered union:** Aug. 1, 1876; rank 38th.

Tourism. Tourist spending: $16.2 bil. **Attractions:** Denver Museum of Nature & Science, Denver Botanic Gardens, Denver Zoo; Red Rocks Park and Amphitheatre, Morrison; Natl. Ctr. for Atmospheric Research, Boulder; Rocky Mountain, Black Canyon of the Gunnison, and Mesa Verde (Anasazi cliff dwellings) Natl. Parks; Aspen, Breckenridge, Steamboat, and Vail ski resorts; Garden of the Gods, Colorado Springs; Great Sand Dunes Natl. Park and Preserve; Dinosaur and Colorado Natl. Monuments; Pikes Peak and Mount Evans; Grand Mesa Natl. Forest; historic mining towns

of Central City, Silverton, Cripple Creek; Bent's Old Fort Natl. Historic Site, near La Junta; Georgetown Loop Historic Mining and Railroad Park; Durango & Silverton Narrow Gauge Railroad Museum, Durango; Cumbres & Toltec Scenic Railroad, Antonito; gambling in Black Hawk, Central City, Cripple Creek and on tribal land in Ignacio and Towaoc. **Information:** Colorado Tourism Office, 1625 Broadway, Ste. 1700, Denver, CO 80202; 1-800-COLORADO; www.colorado.com

History. Paleo-Indians hunted big game in the area at least 11,000 years ago. Anasazi cliff dwellers flourished around Mesa Verde until about 1300 CE; other Native Americans were the Ute, Pueblo, Cheyenne, and Arapaho. The region was claimed by Spain but passed to France, 1800. The U.S. acquired eastern Colorado in the Louisiana Purchase, 1803. Lt. Zebulon M. Pike explored the area, 1806, sighting the peak that bears his name. After the Mexican War, 1846-48, U.S. immigrants settled in the east, former Mexicans in the south. Gold was discovered in 1858, causing a population boom. Congress created Colorado Territory, 1861. Conflict between newcomers and displaced Native Americans led to the Sand Creek Massacre, 1864, in which U.S. soldiers and settlers killed some 150 Cheyenne and Arapaho. U.S. Army troops forced the removal to reservations (mostly in present-day Oklahoma) of most Native Americans in the state, 1867. The 1870s brought statehood, 1876, and rich silver finds that turned Leadville into a boomtown. Federal military and civilian employment in Colorado surged in the 1940s and '50s; since then, tourism and technology have fueled the economy. The state's Hispanic population grew from 5.8% in 1980 to 20.7% in 2010. Colorado became the first state in the U.S. to legalize the sale of recreational marijuana in Jan. 2014.

Famous Coloradans. Tim Allen, Chauncey Billups, Frederick Bonfils, Molly Brown, William N. Byers, M. Scott Carpenter, Lon Chaney, Jack Dempsey, Mamie Eisenhower, Douglas Fairbanks, Barney Ford, Roy Halladay, Chief Ourey, Trey Parker, "Baby Doe" Tabor, Lowell Thomas, Byron R. White, Paul Whiteman.

Website. www.colorado.gov

Connecticut (CT)
Constitution State, Nutmeg State

People. Population: 3,596,080; rank: 29. **Pop. change** (2010-13): 0.6%. **Pop. density:** 742.7 per sq mi. **Racial distribution:** 81.6% white; 11.3% black; 4.3% Asian; 0.5% Amer. Ind.; 0.1% Hawaiian/Pacific Islander; 2 or more races, 2.1%. **Hispanic pop.:** 14.7%.

Geography. Total area: 5,543 sq mi; rank: 48. **Land area:** 4,842 sq mi; rank: 48. **Acres forested:** 1.7 mil. **Location:** New England state in NE corner of U.S. **Climate:** moderate; winters avg. slightly below freezing; warm, humid summers. **Topography:** western upland, the Berkshires, in the NW, highest elevations; narrow central lowland N-S; hilly eastern upland drained by rivers. **Capital:** Hartford. **Chief airport:** Windsor Locks.

Economy. Chief industries: manufacturing, retail trade, government, services, finances, insurance, real estate. **Chief manuf. goods:** aerospace, chemicals, fabricated metals, precision instruments, toiletries, medical equip., printing, plastics. **Chief crops:** nursery stock, Christmas trees, mushrooms, sweet corn, apples, tobacco, hay. **Livestock:** 2.98 mil chickens (excl. broilers), 47,000 cattle/calves. **Nonfuel minerals:** $171 mil; stone (crushed), sand and gravel (construction), clays (common), gemstones (natural). **Commercial fishing:** $20.6 mil. **Chief ports:** New Haven, Bridgeport, New London. **Gross state product:** $249.3 bil. **Sales tax:** 6.35%. **Employment distrib.:** 14.2% govt.; 18.1% trade/trans./util.; 9.7% mfg.; 19.5% ed./health; 12.4% prof./bus. serv.; 9.3% leisure/hosp.; 7.8% finance; 3.4% constr./mining/log.; 1.9% info.; 3.7% other serv. **Unemployment:** 7.8%. **Per cap. pers. income:** $60,847. **New private housing:** 5,424 units/$1.2 bil. **Broadband Internet:** 83.8%. **Commercial banks:** 36; deposits: $74.8 bil. **Savings institutions:** 34; deposits: $32.3 bil. **Lottery:** total sales: $1.1 bil; profit: $314.0 mil.

Federal govt. Fed. civ. employees: 8,845; **avg. salary:** $80,139. **Notable fed. facilities:** U.S. Coast Guard Academy; Naval Sub Base New London.

Higher education. 4-year public coll./univ.: 9; **2-yr. public:** 12; **4-yr. private:** 19.

Energy. Electricity use/cost: 731 kWh, $126.75.

State data. Motto: Qui Transtulit Sustinet (He who transplanted still sustains). **Flower:** Mountain laurel. **Bird:** American robin. **Tree:** White oak. **Song:** "Yankee Doodle." **Fifth** of the 13 original states to ratify the Constitution, Jan. 9, 1788.

Tourism. Tourist spending: $9.7 bil. **Attractions:** Mark Twain House and Museum, Hartford; Yale Univ. Art Gallery, Peabody Museum of Natural History, in New Haven; Mystic Seaport, Mystic Aquarium; Barnum Museum, Bridgeport; Gillette Castle State Park, East Haddam; USS *Nautilus* (1st nuclear-powered submarine) at Submarine Force Library and Museum, Groton; Mashantucket Pequot Museum and Research Ctr.; Foxwoods Resort Casino, Ledyard; Mohegan Sun, Uncasville; Lake Compounce (est. 1846; oldest continuously operating amusement park in U.S.), Bristol; Philip Johnson Glass House, New Canaan. **Information:** Connecticut Commission on Culture and Tourism, One Constitution Plz., 2nd Fl., Hartford, CT 06103; 1-888-CTVISIT, (860) 256-2800; www.ctvisit.com

History. At the time of European contact, inhabitants of the area were Algonquian peoples, including the Mohegan and Pequot. Dutch explorer Adriaen Block was the first European visitor, 1614. By 1634, settlers from Plymouth Bay had started colonies along the Connecticut R.; in 1637 they defeated the Pequots. The Colony of Connecticut was chartered by England, 1662; New Haven colony was added, 1665. A Patriot stronghold in the American Revolution, the state actively supported the antislavery movement and the Union cause in the Civil War. The state economy prospered in the 20th cent. from insurance- and defense-related industries. *Nautilus*, the first nuclear-powered submarine, was launched at Groton, 1954. Connecticut Sen. Joseph Lieberman was the Democratic nominee for vice president in 2000. American Indian casinos, starting with Foxwoods in 1992, were an economic boon to the state, but tourism revenues declined sharply with the recession that began in late 2007. Twenty children and six staff members were killed in a mass shooting at Sandy Hook Elementary School in Newtown, Dec. 14, 2012.

Famous "Nutmeggers." Ethan Allen, P. T. Barnum, Michael Bolton, Glenn Close, Samuel Colt, Ann Coulter, Jonathan Edwards, Nathan Hale, Katharine Hepburn, Isaac Hull, Norman Lear, Seth MacFarlane, John Mayer, Robert Mitchum, J. P. Morgan, Ralph Nader, Israel Putnam, Wallace Stevens, Harriet Beecher Stowe, Mark Twain, Noah Webster, Eli Whitney.

Website. www.ct.gov

Delaware (DE)
First State, Diamond State

People. Population: 925,749; rank: 45. **Pop. change (2010-13):** 3.1%. **Pop. density:** 475.0 per sq mi. **Racial distribution:** 71.1% white; 22.1% black; 3.6% Asian; 0.7% Amer. Ind.; 0.1% Hawaiian/Pacific Islander; 2 or more races, 2.4%. **Hispanic pop.:** 8.7%.

Geography. Total area: 2,489 sq mi; rank: 49. **Land area:** 1,949 sq mi; rank: 50. **Acres forested:** 0.3 mil. **Location:** Delmarva Peninsula on the Atlantic coastal plain. **Climate:** moderate. **Topography:** Piedmont Plateau to the N, sloping to a near sea-level plain. **Capital:** Dover.

Economy. Chief industries: chemicals, agriculture, finance, poultry, shellfish, tourism, auto assembly, food processing, transportation equip. **Chief manuf. goods:** pharmaceuticals, poultry processing, soap and cleaning compounds, precision instruments, basic chemicals, plastics. **Chief crops:** soybeans, corn, greenhouse and nursery, wheat, potatoes, barley, hay, watermelons, lima beans, green peas, pumpkins, mushrooms, cabbage. **Livestock:** 215.6 mil broilers, 16,000 cattle/calves. **Nonfuel minerals:** $15.4 mil; magnesium compounds, sand and gravel (construction), stone (crushed), gemstones (natural). **Commercial fishing:** $7.9 mil. **Chief port:** Wilmington. **Gross state product:** $62.7 bil. **Sales tax:** none. **Employment distrib.:** 15.0% govt.; 17.9% trade/trans./util.; 5.8% mfg.; 16.1% ed./health; 14.0% prof./bus. serv.; 10.8% leisure/hosp.; 10.2% finance; 4.7% constr./mining/log.; 1.2% info.; 4.4% other serv. **Unemployment:** 6.7%. **Per cap. pers. income:** $45,092. **New private housing:** 4,827 units/$592.8 mil. **Broadband Internet:** 82.3%. **Commercial banks:** 35; deposits: $392 bil. **Savings institutions:** 5; deposits: $4.2 bil. **Lottery:** total sales: $631.9 mil; profit: $237.2 mil.

Federal govt. Fed. civ. employees: 3,184; **avg. salary:** $70,490. **Notable fed. facilities:** Dover AFB; Bombay Hook National Wildlife Refuge.

Higher education. 4-year public coll./univ.: 2; **2-yr. public:** 3; **4-yr. private:** 4.

Energy. Electricity use/cost: 942 kWh, $127.92.

State data. Motto: Liberty and independence. **Flower:** Peach blossom. **Bird:** Blue hen chicken. **Tree:** American holly.

Song: "Our Delaware." **First** of original 13 states to ratify the Constitution, Dec. 7, 1787.

Tourism. Tourist spending: $1.7 bil. **Attractions:** Fort Christina (site of founding of colony of New Sweden), Holy Trinity (Old Swedes) Church (erected 1698, oldest church in U.S. still standing as built and in use), Hagley Museum and Library, Nemours Mansion and Gardens, in Wilmington; Winterthur Museum, Garden, and Library, near Wilmington; New Castle Historic District; John Dickinson "Penman of the Revolution" Plantation, First State Heritage Park, Dover Intl. Speedway, in Dover; Rehoboth Beach. **Information:** Delaware Tourism Office, 99 Kings Hwy., Dover, DE 19901; 1-866-2VISITDE; www.visitdelaware.com

History. The Lenni Lenape (Delaware) people lived in the region at the time of European contact. Henry Hudson located the Delaware R., 1609. In 1610, English explorer Samuel Argall entered Delaware Bay and named the area after Virginia's governor, Lord De La Warr. Dutch, Swedish, and Finnish settlers were followed by the British, who took control in 1664. After 1682, Delaware became part of Pennsylvania, and in 1704 it was granted its own assembly. It adopted a constitution as the state of Delaware, 1776, and was the first state to ratify the federal Constitution, 1787. Although it remained in the Union during the Civil War, Delaware retained slavery until the 13th Amendment abolished it in 1865. The DuPont company, founded as a gunpowder mill in 1802, became an industrial giant in the 20th cent. making nylon, Teflon, and other synthetics. Pro-business laws drew many out-of-state firms to incorporate in Delaware. In 2000, Ruth Ann Minner was elected Delaware's first woman governor.

Famous Delawareans. Thomas F. Bayard, Joseph Biden, Henry Seidel Canby, E. I. du Pont, John P. Marquand, Howard Pyle, Caesar Rodney, Susan Stroman.

Website. www.delaware.gov

Florida (FL)
Sunshine State

People. Population: 19,552,860; rank: 4. **Pop. change (2010-13):** 4.0%. **Pop. density:** 364.6 per sq mi. **Racial distribution:** 78.1% white; 16.7% black; 2.7% Asian; 0.5% Amer. Ind.; 0.1% Hawaiian/Pacific Islander; 2 or more races, 1.9%. **Hispanic pop.:** 23.6%.

Geography. Total area: 65,758 sq mi; rank: 22. **Land area:** 53,625 sq mi; rank: 26. **Acres forested:** 17.3 mil. **Location:** peninsula jutting southward 500 mi between the Atlantic and Gulf of Mexico. **Climate:** subtropical N of Bradenton-Lake Okeechobee-Vero Beach line; tropical S of line. **Topography:** land is flat or rolling; highest point is 345 ft in the NW. **Capital:** Tallahassee. **Chief airports:** Clearwater, Fort Lauderdale, Fort Myers, Jacksonville, Miami, Orlando, Pensacola, Sanford, Sarasota, Tampa, West Palm Beach.

Economy. Chief industries: tourism, agriculture, manufacturing, construction, services, international trade. **Chief manuf. goods:** navigational instruments, medical equip., cement, broadcasting equip., beverages, phosphatic fertilizer, preserved fruits and vegetables, structural metal, printing. **Chief crops:** greenhouse and nursery, oranges, sugarcane, tomatoes, green peppers, grapefruit, strawberries, snap beans, sweet corn, potatoes, cucumbers, tangerines. **Livestock:** 10.32 mil chickens (excl. broilers), 64.4 mil broilers, 1.62 mil cattle/calves. **Nonfuel minerals:** $3.8 bil; phosphate rock, stone (crushed), cement (portland), zirconium concentrates, sand and gravel (construction). **Commercial fishing:** $198.9 mil. **Chief ports:** Pensacola, Tampa, Port Manatee, Miami, Port Everglades, Jacksonville, Canaveral. **Gross state product:** $800.5 bil. **Sales tax:** 6.0%. **Employment distrib.:** 14.0% govt.; 20.7% trade/trans./util.; 4.2% mfg.; 14.7% ed./health; 14.8% prof./bus. serv.; 13.9% leisure/hosp.; 6.7% finance; 5.2% constr./mining/log.; 1.7% info.; 4.0% other serv. **Unemployment:** 7.2%. **Per cap. pers. income:** $41,692. **New private housing:** 86,752 units/$18.2 bil. **Broadband Internet:** 90.7%. **Commercial banks:** 253; deposits: $415.8 bil. **Savings institutions:** 28; deposits: $25.3 bil. **Lottery:** total sales: $5.0 bil; profit: $1.4 bil.

Federal govt. Fed. civ. employees: 89,534; **avg. salary:** $72,991. **Notable fed. facilities:** John F. Kennedy Space Ctr.; Eglin AFB; MacDill AFB; Hurlburt Field; Pensacola NAS; Jacksonville NAS; Mayport Naval Sta.

Higher education. 4-year public coll./univ.: 35; **2-yr. public:** 6; **4-yr. private:** 61.

Energy. Electricity use/cost: 1,081 kWh, $123.45.

State data. Motto: In God we trust. **Flower:** Orange blossom. **Bird:** Mockingbird. **Tree:** Sabal palmetto palm. **Song:** "Old Folks at Home." **Entered union:** Mar. 3, 1845; rank: 27th.

Tourism. Tourist spending: $74.8 bil. **Attractions:** Miami Beach; Castillo de San Marcos Natl. Monument, St. Augustine Lighthouse & Museum, Lightner Museum, in St. Augustine (oldest permanent European settlement in U.S.); Walt Disney World Resort, SeaWorld Orlando, Universal Studios, Discovery Cove, in Orlando; Kennedy Space Ctr., U.S. Astronaut Hall of Fame; Everglades Natl. Park; Ringling Museum of Art, Ringling Circus Museum, in Sarasota; Cypress Gardens at Legoland Florida, Winter Haven; Busch Gardens, Big Cat Rescue, in Tampa; Florida Caverns State Park, Marianna; Key West. **Information:** Visit Florida, 2540 W. Executive Center Cir., Ste. 200, Tallahassee, FL 32301; 1-888-7FLA-USA; www.visitflorida.com

History. Florida has been inhabited for at least 12,000 years. Timucua, Apalachee, and Calusa peoples were living in the region when the earliest Europeans came; later the Seminole migrated from Georgia to Florida, becoming dominant there in the early 18th cent. The first European to see Florida was Ponce de León, 1513. France established a colony, Ft. Caroline, on the St. Johns R., 1564. Spain settled St. Augustine, 1565, and Spanish troops massacred most of the French. Britain's Sir Francis Drake burned St. Augustine, 1586. In 1763, Spain ceded Florida to Great Britain, which held the area 20 years before returning it to Spain. Florida was ceded to the U.S. in the Adams-Onís Treaty, 1819. The Seminole War, 1835-42, resulted in the removal of most Native Americans to Indian Territory. Florida joined the Union in 1845, seceded in 1861, and was readmitted in 1868. In the late 19th cent., hotel and railroad builder Henry M. Flagler laid the foundations of the tourism industry. The state experienced phenomenal population growth in the 20th cent., especially after 1950. The first U.S. astronaut was launched into space from Cape Canaveral, 1961. Walt Disney World opened near Orlando, 1971. Hurricane Andrew slammed Florida, 1992, causing at least $25 bil in property damage. A dispute over Florida's presidential vote in 2000 was decided by the U.S. Supreme Court and resulted in George W. Bush's Electoral College victory. Four hurricanes hit the state in 2004, causing more than $40 bil in damages.

Famous Floridians. Edna Buchanan, Jeb Bush, Marjory Stoneman Douglas, Henry Morrison Flagler, Carl Hiaasen, Perez Hilton, Zora Neale Hurston, James Weldon Johnson, Deacon Jones, MacKinlay Kantor, Osceola, Claude Pepper, Tom Petty, Henry B. Plant, A. Philip Randolph, Marjorie Kinnan Rawlings, Janet Reno, Marco Rubio, Deion Sanders, Emmitt Smith, Joseph W. Stilwell, Amar'e Stoudemire, Charles P. Summerall.

Website. www.myflorida.com

Georgia (GA)
Empire State of the South, Peach State

People. Population: 9,992,167; rank: 8. **Pop. change** (2010-13): 3.1%. **Pop. density:** 173.7 per sq mi. **Racial distribution:** 62.5% white; 31.4% black; 3.7% Asian; 0.5% Amer. Ind.; 0.1% Hawaiian/Pacific Islander; 2 or more races, 1.9%. **Hispanic pop.:** 9.2%.

Geography. Total area: 59,425 sq mi; rank: 24. **Land area:** 57,513 sq mi; rank: 21. **Acres forested:** 24.8 mil. **Location:** South Atlantic state. **Climate:** maritime tropical air masses dominate in summer; polar air masses in winter; E central area drier. **Topography:** most southerly of the Blue Ridge Mts. cover NE and N central; central Piedmont extends to the fall line of rivers; coastal plain levels to the coast flatlands. **Capital:** Atlanta. **Chief airports:** Atlanta, Savannah.

Economy. Chief industries: services, manufacturing, retail trade. **Chief manuf. goods:** carpet and rugs, animal slaughtering and processing, motor vehicles and parts, plastics, aircrafts, paper, chemicals, food. **Chief crops:** cotton, greenhouse and nursery, peanuts, pecans, corn, tomatoes, cucumbers, onions, watermelons, tobacco, squash, blueberries, hay, cabbage, soybeans, peaches, snap beans, wheat. **Livestock:** 27.25 mil chickens (excl. broilers), 1.33 bil broilers, 1 mil cattle/calves. **Nonfuel minerals:** $1.5 bil; clays (kaolin), stone (crushed), clays (fuller's earth), cement (portland), sand and gravel (construction). **Commercial fishing:** $16.3 mil. **Chief ports:** Savannah, Brunswick. **Gross state product:** $454.5 bil. **Sales tax:** 4.0%. **Employment distrib.:** 16.5% govt.; 20.9% trade/trans./util.; 8.8% mfg.; 12.5% ed./health; 14.8% prof./bus. serv.; 10.7% leisure/hosp.; 5.6% finance; 3.9% constr./mining/log.; 2.5% info.; 3.8% other serv.

Unemployment: 8.2%. **Per cap. pers. income:** $38,179. **New private housing:** 36,174 units/$5.7 bil. **Broadband Internet:** 83.3%. **Commercial banks:** 249; deposits: $184 bil. **Savings institutions:** 18; deposits: $3.7 bil. **Lottery:** total sales: $3.9 bil; profit: $927.5 mil.

Federal govt. Fed. civ. employees: 76,381; **avg. salary:** $73,605. **Notable fed. facilities:** Ft. Benning; Ft. Stewart; Fed. Law Enforcement Training Ctr., Robins AFB; Ft. Gordon; Naval Sub Base Kings Bay; Moody AFB; Centers for Disease Control; Marine Corps Logistics Base Albany.

Higher education. 4-year public coll./univ.: 30; 2-yr. **public:** 31; 4-yr. **private:** 33.

Energy. Electricity use/cost: 1,098 kWh, $122.73.

State data. Motto: Wisdom, justice, and moderation. **Flower:** Cherokee rose. **Bird:** Brown thrasher. **Tree:** Live oak. **Song:** "Georgia on My Mind." **Fourth** of the 13 original states to ratify the Constitution, Jan. 2, 1788.

Tourism. Tourist spending: $24.0 bil. **Attractions:** Georgia State Capitol, Stone Mountain, Centennial Olympic Park, Six Flags Over Georgia, Martin Luther King Jr. Natl. Historic Site, Jimmy Carter Library and Museum, Atlanta Botanical Garden, Georgia Aquarium (world's largest), in Atlanta; Kennesaw Mountain Natl. Battlefield Park; Chickamauga and Chattanooga Natl. Military Park; Chattahoochee-Oconee Natl. Forest; Dahlonega, site of earliest U.S. gold rush; Brasstown Bald (highest mtn. in state); Franklin D. Roosevelt's Little White House Historic Site, Warm Springs; Callaway Gardens, Pine Mountain; Andersonville Natl. Historic Site (Confederate military prison); Okefenokee Natl. Wildlife Refuge; Jekyll, St. Simons, and Cumberland barrier islands; Savannah Historic District. **Information:** Dept. of Economic Development, 75 Fifth St., NW, Ste. 1200, Atlanta, GA 30308; 1-800-VISITGA; www.exploregeorgia.org

History. Creek and Cherokee peoples were living in the region when Spaniards founded Santa Catalina mission, 1566, on Saint Catherines Island. Gen. James Oglethorpe established a colony at Savannah, 1733, for the poor and religiously persecuted. Oglethorpe defeated a Spanish army from Florida at Bloody Marsh, 1742. Georgia was a battleground in the American Revolution, with the British finally evacuating Savannah in 1782. When Georgia entered the Union, 1788, its plantation economy relied on slaves for rice and cotton growing. The Cherokee were removed to Indian Territory, 1838-39, and thousands died on the long march, known as the Trail of Tears. By 1860 the number of slaves exceeded 462,000 (nearly 44% of the total population). Georgia seceded from the Union, 1861, and was invaded by Union forces, 1864, under Gen. William T. Sherman, who took Atlanta, Sept. 2, and proceeded on his famous "march to the sea," ending in Savannah in Dec. Georgia was readmitted, 1870. Born 1929 in Atlanta, Martin Luther King Jr. made the city his base during the civil rights struggles of the 1960s. Atlanta became the leading city of the "New South," world headquarters of Coca-Cola and CNN, and host of the 1996 Summer Olympic Games. Hispanics are a rapidly growing economic and political force in the state.

Famous Georgians. Kim Basinger, Griffin Bell, James Brown, Erskine Caldwell, Jimmy Carter, Ray Charles, Ty Cobb, James Dickey, Walt Frazier, John C. Fremont, Newt Gingrich, Nancy Grace, Joel Chandler Harris, "Doc" Holliday, Larry Holmes, Holly Hunter, Alan Jackson, Martin Luther King Jr., Gladys Knight, Sidney Lanier, Little Richard, Juliette Gordon Low, Margaret Mitchell, Jessye Norman, Sam Nunn, Flannery O'Connor, Otis Redding, Burt Reynolds, Julia Roberts, Jackie Robinson, Ryan Seacrest, Clarence Thomas, Travis Tritt, Ted Turner, Carl Vinson, Alice Walker, Herschel Walker, Joanne Woodward, Trisha Yearwood, Andrew Young.

Website. www.georgia.gov

Hawai'i (HI)
Aloha State

People. Population: 1,404,054; rank: 40. **Pop. change** (2010-13): 3.2%. **Pop. density:** 218.6 per sq mi. **Racial distribution:** 26.6% white; 2.3% black; 37.7% Asian; 0.4% Amer. Ind.; 10.0% Hawaiian/Pacific Islander; 2 or more races, 23.1%. **Hispanic pop.:** 9.8%.

Geography. Total area: 10,932 sq mi; rank: 43. **Land area:** 6,423 sq mi; rank: 47. **Acres forested:** 1.7 mil. **Location:** Pacific archipelago of hundreds of islands 2,000 mi SW of U.S. mainland. **Climate:** subtropical, with wide variations in rainfall; Mt. Waialeale, on Kaua'i, wettest spot in U.S. (annual rainfall 422 in.). **Topography:** islands are tops of a chain of submerged volcanic mountains; Mauna Loa, Kilauea are active volcanoes. **Capital:** Honolulu. **Chief airports:** Hilo, Honolulu, Kahului, Kailua Kona, Lihue.

Economy. Chief industries: tourism, defense, sugar, pineapples. **Chief manuf. goods:** concrete, printing, baked goods, sugar, preserved fruits and vegetables, apparel. **Chief crops:** flowers and nursery, pineapples, seed crops, sugarcane, macadamia nuts, coffee, algae, papayas, tomatoes, bananas, basil, ginger. **Livestock:** 130,000 cattle/calves.

Nonfuel minerals: $102 mil; stone (crushed), sand and gravel (construction), gemstones (natural). **Commercial fishing:** $112.3 mil. **Chief ports:** Honolulu, Hilo, Barbers Point, Kahului. **Gross state product:** $75.2 bil. **Sales tax:** 4.0%. **Employment distrib.:** 20.7% govt.; 18.6% trade/trans./util.; 2.2% mfg.; 12.7% ed./health; 12.9% prof./bus. serv.; 18.0% leisure/hosp.; 4.4% finance; 4.9% constr./mining/log.; 1.4% info.; 4.2% other serv. **Unemployment:** 4.8%. **Per cap. pers. income:** $45,652. **New private housing:** 3,882 units/$1.0 bil. **Broadband Internet:** 88.8%. **Commercial banks:** 8; deposits: $27.9 bil. **Savings institutions:** 5; deposits: $5.9 bil.

Federal govt. Fed. civ. employees: 24,268; **avg. salary:** $72,670. **Notable fed. facilities:** Joint Base Pearl Harbor-Hickam; Schofield Barracks; Marine Corps Base Hawaii Kaneohe Bay; Tripler Army Med. Ctr.; Ft. Shafter; Wheeler Army Airfield; Prince Kuhio Federal Bldg.

Higher education. 4-year public coll./univ.: 4; **2-yr. public:** 6; **4-yr. private:** 7.

Energy. Electricity use/cost: 544 kWh, $203.15.

State data. Motto: Ua mau ke ea o ka aina i ka pono (The life of the land is perpetuated in righteousness). **Flower:** Yellow hibiscus. **Bird:** Hawaiian goose. **Tree:** Kukui (candlenut). **Song:** "Hawai'i Pono'i" (Hawai'i's Own). **Entered union:** Aug. 21, 1959; rank: 50th.

Tourism. Tourist spending: $18.6 bil. **Attractions:** Oahu Isl.: Natl. Memorial Cemetery of the Pacific, Waikiki Beach, Diamond Head, in Honolulu; USS *Arizona* Memorial, Pearl Harbor; Polynesian Cultural Ctr., Laie; Hanauma Bay; Nu'uanu Pali. Kaua'i Isl.: Waimea Canyon. Maui Isl.: Haleakala Natl. Park. Hawai'i Isl.: Hawaii Volcanoes Natl. Park, Wailoa and Wailuku River State Parks. **Information:** Hawaii Visitors and Conventions Bureau, 2270 Kalakaua Ave., Ste. 801, Honolulu, HI 96815; 1-800-GOHAWAII; www.gohawaii.com

History. Polynesians from islands 2,000 mi to the S settled the Hawaiian Islands, probably 300-600 CE. The first European visitor was British captain James Cook, 1778. King Kamehameha I united the islands by 1810. Christian missionaries arrived, 1819, bringing Western culture. Under the reign, 1825-54, of King Kamehameha III, a constitution, legislature, and public school system were instituted. Sugar production began, 1835, and it became the dominant industry. Queen Liliuokalani was deposed, 1893, and a republic was established, 1894, headed by Sanford B. Dole. Annexation by the U.S. came in 1898. The Japanese attack on Pearl Harbor, Dec. 7, 1941, brought the U.S. into World War II. Hawai'i attained statehood, 1959. Hurricane Iniki pounded Kaua'i, 1992, causing about $1 bil in damage. In 2006, Pres. George W. Bush designated the Northwestern Hawaiian Islands Natl. Monument, a marine area of 140,000 sq mi.

Famous Islanders. Bernice Pauahi Bishop, Tia Carrere, Alexander Cartwright, St. Damien de Veuster, Don Ho, Daniel K. Inouye, Duke Kahanamoku, King Kamehameha, Nicole Kidman, Brook Mahealani Lee, Jason Scott Lee, Queen Liliuokalani, Bruno Mars, Bette Midler, Barack Obama, Ellison S. Onizuka, Michelle Wie.

Website. www.ehawaii.gov

Idaho (ID)
Gem State

People. Population: 1,612,136; rank: 39. **Pop. change (2010-13):** 2.8%. **Pop. density:** 19.5 per sq mi. **Racial distribution:** 93.7% white; 0.8% black; 1.4% Asian; 1.7% Amer. Ind.; 0.2% Hawaiian/Pacific Islander; 2 or more races, 2.2%. **Hispanic pop.:** 11.8%.

Geography. Total area: 83,569 sq mi; rank: 14. **Land area:** 82,643 sq mi; rank: 11. **Acres forested:** 21.5 mil. **Location:** northwestern Mountain state bordering British Columbia. **Climate:** tempered by Pacific westerly winds; drier, colder, continental climate in SE; altitude an important factor. **Topography:** Snake R. plains in the S; central region of mountains, canyons,

gorges (Hells Canyon, 7,900 ft, deepest in N. America); subalpine northern region. **Capital:** Boise. **Chief airport:** Boise.

Economy. Chief industries: manufacturing, agriculture, tourism, lumber, mining, electronics. **Chief manuf. goods:** computers and electronics, preserved fruits and vegetables, cheese, lumber. **Chief crops:** potatoes, wheat, hay, sugar beets, barley, greenhouse and nursery, onions, dry beans, corn, mint, apples, hops, peaches, lentils, peas, cherries, plums and prunes, oats. **Livestock:** 2.19 mil cattle/calves, 250,000 sheep/lambs. **Nonfuel minerals:** $991 mil; molybdenum concentrates, phosphate rock, sand and gravel (construction), silver, stone (crushed). **Chief port:** Lewiston. **Gross state product:** $62.2 bil. **Sales tax:** 6.0%. **Employment distrib.:** 19.0% govt.; 20.2% trade/trans./util.; 9.1% mfg.; 14.4% ed./health; 11.6% prof./bus. serv.; 10.0% leisure/hosp.; 4.8% finance; 6.0% constr./mining/log.; 1.5% info.; 3.4% other serv. **Unemployment:** 6.2%. **Per cap. pers. income:** $35,382. **New private housing:** 8,110 units/$1.5 bil. **Broadband Internet:** 77.2%. **Commercial banks:** 33; deposits: $19.2 bil. **Savings institutions:** 2; deposits: $1 bil. **Lottery:** total sales: $197.4 mil; profit: $48.3 mil.

Federal govt. Fed. civ. employees: 8,469; **avg. salary:** $66,765. **Notable fed. facilities:** Idaho Natl. Lab; Mountain Home AFB.

Higher education. 4-year public coll./univ.: 4; **2-yr. public:** 4; **4-yr. private:** 4.

Energy. Electricity use/cost: 1,010 kWh, $87.52.

State data. Motto: Esto Perpetua (It is perpetual). **Flower:** Syringa. **Bird:** Mountain bluebird. **Tree:** White pine. **Song:** "Here We Have Idaho." **Entered union:** July 3, 1890; rank: 43rd.

Tourism. Tourist spending: $4.1 bil. **Attractions:** Hells Canyon (deepest river gorge in N. America); World Ctr. for Birds of Prey, Boise Art Museum, in Boise; Craters of the Moon Natl. Monument and Preserve; Sun Valley; Shoshone Falls, near Twin Falls; Lava Hot Springs; Lake Coeur d'Alene; Sawtooth Natl. Recreation Area; Frank Church-River of No Return Wilderness Area; Nez Perce Natl. Historical Park. **Information:** Idaho Division of Tourism Development, 700 W. State St., P.O. Box 83720, Boise, ID 83720; 1-800-VISITID; www.visitid.org

History. Paleo-Indian hunters roamed the land over 13,000 years ago; later inhabitants included Shoshone, Northern Paiute, Bannock, and Nez Percé peoples. The Meriwether Lewis and William Clark Expedition took place 1804-06. Next came fur traders, 1809-34, and missionaries, 1830s-50s. Mormons made their first permanent settlement at Franklin, 1860. Idaho's gold rush began the same year and brought thousands of permanent settlers. A series of Indian wars followed, including a remarkable campaign by Chief Joseph and the Nez Percé that ended with his surrender in Montana, 1877. Idaho became a territory, 1863, and a state, 1890. In the 20th cent., it emerged as a leader in potato, lumber, and silver output. The Sun Valley ski resort opened in 1936, boosting tourism. Startup of Lewiston's river port, 1975, opened Idaho to oceangoing trade. Fueled by technology job growth, the state's population jumped 21.2% in 2000-10.

Famous Idahoans. William Borah, Frank Church, Lou Dobbs, Fred Dubois, W. Mark Felt, Chief Joseph, Harmon Killebrew, Ezra Pound, Marilynne Robinson, Sacagawea, Picabo Street, Lana Turner.

Website. www.idaho.gov

Illinois (IL)
Prairie State

People. Population: 12,882,135; rank: 5. **Pop. change (2010-13):** 0.4%. **Pop. density:** 232.0 per sq mi. **Racial distribution:** 77.7% white; 14.7% black; 5.1% Asian; 0.6% Amer. Ind.; 0.1% Hawaiian/Pacific Islander; 2 or more races, 1.8%. **Hispanic pop.:** 16.5%.

Geography. Total area: 57,914 sq mi; rank: 25. **Land area:** 55,519 sq mi; rank: 24. **Acres forested:** 4.9 mil. **Location:** East North Central state; western, southern, and eastern boundaries formed by Mississippi, Ohio, and Wabash Rivers, respectively. **Climate:** temperate; typically cold, snowy winters, hot summers. **Topography:** prairie and fertile plains throughout; open hills in the southern region. **Capital:** Springfield. **Chief airports:** Chicago (2).

Economy. Chief industries: services, manufacturing, travel, wholesale and retail trade, finance, insurance, real estate, construction, health care, agriculture. **Chief manuf. goods:** food, petroleum, plastics, chemicals, agricultural machinery, pharmaceuticals, motor vehicles, printing. **Chief**

crops: corn, soybeans, hay, wheat, greenhouse and nursery, apples, peaches, sorghum. Livestock: 5 mil chickens (excl. broilers), 1.13 mil cattle/calves, 55,000 sheep/lambs, 490,000 hogs/pigs. Nonfuel minerals: $1.2 bil; sand and gravel (industrial), stone (crushed), sand and gravel (construction), cement (portland), tripoli. Chief port: Chicago. Gross state product: $720.7 bil. Sales tax: 6.25%. Employment distrib.: 14.5% govt.; 19.9% trade/trans./util.; 9.8% mfg.; 15.2% ed./health; 15.3% prof./bus. serv.; 9.6% leisure/hosp.; 6.3% finance; 3.6% constr./mining/log.; 1.7% info.; 4.3% other serv. Unemployment: 9.2%. Per cap. pers. income: $46,780. New private housing: 15,545 units/$3.1 bil. Broadband Internet: 87.6%. Commercial banks: 519; deposits: $385.5 bil. Savings institutions: 81; deposits $22 bil. Lottery: total sales: $2.8 bil; profit: $793.5 mil.

Federal govt. Fed. civ. employees: 47,331; avg. salary: $79,176. Notable fed. facilities: Great Lakes Naval Station; Fermi Natl. Accelerator Lab; Argonne Natl. Lab; Scott AFB; Rock Island Arsenal.

Higher education. 4-year public coll./univ.: 12; 2-yr. public: 48; 4-yr. private: 80.

Energy. Electricity use/cost: 767 kWh, $87.20.

State data. Motto: State sovereignty, national union. Flower: Native violet. Bird: Cardinal. Tree: White oak. Song: "Illinois." Entered union: Dec. 3, 1818; rank: 21st.

Tourism. Tourist spending: $33.5 bil. Attractions: Art Institute of Chicago, Field Museum of Natural History, Shedd Aquarium, Millennium Park, Navy Pier, in Chicago; Illinois State Museum, Abraham Lincoln Presidential Library and Museum, in Springfield; Cahokia Mounds State Historic Site, Collinsville; Starved Rock State Park; Crab Orchard Natl. Wildlife Refuge; Forts Kaskaskia, de Chartres, Massac; Shawnee Natl. Forest; Dickson Mounds Museum, Lewistown. Information: Illinois Bureau of Tourism, 100 W. Randolph St., Ste. 3-400, Chicago, IL 60601; 1-800-2CONNECT; www. enjoyillinois.com

History. The region has been inhabited for at least 10,000 years; seminomadic Algonquian peoples, including the Peoria, Illinois, Kaskaskia, and Tamaroa, lived there at the time of European contact. Fur traders were the first Europeans in Illinois, followed shortly by Louis Jolliet and Jacques Marquette, 1673, and René-Robert Cavelier, sieur de La Salle, 1680, who built a fort near present-day Peoria. French priests established the first permanent settlements at Cahokia, near present-day St. Louis, 1699, and Kaskaskia, 1703. France ceded the area to Britain, 1763, and in 1778, American Gen. George Rogers Clark took Kaskaskia from the British without a shot. Illinois became a separate territory, 1809, and a state, 1818. Defeat of Native American tribes in the Black Hawk War, 1832, and canal, rail, and road construction brought rapid change. Mormon settlers at Nauvoo, 1839, met with hostility, and a Carthage mob killed Mormon leader Joseph Smith and his brother, 1844. The Great Chicago Fire, 1871, destroyed the city's downtown. Illinois became a center for the labor movement, leading to bitter conflicts such as the Haymarket riot, 1886, and Pullman strike, 1894. Social reformer Jane Addams founded Hull House, 1889, to aid immigrants and the poor. As manufacturing expanded, 1900-70, many African Americans arrived from the southern U.S. Chicago police violently suppressed antiwar protests at the 1968 Democratic National Convention. Dennis Hastert was the longest serving Republican Speaker of the House, 1999-2007. Barack Obama, elected in 2004, was only the fifth African American to serve in the U.S. Senate; he became the 44th U.S. president in 2009. Political corruption and criminality have plagued the state for decades; since 1960, five former governors have been charged with criminal offenses.

Famous Illinoisans. Jane Addams, Saul Bellow, John Belushi, Jack Benny, Ray Bradbury, Gwendolyn Brooks, St. Frances Xavier Cabrini, Al Capone, Hillary Rodham Clinton, Clarence Darrow, John Deere, Stephen A. Douglas, Katherine Dunham, Wyatt Earp, Roger Ebert, James T. Farrell, Marshall Field, Harrison Ford, Betty Friedan, Benny Goodman, Ulysses S. Grant, Dennis Hastert, Hugh Hefner, Ernest Hemingway, Charlton Heston, Jennifer Hudson, Henry J. Hyde, Abraham Lincoln, Vachel Lindsay, David Mamet, Edgar Lee Masters, Oscar Mayer, Cyrus McCormick, Eliot Ness, Bob Newhart, Michelle Obama, Ronald Reagan, Shonda Rhimes, Donald Rumsfeld, Carl Sandburg, Shel Silverstein, Adlai E. Stevenson, James Watson, Frank Lloyd Wright, Philip K. Wrigley.

Website. www.illinois.gov

Indiana (IN)
Hoosier State

People. Population: 6,570,902; rank: 16. Pop. change (2010-13): 1.3%. Pop. density: 183.4 per sq mi. Racial distribution: 86.3% white; 9.5% black; 1.9% Asian; 0.4% Amer. Ind.; 0.1% Hawaiian/Pacific Islander; 2 or more races, 1.8%. Hispanic pop.: 6.4%.

Geography. Total area: 36,420 sq mi; rank: 38. Land area: 35,826 sq mi; rank: 38. Acres forested: 4.9 mil. Location: East North Central state; Lake Michigan on N border. Climate: four distinct seasons with temperate climate. Topography: hilly southern region; fertile rolling plains of central region; flat, heavily glaciated N; dunes along Lake Michigan shore. Capital: Indianapolis. Chief airport: Indianapolis.

Economy. Chief industries: manufacturing, services, agriculture, government, wholesale and retail trade, transportation and public utilities. Chief manuf. goods: motor vehicles and parts, iron and steel mills, pharmaceuticals, petroleum, plastics, medical equip., printing. Chief crops: corn, soybeans, greenhouse and nursery, wheat, hay, tomatoes, watermelons, apples. Livestock: 35.6 mil chickens (excl. broilers), 870,000 cattle/calves, 50,000 sheep/lambs, 270,000 hogs/pigs. Nonfuel minerals: $821 mil; stone (crushed), cement (portland), sand and gravel (construction), lime, cement (masonry). Chief ports: Burns Harbor-Portage, Mt. Vernon, Jeffersonville. Gross state product: $317.1 bil. Sales tax: 7.0%. Employment distrib.: 14.4% govt.; 19.0% trade/trans./util.; 16.8% mfg.; 14.8% ed./health; 10.7% prof./bus. serv.; 10.3% leisure/hosp.; 4.4% finance; 4.5% constr./mining/log.; 1.2% info.; 4.1% other serv. Unemployment: 7.5%. Per cap. pers. income: $38,812. New private housing: 17,950 units/$3.1 bil. Broadband Internet: 84.4%. Commercial banks: 135; deposits: $98.3 bil. Savings institutions: 38; deposits: $6.9 bil. Lottery: total sales: $934.0 mil; profit: $224.7 mil.

Federal govt. Fed. civ. employees: 23,555; avg. salary: $70,038. Notable fed. facilities: Nav. Surface Warfare Ctr., Crane Div.; Grissom Air Reserve Base.

Higher education. 4-year public coll./univ.: 15; 2-yr. public: 1; 4-yr. private: 39.

Energy. Electricity use/cost: 997 kWh, $104.93.

State data. Motto: Crossroads of America. Flower: Peony. Bird: Cardinal. Tree: Tulip poplar. Song: "On the Banks of the Wabash, Far Away." Entered union: Dec. 11, 1816; rank: 19th.

Tourism. Tourist spending: $10.0 bil. Attractions: Lincoln Boyhood Natl. Memorial, Lincoln City; George Rogers Clark Natl. Historical Park, Vincennes; Tippecanoe Battlefield Museum and Park, Battle Ground; Benjamin Harrison Presidential Site, Indianapolis Motor Speedway and Hall of Fame Museum, Indianapolis Museum of Art, in Indianapolis; Indiana Dunes Natl. Lakeshore, Chesterton; College Football Hall of Fame, Studebaker Natl. Museum, in South Bend; Hoosier Natl. Forest. Information: Indiana Office of Tourism Development, 1 North Capital, Ste. 600, Indianapolis, IN 46204; 1-800-677-9800; www.visitindiana.com.

History. When the Europeans arrived, Miami, Potawatomi, Kickapoo, Piankashaw, Wea, and Shawnee peoples inhabited the region. René-Robert Cavelier, sieur de La Salle, visited the present South Bend area, 1679 and 1681. The first French fort was built near present-day Lafayette, 1717. A French trading post was established, 1731-32, at Vincennes. France ceded the area to Britain, 1763. During the American Revolution, American Gen. George Rogers Clark captured Vincennes, 1778, and defeated British forces, 1779. Indiana became a territory, 1800, and a state, 1816. The Miami were beaten, 1794, at Fallen Timbers, and Gen. William H. Harrison defeated Tecumseh's Indian confederation, 1811, at Tippecanoe. Manufacturing grew rapidly after the Civil War. U.S. Steel founded Gary, 1906. An automotive test track was the site of the first Indianapolis 500 race, 1911. The auto industry remains key to the state economy; in 2008, Honda opened a $550-mil plant near Greensburg. Heavy rain in June 2008 flooded southwest and central Indiana.

Famous "Hoosiers." Larry Bird, Ambrose Burnside, Meg Cabot, Hoagy Carmichael, Jim Davis, James Dean, Eugene V. Debs, John Dillinger, Theodore Dreiser, Paul Dresser, Jeff Gordon, Benjamin Harrison, Gil Hodges, Michael Jackson, David Letterman, Carole Lombard, Marjorie Main, John Mellencamp, Jane Pauley, Cole Porter, Gene Stratton Porter, Ernie Pyle,

Dan Quayle, James Whitcomb Riley, Oscar Robertson, Red Skelton, Tony Stewart, Booth Tarkington, Kurt Vonnegut, Lew Wallace, Ryan White, Wendell L. Willkie, Wilbur Wright. **Website.** www.in.gov

Iowa (IA)
Hawkeye State

People. Population: 3,090,416; rank: 30. **Pop. change** (2010-13): 1.4%. **Pop. density:** 55.3 per sq mi. **Racial distribution:** 92.5% white; 3.3% black; 2.0% Asian; 0.5% Amer. Ind.; 0.1% Hawaiian/Pacific Islander; 2 or more races, 1.6%. **Hispanic pop.:** 5.5%.

Geography. Total area: 56,273 sq mi; rank: 26. **Land area:** 55,857 sq mi; rank: 23. **Acres forested:** 3.0 mil. **Location:** West North Central state bordered by Mississippi R. on the E, Missouri R. on the W. **Climate:** humid, continental. **Topography:** watershed from NW to SE; soil especially rich and sand level in the N central counties. **Capital:** Des Moines. **Chief airports:** Cedar Rapids, Des Moines.

Economy. Chief industries: agriculture, communications, construction, finance, insurance, trade, services, manufacturing. **Chief manuf. goods:** machinery, vegetable oils, animal slaughtering and processing, laundry equip., plastics, motor vehicles and parts. **Chief crops:** corn, soybeans, hay, greenhouse and nursery, oats. **Livestock:** 65.83 mil chickens (excl. broilers), 3.7 mil cattle/calves, 155,000 sheep/lambs, 1 mil hogs/pigs. **Nonfuel minerals:** $670 mil; stone (crushed), cement (portland), sand and gravel (construction), sand and gravel (industrial), lime. **Gross state product:** $165.8 bil. **Sales tax:** 6.0%. **Employment distrib.:** 16.8% govt.; 20.2% trade/trans./util.; 13.8% mfg.; 14.5% ed./health; 8.6% prof./bus. serv.; 9.2% leisure/hosp.; 6.6% finance; 4.8% constr./mining/log.; 1.6% info.; 3.7% other serv. **Unemployment:** 4.6%. **Per cap. pers. income:** $45,114. **New private housing:** 10,877 units/$2.0 bil. **Broadband Internet:** 83.2%. **Commercial banks:** 347; deposits: $70.8 bil. **Savings institutions:** 11; deposits $3.1 bil. **Lottery:** total sales: $339.3 mil; profit: $84.9 mil.

Federal govt. Fed. civ. employees: 9,068; **avg. salary:** $66,625. **Notable fed. facilities:** Ames Lab; Natl. Animal Disease Ctr.

Higher education. 4-year public coll./univ.: 3; **2-yr. public:** 16; **4-yr. private:** 33.

Energy. Electricity use/cost: 873 kWh, $94.50.

State data. Motto: Our liberties we prize, and our rights we will maintain. **Flower:** Wild rose. **Bird:** Eastern goldfinch. **Tree:** Oak. **Song:** "The Song of Iowa." **Entered union:** Dec. 28, 1846; rank: 29th.

Tourism. Tourist spending: $7.8 bil. **Attractions:** Des Moines Art Ctr., Iowa State Fairgrounds, Iowa State Capitol, in Des Moines; Natl. Czech & Slovak Museum & Library, Cedar Rapids; Herbert Hoover Natl. Historic Site, Presidential Library and Museum, in West Branch; Effigy Mounds Natl. Monument, Marquette; Amana Colonies; Figge Art Museum, Davenport; Living History Farms, Urbandale; Adventureland, Altoona; Boone & Scenic Valley Railroad and Museum; riverboat cruises and casino gambling, Mississippi and Missouri Rivers; Iowa Great Lakes, Okoboji; American Gothic House, Eldon; Field of Dreams movie site, Dyersville; Natl. Mississippi River Museum & Aquarium, Dubuque. **Information:** Iowa Tourism Office, Iowa Dept. of Economic Development, 200 E. Grand Ave., Des Moines, IA 50309; 1-888-472-6035; www.traveliowa.com.

History. Early inhabitants were Mound Builders who dwelt on Iowa's fertile plains. Later, Iowa and Yankton Sioux lived in the area. The first Europeans, Jacques Marquette and Louis Jolliet, gave France its claim to the area, 1673. In 1762, France ceded the region to Spain, but Napoleon took it back, 1800. It became part of the U.S. through the Louisiana Purchase, 1803. Native American Sauk and Fox tribes moved into the area but relinquished their land in defeat after the 1832 uprising led by Sauk chieftain Black Hawk. Iowa became a territory in 1838 and entered as a free state, 1846, strongly supporting the Union. Fertile land lured farmers from eastern states, 1850-1900, and the population rose rapidly. Growth slowed in the 20th cent., as farming became mechanized. Surging demand for ethanol fuel from Iowa corn contributed more than $2.6 bil to the state economy in 2005. Severe flooding in eastern Iowa in June 2008 caused billions of dollars in damages and forced the evacuation of thousands of residents.

Famous Iowans. Tom Arnold, Johnny Carson, William F. "Buffalo Bill" Cody, Mamie Dowd Eisenhower, Michael Emerson, Bob Feller, George Gallup, Susan Glaspell, James Norman Hall, Herbert Hoover, Shawn Johnson, Ashton Kutcher, Ann Landers, Cloris Leachman, Glenn Miller, Lillian Russell, Billy Sunday, James A. Van Allen, Abigail Van Buren, Carl Van Vechten, Henry Wallace, Kurt Warner, John Wayne, Meredith Willson, Elijah Wood, Grant Wood. **Website.** www.iowa.gov

Kansas (KS)
Sunflower State

People. Population: 2,893,957; rank: 34. **Pop. change** (2010-13): 1.4%. **Pop. density:** 35.4 per sq mi. **Racial distribution:** 87.1% white; 6.2% black; 2.7% Asian; 1.2% Amer. Ind.; 0.1% Hawaiian/Pacific Islander; 2 or more races, 2.7%. **Hispanic pop.:** 11.2%.

Geography. Total area: 82,278 sq mi; rank: 15. **Land area:** 81,759 sq mi; rank: 13. **Acres forested:** 2.6 mil. **Location:** West North Central state with Missouri R. on E. **Climate:** temperate but continental, with great extremes between summer and winter. **Topography:** hilly Osage Plains in the E; central region level prairie and hills; high plains in the W. **Capital:** Topeka. **Chief airport:** Wichita.

Economy. Chief industries: manufacturing, finance, insurance, real estate, services. **Chief manuf. goods:** animal slaughtering, aerospace, petroleum, plastics, machinery, navigational instruments, printing. **Chief crops:** wheat, corn, soybeans, hay, sorghum, sunflowers, cotton, potatoes. **Livestock:** 5.8 mil cattle/calves, 75,000 sheep/lambs, 170,000 hogs/pigs. **Nonfuel minerals:** $1.2 bil; helium (Grade-A), cement (portland), salt, stone (crushed), sand and gravel (construction). **Chief port:** Kansas City. **Gross state product:** $144.1 bil. **Sales tax:** 6.15%. **Employment distrib.:** 18.9% govt.; 18.7% trade/trans./util.; 11.4% mfg.; 13.7% ed./health; 11.9% prof./bus. serv.; 8.9% leisure/hosp.; 5.4% finance; 5.2% constr./mining/log.; 2.0% info.; 3.8% other serv. **Unemployment:** 5.4%. **Per cap. pers. income:** $43,916. **New private housing:** 8,285 units/$1.5 bil. **Broadband Internet:** 84.7%. **Commercial banks:** 317; deposits $57.6 bil. **Savings institutions:** 15; deposits $6.9 bil. **Lottery:** total sales: $244.8 mil; profit: $74.5 mil.

Federal govt. Fed. civ. employees: 16,925; **avg. salary:** $67,786. **Notable fed. facilities:** Ft. Riley; Leavenworth Fed. Pen.; McConnell AFB; Colmery-O'Neal VA Medical Ctr.; Dwight D. Eisenhower VA Medical Ctr.

Higher education. 4-year public coll./univ.: 8; **2-yr. public:** 24; **4-yr. private:** 22.

Energy. Electricity use/cost: 945 kWh, $106.19.

State data. Motto: Ad Astra per Aspera (To the stars through difficulties). **Flower:** Native sunflower. **Bird:** Western meadowlark. **Tree:** Cottonwood. **Song:** "Home on the Range." **Entered union:** Jan. 29, 1861; rank: 34th.

Tourism. Tourist spending: $6.8 bil. **Attractions:** Eisenhower Presidential Library and Museum, Abilene; Natl. Agricultural Ctr. and Hall of Fame, Bonner Springs; Boot Hill Museum, Dodge City; Old Cowtown Museum, Wichita; Ft. Scott and Ft. Larned Natl. Historic Sites; Kansas Cosmosphere and Space Ctr., Hutchinson; U.S. Cavalry Museum, Ft. Riley; Tallgrass Prairie Natl. Preserve, Strong City; Kansas Speedway, Kansas City. **Information:** Kansas Dept. of Commerce, Travel and Tourism Div., 1000 SW Jackson St., Ste. 100, Topeka, KS 66612; (785) 296-2009; www.travelks.com.

History. Wichita, Pawnee, Kansa, and Osage peoples lived in the area when Francisco de Coronado explored it in 1541. These Native Americans—hunters who also farmed—were joined on the Plains by the nomadic Cheyenne, Arapaho, Comanche, and Kiowa about 1800. France claimed the region, 1682, ceded its claim to Spain, 1762, then regained control, 1800, before selling it to the U.S. in the Louisiana Purchase, 1803. After 1830, thousands of Native Americans were removed from more eastern states to Kansas. Organized as a territory, 1854, the area witnessed violent clashes between pro- and antislavery settlers and became known as "Bleeding Kansas." It entered the Union as a free state, 1861. After the Civil War, rail construction and huge cattle drives from Texas turned Abilene and Dodge City into cowboy capitals. Russian Mennonite immigrants brought a new strain of winter wheat, 1874, transforming Kansas agriculture. Carry Nation launched her anti-saloon crusade in the 1890s. Part of the Dust Bowl, the state experienced drought and depression in the 1930s. Topeka was the focus of the famous Brown v. Board of

Education decision, 1954, that led to desegregation of U.S. public schools. Bob Dole represented Kansas in the U.S. Senate (1969-96) but failed in several efforts to win higher office.

Famous Kansans. Kirstie Alley, Roscoe "Fatty" Arbuckle, Ed Asner, John Brown, Walter P. Chrysler, Glenn Cunningham, John Steuart Curry, Robert Joseph "Bob" Dole, Amelia Earhart, Dwight D. Eisenhower, Melissa Etheridge, Ron Evans, Georgia Neese Clark Gray, Maurice Greene, James Butler "Wild Bill" Hickok, Cyrus K. Holliday, Dennis Hopper, William Inge, Don Johnson, Walter Johnson, Nancy Landon Kassebaum, Buster Keaton, Emmett Kelly, Alfred M. "Alf" Landon, Hattie McDaniel, Oscar Micheaux, Carry Nation, Charlie Parker, Gordon Parks, Jim Ryun, Barry Sanders, Vivian Vance, William Allen White, Jess Willard.

Website. www.kansas.gov

Kentucky (KY)
Bluegrass State

People. Population: 4,395,295; rank: 26. **Pop. change** (2010-13): 1.3%. **Pop. density:** 111.3 per sq mi. **Racial distribution:** 88.5% white; 8.2% black; 1.3% Asian; 0.3% Amer. Ind.; 0.1% Hawaiian/Pacific Islander; 2 or more races, 1.7%. **Hispanic pop.:** 3.3%.

Geography. Total area: 40,408 sq mi; rank: 37. **Land area:** 39,486 sq mi; rank: 37. **Acres forested:** 12.5 mil. **Location:** East South Central state bordered on N by Illinois, Indiana, Ohio; on E by West Virginia and Virginia; on S by Tennessee; on W by Missouri. **Climate:** moderate, with plentiful rainfall. **Topography:** mountainous in E; rounded hills of the Knobs region in the N; Bluegrass region in heart of state; wooded rocky hillsides of the Pennyroyal Plateau; Western Coal Field; the fertile Jackson Purchase region in the SW. **Capital:** Frankfort. **Chief airports:** Greater Cincinnati, Lexington, Louisville.

Economy. Chief industries: manufacturing, services, finance, insurance and real estate, retail trade, public utilities. **Chief manuf. goods:** motor vehicles and parts, aluminum, basic chemicals, plastics, iron and steel, rubber, printing. **Chief crops:** hay, corn, soybeans, tobacco, wheat. **Livestock:** 6.79 mil chickens (excl. broilers), 309 mil broilers, 2.09 mil cattle/calves, 49,000 sheep/lambs. **Nonfuel minerals:** $1 bil; stone (crushed), lime, cement (portland), sand and gravel (construction), clays (common). **Chief ports:** Louisville, Hickman-Fulton County. **Gross state product:** $183.4 bil. **Sales tax:** 6.0%. **Employment distrib.:** 18.4% govt.; 20.0% trade/trans./util.; 12.3% mfg.; 14.0% ed./health; 10.9% prof./bus. serv.; 10.2% leisure/hosp.; 4.6% finance; 4.5% constr./mining/log.; 1.4% info.; 3.6% other serv. **Unemployment:** 8.3%. **Per cap. pers. income:** $36,239. **New private housing:** 8,955 units/$1.2 bil. **Broadband Internet:** 88.0%. **Commercial banks:** 196; deposits: $69.1 bil. **Savings institutions:** 17; deposits: $1.4 bil. **Lottery:** total sales: $846.7 mil; profit: $223.8 mil.

Federal govt. Fed. civ. employees: 25,385; **avg. salary:** $62,385. **Notable fed. facilities:** U.S. Bullion Depository, Ft. Knox; Ft. Campbell; Fed. Medical Ctr., Lexington; Army Corps of Engineers, Louisville District.

Higher education. 4-year public coll./univ.: 8; **2-yr. public:** 16; **4-yr. private:** 27.

Energy. Electricity use/cost: 1,130 kWh, $106.54.

State data. Motto: United we stand, divided we fall. **Flower:** Goldenrod. **Bird:** Cardinal. **Tree:** Tulip poplar. **Song:** "My Old Kentucky Home." **Entered union:** June 1, 1792; rank: 15th.

Tourism. Tourist spending: $8.1 bil. **Attractions:** Churchill Downs (Kentucky Derby), Louisville Slugger Museum and Factory, in Louisville; Land Between the Lakes Natl. Recreation Area (Kentucky and Barkley Lakes); Mammoth Cave Natl. Park (world's longest known cave system); Abraham Lincoln Birthplace Natl. Historical Park, Hodgenville; My Old Kentucky Home State Park, Bardstown; Cumberland Gap Natl. Historical Park, Middlesboro; Kentucky Horse Park, Lexington; Shaker Village of Pleasant Hill, Harrodsburg; Natl. Corvette Museum, Bowling Green. **Information:** Kentucky Dept. of Travel, Capital Plaza Tower, 22nd Fl., 500 Mero St., Frankfort, KY 40601; 1-800-225-8747; www.kentuckytourism.com

History. Paleo-Indians first arrived about 14,000 years ago. Much later, Shawnee, Wyandot, Delaware, and Cherokee peoples also used the area mostly for hunting. Explored by Thomas Walker and Christopher Gist, 1750-51, Kentucky was the first area W of the Alleghenies settled by American pioneers. The first permanent settlement was Harrodsburg, 1774. Daniel Boone blazed the Wilderness Trail through the Cumberland

Gap and founded Ft. Boonesborough, 1775. Clashes with Native Americans were frequent, 1774-94. Virginia dropped its claims to the region, and Kentucky became a state, 1792. Tobacco growing, horse breeding, coal mining, and bourbon whiskey making were major industries in the 19th cent. A slave state, Kentucky tried to stay neutral in the Civil War, but then opted for the Union; many Kentuckians sided with the Confederacy. The U.S. gold depository at Ft. Knox opened, 1937. Prior to the 2008 economic downturn, auto manufacturing had grown in recent decades. An ice storm in southwestern Kentucky in Jan. 2009 killed 14 and caused severe power outages.

Famous Kentuckians. Muhammad Ali, Alben W. Barkley, Ned Beatty, Louis D. Brandeis, John C. Breckinridge, Kit Carson, Albert B. "Happy" Chandler, Henry Clay, George Clooney, Rosemary Clooney, Jefferson Davis, D. W. Griffith, "Casey" Jones, Jennifer Lawrence, Abraham Lincoln, Mary Todd Lincoln, Thomas Hunt Morgan, Carry Nation, Colonel Harland Sanders, Diane Sawyer, Jesse Stuart, Zachary Taylor, Hunter S. Thompson, Robert Penn Warren, Whitney M. Young Jr.

Website. www.kentucky.gov

Louisiana (LA)
Pelican State

People. Population: 4,625,470; rank: 25. **Pop. change** (2010-13): 2.0%. **Pop. density:** 107.1 per sq mi. **Racial distribution:** 63.5% white; 32.4% black; 1.7% Asian; 0.8% Amer. Ind.; 0.1% Hawaiian/Pacific Islander; 2 or more races, 1.5%. **Hispanic pop.:** 4.7%.

Geography. Total area: 52,378 sq mi; rank: 31. **Land area:** 43,204 sq mi; rank: 33. **Acres forested:** 14.9 mil. **Location:** West South Central state on the Gulf Coast. **Climate:** subtropical, affected by continental weather patterns. **Topography:** lowlands of marshes and Mississippi R. floodplain; Red R. Valley lowlands; upland hills in the Florida Parishes; avg. elevation, 100 ft. **Capital:** Baton Rouge. **Chief airport:** Metairie.

Economy. Chief industries: wholesale and retail trade, tourism, manufacturing, construction, transportation, communication, public utilities, finance, insurance, real estate, mining. **Chief manuf. goods:** petroleum, chemicals, plastics material and resin, pesticides and fertilizers, cleaning prods., paper and paperboard, ships, structural metals. **Chief crops:** sugarcane, cotton, rice, soybeans, corn, sweet potatoes. **Livestock:** 2.77 mil chickens (excl. broilers), 790,00 cattle/calves. **Nonfuel minerals:** $395 mil; salt, sand and gravel (construction), stone (crushed), sand and gravel (industrial), lime. **Commercial fishing:** $310.0 mil. **Chief ports:** New Orleans, Baton Rouge, Lake Charles, Port of S. Louisiana (La Place), Shreveport, Plaquemine, St. Bernard, Alexandria. **Gross state product:** $253.6 bil. **Sales tax:** 4.0%. **Employment distrib.:** 17.1% govt.; 19.5% trade/trans./util.; 7.3% mfg.; 14.9% ed./health; 10.8% prof./bus. serv.; 11.3% leisure/hosp.; 4.8% finance; 9.6% constr./mining/log.; 1.2% info.; 3.4% other serv. **Unemployment:** 6.2%. **Per cap. pers. income:** $40,689. **New private housing:** 14,015 units/$2.6 bil. **Broadband Internet:** 88.0%. **Commercial banks:** 131; deposits: $89.1 bil. **Savings institutions:** 23; deposits: $4.5 bil. **Lottery:** total sales: $447.4 mil; profit: $160.2 mil.

Federal govt. Fed. civ. employees: 20,345; **avg. salary:** $68,678. **Notable federal facilities:** Ft. Polk (Joint Readiness Training Ctr.); Barksdale AFB; Strategic Petroleum Reserve, Michoud Assembly Facility, USDA Southern Regional Research Ctr., New Orleans NAS JRB.

Higher education. 4-year public coll./univ.: 17; **2-yr. public:** 18; **4-yr. private:** 10.

Energy. Electricity use/cost: 1,254 kWh, $104.99.

State data. Motto: Union, justice, and confidence. **Flower:** Magnolia. **Bird:** Eastern brown pelican. **Tree:** Cypress. **Song:** "Give Me Louisiana." **Entered union:** Apr. 30, 1812; rank: 18th.

Tourism. Tourist spending: $10.2 bil. **Attractions:** Mardi Gras, French Quarter, Bourbon Street, in New Orleans; Jean Lafitte Natl. Historical Park and Preserve; Longfellow-Evangeline State Historic Site, St. Martinville; Kent Plantation House, Alexandria; Oak Alley Plantation, Vacherie; Hodges Gardens State Park, Florien; USS *Kidd* Veterans Memorial, Baton Rouge. **Information:** Louisiana Office of Tourism, P.O. Box 94291, Baton Rouge, LA 70804-9291; 1-800-677-4082; www.louisianatravel.com

History. Caddo, Tunica, Choctaw, Chitimacha, and Chawash peoples lived in the region at the time of European contact. Spanish explorers in the early 16th cent. reached the mouth of the Mississippi. René-Robert Cavelier, sieur de La Salle, 1682, claimed the region for France. Early French and Spanish settlers were the ancestors of Louisiana Creoles. Cajuns descended from the Acadians, French settlers expelled by the British from Nova Scotia, Canada, in 1755. France ceded the Louisiana region to Spain, 1762, took it back, 1800, and sold it to the U.S., 1803, in the Louisiana Purchase. Admitted as a state in 1812, Louisiana witnessed the Battle of New Orleans, 1815. Cotton and sugar plantations relied on black slaves, who made up close to 47% of the population in 1860, on the eve of the Civil War. Louisiana seceded, 1861, and was readmitted, 1868. Jazz was born in New Orleans in the early 20th cent. As governor (1928-32), Huey Long pushed populist programs. Many tropical storms and floods have battered Louisiana, including Hurricane Katrina and subsequent flooding, 2005, which devastated New Orleans. The offshore oil and gas industry developed after World War II. An oil rig explosion off the state's Gulf coast spilled millions of barrels of oil, damaging coastal wetlands and many of the state's marine-dependent industries in 2010.

Famous Louisianans. Louis Armstrong, Pierre Beauregard, Judah P. Benjamin, Braxton Bragg, Kate Chopin, Harry Connick Jr., Ellen DeGeneres, Fats Domino, George "Buddy" Guy, Lillian Hellman, Grace King, Jerry Lee Lewis, Bob Livingston, Huey Long, Eli Manning, Peyton Manning, Wynton Marsalis, Tim McGraw, Leonidas K. Polk, Anne Rice, Bill Russell, Henry Miller Shreve, Britney Spears, Madam C. J. Walker (Sarah Breedlove), Edward Douglass White Jr.

Website. www.louisiana.gov

Maine (ME)
Pine Tree State

People. Population: 1,328,302; rank: 41. **Pop. change** (2010-13): 0.0%. **Pop. density:** 43.1 per sq mi. **Racial distribution:** 95.2% white; 1.4% black; 1.1% Asian; 0.7% Amer. Ind.; 0.0% Hawaiian/Pacific Islander; 2 or more races, 1.6%. **Hispanic pop.:** 1.4%.

Geography. Total area: 35,380 sq mi; rank: 39. **Land area:** 30,843 sq mi; rank: 39. **Acres forested:** 17.6 mil. **Location:** New England state at northeastern tip of U.S. **Climate:** southern interior and coast influenced by air masses from the S and W; northern clime harsher, avg. over 100 in. snow in winter. **Topography:** Appalachian Mts. extend through state; western borders have rugged terrain; long sand beaches on southern coast; northern coast mainly rocky promontories, peninsulas, fjords. **Capital:** Augusta. **Chief airport:** Portland.

Economy. Chief industries: manufacturing, agriculture, fishing, services, trade, government, finance, insurance, real estate, construction. **Chief manuf. goods:** paper, ships and boats, cardboard, frozen/canned fruits and vegetables, plastics, baked goods. **Chief crops:** potatoes, greenhouse and nursery, wild blueberries, apples, hay, maple syrup. **Livestock:** 3.6 mil chickens (excl. broilers), 85,000 cattle/calves. **Nonfuel minerals:** $131 bil; sand and gravel (construction), stone (crushed), cement (portland), stone (dimension), cement (masonry). **Commercial fishing:** $448.6 mil. **Chief ports:** Searsport, Portland, Eastport. **Gross state product:** $54.8 bil. **Sales tax:** 5.5%. **Employment distrib.:** 16.9% govt.; 19.3% trade/trans./util.; 8.3% mfg.; 20.3% ed./health; 10.1% prof./bus. serv.; 10.6% leisure/hosp.; 5.3% finance; 4.7% constr./mining/log.; 1.2% info.; 3.4% other serv. **Unemployment:** 6.7%. **Per cap. pers. income:** $41,014. **New private housing:** 3,427 units/$618.9 mil. **Broadband Internet:** 85.9%. **Commercial banks:** 11; deposits: $27.4 bil. **Savings institutions:** 21; deposits: $10.4 bil. **Lottery:** total sales: $227.7 mil; profit: $53.5 mil.

Federal govt. Fed. civ. employees: 10,694; **avg. salary:** $67,615. **Notable fed. facilities:** Portsmouth Naval Shipyard.

Higher education. 4-year public coll./univ.: 8; **2-yr. public:** 7; **4-yr. private:** 13.

Energy. Electricity use/cost: 531 kWh, $77.77.

State data. Motto: Dirigo (I direct). **Flower:** White pine cone and tassel. **Bird:** Black-capped chickadee. **Tree:** Eastern white pine. **Song:** "State of Maine Song." **Entered union:** Mar. 15, 1820; rank: 23rd.

Tourism. Tourist spending: $3.3 bil. **Attractions:** Acadia Natl. Park, Bar Harbor, on Mt. Desert Island; Old Orchard Beach; Old Port historic waterfront, Victoria Mansion, Portland; Portland Head Light, Cape Elizabeth; Maine Maritime Museum, Bath; Baxter State Park; L.L. Bean flagship store and outlet shopping, Freeport. **Information:** Maine Office of

Tourism, 59 State House Station, Augusta, ME 04333; 1-888-624-6345; www.visitmaine.com

History. Paleo-Indians arrived about 11,500 years ago. Maine was inhabited by Algonquian peoples including the Abnaki, Penobscot, and Passamaquoddy at the time of European contact. French settled, 1604, at the St. Croix R., English, c. 1607, on the Kennebec; both settlements failed. A royal charter, 1691, made Maine part of Massachusetts. Maine broke off, 1819, and became a separate state, 1820. Drawing on vast forest resources, the pulp and paper industry developed after the Civil War. Bath Iron Works began building U.S. Navy vessels and other ships in the 1890s. Mail-order and retail giant L.L. Bean was founded, 1912. Women have fared well in state politics: Margaret Chase Smith became the first woman to serve in both houses of Congress (House, 1940-49; Senate, 1949-73), and Olympia Snowe and Susan Collins represented Maine in the Senate since the mid-1990s (Snowe retired in Jan. 2013).

Famous "Down Easters." Leon Leonwood (L. L.) Bean, James G. Blaine, Patrick Dempsey, Hannibal Hamlin, Sarah Orne Jewett, Stephen King, Henry Wadsworth Longfellow, Sir Hiram and Hudson Maxim, Edna St. Vincent Millay, George J. Mitchell, Edmund Muskie, Judd Nelson, Edwin Arlington Robinson, Joan Benoit Samuelson, Liv Tyler, Kate Douglas Wiggin, Ben Ames Williams.

Website. www.maine.gov

Maryland (MD)
Old Line State, Free State

People. Population: 5,928,814; rank: 19. **Pop. change** (2010-13): 2.7%. **Pop. density:** 610.8 per sq mi. **Racial distribution:** 60.5% white; 30.1% black; 6.1% Asian; 0.6% Amer. Ind.; 0.1% Hawaiian/Pacific Islander; 2 or more races, 2.6%. **Hispanic pop.:** 9.0%.

Geography. Total area: 12,406 sq mi; rank: 42. **Land area:** 9,707 sq mi; rank: 42. **Acres forested:** 2.4 mil. **Location:** South Atlantic state stretching from the ocean to the Allegheny Mts. **Climate:** continental in the W; humid subtropical in the E. **Topography:** coastal plain on Eastern Shore separated by Chesapeake Bay from coastal plain, Piedmont Plateau, and the Blue Ridge. **Capital:** Annapolis. **Chief airport:** Glen Burnie.

Economy. Chief industries: manufacturing, biotechnology and information technology, services, tourism. **Chief manuf. goods:** navigational instruments, pharmaceutical and medicine, broadcasting equip., plastics, printing, milk and ice cream. **Chief crops:** greenhouse and nursery, corn, soybeans, wheat, hay, tomatoes, watermelons, barley, potatoes, apples. **Livestock:** 3.53 mil chickens (excl. broilers), 305.2 mil broilers, 182,000 cattle/calves. **Nonfuel minerals:** $255 mil; cement (portland), stone (crushed), sand and gravel (construction), cement (masonry), stone (dimension). **Commercial fishing:** $77.9 mil. **Chief port:** Baltimore. **Gross state product:** $342.4 bil. **Sales tax:** 6.0%. **Employment distrib.:** 19.6% govt.; 17.1% trade/trans./util.; 3.9% mfg.; 16.1% ed./health; 16.1% prof./bus. serv.; 10.2% leisure/hosp.; 5.7% finance; 5.8% constr./mining/log.; 1.4% info.; 4.2% other serv. **Unemployment:** 6.6%. **Per cap. pers. income:** $54,259. **New private housing:** 17,918 units/$2.8 bil. **Broadband Internet:** 83.3%. **Commercial banks:** 85; deposits: $115 bil. **Savings institutions:** 35; deposits: $6.3 bil. **Lottery:** total sales: $2.4 bil; profit: $868.7 mil.

Federal govt. Fed. civ. employees: 132,667; **avg. salary:** $98,659. **Notable fed. facilities:** U.S. Naval Academy; Beltsville Agriculture Res. Ctr.; Ft. Meade; Aberdeen Proving Ground; Andrews AFB; Naval Air Sys. Command; Goddard Space Flight Ctr.; Natl. Inst. of Health; Natl. Inst. of Standards & Technology; Food & Drug Admin.; Bureau of the Census; Walter Reed Natl. Military Med. Ctr., Bethesda; Natl. Marine Fisheries Serv.; Natl. Oceanic and Atmospheric Admin.

Higher education. 4-year public coll./univ.: 13; **2-yr. public:** 16; **4-yr. private:** 23.

Energy. Electricity use/cost: 1,005 kWh, $129.

State data. Motto: Fatti Maschii, Parole Femine (Manly deeds, womanly words). **Flower:** Black-eyed Susan. **Bird:** Baltimore oriole. **Tree:** White oak. **Song:** "Maryland, My Maryland." **Seventh** of original 13 states to ratify the Constitution, Apr. 28, 1788.

Tourism. Tourist spending: $15.0 bil. **Attractions:** Ocean City; Ft. McHenry—the defense of which inspired Francis Scott Key to write "The Star-Spangled Banner," Pimlico Race Course (Preakness Stakes), Edgar Allan Poe House and Museum, Oriole Park at Camden Yards, Natl. Aquarium, Inner

Harbor, in Baltimore; Antietam Natl. Battlefield, Sharpsburg; South Mountain State Battlefield, Middletown; U.S. Naval Academy, Maryland State House (oldest in continuous legislative use in U.S.), in Annapolis; Natl. Cryptologic Museum, Ft. Meade. **Information:** Maryland Office of Tourism Development, 401 E. Pratt St., 14th Fl., Baltimore, MD 21202; 1-866-639-3526; www.visitmaryland.org

History. Europeans encountered Algonquian-speaking Nanticoke and Piscataway and Iroquois-speaking Susquehannock when they first visited the area. Italian navigator Giovanni da Verrazano reached the Chesapeake region in the early 16th cent. English Capt. John Smith explored and mapped the area, 1608. William Claiborne set up a trading post on Kent Island in Chesapeake Bay, 1631. King Charles I granted land to Cecilius Calvert, Lord Baltimore, 1632; Calvert's brother Leonard, with about 200 settlers, founded St. Mary's, 1634. During the Revolutionary War, Baltimore (1776-77) and Annapolis (1783-84) served as temporary capitals of the U.S. When a British fleet tried to take Ft. McHenry in the War of 1812, Marylander Francis Scott Key wrote "The Star-Spangled Banner," 1814. Born into slavery at Tuckahoe in 1818, Frederick Douglass became a leading abolitionist. Although a slaveholding state, Maryland stayed in the Union during the Civil War and was the site of the battle of Antietam, 1862. Gov. Spiro Agnew, elected U.S. vice pres., 1968 and 1972, pleaded no contest to tax evasion and resigned, 1973. Israeli and Egyptian leaders reached a historic peace accord at the Camp David presidential retreat, 1978. A major effort is under way to clean up pollution in the Chesapeake Bay watershed.

Famous Marylanders. John Astin, Benjamin Banneker, Tom Clancy, Frederick Douglass, Matthew Henson, Francis Scott Key, H. L. Mencken, Kweisi Mfume, Ogden Nash, Charles Willson Peale, Michael Phelps, William Pinkney, Edgar Allan Poe, Cal Ripken Jr., Babe Ruth, Upton Sinclair, Roger B. Taney, Harriet Tubman, John Waters, Montel Williams.

Website. www.maryland.gov

Massachusetts (MA)
Bay State, Old Colony

People. Population: 6,692,824; rank: 14. **Pop. change** (2010-13): 2.2%. **Pop. density:** 858.1 per sq mi. **Racial distribution:** 83.2% white; 8.1% black; 6.0% Asian; 0.5% Amer. Ind.; 0.1% Hawaiian/Pacific Islander; 2 or more races, 2.1%. **Hispanic pop.:** 10.5%.

Geography. Total area: 10,554 sq mi; rank: 44. **Land area:** 7,800 sq mi; rank: 45. **Acres forested:** 3.0 mil. **Location:** New England state on Atlantic seaboard. **Climate:** temperate, with colder, drier clime in western region. **Topography:** jagged indented coast from Rhode Island around Cape Cod; flat land yields to stony upland pastures near central region and gentle hilly country in W; except in W, land is rocky, sandy, and not fertile. **Capital:** Boston. **Chief airport:** Boston.

Economy. Chief industries: services, trade, manufacturing. **Chief manuf. goods:** electronics and instruments, pharmaceuticals, telecom. and broadcasting equip., plastics, medical equip., printing. **Chief crops:** greenhouse and nursery, cranberries, tomatoes, sweet corn, apples, hay, tobacco. **Livestock:** 126,000 chickens (excl. broilers), 39,000 cattle/calves. **Nonfuel minerals:** $232 mil; stone (crushed), sand and gravel (construction), stone (dimension), lime, clays (common). **Commercial fishing:** $618.2 mil. **Chief ports:** Boston, Fall River. **Gross state product:** $446.3 bil. **Sales tax:** 6.25%. **Employment distrib.:** 13.2% govt.; 16.5% trade/trans./util.; 7.3% mfg.; 21.8% ed./health; 15.1% prof./bus. serv.; 10.0% leisure/hosp.; 6.0% finance; 3.7% constr./mining/log.; 2.5% info.; 3.7% other serv. **Unemployment:** 7.1%. **Per cap. pers. income:** $56,923. **New private housing:** 14,569 units/$3.8 bil. **Broadband Internet:** 82.3%. **Commercial banks:** 69; deposits: $225.6 bil. **Savings institutions:** 112; deposits: $62.8 bil. **Lottery:** total sales: $4.8 bil; profit: $955.8 mil.

Federal govt. Fed. civ. employees: 28,235; **avg. salary:** $80,250. **Notable fed. facilities:** Thomas P. O'Neill Jr. Fed. Bldg.; J.W. McCormack Bldg.; JFK Fed. Bldg.; Hanscom AFB; Army Natick Soldier Systems Ctr.

Higher education. 4-year public coll./univ.: 14; **2-yr. public:** 16; **4-yr. private:** 81.

Energy. Electricity use/cost: 627 kWh, $93.53.

State data. Motto: Ense Petit Placidam Sub Libertate Quietem (By the sword we seek peace, but peace only under liberty). **Flower:** Mayflower. **Bird:** Black-capped chickadee.

Tree: American elm. **Song:** "All Hail to Massachusetts." **Sixth** of original 13 states to ratify the Constitution, Feb. 6, 1788.

Tourism. Tourist spending: $17.7 bil. **Attractions:** Provincetown art colony; Cape Cod; Plymouth Rock, Plimoth Plantation, Mayflower II, in Plymouth; Freedom Trail, Museum of Fine Arts, New England Aquarium, Faneuil Hall, Boston Harbor Isls. Natl. Recreation Area, Boston Public Garden, in Boston; Tanglewood, Hancock Shaker Village, Berkshire Scenic Railway Museum, Norman Rockwell Museum, in the Berkshires region; Peabody Essex Museum, House of the Seven Gables, in Salem; Old Sturbridge Village; Historic Deerfield; Walden Pond, Louisa May Alcott's Orchard House, in Concord; Naismith Memorial Basketball Hall of Fame, Springfield. **Information:** Massachusetts Office of Travel & Tourism, 10 Park Plz., Ste. 4510, Boston, MA 02116; 1-800-227-MASS; www.massvacation.com

History. Early inhabitants were Algonquian peoples: Nauset, Wampanoag, Massachuset, Pennacook, Nipmuc, and Pocumtuc. Pilgrims settled in Plymouth, 1620, giving thanks for their survival with the first Thanksgiving Day, 1621. About 20,000 new settlers arrived, 1630-40. Colonist-Native American relations deteriorated, leading to King Philip's War, 1675-76, which the colonists won. Witch trials at Salem, 1692, led to the execution of 20 people. Demonstrations against British restrictions set off the Boston Massacre, 1770, and the Boston Tea Party, 1773. The first bloodshed of American Revolution was at Lexington, 1775. After statehood, Massachusetts prospered from shipbuilding, seafaring, and the making of textiles, shoes, and metal goods, while artists, writers, and social reformers flourished. The controversial Sacco-Vanzetti case, 1920-27, ended with the execution of two Italian immigrants on murder and robbery charges. After World War II, old industries declined, knowledge-intensive enterprises thrived, and the Kennedys became a dominant political family. The state's highest court ruled, 2003, that same-sex couples could legally marry. Two bombs exploded Apr. 15, 2013, near the finish line of the Boston Marathon, killing three and injuring more than 250.

Famous "Bay Staters." John Adams, John Quincy Adams, Samuel Adams, Louisa May Alcott, Horatio Alger, Susan B. Anthony, Crispus Attucks, Clara Barton, Michael Bloomberg, George H. W. Bush, Steve Carell, John Cheever, E. E. Cummings, Bette Davis, Emily Dickinson, Charles Eliot, Ralph Waldo Emerson, William Lloyd Garrison, Edward Everett Hale, John Hancock, Nathaniel Hawthorne, Oliver Wendell Holmes Jr., Winslow Homer, Elias Howe, John F. Kennedy, Jack Kerouac, John Kerry, Emeril Lagasse, Jack Lemmon, James Russell Lowell, Cotton Mather, Maria Mitchell, Samuel F. B. Morse, Conan O'Brien, Paul Revere, Norman Rockwell, Dr. Seuss (Theodor Seuss Geisel), Henry David Thoreau, Barbara Walters, James Abbott McNeil Whistler, John Greenleaf Whittier.

Website. www.mass.gov

Michigan (MI)
Great Lakes State, Wolverine State

People. Population: 9,895,622; rank: 9. **Pop. change** (2010-13): 0.1%. **Pop. density:** 175.0 per sq mi. **Racial distribution:** 80.1% white; 14.3% black; 2.7% Asian; 0.7% Amer. Ind.; 0.0% Hawaiian/Pacific Islander; 2 or more races, 2.2%. **Hispanic pop.:** 4.7%.

Geography. Total area: 96,714 sq mi; rank: 11. **Land area:** 56,539 sq mi; rank: 22. **Acres forested:** 20.4 mil. **Location:** East North Central state bordering four of the Great Lakes, divided into an Upper and Lower Peninsula by the Straits of Mackinac, which link Lakes Michigan and Huron. **Climate:** well-defined seasons tempered by the Great Lakes. **Topography:** low rolling hills give way to northern tableland of hilly belts in Lower Peninsula; Upper Peninsula is level in the E with swampy areas; western region is higher and more rugged. **Capital:** Lansing. **Chief airports:** Detroit, Grand Rapids.

Economy. Chief industries: manufacturing, services, tourism, agriculture, forestry/lumber. **Chief manuf. goods:** motor vehicles and parts, plastics, metalworking machinery, non-wood office furniture, fabricated metals. **Chief crops:** greenhouse and nursery, soybeans, corn, wheat, sugar beets, apples, blueberries, potatoes, dry beans, cherries, hay, cucumbers, tomatoes, grapes. **Livestock:** 16.22 mil chickens (excl. broilers), 1.12 mil cattle/calves, 81,000 sheep/lambs, 110,000 hogs/pigs. **Nonfuel minerals:** $2.2 bil; iron ore (usable shipped), cement (portland), sand and gravel (construction), stone (crushed), salt. **Commercial fishing:** $9.3 mil. **Chief ports:** Detroit,

Escanaba, Calcite, Port Inland, Muskegon, Port Huron. **Gross state product:** $432.6 bil. **Sales tax:** 6.0%. **Employment distrib.:** 14.4% govt.; 18.1% trade/trans./util.; 13.5% mfg.; 15.3% ed./health; 14.8% prof./bus. serv.; 10.0% leisure/hosp.; 4.8% finance; 3.6% constr./mining/log.; 1.3% info.; 4.1% other serv. **Unemployment:** 8.8%. **Per cap. pers. income:** $39,215. **New private housing:** 15,757 units/$3.3 bil. **Broadband Internet:** 84.7%. **Commercial banks:** 138; deposits: $158.2 bil. **Savings institutions:** 18; deposits: $10.7 bil. **Lottery:** total sales: $2.5 bil; profit: $735.6 mil.

Federal govt. Fed. civ. employees: 29,433; **avg. salary:** $78,331. **Notable fed. facilities:** Detroit Arsenal (Army TACOM Life Cycle Mgmt.); DLA Logistics Info. Service; Selfridge Air Natl. Guard Base; Hart-Dole-Inouye Fed. Ctr.

Higher education. 4-year public coll./univ.: 15; **2-yr. public:** 31; **4-yr. private:** 49.

Energy. Electricity use/cost: 676 kWh, $95.50.

State data. Motto: Si Quaeris Peninsulam Amoenam, Circumspice (If you seek a pleasant peninsula, look about you). **Flower:** Apple blossom. **Bird:** Robin. **Tree:** White pine. **Song:** "Michigan, My Michigan." **Entered union:** Jan. 26, 1837; rank: 26th.

Tourism. Tourist spending: $16.8 bil. **Attractions:** Henry Ford Museum and Greenfield Village, Dearborn; Frederik Meijer Gardens and Sculpture Park, Grand Rapids; Tahquamenon Falls (of Longfellow's poem *Song of Hiawatha*); De Zwaan windmill, Tulip Time Festival, in Holland; Soo Locks (bet. Lakes Superior and Huron), Sault Ste. Marie; Air Zoo, Portage; Mackinac Island; Belle Isle Park, Detroit Institute of Arts, Charles H. Wright Museum of African-American History, Motown Historical Museum, in Detroit. **Information:** Michigan Economic Development Corp., 300 N. Washington Sq., Lansing, MI 48913; 1-888-784-7328; www.michigan.org

History. Hunting and fishing peoples lived in the region as early as 11,000 years ago. Ojibwa, Ottawa, Miami, Potawatomi, and Huron inhabited the area at the time of European contact. French fur traders and missionaries arrived in the 17th cent. and established a settlement at Sault Ste. Marie, 1668. British took over, 1763, and crushed a Native American uprising led by Ottawa chieftain Pontiac. Treaty of Paris ceded the area to U.S., 1783, but the British remained until 1796. Michigan was organized as a territory, 1805. The British seized Ft. Mackinac and Detroit, 1812, but the U.S. regained control, 1814. The opening of the Erie Canal, 1825, and new land laws and Native American cessions led the way for a flood of settlers. Strongly antislavery, Michigan became a state, 1837, and supplied 90,000 soldiers to the Union army in the Civil War. In the 20th cent., automobile manufacturing was the backbone of the economy. Henry Ford launched the Model T car, 1908; the United Auto Workers union was founded, 1935. Motown music flourished in Detroit in the 1960s, but riots in 1967 dealt the city a heavy blow. As the auto industry faltered, Michigan lost more than 20% of its automotive-related jobs in 2002-07. In 2009, the federal government loaned billions of dollars to GM and Chrysler to keep them solvent. Citing massive budget shortfalls, Detroit city officials filed for bankruptcy in July 2013.

Famous Michiganders. Ralph Bunche, Paul de Kruif, Thomas Edison, Eminem (Marshall Mathers), Edna Ferber, Gerald R. Ford, Henry Ford, Aretha Franklin, Edgar Guest, Lee Iacocca, Magic Johnson, Casey Kasem, Will Kellogg, Ring Lardner, Elmore Leonard, Charles Lindbergh, Joe Louis, Madonna, Malcolm X, Terry McMillan, Michael Moore, Larry Page, Pontiac, Gilda Radner, Mitt Romney, Diana Ross, Tom Selleck, Sinbad (David Adkins), John Smoltz, Lily Tomlin, Serena Williams.

Website. www.michigan.gov

Minnesota (MN)
North Star State, Gopher State

People. Population: 5,420,380; rank: 21. **Pop. change** (2010-13): 2.2%. **Pop. density:** 68.1 per sq mi. **Racial distribution:** 86.2% white; 5.7% black; 4.5% Asian; 1.3% Amer. Ind.; 0.1% Hawaiian/Pacific Islander; 2 or more races, 2.3%. **Hispanic pop.:** 5.0%.

Geography. Total area: 86,936 sq mi; rank: 12. **Land area:** 79,627 sq mi; rank: 14. **Acres forested:** 17.4 mil. **Location:** West North Central state bounded on the E by Wisconsin and Lake Superior, on the N by Canada, on the W by the Dakotas, and on the S by Iowa. **Climate:** northern part of state lies in the moist Great Lakes storm belt; the western border lies at the edge of the semiarid Great Plains. **Topography:** central hill and lake region covers approx. half the state; to the NE, rocky ridges and deep lakes; to the NW, flat plain; to the S, rolling plains and deep river valleys. **Capital:** St. Paul. **Chief airport:** Minneapolis.

Economy. Chief industries: agribusiness, forest products, mining, manufacturing, tourism. **Chief manuf. goods:** petroleum and asphalt, computers and electronics, milk and cheese, printing, animal slaughtering, paper and prod., medical equip. **Chief crops:** corn, soybeans, hay, sugar beets, wheat, potatoes, greenhouse and nursery, dry edible beans, green peas, sunflowers. **Livestock:** 14.53 mil chickens (excl. broilers), 48.1 mil broilers, 2.28 mil cattle/calves, 135,000 sheep/lambs, 570,000 hogs/pigs. **Nonfuel minerals:** $4.7 bil; iron ore (usable shipped), sand and gravel (construction), sand and gravel (industrial), stone (crushed), stone (dimension). **Commercial fishing:** $0.3 mil. **Chief ports:** Two Harbors, Silver Bay, Duluth, St. Paul. **Gross state product:** $312.1 bil. **Sales tax:** 6.875%. **Employment distrib.:** 15.0% govt.; 18.0% trade/trans./util.; 11.1% mfg.; 17.7% ed./health; 12.5% prof./bus. serv.; 9.2% leisure/hosp.; 6.3% finance; 4.2% constr./mining/log.; 1.9% info.; 4.2% other serv. **Unemployment:** 5.1%. **Per cap. pers. income:** $47,856. **New private housing:** 17,313 units/$3.7 bil. **Broadband Internet:** 84.0%. **Commercial banks:** 390; deposits: $208 bil. **Savings institutions:** 24; deposits: $4 bil. **Lottery:** total sales: $560.4 mil; profit: $135.2 mil.

Federal govt. Fed. civ. employees: 18,097; **avg. salary:** $73,780. **Notable fed. facilities:** Bishop Henry Whipple Fed. Bldg.; Minneapolis-St. Paul Air Reserve Station.

Higher education. 4-year public coll./univ.: 12; **2-yr. public:** 31; **4-yr. private:** 35.

Energy. Electricity use/cost: 793 kWh, $90.06.

State data. Motto: L'Etoile du Nord (The star of the north). **Flower:** Pink and white lady's-slipper. **Bird:** Common loon. **Tree:** Red pine. **Song:** "Hail! Minnesota." **Entered union:** May 11, 1858; rank: 32nd.

Tourism. Tourist spending: $12.1 bil. **Attractions:** Minneapolis Institute of Arts, Walker Art Center, Minneapolis Sculpture Garden, Minnehaha Falls (in Longfellow's poem *Song of Hiawatha*), Guthrie Theater, in Minneapolis; Mall of America, Bloomington; Ordway Ctr. for the Performing Arts, Science Museum of Minnesota, in St. Paul; Voyageurs Natl. Park; Mayo Clinic, Rochester; North Shore (Lake Superior); Lake Minnetonka; Boundary Waters Canoe Area Wilderness; Superior Natl. Forest; Aerial Lift Bridge, Duluth. **Information:** Explore Minnesota Tourism, Metro Square, 121 7th Pl. E., Ste. 100, St. Paul, MN 55101; 1-888-TOURISM; www.explore minnesota.com

History. Inhabited for at least 10,000 years, the region was home to Dakota Sioux when Europeans arrived. French fur traders Pierre Esprit Radisson and Médard Chouart, sieur des Groseilliers, explored in the mid-17th cent. In 1679, Daniel Greysolon, sieur Duluth, claimed the entire region for France. Ojibwa arrived in the 18th cent. and warred with the Sioux for over 100 years. Britain took the area east of the Mississippi, 1763. The U.S. took over that portion after the American Revolution and gained the western area, 1803, in the Louisiana Purchase. The U.S. built Ft. St. Anthony (now Ft. Snelling), 1819, and bought Native American lands, 1837, spurring an influx of settlers from the east. Minnesota became a territory, 1849, and a state, 1858. Sioux staged a bloody uprising, the Battle of Wood Lake, 1862, and were driven from the state. Railroad construction after the Civil War spurred the growth of the grain, timber, and iron mining industries. The opening of the St. Lawrence Seaway, 1959, aided the port of Duluth. Elected as a reformer, former wrestler Jesse Ventura served as governor, 1999-2003. Two-term Sen. Paul Wellstone, one of a long line of liberal Minnesota Democrats, died when his campaign plane crashed, 2002. The I-35W Mississippi River Bridge in Minneapolis collapsed in 2007, killing 13.

Famous Minnesotans. Andrews Sisters, Warren E. Burger, Ethan and Joel Coen, Bob Dylan, F. Scott Fitzgerald, Al Franken, Judy Garland, Cass Gilbert, Hubert H. Humphrey, Garrison Keillor, Sister Elizabeth Kenny, Jessica Lange, Sinclair Lewis, Paul Manship, E. G. Marshall, William J. and Charles H. Mayo, Eugene McCarthy, Walter F. Mondale, Prince (Prince Rogers Nelson), Charles M. Schulz, Ann Sothern, Harold Stassen, Thorstein Veblen, Jesse Ventura, Lindsey Vonn, Paul Wellstone.

Website. www.minnesota.gov

Mississippi (MS)
Magnolia State

People. Population: 2,991,207; rank: 31. **Pop. change** (2010-13): 0.8%. **Pop. density:** 63.7 per sq mi. **Racial distribution:** 59.8% white; 37.4% black; 1.0% Asian; 0.6% Amer. Ind.; 0.1% Hawaiian/Pacific Islander; 2 or more races, 1.1%. **Hispanic pop.:** 2.9%.

Geography. Total area: 48,432 sq mi; rank: 32. **Land area:** 46,923 sq mi; rank: 31. **Acres forested:** 19.5 mil. **Location:** East South Central state bordered on the W by the Mississippi R., on the S by the Gulf of Mexico. **Climate:** semitropical, with abundant rainfall and long growing season. **Topography:** low, fertile delta between the Yazoo and Mississippi Rivers; loess bluffs stretch around delta border; sandy gulf coastal terraces followed by piney woods and prairie; rugged, high sandy hills in extreme NE followed by Prairie Black Belt, Pontotoc Ridge, and flatwoods into the N central highlands. **Capital:** Jackson. **Chief airport:** Jackson.

Economy. Chief industries: warehousing and distribution, services, manufacturing, government, wholesale and retail trade. **Chief manuf. goods:** petroleum, upholstered furniture, poultry processing, motor vehicle parts, plastics, ships and boats, chemicals. **Chief crops:** cotton, soybeans, rice, hay, corn, sweet potatoes. **Livestock:** 9.43 mil chickens (excl. broilers), 734 mil broilers, 930,000 cattle/calves. **Nonfuel minerals:** $161 mil; sand and gravel (construction), stone (crushed), clays (fuller's earth), clays (ball), clays (bentonite). **Commercial fishing:** $49.3 mil. **Chief ports:** Pascagoula, Vicksburg, Gulfport, Biloxi, Greenville. **Gross state product:** $105.2 bil. **Sales tax:** 7.0%. **Employment distrib.:** 22.0% govt.; 19.4% trade/trans./util.; 12.5% mfg.; 12.0% ed./health; 9.0% prof./bus. serv.; 11.4% leisure/hosp.; 3.9% finance; 5.4% constr./mining/log.; 1.1% info.; 3.4% other serv. **Unemployment:** 8.6%. **Per cap. pers. income:** $34,478. **New private housing:** 6,799 units/$956.1 mil. **Broadband Internet:** 70.2%. **Commercial banks:** 100; deposits: $47.2 bil. **Savings institutions:** 5; deposits: $455 mil.

Federal govt. Fed. civ. employees: 18,609; **avg. salary:** $67,276. **Notable fed. facilities:** Keesler AFB; Meridian NAS; Columbus AFB; NASA Stennis Space Ctr.; Army Corps of Eng. Waterways Experiment Sta.; Naval Constr. Battalion Ctr., Gulfport.

Higher education. 4-year public coll./univ.: 9; **2-yr. public:** 15; **4-yr. private:** 9.

Energy. Electricity use/cost: 1,193 kWh, $122.49.

State data. Motto: Virtute et Armis (By valor and arms). **Flower:** Magnolia. **Bird:** Mockingbird. **Tree:** Magnolia. **Song:** "Go, Mississippi!" **Entered union:** Dec. 10, 1817; rank: 20th.

Tourism. Tourist spending: $6.1 bil. **Attractions:** Vicksburg Natl. Military Park and Cemetery; Natchez Trace Parkway; antebellum home tours in Natchez and other cities; Tupelo Natl. Battlefield, Elvis Presley Birthplace, in Tupelo; Smith Robertson Museum and Cultural Ctr., Mynelle Gardens, Eudora Welty House, in Jackson; Mardi Gras parades on Gulf Coast; Beauvoir (Jefferson Davis Home and Presidential Library), Biloxi; Gulf Islands Natl. Seashore; Delta Blues Museum, Clarksdale. **Information:** Mississippi Division of Tourism, P.O. Box 849, Jackson, MS 39205; 1-866-SEE-MISS; www. visitmississippi.org

History. Choctaw, Chickasaw, and Natchez peoples were living in the region at the time of European contact. The Spaniard Hernando de Soto explored the area, 1540-41. René-Robert Cavelier, sieur de La Salle, traced the Mississippi R. from Illinois to its mouth and claimed the entire Mississippi Valley for France, 1682. The first settlement was the French Ft. Maurepas, 1699, on Biloxi Bay. The region was ceded to Britain, 1763, and claimed by Spain, 1779-98, then became a U.S. territory, 1798, and a state, 1817. Slavery spread along with cotton plantations, and slaves made up 55% of the population, 1860. Mississippi seceded, 1861. In the Civil War, Union forces captured Vicksburg, 1863, and caused extensive damage elsewhere. Mississippi reentered the Union, 1870. For the next 100 years, resistance to desegregation and violence against blacks made the state a battleground for the civil rights movement. Hurricanes Camille, 1969, and Katrina, 2005, caused substantial damage to the Gulf Coast. Since the early 1990s, casino gambling has boosted the economy, but the state's poverty rate remained the highest in the nation in 2010.

Famous Mississippians. Margaret Walker Alexander, Dana Andrews, Jimmy Buffett, Bo Diddley, Medgar Evers, William Faulkner, Brett Favre, Shelby Foote, Morgan Freeman, John Grisham, Fannie Lou Hamer, Jim Henson, Faith Hill, John Lee Hooker, Robert Johnson, James Earl Jones, B. B. King, L. Q. C. Lamar, Trent Lott, Gerald McRaney, Willie Morris, Walter Payton, Elvis Presley, Leontyne Price, Charley Pride, LeAnn Rimes, Robin Roberts, Muddy Waters, Eudora Welty, Tennessee Williams, Oprah Winfrey, Johnny Winter, Richard Wright, Tammy Wynette.

Website. www.ms.gov

Missouri (MO)
Show Me State

People. Population: 6,044,171; rank: 18. **Pop. change** (2010-13): 0.9%. **Pop. density:** 87.9 per sq mi. **Racial distribution:** 83.7% white; 11.7% black; 1.8% Asian; 0.5% Amer. Ind.; 0.1% Hawaiian/Pacific Islander; 2 or more races, 2.0%. **Hispanic pop.:** 3.9%.

Geography. Total area: 69,707 sq mi; rank: 21. **Land area:** 68,742 sq mi; rank: 18. **Acres forested:** 15.5 mil. **Location:** West North Central state near the geographic center of the conterminous U.S.; bordered on the E by Mississippi R., on the NW by Missouri R. **Climate:** continental, susceptible to cold Canadian air; moist, warm Gulf air; and drier SW air. **Topography:** rolling hills, open, fertile plains, and well-watered prairie N of the Missouri R.; S of the river, land is rough and hilly with deep, narrow valleys; alluvial plain in the SE; low elevation in the W. **Capital:** Jefferson City. **Chief airports:** Kansas City, St. Louis.

Economy. Chief industries: agriculture, manufacturing, aerospace, tourism. **Chief manuf. goods:** motor vehicles and parts, aerospace, pharmaceuticals, plastics, soap, animal slaughtering and processing, printing. **Chief crops:** soybeans, corn, hay, cotton and cottonseed, wheat, rice, sorghum. **Livestock:** 11.56 mil chickens (excl. broilers), 277.4 mil broilers, 3.8 mil cattle/calves, 78,000 sheep/lamb, 380,000 hogs/pigs. **Nonfuel minerals:** $2.4 bil; stone (crushed), cement (portland), lead, lime, sand and gravel (construction). **Gross state product:** $276.3 bil. **Sales tax:** 4.225%. **Employment distrib.:** 16.8% govt.; 18.4% trade/trans./util.; 9.3% mfg.; 15.8% ed./health; 12.8% prof./bus. serv.; 10.8% leisure/hosp.; 6.0% finance; 4.0% constr./mining/log.; 2.0% info.; 4.1% other serv. **Unemployment:** 6.5%. **Per cap. pers. income:** $39,897. **New private housing:** 13,708 units/$2.2 bil. **Broadband Internet:** 91.0%. **Commercial banks:** 327; deposits: $126.7 bil. **Savings institutions:** 29; deposits: $23.9 bil. **Lottery:** total sales: $1.1 bil; profit: $280.0 mil.

Federal govt. Fed. civ. employees: 37,551; **avg. salary:** $65,252. **Notable fed. facilities:** Federal Reserve banks; Ft. Leonard Wood; Jefferson Barracks Natl. Cem.; Natl. Personnel Records Ctr.; Whiteman AFB.

Higher education. 4-year public coll./univ.: 13; **2-yr. public:** 14; **4-yr. private:** 53.

Energy. Electricity use/cost: 1,060 kWh, $107.80.

State data. Motto: Salus Populi Suprema Lex Esto (Let the welfare of the people be the supreme law). **Flower:** Hawthorn. **Bird:** Bluebird. **Tree:** Dogwood. **Song:** "Missouri Waltz." **Entered union:** Aug. 10, 1821; rank: 24th.

Tourism. Tourist spending: $12.6 bil. **Attractions:** Silver Dollar City, Branson; Mark Twain Boyhood Home and Museum, Hannibal; Pony Express Natl. Museum, St. Joseph; Harry S. Truman Library and Museum, Independence; Gateway Arch (part of Jefferson Natl. Expansion Memorial), Ulysses S. Grant Natl. Historic Site, St. Louis Zoo, in St. Louis; Worlds of Fun amusement park, Kansas City; Lake of the Ozarks; Ozark Natl. Scenic Riverways; Natl. Churchill Museum, Fulton; State Capitol, Jefferson City; Wilson's Creek Natl. Battlefield; George Washington Carver Natl. Monument, Diamond; Bass Pro Shops Outdoor World, Springfield. **Information:** Missouri Division of Tourism, P.O. Box 1055, Jefferson City, MO 65102; 1-800-519-2100; www.visitmo.com

History. In the 17th cent., when French explorers arrived, Algonquian Sauk, Fox, and Illinois and Siouan Osage, Missouri, Iowa, and Kansa peoples were living in the region; few remained by the 1830s. French hunters and lead miners made the first settlement c. 1735, at Ste. Genevieve. The territory was ceded to Spain by the French, 1762, then returned to France, 1800, and acquired by the U.S. in the Louisiana Purchase, 1803. Powerful earthquakes rocked New Madrid, 1811-12. Missouri became a territory, 1812, and entered the Union as a slave state, 1821. St. Louis became the gateway for pioneers heading West. Though Missouri stayed with the Union, pro- and antislavery forces battled there during the

Civil War. In the late 19th cent. railroad building and the cattle trade made Kansas City a boomtown. The most notable Missourian of the 20th cent., Harry S. Truman, was U.S. president, 1945-53. The state, a political bellwether, voted for the winner in every presidential election from 1960 to 2004. In May 2011, a tornado in Joplin killed about 162.

Famous Missourians. Maya Angelou, Robert Altman, John Ashcroft, Burt Bacharach, Josephine Baker, Scott Bakula, Thomas Hart Benton, Yogi Berra, Chuck Berry, George Caleb Bingham, Daniel Boone, Omar Bradley, William S. Burroughs, Kate Capshaw, Dale Carnegie, George Washington Carver, Bob Costas, Walter Cronkite, Sheryl Crow, Walt Disney, T. S. Eliot, Richard "Dick" Gephardt, John Goodman, Betty Grable, Jon Hamm, Edwin Hubble, Jesse James, Rush Limbaugh, Marianne Moore, Reinhold Niebuhr, J. C. Penney, John J. Pershing, Brad Pitt, Joseph Pulitzer, Ginger Rogers, Bess Truman, Harry S. Truman, Kathleen Turner, Tina Turner, Mark Twain, Dick Van Dyke, Tennessee Williams, Lanford Wilson, Shelley Winters, Jane Wyman.

Website. www.mo.gov

Montana (MT)
Treasure State

People. Population: 1,015,165; rank: 44. **Pop. change** (2010-13): 2.6%. **Pop. density:** 7.0 per sq mi. **Racial distribution:** 89.5% white; 0.6% black; 0.8% Asian; 6.5% Amer. Ind.; 0.1% Hawaiian/Pacific Islander; 2 or more races, 2.5%. **Hispanic pop.:** 3.3%.

Geography. Total area: 147,040 sq mi; rank: 4. **Land area:** 145,546 sq mi; rank: 4. **Acres forested:** 25.6 mil. **Location:** Mountain state bounded on the E by the Dakotas, on the S by Wyoming, on the SSW by Idaho, on the N by Canada. **Climate:** colder, continental climate with low humidity. **Topography:** Rocky Mts. in western third of state; eastern two-thirds gently rolling northern Great Plains. **Capital:** Helena.

Economy. Chief industries: agriculture, timber, mining, tourism, oil and gas. **Chief manuf. goods:** sawmills, softwood veneer and plywood, petroleum. **Chief crops:** wheat, barley, hay, sugar beets, potatoes, dry beans, flaxseed, cherries, corn, oats. **Livestock:** 580,000 chickens (excl. broilers), 2.55 mil cattle/calves, 220,000 sheep/lambs. **Nonfuel minerals:** $1.4 bil; palladium metal, copper, molybdenum concentrates, platinum metal, gold. **Gross state product:** $44.0 bil. **Sales tax:** none. **Employment distrib.:** 20.1% govt.; 20.4% trade/trans./util.; 4.2% mfg.; 15.4% ed./health; 8.9% prof./bus. serv.; 13.0% leisure/hosp.; 5.1% finance; 7.4% constr./mining/log.; 1.5% info.; 4.1% other serv. **Unemployment:** 5.6%. **Per cap. pers. income:** $39,199. **New private housing:** 4,854 units/$792.9 mil. **Broadband Internet:** 71.2%. **Commercial banks:** 68; deposits $19.4 bil. **Savings institutions:** 3; deposits: $498 mil. **Lottery:** total sales: $57.0 mil; profit: $13.1 mil.

Federal govt. Fed. civ. employees: 9,902; **avg. salary:** $65,534. **Notable fed. facilities:** Malmstrom AFB and missile silos; Ft. Peck, Hungry Horse, Libby, Yellowtail, and other dams.

Higher education. 4-year public coll./univ.: 6; **2-yr. public:** 11; **4-yr. private:** 4.

Energy. Electricity use/cost: 842 kWh, $84.88.

State data. Motto: Oro y Plata (Gold and silver). **Flower:** Bitterroot. **Bird:** Western meadowlark. **Tree:** Ponderosa pine. **Song:** "Montana." **Entered union:** Nov. 8, 1889; rank: 41st.

Tourism. Tourist spending: $3.9 bil. **Attractions:** Glacier and Yellowstone Natl. Parks; Museum of the Rockies, Bozeman; Museum of the Plains Indian, Blackfeet Reservation, in Browning; Custer Natl. Cemetery at Little Bighorn Battlefield Natl. Monument; Lewis and Clark Caverns State Park, Whitehall; Lewis and Clark Natl. Historic Trail Interpretive Ctr., Great Falls. **Information:** Travel Montana, Dept. of Commerce, 301 S. Park Ave., P.O. Box 200533, Helena, MT 59601; 1-800-VIS-ITMT; www.visitmt.com

History. Paleo-Indian hunters reached the area over 12,000 years ago. Cheyenne, Blackfoot, Crow, Assiniboin, Salish (Flatheads), Kootenai, and Kalispel peoples lived in the region before Europeans arrived. French explorers visited the region, 1742. The U.S. acquired the area partly through the Louisiana Purchase, 1803, partly through the Lewis and Clark Expedition, 1804-06. Fur traders and missionaries established posts in the early 19th cent. Gold was discovered on Grasshopper Creek, 1862, and Montana Territory was established, 1864. Indian uprisings reached their peak with the defeat of Gen. George Custer at the Battle of Little Bighorn, 1876. Chief Joseph and the Nez Percé tribe surrendered here, 1877, after a long trek across the state. Mining activity and the coming of the Northern Pacific Railway, 1883, brought population growth. Montana became a state, 1889. Copper wealth from the Butte pits resulted in the turn of the century "War of Copper Kings" as feuding factions contended for "the richest hill on earth." During the first half of the 20th cent., the Anaconda Copper firm wielded enormous political influence. Jeannette Rankin, a suffragist and pacifist, was the first woman elected to Congress, 1916. Mike Mansfield served 34 years in Congress and was Senate Democratic leader, 1961-77. An 18-year hunt for notorious "Unabomber" Theodore Kaczynski ended with his arrest, 1996, at his cabin near Lincoln.

Famous Montanans. Dana Carvey, Gary Cooper, Marcus Daly, Chet Huntley, Phil Jackson, Will James, Myrna Loy, David Lynch, Mike Mansfield, Brent Musburger, Jeannette Rankin, Charles M. Russell, Lester Thurow.

Website. www.mt.gov

Nebraska (NE)
Cornhusker State

People. Population: 1,868,516; rank: 37. **Pop. change** (2010-13): 2.3%. **Pop. density:** 24.3 per sq mi. **Racial distribution:** 89.7% white; 4.8% black; 2.1% Asian; 1.3% Amer. Ind.; 0.1% Hawaiian/Pacific Islander; 2 or more races, 2.0%. **Hispanic pop.:** 9.9%.

Geography. Total area: 77,348 sq mi; rank: 16. **Land area:** 76,824 sq mi; rank: 15. **Acres forested:** 1.5 mil. **Location:** West North Central state with the Missouri R. for a border on NE and E. **Climate:** continental semiarid. **Topography:** till plains of the central lowland in the eastern third rises to the Great Plains and hill country of the N central and NW. **Capital:** Lincoln. **Chief airport:** Omaha.

Economy. Chief industries: agriculture, manufacturing. **Chief manuf. goods:** animal slaughtering, grain and oilseed, farm machinery, medical equip., motor vehicle parts, printing, structural metals. **Chief crops:** corn, sorghum, soybeans, hay, wheat, dry beans, oats, potatoes, sugar beets. **Livestock:** 11.42 mil chickens (excl. broilers), 6.15 mil cattle/calves, 76,000 sheep/lambs, 390,000 hogs/pigs. **Nonfuel minerals:** $307 mil; cement (portland), stone (crushed), sand and gravel (construction), sand and gravel (industrial), lime. **Gross state product:** $109.6 bil. **Sales tax:** 5.5%. **Employment distrib.:** 17.4% govt.; 20.6% trade/trans./util.; 9.7% mfg.; 15.1% ed./health; 10.9% prof./bus. serv.; 8.9% leisure/hosp.; 7.3% finance; 4.7% constr./mining/log.; 1.7% info.; 3.8% other serv. **Unemployment:** 3.9%. **Per cap. pers. income:** $46,033. **New private housing:** 7,543 units/$1.2 bil. **Broadband Internet:** 74.8%. **Commercial banks:** 214; deposits: $50.8 bil. **Savings institutions:** 10; deposits $4.4 bil. **Lottery:** total sales: $160.8 mil; profit: $40.0 mil.

Federal govt. Fed. civ. employees: 10,994; **avg. salary:** $69,610. **Notable fed. facilities:** Offutt AFB.

Higher education. 4-year public coll./univ.: 7; **2-yr. public:** 8; **4-yr. private:** 15.

Energy. Electricity use/cost: 1,000 kWh, $100.46.

State data. Motto: Equality before the law. **Flower:** Goldenrod. **Bird:** Western meadowlark. **Tree:** Cottonwood. **Song:** "Beautiful Nebraska." **Entered union:** Mar. 1, 1867; rank: 37th.

Tourism. Tourist spending: $4.4 bil. **Attractions:** Univ. of Nebraska State Museum at Morrill Hall, Nebraska State Capitol, in Lincoln; Stuhr Museum of the Prairie Pioneer, Grand Island; Boys Town; Omaha's Henry Doorly Zoo and Aquarium, Joslyn Art Museum, The Durham Museum, in Omaha; Ashfall Fossil Beds State Hist. Park, near Royal; Strategic Air and Space Museum, Ashland; Arbor Lodge State Historical Park, Nebraska City; Buffalo Bill Ranch State Historical Park, North Platte; Pioneer Village, Minden; Oregon Trail landmarks, incl. at Scotts Bluff Natl. Monument and Chimney Rock Natl. Historic Site; Great Platte River Road Archway, Museum of Nebraska Art, in Kearney. **Information:** Nebraska Division of Travel and Tourism, 301 Centennial Mall S., Lincoln, NE 68508; 1-888-444-1867; www.visitnebraska.com

History. When Europeans arrived, Pawnee, Ponca, Omaha, and Oto peoples lived in the region. Spanish and French explorers visited the area prior to its acquisition in the Louisiana Purchase, 1803. Meriwether Lewis and William Clark passed through, 1804-06. The first permanent settlement was Bellevue, near Omaha, 1823. The 1834 Indian Intercourse Act declared Nebraska Indian country and excluded white settlement, but conflicts with settlers eventually forced Native Americans to move to reservations. Nebraska became a territory, 1854, and a state, 1867. Many Civil War veterans settled under free land terms of the 1862 Homestead Act; as agriculture grew, struggles followed between homesteaders and ranchers. Since the mid-1930s, Nebraska has been the only state with a unicameral legislature. A leader in agribusiness, Nebraska has also become a major telemarketing center. The "Oracle of Omaha," investor Warren Buffett, one of the world's wealthiest men, announced in 2006 he would give most of his $44-bil fortune to charity.

Famous Nebraskans. Grover Cleveland Alexander, Fred Astaire, Marlon Brando, Charles W. Bryan, William Jennings Bryan, Warren Buffett, Johnny Carson, Willa Cather, Dick Cavett, Dick Cheney, Loren Eiseley, Father Edward J. Flanagan, Henry Fonda, Bob Gibson, Rollin Kirby, Harold Lloyd, Malcolm X, J. Sterling Morton, John G. Neihardt, Nick Nolte, George W. Norris, Tom Osborne, Roscoe Pound, Red Cloud, Mari Sandoz, Robert Taylor, Darryl F. Zanuck.
Website. www.nebraska.gov

Nevada (NV)
Sagebrush State, Battle Born State, Silver State

People. Population: 2,790,136; rank: 35. **Pop. change** (2010-13): 3.3%. **Pop. density:** 25.4 per sq mi. **Racial distribution:** 76.7% white; 9.0% black; 8.1% Asian; 1.6% Amer. Ind.; 0.7% Hawaiian/Pacific Islander; 2 or more races, 3.9%. **Hispanic pop.:** 27.5%.

Geography. Total area: 110,572 sq mi; rank: 7. **Land area:** 109,781 sq mi; rank: 7. **Acres forested:** 10.6 mil. **Location:** Mountain state bordered on N by Oregon and Idaho, on E by Utah, on SE by Arizona, and on SW and W by California. **Climate:** semiarid and arid. **Topography:** rugged N-S mountain ranges; highest elevation, Boundary Peak, 13,146 ft; southern area is within the Mojave Desert; lowest elevation, Colorado R., at southern tip of state, 479 ft. **Capital:** Carson City. **Chief airports:** Las Vegas, Reno.

Economy. Chief industries: gaming, tourism, mining, manufacturing, government, retailing, warehousing, trucking. **Chief manuf. goods:** gaming machines, cement and concrete, plastics, printing, architectural and structural metals, electricity instruments. **Chief crops:** hay, onions, potatoes, alfalfa, wheat, garlic, mint, barley. **Livestock:** 455,000 cattle/calves, 80,000 sheep/lambs. **Nonfuel minerals:** $9 bil; gold, copper, silver, lime, sand and gravel (construction). **Gross state product:** $132.0 bil. **Sales tax:** 6.85%. **Employment distrib.:** 12.8% govt.; 18.5% trade/trans./util.; 3.4% mfg.; 9.5% ed./health; 13.2% prof./bus. serv.; 27.6% leisure/hosp.; 4.7% finance; 6.3% constr./mining/log.; 1.0% info.; 2.9% other serv. **Unemployment:** 9.8%. **Per cap. pers. income:** $38,920. **New private housing:** 11,174 units/$1.8 bil. **Broadband Internet:** 89.4%. **Commercial banks:** 38; deposits: $50.9 bil. **Savings institutions:** 8; deposits: $82.9 bil.

Federal govt. Fed. civ. employees: 12,190; **avg. salary:** $67,925. **Notable fed. facilities:** Nevada Natl. Security Site; Hawthorne Army Depot; Creech AFB; Nellis AFB; Fallon NAS; Natl. Wild Horse & Burro Ctr. at Palomino Valley.

Higher education. 4-year public coll./univ.: 6; **2-yr. public:** 1; **4-yr. private:** 3.

Energy. Electricity use/cost: 935 kWh, $110.58.

State data. Motto: All for our country. **Flower:** Sagebrush. **Bird:** Mountain bluebird. **Trees:** Single-leaf piñon and bristlecone pine. **Song:** "Home Means Nevada." **Entered union:** Oct. 31, 1864; rank: 36th.

Tourism. Tourist spending: $30.9 bil. **Attractions:** Legalized gambling, incl. at Lake Tahoe, Reno, Las Vegas, Laughlin, and Elko; Hoover Dam, Lake Mead Natl. Recreation Area, near Boulder City; Great Basin Natl. Park; Valley of Fire State Park; Red Rock Canyon Natl. Conservation Area; Las Vegas Strip, Fremont St., Natl. Atomic Testing Museum, Pinball Hall of Fame; Las Vegas Motor Speedway, in Las Vegas; Natl. Automobile Museum, Reno. **Information:** Commission on Tourism, 401 N. Carson St., Carson City, NV 89701; 1-800-NEVADA-8; www.travelnevada.com

History. Shoshone, Paiute, Bannock, and Washoe peoples lived in the area at the time of European contact. Nevada was first explored by Spaniards, 1776. In the 1820s, fur traders Peter Skene Ogden and Jedediah Smith separately explored the area. It was acquired by the U.S., 1848, at the end of the Mexican War. A trading post at Mormon Station,

now Genoa, was established, 1850. Discovery of the Comstock Lode, rich in gold and silver, 1859, spurred a population boom. Nevada became a territory, 1861, and a state, 1864. Hoover Dam was built, 1931-36. With gambling legal since 1931, a surge in resort casino construction after World War II turned Las Vegas into one of the nation's most popular tourist destinations. An influx of Hispanics and Asians, attracted by service-industry and construction jobs, helped make Nevada the fastest-growing state in the U.S. in 1990-2005 and again in 2007. The recession in recent years has had an equally powerful effect. Nevada had the highest state unemployment and home foreclosure rates in 2011.

Famous Nevadans. Andre Agassi, Kyle Busch, Walter Van Tilburg Clark, George W. G. Ferris, Sarah Winnemucca Hopkins, Paul Laxalt, Dat So La Lee, John William Mackay, Anne Henrietta Martin, Pat McCarran, Key Pittman, William Morris Stewart.
Website. www.nv.gov

New Hampshire (NH)
Granite State

People. Population: 1,323,459; rank: 42. **Pop. change** (2010-13): 0.5%. **Pop. density:** 147.8 per sq mi. **Racial distribution:** 94.2% white; 1.5% black; 2.4% Asian; 0.3% Amer. Ind.; 0.0% Hawaiian/Pacific Islander; 2 or more races, 1.6%. **Hispanic pop.:** 3.2%.

Geography. Total area: 9,349 sq mi; rank: 46. **Land area:** 8,953 sq mi; rank: 44. **Acres forested:** 4.8 mil. **Location:** New England state bounded on S by Massachusetts, on W by Vermont, on N by Canada, on E by Maine and the Atlantic Ocean. **Climate:** highly varied, due to its nearness to high mountains and ocean. **Topography:** low, rolling coast followed by countless hills and mountains rising out of a central plateau. **Capital:** Concord. **Chief airport:** Manchester.

Economy. Chief industries: tourism, manufacturing, agriculture, trade, mining. **Chief manuf. goods:** navigational instruments, circuit boards, electrical equip., fabricated metal, machinery, medical equip., plastics. **Chief crops:** greenhouse and nursery, apples, sweet corn, hay, Christmas trees, berries, maple syrup. **Livestock:** 32,000 cattle/calves. **Nonfuel minerals:** $102 mil; sand and gravel (construction), stone (crushed), stone (dimension), gemstones (natural). **Commercial fishing:** $23.2 mil. **Chief port:** Portsmouth. **Gross state product:** $67.8 bil. **Sales tax:** none. **Employment distrib.:** 14.2% govt.; 21.2% trade/trans./util.; 10.2% mfg.; 18.0% ed./health; 11.2% prof./bus. serv.; 10.3% leisure/hosp.; 5.5% finance; 3.6% constr./mining/log.; 1.9% info.; 3.9% other serv. **Unemployment:** 5.3%. **Per cap. pers. income:** $50,156. **New private housing:** 2,788 units/$566.0 mil. **Broadband Internet:** 77.4%. **Commercial banks:** 16; deposits: $21.1 bil. **Savings institutions:** 25; deposits: $7.1 bil. **Lottery:** total sales: $279.3 mil; profit: $74.3 mil.

Federal govt. Fed. civ. employees: 4,648; **avg. salary:** $82,262. **Notable fed. facilities:** Army Cold Regions Res. and Engineering Lab.

Higher education. 4-year public coll./univ.: 5; **2-yr. public:** 7; **4-yr. private:** 11.

Energy. Electricity use/cost: 615 kWh, $98.80.

State data. Motto: Live free or die. **Flower:** Purple lilac. **Bird:** Purple finch. **Tree:** White birch. **Song:** "Old New Hampshire." **Ninth** of original 13 states to ratify the Constitution, June 21, 1788.

Tourism. Tourist spending: $3.7 bil. **Attractions:** Mt. Washington Cog Railway, Mt. Washington (highest peak in Northeast); Lake Winnipesaukee; Crawford, Franconia, Pinkham Notches (mountain passes); Flume Gorge, Cannon Mountain Aerial Tramway, in White Mountains region; Strawbery Banke Museum, Portsmouth; Canterbury Shaker Village; Saint-Gaudens Natl. Historic Site, Cornish; Mt. Monadnock; Santa's Village, Jefferson. **Information:** Division of Travel & Tourism Development, 172 Pembroke Rd., P.O. Box 1856; Concord, NH 03302; 1-800-FUN-IN-NH; www.visitnh.gov

History. The area has been inhabited for about 10,000 years. Algonquian-speaking peoples, including the Pennacook, lived in the region when the Europeans arrived. The first explorers to visit the area were England's Martin Pring, 1603, and France's Samuel de Champlain, 1605. The first settlement was Odiorne's Point (now part of Rye), 1623. Before the American Revolution, New Hampshire residents raided a British fort at Portsmouth, 1774, and drove the royal governor out, 1775. New Hampshire became the first colony to adopt its own constitution, 1776. After statehood, 1788,

New Hampshire became a textile manufacturing center. The mill towns declined in the first half of the 20th cent., but tourism and technology industries, lured by low taxes, have revived the economy since the 1960s. A state law requires it to hold the first primary of the presidential campaign season.

Famous New Hampshirites. Dan Brown, Salmon P. Chase, Ralph Adams Cram, Mary Baker Eddy, Daniel Chester French, Robert Frost, Horace Greeley, Sarah Josepha Buell Hale, John Irving, Seth Meyers, Bode Miller, Franklin Pierce, Augustus Saint-Gaudens, Adam Sandler, Alan B. Shepard Jr., Sarah Silverman, David H. Souter, Daniel Webster.

Website. www.nh.gov

New Jersey (NJ)
Garden State

People. Population: 8,899,339; rank: 11. **Pop. change** (2010-13): 1.2%. **Pop. density:** 1,210.1 per sq mi. **Racial distribution:** 73.4% white; 14.7% black; 9.2% Asian; 0.6% Amer. Ind.; 0.1% Hawaiian/Pacific Islander; 2 or more races, 2.0%. **Hispanic pop.:** 18.9%.

Geography. Total area: 8,723 sq mi; rank: 47. **Land area:** 7,354 sq mi; rank: 46. **Acres forested:** 2.0 mil. **Location:** Middle Atlantic state bounded on N and E by New York and Atlantic Ocean, on S and W by Delaware and Pennsylvania. **Climate:** moderate, with marked difference between NW and SE extremities. **Topography:** Appalachian Valley in NW also has highest elevation, High Pt., 1,803 ft; Appalachian Highlands, flat-topped NE-SW mountain ranges; Piedmont Plateau, low plains broken by high ridges (Palisades) rising 400-500 ft; Coastal Plain, covering three-fifths of state in SE, rises from sea level to gentle slopes. **Capital:** Trenton. **Chief airports:** Atlantic City, Newark.

Economy. Chief industries: pharmaceuticals, telecommunications, biotechnology, printing and publishing. **Chief manuf. goods:** petroleum, pharmaceuticals, toiletries, chemicals, plastics, printing, navigational instruments, medical equip., paper prod. **Chief crops:** greenhouse and nursery, blueberries, peaches, corn, hay, tomatoes, bell peppers, cranberries, soybeans, apples. **Livestock:** 29,000 cattle/calves. **Nonfuel minerals:** $462 mil; stone (crushed), sand and gravel (construction), sand and gravel (industrial), greensand marl, peat. **Commercial fishing:** $187.7 mil. **Chief ports:** Newark-Elizabeth, Camden. **Gross state product:** $543.1 bil. **Sales tax:** 7.0%. **Employment distrib.:** 15.7% govt.; 21.1% trade/trans./util.; 6.1% mfg.; 16.2% ed./health; 16.2% prof./bus. serv.; 9.1% leisure/hosp.; 6.3% finance; 3.3% constr./mining/log.; 1.8% info.; 4.2% other serv. **Unemployment:** 8.2%. **Per cap. pers. income:** $55,993. **New private housing:** 24,209 units/$3.2 bil. **Broadband Internet:** 81.2%. **Commercial banks:** 93; deposits: $207.9 bil. **Savings institutions:** 65; deposits $68.4 bil. **Lottery:** total sales: $2.8 bil; profit $965.0 mil.

Federal govt. Fed. civ. employees: 25,440; **avg. salary:** $84,893. **Notable fed. facilities:** Joint Base McGuire-Dix-Lakehurst; Picatinny Arsenal; FAA William J. Hughes Technical Ctr.

Higher education. 4-year public coll./univ.: 14; **2-yr. public:** 19; **4-yr. private:** 27.

Energy. Electricity use/cost: 691 kWh, $109.10.

State data. Motto: Liberty and prosperity. **Flower:** Purple violet. **Bird:** Eastern goldfinch. **Tree:** Red oak. **Third of the** original 13 states to ratify the Constitution, Dec. 18, 1787.

Tourism. Tourist spending: $19.9 bil. **Attractions:** 130 mi of beaches, boardwalks on the Jersey Shore at Atlantic City (with gambling), Seaside Heights, Ocean City, Wildwood; Grover Cleveland Birthplace, Caldwell; Cape May Historic District; Thomas Edison Natl. Historical Park, West Orange; Six Flags Great Adventure, Jackson; Liberty State Park, Liberty Science Ctr., in Jersey City; Pine Barrens wilderness; Princeton Univ., Princeton Battlefield State Park, in Princeton; Morristown Natl. Historical Park; Adventure Aquarium, Battleship *New Jersey*, Walt Whitman House, in Camden. **Information:** Dept. of State, Division of Travel and Tourism, P.O. Box 460, Trenton, NJ 08625; 1-800-VISITNJ; www.visitnj.org

History. The Lenni Lenape (Delaware) peoples lived in the region and had mostly peaceful relations with European colonists, who arrived after the explorers Giovanni da Verrazano, 1524, and Henry Hudson, 1609. The first permanent European settlement was Dutch, at Bergen (now Jersey City), 1660. When the British took New Netherland, 1664, the area between the Delaware and Hudson Rivers was given to Lord John Berkeley and Sir George Carteret. During the American

Revolution, New Jersey was the scene of many major battles, including Trenton, 1776; Princeton, 1777; and Monmouth, 1778. New Jersey was the third state to ratify the Constitution, 1787, and the first to approve the Bill of Rights, 1789. In a duel at Weehawken, 1804, Vice Pres. Aaron Burr fatally shot Alexander Hamilton. Canal and railroad building stimulated the growth of cities and industries in the 19th cent. The 20th cent. arrival of large numbers of African Americans, Italians, Irish, European Jews, Puerto Ricans, South Asians, and other groups made New Jersey one of the most diverse states in the U.S. Construction of resort casinos in Atlantic City from the late 1970s revitalized tourism. Gov. James McGreevey resigned, 2004, after acknowledging an extramarital affair with a man identified as his former homeland security adviser. An estimated 37 people in New Jersey were killed when Hurricane Sandy (by then downgraded to a tropical storm) made landfall in 2012. Gov. Chris Christie's presidential aspirations were threatened in 2014 after it was alleged that officials created traffic jams on a toll bridge to punish a political opponent.

Famous New Jerseyans. Buzz Aldrin, Jason Alexander, Samuel Alito, Count Basie, Judy Blume, Jon Bon Jovi, Bill Bradley, Aaron Burr, Grover Cleveland, Stephen Crane, Danny DeVito, Thomas Edison, Albert Einstein, James Gandolfini, Allen Ginsberg, Alexander Hamilton, Ed Harris, Whitney Houston, Joyce Kilmer, Jack Nicholson, Shaquille O'Neal, Thomas Paine, Bill Parcells, Dorothy Parker, Joe Pesci, Molly Pitcher, Paul Robeson, Philip Roth, Antonin Scalia, Wally Schirra, H. Norman Schwarzkopf, Frank Sinatra, Bruce Springsteen, Martha Stewart, Meryl Streep, Dave Thomas, John Travolta, Walt Whitman, William Carlos Williams, Woodrow Wilson.

Website. www.nj.gov

New Mexico (NM)
Land of Enchantment

People. Population: 2,085,287; rank: 36. **Pop. change** (2010-13): 1.3%. **Pop. density:** 17.2 per sq mi. **Racial distribution:** 82.9% white; 2.5% black; 1.6% Asian; 10.4% Amer. Ind.; 0.2% Hawaiian/Pacific Islander; 2 or more races, 2.4%. **Hispanic pop.:** 47.3%.

Geography. Total area: 121,590 sq mi; rank: 5. **Land area:** 121,298 sq mi; rank: 5. **Acres forested:** 24.8 mil. **Location:** southwestern state bounded by Colorado on the N; Oklahoma, Texas, and Mexico on the E and S; and Arizona on the W. **Climate:** dry, with temperatures rising or falling 5°F with every 1,000 ft elevation. **Topography:** eastern third, Great Plains; central third, Rocky Mts. (85% of the state is over 4,000-ft elevation); western third, high plateau. **Capital:** Santa Fe. **Chief airport:** Albuquerque.

Economy. Chief industries: government, services, trade. **Chief manuf. goods:** semiconductors, medical equip., navigational/measuring/medical/control instruments, aircraft, chemicals, jewelry. **Chief crops:** hay, pecans, corn, greenhouse and nursery, chiles, onions, cotton, wheat, peanuts. **Livestock:** 1.29 mil cattle/calves, 85,000 sheep/lambs. **Nonfuel minerals:** $1.5 bil; copper, potash, sand and gravel (construction), molybdenum concentrates, cement (portland). **Gross state product:** $92.2 bil. **Sales tax:** 5.125%. **Employment distrib.:** 23.9% govt.; 16.8% trade/trans./util.; 3.3% mfg.; 15.4% ed./health; 11.9% prof./bus. serv.; 11.0% leisure/hosp.; 4.3% finance; 8.3% constr./mining/log.; 1.6% info.; 3.5% other serv. **Unemployment:** 6.9%. **Per cap. pers. income:** $36,284. **New private housing:** 5,161 units/$831.9 mil. **Broadband Internet:** 80.5%. **Commercial banks:** 55; deposits: $25.8 bil. **Savings institutions:** 8; deposits: $1.4 bil. **Lottery:** total sales: $141.8 mil; profit: $43.7 mil.

Federal govt. Fed. civ. employees: 24,298; **avg. salary:** $70,649. **Notable fed. facilities:** Kirtland, Cannon, Holloman AF Bases; Los Alamos Natl. Lab; White Sands Missile Range; Natl. Solar Observatory; Natl. Radio Astronomy Observatory (Very Large Array); Sandia Natl. Labs.

Higher education. 4-year public coll./univ.: 9; **2-yr. public:** 19; **4-yr. private:** 3.

Energy. Electricity use/cost: 656 kWh, $74.62.

State data. Motto: Crescit Eundo (It grows as it goes). **Flower:** Yucca. **Bird:** Roadrunner. **Tree:** Piñon. **Songs:** "O, Fair New Mexico"; "Asi Es Nuevo Mexico." **Entered union:** Jan. 6, 1912; rank: 47th.

Tourism. Tourist spending: $6.6 bil. **Attractions:** Carlsbad Caverns Natl. Park (with Lechuguilla Cave, among world's longest caves); Petroglyph Natl. Monument, Sandia Peak

Tramway, in Albuquerque; New Mexico History Museum, Museum of Intl. Folk Art, in Santa Fe (oldest U.S. capital); White Sands Natl. Monument (world's largest gypsum dune field); Chaco Culture Natl. Historical Park; Acoma Pueblo, or Sky City, built atop a 367-ft mesa; Taos Art Colony, Taos Ski Valley; Elephant Butte Lake State Park; Shiprock volcanic remnant; Intl. UFO Museum and Research Ctr., Roswell. **Information:** New Mexico Dept. of Tourism, 491 Old Santa Fe Trl., Santa Fe, NM 87501; 1-800-733-6396; www.newmexico.org

History. Inhabited for more than 10,000 years, the region was home to Sandia, Clovis, Folsom, Mogollon, and Anasazi cultures, followed by the Pueblo people, Anasazi descendants; later, nomadic Navajo and Apache came. Franciscan Marcos de Niza and a former black slave, Estevanico, explored the area, 1539, seeking gold; Coronado followed, 1540. First settlements were near San Juan Pueblo, 1598, and at Santa Fe, 1610. Settlers alternately traded and fought with the Apache, Comanche, and Navajo. Trade on the Santa Fe Trail to Missouri started, 1821. After the Mexican War began, 1846, Gen. Stephen Kearny took Santa Fe without firing a shot, and declared New Mexico part of the U.S. All Hispanic New Mexicans and Pueblo became U.S. citizens by terms of the 1848 treaty ending the war. New Mexico became a territory, 1850, but did not attain statehood until 1912. Pancho Villa raided Columbus, 1916, and U.S. troops were sent to the area. The world's first atomic bomb was exploded at a test site near Alamogordo, 1945. An underground nuclear waste depository opened near Carlsbad, 1999. Spaceport America, a state-owned commercial spaceport, hosted its first test launch in 2006.

Famous New Mexicans. Ben Abruzzo, Maxie Anderson, Jeff Bezos, William Bonney (Billy the Kid), Kit Carson, Bob Foster, Neil Patrick Harris, Tony Hillerman, Peter Hurd, Jean Baptiste Lamy, Nancy Lopez, Bill Mauldin, Georgia O'Keeffe, Bill Richardson, Kim Stanley, Al Unser, Bobby Unser.

Website. www.newmexico.gov

New York (NY)
Empire State

People. Population: 19,651,127; rank: 3. **Pop. change** (2010-13): 1.4%. **Pop. density:** 417.0 per sq mi. **Racial distribution:** 70.9% white; 17.5% black; 8.2% Asian; 1.0% Amer. Ind.; 0.1% Hawaiian/Pacific Islander; 2 or more races, 2.3%. **Hispanic pop.:** 18.4%.

Geography. Total area: 54,555 sq mi; rank: 27. **Land area:** 47,126 sq mi; rank: 30. **Acres forested:** 19.0 mil. **Location:** Middle Atlantic state bordered by the New England states, Atlantic Ocean on E; New Jersey and Pennsylvania on S; Lakes Ontario and Erie on W; Canada on N. **Climate:** variable; the SE region moderated by the ocean. **Topography:** highest and most rugged mountains in the NE Adirondack upland; St. Lawrence-Champlain lowlands extend from Lake Ontario NE along the Canadian border; Hudson-Mohawk lowland follows rivers N and W, 10-30 mi wide; Atlantic coastal plain in the SE; Appalachian Highlands, covering half the state westward from the Hudson Valley, include the Catskill Mts., Finger Lakes; plateau of Erie-Ontario lowlands. **Capital:** Albany. **Chief airports:** Albany, Buffalo, Islip, New York (2), Rochester, Syracuse, White Plains.

Economy. Chief industries: manufacturing, finance, communications, tourism, transportation, services. **Chief manuf. goods:** pharmaceuticals, photographic chemicals, electronics, automotive parts, toiletries, printing, plastics, apparel. **Chief crops:** greenhouse and nursery, apples, corn, hay, cabbage, onions, soybeans, potatoes, snap beans, grapes, squash, pumpkins, tomatoes, wheat, cucumbers, green peas. **Livestock:** 5.81 mil chickens (excl. broilers), 1.45 mil cattle/calves, 75,000 sheep/lambs. **Nonfuel minerals:** $1.2 bil; salt, stone (crushed), sand and gravel (construction), cement (portland), wollastonite. **Commercial fishing:** $39.3 mil. **Chief ports:** New York, Buffalo, Albany. **Gross state product:** $1.3 tril. **Sales tax:** 4.0%. **Employment distrib.:** 16.1% govt.; 17.0% trade/trans./util.; 5.0% mfg.; 20.3% ed./health; 13.6% prof./bus. serv.; 9.6% leisure/hosp.; 7.4% finance; 3.8% constr./mining/log.; 2.9% info.; 4.3% other serv. **Unemployment:** 7.7%. **Per cap. pers. income:** $54,063. **New private housing:** 32,581 units/$4.8 bil. **Broadband Internet:** 84.0%. **Commercial banks:** 158; deposits: $1 tril. **Savings institutions:** 59; deposits: $72.1 bil. **Lottery:** total sales: $8.9 bil; profit: $3.0 bil.

Federal govt. Fed. civ. employees: 66,065; **avg. salary:** $76,185. **Notable fed. facilities:** Ft. Drum; West Point Military

Academy; Merchant Marine Academy; NY Fed. Reserve; U.S. Army Watervliet Arsenal; Brookhaven Natl. Lab; U.S. Mission to the United Nations.

Higher education. 4-year public coll./univ.: 43; **2-yr. public:** 35; **4-yr. private:** 164.

Energy. Electricity use/cost: 603 kWh, $106.14.

State data. Motto: Excelsior (Ever upward). **Flower:** Rose. **Bird:** Bluebird. **Tree:** Sugar maple. **Song:** "I Love New York." **Eleventh** of original 13 states to ratify the Constitution, July 26, 1788.

Tourism. Tourist spending: $60.0 bil. **Attractions:** New York City; Adirondack and Catskill Mountains; Watkins Glen State Park; Thousand Islands region; Niagara Falls; Saratoga Race Course, Saratoga Springs; Philipsburg Manor, Old Dutch Church of Sleepy Hollow, in Sleepy Hollow; Washington Irving's Sunnyside, Tarrytown; Corning Museum of Glass; Fenimore Art Museum, Natl. Baseball Hall of Fame and Museum, in Cooperstown; Ft. Ticonderoga; New York State Capitol, Albany; Home of Franklin D. Roosevelt Natl. Historic Site, Hyde Park; Long Island beaches; Sagamore Hill (Theodore Roosevelt's "Summer White House"), Oyster Bay. **Information:** Empire State Development, Travel Information Center, 30 South Pearl St., Albany, NY 12245; 1-800-CALLNYS; www.iloveny.com

History. When Europeans arrived, Algonquians including the Mahican, Wappinger, and Lenni Lenape inhabited the region, as did the Iroquoian Mohawk, Oneida, Onondaga, Cayuga, and Seneca tribes, who established the League of the Five Nations. Giovanni da Verrazano entered New York harbor, 1524. In 1609, Henry Hudson visited the river later named for him, and Samuel de Champlain explored the lake that now bears his name. The first permanent settlement was Dutch, near present-day Albany, 1624. New Amsterdam was settled, 1626, at the southern tip of Manhattan island. A British fleet seized New Netherland, 1664. Key battles of the American Revolution included Saratoga, 1777. In the 19th cent., New York City emerged as one of the world's great metropolitan areas, a center for trade, finance, and arts, and a haven for millions of immigrants. Completion of Erie Canal, 1825, established the state as a gateway to the West. The first women's rights convention was held in Seneca Falls, 1848. Although the state backed the Union in the Civil War, an 1863 military draft triggered three days of riots in New York City. Industry declined in the 20th cent., and California and Texas passed New York in population. Attica was the scene of a bloody prison revolt, 1971. Two jet aircraft hijacked by terrorists on Sept. 11, 2001, destroyed the World Trade Center in lower Manhattan. Gov. Eliot Spitzer resigned in Mar. 2008 after 14 months in office; he was alleged to have patronized a prostitution ring. An estimated 65 people in New York state were killed when Hurricane Sandy (by then downgraded to a tropical storm) made landfall in Oct. 2012.

Famous New Yorkers. Woody Allen, Susan B. Anthony, James Baldwin, Lucille Ball, Ann Bancroft, L. Frank Baum, Milton Berle, Humphrey Bogart, Barbara Boxer, Mel Brooks, Benjamin Cardozo, De Witt Clinton, James Fenimore Cooper, Peter Cooper, Aaron Copland, Francis Ford Coppola, Tom Cruise, Robert De Niro, George Eastman, Jimmy Fallon, Millard Fillmore, Lou Gehrig, George and Ira Gershwin, Ruth Bader Ginsburg, Rudolph Giuliani, Jackie Gleason, Stephen Jay Gould, Julia Ward Howe, Charles Evans Hughes, Washington Irving, Henry and William James, John Jay, Edward Koch, Fiorello LaGuardia, Herman Melville, Arthur Miller, J. Pierpont Morgan Jr., Eddie Murphy, Joyce Carol Oates, Carroll O'Connor, Rosie O'Donnell, Eugene O'Neill, Jerry Orbach, George Pataki, Colin Powell, Nancy Reagan, John Roberts, John D. Rockefeller, Nelson Rockefeller, Richard Rodgers, Ray Romano, Eleanor Roosevelt, Franklin D. Roosevelt, Theodore Roosevelt, Tim Russert, J. D. Salinger, Caroline Kennedy Schlossberg, Jerry Seinfeld, Al Sharpton, Paul Simon, Alfred E. Smith, Elizabeth Cady Stanton, Barbra Streisand, Donald Trump, William (Boss) Tweed, Martin Van Buren, Luther Vandross, Gore Vidal, Denzel Washington, Edith Wharton, Walt Whitman, Mark Zuckerberg.

Website. www.ny.gov

North Carolina (NC)
Tar Heel State, Old North State

People. Population: 9,848,060; rank: 10. **Pop. change** (2010-13): 3.3%. **Pop. density:** 202.6 per sq mi. **Racial distribution:** 71.7% white; 22.0% black; 2.6% Asian; 1.6% Amer. Ind.; 0.1% Hawaiian/Pacific Islander; 2 or more races, 2.0%. **Hispanic pop.:** 8.9%.

Geography. Total area: 53,819 sq mi; rank: 28. **Land area:** 48,618 sq mi; rank: 29. **Acres forested:** 18.6 mil. **Location:** South Atlantic state bounded on N by Virginia, on S by South Carolina, on SW by Georgia, on W by Tennessee, and on E by Atlantic. **Climate:** subtropical in SE, medium-continental in mountain region; tempered by the Gulf Stream and mountains in W. **Topography:** coastal plain and tidewater in two-fifths of state, extending to the fall line of the rivers; Piedmont Plateau in another two-fifths has gentle to rugged hills; southern Appalachian Mts. contain the Blue Ridge and Great Smoky Mts. **Capital:** Raleigh. **Chief airports:** Charlotte, Greensboro, Raleigh.

Economy. Chief industries: manufacturing, agriculture, tourism. **Chief manuf. goods:** transportation, tobacco, pharmaceuticals, toiletries, plastics, animal slaughtering and processing, household furniture, fabric and apparel. **Chief crops:** greenhouse and nursery, tobacco, cotton, soybeans, corn, Christmas trees, sweet potatoes, wheat, peanuts, blueberries, cucumbers, tomatoes, hay, potatoes. **Livestock:** 21.16 mil chickens (excl. broilers), 785.5 mil broilers, 810,000 cattle/calves, 27,000 sheep/lambs, 860,000 hogs/pigs. **Nonfuel minerals:** $1 bil; stone (crushed), phosphate rock, sand and gravel (construction), sand and gravel (industrial), feldspar. **Commercial fishing:** $72.9 mil. **Chief ports:** Morehead City, Wilmington. **Gross state product:** $471.4 bil. **Sales tax:** 4.75%. **Employment distrib.:** 17.6% govt.; 18.6% trade/trans./util.; 10.7% mfg.; 13.6% ed./health; 13.9% prof./bus. serv.; 10.8% leisure/hosp.; 5.0% finance; 4.4% constr./mining/log.; 1.7% info.; 3.7% other serv. **Unemployment:** 8.0%. **Per cap. pers. income:** $38,457. **New private housing:** 51,290 units/$8.3 bil. **Broadband Internet:** 81.0%. **Commercial banks:** 84; deposits: $342.4 bil. **Savings institutions:** 27; deposits: $5.7 bil. **Lottery:** total sales: $1.7 bil; profit: $479.5 mil.

Federal govt. Fed. civ. employees: 44,644; **avg. salary:** $69,681. **Notable fed. facilities:** Ft. Bragg; Camp Lejeune Marine Base, Marine Corps Air Station Cherry Point; NOAA Natl. Climatic Data Ctr.; Natl. Inst. of Environmental Health Sciences, EPA Research and Dev. Labs, all in Research Triangle Park.

Higher education. 4-year public coll./univ.: 16; **2-yr. public:** 59; **4-yr. private:** 48.

Energy. Electricity use/cost: 1,077 kWh, $117.45.

State data. Motto: Esse Quam Videri (To be rather than to seem). **Flower:** Dogwood. **Bird:** Cardinal. **Tree:** Pine. **Song:** "The Old North State." **Twelfth** of the original 13 states to ratify the Constitution, Nov. 21, 1789.

Tourism. Tourist spending: $20.1 bil. **Attractions:** Cape Hatteras and Cape Lookout Natl. Seashores; Great Smoky Mountains Natl. Park; Guilford Courthouse Natl. Military Park; Moore's Creek Natl. Battlefield (1776 victory ended British rule in colony); Bennett Place (site of largest troop surrender of Civil War), Durham; Ft. Raleigh Natl. Historic Site, North Carolina Aquarium, on Roanoke Island; Wright Brothers Natl. Mem., Kill Devil Hills; USS *North Carolina*, Wilmington; North Carolina Zoo, Asheboro; North Carolina Symphony, Marbles Kids Museum, North Carolina Museum of Art, North Carolina Museum of Natural Sciences, in Raleigh; Carl Sandburg Home, Flat Rock; Biltmore House and Gardens, North Carolina Arboretum, in Asheville; U.S. Natl. Whitewater Ctr., Discovery Place, in Charlotte; Fort Macon State Park, Atlantic Beach. **Information:** North Carolina Division of Tourism, Film and Sports Development, 4324 Mail Service Ctr., Raleigh, NC 27699; 1-800-VISIT-NC, (919) 733-8372; www.visitnc.com

History. Algonquian, Siouan, and Iroquoian peoples lived in the region at the time of European contact. Sir Walter Raleigh tried to found a colony, 1584-87; the "Lost Colony" on Roanoke Island, 1587, disappeared without a trace. Permanent settlers came from Virginia in the mid-17th cent. The province's congress was the first to vote for independence, 1776. In the Revolutionary War, Gen. Charles Cornwallis's forces were defeated at Kings Mountain, 1780, and forced out after Guilford Courthouse, 1781. The state ratified the Constitution, 1789, only after Congress passed the Bill of Rights. North Carolina, where one-third of the population was slaves, seceded from the Union, 1861, and provided more troops to the Confederacy than any other state; it was readmitted, 1868. The Wright brothers made the first powered airplane flight at Kitty Hawk, 1903. Sit-ins at segregated Greensboro lunch counters, 1960, drew national attention to the civil rights movement. Long reliant on tobacco, textiles, and wood products, North Carolina has prospered since the 1960s from advanced technologies in the Raleigh-Durham-Chapel Hill

area and banking in Charlotte. The hurricane-prone state was hit hard by Hazel, 1954, Fran, 1996, and Floyd, 1999.

Famous North Carolinians. David Brinkley, Shirley Caesar, John Coltrane, Rick Dees, Elizabeth Hanford Dole, Dale Earnhardt Sr., John Edwards, Ava Gardner, Richard Jordan Gatling, Billy Graham, Andy Griffith, O. Henry, Andrew Jackson, Andrew Johnson, Michael Jordan, William Rufus King, Charles Kuralt, Meadowlark Lemon, Dolley Madison, Thelonious Monk, Edward R. Murrow, Richard Petty, James K. Polk, Charlie Rose, Carl Sandburg, Enos Slaughter, Dean Smith, James Taylor, Thomas Wolfe.

Website. www.nc.gov

North Dakota (ND)
Peace Garden State

People. Population: 723,393; rank: 48. **Pop. change** (2010-13): 7.6%. **Pop. density:** 10.5 per sq mi. **Racial distribution:** 89.6% white; 1.8% black; 1.2% Asian; 5.4% Amer. Ind.; 0.1% Hawaiian/Pacific Islander; 2 or more races, 1.9%. **Hispanic pop.:** 2.9%.

Geography. Total area: 70,698 sq mi; rank: 19. **Land area:** 69,001 sq mi; rank: 17. **Acres forested:** 0.8 mil. **Location:** West North Central state situated exactly in the middle of North America, bounded on the N by Canada, on the E by Minnesota, on the S by South Dakota, on the W by Montana. **Climate:** continental, with a wide range of temperatures and moderate rainfall. **Topography:** Central Lowland in the E comprises the flat Red R. Valley and the Rolling Drift Prairie; Missouri Plateau of the Great Plains on the W. **Capital:** Bismarck.

Economy. Chief industries: agriculture, mining, tourism, manufacturing, telecommunications, energy, food processing. **Chief manuf. goods:** machinery, wood prods., motor vehicles and parts, furniture, processed foods. **Chief crops:** wheat, soybeans, corn, sugar beets, barley, dry beans, sunflowers, canola, potatoes, flaxseed, hay, dry peas, lentils, oats. **Livestock:** 1.77 mil cattle/calves, 66,000 sheep/lamb. **Nonfuel minerals:** $244 mil; sand and gravel (construction), lime, stone (crushed), clays (common), sand and gravel (industrial). **Gross state product:** $56.3 bil. **Sales tax:** 5.0%. **Employment distrib.:** 17.8% govt.; 23.3% trade/trans./util.; 5.4% mfg.; 12.7% ed./health; 7.5% prof./bus. serv.; 8.9% leisure/hosp.; 5.2% finance; 14.3% constr./mining/log.; 1.5% info.; 3.5% other serv. **Unemployment:** 2.9%. **Per cap. pers. income:** $57,084. **New private housing:** 10,532 units/$1.4 bil. **Broadband Internet:** 77.8%. **Commercial banks:** 95; deposits: $21.6 bil. **Savings institutions:** 2; deposits $1.5 bil. **Lottery:** total sales: $27.8 mil; profit: $7.9 mil.

Federal govt. Fed. civ. employees: 6,130; **avg. salary:** $65,179. **Notable fed. facilities:** Minot AFB; Grand Forks AFB; Northern Prairie Wildlife Res. Ctr.; Garrison Dam Natl. Fish Hatchery; Grand Forks Human Nutrition Res. Ctr.

Higher education. 4-year public coll./univ.: 9; **2-yr. public:** 5; **4-yr. private:** 6.

Energy. Electricity use/cost: 1,091 kWh, $98.85.

State data. Motto: Liberty and union, now and forever, one and inseparable. **Flower:** Wild prairie rose. **Bird:** Western meadowlark. **Tree:** American elm. **Song:** "North Dakota Hymn." **Entered union:** Nov. 2, 1889; rank: 39th.

Tourism. Tourist spending: $3.0 bil. **Attractions:** North Dakota Heritage Ctr., North Dakota State Capitol, in Bismarck; Bonanzaville, West Fargo; Ft. Union Trading Post Natl. Historic Site; Intl. Peace Garden, Dunseith; Elkhorn Ranch site, in Theodore Roosevelt Natl. Park; Ft. Abraham Lincoln State Park and Museum, Mandan; Dakota Dinosaur Museum, Dickinson; Knife River Indian Villages Natl. Historic Site; Scandinavian Heritage Park, Minden. **Information:** North Dakota Tourism Division, Century Center, 1600 E. Century Ave., Ste. 2, P.O. Box 2057, Bismarck, ND 58502; 1-800-435-5663; www.ndtourism.com

History. Paleo-Indian peoples hunted in the area at least 11,000 years ago. At the time of European contact, the Ojibwa, Yanktonai and Teton Sioux, Mandan, Arikara, and Hidatsa peoples lived in the region. Pierre de Varennes, sieur de La Vérendrye, was the first French fur trader in the area, 1738, followed by the English at the end of the 18th cent. Lewis and Clark built Ft. Mandan, near present-day Washburn, 1804-05, and wintered there. The first permanent settlement was at Pembina, 1812. Missouri River steamboats reached the area, 1832. Dakota Territory was organized, 1861. The first railroad arrived, 1872. The "bonanza farm" craze of the 1870s-80s led to statehood, 1889. The Nonpartisan League, a farmers' group favoring state ownership of industries, helped elect Lynn Frazier as governor, 1916, but he and others were ousted in a recall vote, 1921. The predominantly agricultural state has one of the nation's lowest unemployment rates, mostly due to surging oil production since late 2008 in the state's Bakken formation.

Famous North Dakotans. Maxwell Anderson, Angie Dickinson, Josh Duhamel, John Bernard Flannagan, Phil Jackson, Louis L'Amour, Peggy Lee, Roger Maris, Eric Sevareid, Vilhjalmur Stefansson, Lawrence Welk.

Website. www.nd.gov

Ohio (OH)
Buckeye State

People. Population: 11,570,808; rank: 7. **Pop. change** (2010-13): 0.3%. **Pop. density:** 283.2 per sq mi. **Racial distribution:** 83.2% white; 12.5% black; 1.9% Asian; 0.3% Amer. Ind.; 0.0% Hawaiian/Pacific Islander; 2 or more races, 2.0%. **Hispanic pop.:** 3.4%.

Geography. Total area: 44,826 sq mi; rank: 34. **Land area:** 40,861 sq mi; rank: 35. **Acres forested:** 8.1 mil. **Location:** East North Central state bounded on the N by Michigan and Lake Erie; on the E and S by Pennsylvania, West Virginia, and Kentucky; on the W by Indiana. **Climate:** temperate but variable; weather subject to much precipitation. **Topography:** generally rolling plain; Allegheny Plateau in E; Lake Erie Plains extend southward; central plains in the W. **Capital:** Columbus. **Chief airports:** Akron, Cleveland, Columbus, Dayton.

Economy. Chief industries: manufacturing, trade, services. **Chief manuf. goods:** motor vehicles and parts, petroleum, plastics and rubber, iron and steel, aircraft, machinery, fabricated metal, printing. **Chief crops:** corn, soybeans, hay, wheat, grapes, potatoes, tomatoes, apples, strawberries, tobacco. **Livestock:** 36.88 mil chickens (excl. broilers), 70.1 mil broilers, 1.25 mil cattle/calves, 117,000 sheep/lambs, 165,000 hogs/pigs. **Nonfuel minerals:** $1 bil; stone (crushed), sand and gravel (construction), salt, lime, cement (portland). **Commercial fishing:** $5.2 mil. **Chief ports:** Cincinnati, Toledo, Conneaut, Cleveland, Ashtabula. **Gross state product:** $565.3 bil. **Sales tax:** 5.75%. **Employment distrib.:** 14.5% govt.; 18.5% trade/trans./util.; 12.6% mfg.; 16.6% ed./health; 13.2% prof./bus. serv.; 10.1% leisure/hosp.; 5.2% finance; 3.8% constr./mining/log.; 1.4% info.; 4.1% other serv. **Unemployment:** 7.4%. **Per cap. pers. income:** $40,865. **New private housing:** 19,903 units/$3.3 bil. **Broadband Internet:** 80.1%. **Commercial banks:** 167; deposits: $225.3 bil. **Savings institutions:** 91; deposits $32.7 bil. **Lottery:** total sales: $2.9 bil; profit: $803.1 mil.

Federal govt. Fed. civ. employees: 51,059; **avg. salary:** $77,962. **Notable fed. facilities:** Wright-Patterson AFB; Defense Supply Ctr., Columbus; NASA Glenn Research Ctr.; Joint Systems Manufacturing Center.

Higher education. 4-year public coll./univ.: 35; **2-yr. public:** 25; **4-yr. private:** 66.

Energy. Electricity use/cost: 895 kWh, $105.23.

State data. Motto: With God, all things are possible. **Flower:** Scarlet carnation. **Bird:** Cardinal. **Tree:** Buckeye. **Song:** "Beautiful Ohio." **Entered union:** Mar. 1, 1803; rank: 17th.

Tourism. Tourist spending: $17.1 bil. **Attractions:** Hopewell Culture Natl. Historical Park, Chillicothe; Cuyahoga Valley Natl. Park; Armstrong Air and Space Museum, Wapakoneta; Natl. Museum of the U.S. Air Force, near Dayton; Pro Football Hall of Fame, First Ladies Natl. Historic Site, in Canton; Kings Island amusement park, Mason; Lake Erie Islands, Cedar Point amusement park, in Sandusky; birthplaces, homes of, and memorials to presidents W. H. Harrison, Grant, Hayes, Garfield, B. Harrison, McKinley, Taft, and Harding; Amish Country, particularly in Holmes County; German Village historic neighborhood, Franklin Park Conservatory and Botanical Gardens, in Columbus; Rock and Roll Hall of Fame and Museum, West Side Market, Cleveland Metroparks Zoo, in Cleveland; Cincinnati Museum Center at Union Terminal; Toledo Zoo. **Information:** Division of Travel and Tourism, P.O. Box 1001, Columbus, OH 43216; 1-800-BUCKEYE; www.discoverohio.com

History. Paleo-Indians hunted in the area about 11,000 years ago; the Adena and Hopewell cultures followed. Wyandot, Delaware, Miami, and Shawnee peoples sparsely occupied the area when the first Europeans arrived. René-Robert Cavelier, sieur de La Salle, visited the region, 1669. France claimed it, 1682, but ceded it to Britain, 1763. After the American Revolution, Ohio became part of the Northwest Territory,

1787. The first permanent settlement was at Marietta, 1788. Cincinnati was also founded, 1788; Cleveland, 1796. Indian warfare abated with the Treaty of Greenville, 1795. Ohio became a state, 1803. In the War of 1812, Oliver Hazard Perry's victory on Lake Erie and William Henry Harrison's invasion of Canada, 1813, ended British incursions. Columbus, founded 1812, became the state capital, 1816. Before the Civil War, Ohioans aided the Underground Railroad, helping runaway slaves. Agricultural for much of the 19th cent., the state became an industrial powerhouse in the 20th. Manufacturing jobs dropped by 24%, 1998-2007. No Republican has ever won the presidency without winning Ohio's electoral votes.

Famous Ohioans. Berenice Abbott, Sherwood Anderson, Neil Armstrong, George Bellows, Halle Berry, Ambrose Bierce, Erma Bombeck, Drew Carey, Hart Crane, George Custer, Clarence Darrow, Paul Laurence Dunbar, Thomas Edison, Clark Gable, John Glenn, Zane Grey, Bob Hope, William Dean Howells, LeBron James, Maya Lin, Toni Morrison, Paul Newman, Jack Nicklaus, Annie Oakley, Jesse Owens, Jack Paar, Pontiac, Eddie Rickenbacker, John D. Rockefeller Sr. and Jr., Roy Rogers, Pete Rose, Arthur Schlesinger Jr., Gen. William Sherman, Steven Spielberg, Gloria Steinem, Harriet Beecher Stowe, Robert A. Taft, William H. Taft, Tecumseh, James Thurber, Ted Turner, Orville and Wilbur Wright.

Website. www.ohio.gov

Oklahoma (OK)
Sooner State

People. Population: 3,850,568; rank: 28. **Pop. change** (2010-13): 2.6%. **Pop. density:** 56.1 per sq mi. **Racial distribution:** 75.4% white; 7.7% black; 2.0% Asian; 9.0% Amer. Ind.; 0.2% Hawaiian/Pacific Islander; 2 or more races, 5.8%. **Hispanic pop.:** 9.6%.

Geography. Total area: 69,899 sq mi; rank: 20. **Land area:** 68,595 sq mi; rank: 19. **Acres forested:** 12.4 mil. **Location:** West South Central state bounded on the N by Colorado and Kansas, on the E by Missouri and Arkansas, on the S and W by Texas and New Mexico. **Climate:** temperate; southern humid belt merging with colder northern continental; humid eastern and dry western zones. **Topography:** high plains predominate in the W, hills and small mountains in the E; the E central region is dominated by the Arkansas R. Basin, and the S by the Red R. Plains. **Capital:** Oklahoma City. **Chief airports:** Oklahoma City, Tulsa.

Economy. Chief industries: manufacturing, mineral and energy exploration and production, agriculture, services. **Chief manuf. goods:** animal slaughtering and processing, petroleum, plastics and rubber, fabricated metals, machinery, motor vehicles and parts. **Chief crops:** wheat, greenhouse and nursery, hay, cotton, corn, soybeans, pecans, sorghum, peanuts. **Livestock:** 4.23 mil chickens (excl. broilers), 206.2 mil broilers, 4.3 mil cattle/calves, 65,000 sheep/lambs, 430,00 hogs/pigs. **Nonfuel minerals:** $755 mil; stone (crushed), cement (portland), sand and gravel (industrial), sand and gravel (construction), iodine. **Chief port:** Catoosa. **Gross state product:** $182.1 bil. **Sales tax:** 4.5%. **Employment distrib.:** 21.3% govt.; 18.0% trade/trans./util.; 8.4% mfg.; 13.9% ed./health; 11.0% prof./bus. serv.; 9.7% leisure/hosp.; 5.0% finance; 8.0% constr./mining/log.; 1.3% info.; 3.6% other serv. **Unemployment:** 5.4%. **Per cap. pers. income:** $41,586. **New private housing:** 13,583 units/$2.3 bil. **Broadband Internet:** 93.8%. **Commercial banks:** 245; deposits: $70.9 bil. **Savings institutions:** 4; deposits: $5 bil. **Lottery:** total sales: $200.2 mil; profit: $70.6 mil.

Federal govt. Fed. civ. employees: 37,450; **avg. salary:** $66,570. **Notable fed. facilities:** Tinker AFB; FAA Mike Monroney Aeronautical Ctr.; Ft. Sill; Altus AFB; McAlester Army Ammunition Plant; Vance AFB; Natl. Severe Storms Lab.

Higher education. 4-year public coll./univ.: 17; **2-yr. public:** 12; **4-yr. private:** 14.

Energy. Electricity use/cost: 1,132 kWh, $107.60.

State data. Motto: Labor Omnia Vincit (Labor conquers all things). **Flower:** Mistletoe. **Bird:** Scissor-tailed flycatcher. **Tree:** Redbud. **Song:** "Oklahoma!" **Entered union:** Nov. 16, 1907; rank: 46th.

Tourism. Tourist spending: $7.3 bil. **Attractions:** Cherokee Heritage Ctr., Tahlequah; Oklahoma City Natl. Memorial and Museum, Natl. Cowboy and Western Heritage Museum, White Water Bay and Frontier City amusement parks, Museum of Osteology, Bricktown neighborhood, in Oklahoma City; Will Rogers Memorial Museums, Claremore and

Oologah; Philbrook Museum of Art, Gilcrease Museum, in Tulsa; Wichita Mountains Wildlife Refuge; Woolaroc Museum and Wildlife Preserve, Price Tower Arts Center, in Bartlesville; Sequoyah's Cabin, Sallisaw; Sam Noble Museum of Natural History, Norman. **Information:** Travel and Tourism Division, 120 N. Robinson, 6th Fl., P.O. Box 52002, Oklahoma City, OK 73152-2002; 1-800-652-6552; www.travelok.com

History. Few Native Americans inhabited the region when the Spanish explorer Coronado arrived, 1541; in the 16th and 17th cent., French traders visited. Part of the Louisiana Purchase, 1803, Oklahoma was known as Indian Country and, from 1834, Indian Territory. It became home to the "Five Civilized Tribes"—Cherokee, Choctaw, Chickasaw, Creek, and Seminole—after the forced removal of Indians from the eastern U.S., 1828-46. The land was also used by Comanche, Osage, and other Plains Indians. As white settlers pressed west, land was opened for homesteading by "runs" and lottery. The first run was in 1889; the most famous run, 1893, was to the Cherokee Outlet. Oklahoma became a state, 1907. In the early 20th cent., oil finds brought wealth to the Tulsa area; the Greenwood section of the city, then known as the "Negro Wall Street," was devastated by a white mob, 1921. Depression and drought drove many "Okies" from the Dust Bowl to California in the 1930s. A truck bomb in Oklahoma City, 1995, destroyed a federal office building, killing 168 people; Timothy McVeigh was executed for the crime, 2001. A tornado in Moore killed 23 people May 20, 2013; the widest tornado on record touched down in El Reno May 31, 2013, killing 10 people.

Famous Oklahomans. Troy Aikman, Carl Albert, Gene Autry, Johnny Bench, William Boyd (Hopalong Cassidy), Garth Brooks, Lon Chaney, Gordon Cooper, Ralph Ellison, John Hope Franklin, James Garner, Vince Gill, Woody Guthrie, Paul Harvey, Ron Howard, Patrick J. Hurley, Ben Johnson, Jeane Kirkpatrick, Louis L'Amour, Shannon Lucid, Wilma Mankiller, Mickey Mantle, Reba McEntire, Wiley Post, Tony Randall, Oral Roberts, Will Rogers, Barry Switzer, Maria Tallchief, Jim Thorpe, Carrie Underwood, J. C. Watts Jr.

Website. www.ok.gov

Oregon (OR)
Beaver State

People. Population: 3,930,065; rank: 27. **Pop. change** (2010-13): 2.6%. **Pop. density:** 40.9 per sq mi. **Racial distribution:** 88.1% white; 2.0% black; 4.1% Asian; 1.8% Amer. Ind.; 0.4% Hawaiian/Pacific Islander; 2 or more races, 3.5%. **Hispanic pop.:** 12.3%.

Geography. Total area: 98,379 sq mi; rank: 9. **Land area:** 95,988 sq mi; rank: 10. **Acres forested:** 29.8 mil. **Location:** Pacific shore bounded on N by Washington, on E by Idaho, on S by Nevada and California, on W by the Pacific. **Climate:** mild and humid on coast; continental dryness and extreme temperatures in the interior. **Topography:** Coast Range of rugged mountains; fertile Willamette R. Valley to E and S; Cascade Mt. Range of volcanic peaks E of the valley; plateau E of Cascades, remaining two-thirds of state. **Capital:** Salem. **Chief airport:** Portland.

Economy. Chief industries: manufacturing, services, trade, finance, insurance, real estate, government, construction. **Chief manuf. goods:** wood prods., frozen produce, printing, computers and electronics, transportation equip., industrial machinery. **Chief crops:** greenhouse and nursery, grass seed, hay, wheat, potatoes, Christmas trees, onions, pears, hazelnuts, corn, grapes, cherries, blackberries, blueberries, peppermint, snap beans, apples, hops. **Livestock:** 2.62 mil chickens (excl. broilers), 1.28 mil cattle/calves, 195,000 sheep/lambs. **Nonfuel minerals:** $328 mil; stone (crushed), sand and gravel (construction), cement (portland), diatomite, perlite (crude). **Commercial fishing:** $128.0 mil. **Chief ports:** Portland, Coos Bay. **Gross state product:** $219.6 bil. **Sales tax:** none. **Employment distrib.:** 17.5% govt.; 18.7% trade/trans./util.; 10.3% mfg.; 14.5% ed./health; 12.5% prof./bus. serv.; 10.7% leisure/hosp.; 5.3% finance; 4.9% constr./mining/log.; 1.9% info.; 3.5% other serv. **Unemployment:** 7.7%. **Per cap. pers. income:** $40,233. **New private housing:** 14,843 units/$2.7 bil. **Broadband Internet:** 85.8%. **Commercial banks:** 49; deposits: $55.8 bil. **Savings institutions:** 8; deposits: $2.8 bil. **Lottery:** total sales $3.0 bil; profit: $530.6 mil.

Federal govt. Fed. civ. employees: 19,686; **avg. salary:** $71,636. **Notable fed. facilities:** Bonneville Power Admin.

Higher education. 4-year public coll./univ.: 9; **2-yr. public:** 17; **4-yr. private:** 24.

Energy. Electricity use/cost: 957 kWh, $93.80.

State data. Motto: She flies with her own wings. **Flower:** Oregon grape. **Bird:** Western meadowlark. **Tree:** Douglas fir. **Song:** "Oregon, My Oregon." **Entered union:** Feb. 14, 1859; rank: 33rd.

Tourism. Tourist spending: $9.2 bil. **Attractions:** John Day Fossil Beds Natl. Monument; Multnomah Falls, Columbia River Gorge; Timberline Lodge, Mount Hood Natl. Forest; Crater Lake Natl. Park; Oregon Dunes Natl. Recreation Area; Ft. Clatsop (Lewis and Clark Natl. Historical Park), Astoria Column, in Astoria; Oregon Caves Natl. Monument; Intl. Rose Test Garden, Lan Su Chinese Garden, Pittock Mansion, Oregon Museum of Science and Industry, in Portland; Oregon Shakespeare Festival, Ashland; High Desert Museum, Bend; "Spruce Goose" (largest aircraft ever built), Evergreen Aviation and Space Museum, McMinnville; Yaquina Head Outstanding Natural Area, Oregon Coast Aquarium, in Newport. **Information:** Travel Oregon, 670 Hawthorne SE, Ste. 240, Salem, OR 97301; 1-800-547-7842; www.traveloregon.com

History. More than 100 Native American tribes inhabited the area at the time of European contact, including the Chinook, Yakima, Cayuse, Modoc, and Nez Percé. Capt. Robert Gray sighted and sailed into the Columbia R., 1792. Lewis and Clark, traveling overland, wintered at its mouth, 1805-06. Fur traders sent by John Jacob Astor established the Astoria trading post in the Columbia River region, 1811. Settlers arrived in the Willamette Valley, 1834. In 1843, the first large wave of settlers arrived via the Oregon Trail. Oregon became a territory, 1848, and a state, 1859. Early in the 20th cent., the "Oregon System"—political reforms that included initiative, referendum, recall, direct primary, and woman suffrage—was adopted. Originally dominated by forest products, the economy diversified after World War II, with technology firms clustering in the "Silicon Forest" area around Portland. Oregonians were the first in the U.S. to pass measures allowing physician-assisted suicide for terminally ill patients, 1994, and establishing an all-mail voting system, 1998.

Famous Oregonians. Ernest Bloch, Bill Bowerman, Ty Burrell, Beverly Cleary, Matt Groening, Ernest Haycox, Chief Joseph, Ken Kesey, Phil Knight, Ursula K. Le Guin, Edwin Markham, Tom McCall, John McLoughlin, Joaquin Miller, Bob Packwood, Linus Pauling, Steve Prefontaine, John "Jack" Reed, Alberto Salazar, Mary Decker Slaney, William Simon U'Ren.

Website. www.oregon.gov

Pennsylvania (PA)
Keystone State

People. Population: 12,773,801; rank: 6. **Pop. change** (2010-13): 0.6%. **Pop. density:** 285.5 per sq mi. **Racial distribution:** 83.2% white; 11.5% black; 3.1% Asian; 0.3% Amer. Ind.; 0.1% Hawaiian/Pacific Islander; 2 or more races, 1.8%. **Hispanic pop.:** 6.3%.

Geography. Total area: 46,054 sq mi; rank: 33. **Land area:** 44,743 sq mi; rank: 32. **Acres forested:** 16.7 mil. **Location:** Middle Atlantic state bordered on the E by the Delaware R., on the S by the Mason-Dixon Line, on the W by West Virginia and Ohio, on the N/NE by Lake Erie and New York. **Climate:** continental with wide fluctuations in seasonal temperatures. **Topography:** Allegheny Mts. run SW-NE, with Piedmont and Coast Plain in the SE triangle; Allegheny Front a diagonal spine across the state's center; N and W rugged plateau falls to Lake Erie Lowland. **Capital:** Harrisburg. **Chief airports:** Harrisburg, Philadelphia, Pittsburgh.

Economy. Chief industries: agribusiness, advanced manufacturing, health care, travel and tourism, depository institutions, biotechnology, printing and publishing, research and consulting, trucking and warehousing, transportation by air, engineering and management, legal services. **Chief manuf. goods:** petroleum, pharmaceuticals, plastics, iron and steel, printing, paper and paperboard, confectionery and snacks, animal slaughtering and processing. **Chief crops:** greenhouse and nursery, mushrooms, corn, hay, soybeans, apples, tomatoes, wheat, grapes, peaches, potatoes, strawberries, tobacco. **Livestock:** 30.26 mil chickens (excl. broilers), 168.8 mil broilers, 1.62 mil cattle/calves, 94,000 sheep/lambs, 100,000 hogs/pigs. **Nonfuel minerals:** $1.4 mil; stone (crushed), cement (portland), lime, sand and gravel (construction), sand and gravel (industrial). **Commercial fishing:** $0.1 mil. **Chief ports:** Philadelphia, Pittsburgh. **Gross state product:** $644.9 bil.

Sales tax: 6.0%. **Employment distrib.:** 12.5% govt.; 19.0% trade/trans./util.; 9.6% mfg.; 20.0% ed./health; 13.1% prof./bus. serv.; 9.7% leisure/hosp.; 5.4% finance; 4.8% constr./mining/ log.; 1.5% info.; 4.4% other serv. **Unemployment:** 7.4%. **Per cap. pers. income:** $45,926. **New private housing:** 21,650 units/$3.7 bil. **Broadband Internet:** 83.3%. **Commercial banks:** 157; deposits: $258.4 bil. **Savings institutions:** 78; deposits: $56.9 bil. **Lottery:** total sales: $3.7 bil; profit: $1.1 bil.

Federal govt. Fed. civ. employees: 65,141; **avg. salary:** $71,461. **Notable fed. facilities:** Army War College, Carlisle Barracks; NAVSUP Weapon Systems Support, Mechanicsburg; Philadelphia Mint, Defense Supply Ctr., Naval Surface Warfare Ctr., in Phila.; DLA Distribution Ctr. Susquehanna, New Cumberland, Mechanicsburg; Tobyhanna Army Depot; Letterkenny Army Depot.

Higher education. 4-year public coll./univ.: 45; **2-yr. public:** 16; **4-yr. private:** 106.

Energy. Electricity use/cost: 837 kWh, $106.78.

State data. Motto: Virtue, liberty, and independence. **Flower:** Mountain laurel. **Bird:** Ruffed grouse. **Tree:** Hemlock. **Song:** "Pennsylvania." **Second** of the original 13 states to ratify the Constitution, Dec. 12, 1787.

Tourism. Tourist spending: $23.2 bil. **Attractions:** Liberty Bell Ctr. at Independence Natl. Historical Park, Franklin Institute, Philadelphia Museum of Art, in Philadelphia; Valley Forge Natl. Historical Park, King of Prussia; Gettysburg Natl. Military Park; Pennsylvania Dutch Country, Lancaster County; Hersheypark, Hershey; Duquesne Incline, Carnegie Museums of Pittsburgh, Heinz Hall for the Performing Arts, in Pittsburgh; Pocono Mountains; Pine Creek Gorge (Pennsylvania Grand Canyon), Allegheny Natl. Forest; Fallingwater (house designed by Frank Lloyd Wright), Mill Run; Johnstown Flood Natl. Memorial; Steamtown Natl. Historic Site, Scranton; U.S. Brig *Niagara*, Erie Maritime Museum, Presque Isle State Park, in Erie; Oil Region Natl. Heritage Area; Longwood Gardens, Kennett Square. **Information:** Pennsylvania Tourism Office, Dept. of Community and Economic Development, Commonwealth Keystone Building, 4th Fl., 400 North St., Harrisburg, PA 17120-0225; 1-800-VISITPA; www.visitpa.com

History. When Europeans came, Algonquian-speaking Lenni Lenape (Delaware) and Shawnee and the Iroquoian Susquehannocks, Erie, and Seneca occupied the region. Swedish explorers made the first permanent settlement, 1643, on Tinicum Island. The Dutch seized the settlement, 1655, but lost it to the British, 1664. The region was given by Charles II to William Penn, 1681. Philadelphia ("brotherly love") was the capital of the colonies during most of the American Revolution and of the U.S., 1790-1800; the Declaration of Independence, 1776, and Constitution, 1787, were signed here. Philadelphia was taken by the British; 1777. George Washington's troops encamped at Valley Forge in the bitter winter of 1777-78. Slavery was abolished, 1780. Union victory at the Battle of Gettysburg, July 1-3, 1863, marked a turning point in the Civil War. A dam collapse at Johnstown, 1889, killed at least 2,200 people. From the late 19th to the mid-20th cent., Pittsburgh prospered from coal and steel; later, heavy industry declined, but the city revived as a hub of finance, health care, and research. The Three Mile Island nuclear plant near Harrisburg had a near-meltdown, 1979. One of four hijacked planes on Sept. 11, 2001, crashed near Shanksville; the Flight 93 national memorial was officially dedicated on the site in 2011.

Famous Pennsylvanians. Marian Anderson, Maxwell Anderson, George Blanda, Kobe Bryant, James Buchanan, Andrew Carnegie, Rachel Carson, Will Chamberlain, Noam Chomsky, Perry Como, Bill Cosby, Cyrus H. K. Curtis, Thomas Eakins, Tina Fey, Stephen Foster, Benjamin Franklin, Robert Fulton, Martha Graham, Milton Hershey, Gene Kelly, Grace Kelly (Princess Grace of Monaco), Dan Marino, George C. Marshall, Chris Matthews, John J. McCloy, Margaret Mead, Andrew W. Mellon, Joe Montana, Stan Musial, Joe Namath, John O'Hara, Arnold Palmer, Robert E. Peary, Mike Piazza, Pink (Alecia Beth Moore), Tom Ridge, Mary Roberts Rinehart, Fred Rogers, Betsy Ross, Will Smith, Jimmy Stewart, Taylor Swift, Jim Thorpe, Johnny Unitas, John Updike, Honus Wagner, Andy Warhol, Benjamin West. **Website.** www.pa.gov

Rhode Island (RI)
Little Rhody, Ocean State

People. Population: 1,051,511; rank: 43. **Pop. change** (2010-13): –0.1%. **Pop. density:** 1,016.9 per sq mi. **Racial distribution:** 85.6% white; 7.5% black; 3.3% Asian; 0.9% Amer. Ind.; 0.2% Hawaiian/Pacific Islander; 2 or more races, 2.5%. **Hispanic pop.:** 13.6%.

Geography. Total area: 1,545 sq mi; rank: 50. **Land area:** 1,034 sq mi; rank: 50. **Acres forested:** 0.4 mil. **Location:** New England state. **Climate:** invigorating and changeable. **Topography:** eastern lowlands of Narragansett Basin; western uplands of flat and rolling hills. **Capital:** Providence. **Chief airport:** Warwick.

Economy. Chief industries: services, manufacturing. **Chief manuf. goods:** plastics, fabricated metals, electrical equip., jewelry. **Chief crops:** greenhouse and nursery, sweet corn, berries, potatoes, apples, hay. **Livestock:** 5,000 cattle/calves. **Nonfuel minerals:** $30.3 mil; sand and gravel (construction), stone (crushed), sand and gravel (industrial), gemstones (natural). **Commercial fishing:** $80.8 mil. **Chief ports:** Providence, Davisville, Newport. **Gross state product:** $53.2 bil. **Sales tax:** 7.0%. **Employment distrib.:** 12.8% govt.; 15.6% trade/trans./util.; 8.5% mfg.; 22.0% ed./health; 12.7% prof./bus. serv.; 11.6% leisure/hosp.; 6.7% finance; 3.6% constr./mining/ log.; 1.8% info.; 4.6% other serv. **Unemployment:** 9.5%. **Per cap. pers. income:** $47,012. **New private housing:** 928 units/$179.9 mil. **Broadband Internet:** 84.3%. **Commercial banks:** 11; deposits: $25.8 bil. **Savings institutions:** 12; deposits: $3 bil. **Lottery:** total sales: $3.7 bil; profit: $379.2 mil.

Federal govt. Fed. civ. employees: 7,196; **avg. salary:** $86,616. **Notable fed. facilities:** Naval War College; Naval Undersea Warfare Ctr.; EPA Atlantic Ecology Div. Lab.

Higher education. 4-year public coll./univ.: 2; **2-yr. public:** 1; **4-yr. private:** 10.

Energy. Electricity use/cost: 597 kWh, $86.04.

State data. Motto: Hope. **Flower:** Violet. **Bird:** Rhode Island red chicken. **Tree:** Red maple. **Song:** "Rhode Island." **Thirteenth** of original 13 states to ratify the Constitution, May 29, 1790.

Tourism. Tourist spending: $1.8 bil. **Attractions:** Block Island; mansions (The Breakers, The Elms, others), Cliff Walk, Intl. Tennis Hall of Fame and Museum, Touro Synagogue (completed 1763, oldest in U.S.), in Newport; First Baptist Church in America, Rhode Island School of Design Museum of Art, WaterFire art installation, in Providence; Slater Mill Historic Site, Pawtucket; Gilbert Stuart Birthplace and Museum, Saunderstown. **Information:** Rhode Island Tourism Division, 315 Iron Horse Way, Ste. 101, Providence, RI 02908; 1-800-556-2484; www.visitrhodeisland.com

History. When Europeans arrived, Narragansett, Niantic, Nipmuc, and Wampanoag peoples lived in the region. Giovanni da Verrazano visited the area, 1524. The first permanent settlement was founded at Providence, 1636, by Roger Williams, who was exiled from the Massachusetts Bay Colony. Anne Hutchinson, also exiled, settled Portsmouth, 1638. Quaker and Jewish immigrants seeking freedom of worship began arriving, 1650s-60s. The colonists broke the power of the Narragansett in the Great Swamp Fight, 1675, the decisive battle in King Philip's War. The colony was the first to formally renounce all allegiance to King George III, May 4, 1776. Initially opposed to joining the Union, Rhode Island was the last of the 13 colonies to ratify the Constitution, 1790. Trade, textiles, and metal goods dominated the economy in the 19th cent., and Newport became a fashionable resort after the Civil War. The U.S. Navy was the state's largest civilian employer, 1945-73, until the destroyer force was relocated from Newport. A nightclub fire in West Warwick killed 100 people in 2003.

Famous Rhode Islanders. Ambrose Burnside, George M. Cohan, Nelson Eddy, Jabez Gorham, Nathanael Greene, Elisabeth Hasselbeck, Christopher and Oliver La Farge, Cormac McCarthy, John McLaughlin, Matthew C. and Oliver Hazard Perry, Gilbert Stuart, Meredith Vieira.

Website. www.ri.gov

South Carolina (SC)
Palmetto State

People. Population: 4,774,839; rank: 24. **Pop. change** (2010-13): 3.2%. **Pop. density:** 158.8 per sq mi. **Racial distribution:** 68.3% white; 27.9% black; 1.5% Asian; 0.5% Amer. Ind.; 0.1% Hawaiian/Pacific Islander; 2 or more races, 1.7%. **Hispanic pop.:** 5.3%.

Geography. Total area: 32,020 sq mi; rank: 40. **Land area:** 30,061 sq mi; rank: 40. **Acres forested:** 13.0 mil. **Location:** South Atlantic state bordered by North Carolina on the N; Georgia on the SW and W; the Atlantic Ocean on the E, SE, and S. **Climate:** humid subtropical. **Topography:** Blue Ridge province in NW has highest peaks; piedmont lies between the mountains and the fall line; coastal plain covers two-thirds of state. **Capital:** Columbia. **Chief airports:** Charleston, Greer, Myrtle Beach.

Economy. Chief industries: tourism, agriculture, manufacturing. **Chief manuf. goods:** chemicals and synthetics, motor vehicles and parts, plastics, paper and paper prods., turbines, rubber, textiles. **Chief crops:** greenhouse and nursery, tobacco, soybeans, cotton, corn, peaches, wheat, tomatoes, peanuts. **Livestock:** 5.72 mil chickens (excl. broilers), 226.5 mil broilers, 360,000 cattle/calves. **Nonfuel minerals:** $538 mil; cement (portland), stone (crushed), sand and gravel (construction), cement (masonry), sand and gravel (industrial). **Commercial fishing:** $24.0 mil. **Chief ports:** Charleston, Georgetown. **Gross state product:** $183.6 bil. **Sales tax:** 6.0%. **Employment distrib.:** 18.4% govt.; 18.9% trade/trans./util.; 11.9% mfg.; 11.5% ed./health; 12.9% prof./bus. serv.; 12.2% leisure/hosp.; 4.9% finance; 4.4% constr./mining/log.; 1.4% info.; 3.6% other serv. **Unemployment:** 7.6%. **Per cap. pers. income:** $35,453. **New private housing:** 24,725 units/$4.9 bil. **Broadband Internet:** 79.0%. **Commercial banks:** 80; deposits: $67.4 bil. **Savings institutions:** 13; deposits: $1.1 bil. **Lottery:** total sales: $1.2 bil; profit: $305.2 mil.

Federal govt. Fed. civ. employees: 22,058; **avg. salary:** $68,862. **Notable fed. facilities:** Ft. Jackson; Joint Base Charleston; Marine Corps Recruit Depot Parris Island; Shaw AFB; USMC Air Station Beaufort; Savannah River Site.

Higher education. 4-year public coll./univ.: 13; 2-yr. public: 20; 4-yr. private: 22.

Energy. Electricity use/cost: 1,119 kWh, $131.64.

State data. Motto: Dum Spiro Spero (While I breathe, I hope). **Flower:** Yellow jessamine. **Bird:** Carolina wren. **Tree:** Palmetto. **Song:** "Carolina." **Eighth** of the original 13 states to ratify the Constitution, May 23, 1788.

Tourism. Tourist spending: $11.8 bil. **Attractions:** Historic Charleston, Waterfront Park, Charleston Museum (est. 1773, oldest in U.S.), Middleton Place, Magnolia Plantation and Gardens, Drayton Hall, in Charleston; Ft. Sumter Natl. Monument (where first shots of Civil War were fired), in Charleston Harbor; Cypress Gardens, Moncks Corner; Boone Hall Plantation and Gardens, Mt. Pleasant; Brookgreen Gardens, Murrells Inlet; Myrtle Beach; Hilton Head Island; Andrew Jackson State Park, Lancaster; South Carolina State Museum, Riverbanks Zoo, in Columbia. **Information:** SC Dept. of Parks, Recreation, and Tourism, 1205 Pendleton St., Columbia, SC 29201; 1-866-224-9339, (803) 734-1700; www.discoversouthcarolina.com.

History. When Europeans arrived, Cherokee, Catawba, and Muskogean peoples lived in the area. Spanish and French came in the 16th cent. The first English colonists settled near the Ashley R., 1670, and moved to the site of present-day Charleston, 1680. The colonists seized the government, 1775, and the royal governor fled. The British took Charleston, 1780, but were defeated at Kings Mountain that same year and at Cowpens, 1781. In the 1830s, South Carolinians, angered by federal protective tariffs, adopted the Nullification Doctrine, holding that a state can void an act of Congress. Plantation agriculture relied on slave labor to cultivate rice and cotton; slaves made up 57% of the population in 1860, when South Carolina was the first state to secede from the Union. Confederate troops fired on and forced the surrender of U.S. troops at Ft. Sumter, in Charleston Harbor, 1861, launching the Civil War. The state was readmitted to the Union, 1868. Strom Thurmond, who ran for president as a segregationist in 1948, later served 48 years in the U.S. Senate (1955-2003). Formerly dependent on textiles, the state has attracted new industries by courting foreign investment.

Famous South Carolinians. Charles F. Bolden Jr., James F. Byrnes, John C. Calhoun, Stephen Colbert, Marian Wright Edelman, Joe Frazier, DuBose Heyward, Ernest F. Hollings, Andrew Jackson, Jesse Jackson, "Shoeless" Joe Jackson, Jasper Johns, Andie MacDowell, Francis Marion, Ronald E. McNair, Charles Pinckney, John Rutledge, Thomas Sumter, Strom Thurmond, John B. Watson.
Website. www.sc.gov

South Carolina (SD)
Coyote State, Mount Rushmore State

People. Population: 844,877; rank: 46. **Pop. change** (2010-13): 3.8%. **Pop. density:** 11.1 per sq mi. **Racial distribution:** 85.9% white; 1.9% black; 1.2% Asian; 8.9% Amer. Ind.; 0.1% Hawaiian/Pacific Islander; 2 or more races, 2.1%. **Hispanic pop.:** 3.4%.

Geography. Total area: 77,116 sq mi; rank: 17. **Land area:** 75,811 sq mi; rank: 16. **Acres forested:** 1.9 mil. **Location:** West North Central state bounded on the N by North Dakota, on the E by Minnesota and Iowa, on the S by Nebraska, on the W by Wyoming and Montana. **Climate:** characterized by extremes of temperature, persistent winds, low precipitation and humidity. **Topography:** Prairie Plains in the E; rolling hills of the Great Plains in the W; the Black Hills, rising 3,500 ft, in the SW corner. **Capital:** Pierre.

Economy. Chief industries: agriculture, services, manufacturing. **Chief manuf. goods:** animal slaughtering, machinery, semiconductors, surgical appliances. **Chief crops:** corn, soybeans, wheat, hay, sunflowers, sorghum, oats, barley. **Livestock:** 3.15 mil chickens (excl. broilers), 3.65 mil cattle/calves, 270,000 sheep/lambs, 175,000 hogs/pigs. **Nonfuel minerals:** $320 mil; sand and gravel (construction), gold, cement (portland), stone (crushed), lime. **Gross state product:** $46.7 bil. **Sales tax:** 4.0%. **Employment distrib.:** 18.7% govt.; 19.9% trade/trans./util.; 9.9% mfg.; 16.0% ed./health; 7.2% prof./bus. serv.; 10.8% leisure/hosp.; 7.0% finance; 5.2% constr./mining/log.; 1.5% info.; 3.8% other serv. **Unemployment:** 3.8%. **Per cap. pers. income:** $45,558. **New private housing:** 5,482 units/$733.7 mil. **Broadband Internet:** 77.8%. **Commercial banks:** 82; deposits: $373.8 bil. **Savings institutions:** 5; deposits: $2.4 bil. **Lottery:** total sales: $637.4 mil; profit: $107.7 mil.

Federal govt. Fed. civ. employees: 8,342; **avg. salary:** $62,465. **Notable fed. facilities:** Ellsworth AFB.

Higher education. 4-year public coll./univ.: 7; 2-yr. public: 5; 4-yr. private: 7.

Energy. Electricity use/cost: 980 kWh, $98.68.

State data. Motto: Under God, the people rule. **Flower:** Pasqueflower. **Bird:** Chinese ring-necked pheasant. **Tree:** Black Hills spruce. **Song:** "Hail, South Dakota." **Entered union:** Nov. 2, 1889; rank: 40th.

Tourism. Tourist spending: $2.7 bil. **Attractions:** Mt. Rushmore Natl. Memorial, Keystone; Harney Peak (tallest E of Rockies); Custer State Park; Crazy Horse Memorial (mtn. carving in progress); Wind Cave Natl. Park, near Hot Springs; Black Hills Natl. Forest; Needles Hwy., part of Peter Norbeck Natl. Scenic Byway; Minuteman Missile Natl. Historic Site; Deadwood (1876 gold rush town); Jewel Cave Natl. Monument, near Custer; Badlands Natl. Park; Great Lakes of South Dakota; Great Plains Zoo and Delbridge Museum of Natural History, Sioux Falls; Corn Palace, Mitchell; Reptile Gardens, Chapel in the Hills, Bear Country USA, in Rapid City. **Information:** Dept. of Tourism and State Development, Capitol Lake Plaza, 711 E. Wells Ave., c/o 500 E. Capitol Ave., Pierre, SD 57501; 1-800-SDAKOTA; www.travelsd.com

History. Paleo-Indians hunted in the region at least 11,500 years ago. At the time of first European contact, Mandan, Hidatsa, Arikara, and Sioux lived in the area. The French Vérendrye brothers explored the region, 1742-43. The U.S. acquired the territory in the Louisiana Purchase, 1803, and Meriwether Lewis and William Clark passed through, 1804-06. In 1817 a trading post opened at what would become Ft. Pierre. Dakota Territory was established, 1861. Gold was discovered, 1874, in the Black Hills on Lakota Sioux land; the "Great Dakota Boom" began in 1879. South Dakota became a state, 1889. Massacre of more than 200 Native American men, women, and children at Wounded Knee, 1890, ended Sioux resistance. Armed supporters of the American Indian Movement, a Native American rights group, occupied the area, leading to a 70-day standoff, 1973. Major economic activities include agribusiness and, since the 1980s, credit card services. Republicans scored a key election victory, 2004, with the defeat of three-term U.S. Sen. Tom Daschle, a national Democratic leader.

Famous South Dakotans. Sparky Anderson, Bob Barker, Black Elk, Tom Brokaw, Crazy Horse, Tom Daschle, Myron Floren, Mary Hart, Cheryl Ladd, Ernest O. Lawrence, George McGovern, Russell Means, Billy Mills, Allen H. Neuharth, Pat O'Brien, Sitting Bull.
Website. www.sd.gov

Tennessee (TN)
Volunteer State

People. Population: 6,495,978; rank: 17. **Pop. change** (2010-13): 2.4%. **Pop. density:** 157.5 per sq mi. **Racial distribution:** 79.1% white; 17.0% black; 1.6% Asian; 0.4% Amer.

Ind.; 0.1% Hawaiian/Pacific Islander; 2.or more races, 1.7%. **Hispanic pop.:** 4.9%.

Geography. Total area: 42,144 sq mi; rank: 36. **Land area:** 41,235 sq mi; rank: 34. **Acres forested:** 13.9 mil. **Location:** East South Central state bounded on the N by Kentucky and Virginia; on the E by North Carolina; on the S by Georgia, Alabama, and Mississippi; on the W by Arkansas and Missouri. **Climate:** humid continental to the N; humid subtropical to the S. **Topography:** rugged country in the E; the Great Smoky Mts. of the Unakas; low ridges of the Appalachian Valley; flat Cumberland Plateau; slightly rolling terrain and knobs of the Interior Low Plateau, the largest region; Eastern Gulf Coastal Plain to the W, laced with streams; Mississippi Alluvial Plain, a narrow strip of swamp and floodplain in the extreme W. **Capital:** Nashville. **Chief airports:** Alcoa, Memphis, Nashville.

Economy. Chief industries: manufacturing, trade, services, tourism, finance, insurance, real estate. **Chief manuf. goods:** motor vehicles and parts, computers and electronics, food, chemicals, plastics, printing, appliances, aluminum. **Chief crops:** greenhouse and nursery, soybeans, cotton, corn, tobacco, hay, tomatoes, wheat. **Livestock.** 2.65 mil chickens (excl. broilers), 172.8 mil broilers, 1.76 mil cattle/calves, 36,000 sheep/lambs. **Nonfuel minerals:** $941 mil; stone (crushed), zinc, cement (portland), sand and gravel (construction), clays (ball). **Chief ports:** Memphis, Nashville, Chattanooga. **Gross state product:** $287.6 bil. **Sales tax:** 7.0%. **Employment distrib.:** 15.0% govt.; 21.0% trade/trans./util.; 11.5% mfg.; 14.2% ed./health; 13.1% prof./bus. serv.; 10.9% leisure/hosp.; 4.9% finance; 4.1% constr./mining/log.; 1.5% info.; 3.8% other serv. **Unemployment:** 8.2%. **Per cap. pers. income:** $39,324. **New private housing:** 23,816 units/$3.9 bil. **Broadband Internet:** 79.0%. **Commercial banks:** 209; deposits: $115 bil. **Savings institutions:** 14; deposits: $3.5 bil. **Lottery:** total sales: $1.4 bil; profit: $339.7 mil.

Federal govt. Fed. civ. employees: 28,418; **avg. salary:** $68,309. **Notable fed. facilities:** Tennessee Valley Authority; Oak Ridge Natl. Lab; Arnold Engineering Development Ctr.; Ft. Campbell; NSA Mid-South, Millington.

Higher education. 4-year public coll./univ.: 9; **2-yr. public:** 13; **4-yr. private:** 45.

Energy. Electricity use/cost: 1,217 kWh; $122.98.

State data. Motto: Agriculture and commerce. **Flower:** Iris. **Bird:** Mockingbird. **Tree:** Tulip poplar. **Songs:** "My Homeland, Tennessee"; "When It's Iris Time in Tennessee"; "My Tennessee"; "Tennessee Waltz"; "Rocky Top"; "Smoky Mountain Rain." **Entered union:** June 1, 1796; rank: 16th.

Tourism. Tourist spending: $16.2 bil. **Attractions:** Lookout Mountain, Tennessee Aquarium, Ruby Falls, in Chattanooga; Great Smoky Mountains Natl. Park; Lost Sea (largest underground lake in U.S.), Sweetwater; Cherokee Natl. Forest; Cumberland Gap Natl. Historical Park; James K. Polk Ancestral Home, Columbia; American Museum of Science and Energy, Oak Ridge; The Hermitage (home of Pres. Andrew Jackson), Country Music Hall of Fame and Museum, Ryman Auditorium, Belle Meade Plantation, Parthenon replica, Grand Ole Opry, in Nashville; Dollywood theme park, Pigeon Forge; Graceland (home of Elvis Presley), Sun Studio, in Memphis; Alex Haley Museum and Interpretive Ctr., Henning; Casey Jones Village, Jackson; Bristol Motor Speedway. **Information:** Dept. of Tourist Development, Wm. Snodgrass/ Tennessee Tower, 312 Rosa L. Parks Ave., 25th Fl., Nashville, TN 37243; 1-800-462-8366; www.tnvacation.com

History. Inhabited for at least 20,000 years, the region was home to Creek and Yuchi peoples when the first Europeans arrived; the Cherokee moved into the region in the early 18th cent. Spanish explorers visited the area, 1540. English traders crossed the Great Smoky Mtns. from the east, while France's Jacques Marquette and Louis Jolliet sailed down the Mississippi on the west, 1673. The first permanent settlement was of Virginians on the Watauga R., 1769. After the American Revolution, in which Tennesseans fought in eastern campaigns, the region became a territory, 1790, and a state, 1796. Slavery was widespread in western Tennessee, where cotton was the main crop, but much less common in the east. The state seceded, 1861, and saw many Civil War engagements; some 187,000 Tennesseans fought for the Confederacy and 51,000 for the Union. Tennessee was readmitted in 1866, the only former Confederate state not to have a postwar military government. The famous Scopes trial, 1925, questioned the teaching of evolution in public schools. In the 1930s, the Tennessee Valley Authority, a federal program, brought electric power to rural areas. Nashville became the capital of country music while Memphis

fostered the blues and, with Elvis Presley in the 1950s, rock 'n' roll. Martin Luther King Jr. was assassinated in Memphis, 1968. Since the 1970s, auto plants have become major employers, as has Federal Express. Al Gore Jr., U.S. vice pres. (1993-2001), lost his 2000 presidential bid partly because he failed to carry his home state of Tennessee. Record amounts of rainfall flooded parts of Tennessee, including Nashville, in May 2010.

Famous Tennesseans. Roy Acuff, Kenny Chesney, Davy Crockett, David Farragut, Ernie Ford, Aretha Franklin, Bill Frist, Al Gore Jr., Alex Haley, William C. Handy, Sam Houston, Cordell Hull, Andrew Jackson, Andrew Johnson, Casey Jones, Estes Kefauver, Grace Moore, Dolly Parton, Minnie Pearl, James Polk, Elvis Presley, Wilma Rudolph, Dinah Shore, Bessie Smith, Fred Thompson, Justin Timberlake, Tina Turner, Hank Williams Jr., Alvin York.

Website. www.tn.gov

Texas (TX)
Lone Star State

People. Population: 26,448,193; rank: 2. **Pop. change** (2010-13): 5.2%. **Pop. density:** 101.2 per sq mi. **Racial distribution:** 80.3% white; 12.4% black; 4.3% Asian; 1.0% Amer. Ind.; 0.1% Hawaiian/Pacific Islander; 2 or more races, 1.8%. **Hispanic pop.:** 38.4%.

Geography. Total area: 268,596 sq mi; rank: 2. **Land area:** 261,232 sq mi; rank: 2. **Acres forested:** 61.8 mil. **Location:** southwestern state bounded on the SE by the Gulf of Mexico; on the SW by Mexico, separated by the Rio Grande; surrounding states are Louisiana, Arkansas, Oklahoma, New Mexico. **Climate:** extremely varied; driest region is the Trans-Pecos; wettest is the NE. **Topography:** Gulf Coast Plain in the S and SE; North Central Plains slope upward with some hills; the Great Plains extend over the Panhandle, are broken by low mountains; the Trans-Pecos is the southern extension of the Rockies. **Capital:** Austin. **Chief airports:** Austin, Dallas, El Paso, Fort Worth, Houston (2), Midland, San Antonio.

Economy. Chief industries: manufacturing, trade, oil and gas extraction, services. **Chief manuf. goods:** petroleum, chemicals and resins, computers and electronics, animal slaughtering and processing, plastics, aerospace. **Chief crops:** cotton, greenhouse and nursery, corn, wheat, sorghum, hay, peanuts, onions, rice, pecans, grapefruit. **Livestock:** 24.88 mil chickens (excl. broilers), 610.1 mil broilers, 10.9 mil cattle/calves, 740,000 sheep/lambs, 100,000 hogs/pigs. **Nonfuel minerals:** $3.7 bil; stone (crushed), cement (portland), sand and gravel (construction), sand and gravel (industrial), lime. **Commercial fishing:** $213.3 mil. **Chief ports:** Houston, Galveston, Brownsville, Beaumont, Port Arthur, Corpus Christi, Texas City, Freeport. **Gross state product:** $1.5 tril. **Sales tax:** 6.25%. **Employment distrib.:** 16.1% govt.; 20.0% trade/trans./util.; 7.6% mfg.; 13.2% ed./health; 13.1% prof./bus. serv.; 10.5% leisure/hosp.; 6.0% finance; 8.2% constr./mining/log.; 1.8% info.; 3.5% other serv. **Unemployment:** 6.3%. **Per cap. pers. income:** $43,552. **New private housing:** 147,460 units/$22.4 bil. **Broadband Internet:** 91.3%. **Commercial banks:** 563; deposits: $584.8 bil. **Savings institutions:** 49; deposits: $67.6 bil. **Lottery:** total sales: $4.4 bil; profit: $1.2 bil.

Federal govt. Fed. civ. employees: 139,777; **avg. salary:** $72,035. **Notable fed. facilities:** Ft. Hood; Ft. Bliss; Sheppard, Dyess, Goodfellow AF Bases; Joint Base San Antonio; NASA Johnson Space Ctr.; Naval Air Training School, Corpus Christi NAS; Red River Army Depot; Western Currency Facility, Ft. Worth.

Higher education. 4-year public coll./univ.: 45; **2-yr. public:** 63; **4-yr. private:** 55.

Energy. Electricity use/cost: 1,168 kWh, $128.27.

State data. Motto: Friendship. **Flower:** Bluebonnet. **Bird:** Mockingbird. **Tree:** Pecan. **Song:** "Texas, Our Texas." **Entered union:** Dec. 29, 1845; rank: 28th.

Tourism. Tourist spending: $58.4 bil. **Attractions:** Big Bend and Guadalupe Mountains Natl. Parks; Fort Davis Natl. Historic Site; Six Flags Over Texas, Arlington; SeaWorld San Antonio, Six Flags Fiesta Texas, The Alamo, San Antonio Missions Natl. Historical Park, San Antonio River Walk, in San Antonio; Natl. Cowgirl Museum and Hall of Fame, Kimbell Art Museum, Ft. Worth Zoo, Bureau of Engraving and Printing, in Ft. Worth; Lyndon B. Johnson Natl. Historical Park, Johnson City; LBJ Presidential Library and Museum, Bullock Texas State History Museum, Austin; George Bush Presidential Library and Museum, College Station; Dallas Arboretum and Botanical Garden, Sixth Floor

Museum at Dealey Plaza, George W. Bush Presidential Library and Museum, in Dallas; USS *Lexington*, Texas State Aquarium, Padre Island Natl. Seashore, in Corpus Christi. **Information:** Texas Tourism, P.O. Box 141009, Austin, TX 78714; 1-800-452-9292, (512) 486-5876; www.traveltex.com

History. Humans have lived in the region for at least 12,000 years. Coahuiltecan, Karankawa, Caddo, Jumano, and Tonkawa peoples were in the area when the first Europeans came; later, Apache, Comanche, Cherokee, and Wichita arrived. Early Spanish explorers included Alonso Alvarez de Pineda, who sailed along the Texas coast, 1519; Cabeza de Vaca, shipwrecked near Galveston along with the former slave Estevanico, 1528; and Coronado, who crossed the Panhandle, 1541. Spaniards made the first settlement at Ysleta, near El Paso, 1682. Americans moved into the land early in the 19th cent. Mexico, of which Texas was a part, won independence from Spain, 1821. Texans rebelled, 1836, losing to Santa Anna at the Alamo but winning decisively under Sam Houston at San Jacinto. With Houston as president, 1836-38 and 1841-44, the Republic of Texas functioned as a nation until admitted to the Union. With a slave population of 30%, Texas seceded, 1861; mostly unscathed by the Civil War, it was readmitted, 1870. In 1900 a powerful hurricane lashed Galveston, killing at least 8,000. Cotton and cattle were dominant until 1901, when the Spindletop gusher, near Beaumont, launched the petroleum and petrochemical industries. By 2000, the state population ranked second in the U.S. With wealth and population came political power, notably in the presidencies of Lyndon B. Johnson (1963-69), George H. W. Bush (1989-93), and George W. Bush (2001-09). Texas was plagued with drought conditions and wildfires starting in late 2010, with almost 4 mil acres burned and close to 3,000 homes destroyed in the 2011 fire season. A fertilizer plant in the town of West exploded Apr. 17, 2013, killing 15 people.

Famous Texans. Lance Armstrong, Stephen F. Austin, Lloyd Bentsen, James Bowie, Drew Brees, Carol Burnett, George H. W. Bush, George W. Bush, Joan Crawford, J. Frank Dobie, Dwight D. Eisenhower, Morgan Fairchild, Farrah Fawcett, Sam Houston, Howard Hughes, Kay Bailey Hutchison, Molly Ivins, Lyndon B. Johnson, Tommy Lee Jones, Janis Joplin, Barbara Jordan, Beyoncé Knowles, Mary Martin, Matthew McConaughey, Chester Nimitz, Sandra Day O'Connor, H. Ross Perot, Katherine Anne Porter, Dan Rather, Sam Rayburn, Ann Richards, Sissy Spacek, George Strait, Babe Didrikson Zaharias. **Website.** www.texas.gov

Utah (UT)
Beehive State

People. Population: 2,900,872; rank: 33. **Pop. change** (2010-13): 5.0%. **Pop. density:** 35.3 per sq mi. **Racial distribution:** 91.6% white; 1.3% black; 2.3% Asian; 1.5% Amer. Ind.; 1.0% Hawaiian/Pacific Islander; 2 or more races, 2.3%. **Hispanic pop.:** 13.4%.

Geography. Total area: 84,897 sq mi; rank: 13. **Land area:** 82,170 sq mi; rank: 12. **Acres forested:** 18.3 mil. **Location:** middle Rocky Mountain state; its SE corner touches Colorado, New Mexico, and Arizona, and is the only spot in the U.S. where four states join. **Climate:** arid; ranges from warm desert in SW to alpine in NE. **Topography:** high Colorado Plateau is cut by brilliantly colored canyons of the SE; broad, flat, desertlike Great Basin of the W; the Great Salt Lake and Bonneville Salt Flats to the NW; Middle Rockies in the NE run E-W; valleys and plateaus of the Wasatch Front. **Capital:** Salt Lake City. **Chief airport:** Salt Lake City.

Economy. Chief industries: services, trade, manufacturing, government, transportation, utilities. **Chief manuf. goods:** food, petroleum, nonferrous metal, motor vehicles and parts, aerospace, sporting goods, fabricated metal, computers and electronics. **Chief crops:** hay, greenhouse and nursery, wheat, cherries, onions, apples, barley, peaches, corn. **Livestock:** 4.69 mil chickens (excl. broilers), 800,000 cattle/calves, 275,000 sheep/lambs, 75,000 hogs/pigs. **Nonfuel minerals:** $3.3 bil; copper, magnesium metal, gold, potash, molybdenum concentrates. **Gross state product:** $141.2 bil. **Sales tax:** 5.95%. **Employment distrib.:** 17.8% govt.; 19.2% trade/trans./util.; 9.2% mfg.; 13.0% ed./health; 13.4% prof./bus. serv.; 9.5% leisure/hosp.; 5.5% finance; 7.0% constr./mining/log.; 2.6% info.; 2.8% other serv. **Unemployment:** 4.4%. **Per cap. pers. income:** $36,274. **New private housing:** 15,818 units/$3.3 bil. **Broadband Internet:** 85.3%. **Commercial banks:** 59; deposits: $344.7 bil. **Savings institutions:** 6; deposits: $47.7 bil.

Federal govt. Fed. civ. employees: 28,496; **avg. salary:** $65,668. **Notable fed. facilities:** Hill AFB; Tooele Army Depot; Army Dugway Proving Ground.

Higher education. 4-year public coll./univ.: 7; **2-yr. public:** 1; **4-yr. private:** 3.

Energy. Electricity use/cost: 793 kWh, $78.70.

State data. Motto: Industry. **Flower:** Sego lily. **Bird:** (California) sea gull. **Tree:** Blue spruce. **Song:** "Utah, This Is the Place." **Entered union:** Jan. 4, 1896; rank: 45th.

Tourism. Tourist spending: $7.3 bil. **Attractions:** Temple Square (site of Mormon Church headquarters), Salt Lake City; Great Salt Lake; Zion, Canyonlands, Bryce Canyon, Arches, and Capitol Reef Natl. Parks; Dinosaur, Rainbow Bridge, Timpanogos Cave, and Natural Bridges Natl. Monuments; Lake Powell; Flaming Gorge Natl. Recreation Area; Utah Olympic Park, Sundance Film Festival, in Park City. **Information:** Utah Office of Tourism, Council Hall/Capitol Hill, 300 N. State St., Salt Lake City, UT 84114; 1-800-200-1160; www.utah.com

History. Ute, Gosiute, Southern Paiute, and Navajo peoples lived in the region at the time of European contact. Spanish Franciscans visited the area, 1776; American fur traders followed. Permanent settlement began with the arrival of the Latter-day Saints, or Mormons, 1847; they made the arid land bloom and created a prosperous economy. Organized in 1849, the State of Deseret asked admission to the Union; instead, Congress established Utah Territory, 1850, and Brigham Young was appointed governor. The Union Pacific and Central Pacific railroads met near Promontory Point, May 10, 1869, creating the first transcontinental railroad. Statehood was not achieved until 1896, after a long controversy over the Mormon practices of economic isolationism and polygamy (the church renounced the latter in 1890). The 20th cent. brought expansion in mining, defense-related industries, and, more recently, information technologies. More than two-thirds of Utahans are Mormons; the church has its world headquarters in Salt Lake City. Utah experienced 60% population growth, 1990-2010, and has the highest birthrate and lowest median age of any state in the U.S.

Famous Utahans. Maude Adams, Roseanne Barr, Ezra Taft Benson, John Moses Browning, Butch Cassidy, Marriner S. Eccles, Philo T. Farnsworth, David M. Kennedy, J. Willard Marriott, Merlin Olsen, the Osmonds, Ivy Baker Priest, George W. Romney, Wallace Stegner, Brigham Young, Loretta Young. **Website.** www.utah.gov

Vermont (VT)
Green Mountain State

People. Population: 626,630; rank: 50. **Pop. change** (2010-13): 0.1%. **Pop. density:** 68.0 per sq mi. **Racial distribution:** 95.2% white; 1.2% black; 1.4% Asian; 0.4% Amer. Ind.; 0.0% Hawaiian/Pacific Islander; 2 or more races, 1.8%. **Hispanic pop.:** 1.7%.

Geography. Total area: 9,616 sq mi; rank: 45. **Land area:** 9,217 sq mi; rank: 43. **Acres forested:** 4.6 mil. **Location:** northern New England state. **Climate:** temperate, with considerable temperature extremes; heavy snowfall in mountains. **Topography:** Green Mts. N-S backbone 20-36 mi wide; avg. altitude 1,000 ft. **Capital:** Montpelier. **Chief airport:** Burlington.

Economy. Chief industries: manufacturing, tourism, agriculture, trade, finance, insurance, real estate, government. **Chief manuf. goods:** dairy, plastics, printing, wood furniture, sporting goods, metalworking machinery. **Chief crops:** greenhouse and nursery, hay, maple syrup, apples, berries, sweet corn. **Livestock:** 143,000 chickens (excl. broilers), 260,000 cattle/calves. **Nonfuel minerals:** $118 mil; stone (crushed), sand and gravel (construction), stone (dimension), talc (crude), gemstones (natural). **Gross state product:** $29.5 bil. **Sales tax:** 6.0%. **Employment distrib.:** 18.5% govt.; 18.1% trade/trans./util.; 10.3% mfg.; 20.4% ed./health; 8.9% prof./bus. serv.; 10.3% leisure/hosp.; 4.0% finance; 5.0% constr./mining/log.; 1.4% info.; 3.2% other serv. **Unemployment:** 4.4%. **Per cap. pers. income:** $45,783. **New private housing:** 1,499 units/$263.0 mil. **Broadband Internet:** 82.2%. **Commercial banks:** 14; deposits: $7.1 bil. **Savings institutions:** 10; deposits: $4.7 bil. **Lottery:** total sales: $102.1 mil; profit: $22.9 mil.

Federal govt. Fed. civ. employees: 4,909; **avg. salary:** $70,666. **Notable fed. facilities:** Law Enforcement Support Ctr.

Higher education. 4-year public coll./univ.: 5; **2-yr. public:** 1; **4-yr. private:** 17.

Energy. Electricity use/cost: 565 kWh, $96.09.

State data. Motto: Freedom and unity. **Flower:** Red clover. **Bird:** Hermit thrush. **Tree:** Sugar maple. **Song:** "These Green Mountains." **Entered union:** Mar. 4, 1791; rank: 14th.

Tourism. Tourist spending: $2.2 bil. **Attractions:** Shelburne Museum; Shelburne Farms; Vermont Marble Museum, Proctor; Bennington Battle Monument; Pres. Calvin Coolidge Homestead, Plymouth; Ben & Jerry's Factory, Waterbury; Stowe, Killington, and Burke ski resorts: Hildene (Robert Todd Lincoln home), Manchester; Marsh-Billings-Rockefeller Natl. Historical Park, Woodstock. **Information:** Vermont Dept. of Tourism and Marketing, Natl. Life Building, 6th Fl., Montpelier, VT 05620; 1-800-VERMONT, (802) 828-3237; www.vermontvacation.com

History. Inhabited for 10,000 years or more, the region attracted Abenaki and Mahican peoples before Europeans arrived. Champlain explored the lake that now bears his name, 1609. The first European settlement was on Isle la Motte in Lake Champlain, 1666. During the American Revolution, Ethan Allen and the Green Mountain Boys captured Ft. Ticonderoga (NY), 1775. Under a constitution that provided for public schools and abolished slavery, settlers declared a republic, 1777. Vermont joined the Union, 1791. Agriculture dominated in the 19th cent. Still mainly rural, the state expanded tourism and manufacturing after World War II, and IBM became the largest private employer. Vermont was the first state to recognize same-sex civil unions (2000) and to enact equal same-sex marriage rights via legislation (2009).

Famous Vermonters. Ethan Allen, Chester A. Arthur, Calvin Coolidge, Howard Dean, John Deere, George Dewey, John Dewey, Stephen A. Douglas, Dorothy Canfield Fisher, James Fisk, James "Jim" Jeffords, Jody Williams.

Website. www.vermont.gov

Virginia (VA)
Old Dominion

People. Population: 8,260,405; rank: 12. **Pop. change** (2010-13): 3.2%. **Pop. density:** 209.2 per sq mi. **Racial distribution:** 70.8% white; 19.7% black; 6.1% Asian; 0.5% Amer. Ind.; 0.1% Hawaiian/Pacific Islander; 2 or more races, 2.7%. **Hispanic pop.:** 8.6%.

Geography. Total area: 42,775 sq mi; rank: 35. **Land area:** 39,490 sq mi; rank: 36. **Acres forested:** 15.9 mil. **Location:** South Atlantic state bounded by the Atlantic Ocean on the E and surrounded by North Carolina, Tennessee, Kentucky, West Virginia, and Maryland. **Climate:** mild and equable. **Topography:** mountain and valley region in the W, including the Blue Ridge Mts.; rolling Piedmont Plateau; tidewater, or coastal plain, including the Eastern Shore. **Capital:** Richmond. **Chief airports:** Arlington, Dulles, Highland Springs, Norfolk.

Economy. Chief industries: services, trade, government, manufacturing, tourism, agriculture. **Chief manuf. goods:** beverages and tobacco, transportation equip., animal slaughtering and processing, plastics, textiles, paper and paper prods., printing, pharmaceuticals, furniture, chemicals. **Chief crops:** greenhouse and nursery, soybeans, tomatoes, corn, tobacco, hay, cotton, apples, wheat, peanuts, potatoes. **Livestock:** 4.03 mil chickens (excl. broilers), 249.6 mil broilers, 1.53 mil cattle/calves, 83,000 sheep/lambs. **Nonfuel minerals:** $1.1 bil; stone (crushed), zirconium concentrates, cement (portland), lime, sand and gravel (construction). **Commercial fishing:** $175.6 mil. **Chief ports:** Norfolk Harbor, Newport News, Richmond, Hopewell. **Gross state product:** $452.6 bil. **Sales tax:** 5.3%. **Employment distrib.:** 18.9% govt.; 16.9% trade/trans./util.; 6.1% mfg.; 13.5% ed./health; 17.6% prof./bus. serv.; 9.9% leisure/hosp.; 5.1% finance; 4.9% constr./mining/log.; 1.9% info.; 5.2% other serv. **Unemployment:** 5.5%. **Per cap. pers. income:** $48,773. **New private housing:** 31,944 units/$4.9 bil. **Broadband Internet:** 82.1%. **Commercial banks:** 137; deposits: $206.7 bil. **Savings institutions:** 8; deposits: $34.1 bil. **Lottery:** total sales: $1.7 bil; profit: $486.5 mil.

Federal govt. Fed. civ. employees: 143,554; **avg. salary:** $88,504. **Notable fed. facilities:** Pentagon; Norfolk Naval Sta., Shipyard, and other Hampton Roads military bases; Ft. Belvoir; Joint Base Langley-Eustis; NASA Langley Res. Ctr.; CIA George Bush Ctr. for Intelligence, Langley; Quantico USMC Base, FBI Academy; Dahlgren Nav. Surface Warfare Ctr. and Lab; USDA Food and Nutrition Serv.; U.S. Geological Survey Natl. Ctr.

Higher education. 4-year public coll./univ.: 16; **2-yr. public:** 24; **4-yr. private:** 37.

Energy. Electricity use/cost: 1,117 kWh., $123.72.

State data. Motto: Sic Semper Tyrannis (Thus always to tyrants). **Flower:** Dogwood. **Bird:** Cardinal. **Tree:** Dogwood. **Song emeritus:** "Carry Me Back to Old Virginia." **Tenth** of original 13 states to ratify the Constitution, June 25, 1788.

Tourism. Tourist spending: $21.7 bil. **Attractions:** Colonial Williamsburg, Busch Gardens Williamsburg, Jamestown Settlement, in Williamsburg; Yorktown Victory Ctr.; Wolf Trap Natl. Park for the Performing Arts, near Vienna; Arlington Natl. Cemetery; George Washington's Mount Vernon; Thomas Jefferson's Monticello, Charlottesville; Stratford Hall (Robert E. Lee birthplace); Appomattox Court House Natl. Historical Park; Shenandoah Natl. Park; Blue Ridge Natl. Parkway; Virginia Beach; Kings Dominion amusement park, Doswell. **Information:** Virginia Tourism Corp., 901 E. Byrd St., Richmond, VA 23219; 1-800-VISITVA; www.virginia.org

History. Cherokee and Susquehanna peoples and the Algonquians of the Powhatan Confederacy were in the region when Europeans arrived. English settlers founded Jamestown, 1607. Virginians were indispensable to the founding of the American republic, and four of the first five U.S. presidents—Washington, Jefferson, Madison, and Monroe—came from there. The conclusive battle of the American Revolution took place at Yorktown, 1781. The state profited from tobacco, cotton, and the slave trade; in 1860, slaves made up nearly one-third of the population. Virginia seceded from the Union, 1861, and Richmond became the capital of the Confederacy. Western counties, loyal to the Union, split off to become West Virginia, 1863. The war ended with Robert E. Lee's surrender to Ulysses S. Grant at Appomattox, 1865, and Virginia was readmitted to the Union, 1870. In the 20th cent., expansion of federal civilian jobs and military facilities transformed the economy. State officials pledged "massive resistance" to racial integration in the mid-1950s, but eventually accommodated. In 1989, L. Douglas Wilder became the first elected black governor in U.S. history. On Sept. 11, 2001, terrorist hijackers crashed a jet into U.S. defense headquarters at the Pentagon, in Arlington. Seven-term Rep. Eric Cantor became the first House majority leader ever to lose a primary in June 2014.

Famous Virginians. Arthur Ashe, Sandra Bullock, Richard E. Byrd, James B. Cabell, Henry Clay, Katie Couric, Gabby Douglas, Jubal Early, Jerry Falwell, William Henry Harrison, Patrick Henry, A. P. Hill, Thomas Jefferson, Joseph E. Johnston, Robert E. Lee, Meriwether Lewis and William Clark, James Madison, John Marshall, George Mason, James Monroe, Sean Parker, George Pickett, Pocahontas, Edgar Allan Poe, John Randolph, Walter Reed, Rev. Pat Robertson, John Smith, J. E. B. Stuart, William Styron, Zachary Taylor, John Tyler, Maggie Walker, Booker T. Washington, George Washington, L. Douglas Wilder, Woodrow Wilson.

Website. www.virginia.gov

Washington (WA)
Evergreen State

People. Population: 6,971,406; rank: 13. **Pop. change** (2010-13): 3.7%. **Pop. density:** 104.9 per sq mi. **Racial distribution:** 81.2% white; 4.0% black; 7.9% Asian; 1.9% Amer. Ind.; 0.7% Hawaiian/Pacific Islander; 2 or more races, 4.4%. **Hispanic pop.:** 11.9%.

Geography. Total area: 71,298 sq mi; rank: 18. **Land area:** 66,456 sq mi; rank: 20. **Acres forested:** 22.3 mil. **Location:** Pacific state bordered by Canada on the N, Idaho on the E, Oregon on the S, and the Pacific Ocean on the W. **Climate:** mild, dominated by the Pacific Ocean and protected by the Cascades. **Topography:** Olympic Mts. on NW peninsula; open land along coast to Columbia R.; flat terrain of Puget Sound Lowland; high peaks of Cascade Mts. to the E; Columbia Basin in central portion; highlands to the NE; mountains to the SE. **Capital:** Olympia. **Chief airports:** Bellingham, Seattle, Spokane.

Economy. Chief industries: advanced technology, aerospace, biotechnology, intl. trade, forestry, tourism, recycling, agriculture and food processing. **Chief manuf. goods:** aerospace, petroleum, food, paper, milled lumber, plastics, structural metals, computers and electronics. **Chief crops:** apples, potatoes, wheat, hay, cherries, greenhouse and nursery, forest products, pears, grapes, onions, hops, sweet corn, Christmas trees, mint, raspberries. **Livestock:** 8.01 mil chickens (excl. broilers), 1.1 mil cattle/calves, 55,000 sheep/lambs. **Nonfuel minerals:** $743 mil; sand and gravel (construction), gold, stone (crushed), cement (portland), diatomite. **Commercial fishing:** $275.6 mil. **Chief ports:** Seattle, Tacoma, Vancouver, Kelso-Longview,

Anacortes. **Gross state product:** $408.0 bil. **Sales tax:** 6.5%. **Employment distrib.:** 18.3% govt.; 18.3% trade/trans./util.; 9.3% mfg.; 14.7% ed./health; 12.0% prof./bus. serv.; 9.8% leisure/hosp.; 5.0% finance; 5.3% constr./mining/log.; 3.5% info.; 3.7% other serv. **Unemployment:** 7.0%. **Per cap. pers. income:** $47,031. **New private housing:** 32,962 units/$6.7 bil. **Broadband Internet:** 86.4%. **Commercial banks:** 82; deposits: $106.6 bil. **Savings institutions:** 16; deposits: $11.2 bil. **Lottery:** total sales: $569.6 mil; profit $139.2 mil.

Federal govt. civ. employees: 55,639; **avg. salary:** $74,362. **Notable fed. facilities:** Bonneville Power Admin.; Lewis-McChord Joint Base; Fairchild AFB; DOE Hanford Nuclear Site; Naval Base Kitsap (Bremerton and Bangor); Whidbey Island NAS; Pacific Northwest Natl. Lab.

Higher education. 4-year public coll./univ.: 17; **2-yr. public:** 26; **4-yr. private:** 23.

Energy. Electricity use/cost: 1,037 kWh, $88.46.

State data. Motto: Alki (By and by). **Flower:** Western rhododendron. **Bird:** Willow goldfinch. **Tree:** Western hemlock. **Song:** "Washington, My Home." **Entered union:** Nov. 11, 1889; rank: 42nd.

Tourism. Tourist spending: $13.8 bil. **Attractions:** Seattle Center, Space Needle, EMP Museum, Museum of Flight, Pike Place Market, Underground Tour, in Seattle; Mount Rainier, Olympic, and North Cascades Natl. Parks; Mount St. Helens Natl. Volcanic Monument; Puget Sound; San Juan Islands; Grand Coulee Dam; Columbia R. Gorge Natl. Scenic Area; Riverfront Park, Spokane; Snoqualmie Falls. **Information:** WA State Tourism Office, 128 10th Ave. SW, P.O. Box 42525, Olympia, WA 98504; 1-866-964-8913; www.experiencewa.com

History. People of the Clovis culture lived in the region 11,000 years ago. At the time of European contact, Native Americans in the area included Nez Percé, Spokane, Yakima, Cayuse, Okanogan, Walla Walla, and Colville peoples in the interior, and Nooksak, Chinook, Nisqually, Clallam, Makah, Quinault, and Puyallup peoples along the coast. Spain's Bruno de Heceta sailed the coast, 1775. In 1792, British naval officer George Vancouver mapped the Puget Sound area, and American Capt. Robert Gray sailed up the Columbia R. Fur traders and missionaries arrived in the first half of the 19th cent. Final agreement on the border of Washington and Canada was made with Britain, 1846. Completion in 1883 of a transcontinental rail link between Puget Sound and the eastern U.S. aided immigration, and Washington became a state in 1889. In the 20th cent., cheap hydroelectric power spurred growth in the aluminum and aircraft industries. Founded in 1975, Microsoft became a computer software giant. Mount St. Helens erupted, 1980. With grunge music, Starbucks coffee, and Amazon.com, Seattle became a national trendsetter in the 1990s. Violent street protests disrupted a World Trade Organization meeting there in 1999. Gary Locke, in office 1997-2005, was the first U.S. governor of Chinese ancestry. A mudslide in Mar. 2014 killed 43 people in a rural area north of Seattle.

Famous Washingtonians. Paul Allen, Glenn Beck, Raymond Carver, Kurt Cobain, Bing Crosby, William O. Douglas, Bill Gates, Jimi Hendrix, Henry M. Jackson, Gary Larson, Mary McCarthy, Robert Motherwell, Edward R. Murrow, Apolo Ohno, Theodore Roethke, Ann Rule, Hope Solo, Hilary Swank, Julia Sweeney, Adam West, Marcus Whitman, Minoru Yamasaki.

Website. access.wa.gov

West Virginia (WV)
Mountain State

People. Population: 1,854,304; rank: 38. **Pop. change** (2010-13): 0.1%. **Pop. density:** 77.1 per sq mi. **Racial distribution:** 93.8% white; 3.6% black; 0.8% Asian; 0.2% Amer. Ind.; 0.0% Hawaiian/Pacific Islander; 2 or more races, 1.5%. **Hispanic pop.:** 1.4%.

Geography. Total area: 24,230 sq mi; rank: 41. **Land area:** 24,038 sq mi; rank: 41. **Acres forested:** 12.2 mil. **Location:** South Atlantic state bounded on the N by Pennsylvania, Maryland; on the S, W, and NW by Virginia, Kentucky, Ohio; on the E by Maryland and Virginia. **Climate:** humid continental climate except for marine modification in the lower panhandle. **Topography:** hilly to mountainous; Allegheny Plateau in the W covers two-thirds of state; mountains here are the highest in the state, over 4,000 ft. **Capital:** Charleston.

Economy. Chief industries: manufacturing, services, mining, tourism. **Chief manuf. goods:** chemicals, aluminum, motor vehicle parts, lumber and plywood, primary and fabricated metals. **Chief crops:** hay, apples, corn, peaches, soybeans, tobacco, wheat. **Livestock:** 2.04 mil chickens (excl. broilers), 96.8 mil broilers, 380,000 cattle/calves, 32,000 sheep/lambs. **Nonfuel minerals:** $313 mil; stone (crushed), cement (portland), lime, sand and gravel (industrial), cement (masonry). **Chief port:** Huntington. **Gross state product:** $74.0 bil. **Sales tax:** 6.0%. **Employment distrib.:** 21.3% govt.; 17.1% trade/trans./util.; 6.1% mfg.; 16.2% ed./health; 8.7% prof./bus. serv.; 9.9% leisure/hosp.; 3.8% finance; 8.5% constr./mining/log.; 1.2% info.; 7.1% other serv. **Unemployment:** 6.5%. **Per cap. pers. income:** $35,613. **New private housing:** 2,575 units/$366.2 mil. **Broadband Internet:** 91.5%. **Commercial banks:** 77; deposits: $29.8 bil. **Savings institutions:** 4; deposits: $801 mil. **Lottery:** total sales: $1.3 bil; profit: $523.0 mil.

Federal govt. Fed. civ. employees: 16,335; **avg. salary:** $70,693. **Notable fed. facilities:** Natl. Radio Astronomy Observatory, Green Bank; Bureau of Public Debt Bldg.; Alderson Fed. Prison Camp; FBI Criminal Justice Information Services.

Higher education. 4-year public coll./univ.: 13; **2-yr. public:** 10; **4-yr. private:** 8.

Energy. Electricity use/cost: 1,078 kWh, $106.15.

State data. Motto: Montani Semper Liberi (Mountaineers are always free). **Flower:** Big rhododendron. **Bird:** Cardinal. **Tree:** Sugar maple. **Songs:** "The West Virginia Hills"; "This Is My West Virginia"; "West Virginia, My Home, Sweet Home." **Entered union:** June 20, 1863; rank: 35th.

Tourism. Tourist spending: $2.9 bil. **Attractions:** Harpers Ferry Natl. Historical Park, Appalachian Trail Conservancy and Visitor Ctr., in Harpers Ferry; Clay Center for the Arts and Sciences and Avampato Discovery Museum, Charleston; The Greenbrier resort, White Sulphur Springs; Berkeley Springs State Park; Seneca Rocks State Park; New River Gorge Natl. River; Beckley Exhibition Coal Mine; Monongahela Natl. Forest; Fenton Art Glass Company, Williamstown; Mountain State Forest Festival, Elkins; Mountain State Art & Craft Fair, Ripley; Natl. Radio Astronomy Observatory in Green Bank (with world's largest fully steerable radio telescope); Cass Scenic Railroad State Park. **Information:** West Virginia Division of Tourism, Capitol Complex, Bldg. 6, Rm. 525, Charleston, WV 25305; 1-800-CALLWVA; www.wvtourism.com

History. Sparsely inhabited at the time of European contact, the area was primarily Native American hunting grounds. British explorers Thomas Batts and Robert Fallam reached the New R., 1671. Coal, discovered in 1742, was mined extensively by the mid-19th cent. White settlement led to conflicts with Native Americans, including a major battle in which settlers defeated an Indian confederacy at Point Pleasant, 1774. The region joined the Union as part of Virginia, 1788. Longstanding tensions between the E and W parts of the state came to a head in 1861, when Virginia seceded. Delegates of western counties, meeting at Wheeling, repudiated the act and created a new state, Kanawha, later renamed West Virginia, which was admitted to the Union in 1863. Poverty has been a problem for much of the state's subsequent history. It continued to rank low in per capita personal income, despite billions of dollars in federal contracts brought to the state by nine-term U.S. Sen. Robert Byrd, who passed away in 2010. Coal mining, though dangerous, continues to be a major industry; nearly 30 miners were killed in a mine explosion in 2010. In Jan. 2014, Gov. Earl Ray Tomblin banned water use for some 300,000 people for up to 10 days after coal processing chemicals leaked into a waterway.

Famous West Virginians. George Brett, Pearl S. Buck, Robert C. Byrd, Henry Louis Gates Jr., Stonewall Jackson, Don Knotts, Michael Joseph Owens, Brad Paisley, Mary Lou Retton, Walter Reuther, Cyrus Vance, Jerry West, Charles "Chuck" Yeager.

Website. www.wv.gov

Wisconsin (WI)
Badger State

People. Population: 5,742,713; rank: 20. **Pop. change** (2010-13): 1.0%. **Pop. density:** 106.0 per sq mi. **Racial distribution:** 88.1% white; 6.5% black; 2.5% Asian; 1.1% Amer. Ind.; 0.0% Hawaiian/Pacific Islander; 2 or more races, 1.7%. **Hispanic pop.:** 6.3%.

Geography. Total area: 65,496 sq mi; rank: 23. **Land area:** 54,158 sq mi; rank: 25. **Acres forested:** 17.1 mil. **Location:** East North Central state bounded on the N by Lake Superior and Upper Michigan, on the E by Lake Michigan, on the S by Illinois, on the W by the St. Croix and Mississippi Rivers.

Climate: long, cold winters and short, warm summers tempered by the Great Lakes. **Topography:** narrow Lake Superior Lowland plain met by Northern Highland, which slopes gently to the sandy crescent Central Plain; Western Upland in the SW; three broad parallel limestone ridges running N-S are separated by wide and shallow lowlands in the SE. **Capital:** Madison. **Chief airports:** Madison, Milwaukee.

Economy. Chief industries: services, manufacturing, trade, government, agriculture, tourism. **Chief manuf. goods:** transportation, dairy, animal slaughtering and processing, paper, printing, plastics, computers and electronics. **Chief crops:** corn, greenhouse and nursery, soybeans, potatoes, cranberries, hay, wheat, snap beans, apples, peas. **Livestock:** 6.81 mil chickens (excl. broilers), 53.1 mil broilers, 3.35 mil cattle/calves, 83,000 sheep/lambs. **Nonfuel minerals:** $935 mil; sand and gravel (industrial), sand and gravel (construction), stone (crushed), lime, stone (dimension). **Commercial fishing:** $5.0 mil. **Chief ports:** Superior, Milwaukee, Green Bay. **Gross state product:** $282.5 bil. **Sales tax:** 5.0%. **Employment distrib.:** 14.8% govt.; 18.1% trade/trans./util.; 16.2% mfg.; 15.0% ed./health; 10.5% prof./bus. serv.; 9.6% leisure/hosp.; 5.5% finance; 3.8% constr./mining/log.; 1.6% info.; 4.9% other serv. **Unemployment:** 6.7%. **Per cap. pers. income:** $43,149. **New private housing:** 13,869 units/$2.5 bil. **Broadband Internet:** 88.5%. **Commercial banks:** 251; deposits: $117.5 bil. **Savings institutions:** 34; deposits: $12.2 bil. **Lottery:** total sales: $566.1 mil; profit: $156.3 mil.

Federal govt. fed. civ. employees: 16,069; **avg. salary:** $68,178. **Notable fed. facilities:** Ft. McCoy; USDA Forest Products Lab.

Higher education. 4-year public coll./univ.: 14; **2-yr. public:** 17; **4-yr. private:** 30.

Energy. Electricity use/cost: 703 kWh, $92.79.

State data. Motto: Forward. **Flower:** Wood violet. **Bird:** Robin. **Tree:** Sugar maple. **Song:** "On, Wisconsin!" **Entered union:** May 29, 1848; rank: 30th.

Tourism. Tourist spending: $10.0 bil. **Attractions:** Wade House, Greenbush; Villa Louis, Prairie du Chien; Circus World Museum, Baraboo; Wisconsin Dells; Old World Wisconsin, Eagle; shoreline and state parks of Door County; Chequamegon-Nicolet Natl. Forest; House on the Rock, Taliesin, in Spring Green; Monona Terrace Community and Convention Ctr., Madison; Milwaukee Art Museum, Pabst Mansion, in Milwaukee. **Information:** Wisconsin Dept. of Tourism, 201 W. Washington Ave., P.O. Box 8690, Madison, WI 53708; 1-800-432-TRIP; www.travelwisconsin.com

History. At the time of European contact, Ojibwa, Menominee, Winnebago, Kickapoo, Sauk, Fox, and Potawatomi peoples inhabited the area. French explorer Jean Nicolet reached Green Bay, 1634; French missionaries and fur traders followed. The British took over, 1763. The U.S. won the land after the American Revolution but did not wield control until forts were established at Green Bay and Prairie du Chien, 1816. Native Americans rebelled against the seizure of tribal lands in the Black Hawk War, 1832, but were defeated and relocated to reservations. Wisconsin became a territory, 1836, and a state, 1848. Some 96,000 soldiers served the Union cause during the Civil War. Many immigrants arrived from Germany, Poland, and Scandinavia. Wisconsin agriculture focused on dairy; Milwaukee became a manufacturing center. As governor, 1901-06, Robert La Follette pushed Progressive reforms such as direct primary voting and consumer protection laws. An era of "McCarthyism" ended when anti-Communist crusader U.S. Sen. Joseph McCarthy was censured by the Senate, 1954. After weeks of protests in Madison, the Republican-controlled state legislature passed controversial measures in 2011 to restrict collective bargaining by some 170,000 public-sector employees.

Famous Wisconsinites. Don Ameche, Carrie Chapman Catt, Willem Dafoe, Edna Ferber, Hamlin Garland, King Camp Gillette, Harry Houdini, Robert La Follette, (Vladzio Valentino) Liberace, Alfred Lunt, Pat O'Brien, Georgia O'Keeffe, Danica Patrick, Les Paul, William H. Rehnquist, John Ringling, Donald K. "Deke" Slayton, Spencer Tracy, Orson Welles, Laura Ingalls Wilder, Thornton Wilder, Frank Lloyd Wright.

Website. www.wisconsin.gov

Wyoming (WY)
Equality State, Cowboy State

People. Population: 582,658; rank: 51. **Pop. change** (2010-13): 3.4%. **Pop. density:** 6.0 per sq mi. **Racial distribution:** 92.7% white; 1.7% black; 0.9% Asian; 2.6% Amer. Ind.; 0.1% Hawaiian/Pacific Islander; 2 or more races, 1.9%. **Hispanic pop.:** 9.7%.

Geography. Total area: 97,813 sq mi; rank: 10. **Land area:** 97,093 sq mi; rank: 9. **Acres forested:** 10.4 mil. **Location:** Mountain state in the high western plateaus of the Great Plains. **Climate:** semidesert conditions throughout; true desert in the Bighorn and Great Divide Basins. **Topography:** eastern Great Plains rise to the foothills of the Rocky Mts.; the Continental Divide crosses the state from the NW to the SE. **Capital:** Cheyenne.

Economy. Chief industries: mineral extraction, oil, natural gas, tourism and recreation, agriculture. **Chief manuf. goods:** petroleum, chemicals, fabricated metal, beet sugar, lumber. **Chief crops:** hay, sugar beets, barley, dry beans, wheat, corn, greenhouse and nursery, oats. **Livestock:** 13,000 chickens (excl. broilers), 1.27 mil cattle/calves, 355,000 sheep/lambs. **Nonfuel minerals:** $2.5 bil; soda ash, clays (bentonite), helium (Grade-A), sand and gravel (construction), cement (portland). **Gross state product:** $45.4 bil. **Sales tax:** 4.0%. **Employment distrib.:** 25.1% govt.; 18.9% trade/trans./util.; 3.2% mfg.; 9.2% ed./health; 6.3% prof./bus. serv.; 11.4% leisure/hosp.; 3.8% finance; 16.8% constr./mining/log.; 1.3% info.; 3.9% other serv. **Unemployment:** 4.6%. **Per cap. pers. income:** $50,924. **New private housing:** 2,300 units/$535.9 mil. **Broadband Internet:** 74.3%. **Commercial banks:** 43; deposits: $13 bil. **Savings institutions:** 3; deposits: $498 mil.

Federal govt. Fed. civ. employees: 5,738; **avg. salary:** $62,592. **Notable fed. facilities:** Warren AFB.

Higher education. 4-year public coll./univ.: 1; **2-yr. public:** 7; **4-yr. private:** 0.

Energy. Electricity use/cost: 867 kWh, $85.35.

State data. Motto: Equal rights. **Flower:** Indian paintbrush. **Bird:** Western meadowlark. **Tree:** Plains cottonwood. **Song:** "Wyoming." **Entered union:** July 10, 1890; rank: 44th.

Tourism. Tourist spending: $3.0 bil. **Attractions:** Yellowstone Natl. Park (est. 1872, first U.S. national park); Grand Teton Natl. Park; Natl. Elk Refuge, Jackson; Devils Tower Natl. Monument; Ft. Laramie Natl. Historic Site; Oregon Trail ruts, Guernsey; Buffalo Bill Historical Ctr., Cody; Cheyenne Frontier Days. **Information:** Wyoming Travel and Tourism, 1520 Etchepare Cir., Cheyenne, WY 82007; 1-800-225-5996; www.wyomingtourism.org

History. Inhabited for at least 12,000 years, the region supported Shoshone, Crow, Cheyenne, Oglala Sioux, and Arapaho peoples when Europeans arrived. France's Vérendrye brothers were the first Europeans to see the region, 1742-43. John Colter, an American, traversed the Yellowstone area, 1807-08. Trappers and fur traders followed in the 1820s. Forts Laramie and Bridger became important stops on trails to the West Coast. Population grew after the Union Pacific crossed the state, 1867-68. Wyoming became a territory, 1868, and the first to extend full voting rights to women, 1869. Statehood was attained, 1890. Disputes between large landowners and small ranchers culminated in the Johnson County Cattle War, 1892; federal troops were called in to restore order. Nellie Tayloe Ross was the first woman governor to take office in the U.S., 1925. Wyoming, the least populous state, has relied on the energy, tourism, and ranching industries in recent decades. Dick Cheney, Wyoming's representative in the U.S. House, 1979-89, served as U.S. vice pres. (2001-09).

Famous Wyomingites. James Bridger, Dick Cheney, William F. "Buffalo Bill" Cody, Curt Gowdy, Esther Hobart Morris, Nellie Tayloe Ross.

Website. www.wyoming.gov

District of Columbia (DC)

People. Population: 646,449; rank: 49. **Pop. change** (2010-13): 7.4%. **Pop. density:** 10,597.5 per sq mi. **Racial distribution:** 43.4% white; 49.5% black; 3.9% Asian; 0.6% Amer. Ind.; 0.1% Hawaiian/Pacific Islander; 2 or more races, 2.6%. **Hispanic pop.:** 10.1%.

Geography. Total area: 68 sq mi; rank: 51. **Land area:** 61 sq mi; rank: 51. **Acres forested:** NA. **Location:** at the confluence of the Potomac and Anacostia Rivers, flanked by Maryland on the N, E, and SE and by Virginia on the SW. **Climate:** hot humid summers, mild winters. **Topography:** low hills rise toward the N away from the Potomac R. and slope to the S; highest elevation, 410 ft; lowest on Potomac R., 1 ft.

Economy. Chief industries: government, legal, publishing, medical, service, tourism. **Gross state product:** $113.4 bil. **Sales tax:** 5.75%. **Employment distrib.:** 33.2% govt.; 3.7% trade/trans./util.; 0.2% mfg.; 16.1% ed./health;

20.5% prof./bus. serv.; 9.0% leisure/hosp.; 3.7% finance; 1.8% constr./mining/log.; 2.5% info.; 9.4% other serv. **Unemployment:** 8.3%. **Per cap. pers. income:** $74,513. **New private housing:** 3,255 units/$279.9 mil. **Broadband Internet:** 79.4%. **Commercial banks:** 30; deposits: $36.3 bil. **Savings institutions:** 5; deposits: $168 mil. **Lottery:** total sales: $242.7 mil; profit: $70.0 mil.

Federal govt. Fed. civ. employees: 158,664; **avg. salary:** $108,830.

Higher education. 4-year public coll./univ.: 2; **2-yr. public:** 0; **4-yr. private:** 14.

Energy. Electricity use/cost: 721 kWh, $88.51.

District data. Motto: *Justitia omnibus* (Justice for all). **Flower:** American beauty rose. **Bird:** Wood thrush. **Tree:** Scarlet oak.

Tourism. Tourist spending: $9.4 bil. **Attractions:** See Attractions in and around Washington, DC, pp. 444-45. **Information:** Destination DC, 901 7th St. NW, 4th Fl., Washington, DC, 20001-3719; 1-800-422-8644; www.washington.org

History. The District of Columbia, coextensive with the city of Washington, is the seat of the U.S. federal government. It lies on the west central edge of Maryland on the Potomac R., opposite Virginia. The Piscataway, an Algonquian-speaking people, were living in the region when Europeans arrived in the 17th cent. Proposals for a "federal town" for the deliberations of the Continental Congress were made in 1783. Authorized by Congress, 1790, Pres. George Washington chose the Potomac site and persuaded landowners to sell their holdings to the government. Its area was originally 100 sq mi taken from the sovereignty of Maryland and Virginia. Virginia's portion south of the Potomac was given back to that state in 1846.

Pres. Washington chose Pierre Charles L'Enfant, a Frenchman, to plan the capital. Surveyor Andrew Ellicott finished the official map and design of the city, assisted by Benjamin Banneker, a black architect and astronomer. Washington laid the cornerstone of the north wing of the Capitol building, 1793, and Pres. John Adams moved to the new national capital, 1800. The City of Washington was incorporated, 1802. British troops invaded, 1814, setting fire to the Capitol, the President's House (as the White House was then called), and other buildings. Pres. Abraham Lincoln ended slavery in the district, 1862. Many African Americans arrived after the Civil War, but racial segregation remained legal until the mid-20th cent. After federal government expansion spurred population growth, 1930-50, an exodus to the suburbs shrank the city's population, 1950-2005.

The 23rd Amendment (1961) granted residents the right to vote for president and vice president. Congress, which has legislative authority over the District under the Constitution, approved legislation in 1970 giving the District one delegate to the House of Representatives, who could vote in committee but not on the floor. Voters approved, 1974, a congressionally drafted charter giving them the right to elect their own mayor and city council. The district won the right to levy taxes, but Congress retained power to veto council actions and approve the city budget. Security measures were dramatically increased after terrorists attacked the U.S. on Sept. 11, 2001. After a 34-year absence, major league baseball returned to the city in 2005.

Famous Washingtonians. Edward Albee, Michael Chabon, Frederick Douglass, John Foster Dulles, Kevin Durant, Edward Kennedy "Duke" Ellington, Marvin Gaye, Katharine Graham, Goldie Hawn, J. Edgar Hoover, Bill Nye, Pete Sampras, John Philip Sousa.

Website. www.dc.gov

OUTLYING U.S. AREAS

American Samoa (AS)

People. Population (2014 est.): 54,517. **Pop. change** (2010-14): -1.8%. **Pop. density:** 708.0 per sq mi. **Racial distribution** (2000): 91.6% Pac. Isl.; 2.8% Asian; 1.1% white; 2 or more races, 4.2%. **Languages:** Samoan, English, Tongan.

Geography. Total area: 77 sq mi. **Land area:** 77 sq mi. **Acres forested:** 43,631. **Location:** most southerly of all lands under U.S. sovereign, about 2,300 mi SW of Honolulu. It is an unincorporated territory consisting of seven small islands of the Samoan group: **Tutuila** (52.59 sq mi); **Aunu'u** (0.59 sq mi); Manu'a group: **Ta'u** (17.57 sq mi), **Olosega** (2.03 sq mi), **Ofu** (2.83 sq mi), and the atolls **Rose** (0.03 sq mi) and **Swains** (1.38 sq mi). **Climate:** marine tropical, avg. temp 82°F with little seasonal variation; avg. annual rainfall about 36 in. **Topography:** volcanic islands, rugged peaks, and limited coastal plains. About 70% of the land is bush and mountains. **Capital:** Pago Pago on Tutuila. **Airport:** Pago Pago.

Economy. Chief industries: tuna fishing and processing, trade, services, tourism. **Chief crops:** giant taro, taro, yams, coconuts, breadfruits, bananas, papayas. **Livestock** (2008): 35,709 chickens, 16,904 hogs/pigs. **Nonfuel minerals:** crushed stone, traprock. **Commercial fishing** (2008): $9.7 mil. **Unemployment** (2007): 29.8%. **Gross domestic product** (2012 est.): $725.0 mil. **Commercial banks:** 2; deposits: $175 mil.

Higher education. 4-year public coll./univ.: 1; **2-yr. public:** 0; **4-yr. private:** 0.

Energy. Electricity production (2011 est.): 155 mil kWh. **Fed. civ. employees** (Mar. 2014): 106; **avg. salary:** $57,024.

Misc. data. Motto: Samoa Muamua le Atua (In Samoa, God is first). **Flower:** Paogo (Ula-fala). **Plant:** Ava. **Song:** "Amerika Samoa."

Tourism. Attractions: Natl. Park of American Samoa; Natl. Marine Sanctuary of American Samoa; Jean P. Haydon Museum. **Information:** Office of Tourism, Dept. of Commerce, American Samoa Govt., P.O. Box 1147, Pago Pago, AS 96799; (684) 699-9411; www.amsamoatourism.com

History. A tripartite agreement between Great Britain, Germany, and the U.S. in 1899 gave the U.S. sovereignty over the eastern islands of the Samoan group; these islands became American Samoa. Local chiefs ceded Tutuila and Aunu'u to the U.S. in 1900 and the Manu'a group and Rose Island in 1904; Swains Island was annexed in 1925. Samoa (Western), comprising the larger islands of the Samoan group, was a New Zealand mandate and UN Trusteeship until it became independent Jan. 1, 1962 (now called Samoa).

From 1900 to 1951, American Samoa was under the jurisdiction of the U.S. Navy. Since 1951, it has been under the Interior Dept. On Jan. 3, 1978, the first popularly elected Samoan governor and lieutenant governor were inaugurated. Previously, the governor was appointed by the Sec. of the Interior. American Samoa has a bicameral legislature and elects a delegate to the U.S. House of Representatives who has a voice but no vote, except in committees.

Five of the seven islands are volcanoes. Scientists discovered a rapidly growing volcano, Vailulu'u, between Ta'u and Rose in 1975.

The tuna canning industry has been the backbone of the economy since the 1950s, but one of the two canneries closed in 2009. An 8.1-magnitude earthquake in Sept. 2009 triggered a tsunami that severely damaged Tutuila.

American Samoans are of Polynesian origin. They are nationals of the U.S. As of 2010, 109,637 lived in the U.S., including 18,287 in Hawaii and 40,100 in California.

Website. www.americansamoa.gov

Guam (GU)

People. Population (2014 est.): 161,001. **Pop change** (2010-14): 1.0%. **Pop. density:** 759.4 per sq mi. **Racial/ethnic distribution** (2010 est.): 37.3% Chamorro; 26.3% Filipino; 12.0% other Pac. Isl.; 7.1% white. **Languages:** English, Chamorro, Philippine/other Pacific Island languages.

Geography. Total area: 212 sq mi. **Land area:** 212 sq mi. **Acres forested:** 63,830. **Location:** largest and southernmost of the Mariana Islands in the West Pacific, 3,700 mi W of Hawaii. **Climate:** tropical, with temperatures from 70° to 90°F; rainy July to Nov., avg. annual rainfall about 80-100 in. **Topography:** coralline limestone plateau in the N; southern chain of low volcanic mountains slope gently to the W, more steeply to coastal cliffs on the E; general elevation, 500 ft; highest point, Mt. Lamlam, 1,332 ft. **Capital:** Hagåtña. **Chief airport:** Tamuning.

Economy. Chief industries: U.S. military, tourism, construction, shipping, concrete products, printing and publishing. **Chief manuf. goods:** textiles, foods. **Chief crops:** watermelons, cucumbers, eggplant, long beans, bananas, corn. **Livestock** (2007): 533 chickens, 112 cattle, 635 hogs/pigs, 124 goats. **Nonfuel minerals** (2008): $3.8 mil; crushed stone. **Commercial fishing** (2008): $499,095. **Chief port:** Apra Harbor. **Gross domestic product** (2012 est.): $4.8 bil. **Employment distrib.** (Dec. 2012): 30.2% trade/trans; 26.7% serv.; 25.5% govt.; 10.6% constr.; 2.7% mfg.; 0.2% agric. **Unemployment** (2012): 10.7%. **Per capita income** (2010): $12,864.

Broadband Internet: 98.6%. **Commercial banks:** 5; deposits: $2.2 bil. **Savings institutions:** 1; deposits: $92 mil.

Higher education. 4-year public coll./univ.: 1; **2-yr. public:** 1; **4-yr. private:** 1.

Energy. Electricity production (2011 est.): 1.7 bil kWh. **Federal govt. Fed. employees** (Mar. 2014): 2,801; **avg. salary:** $59,670. **Notable fed. facilities:** Andersen AFB.

Misc. data. Motto: Where America's day begins. **Flower:** Puti Tai Nobio (Bougainvillea). **Bird:** Ko'ko (Guam rail). **Tree:** Ifit (Intsia bijuga). **Song:** "Stand Ye Guamanians."

Tourism. Attractions: Ritidian Point, Guam Natl. Wildlife Refuge; War in the Pacific Natl. Historical Park; Chamorro Village; Two Lovers Point. **Information:** Guam Visitors Bureau, 401 Pale San Vitores Rd., Tumon, Guam 96913; (671) 646-5278; www.visitguam.org

History. Guam was probably settled by voyagers from the Indonesian-Philippine archipelago by 3rd cent. BCE. Pottery, rice cultivation, and megalithic technology show strong East Asian cultural influence. Centralized, village clan-based communities engaged in agriculture and offshore fishing. The estimated population by the early 16th cent. was 50,000–75,000. Ferdinand Magellan arrived in the Marianas Mar. 6, 1521. They were colonized in 1668 by Spanish missionaries, who named them the Mariana Islands in honor of Maria Anna, queen of Spain. When Spain ceded Guam to the U.S., it sold the other Marianas to Germany. Japan obtained a League of Nations mandate over the German islands in 1919; in Dec. 1941 it seized Guam, which was retaken by the U.S. in July-Aug. 1944.

Guam is a self-governing organized unincorporated U.S. territory. The Organic Act of 1950 provided for a governor, elected to a four-year term, and a 21-member unicameral legislature, elected biennially by the residents, who are American citizens. In 1970, the first governor was elected. In 1972, a U.S. law gave Guam one delegate to the U.S. House of Representatives who has a voice but no vote, except in committees.

Guam's quest to change its status to a U.S. commonwealth began in the late 1970s. The Guam Commission on Self-Determination, created in 1984, developed a draft Commonwealth Act. In 1993, legislation proposing a change of status was submitted to the U.S. Congress. In 1994, the U.S. Congress passed legislation transferring 3,200 acres of land on Guam from federal to local control. The U.S. plans to move 8,000 Marines stationed in Okinawa, Japan, to Guam by 2015.

Website. www.guam.gov

Commonwealth of the Northern Mariana Islands (MP)

People. Population (2014 est.): 51,483; **Pop. change** (2010-14): −4.5%. **Pop. density:** 50.0 per sq mi. **Racial/ethnic distribution** (2010 est.): 50.0% Asian; 34.9% Pac. Isl.; 1.8% white; 2.5% other; 2 or more races/ethnicities, 12.7%. **Languages:** Philippine languages, Chinese, Chamorro, English other Pacific Island langs.

Geography. Total area: 184 sq mi. **Land area:** 184 sq mi. **Acres forested:** 50,218. **Location:** between Guam and the Tropic of Cancer, the 14 islands of the Northern Marianas form a 300-mi long archipelago. The indigenous population is concentrated on the three largest of the six inhabited islands: **Saipan,** the seat of government and commerce, **Rota,** and **Tinian. Climate:** tropical, with avg. temperature around 82°F, moderated by NE trade winds; avg. annual rainfall 80-100 in. **Topography:** limestone southern islands with even terraces, coral reefs; volcanic northern isles. **Capital:** Saipan. **Airport:** Saipan.

Economy. Chief industries: banking, construction, fishing, mining, tourism, apparel manufacturing, retail. **Chief manuf. goods:** apparel, stone, clay and glass prods. **Chief crops:** bananas, cucumbers, sweet potatoes, taro, watermelons. **Livestock** (2007): 9,700 chickens, 1,395 cattle, 1,483 hogs/pigs. **Commercial fishing** (2010 est.): $608,971. **Chief port:** Saipan. **Gross domestic product** (2012 est.): $701.0 mil. **Unemployment** (2010): 11.2%. **Commercial banks:** 3; deposits: $524 mil.

Higher education. 4-year public coll./univ.: 1; **2-yr. public:** 0; **4-yr. private:** 0.

Energy. Electricity production (2009): 60,600 kWh. **Federal govt. Fed. civ. employees** (Mar. 2014): 186; **avg. salary:** $54,256.

Misc. data. Flower: Plumeria. **Bird:** Mariana fruit-dove. **Tree:** Flame tree. **Song:** "Gi Talo Gi Halom Tasi" (In the Middle of the Sea).

Tourism. Attractions: House of Taga; American Memorial Park; Banzai Cliff. **Information:** Marianas Visitors Authority, P.O. Box 500861, Saipan, MP 96950; (670) 664-3200; www.mymarianas.com

History. The people of the Northern Marianas are predominantly of Chamorro cultural extraction, although Carolinians and immigrants from other areas of E. Asia and Micronesia have also settled in the islands. English is among the several languages commonly spoken.

The German-controlled Northern Marianas were placed under Japanese control by a League of Nations mandate after World War I. The U.S. captured the islands during World War II. From July 18, 1947, the U.S. had administered the Northern Marianas under a trusteeship agreement with the UN Security Council. In 1975, the residents voted to become a U.S. commonwealth.

The Northern Mariana Islands has been self-governing since 1978, when a constitution drafted and adopted by the people became effective and a popularly elected bicameral legislature (two-year term), with offices of governor (four-year term) and lieut. governor, was inaugurated. Pres. Ronald Reagan proclaimed the Northern Marianas a commonwealth, 1986, and the UN formally ended its trusteeship, 1990. In 2008, U.S. law gave the islands one delegate to the U.S. House of Representatives who has a voice but no vote, except in committees.

Under the 1976 Commonwealth Covenant with the U.S., the islands are exempt from federal immigration and import laws, and minimum wage is lower than on the mainland. The garment-making industry, which has since boomed, has drawn accusations of sweatshop conditions from some critics. Legislation passed in 2007 will raise the minimum wage to the federal rate by 2015.

Website. gov.mp

Commonwealth of Puerto Rico (PR)
(Estado Libre Asociado de Puerto Rico)

People. Population (2014 est.): 3,620,897 (about 4.6 mil additional Puerto Ricans reside in the mainland U.S.). **Pop. change** (2010-14): −2.8%. **Pop. density:** 1,057.5 per sq mi. **Racial distribution:** 75.8% white; 12.4% black; 0.2% Asian; 0.5% Amer. Ind.; <0.05% Pac. Isl.; 2 or more races, 3.3%. **Hispanic pop.:** 99.0%. **Languages:** Spanish and English are joint official languages.

Geography. Total area: 5,325 sq mi. **Land area:** 3,424 sq mi. **Acres forested:** 1.2 mil. **Location:** island lying between the Atlantic to the N and the Caribbean to the S; it is easternmost of the West Indies group called the Greater Antilles, of which Cuba, Hispaniola, and Jamaica are the larger islands. **Climate:** mild, with a mean temperature of 77°F. **Topography:** mountainous throughout three-fourths of its rectangular area, surrounded by a broken coastal plain; highest peak, Cerro de Punta, 4,390 ft. **Capital:** San Juan. **Chief airport:** San Juan.

Economy. Chief industries: manufacturing, service, tourism. **Chief manuf. goods:** pharmaceuticals, medical equip., electronics, apparel, food products. **Chief crops:** pumpkins, coffee, watermelons, plantains, yams, oranges, pineapples, sugarcane, bananas. **Livestock** (2007): 1.4 mil chickens, 5.1 mil broilers, 490,817 cattle, 11,137 sheep, 69,892 hogs/pigs. **Nonfuel minerals** (2008): $164 mil; crushed stone, lime, salt, cement (portland), clays (common). **Commercial fishing** (2008): $3.8 mil. **Chief ports:** San Juan, Ponce, Mayaguez. **Gross domestic product** (2012): $101.5 bil. **Employment distrib.:** 26.0% govt.; 18.9% trade/trans./util.; 8.1% mfg.; 13.6% ed./health; 12.7% prof./bus. serv.; 8.7% leisure/hosp.; 4.7% finance; 3.3% constr./mining/log.; 2.1% info.; 1.9% other serv. **Unemployment** (2012): 14.2%. **Per capita pers. income** (est. 2009): $14,905. **Broadband Internet:** 92.4%. **Commercial banks:** 8; deposits: $52.5 bil. **Lottery** (2009): total sales: $421.2 mil; profit: $146.9 mil.

Federal govt. Fed. civ. employees (Mar. 2014): 10,788; **avg. salary:** $65,130. **Notable fed. facilities:** PR Natl. Guard Training Area at Camp Santiago; Ft. Buchanan; Intl. Inst. of Tropical Forestry; Vieques Natl. Wildlife Refuge; USGS Caribbean Water Science Ctr.

Higher education. 4-year public coll./univ.: 14; **2-yr. public:** 4; **4-yr. private:** 45.

Energy. Electricity production (2011 est.): 20.0 bil kWh. **Misc. data. Motto:** Joannes Est Nomen Eius (John is his name). **Flower:** Maga. **Bird:** Reinita. **Tree:** Ceiba. **Anthem:** "La Borinqueña."

Tourism. Attractions: Museo de Arte de Ponce; San Felipe del Morro and San Cristóbal forts, San Juan Natl. Historic Site, Walled City of Old San Juan, Casa Blanca in San Juan; Arecibo Observatory; Cordillera Central mtn. range; El Yunque Natl. Forest (only tropical rain forest in Natl. Forest system); Cathedral of San Juan Bautista; Porta Coeli (Doorway to Heaven) Church and Religious Art Museum, San Germán; Rio Camuy Cave Park, Camuy; Mosquito Bay. **Information:** The Puerto Rico Tourism Company, La Princesa Bldg. #2, Paseo La Princesa, Old San Juan, PR 00902; (800) 866-7827; www.seepuertorico.com.

History. Puerto Rico (or Borinquen, after the original Arawak Indian name, Boriquen) was visited by Christopher Columbus on his second voyage, Nov. 19, 1493. In 1508, the Spanish arrived.

Sugarcane was introduced, 1515, and slaves were imported three years later. Gold mining petered out, 1570. Spaniards fought off a series of British and Dutch attacks; slavery was abolished, 1873. Under the Treaty of Paris, Puerto Rico was ceded to the U.S. after the Spanish-American War, 1898. In 1952 the people voted in favor of commonwealth status.

The Commonwealth of Puerto Rico is a self-governing part of the U.S. with a primarily Hispanic culture. The island's citizens have virtually the same control over their internal affairs as do the 50 states of the U.S. However, they do not vote in national general elections, only in national primaries.

Puerto Rico is represented in the U.S. House of Representatives by a Resident Commissioner who has a voice but no vote, except in committees.

No federal income tax is collected from residents on income earned from local sources in Puerto Rico. Nevertheless, as part of the U.S. legal system, Puerto Rico is subject to the provisions of the U.S. Constitution; most federal laws apply as they do in the 50 states.

Puerto Rico's famous "Operation Bootstrap," begun in the late 1940s, succeeded in changing the island from the "Poorhouse of the Caribbean" to an area with the highest per capita income in Latin America. This program encouraged manufacturing and development of the tourist trade by selective tax exemption, low-interest loans, and other incentives. Despite the marked success of Puerto Rico's development efforts over an extended period of time, per capita income in Puerto Rico is low in comparison to that of the 50 states.

In plebiscites held in 1967, 1993, and 1998, voters chose to retain commonwealth status. Protests mounted in the late-1990s over the U.S. Navy's use of Vieques Island for live ammunition training; official military exercises there were terminated, 2003.

Cultural facilities and events. Festival Casals classical music concerts, mid-June; Puerto Rico Symphony Orchestra at Music Conservatory; Botanical Garden and Museum of Anthropology, Art, and History at the Univ. of Puerto Rico; Institute of Puerto Rican Culture, at the Dominican Convent.

Famous Puerto Ricans. Julia de Burgos, Marta Casals Istomin, Pablo Casals, José Celso Barbosa, Orlando Cepeda, Roberto Clemente, José de Diego, José Feliciano, Doña Felisa Rincón de Gautier, Luis A. Ferré, José Ferrer, Commodore Diégo E. Hernández, Miguel Hernández Agosto, Rafael Hernández (El Jibarito), Rafael Hernández Colón, Raúl Julía, René Marqués, Ricky Martin, Concha Meléndez, Rita Moreno, Luis Muñoz Marín, Luis Palés Matos, Joaquin Phoenix, Adm. Horacio Rivero.

Website. www.pr.gov (in Spanish)

Virgin Islands (VI)
St. John, St. Croix, St. Thomas

People. Population (2014 est.): 104,170. **Pop. change** (2010-14): –2.1%. **Pop. density** (2000): 771.6 per sq mi. **Racial distribution** (2000): 76.2% black; 13.1% white; 1.1% Asian; 6.1% other races; 2 or more races, 3.5%. **Languages:** English (official), Spanish, Creole.

Geography. Total area: 136 sq mi. **Land area:** 135 sq mi. **Acres forested:** 45,163. **Location:** 3 larger and 50 smaller islands and cays in the S and W of the V.I. group (British V.I. colony to the N and E), which is situated 70 mi E of Puerto Rico; located W of Anegada Passage, a major channel connecting the Atlantic Ocean and Caribbean Sea. **Climate:** subtropical; sun tempered by gentle trade winds; humidity is low; avg. temperature 78°F. **Topography:** St. Thomas is mainly a ridge of hills running E-W and has little tillable land; St. Croix

rises abruptly in the N but slopes to flatlands and lagoons in the S; St. John has steep, lofty hills and valleys with little level tillable land. **Capital:** Charlotte Amalie on St. Thomas. **Chief airport:** Charlotte Amalie.

Economy. Chief industries: retail, petroleum, tourism, prof. consulting. **Chief manuf. goods:** rum, stone, glass and clay products, electronics, textiles. **Chief crops:** cucumbers, coconuts, mangoes, tomatoes, bananas. **Livestock** (2007): 699 chickens, 776 cattle, 2,981 sheep, 1,125 hogs/pigs, 2,331 goats. **Nonfuel minerals:** crushed stone, limestone, traprock. **Commercial fishing** (2011): $7.1 mil. **Chief port:** Charlotte Amalie. **Gross domestic product** (2012 est.): $4.2 bil. **Employment distrib.:** 28.2% govt.; 21.1% trade/trans./util.; 1.8% mfg.; 6.3% ed./health; 8.9% prof./bus. serv.; 19.1% leisure/hosp.; 5.7% finance; 4.2% constr./mining/log.; 2.1% info.; 2.6% other serv. **Unemployment** (June 2011): 9.4%. **Per capita pers. income** (2007): $19,787. **Broadband Internet:** 91.1%. **Commercial banks:** 4; deposits: $1.8 bil.

Higher education. 4-year public coll./univ.: 1; **2-yr. public:** 0; **4-yr. private:** 0.

Energy. Electricity production (2011 est.): 794 mil kWh.

Federal govt. Fed. civ. employees (Mar. 2013): 665; **avg. salary:** $60,079.

Misc. data. Motto: United in pride and hope. **Flower:** Yellow cedar. **Bird:** Yellow breast. **Song:** "Virgin Islands March."

Tourism. Attractions: St. Croix Isl.: Salt River Bay Natl. Historic Park and Ecological Preserve, Christiansted Natl. Historic Site. St. John and Hassel Isls.: Virgin Islands Natl. Park. St. Thomas Isl.: Blackbeard's Castle, Coral World Ocean Park, Magens Bay, 99 Steps. **Information:** USVI Division of Tourism, P.O. Box 6400, St. Thomas 00804; 1-800-372-USVI; www.visitusvi.com

History. The islands were visited by Columbus in 1493. Spanish forces, 1555, defeated the Caribes and claimed the territory; by 1596 the native population was annihilated. The first permanent settlement in the U.S. territory, 1672, was by the Danes; U.S. purchased the islands, 1917, for defense purposes.

The Virgin Islands has a republican form of government, headed by a governor and lieut. governor elected, since 1970, by popular vote for four-year terms. There is a 15-member unicameral legislature, elected by popular vote for a two-year terms. Residents of the V.I. have been U.S. citizens since 1927. Since 1973 they have elected a delegate to the U.S. House of Representatives, who has a voice but no vote, except in committees.

Website. www.gov.vi

Other Islands

Navassa lies between Haiti and Jamaica, 100 mi S of Guantánamo Bay, Cuba, in the Caribbean; it covers 1,147 acres, and is uninhabited. Claimed 1857, a USCG lighthouse was built 1917, now inoperative. Natl. Wildlife Refuge since 1999. Administered by the Dept. of Interior.

The three coral islands of **Wake Atoll—Wake, Wilkes,** and **Peale—**lie in the Pacific Ocean on a direct route from Hawaii to Hong Kong, about 2,300 mi W of Honolulu and 1,500 mi NE of Guam. The group is 4.5 mi long, 1.5 mi wide. Land area totals 2.5 sq mi. The U.S. annexed Wake Atoll Jan. 17, 1899. Japan occupied Wake 1941-45. Designated a National Historic Landmark in 1985. Wake is owned by the U.S. Air Force, administered by the Dept. of Interior, but used by the Army as a missile launch facility. The population consists of military personnel and contractors. Most infrastructure was damaged by super typhoon Ioke in 2006.

The following mostly uninhabited islands are part of the **Pacific/Remote Islands National Wildlife Refuge Complex,** along with Wake Atoll, administered by the Dept. of Interior: **Midway Atoll,** acquired in 1867, has three main islands—Sand, Spit, and Eastern—1,250 mi WNW of Honolulu, with an area of about 1,500 acres. Naval activity ended in 1997. Has the world's largest colony of Laysan albatross. **Johnston Atoll,** 800 mi WSW of Honolulu, is two natural and two artificial islands across 107 sq mi administered by the Navy. Johnston was a nuclear test site in 1958, 1962; the Army disposed of chemical weapons 1990-2000. Cleanup ended in 2005. **Kingman Reef** is a barren, coral atoll 932 mi S of Hawaii, annexed 1922. **Palmyra Atoll** is 54 islets over 753 sq mi, 1,052 mi S of Hawaii; annexed with Hawaii in 1898. Part privately owned by the Nature Conservancy. **Jarvis Island** covers 1,086 acres, 1,330 mi S of Honolulu near the equator. West of Jarvis are **Howland and Baker Islands,** 36 mi apart and about 1,600 mi SW of Honolulu.

Sources: Population: Decennial Census and Population Estimates Program, U.S. Census Bureau, U.S. Dept. of Commerce. Population is as of July 1, 2013; population rank is indicated within parentheses. **Pop. density** specifies the number of persons per square mile (sq mi) of land area. Unless otherwise noted, **all other figures** are estimates for 2008-12 from the American Community Survey, U.S. Census Bureau. **Racial distribution** categories are abbreviated; their full forms are white, black or African American, Asian, American Indian and Alaska Native, Native Hawaiian and Other Pacific Islander, some other race, two or more races. **Hispanic** or Latino persons may be of any race. **Language** is what is spoken at home; languages other than Spanish spoken by less than 5% of the population over age 5 are omitted. **Employment:** Bureau of Labor Statistics, U.S. Dept. of Labor, for 2013. **Per capita income:** Bureau of Economic Analysis, U.S. Dept. of Commerce; figures apply to MSAs for 2012. **Educational attainment** is the percentage of persons ages 25 and up who have graduated high school (HS) and who have a bachelor's degree or higher. **Avg. commute** is the time it takes for workers 16 years and over to travel from home to work. "Drive" includes only those who drive to work alone. Forms of transport used by less than 10% are omitted. **Avg. home:** National Association of Realtors®. Figures represent median 2013 sales price of existing single-family homes in the metropolitan area; data not available for all cities. **Avg. rent** is the median gross rent (rent asked plus est. avg. cost of utilities) per month. **Mayor** (or other city leader) and **website:** World Almanac research as of mid-2014; subject to change. A nonpartisan mayor is one whose party affiliation was not indicated on the ballot.

Included here are the 100 most populous U.S. cities, according to U.S. Census Bureau estimates released in May 2014. Most data are for the city proper; some, where noted, apply to the Metropolitan Statistical Area (MSA). Inc. = incorporated; est. = established.

Albuquerque, New Mexico

Population: 556,495 (32). **Pop. density:** 2,958. **Pop. change (2010-13):** 1.7%. **Area:** 188.1 sq mi. **Racial distribution:** 69.8% white; 3.3% black; 2.6% Asian; 4.4% Amer. Ind.; 0.1% Pac. Isl.; 16.0% other; 2+ races 3.9%. **Hispanic pop.:** 46.5%. **Foreign born:** 10.9%. **U.S. citizens:** 92.9%. **Language:** 70.1% English only; 24.4% Spanish.
Employment: 235,410 employed; 6.6% unemployed. **Per capita income:** $36,272; change (2011-12): 2.1%. **Below poverty level:** 17.3%; 13.4% of families. **Educational attainment:** 88.1% HS; 32.6% bachelor's. **Avg. commute:** 21.4 min. 79.4% drive; 10.1% carpool. **Housing units:** 239,718; 92.9% occupied. **Home ownership:** 60.4%. **Avg. home:** $174,300; change (2011-13): 3.8%. **Avg. rent:** $758.
Mayor: Richard J. Berry, nonpartisan
History: Founded 1706 by the Spanish; inc. 1890.
Website: www.cabq.gov

Anaheim, California

Population: 345,012 (56). **Pop. density:** 6,903. **Pop. change (2010-13):** 2.3%. **Area:** 50.0 sq mi. **Racial distribution:** 61.1% white; 2.6% black; 15.0% Asian; 0.3% Amer. Ind.; 0.5% Pac. Isl.; 17.5% other; 2+ races 3.0%. **Hispanic pop.:** 52.8%. **Foreign born:** 37.7%. **U.S. citizens:** 78.0%. **Language:** 39.1% English only; 44.4% Spanish.
Employment: 161,489 employed; 8.0% unemployed. **Per capita income:** $46,337; change (2011-12): 3.5%. **Below poverty level:** 15.6%; 12.7% of families. **Educational attainment:** 73.8% HS; 23.8% bachelor's. **Avg. commute:** 26.7 min. 75.6% drive; 12.7% carpool. **Housing units:** 104,323; 94.4% occupied. **Home ownership:** 48.4%. **Avg. home:** $405,580; change (2011-13): 31.8%. **Avg. rent:** $1,339.
Mayor: Tom Tait, nonpartisan
History: Founded 1857; inc. 1870. Home of Disneyland, the Anaheim Ducks, and the Los Angeles Angels.
Website: www.anaheim.net

Anchorage, Alaska

Population: 300,950 (63). **Pop. density:** 177. **Pop. change (2010-13):** 2.6%. **Area:** 1,704.8 sq mi. **Racial distribution:** 66.8% white; 5.8% black; 8.0% Asian; 6.6% Amer. Ind.; 2.0% Pac. Isl.; 1.5% other; 2+ races 9.3%. **Hispanic pop.:** 7.7%. **Foreign born:** 9.3%. **U.S. citizens:** 95.7%. **Language:** 82.8% English only; 4.7% Spanish.
Employment: 147,796 employed; 5.0% unemployed. **Per capita income:** $52,360; change (2011-12): 3.1%. **Below poverty level:** 7.7%; 5.5% of families. **Educational attainment:** 92.3% HS; 32.8% bachelor's. **Avg. commute:** 19.0 min. 75.4% drive; 13.0% carpool. **Housing units:** 113,070; 93.3% occupied. **Home ownership:** 61.3%. **Avg. rent:** $1,104.
Mayor: Dan Sullivan, Republican
History: Founded 1914 as a construction camp for railroad; HQ of Alaska Defense Command, WWII. Severely damaged in earthquake, 1964. Current population center of Alaska.
Website: www.muni.org

Arlington, Texas

Population: 379,577 (50). **Pop. density:** 3,958. **Pop. change (2010-13):** 3.6%. **Area:** 95.9 sq mi. **Racial distribution:** 64.4% white; 19.3% black; 7.2% Asian; 0.5% Amer. Ind.; 0.1% Pac. Isl.; 6.4% other; 2+ races 2.2%. **Hispanic pop.:** 28.0%. **Foreign born:** 19.8%. **U.S. citizens:** 87.0%. **Language:** 67.7% English only; 22.3% Spanish.
Employment: 195,202 employed; 5.9% unemployed. **Per capita income:** $46,136; change (2011-12): 3.4%. **Below poverty level:** 15.9%; 12.6% of families. **Educational attainment:** 84.2% HS; 28.7% bachelor's. **Avg. commute:** 25.7 min. 80.6% drive; 12.5% carpool. **Housing units:** 145,750; 90.7% occupied. **Home ownership:** 57.7%. **Avg. home:** $175,600; change (2011-13): 17.9%. **Avg. rent:** $835.
Mayor: Robert N. Cluck, nonpartisan
History: Settled in 1840s; inc. 1884.
Website: www.arlingtontx.gov

Atlanta, Georgia

Population: 447,841 (40). **Pop. density:** 3,365. **Pop. change (2010-13):** 5.9%. **Area:** 133.1 sq mi. **Racial distribution:** 39.0% white; 53.8% black; 3.3% Asian; 0.2% Amer. Ind.; <0.05% Pac. Isl.; 1.8% other; 2+ races 1.8%. **Hispanic pop.:** 5.4%. **Foreign born:** 7.8%. **U.S. citizens:** 94.4%. **Language:** 89.2% English only; 5.1% Spanish.
Employment: 175,847 employed; 10.1% unemployed. **Per capita income:** $40,963; change (2011-12): 2.7%. **Below poverty level:** 24.3%; 19.9% of families. **Educational attainment:** 87.4% HS; 46.2% bachelor's. **Avg. commute:** 25.5 min. 66.9% drive; 11.3% public trans. **Housing units:** 224,615; 79.7% occupied. **Home ownership:** 46.0%. **Avg. home:** $139,500; change (2011-13): 41.5%. **Avg. rent:** $931.
Mayor: Kasim Reed, nonpartisan
History: Founded as Terminus 1837; renamed Atlanta 1845; inc. 1847. Played major role in Civil War; became permanent state capital 1877. Birthplace of civil rights movement. Host to 1996 Centennial Olympic Games.
Website: www.atlantaga.gov

Aurora, Colorado

Population: 345,803 (55). **Pop. density:** 2,248. **Pop. change (2010-13):** 6.1%. **Area:** 153.9 sq mi. **Racial distribution:** 66.1% white; 15.7% black; 4.8% Asian; 1.2% Amer. Ind.; 0.3% Pac. Isl.; 7.0% other; 2+ races 4.9%. **Hispanic pop.:** 28.5%. **Foreign born:** 20.7%. **U.S. citizens:** 85.4%. **Language:** 68.4% English only; 21.2% Spanish.
Employment: 169,275 employed; 7.1% unemployed. **Per capita income:** $50,936; change (2011-12): 3.7%. **Below poverty level:** 16.2%; 12.8% of families. **Educational attainment:** 85.6% HS; 26.6% bachelor's. **Avg. commute:** 28.3 min. 76.3% drive; 11.9% carpool. **Housing units:** 132,023; 92.5% occupied. **Home ownership:** 59.9%. **Avg. home:** $280,600; change (2011-13): 21.3%. **Avg. rent:** $916.
Mayor: Steve Hogan, nonpartisan
History: Founded 1891; originally called Fletcher; renamed Aurora 1907; inc. 1929. Early growth stimulated by presence of military bases; fast-growing trade, technology, and med. science center.
Website: www.auroragov.org

Austin, Texas

Population: 885,400 (11). **Pop. density:** 2,855. **Pop. change (2010-13):** 8.6%. **Area:** 310.2 sq mi. **Racial distribution:** 71.0% white; 8.2% black; 6.2% Asian; 0.6% Amer. Ind.; 0.1% Pac. Isl.; 11.3% other; 2+ races 2.6%. **Hispanic pop.:** 35.2%. **Foreign born:** 19.1%. **U.S. citizens:** 85.4%. **Language:** 66.8% English only; 25.7% Spanish.
Employment: 455,664 employed; 4.9% unemployed. **Per capita income:** $42,902; change (2011-12): 3.0%. **Below poverty level:** 19.4%; 13.8% of families. **Educational attainment:** 86.1% HS; 44.8% bachelor's. **Avg. commute:** 22.8 min. 71.7% drive; 10.9% carpool. **Housing units:** 354,901; 91.9% occupied. **Home ownership:** 45.1%. **Avg. home:** $222,900; change (2011-13): 15.4%. **Avg. rent:** $950.
Mayor: Lee Leffingwell, nonpartisan
History: First permanent settlement 1835; capital of Rep. of Texas 1839; named after Stephen Austin; inc. 1840.
Website: www.austintexas.gov

Bakersfield, California

Population: 363,630 (52). **Pop. density:** 2,449. **Pop. change (2010-13):** 4.2%. **Area:** 148.5 sq mi. **Racial distribution:** 64.5% white; 8.3% black; 6.1% Asian; 1.2% Amer. Ind.; 0.1% Pac. Isl.; 15.3% other; 2+ races 4.6%. **Hispanic pop.:** 45.2%. **Foreign born:** 18.6%. **U.S. citizens:** 88.5%. **Language:** 62.9% English only; 30.4% Spanish.
Employment: 152,568 employed; 8.2% unemployed. **Per capita income:** $34,453; change (2011-12): 5.1%. **Below**

poverty level: 19.3%; 15.4% of families. Educational attainment: 78.2% HS; 19.9% bachelor's. Avg. commute: 22.7 min. 78.9% drive; 13.9% carpool. Housing units: 118,222; 92.6% occupied. Home ownership: 58.1%. Avg. rent: $970.
Mayor: Harvey L. Hall, nonpartisan
History: Named after Col. Thomas Baker, an early settler; inc. 1898.
Website: www.bakersfieldcity.us

Baltimore, Maryland

Population: 622,104 (26). Pop. density: 7,686. Pop. change (2010-13): 0.1%. Area: 80.9 sq mi. Racial distribution: 30.1% white; 63.7% black; 2.4% Asian; 0.3% Amer. Ind.; <0.05% Pac. Isl.; 1.3% other; 2+ races 2.2%. Hispanic pop.: 4.1%. Foreign born: 7.4%. U.S. citizens: 95.4%. Language: 91.1% English only; 3.7% Spanish.
Employment: 250,660 employed; 9.6% unemployed. Per capita income: $54,201; change (2011-12): 3.4%. Below poverty level: 23.4%; 18.8% of families. Educational attainment: 79.6% HS; 26.1% bachelor's. Avg. commute: 30.0 min. 59.6% drive; 18.2% public trans.; 10.7% carpool. Housing units: 296,437; 81.2% occupied. Home ownership: 48.8%. Avg. home: $251,900; change (2011-13): 9.5%. Avg. rent: $909.
Mayor: Stephanie C. Rawlings-Blake, Democrat
History: Founded by Maryland legislature 1729; inc. 1797. War of 1812 British artillery barrage of Ft. McHenry (1814) inspired Francis Scott Key to write "Star-Spangled Banner." Birthplace of America's railroads 1828; rebuilt after fire 1904. Site of National Aquarium.
Website: www.baltimorecity.gov

Baton Rouge, Louisiana

Population: 229,426 (93). Pop. density: 2,963. Pop. change (2010-13): -0.1%. Area: 77.4 sq mi. Racial distribution: 39.6% white; 54.7% black; 3.3% Asian; 0.2% Amer. Ind.; <0.05% Pac. Isl.; 0.8% other; 2+ races 1.5%. Hispanic pop.: 3.5%. Foreign born: 5.2%. U.S. citizens: 96.7%. Language: 91.8% English only; 3.0% Spanish.
Employment: 102,605 employed; 6.7% unemployed. Per capita income: $40,245; change (2011-12): 4.2%. Below poverty level: 24.7%; 17.1% of families. Educational attainment: 84.8% HS; 32.7% bachelor's. Avg. commute: 20.4 min. 78.3% drive; 12.0% carpool. Housing units: 100,091; 87.4% occupied. Home ownership: 51.5%. Avg. home: $170,000; change (2011-13): 4.0%. Avg. rent: $773.
Mayor-President: Melvin "Kip" Holden, Democrat
History: Claimed by Spain at time of Louisiana Purchase 1803; independence by rebellion 1810; inc. as town 1817. Became state capital 1849; Union-held most of Civil War.
Website: www.brgov.com

Boise, Idaho

Population: 214,237 (98). Pop. density: 2,662. Pop. change (2010-13): 3.8%. Area: 80.5 sq mi. Racial distribution: 90.3% white; 1.3% black; 3.6% Asian; 0.7% Amer. Ind.; 0.1% Pac. Isl.; 1.1% other; 2+ races 2.7%. Hispanic pop.: 7.0%. Foreign born: 7.6%. U.S. citizens: 95.5%. Language: 89.9% English only; 4.3% Spanish.
Employment: 105,307 employed; 5.6% unemployed. Per capita income: $35,354; change (2011-12): 2.4%. Below poverty level: 14.7%; 9.8% of families. Educational attainment: 93.5% HS; 37.4% bachelor's. Avg. commute: 17.5 min. 78.6% drive. Housing units: 91,747; 93.8% occupied. Home ownership: 60.8%. Avg. home: $163,700; change (2011-13): 41.9%. Avg. rent: $780.
Mayor: David H. Bieter, nonpartisan
History: Gold discovered in area 1862; inc., proclaimed capital of Idaho Terr. 1864; on Oregon Trail.
Website: www.cityofboise.org

Boston, Massachusetts

Population: 645,966 (24). Pop. density: 13,356. Pop. change (2010-13): 4.1%. Area: 48.4 sq mi. Racial distribution: 53.8% white; 25.4% black; 9.1% Asian; 0.3% Amer. Ind.; <0.05% Pac. Isl.; 7.1% other; 2+ races 4.2%. Hispanic pop.: 17.4%. Foreign born: 26.7%. U.S. citizens: 85.3%. Language: 63.9% English only; 15.4% Spanish.
Employment: 301,078 employed; 6.8% unemployed. Per capita income: $60,387; change (2011-12): 3.1%. Below poverty level: 21.2%; 15.7% of families. Educational attainment: 84.5% HS; 43.4% bachelor's. Avg. commute: 28.7 min. 38.5% drive; 33.0% public trans.; 15.1% walk. Housing units: 272,587; 91.2% occupied. Home ownership: 34.2%. Avg. home: $375,900; change (2011-13): 8.6%. Avg. rent: $1,265.
Mayor: Martin J. Walsh, Democrat
History: Settled 1630 by John Winthrop; capital of Mass. Bay Colony. Figured strongly in American Revolution, earning distinction as the "Cradle of Liberty"; inc. 1822.
Website: www.cityofboston.gov

Buffalo, New York

Population: 258,959 (73). Pop. density: 6,412. Pop. change (2010-13): -0.8%. Area: 40.4 sq mi. Racial distribution: 51.4% white; 37.9% black; 3.3% Asian; 0.6% Amer. Ind.; <0.05% Pac. Isl.; 3.7% other; 2+ races 3.1%. Hispanic pop.: 9.3%. Foreign born: 7.7%. U.S. citizens: 95.7%. Language: 85.2% English only; 6.7% Spanish.
Employment: 103,138 employed; 9.7% unemployed. Per capita income: $42,788; change (2011-12): 3.1%. Below poverty level: 30.1%; 26.4% of families. Educational attainment: 81.7% HS; 23.4% bachelor's. Avg. commute: 20.4 min. 67.1% drive; 12.6% public trans. Housing units: 135,623; 82.7% occupied. Home ownership: 42.3%. Avg. home: $131,000; change (2011-13): 9.3%. Avg. rent: $672.
Mayor: Byron W. Brown, Democrat
History: Settled 1780 by Seneca Indians; raided twice by British in War of 1812. Served as western terminus for Erie Canal; became a center for trade and manufacturing; inc. 1832. A last stop on the Underground Railroad. Key point for Canada-U.S. political, trade, and social relations.
Website: www.ci.buffalo.ny.us

Chandler, Arizona

Population: 249,146 (79). Pop. density: 3,857. Pop. change (2010-13): 5.3%. Area: 64.6 sq mi. Racial distribution: 79.0% white; 5.3% black; 7.9% Asian; 1.2% Amer. Ind.; 0.1% Pac. Isl.; 2.6% other; 2+ races 3.8%. Hispanic pop.: 23.1%. Foreign born: 13.9%. U.S. citizens: 92.7%. Language: 77.5% English only; 13.2% Spanish.
Employment: 126,448 employed; 5.7% unemployed. Per capita income: $38,006; change (2011-12): 2.2%. Below poverty level: 8.6%; 6.4% of families. Educational attainment: 92.0% HS; 39.7% bachelor's. Avg. commute: 23.8 min. 78.8% drive; 11.5% carpool. Housing units: 95,000; 91.0% occupied. Home ownership: 64.7%. Avg. home: $183,600; change (2011-13): 59.0%. Avg. rent: $1,068.
Mayor: Jay Tibshraeny, nonpartisan
History: Formed 1912; population doubled in 1990s as "the high-tech oasis of the Silicon Desert."
Website: www.chandleraz.gov

Charlotte, North Carolina

Population: 792,862 (16). Pop. density: 2,613. Pop. change (2010-13): 7.3%. Area: 303.4 sq mi. Racial distribution: 53.1% white; 34.6% black; 5.1% Asian; 0.4% Amer. Ind.; 0.1% Pac. Isl.; 4.3% other; 2+ races 2.5%. Hispanic pop.: 13.1%. Foreign born: 15.1%. U.S. citizens: 89.4%. Language: 80.4% English only; 11.5% Spanish.
Employment: 371,062 employed; 7.1% unemployed. Per capita income: $40,465; change (2011-12): 4.0%. Below poverty level: 16.0%; 12.4% of families. Educational attainment: 88.0% HS; 39.4% bachelor's. Avg. commute: 24.4 min. 76.2% drive; 11.2% carpool. Housing units: 322,318; 90.6% occupied. Home ownership: 57.6%. Avg. home: $174,200; change (2011-13): 17.0%. Avg. rent: $868.
Mayor: Anthony R. Foxx, Democrat
History: Settled by Scotch-Irish immigrants 1740s; inc. 1768 and named after Queen Charlotte, wife of English King George III. Scene of first major U.S. gold discovery 1799.
Website: charmeck.org

Chesapeake, Virginia

Population: 230,571 (91). Pop. density: 677. Pop. change (2010-13): 3.1%. Area: 340.8 sq mi. Racial distribution: 62.6% white; 29.9% black; 3.1% Asian; 0.4% Amer. Ind.; 0.1% Pac. Isl.; 1.4% other; 2+ races 2.5%. Hispanic pop.: 4.4%. Foreign born: 4.8%. U.S. citizens: 97.9%. Language: 92.7% English only; 3.3% Spanish.
Employment: 112,498 employed; 5.7% unemployed. Per capita income: $44,321; change (2011-12): 2.9%. Below poverty level: 8.3%; 6.7% of families. Educational attainment: 89.6% HS; 28.4% bachelor's. Avg. commute: 24.4 min. 86.2% drive. Housing units: 83,541; 95.0% occupied. Home ownership: 72.9%. Avg. home: $193,000; change (2011-13): 5.5%. Avg. rent: $1,113.
Mayor: Alan P. Krasnoff, Independent
History: Region settled in 1620s with first English colonies on banks of Elizabeth R. Home to Great Dismal Swamp Canal, first envisioned by George Washington in 1763. Battle of Great Bridge fought here Dec. 1775; inc. 1963.
Website: www.cityofchesapeake.net

Chicago, Illinois

Population: 2,718,782 (3). Pop. density: 11,942. Pop. change (2010-13): 0.8%. Area: 227.7 sq mi. Racial distribution: 47.0% white; 32.9% black; 5.6% Asian; 0.3% Amer. Ind.; <0.05% Pac. Isl.; 12.3% other; 2+ races 1.9%. Hispanic pop.: 28.4%. Foreign born: 21.2%. U.S. citizens: 87.4%. Language: 64.2% English only; 24.4% Spanish.

Employment: 1,143,944 employed; 10.5% unemployed. **Per capita income:** $48,305; change (2011-12): 4.3%. **Below poverty level:** 22.1%; 18.3% of families. **Educational attainment:** 80.5% HS; 33.6% bachelor's. **Avg. commute:** 33.5 min. 50.3% drive; 26.7% public trans. **Housing units:** 1,197,248; 86.0% occupied. **Home ownership:** 46.1%. **Avg. home** $191,300; change (2011-13): 8.4%. **Avg. rent:** $935.
Mayor: Rahm Emanuel, nonpartisan
History: Site acquired from Indians 1795; significant white settlement began with completion of Erie Canal 1825; chartered as city 1837. Boomed with arrival of railroads and canal to Mississippi R.; one-third of city destroyed by fire 1871.
Website: www.cityofchicago.org

Chula Vista, California

Population: 256,780 (75). **Pop. density:** 5,174. **Pop. change (2010-13):** 4.9%. **Area:** 49.6 sq mi. **Racial distribution:** 67.1% white; 4.8% black; 14.4% Asian; 0.7% Amer. Ind.; 0.4% Pac. Isl.; 7.7% other; 2+ races 4.9%. **Hispanic pop.:** 57.0%. **Foreign born:** 30.7%. **U.S. citizens:** 86.2%. **Language:** 43.9% English only; 45.3% Spanish; 6.3% Tagalog.
Employment: 84,910 employed; 8.8% unemployed. **Per capita income:** $49,719; change (2011-12): 3.4%. **Below poverty level:** 10.4%; 8.9% of families. **Educational attainment:** 81.9% HS; 27.1% bachelor's. **Avg. commute:** 26.4 min. 78.8% drive; 11.1% carpool. **Housing units:** 82,811; 89.9% occupied. **Home ownership:** 59.8%. **Avg. home:** $464,280; change (2011-13): 25.4%. **Avg. rent:** $1,242.
Mayor: Cheryl Cox, nonpartisan
History: Visited by Spanish in 1542; became part of Spanish land grant in 1795; brought into the U.S. during the Mexican War in 1847; inc. 1911. WWII brought aircraft industry and growth.
Website: www.chulavistaca.gov

Cincinnati, Ohio

Population: 297,517 (65). **Pop. density:** 3,817. **Pop. change (2010-13):** 0.2%. **Area:** 77.9 sq mi. **Racial distribution:** 50.5% white; 44.1% black; 1.8% Asian; 0.3% Amer. Ind.; <0.05% Pac. Isl.; 0.9% other; 2+ races 2.4%. **Hispanic pop.:** 2.9%. **Foreign born:** 5.0%. **U.S. citizens:** 96.7%. **Language:** 92.6% English only; 3.0% Spanish.
Employment: 131,067 employed; 7.9% unemployed. **Per capita income:** $23,454; change (2011-12): 4.1%. **Below poverty level:** 29.4%; 23.7% of families. **Educational attainment:** 83.9% HS; 31.3% bachelor's. **Avg. commute:** 22.4 min. 70.6% drive; 10.3% carpool. **Housing units:** 164,784; 78.9% occupied. **Home ownership:** 40.5%. **Avg. home** $135,500; change (2011-13): 10.8%. **Avg. rent:** $630.
Mayor: John Cranley, nonpartisan
History: Founded 1788; named after the Society of Cincinnati, an organization of Revolutionary War officers; chartered as village 1802; inc. 1819.
Website: www.cincinnati-oh.gov

Cleveland, Ohio

Population: 390,113 (48). **Pop. density:** 5,020. **Pop. change (2010-13):** −1.5%. **Area:** 77.7 sq mi. **Racial distribution:** 40.6% white; 52.6% black; 1.7% Asian; 0.3% Amer. Ind.; <0.05% Pac. Isl.; 2.0% other; 2+ races 2.7%. **Hispanic pop.:** 9.7%. **Foreign born:** 4.6%. **U.S. citizens:** 97.6%. **Language:** 88.1% English only; 7.3% Spanish.
Employment: 145,026 employed; 9.8% unemployed. **Per capita income:** $44,775; change (2011-12): 4.1%. **Below poverty level:** 34.2%; 29.5% of families. **Educational attainment:** 76.7% HS; 14.0% bachelor's. **Avg. commute:** 24.2 min. 69.9% drive; 11.1% public trans. **Housing units:** 214,504; 78.3% occupied. **Home ownership:** 45.3%. **Avg. home:** $117,700; change (2011-13): 12.0%. **Avg. rent:** $656.
Mayor: Frank G. Jackson, nonpartisan
History: Surveyed in 1796; given recognition as village 1815; inc. 1836; annexed Ohio City 1854.
Website: www.city.cleveland.oh.us

Colorado Springs, Colorado

Population: 439,886 (41). **Pop. density:** 2,257. **Pop. change (2010-13):** 4.7%. **Area:** 194.9 sq mi. **Racial distribution:** 80.7% white; 6.5% black; 2.8% Asian; 0.8% Amer. Ind.; 0.3% Pac. Isl.; 4.3% other; 2+ races 4.8%. **Hispanic pop.:** 16.3%. **Foreign born:** 8.1%. **U.S. citizens:** 95.7%. **Language:** 87.4% English only; 7.7% Spanish.
Employment: 192,009 employed; 7.9% unemployed. **Per capita income:** $40,980; change (2011-12): 2.2%. **Below poverty level:** 13.7%; 9.9% of families. **Educational attainment:** 92.8% HS; 36.3% bachelor's. **Avg. commute:** 20.9 min. 79.2% drive; 10.2% carpool. **Housing units:** 178,842; 92.8% occupied. **Home ownership:** 59.8%. **Avg. home:** $216,800; change (2011-13): 15.8%. **Avg. rent:** $842.
Mayor: Steve Bach, nonpartisan
History: Founded 1871 at the foot of Pike's Peak; inc. 1872.
Website: coloradosprings.gov

Columbus, Ohio

Population: 822,553 (15). **Pop. density:** 3,775. **Pop. change (2010-13):** 4.1%. **Area:** 217.9 sq mi. **Racial distribution:** 62.6% white; 27.7% black; 4.2% Asian; 0.3% Amer. Ind.; <0.05% Pac. Isl.; 1.9% other; 2+ races 3.3%. **Hispanic pop.:** 5.4%. **Foreign born** 10.5%. **U.S. citizens:** 93.3%. **Language:** 86.6% English only; 4.4% Spanish.
Employment: 410,359 employed; 6.2% unemployed. **Per capita income:** $42,728; change (2011-12): 4.1%. **Below poverty level:** 22.0%; 16.8% of families. **Educational attainment:** 88.2% HS; 32.9% bachelor's. **Avg. commute:** 21.2 min. 80.8% drive. **Housing units:** 374,446; 86.3% occupied. **Home ownership:** 47.8%. **Avg. home:** $142,800; change (2011-13): 15.3%. **Avg. rent:** $794.
Mayor: Michael B. Coleman, Democrat
History: First settlement 1797; laid out as new state capital 1812 with current name; inc. 1834.
Website: www.columbus.gov

Corpus Christi, Texas

Population: 316,381 (60). **Pop. density:** 1,971. **Pop. change (2010-13):** 3.6%. **Area:** 160.5 sq mi. **Racial distribution:** 85.4% white; 4.5% black; 1.7% Asian; 0.3% Amer. Ind.; <0.05% Pac. Isl.; 5.9% other; 2+ races 2.1%. **Hispanic pop.:** 59.8%. **Foreign born:** 7.8%. **U.S. citizens:** 95.4%. **Language:** 60.8% English only; 36.6% Spanish.
Employment: 152,661 employed; 5.6% unemployed. **Per capita income:** $40,796; change (2011-12): 3.9%. **Below poverty level:** 18.0%; 14.1% of families. **Educational attainment:** 80.0% HS; 20.7% bachelor's. **Avg. commute:** 19.2 min. 78.8% drive; 11.3% carpool. **Housing units:** 124,756; 88.3% occupied. **Home ownership:** 58.1%. **Avg. home:** $152,600; change (2011-13): 13.7%. **Avg. rent:** $840.
Mayor: Nelda Martinez, nonpartisan
History: Settled 1839; inc. 1852. One of the largest U.S. ports.
Website: www.cctexas.com

Dallas, Texas

Population: 1,257,676 (9). **Pop. density:** 3,684. **Pop. change (2010-13):** 4.8%. **Area:** 341.4 sq mi. **Racial distribution:** 55.8% white; 24.6% black; 2.9% Asian; 0.3% Amer. Ind.; <0.05% Pac. Isl.; 14.3% other; 2+ races 2.0%. **Hispanic pop.:** 42.0%. **Foreign born** 24.5%. **U.S. citizens:** 80.6%. **Language:** 57.6% English only; 37.5% Spanish.
Employment: 548,575 employed; 6.8% unemployed. **Per capita income:** $46,136; change (2011-12): 3.4%. **Below poverty level:** 23.6%; 20.1% of families. **Educational attainment:** 73.8% HS; 29.0% bachelor's. **Avg. commute:** 25.1 min. 77.3% drive; 11.2% carpool. **Housing units:** 520,384; 87.8% occupied. **Home ownership:** 44.4%. **Avg. home:** $175,600; change (2011-13): 17.9%. **Avg. rent:** $822.
Mayor: Mike Rawlings, nonpartisan
History: First settled 1841; platted 1846; inc. 1871. Developed as financial and commercial center of Southwest; headquarters of regional Federal Reserve Bank; major center for distribution and high-tech manufacturing.
Website: www.dallascityhall.com

Denver, Colorado

Population: 649,495 (22). **Pop. density:** 4,244. **Pop. change (2010-13):** 7.6%. **Area:** 153.0 sq mi. **Racial distribution:** 73.6% white; 10.1% black; 3.4% Asian; 1.2% Amer. Ind.; 0.1% Pac. Isl.; 8.4% other; 2+ races 3.2%. **Hispanic pop.:** 31.8%. **Foreign born:** 16.1%. **U.S. citizens:** 88.9%. **Language:** 72.7% English only; 20.6% Spanish.
Employment: 310,758 employed; 7.0% unemployed. **Per capita income:** $50,936; change (2011-12): 3.7%. **Below poverty level:** 18.9%; 14.2% of families. **Educational attainment:** 85.1% HS; 42.2% bachelor's. **Avg. commute:** 24.8 min. 69.1% drive. **Housing units:** 285,495; 91.7% occupied. **Home ownership:** 50.4%. **Avg. home:** $280,600; change (2011-13): 21.3%. **Avg. rent:** $863.
Mayor: Michael B. Hancock, nonpartisan
History: Settled 1858 by gold prospectors and miners; inc. 1861; became territorial capital 1867. Growth spurred by gold and silver boom. Became financial, industrial, cultural center of Rocky Mt. region.
Website: www.denvergov.org

Detroit, Michigan

Population: 688,701 (18). **Pop. density:** 4,964. **Pop. change (2010-13):** −3.2%. **Area:** 138.8 sq mi. **Racial distribution:** 11.6% white; 82.2% black; 1.2% Asian; 0.3% Amer. Ind.; <0.05% Pac. Isl.; 2.8% other; 2+ races 1.9%. **Hispanic pop.:** 6.9%. **Foreign born:** 5.1%. **U.S. citizens:** 96.5%. **Language:** 90.5% English only; 5.8% Spanish.
Employment: 284,587 employed; 16.9% unemployed. **Per capita income:** $42,261; change (2011-12): 3.6%. **Below poverty level:** 38.1%; 33.0% of families. **Educational attainment:** 77.2% HS; 12.3% bachelor's. **Avg. commute:** 26.4 min. 70.9%

drive; 11.9% carpool. **Housing units:** 363,010; 71.3% occupied. **Home ownership:** 52.6%. **Avg. home:** $63,400 (2012). **Avg. rent:** $762.
Mayor: Mike Duggan, nonpartisan
History: Founded by French 1701; controlled by British 1760; acquired by U.S. 1796. Destroyed by fire 1805; fought over during War of 1812; inc. 1815; capital of state 1837-47. Auto manufacturing began 1890.
Website: www.detroitmi.gov

Durham, North Carolina

Population: 245,475 (82). **Pop. density:** 2,262. **Pop. change (2010-13):** 7.1%. **Area:** 108.5 sq mi. **Racial distribution:** 45.5% white; 40.2% black; 4.8% Asian; 0.4% Amer. Ind.; <0.05% Pac. Isl.; 6.1% other; 2+ races 3.0%. **Hispanic pop.:** 13.5%. **Foreign born:** 14.5%. **U.S. citizens:** 89.2%. **Language:** 79.8% English only; 12.7% Spanish.
Employment: 115,682 employed; 6.0% unemployed. **Per capita income:** $44,294; change (2011-12): 2.7%. **Below poverty level:** 19.4%; 13.6% of families. **Educational attainment:** 86.6% HS; 46.6% bachelor's. **Avg. commute:** 21.1 min. 74.1% drive; 13.3% carpool. **Housing units:** 104,554; 90.5% occupied. **Home ownership:** 50.6%. **Avg. home:** $192,700; change (2011-13): 5.1%. **Avg. rent:** $833.
Mayor: William V. Bell, nonpartisan
History: Inc. 1869. Trinity College moved to Durham in 1892, renamed Duke Univ. in 1924.
Website: durhamnc.gov

El Paso, Texas

Population: 674,433 (19). **Pop. density:** 2,630. **Pop. change (2010-13):** 3.5%. **Area:** 256.4 sq mi. **Racial distribution:** 81.1% white; 3.3% black; 1.2% Asian; 0.5% Amer. Ind.; 0.1% Pac. Isl.; 11.3% other; 2+ races 2.4%. **Hispanic pop.:** 80.1%. **Foreign born:** 25.1%. **U.S. citizens:** 86.1%. **Language:** 28.4% English only; 69.4% Spanish.
Employment: 251,852 employed; 8.1% unemployed. **Per capita income:** $30,186; change (2011-12): 3.0%. **Below poverty level:** 22.3%; 19.2% of families. **Educational attainment:** 75.9% HS; 22.4% bachelor's. **Avg. commute:** 22.4 min. 79.7% drive; 11.1% carpool. **Housing units:** 230,031; 93.1% occupied. **Home ownership:** 60.0%. **Avg. home:** $141,200; change (2011-13): 5.1%. **Avg. rent:** $697.
Mayor: Oscar Leeser, nonpartisan
History: First settled 1598; inc. 1873. Arrival of railroad, 1881, boosted city's population and industries.
Website: www.elpasotexas.gov

Fort Wayne, Indiana

Population: 256,496 (76). **Pop. density:** 2,318. **Pop. change (2010-13):** 1.1%. **Area:** 110.6 sq mi. **Racial distribution:** 74.7% white; 15.8% black; 3.0% Asian; 0.4% Amer. Ind.; 0.1% Pac. Isl.; 3.0% other; 2+ races 3.2%. **Hispanic pop.:** 7.8%. **Foreign born:** 7.2%. **U.S. citizens:** 95.4%. **Language:** 89.7% English only; 5.7% Spanish.
Employment: 112,227 employed; 7.7% unemployed. **Per capita income:** $37,226; change (2011-12): 4.6%. **Below poverty level:** 17.5%; 13.5% of families. **Educational attainment:** 88.0% HS; 25.6% bachelor's. **Avg. commute:** 19.7 min. 84.9% drive. **Housing units:** 113,988; 88.7% occupied. **Home ownership:** 64.1%. **Avg. home:** $106,600; change (2011-13): 11.7%. **Avg. rent:** $644.
Mayor: Tom Henry, Democrat
History: French fort 1680; U.S. fort 1794; settled by 1832; inc. 1840 prior to Wabash-Erie Canal completion in 1843.
Website: www.cityoffortwayne.org

Fort Worth, Texas

Population: 792,727 (17). **Pop. density:** 2,327. **Pop. change (2010-13):** 6.3%. **Area:** 340.7 sq mi. **Racial distribution:** 65.2% white; 18.8% black; 3.7% Asian; 0.6% Amer. Ind.; 0.1% Pac. Isl.; 9.3% other; 2+ races 2.3%. **Hispanic pop.:** 34.0%. **Foreign born:** 17.7%. **U.S. citizens:** 87.2%. **Language:** 67.3% English only; 27.5% Spanish.
Employment: 344,581 employed; 6.3% unemployed. **Per capita income:** $46,136; change (2011-12): 3.4%. **Below poverty level:** 18.7%; 14.9% of families. **Educational attainment:** 78.9% HS; 26.0% bachelor's. **Avg. commute:** 25.9 min. 81.4% drive; 11.3% carpool. **Housing units:** 291,697; 89.7% occupied. **Home ownership:** 59.1%. **Avg. home:** $175,600; change (2011-13): 17.9%. **Avg. rent:** $843.
Mayor: Betsy Price, nonpartisan
History: Established as military post 1849; inc. 1873; oil discovered 1917.
Website: fortworthtexas.gov

Fremont, California

Population: 224,922 (97). **Pop. density:** 2,904. **Pop. change (2010-13):** 4.8%. **Area:** 77.5 sq mi. **Racial distribution:** 31.9% white; 3.6% black; 50.3% Asian; 0.6% Amer. Ind.; 0.4% Pac. Isl.;

7.4% other; 2+ races 5.7%. **Hispanic pop.:** 14.9%. **Foreign born:** 43.3%. **U.S. citizens:** 81.0%. **Language:** 42.3% English only; 15.9% Chinese; 9.8% Spanish; 6.9% Hindi.
Employment: 107,439 employed; 5.3% unemployed. **Per capita income:** $66,591; change (2011-12): 5.8%. **Below poverty level:** 5.8%; 3.6% of families. **Educational attainment:** 90.5% HS; 49.5% bachelor's. **Avg. commute:** 29.4 min. 74.8% drive; 10.9% carpool. **Housing units:** 74,961; 93.3% occupied. **Home ownership:** 63.5%. **Avg. home:** $679,240; change (2011-13): 40.5%. **Avg. rent:** $1,514.
Mayor: Bill Harrison, nonpartisan
History: Area first settled by Spanish 1769; inc. 1956 with consolidation of five communities.
Website: www.fremont.gov

Fresno, California

Population: 509,924 (34). **Pop. density:** 4,504. **Pop. change (2010-13):** 2.6%. **Area:** 113.2 sq mi. **Racial distribution:** 53.2% white; 7.7% black; 12.6% Asian; 0.9% Amer. Ind.; 0.2% Pac. Isl.; 20.8% other; 2+ races 4.6%. **Hispanic pop.:** 46.8%. **Foreign born:** 21.2%. **U.S. citizens:** 86.5%. **Language:** 57.9% English only; 28.6% Spanish.
Employment: 207,183 employed; 12.1% unemployed. **Per capita income:** $34,074; change (2011-12): 2.8%. **Below poverty level:** 27.5%; 22.4% of families. **Educational attainment:** 74.7% HS; 20.1% bachelor's. **Avg. commute:** 21.5 min. 77.3% drive; 11.7% carpool. **Housing units:** 171,841; 91.7% occupied. **Home ownership:** 48.4%. **Avg. home:** $874.
Mayor: Ashley Swearengin, nonpartisan
History: Founded 1872; inc. 1885.
Website: www.fresno.gov

Garland, Texas

Population: 234,566 (88). **Pop. density:** 4,113. **Pop. change (2010-13):** 3.2%. **Area:** 57.0 sq mi. **Racial distribution:** 45.9% white; 13.4% black; 10.1% Asian; 0.4% Amer. Ind.; 0.1% Pac. Isl.; 23.8% other; 2+ races 6.2%. **Hispanic pop.:** 38.9%. **Foreign born:** 27.3%. **U.S. citizens:** 82.4%. **Language:** 54.1% English only; 33.9% Spanish.
Employment: 109,612 employed; 6.6% unemployed. **Per capita income:** $46,136; change (2011-12): 3.4%. **Below poverty level:** 14.7%; 11.5% of families. **Educational attainment:** 76.8% HS; 21.6% bachelor's. **Avg. commute:** 27.7 min. 78.0% drive; 14.9% carpool. **Housing units:** 78,222; 93.1% occupied. **Home ownership:** 65.2%. **Avg. home:** $175,600; change (2011-13): 17.9%. **Avg. rent:** $924.
Mayor: Douglas Athas, nonpartisan
History: Settled 1850s; inc. 1891.
Website: www.garlandtx.gov

Gilbert, Arizona

Population: 229,972 (92). **Pop. density:** 3,390. **Pop. change (2010-13):** 9.8%. **Area:** 67.8 sq mi. **Racial distribution:** 83.3% white; 3.7% black; 6.0% Asian; 0.6% Amer. Ind.; 0.2% Pac. Isl.; 2.6% other; 2+ races 3.6%. **Hispanic pop.:** 14.7%. **Foreign born:** 9.0%. **U.S. citizens:** 96.1%. **Language:** 84.8% English only; 7.8% Spanish.
Employment: 111,972 employed; 5.2% unemployed. **Per capita income:** $38,006; change (2011-12): 2.2%. **Below poverty level:** 6.4%; 5.1% of families. **Educational attainment:** 95.9% HS; 38.6% bachelor's. **Avg. commute:** 26.7 min. 78.1% drive; 12.3% carpool. **Housing units:** 74,009; 92.7% occupied. **Home ownership:** 72.0%. **Avg. home:** $183,600; change (2011-13): 59.0%. **Avg. rent:** $1,270.
Mayor: John Lewis, nonpartisan
History: Est. 1891; inc. 1920.
Website: www.gilbertaz.gov

Glendale, Arizona

Population: 234,632 (87). **Pop. density:** 4,011. **Pop. change (2010-13):** 3.7%. **Area:** 58.5 sq mi. **Racial distribution:** 76.2% white; 5.8% black; 3.8% Asian; 1.3% Amer. Ind.; 0.1% Pac. Isl.; 9.4% other; 2+ races 3.3%. **Hispanic pop.:** 36.6%. **Foreign born:** 16.3%. **U.S. citizens:** 89.6%. **Language:** 69.5% English only; 24.3% Spanish.
Employment: 107,713 employed; 6.9% unemployed. **Per capita income:** $38,006; change (2011-12): 2.2%. **Below poverty level:** 18.2%; 14.0% of families. **Educational attainment:** 83.5% HS; 21.5% bachelor's. **Avg. commute:** 26.5 min. 74.6% drive; 15.1% carpool. **Housing units:** 90,372; 87.5% occupied. **Home ownership:** 59.8%. **Avg. home:** $183,600; change (2011-13): 59.0%. **Avg. rent:** $857.
Mayor: Jerry Weiers, nonpartisan
History: Est. 1892; inc. 1910.
Website: www.glendaleaz.com

Greensboro, North Carolina

Population: 279,639 (68). **Pop. density:** 2,208. **Pop. change (2010-13):** 3.7%. **Area:** 126.7 sq mi. **Racial distribution:** 49.8% white; 40.7% black; 4.1% Asian; 0.4% Amer. Ind.; <0.05%

Pac. Isl.; 2.7% other; 2+ races 2.2%. **Hispanic pop.:** 7.2%. **Foreign born:** 10.5%. **U.S. citizens:** 93.1%. **Language:** 86.5% English only; 6.6% Spanish.

Employment: 128,606 employed; 7.8% unemployed. **Per capita income:** $36,645; change (2011-12): 3.5%. **Below poverty level:** 18.8%; 13.7% of families. **Educational attainment:** 87.4% HS; 35.4% bachelor's. **Avg. commute:** 19.9 min. 81.1% drive. **Housing units:** 125,087; 88.3% occupied. **Home ownership:** 54.6%. **Avg. home:** $131,000; change (2011-13): 5.8%. **Avg. rent:** $732.

Mayor: Nancy Vaughan, nonpartisan

History: Settled 1749; site of 1781 Revolutionary War conflict between Generals Nathanael Greene and Lord Charles Cornwallis; inc. 1807. Origin of civil rights sit-in movement.

Website: www.greensboro-nc.gov

Henderson, Nevada

Population: 270,811 (71). **Pop. density:** 2,588. **Pop. change (2010-13):** 5.0%. **Area:** 104.7 sq mi. **Racial distribution:** 79.1% white; 5.9% black; 7.5% Asian; 0.5% Amer. Ind.; 0.5% Pac. Isl.; 3.0% other; 2+ races 3.7%. **Hispanic pop.:** 14.2%. **Foreign born:** 11.5%. **U.S. citizens:** 95.8%. **Language:** 83.2% English only; 8.4% Spanish.

Employment: 130,151 employed; 9.4% unemployed. **Per capita income:** $36,676; change (2011-12): 2.2%. **Below poverty level:** 8.9%; 6.1% of families. **Educational attainment:** 92.4% HS; 30.8% bachelor's. **Avg. commute:** 23.0 min. 81.9% drive. **Housing units:** 113,180; 88.2% occupied. **Home ownership:** 65.4%. **Avg. home:** $173,800; change (2011-13): 39.4%. **Avg. rent:** $1,185.

Mayor: Andy A. Hafen, nonpartisan

History: Early growth spurred by WWII magnesium mining; inc. 1953.

Website: www.cityofhenderson.com

Hialeah, Florida

Population: 233,394 (89). **Pop. density:** 10,889. **Pop. change (2010-13):** 3.6%. **Area:** 21.4 sq mi. **Racial distribution:** 93.5% white; 2.2% black; 0.4% Asian; 0.1% Amer. Ind.; <0.05% Pac. Isl.; 2.9% other; 2+ races 0.9%. **Hispanic pop.:** 95.1%. **Foreign born:** 73.0%. **U.S. citizens:** 61.8%. **Language:** 6.9% English only; 92.5% Spanish.

Employment: 93,495 employed; 10.3% unemployed. **Per capita income:** $44,222; change (2011-12): 2.6%. **Below poverty level:** 22.6%; 19.7% of families. **Educational attainment:** 69.2% HS; 13.4% bachelor's. **Avg. commute:** 24.3 min. 77.7% drive. **Housing units:** 75,237; 94.8% occupied. **Home ownership:** 51.4%. **Avg. home:** $246,000; change (2011-13): 35.8%. **Avg. rent:** $981.

Mayor: Carlos Hernandez, nonpartisan

History: Founded 1917; inc. 1925. Industrial and residential city NW of Miami; site of Hialeah Park racetrack.

Website: www.hialeahfl.gov

Honolulu, Hawaii

Population: 347,884 (54). **Pop. density:** 5,748. **Pop. change (2010-13):** 2.7%. **Area:** 60.5 sq mi. **Racial distribution:** 18.0% white; 1.6% black; 55.1% Asian; 0.2% Amer. Ind.; 8.0% Pac. Isl.; 0.6% other; 2+ races 16.5%. **Hispanic pop.:** 5.5%. **Foreign born:** 28.1%. **U.S. citizens:** 86.8%. **Language:** 63.0% English only; 7.3% Chinese; 6.8% Japanese; 5.3% Tagalog; 8.2% other Pac. Isl. languages; 1.4% Spanish.

Employment: 437,230 employed; 4.3% unemployed. **Per capita income:** $48,529; change (2011-12): 2.7%. **Below poverty level:** 12.0%; 7.9% of families. **Educational attainment:** 88.1% HS; 33.8% bachelor's. **Avg. commute:** 22.3 min. 57.7% drive; 12.9% carpool; 12.3% public trans. **Housing units:** 143,333; 89.1% occupied. **Home ownership:** 44.2%. **Avg. home:** $661,500; change (2011-13): 10.8%. **Avg. rent:** $1,231.

Mayor: Kirk Caldwell, nonpartisan

History: Europeans entered harbor 1778; declared capital of kingdom by King Kamehameha III 1850. Pearl Harbor naval base attacked by Japanese Dec. 7, 1941.

Website: www.honolulu.gov

Houston, Texas

Population: 2,195,914 (4). **Pop. density:** 3,662. **Pop. change (2010-13):** 4.4%. **Area:** 599.7 sq mi. **Racial distribution:** 57.3% white; 23.6% black; 6.1% Asian; 0.4% Amer. Ind.; <0.05% Pac. Isl.; 11.0% other; 2+ races 1.5%. **Hispanic pop.:** 43.5%. **Foreign born:** 28.3%. **U.S. citizens:** 79.4%. **Language:** 53.8% English only; 37.6% Spanish.

Employment: 979,408 employed; 6.3% unemployed. **Per capita income:** $51,004; change (2011-12): 4.5%. **Below poverty level:** 22.2%; 18.8% of families. **Educational attainment:** 74.8% HS; 28.7% bachelor's. **Avg. commute:** 25.8 min. 75.4% drive; 12.6% carpool. **Housing units:** 902,153; 85.7% occupied. **Home ownership:** 45.9%. **Avg. home:** $181,300; change (2011-13): 16.4%. **Avg. rent:** $837.

Mayor: Annise D. Parker, Democrat

History: Founded 1836; inc. 1837; capital of Rep. of Texas 1837-39. Developed rapidly after completion of channel to Gulf of Mexico 1914. World center of oil, natural gas technology.

Website: www.houstontx.gov

Indianapolis, Indiana

Population: 843,393 (12). **Pop. density:** 2,333. **Pop. change (2010-13):** 2.6%. **Area:** 361.5 sq mi. **Racial distribution:** 63.1% white; 27.5% black; 2.1% Asian; 0.2% Amer. Ind.; <0.05% Pac. Isl.; 4.3% other; 2+ races 2.8%. **Hispanic pop.:** 9.2%. **Foreign born:** 8.4%. **U.S. citizens:** 93.7%. **Language:** 87.8% English only; 8.2% Spanish.

Employment: 392,679 employed; 7.7% unemployed. **Per capita income:** $42,342; change (2011-12): 4.6%. **Below poverty level:** 19.9%; 15.5% of families. **Educational attainment:** 84.2% HS; 27.5% bachelor's. **Avg. commute:** 22.6 min. 81.9% drive; 10.0% carpool. **Housing units:** 380,830; 85.7% occupied. **Home ownership:** 56.2%. **Avg. home:** $136,700; change (2011-13): 10.3%. **Avg. rent:** $753.

Mayor: Gregory A. Ballard, Republican

History: Settled 1820; became state capital 1825.

Website: www.indy.gov

Irvine, California

Population: 236,716 (85). **Pop. density:** 3,610. **Pop. change (2010-13):** 10.9%. **Area:** 65.6 sq mi. **Racial distribution:** 52.6% white; 1.8% black; 38.3% Asian; 0.4% Amer. Ind.; 0.3% Pac. Isl.; 2.1% other; 2+ races 4.5%. **Hispanic pop.:** 9.8%. **Foreign born:** 35.6%. **U.S. citizens:** 84.9%. **Language:** 55.8% English only; 9.8% Chinese; 6.6% Korean; 5.9% Spanish.

Employment: 80,296 employed; 4.7% unemployed. **Per capita income:** $46,323; change (2011-12): 3.5%. **Below poverty level:** 11.4%; 5.7% of families. **Educational attainment:** 96.6% HS; 65.7% bachelor's. **Avg. commute:** 23.1 min. 77.8% drive. **Housing units:** 83,090; 94.0% occupied. **Home ownership:** 50.3%. **Avg. home:** $405,580; change (2011-13): 31.8%. **Avg. rent:** $1,832.

Mayor: Steven S. Choi, nonpartisan

History: Univ. of CA–Irvine campus announced 1959; planned city developed around campus 1960s; inc. 1971.

Website: www.cityofirvine.org

Irving, Texas

Population: 228,653 (94). **Pop. density:** 3,411. **Pop. change (2010-13):** 5.4%. **Area:** 67.0 sq mi. **Racial distribution:** 57.8% white; 12.1% black; 14.5% Asian; 0.7% Amer. Ind.; <0.05% Pac. Isl.; 12.5% other; 2+ races 2.4%. **Hispanic pop.:** 41.2%. **Foreign born:** 33.3%. **U.S. citizens:** 75.4%. **Language:** 47.9% English only; 35.9% Spanish.

Employment: 117,218 employed; 5.8% unemployed. **Per capita income:** $46,136; change (2011-12): 3.4%. **Below poverty level:** 16.2%; 13.2% of families. **Educational attainment:** 78.9% HS; 33.4% bachelor's. **Avg. commute:** 22.3 min. 79.4% drive; 12.1% carpool. **Home ownership:** 39.2%. **Avg. home:** $175,600; change (2011-13): 17.9%. **Avg. rent:** $885.

Mayor: Beth Van Duyne, nonpartisan

History: Founded 1903; inc. 1914; remained small until 1950s.

Website: www.ci.irving.tx.us

Jacksonville, Florida

Population: 842,583 (13). **Pop. density:** 1,128. **Pop. change (2010-13):** 2.3%. **Area:** 747.3 sq mi. **Racial distribution:** 60.5% white; 30.5% black; 4.3% Asian; 0.3% Amer. Ind.; 0.1% Pac. Isl.; 1.4% other; 2+ races 2.9%. **Hispanic pop.:** 7.8%. **Foreign born:** 9.5%. **U.S. citizens:** 95.4%. **Language:** 86.5% English only; 6.0% Spanish.

Employment: 392,982 employed; 7.2% unemployed. **Per capita income:** $41,900; change (2011-12): 2.9%. **Below poverty level:** 16.1%; 12.5% of families. **Educational attainment:** 87.2% HS; 24.7% bachelor's. **Avg. commute:** 23.5 min. 80.9% drive; 10.4% carpool. **Housing units:** 366,462; 85.0% occupied. **Home ownership:** 62.4%. **Avg. home:** $160,800; change (2011-13): 30.1%. **Avg. rent:** $920.

Mayor: Alvin Brown, Democrat

History: Settled 1816 as Cowford; renamed after Andrew Jackson 1822; inc. 1832; rechartered 1851. Scene of conflicts in Seminole and Civil Wars.

Website: www.coj.net

Jersey City, New Jersey

Population: 257,342 (74). **Pop. density:** 17,396. **Pop. change (2010-13):** 3.6%. **Area:** 14.8 sq mi. **Racial distribution:** 34.9% white; 26.1% black; 23.9% Asian; 0.5% Amer. Ind.; <0.05% Pac. Isl.; 11.8% other; 2+ races 2.8%. **Hispanic pop.:** 27.9%. **Foreign born:** 38.6%. **U.S. citizens:** 78.6%. **Language:** 47.5% English only; 23.4% Spanish; 5.4% Tagalog.

Employment: 106,650 employed; 9.7% unemployed. **Per capita income:** $58,403; change (2011-12): 2.6%. **Below poverty level:** 17.6%; 15.1% of families. **Educational attainment:** 84.5% HS; 41.5% bachelor's. **Avg. commute:** 35.0 min. 46.0%

public trans.; 33.8% drive. **Housing units:** 109,003; 87.6% occupied. **Home ownership:** 30.4%. **Avg. home:** $391,800; change (2011-13): 3.5%. **Avg. rent:** $1,157.
Mayor: Steven M. Fulop, nonpartisan
History: Site bought from Indians 1630; chartered as town by British 1668; scene of Revolutionary War conflict 1779; chartered under present name 1838. Important station on Underground Railroad.
Website: www.cityofjerseycity.com

Kansas City, Missouri

Population: 467,007 (37). **Pop. density:** 1,483. **Pop. change (2010-13):** 1.4%. **Area:** 314.9 sq mi. **Racial distribution:** 59.8% white; 29.8% black; 2.5% Asian; 0.5% Amer. Ind.; 0.2% Pac. Isl.; 3.8% other; 2+ races 3.4%. **Hispanic pop.:** 9.9%. **Foreign born:** 7.6%. **U.S. citizens:** 95.3%. **Language:** 88.1% English only; 7.0% Spanish.
Employment: 210,838 employed; 7.4% unemployed. **Per capita income:** $44,766; change (2011-12): 3.3%. **Below poverty level:** 18.8%; 14.4% of families. **Educational attainment:** 87.1% HS; 30.9% bachelor's. **Avg. commute:** 21.3 min. 80.5% drive. **Housing units:** 224,765; 85.4% occupied. **Home ownership:** 56.8%. **Avg. home:** $154,800; change (2011-13): 16.2%. **Avg. rent:** $772.
Mayor: Sly James, nonpartisan
History: Settled by 1838 at confluence of Missouri and Kansas Rivers; inc. 1850.
Website: www.kcmo.org

Laredo, Texas

Population: 248,142 (80). **Pop. density:** 2,689. **Pop. change (2010-13):** 4.7%. **Area:** 92.3 sq mi. **Racial distribution:** 92.9% white; 0.3% black; 0.8% Asian; 0.3% Amer. Ind.; <0.05% Pac. Isl.; 4.9% other; 2+ races 0.8%. **Hispanic pop.:** 95.5%. **Foreign born:** 28.3%. **U.S. citizens:** 79.8%. **Language:** 8.1% English only; 91.1% Spanish.
Employment: 90,823 employed; 6.3% unemployed. **Per capita income:** $26,120; change (2011-12): 2.0%. **Below poverty level:** 29.8%; 25.1% of families. **Educational attainment:** 65.2% HS; 17.4% bachelor's. **Avg. commute:** 21.2 min. 78.7% drive; 14.1% carpool. **Housing units:** 68,650; 92.6% occupied. **Home ownership:** 62.9%. **Avg. rent:** $741.
Mayor: Raul G. Salinas, nonpartisan
History: Founded by Spanish colonists in 1755; part of U.S. from 1848. Fast growth fueled by immigration. Principal port of entry into Mexico.
Website: www.cityoflaredo.com

Las Vegas, Nevada

Population: 603,488 (30). **Pop. density:** 4,534. **Pop. change (2010-13):** 3.3%. **Area:** 133.1 sq mi. **Racial distribution:** 70.1% white; 10.9% black; 6.3% Asian; 0.6% Amer. Ind.; 0.5% Pac. Isl.; 7.4% other; 2+ races 4.2%. **Hispanic pop.:** 31.7%. **Foreign born:** 21.8%. **U.S. citizens:** 86.0%. **Language:** 66.5% English only; 25.1% Spanish.
Employment: 257,321 employed; 10.3% unemployed. **Per capita income:** $36,676; change (2011-12): 2.2%. **Below poverty level:** 16.2%; 12.0% of families. **Educational attainment:** 82.1% HS; 21.3% bachelor's. **Avg. commute:** 25.2 min. 77.8% drive; 11.4% carpool. **Housing units:** 246,979; 85.8% occupied. **Home ownership:** 54.8%. **Avg. home:** $173,800; change (2011-13): 39.4%. **Avg. rent:** $1,009.
Mayor: Carolyn G. Goodman, nonpartisan
History: Occupied by Mormons 1855-57; bought by railroad 1903; inc. 1911. Gambling legalized 1931.
Website: www.lasvegasnevada.gov

Lexington, Kentucky

Population: 308,428 (61). **Pop. density:** 1,087. **Pop. change (2010-13):** 4.0%. **Area:** 283.6 sq mi. **Racial distribution:** 76.5% white; 14.2% black; 3.4% Asian; 0.2% Amer. Ind.; 0.1% Pac. Isl.; 2.9% other; 2+ races 2.6%. **Hispanic pop.:** 6.7%. **Foreign born:** 8.6%. **U.S. citizens:** 93.5%. **Language:** 88.6% English only; 6.2% Spanish.
Employment: 146,664 employed; 6.5% unemployed. **Per capita income:** $39,925; change (2011-12): 2.8%. **Below poverty level:** 18.2%; 11.8% of families. **Educational attainment:** 88.7% HS; 39.9% bachelor's. **Avg. commute:** 19.6 min. 79.9% drive; 10.1% carpool. **Housing units:** 134,977; 91.0% occupied. **Home ownership:** 56.3%. **Avg. home:** $143,800; change (2011-13): 3.8%. **Avg. rent:** $731.
Mayor: Jim Gray, nonpartisan
History: Site founded and named in 1775 after site of the Revolutionary War's opening battle at Lexington, MA; settled 1779; chartered 1782; inc. 1832.
Website: www.lexingtonky.gov

Lincoln, Nebraska

Population: 268,738 (72). **Pop. density:** 2,972. **Pop. change (2010-13):** 3.7%. **Area:** 90.4 sq mi. **Racial distribution:** 87.8% white; 4.0% black; 4.0% Asian; 0.7% Amer. Ind.; 0.1% Pac. Isl.;

0.9% other; 2+ races 2.6%. **Hispanic pop.:** 6.2%. **Foreign born:** 7.3%. **U.S. citizens:** 95.8%. **Language:** 88.6% English only; 4.3% Spanish.
Employment: 146,634 employed; 3.4% unemployed. **Per capita income:** $41,584; change (2011-12): 3.9%. **Below poverty level:** 15.5%; 9.4% of families. **Educational attainment:** 93.3% HS; 35.9% bachelor's. **Avg. commute:** 17.6 min. 80.9% drive. **Housing units:** 110,530; 94.0% occupied. **Home ownership:** 58.4%. **Avg. home:** $143,300; change (2011-13): 7.7%. **Avg. rent:** $700.
Mayor: Chris Beutler, nonpartisan
History: Originally called Lancaster; chosen state capital, 1867, and renamed after Abraham Lincoln; inc. 1869.
Website: lincoln.ne.gov

Long Beach, California

Population: 469,428 (36). **Pop. density:** 9,332. **Pop. change (2010-13):** 1.5%. **Area:** 50.3 sq mi. **Racial distribution:** 52.0% white; 13.4% black; 12.8% Asian; 0.6% Amer. Ind.; 0.8% Pac. Isl.; 14.4% other; 2+ races 6.0%. **Hispanic pop.:** 40.8%. **Foreign born:** 26.4%. **U.S. citizens:** 84.8%. **Language:** 54.9% English only; 32.2% Spanish.
Employment: 214,146 employed; 10.9% unemployed. **Per capita income:** $46,337; change (2011-12): 3.5%. **Below poverty level:** 20.2%; 16.3% of families. **Educational attainment:** 79.0% HS; 28.6% bachelor's. **Avg. commute:** 28.3 min. 72.2% drive; 11.1% carpool. **Housing units:** 174,259; 92.7% occupied. **Home ownership:** 40.8%. **Avg. home:** $405,580; change (2011-13): 31.8%. **Avg. rent:** $1,093.
Mayor: Robert Garcia, nonpartisan
History: Settled as early as 1784 by Spanish; by 1884, present site developed on harbor; inc. 1888. Oil discovered 1921.
Website: www.longbeach.gov

Los Angeles, California

Population: 3,884,307 (2). **Pop. density:** 8,288. **Pop. change (2010-13):** 2.3%. **Area:** 468.7 sq mi. **Racial distribution:** 52.5% white; 9.5% black; 11.4% Asian; 0.5% Amer. Ind.; 0.2% Pac. Isl.; 22.7% other; 2+ races 3.2%. **Hispanic pop.:** 48.4%. **Foreign born:** 39.1%. **U.S. citizens:** 76.9%. **Language:** 39.8% English only; 43.0% Spanish.
Employment: 1,728,456 employed; 10.9% unemployed. **Per capita income:** $46,337; change (2011-12): 3.5%. **Below poverty level:** 21.2%; 17.2% of families. **Educational attainment:** 74.2% HS; 30.8% bachelor's. **Avg. commute:** 29.2 min. 67.0% drive; 11.1% public trans.; 10.3% carpool. **Housing units:** 1,419,626; 92.8% occupied. **Home ownership:** 38.0%. **Avg. home:** $405,580; change (2011-13): 31.8%. **Avg. rent:** $1,156.
Mayor: Eric Garcetti, nonpartisan
History: Founded by Spanish 1781; captured by U.S. 1846; inc. 1850; grew rapidly after coming of railroads, 1876 and 1885. Hollywood is a district of Los Angeles.
Website: www.lacity.org

Louisville, Kentucky

Population: 609,893 (28). **Pop. density:** 2,312. **Pop. change (2010-13):** 2.0%. **Area:** 263.8 sq mi. **Racial distribution:** 71.5% white; 22.7% black; 2.2% Asian; 0.2% Amer. Ind.; <0.05% Pac. Isl.; 0.9% other; 2+ races 2.5%. **Hispanic pop.:** 4.4%. **Foreign born:** 6.4%. **U.S. citizens:** 95.8%. **Language:** 91.7% English only; 3.8% Spanish.
Employment: 339,429 employed; 8.1% unemployed. **Per capita income:** $40,970; change (2011-12): 4.4%. **Below poverty level:** 18.2%; 14.2% of families. **Educational attainment:** 86.7% HS; 26.5% bachelor's. **Avg. commute:** 22.2 min. 80.9% drive. **Housing units:** 272,287; 89.2% occupied. **Home ownership:** 61.9%. **Avg. home:** $139,500; change (2011-13): 7.0%. **Avg. rent:** $682.
Mayor: Greg Fischer, Democrat
History: Settled 1778; named for Louis XVI of France; inc. 1828. Base for Union forces in Civil War.
Website: www.louisvilleky.gov

Lubbock, Texas

Population: 239,538 (84). **Pop. density:** 1,957. **Pop. change (2010-13):** 3.9%. **Area:** 122.4 sq mi. **Racial distribution:** 78.1% white; 7.9% black; 2.4% Asian; 0.5% Amer. Ind.; 0.2% Pac. Isl.; 7.8% other; 2+ races 3.2%. **Hispanic pop.:** 32.6%. **Foreign born:** 5.8%. **U.S. citizens:** 96.4%. **Language:** 77.9% English only; 18.9% Spanish.
Employment: 115,515 employed; 4.9% unemployed. **Per capita income:** $36,074; change (2011-12): 4.4%. **Below poverty level:** 21.2%; 13.9% of families. **Educational attainment:** 84.8% HS; 29.3% bachelor's. **Avg. commute:** 15.4 min. 82.3% drive; 10.0% carpool. **Housing units:** 97,210; 91.0% occupied. **Home ownership:** 56.0%. **Avg. rent:** $772.
Mayor: Glen Robertson, nonpartisan
History: Settled 1879; laid out 1891; inc. 1909 through merger of two towns.
Website: www.ci.lubbock.tx.us

Madison, Wisconsin

Population: 243,344 (83). **Pop. density:** 3,170. **Pop. change (2010-13):** 4.1%. **Area:** 76.8 sq mi. **Racial distribution:** 80.7% white; 7.4% black; 7.5% Asian; 0.3% Amer. Ind.; <0.05% Pac. Isl.; 1.2% other; 2+ races 3.0%. **Hispanic pop.** 6.5%. **Foreign born:** 10.4%. **U.S. citizens:** 93.1%. **Language:** 85.5% English only; 5.2% Spanish.
Employment: 141,888 employed; 4.6% unemployed. **Per capita income:** $48,026; change (2011-12): 3.3%. **Below poverty level:** 18.5%; 8.9% of families. **Educational attainment:** 94.8% HS; 53.3% bachelor's. **Avg. commute:** 19.1 min. 63.7% drive. **Housing units:** 107,592; 94.3% occupied. **Home ownership:** 50.1%. **Avg. home:** $221,500; change (2011-13): 3.9%. **Avg. rent:** $890.
Mayor: Paul R. Soglin, nonpartisan
History: Settled 1832; selected as site for state capital and named after James Madison, 1836; chartered 1856.
Website: www.cityofmadison.com

Memphis, Tennessee

Population: 653,450 (20). **Pop. density:** 2,074. **Pop. change (2010-13):** 0.9%. **Area:** 315.1 sq mi. **Racial distribution:** 30.6% white; 63.0% black; 1.6% Asian; 0.3% Amer. Ind.; <0.05% Pac. Isl.; 2.8% other; 2+ races 1.7%. **Hispanic pop.:** 6.3%. **Foreign born:** 6.1%. **U.S. citizens:** 95.4%. **Language:** 91.0% English only; 5.9% Spanish.
Employment: 254,298 employed; 10.8% unemployed. **Per capita income:** $40,288; change (2011-12): 4.3%. **Below poverty level:** 26.2%; 21.4% of families. **Educational attainment:** 82.3% HS; 23.4% bachelor's. **Avg. commute:** 21.5 min. 78.8% drive. 13.1% carpool. **Housing units:** 294,777; 83.0% occupied. **Home ownership:** 52.1%. **Avg. home:** $129,400; change (2011-13): 15.2%. **Avg. rent:** $805.
Mayor: A. C. Wharton, nonpartisan
History: French, Spanish, and U.S. forts by 1797; settled by 1819; inc. as town 1826, as city 1840; surrendered charter to state, 1879, after yellow fever epidemics; rechartered as city 1893.
Website: www.cityofmemphis.org

Mesa, Arizona

Population: 457,587 (38). **Pop. density:** 3,349. **Pop. change (2010-13):** 4.0%. **Area:** 136.6 sq mi. **Racial distribution:** 83.3% white; 3.2% black; 2.1% Asian; 2.3% Amer. Ind.; 0.3% Pac. Isl.; 6.2% other; 2+ races 2.7%. **Hispanic pop.** 25.9%. **Foreign born:** 12.6%. **U.S. citizens:** 90.8%. **Language:** 78.5% English only; 17.8% Spanish.
Employment: 207,826 employed; 6.6% unemployed. **Per capita income:** $38,000; change (2011-12): 2.2%. **Below poverty level:** 14.8%; 10.9% of families. **Educational attainment:** 87.0% HS; 24.2% bachelor's. **Avg. commute:** 24.9 min. 76.2% drive, 13.5% carpool. **Housing units:** 198,290; 84.1% occupied. **Home ownership:** 63.1%. **Avg. home:** $183,600; change (2011-13): 59.0%. **Avg. rent:** $872.
Mayor: Alex Finter, nonpartisan
History: Founded by Mormons 1878; inc. 1883. Population boomed fivefold 1960-80.
Website: www.mesaaz.gov

Miami, Florida

Population: 417,650 (44). **Pop. density:** 11,637. **Pop. change (2010-13):** 4.2%. **Area:** 35.9 sq mi. **Racial distribution:** 74.6% white, 20.1% black; 0.9% Asian; 0.1% Amer. Ind.; <0.05% Pac. Isl.; 3.2% other; 2+ races 1.1%. **Hispanic pop.** 70.3%. **Foreign born:** 58.1%. **U.S. citizens:** 66.4%. **Language:** 22.6% English only; 69.9% Spanish.
Employment: 164,695 employed; 9.3% unemployed. **Per capita income:** $44,222; change (2011-12): 2.6%. **Below poverty level:** 29.5%; 24.6% of families. **Educational attainment:** 69.6% HS; 22.9% bachelor's. **Avg. commute:** 26.4 min. 69.1% drive, 11.4% public trans.; 10.4% carpool. **Housing units:** 187,869; 80.4% occupied. **Home ownership:** 33.8%. **Avg. home:** $246,000; change (2011-13): 35.8%. **Avg. rent:** $925.
Mayor: Tomás Regalado, nonpartisan
History: Site of fort 1836; settlement began 1870; inc. 1896. Land speculation in 1920s added to city's growth, as did Cuban, Central and South American, and Haitian immigration since 1960.
Website: www.miamigov.com

Milwaukee, Wisconsin

Population: 599,164 (31). **Pop. density:** 6,230. **Pop. change (2010-13):** 0.7%. **Area:** 96.2 sq mi. **Racial distribution:** 47.9% white; 39.4% black; 3.6% Asian; 0.6% Amer. Ind.; 0.1% Pac. Isl.; 5.1% other; 2+ races 3.4%. **Hispanic pop.** 17.1%. **Foreign born:** 10.0%. **U.S. citizens:** 93.0%. **Language:** 80.7% English only; 13.6% Spanish.
Employment: 244,362 employed; 10.0% unemployed. **Per capita income:** $46,943; change (2011-12): 3.2%. **Below poverty level:** 28.3%; 23.8% of families. **Educational attainment:** 80.8% HS; 21.7% bachelor's. **Avg. commute:** 21.9 min. 70.9% drive; 11.9% carpool. **Housing units:** 258,284; 88.9% occupied. **Home ownership:** 44.5%. **Avg. home:** $200,700; change (2011-13): 8.4%. **Avg. rent:** $768.
Mayor: Tom Barrett, Democrat
History: Indian trading post by 1674; settlement began 1835; inc. 1848. Famous beer industry.
Website: city.milwaukee.gov

Minneapolis, Minnesota

Population: 400,070 (46). **Pop. density:** 7,408. **Pop. change (2010-13):** 4.5%. **Area:** 54.0 sq mi. **Racial distribution:** 68.3% white; 17.5% black; 5.5% Asian; 1.6% Amer. Ind.; <0.05% Pac. Isl.; 2.9% other; 2+ races 4.1%. **Hispanic pop.:** 9.9%. **Foreign born:** 14.6%. **U.S. citizens:** 90.6%. **Language:** 80.1% English only; 8.4% Spanish.
Employment: 206,897 employed; 4.9% unemployed. **Per capita income:** $50,260; change (2011-12): 2.9%. **Below poverty level:** 22.5%; 15.7% of families. **Educational attainment:** 88.0% HS; 45.5% bachelor's. **Avg. commute:** 22.2 min. 61.6% drive, 13.9% public trans. **Housing units:** 181,196; 91.7% occupied. **Home ownership:** 50.0%. **Avg. home:** $196,200; change (2011-13): 26.8%. **Avg. rent:** $817.
Mayor: Betsy Hodges, Democrat (DFL)
History: Site visited by French missionary Louis Hennepin 1680; included in area of military reservations 1819; inc. 1867.
Website: www.ci.minneapolis.mn.us

Nashville, Tennessee

Population: 634,464 (25). **Pop. density:** 1,332. **Pop. change (2010-13):** 4.9%. **Area:** 476.2 sq mi. **Racial distribution:** 62.0% white; 28.5% black; 3.2% Asian; 0.2% Amer. Ind.; <0.05% Pac. Isl.; 3.9% other; 2+ races 2.1%. **Hispanic pop.:** 9.8%. **Foreign born:** 12.0%. **U.S. citizens:** 91.7%. **Language:** 84.1% English only; 8.6% Spanish.
Employment: 312,906 employed; 6.5% unemployed. **Per capita income:** $45,213; change (2011-12): 6.1%. **Below poverty level:** 19.0%; 14.5% of families. **Educational attainment:** 85.6% HS; 34.3% bachelor's. **Avg. commute:** 23.2 min. 79.4% drive; 10.6% carpool. **Housing units:** 274,594; 89.9% occupied. **Home ownership:** 54.9%. **Avg. home:** $176,400; change (2011-13): 16.1%. **Avg. rent:** $816.
Mayor: Karl Dean, nonpartisan
History: Settled 1779; first chartered 1806; became permanent state capital 1843. Home of Grand Ole Opry.
Website: www.nashville.gov

New Orleans, Louisiana

Population: 378,715 (51). **Pop. density:** 2,235. **Pop. change (2010-13):** 8.8%. **Area:** 169.4 sq mi. **Racial distribution:** 33.5% white; 60.2% black; 2.9% Asian; 0.3% Amer. Ind.; 0.1% Pac. Isl.; 1.5% other; 2+ races 1.4%. **Hispanic pop.:** 5.2%. **Foreign born:** 5.8%. **U.S. citizens:** 96.8%. **Language:** 90.2% English only; 4.7% Spanish.
Employment: 144,753 employed; 7.3% unemployed. **Per capita income:** $43,936; change (2011-12): 2.2%. **Below poverty level:** 27.2%; 21.8% of families. **Educational attainment:** 84.7% HS; 33.0% bachelor's. **Avg. commute:** 22.8 min. 69.7% drive; 11.2% carpool. **Housing units:** 186,987; 76.9% occupied. **Home ownership:** 47.6%. **Avg. home:** $164,700; change (2011-13): 7.6%. **Avg. rent:** $922.
Mayor: Mitchell J. Landrieu, Democrat
History: Founded by French 1718; became major seaport on Mississippi R.; acquired by U.S. as part of Louisiana Purchase 1803; inc. 1805. Americans defeated British forces at Battle of New Orleans in 1815.
Website: www.nola.gov

New York, New York

Population: 8,405,837 (1). **Pop. density:** 27,781. **Pop. change (2010-13):** 2.6%. **Area:** 302.6 sq mi. **Racial distribution:** 44.5% white; 25.1% black; 12.9% Asian; 0.4% Amer. Ind.; <0.05% Pac. Isl.; 14.3% other; 2+ races 2.9%. **Hispanic pop.:** 28.6%. **Foreign born:** 36.9%. **U.S. citizens:** 82.2%. **Language:** 51.3% English only; 24.6% Spanish; 5.6% Chinese.
Employment: 3,702,239 employed; 8.7% unemployed. **Per capita income:** $58,403; change (2011-12): 2.6%. **Below poverty level:** 19.9%; 16.9% of families. **Educational attainment:** 79.4% HS; 34.0% bachelor's. **Avg. commute:** 39.1 min. 55.6% public trans.; 22.7% drive; 10.3% walk. **Housing units:** 3,371,464; 90.9% occupied. **Home ownership:** 32.3%. **Avg. home:** $391,800; change (2011-13): 3.5%. **Avg. rent:** $1,167.
Mayor: Bill de Blasio, Democrat
History: Trading post est. 1624; British took control from Dutch, 1664, and named city New York. Briefly U.S. capital; under new charter, 1898, city expanded to include five boroughs: Bronx, Brooklyn, Queens, and Staten Island, as well as Manhattan. Sept. 11, 2001, terrorist attacks destroyed World Trade Center, killed more than 2,750.
Website: www.nyc.gov

Newark, New Jersey

Population: 278,427 (69). **Pop. density:** 11,509. **Pop. change (2010-13):** 0.3%. **Area:** 24.2 sq mi. **Racial distribution:** 27.6% white; 52.0% black; 1.6% Asian; 0.4% Amer. Ind.; 0.1% Pac. Isl.; 12.3% other; 2+ races 6.0%. **Hispanic pop.:** 33.3%. **Foreign born:** 26.9%. **U.S. citizens:** 82.1%. **Language:** 55.0% English only; 30.3% Spanish; 8.1% Portuguese.
Employment: 91,781 employed; 13.4% unemployed. **Per capita income:** $58,403; change (2011-12): 2.6%. **Below poverty level:** 28.0%; 25.3% of families. **Educational attainment:** 70.1% HS; 12.5% bachelor's. **Avg. commute:** 31.3 min. 48.5% drive; 26.9% public trans.; 12.5% carpool. **Housing units:** 110,058; 83.9% occupied. **Home ownership:** 23.5%. **Avg. home:** $391,800; change (2011-13): 3.5%. **Avg. rent:** $954.
Mayor: Ras J. Baraka, nonpartisan
History: Settled by Puritans 1666; used as supply base by Washington 1776; inc. as town 1833, as city 1836.
Website: www.ci.newark.nj.us

Norfolk, Virginia

Population: 246,139 (81). **Pop. density:** 4,551. **Pop. change (2010-13):** 1.3%. **Area:** 54.1 sq mi. **Racial distribution:** 48.0% white; 43.2% black; 3.4% Asian; 0.5% Amer. Ind.; 0.2% Pac. Isl.; 1.7% other; 2+ races 3.1%. **Hispanic pop.:** 6.7%. **Foreign born:** 6.6%. **U.S. citizens:** 96.3%. **Language:** 90.7% English only; 4.6% Spanish.
Employment: 97,473 employed; 7.0% unemployed. **Per capita income:** $44,321; change (2011-12): 2.9%. **Below poverty level:** 18.2%; 14.4% of families. **Educational attainment:** 85.3% HS; 25.4% bachelor's. **Avg. commute:** 21.9 min. 69.7% drive; 11.1% carpool. **Housing units:** 95,093; 89.6% occupied. **Home ownership:** 45.6%. **Avg. home:** $193,000; change (2011-13): 5.5%. **Avg. rent:** $920.
Mayor: Paul D. Fraim, nonpartisan
History: Founded 1682; burned by colonists to prevent capture by British during Revolutionary War; rebuilt and inc. as town 1805, as city 1845. Site of world's largest naval base; major East Coast commercial port and cruise terminal.
Website: www.norfolk.gov

North Las Vegas, Nevada

Population: 226,877 (96). **Pop. density:** 2,313. **Pop. change (2010-13):** 4.6%. **Area:** 98.1 sq mi. **Racial distribution:** 55.8% white; 19.9% black; 5.7% Asian; 0.5% Amer. Ind.; 1.0% Pac. Isl.; 12.2% other; 2+ races 4.9%. **Hispanic pop.:** 39.2%. **Foreign born:** 23.2%. **U.S. citizens:** 84.7%. **Language:** 60.0% English only; 33.3% Spanish.
Employment: 85,259 employed; 11.7% unemployed. **Per capita income:** $36,676; change (2011-12): 2.2%. **Below poverty level:** 15.4%; 12.2% of families. **Educational attainment:** 76.3% HS; 15.2% bachelor's. **Avg. commute:** 27.6 min. 81.9% drive; 10.6% carpool. **Housing units:** 76,029; 86.4% occupied. **Home ownership:** 59.6%. **Avg. home:** $173,800; change (2011-13): 39.4%. **Avg. rent:** $1,140.
Mayor: John J. Lee, nonpartisan
History: Inc. 1946.
Website: www.cityofnorthlasvegas.com

Oakland, California

Population: 406,253 (45). **Pop. density:** 7,268. **Pop. change (2010-13):** 3.7%. **Area:** 55.9 sq mi. **Racial distribution:** 39.0% white; 27.3% black; 16.7% Asian; 0.6% Amer. Ind.; 0.6% Pac. Isl.; 10.7% other; 2+ races 5.1%. **Hispanic pop.:** 25.4%. **Foreign born:** 27.5%. **U.S. citizens:** 84.1%. **Language:** 59.8% English only; 21.9% Spanish; 7.8% Chinese.
Employment: 182,652 employed; 11.3% unemployed. **Per capita income:** $66,591; change (2011-12): 5.8%. **Below poverty level:** 20.3%; 16.9% of families. **Educational attainment:** 79.7% HS; 37.9% bachelor's. **Avg. commute:** 28.0 min. 56.3% drive; 17.9% public trans.; 10.7% carpool. **Housing units:** 172,017; 89.7% occupied. **Home ownership:** 41.0%. **Avg. home:** $679,240; change (2011-13): 40.5%. **Avg. rent:** $1,078.
Mayor: Jean Quan, nonpartisan
History: Area settled by Spanish 1820; inc. 1854.
Website: www.oaklandnet.com

Oklahoma City, Oklahoma

Population: 610,613 (27). **Pop. density:** 1,006. **Pop. change (2010-13):** 4.9%. **Area:** 606.7 sq mi. **Racial distribution:** 66.6% white; 14.6% black; 3.9% Asian; 3.1% Amer. Ind.; 0.1% Pac. Isl.; 4.9% other; 2+ races 6.8%. **Hispanic pop.:** 17.1%. **Foreign born:** 11.9%. **U.S. citizens:** 91.6%. **Language:** 81.4% English only; 13.6% Spanish.
Employment: 261,687 employed; 5.1% unemployed. **Per capita income:** $43,337; change (2011-12): 3.9%. **Below poverty level:** 17.6%; 13.6% of families. **Educational attainment:** 85.0% HS; 28.0% bachelor's. **Avg. commute:** 20.2 min. 82.2% drive; 11.3% carpool. **Housing units:** 257,492; 88.1% occupied. **Home ownership:** 60.4%. **Avg. home:** $153,100; change (2011-13): 8.1%. **Avg. rent:** $726.
Mayor: Mick Cornett, nonpartisan
History: Settled during land rush in Midwest 1889; inc. 1890; became state capital 1910. Oil discovered 1928. Bomb in 1995 terrorist attack destroyed federal office bldg., killed 168 people.
Website: www.okc.gov

Omaha, Nebraska

Population: 434,353 (42). **Pop. density:** 3,375. **Pop. change (2010-13):** 3.8%. **Area:** 128.7 sq mi. **Racial distribution:** 75.3% white; 13.1% black; 2.4% Asian; 0.8% Amer. Ind.; <0.05% Pac. Isl.; 5.2% other; 2+ races 3.2%. **Hispanic pop.:** 12.9%. **Foreign born:** 9.5%. **U.S. citizens:** 93.2%. **Language:** 85.2% English only; 10.1% Spanish.
Employment: 209,454 employed; 4.4% unemployed. **Per capita income:** $46,575; change (2011-12): 4.1%. **Below poverty level:** 16.4%; 11.7% of families. **Educational attainment:** 88.1% HS; 32.5% bachelor's. **Avg. commute:** 18.0 min. 80.3% drive; 11.3% carpool. **Housing units:** 179,349; 91.6% occupied. **Home ownership:** 58.8%. **Avg. home:** $145,700; change (2011-13): 7.4%. **Avg. rent:** $757.
Mayor: Jean Stothert, nonpartisan
History: Founded 1854; inc. 1857. Large food-processing, telecommunications, information-processing center.
Website: www.cityofomaha.org

Orlando, Florida

Population: 255,483 (77). **Pop. density:** 2,488. **Pop. change (2010-13):** 6.7%. **Area:** 102.7 sq mi. **Racial distribution:** 58.0% white; 28.9% black; 3.3% Asian; 0.3% Amer. Ind.; <0.05% Pac. Isl.; 7.0% other; 2+ races 2.4%. **Hispanic pop.:** 25.8%. **Foreign born:** 18.6%. **U.S. citizens:** 89.1%. **Language:** 67.1% English only; 22.4% Spanish.
Employment: 130,244 employed; 6.7% unemployed. **Per capita income:** $36,412; change (2011-12): 2.7%. **Below poverty level:** 18.4%; 14.3% of families. **Educational attainment:** 87.6% HS; 32.1% bachelor's. **Avg. commute:** 24.5 min. 79.0% drive. **Housing units:** 120,519; 82.1% occupied. **Home ownership:** 39.6%. **Avg. home:** $160,400; change (2011-13): 28.4%. **Avg. rent:** $973.
Mayor: Buddy Dyer, nonpartisan
History: Ft. Gatlin built just south of present-day Orlando in 1838; name changed from Jernigan 1856; inc. 1875. Walt Disney World opened in 1971.
Website: www.cityoforlando.net

Philadelphia, Pennsylvania

Population: 1,553,165 (5). **Pop. density:** 11,581. **Pop. change (2010-13):** 1.6%. **Area:** 134.1 sq mi. **Racial distribution:** 41.4% white; 43.4% black; 6.4% Asian; 0.3% Amer. Ind.; 0.1% Pac. Isl.; 6.0% other; 2+ races 2.4%. **Hispanic pop.:** 12.3%. **Foreign born:** 11.8%. **U.S. citizens:** 94.0%. **Language:** 78.8% English only; 9.8% Spanish.
Employment: 590,679 employed; 10.0% unemployed. **Per capita income:** $51,519; change (2011-12): 2.7%. **Below poverty level:** 26.2%; 21.0% of families. **Educational attainment:** 80.4% HS; 23.2% bachelor's. **Avg. commute:** 31.8 min. 50.2% drive; 26.3% public trans. **Housing units:** 669,244; 86.7% occupied. **Home ownership:** 54.1%. **Avg. home:** $220,300; change (2011-13): 4.9%. **Avg. rent:** $872.
Mayor: Michael A. Nutter, Democrat
History: First settled by Swedes 1638; Swedes surrendered to Dutch 1654; settled by English and Scottish Quakers 1678; named Philadelphia 1682; chartered 1701. Continental Congresses convened 1774, 1775; Declaration of Independence signed here 1776; national capital 1790-1800; state capital 1683-1799.
Website: www.phila.gov

Phoenix, Arizona

Population: 1,513,367 (6). **Pop. density:** 2,924. **Pop. change (2010-13):** 4.4%. **Area:** 517.5 sq mi. **Racial distribution:** 78.4% white; 6.5% black; 3.1% Asian; 1.9% Amer. Ind.; 0.2% Pac. Isl.; 7.3% other; 2+ races 2.6%. **Hispanic pop.:** 40.1%. **Foreign born:** 20.0%. **U.S. citizens:** 84.8%. **Language:** 63.5% English only; 30.6% Spanish.
Employment: 675,630 employed; 7.0% unemployed. **Per capita income:** $38,006; change (2011-12): 2.2%. **Below poverty level:** 21.8%; 17.1% of families. **Educational attainment:** 80.1% HS; 25.9% bachelor's. **Avg. commute:** 24.4 min. 74.8% drive; 12.6% carpool. **Housing units:** 599,325; 86.1% occupied. **Home ownership:** 56.8%. **Avg. home:** $183,600; change (2011-13): 59.0%. **Avg. rent:** $871.
Mayor: Greg Stanton, nonpartisan
History: Founded 1867; inc. 1881; became territorial capital 1889.
Website: www.phoenix.gov

Pittsburgh, Pennsylvania

Population: 305,841 (62). **Pop. density:** 5,523. **Pop. change (2010-13):** 0.1%. **Area:** 55.4 sq mi. **Racial distribution:** 66.1% white; 25.7% black; 4.5% Asian; 0.1% Amer. Ind.; 0.1% Pac. Isl.; 0.6% other; 2+ races 2.8%. **Hispanic pop.:** 2.5%.

Foreign born: 7.1%. **U.S. citizens:** 95.5%. **Language:** 90.2% English only; 2.0% Spanish.
Employment: 143,329 employed; 6.9% unemployed. **Per capita income:** $47,862; change (2011-12): 3.8%. **Below poverty level:** 22.5%; 15.7% of families. **Educational attainment:** 89.8% HS; 35.0% bachelor's. **Avg. commute:** 23.2 min. 53.8% drive; 18.8% public trans.; 11.3% walk; 10.3% carpool. **Housing units:** 157,228; 84.7% occupied. **Home ownership:** 49.0%. **Avg. rent:** $749.
Mayor: Bill Peduto, Democrat
History: Settled around Ft. Pitt 1758; inc. 1816. Became an inland port; by Civil War, already a center for iron production.
Website: pittsburghpa.gov

Plano, Texas

Population: 274,409 (70). **Pop. density:** 3,829. **Pop. change (2010-13):** 5.1%. **Area:** 71.7 sq mi. **Racial distribution:** 70.2% white; 7.1% black; 17.8% Asian; 0.4% Amer. Ind.; 0.1% Pac. Isl.; 1.7% other; 2+ races 2.7%. **Hispanic pop.:** 15.0%. **Foreign born:** 24.1%. **U.S. citizens:** 86.5%. **Language:** 67.3% English only; 12.3% Spanish.
Employment: 143,327 employed; 5.7% unemployed. **Per capita income:** $46,136; change (2011-12): 3.4%. **Below poverty level:** 7.4%; 5.5% of families. **Educational attainment:** 92.9% HS; 54.0% bachelor's. **Avg. commute:** 25.6 min. 82.4% drive. **Housing units:** 104,112; 94.5% occupied. **Home ownership:** 64.8%. **Avg. home:** $175,600; change (2011-13): 17.9%. **Avg. rent:** $1,051.
Mayor: Harry LaRosiliere, nonpartisan
History: Settled 1846; inc. 1873.
Website: www.plano.gov

Portland, Oregon

Population: 609,456 (29). **Pop. density:** 4,567. **Pop. change (2010-13):** 4.1%. **Area:** 133.5 sq mi. **Racial distribution:** 77.5% white; 6.5% black; 7.2% Asian; 0.8% Amer. Ind.; 0.6% Pac. Isl.; 3.1% other; 2+ races 4.3%. **Hispanic pop.:** 9.3%. **Foreign born:** 13.5%. **U.S. citizens:** 92.1%. **Language:** 81.2% English only; 7.1% Spanish.
Employment: 298,856 employed; 6.8% unemployed. **Per capita income:** $43,103; change (2011-12): 4.3%. **Below poverty level:** 17.2%; 11.8% of families. **Educational attainment:** 90.3% HS; 43.1% bachelor's. **Avg. commute:** 24.2 min. 59.5% drive; 11.9% public trans. **Housing units:** 265,875; 93.5% occupied. **Home ownership:** 53.8%. **Avg. home:** $265,500; change (2011-13): 21.0%. **Avg. rent:** $885.
Mayor: Charlie Hales, nonpartisan
History: Settled by pioneers 1845; developed as trading center, aided by California Gold Rush of 1849; chartered 1851.
Website: www.portlandoregon.gov

Raleigh, North Carolina

Population: 431,746 (43). **Pop. density:** 2,996. **Pop. change (2010-13):** 6.3%. **Area:** 144.1 sq mi. **Racial distribution:** 60.2% white; 30.2% black; 4.3% Asian; 0.2% Amer. Ind.; <0.05% Pac. Isl.; 3.4% other; 2+ races 1.7%. **Hispanic pop.:** 11.0%. **Foreign born:** 13.8%. **U.S. citizens:** 90.3%. **Language:** 82.4% English only; 9.6% Spanish.
Employment: 211,605 employed; 5.7% unemployed. **Per capita income:** $42,709; change (2011-12): 3.5%. **Below poverty level:** 16.3%; 11.7% of families. **Educational attainment:** 90.4% HS; 46.8% bachelor's. **Avg. commute:** 21.4 min. 79.4% drive. **Housing units:** 176,564; 90.6% occupied. **Home ownership:** 53.6%. **Avg. home:** $196,900; change (2011-13): 6.3%. **Avg. rent:** $875.
Mayor: Nancy McFarlane, nonpartisan
History: Named after Sir Walter Raleigh; site chosen for state capital 1788; laid out 1792; inc. 1795. Occupied by Union Gen. William Sherman 1865.
Website: www.raleighnc.gov

Reno, Nevada

Population: 233,294 (90). **Pop. density:** 2,176. **Pop. change (2010-13):** 3.0%. **Area:** 107.2 sq mi. **Racial distribution:** 79.9% white; 3.1% black; 6.4% Asian; 0.9% Amer. Ind.; 0.7% Pac. Isl.; 5.6% other; 2+ races 3.4%. **Hispanic pop.:** 24.3%. **Foreign born:** 16.8%. **U.S. citizens:** 89.7%. **Language:** 75.0% English only; 17.5% Spanish.
Employment: 106,550 employed; 9.7% unemployed. **Per capita income:** $43,317; change (2011-12): 1.9%. **Below poverty level:** 17.7%; 13.1% of families. **Educational attainment:** 85.5% HS; 28.2% bachelor's. **Avg. commute:** 19.4 min. 75.9% drive; 10.6% carpool. **Housing units:** 101,279; 88.2% occupied. **Home ownership:** 48.0%. **Avg. home:** $218,400; change (2011-13): 38.2%. **Avg. rent:** $874.
Mayor: Robert Cashell, nonpartisan
History: Founded 1857; originally named Lakes Crossing; name changed to Reno, after a Union Civil War general, 1868, with arrival of transcontinental railroad.
Website: www.reno.gov

Richmond, Virginia

Population: 214,114 (99). **Pop. density:** 3,579. **Pop. change (2010-13):** 4.8%. **Area:** 59.8 sq mi. **Racial distribution:** 43.1% white; 49.9% black; 2.2% Asian; 0.3% Amer. Ind.; <0.05% Pac. Isl.; 1.3% other; 2+ races 3.1%. **Hispanic pop.:** 6.1%. **Foreign born:** 7.4%. **U.S. citizens:** 94.4%. **Language:** 89.9% English only; 5.7% Spanish.
Employment: 95,931 employed; 6.9% unemployed. **Per capita income:** $45,194; change (2011-12): 3.1%. **Below poverty level:** 26.7%; 20.5% of families. **Educational attainment:** 80.6% HS; 33.8% bachelor's. **Avg. commute:** 21.7 min. 70.3% drive; 11.1% carpool. **Housing units:** 98,318; 85.2% occupied. **Home ownership:** 44.1%. **Avg. home:** $207,500; change (2011-13): 10.9%. **Avg. rent:** $863.
Mayor: Dwight C. Jones, nonpartisan
History: First settled 1607; became capital of Virginia 1779; attacked by British under Benedict Arnold 1781; inc. as city 1782; capital of Confederate States of America 1861-65.
Website: www.richmondgov.com

Riverside, California

Population: 316,619 (59). **Pop. density:** 3,900. **Pop. change (2010-13):** 3.6%. **Area:** 81.2 sq mi. **Racial distribution:** 65.9% white; 6.9% black; 6.7% Asian; 1.0% Amer. Ind.; 0.3% Pac. Isl.; 14.7% other; 2+ races 4.6%. **Hispanic pop.:** 50.3%. **Foreign born:** 23.7%. **U.S. citizens:** 85.3%. **Language:** 56.5% English only; 36.0% Spanish.
Employment: 150,252 employed; 10.4% unemployed. **Per capita income:** $31,900; change (2011-12): 2.6%. **Below poverty level:** 17.5%; 12.2% of families. **Educational attainment:** 77.6% HS; 22.2% bachelor's. **Avg. commute:** 28.4 min. 76.8% drive; 12.0% carpool. **Housing units:** 99,144; 91.2% occupied. **Home ownership:** 57.4%. **Avg. home:** $241,620; change (2011-13): 40.2%. **Avg. rent:** $1,126.
Mayor: Rusty Bailey, nonpartisan
History: Founded 1870; inc. 1886. Known for its citrus industry; home of the parent navel orange tree, historic Mission Inn resort.
Website: www.riversideca.gov

Sacramento, California

Population: 479,686 (35). **Pop. density:** 4,899. **Pop. change (2010-13):** 2.6%. **Area:** 97.9 sq mi. **Racial distribution:** 49.5% white; 13.9% black; 19.0% Asian; 1.0% Amer. Ind.; 1.3% Pac. Isl.; 8.4% other; 2+ races 6.8%. **Hispanic pop.:** 26.3%. **Foreign born:** 22.1%. **U.S. citizens:** 89.0%. **Language:** 63.2% English only; 17.0% Spanish.
Employment: 192,684 employed; 10.3% unemployed. **Per capita income:** $44,641; change (2011-12): 3.6%. **Below poverty level:** 20.2%; 15.6% of families. **Educational attainment:** 82.1% HS; 29.4% bachelor's. **Avg. commute:** 23.7 min. 72.6% drive; 12.8% carpool. **Housing units:** 192,715; 91.4% occupied. **Home ownership:** 49.1%. **Avg. home:** $239,520; change (2011-13): 44.2%. **Avg. rent:** $990.
Mayor: Kevin Johnson, nonpartisan
History: Settled 1839; important trading center during California Gold Rush in 1840s; became state capital 1854.
Website: www.cityofsacramento.org

St. Louis, Missouri

Population: 318,416 (58). **Pop. density:** 5,140. **Pop. change (2010-13):** -0.3%. **Area:** 62.0 sq mi. **Racial distribution:** 44.5% white; 48.9% black; 2.7% Asian; 0.2% Amer. Ind.; <0.05% Pac. Isl.; 0.9% other; 2+ races 2.8%. **Hispanic pop.:** 3.5%. **Foreign born:** 6.8%. **U.S. citizens:** 95.3%. **Language:** 90.7% English only; 3.0% Spanish.
Employment: 126,964 employed; 9.1% unemployed. **Per capita income:** $44,625; change (2011-12): 3.9%. **Below poverty level:** 27.0%; 21.6% of families. **Educational attainment:** 82.3% HS; 28.5% bachelor's. **Avg. commute:** 24.2 min. 70.5% drive; 10.5% carpool. **Housing units:** 175,855; 79.5% occupied. **Home ownership:** 45.6%. **Avg. home:** $134,300; change (2011-13): 10.3%. **Avg. rent:** $711.
Mayor: Francis Slay, Democrat
History: Founded 1764 as fur trading post by French; acquired by U.S. 1803; chartered as city 1822; became independent city 1876. Lies on Mississippi R., near confluence with Missouri R.
Website: www.stlouis-mo.gov

St. Paul, Minnesota

Population: 294,873 (66). **Pop. density:** 5,673. **Pop. change (2010-13):** 3.3%. **Area:** 52.0 sq mi. **Racial distribution:** 62.3% white; 15.2% black; 15.1% Asian; 0.9% Amer. Ind.; 0.1% Pac. Isl.; 2.3% other; 2+ races 4.2%. **Hispanic pop.:** 9.7%. **Foreign born:** 17.5%. **U.S. citizens:** 89.9%. **Language:** 73.8% English only; 8.9% Hmong; 7.3% Spanish.
Employment: 139,210 employed; 5.3% unemployed. **Per capita income:** $50,260; change (2011-12): 2.9%. **Below poverty level:** 22.8%; 17.2% of families. **Educational attainment:** 86.2% HS; 37.8% bachelor's. **Avg. commute:** 22.1 min. 69.8%

drive; 10.7% carpool. **Housing units:** 120,653; 92.7% occupied. **Home ownership:** 51.2%. **Avg. home:** $196,200; change (2011-13): 26.8%. **Avg. rent:** $786.
Mayor: Chris Coleman, nonpartisan
History: Founded in early 1840s as Pig's Eye Landing; became capital of Minnesota territory 1849; chartered as St. Paul 1854.
Website: www.stpaul.gov

St. Petersburg, Florida

Population: 249,688 (78). **Pop. density:** 4,043. **Pop. change (2010-13):** 1.7%. **Area:** 61.8 sq mi. **Racial distribution:** 69.4% white; 23.9% black; 2.3% Asian; 0.2% Amer. Ind.; 0.1% Pac. Isl.; 1.0% other; 2+ races 2.2%. **Hispanic pop.:** 6.7%. **Foreign born:** 10.3%. **U.S. citizens:** 95.2%. **Language:** 88.4% English only; 4.9% Spanish.
Employment: 113,478 employed; 7.1% unemployed. **Per capita income:** $40,862; change (2011-12): 3.7%. **Below poverty level:** 16.1%; 11.1% of families. **Educational attainment:** 87.8% HS; 28.1% bachelor's. **Avg. commute:** 21.9 min. 80.2% drive. **Housing units:** 127,245; 82.1% occupied. **Home ownership:** 61.6%. **Avg. home:** $142,800; change (2011-13): 11.7%. **Avg. rent:** $908.
Mayor: Rick Kriseman, nonpartisan
History: Founded 1888; inc. 1903. Site of Salvador Dali Museum.
Website: www.stpete.org

San Antonio, Texas

Population: 1,409,019 (7). **Pop. density:** 3,057. **Pop. change (2010-13):** 5.6%. **Area:** 461.0 sq mi. **Racial distribution:** 75.0% white; 6.8% black; 2.2% Asian; 0.7% Amer. Ind.; 0.1% Pac. Isl.; 12.4% other; 2+ races 2.7%. **Hispanic pop.:** 63.0%. **Foreign born:** 13.9%. **U.S. citizens:** 91.4%. **Language:** 54.4% English only; 42.1% Spanish.
Employment: 603,928 employed; 5.9% unemployed. **Per capita income:** $39,019; change (2011-12): 2.3%. **Below poverty level:** 20.1%; 15.9% of families. **Educational attainment:** 80.0% HS; 24.2% bachelor's. **Avg. commute:** 23.4 min. 78.9% drive; 11.4% carpool. **Housing units:** 524,522; 89.9% occupied. **Home ownership:** 57.0%. **Avg. home:** $171,000; change (2011-13): 12.1%. **Avg. rent:** $798.
Mayor: Julián Castro, nonpartisan
History: First Spanish garrison 1718; Battle of the Alamo 1836; city subsequently captured by Texans; inc. 1837; first town meeting in Texas took place here in 1845.
Website: www.sanantonio.gov

San Bernardino, California

Population: 213,708 (100). **Pop. density:** 3,475. **Pop. change (2010-13):** 1.7%. **Area:** 61.5 sq mi. **Racial distribution:** 46.6% white; 14.3% black; 4.3% Asian; 0.9% Amer. Ind.; 0.3% Pac. Isl.; 28.7% other; 2+ races 4.8%. **Hispanic pop.:** 59.7%. **Foreign born:** 23.1%. **U.S. citizens:** 84.6%. **Language:** 53.2% English only; 41.5% Spanish.
Employment: 73,039 employed; 13.6% unemployed. **Per capita income:** $31,900; change (2011-12): 2.6%. **Below poverty level:** 30.6%; 25.6% of families. **Educational attainment:** 67.9% HS; 11.8% bachelor's. **Avg. commute:** 26.9 min. 74.4% drive; 15.2% carpool. **Housing units:** 64,977; 91.0% occupied. **Home ownership:** 50.7%. **Avg. home:** $241,620; change (2011-13): 40.2%. **Avg. rent:** $929.
Mayor: R. Carey Davis, nonpartisan
History: Named by Spanish Franciscan missionaries 1810; major Mormon settlement in the 1850s, though Mormons were later recalled to Utah; inc. 1854. Population grew in 1860s when gold was discovered nearby; later became transportation hub.
Website: www.ci.san-bernardino.ca.us

San Diego, California

Population: 1,355,896 (8). **Pop. density:** 4,170. **Pop. change (2010-13):** 3.8%. **Area:** 325.2 sq mi. **Racial distribution:** 65.2% white; 6.8% black; 16.2% Asian; 0.6% Amer. Ind.; 0.6% Pac. Isl.; 6.1% other; 2+ races 4.5%. **Hispanic pop.:** 28.9%. **Foreign born:** 26.0%. **U.S. citizens:** 87.1%. **Language:** 60.5% English only; 22.4% Spanish.
Employment: 656,247 employed; 7.5% unemployed. **Per capita income:** $49,719; change (2011-12): 3.4%. **Below poverty level:** 15.4%; 10.6% of families. **Educational attainment:** 86.6% HS; 41.4% bachelor's. **Avg. commute:** 22.2 min. 75.3% drive. **Housing units:** 514,515; 92.0% occupied. **Home ownership:** 48.3%. **Avg. home:** $464,280; change (2011-13): 25.4%. **Avg. rent:** $1,312.
Mayor: Kevin L. Faulconer, nonpartisan
History: Claimed by Spanish 1542; first mission est. 1769; scene of conflict during Mexican-American War 1846; inc. 1850.
Website: www.sandiego.gov

San Francisco, California

Population: 837,442 (14). **Pop. density:** 17,859. **Pop. change (2010-13):** 3.9%. **Area:** 46.9 sq mi. **Racial distribution:** 50.7% white; 6.0% black; 33.5% Asian; 0.5% Amer. Ind.; 0.4% Pac. Isl.; 4.8% other; 2+ races 4.1%. **Hispanic pop.:** 15.1%. **Foreign born:** 35.7%. **U.S. citizens:** 86.1%. **Language:** 54.8% English only; 18.7% Chinese; 11.6% Spanish.
Employment: 459,341 employed; 5.7% unemployed. **Per capita income:** $66,591; change (2011-12): 5.8%. **Below poverty level:** 13.2%; 8.1% of families. **Educational attainment:** 85.9% HS; 52.0% bachelor's. **Avg. commute:** 29.9 min. 37.3% drive; 32.4% public trans. **Housing units:** 375,861; 90.7% occupied. **Home ownership:** 36.9%. **Avg. home:** $679,240; change (2011-13): 40.5%. **Avg. rent:** $1,447.
Mayor: Edwin M. Lee, nonpartisan
History: Nearby Farallon Islands sighted by Spanish 1542; city settled by 1776; claimed by U.S. 1846. Became major city during California Gold Rush of 1849; inc. 1850. Devastated by earthquake 1906.
Website: www.sfgov.org

San Jose, California

Population: 998,537 (10). **Pop. density:** 5,655. **Pop. change (2010-13):** 4.5%. **Area:** 176.6 sq mi. **Racial distribution:** 47.0% white; 3.1% black; 32.6% Asian; 0.6% Amer. Ind.; 0.4% Pac. Isl.; 11.9% other; 2+ races 4.4%. **Hispanic pop.:** 33.0%. **Foreign born:** 38.2%. **U.S. citizens:** 82.0%. **Language:** 44.7% English only; 23.4% Spanish; 9.9% Vietnamese; 6.2% Chinese.
Employment: 446,428 employed; 7.6% unemployed. **Per capita income:** $65,679; change (2011-12): 6.2%. **Below poverty level:** 11.7%; 8.4% of families. **Educational attainment:** 82.4% HS; 37.2% bachelor's. **Avg. commute:** 25.6 min. 77.8% drive; 10.8% carpool. **Housing units:** 317,592; 95.7% occupied. **Home ownership:** 58.7%. **Avg. home:** $780,000; change (2011-13): 36.8%. **Avg. rent:** $1,435.
Mayor: Chuck Reed, nonpartisan
History: Founded by Spanish 1777, between San Francisco and Monterey; state capital 1849-51; inc. 1850.
Website: www.sanjoseca.gov

Santa Ana, California

Population: 334,227 (57). **Pop. density:** 12,314. **Pop. change (2010-13):** 2.7%. **Area:** 27.1 sq mi. **Racial distribution:** 44.6% white; 1.3% black; 9.8% Asian; 0.7% Amer. Ind.; 0.1% Pac. Isl.; 42.1% other; 2+ races 1.6%. **Hispanic pop.:** 79.0%. **Foreign born:** 48.6%. **U.S. citizens:** 66.4%. **Language:** 17.0% English only; 73.1% Spanish; 6.9% Vietnamese.
Employment: 144,249 employed; 10.0% unemployed. **Per capita income:** $46,337; change (2011-12): 3.5%. **Below poverty level:** 20.7%; 17.7% of families. **Educational attainment:** 52.9% HS; 11.6% bachelor's. **Avg. commute:** 24.7 min. 69.8% drive; 17.1% carpool. **Housing units:** 76,251; 95.3% occupied. **Home ownership:** 47.2%. **Avg. home:** $405,580; change (2011-13): 31.8%. **Avg. rent:** $1,283.
Mayor: Miguel Pulido, nonpartisan
History: Founded 1769; inc. 1869.
Website: www.ci.santa-ana.ca.us

Scottsdale, Arizona

Population: 226,918 (95). **Pop. density:** 1,234. **Pop. change (2010-13):** 4.3%. **Area:** 183.9 sq mi. **Racial distribution:** 90.5% white; 1.9% black; 3.8% Asian; 1.0% Amer. Ind.; 0.1% Pac. Isl.; 1.5% other; 2+ races 1.3%. **Hispanic pop.:** 9.3%. **Foreign born:** 11.1%. **U.S. citizens:** 94.6%. **Language:** 85.3% English only; 6.6% Spanish.
Employment: 112,990 employed; 5.6% unemployed. **Per capita income:** $38,006; change (2011-12): 2.2%. **Below poverty level:** 8.3%; 5.3% of families. **Educational attainment:** 95.9% HS; 52.7% bachelor's. **Avg. commute:** 22.3 min. 77.4% drive. **Housing units:** 124,724; 80.2% occupied. **Home ownership:** 69.4%. **Avg. home:** $183,600; change (2011-13): 59.0%. **Avg. rent:** $1,127.
Mayor: W. J. "Jim" Lane, nonpartisan
History: Founded 1888 by Army Chaplain Winfield Scott; inc. 1951; slogan "West's Most Western Town" adopted same year.
Website: www.scottsdaleaz.gov

Seattle, Washington

Population: 652,405 (21). **Pop. density:** 7,782. **Pop. change (2010-13):** 6.9%. **Area:** 83.8 sq mi. **Racial distribution:** 70.6% white; 7.8% black; 14.0% Asian; 0.8% Amer. Ind.; 0.4% Pac. Isl.; 1.5% other; 2+ races 4.9%. **Hispanic pop.:** 6.2%. **Foreign born:** 17.5%. **U.S. citizens:** 91.9%. **Language:** 77.9% English only; 4.4% Spanish.
Employment: 363,803 employed; 4.9% unemployed. **Per capita income:** $53,328; change (2011-12): 4.1%. **Below poverty level:** 13.2%; 6.5% of families. **Educational attainment:** 92.9% HS; 56.5% bachelor's. **Avg. commute:** 25.1 min. 52.0% drive; 18.5% public trans. **Housing units:** 306,694; 93.1% occupied. **Home ownership:** 47.3%. **Avg. home:** $336,300; change (2011-13): 18.0%. **Avg. rent:** $1,051.
Mayor: Ed Murray, nonpartisan

History: Settled 1851; inc. 1869. Suffered severe fire 1889; played prominent role during Klondike Gold Rush beginning in 1897; growth followed opening of Panama Canal 1914. Center of aircraft industry during WWII.
Website: www.seattle.gov

Stockton, California

Population: 298,118 (64). **Pop. density:** 4,834. **Pop. change (2010-13):** 1.9%. **Area:** 61.7 sq mi. **Racial distribution:** 45.8% white; 11.8% black; 21.8% Asian; 1.1% Amer. Ind.; 0.6% Pac. Isl.; 12.2% other; 2+ races 6.8%. **Hispanic pop.:** 40.0%. **Foreign born:** 26.1%. **U.S. citizens:** 85.6%. **Language:** 54.9% English only; 26.2% Spanish.
Employment: 105,841 employed; 15.6% unemployed. **Per capita income:** $33,024; change (2011-12): 2.7%. **Below poverty level:** 23.3%; 19.1% of families. **Educational attainment:** 73.7% HS; 17.5% bachelor's. **Avg. commute:** 26.4 min. 74.8% drive; 16.3% carpool. **Housing units:** 100,330; 90.2% occupied. **Home ownership:** 51.9%. **Avg. rent:** $946.
Mayor: Anthony Silva, nonpartisan
History: Site purchased 1842; settled 1849; inc. 1850. Chief distribution point for agric. products of San Joaquin Valley.
Website: www.stocktongov.com

Tampa, Florida

Population: 352,957 (53). **Pop. density:** 3,113. **Pop. change (2010-13):** 4.8%. **Area:** 113.4 sq mi. **Racial distribution:** 64.6% white; 26.0% black; 3.3% Asian; 0.7% Amer. Ind.; 0.1% Pac. Isl.; 2.4% other; 2+ races 2.9%. **Hispanic pop.:** 23.4%. **Foreign born:** 15.1%. **U.S. citizens:** 91.6%. **Language:** 74.8% English only; 18.4% Spanish.
Employment: 151,088 employed; 7.7% unemployed. **Per capita income:** $40,862; change (2011-12): 3.7%. **Below poverty level:** 21.1%; 16.8% of families. **Educational attainment:** 85.5% HS; 32.9% bachelor's. **Avg. commute:** 22.4 min. 77.0% drive. **Housing units:** 158,239; 85.7% occupied. **Home ownership:** 51.7%. **Avg. home:** $142,800; change (2011-13): 11.7%. **Avg. rent:** $929.
Mayor: Bob Buckhorn, nonpartisan
History: U.S. army fort on site 1824; inc. 1851. Ybor City, Tampa's Latin Quarter, a Natl. Historical Landmark District.
Website: www.tampagov.net

Toledo, Ohio

Population: 282,313 (67). **Pop. density:** 3,497. **Pop. change (2010-13):** −1.6%. **Area:** 80.7 sq mi. **Racial distribution:** 65.9% white; 27.2% black; 1.1% Asian; 0.3% Amer. Ind.; 0.1% Pac. Isl.; 1.9% other; 2+ races 3.5%. **Hispanic pop.:** 7.3%. **Foreign born:** 3.1%. **U.S. citizens:** 98.3%. **Language:** 93.8% English only; 3.3% Spanish.
Employment: 118,830 employed; 9.1% unemployed. **Per capita income:** $37,693; change (2011-12): 2.5%. **Below poverty level:** 26.8%; 21.8% of families. **Educational attainment:** 85.0% HS; 17.1% bachelor's. **Avg. commute:** 19.0 min. 82.0% drive. **Housing units:** 138,719; 85.6% occupied. **Home ownership:** 55.9%. **Avg. home:** $81,700; change (2011-13): 7.9%. **Avg. rent:** $623.
Mayor: D. Michael Collins, nonpartisan
History: Site of Ft. Industry 1794; Battle of Ft. Meigs 1812; figured in Toledo War 1835-36 between OH and MI over borders; inc. 1837.
Website: toledo.oh.gov

Tucson, Arizona

Population: 526,116 (33). **Pop. density:** 2,279. **Pop. change (2010-13):** 0.9%. **Area:** 230.8 sq mi. **Racial distribution:** 76.5% white; 4.9% black; 2.6% Asian; 2.6% Amer. Ind.; 0.1% Pac. Isl.; 10.0% other; 2+ races 3.3%. **Hispanic pop.:** 41.8%. **Foreign born:** 15.2%. **U.S. citizens:** 90.5%. **Language:** 66.5% English only; 28.6% Spanish.
Employment: 223,276 employed; 7.5% unemployed. **Per capita income:** $36,335; change (2011-12): 2.7%. **Below poverty level:** 24.4%; 17.9% of families. **Educational attainment:** 84.0% HS; 24.2% bachelor's. **Avg. commute:** 21.7 min. 73.5% drive; 10.7% carpool. **Housing units:** 231,026; 88.0% occupied. **Home ownership:** 51.7%. **Avg. home:** $169,600; change (2011-13): 26.1%. **Avg. rent:** $726.
Mayor: Jonathan Rothschild, Democrat
History: Settled 1775 by Spanish as a presidio; acquired by U.S. in Gadsden Purchase 1853; inc. 1877.
Website: www.tucsonaz.gov

Tulsa, Oklahoma

Population: 398,121 (47). **Pop. density:** 2,022. **Pop. change (2010-13):** 1.4%. **Area:** 196.9 sq mi. **Racial distribution:** 67.3% white; 15.1% black; 2.4% Asian; 4.2% Amer. Ind.; 0.1% Pac. Isl.; 4.0% other; 2+ races 6.9%. **Hispanic pop.:** 14.0%. **Foreign born:** 9.9%. **U.S. citizens:** 92.9%. **Language:** 85.1% English only; 11.1% Spanish.
Employment: 180,202 employed; 5.3% unemployed. **Per capita income:** $45,350; change (2011-12): 4.4%. **Below poverty**

level: 19.7%; 15.5% of families. **Educational attainment:** 86.6% HS; 29.8% bachelor's. **Avg. commute:** 18.3 min. 80.6% drive; 11.3% carpool. **Housing units:** 186,258; 88.0% occupied. **Home ownership:** 53.8%. **Avg. home:** $143,100; change (2011-13): 10.3%. **Avg. rent:** $712.
Mayor: Dewey F. Bartlett Jr., Republican
History: Settled in 1836 by Creek Indians; modern town founded 1882; inc. 1898; oil discovered early 20th century. Emerging telecommunications hub.
Website: www.cityoftulsa.org

Virginia Beach, Virginia

Population: 448,479 (39). **Pop. density:** 1,798. **Pop. change (2010-13):** 2.1%. **Area:** 249.4 sq mi. **Racial distribution:** 68.7% white; 19.2% black; 6.3% Asian; 0.3% Amer. Ind.; 0.1% Pac. Isl.; 1.1% other; 2+ races 4.3%. **Hispanic pop.:** 6.7%. **Foreign born:** 8.7%. **U.S. citizens:** 96.5%. **Language:** 88.6% English only; 3.8% Spanish.
Employment: 217,138 employed; 5.3% unemployed. **Per capita income:** $44,321; change (2011-12): 2.9%. **Below poverty level:** 7.4%; 5.7% of families. **Educational attainment:** 93.1% HS; 32.3% bachelor's. **Avg. commute:** 22.7 min. 82.1% drive. **Housing units:** 177,945; 92.3% occupied. **Home ownership:** 64.9%. **Avg. home:** $193,000; change (2011-13): 5.5%. **Avg. rent:** $1,224.
Mayor: William D. Sessoms Jr., nonpartisan
History: Area founded by Capt. John Smith 1607; formed by merger with Princess Anne Co. 1963.
Website: www.vbgov.com

Washington, District of Columbia

Population: 646,449 (23). **Pop. density:** 10,574. **Pop. change (2010-13):** 6.8%. **Area:** 61.1 sq mi. **Racial distribution:** 39.5% white; 51.1% black; 3.5% Asian; 0.4% Amer. Ind.; 0.1% Pac. Isl.; 3.4% other; 2+ races 2.1%. **Hispanic pop.:** 9.3%. **Foreign born:** 13.5%. **U.S. citizens:** 91.6%. **Language:** 85.1% English only; 7.1% Spanish.
Employment: 339,708 employed; 8.3% unemployed. **Per capita income:** $61,743; change (2011-12): 1.5%. **Below poverty level:** 18.5%; 14.2% of families. **Educational attainment:** 87.5% HS; 51.2% bachelor's. **Avg. commute:** 29.6 min. 37.8% public trans.; 34.7% drive; 12.1% walk. **Housing units:** 296,671; 88.0% occupied. **Home ownership:** 42.4%. **Avg. home:** $381,900; change (2011-13): 17.4%. **Avg. rent:** $1,200.
Mayor: Vincent C. Gray, Democrat
History: U.S. capital; site on Potomac R. chosen by George Washington, 1790, on land ceded from VA and MD (portion S of Potomac returned to VA 1846). Congress first met 1800; inc. 1802; sacked by British, War of 1812. 125 killed in Sept. 11, 2001, terrorist attack on the Pentagon.
Website: dc.gov

Wichita, Kansas

Population: 386,552 (49). **Pop. density:** 2,409. **Pop. change (2010-13):** 1.0%. **Area:** 160.4 sq mi. **Racial distribution:** 74.2% white; 10.9% black; 4.9% Asian; 0.9% Amer. Ind.; 0.1% Pac. Isl.; 4.5% other; 2+ races 4.5%. **Hispanic pop.:** 14.9%. **Foreign born:** 9.8%. **U.S. citizens:** 94.1%. **Language:** 84.1% English only; 10.2% Spanish.
Employment: 173,234 employed; 6.6% unemployed. **Per capita income:** $41,152; change (2011-12): 2.8%. **Below poverty level:** 16.5%; 12.3% of families. **Educational attainment:** 87.1% HS; 28.3% bachelor's. **Avg. commute:** 17.5 min. 84.7% drive. **Housing units:** 167,191; 90.3% occupied. **Home ownership:** 61.6%. **Avg. home:** $122,200; change (2011-13): 5.7%. **Avg. rent:** $675.
Mayor: Carl Brewer, nonpartisan
History: Founded 1864; inc. 1871. Established itself as aircraft manufacturing hub between WWI and WWII.
Website: www.wichita.gov

Winston-Salem, North Carolina

Population: 236,441 (86). **Pop. density:** 1,785. **Pop. change (2010-13):** 2.8%. **Area:** 132.5 sq mi. **Racial distribution:** 55.5% white; 34.9% black; 2.1% Asian; 0.2% Amer. Ind.; <0.05% Pac. Isl.; 5.5% other; 2+ races 1.9%. **Hispanic pop.:** 14.8%. **Foreign born:** 11.1%. **U.S. citizens:** 91.4%. **Language:** 82.8% English only; 13.7% Spanish.
Employment: 103,788 employed; 7.3% unemployed. **Per capita income:** $37,625; change (2011-12): 4.3%. **Below poverty level:** 22.0%; 16.9% of families. **Educational attainment:** 85.5% HS; 32.0% bachelor's. **Avg. commute:** 19.1 min. 82.2% drive. **Housing units:** 104,299; 87.0% occupied. **Home ownership:** 57.2%. **Avg. home:** $128,700; change (2011-13): 2.2%. **Avg. rent:** $693.
Mayor: Allen Joines, Democrat
History: Salem founded 1766; Winston founded 1849; became Winston-Salem 1913. The Reynolds Building, completed 1929, used as model for Empire State Building (designed by same architects).
Website: www.cityofws.org

UNITED STATES POPULATION

Census Origins and Methods

A census is conducted in the U.S. every 10 years. The primary purpose is to apportion seats in the House of Representatives. Census data is also used to determine the boundaries of state legislative districts and the distribution of federal funds to local, state, and tribal governments.

The first U.S. census, mandated by Article 1, Section 2 of the Constitution, was conducted in 1790, a little more than a year after George Washington became president. It counted the numbers of free white males ages 16 and over (as a measure of available workers and military personnel), free white males under 16, free white females, all other free persons, and slaves. The data was collected over 18 months, at a cost of about $44,000, or $1.1 million in current dollars. The 1790 census counted a total of 3.9 million people, resulting in an increase from 65 to 105 seats in the House of Representatives.

As the nation grew, so did the scope of the census. The first inquiries on manufacturing were made in 1810. Questions on "the pursuits, industry, education, and resources of the country" were added to the 1840 census. It took a full 10 years to publish the results of the 1880 and 1890 censuses because of the number of questions asked. Because of those delays, Congress limited the 1900 census to questions on population, mortality, agriculture, and manufacturing.

Today, the secretary of commerce and the Census Bureau are directed by law to collect data on population, housing, employment, agriculture, manufacturing, trade, construction, transportation, and governments, among other things, at stated intervals. They also conduct smaller-scale surveys on behalf of other federal agencies.

U.S. marshals administered the earliest decennial censuses by visiting each household and reporting to the president (1790), to the secretary of state (1800-40), or to the secretary of the interior (1850-70). Trained census-takers were hired for the 1880 census and thereafter. In 1902, Congress authorized a permanent Census Office within the Interior Department. In 1903, the agency was transferred to the new Department of Commerce and Labor. When a separate labor department was created in 1913, the Census Bureau remained with the Commerce Department.

The 1790 through 1820 decennial censuses were conducted on the first Monday in Aug. The 1830-80 and 1900 censuses were on June 1 while the 1890 census was as of June 2. The 1910 census was on Apr. 15, the 1920 census on Jan. 1, and every census since 1930 has been as of Apr. 1.

The Census Bureau began using statistical sampling techniques in the 1940s, the first modern computer in the 1950s, and enumeration by mail in the 1960s. These innovations allowed the Bureau to publish data more quickly, at a lower cost and with less burden on the public. Any personally identifiable information that it gathers is withheld from the public for 72 years, after which it can be accessed through the National Archives. The 1940 Census records can now be accessed using various commercial and government websites, including 1940census.archives.gov.

Prior to 2010, about five in six households responded to the short-form census while one in six households answered a long-form questionnaire, which asked about details such as ancestry, marital status, and occupation. The 2005 implementation of the American Community Survey (ACS) made the long-form questionnaire no longer necessary. Conducted yearly on a random sample of the population, the ACS gathers demographic, economic, and housing information on communities across the country.

U.S. Population by State and Region, 2000, 2013

Source: Population Estimates Program, Decennial Census, U.S. Census Bureau, U.S. Dept. of Commerce

(ranked by 2013 resident population)

Rank	State	2013[1]	2000[2]	% change, 2000-13	Rank	State	2013[1]	2000[2]	% change, 2000-13
1.	California	38,332,521	33,871,648	13.2%	29.	Connecticut	3,596,080	3,405,565	5.6%
2.	Texas	26,448,193	20,851,820	26.8	30.	Iowa	3,090,416	2,926,324	5.6
3.	New York	19,651,127	18,976,457	3.6	31.	Mississippi	2,991,207	2,844,658	5.2
4.	Florida	19,552,860	15,982,378	22.3	32.	Arkansas	2,959,373	2,673,400	10.7
5.	Illinois	12,882,135	12,419,293	3.7	33.	Utah	2,900,872	2,233,169	29.9
6.	Pennsylvania	12,773,801	12,281,054	4.0	34.	Kansas	2,893,957	2,688,418	7.6
7.	Ohio	11,570,808	11,353,140	1.9	35.	Nevada	2,790,136	1,998,257	39.6
8.	Georgia	9,992,167	8,186,453	22.1	36.	New Mexico	2,085,287	1,819,046	14.6
9.	Michigan	9,895,622	9,938,444	-0.4	37.	Nebraska	1,868,516	1,711,263	9.2
10.	North Carolina	9,848,060	8,049,313	22.3	38.	West Virginia	1,854,304	1,808,344	2.5
11.	New Jersey	8,899,339	8,414,350	5.8	39.	Idaho	1,612,136	1,293,953	24.6
12.	Virginia	8,260,405	7,078,515	16.7	40.	Hawaii	1,404,054	1,211,537	15.9
13.	Washington	6,971,406	5,894,121	18.3	41.	Maine	1,328,302	1,274,923	4.2
14.	Massachusetts	6,692,824	6,349,097	5.4	42.	New Hampshire	1,323,459	1,235,786	7.1
15.	Arizona	6,626,624	5,130,632	29.2	43.	Rhode Island	1,051,511	1,048,319	0.3
16.	Indiana	6,570,902	6,080,485	8.1	44.	Montana	1,015,165	902,195	12.5
17.	Tennessee	6,495,978	5,689,283	14.2	45.	Delaware	925,749	783,600	18.1
18.	Missouri	6,044,171	5,595,211	8.0	46.	South Dakota	844,877	754,844	11.9
19.	Maryland	5,928,814	5,296,486	11.9	47.	Alaska	735,132	626,932	17.3
20.	Wisconsin	5,742,713	5,363,675	7.1	48.	North Dakota	723,393	642,200	12.6
21.	Minnesota	5,420,380	4,919,479	10.2	49.	District of Columbia	646,449	572,059	13.0
22.	Colorado	5,268,367	4,301,261	22.5	50.	Vermont	626,630	608,827	2.9
23.	Alabama	4,833,722	4,447,100	8.7	51.	Wyoming	582,658	493,782	18.0
24.	South Carolina	4,774,839	4,012,012	19.0		United States	316,128,839	281,421,906	12.3
25.	Louisiana	4,625,470	4,468,976	3.5		Northeast[3]	55,943,073	53,594,378	4.4
26.	Kentucky	4,395,295	4,041,769	8.7		Midwest[4]	67,547,890	64,392,776	4.9
27.	Oregon	3,930,065	3,421,399	14.9		South[5]	118,383,453	100,236,820	18.1
28.	Oklahoma	3,850,568	3,450,654	11.6		West[6]	74,254,423	63,197,932	17.5

Note: The U.S. resident population consists of individuals whose usual residence, or where they live and sleep most of the time, is in one of the 50 states or DC. It excludes overseas U.S. military personnel and civilian U.S. citizens living abroad. (1) Estimates are as of July 1. (2) Figures are for Apr. 1 of decennial census year. (3) Incl. the states of the New England (Connecticut, Maine, Massachusetts, New Hampshire, Rhode Island, Vermont) and Middle Atlantic (New Jersey, New York, Pennsylvania) divisions. (4) Incl. the states of the East North Central (Illinois, Indiana, Michigan, Ohio, Wisconsin) and West North Central (Iowa, Kansas, Minnesota, Missouri, Nebraska, North Dakota, South Dakota) divisions. (5) Incl. the states of the South Atlantic (Delaware, DC, Florida, Georgia, Maryland, North Carolina, South Carolina, Virginia, West Virginia), East South Central (Alabama, Kentucky, Mississippi, Tennessee), and West South Central (Arkansas, Louisiana, Oklahoma, Texas) divisions. (6) Incl. the states of the Mountain (Arizona, Colorado, Idaho, Montana, Nevada, New Mexico, Utah, Wyoming) and Pacific (Alaska, California, Hawaii, Oregon, Washington) divisions.

U.S. Population by Official

Source: Decennial Censuses, U.S. Census Bureau,
(population figures for 1790-1860)

State	1790	1800	1810	1820	1830	1840	1850	1860	1870	1880	1890	1900	1910	1920
AL[1]	—	1	9	128	310	591	772	964	996,992	1,262,505	1,513,401	1,828,697	2,138,093	2,348,174
AK	—	—	—	—	—	—	—	—	—	33,426	32,052	63,592	64,356	55,036
AZ[2]	—	—	—	—	—	—	—	—	9,658	40,440	88,243	122,931	204,354	334,162
AR	—	—	1	14	30	98	210	435	484,471	802,525	1,128,211	1,311,564	1,574,449	1,752,204
CA	—	—	—	—	—	—	93	380	560,247	864,694	1,213,398	1,485,053	2,377,549	3,426,861
CO[2]	—	—	—	—	—	—	—	34	39,864	194,327	413,249	539,700	799,024	939,629
CT	238	251	262	275	298	310	371	460	537,454	622,700	746,258	908,420	1,114,756	1,380,631
DE	59	64	73	73	77	78	92	112	125,015	146,608	168,493	184,735	202,322	223,003
DC	—	8	16	23	30	34	52	75	131,700	177,624	230,392	278,718	331,069	437,571
FL	—	—	—	—	35	54	87	140	187,748	269,493	391,422	528,542	752,619	968,470
GA	83	163	252	341	517	691	906	1,057	1,184,109	1,542,180	1,837,353	2,216,331	2,609,121	2,895,832
HI[3]	—	—	—	—	—	—	—	—	—	—	—	154,001	191,909	255,912
ID[3]	—	—	—	—	—	—	—	—	14,999	32,610	88,548	161,772	325,594	431,866
IL	—	—	12	55	157	476	851	1,712	2,539,891	3,077,871	3,826,352	4,821,550	5,638,591	6,485,280
IN	—	6	25	147	343	686	988	1,350	1,680,637	1,978,301	2,192,404	2,516,462	2,700,876	2,930,390
IA	—	—	—	—	—	43	192	675	1,194,020	1,624,615	1,912,297	2,231,853	2,224,771	2,404,021
KS	—	—	—	—	—	—	—	107	364,399	996,096	1,428,108	1,470,495	1,690,949	1,769,257
KY	74	221	407	564	688	780	982	1,156	1,321,011	1,648,690	1,858,635	2,147,174	2,289,905	2,416,630
LA	—	—	77	153	216	352	518	708	726,915	939,946	1,118,588	1,381,625	1,656,388	1,798,509
ME[4]	97	152	229	298	399	502	583	628	626,915	648,936	661,086	694,466	742,371	768,014
MD	320	342	381	407	447	470	583	687	780,894	934,943	1,042,390	1,188,044	1,295,346	1,449,661
MA[4]	379	423	472	523	610	738	995	1,231	1,457,351	1,783,085	2,238,947	2,805,346	3,366,416	3,852,356
MI	—	—	5	9	32	212	398	749	1,184,059	1,636,937	2,093,890	2,420,982	2,810,173	3,668,412
MN	—	—	—	—	—	—	6	172	439,706	780,773	1,310,283	1,751,394	2,075,708	2,387,125
MS[1]	—	8	31	75	137	376	607	791	827,922	1,131,597	1,289,600	1,551,270	1,797,114	1,790,618
MO	—	—	20	67	140	384	682	1,182	1,721,295	2,168,380	2,679,185	3,106,665	3,293,335	3,404,055
MT[3]	—	—	—	—	—	—	—	—	20,595	39,159	142,924	243,329	376,053	548,889
NE	—	—	—	—	—	—	—	29	122,993	452,402	1,062,656	1,066,300	1,192,214	1,296,372
NV[2]	—	—	—	—	—	—	—	7	42,491	62,266	47,355	42,335	81,875	77,407
NH	142	184	214	244	269	285	318	326	318,300	346,991	376,530	411,588	430,572	443,083
NJ	184	211	246	278	321	373	490	672	906,096	1,131,116	1,444,933	1,883,669	2,537,167	3,155,900
NM[2]	—	—	—	—	—	—	62	94	91,874	119,565	160,282	195,310	327,301	360,350
NY	340	589	959	1,373	1,919	2,429	3,097	3,881	4,382,759	5,082,871	6,003,174	7,268,894	9,113,614	10,385,227
NC	394	478	556	639	736	753	869	993	1,071,361	1,399,750	1,617,949	1,893,810	2,206,287	2,559,123
ND[5]	—	—	—	—	—	—	—	—	2,405	36,909	190,983	319,146	577,056	646,872
OH	—	45	231	581	938	1,519	1,980	2,340	2,665,260	3,198,062	3,672,329	4,157,545	4,767,121	5,759,394
OK	—	—	—	—	—	—	—	—	—	258,657	790,391	1,657,155	2,028,283
OR[6]	—	—	—	—	—	—	12	52	90,923	174,768	317,704	413,536	672,765	783,389
PA	434	602	810	1,049	1,348	1,724	2,312	2,906	3,521,951	4,282,891	5,258,113	6,302,115	7,665,111	8,720,017
RI	69	69	77	83	97	109	148	175	217,353	276,531	345,506	428,556	542,610	604,397
SC	249	346	415	503	581	594	669	704	705,606	995,577	1,151,149	1,340,316	1,515,400	1,683,724
SD[5]	—	—	—	—	—	—	—	5	11,776	98,268	348,600	401,570	583,888	636,547
TN	36	106	262	423	682	829	1,003	1,110	1,258,520	1,542,359	1,767,518	2,020,616	2,184,789	2,337,885
TX	—	—	—	—	—	—	213	604	818,579	1,591,749	2,235,527	3,048,710	3,896,542	4,663,228
UT	—	—	—	—	—	—	11	40	86,786	143,963	210,779	276,749	373,351	449,396
VT	85	154	218	236	281	292	314	315	330,551	332,286	332,422	343,641	355,956	352,428
VA[7]	692	808	878	938	1,044	1,025	1,120	1,220	1,225,163	1,512,565	1,655,980	1,854,184	2,061,612	2,309,187
WA[3,6]	—	—	—	—	—	—	—	12	23,955	75,116	357,232	518,103	1,141,990	1,356,621
WV[7]	56	79	105	137	177	225	302	377	442,014	618,457	762,794	958,800	1,221,119	1,463,701
WI	—	—	—	—	—	31	305	776	1,054,670	1,315,497	1,693,330	2,069,042	2,333,860	2,632,067
WY[3]	—	—	—	—	—	—	—	—	9,118	20,789	62,555	92,531	145,965	194,402
U.S.[8]	3,929	5,308	7,240	9,638	12,866	17,063	23,192	31,443	38,558,371	50,189,209	62,979,766	76,212,168	92,228,531	106,021,568

Note: Unless otherwise noted, pop. shown is for a state's present-day area. Excl. overseas U.S. military personnel and civilian U.S. citizens living abroad. (1) 1800-10 figures for MS are for those areas of Mississippi Territory now part of present-day AL and MS. (2) 1850 figure for NM incl. parts of New Mexico Territory now part of present-day AZ, NM, CO, and NV; 1860 figure incl. parts taken in formation of Arizona Territory in 1863. (3) 1860 figure for WA incl. pop. in present-day ID and parts of MT and WY. (4) 1790-1810 figures for MA do not incl. district taken to form state of ME in 1820. (5) 1860 figure is for Dakota Territory, which comprised present-day ND and SD; 1870-80 figures are for parts of territory that became the two states in 1889. (6) Parts of Oregon Territory went to Washington Territory in 1853 and 1859. 1850 pop. in those areas are listed under WA, not OR. (7) 1790-1860 figures for VA do not incl. areas taken in creation of WV in 1863. (8) 1830-40 totals incl. persons (5,318 in 1830; 6,100 in 1840) on public ships in service of the U.S. not credited to any state.

Estimated Population of American Colonies, 1630-1780

Source: U.S. Census Bureau, U.S. Dept. of Commerce
(numbers in thousands)

Colony	1630	1650	1670	1690	1700	1720	1740	1750	1760	1770	1780
Total	4.6	50.4	111.9	210.4	250.9	466.2	905.6	1,170.8	1,593.6	2,148.1	2,780.4
Connecticut	—	4.1	12.6	21.6	26.0	58.8	89.6	111.3	142.5	183.9	206.7
Delaware	—	0.2	0.7	1.5	2.5	5.4	19.9	28.7	33.3	35.5	45.4
Georgia	—	—	—	—	—	—	2.0	5.2	9.6	23.4	56.1
Kentucky[1]	—	—	—	—	—	—	—	—	—	15.7	45.0
Maine (counties)[2]	0.4	1.0									
Maryland	—	4.5	13.2	24.0	29.6	66.1	116.1	141.1	162.3	202.6	245.5
Massachusetts and Plymouth[2,3]	0.9	15.6	35.3	56.9	55.9	91.0	151.6	188.0	202.6	235.3	268.6
New Hampshire	0.5	1.3	1.8	4.2	5.0	9.4	23.3	27.5	39.1	62.4	87.8
New Jersey	—	—	1.0	8.0	14.0	29.8	51.4	71.4	93.8	117.4	139.6
New York	0.4	4.1	5.8	13.9	19.1	36.9	63.7	76.7	117.1	162.9	210.5
North Carolina	—	—	3.9	7.6	10.7	21.3	51.8	73.0	110.4	197.2	270.1
Pennsylvania	—	—	—	11.4	18.0	31.0	85.6	119.7	183.7	240.1	327.3
Rhode Island	—	0.8	2.2	4.2	5.9	11.7	25.3	33.2	45.5	58.2	52.9
South Carolina	—	—	0.2	3.9	5.7	17.0	45.0	64.0	94.1	124.2	180.0
Tennessee[4]	—	—	—	—	—	—	—	—	—	1.0	10.0
Vermont[5]	—	—	—	—	—	—	—	—	—	10.0	47.6
Virginia	2.5	18.7	35.3	53.0	58.6	87.8	180.4	231.0	339.7	447.0	538.0

Note: With the exception of KY, ME, Plymouth, TN, and VT, colonies shown are the original 13 states. (1) Admitted as state 1792. (2) For 1660-1750, the pop. of ME counties are included with MA. ME was annexed by MA in the 1650s but became a separate state in 1820. (3) Plymouth became part of Prov. of Massachusetts in 1691. (4) Admitted as state 1796. (5) Admitted as state 1791.

Census, 1790-2010

U.S. Dept. of Commerce
only are in thousands)

1930	1940	1950	1960	1970	1980	1990	2000	2010	State
2,646,248	2,832,961	3,061,743	3,266,740	3,444,165	3,893,888	4,040,587	4,447,100	4,779,736	AL
59,278	72,524	128,643	226,167	300,382	401,851	550,043	626,932	710,231	AK
435,573	499,261	749,587	1,302,161	1,770,900	2,718,215	3,665,228	5,130,632	6,392,017	AZ
1,854,482	1,949,387	1,909,511	1,786,272	1,923,295	2,286,435	2,350,725	2,673,400	2,915,918	AR
5,677,251	6,907,387	10,586,223	15,717,204	19,953,134	23,667,902	29,760,021	33,871,648	37,253,956	CA
1,035,791	1,123,296	1,325,089	1,753,947	2,207,259	2,889,964	3,294,394	4,301,261	5,029,196	CO
1,606,903	1,709,242	2,007,280	2,535,234	3,031,709	3,107,576	3,287,116	3,405,565	3,574,097	CT
238,380	266,505	318,085	446,292	548,104	594,338	666,168	783,600	897,934	DE
486,869	663,091	802,178	763,956	756,510	638,333	606,900	572,059	601,723	DC
1,468,211	1,897,414	2,771,305	4,951,560	6,789,443	9,746,324	12,937,926	15,982,378	18,801,310	FL
2,908,506	3,123,723	3,444,578	3,943,116	4,589,575	5,463,105	6,478,216	8,186,453	9,687,653	GA
368,336	422,330	499,794	632,772	768,561	964,691	1,108,229	1,211,537	1,360,301	HI
445,032	524,873	588,637	667,191	712,567	943,935	1,006,749	1,293,953	1,567,582	ID
7,630,654	7,897,241	8,712,176	10,081,158	11,113,976	11,426,518	11,430,602	12,419,293	12,830,632	IL
3,238,503	3,427,796	3,934,224	4,662,498	5,193,669	5,490,224	5,544,159	6,080,485	6,483,802	IN
2,470,939	2,538,268	2,621,073	2,757,537	2,824,376	2,913,808	2,776,755	2,926,324	3,046,355	IA
1,880,999	1,801,028	1,905,299	2,178,611	2,246,578	2,363,679	2,477,574	2,688,418	2,853,118	KS
2,614,589	2,845,627	2,944,806	3,038,156	3,218,706	3,660,777	3,685,296	4,041,769	4,339,367	KY
2,101,593	2,363,880	2,683,516	3,257,022	3,641,306	4,205,900	4,219,973	4,468,976	4,533,372	LA
797,423	847,226	913,774	969,265	992,048	1,124,660	1,227,928	1,274,923	1,328,361	ME
1,631,526	1,821,244	2,343,001	3,100,689	3,922,399	4,216,975	4,781,468	5,296,486	5,773,552	MD
4,249,614	4,316,721	4,690,514	5,148,578	5,689,170	5,737,037	6,016,425	6,349,097	6,547,629	MA
4,842,325	5,256,106	6,371,766	7,823,194	8,875,083	9,262,078	9,295,297	9,938,444	9,883,640	MI
2,563,953	2,792,300	2,982,483	3,413,864	3,804,971	4,075,970	4,375,099	4,919,479	5,303,925	MN
2,009,821	2,183,796	2,178,914	2,178,141	2,216,912	2,520,638	2,573,216	2,844,658	2,967,297	MS
3,629,367	3,784,664	3,954,653	4,319,813	4,676,501	4,916,686	5,117,073	5,595,211	5,988,927	MO
537,606	559,456	591,024	674,767	694,409	786,690	799,065	902,195	989,415	MT
1,377,963	1,315,834	1,325,510	1,411,330	1,483,493	1,569,825	1,578,385	1,711,263	1,826,341	NE
91,058	110,247	160,083	285,278	488,738	800,493	1,201,833	1,998,257	2,700,551	NV
465,293	491,524	533,242	606,921	737,681	920,610	1,109,252	1,235,786	1,316,470	NH
4,041,334	4,160,165	4,835,329	6,066,782	7,168,164	7,364,823	7,730,188	8,414,350	8,791,894	NJ
423,317	531,818	681,187	951,023	1,016,000	1,302,894	1,515,069	1,819,046	2,059,179	NM
12,588,066	13,479,142	14,830,192	16,782,304	18,236,967	17,558,072	17,990,455	18,976,457	19,378,102	NY
3,170,276	3,571,623	4,061,929	4,556,155	5,082,059	5,881,766	6,628,637	8,049,313	9,535,483	NC
680,845	641,935	619,636	632,446	617,761	652,717	638,800	642,200	672,591	ND
6,646,697	6,907,612	7,946,627	9,706,397	10,652,017	10,797,630	10,847,115	11,353,140	11,536,504	OH
2,396,040	2,336,434	2,233,351	2,328,284	2,559,229	3,025,290	3,145,585	3,450,654	3,751,351	OK
953,786	1,089,684	1,521,341	1,768,687	2,091,385	2,633,105	2,842,321	3,421,399	3,831,074	OR
9,631,350	9,900,180	10,498,012	11,319,366	11,793,909	11,863,895	11,881,643	12,281,054	12,702,379	PA
687,497	713,346	791,896	859,488	949,723	947,154	1,003,464	1,048,319	1,052,567	RI
1,738,765	1,899,804	2,117,027	2,382,594	2,590,516	3,121,820	3,486,703	4,012,012	4,625,364	SC
692,849	642,961	652,740	680,514	665,507	690,768	696,004	754,844	814,180	SD
2,616,556	2,915,841	3,291,718	3,567,089	3,923,687	4,591,120	4,877,185	5,689,283	6,346,105	TN
5,824,715	6,414,824	7,711,194	9,579,677	11,196,730	14,229,191	16,986,510	20,851,820	25,145,561	TX
507,847	550,310	688,862	890,627	1,059,273	1,461,037	1,722,850	2,233,169	2,763,885	UT
359,611	359,231	377,747	389,881	444,330	511,456	562,758	608,827	625,741	VT
2,421,851	2,677,773	3,318,680	3,966,949	4,648,494	5,346,818	6,187,358	7,078,515	8,001,024	VA
1,563,396	1,736,191	2,378,963	2,853,214	3,409,169	4,132,156	4,866,692	5,894,121	6,724,540	WA
1,729,205	1,901,974	2,005,552	1,860,421	1,744,237	1,949,644	1,793,477	1,808,344	1,852,994	WV
2,939,006	3,137,587	3,434,575	3,951,777	4,417,731	4,705,767	4,891,769	5,363,675	5,686,986	WI
225,565	250,742	290,529	330,066	332,416	469,557	453,588	493,782	563,626	WY
123,202,660	132,164,569	151,325,798	179,323,175	203,211,926	226,545,805	248,709,873	281,421,906	308,745,538	U.S.

U.S. Center of Population, 1790-2010

Source: Decennial Censuses, Geography Division, U.S. Census Bureau, U.S. Dept. of Commerce

The country's (**mean**) **center of population** is the center of population gravity. In other words, it is the point upon which the U.S. would balance if the country were a rigid, weightless plane and its population was distributed thereon, with each individual assuming an equal weight.

Census year	N Lat °	'	"	W Long °	'	"	Approximate location
1790	39	16	30	76	11	12	Kent Co., MD, 23 miles east of Baltimore
1800	39	16	6	76	56	30	Howard Co., MD, 18 miles west of Baltimore
1810	39	11	30	77	37	12	Loudoun Co., VA, 40 miles northwest by west of Washington, DC
1820	39	5	42	78	33	0	Hardy Co., WV[1], 16 miles east of Moorefield
1830	38	57	54	79	16	54	Grant Co., WV[1], 19 miles west-southwest of Moorefield
1840	39	2	0	80	18	0	Upshur Co., WV[1], 16 miles south of Clarksburg
1850	38	59	0	81	19	0	Wirt Co., WV[1], 23 miles southeast of Parkersburg
1860	39	0	24	82	48	48	Pike Co., OH, 20 miles south by east of Chillicothe
1870	39	12	0	83	35	42	Highland Co., OH, 48 miles east by north of Cincinnati
1880	39	4	8	84	39	40	Boone Co., KY, 8 miles west by south of Cincinnati, OH
1890	39	11	56	85	32	53	Decatur Co., IN, 20 miles east of Columbus
1900	39	9	36	85	48	54	Bartholomew Co., IN, 6 miles southeast of Columbus
1910	39	10	12	86	32	20	Monroe Co., IN, in the city of Bloomington
1920	39	10	21	86	43	15	Owen Co., IN, 8 miles south-southeast of Spencer
1930	39	3	45	87	8	6	Greene Co., IN, 3 miles northeast of Linton
1940	38	56	54	87	22	35	Sullivan Co., IN, 2 miles southeast by east of Carlisle
1950	38	50	21	88	9	33	Richland Co., IL, 8 miles north-northwest of Olney
1950[2]	38	48	15	88	22	8	Clay Co., IL, 3 miles northeast of Louisville
1960[2]	38	35	58	89	12	35	Clinton Co., IL, 6.5 miles northwest of Centralia
1970[2]	38	27	47	89	42	22	St. Clair Co., IL, 5 miles east-southeast of Mascoutah
1980[2]	38	8	13	90	34	26	Jefferson Co., MO, 0.25 mile west of DeSoto
1990[2]	37	52	20	91	12	55	Crawford Co., MO, 9.7 miles southeast of Steelville
2000[2]	37	41	49	91	48	34	Phelps Co., MO, 2.8 miles east of Edgar Springs
2010[2]	37	31	3	92	10	23	Texas Co., MO, 2.7 miles northeast of Plato

(1) Pres. Lincoln signed a bill Dec. 31, 1862, approving statehood for West Virginia (made up of former Virginia counties). It was admitted to the Union June 20, 1863. (2) Incl. Alaska and Hawaii.

Density of U.S. Population by State, 1930-2010

Source: Decennial Censuses, U.S. Census Bureau, U.S. Dept. of Commerce

(per square mile of land area)

State	1930	1950	1970	1990	2010	State	1930	1950	1970	1990	2010
AL......	52.3	60.5	68.0	79.8	94.4	MT	3.7	4.1	4.8	5.5	6.8
AK......	0.1	0.2	0.5	1.0	1.2	NE......	17.9	17.3	19.3	20.5	23.8
AZ......	3.8	6.6	15.6	32.3	56.3	NV......	0.8	1.5	4.5	10.9	24.6
AR......	35.6	36.7	37.0	45.2	56.0	NH......	52.0	59.6	82.4	123.9	147.0
CA......	36.4	68.0	128.1	191.0	239.1	NJ......	549.5	657.5	974.7	1,051.1	1,195.5
CO......	10.0	12.8	21.3	31.8	48.5	NM......	3.5	5.6	8.4	12.5	17.0
CT......	331.8	414.5	626.1	678.8	738.1	NY......	267.1	314.7	387.0	381.7	411.2
DE......	122.3	163.2	281.3	341.9	460.8	NC......	65.2	83.5	104.5	136.3	196.1
DC 7,975.1		13,140.0	12,392.0	9,941.3	9,856.5	ND	9.9	9.0	9.0	9.3	9.7
FL.......	27.4	51.7	126.6	241.3	350.6	OH......	162.7	194.5	260.7	265.5	282.3
GA......	50.6	59.9	79.8	112.6	168.4	OK	34.9	32.6	37.3	45.9	54.7
HI	57.3	77.8	119.7	172.6	211.8	OR	9.9	15.8	21.8	29.6	39.9
ID	5.4	7.1	8.6	12.2	19.0	PA......	215.3	234.6	263.6	265.6	283.9
IL.......	137.4	156.9	200.2	205.9	231.1	RI	665.0	766.0	915.8	970.6	1,018.1
IN	90.4	109.8	145.0	154.8	181.0	SC......	57.8	70.4	86.2	116.0	153.9
IA	44.2	46.9	50.6	49.7	54.5	SD......	9.1	8.6	8.8	9.2	10.7
KS......	23.0	23.3	27.5	30.3	34.9	TN......	63.5	79.8	95.2	118.3	153.9
KY......	66.2	74.6	81.5	93.3	109.9	TX......	22.3	29.5	42.9	65.0	96.3
LA......	48.6	62.1	84.3	97.7	104.9	UT......	6.2	8.4	12.9	21.0	33.6
ME	25.9	29.6	32.2	39.8	43.1	VT........	39.0	41.0	48.2	61.1	67.9
MD	168.1	241.4	404.1	492.6	594.8	VA	61.3	84.0	117.7	156.7	202.6
MA	544.8	601.3	729.4	771.3	839.4	WA	23.5	35.8	51.3	73.2	101.2
MI	85.6	112.7	157.0	164.4	174.8	WV......	71.9	83.4	72.6	74.6	77.1
MN	32.2	37.5	47.8	54.9	66.6	WI.......	54.3	63.4	81.6	90.3	105.0
MS	42.8	46.4	47.2	54.8	63.2	WY......	2.3	3.0	3.4	4.7	5.8
MO	52.8	57.5	68.0	74.4	87.1	U.S.	34.7	42.6	57.5	70.4	87.4

Note: For the sake of comparison, the densities of Alaska and Hawaii in 1930 and 1950 are included though they were not yet states.

U.S. Area and Population, 1790-2010

Source: Decennial Censuses, U.S. Census Bureau, U.S. Dept. of Commerce

Census date	AREA (square miles)			RESIDENT POPULATION			
	Total area[1]	Land area	Water area[1]	Number	Per sq mi of land	Increase over preceding census Number	%
1790 (Aug. 2)	891,364	864,746	24,065	3,929,214	4.5	—	—
1800 (Aug. 4)	891,364	864,746	24,065	5,308,483	6.1	1,379,269	35.1%
1810 (Aug. 6)	1,722,685	1,681,828	34,175	7,239,881	4.3	1,931,398	36.4
1820 (Aug. 7)	1,792,552	1,749,462	38,544	9,638,453	5.5	2,398,572	33.1
1830 (June 1)	1,792,552	1,749,462	38,544	12,866,020	7.4	3,227,567	33.5
1840 (June 1)	1,792,552	1,749,462	38,544	17,069,453	9.8	4,203,433	32.7
1850 (June 1)	2,991,655	2,940,042	52,705	23,191,876	7.9	6,122,423	35.9
1860 (June 1)	3,021,295	2,969,640	52,747	31,443,321	10.6	8,251,445	35.6
1870 (June 1)	3,612,299	3,540,705	68,082	39,818,449	11.2	8,375,128	26.6
1880 (June 1)	3,612,299	3,540,705	68,082	50,189,209	14.2	10,370,760	26.0
1890 (June 1)	3,612,299	3,540,705	68,082	62,979,766	17.8	12,790,557	25.5
1900 (June 1)	3,618,770	3,547,314	67,901	76,212,168	21.5	13,232,402	21.0
1910 (Apr. 15)	3,618,770	3,547,045	68,170	92,228,496	26.0	16,016,328	21.0
1920 (Jan. 1)	3,618,770	3,546,931	68,284	106,021,537	29.9	13,793,041	15.0
1930 (Apr. 1)	3,618,770	3,554,608	60,607	123,202,624	34.7	17,181,087	16.2
1940 (Apr. 1)	3,618,770	3,554,608	60,607	132,164,569	37.2	8,961,945	7.3
1950 (Apr. 1)	3,618,770	3,552,206	63,005	151,325,798	42.6	19,161,229	14.5
1960 (Apr. 1)	3,618,770	3,540,911	74,212	179,323,175	50.6	27,997,377	18.5
1970 (Apr. 1)	3,618,770	3,536,855	78,444	203,302,031	57.5	23,978,856	13.4
1980 (Apr. 1)	3,618,770	3,539,289	79,481	226,542,199	64.0	23,240,168	11.4
1990 (Apr. 1)	3,717,796	3,536,278	181,518	248,718,302	70.3	22,176,103	9.8
2000 (Apr. 1)	3,794,083	3,537,438	256,645	281,424,603	79.6	32,706,301	13.1
2010 (Apr. 1)	3,796,742	3,531,905	264,837	308,745,538	87.4	27,320,935	9.7

Note: Area and population density figures represent the area within the boundaries of the U.S. under its jurisdiction on the date in question including, in some cases, considerable areas not organized or settled and not covered by the census. Beginning in 1870, area data include Alaska; from 1900 on, data include Hawaii. Population figures may reflect corrections made to initial tabulated census counts. (1) Figures for 1790-1980 cover inland water only. Figures for 1990 include inland, coastal, and Great Lakes water. Figures for 2000-10 include additional territorial water.

U.S. Congressional Apportionment by Census Year, 1850-2010
Source: Decennial Censuses, U.S. Census Bureau, U.S. Dept. of Commerce

The U.S. Constitution, in Article 1, Section 2, mandates that the population be counted every 10 years so that the number of U.S. representatives can be apportioned among the states. Every state is entitled to at least one House seat. The size of a state's resident population, both citizens and noncitizens, determines if it may send additional representatives to Congress. A congressional apportionment has been made after every decennial census except for that of 1920. Prior to 1870, slaves were counted as being only three-fifths of a person in the apportionment population. Since the 1970 census (excluding 1980), overseas military personnel and federal civilian employees as well as their dependents have been allocated to a home state for apportionment purposes. District of Columbia residents lack voting representation in Congress.

Under a law approved in 1941, House seats are allocated using the Huntington-Hill, or equal proportions, method. It allows for the least possible variation in the average number of people each House member represents.

The first House of Representatives, in 1789, had 65 members as provided by the Constitution. The states with the most representatives were Virginia (10), Massachusetts (8), and Pennsylvania (8). As the nation's population grew, the number of representatives was increased. A 1911 act fixed the total membership of the House at 435. (Alaska and Hawaii each gained one House seat when they became states, temporarily raising the total to 437 representatives until after the 1960 census was conducted.)

State	2010	2000	1990	1970	1950	1900	1850	State	2010	2000	1990	1970	1950	1900	1850
AL	7	7	7	7	9	9	7	NE	3	3	3	3	4	6	NA
AK	1	1	1	1	1	NA	NA	NV	4	3	2	1	1	1	NA
AZ	9	8	6	4	2	NA	NA	NH	2	2	2	2	2	2	3
AR	4	4	4	4	6	7	2	NJ	12	13	13	15	14	10	5
CA	53	53	52	43	30	8	2	NM	3	3	3	2	2	NA	NA
CO	7	7	6	5	4	3	NA	NY	27	29	31	39	43	37	33
CT	5	5	6	6	6	5	4	NC	13	13	12	11	12	10	8
DE	1	1	1	1	1	1	1	ND	1	1	1	1	2	2	NA
FL	27	25	23	15	8	3	1	OH	16	18	19	23	23	21	21
GA	14	13	11	10	10	11	8	OK	5	5	6	6	6	5	NA
HI	2	2	2	2	1	NA	NA	OR	5	5	5	4	4	2	1
ID	2	2	2	2	2	1	NA	PA	18	19	21	25	30	32	25
IL	18	19	20	24	25	25	9	RI	2	2	2	2	2	2	2
IN	9	9	10	11	11	13	11	SC	7	6	6	6	6	7	6
IA	4	5	5	6	8	11	2	SD	1	1	1	2	2	2	NA
KS	4	4	4	5	6	8	NA	TN	9	9	9	8	9	10	10
KY	6	6	6	7	8	11	10	TX	36	32	30	24	22	16	2
LA	6	7	7	8	8	7	4	UT	4	3	3	2	2	1	NA
ME	2	2	2	2	3	4	6	VT	1	1	1	1	1	2	3
MD	8	8	8	8	7	6	6	VA	11	11	11	10	10	10	13
MA	9	10	10	12	14	14	11	WA	10	9	9	7	7	3	NA
MI	14	15	16	19	18	12	4	WV	3	3	3	4	6	5	NA
MN	8	8	8	8	9	9	2	WI	8	8	9	9	10	11	3
MS	4	4	5	5	6	8	5	WY	1	1	1	1	1	1	NA
MO	8	9	9	10	11	16	7								
MT	1	1	1	2	2	1	NA	Total	435	435	435	435	437	391	237

NA = Not applicable.

U.S. Slave and "Free Colored" Population, 1790, 1820, 1860
Source: Decennial Censuses, U.S. Census Bureau, U.S. Dept. of Commerce

	1790 census			1820 census			1860 census		
	Slaves	% slaves[1]	Free colored	Slaves	% slaves[1]	Free colored	Slaves	% slaves[1]	Free colored
Northern states[2]	**40,354**	**2.1%**	**27,070**	**19,108**	**0.4%**	**99,307**	**18**	**0.0%**	**225,224**
Connecticut	2,764	1.2	2,808	97	0.0	7,870	0	0.0	8,627
New Jersey	11,423	6.2	2,762	7,557	2.7	12,460	18	0.0	25,318
New York	21,324	6.3	4,654	10,088	0.7	29,279	0	0.0	49,005
Pennsylvania	3,737	0.9	6,537	211	0.0	30,202	0	0.0	56,949
Border/disputed states	**124,353**	**27.5**	**12,056**	**248,860**	**22.4**	**55,794**	**429,403**	**13.2**	**118,652**
Delaware	8,887	15.0	3,899	4,509	6.2	12,958	1,798	1.6	19,829
Kansas	—	—	—	—	—	—	2	0.0	625
Kentucky	12,430	16.9	114	126,732	22.5	2,759	225,483	19.5	10,684
Maryland	103,036	32.2	8,043	107,397	26.4	39,730	87,189	12.7	83,942
Missouri	—	—	—	10,222	15.4	347	114,931	9.7	3,572
Southern states	**532,974**	**35.3**	**20,401**	**1,265,534**	**37.8**	**75,775**	**3,521,110**	**38.7**	**132,760**
Alabama	—	—	—	41,879	32.7	571	435,080	45.1	2,690
Arkansas	—	—	—	1,617	11.3	59	111,115	25.5	144
Florida	—	—	—	—	—	—	61,745	44.0	932
Georgia	29,264	35.5	398	149,656	43.9	1,763	462,198	43.7	3,500
Louisiana	—	—	—	69,064	45.0	10,476	331,726	46.9	18,647
Mississippi	—	—	—	32,814	43.5	458	436,631	55.2	773
North Carolina	100,572	25.5	4,975	204,917	32.1	14,712	331,059	33.4	30,463
South Carolina	107,094	43.0	1,801	258,475	51.4	6,826	402,406	57.2	9,914
Tennessee	3,417	9.6	361	80,107	18.9	2,737	275,719	24.8	7,300
Texas	—	—	—	—	—	—	182,566	30.2	355
Virginia	292,627	39.1	12,866	427,005	39.7	38,173	490,865	30.7	58,042
Total territories[3]	—	—	—	**4,520**	**19.4**	**2,758**	**3,229**	**1.1**	**11,434**
Total states and territories	**697,681**	**17.8**	**59,527**	**1,538,022**	**16.0**	**233,634**	**3,953,760**	**12.6**	**488,070**

Note: "Free colored" was an official Census Bureau designation in these decades. States are grouped roughly by allegiance in the Civil War. (1) Percentage of total pop., all races. (2) The following states are not listed separately but are included in totals for Northern states (relevant census years in parentheses): CA (1860), IL (1820, 1860), IN (1820, 1860), IA (1860), ME (1790, 1820, 1860), MA (1790, 1820, 1860), MI (1820, 1860), MN (1820, 1860), NH (1790, 1820, 1860), OH (1820, 1860), OR (1860), RI (1790, 1820, 1860), VT (1790, 1820, 1860), WI (1820, 1860). (3) Incl. AZ (1860), CO (1860), Dakota (1860), DC (1820, 1860), NE (1860), NV (1860), NM (1860), UT (1860), WA (1860).

Largest U.S. Metropolitan Areas by Population, 2000-13

Source: Population Estimates Program, Decennial Censuses, U.S. Census Bureau, U.S. Dept. of Commerce
(ranked by 2013 population; 2013 estimates are as of July 1; 2000 and 2010 decennial census figures are for Apr. 1)

Metropolitan Statistical Areas (MSAs) are defined, or delineated geographically, for federal statistical use by the Office of Management and Budget (OMB) with technical assistance from the Census Bureau. The standards used to define metropolitan areas are revised before each decennial census. Areas are delineated using the most recently issued standards and are updated between census years.

An MSA consists of at least one urbanized area of 50,000 or more inhabitants, plus adjacent territory closely integrated socially and economically with the core as measured by commuting ties. The OMB's most recent definitions, issued in Feb. 2013, designates 381 MSAs in the U.S. About 85% of the resident population resides in an MSA.

Rank	Metropolitan Statistical Area	Population 2013	Population 2010	Population 2000	Percent change 2010-13	Percent change 2000-13
1.	New York-Newark-Jersey City, NY-NJ-PA	19,949,502	19,567,410	18,944,519	2.0%	5.3%
2.	Los Angeles-Long Beach-Anaheim, CA	13,131,431	12,828,837	12,365,627	2.4	6.2
3.	Chicago-Naperville-Elgin, IL-IN-WI	9,537,289	9,461,105	9,098,316	0.8	4.8
4.	Dallas-Fort Worth-Arlington, TX	6,810,913	6,426,214	5,204,126	6.0	30.9
5.	Houston-The Woodlands-Sugar Land, TX	6,313,158	5,920,416	4,693,161	6.6	34.5
6.	Philadelphia-Camden-Wilmington, PA-NJ-DE-MD	6,034,678	5,965,343	5,687,147	1.2	6.1
7.	Washington-Arlington-Alexandria, DC-VA-MD-WV	5,949,859	5,636,232	4,837,428	5.6	23.0
8.	Miami-Fort Lauderdale-West Palm Beach, FL	5,828,191	5,564,635	5,007,564	4.7	16.4
9.	Atlanta-Sandy Springs-Roswell, GA	5,522,942	5,286,728	4,263,438	4.5	29.5
10.	Boston-Cambridge-Newton, MA-NH	4,684,299	4,552,402	4,391,344	2.9	6.7
11.	San Francisco-Oakland-Hayward, CA	4,516,276	4,335,391	4,123,740	4.2	9.5
12.	Phoenix-Mesa-Scottsdale, AZ	4,398,762	4,192,887	3,251,876	4.9	35.3
13.	Riverside-San Bernardino-Ontario, CA	4,380,878	4,224,851	3,254,821	3.7	34.6
14.	Detroit-Warren-Dearborn, MI	4,294,983	4,296,250	4,452,557	0.0	-3.5
15.	Seattle-Tacoma-Bellevue, WA	3,610,105	3,439,809	3,043,878	5.0	18.6
16.	Minneapolis-St. Paul-Bloomington, MN-WI	3,459,146	3,348,859	3,031,918	3.3	14.1
17.	San Diego-Carlsbad, CA	3,211,252	3,095,313	2,813,833	3.7	14.1
18.	Tampa-St. Petersburg-Clearwater, FL	2,870,569	2,783,243	2,395,997	3.1	19.8
19.	St. Louis, MO-IL	2,801,056	2,787,701	2,675,343	0.5	4.7
20.	Baltimore-Columbia-Towson, MD	2,770,738	2,710,489	2,552,994	2.2	8.5
21.	Denver-Aurora-Lakewood, CO	2,697,476	2,543,482	2,179,240	6.1	23.8
22.	Pittsburgh, PA	2,360,867	2,356,285	2,431,087	0.2	-2.9
23.	Charlotte-Concord-Gastonia, NC-SC	2,335,358	2,217,012	1,717,372	5.3	36.0
24.	Portland-Vancouver-Hillsboro, OR-WA	2,314,554	2,226,009	1,927,881	4.0	20.1
25.	San Antonio-New Braunfels, TX	2,277,550	2,142,508	1,711,703	6.3	33.1
26.	Orlando-Kissimmee-Sanford, FL	2,267,846	2,134,411	1,644,561	6.3	37.9
27.	Sacramento-Roseville-Arden-Arcade, CA	2,215,770	2,149,127	1,796,857	3.1	23.3
28.	Cincinnati, OH-KY-IN	2,137,406	2,114,580	1,994,830	1.1	7.1
29.	Cleveland-Elyria, OH	2,064,725	2,077,240	2,148,143	-0.6	-3.9
30.	Kansas City, MO-KS	2,054,473	2,009,342	1,811,254	2.2	13.4
31.	Las Vegas-Henderson-Paradise, NV	2,027,868	1,951,269	1,375,765	3.9	47.4
32.	Columbus, OH	1,967,066	1,901,974	1,675,013	3.4	17.4
33.	Indianapolis-Carmel-Anderson, IN	1,953,961	1,887,877	1,658,462	3.5	17.8
34.	San Jose-Sunnyvale-Santa Clara, CA	1,919,641	1,836,911	1,735,819	4.5	10.6
35.	Austin-Round Rock, TX	1,883,051	1,716,289	1,249,763	9.7	50.7
36.	Nashville-Davidson--Murfreesboro--Franklin, TN	1,757,912	1,670,890	1,381,287	5.2	27.3
37.	Virginia Beach-Norfolk-Newport News, VA-NC	1,707,369	1,676,822	1,580,057	1.8	8.1
38.	Providence-Warwick, RI-MA	1,604,291	1,600,852	1,582,997	0.2	1.3
39.	Milwaukee-Waukesha-West Allis, WI	1,569,659	1,555,908	1,500,741	0.9	4.6
40.	Jacksonville, FL	1,394,624	1,345,596	1,122,750	3.6	24.2
41.	Memphis, TN-MS-AR	1,341,746	1,324,829	1,213,230	1.3	10.6
42.	Oklahoma City, OK	1,319,677	1,252,987	1,095,421	5.3	20.5
43.	Louisville-Jefferson County, KY-IN	1,262,261	1,235,708	1,121,109	2.1	12.6
44.	Richmond, VA	1,245,764	1,208,101	1,055,683	3.1	18.0
45.	New Orleans-Metairie, LA	1,240,977	1,189,866	1,337,726	4.3	-7.2
46.	Hartford-West Hartford-East Hartford, CT	1,215,211	1,212,381	1,148,618	0.2	5.8
47.	Raleigh, NC	1,214,516	1,130,490	797,071	7.4	52.4
48.	Salt Lake City, UT	1,140,483	1,087,873	939,122	4.8	21.4
49.	Birmingham-Hoover, AL	1,140,300	1,128,047	1,052,238	1.1	8.4
50.	Buffalo-Cheektowaga-Niagara Falls, NY	1,134,115	1,135,509	1,170,111	-0.1	-3.1
51.	Rochester, NY	1,083,278	1,079,671	1,062,452	0.3	2.0
52.	Grand Rapids-Wyoming, MI	1,016,603	988,938	930,670	2.8	9.2
53.	Tucson, AZ	996,554	980,263	843,746	1.7	18.1
54.	Urban Honolulu, HI	983,429	953,207	876,156	3.2	12.2
55.	Tulsa, OK	961,561	937,478	859,532	2.6	11.9
56.	Fresno, CA	955,272	930,450	799,407	2.7	19.5
57.	Bridgeport-Stamford-Norwalk, CT	939,904	916,829	882,567	2.5	6.5
58.	Worcester, MA-CT	926,710	916,980	860,054	1.1	7.8
59.	Albuquerque, NM	902,797	887,077	729,649	1.8	23.7
60.	Omaha-Council Bluffs, NE-IA	895,151	865,350	767,041	3.4	16.7
61.	Albany-Schenectady-Troy, NY	877,905	870,716	825,875	0.8	6.3
62.	Bakersfield, CA	864,124	839,631	661,645	2.9	30.6
63.	New Haven-Milford, CT	862,287	862,477	824,008	0.0	4.6
64.	Knoxville, TN	852,715	837,571	748,259	1.8	14.0
65.	Greenville-Anderson-Mauldin, SC	850,965	824,112	725,680	3.3	17.3
66.	Oxnard-Thousand Oaks-Ventura, CA	839,620	823,318	753,197	2.0	11.5
67.	El Paso, TX	831,036	804,123	682,966	3.3	21.7
68.	Allentown-Bethlehem-Easton, PA-NJ	827,048	821,173	740,395	0.7	11.7
69.	Baton Rouge, LA	820,159	802,484	705,973	2.2	16.2
70.	McAllen-Edinburg-Mission, TX	815,996	774,769	569,463	5.3	43.3
71.	Dayton, OH	802,489	799,232	805,816	0.4	-0.4
72.	Columbia, SC	793,779	767,598	647,158	3.4	22.7

Largest U.S. Cities by Population, 1850-2013

Source: Population Estimates Program, Decennial Censuses, U.S. Census Bureau, U.S. Dept. of Commerce
(ranked by 2013 population)

Rank	City	2013	2000	1990	1980	1970	1950	1900	1850
1.	New York, NY	8,405,837	8,008,278	7,322,564	7,071,639	7,895,563	7,891,957	3,437,202	696,115
2.	Los Angeles, CA	3,884,307	3,694,820	3,485,398	2,968,528	2,811,801	1,970,358	102,479	1,610
3.	Chicago, IL	2,718,782	2,896,016	2,783,726	3,005,072	3,369,357	3,620,962	1,698,575	29,963
4.	Houston, TX	2,195,914	1,953,631	1,630,553	1,595,138	1,233,535	596,163	44,633	2,396
5.	Philadelphia, PA	1,553,165	1,517,550	1,585,577	1,688,210	1,949,996	2,071,605	1,293,697	121,376
6.	Phoenix, AZ	1,513,367	1,321,045	983,403	789,704	584,303	106,818	5,544	—
7.	San Antonio, TX	1,409,019	1,144,646	935,933	785,940	654,153	408,442	53,321	3,488
8.	San Diego, CA	1,355,896	1,223,400	1,110,549	875,538	697,471	334,387	17,700	—
9.	Dallas, TX	1,257,676	1,188,580	1,006,877	904,599	844,401	434,462	42,638	—
10.	San Jose, CA	998,537	894,943	782,248	629,400	459,913	95,280	21,500	—
11.	Austin, TX	885,400	656,562	465,622	345,890	253,539	132,459	22,258	629
12.	Indianapolis, IN[1]	843,393	781,870	741,952	700,807	736,856	427,173	169,164	8,091
13.	Jacksonville, FL	842,583	735,617	635,230	540,920	504,265	204,517	28,429	1,045
14.	San Francisco, CA	837,442	776,733	723,959	678,974	715,674	775,357	342,782	34,776
15.	Columbus, OH	822,553	711,470	632,910	565,021	540,025	375,901	125,560	17,882
16.	Charlotte, NC	792,862	540,828	395,934	315,474	241,420	134,042	18,091	1,065
17.	Fort Worth, TX	792,727	534,694	447,619	385,164	393,455	278,778	26,688	—
18.	Detroit, MI	688,701	951,270	1,027,974	1,203,368	1,514,063	1,849,568	285,704	21,019
19.	El Paso, TX	674,433	563,662	515,342	425,259	322,261	130,485	15,906	—
20.	Memphis, TN	653,450	650,100	610,337	646,174	623,988	396,000	102,320	8,841
21.	Seattle, WA	652,405	563,374	516,259	493,846	530,831	467,591	80,671	—
22.	Denver, CO	649,495	554,636	467,610	492,686	514,678	415,786	133,859	—
23.	Washington, DC	646,449	572,059	606,900	638,432	756,668	802,178	278,718	40,001
24.	Boston, MA	645,966	589,141	574,283	562,994	641,071	801,444	560,892	136,881
25.	Nashville-Davidson, TN[1]	634,464	545,524	510,784	455,651	426,029	174,307	80,865	10,165
26.	Baltimore, MD	622,104	651,154	736,014	786,741	905,787	949,708	508,957	169,054
27.	Oklahoma City, OK	610,613	506,132	444,719	404,014	368,164	243,504	10,037	—
28.	Louisville-Jefferson Co., KY[1]	609,893	256,231	269,063	298,694	361,706	369,129	204,731	43,194
29.	Portland, OR	609,456	529,121	437,319	368,148	379,967	373,628	90,426	—
30.	Las Vegas, NV	603,488	478,434	258,295	164,674	125,787	24,624	—	—
31.	Milwaukee, WI	599,164	596,974	628,088	636,297	717,372	637,392	285,315	20,061
32.	Albuquerque, NM	556,495	448,607	384,736	332,920	244,501	96,815	6,238	—
33.	Tucson, AZ	526,116	486,699	405,390	330,537	262,933	45,454	7,531	—
34.	Fresno, CA	509,924	427,652	354,202	217,491	165,655	91,669	12,470	—
35.	Sacramento, CA	479,686	407,018	369,365	275,741	257,105	137,572	29,282	6,820
36.	Long Beach, CA	469,428	461,522	429,433	361,498	358,879	250,767	2,252	—
37.	Kansas City, MO	467,007	441,545	435,146	448,028	507,330	456,622	163,752	—
38.	Mesa, AZ	457,587	396,375	288,091	152,404	63,049	16,790	722	—
39.	Virginia Beach, VA	448,479	425,257	393,069	262,199	172,106	5,390	—	—
40.	Atlanta, GA	447,841	416,474	394,017	425,022	495,039	331,314	89,872	2,572
41.	Colorado Springs, CO	439,886	360,890	281,140	215,105	135,517	45,472	21,085	—
42.	Omaha, NE	434,353	390,007	335,795	313,939	346,929	251,117	102,555	—
43.	Raleigh, NC	431,746	276,093	207,951	150,255	122,830	65,679	13,643	4,518
44.	Miami, FL	417,650	362,470	358,548	346,681	334,859	249,276	1,681	—
45.	Oakland, CA	406,253	399,484	372,242	339,337	361,561	384,575	66,960	—
46.	Minneapolis, MN	400,070	382,618	368,383	370,951	434,400	521,718	202,718	—
47.	Tulsa, OK	398,121	393,049	367,302	360,919	330,350	182,740	1,390	—
48.	Cleveland, OH	390,113	478,403	505,616	573,822	750,879	914,808	381,768	17,034
49.	Wichita, KS	386,552	344,284	304,011	279,838	276,554	168,279	24,671	—
50.	Arlington, TX	379,577	332,969	261,721	160,113	90,229	7,692	1,079	—
51.	New Orleans, LA	378,715	484,674	496,938	557,927	593,471	570,445	287,104	116,375
52.	Bakersfield, CA	363,630	247,057	174,820	105,611	69,515	34,784	4,836	—
53.	Tampa, FL	352,957	303,447	280,015	271,577	277,714	124,681	15,839	—
54.	Honolulu, HI[2]	347,884	371,657	365,272	365,048	324,871	248,034	39,306	—
55.	Aurora, CO	345,803	276,393	222,103	158,588	74,974	11,421	202	—
56.	Anaheim, CA	345,012	328,014	266,406	219,494	166,408	14,556	1,456	—
57.	Santa Ana, CA	334,227	337,977	293,742	204,023	155,710	45,533	4,933	—
58.	St. Louis, MO	318,416	348,189	396,685	452,801	622,236	856,796	575,238	77,860
59.	Riverside, CA	316,619	255,166	226,505	170,591	140,089	46,764	7,973	—
60.	Corpus Christi, TX	316,381	277,454	257,453	232,134	204,525	108,287	4,703	—
61.	Lexington-Fayette, KY	308,428	260,512	225,366	204,165	108,137	55,534	26,369	8,159
62.	Pittsburgh, PA	305,841	334,563	369,879	423,959	520,089	676,806	321,616	46,601
63.	Anchorage, AK	300,950	260,283	226,338	174,431	48,081	11,254	—	—
64.	Stockton, CA	298,118	243,771	210,943	148,283	109,963	70,853	17,506	—
65.	Cincinnati, OH	297,517	331,285	364,040	385,409	453,514	503,998	325,902	115,435
66.	St. Paul, MN	294,873	287,151	272,235	270,230	309,866	311,349	163,065	1,112
67.	Toledo, OH	282,313	313,619	332,943	354,635	383,062	303,616	131,822	3,829
68.	Greensboro, NC	279,639	223,891	183,521	155,642	144,076	74,389	10,035	—
69.	Newark, NJ	278,427	273,546	275,221	329,248	381,930	438,776	246,070	38,894
70.	Plano, TX	274,409	222,030	128,713	72,331	17,872	2,126	1,304	—
71.	Henderson, NV	270,811	175,381	64,942	23,376	16,400	5,717	—	—
72.	Lincoln, NE	268,738	225,581	191,972	171,932	149,518	98,884	40,169	—
73.	Buffalo, NY	258,959	292,648	328,123	357,870	462,768	580,132	352,387	42,261
74.	Jersey City, NJ	257,342	240,055	228,537	223,532	260,350	299,017	206,433	6,856
75.	Chula Vista, CA	256,780	173,556	135,163	83,927	67,901	31,339	—	—
76.	Fort Wayne, IN	256,496	205,727	173,072	172,391	178,269	133,607	45,115	4,282
77.	Orlando, FL	255,483	185,951	164,693	128,394	99,006	52,367	2,481	—
78.	St. Petersburg, FL	249,688	248,232	238,629	238,647	216,159	96,738	1,575	—
79.	Chandler, AZ	249,146	176,581	89,862	29,673	13,763	3,799	—	—
80.	Laredo, TX	248,142	176,576	122,899	91,449	69,024	51,910	13,429	—

Rank City	2013	2000	1990	1980	1970	1950	1900	1850
81. Norfolk, VA	246,139	234,403	261,229	266,979	307,951	213,513	46,624	14,326
82. Durham, NC	245,475	187,035	136,611	100,831	95,438	71,311	6,679	—
83. Madison, WI	243,344	208,054	191,262	170,616	171,809	96,056	19,164	1,525
84. Lubbock, TX	239,538	199,564	186,206	174,361	149,101	71,747	—	—
85. Irvine, CA	236,716	143,072	110,330	62,134	—	—	—	—
86. Winston-Salem, NC	236,441	185,776	143,485	131,885	133,683	87,811	13,650	—
87. Glendale, AZ	234,632	218,812	148,134	96,988	36,228	8,179	—	—
88. Garland, TX	234,566	215,768	180,650	138,857	81,437	10,571	819	—
89. Hialeah, FL	233,394	226,419	188,004	145,254	102,452	19,676	—	—
90. Reno, NV	233,294	180,480	134,230	100,756	72,863	32,497	4,500	—
91. Chesapeake, VA	230,571	199,184	151,976	114,486	89,580	—	—	—
92. Gilbert, AZ	229,972	109,697	29,188	5,717	1,971	—	—	—
93. Baton Rouge, LA	229,426	227,818	219,531	220,394	165,921	125,629	11,269	3,905
94. Irving, TX	228,653	191,615	155,037	109,943	97,260	2,621	—	—
95. Scottsdale, AZ	226,918	202,705	130,069	88,364	67,823	2,032	—	—
96. North Las Vegas, NV	226,877	115,488	47,707	42,739	46,067	—	—	—
97. Fremont, CA	224,922	203,413	173,339	131,945	100,869	—	—	—
98. Boise City, ID	214,237	185,787	125,738	102,451	74,990	34,393	5,957	—
99. Richmond, CA	214,114	197,790	203,056	219,214	249,621	230,310	85,050	27,570
100. San Bernardino, CA	213,708	185,401	164,164	117,490	104,251	63,058	6,150	—

Note: 2013 population estimates are as of July 1. Decennial census figures for 1950-2010 are for Apr. 1; 1850 and 1900 are for June 1. Cities are incorporated places unless otherwise noted. (1) Consolidated city. Population figures are for the primary incorporated place only, i.e., exclude the populations of semi-independent incorporated places within the consolidated city. For years predating consolidation, city population figures are shown. (2) Census designated place. Although not incorporated, it is recognized as a statistical equivalent by the Census Bureau.

Largest U.S. Counties by Population, 2000, 2013

Source: Population Estimates Program, Decennial Census, U.S. Census Bureau, U.S. Dept. of Commerce
(ranked by 2013 population; 2013 estimates are as of July 1; 2000 decennial census figures are for Apr. 1)

Rank County	2013	2000	% change, 2000-13	Rank County	2013	2000	% change, 2000-13
1. Los Angeles Co., CA..	10,017,068	9,519,338	5.2%	16. Santa Clara Co., CA ..	1,862,041	1,682,585	10.7%
2. Cook Co., IL	5,240,700	5,376,741	−2.5	17. Broward Co., FL	1,838,844	1,623,018	13.3
3. Harris Co., TX........	4,336,853	3,400,578	27.5	18. Bexar Co., TX	1,817,610	1,392,931	30.5
4. Maricopa Co., AZ	4,009,412	3,072,149	30.5	19. Wayne Co., MI	1,775,273	2,061,162	−13.9
5. San Diego Co., CA ...	3,211,252	2,813,833	14.1	20. New York Co., NY ...	1,626,159	1,537,195	5.8
6. Orange Co., CA	3,114,363	2,846,289	9.4	21. Alameda Co., CA	1,578,891	1,443,741	9.4
7. Miami-Dade Co., FL ..	2,617,176	2,253,362	16.1	22. Philadelphia Co., PA..	1,553,165	1,517,550	2.3
8. Kings Co., NY	2,592,149	2,465,326	5.1	23. Middlesex Co., MA ...	1,552,802	1,465,396	6.0
9. Dallas Co., TX.......	2,480,331	2,218,899	11.8	24. Suffolk Co., NY	1,499,738	1,419,369	5.7
10. Queens Co., NY	2,296,175	2,229,379	3.0	25. Sacramento Co., CA..	1,462,131	1,223,499	19.5
11. Riverside Co., CA	2,292,507	1,545,387	48.3	26. Bronx Co., NY.......	1,418,733	1,332,650	6.5
12. San Bernardino Co., CA..	2,088,371	1,709,434	22.2	27. Palm Beach Co., FL ..	1,372,171	1,131,184	21.3
13. King Co., WA	2,044,449	1,737,034	17.7	28. Nassau Co., NY	1,352,146	1,334,544	1.3
14. Clark Co., NV	2,027,868	1,375,765	47.4	29. Hillsborough Co., FL..	1,291,578	998,948	29.3
15. Tarrant Co., TX	1,911,541	1,446,219	32.2	30. Cuyahoga Co., OH ...	1,263,154	1,393,978	−9.4

Note: The 10 smallest counties by estimated 2013 population: (1) Kalawao Co., HI (pop. 90); (2) Loving Co., TX (95); (3) King Co., TX (285); (4) Kenedy Co., TX (412); (5) Arthur Co., NE (458); (6) Blaine Co., NE (482); (7) Petroleum Co., MT (506); (8) McPherson Co., NE (526); (9) Loup Co., NE (576); and (10) Grant Co., NE (633).

Mobility of U.S. Population by Selected Characteristics, 2012-13

Source: Annual Social and Economic Supplement, Current Population Survey (CPS), U.S. Census Bureau, U.S. Dept. of Commerce
(numbers in thousands)

	Total movers	Same county	Diff. county, same state	Diff. state	Abroad		Total movers	Same county	Diff. county, same state	Diff. state	Abroad
Age						**Marital status[1]**					
1 to 14 years.........	7,877	5,377	1,337	943	220	Married, spouse present	9,373	5,473	1,978	1,579	342
15 years and older	28,041	17,773	5,625	3,827	816	Married, spouse absent	620	348	97	116	60
25 years and older	20,226	12,647	4,095	2,870	614	Widowed..............	733	465	162	99	7
65 years and older	1,580	896	383	269	33	Divorced..............	3,352	2,229	691	393	39
85 years and older	209	116	55	30	8	Separated.............	997	689	186	105	17
Income[1]						Never married.........	12,965	8,569	2,511	1,535	351
Without income........	4,225	2,747	708	500	269	**Educational attainment[2]**					
Under $5,000 or loss ...	2,506	1,517	500	362	128	Not a h.s. graduate	2,579	1,840	403	231	106
$5,000 to $9,999.	2,626	1,655	551	350	69	High school graduate ...	5,776	3,707	1,296	673	100
$10,000 to $19,999....	5,050	3,329	982	652	90	Some college or associate degree ...	5,639	3,647	1,163	748	80
$20,000 to $29,999....	3,984	2,634	809	471	70	Bachelor's degree......	4,189	2,365	850	790	183
$30,000 to $39,999....	2,856	1,782	632	405	38	Prof. or grad. degree ...	2,045	1,090	383	427	145
$40,000 to $59,999....	3,370	2,152	696	467	54	**Tenure**					
$60,000 to $74,999....	1,292	765	287	206	33	In owner-occupied unit ..	10,461	6,342	2,308	1,595	215
$75,000 to $99,999....	978	558	201	190	29	In renter-occupied unit[3]..	25,459	16,808	4,653	3,175	822
$100,000 and over	1,154	634	258	226	36	Total movers	35,918	23,150	6,961	4,770	1,036

Note: Total movers consists of persons ages 1 and older who moved to a new residence in the 12 months preceding the administering of the survey. Figures may not add up to totals due to rounding. (1) Ages 15 and older. (2) Ages 25 and older. (3) Includes units occupied without payment of cash rent.

Persons Granted Lawful Permanent Resident Status by State, 2013

Source: Office of Immigration Statistics, U.S. Dept. of Homeland Security
(ranked by fiscal year 2013 number)

State/territory	Number	State/territory	Number	State/territory	Number	State/territory	Number
Total	990,553	North Carolina	16,798	Kentucky	5,159	New Hampshire	2,227
California	191,806	Arizona	16,097	Kansas	5,000	Idaho	2,120
New York	133,601	Ohio	13,819	Oklahoma	4,648	Mississippi	1,716
Florida	102,939	Minnesota	12,781	Louisiana	4,355	Alaska	1,460
Texas	92,674	Colorado	11,108	South Carolina	4,266	North Dakota	1,234
New Jersey	53,082	Connecticut	10,985	Nebraska	4,141	South Dakota	1,231
Illinois	35,988	Nevada	9,886	Iowa	4,105	Guam	1,210
Massachusetts	29,482	Tennessee	8,380	Alabama	3,848	Maine	1,208
Virginia	27,861	Indiana	7,668	New Mexico	3,664	Vermont	838
Maryland	25,361	Oregon	7,171	Rhode Island	3,337	West Virginia	760
Pennsylvania	24,720	Missouri	6,345	District of Columbia	2,981	Wyoming	522
Georgia	24,387	Hawaii	6,226	Puerto Rico	2,942	Montana	445
Washington	22,994	Wisconsin	5,918	Arkansas	2,900	Other[1]	1,379
Michigan	16,952	Utah	5,503	Delaware	2,325		

Note: Applicants for lawful permanent resident (LPR) status, or "green cards," may already live in the U.S. They include refugees and asylees, temporary workers, foreign students, family members of U.S. citizens, and unauthorized immigrants. Applicants from outside the U.S. enter on a visa and are granted LPR status upon admittance. (1) Includes other U.S. territories and armed forces posts.

Persons Granted Lawful Permanent Resident Status by Top Areas of Residence, 2013

Source: Office of Immigration Statistics, U.S. Dept. of Homeland Security
(ranked by fiscal year 2013 number)

Core Based Statistical Area (CBSA)[1]	Number	% of total	Core Based Statistical Area (CBSA)[1]	Number	% of total
Total	990,553	100.0%	Portland-Vancouver-Hillsboro, OR-WA	5,934	0.6%
New York-Northern New Jersey-Long Island, NY-NJ-PA	167,393	16.9	El Paso, TX	5,261	0.5
Los Angeles-Long Beach-Santa Ana, CA	79,893	8.1	San Antonio-New Braunfels, TX	5,082	0.5
Miami-Fort Lauderdale-Pompano Beach, FL	66,636	6.7	Charlotte-Gastonia-Rock Hill, NC-SC	5,053	0.5
Washington-Arlington-Alexandria, DC-VA-MD-WV	39,170	4.0	Columbus, OH	4,868	0.5
Chicago-Joliet-Naperville, IL-IN-WI	32,819	3.3	Honolulu, HI	4,656	0.5
Houston-Sugar Land-Baytown, TX	31,953	3.2	Bridgeport-Stamford-Norwalk, CT	4,468	0.5
San Francisco-Oakland-Fremont, CA	30,600	3.1	Nashville-Davidson–Murfreesboro–Franklin, TN	4,275	0.4
Dallas-Fort Worth-Arlington, TX	26,760	2.7	Providence-New Bedford-Fall River, RI-MA	4,263	0.4
Boston-Cambridge-Quincy, MA-NH	23,867	2.4	Indianapolis-Carmel, IN	3,944	0.4
Atlanta-Sandy Springs-Marietta, GA	20,054	2.0	Raleigh-Cary, NC	3,798	0.4
Philadelphia-Camden-Wilmington, PA-NJ-DE-MD	18,121	1.8	Kansas City, MO-KS	3,696	0.4
Seattle-Tacoma-Bellevue, WA	17,865	1.8	Salt Lake City, UT	3,403	0.3
San Jose-Sunnyvale-Santa Clara, CA	17,292	1.7	Hartford-West Hartford-East Hartford, CT	3,373	0.3
San Diego-Carlsbad-San Marcos, CA	16,567	1.7	McAllen-Edinburg-Mission, TX	3,267	0.3
Riverside-San Bernardino-Ontario, CA	14,026	1.4	St. Louis, MO-IL	3,187	0.3
Detroit-Warren-Livonia, MI	11,131	1.1	Jacksonville, FL	3,170	0.3
Phoenix-Mesa-Glendale, AZ	11,025	1.1	Cleveland-Elyria-Mentor, OH	3,076	0.3
Minneapolis-St. Paul-Bloomington, MN-WI	10,478	1.1	Fresno, CA	2,853	0.3
Orlando-Kissimmee-Sanford, FL	10,200	1.0	Worcester, MA	2,853	0.3
Baltimore-Towson, MD	8,599	0.9	Oxnard-Thousand Oaks-Ventura, CA	2,801	0.3
Las Vegas-Paradise, NV	8,381	0.8	Cincinnati-Middletown, OH-KY-IN	2,762	0.3
Tampa-St. Petersburg-Clearwater, FL	8,360	0.8	San Juan-Caguas-Guaynabo, PR	2,706	0.3
Sacramento–Arden-Arcade–Roseville, CA	7,504	0.8	Milwaukee-Waukesha-West Allis, WI	2,686	0.3
Denver-Aurora-Broomfield, CO	7,498	0.8	Pittsburgh, PA	2,645	0.3
Austin-Round Rock-San Marcos, TX	6,015	0.6	Other CBSAs	191,377	19.3
			Non-CBSA or unknown	12,889	1.3

Note: Applicants for lawful permanent resident (LPR) status, or "green cards," may already live in the U.S. They include refugees and asylees, temporary workers, foreign students, family members of U.S. citizens, and unauthorized immigrants. Applicants from outside the U.S. enter on a visa and are granted LPR status upon admittance. (1) CBSAs refer collectively to metropolitan and micropolitan statistical areas. These areas are defined for federal statistical use by the Office of Management and Budget with technical assistance from the Census Bureau.

Unauthorized Immigrant Population in the U.S., 2000, 2012

Source: Office of Immigration Statistics, U.S. Dept. of Homeland Security
(ranked by 2012 est. population; as of Jan. of given year)

	Country of Birth				State of Residence		
	Est. population		% change,		Est. population		% change,
Country	2012	2000	2000-12	State	2012	2000	2000-12
All countries	11,430,000	8,460,000	35.1%	All states	11,430,000	8,460,000	35.1%
Mexico	6,720,000	4,680,000	43.6	California	2,820,000	2,510,000	12.4
El Salvador	690,000	430,000	60.5	Texas	1,830,000	1,090,000	67.9
Guatemala	560,000	290,000	93.1	Florida	730,000	800,000	–8.8
Honduras	360,000	160,000	125.0	New York	580,000	540,000	7.4
Philippines	310,000	200,000	55.0	Illinois	540,000	440,000	22.7
India	260,000	120,000	116.7	New Jersey	430,000	350,000	22.9
Korea[1]	230,000	180,000	27.8	Georgia	400,000	220,000	81.8
China	210,000	190,000	10.5	North Carolina	360,000	260,000	38.5
Ecuador	170,000	110,000	54.5	Arizona	350,000	330,000	6.1
Vietnam	160,000	160,000	0.0	Washington	270,000	170,000	58.8
Other countries	1,760,000	1,940,000	–9.3	Other states	3,110,000	1,750,000	77.7

Note: Unauthorized immigrant population estimates are made using the residual method. The estimated size of the legally resident foreign-born pop. (i.e., lawful permanent residents, asylees, refugees, and nonimmigrants such as temporary workers) is subtracted from the total foreign-born pop. Numbers may not add up to totals because of rounding. (1) Incl. North and South Korea.

U.S. Foreign-Born Population

Source: Annual Social and Economic Supplements, Current Population Surveys (CPS), U.S. Census Bureau, U.S. Dept. of Commerce

Percentage of Population That Is Foreign-Born, 1900-2012

Foreign-Born Population by Region of Birth, 1995-2012

(numbers in thousands)

Region	2012[1] No.	%	2000	1995
Asia.	11,587	29.0%	7,246	6,121
Under 18.	843	32.3	657	767
Europe	4,546	11.4	4,355	3,937
Under 18.	214	8.2	250	232
Latin America . . . ,	21,034	52.6	14,477	11,777
Under 18.	1,278	48.9	1,684	1,481
Other[2]	2,809	7.0	2,301	2,658
Under 18.	277	10.6	245	275
All regions.	**39,976**	**100.0**	**28,379**	**24,493**
Under 18.	2,612	100.0	2,837	2,726

(1) Figures are percentage of total foreign-born population or of all foreign-born under 18 years of age. (2) Including those born at sea.

U.S. Foreign-Born Population: Top Countries of Origin, 1880-2013

Source: American Community Survey (ACS), Decennial Censuses, U.S. Census Bureau, U.S. Dept. of Commerce

(numbers in thousands; percentage is of all foreign-born)

1880 Country	No.	%	1920 Country	No.	%	1960 Country	No.	%	2000 Country	No.	%	2013[4] Country	No.	%
Germany	1,967	29.4	Germany	1,686	12.1	Italy	1,257	12.9	Mexico	9,177	29.5	Mexico	11,585	28.0
Ireland	1,855	27.8	Italy	1,610	11.6	Germany	990	10.2	China[2]	1,519	4.9	China[2]	2,384	5.8
UK	918	13.7	U.S.S.R.	1,400	10.1	Canada	953	9.8	Philippines	1,369	4.4	India	2,035	4.9
Canada	717	10.7	Poland	1,140	8.2	UK	765	7.9	India	1,023	3.3	Philippines	1,844	4.5
Sweden	194	2.9	Canada	1,138	8.2	Poland	748	7.7	Vietnam	988	3.2	Vietnam	1,281	3.1
Norway	182	2.7	UK	1,135	8.2	U.S.S.R.	691	7.1	Cuba	873	2.8	El Salvador	1,252	3.0
France	107	1.6	Ireland	1,037	7.5	Mexico	576	5.9	Korea[3]	864	2.8	Cuba	1,144	2.8
China[1]	104	1.6	Sweden	626	4.5	Ireland	339	3.5	Canada	821	2.6	Korea[3]	1,070	2.6
Switzerland	89	1.3	Austria	576	4.1	Austria	305	3.1	El Salvador	817	2.6	Dominican Republic	991	2.4
Czech.	85	1.3	Mexico	486	3.5	Hungary	245	2.5	Germany	707	2.3	Guatemala	902	2.2
Total	**6,680**	**100.0**	**Total**	**13,921**	**100.0**	**Total**	**9,738**	**100.0**	**Total**	**31,108**	**100.0**	**Total**	**41,348**	**100.0**

(1) Incl. Taiwan. (2) Incl. Hong Kong and Taiwan. (3) North and South Korea. (4) Data based on sample and subject to sampling variability. The Census Bureau collects data from foreign-born persons regardless of their legal status, so data implicitly incl. unauthorized migrants.

Language Spoken at Home by the U.S. Population, 2013

Source: American Community Survey (ACS), U.S. Census Bureau, U.S. Dept. of Commerce

(number of speakers ages 5 and older, by major language group)

Language	Number (thous.)	% of tot. pop.	% English inability[1]	Language	Number (thous.)	% of tot. pop.	% English inability[1]
Total population	296,358.8	100.00%	8.5%	Other Slavic languages	314.0	0.11%	38.0%
Speak only English.	234,610.0	79.16	NA	Other West Germanic langs. . .	316.4	0.11	24.9
Speak another language	61,748.7	20.84	40.7	Other Indo-European langs. . . .	455.6	0.15	36.3
Spanish				**Asian and Pacific Island languages**			
Spanish or Spanish Creole	38,417.2	12.96	42.2	Chinese	3,029.0	1.02	55.4
Other Indo-European languages				Hmong	229.0	0.08	45.2
Armenian	236.6	0.08	44.8	Japanese	455.0	0.15	42.5
French (incl. Patois, Cajun)	1,251.8	0.42	19.5	Korean	1,100.9	0.37	53.8
French Creole	783.0	0.26	42.0	Laotian	153.1	0.05	48.8
German	984.7	0.33	15.6	Mon-Khmer, Cambodian.	220.9	0.07	50.4
Greek	294.5	0.10	25.4	Tagalog	1,612.5	0.54	32.0
Gujarati.	372.1	0.13	33.5	Thai.	151.1	0.05	48.7
Hindi	654.1	0.22	19.4	Vietnamese.	1,428.4	0.48	58.4
Italian	641.3	0.22	28.2	Other Asian languages	1,016.9	0.34	31.3
Persian	399.0	0.13	37.8	Other Pacific Island langs.	422.4	0.14	37.9
Polish	549.7	0.19	40.8	**All other languages**			
Portuguese or				African languages.	967.9	0.33	31.3
Portuguese Creole	677.3	0.23	37.9	Arabic	1,052.9	0.36	36.7
Russian	895.9	0.30	45.6	Hebrew	210.9	0.07	16.2
Scandinavian languages	122.1	0.04	10.9	Hungarian	82.7	0.03	29.5
Serbo-Croatian	255.6	0.09	38.1	Navajo.	160.3	0.05	19.1
Urdu	439.1	0.15	29.9	Other Native North American			
Yiddish	157.2	0.05	35.7	languages	199.1	0.07	13.6
Other Indic languages	886.0	0.30	40.4	Other and unspecified langs. . . .	152.7	0.05	41.1

NA = Not applicable/available. **Note:** Data based on sample and subject to sampling variability. (1) Speakers of other languages were asked how well they spoke English. Respondents who indicated that they spoke English less than "very well" are given as a percentage of their subgroup. (For example, 44.8% of respondents who use Armenian at home do not speak English very well.)

U.S. Population by Age, Sex, and Household, 2013
Source: American Community Survey (ACS), U.S. Census Bureau, U.S. Dept. of Commerce

	Number	% of tot.		Number	% of tot.
Total population[1]	316,128,839	100.0%	Sex		
Age			Male	155,627,698	49.2%
Under 5 years	19,770,079	6.3	Female	160,501,141	50.8
5 to 14 years	41,341,594	13.1	Total households[2]	116,291,033	100.0%
15 to 17 years	12,474,939	3.9	Family households	76,680,463	65.9
15 to 44 years	127,341,341	40.3	2-person household	33,221,015	28.6
18 years and over	242,542,227	76.7	3-person household	17,392,132	15.0
Male	117,977,584	37.3	4-person household	14,757,229	12.7
Female	124,564,643	39.4	5-or-more person household	11,310,087	9.7
18 to 24 years	31,631,612	10.0	Married-couple family	55,858,808	48.0
25 to 34 years	42,626,551	13.5	Female HH, no husband present	15,201,756	13.1
35 to 44 years	40,608,235	12.8	Male HH, no wife present	5,619,899	4.8
45 to 54 years	43,674,983	13.8	Nonfamily households	39,610,570	34.1
55 to 64 years	39,336,852	12.4	1-person household	32,242,369	27.7
65 years and over	44,663,990	14.1	HH 65 years and over	11,725,373	10.1
75 years and over	19,450,244	6.2	2-person household	5,976,363	5.1
85 years and over	5,984,754	1.9	3-or-more person household	1,391,838	1.2
Median age (years)	37.5	NA	Average household size	2.65	NA

NA = Not applicable. HH = Householder, or person in whose name a home is owned or rented. **Note:** Data based on sample and subject to sampling variability. (1) Includes population living in group quarters (institutional and noninstitutional, e.g., correctional facilities, university housing). (2) Number of occupied housing units, not household members. Group quarters are not considered households.

Elderly U.S. Population, 1900-2050
Source: Decennial Censuses, Population Projections Program, U.S. Census Bureau, U.S. Dept. of Commerce
(numbers of resident population in thousands)

Year	65 and over Number	% tot. pop.	85 and over Number	% tot. pop.	Year	65 and over Number	% tot. pop.	85 and over Number	% tot. pop.
1900[1]	3,080	4.1%	122	0.2%	2010	40,268	13.0%	5,493	1.8%
1920[1]	4,933	4.7	210	0.2	2015	47,695	14.8	6,306	2.0
1940[1]	9,019	6.8	365	0.3	2020	55,969	16.8	6,693	2.0
1960	16,560	9.2	929	0.5	2030	72,774	20.3	8,946	2.5
1980	25,549	11.3	2,240	1.0	2040	79,719	21.0	14,115	3.7
2000	34,992	12.4	4,240	1.5	2050	83,739	21.0	17,978	4.5

Note: 1900 figures are for June 1; 1920 figures are for Jan. 1; and 1940-2010 figures are for Apr. 1. 2015-50 projections are as of July 1. (1) Excludes Alaska and Hawaii.

U.S. Population Projections by Age, 2015-50
Source: Population Projections Program, U.S. Census Bureau, U.S. Dept. of Commerce
(numbers of resident population in thousands)

Age	2015 No.	% distrib.	2020 No.	% distrib.	2030 No.	% distrib.	2040 No.	% distrib.	2050 No.	% distrib.
Total	321,363	100.0%	333,896	100.0%	358,471	100.0%	380,016	100.0%	399,803	100.0%
Under 5 years	21,051	6.6	21,808	6.5	22,252	6.2	23,004	6.1	24,115	6.0
5 to 13 years	36,772	11.4	37,769	11.3	40,366	11.3	41,190	10.8	42,951	10.7
14 to 17 years	16,695	5.2	16,582	5.0	17,730	4.9	18,427	4.8	18,852	4.7
18 to 24 years	30,983	9.6	30,028	9.0	30,605	8.5	33,199	8.7	33,967	8.5
25 to 44 years	84,327	26.2	88,501	26.5	93,878	26.2	96,078	25.3	101,609	25.4
45 to 64 years	83,839	26.1	83,238	24.9	80,865	22.6	88,398	23.3	94,570	23.7
65 years and over	47,695	14.8	55,969	16.8	72,774	20.3	79,719	21.0	83,739	20.9
85 years and over	6,306	2.0	6,693	2.0	8,946	2.5	14,115	3.7	17,978	4.5
100 years and over	78	0.0	106	0.0	168	0.0	230	0.1	442	0.1

Note: Projections are as of July 1 of given year. They are based on assumptions about future births, deaths, and net international migration. Numbers exclude overseas U.S. military personnel and civilian U.S. citizens living abroad.

Disability Status of U.S. Population by Age, 2013
Source: American Community Survey (ACS), U.S. Census Bureau, U.S. Dept. of Commerce
(numbers in thousands, by disability type)

Characteristic	Number	% of pop.	Characteristic	Number	% of pop.
Total population	311,158	100.00%	Total population (5 and over)	291,389	100.00%
With a disability[1]	39,138	12.58	With a cognitive difficulty[2]	14,637	5.02
Under 5 years	161	0.05	5 to 17 years	2,180	0.75
Under 18 years	3,040	0.98	18 to 64 years	8,463	2.90
18 to 64 years	20,322	6.53	65 years and over	3,993	1.37
65 years and over	15,776	5.07	With an ambulatory difficulty[3]	20,630	7.08
With a hearing difficulty	11,097	3.57	5 to 17 years	339	0.12
Under 5 years	106	0.03	18 to 64 years	10,201	3.50
Under 18 years	440	0.14	65 years and over	10,090	3.46
18 to 64 years	4,085	1.31	With a self-care difficulty[4]	7,790	2.67
65 years and over	6,572	2.11	5 to 17 years	483	0.17
With a vision difficulty	7,311	2.35	18 to 64 years	3,619	1.24
Under 5 years	96	0.03	65 years and over	3,688	1.27
Under 18 years	557	0.18			
18 to 64 years	3,787	1.22	Total population (18 and over)	237,712	100.00%
65 years and over	2,967	0.95	With an independent living difficulty[5]	13,771	5.79
			18 to 64 years	7,079	2.98
			65 years and over	6,692	2.82

Note: Data based on sample and subject to sampling variability. Does not include military personnel and civilian non-institutionalized population (i.e., those under formal supervision or custody in a facility). (1) Identified by the ACS as persons "who exhibit difficulty with specific functions and may, in absence of accommodation, have a disability." (2) Concentrating, remembering, or making decisions. (3) Walking or climbing stairs. (4) Dressing or bathing. (5) Doing errands alone, such as visiting a doctor's office or shopping.

Marital Status of the U.S. Population, 1960-2013

Source: Annual Social and Economic Supplements, Current Population Surveys (CPS), U.S. Census Bureau, U.S. Dept. of Commerce
(numbers in millions)

Marital status	Both sexes				Male				Female			
	2013	2000	1980	1960	2013	2000	1980	1960	2013	2000	1980	1960
Total................	249.9	213.8	171.9	124.9	121.1	103.1	81.9	60.3	128.8	110.7	89.9	64.6
Married[1]............	131.7	120.2	104.8	84.4	65.4	59.7	51.8	41.8	66.3	60.5	53.0	42.6
Never married........	78.5	60.0	44.5	27.5	41.6	32.3	24.2	15.3	36.9	27.8	20.2	12.3
Divorced	25.4	19.9	9.9	2.8	11.0	8.6	3.9	1.1	14.4	11.3	6.0	1.7
Widowed	14.3	13.7	12.7	10.2	3.1	2.6	2.0	2.1	11.2	11.1	10.8	8.1
% of total or subset pops.												
Married[1]............	52.7%	56.2%	61.0%	67.6%	54.0%	57.9%	63.2%	69.3%	51.5%	54.7%	58.9%	65.9%
Never married........	31.4	28.1	25.9	22.0	34.4	31.3	29.6	25.3	28.6	25.1	22.5	19.0
Divorced	10.2	9.3	5.8	2.3	9.0	8.3	4.8	1.8	11.2	10.2	6.6	2.6
Widowed............	5.7	6.4	7.4	8.1	2.6	2.5	2.4	3.5	8.7	10.0	12.0	12.5

Note: Total population for 1980, 2000, and 2013 is persons ages 15 and older and for 1960, persons ages 14 and older. Data is based on sample of occupied households in the civilian noninstitutional population. Figures may not add up to totals due to rounding. (1) Comprises subcategories Married, spouse present; Married, spouse absent; and Separated.

Living Arrangements of Children in the U.S. by Parental Presence, 1970-2013

Source: Annual Social and Economic Supplements, Current Population Surveys (CPS), U.S. Census Bureau, U.S. Dept. of Commerce

		% of children (within selected population at left) living with—							
	No. of			Mother only—					
Race and Hispanic origin/year	children (thous.)	Both parents[4]	Total[5]	Married spouse absent	Divorced	Widowed	Never married	Father only	Neither parent
All children									
2013	73,910	69%	24%	1%	7%	1%	11%	4%	4%
White alone[1]									
1970	58,791	90	8	3	3	2	Z	1	2
1980	52,242	83	14	4	7	2	1	1	2
1990	51,390	79	16	4	8	1	3	3	2
2000	56,455	75	17	NA	NA	NA	NA	4	3
2013	54,227	74	18	1	7	1	7	4	3
Black alone[1]									
1970	9,422	58	30	16	5	4	4	2	10
1980	9,375	42	44	16	11	4	13	2	12
1990	10,018	38	51	12	10	2	27	4	8
2000	11,412	38	49	NA	NA	NA	NA	4	9
2013	11,086	39	51	2	8	1	34	5	6
Hispanic[2]									
1970[3]	4,006	78	NA	NA	NA	NA	NA	NA	NA
1980	5,459	75	20	8	6	2	4	2	3
1990	7,174	67	27	10	7	2	8	3	3
2000	11,613	65	25	NA	NA	NA	NA	4	5
2013	17,709	65	28	2	6	1	14	3	4

NA = Not available. Z = Less than 1%. **Note:** Children are defined as all persons under 18 years of age excluding those who are a family reference person or spouse. Data based on sample of occupied households in the civilian noninstitutional population. (1) One race only, not in combination with another race. (2) May be of any race. (3) Data based on 1970 decennial census. (4) Includes married and unmarried couples. (5) Includes children whose mothers are separated, a subcategory not shown in detail here.

Children in the U.S. by Parental Presence, 2013

Source: Annual Social and Economic Supplement, Current Population Survey (CPS), U.S. Census Bureau, U.S. Dept. of Commerce
(numbers in thousands)

	Number	% of total		Number	% of total
Total children	73,910	100.0%	Living with 1 parent............	20,531	27.8%
			Mother only..................	17,532	23.7
Living with 2 parents...............	50,646	68.5	Biological mother	17,182	23.2
Married parents	47,611	64.4	Father only..................	2,999	4.1
Unmarried parents	3,034	4.1	Biological father	2,863	3.9
Biological mother and father........	45,814	62.0	Living with no parents...........	2,733	3.7
Married parents	43,230	58.5	Grandparents only	1,431	1.9
Biological mother and stepfather	2,837	3.8	Other relatives only	649	0.9
Biological father and stepmother	896	1.2	Nonrelatives only	525	0.7
Biological mother and adoptive father	147	0.2	Other arrangement	127	0.2
Biological father and adoptive mother	34	0.0	Living with at least 1 biological parent ..	69,772	94.4
Adoptive mother and father	695	0.9	Living with at least 1 stepparent	4,117	5.6
Other[1]........................	224	0.3	Living with at least 1 adoptive parent ...	1,216	1.6

Note: Children are defined as all persons under 18 years of age excluding those who are a family reference person or spouse. Data based on sample of occupied households in the civilian noninstitutional population. (1) Includes children living with one adoptive parent and one stepparent, or two stepparents.

Unmarried-Partner Households in the U.S. by Sex of Partners, 2013

Source: American Community Survey (ACS), U.S. Census Bureau, U.S. Dept. of Commerce

Household	Number	% of total	% of cat.	Household	Number	% of total	% of cat.
Total households	116,291,033	100.0%	—	Female HH, female partner	239,816	0.2%	3.4%
Unmarried-partner households...	7,046,164	6.1	100.0%	Male HH, male partner	235,089	0.2	3.3
Male HH, female partner	3,302,287	2.8	46.9	All other households..........	109,244,869	93.9	100.0
Female HH, male partner	3,268,972	2.8	46.4				

HH = Householder, or person in whose name a home is owned or rented. **Note:** Data based on sample and subject to sampling variability. A household is defined as an occupied housing unit; the household population thus does not include people living in group quarters (e.g., correctional facilities, university housing).

U.S. Population by Sex, Race, Residence, and Median Age, 1790-2010

Source: Decennial Censuses, U.S. Census Bureau, U.S. Dept. of Commerce

(numbers in thousands, unless otherwise noted)

Census date	SEX Male	SEX Female	RACE[2] White	RACE[2] Black Number	RACE[2] Black % tot. pop	RACE[2] Other	RESIDENCE Urban[3]	RESIDENCE Rural	MEDIAN AGE (years) All races	MEDIAN AGE (years) White[2]	MEDIAN AGE (years) Black[2]
Conterminous U.S.[1]											
1790 (Aug. 2)	NA	NA	3,172	757	19.3%	NA	202	3,728	NA	NA	NA
1810 (Aug. 6)	NA	NA	5,862	1,378	19.0	NA	525	6,714	NA	16.0	NA
1820 (Aug. 7)	4,897	4,742	7,867	1,772	18.4	NA	693	8,945	16.7	16.6	17.2
1840 (June 1)	8,689	8,381	14,196	2,874	16.8	NA	1,845	15,218	17.8	17.9	17.6
1850 (June 1)	11,838	11,354	19,553	3,639	15.7	NA	3,574	19,617	18.9	19.2	17.4
1860 (June 1)	16,085	15,358	26,923	4,442	14.1	79	6,217	25,227	19.4	19.7	17.5
1870 (June 1)	19,494	19,065	33,589	4,880	12.7	89	9,902	28,656	20.2	20.4	18.5
1880 (June 1)	25,519	24,637	43,403	6,581	13.1	172	14,130	36,059	20.9	21.4	18.0
1890 (June 1)	32,237	30,711	55,101	7,489	11.9	358	22,106	40,874	22.0	22.5	17.8
1900 (June 1)	38,816	37,178	66,809	8,834	11.6	351	30,215	45,997	22.9	23.4	19.4
1910 (Apr. 15).......	47,332	44,640	81,732	9,828	10.7	413	42,064	50,164	24.1	24.5	20.8
1920 (Jan. 1)	53,900	51,810	94,821	10,463	9.9	427	54,253	51,768	25.3	25.5	22.3
1930 (Apr. 1).......	62,137	60,638	110,287	11,891	9.7	597	69,161	54,042	26.5	26.9	23.5
1940 (Apr. 1).......	66,062	65,608	118,215	12,866	9.8	589	74,705	57,459	29.0	29.5	25.3
United States											
1950 (Apr. 1).......	74,833	75,864	135,150	15,045	10.0	713	96,847	54,479	30.2	30.8	26.1
1960 (Apr. 1).......	88,331	90,992	158,832	18,872	10.5	1,620	125,269	54,054	29.5	30.3	23.5
1970 (Apr. 1).......	98,926	104,309	178,098	22,581	11.1	2,557	149,647	53,565	28.1	28.9	22.4
1980 (Apr. 1).......	110,053	116,493	194,713	26,683	11.8	5,150	167,051	59,495	30.0	30.9	24.9
1990 (Apr. 1).......	121,284	127,507	208,741	30,517	12.3	9,533	187,053	61,656	32.8	33.7	27.9
2000 (Apr. 1).......	138,056	143,368	195,577	35,705	12.7	13,716	222,361	59,061	35.3	38.6	30.0
2010 (Apr. 1).......	151,781	156,964	196,818	38,929	12.2	18,147	249,253	59,492	37.2	42.0	32.4

NA = Not available. (1) Excludes Alaska and Hawaii. (2) New race categories were introduced in the 2000 census. Race data for 2000 and on are for one race alone, not in combination with one or more other races. "White" does not include people who reported being of Hispanic origin. "Other" comprises Asians, Native Hawaiians and other Pacific Islanders, and American Indians and Alaska Natives. Because of these changes, race data from 2000 on are not comparable to figures from previous years. (3) The Census Bureau's definition of "urban" has changed over time. Figures for 2000 and 2010 include residents of so-called urban areas (50,000 or more inhabitants) and urban clusters (at least 2,500 but fewer than 50,000 inhabitants).

U.S. Population by Race and Hispanic Origin, 2000-10

Source: Decennial Censuses, U.S. Census Bureau, U.S. Dept. of Commerce

	2010 One race alone	2010 One or more races[1]	2000 One race alone	2000 One or more races[1]	% change, 2000-10[2] One race alone	% change, 2000-10[2] One or more races
Total population	299,736,465	308,745,538	274,595,678	281,421,906	9.2%	9.7%
Race						
White..........................	223,553,265	231,040,398	211,460,626	216,930,975	5.7	6.5
Black or African American...........	38,929,319	42,020,743	34,658,190	36,419,434	12.3	15.4
Asian............................	14,674,252	17,320,856	10,242,998	11,898,828	43.3	45.6
American Indian and Alaska Native	2,932,248	5,220,579	2,475,956	4,119,301	18.4	26.7
Native Hawaiian and other Pac. Isl.	540,013	1,225,195	398,835	874,414	35.4	40.1
Some other race	19,107,368	21,748,084	15,359,073	18,521,486	24.4	17.4
Hispanic origin and race						
Hispanic or Latino, any race	47,435,002	50,477,594	33,081,736	35,305,818	43.4	43.0
Not Hispanic or Latino..............	252,301,463	258,267,944	241,513,942	246,116,088	4.5	4.9
White........................	196,817,552	201,856,108	194,552,774	198,177,900	1.2	1.9
Black or African American	37,685,848	40,123,525	33,947,837	35,383,751	11.0	13.4
Asian........................	14,465,124	16,722,710	10,123,169	11,579,494	42.9	44.4
American Indian and Alaska Native..	2,247,098	4,029,675	2,068,883	3,444,700	8.6	17.0
Native Hawaiian and other Pac. Isl.	481,576	1,014,888	353,509	748,149	36.2	35.7
Some other race	604,265	1,033,866	467,770	1,770,645	29.2	−41.6

(1) Alone or in combination with one or more of the other races listed. Numbers may not add up to totals because of individuals reporting more than one race. (2) Columns 5 and 6 provide, respectively, a minimum-maximum range for the percent change in the population of each race.

U.S. Population by Ancestry Reported, 2013

Source: American Community Survey (ACS), U.S. Census Bureau, U.S. Dept. of Commerce
(numbers in thousands; ranked by number)

Ancestry	Number	% of total	Ancestry	Number	% of total	Ancestry	Number	% of total
Total population	316,129	100.0%	Norwegian	4,484	1.4%	French Canadian	2,101	0.7%
German	46,163	14.6	Dutch	4,272	1.4	Arab[4]...............	1,823	0.6
Irish.................	33,348	10.5	Swedish	3,913	1.2	Welsh	1,777	0.6
English	24,483	7.7	European	3,520	1.1	Czech..............	1,441	0.5
American	22,218	7.0	Sub-Saharan African[1]..	3,077	1.0	Hungarian	1,438	0.5
Italian	17,222	5.4	Scotch-Irish[2]........	2,977	0.9	Other ancestry not		
Polish	9,383	3.0	Russian.............	2,845	0.9	shown here	137,924	43.6
French (excl. Basque)..	8,228	2.6	West Indian (excl.			Unclassified or not		
Scottish.............	5,310	1.7	Hispanic groups)[3]...	2,821	0.9	reported	47,088	14.9

Note: Data based on sample and subject to sampling variability. Because respondents could self-identify with more than one ancestry, numbers do not add up to total. (1) Incl. Cabo Verdean, Ethiopian, Ghanian, Kenyan, Liberian, Nigerian, Senegalese, Sierra Leonean, Somalian, South African, Sudanese, Ugandan, Zimbabwean, African, and other Sub-Saharan African. (2) Persons reporting Irish-Scotch ancestry are incl. in "Other ancestry not shown here." (3) Incl. Bahamian, Barbadian, Belizean, Bermudan, British or Dutch West Indian, Haitian, Jamaican, Trinidadian and Tobagonian, U.S. Virgin Islander, West Indian, and other West Indian. (4) Incl. Egyptian, Iraqi, Jordanian, Lebanese, Moroccan, Palestinian, Syrian, Arab, and other Arab.

U.S. Race and Minority Group Populations by Age, 2013

Source: American Community Survey (ACS), U.S. Census Bureau, U.S. Dept. of Commerce

Race and origin/age	Number	% of race	Race and origin/age	Number	% of race
White (not Hispanic or Latino)	197,392,411	100.0%	Native Hawaiian and other		
Under 5 years...............	9,884,145	5.0	Pacific Islander	525,750	100.0%
Under 18 years...............	38,396,423	19.5	Under 5 years..............	38,328	7.3
18 to 64 years...............	123,780,531	62.7	Under 18 years.............	146,463	27.9
65 years and over............	35,215,457	17.8	18 to 64 years.............	341,791	65.0
85 years and over............	4,968,850	2.5	65 years and over..........	37,496	7.1
Black or African American.....	39,919,371	100.0	85 years and over..........	2,578	0.5
Under 5 years...............	2,789,535	7.0	Some other race	14,811,025	100.0
Under 18 years...............	10,461,597	26.2	Under 5 years..............	1,300,656	8.8
18 to 64 years...............	25,582,523	64.1	Under 18 years.............	4,588,114	31.0
65 years and over............	3,875,251	9.7	18 to 64 years.............	9,524,575	64.3
85 years and over............	422,893	1.1	65 years and over..........	698,336	4.7
Asian	16,012,120	100.0	85 years and over..........	66,538	0.4
Under 5 years...............	900,214	5.6	Two or more races	9,369,541	100.0
Under 18 years...............	3,372,183	21.1	Under 5 years..............	1,407,605	15.0
18 to 64 years...............	10,923,337	68.2	Under 18 years.............	4,360,528	46.5
65 years and over............	1,716,600	10.7	18 to 64 years.............	4,561,715	48.7
85 years and over............	189,230	1.2	65 years and over..........	447,298	4.8
American Indian and Alaska Native	2,521,131	100.0	85 years and over..........	47,004	0.5
Under 5 years...............	176,476	7.0	Hispanic or Latino (any race)	53,986,412	100.0
Under 18 years...............	700,606	27.8	Under 5 years..............	5,091,351	9.4
18 to 64 years...............	1,601,223	63.5	Under 18 years.............	17,721,576	32.8
65 years and over............	219,302	8.7	18 to 64 years.............	32,966,650	61.1
85 years and over............	17,585	0.7	65 years and over..........	3,298,186	6.1
			85 years and over..........	350,771	0.6

Note: Data based on sample and subject to sampling variability. Categories are for one race alone, not in combination with any other race, unless otherwise noted.

Educational Attainment of the U.S. Population, 2013

Source: American Community Survey (ACS), U.S. Census Bureau, U.S. Dept. of Commerce
(numbers in thousands; population 25 years of age and over)

Race and origin/highest ed. completed	Number	% of race	Race and origin/highest ed. completed	Number	% of race
White (not Hispanic or Latino)	141,478	100.0%	Native Hawaiian and other		
Less than H.S. diploma	11,779	8.3	Pacific Islander	317	100.0%
H.S. diploma or equiv. credential	40,169	28.4	Less than H.S. diploma	43	13.6
Some college or associate's degree.....	42,737	30.2	H.S. diploma or equiv. credential	114	35.9
Bachelor's degree or higher	46,794	33.1	Some college or associate's degree.....	109	34.5
Black or African American.............	24,615	100.0	Bachelor's degree or higher...........	51	16.0
Less than H.S. diploma	4,020	16.3	Some other race	8,328	100.0
H.S. diploma or equiv. credential	7,648	31.1	Less than H.S. diploma	3,430	41.2
Some college or associate's degree.....	8,194	33.3	H.S. diploma or equiv. credential	2,288	27.5
Bachelor's degree or higher	4,753	19.3	Some college or associate's degree.....	1,755	21.1
Asian	11,043	100.0	Bachelor's degree or higher...........	856	10.3
Less than H.S. diploma	1,528	13.8	Two or more races	3,805	100.0
H.S. diploma or equiv. credential	1,688	15.3	Less than H.S. diploma	532	14.0
Some college or associate's degree.....	2,160	19.6	H.S. diploma or equiv. credential	898	23.6
Bachelor's degree or higher	5,667	51.3	Some college or associate's degree.....	1,295	34.0
American Indian and Alaska Native	1,521	100.0	Bachelor's degree or higher...........	1,080	28.4
Less than H.S. diploma	313	20.6	Hispanic or Latino (any race)	29,673	100.0
H.S. diploma or equiv. credential	479	31.5	Less than H.S. diploma	10,479	35.3
Some college or associate's degree.....	518	34.0	H.S. diploma or equiv. credential	8,056	27.1
Bachelor's degree or higher	211	13.9	Some college or associate's degree.....	6,988	23.5
			Bachelor's degree or higher...........	4,151	14.0

H.S. = High school. Note: Data based on sample and subject to sampling variability. Categories are for one race alone, not in combination with any other race, unless otherwise noted.

U.S. Population Growth by Race and Hispanic Origin, 1970-2030

Source: Decennial Censuses, Population Projections Program, U.S. Census Bureau, U.S. Dept. of Commerce
(numbers in millions)

*Projected. **Note:** Because of changes in census questions and methods, data on race and Hispanic origin are not wholly comparable over time. (1) Includes American Indians and Alaska Natives as well as other races not shown. For 2000 and on, this category also includes Native Hawaiians and other Pacific Islanders along with persons reporting two or more races. (2) Figures for 1970-90 include Pacific Islanders. (3) May be of any race.

U.S. Race and Minority Group Percentages by State, 2010

Source: Decennial Census, U.S. Census Bureau, U.S. Dept. of Commerce
(percentage of state or country's total population)

| State | One race alone[1] (%) | | | | | | Two or more races[1] (%) | Hispanic or Latino, any race (%) |
	White	Black or African American	Asian	American Indian and Alaska Native	Native Hawaiian and other Pacific Islander	Some other race		
Alabama	67.0%	26.0%	1.1%	0.5%	0.04%	0.08%	1.3%	3.9%
Alaska	64.1	3.1	5.3	14.4	1.02	0.16	6.4	5.5
Arizona	57.8	3.7	2.7	4.0	0.17	0.13	1.8	29.6
Arkansas	74.5	15.3	1.2	0.7	0.19	0.07	1.6	6.4
California	40.1	5.8	12.8	0.4	0.35	0.23	2.6	37.6
Colorado	70.0	3.8	2.7	0.6	0.11	0.15	2.0	20.7
Connecticut	71.2	9.4	3.8	0.2	0.03	0.34	1.7	13.4
Delaware	65.3	20.8	3.2	0.3	0.03	0.17	2.0	8.2
District of Columbia	34.8	50.0	3.5	0.2	0.04	0.24	2.1	9.1
Florida	57.9	15.2	2.4	0.3	0.05	0.26	1.5	22.5
Georgia	55.9	30.0	3.2	0.2	0.05	0.20	1.6	8.8
Hawaii	22.7	1.5	37.7	0.2	9.43	0.14	19.4	8.9
Idaho	84.0	0.6	1.2	1.1	0.14	0.10	1.7	11.2
Illinois	63.7	14.3	4.5	0.1	0.02	0.12	1.4	15.8
Indiana	81.5	9.0	1.6	0.2	0.03	0.13	1.5	6.0
Iowa	88.7	2.9	1.7	0.3	0.06	0.07	1.4	5.0
Kansas	78.2	5.7	2.3	0.8	0.07	0.10	2.3	10.5
Kentucky	86.3	7.7	1.1	0.2	0.05	0.11	1.5	3.1
Louisiana	60.3	31.8	1.5	0.6	0.03	0.15	1.3	4.2
Maine	94.4	1.1	1.0	0.6	0.02	0.08	1.4	1.3
Maryland	54.7	29.0	5.5	0.2	0.04	0.21	2.2	8.2
Massachusetts	76.1	6.0	5.3	0.2	0.02	0.94	1.9	9.6
Michigan	76.6	14.0	2.4	0.6	0.02	0.10	1.9	4.4
Minnesota	83.1	5.1	4.0	1.0	0.04	0.11	1.9	4.7
Mississippi	58.0	36.9	0.9	0.5	0.03	0.06	0.9	2.7
Missouri	81.0	11.5	1.6	0.4	0.10	0.09	1.8	3.5
Montana	87.8	0.4	0.6	6.1	0.06	0.05	2.2	2.9
Nebraska	82.1	4.4	1.7	0.8	0.05	0.12	1.6	9.2
Nevada	54.1	7.7	7.1	0.9	0.57	0.18	2.9	26.5
New Hampshire	92.3	1.0	2.1	0.2	0.02	0.14	1.4	2.8
New Jersey	59.3	12.8	8.2	0.1	0.02	0.31	1.5	17.7
New Mexico	40.5	1.7	1.3	8.5	0.06	0.18	1.4	46.3
New York	58.3	14.4	7.3	0.3	0.03	0.42	1.7	17.6
North Carolina	65.3	21.2	2.2	1.1	0.06	0.16	1.6	8.4
North Dakota	88.9	1.1	1.0	5.3	0.04	0.05	1.5	2.0
Ohio	81.1	12.0	1.7	0.2	0.03	0.13	1.8	3.1
Oklahoma	68.7	7.3	1.7	8.2	0.11	0.08	5.1	8.9
Oregon	78.5	1.7	3.6	1.1	0.33	0.14	2.9	11.7
Pennsylvania	79.5	10.4	2.7	0.1	0.02	0.13	1.4	5.7
Rhode Island	76.4	4.9	2.8	0.4	0.03	0.84	2.2	12.4
South Carolina	64.1	27.7	1.3	0.4	0.05	0.12	1.4	5.1
South Dakota	84.7	1.2	0.9	8.5	0.04	0.06	1.8	2.7
Tennessee	75.6	16.5	1.4	0.3	0.04	0.10	1.4	4.6
Texas	45.3	11.5	3.8	0.3	0.07	0.14	1.3	37.6
Utah	80.4	0.9	2.0	1.0	0.87	0.13	1.8	13.0
Vermont	94.3	0.9	1.3	0.3	0.02	0.09	1.6	1.5
Virginia	64.8	19.0	5.5	0.3	0.06	0.19	2.3	7.9
Washington	72.5	3.4	7.1	1.3	0.58	0.18	3.7	11.2
West Virginia	93.2	3.4	0.7	0.2	0.02	0.06	1.3	1.2
Wisconsin	83.3	6.2	2.3	0.9	0.03	0.07	1.4	5.9
Wyoming	85.9	0.8	0.8	2.1	0.06	0.08	1.5	8.9
United States	63.7	12.2	4.7	0.7	0.16	0.20	1.9	16.3

(1) Not Hispanic or Latino.

American Indian and Alaska Native Population by State, 2010

Source: Decennial Census, U.S. Census Bureau, U.S. Dept. of Commerce
(ranked by one race alone)

Rank	State	One race alone[1]	More than one race[2]	Rank	State	One race alone[1]	More than one race[2]
1.	California	362,801	360,424	27.	Kansas	28,150	30,980
2.	Oklahoma	321,687	161,073	28.	Missouri	27,376	45,000
3.	Arizona	296,529	56,857	29.	Pennsylvania	26,843	54,249
4.	New Mexico	193,222	26,290	30.	Ohio	25,292	64,832
5.	Texas	170,972	144,292	31.	Arkansas	22,248	25,340
6.	North Carolina	122,110	61,972	32.	Idaho	21,441	14,944
7.	New York	106,906	114,152	33.	Maryland	20,420	38,237
8.	Alaska	104,871	33,441	34.	Tennessee	19,994	34,880
9.	Washington	103,869	95,129	35.	South Carolina	19,524	22,647
10.	South Dakota	71,817	10,256	36.	Massachusetts	18,850	31,855
11.	Florida	71,458	91,104	37.	Indiana	18,462	31,276
12.	Montana	62,555	16,046	38.	Nebraska	18,427	11,389
13.	Michigan	62,007	77,088	39.	Mississippi	15,030	10,880
14.	Minnesota	60,916	40,984	40.	Wyoming	13,336	5,260
15.	Colorado	56,010	51,822	41.	Connecticut	11,256	19,884
16.	Wisconsin	54,526	31,702	42.	Iowa	11,084	13,427
17.	Oregon	53,203	56,020	43.	Kentucky	10,120	21,235
18.	Illinois	43,963	57,488	44.	Maine	8,568	9,914
19.	North Dakota	36,591	6,405	45.	Rhode Island	6,058	8,336
20.	Utah	32,927	17,137	46.	Delaware	4,181	5,718
21.	Georgia	32,151	51,873	47.	Hawaii	4,164	29,306
22.	Nevada	32,062	23,883	48.	West Virginia	3,787	9,527
23.	Louisiana	30,579	24,500	49.	New Hampshire	3,150	7,374
24.	Virginia	29,225	51,699	50.	Vermont	2,207	5,172
25.	New Jersey	29,026	41,690	51.	District of Columbia	2,079	4,442
26.	Alabama	28,218	28,900		United States	2,932,248	2,288,331

(1) Respondents who self-identified as American Indian and Alaska Native (AIAN) alone. (2) Respondents who self-identified as AIAN in combination with one or more other races.

American Indian and Alaska Native Population by Selected Tribal Groupings, 2010

Source: Decennial Census, U.S. Census Bureau, U.S. Dept. of Commerce
(ranked by American Indian and Alaska Native [AIAN] alone, one tribal grouping alone)

Tribal grouping	AIAN alone — One tribal grouping alone[1]	AIAN alone — One or more tribal groupings[2]	AIAN alone or in combination — One or more tribal groupings[3]	Tribal grouping	AIAN alone — One tribal grouping alone[1]	AIAN alone — One or more tribal groupings[2]	AIAN alone or in combination — One or more tribal groupings[3]
Total	2,879,638	2,932,248	5,220,579	Crow	10,332	10,860	15,203
AIAN tribes, not specified	693,709	693,709	1,545,963	Kiowa	9,437	10,355	13,787
				Paiute	9,340	10,205	13,767
Amer. Ind. tribes, specified	1,935,363	2,032,133	3,397,251	Osage	8,938	10,063	18,576
Navajo	286,731	295,016	332,129	Yakama	8,786	9,096	11,527
Cherokee	284,247	300,463	819,105	Menominee	8,374	8,627	11,133
Mexican Amer. Ind.	121,221	123,550	175,494	Houma	8,169	8,240	10,768
Chippewa	112,757	115,402	170,742	Colville	8,114	8,314	10,549
Sioux	112,176	116,477	170,110	Arapaho	8,014	8,402	10,861
Choctaw	103,910	110,308	195,764	Shoshone	7,852	8,462	13,002
Apache	63,193	69,694	111,810	Delaware	7,843	8,215	18,264
Lumbee	62,306	62,957	73,691	Yuman	7,727	8,278	10,089
Pueblo	49,695	52,026	62,540	Ute	7,435	8,220	11,491
Creek	48,352	52,948	88,332	Ottawa	7,272	8,048	13,033
Iroquois	40,570	42,461	81,002	Canadian and French Amer. Ind.	6,433	7,051	14,822
Chickasaw	27,973	30,206	52,278	Cree	2,211	2,950	7,983
Blackfeet	27,279	31,798	105,304	All other tribes	270,141	282,747	429,629
Pima	22,040	23,205	26,655	Amer. Ind. tribes, not specified	131,943	132,060	234,320
Yaqui	21,679	23,195	32,595	AK Native tribes, specified	98,892	103,086	138,850
S. Amer. Ind.	20,901	21,380	47,233	Yup'ik	28,927	29,618	33,889
Potawatomi	20,412	20,874	33,771	Inupiat[4]	24,859	25,736	33,360
Tohono O'Odham	19,522	20,247	23,478	Alaskan Athabascan	15,623	16,427	22,484
Central Amer. Ind.	15,882	16,454	27,844	Tlingit-Haida	15,256	16,115	26,080
Puget Sound Salish	14,320	14,535	20,260	Aleut	11,920	12,643	19,282
Seminole	14,080	16,448	31,971	Tsimshian	2,307	2,547	3,755
Spanish Amer. Ind.	13,460	13,758	19,951	AK Native tribes, not specified	19,731	19,904	29,933
Hopi	12,580	14,634	18,327				
Comanche	12,284	13,471	23,330				
Cheyenne	11,375	12,493	19,051				

Note: This table measures the number of responses, not respondents. Respondents who self-identified with multiple tribal groupings are counted more than once. A tribal grouping refers to combined individual tribes (e.g., Fort Sill Apache and San Carlos Apache as Apache or King Salmon Tribe and Native Village of Kanatak as Aleut). (1) Respondents who self-identified with one tribal grouping alone (e.g., Navajo or Alaskan Athabascan. (2) As in footnote 1 or in combination with other tribal groupings (e.g., Yakama and Aleut). (3) As in footnotes 1 or 2 or in combination with another race (e.g., Apache, Navajo, and white; or Inupiat, white, and black). (4) Eskimo in previous censuses.

Populations, ZIP, and Area Codes for U.S. Places of 10,000 or More

Source: Decennial Census and Population Estimates Program, U.S. Census Bureau, U.S. Dept. of Commerce; NeuStar Inc.; www.usps.com

The following is a list of places of 10,000 or more residents according to the U.S. Census Bureau's population estimates for 2013 and the results of the 2010 census.

Census designated places (CDPs) are marked with a (c). These are unincorporated areas that the Census Bureau has delineated, in cooperation with state and local officials, for statistical purposes. Unless an exception is noted, the Census Bureau does not include CDPs in its estimates program. This list includes **places incorporated** under state law as cities, boroughs, towns, or villages. **Townships are not included.** This list also includes, in *italics*, **minor civil divisions (MCDs)** for Connecticut, Maine, Massachusetts, New Hampshire, Rhode Island, and Vermont. MCDs are not incorporated and not automatically recognized as CDPs, but are often the primary political or administrative divisions of a county. (Balance) indicates that the population given is for a consolidated area minus the residents of any incorporated places within.

An asterisk (*) denotes that the ZIP code given is for general delivery; mail routes and/or P.O. boxes within the place may use a different one. Telephone **area codes** are given in parentheses. New phone numbers may be assigned a different area code from that of existing phone numbers in an area. These areas of overlay are noted. When two or more area codes are listed for one place, consult local operators for assistance. Area codes based on latest information as of Sept. 2014. — = Not available.

Alabama

Area code 938 overlays area code 256.

ZIP	Place	Area code	2010 population	2013 estimate
*35007	Alabaster	(205)	30,352	31,342
*35950	Albertville	(256)	21,160	21,556
*35010	Alexander City	(256)	14,875	14,876
*36201	Anniston	(256)	23,106	22,666
*35611	Athens	(256)	21,897	24,000
*36502	Atmore	(251)	10,194	10,113
*36830	Auburn	(334)	53,380	58,582
*35020	Bessemer	(205)	27,456	27,053
*35203	Birmingham	(205)	212,237	212,113
35040	Calera	(205)	11,620	12,756
*35215	Center Point	(205)	16,921	16,864
35043	Chelsea	(205)	10,183	11,277
*35055	Cullman	(256)	14,775	15,030
36526	Daphne	(251)	21,570	23,633
*35601	Decatur	(256)	55,683	55,816
*36301	Dothan	(334)	65,496	68,001
*36330	Enterprise	(334)	26,562	27,775
*36027	Eufaula	(334)	13,137	12,914
35064	Fairfield	(205)	11,117	10,952
*36532	Fairhope	(251)	15,326	17,386
*35630	Florence	(256)	39,319	40,059
*36535	Foley	(251)	14,618	15,818
35214	Forestdale (c)	(205)	10,162	—
*35967	Fort Payne	(256)	14,012	14,136
*35901	Gadsden	(256)	36,856	36,542
35071	Gardendale	(205)	13,893	13,735
36542	Gulf Shores	(251)	9,741	10,765
*35640	Hartselle	(256)	14,255	14,466
*35080	Helena	(205)	16,793	17,560
35209	Homewood	(205)	25,167	25,750
*35023	Hueytown	(205)	16,105	15,866
*35801	Huntsville	(256)	180,105	186,254
35210	Irondale	(205)	12,349	12,379
36265	Jacksonville	(256)	12,548	12,484
*35501	Jasper	(205)	14,352	14,222
35094	Leeds	(205)	11,773	11,907
*35758	Madison	(256)	42,938	45,799
36054	Millbrook	(334)	14,640	15,112
*36602	Mobile	(251)	195,111	194,899
*36104	Montgomery	(334)	205,764	201,332
35004	Moody	(205)	11,726	12,390
*35223	Mountain Brook	(205)	20,413	20,359
*35661	Muscle Shoals	(256)	13,146	13,506
*35476	Northport	(205)	23,330	24,497
*36801	Opelika	(334)	26,477	28,655
36203	Oxford	(256)	21,348	21,232
*36360	Ozark	(334)	14,907	14,860
35124	Pelham	(205)	21,352	22,289
*35125	Pell City	(205)	12,695	13,367
*36867	Phenix City	(334)	32,822	37,498
35127	Pleasant Grove	(205)	10,110	10,361
*36066	Prattville	(334)	33,960	35,229
36610	Prichard	(251)	22,659	22,399
36206	Saks (c)	(256)	10,744	—
36571	Saraland	(251)	13,405	13,710
*35768	Scottsboro	(256)	14,770	14,831
*36701	Selma	(334)	20,756	19,912
*35150	Sylacauga	(256)	12,749	12,736
*35160	Talladega	(256)	15,676	15,846
36619	Tillman's Corner (c)	(251)	17,398	—
*36081	Troy	(334)	18,033	18,919
35173	Trussville	(205)	19,933	20,368
*35401	Tuscaloosa	(205)	90,468	95,334
*35216	Vestavia Hills	(205)	34,033	34,018

Alaska

Area code 907 applies to the entire state.

ZIP	Place	2010 population	2013 estimate
*99501	Anchorage	291,826	300,950
99711	Badger (c)	19,482	—
*99708	College (c)	12,964	—
*99701	Fairbanks	31,535	32,324
*99801	Juneau	31,275	32,660
99654	Knik-Fairview (c)	14,923	—

Arizona

ZIP	Place	Area code	2010 population	2013 estimate
85086	Anthem (c)	(623)	21,700	—
*85120	Apache Junction	(480)	35,840	37,130
85123	Arizona City (c)	(520)	10,475	—
*85323	Avondale	(623)	76,238	78,822
*85326	Buckeye	(623)	50,876	56,683
86442	Bullhead City	(928)	39,540	39,383
86322	Camp Verde	(928)	10,873	11,018
*85122	Casa Grande	(520)	48,571	50,111
85740	Casas Adobes (c)	(520)	66,795	—
85718	Catalina Foothills (c)	(520)	50,796	—
*85225	Chandler	(480)	236,123	249,146
86323	Chino Valley	(928)	10,817	10,943
85128	Coolidge	(520)	11,825	11,887
86326	Cottonwood	(928)	11,265	11,424
*85607	Douglas	(520)	17,378	16,915
85746	Drexel Heights (c)	(520)	27,749	—
85335	El Mirage	(623)	31,797	32,998
85131	Eloy	(520)	16,631	16,996
*86004	Flagstaff	(928)	65,870	68,667
85132	Florence	(520)	25,536	25,428
85705	Flowing Wells (c)	(520)	16,419	—
*86427	Fort Mohave (c)	(928)	14,364	—
85367	Fortuna Foothills (c)	(928)	26,265	—
*85268	Fountain Hills	(480)	22,489	23,235
*85234	Gilbert	(480)	208,453	229,972
*85302	Glendale	(623)	226,721	234,632
85118	Gold Canyon (c)	(480)	10,159	—
*85338	Goodyear	(623)	65,275	72,864
*85622	Green Valley (c)	(520)	21,391	—
*86401	Kingman	(928)	28,068	28,393
*86403	Lake Havasu City	(928)	52,527	52,844
*85653	Marana	(520)	34,961	38,290
85139	Maricopa	(520)	43,482	45,508
*85201	Mesa	(480)	439,041	457,587
86401	New Kingman-Butler (c)	(928)	12,134	—
*85087	New River (c)	(623)	14,952	—
*85621	Nogales	(520)	20,837	20,456
*85737	Oro Valley	(520)	41,011	41,627
*85253	Paradise Valley	(480)	12,820	13,387
*85541	Payson	(928)	15,301	15,245
*85345	Peoria	(623)	154,065	162,592
*85034	Phoenix	(480)/(602)/(623)	1,445,632	1,513,367
*85301	Prescott	(928)	39,843	40,590
*86314	Prescott Valley	(928)	38,822	39,791
*85142	Queen Creek	(480)	26,361	29,673
85648	Rio Rico (c)	(520)	18,962	—
*85629	Sahuarita	(520)	25,259	26,870
85349	San Luis	(928)	25,505	31,180
*85142	San Tan Valley (c)	(480)	81,321	—
*85251	Scottsdale	(480)	217,385	226,918
86336	Sedona	(928)	10,031	10,111
*85901	Show Low	(928)	10,660	10,730
*85635	Sierra Vista	(520)	43,888	45,129
85650	Sierra Vista Southeast (c)	(520)	14,797	—
85350	Somerton	(928)	14,287	14,994
*85351	Sun City (c)	(623)	37,499	—
*85375	Sun City West (c)	(623)	24,535	—
85248	Sun Lakes (c)	(480)	13,975	—
*85374	Surprise	(623)	117,517	123,546
85749	Tanque Verde (c)	(520)	16,901	—
*85282	Tempe	(480)	161,719	168,228
*85701	Tucson	(520)	520,116	526,116
85735	Tucson Estates (c)	(520)	12,192	—
85641	Vail (c)	(520)	10,208	—
86326	Verde Village (c)	(928)	11,605	—
*85364	Yuma	(928)	93,064	91,923

Arkansas

ZIP	Place	Area code	2010 population	2013 estimate
*71923	Arkadelphia	(870)	10,714	10,716
*72501	Batesville	(870)	10,248	10,490
*72714	Bella Vista	(479)	26,461	27,642
*72015	Benton	(501)	30,681	33,155
72712	Bentonville	(479)	35,301	40,167

ZIP	Place	Area code	2010 population	2013 estimate
*72315	Blytheville	(870)	15,620	15,120
*72022	Bryant	(501)	16,688	19,340
72023	Cabot	(501)	23,776	25,434
*71701	Camden	(870)	12,183	11,674
*72719	Centerton	(479)	9,515	10,556
*72032	Conway	(501)	58,908	63,816
*71730	El Dorado	(870)	18,884	18,539
*72701	Fayetteville	(479)	73,580	78,960
*72335	Forrest City	(870)	15,371	15,016
*72901	Fort Smith	(479)	86,209	87,650
*72601	Harrison	(870)	12,943	13,224
72342	Helena-West Helena	(870)	12,282	11,572
*71801	Hope	(870)	10,095	10,095
*71901	Hot Springs	(501)	35,193	35,680
*71909	Hot Springs Village (c)	(501)	12,807	—
*72076	Jacksonville	(501)	28,364	28,749
*72401	Jonesboro	(870)	67,263	71,551
*72201	Little Rock	(501)	193,524	197,357
*71753	Magnolia	(870)	11,577	11,574
*72104	Malvern	(501)	10,318	10,902
72364	Marion	(870)	12,345	12,327
*72113	Maumelle	(501)	17,163	17,736
72653	Mountain Home	(870)	12,448	12,284
*72114	North Little Rock	(501)	62,304	66,075
*72450	Paragould	(870)	26,113	27,078
*71601	Pine Bluff	(870)	49,083	46,094
*72756	Rogers	(479)	55,964	60,112
*72801	Russellville	(479)	27,920	28,533
*72143	Searcy	(501)	22,858	23,768
*72120	Sherwood	(501)	29,523	30,045
72761	Siloam Springs	(479)	15,039	15,856
*72764	Springdale	(479)	69,797	75,229
71854	Texarkana	(870)	29,919	30,016
*72956	Van Buren	(479)	22,791	23,059
*72301	West Memphis	(870)	26,245	25,545

California

Area code 424 overlays area code 310. Area code 442 overlays area code 760. Area code 628 overlays area code 415 effective Mar. 21, 2015. Area code 657 overlays area code 714. Area code 669 overlays area code 408. Area code 747 overlays area code 818.

ZIP	Place	Area code	2010 population	2013 estimate
92301	Adelanto	(760)	31,765	31,304
*91301	Agoura Hills	(818)	20,330	20,681
*94501	Alameda	(510)	73,812	76,419
94507	Alamo (c)	(925)	14,570	—
94706	Albany	(510)	18,539	19,192
*91801	Alhambra	(626)	83,089	84,577
92656	Aliso Viejo	(949)	47,823	50,175
*91901	Alpine (c)	(619)	14,236	—
*91001	Altadena (c)	(626)	42,777	—
95127	Alum Rock (c)	(408)	15,536	—
*94503	American Canyon	(707)	19,454	20,208
*92805	Anaheim	(714)	336,265	345,012
96007	Anderson	(530)	9,932	10,128
95843	Antelope (c)	(916)	45,770	—
*94509	Antioch	(925)	102,372	107,100
92307	Apple Valley	(760)	69,135	70,924
*91006	Arcadia	(626)	56,364	57,639
*95521	Arcata	(707)	17,231	17,697
*95825	Arden-Arcade (c)	(916)	92,186	—
*93420	Arroyo Grande	(805)	17,252	17,716
*90701	Artesia	(562)	16,522	16,736
93203	Arvin	(661)	19,304	20,298
94577	Ashland (c)	(510)	21,925	—
*93422	Atascadero	(805)	28,310	29,096
95301	Atwater	(209)	28,168	28,818
*95603	Auburn	(530)	13,330	13,905
93204	Avenal	(559)	15,505	14,176
91746	Avocado Heights (c)	(626)	15,411	—
91702	Azusa	(626)	46,361	47,842
*93301	Bakersfield	(661)	347,483	363,630
91706	Baldwin Park	(626)	75,390	76,635
92220	Banning	(951)	29,603	30,506
*92310	Barstow	(760)	22,639	23,219
94565	Bay Point (c)	(925)	21,349	—
92223	Beaumont	(951)	36,877	40,481
*90201	Bell	(323)	35,477	35,948
*90201	Bell Gardens	(213)/(323)/(562)	42,072	42,889
*90706	Bellflower	(562)	76,616	77,593
94002	Belmont	(650)	25,835	26,731
94510	Benicia	(707)	26,997	27,618
*94704	Berkeley	(510)	112,580	116,768
*90210	Beverly Hills	(213)/(310)/(323)	34,109	34,658
*92314	Big Bear City (c)	(909)	12,304	—
92316	Bloomington (c)	(951)	23,851	—
*92225	Blythe	(760)	20,817	19,832
*91902	Bonita (c)	(619)	12,538	—
92021	Bostonia (c)	(619)	15,379	—
92227	Brawley	(760)	24,953	25,558
*92821	Brea	(562)/(714)	39,282	40,963
94513	Brentwood	(925)	51,481	55,000
*90620	Buena Park	(714)	80,530	82,882

ZIP	Place	Area code	2010 population	2013 estimate
*91510	Burbank	(818)	103,340	104,709
*94010	Burlingame	(650)	28,806	29,892
91301	Calabasas	(818)	23,058	24,153
*92231	Calexico	(760)	38,572	39,389
*93505	California City	(760)	14,120	13,223
*93010	Camarillo	(805)	65,201	66,086
95682	Cameron Park (c)	(530)	18,228	—
92058	Camp Pendleton South (c)	(760)	10,616	—
*95008	Campbell	(408)	39,349	40,584
92587	Canyon Lake	(951)	10,561	10,911
95010	Capitola	(831)	9,918	10,093
*92008	Carlsbad	(760)	105,328	110,972
*95608	Carmichael (c)	(916)	61,762	—
*93013	Carpinteria	(805)	13,040	13,532
90745	Carson	(310)	91,714	92,599
92077	Casa de Oro-Mt. Helix (c)	(619)	18,762	—
*91384	Castaic (c)	(661)	19,015	—
*94546	Castro Valley (c)	(510)	61,388	—
*92234	Cathedral City	(760)	51,200	52,977
95307	Ceres	(209)	45,417	46,714
90703	Cerritos	(562)	49,041	49,707
94541	Cherryland (c)	(510)	14,728	—
*95926	Chico	(530)	86,187	88,077
*91708	Chino	(909)	77,983	80,988
91709	Chino Hills	(909)	74,799	76,572
93610	Chowchilla	(559)	18,720	17,383
*91910	Chula Vista	(619)	243,916	256,780
91702	Citrus (c)	(626)	10,866	—
*95610	Citrus Heights	(916)	83,301	85,285
91711	Claremont	(909)	34,926	35,824
94517	Clayton	(925)	10,897	11,505
95422	Clearlake	(707)	15,250	14,985
*93612	Clovis	(559)	95,631	99,769
92236	Coachella	(760)	40,704	43,092
93210	Coalinga	(559)	13,380	16,755
92324	Colton	(909)	52,154	53,243
90040	Commerce	(323)	12,823	12,993
*90221	Compton	(310)	96,455	97,877
*94520	Concord	(925)	122,067	125,880
*93212	Corcoran	(559)	24,813	23,320
*92882	Corona	(951)	152,374	159,503
*92118	Coronado	(619)	18,912	23,511
92626	Costa Mesa	(714)/(949)	109,960	112,174
92679	Coto de Caza (c)	(949)	14,866	—
*91722	Covina	(626)	47,796	48,508
92325	Crestline (c)	(909)	10,770	—
90201	Cudahy	(323)	23,805	24,103
*90230	Culver City	(310)	38,883	39,428
95014	Cupertino	(408)	58,302	60,189
90630	Cypress	(714)	47,802	49,087
*94015	Daly City	(415)/(650)	101,123	104,739
92629	Dana Point	(949)	33,351	34,062
94526	Danville	(925)	42,039	43,341
*95616	Davis	(530)	65,622	66,205
90250	Del Aire (c)	(310)/(323)	10,001	—
*93215	Delano	(661)	53,041	52,403
95315	Delhi (c)	(209)	10,755	—
*92240	Desert Hot Springs	(760)	25,938	27,902
91765	Diamond Bar	(909)	55,544	56,449
95619	Diamond Springs (c)	(530)	11,037	—
93618	Dinuba	(559)	21,453	23,347
94514	Discovery Bay (c)	(925)	13,352	—
95620	Dixon	(707)	18,351	18,963
*90240	Downey	(562)	111,772	113,242
91008	Duarte	(626)	21,321	21,724
94568	Dublin	(925)	46,036	52,105
92343	East Hemet (c)	(951)	17,418	—
90022	East Los Angeles (c)	(323)	126,496	—
94303	East Palo Alto	(650)	28,155	29,143
90221	East Rancho Dominguez (c)	(310)/(323)	15,135	—
*91775	East San Gabriel (c)	(626)	14,874	—
*91752	Eastvale[1]	(909)/(951)	53,668	55,191
*92020	El Cajon	(619)	99,478	102,211
*92243	El Centro	(760)	42,598	43,363
94530	El Cerrito	(510)	23,549	24,316
95762	El Dorado Hills (c)	(916)	42,108	—
*91731	El Monte	(626)	113,475	115,708
*93446	El Paso de Robles (Paso Robles)	(805)	29,793	30,857
90245	El Segundo	(310)	16,654	16,924
*94803	El Sobrante (c) (Contra Costa Co.)	(510)	12,669	—
92503	El Sobrante (c) (Riverside Co.)	(714)/(909)	12,723	—
*95624	Elk Grove	(916)	153,015	161,007
*94608	Emeryville	(510)	10,080	10,777
92024	Encinitas	(760)	59,518	61,588
*92025	Escondido	(760)	143,911	148,738
95501	Eureka	(707)	27,191	26,913
93221	Exeter	(559)	10,334	10,489
95628	Fair Oaks (c)	(916)	30,912	—
*94533	Fairfield	(707)	105,321	109,320
94541	Fairview (c)	(510)	10,003	—
*92028	Fallbrook (c)	(760)	30,534	—
93223	Farmersville	(559)	10,588	10,720

ZIP	Place	Area code	2010 population	2013 estimate
*93015	Fillmore	(805)	15,002	15,255
90001	Florence-Graham (c)	(323)	63,387	—
95828	Florin (c)	(916)	47,513	—
*95630	Folsom	(916)	72,203	73,098
*92335	Fontana	(909)	196,069	203,003
95841	Foothill Farms (c)	(916)	33,121	—
95540	Fortuna	(707)	11,926	11,788
94404	Foster City	(650)	30,567	32,377
*92704	Fountain Valley	(714)	55,313	56,707
*94536	Fremont	(510)	214,089	224,922
92563	French Valley (c)	(951)	23,067	—
*93706	Fresno	(559)	494,665	509,924
*92831	Fullerton	(714)	135,161	138,981
95632	Galt	(209)	23,647	24,472
95215	Garden Acres (c)	(209)	10,648	—
*92843	Garden Grove	(714)	170,883	175,140
*90247	Gardena	(310)	58,829	59,957
*95020	Gilroy	(408)	48,821	51,701
92509	Glen Avon (c)	(951)	20,199	—
*91201	Glendale	(818)	191,719	196,021
*91741	Glendora	(626)	50,073	51,074
*93117	Goleta	(805)	29,888	30,525
*92313	Grand Terrace	(951)	12,040	12,337
95746	Granite Bay (c)	(916)	20,402	—
*95945	Grass Valley	(530)	12,860	12,793
93927	Greenfield	(831)	16,330	16,869
*93433	Grover Beach	(805)	13,156	13,432
91745	Hacienda Heights (c)	(626)	54,038	—
94019	Half Moon Bay	(650)	11,324	12,013
*93230	Hanford	(559)	53,967	54,686
90716	Hawaiian Gardens	(562)	14,254	14,446
*90250	Hawthorne	(310)/(323)	84,293	86,199
*94544	Hayward	(510)	144,186	151,574
95448	Healdsburg	(707)	11,254	11,517
*92543	Hemet	(951)	78,657	81,750
94547	Hercules	(510)	24,060	24,848
90254	Hermosa Beach	(310)	19,506	19,801
*92344	Hesperia	(760)	90,173	92,147
92346	Highland	(909)	53,104	54,291
94010	Hillsborough	(650)	10,825	11,273
*95023	Hollister	(831)	34,928	36,589
92879	Home Gardens (c)	(909)	11,570	—
*92647	Huntington Beach	(714)	189,992	197,575
90255	Huntington Park	(323)	58,114	58,879
92251	Imperial	(760)	14,758	16,184
*91932	Imperial Beach	(619)	26,324	27,063
*92201	Indio	(760)	76,036	83,539
*90301	Inglewood	(310)/(323)	109,673	111,542
*92602	Irvine	(714)/(949)	212,375	236,716
93117	Isla Vista (c)	(805)	23,096	—
*91752	Jurupa Valley[2]	(951)	95,004	98,030
93630	Kerman	(559)	13,544	14,349
93930	King City	(831)	12,874	13,248
93631	Kingsburg	(559)	11,382	11,695
*91011	La Cañada Flintridge	(818)	20,246	20,553
91214	La Crescenta-Montrose (c)	(818)	19,653	—
*90631	La Habra	(562)/(714)	60,239	61,653
*91941	La Mesa	(619)	57,065	58,642
*90638	La Mirada	(562)/(714)	48,527	49,133
90623	La Palma	(562)/(714)	15,568	15,892
91977	La Presa (c)	(619)	34,169	—
*91744	La Puente	(626)	39,816	40,435
*92253	La Quinta	(760)	37,467	39,331
95401	La Riviera (c)	(916)	10,802	—
91750	La Verne	(909)	31,063	31,868
92694	Ladera Ranch (c)	(949)	22,980	—
94549	Lafayette	(925)	23,893	25,053
*92652	Laguna Beach	(949)	22,723	23,250
*92653	Laguna Hills	(949)	30,344	30,880
92677	Laguna Niguel	(949)	62,979	64,652
92637	Laguna Woods	(949)	16,192	16,400
92352	Lake Arrowhead (c)	(909)	12,424	—
*92530	Lake Elsinore	(951)	51,821	57,525
92630	Lake Forest	(949)	77,264	79,312
*93535	Lake Los Angeles (c)	(661)	12,328	—
92530	Lakeland Village (c)	(909)/(951)	11,541	—
92040	Lakeside (c)	(619)	20,648	—
*90714	Lakewood	(562)	80,048	81,121
93241	Lamont (c)	(661)	15,120	—
*93534	Lancaster	(661)	156,633	159,523
*94939	Larkspur	(415)	11,926	12,204
95330	Lathrop	(209)	18,023	19,626
*90260	Lawndale	(310)	32,769	33,230
*91945	Lemon Grove	(619)	25,320	26,141
95824	Lemon Hill (c)	(916)	13,729	—
93245	Lemoore	(559)	24,531	24,973
90304	Lennox (c)	(310)	22,753	—
95648	Lincoln	(916)	42,819	45,237
95901	Linda (c)	(530)	17,773	—
93247	Lindsay	(559)	11,768	12,974
95062	Live Oak (c)	(831)	17,158	—
*94550	Livermore	(925)	80,968	85,156
95334	Livingston	(209)	13,058	13,571
*95240	Lodi	(209)	62,134	63,338
92354	Loma Linda	(951)	23,261	23,704

ZIP	Place	Area code	2010 population	2013 estimate
90717	Lomita	(310)	20,256	20,596
*93436	Lompoc	(805)	42,434	43,509
*90802	Long Beach	(310)/(562)	462,257	469,428
*90720	Los Alamitos	(562)/(949)	11,449	11,652
94022	Los Altos	(650)	28,976	30,010
*90086	Los Angeles	(213)/(310)/(323)	3,792,621	3,884,307
93635	Los Banos	(209)	35,972	36,822
*95030	Los Gatos	(408)	29,413	30,391
93402	Los Osos (c)	(805)	14,276	—
90262	Lynwood	(213)/(310)/(323)	69,772	71,371
93638	Madera	(559)	61,416	63,105
95954	Magalia (c)	(530)	11,310	—
90265	Malibu	(310)	12,645	12,861
*90266	Manhattan Beach	(310)	35,135	35,726
95336	Manteca	(209)	67,096	71,948
93933	Marina	(831)	19,718	20,370
94553	Martinez	(925)	35,824	37,165
95901	Marysville	(530)	12,072	12,213
90270	Maywood	(323)	27,395	27,748
93250	McFarland	(661)	12,707	12,420
*95521	McKinleyville (c)	(707)	15,177	—
92570	Mead Valley (c)	(951)	18,510	—
93640	Mendota	(559)	11,014	11,420
*92586	Menifee	(951)	77,519	83,447
*94025	Menlo Park	(650)	32,026	33,071
*95340	Merced	(209)	78,958	81,102
94941	Mill Valley	(415)	13,903	14,311
94030	Millbrae	(650)	21,532	22,424
95035	Milpitas	(408)	66,790	69,783
91752	Mira Loma (c)	(951)	21,930	—
92691	Mission Viejo	(949)	93,305	96,346
*95350	Modesto	(209)	201,165	204,933
91016	Monrovia	(626)	36,590	37,101
91763	Montclair	(909)	36,664	38,027
90640	Montebello	(323)	62,500	63,495
*93940	Monterey	(831)	27,810	28,294
*91754	Monterey Park	(323)/(626)/(818)	60,269	61,085
93021	Moorpark	(805)	34,421	35,149
*94556	Moraga	(925)	16,016	16,771
92551	Moreno Valley	(951)	193,365	201,175
*95037	Morgan Hill	(408)	37,882	40,836
93442	Morro Bay	(805)	10,234	10,461
*94041	Mountain View	(650)	74,066	77,846
92562	Murrieta	(951)	103,466	107,479
92407	Muscoy (c)	(909)	10,644	—
*94558	Napa	(707)	76,915	79,068
*91950	National City	(619)	58,582	59,834
94560	Newark	(510)	42,573	44,096
95360	Newman	(209)	10,224	10,639
92657	Newport Beach	(949)	85,186	87,273
93444	Nipomo (c)	(805)	16,714	—
92860	Norco	(951)	27,063	26,966
95603	North Auburn (c)	(530)	13,022	—
94025	North Fair Oaks (c)	(650)	14,687	—
95660	North Highlands (c)	(916)	42,694	—
92705	North Tustin (c)	(714)/(949)	24,917	—
*90650	Norwalk	(562)	105,549	106,589
94947	Novato	(415)	51,904	54,194
*91377	Oak Park (c)	(805)/(818)	13,811	—
95361	Oakdale	(209)	20,675	21,469
*94601	Oakland	(510)	390,724	406,253
94561	Oakley	(925)	35,432	38,194
*92056	Oceanside	(760)	167,086	172,794
93308	Oildale (c)	(661)	32,684	—
95961	Olivehurst (c)	(530)	13,656	—
91761	Ontario	(909)	163,924	167,500
*92868	Orange	(714)	136,416	139,969
95662	Orangevale (c)	(916)	33,960	—
93455	Orcutt (c)	(805)	28,905	—
94563	Orinda	(925)	17,643	18,681
95965	Oroville	(530)	15,546	16,061
93030	Oxnard	(805)	197,899	203,007
93950	Pacific Grove	(831)	15,041	15,504
94044	Pacifica	(650)	37,234	38,606
*92260	Palm Desert	(760)	48,445	50,508
92262	Palm Springs	(760)	44,552	46,281
*93550	Palmdale	(661)	152,750	157,161
94303	Palo Alto	(650)	64,403	66,642
*90274	Palos Verdes Estates	(310)	13,438	13,623
95969	Paradise	(530)	26,218	26,283
90723	Paramount	(562)	54,098	54,980
95823	Parkway (c)	(916)	14,670	—
93648	Parlier	(559)	14,494	14,865
*91101	Pasadena	(323)/(626)/(818)	137,122	139,731
	Paso Robles. See El Paso de Robles			
95363	Patterson	(209)	20,413	20,868
92509	Pedley (c)	(951)	12,672	—
92570	Perris	(951)	68,386	72,326
*94952	Petaluma	(707)	57,941	59,440
93260	Phelan (c)	(760)	14,304	—
*90660	Pico Rivera	(562)	62,942	63,771
*94611	Piedmont	(510)	10,667	11,082
94564	Pinole	(510)	18,390	18,902
94565	Pittsburg	(925)	63,264	66,695
*92870	Placentia	(714)	50,533	52,206

ZIP	Place	Area code	2010 population	2013 estimate
95667	Placerville	(530)	10,389	10,464
94523	Pleasant Hill	(925)	33,152	34,127
*94566	Pleasanton	(925)	70,285	74,110
*91765	Pomona	(909)	149,058	151,348
*93041	Port Hueneme	(805)	21,723	22,138
*93257	Porterville	(559)	54,165	55,174
*92064	Poway	(858)	47,811	49,417
93907	Prunedale (c)	(831)	17,560	—
*93536	Quartz Hill (c)	(661)	10,912	—
92065	Ramona	(760)	20,292	—
*95670	Rancho Cordova	(916)	64,776	67,911
*91730	Rancho Cucamonga	(909)	165,269	171,386
92270	Rancho Mirage	(760)	17,218	17,799
90275	Rancho Palos Verdes	(310)	41,643	42,448
91941	Rancho San Diego (c)	(619)	21,208	—
92688	Rancho Santa Margarita	(949)	47,853	49,228
96080	Red Bluff	(530)	14,076	14,104
*96001	Redding	(530)	89,861	91,119
*92373	Redlands	(909)	68,747	69,999
*90277	Redondo Beach	(310)	66,748	67,815
*94063	Redwood City	(650)	76,815	80,872
93654	Reedley	(559)	24,194	25,010
*92377	Rialto	(909)	99,171	101,910
*94801	Richmond	(510)	103,701	107,571
*93555	Ridgecrest	(760)	27,616	28,600
95673	Rio Linda (c)	(916)	15,106	—
95366	Ripon	(209)	14,297	14,754
95367	Riverbank	(209)	22,678	23,504
*92501	Riverside	(951)	303,871	316,619
95677	Rocklin	(916)	56,974	59,738
*94928	Rohnert Park	(707)	40,971	41,398
93560	Rosamond (c)	(661)	18,150	—
93314	Rosedale (c)	(661)	14,058	—
*91770	Rosemead	(626)	53,764	54,561
95826	Rosemont (c)	(916)	22,681	—
95678	Roseville	(916)	118,788	127,035
90720	Rossmoor (c)	(714)	10,244	—
91748	Rowland Heights (c)	(626)	48,993	—
*92519	Rubidoux (c)	(951)	34,280	—
*95814	Sacramento	(916)	466,488	479,686
95368	Salida (c)	(209)	13,722	—
93907	Salinas	(831)	150,441	155,662
*94960	San Anselmo	(415)	12,336	12,605
*92401	San Bernardino	(909)	209,924	213,708
94066	San Bruno	(650)	41,114	42,443
*93001	San Buenaventura (Ventura)	(805)	106,433	108,817
94070	San Carlos	(650)	28,406	29,387
*92672	San Clemente	(949)	63,522	65,040
*92101	San Diego	(619)/(858)	1,307,402	1,355,896
92065	San Diego Country Estates (c)	(760)	10,109	—
91773	San Dimas	(909)	33,371	33,840
*91340	San Fernando	(818)	23,645	24,220
*94102	San Francisco	(415)	805,235	837,442
91775	San Gabriel	(626)	39,718	40,275
*92582	San Jacinto	(951)	44,199	45,851
*95113	San Jose	(408)	945,942	998,537
*92675	San Juan Capistrano	(949)	34,593	35,852
*94577	San Leandro	(510)	84,950	87,965
94580	San Lorenzo (c)	(510)	23,452	—
*93401	San Luis Obispo	(805)	45,119	46,377
*92069	San Marcos	(760)	83,781	89,387
*91108	San Marino	(626)	13,147	13,327
*94402	San Mateo	(650)	97,207	101,128
94806	San Pablo	(510)	29,139	29,685
*94901	San Rafael	(415)	57,713	58,994
*94583	San Ramon	(925)	72,148	74,513
93657	Sanger	(559)	24,270	24,681
*92701	Santa Ana	(714)/(949)	324,528	334,227
*93101	Santa Barbara	(805)	88,410	90,412
*95050	Santa Clara	(408)	116,468	120,245
*91350	Santa Clarita	(661)	176,320	179,590
*95060	Santa Cruz	(831)	59,946	62,864
90670	Santa Fe Springs	(562)	16,223	17,053
*93454	Santa Maria	(805)	99,553	102,216
*90401	Santa Monica	(310)	89,736	92,472
*93060	Santa Paula	(805)	29,321	30,091
*95401	Santa Rosa	(707)	167,815	171,990
*92071	Santee	(619)	53,413	56,105
*95070	Saratoga	(408)	29,926	30,907
*95066	Scotts Valley	(831)	11,580	11,755
90740	Seal Beach	(562)	24,168	24,605
93955	Seaside	(831)	33,025	34,095
93662	Selma	(559)	23,219	24,182
93263	Shafter	(661)	16,988	17,197
*96019	Shasta Lake	(916)	10,164	10,139
*91024	Sierra Madre	(626)	10,917	11,056
*90755	Signal Hill	(562)	11,016	11,332
*93065	Simi Valley	(805)	124,237	126,181
92075	Solana Beach	(858)	12,867	13,236
93960	Soledad	(831)	25,738	25,849
95476	Sonoma	(707)	10,648	10,892
91733	South El Monte	(626)	20,116	20,398

ZIP	Place	Area code	2010 population	2013 estimate
90280	South Gate	(323)/(562)	94,396	95,677
*96150	South Lake Tahoe	(530)	21,403	21,387
91030	South Pasadena	(213)/(323)/(626)/(818)	25,619	25,959
*94080	South San Francisco	(650)	63,632	66,174
91744	South San Jose Hills (c)	(626)	20,551	—
90605	South Whittier (c)	(562)	57,156	—
*91977	Spring Valley (c) (San Diego Co.)	(619)	28,205	—
*94305	Stanford (c)	(650)	13,809	—
90680	Stanton	(714)	38,186	38,623
91381	Stevenson Ranch (c)	(661)	17,557	—
*95202	Stockton	(209)	291,707	298,118
*94585	Suisun City	(707)	28,111	28,819
93543	Sun Village (c)	(661)	11,565	—
*94086	Sunnyvale	(408)	140,081	147,559
*96130	Susanville	(530)	17,947	15,546
94941	Tamalpais-Homestead Valley (c)	(415)	10,735	—
*93561	Tehachapi	(661)	14,414	13,258
*92590	Temecula	(951)	100,097	106,780
92883	Temescal Valley (c)	(951)	22,535	—
91780	Temple City	(626)	35,558	36,133
*91360	Thousand Oaks	(805)	126,683	128,731
90503	Torrance	(310)	145,438	147,478
*95076	Tracy	(209)	82,922	84,691
*96161	Truckee	(916)	16,180	16,165
93274	Tulare	(559)	59,278	61,170
*95380	Turlock	(209)	68,549	70,365
*92780	Tustin	(714)/(949)	75,540	78,327
*92277	Twentynine Palms	(760)	25,048	25,768
*95482	Ukiah	(707)	16,075	15,871
94587	Union City	(510)	69,516	72,528
*91784	Upland	(909)	73,732	75,413
*95687	Vacaville	(707)	92,428	94,275
91744	Valinda (c)	(626)	22,822	—
92343	Valle Vista (c)	(951)	14,578	—
*94590	Vallejo	(707)	115,942	118,837
	Ventura. See San Buenaventura			
*92393	Victorville	(760)	115,903	121,096
90043	View Park-Windsor Hills (c)	(310)	11,075	—
91722	Vincent (c)	(925)	15,922	—
95829	Vineyard (c)	(916)	24,836	—
*93291	Visalia	(559)	124,442	127,763
*92083	Vista	(760)	93,834	96,929
*91789	Walnut	(626)	29,172	30,065
*94596	Walnut Creek	(925)	64,173	66,900
90255	Walnut Park (c)	(213)	15,966	—
93380	Wasco	(661)	25,545	25,945
*95076	Watsonville	(831)	51,199	52,477
90502	West Carson (c)	(310)	21,699	—
*91790	West Covina	(626)	106,098	107,740
*90069	West Hollywood	(310)/(323)	34,399	35,288
91746	West Puente Valley (c)	(626)	22,636	—
*95691	West Sacramento	(916)	48,744	49,891
90606	West Whittier-Los Nietos (c)	(562)	25,540	—
*92683	Westminster	(714)	89,701	91,739
90047	Westmont (c)	(323)	31,853	—
*90605	Whittier	(562)	85,331	86,635
92595	Wildomar	(951)	32,176	33,620
90222	Willowbrook (c)	(323)	35,983	—
95492	Windsor	(707)	26,801	27,243
92040	Winter Gardens (c)	(619)	20,631	—
95388	Winton (c)	(209)	10,613	—
92504	Woodcrest (c)	(909)/(951)	14,347	—
*95695	Woodland	(530)	55,468	56,590
92886	Yorba Linda	(714)	64,234	67,032
*95991	Yuba City	(530)	64,925	65,416
92399	Yucaipa	(909)	51,367	52,536
*92284	Yucca Valley	(760)	20,700	21,132

(1) Place was incorporated after the 2010 Census was conducted. Data in 2010 column is for Eastvale CDP. (2) Place was incorporated after the 2010 Census was conducted. Data in 2010 column is Census Bureau estimate.

Colorado
Area code 720 overlays area code 303.

ZIP	Place	Area code	2010 population	2013 estimate
*80003	Arvada	(303)	106,433	111,707
*80010	Aurora	(303)	325,078	345,803
80221	Berkley (c)	(970)	11,207	—
*80908	Black Forest (c)	(719)	13,116	—
*80302	Boulder	(303)	97,385	103,166
80601	Brighton	(303)	33,352	35,719
*80020	Broomfield	(303)	55,889	59,471
81212	Cañon City	(719)	16,400	16,318
80108	Castle Pines[1]	(303)	10,360	10,726
*80104	Castle Rock	(303)	48,231	53,063
*80015	Centennial	(303)	100,377	106,114
80111	Cherry Creek (c)	(303)	11,120	—
81222	Cimarron Hills (c)	(719)	16,161	—

ZIP	Place	Area code	2010 population	2013 estimate
81520	Clifton (c)	(970)	19,889	—
*80903	Colorado Springs	(719)	416,427	439,886
80120	Columbine (c)	(303)	24,280	—
80022	Commerce City	(303)	45,913	49,799
80304	Dakota Ridge (c)	(303)	32,005	—
*80202	Denver	(303)	600,158	649,495
*81301	Durango	(970)	16,887	17,557
81632	Edwards (c)	(970)	10,266	—
*80110	Englewood	(303)	30,255	31,516
80516	Erie	(303)	18,135	19,723
80620	Evans	(970)	18,537	19,944
80221	Federal Heights	(303)	11,467	11,973
*80520	Firestone	(303)	10,147	11,175
80913	Fort Carson (c)	(719)	13,813	—
*80525	Fort Collins	(970)	143,986	152,061
*80701	Fort Morgan	(970)	11,315	11,407
80817	Fountain	(719)	25,846	27,265
*80530	Frederick	(303)	8,679	10,196
*81521	Fruita	(970)	12,646	12,724
*80401	Golden	(303)	18,867	19,393
*81501	Grand Junction	(970)	58,566	59,778
*80631	Greeley	(970)	92,889	96,539
*80111	Greenwood Village	(303)	13,925	14,652
*80126	Highlands Ranch (c)	(303)	96,713	—
80534	Johnstown	(970)	9,887	12,093
80127	Ken Caryl (c)	(303)	32,438	—
80026	Lafayette	(303)	24,453	26,784
*80226	Lakewood	(303)	142,980	147,214
*80126	Littleton	(303)	41,737	44,275
*80124	Lone Tree	(303)	10,218	13,267
*80501	Longmont	(303)	86,270	89,919
80027	Louisville	(303)	18,376	19,588
*80538	Loveland	(970)	66,859	71,334
*81401	Montrose	(970)	19,132	19,015
*80233	Northglenn	(303)	35,789	37,499
*80134	Parker	(303)	45,297	48,608
*81003	Pueblo	(719)	106,595	108,249
81007	Pueblo West (c)	(719)	29,637	—
80911	Security-Widefield (c)	(719)	32,882	—
*80221	Sherrelwood (c)	(303)	18,287	—
*80487	Steamboat Springs	(970)	12,088	12,100
*80751	Sterling	(970)	14,777	14,637
80027	Superior	(303)	12,483	12,865
*80134	The Pinery (c)	(303)	10,517	—
*80229	Thornton	(303)	118,772	127,359
80229	Welby (c)	(303)	14,846	—
*80030	Westminster	(303)	106,114	110,945
*80033	Wheat Ridge	(303)	30,166	30,920
*80550	Windsor	(970)	18,644	20,422

(1) Place was incorporated after the 2010 Census was conducted. Data in 2010 column is Census Bureau estimate.

Connecticut

Area code 475 overlays area code 203. Area code 959 overlays area code 860. See introductory note.

ZIP	Place	Area code	2010 population	2013 estimate
06401	Ansonia	(203)	19,249	19,020
06001	Avon	(860)	18,098	18,386
06037	Berlin	(860)	19,866	20,590
06801	Bethel	(203)	18,584	19,264
06002	Bloomfield	(860)	20,486	20,673
06405	Branford	(203)	28,026	27,988
*06604	Bridgeport	(203)	144,229	147,216
*06010	Bristol	(860)	60,477	60,568
06804	Brookfield	(203)	16,452	16,860
06019	Canton	(860)	10,292	10,357
*06410	Cheshire	(203)	29,261	29,150
06413	Clinton	(860)	13,260	13,180
*06415	Colchester	(860)	16,068	16,210
06238	Coventry	(860)	12,435	12,411
06416	Cromwell	(860)	14,005	14,178
*06810	Danbury	(203)	80,893	83,684
06820	Darien	(203)	20,732	21,330
06418	Derby	(203)	12,902	12,801
*06424	East Hampton	(860)	12,959	12,912
*06108	East Hartford	(860)	51,252	51,199
*06512	East Haven	(203)	29,257	29,121
06333	East Lyme	(860)	19,159	18,937
*06088	East Windsor	(860)	11,162	11,406
06029	Ellington	(860)	15,602	15,786
*06082	Enfield	(860)	44,654	44,748
*06825	Fairfield	(203)	59,404	60,855
*06032	Farmington	(860)	25,340	25,613
06033	Glastonbury	(860)	34,427	34,768
06035	Granby	(860)	11,282	11,323
*06830	Greenwich	(203)	61,171	62,396
*06830	Greenwich (c)	(203)	12,942	—
06351	Griswold	(860)	11,951	11,959
06340	Groton	(860)	40,115	40,176
06437	Guilford	(203)	22,375	22,417
*06514	Hamden	(203)	60,960	61,607

ZIP	Place	Area code	2010 population	2013 estimate
*06101	Hartford	(860)	124,775	125,017
*06239	Killingly	(860)	17,370	17,233
06339	Ledyard	(860)	15,051	15,094
06443	Madison	(203)	18,269	18,297
*06040	Manchester	(860)	58,241	58,211
*06040	Manchester (c)	(860)	30,577	—
*06250	Mansfield	(860)	26,543	25,774
*06450	Meriden	(203)	60,868	60,456
06457	Middletown	(860)	47,648	47,333
*06460	Milford (balance)	(203)	51,271	51,644
*06460	Milford	(203)	52,759	53,137
06468	Monroe	(203)	19,479	19,834
06353	Montville	(860)	19,571	19,713
06770	Naugatuck	(203)	31,862	31,707
*06051	New Britain	(860)	73,206	72,939
*06840	New Canaan	(203)	19,738	20,194
06812	New Fairfield	(203)	13,881	14,145
*06511	New Haven	(203)	129,779	130,660
06320	New London	(860)	27,620	27,545
06776	New Milford	(860)	28,142	27,767
*06111	Newington	(860)	30,562	30,756
06470	Newtown	(203)	27,560	28,113
06471	North Branford	(203)	14,407	14,353
06473	North Haven	(203)	24,093	23,939
*06850	Norwalk	(203)	85,603	87,776
06360	Norwich	(860)	40,493	40,347
06475	Old Saybrook	(860)	10,242	10,246
06477	Orange	(203)	13,956	13,953
06478	Oxford	(203)	12,683	12,874
06374	Plainfield	(860)	15,405	15,228
06062	Plainville	(860)	17,716	17,820
06782	Plymouth	(860)	12,243	12,047
06877	Ridgefield	(203)	24,638	25,164
06067	Rocky Hill	(860)	19,709	19,915
*06483	Seymour	(203)	16,540	16,571
06484	Shelton	(203)	39,559	40,999
*06070	Simsbury	(860)	23,511	23,824
06071	Somers	(860)	11,444	11,320
*06074	South Windsor	(860)	25,709	25,846
06488	Southbury	(203)	19,904	19,859
06489	Southington	(860)	43,069	43,661
*06075	Stafford	(860)	12,087	11,928
*06901	Stamford	(203)	122,643	126,456
06378	Stonington	(860)	18,545	18,541
*06268	Storrs (c)	(860)	15,344	—
*06614	Stratford	(203)	51,384	52,112
*06078	Suffield	(860)	15,735	15,788
06084	Tolland	(860)	15,052	14,915
*06790	Torrington	(860)	36,383	35,611
06611	Trumbull	(203)	36,018	36,571
06066	Vernon	(860)	29,179	29,161
*06492	Wallingford	(203)	45,135	45,141
06492	Wallingford Center (c)	(203)	18,209	—
*06702	Waterbury	(203)	110,366	109,676
*06385	Waterford	(860)	19,517	19,505
06795	Watertown	(860)	22,514	22,228
*06105	West Hartford	(860)	63,268	63,371
06516	West Haven	(203)	55,564	55,046
06883	Weston	(203)	10,179	10,372
*06880	Westport	(203)	26,391	27,308
*06109	Wethersfield	(860)	26,668	26,510
06226	Willimantic (c)	(860)	17,737	—
06897	Wilton	(203)	18,062	18,657
*06094	Winchester	(860)	11,242	11,013
*06280	Windham	(860)	25,268	25,213
*06095	Windsor	(860)	29,044	29,142
06096	Windsor Locks	(860)	12,498	12,573
*06716	Wolcott	(203)	16,680	16,725

Delaware

Area code 302 applies to the entire state.

ZIP	Place	2010 population	2013 estimate
19701	Bear (c)	19,371	—
19713	Brookside (c)	14,353	—
*19901	Dover	36,047	37,366
19702	Glasgow (c)	14,303	—
19707	Hockessin (c)	13,527	—
19709	Middletown	18,871	19,600
19963	Milford	9,559	10,122
*19711	Newark	31,454	32,549
19808	Pike Creek Valley (c)	11,217	—
19977	Smyrna	10,023	10,960
*19801	Wilmington	70,851	71,525

District of Columbia

Area code 202 applies to the entire district.

ZIP	Place	2010 population	2013 estimate
*20001	Washington	601,723	646,449

Florida

Part of area code 321 overlays area code 407. Area code 754 overlays area code 954. Area code 786 overlays area code 305.

ZIP	Place	Area code	2010 population	2013 estimate
*32828	Alafaya (c)	(407)	78,113	—
*32714	Altamonte Springs	(407)	41,496	42,150
33572	Apollo Beach (c)	(813)	14,055	—
*32712	Apopka	(407)	41,542	45,587
32233	Atlantic Beach	(904)	12,655	12,895
33823	Auburndale	(863)	13,507	14,261
*33160	Aventura	(305)	35,762	37,199
32807	Azalea Park (c)	(407)	12,556	—
*33830	Bartow	(863)	17,298	17,996
34667	Bayonet Point (c)	(727)	23,467	—
33507	Bayshore Gardens (c)	(941)	16,323	—
*33756	Bellair-Meadowbrook Terrace (c)	(904)	13,343	—
33430	Belle Glade	(561)	17,467	17,839
*34420	Belleview (c)	(352)	23,355	—
*33509	Bloomingdale (c)	(813)	22,711	—
*33431	Boca Raton	(561)	84,392	89,407
*34135	Bonita Springs	(239)	43,914	47,547
*33436	Boynton Beach	(561)	68,217	71,097
*34201	Bradenton	(941)	49,546	51,763
*33510	Brandon (c)	(813)	103,483	—
32503	Brent (c)	(850)	21,804	—
33142	Brownsville (c)	(305)	15,313	—
34743	Buenaventura Lakes (c)	(407)	26,079	—
32404	Callaway	(850)	14,405	14,732
*33914	Cape Coral	(239)	154,305	165,831
*33618	Carrollwood (c)	(813)	33,365	—
*32707	Casselberry	(407)	26,241	26,566
33558	Cheval (c)	(813)	10,702	—
33624	Citrus Park (c)	(813)	24,252	—
*33755	Clearwater	(727)	107,685	109,703
*34711	Clermont	(352)	28,742	30,033
*32922	Cocoa	(321)	17,140	17,262
32931	Cocoa Beach	(321)	11,231	11,325
*33063	Coconut Creek	(954)	52,909	56,792
32809	Conway (c)	(407)	13,467	—
*33328	Cooper City	(954)	28,547	34,128
33114	Coral Gables	(305)	46,780	49,631
*33065	Coral Springs	(954)	121,096	126,604
33157	Coral Terrace (c)	(305)	24,376	—
33015	Country Club (c)	(305)	47,105	—
33196	Country Walk (c)	(305)	15,997	—
*32536	Crestview	(850)	20,978	22,785
33189	Cutler Bay	(305)	40,286	43,328
33919	Cypress Lake (c)	(239)	11,846	—
*33004	Dania Beach	(954)	29,639	30,731
*33314	Davie	(954)	91,992	96,830
*32114	Daytona Beach	(386)	61,005	62,316
*32713	DeBary	(386)	19,320	19,447
*33441	Deerfield Beach	(954)	75,018	78,041
*32720	DeLand	(386)	27,031	28,237
*33444	Delray Beach	(561)	60,522	64,072
32738	Deltona	(407)	85,182	86,290
*32541	Destin	(850)	12,305	13,264
32836	Doctor Phillips (c)	(407)	10,981	—
*33178	Doral	(305)	45,704	50,213
*34698	Dunedin	(727)	35,321	35,690
33610	East Lake (c)	(813)	30,962	—
33619	East Lake-Orient Park (c)	(813)	22,753	—
32583	East Milton (c)	(850)	11,074	—
*32132	Edgewater	(386)	20,750	20,938
33614	Egypt Lake-Leto (c)	(813)	35,282	—
34680	Elfers (c)	(727)	13,986	—
*34223	Englewood (c)	(941)	14,863	—
32534	Ensley (c)	(850)	20,602	—
*33928	Estero (c)	(239)	22,612	—
*32726	Eustis	(352)	18,558	19,214
32804	Fairview Shores (c)	(305)	10,239	—
*32034	Fernandina Beach	(904)	11,487	11,952
32514	Ferry Pass (c)	(850)	28,921	—
33547	Fish Hawk (c)	(813)	14,087	—
32003	Fleming Island (c)	(904)	27,126	—
33034	Florida City	(305)	11,245	11,977
32960	Florida Ridge (c)	(772)	18,164	—
32714	Forest City (c)	(407)	13,854	—
*33301	Fort Lauderdale	(954)	165,521	172,389
*33901	Fort Myers	(239)	62,298	68,190
34981	Fort Pierce	(772)	41,590	43,074
*32548	Fort Walton Beach	(850)	19,507	20,597
33172	Fountainbleau (c)	(305)	59,764	—
34747	Four Corners (c)	(863)	26,116	—
*32259	Fruit Cove (c)	(904)	29,362	—
34232	Fruitville (c)	(941)	13,224	—
*32601	Gainesville	(352)	124,354	127,488
33534	Gibsonton (c)	(813)	14,234	—
33138	Gladeview (c)	(954)	11,535	—
33143	Glenvar Heights (c)	(305)	16,898	—
34116	Golden Gate (c)	(239)	23,961	—
33055	Golden Glades (c)	(305)	33,145	—
32733	Goldenrod (c)	(407)	12,039	—
32560	Gonzalez (c)	(850)	13,273	—
33170	Goulds (c)	(305)	10,103	—
*33454	Greenacres	(561)	37,573	38,696
33581	Gulf Gate Estates (c)	(941)	10,911	—
*33737	Gulfport	(727)	12,029	12,164
*33844	Haines City	(863)	20,535	21,490
*33009	Hallandale Beach	(305)/(954)	37,113	38,632
*33010	Hialeah	(305)	224,669	233,394
*33016	Hialeah Gardens	(305)	21,744	22,642
33846	Highland City (c)	(863)	10,834	—
*33455	Hobe Sound (c)	(772)	11,521	—
*34690	Holiday (c)	(727)	22,403	—
*32125	Holly Hill	(386)	11,659	11,679
*33019	Hollywood	(954)	140,768	146,526
*33030	Homestead	(305)	60,512	64,079
34447	Homosassa Springs (c)	(352)	13,791	—
34787	Horizon West (c)	(352)	14,000	—
34667	Hudson (c)	(727)	12,158	—
32837	Hunters Creek (c)	(407)	14,321	—
*34142	Immokalee (c)	(239)	24,154	—
33908	Iona (c)	(239)	15,369	—
33162	Ives Estates (c)	(305)	19,525	—
*33210	Jacksonville	(904)	821,784	842,583
*33250	Jacksonville Beach	(904)	21,362	21,823
33568	Jasmine Estates (c)	(727)	18,989	—
*34957	Jensen Beach (c)	(772)	11,707	—
*33458	Jupiter	(561)	55,156	58,298
33478	Jupiter Farms (c)	(561)	11,994	—
33183	Kendale Lakes (c)	(305)	56,148	—
33156	Kendall (c)	(305)	75,371	—
33193	Kendall West (c)	(305)	36,154	—
33149	Key Biscayne	(305)	12,344	12,832
33037	Key Largo (c)	(305)	10,433	—
*33040	Key West	(305)	24,649	25,550
33556	Keystone (c)	(813)	24,039	—
*34744	Kissimmee	(407)	59,682	65,173
*32159	Lady Lake	(352)	13,926	14,247
32054	Lake Butler (c)	(386)	15,400	—
32055	Lake City	(386)	12,046	12,107
33612	Lake Magdalene (c)	(813)	28,509	—
*32746	Lake Mary	(407)	13,822	14,807
*33853	Lake Wales	(863)	14,225	14,916
33461	Lake Worth	(561)	34,910	36,000
*33801	Lakeland	(863)	97,422	100,710
33801	Lakeland Highlands (c)	(863)	11,056	—
32073	Lakeside (c)	(904)	30,943	—
34951	Lakewood Park (c)	(772)	11,323	—
*34639	Land O'Lakes (c)	(813)	31,996	—
*33465	Lantana	(561)	10,423	10,867
*33770	Largo	(727)	77,648	78,409
*33313	Lauderdale Lakes	(954)	32,593	34,062
*33313	Lauderhill	(954)	66,887	69,813
33714	Lealman (c)	(727)	19,879	—
*34748	Leesburg	(352)	20,117	21,142
*33936	Lehigh Acres (c)	(239)	86,784	—
*33033	Leisure City (c)	(305)	22,655	—
*33074	Lighthouse Point	(954)	10,344	10,826
32810	Lockhart (c)	(407)	13,060	—
*32750	Longwood	(407)	13,657	13,822
*33549	Lutz (c)	(813)	19,344	—
32444	Lynn Haven	(850)	18,493	19,360
*32751	Maitland	(407)	15,751	16,464
33550	Mango (c)	(813)	11,313	—
*34145	Marco Island	(239)	16,413	17,163
*33093	Margate	(954)	53,284	55,456
32824	Meadow Woods (c)	(407)	25,558	—
*32901	Melbourne	(321)	76,068	77,508
*32953	Merritt Island (c)	(321)	34,743	—
*33125	Miami	(305)	399,457	417,650
*33140	Miami Beach	(305)	87,779	91,026
*33014	Miami Gardens	(305)	107,167	111,378
*33014	Miami Lakes	(305)	29,361	30,571
33138	Miami Shores	(305)	10,493	10,654
33266	Miami Springs	(305)	13,809	14,316
*32068	Middleburg (c)	(904)	13,008	—
32563	Midway (c) (Santa Rosa Co.)	(850)	16,115	—
*32751	Minneola	(352)	9,403	10,037
*33023	Miramar	(954)	122,041	130,288
32757	Mount Dora	(352)	12,370	12,895
32526	Myrtle Grove (c)	(850)	15,870	—
*34102	Naples	(239)	19,537	20,537
32566	Navarre (c)	(850)	31,378	—
*34653	New Port Richey	(727)	14,911	15,087
34653	New Port Richey East (c)	(727)	10,036	—
*32168	New Smyrna Beach	(386)	22,464	23,230
*32578	Niceville	(850)	12,749	14,058
*33917	North Fort Myers (c)	(239)	39,407	—
*33068	North Lauderdale	(954)	41,023	42,757
*33261	North Miami	(305)	58,786	61,007
*33160	North Miami Beach	(305)	41,523	43,250
*33408	North Palm Beach	(561)	12,015	12,348

ZIP	Place	Area code	2010 population	2013 estimate
*34287	North Port	(941)	57,357	59,212
33624	Northdale (c)	(813)	22,079	—
33860	Oak Ridge (c)	(407)	22,685	—
33307	Oakland Park	(305)	41,363	43,286
32065	Oakleaf Plantation (c)	(904)	20,315	—
*34470	Ocala	(352)	56,315	57,468
34761	Ocoee	(407)	35,579	39,172
*33163	Ojus (c)	(305)	18,036	—
34677	Oldsmar	(813)	13,591	13,796
*33265	Olympia Heights (c)	(305)	13,488	—
33054	Opa-Locka	(305)	15,219	15,967
*32763	Orange City	(386)	10,599	10,942
32801	Orlando	(407)	238,300	255,483
32174	Ormond Beach	(386)	38,137	38,661
32765	Oviedo	(407)	33,342	36,648
32571	Pace (c)	(850)	20,039	—
32177	Palatka	(386)	10,558	10,482
*32905	Palm Bay	(321)	103,190	104,898
33408	Palm Beach Gardens	(561)	48,452	50,699
*34990	Palm City (c)	(772)	23,120	—
32137	Palm Coast	(386)	75,180	78,740
*34683	Palm Harbor (c)	(727)	57,439	—
*33601	Palm River-Clair Mel (c)	(813)	21,024	—
*33406	Palm Springs	(561)	18,928	20,872
32082	Palm Valley (c)	(904)	20,019	—
*34221	Palmetto	(941)	12,606	12,964
33157	Palmetto Bay	(305)	23,410	24,339
33157	Palmetto Estates (c)	(305)	13,535	—
32401	Panama City	(850)	36,484	36,877
32417	Panama City Beach	(850)	12,018	12,064
33067	Parkland	(954)	23,962	26,518
33029	Pembroke Pines	(954)	154,750	162,329
32502	Pensacola	(850)	51,923	52,703
32809	Pine Castle (c)	(407)	10,805	—
32858	Pine Hills (c)	(407)	60,076	—
33156	Pinecrest	(305)	18,223	19,046
*33781	Pinellas Park	(727)	49,079	49,998
33168	Pinewood (c)	(305)	16,520	—
*33566	Plant City	(813)	34,721	36,097
*33311	Plantation	(954)	84,955	90,268
*34758	Poinciana (c)	(407)	53,193	—
33060	Pompano Beach	(954)	99,845	104,410
*33952	Port Charlotte (c)	(941)	54,392	—
32129	Port Orange	(904)	56,048	57,203
32927	Port St. John (c)	(321)	12,267	—
*34953	Port St. Lucie	(772)	164,603	171,016
34992	Port Salerno (c)	(772)	10,091	—
*33032	Princeton (c)	(305)	22,038	—
*33950	Punta Gorda	(941)	16,641	17,172
33177	Richmond West (c)	(305)	31,973	—
*33569	Riverview (c)	(813)	71,050	—
*33419	Riviera Beach	(561)	32,488	33,263
*32955	Rockledge	(321)	24,926	25,624
*33411	Royal Palm Beach	(561)	34,140	36,306
*33570	Ruskin (c)	(813)	17,208	—
*34695	Safety Harbor	(727)	16,884	17,139
32084	Saint Augustine	(904)	12,975	13,679
*34769	Saint Cloud	(407)	35,183	40,918
*33701	Saint Petersburg	(727)	244,769	249,688
33912	San Carlos Park (c)	(239)	16,824	—
32771	Sanford	(407)	53,570	56,002
*34231	Sarasota	(941)	51,917	53,326
33577	Sarasota Springs (c)	(941)	14,395	—
32937	Satellite Beach	(321)	10,109	10,333
*32958	Sebastian	(772)	21,929	22,699
*33870	Sebring	(863)	10,491	10,331
*33770	Seminole	(813)	17,233	17,830
34610	Shady Hills (c)	(727)	11,523	—
33505	South Bradenton (c)	(941)	22,178	—
32121	South Daytona	(386)	12,252	12,279
*33243	South Miami	(305)	11,657	12,088
33157	South Miami Heights (c)	(305)	35,696	—
33595	South Venice (c)	(941)	13,949	—
32824	Southchase (c)	(407)	15,921	—
*34604	Spring Hill (c)	(352)	98,621	—
*34994	Stuart	(772)	15,593	16,078
*33573	Sun City Center (c)	(813)	19,258	—
33160	Sunny Isles Beach	(305)	20,832	21,720
*33325	Sunrise	(954)	84,439	90,116
*33283	Sunset (c)	(305)	16,389	—
33144	Sweetwater	(305)	13,499	20,575
*32301	Tallahassee	(850)	181,376	186,411
33320	Tamarac	(954)	60,427	63,155
33144	Tamiami (c)	(305)	55,271	—
*33602	Tampa	(813)	335,709	352,957
*34689	Tarpon Springs	(727)	23,484	23,871
32778	Tavares	(352)	13,951	14,411
*33687	Temple Terrace	(813)	24,541	25,179
33412	The Acreage (c)	(561)	38,704	—
33186	The Crossings (c)	(305)	22,758	—
33196	The Hammocks (c)	(305)	51,003	—
*32162	The Villages (c)	(352)	51,442	—
33186	Three Lakes (c)	(305)	15,047	—

ZIP	Place	Area code	2010 population	2013 estimate
*32780	Titusville	(321)	43,761	44,206
32615	Town 'n' Country (c)	(813)	78,442	—
34655	Trinity (c)	(813)	10,907	—
33613	University (c)			
	(Hillsborough Co.)	(813)	41,163	—
32826	University (c) (Orange Co.)	(407)	31,084	—
33165	University Park (c)	(305)	26,995	—
32401	Upper Grand Lagoon (c)	(850)	13,963	—
*33594	Valrico (c)	(813)	35,545	—
*34285	Venice	(941)	20,748	21,253
*32960	Vero Beach	(772)	15,220	15,749
32960	Vero Beach South (c)	(772)	23,092	—
32955	Viera East (c)	(321)	10,757	—
33901	Villas (c)	(239)	11,569	—
32507	Warrington (c)	(850)	14,531	—
32779	Wekiwa Springs (c)	(407)	21,998	—
*33414	Wellington	(561)	56,508	60,202
*33544	Wesley Chapel (c)	(813)	44,092	—
33714	West Lealman (c)	(727)	15,651	—
33138	West Little River (c)	(305)	34,699	—
*32912	West Melbourne	(321)	18,355	19,667
*33401	West Palm Beach	(561)	99,919	102,436
33023	West Park	(954)	14,156	14,758
32505	West Pensacola (c)	(850)	21,339	—
33626	Westchase (c)	(813)	21,747	—
33165	Westchester (c)	(305)	29,862	—
*33326	Weston	(954)	65,333	68,388
33165	Westwood Lakes (c)	(305)	11,838	—
*33305	Wilton Manors	(954)	11,632	12,108
*34787	Winter Garden	(407)	34,568	37,711
*33880	Winter Haven	(863)	33,874	35,531
*32789	Winter Park	(407)	27,852	29,203
*32707	Winter Springs	(407)	33,282	33,871
32092	World Golf Village (c)	(904)	12,310	—
32547	Wright (c)	(850)	23,127	—
*32097	Yulee (c)	(904)	11,491	—
*33540	Zephyrhills	(813)	13,288	14,012

Georgia

Area codes 470/678 overlay area code 770. Area code 762 overlays area code 706.

ZIP	Place	Area code	2010 population	2013 estimate
*30101	Acworth	(770)	20,425	21,476
*31701	Albany	(229)	77,434	76,185
30004	Alpharetta	(770)	57,551	62,298
*31709	Americus	(229)	17,041	16,359
30601	Athens-Clarke Co.			
	(balance)	(706)	115,452	119,980
*30301	Atlanta	(404)	420,003	447,841
*30901	Augusta-Richmond Co.			
	(balance)	(706)	195,844	197,350
*39817	Bainbridge	(229)	12,697	12,597
30032	Belvedere Park (c)	(404)	15,152	—
30326	Brookhaven[1]	(404)	49,217	50,603
*31520	Brunswick	(912)	15,383	15,813
*30518	Buford	(404)	12,225	12,962
*30701	Calhoun	(706)	15,650	15,899
30032	Candler-McAfee (c)	(404)	23,025	—
*30114	Canton	(770)	22,958	24,163
30117	Carrollton	(770)	24,388	25,124
30120	Cartersville	(770)	19,731	20,001
30341	Chamblee	(770)	9,892	15,948
30337	College Park	(404)	13,942	14,621
*31907	Columbus	(706)	189,885	202,824
*30013	Conyers	(404)	15,195	15,618
31015	Cordele	(229)	11,147	11,187
*30014	Covington	(770)	13,118	13,452
31805	Cusseta-Chattahoochee			
	Co.	(706)	11,267	12,842
*30132	Dallas	(770)	11,544	12,415
*30720	Dalton	(706)	33,128	33,414
*30030	Decatur	(404)	19,335	20,086
*30340	Doraville	(770)	8,330	10,603
*31533	Douglas	(912)	11,589	11,872
*30134	Douglasville	(404)	30,961	31,890
30333	Druid Hills (c)	(404)	14,568	—
*31021	Dublin	(478)	16,201	16,379
*30096	Duluth	(404)	26,600	28,404
*30338	Dunwoody	(770)	46,267	47,591
*30344	East Point	(404)	33,712	35,512
30809	Evans (c)	(706)	29,011	—
30213	Fairburn	(770)	12,950	13,693
*30214	Fayetteville	(404)	15,945	16,370
*30297	Forest Park	(404)	18,468	18,779
*30501	Gainesville	(770)	33,804	35,533
39854	Georgetown (c)	(912)	11,823	—
*30223	Griffin	(770)	23,643	23,344
30813	Grovetown	(706)	11,216	12,389
*31313	Hinesville	(912)	33,437	34,227
*31546	Jesup	(912)	10,214	10,302
30022	Johns Creek	(770)	76,728	82,788

ZIP	Place	Area code	2010 population	2013 estimate
*30144	Kennesaw	(404)	29,783	32,001
31548	Kingsland	(912)	15,946	16,240
*30240	LaGrange	(706)	29,588	30,452
*30045	Lawrenceville	(404)	28,546	29,868
*30047	Lilburn	(404)	11,596	12,425
30122	Lithia Springs (c)	(770)	15,491	—
30052	Loganville	(770)	10,458	10,815
30126	Mableton (c)	(404)	37,115	—
*31201	Macon	(478)	91,351	89,981
*30060	Marietta	(404)	56,579	59,089
30907	Martinez (c)	(706)	35,795	—
*30253	McDonough	(770)	22,084	22,834
*31061	Milledgeville	(478)	17,715	19,256
*30004	Milton	(770)	32,661	35,907
*30655	Monroe	(770)	13,234	13,466
*31768	Moultrie	(229)	14,268	14,622
30087	Mountain Park (c)	(404)	11,554	—
*30263	Newnan	(770)	33,039	34,847
*30071	Norcross	(770)	9,116	16,131
30319	North Atlanta (c)	(404)	40,456	—
30033	North Decatur (c)	(404)	16,698	—
30033	North Druid Hills (c)	(404)	18,947	—
*30269	Peachtree City	(404)	34,364	34,893
*30092	Peachtree Corners[1]	(770)	38,011	40,059
31069	Perry	(478)	13,839	14,926
31322	Pooler	(912)	19,140	21,187
30127	Powder Springs	(404)	13,940	14,411
30074	Redan (c)	(404)	33,015	—
31324	Richmond Hill	(912)	9,281	10,919
*30274	Riverdale	(404)	15,134	15,537
*30161	Rome	(706)	36,303	35,973
*30077	Roswell	(404)	88,346	94,034
31558	Saint Marys	(912)	17,121	17,755
31522	Saint Simons (c)	(912)	12,743	—
*30328	Sandy Springs	(404)	93,853	99,770
*31401	Savannah	(912)	136,286	142,772
30079	Scottdale (c)	(404)	10,631	—
*30080	Smyrna	(404)	51,271	53,438
*30078	Snellville	(404)	18,242	19,245
*30458	Statesboro	(912)	28,422	29,937
30281	Stockbridge	(404)	25,636	27,265
30518	Sugar Hill	(404)	18,522	20,153
30024	Suwanee	(770)	15,355	17,688
*31792	Thomasville	(229)	18,413	18,718
*31794	Tifton	(229)	16,350	16,405
*30084	Tucker (c)	(404)	27,581	—
30291	Union City	(404)	19,456	20,458
*31601	Valdosta	(229)	54,518	56,481
30474	Vidalia	(912)	10,473	10,674
30180	Villa Rica	(770)	13,956	14,452
*31088	Warner Robins	(478)	66,588	72,531
*31501	Waycross	(912)	14,649	14,250
31410	Wilmington Island (c)	(912)	15,138	—
30680	Winder	(770)	14,099	14,679
*30188	Woodstock	(770)	23,896	26,890

(1) Place was incorporated after the 2010 Census was conducted. Data in 2010 column is Census Bureau estimate.

Hawaii

Area code 808 applies to the entire state.

ZIP	Place	2000 population	2010 population
96821	East Honolulu (c)	—	49,914
96706	Ewa Beach (c)	14,650	14,955
96706	Ewa Gentry (c)	4,939	22,690
96701	Halawa (c)	13,891	14,014
96749	Hawaiian Paradise Park (c)	7,051	11,404
*96720	Hilo (c)	40,759	43,263
*96813	Honolulu, urban (c)	371,657	347,884[1]
*96732	Kahului (c)	20,146	26,337
96740	Kailua (c) (Hawaii Co.)	9,870	11,975
96734	Kailua (c) (Honolulu Co.)	36,513	38,635
96744	Kaneohe (c)	34,970	34,597
96746	Kapaa (c)	9,472	10,699
*96707	Kapolei (c)	—	15,186
96753	Kihei (c)	16,749	20,881
*96761	Lahaina (c)	9,118	11,704
96707	Makakilo (c)	13,156	18,248
96789	Mililani Mauka (c)	—	21,039
96789	Mililani Town (c)	28,608	27,629
96792	Nanakuli (c)	10,814	12,666
96782	Pearl City (c)	30,976	47,698
96797	Royal Kunia (c)	—	14,525
96857	Schofield Barracks (c)	14,428	16,370
96786	Wahiawa (c)	16,151	17,821
96792	Waianae (c)	10,506	13,177
96793	Wailuku (c)	12,296	15,313
96701	Waimalu (c)	29,371	13,730
96797	Waipahu (c)	33,108	38,216
96797	Waipio (c)	11,672	11,674

(1) 2013 estimate.

Idaho

Area code 208 applies to the entire state.

ZIP	Place	2010 population	2013 estimate
*83401	Ammon	13,816	14,460
83221	Blackfoot	11,899	11,854
*83704	Boise	205,671	214,237
83318	Burley	10,345	10,456
*83605	Caldwell	46,237	48,957
83202	Chubbuck	13,922	14,125
*83814	Coeur d'Alene	44,137	46,402
83616	Eagle	19,908	21,646
*83714	Garden City	10,972	11,260
83835	Hayden	13,294	13,681
*83402	Idaho Falls	56,813	58,292
83338	Jerome	10,890	11,038
83634	Kuna	15,210	16,532
83501	Lewiston	31,894	32,401
*83642	Meridian	75,092	83,596
83843	Moscow	23,800	24,534
83647	Mountain Home	14,206	13,805
*83651	Nampa	81,557	86,518
*83201	Pocatello	54,255	54,350
*83854	Post Falls	27,574	29,357
83440	Rexburg	25,484	26,520
*83301	Twin Falls	44,125	45,981

Illinois

Area code 224 overlays area code 847. Area code 331 overlays area code 630. Area code 779 overlays area code 815. Area code 872 overlays area codes 312/773.

ZIP	Place	Area code	2010 population	2013 estimate
60101	Addison	(630)	36,942	37,385
*60102	Algonquin	(847)	30,046	30,467
60803	Alsip	(708)	19,277	19,453
62002	Alton	(618)	27,865	27,290
60002	Antioch	(847)	14,430	14,410
*60005	Arlington Heights	(847)	75,101	75,994
60505	Aurora	(630)	197,899	199,963
*60010	Barrington	(847)	10,327	10,361
60103	Bartlett	(630)	41,208	41,679
60510	Batavia	(630)	26,045	26,394
60083	Beach Park	(847)	13,638	13,787
*62220	Belleville	(618)	44,478	42,895
60104	Bellwood	(708)	19,071	19,161
61008	Belvidere	(815)	25,585	25,339
*60106	Bensenville	(630)	18,352	18,535
60402	Berwyn	(708)	56,657	56,758
*60108	Bloomingdale	(630)	22,018	22,346
*61701	Bloomington	(309)	76,610	78,902
60406	Blue Island	(708)	23,706	23,793
*60440	Bolingbrook	(630)	73,366	73,936
60914	Bourbonnais	(815)	18,631	18,583
60915	Bradley	(815)	15,895	15,793
60455	Bridgeview	(708)	16,446	16,471
60513	Brookfield	(708)	18,978	19,039
60089	Buffalo Grove	(847)	41,496	41,778
60459	Burbank	(708)	28,925	29,210
60527	Burr Ridge	(630)	10,559	10,749
62206	Cahokia	(618)	15,241	14,737
60409	Calumet City	(708)	37,042	37,240
*60119	Campton Hills	(630)/(847)	11,131	11,305
61520	Canton	(309)	14,704	14,437
*62901	Carbondale	(618)	25,902	26,363
*60188	Carol Stream	(630)	39,711	40,379
60110	Carpentersville	(847)	37,691	38,241
60013	Cary	(847)	18,271	18,025
62801	Centralia	(618)	13,032	12,787
*61821	Champaign	(217)	81,055	83,424
60410	Channahon	(815)	12,560	12,600
61920	Charleston	(217)	21,838	21,961
62629	Chatham	(217)	11,500	12,077
*60607	Chicago	(312)/(773)	2,695,598	2,718,782
*60411	Chicago Heights	(708)	30,276	30,423
60415	Chicago Ridge	(708)	14,305	14,403
60804	Cicero	(708)	83,891	84,100
62234	Collinsville	(618)	25,579	25,059
60478	Country Club Hills	(708)	16,541	16,886
60435	Crest Hill	(815)	20,837	20,783
60445	Crestwood	(708)	10,950	11,039
*60014	Crystal Lake	(815)	40,743	40,388
61832	Danville	(217)	33,027	32,523
60561	Darien	(630)	22,086	22,360
*62521	Decatur	(217)	76,122	74,710
60015	Deerfield	(847)	18,225	18,297
60115	DeKalb	(815)	43,862	43,849
*60018	Des Plaines	(847)	58,364	58,918
61021	Dixon	(815)	15,733	15,333
60419	Dolton	(708)	23,153	23,333
*60515	Downers Grove	(630)	47,833	49,670
61244	East Moline	(309)	21,302	21,360
*61611	East Peoria	(309)	23,402	23,503
*62201	East St. Louis	(618)	27,006	26,598

ZIP	Place	Area code	2010 population	2013 estimate
*62025	Edwardsville	(618)	24,293	24,663
62401	Effingham	(217)	12,328	12,558
*60120	Elgin	(847)	108,188	110,145
*60007	Elk Grove Village	(847)	33,127	33,419
60126	Elmhurst	(630)	44,121	45,556
60707	Elmwood Park	(708)	24,883	24,985
*60201	Evanston	(847)	74,486	75,570
60805	Evergreen Park	(708)	19,852	19,957
*62208	Fairview Heights	(618)	17,078	16,929
*60130	Forest Park	(708)	14,167	14,213
60020	Fox Lake	(847)	10,579	10,537
60423	Frankfort	(815)	17,782	18,168
*60131	Franklin Park	(847)	18,333	18,427
61032	Freeport	(815)	25,638	25,035
60030	Gages Lake (c)	(847)	10,198	—
*61401	Galesburg	(309)	32,195	31,665
60134	Geneva	(630)	21,495	21,694
62034	Glen Carbon	(618)	12,934	12,947
*60137	Glen Ellyn	(630)	27,450	27,761
*60139	Glendale Heights	(630)	34,208	34,620
*60025	Glenview	(847)	44,692	45,417
62035	Godfrey	(618)	17,982	17,874
62040	Granite City	(618)	29,849	29,375
60030	Grayslake	(847)	20,957	21,101
60031	Gurnee	(847)	31,295	31,284
60133	Hanover Park	(630)	37,973	38,510
*60426	Harvey	(708)	25,282	25,361
60429	Hazel Crest	(708)	14,100	14,200
62948	Herrin	(618)	12,501	12,838
*60457	Hickory Hills	(708)	14,049	14,179
*60035	Highland Park	(847)	29,763	29,902
*60521	Hinsdale	(630)	16,816	17,261
*60195	Hoffman Estates	(847)	51,895	52,398
*60491	Homer Glen	(708)	24,220	24,320
*60430	Homewood	(708)	19,323	19,443
60142	Huntley	(847)	24,291	25,267
*62650	Jacksonville	(217)	19,446	19,230
*60436	Joliet	(815)	147,433	147,806
60458	Justice	(708)	12,926	13,031
60901	Kankakee	(815)	27,537	27,126
61443	Kewanee	(309)	12,916	12,676
60525	La Grange	(708)	15,550	15,732
60526	La Grange Park	(708)	13,579	13,659
60045	Lake Forest	(847)	19,375	19,352
*60102	Lake in the Hills	(847)	28,965	28,939
*60047	Lake Zurich	(847)	19,631	19,984
60438	Lansing	(708)	28,331	28,508
*60439	Lemont	(630)	16,000	16,517
*60048	Libertyville	(847)	20,315	20,431
62656	Lincoln	(217)	14,504	14,284
*60645	Lincolnwood	(847)	12,590	12,697
60046	Lindenhurst	(847)	14,462	14,513
60532	Lisle	(630)	22,390	22,757
*60441	Lockport	(815)	24,839	25,023
*60148	Lombard	(630)	43,165	43,907
*61130	Loves Park	(815)	23,996	23,703
60534	Lyons	(708)	10,729	10,781
*61115	Machesney Park	(815)	23,499	23,205
61455	Macomb	(309)	19,288	19,265
62959	Marion	(618)	17,193	17,413
*60426	Markham	(708)	12,508	12,671
*60443	Matteson	(708)	19,009	19,150
61938	Mattoon	(217)	18,555	18,368
*60153	Maywood	(708)	24,090	24,160
*60050	McHenry	(815)	26,992	26,676
*60160	Melrose Park	(708)	25,411	25,518
60445	Midlothian	(708)	14,819	14,924
60447	Minooka	(815)	10,924	11,129
60448	Mokena	(708)	18,740	19,172
*61265	Moline	(309)	43,483	43,116
60538	Montgomery	(630)	18,438	19,129
60450	Morris	(815)	13,636	13,926
61550	Morton	(309)	16,267	16,525
60053	Morton Grove	(847)	23,270	23,519
60056	Mount Prospect	(847)	54,167	54,771
62864	Mount Vernon	(618)	15,277	15,239
60060	Mundelein	(847)	31,064	31,395
*60540	Naperville	(630)	141,853	144,864
60451	New Lenox	(815)	24,394	24,962
60714	Niles	(847)	29,803	30,022
*61761	Normal	(309)	52,497	54,664
*60634	Norridge	(708)	14,572	14,686
60542	North Aurora	(630)	16,760	17,130
*60064	North Chicago	(847)	32,574	30,038
*60062	Northbrook	(708)	33,170	33,600
60164	Northlake	(708)	12,323	12,431
60452	Oak Forest	(708)	27,962	28,198
*60453	Oak Lawn	(708)	56,690	57,073
*60301	Oak Park	(708)	51,878	52,066
62269	O'Fallon	(618)	28,281	31,461
*60462	Orland Park	(708)	56,767	58,590
60543	Oswego	(630)	30,355	32,174
61350	Ottawa	(815)	18,768	18,562
*60067	Palatine	(847)	68,557	69,350

ZIP	Place	Area code	2010 population	2013 estimate
60463	Palos Heights	(708)	12,515	12,611
60465	Palos Hills	(708)	17,484	17,638
60466	Park Forest	(708)	21,975	22,056
60068	Park Ridge	(847)	37,480	37,839
*61554	Pekin	(309)	34,094	34,081
*61602	Peoria	(309)	115,007	116,513
61354	Peru	(815)	10,295	10,107
*60544	Plainfield	(815)	39,581	41,734
60545	Plano	(630)	10,856	11,097
61764	Pontiac	(815)	11,931	11,688
.60070	Prospect Heights	(847)	16,256	16,408
*62301	Quincy	(217)	40,633	40,915
61866	Rantoul	(217)	12,941	13,037
60471	Richton Park	(708)	13,646	13,765
60305	River Forest	(708)	11,172	11,210
60171	River Grove	(708)	10,227	10,279
60827	Riverdale	(708)	13,549	13,624
*61201	Rock Island	(309)	39,018	38,877
*61101	Rockford	(815)	152,871	150,251
60008	Rolling Meadows	(847)	24,099	24,289
*60446	Romeoville	(815)	39,680	39,650
61073	Roscoe	(815)	10,785	10,680
60172	Roselle	(630)	22,763	23,026
60073	Round Lake	(847)	18,289	18,481
60073	Round Lake Beach	(847)	28,175	28,093
*60174	Saint Charles	(630)	32,974	33,264
60411	Sauk Village	(708)	10,506	10,549
*60194	Schaumburg	(847)	74,227	74,907
*60176	Schiller Park	(847)	11,793	11,874
*62269	Shiloh	(618)	12,651	12,882
*60436	Shorewood	(815)	15,615	16,327
*60077	Skokie	(847)	64,784	65,176
60177	South Elgin	(847)	21,985	22,201
60473	South Holland	(708)	22,030	22,170
*62703	Springfield	(217)	116,250	117,006
61081	Sterling	(815)	15,370	15,152
60107	Streamwood	(630)	39,858	40,351
61364	Streator	(815)	13,710	13,422
60501	Summit	(708)	11,054	11,458
*62221	Swansea	(618)	13,430	13,712
60178	Sycamore	(815)	17,519	17,534
62568	Taylorville	(217)	11,246	11,093
*60477	Tinley Park	(708)	56,703	57,282
*61801	Urbana	(217)	41,250	41,752
60061	Vernon Hills	(847)	25,113	25,613
60181	Villa Park	(630)	21,904	22,093
60555	Warrenville	(630)	13,140	13,358
61571	Washington	(309)	15,134	15,716
62298	Waterloo	(618)	9,811	10,140
60084	Wauconda	(847)	13,603	13,823
*60085	Waukegan	(847)	89,078	88,826
*60185	West Chicago	(630)	27,086	27,554
60154	Westchester	(708)	16,718	16,825
60558	Western Springs	(708)	12,975	13,171
60559	Westmont	(630)	24,685	24,974
*60187	Wheaton	(630)	52,894	53,648
60090	Wheeling	(847)	37,648	38,015
60091	Wilmette	(847)	27,087	27,363
60093	Winnetka	(847)	12,187	12,422
*60191	Wood Dale	(630)	13,770	13,969
62095	Wood River	(618)	10,657	10,424
60517	Woodridge	(630)	32,971	33,408
60098	Woodstock	(815)	24,770	25,146
60482	Worth	(708)	10,789	10,846
60560	Yorkville	(630)	16,921	17,742
60099	Zion	(847)	24,413	24,339

Indiana
Area code 930 overlays area code 812.

ZIP	Place	Area code	2010 population	2013 estimate
*46011	Anderson	(765)	56,129	55,670
46706	Auburn	(260)	12,731	12,788
46123	Avon	(317)	12,446	13,708
47421	Bedford	(812)	13,413	13,380
46107	Beech Grove	(317)	14,192	14,470
*47408	Bloomington	(812)	80,405	82,575
46112	Brownsburg	(317)	21,285	23,160
*46032	Carmel	(317)	79,191	85,927
46303	Cedar Lake	(219)	11,560	11,706
46304	Chesterton	(219)	13,068	13,315
*47129	Clarksville	(812)	21,724	21,838
*47201	Columbus	(812)	44,061	45,775
47331	Connersville	(765)	13,481	13,253
47933	Crawfordsville	(765)	15,915	15,995
*46307	Crown Point	(219)	27,317	28,412
*46311	Dyer	(219)	16,390	16,277
46312	East Chicago	(219)	29,698	29,212
*46514	Elkhart	(574)	50,949	51,265
*47708	Evansville	(812)	117,429	120,310
*46038	Fishers	(317)	76,794	83,891
*46802	Fort Wayne	(260)	253,691	256,496

ZIP	Place	Area code	2010 population	2013 estimate
*46041	Frankfort	(765)	16,422	16,249
46131	Franklin	(317)	23,712	24,194
*46402	Gary	(219)	80,294	78,450
*46526	Goshen	(574)	31,719	32,219
46530	Granger (c)	(574)	30,465	—
46135	Greencastle	(765)	10,326	10,310
46140	Greenfield	(317)	20,602	21,249
47240	Greensburg	(812)	11,492	11,747
*46142	Greenwood	(317)	49,791	53,665
46319	Griffith	(219)	16,893	16,619
*46320	Hammond	(219)	80,830	78,967
*46322	Highland	(219)	23,727	23,285
46342	Hobart	(219)	29,059	28,519
46750	Huntington	(260)	17,391	17,210
*46201	Indianapolis (balance)	(317)	820,445	843,393
*47546	Jasper	(812)	15,038	15,309
*47130	Jeffersonville	(812)	44,953	45,929
*46902	Kokomo	(765)	45,468	56,895
*46350	La Porte	(219)	22,053	22,010
*47901	Lafayette	(765)	67,140	70,373
46405	Lake Station	(219)	12,572	12,247
46226	Lawrence	(317)	46,001	47,135
46052	Lebanon	(765)	15,792	15,781
46947	Logansport	(574)	18,396	18,034
47250	Madison	(812)	11,967	12,049
*46952	Marion	(765)	29,948	29,558
46151	Martinsville	(765)	11,828	11,855
*46410	Merrillville	(219)	35,246	35,622
*46360	Michigan City	(219)	31,479	31,494
*46544	Mishawaka	(574)	48,252	47,989
*47302	Muncie	(765)	70,085	70,316
46321	Munster	(219)	23,603	23,270
*47150	New Albany	(812)	36,372	36,803
47362	New Castle	(765)	18,114	17,694
46774	New Haven	(260)	14,794	15,474
*46060	Noblesville	(317)	51,969	56,540
*46970	Peru	(765)	11,417	11,155
*46168	Plainfield	(317)	27,631	30,097
46563	Plymouth	(574)	10,033	10,034
46368	Portage	(219)	36,828	36,812
47907	Purdue University (c)	(765)	12,183	—
*47374	Richmond	(765)	36,812	36,345
46373	Saint John	(219)	14,850	15,677
46375	Schererville	(219)	29,243	29,010
47274	Seymour	(812)	17,503	18,866
46176	Shelbyville	(765)	19,191	19,253
*46601	South Bend	(574)	101,168	100,886
46224	Speedway	(317)	11,812	12,060
*47802	Terre Haute	(812)	60,785	61,025
*46383	Valparaiso	(219)	31,730	32,261
47591	Vincennes	(812)	18,423	18,069
46992	Wabash	(260)	10,666	10,491
*46580	Warsaw	(574)	13,559	14,042
*47501	Washington	(812)	11,509	11,887
*47906	West Lafayette	(765)	29,596	30,875
*46074	Westfield	(317)	30,068	33,382
47396	Yorktown	(765)	9,405	11,270
46077	Zionsville	(317)	14,160	25,115

Iowa

ZIP	Place	Area code	2010 population	2013 estimate
50009	Altoona	(515)	14,541	15,653
*50010	Ames	(515)	58,965	61,792
*50021	Ankeny	(515)	45,582	51,567
52722	Bettendorf	(563)	33,217	34,707
*50036	Boone	(515)	12,661	12,629
52601	Burlington	(319)	25,663	25,725
51401	Carroll	(712)	10,103	10,013
*50613	Cedar Falls	(319)	39,260	40,566
*52401	Cedar Rapids	(319)	126,326	128,429
*52732	Clinton	(563)	26,885	26,473
50325	Clive	(515)	15,447	16,590
52241	Coralville	(319)	18,907	20,092
*51501	Council Bluffs	(712)	62,230	61,969
*52802	Davenport	(563)	99,685	102,157
*50315	Des Moines	(515)	203,433	207,510
*52001	Dubuque	(563)	57,637	58,253
50501	Fort Dodge	(515)	25,206	24,639
52627	Fort Madison	(319)	11,051	11,043
50125	Indianola	(515)	14,782	15,108
*52240	Iowa City	(319)	67,862	71,591
50131	Johnston	(515)	17,278	19,798
52632	Keokuk	(319)	10,780	10,769
52302	Marion	(319)	34,768	36,147
*50401	Mason City	(641)	28,079	27,704
52761	Muscatine	(563)	22,886	23,034
50208	Newton	(641)	15,254	15,136
52317	North Liberty	(319)	13,374	14,971
52577	Oskaloosa	(641)	11,463	11,568
52501	Ottumwa	(641)	25,023	24,840
50219	Pella	(641)	10,352	10,344

ZIP	Place	Area code	2010 population	2013 estimate
*51101	Sioux City	(712)	82,684	82,459
51301	Spencer	(712)	11,233	11,150
50588	Storm Lake	(712)	10,600	10,790
*50322	Urbandale	(515)	39,463	41,776
*50701	Waterloo	(319)	68,406	68,366
50263	Waukee	(515)	13,790	17,077
50677	Waverly	(319)	9,874	10,070
*50265	West Des Moines	(515)	56,609	61,255

Kansas

ZIP	Place	Area code	2010 population	2013 estimate
67002	Andover	(316)	11,791	12,265
67005	Arkansas City	(620)	12,415	12,305
66002	Atchison	(913)	11,021	10,925
67037	Derby	(316)	22,158	23,047
*67801	Dodge City	(620)	27,340	28,159
67042	El Dorado	(316)	13,021	12,852
66801	Emporia	(620)	24,916	24,799
*67846	Garden City	(620)	26,658	26,966
*66030	Gardner	(913)	19,123	20,473
67530	Great Bend	(620)	15,995	15,901
*67601	Hays	(785)	20,510	21,038
67060	Haysville	(316)	10,826	11,004
*67501	Hutchinson	(620)	42,080	41,889
*66441	Junction City	(785)	23,353	25,388
*66102	Kansas City	(913)	145,786	148,483
66043	Lansing	(913)	11,265	11,642
*66044	Lawrence	(785)	87,643	90,811
66048	Leavenworth	(913)	35,251	35,891
*66209	Leawood	(913)	31,867	32,991
66214	Lenexa	(913)	48,190	50,344
*67901	Liberal	(620)	20,525	20,956
*66502	Manhattan	(785)	52,281	56,143
67460	McPherson	(620)	13,155	13,322
66202	Merriam	(913)	11,003	11,281
*67114	Newton	(316)	19,132	19,117
*66061	Olathe	(913)	125,872	131,885
66067	Ottawa	(785)	12,649	12,482
*66204	Overland Park	(913)	173,372	181,260
67357	Parsons	(620)	10,500	10,164
*66762	Pittsburg	(620)	20,233	20,398
*66208	Prairie Village	(913)	21,447	21,892
*67401	Salina	(785)	47,707	47,846
*66203	Shawnee	(913)	62,209	64,323
*66603	Topeka	(785)	127,473	127,679
*67202	Wichita	(316)	382,368	386,552
67156	Winfield	(620)	12,301	12,333

Kentucky
Area code 364 overlays area code 270.

ZIP	Place	Area code	2010 population	2013 estimate
*41101	Ashland	(606)	21,684	21,407
40004	Bardstown	(502)	11,700	12,933
*40403	Berea	(859)	13,561	14,374
*42101	Bowling Green	(270)	58,067	61,488
41005	Burlington (c)	(859)	15,926	—
*42718	Campbellsville	(270)	9,108	10,803
*41011	Covington	(859)	40,640	40,956
*40422	Danville	(859)	16,218	16,411
*42701	Elizabethtown	(270)	28,531	29,948
*41018	Erlanger	(859)	18,082	18,526
*41042	Florence	(859)	29,951	31,423
42223	Fort Campbell North (c)	(270)	13,685	—
40121	Fort Knox (c)	(270)	10,124	—
41075	Fort Thomas	(859)	16,325	16,225
*40601	Frankfort	(502)	25,527	27,453
40324	Georgetown	(502)	29,098	30,872
*42141	Glasgow	(270)	14,028	14,261
*42420	Henderson	(270)	28,757	28,832
*42240	Hopkinsville	(270)	31,577	32,582
41051	Independence	(859)	24,757	26,110
*40269	Jeffersontown	(502)	26,595	27,027
40342	Lawrenceburg	(502)	10,505	11,081
*40507	Lexington-Fayette	(859)	295,803	308,428
*40202	Louisville-Jefferson Co. (balance)	(502)	597,337	609,893
*40252	Lyndon	(502)	11,002	11,278
42431	Madisonville	(270)	19,591	19,791
42066	Mayfield	(270)	10,024	10,113
40047	Mount Washington	(502)	9,117	12,083
42071	Murray	(270)	17,741	18,106
*41071	Newport	(859)	15,273	15,382
*40356	Nicholasville	(859)	28,015	28,730
*42301	Owensboro	(270)	57,265	58,416
*42003	Paducah	(270)	25,024	25,018
*40160	Radcliff	(502)	21,688	23,113
*40475	Richmond	(859)	31,364	32,550
*40207	Saint Matthews	(502)	17,472	17,854
*40066	Shelbyville	(502)	14,045	14,761

ZIP	Place	Area code	2010 population	2013 estimate
40165	Shepherdsville	(502)	11,222	11,696
*40216	Shively	(502)	15,264	15,592
*42501	Somerset	(606)	11,196	11,447
*40391	Winchester	(859)	18,368	18,383

Louisiana

ZIP	Place	Area code	2010 population	2013 estimate
*70510	Abbeville	(337)	12,257	12,440
*71301	Alexandria	(318)	47,723	48,426
70714	Baker	(225)	13,895	13,830
71220	Bastrop	(318)	11,365	10,949
*70801	Baton Rouge	(225)	229,493	229,426
70360	Bayou Blue (c)	(985)	12,352	—
*70364	Bayou Cane (c)	(985)	19,355	—
*70037	Belle Chasse (c)	(504)	12,679	—
*70427	Bogalusa	(985)	12,232	12,008
*71111	Bossier City	(318)	61,315	66,333
70837	Central	(225)	26,864	27,743
*70043	Chalmette (c)	(504)	16,751	—
70433	Claiborne (c)	(985)	11,507	—
*70526	Crowley	(337)	13,265	13,219
*70726	Denham Springs	(225)	10,215	10,148
70634	DeRidder	(337)	10,578	10,793
70047	Destrehan (c)	(985)	11,535	—
70072	Estelle (c)	(504)	16,377	—
70535	Eunice	(337)	10,398	10,344
70810	Gardere (c)	(225)	10,580	—
*70737	Gonzales	(225)	9,781	10,301
*70053	Gretna	(504)	17,736	17,802
*70401	Hammond	(985)	20,019	20,337
*70058	Harvey (c)	(504)	20,348	—
*70360	Houma	(985)	33,727	34,040
70121	Jefferson (c)	(504)	11,193	—
70546	Jennings	(337)	10,383	10,188
*70062	Kenner	(504)	66,702	66,975
*70501	Lafayette	(337)	120,623	124,276
*70601	Lake Charles	(337)	71,993	74,024
*70068	LaPlace (c)	(985)	29,872	—
70070	Luling (c)	(985)	12,119	—
*70471	Mandeville	(985)	11,560	12,193
*70072	Marrero (c)	(504)	33,141	—
*70001	Metairie (c)	(504)	138,481	—
*71055	Minden	(318)	13,082	12,954
*71201	Monroe	(318)	48,815	49,761
*70380	Morgan City	(985)	12,404	12,091
70611	Moss Bluff (c)	(337)	11,557	—
*71457	Natchitoches	(318)	18,323	18,275
*70560	New Iberia	(337)	30,617	30,797
*70112	New Orleans	(504)	343,829	378,715
*70570	Opelousas	(337)	16,634	16,493
*71360	Pineville	(318)	14,555	14,475
70769	Prairieville (c)	(225)	26,895	—
*70394	Raceland (c)	(985)	10,193	—
70123	River Ridge (c)	(504)	13,494	—
*71270	Ruston	(318)	21,859	22,287
70817	Shenandoah (c)	(318)	18,399	—
*71102	Shreveport	(318)	199,311	200,327
*70458	Slidell	(985)	27,068	27,526
*70663	Sulphur	(337)	20,410	20,155
70056	Terrytown (c)	(504)	23,319	—
*70301	Thibodaux	(985)	14,566	14,565
70056	Timberlane (c)	(504)	10,243	—
70094	Waggaman (c)	(504)	10,015	—
*71291	West Monroe	(318)	13,065	13,094
*70058	Woodmere (c)	(504)	12,080	—
70791	Zachary	(225)	14,960	15,894

Maine

Area code 207 applies to the entire state. See introductory note.

ZIP	Place	2010 population	2013 estimate
*04210	Auburn	23,055	22,987
*04330	Augusta	19,136	18,793
*04401	Bangor	33,039	32,673
*04005	Biddeford	21,277	21,297
04011	Brunswick	20,278	20,332
04011	Brunswick (c)	15,175	—
04105	Falmouth	11,185	11,505
04038	Gorham	16,381	16,839
04043	Kennebunk	10,798	11,039
*04240	Lewiston	36,592	36,437
*04473	Orono	10,362	10,673
*04101	Portland	66,194	66,318
04072	Saco	18,482	18,877
04073	Sanford	20,798	20,836
*04074	Scarborough	18,919	19,343
*04106	South Portland	25,002	25,255
*04901	Waterville	15,722	15,962
*04092	Westbrook	17,494	17,743
*04062	Windham	17,001	17,443
03909	York	12,529	12,697

Maryland

Area code 240 overlays area code 301. Area codes 443/667 overlay area code 410.

ZIP	Place	Area code	2010 population	2013 estimate
21001	Aberdeen	(410)	14,959	15,120
20607	Accokeek (c)	(301)	10,573	—
*20783	Adelphi (c)	(301)	15,086	—
*21401	Annapolis	(410)	38,394	38,722
21403	Annapolis Neck (c)	(410)	10,950	—
21227	Arbutus (c)	(410)	20,483	—
21012	Arnold (c)	(410)	23,106	—
*20906	Aspen Hill (c)	(301)	48,759	—
21220	Ballenger Creek (c)	(410)	18,274	—
21201	Baltimore	(410)	620,961	622,104
*21014	Bel Air	(410)	10,120	10,307
21050	Bel Air North (c)	(410)	30,568	—
21014	Bel Air South (c)	(410)	47,709	—
*20705	Beltsville (c)	(301)	16,772	—
20603	Bensville (c)	(301)	11,923	—
*20814	Bethesda (c)	(301)	60,858	—
*20715	Bowie	(301)	54,727	56,759
21225	Brooklyn Park (c)	(410)	14,373	—
20619	California (c)	(301)	11,857	—
20705	Calverton (c)	(301)	17,724	—
21613	Cambridge	(410)	12,326	12,620
*20748	Camp Springs (c)	(301)	19,096	—
21234	Carney (c)	(410)	29,941	—
*21228	Catonsville (c)	(410)	41,567	—
20657	Chesapeake Ranch Estates (c)	(301)	10,519	—
20782	Chillum (c)	(301)	33,513	—
20871	Clarksburg (c)	(301)	13,766	—
20735	Clinton (c)	(301)	35,970	—
20904	Cloverly (c)	(301)	15,126	—
21030	Cockeysville (c)	(410)	20,776	—
*20904	Colesville (c)	(301)	14,647	—
*20740	College Park (c)	(301)	30,413	31,274
21045	Columbia (c)	(410)	99,615	—
21114	Crofton (c)	(410)	27,348	—
*21502	Cumberland	(301)	20,859	20,452
20872	Damascus (c)	(301)	15,257	—
21222	Dundalk (c)	(410)	63,597	—
20737	East Riverdale (c)	(301)	15,509	—
*21601	Easton	(410)	15,945	16,687
21040	Edgewood (c)	(410)	25,562	—
21784	Eldersburg (c)	(410)	30,531	—
21075	Elkridge (c)	(410)	15,593	—
*21921	Elkton	(410)	15,443	15,718
*21043	Ellicott City (c)	(410)	65,834	—
21221	Essex (c)	(410)	39,262	—
20904	Fairland (c)	(301)	23,681	—
21061	Ferndale (c)	(410)	16,746	—
*20747	Forestville (c)	(301)	12,353	—
*20744	Fort Washington (c)	(301)	23,717	—
*21701	Frederick	(301)	65,239	66,893
20877	Gaithersburg	(301)	59,933	65,690
*20874	Germantown (c)	(301)	86,395	—
20745	Glassmanor (c)	(301)	17,295	—
*21061	Glen Burnie (c)	(410)	67,639	—
20906	Glenmont (c)	(301)	13,529	—
20769	Glenn Dale (c)	(301)	13,466	—
*20770	Greenbelt (c)	(301)	23,068	23,753
*21740	Hagerstown	(301)	39,662	40,612
21740	Halfway (c)	(301)	10,701	—
21078	Havre de Grace	(410)	12,952	13,501
20748	Hillcrest Heights (c)	(301)	16,469	—
*20781	Hyattsville	(301)	17,557	18,045
21043	Ilchester (c)	(410)	23,476	—
21085	Joppatowne (c)	(410)	12,616	—
20902	Kemp Mill (c)	(301)	12,564	—
*20774	Kettering (c)	(301)	12,790	—
*21122	Lake Shore (c)	(410)	19,477	—
20785	Landover (c)	(301)	23,078	—
*20787	Langley Park (c)	(301)	18,755	—
*20706	Lanham (c)	(301)	10,157	—
*20774	Largo (c)	(301)	10,709	—
20707	Laurel	(301)	25,115	25,800
20653	Lexington Park (c)	(410)	11,626	—
21090	Linthicum (c)	(410)	10,324	—
21207	Lochearn (c)	(410)	25,333	—
20724	Maryland City (c)	(301)	16,093	—
21093	Mays Chapel (c)	(410)	11,420	—
21220	Middle River (c)	(410)	25,191	—
21207	Milford Mill (c)	(410)	29,042	—
*20716	Mitchellville (c)	(301)	10,967	—
*20886	Montgomery Village (c)	(301)	32,032	—
20784	New Carrollton (c)	(301)	12,135	12,514
*20852	North Bethesda (c)	(301)	43,828	—
20878	North Potomac (c)	(301)	24,410	—
21811	Ocean Pines (c)	(410)	11,710	—
21113	Odenton (c)	(410)	37,132	—
*20832	Olney (c)	(301)	33,844	—
21236	Overlea (c)	(410)	12,275	—
21117	Owings Mills (c)	(410)	30,622	—

ZIP	Place	Area code	2010 population	2013 estimate
*20745	Oxon Hill (c)	(301)	17,722	—
21234	Parkville (c).	(410)	30,734	—
21401	Parole (c)	(410)	15,922	—
*21122	Pasadena (c)	(410)	24,287	—
21128	Perry Hall (c)	(410)	28,474	—
*21207	Pikesville (c)	(410)	30,764	—
*20850	Potomac (c)	(301)	44,965	—
21133	Randallstown (c).	(301)	32,430	—
20855	Redland (c)	(301)	17,242	—
*21136	Reisterstown (c)	(410)	25,968	—
*21122	Riviera Beach (c)	(410)	12,677	—
*20850	Rockville	(301)	61,209	64,072
20772	Rosaryville (c)	(301)	10,697	—
21237	Rosedale (c).	(410)	19,257	—
21221	Rossville (c)	(410)	15,147	—
*21801	Salisbury	(410)	30,343	31,507
20723	Scaggsville (c)	(301)	24,333	—
*20706	Seabrook (c)	(301)	17,287	—
21144	Severn (c)	(410)	44,231	—
21146	Severna Park (c).	(410)	37,634	—
*20901	Silver Spring (c)	(301)	71,452	—
20707	South Laurel (c)	(301)	26,112	—
*20746	Suitland (c)	(301)	25,825	—
21842	Summerfield (c)	(301)	10,898	—
*20912	Takoma Park	(301)	16,715	17,721
*21204	Towson (c)	(410)	55,197	—
20854	Travilah (c)	(301)	12,159	—
*20602	Waldorf (c)	(301)	67,752	—
20743	Walker Mill (c)	(301)	11,302	—
*21157	Westminster	(410)	18,590	18,645
*20902	Wheaton (c)	(301)	48,284	—
20904	White Oak (c)	(301)	17,403	—
21207	Woodlawn (c)			
	(Baltimore Co.)	(410)	37,879	—

Massachusetts

Area code 339 overlays area code 781. Area code 351 overlays area code 978. Area code 774 overlays area code 508. Area code 857 overlays area code 617. See introductory note.

ZIP	Place	Area code	2010 population	2013 estimate
02351	Abington	(781)	15,985	16,124
*01720	Acton	(978)	21,924	22,891
*02743	Acushnet	(508)	10,303	10,350
01001	Agawam	(413)	28,438	28,705
01913	Amesbury	(978)	16,283	16,650
*01002	Amherst	(413)	37,819	38,919
*01002	Amherst Center (c)	(413)	19,065	—
*01810	Andover	(978)	33,201	34,477
*02205	Arlington	(781)	42,844	44,028
01721	Ashland	(508)	16,593	17,150
*01331	Athol	(978)	11,584	11,619
02703	Attleboro	(508)	43,593	43,886
01501	Auburn	(508)	16,188	16,315
02630	Barnstable	(508)	45,193	44,641
*01730	Bedford	(781)	13,320	13,975
01007	Belchertown	(413)	14,649	14,735
02019	Bellingham	(508)	16,332	16,675
*02478	Belmont	(781)	24,729	25,332
01915	Beverly	(978)	39,502	40,664
*01821	Billerica	(978)	40,243	41,888
*02108	Boston	(617)	617,594	645,966
*02532	Bourne	(508)	19,754	19,733
*02185	Braintree	(781)	35,744	36,727
*02324	Bridgewater	(508)	26,563	26,506
*02301	Brockton	(508)	93,810	94,089
*02446	Brookline	(617)	58,732	59,128
*01803	Burlington	(781)	24,498	25,463
*02139	Cambridge	(617)	105,162	107,289
02021	Canton	(781)	21,561	22,221
*02330	Carver	(508)	11,509	11,494
01507	Charlton	(508)	12,981	13,175
01824	Chelmsford	(978)	33,802	34,722
02150	Chelsea	(617)	35,177	37,670
*01020	Chicopee	(413)	55,298	55,717
01510	Clinton	(978)	13,606	13,697
01742	Concord	(978)	17,668	19,285
01923	Danvers	(978)	26,493	27,483
*02714	Dartmouth	(508)	34,032	34,557
*02026	Dedham	(781)	24,729	25,299
02638	Dennis	(508)	14,207	14,067
01826	Dracut	(978)	29,457	30,687
01571	Dudley	(508)	11,390	11,516
*02332	Duxbury	(781)	15,059	15,288
02333	East Bridgewater	(508)	13,794	14,090
*01028	East Longmeadow	(413)	15,720	16,022
01027	Easthampton	(413)	16,053	15,971
*02334	Easton	(508)	23,112	23,753
02149	Everett	(617)	41,667	42,935
02719	Fairhaven	(508)	15,873	16,065
*02720	Fall River	(508)	88,857	88,697
*02540	Falmouth	(508)	31,531	31,644
01420	Fitchburg	(978)	40,318	40,383

ZIP	Place	Area code	2010 population	2013 estimate
02035	Foxborough	(508)	16,865	17,257
*01701	Framingham	(508)	68,318	70,441
02038	Franklin	(508)	31,635	32,581
*01440	Gardner	(978)	20,228	20,354
*01930	Gloucester	(978)	28,789	29,393
01519	Grafton	(508)	17,765	18,155
*01301	Greenfield	(413)	17,456	17,492
*01450	Groton	(978)	10,646	11,115
*02339	Hanover	(781)	13,879	14,280
*02341	Hanson	(781)	10,209	10,324
02645	Harwich	(508)	12,243	12,202
*01830	Haverhill	(978)	60,879	62,088
*02043	Hingham	(781)	22,157	22,740
02343	Holbrook	(781)	10,791	10,952
01520	Holden	(508)	17,346	17,995
01746	Holliston	(508)	13,547	14,162
*01040	Holyoke	(413)	39,880	40,249
01748	Hopkinton	(508)	14,925	15,918
01749	Hudson	(978)	19,063	19,586
01749	Hudson (c)	(978)	14,907	—
02045	Hull	(781)	10,293	10,332
01938	Ipswich	(978)	13,175	13,574
02364	Kingston	(781)	12,629	12,819
02347	Lakeville	(508)	10,602	11,144
*01840	Lawrence	(978)	76,377	77,657
01524	Leicester	(508)	10,970	11,243
01453	Leominster	(978)	40,759	41,002
*02420	Lexington	(781)	31,394	32,650
*01028	Longmeadow	(413)	15,784	15,882
*01850	Lowell	(978)	106,519	108,861
*01056	Ludlow	(413)	21,103	21,451
*01462	Lunenburg	(978)	10,086	10,969
*01901	Lynn	(781)	90,329	91,589
01940	Lynnfield	(781)	11,596	12,395
02148	Malden	(781)	59,450	60,509
*02048	Mansfield	(508)	23,184	23,566
01945	Marblehead	(781)	19,808	20,187
01752	Marlborough	(508)	38,499	39,414
*02050	Marshfield	(781)	25,132	25,509
02649	Mashpee	(508)	14,006	14,068
01754	Maynard	(978)	10,106	10,370
02052	Medfield	(508)	12,024	12,313
*02155	Medford	(781)	56,173	57,170
02053	Medway	(508)	12,752	13,053
02176	Melrose	(781)	26,983	27,690
01844	Methuen	(978)	47,255	48,514
*02346	Middleborough	(508)	23,116	23,601
01757	Milford	(508)	27,999	28,288
01757	Milford (c)	(508)	25,055	—
*01527	Millbury	(508)	13,261	13,399
02186	Milton	(617)	27,003	27,270
*02584	Nantucket	(508)	10,172	10,399
01760	Natick	(508)	33,006	35,214
*02494	Needham	(781)	28,886	29,736
02740	New Bedford	(508)	95,072	95,078
01950	Newburyport	(978)	17,416	17,800
02456	Newton	(617)	85,146	87,971
02056	Norfolk	(508)	11,227	11,689
01247	North Adams	(413)	13,708	13,533
01845	North Andover	(978)	28,352	29,217
*02760	North Attleborough	(508)	28,712	28,801
*01864	North Reading	(978)	14,892	15,377
*01060	Northampton	(413)	28,549	28,495
01532	Northborough	(508)	14,155	14,762
01534	Northbridge	(508)	15,707	16,103
*02766	Norton	(508)	19,031	19,367
02061	Norwell	(781)	10,506	10,723
02062	Norwood	(781)	28,602	28,951
01540	Oxford	(508)	13,709	13,806
01069	Palmer	(413)	12,140	12,157
*01960	Peabody	(978)	51,251	52,044
*02359	Pembroke	(781)	17,837	18,097
01463	Pepperell	(978)	11,497	11,876
*01201	Pittsfield	(413)	44,737	44,057
*02360	Plymouth	(508)	56,468	57,826
*02169	Quincy	(617)	92,271	93,494
02368	Randolph	(781)	32,112	33,456
*02767	Raynham	(508)	13,383	13,554
01867	Reading	(781)	24,747	25,327
02769	Rehoboth	(508)	11,608	11,837
02151	Revere	(781)	51,755	53,756
02370	Rockland	(781)	17,489	17,632
*01970	Salem	(978)	41,340	42,544
*02563	Sandwich	(508)	20,675	20,589
01906	Saugus	(781)	26,628	27,735
*02066	Scituate	(781)	18,133	18,297
02771	Seekonk	(508)	13,722	14,366
02067	Sharon	(781)	17,612	18,027
*01545	Shrewsbury	(508)	35,608	36,309
*02725	Somerset	(508)	18,165	18,290
*02143	Somerville	(617)	75,754	78,804
01075	South Hadley	(413)	17,514	17,740
02664	South Yarmouth (c)	(508)	11,092	—
01550	Southbridge	(508)	16,719	16,793

ZIP	Place	Area code	2010 population	2013 estimate
01562	Spencer	(508)	11,688	11,766
*01103	Springfield	(413)	153,060	153,703
02180	Stoneham	(781)	21,437	21,734
02072	Stoughton	(781)	26,962	28,106
01776	Sudbury	(978)	17,659	18,367
01907	Swampscott	(781)	13,787	13,951
02777	Swansea	(508)	15,865	16,079
*02780	Taunton	(508)	55,874	56,069
01876	Tewksbury	(978)	28,961	30,107
01879	Tyngsborough	(978)	11,292	12,054
01569	Uxbridge	(508)	13,457	13,647
01880	Wakefield	(781)	24,932	26,080
02081	Walpole	(508)	24,070	24,818
*02451	Waltham	(781)	60,632	62,227
02571	Wareham	(508)	21,822	22,384
*02471	Watertown	(781)	31,915	32,996
01778	Wayland	(508)	12,994	13,444
01570	Webster	(508)	16,767	16,811
01570	Webster (c)	(508)	11,412	—
*02457	Wellesley	(781)	27,982	29,090
*01089	West Springfield	(413)	28,391	28,684
*01581	Westborough	(508)	18,272	18,630
*01085	Westfield	(413)	41,094	41,301
01886	Westford	(978)	21,951	23,265
02493	Weston	(781)	11,261	11,853
02790	Westport	(508)	15,532	15,700
02090	Westwood	(781)	14,618	14,876
*02188	Weymouth	(781)	53,743	55,419
02382	Whitman	(781)	14,489	14,696
01095	Wilbraham	(413)	14,219	14,477
01887	Wilmington	(978)	22,325	23,147
01475	Winchendon	(978)	10,300	10,542
01890	Winchester	(781)	21,374	22,079
02152	Winthrop	(617)	17,497	18,111
*01801	Woburn	(781)	38,120	39,083
*01602	Worcester	(508)	181,045	182,544
*02093	Wrentham	(508)	10,955	11,268
*02675	Yarmouth	(508)	23,793	23,651

Michigan

Area code 947 overlays area code 248.

ZIP	Place	Area code	2010 population	2013 estimate
49221	Adrian	(517)	21,133	20,861
*48101	Allen Park	(313)	28,210	27,668
49401	Allendale (c)	(616)	17,579	—
49707	Alpena	(989)	10,483	10,295
*48103	Ann Arbor	(734)	113,934	117,025
*48321	Auburn Hills	(248)	21,412	21,769
*49014	Battle Creek	(269)	52,347	51,848
*48707	Bay City	(906)	34,932	34,424
48505	Beecher (c)	(810)	10,232	—
*49022	Benton Harbor	(269)	10,038	10,020
48072	Berkley	(248)	14,970	15,253
48025	Beverly Hills	(248)	10,267	10,448
49307	Big Rapids	(231)	10,601	10,517
*48012	Birmingham	(248)	20,103	20,504
*48509	Burton	(810)	29,999	29,181
49601	Cadillac	(231)	10,355	10,281
*48017	Clawson	(248)	11,825	12,048
49036	Coldwater	(517)	10,945	10,846
49321	Comstock Park (c)	(616)	10,088	—
49508	Cutlerville (c)	(616)	14,370	—
*48120	Dearborn	(313)	98,153	95,884
*48127	Dearborn Heights	(313)	57,774	56,620
*48201	Detroit	(313)	713,777	688,701
*49506	East Grand Rapids	(616)	10,694	11,182
*48823	East Lansing	(517)	48,579	48,554
48021	Eastpointe	(586)	32,442	32,627
49829	Escanaba	(906)	12,616	12,562
*48333	Farmington	(248)	10,372	10,557
*48331	Farmington Hills	(248)	79,740	81,295
48430	Fenton	(810)	11,756	11,574
48220	Ferndale	(248)	19,900	20,257
*48502	Flint	(810)	102,434	99,763
49506	Forest Hills (c)	(616)	25,867	—
48026	Fraser	(586)	14,480	14,602
*48135	Garden City	(734)	27,692	27,153
49417	Grand Haven	(616)	10,412	10,895
*49503	Grand Rapids	(616)	188,040	192,294
*49418	Grandville	(616)	15,378	15,738
48230	Grosse Pointe Park	(313)	11,555	11,330
48230	Grosse Pointe Woods	(313)	16,135	15,862
*48212	Hamtramck	(313)	22,423	22,099
48225	Harper Woods	(313)	14,236	13,958
48840	Haslett (c)	(517)	19,220	—
48030	Hazel Park	(248)	16,422	16,615
48203	Highland Park	(313)	11,776	10,441
*49423	Holland	(616)	33,051	33,481
48842	Holt (c)	(517)	23,973	—
48141	Inkster	(313)/(734)	25,369	24,857
48846	Ionia	(616)	11,394	11,424
*49201	Jackson	(517)	33,534	33,423

ZIP	Place	Area code	2010 population	2013 estimate
*49428	Jenison (c)	(616)	16,538	—
*49001	Kalamazoo	(269)	74,262	75,548
*49508	Kentwood	(616)	48,707	50,233
*48915	Lansing	(517)	114,297	113,972
48146	Lincoln Park	(313)	38,144	37,313
48150	Livonia	(734)	96,942	95,208
48071	Madison Heights	(248)	29,694	30,226
49855	Marquette	(906)	21,355	21,491
48122	Melvindale	(313)	10,715	10,480
48640	Midland	(906)	41,863	42,181
48161	Monroe	(734)	20,733	20,405
48046	Mount Clemens	(586)	16,314	16,399
*48858	Mount Pleasant	(989)	26,016	26,185
49440	Muskegon	(231)	38,401	37,213
49444	Muskegon Heights	(231)	10,856	10,831
48047	New Baltimore	(586)	12,084	12,211
*49120	Niles	(269)	11,600	11,430
49505	Northview (c)	(616)	14,541	—
*49441	Norton Shores	(231)	23,994	23,998
48374	Novi	(248)	55,224	57,960
48237	Oak Park	(248)	29,319	29,842
48805	Okemos (c)	(517)	21,369	—
*48867	Owosso	(906)	15,194	14,784
48340	Pontiac	(248)	59,515	59,887
*48060	Port Huron	(810)	30,184	29,331
49024	Portage	(269)	46,292	47,523
48192	Riverview	(734)	12,486	12,255
*48308	Rochester	(248)	12,711	12,988
48306	Rochester Hills	(248)	70,995	72,952
48174	Romulus	(313)/(734)	23,989	23,519
48066	Roseville	(586)	47,299	47,555
48068	Royal Oak	(248)	57,236	58,946
48601	Saginaw	(989)	51,508	50,303
*48080	Saint Clair Shores	(313)	59,715	60,070
*49783	Sault Sainte Marie	(906)	14,144	14,098
48178	South Lyon	(248)	11,327	11,626
48033	Southfield	(248)	71,739	73,006
48195	Southgate	(734)	30,047	29,487
*48310	Sterling Heights	(586)	129,699	131,224
49091	Sturgis	(269)	10,994	10,928
*48180	Taylor	(313)/(734)	63,131	61,817
*49684	Traverse City	(231)	14,674	15,018
48183	Trenton	(734)	18,853	18,485
*48083	Troy	(248)	80,980	82,821
49534	Walker	(616)	23,537	24,259
*48088	Warren	(586)	134,056	134,873
48917	Waverly (c)	(517)	23,925	—
48184	Wayne	(734)	17,593	17,163
*48185	Westland	(313)/(734)	84,094	82,578
48393	Wixom	(248)	13,498	13,743
48183	Woodhaven	(734)	12,875	12,636
*48192	Wyandotte	(734)	25,883	25,225
49509	Wyoming	(616)	72,125	74,100
*48197	Ypsilanti	(734)	19,435	19,809

Minnesota

ZIP	Place	Area code	2010 population	2013 estimate
56007	Albert Lea	(507)	18,016	17,881
56308	Alexandria	(320)	11,070	11,580
*55304	Andover	(763)	30,598	31,709
*55303	Anoka	(612)	17,142	17,268
55124	Apple Valley	(952)	49,084	50,201
55912	Austin	(507)	24,718	24,763
*56601	Bemidji	(218)	13,431	14,435
55309	Big Lake	(763)	10,060	10,298
55014	Blaine	(651)	57,186	60,407
*55420	Bloomington	(952)	82,893	86,319
*55429	Brainerd	(218)	13,590	13,487
55601	Brooklyn Center	(763)	30,104	30,712
*55443	Brooklyn Park	(763)	75,781	78,373
55313	Buffalo	(763)	15,453	15,825
*55337	Burnsville	(651)	60,306	61,434
55316	Champlin	(763)	23,089	23,797
55317	Chanhassen	(952)	22,952	24,432
55318	Chaska	(952)	23,770	24,444
55720	Cloquet	(218)	12,124	12,050
55421	Columbia Heights	(612)	19,496	19,674
*55433	Coon Rapids	(763)	61,476	62,103
55016	Cottage Grove	(651)	34,589	35,399
*55428	Crystal	(763)	22,151	22,588
*55806	Duluth	(218)	86,265	86,128
*55121	Eagan	(651)	64,206	65,453
55005	East Bethel	(763)	11,626	11,607
*55344	Eden Prairie	(612)	60,797	62,603
*55424	Edina	(952)	47,941	49,376
55330	Elk River	(763)	22,974	23,447
*56031	Fairmont	(507)	10,666	10,434
55021	Faribault	(507)	23,352	23,414
55024	Farmington	(651)	21,086	22,167
*56537	Fergus Falls	(218)	13,138	13,351
55025	Forest Lake	(651)	18,375	19,132
*55432	Fridley	(763)	27,208	27,667

ZIP	Place	Area code	2010 population	2013 estimate
*55427	Golden Valley	763	20,371	20,845
*55744	Grand Rapids	218	10,869	10,989
*55304	Ham Lake	763	15,296	15,733
55033	Hastings	651	22,172	22,424
*55746	Hibbing	218	16,361	16,301
*55343	Hopkins	952	17,591	18,025
55038	Hugo	651	13,332	14,082
55350	Hutchinson	320	14,178	13,871
*55076	Inver Grove Heights	651	33,880	34,344
55044	Lakeville	952	55,954	58,562
*55014	Lino Lakes	651	20,216	20,862
*55109	Little Canada	651	9,773	10,102
*56001	Mankato	507	39,309	40,641
*55311	Maple Grove	763	61,567	65,415
*55109	Maplewood	651	38,018	39,765
56258	Marshall	507	13,680	13,483
*55118	Mendota Heights	651	11,071	11,172
*55401	Minneapolis	612	382,578	400,070
*55345	Minnetonka	952	49,734	51,368
*55362	Monticello	763	12,759	13,029
*56560	Moorhead	218	38,065	39,398
55112	Mounds View	763	12,155	12,525
55112	New Brighton	651	21,456	22,073
*54427	New Hope	763	20,339	20,787
56073	New Ulm	507	13,522	13,210
55056	North Branch	651	10,125	10,087
*56002	North Mankato	507	13,394	13,439
55109	North Saint Paul	651	11,460	11,830
55057	Northfield	507	20,007	20,581
*55128	Oakdale	651	27,378	27,780
*55330	Otsego	763	13,571	14,524
55060	Owatonna	507	25,599	25,546
*55446	Plymouth	763	70,576	73,987
55372	Prior Lake	952	22,796	24,408
55303	Ramsey	763	23,668	24,935
55066	Red Wing	651	16,459	16,513
55423	Richfield	612	35,228	36,175
55422	Robbinsdale	763	13,953	14,302
*55901	Rochester	507	106,769	110,742
55374	Rogers	763	8,597	11,983
55068	Rosemount	651	21,874	22,666
*55113	Roseville	651	33,660	34,934
*56301	Saint Cloud	320	65,842	66,297
*55426	Saint Louis Park	952	45,250	47,411
55376	Saint Michael	763	16,399	16,921
*55101	Saint Paul	651	285,068	294,873
56082	Saint Peter	507	11,196	11,439
56377	Sartell	320	15,876	16,277
56379	Sauk Rapids	320	12,773	13,270
55378	Savage	952	26,911	28,639
55379	Shakopee	612	37,076	39,167
55126	Shoreview	651	25,043	25,931
55075	South Saint Paul	651	20,160	20,436
*55082	Stillwater	651	18,225	18,674
*55127	Vadnais Heights	651	12,302	12,983
*55387	Waconia	952	10,697	11,490
*55118	West Saint Paul	651	19,540	19,756
*55110	White Bear Lake	651	23,797	24,555
56201	Willmar	320	19,610	19,680
*55987	Winona	507	27,592	27,546
*55125	Woodbury	651	61,961	65,656
56187	Worthington	507	12,764	12,943

Mississippi

Area code 769 overlays area code 601.

ZIP	Place	Area code	2010 population	2013 estimate
39520	Bay Saint Louis	228	9,260	10,822
*39530	Biloxi	228	44,054	44,820
*39042	Brandon	601	21,705	22,498
*39601	Brookhaven	601	12,513	12,515
39272	Byram	601	11,489	11,603
39046	Canton	601	13,189	13,263
*38614	Clarksdale	662	17,962	17,282
*38732	Cleveland	662	12,334	12,438
*39056	Clinton	601	25,216	25,305
*39701	Columbus	662	23,640	23,518
*38834	Corinth	662	14,573	14,870
39540	D'Iberville	228	9,486	10,390
39553	Gautier	228	18,572	18,544
*38701	Greenville	662	34,400	33,203
*38930	Greenwood	662	15,205	15,860
38901	Grenada	662	13,092	12,942
*39501	Gulfport	228	67,793	71,012
*39401	Hattiesburg	601	45,989	47,556
38632	Hernando	662	14,090	15,000
38637	Horn Lake	662	26,066	26,635
*38751	Indianola	662	10,683	10,271
*39201	Jackson	601	173,514	172,638
*39440	Laurel	601	18,540	18,978
39560	Long Beach	228	14,792	15,416
*39110	Madison	601	24,149	25,304
*39648	McComb	601	12,790	12,747
*39301	Meridian	601	41,148	40,921
*39563	Moss Point	228	13,704	13,682
*39120	Natchez	601	15,792	15,513
39564	Ocean Springs	228	17,442	17,493
38654	Olive Branch	662	33,484	34,963
38655	Oxford	662	18,916	20,865
*39567	Pascagoula	228	22,392	22,240
39288	Pearl	601	25,092	26,262
39465	Petal	601	10,454	10,815
39466	Picayune	601	10,878	10,813
*39157	Ridgeland	601	24,047	24,427
38671	Southaven	662	48,982	50,997
*39759	Starkville	662	23,888	24,775
*38801	Tupelo	662	34,546	35,827
*39180	Vicksburg	601	23,856	23,542
39773	West Point	662	11,307	11,217
39194	Yazoo City	662	11,403	11,419

Missouri

ZIP	Place	Area code	2010 population	2013 estimate
63123	Affton (c)	314	20,307	—
63010	Arnold	636	20,808	21,134
*63011	Ballwin	636	30,404	30,498
63137	Bellefontaine Neighbors	314	10,860	10,823
64002	Belton	816	23,116	23,175
*64015	Blue Springs	816	52,575	53,294
*65613	Bolivar	417	10,325	10,487
*65616	Branson	417	10,520	11,064
63044	Bridgeton	314	11,550	11,686
*63701	Cape Girardeau	573	37,941	38,816
64836	Carthage	417	14,378	14,232
*63017	Chesterfield	636	47,484	47,749
*63105	Clayton	314	15,939	15,884
*65201	Columbia	573	108,500	115,276
*63128	Concord (c)	314	16,421	—
63126	Crestwood	314	11,912	11,942
*63011	Creve Coeur	314	17,833	17,865
*63366	Dardenne Prairie	636	11,494	12,324
63025	Eureka	636	10,189	10,467
64024	Excelsior Springs	816	11,084	11,418
63640	Farmington	573	16,240	17,796
63135	Ferguson	314	21,203	21,111
63028	Festus	636	11,602	11,829
63033	Florissant	314	52,158	52,363
65473	Fort Leonard Wood (c)	573	15,061	—
65251	Fulton	573	12,790	12,760
*64118	Gladstone	816	25,410	26,157
64029	Grain Valley	816	12,854	13,125
64030	Grandview	816	24,475	25,307
63401	Hannibal	573	17,916	17,883
64701	Harrisonville	816	10,019	10,001
*63042	Hazelwood	314	25,703	25,668
*64050	Independence	816	116,830	117,240
63755	Jackson	573	13,758	14,386
*65101	Jefferson City	573	43,079	43,330
63136	Jennings	314	14,712	14,756
*64801	Joplin	417	50,150	50,789
64106	Kansas City	816	459,787	467,007
63857	Kennett	573	10,932	10,916
63501	Kirksville	660	17,505	17,577
63122	Kirkwood	314	27,540	27,596
63367	Lake Saint Louis	636	14,545	14,831
65536	Lebanon	417	14,474	14,759
*64063	Lee's Summit	816	91,364	93,184
63125	Lemay (c)	314	16,645	—
*64068	Liberty	816	29,149	30,096
*63011	Manchester	636	18,094	18,186
65540	Marshall	660	13,065	13,010
63043	Maryland Heights	314	27,472	27,436
64468	Maryville	660	11,972	12,062
63129	Mehlville (c)	314	28,380	—
65265	Mexico	573	11,543	11,530
65270	Moberly	660	13,974	13,746
*64850	Neosho	417	11,835	12,157
65714	Nixa	417	19,022	20,195
63129	Oakville (c)	314	36,143	—
*63366	O'Fallon	636	79,329	82,809
63034	Old Jamestown (c)	314	19,184	—
63114	Overland	314	16,062	16,008
65721	Ozark	417	17,820	18,606
*63901	Poplar Bluff	573	17,023	17,287
64083	Raymore	816	19,206	19,754
*64133	Raytown	816	29,526	29,510
65738	Republic	417	14,751	15,590
*65401	Rolla	573	19,559	19,831
63074	Saint Ann	314	13,020	12,971
*63301	Saint Charles	636	65,794	67,569
*64501	Saint Joseph	816	76,780	77,147
*63101	Saint Louis	314	319,294	318,416
*63376	Saint Peters	636	52,575	54,842
65301	Sedalia	660	21,387	21,492
63801	Sikeston	573	16,318	16,494
63138	Spanish Lake (c)	314	19,650	

ZIP	Place	Area code	2010 population	2013 estimate
*65804	Springfield.............	(417)	159,498	164,122
63017	Town and Country.......	(314)	10,815	10,922
63379	Troy...................	(314)	10,540	11,211
63084	Union	(636)	10,204	10,577
63130	University City.........	(314)	35,371	35,148
64093	Warrensburg...........	(660)	18,838	19,927
63090	Washington............	(636)	13,982	14,031
64870	Webb City.............	(417)	10,996	10,989
63119	Webster Groves	(314)	22,995	23,203
63385	Wentzville.............	(636)	29,070	32,509
*65775	West Plains............	(417)	11,986	12,268
*63011	Wildwood	(314)	35,517	35,787

Montana
Area code 406 applies to the entire state.

ZIP	Place	2010 population	2013 estimate
*59101	Billings	104,170	109,059
*59715	Bozeman	37,280	39,860
*59701	Butte-Silver Bow (balance)	33,525	33,854
*59401	Great Falls	58,505	59,351
*59601	Helena	28,190	29,596
*59901	Kalispell	19,927	20,972
*59801	Missoula	66,788	69,122

Nebraska
Area code 531 overlays area code 402.

ZIP	Place	Area code	2010 population	2013 estimate
68310	Beatrice	(402)	12,459	12,157
*68005	Bellevue	(402)	50,137	53,663
68138	Chalco (c)..............	(402)	10,994	—
*68601	Columbus	(402)	22,111	22,533
*68025	Fremont	(402)	26,397	26,340
*68801	Grand Island	(308)	48,520	50,550
*68901	Hastings	(402)	24,907	25,093
*68847	Kearney	(308)	30,787	32,174
*68128	La Vista	(402)	15,758	17,562
68850	Lexington	(308)	10,230	10,204
*68502	Lincoln	(402)	258,379	268,738
*68701	Norfolk	(402)	24,210	24,523
*69101	North Platte............	(308)	24,733	24,534
*68104	Omaha	(402)	408,958	434,353
*68046	Papillion	(402)	18,894	21,921
*69361	Scottsbluff	(308)	15,039	15,023
68776	South Sioux City	(402)	13,353	13,424

Nevada
Area code 725 overlays area code 702.

ZIP	Place	Area code	2010 population	2013 estimate
*89005	Boulder City	(702)	15,023	15,189
*89701	Carson City............	(775)	55,274	54,080
*89801	Elko...................	(775)	18,297	20,074
89124	Enterprise (c)	(702)	108,481	—
89408	Fernley	(775)	19,368	19,193
89410	Gardnerville Ranchos (c)	(775)	11,312	—
*89015	Henderson	(702)	257,729	270,811
*89101	Las Vegas..............	(702)	583,756	603,488
*89027	Mesquite	(702)	15,276	16,439
*89030	North Las Vegas	(702)	216,961	226,877
*89048	Pahrump (c)	(775)	36,441	—
89109	Paradise (c)	(702)	223,167	—
*89501	Reno	(775)	225,221	233,294
*89441	Spanish Springs (c)	(775)	15,064	—
*89431	Sparks	(775)	90,264	93,282
89815	Spring Creek (c)	(702)	12,361	—
89147	Spring Valley (c)	(702)	178,395	—
89135	Summerlin South (c).....	(702)	24,085	—
*89433	Sun Valley (c)	(775)	189,372	—
89110	Sunrise Manor (c).......	(702)	19,299	—
89122	Whitney (c)............	(702)	38,585	—
89101	Winchester (c)..........	(702)	27,978	—

New Hampshire
Area code 603 applies to the entire state. See introductory note.

ZIP	Place	2010 population	2013 estimate
03031	Amherst	11,201	11,261
03110	Bedford	21,203	21,610
03743	Claremont.................	13,355	13,051
*03301	Concord	42,695	42,419
03818	Conway	10,115	10,023
03038	Derry....................	33,109	33,251
03038	Derry (c)..................	22,015	—
*03820	Dover	29,987	30,510
03824	Durham	14,638	15,380
03824	Durham (c)................	10,345	—
03833	Exeter	14,306	14,531
03045	Goffstown	17,651	17,802

ZIP	Place	2010 population	2013 estimate
*03842	Hampton..................	15,430	15,177
03755	Hanover	11,260	11,320
03106	Hooksett..................	13,451	13,716
03051	Hudson...................	24,467	24,645
*03431	Keene....................	23,409	23,419
*03246	Laconia...................	15,951	16,010
*03766	Lebanon	13,151	13,599
03053	Londonderry...............	24,129	24,308
03053	Londonderry (c)............	11,037	—
*03103	Manchester	109,565	110,378
03054	Merrimack	25,494	25,599
03055	Milford	15,115	15,137
*03060	Nashua...................	86,494	87,137
03076	Pelham...................	12,897	13,088
*03801	Portsmouth................	20,779	21,440
03077	Raymond	10,138	10,216
*03867	Rochester.................	29,752	29,745
03079	Salem....................	28,776	28,866
03878	Somersworth	11,766	11,741
03087	Windham	13,592	14,113

New Jersey
Area code 551 overlays area code 201. Area code 848 overlays area code 732. Area code 862 overlays area code 973.

ZIP	Place	Area code	2010 population	2013 estimate
07712	Asbury Park	(732)	16,116	15,855
*08401	Atlantic City	(609)	39,558	39,551
07001	Avenel (c)	(732)	17,011	—
07002	Bayonne...............	(201)	63,024	65,028
08722	Beachwood............	(732)	11,045	11,172
*08031	Bellmawr..............	(856)	11,583	11,540
07621	Bergenfield	(201)	26,764	27,191
08805	Bound Brook	(732)	10,402	10,487
08807	Bradley Gardens (c)....	(908)	14,206	—
08302	Bridgeton	(856)	25,349	25,252
08015	Browns Mills (c)	(609)	11,223	—
*08101	Camden	(856)	77,344	76,903
08002	Cherry Hill Mall (c)	(856)	14,171	—
07008	Carteret...............	(732)	22,844	23,994
07010	Cliffside Park..........	(201)	23,594	25,209
*07015	Clifton	(973)	84,136	85,390
*08108	Collingswood	(856)	13,926	13,850
07067	Colonia (c)	(732)	17,795	—
*07801	Dover	(973)	18,157	18,367
07628	Dumont...............	(201)	17,479	17,757
*07019	East Orange	(973)	64,270	64,544
*07724	Eatontown............	(732)	12,709	12,262
08043	Echelon (c)............	(856)	10,743	—
07020	Edgewater............	(201)	11,513	12,148
*07207	Elizabeth.............	(908)	124,969	127,558
07407	Elmwood Park	(201)	19,403	20,094
*07631	Englewood	(201)	27,147	27,533
07410	Fair Lawn	(201)/(973)	32,457	32,998
07022	Fairview	(201)	13,835	14,237
07932	Florham Park	(973)	11,696	11,831
08863	Fords (c)	(732)	15,187	—
07024	Fort Lee	(201)	35,345	36,014
07417	Franklin Lakes	(201)	10,590	10,759
08823	Franklin Park (c)	(732)	13,295	—
07728	Freehold	(732)	12,052	12,047
07026	Garfield	(973)	30,487	31,199
08028	Glassboro	(856)	18,579	18,953
07452	Glen Rock	(201)	11,601	11,838
08030	Gloucester City	(856)	11,456	11,402
*08053	Greentree (c)	(856)	11,367	—
07093	Guttenberg	(201)	11,176	11,429
*07602	Hackensack	(201)	43,010	44,113
08033	Haddonfield	(856)	11,593	11,507
08690	Hamilton Square (c) ...	(609)	12,784	—
08037	Hammonton	(609)	14,791	14,799
07029	Harrison	(973)	13,620	15,227
07604	Hasbrouck Heights	(201)	11,842	12,022
*07506	Hawthorne	(973)	18,791	18,987
08904	Highland Park	(732)	13,982	14,361
07642	Hillsdale	(201)	10,219	10,424
07030	Hoboken	(201)	50,005	52,575
*08753	Holiday City-Berkeley (c)	(732)	12,831	—
07843	Hopatcong	(973)	15,147	14,806
08830	Iselin (c)	(732)	18,695	—
*07303	Jersey City	(201)	247,597	257,342
07734	Keansburg	(732)	10,105	10,014
*07032	Kearny	(201)/(973)	40,684	41,664
07405	Kinnelon	(973)	10,248	10,400
08701	Lakewood (c)	(732)	53,805	—
07035	Lincoln Park	(973)	10,521	10,470
07036	Linden	(732)/(908)	40,499	41,301
08021	Lindenwold	(856)	17,613	17,501
07643	Little Ferry	(201)	10,626	10,806
07644	Lodi..................	(201)/(973)	24,136	24,522
07740	Long Branch	(732)	30,719	30,390
07940	Madison	(973)	15,845	16,274

ZIP	Place	Area code	2010 population	2013 estimate
08835	Manville	(908)	10,344	10,424
08053	Marlton (c)	(856)	10,133	—
08836	Martinsville (c)	(908)	11,980	—
08619	Mercerville (c)	(609)	13,230	—
08840	Metuchen	(732)	13,574	13,756
08846	Middlesex	(732)	13,635	13,812
08332	Millville	(856)	28,400	28,711
08057	Moorestown-Lenola (c)	(856)	14,217	—
*07960	Morristown	(973)	18,411	18,529
*08901	New Brunswick	(732)	55,181	55,831
07646	New Milford	(201)	16,341	16,572
07974	New Providence	(908)	12,171	12,332
*07102	Newark	(973)	277,140	278,427
07031	North Arlington	(201)	15,392	15,632
*07060	North Plainfield	(908)	21,936	22,056
07436	Oakland	(201)	12,754	12,959
*08050	Ocean Acres (c)	(609)	16,142	—
08226	Ocean City	(609)	11,701	11,451
08857	Old Bridge (c)	(732)	23,753	—
07650	Palisades Park	(201)	19,622	20,288
*07652	Paramus	(201)	26,342	26,674
07055	Passaic	(973)	69,781	70,868
*07510	Paterson	(973)	146,199	145,948
08070	Pennsville (c)	(856)	11,888	—
*08861	Perth Amboy	(732)	50,814	51,982
08865	Phillipsburg	(908)	14,950	14,655
08021	Pine Hill	(856)	10,233	10,496
*07061	Plainfield	(908)	49,808	50,588
*08232	Pleasantville	(609)	20,249	20,520
08742	Point Pleasant	(732)	18,392	18,521
07442	Pompton Lakes	(973)	11,097	11,148
*08540	Princeton	(609)	12,307	29,008
08536	Princeton Meadows (c)	(609)	13,834	—
07065	Rahway	(732)	27,346	28,394
07446	Ramsey	(201)	14,473	14,706
*07701	Red Bank	(732)	12,206	12,213
07657	Ridgefield	(201)	11,032	11,218
07660	Ridgefield Park	(201)	12,729	12,925
*07451	Ridgewood	(201)/(973)	24,958	25,352
07456	Ringwood	(973)	12,228	12,335
07661	River Edge	(201)	11,340	11,515
07751	Robertsville (c)	(732)	11,297	—
07203	Roselle	(908)	21,085	21,449
07204	Roselle Park	(908)	13,297	13,525
07070	Rutherford	(201)	18,061	18,358
*08872	Sayreville	(732)	42,704	44,412
*07094	Secaucus	(201)	16,264	18,311
07078	Short Hills (c)	(973)	13,165	—
08244	Somers Point	(609)	10,795	10,785
*08873	Somerset (c)	(732)	22,083	—
08876	Somerville	(908)	12,098	12,171
07080	South Plainfield	(732)/(908)	23,385	23,784
*08882	South River	(732)	16,008	16,236
08003	Springdale (c)	(856)	14,518	—
*07901	Summit	(908)	21,457	21,988
07670	Tenafly	(201)	14,488	14,704
*07724	Tinton Falls	(732)	17,892	17,976
*08753	Toms River (c)	(732)	88,791	—
*07512	Totowa	(973)	10,804	10,907
*08650	Trenton	(609)	84,913	84,349
07087	Union City	(201)	66,455	68,247
07043	Upper Montclair (c)	(973)	11,565	—
08406	Ventnor City	(609)	10,650	10,630
*08360	Vineland	(856)	60,724	61,050
07057	Wallington	(201)/(973)	11,335	11,545
07465	Wanaque	(201)/(973)	11,116	11,208
07728	West Freehold (c)	(732)/(908)	13,613	—
07093	West New York	(201)	49,708	52,122
*07091	Westfield	(732)/(908)	30,316	30,851
*07675	Westwood	(201)	10,908	11,075
08094	Williamstown (c)	(609)/(856)	15,567	—
07095	Woodbridge (c)	(732)/(908)	19,265	—
*08096	Woodbury	(856)	10,174	10,078
07424	Woodland Park	(973)	11,819	12,274

New Mexico

ZIP	Place	Area code	2010 population	2013 estimate
*88310	Alamogordo	(575)	30,403	31,368
*87101	Albuquerque	(505)	545,852	556,495
*88210	Artesia	(575)	11,301	11,484
*88220	Carlsbad	(575)	26,138	27,653
*88021	Chaparral (c)	(575)	14,631	—
*88101	Clovis	(575)	37,775	39,508
*88030	Deming	(575)	14,855	14,609
*87532	Española	(505)	10,224	10,190
*87401	Farmington	(505)	45,877	45,426
*87301	Gallup	(505)	21,678	22,261
*88240	Hobbs	(575)	34,122	36,041
*88001	Las Cruces	(575)	97,618	101,324
*87701	Las Vegas	(505)	13,753	13,691
*87544	Los Alamos (c)	(505)	12,019	—
87031	Los Lunas	(505)	14,835	15,308

ZIP	Place	Area code	2010 population	2013 estimate
*88260	Lovington	(575)	11,009	11,550
87107	North Valley (c)	(505)	11,333	—
*88130	Portales	(575)	12,280	12,497
*87124	Rio Rancho	(505)	87,521	91,956
*88201	Roswell	(575)	48,366	48,611
*87501	Santa Fe	(505)	67,947	69,976
*88061	Silver City	(575)	10,315	10,273
87105	South Valley (c)	(505)	40,976	—
*88063	Sunland Park	(575)	14,106	15,069

New York

Area codes 347/929 overlay area code (718). Area codes 646/917 overlay area code 212.

ZIP	Place	Area code	2010 population	2013 estimate
*12202	Albany	(518)	97,856	98,424
12010	Amsterdam	(518)	18,620	18,206
*13021	Auburn	(315)	27,687	27,381
11702	Babylon	(631)	12,166	12,153
11510	Baldwin	(516)	24,033	—
*14020	Batavia	(585)	15,465	15,269
11706	Bay Shore (c)	(631)	26,337	—
12508	Beacon	(845)	15,541	14,389
11710	Bellmore (c)	(516)	16,218	—
11714	Bethpage (c)	(516)	16,429	—
*13901	Binghamton	(607)	47,376	46,444
11716	Bohemia (c)	(631)	10,180	—
11717	Brentwood (c)	(631)	60,664	—
*14610	Brighton (c)	(585)	36,609	—
*14201	Buffalo	(716)	261,310	258,959
*14424	Canandaigua	(585)	10,545	10,471
11720	Centereach (c)	(631)	31,578	—
*11722	Central Islip (c)	(516)	34,450	—
14225	Cheektowaga (c)	(716)	75,178	—
12047	Cohoes	(518)	16,168	16,193
11725	Commack (c)	(631)	36,124	—
11726	Copiague (c)	(516)	22,993	—
11727	Coram (c)	(631)	39,113	—
*14830	Corning	(607)	11,183	11,068
13045	Cortland	(607)	19,204	19,059
11729	Deer Park (c)	(631)	27,745	—
14043	Depew	(716)	15,303	15,219
*11746	Dix Hills (c)	(631)	26,892	—
10522	Dobbs Ferry	(914)	10,875	11,059
*14048	Dunkirk	(716)	12,563	12,328
11730	East Islip (c)	(631)	14,475	—
11758	East Massapequa (c)	(516)	19,069	—
11554	East Meadow (c)	(516)	38,132	—
11731	East Northport (c)	(631)	20,217	—
11772	East Patchogue (c)	(631)	22,469	—
10709	Eastchester (c)	(914)	19,554	—
14226	Eggertsville (c)	(716)	15,019	—
*14901	Elmira	(607)	29,200	28,899
11003	Elmont (c)	(516)	33,198	—
11731	Elwood (c)	(631)	11,177	—
*13760	Endicott	(607)	13,392	13,151
13762	Endwell (c)	(607)	11,446	—
13219	Fairmount (c)	(315)	10,224	—
11738	Farmingville (c)	(631)	15,481	—
*11001	Floral Park	(516)	15,863	15,907
13603	Fort Drum (c)	(315)	12,955	—
11768	Fort Salonga (c)	(631)	10,008	—
11010	Franklin Square (c)	(516)	29,320	—
14063	Fredonia	(716)	11,230	10,909
11520	Freeport	(516)	42,860	43,167
13069	Fulton	(315)	11,896	11,744
*11530	Garden City	(516)	22,371	22,552
14456	Geneva	(315)	13,261	13,199
11542	Glen Cove	(516)	26,964	27,191
12801	Glens Falls	(518)	14,700	14,552
12078	Gloversville	(518)	15,665	15,315
*11022	Great Neck	(516)	9,989	10,088
14616	Greece (c)	(585)	14,519	—
11740	Greenlawn (c)	(631)	13,742	—
11946	Hampton Bays (c)	(631)	13,603	—
10528	Harrison	(914)	27,472	28,005
10927	Haverstraw	(845)	11,910	12,102
*11550	Hempstead	(516)	53,891	55,361
*11801	Hicksville (c)	(516)	41,547	—
11741	Holbrook (c)	(631)	27,195	—
11742	Holtsville (c)	(631)	19,714	—
11743	Huntington (c)	(631)	18,046	—
11746	Huntington Station (c)	(631)	33,029	—
*14617	Irondequoit (c)	(585)	51,692	—
11751	Islip (c)	(631)	18,689	—
*14850	Ithaca	(607)	30,014	30,515
*14701	Jamestown	(716)	31,146	30,737
10535	Jefferson Valley-Yorktown (c)	(914)	14,142	—
11753	Jericho (c)	(516)	13,567	—
13790	Johnson City	(607)	15,174	14,890
*14217	Kenmore (c)	(716)	15,423	15,254
11754	Kings Park (c)	(631)	17,282	—

ZIP	Place	Area code	2010 population	2013 estimate
*12401	Kingston	(845)	23,893	23,731
10950	Kiryas Joel	(845)	20,175	21,894
14218	Lackawanna	(716)	18,141	17,970
11755	Lake Grove	(631)	11,163	11,197
11779	Lake Ronkonkoma (c)	(631)	20,155	—
*14086	Lancaster	(716)	10,352	10,279
11756	Levittown (c)	(516)	51,881	—
11757	Lindenhurst	(631)	27,253	27,283
*14094	Lockport	(716)	21,165	20,870
11561	Long Beach	(516)	33,275	33,552
11563	Lynbrook	(516)	19,427	19,493
10543	Mamaroneck	(914)	18,929	19,237
11949	Manorville (c)	(631)	14,314	—
11758	Massapequa (c)	(516)	21,685	—
11762	Massapequa Park	(516)	17,008	17,150
13662	Massena	(315)	10,936	10,813
11950	Mastic (c)	(631)	15,481	—
11951	Mastic Beach[1]	(631)	12,930	14,860
11763	Medford (c)	(631)	24,142	—
11747	Melville (c)	(631)	18,985	—
11566	Merrick (c)	(516)	22,097	—
11953	Middle Island (c)	(631)	10,483	—
*10940	Middletown	(845)	28,086	27,783
11764	Miller Place (c)	(631)	12,339	—
11501	Mineola	(516)	18,799	18,957
10952	Monsey (c)	(845)	18,412	—
10549	Mount Kisco	(914)	10,877	11,067
11766	Mount Sinai (c)	(631)	12,118	—
*10550	Mount Vernon	(914)	67,292	68,224
10954	Nanuet (c)	(845)	17,882	—
11767	Nesconset (c)	(631)	13,387	—
11590	New Cassel (c)	(516)	14,059	—
10956	New City (c)	(845)	33,559	—
*10801	New Rochelle	(914)	77,062	79,446
*10001	New York	(212)/(718)	8,175,133	8,405,837
*12550	Newburgh	(845)	28,866	28,480
*14301	Niagara Falls	(716)	50,193	49,468
11701	North Amityville (c)	(631)	17,862	—
11703	North Babylon (c)	(631)	17,509	—
11706	North Bay Shore (c)	(631)	18,944	—
11710	North Bellmore (c)	(516)	19,941	—
11713	North Bellport (c)	(631)	11,545	—
11757	North Lindenhurst (c)	(631)	11,652	—
11758	North Massapequa (c)	(516)	17,886	—
11566	North Merrick (c)	(516)	12,272	—
11040	North New Hyde Park (c)	(516)	14,899	—
14120	North Tonawanda	(716)	31,568	31,097
11580	North Valley Stream (c)	(516)	16,628	—
11793	North Wantagh (c)	(516)	11,960	—
11572	Oceanside (c)	(516)	32,109	—
13669	Ogdensburg	(315)	11,128	11,011
14760	Olean	(585)/(716)	14,452	14,152
13421	Oneida	(315)	11,393	11,262
13820	Oneonta	(607)	13,901	13,946
10562	Ossining	(914)	25,060	25,382
13126	Oswego	(315)	18,142	18,126
11772	Patchogue	(631)	11,798	12,253
10965	Pearl River (c)	(845)	15,876	—
10566	Peekskill	(914)	23,583	23,988
11803	Plainview (c)	(516)	26,217	—
*12901	Plattsburgh	(518)	19,989	19,898
10573	Port Chester	(914)	28,967	29,410
11050	Port Washington (c)	(516)	15,846	—
*12601	Poughkeepsie	(845)	32,736	30,639
11961	Ridge (c)	(631)	13,336	—
11901	Riverhead (c)	(631)	13,299	—
*14604	Rochester	(585)	210,565	210,358
11571	Rockville Centre	(516)	24,023	24,110
11778	Rocky Point (c)	(631)	14,014	—
*13440	Rome	(315)	33,725	32,837
11779	Ronkonkoma (c)	(631)	19,082	—
11575	Roosevelt (c)	(516)	16,258	—
12303	Rotterdam (c)	(518)	20,652	—
10580	Rye	(914)	15,720	15,960
11780	Saint James (c)	(631)	13,338	—
13454	Salisbury (c)	(315)	12,093	—
12866	Saratoga Springs	(518)	26,586	27,315
11782	Sayville (c)	(631)	16,853	—
*10583	Scarsdale	(914)	17,166	17,605
*12305	Schenectady	(518)	66,135	65,902
11783	Seaford (c)	(516)	15,294	—
11784	Selden (c)	(631)	19,851	—
11733	Setauket-East Setauket (c)	(631)	15,477	—
11967	Shirley (c)	(631)	27,854	—
10591	Sleepy Hollow (c)	(914)	9,870	10,017
11787	Smithtown (c)	(631)	26,470	—
11735	South Farmingdale (c)	(516)	14,486	—
10977	Spring Valley	(845)	31,347	32,359
*11790	Stony Brook (c)	(631)	13,740	—
10980	Stony Point (c)	(845)	12,147	—
*10901	Suffern (c)	(845)	10,723	10,929
11791	Syosset (c)	(516)	18,829	—
*13202	Syracuse	(315)	145,170	144,669
10591	Tarrytown	(914)	11,277	11,483
11776	Terryville (c)	(631)	11,849	—

ZIP	Place	Area code	2010 population	2013 estimate
*14150	Tonawanda	(716)	15,130	14,990
*14150	Tonawanda (c)	(716)	58,144	—
*12180	Troy	(518)	50,129	49,974
11553	Uniondale (c)	(516)	24,759	—
*13501	Utica	(315)	62,235	61,808
*11580	Valley Stream	(516)	37,511	37,659
11793	Wantagh (c)	(516)	18,871	—
*13601	Watertown	(315)	27,023	27,823
12189	Watervliet	(518)	10,254	10,236
*11704	West Babylon (c)	(631)	43,213	—
10993	West Haverstraw	(845)	10,165	10,359
11552	West Hempstead (c)	(516)	18,862	—
11795	West Islip (c)	(631)	28,335	—
*14224	West Seneca (c)	(716)	44,711	—
*11590	Westbury	(516)	15,146	15,242
10601	White Plains	(914)	56,853	57,866
11797	Woodbury (c)	(516)	10,686	10,730
11598	Woodmere (c)	(516)	17,121	—
11798	Wyandanch (c)	(631)	11,647	—
*10701	Yonkers	(914)	195,976	199,766

(1) Place was incorporated after the 2010 Census was conducted. Data in 2010 column is for Mastic Beach CDP.

North Carolina

Area code 980 overlays area code 704. Area code 984 overlays area code 919.

ZIP	Place	Area code	2010 population	2013 estimate
28315	Albemarle	(910)	15,903	16,007
*27502	Apex	(919)	37,476	42,214
27263	Archdale	(336)	11,415	11,554
*27203	Asheboro	(336)	25,012	25,913
*28801	Asheville	(828)	83,393	87,236
28012	Belmont	(704)	10,076	10,412
*28607	Boone	(828)	17,122	18,211
*27215	Burlington	(336)	49,963	51,510
27510	Carrboro	(919)	19,582	20,908
*27511	Cary	(919)	135,234	151,088
*27514	Chapel Hill	(919)	57,233	59,635
*28204	Charlotte	(704)	731,424	792,862
27520	Clayton	(919)	16,116	17,694
27012	Clemmons	(336)	18,627	19,329
*28025	Concord	(704)	79,066	83,506
28031	Cornelius	(704)	24,866	26,898
*28036	Davidson	(704)	10,944	11,750
*27701	Durham	(919)	228,330	245,475
*27288	Eden	(336)	15,527	15,488
*27909	Elizabeth City	(252)	18,683	18,266
*28301	Fayetteville	(910)	200,564	204,408
27526	Fuquay-Varina	(919)	17,937	21,277
27529	Garner	(919)	25,745	26,772
*28052	Gastonia	(704)	71,741	73,209
27530	Goldsboro	(919)	36,437	36,306
27253	Graham	(336)	14,153	14,280
*27401	Greensboro	(336)	269,666	279,639
*27834	Greenville	(252)	84,554	89,130
28075	Harrisburg	(704)	11,526	13,788
*28532	Havelock	(252)	20,735	20,940
27536	Henderson	(252)	15,368	15,345
*28739	Hendersonville	(828)	13,137	13,466
*28601	Hickory	(828)	40,010	40,361
*27260	High Point	(336)	104,371	107,741
27540	Holly Springs	(919)	24,661	28,915
28348	Hope Mills (c)	(910)	15,176	16,248
*28078	Huntersville	(704)	46,773	50,458
28079	Indian Trail	(704)	33,518	35,494
*28540	Jacksonville	(910)	70,145	69,079
*28081	Kannapolis	(704)	42,625	44,359
*27284	Kernersville	(336)	23,123	23,567
28086	Kings Mountain	(704)	10,296	10,649
*28502	Kinston	(252)	21,677	21,641
27545	Knightdale	(919)	11,401	13,291
*28352	Laurinburg	(910)	15,962	15,774
28451	Leland	(910)	13,527	16,022
*28645	Lenoir	(828)	18,228	18,042
27023	Lewisville	(336)	12,639	13,216
*27292	Lexington	(336)	18,931	18,993
28092	Lincolnton	(704)	10,486	10,743
28358	Lumberton	(910)	21,542	21,823
28105	Matthews	(704)	27,198	29,384
27302	Mebane	(919)	11,393	12,981
28227	Mint Hill	(704)	22,722	24,543
*28110	Monroe	(704)	32,797	33,975
28115	Mooresville	(704)	32,711	34,887
*28655	Morganton	(828)	16,918	16,807
27560	Morrisville	(919)	18,576	21,932
*27030	Mount Airy	(336)	10,388	10,417
28120	Mount Holly	(704)	13,656	13,904
28411	Murraysville (c)	(910)	14,215	—
*28562	New Bern	(252)	29,524	30,242
28658	Newton	(828)	12,968	13,043
*28374	Pinehurst	(910)	13,124	15,255
28399	Piney Green (c)	(910)	13,293	—
*27601	Raleigh	(919)	403,892	431,746

ZIP	Place	Area code	2010 population	2013 estimate
*27320	Reidsville	(336)	14,520	14,162
27870	Roanoke Rapids	(252)	15,754	15,623
*27801	Rocky Mount	(252)	57,477	56,954
*28144	Salisbury	(704)	33,662	33,604
*27330	Sanford	(919)	28,094	29,470
*28150	Shelby	(704)	20,323	20,325
27577	Smithfield	(919)	10,966	11,560
*28387	Southern Pines	(910)	12,334	13,005
*28390	Spring Lake	(910)	11,964	13,037
28104	Stallings	(704)	13,831	14,645
*28677	Statesville	(704)	24,532	25,432
27358	Summerfield	(336)	10,232	10,614
27886	Tarboro	(252)	11,415	11,348
*27360	Thomasville	(336)	26,757	26,968
*27587	Wake Forest	(919)	30,117	34,752
28173	Waxhaw	(704)	9,859	11,295
28104	Weddington	(704)	9,459	10,101
*28401	Wilmington	(910)	106,476	112,067
*27893	Wilson	(252)	49,167	49,628
*27101	Winston-Salem	(336)	229,617	236,441

North Dakota
Area code 701 applies to the entire state.

ZIP	Place	2010 population	2013 estimate
*58501	Bismarck	61,272	67,034
*58601	Dickinson	17,787	20,826
*58102	Fargo	105,549	113,658
*58201	Grand Forks	52,838	54,932
*58401	Jamestown	15,427	15,440
58554	Mandan	18,331	19,887
*58701	Minot	40,888	46,321
58078	West Fargo	25,830	29,878
*58801	Williston	14,716	20,850

Ohio
Area code 220 overlays area code 740 as of Apr. 22, 2015. Area code 234 overlays area code 330. Area code 567 overlays area code 419.

ZIP	Place	Area code	2010 population	2013 estimate
*44301	Akron	(330)	199,110	198,100
44601	Alliance	(330)	22,322	22,213
44001	Amherst	(440)	12,021	12,112
44805	Ashland	(419)	20,362	20,337
*44004	Ashtabula	(440)	19,124	18,673
45701	Athens	(740)	23,832	24,122
44202	Aurora	(330)	15,548	15,577
44515	Austintown (c)	(330)	29,677	—
44011	Avon	(440)	21,193	22,017
44012	Avon Lake	(440)	22,581	22,998
44203	Barberton	(330)	26,550	26,337
44140	Bay Village	(440)	15,651	15,474
44122	Beachwood	(216)	11,953	11,837
45434	Beavercreek	(937)	45,193	45,712
44146	Bedford	(216)/(440)	13,074	12,875
*44146	Bedford Heights	(216)/(440)	10,751	10,693
43311	Bellefontaine	(937)	13,370	13,193
44017	Berea	(440)	19,093	19,015
43209	Bexley	(614)	13,057	13,445
*45242	Blue Ash	(513)	12,114	12,139
*44512	Boardman (c)	(330)	35,376	—
*43402	Bowling Green	(419)	30,028	31,802
44141	Brecksville	(440)	13,656	13,533
45211	Bridgetown (c)	(513)	14,407	—
44147	Broadview Heights	(440)	19,400	19,330
44142	Brook Park	(216)/(440)	19,212	18,986
44144	Brooklyn	(216)	11,169	11,001
44212	Brunswick	(330)	34,255	34,544
44820	Bucyrus	(419)	12,362	12,077
*43725	Cambridge	(740)	10,635	10,518
*44703	Canton	(330)	73,007	72,535
*45822	Celina	(419)	10,400	10,376
*45458	Centerville	(937)	23,999	23,965
45601	Chillicothe	(740)	21,901	21,899
*45202	Cincinnati	(513)	296,943	297,517
43113	Circleville	(740)	13,314	13,444
45315	Clayton	(937)	13,209	13,213
*44102	Cleveland	(216)	396,815	390,113
44118	Cleveland Heights	(216)	46,121	45,394
*43201	Columbus	(614)	787,033	822,553
44030	Conneaut	(440)	12,841	12,877
43812	Coshocton	(740)	11,216	11,204
44221	Cuyahoga Falls	(330)	49,652	49,267
*45401	Dayton	(937)	141,527	143,355
43512	Defiance	(419)	16,494	16,836
43015	Delaware	(740)	34,753	36,459
*45247	Dent (c)	(513)	10,497	—
44622	Dover	(330)	12,826	12,854
*43016	Dublin	(614)/(740)	41,751	43,607
*44112	East Cleveland	(216)	17,843	17,520
43920	East Liverpool	(330)	11,195	11,010
*44095	Eastlake	(440)	18,577	18,418
*44035	Elyria	(440)	54,533	53,956
45322	Englewood	(937)	13,465	13,470
*44117	Euclid	(216)	48,920	48,139
45324	Fairborn	(937)	32,352	33,213
*45011	Fairfield	(513)	42,510	42,635
44126	Fairview Park	(440)	16,826	16,571
*45839	Findlay	(419)	41,202	41,512
*45224	Finneytown (c)	(513)	12,741	—
45240	Forest Park	(513)	18,720	18,721
45230	Forestville (c)	(513)	10,532	—
44830	Fostoria	(419)	13,441	13,244
45005	Franklin	(513)	11,771	11,829
43420	Fremont	(419)	16,734	16,446
43230	Gahanna	(614)	33,248	34,051
44833	Galion	(419)	10,512	10,273
*44125	Garfield Heights	(216)	28,849	28,378
44232	Green	(330)	25,699	25,943
45331	Greenville	(937)	13,227	13,073
43123	Grove City	(614)	35,575	37,490
*45011	Hamilton	(513)	62,477	62,258
45030	Harrison	(513)	9,897	10,292
43056	Heath	(740)	10,310	10,452
43026	Hilliard	(614)/(740)	28,435	31,012
45424	Huber Heights	(937)	38,101	38,142
*44236	Hudson	(330)	22,262	22,474
45638	Ironton	(740)	11,129	11,062
*44240	Kent	(330)	28,904	32,345
*45429	Kettering	(937)	56,163	55,870
44107	Lakewood	(216)	52,131	51,143
43130	Lancaster	(740)	38,780	39,325
45036	Lebanon	(513)	20,033	20,476
*45801	Lima	(419)	38,771	38,355
*44052	Lorain	(440)	64,097	63,710
*45140	Loveland	(513)	12,081	12,326
44124	Lyndhurst	(216)/(440)	14,001	13,791
*44056	Macedonia	(330)	11,188	11,478
*45248	Mack (c)	(513)	11,585	—
*44901	Mansfield	(419)	47,821	46,454
*44137	Maple Heights	(216)	23,138	22,784
45750	Marietta	(740)	14,085	14,053
*43302	Marion	(740)	36,837	36,772
*43040	Marysville	(937)	22,094	22,396
45040	Mason	(513)	30,712	31,282
*44646	Massillon	(330)	32,149	32,183
43537	Maumee	(419)	14,286	14,104
44124	Mayfield Heights	(440)	19,155	18,938
*44256	Medina	(330)	26,678	26,570
*44060	Mentor	(440)	47,159	46,979
*45343	Miamisburg	(937)	20,181	20,129
44130	Middleburg Heights	(216)/(440)	15,946	15,802
*45042	Middletown	(513)	48,694	48,630
45211	Monfort Heights (c)	(513)	11,948	—
*45050	Monroe	(513)	12,442	13,061
45242	Montgomery	(513)	10,251	10,366
43050	Mount Vernon	(740)	16,990	16,798
44216	New Franklin	(330)	14,227	14,307
44663	New Philadelphia	(330)	17,288	17,396
43055	Newark	(740)	47,573	47,777
44446	Niles	(330)	19,266	18,924
44720	North Canton	(330)	17,488	17,496
44070	North Olmsted	(440)	32,718	32,292
44039	North Ridgeville	(440)	29,465	31,269
44133	North Royalton	(440)	30,444	30,367
45239	Northbrook (c)	(513)	10,668	—
44203	Norton	(330)	12,085	12,050
44857	Norwalk	(419)	17,012	16,833
*45212	Norwood	(513)	19,207	19,059
*43616	Oregon	(419)	20,291	20,233
45056	Oxford	(513)	21,371	21,470
44077	Painesville	(440)	19,563	19,933
*44129	Parma	(216)/(440)	81,601	80,429
44130	Parma Heights	(216)/(440)	20,718	20,437
43062	Pataskala	(740)	14,962	15,160
*43551	Perrysburg	(419)	20,623	21,377
43147	Pickerington	(614)/(740)	18,291	19,085
45356	Piqua	(937)	20,522	20,699
*45662	Portsmouth	(740)	20,226	20,430
43065	Powell	(614)	11,500	12,237
44266	Ravenna	(330)	11,724	11,556
*45215	Reading	(513)	10,385	10,354
43068	Reynoldsburg	(614)/(740)	35,893	36,526
44143	Richmond Heights	(216)/(440)	10,546	10,504
45431	Riverside	(937)	25,201	25,101
44116	Rocky River	(440)	20,213	19,988
44460	Salem	(330)	12,303	12,130
*44870	Sandusky	(419)	25,793	25,340
44131	Seven Hills	(216)/(440)	11,804	11,730
*44122	Shaker Heights	(216)	28,448	27,935
45241	Sharonville	(513)	13,560	13,519
*45365	Sidney	(937)	21,229	21,006
44139	Solon	(440)	23,348	23,155
44121	South Euclid	(216)	22,295	21,968
45066	Springboro	(513)	17,409	17,860
45246	Springdale	(513)	11,223	11,216
*45501	Springfield	(937)	60,608	59,357

ZIP	Place	Area code	2010 population	2013 estimate
*43952	Steubenville	(740)	18,659	18,355
44224	Stow	(330)	34,837	34,768
44241	Streetsboro	(330)	16,028	16,130
*44136	Strongsville	(440)	44,750	44,730
44471	Struthers	(330)	10,713	10,498
43560	Sylvania	(419)	18,965	18,935
44278	Tallmadge	(330)	17,537	17,536
44883	Tiffin	(419)	17,963	17,832
*43601	Toledo	(419)	287,208	282,313
45067	Trenton	(513)	11,869	12,191
*45426	Trotwood	(937)	24,431	24,246
*45373	Troy	(937)	25,058	25,445
44087	Twinsburg	(330)	18,795	18,864
*44122	University Heights	(216)	13,539	13,394
*43221	Upper Arlington	(614)	33,771	34,420
43078	Urbana	(937)	11,793	11,629
45891	Van Wert	(419)	10,846	10,774
45377	Vandalia	(937)	15,246	15,175
*44089	Vermilion	(440)	10,594	10,490
*44281	Wadsworth	(330)	21,567	21,842
*44481	Warren	(330)	41,557	40,768
*44122	Warrensville Heights	(216)	13,542	13,350
43160	Washington Court House	(740)	14,192	14,095
*45449	West Carrollton	(937)	13,143	13,054
*43081	Westerville	(614)	36,120	37,530
44145	Westlake	(440)	32,729	32,471
*45239	White Oak (c)	(513)	19,167	—
43213	Whitehall	(614)	18,062	18,503
44092	Wickliffe	(440)	12,750	12,640
*44094	Willoughby	(440)	22,268	22,458
44095	Willowick	(440)	14,171	14,061
45177	Wilmington	(937)	12,520	12,459
44691	Wooster	(330)	26,119	26,384
43085	Worthington	(614)	13,575	13,837
45385	Xenia	(937)	25,719	25,879
*44501	Youngstown	(330)	66,982	65,184
*43701	Zanesville	(740)	25,487	25,435

Oklahoma
Area code 539 overlays area code 918.

ZIP	Place	Area code	2010 population	2013 estimate
*74820	Ada	(580)	16,810	17,140
*73521	Altus	(580)	19,813	19,591
*73401	Ardmore	(580)	24,283	24,950
*74003	Bartlesville	(918)	35,750	36,258
73008	Bethany	(405)	19,051	19,563
74008	Bixby	(918)	20,884	23,228
*74012	Broken Arrow	(918)	98,850	103,500
*73018	Chickasha	(405)	16,036	16,374
73020	Choctaw	(405)	11,146	11,843
*74017	Claremore	(918)	18,581	19,032
*73115	Del City	(405)	21,332	21,990
*73533	Duncan	(580)	23,431	23,400
*74701	Durant	(580)	15,856	16,891
*73034	Edmond	(405)	81,405	87,004
*73036	El Reno	(405)	16,749	17,857
*73644	Elk City	(580)	11,693	12,606
*73701	Enid	(580)	49,379	50,725
*74033	Glenpool	(918)	10,808	11,617
73044	Guthrie	(405)	10,191	10,908
73942	Guymon	(580)	11,442	12,272
74037	Jenks	(918)	16,924	18,670
*73501	Lawton	(580)	96,867	97,151
*74501	McAlester	(918)	18,383	18,301
*74354	Miami	(918)	13,570	13,758
*73110	Midwest City	(405)	54,371	56,756
*73160	Moore	(405)	55,081	58,414
*74401	Muskogee	(918)	39,223	38,863
73064	Mustang	(405)	17,395	19,097
*73069	Norman	(405)	110,925	118,197
*73102	Oklahoma City	(405)	579,999	610,613
74447	Okmulgee	(918)	12,321	12,373
*74055	Owasso	(918)	28,915	32,472
*74601	Ponca City	(580)	25,387	24,879
74063	Sand Springs	(918)	18,906	19,339
*74066	Sapulpa	(918)	20,544	20,836
*74801	Shawnee	(405)	29,857	30,975
*74074	Stillwater	(405)	45,688	47,186
*74464	Tahlequah	(918)	15,753	16,359
*74103	Tulsa	(918)	391,906	398,121
*73112	Warr Acres	(405)	10,043	10,380
73096	Weatherford	(580)	10,833	11,862
*73801	Woodward	(580)	12,051	12,758
*73099	Yukon	(405)	22,709	24,826

Oregon
Area code 458 overlays area code 541. Area code 971 overlays area code 503.

ZIP	Place	Area code	2010 population	2013 estimate
*97321	Albany	(541)	50,158	51,583
*97006	Aloha (c)	(503)	49,425	—
97601	Altamont (c)	(541)	19,257	—
97520	Ashland	(541)	20,078	20,713
*97005	Beaverton	(503)	89,803	93,542
*97701	Bend	(541)	76,639	81,236
97229	Bethany (c)	(503)	20,646	—
97013	Canby	(503)	15,829	16,866
97291	Cedar Mill (c)	(503)	14,546	—
97502	Central Point	(541)	17,169	17,600
97420	Coos Bay	(541)	15,967	15,946
97113	Cornelius	(503)	11,869	12,161
*97333	Corvallis	(541)	54,462	55,298
97338	Dallas	(503)	14,583	14,807
*97009	Damascus	(503)	10,539	10,743
*97401	Eugene	(541)	156,185	159,190
97116	Forest Grove	(503)	21,083	22,419
97301	Four Corners (c)	(503)	15,947	—
97027	Gladstone	(503)	11,497	11,724
*97526	Grants Pass	(541)	34,533	35,076
*97030	Gresham	(503)	105,594	109,397
*97015	Happy Valley	(503)	13,903	16,321
97303	Hayesville (c)	(503)	19,936	—
97838	Hermiston	(541)	16,745	17,107
*97123	Hillsboro	(503)	91,611	97,368
97307	Keizer	(503)	36,478	37,064
*97601	Klamath Falls	(541)	20,840	21,207
97850	La Grande	(541)	13,082	13,074
*97034	Lake Oswego	(503)	36,619	37,610
97355	Lebanon	(541)	15,518	15,930
97741	McMinnville	(541)	32,187	33,131
*97501	Medford	(541)	74,907	77,677
*97269	Milwaukie	(503)	20,291	20,512
97132	Newberg	(503)	22,068	22,508
97365	Newport	(541)	9,989	10,117
97268	Oak Grove (c)	(503)	16,629	—
97006	Oak Hills (c)	(503)	11,333	—
97267	Oatfield (c)	(503)	13,415	—
97914	Ontario	(541)	11,366	11,091
97045	Oregon City	(503)	31,859	34,622
97801	Pendleton	(541)	16,612	16,935
*97201	Portland	(503)	583,776	609,456
97756	Redmond	(541)	26,215	27,427
97470	Roseburg	(541)	21,181	21,968
97051	Saint Helens	(503)	12,883	13,060
*97301	Salem	(503)	154,637	160,614
97055	Sandy	(503)	9,570	10,014
97140	Sherwood	(503)	18,194	18,884
*97477	Springfield	(541)	59,403	60,177
*97058	The Dalles	(541)	13,620	15,158
*97223	Tigard	(503)	48,035	50,444
97060	Troutdale	(503)	15,962	16,487
97062	Tualatin	(503)	26,054	26,879
97068	West Linn	(503)	25,109	25,992
97070	Wilsonville	(503)	19,509	21,484
97071	Woodburn	(503)	24,080	24,395

Pennsylvania
Area code 267 overlays area code 215. Area code 272 overlays area code 570. Area code 484 overlays area code 610. Area code 878 overlays area code 412.

ZIP	Place	Area code	2010 population	2013 estimate
*18101	Allentown	(610)	118,032	118,577
15101	Allison Park (c)	(412)/(724)	21,552	—
*16601	Altoona	(814)	46,320	45,796
19003	Ardmore (c)	(610)	12,455	—
15234	Baldwin	(412)	19,767	19,812
18603	Berwick	(570)	10,477	10,343
15102	Bethel Park	(412)	32,313	32,391
*18016	Bethlehem	(610)	74,982	75,018
*17815	Bloomsburg	(570)	14,855	14,519
19008	Broomall (c)	(610)	10,789	—
*16001	Butler	(724)	13,757	13,562
*17013	Carlisle	(717)	18,682	18,927
15108	Carnot-Moon (c)	(412)	11,372	—
17201	Chambersburg	(717)	20,268	20,508
*19013	Chester	(610)	33,972	34,046
19320	Coatesville	(610)	13,100	13,133
17109	Colonial Park (c)	(717)	13,229	—
17512	Columbia	(717)	10,400	10,382
19023	Darby	(610)	10,687	10,687
19026	Drexel Hill (c)	(610)	28,043	—
*18512	Dunmore	(570)	14,057	13,966
*18042	Easton	(610)	26,800	27,073
17022	Elizabethtown	(717)	11,545	11,648
*18049	Emmaus	(610)	11,211	11,296
17522	Ephrata	(717)	13,394	13,516
*16501	Erie	(814)	101,786	100,671
16063	Fernway (c)	(724)	12,414	—
15237	Franklin Park	(412)	13,470	14,030
18052	Fullerton (c)	(610)	14,925	—
*15601	Greensburg	(724)	14,892	14,660
*17331	Hanover	(717)	15,289	15,365

ZIP	Place	Area code	2010 population	2013 estimate
*17101	Harrisburg	(717)	49,528	49,188
*18201	Hazleton	(570)	25,340	25,083
16148	Hermitage	(724)	16,220	16,190
17033	Hershey (c)	(717)	14,257	—
19044	Horsham (c)	(215)	14,842	—
*15701	Indiana	(724)	13,975	14,055
15025	Jefferson Hills	(412)	10,619	11,121
*15901	Johnstown	(814)	20,978	20,402
*19406	King of Prussia (c)	(610)	19,936	—
18704	Kingston	(570)	13,182	13,074
*17601	Lancaster	(717)	59,322	59,325
19446	Lansdale	(215)	16,269	16,408
19050	Lansdowne	(610)	10,620	10,627
*17042	Lebanon	(717)	25,477	25,524
*19055	Levittown (c)	(215)	52,983	—
17745	Lock Haven	(570)	9,772	10,025
15068	Lower Burrell	(724)	11,761	11,629
*15134	McKeesport	(412)	19,731	19,645
*16335	Meadville	(814)	13,388	13,265
*15146	Monroeville	(412)/(724)	28,386	28,400
18936	Montgomeryville (c)	(215)	12,624	—
18707	Mountain Top (c)	(570)	10,982	—
15120	Munhall	(412)	11,406	11,356
*15668	Murraysville	(412)/(724)	20,079	20,253
18634	Nanticoke	(570)	10,465	10,366
*16108	New Castle	(724)	23,273	22,748
15068	New Kensington	(724)	13,116	12,911
*19403	Norristown	(610)	34,324	34,432
16301	Oil City	(814)	10,557	10,321
*19104	Philadelphia	(215)	1,526,006	1,553,165
*19460	Phoenixville	(610)	16,440	16,520
*15201	Pittsburgh	(412)	305,704	305,841
15239	Plum	(412)	27,126	27,505
*19464	Pottstown	(610)	22,377	22,562
17901	Pottsville	(570)	14,324	14,095
*19601	Reading	(610)	88,082	87,893
15857	Saint Marys	(814)	13,070	12,909
*18505	Scranton	(570)	76,089	75,806
*16146	Sharon	(724)	14,038	13,760
17404	Shiloh (c)	(717)	11,218	—
15129	South Park Twp. (c)	(814)	13,416	—
*16801	State College	(814)	42,034	41,757
15401	Uniontown	(724)	10,372	10,182
15241	Upper Saint Clair (c)	(412)	19,229	—
15301	Washington	(724)	13,663	13,725
*17268	Waynesboro	(717)	10,568	10,714
17315	Weigelstown (c)	(717)	12,875	—
*19380	West Chester	(610)	18,461	18,968
*15122	West Mifflin	(412)	20,313	20,253
18052	Whitehall	(412)	13,944	13,935
*18701	Wilkes-Barre	(570)	41,498	41,108
15221	Wilkinsburg	(412)	15,930	15,882
*17701	Williamsport	(570)	29,381	29,349
19090	Willow Grove (c)	(215)	15,726	—
19610	Wyomissing	(610)	10,461	10,481
19050	Yeadon	(610)	11,443	11,510
*17401	York	(717)	43,718	43,935

Rhode Island

Area code 401 applies to the entire state. See introductory note.

ZIP	Place	2010 population	2013 estimate
02806	Barrington	16,310	16,293
02809	Bristol	22,954	22,385
*02830	Burrillville	15,955	16,109
02863	Central Falls	19,376	19,416
*02816	Coventry	35,014	34,935
*02905	Cranston	80,387	80,566
02864	Cumberland	33,506	34,055
02818	East Greenwich	13,146	13,131
02914	East Providence	47,037	47,149
02919	Johnston	28,769	29,045
*02865	Lincoln	21,105	21,299
02842	Middletown	16,150	16,154
*02882	Narragansett	15,868	15,706
*02840	Newport	24,672	24,027
02843	Newport East (c)	11,769	—
02852	North Kingstown	26,486	26,184
*02908	North Providence	32,078	32,238
02896	North Smithfield	11,967	12,178
*02860	Pawtucket	71,148	71,172
02871	Portsmouth	17,389	17,383
*02904	Providence	178,042	177,994
02857	Scituate	10,329	10,433
*02917	Smithfield	21,430	21,410
*02879	South Kingstown	30,639	30,615
02878	Tiverton	15,780	15,858
*02864	Valley Falls (c)	11,547	—
02885	Warren	10,611	10,542
*02886	Warwick	82,672	81,971
02893	West Warwick	29,191	28,893
02891	Westerly	22,787	22,657

ZIP	Place	2010 population	2013 estimate
02891	Westerly (c)	17,936	—
02895	Woonsocket	41,186	41,026

South Carolina

Area code 854 overlays area code 843 effective Oct. 19, 2015.

ZIP	Place	Area code	2010 population	2013 estimate
*29801	Aiken	(803)	29,524	30,296
*29621	Anderson	(864)	26,686	26,985
*29906	Beaufort	(843)	12,361	12,967
29611	Berea (c)	(864)	14,295	—
*29910	Bluffton	(843)	12,530	13,606
29033	Cayce	(803)	12,528	12,860
*29401	Charleston	(843)	120,083	127,999
*29631	Clemson	(864)	13,905	14,276
*29201	Columbia	(803)	129,272	133,358
*29526	Conway	(843)	17,103	19,300
29204	Dentsville (c)	(803)	14,062	—
*29640	Easley	(864)	19,993	20,300
*29681	Five Forks (c)	(864)	14,140	—
*29501	Florence	(843)	37,056	37,792
29206	Forest Acres	(803)	10,361	10,560
*29715	Fort Mill	(803)	10,811	12,419
*29341	Gaffney	(864)	12,414	12,657
29605	Gantt (c)	(864)	14,229	—
*29445	Goose Creek	(843)	35,938	39,823
*29601	Greenville	(864)	58,409	61,397
*29646	Greenwood	(864)	23,222	23,379
*29650	Greer	(864)	25,515	27,167
*29406	Hanahan	(843)	17,997	19,597
*29928	Hilton Head Island	(843)	37,099	39,412
29063	Irmo	(803)	11,097	11,742
29412	James Island[1]	(843)	11,187	11,542
*29456	Ladson (c)	(843)	13,790	—
*29072	Lexington	(803)	17,870	19,576
29662	Mauldin	(864)	22,889	24,525
*29464	Mount Pleasant	(843)	67,843	74,885
*29575	Myrtle Beach	(843)	27,109	29,175
29108	Newberry	(803)	10,277	10,256
*29841	North Augusta	(803)	21,348	22,229
*29410	North Charleston	(843)	97,471	104,054
*29582	North Myrtle Beach	(843)	13,752	14,827
29073	Oak Grove (c)	(803)	10,291	—
*29115	Orangeburg	(803)	13,964	13,891
29611	Parker (c)	(864)	11,431	—
29935	Port Royal	(843)	10,678	11,542
29020	Red Hill (c)	(843)	13,223	—
*29730	Rock Hill	(803)	66,154	69,103
29417	Saint Andrews (c)	(843)	20,493	—
29210	Seven Oaks (c)	(803)	15,144	—
*29681	Simpsonville	(864)	18,238	19,615
29577	Socastee (c)	(843)	19,952	—
*29306	Spartanburg	(864)	37,013	37,647
*29483	Summerville	(843)	43,392	46,074
*29150	Sumter	(803)	40,524	41,190
29687	Taylors (c)	(864)	21,617	—
29607	Wade Hampton (c)	(864)	20,622	—
*29169	West Columbia	(803)	14,988	15,824

(1) Place was incorporated after the 2010 Census was conducted. Data in 2010 column is Census Bureau estimate.

South Dakota

Area code 605 applies to the entire state.

ZIP	Place	2010 population	2013 estimate
*57401	Aberdeen	26,091	27,333
*57006	Brookings	22,056	22,943
*57350	Huron	12,592	13,097
57301	Mitchell	15,254	15,539
57501	Pierre	13,646	13,984
*57701	Rapid City	67,956	70,812
*57103	Sioux Falls	153,888	164,676
*57783	Spearfish	10,494	11,107
57069	Vermillion	10,571	10,692
57201	Watertown	21,482	21,995
57078	Yankton	14,454	14,591

Tennessee

Area code 629 overlays area code 615 effective Mar. 28, 2015.

ZIP	Place	Area code	2010 population	2013 estimate
38002	Arlington	(901)	11,517	11,664
*37303	Athens	(423)	13,458	13,623
*38133	Bartlett	(901)	54,613	58,226
*37027	Brentwood	(615)	37,060	40,021
*37620	Bristol	(423)	26,702	26,626
38012	Brownsville	(731)	10,292	10,022
*37402	Chattanooga	(423)	167,674	173,366

ZIP	Place	Area code	2010 population	2013 estimate
*37040	Clarksville	(931)	132,929	142,357
*37311	Cleveland	(423)	41,285	42,774
*38017	Collierville	(901)	43,965	47,333
*38401	Columbia	(931)	34,681	35,558
*38501	Cookeville	(931)	30,435	31,135
*38555	Crossville	(931)	10,795	11,246
*37055	Dickson	(615)	14,538	14,952
*38024	Dyersburg	(731)	17,145	17,002
37412	East Ridge	(423)	20,979	21,382
*37643	Elizabethton	(423)	14,176	14,359
*37922	Farragut	(865)	20,676	21,390
*37064	Franklin	(615)	62,487	68,886
37066	Gallatin	(615)	30,278	32,307
*38138	Germantown	(901)	38,844	39,375
*37072	Goodlettsville	(615)	15,921	16,813
*37743	Greeneville	(423)	15,062	15,020
*37075	Hendersonville	(615)	51,372	54,068
38301	Jackson	(731)	65,211	67,685
*37601	Johnson City	(423)	63,152	65,123
*37660	Kingsport	(423)	48,205	52,962
*37902	Knoxville	(865)	178,874	183,270
*37086	La Vergne	(615)	32,588	34,077
38002	Lakeland	(901)	12,430	12,590
38464	Lawrenceburg	(931)	10,428	10,446
*37087	Lebanon	(615)	26,190	28,408
37091	Lewisburg	(931)	11,100	11,339
37355	Manchester	(931)	10,102	10,261
38237	Martin	(731)	11,473	11,359
37801	Maryville	(865)	27,465	27,992
*37110	McMinnville	(931)	13,605	13,669
*38103	Memphis	(901)	646,889	653,450
37343	Middle Valley (c)	(423)	12,684	—
*38053	Millington	(901)	10,176	11,107
*37813	Morristown	(423)	29,137	29,324
*37122	Mount Juliet	(615)	23,671	28,222
*37130	Murfreesboro	(615)	108,755	117,044
*37201	Nashville-Davidson (balance)	(615)	601,222	634,464
*37830	Oak Ridge	(865)	29,330	29,419
38242	Paris	(731)	10,156	10,166
37148	Portland	(615)	11,480	11,993
37415	Red Bank	(423)	11,651	11,830
*37862	Sevierville	(865)	14,807	16,011
*37865	Seymour (c)	(865)	10,919	—
*37160	Shelbyville	(931)	20,335	20,764
37167	Smyrna	(615)	39,974	43,060
*37379	Soddy-Daisy	(423)	12,714	13,118
37174	Spring Hill	(931)	29,036	32,576
37172	Springfield	(615)	16,440	16,659
*37388	Tullahoma	(931)	18,655	18,837
*38261	Union City	(731)	10,895	10,749
37188	White House	(615)	10,255	10,752

Texas

Area code 346 overlays area codes 281/713/832. Area code 430 overlays area code 903. Area codes 469/972 overlay area code 214. Area code 682 overlays area code 817. Area code 737 overlays area code 512.

ZIP	Place	Area code	2010 population	2013 estimate
*79603	Abilene	(325)	117,063	120,099
75001	Addison	(214)	13,056	15,407
78516	Alamo	(956)	18,353	18,965
77039	Aldine (c)	(713)	15,869	—
*78332	Alice	(361)	19,104	19,576
*75002	Allen	(214)	84,246	92,020
78573	Alton	(956)	12,341	15,050
*77511	Alvin	(713)	24,236	25,057
*79109	Amarillo	(806)	190,695	196,429
79714	Andrews	(432)	11,088	12,718
*77515	Angleton	(979)	18,862	18,988
*76001	Arlington	(817)	365,438	379,577
77346	Atascocita (c)	(281)	65,844	—
*75751	Athens	(903)	12,710	12,803
*78712	Austin	(512)	790,390	885,400
*76020	Azle	(817)	10,947	11,334
*75180	Balch Springs	(214)	23,728	25,024
*77414	Bay City	(979)	17,614	17,509
*77520	Baytown	(713)	71,802	75,418
*77707	Beaumont	(409)	118,296	117,796
76021	Bedford	(817)	46,979	48,592
*78102	Beeville	(361)	12,863	13,290
*77401	Bellaire	(713)	16,855	17,849
*76704	Bellmead	(254)	9,901	10,047
76513	Belton	(254)	18,216	19,572
*76126	Benbrook	(817)	21,234	22,206
*79720	Big Spring	(432)	27,282	28,125
78006	Boerne	(830)	10,471	12,384
75418	Bonham	(903)	10,127	10,005
*79007	Borger	(806)	13,251	13,024
77833	Brenham	(979)	15,716	16,101
*78520	Brownsville	(956)	175,023	181,860
76801	Brownwood	(325)	19,288	18,965
78717	Brushy Creek (c)	(903)	21,764	—

ZIP	Place	Area code	2010 population	2013 estimate
*77801	Bryan	(979)	76,201	78,709
78610	Buda	(512)	7,295	10,209
76354	Burkburnett	(940)	10,811	10,992
*76028	Burleson	(817)	36,690	40,714
*79015	Canyon	(806)	13,303	13,913
*78130	Canyon Lake (c)	(830)	21,262	—
*75006	Carrollton	(214)	119,097	126,700
*75104	Cedar Hill	(214)	45,028	46,663
*78613	Cedar Park	(512)	48,937	61,238
77530	Channelview (c)	(713)	38,289	—
78108	Cibolo	(210)	15,349	23,890
77450	Cinco Ranch (c)	(281)	18,274	—
*76001	Cleburne	(817)	29,337	29,747
77015	Cloverleaf (c)	(713)	22,942	—
77531	Clute	(979)	11,211	11,287
*77840	College Station	(979)	93,857	100,050
76034	Colleyville	(817)	22,807	24,500
*77301	Conroe	(936)	56,207	63,032
78109	Converse	(210)	18,198	20,323
*75019	Coppell	(214)	38,659	40,342
76522	Copperas Cove	(254)	32,032	33,122
*76205	Corinth	(940)	19,935	20,618
*78401	Corpus Christi	(361)	305,215	316,381
*75110	Corsicana	(903)	23,770	23,937
76036	Crowley	(817)	12,838	14,102
*75201	Dallas	(214)	1,197,816	1,257,676
77536	Deer Park	(713)	32,010	33,237
*78840	Del Rio	(830)	35,591	35,589
*75020	Denison	(903)	22,682	22,816
*76201	Denton	(940)	113,383	123,099
*75115	DeSoto	(214)	49,047	51,483
77539	Dickinson	(281)	18,680	19,293
78537	Donna	(956)	15,798	16,270
79029	Dumas	(806)	14,691	14,958
*75138	Duncanville	(214)	38,524	39,605
*78852	Eagle Pass	(830)	26,248	27,708
*78539	Edinburg	(956)	77,100	80,836
77437	El Campo	(979)	11,602	11,486
*79910	El Paso	(915)	649,121	674,433
*75119	Ennis	(214)	18,513	18,711
76039	Euless	(817)	51,277	53,224
*75381	Farmers Branch	(214)	28,616	31,664
*75022	Flower Mound	(214)	64,669	68,609
76119	Forest Hill	(817)	12,355	12,700
75126	Forney	(214)	14,661	16,650
76544	Fort Hood	(254)	29,589	—
*76133	Fort Worth	(817)	741,206	792,727
77498	Four Corners (c)	(281)	12,382	—
78624	Fredericksburg	(830)	10,530	10,829
*77541	Freeport	(979)	12,049	12,093
77545	Fresno (c)	(281)	19,069	—
*77546	Friendswood	(281)	35,805	37,587
*75034	Frisco	(214)	116,989	136,791
*76240	Gainesville	(940)	16,002	16,030
77547	Galena Park	(713)	10,887	11,113
*77550	Galveston	(409)	47,743	48,733
*75040	Garland	(214)	226,876	234,566
*76528	Gatesville	(254)	15,751	15,945
*78626	Georgetown	(512)	47,400	54,898
75154	Glenn Heights	(214)	11,278	11,763
*75051	Grand Prairie	(214)	175,396	183,372
*76051	Grapevine	(817)	46,334	50,195
77479	Greatwood (c)	(281)	11,538	—
*75401	Greenville	(903)	25,557	25,917
77619	Groves	(409)	16,144	15,804
*76117	Haltom City	(817)	42,409	43,580
*76548	Harker Heights	(254)	26,700	28,169
*78550	Harlingen	(956)	64,849	65,665
*75652	Henderson	(903)	13,712	13,700
79045	Hereford	(806)	15,370	15,210
76643	Hewitt	(254)	13,549	14,054
78557	Hidalgo	(956)	11,198	13,273
75067	Highland Village	(214)	15,056	15,747
*79927	Horizon City	(915)	16,735	18,997
*77002	Houston	(713)	2,099,451	2,195,914
*77338	Humble	(713)	15,133	15,500
*76053	Hurst	(817)	37,337	38,448
78634	Hutto	(512)	14,698	19,728
*75062	Irving	(214)	216,290	228,653
77029	Jacinto City	(281)	10,553	10,749
75766	Jacksonville	(903)	14,544	14,713
78729	Jollyville (c)	(512)	16,151	—
*77449	Katy	(713)	14,102	15,013
*76248	Keller	(817)	39,627	42,907
*78028	Kerrville	(830)	22,347	22,663
*75662	Kilgore	(903)	12,975	14,518
*76541	Killeen	(254)	127,921	137,147
*78363	Kingsville	(361)	26,213	26,312
78640	Kyle	(512)	28,016	31,760
78572	La Homa (c)	(956)	11,985	—
*77568	La Marque	(409)	14,509	15,154
*77571	La Porte	(713)	33,800	34,654
*77566	Lake Jackson	(979)	26,849	27,394
*78734	Lakeway	(512)	11,391	13,168

ZIP	Place	Area code	2010 population	2013 estimate
*75146	Lancaster	(214)	36,361	38,071
*78041	Laredo	(956)	236,091	248,142
*77573	League City	(281)	83,560	90,983
*78641	Leander	(512)	26,521	31,717
*78268	Leon Valley	(210)	10,151	10,808
*79336	Levelland	(806)	13,542	13,929
*75067	Lewisville	(214)	95,290	101,074
*75068	Little Elm	(214)	25,898	32,701
*78233	Live Oak	(210)	13,131	14,751
*78644	Lockhart	(512)	12,698	13,098
*75601	Longview	(903)	80,455	81,443
*79401	Lubbock	(806)	229,573	239,538
*75901	Lufkin	(936)	35,067	36,085
77657	Lumberton	(409)	11,943	12,184
76063	Mansfield	(817)	56,368	60,872
*75670	Marshall	(903)	23,523	24,501
*78501	McAllen	(956)	129,877	136,639
*75070	McKinney	(214)	131,117	148,559
78570	Mercedes	(956)	15,570	16,352
*75149	Mesquite	(214)	139,824	143,484
*79701	Midland	(432)	111,147	123,933
76065	Midlothian	(214)	18,037	19,891
*76067	Mineral Wells	(940)	16,788	16,773
*78572	Mission	(956)	77,058	81,050
77083	Mission Bend (c)	(713)	36,501	—
*77489	Missouri City	(713)	67,358	70,185
*75455	Mount Pleasant	(903)	15,564	16,113
*75094	Murphy	(214)	17,708	19,515
*75961	Nacogdoches	(936)	32,996	33,868
77627	Nederland	(409)	17,547	17,563
*78130	New Braunfels	(830)	57,740	63,279
77479	New Territory (c)	(281)	15,186	—
*76117	North Richland Hills	(817)	63,343	67,317
*79761	Odessa	(432)	99,940	110,720
*77630	Orange	(409)	18,595	18,922
*75801	Palestine	(903)	18,712	18,617
*79065	Pampa	(806)	17,994	18,401
*75460	Paris	(903)	25,171	24,912
*75506	Pasadena	(713)	149,043	152,735
*77581	Pearland	(713)	91,252	100,065
78721	Pecan Grove (c)	(254)	15,963	—
*78660	Pflugerville	(512)	46,936	53,752
78577	Pharr	(956)	70,400	73,790
*79072	Plainview	(806)	22,194	21,860
*75074	Plano	(214)	259,841	274,409
*77640	Port Arthur	(409)	53,818	54,135
77979	Port Lavaca	(361)	12,248	12,374
77651	Port Neches	(409)	13,040	12,784
78374	Portland	(361)	15,099	15,711
75078	Prosper	(214)	9,423	12,943
*78580	Raymondville	(965)	11,284	11,153
75154	Red Oak	(214)	10,769	11,245
76140	Rendon (c)	(817)	12,552	—
*75080	Richardson	(214)	99,223	104,475
*77469	Richmond	(713)	11,679	11,863
78582	Rio Grande City	(956)	13,834	14,021
76701	Robinson	(254)	10,509	11,300
78380	Robstown	(361)	11,487	11,688
*78382	Rockport	(361)	8,766	10,036
*75087	Rockwall	(214)	37,490	40,922
77471	Rosenberg	(713)	30,618	33,188
*78681	Round Rock	(512)	99,887	109,821
*75088	Rowlett	(214)	56,199	58,043
*75189	Royse City	(214)	9,349	10,275
75048	Sachse	(214)	20,329	22,026
*76179	Saginaw	(817)	19,806	21,257
*76901	San Angelo	(325)	93,200	97,492
*78201	San Antonio	(210)	1,327,407	1,409,019
78586	San Benito	(956)	24,250	24,374
79849	San Elizario (c)	(915)	13,603	—
78589	San Juan	(956)	33,856	35,593
*78666	San Marcos	(512)	44,894	54,076
*77510	Santa Fe	(409)	12,222	12,637
*78154	Schertz	(210)	31,465	35,929
77586	Seabrook	(281)	11,952	12,649
75159	Seagoville	(214)	14,835	15,519
*78155	Seguin	(830)	25,175	26,660
*75090	Sherman	(903)	38,521	39,296
77459	Sienna Plantation (c)	(281)	13,721	—
*79549	Snyder	(325)	11,202	11,532
79927	Socorro	(915)	32,013	32,517
77587	South Houston	(713)	16,983	17,397
76092	Southlake	(817)	26,575	28,234
*77373	Spring (c)	(713)	54,298	—
*77477	Stafford	(713)	17,693	18,126
*77601	Stephenville	(254)	17,123	18,561
*77478	Sugar Land	(713)	78,817	83,860
*75482	Sulphur Springs	(903)	15,449	15,868
79556	Sweetwater	(325)	10,906	10,762
76574	Taylor	(512)	15,191	16,233
*76501	Temple	(254)	66,102	70,190
*75160	Terrell	(214)	15,816	16,347
*77501	Texarkana	(903)	36,411	37,442
*77590	Texas City	(409)	45,099	46,081

ZIP	Place	Area code	2010 population	2013 estimate
*75056	The Colony	(214)	36,328	39,458
*77382	The Woodlands (c)	(713)	93,847	—
78260	Timberwood Park (c)	(830)	13,447	—
*77375	Tomball	(713)	10,753	11,124
76262	Trophy Club	(817)	8,024	10,459
*75702	Tyler	(903)	96,900	100,223
*78148	Universal City	(830)	18,530	19,372
75205	University Park	(214)	23,068	23,992
*78801	Uvalde	(830)	15,751	16,284
*76384	Vernon	(940)	11,002	10,665
*77901	Victoria	(361)	62,592	65,098
*77662	Vidor	(409)	10,579	10,906
*76704	Waco	(254)	124,805	129,030
76148	Watauga	(817)	23,497	24,187
*75165	Waxahachie	(214)	29,621	31,591
*76086	Weatherford	(817)	25,250	27,021
*77598	Webster	(281)	10,400	11,006
78728	Wells Branch (c)	(512)	12,120	—
*78596	Weslaco	(956)	35,670	37,093
79764	West Odessa (c)	(432)	22,707	—
77005	West University Place	(713)	14,787	15,369
76108	White Settlement	(817)	16,116	16,714
*76301	Wichita Falls	(940)	104,553	104,898
75098	Wylie	(214)	41,427	44,575

Utah

Area code 385 overlays area code 801.

ZIP	Place	Area code	2010 population	2013 estimate
84004	Alpine	(801)	9,555	10,024
*84003	American Fork	(801)	26,263	27,813
*84010	Bountiful	(801)	42,552	43,023
84302	Brigham City	(435)	17,899	18,454
*84720	Cedar City	(435)	28,857	29,162
84062	Cedar Hills	(801)	9,796	10,179
84014	Centerville	(801)	15,335	16,624
*84015	Clearfield	(801)	30,112	30,467
*84015	Clinton	(801)	20,426	20,924
84121	Cottonwood Heights	(801)	33,433	34,238
84020	Draper	(801)	42,274	45,285
84043	Eagle Mountain	(801)	21,415	24,217
84025	Farmington	(801)	18,275	21,599
*84032	Heber City	(435)	11,362	12,911
84065	Herriman	(801)	21,785	26,362
84003	Highland	(801)	15,523	17,011
*84117	Holladay	(801)	26,472	27,137
84737	Hurricane	(435)	13,748	14,576
84037	Kaysville	(801)	27,300	28,876
84118	Kearns (c)	(801)	35,731	—
*84041	Layton	(801)	67,311	70,790
*84043	Lehi	(801)	47,407	54,382
84042	Lindon	(801)	10,070	10,611
*84321	Logan	(435)	48,174	48,913
84044	Magna (c)	(801)	26,505	—
84047	Midvale	(801)	27,964	30,764
84109	Millcreek (c)	(801)	62,139	—
*84107	Murray	(801)	46,746	48,612
*84404	North Ogden	(801)	17,357	18,019
84054	North Salt Lake	(801)	16,322	17,017
*84401	Ogden	(801)	82,825	84,249
*84057	Orem	(801)	88,328	91,648
84651	Payson	(801)	18,294	19,154
84062	Pleasant Grove	(801)	33,509	34,988
*84601	Provo	(801)	112,488	116,288
*84065	Riverton	(801)	38,753	40,921
*84067	Roy	(801)	36,884	37,733
*84770	Saint George	(435)	72,897	76,817
*84101	Salt Lake City	(801)	186,440	191,180
*84070	Sandy	(801)	87,461	90,231
84043	Saratoga Springs	(801)	17,781	22,749
84335	Smithfield	(435)	9,495	10,466
*84095	South Jordan	(801)	50,418	59,366
84403	South Ogden	(801)	16,532	16,789
84165	South Salt Lake	(801)	23,617	24,702
84660	Spanish Fork	(801)	34,691	36,956
84663	Springville	(801)	29,466	31,205
84075	Syracuse	(801)	24,331	25,775
*84118	Taylorsville	(801)	58,652	60,519
84074	Tooele	(435)	31,605	32,342
*84078	Vernal	(435)	9,089	10,344
84780	Washington	(435)	18,761	21,890
84401	West Haven	(801)	10,272	11,248
*84084	West Jordan	(801)	103,712	110,077
*84128	West Valley City	(801)	129,480	133,579
*84010	Woods Cross	(801)	9,761	10,756

Vermont

Area code 802 applies to the entire state. See introductory note.

ZIP	Place	2010 population	2013 estimate
05201	Bennington	15,764	15,519
*05301	Brattleboro	12,046	11,798
*05401	Burlington	42,417	42,284

ZIP	Place	2010 population	2013 estimate
*05446	Colchester	17,067	17,299
*05452	Essex	19,587	20,526
05468	Milton	10,352	10,572
*05701	Rutland	16,495	16,126
*05403	South Burlington	17,904	18,612

Virginia
Area code 571 overlays area code 703.

ZIP	Place	Area code	2010 population	2013 estimate
*22314	Alexandria	(703)	139,966	148,892
22003	Annandale (c)	(703)	41,008	—
*22201	Arlington (c)	(703)	207,627	—
*20146	Ashburn (c)	(703)	43,511	—
22041	Bailey's Crossroads (c)	(540)	23,643	—
*24060	Blacksburg	(540)	42,620	43,609
23235	Bon Air (c)	(804)	16,366	—
23112	Brandermill (c)	(804)	13,173	—
*24201	Bristol	(276)	17,835	17,341
20148	Broadlands (c)	(703)	12,313	—
20111	Buckhall (c)	(703)	16,293	—
20109	Bull Run (c)	(703)	14,983	—
*22015	Burke (c)	(703)	41,055	—
22015	Burke Centre (c)	(703)	17,326	—
*20165	Cascades (c)	(434)	11,912	—
24018	Cave Spring (c)	(540)	24,922	—
*20120	Centreville (c)	(703)	71,135	—
*20151	Chantilly (c)	(703)	23,039	—
*22901	Charlottesville	(434)	43,475	44,349
22026	Cherry Hill (c)	(703)	16,000	—
*23320	Chesapeake	(757)	222,209	230,571
*23831	Chester (c)	(804)	20,987	—
*24073	Christiansburg	(540)	21,041	21,533
23834	Colonial Heights	(804)	17,411	17,634
20165	Countryside (c)	(703)	10,072	—
22701	Culpeper	(540)	16,379	17,145
22193	Dale City (c)	(703)	65,969	—
*24541	Danville	(434)	43,055	42,907
20170	Dranesville (c)	(703)	11,921	—
23222	East Highland Park (c)	(804)	14,796	—
22033	Fair Oaks (c)	(703)	30,223	—
*22030	Fairfax	(703)	22,565	23,973
22039	Fairfax Station (c)	(703)	12,030	—
*22046	Falls Church	(703)	12,332	13,508
22308	Fort Hunt (c)	(703)	16,045	—
*22310	Franconia (c)	(703)	18,245	—
20171	Franklin Farm (c)	(703)	19,288	—
*22401	Fredericksburg	(540)	24,286	28,132
22630	Front Royal	(540)	14,440	14,899
20155	Gainesville (c)	(703)	11,481	—
*23060	Glen Allen (c)	(804)	14,774	—
22066	Great Falls (c)	(703)	15,427	—
22306	Groveton (c)	(703)	14,598	—
*23666	Hampton	(757)	137,436	136,699
*22801	Harrisonburg	(540)	48,914	51,395
*20170	Herndon	(703)	23,292	24,446
23075	Highland Springs (c)	(804)	15,711	—
24019	Hollins (c)	(540)	14,673	—
23860	Hopewell	(804)	22,591	22,163
22303	Huntington (c)	(703)	11,267	—
22306	Hybla Valley (c)	(703)	15,801	—
22043	Idylwood (c)	(703)	17,288	—
22038	Kings Park West (c)	(703)	13,390	—
22315	Kingstowne (c)	(703)	15,556	—
22192	Lake Ridge (c)	(540)	41,058	—
23228	Lakeside (c)	(804)	11,849	—
20176	Lansdowne (c)	(703)	11,253	—
23060	Laurel (c)	(804)	16,713	—
*20175	Leesburg	(703)	42,616	47,673
22312	Lincolnia (c)	(703)	22,855	—
20136	Linton Hall (c)	(703)	35,725	—
*22079	Lorton (c)	(703)	18,610	—
20165	Lowes Island (c)	(703)	10,756	—
*24501	Lynchburg	(434)	75,568	78,014
24572	Madison Heights (c)	(434)	11,285	—
*20110	Manassas	(703)	37,821	41,705
*20111	Manassas Park	(703)	14,273	16,149
23235	Manchester (c)	(804)	10,804	—
*24112	Martinsville	(276)	13,821	13,755
22191	Marumsco (c)	(703)	35,036	—
*22101	McLean (c)	(703)	48,115	—
20171	McNair (c)	(703)	17,513	—
23234	Meadowbrook (c)	(804)	18,312	—
*23111	Mechanicsville (c)	(804)	36,348	—
22081	Merrifield (c)	(703)	15,212	—
22025	Montclair (c)	(703)	19,570	—
22121	Mount Vernon (c)	(703)	12,416	—
22191	Neabsco (c)	(703)	12,068	—
22122	Newington (c)	(703)	12,943	—
22153	Newington Forest (c)	(703)	12,442	—
23502	Newport News	(757)	180,719	182,020
*23502	Norfolk	(757)	242,803	246,139
22124	Oakton (c)	(703)	34,166	—
*23801	Petersburg	(804)	32,420	32,538
23662	Poquoson	(757)	12,150	12,104
*23707	Portsmouth	(757)	95,535	96,205
24141	Radford	(540)	16,408	17,184
*20190	Reston (c)	(703)	58,404	—
23232	Richmond	(804)	204,214	214,114
*24017	Roanoke	(540)	97,032	98,465
24281	Rose Hill (c) (Fairfax Co.)	(276)	20,226	—
*24153	Salem	(540)	24,802	25,299
23233	Short Pump (c)	(804)	24,729	—
20152	South Riding (c)	(703)	24,256	—
*22150	Springfield (c)	(703)	30,484	—
*24401	Staunton	(540)	23,746	24,350
*20164	Sterling (c)	(703)	27,822	—
20109	Sudley (c)	(703)	16,203	—
*23434	Suffolk	(757)	84,585	85,728
20164	Sugarland Run (c)	(703)	11,799	—
24502	Timberlake (c)	(434)	12,183	—
23229	Tuckahoe (c)	(804)	44,990	—
*22102	Tysons Corner (c)	(703)	19,627	—
22180	Vienna	(703)	15,687	16,370
*23450	Virginia Beach	(757)	437,994	448,479
23888	Wakefield (c)	(757)	11,275	—
22980	Waynesboro	(540)	21,006	21,263
22042	West Falls Church (c)	(703)	29,207	—
22152	West Springfield (c)	(703)	22,460	—
*23185	Williamsburg	(757)	14,068	15,206
*22601	Winchester	(540)	26,203	27,216
24592	Wolf Trap (c)	(703)	16,131	—
24381	Woodlawn (c) (Fairfax Co.)	(276)	20,804	—

Washington

ZIP	Place	Area code	2010 population	2013 estimate
98520	Aberdeen	(360)	16,896	16,371
*98221	Anacortes	(360)	15,778	16,048
98223	Arlington	(360)	17,926	18,664
98335	Artondale (c)	(253)	12,653	—
*98002	Auburn	(253)	70,180	74,860
98110	Bainbridge Island	(206)	23,025	23,196
98604	Battle Ground	(360)	17,571	18,305
*98004	Bellevue	(425)	122,363	133,992
*98225	Bellingham	(360)	80,885	82,631
*98390	Bonney Lake	(360)	17,374	18,289
*98011	Bothell	(425)	33,505	35,576
98036	Bothell West (c)	(425)	16,607	—
*98337	Bremerton	(360)	37,729	39,056
*98178	Bryn Mawr-Skyway (c)	(206)	15,645	—
*98166	Burien	(206)	33,313	49,858
98607	Camas	(360)	19,355	20,907
98531	Centralia	(360)	16,336	16,660
99004	Cheney	(509)	10,590	11,251
98072	Cottage Lake (c)	(206)	22,494	—
98042	Covington	(253)	17,575	18,830
*98198	Des Moines	(206)	29,673	30,687
98031	East Hill-Meridian (c)	(253)/(425)	29,878	—
98056	East Renton Highlands (c)	(425)	11,140	—
98802	East Wenatchee	(509)	13,190	13,477
98204	Eastmont (c)	(425)	20,101	—
*98020	Edmonds	(425)	39,709	40,727
98387	Elk Plain (c)	(253)	14,205	—
*98026	Ellensburg	(509)	18,174	18,363
98022	Enumclaw	(360)	10,669	11,479
*98201	Everett	(425)	103,019	105,370
98058	Fairwood (c) (King Co.)	(253)/(425)	19,102	—
*98001	Federal Way	(253)	89,306	92,734
98248	Ferndale	(360)	11,415	12,343
98597	Five Corners (c)	(360)	18,159	—
98433	Fort Lewis (c)	(253)	11,046	—
98375	Frederickson (c)	(253)	18,719	—
98338	Graham (c)	(253)	23,491	—
98930	Grandview	(509)	10,862	11,117
98665	Hazel Dell (c)	(360)	19,435	—
98011	Inglewood-Finn Hill (c)	(425)	22,707	—
*98027	Issaquah	(425)	30,434	33,566
98626	Kelso	(360)	11,925	11,810
98028	Kenmore	(425)	20,460	21,611
*99336	Kennewick	(509)	73,917	76,762
*98031	Kent	(253)/(425)	92,411	124,435
98033	Kingsgate (c)	(425)	13,065	—
*98033	Kirkland	(425)	48,787	84,430
98029	Klahanie (c)	(425)	10,674	—
*98503	Lacey	(360)	42,393	44,919
98155	Lake Forest Park	(206)	12,598	13,091
98042	Lake Morton-Berrydale (c)	(253)/(425)	10,160	—
98258	Lake Stevens	(425)	28,069	29,949
98391	Lake Tapps (c)	(253)	11,859	—
98002	Lakeland North (c)	(253)	12,942	—
98002	Lakeland South (c)	(253)	11,574	—
*98498	Lakewood	(253)	58,163	59,097
98632	Longview	(360)	36,648	36,530

ZIP	Place	Area code	2010 population	2013 estimate
98264	Lynden	(360)	11,951	12,902
*98046	Lynnwood	(425)	35,836	36,485
98290	Maltby (c)	(360)/(425)	10,830	—
98038	Maple Valley	(425)	22,684	24,804
98012	Martha Lake (c)	(425)	15,473	—
*98270	Marysville	(360)	60,020	63,269
98040	Mercer Island	(206)	22,699	24,098
*98082	Mill Creek	(425)	18,244	18,828
98012	Mill Creek East (c)	(425)	15,709	—
98272	Monroe	(360)	17,304	17,724
98837	Moses Lake	(509)	20,366	21,360
*98273	Mount Vernon	(360)	31,743	32,600
98043	Mountlake Terrace	(425)	19,909	20,674
98275	Mukilteo	(425)	20,254	20,860
*98059	Newcastle	(425)	10,380	11,062
98037	North Lynnwood (c)	(425)	16,574	—
*98277	Oak Harbor	(360)	22,075	22,136
*98501	Olympia	(360)	46,478	48,338
98662	Orchards (c)	(360)	19,556	—
98444	Parkland (c)	(253)	35,803	—
*99301	Pasco	(509)	59,781	67,599
*98362	Port Angeles	(360)	19,038	19,190
*98366	Port Orchard	(360)	11,144	12,959
98390	Prairie Ridge (c)	(360)	11,464	—
*99163	Pullman	(509)	29,799	31,395
*98371	Puyallup	(253)	37,022	38,609
*98052	Redmond	(425)	54,144	57,530
*98058	Renton	(425)	90,927	97,003
*99352	Richland	(509)	48,058	52,413
98686	Salmon Creek (c)	(360)	19,686	—
*98074	Sammamish	(425)	45,780	50,169
*98148	SeaTac	(206)	26,909	27,875
*98101	Seattle	(206)/(425)	608,660	652,405
98284	Sedro-Woolley	(360)	10,540	10,645
*98133	Shoreline	(206)	53,007	54,790
98208	Silver Firs (c).	(206)/(425)	20,891	—
*98315	Silverdale (c).	(360)	19,204	—
*98065	Snoqualmie	(425)	10,670	12,018
*98373	South Hill (c)	(253)	52,431	—
98387	Spanaway (c)	(253)	27,227	—
*99201	Spokane	(509)	208,916	210,721
*99216	Spokane Valley	(509)	89,755	91,113
98944	Sunnyside	(509)	15,858	16,066
*98402	Tacoma	(253)	198,397	203,446
*98138	Tukwila	(206)	19,107	19,765
*98501	Tumwater	(360)	17,371	18,511
98053	Union Hill-Novelty Hill (c)	(425)	18,805	—
*98467	University Place	(253)	31,144	32,040
*98661	Vancouver	(360)	161,791	167,405
*98013	Vashon (c)	(206)	10,624	—
99362	Walla Walla	(509)	31,731	31,825
*98671	Washougal	(360)	14,095	14,750
*98801	Wenatchee	(509)	31,925	32,701
*99353	West Richland	(509)	11,811	13,003
98166	White Center (c)	(206)	13,495	—
*98072	Woodinville	(425)	10,938	11,318
*98903	Yakima	(509)	91,067	93,257

West Virginia

Area code 681 overlays area code 304; both apply to the entire state.

ZIP	Place	2010 population	2013 estimate
*25801	Beckley	17,614	17,607
24701	Bluefield	10,447	10,473
*25301	Charleston	51,400	50,821
*26301	Clarksburg	16,578	16,360
*26554	Fairmont	18,704	18,815
*25701	Huntington	49,138	49,177
25401	Martinsburg	17,227	17,668
*26505	Morgantown	29,660	30,666
26101	Parkersburg	31,492	31,186
25177	Saint Albans	11,044	10,950
25303	South Charleston	13,450	13,471
*25526	Teays Valley (c)	13,175	—
*26105	Vienna	10,749	10,633
26062	Weirton	19,746	19,525
26003	Wheeling	28,486	28,009

Wisconsin

Area code 534 overlays area code 715.

ZIP	Place	Area code	2010 population	2013 estimate
54301	Allouez	(920)	13,975	13,967
*54911	Appleton	(920)	72,623	73,596
*54304	Ashwaubenon	(920)	16,963	17,116
53913	Baraboo	(608)	12,048	12,100
53916	Beaver Dam	(920)	16,214	16,345
54311	Bellevue	(920)	14,570	14,964
*53511	Beloit	(608)	36,966	36,888
*53045	Brookfield	(262)	37,920	37,999
*53209	Brown Deer	(414)	11,999	12,102
53105	Burlington	(262)	10,464	10,523
53108	Caledonia	(262)	24,705	24,737
53012	Cedarburg	(262)	11,412	11,475
*54729	Chippewa Falls	(715)	13,661	13,718
53110	Cudahy	(414)	18,267	18,340
54115	De Pere	(920)	23,800	24,359
*54703	Eau Claire	(715)	65,883	67,545
*53711	Fitchburg	(608)	25,260	26,380
*54935	Fond du Lac	(920)	43,021	42,970
53538	Fort Atkinson	(920)	12,368	12,482
53132	Franklin	(414)	35,451	36,310
53022	Germantown	(262)	19,749	19,788
*53209	Glendale	(414)	12,872	12,920
53024	Grafton	(262)	11,459	11,524
*54303	Green Bay	(920)	104,057	104,779
53129	Greendale	(414)	14,046	14,340
*53220	Greenfield	(414)	36,720	37,159
53027	Hartford	(262)	14,223	14,251
*54303	Howard	(920)	17,399	18,671
*54016	Hudson	(715)	12,719	13,179
*53545	Janesville	(608)	63,575	63,820
54130	Kaukauna	(920)	15,462	15,725
*53140	Kenosha	(262)	99,218	99,889
*54601	La Crosse	(608)	51,320	51,522
54140	Little Chute	(920)	10,449	10,491
*53714	Madison	(608)	233,209	243,344
*54220	Manitowoc	(920)	33,736	33,335
54143	Marinette	(715)	10,968	10,930
*54449	Marshfield	(715)	19,118	18,750
54952	Menasha	(920)	17,353	17,588
*53051	Menomonee Falls	(262)	35,626	35,924
54751	Menomonie	(715)	16,264	16,156
*53097	Mequon	(262)	23,132	23,334
53562	Middleton	(608)	17,442	18,411
*53202	Milwaukee	(414)	594,833	599,164
53566	Monroe	(608)	10,827	10,832
53406	Mount Pleasant	(262)	26,197	26,224
53150	Muskego	(414)	24,135	24,555
*54956	Neenah	(920)	25,501	25,892
*53186	New Berlin	(262)	39,584	39,834
53154	Oak Creek	(414)	34,451	35,008
53066	Oconomowoc	(262)	15,759	16,230
54650	Onalaska	(608)	17,736	18,312
*54901	Oshkosh	(920)	66,083	66,778
53072	Pewaukee	(262)	13,195	13,827
53818	Platteville	(608)	11,224	11,384
*53158	Pleasant Prairie	(262)	19,719	20,173
54467	Plover	(715)	12,123	12,274
53074	Port Washington	(262)	11,250	11,343
53901	Portage	(608)	10,324	10,183
*53402	Racine	(262)	78,860	78,199
*53076	Richfield	(262)	11,300	11,382
54022	River Falls	(715)	15,000	15,209
*53081	Sheboygan	(920)	49,288	48,725
53211	Shorewood	(414)	13,162	13,337
53172	South Milwaukee	(414)	21,156	21,239
*54481	Stevens Point	(715)	26,717	26,670
53589	Stoughton	(608)	12,611	12,945
*54173	Suamico	(920)	11,346	11,731
*53590	Sun Prairie	(608)	29,364	30,871
54880	Superior	(715)	27,244	26,869
53089	Sussex	(262)	10,518	10,695
*54241	Two Rivers	(920)	11,712	11,525
53593	Verona	(608)	10,619	11,775
*53094	Watertown	(920)	23,861	23,929
*53186	Waukesha	(262)	70,718	71,016
53597	Waunakee	(608)	12,097	12,840
53963	Waupun	(920)	11,340	11,330
*54403	Wausau	(715)	39,106	39,309
*53213	Wauwatosa	(414)	46,396	47,134
*53214	West Allis	(414)	60,411	60,697
*53095	West Bend	(262)	31,078	31,550
*54476	Weston	(715)	14,868	14,934
*53217	Whitefish Bay	(414)	14,110	14,125
53190	Whitewater	(262)	14,390	14,732
*54494	Wisconsin Rapids	(715)	18,367	18,039

Wyoming

Area code 307 applies to the entire state.

ZIP	Place	2010 population	2013 estimate
*82609	Casper	55,316	59,628
*82009	Cheyenne	59,466	62,448
*82930	Evanston	12,359	12,295
*82716	Gillette	29,087	31,797
*82935	Green River	12,515	12,752
*83001	Jackson	9,577	10,135
*82072	Laramie	30,816	31,814
82501	Riverton	10,615	10,990
*82901	Rock Springs	23,036	24,138
82801	Sheridan	17,444	17,828

Note: In this section, the notation BCE (before the common era) is applied to years dating to the traditional BC (before Christ) era, and CE (common era) is applied to AD (anno domini) dates. This notation is now preferred in scientific and academic publications. The traditional Gregorian Calendar system and its dates and years are unaltered except by these labels.

Other abbreviations used in this chapter include the following: KYA = thousand years ago, MYA = million years ago, c. = circa, fl. = flourished, r. = ruled, b. = born, d. = died.

Prehistory: Our Ancestors Emerge
Reviewed by Albert Rolls, Ph.D., June 2013

Evidence of the origins of *Homo sapiens sapiens*, the genus, species, and subspecies to which all living humans belong, comes from a small but increasing number of fossils, from genetic and anatomical studies, and from interpretation of the geological and archaeological records. The latest evidence suggests that humans evolved from apelike primate ancestors that lived in eastern and central Africa 7 to 5 million years ago (MYA). Although all humans living today are members of a single species, the fossil record confirms that our ancestors coexisted with a number of similar species throughout our evolutionary history. Current theories trace the first hominin[1] (upright, bipedal, humanlike primate) to Africa, where several distinct genera appeared 6-4 MYA. They lived in a variety of environments throughout most of the continent, including swampy forest margins, woodlands, and open savannas (usually near lakes or springs). In addition to *Australopithecus afarensis*—better known as "Lucy," a 3.2 MYA Ethiopian specimen found in 1974—these earliest hominins include such recent discoveries as *Sahelanthropus* (c. 6.5 MYA, from Chad), *Ardipithecus* (c. 5 MYA, Kenya), *Kenyanthropus* (c. 3.5 MYA, Kenya), and *Orrorin* (c. 5 MYA, Kenya). Later, between 4 and 3 MYA, these earliest hominins gave rise to at least two groups of savanna/lake-edge adapted "man-apes." Called australopithecines, they are divided into "gracile" and "robust" lineages, both containing a number of species. The robust australopithecines were characterized by enormous molar and premolar teeth; they probably went extinct around 1 MYA or slightly thereafter. Although it is uncertain from which australopithecine species humans descended, the most likely species are usually assigned to the gracile lineage.

Our genus, *Homo*, arose 3-2 MYA, when hominins began to produce primitive stone tools. The oldest tools are dated to c. 2.5 MYA from the Kada Gona site, in Ethiopia, and were used for scraping and cutting meat, sinew, and wood. It is not known whether these early hominins had the ability to speak, but they were social animals, lived in groups of 12-20 individuals, aggregated and dispersed seasonally, had campsites, and subsisted by gathering plants and small animals and by scavenging other kills. A closer ancestor, *Homo ergaster*, appeared in E Africa around 1.9 MYA and was the first to leave the continent, spreading throughout Eurasia by c. 1.8 MYA. *H. ergaster* is sometimes grouped with *H. erectus*, a species first identified in the 1890s on the island of Java. It was capable of hunting large and medium-sized hoofed animals, such as antelopes and horses, learned to make and control fire—by c. 500 thousand years ago (KYA) in Europe, possibly earlier in Africa—and almost certainly had primitive language skills.

After about 350 KYA, Europe provides a particularly rich set of fossil evidence usually assigned to *H. erectus*. By a near-universal standard, this species gave rise to the Neanderthals, who appeared c. 200 KYA. Neanderthals were humanlike in most respects: they could speak, were proficient hunters of large game, had sophisticated tools and weapons and a developed social organization, and were well adapted to the harsh climates of Ice Age Europe. Recent advances in molecular biology support the theory that Neanderthals were a distinct population or species that in some places coexisted and may have interbred with early modern humans (also called Crô-Magnons). *H. antecessor*, a new species (c. 870 KYA) identified at the Trinchera Dolina site in north-central Spain, might help clarify the relationship between the earliest representatives of *Homo* in western Europe, and the Neanderthals. A similar situation may have occurred in E Asia, where more primitive *Homo* species coexisted with early modern humans after c. 40 KYA, and possibly as recently as 18 KYA, on the island of Flores, in Indonesia.

Genetic evidence indicates that the first *Homo sapiens* originated in E Africa between 200 and 100 KYA. The oldest modern human fossils date to c. 160 KYA and were found at the Herto site in Ethiopia's Middle Awash Valley. The species quickly spread, displacing, extinguishing, outcompeting, and/or genetically swamping the archaic humans it encountered. Modern humans were living in Israel by c. 100 KYA, and in Romania by c. 35 KYA. Migration from Asia to Australia took place as early as 60 KYA. First confirmation for the crossing from Asia to the Americas by the Bering land bridge dates to the end of the last Ice Age, at 14 KYA. However, genetic data suggests that small, isolated groups of hunter-gatherers arrived in the Americas up to 10,000 years earlier, settling in both continents. Their arrival was rapidly followed by the extinction of the indigenous Pleistocene megafauna (e.g., mammoths, mastodons), due either to overexploitation by humans, an extraterrestrial impact c. 12,900 years ago, or a combination of both.

As human cognitive capacities slowly expanded over the Pleistocene (1.7-0.01 MYA), a variety of behavioral modes—in toolmaking, diet, shelter, social arrangements, and spiritual expression—arose as humans adapted to different geographic and climatic zones. By about 13,000 years ago, sites from all over the world show seasonal migration patterns and efficient exploitation of a wide range of plant and animal foods, some of which were eventually domesticated.

The ability to make fire at will enormously expanded the human food niche. Fire-making possibly began as early as 1 MYA in Africa and is clearly documented throughout Eurasia after c. 500 KYA. Hearths were found in northern Israel by c. 750 KYA, and by 465 KYA in southwestern France. Fire-hardened wooden throwing spears about 3 m long were fashioned by big-game hunters 400 KYA at the Schoeningen lignite mine in Germany. Scraping tools, dated after 750 KYA in Europe, N Africa, the Middle East, and Central Asia, suggest the preparation of hides for clothing. The oldest relatively unambiguous evidence of personal adornment—perforated shell beads—dates to c. 120 KYA at Skhul Cave on Mount Carmel in Israel. Although they were probably invented much earlier, impressions in burnt clay from the Czech Republic document the ability to weave cloth baskets and nets by 28 KYA. By the time Australia was settled, human ancestors had learned to navigate in boats over considerable distances in open water. The earliest-known bone tools were fashioned some 90 KYA at Semliki, in the Congo basin, by fishermen who crafted sophisticated bone harpoons to catch giant catfish.

About 60 KYA, the earliest immigrants to Australia carved and painted designs on rocks. Although the painted caves of Cosquer and Chauvet in southern France have (contested) radiocarbon dates of c. 32 KYA, painting, engraving, and bodily decoration flourished in Europe 15 KYA, along with stone and ivory sculpture. More than 200 western European caves show remarkable examples of naturalistic wall painting. A few musical instruments—bone flutes with precisely bored holes—have been found in sites dated after 40 KYA. Over the course of the Upper Pleistocene (c. 130-12 KYA), the number of people who survived to become grandparents slowly increased. With more adults available to provide child care, humans began to develop more complex, multigenerational social systems.

Cave paintings in Lascaux, France, discovered in 1940, have been carbon-dated to 11,000 to 30,000 years before the present.

The reach of social memory increased accordingly. Shortly after 12 KYA, among widely separated foraging communities in both hemispheres, a series of dramatic technological and social changes occurred, marking the Neolithic, or New Stone, Age. As the world climate became drier and warmer, population/resource imbalances ensued, creating the conditions that allowed for increased human interference in the life cycles of certain plants and animals. This interference ultimately resulted in the appearance of domestication economies, initially in the northern Middle East. Domesticated plants and animals encouraged population growth and the appearance of permanent settlements, which in turn reduced birth spacing and spurred more population growth. Agricultural economies increasingly replaced hunting and gathering. Reliance upon domesticated plants and animals, coupled with technological advances like pottery-making, precipitated a dramatic increase in world population and social complexity. Genetic research suggests that mutations related to traits currently found in some human populations, such as Europeans' unusually light skin pigmentation and ability to process lactose, arose after c. 12 KYA.

Sites in the Americas, SE Europe, and the Middle East show roughly contemporaneous (12-6 KYA) evidence of Neolithic

domestication economies; similar evidence of E and S Asian, W European, and sub-Saharan African Neolithic adaptations dates to 10-7 KYA. From W Asian sources, farming and the herding of sheep and goats spread rapidly throughout the Mediterranean Basin, perhaps in as short a time interval as 100-200 years. The variety of crops—wheat, barley, rice, maize, squash, beans, and tubers—and a mix of other characteristics suggest that this adaptation occurred independently in as many as 12 or 13 places in both hemispheres. Evidence for fermented beverages likewise coincides with the early Neolithic settled farming lifestyle. Northern Chinese farmers concocted a wine-like drink from rice, honey, and fruit between 9 and 8 KYA. In highland W Asia, in what is today Iran, vintners were fermenting grapes and making wine by c. 7.4 KYA. The plants and animals associated with the Neolithic Revolution provided the basis for all subsequent social and cultural evolution worldwide.

(1) Although "hominid" was standard usage several decades ago, "hominin" is now more commonly used in reference to human ancestors because of new developments in the interpretation of primate evolution.

Earliest Civilizations: 4000-1000 BCE

Mesopotamia. If history began with writing, the first chapter opened in Mesopotamia, the Tigris-Euphrates river valley. The Sumerians used clay tablets with pictographs to keep records after 4000 BCE. A **cuneiform** (wedge-shaped) script evolved by 3000 BCE as a full syllabic alphabet. Neighboring peoples adapted the script for their own use.

Sumerian life centered, from 4000 BCE, on large cities (Eridu, Ur, Uruk, Nippur, Kish, and Lagash) organized around temples and priestly bureaucracies, with surrounding plains watered by vast irrigation works and worked with traction plows. Sailboats, wheeled vehicles, potter's wheels, and kilns were used. Copper was smelted and tempered from c. 4000 BCE; bronze was produced not long after. Ores, as well as precious stones and metals, were obtained through long-distance ship and caravan trade. Iron was used from c. 2000 BCE. Improved ironworking, developed partly by the Hittites, became widespread by 1200 BCE.

Sumerian political primacy passed among cities and their kingly dynasties. Semitic-speaking peoples, with cultures derived from the Sumerian, founded a succession of dynasties that ruled in Mesopotamia and neighboring areas for most of 1,800 years. Among them were the **Akkadians** (first under Sargon I, c. 2350 BCE), the Amorites (whose laws, codified by **Hammurabi**, c. 1792-1750 BCE, have biblical parallels), and the Assyrians, with interludes of rule by the Hittites, Kassites, and Mitanni.

Mesopotamian learning, preserved in vast libraries, was practically oriented. Scribes maintained lists of astronomical phenomena, plants, animals, and stones. Medical texts listed ailments and herbal cures. The Sumerians worshipped anthropomorphic gods representing natural forces. Sacrifices were made at **ziggurats**, or huge stepped temples.

The Syria-Palestine area, site of some of the earliest urban remains (Jericho, 7000 BCE) and of the recently uncovered **Ebla** civilization (fl. 2500 BCE), experienced Egyptian cultural and

political influence along with Mesopotamian. The **Phoenician** coast was an active commercial center. A phonetic alphabet was invented here before 1600 BCE. It became the ancestor of many other alphabets.

Egypt. Agricultural villages along the Nile R. were united by around 3300 BCE into two kingdoms, Upper and Lower Egypt. They were unified (c. 3100 BCE) under the pharaoh Menes. A bureaucracy supervised construction of canals and monuments (**pyramids** starting 2700 BCE). Control over Nubia to the S was asserted from 2600 BCE. Brilliant **Old Kingdom** period achievements in architecture, sculpture, and painting reached their height during the 3rd and 4th dynasties. **Hieroglyphic writing** appeared by 3200 BCE, recording a sophisticated literature that included religious writings, philosophy, history, and science. An ordered hierarchy of gods, including totemistic animal elements, was served by a powerful priesthood in Memphis. The pharaoh was identified with the falcon god Horus. Other trends included belief in an afterlife and short-lived quasi-monotheistic reforms introduced by the pharaoh **Akhenaton** (c. 1379-1362 BCE), who was married to Nefertiti.

After a period of dominance by Semitic Hyksos from Asia (c. 1700-1550 BCE), the **New Kingdom** established an empire in Syria. Egypt became increasingly embroiled in Asiatic wars and diplomacy. Conquered by Persia in 525 BCE, it eventually faded away as an independent culture.

India. An urban civilization with an as-yet undeciphered writing system stretched across the Indus Valley along the Arabian Sea c. 3000-1500 BCE. Major sites are Harappa and **Mohenjo-Daro** in Pakistan, well-planned geometric cities with underground sewers and vast granaries. The entire region may have been ruled as a single state. Bronze was used, and arts and crafts were well developed. Religious life apparently took the form of fertility cults. Indus civilization was in decline before the arrival of **Aryan** migrants who arrived from the NW, speaking an Indo-European language. Led by a warrior aristocracy whose legendary deeds are in the **Rig Veda**, the Aryans spread E and S, bringing their sky gods, priestly (Brahman) ritual, and the beginnings of the caste system. Local customs and beliefs were assimilated by the conquerors.

Europe. On Crete, the Bronze Age **Minoan civilization** emerged c. 2500 BCE. A prosperous economy and richly decorative art was supported by seaborne commerce. Mycenae and other cities in mainland Greece and Asia Minor (e.g., **Troy**) preserved elements of the culture until c. 1200 BCE. Cretan Linear A script (c. 2000-1700 BCE) remains undeciphered; Linear B script (c. 1300-1200 BCE) records an early Greek dialect. The possible connection between Mycenaean monumental stonework and the megalithic monuments of Western Europe, Iberia, and Malta (c. 4000-1500 BCE) is unclear.

China. Proto-Chinese Neolithic cultures had long covered N and SE China when the first large political state was organized in the N by the **Shang dynasty** (c. 1523 BCE). Shang kings

The Great Sphinx of Giza is believed to have been built during Egypt's 4th dynasty (c. 2575-2465 BCE).

called themselves Sons of Heaven, and they presided over a cult of human and animal sacrifice to ancestors and nature gods. The Chou dynasty, starting c. 1027 BCE, expanded the area of the Sons of Heaven's dominion, but feudal states exercised most temporal power. A writing system with 2,000 characters was already in use under the Shang, with **pictographs** later supplemented by phonetic characters. Many of its principles and symbols, despite changes in spoken Chinese, were preserved in later writing systems. Technical advances allowed urban specialists to create fine ceramic and jade products, and bronze casting

after 1500 BCE was the most advanced in the world. Bronze artifacts discovered in northern Thailand date from 3600 BCE, hundreds of years before similar Middle Eastern finds.

Americas. Olmecs settled (1500 BCE) on the Gulf coast of Mexico and developed the first known civilization in the Western Hemisphere. Temple cities and huge stone sculptures date from 1200 BCE. A rudimentary calendar and writing system existed. Olmec religion—centered on a jaguar god—and art forms influenced later Mesoamerican cultures.

Formation of Classical Societies: 1000–400 BCE

Greece. After a period of decline during the Dorian Greek invasions (1200-1000 BCE), the Aegean area developed a unique civilization. Drawing on Mycenaean traditions, Mesopotamian learning (weights and measures, lunisolar calendar, astronomy, musical scales), the Phoenician alphabet (modified for Greek), and Egyptian art, **Greek city-states** saw a rich elaboration of intellectual life. The two great epic poems attributed to **Homer**, the *Iliad* and the *Odyssey*, were probably composed around the 8th cent. BCE. Long-range commerce was aided by metal coinage (introduced by the Lydians in Asia Minor before 700 BCE). Colonies were founded around the Mediterranean (Cumae in Italy in 760 BCE; Massalia in France c. 600 BCE) and Black Sea shores.

Philosophy, starting with Ionian speculation on the nature of matter (Thales, c. 634-546 BCE), continued by later "Pre-Socratics" (e.g., Heraclitus, c. 535-415 BCE; Parmenides, b. c. 515 BCE), reached a high point in Athens in the rationalist idealism of **Plato** (c. 428-347 BCE), a disciple of **Socrates** (c. 469-399 BCE; executed for alleged impiety), and in **Aristotle** (384-322 BCE), a pioneer in many fields, from natural sciences to logic, ethics, and metaphysics. The **arts** were highly valued. Architecture culminated in the **Parthenon** (438 BCE) by Phidias (fl. 490-430 BCE). Poetry (Sappho, c. 610-580 BCE; Pindar, c. 518-438 BCE) and **drama** (Aeschylus, 525-456 BCE; Sophocles, c. 496-406 BCE; Euripides, c. 484-406 BCE) thrived. Male beauty and strength, a chief artistic theme, were celebrated at the national games at Olympia.

Ruled by local tyrants or **oligarchies**, the Greeks were not politically united but managed to resist inclusion in the Persian Empire. Persian king Darius was defeated at Marathon (490 BCE), his son Xerxes at Salamis (480 BCE), and the Persian army at Plataea (479 BCE). Democracy sprouted in Athens as statesman Pericles (495-429 BCE) sought participation in government from all citizens. Local warfare was common; the **Peloponnesian Wars** (431-404 BCE) ended in Sparta's victory over Athens. Greek political power subsequently waned, but Greek cultural forms spread far and wide.

Hebrews. Nomadic Hebrew tribes entered Canaan before 1200 BCE, settling among other Semitic peoples speaking the same language. They brought from the desert a **monotheistic** faith said to have been revealed to Abraham in Canaan c. 1800 BCE and Moses at Mt. Sinai c. 1250 BCE, after the Hebrews' escape from bondage in Egypt. David (r. 1000-961 BCE) and Solomon (r. 961-922 BCE) united them in a kingdom that briefly dominated the area. **Phoenicians** to the N founded Mediterranean colonies (Carthage, c. 814 BCE) and sailed into the Atlantic.

A temple in Jerusalem became the national religious center, with sacrifices performed by a hereditary priesthood. Polytheistic influences, especially of the fertility cult of Baal, were opposed by **prophets** (Elijah, Amos, Isaiah).

Divided into **two kingdoms** after Solomon, the Hebrews were unable to resist the revived Assyrian empire, which conquered Israel, the northern kingdom, in 722 BCE. Judah, the southern kingdom, was conquered in 586 BCE by the Babylonians under Nebuchadnezzar II. With the fixing of most of the biblical canon by the mid-4th cent. BCE and the emergence of rabbis, Judaism successfully survived the loss of Hebrew autonomy. A Jewish kingdom was revived under the Hasmoneans (168-42 BCE).

China. During the **Eastern Zhou** dynasty (770-256 BCE), Chinese culture spread E to the sea and S to the Yangtze R. Large feudal states on the periphery of the empire contended for preeminence but continued to recognize the Son of Heaven (king), who retained a purely ritual role enriched with courtly music and dance. In the Age of Warring States (403-221 BCE),

when the first sections of the **Great Wall** were built, the Ch'in state in the W gained supremacy and finally united all of China.

Iron tools entered China c. 500 BCE. Casting techniques were advanced, aiding agriculture. Peasants owned their land and owed civil and military service to nobles. China's cities grew in number and size; barter remained the chief trade medium.

Intellectual ferment among noble scribes and officials produced a classical age of Chinese literature and philosophy. **Confucius** (551-479 BCE) urged a restoration of a supposedly harmonious social order of the past through proper conduct in accordance with one's station and through filial and ceremonial piety. The *Analects* attributed to him are revered throughout E Asia.

Among other thinkers, **Mencius** (d. 289 BCE) added the view that the Mandate of Heaven can be removed from an unjust dynasty. The Legalists sought to curb the supposed natural wickedness of people through new institutions and harsh laws. The Naturalists emphasized the balance of opposites—yin, yang—in the world. **Daoists** sought mystical knowledge through meditation and disengagement.

India. The political and cultural center of India shifted from the Indus to the Ganges River Valley. Buddhism, Jainism, and mystical revisions of orthodox Vedism all developed c. 500-300 BCE. The *Upanishads*, last part of the *Veda*, urged escape from the cycle of rebirth into the physical world. Vedism remained the preserve of the Brahman caste.

In contrast, **Buddhism**, founded by Siddhartha Gautama (c. 563-c. 483 BCE)—Buddha ("Enlightened One")—appealed to merchants in the urban centers and took hold at first (and most lastingly) on the geographic fringes of Indian civilization. The classic Indian epics were composed in this era: the *Ramayana* perhaps c. 300 BCE, the *Mahabharata* over a period starting around 400 BCE.

Northern India was divided into a large number of monarchies and aristocratic republics, probably derived from tribal groupings, when the Magadha kingdom was formed in Bihar c. 542 BCE. It soon became the dominant power. The **Maurya** dynasty, founded by Chandragupta c. 321 BCE, expanded the kingdom, uniting most of Northern India in a centralized bureaucratic empire. The third Mauryan king, **Asoka** (reigned c. 274-236 BCE), conquered most of the subcontinent. He converted to Buddhism, inscribed its tenets on pillars throughout India, and downplayed the caste system.

China's Great Wall, first built during the Age of Warring States (403-221 BCE), was rebuilt, extended, and modified over thousands of years to protect China from invaders.

Before its final decline in India, Buddhism developed into a popular worship of heavenly Bodhisattvas ("enlightened beings"), and it produced a refined architecture (the Great Stupa [shrine] at Sanchi, 100 CE) and sculpture (Gandhara reliefs, 1-400 CE).

Persia. Aryan peoples (Persians, Medes) dominated the area of present Iran by the beginning of the 1st millennium BCE. The prophet **Zoroaster** (b. c. 628 BCE) introduced a dualistic religion in which the forces of good (Ahura Mazda, "Lord of Wisdom") and evil (Ahriman) battle for dominance; individuals are judged by their actions and earn damnation or salvation. Zoroaster's hymns (*Gathas*) are included in the *Avesta*, the Zoroastrian

scriptures. A version of this faith became the established religion of the Persian Empire.

Africa. Nubia, periodically occupied by Egypt since about 2600 BCE, ruled Egypt c. 750-661 BCE and survived as an independent Egyptianized kingdom (**Kush**; capital Meroe) for 1,000 years. The Iron Age Nok culture flourished c. 500 BCE-200 CE on the Benue Plateau of **Nigeria**.

Americas. The Chavin culture controlled Northern Peru c. 900 BCE to 200 BCE. Its ceremonial centers, featuring the jaguar god, survived long after. Its architecture, ceramics, and textiles had influenced other Peruvian cultures. **Mayan civilization** began to develop in Central America as early as 1500 BCE.

Great Empires Unite the Classical World: 400 BCE-400 CE

Persia and the Mediterranean. Cyrus, ruler of a small kingdom in Persia from 559 BCE, united the Persians and Medes within 10 years and conquered Asia Minor and Babylonia in another 10. His son Cambyses, followed by **Darius** (r. 522-486 BCE), added vast lands to the E and N as far as the Indus Valley and Central Asia, as well as Egypt and Thrace. The whole empire was ruled by an international bureaucracy and army, with Persians holding the chief positions. The resources and styles of all the subject civilizations were exploited to create a rich syncretic art.

The kingdom of Macedon, which under Philip II dominated the Greek world and Egypt, was passed on to Philip's son **Alexander** in 336 BCE. Within 13 years, Alexander had conquered all the Persian dominions. Imbued with his tutor Aristotle with Greek ideals, Alexander encouraged colonization, and Greek-style cities were founded. After his death in 323 BCE, wars of succession divided the empire into three significant dynasties—the **Antigonids** in Asia Minor and Macedon, the **Ptolemies** in Egypt, and the **Seleucids** in Mesopotamia. In the ensuing 300 years (the **Hellenistic Era**), a cosmopolitan Greek-oriented culture permeated the ancient world from Western Europe to the borders of India, absorbing native elites everywhere.

Hellenistic philosophy stressed the private individual's search for happiness. The Cynics followed Diogenes (c. 372-287 BCE), who stressed self-sufficiency and restriction of desires and expressed contempt for luxury and social convention. Zeno (c. 335-c. 263 BCE) and the **Stoics** exalted reason, identified it with virtue, and counseled an ascetic disregard for misfortune. The **Epicureans** tried to build lives of moderate pleasure without political or emotional involvement. Hellenistic arts imitated life realistically, especially in sculpture and literature (comedies of Menander, 342-292 BCE).

The sciences thrived, especially at Alexandria, where the Ptolemies financed a great library and museum. Fields of study included mathematics (**Euclid**'s geometry, c. 300 BCE); astronomy (heliocentric theory of Aristarchus, 310-230 BCE; Julian calendar, 45 BCE; **Ptolemy**'s *Almagest*, c. 150 CE); geography (world map of Eratosthenes, 276-194 BCE); hydraulics (**Archimedes**, 287-212 BCE); medicine (Galen, 130-200 CE); and chemistry. Inventors refined uses for siphons, valves, gears, springs, screws, levers, cams, and pulleys.

A restored Persian empire under the **Parthians** (northern Iranian tribesmen) controlled the eastern Hellenistic world from 250 BCE to 229 CE. The Parthians and the succeeding **Sassanian dynasty** (c. 224-651 CE) fought with Rome periodically. The Sassanians revived Zoroastrianism as a state religion and patronized a nationalistic artistic and scholarly renaissance.

Rome. The city of Rome was founded, according to legend, by Romulus in 753 BCE. Through military expansion and colonization, and by granting citizenship to leading members of conquered tribes, the city annexed all of Italy S of the Po R. in the 100-year period before 268 BCE. The Latin and other Italic tribes were annexed first, followed by the **Etruscans** (founders of a great civilization N of Rome) and Greek colonies in the S. With a large standing army and reserve forces of several hundred thousand, Rome was able to defeat **Carthage** in the three **Punic Wars** (264-241 BCE, 218-201 BCE, 149-146 BCE), despite the invasion of Italy by **Hannibal** (218 BCE), thus gaining Sicily and territory in Spain and N Africa.

Rome exploited local disputes to conquer Greece and Asia Minor in the 2nd cent. and Egypt in the 1st (after the defeat and suicide of **Antony and Cleopatra**, 30 BCE). The Mediterranean civilized world, up to the disputed Parthian border, was now Roman and remained so for 500 years. Less civilized

regions were added to the Empire: Gaul (conquered by **Julius Caesar**, 58-51 BCE), Britain (43 CE), and Dacia NE of the Danube (107 CE).

The original aristocratic republican government, with democratic features added in the 5th and 4th cent. BCE, deteriorated under the pressures of empire and class conflict (**Gracchus** brothers, social reformers, murdered in 133 BCE and 121 BCE; slave revolts in 135 BCE and 73 BCE). After a series of civil wars (Marius vs. Sulla, 88-82 BCE; Caesar vs. **Pompey**, 49-45 BCE; triumvirate vs. Caesar's assassins, 44-43 BCE; Antony vs. Octavian, 32-30 BCE), the empire came under the rule of a deified monarch (first emperor, **Augustus**, 27 BCE-14 CE).

Provincials (nearly all granted citizenship by Caracalla, 212 CE) came to dominate the army and civil service. Traditional **Roman law**, systematized and interpreted by independent jurists, and local self-rule in provincial cities were supplanted by a vast tax-collecting bureaucracy in the 3rd and 4th cent. The legal rights of women, children, and slaves were strengthened.

Roman innovations in **civil engineering** included water mills, windmills, and rotary mills and the use of cement that hardened under water. Monumental architecture (baths, theaters, temples) relied on the arch and the dome. A network of roads (some still standing) stretched 53,000 mi, passing through mountain tunnels as long as 3.5 mi. Aqueducts brought water to cities; underground sewers removed waste.

Roman art and literature were derivative of Greek models. Innovations were made in sculpture (naturalistic busts, equestrian statues), decorative wall painting (as at Pompeii), satire (**Juvenal**, 60-127 CE), history (**Tacitus**, 56-120 CE), and prose romance (**Petronius**, d. 66 CE). Gladiatorial contests dominated public amusements, which were supported by the state.

India. The **Gupta** monarchs reunited Northern India c. 320 CE. Their peaceful and prosperous reign saw a revival of Hindu religious thought and Brahman power. The old Vedic traditions were combined with devotion to many indigenous deities (who were seen as manifestations of Vedic gods). Caste lines were reinforced, and Buddhist practices gradually disappeared or were integrated with **Hindu** traditions. The art (often erotic), architecture, and literature of the period, patronized by the Gupta court, are considered among India's

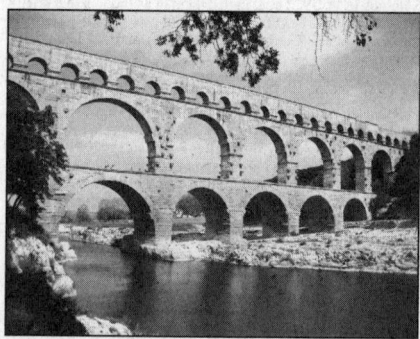

Pont du Gard, an aqueduct bridge built by Romans c. 1st century CE, is believed to have brought water to Nîmes through at least the 6th century.

finest achievements (Kalidasa, poet and dramatist, fl. c. 400 CE). Mathematical innovations included the use of zero and decimal numbers. Invasions by White Huns from the NW led to the empire's destruction c. 550 CE. Rich cultures also developed in Southern India during this period. Emotional Tamil religious poetry contributed to the Hindu revival. The Pallava kingdom controlled much of Southern India c. 350-880 CE and helped to spread Indian civilization to SE Asia.

China. The Ch'in ruler Shih Huang Ti (r. 221-210 BCE), known as the First Emperor, centralized political authority; standardized the written language, laws, weights, measures, and coinage; and conducted a census. But he tried to destroy most philosophical texts. The **Han** dynasty (202 BCE-220 CE) instituted the Mandarin bureaucracy, which lasted 2,000 years. Local officials were selected by examination in Confucian classics and trained at the imperial university and provincial schools.

The invention of **paper** facilitated this bureaucratic system. Agriculture was promoted, but peasants bore most of the tax burden. Irrigation was improved, water clocks and sundials were used, astronomy and mathematics thrived, and landscape painting was perfected.

With the expansion S and W (to nearly the present borders of today's China), trade was opened with India, SE Asia, and the Middle East over sea and caravan routes. Indian missionaries brought Mahayana Buddhism to China by the 1st cent. CE and Daoism was revived and merged with popular superstitions. **Daoist and Buddhist monasteries** and convents multiplied in the turbulent centuries after the collapse of the Han dynasty in 220 CE.

Monotheism Spreads: 1-750 CE

Roman Empire. Polytheism was practiced in the Roman Empire, and religions indigenous to particular Middle Eastern nations became international. Roman citizens worshiped **Isis** of Egypt, **Mithras** of Persia, **Demeter** of Greece, and the great mother **Cybele** of Phrygia. Their cults centered on mysteries (secret ceremonies) and the promise of an afterlife, symbolized by the death and rebirth of the god. The Jews of the empire preserved their monotheistic religion, Judaism, the world's oldest (c. 1300 BCE) continuous religion. Its teachings are contained in the Bible (the Old Testament). 1st-cent. CE Judaism embraced several sects, including the **Sadducees**, mostly drawn from the Temple priesthood, who were culturally Hellenized; the **Pharisees**, who upheld the full range of traditional customs and practices as of equal weight to literal scriptural law and elaborated synagogue worship; and the **Essenes**, an ascetic, millenarian sect. Messianic fervor led to repeated, unsuccessful rebellions against Rome (66-70, 135 CE). As a result, the Temple in Jerusalem was destroyed and the population decimated; this event marked the beginning of the Diaspora (living in exile). To preserve the faith, codification of law was begun at the academy of Yavneh. The work continued for some 500 years in Palestine and in Babylonia, ending in the final redaction (c. 600) of the **Talmud**, a huge collection of legal and moral debates, rulings, liturgy, biblical exegesis, and legendary materials.

Christianity. Emerging as a distinct sect by the second half of the 1st cent. CE, Christianity is based on the teachings of **Jesus**, whom believers considered the Savior (Messiah or Christ) and son of God. Missionary activities of the Apostles and such early leaders as **Paul of Tarsus** spread the faith. Intermittent persecution, as in Rome under Nero in 64 CE, on grounds of suspected disloyalty, failed to disrupt Christian communities. Each congregation, generally urban and of plebeian character, was tightly organized under a leader (bishop), elders (presbyters or priests), and assistants (deacons). The four **Gospels** (accounts of the life and teachings of Jesus) and the Acts of the Apostles were written down in the late 1st and early 2nd cent. and circulated along with letters of Paul and other Christian leaders. An authoritative canon of these writings was not fixed until the 4th cent.

A school for priests was established at Alexandria in the 2nd cent. Its teachers (**Origen**, c. 182-251) helped define doctrine and promote the faith in Greek-style philosophical works. Neoplatonism underwent Christian coloration in the writings of Church Fathers such as **Augustine** (354-430). Christian hermits began to associate in monasteries, first in Egypt (St. Pachomius, c. 290-345), then in other eastern lands, then in the W (**St. Benedict's rule**, 529). Devotion to saints, especially Mary, mother of Jesus, spread. Under **Constantine** (r. 306-37), Christianity became in effect the established religion of the Empire. Pagan temples were expropriated, state funds were used to build churches and support the hierarchy, and laws were adjusted in accordance with Christian ideas. Pagan worship was banned by the end of the 4th cent., and severe restrictions were placed on Judaism.

The newly established church was rocked by doctrinal disputes, often exacerbated by regional rivalries. Chief heresies (as defined by church councils, backed by imperial authority) were **Arianism**, which denied the divinity of Jesus; **Monophysitism**, denying the human nature of Christ; **Donatism**, which regarded as invalid any sacraments administered by sinful clergy; and **Pelagianism**, which denied the necessity of unmerited divine aid (grace) for salvation.

Islam. The earliest Arab civilization emerged by the end of the 2nd millennium BCE in the watered highlands of Yemen. Seaborne and caravan trade in frankincense and myrrh connected the area with the Nile and Fertile Crescent. The Minaean, Sabean (Sheba), and Himyarite states successively held sway. By Muhammad's time (7th cent. CE), the region was a province of Sassanian Persia. In the N, the Nabataean kingdom at Petra and the kingdom of Palmyra were Aramaicized, Romanized, and finally absorbed, as neighboring Judea had been, into the Roman Empire. Nomads shared the central region with a few trading towns and oases. Wars between tribes and raids on communities were common and were celebrated in a poetic tradition that by the 6th cent. helped establish a classic literary Arabic.

About 610, **Muhammad**, a 40-year-old Arab man of Mecca, emerged as a prophet. He proclaimed a revelation from the one true God, calling on contemporaries to abandon idolatry and restore the faith of Abraham. He introduced his religion as **Islam**, meaning "submission" to the one God, Allah, as a continuation of the biblical faith of Abraham, Moses, and Jesus, all respected as prophets in this system. His teachings, recorded in the **Koran** (al-Qur'an in Arabic), in many ways were inclusive of Abrahamic monotheistic ideas known to the Jews and Christians in Arabia. A key aspect of the Abrahamic connection was insistence on justice in society, which led to severe opposition among the aristocrats in Mecca. As conditions worsened for Muhammad and his followers, he decided in 622 to make a *hegira* (flight) to Medina, 200 mi to the N. This event marks the beginning of the Muslim lunar calendar. Hostilities between Mecca and Medina increased, and in 629 Muhammad conquered Mecca. By the time he died in 632, nearly all the Arabian peninsula accepted his political and religious leadership.

After his death the majority of Muslims (later known as **Sunni** Muslims) recognized the leadership of the **caliph** (successor) Abu Bakr (632-34), followed by Umar (634-44), Uthman (644-56), and Ali (656-60). A minority, the **Shiites**, insisted instead on the leadership of Ali, Muhammad's cousin and son-in-law. By 644, **Muslim rule** over Arabia was

The now-typical use of a minaret as the location for the Muslim call to prayer began at the Mosque of Uqba, or Great Mosque of Kairouan, built from 670 CE in present-day Tunisia.

confirmed. Muslim armies had threatened the Byzantine and Persian empires, which were weakened by wars and disaffection among subject peoples (including Coptic and Syriac Christians opposed to the Byzantine Orthodox establishment). Syria, Palestine, Egypt, Iraq, and Persia fell to Muslim armies. The new administration assimilated existing systems in the region; hence the conquered peoples participated in running the empire. The Koran recognized the so-called Peoples of the Book, i.e., Christians, Jews, and Zoroastrians, as tolerated monotheists, and Muslim policy was relatively tolerant to minorities living as "protected" peoples. An expanded tax system, based on conquests of the Persian and Byzantine empires, provided revenue to organize campaigns against neighboring non-Muslim regions.

Under the **Umayyads** (661-750) and **Abbasids** (750-1256), territorial expansion led Muslim armies across N Africa and into Spain (711). Muslim armies in the W were stopped at Tours, France, in 732 by the Frankish ruler **Charles Martel**. Asia Minor, the Indus Valley, and Transoxiana were conquered in the E. The conversion of conquered peoples to Islam was gradual. In many places the official Arabic language supplanted the local tongues. But in the eastern regions the Arab rulers and their armies adopted Persian cultures and language as part of their Muslim identity.

Disputes over succession and pious opposition to injustices in society led to a number of oppositional movements, which led to the factionalization of Muslim community. The **Shiites** supported leadership candidates descended from Muhammad, believing them to be carriers of some kind of divine authority. The **Kharijites** supported an egalitarian system derived from the Koran, opposing and even engaging in battle against those who did not agree with them.

New Peoples Enter World History: 400-900 CE

Barbarian invasions and fall of Rome. Germanic tribes infiltrated S and E from their Baltic homeland during the 1st millennium BCE, reaching southern Germany by 100 BCE and the Black Sea by 214 CE. Organized into large federated tribes under elected kings, most resisted Roman domination and raided the empire in times of civil war (Goths took Dacia in 214, raided Thrace in 251-69). Germanic troops and commanders dominated the Roman armies by the end of the 4th cent. **Huns**, invaders from Asia, entered Europe in 372, driving more Germans into the empire. Emperor Valens allowed Visigoths to cross the Danube in 376. Huns under Attila (d. 453) raided Gaul, Italy, and the Balkans.

The western empire, weakened by overtaxation and social stagnation, was overrun in the 5th cent. Gaul was effectively lost in 406-07, Spain in 409, Britain in 410, and Africa in 429-39. Rome was sacked in 410 by Visigoths under Alaric and in 455 by Vandals. The **last western emperor**, Romulus Augustulus, was deposed in 476 by the Germanic chief Odovacar.

Celts. Celtic cultures, which in pre-Roman times covered most of W Europe, were confined almost entirely to the British Isles after the Germanic invasions. **St. Patrick** completed (c. 457-92) the conversion of Ireland and a strong monastic tradition took hold. Irish monastic missionaries in Scotland, England, and on the continent (Columba, c. 521-97; Columbanus, c. 543-615) helped restore Christianity after the Germanic invasions. **Monasteries** became centers of classic and Christian learning and presided over the recording of a Christianized Celtic mythology, elaborated by secular writers and bards. An intricate decorative art style developed, especially in book illumination (Lindisfarne Gospels, c. 700; Book of Kells, 8th cent.).

Successor states. The Visigothic kingdom in Spain (from 419) and much of France (to 507) saw continuation of Roman administration, language, and law (Breviary of Alaric, 506) until its destruction by the Muslims (711). The Vandal kingdom in Africa (from 429) was conquered by the Byzantines in 533. Italy was ruled successively by an Ostrogothic kingdom under Byzantine suzerainty (489-554), direct Byzantine government, and German Lombards (568-774). The Lombards divided the peninsula with the Byzantines and papacy under the dynamic reformer **Pope Gregory the Great** (590-604) and successors.

King Clovis (r. 481-511) united the Franks on both sides of the Rhine and, after his conversion to Christianity, defeated the Arian heretics, Burgundians (after 500), and Visigoths (507) with the support of native clergy and the papacy. Under the **Merovingian** kings, a feudal system emerged: power was fragmented among hierarchies of military landowners. Social stratification, which in late Roman times had acquired legal, hereditary sanction, was reinforced.

The Carolingians (747-987) expanded the kingdom and restored central power. **Charlemagne** (r. 768-814) conquered nearly all the Germanic lands, including Lombard Italy. He was crowned emperor by Pope Leo III in Rome in 800. A centuries-long decline in commerce and arts was reversed under Charlemagne's patronage. He welcomed Jews to his kingdom, which became a center of Jewish learning (Rashi, 1040-1105). He sponsored the Carolingian Renaissance of learning under the Anglo-Latin scholar Alcuin (c. 732-804), who reformed church liturgy.

Byzantine Empire. Under **Diocletian** (r. 284-305) the Roman empire had been divided into two parts to facilitate administration and defense. **Constantine** founded (330) **Constantinople** (at old Byzantium) as a fully Christian city. Commerce and taxation financed a sumptuous, orientalized court, a class of hereditary bureaucratic families, and magnificent urban construction (Hagia Sophia, 532-37). The city's fortifications and naval innovations repelled assaults by Goths, Huns, Slavs, Bulgars, Avars, Arabs, and Scandinavians. Greek replaced Latin as the official language by c. 700. **Byzantine art**, a solemn, sacral, and stylized variation of late classical styles (mosaics at the Church of San Vitale, Ravenna, Italy, 526-48), was a starting point for medieval art in Eastern and Western Europe.

Justinian (r. 527-65) briefly reconquered parts of Spain, N Africa, and Italy, codified **Roman law** (Codex Justinianus [529] was medieval Europe's chief legal text), closed the Platonic Academy at Athens, and ordered all pagans to convert. Lombards in Italy and Arabs in Africa retook most of his conquests. The Isaurian dynasty from Anatolia (from 717) and the Macedonian dynasty (867-1054) restored military and commercial power. The Iconoclast controversy (726-843) over the permissibility of images helped alienate the Eastern Church from the papacy.

Abbasid Empire. Baghdad (established 762) became seat of the **Abbasid dynasty** (established 750), while Umayyads continued to rule in Spain. A brilliant cosmopolitan civilization emerged, inaugurating a Muslim-Arab golden age. Arabic was the lingua franca of the empire; intellectual sources from Persian, Sanskrit, Greek, and Syriac were rendered into Arabic. Christians and Jews equally participated in this translation movement, which also involved interaction between Jewish legal thought and Islamic law, as much as between Christian theology and Muslim scholasticism. Persian-style court life, with art and music, flourished at the court of **Harun al-Rashid** (786-809), celebrated in the masterpiece known to English readers as *The Arabian Nights*. The sciences, medicine, and mathematics were pursued at Baghdad, Cordova, and Cairo (c. 969). The culmination of this intellectual synthesis in Islamic civilization came with the scientific and philosophical works of **Avicenna** (Ibn Sina, 980-1037), **Averroes** (Ibn Rushd, 1126-98), and **Maimonides** (1135-1204), a Jew who wrote in Arabic. This intellectual tradition was translated into Latin and opened a new period in Christian thought.

The decentralization of the Abbasid empire, from 874, led to the establishment of various Muslim dynasties under different ethnic groups. Persians, Berbers, and Turks ruled different regions, retaining connection with the Abbasid caliph at the religious level. The Abbasid period also saw various religious movements against the orthodox position held by governing authorities. This situation in Muslim religion led to the establishment of different legal, theological, and mystical schools of thought. The most influential mass movement was **Sufism**, which aimed at the reaching out of the average individual in quest of a spiritual path. Al-Ghazali (1058-1111) is credited with reconciling personal Sufism with orthodox Sunni tradition.

Africa. Immigrants from Saba in S Arabia helped set up the **Axum** kingdom in Ethiopia in the 1st cent. (their language, Ge'ez, is preserved by the Ethiopian Church). In the 3rd cent., when the kingdom became Christianized, it defeated Kushite Meroe and expanded its influence into Yemen. Axum was the center of a vast ivory trade and controlled the Red Sea coast until c. 1100. Arab conquest in Egypt cut Axum's political and economic ties with Byzantium.

The pyramid of Kukulkan (El Castillo) at Chichen Itza is one of the preeminent existing examples of Mayan architecture in present-day Mexico.

The Iron Age entered W Africa by the end of the 1st millennium BCE. **Ghana**, the first known sub-Saharan state, ruled in the upper Senegal-Niger region c. 400-1240, controlling the trade of gold from mines in the S to trans-Sahara caravan routes to the N. The **Bantu** peoples, probably of W African origin, began to spread E and S perhaps 2,000 years ago, displacing the Pygmies and Bushmen of central and southern Africa during a 1,500-year period.

Japan. The advanced Neolithic Yayoi period, when irrigation, rice farming, and iron and bronze casting techniques were introduced from China or Korea, persisted to c. 400 CE. The myriad Japanese states were then united by the **Yamato** clan, under an emperor who acted as chief priest of the animistic Shinto cult. Japanese political and military intervention by the 6th cent. in Korea, then under strong Chinese influence, quickened a Chinese cultural invasion of Japan, bringing Buddhism, the Chinese language (which long remained a literary and governmental medium), Chinese ideographs, and Buddhist styles in painting, sculpture, literature, and architecture (7th cent., Horyuji temple at Nara). The Taika Reforms (646) tried unsuccessfully to centralize Japan according to Chinese bureaucratic and Buddhist philosophical values.

A nativist reaction against the Buddhist **Nara** period (710-94) ushered in the **Heian** period (794-1185) centered at the new capital, Kyoto. Japanese elegance and simplicity modified Chinese styles in architecture, scroll painting, and literature; the writing system was also simplified. The courtly novel *Tale of Genji* (1010-20) testifies to the enhanced role of women in medieval Japanese literature and culture.

Southeast Asia. The historic peoples of SE Asia began arriving some 2,500 years ago from China and Tibet, displacing scattered aborigines. Their agriculture relied on rice and yams. Indian cultural influences were strongest; literacy and Hindu and Buddhist ideas followed the S India-China trade route. From the southern tip of Indochina, the kingdom of **Funan** (1st-7th cent.) traded as far W as Persia. It was absorbed by Chenla, itself conquered by the **Khmer** empire (600-1300). The Khmers, under Hindu god-kings (Suryavarman II, 1113-c. 1150), built the monumental Angkor Wat temple center for the royal phallic cult. The **Nam-Viet** kingdom in Annam, dominated by China and Chinese culture for 1,000 years, emerged in the 10th cent., growing at the expense of the Khmers, who also lost ground in the NW to the new, highly organized **Thai** kingdom. On Sumatra, the **Srivijaya** empire controlled vital sea lanes (7th-10th cent.). A Buddhist dynasty, the Sailendras, ruled central **Java** (8th-9th cent.), building at Borobudur one of the largest stupas (dome-shaped Buddhist shrines) in the world.

China. The Sui dynasty (581-618) ushered in a period of commercial, artistic, and scientific achievement in China, which continued under the **Tang** dynasty (618-906). Inventions like the magnetic compass, gunpowder, the abacus, and printing were introduced or perfected. Medical innovations included cataract surgery. The state, from its cosmopolitan capital, Chang-an, supervised foreign trade, which exchanged Chinese silks, porcelains, and art for spices and ivory over Central Asian caravan routes and sea routes reaching Africa. A golden age of poetry bequeathed valuable works to later generations (Tu Fu, 712-70; Li Po, 701-62). Landscape painting flourished.

Commercial and industrial expansion continued under the **Northern Sung** dynasty (960-1126), facilitated by paper money and credit notes. But commerce never achieved full respectability; government monopolies expropriated successful merchants. The population, long stable at 50 million, doubled in 200 years with the introduction of early-ripening rice and the double harvest. In art, native Chinese styles were revived.

Americas. From 300 to 600, a Native American empire stretched from the Valley of Mexico to Guatemala, centering on the huge city **Teotihuacán** (founded 100 BCE). To the S, in Guatemala, a high **Mayan** civilization developed (150-900) around hundreds of rural ceremonial centers. The Mayans improved on Olmec writing and the calendar and pursued astronomy and mathematics. In South America, a widespread pre-Inca culture grew from **Tiahuanaco**, Bolivia, near Lake Titicaca (Gateway of the Sun doorway, c. 700).

Christian Europe Regroups and Expands: 900-1300

Scandinavia. Pagan Danish and Norse (Viking) adventurers, traders, and pirates raided the coasts of the British Isles (Dublin, c. 831), France, and even the Mediterranean for over 200 years beginning in the late 8th cent. Inland settlement in the W was limited to Great Britain (King Canute, 994-1035) and Normandy, settled (911) under Rollo, as a fief of France. Vikings also reached Iceland (874), Greenland (c. 986), and North America (**Leif Ericson** and others, c. 1000). Norse traders (**Varangians**) developed Russian river commerce from the 8th to the 11th cent. and helped set up a state at Kiev in the late 9th cent. Conversion to Christianity occurred in the 10th cent., reaching Sweden 100 years later. In the 11th cent. Norman bands conquered Southern Italy and Sicily, and Duke **William of Normandy** conquered (1066) England, bringing feudal government and the French language, essential elements in later English civilization.

Central and East Europe. Slavs began to expand from about 150 CE in all directions in Europe. By the 7th cent. they reached as far S as the Adriatic and Aegean seas. In the Balkan Peninsula they dislocated Romanized local populations or assimilated newcomers (Bulgarians, a Turkic people). The first **Slavic** states were Moravia (628) in Central Europe and the Bulgarian state (680) in the Balkans. Byzantine missions of St. Methodius and Cyril (whose Greek-based cyrillic alphabet is still used by some Southern and Eastern Slavs) converted (863) Moravia.

The Eastern Slavs, part-civilized under the overlordship of the Turkish-Jewish **Khazar** trading empire (7th-10th cent.), gravitated toward Constantinople by the 9th cent. The **Kievan** state adopted (989) Eastern Christianity under Prince Vladimir. King Boleslav I (992-1025) began **Poland**'s long history of conquest. The Magyars (**Hungarians**), in present-day Hungary since 896, accepted (1001) Latin Christianity.

Germany. The German kingdom that emerged after the breakup of Charlemagne's Western Empire remained a confederation of largely autonomous states. Otto I, a Saxon who was king from 936, established the **Holy Roman Empire**—a union of Germany and Northern Italy—in alliance with Pope John XII, who crowned (962) him emperor; he defeated (955) the Magyars. Imperial power was greatest under the **Hohenstaufens** (1138-1254), despite the growing opposition of the papacy, which ruled central Italy, and the Lombard League cities. Frederick II (1194-1250) improved administration and patronized the arts. After his death, German influence was removed from Italy.

Christian Spain. From its northern mountain redoubts, Christian rule slowly migrated S through the 11th cent., when Muslim unity collapsed. After the capture (1085) of **Toledo**, the kingdoms of Portugal, Castile, and Aragon undertook repeated crusades of reconquest, finally completed in 1492. Elements of Islamic civilization persisted in recaptured areas, influencing all Western Europe.

Crusades. Pope Urban II called for a crusade (1095) to restore Asia Minor to Byzantium and the Holy Land to Christendom. This first crusade captured Jerusalem and led to the foundation of four Frankish states in the Levant. The defeat inflicted upon crusaders at the Battle of Hattin (1187) by **Saladin** (c. 1137-93), the Kurdish ruler of Egypt and Syria, effectively negated territorial gains. Many crusades followed until 1291. The 4th crusade sacked Constantinople (1204). Other crusades were launched against Christian heretics (Albigensian Crusade, 1229), pagans, and enemies of the papacy.

Economy. The agricultural base of European life benefited from improvements in **plow design** (c. 1000) and by the draining of lowlands and clearing of forests, leading to a rural population increase. Towns grew in Northern Italy, Flanders, and Northern Germany (Hanseatic League). Improvements in **loom design** permitted factory textile production. **Guilds** dominated urban trades from the 12th cent. Banking (centered in Italy, 12th-15th cent.) facilitated long-distance trade.

Christianity. The split between the Eastern and Western churches was formalized in 1054. Western and Central Europe was divided into 500 bishoprics under one united hierarchy, but conflicts between secular and church authorities were frequent (German **Investiture Controversy**, 1075-1122). Clerical power was first strengthened through the international monastic reform begun at Cluny in 910. Popular religious enthusiasm often expressed itself in heretical movements (Waldensians from 1173), but was channeled by the **Dominican** (1215) and **Franciscan** (1223) friars into the religious mainstream.

Arts. Romanesque architecture (9th to mid-12th cent.) expanded on late Roman models, using the rounded arch and massed stone to support enlarged basilicas. Painting and sculpture followed Byzantine models. The literature of **chivalry** was exemplified by the epic (*Chanson de Roland*, c. 1100) and by courtly love poems of the troubadours of Provence and minnesingers of Germany. **Gothic** architecture emerged in France (choir of St. Denis, c. 1140) and spread along with French cultural influence. Rib vaulting and pointed arches were used to combine soaring heights with delicacy, and they freed walls for display of stained glass. Exteriors were covered with painted relief sculpture and embellished with elaborate architectural detail.

Learning. Law, medicine, and philosophy were advanced at independent **universities** (Bologna, Paris, 12th cent.), originally corporations of students and masters. Twelfth-cent. translations of Greek classics, especially by Aristotle, encouraged an analytic approach. Scholastic philosophy, from Anselm (1033-1109) to **Aquinas** (1225-74), attempted to understand revelation through reason.

Apogee of Central Asian Power and the Spread of Islam: 1250-1500

Turks. Turkic peoples, of Central Asian ancestry, were a military threat to the Byzantine and Persian Empires from the 6th cent. After several waves of invasions, during which most of the Turks adopted Islam, the **Seljuk Turks** took (1055) Baghdad. They ruled Persia, Iraq, and, after 1071, Asia Minor, where massive numbers of Turks settled. The empire was divided in the 12th cent. into smaller states ruled by Seljuks, Kurds, and Mamluks (a military caste of former Turk, Kurd, and Circassian slaves), which governed Egypt and the Middle East until the Ottoman era (c. 1290-1922).

Osman I (r. c. 1290-1326) and succeeding sultans united Anatolian Turkish warriors in a militaristic state that waged holy war against Byzantine and Balkan Christians. Most of the Balkans had been subdued and Anatolia united when Constantinople fell (1453). By the mid-16th cent., Hungary, the Middle East, and N Africa had been conquered. The Turkish advance was stopped at Vienna (1529) and at the naval battle of Lepanto (1571) by Spain, Venice, and the papacy.

The **Ottoman state** was governed in accordance with orthodox Muslim law. Greek, Armenian, and Jewish communities were segregated and were ruled by religious leaders responsible for taxation; they dominated trade. Many state offices and most army ranks were filled by slaves, in part through a system of child conscription among Christians.

India. Mahmud of Ghazni (971-1030) led repeated Turkish raids into N India. Turkish power was consolidated in 1206 with the start of the **Sultanate at Delhi**. Centralization of state power under the early Delhi sultans went far beyond traditional Indian practice. Muslim rule of much of the subcontinent lasted until the British conquest 600 years later, though Hinduism remained the majority religion.

Mongols. Genghis Khan (c. 1167-1227) first united the feuding Mongol tribes and built their armies into an effective offensive force around a core of highly mobile cavalry. He and his immediate successors created the largest land empire in history; by 1279 it stretched from the E coast of Asia to the Danube and from the Siberian steppes to the Arabian Sea. East-West trade and contacts were facilitated (Marco Polo, c. 1254-1324). The western Mongols were Islamized by 1295; successor states soon lost their Mongol character by assimilation. They were briefly reunited under the Turk Tamerlane (1336-1405).

Kublai Khan ruled China from his new capital Beijing (established c. 1264). Naval campaigns against Japan (1274, 1281) and Java (1293) were defeated, the latter by the Hindu-Buddhist maritime kingdom of Majapahit. The **Yuan** dynasty used Mongols and other foreigners (including Europeans) in official posts and tolerated the return of Nestorian Christianity (suppressed 841-45) and the spread of Islam in the S and W. A native reaction expelled the Mongols in 1367-68.

Russia. The Kievan state in Russia, weakened by the decline of Byzantium and the rise of the Catholic Polish-Lithuanian state, was overrun (1238-40) by the Mongols. Only the northern trading republic of Novgorod remained independent. The grand dukes of Moscow emerged as leaders of a coalition of princes that eventually (by 1481) defeated the Mongols. After the fall of Constantinople in 1453, the **Tsars** (Caesars) at Moscow (from Ivan III, r. 1462-1505) set up an independent Russian Orthodox Church. Commerce failed to revive. The isolated Russian state remained agrarian with the peasant class falling into serfdom.

Persia. A revival of Persian literature, making use of the Arab alphabet and literary forms, began in the 10th cent. (epic of Firdausi, 935-1020). An art revival, influenced by Chinese styles introduced after the Mongols came to power in Iran, began in the 13th cent. Persian cultural and political forms, and often the Persian language, were used for centuries by Turkish and Mongol elites from the Balkans to India. Persian mystics from Rumi (1207-73) to Jami (1414-92) promoted Sufism in their poetry.

Africa. Two militant Islamic Berber dynasties emerged from the Sahara to carve out empires from the Sahel to central Spain—the **Almoravids** (c. 1050-1140) and the fanatical **Almohads** (c. 1125-1269). The Ghanaian empire was replaced in the upper Niger by Mali (c. 1230-1340), whose Muslim rulers

Born Temüjin, Genghis Khan was proclaimed ruler of the unified Mongol empire in 1206.

imported Egyptians to help make **Timbuktu** a center of commerce (in gold, leather, and slaves) and learning. The Songhay empire (to 1590) replaced Mali. To the S, forest kingdoms produced refined artworks (Ife terra cotta, **Benin** bronzes).

Other **Muslim states** in Nigeria (Hausas) and Chad originated in the 11th cent. and continued in some form until the 19th-cent. European conquest. Less-developed Bantu kingdoms existed across central Africa.

Some 40 Muslim Arab-Persian trading colonies and city-states were established all along the E African coast from the 10th cent. (Kilwa, Mogadishu). The interchange with Bantu peoples produced the **Swahili** language and culture. Gold, palm oil, and slaves were brought from the interior, stimulating the growth of the Monamatapa kingdom of the Zambezi (15th cent.). The Christian Ethiopian empire (from 13th cent.) continued the traditions of Axum.

Southeast Asia. Islam was introduced into Malaya and the Indonesian islands by Arab, Persian, and Indian traders. Coastal Muslim cities and states (starting before 1300) soon dominated the interior. Chief among these was the **Malacca** state (c. 1400-1511), on the Malay peninsula.

Arts and Statecraft Thrive in Europe; New Asian Empires Rise: 1350-1600

Italy. Distinctive Italian achievements in literature and fine arts during the late Middle Ages (**Dante**, 1265-1321; Giotto, 1276-1337) led to the vigorous new styles of the Renaissance (14th-16th cent.). Patronized by the rulers of the quarreling petty states of Italy (**Medicis** in Florence and the papacy, c. 1400-1737), the plastic arts perfected realistic techniques, including **perspective** (Masaccio, 1401-28; Leonardo **da Vinci**, 1452-1519). Classical motifs were used in architecture, and increased talent and expense were put into secular buildings. The Florentine dialect was refined as a national literary language (**Petrarch**, 1304-74). Greek refugees from the E strengthened the respect of humanist scholars for the classic sources. Soon an international movement aided by the spread of **printing** (Gutenberg, c. 1397-1468), **humanism** was optimistic about the power of human reason (Erasmus of Rotterdam, 1466-1536, More's *Utopia*, 1516) and valued individual effort in the arts and in politics (**Machiavelli**, 1469-1527).

France. The French monarchy, strengthened in its repeated struggles with powerful nobles (Burgundy, Flanders, Aquitaine) by alliances with the growing commercial towns, consolidated bureaucratic control under Philip IV (r. 1285-1314) and extended French influence into Germany and Italy (popes at Avignon, France, 1309-1417). The **Hundred Years War** (1337-1453) ended English dynastic claims in France (battles of Crécy, 1346, and Poitiers, 1356; Joan of Arc executed, 1431). A French Renaissance, dating from royal invasions (1494, 1499) of Italy, was encouraged at the court of Francis I (r. 1515-47), who centralized taxation and law. French vernacular literature consciously asserted its independence (La Pléiade, 1549).

England. The evolution of England's political institutions began with the **Magna Carta** (1215), by which King John guaranteed the privileges of nobles and church against the monarchy and assured jury trial. After the **Wars of the Roses** (1455-85), the **Tudor** dynasty reasserted royal prerogatives (Henry VIII, r. 1509-47), but the trend toward independent departments and ministerial government also continued. English trade (wool exports from c. 1340) was protected by the nation's growing maritime power (**Spanish Armada** destroyed, 1588).

English replaced French and Latin in the late 14th cent. in law and literature (**Chaucer**, c. 1340-1400), and English translation of the Bible began (Wycliffe, 1380s). **Elizabeth I** (r. 1558-1603) presided over the development of poetry (Spenser, 1552-99), drama (**Shakespeare**, 1564-1616), and music.

The Magna Carta, granted by England's King John to his rebellious barons in 1215, is considered a foundational document for constitutional liberties.

German Empire. From among a welter of minor feudal states, church lands, and independent cities, the **Habsburgs** assembled a far-flung territorial domain, based in Austria from 1276. Family members held the title of Holy Roman Emperor from 1438 to the Empire's dissolution in 1806 but failed to centralize its domains, leaving Germany disunited for centuries. Resistance to Turkish expansion brought Hungary under Austrian control from the 16th cent. The Netherlands, Luxembourg, and Burgundy were added in 1477, curbing French expansion.

The Flemish painting tradition of naturalism, technical proficiency, and bourgeois subject matter began in the 15th cent. (Jan van Eyck, c. 1390-1441), the earliest northern manifestation of the Renaissance. Albrecht Dürer (1471-1528) typified the merging of late Gothic and Italian trends in 16th-cent. German art. Imposing civic architecture flourished in the prosperous commercial cities.

Black Death. The bubonic plague reached Europe from the E in 1348, killing up to half the population by 1350 (and recurring periodically in most areas until the early 18th cent.). Labor scarcity forced wages to rise and brought greater freedom to the peasantry, making possible **peasant uprisings** (Jacquerie in France, 1358; Wat Tyler's rebellion in England, 1381).

Spain. Despite the unification of Castile and Aragon in 1479, the two countries retained separate governments, and the nobility, especially in Aragon and Catalonia, retained many privileges. Spanish lands in Italy (Naples, Sicily) and the Netherlands entangled the country in European wars through the mid-17th cent., while explorers, traders, and conquerors built up a Spanish empire in the Americas and the Philippines.

From the late 15th cent., a **golden age** of literature and art produced works of social satire (plays of Lope de Vega, 1562-1635; **Cervantes**, 1547-1616), as well as spiritual intensity (**El Greco**, 1541-1614; **Velázquez**, 1599-1660).

Explorations. Organized European maritime exploration began, seeking to evade the Venice-Ottoman monopoly of eastern trade and to promote Christianity. A key goal was to satisfy a growing taste for Asian goods. Beginning in 1418, expeditions from Portugal explored the W coast of Africa, until Vasco da Gama rounded the Cape of Good Hope in 1497 and reached India. A Portuguese trading empire was consolidated by the seizure of Goa (1510) and Malacca (1551). Japan was reached in 1542. The voyages of Christopher **Columbus** (1492-1504) uncovered a world new to Europeans, which Spain hastened to subdue. Navigation schools in Spain and Portugal, the development of large sailing ships (carracks) mounted with cannons, and the invention (c. 1475) of the rifle aided European penetration.

Mughals and Safavids. E of the Ottoman Empire, two Muslim dynasties ruled unchallenged in the 16th and 17th cent. The Mughal dynasty of India, founded by Persianized Turkish invaders from the NW under Babur, dates from their 1526 conquest of the Delhi Sultanate. The dynasty ruled most of India for more than 200 years, surviving nominally until 1857. **Akbar** (r. 1556-1605) consolidated administration at his glorious court, where the Urdu language (Persian-influenced Hindi) developed. Trade relations with Europe increased. Under Shah Jahan (1629-58), a secularized art fusing Hindu and Muslim elements flourished in miniature painting and in architecture (**Taj Mahal**). **Sikhism** (founded late 15th cent.) combined elements of both faiths. Suppression of Hindus and Shiite Muslims in S India in the late 17th cent. weakened the empire.

Intense devotion to the Shiite sect characterized the Safavids (1502-1736) of Persia and led to hostilities with the Sunni Ottomans for more than a century. The prosperity and the strength of the empire are evidenced by the mosques at its capital city, **Isfahan.** The Safavids enhanced Iranian national consciousness.

China. The **Ming** emperors (1368-1644), the last native dynasty in China, wielded strong personal power. European trade (Portuguese monopoly through **Macao** from 1557) was strictly controlled. Jesuit scholars and scientists (Matteo Ricci, 1552-1610) introduced some Western science; their writings familiarized the West with China. The arts thrived, especially in the areas of painting and ceramics. Chinese manufacturing boomed, bringing in new profits from world trade.

Japan. After the decline of the first hereditary *shogunate* (chief generalship) at **Kamakura** (1185-1333), fragmentation

of power accelerated, as did the consequent social mobility. Under Kamakura and the Ashikaga shogunate (1338-1573), the *daimyos* (lords) and *samurai* (warriors) grew more powerful and promoted a martial ideology. Japanese pirates and traders plied the China coast. Popular Buddhist movements included the nationalist Nichiren sect (from c. 1250) and **Zen** (brought from China, 1191), which stressed meditation and a disciplined aesthetic (tea ceremony, gardening, martial arts, *No* drama).

Change and Expansion in Europe: 1500-1700

Reformation. Theological debate and protests against real and perceived clerical corruption existed in the medieval Christian world, expressed by such dissenters as John **Wycliffe** (c. 1320-84) and his followers (the Lollards) in England, and **Huss** (burned as a heretic, 1415) in Bohemia.

Martin **Luther** (1483-1546) preached that faith alone, without the mediation of clergy or good works, leads to salvation. He attacked the authority of the pope, rejected priestly celibacy, and recommended individual study of the Bible (which he translated into German c. 1525). His 95 Theses (1517) led to his excommunication (1521). John **Calvin** (1509-64) said that God's elect were predestined for salvation and all others for damnation; good conduct and success were signs of election. Calvin in Geneva and John **Knox** (1505-72) in Scotland established theocratic states.

Henry VIII asserted English national authority and secular power by breaking away (1534) from the Catholic Church, creating what would become the Anglican Church. Monastic property was confiscated, and some Protestant doctrines given official sanction.

Religious wars. A century and a half of religious wars began with a southern German peasant uprising (1524), repressed with Luther's support. Radical sects—democratic, pacifist, millenarian—arose (Anabaptists ruled Münster, 1534-35) and were suppressed violently. Civil war in France from 1562 between **Huguenots** (Protestant nobles and merchants) and Catholics ended with the 1598 **Edict of Nantes**, tolerating Protestants (revoked 1685). Habsburg attempts to restore Catholicism in Germany were resisted in 25 years of fighting. The 1555 Peace of Augsburg guarantee of religious independence to local princes and cities was confirmed only after the **Thirty Years' War** (1618-48), when much of Germany was devastated by local and foreign armies (Sweden, France).

A Catholic Reformation, or **Counter-Reformation,** met the Protestant challenge, defining an official theology at the Council of Trent (1545-63). The **Jesuit** order (Society of Jesus), founded in 1534 by Ignatius Loyola (1491-1556), helped reconvert large areas of Poland, Hungary, and S Germany and sent missionaries to the New World, India, and China. The **Inquisition** suppressed heresy in Catholic countries. A revival of religious fervor appeared in devotional literature (Teresa of Avila, 1515-82) and in grandiose **Baroque** art (Bernini, 1598-1680).

Scientific Revolution. The late nominalist thinkers (Ockham, c. 1300-49) of Paris and Oxford challenged Aristotelian orthodoxy, allowing for a freer scientific approach. At the same time, metaphysical values, such as the Neoplatonic faith in an orderly, mathematical cosmos, still motivated and directed inquiry. Nicolaus **Copernicus** (1473-1543) promoted the heliocentric theory, which was confirmed when Johannes **Kepler** (1571-1630) discovered the mathematical laws describing the elliptical orbits of the planets. The traditional Christian-Aristotelian belief that the heavens and the Earth were fundamentally different collapsed when **Galileo** Galilei (1564-1642) discovered moving sunspots, irregular moon topography, and moons around Jupiter, but he faced religious opposition (Galileo's retraction, 1633). He and Sir Isaac **Newton** (1642-1727) developed a mechanics that unified cosmic and earthly phenomena. Newton and Gottfried von **Leibniz** (1646-1716) invented calculus. René **Descartes** (1596-1650), best known for his influential philosophy, also invented analytic geometry.

An explosion of **observational science** included the discovery of blood circulation (Harvey, 1578-1657) and microscopic life (Leeuwenhoek, 1632-1723) and advances in anatomy (Vesalius, 1514-64, dissected corpses) and chemistry (Boyle, 1627-91). Scientific research institutes were founded in Florence (1657), London (**Royal Society**, 1660), and Paris (1666). Inventions proliferated (Savery's steam engine, 1696).

Arts. Mannerist trends of the High Renaissance (**Michelangelo,** 1475-1564) exploited virtuosity, grace, novelty, and exotic subjects and poses. The notion of artistic genius was promoted. Private connoisseurs entered the art market. These trends were elaborated in the 17th cent. **Baroque** era on a grander scale. Dynamic movement in painting and sculpture was emphasized by sharp lighting effects, rich materials (colored marble, gilt), and realistic details. Curved facades, broken lines, rich detail, and ceiling decoration characterized Baroque architecture. Monarchs, princes, and prelates, usually Catholic, used Baroque art to enhance and embellish their authority, as in royal portraits (Velázquez, 1599-1660; Van Dyck, 1599-1641).

National styles emerged. In France, a taste for rectilinear order and serenity (Poussin, 1594-1665), linked to the new rational philosophy, was expressed in classical forms. The influence of **classical values** in French literature (tragedies of **Racine,** 1639-99) gave rise to the "battle of the Ancients and Moderns." New forms included the essay (**Montaigne,** 1533-92) and novel (*Princesse de Clèves,* La Fayette, 1678).

Dutch painting of the 17th cent. was unique in its wide social distribution. The Flemish tradition of undemonstrative realism reached its peak in **Rembrandt** (1606-69) and Jan Vermeer (1632-75).

Economy. European economic expansion, known as the **commercial revolution,** was stimulated by new trade with the East, by New World gold and silver, and by a doubling of population (50 million in 1450, 100 million in 1600). **New business and financial techniques** were developed and refined, such as joint-stock companies, insurance, and letters of credit and exchange. The Bank of Amsterdam (1609) and the Bank of England (1694) broke the old monopoly of private banking families. The rise of a business mentality was typified by the spread of clock towers in cities in the 14th cent. By the mid-15th cent., portable clocks were available; the first watch was invented in 1502.

By 1650, most governments had adopted the **mercantile system,** in which they sought to amass metallic wealth by protecting merchants' foreign and colonial trade monopolies. The rise in prices and the new coin-based economy undermined craft guild and feudal manorial systems. Expanding industries (clothweaving, mining) benefited from technical advances. Coal began to replace wood as the chief fuel; it was used to fuel new 16th-cent. blast furnaces making cast iron.

New World. The **Aztecs** united much of the Mesoamerican area in a militarist empire by 1519 from their capital, Tenochtitlán

Nicolaus Copernicus's theory of heliocentricity (1533) was later proven by Johannes Kepler, but the concept of a moving Earth was too outlandish for many 16th-century thinkers.

(pop. 300,000), which was the center of a cult requiring ritual human sacrifice. Most of the civilized areas of South America were ruled by the centralized Inca Empire (1476-1534), stretching 2,000 mi from Ecuador to NW Argentina. Lavish and sophisticated traditions in pottery, weaving, sculpture, and architecture were maintained in both regions.

These empires, beset by revolts, fell in two short campaigns to gold-seeking Spanish forces based in the Antilles and Panama. Hernán Cortés took Mexico (1519-21); Francisco Pizarro, Peru (1532-35). From these centers, land and sea expeditions claimed most of North and South America for Spain. The indigenous high cultures did not survive the impact of Christian missionaries and the new upper class of whites. Although the Spanish administration intermittently concerned itself with their welfare, the population was devastated by European diseases and remained impoverished at most levels. New World silver and such native products as potatoes, tobacco, corn, peanuts, chocolate, and rubber exercised a major economic influence on Europe.

Brazil, which the Portuguese reached in 1500 and settled after 1530, and the Caribbean colonies of several European nations developed a plantation economy where sugarcane, tobacco, cotton, coffee, rice, indigo, and lumber were grown by slaves. From the early 16th to late 19th cent., 10 million Africans were transported to slavery in the Americas and Caribbean islands.

Netherlands. The urban, Calvinist northern provinces of the Netherlands rebelled (1568) against Habsburg Spain and founded an oligarchic mercantile republic. Their control of the Baltic grain market enabled them to exploit Mediterranean food shortages. Religious refugees—French and Belgian Protestants, Iberian Jews—added to the commercial talent pool. After Spain absorbed Portugal (1580), the Dutch seized Portuguese possessions and created a vast commercial empire ultimately centered in parts of the Caribbean and in Indonesia. The Dutch also challenged or supplanted Portuguese traders in China and Japan. Revolution in 1640 restored Portuguese independence.

England. Anglicanism became firmly established under Elizabeth I after a brief Catholic interlude under "Bloody Mary" (1553-58). But religious and political conflicts led to a rebellion (1642) by Parliament. Forces of the Roundheads (Puritans) defeated the Cavaliers (Royalists); Charles I was beheaded (1649). The new Commonwealth was ruled as a military dictatorship by Oliver Cromwell, who also brutally crushed (1649-51) an Irish rebellion. Conflicts within the Puritan camp (democratic Levelers defeated, 1649) aided the Stuart restoration (1660), but Parliament was strengthened and the peaceful "Glorious Revolution" (1688) advanced political and religious liberties (writings of Locke, 1632-1704). British privateers (Drake, 1540-96) challenged Spanish control of the

New World and penetrated Asian trade routes (Madras taken, 1639). North American colonies (Jamestown, 1607; Plymouth, 1620) provided an outlet for private enterprise and religious dissenters from Europe. The British East India company gained growing sway in 18th-cent. India, as Mughal power declined.

France. Emerging from the religious civil wars in 1628, France regained military and commercial great power status (under the ministries of Richelieu, Mazarin, and Colbert). Under Louis XIV (r. 1643-1715), royal absolutism triumphed over nobles and local parlements (defeat of Fronde, 1648-53). Durable colonies were founded in Canada (1608), the Caribbean (1626), and India (1674).

Sweden. Sweden seceded from the Scandinavian Union in 1523. The thinly populated agrarian state (with copper, iron, and timber exports) was united by the Vasa kings, whose conquests by the mid-17th cent. made Sweden the dominant Baltic power. The empire collapsed in the Great Northern War (1700-21).

Poland. After the union with Lithuania in 1447, Poland ruled vast territories from the Baltic to the Black Sea, resisting German and Turkish incursions. Catholic nobles failed to gain the loyalty of their Orthodox Christian subjects in the E; commerce and trades were practiced by German and Jewish immigrants. The bloody 1648-49 Cossack uprising began the kingdom's dismemberment.

Russia. Growing authority of the tsars continued with advancing serfdom. Around 1700, Peter the Great imported new Western styles and technologies. Steady territorial expansion created a vast territory touching China, the Ottoman Empire, and east-central Europe.

China. A new dynasty, the Manchus, invaded from the NE, seized power in 1644, and expanded Chinese control to its greatest extent in Central and SE Asia. Trade and diplomatic contact with Europe grew, carefully controlled by China. New crops (sweet potato, maize, peanut) allowed economic and population growth (pop. 300 million, in 1800). Traditional arts and literature were pursued with increased sophistication (Dream of the Red Chamber, novel, mid-18th cent.).

Japan. Tokugawa Ieyasu, shogun from 1603, finally unified and pacified feudal Japan. Hereditary nobles (daimyos and samurai) monopolized government office and the professions. An urban merchant class grew, literacy spread, and a cultural renaissance occurred (haiku, a verse innovation of the poet Basho, 1644-94). Fear of European domination led to persecution of Christian converts from 1597 and to substantial isolation from outside contact from 1640.

Philosophy, Industry, and Revolution: 1700-1800

Science and reason. Greater faith in reason and empirical observation, instead of tradition and religious beliefs, espoused since the Renaissance (Francis Bacon, 1561-1626), was bolstered by scientific discoveries. René Descartes (1596-1650) used a rationalistic approach modeled on geometry and introspection to discover "self-evident" truths as a foundation of knowledge. Sir Isaac Newton emphasized induction from experimental observation. Baruch de Spinoza (1632-77), who called for political and intellectual freedom, developed a systematic rationalistic philosophy in his classic work Ethics.

French philosophers assumed leadership of the Enlightenment in the 18th cent. Montesquieu (1689-1755) used British history to support his notions of limited government. Voltaire's (1694-1778) diaries and novels of exotic travel illustrated the intellectual trends toward secular ethics and relativism. Jean-Jacques Rousseau's (1712-78) radical concepts of the social contract and of the inherent goodness of the common man gave impetus to antimonarchical republicanism. The Encyclopedia (1751-72, edited by Diderot and d'Alembert), designed as a monument to reason, was largely devoted to practical technology.

In England, ideals of liberty were connected with empiricist philosophy and science in the followers of John Locke. But British empiricism, especially as developed by the skeptical David Hume (1711-76), radically reduced the role of reason in philosophy, as did the evolutionary approach to law and politics of Edmund Burke (1729-97) and the utilitarian ethics of Jeremy Bentham (1748-1832). Adam Smith (1723-90) and other economists called for a rationalization of economic activity

by removing artificial barriers to a supposedly natural free exchange of goods known as laissez-faire.

German writers participated in the new philosophical trends popularized by Christian von Wolff (1679-1754). Immanuel Kant's (1724-1804) transcendental idealism, unifying an empirical epistemology with a priori moral and logical concepts, directed German thought away from skepticism. Italian contributions included work on electricity (Galvani, 1737-98; Volta, 1745-1827), the pioneer historiography of Vico (1668-1744), and writings on penal reform (Beccaria, 1738-94). Benjamin Franklin (1706-90) was celebrated in Europe for his varied achievements.

The growth of the press (Spectator, 1711-12) and the wide distribution of sentimental novels attested to the increase of a large bourgeois public.

Arts. Rococo art, characterized by extravagant decorative effects, asymmetries copied from organic models, and artificial pastoral subjects, was favored by the continental aristocracy for most of the century (Watteau, 1684-1721) and had musical analogies in the ornamentalized polyphony of late Baroque. The Neoclassical art after 1750, associated with the new scientific archaeology, was more streamlined and was infused with the supposed moral and geometric rectitude of the Roman Republic (David, 1748-1825). In England, town planning on a grand scale began.

Industrial Revolution in England. Agricultural improvements, such as the sowing drill (1701) and livestock breeding, were implemented on the large fields provided by enclosure of common lands by private owners. Profits from agriculture and

Catherine II (called the Great) ruled Russia for more than three decades (1762-96); she ascended the throne after husband Peter III was murdered, possibly at her behest.

from colonial and foreign trade (1800 volume, £54 mil) were channeled through hundreds of banks and the **Stock Exchange** (est. 1773) into new industrial processes.

The Newcomen steam pump (1712) aided coal mining. Coal fueled the new efficient steam engines patented by James Watt in 1769, and coke-smelting produced cheap, sturdy iron for machinery by the 1730s. The **flying shuttle** (1733) and **spinning jenny** (c. 1764) were used in the large new cotton textile factories, where women and children were much of the workforce. Goods were transported cheaply over **canals** (2,000 mi; built 1760-1800). By the early 19th cent., industrialization spread in Western Europe and North America.

American Revolution. The British colonies in North America attracted a mass immigration of religious dissenters and poor people throughout the 17th and 18th cent., coming from the British Isles, Germany, the Netherlands, and other countries including imported African slaves. The population reached 3 million non-natives by the 1770s. The indigenous population was greatly reduced by European diseases and by wars with the various colonies. British attempts to control colonial trade and to tax the colonists to pay for the costs of colonial administration and defense clashed with local self-government and eventually provoked the colonies to a successful rebellion.

Central and East Europe. The monarchs of the three states that dominated E Europe—Austria, Prussia, and Russia—expanded royal power and centralized institutions in their kingdoms, which were enlarged by the division (1772-95) of Poland.

Under **Frederick II** (called the Great) (r. 1740-86) Prussia, with its efficient modern army, doubled in size. State monopolies and tariff protection fostered industry, and some legal reforms were introduced. Austria's heterogeneous realms were unified under **Maria Theresa** (r. 1740-80) and **Joseph II** (r. 1780-90). Reforms in education, law, and religion were enacted, and the Austrian serfs were freed (1781). With its defeat in the Seven Years' War in 1763, Austria failed to regain Silesia, which had been seized by Prussia, but it was compensated by expansion to the E and S (Hungary, Slavonia, 1699; Galicia, 1772).

Russia, whose borders continued to expand, adopted some Western bureaucratic and economic policies under **Peter I** (r. 1682-1725) and **Catherine II** (r. 1762-96). Trade and cultural contacts with the West multiplied from the new Baltic Sea capital, **St. Petersburg** (est. 1703).

French Revolution. The growing French middle class lacked political power and resented aristocratic tax privileges, especially in light of the successful American Revolution. Peasants lacked adequate land and were burdened with feudal obligations to nobles. War with Britain led to the loss of French Canada and drained the treasury, finally forcing the king to call the **Estates-General** in 1789 for the first time since 1614, in an atmosphere of food riots (poor crop in 1788).

Aristocratic resistance to absolutism was soon overshadowed by the reformist Third Estate (middle class), which proclaimed itself the **National Constituent Assembly** June 17 and took the "Tennis Court oath" on June 20 to secure a constitution. The storming of the **Bastille** on July 14, 1789, by Parisian artisans was followed by looting and the seizure of aristocratic property throughout France. Assembly reforms included abolition of class and regional privileges, a Declaration of Rights, suffrage by taxpayers (75% of male population), and the **Civil Constitution of the Clergy** providing for election and loyalty oaths for priests. A republic was declared Sept. 22, 1792, in spite of royalist pressure from Austria and Prussia, which had declared war in Apr. (joined by Britain the next year). Louis XVI was beheaded Jan. 21, 1793, and Queen Marie Antoinette was beheaded Oct. 16, 1793.

Royalist uprisings in La Vendée and military reverses led to institution of a **reign of terror** in which tens of thousands of opponents of the Revolution and criminals were executed. Radical reforms in the **Convention** period (Sept. 1793-Oct. 1795) included the abolition of colonial slavery, economic measures to aid the poor, support of public education, and a short-lived de-Christianization.

Division among radicals (execution of Hebert, Danton, and Robespierre, 1794) aided the ascendancy of a moderate **Directory**, which consolidated military victories. **Napoleon Bonaparte** (1769-1821), a popular young general, exploited political divisions and participated in a coup Nov. 9, 1799, making himself first consul (dictator).

India. Sikh and Hindu rebels (Rajputs, Marathas) and Afghans destroyed the power of the Mughals during the 18th cent. After France's defeat (1763) in the Seven Years' War, Britain was the primary European trade power in India. Its control of inland **Bengal** and **Bihar** was recognized (1765) by the Mughal shah, who granted the **British East India Co.** (under Clive, 1725-74) the right to collect land revenue there. Despite objections from Parliament (1784 India Act), the company's involvement in local wars and politics led to repeated acquisitions of new territory. The company exported Indian textiles, sugar, and indigo, but industry was discouraged to promote British imports.

Nationalism Gathers Momentum: 1800-40

French ideals and empire spread. Inspired by the ideals of the French Revolution, and supported by the expanding French armies, new republican regimes arose near France: the **Batavian** Republic in the Netherlands (1795-1806), the **Helvetic** Republic in Switzerland (1798-1803), the **Cisalpine** Republic in Northern Italy (1797-1805), the **Ligurian** Republic in Genoa (1797-1805), and the **Parthenopean** Republic in Southern Italy (1799). A Roman Republic existed briefly in 1798 after Pope Pius VI was arrested by French troops. In Italy and Germany, new nationalist sentiments were stimulated both in imitation of and in reaction to developments in France (anti-French and anti-Jacobin peasant uprisings in Italy, 1796-99).

From 1804, when Napoleon declared himself emperor, to 1812, a succession of military victories (Austerlitz, 1805; Jena, 1806) extended his control over most of Europe through puppet states (**Confederation of the Rhine** united W German states for the first time and **Grand Duchy of Warsaw** revived Polish national hopes), expansion of the empire, and alliances.

Among the lasting reforms initiated under Napoleon's absolutist reign were establishment of the Bank of France, centralization of tax collection, codification of law along Roman models (Code Napoléon), and reform and extension of secondary and university education. In an 1801 concordat, the papacy recognized the effective autonomy of the French Catholic Church.

Napoleon's continental successes were offset by a British victory under Adm. Horatio Nelson in the **Battle of Trafalgar** (1805). Some 400,000 French soldiers were killed in the Napoleonic Wars, along with about 600,000 foreign troops.

Last gasp of old regimes. The disastrous 1812 invasion of Russia exposed Napoleon's overextension. After Napoleon's 1814 exile at Elba, his armies were defeated (1815) at **Waterloo** by British and Prussian troops.

At the **Congress of Vienna**, the monarchs and princes of Europe redrew their boundaries, to the advantage of Prussia (in Saxony and the Ruhr), Austria (in Illyria and Venetia), and Russia (in Poland and Finland). British conquest of Dutch and French colonies (S Africa, Ceylon, Mauritius) was recognized. France, under the restored Bourbons, retained its expanded 1792 borders. The settlement brought 50 years of international peace to Europe.

But the Congress was unable to check the advance of liberal ideals and of nationalism among the smaller European nations. The 1825 **Decembrist** uprising by liberal officers in Russia was easily suppressed. But an independence movement in **Greece**, stirred by commercial prosperity and a cultural revival, succeeded in expelling Ottoman rule by 1831, with the aid of Britain, France, and Russia.

A constitutional monarchy was secured in France by the **1830 Revolution**; Louis Philippe became king. The revolutionary contagion spread to **Belgium**, which gained its independence (1830) from the Dutch monarchy, and to **Poland**, whose rebellion was defeated (1830-31) by Russia, and to Germany.

Romanticism. A new style in intellectual and artistic life replaced Neoclassicism and Rococo after the mid-18th cent. By the early 19th cent., Romanticism prevailed in Europe.

Rousseau had begun the reaction against rationalism; in education (*Émile*, 1762) he stressed subjective spontaneity over regularized instruction. German writers (Lessing, 1729-81; Herder, 1744-1803) favorably compared the German folk song to classical forms and began a cult of Shakespeare, whose passion and "natural" wisdom was a model for the romantic *Sturm und Drang* (Storm and Stress) movement. **Goethe's** *Sorrows of Young Werther* (1774) set the model for the tragic, passionate genius.

A new interest in **Gothic architecture** in England after 1760 (Walpole, 1717-97) spread through Europe, associated with an aesthetic Christian and mystic revival (**Blake**, 1757-1827).

Celtic, Norse, and German mythology and folk tales were revived or imitated (Grimm's Fairy Tales, 1812-22). The medieval revival (Scott's *Ivanhoe*, 1819) led to a new interest in history, stressing national differences and organic growth (**Carlyle**, 1795-1881; Michelet, 1798-1874), corresponding to theories of natural evolution (Lamarck's *Philosophie Zoologique*, 1809; Lyell's *Geology*, 1830-33). A reaction against classicism characterized the English **romantic poets** (beginning with **Wordsworth**, 1770-1850). Revolution and war fed an emphasis on freedom and conflict, expressed by both poets (**Byron**, 1788-1824; **Hugo**, 1802-85) and philosophers (**Hegel**, 1770-1831).

Wild gardens replaced the formal French variety, and painters favored rural, stormy, and mountainous landscapes (**Turner**, 1775-1851; **Constable**, 1776-1837). Clothing became freer, with wigs, hoops, and ruffles discarded. Originality and genius were expected in the life and work of inspired artists (Murger's *Scenes From Bohemian Life*, 1847-49). Exotic locales and themes (as in Gothic horror stories) were used in art and literature (Delacroix, 1798-1863; **Poe**, 1809-49). Music exhibited the new dramatic style and a breakdown of classical forms (**Beethoven**, 1770-1827). The use of folk melodies and modes aided the growth of distinct national traditions (Glinka in Russia, 1804-57).

Latin America. François **Toussaint L'Ouverture** led a successful slave revolt in Haiti, which subsequently became the first Caribbean state to achieve independence (1804). The mainland Spanish colonies won their independence (1810-24) under such leaders as Simón **Bolívar** (1783-1830). Brazil became an independent empire (1822) under the Portuguese prince regent. A new class of military officers divided power with large landholders and the church.

United States. Territory under U.S. control nearly doubled in size with the **Louisiana Purchase** (1803). Heavy immigration and exploitation of ample natural resources fueled rapid economic growth. The spread of the franchise, public education, and antislavery sentiment were signs of a widespread democratic ethic.

China. Failure to keep pace with Western arms technology exposed China to greater European influence and hampered efforts to bar imports of opium, which had damaged Chinese society and drained wealth overseas. In the **Opium War** (1839-42), Britain forced China to expand trade opportunities and to cede Hong Kong.

New Complexities: Reforms and Imperialism: 1840-80

Idea of progress. As a result of the cumulative scientific, economic, and political changes of the preceding eras, the idea took hold among literate people in the West that continuing growth and improvement constituted the usual state of human and natural life.

Charles **Darwin's** statement of the **theory of evolution** and survival of the fittest (*On the Origin of Species*, 1859), defended by intellectuals and scientists against theological objections, was taken as confirmation that progress was the natural direction of life. The controversy helped define popular ideas of the dedicated scientist and of science's increasing control over the world (Foucault's demonstration of Earth's rotation, 1851; **Pasteur's** germ theory, 1861).

Liberals following Ricardo (1772-1823) in their faith that unrestrained competition would bring continuous economic expansion sought to adjust political life to new social realities and believed that unregulated competition of ideas would yield truth (**Mill**, 1806-73). In England, successive reform bills (1832, 1867, 1884) gave representation to the new industrial towns and extended the franchise to the middle and lower classes and to Catholics, Dissenters, and Jews. On both sides of the Atlantic, reformists tried to improve conditions for the mentally ill (**Dix**, 1802-87), women (Anthony, 1820-1906), and prisoners. Slavery was barred in the British Empire (1833), the U.S. (1865), and Brazil (1888).

Socialist theories based on ideas of human perfectibility or progress were widely disseminated. Utopian socialists such as Saint-Simon (1760-1825) envisaged an orderly, just society directed by a technocratic elite. A model factory town, New Lanark, Scotland, was set up by utopian Robert Owen (1771-1858), and communal experiments were tried in the U.S. (Brook Farm, MA, 1841-47). Bakunin's (1814-76) anarchism represented the opposite extreme of total freedom. Karl **Marx** (1818-83) posited the inevitable triumph of socialism in industrial countries through a dialectical process of class conflict.

Effective development of oceanic steamship lines (Cunard Lines, 1840s) and the opening of the **Suez Canal** accelerated shipping and commerce. Telegraph lines (Australia-Europe, 1871) sped communication. International organizations included the General (later Universal) Postal Union (1874) and conferences to limit epidemics like cholera. The initial **Geneva Convention** (1864) regulated treatment of prisoners of war.

Spread of industry. The technical processes and managerial innovations of the English industrial revolution spread to Europe (especially Germany) and the U.S., causing an explosion of industrial production, demand for raw materials, and

Louis Daguerre's 10-minute exposure of Boulevard du Temple in Paris (1838) omits moving traffic but includes the earliest candid image of a person: a man having his shoes polished.

competition for markets. Inventors, both trained and self-taught, provided means for larger-scale production (Bessemer steel, 1856; sewing machine, 1846). Many inventions were shown at the universal prosperity-themed 1851 London Great Exhibition at the **Crystal Palace**.

Local specialization and long-distance trade were aided by a revolution in transportation and communication. Railroads were first introduced in the 1820s in England and the U.S. Over 150,000 mi of track had been laid worldwide by 1880, with another 100,000 mi laid in the next decade. Steamships were improved (*Savannah* crossed Atlantic, 1819). The **telegraph**, perfected by 1844 (Morse), connected the Old and New Worlds by cable in 1866 and quickened the pace of international commerce and politics. The first commercial **telephone** exchange went into operation in the U.S. in 1878.

The new class of industrial workers, uprooted from their rural homes, lacked job security and suffered from dangerous overcrowding at work and at home. Many responded by organizing **trade unions** (legalized in England, 1824; France, 1884). The U.S. Knights of Labor had 700,000 members by 1886. The First International (1864-76) tried to unite workers worldwide around a Marxist program. The quasi-Socialist Paris Commune uprising (1871) was violently suppressed. Acts to reduce child labor and regulate conditions were passed (1833-50 in England). Social security measures were introduced by the Bismarck regime (1883-89) in Germany.

Revolutions of 1848. Among the causes of the continent-wide revolutions were an international collapse of credit and resulting unemployment, bad harvests in 1845-47, and a cholera epidemic. The new urban proletariat and expanding bourgeoisie demanded greater political roles. Republics were proclaimed in France, Rome, and Venice. Nationalist feelings reached fever pitch in the Habsburg empire, as Hungary declared independence under Kossuth, a Slav Congress demanded equality, and Piedmont tried to drive Austria from Lombardy. A national liberal assembly at Frankfurt called for German unification.

But riots fueled bourgeois fear of socialism (**Marx** and **Engels**, *Communist Manifesto*, 1848), and peasants remained conservative. The old establishment—the Papacy, the Habsburgs with the help of the Tsarist Russian army—was able to rout the revolutionaries by 1849. The French Republic succumbed to a renewed monarchy by 1852 (Emperor Napoleon III).

Great nations unified. Using the "blood and iron" tactics of Bismarck from 1862, Prussia controlled N Germany by 1867 (war with Denmark, 1864; Austria, 1866). After defeating France in 1870 (annexation of Alsace-Lorraine), it won the allegiance of S German states. A new **German Empire** was proclaimed (1871). **Italy**, inspired by Giuseppe Mazzini (1805-72)

and Giuseppe Garibaldi (1807-82), was unified by the reformed Piedmont kingdom through uprisings, plebiscites, and war.

The **United States** expanded its area after the 1846-48 Mexican War and defeated (1861-65) a secession attempt by Southern states in the **Civil War**. Canadian provinces were united in an autonomous **Dominion of Canada** (1867). Control in **India** was removed from the East India Co. and centralized under British administration after the 1857-58 Sepoy rebellion, laying the groundwork for the modern Indian state. Queen Victoria was named Empress of India (1876).

Europe dominates Asia. The Ottoman Empire began to weaken in the face of Balkan nationalisms and European imperial incursions in N Africa (**Suez Canal**, 1869). The Ottomans had lost control of most of both regions by 1882. Russia completed its expansion S by 1884 (despite the temporary setback of the **Crimean War** with Turkey, Britain, and France, 1853-56), taking Turkestan, all the Caucasus, and Chinese areas in the E and sponsoring Balkan Slavs against the Turks. A succession of reformist and reactionary regimes presided over a slow modernization (serfs freed, 1861). Persian independence suffered as Russia and British India competed for influence.

China was forced to sign a series of unequal treaties with European powers and Japan. Overpopulation and an inefficient dynasty brought misery and caused rebellions (Taiping, Muslims) leaving tens of millions dead. **Japan** was forced by the U.S. (Commodore Perry's visits, 1853-54) and Europe to end its isolation. The Meiji restoration (1868) gave power to a Westernizing oligarchy, abolishing feudalism and expanding education. Intensified empire-building gave Burma to Britain (1824-85) and Indochina to France (1862-95). Christian missionary activity followed imperial and trade expansion in Asia.

Arts. The official **Beaux Arts** school in Paris set an international style of imposing public buildings (Paris Opera, 1861-74; Vienna Opera, 1861-69) and uplifting statues (Bartholdi's Statue of Liberty, 1884). Realist painting, influenced by photography (Daguerre, 1837), appealed to a new mass audience with social or historical narrative (Wilkie, 1785-1841; Poynter, 1836-1919) or with serious religious, moral, or social messages (pre-Raphaelites, Millet's *Angelus*, 1858), often drawn from ordinary life. The **Impressionists** (Monet, 1840-1926; Pissarro, 1830-1903; Renoir, 1841-1919) rejected the formalism, sentimentality, and precise techniques of academic art in favor of a spontaneous, undetailed rendering of the world through careful representation of the effect of natural light on objects. They were strongly influenced by Asian and African styles.

Realistic **novelists** presented the full panorama of social classes and personalities but retained sentimentality and moral judgment (**Dickens**, 1812-70; **Eliot**, 1819-80; **Tolstoy**, 1828-1910; **Balzac**, 1799-1850).

Veneer of Stability: 1880-1900

Imperialism triumphant. The vast **African** interior, visited by European explorers (Barth, 1821-65; Livingstone, 1813-73), was conquered by the European powers in rapid, competitive thrusts from their coastal bases after 1880, mostly for domestic political and international strategic reasons. W African Muslim kingdoms (Fulani), Arab slave traders (Zanzibar), and Bantu military confederations (Zulu) were alike subdued. Only Christian Ethiopia (defeat of Italy, 1896) and Liberia resisted successfully. France (W Africa) and Britain ("Cape to Cairo," **Boer War**, 1899-1902) were the major beneficiaries. The ideology of "the white man's burden" (Kipling, *Barrack Room Ballads*, 1892) justified the conquests, which in fact reflected Europe's weapons superiority.

W European foreign capital investment soared to nearly $40 bil by 1914, but most was in E Europe (France, Germany), the Americas (Britain), and Europe's colonies. The foundation of the modern interdependent world economy was laid, with cartels dominating raw material trade. Global developments included a new agreement on international patents (1883), the modern Olympics (1896), and the global spread of department stores.

An industrious world. Industrial and technological proficiency characterized the two new great powers—Germany and the U.S. Coal and iron deposits enabled Germany to reach second- or third-place status in iron, steel, and shipbuilding by the 1900s. German electrical and chemical industries were world leaders. The U.S. post-Civil War boom (interrupted by financial panics—1884, 1893, 1896) was shaped by massive

immigration from S and E Europe from 1880, government subsidy of railroads, and huge private monopolies (Standard Oil, 1870; U.S. Steel, 1901). The **Spanish-American War**, 1898 (Philippine Insurrection, 1899-1902), and the **Open Door policy** in China (1899) made the U.S. a world power.

England led in **urbanization**, with London the world capital of finance, insurance, and shipping. Sewer systems (Paris, 1850s), electric subways (London, 1890), parks, and bargain department stores helped improve living standards for most of the urban population of the industrial world. Birthrates declined in the West while infant mortality rates plunged (demographic transition, 1880-1920).

Upheavals in Asia. Asian reaction to European economic, military, and religious incursions took the form of imitation of Western techniques and adoption of Western ideas of progress and freedom. The Chinese "self-strengthening" movement of the 1860s and 1870s included rail, port, and arsenal improvements and metal and textile mills. Reformers such as **K'ang** Yu-wei (1858-1927) won liberalizing reforms in 1898, right after the European and Japanese "scramble for concessions."

A universal education system in Japan and importation of foreign industrial, scientific, and military experts aided Japan's rapid modernization after 1868 under the authoritarian Meiji regime. Japan's victory in the **Sino-Japanese War** (1894-95) put Formosa and Korea in its power. Industrialization began in earnest by 1890.

In India, the British alliance with the remaining princely states masked reform sentiment among the Westernized urban elite; higher education had been conducted largely in English for 50 years. The **Indian National Congress**, founded in 1885, demanded a larger government role for Indians.

Fin-de-siècle **sophistication.** **Naturalist** writers pushed realism to its extreme limits, adopting a quasi-scientific attitude and writing about formerly taboo subjects such as sex, crime, extreme poverty, and corruption (Flaubert, 1821-80; Zola, 1840-1902; Hardy, 1840-1928). Unseen or repressed psychological motivations were explored in the clinical and theoretical works of Sigmund **Freud** (1856-1939) and in works of fiction (**Dostoyevsky**, 1821-81; Henry James, 1843-1916; Schnitzler, 1862-1931).

A contempt for bourgeois life or a desire to shock a complacent audience was shared by the French **symbolist** poets (Verlaine, 1844-96; Rimbaud, 1854-91), by neopagan English writers (Swinburne, 1837-1909), by continental dramatists (**Ibsen**, 1828-1906), and by satirists (**Wilde**, 1854-1900). The

German philosopher Friedrich **Nietzsche** (1844-1900) was influential in his elitism and pessimism.

Postimpressionist art neglected long-cherished conventions of representation (**Cézanne**, 1839-1906) and showed a willingness to learn from primitive and non-European art (**Gauguin**, 1848-1903; Japanese prints).

Racism. Gobineau (1816-82) gave a pseudobiological foundation to modern racist theories, which spread in Europe in the latter 19th cent., along with **Social Darwinism**, the belief that societies are and should be organized as a struggle for survival of the fittest. The medieval period was interpreted as an era of natural Germanic rule (Chamberlain, 1855-1927), and notions of racial superiority were associated with German national aspirations (Treitschke, 1834-96). **Anti-Semitism**, with a new racist rationale, became a significant political force in Germany (Anti-Semitic Petition, 1880), Austria (Lueger, 1844-1910), and France (**Dreyfus affair**, 1894-1906).

Imperialism's High Point: 1900-09

Alliances. While the peace of Europe (and its dependencies) continued to hold (1907 **Hague Conference** extended the rules of war and international arbitration procedures), imperial rivalries, protectionist trade practices (in Germany and France), and the escalating arms race (British *Dreadnought* battleship launched; Germany widens Kiel canal, 1906) exacerbated minor disputes (German-French Moroccan "crises," 1905, 1911).

Security was sought through balance-of-power alliances: **Triple Alliance** (Germany, Austria-Hungary, Italy; renewed in 1902 and 1907); Anglo-Japanese Alliance (1902), Franco-Russian Alliance (1899), **Entente Cordiale** (Britain, France, 1904), Anglo-Russian Treaty (1907), German-Ottoman friendship. Global developments included the establishment of an International Court in The Hague, the first transatlantic radio transmission (1901), and the creation of the first international association for European football (1904).

Ottomans decline. The Ottoman government was unable to resist further loss of territory, and earlier reform efforts gave way to greater authoritarianism. Nearly all European lands were lost in 1912 to Serbia, Greece, Montenegro, and Bulgaria. Italy took Libya and the Dodecanese islands the same year. Britain took Kuwait (1899) and the Sinai (1906). The **Young Turk** revolution in 1908 forced the sultan to restore a constitution, and it introduced some social reform and secularization.

British Empire. British trade and cultural influence remained dominant in the empire, but constitutional reforms presaged its eventual dissolution. The colonies of **Australia** were united in 1901 under a self-governing commonwealth. **New Zealand** acquired dominion status in 1907. The old Boer republics joined Cape Colony and Natal in the self-governing Union of **South Africa** in 1910.

The 1909 Indian Councils Act enhanced the role of elected province legislatures in **India**. The Muslim League (founded 1906) sought separate communal representation.

East Asia. Japan exploited its growing industrial power to expand its empire. Victory in the 1904-05 war against Russia (naval battle of Tsushima, 1905) assured Japan's domination of **Korea** (annexed 1910) and Manchuria (Port Arthur taken, 1905).

In China, central authority began to crumble (empress died, 1908). Reforms (Confucian exam system ended 1905, modernization of the army, building of railroads) were inadequate, and secret societies of reformers and nationalists, inspired by the Westernized **Sun** Yat-sen (1866-1925), fomented periodic uprisings in the S.

Siam, whose independence had been guaranteed by Britain and France in 1896, was split into spheres of influence by those countries in 1907.

Russia. The population of the Russian Empire approached 150 million in 1900. Reforms in education, in law, and in local institutions (*zemstvos*) and an industrial boom starting in the 1880s (oil, railroads) created the beginnings of a modern society, despite the autocratic tsarist regime. Liberals (1903 Union of Liberation), Socialists (Social Democrats founded 1898, Bolsheviks split off 1903), and populists (Social Revolutionaries founded 1901) were periodically repressed, and national minorities were persecuted (anti-Jewish pogroms, 1903, 1905-06).

An industrial crisis after 1900 and harvest failures aggravated poverty among urban workers, and the 1904-05 defeat

by Japan (which checked Russia's Asian expansion) sparked the **Revolution of 1905-06**. A **Duma** (parliament) was created under Tsar Nicholas II. Agricultural reform (under Stolypin, prime minister, 1906-11) created a large class of land-owning peasants (*kulaks*).

The world shrinks. Developments in transportation and communication and mass population movements helped create an awareness of an interdependent world. Early **automobiles** (Daimler, Benz, 1885) were experimental or were designed as luxuries. Assembly-line mass production (Ford Motor Co., 1903) made the invention practical, and by 1910 nearly 500,000 motor vehicles were registered in the U.S. alone. **Heavier-than-air flights** began in 1903 in the U.S. (Wright brothers' *Flyer*), preceded by glider, balloon, and model plane advances in several countries. Trade was advanced by improvements in **ship design** (gyrocompass, 1910), speed (*Lusitania* crossed Atlantic in five days, 1907), and reach (Panama Canal begun, 1904).

The first transatlantic **radio** telegraphic transmission occurred in 1901, six years after Marconi discovered radio. Radio transmission of human speech had been made in 1900. Telegraphic transmission of photos was achieved in 1904, lending immediacy to news reports. **Phonographs**, popularized by Caruso's recordings (starting 1902), made for quick international spread of musical styles (ragtime). **Motion pictures**, perfected in the 1890s (Dickson, Lumière brothers), became a popular and artistic medium after 1900; newsreels appeared in 1909.

Emigration from crowded European centers soared in the decade: 9 million migrated to the U.S., and millions more went to Siberia, Canada, Argentina, Australia, South Africa, and Algeria. Some 70 million Europeans emigrated in the century before 1914. Several million Chinese, Indians, and Japanese migrated to SE Asia, where their urban skills often enabled them to take a predominant economic role.

Social reform. The social and economic problems of the poor were kept in the public eye by realist fiction writers (Dreiser's *Sister Carrie*, 1900; Gorky's *Lower Depths*, 1902; Sinclair's *The Jungle*, 1906), journalists (U.S. **muckrakers**—

Mass production of automobiles on an assembly line, introduced by Henry Ford in 1903, enabled quick production and lowered costs for consumers.

Steffens, Tarbell), and artists (Ashcan school). Frequent labor strikes and occasional assassinations by anarchists or radicals (Empress Elizabeth of Austria, 1898; King Umberto I of Italy, 1900; U.S. Pres. McKinley, 1901; Russian Interior Min. Plehve, 1904; Portugal's King Carlos, 1908) added to social tension and fear of revolution. Feminist agitators for the vote surfaced in several countries.

But democratic reformism responded in part. In Germany, Bernstein's (1850-1932) **revisionist Marxism**, downgrading revolution, was accepted by the powerful Social Democrats and trade unions. The British Fabian Society (the Webbs, Shaw) and the Labour Party (founded 1906) worked for reforms such as social security and union rights (1906), while woman suffragists grew more militant. U.S. **progressives** fought big business (Pure Food and Drug Act, 1906). In France, the 10-hour workday (1904) and separation of church and state (1905) were reform victories, as was universal suffrage in Austria (1907).

Arts. An unprecedented period of experimentation, centered in France, produced several **new painting styles**: Fauvism exploited bold color areas (Matisse, *Woman With Hat*, 1905); expressionism reflected powerful inner emotions (Brücke group, 1905); Cubism combined several views of an object on one flat surface (Picasso, *Demoiselles*, 1906-07); futurism tried to depict speed and motion (Italian Futurist Manifesto, 1910). **Architects** explored new uses of steel structures, with facades either neoclassical (Adler and Sullivan in U.S.), curvilinear Art Nouveau (Gaudi's Casa Mila, 1905-10), or functionally streamlined (Wright's Robie House, 1909).

Music and dance shared the experimental spirit. Ruth St. Denis (1877-1968) and Isadora Duncan (1878-1927) pioneered modern dance, while Sergei Diaghilev in Paris revitalized classic ballet from 1909. Composers explored atonal music (Debussy, 1862-1918) and dissonance (Schoenberg, 1874-1951) or revolutionized classical forms (Stravinsky, 1882-1971), often showing jazz or folk music influences.

War and Revolution: 1910-19

War threatens. Germany under Wilhelm II sought a political and imperial role consonant with its industrial strength, challenging Britain's world supremacy and threatening France, which was still resenting the loss (1871) of Alsace-Lorraine. Austria wanted to curb an expanded Serbia (after 1912) and the threat it posed to its own Slav lands. Russia feared Austrian and German political and economic aims in the Balkans and Turkey.

An accelerated arms race resulted from these circumstances. The German standing army rose to more than 2 million men by 1914. Russia and France had more than a million each, and Austria and the British Empire nearly a million each. Dozens of enormous battleships were built by the powers after 1906.

The **assassination of Austrian Archduke Franz Ferdinand** by a Serbian nationalist, June 28, 1914, was the trigger for war. The system of alliances made the conflict Europe-wide; Germany's invasion of Belgium to outflank France forced Britain to enter the war. Patriotic fervor was nearly unanimous among all classes in most countries.

World War I. German forces were stopped in France in one month. The rival armies dug **trench networks**. Artillery and improved machine guns prevented either side from any lasting advance despite repeated assaults (600,000 dead at **Verdun**, Feb.-July 1916). Poison gas, used by Germany in 1915, proved ineffective. The entrance of more than 1 million U.S. troops tipped the balance after mid-1917, forcing Germany to sue for peace the next year. The formal armistice was signed on Nov. 11, 1918, and the German emperor abdicated.

In the E, the Russian armies were thrown back (battle of **Tannenberg**, Aug. 20, 1914), and the war grew unpopular in Russia. An allied attempt to relieve Russia through Turkey failed (**Gallipoli**, 1915). The **Russian Revolution** (1917) abolished the monarchy. The new Bolshevik regime signed the capitulatory Brest-Litovsk peace in Mar. 1918. Italy entered the war on the allied side in May 1915 but was pushed back by Oct. 1917. A renewed offensive with Allied aid in Oct.-Nov. 1918 forced Austria to surrender.

The British Navy successfully blockaded Germany, which responded with submarine U-boat attacks; **unrestricted submarine warfare** against neutrals after Jan. 1917 helped bring the U.S. into the war. Other battlefields included Palestine and Mesopotamia, both of which Britain wrested from the Turks in 1917, and the African and Pacific colonies of Germany, most of which fell to Britain, France, Australia, Japan, and South Africa.

Settlement. At the **Paris Peace Conference** (Jan.-June 1919), concluded by the **Treaty of Versailles**, and in subsequent negotiations and local wars (Russian-Polish War, 1920), the **map of Europe** was redrawn with a nod to U.S. Pres. Woodrow Wilson's principle of self-determination. Austria and Hungary were separated, and much of their land was given to Yugoslavia (formerly Serbia), Romania, Italy, and the newly independent Poland and Czechoslovakia. Germany lost territory in the W, N, and E, while Finland and the Baltic states were detached from Russia. The Ottoman Empire ended (1922) and most of its Arab lands went to British-sponsored Arab states or to direct French and British rule. Belgium's sovereignty was recognized.

From 1916, the civilian populations and economies of both sides were mobilized to an unprecedented degree. Hardships intensified among fighting nations in 1917 (French mutiny crushed in May). More than 10 million soldiers died in the war.

A huge **reparations** burden and partial demilitarization were imposed on Germany. Pres. Wilson obtained approval for a League of Nations, but the U.S. Senate refused to allow the U.S. to join.

Russian revolution. Military defeats and high casualties caused a contagious lack of confidence in Tsar Nicholas, who was forced to abdicate Mar. 1917. A liberal provisional government failed to end the war, and massive desertions, riots, and fighting between factions followed. A moderate socialist government under Aleksandr Kerensky was overthrown (Nov. 1917) in a violent coup by the **Bolsheviks** in Petrograd under **Lenin**, who later disbanded the elected Constituent Assembly.

The Bolsheviks brutally suppressed all opposition and ended the war with Germany in Mar. 1918. **Civil war** broke out in the summer between the Red Army (the Bolsheviks and their supporters), and monarchists, anarchists, minority nationalities (Ukrainians, Georgians, Poles), and others. Small U.S., British, French, and Japanese units also opposed the Bolsheviks (1918-19; Japan in Vladivostok to 1922). The civil war, anarchy, and pogroms devastated the country until the 1920 Red Army victory. The **Communist Party** leadership retained absolute power.

Other European revolutions. An unpopular monarchy in **Portugal** was overthrown in 1910. The new republic took severe anticlerical measures in 1911.

After a century of Home Rule agitation, during which **Ireland** was devastated by famine (1 million dead, 1846-47) and emigration, republican militants staged an unsuccessful uprising in Dublin during **Easter 1916**. The execution of the leaders and mass arrests by the British won popular support for the rebels. The **Irish Free State**, comprising all but the six northern counties, achieved dominion status in 1922.

In the aftermath of the world war, radical revolutions were attempted in Germany (**Spartacist** uprising, Jan. 1919), **Hungary** (Kun regime, 1919), and elsewhere. All were suppressed or failed for lack of support.

The total number of fatalities in World War I includes about 10 million military and 7 million civilians, making the conflict one of the deadliest in world history.

Chinese revolution. The Manchu Dynasty was overthrown and a republic proclaimed in Oct. 1911. First Pres. Sun Yat-sen resigned in favor of strongman Yuan Shih-k'ai. Sun organized the parliamentarian **Kuomintang** party.

Students launched protests on May 4, 1919, against League of Nations concessions in China to Japan. Nationalist, liberal, and socialist ideas and political groups spread. The **Communist Party** was founded in 1921. A Communist regime took power in Mongolia with Soviet support in 1921.

India restive. Indian objections to British rule erupted in nationalist riots as well as in the nonviolent tactics of Mahatma **Gandhi** (1869-1948). Nearly 400 unarmed demonstrators were shot at **Amritsar** in Apr. 1919. Britain approved limited self-rule that year.

Mexican revolution. Under the long Diaz dictatorship (1877-1911) the economy advanced, but Indian and mestizo lands were confiscated, and concessions to foreigners (mostly U.S.) damaged the middle class. A revolution in 1910 led to civil wars and U.S. intervention (1914, 1916-17). Land reform and a more democratic constitution (1917) were achieved.

Sciences. Scientific specialization prevailed by the 20th cent. Advances in knowledge and technological aptitude increased with the geometric rise in the number of practitioners. Physicists challenged common-sense views of causality, observation, and a mechanistic universe, putting science further beyond popular grasp (**Einstein**'s general theory of relativity, 1916; Bohr's quantum mechanics, 1913; Heisenberg's uncertainty principle, 1927).

Aftermath of War: 1920-29

U.S. Easy credit, technological ingenuity, and war-related industrial decline in Europe caused a long economic boom, in which ownership of new products—**autos, phones, radios**—became more democratized. **Prosperity**, an increase in women workers, women's suffrage (19th Amendment ratified, 1920), and drastic change in fashion (**flappers**, mannish bob for women, clean-shaven men) created a wide perception of social change despite prohibition of alcoholic beverages (1919-33). Union membership and strikes increased. Fear of radicals led to Palmer raids (1919-20) and the Sacco-Vanzetti case (1921-27).

Europe sorts itself out. Germany's liberal **Weimar constitution** (1919) could not guarantee a stable government in the face of rightist violence (Rathenau assassinated, 1922) and Communist refusal to cooperate with Socialists. Reparations and Allied occupation of the Rhineland caused staggering inflation that destroyed middle-class savings, but economic expansion resumed after mid-decade, aided by U.S. loans. A sophisticated, **innovative culture** developed in architecture and design (Bauhaus, 1919-28), film (Lang, *M*, 1931), painting (Grosz), music (Weill, *Threepenny Opera*, 1928), theater (Brecht, *A Man's a Man*, 1926), criticism (Benjamin), philosophy (Jung), and fashion. This culture was considered decadent and socially disruptive by rightists.

England elected its first Labour governments (Jan. 1924, June 1929). A 10-day general strike in support of coal miners failed in May 1926. In **Italy**, strikes, political chaos, and violence by small Fascist bands culminated in the Oct. 1922 Fascist March on Rome, which established **Mussolini**'s dictatorship. Strikes were outlawed (1926), and Italian influence was pressed in the Balkans (Albania made a protectorate, 1926). A conservative dictatorship was also established in **Portugal** in a 1926 military coup.

Czechoslovakia, the only stable democracy to emerge from the war in Central or E Europe, faced opposition from Germans (in the Sudetenland), Ruthenians, and some Slovaks. As the industrial heartland of the old Habsburg empire, it remained fairly prosperous. With French backing, it formed the Little Entente with Yugoslavia (1920) and **Romania** (1921) to block Austrian or Hungarian irredentism. Croats and Slovenes in **Yugoslavia** demanded a federal state until King Alexander I proclaimed (1929) a royal dictatorship. Poland faced internal nationality problems as well (Germans, Ukrainians, Jews); Pilsudski ruled as dictator from 1926. The Baltic states were threatened by traditionally dominant ethnic Germans and by Soviet-supported Communists.

An economic collapse and famine in **Russia** (1921-22) claimed 5 million lives. The New Economic Policy (1921) allowed land ownership by peasants and some private commerce and industry. **Stalin** was absolute ruler within four years of Lenin's death (1924). He inaugurated a brutal collectivization program (1929-32) and used foreign Communist parties for Soviet state advantage. Industrialization advanced rapidly.

Internationalism. Revulsion against World War I led to pacifist agitation, to the Kellogg-Briand Pact renouncing

aggressive war (1928), and to **naval disarmament** pacts (Washington, 1922; London, 1930). But the League of Nations was able to arbitrate only minor disputes (Greece-Bulgaria, 1925). A number of countries pulled back from global contacts, as with American isolationism and Russia's separation from international capitalism.

Middle East. Mustafa Kemal (**Ataturk**) led **Turkish** nationalists in resisting Italian, French, and Greek military advances (1919-23). The sultanate was abolished (1922), and elaborate reforms were passed, including secularization of law and adoption of the Latin alphabet. Ethnic conflict led to persecution of **Armenians** (more than 1 million dead in 1915, 1 million expelled), Greeks (forced Greek-Turk population exchange, 1923), and Kurds (1925 uprising).

With evacuation of the Turks from **Arab** lands, the puritanical Wahabi dynasty of E Arabia conquered (1919-25) what is now Saudi Arabia. British, French, and Arab dynastic and nationalist maneuvering resulted in the creation of two more Arab monarchies in 1921—Iraq and Transjordan (both under British control)—and two French mandates—Syria and Lebanon. Jewish immigration into British-mandated **Palestine**, inspired by the Zionist movement, was resisted by Arabs, at times violently (1921, 1929 massacres).

Reza Khan ruled **Persia** after his 1921 coup (shah from 1925), centralized control, and created the trappings of a modern secular state.

In 1922, English archaeologist Howard Carter discovered the tomb of the boy pharaoh **Tutankhamen** in the Valley of the Kings in Egypt.

China. The Kuomintang under **Chiang Kai-shek** (1887-1975) subdued the warlords by 1928. The Communists were brutally suppressed after their alliance with the Kuomintang was broken in 1927. Relative peace thereafter allowed for industrial and financial improvements, with some Russian, British, and U.S. cooperation.

Arts. Nearly all bounds of subject matter, style, and attitude were broken in the arts of the period. **Abstract art** first took inspiration from natural forms or narrative themes (Kandinsky from 1911) and then worked free of any representational aims (Malevich's suprematism, 1915-19; Mondrian's geometric style from 1917). The **Dada** movement (from 1916) mocked artistic pretension with absurd collages and constructions. Paradox, illusion, and psychological taboos were exploited by **surrealists** by the late 1920s (Dali, Magritte). Architectural schools celebrated industrial values, whether vigorous abstract constructivism (Tatlin, *Monument to the Third International*, 1919) or the machined, streamlined **Bauhaus** style, which was extended to many design fields (Helvetica typeface).

Prose writers explored revolutionary narrative modes related to dreams (Kafka's *Trial*, 1925), internal monologue (Joyce's *Ulysses*, 1922), and word play (Stein's *Making of Americans*, 1925). Poets and novelists wrote of modern alienation (Eliot's *Waste Land*, 1922) and aimlessness ("The Lost Generation").

Rise of Totalitarians: 1930-39

Depression. A worldwide financial panic and economic depression began with the Oct. 1929 U.S. stock market crash and the May 1931 failure of the Austrian Credit-Anstalt. A credit crunch caused international bankruptcies and **unemployment**: 12 million jobless by 1932 in the U.S., 5.6 million in Germany, 2.7 million in England. Governments responded with **tariff restrictions** (Smoot-Hawley Act, 1930; Ottawa Imperial Conference,

1932), which dried up world trade. Government public works programs were vitiated by deflationary budget balancing.

Germany. Years of agitation by violent extremists were brought to a head by the Depression. Nazi leader Adolf Hitler was named chancellor in Jan. 1933 and given dictatorial power by the Reichstag in Mar. Opposition parties were disbanded, strikes

Italy's Benito Mussolini and Germany's Adolf Hitler affirmed their total political and military alliance with 1939's Pact of Steel.

banned, and all aspects of economic, cultural, and religious life were brought under central government and Nazi party control and manipulated by sophisticated propaganda. Severe persecution of Jews began (**Nuremberg Laws**, Sept. 1935). Many Jews, political opponents, and others were sent to concentration camps (Dachau, 1933), where thousands died or were killed. Public works, renewed conscription (1935), arms production, and a four-year plan (1936) all but ended unemployment.

Hitler's expansionism started with reincorporation of the Saar (1935), occupation of the **Rhineland** (Mar. 1936), and annexation of Austria (Mar. 1938). At **Munich** (Sept. 1938) Britain and France attempted to appease Hitler and avoid war by successfully encouraging Czechoslovakia's surrender of the Sudetenland territory.

Russia. Rapid industrialization was achieved through successive **five-year plans** starting in 1928, using severe labor discipline and mass forced labor. Industry was financed by exploitation of agriculture, which was almost totally collectivized by the early 1930s (*kolkhoz* [collective farm]; *sovkhoz* [state farm], often in newly worked lands). Millions perished in a series of manufactured disasters: extermination (1929-34) of kulaks (peasant landowners), severe famine (1932-33), party purges and show trials (Great Purge, 1936-38), suppression of nationalities, and poor conditions in labor camps. Purges also increased Stalin's power in the Communist party.

Spain. An industrial revolution during World War I created an urban proletariat, which was attracted to socialism and anarchism; Catalan nationalists challenged central authority. The five years after King Alfonso left Spain in Apr. 1931 was dominated by tension between intermittent leftist and anticlerical governments and clericals, monarchists, and other rightists. Anarchist and Communist rebellions were crushed, but a July

1936 extreme right rebellion led by Gen. Francisco **Franco** and aided by Nazi Germany and Fascist Italy succeeded after a three-year **civil war** (more than 1 million dead in battles and atrocities). The war polarized international public opinion.

Italy. Despite propaganda for the ideal of the Corporate State, few domestic reforms were attempted. An entente with Hungary and Austria (Mar. 1934), a pact with Germany and Japan (Nov. 1937), and intervention by 50,000-75,000 troops in Spain (1936-39) sealed Italy's identification with the fascist bloc (anti-Semitic laws after Mar. 1938). Ethiopia was conquered (1935-36) and Albania annexed (Jan. 1939) in conscious imitation of ancient Rome.

Eastern Europe. Repressive regimes fought for power against an active opposition (liberals, socialists, Communists, peasants, Nazis). Minority groups and Jews were restricted within national boundaries that did not coincide with ethnic population patterns. In the destruction of **Czechoslovakia**, Hungary occupied S Slovakia (Nov. 1938) and Ruthenia (Mar. 1939), and a pro-Nazi regime took power in the rest of Slovakia. Other boundary disputes (e.g., Poland-Lithuania, Yugoslavia-Bulgaria, and Romania-Hungary) doomed attempts to build joint fronts against Germany or Russia. Economic depression was severe.

East Asia. After a period of liberalism in **Japan**, nativist militarists dominated the government with peasant support. Manchuria was seized (Sept. 1931-Feb. 1932), and a puppet state was set up (Manchukuo). Adjacent Jehol (Inner Mongolia) was occupied in 1933. **China** proper was invaded in July 1937; large areas were conquered by Oct. 1938. Hundreds of thousands of rapes, murders, and other atrocities were attributed to the Japanese.

Communist forces left Kuomintang-besieged strongholds in the S of China in a Long March (1934-35) to the N. The Kuomintang-Communist civil war was suspended in Jan. 1937 in the face of threatening Japan.

Democracies. The Roosevelt Administration, in office Mar. 1933, embarked on an extensive program of **New Deal** social reform and economic stimulation, including protection for labor unions (heavy industries organized), Social Security, public works, wage-and-hour laws, and assistance to farmers. Isolationist sentiment (1937 Neutrality Act) prevented U.S. intervention in Europe, but military expenditures were increased in 1939.

French political instability and polarization prevented resolution of economic and international security questions. The **Popular Front** government under Leon Blum (June 1936-Apr. 1938) passed social reforms (40-hour work week) and raised arms spending. National coalition governments, which ruled Britain from Aug. 1931, brought economic recovery but failed to define a consistent international policy until Chamberlain's government (from May 1937), which practiced **appeasement** of Germany and Italy.

India. Twenty years of agitation for autonomy and then for independence (Gandhi's **salt march**, 1930) achieved some constitutional reform (extended provincial powers, 1935) despite Muslim-Hindu strife. Social issues assumed prominence in peasant uprisings (1921), strikes (1928), Gandhi's efforts for untouchables (1932 "fast unto death"), and social and agrarian reform by the provinces after 1937.

Arts. The streamlined, geometric design motifs of Art Deco (from 1925) prevailed through the 1930s. Abstract art flourished (Moore sculptures from 1931) alongside a new realism related to social and political concerns (Socialist Realism, the official Soviet style from 1934; Mexican muralist Rivera, 1886-1957; and Orozco, 1883-1949), which were also expressed in fiction and poetry (Steinbeck's *Grapes of Wrath*, 1939; Sandburg's *The People, Yes*, 1936). Modern architecture (International Style, 1932) was unchallenged in its use of artificial materials (concrete, glass), lack of decoration, and monumentality (Rockefeller Center, 1929-40). Larger-than-life U.S.-made films captured a worldwide audience (*Gone With the Wind, The Wizard of Oz*, both 1939).

War, Hot and Cold: 1940-49

War in Asia-Pacific. Japan occupied Indochina in Sept. 1940, dominated Thailand in Dec. 1941, and attacked Hawaii (**Pearl Harbor**), the Philippines, Hong Kong, and Malaya on Dec. 7, 1941 (precipitating U.S. entrance into the war). Indonesia was attacked in Jan. 1942, and Burma was conquered in Mar. 1942. The Battle of **Midway** (June 1942) turned back the Japanese advance. "Island-hopping" battles (**Guadalcanal**, Aug. 1942-Jan. 1943; **Leyte Gulf**, Oct. 1944; **Iwo Jima**,

Feb.-Mar. 1945; **Okinawa**, Apr. 1945) and massive bombing raids on Japan from June 1944 wore out Japanese defenses. U.S. atom bombs, dropped Aug. 6 and 9 on **Hiroshima** and **Nagasaki**, forced Japan to agree, on Aug. 14, to surrender; formal surrender was on Sept. 2, 1945.

War in Europe. The Nazi-Soviet nonaggression pact (Aug. 1939) freed Germany to attack Poland (Sept. 1939). Britain and France, which had guaranteed Polish independence,

The U.S. bombing of Hiroshima and Nagasaki, Japan, in 1945 demonstrated the deadly, destructive power of atomic weapons and forced an end to World War II.

declared war on Germany. Russia seized E Poland (Sept. 1939), attacked Finland (Nov. 1939), and took the Baltic states (July 1940). Mobile German forces staged *blitzkrieg* attacks during Apr.-June 1940, conquering neutral Denmark, Norway, and the Low Countries and defeating France; 350,000 British and French troops were evacuated at **Dunkirk**, France (May). The **Battle of Britain** (June-Dec. 1940) denied Germany air superiority. German-Italian campaigns won the Balkans by Apr. 1941. Three million Axis troops **invaded Russia** in June 1941, marching through Ukraine to the Caucasus, and through White Russia and the Baltic republics to Moscow and Leningrad.

Russian winter counterthrusts (1941-42 and 1942-43) stopped the German advance (**Stalingrad**, Sept. 1942-Feb. 1943). Sustaining great casualties, the Russians drove the Axis from all E Europe and the Balkans in the next two years. Invasions of N Africa (Nov. 1942), Italy (Sept. 1943), and **Normandy** (launched on D-Day, June 6, 1944) brought U.S., British, Free French, and allied troops to Germany by spring 1945. In Feb. 1945, the three Allied leaders, Winston **Churchill** (Britain), Joseph **Stalin** (USSR), and Franklin D. **Roosevelt** (U.S.), met in Yalta to discuss strategy and resolve political issues, including the postwar Allied occupation of Germany. Germany surrendered May 7, 1945.

Atrocities. The war brought 20th-cent. cruelty to its peak. The Nazi regime systematically killed an estimated 5-6 million Jews, including some 3 million who died in death camps (e.g., **Auschwitz**). Gypsies, political opponents, people with mental or physical disabilities, and others deemed undesirable were also murdered by the Nazis, as were vast numbers of Slavs.

German bombs killed 70,000 British civilians. More than 100,000 Chinese civilians were killed by Japanese forces in the capture and occupation of Nanking. Severe retaliation by the Soviet army, E European partisans, Free French, and others took a heavy toll. U.S. and British bombing of Germany killed hundreds of thousands, as did U.S. bombing of Japan (80,000-200,000 at Hiroshima alone). Some 45 million people died in the war.

Settlement. The **United Nations** charter was signed in San Francisco on June 26, 1945, by 50 nations. The International Tribunal at **Nuremberg** convicted 22 German leaders for war crimes in Sept. 1946; 23 Japanese leaders were convicted in

Nov. 1948. Postwar border changes included large gains in territory for the USSR, losses for Germany, a shift to the W in Polish borders, and minor losses for Italy. Communist regimes, supported by Soviet troops, took power in most of Eastern Europe, including Soviet-occupied Germany (GDR, aka East Germany, proclaimed Oct. 1949). Japan lost all overseas lands. Global developments involved establishing new economic coordinating bodies like the International Monetary Fund (1944) and the Universal Declaration of Human Rights (1948).

Recovery. Basic political and social changes were imposed on Japan and W Germany by the Western allies (Japan constitution adopted, Nov. 1946; W German basic law, May 1949). U.S. **Marshall Plan** aid ($12 bil, 1947-51) spurred W European economic recovery after a period of severe inflation and strikes in Europe and the U.S. The British Labour Party introduced a national health service and nationalized basic industries in 1946.

Cold War. Western fears of further Soviet advances (Cominform formed in Oct. 1947; Czechoslovakia coup, Feb. 1948; Berlin blockade, Apr. 1948-Sept. 1949) led to the formation of **NATO**. Civil war in Greece and Soviet pressure on Turkey led to U.S. aid under the **Truman Doctrine** (Mar. 1947). Other anti-Communist security pacts were the Organization of American States (Apr. 1948) and the SE Asia Treaty Organization (Sept. 1954). A new wave of **Soviet purges** and repression intensified in the last years of Stalin's rule, extending to E Europe (Slansky trial in Czechoslovakia, 1951). Only Yugoslavia resisted Soviet control (expelled by Cominform, June 1948; U.S. aid, June 1949).

China, Korea. Communist forces emerged from World War II strengthened by the Soviet takeover of industrial Manchuria. In four years of fighting, the Kuomintang was driven from the mainland; the People's Republic of China was proclaimed Oct. 1, 1949. Korea was divided by USSR and U.S. occupation forces. Separate republics were proclaimed in the two zones in Aug.-Sept. 1948.

India. India and Pakistan became independent dominions on Aug. 15, 1947. Millions of Hindu and Muslim refugees were created by the partition. Riots (1946-47) took hundreds of thousands of lives. Mahatma **Gandhi** was assassinated in Jan. 1948. Burma became completely independent in Jan. 1948; Ceylon took dominion status in Feb.

Middle East. The UN approved partition of Palestine into Jewish and Arab states. **Israel** was proclaimed a state, May 14, 1948. Arabs rejected partition, but failed to defeat Israel in war (May 1948-July 1949). Immigration from Europe and the Middle East swelled Israel's Jewish population. British and French forces left Lebanon and Syria in 1946. Transjordan occupied most of Arab Palestine.

Southeast Asia. Communists and others fought against restoration of French rule in **Indochina** from 1946; a non-Communist government was recognized by France in Mar. 1949, but fighting continued. Both Indonesia and the Philippines became independent; the former in 1949 after four years of war with the Netherlands, the latter in 1946. Philippine economic and military ties with the U.S. remained strong; a Communist-led peasant rising was checked in 1948.

Arts. New York became the center of the world art market; **abstract expressionism** was the chief mode (Pollock from 1943, de Kooning from 1947). Literature and philosophy explored **existentialism** (Camus's *The Stranger*, 1942; Sartre's *Being and Nothingness*, 1943). Non-Western attempts to revive or create regional styles (Senghor's Négritude, Mishima's novels) were responses to global cultural influences. Radio and phonograph records spread American popular music (swing, bebop) around the world.

The Cold War Decade: 1950-59

Decolonization. The relatively peaceful decline of European political and military power in Asia and Africa accelerated in the 1950s. Nearly all of **N Africa** was freed by 1956, but France fought a bitter war to retain Algeria, with its large European minority, until 1962. **Ghana**, independent in 1957, led a parade of new black African nations (more than two dozen by 1962), which altered the political character of the UN. Ethnic disputes often exploded in the new nations after decolonization (UN troops in Cyprus, 1964; **Nigerian civil war**, 1967-70). Leaders of the new states, mostly sharing socialist ideologies, tried to create an Afro-Asian bloc (Bandung Conference, 1955), but Western economic

influence and U.S. political ties remained strong (Baghdad Pact, 1955).

Trade. World trade volume soared, in an atmosphere of monetary stability assured by international accords (**Bretton Woods**, 1944). In Europe, economic integration advanced (**European Economic Community**, 1957; European Free Trade Association, 1960). Comecon (1949) coordinated the economies of Soviet-bloc countries. Global developments included transcontinental jet travel (first South Africa to Britain flight, 1952; introduction of term "jet lag," 1965) and the increasing spread of English in global business, sports, and transportation.

Cuban revolutionary leader Fidel Castro established diplomatic ties with the USSR and Soviet Premier Nikita Khrushchev in 1959; the two nations quickly developed close economic ties.

U.S. Economic growth produced an abundance of consumer goods (9.3 million motor vehicles sold, 1955). Suburban housing changed life patterns for middle and working classes (Levittown, NY, 1947-51). Pres. Dwight **Eisenhower**'s landslide election victories (1952, 1956) reflected consensus politics. A system of alliances and military bases bolstered U.S. influence on all continents. Trade and payments surpluses were balanced by overseas investments and foreign aid ($50 bil, 1950-59).

USSR. In the "thaw" after Stalin's death in 1953, relations with the West improved (evacuation of Vienna, Geneva summit conference, both 1955). Repression of scientific and cultural life eased, and many prisoners were freed culminating in de-Stalinization (1956). Nikita **Khrushchev**'s leadership aimed at consumer sector growth, but farm production lagged, despite the virgin lands program (from 1954). Soviet crushing of the 1956 Hungarian revolution, the 1960 U-2 spy plane episode, and other incidents renewed E-W tension and domestic curbs.

Eastern Europe. Resentment of Russian domination and Stalinist repression combined with nationalist, economic, and religious factors to produce periodic violence. E Berlin workers rioted (1953), Polish workers rioted in Poznan (June 1956), and a broad-based **revolution** broke out in **Hungary** (Oct. 1956). All were suppressed by Soviet force or threats (at least 7,000 dead in Hungary), but Poland was allowed to restore private ownership of farms, and a degree of personal and economic freedom

returned to Hungary. Yugoslavia experimented with worker self-management and a market economy.

Korea. The 1945 division of Korea along the 38th parallel left industry in the N, which was organized into a militant regime and armed by the USSR. The S was politically disunited. More than 60,000 N Korean troops invaded the S on June 25, 1950. The U.S., backed by the UN Security Council, sent troops. **UN troops** reached the Chinese border in Nov. Some 200,000 Chinese troops crossed the Yalu R. and drove back UN forces. By spring 1951, battle lines had become stabilized near the original 38th parallel border, but heavy fighting continued. Finally, an armistice was signed on July 27, 1953. U.S. troops remained in the S, and U.S. economic and military aid continued. The war stimulated rapid economic recovery in Japan.

China. Starting in 1952, industry, agriculture, and social institutions were forcibly collectivized. In a massive purge, as many as several million people were executed as Kuomintang supporters or as class and political enemies. The **Great Leap Forward** (1958-60) unsuccessfully tried to force the pace of development by substituting labor for investment.

Indochina. Ho Chi Minh's forces, aided by the USSR and the new Chinese Communist government, fought French and pro-French Vietnamese forces to a standstill and captured the strategic **Dien Bien Phu** camp in May 1954. The Geneva Agreements divided Vietnam in half pending elections (never held) and recognized Laos and Cambodia as independent. The U.S. aided the anti-Communist Republic of Vietnam in the S.

Middle East. Arab revolutions placed leftist, militantly nationalist regimes in power in Egypt (1952) and Iraq (1958). But Arab unity attempts failed (United Arab Republic joined Egypt, Syria, Yemen, 1958-61). Arab refusal to recognize Israel (Arab League economic blockade began Sept. 1951) led to a permanent **state of war**, with repeated incidents (Gaza, 1955). Israel occupied Sinai, and Britain and France took (Oct. 1956) the Suez Canal, but were replaced by the UN Emergency Force. The Mossadegh government in Iran nationalized (May 1951) the British-owned oil industry in May, but was overthrown (Aug. 1953) in a U.S.-aided coup.

Latin America. Argentinian dictator Juan **Perón**, in office 1946, crushed opposition and enforced land reform, some nationalization, welfare state measures, and curbs on the Roman Catholic Church. A Sept. 1955 coup deposed Perón. The 1952 revolution in Bolivia brought land reform, nationalization of tin mines, and improvement in the status of Native Americans, who nevertheless remained poor. The Batista regime in Cuba was overthrown (Jan. 1959) by Fidel **Castro**, who imposed a Communist dictatorship, aligned Cuba with the USSR and improved education and health care. A U.S.-backed anti-Castro invasion (**Bay of Pigs**, Apr. 1961) was crushed. Self-government advanced in the British Caribbean.

Technology. Large outlays on research and development in the U.S. and the USSR focused on military applications (H-bomb in U.S., 1952; USSR, 1953; Britain, 1957; intercontinental missiles, late 1950s). Soviet launching of the **Sputnik** satellite (Oct. 4, 1957) spurred increases in U.S. science education funds (National Defense Education Act).

Literature and film. Alienation from social and literary conventions reached an extreme in the theater of the absurd (Beckett's *Waiting for Godot*, 1952), the "new novel" (Robbe-Grillet's *Voyeur*, 1955), and avant-garde film (Antonioni's *L'Avventura*, 1960). U.S. beatniks (Kerouac's *On the Road*, 1957) and others rejected the supposed conformism of Americans (Riesman's *The Lonely Crowd*, 1950).

Rising Expectations and New Protests: 1960-69

Global economy. The longest sustained economic boom on record spanned almost the entire decade in the capitalist world; the closely watched GNP figure doubled (1960-70) in the U.S., fueled by Vietnam War-related budget deficits. The **General Agreement on Tariffs and Trade** (1967) stimulated Western European prosperity, which spread to peripheral areas (Spain, Italy, E Germany). Japan became a top economic power. Foreign investment aided the industrialization of Brazil. There were limited Soviet economic reform attempts. Outside the Soviet zone the global economy was marked by the growing role of multinational corporations (3,000 in 1914; 6,000 by 1970). International nongovernmental organizations (NGOs) also multiplied rapidly (Amnesty International, 1961). The United Nations began sponsoring international "Years of Women" (1964).

Reform and radicalization. Pres. John F. **Kennedy**, inaugurated 1961, emphasized youthful idealism and vigor; his assassination Nov. 22, 1963, was a national trauma. A series of political and social reform movements took root in the U.S. and other countries. Blacks demonstrated nonviolently and with partial success against segregation and poverty (1963 March on Washington; 1964 **Civil Rights Act**), but some urban areas erupted in extensive riots (Watts, 1965; Detroit, 1967; **Martin Luther King Jr.** assassination, Apr. 4, 1968). New concern for the poor (Harrington's *Other America*, 1963) helped lead to Pres. Lyndon Johnson's **"Great Society"** programs (Medicare, Water Quality Act, Higher Education Act, all 1965). Concern for the **environment** surged (Carson's *Silent Spring*, 1962).

Feminism revived as a cultural and political movement (Friedan's *Feminine Mystique*, 1963; National Organization for Women founded, 1966), and a movement for homosexual rights emerged (Stonewall riot in NYC, 1969). Pope John XXIII called the **Second Vatican Council** (1962-65), which liberalized Roman Catholic liturgy and some other aspects of Catholicism.

Opposition to U.S. involvement in Vietnam, especially among university students (**Moratorium** protest, Nov. 1969), turned violent (Weatherman Chicago riots, Oct. 1969). **New Left** and Marxist theories became popular, and membership in radical groups (Students for a Democratic Society, Black Panthers) increased. Maoist groups, especially in Europe, called for total transformation of society. In France, students sparked a nation-wide strike affecting 10 million workers in May-June 1968, but an electoral reaction barred revolutionary change.

China. China's revolutionary militancy under **Mao Zedong** caused disputes with the USSR under "revisionist" Khrushchev, starting in 1960. The two powers exchanged fire in 1969 border disputes. China used force to capture (1962) areas disputed with India. The **"Great Proletarian Cultural Revolution"** tried to impose a utopian egalitarian program in China and spread revolution abroad; political struggle, often violent, convulsed China in 1965-68.

Indochina. Communist-led guerrillas aided by N Vietnam fought from 1960 against the S Vietnam government of Ngo Dinh Diem (killed 1963). The U.S. military role increased after the 1964 **Tonkin Gulf** incident. U.S. forces there peaked at 543,400 in Apr. 1969. Massive numbers of N Vietnamese troops also fought. Laotian and Cambodian neutrality were threatened by Communist insurgencies, with N Vietnamese aid, and U.S. intrigues.

Developing world. A bloc of authoritarian leftist regimes among the newly independent nations emerged in political opposition to the U.S.-led Western alliance and came to dominate the conference of nonaligned nations (Belgrade, 1961; Cairo, 1964; Lusaka, 1970). Soviet political ties and military bases were established in Cuba, Egypt, Algeria, Guinea, and other countries whose leaders were regarded as revolutionary heroes by opposition groups in pro-Western or colonial countries. Some leaders were ousted in coups by pro-Western groups—Dem. Rep. of the Congo's Patrice Lumumba (killed 1961), Ghana's Kwame Nkrumah (exiled 1966), and Indonesia's Sukarno (effectively ousted in 1965 after a Communist coup failed).

Middle East. Arab-Israeli tension erupted into a brief war June 1967. Israel emerged from the war as a major regional power. Military shipments before and after the war increased Soviet influence in much of the Arab world. Most Arab states broke U.S. diplomatic ties, while Communist countries cut their ties to Israel. Intra-Arab disputes continued: Egypt and Saudi Arabia supported rival factions in a bloody Yemen civil war 1962-70; Lebanese troops fought Palestinian commandos 1969.

Eastern Europe. To stop the large-scale exodus of citizens, E German authorities built (Aug. 1961) a fortified

American astronauts walked on the moon (1969) just a dozen years after the Soviet Union launched the first human-made satellite into orbit.

wall across Berlin. Soviet sway in the Balkans was weakened by Albania's support of China (USSR broke ties in Dec. 1961) and Romania's assertion (1964) of industrial and foreign policy autonomy. Liberalization (spring 1968) in Czechoslovakia was crushed with massive force by troops of five Warsaw Pact countries. W German treaties (1970) with the USSR and Poland facilitated the transfer of German technology and confirmed postwar boundaries.

Arts and styles. The boundary between fine and popular arts was blurred to some extent by Pop Art (Warhol) and rock musicals (*Hair*, 1968). Informality and exaggeration prevailed in fashion (beards, miniskirts). A nonpolitical "counterculture" developed, rejecting traditional bourgeois life goals and personal habits, and use of marijuana and hallucinogens spread (**Woodstock** festival, Aug. 1969). Indian influence was felt in religion (Ram Dass) and fashion, and **The Beatles**, who brought unprecedented sophistication to rock music, became for many a symbol of the decade.

Science. Achievements in space (**humans on the moon**, July 1969) and electronics (lasers, integrated circuits) encouraged a faith in scientific solutions to problems in agriculture ("green revolution"), medicine (heart transplants, 1967), and other areas. Harmful technology, it was believed, could be controlled (1963 Limited Test Ban Treaty, 1968 Nuclear Nonproliferation Treaty).

New Global Balances and Religious Revivals: 1970-79

U.S.: Caution and neoconservatism. A relatively sluggish economy, energy shortages, and environmental problems contributed to a **"limits of growth"** philosophy. Suspicion of science and technology killed or delayed major projects (supersonic transport dropped, 1971) and was fed by the Three Mile Island nuclear reactor accident (Mar. 1979).

There were signs of growing mistrust of government and less support for new policies. School busing and racial quotas were opposed (Bakke decision, June 1978); the Equal Rights Amendment for women languished; civil rights legislation aimed at protecting homosexuals was opposed (Dade County referendum, June 1977).

Completion of Communist forces' takeover of **South Vietnam** (evacuation of U.S. civilians, Apr. 1975), revelations of Central Intelligence Agency misdeeds (Rockefeller Commission report, June 1975), and **Watergate** scandals (Nixon resigned in Aug. 1974) reduced faith in U.S. moral and material capacity to influence world affairs. Revelations of Soviet crimes (Solzhenitsyn's *Gulag Archipelago*, 1974) and Soviet intervention in Africa helped foster a revival of anti-Communist sentiment.

Economy sluggish. The 1960s boom faltered in the 1970s; a severe recession in the U.S. and Europe (1974-75) followed a huge oil price hike (Dec. 1973). Monetary instability

(U.S. cut ties to gold in Aug. 1971), the decline of the dollar, and protectionist moves by industrial countries (1977-78) threatened trade. Business investment and spending for research declined. Severe inflation plagued many countries (25% in Britain, 1975; 18% in U.S., 1979).

China readjusts. After the 1976 deaths of Mao Zedong and Zhou Enlai, struggle for the leadership succession was won by pragmatists. A nationwide purge of orthodox Maoists was carried out, and the **Gang of Four**, led by Mao's widow, Chiang Ching, was arrested. The new leaders freed more than 100,000 political prisoners and reduced public adulation of Mao. Political and trade ties were expanded with Japan, Europe, and the U.S. in the late 1970s, as relations worsened with the USSR, Cuba, and Vietnam (four-week invasion by China, 1979). Ideological guidelines in industry, science, education, and the armed forces, which the ruling faction said had caused chaos and decline, were reversed (bonuses to workers, Dec. 1977; exams for college entrance, Oct. 1977. Severe restrictions on cultural expression were eased.

Europe. European unity moves (EEC-EFTA trade accord, 1972) faltered as economic problems appeared (Britain floated pound, 1972; France floated franc, 1974). Germany and Switzerland curbed guest workers from S Europe. Greece and Turkey quarreled over Cyprus and Aegean oil rights.

The Vietnam War, in which an estimated 2 million Vietnamese and 50,000 Americans died, also engulfed Laos and Cambodia.

All non-Communist Europe was under democratic rule after free elections (June 1976) in **Spain** seven months after the death of Franco. The conservative, colonialist regime in **Portugal** was overthrown in Apr. 1974. In **Greece** the seven-year military dictatorship yielded power in 1974. N Europe, though ruled mostly by Socialists, became more conservative. The **British** Labour government imposed (1975) wage curbs and suspended nationalization schemes. Terrorism in **Germany** (1972 Munich Olympics killings) led to laws curbing some civil liberties. **French** "new philosophers" rejected leftist ideologies, and the Socialist-Communist coalition lost a 1978 election bid.

Religion and politics. The improvement in **Muslim** countries' political fortunes by the 1950s (with the exception of Central Asia under Soviet and Chinese rule) and the growth of Arab oil wealth were followed by a resurgence of traditional religious fervor. Libyan dictator Muammar al-Qaddafi mixed Islamic laws with socialism. The illegal Muslim Brotherhood in **Egypt** was accused of violence, while extreme groups bombed (1977) theaters to protest Western and secular values.

In **Turkey**, the National Salvation Party was the first Islamic group to share (1974) power since secularization in the 1920s. In **Iran**, Ayatollah Ruhollah **Khomeini** led a revolution that deposed the secular shah (Jan. 1979) and created an Islamic republic. Religiously motivated Muslims took part in an insurrection in Saudi Arabia that briefly seized (1979) the Grand Mosque in Mecca. Muslim puritan opposition to **Pakistan** Pres. Zulfikar Ali-Bhutto helped lead to his overthrow in July 1977. Muslim solidarity, however, could not prevent Pakistan's eastern province (**Bangladesh**) from declaring (Dec. 1971) independence after a bloody civil war.

Muslim and Hindu resentment of coerced sterilization in **India** helped defeat the Indira Gandhi government, and a coalition including religious Hindu parties replaced it (Mar. 1977). Muslims in the S **Philippines**, aided by Libya, rebelled against

central rule from 1973. The Buddhist Soka Gakkai movement launched (1964) the Komeito party in **Japan**, which became a major opposition party in 1972 and 1976 elections.

Evangelical Protestant groups grew in the U.S. A revival of interest in Orthodox Christianity occurred among **Russian** intellectuals (Solzhenitsyn). The secularist **Israeli** Labor party, after decades of rule, was ousted in 1977 by conservatives led by Menachem Begin; religious militants founded settlements on the disputed West Bank, part of biblically promised Israel. Reform Judaism in U.S. revived many previously discarded traditional practices.

Religious wars raged intermittently in **Northern Ireland** (Catholic vs. Protestant, 1969-97) and **Lebanon** (Christian vs. Muslim, 1975-90), while religious militancy complicated the Israel-Arab dispute (1973 Israel-Arab war). The Camp David Accords in 1978, negotiated by Egyptian Pres. Anwar al-Sadat, Israeli Prime Min. Menachem Begin, and U.S. Pres. Jimmy Carter, facilitated the landmark 1979 **Egypt-Israel peace treaty**, but increased militancy on the West Bank impeded further progress.

Latin America. Repressive conservative regimes strengthened their hold, with a violent coup against the elected (Sept. 1973) Allende government in **Chile**, military coup in **Argentina** (1976), and coups against reformist regimes in **Bolivia** (1971, 1979) and **Peru** (1976). In Central America, increasing liberal and leftist militancy led to the ouster (1979) of the Somoza regime of **Nicaragua** and to civil conflict in **El Salvador**.

Indochina. Communist victories in Vietnam, Cambodia, and Laos by May 1975 led to new turmoil. The **Pol Pot** regime ordered millions to resettle in rural areas, in a program of forced labor and terrorism that cost more than 1 million lives (1975-79) and caused hundreds of thousands to flee. The Vietnamese invasion of Cambodia (1979) swelled the refugee population and contributed to widespread starvation.

Russian expansion. Soviet influence, checked in some countries (troops ousted by Egypt, 1972), was projected farther afield, often with the use of Cuban troops (Angola, 1975-89; Ethiopia, 1977-88) and aided by a growing navy, a merchant fleet, and international banking ability. Détente with the West— 1972 Berlin pact, 1972 strategic arms pact (**SALT**)—gave way to a more antagonistic relationship in the late 1970s, exacerbated by the Soviet invasion (1979) of **Afghanistan**.

Africa. The last remaining European colonies were granted independence (**Spanish Sahara**, 1976; **Djibouti**, 1977) and, after 10 years of civil war, a black government took over (1979) in Zimbabwe (Rhodesia); white domination remained in **South Africa**. European involvement in local wars (Russia in **Angola**, **Ethiopia**; France in **Chad**, **Zaire**, **Mauritania**) and the use of tens of thousands of Cuban troops were denounced by some African leaders. Ethnic or tribal clashes made Africa a locus of sustained warfare during the late 1970s.

Arts. Traditional modes of painting, architecture, and music received increased popular and critical attention in the 1970s. These more conservative styles coexisted with modernist works in an atmosphere of increased variety and tolerance.

End of the Cold War and Demand for Democracy: 1980-89

Global developments. International contacts accelerated thanks to new openness in China (1978) and USSR (1985); global consumerism was symbolized by the rapid spread of McDonald's restaurants (Japan, 1971; Russia, 1990).

USSR, Eastern Europe. The late 1980s saw the remaking of the Soviet state and the beginning of the disintegration of the Soviet empire. After the deaths of Gen. Sec. Leonid Brezhnev (1982) and two successors, the harsh treatment of dissent and restriction of emigration, and the Soviet invasion (Dec. 1979) of Afghanistan, Gen. Sec. Mikhail Gorbachev (in office 1985-91) promoted *glasnost* and *perestroika*—economic, political, and social reform. Supported by the Communist Party (July 1988), he signed (Dec. 1987) the INF disarmament treaty. Military withdrawal from Afghanistan was completed in Feb. 1989, and the Soviet people chose (Mar. 1989) part of the new Congress of People's Deputies from competing candidates. By decade's end the Cold War appeared to be fading away.

In **Poland**, Solidarity, the labor union founded (1980) by Lech Walesa, was outlawed in 1982 and then legalized in 1988, after years of unrest. Poland's first free election since the Communist takeover brought **Solidarity** victory (June 1989); Tadeusz Mazowiecki, a Walesa adviser, became (Aug. 1989)

prime minister in a government with the Communists. In the fall of 1989 the failure of Marxist economies in Hungary, **East Germany**, **Czechoslovakia**, **Bulgaria**, and **Romania** brought the collapse of the Communist monopoly and a demand for democracy. In a historic step, the **Berlin Wall** was opened in Nov. 1989.

U.S. The "**Reagan Years**" (1981-88) featured new economic policies via budget and tax cuts, deregulation, "junk bond" financing, leveraged buyouts, and mergers. However, there was a stock market crash (Oct. 1987), and federal budget deficits and the trade deficit increased. Foreign policy showed a **strong anti-Communist stance**, via increased defense spending, aid to anti-Communists in Central America, invasion of Cuba-threatened Grenada, and championing of the "Star Wars" missile defense program. Four Reagan-Gorbachev summits (1985-88) climaxed in the INF treaty (1987), as the Cold War began to wind down. The **Iran-Contra affair** (Oliver North's testimony, July 1987) was a major political scandal. In 1988, Vice Pres. George H. W. Bush was elected to succeed Ronald Reagan as president.

Middle East. The Middle East remained militarily unstable, with sharp divisions along economic, political, racial,

The Chinese government responded to pro-democracy demonstrations in Tiananmen Square with force (1989).

and religious lines. In **Iran**, the Islamic revolution of 1979 created a strong anti-U.S. stance (hostage crisis, Nov. 1979-Jan. 1981). In Sept. 1980, **Iraq** repudiated its border agreement with Iran and began major hostilities that led to an eight-year war in which hundreds of thousands were killed.

Libya's support for international terrorism induced the U.S. to close (May 1981) its diplomatic mission there and embargo (Mar. 1982) Libyan oil. The U.S. accused Libyan leader Muammar al-Qaddafi of aiding (Dec. 1985) terrorists. Following an attack on a West Berlin disco frequented by U.S. military, U.S. bombed targets in Libya (Apr. 1986).

Israel affirmed (July 1980) all Jerusalem as its capital, destroyed (June 1981) an Iraqi atomic reactor, and invaded Lebanon, citing terrorism from the Palestine Liberation Organization; PLO withdrew after cease-fire. A **Palestinian uprising** began (Dec. 1987) in Israeli-occupied Gaza and spread to the West Bank; troops responded with force, killing 300 by the end of 1988, with 6,000 more in detention camps. Israeli withdrawal from **Lebanon** began in Feb. 1985 and ended in June 1985, as Lebanon continued to be torn by military and political conflict. Artillery duels (Mar.-Apr. 1989) between Christian East Beirut and Muslim West Beirut left 200 dead and 700 wounded.

Latin America. In **Nicaragua**, the leftist Sandinista National Liberation Front, in power after the 1979 civil war, faced problems as a result of Nicaragua's military aid to leftist guerrillas in El Salvador and U.S. backing of antigovernment contras. The CIA admitted (1984) having directed the mining of Nicaraguan ports, and the U.S. sent humanitarian (1985) and military (1986) aid. Profits from **secret arms sales** to Iran were found (1987) diverted to contras. Cease-fire talks between the Sandinista government and contras came in 1988, and elections were held in Nicaragua in Feb. 1990.

In **El Salvador**, a military coup (Oct. 1979) failed to halt extremist terrorism. Archbishop Oscar Romero was assassinated in Mar. 1980; from Jan. to June some 4,000 civilians were killed in the civil unrest. In 1984, newly elected Pres. José Napoleon Duarte worked to stem human rights abuses, but violence continued.

In **Chile**, Gen. Augusto Pinochet yielded the presidency after a democratic election (Dec. 1989), but remained as head of the army. He had ruled the country since 1973, imposing harsh measures against leftists and dissidents.

Africa. The 1980s saw continuing economc decline in virtually all African countries, a result of accelerating desertification, the world economic recession, heavy indebtedness to overseas creditors, rapid population growth, and political instability. Some 60 million Africans faced prolonged hunger in 1981. Much of Africa had one of the worst **droughts** ever in 1983, and by year's end, one-third of the population, or about 150 million, were near **famine**. Live Aid, a marathon rock concert, was presented in July 1985, and the U.S. and Western nations sent aid in Sept. 1985. Wars in Ethiopia and Sudan and military strife in several other nations continued. **HIV/AIDS** took a heavy toll.

Anti-apartheid sentiment gathered force in **South Africa** as demonstrations and violent police response grew. White voters approved (Nov. 1983) the first constitution to give "Coloureds" (people of mixed-race background) and Asians a voice, while still excluding blacks (70% of the population). The U.S. imposed economic sanctions in Aug. 1985, and 11 Western nations followed in Sept. Pres. P. W. **Botha** was succeeded by F. W. **de Klerk**, in Sept. 1989, who promised "evolutionary" change via negotiation with the black population.

Asia and the Pacific. Benazir **Bhutto** became the first woman to lead a majority-Muslim nation as prime minister of **Pakistan** (Dec. 1988). The "people power" revolt in the **Philippines** ousted Ferdinand **Marcos** (Feb. 1986) after two decades as president; he was replaced by Corazon **Aquino**.

During the 1980s **China**'s Communist government and paramount leader **Deng Xiaoping** pursued far-reaching changes, expanding commercial and technical ties to the industrialized world and increasing the role of market forces in stimulating urban development. Apr. 1989 brought new demands for political reforms; student demonstrators camped out in **Tiananmen Square**, Beijing, in a massive peaceful protest. Some 100,000 students and workers marched, and at least 20 other cities saw protests. In response, martial law was imposed. Army troops crushed the demonstration in and around Tiananmen Square on June 3-4, with death toll estimates of 500-7,000, up to 10,000 dissidents arrested, and 31 people tried and executed. The conciliatory Communist Party chief was ousted; the Politburo adopted (July 1989) reforms against official corruption.

Japan's relations with other nations, especially the U.S., were dominated by **trade imbalances** favoring Japan. Western Europe and the U.S. accused Japan of restrictive trade policies.

Europe. With the addition of Greece, Portugal, and Spain, the European Community became a common market of more than 300 million people. Margaret **Thatcher** became the first British prime minister in the 20th cent. to win a third consecutive term (1987). **France** elected (1981) its first socialist president, François **Mitterrand**, who was reelected in 1988. Elections in 1983 saw **Italy** its first socialist premier, Bettino **Craxi**.

International terrorism. With the 1979 **overthrow of the shah** of Iran and with instablity in the Middle East, terrorism became a prominent tactic. In 1979-81, Iranian militants held 52 **U.S. hostages in Iran** for 444 days; in 1983 a TNT-laden suicide terrorist blew up U.S. Marine headquarters in Beirut, killing 241 Americans, and a truck bomb blew up a French paratroop barracks, killing 58. The **Achille Lauro** cruise ship was hijacked in 1985, and an American passenger killed; the U.S. subsequently intercepted the Egyptian plane flying the terrorists to safety. Incidents rose to 700 in 1985 and to 1,000 in 1988. **Assassinated leaders** included Egypt's Pres. Anwar al-**Sadat** (1981), India's Prime Min. Indira **Gandhi** (1984), and Lebanese Prem. Rashid **Karami** (1987).

New Regional Tensions in the Post-Cold War World: 1990-99

Global developments. Nations in the 1990s made post-Cold War adjustments; a growing awareness of globalization developed with further spread of democracy and growth of the Internet (1990). Efforts to deal with environmental change intensified with tentative agreements in Kyoto, Japan (1997). A milestone protest against global economic trends burst forth in a World Bank meeting in Seattle (1999).

Soviet Empire breakup. The breakup of the Soviet Union into 15 independent states began with declarations of independence by the Baltic republics of **Lithuania**, **Latvia**, and **Estonia** during an abortive coup against Mikhail **Gorbachev** (Aug. 1991). Other republics soon took the same step. In Dec. 1991, **Russia**, **Ukraine**, and **Belarus** declared the Soviet Union dead; Gorbachev resigned, and the Soviet Parliament went out of existence. The Warsaw Pact and the Council for Mutual Economic Assistance (Comecon) were disbanded. Most of the former Soviet republics joined in a loose confederation called the **Commonwealth of Independent States**. Russia's people suffered severe economic hardship as the nation, under Pres. Boris **Yeltsin**, moved to reboot the economy under a free market system. In Oct. 1993, anti-Yeltsin forces occupied the Parliament building and were ousted by the army.

The Muslim republic of **Chechnya** declared independence from the rest of Russia, but this was met with an invasion by Russian troops (Dec. 1994). A cease-fire took hold in 1996, and the Russians withdrew. In 1999 Russia forcibly suppressed Muslim insurgents in Dagestan and entered Chechnya, again fighting separatist rebels there. Yeltsin resigned Dec. 31, 1999, to be replaced by Vladimir **Putin** (elected in his own right, Mar. 2000).

Europe. Yugoslavia broke apart, and hostilities ensued along ethnic and religious lines. **Croatia, Slovenia,** and **Macedonia** declared independence (1991), followed by **Bosnia-Herzegovina** (1992). **Serbia** and **Montenegro** remained as the republic of Yugoslavia. Bitter fighting followed, especially in Bosnia, where Serbs reportedly engaged in **"ethnic cleansing"** of the Muslim population; a peace plan (Dayton accord, 1995), brokered by the U.S., was signed by **Bosnia, Serbia,** and **Croatia,** with **NATO** responsible for policing its implementation. In spring 1999, NATO conducted a bombing campaign aimed at stopping Yugoslavia from driving out ethnic Albanians from the **Kosovo** region; a peace accord was reached in June under which NATO peacekeeping troops entered Kosovo.

The **two Germanys were reunited** after 45 years (Oct. 1990). The union was greeted with jubilation, but economic stresses followed. West German chancellor Helmut **Kohl,** a Christian Democrat, lost power after 16 years, in Sept. 1998 elections; Gerhard **Schröder,** a Social Democrat, took over. Czechoslovakia broke apart peacefully (Jan. 1993), becoming the **Czech Republic** and **Slovakia.** In Poland, Lech **Walesa** was elected president (Dec. 1991) but was defeated in his bid for a second term (Nov. 1995).

NATO approved the **Partnership for Peace** Program (Jan. 1994) coordinating the defense of E and Central European countries; Russia joined the program later that year. NATO signed a pact with **Russia** (1997) providing for NATO expansion into the former Soviet-bloc countries; a similar treaty was set up with **Ukraine.** The Czech Republic, Hungary, and Poland became members in Jan. 1999. Efforts toward European unity continued with adoption of a single market (Jan. 1993) and conversion of the European Community to the **European Union** as the Maestricht Treaty took effect (Nov. 1993). Agreement was reached for 11 EU members to participate in Economic and Monetary Union, adopting a common currency **(euro)** in Jan. 1999.

An intraparty revolt forced Margaret **Thatcher** out as prime minister of **Great Britain,** to be succeeded by John **Major** (Nov. 1990); seven years later, Labour was returned to power under Tony **Blair** (May 1997). The divorce of Prince **Charles and Diana,** followed by the death of Diana in a car accident (Aug. 1997), made headlines around the world. Talks on peace in **Northern Ireland** that included participation of Sinn Fein, political arm of the IRA, led to a peace plan, approved in an all-Ireland vote (May 1998). In Dec. 1999, Northern Ireland was granted home rule. In **Scotland** voters overwhelmingly approved establishment of a regional legislature (1997), and in **Wales** voters narrowly approved establishment of a local assembly (1997). In a historic innovation, the Church of England ordained women as priests (1994).

Middle East. In Aug. 1990, **Iraq**'s Saddam Hussein ordered troops to invade **Kuwait.** The UN approved military action (Nov. 1990), and an international military force led by the U.S. bombed Iraq (Jan. 1991) and launched a land attack, crushing the invasion (Feb. 1991). Iraq accepted the terms of a cease-fire (Apr. 1991), and U.S. troops withdrew, but "no-fly" zones were set up over some regions to protect Kurds and Shiite Muslims. The UN imposed **sanctions** on Iraq for failure to abide by the cease-fire. Iraq's repeated failure to cooperate with UN inspectors seeking to eliminate **"weapons of mass destruction"** led to air strikes by the U.S. and Britain (1998, 2001).

The last Western hostages were freed in **Lebanon,** June 1992. **Israel** and the **PLO** signed a peace accord (Sept. 1993) providing for Palestinian self-government in the West Bank and Gaza Strip. Prime Min. Yitzhak **Rabin** and Foreign Min. Shimon **Peres** of Israel and Yasir **Arafat** of the PLO received the Nobel Peace Prize for their efforts (1994). Six Arab nations relaxed boycott against Israel (1994), and Israel and **Jordan** signed a peace treaty (Oct. 1994). Rabin was assassinated (Nov. 1995) by an Israeli opponent of the peace process. Benjamin **Netanyahu** became prime minister (May 1996). Arafat was elected to the presidency of the Palestinian Authority (Jan. 1996). A Labour government under Ehud **Barak** took power after Israel's May 1999 elections.

Asia and the Pacific. Hong Kong was returned to China (July 1997) after 156 years as a British colony, and **Macao** reverted to China (Dec. 1999) after over 400 years of Portuguese rule. Both were to retain their legal and economic systems for 50 years. **Jiang** Zemin, general secretary of the Chinese Communist Party, assumed the additional post of president of China (Mar. 1993) and emerged as the key leader after the death of **Deng** Xiaoping (Feb. 1997). China released from prison—and exiled—some well-known dissidents but continued to earn criticism for **human rights abuses.** In Nov. 1999 the U.S. and

Margaret Thatcher, Britain's longest-serving prime minister of the 20th century, was replaced in 1990 by John Major, a member of her own Conservative Party.

China signed a landmark pact normalizing trade relations. China's annual economic growth approached and even eclipsed 10% during the decade.

After years of prosperity, **Thailand, Indonesia,** and **South Korea** in 1997 began to suffer economic reverses that had a worldwide ripple effect. All three received IMF bailout packages. In **Indonesia,** protests over mismanagement led to the resignation of Pres. Suharto (May 1998) after 32 years of nearly autocratic rule. Abdurraham Wahid was elected (Oct. 1999) in the country's first fully democratic elections. In a referendum (Aug. 1999), **East Timor** voted overwhelmingly for independence from Indonesia; pro-Indonesian militias rampaged through the territory, but a multinational **peacekeeping force** helped restore order (Sept. 1999). In South Korea, former dissident **Kim** Dae-jung was elected president (Dec. 1997).

In Japan members of a religious cult released the nerve gas sarin on five **Tokyo subway** cars, killing 12 people and injuring more than 5,500 (Mar. 1995). Tamil rebels continued their armed conflict in **Sri Lanka.** In **Afghanistan** the **Taliban,** an extreme Islamic fundamentalist group, gained control of Kabul (Sept. 1996) and, eventually, most of the country. In **North Korea,** longtime dictator **Kim Il Sung** died (July 1994), to be succeeded by his son, **Kim Jong Il.** In the same year the country signed an agreement with the U.S. setting a timetable for North Korea to eliminate its **nuclear program.** The country also suffered from severe drought and famine conditions.

India was beset by riots following destruction of a mosque by Hindu militants (Dec. 1992); Indian army troops repeatedly clashed with pro-independence demonstrators in the disputed Muslim region of **Kashmir,** exacerbating relations with **Pakistan.** Uneasy relations between India and Pakistan reached a new level when both nations conducted nuclear tests in 1998. Conflict in Pakistan between government and the military led to a bloodless coup (Oct. 1999).

Africa. South Africa's Pres. F. W. **de Klerk** released dissident Nelson **Mandela** from prison (Feb. 1990) after 27 years, and lifted a ban on the black nationalist African National Congress. The white minority government repealed apartheid laws (1990, 1991). Mandela was elected president (Apr. 1994), and a new nonracial constitution became law (Dec. 1996). In **Nigeria,** Gen. Olusegun Obasanjo was elected president (Feb. 1999), to become the country's first civilian leader in 15 years. The decades-long rule of **Mobutu** Sese Seko in **Zaire** came to an end (May 1997) at the hands of rebel forces led by Laurent **Kabila;** an ailing Mobutu fled the country and soon after died. Kabila changed the country's name back to **Democratic Republic of the Congo;** conditions remained unstable.

After the presidents of **Burundi** and **Rwanda** were killed in an airplane crash (Apr. 1994), violence erupted in Rwanda between Hutu and Tutsi factions; hundreds of thousands were slain in genocidal fashion. The conflict spread to refugee camps in neighboring Zaire and Burundi. Factional fighting also erupted in **Somalia** (Jan. 1991). The UN sent a U.S.-led **peacekeeping force,** but it was unsuccessful in restoring order. The UN ended its mission (Mar. 1995) with no durable government in place. **Liberia** endured factional fighting that lasted almost five years and claimed over 150,000 lives; a cease-fire was concluded in Aug. 1995. The World Health Organization reported (1995) that Africa accounted for 70% of **AIDS** cases worldwide.

South African antiapartheid activist Nelson Mandela served over 27 years in jail before his 1990 release; he was elected president of South Africa four years later.

A 16-year civil war appeared to end in **Angola** (May 1991) when the government signed a peace accord with the rebel UNITA faction. Despite the inauguration of a national unity government (Apr. 1997), insurgents continued to fight. **Namibia** officially became independent in Mar. 1990 after almost 20 years under UN trusteeship. In **Algeria**, the army cancelled a second round of parliamentary elections (Jan. 1992) after the Islamic party won a first round. Ensuing violence by **Islamic fundamentalists** claimed thousands of lives; a peace plan was worked out in 1999.

North America. The **North American Free Trade Agreement** (NAFTA), liberalizing trade between the U.S., Canada, and Mexico, went into effect Jan. 1, 1994. In **Canada**, the Progressive Conservative Party suffered a crushing defeat in general elections (Oct. 1993), and liberal Jean **Chrétien** became prime minister. The map of Canada was altered in Apr. 1999 to create a new territory, **Nunavut**, out of an area that had been part of Northwest Territories.

In the **U.S.**'s 1992 presidential election, Bill **Clinton** (D) defeated Pres. George H. W. Bush (R), and won reelection in 1996. He proposed (Feb. 1998) the first balanced federal budget in nearly 30 years. In Dec. 1998 Clinton was **impeached** by the U.S. House on charges related to the Monica Lewinsky scandal; he was acquitted by the Senate in Feb. 1999.

In **Mexico**, Ernesto Zedillo of the ruling PRI party was elected president (July 1994) after the party's first candidate was assassinated. The country soon faced a crisis affecting the value of the peso, but recovered with the help of a bailout package from the U.S. A peasant revolt spearheaded by the **Zapatista National Liberation Army** erupted in the state of Chiapas (Jan. 1994) and was suppressed.

Central America and the Caribbean. In **Haiti**, Jean-Bertrand **Aristide** was elected president (Dec. 1990) but was ousted in a military coup after nine months. A delegation headed by former U.S. Pres. Jimmy Carter arranged (Sept. 1994) for the junta to step aside for Aristide, who served until 1996. In **Nicaragua**, Violeta Chamorro defeated Daniel **Ortega** in the presidential election (Feb. 1990), thus ousting the Sandinistas. In **Panama**, U.S. troops invaded and overthrew the government of Manuel **Noriega** (Dec. 1989). Noriega was captured Jan. 1990; convicted and jailed on drug-related charges in U.S. in 1992, and in France in 2010. On Dec. 31, 1999, Panama assumed full control of the **Panama Canal**, in accord with a treaty with the U.S. In **El Salvador** (1992) and **Guatemala** (1996) the governments signed agreements with rebel factions.

South America. Alberto **Fujimori** was elected president of **Peru** in June 1990 and, despite his suppression of the constitution (1992), was reelected in 1995. Peru succeeded in capturing (Sept. 1992) the leader of the Shining Path guerrilla movement. Leftist guerrillas took hostages at an ambassador's residence in Lima (Dec. 1996); one hostage was killed during a government assault rescuing the rest (Apr. 1997). Peronist Pres. Carlos Saúl **Menem** served as **Argentina**'s president for much of the decade (elected 1989, reelected 1995), imposing economic austerity.

Former Chilean Pres. Augusto **Pinochet** continued to head the army until Mar. 1998; he was arrested in London (Oct. 1998) on human rights charges but judged unfit for trial and returned to Chile (Mar. 2000). In **Brazil**, Fernando Henrique **Cardoso** was elected president (Oct. 1994) and reelected in 1998 despite an economic slump; the IMF announced a $42-bil aid package (Nov. 1998). In **Venezuela** two coup attempts were thwarted (1992); coup leader Hugo **Chávez**, a leftist populist, was elected president in Dec. 1998.

Terrorism. The U.S. was a prominent target of terrorism linked to Middle Eastern sources. A bomb exploded in a garage beneath New York City's **World Trade Center**, killing six people (Feb. 1993). Bombs set off outside **U.S. embassies** in Kenya and Tanzania killed over 220 people (Aug. 1998); the U.S. retaliated with missiles fired at alleged terrorist-linked sites in Afghanistan and Sudan and four Islamists linked to **al-Qaeda** were convicted of involvement in the bombings in U.S. (May 2001). In the U.S.'s deadliest instance of domestic terrorism, 168 people were killed in the bombing of a federal building in **Oklahoma City**, OK (Apr. 1995).

Science and technology. The powerful **Hubble Space Telescope** was launched in Apr. 1990. U.S. space shuttle *Atlantis* docked with the orbiting Russian space station *Mir* (June 1995) in first of several joint missions. In Nov. 1998 the first component for a new **International Space Station** was launched into space from Kazakhstan.

Scottish scientist Ian Wilmut announced (Feb. 1997) the **cloning** of a sheep, named Dolly—the first mammal successfully cloned from a cell from an adult animal.

Tim Berners-Lee launched the first **World Wide Web** server (1990). User-friendly graphical browsers (Mosaic, 1993; Netscape, 1994) and affordable Internet service providers followed, expanding the reach of the **Internet**.

Globalization and Global Realignments: 2000-09

Terrorism and crime. The first decade of the new century saw a dramatic surge in international terrorism, often associated with radical **Islam**. In Oct. 2000, 17 American sailors were killed aboard the USS *Cole* in Aden, **Yemen**, when a small boat exploded alongside it in a suicide bombing tied to the **al-Qaeda** terrorist network based in Afghanistan. Terrorism reached a new level on **Sept. 11, 2001**, when hijackers crashed two jetliners into the twin towers of the **World Trade Center** in New York City and another into the **Pentagon** outside Washington, DC, with a fourth plane crashing in a Pennsylvania field. The attacks, linked to al-Qaeda and its leader **Osama bin Laden**, destroyed both towers, damaged the Pentagon, and killed about 3,000 people.

Among other incidents tied to Islamic radicals, a car bomb on the Indonesian island of **Bali** (Oct. 2002) killed about 200. **Commuter trains** were bombed in **Madrid**, Spain, killing 191 (Mar. 2004); elections a week later ousted Spain's premier. Subway trains and a bus were bombed in **London** (July 2005); 56 people died. Eight explosions killed 207 on commuter trains in **Mumbai**, India (July 2006); also in Mumbai (Nov. 2008),

terrorists launched coordinated attacks on sites frequented by foreigners, killing some 170. **Chechen** separatist guerrillas were implicated in an attack on a **Moscow** movie theater (Oct. 2002; over 100 hostages died), bombings in Moscow's subways (Feb. 2004), explosions on two Russian planes (Aug. 2004; 89 died), and takeover of a school in Beslan (Aug.-Sept. 2004; over 330 died).

Other attacks were foiled, as when a Nigerian man, reportedly aided by al-Qaeda in Yemen, tried to ignite explosives in his underwear on a Detroit-bound international flight (Dec. 2009).

Global economic crisis. Rapid economic growth in China and other developing countries contrasted with sluggish rates in traditional economic powers; efforts at international economic coordination expanded to include rising economies (Group of 20, 2008). A global **recession**, beginning in late 2007, led to a **financial meltdown** (Sept. 2008) with ripple effects. **Iceland**'s banking system collapsed (Oct. 2008), rescued by loans and austerity measures. **Dubai**'s state-controlled investment company Dubai World could not meet debt payments; bailed out (Dec. 2009) by loan from Abu Dhabi. Soaring food and **fuel**

prices led to unrest, including an attempted general strike in **Egypt** and riots in **Haiti** (Apr. 2008). Spending cuts, pension reforms, tax hikes, and other **austerity** measures spurred protests in several European countries.

War in Iraq and Afghanistan. The U.S., with Great Britain, invaded **Iraq** (Mar. 2003) to oust the regime of Saddam **Hussein**. Troops took control of Baghdad and other cities, and Pres. George W. **Bush** declared major combat ended by May 1, but insurgents caused continuing casualties. Interim government installed, June 2004. No **weapons of mass destruction**, cited as major grounds for the invasion, were found. Hussein was captured by U.S. troops (Dec. 2003) and convicted and executed by Iraqi authorities for crimes against humanity (Dec. 2006). Iraqis voted in **elections** for a transitional assembly (Jan. 2005), democratic constitution (Oct. 2005), and parliament (Dec. 2005); negotiations produced a Shiite coalition government under Prime Min. Nouri **al-Maliki** (May 2006). With sectarian and **insurgent violence** intensifying, Bush announced (Jan. 2007) a **"surge"** of additional U.S. troops; casualties fell sharply after mid-2007, aided by a cease-fire with Shiite militias and a shift by minority Sunni clans away from support for al-Qaeda.

In **Afghanistan**, a U.S.-led military coalition ousted the **Taliban** regime. A transitional government was installed (Dec. 2001), but the Taliban remained strong in many areas as NATO assumed control of multinational forces in Aug. 2003. Afghans elected Hamid **Karzai** as president (Nov. 2004); he retained office after Aug. 2009 election marked by **vote-rigging**. From 2007, Taliban and other Islamist militants stepped up activities, often operating from safe havens inside Pakistan. The U.S. increased its troop strength in Afghanistan (2009) and expanded use of **drones**.

Asia. Gen. Pervez **Musharraf**, brought to power in a 1999 coup, assumed **Pakistan**'s presidency (June 2001) and retained office through elections denounced by protesters. After the Sept. 11, 2001, terrorist attacks, Pakistan agreed to cooperate in fighting **Taliban** and **al-Qaeda** militants. Pakistan and **India** restored ties (May 2003) and declared a cease-fire in disputed territory (Nov. 2003); relations remained tense. After former Pakistani Prime Min. Benazir **Bhutto** was assassinated in a bombing (Dec. 2007), her party won parliamentary elections (Feb. 2008), and her widower, Asif Ali **Zardari**, was elected president (Sept. 2008). In May 2009, the government launched a major offensive against Taliban insurgents in the Swat Valley.

The UN Intl. Atomic Energy Agency censured **Iran** (Dec. 2003) for covering up aspects of its **nuclear** program. Iran continued enriching uranium in defiance of IAEA deadlines and tested missiles said to be capable of reaching Israel. Pres. Mahmoud **Ahmadinejad** was declared landslide winner in June 2009 elections widely perceived as rigged; massive **protests** were crushed by police and Basij paramilitaries (at least 30 killed; thousands arrested). In **Kyrgyzstan**, protests (Mar. 2005) against election fraud brought down Pres. Askar Akayev in a **"tulip revolution."** leading to the election of Kurmanbek **Bakiyev**.

South Korean Pres. Kim Dae-jung and **North Korean** ruler Kim Jong Il agreed to seek peace and reunification at a summit (June 2000), but tensions rose after North Korea admitted to a covert **nuclear weapons** development program (Oct. 2002). At multination talks in Beijing, North Korea agreed (Feb. 2007) to end its nuclear program in exchange for aid but reneged, conducting tests in Apr.-May 2009.

A **tsunami** (Dec. 2004) swept ashore in Indian Ocean nations, leaving some 228,000 dead. **Earthquakes** struck Kashmir and other parts of Pakistan and India (Oct. 2005), killing nearly 80,000, and hit China's Sichuan province (May 2008), killing nearly 70,000. With the retirement of **China**'s Pres. Jiang Zemin, **Hu** Jintao was named Communist party chief (Nov. 2002) and president (Mar. 2003). In **Japan**, Liberal Democrats, in virtually uninterrupted power since the 1950s, were dispatched in parliamentary elections (Aug. 2009).

Myanmar's military junta cracked down on hundreds of thousands of protesters (Sept. 2007). More than 80,000 people were killed in a **cyclone** in Myanmar (May 2008); the regime thwarted aid agencies. **Sri Lanka** government forces stepped-up an offensive in 2008 against **Tamil guerrillas**, leading them to declare an end (May 2009) to a rebellion that since 1983 had claimed at least 80,000 lives. The military carried out a bloodless coup in **Thailand** (Sept. 2006), ousting Prem. Thaksin Shinawatra; civilian rule was restored after Dec. 2007 elections, but unrest continued.

Middle East. Violence between Israelis and Palestinians escalated, with **suicide bombings** by Palestinians and retaliation by Israelis. Israel launched major **West Bank offensive**

(Mar. 2002) and withdrew in early May but, after more suicide bombings, reoccupied much of the West Bank. The U.S., Russia, UN, and EU initiated (Apr. 2003) a **"road map"** for peace negotiations; little progress was made. After Palestinian leader Yasir **Arafat** died (Nov. 2004), Mahmoud **Abbas** was elected in his place. Israeli Prime Min. Ariel **Sharon** decided in 2005 to pull troops and settlers out of the **Gaza Strip**, angering his party's right wing. He formed a new party but suffered a stroke (Jan. 2006); he was succeeded by ally Ehud **Olmert**, who led a coalition government following elections (Apr. 2006). The militant Palestinian party **Hamas** won a parliamentary majority over the long-ruling **Fatah** party (Jan. 2006).

Israel launched attacks on **Lebanon** (July 2006) after a raid into N Israel by Lebanon-based **Hezbollah** guerrillas; a cease-fire was declared a month later. In reaction to Hamas rocket and mortar attacks, Israel launched an offensive in the **Gaza Strip** (Dec. 2008), which killed an estimated 1,300 Palestinians. Olmert resigned as prime minister (effective Sept. 2008) amid corruption inquiries; Feb. 2009 elections led to a coalition government headed by former Prime Min. Benjamin **Netanyahu**, a conservative.

Europe. The EU admitted 10 East European nations in May 2004; two more joined in Jan. 2007, for a total of 27 members. By 2008 the **euro** was the common currency in 15 EU nations. Voters in France and the Netherlands rejected a treaty to establish a new **EU constitution** (May-June 2005). A modified plan (called the **Treaty of Lisbon**) came into force (Dec. 2009) after Irish voters approved it (Oct. 2009).

In Oct. 2000, Yugoslav strongman Slobodan **Milosevic** yielded power to Vojislav **Kostunica**, who had declared himself president after a disputed election. Milosevic surrendered to Serbian authorities; he went on trial in the Hague (Feb. 2002) for **war crimes** during 1990s ethnic conflicts in the Balkans but died (Mar. 2006) before a verdict. Former Bosnian Serb leader Radovan **Karadzic** was arraigned on war crimes charges (July 2008). **Kosovo** unilaterally declared independence (Feb. 2008).

Germany elected its first East German and first woman chancellor (Nov. 2005) in Angela **Merkel**, a Christian Democrat. Rioting shook France's immigrant communities in 300 cities and towns (Nov. 2005). A Danish newspaper's publication of cartoon **caricatures of Muhammad** sparked violent worldwide protests by Muslims (Jan.-Feb. 2006).

British Prime Min. Tony **Blair** won reelection twice (2001, 2005), becoming the first Labour prime minister to earn three straight terms. He stepped down in June 2007, to be succeeded

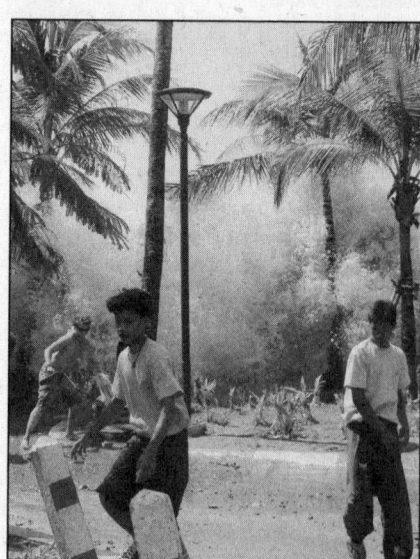

One of the deadliest natural disasters in recorded history, a 2004 tsunami killed more than 200,000 people in African and Asian countries.

The conventional military combat phase of the Iraq War (2003-10) was over quickly, but violence stretched on, killing nearly 5,000 coalition troops and an estimated 100,000 Iraqi civilians.

by fellow Labourite Gordon **Brown**. **France** saw the election (May 2007) of conservative Nicolas **Sarkozy** as president and rejoined NATO's military command (Apr. 2009) after more than 40 years. Vladimir **Putin**, in power in Russia since 1999, was constitutionally barred from a new presidential term in 2008; his protégé, Dmitri **Medvedev**, was elected (May 2008). In **Ukraine**, a tainted presidential runoff election (Nov. 2004) led to the country's "**orange revolution**"; a recount gave power to nationalist Viktor **Yushchenko**.

Africa. Ethiopia and Eritrea signed a peace treaty (Dec. 2000). Laurent **Kabila**, president of **Dem. Rep. of the Congo**, was assassinated (Jan. 2001). Liberian Pres. Charles **Taylor** went into exile (Aug. 2003) as part of a deal to end a 14-year civil war; other accords were reached aimed at ending civil wars in **Angola** (Apr. 2002) and **Côte d'Ivoire** (Jan. 2003).

A peace agreement in Dem. Rep. of the Congo (Apr. 2003) did not end violence there; the nation agreed to work with Rwanda to disarm Hutu rebels (Nov. 2007). In **Sudan** a powersharing accord between the Muslim-led government and rebels from the Christian south was signed, Jan. 2005, giving the south limited autonomy. Rebellion in the **Darfur** area of western Sudan led to large-scale violence. Arab militias (**janjaweed**), reportedly backed by the government, were accused of displacing over 2 million people in acts bordering on **genocide**; by the end of 2009 over 300,000 people had been killed. The Intl. Criminal Court issued an arrest warrant for Sudanese Pres. Omar Hassan Ahmad al-**Bashir**, for war crimes (Mar. 2009); he remained in power.

Disputed elections sparked violence in **Kenya** (Jan. 2008) and **Zimbabwe** (Apr. 2008). Under Pres. Robert Mugabe's rule, unemployment in Zimbabwe topped 90% and hyperinflation left the currency virtually worthless. **Guinea-Bissau**'s defense chief and then its president were assassinated in turn by rival groups (Mar. 2009).

Americas and the Caribbean. In Jan. 2001, Republican George W. **Bush** was inaugurated as **U.S. president**, after one of the closest elections in U.S. history; he was reelected in Nov. 2004. Democrats claimed the White House with the

Nov. 2008 election of Barack **Obama**, first-ever black U.S. president. The long-supreme **Institutional Revolutionary Party** lost power in **Mexico** with the election of two successive presidents from a center-right party, Vicente **Fox** and Felipe **Calderón** (July 2000, July 2006). Calderón launched a crackdown on drug trafficking (Dec. 2006); from then through the end of 2010, more than 30,000 people were killed in violence fueled by **drug cartels**.

In **Brazil**, reformist candidate Luiz Inácio **Lula da Silva**, won a runoff (Oct. 2002) to become president; he was reelected in 2006. **Chile** was ruled by Socialist governments under Ricardo Lagos Escobar (from 2000) and Michelle **Bachelet** (from 2006). In **Venezuela**, leftist populist Pres. Hugo **Chávez** regained power after a 48-hour coup (Dec. 2002) and consolidated it, in part through a referendum (Feb. 2009) that eliminated presidential term limits. In **Bolivia**, Evo **Morales**, another leftist populist, won election as president (Dec. 2005) and passage of a new constitution (Jan. 2009) that increased his power. In **Honduras**, leftist opposition leader Manuel **Zelaya** was elected president (Nov. 2005) but was ousted by the military (June 2009) after he had sought constitutional changes; conservative Porfirio (Pepe) **Lobo** was elected (Nov. 2009) to succeed him.

Peronist Nestor **Kirchner** won election as president of **Argentina** (Apr. 2003); his wife, Cristina Kirchner, was elected (Oct. 2007) to succeed him. **Haiti** was wracked by antigovernment protests, leading to the resignation of Jean-Bertrand **Aristide** in Feb. 2004; a UN peacekeeping mission was brought in. **Canada**'s Liberal Party was defeated in Jan. 2006 elections; Conservative Stephen Harper became prime minister. Pres. Fidel **Castro**, Cuba's leader since 1959, ceded powers to his brother, Raúl, to undergo surgery (July 2006); he formally resigned in Feb. 2008.

Religion. Pope **John Paul II** died, Apr. 2005, after 26 years in the papacy; German Cardinal Joseph Ratzinger was elected as his successor, taking the name **Benedict XVI**. During the decade, reports of **sexual abuse** by Catholic priests going back generations and evidence of inaction by church officials emerged.

Science and technology. The U.S. **space shuttle** *Columbia* broke up on reentering Earth's atmosphere (Feb. 2003), killing all seven crew members; space shuttle program suspended, resuming July 2005. NASA landed two rovers, *Spirit* and *Opportunity*, on Mars (Jan. 2004), and Phoenix Mars Lander verified the presence of water ice on the planet (June 2008). China launched its first manned space flight, Oct. 2003. China, Oct. 2010, unveiled the Tianhe-1A **supercomputer**, said to be the world's fastest. **Internet** penetration and access to technology expanded exponentially. More than one-fifth of the world's population had regular web access by decade's end, and online commerce, social networking (Facebook, 2004; Twitter, 2006), and file-sharing services became commonplace.

Environment and health. Under the **Kyoto Protocol**, which took effect Feb. 2005, most industrialized nations, other than the U.S., agreed to specific reductions in emissions of **greenhouse gases** linked to global warming by 2012. A NASA report (Jan. 2010) found that 2000-09 had the warmest average global temperatures since modern records began in the 1880s.

Worldwide AIDS estimates were revised downward (Nov. 2007) to show new infections had peaked in the late 1990s. An epidemic of **swine flu**, or influenza A (H1N1), broke out in Mexico (Apr. 2009) and spread around the globe, killing more than 18,000.

Searching for Resolutions: 2010-14

Terrorism. Early in the decade, the core **al-Qaeda** leadership showed signs of weakening. U.S. forces raided the secret compound of Osama **bin Laden** in Pakistan, killing the al-Qaeda leader (May 2011). However, radical Islamist groups were gaining ground and influence in a number of countries and the threat of terrorism lingered. Bombs in Kampala, **Uganda**, killed more than 70 gathered to watch World Cup soccer (July 2010); **al-Shabab** militants based in Somalia and linked to al-Qaeda claimed responsibility. An al-Qaeda-inspired terrorist killed seven in two French towns (Mar. 2012). The U.S. ambassador and three other Americans were killed, Sept. 11, 2012, when Islamic militants attacked U.S. consulate in **Benghazi, Libya**. Two U.S. immigrants from Chechnya set off bombs, killing three and injuring 264, at the finish line of the **Boston Marathon** (Apr. 2013). In Sept. 2013, some 70 were killed by al-Shabaab militants at a shopping mall in Nairobi, Kenya. Al-Qaeda in the Arabian Peninsula launched attacks in **Yemen**, including one on a hospital, Dec. 2013, that killed more than 50. The radical Islamist group **Boko Haram**, increasingly active in Nigeria, was responsible for kidnappings (including abduction of over 200 schoolgirls, Apr. 2014), bombings, and massacres.

In other outbreaks of terrorism, an anti-Muslim extremist in **Norway** killed 77 people in a rampage, July 2011.

War in Iraq and Afghanistan. The last U.S. combat unit withdrew from **Iraq**, Aug. 2010, and the U.S. military left in Dec. 2011, with no residual force remaining. Death toll: about 4,500 U.S. service members, 300 from allied countries, with Iraqi civilian deaths estimated at over 100,000. Sectarian violence accelerated in 2013 (some 8,000 deaths).

As Sunni disaffection grew, the increasingly powerful Sunni Islamic State of Iraq and Syria (**ISIS**), an al-Qaeda offshoot incubated in Syria, gained ground (**Fallujah** takeover, Jan. 2014). Prime Min. Nouri al-Maliki's Shiite party won a plurality in general elections, Apr. 2014. With Iraqi government troops often abandoning positions, ISIS, aided by other Sunni rebels, took over **Mosul** and other territory, declaring an Islamic state in a large part of Iraq and Syria (June 2014), while separatist Kurds controlled another sector of Iraq.

Pres. Barack Obama outlined plans (May 2014) to withdraw all U.S. forces from Afghanistan by the end of 2016; the sole U.S. prisoner in **Taliban** custody there was freed (May 2014) in exchange for five high-level Taliban prisoners in Guantanamo.

Taliban remained active and showed strength in assault on the Karachi, Pakistan, international airport (June 2014).

Arab upheavals. Poverty, religious and ethnic conflict, and government corruption and repression fueled revolts (so-called **Arab Spring**) that challenged several entrenched Arab regimes, with varying results. Protests forced the ouster of **Tunisian** Pres. Zine al-Abidine Ben Ali (Jan. 2011); elections followed and a new constitution (Jan. 2014) recognized civil liberties. But in **Egypt**, after mass protests led to the overthrow of longtime Pres. Hosni **Mubarak** (Feb. 2011), the **Muslim Brotherhood**-dominated government (elected June 2012) provoked protests and fell in a military coup (July 2013). Raids (over 600 killed, Aug. 2013) and mass arrests followed. The coup leader, Abdel Fattah **al-Sisi**, was elected president, May 2014.

In **Libya**, insurgents with NATO military backing overthrew dictator Muammar al-Qaddafi, who was killed (Oct. 2011); the situation remained unstable. In **Syria**, Pres. Bashar al-Assad launched a ferocious offensive against antigovernment protesters, giving rise to civil war; well over 100,000 people were killed by the end of 2013, as regime forces fought rebel groups, including the dominant **ISIS**. After about 1,400 people were killed in chemical attacks (Aug. 2013), the government accepted a Russian-backed plan for surrender of its chemical weapons.

Europe. The EU, with IMF help, provided **loan packages** to bail out **Greece** (May 2010; additional pledges later) and Ireland (Nov. 2010). The **European Central Bank** bailed out Portugal (May 2011). The EU provided a bank bailout for **Spain** (June 2012) and reached a bailout agreement with Cyprus (Mar. 2013). Far-right parties scored big gains in **European Parliament** elections (May 2014).

Polish Pres. Lech **Kaczynski** and 95 others were killed in a plane crash (Apr. 2010); Bronisław **Komorowski** was elected to replace him (July 2010). In **Britain**, conservatives were returned to power in a coalition government under David **Cameron** (May 2010). In **France**, socialist François Hollande defeated Nicolas **Sarkozy** to become president (May 2012).

Amid accusations of corruption and voter fraud, Vladimir **Putin** won a third term as **Russia**'s president (Mar. 2012). He gave asylum to fugitive U.S. secrets leaker Edward Snowden (Aug. 2013) and strengthened ties to China with a 30-year natural gas deal (May 2014). In **Ukraine**, the pro-Russian Viktor **Yanukovich** was elected president (Feb. 2010), but his rebuff to EU integration (Nov. 2013) led to mass protests, with protesters fired on; he fled and was removed by Parliament. Claiming a danger to ethnic Russians, Putin sent troops to **Crimea** and, in Mar. 2014, annexed the region. With pro-Russian separatists fighting for control of East Ukraine, a pro-European moderate, Petro **Poroshenko**, was elected Ukraine's president (May 2014); he signed EU trade agreement, June 2014.

Asia and the Pacific. Monsoon **floods** (July-Aug. 2010) in **Pakistan** left millions homeless. An earthquake and tsunami (Mar. 2011) struck Japan, killing more than 16,000 and leading to meltdowns at nuclear reactors. A **Malaysian airliner** en route to Beijing with 239 aboard veered off course and vanished (Mar. 2014); a massive search effort followed. A **South Korean** ferry with over 470 aboard capsized (Apr. 2014); an estimated 304 died.

In **Kyrgyzstan**, Kumanbek **Bakiyeve** was ousted (Apr. 2010), after clashes with protesters left at least 85 people dead. Despite ethnic violence (up to 2,000 killed), a referendum was held (June 2010) and new constitution approved. Almazbek **Atambayev** was elected president (Oct. 2011). **North Korean** dictator **Kim Jong Il** died (Dec. 2011) and was succeeded by youngest son **Kim Jong Un**, who threatened the U.S. with a preemptive nuclear strike (Mar. 2013) and fired missiles in the Sea of Japan (Mar. 2014). Reformist-minded cleric Hassan **Rouhani** won the June 2013 presidential election in **Iran**, which agreed to limited cutbacks in its nuclear program (Nov. 2013).

Myanmar's military junta was dissolved (Mar. 2011) following the country's first election in 20 years (Nov. 2010), which brought the military-backed USDP party to power; the party led by pro-democracy dissident Aung San **Suu Kyi** did not participate but won 43 seats, including one for Suu Kyi, in interim elections (Apr. 2012). Violence against the segregated Muslim Rohingya minority continued. After mass protests in **Thailand**, the government of Prime Min. Yingluck Shinawatra was ousted (May 2014) in the country's 12th military coup.

Upon Chinese Pres. **Hu** Jintao's retirement, **Xi** Jinping was named Communist party chief (Nov. 2012) and president (Mar. 2013). Liberal Democrats in **Japan** regained control in

Dec. 2012 elections. In **Australia**, Prime Min. Kevin Rudd was temporarily displaced (June 2010) by his deputy, Julia **Gillard**, who became Australia's first female prime minister; Rudd ousted her and again became prime minister in June 2013. The Hindu nationalist Bharatiya Janata party won a majority in May 2014 elections in **India**, ousting the dominant Indian Congress Party; Narendra **Modi** became prime minister.

Africa. Coups ousted **Niger**'s president (Feb. 2010) and ended elections in **Guinea-Bissau** (Apr. 2012); in both cases, civilian rule returned following new elections. In a referendum, southern Sudanese (mostly Christian or indigenous beliefs) voted overwhelmingly for separation from the north (mostly Arab Muslim), and **South Sudan** was granted independence as of July 2011. Low-level soldiers staged a coup in **Mali** (Mar. 2012). The junta ceded power to civilians, but Islamic rebels seized control in the north. French and West African forces intervened; a peace deal was reached (June 2013) but proved fragile. An outbreak of **Ebola** virus in W Africa killed about 2,600 people by mid-Sept. 2014.

Middle East. UN General Assembly voted to grant non-member observer state status to **Palestine** (Nov. 2012). Arab-Israeli **peace talks** resumed (July 2013), but foundered, Apr. 2014, as Fatah and militant Hamas factions agreed to aim at unification. Israel began air strikes on Gaza (July 2014) ostensibly in response to rocket attacks by Hamas-affiliated groups; at least 2,000 Palestinians and 60 Israeli soldiers were dead by the end of Aug. 2014, when an open-ended ceasefire was established.

Americas and the Caribbean. **Haiti** was devastated by an earthquake (Jan. 2010) that killed more than 200,000; a massive international relief effort was launched. A **cholera** epidemic developed, with over 8,000 dead by the end of 2013. **Mexico**'s Institutional Revolutionary Party regained power with the election of Enrique **Peña Nieto** (July 2012). In **Brazil**, Pres. Lula da Silva's chosen successor, Dilma **Rousseff**, was elected (Oct. 2010); she faced mass protests (June 2013) over plan to raise bus fares and spending on World Cup (2014). In **Venezuela**, Pres. Hugo **Chávez** was reelected (Oct. 2012) but died (Mar. 2013) before he could be inaugurated; Nicolás **Maduro** Moros, Chávez's chosen successor and vice president, was elected to replace him (Apr. 2013); more than 40 killed and hundreds arrested in antigovernment protests starting Feb. 2014.

Religion. **Benedict XVI** resigned after eight years as pope (Feb. 2013); Argentinean Cardinal Jorge Mario Bergoglio succeeded him, taking the name **Francis** and becoming the first pope from the Americas. The U.S. Commission on International Religious Freedom cited (Apr. 2014) 16 countries for severe violations of religious freedom.

Science and technology. **WikiLeaks**, a nonprofit group formed in 2007 to expose government secrets, began disseminating secret documents related to Iraq and Afghanistan wars (Apr., July 2010). After 30 years, NASA's space shuttle program ended with return of *Atlantis* to Earth (July 2011). NASA's rover *Curiosity* landed on Mars, Aug. 2012. China landed unmanned *Yulu* rover on the Moon, Dec. 2013.

Environment. The UN-sponsored Intergovernmental Panel on Climate Change, in reports issued in 2013-14, stressed "human influence" as "dominant cause" of **global warming** and recommended steps to be taken by governments.

Pope Benedict XVI (right), the leader of the world's 1.1 billion Roman Catholics, resigned in 2013 and was replaced by Pope Francis, the first pontiff from the Americas.

Note: Information accurate as of Sept. 2014.

Ancient Greeks and Romans

Greeks

Aeschines, orator, 389-314 BCE
Aeschylus, dramatist, 525-456 BCE
Aesop, fableist, c. 620-c. 560 BCE
Alcibiades, politician, 450-404 BCE
Anacreon, poet, c. 582-c. 485 BCE
Anaxagoras, philosopher, c. 500-428 BCE
Anaximander, philosopher, 611-546 BCE
Anaximenes, philosopher, c. 570-500 BCE
Antiphon, speechwriter, c. 480-411 BCE
Apollonius, mathematician, c. 265-170 BCE
Archimedes, mathematician, 287-212 BCE
Aristophanes, dramatist, c. 448-380 BCE
Aristotle, philosopher, 384-322 BCE
Athenaeus, scholar, fl. c. 200
Callicrates, architect, fl. 5th cent. BCE
Callimachus, poet, c. 305-240 BCE
Cratinus, comic dramatist, 520-421 BCE
Democritus, philosopher, c. 460-370 BCE
Demosthenes, orator, 384-322 BCE
Diodorus, historian, fl. 20 BCE
Diogenes, philosopher, 372-c. 287 BCE
Dionysius, historian, d. c. 7 BCE
Empedocles, philosopher, c. 490-430 BCE
Epicharmus, dramatist, c. 530-440 BCE
Epictetus, philosopher, c. 55-c. 135
Epicurus, philosopher, 341-270 BCE
Eratosthenes, scientist, 276-194 BCE
Euclid, mathematician, fl. c. 300 BCE
Euripides, dramatist, c. 484-406 BCE
Galen, physician, 129-216
Heraclitus, philosopher, c. 540-c. 475 BCE
Herodotus, historian, c. 484-420 BCE

Hesiod, poet, 8th cent. BCE
Hippocrates, physician, c. 460-377 BCE
Homer, poet, fl. c. 8th cent. BCE
Isocrates, orator, 436-338 BCE
Menander, dramatist, 342-292 BCE
Parmenides, philosopher, b. c. 515 BCE
Pericles, statesman, c. 495-429 BCE
Phidias, sculptor, c. 500-435 BCE
Pindar, poet, c. 518-c. 438 BCE
Plato, philosopher, c. 428-347 BCE
Plutarch, biographer, c. 46-120
Polybius, historian, c. 200-c. 118 BCE
Praxiteles, sculptor, 400-330 BCE
Pythagoras, phil., math., c. 580-c. 500 BCE
Sappho, poet, c. 610-c. 580 BCE
Simonides, poet, 556-c. 468 BCE
Socrates, philosopher, 469-399 BCE
Solon, statesman, 640-560 BCE
Sophocles, dramatist, c. 496-406 BCE
Strabo, geographer, c. 63 BCE-24 CE
Thales, philosopher, c. 634-546 BCE
Themistocles, politician, c. 524-c. 460 BCE
Theocritus, poet, c. 310-250 BCE
Theophrastus, phil., c. 372-c. 287 BCE
Thucydides, historian, fl. 5th cent. BCE
Timon, philosopher, c. 320-c. 230 BCE
Xenophon, historian, c. 434-c. 355 BCE
Zeno, philosopher, c. 335-c. 263 BCE

Romans

Ammianus, historian, c. 330-395
Apuleius, satirist, c. 124-c. 170
Boethius, scholar, c. 480-524
Caesar, Julius, leader, 100-44 BCE

Catiline, politician, c. 108-62 BCE
Cato (Elder), statesman, 234-149 BCE
Catullus, poet, c. 84-54 BCE
Cicero, orator, 106-43 BCE
Claudian, poet, c. 370-c. 404
Ennius, poet, 239-170 BCE
Gellius, author, c. 130-c. 165
Horace, poet, 65-8 BCE
Juvenal, satirist, 60-127
Livy, historian, 59 BCE-17 CE
Lucan, poet, 39-65
Lucilius, poet, c. 180-c.102 BCE
Lucretius, poet, c. 99-c. 55 BCE
Martial, epigrammatist, c. 38-c. 103
Nepos, historian, c. 100-c. 25 BCE
Ovid, poet, 43 BCE-17 CE
Persius, satirist, 34-62
Plautus, dramatist, c. 254-c. 184 BCE
Pliny the Elder, scholar, 23-79
Pliny the Younger, author, 62-113
Quintilian, rhetorician, c. 35-c. 97
Sallust, historian, 86-34 BCE
Seneca, philosopher, 4 BCE-65 CE
Silius, poet, c. 25-101
Statius, poet, c. 45-c. 96
Suetonius, biographer, c. 69-c. 122
Tacitus, historian, 56-120
Terence, dramatist, 195/185-c. 159 BCE
Tibullus, poet, c. 55-c. 19 BCE
Vergil, poet, 70-19 BCE
Vitruvius, architect, fl. 1st cent. BCE

Roman Rulers

From Romulus to the end of the Empire in the West (Rome). Rulers in the East sat in Constantinople and, for a brief period, in Nicaea, until the capture of Constantinople by the Turks in 1453, when Byzantium was succeeded by the Ottoman Empire.

The Kingdom

BCE
753 Romulus (Quirinus)
715 Numa Pompilius
673 Tullus Hostilius
641 Ancus Marcius
616 L. Tarquinius Priscus
579 Servius Tullius
534 L. Tarquinius Superbus

The Republic

509 Consulate established; Quaestorship instituted
498 Dictatorship introduced
494 Plebeian Tribunate created; Plebeian Aedileship created
444 Consular Tribunate organized
435 Censorship instituted
366 Praetorship established; Curule Aedileship created
362 Military Tribunate elected
326 Proconsulate introduced
311 Naval Duumvirate elected
217 Dictatorship of Fabius Maximus
133 Tribunate of Tiberius Gracchus
123 Tribunate of Gaius Gracchus
82 Dictatorship of Sulla
60 First Triumvirate formed (Caesar, Pompeius, Crassus)
47 Dictatorship of Caesar
43 Second Triumvirate formed (Octavianus, Antonius, Lepidus)

The Empire

27 Augustus (or Octavian)
CE
14 Tiberius
37 Caligula
41 Claudius
54 Nero
68 Galba
69 Otho; Vitellius; Vespasian, established Flavian Dynasty
79 Titus
81 Domitian, end of Flavian Dynasty

96 Nerva
98 Trajan
117 Hadrian
138 Antoninus Pius
161 Marcus Aurelius and Lucius Verus
169 Marcus Aurelius (alone)
177 Marcus Aurelius and Commodus
180 Commodus
193 Pertinax
193 Didius Julianus
193 Septimius Severus, founded Severan Dynasty
211 Caracalla and Geta
212 Caracalla (alone)
217 Macrinus
218 Elagabalus (or Heliogabalus)
222 Alexander Severus, end of dynasty
235 Maximinus (the Thracian)
238 Gordian I and Gordian II
238 Pupienus and Balbinus
238 Gordian III
244 Philip (the Arabian)
249 Decius
251 Gallus and Volusianus
253 Aemilian
253 Valerian and Gallienus
258 Gallienus (alone)
268 Claudius II (or Claudius Gothicus)
270 Quintillus
270 Aurelian
275 Tacitus
276 Florian
276 Probus
282 Carus
283 Carinus and Numerian
284 Diocletian
286 Diocletian and Maximian
305 Galerius and Constantius I
306 Galerius, Maximinus (or Maximinus Daia), Severus
307 Galerius, Maximinus (Daia), Constantine I, Licinius, Maxentius
311 Maximinus (Daia), Constantine I, Licinius, Maxentius

314 Constantine I, Licinius
324 Constantine I (the Great), first Christian emperor
337 Constantine II, Constans I, Constantius II
340 Constantius II and Constans I
353 Constantius II (alone)
361 Julian (the Apostate)
363 Jovian

West (Rome) and East (Constantinople)

364 Valentinian I (West), Valens (East)
367 Valentinian I with Gratian (W), Valens (E)
375 Gratian with Valentinian II (W), Valens (E)
379 Gratian with Valentinian II (W), Theodosius I (E)
383 Magnus Maximus and Valentinian II (W), Theodosius I (E)
388 Valentinian II (W), Theodosius I (E)
392 Eugenius (W), Theodosius I (E)
394 Theodosius I (the Great)
395 Honorius (W), Arcadius (E)
408 Honorius (W), Theodosius II (E)
423 Valentinian III (W), Theodosius II (E)
450 Valentinian III (W), Marcian (E)
455 Petronius Maximus (W), Marcian (E)
455 Avitus (W), Marcian (E)
457 Majorian (W), Leo I (E)
461 Libius Severus (W), Leo I (E)
467 Anthemius (W), Leo I (E)
472 Olybrius (W), Leo I (E)
473 Glycerius (W), Leo I (E)
474 Julius Nepos (W), Leo II (E)
475 Romulus Augustulus (W), Zeno (E)
476 End of Empire in W when Romulus Augustulus deposed by Germanic chief Odoacer, who was later murdered by King Theodoric of Ostrogoths, 493

Rulers of England and Great Britain

Reign began	Name	Age at death[1]
	England: Saxons and Danes	
829	Egbert, king of Wessex, won allegiance of all English	NA
839	Ethelwulf, son of Egbert, king of Wessex, Sussex, Kent, Essex.	NA
858	Ethelbald, eldest son of Ethelwulf, displaced father in Wessex.	NA
860	Ethelbert, 2nd son of Ethelwulf, united Kent and Wessex.	NA
866	Ethelred I, 3rd son of Ethelwulf, king of Wessex, fought Danes	NA
871	Alfred (the Great), 4th son of Ethelwulf, defeated Danes, fortified London	52
899	Edward (the Elder), son of Alfred, united English, claimed Scotland	55
924	Athelstan (the Glorious), eldest son of Edward, king of Mercia, Wessex	45
940	Edmund, 3rd son of Edward, king of Wessex, Mercia.	25
946	Edred, 4th son of Edward	32
955	Edwy (the Fair), eldest son of Edmund, king of Wessex.	18
959	Edgar (the Peaceful), 2nd son of Edmund, ruled all English.	32
975	Edward (the Martyr), eldest son of Edgar, murdered by stepmother.	17
978; 1014[2]	Ethelred II (the Unready), 2nd son of Edgar, married Emma of Normandy.	48
1016	Edmund II (Ironside), son of Ethelred II, king of London.	27
1016	Canute (the Dane), son of Sweyn, who conquered English territory; gave Wessex to Edmund II; married Emma, Ethelred II's widow.	40
1035	Harold I (Harefoot), illegitimate son of Canute	NA
1040	Hardecanute, son of Canute by Emma, also king of Denmark	24
1042	Edward (the Confessor), son of Ethelred II, canonized 1161	62
1066	Harold II, Edward's brother-in-law, last Saxon king.	44
	England: House of Normandy	
1066	William I (the Conqueror), son of Duke Robert I of Normandy, defeated Harold II at Hastings	60
1087	William II (Rufus), 3rd son of William I, killed by arrow while hunting in possible assassination	43
1100	Henry I (Beauclerc), youngest son of William I	67
	England: House of Blois	
1135	Stephen, son of Adela, daughter of William I, and Count of Blois.	50
	England: House of Plantagenet	
1154	Henry II, son of Geoffrey Plantagenet (Angevin) by Matilda, daughter of Henry I. . .	56
1189	Richard I (Coeur de Lion), son of Henry II, crusader.	42
1199	John (Lackland), son of Henry II, approved Magna Carta, 1215.	50
1216	Henry III, son of John, acceded at 9, under regency until 1227	65
1272	Edward I (Longshanks), son of Henry III	68
1307	Edward II, son of Edward I, deposed by Parliament	43
1327	Edward III (of Windsor), son of Edward II	65
1377	Richard II, grandson of Edward III, deposed.	33
	England: House of Lancaster	
1399	Henry IV (of Bolingbroke), son of John of Gaunt, duke of Lancaster, son of Edward III . .	47
1413	Henry V, son of Henry IV, victor over French at Agincourt	34
1422; 1470	Henry VI, son of Henry V, overthrown by Edward IV in 1461 but was returned to throne in 1470. Deposed, died in Tower of London, 1471	49
	England: House of York	
1461; 1471	Edward IV, great-great-grandson of Edward III, son of duke of York. Acclaimed king by Parliament, 1461. Driven into exile in 1470 but regained throne, 1471	40
1483	Edward V, son of Edward IV, murdered in Tower of London	13
1483	Richard III, brother of Edward IV, fell in battle at Bosworth Field against Henry Tudor	32
	England: House of Tudor	
1485	Henry VII, son of Edmund Tudor, earl of Richmond, whose father had married Henry V's widow. Descended from Edward III through mother, Margaret Beaufort, via John of Gaunt. Married Elizabeth of York, eldest daughter of Edward IV, to unite Lancaster and York.	53
1509	Henry VIII, 2nd son of Henry VII, by Elizabeth	56
1547	Edward VI, son of Henry VIII, by Jane Seymour, his 3rd queen. Ruled under regents, was forced to name Lady Jane Grey his successor. Council of State proclaimed her queen, July 10, 1553. Mary Tudor won Council, was proclaimed queen, July 19. Mary had Jane beheaded for treason, 1554.	16
1553	Mary I, daughter of Henry VIII, by his 1st wife, Catherine of Aragon.	43
1558	Elizabeth I, daughter of Henry VIII, by his 2nd wife, Anne Boleyn.	69
	Great Britain: House of Stuart	
1603	James I (James VI of Scotland), son of Mary, Queen of Scots. First to call self king of Great Britain; this became official with Act of Union, 1707.	59
1625	Charles I, only surviving son of James I.	48
	Great Britain: Commonwealth	
1649	Declared upon execution of Charles I	
	Great Britain: Protectorate	
1653	Oliver Cromwell, served on Council of State, executive body of Commonwealth, following overthrow of monarchy. Named Lord Protector upon creation of Protectorate by 1653 Instrument of Government	59
1658	Richard Cromwell, 3rd son of Oliver Cromwell. Resigned as Lord Protector amid civil war, 1659.	86
	Great Britain: House of Stuart (restored)	
1660	Charles II, eldest son of Charles I, Restoration put him back on throne, died without issue	55
1685	James II, 2nd son of Charles I, deposed 1688	68
1689	William III, son of William, Prince of Orange, by Mary, daughter of Charles I. Offered joint rule of throne with wife by Parliament	51
1689	Mary II, eldest daughter of James II and wife of William III, died 1694	33
1702	Anne, 2nd daughter of James II, sister-in-law of William III, assumed throne on William's death . . .	49
	Great Britain: House of Hanover	
1714	George I, son of Elector of Hanover by Sophia, granddaughter of James I	67
1727	George II, only son of George I, married Caroline of Brandenburg.	77
1760	George III, grandson of George II, married Charlotte of Mecklenburg	81
1820	George IV, eldest son of George III, prince regent from Feb. 1811	67
1830	William IV, 3rd son of George III, married Adelaide of Saxe-Meiningen	71
1837	Victoria, daughter of Edward, 4th son of George III; married Prince Albert of Saxe-Coburg and Gotha, 1840 . . .	81
	Great Britain: House of Saxe-Coburg and Gotha	
1901	Edward VII, eldest son of Victoria, married Alexandra, Princess of Denmark.	68

Reign began	Great Britain: House of Windsor[3]	Age at death[1]
1910	George V, 2nd son of Edward VII, married Princess Mary of Teck	70
1936	Edward VIII, eldest son of George V, acceded Jan. 20, abdicated Dec. 11.	77
1936	George VI, 2nd son of George V, married Lady Elizabeth Bowes-Lyon	56
1952	Elizabeth II, elder daughter of George VI, acceded Feb. 6	

NA = Age/birth date not certain. (1) Except where noted, year of death is year of accession of succeeding ruler. (2) King Sweyn I of Denmark invaded England in 1013 and declared himself king. Ethelred II reclaimed the throne upon Sweyn's death in 1014. (3) Name adopted by proclamation of George V, July 17, 1917.

Rulers of Scotland

Reign began	Name	Reign began	Name
846	Kenneth I, first Scot to rule both Scots and Picts	1306	Robert I (the Bruce), victor at Bannockburn, 1314. Treaty with England and secured throne, 1328
1005	Malcolm II, son of Kenneth II		
1034	Duncan I, grandson, first general ruler	1329	David II, only surviving son
1040	Macbeth, seized kingdom, slain by Malcolm Canmore	1371	Robert II (the Steward), son of Robert I's daughter Marjorie and Walter, steward of Scotland. First of Stewart line
1057	Malcolm III (Canmore), eldest son of Duncan I	1390	Robert III, son
1093	Donald III (the Fair), younger brother	1406	James I, son, assassinated
1094	Duncan II, eldest son of Malcolm III by first wife	1437	James II, son
1095	Donald III (restored)	1460	James III, eldest son, possibly assassinated
1097	Edgar, 4th son of Malcolm III and Queen Margaret	1488	James IV, eldest son
1107	Alexander I, brother	1513	James V, eldest son, died at Battle of Flodden
1124	David I, brother	1542	Mary (Queen of Scots), daughter, became queen before she was 1 week old. Married Francis II (d. 1560), son of King Henry II of France, 1558. Married her cousin, Henry Stewart, Lord Darnley (d. 1567), 1565. Married James Hepburn, Earl of Bothwell, 1567. Imprisoned by Elizabeth I, 1568; beheaded, 1587
1153	Malcolm IV (the Maiden), grandson		
1165	William (the Lion), brother		
1214	Alexander II, son		
1249	Alexander III, son		
1286	Margaret (Maid of Norway), granddaughter; died 1290 at age 8. (Interregnum, 1290-92)	1567	James VI, son of Mary and Lord Darnley, became James I, king of England, on Elizabeth's death, 1603. (Legislative union of Scotland and England as United Kingdom of Great Britain not official until Act of Union, 1707)
1292	John Balliol, proclaimed king of Scotland by Edward I of England. (Interregnum, 1296-1306[1])		

Note: Not all rulers before 1005 are shown. (1) Edward I decreed annexation of Scotland to England, 1296, after defeating Balliol in battle. William Wallace led resistance, 1297-1305.

Prime Ministers of Great Britain

Cl. = Coalition; C = Conservative; La. = Labour; Li. = Liberal; P = Peelite; T = Tory; W = Whig

Entered office	Name	Entered office	Name	Entered office	Name
1721	Sir Robert Walpole (W)[1]	1830	Earl Grey (W)	1915	Herbert H. Asquith (Cl.)
1742	Earl of Wilmington (W)	1834	Viscount Melbourne (W)	1916	David Lloyd George (Cl.)
1743	Henry Pelham (W)	1834	Sir Robert Peel (C)	1922	Andrew Bonar Law (C)
1754	Duke of Newcastle (W)	1835	Viscount Melbourne (W)	1923	Stanley Baldwin (C)
1756	Duke of Devonshire (W)	1841	Sir Robert Peel (C)	1924	James Ramsay MacDonald (La.)
1757	Duke of Newcastle (W)	1846	Lord (later Earl) John Russell (W)	1924	Stanley Baldwin (C)
1762	Earl of Bute (T)	1852	Earl of Derby (C)	1929	James Ramsay MacDonald (La.)
1763	George Grenville (W)	1852	Earl of Aberdeen (P)	1931	James Ramsay MacDonald (Cl.)
1765	Marquess of Rockingham (W)	1855	Viscount Palmerston (Li.)	1935	Stanley Baldwin (Cl.)
1766	William Pitt the Elder (Earl of Chatham) (W)	1858	Earl of Derby (C)	1937	Neville Chamberlain (Cl.)
		1859	Viscount Palmerston (Li.)	1940	Winston Churchill (Cl.)
1768	Duke of Grafton (W)	1865	Earl Russell (Li.)	1945	Winston Churchill (C)
1770	Frederick North (Lord North) (T)	1866	Earl of Derby (C)	1945	Clement Attlee (La.)
1782	Marquess of Rockingham (W)	1868	Benjamin Disraeli (C)	1951	Sir Winston Churchill (C)
1782	Earl of Shelburne (W)	1868	William E. Gladstone (Li.)	1955	Sir Anthony Eden (C)
1783	Duke of Portland (T)	1874	Benjamin Disraeli (C)	1957	Harold Macmillan (C)
1783	William Pitt the Younger (T)	1880	William E. Gladstone (Li.)	1963	Sir Alec Douglas-Home (C)
1801	Henry Addington (T)	1885	Marquess of Salisbury (C)	1964	Harold Wilson (La.)
1804	William Pitt the Younger (T)	1886	William E. Gladstone (Li.)	1970	Edward Heath (C)
1806	William Wyndham Grenville, Baron Grenville (W)	1886	Marquess of Salisbury (C)	1974	Harold Wilson (La.)
		1892	William E. Gladstone (Li.)	1976	James Callaghan (La.)
1807	Duke of Portland (T)	1894	Earl of Rosebery (Li.)	1979	Margaret Thatcher (C)
1809	Spencer Perceval (T)	1895	Marquess of Salisbury (C)	1990	John Major (C)
1812	Earl of Liverpool (T)	1902	Arthur J. Balfour (C)	1997	Tony Blair (La.)
1827	George Canning (T)	1905	Sir Henry Campbell-Bannerman (Li.)	2007	Gordon Brown (La.)
1827	Viscount Goderich (T)			2010	David Cameron (Cl.)
1828	Duke of Wellington (T)	1908	Herbert H. Asquith (Li.)		

Note: The Conservative Party was formed in 1834, an outgrowth of the Tory party. (1) Walpole is commonly regarded as the first prime minister of Britain, though the title was not commonly used then and did not become official until 1905.

Prime Ministers of Canada

C = Conservative; Li. = Liberal; PC = Progressive Conservative; U = Unionist

Entered office	Name (party)	Entered office	Name (party)	Entered office	Name (party)
1867	Sir John A. Macdonald (C)	1920	Arthur Meighen (U)	1968	Pierre Elliott Trudeau (Li.)
1873	Alexander Mackenzie (Li.)	1921	W. L. Mackenzie King (Li.)	1979	Joe Clark (PC)
1878	Sir John A. Macdonald (C)	1926[3]	Arthur Meighen (C)	1980	Pierre Elliott Trudeau (Li.)
1891	Sir John J. C. Abbott (C)	1926	W. L. Mackenzie King (Li.)	1984[3]	John Napier Turner (Li.)
1892	Sir John S. D. Thompson (C)	1930	Richard Bedford Bennett (C)	1984	Brian Mulroney (PC)
1894	Sir Mackenzie Bowell (C)	1935	W. L. Mackenzie King (Li.)	1993[4]	Kim Campbell (PC)
1896[1]	Sir Charles Tupper (C)	1948	Louis St. Laurent (Li.)	1993	Jean Chrétien (Li.)
1896	Sir Wilfrid Laurier (Li.)	1957	John G. Diefenbaker (PC)	2003	Paul Martin (Li.)
1911	Sir Robert Laird Borden (C/U)[2]	1963	Lester Bowles Pearson (Li.)	2006	Stephen Harper (C)

(1) May-July. (2) Conservative 1911-17, Unionist 1917-20. (3) June-Sept. (4) June-Oct.

Rulers of France

Caesar to Charlemagne

Julius Caesar subdued the Gauls, native tribes of Gaul (France), 58 to 51 BCE. The Romans ruled 500 years. The Franks, a Teutonic tribe, reached the Somme from the east c. 250 CE. By the 5th cent., the Merovingian Franks ousted the Romans. In 451, with the help of Visigoths, Burgundians, and others, they defeated Attila and the Huns at Châlons-sur-Marne.

Childeric I became leader of the Merovingians, 458. His son Clovis I, crowned 481, founded the dynasty. After defeating the Alemanni (Germans), 496, he was baptized a Christian and made Paris his capital. His line ruled until Childeric III was deposed, 751.

The West Merovingians were called Neustrians, the eastern Austrasians. Pepin of Herstal (687-714), major domus (head of the palace) of Austrasia, took over Neustria as dux (leader) of the Franks. Pepin's son, Charles, called Martel (the Hammer), defeated the Saracens at Tours-Poitiers, 732; was succeeded by his son, Pepin the Short, 741, who deposed Childeric III and ruled as king until 768.

His son, Charlemagne, or Charles the Great (742-814), became king of the Franks, 768, with his brother Carloman (751-71). Charlemagne ruled France, Germany, parts of Italy, Spain, and Austria, and enforced Christianity. Crowned Emperor of the Romans by Pope Leo III in Rome, Dec. 25, 800. Succeeded by son, Louis I (the Pious), 814. At death, 840, Louis left empire to sons Lothair (Roman emperor), Pepin I (king of Aquitaine), Louis II (the German), and Charles II (the Bald, of France). They quarreled and, by the Treaty of Verdun, 843, divided the empire.

The date preceding each entry is year of accession.

Carolingian Dynasty

843 Charles I (the Bald), Roman emperor, 875
877 Louis II (the Stammerer), son
879 Louis III (d. 882) and brother Carloman
885 Charles II (the Fat), Roman emperor, 881
888 Eudes (Odo), elected by nobles
898 Charles III (the Simple), son of Louis II, defeated by Robert
922 Robert, brother of Eudes, killed in war
923 Rudolph (Raoul), duke of Burgundy
936 Louis IV, son of Charles III
954 Lothair, son, aged 13, defeated by Capet
986 Louis V (the Sluggard), left no heirs

House of Capet

987 Hugh Capet, son of Hugh the Great
996 Robert II (the Pious), son
1031 Henry I, son
1060 Philip I (the Fair), son
1108 Louis VI (the Fat), son
1137 Louis VII (the Younger), son
1180 Philip II (Augustus), son, crowned at Reims
1223 Louis VIII (the Lion), son
1226 Louis IX, son, arbitrated disputes with English King Henry III; led crusades, 1248 (captured in Egypt, 1250) and 1270, when he died of plague in Tunis. Canonized as St. Louis, 1297
1270 Philip III (the Hardy), son
1285 Philip IV (the Fair), son, king at 17
1314 Louis X (the Headstrong), son. His posthumous son, John I, lived and reigned only five days.
1316 Philip V (the Tall), brother of Louis X
1322 Charles IV (the Fair), brother of Louis X

House of Valois

1328 Philip VI (of Valois), grandson of Philip III
1350 John II (the Good), son, retired to England
1364 Charles V (the Wise), son
1380 Charles VI (the Beloved), son
1422 Charles VII (the Victorious), son. In 1429, Joan of Arc (Jeanne d'Arc) defeated English at Orleans and Patay and had Charles crowned at Reims, July 17. Joan was captured May 24, 1430, and executed May 30, 1431, at Rouen for heresy. Charles ordered her rehabilitation, effected 1455.
1461 Louis XI (the Cruel), son, civil reformer
1483 Charles VIII (the Affable), son
1498 Louis XII, great-grandson of Charles V
1515 Francis I, of Angouleme, nephew, son-in-law. Fought four major wars, was patron of the arts
1547 Henry II, son, killed at joust. Husband of Catherine de Médicis and lover of Diane de Poitiers. Catherine was daughter of Lorenzo de Medici. By marriage to Henry II, she became the mother of Francis II, Charles IX, Henry III, and Queen Margaret (Reine Margot), wife of Henry IV (of Navarre).

1559 Francis II, son. Betrothed in 1548 at age 4 to Mary, Queen of Scots, aged 6; they were married 1558. Francis died 1560, aged 16. Mary returned to rule Scotland, 1561.
1560 Charles IX, brother
1574 Henry III, brother, assassinated

House of Bourbon

1589 Henry IV (of Navarre), grandson of Queen Margaret of Navarre. Made enemies when he gave tolerance to Protestants by Edict of Nantes, 1598. Married Margaret of Valois, daughter of Henry II and Catherine de Médicis; was divorced. Married Marie de Médicis, 1600. She became regent upon Henry's assassination, 1610-17, for her son, Louis XIII; she was exiled by Richelieu, 1631.
1610 Louis XIII (the Just), son, married Anne of Austria. His chief minister (1622-42), Cardinal Richelieu, determined his policies.
1643 Louis XIV (the Sun King), son; was king 72 years. Until 1661, Anne of Austria was regent with Cardinal Mazarin as chief minister; Louis then ruled absolutely. Known for his lavish court and arts patronage, he exhausted a prosperous country in wars for thrones and territory.
1715 Louis XV (the Beloved), great-grandson. His favorite mistresses, Mme. de Pompadour and Mme. Du Barry, influenced policies. Mme. Pompadour's saying "Après moi, le déluge" (After me, the deluge) often incorrectly attributed to Louis XV
1774 Louis XVI, grandson, married Marie Antoinette, daughter of Empress Maria Therese of Austria. King and queen beheaded by Revolution, 1793. Their son, called Louis XVII, died in prison, never ruled

First Republic

1792 National Convention of the French Revolution
1795 Directory, under Barras and others
1799 Consulate, Napoleon Bonaparte, first consul. Elected consul for life, 1802

First Empire

1804 Napoleon I (Napoleon Bonaparte), emperor. Josephine (de Beauharnais), empress, 1804-09; Marie Louise, empress, 1810-14. Son, Napoleon II (1811-32), titular king of Rome, later duke of Reichstadt, never ruled. Napoleon I abdicated 1814; died in exile, 1821.

House of Bourbon (restored)

1814 Louis XVIII, brother of Louis XVI, king
1824 Charles X, brother, reactionary, deposed by the July Revolution, 1830

House of Orleans

1830 Louis-Philippe (the Citizen King)

Second Republic

1848 Louis Napoleon Bonaparte, nephew of Napoleon I, president

Second Empire

1852 Napoleon III (Louis Napoleon Bonaparte), emperor; Eugenie (de Montijo), empress. Lost Franco-Prussian war, deposed 1870. Son, Prince Imperial (1856-79), died in Zulu War. Eugenie died 1920.

Third Republic

1871 Louis Adolphe Thiers (1797-1877), president
1873 Marshal Patrice M. de MacMahon (1808-93)
1879 Paul J. Grevy (1807-91)
1887 M. Sadi-Carnot (1837-94), assassinated
1894 Jean P. P. Casimir-Perier (1847-1907)
1895 François Felix Faure (1841-99)
1899 Emile Loubet (1838-1929)
1906 C. Armand Fallieres (1841-1931)
1913 Raymond Poincaré (1860-1934)
1920 Paul Deschanel (1856-1922)
1920 Alexandre Millerand (1859-1943)
1924 Gaston Doumergue (1863-1937)
1931 Paul Doumer (1857-1932), assassinated
1932 Albert Lebrun (1871-1950), resigned 1940

Vichy Regime

1940 Henri Philippe Petain (1856-1951), chief of state, 1940-44, under German armistice

Provisional Government

1944 Charles Andre J. M. de Gaulle (1890-1970)
1946 Felix Gouin (1884-1977)
1946 Georges Bidault (1899-1983)

Fourth Republic

1947 Vincent Auriol (1884-1966), president
1954 Rene Coty (1882-1962)

Fifth Republic

1959 Charles Andre J. M. De Gaulle (1890-1970), president
1969 Georges Pompidou (1911-74)
1974 Valéry Giscard d'Estaing (1926-)
1981 François Mitterrand (1916-96)
1995 Jacques Chirac (1932-)
2007 Nicolas Sarkozy (1955-)
2012 François Hollande (1954-)

Rulers of Middle Europe and Germany

Carolingian Dynasty

Charles I (the Great), or Charlemagne, made Roman emperor by pope in Rome, 800. Ruled France, Italy, and Middle Europe; established Ostmark (later Austria). Died 814.

Louis I (Ludwig) (the Pious), son, crowned co-emperor by Charlemagne, 813. Divided empire among sons. Died 840; sons fought for control.

Louis II (the German), son, succeeded to East Francia (Germany), 843-76, with Treaty of Verdun.

Charles III (the Fat), son, inherited Swabia, 876. With brothers' deaths, acquired East Francia and West Francia (France), reuniting empire. Crowned emperor by pope, 881; deposed 887.

Arnulf, nephew, 887-99, took over East Francia; partition of empire.

Louis IV (the Child), son, 900-11, last direct descendant of Charlemagne.

Conrad I, duke of Franconia, first elected German king, 911-18.

Saxon Dynasty; First Reich

Henry I (the Fowler), duke of Saxony, elected king 919-36.

Otto I (the Great), son, 936-73, crowned Holy Roman Emperor by pope, 962.

Otto II, son, 961-83, ruled with Otto I as king, then emperor, 967.

Otto III, son, 983-1002, crowned Holy Roman Emperor, 996.

Henry II (the Saint), great-grandson of Otto the Great, duke of Bavaria, 1002-24. Crowned emperor, 1014.

Salian Dynasty

Conrad II, 1024-39, elected king of Germany.

Henry III (the Black), son, 1039-56, deposed three popes; annexed Burgundy.

Henry IV, son, 1056-1106, with mother, Agnes of Poitou, as regent in early years. He and Pope Gregory VII tried to depose each other. Civil war lasted about 20 years.

Henry V, son, 1106-25, last of Salian Dynasty.

Lothair, duke of Saxony, elected king 1125-37. Crowned emperor in Rome, 1133.

Hohenstaufen Dynasty

Conrad III, duke of Franconia, 1138-52, in Second Crusade.

Frederick I (Barbarossa, Italian for "Redbeard"), nephew, 1152-90.

Henry VI, son, 1190-97, gained kingdom of Sicily through marriage.

Philip of Swabia, brother, 1197-1208. Otto IV, nephew of King Richard I of England, 1198-1215, was elected rival king. Philip's murder, in 1208, led to Otto's win in new election same year. Civil war followed before Otto was deposed, 1215.

Frederick II, son of Henry VI, elected 1212-50. Had earlier succeeded father as king of Sicily; crowned himself king of Jerusalem, 1229, in Sixth Crusade.

Conrad IV, son, 1250-54. Conquered Naples.

(Interregnum, 1254-73. Conradin, son of Conrad IV and last legitimate Hohenstaufen, defeated by Charles of Anjou—brother of King Louis IX of France—and executed, 1268. Rise of electors of German monarch.)

Transition

Rudolf I, of Hapsburg, 1273-91, defeated King Ottocar II of Bohemia, 1278. Bequeathed duchies of Austria and Styria to sons.

Adolf of Nassau, 1292-98, killed in war with Albert I.

Albert I, elder son of Rudolf I, 1298-1308, assassinated.

Henry VII, of Luxembourg, 1308-13. Gained Bohemia, 1310; crowned Holy Roman Emperor, 1312.

Louis IV, of Wittelsbach, 1314-46. Also elected was a son of Albert I, Frederick of Austria, whom Louis defeated in 1322. Rejected need for papal confirmation of elected German king.

Charles IV, of Luxembourg, grandson of Henry VII, 1346-78. Took Brandenburg.

Wenceslaus, son, 1378-1400; deposed.

Rupert, of Wittelsbach, elector palatine, 1400-10.

Sigismund, brother of Wenceslaus, 1410-37.

Hapsburg Dynasty

Albert II, duke of Austria, son-in-law of Sigismund, elected German king, 1438-39; king of Hungary and Holy Roman Emperor.

Frederick III, cousin, 1440-93, fought Turks.

Maximilian I, son, 1493-1519, archduke of Austria.

Charles V, grandson, 1519-58. King of Spain; assumed title of Holy Roman Emperor. Martin Luther, who had been excommunicated by pope, appeared at Diet of Worms, 1521. Charles attempted church reform and conciliation between Catholicism and Protestantism; abdicated.

Ferdinand I, brother, 1558-64; king of Hungary and Bohemia, 1526 (successive leaders through Maria Theresa will rule these lands as well).

Maximilian II, son, 1564-76.

Rudolf II, son, 1576-1612.

Matthias, brother, 1612-19.

Ferdinand II, grandson of Ferdinand I, 1619-37. Bohemian Protestants, unhappy with Ferdinand's support of Catholic Counter-Reformation, crowned Frederick V, elector palatine. Frederick became known as "Winter King" with defeat in battle, 1620; start of Thirty Years' War.

Ferdinand III, son, 1637-57. Treaties signed, 1648, in Peace of Westphalia ended war.

Leopold I, son, 1658-1705.

Joseph I, son, 1705-11.

Charles VI, brother, 1711-40; died without male heir.

Maria Theresa, daughter, 1740-80. Appointed husband, Francis Stephen of Lorraine, co-regent. Dispute over her inheritance led to War of the Austrian Succession. Charles VII, also known as Charles Albert, elected in opposition to Francis, 1742-45. After Charles's death, she obtained election of her husband as Holy Roman Emperor Francis I, 1745-65. Fought Seven Years' War with Frederick II of Prussia.

Hapsburg-Lorraine Dynasty

Joseph II, son, 1765-90, reformer. Ruled jointly with Maria Theresa until her death. Participated in first partition of Poland, with Prussia and Russia.

Leopold II, brother, 1790-92; king of Hungary and Bohemia.

Francis II, son, 1792-1806; king of Hungary and Bohemia. Proclaimed first emperor of Austria, 1804-35. Unsuccessfully fought against Napoleon; forced to abdicate, 1806, as Holy Roman Emperor, last use of title.

Ferdinand, son, 1835-48, emperor of Austria; king of Hungary and Bohemia. Abdicated in favor of nephew after revolution broke out in Vienna.

Austro-Hungarian Monarchy

Francis Joseph I, nephew, 1848-1916, emperor of Austria and king of Hungary. Defeated in Austro-Prussian War, 1866. Formed dual monarchy of Austria-Hungary, 1867. After Serbian nationalist assassinated Francis Joseph's nephew and heir, Archduke Francis Ferdinand, June 28, 1914, Austrian diplomacy precipitated World War I.

Charles I, grandnephew, 1916-18, last emperor of Austria and king of Hungary. Abdicated Nov. 1918; died in exile, 1922.

Second and Third Reichs

William I, brother of Frederick William IV, 1861-88, king of Prussia. Appointed Otto von Bismarck chancellor, 1862. Franco-Prussian War, also known as Franco-German War, 1870-71, unified German states. William proclaimed German emperor, 1871; beginning of Second Reich.

Frederick III, son, 1888.

William II, son, 1888-1918, led Germany into World War I. Abdicated Nov. 1918; died in exile in the Netherlands, 1941.

Germany adopted constitution at Weimar, July 1, 1919, setting up Weimar Republic. Presidents included Friedrich Ebert, 1919-25, and Paul von Hindenburg, 1925-34, field marshal in World War I. Hindenburg appointed Adolf Hitler chancellor, 1933, at beginning of Third Reich. Following Hindenburg's death, Hitler succeeded as Führer and chancellor, 1934-45, with dictatorial powers. Annexed Austria, 1938. Precipitated World War II, 1939-45. Hitler committed suicide, 1945.

Germany After 1945

After World War II, Germany was split between democratic West and Soviet-dominated East. West German chancellors: Konrad Adenauer, 1949-63; Ludwig Erhard, 1963-66; Kurt Georg Kiesinger, 1966-69; Willy Brandt, 1969-74; Helmut Schmidt, 1974-82; Helmut Kohl, 1982-90. East German Communist party leaders: Walter Ulbricht, 1950-71; Erich Honecker, 1971-89; Egon Krenz, 1989.

Germany reunited Oct. 3, 1990. Post-reunification chancellors: Helmut Kohl, 1990-98; Gerhard Schröder, 1998-2005; Angela Merkel, 2005- .

Rulers of Hungary

The first king of Hungary was Stephen I, of the Arpad Dynasty, 1000-38. Feuds followed his death.

Charles I, also known as Charles Robert, became king, 1308-42.

Louis I (the Great), son, 1342-82. Succeeded uncle Casimir III as ruler of Poland, 1370.

Mary, elder daughter, 1382-95, ruled with husband, Sigismund of Luxemburg, 1387-1437, who also became king of Bohemia, Germany and Holy Roman Emperor. Hedwig (Jadwiga), younger daughter of Louis I, became queen of Poland. (See **Rulers of Poland**.)

Albert II, duke of Austria, son-in-law of Sigismund, 1438-39. Also king of Germany and Holy Roman Emperor.

Vladislaus I, 1440-44, king of Poland.

Ladislaus V, posthumous son of Albert II, 1444-57, not crowned until 1453. Janos Hunyadi acted as governor under young king, 1446-52; fought Turks.

Matthias I (Corvinus), son of Janos Hunyadi, 1458-90. Shared title of king of Bohemia. Captured Vienna, 1485; annexed Styria, Carinthia.

Vladislaus II, 1490-1516, king of Bohemia.

Louis II, son, 1516-26. Died in Battle of Mohács against Suleiman (the Magnificent), head of Ottoman Empire.

Ferdinand I, of Austria, brother-in-law, and John I, also known as John Zapolya of Transylvania, elected rival kings. Suleiman claimed part of Hungary for Ottoman Empire. Hungary partitioned. (Refer to **Hapsburg Dynasty** for continuation.)

Rulers of Prussia

Nucleus of Prussia was the margravate of Brandenburg, an electorate of the Holy Roman Empire. Frederick VI, burgrave of Nuremberg, was made elector of Brandenburg, 1415. Rise of Hohenzollern Dynasty in territory that included Brandenburg and duchy of Prussia.

Frederick William (the Great Elector), 1640-88, elector of Brandenburg.

Frederick III, son, 1688-1713, elector of Brandenburg. Crowned Frederick I, king in Prussia, 1701.

Frederick William I, son, 1713-40.

Frederick II (the Great), son, 1740-86; military strategist who expanded Prussia's holdings.

Frederick William II, nephew, 1786-97.

Frederick William III, son, 1797-1840; Napoleonic Wars.

Frederick William IV, son, 1840-61. Revolution of 1848; constitution adopted, 1850. (Refer to **Second and Third Reichs** for continuation.)

Rulers of Poland

House of Piast

Mieszko I, c. 963-92, duke of Poland; Poland Christianized, 966. Expansion under three with name Boleslaus (reigns not consecutive): Boleslaus I (the Brave), son, 992-1025, crowned first king of Poland, 1025; Boleslaus II (the Bold), great-grandson, 1058-79, exiled after killing bishop of Krakow, Stanislaus (who became a patron saint of Poland); Boleslaus III (the Wry-Mouthed), nephew, 1102-38, divided Poland among four sons with oldest also in control of crown. Period of feudal division followed.

A Polish duke, Conrad of Masovia, asked the Teutonic Knights—a German military religious order—to crusade against Prussia, 1226. Teutonic Knights conquered lands; thereafter warred with Poland. Mongols/Tatars invaded Poland, 1241.

Vladislaus I, 1306-33, reunited most Polish territories; crowned king, 1320. Casimir III (the Great), son, 1333-70, developed economy, cultural life, foreign policy. No male heir. Succeeded by Louis I, nephew, 1370-82, who was also Louis I (the Great) of Hungary.

Jadwiga, daughter, 1384-99.

House of Jagiello

Vladislaus Jagiello, grand duke of Lithuania, married Jadwiga, 1386, and ruled jointly as Vladislaus II, 1386-1434. Poland and Lithuania united; Lithuania converted to Christianity. Defeated Teutonic Knights at Grunwald (Tannenberg), 1410.

Vladislaus III, son, 1434-44, also king of Hungary. Fought Turks; killed in Battle of Varna, 1444.

Casimir IV, brother, 1447-92, put son Vladislaus on throne of Bohemia and Hungary. Victorious over Teutonic Knights; signed treaty, 1466, after 13-year war.

John I, son, 1492-1501.

Alexander I, brother, 1501-05.

Sigismund I, brother, 1506-48, patronized sciences and arts; his and son's reign were golden age. Grand Master of Teutonic Order, Albert Hohenzollern, converted to Protestantism; secularized his state and made first duke of Prussia by Sigismund, 1525.

Sigismund II, son, 1548-72; Union of Lublin, 1569, established dual state of Poland and Lithuania. No male heir.

Elective Kings

Henry of Valois, 1573-74, first king elected by nobility. Left Poland to assume crown of France after brother's death. Interregnum.

Stephen Bathory, 1576-86, prince of Transylvania, married Anna, sister of Sigismund II. Fought Russians.

Sigismund III Vasa, nephew of Sigismund II and son of king of Sweden, 1587-1632. Fought to reclaim Swedish crown, which he'd lost because of his Catholicism; battled Russians and Turks.

Vladislaus IV Vasa, son, 1632-48.

John II Casimir Vasa, brother, 1648-68. Fought Cossacks, Swedish, Russians, Turks, Tatars; period of invasions known as "the Deluge."

Michael Korybut Wisniowiecki, 1669-73.

John III Sobieski, 1674-96, freed Vienna from besieging Turks, 1683.

Augustus II (the Strong), 1697-1733, elector of Saxony.

Augustus III, son, 1733-63, elector of Saxony.

Stanislaus II, 1764-95, last king. Encouraged reforms; first modern constitution in Europe, 1791. Poland lost territory to Russia, Austria, and Prussia in three partitions (1772, 1793, 1795). Thaddeus Kosciusko, American-Polish general, attempted unsuccessful insurrection, 1794.

Poland Under Foreign Rule

Grand duchy of Warsaw created by Napoleon I out of Prussian (formerly Polish) territory. Frederick Augustus I, king of Saxony, ruled grand duchy, 1807-15. Defeat of Napoleon led to Congress of Vienna, 1814-15; part of Poland claimed as kingdom by Russia. Polish uprisings against Russia (1830, 1863) repressed. Poland regained independence following World War I.

Second Republic

Jozef Pilsudski, 1918-22, head of state. Presidents: Gabriel Narutowicz, 1922, assassinated by extremist; Stanislaus Wojciechowski, 1922-26, resigned after coup d'état by Pilsudski; Ignacy Moscicki, 1926-39, ruled with Pilsudski (d. 1935) and Pilsudski's military colleagues as virtual dictator during what came to be known as Sanacja (meaning "cleansing" or "healing") regime.

Poland Under Foreign Occupation, Influence

After Hitler and Stalin signed nonaggression pact, Germany invaded Poland Sept. 1, 1939; Russia invaded Sept. 17. Polish government-in-exile was in France, then England. Vladislaus Raczkiewicz, 1939-47, president; Gen. Vladislaus Sikorski, 1939-43, and Stanislaus Mikolajczyk, 1943-44, prime ministers. Polish residents were sent to German concentration camps and Soviet labor camps; about 3 million Jewish Poles were killed in the Holocaust. Thousands of Polish prisoners of war, mostly military officers, massacred in Katyn Forest by Soviet secret police, 1940. Soviet-sponsored Polish Committee of National Liberation took formative role in new government, 1945, renamed Polish People's Republic in 1952. Communist Polish United Workers' Party ruled the country. Brief period of liberalization followed Stalin's death in 1953. Vladislaus Gomulka, 1956-70, and Edward Gierek, 1970-80, led country as first secretary of Polish United Workers' Party.

Election of Cardinal Karol Wojtyla, archbishop of Krakow, as pope (John Paul II) inspired Poles, 1978. Strikes in 1980 prompted creation of Solidarity, an independent trade union headed by Lech Walesa. Solidarity gained control of government in partly free elections, 1985.

Third Republic

Presidents: Lech Walesa, 1990-95; Aleksander Kwasniewski, 1995-2005; Lech Kaczynski, 2005-10, died in plane crash; Bronislaus Komorowski and Grzegorz Schetyna, acting, 2010; Komorowski, 2010- .

Rulers of Denmark, Sweden, Norway

Denmark

Canute (the Great) ruled area that included England, Denmark, and Norway, 1016-35. Valdemar IV Atterdag reunited Denmark, 1361. Margaret I, daughter, married to Haakon VI, king of Norway, 1363. After Valdemar's death, Olaf, Margaret's infant son, made king of Denmark, 1375. He was also crowned king of Norway after death of Haakon, 1380. Following Olaf's death, 1387, Margaret served as regent of Denmark, Norway, and Sweden. She effected the Union of Kalmar of the three kingdoms, 1397. She had her grandnephew, Eric of Pomerania, crowned (she held actual power until her death, 1412).

Succeeding rulers were unable to enforce their claims on Sweden until Christian II, 1512-23, conquered the country, 1520. He was soon deposed; accession of Christian I as king of Sweden, 1523, ended Kalmar Union. Denmark continued to dominate Norway until the Napoleonic Wars when Frederick VI, 1808-39, allied with Napoleon I after Danish fleet was attacked by Britain, 1807. By 1814 treaty, Denmark was forced to cede Norway to Sweden.

Succession: House of Oldenborg (began with Christian I, 1448): Christian VIII, 1839-48; Frederick VII, son, 1848-63. House of Glücksborg: Christian IX, 1863-1906; Frederick VIII, son, 1906-12; Christian X, son, 1912-47; Frederick IX, son, 1947-72; Margrethe II, daughter, 1972- .

Sweden

Under King Magnus Ladulas, hereditary nobility established around 1280. Swedish nobles opposed to Albert of Mecklenburg accepted Margaret I, regent of Denmark, as ruler, 1389. Sweden joined Kalmar Union, 1397. After internal unrest, Sweden was conquered anew by Denmark's Christian II, 1520. Execution of Christian's opponents in "Stockholm Bloodbath" led to uprising under Gustavus Vasa, who was elected Swedish king, 1523-60. Gustavus established an independent kingdom with centralized power, state church, and hereditary throne. Gustavus II

Adolphus, 1611-32, fought Russia, Poland, Germany and was called the Lion of the North; died in battle.

Later rulers: Christina, daughter, 1632-54, abdicated; Charles X Gustavus, cousin, 1654-60; Charles XI, son, 1660-97; Charles XII, son, 1697-1718; Ulrika Eleonora, sister, 1718-20, abdicated; Frederick I, husband, 1720-51; Adolphus Frederick, 1751-71; Gustavus III, son, 1771-92; Gustavus IV Adolphus, son, 1792-1809, deposed; Charles XIII, uncle, 1809-18. Charles XIV John (born Jean Baptiste Bernadotte, a general under Napoleon I), 1818-44, founded House of Bernadotte.

Succession: Oscar I, son, 1844-59; Charles XV, son, 1859-72; Oscar II, brother, 1872-1907; Gustavus V, son, 1907-50; Gustavus VI Adolf, son, 1950-73; Carl XVI Gustavus, grandson, 1973- .

Norway

Harald I (Fairhair) overcame rivals to become first king of Norway, c. 885-c. 933. Olaf II Haraldsson, 1015-28, Christianized country; became patron saint of Norway. Haakon V Magnusson, 1299-1319, died without male heir. His daughter Ingeborg was married to Erik, a son of the Norwegian king; their son Magnus VII Eriksson became ruler of Norway, 1319-55, and Sweden, 1319-63. Haakon VI Magnusson, son, 1355-80, married Margaret of Denmark. Olaf IV, son, became king of Norway, 1380-87, and Denmark, 1375-87, with mother as regent. Margaret took over rule upon his death, 1387. Union of Kalmar, 1397, united Norway, Denmark, and Sweden.

After Napoleonic Wars, Denmark ceded Norway to Sweden, 1814. A strong nationalist movement forced Sweden to recognize Norway as an independent kingdom under the Swedish kings. Norwegian constitution, adopted 1814, allowed for creation of the Storting (Norwegian parliament), which governed country domestically. In 1905, the union was dissolved. Prince Charles of Denmark elected king of Norway as Haakon VII, 1905-57; founded House of Glücksburg. Succession: Olav V, son, 1957-91; Harald V, son, 1991- .

Rulers of the Netherlands and Belgium

The Netherlands

William I, son of Prince William V of Orange, came to power after French rule ended in the Netherlands, 1813; crowned king with approval of Congress of Vienna, 1815. Started House of Orange-Nassau. Northern Netherlands was known as Holland. Belgians, in southern Netherlands, rebelled against the Dutch and seceded, Oct. 4, 1830. Dutch formally recognized Belgian independence, Apr. 19, 1839. William I abdicated, 1840.

Succession: William II, son, 1840-49; William III, son, 1849-90; Wilhelmina, daughter, 1890-1948; Juliana, daughter,

1948-80; Beatrix, daughter, 1980-2013; Willem-Alexander, son, 2013- .

Belgium

A national congress elected Prince Leopold of Saxe-Coburg as king. He took the throne July 21, 1831, as Leopold I.

Succession: Leopold II, son, 1865-1909; Albert I, nephew, 1909-34; Leopold III, son, 1934-51, in exile after Germany invaded Belgium, later abdicated; Prince Charles, brother, acted as regent 1944-50; Baudouin I, son of Leopold III, 1951-93; Albert II, brother, 1993-2013; Philippe, son, 2013- .

Rulers of Modern Italy

After the fall of Napoleon, the Congress of Vienna, 1814-15, restored Italy as a political patchwork, comprising the Kingdom of the Two Sicilies (Naples and Sicily), the Papal States, and smaller units. King Victor Emmanuel I of Savoy ruled Sardinia, Piedmont, and Genoa.

Victor Emmanuel I abdicated 1821. Charles Felix, brother, 1821-31, died without issue. Succeeded by Charles Albert, 1831-49; he abdicated upon defeat by the Austrians. Succeeded by Victor Emmanuel II, son, 1849-61. United Italy emerged under Camillo Benso di Cavour, prime minister of the Kingdom of Sardinia, 1852-61. Giuseppe Mazzini and Giuseppe Garibaldi were also figures in Risorgimento ("resurgence") period before Italy's unification.

In 1859, France forced Austria to cede Lombardy to Sardinia. In 1860, Garibaldi led more than 1,000 volunteers in a campaign against King Francis II of the Two Sicilies, taking Sicily and Naples. The House of Savoy subsequently annexed the Two Sicilies, Tuscany, Parma, Modena, Romagna, the Marches, and Umbria. Victor Emmanuel II assumed leadership of a united Kingdom of Italy, Mar. 17, 1861.

In 1866, Victor Emmanuel II allied with Prussia and, in the Austro-Prussian War and, with Prussia's victory, received

Venetia. On Sept. 20, 1870, Italian troops entered Rome, ending the temporal power of the Roman Catholic Church. (The 1929 Lateran Treaty established papal sovereignty in Vatican City.)

Succession: Umberto I, son, 1878-1900, assassinated; Victor Emmanuel III, son, 1900-46; Umberto II, son, 1946, ruled a month. In 1919, Benito Mussolini helped found the nationalist Fasci di Combattimento ("Fighting Leagues"), or Fascists. After Mussolini organized March on Rome, 1922, Victor Emmanuel III agreed to a coalition government. Mussolini eventually became dictator (Il Duce). He entered World War II as an ally of Hitler, 1940. He was dismissed by the king, 1943; executed, 1945.

At a plebiscite, 1946, voters approved a republic. Prime minister Alcide de Gasperi was chief of state, 1945-53; Enrico de Nicola was provisional president. Successive presidents: Luigi Einaudi, 1948-55; Giovanni Gronchi, 1955-62; Antonio Segni, 1962-64; Giuseppe Saragat, 1964-71; Giovanni Leone, 1971-78; Alessandro Pertini, 1978-85; Francesco Cossiga, 1985-92; Oscar Luigi Scalfaro, 1992-99; Carlo Azeglio Ciampi, 1999-2006; Giorgio Napolitano, 2006- .

Rulers of Spain

From 8th to 11th centuries, Spain was dominated by the Moors (Muslims from North Africa of Arab and Berber origin). A number of small kingdoms—Aragon, Asturias, Castile, Catalonia, Leon, Navarre, and Valencia—undertook a Christian reconquest. In 1474, Isabella became Queen of Castile and Leon. Her husband, Ferdinand V, acceded to the throne of Aragon, 1479. By the Catholic Monarchs' request, Pope Sixtus IV authorized the

Inquisition, 1478. Last Moorish kingdom, Granada, seized 1492. Spain sponsored Christopher Columbus, who opened New World, 1492. Isabella was succeeded by daughter, Joanna (the Mad), but Ferdinand acted as regent until his death, 1516.

Charles I, son of Joanna and grandson of Hapsburg Emperor Maximilian I, became Holy Roman Emperor as Charles V, 1520; abdicated 1556. Philip II, son, 1556-98, inherited only part of empire. He conquered Portugal, fought against Ottoman Empire, sent Armada in unsuccessful invasion of England. Succession: Philip III, son, 1598-1621; Philip IV, son, 1621-65; Charles II, son, 1665-1700, no issue, left Spain to Philip of Anjou, grandson of Louis XIV of France. As Philip V, he was first of Bourbon dynasty in Spain, 1700-46 (his son Louis ruled briefly in 1724); Ferdinand VI, son, 1746-59; Charles III, brother, 1759-88; Charles IV, son, 1788-1808, abdicated.

Joseph Bonaparte made king of Spain, 1808-13, by his brother Napoleon. Ferdinand VII, son of Charles IV, 1808, 1814-33, lost American colonies except Cuba, Puerto Rico. Maria Christina of the Two Sicilies, wife, was regent until 1843 for Isabella II, daughter, who was driven into exile by revolution, 1868. Amadeo of Savoy elected king by the Cortes (parliament), 1870-73. First

Republic, 1873-74. Alfonso XII, son of Isabella II, 1875-85; Alfonso XIII, posthumous son, 1901-31, with mother Maria Christina as regent before he assumed throne. Spain ceded territory after loss in Spanish-American War, 1898. Primo de Rivera ruled as dictator after military coup but was forced to resign after losing support, 1923-30. Alfonso agreed to exile without formal abdication. Monarchy abolished; Second Republic established with socialist backing. Presidents: Niceto Alcala Zamora, 1931-36; Manuel Azaña, 1936-39.

Revolt by military started Spanish Civil War, 1936-39. Gen. Francisco Franco ruled as head of Nationalist regime, 1939-73. Monarchy restored after 1947 referendum. Juan Carlos, grandson of Alfonso XIII, acceded to throne after Franco's death in 1975; abdicated, 2014. Felipe, son, 2014- .

Leaders in the South American Wars of Liberation

Francisco de Miranda, José de San Martín, and Simón Bolívar led early 19th-cent. struggles of South American nations to free themselves from Spain.

Miranda (1750-1816), a Venezuelan, served as an officer in the Spanish army. After a dispute with the army, he fled to U.S., 1783, where he met leaders of American Revolution. He traveled seeking support for South American independence from other world leaders. Miranda unsuccessfully attempted a revolt in Venezuela, 1806. Napoleon's invasion of Spain, 1808, prompted the start of a revolution in Venezuela. Miranda returned, 1810, and headed the revolution with dictatorial powers. Venezuela declared independence, 1811. Overcome by royalist forces, 1812, Miranda surrendered and was arrested; he died in a Spanish prison.

San Martín (1778-1850) was born in present-day Argentina. He served in Spanish campaigns in Europe until 1811. He returned to Argentina and joined the independence movement, 1812. In 1817, he invaded Chile through the Andean mountain passes. He and Bernardo O'Higgins defeated the Spanish at Chacabuco, 1817. Chile gained independence, 1819; O'Higgins became first director of Chile, 1817-23. In 1821, San Martín entered Lima and took the port of Callao; he became protector of an independent Peru.

Bolívar (1783-1830) was born into an aristocratic family in Venezuela. He served under Miranda until Miranda's surrender

in 1812. Bolívar continued to fight; he captured Caracas and was named Liberator, 1813. But he was forced to flee by royalist forces, 1814. In 1817, Bolívar again fought for control of Venezuela. With Francisco de Paula Santander and José Antonio Páez, he defeated Spanish at Battle of Boyacá, 1819, freeing New Granada (present-day Colombia). New Granada, Venezuela, and the area that is now Panama and Ecuador were joined as the Republic of Colombia, or Gran Colombia, with Bolívar as president later that same year, though parts of the republic remained under Spanish control. He decisively defeated the Spanish in the Battle of Carabobo in Venezuela, 1821.

Antonio José de Sucre, Bolívar's chief lieutenant, overcame Spanish forces at the Battle of Pichincha in Ecuador, 1822. Bolívar convinced San Martín to resign as protector of Peru. Peru was declared independent after Bolívar and Sucre won the Battle of Junín, Aug. 1824, and Sucre triumphed at the Battle of Ayacucho, Dec. 1824.

Sucre organized Upper Peru as Republica Bolívar (now Bolivia), 1825, and acted as president in place of Bolívar, who wrote its constitution.

Civil strife caused the Colombian federation to break apart. Bolívar gave up the presidency, 1830.

Rulers of Russia; Leaders of the USSR and Russian Federation

The Varangian (Viking) prince Rurik is considered to be the first leader of the Russians; he established himself at Novgorod, c. 862 CE. His successor, Oleg, and those who followed Oleg ruled as princes of Kiev. Vladimir I, or Saint Vladimir, married sister of Byzantine emperor and converted to Christianity, 988. Yaroslav I (the Wise), brother, 1019-54, was important organizer and lawgiver; his daughters married kings of Norway, Hungary, and France. In 1169, Andrew Bogolyubsky conquered Kiev and began the line of Vladimir.

Daniel, a son of grand prince of Vladimir, Alexander Nevsky, was first to be called prince of Muscovy (Moscow), 1263-1303. Dmitri Ivanovich (Donskoi), prince of Moscow, defeated the Tatars at the Battle of Kulikovo, 1380. His successors were grand princes of Moscow. Ivan III (the Great), 1462-1505, achieved considerable territorial expansion.

Ivan III married Sofia Palaeologus, niece of the last Byzantine emperor. Succession: Vasily III, son. Ivan IV (the Terrible), son, crowned 1547 as Tsar of Russia, ruled until 1584. Fyodor I, son, 1584-98, was weak; Boris Godunov had control before becoming tsar, 1598-1605. After years of internal strife ("Time of Troubles"), the Russians united under 16-year-old Michael Romanov, distantly related to Ivan IV's first wife. He ruled 1613-45, establishing the Romanov line.

Tsars, or emperors, of Russia (Romanovs): Peter I (the Great), 1682-1725, with Ivan V, brother, as co-ruler, 1682-96. Catherine I, his widow, 1725-27. Peter II, grandson of Peter I, 1727-30. Anna, daughter of Ivan V and niece of Peter I, 1730-40. Ivan VI, nephew, 1740-41; deposed by Elizabeth, daughter of Peter I, 1741-62. Peter III, nephew, 1762; deposed by his wife, Catherine II (the Great), former princess of Anhalt Zerbst (Germany), 1762-96. Paul I, son, 1796-1801, assassinated. Alexander I, son, 1801-25, defeated Napoleon. Nicholas I, brother, 1825-55. Alexander II, son, 1855-81, assassinated. Alexander III, son, 1881-94. Nicholas II, son, 1894-1917, last tsar of Russia, was forced to abdicate by revolutionaries following losses to Germany in WWI. The tsar, empress, tsarevich (crown prince), and tsar's four daughters were murdered by the Bolsheviks, July 1918.

Premiers of provisional government: Prince Georgi Lvov, followed by Alexander Kerensky, 1917.

Union of Soviet Socialist Republics

Bolshevik Revolution, Nov. 7, 1917, removed Kerensky from power; council of People's Commissars formed. Lenin (Vladimir Ilyich Ulyanov) served as premier, 1917-24. Aleksei Rykov (executed 1938) and V. M. Molotov held the office, but actual ruler was Joseph Stalin (Joseph Vissarionovich Dzhugashvili), general secretary of the Central Committee of the Communist Party. Stalin became chairman of the Council of Ministers (premier) May 1941; died Mar. 1953. Succeeded by Georgi Malenkov, who also briefly served as first secretary of Central Committee before giving position to Nikita S. Khrushchev. Malenkov was forced to resign as premier, 1955, and was dropped from Central Committee, 1957. Nikolai A. Bulganin was premier, 1955-58, until his replacement by Khrushchev.

Khrushchev, 1958-64, was ousted and replaced by Leonid I. Brezhnev as first secretary of the party and by Aleksei N. Kosygin as premier. Brezhnev also president, 1977-82. The Central Committee elected former KGB (state security) head Yuri V. Andropov president, 1982-84. Konstantin U. Chernenko was chosen by Central Committee as its general secretary. Upon Chernenko's death, 1985, he was succeeded by Mikhail Gorbachev, who replaced Andrei Gromyko as president in 1988. Gorbachev resigned Dec. 25, 1991, and the Soviet Union officially disbanded the next day. Each of the 15 former Soviet constituent republics became independent.

Post-Soviet Russia

Boris Yeltsin was sworn in July 10, 1991, as Russia's first elected president. With the Dec. 1991 dissolution of the Soviet Union, the Russian Federation became a founding member of the Commonwealth of Independent States. Presidents: Yeltsin, 1991-99; Vladimir Putin, 2000-08; Dmitry Medvedev, 2008-12; Putin, 2012- .

Governments of China

Where dynastic dates overlap, the rulers or events referred to appeared in different areas of China.

Years in power	Government
c. 1994–c. 1766 BCE	Hsia dynasty, first hereditary Chinese dynasty
c. 1766–c. 1027 BCE	Shang dynasty
c. 1027–770 BCE	Western Chou dynasty, capital near present-day Xi'an
770–256 BCE	Eastern Chou dynasty, new capital established at Luoyang
403–221 BCE	Period of the Warring States
221–206 BCE	Ch'in dynasty, quasi-feudal states unified for first time; name of China derived from this dynasty
206 BCE–9 CE	Earlier, or Western Han dynasty, founded by rebel leader Liu Pang; Chinese state expanded under Emperor Wu Ti, 140-87 BCE, who represented zenith of power
9–23	Hsin dynasty, established by courtier Wang Mang, who deposed infant emperor for whom he had been acting as regent
25–220	Later, or Eastern Han dynasty
220–265[1]	Wei dynasty, established by son of Han general Ts'ao Ts'ao
221–263[1]	Shu Han dynasty in SW China
222–280[1]	Wu dynasty in SE China
265–317	Western Chin dynasty, established by Ssu-ma Yen, Wei dynasty general
317–420	Eastern Chin dynasty, established by prince of Ssu-ma family
420–589	Southern dynasties, four short-lived dynasties with capital at Chien-k'ang (present-day Nanjing)
589–618	Sui dynasty, reunified China; first emperor was Yang Chien, military servant who usurped throne of non-Chinese Northern Chou, 581
618–906	T'ang dynasty, founded by Li Yuan, who led rebellion against the Sui. Early rulers included former imperial concubine Empress Wu, 683-705; Hsuan Tsung, 712-56
907–960	Five Dynasties, period of disunion with short-lived dynasties in N, 10 independent states mostly in S
907–1125	Liao dynasty, of Khitan Mongols, capital at Yen-ching (present-day Beijing)
960–1126	Northern Sung dynasty, established by military leader Chao K'uang-yin, capital at Kaifeng
1122–1234	Chin dynasty, of Juchen people of Manchuria; drove Sung out of N China
1127–1279	Southern Sung dynasty, capital at Lin-an (present-day Hangzhou)
1279–1368	Yuan dynasty, of Mongols; Kublai Khan, grandson of Genghis Khan, high point of Mongol power
1368–1644	Ming dynasty, founded by rebel leader Chu Yuan-chang, former Buddhist monk. Country again under Chinese rule, capital in present-day Nanjing, then Beijing after defeat of Mongolian tribes
1644–1912	Manchu, or Ch'ing dynasty, under Manchu rule with capital at Chiang-ning (present-day Nanjing). Power of Chinese empire reached highest point in its 2,000-year history. Last imperial dynasty; Hsuan T'ung, or Pu Yi, last emperor. Sun Yat-sen led revolution, 1911. Republic of China formed, 1912
1912–1949	Rep. of China, Gen. Yüan Shih-k'ai elected first president. Power passed to provincial warlords upon his death, 1916. Gen. Chiang Kai-shek sought to reunify China under Kuomintang (Nationalist party), with new national government at Nanjing, 1928. War with Japan, then civil war, led to Nationalist authority collapse, Communist declaration of People's Rep. of China, 1949

(1) Also known as the period of the Three Kingdoms because of warfare between the Wei, Shu Han, and Wu dynasties.

Leaders of People's Republic of China

Name	Title/position, years in power
Mao Zedong	Chairman, 1949-59; Communist Party of China (CPC) Chairman, 1949-76
Zhou Enlai	Premier, 1949-76; foreign minister, 1949-76
Deng Xiaoping	Deputy Premier, 1952-66, 1973-76; "paramount leader," 1977-97
Liu Shaoqi	Chairman, 1959-68
Hua Guofeng	Premier, 1976-80; CPC Chairman, 1976-81
Hu Yaobang	CPC General Secretary, 1980-87; CPC Chairman 1981-82
Zhao Ziyang	Premier, 1980-87; CPC General Secretary, 1987-89
Li Xiannian	President, 1983-88
Yang Shangkun	President, 1988-93
Li Peng	Premier, 1988-98
Jiang Zemin	CPC General Secretary, 1989-2002; President, 1993-2003
Zhu Rongji	Premier, 1998-2003
Hu Jintao	CPC General Secretary, 2002-12; President, 2003-13
Wen Jiabao	Premier, 2003-13
Xi Jinping	CPC General Secretary, 2012- ; President, 2013-
Li Keqiang	Premier, 2013-

Historical Periods of Japan

Years in power	Period	Founding event
c. 300-592	Yamato	Conquest of Yamato plain
592-710	Asuka	Accession of Empress Suiko
710-794	Nara	Heijo (Nara) completed; capital moved to Nagaoka, 784
794-1185	Heian	Heian (Kyoto) completed
858-1160	Fujiwara	Fujiwara-no-Yoshifusa became regent
1160-1185	Taira	Taira-no-Kiyomoro assumed control; Minamoto-no-Yoritomo victor over Taira, 1185
1192-1333	Kamakura	Yoritomo became shogun
1334-1392	Namboku	Emperor Godaigo restored; established Southern Court at Yoshino, 1336
1392-1573	Muromachi	Unification of Southern and Northern Courts
1467-1600	Sengoku	Onin war began
1573-1603	Momoyama	Oda Nobunaga entered Kyoto, 1568, deposed last Ashikaga shogun, 1573. Tokugawa Ieyasu victor at Sekigahara, 1600
1603-1867	Edo	Ieyasu became shogun
1868-1912	Meiji	Meiji (Mutsuhito) ascended throne in Meiji Restoration; Charter Oath, 1868, led to Westernization
1912-1926	Taisho	Accession of Emperor Taisho (Yoshihito)
1926-1989	Showa	Accession of Emperor Hirohito
1989-	Heisei	Accession of Emperor Akihito

WORLD EXPLORATION AND GEOGRAPHY

Early Explorers of the Western Hemisphere

Reviewed by G. A. Clark, Ph.D., Aug. 2008

Genetic evidence suggests that beginning around 14,000 years before the present (BP), the earliest immigrants crossed a 1,000-km wide land bridge between Siberia and Alaska in small groups and spread rapidly south through the Americas, arriving at S America's southern tip by c. 10,700 BP. Kennewick Man, found in 1996 in Washington's Columbia River, dates to 9,600-9,200 BP, and Luzia, dating to 11,500 BP from Brazil, are examples of these early arrivals. Modern Native Americans appear to be descended from peoples indigenous to N and Central Asia who arrived in subsequent waves of migration. A growing body of genetic, skeletal, and linguistic evidence documents their migration throughout the Americas.

Archaeologists have confirmed evidence of habitation by 12,900 BP at sites located on the shores of ancient lakes at an elevation of 17,400 ft in Chile's Atacama Desert. There is also growing support for the settlement of Chile's Monte Verde site, c. 12,500 BP, and eight other 13th-millennium sites in Brazil, Chile, and Argentina. One theory on their migration holds that a glacier covered much of N America from c. 20,000 to 13,000 BP, so those who settled in S America might have traveled there in small boats skirting the pack ice along the W coast, or spread from N to S America through an ice-free corridor in what today is western Canada. Other theories hold that they arrived before continental glaciation blocked migration from the north, or migrated from Iberia in skin boats. Controversial skeletal evidence from a burial at Santana do Riacho in Brazil (9,460 BP) suggests that some of the early immigrants who came via the land bridge from Siberia may have originated in Africa.

Long before Europeans arrived, the Americas were—for the most part—populated by hunter-gatherers and small-scale horticulturalists. In a few areas (SE U.S., Mesoamerica, coastal Peru and Chile), complex chiefdoms and state-level societies had appeared. Irrigation canals dating to 4,700 BP provide evidence for the origins of large-scale agriculture along the western slopes of Peru's Andes Mountains. The earliest known state in the Americas occupied a 700-sq-mi area spanning four river valleys in coastal Peru between 3,500 and 500 BP.

The Norse (Vikings sailing out of Iceland and Greenland), led by Leif Ericson, are usually credited with having been the first Europeans to reach America, with at least five voyages occurring about 1000 CE to areas they called Helluland, Markland, and Vinland—possibly what are known today as Baffin Island, Labrador, and either Newfoundland or somewhere farther south in New England. L'Anse aux Meadows, on the northern tip of Newfoundland, is the only documented settlement, with evidence of a small village with workshops and a forge dating to c. 1000 CE. The Norse tried to import farming and herding economies, but these efforts failed after a few centuries, and Greenland and Newfoundland were abandoned by Europeans.

Sustained contact between the hemispheres began with the first voyage of Christopher Columbus (born Cristoforo Colombo, c. 1451, near Genoa, Italy). Columbus made four voyages to the New World while sailing for the Spanish monarchs Ferdinand II and Isabella. He left Palos, Spain, Aug. 3, 1492, with 88 men and landed at San Salvador (Watling Islands, The Bahamas), Oct. 12, 1492. His fleet included three vessels, the Niña, Pinta, and Santa María. He also visited Cuba, Hispaniola, and many smaller Caribbean islands, then populated by the Taíno Indians. A second expedition left Cadíz, Spain, Sept. 25, 1493, with 17 ships and 1,400 men, reaching the island of Dominica in the Lesser Antilles on Nov. 3, 1493. His third voyage took him from Sanlucar, Spain (May 30, 1498, with six ships), to the island of Trinidad and to the adjacent coast of S America, where he made landfall at the mouth of the Orinoco River. A fourth voyage departed Cadíz on May 9, 1502, and reached the E coast of Mexico, Honduras, Panama, and what he christened Santiago (the present-day island of Jamaica). Columbus died in Valladolid, Spain, on May 20, 1506, still convinced he had reached Asia by sailing west.

In N America, John and Sebastian Cabot, Italian explorers sailing for the English crown, reached Newfoundland and possibly Nova Scotia in 1497. John's second voyage (1498), seeking the fabled Northwest Passage, a new trade route to Asia, resulted in the loss of his entire fleet. For most of the 16th cent., exploration of the New World was dominated by the empires of Spain and Portugal.

In 1497 and 1499, Amerigo Vespucci (for whom the Americas are named), an Italian explorer sailing for Spain, passed along the N and E coasts of S America. He was the first to argue that these lands were previously unknown and not part of Asia.

Other early explorations are listed below.

Year	Explorer	Nationality (sponsor, if different)	Area reached or explored
1497-98	Vasco da Gama	Portuguese	Cape of Good Hope (Africa), India
1499	Alonso de Ojeda	Spanish	Northern S Amer. coast, Venezuela
1500	Vicente Yañez Pinzón	Spanish	S American coast, Amazon R.
1500	Pedro Álvarez Cabral	Portuguese	Brazil
1501	Rodrigo de Bastidas	Spanish	Central America
1513	Vasco Núñez de Balboa	Spanish	Panama, Pacific Ocean
1513	Juan Ponce de León	Spanish	Florida, Yucatán Peninsula
1515	Juan de Solis	Spanish	Río de la Plata
1519	Alonso de Pineda	Spanish	Mouth of Mississippi R.
1519	Hernán Cortés	Spanish	Mexico
1519-20	Ferdinand Magellan	Portuguese (Spanish)	Straits of Magellan, Tierra del Fuego
1524	Giovanni da Verrazano	Italian (French)	Atlantic coast, incl. New York Harbor
1528	Álvar Núñez Cabeza de Vaca	Spanish	Texas coast and interior
1532	Francisco Pizarro	Spanish	Peru
1534	Jacques Cartier	French	Canada, Gulf of St. Lawrence
1536	Pedro de Mendoza	Spanish	Buenos Aires
1539	Francisco de Ulloa	Spanish	California coast
1539-41	Hernando de Soto	Spanish	Mississippi R., near Memphis, TN
1539	Marcos de Niza	Italian (Spanish)	SW United States
1540	Francisco de Coronado	Spanish	SW United States
1540	Hernando de Alarcón	Spanish	Colorado R.
1540	Garcia Lopez de Cárdenas	Spanish	Colorado, Grand Canyon
1541	Francisco de Orellana	Spanish	Amazon R.
1542	Juan Rodriguez Cabrillo	Portuguese (Spanish)	Western Mexico, San Diego Harbor
1565	Pedro Menéndez de Avilés	Spanish	St. Augustine, FL
1576	Sir Martin Frobisher	English	Frobisher Bay, Canada
1577-80	Sir Francis Drake	English	California coast
1582	Antonio de Espejo	Spanish	SW U.S. (New Mexico)
1584	Philip Amadas and Arthur Barlowe (for Raleigh)	English	Virginia
1585-87	Sir Walter Raleigh's men	English	Roanoke Isl., NC
1595	Sir Walter Raleigh	English	Orinoco R.
1603-09	Samuel de Champlain	French	Canadian interior, Lake Champlain
1607	John Smith	English	Atlantic coast
1609-10	Henry Hudson	English (Dutch)	Hudson R., Hudson Bay
1634	Jean Nicolet	French	Lake Michigan, Wisconsin
1673	Jacques Marquette and Louis Jolliet	French	Mississippi R., south to Arkansas
1682	René-Robert Cavelier, sieur de La Salle	French	Mississippi R., south to Gulf of Mexico
1727-29	Vitus Bering	Danish (Russian)	Bering Strait, Alaska
1789	Sir Alexander Mackenzie	Canadian	NW Canada
1804-06	Meriwether Lewis and William Clark	American	Missouri R., Rocky Mts., Columbia R.

Arctic Exploration

Early Explorers

1587: John Davis (Eng.) traveled Davis Strait to Sanderson's Hope, 72°12′N.

1596: Willem Barents and Jacob van Heemskerck (Dutch) discovered Bear Isl., touched NW tip of Spitsbergen, 79°49′N, rounded Novaya Zemlya, wintered at Ice Haven.

1607: Henry Hudson (Eng.) went north along Greenland's E coast to Cape Hold-with-Hope, 73°30′, then north of Spitsbergen to 80°23′. Explored Hudson's Touches (Jan Mayen).

1616: William Baffin and Robert Bylot (Eng.) traveled Baffin Bay to Smith Sound.

1728: Vitus Bering (Dan./Russ.) sailed through strait (Bering), proving Asia and America are separate.

1733-40: Great Northern Expedition (Russ.) surveyed Siberian Arctic coast.

1741: Vitus Bering (Dan./Russ.) sighted Alaska, named Mount St. Elias. His lieutenant, Aleksei Chirikof, explored coast.

1771: Samuel Hearne (Brit., Hudson's Bay Co.) went overland from Prince of Wales Fort (Churchill) on Hudson Bay to mouth of Coppermine R.

1778: James Cook (Brit.) sailed through Bering Strait to Icy Cape, AK, and North Cape, Siberia.

1789: Sir Alexander Mackenzie (Scot., North West Co.). Montreal to mouth of Mackenzie R.

1806: William Scoresby (Brit.). North of Spitsbergen to 81°30′.

1820-23: Ferdinand von Wrangel (Russ.) surveyed Siberian Arctic coast. His exploration joined James Cook's at North Cape, confirming separation of the continents.

1878-79: Baron Nils Adolf Erik Nordenskiöld (Swed.) was first to navigate the Northeast Passage—an ocean route connecting Europe's North Sea, along the Arctic coast of Asia and through the Bering Sea, to the Pacific Ocean.

1881: The U.S. steamer *Jeannette*, led by Lt. Cmdr. George W. DeLong, was trapped in ice and crushed, June. DeLong and 11 others died; 12 survived.

1888: Fridtjof Nansen (Nor.) crossed Greenland icecap.

1893-96: Nansen in *Fram* drifted from New Siberian Isls. to Spitsbergen; tried polar dash in 1895, reached Franz Josef Land, 86°14′N.

1897: Salomon A. Andrée (Swed.) and two others started in balloon from Spitsbergen, July 11; they drifted across pole to U.S. before reaching Pacific. Their bodies were found, Aug. 6, 1930, on White Isl., 82°57′N, 29°52′E.

1903-06: Roald Amundsen (Nor.) was first to sail whole length of Northwest Passage—ocean route linking the Atlantic Ocean to the Pacific via Canada's marine waterways.

North Pole Exploration

Robert E. Peary (U.S.) explored Greenland's coast, 1891-92; tried for North Pole, 1893. In 1900, he reached northern limit of Greenland and 83°50′N; in 1902, he reached 84°17′N; in 1906, he went from Ellesmere Isl. to 87°06′N. He sailed in the *Roosevelt*, July 1908, to winter off Cape Sheridan, Grant Land. The dash for the North Pole began Mar. 1 from Cape Columbia, Ellesmere Isl. Peary reportedly reached the pole, 90°N, Apr. 6, 1909; recent research suggests he may have fallen short of his goal by c. 30-60 mi. (Dr. Frederick Cook claimed to have reached the North Pole in 1908.) The first surface expedition

independently confirmed to have reached the North Pole was that of Ralph Plaisted in 1968 (see below).

Peary had several support groups carrying supplies until the last group turned back at 87°47′N. Peary, Matthew Henson, and four Eskimos (or Inuit) proceeded with dog teams and sleds. They were said to have crossed the pole several times, then built an igloo there and rested before returning south.

1914: Donald MacMillan (U.S.) traveled 200 mi from Axel Heiberg Isl. in search of Peary-named Crocker Land; MacMillan realized Peary had seen a Fata Morgana, mirage whereby pack ice in distance appears to be land.

1915-17: Vilhjalmur Stefansson (Can.) discovered Borden, Brock, Meighen, and Lougheed Isls.

1918-20: Roald Amundsen (Nor.) sailed Northeast Passage.

1925: Amundsen and Lincoln Ellsworth (U.S.) reached 87°44′N in attempt to fly to North Pole from Spitsbergen.

1926: Richard E. Byrd and Floyd Bennett (U.S.) reputedly flew over North Pole, May 9.

Amundsen, Ellsworth, and Umberto Nobile (Ital.) flew over North Pole May 12 in dirigible *Norge*.

1928: Nobile crossed North Pole in airship, May 24; crashed, May 25. Amundsen died attempting rescue.

North Pole Exploration Records

1958: Nuclear-powered submarine USS *Nautilus*, under Cmdr. William R. Anderson, crossed the North Pole beneath the ice, Aug. 3.

1960: In Aug., the nuclear submarine USS *Seadragon* (Cmdr. George P. Steele II) made the first E-W underwater transit through Northwest Passage. Traveling mostly submerged, it made the 850-mi trek from Baffin Bay to the Beaufort Sea in six days.

1968: Ralph Plaisted (U.S.) and three amateur explorers on snowmobiles became first independently confirmed surface expedition to reach North Pole, Apr. 19.

1977: Soviet nuclear icebreaker *Arktika* became first surface ship to reach North Pole, Aug. 16.

1978: On Apr. 30, Naomi Uemura (Jpn.) became first person to reach the North Pole alone, traveling by dog sled in a 54-day, 600-mi trek over the frozen Arctic.

1982: In Apr., Sir Ranulph Fiennes and Charles Burton, Brit. explorers, reached the North Pole and became first to circle the Earth from pole to pole. They had reached the South Pole 16 months earlier. The 52,000-mi trek took three years, involved 23 people, and cost an estimated $18 mil.

1986: Six explorers reached the North Pole assisted only by dogs, May 2. They became first to reach the pole without aerial logistics support since at least 1909. The explorers—Americans Will Steger, Paul Schurke, Ann Bancroft, and Geoff Carroll and Canadians Brent Boddy and Richard Weber—completed the 500-mi journey in 56 days.

1995: Weber and Mikhail Malakhov (Russ.) became first pair to make it to North Pole and back without any mechanical assistance, June 15. The 940-mi trip, made entirely on skis, took 121 days.

2003: Pen Hadow (Brit.) became first to reach North Pole from Canada, solo and without resupply, May 20. The 377-mi journey across the ice took 64 days.

2006: Prince Albert II of Monaco became first royal to reach North Pole, Apr. 16.

Antarctic Exploration

Antarctica has been approached since 1773-75, when Capt. James Cook (Brit.) reached 71°10′S. Many seas and landmarks bear the names of early explorers. Fabian von Bellingshausen (Russ.) discovered Peter I and Alexander I Isls., 1819-21. Nathaniel Palmer (U.S.) traveled throughout Palmer Peninsula, 60°W, 1820. Capt. John Davis (U.S.) made the first known Antarctic landing on Feb. 7, 1821. In 1823, James Weddell (Brit.) found Weddell Sea, 74°15′S, the southernmost point that had been reached.

First to announce existence of the continent of Antarctica was Charles Wilkes (U.S.), who followed the coast for 1,500 mi, 1840. Adelie Coast, 140°E, was found by Dumont d'Urville (Fr.), 1840. Ross Ice Shelf was found by James Clark Ross (Brit.), 1841-42.

1895: Leonard Kristensen (Nor.) landed a party on the coast of Victoria Land. They were first ashore on main continental mass. C. E. Borchgrevink, a member of that party, returned in 1899 with a Brit. expedition, first to winter on Antarctica.

1902-04: Robert Falcon Scott (Brit.) explored Edward VII Peninsula to 82°17′S, 146°33′E from McMurdo Sound.

1908-09: Ernest Shackleton (Brit.) was first to use Manchurian ponies in Antarctic sledging. He reached 88°23′S, discovering route onto plateau by way of Beardmore Glacier and pioneering the way to the pole.

1911: Roald Amundsen (Nor.) with four men and dog teams reached South Pole, Dec. 14.

1912: Scott reached the pole from Ross Isl., Jan. 18, with four companions. None survived. Their bodies and expedition notes were found, Nov. 12.

1928: Sir George Hubert Wilkins (Austral.) was first to use airplane over Antarctica.

1929: Richard E. Byrd (U.S.) established Little America on Bay of Whales. On 1,600-mi airplane flight begun Nov. 28, he crossed South Pole, Nov. 29, with three others.

1934-35: Byrd led second expedition to Little America, explored 450,000 sq mi, wintered alone at 80°08´S.

1934-37: John Rymill (Austral.) led British Graham Land Expedition; discovered Palmer Peninsula was part of mainland.

1935: Lincoln Ellsworth (U.S.) flew south along E Coast of Palmer Peninsula, then crossed continent to Little America, making four landings.

1939-41: U.S. Navy planes discovered about 150,000 sq mi of new land.

1940: Byrd charted most of coast between Ross Sea and Palmer Peninsula.

1946-47: U.S. Navy undertook Operation Highjump, commanded by Byrd, which included 13 ships and 4,000 men. Airplanes photomapped coastline and penetrated beyond pole.

1946-48: Ronne Antarctic Research Expedition Cmdr. Finn Ronne, USNR, determined Antarctic to be only one continent with no strait between Weddell Sea and Ross Sea; explored 250,000 sq mi of land by flights to 79°S.

1955-57: U.S. Navy's Operation Deep Freeze led by Byrd. Supporting U.S. scientific efforts for International Geophysical Year (IGY), the operation established five coastal stations fronting Indian, Pacific, and Atlantic Oceans and three interior stations; explored more than 1 mil sq mi in Wilkes Land.

1957-58: During IGY, July 1957 through Dec. 1958, scientists from 12 countries conducted research within network of some 60 stations on Antarctica.

Dr. Vivian E. Fuchs (Brit.) led 12-person Trans-Antarctic Expedition on first land crossing of Antarctica. Starting from the Weddell Sea, they reached Scott Station, Mar. 2, 1958, after traveling 2,158 mi in 99 days.

1958: A group of five U.S. scientists led by seismologist Edward C. Thiel, moving by tractor from Ellsworth Station on Weddell Sea, identified a mountain range 5,000 ft above the ice sheet and 9,000 ft above sea level. The range, originally seen by a Navy plane, was named Dufek Massif, for Rear Adm. George Dufek.

1959: Argentina, Australia, Belgium, Chile, France, Japan, New Zealand, Norway, South Africa, USSR, UK, and U.S. signed a treaty suspending territorial claims for 30 years and reserving the continent south of 60°S for research.

1961-62: Scientists discovered Bentley Trench, running from Ross Ice Shelf into Marie Byrd Land, near the end of the Ellsworth Mts., toward Weddell Sea.

1962: U.S. nuclear power plant went online at McMurdo Sound; in operation until 1972.

1963: On Feb. 22, a U.S. plane made the region's longest nonstop flight from McMurdo Station south past the pole to Shackleton Mts., southeast to "area of inaccessibility," and back to McMurdo Station, covering 3,600 mi in 10 hours.

1964: New Zealanders mapped the mountain area from Cape Adare west some 400 mi to Pennell Glacier.

1985: Researcher Igor A. Zotikov (Russ.) discovered sediments in Ross Ice Shelf that seem to support continental drift theory. Ocean Drilling Project finds that the ice sheets of E Antarctica are 37 mil years old.

1989: Victoria Murden and Shirley Metz became first women as well as first Americans to reach South Pole overland when they arrived with nine others, Jan. 17.

1991: 24 nations approved a protocol to 1959 Antarctica Treaty, Oct. 4. New conservation provisions include banning oil and other mineral exploration for 50 years.

1994: On Dec. 25, after 50-day trek, Liv Arnesen (Nor.) became first woman to ski alone and unaided to South Pole.

1995: Borge Ousland (Nor.) reached South Pole on skis, Dec. 22, becoming first to reach both N and S Poles solo.

1996-97: Ousland became first to traverse Antarctica alone; reached South Pole Dec. 19, 1996. Traveled 1,675 mi in 64 days, ending Jan. 18, 1997.

2000-01: Ann Bancroft (U.S.) and Arnesen became first women to ski unaided across Antarctica, Feb. 11, 2001. The 1,717-mi journey took 94 days.

2008: Norwegians Christian Eide, Rune Midtgaard, Morten Andvig, and Mads Agerup reached the South Pole unaided, Dec. 26, in record 24 days, 8 hr., 50 min.

Volcanoes

Source: *Volcanoes of the World*, Geoscience Press; Global Volcanism Program, Smithsonian Institution

Eruptions have been documented in about 550 volcanoes. More than half to three-quarters of these historically active volcanoes can be found on the so-called **Ring of Fire**, which runs along the W coast of the Americas from the southern tip of Chile to Alaska, down the E coast of Asia from Kamchatka to Indonesia, and continues from New Guinea to New Zealand. The Ring of Fire marks the boundaries between tectonic plates underlying the Pacific Ocean and those of the surrounding continents. Volcanic activity also occurs along rift zones like Iceland, where plates pull apart, or over hot spots such as Hawaii, where plumes of molten material rise from the mantle to the Earth's crust. The majority of Earth's volcanism takes place at submarine rift zones, on the seafloor. For more information on volcanoes, see the Smithsonian Institution's global volcanism website at www.volcano.si.edu.

Notable Volcanic Eruptions

In approximately 5,700 BC, Mount Mazama, in southern Oregon, erupted violently, ejecting large amounts of ash and pumice and sending out pyroclastic flows (mixture of volcanic debris and gases). The ash spread over the northwestern U.S. and southern Canada. The eruption collapsed the top of the mountain, leaving a caldera about 6 mi across and 1 mi deep. This depression filled with water from rain and snow to form what is now called Crater Lake.

In 79 CE, Mount Vesuvius, a volcano overlooking Naples Bay, became active after several centuries of apparent inactivity. On Aug. 24 of that year, heated mud and ash swept down the mountain, engulfing the cities of Pompeii, Herculaneum, and Stabiae with debris more than 60 ft deep. About 10% of the population of the three towns were killed.

In 1883, an eruption similar to the Mazama eruption occurred on the island of Krakatau. At least 2,000 people died in pyroclastic flows on Aug. 26. The next day, the 2,640-ft peak of the volcano collapsed to 1,000 ft below sea level, sinking most of the island and killing over 3,000. The eruptions and collapse generated a series of tsunamis that killed more than 31,000 people in Java and Sumatra. Ash from the eruption colored sunsets around the world for two years.

Date	Volcano	Est. deaths	Date	Volcano	Est. deaths
Aug. 24, 79 CE	Vesuvius, Italy	16,000	Jan. 30, 1911	Taal, Philippines	1,400
1586	Kelut, Java, Indon.	10,000	June 6-8, 1912	Novarupta, AK, U.S.[4]	1
Dec. 15, 1631	Vesuvius, Italy	4,000	May 19, 1919	Kelut, Java, Indon.	5,000
Aug. 12, 1772	Papandayan, Java, Indon.	3,000	Jan. 17-21, 1951	Lamington, New Guinea	3,000
June 8, 1783	Laki, Iceland	9,350	May 18, 1980	St. Helens, WA, U.S.	57
May 21, 1792	Unzen, Japan	14,500	Mar. 28, 1982	El Chichon, Mexico	1,880
Apr. 10-12, 1815	Tambora, Sumbawa, Indon.	92,000[1]	Nov. 13, 1985	Nevado del Ruiz, Colombia	23,000
Aug. 26-27, 1883	Krakatau, Indon.	36,000[2]	Aug. 21, 1986	Lake Nyos, Cameroon	1,700[5]
Apr. 24, 1902	Santa María, Guatemala	1,000[3]	June 15, 1991	Pinatubo, Luzon, Philippines	800[6]
May 8, 1902	Pelée, Martinique	28,000			

(1) Of these, 10,000 were directly related to the eruption; additional deaths were the result of starvation and disease brought on by the event. (2) Collapse of volcano generated tsunamis, which were responsible for the majority of deaths. (3) An additional 3,000 deaths due to a malaria outbreak are sometimes attributed to the eruption. (4) Biggest eruption of 20th cent. by volume. (5) Caused by release of massive amount of carbon dioxide from crater lake. (6) Of these, about 500 were associated with post-eruption lahars (volcanic mudflows).

Notable Active Volcanoes

Source: Global Volcanism Program, Smithsonian Institution; Volcano Hazards Program, U.S. Geological Survey, U.S. Dept. of the Interior

Active volcanoes display a wide range of activity, including the production of ash plumes and seismic swarms. An eruption may involve the explosive ejection of fragmental material and escape of liquid lava. Year of a volcano's last known or confirmed eruption, as of June 2014, is given. Volcanoes are listed by height, which does not reflect eruptive magnitude. Submarine volcanoes are not included.

Volcano (latest eruption)	Location	Height (ft)
Africa		
Cameroon (2000)	Cameroon	13,435
Nyiragongo (2013)	Dem. Rep. of the Congo	11,385
Nyamuragira (2012)	Dem. Rep. of the Congo	10,033
Ol Doinyo Lengai (2013)	Tanzania	9,718
Fogo (1995)	Cape Verde Isls.	9,281
Piton de la Fournaise (2010)	Réunion Isl. (Fr.), Indian O.	8,635
Karthala (2007)	Comoros	7,746
Nabro (2011)	Eritrea	7,277
Antarctica		
Erebus (2011)	Ross Isl.	12,448
Michael (2006)	Saunders Isl. (UK)	3,248
Asia and Oceania		
Kliuchevskoi (2013)	Kamchatka, Russia	15,863
Kerinci (2009)	Sumatra, Indon.	12,467
Fuji (1708)	Honshu, Japan	12,388
Rinjani (2010)	Lombok, Indon.	12,224
Tolbachik (2013)	Kamchatka, Russia	12,080
Semeru (2012)	Java, Indon.	12,060
Koryaksky (2009)	Kamchatka, Russia	11,339
Slamet (2009)	Java, Indon.	11,247
Raung (2008)	Java, Indon.	10,932
Shiveluch (2014)	Kamchatka, Russia	10,771
Ontake (1980)	Honshu, Japan	10,062
Merapi (2013)	Java, Indon.	9,738
Marapi (2012)	Sumatra, Indon.	9,485
Bezymianny (2013)	Kamchatka, Russia	9,455
Peuet Sague (2000)	Sumatra, Indon.	9,190
Ruapehu (2007)	New Zealand	9,177
Heard (2013)	Australia	9,006
Changbaishan (1903)	China-North Korea	9,003
Papandayan (2002)	Java, Indon.	8,743
Asama (2009)	Honshu, Japan	8,425
Dieng Volcanic Complex (2009)	Java, Indon.	8,415
Mayon (2013)	Luzon, Philippines	8,077
Sinabung (2014)	Sumatra, Indon.	8,071
Kanlaon (2006)	Negros Isl., Philippines	7,989
Niigata-Yakeyama (1998)	Honshu, Japan	7,874
Kizimen (2013)	Kamchatka, Russia	7,795
Alaid (2012)	Kuril Isls., Russia	7,674
Ulawun (2013)	Papua New Guinea	7,657
Tengger Caldera (2012)	Java, Indon.	7,641
Chokai (1974)	Honshu, Japan	7,336
Galunggung (1984)	Java, Indon.	7,113
Tangkubanparahu (2013)	Java, Indon.	6,837
Tongariro (2012)	New Zealand	6,490
Azuma (1977)	Honshu, Japan	6,394
Sangeang Api (1999)	Lesser Sunda Isls., Indon.	6,394
Nasu (1963)	Honshu, Japan	6,283
Karkar (2013)	Papua New Guinea	6,033
Gorely (2010)	Kamchatka, Russia	6,001
Chachadake (Tiatia) (1981)	Kunashir Isl., Japan-admin. by Russia	5,978
Bandai (1888)	Honshu, Japan	5,958
Chikurachki (2008)	Paramushir Isl., Russia	5,958
Manam (2013)	Papua New Guinea	5,928
Kuju (1996)	Kyushu, Japan	5,876
Karangetang (Api Siau) (2013)	Sangihe Isls., Indon.	5,853
Soputan (2012)	Sulawesi, Indon.	5,853
Bagana (2013)	Papua New Guinea	5,741
Kelut (2008)	Java, Indon.	5,679
Adatara (1996)	Honshu, Japan	5,669
Gamalama (2012)	Halmahera, Indon.	5,627
Kirishima (2011)	Kyushu, Japan	5,577
Gamkonora (2007)	Halmahera, Indon.	5,364
Aso (2011)	Kyushu, Japan	5,223
Lokon-Empung (2013)	Sulawesi, Indon.	5,184
Bulusan (2011)	Luzon, Philippines	5,135
Karymsky (2014)	Kamchatka, Russia	5,039
Akan (2008)	Hokkaido, Japan	4,918
Aoba (2011)	Vanuatu	4,908
Sarychev Peak (2009)	Kuril Isls., Russia	4,908
Pinatubo (1993)	Luzon, Philippines	4,875
Unzen (1996)	Kyushu, Japan	4,865
Lopevi (2007)	Vanuatu	4,636
Akita-Yakeyama (1997)	Honshu, Japan	4,482
Dukono (2014)	Halmahera, Indon.	4,380
Ambrym (2013)	Vanuatu	4,377
Langila (2012)	Papua New Guinea	4,364
Ibu (2013)	Halmahera Isl., Indon.	4,347
Awu (2004)	Sangihe Isls., Indon.	4,331
Ekarma (2010)	Kuril Isls., Russia	3,839
Etorofu-Yakeyama (Grozny Group) (2013)	Iturup Isl., Japan-admin. by Russia	3,799
Ebeko (2010)	Kuril Isls., Russia	3,793

Volcano (latest eruption)	Location	Height (ft)
Central America and Caribbean		
Tacaná (1986)	Mexico-Guatemala	13,320
Acatenango (1972)	Guatemala	13,045
Santa María (2013)	Guatemala	12,375
Fuego (2013)	Guatemala	12,346
Irazú (1994)	Costa Rica	11,260
Turrialba (2013)	Costa Rica	10,958
Poás (2013)	Costa Rica	8,885
Pacaya (2013)	Guatemala	8,373
Santa Ana (2005)	El Salvador	7,812
San Miguel (2002)	El Salvador	6,988
Rincón de la Vieja (2012)	Costa Rica	6,286
San Cristóbal (2013)	Nicaragua	5,725
Concepción (2011)	Nicaragua	5,577
Arenal (2010)	Costa Rica	5,479
Soufrière Guadeloupe (1977)	Guadeloupe Isl. (France)	4,813
Pelée (1932)	Martinique (France)	4,573
Momotombo (1905)	Nicaragua	4,255
North America		
Pico de Orizaba (1846)	Mexico	18,619
Popocatépetl (2013)	Mexico	17,802
Rainier (1894)	Washington	14,409
Shasta (1786)	California	14,163
Wrangell (2002)	Alaska	14,163
Colima (2013)	Mexico	12,631
Spurr (1992)	Alaska	11,070
Lassen Peak (1917)	California	10,456
Redoubt (2009)	Alaska	10,197
Iliamna (1876)	Alaska	10,016
Shishaldin (2004)	Aleutian Isls., AK	9,373
St. Helens (2008)	Washington	8,363
Pavlof (2013)	Alaska	8,264
Veniaminof (2013)	Alaska	8,225
Katmai (1912)	Alaska	6,716
Makushin (1995)	Alaska	5,906
Great Sitkin (1974)	Aleutian Isls., AK	5,709
Cleveland (2014)	Aleutian Isls., AK	5,676
Gareloi (1989)	Aleutian Isls., AK	5,161
Korovin (2007)	Aleutian Isls., AK	5,030
South America		
Llullaillaco (1877)	Chile-Argentina	22,110
San Pedro (1960)	Chile	20,161
Guallatiri (1960)	Chile	19,918
Sabancaya (2003)	Peru	19,577
Cotopaxi (1940)	Ecuador	19,393
El Misti (1985)	Peru	19,101
Tupungatito (1987)	Chile-Argentina	18,570
Láscar (2014)	Chile	18,346
Nevado del Huila (2012)	Colombia	17,598
Nevado del Ruiz (2013)	Colombia	17,457
Sangay (2013)	Ecuador	17,159
Irruputuncu (1995)	Chile-Bolivia	16,939
Tungurahua (2014)	Ecuador	16,480
Guagua Pichincha (2002)	Ecuador	15,696
Puracé (1977)	Colombia	15,256
Galeras (2013)	Colombia	14,029
Planchón-Peteroa (2011)	Chile	13,474
Lautaro (1979)	Chile	11,834
Reventador (2013)	Ecuador	11,686
Arenales (1979)	Chile	11,276
Llaima (2009)	Chile	10,253
Copahue (2013)	Chile-Argentina	9,688
Villarrica (2014)	Chile	9,341
Europe		
Etna (2014)	Italy	10,925
Vesuvius (1944)	Italy	4,203
Stromboli (2013)	Italy	3,031
Santorini (1950)	Greece	1,204
Mid-Atlantic		
Jan Mayen (1985)	N Atlantic O. (Norway)	7,470
Grímsvötn (2011)	Iceland	5,659
Eyjafjallajökull (2010)	Iceland	5,466
Katla (2011)	Iceland	4,961
Hekla (2000)	Iceland	4,892
Mid-Pacific		
Mauna Loa (1984)	Hawaii, HI	13,681
Haleakala (1750)	Maui, HI	10,023
Kilauea (2014)	Hawaii, HI	4,009

Mountains
North America

Source: U.S. Geological Survey, U.S. Dept. of the Interior; Natural Resources Canada. Survey dates and elevation sources may differ.

Peak, state/prov., country	Height (ft)	Peak, state/prov., country	Height (ft)	Peak, state/prov., country	Height (ft)
McKinley (Denali), AK	20,320	Hunter, AK	14,573	Cameron, CO	14,238
Logan, Yukon, Canada	19,551	Browne Tower, AK	14,530	Shavano, CO	14,231
Pico de Orizaba, Mexico	18,619	Whitney, CA	14,505	Princeton, CO	14,204
St. Elias, AK-YT, U.S.-Can.	18,009	Alverstone, AK-YT, U.S.-Can.	14,500	Belford, CO	14,203
Popocatépetl, Mexico	17,802	University Peak, AK	14,470	Yale, CO	14,200
Foraker, AK	17,400	Elbert, CO	14,440	Crestone Needle, CO	14,197
Iztaccíhuatl, Mexico	17,154	Massive, CO	14,421	Bross, CO	14,172
Lucania, YT, Canada	17,146	Harvard, CO	14,421	Kit Carson, CO	14,165
King, YT, Canada	16,972	Rainier, WA	14,410	Point Success, WA	14,164
Steele, YT, Canada	16,624	Williamson, CA	14,376	Shasta, CA	14,163
Bona, AK	16,500	Blanca Peak, CO	14,345	Wrangell, AK	14,163
Blackburn, AK	16,390	La Plata Peak, CO	14,336	Maroon Peak, CO	14,163
Sanford, AK	16,237	Uncompahgre Peak, CO	14,321	Tabeguache, CO	14,162
Vancouver, AK-YT, U.S.-Can.	15,699	Crestone Peak, CO	14,294	Oxford, CO	14,160
South Buttress, AK	15,885	Lincoln, CO	14,293	El Diente Peak, CO	14,159
Wood, YT, Canada	15,873	Castle Peak, CO	14,279	Sill, CA	14,159
Churchill, AK	15,638	Grays Peak, CO	14,278	Democrat, CO	14,155
Nevado de Toluca (Xinantécatl),		Antero, CO	14,276	Sneffels, CO	14,150
Mexico	15,350	Torreys Peak, CO	14,275	Capitol Peak, CO	14,130
Fairweather, AK-BC, U.S.-Can.	15,299	Quandary Peak, CO	14,271	Liberty Cap, WA	14,118
MacAulay, YT, Canada	15,299	Evans, CO	14,265	Pikes Peak, CO	14,115
Slaggard, YT, Canada	15,299	Longs Peak, CO	14,259	Snowmass, CO	14,099
Hubbard, AK-YT, U.S.-Can.	15,016	McArthur, YT, Canada	14,253	Russell, CA	14,094
Bear, AK	14,831	White Mountain Peak, CA	14,252	Eolus, CO	14,083
Walsh, YT, Canada	14,780	North Palisade, CA	14,248	Windom, CO	14,082
East Buttress, AK	14,730	Wilson, CO	14,246	Challenger Point, CO	14,081
Matlalcueyetl, Mexico	14,636				

Note: The highest point in the West Indies is Pico Duarte (10,417 ft), in the Dominican Republic.

Other Notable U.S. Mountains

Peak, state	Height (ft)	Peak, state	Height (ft)	Peak, state	Height (ft)
Gannett Peak, WY	13,810	Adams, WA	12,281	Clingmans Dome, NC-TN	6,643
Grand Teton, WY	13,775	San Gorgonio, CA	11,503	Washington, NH	6,289
Kings, UT	13,534	Hood, OR	11,240	Rogers, VA	5,729
Cloud, WY	13,171	Lassen, CA	10,461	Marcy, NY	5,344
Wheeler, NM	13,166	Granite, CA	10,325	Katahdin, ME	5,269
Boundary, NV	13,146	Guadalupe, TX	8,751	Spruce Knob, WV	4,863
Granite, MT	12,804	Olympus, WA	7,973	Mansfield, VT	4,393
Borah, ID	12,661	Harney, SD	7,244	Black Mountain, KY	4,145
Humphreys, AZ	12,637	Mitchell, NC	6,683		

South America

Peak, country	Height (ft)	Peak, country	Height (ft)	Peak, country	Height (ft)
Aconcagua, Argentina	22,831	Coropuna, Peru	21,083	Solo, Argentina	20,492
Ojos del Salado, Arg.-Chile	22,595	Laudo, Argentina	20,997	Polleras, Argentina	20,456
Bonete, Argentina	22,546	Ancohuma, Bolivia	20,958	Pular, Chile	20,423
Tupungato, Argentina-Chile	22,310	Ausangate, Peru	20,945	Chani, Argentina	20,341
Pissis, Argentina	22,241	Toro, Argentina-Chile	20,932	Aucanquilcha, Chile	20,295
Mercedario, Argentina	22,211	Illampu, Bolivia	20,873	Juncal, Argentina-Chile	20,276
Huascarán, Peru	22,205	Tres Cruces, Argentina-Chile	20,853	Negro, Argentina	20,184
Llullaillaco, Argentina-Chile	22,109	Huandoy, Peru	20,852	Quela, Argentina	20,128
El Libertador, Argentina	22,047	Parinacota, Bolivia-Chile	20,768	Condoriri, Bolivia	20,095
Cachi, Argentina	22,047	Tortolas, Argentina-Chile	20,745	Palermo, Argentina	20,079
Yerupajá, Peru	21,765	Ampato, Peru	20,702	Solimana, Peru	20,068
Incahuasi, Argentina-Chile	21,720	Chimborazo, Ecuador	20,702	San Juan, Argentina-Chile	20,049
Galan, Argentina	21,654	El Condor, Argentina	20,669	Sierra Nevada, Argentina-Chile	20,023
El Muerto, Argentina-Chile	21,457	Salcantay, Peru	20,574	Antofalla, Argentina	20,013
Sajama, Bolivia	21,391	Huancarhuas, Peru	20,531	Marmolejo, Argentina-Chile	20,013
Nacimiento, Argentina	21,302	Famatina, Argentina	20,505	Chachani, Peru	19,931
Illimani, Bolivia	21,201	Pumasillo, Peru	20,492		

Africa

Peak, country	Height (ft)	Peak, country	Height (ft)	Peak, country	Height (ft)
Kilimanjaro, Tanzania	19,341	Meru, Tanzania	14,977	Guna, Ethiopia	13,881
Kenya, Kenya	17,057	Karisimbi, Congo-Rwanda	14,787	Gughe, Ethiopia	13,780
Margherita Pk., Uganda-Congo	16,763	Elgon, Kenya-Uganda	14,178	Toubkal, Morocco	13,661
Ras Dashan, Ethiopia	15,158	Batu, Ethiopia	14,131	Cameroon, Cameroon	13,435

Australia, New Zealand, SE Asian Islands

Peak, country	Height (ft)	Peak, country	Height (ft)	Peak, country	Height (ft)
Jaya, New Guinea	16,500	Wilhelm, New Guinea	14,793	Cook/Aoraki, New Zealand	12,218
Trikora, New Guinea	15,585	Kinabalu, Malaysia	13,455	Semeru, Java, Indonesia	12,060
Mandala, New Guinea	15,420	Kerinci, Sumatra, Indon.	12,467	Kosciusko, Australia	7,310

Height of Mount Everest

Mt. Everest, the world's highest mountain, was considered 29,002 ft when Edmund Hillary and Tenzing Norgay became the first to scale it, in 1953. In 1954, the Surveyor General of the Republic of India set the height at 29,028 ft, plus or minus 10 ft because of snow. In 1999, a team of climbers sponsored by Boston's Museum of Science and the National Geographic Society measured the height at the summit using satellite-based technology. The new measurement, of 29,035 ft, was accepted by other authorities, including the U.S. National Imagery and Mapping Agency.

Climbers typically ascend Everest on its north (Tibet) or south face (Nepal). By the end of the 2013 climbing season, which runs from April through May, there were about 6,800 successful ascents; an estimated 242 climbers had died in the attempt. The 2014 climbing season on the south face was unofficially canceled after 16 Sherpas were killed in an avalanche triggered by falling ice Apr. 18, 2014. It was the deadliest day on the mountain to date. The Sherpas, members of a Himalayan ethnic group, were employed by tour operators to fix ropes and carry supplies for Western clients. Concerns about additional avalanches, the increasing number of tourists on Everest, and fair worker compensation also contributed to the decision by most tour operators to cancel.

Europe

Peak, country	Height (ft)
Alps	
Mont Blanc, France-Italy	15,781
Monte Rosa (highest peak of group), Switzerland	15,203
Dom, Switzerland	14,911
Liskamm, It.-Switzerland	14,852
Weisshorn, Switzerland	14,780
Taschhorn, Switzerland	14,733
Matterhorn, It.-Switzerland	14,692
Dent Blanche, Switzerland	14,293
Nadelhorn, Switzerland	14,196
Grand Combin, Switzerland	14,154
Lenzpitze, Switzerland	14,088
Finsteraarhorn, Switzerland	14,022
Castor, Switzerland	13,865
Zinalrothorn, Switzerland	13,849
Hohberghorn, Switzerland	13,842
Alphubel, Switzerland	13,799
Rimpfischhorn, Switzerland	13,776
Aletschorn, Switzerland	13,763
Strahlhorn, Switzerland	13,747

Peak, country	Height (ft)
Dent D'Herens, Switzerland	13,686
Breithorn, It.-Switzerland	13,665
Bishorn, Switzerland	13,645
Jungfrau, Switzerland	13,642
Ecrins, France	13,461
Monch, Switzerland	13,448
Pollux, Switzerland	13,422
Schreckhorn, Switzerland	13,379
Ober Gabelhorn, Switzerland	13,330
Gran Paradiso, Italy	13,323
Bernina, It.-Switzerland	13,284
Fiescherhorn, Switzerland	13,283
Grunhorn, Switzerland	13,266
Lauteraarhorn, Switzerland	13,261
Durrenhorn, Switzerland	13,238
Allalinhorn, Switzerland	13,213
Weissmies, Switzerland	13,199
Lagginhorn, Switzerland	13,156
Zupo, Switzerland	13,120
Fletschhorn, Switzerland	13,110
Adlerhorn, Switzerland	13,081
Gletscherhorn, Switzerland	13,068

Peak, country	Height (ft)
Schalihorn, Switzerland	13,040
Scerscen, Switzerland	13,028
Eiger, Switzerland	13,025
Jagerhorn, Switzerland	13,024
Rottalhorn, Switzerland	13,022
Pyrenees	
Aneto, Spain	11,168
Posets, Spain	11,073
Perdido, Spain	11,007
Vignemale, France-Spain	10,820
Long, Spain	10,479
Estats, Spain	10,304
Montcalm, Spain	10,105
Caucasus (Europe-Asia)	
Elbrus, Russia	18,510
Shkhara, Georgia	17,064
Dykh Tau, Russia	17,054
Kashtan Tau, Russia	16,877
Janqi, Georgia	16,565
Kazbek, Georgia	16,558

Asia (Mainland)

Peak, country/region	Height (ft)
Everest, Nepal-Tibet	29,035
K2 (Godwin Austen), Kashmir	28,251
Kanchenjunga, India-Nepal	28,169
Lhotse I (Everest), Nepal-Tibet	27,923
Makalu I, Nepal-Tibet	27,824
Lhotse II (Everest), Nepal-Tibet	27,560
Dhaulagiri, Nepal	26,795
Manaslu I, Nepal	26,781
Cho Oyu, Nepal-Tibet	26,750
Nanga Parbat, Kashmir	26,660
Annapurna I, Nepal	26,545
Annapurna II, Nepal	26,545
Gasherbrum, Kashmir	26,470
Broad, Kashmir	26,400
Gosainthan, Nepal-Tibet	26,287
Gyachung Kang, Nepal-Tibet	25,910
Disteghil Sar, Kashmir	25,868
Himalchuli, Nepal	25,801
Nuptse (Everest), Nepal-Tibet	25,726
Masherbrum, Kashmir	25,660
Nanda Devi, India	25,645
Rakaposhi, Kashmir	25,550
Kamet, India-Tibet	25,447
Namcha Barwa, Tibet	25,445
Gurla Mandhata, Tibet	25,355
Ulugh Muztagh, Xinjiang, China-Tibet	25,340
Kungur, Xinjiang, China	25,325

Peak, country/region	Height (ft)
Tirich Mir, Pakistan	25,230
Makalu II, Nepal-Tibet	25,120
Minya Konka, China	24,900
Annapurna III, Nepal	24,786
Kula Gangri, Bhutan-Tibet	24,784
Changtse (Everest), Nepal-Tibet	24,780
Muztagh Ata, Xinjiang, China	24,757
Skyang Kangri, Kashmir	24,750
Annapurna IV, Nepal	24,688
Ismail Samani Peak, Tajikistan	24,590
Jongsong Peak, India-Nepal-China	24,472
Jengish Chokusu, Xinjiang, China-Kyrgyzstan	24,406
Sia Kangri, Kashmir	24,350
Haramosh Peak, Pakistan	24,270
Istoro Nal, Pakistan	24,240
Kirat Chuli, India-Nepal	24,165
Chomo Lhari, Bhutan-Tibet	24,040
Chamlang, Nepal	24,012
Kabru, India-Nepal	24,002
Alung Gangri, Tibet	24,000
Baltoro Kangri, Kashmir	23,990
Mana, India	23,860
Baruntse, Nepal	23,688
Nepal Peak, India-Nepal	23,500
Amne Machin, China	23,490
Gauri Sankar, Nepal-Tibet	23,440

Peak, country/region	Height (ft)
Badrinath, India	23,420
Nunkun, Kashmir	23,410
Lenin Peak, Tajikistan	23,406
Pyramid, India-Nepal	23,400
Api, Nepal	23,399
Pauhunri, India-Tibet	23,385
Trisul, India	23,360
Kangto, India-Tibet	23,260
Nyenchen Thanglha, Tibet	23,255
Trisuli, India	23,210
Pumori, Nepal-Tibet	23,190
Dunagiri, India	23,184
Lombo Kangra, Tibet	23,165
Saipal, Nepal	23,100
Macha Pucchare, Nepal	22,958
Khan Tengri, Kazakhstan-Kyrgyzstan-Xinjiang, China	22,949
Numbar, Nepal	22,817
Kanjiroba, Nepal	22,580
Ama Dablam, Nepal	22,350
Cho Polu, Nepal	22,093
Lingtren, Nepal-Tibet	21,972
Khumbutse, Nepal-Tibet	21,785
Hlako Gangri, Tibet	21,266
Grosvenor, China	21,190
Thagchhab Gangri, Tibet	20,970
Damavand, Iran	18,406
Ararat, Turkey	16,854

Antarctica

Peak	Height (ft)
Vinson Massif	16,066
Tyree	15,919
Shinn	15,750
Gardner	15,375
Epperly	15,100
Kirkpatrick	14,855
Elizabeth	14,698
Markham	14,290
Bell	14,117
Mackellar	14,098
Anderson	13,957
Bentley	13,934
Kaplan	13,878
Andrew Jackson	13,750
Sidley	13,720
Ostenso	13,710

Peak	Height (ft)
Minto	13,668
Miller	13,650
Long Gables	13,620
Dickerson	13,517
Giovinetto	13,412
Wade	13,400
Fisher	13,386
Fridtjof Nansen	13,350
Wexler	13,202
Lister	13,200
Shear	13,100
Odishaw	13,008
Donaldson	12,894
Ray	12,808
Sellery	12,779
Waterman	12,730

Peak	Height (ft)
Anne	12,703
Press	12,566
Falla	12,549
Rucker	12,520
Goldthwait	12,510
Morris	12,500
Erebus	12,450
Campbell	12,434
Don Pedro Christophersen	12,355
Lysaght	12,326
Huggins	12,247
Sabine	12,200
Astor	12,175
Mohl	12,172
Frankes	12,064
Jones	12,040

Notable Islands and Their Areas

Figures are for total area in square miles. Boldface figures in parentheses show rank among the world's 10 largest individual islands. Only the largest islands in an island group are shown. Table does not include islands smaller than 10 sq mi in area. Canada's Manitoulin Island (1,068 sq mi), in Lake Huron, is the world's largest island in a freshwater lake.

Antarctica

Adelaide	1,400
Alexander	16,700
Berkner	18,500
Roosevelt	2,900

Arctic Ocean

Amund Ringnes, NU, Can.	2,029
Axel Heiberg, NU, Can.	16,671
Baffin, NU, Can. (5)	195,928
Banks, NT, Can.	27,038
Bathurst, NU, Can.	6,194
Bolshoy Lyakhovsky, Russia	1,776
Borden, NT-NU, Can.	1,079
Bylot, NU, Can.	4,273
Coats, NU, Can.	2,123
Cornwallis, NU, Can.	2,701
Devon, NU, Can.	21,331
Disko, Greenland, Denmark	3,312
Ellef Ringnes, NU, Can.	4,361
Ellesmere, NU, Can. (10)	75,767
Faddayevskiy, Russia	1,930
Franz Josef Land, Russia	8,000
Iturup (Etorofu), Russia	2,596
King William, NU, Can.	5,062
Kotelny, Russia	4,504
Mackenzie King, NT, Can.	1,949
Melville, NT-NU, Can.	16,274
Milne Land, Greenland, Den.	1,400
New Siberian Isls., Russia	14,500
Novaya Zemlya, Russia (2 isls.)	31,730
Prince Charles, NT, Can.	3,676
Prince Patrick, NT, Can.	6,119
Prince of Wales, NU, Can.	12,872
Severnaya Zemlya, Russia (tot. group)	14,175
Bol'shevik	4,368
Komsomolets	3,477
Oktyabr'skoy Revolyutsii	5,471
Somerset, NU, Can.	9,570
Southampton, NU, Can.	15,913
Svalbard, Norway (tot. group)	23,561
Nordaustlandet	5,410
Spitsbergen	14,546
Traill, Greenland, Denmark	1,300
Victoria, NT-NU, Can. (8)	83,897
Wrangel, Russia	2,800

Atlantic Ocean

Anticosti, QC, Can.	3,066
Ascension, UK	35
Azores, Portugal (tot. group)	868
Faial	67
San Miguel	291
Bahama Isls. (tot. group)	5,382
Andros	2,300
Bermuda Isls., UK (tot. group)	21
Bioko Isl., Equatorial Guinea	785
Block Island, RI, U.S.	21
Cabo Verde	1,557
Canary Isls., Spain (tot. group)	2,807
Fuerteventura	688
Gran Canaria	592
Tenerife	795
Cape Breton, NS, Can.	3,981
Caviana, Pará, Brazil	1,918
Channel Isls., UK (tot. group)	75
Guernsey	24
Jersey	45
Falkland Isls., UK (tot. group)	4,700
East Falkland	2,550
West Falkland	1,750
Faroe Isls., Denmark	539
Great Britain, UK (9)	80,823
Greenland, Denmark (1)	836,330
Gurupá, Pará, Brazil	1,878
Hebrides, Scotland, UK	2,744
Iceland	39,938
Ireland, Ireland-UK	32,589
Isle of Man, UK	221
Isle of Wight, England, UK	147
Long Island, NY, U.S.	1,320
Madeira Islands, Portugal	306
Marajo, Brazil	15,444
Martha's Vineyard, MA, U.S.	89

Atlantic Ocean (cont.)

Mount Desert, ME, U.S.	104
Nantucket, MA, U.S.	45
Newfoundland, Canada	42,031
Orkney Isls., Scotland, UK	383
Prince Edward Isl. (main), Can.	2,170
St. Helena, UK	47
Shetland Isls., Scotland, UK	555
Skye, Scotland, UK	647
South Georgia, UK	1,450
Tierra del Fuego, Chile-Arg.	18,800
Tristan da Cunha, UK	38

Baltic Sea

Aland Isls., Finland	610
Bornholm, Denmark	228
Funen, Denmark	1,154
Gotland, Sweden	1,159
Zealand, Denmark	2,722

Caribbean Sea

Antigua	108
Aruba, Netherlands	69
Barbados	166
Cuba	42,804
Isle of Youth	926
Cayman Isls., UK	100
Curaçao, Netherlands	171
Dominica	290
Guadeloupe, France	687
Hispaniola (Haiti and Dominican Rep.)	29,389
Jamaica	4,244
Martinique, France	436
Puerto Rico, U.S.	3,425
Tobago	116
Trinidad	1,864
Virgin Isls., UK	59
Virgin Isls., U.S.	134

East Indies

Bali, Indonesia	2,171
Bangka, Indonesia	4,375
Borneo, Indonesia-Malaysia-Brunei (3)	290,321
Bougainville, Papua New Guinea	3,880
Buru, Indonesia	3,670
Celebes, Indonesia	69,000
Flores, Indonesia	5,500
Halmahera, Indonesia	6,865
Java (Jawa), Indonesia	48,900
Madura, Indonesia	2,113
Moluccas, Indonesia	32,307
New Britain, Papua New Guinea	14,093
New Guinea, Indon.-PNG (2)	303,381
New Ireland, PNG.	3,707
Seram, Indonesia	6,621
Sumatra, Indonesia (6)	182,543
Sumba, Indonesia	4,306
Sumbawa, Indonesia	5,965
Timor, Indon.–Timor-Leste	13,094
Yos Sudarsa, Indonesia	4,500

Indian Ocean

Andaman Isls., India	2,500
Kerguelen, France	2,247
Madagascar (4)	226,917
Mauritius	720
Pemba, Tanzania	380
Réunion, France	970
Seychelles	176
Sri Lanka	25,332
Zanzibar, Tanzania	640

Mediterranean Sea

Balearic Isls., Spain	1,927
Corfu, Greece	229
Corsica, France	3,369
Crete, Greece	3,189
Cyprus	3,572
Elba, Italy	86
Euboea, Greece	1,411
Malta	95
Rhodes, Greece	540
Sardinia, Italy	9,301
Sicily, Italy	9,926

Pacific Ocean

Admiralty, AK, U.S.	1,709
Aleutian Isls., AK, U.S. (tot. group)	6,912
Adak	275
Amchitka	116
Attu	350
Kanaga	142
Kiska	106
Tanaga	195
Umnak	686
Unalaska	1,051
Unimak	1,571
Baranof, AK, U.S.	1,636
Chichagof, AK, U.S.	2,062
Chiloe, Chile	3,241
Diomede (Big), Russia	11
Easter Isl. (Rapa Nui), Chile	63
Fiji (tot. group)	7,056
Vanua Levu	2,242
Viti Levu	4,109
Galapagos Isls., Ecuador	3,043
Graham Isl., BC, Can.	2,456
Guadalcanal, Solomon Isls.	2,180
Guam, U.S.	210
Hainan, China	13,000
Hawaiian Isls., HI, U.S. (tot. group)	6,428
Hawaii	4,028
Oahu	597
Hong Kong, China	31
Hoste, Chile	1,590
Japan (tot. group)	145,931
Hokkaido	30,110
Honshu (7)	88,022
Kyushu	14,190
Okinawa	466
Shikoku	7,066
Kangaroo, South Australia	1,705
Kiritimati (Christmas), Kiribati	150
Kodiak, AK, U.S.	3,485
Kupreanof, AK, U.S.	1,084
Marquesas Isls., France	492
Marshall Islands	70
Melville, Northern Terr., Australia	2,234
Micronesia	271
New Caledonia, France	6,530
New Zealand (tot. group)	103,362
Chatham Isls.	372
North	44,075
South	58,076
Stewart	649
Northern Mariana Isls., U.S.	179
Nunivak, AK, U.S.	1,600
Palau	188
Philippines (tot. group)	115,831
Leyte	2,787
Luzon	40,680
Mindanao	36,775
Mindoro	3,690
Negros	4,907
Palawan	4,554
Panay	4,446
Samar	5,050
Prince of Wales, AK, U.S.	2,770
Revillagigedo, AK, U.S.	1,134
Riesco, Chile	1,973
St. Lawrence, AK, U.S.	1,780
Sakhalin, Russia	29,500
Samoa Isls. (tot. group)	1,177
American Samoa, U.S.	77
Savaii, Samoa	659
Tutuila, U.S.	55
Upolu, Samoa	432
Santa Catalina, CA, U.S.	75
Santa Ines, Chile	1,407
Tahiti, France	402
Taiwan (tot. group)	13,892
Jinmen Dao (Quemoy)	56
Tasmania, Australia	26,178
Tonga	288
Vancouver Isl., BC, Can.	12,079
Vanuatu	4,707
Wellington, Chile	2,549

Persian Gulf

Bahrain	295

Notable Deserts of the World

Deserts are defined as regions of the Earth receiving less than 10 in. of precipitation annually, usually in combination with an evaporation rate exceeding precipitation.

In addition to areas listed below, the continent of Antarctica, with an area of about 5.4 mil sq mi (roughly doubled by ice in winter), is generally considered a desert. Annual precipitation averages 8 in. along the coast and far less in the deep interior; however, there is little evaporation.

Arabian (Eastern), 86,000 sq mi in Egypt between the Nile R. and Red Sea, extending S into Sudan
Atacama, 600-mi-long area rich in nitrate and copper deposits in northern Chile
Chihuahuan, 140,000 sq mi in TX, NM, AZ, and Mexico
Dasht-e Kavir, approx. 500 mi long by 200 mi wide in north-central Iran
Dasht-e Lut, approx. 300 mi long by 200 mi wide in south-central Iran
Death Valley, 3,300 sq mi in CA and NV
Gibson, 120,000 sq mi in the interior of western Australia
Gobi, 500,000 sq mi in Mongolia and China
Great Sandy, 103,186 sq mi in western Australia
Great Victoria, 134,653 sq mi in southwestern Australia
Kalahari, 275,000 sq mi in southern Africa
Kara Kum, 115,000 sq mi in Turkmenistan
Kyzyl Kum, 115,000 sq mi in Kazakhstan and Uzbekistan
Libyan, 425,000 sq mi in the Sahara, extending from Libya through southwestern Egypt into Sudan

Mojave, 15,000 sq mi in southern CA
Namib, long narrow area (varies 30-100 mi wide) extending 800 mi along SW coast of Africa
Nubian, 157,000 sq mi in the Sahara in northeastern Sudan
Painted Desert, section of high plateau in northern AZ extending 200 mi SE from Grand Canyon
Patagonia, 300,000 sq mi in southern Argentina
Rub al-Khali (Empty Quarter), 225,000 sq mi in the S Arabian Peninsula
Sahara, 3,500,000 sq mi in N Africa, extending W to the Atlantic. Largest desert in the world
Sonoran, 70,000 sq mi in southwestern AZ and southeastern CA extending into NW Mexico
Syrian, 100,000-sq-mi area extending over much of northern Saudi Arabia, eastern Jordan, southern Syria, and western Iraq
Taklamakan, 140,000 sq mi in Xinjiang Prov., China
Thar (Great Indian), 100,000-sq-mi area extending 400 mi along India-Pakistan border

Areas and Average Depths of Oceans, Seas, and Gulfs

Geographers and mapmakers recognize at least four major bodies of water: the Pacific, Atlantic, Indian, and Arctic Oceans. The Atlantic and Pacific Oceans are considered divided at the equator into the N and S Atlantic and the N and S Pacific. The Arctic Ocean is the name for waters north of the continental landmasses in the region of the Arctic Circle. The International Hydrographic Organization delimited a fifth world ocean in 2000. The Southern Ocean extends from the coast of Antarctica north to 60°S latitude, encompassing portions of the Atlantic, Indian, and Pacific Oceans.

Body of water	Area (sq mi)	Avg. depth (ft)	Body of water	Area (sq mi)	Avg. depth (ft)
Pacific Ocean	60,060,869	14,040	Sea of Japan	391,100	5,468
Atlantic Ocean	29,637,962	11,810	Hudson Bay	281,900	305
Indian Ocean	26,469,609	12,800	East China Sea	256,600	620
Southern Ocean	7,848,295	14,450	Andaman Sea	218,100	3,667
Arctic Ocean	5,427,050	4,300	Black Sea	196,100	3,906
South China Sea	1,148,500	4,802	Red Sea	174,900	1,764
Caribbean Sea	971,400	8,448	North Sea	164,900	308
Mediterranean Sea	969,100	4,926	Baltic Sea	147,500	180
Bering Sea	873,000	4,893	Yellow Sea	113,500	121
Gulf of Mexico	582,100	5,297	Persian Gulf	88,800	328
Sea of Okhotsk	537,500	3,192	Gulf of California	59,100	2,375

Principal Ocean Depths

Source: National Geospatial-Intelligence Agency, U.S. Dept. of Defense

Body of water	Location (lat.)	Location (long.)	Depth (meters)	Depth (fathoms)	(feet)
Pacific Ocean					
Mariana Trench	11°22′ N	142°36′ E	10,994	6,012	36,069
Tonga Trench	23°16′ S	174°44′ W	10,800	5,906	35,433
Philippine Trench	10°38′ N	126°36′ E	10,057	5,499	32,995
Kermadec Trench	31°53′ S	177°21′ W	10,047	5,494	32,963
Bonin Trench	24°30′ N	143°24′ E	9,994	5,464	32,788
Kuril Trench	44°15′ N	150°34′ E	9,750	5,331	31,988
Izu Trench	31°05′ N	142°10′ E	9,695	5,301	31,808
New Britain Trench	06°19′ S	153°45′ E	8,940	4,888	29,331
Yap Trench	08°33′ N	138°02′ E	8,527	4,663	27,976
Japan Trench	36°08′ N	142°43′ E	8,412	4,600	27,599
Peru-Chile Trench	23°18′ S	71°14′ W	8,064	4,409	26,457
Palau Trench	07°52′ N	134°56′ E	8,054	4,404	26,424
Aleutian Trench	50°51′ N	177°11′ E	7,679	4,199	25,194
New Hebrides Trench	20°36′ S	168°37′ E	7,570	4,139	24,836
North Ryukyu Trench	24°00′ N	126°48′ E	7,181	3,927	23,560
Middle America Trench	14°02′ N	93°39′ W	6,662	3,643	21,857
Atlantic Ocean					
Puerto Rico Trench	19°55′ N	65°27′ W	8,605	4,705	28,232
South Sandwich Trench	55°42′ S	25°56′ W	8,325	4,552	27,313
Romanche Gap	0°13′ S	18°26′ W	7,728	4,226	25,354
Cayman Trench	19°12′ N	80°00′ W	7,535	4,120	24,721
Brazil Basin	09°10′ S	23°02′ W	6,119	3,346	20,076
Indian Ocean					
Java Trench	10°19′ S	109°58′ E	7,125	3,896	23,376
Ob' Trench	09°45′ S	67°18′ E	6,874	3,759	22,553
Diamantina Trench	35°50′ S	105°14′ E	6,602	3,610	21,660
Vema Trench	09°08′ S	67°15′ E	6,402	3,501	21,004
Agulhas Basin	45°20′ S	26°50′ E	6,195	3,387	20,325
Arctic Ocean					
Eurasia Basin	82°23′ N	19°31′ E	5,450	2,980	17,881
Mediterranean Sea					
Ionian Basin	36°32′ N	21°06′ E	5,150	2,816	16,896

Note: Greater depths have been reported in some areas but have not been officially confirmed by research vessels.

Major World Rivers

North American rivers are listed in a separate table.

River	Source or upper limit of length	Outflow	Length (mi)
Africa			
Chari	Bamingui-Bangoran region, Central African Republic	Lake Chad	650
Congo	Junction of Lualaba and Luvua Rivers, Dem. Rep. of Congo	Atlantic Ocean	2,720
Cubango (fmr. Okavango)	Central Angola	Okavango Delta	1,000
Gambia	Fouta Djallon, Guinea	Atlantic Ocean	700
Kasai	Central Angola	Congo River	1,100
Limpopo	Junction of Marico and Ngotwane Rivers, South Africa	Indian Ocean	1,100
Lualaba	Southeastern Dem. Rep. of Congo	Congo River	1,100
Niger	Fouta Djallon, Guinea	Gulf of Guinea	2,600
Nile	Luvironza River, Burundi	Mediterranean Sea	4,160
Orange	Maluti Mountains, northern Lesotho	Atlantic Ocean	1,300
Sénégal	Junction of Bafing and Bakoy Rivers, Mali	Atlantic Ocean	1,000
Ubangi	Junction of Uele and Bomu Rivers, Dem. Rep. of Congo	Congo River	700
Zambezi	Northwestern Zambia	Indian Ocean	1,700
Asia			
Amu Darya	Junction of Wakhsh and Panj Rivers, Tajikistan	Aral Sea	1,660
Amur	Junction of Shilka and Argun Rivers, China-Russia	Tartar Strait	1,780
Angara	Lake Baykal, Russia	Yenisei River	1,150
Ayeyarwady (fmr. Irrawaddy)	Junction of Mali and Nmai Rivers, Myanmar	Andaman Sea	1,000
Brahmaputra	Kailas Range, Himalayas, southwestern Tibet	Bay of Bengal	1,800
Chang-Jiang	Tibetan Plateau, southwestern Qinghai, China	East China Sea	3,450
Euphrates	Junction of Kara (Sarasu) and Murat Rivers, Turkey	Shatt al-Arab	1,700
Ganges	Gangotri glacier, Himalayas, India	Bay of Bengal	1,560
Godavari	Western Ghats, Maharashtra, India	Bay of Bengal	900
Hsi (see Xi He)			
Huang-He	Kunlun Mountains, Qinghai, China	Yellow Sea	3,000
Indus	Kailas Range, Himalayas, Tibet	Arabian Sea	1,900
Irtysh	Kazakhstan-Russia	Ob River	2,650
Jordan	Junction of Dan, Banias, and Hazbani streams, Israel	Dead Sea	200
Kolyma	Kolyma and Cherskogo Ranges, Russia	Arctic Ocean	1,500
Krishna	Western Ghats, Maharashtra, India	Bay of Bengal	800
Kura	Northeastern Turkey	Caspian Sea	950
Lena	Western Baikal Range, Russia	Laptev Sea	2,648
Mekong	Eastern Tibetan Plateau, China	South China Sea	2,700
Narmada	Madhya Pradesh, India	Arabian Sea	775
Ob	Junction of Biya and Katun Rivers, Russia	Gulf of Ob	2,300
Salween	Eastern Tibet, China	Gulf of Martaban	1,750
Songhua Jiang	Changbai Mountains, Jilin, China	Amur River	1,150
Sungari (see Songhua Jiang)			
Sutlej	Kailas Range, Himalayas, Tibet	Indus River	900
Syr	Junction of Naryn and Kara Darya Rivers, Uzbekistan	Aral Sea	1,380
Tarim	Junction of Kashi and Yarkant Rivers, China	Lop Nor	1,300
Tigris	Taurus Mountains, Turkey	Shatt al-Arab	1,150
Xi He	Eastern Yunnan, China	South China Sea	1,250
Yamuna	Uttarakhand, India	Ganges River	850
Yangtze (see Chang-Jiang)			
Yellow (see Huang-He)			
Yenisei	Kyzyl, Tuva Republic, Russia	Kara Sea	2,500
Australia			
Darling	Eastern Highlands, NE New South Wales/SE Queensland	Murray River	1,702
Murray	Australian Alps, SE New South Wales	Southern Ocean	1,558
Murrumbidgee	Australian Alps, SE New South Wales	Murray River	923
Europe			
Buh, Southern	NW of Khmel'nyts'kyy, Ukraine	Black Sea	532
Buh, Western	ENE of Zolochiv, Ukraine	Wisla River	500
Danube	Brege and Brigach Rivers, Black Forest, southwestern Germany	Black Sea	1,770
Dnieper	W of Sychevka, Smolensk, Russia	Black Sea	1,420
Dniester	Carpathian Mountains, Ukraine	Black Sea	850
Don	SE of Tula, Russia	Sea of Azov	1,200
Drava	Carnic Alps, northern Italy	Danube River	450
Dvina, North	Near Veliki Ustyug, Vologda, Russia	White Sea	465
Dvina, West	Valdai Hills, Russia	Gulf of Riga	635
Ebro	Cantabrian Mountains, northern Spain	Mediterranean Sea	575
Elbe	Giant Mountains, northwestern Czech Republic	North Sea	725
Garonne	Central Pyrenees, Spain	Bay of Biscay	402
Kama	Ural Mountains, N of Kuliga, Russia	Volga River	1,260
Loire	Mt. Gerbier-de-Jonc, Vivrais Mountains, France	Atlantic Ocean	630
Marne	Langres Plateau, northeastern France	Seine River	325
Meuse	Langres Plateau, northeastern France	North Sea	560
Oder	Sudetes Mountains, northeastern Czech Republic	Baltic Sea	562
Oka	S of Orël, Russia	Volga River	925
Pechora	Northern Ural Mountains, Russia	Barents Sea	1,120
Po	Cottian Alps, Piedmont, northwestern Italy	Adriatic Sea	405
Rhine	Swiss Alps	North Sea	820

River	Source or upper limit of length	Outflow	Length (mi)
Rhône	Rhône glacier, northeastern Valais, Switzerland	Mediterranean Sea	505
Seine	Langres Plateau, northern Burgundy, France	English Channel	480
Shannon	Near Cuilcagh Mountain, northwestern Cavan County, Ireland	Atlantic Ocean	240
Tagus	E of Madrid, Spain	Atlantic Ocean	585
Thames	4 headstreams in the Cotswold Hills, Gloucestershire, England, UK	North Sea	215
Tiber	Etruscan Apennines, Italy	Tyrrhenian Sea	251
Tisza	N of Rakhiv, western Ukraine	Danube River	700
Ural	Southern Ural Mountains, northeastern Bashkortostan, Russia	Caspian Sea	1,580
Volga	Valdai Hills, Smolensk, Russia	Caspian Sea	2,290
Weser	Junction of Fulda and Werra Rivers, Germany	North Sea	273
Wisla	W Beskid range, Carpathian Mountains, southwestern Poland	Gulf of Gdansk	665

South America

River	Source or upper limit of length	Outflow	Length (mi)
Amazon	Junction of Ucayali and Marañón Rivers, Andes Mountains, Peru	Atlantic Ocean	3,900
Araguaía	Serra das Araras, Goiás-Mato Grosso, Brazil	Tocantins River	1,100
Beni	Cordillera Real, La Paz, Bolivia	Madeira River	1,000
Caquetá-Japura	Andes Mountains, southwestern Colombia	Amazon River	1,750
Juruá	Cerros de Canchyuaya, eastern Peru	Amazon River	1,500
Madeira	Junction of Beni and Mamoré Rivers, Bolivia	Amazon River	2,100
Magdalena	Cordillera Central, southwestern Colombia	Caribbean Sea	1,000
Negro	Southeastern Colombia	Amazon River	1,400
Orinoco	Near Mt. Delgado Chalbaud, Guiana Highlands, S Venezuela	Atlantic Ocean	1,600
Paraguay	Central Mato Grosso highlands, Brazil	Paraná River	1,584
Paraná	Junction of Paranaíba and Rio Grande Rivers, SE Brazil	Rio de la Plata	2,485
Pilcomayo	E of Lake Poopó, Bolivia	Paraguay River	1,000
Purus	Andes Mountains, eastern Peru	Amazon River	2,100
Putumayo	Andes Mountains, southern Colombia	Amazon River	1,000
Rio de la Plata	Estuary of Paraná and Uruguay Rivers, Argentina-Uruguay	Atlantic Ocean	170
São Francisco	Serra de Canastra, southwestern Minas Gerais, Brazil	Atlantic Ocean	1,800
Tocantins	South-central Goiás, Brazil	Para River	1,640
Ucayali	Junction of Apurímac and Urubamba Rivers, eastern Peru	Marañón River	1,000
Uruguay	Southern Brazil	Rio de la Plata	1,000
Xingu	Central Mato Grosso, Brazil	Amazon River	1,230

Major Rivers in North America

River	Source or upper limit of length	Outflow	Length (mi)
Alabama	Gilmer County, GA	Mobile River	729
Albany	Lake St. Joseph, ON, Can.	James Bay	610
Allegheny	Potter County, PA.	Ohio River	325
Altamaha-Ocmulgee	Junction of Yellow and South Rivers, Newton Co., GA	Atlantic Ocean	392
Apalachicola-Chattahoochee	Towns County, GA	Gulf of Mexico	524
Arkansas	Lake County, CO	Mississippi River	1,459
Assiniboine	Eastern Saskatchewan, Can.	Red River	450
Attawapiskat	Attawapiskat, ON, Can.	James Bay	465
Back (NT)	Contwoyto Lake, NT, Can.	Chantrey Inlet, Arctic Ocean	605
Big Black	Webster County, MS	Mississippi River	330
Brazos	Junction of Salt and Double Mountain Forks, Stonewall Co., TX.	Gulf of Mexico	1,280
Canadian	Las Animas County, CO	Arkansas River	906
Cedar (IA)	Dodge County, MN	Iowa River	329
Cheyenne	Junction of Antelope Creek and Dry Fork, Converse Co., WY	Missouri River	290
Churchill, Labrador	Lake Ashuanipi, NL, Can.	Atlantic Ocean	532
Churchill, Manitoba	Methy Lake, SK, Can.	Hudson Bay	1,000
Cimarron	Colfax County, NM	Arkansas River	600
Colorado (AZ)	Rocky Mountain Natl. Park, CO	Gulf of California	1,450
Colorado (TX)	Dawson County, TX	Matagorda Bay	862
Columbia	Columbia Lake, BC, Can.	Pacific Ocean, bet. OR and WA	1,243
Columbia, Upper	Columbia Lake, BC, Can.	Mouth of Snake River	890
Connecticut	Third Connecticut Lake, NH	Long Island Sound, CT	407
Coppermine	Lac de Gras, NT, Can.	Coronation Gulf, Arctic Ocean	525
Cumberland	Letcher County, KY	Ohio River	720
Delaware	Schoharie County, NY	Liston Point, Delaware Bay	390
Fraser	Near Mount Robson (on Continental Divide)	Strait of Georgia	850
Gila	Catron County, NM	Colorado River	649
Green (UT-WY)	Junction of Wells and Trail Creeks, Sublette County, WY	Colorado River	730
Hudson	Henderson Lake, Essex County, NY	Upper New York Bay	306
Illinois	St. Joseph County, IN.	Mississippi River	420
James (ND-SD)	Wells County, ND	Missouri River	710
James (VA)	Junction of Jackson and Cowpasture Rivers, Botetourt Co., VA	Hampton Roads	340
Kanawha-New	Junction of North and South Forks of New River, NC	Ohio River	352
Kentucky	Junction of North and Middle Forks, Lee County, KY	Ohio River	259
Klamath	Lake Ewauna, Klamath Falls, OR.	Pacific Ocean	250

River	Source or upper limit of length	Outflow	Length (mi)
Kootenay	Kootenay Lake, BC, Can.	Columbia River	485
Koyukuk	Endicott Mountains, AK	Yukon River	470
Kuskokwim	Alaska Range	Kuskokwim Bay	724
Liard	Southern Yukon, AK	Mackenzie River	693
Little Missouri	Crook County, WY	Missouri River	560
Mackenzie	Great Slave Lake, NT, Can.	Arctic Ocean	2,635
Milk	Junction of North and South Forks, AB, Can.	Missouri River	625
Minnesota	Big Stone Lake, MN	Mississippi River	332
Mississippi	Lake Itasca, Clearwater County, MN	Gulf of Mexico	2,340
Mississippi-Missouri-Red Rock	Source of Red Rock, Beaverhead County, MT	Gulf of Mexico	3,710
Missouri	Junction of Jefferson, Madison, and Gallatin Rivers, Gallatin County, MT	Mississippi River	2,315
Missouri-Red Rock	Source of Red Rock, Beaverhead County, MT	Mississippi River	2,540
Mobile-Alabama-Coosa	Gilmer County, GA	Mobile Bay	774
Nelson	Lake Winnipeg, MB, Can.	Hudson Bay	410
Neosho	Morris County, KS	Arkansas River, OK	460
Niobrara	Niobrara County, WY	Missouri River, NE	431
North Canadian	Union County, NM	Canadian River, OK	800
North Platte	Junction of Grizzly and Little Grizzly Creeks, Jackson Co., CO	Platte River, NE	618
Ohio	Junction of Allegheny and Monongahela Rivers, Pittsburgh, PA	Mississippi River	981
Ohio-Allegheny	Potter County, PA.	Mississippi River	1,310
Osage	East-central Kansas	Missouri River	500
Ottawa	Lake Capimitchigama, QC, Can.	St. Lawrence River	790
Ouachita	Polk County, AR	Black River	605
Peace	Junction of Finlay and Parsnip Rivers, BC, Can.	Slave River	1,210
Pearl	Neshoba County, MS	Gulf of Mexico	411
Pecos	Mora County, NM	Rio Grande	926
Pee Dee-Yadkin	Watauga County, NC	Winyah Bay	435
Pend Oreille-Clark Fork	Near Butte, MT	Columbia River	531
Platte	Junction of North Platte and South Platte Rivers, NE.	Missouri River	310
Porcupine	Ogilvie Mountains, AK	Yukon River, AK	569
Potomac	Garrett County, MD	Chesapeake Bay	383
Powder	Junction of South and Middle Forks, WY	Yellowstone River	375
Red (River of the South)	Curry County, NM.	Atchafalaya River, LA	1,290
Red River of the North	Junction of Otter Tail and Bois de Sioux Rivers, Wilkin Co., MN	Lake Winnipeg	545
Republican	Junction of North Fork and Arikaree Rivers, NE.	Kansas River	445
Rio Grande (Rio Bravo)	San Juan County, CO.	Gulf of Mexico	1,900
Roanoke	Junction of North and South Forks, Montgomery Co., VA	Albemarle Sound	380
Rock (IL-WI)	Dodge County, WI	Mississippi River	300
Sabine	Junction of South and Caddo Forks, Hunt Co., TX	Sabine Lake	380
Sacramento	Siskiyou County, CA.	Suisun Bay	377
St. Francis	Iron County, MO.	Mississippi River	425
St. John	Northwestern Maine	Bay of Fundy	418
St. Lawrence	Lake Ontario, ON-NY	Gulf of St. Lawrence, Atlantic Ocean	800
Saguenay	Lake St. John, QC, Can.	St. Lawrence River	434
Salmon (ID)	Custer County, ID.	Snake River	420
San Joaquin	Junction of South and Middle Forks, Madera Co., CA	Suisun Bay	350
San Juan	Silver Lake, Archuleta County, CO.	Colorado River	360
Santee-Wateree-Catawba	McDowell County, NC	Atlantic Ocean	538
Saskatchewan, North	Rocky Mountains, AB, Can.	Saskatchewan R.	800
Saskatchewan, South	Rocky Mountains, AB, Can.	Saskatchewan R.	865
Savannah	Junction of Seneca and Tugaloo Rivers, Anderson Co., SC	Atlantic Ocean, GA-SC	314
Severn (ON)	Sandy Lake, ON, Can.	Hudson Bay	610
Smoky Hill	Cheyenne County, CO	Kansas River, KS	540
Snake	Teton County, WY	Columbia River, WA	1,038
South Platte	Junction of South and Middle Forks, Park County, CO	Platte River	424
Susitna	Alaska Range	Cook Inlet	313
Susquehanna	Otsego Lake, Otsego County, NY	Chesapeake Bay	447
Tallahatchie	Tippah County, MS.	Yazoo River	301
Tanana	Wrangell Mountains, AK	Yukon River	659
Tennessee	Junction of French Broad and Holston Rivers, TN	Ohio River	652
Tennessee-French Broad	Courthouse Creek, Transylvania County, NC	Ohio River	886
Tombigbee	Prentiss County, MS.	Mobile River	525
Trinity	N of Dallas, TX	Galveston Bay	360
Usumacinta	Junction of Pasión and Chixoy Rivers, Guatemala	Bay of Campeche, Mex.	600
Wabash	Darke County, OH	Ohio River	512
Washita	Hemphill County, TX.	Red River, OK	500
White (AR-MO)	Madison County, AR.	Mississippi River	722
Willamette	Douglas County, OR.	Columbia River	309
Wind-Bighorn	Junction of Wind and Little Wind Rivers, Fremont Co., WY (source of Wind R. is Togwotee Pass, Teton Co., WY)	Yellowstone River	338
Wisconsin	Lac Vieux Desert, Vilas County, WI	Mississippi River	430
Yellowstone	Park County, WY	Missouri River	682
Yukon	McNeil River, YT, Can.	Bering Sea	1,979

Major Natural Lakes of the World

Source: U.S. Geological Survey, U.S. Dept. of the Interior; Natural Resources Canada

A lake is generally defined as a body of water surrounded by land. By this definition some bodies of water that are called seas, such as the Caspian Sea and the Aral Sea, are really lakes. In the following table, the word "lake" is omitted when it is part of the name.

Name	Continent	Area (sq mi)	Length (mi)	Maximum depth (ft)	Elevation (ft)
Caspian Sea[1]	Asia-Europe	143,244	760	3,363	−92
Superior	North America	31,700	350	1,330	600
Victoria	Africa	26,828	250	270	3,720
Huron	North America	23,000	206	750	579
Michigan	North America	22,300	307	923	579
Aral Sea[1]	Asia	13,000[2]	260	180	125
Tanganyika	Africa	12,700	420	4,823	2,534
Baykal	Asia	12,162	395	5,315	1,493
Great Bear	North America	12,096	192	1,463	512
Nyasa (Malawi)	Africa	11,150	360	2,280	1,550
Great Slave	North America	11,030	298	2,014	512
Erie	North America	9,910	241	210	570
Winnipeg	North America	9,416	266	200	712
Ontario	North America	7,340	193	802	245
Balkhash[1]	Asia	7,115	376	85	1,115
Ladoga	Europe	6,835	124	738	13
Maracaibo	South America	5,217	133	115	sea level
Onega	Europe	3,710	145	328	108
Eyre[1]	Australia	3,600[3]	90	4	−52
Titicaca	South America	3,200	122	922	12,500
Nicaragua	North America	3,100	102	230	102
Athabasca	North America	3,064	208	407	699
Reindeer	North America	2,568	143	720	1,106
Tonle Sap	Asia	2,500[3]	70	45	NA
Turkana (Rudolf)	Africa	2,473	154	240	1,230
Issyk Kul[1]	Asia	2,355	115	2,303	5,279
Torrens[1]	Australia	2,230[3]	130	(3)	92
Vänern	Europe	2,181	91	328	144
Nettilling	North America	2,140	67	(3)	98
Winnipegosis	North America	2,075	141	38	833
Albert	Africa	2,075	100	168	2,030
Nipigon	North America	1,872	72	540	853
Gairdner[1]	Australia	1,840[3]	90	(3)	112
Urmia[1]	Asia	1,815	90	49	4,180
Manitoba	North America	1,799	140	21	813
Chad	Africa	500+[4]	175	24	787

NA = Not available. (1) Salt lake. (2) The diversion of feeder rivers since the 1960s has devastated the Aral—once the world's fourth-largest lake (26,000 sq mi). By 2000, the Aral had effectively become three lakes, with the total area shown. (3) Subject to great seasonal variation. (4) Once fourth-largest lake in Africa (about 10,000 sq mi in the 1960s), Chad had shrunk to around 5% of its original size by 2006 as a result of irrigation and long-term drought.

The Great Lakes

Source: National Ocean Service, National Oceanic and Atmospheric Administration, U.S. Dept. of Commerce

The Great Lakes form the world's **largest freshwater body** (in surface area) and with their connecting waterways are the largest inland water transportation unit. Draining the north-central basin of the U.S., they enable shipping to get to the Atlantic via their outlet, the St. Lawrence R.; the Gulf of Mexico can be reached via the Illinois Waterway, between Lake Michigan and the Mississippi R. A third outlet connects with the Hudson R. and then the Atlantic via the New York State Barge Canal System. Illinois Waterway and NYS Barge Canal System traffic is limited to recreational boating and small shipping vessels.

Only Lake Michigan is wholly in the U.S.; the other lakes are shared with Canada. Ships move from the shores of Lake Superior to Whitefish Bay in the east, then through the Soo Locks in Sault Ste. Marie, MI, onto St. Mary's R. and into Lake Huron. To reach the Port of Indiana-Burns Harbor and South Chicago, IL, ships travel west from Lake Huron to Lake Michigan through the Straits of Mackinac. Low water datum is based on the International Great Lakes Datum (1985), with Rimouski, Quebec, as the reference zero point. The distance between Duluth, MN, and Lake Ontario's east end is 1,156 mi.

	Superior	Michigan	Huron	Erie	Ontario
Length (mi)	350	307	206	241	193
Breadth (mi)	160	118	183	57	53
Deepest soundings (ft)	1,333	923	750	210	802
Volume of water (cu mi)	2,935	1,180	850	116	393
Area (sq mi) water surface—U.S.	20,600	22,300	9,100	4,980	3,460
Canada	11,100	NA	13,900	4,930	3,880
Area (sq mi) entire drainage basin—U.S.	16,900	45,600	16,200	18,000	15,200
Canada	32,400	NA	35,500	4,720	12,100
Total area (sq mi), U.S. and Canada	**81,000**	**67,900**	**74,700**	**32,630**	**34,850**
Low water datum above mean water level at Rimouski, QC, avg. level (ft)	601.10	577.50	577.50	569.20	243.30
Latitude, N	46°25´	41°37´	43°00´	41°23´	43°11´
	49°00´	46°06´	46°17´	42°52´	44°15´
Longitude, W	84°22´	84°45´	79°43´	78°51´	76°03´
	92°06´	88°02´	84°45´	83°29´	79°53´
National boundary line (mi)	282.8	NA	260.8	251.5	174.6
U.S. shoreline (mainland only) (mi)	863	1,400	580	431	300

NA = Not applicable.

Notable Waterfalls

Source: National Geographic Society

The Earth has thousands of waterfalls, some of considerable magnitude. Magnitude is determined not only by height but also by volume of flow, steadiness of flow, crest width, whether the water drops sheerly or over a sloping surface, and whether it descends in one leap or a succession of leaps. A series of low falls flowing over a considerable distance is known as a cascade. Waterfalls are highly variable and few authoritative figures exist. For more information and some alternative measurements, see the World Waterfall Database at www.worldwaterfalldatabase.com.

Estimated mean annual flow (ft³/sec) of major waterfalls: Niagara, 212,200; Paulo Afonso, 100,000; Iguazú, 61,000; Victoria, 35,400; and Kaieteur, 23,400.

Height is total drop in feet in one or more leaps. If river name is not shown, it is the same as the waterfall. # = more than one leap; * = diminishes greatly seasonally; ** = reduces to a trickle or is dry for part of each year; R. = river; (C) = cascade.

Name, location	Height (ft)
Africa	
Angola	
Ruacana, Cunene R.	406
Lesotho	
Maletsunyane*	630
South Africa	
Augrabies, Orange R.*	480
Tugela#.	2,800
Tanzania-Zambia	
Kalambo*	704
Zimbabwe-Zambia	
Victoria, Zambezi R.*	343
Asia and Oceania	
Australia	
New South Wales	
Wentworth	614
Wollomombi	722
Queensland	
Tully**	984
Wallaman, Stony Creek#	1,137
India	
Sivasamudram	320
Jog, Sharavati R.*	830
Japan	
Kegon, Lake Chuzenji*	350
New Zealand	
Helena	722
Sutherland, Arthur R.#	1,904
Europe	
Austria	
Gastein#	487
Krimml#	1,246
France	
Gavarnie*	1,385
Italy	
Toce (C)	470
Norway	
Mardalsfossen#**	2,154
Skykje**	984
Vetti, Morka-Koldedola R.	900

Name, location	Height (ft)
Sweden	
Handol#	345
Switzerland	
Giessbach (C).	984
Reichenbach#.	820
Staubbach	984
Trümmelbach#	1,312
United Kingdom	
Scotland	
Glomach.	370
Wales	
Pistyll Rhaeadr.	240
North America	
Canada	
Alberta	
Panther, Nigel Creek	600
British Columbia	
Della#.	1,444
Takakkaw, Daly Glacier#	833
Québec	
Montmorency	276
Canada-United States	
Niagara (American)	194
Niagara (Horseshoe)	187
United States	
Alabama	
Noccalula Falls	90
California	
Feather*	640
Yosemite National Park	
Bridalveil*	620
Illilouette*	370
Nevada, Merced R.*	594
Ribbon**	1,612
Silver Strand,	
Meadow Brook**	574
Vernal, Merced R.*	317
Yosemite#**	2,425
Colorado	
Seven Falls,	
S. Cheyenne Creek#	300
Hawaii	
Akaka, Kolekole Stream	420

Name, location	Height (ft)
Idaho	
Shoshone, Snake R.**	212
Kentucky	
Cumberland	68
Maryland	
Great, Potomac R. (C)*	76
Minnesota	
Minnehaha**	53
New Jersey	
Great, Passaic R.	70
New York	
Taughannock*	215
Oregon	
Multnomah#	850
Tennessee	
Fall Creek	256
Washington	
Sluiskin, Paradise R.	300
Snoqualmie**	268
Wisconsin	
Big Manitou, Black R. (C)*	165
Wyoming	
Tower	132
Yellowstone (lower)*.	308
Yellowstone (upper)*	109
South America	
Argentina-Brazil	
Iguazú.	269
Brazil	
Cachoeira da Fumaça*.	1,312
Paulo Afonso, São Francisco R.	275
Colombia	
Tequendama, Bogota R.*	482
Ecuador	
Agoyan, Pastaza R.*	200
Guyana	
Kaieteur, Potaro R.	741
King George VI, Kamarang R.	1,600
Marina, Ipobe R.#.	500
Venezuela	
Angel#*.	3,212
Cuquenan.	2,000

Latitude, Longitude, and Elevation of U.S. and Canadian Cities

Source: U.S. geographic positions and altitudes provided by U.S. Geological Survey, U.S. Dept. of the Interior. Canadian geographic positions and altitudes provided by Natural Resources Canada.

City, state/province	Lat. N °	′	″	Long. W °	′	″	Elev. (ft)	City, state/province	Lat. N °	′	″	Long. W °	′	″	Elev. (ft)
Abilene, TX.	32	26	55	99	43	59	1,719	Belleville, ON	44	15	24	77	22	11	320
Akron, OH.	41	4	53	81	31	8	961	Bellingham, WA.	48	45	35	122	29	13	100
Albany, NY	42	39	9	73	45	22	148	Berkeley, CA.	37	52	18	122	16	18	150
Albuquerque, NM.	35	5	4	106	39	4	4,954	Billings, MT.	45	47	0	108	30	0	3,124
Alert, NU.	82	30	0	62	22	0	100	Biloxi, MS.	30	23	45	88	53	7	25
Allentown, PA.	40	36	30	75	29	26	350	Binghamton, NY.	42	5	55	75	55	6	865
Amarillo, TX	35	13	19	101	49	53	3,668	Birmingham, AL.	33	31	14	86	48	9	600
Anchorage, AK.	61	13	5	149	54	1	101	Bismarck, ND.	46	48	30	100	47	0	1,700
Ann Arbor, MI.	42	16	15	83	43	35	880	Bloomington, IL.	40	29	3	88	59	37	829
Asheville, NC.	35	36	3	82	33	14	2,129	Boise, ID.	43	36	49	116	12	9	2,730
Ashland, KY.	38	28	42	82	38	17	558	Boston, MA.	42	21	30	71	3	37	20
Atlanta, GA.	33	44	56	84	23	17	1,050	Bowling Green, KY.	36	59	25	86	26	37	510
Atlantic City, NJ	39	21	51	74	25	24	8	Brandon, MB.	49	50	49	99	57	8	1,343
Augusta, GA.	33	28	15	81	58	29	141	Brantford, ON.	43	9	25	80	15	27	815
Augusta, ME.	44	18	38	69	46	48	45	Brattleboro, VT.	42	51	3	72	33	30	240
Austin, TX.	30	16	1	97	44	34	501	Bridgeport, CT.	41	10	1	73	12	19	10
Bakersfield, CA.	35	22	24	119	1	4	408	Brockton, MA.	42	5	0	71	1	8	112
Baltimore, MD.	39	17	25	76	36	45	100	Buffalo, NY.	42	53	11	78	52	43	585
Bangor, ME.	44	48	4	68	46	42	158	Burlington, ON.	43	22	12	79	48	51	640
Baton Rouge, LA.	30	27	2	91	9	16	53	Burlington, VT.	44	28	33	73	12	45	113
Battle Creek, MI.	42	19	16	85	10	47	820	Butte, MT.	46	0	14	112	32	2	5,549
Bay City, MI.	43	35	40	83	53	20	595	Calgary, AB.	51	2	45	114	3	27	3,557
Beaumont, TX.	30	5	9	94	6	6	20	Cambridge, MA.	42	22	30	71	6	22	30

City, state/province	Lat. N °	'	"	Long. W °	'	"	Elev. (ft)
Canton, OH	40	47	56	81	22	43	1,100
Carson City, NV	39	9	50	119	45	59	4,730
Cedar Rapids, IA	42	0	30	91	38	38	730
Central Islip, NY	40	47	26	73	12	8	88
Champaign, IL	40	6	59	88	14	36	740
Charleston, SC	32	46	35	79	55	52	118
Charleston, WV	38	20	59	81	37	58	606
Charlotte, NC	35	13	37	80	50	36	850
Charlottetown, PE	46	14	25	63	8	5	160
Chattanooga, TN	35	2	44	85	18	35	685
Cheyenne, WY	41	8	24	104	49	11	6,067
Chicago, IL	41	51	0	87	39	0	596
Churchill, MB	58	46	51	94	11	13	94
Cincinnati, OH	39	9	43	84	27	25	683
Cleveland, OH	41	29	58	81	41	44	690
Colorado Springs, CO	38	50	2	104	49	15	6,008
Columbia, MO	38	57	6	92	20	2	758
Columbia, SC	34	0	2	81	2	6	314
Columbus, GA	32	27	39	84	59	16	300
Columbus, OH	39	57	40	82	59	56	800
Concord, NH	43	12	29	71	32	17	288
Corpus Christi, TX	27	48	1	97	23	46	35
Dallas, TX	32	47	0	96	48	0	463
Dawson, YT	64	3	36	139	25	55	1,214
Dayton, OH	39	45	32	84	11	30	750
Daytona Beach, FL	29	12	38	81	1	23	10
Decatur, IL	39	50	25	88	57	17	670
Denver, CO	39	44	21	104	59	3	5,260
Des Moines, IA	41	36	2	93	36	32	803
Detroit, MI	42	19	53	83	2	45	585
Dodge City, KS	37	45	10	100	1	0	2,550
Dubuque, IA	42	30	2	90	39	52	620
Duluth, MN	46	47	0	92	6	23	610
Durham, NC	35	59	38	78	53	56	394
Eau Claire, WI	44	48	41	91	29	54	850
Edmonton, AB	53	32	4	113	29	25	2,200
El Paso, TX	31	45	31	106	29	11	3,695
Elizabeth, NJ	40	39	50	74	12	40	38
Enid, OK	36	23	44	97	52	41	1,246
Erie, PA	42	7	45	80	5	7	650
Eugene, OR	44	3	8	123	5	8	419
Eureka, CA	40	48	8	124	9	45	44
Evansville, IN	37	58	29	87	33	21	388
Fairbanks, AK	64	50	16	147	42	59	440
Fall River, MA	41	42	5	71	9	20	200
Fargo, ND	46	52	38	96	47	22	900
Flagstaff, AZ	35	11	53	111	39	2	6,900
Flint, MI	43	0	45	83	41	15	750
Ft. Smith, AR	35	23	9	94	23	54	446
Ft. Wayne, IN	41	7	50	85	7	44	781
Ft. Worth, TX	32	43	31	97	19	14	670
Fredericton, NB	45	56	43	66	40	0	67
Fresno, CA	36	44	52	119	46	17	296
Gadsden, AL	34	0	51	86	0	24	554
Gainesville, FL	29	39	5	82	19	30	183
Gallup, NM	35	31	41	108	44	31	6,508
Galveston, TX	29	18	4	94	47	51	10
Gary, IN	41	35	36	87	20	47	600
Grand Junction, CO	39	3	50	108	33	0	4,597
Grand Rapids, MI	42	57	48	85	40	5	610
Great Falls, MT	47	30	1	111	18	0	3,334
Green Bay, WI	44	31	9	88	1	11	594
Greensboro, NC	36	4	21	79	47	32	770
Greenville, SC	34	51	9	82	23	39	966
Guelph, ON	43	32	9	80	13	44	1,100
Gulfport, MS	30	22	2	89	5	34	25
Halifax, NS	44	52	0	63	42	58	477
Hamilton, OH	39	23	58	84	33	41	600
Hamilton, ON	43	14	34	79	59	22	780
Harrisburg, PA	40	16	25	76	53	5	320
Hartford, CT	41	45	49	72	41	8	40
Helena, MT	46	35	34	112	2	7	4,090
Hilo, HI	19	43	47	155	5	24	38
Honolulu, HI	21	18	25	157	51	30	18
Houston, TX	29	45	47	95	21	47	40
Huntsville, AL	34	43	49	86	35	10	641
Indianapolis, IN	39	46	6	86	9	29	717
Iowa City, IA	41	39	40	91	31	48	685
Jackson, MI	42	14	45	84	24	5	940
Jackson, MS	32	17	55	90	11	5	294
Jacksonville, FL	30	19	55	81	39	21	12
Jersey City, NJ	40	43	41	74	4	41	83
Johnstown, PA	40	19	36	78	55	20	1,200
Joplin, MO	37	5	3	94	30	47	990
Juneau, AK	58	18	7	134	25	11	50
Kalamazoo, MI	42	17	30	85	35	14	755
Kansas City, KS	39	6	51	94	37	50	750
Kansas City, MO	39	5	59	94	34	42	740
Kenosha, WI	42	35	5	87	49	16	610
Key West, FL	24	33	19	81	46	58	8
Kingston, ON	44	18	24	76	24	59	305
Kitchener, ON	43	25	7	80	28	22	1,040
Knoxville, TN	35	57	38	83	55	15	889
Lafayette, IN	40	25	0	86	52	31	567
Lancaster, PA	40	2	16	76	18	21	368
Lansing, MI	42	43	57	84	33	20	830
Laredo, TX	27	30	22	99	30	26	414
Las Vegas, NV	36	10	30	115	8	11	2,000
Lawrence, MA	42	42	25	71	9	49	50
Lethbridge, AB	49	41	37	112	50	31	3,047
Lexington, KY	37	59	19	84	28	40	955
Lihue, HI	21	58	52	159	22	16	206
Lima, OH	40	44	33	84	6	19	875
Lincoln, NE	40	48	0	96	40	0	1,150
Little Rock, AR	34	44	47	92	17	22	350
London, ON	42	58	3	81	13	57	875
Los Angeles, CA	34	3	8	118	14	34	330
Louisville, KY	38	15	15	85	45	34	462
Lowell, MA	42	38	0	71	19	0	102
Lubbock, TX	33	34	40	101	51	17	3,195
Macon, GA	32	50	26	83	37	57	400
Madison, WI	43	4	23	89	24	4	863
Manchester, NH	42	59	44	71	27	19	175
Marshall, TX	32	32	41	94	22	2	410
Medicine Hat, AB	50	2	27	110	40	36	2,352
Memphis, TN	35	8	58	90	2	56	254
Meriden, CT	41	32	17	72	48	27	190
Miami, FL	25	46	26	80	11	38	11
Milwaukee, WI	43	2	20	87	54	23	634
Minneapolis, MN	44	58	48	93	15	49	815
Minot, ND	48	13	57	101	17	45	1,555
Mobile, AL	30	41	39	88	2	35	16
Moncton, NB	46	5	58	64	47	59	232
Montgomery, AL	32	22	0	86	18	0	250
Montpelier, VT	44	15	36	72	34	33	525
Montréal, QC	45	31	0	73	39	0	221
Moose Jaw, SK	50	23	36	105	33	7	1,892
Muncie, IN	40	11	36	85	23	11	952
Nashville, TN	36	9	57	86	47	4	440
Natchez, MS	31	33	37	91	24	11	230
New Britain, CT	41	39	40	72	46	48	200
New Haven, CT	41	18	29	72	55	43	40
New Orleans, LA	29	57	16	90	4	30	11
New York, NY	40	42	51	74	0	23	55
Newark, NJ	40	44	8	74	10	22	95
Niagara Falls, ON	43	3	36	79	6	24	589
Nome, AK	64	30	4	165	24	23	25
Norfolk, VA	36	50	48	76	17	8	10
North Bay, ON	46	18	52	79	27	33	1,200
Oakland, CA	37	48	16	122	16	11	42
Ogden, UT	41	13	23	111	58	23	4,299
Oklahoma City, OK	35	28	3	97	30	58	1,195
Omaha, NE	41	15	31	95	56	15	1,040
Orlando, FL	28	32	17	81	22	46	106
Ottawa, ON	45	20	0	75	35	3	382
Paducah, KY	37	5	0	88	36	0	345
Pasadena, CA	34	8	52	118	8	37	865
Paterson, NJ	40	55	0	74	10	20	70
Pensacola, FL	30	25	16	87	13	1	32
Peoria, IL	40	41	37	89	35	20	470
Peterborough, ON	44	18	4	78	20	0	628
Philadelphia, PA	39	57	8	75	9	51	40
Phoenix, AZ	33	26	54	112	4	24	1,090
Pierre, SD	44	22	6	100	21	2	1,484
Pittsburgh, PA	40	26	26	79	59	46	770
Pittsfield, MA	42	27	0	73	14	45	1,039
Pocatello, ID	42	52	17	112	26	41	4,464
Pt. Arthur, TX	29	53	55	93	55	43	10
Portland, ME	43	39	41	70	15	21	25
Portland, OR	45	31	25	122	40	30	50
Portsmouth, NH	43	4	18	70	45	47	21
Portsmouth, VA	36	50	7	76	17	55	10
Prince Rupert, BC	54	18	46	130	19	31	116
Providence, RI	41	49	26	71	24	48	80
Provo, UT	40	14	2	111	39	28	4,549
Pueblo, CO	38	15	16	104	36	31	4,662
Québec, QC	46	49	0	71	13	0	244
Racine, WI	42	43	34	87	46	58	630
Raleigh, NC	35	46	19	78	38	20	350
Rapid City, SD	44	4	50	103	13	50	3,247
Reading, PA	40	20	8	75	55	38	266
Regina, SK	50	27	17	104	36	24	1,894

City, state/province	Lat. N °	'	''	Long. W °	'	''	Elev. (ft)
Reno, NV	39	31	47	119	48	46	4,498
Richmond, VA	37	33	13	77	27	38	190
Roanoke, VA	37	16	15	79	56	30	940
Rochester, MN	44	1	18	92	28	11	990
Rochester, NY	43	9	17	77	36	57	515
Rockford, IL	42	16	16	89	5	38	715
Sacramento, CA	38	34	54	121	29	36	20
Saginaw, MI	43	25	10	83	57	3	595
St. Catharines, ON	43	9	56	79	15	12	321
St. Cloud, MN	45	33	39	94	9	44	1,040
St. John, NB	45	15	33	66	2	20	357
St. John's, NL	47	28	56	52	47	49	461
St. Joseph, MO	39	46	7	94	50	47	850
St. Louis, MO	38	37	38	90	11	52	455
St. Paul, MN	44	56	40	93	5	35	780
St. Petersburg, FL	27	46	14	82	40	46	44
Salem, OR	44	56	35	123	2	2	154
Salina, KS	38	50	25	97	36	40	1,225
Salt Lake City, UT	40	45	39	111	53	25	4,266
San Antonio, TX	29	25	26	98	29	36	650
San Bernardino, CA	34	6	30	117	17	20	1,200
San Diego, CA	32	42	55	117	9	23	40
San Francisco, CA	37	46	30	122	25	6	63
San Jose, CA	37	20	22	121	53	38	87
San Juan, PR	18	28	6	66	6	22	8
Santa Barbara, CA	34	25	15	119	41	50	50
Santa Cruz, CA	36	58	27	122	1	47	20
Santa Fe, NM	35	41	13	105	56	14	6,989
Sarasota, FL	27	20	10	82	31	51	27
Saskatoon, SK	52	8	23	106	41	10	1,653
Sault Ste. Marie, ON	46	33	32	84	20	49	630
Savannah, GA	32	5	0	81	6	0	42
Schenectady, NY	42	48	51	73	56	24	245
Seattle, WA	47	36	23	122	19	51	350
Sheboygan, WI	43	45	3	87	42	52	630
Sherbrooke, QC	45	24	0	71	54	0	792
Sheridan, WY	44	47	50	106	57	20	3,742
Shreveport, LA	32	31	30	93	45	0	209
Sioux City, IA	42	30	0	96	24	0	1,117
Sioux Falls, SD	43	32	48	96	43	48	1,442
South Bend, IN	41	41	0	86	15	0	725
Spartanburg, SC	34	56	58	81	55	56	816
Spokane, WA	47	39	32	117	25	30	2,000
Springfield, IL	39	48	6	89	38	37	610
Springfield, MA	42	6	5	72	35	25	70
Springfield, MO	37	12	55	93	17	53	1,300
Springfield, OH	39	55	27	83	48	32	1,000
Stamford, CT	41	3	12	73	32	21	35
Steubenville, OH	40	22	11	80	38	3	1,060
Stockton, CA	37	57	28	121	17	23	15
Sudbury, ON	46	31	28	80	54	4	1,140
Superior, WI	46	43	15	92	6	14	642
Sydney, NS	46	8	17	60	11	45	203
Syracuse, NY	43	2	53	76	8	52	400
Tacoma, WA	47	15	11	122	26	35	380
Tallahassee, FL	30	26	17	84	16	51	188
Tampa, FL	27	56	50	82	27	31	48
Terre Haute, IN	39	28	0	87	24	50	501
Texarkana, TX	33	25	30	94	2	51	324
Thunder Bay, ON	48	24	5	89	16	4	653
Timmins, ON	48	28	18	81	19	53	967
Toledo, OH	41	39	50	83	33	19	615
Topeka, KS	39	2	54	95	40	40	1,000
Toronto, ON	43	44	30	79	22	24	251
Trenton, NJ	40	13	1	74	44	36	54
Trois-Rivières, QC	46	21	0	72	33	0	198
Troy, NY	42	43	42	73	41	32	35
Tucson, AZ	32	13	18	110	55	33	2,390
Tulsa, OK	36	9	14	95	59	33	804
Urbana, IL	40	6	38	88	12	26	725
Utica, NY	43	6	3	75	13	59	415
Vancouver, BC	49	15	40	123	6	50	14
Victoria, BC	48	25	42	123	21	53	63
Waco, TX	31	32	57	97	8	47	405
Walla Walla, WA	46	3	53	118	20	31	1,000
Washington, DC	38	53	42	77	2	11	23
Waterloo, IA	42	29	34	92	20	34	850
West Palm Beach, FL	26	42	54	80	3	13	21
Wheeling, WV	40	3	50	80	43	16	672
White Plains, NY	41	2	2	73	45	48	220
Whitehorse, YT	60	41	46	135	4	51	2,305
Wichita, KS	37	41	32	97	20	14	1,305
Wilkes-Barre, PA	41	14	45	75	52	54	550
Wilmington, DE	39	44	45	75	32	49	100
Wilmington, NC	34	13	32	77	56	42	50
Windsor, ON	42	18	8	82	59	37	622
Winnipeg, MB	49	53	4	97	8	47	783
Winston-Salem, NC	36	5	59	80	14	40	912
Worcester, MA	42	15	45	71	48	10	480
Yakima, WA	46	36	8	120	30	17	1,066
Yellowknife, NT	62	27	13	114	22	12	675
Youngstown, OH	41	5	59	80	38	59	861
Yuma, AZ	32	43	31	114	37	25	160
Zanesville, OH	39	56	25	82	0	47	676

Latitude and Longitude of World Cities

Source: National Geospatial-Intelligence Agency, U.S. Dept. of Defense

City, country	Lat. °	''	Long. °	''
Athens, Greece	37	59 N	23	44 E
Bangkok, Thailand	13	45 N	100	31 E
Beijing, China	39	55 N	116	23 E
Berlin, Germany	52	31 N	13	24 E
Bogotá, Colombia	4	38 N	74	3 W
Buenos Aires, Argentina	34	35 S	58	40 W
Cairo, Egypt	30	4 N	31	17 E
Jakarta, Indonesia	6	10 S	106	49 E
Jerusalem, Israel	31	45 N	35	0 E
Johannesburg, South Africa	26	12 S	28	2 E
Kathmandu, Nepal	27	43 N	85	19 E
Kiev, Ukraine	50	26 N	30	31 E
London, UK (Greenwich)	51	28 N	0	0
Manila, Philippines	14	35 N	121	0 E
Mexico City, Mexico	19	26 N	99	8 W
Moscow, Russia	55	45 N	37	36 E
Mumbai (Bombay), India	18	59 N	72	50 E
New Delhi, India	28	36 N	77	12 E
Panama City, Panama	8	58 N	79	32 W
Paris, France	48	52 N	2	20 E
Quito, Ecuador	0	11 S	78	29 W
Rio de Janeiro, Brazil	22	52 S	43	16 W
Rome, Italy	41	54 N	12	29 E
Santiago, Chile	33	27 S	70	40 W
Seoul, South Korea	37	35 N	127	0 E
Sydney, Australia	33	51 S	151	12 E
Tehran, Iran	35	40 N	51	25 E
Tokyo, Japan	35	41 N	139	45 E
Warsaw, Poland	52	15 N	21	0 E
Wellington, New Zealand	41	18 S	174	47 E

Highest and Lowest Continental Elevations

Source: National Geographic Society

Continent	Highest point	Elev. (ft)
Asia	Everest, Nepal-Tibet	29,035
South America	Aconcagua, Argentina	22,834
North America	McKinley (Denali), Alaska	20,320
Africa	Kilimanjaro, Tanzania	19,341
Europe	Elbrus, Russia	18,510
Antarctica	Vinson Massif	16,066
Australia	Kosciusko, New South Wales	7,310

Continent	Lowest point	Ft below sea level
Antarctica	Bentley Subglacial Trench	8,333[1]
Asia	Dead Sea, Israel-Jordan	1,348
Africa	Lake Assal, Djibouti	512
North America	Death Valley, California	282
South America	Valdes Peninsula, Argentina	131
Europe	Caspian Sea, Russia, Azerbaijan	92
Australia	Lake Eyre, South Australia	49

(1) Estimated level of the continental floor. Lower points that have yet to be discovered may exist beneath the ice.

RELIGION

Religious Group Membership in the U.S.

Source: Todd M. Johnson, ed. *World Christian Database* (Leiden/Boston: Brill, Aug. 2014), except where indicated.

Figures are latest available from the source and generally are based on collected reports made by each denomination and include only persons affiliated with a congregation of the denomination. Reporting practices vary from one denomination to another, but generally include all members, not only full communicants. Religious groups with fewer than 40,000 members not generally shown. Broad religious groups indicated in **boldface** are estimates for adherents, based on self-identification in surveys and other data, and are updated on a continuing basis.

Group (congregations)	Members
African Methodist Episcopal Church (8,915)	2,697,000
African Methodist Episcopal Zion Church (3,305)	1,596,000
Agnosticism (NA)	**47,927,808**
American Baptist Assn. (1,720)	349,000
American Baptist Churches in the USA (5,724)	1,692,000
American Evangelistic Assn. (560)	270,000
Antiochian Orthodox Christian, North America (247)	450,000
Apostolic Assemblies of Christ Intl. (300)	45,600
Apostolic Assembly of the Faith in Christ Jesus (759)	90,000
Armenian Apostolic Church of America (37)	350,000
Armenian Church of North America (94)	370,000
Armenian Evangelical Union of Churches (58)	44,100
Assemblies of God Fellowship Intl. (853)	820,000
Assemblies of God USA (12,516)	3,102,000
Assemblies of the Lord Jesus Christ (300)	50,000
Associate Reformed Presbyterian Church (275)	48,700
Assn. of Faith Churches and Ministries (1,111)	202,000
Assn. of Free Lutheran Congregations (271)	44,500
Assn. of Intl. Gospel Assemblies (260)	270,000
Assyrian Church of the East (22)	114,000
Atheism (NA)	**1,371,097**
Baha'i Faith (NA)	**549,907**
Baptist Bible Fellowship Intl. (4,500)	1,669,000
Baptist General Conference (1,200)	180,000
Baptist Missionary Assn. of America (1,250)	230,000
Bible Way Churches of Our Lord Jesus Christ World-Wide (1,400)	340,000
Brethren in Christ Church (222)	46,300
Buddhism (NA)	**4,142,782**
Calvary Chapels Intl. (1,111)	500,000
Charismatic Episcopal Church of N. America (85)	40,000
Chinese Folk Religions[1] (NA)	**113,795**
Christian and Missionary Alliance (2,021)	432,471
Christian Brethren (Open) (1,200)	110,000
Christian Church (Disciples of Christ) (3,691)	658,869
Christian Churches and Churches of Christ (5,007)	1,174,000
Christian Congregation (1,550)	125,000
Christian Methodist Episcopal Church (3,592)	919,000
Christian Reformed Church in N. America (1,062)	269,000
Christianity (all)[2] (NA)	**256,295,282**
Church of Christ, Scientist (2,206)	848,000
Church of God (Anderson, IN) (2,305)	259,000
Church of God (Cleveland, OH) (6,752)	1,144,000
Church of God (Huntsville, AL) (1,645)	84,800
Church of God in Christ (22,401)	8,016,000
Church of God of Prophecy (1,841)	98,800
Church of Jesus Christ (655)	150,000
Church of Jesus Christ of Latter-day Saints (13,601)	6,144,582
Church of Our Lord Jesus Christ of Apostolic Faith (535)	650,000
Church of the Brethren (1,047)	152,000
Church of the Living God (170)	42,000
Church of the Nazarene (5,130)	793,000
Churches of Christ (Non-Instrumental) (13,067)	1,402,000
Churches of God General Conference (320)	40,000
Churches on the Rock Intl. (188)	206,000
Congregational Christian Churches (400)	67,000
Conservative Baptist Assn. of America (1,250)	245,000
Conservative Congregational Christian Conference (296)	42,296
Coptic Orthodox Church (170)	130,000
Covenant Ministries Intl. (31)	101,000
Cumberland Presbyterian Church (740)	76,500
Czechoslovak Hussite Church (38)	59,900
Elim Assemblies Fellowship (240)	41,000
Episcopal Church in the USA (5,007)	2,191,000
Ethiopian Orthodox Church in the USA (77)	80,200
Ethnoreligious[1] (NA)	**1,136,159**
Evangelical Covenant Church of America (850)	150,000
Evangelical Fellowship Intl. (270)	80,000
Evangelical Free Church of America (1,355)	396,000
Evangelical Lutheran Church in America (10,498)	4,603,000
Evangelical Presbyterian Church (271)	113,762
Evangelistic Messengers Assn. (556)	131,000
Faith Christian Fellowship Intl. (331)	230,000

Group (congregations)	Members
Free Methodist Church of North America (1,053)	75,586
Full Gospel Baptist Church Fellowship (500)	165,000
Full Gospel Fellowship of Churches and Ministries (1,273)	432,632
General Assn. of General Baptists (840)	98,000
General Assn. of Regular Baptist Churches (1,321)	132,700
General Conference of Mennonite Brethren Churches (464)	111,000
Global Network of Christian Ministries (270)	40,000
Grace Gospel Fellowship (Network of Ministers) (41)	44,300
Grace Intl. (102)	120,000
Greater Emmanuel Intl. Fellowship of Churches and Ministries (47)	47,800
Greek Orthodox Archdiocese of America (525)	1,500,000
Hinduism (NA)	**1,513,403**
Independent Assemblies Fellowship (457)	91,200
Independent Assemblies of God Intl. (300)	120,000
Independent Churches of the Latter Rain Revival (706)	70,400
Independent Fundamental Churches of America (630)	59,000
Indian Pentecostal Church of America (361)	220,000
Interdenominational Ministries Intl. (163)	45,600
Intl. Church of the Foursquare Gospel (1,971)	480,000
Intl. Churches of Christ (142)	45,000
Intl. Convention of Faith Ministries (410)	100,000
Intl. Council of Community Churches (137)	69,276
Intl. Evangelical Church (100)	50,000
Intl. Evangelism Crusades (65)	65,000
Intl. Fellowship of Faith Ministries (2,618)	261,000
Intl. Gospel Assemblies (655)	460,000
Intl. Ministers Forum (492)	170,000
Intl. Pentecostal Holiness Church (2,024)	330,054
Islam[3] (NA)	**4,419,131**
Jainism (NA)	**89,410**
Jehovah's Witnesses (13,355)	2,510,000
Jesus Is Lord Church (245)	40,700
Judaism[4] (NA)	**5,243,246**
Korean American Presbyterian Church (817)	81,500
Korean Full Gospel Churches of America (914)	293,000
Korean Presbyterian Church of America (1,793)	569,000
Latin American Council of Christian Churches (226)	117,000
Lighthouse Gospel Fellowship (425)	50,500
Living Faith Christian Centers (533)	53,200
Lutheran Church-Missouri Synod (6,138)	2,327,000
Malankara Orthodox Syrian Church of the East (92)	45,000
Mennonite Church USA (920)	140,000
Ministers Fellowship Intl. (723)	65,300
Missionary Church (361)	52,200
Missionary Gospel Church Intl. (750)	45,000
Moravian Church in America (170)	42,200
Natl. Assn. of Free Will Baptists (2,400)	233,000
Natl. Baptist Convention, USA (40,000)	9,364,000
Natl. Baptist Convention of America (12,300)	4,200,000
Natl. Baptist Evangelical Life and Soul Saving Assembly (287)	85,800
Natl. David Spiritual Temple of Christ (73)	67,900
Natl. Missionary Baptist Conv. of America (280)	449,000
Natl. Primitive Baptist Convention (1,565)	600,000
Native American Church of North America (400)	200,000
Network of Kingdom Churches (1,210)	291,000
Network of Restoration Churches (163)	40,700
New Apostolic Church USA (320)	50,000
New Religionist[1] (NA)	**1,699,954**
North American Baptist Conference (422)	90,900
North American Old Roman Catholic Church (137)	65,200
Old Order Amish Mennonite Church (950)	115,000
Open Bible Standard Churches (330)	40,000
Orthodox Church in America (551)	2,700,000
Pentecostal Assemblies of the Apostolic Faith (77)	59,400
Pentecostal Assemblies of the World (1,650)	1,300,000
Pentecostal Church of God (1,134)	98,579
Pentecostal Churches of the Apostolic Faith (246)	72,000
Presbyterian Church (USA) (10,746)	2,749,000

Group (congregations)	Members	Group (congregations)	Members
Presbyterian Church in America (1,365)	377,000	United Evangelical Churches (294)	78,800
Primitive Baptists (2,897)	132,000	United Free Will Baptist Church (706)	104,000
Progressive Natl. Baptist Convention (1,200)	2,087,000	United House of Prayer for All People (161)	1,632,000
Reformed Church in America (896)	250,938	United Methodist Church (33,869)	7,799,000
Reorganized Church of Jesus Christ of Latter-Day		United Pentecostal Church Intl. (4,748)	830,000
Saints (920)	175,000	Unity School of Christianity (661)	115,000
Rhema Bible Churches (560)	170,000	Universal Fellowship of Metropolitan Community	
Roman Catholic Church 5 (18,538)	70,655,599	Churches (220)	40,000
Romanian Orthodox Episcopate of America (37)	105,000	Victory Fellowship of Ministries (160)	57,000
Russian Orthodox Church Outside Russia (221)	90,100	Vineyard Churches (USA) (556)	189,000
Salvation Army (1,228)	377,000	Volunteers of America (300)	45,400
Serbian Orthodox Church in N. and S. America		Way of the Cross Church of Christ (72)	75,000
(123)	68,760	Wesleyan Church (1,716)	139,008
Seventh-day Adventist Church (4,917)	1,241,000	Willow Creek Assn. of Churches (2,000)	400,000
Shintoism (NA)	**65,666**	Wisconsin Evangelical Lutheran Synod (1,297)	382,000
Sikhism (NA)	**292,615**	Word of Faith Fellowship/Ministries (25)	45,600
Southern Baptist Convention (45,854)	20,678,000	World Council of Independent Christian Churches	
Spanish Christian Churches (346)	85,100	(327)	54,700
Spiritism (NA)	**235,911**	World Harvest Ministerial Alliance (163)	59,000
Taoism (or Daoism) (NA)	**13,005**	World Ministry Fellowship (290)	50,000
Trinity Church Network (20)	131,000	World Missionary Church (163)	40,700
Unitarian Universalist Assn. (1,048)	221,367	World Salt (82)	50,500
United Baptist Churches (410)	56,800	Worldwide Missionary Evangelism (231)	45,600
United Church of Christ (5,232)	1,086,000	Worldwide/Last Churches (220)	156,000
United Church of Jesus Christ (Apostolic) (114)	131,000	**Zoroastrianism (NA)**	**18,474**

(1) See definition in World Adherents table on p. 700. (2) 2015 estimate. Self-identified; affiliated Christians in the U.S. were estimated at 209,754,502 in 2015. (3) Other sources vary. The Council on American-Islamic Relations estimates a total of 2,000 mosques and 6-7 mil Muslims in the U.S. (4) Includes congregations of Jewish Reconstructionist Federation (about 100), Union of Orthodox Jewish Congregations of America (1,930), Union for Reform Judaism (850), and United Synagogue of Conservative Judaism (600). Among Jewish adherents in the U.S., about 35% classify themselves as Reform, 18% as Conservative, 10% as Orthodox, 2% as Reconstructionist, the rest as "just Jewish." Source: Ira M. Sheskin and Arnold Dashefsky, "Jewish Population of the United States," in *The American Jewish Year Book,* (Dordrecht: Springer, 2014). (This source estimates the total American Jewish population at 6.7 mil.) (5) According to another estimate, by the U.S. Center for Research in the Apostolate, there were 76.7 mil self-identified Roman Catholics in the U.S. in 2014. *The Official Catholic Directory* reported a total of 17,483 Roman Catholic parishes in 2014, with 66.6 mil parish-connected Catholics.

World Adherents of Religions by Continental Area, 2013

Source: *2014 Encyclopædia Britannica Book of the Year.* All figures are midyear estimates.

Religion (no. of countries)	Africa	Asia	Europe	Latin America	Northern America	Oceania	World
Baha'is (222)	2,306,000	3,552,000	162,000	941,000	583,000	118,000	7,662,000
Buddhists (152)	265,000	500,968,000	1,811,000	785,000	4,593,000	624,000	509,046,000
Chinese folk religionists (120)	140,000	434,478,000	449,000	196,000	806,000	110,000	436,179,000
Christians (232)	532,591,000	364,780,000	581,368,000	562,947,000	277,275,000	28,210,000	2,347,171,000
Roman Catholics (232)	192,585,000	144,065,000	277,522,000	495,363,000	88,218,000	9,237,000	1,206,990,000
Protestants (229)	203,136,000	91,977,000	93,932,000	62,052,000	62,085,000	12,838,000	526,020,000
Independents (229)	115,303,000	143,285,000	14,940,000	53,003,000	71,260,000	2,002,000	399,793,000
Orthodox (137)	45,945,000	18,710,000	204,339,000	1,087,000	7,697,000	1,029,000	278,807,000
Confucianists (17)	20,600	8,156,000	15,900	500	0	52,000	8,245,000
Ethnoreligionists (146)	92,758,000	149,391,000	1,171,000	3,724,000	1,235,000	386,000	248,665,000
Hindus (144)	3,092,000	979,966,000	1,215,000	777,000	1,930,000	533,000	987,513,000
Jains (19)	101,000	5,375,800	19,600	1,500	104,000	3,100	5,605,000
Jews (146)	119,000	6,288,000	1,460,000	436,000	5,439,000	120,000	13,862,000
Muslims (213)	455,521,000	1,128,271,000	42,017,000	1,576,000	5,195,000	593,000	1,633,173,000
Sunnis (211)	448,413,000	930,444,000	39,849,000	1,144,000	3,570,000	489,000	1,423,954,000
Shi'ites (147)	2,792,000	189,071,000	2,076,000	420,000	1,018,000	99,000	195,476,000
New religionists (119)	208,000	59,601,000	644,000	1,912,000	2,442,000	122,000	64,929,000
Shintoists (8)	0	2,699,000	0	8,000	64,000	0	2,771,000
Sikhs (64)	78,700	23,807,000	579,000	7,300	626,000	52,000	25,150,000
Spiritists (57)	3,000	2,000	145,000	13,638,000	252,000	8,000	14,048,000
Taoists (6)	0	8,622,000	0	0	12,600	4,200	8,639,000
Zoroastrians (27)	1,000	165,300	5,800	0	21,300	2,600	196,000
All religious adherents (232)	1,087,204,000	3,676,122,000	631,063,000	586,949,000	300,577,000	30,937,000	6,312,852,000
Nonreligious (231)	7,533,000	616,694,000	109,814,000	22,737,000	53,043,000	7,340,000	817,161,000
Agnostics (231)	6,933,000	502,947,000	94,587,000	19,698,000	50,779,000	6,804,000	680,848,000
Atheists (221)	600,000	114,647,000	15,227,000	3,039,000	2,264,000	536,000	136,313,000

Note: Figures may not add up to totals due to rounding. "Religious adherents," or those who indicate attachment to religion, may or may not consider themselves as belonging to a particular religious denomination. They are estimated to make up 88.5% of the world population. Figures shown for adherents to specific religious groups are estimates generally based on self-definition as reported in censuses, surveys, and other data; these people may not all be actually affiliated with a particular congregation as members. Some individuals report attachment to more than one religious group, and subdivisions shown in this table are not necessarily exhaustive. Continental areas are as per UN demographic terminology; "Asia" is defined to include the former Soviet Central Asian states, while "Europe" includes all of Russia, extending to the Pacific coast. Figures in parentheses indicate the number of countries where the religion or type of belief has a significant following. **Buddhists** include Mahayana (56%), Theravada or Hinayana (38%), and Tantrayana or Lamaism (6%). **Chinese folk religionists** are followers of traditional Chinese religion; it may involve worship of local deities, ancestor veneration, Confucian ethics, divination, and Buddhist or Taoist elements, among other beliefs and practices. **Christians** are usually baptized members of a church belonging to one of the major Christian mainstream institutionalized Christianity; these include groups such as Unitarians, Mormons, Jehovah's Witnesses, and Christian Science adherents. **Confucianists** are followers of Confucius, mostly living in China or elsewhere in East/Southeast Asia. **Ethnoreligionists** are followers of local, tribal, animistic, or shamanistic religions, generally belonging to a single ethnic group. **Hindus** include Vaishnavites (68%), Shaivites (27%), and 2% non-Hindi and reformed Hindi. **New religionists** include followers of Asian new religions, radical new crisis religions, and non-Christian syncretistic mass religions.

Episcopal Church Liturgical Colors and Calendar, 2014-18

The most common liturgical colors in the Episcopal Church are as follows: **White**—Christmas Day through first Sunday after Epiphany; Maundy Thursday (as an alternative to crimson at the Eucharist); from the Vigil of Easter to the Day of Pentecost (Whit-sunday); Trinity Sunday; Feasts of the Lord (except Holy Cross Day); the Confession of St. Peter; the Conversion of St. Paul; St. Joseph; St. Mary Magdalene; St. Mary the Virgin; St. Michael and All Angels; All Saints' Day; St. John the Evangelist; memorials of other saints who were not martyred; Independence Day and Thanksgiving Day; weddings and funerals. **Red**—the Day of Pentecost; Holy Cross Day; feasts of apostles and evangelists (except those previously mentioned); feasts and memorials of martyrs (including Holy Innocents' Day). **Violet**—Advent and Lent. **Crimson** or oxblood (dark red)—Holy Week. **Green**—the seasons after Epiphany and after Pentecost. **Black**—optional alternative for funerals and Good Friday.

The days of fasting are Ash Wednesday and Good Friday. Other days of special devotion (penitence) include the 40 days of Lent. Ember days are days of prayer for the church's ministry. They fall on the Wednesday, Friday, and Saturday after the first Sunday in Lent, the Day of Pentecost, Holy Cross Day, and Dec. 13. Rogation Days, the three days before Ascension Day, are days of prayer for God's blessing on the crops, on commerce and industry, and for conservation of the Earth's resources.

Holy days and other variables	2014	2015	2016	2017	2018
Golden Number	1	2	3	4	5
Sunday Letter	E	D	C/B	A	G
Sundays after Epiphany	8	6	5	8	6
Ash Wednesday	Mar. 5	Feb. 18	Feb. 10	Mar. 1	Feb. 14
First Sunday in Lent	Mar. 9	Feb. 22	Feb. 14	Mar. 5	Feb. 18
Passion/Palm Sunday	Apr. 13	Mar. 29	Mar. 20	Apr. 9	Mar. 25
Good Friday	Apr. 18	Apr. 3	Mar. 25	Apr. 14	Mar. 30
Easter Day	Apr. 20	Apr. 5	Mar. 27	Apr. 16	Apr. 1
Ascension Day	May 29	May 14	May 5	May 25	May 10
Day of Pentecost	June 8	May 24	May 15	June 4	May 20
Trinity Sunday	June 15	May 31	May 22	June 11	May 27
Numbered Proper of 2 Pentecost	#7	#5	#4	#6	#4
First Sunday of Advent	Nov. 30	Nov. 29	Nov. 27	Dec. 3	Dec. 2

Greek Orthodox Movable Ecclesiastical Dates, 2014-18

Feast days and fasting days are determined annually on the basis of the date of Holy Pascha (Easter). This ecclesiastical cycle begins with the first day of the Triodion and ends with the Sunday of All Saints, a total of 18 weeks.

Holy days and observances	2014	2015	2016	2017	2018
Triodion begins	Feb. 9	Feb. 1	Feb. 21	Feb. 5	Jan. 28
1st Saturday of Souls	Feb. 22	Feb. 14	Mar. 5	Feb. 18	Feb. 10
Meat-Fare Sunday	Feb. 23	Feb. 15	Mar. 6	Feb. 19	Feb. 11
2nd Saturday of Souls	Mar. 1	Feb. 21	Mar. 12	Feb. 25	Feb. 17
Lent begins	Mar. 3	Feb. 23	Mar. 14	Feb. 27	Feb. 19
St. Theodore—3rd Saturday of Souls	Mar. 8	Feb. 28	Mar. 19	Mar. 4	Feb. 24
Sunday of Orthodoxy	Mar. 9	Mar. 1	Mar. 20	Mar. 5	Feb. 25
Saturday of Lazarus	Apr. 12	Apr. 4	Apr. 23	Apr. 8	Mar. 31
Palm Sunday	Apr. 13	Apr. 5	Apr. 24	Apr. 9	Apr. 1
Holy (Good) Friday	Apr. 18	Apr. 10	Apr. 29	Apr. 14	Apr. 6
Western Easter	Apr. 20	Apr. 5	Mar. 27	Apr. 16	Apr. 1
Orthodox Easter	Apr. 20	Apr. 12	May 1	Apr. 16	Apr. 8
Ascension	May 29	May 21	June 9	May 25	May 17
Saturday of Souls	June 7	May 30	June 18	June 3	May 26
Pentecost	June 8	May 31	June 19	June 4	May 27
All Saints	June 15	June 7	June 26	June 11	June 3
Fast of Holy Apostles (first day)	June 16	June 8	June 27	June 12	June 4

Jewish Holy Days, 5774-5778 (2013-18)

The Jewish calendar consists of 12 lunar months, alternating between 29 and 30 days. It is lunisolar and adjusts for the solar cycle by adding an extra month (Adar II) in the 3rd, 6th, 8th, 11th, 14th, 17th, and 19th years of a 19-year cycle. The calendar starts on the day of Creation, reckoned in the 2nd-3rd cent. BCE as Tishrei 1, 3,761 years before the common era.

The religious calendar begins with the month Nisan, from which all other months are counted, and the civil calendar with Tishrei. The months are 1) Nisan, 2) Iyar, 3) Sivan, 4) Tammuz, 5) Av (also Abh), 6) Elul, 7) Tishrei, 8) Cheshvan (also Marcheshvan), 9) Kislev, 10) Tevet (also Tebeth), 11) Shevat (also Shebhat), 12) Adar, and 12a) Adar Sheni (II), added in leap years.

All holidays listed below begin at sunset of the previous day and end at nightfall on the last day shown.

Holiday	Date on Jewish cal.	(5774) 2013-14		(5775) 2014-15		(5776) 2015-16		(5777) 2016-17		(5778) 2017-18	
Rosh Hashanah (New Year)	Tishrei 1	Sept. 5	Thu.	Sept. 25	Thu.	Sept. 14	Mon.	Oct. 3	Mon.	Sept. 21	Thu.
	Tishrei 2	Sept. 6	Fri.	Sept. 26	Fri.	Sept. 15	Tue.	Oct. 4	Tue.	Sept. 22	Fri.
Yom Kippur (Day of Atonement)	Tishrei 10	Sept. 14	Sat.	Oct. 4	Sat.	Sept. 23	Wed.	Oct. 12	Wed.	Sept. 30	Sat.
Sukkot	Tishrei 15	Sept. 19	Thu.	Oct. 9	Thu.	Sept. 28	Mon.	Oct. 17	Mon.	Oct. 5	Thu.
	Tishrei 21	Sept. 25	Wed.	Oct. 15	Wed.	Oct. 4	Sun.	Oct. 23	Sun.	Oct. 11	Wed.
Shemini Atzeret	Tishrei 22	Sept. 26	Thu.	Oct. 16	Thu.	Oct. 5	Mon.	Oct. 24	Mon.	Oct. 12	Thu.
Simchat Torah	Tishrei 23	Sept. 27	Fri.	Oct. 17	Fri.	Oct. 6	Tue.	Oct. 25	Tue.	Oct. 13	Fri.
Hanukkah	Kislev 25	Nov. 28	Thu.	Dec. 17	Wed.	Dec. 7	Mon.	Dec. 25	Sun.	Dec. 13	Wed.
	Tevet 2 or 3	Dec. 5	Thu.	Dec. 24	Wed.	Dec. 14	Mon.	Jan. 1	Sun.	Dec. 20	Wed.
Purim	Adar 14	Mar. 16	Sun.	Mar. 5	Thu.	Mar. 24	Thu.	Mar. 12	Sun.	Mar. 1	Thu.
Pesach (Passover)	Nisan 15	Apr. 15	Tue.	Apr. 4	Sat.	Apr. 23	Sat.	Apr. 11	Tue.	Mar. 31	Sat.
	Nisan 22	Apr. 22	Tue.	Apr. 11	Sat.	Apr. 30	Sat.	Apr. 18	Tue.	Apr. 7	Sat.
Shavuot (Pentecost)	Sivan 6	June 4	Wed.	May 24	Sun.	June 12	Sun.	May 31	Wed.	May 20	Sun.
	Sivan 7	June 5	Thu.	May 25	Mon.	June 13	Mon.	June 1	Thu.	May 21	Mon.
Fast of the 9th of Av	Av 9	Aug. 5	Tue.	July 26	Sun.*	Aug. 14	Sun.*	Aug. 1	Tue.	July 22	Sun.*

*Date changed to avoid Sabbath.

Hindu Festivals, 2014-18

There are various traditional lunisolar Hindu calendars. Most have similar names for the 12 lunar months, with days beginning at dawn or sunrise, but they differ in various ways, including the numbering of years and the starting point of months. The Indian civil (Saka) calendar, adopted in 1957, is solar-based, and begins Mar. 22 (Mar. 21 in leap years). The year 1937 on the Saka calendar begins Mar. 22, 2015. There are many Hindu holidays and festivals; some are observed only in certain regions. Below are three of the most widely observed.

Festival	2014	2015	2016	2017	2018
Maha Shivaratri (Night of Shiva)[1]	Feb. 28	Feb. 17	Mar. 8	Feb. 25	Feb. 14
Holi (Festival of Color)	Mar. 17	Mar. 6	Mar. 23	Mar. 13	Mar. 2
Diwali (Festival of Lights)	Oct. 23	Nov. 11	Oct. 30	Oct. 19	Nov. 7
(1) Begins the night of the previous day.					

Islamic Holy Days, 1435-39 AH (late 2013-18)

The Islamic calendar is a strict lunar calendar reckoned from the year of the Hijra (anno Hegirae, or AH)—Muhammad's flight from Mecca to Medina, in 622 CE. Each year consists of 12 lunar months of 29 or 30 days beginning and ending with each new moon's visible crescent. Common years have 354 days; leap years have 355 days. Some Muslim countries employ a conventionalized calendar with the leap day added to the last month, Dhu'l-Hijja, but for religious purposes the leap date is taken into account by tracking each new moon sighting.

Holy days begin at sunset of the day previous to the day cited. The actual dates may vary slightly from what is shown below, depending on the locality and the times of actual moon sightings as determined by different authorities.

Holy day (date)	(1435) 2013-14	(1436) 2014-15	(1437) 2015-16	(1438) 2016-17	(1439) 2017-18
New Year's Day (Muharram 1)	Nov. 4, 2013	Oct. 25 2014	Oct. 14, 2015	Oct. 2, 2016	Sept. 21, 2017
Ashura (Muharram 10)	Nov. 13, 2013	Nov. 3, 2014	Oct. 23, 2015	Oct. 11, 2016	Sept. 30, 2017
Mawlid (Rabi' I 12)	Jan. 13, 2014	Jan. 3, 2015	Dec. 23, 2015	Dec. 12, 2016	Dec. 1, 2017
Ramadan begins (Ramadan 1)	June 28, 2014	June 18, 2015	June 6, 2016	May 27, 2017	May 16, 2018
Eid al-Fitr (Shawwal 1)	July 29, 2014	July 17, 2015	July 7, 2016	June 26, 2017	June 15, 2018
Eid al-Adha (Dhu'l-Hijja 10)	Oct. 4, 2014	Sept. 23, 2015	Sept. 11, 2016	Sept. 1, 2017	Aug. 22, 2018

Ash Wednesday and Easter Sunday (Western Churches), 2001-2100

Year	Ash Wed.	Easter Sunday	Year	Ash Wed.	Easter Sunday	Year	Ash Wed.	Easter Sunday	Year	Ash Wed.	Easter Sunday	Year	Ash Wed.	Easter Sunday
2001	Feb. 28	Apr. 15	2021	Feb. 17	Apr. 4	2041	Mar. 6	Apr. 21	2061	Feb. 23	Apr. 10	2081	Feb. 12	Mar. 30
2002	Feb. 13	Mar. 31	2022	Mar. 2	Apr. 17	2042	Feb. 19	Apr. 6	2062	Feb. 8	Mar. 26	2082	Mar. 4	Apr. 19
2003	Mar. 5	Apr. 20	2023	Feb. 22	Apr. 9	2043	Feb. 11	Mar. 29	2063	Feb. 28	Apr. 15	2083	Feb. 17	Apr. 4
2004	Feb. 25	Apr. 11	2024	Feb. 14	Mar. 31	2044	Mar. 2	Apr. 17	2064	Feb. 20	Apr. 6	2084	Feb. 9	Mar. 26
2005	Feb. 9	Mar. 27	2025	Mar. 5	Apr. 20	2045	Feb. 22	Apr. 9	2065	Feb. 11	Mar. 29	2085	Feb. 28	Apr. 15
2006	Mar. 1	Apr. 16	2026	Feb. 18	Apr. 5	2046	Feb. 7	Mar. 25	2066	Feb. 24	Apr. 11	2086	Feb. 13	Mar. 31
2007	Feb. 21	Apr. 8	2027	Feb. 10	Mar. 28	2047	Feb. 27	Apr. 14	2067	Feb. 16	Apr. 3	2087	Mar. 5	Apr. 20
2008	Feb. 6	Mar. 23	2028	Mar. 1	Apr. 16	2048	Feb. 19	Apr. 5	2068	Mar. 7	Apr. 22	2088	Feb. 25	Apr. 11
2009	Feb. 25	Apr. 12	2029	Feb. 14	Apr. 1	2049	Mar. 3	Apr. 18	2069	Feb. 27	Apr. 14	2089	Feb. 16	Apr. 3
2010	Feb. 17	Apr. 4	2030	Mar. 6	Apr. 21	2050	Feb. 23	Apr. 10	2070	Feb. 12	Mar. 30	2090	Mar. 1	Apr. 16
2011	Mar. 9	Apr. 24	2031	Feb. 26	Apr. 13	2051	Feb. 15	Apr. 2	2071	Mar. 4	Apr. 19	2091	Feb. 21	Apr. 8
2012	Feb. 22	Apr. 8	2032	Feb. 11	Mar. 28	2052	Mar. 6	Apr. 21	2072	Feb. 24	Apr. 10	2092	Feb. 13	Mar. 30
2013	Feb. 13	Mar. 31	2033	Mar. 2	Apr. 17	2053	Feb. 19	Apr. 6	2073	Feb. 8	Mar. 26	2093	Feb. 25	Apr. 12
2014	Mar. 5	Apr. 20	2034	Feb. 22	Apr. 9	2054	Feb. 11	Mar. 29	2074	Feb. 28	Apr. 15	2094	Feb. 17	Apr. 4
2015	Feb. 18	Apr. 5	2035	Feb. 7	Mar. 25	2055	Mar. 3	Apr. 18	2075	Feb. 20	Apr. 7	2095	Mar. 9	Apr. 24
2016	Feb. 10	Mar. 27	2036	Feb. 27	Apr. 13	2056	Feb. 16	Apr. 2	2076	Mar. 4	Apr. 19	2096	Feb. 29	Apr. 15
2017	Mar. 1	Apr. 16	2037	Feb. 18	Apr. 5	2057	Mar. 7	Apr. 22	2077	Feb. 24	Apr. 11	2097	Feb. 13	Mar. 31
2018	Feb. 14	Apr. 1	2038	Mar. 10	Apr. 25	2058	Feb. 27	Apr. 14	2078	Feb. 16	Apr. 3	2098	Mar. 5	Apr. 20
2019	Mar. 6	Apr. 21	2039	Feb. 23	Apr. 10	2059	Feb. 12	Mar. 30	2079	Mar. 8	Apr. 23	2099	Feb. 25	Apr. 12
2020	Feb. 26	Apr. 12	2040	Feb. 15	Apr. 1	2060	Mar. 3	Apr. 18	2080	Feb. 21	Apr. 7	2100	Feb. 10	Mar. 28

Roman Catholic Church Hierarchy

The Roman Catholic Church is headed by the pope, or bishop of Rome. He is assisted and advised by members of the College of Cardinals. The church is governed through a central administrative body, the Roman Curia. Dioceses around the world are headed by bishops appointed by the pope; collectively they also play a part in leadership of the church as a whole.

The Papacy

Roman Catholics consider Peter the Apostle to have been the first bishop of Rome and first in a line of popes extending to the present. He is said to have arrived in Rome c. 42 CE and to have been martyred there c. 67; he was later canonized as a saint. Popes through history have had both religious and secular roles. The pope today is the head of state of Vatican City as well as leader of the church.

German-born Pope **Benedict XVI**, formerly Cardinal Joseph Ratzinger, who was elected in Apr. 2005, resigned effective Feb. 28, 2013, citing his age (85) and declining health. Assuming the title of supreme pontiff emeritus, he took up residence in a restored convent near the Vatican.

At a papal conclave in Mar. 2013, 115 cardinals from 48 countries chose Argentinean Cardinal Jorge Mario Bergoglio as pope. He took the name **Francis**, after St. Francis of Assisi (1182-1226), known for his life of poverty and devotion to the poor. Pope Francis was the first member of the Society of Jesus (Jesuits) to become pope, and the first born outside Europe since Syrian-born Gregory III, who died in 741.

Chronological List of Popes

Source: *Annuario Pontificio*

Table lists year of accession of each pope. * = antipope, an illegitimate claimant to the papal throne.

Year	Pope	Year	Pope	Year	Pope	Year	Pope	Year	Pope
	St. Peter	530	Boniface II	882	Marinus I	1102	Albert*	1431	Eugene IV
67	St. Linus	530	Dioscorus*	884	St. Adrian III	1105	Sylvester IV*	1439	Felix V*
76	St. Anacletus or Cletus	533	John II	885	Stephen V (VI)	1118	Gelasius II	1447	Nicholas V
88	St. Clement I	535	St. Agapitus I	891	Formosus	1118	Gregory VIII*	1455	Callistus III
97	St. Evaristus	536	St. Silverius, Martyr	896	Boniface VI	1119	Callistus II	1458	Pius II
105	St. Alexander I	537	Vigilius	896	Stephen VI (VII)	1124	Honorius II	1464	Paul II
115	St. Sixtus I	556	Pelagius I	897	Romanus	1124	Celestine II*	1471	Sixtus IV
125	St. Telesphorus	561	John III	897	Theodore II	1130	Innocent II	1484	Innocent VIII
136	St. Hyginus	575	Benedict I	898	John IX	1130	Anacletus II*	1492	Alexander VI
140	St. Pius I	579	Pelagius II	900	Benedict IV	1138	Victor IV*	1503	Pius III
155	St. Anicetus	590	St. Gregory I	903	Leo V	1143	Celestine II	1503	Julius II
166	St. Soter	604	Sabinian	903	Christopher*	1144	Lucius II	1513	Leo X
175	St. Eleutherius	607	Boniface III	904	Sergius III	1145	Bl. Eugene III	1522	Adrian VI
189	St. Victor I	608	St. Boniface IV	911	Anastasius III	1153	Anastasius IV	1523	Clement VII
199	St. Zephyrinus	615	St. Deusdedit or Adeodatus	913	Landus	1154	Adrian IV	1534	Paul III
217	St. Callistus I	619	Boniface V	914	John X	1159	Alexander III	1550	Julius III
217	St. Hippolytus*	625	Honorius I	928	Leo VI	1159	Victor IV*	1555	Marcellus II
222	St. Urban I	640	Severinus	928	Stephen VII (VIII)	1164	Paschal III*	1555	Paul IV
230	St. Pontian	640	John IV	931	John XI	1168	Callistus III*	1559	Pius IV
235	St. Anterus	642	Theodore I	936	Leo VII	1179	Innocent III*	1566	St. Pius V
236	St. Fabian	649	St. Martin I, Martyr	939	Stephen VIII (IX)	1181	Lucius III	1572	Gregory XIII
251	St. Cornelius	654	St. Eugene I	942	Marinus II	1185	Urban III	1585	Sixtus V
251	Novatian*	657	St. Vitalian	946	Agapitus II	1187	Gregory VIII	1590	Urban VII
253	St. Lucius I	672	Adeodatus II	955	John XII	1187	Clement III	1590	Gregory XIV
254	St. Stephen I	676	Donus	963	Leo VIII	1191	Celestine III	1591	Innocent IX
257	St. Sixtus II	678	St. Agatho	964	Benedict V	1198	Innocent III	1592	Clement VIII
259	St. Dionysius	682	St. Leo II	965	John XIII	1216	Honorius III	1605	Leo XI
269	St. Felix I	684	St. Benedict II	973	Benedict VI	1227	Gregory IX	1605	Paul V
275	St. Eutychian	685	John V	974	Boniface VII*	1241	Celestine IV	1621	Gregory XV
283	St. Caius	686	Conon	974	Benedict VII	1243	Innocent IV	1623	Urban VIII
296	St. Marcellinus	687	Theodore*	983	John XIV	1254	Alexander IV	1644	Innocent X
308	St. Marcellus I	687	Paschal*	985	John XV	1261	Urban IV	1655	Alexander VII
309	St. Eusebius	687	St. Sergius I	996	Gregory V	1265	Clement IV	1667	Clement IX
311	St. Melchiades	701	John VI	997	John XVI*	1271	Bl. Gregory X	1670	Clement X
314	St. Sylvester I	705	John VII	999	Sylvester II	1276	Bl. Innocent V	1676	Bl. Innocent XI
336	St. Marcus	708	Sisinnius	1003	John XVII	1276	Adrian V	1689	Alexander VIII
337	St. Julius I	708	Constantine	1004	John XVIII	1276	John XXI	1691	Innocent XII
352	Liberius	715	St. Gregory II	1009	Sergius IV	1277	Nicholas III	1700	Clement XI
355	Felix II*	731	St. Gregory III	1012	Benedict VIII	1281	Martin IV	1721	Innocent XIII
366	St. Damasus I	741	St. Zachary	1012	Gregory*	1285	Honorius IV	1724	Benedict XIII
366	Ursinus*	752	Stephen II (III)[1]	1024	John XIX	1288	Nicholas IV	1730	Clement XII
384	St. Siricius	757	St. Paul I	1032	Benedict IX	1294	St. Celestine V	1740	Benedict XIV
399	St. Anastasius I	767	Constantine*	1045	Sylvester III	1294	Boniface VIII	1758	Clement XIII
401	St. Innocent I	768	Philip*	1045	Benedict IX	1303	Bl. Benedict XI	1769	Clement XIV
417	St. Zosimus	768	Stephen III (IV)	1045	Gregory VI	1305	Clement V	1775	Pius VI
418	St. Boniface I	772	Adrian I	1046	Clement II	1316	John XXII	1800	Pius VII
418	Eulalius*	795	St. Leo III	1047	Benedict IX	1328	Nicholas V*	1823	Leo XII
422	St. Celestine I	816	Stephen IV (V)	1048	Damasus II	1334	Benedict XII	1829	Pius VIII
432	St. Sixtus III	817	St. Paschal I	1049	St. Leo IX	1342	Clement VI	1831	Gregory XVI
440	St. Leo I	824	Eugene II	1055	Victor II	1352	Innocent VI	1846	Pius IX
461	St. Hilary	827	Valentine	1057	Stephen IX (X)	1362	Bl. Urban V	1878	Leo XIII
468	St. Simplicius	827	Gregory IV	1058	Benedict X*	1370	Gregory XI	1903	St. Pius X
483	St. Felix III (II)	844	John*	1059	Nicholas II	1378	Urban VI	1914	Benedict XV
492	St. Gelasius I	844	Sergius II	1061	Alexander II	1378	Clement VII*	1922	Pius XI
496	Anastasius II	847	St. Leo IV	1061	Honorius II*	1389	Boniface IX	1939	Pius XII
498	St. Symmachus	855	Benedict III	1073	St. Gregory VII	1394	Benedict XIII*	1958	St. John XXIII
498	Lawrence* (also in 501-505)	855	Anastasius*	1080	Clement III*	1404	Innocent VII	1963	Paul VI
514	St. Hormisdas	858	St. Nicholas I	1086	Bl. Victor III	1406	Gregory XII	1978	John Paul I
523	St. John I, Martyr	867	Adrian II	1088	Bl. Urban II	1409	Alexander V*	1978	St. John Paul II
526	St. Felix IV (III)	872	John VIII	1099	Paschal II	1410	John XXIII*	2005	Benedict XVI
				1100	Theodoric*	1417	Martin V	2013	Francis

Bl. = Blessed. (1) After St. Zachary, a Roman priest named Stephen was elected who died before assuming the papacy. Another Stephen was then elected to succeed Zachary as Stephen II. He is sometimes listed as Stephen III.

Pope Francis

Pope Francis was born Jorge Mario Bergoglio in Buenos Aires, Argentina, Dec. 17, 1936; his parents were Italian immigrants. He joined the Jesuits in 1958 and was ordained a priest in 1969. Bergoglio served as a parish priest, theology professor, college administrator, and head of the Jesuit province covering Argentina and Uruguay. Ordained a bishop in 1992, he was named archbishop of Buenos Aires in 1998 and made a cardinal in 2001. He was said to have placed second in the balloting for pope in 2005.

Soon after his election in 2013, Francis took steps to illustrate his commitment to the ideals of St. Francis; for example, he chose to live in a modest apartment in a Vatican guest house, rather than in the elaborate papal suite overlooking St. Peter's Square. He named an eight-member Council of Cardinals as close advisers in church governance and approved measures for reform of the scandal-ridden Institute for the Works of Religion (Vatican Bank). He also established a Pontifical Commission for the Protection of Minors to advise on dealing with clerical sex abuse. In Feb. 2014 he installed 19 new cardinals, including five from Latin America, two from Africa, and two from Asia.

College of Cardinals

Members of the Sacred College of Cardinals are chosen by the pope to be his chief assistants and advisers in the administration of the church. Among their duties is the election of the pope.

In its present form, the College of Cardinals dates from the 12th century. The first cardinals, from about the 6th century, were deacons and priests of the leading churches of Rome and were bishops of neighboring dioceses. The title of cardinal was limited to members of the college in 1567. The number of cardinals was set at 70 in 1586. Pope John XXIII began to increase the number in 1959; however, the number eligible to participate in papal elections was limited to 120. Previous limitations were set aside by Pope John Paul II when he created new cardinals. In 1918, the Code of Canon Law specified that all cardinals must be priests. Pope John XXIII in 1962 ruled that cardinals must ordinarily be bishops. In 1971, Pope Paul VI decreed that at age 80, cardinals must retire from curial departments and offices and cannot be summoned to participate in papal elections.

As of Sept. 2014, there were 210 cardinals from 67 countries, of whom 114, from 52 countries, remained eligible to vote.

North American Cardinals

Name	Office	Born	Named cardinal
William W. Baum[1]	Archbishop emeritus of Washington, DC	1926	1976
Raymond L. Burke	Prefect, Supreme Tribunal of the Apostolic Signature	1948	2010
Thomas C. Collins[2]	Archbishop of Toronto, ON, Canada	1947	2012
Daniel N. DiNardo[3]	Archbishop of Galveston-Houston	1949	2007
Timothy M. Dolan	Archbishop of New York	1950	2012
Edward M. Egan[1]	Archbishop emeritus of New York	1932	2001
Francis E. George	Archbishop of Chicago	1937	1998
James M. Harvey	Archpriest of St. Paul Outside-the-Walls	1949	2012
William Henry Keeler[1]	Archbishop emeritus of Baltimore	1931	1994
Gérald Cyprien Lacroix	Archbishop of Quebec, Canada	1957	2014
Bernard F. Law[1]	Archbishop emeritus of Boston	1931	1985
William Levada	Archbishop emeritus of San Francisco	1936	2006
Javier Lozano Barragán[1]	Archbishop emeritus of Zacatecas, Mexico	1933	2003
Roger Mahony	Archbishop emeritus of Los Angeles	1936	1991
Adam Joseph Maida[1]	Archbishop emeritus of Detroit	1930	1994
Theodore McCarrick[1]	Archbishop emeritus of Washington, DC	1930	2001
Edwin F. O'Brien	Grand Master of the Knights of the Holy Sepulcher	1939	2012
Sean O'Malley[4]	Archbishop of Boston	1944	2006
Marc Ouellet	Prefect, Congregation for Bishops; archbishop emeritus of Quebec, Canada	1944	2003
Justin F. Rigali	Archbishop emeritus of Philadelphia	1935	2003
Norberto Rivera Carrera[3]	Archbishop of Mexico City, Mexico	1942	1998
José Francisco Robles Ortega	Archbishop of Guadalajara, Mexico	1949	2007
Juan Sandoval Íñiguez[1]	Archbishop emeritus of Guadalajara, Mexico	1933	1994
James F. Stafford[1]	Archbishop emeritus of Denver	1932	1998
Jean-Claude Turcotte	Archbishop emeritus of Montréal, QC, Canada	1936	1994
Donald W. Wuerl	Archbishop of Washington, DC	1940	2010

(1) Ineligible to vote in a papal conclave because of age. (2) Member, Commission of Cardinals Overseeing the Institute for Works of Religion (Vatican Bank). (3) Member, Council for the Economy. (4) Member, Council of Cardinals and Pontifical Commission for the Protection of Minors.

The Ten Commandments

In the Hebrew Bible (Old Testament) the Ten Commandments (also called the Decalogue, from the Greek meaning "ten words") were revealed by God to Moses on Mt. Sinai. They form the covenant between God and the Israelites and the moral code that is the basis for Jewish and Christian religions. The Ten Commandments appear in two places in the Old Testament—Exodus 20:1-17 and Deuteronomy 5:6-21.

Most Protestant, Anglican, and Orthodox Christians follow Jewish tradition, as shown here, which considers the introduction ("I am the Lord …") the first commandment and makes the prohibition against idolatry the second. Roman Catholic and Lutheran traditions combine I and II and split the last commandment into two that separately prohibit coveting of a neighbor's wife and of a neighbor's goods. This arrangement alters the numbering of the other commandments by one.

Following is the text as it appears in Exodus 20:1-17, in the King James version of the Bible [Roman numerals added]:

And God spake all these words, saying,

I. I *am* the LORD thy God, which have brought thee out of the land of Egypt, out of the house of bondage. Thou shalt have no other gods before me.

II. Thou shalt not make unto thee any graven image, or any likeness of *any thing* that *is* in heaven above, or that *is* in the earth beneath, or that *is* in the water under the earth. Thou shalt not bow down thyself to them, nor serve them: for I the LORD thy God *am* a jealous God, visiting the iniquity of the fathers upon the children unto the third and fourth *generation* of them that hate me; and shewing mercy unto thousands of them that love me, and keep my commandments.

III. Thou shalt not take the name of the LORD thy God in vain: for the LORD will not hold him guiltless that taketh his name in vain.

IV. Remember the sabbath day, to keep it holy. Six days shalt thou labour, and do all thy work: but the seventh day *is* the sabbath of the LORD thy God: *in it* thou shalt not do any work, thou, nor thy son, nor thy daughter, thy manservant, nor thy maidservant, nor thy cattle, nor thy stranger that *is* within thy gates: for in six days the LORD made heaven and earth, the sea, and all that in them *is*, and rested the seventh day: wherefore the LORD blessed the sabbath day, and hallowed it.

V. Honour thy father and thy mother: that thy days may be long upon the land which the LORD thy God giveth thee.

VI. Thou shalt not kill.

VII. Thou shalt not commit adultery.

VIII. Thou shalt not steal.

IX. Thou shalt not bear false witness against thy neighbour.

X. Thou shalt not covet thy neighbour's house, thou shalt not covet thy neighbour's wife, nor his manservant, nor his maidservant, nor his ox, nor his ass, nor any thing that *is* thy neighbour's.

Books of the Bible

Old Testament—Standard Protestant List

Genesis	I Kings	Ecclesiastes	Obadiah
Exodus	II Kings	Song of Solomon	Jonah
Leviticus	I Chronicles	Isaiah	Micah
Numbers	II Chronicles	Jeremiah	Nahum
Deuteronomy	Ezra	Lamentations	Habakkuk
Joshua	Nehemiah	Ezekiel	Zephaniah
Judges	Esther	Daniel	Haggai
Ruth	Job	Hosea	Zechariah
I Samuel	Psalms	Joel	Malachi
II Samuel	Proverbs	Amos	

New Testament List

Matthew	Ephesians	Hebrews
Mark	Philippians	James
Luke	Colossians	I Peter
John	I Thessalonians	II Peter
Acts	II Thessalonians	I John
Romans	I Timothy	II John
I Corinthians	II Timothy	III John
II Corinthians	Titus	Jude
Galatians	Philemon	Revelation

The standard Protestant Old Testament consists of the same 39 books as in the Bible of Judaism, but the latter is organized differently. The Old Testament used by Roman Catholics has 7 additional deuterocanonical books, plus some additional parts of books. The 7 are **Tobit, Judith, Wisdom, Sirach (Ecclesiasticus), Baruch, I Maccabees,** and **II Maccabees.** Both Catholic and Protestant versions of the New Testament have 27 books with the same names.

Figures in the Hebrew Bible (Old Testament)

Aaron: First of Hebrew high priests; brother of Moses and Miriam.

Abel: Second son of Adam and Eve; slain by Cain.

Abraham: Founder of monotheism; patriarch; also called Abram.

Adam: First human according to Genesis.

Amos: Herdsman; prophesized against social injustice and oppression of the poor.

Bathsheba: Seduced by King David; mother of King Solomon.

Cain: First son of Adam and Eve; killed his brother Abel.

Cyrus: Persian ruler; sent Jews home from exile.

Daniel: Cast into lion's den for violating decree of King Darius; saved.

David: Israel's greatest king; shepherd, warrior, musician, psalmist.

Deborah: Prophet and judge; ruled over Israel.

Elijah: Great prophet; was victorious over the priests of the Phoenician god Baal.

Elisha: Prophet; successor to Elijah.

Esther: Jewish wife of the king of Persia; saved Jews from annihilation.

Eve: First woman according to Genesis.

Ezekiel: Visionary; prophesized hope to exiled Jews in Babylon.

Ezra: Great Jewish leader; rededicated worship and Torah law after exile.

Goliath: Giant Philistine warrior; slain by David.

Hannah: Childless; promised child to God; mother to the prophet Samuel.

Hosea: Enacted prophecy; asked God's forgiveness for Israel's unfaithfulness.

Isaac: Son of Abraham and Sarah; saved from sacrificial altar.

Isaiah: Highly educated prophet; avoided war with Assyria; Israel destroyed; Jerusalem survived.

Jacob: Son of Isaac; father of the Twelve Tribes; renamed "Israel" by angel.

Jeremiah: Confronted leaders; urged surrender to Babylon.

Jezebel: Phoenician queen of King Ahab; had Israelite prophets killed.

Job: "Blameless" man; allowed by God to lose family, health, and possessions in a test of his faith.

Jonah: Swallowed by a great fish; prophesied destruction of Nineveh, averted when the people repented.

Jonathan: Son of King Saul; friend of David.

Joseph: Favorite of Jacob; interpreted Pharaoh's dreams; brought Hebrews to Egypt.

Joshua: Successor of Moses; led Hebrews into Canaan.

Josiah: Reformist king; repaired Solomon's Temple; restored worship; reintroduced Passover.

Leah: Matriarch; older sister of Rachel; Jacob's wife.

Micah: Prophet; predicted the end of war and beginning of peace.

Miriam: Prophet and great leader of the Hebrews; sister to Moses and Aaron.

Moses: Most important Hebrew prophet; leader of the Israelites; received the Torah.

Nathan: Prophet; confronted King David over his seduction of Bathsheba.

Nebuchadnezzar: Babylonian king; destroyed Jerusalem.

Nehemiah: Led Jews back to Jerusalem from Babylonian exile.

Noah: Man of great faith who, according to Genesis, saved his family and two of every living thing on Earth from a great flood.

Rachel: Matriarch; younger sister of Leah; Jacob's wife; Joseph's mother.

Rebecca: Matriarch; wife of Isaac; mother of Jacob.

Ruth: Moabite convert; ancestor of David.

Samson: Judge and military leader of Israel; possessed super-human strength.

Samuel: Prophet; anointed Saul king of Israel and later anointed David to succeed him.

Sarah: First matriarch of Israel; wife of Abraham; mother of Isaac.

Saul: First king of Israel; father of Jonathan.

Solomon: King of Israel at its zenith; known for great wisdom.

Zechariah: Prophet; encouraged rebuilding of Solomon's Temple destroyed by Babylonians.

Figures in the New Testament

Andrew: One of the Twelve Apostles; brother of Peter and former fisherman; one of the first disciples.

Barabbas: Imprisoned with Jesus; set free by Pilate on Passover.

Barnabas: Disciple of Jesus; closely connected with Paul.

Bartholomew: A lesser-known member of the Twelve Apostles; cheerful and prayed often.

Cornelius: A Roman convert; defended by Peter, allowing Gentiles to become Christians.

Elizabeth: Mother of John the Baptist; relation of the Virgin Mary.

Gabriel: Archangel; appeared to the Virgin Mary to announce that she was to give birth to the Messiah.

Herod: May refer to Herod the Great, who ordered the death of children after Jesus's birth, or to his son, Herod, who had John the Baptist beheaded.

James: May refer to either of two apostles: James, son of Zebedee, brother of John the Apostle, or the lesser-known James, son of Alphaeus.

Jesus: Central figure of the Gospels; believed to be the Messiah and son of God; crucified by the Romans.

John (Apostle): Beloved disciple of Jesus; one of the Twelve; possible author of fourth Gospel; brother of James.

John (Baptist): Known as John the Baptist; important prophet and forerunner to Jesus; relation of the Virgin Mary.

Joseph: Husband of the Virgin Mary; descendant of King David.

Judas Iscariot: Betrayer of Jesus; prominent member of the Apostles; committed suicide.

Judas Thaddeus: One of the Twelve; also called Jude to distinguish him from Judas Iscariot.

Lazarus: Brother of the disciples Martha and Mary of Bethany; raised from the dead at their request; possibly the same Lazarus who appears in Jesus's parable of the rich man.

Luke: Traditional author of the Gospel of Luke; possibly a follower of Paul.

Mark: Traditional author of the Gospel of Mark; possibly a disciple of Peter.

Mary, the mother of Jesus: Traditionally believed to be a virgin who conceived without sin; wife of Joseph.

Mary Magdalene: Important female disciple of Jesus; witness to his death and resurrection.

Matthew: One of the Twelve; possible author of the Gospel of Matthew; former tax collector.

Matthias: Often included on lists of the Twelve Apostles as the apostle who replaced Judas Iscariot after his betrayal.

Paul (Saul): Writer of nearly a quarter of the New Testament; a former persecutor of Christians, converted after a vision; played a significant role in spreading Christianity.

Peter: Considered the foremost of the Twelve Apostles; traditionally the first pope and "rock" of the Christian church; author of epistles; also called Simon and Simon Peter.

Philip: One of the Twelve; considered pragmatic and sensible.

Pilate, Pontius: A Roman prefect; played large role in the trial and crucifixion of Jesus.

Simon: One of the Twelve; known as "the Zealot" to distinguish from Simon Peter.

Stephen: Fervently preached that Jesus was the Messiah; stoned to death by angry mob, including Saul; important figure in Saul's conversion.

Thomas: One of the Twelve; known as "Doubting Thomas" because he did not believe Jesus was risen until he could touch him.

Timothy: A disciple closely connected with Paul; recipient of epistles.

Zacharias: Father of John the Baptist; husband of Elizabeth; struck dumb when he doubted his barren wife could become pregnant.

Major Christian Denominations:

Brackets indicate some features that tend to

Denomination	Origins	Organization	Authority	Special rites
Baptists	In radical Reformation, objections to infant baptism, demands for church and state separation; John Smyth, English Separatist, in 1609; Roger Williams, 1638, Providence, RI.	Congregational; each local church is autonomous.	Scripture; some Baptists, particularly in the South, interpret the Bible literally.	[Baptism, usually early teen years and after, by total immersion]; Lord's Supper.
Church of Christ (Disciples)	Among evangelical Presbyterians in KY (1804) and PA (1809), in distress over Protestant factionalism and decline of fervor; organized in 1832.	Congregational.	["Where the Scriptures speak, we speak; where the Scriptures are silent, we are silent."]	Adult baptism; Lord's Supper (weekly).
Episcopalians	Henry VIII separated English Catholic Church from Rome, 1534, for political reasons; Protestant Episcopal Church in U.S. founded in 1789.	[Diocesan bishops, in apostolic succession, are elected by parish representatives; the national Church is headed by General Convention and Presiding Bishop; part of the Anglican Communion.]	Scripture as interpreted by tradition, especially 39 Articles (1563); tri-annual convention of bishops, priests, and lay people.	Infant baptism, Eucharist, and other sacraments; sacrament taken to be symbolic, but as having real spiritual effect.
Jehovah's Witnesses	Founded in 1870 in PA by Charles Taze Russell; incorporated as Watch Tower Bible and Tract Society of PA, 1884; name Jehovah's Witnesses adopted in 1931.	A governing body located in NY coordinates worldwide activities; each congregation cared for by a body of elders; each Witness considered a minister.	The Bible.	Baptism by immersion; annual Lord's Meal ceremony.
Latter-day Saints (Mormons)	In a vision of the Father and the Son reported by Joseph Smith (1820s) in NY; Smith also reported receiving new scripture on golden tablets: the Book of Mormon.	Theocratic; 1st Presidency (church president, two counselors), 12 Apostles preside over international church; local congregations headed by lay priesthood leaders.	Revelation to living prophet (church president). The Bible, Book of Mormon, and other revelations to Smith and his successors.	Baptism at age 8; laying on of hands (which confers the gift of the Holy Ghost); Lord's Supper; temple rites: baptism for the dead, marriage for eternity, others.
Lutherans	Begun by Martin Luther in Wittenberg, Germany, in 1517; objection to Catholic doctrine of salvation and sale of indulgences; break complete, 1519.	Varies from congregational to episcopal; in U.S., a combination of regional synods and congregational polities is most common.	Scripture alone; the Book of Concord (1580), which includes the three Ecumenical Creeds, is subscribed to as a correct exposition of Scripture.	Infant baptism; Lord's Supper; Christ's true body and blood present "in, with, and under the bread and wine."
Methodists	Rev. John Wesley began movement in 1738, within Church of England; first U.S. denomination in Baltimore (1784).	Conference and superintendent system; [in United Methodist Church, general superintendents are bishops—not a priestly order, only an office—who are elected for life].	Scripture as interpreted by tradition, reason, and experience.	Baptism of infants or adults; Lord's Supper commanded; other rites: marriage, ordination, solemnization of personal commitments.
Orthodox	Developed in original Christian proselytizing; broke with Rome in 1054 after centuries of doctrinal disputes and diverging traditions.	Synods of bishops in autonomous, usually national, churches elect a patriarch, archbishop, or metropolitan; these men, as a group, are the heads of the church.	Scripture, tradition, and the first seven church councils up to Nicaea II in 787; bishops in council have authority in doctrine and policy.	Seven sacraments: infant baptism and anointing, Eucharist, ordination, penance, marriage, and anointing of the sick.
Pentecostal	In Topeka, KS (1901) and Los Angeles (1906), in reaction to perceived loss of evangelical fervor among Methodists and others.	Originally a movement, not a formal organization, Pentecostalism now has a variety of organized forms and continues also as a movement.	Scripture; individual charismatic leaders, the teachings of the Holy Spirit.	[Spirit baptism, especially as shown in "speaking in tongues"; healing and sometimes exorcism]; adult baptism; Lord's Supper.
Presbyterians	In 16th-cent. Calvinist reformation; differed with Lutherans over sacraments, church government; John Knox founded Scotch Presbyterian church about 1560.	[Highly structured representational system of ministers and lay persons (presbyters) in local, regional, and national bodies (synods).]	Scripture.	Infant baptism; Lord's Supper; bread and wine symbolize Christ's spiritual presence.
Roman Catholics	Traditionally, founded by Jesus who named St. Peter the first vicar; developed in early Christian proselytizing, especially after the conversion of imperial Rome in the 4th cent.	[Hierarchy with supreme power vested in pope elected by cardinals]; councils of bishops advise on matters of doctrine and policy.	[The pope, when speaking for the whole church in matters of faith and morals, and tradition (which is expressed in church councils and in part contained in Scripture).]	Mass; seven sacraments: baptism, reconciliation, Eucharist, confirmation, marriage, ordination, and anointing of the sick (unction).
United Church of Christ	[By ecumenical union, in 1957, of Congregationalists and Evangelical and Reformed, representing both Calvinist and Lutheran traditions.]	Congregational; a General Synod, representative of all congregations, sets general policy.	Scripture.	Infant baptism; Lord's Supper.

How Do They Differ?

distinguish a denomination sharply from others.

Practice	Ethics	Doctrine	Other	Denomination
Worship style varies from staid to evangelistic; extensive missionary activity.	Usually opposed to alcohol and tobacco; some tendency toward a perfectionist ethical standard.	[No creed; true church is of believers only, who are all equal.]	Believing no authority can stand between the believer and God, the Baptists are strong supporters of church and state separation.	Baptists
Tries to avoid any rite not considered part of the 1st-cent. church; some congregations may reject instrumental music.	Some tendency toward perfectionism; increasing interest in social action programs.	Simple New Testament faith; avoids any elaboration not firmly based on Scripture.	Highly tolerant in doctrinal and religious matters; strongly supportive of scholarly education.	Church of Christ (Disciples)
Formal, based on *Book of Common Prayer*, updated 1979; services range from austerely simple to highly liturgical.	Tolerant, sometimes permissive; some social action programs.	Scripture; the "historic creeds," which include the Apostles, Nicene, and Athanasian, and the *Book of Common Prayer*; ranges from Anglo-Catholic to low church, with Calvinist influences.	Strongly ecumenical, holding talks with many branches of Christendom.	Episcopalians
Meetings are held in Kingdom Halls and members' homes for study and worship; [extensive door-to-door visitations].	High moral code; stress on marital fidelity and family values; avoidance of tobacco and blood transfusions.	[God, by his first creation, Christ, will soon destroy all wickedness; 144,000 faithful ones will rule in heaven with Christ over others on a paradise earth.]	Total allegiance proclaimed only to God's kingdom or heavenly government by Christ; main periodical, *The Watchtower*, is printed in 204 languages.	Jehovah's Witnesses
Simple service with prayers, hymns, sermon; private temple ceremonies may be more elaborate.	Temperance; strict moral code; [tithing]; a strong work ethic with communal self-reliance; [strong missionary activity]; family emphasis.	Jesus Christ is the Son of God, the Eternal Father. Jesus's atonement saves all humans; those who are obedient to God's laws may become joint-heirs with Christ in God's kingdom.	Mormons believe theirs is the true church of Jesus Christ, restored by God through Joseph Smith. Official name: The Church of Jesus Christ of Latter-day Saints.	Latter-day Saints (Mormons)
Relatively simple, formal liturgy with emphasis on the sermon.	Generally conservative in personal and social ethics; doctrine of "two kingdoms" (worldly and holy) supports conservatism in secular affairs.	Salvation by grace alone through faith; Lutheranism has made major contributions to Protestant theology.	Though still somewhat divided along ethnic lines (German, Swedish, etc.), main divisions are between fundamentalists and liberals.	Lutherans
Worship style varies widely by denomination, local church, geography.	Originally pietist and perfectionist; always strong social activist elements.	No distinctive theological development; 25 articles abridged from Church of England's 39, not binding.	In 1968, The United Methodist Church was formed by the union of The Methodist Church and The Evangelical United Brethren Church.	Methodists
Elaborate liturgy, usually in the vernacular, though extremely traditional; the liturgy is the essence of Orthodoxy; veneration of icons.	Tolerant; little stress on social action; divorce, remarriage permitted in some cases; bishops are celibate; priests need not be.	Emphasis on Christ's resurrection, rather than crucifixion; the Holy Spirit proceeds from God the Father only.	Orthodox Church in America originally under Patriarch of Moscow, was granted autonomy in 1970; Greek Orthodox do not recognize this autonomy.	Orthodox
Loosely structured service with rousing hymns and sermons, culminating in spirit baptism.	Usually, emphasis on perfectionism, with varying degrees of tolerance.	Simple traditional beliefs, usually Protestant, with emphasis on the immediate presence of God in the Holy Spirit.	Once confined to lower-class "holy rollers," Pentecostalism now appears in mainline churches and has established middle-class congregations.	Pentecostal
A simple, sober service in which the sermon is central.	Traditionally, a tendency toward strictness, with firm church- and self-discipline; otherwise tolerant.	Emphasizes the sovereignty and justice of God; no longer dogmatic.	Although traces of belief in predestination (that God has foreordained salvation for the "elect") remain, this idea is no longer a central element in Presbyterianism.	Presbyterians
Relatively elaborate ritual centered on the Mass; also rosary recitation, novenas, etc.	Traditionally strict but increasingly tolerant in practice; divorce and remarriage not accepted, but annulments sometimes granted; celibate clergy, except in Eastern rite.	Highly elaborated; salvation by merit gained through grace; dogmatic; special veneration of Mary, the mother of Jesus.	Relatively rapid change followed Vatican Council II; Mass now in vernacular instead of Latin; more stress on social action, tolerance, ecumenism.	Roman Catholics
Usually simple service with emphasis on the sermon.	Tolerant; some social action emphasis.	Standard Protestant; "Statement of Faith" (1959) is not binding.	Two main churches in the 1957 union represented earlier unions with small groups of almost every Protestant denomination.	United Church of Christ

Major Non-Christian Religions

Source: Baha'i reviewed by the Baha'i Community Relations Center; Islam reviewed by Natana Delong-Bas, Lecturer in Islamic Studies, Boston Coll.; Hinduism and Judaism reviewed by Anthony Padovano, PhD, STD, Prof. of Literature & Relig. Studies, Ramapo College, NJ, Adj. Prof. of Theol., Fordham Univ.; Sikhism reviewed by The Sikh Coalition of New York, NY.

Islam

Founded: Muhammad received his first revelation in 610 CE.

Founder: Muhammad (c. 570-632 CE), the Prophet.

Sacred texts: Two texts constitute the Muslim sacred canon, the *Qur'an* (Koran) and the *Hadith*. The Koran provides the foundation for Islamic religion and culture. It is regarded as the final, perfect, and complete word of God as revealed to Muhammad over the course of his life. Received by Muhammad in the Arabic language, it is memorized in Arabic by adherents regardless of their native language. It is divided into 114 chapters of unequal length, the shortest containing only 3 verses, and the longest containing 286 verses. The Koran is the ultimate source of everything Islamic, from metaphysics to theology to sacred history, to ethics and law, to art. The Hadith, which describes Muhammad's actions, attitudes, and teachings, complements the Koran. Due to its long history of oral transmission, the Hadith's lessons are seen as somewhat vulnerable to human error. It is not said to contain God's unadulterated voice as is the Koran but functions as a powerful spiritual and behavioral code nonetheless.

Organization: Muhammad was both the last prophet and a statesman. Muslim leaders have often assumed both civil and moral functions within Islamic states. Within the larger community, there are cultural and national groups, held together by a common religious law, the *Sharia*. Muslims believe that God is the ultimate lawgiver and that human beings cannot devise laws that oppose divine laws. Still, the Sharia is approached differently in different parts of the Islamic world. Over the centuries, Sunnis have developed four major schools of law: the Hanafi, the Shafi'i, the Hanbali, and the Maliki. The Ja'fari is the most important and well-known Shiite school. Before the 20th century, religious scholars known as the *ulama* held much legal power. Judges (*qadis*) and law-interpreters (*muftis*) are people learned in religious law who lead congregational prayers in mosques and perform other religious duties.

Practice: Five duties (of both men and women), known as the Pillars of Islam, are regarded as cardinal in Islam and as central to the life of the Islamic community. In accordance with Islam's absolute commitment to monotheism, the first duty is the profession of faith (the *Shahadah*): "There is no God but Allah and Muhammad is His Prophet." A Muslim must profess this belief publicly at least once in his or her lifetime; it defines the membership of an individual in the Islamic community. The second duty is that of five daily prayers organized in intervals throughout the day: sunrise, early afternoon, late afternoon, immediately after sunset, and before midnight. During prayer, Muslims face the Kaaba, a small, cube-shaped structure in the courtyard of al-Haram (the "inviolate place"), at the Grand Mosque of Mecca. All five prayers in Islam are congregational and are to be offered in a mosque, but they may be offered individually if one cannot be present with a congregation. Congregational prayer is required only at the early afternoon prayer on Friday for men. The third cardinal duty of a Muslim is to pay alms, or *zakat*, which should be 2.5% of one's total wealth. This was originally the tax levied by Muhammad on the wealthy members of the community, primarily to help the poor. Only when zakat has been paid is the rest of a Muslim's property considered purified and legitimate. The fourth duty is the fast of the lunar month of Ramadan. During the fasting month, one must abstain from eating, drinking, smoking, impure thoughts, and sexual intercourse from dawn until sunset, and feed at least one poor person, if able. The fifth duty is the pilgrimage to the Kaaba, which a Muslim must undertake, with exceptions for poverty and ill health, at least once during his or her lifetime.

Divisions: There are two major groups: the majority Sunni (84% of the worldwide Muslim population) and the minority Shiites (14%). Sects first appeared in Islam at the time of Muhammad's death. The group that came to be known as Sunni accepted Abu Bakr, an early convert, as his successor (caliph), while a smaller number, which became the Shia, believed that Ali ibn Abi Talib, the son-in-law and first cousin of the prophet, should have become his successor (Imam). Imams are believed to interpret the Koran infallibly. **Shiites** fall into three major branches: Fivers, Seveners, and Twelvers, reflecting the number of Imams they recognize. Twelvers believe that the 12th Imam has lived an invisible existence since 874, and will return as the Mahdi (a messiah figure) who will usher in a 1,000-year reign of peace and justice. **Sufism** (mystical dimension of Islam) emphasizes personal relation to God and obedience informed by love of God; it is prevalent among both Sunni and Shiites.

Location: W Africa to Philippines, across a band including E Africa, Central Asia and western China, India, Malaysia, Indonesia. Islam has several million adherents in North America and about 30 mil in Europe.

Beliefs: Strictly monotheistic. God is creator of the universe, omnipotent, omniscient, just, forgiving, and merciful. God revealed the Koran to Muhammad to guide humanity to truth and justice. Those who sincerely "submit" (literal meaning of "Islam") to God attain salvation.

World's Largest Muslim Populations

Source: "Global Religious Landscape," Pew Research Center's Forum on Religion & Public Life, Dec. 2012; based on 2010 ests.

Rank	Country	Muslim population	% of country's pop.
1.	Indonesia	209,120,000	87.2%
2.	India	176,190,000	14.4
3.	Pakistan	167,410,000	96.4
4.	Bangladesh	133,540,000	89.8
5.	Nigeria	77,300,000	48.8
6.	Egypt	76,990,000	94.9
7.	Iran	73,570,000	99.0+
8.	Turkey	71,330,000	98.0
9.	Algeria	34,730,000	97.9
10.	Morocco	31,940,000	99.0+
11.	Iraq	31,340,000	99.0
12.	Afghanistan	31,330,000	99.0+
13.	Sudan[1]	30,490,000	90.7
14.	Ethiopia	28,680,000	34.6
15.	Uzbekistan	26,550,000	96.7
16.	Saudi Arabia	25,520,000	93.0
17.	China	24,690,000	1.8
18.	Yemen	23,830,000	99.0+
19.	Syria	18,930,000	92.8
20.	Malaysia	18,100,000	63.7

(1) Excluding what is now South Sudan.

Baha'i

Founded: Mid-19th century.

Founder: Mirza Husayn-Ali Nuri (1817-92), later known as Baha'u'llah (Arabic for "Glory of God").

Sacred texts: The writings of Baha'u'llah and of his herald the Bab (Siyyid Ali-Muhammad, 1819-50). The primary text is *Kitab-i-Aqdas* (Most Holy Book).

Organization: The Baha'i administrative system consists of elected nine-member councils at the local, national, and international levels. There are also more than 180 National Spiritual Assemblies and an elected, international governing body known as the Universal House of Justice.

Practice: Prayer, meditation, and fasting are key components of the Baha'i Faith. Work performed in a spirit of service to humanity is considered an important form of worship. The Baha'i Faith has no clergy and minimal ritual and congregational worship.

Divisions: In a religion in which unity is perhaps the central spiritual value, the Baha'i Faith has avoided separating into sects with differentiated theologies and practices.

Location: Worldwide.

Beliefs: God has progressively revealed His will and purpose through a series of Divine manifestations including Jesus, Buddha, Muhammad, Zoroaster, and Baha'u'llah. Baha'u'llah's teachings include the oneness of humanity, the equality of men and women, the harmony of science and religion, and the need to abandon all forms of prejudice and eliminate extremes of poverty and wealth.

Buddhism

Founded: About 525 BCE, reportedly near Benares, India.

Founder: Gautama Siddhartha (c. 563-483 BCE), the Buddha, who achieved enlightenment through intense meditation.

Sacred texts: The *Tripitaka*, a collection of the Buddha's teachings, rules of monastic life, and philosophical commentaries on the teachings; also a vast body of Buddhist teachings and commentaries, many of which are called *sutras*.

Organization: The basic institution is the *sangha*, or monastic order, through which traditions are passed down. Monastic life tends to be democratic and antiauthoritarian.

Practice: Varies widely according to the sect and ranges from austere meditation to magical chanting and elaborate temple rites. Many practices, such as exorcism of devils, reflect pre-Buddhist beliefs.

Divisions: A variety of sects grouped into three primary branches: Theravada, which emphasizes the importance of pure thought and deed; Mahayana (includes Zen and Soka-gakkai), which ranges from philosophical schools to belief in the saving grace of higher beings or ritual practices and to practical meditative disciplines; and Vajrayana, or Tantrism, a combination of belief in ritual magic and sophisticated philosophy.

Location: Mainly in Asia, from Sri Lanka to Japan.

Beliefs: Life is suffering, and there is no ultimate reality behind it. The cycle of birth and rebirth continues because of desire and attachment to the unreal "self." Meditation and deeds will end the cycle and achieve Nirvana (nothingness, enlightenment).

Hinduism

Founded: About 1500 BCE by Aryans who migrated to India, where their Vedic religion intermixed with the practices and beliefs of the native peoples.

Sacred texts: The *Veda*, including the *Upanishads*, a collection of rituals and commentaries; a vast number of epic stories about gods, heroes, and saints, including the *Bhagavadgita*, a part of the *Mahabharata*, and the *Ramayana*.

Organization: None, strictly speaking. Generally, rituals should be performed or assisted by Brahmins, the priestly caste, but in practice, simpler rituals can be performed by anyone. Brahmins are the final judges of ritual purity, the vital element in Hindu life. Temples and religious organizations are usually presided over by Brahmins.

Practice: Primarily passage rites (e.g., initiation, marriage, death) and daily devotions. Of the public rites, the *puja*, a ceremonial dinner for a god, is the most common.

Divisions: There is no concept of orthodoxy in Hinduism, which presents a variety of sects. The three major living traditions are those devoted to the gods Vishnu and Shiva and to the goddess Shakti. Numerous folk beliefs and practices, often in amalgamation with the above groups, exist side by side with philosophical schools.

Location: Mainly India, Nepal, Malaysia, Guyana, Suriname, and Sri Lanka.

Beliefs: There is only one divine principle; the many gods are only aspects of that unity. Life in all its forms is an aspect of the divine, but it appears as a separation from the divine, a meaningless cycle of birth and rebirth (*samsara*) determined by the purity or impurity of past deeds (*karma*). To improve one's karma or escape samsara by pure acts, thought, and/or devotion is the aim of every Hindu.

Judaism

Founded: About 2000 BCE.

Founder: Abraham is regarded as the founding patriarch.

Sacred texts: The five books of Moses (the Torah), the basic source of teachings.

Organization: Originally theocratic, Judaism has evolved into a congregational polity. The basic institution is the local synagogue or temple, operated by the congregation and led by a rabbi of their choice. Chief rabbis in France and Great Britain have authority only over those who accept it; in Israel, the two chief rabbis have civil authority in family law.

Practice: Among traditional practitioners, almost all areas of life are governed by strict discipline. Sabbath and holidays are marked by observances, and attendance at public worship is considered especially important. Chief annual observances are Passover, celebrating liberation of the Israelites from Egypt and marked by the Seder meal in homes, and the 10 days from Rosh Hashanah (New Year) to Yom Kippur (Day of Atonement), a period of penitence.

Divisions: Judaism is an unbroken spectrum from ultraconservative to ultraliberal, largely reflecting different points of view regarding the binding character of the prohibitions and duties—particularly the dietary and Sabbath observations—traditionally prescribed for the daily life of the Jew.

Location: Mainly in Israel and the U.S.

Beliefs: Strictly monotheistic. God is the creator and ruler of the universe. God established a particular relationship with the Hebrew people: by obeying a divine law God gave them, they would be a special witness to God's mercy and justice. Judaism stresses ethical behavior (and, among the traditional, careful ritual obedience) as true worship of God.

Sikhism

Founded: Late 15th century in South Asia.

Founder: Guru Nanak Dev ji, Sikhism's first Guru.

Sacred texts: The *Guru Granth Sahib* was compiled by the Sikh Gurus and contains their experiences of the Divine. It also contains writings by other saintly figures of different faiths.

Organization: Each Sikh must make her or his own spiritual journey and not depend on clergy. Congregational prayer led by both men and women takes place in local *Gurdwaras*. Harmandir Sahib in Amritsar, Punjab (northern India), is the central place of worship.

Practice: Prayers are required in the morning, evening, and before sleeping. The most important mode of congregational prayer is the singing of hymns from the Guru Granth Sahib. The "Five Ks" are five articles of faith required of all Sikhs: *Kes* (uncut hair), *Kangha* (comb), *Kara* (steel bracelet), *Kirpan* (sword), and *Kaccha* (short pants).

Divisions: The last living Guru, Guru Gobind Singh (1666-1708) crystallized the practices and beliefs of the faith and determined that no future living Guru was needed. Today the religion is guided by joint sovereignty of Guru Granth and Guru Panth. Guru Granth is the Sikh scripture, as the spiritual manifestation of the Guru, while the Guru Panth is the collectivity of all initiated Sikhs worldwide, as the physical manifestation of the Guru.

Location: Many Sikhs have Punjabi backgrounds. The Punjab region was divided between India and Pakistan with the end of British rule.

Beliefs: Sikhism preaches a message of devotion, remembrance of God at all times, truthful living, equality between all human beings, and social justice, while denouncing what is considered superstition and blind ritualism. Sikhism is a monotheistic religion based on revelation.

LANGUAGE

New Words in English

The following words and definitions were provided by Merriam-Webster Inc., publishers of *Merriam-Webster's Collegiate Dictionary, Eleventh Edition*, released in 2003. The words are among those that the Merriam-Webster editors decided had achieved enough currency in English to be added to the latest (2014) printing of the dictionary.

Arab Spring: a series of antigovernment uprisings affecting Arab countries of North Africa and the Middle East beginning in 2010

baby bump: the enlarged abdomen of a pregnant woman

beatbox: an electronic device that adds a backbeat, manipulates sounds, and mimics musical instruments

beer goggles: the effects of alcohol thought of metaphorically as a pair of goggles that alter a person's perceptions especially by making others appear more attractive than they actually are

brain fog: a usually temporary state of diminished mental capacity marked by inability to concentrate or to think or reason clearly

bullet point: an item in a list that has a large dot in front of it to signify its importance; *broadly*: any point or statement given special emphasis (as in a speech)

cringeworthy: so embarrassing, awkward, or upsetting as to cause one to cringe

crowdfunding: the practice of soliciting financial contributions from a large number of people especially from the online community

crudo: a dish of sliced, seasoned, uncooked seafood often served with a sauce

derecho: a large fast-moving complex of thunderstorms with powerful straight-line winds that cause widespread destruction

dubstep: a type of electronic dance music having prominent bass lines and syncopated drum patterns

eurozone: the geographical area comprising the countries that use the euro as the official currency

exoplanet: a planet orbiting a star that is not our sun

fist pump: a celebratory gesture (as by a sports player) in which the fist is raised in front of the body and then quickly and vigorously drawn back

flash drive: a data storage device that uses flash memory; *specifically*: a small rectangular device that is designed to be plugged directly into a USB port on a computer and is often used for transferring files from one computer to another

fracking: the injection of fluid into shale beds at high pressure in order to free up petroleum resources (such as oil or natural gas)

hashtag: a word or phrase preceded by the symbol # that classifies or categorizes the accompanying text (such as a tweet)

manscaping: the trimming or shaving of a man's body hair so as to enhance his appearance

meh: used to express indifference or mild disappointment

motion capture: a technology for digitally recording specific movements of a person (as an actor) and translating them into computer-animated images

paywall: a system that prevents Internet users from accessing certain Web content without a paid subscription

selfie: an image of oneself taken by oneself using a digital camera especially for posting on social networks

sous vide: relating to or denoting a method of cooking food slowly in a vacuum-sealed pouch at a low temperature so as to retain most of the juice and aroma

spoiler alert: a reviewer's warning that a plot spoiler is about to be revealed

steampunk: science fiction dealing with 19th-century societies dominated by historical or imagined steam-powered technology

terroir: the combination of factors including soil, climate, and sunlight that gives wine grapes their distinctive character

turducken: a boneless chicken stuffed into a boneless duck stuffed into a boneless turkey

tweep: a person who uses the Twitter online message service to send and receive tweets

vodcast: a video podcast

voluntourism: the act or practice of doing volunteer work as needed in the community where one is vacationing

Words About Words

alliteration: repetition of same, initial consonant sounds of two or more words in sequence or in short intervals. Ex.: "I have stood still and stopped the sound of feet."—Robert Frost, "Acquainted With the Night"

anagram: word or word sequence that is a rearrangement, typically clever, of letters in another word or word sequence. Ex: The Leaning Tower of Pisa = I spot one giant flaw here.

assonance: repetition of same or similar vowel sounds in words located near each other. Ex.: "Green as a dream, and deep as death."—Rupert Brooke, "The Old Vicarage, Grantchester"

back-formation: creation of a word from an existing word, whose forms seem to suggest that the previously existing word derived from the newer word. Ex.: The verb "edit" is a back-formation of the word "editor."

cliché: a saying or expression that has been used so often it has lost its effect. Ex.: work like a dog

euphemism: a mild, indirect expression used instead of a plainer one that might be harsh, unpleasant, or offensive. Ex.: restroom instead of toilet; pass away, or pass, instead of die

hyperbole: exaggeration for emphasis or effect. Ex.: "And fired the shot heard round the world." —Ralph Waldo Emerson, "Concord Hymn"

irony: deliberate use of an expression in which the literal or surface meaning is contrary to a hidden intended, often opposite meaning that can be inferred. Ex.: "Yet Brutus says he was ambitious; / And Brutus is an honorable man."—William Shakespeare, *Julius Caesar*

litotes: intentional understatement made by negating the opposite of what is meant. Ex.: This was no small matter.

metaphor: a stated equivalence between two dissimilar things or a reference to one thing rather than another, so as to imply a comparison. Ex.: "Life is a tale told by an idiot, full of sound and fury, signifying nothing." —William Shakespeare, *Macbeth*

metonymy: substitution of one word for another that it suggests. Ex.: The pen is mightier than the sword.

onomatopoeia: words that imitate the sounds they describe. Ex.: buzz, murmur

oxymoron: expression containing seemingly contradictory words. Ex.: deafening silence

palindrome: word or phrase that reads the same backward and forward. Ex: radar, Hannah, "Madam, I'm Adam"

paradox: a statement that is phrased to seem contradictory, odd, or opposed to common sense or expectation, while being presented as true. Ex.: "What a pity that youth must be wasted on the young." —George Bernard Shaw

personification: treatment of objects or abstractions as if they were persons. Ex.: "Because I could not stop for Death—/ He kindly stopped for me."—Emily Dickinson, "Because I Could Not Stop for Death"

simile: a comparison between two dissimilar things using the words "like" or "as." Ex.: "My love is like a red, red rose" —Robert Burns, "A Red, Red Rose"

spoonerism: play on words in which the initial sounds of two or more words are transposed, creating different phrases whose meanings when compared can be humorous. Ex.: blushing crow instead of crushing blow

synecdoche: a form of metonymy; the use of a part for the whole, or the whole for the part. Ex.: All hands on deck!

tautology: useless, often unwitting repetition of the same idea in different wording. Ex.: close proximity. In logic, a proposition that would be self-contradictory to deny. Ex.: All bachelors are male.

National Spelling Bee

The annual Scripps National Spelling Bee competition, conducted by The E.W. Scripps Company and other newspapers since 1941, was instituted by *The Courier-Journal* of Louisville, KY, in 1925. Students under 16 who are not beyond the 8th grade are eligible to compete at the local level for a chance to advance to the national competition in Washington, DC. In 2014, for the first time since 1962, there was a tie for first place. The co-winners were Sriram Hathwar of Painted Post, NY, and Ansun Sujoe of Fort Worth, TX. They both correctly spelled the last words available in the final round.

Here are the last words given and spelled correctly at the National Spelling Bee in recent years.

1981	sarcophagus	1988	elegiacal	1995	xanthosis	2002	prospicience	2009	Laodicean
1982	psoriasis	1989	spoliator	1996	vivisepulture	2003	pococurante	2010	stromuhr
1983	Purim	1990	fibranne	1997	euonym	2004	autochthonous	2011	cymotrichous
1984	luge	1991	antipyretic	1998	chiaroscurist	2005	appoggiatura	2012	guetapens
1985	milieu	1992	lyceum	1999	logorrhea	2006	Ursprache	2013	knaidel
1986	odontalgia	1993	kamikaze	2000	demarche	2007	serrefine	2014	feuilleton
1987	staphylococci	1994	antediluvian	2001	succedaneum	2008	guerdon		stichomythia

Commonly Misspelled English Words

a lot	cemetery	eighth	inoculate	miscellaneous	potatoes	sincerely
accidentally	changeable	eligible	irresistible	Mississippi	precede	success
accommodate	Cincinnati	embarrass	jewelry	misspelled	preferred	supersede
accumulate	collectible	environment	judgment	mnemonic	prescient	temperament
acknowledgment	commission	existence	laboratory	mysterious	privilege	temperature
acquainted	commitment	fascinating	leisure	necessary	propaganda	thorough
acquire	committee	February	liaison	noticeable	questionnaire	transferred
all right	connoisseur	fluorescent	license	occasionally	raspberry	transsexual
already	conscience	forty	lieutenant	occurrence	receipt	truly
amateur	conscious	gauge	lightning	omitted	receive	twelfth
appearance	convenience	government	liquefy	opportunity	recommend	vaccinate
appropriate	deceive	grammar	maintenance	parallel	rhythm	vacillate
assimilate	defendant	harass	management	patience	ridiculous	vacuum
broccoli	definitely	humorous	marriage	performance	sacrilegious	vicious
bureau	desirable	incidentally	Massachusetts	permanent	seize	Wednesday
business	desperate	independent	medieval	permissible	separate	weird
calendar	deterrent	indispensable	millennium	perseverance	sergeant	wholly
Caribbean	doesn't	innocuous	miniature	personnel	sheriff	

Foreign Words and Phrases

(A = Arabic; F = French; Ger = German; Gr = Greek; I = Italian; J = Japanese; L = Latin; R = Russian; S = Spanish; Y = Yiddish)

ad hoc (L; ad-HOK): for the end or purpose at hand; impromptu

ad hominem (L; ad-HOH-mee-nem): argument that criticizes an opponent, often unfairly, rather than addressing an issue directly

al fresco (I; ahl-FRAYS-koh): outdoors

anime (J: A-nuh-may): Japanese-style animation

antebellum (L; AHN-teh-BEL-lum): pre-war

aperçu (F; ah-per-SOO): first perception or insight; outline

au courant (F; oh-koo-RAHN): up-to-date, fashionable

belles lettres (F; bel-LET-truh): writing aspiring to artistic merit

bête noire (F; bet-NWAHR): a thing or person viewed with particular dislike or fear

bildungsroman (Ger; BIL-doongs-roh-mahn): novel embodying coming-of-age story

bodega (S; boh-DAY-gah): grocery store

bon vivant (F; bon-vee-VAHN): a person with refined tastes, especially for food and drink

bonhomie (F; boh-noh-MEE): friendliness

bourgeois (F; boo-ZHWAH): middle-class; materialistic

carte blanche (F; kahrt-BLANSH): full discretionary power

cause célèbre (F; kawz-suh-LEB): a notorious incident

chutzpah (Y, HUHTS-pah): audacity, nerve

comme il faut (F; cum-eel-FOH): proper; as it should be

contretemps (F; kon-truh-TAHN): awkward situation

coup de grâce (F; kooh-duh-GRAHS): the decisive final blow

cum laude/magna cum laude/summa cum laude (L; kuhm-LOU-day; MAG-na ... ; SOO-ma ...): with praise or honor/with great praise or honor/with the highest praise or honor

de facto (L; day-FAK-toh): in fact, if not by law

de jure (L; dee-JOOR-ee, day-YOOR-ay): by right or by law

de rigueur (F; duh-ree-GUR): required by convention or etiquette

détente (F; day-TAHNT): an easing of strained relations

deus ex machina (L; DAY-uhs-eks-MAH-keh-nah): person/event that provides a solution unexpectedly or suddenly, espec. (in literature) a contrived solution to a plot

doppelgänger (Ger; DAH-pul-gang-ur): a double or ghostly counterpart of a person

double entendre (F; DOO-blahn-TAHN-druh): expression with a double meaning, one meaning of which is often risqué

e pluribus unum (L; eh-PLOO-ree-boos-OO-noom): out of many, one (U.S. motto)

éminence grise (F; ay-meh-nahns-GREEZ): one who wields power behind the scenes

ennui (F; ah-NOOEE): boredom; world-weariness; annoyance

ersatz (Ger; EHR-zats): artificial; being a (usually inferior) substitute

ex post facto (L; eks-pohst-FAK-toh): retroactive(ly)

fait accompli (F; fayt-uh-kom-PLEE): an accomplished fact

fatwa (A; FAHT-wah): in Islam, a legal or religious decree

faux pas (F; foh-PAH): false step; breach of etiquette

habeas corpus (L; HAY-bee-ahs-KOR-pus): an order for a prisoner to be brought to court to challenge his or her detention

hoi polloi (Gr; hoy-puh-LOY): the masses

impresario (I; im-prah-SAH-ri-oh): manager, promoter, or sponsor of a musical or theatrical program or company

imprimatur (L; im-prah-MAH-toor): approval or official permission to print, espec. by the Roman Catholic church

in loco parentis (L; in-LOH-koh-puh-REN-tis): in place of parent

in medias res (L; in-MAY-dee-oos-rays): into the middle of things

intelligentsia (R; in-te-luh-JEN-see-uh): elite social class made up of intellectuals and educated people

ipso facto (L; ip-soh-FAK-toh): by that fact itself

je ne sais quoi (F; zhuh-nuh-say-KWAH): literally, "I don't know what"; the little something that eludes description

jihad (A; jih-HAHD): Islamic holy war; struggle in devotion to Islam

joie de vivre (F; zhwah-duh-VEEV-ruh): zest for life.

kvetch (Y; Kuh-VETCH): complain, gripe

leitmotif (Ger; lyt-moh-TEEF): the central theme or idea, particularly in art and literature

mano a mano (S; MAH-noh-ah-MAH-noh): hand to hand; in direct combat

mea culpa (L; MAY-uh-CUL-puh): through my fault

mensch (Y; MENTSCH): an upright, noble, admirable person

modus operandi (L; MOH-duhs-op-uh-RAN-dee): method of operation

mujahedeen (A; moo-jah-ha-DEEN): Islamic holy warrior

noblesse oblige (F; noh-BLES-oh-BLEEZH): the obligation of nobility to help the less fortunate

nolo contendere (L; NOH-loh-kohn-TEN-duh-ree): a plea of no contest to charges, without admitting guilt

non compos mentis (L; non-KOM-puhs-MEN-tis): not of sound mind

non sequitur (L; non-SEH-kwi-tour): a conclusion that does not logically follow from what preceded it

nouveau riche (F; noo-voh-REESH): a newly rich person, espec. one who spends money conspicuously

ombudsman (Swedish; AHM-budz-muhn): person who receives, investigates, and settles complaints

par excellence (F; par-ek-seh-LANS): best of all; incomparable

parvenu (F; par-vuh-NOO): upstart

persona non grata (L; per-SOH-nah-non-GRAH-tah): unwelcome person

pièce de résistance (F; pee-es-duh-ray-ZEES-tonz): the outstanding item in a series or group

prima facie (L; pry-muh-FAY-shee-ee; pry-muh-FAY-shuh): true at first glance; presumptively valid

pro bono (L; proh-BOH-noh): (work) donated for the public good

quid pro quo (L; kwid-proh-KWOH): something given or received for something else

raison d'être (F; RAY-zohnn-DET-ruh): reason for being

savoir faire (F; sav-wahr-FAIR): dexterity in social affairs

schadenfreude (Ger; SHAH-duhn-froy-deh): joy at another's misfortune

semper fidelis (L; SEM-puhr-fee-DAY-lis): always faithful

sobriquet (F; SOH-bri-kay): nickname or informal descriptive name for someone

sotto voce (I; sah-toh-VOH-chee); in a low voice

sui generis (L; soo-ee-JEN-er-is); unique; one of a kind

terra firma (L; TER-uh-FUR-muh): solid ground

verboten (Ger; ver-BOH-ten): forbidden

vis-à-vis (F; vee-zuh-VEE): compared with; with regard to

voir dire (F; vwar-DEER): examination by lawyers or judge to determine the suitability of a witness or a prospective juror

zeitgeist (Ger; ZITE-gyste): the general intellectual, moral, and cultural climate of an era

Names for Animal Young

calf: cattle, elephant, hippo, camel, others
cheeper: grouse, partridge, quail
chick: chicken, penguin, other birds
cockerel: rooster
codling, sprag: codfish
colt: horse, zebra (male)
cria: llama, alpaca
cub: lion, bear, shark, fox, others
cygnet: swan
duckling: duck
elver: eel
ephyra: jellyfish
eyas: hawk, others
fawn: deer, antelope

filly: horse, zebra (female)
fingerling, fry: fish generally
fledgling, nestling: birds generally
foal: horse, zebra, others
gosling: goose
heifer: cow
hoglet: hedgehog
joey: kangaroo, opossum, wombat
kid: goat
kit: beaver, rabbit, ferret, others
kitten: cat, other small mammals
lamb: sheep
larva: frog, sea urchin, insects generally

parr, smolt, grilse: salmon
piglet, shoat, farrow, suckling: pig
polliwog, tadpole: frog
poult: turkey
pullet: hen
pup: dog, fox, seal, rat, others
spat: oyster, other bivalves
spiderling: spider
spike, blinker, tinker: mackerel
squab: pigeon
whelp: dog, tiger, other carnivorous mammals
yearling: cattle, sheep, horse, others

Names for Animal Collectives

alligators: congregation
ants: army, colony, swarm
apes: shrewdness, troop
bats: colony
bears: sleuth, sloth
bees: colony, swarm, hive, grist
birds: flight, volery
boars/swine: singular, sounder
buffalo: gang, obstinacy
butterflies: flutter
buzzards: wake
camels: caravan, flock, train
cats: clowder, cluster, pounce
cattle: drove
cheetahs: coalition
clams, oysters: bed
cockroaches: intrusion
cranes: sedge, siege

crocodiles: bask, nest, float
crows: murder, horde
dolphins: pod
doves: dule, pitying
ducks: brace, team
eagles: convocation, aerie
ferrets: business
finches: charm
fish: school, shoal
flamingos: stand, flamboyance
foxes: skulk
geese: flock, gaggle, skein
giraffes: corps, herd, tower
goats: tribe, trip
gorillas: band, whoop
grasshoppers: cloud
hawks: cast, kettle
hedgehogs: array, prickle
hippopotamuses: bloat

horses: pair, team
hounds: cry, mute, pack
hyenas: cackle
iguanas: mess
jellyfish: smack
kangaroos: mob, troop
larks: exaltation
leopards: leap
lions: pride
locusts: plague, swarm
moles: labor
monkeys: troop
mules: barren, span
nightingales: watch
otters: romp
owls: parliament
oxen: yoke
peacocks: muster
pheasants: nest, nide, bouquet

ponies: string
raccoons: gaze
ravens: unkindness
rhinoceroses: crash
seals: pod
sheep: flock, drove, hurtle
snakes: nest
squirrels: dray, scurry
starlings: flock, murmuration
swans: bevy
tigers: streak
toads: knot
trout: hover
turkeys: rafter
turtles: bale
vultures: committee
whales: gam, herd, pod
woodchucks: fall
woodpeckers: descent
zebras: herd, zeal

Some Common Abbreviations and Acronyms

Acronyms are pronounceable words formed from first letters (or syllables) of other words. Some abbreviations below (e.g., AIDS, NATO) are thus acronyms. Some acronyms are words coined as abbreviations and written in lowercase (e.g., sonar, yuppie). Capitalization usage may vary from what is shown here. Some acronyms may have other meanings not given here. Italicized words preceding parenthetical definitions below are Latin unless otherwise noted.

AA: Alcoholics Anonymous; Associate in Arts; administrative assistant
ABA: American Bar Association
AC: alternating current; air-conditioning
ACA: Affordable Care Act
ACLU: American Civil Liberties Union
AD: *anno Domini* (in the year of the Lord)
ADD: attention deficit disorder
AFL-CIO: American Federation of Labor and Congress of Industrial Organizations
AFSCME: American Federation of State, County, and Municipal Employees
AFT: American Federation of Teachers
AI: artificial intelligence
AIDS: acquired immune deficiency syndrome
ALA: American Library Association
a.m. or **AM:** *ante meridiem* (before noon)
AP: Associated Press
APO: army post office
APR: annual percentage rate
ARM: adjustable rate mortgage
ASCAP: American Society of Composers, Authors, and Publishers
ASCII: American Standard Code for Information Interchange
ATM: automated teller machine
Ave.: Avenue
AWOL: absent without leave
BA: Bachelor of Arts
bbl: barrel(s)
BC: before Christ
BCE: before the Common Era; before the Christian Era
bpd: barrels per day
BS: Bachelor of Science
Btu: British thermal unit(s)
bu: bushel(s)
BYOB: bring your own bottle
C: Celsius, centigrade
c: *circa* (about); copyright
CAT: computerized axial tomography
CD: compact disc
CDC: Centers for Disease Control and Prevention; Community Development Corporation
CE: Common Era; Christian Era
CEO: chief executive officer
CFO: chief financial officer
CIA: Central Intelligence Agency
CIF: cost, insurance, and freight
COBRA: Consolidated Omnibus Budget Reconciliation Act (health insurance continuation)
COD: cash (or collect) on delivery
COL or **Col.:** Colonel
COLA: cost of living adjustment
COO: chief operating officer

CPA: certified public accountant
CPI: consumer price index
CPL or **Cpl.:** Corporal
CPR: cardiopulmonary resuscitation
CPU: central processing unit
CST: central standard time
CV: curriculum vitae
DA: district attorney
DC: direct current
DD: Doctor of Divinity
DDS: Doctor of Dental Surgery
DEA: Drug Enforcement Agency
DHS: Department of Homeland Security
DMD: Doctor of Dental Medicine
DMZ: demilitarized zone
DNA: deoxyribonucleic acid
DNC: Democratic National Committee
DNR: do not resuscitate
DOA: dead on arrival
DOB: date of birth
DoD: Department of Defense
dpi: dots per inch
DPT: diphtheria, pertussis, tetanus
DUI: driving under the influence
DVD: digital video disc
DVM: Doctor of Veterinary Medicine
DWI: driving while intoxicated
ed.: edited; edition; editor
EEG: electroencephalogram
e.g.: *exempli gratia* (for example)
EKG: electrocardiogram
EOE: equal opportunity employer
EP: extended play
EPA: Environmental Protection Agency
ERA: Equal Rights Amendment; earned run average
ESL: English as a second language
ESP: extrasensory perception
Esq.: Esquire
EST: eastern standard time
et al.: *et alii* (and others)
etc.: *et cetera* (and so forth)
EU: European Union
F: Fahrenheit
Fannie Mae: Federal National Mortgage Association
FAQ: frequently asked questions
FBI: Federal Bureau of Investigation
FDA: Food and Drug Administration
FDIC: Federal Deposit Insurance Corporation
FEC: Federal Election Commission
FEMA: Federal Emergency Management Agency
ff.: and those following
FICA: Federal Insurance Contributions Act (Social Security)
FIFA: Fédération Internationale de Football Association

fl.: *floruit* (flourished), used for historical figures when life dates uncertain
Freddie Mac: Federal Home Loan Mortgage Corporation
FTP: file transfer protocol
FY: fiscal year
FYI: for your information
GATT: General Agreement on Tariffs and Trade
GB: gigabyte(s)
GDP: gross domestic product
GED: general equivalency diploma; General Educational Development (tests)
GMT: Greenwich mean time
GOP: Grand Old Party (Republican Party)
GPS: Global Positioning System
GUI: graphical user interface
hazmat: HAZardous MATerial
HDTV: high-definition television
HIV: human immunodeficiency virus
HMO: health maintenance organization
HMS: His/Her Majesty's Ship (UK)
Hon.: the Honorable
HOV: high-occupancy vehicle
HRH: Her (His) Royal Highness (UK)
HTML: hypertext markup language
HTTP: hypertext transfer protocol
HUD: Department of Housing and Urban Development
HVAC: heating, ventilating, and air-conditioning
Hz: hertz
ibid: *ibidem* (in the same place)
ICU: intensive care unit
i.e.: *id est* (that is)
IM: instant messaging
IMF: International Monetary Fund
INS: Immigration and Naturalization Service
IPO: initial public offering
IQ: intelligence quotient
IRA: individual retirement account; Irish Republican Army
IRS: Internal Revenue Service
ISBN: International Standard Book Number
ISP: Internet service provider
IVF: in vitro fertilization
JD: *Juris Doctor* (Doctor of Law)
k: karat
K: kelvin
kWh: kilowatt-hour(s)
laser: Light Amplification by Stimulated Emission of Radiation
LGBT: lesbian, gay, bisexual, and transgender
LLP: limited liability partnership
loc. cit.: *loco citato* (in the place cited)
LSAT: Law School Admission Test

LT or **Lt.:** Lieutenant
MA: Master of Arts
MB: megabyte(s)
MBA: Master of Business Administration
MCAT: Medical College Admission Test
MD: *Medicinae Doctor* (Doctor of Medicine)
MIA: missing in action
modem: MOdulator-DEModulator
MP: member of Parliament (UK)
mph: miles per hour
MRI: magnetic resonance imaging
ms, mss: manuscript(s)
MS: Master of Science; multiple sclerosis
MSG: monosodium glutamate
MST: mountain standard time
MVP: most valuable player
NA: not applicable; not available
NAACP: National Association for the Advancement of Colored People
NAFTA: North American Free Trade Agreement
NASA: National Aeronautics and Space Administration
NATO: North Atlantic Treaty Organization
NB or **n.b.:** *nota bene* (note carefully)
NCAA: National Collegiate Athletic Association
NEA: National Education Association
NIH: National Institutes of Health
NOW: National Organization for Women
NPR: National Public Radio
NRA: National Rifle Association
NSA: National Security Agency
obs.: obsolete
OED: Oxford English Dictionary
OMB: Office of Management and Budget
op: *opus* (work)
OPEC: Organization of Petroleum Exporting Countries
OTC: over-the-counter
p, pp: page(s)

PA: public address
PAC: political action committee
PC: personal computer; politically correct
PDA: Personal Digital Assistant
PETA: People for the Ethical Treatment of Animals
PhD: *Philosophiae Doctor* (Doctor of Philosophy)
PIN: personal identification number
p.m. or **PM:** *post meridiem* (after noon)
POTUS: President of the United States
PPO: preferred provider organization, a type of healthcare provider network
PS: *post scriptum* (postscript)
PST: Pacific standard time
pt: part(s); pint(s); point(s)
PVT or **Pvt.:** Private
QC: Queen's Council (UK)
QED: *quod erat demonstrandum* (which was to be demonstrated)
q.v.: *quod vide* (which see)
radar: RAdio Detecting And Ranging
RAM: random access memory
RCMP: Royal Canadian Mounted Police
REM: rapid eye movement
Rev.: Reverend
rev.: revised; reviewed
RIP: *requiescat in pace* (may he/she rest in peace)
RN: Registered Nurse
RNA: ribonucleic acid
RNC: Republican National Committee
ROM: read only memory
ROTC: Reserve Officers' Training Corps
rpm: revolutions per minute
RSVP: *répondez s'il vous plaît* (Fr.) (please reply)
SARS: severe acute respiratory syndrome
SASE: self-addressed stamped envelope
SEC: Securities and Exchange Commission

SETI: Search for Extraterrestrial Intelligence
SGT or **Sgt.:** Sergeant
SIDS: sudden infant death syndrome
SJ: Society of Jesus (Jesuits)
sonar: SOund NAvigation and Ranging
SPCA: Society for the Prevention of Cruelty to Animals
SSI: Supplementary Security Income
St.: Saint; Street
TB: tuberculosis; terabyte(s)
TBA: to be announced
TBD: to be determined
TEFL: teaching English as a foreign language
TSA: Transportation Security Administration
UFO: unidentified flying object
UPC: Universal Product Code
URL: Universal Resource Locator
USDA: United States Department of Agriculture
USS: United States ship
UTC: coordinated universal time
VA: Department of Veterans Affairs
var.: variant
VAT: value-added tax
VCR: videocassette recorder
viz: *videlicet* (namely)
VP: vice president
W: watt(s)
WHO: World Health Organization
WMD: weapon of mass destruction
WPM: words per minute
WWW: World Wide Web
YMCA/YWCA: Young Men's/Women's Christian Association
YTD: year to date
yuppie: young urban professional
ZIP: zone improvement plan (U.S. Postal Service)

Top 10 First Names of Americans by Decade or Year of Birth

Source: U.S. Social Security Administration

All names are from Social Security card applications for births that occurred in the United States after 1879. Rankings are based on one spelling of the name; variant spellings and similar names are considered separate names.

BOYS

Decade/Year	Names
1880-1889	John, William, James, George, Charles, Frank, Joseph, Henry, Robert, Thomas
1890-1899	John, William, James, George, Charles, Joseph, Frank, Robert, Edward, Henry
1900-1909	John, William, James, George, Charles, Robert, Joseph, Frank, Edward, Thomas
1910-1919	John, William, James, Robert, Joseph, George, Charles, Edward, Frank, Thomas
1920-1929	Robert, John, James, William, Charles, George, Joseph, Richard, Edward, Donald
1930-1939	Robert, James, John, William, Richard, Charles, Donald, George, Thomas, Joseph
1940-1949	James, Robert, John, William, Richard, David, Charles, Thomas, Michael, Ronald
1950-1959	Michael, David James, John, Robert, Mark, William, Richard, Thomas, Jeffrey
1960-1969	Michael, David, John, James, Robert, Mark, William, Richard, Thomas, Jeffrey
1970-1979	Michael, Christopher, Jason, David, James, John, Robert, Brian, William, Matthew
1980-1989	Michael, Christopher, Matthew, Joshua, David, James, Daniel, Robert, John, Joseph
1990-1999	Michael, Christopher, Matthew, Joshua, Jacob, Nicholas, Andrew, Daniel, Tyler, Joseph
2000-2009	Jacob, Michael, Joshua, Matthew, Daniel, Christopher, Andrew, Ethan, Joseph, William
2013	Noah, Liam, Jacob, Mason, William, Ethan, Michael, Alexander, Jayden, Daniel

GIRLS

Decade/Year	Names
1880-1889	Mary, Anna, Emma, Elizabeth, Margaret, Minnie, Ida, Bertha, Clara, Alice
1890-1899	Mary, Anna, Margaret, Helen, Elizabeth, Ruth, Florence, Ethel, Emma, Marie
1900-1909	Mary, Helen, Margaret, Anna, Ruth, Elizabeth, Dorothy, Marie, Florence, Mildred
1910-1919	Mary, Helen, Dorothy, Margaret, Ruth, Mildred, Anna, Elizabeth, Frances, Virginia
1920-1929	Mary, Dorothy, Helen, Betty, Margaret, Ruth, Virginia, Doris, Mildred, Frances
1930-1939	Mary, Betty, Barbara, Shirley, Patricia, Dorothy, Joan, Margaret, Nancy, Helen
1940-1949	Mary, Linda, Barbara, Patricia, Carol, Sandra, Nancy, Sharon, Judith, Susan
1950-1959	Mary, Linda, Patricia, Susan, Deborah, Barbara, Debra, Karen, Nancy, Donna
1960-1969	Lisa, Mary, Susan, Karen, Kimberly, Patricia, Linda, Donna, Michelle, Cynthia
1970-1979	Jennifer, Amy, Melissa, Michelle, Kimberly, Lisa, Angela, Heather, Stephanie, Nicole
1980-1989	Jessica, Jennifer, Amanda, Ashley, Sarah, Stephanie, Melissa, Nicole, Elizabeth, Heather
1990-1999	Jessica, Ashley, Emily, Sarah, Samantha, Amanda, Brittany, Elizabeth, Taylor, Megan
2000-2009	Emily, Madison, Emma, Olivia, Hannah, Abigail, Isabella, Samantha, Elizabeth, Ashley
2013	Sophia, Emma, Olivia, Isabella, Ava, Mia, Emily, Abigail, Madison, Elizabeth

Origins of Popular American Given Names

Source: World Almanac research

Some names are commonly used for either sex but are listed here under the more traditionally associated sex. Some names listed here have variant spellings that are not shown.

Boys

Aiden: Gaelic *Aodhan*, "little fire," from name of Celtic sun god

Alexander: Gr. *Alexandros*, "defender of man"

Andrew: Gr. *andreios*, "manly"

Anthony: Roman *Antonius*, possibly from Gr. *anthos*, "flower"

Benjamin: Heb. *Binyamin*, "son of the right hand"

Brandon: Eng. place name, "gorse-covered hill"

Brian: Irish, perhaps Celtic *Brigonos*, "high" or "noble"

Charles: Ger. *ceorl*, "free man"

Christopher: Gr. *Christophoros*, "bearing Christ"

Daniel: Heb. "God is my judge"

David: Heb. *Dodavehu*, perhaps "darling"

Edward: Old Eng. *Eadweard*, "wealth-guard"

Elijah: Heb. "the Lord is my God"

Ethan: Heb. "solid, firm"

Francis, Frank: Late Lat. *Franciscus*, "Frenchman"

George: Gr. *georgos*, "soil tiller, farmer"

Henry: Ger. *Haimric*, "home-power"

Jack: nickname for or variant of John

Jacob: Heb. *Yaakov*, "God protects" or "supplanter"

James: Late Lat. *Iacomus*, form of Jacob

Jason: Gr. *Iason*, "healer"

Jayden: prob. from Jay (short form for many *J* names) and Hayden (Old Eng. "little hollow")

Jeffrey: Norman Fr., from Ger. *Gaufrid*, "land-peace," or *Gisfrid*, "pledge-peace"

John: Heb. *Yohanan*, "God is gracious"

Jonathan: Heb. "God has given"

José: Heb. and Aramaic *Yose*, variant of Joseph

Joseph: Heb. *Yosef*, "[God] shall add"

Joshua: Heb. *Yoshua*, "God saves"

Liam: Gaelic form of William

Logan: Scot. "little hollow"

Mark: Lat. *Marcus*, perhaps from Mars, Roman god of war

Mason: Fr. "stone worker," related to Old Eng. "work"

Matthew: Heb. *Mattathia*, "gift of God"

Michael: Heb. "who could ever be like God?"

Nathan: Heb. "God has given"; modern short form of Nathaniel or Jonathan

Nicholas: Gr. *Nikolaos*, "victory-people"

Noah: Heb. "rest"

Patrick: Lat. *Patricius*, "of noble origin"

Richard: Ger. "power-hardy"

Robert: Ger. *Hrodberht*, "fame-bright"

Ryan: prob. from Irish surname, Gaelic "king"

Samuel: Heb. *Shemuel*, "God heard"

Sean: Gaelic form of John

Steven: Gr. *stephanos*, "crown" or "garland"

Thomas: Aramaic "twin"

Tyler: Old Eng. *tigeler*, "tile layer"

William: Ger. *Wilhelm*, "will-helmet"

Girls

Abigail: Heb. "my father is joy"

Addison: Eng. "son of Adam"

Alexandra, Sandra: fem. forms of Alexander

Alexis: Gr. "helper" or "defender"

Alyssa: variant of Alicia (Eng., Sp.) or Alice (Eng., Fr.); may mean "noble"

Amanda: 17th-cent. invention from Lat. "lovable"

Amelia: Ger. "hard-working," or from Lat. *aemulus*, "striving"

Amy: Old Fr. *Amee*, "beloved"

Andrea: fem. form of Andrew

Angela: Gr. *angelos*, "messenger [of God]"

Anna: Lat., Gr. form of Hannah; variants include Ann (Eng.), Ana (Sp.), Anne (Eng., Fr., Ger.)

Ashley: Eng. place name, "ash grove"

Aubrey: Fr., orig. from Ger. *Alberic*, "king of elves"

Ava: prob. modern form of Eva, Lat. form of Heb. *Eve*

Avery: Eng., common place name; may also mean "elf counsel" or "elf ruler"

Barbara: Gr. *barbarus*, "foreign"

Brianna: modern fem. form of Brian

Carol, Charlotte: fem. forms of Charles

Chloe: Gr. "young shoot," "blooming"

Claire, Clara: Lat. *clarus*, "famous"

Deborah: Heb. "bee"

Donna: Ital. "lady"

Dorothy: Gr. *Dorothea*, "gift of God"

Elizabeth: Heb. *Elisheba*, perhaps "God is my oath" or "God is good fortune"

Ella: prob. variant or nickname for Ellen or Eleanor

Emily: see Amelia

Emma: Ger. *ermen*, "whole" or "entire"

Eve, Evelyn: Heb. "life-giving"

Grace: Lat. *gratia*, "grace, blessing"

Hailey: Eng. place name, "hay clearing"

Hannah: Heb. "He has favored me"

Harper: Old Eng. "harp player"

Heather: Middle Eng. *hathir*, "heather"

Helen: Gr. *Helene*, possibly "sunbeam"

Isabella, Isabel: Lat., Sp. variant of Elizabeth

Jennifer: Cornish form of Welsh *Gwenhwyfar*, "fair-smooth"

Jessica: Shakesp. invention, prob. fem. form of *Jesse*, Heb. "God exists"

Judith: Heb. "Jewish woman"

Julia: fem. form of Julius, Roman family name, or Lat. "youthful"

Kaitlyn: American spelling of Caitlin, the Irish form of Katherine

Karen: Danish form of Katherine

Katherine: Egyptian *Aikaterine*, later modified to resemble Gr. *katharos*, "pure"

Kelly: Irish Gaelic *Ceallagh*, perhaps "churchgoer" or "bright-headed"

Kimberly: Eng. place name, "Cyneburgh's clearing"

Laura: Lat. *laurus*, "laurel"

Lily: for the flower, symbol of purity

Linda: Sp. "pretty" or Ger. "tender"

Lisa: nickname for Elizabeth

Madison: Middle Eng. surname, "son of Madeline or Maud"

Margaret: Gr. *margaron*, "pearl"

Maria, Marie, Mary: Lat., Fr., Eng. forms for Heb. *Maryam*, perhaps "seeress" or "wished-for child"

Megan: Welsh form of Margaret

Melissa: Gr. "bee"

Mia: Nordic or Ital., short for Maria, etc.

Michelle: Fr. fem. form of Michael

Nancy: medieval Eng. nickname for Agnes (Gr. *hagnos*, "holy"), later also for Ann

Natalie: Fr., from Lat. *natalia*, "birthday [of Christ]"

Nicole: Fr. fem. form of Nicholas

Olivia: Lat. *oliva*, "olive tree"

Patricia: Lat. fem. form of Patrick

Rachel: Heb. "ewe"

Rose, Rosa: for the flower, suggesting beauty

Ruth: Heb., perhaps "companion"

Samantha: colonial American invention, prob. combining Sam from Samuel with *-antha* from Gr. *anthos*, "flower"

Sarah: Heb. "princess"

Sharon: Biblical place name, Heb. "plain"

Sofia, Sophia: Gr. "wisdom"

Stephanie: Fr. fem. form of Steven

Susan: Eng. form of Heb. *Shoshana*, "lily"

Teresa: Sp., perhaps "woman from Therasia"

Victoria: Lat. *victoria*, "victory"

Eponyms

(words named for people)

boycott: to avoid trade or dealings with, as a protest; after Charles C. Boycott, an English land agent in County Mayo, Ireland, ostracized in 1880 for refusing to reduce rents

derrick: a type of crane consisting of a boom connected to the base of an upright mast; after Derrick, early 17th-cent. English hangman who used a gallows that operated via cables and pulleys

draconian: harsh or severe; after Draco, statesman who codified the laws in Athens in 621 BCE

gerrymander: to draw an election district in such a way as to favor a political party; after Elbridge Gerry, who created (1812) just such an election district (shaped like a salamander) during his governorship of Massachusetts

guillotine: a machine for beheading; after Joseph Guillotin, French physician who proposed its use in 1789 as more humane than hanging

Luddite: one who opposes new technology; from Ned Ludd, leader of a group of textile workers in England who destroyed machinery in the early 1800s

maudlin: excessively sentimental; from scriptural figure Mary Magdalene, who is often shown weeping in depictions

milquetoast: a timid, unassertive person; after Caspar Milquetoast, comic strip character created by American cartoonist Harold Tucker Webster in 1924

salmonella: bacteria that can cause infections when contaminated food or water is consumed; named after Daniel Elmer Salmon, American veterinarian and public health official

sandwich: two or more slices of bread with a filling in-between; after John Montagu, 4th Earl of Sandwich (1718-92), who supposedly ate these at the gaming table

shrapnel: originally, a projectile with lead balls designed to inflict maximum damage in explosions, later pieces of metal casings; from Henry Shrapnel (1761-1842), British artillery officer who designed the projectile

silhouette: an outline image; from Étienne de Silhouette (1709-67), a stingy French finance minister

Zamboni: an ice resurfacing machine; after American inventor Frank Zamboni, who owned an ice skating rink

American Manual Alphabet

In the American Manual Alphabet, each letter of the alphabet is represented by a position of the fingers. This system was originally developed in France by Charles-Michel de l'Épée in the 1700s. Laurent Clerc and Thomas Gallaudet further refined it into the American Manual Alphabet, which a person may use to spell out a word with no American Sign Language equivalent.

Words and Expressions in Common Languages

English	Arabic	Chinese[1]	French	German	Hebrew	Russian	Spanish
Hello/hi	Salam	Ni hao	Bonjour	Hallo	Shalom	Privet (informal)	Hola
Good morning	Sabah el kheer	Zao shang hao	Bonjour	Guten Morgen	Boker tov	Dobraye utra	Buenos días
Good night	Tosbeho 'ala khair	Wan an	Bonne nuit	Gute Nacht	Layla tov	Spakoynay noci	Buenas noches
Good-bye	Ma'a salama	Zai jian	Au revoir	Auf wiedersehen	Lehitraot	Da svidan'ya	Adiós
Please	Men fadlek	Qing	S'il vous plaît	Bitte	Bevakasha	Pazhalusta	Por favor
Thank you very much	Shokran jazeelan	Xie xie	Merci beaucoup	Danke schön	Toda raba	Spasiba	Muchas gracias
You're welcome	Al' afw	Huan ying	De rien/pas de quoi	Keine Ursache	Bevakasha	Pazhalusta	De nada
How are you?	Kaifa haloka?	Ni hao?	Comment allez-vous?	Wie geht's dir/Ihnen?	Ma shelomkha?	Kak dela?	Cómo estás?
I'm fine	Ana bekhair	Hen hao	Je vais bien	Mir geht's gut	Tov	Harasho	Estoy bien
I'm sorry	Aasef	Bao qian	Je suis désolé	Entschuldigung	Ani mamash mitstaer	Prastite	Lo siento
Excuse me	Alma'derah	Bao qian	Pardon	Darf ich mal vorbei?	Selikha	Izvinite	Perdone
yes	na'am	shi [it is so]	oui	ja	ken	da	si
no	laa	bu [not]	non	nein	lo	nyet	no
one	wahed	yi	un	eins	ekhad	adin	uno
two	ithnaan	er	deux	zwei	shenayim	dva	dos
three	thalatha	san	trois	drei	shelosha	tri	tres
four	arba'a	si	quatre	vier	arbaa	chityri	cuatro
five	khamsa	wu	cinq	fünf	khamisha	p'at	cinco

Note: Actual form or usage of some words and expressions may vary depending on dialect, grammar, or circumstances. Transliterations for languages not in Latin alphabet vary. (1) Mandarin.

Language Diversity

Source: *Ethnologue: Languages of the World, 17th Edition*; United Nations Educational, Scientific, and Cultural Organization (UNESCO); World Almanac research

There are more than 7,100 individual languages spoken somewhere in the world. But more than 40% of the world's people speak one of the eight most common languages as their native tongue, and more than 75% speak one of the top 85 languages. Some 3,700 languages have fewer than 10,000 native speakers, and about 700 languages have fewer than 100.

Using classifications developed by linguists, about 2,400 languages spoken today are said to be at least threatened or unsustainably losing speakers. In some cases, people of the childbearing generation still use the language but do not transmit it to their children. In others, only those in the grandparent generation or older use a language, though they may have little occasion to do so. *Ethnologue* classifies 432 languages as nearly extinct and another 188 as dormant—that is, having no speakers with more than a "symbolic proficiency." Some languages disappear when the last native speaker dies.

Some say communities should determine whether a language remains worth using; a language should be allowed to die naturally. Others give more value to language preservation in the name of cultural diversity. Some experts have concluded that as languages die out, knowledge of the local environment and physical world is lost. A recent study of the Amesha tribe in the Peruvian Amazon found that as their severely endangered language faded, crop diversity decreased.

UNESCO supports efforts to preserve various endangered languages. In one, experts created a system for writing down words in the Khang (spoken in parts of northwest Vietnam), which had no written version. In addition, they produced recordings, word lists, grammars, and other materials for use in language classes aimed at reviving and perpetuating the use of Khang.

Principal Languages of the World

Source: Lewis, M. Paul, Gary F. Simons, Charles D. Fennig (eds.). *Ethnologue: Languages of the World, 17th Edition.* www.ethnologue.com. As updated 2014. Used by permission. © SIL International.

Languages shown in italics are macrolanguages, or language groups that are equivalent in some ways to individual languages. Each language group consists of a number of variants, which may be mutually unintelligible; these variants, when they have 2.5 million speakers or more, will also appear in the larger table below, and occasionally have the same name as the macrolanguage. Numbers are estimates and count only speakers for whom the language is a first language, or mother tongue.

Languages Spoken by the Most People

Language	Speakers (mil)	Language	Speakers (mil)	Language	Speakers (mil)
Chinese	1,197	Japanese	122	Turkish	71
Spanish	414	Javanese	84	Tamil	69
English	335	*Lahnda*	83	Vietnamese	68
Hindi	260	German (standard)	78	Urdu	64
Arabic	237	Korean	77	Italian	64
Portuguese	203	French	75	Panjabi (Western)	63
Bengali	193	Telugu	74	*Malay*	60
Russian	167	Marathi	72		

Languages With at Least 2.5 Million Speakers

Primary country is country of origin, not necessarily the country where the most speakers reside (e.g., Portugal is the primary country for Portuguese, but more Portuguese speakers live in Brazil). Number of speakers is worldwide total for each language.

Primary country	Language	Countries	Speakers (mil)	Primary country	Language	Countries	Speakers (mil)
Afghanistan	Pashto, Southern	4	10.8	Ethiopia	Amharic	2	21.8
	Dari	2	9.6		*Oromo*	4	17.5
	Uzbek, Southern	2	3.0		Oromo, West Central	1	8.9
Albania	*Albanian*	17	5.4		Tigrigna	3	6.9
Algeria	Arabic, Algerian Spoken	1	28.0		Oromo, Eastern	1	4.5
	Kabyle	1	5.6		Sidamo	1	3.0
Angola	Umbundu	1	6.0	Finland	Finnish	3	5.4
	Kimbundu	1	4.0	France	French	51	75.0
Armenia	Armenian	14	5.9	Georgia	Georgian	3	4.2
Austria	Bavarian	4	14.1	Germany	German, Standard	18	78.2
Azerbaijan	Azerbaijani, North	4	7.3		Mainfränkisch	1	4.9
Bangladesh	Bengali	4	193.0	Ghana	Akan	1	8.3
	Rangpuri	2	15.0		Ghanaian Pidgin English	1	5.0
	Chittagonian	1	13.0		Éwé	2	3.1
	Sylheti	2	10.3	Greece	Greek	9	13.4
Belarus	Belarusan	4	3.3	Guinea	*Mandingo*	7	6.5
Bolivia	*Aymara*	4	2.8		Maninkakan, Eastern	3	3.5
	Quechua, South Bolivian	2	2.8		Pular	4	2.9
	Aymara, Central	4	2.6	Haiti	Haitian	2	7.7
Botswana	Tswana	4	5.2	Hungary	Hungarian	9	12.6
Brazil	Hunsrik	1	3.0	India	Hindi	4	260.0
Bulgaria	Bulgarian	8	8.2		Telugu	2	74.0
Burkina Faso	Mòoré	3	5.1		Marathi	1	71.8
Burundi	Rundi	1	10.2		Tamil	6	68.8
Cambodia	Khmer, Central	2	14.2		Gujarati	6	46.6
China	*Chinese*	33	1,197.0		Bhojpuri	3	39.7
	Chinese, Mandarin	13	848.0		Kannada	1	37.7
	Chinese, Wu	1	77.2		Maithili	2	33.9
	Chinese, Yue	10	62.2		Malayalam	2	33.6
	Chinese, Min Nan	10	46.6		*Oriya*	4	32.7
	Chinese, Jinyu	1	45.0		Oriya	1	32.1
	Chinese, Xiang	1	36.0		Panjabi, Eastern	3	29.5
	Chinese, Hakka	13	30.1		*Marwari*	3	19.7
	Chinese, Gan	1	20.6		Magahi	1	14.0
	Zhuang	2	14.9		Chhattisgarhi	1	13.3
	Chinese, Min Bei	2	10.3		Assamese	1	12.8
	Chinese, Min Dong	6	9.1		Deccan	1	12.8
	Uyghur	4	8.8		*Rajasthani*	3	12.4
	Hmong	10	7.7		Kanauji	1	9.5
	Chinese, Huizhou	1	4.6		Haryanvi	1	8.0
	Mongolian, Peripheral	2	3.4		Varhadi-Nagpuri	1	7.0
	Chinese, Min Zhong	1	3.1		Santhali	3	6.2
	Bouyei	2	2.7		Konkani	4	6.1
	Chinese, Pu-Xian	3	2.6		Marwari	2	5.6
Congo, Dem. Rep. of	Luba-Kasai	1	6.3		Kashmiri	2	5.6
	Kongo	3	5.6		Malvi	1	5.6
	Koongo	3	5.0		Mewari	1	5.1
	Kituba	1	4.2		Lambadi	1	4.2
Côte d'Ivoire	Jula	3	2.6		*Dogri*	1	4.0
	Baoulé	1	2.1		Merwari	1	3.9
Croatia	Croatian	8	5.8		Mina	1	3.8
Czech Republic	Czech	6	10.6		Konkani, Goan	2	3.6
Denmark	Danish	3	5.5		Bhili	1	3.3
Egypt	Arabic, Egyptian Spoken	1	54.0		Sadri	2	3.3
	Arabic, Sa'idi Spoken	1	19.0				

Primary country	Language	Countries	Speakers (mil)
India (cont.)	Bundeli	1	3.1
	Awadhi	2	3.0
	Shekhawati	1	3.0
	Godwari	1	3.0
	Garhwali	1	2.9
	Bagheli	2	2.9
	Indian Sign Language	2	2.7
	Wagdi	1	2.5
Indonesia	Javanese	3	84.3
	Sunda	1	34.0
	Indonesian	1	23.2
	Madura	2	6.8
	Minangkabau	1	5.5
	Bugis	2	5.0
	Betawi	1	5.0
	Banjar	2	3.5
	Aceh	1	3.5
	Bali	1	3.3
	Musi	1	3.1
Iran	Persian	29	56.6
	Persian, Iranian	6	47.0
	Azerbaijani	15	24.2
	Azerbaijani, South	4	16.9
	Domari	13	4.0
	Gilaki	1	3.3
	Mazanderani	1	3.3
	Kurdish, Southern	2	3.0
Iraq	Kurdish	31	30.0
	Arabic, Mesopotamian Spoken	4	15.1
	Kurdish, Central	2	6.8
	Arabic, North Mesopotamian Spoken	3	6.3
Israel	Hebrew	1	5.3
Italy	Italian	10	63.7
	Napoletano-Calabrese	1	5.7
	Sicilian	1	4.7
	Lombard	2	3.9
	Venetian	4	3.9
Jamaica	Jamaican Creole English	3	3.2
Japan	Japanese	3	122.0
Jordan	Arabic, South Levantine Spoken	3	6.2
Kazakhstan	Kazakh	6	8.1
Kenya	Gikuyu	1	6.6
	Oluluyia	3	5.2
	Kalenjin	3	5.1
	Dholuo	2	4.2
	Kamba	1	3.9
Korea	Korean	5	77.2
Kyrgyzstan	Kyrgyz	5	2.9
Laos	Lao	3	3.3
Lesotho	Sotho, Southern	2	5.6
Libya	Arabic, Libyan Spoken	3	4.3
Lithuania	Lithuanian	1	3.0
Madagascar	Malagasy	5	16.7
	Malagasy, Plateau	2	7.5
Malawi	Chichewa	4	10.0
	Yao	4	3.1
	Tumbuka	2	2.6
Malaysia	Malay	13	59.5
	Malay	3	15.8
	Malay, Kedah	2	2.6
Mali	Bamanankan	2	4.1
Mauritania	Hassaniyya	7	3.3
Mongolia	Mongolian	6	5.8
Morocco	Arabic, Moroccan Spoken	2	21.0
	Tachelhit	2	3.9
Mozambique	Makhuwa	1	3.1
Myanmar (Burma)	Burmese	1	32.0
	Shan	3	3.3
Nepal	Nepali	5	16.1
	Nepali	3	15.4
Netherlands	Dutch	7	21.9
Nigeria	Hausa	8	25.0
	Yoruba	2	19.4
	Igbo	1	18.0
	Fulfulde, Nigerian	3	11.6
	Kanuri	6	3.8

Primary country	Language	Countries	Speakers (mil)
Nigeria (cont.)	Kanuri, Central	5	3.2
	Tiv	2	2.2
Norway	Norwegian	1	4.7
Pakistan	Lahnda	6	82.6
	Urdu	6	63.9
	Panjabi, Western	2	62.6
	Pushto	9	37.9
	Pashto, Northern	3	20.5
	Sindhi	3	20.3
	Seraiki	2	14.0
	Baluchi	8	7.0
	Pashto, Central	1	6.5
	Brahui	3	4.2
	Balochi, Southern	4	3.4
	Pahari-Potwari	1	2.5
Paraguay	Guarani	5	4.9
	Guaraní, Paraguayan	1	4.9
Peru	Quechua	6	8.9
Philippines	Tagalog	3	24.2
	Cebuano	1	15.8
	Ilocano	1	7.0
	Hiligaynon	1	5.8
	Bikol	1	3.7
	Waray-Waray	1	2.6
	Bikol, Central	1	2.5
Poland	Polish	9	38.7
Portugal	Portuguese	12	203.0
Romania	Romanian	6	23.8
	Romany	41	2.6
Russia	Russian	16	167.0
	Tatar	4	5.4
Rwanda	Rwanda	3	7.2
Saudi Arabia	Arabic	60	237.0
	Arabic, Najdi Spoken	4	9.7
	Arabic, Hijazi Spoken	2	6.0
Senegal	Fulah	20	22.3
	Wolof	2	4.0
	Pulaar	6	3.7
Serbia	Serbo-Croatian	27	17.1
	Serbian	10	9.0
	Albanian, Gheg	6	3.5
Slovakia	Slovak	9	5.2
Somalia	Somali	4	14.7
South Africa	Zulu	5	12.0
	Xhosa	2	8.2
	Afrikaans	6	7.1
	Sotho, Northern	1	4.6
	Tsonga	4	4.0
Spain	Spanish	31	414.0
	Catalan	4	4.1
Sri Lanka	Sinhala	2	15.6
Sudan	Arabic, Sudanese Spoken	3	16.8
Sweden	Swedish	3	9.2
Switzerland	German, Swiss	5	6.5
Syria	Arabic, North Levantine Spoken	2	14.4
Tajikistan	Tajiki	4	4.5
Tanzania	Swahili	15	15.5
	Swahili	8	15.5
	Sukuma	1	5.4
Thailand	Thai	2	20.4
	Thai, Northeastern	1	15.0
	Thai, Northern	2	6.0
	Thai, Southern	1	4.5
Tunisia	Arabic, Tunisian Spoken	1	9.4
Turkey	Turkish	8	70.8
	Kurdish, Northern	9	20.2
Turkmenistan	Turkmen	4	7.6
Uganda	Ganda	1	4.1
Ukraine	Ukrainian	9	36.0
United Kingdom	English	99	335.0
Uzbekistan	Uzbek	14	21.9
	Uzbek, Northern	6	19.0
Vietnam	Vietnamese	3	67.8
Yemen	Arabic, Sanaani Spoken	1	7.6
	Arabic, Ta'izzi-Adeni Spoken	2	7.1
Zambia	Bemba	2	4.1
Zimbabwe	Shona	3	10.7

BUILDINGS, BRIDGES, AND TUNNELS

100 Tallest Buildings in the World

Source: Phorio, phorio.com; Council on Tall Buildings and Urban Habitat (CTBUH), Illinois Inst. of Technology, www.ctbuh.org

Structures under construction and topped out architecturally are denoted by an asterisk (*). Year in parentheses is date of completion or projected completion. Only buildings that are completed or under construction and topped out as of Oct. 2014 are included here. Height is generally measured from the lowest significant open-air pedestrian entrance to the architectural top, including penthouses, spires, and other decorative features that are an integral part of the design. Stories generally counted from street level. NA = Not available.

Building	Ht. (ft)	Stories	Building	Ht. (ft)	Stories
Burj Khalifa, Dubai, United Arab Emirates (2010)	2,717	163	Rose Rayhaan by Rotana, Dubai, UAE (2007)	1,093	71
*Shanghai Tower, Shanghai, China (2015)	2,074	128	Minsheng Bank Building, Wuhan, China (2008)	1,087	68
Makkah Royal Clock Tower Hotel, Mecca, Saudi Arabia (2013)	1,972	120	*Ryugyong Hotel, Pyongyang, North Korea (NA)	1,083	105
*One World Trade Center, New York, NY, U.S. (2014)	1,776	92	China World Tower, Beijing, China (2009)	1,083	74
*CTF Finance Center, Guangzhou, China (2016)	1,739	111	Longxi International Hotel, Jiangyin, China (2011)	1,076	72
Taipei 101, Taipei, Taiwan (2004)	1,667	101	Al Yaqoub Tower, Dubai, UAE (2013)	1,076	69
Shanghai World Financial Center, Shanghai, China (2008)	1,614	101	*Wuxi Suning Plaza 1, Wuxi, China (2014)	1,076	68
International Commerce Centre, Hong Kong, China (2010)	1,588	108	The Index, Dubai, UAE (2010)	1,070	80
Petronas Tower I, Kuala Lumpur, Malaysia (1998)	1,483	88	The Landmark, Abu Dhabi, UAE (2013)	1,063	72
Petronas Tower II, Kuala Lumpur, Malaysia (1998)	1,483	88	Deji Plaza Phase 2, Nanjing, China (2013)	1,063	62
Zifeng Tower, Nanjing, China (2010)	1,476	66	*Yantai Shimao No. 1 The Harbour, Yantai, China (2015)	1,060	59
Willis (formerly Sears) Tower, Chicago, IL, U.S. (1974)	1,451	108	Q1, Gold Coast, Australia (2005)	1,058	78
KK100, Shenzhen, China (2011)	1,449	100	Wenzhou Trade Center, Wenzhou, China (2011)	1,056	68
Guangzhou International Finance Center, Guangzhou, China (2010)	1,439	103	Burj Al Arab Hotel, Dubai, UAE (1999)	1,053	56
Trump International Hotel & Tower, Chicago, IL, U.S. (2009)	1,389	98	Nina Tower I, Hong Kong, China (2007)	1,046	80
Jin Mao Tower, Shanghai, China (1999)	1,380	88	Chrysler Building, New York, NY, U.S. (1930)	1,046	77
Princess Tower, Dubai, UAE (2012)	1,356	101	New York Times Tower, New York, NY, U.S. (2007)	1,046	52
Al Hamra Tower, Kuwait City, Kuwait (2011)	1,354	80	United International Mansion, Chongqing, China (2013)	1,043	67
Two International Finance Centre, Hong Kong, China (2003)	1,352	88	*Riverside Century Plaza Main Tower, Wuhu, China (2015)	1,043	66
23 Marina, Dubai, UAE (2012)	1,289	90	HHHR Tower, Dubai, UAE (2010)	1,042	72
CITIC Plaza, Guangzhou, China (1997)	1,280	80	*Youth Olympics Center Tower 1, Nanjing, China (2015)	1,032	68
*Capital Market Authority Headquarters, Riyadh, Saudi Arabia (2015)	1,260	77	Bank of America Plaza, Atlanta, GA, U.S. (1992)	1,023	55
Shun Hing Square, Shenzhen, China (1996)	1,260	69	*Moi Center Tower A, Shenyang, China (2014)	1,020	75
*Eton Place Dalian Tower 1, Dalian, China (2015)	1,257	80	US Bank Tower, Los Angeles, CA, U.S. (1990)	1,018	73
World Trade Center Abu Dhabi-The Residences, Abu Dhabi, UAE (2014)	1,251	88	Ocean Heights, Dubai, UAE (2010)	1,017	83
Empire State Building, New York, NY, U.S. (1931)	1,250	102	Menara Telekom Headquarters, Kuala Lumpur, Malaysia (2001)	1,017	59
Elite Residence, Dubai, UAE (2012)	1,248	87	Pearl River Tower, Guangzhou, China (2012)	1,015	71
Central Plaza, Hong Kong, China (1992)	1,227	78	*Guangzhou Fortune Center, Guangzhou, China (2015)	1,015	68
Bank of China Tower, Hong Kong, China (1990)	1,205	72	Jumeirah Emirates Towers Hotel, Dubai, UAE (2000)	1,014	56
Bank of America Tower, New York, NY, U.S. (2009)	1,200	55	*Eurasia, Moscow, Russia (2014)	1,013	72
Almas Tower, Dubai, UAE (2008)	1,181	68	Burj Rafal, Riyadh, Saudi Arabia (2014)	1,010	68
The Pinnacle, Guangzhou, China (2012)	1,181	60	Cayan Tower, Dubai, UAE (2013)	1,008	73
JW Marriott Marquis Hotel Dubai Tower 1, Dubai, UAE (2012)	1,166	82	Franklin Center-North Tower, Chicago, IL, U.S. (1989)	1,007	60
JW Marriott Marquis Hotel Dubai Tower 2, Dubai, UAE (2013)	1,166	82	One57, New York, NY, U.S. (2014)	1,005	79
Emirates Office Tower, Dubai, UAE (2000)	1,163	54	East Pacific Center Tower A, Shenzhen, China (2013)	1,004	85
*OKO-South Tower, Moscow, Russia (2015)	1,155	85	The Shard, London, United Kingdom (2013)	1,004	73
*Forum 66 Tower 2, Shenyang, China (2015)	1,150	68	Etihad Towers 2, Abu Dhabi, UAE (2011)	1,002	70
Tuntex Sky Tower, Kaohsiung, Taiwan (1998)	1,140	85	JPMorganChase Tower, Houston, TX, U.S. (1982)	1,002	75
Aon Center, Chicago, IL, U.S. (1973)	1,136	83	NE Asia Trade Tower, New Songdo City, Incheon, South Korea (2011)	1,001	68
The Center, Hong Kong, China (1998)	1,135	73	Baiyoke Tower II, Bangkok, Thailand (1997)	997	85
John Hancock Center, Chicago, IL, U.S. (1969)	1,128	100	Maoye City-Marriott Hotel, Wuxi, China (2014)	997	68
*Ahmed Abdul Rahim Al Attar Tower, Dubai, UAE (2015)	1,122	76	Two Prudential Plaza, Chicago, IL, U.S. (1990)	995	64
*ADNOC Headquarters, Abu Dhabi, UAE (2015)	1,122	65	*KAFD World Trade Center, Riyadh, Saudi Arabia (2015)	994	67
*Chongqing World Financial Center, Chongqing, China (2014)	1,112	73	*Jiangxi Nanchang Greenland Central Plaza 1, Nanchang, China (2015)	994	59
Mercury City Tower, Moscow, Russia (2013)	1,112	75	*Jiangxi Nanchang Greenland Central Plaza 2, Nanchang, China (2015)	994	59
Tianjin World Financial Center, Tianjin, China (2011)	1,105	75	*Diwang International Fortune Center, Liuzhou, China (2015)	993	75
The Torch, Dubai, UAE (2011)	1,105	79	Leatop Plaza, Guangzhou, China (2011)	993	64
Hanoi Landmark Tower, Hanoi, Vietnam (2012)	1,103	72	Wells Fargo Plaza, Houston, TX, U.S. (1983)	992	71
Shanghai Shimao International Plaza, Shanghai, China (2006)	1,094	60	Kingdom Centre, Riyadh, Saudi Arabia (2002)	992	41
			The Address Downtown Dubai, Dubai, UAE (2008)	991	63
			*Gate of the Orient, Suzhou, China (2014)	990	68

Tallest Free-Standing Towers in the World

Source: Phorio, phorio.com; Council on Tall Buildings and Urban Habitat (CTBUH), Illinois Inst. of Technology, www.ctbuh.org
Year is date of completion. As of Oct. 2014.

Tower	Ht. (ft)	Year	Tower	Ht. (ft)	Year
Tokyo Sky Tree, Tokyo, Japan	2,080	2012	Central Radio & TV Tower, Beijing, China	1,268	1992
Canton Tower, Guangzhou, China	1,969	2010	Kiev TV Tower, Kiev, Ukraine	1,263	1974
CN Tower, Toronto, ON, Canada	1,815	1976	Tashkent Tower, Tashkent, Uzbekistan	1,230	1985
Ostankino Tower, Moscow, Russia	1,772	1967	Liberation Tower, Kuwait City, Kuwait	1,220	1996
Oriental Pearl Television Tower, Shanghai, China	1,535	1995	Alma-Ata Tower, Almaty, Kazakhstan	1,217	1982
Milad Tower, Tehran, Iran	1,427	2008	TV Tower, Riga, Latvia	1,208	1987
Manara Kuala Lumpur, Kuala Lumpur, Malaysia	1,379	1996	Berliner Fernsehturm, Berlin, Germany	1,207	1969
Tianjin Radio & TV Tower, Tianjin, China	1,362	1991	Stratosphere Tower, Las Vegas, NV, U.S.	1,149	1996
Henan Province Radio & Television Emission Tower, Zhengzhou, China	1,273	2010	West Pearl Tower, Chengdu, China	1,112	2004
			Macau Tower, Macau, China	1,109	2001
			Europaturm, Frankfurt, Germany	1,106	1979

Tall Buildings in Selected North American Cities

Source: Phorio, phorio.com; Council on Tall Buildings and Urban Habitat (CTBUH), Illinois Inst. of Technology, www.ctbuh.org
List includes freestanding towers and other structures that do not have stories and are not technically considered buildings. Structures still under construction as of Oct. 2014 are denoted by an asterisk (*). Year in parentheses is date of completion or projected completion. Height is generally measured from the lowest significant open-air pedestrian entrance to the architectural top, including penthouses, spires, and other decorative features that are an integral part of the design. Stories generally counted from street level.
NA = Not applicable/available.

Building/structure	Ht. (ft)	Stories
Atlanta, GA		
Bank of America Plaza (incl. spire),		
600 Peachtree St. NE (1992)	1,023	55
SunTrust Plaza, 303 Peachtree St. NE (1993)[1] . . .	867	60
One Atlantic Center, 1201 W. Peachtree St. (1987)	820	50
191 Peachtree Tower (1991)	770	50
Westin Peachtree Plaza, 210 Peachtree St. NW		
(1976)[2]	723	73
Georgia Pacific Tower, 133 Peachtree St. NE (1981)	697	51
Promenade II (incl. spire), 1230 Peachtree St. NE		
(1989)	691	40
AT&T Building, 675 W. Peachtree St. (1980).	677	47
Sovereign, 3344 Peachtree (2008)	665	48
1180 Peachtree (2006)	657	41
GLG Grand/Four Seasons Hotel, 75 14th St. NE		
(1992)	609	53
The Mansion on Peachtree, 3376 Peachtree Rd.		
NE (2008)	580	42
Atlantic, 270 17th St. NW (2009)	577	46
State of Georgia Building, 2 Peachtree St. NW		
(1967)[3]	556	44
Marriott Marquis, 265 Peachtree Center Ave. NE		
(1985)	554	52
Viewpoint, 855 Peachtree St. NE (2008)	501	36
(1) 902 ft incl. antenna. (2) 883 ft incl. antenna. (3) 599 ft incl. antenna.		
Austin, TX		
Austonian, 200 Congress Ave. (2010).	683	56
360 Condominiums (incl. spire), 360 Nueces St.		
(2008)	581	45
Frost Bank Tower, 401 N. Congress Ave. (2004). . .	516	33
Boston, MA		
Hancock Place, 200 Clarendon St. (1976)	790	62
Prudential Tower, 800 Boylston St. (1964)[1]	750	52
*Millennium Tower, Washington St. (2016)	606	54
Federal Reserve Bldg., 600 Atlantic Ave. (1978). . .	604	32
BNY Mellon Center at One Boston Place,		
201 Washington St. (1970)	602	41
One International Place, 100 Oliver St. (1987).	600	46
100 Federal St. (1971)	591	37
One Financial Center, 10 Dewey Square (1984) . .	590	46
111 Huntington Ave. (2002)	564	36
Two International Place (1993)	538	35
One Post Office Square (1981)	525	40
1 Federal St. (1975)	520	38
Exchange Place, 53 State St. (1984)	510	39
Sixty State St. (1977)	509	38
1 Beacon St. (1972)	507	36
State Street Financial Center (incl. spire),		
1 Lincoln St. (2003)	503	36
28 State St. (1970)	500	40
(1) 920 ft incl. antenna.		
Calgary, AB, Canada		
*Brookfield Place Tower One, 225 6th Ave. (2018)	810	56
The Bow, 510 Centre St. (2012)	779	57
Petro Canada Centre West Tower,		
150 6th Ave. SW (1984)	705	53
Eighth Avenue Place East Tower, 8th Ave.		
and 5th St. SW (2011)	696	49
Bankers Hall West Tower, 888 3rd St. SW (2000). .	645	50
Bankers Hall East Tower, 855 2nd St. SW (1989). .	645	50
Calgary Tower, 101 9th Ave. SW (1967)	626	NA
Centennial Place 1 (incl. spire), 520 3rd Ave. SW		
(2010)	599	40
*Eighth Avenue Place West Tower, 8th Ave. and		
5th St. SW (2014)	581	41
TransCanada Tower, 450 1st St. SW (2001)	581	38
Canterra Tower, 400 3rd Ave. SW (1988)	580	46
Jamieson Place (incl. spires), 302 4th Ave. SW (2009)	568	38
First Canadian Centre, 350 7th Ave. SW (1982). . .	547	41
Western Canadian Place-North Tower,		
707 6th St. SW (1983)	538	41
Canada Trust, Calgary Eatons Centre,		
421 7th Ave. SW (1991)	530	40
*City Centre I, 339 2nd Ave. SW (2015)	530	41
Scotia Square, 700 2nd St. SW (1976).	509	41
Nexen Building, 801 7th Ave. SW (1982)	500	37
Charlotte, NC		
Bank of America Corporate Center, 100 N. Tryon		
St. (1992)	871	60
Duke Energy Center, 534 S. Tryon St. (2010)	786	48

Building/structure	Ht. (ft)	Stories
Hearst Tower, 214 N. Tryon St. (2002)	659	47
One Wells Fargo Center, 301 S. College St. (1988)	588	42
The Vue, 400 W. 5th St. (2010)	574	50
Bank of America Plaza, 101 S. Tryon St. (1974). . .	503	40
Chicago, IL		
Willis (fmr. Sears) Tower, 233 S. Wacker Dr. (1974)[1]	1,451	108
Trump International Hotel & Tower (incl. spire),		
401 N. Wabash Ave. (2009)	1,389	98
Aon Center, 200 E. Randolph St. (1973).	1,136	83
John Hancock Center, 875 N. Michigan Ave.		
(1969)[2]	1,128	100
Franklin Center-North Tower (incl. spires),		
227 W. Monroe St. (1989).	1,007	60
Two Prudential Plaza (incl. spire), 180 N. Stetson		
Ave. (1990)	995	64
311 S. Wacker Dr. (1990).	961	65
900 N. Michigan Ave. (1989)	871	66
Aqua, 225 N. Columbus Dr. (2009)	859	86
Water Tower Place, 845 N. Michigan Ave. (1976) . .	859	74
Chase Tower, 21 S. Clark St. (1969)	850	60
Park Tower, 800 N. Michigan Ave. (2000)	844	68
The Legacy at Millennium Park, 21-39 S. Wabash		
(2010)	818	73
300 N. LaSalle (2009).	785	60
3 First National Plaza, 70 W. Madison St. (1981). .	767	57
Chicago Title & Trust Center, 161 N. Clark St. (1992)	756	50
Blue Cross HQ, 300 E. Randolph St. (2010).	744	54
*River Point, 444 W. Lake St. (2017).	732	50
Olympia Centre, 737 N. Michigan Ave. (1986)	731	63
One Museum Park, 1215 S. Prairie Ave. (2009) . . .	726	62
AMA Plaza, 330 N. Wabash Ave. (1973).	695	52
Waldorf Astoria Chicago, 940 N. Rush St. (2009)	686	60
111 S. Wacker Dr. (2005).	681	51
181 W. Madison St. (1990).	680	50
Hyatt Center, 71 S. Wacker (2005)	679	48
One Magnificent Mile, 980 N. Michigan Ave.		
(1983)	673	57
340 on the Park, 340 W. Randolph St. (2007).	672	64
United Bldg., 77 W. Wacker Dr. (1992)	668	49
*150 North Riverside (2017)	665	49
UBS Tower, 1 N. Wacker Dr. (2001)	652	50
Daley Center, 55 W. Washington St. (1965)	648	32
55 E. Erie St. (2004)	647	56
Lake Point Tower, 505 N. Lake Shore Dr. (1968) . .	645	70
River East Center, 350 E. Illinois St. (2001)	644	58
Grand Plaza I (incl. spire), 540 N. State St. (2003)	641	57
155 N. Wacker Dr. (2009)	638	45
Leo Burnett Bldg., 35 W. Wacker Dr. (1989)	635	46
The Heritage at Millennium Park, 125 N. Wabash		
Ave. (2005)	631	57
NBC Tower (incl. spire), 455 N. Cityfront Plaza Dr.		
(1989)	627	37
353 N. Clark (2009)	623	44
OneEleven, 111 W. Wacker (2014).	616	58
Millennium Centre, 33 W. Ontario St. (2003).	610	58
Board of Trade (incl. statue), 141 W. Jackson Blvd.		
(1930).	609	44
Chicago Place, 700 N. Michigan Ave. (1991)	608	49
CNA Plaza, 325 S. Wabash St. (1972).	601	44
One Prudential Plaza, 130 E. Randolph St.		
(1955)[3]	601	41
Heller International Tower, 500 W. Monroe St.		
(1992)	600	45
One Madison Plaza, 200 W. Madison St. (1982) . .	599	44
One Museum Park West, 201 E. Roosevelt Rd.		
(2010)	595	54
1000 Lake Shore Plaza (1964)	590	55
The Clare at Water Tower, 55 East Pearson St.		
(2008)	589	52
Citigroup Center, 500 W. Madison St. (1987)	588	42
The Park Monroe, 65 E. Monroe St. (1972)	583	49
Crain Communications Bldg., 150 N. Michigan Ave.		
(1983)	582	41
North Pier Apts., 474 N. Lake Shore Dr. (1990) . . .	581	61
Citadel Center, 131 S. Dearborn St. (2003)	580	37
The Fordham, 25 E. Superior St. (2003)	574	52
190 S. LaSalle St. (1987)	573	40
One S. Dearborn (2005)	571	39
Onterie Center, 446 E. Ontario St. (1986).	570	58
*Loews North Park Drive, 455 North Park Dr.		
(2015)	569	49

Building/structure	Ht. (ft)	Stories
Chicago Temple, 77 W. Washington St. (1924)....	568	23
Palmolive Building (incl. beacon), 919 N. Michigan Ave. (1929)...........................	565	37
Marina City I, 300 N. State St. (1964)...........	562	61
Marina City II, 301 N. Dearborn St. (1964).......	562	61
Huron Plaza Apts., 30 E. Huron St. (1983).......	560	56
Boeing International Headquarters, 100 N. Riverside Plz. (1990).................	560	36
The Parkshore, 195 N. Harbor Dr. (1991)........	556	56
North Harbor Tower, 175 N. Harbor Dr. (1988)....	556	55
Civic Opera Bldg., 20 N. Wacker Dr. (1929)......	555	45
Streeter Place, 351 E. Ohio St. (2009)..........	554	55
Harbor Point, 155 N. Harbor Dr. (1975)..........	554	54
Newberry Plaza, 1000 N. State St. (1974)........	553	53
Michigan Plaza South, 205 N. Michigan Ave. (1985)	553	46
30 N. LaSalle St. (1975).......................	553	44
Pittsfield Building, 55 E. Washington St. (1927)...	551	38
One S. Wacker Dr. (1982)......................	550	40
Kluczynski Federal Building, 230 S. Dearborn St. (1975).......................................	545	45
Park Millennium, 222 N. Columbus Dr. (2002)....	544	57
AMLI River North, 401 N. Clark St. (2013).......	543	49
Franklin Center-South Tower, 125 S. Franklin St. (1992)......................................	538	35
The Pinnacle, 21 E. Huron St. (2004)............	535	48
LaSalle National Bank, 135 S. LaSalle St. (1934). .	535	45
Park Place Tower, 655 W. Irving Park Rd. (1971) . .	531	56
One N. LaSalle St. (1930)......................	530	48
The Elysees, 111 E. Chestnut St. (1973).........	529	56
River Plaza, 405 N. Wabash St. (1977)..........	524	56
35 E. Wacker Drive (1927).....................	523	40
Kemper Building, 1 E. Wacker Dr. (1962)........	522	41
Mather Tower, 75 E. Wacker Dr. (1928).........	521	41
Chicago Mercantile Exchange, 10 S. Wacker Dr. (1987)......................................	520	40
Chicago Mercantile Exchange, 30 S. Wacker Dr. (1983)......................................	520	40
The Columbian, 1180 S. Michigan Ave. (2008)....	517	47
*200 N. Michigan (2016).......................	517	44
191 N. Wacker Drive (2002).....................	516	37
401 E. Ontario St. (1990)......................	515	51
One Financial Place, 440 S. LaSalle St. (1985) ...	515	39
The Streeter, 345 E. Ohio St. (2006)............	514	50
Park Tower Condominiums, 5415 N. Sheridan Rd. (1973)......................................	513	54
600 North Lake Shore Drive-South Tower (2009). .	513	47
LaSalle-Wacker Building, 221 N. LaSalle St. (1930)......................................	512	41
Harris Bank III, 115 S. LaSalle St. (1974)........	510	41
321 N. Clark St. (1987)........................	510	35
215 West, 215 W. Washington St. (2010).........	509	50
400 E. Ohio St. (1982)........................	505	50
Carbide & Carbon Bldg., 230 N. Michigan Ave. (1929)......................................	503	37
One Superior Place, 1 W. Superior St. (1999).....	502	52
120 N. LaSalle St. (1992)......................	501	39
10 S. LaSalle St. (1986).......................	501	37
The Tides, 360 E. South Water St. (2008)........	500	51
200 S. Wacker Drive (1981)....................	500	41

(1) 1,729 ft incl. antenna. (2) 1,499 ft incl. antenna. (3) 912 ft incl. antenna.

Cleveland, OH

Key Tower (incl. spire), 127 Public Sq. (1991).....	947	57
Terminal Tower, 50 Public Sq. (1928)[1].........	708	52
200 Public Sq. (1985).........................	658	46
Tower at Erieview, 1301 E. 9th St. (1964)........	529	40

(1) 771 ft incl. flagpole.

Columbus, OH

James A. Rhodes State Office Tower, 30 E. Broad St. (1973)...................................	624	41
Leveque-Lincoln Tower, 50 W. Broad St. (1927)...	555	47
William Green Building, 30 W. Spring St. (1990)...	530	33
Huntington Center, 41 S. High St. (1983)........	512	37
Vern Riffe State Office Tower, 77 S. High St. (1988)	503	33

Dallas, TX

Bank of America Plaza, 901 Main St. (1985)......	921	72
Renaissance Tower (incl. spire), 1201 Elm St. (1974)	886	56
Comerica Bank Tower, 1717 Main St. (1987).....	787	60
JPMorgan Chase Tower, 2200 Ross Ave. (1987)..	738	55
Fountain Place, 1445 Ross Ave. (1986)..........	720	58
Trammel Crow Center, 2001 Ross Ave. (1984)....	686	50
1700 Pacific Ave. (1983)......................	655	50
Thanksgiving Tower, 1600 Pacific Ave. (1982)	645	50
Energy Plaza, 1601 Bryan St. (1983)............	629	49
Elm Place, 1401 Elm St. (1965)................	628	52
Gables Republic Tower (incl. spire), 300 N. Ervay (1954)......................................	602	36
Republic Center Tower II, 325 N. St. Paul (1964) ..	598	50
One AT&T Plaza, 208 S. Akard St. (1984)	580	37

Building/structure	Ht. (ft)	Stories
Ross Tower, 500 N. Akard St. (1984)............	579	45
Museum Tower, 2112 Flora St. (2013)	560	42
Cityplace Center East, 2711 N. Haskell Ave. (1989)	560	42
Reunion Tower, 300 Reunion Blvd. (1976)	560	NA
Sheraton Dallas Hotel Center Tower, 400 Olive St. (1959)	550	42
Mercantile Bldg. (incl. spire), 1700 Main St. (1943)	523	31
Bryan Tower, 2001 Bryan St. (1973)............	512	40

Denver, CO

Republic Plaza, 330 17th St. (1984)............	714	56
1801 California St. (1982).....................	709	52
Wells Fargo Center, 1700 Lincoln Ave. (1983)	698	50
Four Seasons Hotel and Private Residences, 1111 14th St. (2010)......................	639	45
1999 Broadway (1985)........................	544	43
707 17th St. (1981)...........................	522	42
555 17th St. (1978)...........................	507	40

Detroit, MI

Marriott Hotel, Renaissance Center I (1977)[1]....	727	70
One Detroit Center, 500 Woodward Ave. (1991)...	619	43
Penobscot Building, 633 Griswold Ave. (1928)[2]..	565	47
Renaissance Center 100 Tower (1976)...........	508	39
Renaissance Center 200 Tower (1976)...........	508	39
Renaissance Center 300 Tower (1976)...........	508	39
Renaissance Center 400 Tower (1976)...........	508	39

(1) 755 ft incl. antenna. (2) 665 ft incl. antenna.

Fort Worth, TX

Burnett Plaza, 801 Cherry St. (1983)............	567	40
D.R. Horton Tower, 301 Commerce St. (1984)	547	38
Carter Burgess Plaza, 777 Main St. (1982)	525	40

Hartford, CT

City Place I, 185 Asylum St. (1980).............	535	38
Travelers Tower, 26 Grove St. (1919)............	527	24
Goodwin Square, 225 Asylum St. (1990).........	522	30

Houston, TX

JPMorganChase Tower, 600 Travis St. (1982)	1,002	75
Wells Fargo Plaza, 1000 Louisiana St. (1983)	992	71
Williams Tower, 2800 Post Oak Blvd. (1982)	901	64
Bank of America Center, 700 Louisiana St. (1983)	780	56
Texaco Heritage Plaza, 1111 Bagby St. (1987) ...	762	53
*609 Main at Texas (2017)	757	49
Enterprise Plaza, 1100 Louisiana St. (1980)[1]....	756	55
Centerpoint Energy Plaza, 1111 Louisiana St. (1996)	741	47
Continental Center I, 1600 Smith St. (1984)......	732	47
Fulbright Tower, 1301 McKinney St. (1982)	725	52
One Shell Plaza, 900 Louisiana St. (1970)[2].....	714	50
1400 Smith St. (1983).........................	691	50
3 Allen Center, 333 Clay St. (1980).............	685	50
LyondellBassell Tower, 1221 McKinney St. (1978)	678	47
First City Tower, 1001 Fannin St. (1984).........	662	47
BG Group Place, 811 Main St. (2011)	632	46
San Felipe Plaza, 5847 San Felipe Blvd. (1984) ..	625	45
ExxonMobil Building, 800 Bell Ave. (1962).......	606	44
1500 Louisiana St. (2002)......................	600	40
America General Center, 2929 Allen Pkwy. (1983)	590	42
Two Houston Center, 909 Fannin St. (1974)......	579	40
San Jacinto Column, La Porte	570	NA
Marathon Oil Tower, 5555 San Felipe Blvd. (1983)	562	41
Wedge International Tower, 1415 Louisiana St. (1983)......................................	550	44
KBR Tower, 601 Jefferson St. (1973)	550	40
*2929 Weslayan (2015)	533	40
Pennzoil Place I, 700 Main St. (1976)...........	523	36
Pennzoil Place II, 700 Louisiana St. (1976)	523	36
Devon Energy Center, 1200 Smith St. (1978).....	521	36
RRI Energy Plaza, 1000 Main St. (2003).........	518	36
Total Plaza, 1201 Louisiana St. (1971)..........	518	35
The Huntington, 2121 Kirby Dr. (1982)..........	503	34
El Paso Energy Building, 1010 Milam St. (1962) ..	502	33
One Park Place, 1500 McKinney St. (2009).......	501	37
Memorial Hermann Tower, 929 Gessner Rd. (2009)	500	35

(1) 782 ft incl. antenna. (2) 999 ft incl. antenna.

Indianapolis, IN

Chase Tower, 111 Monument Cir. (1990)[1]......	701	49
One America Tower, 200 N. Illinois St. (1982).....	533	38
One Indiana Square, 200 N. Delaware St. (1970). .	504	36

(1) 811 ft incl. antenna.

Jersey City, NJ

30 Hudson St. (2004)..........................	781	42
*URL Harborside Tower 1 (2016)................	700	71
101 Hudson St. (1992)	548	42
Trump Plaza I, 88 Morgan St. (2008)	532	55
Newport Tower, 525 Washington Blvd. (1990)	531	37
Exchange Place Center, 10 Exchange Pl. (incl. spire) (1990).........................	516	32

Building/structure	Ht. (ft)	Stories
Hudson Green East Tower, 77 Hudson St. (2009)	509	48
Hudson Green West Tower, 77 Hudson St. (2010)	501	48

Las Vegas, NV

Building/structure	Ht. (ft)	Stories
Stratosphere Tower, 2000 Las Vegas Blvd. S. (1996)	1,149	NA
*Fontainebleau Resort Hotel, 2755 Las Vegas Blvd. S. (NA)	735	63
The Palazzo, 3339 Las Vegas Blvd. S. (2007)	642	53
Encore at Wynn Las Vegas, 3145 Las Vegas Blvd. S. (2008)	631	52
Trump International Hotel and Tower 1, 3128 Las Vegas Blvd. S. (2008)	622	64
Wynn Las Vegas, 3145 Las Vegas Blvd. S. (2005)	613	45
Cosmopolitan Casino Spa Tower, Las Vegas Blvd. and Harmon Ave. (2010)	603	52
Cosmopolitan Beach Resort Tower, Las Vegas Blvd. and Harmon Ave. (2010)	603	50
Aria Resort and Casino, 3730 Las Vegas Blvd. S. (2009)	600	60
Planet Hollywood Towers, 3667 Las Vegas Blvd. S. (2009)	597	50
VDARA, 2551 W. Harmon Ave. (2009)	556	55
Eiffel Tower, Paris Hotel and Casino, 3645 Las Vegas Blvd. S. (1998)	540	NA
Mandarin Oriental Hotel Las Vegas, 3750 Las Vegas Blvd. S. (2009)	539	47
New York, New York Hotel and Casino, 3790 Las Vegas Blvd. S. (1997)	529	48
Palms Place, 4321 W. Flamingo Rd. (2008)	518	50
Bellagio Hotel and Casino, 3600 Las Vegas Blvd. S. (1998)	508	36
Sky Las Vegas, 2780 Las Vegas Blvd. S. (2007)	500	45

Los Angeles, CA

Building/structure	Ht. (ft)	Stories
*Wilshire Grand Tower (2017)	1,100	73
US Bank Tower, 633 W. 5th St. (1990)	1,018	73
Aon Center, 707 Wilshire Blvd. (1974)	858	62
Two California Plaza, 350 S. Grand Ave. (1992)	750	52
Gas Company Tower, 555 W. 5th St. (1991)	749	52
Bank of America Plaza, 333 South Hope St. (1975)	735	55
777 Tower, 777 S. Figueroa St. (1991)	725	53
Wells Fargo Tower, 333 S. Grand Ave. (1983)	723	54
Figueroa at Wilshire, 601 S. Figueroa St. (1989)	717	52
Paul Hastings Tower, 515 S. Flower St. (1971)	699	52
City National Tower, 555 S. Flower St. (1971)	699	52
L.A. Live Hotel and Condominiums, 900 W. Olympic Blvd. (2010)	667	54
Citigroup Center, 444 S. Flower St. (1979)	625	48
611 Place, 611 W. 6th St. (1967)	620	42
KPMG Tower, 355 S. Grand Ave. (1984)	606	45
One California Plaza, 300 S. Grand Ave. (1985)	578	42
Century Plaza Tower 1, 2029 Century Park East (1973)	571	44
Century Plaza Tower 2, 2049 Century Park East (1973)	571	44
Ernst & Young, LLP Plaza, 725 S. Figueroa St. (1986)	534	41
AIG-SunAmerica Ctr., 1999 Ave. of the Stars (1989)	533	39
TCW Tower, 865 S. Figueroa St. (1990)	517	37
Union Bank Plaza, 445 S. Figueroa St. (1968)	516	40
10 Universal City Plaza (1984)	506	36

Mexico City, Mexico

Building/structure	Ht. (ft)	Stories
*Torre Reforma, Paseo de la Reforma 483 (2015)	800	57
*Punto Chapultepec, Reforma 509 (2016)	780	59
*Torre BBVA Bancomer, Paseo de la Reforma 506 (2015)	771	50
*Torre Paradox, Av. Santa Fe 483 (2017)	768	62
*Torre Mayor, Paseo de la Reforma 505 (2003)	738	55
*Torre BBVA Bancomer, Paseo de la Reforma 506 (2014)	738	50
Torre Ejecutiva Pemex, Marina Nacional 329 Col. Huasteca (1984)	693	51
Torre Altus, Paseo de los Laureles 416 (1999)	640	44
Torre Latino Americana (incl. spire), Eje Central Lazaro Cardenas 2 (1956)	597	45
*Torre Cuarzo, Paseo de la Reforma 26 (2016)	591	40
World Trade Center, Montecito 38 Col. Napoles (1972)	565	50
*Siroco Elite Residences, Av. Santa Fe 482 (2014)	561	43
*Torre Punta Reforma, Paseo de la Reforma 180 (2014)	558	37
Peninsula Tower, Av. Santa Fe 1240 (2014)	539	50
Arcos Torre II, Paseo de los Tamarindos 400 (2008)	529	35
Arcos Torre I, Paseo de los Tamarindos 400 (1997)	529	35
*Torre Diana, Rio Lerma 232 (2016)	519	33

Miami, FL

Building/structure	Ht. (ft)	Stories
*Panorama Tower, 1101 Brickell Ave. (2017)	831	83
Four Seasons Hotel & Tower, 1441 Brickell Ave. (2003)	789	64
Wachovia Financial Ctr., 200 S. Biscayne Blvd. (1983)	764	55
900 Biscayne Bay, 900 Biscayne Blvd. (2008)	712	65
Marquis, 1100 Biscayne Blvd. (2009)	679	63
Met 2 Office Tower, 200 SE 3rd St. (2010)	655	47
*Brickell CityCentre Office Tower 3 (2016)	634	45
Mint at Riverfront, 90 SW 3rd St. (2009)	631	55
Infinity at Brickell, 60 W. 13th St. (2008)	630	52
Miami Tower, 100 SE 2nd St. (1987)	625	47
Marinablue, 888 Biscayne Blvd. (2007)	615	57
Plaza on Brickell Tower I, 901 Brickell Ave. (2007)	610	56
Epic Residences & Hotel, 300 Biscayne Blvd. Way (2008)	601	54
*SLS Brickell, 1300 S. Miami Ave. (2016)	599	52
Icon Brickell North Tower, 495 Brickell Ave. (2008)	586	58
Icon Brickell South Tower, 495 Brickell Ave. (2008)	586	58
Ten Museum Park, 1040 Biscayne Blvd. (2007)	585	50
Paramount at Edgewater Square, 2066 N. Bayshore Dr. (2009)	555	47
50 Biscayne Blvd. (2007)	554	55
Quantum on the Bay South Tower, 1900 N. Bayshore Dr. (2008)	554	51
*Biscayne Beach, 701 NE 29th St. (2016)	550	51
*Brickell Heights North Tower, 850 S. Miami Ave. (2016)	549	52
*Paraiso Bay Tower 1, 600 NE 31st St. (2017)	548	55
*Paraiso Bay Tower 2, 600 NE 31st St. (2017)	548	55
Opera Tower, 1750 N. Bayshore Dr. (2007)	543	56
Everglades on the Bay North Tower, 244 Biscayne Blvd. (2008)	538	49
Everglades on the Bay South Tower, 244 Biscayne Blvd. (2008)	538	49
Quantum on the Bay North Tower, 1900 N. Bayshore Dr. (2008)	536	44
*Brickell Heights South Tower, 850 S. Miami Ave. (2016)	529	52
Jade at Brickell Bay, 1331 Brickell Bay Dr. (2004)	528	49
Plaza on Brickell Tower II, 901 Brickell Ave. (2007)	525	48
*Brickell House, 1300 Brickell Bay Dr. (2014)	524	46
*Brickell CityCentre Condo Tower 3 (2016)	522	48
Santa Maria, 1643 Brickell Ave. (1997)	520	51
*Brickell CityCentre Condo Tower 2 (2015)	520	45
*Brickell CityCentre Hotel Tower (2015)	516	41
The Ivy, 90-95 SW 3rd St. (2008)	512	45
Stephen P. Clark Center, 111 NW 1st St. (1985)	510	28
*Brickell CityCentre Condo Tower 1 (2015)	503	44
Met 2 Marriott Marquis, 200 SE 3rd St. (2010)	502	41
Wind, 330 S. Miami Ave. (2008)	501	41
1450 Brickell (2010)	500	34

Minneapolis, MN

Building/structure	Ht. (ft)	Stories
IDS Tower, 80 S. 8th St. (1973)[1]	792	55
Capella Tower, 225 S. 6th St. (1992)	776	56
Wells Fargo Center, 90 S. 7th St. (1988)	775	56
33 South 6th St. (1983)	668	52
Campbell Mithun Tower, 222 S. 9th St. (1985)	582	42
US Bank Plaza I, 200 S. 6th St. (1981)	561	40
RBC Plaza, 60 S. 6th St. (1992)	539	40
Fifth Street Towers II, 150 S. 5th St. (1988)	504	36
(1) 910 ft incl. antenna.		

Monterrey, Mexico

Building/structure	Ht. (ft)	Stories
*Torre Koi, San Pedro Garza Garcia (2016)	906	67
*Metropolitan Center Torre III, San Pedro Garza Garcia (2016)	689	50
*Pabellon M (2015)	682	47
Torre Avalanz, San Pedro Garza Garcia (2000)	597	43
*Metropolitan Center Torre II, San Pedro Garza Garcia (2016)	594	52
Centro de Gobierno Plaza Civica (2010)	591	36
Torre Helicon, San Pedro Garza Garcia (2012)	512	33

Montréal, QC, Canada

Building/structure	Ht. (ft)	Stories
1250 Boulevard Rene Levesque (incl. spire) (1992)	743	47
1000 Rue de la Gauchetiere (1992)	673	51
Tour de la Bourse, 800 Place Victoria (1964)	624	47
1 Place Villa Marie (1962)	616	43
La Tour CIBC, 1155 Rene Levesque Blvd. (1962)[1]	604	45
*L'Avenue (2017)	574	50
Montreal Tower (1987)	574	NA
*Tour Avenue des Canadiens (2016)	548	50
Tour McGill College, 1501 McGill College (1992)	519	38
(1) 740 ft incl. antenna.		

New Orleans, LA

Building/structure	Ht. (ft)	Stories
One Shell Square, 701 Poydras St. (1972)	697	51
CapitalOne Center, 201 St. Charles Ave. (1985)	645	53
Plaza Tower, 1001 Howard Ave. (1969)	531	45
Energy Centre, 1100 Poydras St. (1984)	530	39

New York, NY

Building/structure	Ht. (ft)	Stories
*One World Trade Center (incl. spire) (2014)	1,776	94
*Nordstrom Tower, 217 West 57th Street (2018)	1,775	92
*432 Park Avenue (2015)	1,397	85
Empire State Building, 350 5th Ave. (1931)[1]	1,250	102

Building/structure	Ht. (ft)	Stories
Bank of America (incl. spire), One Bryant Park (2009)	1,200	55
*Three World Trade Center (incl. spires), 175 Greenwich St. (2018)	1,171	80
Chrysler Building. (incl. spire), 405 Lexington Ave. (1930)	1,046	77
New York Times Tower (incl. spire), 620 8th Ave. (2007)	1,046	52
One57, 157 W. 57th St. (2014)	1,005	75
4 World Trade Center, 150 Greenwich St. (2014)	977	65
American International Building (incl. spire), 70 Pine St. (1932)	952	67
*220 Central Park South (2017)	950	66
*30 Park Place, 99 Church St. (2016)	937	67
The Trump Bldg., 40 Wall St. (1930)	927	71
Citigroup Center, 153 E. 53rd St. (1977)	915	59
*10 Hudson Yards (2015)	895	47
New York by Gehry at Eight Spruce Street (2011)	870	76
Trump World Tower, 845 UN Plaza (2001)	861	72
GE Building, 30 Rockefeller Center (1933)	850	70
*56 Leonard Street (2016)	821	57
Cityspire Center, 150 W. 56th St. (1989)	814	75
One Chase Manhattan Plaza (1960)	813	60
4 Times Square (1999)[2]	809	48
MetLife Building, 200 Park Ave. (1963)	808	59
Bloomberg Tower, 731 Lexington Ave. (2005)[3]	806	54
Woolworth Building, 233 Broadway (1913)	792	57
*520 Park Avenue (2017)	781	54
*50 West, 50 West St. (2017)	778	64
1 Worldwide Plaza, 935 8th Ave. (1989)	778	47
Carnegie Hall Tower, 152 W. 57th St. (1991)	757	60
383 Madison Avenue (2001)	755	47
1717 Broadway (2013)	753	67
AXA Center, 787 7th Ave. (1985)	752	51
One Penn Plaza, 250 W. 34th St. (1972)	750	57
1251 Avenue of the Americas (1971)	750	54
Time Warner Center North Tower, 10 Columbus Cir. (2004)	749	55
Time Warner Center South Tower, 10 Columbus Cir. (2004)	749	55
Goldman Sachs HQ, 200 Murray St. (2010)	749	44
60 Wall Street (1989)	745	55
One Astor Plaza, 1515 Broadway (1970)	745	54
1 Liberty Plaza, 165 Broadway (1973)	743	54
7 World Trade Center (2006)	743	49
20 Exchange Place (1931)	741	57
Three World Financial Center, 200 Vesey St. (1986)	739	51
1540 Broadway (incl. spire) (1990)	732	42
Times Square Tower, 1459 Broadway (2004)	726	47
Metropolitan Tower, 142 W. 57th St. (1985)	716	68
*250 E. 57th Street (2017)	715	59
*610 Lexington Avenue (2017)	712	66
JPMorganChase World Headquarters, 270 Park Ave. (1960)	707	52
General Motors Building, 767 5th Ave. (1968)	705	50
Metropolitan Life Tower, 1 Madison Ave. (1909)	700	50
500 5th Avenue (1931)	697	60
Americas Tower, 1177 Ave. of the Americas (1992)	692	48
Solow Building, 9 W. 57th St. (1974)	689	49
HSBC Bank Building, 140 Broadway (1967)	688	52
55 Water Street (1972)	687	53
277 Park Avenue (1963)	687	50
*The Beekman Hotel & Residences, 5 Beekman St. (2016)	687	47
1585 Broadway (1989)	685	42
Random House/Park Imperial, 1739 Broadway (2003)	684	52
Four Seasons Hotel, 57 E. 57th St. (1993)	682	52
McGraw-Hill Building, 1221 Ave. of the Americas (1972)	674	51
Barclay Tower, 10 Barclay St. (2007)	673	56
One Grand Central Place, 60 E. 42nd St. (1930)	673	53
Citigroup Building, 1 Court Sq., Queens (1990)	673	50
Paramount Plaza, 1633 Broadway (1970)	670	48
Trump Tower, 725 5th Ave. (1982)	664	58
*Atelier II, 605 W. 42nd St. (2015)	656	61
Bank of New York Building, 1 Wall St. (1932)	654	50
Silver Towers East, 600 W. 42nd St. (2009)	653	58
Silver Towers West, 600 W. 42nd St. (2009)	653	58
599 Lexington Avenue (1986)	653	51
712 5th Avenue (1990)	650	53
Chanin Building, 122 E. 42nd St. (1929)	649	56
245 Park Avenue (1967)	648	47
550 Madison Avenue (1983)	647	37
Two World Financial Center, 225 Liberty St. (1986)	645	44
1095 Avenue of the Americas (1970)	645	43
570 Lexington Avenue (1931)	642	50
1 New York Plaza, 1 Water St. (1969)	640	50
1 MiMA, 450 W. 42nd St. (2011)	638	63
1 Dag Hammarskjold Plaza, 885 2nd Ave. (1972)	637	48
345 Park Avenue (1968)	634	44
400 5th Avenue (2010)	632	58
Mercantile Bldg., 10 E. 40th St. (1929)	632	48
W New York Downtown Hotel & Residences, 123 Washington St. (2010)	631	57
Grace Plaza, 1114 Ave. of the Americas (1972)	630	50
Home Insurance Plaza, 59 Maiden Ln. (1966)	630	44
101 Park Avenue (1982)	629	49
Central Park Place, 301 W. 57th St. (1988)	628	56
888 7th Avenue (1971)	628	45
Burlington House, 1345 Ave. of the Americas (1969)	625	50
Waldorf Astoria New York, 301 Park Ave. (1931)	625	47
Trump Palace, 200 E. 69th St. (1991)	623	54
One Madison Park, 20 E. 23rd St. (2010)	621	51
Olympic Tower, 645 5th Ave. (1976)	620	51
425 Fifth Avenue (2003)	618	55
The Epic, 125 W. 31st St. (2007)	615	58
919 3rd Avenue (1970)	615	47
Tower 49, 12 E. 49th St. (1985)	615	44
750 7th Avenue (incl. spire) (1989)	615	35
New York Life, 51 Madison Ave. (1928)	615	33
Eventi, 851 6th Ave. (2010)	614	46
Credit Lyonnais Building, 1301 Ave. of the Americas (1964)	609	46
*Baccarat Hotel & Residences, 20 West 53rd St. (2014)	606	50
The Orion, 350 W. 42nd St. (2006)	604	58
590 Madison Avenue (1983)	603	41
250 W. 55th Street (2013)	602	40
Eleven Times Square, 644 8th Ave. (2011)	601	40
1166 Avenue of the Americas (1974)	600	44
*160 West 62nd Street (2014)	598	54
Hearst Magazine Tower, 959 8th Ave. (2006)	597	46
*Avalon Willoughby West, 100 Willoughby St. (2015)	596	57
3 Lincoln Center, 160 W. 66th St. (1993)	595	60
Celanese Building, 1211 Ave. of the Americas (1973)	592	45
The London NYC, 151 W. 54th St. (1990)	590	54
388 Bridge Street, Brooklyn (2014)	590	51
Thurgood Marshall U.S. Courthouse, 505 Pearl St. (1936)	590	37
The Millenium Hilton Hotel, 55 Church St. (1992)	588	58
Sky House, 11 E. 29th St. (2008)	588	55
Museum Tower Apts., 21 W. 53rd St. (1985)	588	52
Time-Life Building, 1271 Ave. of the Americas (1959)	587	48
Jacob K. Javits Federal Bldg., 26 Federal Plz. (1967)	587	41
W Times Square, 1567 Broadway (2000)	584	53
Trump International Hotel & Tower, 15 Columbus Cir. (1970)	583	44
Stevens Tower, 1185 Ave. of the Americas (1971)	580	42
Municipal Building, 1 Centre St. (1914)	580	34
520 Madison Avenue (1981)	577	43
One World Financial Center, 200 Liberty St. (1985)	577	37
Merchandise Mart, 41 Madison Ave. (1973)	576	42
Park Avenue Plaza, 55 E. 52nd St. (1981)	575	44
300 Madison Avenue (2003)	575	38
Lehman Building, 745 7th Ave. (2001)	575	38
One Financial Square, 33 Old Slip (1987)	575	37
Marriott Marquis Times Square, 1531 Broadway (1985)	574	50
299 Park Avenue (1967)	574	42
5 Times Square, 590 7th Ave. (2002)	574	40
Socony Mobil Building, 150 E. 42nd St. (1956)	572	42
1290 Avenue of the Americas (1963)	571	43
780 3rd Avenue (1983)	570	49
600 3rd Avenue (1971)	570	42
450 Lexington Avenue (1991)	568	38
Paramount Tower, 240 E. 39th St. (1998)	567	51
230 Park Avenue (1928)	565	35
*The Hub, 333 Schermerhorn St., Brooklyn (2016)	563	52
New York Palace Hotel, 455 Madison Ave. (1980)	563	51
Continental Bank Building, 30 Broad St. (1932)	562	48
Park Avenue Tower, 65 E. 55th St. (1986)	561	36
Nelson Tower, 450 7th Ave. (1931)	560	46
Sherry-Netherland, 781 5th Ave. (1927)	560	40
623 5th Avenue (1990)	560	36
South Park Tower, 124 W. 60th St. (1986)	558	51
100 UN Plaza, 327 E. 48th St. (1986)	557	52
Continental Can, 633 3rd Ave. (1962)	557	39
*551 10th Avenue (2016)	556	52
3 Park Avenue (1975)	556	42
Continental Center, 180 Maiden Ln. (1983)	555	41
Sperry & Hutchinson Bldg., 330 Madison Ave. (1964)	555	41
Reuters Building, 3 Times Sq. (2001)[4]	555	30
Tower 111, 885 6th Ave. (2011)	554	48
The Belvedere, 10 E. 29th St. (1999)	554	48
Inmont Bldg., 1133 Ave. of the Americas (1970)	552	45
Downtown by Philippe Starck, 15 Broad St. (1927)	551	42
Hyatt Times Square, 135 W. 45th St. (2013)	550	53
Biltmore Tower, 267 W. 47th St. (2003)	550	51

Building/structure	Ht. (ft)	Stories
Unisys Building, 605 3rd Ave. (1963)	550	44
2 Grand Central Tower, 140 E. 45th St. (1982)	550	43
The Tower at 15 Central Park West (2008)	550	35
AT&T Long Lines Building, 33 Thomas St. (1974)	550	29
*50 UN Plaza, 345 E. 46th St. (2015)	548	44
Bankers Trust, 33 E. 48th St. (1971)	547	41
The Corinthian, 330 E. 38th St. (1988)	546	55
Transportation Building, 225 Broadway (1928)	546	44
MillenniumTower, 101 W. 67th St. (1995)	545	54
Equitable Building, 120 Broadway (1915)	545	36
The Galleria, 117 E. 57th St. (1975)	544	56
2 Gold Street (2005)	543	51
220 Riverside Blvd. at Trump Place (2003)	542	49
17 State Street (1988)	542	41
Grand Central Plaza, 622 3rd Ave. (1973)	542	38
*616 1st Avenue West Tower (2016)	540	46
New York Telephone, 375 Pearl St. (1976)	540	42
1285 Avenue of the Americas (1960)	540	42
Ritz Tower, 109 E. 57th St. (1925)	540	41
14 Wall Street (1912)	540	29
Tribeca Tower, 105 Duane St. (1990)	537	53
Lefcourt Colonial Building, 295 Madison Ave. (1929)	537	45
*175 W. 60th Street (2016)	533	48
1700 Broadway (1969)	533	41
Westin Hotel New York, 43rd St. and 8th Ave. (2002)	532	45
515 Park Avenue (1999)	532	43
DuMont Building, 515 Madison Ave. (1931)	532	42
The Brooklyner, 111 Lawrence St., Brooklyn (2010)	531	52
One East River Place, 525 E. 72nd St. (1989)	530	49
*21 West End Avenue (2016)	529	45
The Metropolis, 150 E. 44th St. (2001)	528	50
William Beaver House, 15 William St. (2010)	528	47
North American Plywood, 800 3rd Ave. (1972)	526	41
Hotel Pierre, 2 E. 61st St. (1928)	525	44
767 3rd Avenue (1980)	525	39
Citibank, 399 Park Ave. (1961)	524	41
Random House, 825 3rd Ave. (1969)	522	40
Atelier, 625 W. 42nd St. (2007)	521	46
26 Broadway (1924)	520	31
Newsweek Building, 444 Madison Ave. (1931)	518	42
The Downtown Club, 19 West St. (1930)	518	39
Architects and Designers Bldg., 964 3rd Ave. (1969)	518	39
785 8th Avenue (2009)	517	42
High Point Condominium, 250 E. 40th St. (1988)	516	49
House of Seagram, 375 Park Ave. (1958)	516	38
Sterling Drug Bldg., 90 Park Ave. (1964)	515	41
Millennium Towers North, 512 7th Ave. (1930)	513	44
1214 Fifth Avenue (2012)	513	42
Bank of New York, 48 Wall St. (1927)	513	31
The Belaire, 524 E. 72nd St. (1988)	512	50
One Hanson Place, Brooklyn (1929)	512	42
1407 Broadway Realty Corp. (1950)	512	41
International Building, Rockefeller Center, 630 5th Ave. (1935)	512	41
ITT-American, 437 Madison Ave. (1967)	512	40
Continental Building, 1450 Broadway (1931)	511	42
1155 Avenue of the Americas (1984)	511	40
Liberty Plaza, 10 Liberty St. (2004)	510	45
810 7th Avenue (1970)	506	41
United Nations Secretariat Building, 405 E. 42nd St. (1953)	506	39
The Sheffield Apartments, 325 W. 56th St. (1978)	505	50
2 UN Plaza (1981)	505	39
1 UN Plaza (1975)	505	39
2 New York Plaza, 125 Broad St. (1970)	504	40
Johns-Manville Building, 22 E. 40th St. (1931)	503	43
60 Broad Street (1962)	503	39
Lefcourt National Building, 521 5th Ave. (1928)	503	37
1325 Ave. of the Americas (1989)	502	35
Sheraton Centre, 811 7th Ave. (1962)	501	51
World Apparel Center, 1411 Broadway (1969)	501	39
International Gem Tower, 44 W. 47th St. (2013)	501	34
Bristol Plaza, 200 E. 65th St. (1987)	500	50
One Columbus Place Tower I, 400 W. 59th St. (1999)	500	49
One Columbus Place Tower II, 400 W. 59th St. (1999)	500	49
Four World Financial Center, 250 Vesey St. (1986)	500	34

(1) 1,455 ft incl. antenna. (2) 1,118 ft incl. antenna. (3) 941 ft incl. antenna. (4) 659 ft incl. antenna.

Philadelphia, PA

Building/structure	Ht. (ft)	Stories
*Comcast Innovation and Technology Center, 1800 Arch St. (2018)	1,121	59
Comcast Center, 1701 JFK Blvd. (2008)	974	57
One Liberty Place (incl. spire), 1650 Market St. (1987)	945	61
Two Liberty Place (incl. spire), 1601 Chestnut St. (1989)	848	58
Mellon Bank Center, 1735 Market St. (1990)	792	54
Three Logan, 1717 Arch St. (1991)	739	55
*FMC Tower at Cira Centre South (2017)	730	49

Building/structure	Ht. (ft)	Stories
G. Fred DiBona Jr. Building, 1901 Market St. (1990)	625	45
Commerce Square #2, 2001 Market St. (1992)	572	40
Commerce Square #1, 2005 Market St. (1990)	572	40
City Hall (incl. statue) (1901)	548	7
Residences at Ritz-Carlton, 1416 S. Penn Sq. (2009)	518	46
1818 Market St. (1974)	500	40

Pittsburgh, PA

Building/structure	Ht. (ft)	Stories
US Steel Tower, 600 Grant St. (1970)	841	64
One Mellon Bank Center, 500 Grant St. (1983)	725	54
One PPG Place (1984)	635	40
Fifth Avenue Place, 120 5th Ave. (1987)	616	32
One Oxford Centre, 301 Grant St. (1982)	615	46
Gulf Tower, 707 Grant St. (1932)	582	44
*The Tower at PNC Plaza (2015)	564	33
University of Pittsburgh Cathedral of Learning, 4200 5th Ave. (1936)	535	42
3 Mellon Bank Center, 525 Wm. Penn Way (1951)	520	41
K&L Gates Center, 210 6th Ave. (1968)	511	39

Portland, OR

Building/structure	Ht. (ft)	Stories
Wells Fargo Center, 1300 SW 5th Ave. (1973)	546	40
U.S. Bancorp Tower, 111 SW 5th Ave. (1983)	536	42
*Park Avenue West, 728 SW 9th Ave. (2015)	515	33
Koin Center, 222 SW Columbia St. (1984)	509	31

St. Louis, MO

Building/structure	Ht. (ft)	Stories
Gateway Arch (1965)	630	NA
Metropolitan Square Tower, 211 N. Broadway (1988)	593	42
AT&T Center, 900 Pine St. (1984)	588	44
Thomas F. Eagleton Federal Courthouse, 111 S. 10th St. (2000)	557	29

San Francisco, CA

Building/structure	Ht. (ft)	Stories
*Salesforce Tower, 415 Mission St. (2017)	1,070	61
Sutro Tower (1972)	977	NA
Transamerica Pyramid, 600 Montgomery St. (1972)	853	48
*181 Fremont (2016)	802	54
555 California St. (1969)	779	52
345 California Center (1986)	695	48
Millennium Tower, 301 Mission St. (2009)	645	58
One Rincon Hill South Tower, 425 First St. (2008)	605	54
101 California Street (1982)	600	48
50 Fremont Center (1985)	600	43
Chevron Tower, 575 Market St. (1975)	573	40
Four Embarcadero Center, 55 Clay St. (1984)	570	45
One Embarcadero Center, 355 Clay St. (1970)	569	45
44 Montgomery St. (1967)	565	43
Spear Tower, 1 Market St. (1976)	565	42
One Sansome Street (1984)	550	43
*One Rincon Hill North Tower, 425 First St. (2014)	541	45
Shaklee Terrace Building, 444 Market St. (1982)	537	38
First Market Tower, 525 Market St. (1972)	529	38
McKesson Plaza, 1 Post St. (1969)	529	38
425 Market Street (1973)	524	38
Telsis Tower, 1 Montgomery St. (1982)	500	38

Seattle, WA

Building/structure	Ht. (ft)	Stories
Columbia Center, 701 5th Ave. (1985)	933	76
1201 Third Avenue Tower, 1201 3rd Ave. (1988)	772	55
Two Union Square, 601 Union St. (1989)	740	56
Seattle Municipal Tower, 700 5th Ave. (1990)	722	57
Safeco Plaza, 1001 4th Ave. (1969)	630	50
City Centre, 1420 5th Ave. (1989)	606	44
Space Needle, 203 6th Ave. (1962)	605	NA
Russell Investments Center, 1301 2nd Ave. (2006)	598	42
Wells Fargo Center, 999 3rd Ave. (1983)	574	47
Bank of America Fifth Ave. Plz., 800 5th Ave. (1981)	543	42
901 5th Ave. (1973)	536	41
*Amazon Tower I, 2021 7th Ave. (2016)	524	37
*Amazon Tower II, 2021 7th Ave. (2017)	521	37
Rainier Tower, 1301 5th Ave. (1977)	514	31
Fourth & Madison Building, 915 4th Ave. (2003)	512	40
1918 8th Avenue (2009)	500	36

Sunny Isles Beach, FL

Building/structure	Ht. (ft)	Stories
*Mansions at Acqualina, 17749 Collins Ave. (2015)	643	46
*Porsche Design Tower, 18555 Collins Ave. (2016)	641	57
*Jade Signature, 16901 Collins Ave. (2017)	636	55
Jade on the Beach Condominiums, 17001 Collins Ave. (2008)	574	51
Trump Royale, 18201 Collins Ave. (2008)	551	43
Trump Palace, 18101 Collins Ave. (2005)	551	43
Acqualina Ocean Residences, 17875 Collins Ave. (2004)	550	51
Jade Ocean, 17121 Collins Ave. (2009)	543	51

Tampa, FL

Building/structure	Ht. (ft)	Stories
Regions Building, 100 N. Tampa St. (1992)	579	42
Bank of America Plaza, 101 E. Kennedy Blvd. (1986)	577	42
One Tampa City Center, 201 N. Franklin St. (1981)	537	39
SunTrust Financial Center, 401 E. Jackson St. (1992)	525	36

Toronto, ON, Canada

Building/structure	Ht. (ft)	Stories
CN Tower, 310 Front St. West (1976)	1,815	NA
First Canadian Place, 100 King St. West (1975)[1]	978	72
Trump International Hotel & Tower (incl. spire), 325 Bay St. (2012)	908	63
Scotia Tower, 40 King St. West (1989)	902	68
*Aura at College Park, 388 Yonge St. (2014)	892	78
Brookfield Place (incl. spire), 161 Bay St. (1990)	856	53
*Number One Bloor, 1 Bloor St. East (2016)	844	75
Commerce Court West, 199 Bay St. (1973)[2]	784	57
*Ice Condos at York Centre 2, 16 York St. (2014)	768	67
*Harbour Plaza Res. East, 90 Harbour St. (2017)	764	66
*Ten York (2017)	735	65
*Harbour Plaza Res. West, 90 Harbour St. (2017)	735	62
TD Centre-Toronto Dominion Bank Tower, 66 Wellington St. West (1967)	730	56
Bay-Adelaide Center West Tower, 335 Bay St. (2010)	704	52
Living Shangri-La Toronto, 180 University Ave. (2012)	702	65
Ritz-Carlton Hotel and Residences, 185 Wellington St. West (2011)	687	54
BCE Place, Bay-Wellington Tower, 181 Bay St. (1991)	679	49
*L Tower, 1 Front St. (2014)	673	58
*88 Scott St. (2017)	669	58
Four Seasons Private Residences West, 48 Yorkville Ave. (2012)	669	55
*Ice Condos at York Centre 1, 16 York St. (2014)	663	57
*Bay-Adelaide Center East Tower, 40 Adelaide St. (2016)	643	44
*EY Tower, 100 Adelaide St. West (2017)	617	40
RBC Centre, 155 Wellington St. West (2009)	607	42
*CASA II, 42 Charles St. East (2016)	605	57
*U Condominiums West Tower, 50 St. Joseph St. (2014)	604	55
TD North Tower, 77 King St. West (1969)	600	46
Maple Leaf Square North Tower, 65 Bremner Blvd. (2010)	595	54
*INDX Condominiums, 70 Temperance St. (2016)	587	54
1 King West (2005)	578	51
Success Tower 2, 33 Bay St. (2010)	569	55
*One York Street (2016)	569	35
Royal Bank Plaza-South Tower, 200 Bay St. (1976)	567	41
Maple Leaf Square South Tower, 55 Bremner Blvd. (2010)	562	50
*Hullmark Centre I, 4789 Yonge St. (2014)	561	45
*Lago at the Waterfront, 2151 Lake Shore Blvd. West, Etobicoke (2016)	550	49
44 Charles Street West (1974)	545	51
*Karma, 9 Grenville St. (2015)	544	50
Quantum 2, 2195 Yonge St. (2008)	541	51
Residences @ College Park I, 763 Bay St. (2006)	535	51
Burano, 832 Bay St. (2012)	535	50
Success Tower 1, 18 Harbour St. (2011)	531	52
*X2, 580 Jarvis St. (2014)	529	44
*FIVE, 606 Yonge St. (2014)	528	48
*Southcore Financial Centre Delta Hotel (2014)	524	47
Three Hundred, 300 Front St. West (2014)	518	52
The Uptown, 35 Balmuto St. (2011)	518	48
*Theatre Park, 224 King St. West (2014)	515	47
Festival Tower, 330 King St. West (2011)	514	42
*U Condominiums East Tower, 50 St. Joseph St. (2014)	505	45
TD South Tower, 79 Wellington St. West (1985)	504	39
35 Mariner (2008)	503	49
*Westlake Village 1 (2014)	503	48
Montage, 20 Fort York Blvd. (2014)	502	48

(1) 1,116 ft incl. antenna. (2) 942 ft incl. antenna.

Tulsa, OK

Building/structure	Ht. (ft)	Stories
BOK Tower, 1 E. 2nd St. (1975)	667	52
Cityplex Central Tower, 2448 E. 81st St. (1979)	648	60

Building/structure	Ht. (ft)	Stories
First Place Tower, 15 E. 5th St. (1973)	516	40
Mid-Continent Tower, 401 S. Boston St. (1984)	513	36

Vancouver, BC, Canada

Building/structure	Ht. (ft)	Stories
Shangri-La Vancouver, 1120 W. Georgia St. (2009)	659	59
*Trump International Hotel & Tower, 1153 W. Georgia (2016)	616	58
*Telus Garden Residential Tower (2016)	550	53
Hotel Georgia, 667 Howe St. (2012)	520	50

Other Tall Buildings in North America

Building/structure	City	Ht. (ft)	Stories
Devon Energy Center (2012)	Oklahoma City, OK	844	52
RSA Battle House Tower (incl. spire) (2007)	Mobile, AL	745	35
Revel Hotel (2012)	Atlantic City, NJ	718	53
Hotel Riu Plaza Guadalajara (2011)	Guadalajara, Mex.	705	44
Great American Tower at Queen City Square (2011)	Cincinnati, OH	665	40
The Tower at First National Center (2002)	Omaha, NE	634	45
801 Grand (1991)	Des Moines, IA	630	44
One Kansas City Place (incl. spire) (1988)	Kansas City, MO	623	42
Tower of the Americas (1968)	San Antonio, TX	622	NA
Bank of America Tower (1990)	Jacksonville, FL	617	42
AT&T Building (1994)	Nashville TN	617	33
*Solo District-Altus (2016)	Burnaby, BC, Can.	602	48
U.S. Bank Center (1973)	Milwaukee, WI.	601	42
Town Pavilion (1986)	Kansas City, MO.	591	38
Erastus Corning II Tower (1973)	Albany, NY	589	44
Niagara Falls Hilton Phase 2 (2009)	Niagara Falls, ON, Can.	581	58
Absolute World 56 (2012)	Mississauga, ON, Can.	576	56
Carew Tower (1931)[1]	Cincinnati, OH	574	49
*Torre NVBOLA (2016)	Puebla, Mex.	574	43
Concourse Corporate Ctr. V (incl. spire) (1988)	Sandy Springs, GA	570	34
Torre Aura Altitude (2008)	Zapopan, Mex.	563	44
Blue Diamond Tower (2000)	Miami Beach, FL.	559	44
Green Diamond Tower (2000)	Miami Beach, FL.	559	44
Washington Monument (1884)	Washington, DC	555	NA
Concourse Corporate Ctr. VI (incl. spire) (1991)	Sandy Springs, GA	553	34
100 E. Wisconsin Ave. (1989)	Milwaukee, WI.	549	37
AEGON Center (1992)	Louisville, KY	549	35
Metropolitan Tower (1986)	Little Rock, AK	546	40
Marriott Rivercenter (incl. spires) (1988)	San Antonio, TX	546	38
RBC Plaza (incl. spire) (2008)	Raleigh, NC	538	32
Modis Tower (1975)	Jacksonville, FL	535	37
Legg Mason Building (1973)	Baltimore, MD.	529	40
One Seneca Tower (1970)	Buffalo NY.	529	38
Vehicle Assembly Building (1965)	Cape Canaveral, FL	526	40
Harrah's Waterfront Tower (2008)	Atlantic City, NJ	525	44
Skylon (1965)	Niagara Falls, ON, Can.	520	NA
Absolute World 50 (2012)	Mississauga, ON, Can.	518	50
*Sovereign (2014)	Burnaby, BC, Can.	511	45
Bank of America (1924)	Baltimore, MD.	509	37
The Westin Virginia Beach Town Center and Residences (2007)	Virginia Beach, VA	508	38
The Beach Club Tower 2 (2006)	Hallandale Beach, FL.	505	50
Chase Tower (1971)	Oklahoma City, OK	500	36
One American Plaza (1991)	San Diego, CA	500	34

(1) 623 ft incl. antenna.

Selected Bridge Styles

Bridges support weight through tension (pulling), compression (pushing), or a combination of both. **Suspension** and **cable-stayed** bridges are characterized by cables under tension. While the deck of a suspension bridge hangs from suspenders, that of a cable-stayed bridge ties directly to a bridge tower. The elements of a **truss** form triangles, which distribute the forces of tension and compression. Truss bridges can thus carry more weight than beam bridges. Steel plates can be welded or bolted together to make a **plate girder**, a kind of beam. A common form is the **box girder**.

A bridge can have a **simple** configuration, whereby its load is supported at both ends. If a bridge is **continuous**, its load extends across multiple supports. In a **cantilever** configuration, structural elements (e.g., trusses or girders) supported at one end project out, or cantilever, to carry a span.

Notable North American Bridges

Source: World Almanac research; Office of Bridge Technology, Federal Highway Administration, U.S. Dept. of Transportation Asterisk (*) designates a bridge that carries railroads only. All other bridges carry roads or roads and rail unless otherwise noted. Year is date of completion or projected completion. Span of bridge is the distance between its main supports. As of mid-2014.

Year Bridge	Location	Main span (ft)
Suspension		
1964 Verrazano-Narrows	New York, NY	4,260
1937 Golden Gate	San Francisco Bay, CA	4,200
1957 Mackinac	Straits of Mackinac, MI	3,800
1931 George Washington	New York, NY-Fort Lee, NJ	3,500
1950/Tacoma Narrows		
2007 (twin)	Tacoma, WA	2,800
2003 Al Zampa Memorial (New Carquinez) (westbound)	Carquinez Strait, CA	2,388
1936 San Francisco-Oakland Bay (West Span)[1]	San Francisco-Yerba Buena Isl., CA	2,310
1939 Bronx-Whitestone	East R., New York, NY	2,300
1970 Pierre Laporte	Quebec City, QC, Can.	2,190
1951/Delaware Mem. (twin) 68	Pennsville, NJ-New Castle, DE	2,150
1957 Walt Whitman	Philadelphia, PA	2,000
1929 Ambassador	Detroit, MI-Windsor, ON, Can.	1,850
1961 Throgs Neck	New York, NY	1,801
1926 Benjamin Franklin	Phila., PA-Camden, NJ	1,750
1924 Bear Mountain	Hudson R., Peekskill, NY	1,632
1969 Claiborne Pell/Newport	Narragansett Bay, RI	1,600
1952/William Preston Lane Jr. 73 Memorial (twin)	Sandy Point, MD	1,600
1903 Williamsburg	East R., New York, NY	1,600
1883 Brooklyn	East R., New York, NY	1,596
1938 Lions Gate	Vancouver, BC, Can.	1,550
1963 Vincent Thomas	L.A. Harbor, CA	1,500
1930 Mid-Hudson	Poughkeepsie, NY	1,495
1909 Manhattan	East R., New York, NY	1,470
1955 Angus L. Macdonald	Halifax, NS, Can.	1,447
1970 A. Murray MacKay	Halifax, NS, Can.	1,400
1936 Triborough (Harlem R. Lift/Bronx Crossing/ East R. Suspension)	East R., New York, NY	1,380
2013 San Francisco-Oakland Bay (SAS)[2]	San Francisco Bay, CA	1,263
Cantilever		
1917 Quebec	Quebec City, QC, Can.	1,800
1974 Commodore Barry	Chester, PA-Bridgeport, NJ	1,644
1958/Crescent City Connection 88 (twin)	Mississippi R., New Orleans, LA	1,575
1995 Veterans Memorial	Gramercy, LA	1,460
1968 Baton Rouge	Mississippi R., LA	1,235
1955 Tappan Zee (I-287)	Hudson R., Tarrytown, NY	1,212
1930 Lewis and Clark	Longview, WA-Rainier, OR	1,200
1909 Queensboro	East R., New York, NY	1,182
1958 Carquinez (eastbound)	San Francisco Bay, CA	1,100
1930 Jacques Cartier	Montreal, QC, Can.	1,097
1968 Isaiah D. Hart	Jacksonville, FL	1,088
1956 Richmond-San Rafael (twin)	San Francisco Bay, CA	1,070
1963/ 80 Newburgh-Beacon (twin)	Hudson R., NY	1,000
Truss		
1966 Astoria	Columbia R., OR-WA	1,232
1976 Francis Scott Key	Baltimore, MD	1,200
1981 Ravenswood	Ohio R., Ravenswood, WV	902
1995 Taylor-Southgate, Ohio R.	Cincinnati, OH-Newport, KY	850
1943 Julien Dubuque (U.S. 20)	Mississippi R., IA-IL	845
1966 Charles Braga	Fall River, MA	840
1956 Shawneetown (KY 56) (twin)	Ohio R., IL-KY	825
1953 John E. Mathews	Jacksonville, FL	810
1992 Cooper R.	Charleston, SC	800
1957 Kingston-Rhinecliff	Hudson R., NY	800
1950 Maurice J. Tobin	Boston, MA	800
1940 Gov. Nice Mem.	Newburg, MD-Dahlgren, VA	800
1986 Rochester-Monaca	Rochester-Monaca, PA	780
1973/Atchafalaya R. (U.S. 190) 88 (twin)	Krotz Springs, LA	780
1988 Phil G. McDonald (Glade Creek)	Beckley, WV	784
1917 *Sciotoville RR (twin)	Sciotoville, OH-KY	775
1981 Sewickley	Sewickley, PA	750
1977 Jennings Randolph	Chester, WV-E. Liverpool, OH	750
1974 Carroll C. Cropper (I-275)	Ohio R., IN-KY	750
1940 Glover Cary	Ohio R., Owensboro, KY-IN	750
1984 13th Street	Ohio R., Ashland, KY-OH	740
1959 Monaca-E. Rochester	Monaca-E. Rochester, PA	730
1976 Betsy Ross	Philadelphia, PA	729
2013 Milton-Madison (U.S. 421)	Ohio R., KY-IN	727
1967 Matthew E. Welsh	Ohio R., Mauckport, IN-KY	725
1994 Robert C. Byrd	Huntington, WV.	720
1971 Atchafalaya R. (LA 1)	Simmesport, LA	720
1962 U.S. 41 Twin	Ohio R., Evansville, IN-Henderson, KY	720
1929 Irvin S. Cobb (U.S. 45)	Ohio R., Brookport, IL-Paducah, KY	716
1970 Vanport	Vanport, PA	715
1962 Champlain	Montreal, QC, Can.	707
1973 Girard Point	Philadelphia, PA	700
1963 John F. Kennedy (I-65)	Ohio R., Louisville, KY-Jeffersonville, IN	700
1923 *Mears Mem., Tanana R.	Nenana, AK	700
Plate and Box Girder		
1997 Confederation[3]	Prince Edward Isl.-NB, Can.	820
1978 Shubenacadie R.	S. Maitland, NS, Can.	790
2010 Kanawha R. (I-64)	S. Charleston-Dunbar, WV	760
1982 Jesse H. Jones Mem.	Houston, TX	750
1977 LA 27, Intracoastal Canal.	Gibbstown, LA	750
1976 LA 82, Intracoastal Canal.	Forked Isl., LA	750
1967 San Mateo-Hayward	San Francisco Bay, CA	750
1992 Jamestown-Verrazano	Narragansett Bay, RI	674
2002 Vietnam Veterans Memorial	James R., Richmond, VA	672
1986 Umatilla	Columbia R., OR-WA	660
1969 San Diego-Coronado (twin)	San Diego Bay, CA	660
2007 Benicia-Martinez (new)	Carquinez Strait, CA	659
1967 Poplar St./William L. Clay Sr.	Miss. R., St. Louis, MO-IL	647
1978 Stanislaus R.	Parrots Ferry, CA	640
1992/94 Acosta (twin)	Jacksonville, FL	630
1973 Loop 610/Sidney Sherman	Houston, TX	630
1981 Juneau-Douglas	Gastineau Channel, AK	620
1981 Glenn Jackson (I-205)	Columbia R., OR-WA	600
Cable-Stayed		
2012 Baluarte Bicentennial	Sinaloa-Durango states, Mex.	1,706
2011 John James Audubon	Pointe Coupee-West Feliciana, LA	1,583
2005 Arthur Ravenel Jr.	Charleston, SC	1,546
2012 Port Mann	Vancouver, BC, Can.	1,542
1986 Alex Fraser	Vancouver, BC, Can.	1,526
2014 Stan Musial Veterans Mem. (I-70)	Miss. R., St. Louis, MO-IL	1,500
2010 U.S. 82, Mississippi R.	Greenville, MS-Lake Village, AR	1,378
1994 Clark	Alton, IL-MO	1,360
1989 Dames Point	Jacksonville, FL	1,300
2003 Sidney Lanier	Brunswick, GA	1,250
1995 Fred Hartman	Houston Ship Channel, Baytown, TX	1,250
2007 Veterans' Glass City Skyway	Maumee R., Toledo, OH	1,225
1983 Hale Boggs Memorial	Luling, LA	1,222
2016/New NY (I-287) 18 (twin)	Hudson R., Tarrytown, NY	1,200
2002 William Natcher, Ohio R.	Owensboro, KY-IN	1,200
1987 Sunshine Skyway (I-275)	Tampa Bay, FL	1,200
2012 Margaret Hunt Hill	Trinity R., Dallas, TX	1,197
1988 Tampico	Panuco R., Mex.	1,181
2006 Penobscot Narrows	Bucksport, ME	1,161
2003 Bill Emerson Memorial	Cape Girardeau, MO-IL	1,150
1988 Skybridge[4]	Vancouver, BC, Can.	1,115
1991 Talmadge Memorial	Savannah, GA	1,100
2000 Maysville (Wm. H. Harsha)	Savannah, GA	1,050
Steel Arch		
1977 New River Gorge	Fayetteville, WV	1,700
1931 Bayonne (Kill Van Kull)	Bayonne, NJ-New York, NY	1,675
1973 Fremont	Portland, OR	1,255
1964 Port Mann	Vancouver, BC, Can.	1,200
1967 Laviolette	Trois-Rivières, QC, Can.	1,100
1990 Roosevelt Lake	Roosevelt Lake, AZ	1,080

Year	Bridge	Location	Main span (ft)
1959	Glen Canyon	Page, AZ	1,028
1962	Lewiston-Queenston	NY-ON, Can.	1,001
1976	Perrine	Twin Falls, ID	993
1916	*Hell Gate	East R., New York, NY	978
1941	Rainbow	Niagara Falls, NY-ON, Can.	950
1997	Second Blue Water	Port Huron, MI-ON, Can.	922
1977	Moundsville	Ohio R., WV	912
1983/Jefferson Barracks (I-255)			
92	(twin)	Mississippi R., IL-MO	910
1973	Hernando DeSoto (I-40) (two spans)	Mississippi R., AR-TN	900
2008	Blennerhassett (U.S. 50)	Parkersburg, WV-OH	878
1936	Henry Hudson	Harlem R., New York, NY	840
1966	Bob Cummings Lincoln Trail Ohio R.	IN-KY	825
1978	I-57, Mississippi R.	Cairo, IL	821
1980	I-65, Mobile R.	Mobile, AL	800
1961	Sherman Minton (I-64)	New Albany, IN-Louisville, KY	800
1978	I-470, Ohio R.	Wheeling, WV	780
1932	West End	Pittsburgh, PA	780
1971	Piscataqua R. (I-95 High Level)	Portsmouth, NH-Kittery, ME	756
1995	Navajo	Marble Canyon, AZ	726

Movable Bridges
Vertical Lift

Year	Bridge	Location	Main span (ft)
1959	*Arthur Kill	New York, NY-Elizabeth, NJ	558
1935	*Cape Cod Canal	Buzzards Bay, MA	544

Year	Bridge	Location	Main span (ft)
1896	*Delair	Pennsauken, NJ-Phila., PA	542
1937	Marine Pkwy. Gil Hodges Mem.	Jamaica Bay, New York, NY	540
1931	Burlington-Bristol	Delaware R., NJ-PA	540
1908	*Burlington Northern RR[5]	Portland, OR	516
1968	*Second Narrows Railway	Vancouver, BC, Can.	499
1911	*Armour-Swift-Burlington	Missouri R., Kansas City, MO	428
1945	*Harry S Truman	Kansas City, MO	427

Bascule

Year	Bridge	Location	Main span (ft)
1940	Charles Berry Memorial	Lorain, OH	333
1917	Market St./Ch. John Ross	Chattanooga, TN	310
2003	SW 2nd Avenue	Miami, FL	302

Swing

Year	Bridge	Location	Main span (ft)
1927	Fort Madison (Santa Fe)	Mississippi R., IA	525
1952	George P. Coleman Mem.	Yorktown, VA	500
1991	SW Spokane St.	Seattle, WA	480
1899	*Illinois Central RR	Chicago, IL	479
1914	*Coos Bay RR	Coos Bay, OR	458
1913	East Haddam (Rt. 82)	Connecticut R., CT	456

Floating Pontoon[6]

Year	Bridge	Location	Main span (ft)
1963	Evergreen Pt. (SR 520)[7]	Seattle, WA	7,578
1961	Hood Canal (SR 104)	Kitsap Co.-Jefferson Co., WA	7,450
1993	Lacey V. Murrow (I-90)	Seattle, WA	6,561
1989	Homer M. Hadley (I-90)	Seattle, WA	5,736

Other Notable North American Bridges

Year	Bridge	Type	Location	Tot. length (ft)
1956/69	Lake Pontchartrain Causeway[8]	Twin concrete trestle	Metairie-Mandeville, LA	126,055
1979	Manchac Swamp	Twin concrete trestle	Manchac, LA	120,384
1973	Atchafalaya Basin (I-10)	Twin concrete trestle	Baton Rouge, LA	95,040
1982	Seven Mile (Overseas Hwy, U.S. 1)	Segmental concrete	Florida Keys	35,867
2009/11	I-10 Twin Spans	Twin concrete trestle	Slidell-New Orleans, LA	29,040
2002	Croatan Sound	Continuous post-tensioned girder	Manteo, NC	27,000
1993	Choctawhatchee Mid-Bay	Segmental concrete	Destin-Niceville, FL	19,265
1962	International	Arch truss	Sault Ste. Marie, MI-ON, Can.	9,278
2009	Walkway Over the Hudson[9]	Pedestrian	Poughkeepsie-Highland, NY	6,768
1874	Eads, Mississippi R.[10]	Steel arch	St. Louis, MO-IL	6,442
1987	Powder Point	Tropical hardwood	Duxbury, MA	2,200
1969	Silver Memorial, Ohio R.[12]	Cantilever	Pt. Pleasant, WV-OH	1,964
2010	Mike O'Callaghan-Pat Tillman Mem. (U.S. 93)[11]	Concrete arch	Colorado R., AZ-NV	1,900
1994	Natchez Trace Parkway	Concrete arch	Franklin, TN	1,572
1901	Hartland[13]	Covered	St. John R., Hartland, NB, Can.	1,282

(1) Two complete bridges each 2,310-ft long, which share an anchor point. (2) Self-Anchored Suspension Span (SAS; the world's longest single-tower, self-anchored suspension bridge. (3) World's longest bridge crossing ice-covered water, with total length of 8 mi. (4) World's longest cable-stayed bridge carrying mass transit only. (5) Vertical lift replaced swing span in 1989. (6) Length listed is of bridge's floating section. (7) To be replaced by new, wider SR 520 floating pontoon, with expected opening in 2016. (8) World's second-longest bridge over water, behind China's Qingdao Bay Bridge (25.8 mi). (9) Originally opened in 1889 as a railroad bridge. (10) World's first major structure made of alloy steel. (11) Longest single-span concrete arch in Western Hemisphere. (12) Replaced Silver Bridge, the collapse of which in 1967 led to the creation of National Bridge Inspection Standards in the U.S. (13) World's longest covered bridge.

Oldest U.S. Bridges in Continuous Use

Built in 1697, the stone-arch Frankford Ave. Bridge (U.S. 13) crosses Pennypack Creek in Philadelphia, PA. It consists of three spans and has a total length of 154 ft. The bridge was constructed as part of the King's Road, which connected Philadelphia to New York.

The oldest covered bridge, completed in 1829, is the double-span, 256-ft-long Bath-Haverhill Bridge, which spans the Ammonoosuc River between the towns of Bath and Haverhill, NH. The bridge was bypassed in 1999. It has since reopened to pedestrian traffic only.

Notable World Bridges

Source: World Almanac research; Laboratory of Bridge Engineering, Aalto Univ. School of Science and Technology
Year is date of completion or projected completion. Span of bridge is the distance between its main supports. As of mid-2014.

Year	Bridge	Location	Main span (ft)
	Suspension		
1998	Akashi Kaikyo	Japan	6,532
2009	Xihoumen	China	5,413
1998	Storebælt (Great Belt, East Bridge)	Denmark	5,328
2012	Yi Sun-sin (Gwangyang)	South Korea	5,069
2005	Runyang Yangtze R. (south)	China	4,888
2012	Nanjing Fourth Yangtze R.	China	4,652
1981	Humber	England	4,626
2015	Yavuz Sultan Selim (Third Bosphorus)	Turkey	4,619
1999	Jiangyin Yangtze R.	China	4,544
1997	Tsing Ma	China	4,518
2013	Hardanger	Norway	4,298
2007	Yangluo Yangtze R.	China	4,199
1997	Höga Kusten	Sweden	3,970
2012	Aizhai	China	3,858
2015	Ulsan Grand	South Korea	3,773
2008	Huangpu	China	3,635
1988	Minami Bisan-Seto	Japan	3,609
1988	Fatih Sultan Mehmet (Bosphorus II)	Turkey	3,576

Year	Bridge	Location	Main span (ft)
2010	Baling R.	China	3,570
2012	Taizhou Yangtze R.[1]	China	3,543
1973	Bosphorus	Turkey	3,524
1999	Kurushima III	Japan	3,379
1999	Kurushima II	Japan	3,346
1966	Ponte 25 de Abril, Tagus R.	Portugal	3,323
1964	Forth Road	Scotland	3,300

(1) Two consecutive spans of equal length.

	Steel Arch		
2009	Chaotianmen Yangtze R.	China	1,811
2003	Lupu	China	1,804
1932	Sydney Harbour	Australia	1,650
2005	Wushan Yangtze R.	China	1,614
2016	Chenab (rail)[1]	India	1,532
2013	Xijiang (rail)	China	1,476
2007	Xinguang	China	1,404
2007	Caiyuanba	China	1,378
2010	Daning R.	China	1,312
2008	Hiroshima Airport	Japan	1,247

Year Bridge	Location	Main span (ft)
1959 Sloboda	Croatia	1,224
2000 Yajisha	China	1,181
1962 Bridge of the Americas	Panama	1,128
1967 Zdakov	Czech Republic	1,083
1961 Runcorn-Widnes	England	1,082
1935 Birchenough	Zimbabwe	1,080

(1) Will be world's highest rail bridge (1,178 ft) upon completion.

Concrete Arch

Year Bridge	Location	Main span (ft)
1997 Wanxian Yangtze R.	China	1,378
2015 Nanpanjiang (rail)	China	1,365
1980 Krk I	Croatia	1,280
2015 Almonte Viaduct	Spain	1,260
2012 Zhaohua Jialing R.	China	1,194
1995 Jiangjiehe	China	1,083
2015 Tajo Railway	Spain	1,063
1996 Yongjiang	China	1,024
1964 Gladesville	Australia	1,000

Cantilever

Year Bridge	Location	Main span (ft)
1890 Forth Rail[1]	Scotland	1,710
1974 Minato	Japan	1,673
1943 Rabindra Setu (Howrah)	India	1,500

(1) Two spans of equal length.

Plate and Box Girder

Year Bridge	Location	Main span (ft)
2006 Shibanpo	China	1,083
1998 Stolmasundet	Norway	988
1998 Raftsundet	Norway	978
1974 Pres. Costa e Silva (Rio-Niterói)	Brazil	984
1978 Neckar Valley Viaduct, Weitingen	Germany	863
1956 Branko's	Serbia	856
1989 Third	Brazil	853
1966 Zoobrücke	Germany	850

Cable-Stayed

Year Bridge	Location	Main span (ft)
2012 Russky Island	Russia	3,622
2008 Sutong Yangtze R.	China	3,570
2009 Stonecutters	China	3,340
2009 Edong	China	3,038
1999 Tatara	Japan	2,920
1995 Normandy	France	2,808

Year Bridge	Location	Main span (ft)
2010 Jingyue Yangtze R.	China	2,677
2009 Incheon	South Korea	2,625
2012 Zolotoy Rog	Russia	2,418
2009 Shanghai Yangtze R.	China	2,395
2009 Minpu	China	2,323
2005 Third Nanjing Yangtze R.	China	2,126
2001 Second Nanjing Yangtze R.	China	2,060
2000 Third Wuhan Yangtze R. (Baishazhou)	China	2,028
2002 Qingzhou Minjiang R.	China	1,985
1993 Yangpu	China	1,975
1998 Meiko Chuo	Japan	1,936
1997 Xupu	China	1,936
2004 Rion-Antirion	Greece	1,837
2014 Bukhang	South Korea	1,772
1991 Skarnsundet	Norway	1,739
1999 Shantou Queshi	China	1,699
1995 Tsurumi Tsubasa	Japan	1,673
2008 Tianxingzhou Yangtze R.	China	1,654
2012 Mokpo	South Korea	1,640
2007 Kanchanaphisek	Thailand	1,640
2002 Jingsha	China	1,640
2000 Øresund	Denmark-Sweden	1,608
1991 Ikuchi	Japan	1,608
1994 Higashi Kobe	Japan	1,591
2011 Geo Geum	South Korea	1,575
1998 Zhanjiang	China	1,575
1997 Ting Kau	China	1,558
1999 Seohae Grand	South Korea	1,542
1989 Yokohama Bay	Japan	1,509

Other Notable World Bridges[1]

Year Bridge	Location	Main span (ft)
2011 Danyang-Kunshan Grand (rail)[2]	China	538,000
2000 Bang Na Espressway[3]	Thailand	180,446
2011 Qingdao Bay[4]	China	136,417
2007 Hangzhou Bay	China	118,000
2005 Donghai	China	106,627
2013 Jiashao	China	33,136
1978 Demerara Harbour (floating)	Guyana	6,074
1994 Nordhordland (floating)	Norway	4,088

(1) Length listed is total length of bridge. (2) World's longest bridge. (3) World's longest road bridge. (4) World's longest oversea bridge.

World's Longest Railway Tunnels

Source: World Almanac research
Year is date of opening or projected opening unless otherwise noted. As of mid-2014.

Year	Tunnel	Location	Operating railway	Length (mi)
2016	Gotthard Base (twin)	Switzerland-Italy	Swiss Federal Railways (SBB)	35.4/35.5
1988	Seikan	Japan	Japan Railways Group	33.5
1994	English Channel (Chunnel) (twin)	UK-France	Eurotunnel	31.1
2007	Lötschberg Base (twin)	Switzerland	BLS Lötschbergbahn AG	21.0
2007	Guadarrama (twin)	Spain	Renfe	17.6
2009	Taihang (twin)	China	China's Ministry of Railways	17.3
2005	Hakkoda	Japan	Japan Railways Group	16.4
2017	Guangzhou-Shenzhen-Hong Kong Express Rail Link (XRL), Hong Kong section	China	MTR Corporation	16.2
2002	Iwate-Ichinohe	Japan	Japan Railways Group	16.0
2012-13[1]	Pajares (twin)	Spain	Renfe	15.3
2015	Iiyama	Japan	Japan Railways Group	13.8
1982	Daishimizu	Japan	Japan Railways Group	13.8
2008-09	Geumjeong	South Korea	Korea Railroad Corporation	12.6
2006	Wushaoling (twin)	China	China's Ministry of Railways	12.5
1906/22	Simplon No. 1 and 2	Switzerland-Italy	BLS Lötschbergbahn AG	12.3
1999	Vereina	Switzerland	Rhätische Bahn (RhB)	11.8
2007	High Speed 1 (Channel Tunnel Rail Link, or CTRL) (twin)	UK-France	London & Continental Railways (LCR)	11.8
1975	Shin-Kanmon (twin)	Japan	Japan Railways Group	11.6
1934	Apennine	Italy	Ferrovie dello Stato (FS)	11.5
2002	Qinling (twin)	China	China's Ministry of Railways	10.4
2006	Vaglia	Italy	Ferrovie dello Stato (FS)	10.4
2014	West Qinling (twin)	China	China's Ministry of Railways	10.3
1972	Rokko	Japan	Japan Railways Group	10.1

(1) Tunnels have been dug but are not yet in operation.

Underwater Vehicular Tunnels in North America

Source: World Almanac research
(more than 5,000 ft in length; year is date of opening)

Year	Name	Location	Waterway	Length (ft)
1950	Brooklyn Battery (twin)	New York, NY	East River	9,117
1927	Holland (twin)	New York, NY-Jersey City, NJ	Hudson River	8,558/8,371
1937/45/57	Lincoln (center/north/south tubes)	New York, NY-Weehawken, NJ	Hudson River	8,216/7,482/8,006
1985	Fort McHenry (twin)	Baltimore, MD	Patapsco River	7,920
1957/76	Hampton Roads (twin)	Hampton, VA	Hampton Roads	7,479
1957	Baltimore Harbor (twin)	Baltimore, MD	Baltimore Harbor	7,392
1940	Queens Midtown (twin)	New York, NY	East River	6,414
1934	Sumner	Boston, MA	Boston Harbor	5,653
1964	Thimble Shoal	Northampton Co., VA	Chesapeake Bay	5,552
1964	Chesapeake Channel	Northampton Co., VA	Chesapeake Bay	5,237
1930	Detroit-Windsor	Detroit, MI-Windsor, ON, Canada	Detroit River	5,160
1961	Callahan	Boston, MA	Boston Harbor	5,070

Land Vehicular Tunnels in the U.S.

Source: World Almanac research; Federal Highway Administration, U.S. Dept. of Transportation
(3,400 ft or more in length)

Name	Location	Length (ft)
Anton Anderson Memorial[1]	Whittier, AK	13,300
Edwin C. Johnson Memorial (eastbound)	I-70, Clear Creek Co.-Summit Co., CO	8,960
Eisenhower Mem. (westbound)	I-70, Clear Creek Co.-Summit Co., CO	8,939
Ted Williams[2]	MA Turnpike, Boston, MA	8,448
Thomas P. O'Neill Jr.	I-93, Boston, MA	7,920
Allegheny (twin)	PA Turnpike	6,070
Liberty (twin)	Pittsburgh, PA	5,920
Zion-Mount Carmel	Zion Natl. Park, UT	5,808
East River Mountain (twin)	I-77, Rocky Gap, VA-Bluefield, WV	5,412
Tuscarora Mountain (twin)	PA Turnpike	5,326
Tetsuo Harano (twin)	H-3 Freeway, HI	5,165
Kittatinny Mountain (twin)	PA Turnpike	4,727
Cumberland Gap (twin)	U.S. 25E, KY-TN	4,600
Lehigh (twin)	PA Tpke., NE Extension	4,461/4,380
Blue Mountain (twin)	PA Turnpike	4,339
Wawona	Yosemite Natl. Pk., CA	4,233
Big Walker Mountain (twin)	Bland Co., VA	4,229
Squirrel Hill	Pittsburgh, PA	4,225
Tom Lantos/Devil's Slide (twin)	San Mateo Co., CA	4,200
Hanging Lake (twin)	Glenwood Canyon, CO	4,000
Caldecott (4 tubes)	Oakland, CA	3,771/3,610/3,610/3,389
Fort Pitt (twin)	Pittsburgh, PA	3,614
Mount Baker	Seattle, WA	3,456
Dingess	Mingo Co., WV	3,400
Mall	Washington, DC	3,400

(1) Vehicles and trains take turns using the tunnel's one lane. (2) Total length of tunnel is 8,448 ft, 3,960 ft of which is underwater.

Major U.S. Dams and Reservoirs

Source: 2013 National Inventory of Dams, U.S. Army Corps of Engineers

Highest U.S. Dams

Rank	Dam	River	State	Type	Height Feet	Height Meters	Year completed
1.	Oroville	Feather	California	E	770	235	1968
2.	Hoover	Colorado	Nevada	A-G	730	221	1935
3.	Dworshak	N. Fork Clearwater	Idaho	G	717	219	1973
4.	Glen Canyon	Colorado	Arizona	A	710	216	1963
5.	New Bullards Bar	North Yuba	California	A	645	197	1970
6.	Mossyrock	Cowlitz	Washington	A	606	185	1968
7.	Shasta	Sacramento	California	G	602	183	1945
8.	Don Pedro	Tuolumne	California	E	585	178	1971
9.	New Melones	Stanislaus	California	E-R	578	176	1979
10.	Hungry Horse	S. Fork Flathead	Montana	A	564	172	1952

A = Arch; E = Embankment, earthfill; R = Embankment, rockfill; G = Gravity. **Note:** The height of a dam is the vertical distance between the original streambed or excavated foundation and the dam's crest, parapet wall, or maximum design water level. Tailings and other mining dams (i.e., dams built from the waste generated by mining operations) are not included in this list.

Largest U.S. Embankment Dams

Rank	Dam	River	State	Volume Cubic yards (thousands)	Volume Cubic meters (thousands)	Year completed
1.	Fort Peck	Missouri	Montana	125,628	96,049	1957
2.	Oahe	Missouri	South Dakota	92,000	70,339	1966
3.	Oroville	Feather	California	80,000	61,164	1968
4.	B. F. Sisk	San Luis Creek	California	77,670	59,383	1967
5.	Garrison	Missouri	North Dakota	66,500	50,843	1953
6.	Scotts Flat	Deer Creek	California	66,300	50,690	1948
7.	Cochiti	Rio Grande	New Mexico	65,000	49,696	1975
8.	Herbert Hoover	North New River Canal	Florida	54,700	41,821	1965
9.	Fort Randall	Missouri	South Dakota	50,200	38,381	1954
10.	Castaic	Castaic Creek	California	44,000	33,640	1973

Note: An embankment dam is any dam constructed with excavated material, including earth, rocks, and mining or other industrial waste. (In contrast, gravity, arch, and buttress dams are generally made out of concrete or masonry.) The majority of the world's dams are embankment dams. All dams in this list are earthfill, or formed primarily out of layers of compacted earth.

Largest-Capacity U.S. Reservoirs

Rank	Dam	Reservoir	State	Max. reservoir capacity Acre feet (thousands)	Max. reservoir capacity Cubic meters (thousands)	Year completed
1.	Hoover	Lake Mead	Nevada	30,237	37,296,790	1935
2.	Glen Canyon	Lake Powell	Arizona	29,875	36,850,270	1963
3.	Garrison	Lake Sakakawea	North Dakota	24,500	30,220,305	1953
4.	Oahe	Lake Oahe	South Dakota	23,600	29,110,172	1966
5.	Fort Peck	Fort Peck Lake	Montana	19,100	23,559,503	1957
6.	Grand Coulee	Lake Roosevelt	Washington	9,562	11,794,553	1941
7.	Herbert Hoover	Lake Okeechobee	Florida	8,519	10,508,032	1965
8.	Kentucky	Kentucky Lake	Kentucky	7,535	9,294,779	1944
9.	Sam Rayburn	Sam Rayburn Lake	Texas	6,520	8,042,302	1965
10.	Wright Patman	Wright Patman Lake	Texas	6,505	8,023,799	1954

Note: A reservoir is a body of water created by a dam for storage. This water may serve a single or multiple purposes, such as irrigation, flood reduction, and electricity generation.

Major Dams and Reservoirs of the World

Source: World Register of Dams, Intl. Commission on Large Dams (ICOLD).
Asterisk (*) designates structure is planned or under construction as of mid-2014.

World's Highest Dams

Rank	Dam	Country	Height above lowest formation Meters	Feet
1.	*Rogun	Tajikistan	335	1,099
2.	*Bakhtiari	Iran	315	1,033
3.	Jinping	China	305	1,001
4.	Nurek	Tajikistan	300	984
5.	Xiaowan (Yunnan Gorge)	China	292	958
6.	Grand Dixence	Switzerland	285	935
7.	Xiluodu	China	278	912
8.	Inguri	Georgia	272	892
9.	Chicoasén	Mexico	262	860
10.	Vajont	Italy	262	860
11.	Khersan 2	Iran	260	853
12.	Tehri	India	260	853
13.	Badoosh	Iraq	256	840
14.	Mauvoisin	Switzerland	250	820
15.	Kalat e Dehdasht	Iran	250	820

World's Largest Embankment Dams

Rank	Dam	Country	Volume cubic meters (thousands)
1.	Tarbela	Pakistan	129,200
2.	Fort Peck	U.S.	96,049
3.	Ataturk	Turkey	84,500
4.	Yacyreta	Argentina/Paraguay	81,000
5.	Tucurui	Brazil	80,865
6.	*Rogun	Tajikistan	75,500
7.	Oahe	U.S.	70,339
8.	Guri	Venezuela	70,000
9.	Parambikulam	India	69,165
10.	High Island West	China	67,000
11.	Gardiner	Canada	65,440
12.	Mangla	Pakistan	64,991
13.	Afsluitdijk	Netherlands	63,400
14.	Oroville	U.S.	61,164
15.	B. F. Sisk	U.S.	59,378

World's Largest-Capacity Reservoirs

Rank	Dam	Country	Max. capacity cubic meters (millions)
1.	Tehri	India	260,000
2.	Kariba	Zimbabwe/Zambia	180,600
3.	Bratsk	Russia	169,000
4.	High Aswan	Egypt	162,000
5.	Akosombo (Lake Volta)	Ghana	150,000
6.	Daniel-Johnson	Canada	141,851
7.	Guri	Venezuela	135,000
8.	W. A. C. Bennett	Canada	74,300
9.	Krasnoyarsk	Russia	73,300
10.	Zeya	Russia	68,400
11.	*Hidase	Ethiopia	63,000
12.	Robert-Bourassa (La Grande 2)	Canada	61,715
13.	La Grande 3	Canada	60,020
14.	Ust-Ilim	Russia	59,300
15.	Boguchany	Russia	58,200

World's Largest-Capacity Hydro Plants

Rank	Dam	Country	Installed capacity (MW)
1.	San Xia (Three Gorges Dam)	China	18,200
2.	Dnieper	Ukraine	15,031
3.	Itaipu	Brazil/Paraguay	14,000
4.	Wangjiahe	China	12,630
5.	Xiluodu	China	12,600
6.	*Belo Monte	Brazil	11,234
7.	Guri	Venezuela	10,000
8.	Grand Coulee	U.S.	6,809
9.	Sayano-Shushenskaya	Russia	6,400
10.	Qilinguan	China	6,400
11.	Krasnoyarsk	Russia	6,000
12.	Xiangjiaba	China	6,000
13.	Robert-Bourassa	Canada	5,616
14.	Longtan (Guangxi, Tian'e)	China	5,400
15.	*Hidase	Ethiopia	5,250

Timeline of Selected Architectural Styles and Structures

Asterisk (*) denotes part of a UNESCO World Heritage site.

Style and period	Location; characteristics; significant examples
Mesopotamian c. 3500-539 BCE	City-states of Sumer, Akkad, Babylon, Assyria (modern-day Iraq). Mud-brick rectangular temples on oval platforms with simple corbel vaults, later ziggurats. Painted terra-cotta mosaics and murals; carved reliefs on columns and walls. **Ziggurat of Nanna**, Ur (Muqayyar, Iraq), ordered by Ur-Nammu, c. 2100 BCE **Anu Ziggurat and White Temple**, Uruk (Warka, Iraq), c. 3000 BCE
Egyptian c. 3000-30 BCE	Along Nile R. Mud-brick and limestone tombs and massive, geometric pyramids, post-and-lintel construction. Highly decorative with colorful hieroglyphics, carvings, columns, obelisks, paintings, and sculpture. ***Stepped Pyramid of Pharaoh Djoser** (Saqqara, Egypt), by Imhotep, c. 2737-2717 BCE ***Great Pyramid of Khufu** (Giza, Egypt), c. 2250 BCE ***Great Temple of Amon-Ra** (Karnak, Egypt), c. 1530-300 BCE ***Mortuary Temple of Queen Hatshepsut**, Deir el-Bahari (Thebes, Egypt), by Senenmut, c. 1479-1458 BCE
Three Dynasties c. 2100-221 BCE	China. Single-level mud-brick or mud-smeared timber structures on earthen platforms with thatched roofs. Later, bracketed wooden-framed structures with brick-tiled floors, roofs with overhanging eaves. **City of Erlitou** (Yanshi, China), c. 1900-1500 BCE
Minoan c. 1800-1450 BCE	Crete. Palaces, tombs in monumental style adapted from Mesopotamia and Egypt. Multilevel stone palaces with large central court, no fortifications. Walls made of doors (*polythyron*); stone porticoes and lintels; wooden ceilings and columns; beehive-shaped tombs (*tholi*). **Palace at Knossos** (Heraklion, Crete, Greece), c. 1700 BCE
Mycenaean c. 1600-1100 BCE	Greece. Adapted Minoan style, with large stone masonry, huge walls, and fortified citadels with complex palaces (*megaron*). ***Treasury of Atreus** (Mycenae, Greece), c. 1250 BCE
Olmec c. 1200-400 BCE	Mexico Gulf Coast. Many religious structures, including stone temple-pyramids centered in cities; also large stone sculptures and mosaic pavement with natural and animistic themes. **Great Pyramid** (La Venta, Mexico), c. 800-400 BCE
Mayan c. 900 BCE-900 CE	Central America. Religious structures with plaster-surfaced stone temple-pyramids with stairs containing tombs. Decorative animistic and geometric relief sculptures, lintels, and stone monuments with hieroglyphics. ***Pyramid of the Magician** (Uxmal, Mexico), c. 700-910 CE ***North Acropolis** (Tikal, Guatemala), c. 200 BCE

Style and period	Location; characteristics; significant examples
Greek c. 750-323 BCE	Greek peninsula, Asia Minor, North Africa, western Mediterranean. Religious, civic buildings in monumental style, inspired by Egypt, based on strict rules of form and human proportion; many ornamental details. Marble and limestone structures (including rectangular temples) with pediment, colonnaded porticoes in diverse regional styles, defined by orders of architecture like Ionic, Doric, Corinthian. Most early buildings with timber supports; solid stone in later temples. ***Parthenon, Acropolis** (Athens, Greece), by Ictinus and Callicrates, 447-436 BCE ***Temple of Zeus** (Olympia, Greece), by Libon of Elis, mid-5th cent. BCE **Mausoleum of Halicarnassus** (Bodrum, Turkey), by Pythis, c. 353 BCE (destroyed) ***Temple of Apollo Epicurius** (Bassae, Greece), by Ictinus, c. 420 BCE
Achaemenid c. 550-334 BCE	Persian Empire (Eastern Mediterranean to Indus R.). Palatial complexes influenced by cultures absorbed by the empire; limestone and mud-brick complexes on raised stone terraces with ornamental stairways, rectangular pillared audience halls with porticoes and corner towers; pleasure gardens (*bâgh*) as focal point of architecture. ***Pasargadae** (Iran), founded by Cyrus II, after 547 BCE ***Persepolis** (Iran), founded by Darius I, around 518 BCE
Roman c. 500 BCE-400 CE	Roman Empire. Civic and religious structures with grandiose limestone brick and concrete construction in systematic, practical layout. Adapted Greek orders in many structures, including circular temples and large covered halls (basilica), but emphasized movement with rounded arches and domes, geometric vaults. ***Pantheon** (Rome, Italy), ordered by Emperor Hadrian, 118-128 CE ***Colosseum** (Rome, Italy), ordered by Emperor Vespasian, 70-82 CE ***Roman Forum** (Rome, Italy), 500s BCE-608 CE
Qin and Han c. 221 BCE-220 CE	China. Massive public works, palaces, tombs, and planned cities; systematic layout and design determined by divination techniques (geomancy). Multistoried timber palace complexes with gardens, courtyards laid along a long hall with a south-north axis for weather; decorative roof with overhanging eaves. ***The Great Wall** (China), ordered by Qin Shi Huang, 220 BCE-c. 1600 CE ***Mausoleum of the First Qin Emperor** (Xianyang [Xi'an], China), c. 210 BCE
Sassanian 226-651	Iran. Mud-brick, mortared rubble, and stone palaces on platforms. Tall, vaulted entry chambers with one open side (*iwans*). Three-aisled hall chambers covered with rudimentary barrel vaults. Parabolic domes abandoned for square courtyards in later Sassanian period. **Palace of Ardashir I** (Firuzabad, Iran), c. 224 **Taq-i Kisra** [Arch of Khosrau] (Ctesiphon, Iraq), c. 260 or c. 550
Byzantine 330-1453	Byzantine Empire, Italy, Russia. Religious structures with masonry construction based on Roman architecture, many salvaged pieces. Centralized cross-in-square layout, with large central dome supported by vaults. Highly decorative, with iconographic frescoes, glass mosaics. ***Hagia Sophia** (Istanbul, Turkey), by Anthemius and Isidorus, 532-37 ***St. Mark's Basilica** (Venice, Italy), ordered by Domenico Contarini, 1063-94
Sui and Tang 581-906	China. Includes influences from other cultures; geomancy used to enhance harmony and social status. Rectangular, multistory modular timber structures with interlinking corridors; single-eaved roofs with exposed beams. **Daming Palace** (Xi'an, China), 634 (destroyed) ***Hall of the Great Buddha**, Foguang Temple (Mount Wutai, China), ordered rebuilt by Xuan Zhong, 857
Early Islamic (Umayyad) 692-c. 1000	Syria, Middle East, North Africa, southern Spain. Mosques in adapted Sassanian style. Austere exteriors; simple columned halls with minarets and mihrabs (prayer niches), walled courtyards and gardens, onion domes. Highly decorative interiors with patterned marble, mosaics. **Dome of the Rock** [Qubbat al-Sakhra] (Jerusalem), ordered by Abd al-Malik, 692 ***Great Mosque of Córdoba** (Spain), ordered by Abd al-Rahman I, 784-86
Khmer c. 880-1200s	Indochina. Hindu or Buddhist temple complexes, including brick, later sandstone beehive-shaped shrines with arches atop terraced temple "mountains" symbolizing Mount Meru, Hindu and Buddhist center of the universe, where the gods dwell. Concentric layout of structures mimics the cosmos, relating religious narrative in carved reliefs. ***Angkor Wat** (Cambodia), ordered by Suryavarman II, 12th cent.
Romanesque (Norman) c. 900s-1100s	Western Europe. Churches and monasteries in localized Roman style; many reused material from Roman structures. Austere, heavy, simple masonry construction with thick walls, concealed buttresses, small windows, barrel arches, and vaults. Churches like Roman basilica with arched central nave, lower side aisles, apse, transept formed Latin cross. Monumental art and ornaments with Christian narrative throughout, especially on façade and portals. ***Durham Cathedral** (England, UK), ordered by Bishop William de Saint-Calais, 1093-1133 ***Cathedral, Baptistery, and "Leaning" Tower** (Pisa, Italy), by various architects, begun in 1063, tower not completed until 1372
Gothic c. 1100s-1500s	France, Europe. Cathedrals meant to inspire spirituality with design like Roman basilica: pointed arches and spires that reach toward heavens, skeletal masonry, revealed structure like flying buttresses, ribbed vaults to allow better lighting, large stained-glass windows. **Abbey Church of Saint-Denis** (France), ordered by Abbot Suger, 1136-47 ***Cathedral of Notre-Dame** (Paris, France), ordered by Bishop Maurice de Sully, 1163-1351 ***Chartres Cathedral** (France), 1194-1260 ***Cologne Cathedral** (Cologne, Germany), ordered by Archbishop Konrad von Hochstaden, 1248-1880 ***St. Vitus Cathedral** (Prague, Czech Republic), by Matthias of Arras, later Peter Parler, 1344-1929
Yuan and Ming 1279-1644	China. Mongol-influenced timber and some brick structures influenced by geomancy. Emphasized monumental mass in low-lying, sprawling structures with simple rectangular pavilions, great halls, elaborate wooden latticework, carved and painted details. ***Forbidden City** (Beijing, China), ordered by Emperor Yongle, 1406-20
Renaissance 1420s-1520s	Italy. The rebirth or rediscovery of ancient Roman design, grounded in a scholarly approach to architecture. Followed rules of proportion in perspective and symmetry, classical orders, and simple but perfected geometric forms; emphasis on human scale. ***Pazzi Chapel** (Florence, Italy), by Filippo Brunelleschi, 1429-61 ***Palazzo Medici-Riccardi** (Florence, Italy), by Michelozzo di Bartolomeo, 1444-60 ***Tempietto San Pietro** (Rome, Italy), by Donato Bramante, 1502-10 ***Villa Almerico Capra, or La Rotonda** (near Vicenza, Italy), by Andrea Palladio, later Vincenzo Scamozzi, 1566-1610

Style and period	Location; characteristics; significant examples
Mughal 1526-1858	India. Monumental palaces and mosques blending Hindu and Islamic architecture. Sandstone with marble inlay; highly decorative, with semiprecious stones, vegetal and Koranic motifs. Formulaic four-part pleasure gardens (*charbâgh*), exemplified by grounds of Taj Mahal. ***Humayun's Tomb** (Delhi, India), by Sayyid Muhammad, 1562-72 ***Taj Mahal** (Agra, India), ordered by Emperor Shah Jahan, 1631-48
Baroque 1630s-1700s	Italy, later Western Europe. Elaborate and theatrical religious and civic structures, focused on dramatic overall effect. Complex geometric shapes and elaborate sculptures meant to be viewed from many angles. **St. Carlo alle Quattro Fontane** (Rome, Italy), by Francesco Borromini, 1638-41 ***Palace of Versailles** (Versailles, France), royal hunting lodge (built 1631-34) expanded under Louis XIV, 1661-1710 **Church of San Lorenzo** (Turin, Italy), by Guarino Guarini, 1666-79 **Church of St. John of Nepomuk, or Asamkirche** (Munich, Germany), by Cosmas Damian and Egid Quirin Asam, 1733-46
Rococo 1690s-1700s	Europe. Mostly interior, simplified but still fanciful Baroque designs; ornate with natural motifs, gold trim, light and creamy colors, asymmetrical designs, and unusual materials. ***Sanssouci Palace** (Potsdam, Germany), by Georg Wenzeslaus von Knobelsdorff, 1745-47
Neoclassicism 1750-1830	Europe, Americas. Civic, commercial, and religious structures; chaste, non-decorative designs in reaction to Baroque excess. Grounded in Enlightenment-era principles and simple, strict adherence to classic (Greek, Roman, Renaissance) forms and details. Palladian style in England, Federal style in U.S. **Chiswick House** (Chiswick, England, UK), by Richard Boyle, 1725-29 ***Monticello** (Charlottesville, VA), by Thomas Jefferson, 1768-1809
Neo-Gothic 1837-1900s	Britain, U.S. Civic, commercial, and religious structures utilizing Gothic forms in new commercial enterprises like railway stations and hotels. Traditional masonry façade disguised modern structural material like iron and glass. ***Westminster Palace** (London, England, UK), by Charles Barry and A.W.N. Pugin, 1840-47 **Hotel fronting St. Pancras Railway Station** (London, England, UK), by George Gilbert Scott, 1865-71
Arts and Crafts 1850s-1930s	England, U.S. Residential structures made of brick and other indigenous materials with pastoral and traditional elements like gabled roofs. Conceived as a reaction against homogenization of style following the Industrial Revolution. **Red House** (Bexley Heath, England, UK), by Philip Webb, 1859 **Tigbourne Court** (Surrey, England, UK), by Edwin Lutyens, 1898
Beaux-Arts 1870s-1930s	France, U.S. Grandiose, highly decorative style, using a mix of classical forms taught at the École des Beaux-Arts (School of Fine Arts) in Paris: columns, wall projections, elaborate rooftops, high-relief decoration. **Boston Public Library** (Boston, MA), by McKim, Mead, and White, 1888-95 **Grand Central Terminal** (New York, NY), Reed & Stem and Warren & Wetmore, 1903-13
Art Nouveau 1884-1905	Europe (esp. Brussels, Belgium; France). Civic and residential structures using industrial products like metal and glass to mimic natural forms; airy, fluid, and ornate. ***Hôtel Tassel** (Brussels, Belgium), by Victor Horta, 1892-93 **Entrances to Métro (subway)** (Paris, France), by Hector Guimard, 1900
Prairie 1893-1917	U.S. Mostly residences, some civic buildings in adapted Arts and Crafts style. Inspired by American Midwest and small-town values. Frank Lloyd Wright most notable architect of the style. Buildings centered on chimney, with overhanging eaves and horizontal emphasis, long bands of windows. **Robie House** (Chicago, IL), by Frank Lloyd Wright, 1908-10 **National Farmer's Bank** (Owatonna, MN), by Louis Sullivan, 1906-08
Futurism 1913-14	Italy. Purely theoretical style that produced no actual structures. Emphasized concrete, glass, and steel construction; pure geometric forms and straight lines; and exposed structure and utilities. **La Città Nuova (The New City)** (sketches), by Antonio Sant'Elia, 1913
Constructivism 1914-20s	Russia, Europe. Public buildings based on socialist philosophies. Purely utilitarian industrial design, modern materials. **Rusakov Club** (Moscow, Russia), by Konstantin Melnikov, 1927-28
De Stijl 1917-31	Netherlands. Building and fixtures designed as a complete, sculpture-like piece of art; emphasis on primary colors, simple but asymmetrical geometry. Name is Dutch for "The Style." ***Schröder House** (Utrecht, Netherlands), by Gerrit Thomas Rietveld, 1924
Bauhaus 1919-33	Weimar Republic Germany. Art and design school founded by Walter Gropius with philosophy that the machine is the modern medium. Concrete, glass, and steel construction that united industrial crafts and fine arts with simple geometric forms and colors. ***Bauhaus** (Dessau, Germany), by Walter Gropius, 1925-26
International Style 1920s-70s	Asia, Europe, North America. Reinforced concrete and steel structures, mostly commercial buildings with some residences and civic structures. Post-and-slab construction meant walls no longer supported weight so façades could be continuous strip (ribbon) glass "curtain-walls" with modular interiors. Emphasis on simple forms; glass, marble, and stainless steel; minimal decoration. **Philadelphia Savings Fund Society Building** (Philadelphia, PA), by George Howe and William Lescaze, 1926-32 **Villa Savoye** (Poissy, France), by Le Corbusier, 1928-31 **Seagram Building** (New York, NY), by Ludwig Mies Van Der Rohe with Philip Johnson, 1954-58
Art Deco 1925-30s	Europe, U.S. Traditional, symmetric, elegant construction like Beaux-Arts whimsically mixed with modern styles like geometric forms and steel or chrome features. **Chrysler Building** (New York, NY), by William van Alen, 1928-30 **Empire State Building** (New York, NY), by Shreve, Lamb, & Harmon, 1930-31
Postmodernism 1970s-present	Asia, Europe, North America. Playful reaction against generic, mainstream "orthodox modern architecture," according to Robert Venturi. Token references to traditional architectural elements like pediments or gables on houses; aim to present, Venturi wrote, "old clichés in new settings." **Vanna Venturi House** (Philadelphia, PA), by Robert Venturi, 1962 **Public Service Building** (Portland, OR), by Michael Graves, 1980-82

World Population Growth

The global population in ancient times can only be very roughly estimated, but there were perhaps 50 mil people in the world in 1000 BCE. The United Nations (UN) Population Division estimates a figure of 300 mil for 1 CE. This diagram shows estimated population growth since then.

Although different sources may provide varying estimates, they agree that the world's population began growing more rapidly in the 18th and 19th centuries and increased at an even greater rate in the 20th century. According to the UN, the total population reached 1 bil in 1804; rose to 2 bil 123 years later, in 1927; to 3 bil 33 years after that, in 1960; to 4 bil in 1974; to 5 bil in 1987; and to 6 bil in 1999.

The U.S. Census Bureau, which also issues estimates and projections, put the world population in mid-2014 at about 7.2 bil. It projects that the population will reach 8 bil by 2026.

```
                                    2011
                                    7 bil
                              1999
                              6 bil
                        1987
                        5 bil
                    1974
                    4 bil
              1960
              3 bil
          1927
          2 bil
      1804
      1 bil
1 CE            1250    1500
300 mil        400 mil  500 mil
```

Area and Population of the World by Continent/Region

Source: International Data Base, International Programs Center, U.S. Census Bureau, U.S. Dept. of Commerce; *The World Factbook*, Central Intelligence Agency (CIA)

Composition of geographical (continental) regions are as defined by the United Nations. Land area figures are from *The World Factbook*. Figures may not add up to totals due to rounding.

Continent/ region	Land area (sq mi)	(sq km)	% of Earth's land	Population (midyear) 1950	1975	2000	2014	% of world total, 2014	2025[1]
Asia	12,015,259	31,119,378	21.3	1,437,565,483	2,413,261,390	3,694,627,895	4,306,685,522	60.0	4,712,851,182
Africa	11,494,762	29,771,296	20.4	229,058,740	416,195,934	803,528,244	1,124,638,963	15.7	1,429,635,911
Europe[2]	8,559,255	22,168,368	15.2	547,140,324	678,635,710	730,597,540	743,008,093	10.4	745,416,114
N. America	7,879,373	20,407,482	14.0	165,945,185	238,783,486	313,388,332	353,860,227	4.9	384,101,059
Latin America[3]	7,762,306	20,104,280	13.8	165,442,794	320,629,690	517,756,498	611,121,722	8.5	673,313,198
Oceania	3,278,295	8,490,744	5.8	12,476,128	21,114,852	30,420,890	36,708,528	0.5	41,266,804
Antarctica[4]	5,405,430	14,000,000	9.6	NA	NA	NA	NA	NA	NA
World	**56,394,679**	**146,061,547**	**100.0**	**2,557,628,654**	**4,088,621,062**	**6,090,319,399**	**7,176,023,055**	**100.0**	**7,986,584,268**

NA = Not applicable. (1) Projected. (2) Includes all of Russia. (3) Includes the Caribbean. (4) Antarctica has no indigenous inhabitants, though people are present at permanent and seasonal research stations.

Current Population and Projections for Countries and Other Areas

Source: International Data Base, International Programs Center, U.S. Census Bureau, U.S. Dept. of Commerce; *The World Factbook*, Central Intelligence Agency (CIA)

(midyear figures)

Country/area	2014	2025	2050
Afghanistan	31,822,848	41,117,073	63,795,418
Albania	3,020,209	3,104,932	2,824,012
Algeria	38,813,722	45,841,317	55,444,735
American Samoa	54,517	53,316	49,308
Andorra	85,458	85,112	74,765
Angola	19,088,106	25,673,282	45,888,061
Anguilla	16,086	19,749	26,980
Antigua and Barbuda	91,295	103,830	122,930
Argentina	43,024,374	47,164,630	53,511,279
Armenia	3,060,927	2,968,203	2,495,868
Aruba	110,663	126,130	150,730
Australia	22,507,617	25,053,669	29,012,740
Austria	8,223,062	8,189,560	7,520,950
Azerbaijan	9,686,210	10,533,598	11,209,644
Bahamas, The	321,834	349,116	371,219
Bahrain	1,314,089	1,579,899	1,847,072
Bangladesh	166,280,712	197,673,655	250,155,274
Barbados	289,680	297,015	282,041
Belarus	9,608,058	9,325,020	8,339,664
Belgium	10,449,361	10,453,261	9,882,599
Belize	340,844	411,007	543,690
Benin	10,160,556	13,564,964	22,118,545
Bermuda	69,839	72,851	69,874
Bhutan	733,643	820,143	951,873
Bolivia	10,631,486	12,463,434	16,003,638
Bosnia and Herzegovina	3,871,643	3,787,402	3,216,039
Botswana	2,155,784	2,425,114	2,871,345
Brazil	202,656,788	218,259,140	232,304,177
Brunei	422,675	498,756	638,157
Bulgaria	6,924,716	6,257,716	4,651,477
Burkina Faso	18,365,123	25,384,628	47,429,509
Burundi	10,395,931	14,791,662	30,391,856
Cabo Verde	538,535	619,168	741,842
Cambodia	15,458,332	18,037,946	22,338,891
Cameroon	23,130,708	30,508,842	51,912,309

Country/area	2014	2025	2050
Canada	34,834,841	37,558,781	41,135,648
Cayman Islands	54,914	67,661	91,118
Central African Republic	5,277,959	6,637,613	10,338,863
Chad	11,412,107	13,914,726	20,473,601
Chile	17,363,894	18,764,737	19,688,474
China	1,355,692,576	1,394,638,699	1,303,723,332
Colombia	46,245,297	51,194,904	56,227,630
Comoros	766,865	905,545	1,169,893
Congo, Dem. Rep. of	77,433,744	99,162,003	144,805,434
Congo Republic	4,662,446	5,947,999	10,201,971
Cook Islands	10,134	7,621	5,460
Costa Rica	4,755,234	5,353,218	6,065,989
Côte d'Ivoire	22,848,945	27,651,498	37,111,782
Croatia	4,470,534	4,374,007	3,864,201
Cuba	11,047,251	10,784,894	9,161,479
Curaçao	147,695	153,501	150,128
Cyprus	1,172,458	1,329,908	1,392,078
Czech Republic	10,627,448	10,696,842	10,209,638
Denmark	5,569,077	5,697,913	5,575,147
Djibouti	810,179	1,016,919	1,395,810
Dominica	73,449	74,374	64,772
Dominican Republic	10,349,741	11,702,846	13,690,264
Ecuador	15,654,411	17,867,616	21,102,550
Egypt	86,895,099	103,742,157	137,872,522
El Salvador	6,125,512	6,288,430	6,181,181
Equatorial Guinea	722,254	935,553	1,428,139
Eritrea	6,380,803	7,987,458	11,381,250
Estonia	1,257,921	1,149,245	861,913
Ethiopia	96,633,458	131,260,566	228,066,276
Faroe Islands	49,947	53,220	57,112
Fiji	903,207	956,003	1,013,636
Finland	5,268,799	5,251,272	4,819,615
France	66,259,012	68,860,202	69,484,481
French Polynesia	280,026	305,484	324,712
Gabon	1,672,597	2,063,339	3,229,741
Gambia, The	1,925,527	2,369,298	3,210,223

Country/area	2014	2025	2050
Gaza Strip	1,816,379	2,350,255	3,392,849
Georgia	4,935,880	4,929,789	4,714,548
Germany	80,996,685	79,226,209	71,541,906
Ghana	25,758,108	32,610,058	52,415,526
Gibraltar	29,185	29,753	28,423
Greece	10,775,557	10,670,697	10,035,935
Greenland	57,728	57,174	49,356
Grenada	110,152	114,741	114,205
Guam	161,001	176,770	201,610
Guatemala	14,647,083	17,564,073	22,995,434
Guernsey	65,849	67,710	66,521
Guinea	11,474,383	15,240,839	26,407,254
Guinea-Bissau	1,693,398	2,061,262	2,894,545
Guyana	735,554	781,231	878,028
Haiti	9,996,731	11,252,370	13,352,710
Honduras	8,598,561	10,143,828	12,948,839
Hong Kong	7,112,688	7,296,877	6,623,263
Hungary	9,919,128	9,615,020	8,489,811
Iceland	317,351	337,632	350,922
India	1,236,344,631	1,396,046,308	1,656,553,632
Indonesia	253,609,643	276,746,433	300,183,166
Iran	80,840,713	90,481,226	100,044,564
Iraq	32,585,692	40,387,147	56,316,329
Ireland	4,832,765	5,417,947	6,333,836
Isle of Man	86,866	92,606	92,840
Israel	7,821,850	8,984,285	10,828,462
Italy	61,680,122	62,591,055	61,415,852
Jamaica	2,930,050	3,151,611	3,554,571
Japan	127,103,388	123,385,521	107,209,536
Jersey	96,513	104,140	107,581
Jordan	6,528,061	7,945,150	11,243,177
Kazakhstan	17,948,816	19,809,426	22,237,156
Kenya	45,010,056	53,196,255	70,755,460
Kiribati	104,488	117,779	139,738
Korea, North	24,851,627	26,242,210	26,969,396
Korea, South	49,039,986	49,372,307	43,368,983
Kosovo	1,859,203	1,999,461	2,222,619
Kuwait	2,742,711	3,169,497	3,863,453
Kyrgyzstan	5,604,212	6,218,713	7,063,351
Laos	6,803,699	7,971,675	10,068,995
Latvia	2,165,165	1,992,516	1,544,073
Lebanon	4,136,895	4,307,087	4,155,101
Lesotho	1,942,008	1,970,540	1,920,225
Liberia	4,092,310	5,283,774	8,192,118
Libya	6,244,174	7,374,566	8,970,664
Liechtenstein	37,313	40,505	43,610
Lithuania	3,505,738	3,355,985	2,787,516
Luxembourg	520,672	586,296	720,603
Macao	587,914	630,434	620,184
Macedonia	2,091,719	2,119,511	1,990,728
Madagascar	23,201,926	30,182,920	45,807,534
Malawi	17,241,754	22,859,677	37,406,745
Malaysia	30,073,353	34,683,300	42,928,546
Maldives	393,595	388,681	444,429
Mali	16,455,903	22,533,811	38,395,414
Malta	412,655	421,239	395,639
Marshall Islands	70,983	83,203	103,092
Mauritania	3,516,806	4,425,089	6,536,272
Mauritius	1,331,155	1,412,384	1,441,100
Mexico	120,286,655	134,828,700	150,567,503
Micronesia	105,681	98,948	74,483
Moldova	3,583,288	3,176,863	2,261,208
Monaco	30,508	31,706	29,810
Mongolia	2,953,190	3,301,176	3,669,264
Montenegro	650,036	635,537	577,654
Montserrat	5,215	5,529	5,707
Morocco	32,987,206	36,484,418	42,026,448
Mozambique	24,692,144	32,306,018	58,998,457
Myanmar (Burma)	55,746,253	61,747,758	70,673,160
Namibia	2,198,406	2,283,845	2,149,815
Nauru	9,488	10,008	11,995
Nepal	30,986,975	36,622,606	45,984,605
Netherlands	16,877,351	17,572,113	17,906,594
New Caledonia	267,840	307,452	370,511
New Zealand	4,401,916	4,775,930	5,198,992
Nicaragua	5,848,641	6,493,913	7,233,620
Niger	17,466,172	24,618,828	44,221,854
Nigeria	177,155,754	230,570,741	391,296,754
Northern Mariana Islands	51,483	61,985	77,842
Norway	5,147,792	5,682,068	6,364,008
Oman	3,219,775	3,981,057	5,401,957
Pakistan	196,174,380	228,385,138	290,847,790
Palau	21,186	22,102	22,894
Panama	3,608,431	4,117,882	4,859,334
Papua New Guinea	6,552,730	7,823,210	10,110,027
Paraguay	6,703,860	7,602,853	8,840,105
Peru	30,147,935	33,283,408	36,943,693
Philippines	107,668,231	128,921,424	171,964,187
Poland	38,346,279	37,349,696	32,084,570
Portugal	10,813,834	10,806,202	9,933,334
Puerto Rico	3,620,897	3,476,473	2,984,291
Qatar	2,123,160	2,562,764	2,558,854
Romania	21,729,871	20,872,127	18,060,354
Russia	142,470,272	140,139,049	129,908,086
Rwanda	12,337,138	16,080,729	27,506,207
Saint Barthélemy	7,267	7,056	6,527
Saint Helena	7,776	7,888	7,296
Saint Kitts and Nevis	51,538	55,405	56,362
Saint Lucia	163,362	168,519	162,356
Saint Martin	31,530	33,048	34,601
Saint Pierre and Miquelon	5,716	5,030	3,516
Saint Vincent and the Grenadines	102,918	100,409	93,507
Samoa	196,628	210,369	245,010
San Marino	32,742	35,203	35,178
São Tomé and Príncipe	190,428	227,395	309,457
Saudi Arabia	27,345,986	31,877,311	40,250,628
Senegal	13,635,927	17,580,816	27,244,158
Serbia	7,209,764	6,845,638	5,869,146
Seychelles	91,650	98,843	100,391
Sierra Leone	5,743,725	7,500,140	13,593,862
Singapore	5,567,301	6,732,999	8,609,518
Sint Maarten	40,289	46,560	53,001
Slovakia	5,492,677	5,458,581	4,943,616
Slovenia	1,988,292	1,907,560	1,596,947
Solomon Islands	609,883	747,001	1,015,731
Somalia	10,428,043	13,274,251	22,626,120
South Africa	48,375,645	48,714,478	49,400,628
South Sudan	11,562,695	16,615,122	26,843,710
Spain	47,737,941	51,415,437	52,490,640
Sri Lanka	21,866,445	23,563,343	25,166,733
Sudan	35,482,233	42,733,103	59,129,521
Suriname	573,311	636,782	717,936
Swaziland	1,419,623	1,585,439	1,834,151
Sweden	9,723,809	10,587,441	12,011,256
Switzerland	8,061,516	8,665,531	9,539,097
Syria	22,597,531	26,536,400	33,657,629
Taiwan	23,359,928	23,642,264	20,834,040
Tajikistan	8,051,512	9,510,130	12,132,365
Tanzania	49,639,138	66,904,889	118,586,412
Thailand	67,741,401	69,588,429	66,063,997
Timor-Leste	1,201,542	1,539,173	2,191,749
Togo	7,351,374	9,741,450	16,583,950
Tonga	106,440	104,648	78,995
Trinidad and Tobago	1,223,916	1,183,838	1,023,741
Tunisia	10,937,521	11,849,537	12,180,271
Turkey	81,619,392	90,498,016	100,955,188
Turkmenistan	5,171,943	5,800,391	6,607,083
Turks and Caicos Islands	49,070	61,293	84,240
Tuvalu	10,782	11,759	13,423
Uganda	35,918,915	50,692,201	93,476,229
Ukraine	44,291,413	41,037,583	33,573,842
United Arab Emirates	5,628,805	7,063,346	8,018,904
United Kingdom	63,742,977	67,243,723	71,153,797
United States	318,892,103	346,407,223	399,803,369
Uruguay	3,332,972	3,431,610	3,495,238
Uzbekistan	28,929,716	31,823,964	35,116,374
Vanuatu	266,937	323,464	432,658
Vatican City	842	NA	NA
Venezuela	28,868,486	33,188,608	40,255,592
Vietnam	93,421,835	102,458,828	111,173,583
Virgin Islands, British	32,680	41,324	59,618
Virgin Islands, U.S.	104,170	95,902	68,933
Wallis and Futuna	15,561	16,023	15,598
West Bank	2,731,052	3,328,248	4,376,251
Western Sahara	554,795	735,697	1,173,350
Yemen	26,052,966	32,822,216	46,080,625
Zambia	14,638,505	20,104,997	38,992,619
Zimbabwe	13,771,721	17,370,260	25,198,196
World[1]	7,176,023,055	7,986,584,268	9,376,416,975

NA = Not available. **Note:** Figures for countries do not include the population of any dependencies listed separately in this table. For example, China's population estimate and projections do not include Hong Kong nor Macao. (1) Total projected populations do not include countries for which projections were not available.

Population of the World's Largest Urban Areas

Source: *World Urbanization Prospects*, Dept. of Economic and Social Affairs, UN Population Division

Population figures are midyear estimates for urban agglomerations, i.e., whole metropolitan areas comprising an urban center and surrounding settlements of lower density. The UN releases an update every two years. Population counts for 2030 are projections. Data may differ from figures elsewhere in *The World Almanac*. MMA = Major Metropolitan Area.

(ranked by mid-2014 population)

		Population (thous.)				Rate of change (%)			Pop. of urban area as % of country's 2014 pop.
Rank	Urban area, country	1975	2000	2014	2030	1975-2000	2000-14	2014-30	
1.	Tokyo, Japan	26,614.7	34,449.9	37,832.9	37,190.5	29.4%	9.8%	−1.7%	29.8%
2.	Delhi, India	4,426.0	15,732.3	24,953.3	36,060.1	255.5	58.6	44.5	2.0
3.	Shanghai, China	5,626.6	13,959.0	22,991.1	30,750.7	148.1	64.7	33.8	1.6
4.	Mexico City, Mexico	10,733.9	18,457.0	20,843.5	23,864.7	72.0	12.9	14.5	16.8
5.	São Paulo, Brazil	9,614.0	17,014.1	20,830.9	23,444.4	77.0	22.4	12.5	10.3
6.	Mumbai (Bombay), India	7,082.0	16,366.8	20,740.8	27,796.6	131.1	26.7	34.0	1.6
7.	Kinki MMA (Osaka), Japan	16,298.1	18,660.0	20,122.7	19,975.7	14.5	7.8	−0.7	15.8
8.	Beijing, China	4,827.9	10,162.4	19,520.3	27,706.0	110.5	92.1	41.9	1.4
9.	New York-Newark, NY-NJ, U.S.	15,880.3	17,813.4	18,590.7	19,885.3	12.2	4.4	7.0	5.8
10.	Cairo, Egypt	6,449.9	13,625.6	18,419.1	24,502.2	111.3	35.2	33.0	22.1
11.	Dhaka, Bangladesh	2,221.1	10,284.9	16,982.4	27,373.6	363.1	65.1	61.2	10.7
12.	Karachi, Pakistan	3,989.2	10,031.7	16,125.9	24,837.9	151.5	60.7	54.0	8.7
13.	Buenos Aires, Argentina	8,744.6	12,406.8	15,023.8	16,956.5	41.9	21.1	12.9	35.9
14.	Kolkata (Calcutta), India	7,887.8	13,058.1	14,766.1	19,092.5	65.5	13.1	29.3	1.2
15.	Istanbul, Turkey	3,600.3	8,743.9	13,953.7	16,694.3	142.9	59.6	19.6	18.4

National Rankings by Population, Area, Population Density, 2014

Source: International Data Base, International Programs Center, U.S. Census Bureau, U.S. Dept. of Commerce; *The World Factbook*, Central Intelligence Agency (CIA)

Population figures are for midyear. The world had an estimated population of 7.2 bil in mid-2014. China was the most populous nation, with nearly one-fifth of the world total. A country's land area does not include inland water. Refer to Nations of the World for a country's total area. Population density is calculated using land area.

Largest Populations

Rank	Country	Population
1.	China[1]	1,355,692,576
2.	India	1,236,344,631
3.	United States	318,892,103
4.	Indonesia	253,609,643
5.	Brazil	202,656,788
6.	Pakistan	196,174,380
7.	Nigeria	177,155,754
8.	Bangladesh	166,280,712
9.	Russia	142,470,272
10.	Japan	127,103,388

Smallest Populations

Rank	Country	Population
1.	Vatican City	842
2.	Nauru	9,488
3.	Tuvalu	10,782
4.	Palau	21,186
5.	Monaco	30,508
6.	San Marino	32,742
7.	Liechtenstein	37,313
8.	Saint Kitts and Nevis	51,538
9.	Marshall Islands	70,983
10.	Dominica	73,449

Largest Land Areas

Rank	Country	Area (sq mi)	Area (sq km)
1.	Russia	6,323,482	16,377,742
2.	China	3,694,959	9,569,901
3.	United States	3,531,905	9,147,593
4.	Canada	3,511,023	9,093,507
5.	Brazil	3,266,199	8,459,417
6.	Australia	2,966,153	7,682,300
7.	India	1,147,956	2,973,193
8.	Argentina	1,056,642	2,736,690
9.	Kazakhstan	1,042,360	2,699,700
10.	Algeria	919,595	2,381,741

Smallest Land Areas

Rank	Country	Area (sq mi)	Area (sq km)
1.	Vatican City	0.17	0.44
2.	Monaco	0.77	2
3.	Nauru	8.1	21
4.	Tuvalu	10	26
5.	San Marino	24	61
6.	Liechtenstein	62	160
7.	Marshall Islands	70	181
8.	Saint Kitts and Nevis	101	261
9.	Maldives	115	298
10.	Malta	122	316

Most Densely Populated

Rank	Country	Persons per sq mi	Persons per sq km
1.	Monaco	39,507.7	15,254.0
2.	Singapore	20,988.7	8,103.8
3.	Vatican City	4,956.3	1,913.6
4.	Bahrain	4,478.3	1,729.1
5.	Maldives	3,420.8	1,320.8
6.	Malta	3,382.2	1,305.9
7.	Bangladesh	3,308.5	1,277.4
8.	Taiwan	1,875.4	724.1
9.	Barbados	1,744.8	673.7
10.	Mauritius	1,698.4	655.7

Most Sparsely Populated

Rank	Country	Persons per sq mi	Persons per sq km
1.	Mongolia	4.9	1.9
2.	Namibia	6.9	2.7
3.	Australia	7.6	2.9
4.	Iceland	8.2	3.2
5.	Mauritania	8.8	3.4
6.	Libya	9.2	3.5
7.	Suriname	9.5	3.7
8.	Guyana	9.7	3.7
9.	Botswana	9.9	3.8
10.	Canada	9.9	3.8

(1) Does not include mid-2014 population of Hong Kong (7,112,688) and Macao (587,914).

Countries Ranked by Gross Domestic Product and Per Capita GDP, 2013

Source: *The World Factbook*, Central Intelligence Agency (CIA)

Estimates of gross domestic product (GDP)—the value of all final goods and services that a country produced in a year—were made based on purchasing power parity exchange rates. Per capita GDP is calculated using the estimated population size as of July 1 in a given year. Data may differ from estimates made by the U.S. Bureau of Economic Analysis. GDP figures are for 2013 unless otherwise noted.

GDP (in mil)		Per capita GDP	
Highest	**Lowest**	**Highest**	**Lowest**
1. U.S. $16,720,000	1. Tuvalu............ $40	1. Qatar............$102,100	1. Congo, Dem. Rep. of $400
2. China[1] 13,390,000	2. Nauru[2] 60	2. Liechtenstein[4]..... 89,400	2. Zimbabwe...... 600
3. India 4,990,000	3. Palau 246	3. Monaco[5]........ 85,500	Somalia[7]....... 600
4. Japan 4,729,000	4. São Tomé and Príncipe 421	4. Luxembourg 77,900	Burundi......... 600
5. Germany.... 3,227,000	5. Marshall Islands ... 486	5. Singapore 62,400	5. Central African Republic 700
6. Russia....... 2,553,000	6. Kiribati 698	6. Norway 55,400	Liberia........ 700
7. Brazil....... 2,416,000	7. Micronesia[3]...... 754	7. Switzerland........ 54,800	7. Niger.......... 800
8. UK........ 2,387,000	8. Tonga 846	Brunei....... 54,800	8. Malawi 900
9. France....... 2,276,000	9. Comoros 911	9. U.S........... 52,800	9. Madagascar 1,000
10. Mexico 1,845,000	10. St. Kitts and Nevis.... 952	10. Netherlands[6]...... 43,300	10. Guinea 1,100
11. Italy........ 1,805,000	11. Dominica 1,015	11. Canada 43,100	Togo 1,100
12. Korea, South 1,666,000	12. Samoa 1,145	12. Australia 43,000	Mali...........1,100
13. Canada..... 1,518,000	13. Vanuatu 1,270	13. Austria 42,600	Afghanistan.....1,100
14. Spain 1,389,000	14. San Marino 1,306	14. Kuwait........... 42,100	14. Guinea-Bissau ...1,200
15. Indonesia ... 1,285,000	15. St. Vincent and the Grenadines.......1,335	15. Ireland........ 41,300	Mozambique....1,200 Eritrea.......1,200
16. Turkey..... 1,167,000	16. Grenada 1,458	16. Sweden........ 40,900	
17. Australia 998,300	17. Antigua and Barbuda .1,610	17. Iceland........ 40,700	17. Ethiopia........1,300
18. Iran........ 987,100	18. Solomon Islands.....1,958	18. Taiwan 39,600	Comoros........1,300
19. Saudi Arabia 927,800	19. Guinea-Bissau 2,005	19. Germany........ 39,500	Haiti 1,300
20. Taiwan 926,400	20. St. Lucia 2,216	20. Belgium........ 37,800	20. Sierra Leone....1,400 South Sudan....1,400

(1) Does not include Hong Kong ($381.3 bil GDP) or Macao ($51.7 bil GDP). (2) 2005 est. (3) Supplemented by grant aid, averaging perhaps $100 mil annually. (4) 2009 est. (5) 2011. (6) 2012 est. (7) 2010 est.

Gold Reserves of Selected Central Banks and Governments, 1975-2013

Source: *International Financial Statistics*, International Monetary Fund (IMF)

(in mil fine troy ounces)

Year end	All countries	Canada	China[1]	France	Germany[2]	India	Italy	Japan	Netherlands	Russia	Switzerland	UK	U.S.
1975	1,188.0	22.0	NA	100.9	117.6	7.0	82.5	21.1	54.3	NA	83.2	21.0	274.7
1980	1,152.2	21.0	12.8	81.9	95.2	8.6	66.7	24.2	43.9	NA	83.3	18.8	264.3
1985	1,147.4	20.1	12.7	81.9	95.2	9.4	66.7	24.2	43.9	NA	83.3	19.0	262.7
1990	1,144.2	14.8	12.7	81.9	95.2	10.7	66.7	24.2	43.9	NA	83.3	18.9	261.9
1995	1,114.4	3.4	12.7	81.9	95.2	12.8	66.7	24.2	34.8	9.4	83.3	18.4	261.7
2000	1,066.0	1.2	12.7	97.2	111.5	11.5	78.8	24.5	29.3	12.4	77.8	15.7	261.6
2002	1,045.2	0.6	19.3	97.2	110.8	11.5	78.8	24.6	27.4	12.5	61.6	10.1	262.0
2003	1,027.4	0.1	19.3	97.2	110.6	11.5	78.8	24.6	25.0	12.5	52.5	10.1	261.5
2004	1,010.7	0.1	19.3	96.0	110.4	11.5	78.8	24.6	25.0	12.4	43.5	10.0	261.6
2005	991.4	0.1	19.3	90.9	110.2	11.5	78.8	24.6	22.3	12.4	41.5	10.0	261.6
2006	979.6	0.1	19.3	87.4	110.0	11.5	78.8	24.6	20.6	12.9	41.5	10.0	261.5
2007	963.3	0.1	19.3	83.7	109.9	11.5	78.8	24.6	20.0	14.5	36.8	10.0	261.5
2008	963.9	0.1	19.3	80.1	109.7	11.5	78.8	24.6	19.7	16.7	33.4	10.0	261.5
2009	981.2	0.1	33.9	78.3	109.5	17.9	78.8	24.6	19.7	20.9	33.4	10.0	261.5
2010	992.0	0.1	33.9	78.3	109.3	17.9	78.8	24.6	19.7	25.4	33.4	10.0	261.5
2011	1,003.8	0.1	33.9	78.3	109.2	17.9	78.8	24.6	19.7	28.4	33.4	10.0	261.5
2012	1,019.4	0.1	33.9	78.3	109.0	17.9	78.8	24.6	19.7	30.8	33.4	10.0	261.5
2013	1,025.3	0.1	33.9	78.3	108.9	17.9	78.8	24.6	19.7	33.3	33.4	10.0	261.5

NA = Not available. (1) Figures are for mainland China only and do not include Hong Kong (0.07 mil oz t in 2013) or Macao. (2) West Germany prior to 1991.

Consumer Price Changes in Selected Countries, 1975-2013

Source: International Monetary Fund (IMF); World Development Indicators, The World Bank

(annual average % change)

Country	1975-80	1980-85	1985-90	1990-95	1997-98	2000-01	2004-05	2006-07	2008-09	2009-10	2010-11	2011-12	2012-13
Canada..........	8.7%	7.5%	4.5%	2.3%	1.0%	2.5%	2.2%	2.1%	0.3%	1.8%	2.9%	1.5%	0.9%
China[1]..........	NA	NA	9.5	13.1	-0.8	0.7	1.8	4.8	-0.7	3.3	5.4	2.7	2.6
France..........	10.5	9.7	3.1	2.2	0.6	1.6	1.7	1.5	0.1	1.5	2.1	2.0	0.9
Germany..........	NA	NA	NA	2.8	0.9	2.0	1.5	2.3	0.3	1.1	2.1	2.0	1.5
Italy..........	16.4	13.8	5.7	5.0	2.0	2.8	2.0	1.8	0.8	1.5	2.7	3.0	1.2
Japan..........	6.6	2.8	1.3	1.4	0.7	-0.8	-0.3	0.1	-1.3	-0.7	-0.3	-0.03	0.4
Spain..........	18.6	12.2	6.5	5.2	1.8	3.6	3.4	2.8	-0.3	1.8	3.2	2.4	1.4
Sweden..........	10.5	9.0	6.2	4.2	-0.1	2.4	0.5	2.2	-0.5	1.2	3.0	0.9	-0.04
Switzerland..........	2.3	4.3	2.5	3.2	0.02	1.0	1.2	0.7	-0.5	0.7	0.2	-0.7	-0.2
United Kingdom....	NA	NA	2.4	3.8	1.6	1.2	2.0	2.3	2.2	3.3	4.5	2.8	2.6
United States	8.9	5.5	4.0	3.1	1.6	2.8	3.4	2.9	-0.4	1.6	3.2	2.1	1.5

NA = Not available. (1) Figures are for mainland China only and do not include Hong Kong (4.4% in 2012-13) or Macao (5.5% in 2012-13).

Hourly Compensation Costs in Manufacturing in Selected Countries, 1996-2012

Source: International Labor Comparisons Program, U.S. Bureau of Labor Statistics, U.S. Dept. of Labor
For all workers in manufacturing, including part-time and temporary employees. Compensation costs, or employer labor costs, include direct pay (pay for time worked and directly-paid benefits), social insurance expenditures, and labor-related taxes.
(in U.S. dollars)

Country	1996	2000	2003	2006	2009	2012
Argentina	7.43	8.16	3.65	6.63	10.23	18.87
Australia	19.17	16.45	22.65	29.17	33.42	47.68
Austria	28.12	21.97	28.38	33.63	42.62	41.53
Belgium	32.71	26.14	35.01	42.49	52.27	52.19
Brazil	7.11	4.35	3.23	5.99	8.13	11.20
Canada	18.62	18.33	21.08	28.58	29.40	36.59
Czech Republic	3.38	3.40	5.65	8.16	11.42	11.95
Denmark	NA	22.21	31.70	38.23	48.60	48.47
Estonia	NA	2.55	4.11	6.53	10.03	10.41
Finland	25.01	19.87	28.12	35.19	44.25	42.60
France	27.82	21.37	28.46	33.85	40.37	39.81
Germany	33.22	25.41	34.00	39.37	45.76	45.79
Greece	12.61	9.94	13.72	16.60	22.72	19.41
Hungary	3.11	2.96	5.19	6.85	8.62	8.95
Ireland	16.87	15.76	23.64	30.41	41.21	38.17
Israel	10.90	12.25	12.47	13.86	17.55	20.14
Italy	21.00	16.64	23.42	28.53	34.32	34.18
Japan	23.67	25.02	23.41	24.03	30.03	35.34
Korea, South	9.54	9.62	11.33	17.37	15.06	20.72
Mexico	3.05	4.70	5.31	5.88	5.70	6.36
Netherlands	NA	21.04	29.66	34.37	41.39	39.62
New Zealand	12.11	9.00	12.62	15.75	17.47	24.77
Norway	NA	24.50	35.59	44.57	53.39	63.36
Philippines	1.36	1.00	1.03	1.35	1.71	2.10
Poland	NA	3.41	4.40	6.18	7.72	8.25
Portugal	7.13	5.94	8.19	9.96	12.34	12.10
Singapore	11.93	11.71	12.74	13.77	17.54	24.16
Slovakia	2.73	2.60	4.38	6.56	11.24	11.30
Spain	15.48	12.40	17.42	21.80	27.86	26.83
Sweden	27.15	23.40	31.01	36.55	40.92	49.80
Switzerland	35.52	26.92	36.79	40.91	50.54	57.79
Taiwan	7.10	7.30	6.97	8.05	7.77	9.46
United Kingdom	17.78	20.67	25.15	31.23	29.47	31.23
United States	22.47	24.96	28.57	30.48	34.19	35.67
OECD countries[1]	NA	16.57	19.92	24.36	27.18	30.53

NA = Not available. **Note:** China and India are not shown here because data for those countries are not comparable. (1) The Organisation for Economic Co-operation and Development (OECD) includes Australia, Canada, Israel, Japan, South Korea, Mexico, New Zealand, U.S., and all European countries covered in this table.

Unemployment Rates in Selected Countries, 1970-2014

Source: International Labor Comparisons Program, U.S. Bureau of Labor Statistics, U.S. Dept. of Labor; The Conference Board

Year	U.S.	Australia	Canada	France	Germany[1]	Italy	Japan	Netherlands	Sweden	UK
1970	4.9%	1.7%	5.7%	2.5%	0.5%	3.2%	1.2%	NA	1.5%	NA
1975	8.5	4.9	6.9	3.6	3.4	3.4	1.9	5.1%	1.6	4.5%
1980	7.1	6.1	7.3	5.6	2.8	4.4	2.0	6.0	2.0	6.8
1985	7.2	8.3	10.1	9.0	7.2	6.0	2.5	9.6	2.8	11.4
1990	5.6	6.9	7.7	8.0	5.0	7.0	2.0	7.6	1.8	7.1
1995	5.6	8.5	8.6	10.2	8.2	11.3	2.9	7.1	9.1	8.7
1997	4.9	8.5	8.4	10.8	9.9	11.3	3.1	5.6	10.1	7.0
1999	4.2	6.9	7.0	10.1	8.5	11.0	4.2	3.5	7.1	6.0
2000	4.0	6.3	6.1	8.6	7.8	10.1	4.4	3.1	5.8	5.5
2001	4.7	6.8	6.5	7.8	7.9	9.1	4.5	2.5	5.0	5.1
2002	5.8	6.4	7.0	8.0	8.6	8.6	4.9	3.0	5.1	5.2
2003	6.0	5.9	6.9	8.6	9.3	8.5	4.6	4.1	5.8	5.0
2004	5.5	5.4	6.4	9.0	10.3	8.1	4.2	5.0	6.6	4.9
2005	5.1	5.0	6.0	9.0	11.2	7.8	3.8	5.2	7.7	4.9
2006	4.6	4.8	5.5	8.9	10.3	6.9	3.6	4.3	7.0	5.5
2007	4.6	4.4	5.2	8.1	8.7	6.2	3.6	3.5	6.1	5.4
2008	5.8	4.2	5.3	7.5	7.6	6.8	3.7	3.0	6.1	5.7
2009	9.3	5.6	7.3	9.2	7.8	7.9	4.8	3.7	8.3	7.6
2010	9.6	5.2	7.1	9.4	7.1	8.5	4.7	4.5	8.5	7.9
2011	8.9	5.1	6.5	9.3	5.9	8.5	4.2	4.5	7.7	8.1
2012	8.1	5.2	6.3	10.0	5.5	10.8	3.9	5.3	7.9	8.0
2013[2]	7.5	5.7	6.2	10.0	5.3	12.4	3.5	6.9	8.0	7.7
2014[2]	6.1	6.0	6.1	9.8	5.1	12.5	3.3	6.8	7.9	NA

NA = Not available. **Note:** Unemployment rates are for the civilian working-age population. Data from other countries have been adjusted to U.S. concepts so that comparisons can be made. Because of changes in survey methodology, some data may not be fully comparable over time. (1) For former West Germany only through 1990; data after 1991 are for unified Germany. (2) June monthly unemployment rate.

Personal Tax Payments in Selected Countries, 2013

Source: *Taxing Wages*, Organisation for Economic Co-operation and Development (OECD)
Rates are averages for a single person without children at an average earnings level.
(as % of gross wage earnings before taxes, in U.S. dollars with equal purchasing power; ranked by total payment rate)

Country	Total payment rate[1]	Income tax	Employee soc. sec. contribs.	Gross earnings	Country	Total payment rate[1]	Income tax	Employee soc. sec. contribs.	Gross earnings
Belgium	42.6%	28.6	14.0%	$56,171	United States	24.6%	16.9%	7.7%	$48,463
Germany	39.6	19.1	20.4	57,818	United Kingdom	24.1	14.7	9.4	51,255
Denmark	38.6	35.8	2.7	51,772	Australia	23.1	23.1	0.0	52,639
Hungary	34.5	16.0	18.5	22,930	Spain	22.9	16.6	6.4	38,278
Austria	34.3	16.2	18.1	50,322	Czech Republic	22.8	11.8	11.0	22,460
Slovenia	33.1	11.0	22.1	29,528	Slovakia	22.8	9.4	13.4	19,716
Netherlands	31.2	15.7	15.5	58,252	Canada	22.7	15.3	7.4	38,948
Italy	31.0	21.5	9.5	39,430	Japan	21.6	7.7	13.9	47,771
Finland	30.2	22.5	7.6	46,748	Estonia	19.5	17.5	2.0	21,217
Luxembourg	29.3	17.0	12.3	57,591	Ireland	18.7	14.7	4.0	40,175
Norway	29.2	21.4	7.8	59,548	Switzerland	17.1	10.9	6.3	64,298
Turkey	28.5	13.5	15.0	29,436	New Zealand	16.9	16.9	0.0	36,381
France	28.4	14.6	13.8	43,984	Israel	16.7	8.8	7.9	32,419
Iceland	28.3	27.9	0.5	44,883	South Korea	13.4	5.1	8.3	47,005
Portugal	27.2	16.2	11.0	28,696	Mexico	9.8	8.4	1.4	12,501
Greece	25.5	9.0	16.5	31,892	Chile	7.0	0.0	7.0	18,989
Sweden	25.0	18.0	7.0	45,388	OECD countries[2]	35.9	15.6	9.9	40,292
Poland	24.7	6.9	17.8	22,968					

(1) Figures may not add up to totals due to rounding. (2) Includes Australia, Canada, Israel, Japan, South Korea, Mexico, New Zealand, U.S., and all European countries in this table.

Refugees and People in a Refugee-Like Situation, 2013

Source: *UNHCR Global Trends*, United Nations High Commissioner for Refugees (UNHCR)

Refugees are persons recognized under the 1951 UN Refugee Convention/1967 Protocol or the 1969 OAU (Org. of African Unity) Refugee Convention; those recognized in accordance with the UNHCR Statute; and persons granted or receiving protection. Persons outside of their country or territory of origin who face protection risks—but whose refugee status has not been ascertained—are described as being in a refugee-like situation. Only countries hosting 50,000 or more refugees and people in a refugee-like situation are shown. Only places originating 5,000 or more refugees and people in a refugee-like situation are shown, in decreasing order. As of year-end.

Place of asylum	Origin of most refugees (excl. asylum seekers with pending cases)	Number
Africa		**3,377,618**
Algeria	Western Sahara	94,150
Cameroon	Central African Republic, Nigeria	114,753
Chad	Sudan, Central African Republic	434,479
Congo, Dem. Rep. of	Central African Republic, Rwanda, Burundi	113,362
Congo Republic	Dem. Rep. of the Congo, Central African Republic, Rwanda	51,037
Egypt	Syria, Palestinian[1], Sudan, Somalia, Iraq	230,086
Ethiopia	Somalia, Eritrea, South Sudan, Sudan	433,936
Kenya	Somalia, Ethiopia, South Sudan, Dem. Rep. of the Congo	534,938
Liberia	Côte d'Ivoire	53,253
Mauritania	Mali, Western Sahara	92,767
Niger	Mali, Nigeria	57,661
Rwanda	Dem. Rep. of the Congo	73,349
South Africa	Somalia, Dem. Rep. of the Congo, Ethiopia	65,881
South Sudan	Sudan, Dem. Rep. of the Congo, Ethiopia	229,587
Sudan	Eritrea, Chad, Ethiopia	159,857
Tanzania	Dem. Rep. of the Congo, Burundi	102,099
Uganda	Dem. Rep. of the Congo, South Sudan, Rwanda, Somalia, Burundi	220,555
Asia		**6,317,585**
Bangladesh	Myanmar (Burma)	231,145
China (incl. HK, Macao)	Vietnam	301,047
India	China, Sri Lanka, Myanmar (Burma), Afghanistan	188,395
Iran	Afghanistan, Iraq	857,354
Iraq	Syria, Turkey, Palestinian[1], Iran	246,298
Jordan	Syria, Iraq	641,915
Lebanon	Syria	856,546
Malaysia	Myanmar (Burma)	97,513
Pakistan	Afghanistan	1,616,507
Syria	Iraq	149,292
Thailand	Myanmar (Burma)	136,499
Turkey	Syria, Iraq	609,938
Yemen	Somalia, Ethiopia	241,288
Europe		**1,156,721**
Austria	Russia, Afghanistan	55,598
France	Sri Lanka, Dem. Rep. of the Congo, Russia, Cambodia, Serbia-Kosovo, Turkey, Vietnam, Laos, Mauritania	232,487
Germany	Iraq, Turkey, Afghanistan, Syria, Iran, Serbia-Kosovo	187,567
Italy	Eritrea, Somalia, Afghanistan	78,061
Netherlands	Somalia, Iraq, Afghanistan	74,707
Serbia-Kosovo	Croatia, Bosnia and Herzegovina	57,083
Sweden	Iraq, Somalia, Syria, Afghanistan, Eritrea, stateless[2]	114,175
Switzerland	Eritrea	52,464
United Kingdom	Iran, Somalia, Zimbabwe, Eritrea, Afghanistan, Pakistan	126,055
Latin America and the Caribbean		**381,949**
Ecuador	Colombia	123,133
Venezuela	Colombia	204,340
North America		**424,011**
Canada	Colombia, China, Sri Lanka, Pakistan, Haiti, Mexico	160,349
United States	China, Haiti, Colombia, Ethiopia, Egypt, El Salvador, Venezuela, Russia, Nepal, Cameroon, Guatemala	263,662
TOTAL		**11,703,179**

(1) Palestinians under the UNHCR mandate only. (2) Persons not considered nationals under any state under the operation of its laws.

Internally Displaced Persons, 2013

Source: Internal Displacement Monitoring Centre, Norwegian Refugee Council

Internally displaced persons (IDPs) are people who have been forced to flee due to armed conflict or human rights violations but who have not crossed into another country. As such, they are not protected by international refugee law and legally remain under the protection of their home country. Estimates are as of year-end 2013 and may comprise only registered IDPs or those displaced from a certain area of a country.

Country	Number	Country	Number	Country	Number
Afghanistan	631,000+	India	526,000+	Philippines	115,800+
Angola	<20,000	Indonesia	90,000+	Russia	34,900+
Armenia	<8,400	Iraq	<2.1 mil	Senegal	<24,000
Azerbaijan	<543,400	Kenya	412,000	Serbia	97,300
Bangladesh	<280,000	Kosovo	17,300+	Somalia	1.1 mil
Bosnia and Herzegovina	103,400	Laos	<4,500	South Sudan[3]	383,000+
Burundi	<78,900	Lebanon	20,000+	Sri Lanka	<90,000
Central African Republic	935,000	Liberia	<23,000	Sudan[3]	2.4 mil+
Chad	<90,000	Libya	59,400+	Syria	6.5 mil+
Colombia[1]	5.7 mil	Macedonia	330+	Thailand	35,000+
Congo, Dem. Rep. of	2.9 mil+	Mali	218,000+	Timor-Leste	900+
Congo Republic	<7,800	Mexico	160,000	Togo	<10,000
Côte d'Ivoire	70,000+	Myanmar (Burma)	640,900	Turkey	953,700+
Cyprus	<212,400	Nepal	<50,000	Turkmenistan	4,000+
Eritrea	<10,000	Niger	<11,000	Uganda	<29,800
Ethiopia	316,000	Nigeria	3.3 mil	Uzbekistan	3,400+
Georgia	<206,600	Pakistan	746,700+	Yemen	307,000
Guatemala	242,000	Palestine[2]	146,000+	Zimbabwe	36,000
Honduras	17,000	Peru	150,000	**Total**	**33.3 mil**

Note: The number of IDPs in Algeria, Israel, and Rwanda was undetermined. (1) Cumulative since 1985. (2) Occupied Palestinian Territory. (3) Number does not incl. an est. 20,000+ IDPs from Abyei Area, disputed territory between Sudan and South Sudan.

Estimated HIV Infection and Reported AIDS Cases, 2013
Source: Joint United Nations Programme on HIV/AIDS (UNAIDS)

In 2013, about 2.1 mil people were newly infected with HIV. Changes in behavior among young people, intravenous drug users, and other at-risk populations have contributed to the decline in infections, as has increased access to HIV prevention services. About 35 mil people worldwide were living with HIV/AIDS in 2013, 70.6% of whom were in sub-Saharan Africa. Thirty-seven percent of those with HIV/AIDS had access to antiretroviral therapy. The number of AIDS-related deaths fell to 1.5 mil in 2013. Tuberculosis remained the leading cause of death among those living with HIV/AIDS.

Worldwide in 2013, $19.1 bil was spent on the HIV/AIDS epidemic. UNAIDS estimates that between $22 bil and $24 bil would be needed yearly if it is to meet targets it has set for 2015, including the elimination of new infections in children. As of mid-2014, 38 countries and territories still restricted the right of those living with HIV/AIDS to enter or stay.

Current and New HIV/AIDS Cases and Deaths by Region, 2013

Region	Number living with HIV/AIDS	Percent of world total[1]	New HIV infections	AIDS-related deaths
Sub-Saharan Africa	24,700,000	70.6%	1,500,000	1,100,000
Asia and the Pacific	4,800,000	13.7	350,000	250,000
Latin America	1,600,000	4.6	94,000	47,000
Western and Central Europe and North America	2,300,000	6.6	88,000	27,000
Eastern Europe and Central Asia	1,100,000	3.1	110,000	53,000
Caribbean	250,000	0.7	12,000	11,000
Middle East and North Africa	230,000	0.7	25,000	15,000
World[2]	35,000,000	100.0	2,100,000	1,500,000

(1) Population within a region living with HIV/AIDS as a percentage of population worldwide living with HIV/AIDS. (2) Figures may not add up to totals because of rounding.

Sanitation and Drinking Water, 2012
Source: World Health Organization (WHO); United Nations Children's Fund (UNICEF)

By year-end 2012, 89% of the world's population had access to improved drinking-water sources, although service and water quality was inconsistent. Meanwhile, the UN's Millennium Development Goal for access to improved sanitation has yet to be reached. As of the end of 2012, only 64% of all people worldwide relied on improved sanitation facilities. The population in areas without access are at increased risk of contracting a variety of infectious and parasitic diseases such as diarrhea, malaria, and hepatitis A. With the exception of Russia, the G8 countries have near-universal (99% or greater) access to improved sanitation and water. In 2012, 74% of Russia's population had access to improved sanitation, and 97% had access to improved drinking-water sources. In China, the figures were 52% and 92%, respectively.

Lowest Access to Improved Sanitation Facilities
Sanitation facilities are considered improved if they are private and not shared with other households, incl. sewer or septic system connections, ventilated improved pit latrines, and composting toilets.

Rank	Country	% of pop. with access
1.	Niger	9%
	South Sudan	9
2.	Malawi	10
3.	Togo	11
4.	Chad	12
	Tanzania	12
5.	Sierra Leone	13
6.	Benin	14
	Ghana	14
	Madagascar	14
7.	Congo	15
8.	Liberia	17
9.	Burkina Faso	19
	Guinea	19
	Papua New Guinea	19
10.	Guinea-Bissau	20

Lowest Access to Improved Drinking-Water Sources
Improved drinking-water sources protect from outside contamination and incl. household connections, public taps or standpipes, dug wells, and rainwater collection.

Rank	Country	% of pop. with access
1.	Papua New Guinea	40%
2.	Congo, Dem. Rep. of	46
3.	Mozambique	49
4.	Madagascar	50
	Mauritania	50
5.	Chad	51
6.	Ethiopia	52
	Niger	52
7.	Tanzania	53
8.	Angola	54
9.	Sudan	55
	Yemen	55
10.	South Sudan	57

Mortality Rate by Cause of Death in Selected Nations, 2012
Source: World Health Organization (WHO)
(per 100,000 population; ranked by deaths from communicable, maternal, neonatal, and nutritional conditions)

Rank	Country	Communicable, maternal, neonatal, and nutritional conditions	Non-communicable diseases	Injuries	All causes
1.	Sierra Leone	1,327.4	963.5	149.5	2,440.4
2.	Central African Republic	1,212.1	550.8	107.9	1,870.9
3.	Lesotho	1,110.5	671.8	142.5	1,924.7
4.	Chad	1,070.9	712.6	114.5	1,897.9
5.	Mozambique	998.1	593.7	175.3	1,767.0
6.	Somalia	927.2	550.7	188.5	1,666.3
7.	Congo, Dem. Rep. of	920.7	724.4	137.1	1,782.2
8.	Swaziland	884.3	702.4	119.5	1,706.2
9.	Angola	873.3	768.4	137.8	1,779.4
10.	Guinea-Bissau	869.8	764.7	111.6	1,746.2
96.	Russia	73.8	790.3	102.8	966.9
121.	China	41.4	576.3	50.4	668.2
129.	Japan	33.9	244.2	40.5	318.6
133.	United States	31.3	412.8	44.2	488.4
138.	United Kingdom	28.5	358.8	21.5	408.8
149.	Canada	22.6	318.0	31.3	372.0
151.	Germany	21.6	365.1	23.0	409.7
153.	France	21.4	313.2	34.6	369.1
165.	Italy	15.5	303.6	20.1	339.2
170.	Austria	12.6	359.5	30.6	402.7

Foreign Development Aid Donors, 2012-13

Source: Development Assistance Committee (DAC), Organisation for Economic Co-operation and Development (OECD)

Listed below is the amount of official development assistance (ODA)—in the form of grants or loans—each DAC member country disbursed in a given year to developing countries. The numbers are net flows, or amounts disbursed less repayments on earlier loans. Both bilateral ODA (made directly to an aid recipient) and multilateral ODA (made to an agency like the World Bank) are included.

(ranked by size of ODA as % of 2013 gross national income [GNI]; 2013 figures are prelim.)

Rank	Donor	ODA as % of GNI 2012	2013	ODA in mil of current U.S. dollars 2012	2013	Rank	Donor	ODA as % of GNI 2012	2013	ODA in mil of current U.S. dollars 2012	2013
1.	Norway	0.93%	1.07%	$4,752.99	$5,581.36	18.	Japan	0.17%	0.23%	$10,604.51	$11,786.11
2.	Sweden	0.97	1.02	5,239.79	5,831.20	19.	Portugal	0.28	0.23	580.78	484.05
3.	Luxembourg	1.00	1.00	399.03	430.68	20.	United States	0.19	0.19	30,686.96	31,545.25
4.	Denmark	0.83	0.85	2,692.59	2,928.46	21.	Spain	0.16	0.16	2,037.33	2,198.64
5.	United Kingdom	0.56	0.72	13,891.44	17,881.48	22.	Italy	0.14	0.16	2,737.13	3,252.64
6.	Netherlands	0.71	0.67	5,522.84	5,435.28	23.	Korea, South	0.14	0.13	1,597.45	1,743.64
7.	Finland	0.53	0.55	1,319.71	1,435.36	24.	Slovenia	0.13	0.13	58.45	60.23
8.	Switzerland	0.47	0.47	3,055.59	3,197.86	25.	Greece	0.13	0.13	327.41	305.02
9.	Belgium	0.47	0.45	2,314.86	2,281.29	26.	Czech Rep.	0.12	0.11	219.63	212.32
10.	Ireland	0.47	0.45	808.36	821.96	27.	Poland	0.09	0.10	421.06	474.31
11.	France	0.45	0.41	12,028.27	11,376.00	28.	Slovakia	0.09	0.09	79.68	85.38
12.	Germany	0.37	0.38	12,939.49	14,059.45		**Total DAC**	**0.29**	**0.30**	**126,949.28**	**134,838.33**
13.	Australia	0.36	0.34	5,402.70	4,851.05		Avg. country				
14.	Austria	0.28	0.28	1,105.75	1,171.61		effort	0.39	0.40		
15.	Canada	0.32	0.27	5,650.26	4,911.14		G7 countries[1]	0.25	0.27	88,538.06	94,812.07
16.	New Zealand	0.28	0.26	449.10	461.33		EU institutions	NA	NA	17,479.05	15,925.05
17.	Iceland	0.22	0.26	26.12	35.23						

NA = Not applicable/available. (1) Canada, France, Germany, Italy, Japan, the UK, and the U.S.

Recipients of U.S. Official Development Assistance, 2011-12

Source: Development Assistance Committee (DAC), Organisation for Economic Co-operation and Development (OECD)

(net flows of total official development assistance in mil of current U.S. dollars; ranked by 2012 numbers)

Rank	Country	2011	2012	Rank	Country	2011	2012
1.	Afghanistan	$3,075.00	$2,773.13	12.	Nigeria	$409.23	$419.11
2.	Kenya	715.42	817.83	13.	Uganda	397.92	394.25
3.	South Sudan	707.42	773.34	14.	Mali	273.84	348.24
4.	Ethiopia	706.66	732.61	15.	Colombia	500.64	326.93
5.	Pakistan	1,273.85	624.76	16.	Lebanon	86.66	323.87
6.	Iraq	1,268.43	582.80	17.	Zambia	276.69	305.09
7.	Tanzania	541.27	568.74	18.	Congo, Dem. Rep. of	1,293.20	291.76
8.	Jordan	450.13	556.64	19.	West Bank and Gaza Strip	625.04	288.27
9.	South Africa	564.03	505.27	20.	Ghana	314.41	220.61
10.	Mozambique	397.90	435.49		**All developing countries**	**27,212.81**	**25,471.15**
11.	Haiti	620.18	427.64				

Nuclear Powers of the World

As of Aug. 2014, eight countries were acknowledged nuclear powers: the **UK**, **France**, **China**, **India**, **Pakistan**, **Russia**, **North Korea**, and the **U.S. Israel** was presumed to have an arsenal. **Iran** was suspected of developing nuclear weapons. More than 40 nations have the knowledge or technology to produce nuclear weapons. All—except Israel, India, and Pakistan—have signed the Nuclear Non-Proliferation Treaty (NPT). North Korea announced its withdrawal Jan. 10, 2003, after expelling Intl. Atomic Energy Agency (IAEA) inspectors in 2002.

North Korea conducted its first nuclear test Oct. 9, 2006. After a new round of talks in 2007, it agreed to close its main nuclear facility and take steps toward disabling its nuclear weapons program in exchange for economic aid and diplomatic recognition. But the next round of talks, in 2008, ended in deadlock. North Korea conducted a second nuclear test May 25, 2009. The state-run media reported a third test took place Feb. 12, 2013.

In 2009, the U.S., France, and the UK accused Iran of building a secret uranium enrichment facility near the city of Qom. Iran acknowledged the existence of the facility as a backup to its main enrichment site, at Natanz. Iranian president Hassan Rouhani, elected in June 2013, expressed his willingness to enter new talks. Iran agreed to suspend its enrichment activities in return for a lifting of sanctions in a Jan. 2014 deal. Iran had argued previously that as an NPT signatory, it had a right to pursue the peaceful application of nuclear technology. The IAEA maintained the country had withheld information on the extent of its nuclear activities.

Several countries abandoned their nuclear ambitions. **South Africa** announced in 1993 that it had built seven fission weapons (one was under construction) but had dismantled all of them. In the 1980s, **Argentina** and **Brazil** had active nuclear weapons programs but abandoned them by mutual treaty.

Estimated Numbers of Nuclear Weapons by Country, 1945-2014

Source: *Bulletin of the Atomic Scientists*; Carnegie Endowment for International Peace; Federation of American Scientists (FAS); Natural Resources Defense Council (NRDC); Nuclear Threat Initiative (NTI); Stockholm International Peace Research Institute (SIPRI)

Year	United States	USSR/Russia	United Kingdom	France	China	Israel[1]	India	Pakistan	Total[2]
1945	6	—	—	—	—	—	—	—	6
1950	369	5	—	—	—	—	—	—	374
1960	20,434	1,605	30	—	—	—	—	—	22,069
1970	26,662	11,643	280	36	75	8	—	—	38,696
1980	24,304	30,062	350	250	280	31	—	—	55,246
1990	21,004	37,000	300	505	430	53	—	—	59,239
2000	10,577	21,000	185	470	400	72	—	—	32,632
2010	9,400	12,300	225	300	240	60-80	60-80	70-90	22,400
2014	7,315	8,000	225	300	250	80	90-110	100-120	16,400

(1) Israel is widely presumed to have a nuclear stockpile although it has never confirmed nor denied its nuclear status. (2) Numbers may not add up to total due to rounding and uncertainty over size of stockpiles and operational status of warheads.

Nuclear Arms Treaties and Negotiations: A Historical Overview

Aug. 5, 1963: Partial (Limited) Test Ban Treaty signed by the UK, U.S., and USSR, went into effect Oct. 10, 1963. Prohibits its parties from testing or participating in the testing of nuclear weapons in the atmosphere, in outer space, and under water.

July 1, 1968: Nuclear Non-Proliferation Treaty (NPT) opened to signatures, went into effect Mar. 5, 1970. With the UK, U.S., and USSR as major signers, the parties agree not to help non-nuclear nations get or make nuclear weapons, though such nations can pursue the peaceful application of nuclear energy.

On May 11, 1995, parties to the treaty voted to extend it indefinitely. As of Aug. 2014, 190 countries were party to the treaty, not including North Korea, which withdrew in 2003. Israel, India, and Pakistan were not signatories.

May 26, 1972: The **Strategic Arms Limitation Talks (SALT I)** led to the signing of two agreements by the U.S. and USSR: the **Treaty on the Limitation of Anti-Ballistic Missile Systems** (or **ABM Treaty**) and an interim agreement. These treaties cap the numbers of intercontinental ballistic missile (ICBM) launchers and submarine-launched ballistic missile (SLBM) launchers.

July 3, 1974: Treaty on the Limitation of Underground Nuclear Weapon Tests (or **Threshold Test Ban Treaty**) signed by the U.S. and USSR. Limits underground testing of nuclear weapons to yields of 150 kilotons or less. On May 28, 1976, U.S. and Russia signed the **Peaceful Nuclear Explosions Treaty**, governing explosions outside weapons test sites. Both treaties entered into force Dec. 11, 1990.

June 18, 1979: Strategic Offensive Arms Limitation Treaty (or **SALT II**) signed by the U.S. and USSR. Limited each side to 2,400 missile launchers and heavy bombers; ceiling to apply until Jan. 1, 1985. Treaty also set a sub-ceiling of 1,320 ICBMs and SLBMs with multiple warheads on each side. Following Dec. 1979 Soviet invasion of Afghanistan, U.S. Pres. Jimmy Carter withdrew SALT II from Senate consideration for ratification.

Dec. 8, 1987: Intermediate-Range Nuclear Forces (INF) Treaty signed by the U.S. and USSR. Eliminates all U.S. and Soviet intermediate- and shorter-range nuclear missiles from Europe and Asia. Entered into force June 1, 1988.

July 31, 1991: Strategic Arms Reduction Treaty (START I) signed by the USSR and U.S. to reduce strategic offensive arms by about 30% in three phases over seven years. This was the first treaty to mandate reductions by the superpowers.

With the Soviet Union breakup in Dec. 1991, four former republics became independent nations with strategic nuclear weapons: Russia, Ukraine, Kazakhstan, and Belarus. Under the **Lisbon Protocol** of May 1992, Ukraine, Kazakhstan, and Belarus agreed to accede to the NPT as non-nuclear-weapon states, to destroy or transfer their nuclear weapons to Russia, and to ratify START I. START I expired on Dec. 5, 2009.

Jan. 3, 1993: START II signed by the U.S. and Russia, ratified by the two on Jan. 26, 1996, and Apr. 14, 2000, respectively. Called for reductions in their long-range nuclear arsenals. Both sides withdrew from the treaty before it went into force.

Sept. 24, 1996: Comprehensive Nuclear-Test-Ban Treaty (CTBT) signed by the U.S. and Russia. The CTBT bans all nuclear explosions. It is intended to prevent the nuclear powers from developing more advanced weapons while limiting the ability of other states to acquire such devices. As of Aug. 2014, the CTBT had been signed by 183 nations. It had been ratified by 162, including France, Russia, and the UK but neither the U.S. nor China. It will enter into force only after ratification by all Annex 2 states—the 44 states with nuclear technology capabilities at the time of the treaty's final negotiations. Only 36 have done so.

Dec. 13, 2001: The U.S. announced its intention to withdraw from the **ABM Treaty** in 180 days, arguing that it hindered the government in protecting itself from "future terrorist or rogue state missile attacks." Russia responded by withdrawing from **START II**, stating that U.S. withdrawal from the ABM Treaty effectively invalidated START II.

May 24, 2002: Strategic Offensive Reductions Treaty (SORT or **Moscow Treaty)** signed by the U.S. and Russia, entered into force June 1, 2003. Committed both countries to cutting nuclear arsenals to 1,700-2,200 warheads each, down from about 6,000, by Dec. 31, 2012. SORT terminated upon entry into force of the New START Treaty.

Apr. 8, 2010: New START Treaty signed by the U.S. and Russia, entered into force Feb. 5, 2011. It limits each country's arsenal of deployed strategic nuclear warheads to 1,550 by 2018.

Major International Organizations

African Union (AU), inaugurated July 9, 2002, in Durban, South Africa, following disbanding of the Organization of African Unity (OAU). All of Africa's countries, with the exception of Morocco, make up its 54 members. (Morocco withdrew after the OAU admitted Western Sahara [Sahrawi Arab Dem. Rep.], a territory claimed by Morocco.) The AU is focused on achieving greater socioeconomic integration and unity among its member states. The AU's founding document authorized the organization to intervene to stop genocide, war crimes, or human rights abuses within individual member nations. **Headquarters:** Addis Ababa, Ethiopia. **Website:** www.au.int

Asia-Pacific Economic Cooperation (APEC), founded Nov. 1989 as a forum to further cooperation on trade and investment between nations of the region and the rest of the world. Its 21 members are Australia, Brunei, Canada, Chile, China, Hong Kong, Indonesia, Japan, Malaysia, Mexico, New Zealand, Papua New Guinea, Peru, Philippines, Russia, Singapore, South Korea, Taiwan, Thailand, the U.S., and Vietnam. **Headquarters:** Singapore. **Website:** www.apec.org

Association of Southeast Asian Nations (ASEAN), formed Aug. 8, 1967, to promote economic, social, and cultural cooperation and development among states of the Southeast Asian region. Its members are Brunei, Cambodia, Indonesia, Laos, Malaysia, Myanmar, Philippines, Singapore, Thailand, and Vietnam. **Headquarters:** Jakarta, Indonesia. **Website:** www.asean.org

Caribbean Community and Common Market (CARICOM), established Aug. 1, 1973. Its aim is to increase cooperation in economics, health, education, culture, science and technology, and tax administration, as well as the coordination of foreign policy. Its 15 members are Antigua and Barbuda, The Bahamas, Barbados, Belize, Dominica, Grenada, Guyana, Haiti, Jamaica, Montserrat, St. Kitts and Nevis, St. Lucia, St. Vincent and the Grenadines, Suriname, and Trinidad and Tobago. Anguilla, Bermuda, British Virgin Islands, Cayman Islands, and Turks and Caicos Islands are associate members. **Headquarters:** Georgetown, Guyana. **Website:** www.caricom.org

The Commonwealth, originally called the British Commonwealth of Nations, then the Commonwealth of Nations, is an association of nations and dependencies that were part of the former British Empire. The British monarch is the symbolic head of the Commonwealth.

There are 53 independent nations in the Commonwealth. Regular members include the UK and 15 other nations recognizing the British monarch, represented by a governor-general, as their head of state, and member countries in good standing with their own heads of state. In 2009, Fiji's military regime was suspended. **Headquarters:** London, UK. **Website:** www.thecommonwealth.org

Commonwealth of Independent States (CIS), an alliance established in Dec. 1991, made up of former Soviet constituent republics. Its members are Armenia, Azerbaijan, Belarus, Kazakhstan, Kyrgyzstan, Moldova, Russia, Tajikistan, Turkmenistan, Ukraine, and Uzbekistan. Georgia withdrew from the organization in 2009 following fighting with Russia over disputed territory. Policy is set through coordinating bodies such as the Council of the Heads of States and Council of the Heads of Governments. **Headquarters:** Minsk, Belarus. **Website:** www.cis.minsk.by or www.cisstat.com/eng/

European Free Trade Association (EFTA), created May 3, 1960, to promote expansion of free trade. Members entered into free trade agreements with the EU in 1972-73. In 1992, EFTA and EU agreed to create a single market—with free flow of goods, services, capital, and labor—among nations of the two organizations. Its members are Iceland, Liechtenstein, Norway, and Switzerland. **Headquarters:** Geneva, Switzerland. **Website:** www.efta.int

European Union (EU), known as the European Community (EC) until 1994, comprises three organizations with common membership: the European Economic Community (EEC, or Common Market), the European Coal and Steel Community, and the European Atomic Energy Community (Euratom). A merger of the three communities' executives went into effect in 1967. As of Aug. 2014, there were 28 EU members: the 12 original members (Belgium, Denmark, France, Germany, Greece, Ireland, Italy, Luxembourg, Netherlands, Portugal, Spain, and UK), three that entered in 1995 (Austria, Finland, Sweden), 10 that joined in 2004 (Cyprus, Czech Republic, Estonia, Hungary, Latvia, Lithuania, Malta, Poland, Slovakia, Slovenia), two that joined in 2007 (Bulgaria, Romania), and one that joined in 2013 (Croatia). Albania, Iceland, Macedonia, Montenegro, Serbia, and Turkey were candidate countries. Some 70 countries and territories in Africa, the Caribbean, and the Pacific are affiliated under the Lomé Convention. **Headquarters:** Brussels, Belgium. **Website:** europa.eu

The EU aims to integrate the economies, coordinate social developments, and bring about political union of the member states. As of year-end 1992, there are no restrictions on the movement of goods, services, capital, workers, and tourists within the EU. There are also common agricultural, fisheries, and nuclear research policies.

Leaders of the member nations (12 at the time) met Dec. 9-11, 1991, in Maastricht, the Netherlands, and signed a treaty. The Maastricht treaty, which went into effect in 1993, committed the organization to launching a common currency; establishing common foreign policies; and taking a leading role in social policy among other issues. The European Central Bank was established in 1998. In 1999, 11 of the then-15 EU countries began using the euro. By 2002, national currencies in those 11 countries and Greece were removed from circulation and replaced with the euro as the only currency of legal tender. EU peacekeeping forces replaced NATO troops in Macedonia, 2003, the first such mission for the organization. A Treaty Establishing a Constitution for Europe was signed in 2004 by EU members but was never ratified.

Group of Eight (G8), forum of major industrialized countries. France, Germany, Italy, Japan, the UK, and the U.S. first met in 1975 as the Group of Six. Canada joined in 1976 and Russia in 1998. The EU is also represented at summits. In Mar. 2014, group members condemned Russia for its annexation of Crimea, a region of Ukraine. They boycotted a planned G8 summit in Russia and met instead as the Group of Seven in June 2014.

International Criminal Police Organization (INTERPOL), created 1923 as the International Criminal Police Commission before changing its name in 1956, is the world's largest international police organization. There were 190 member nations as of Aug. 2014. **Headquarters:** Lyon, France. **Website:** www.interpol.int

League of Arab States (Arab League), created Mar. 22, 1945. The League promotes economic, social, political, and military cooperation, mediates disputes, and represents Arab states in certain international negotiations. Its members are Algeria, Bahrain, Comoros, Djibouti, Egypt, Iraq, Jordan, Kuwait, Lebanon, Libya, Mauritania, Morocco, Oman, Palestine (considered an independent state by the League), Qatar, Saudi Arabia, Somalia, Sudan, Syria, Tunisia, United Arab Emirates, and Yemen. **Headquarters:** Cairo, Egypt. **Website:** www.lasportal.org

North Atlantic Treaty Organization (NATO), created by treaty (signed Apr. 4, 1949; in effect Aug. 24, 1949). Its 28 members as of Aug. 2014 are Albania, Belgium, Bulgaria, Canada, Croatia, Czech Republic, Denmark, Estonia, France, Germany, Greece, Hungary, Iceland, Italy, Latvia, Lithuania, Luxembourg, Netherlands, Norway, Poland, Portugal, Romania, Slovakia, Slovenia, Spain, Turkey, UK, and U.S. Several of these states are former Warsaw Pact Eastern European nations.

Members have agreed to settle disputes by peaceful means, to develop their capacity to resist armed attack, to regard an attack on one as an attack on all, and to take necessary action to repel an attack under Article 51 of the UN Charter. **Headquarters:** Brussels, Belgium. **Website:** www.nato.int

The NATO structure consists of the North Atlantic Council (NAC), the Defense Planning Committee, the Military Committee (realigned in June 2003 and consisting of two commands: Allied Command Operations and Allied Command Transformation), the Nuclear Planning Group, and the Canada-U.S. Regional Planning Group. France detached itself from the military command structure in 1966.

With the end of the Cold War in the early 1990s, members put greater stress on political action and on creating a rapid deployment force to react to local crises. By the mid-1990s, 27 nations, including Russia and other former Soviet republics, had joined with NATO in the so-called Partnership for Peace (PfP; drafted Dec. 1993), which provided for limited joint military exercises and peacekeeping missions. NATO has proceeded gradually toward extending full membership to former Eastern bloc nations. Three former Warsaw Pact members, Hungary, Poland, and the Czech Republic, formally became members in 1999. NATO and Russia signed a cooperation pact in 2002, forming a NATO-Russia Council; NATO that same year invited seven former Eastern-bloc nations to join the alliance.

A NATO-led multinational force was deployed to help keep the peace in Bosnia and Herzegovina in 1995. In 1999, another force was deployed in Kosovo. Following the Sept. 2001 terrorist attacks on the U.S., the NATO Council agreed to invoke for the first time Article 5 of the treaty, which stipulates mutual defense of alliance members. NATO assumed control of the International Security Assistance Force in Afghanistan (ISAF), Aug. 2003, marking the first time NATO led a mission outside Europe.

Organization of American States (OAS), formed in Bogotá, Colombia, Apr. 30, 1948. It has a Permanent Council, Inter-American Council for Integral Development, Juridical Committee, and Commission on Human Rights. A general assembly meets annually.

Its 35 members are Antigua and Barbuda, Argentina, The Bahamas, Barbados, Belize, Bolivia, Brazil, Canada, Chile, Colombia, Costa Rica, Cuba, Dominica, Dominican Republic, Ecuador, El Salvador, Grenada, Guatemala, Guyana, Haiti, Honduras, Jamaica, Mexico, Nicaragua, Panama, Paraguay, Peru, St. Kitts and Nevis, St. Lucia, St. Vincent and the Grenadines, Suriname, Trinidad and Tobago, U.S., Uruguay, and Venezuela. **Headquarters:** Washington, DC. **Website:** www.oas.org

Organization for Economic Cooperation and Development (OECD), established Dec. 14, 1960, to promote the economic and social welfare of all its member countries and to stimulate efforts on behalf of developing nations. Its 34 members are Australia, Austria, Belgium, Canada, Chile, Czech Republic, Denmark, Estonia, Finland, France, Germany, Greece, Hungary, Iceland, Ireland, Israel, Italy, Japan, Luxembourg, Mexico, Netherlands, New Zealand, Norway, Poland, Portugal, Slovakia, Slovenia, South Korea, Spain, Sweden, Switzerland, Turkey, UK, and the U.S. **Headquarters:** Paris, France. **Website:** www.oecd.org

Organization of Petroleum Exporting Countries (OPEC), created Sept. 14, 1960, by Iran, Iraq, Kuwait, Saudi Arabia, and Venezuela. This group made up of most but not all the major petroleum exporting nations seeks to stabilize the oil market and set world oil prices by controlling production. In addition to the founding countries, members include Algeria, Angola, Ecuador, Indonesia (suspended membership starting in Jan. 2009), Libya, Nigeria, Qatar, and United Arab Emirates. Gabon is a former member. **Headquarters:** Vienna, Austria. **Website:** www.opec.org

Organization for Security and Cooperation in Europe (OSCE), established in 1972 as the Conference on Security and Cooperation in Europe; current name adopted 1995. The group, formed by NATO and Warsaw Pact members, seeks improved East-West relations through a commitment to nonaggression and human rights, and cooperation in economics, science and technology, cultural exchange, and environmental protection. There were 57 member states as of Aug. 2014, making it the world's largest regional security organization. **Headquarters:** Vienna, Austria. **Website:** www.osce.org

United Nations

The 69th regular session of the United Nations General Assembly convened Sept. 16, 2014, attended by world leaders and other delegates from 193 nations. The UN headquarters is located on 18 acres, considered international territory, in New York, NY.

Proposals to establish an organization for maintenance of world peace led to the convening of the United Nations Conference on International Organization in San Francisco, Apr. 25-June 26, 1945, where the UN charter was drawn. It was signed June 26 by 50 nations and on Oct. 15 by Poland. It went into effect Oct. 24, 1945, upon ratification by the permanent members of the Security Council and a majority of the other signatories.

Purposes. To maintain international peace and security; to develop friendly relations among nations; to achieve international cooperation in solving economic, social, cultural, and humanitarian problems and in promoting respect for human rights and basic freedoms; to be a center for harmonizing the actions of nations in attaining these common ends.

Visitors to the UN. The UN headquarters is open every day except New Year's Day, President's Day, Good Friday, Memorial Day, Independence Day, Eid al-Fitr, Labor Day, Eid al-Adha, Thanksgiving, and Christmas. It may also close on short notice when meetings of heads of state and government are held. Because of ongoing renovations, to be completed in 2015, only visitors with tickets for a guided tour may enter the UN on weekdays. Reservations are not required for weekend visitors.

Guided one-hour tours are conducted on weekdays. Tickets must be purchased in advance online. Groups of 46 or more can make reservations directly with the UN by emailing unitg@un.org. For safety reasons, children under 5 years of age are not admitted on tours.

United Nations Secretaries General

Took office	Secretary, nation
1946	Trygve Lie, Norway
1953	Dag Hammarskjöld, Sweden
1961	U Thant, Burma (Myanmar)
1972	Kurt Waldheim, Austria

Took office	Secretary, nation
1982	Javier Pérez de Cuéllar, Peru
1992	Boutros Boutros-Ghali, Egypt
1997	Kofi Annan, Ghana
2007	Ban Ki-moon, South Korea

Six Main Organs of the United Nations

The United Nations consists of six principal organs, 15 agencies, and many programs and other bodies. The six principal organs are the General Assembly, the Security Council, the Secretariat, the Economic and Social Council, the International Court of Justice, and the Trusteeship Council.

General Assembly. The General Assembly is composed of representatives of all the member nations. Each nation is entitled to one vote. The General Assembly meets in regular annual sessions and in special session when convoked at the request of the Security Council or a majority of UN members. On important questions a two-thirds majority of members present and voting is required; on other questions a simple majority is sufficient.

The General Assembly must approve the UN budget and apportion expenses among members. A member in arrears can lose its vote if the amount of arrears equals or exceeds the amount of the contributions due for the preceding two full years. **Website:** www.un.org/en/ga/

Security Council. The Security Council consists of 15 members, five with permanent seats. The remaining 10 are elected for two-year terms by the General Assembly.

The permanent members of the Council are China, France, Russia, United Kingdom, and the United States. Nonpermanent members with terms expiring Dec. 31, 2014, are Argentina, Australia, South Korea, Luxembourg, and Rwanda; those with terms expiring Dec. 31, 2015, are Chad, Chile, Jordan, Lithuania, and Nigeria.

The Security Council has the primary responsibility within the UN for maintaining international peace and security. The Council may investigate any dispute that threatens international peace and security.

Any UN member may participate in Council discussions at its invitation. Decisions on procedural questions are made by an affirmative vote of nine members. On all other matters the affirmative vote of nine members must include the concurring votes of all permanent members (giving them veto power).

The Security Council directs the various peacekeeping forces deployed throughout the world. **Website:** www.un.org/en/sc/

Secretariat. The Secretariat is responsible for the UN's day-to-day operations. It is headed by the secretary-general, who is the chief administrative officer of the UN. This person is appointed by the General Assembly, on the recommendation of the Security Council, for a five-year, renewable term. The secretary-general reports to the General Assembly and may bring to the attention of the Security Council any matter that threatens international peace. The Secretariat maintains an international staff of about 43,000. **Website:** www.un.org/en/mainbodies/secretariat/

Economic and Social Council. The Economic and Social Council consists of 54 members elected by the General Assembly to overlapping three-year terms. The council is responsible for economic, social, and environmental matters. It meets with academics, non-governmental organizations, and private-sector representatives throughout the year. A month-long substantive session takes place each July. These sessions are alternately held in New York and Geneva, Switzerland. **Website:** www.un.org/en/ecosoc/

International Court of Justice (World Court). The International Court of Justice is the principal judicial organ of the UN. The Court has jurisdiction over cases that UN members or parties to the court's statute submit to it. In addition to rendering judgments, the Court gives advisory opinions.

The court's 15 judges are elected to nine-year terms by the General Assembly and the Security Council. No two judges come from the same nation, and they represent the world's principal legal systems. Once elected, the judges no longer act as representatives of a government. The Court remains permanently in session, except during vacations. All questions are decided by a majority. The International Court of Justice sits in The Hague, Netherlands. **Website:** www.icj-cij.org

Trusteeship Council. The Trusteeship Council, made up of the five permanent Security Council members, supervised the administration of UN trust territories. All 11 trust territories have since attained their right to self-determination. The Council formally suspended its work on Nov. 1, 1994, with Palau's independence. **Website:** www.un.org/en/mainbodies/trusteeship/

The text of the **UN Charter** is online at www.un.org/en/documents/charter/index.shtml.

Selected Specialized and UN-Related Agencies

These specialized and related agencies are autonomous, with their own memberships and organs. They have a functional relationship or working agreement with the UN except for UNICEF and UNHCR, which report directly to the General Assembly. The location in parentheses is the primary office or headquarters.

Food and Agriculture Org. (FAO) helps countries modernize farms, forests, and fisheries; improves food distribution; and raises levels of nutrition. (Rome, Italy) **Website:** www.fao.org

International Atomic Energy Agency (IAEA) aims to promote safe, peaceful uses of atomic energy. (Vienna, Austria) **Website:** www.iaea.org

International Civil Aviation Org. (ICAO) promotes international civil aviation standards and regulations. (Montréal, Quebec, Canada) **Website:** www.icao.int

International Fund for Agricultural Development (IFAD) seeks to alleviate poverty in rural areas of developing countries. (Rome, Italy) **Website:** www.ifad.org

International Labor Org. (ILO) aims to promote decent and productive employment practices, the improvement of labor conditions, social security, and vocational training. (Geneva, Switzerland) **Website:** www.ilo.org

International Maritime Org. (IMO) aims to promote cooperation on technical matters affecting international shipping. (London, England, UK) **Website:** www.imo.org

International Monetary Fund (IMF) aims to promote international monetary cooperation, currency stabilization, and the expansion of international trade. (Washington, DC) **Website:** www.imf.org

International Telecommunication Union (ITU) regulates all aspects of global communication, including setting standards for radio, telegraph, telephone, and space radio-communications, and allocating radio frequencies. (Geneva, Switzerland) **Website:** www.itu.int

Office of the United Nations High Commissioner for Refugees (UNHCR) safeguards the rights of and provides essential assistance for refugees. (Geneva, Switzerland) **Website:** www.unhcr.org

United Nations Children's Fund (UNICEF) provides financial aid and development assistance to programs for children and mothers in developing countries. (New York, NY) **Website:** www.unicef.org

United Nations Educational, Scientific, and Cultural Org. (UNESCO) aims to promote collaboration among nations through education, science, and culture. (Paris, France) **Website:** www.unesco.org

United Nations Industrial Development Org. (UNIDO) helps developing and transitional nations pursue sustainable industrial development while promoting international industrial cooperation. (Vienna, Austria) **Website:** www.unido.org

Universal Postal Union (UPU) aims to perfect postal services and promote international collaboration. (Berne, Switzerland) **Website:** www.upu.int

World Bank Group encompasses two development institutions and three affiliates focused on worldwide poverty reduction. The **International Bank for Reconstruction and Development (IBRD)** provides loans and technical assistance for projects in developing member countries and encourages co-financing for projects from other sources. The **International Development Assn. (IDA)** provides funds for development projects on concessionary terms to poorer developing member countries. The **International Finance Corp. (IFC)** promotes private-sector growth in developing member countries; encourages the development of local capital markets; and stimulates the international flow of private capital. The **Multilateral Investment Guarantee Agency (MIGA)** promotes investment in developing countries; guarantees investments to protect investors from noncommercial risks, such as nationalization; and advises governments on attracting private investment. The **International Center for Settlement of Investment Disputes (ICSID)** provides conciliation and arbitration services for disputes between foreign investors and host governments that arise out of an investment. (Washington, DC) **Website:** www.worldbank.org, www.ifc.org, www.miga.org

World Health Org. (WHO) aims for the attainment of the highest possible level of health. (Geneva, Switzerland) **Website:** www.who.int

World Intellectual Property Org. (WIPO) seeks to protect, literary, industrial, scientific, and artistic works through international cooperation. (Geneva, Switzerland) **Website:** www.wipo.int

World Meteorological Org. (WMO) aims to coordinate and improve world meteorological work. (Geneva, Switzerland) **Website:** www.wmo.int

World Tourism Org. (UNWTO) promotes responsible, sustainable, and universally accessible tourism with the aim of fostering economic development and international understanding. (Madrid, Spain) **Website:** www.unwto.org

World Trade Org. (WTO) administers trade agreements and treaties between nations, examines members' trade regimes, keeps track of trade measures and statistics, and attempts to settle disputes. (Geneva, Switzerland) **Website:** www.wto.org

Ongoing UN Peacekeeping Missions, 2014

Source: Dept. of Peacekeeping Operations (DPKO), Dept. of Field Support, Dept. of Management; United Nations Secretariat
Unless otherwise noted, numbers are for peacekeeping operations only, as of July 31, 2014. Year given in graphic is the year each mission started.

Uniformed personnel (troops, police, military observers)	96,535	Total personnel serving in 17 DPKO-led peace operations (16 peacekeeping, 1 political mission)	117,184
Countries contributing uniformed personnel	122	Approved budget for July 1, 2014-June 30, 2015	$7.06 bil
Civilian personnel:		Peacekeeping operations since 1948	69
International	5,323	Total fatalities in peace operations since 1948	3,250
Local	11,954	Est. total cost of operations, 1948 to June 30, 2010	$69 bil

*Political mission directed and supported by the Dept. of Peacekeeping Operations.

Roster of the United Nations

Listed below are the 193 members of the United Nations, with the years in which they were admitted (as of Aug. 2014). Vatican City, Kosovo, and China (Taiwan)[1] are not members. Taiwan's repeated bids for UN membership have so far been unsuccessful. Vatican City is a permanent observer.

Member	Year	Member	Year	Member	Year	Member	Year
Afghanistan	1946	Dominica	1978	Libya	1955	Saint Vincent and the Grenadines	1980
Albania	1955	Dominican Republic	1945	Liechtenstein	1990	Samoa	1976
Algeria	1962	Ecuador	1945	Lithuania	1991	San Marino	1992
Andorra	1993	Egypt[4]	1945	Luxembourg	1945	São Tomé and Príncipe	1975
Angola	1976	El Salvador	1945	Macedonia[2,7]	1993	Saudi Arabia	1945
Antigua and Barbuda	1981	Equatorial Guinea	1968	Madagascar	1960	Senegal	1960
Argentina	1945	Eritrea	1993	Malawi	1964	Serbia[2,9]	2000
Armenia	1992	Estonia	1991	Malaysia[8]	1957	Seychelles	1976
Australia	1945	Ethiopia	1945	Maldives	1965	Sierra Leone	1961
Austria	1955	Fiji	1970	Mali	1960	Singapore[8]	1965
Azerbaijan	1992	Finland	1955	Malta	1964	Slovakia[3]	1993
Bahamas, The	1973	France	1945	Marshall Islands	1991	Slovenia[2]	1992
Bahrain	1971	Gabon	1960	Mauritania	1961	Solomon Islands	1978
Bangladesh	1974	Gambia, The	1965	Mauritius	1968	Somalia	1960
Barbados	1966	Georgia	1992	Mexico	1945	South Africa[11]	1945
Belarus	1945	Germany[5]	1973	Micronesia	1991	South Sudan[12]	2011
Belgium	1945	Ghana	1957	Moldova	1992	Spain	1955
Belize	1981	Greece	1945	Monaco	1993	Sri Lanka	1955
Benin	1960	Grenada	1974	Mongolia	1961	Sudan[12]	1956
Bhutan	1971	Guatemala	1945	Montenegro[2,9]	2006	Suriname	1975
Bolivia	1945	Guinea	1958	Morocco	1956	Swaziland	1968
Bosnia and Herzegovina[2]	1992	Guinea-Bissau	1974	Mozambique	1975	Sweden	1946
Botswana	1966	Guyana	1966	Myanmar (Burma)	1948	Switzerland	2002
Brazil	1945	Haiti	1945	Namibia	1990	Syria[3]	1945
Brunei	1984	Honduras	1945	Nauru	1999	Tajikistan	1992
Bulgaria	1955	Hungary	1955	Nepal	1955	Tanzania[13]	1961
Burkina Faso	1960	Iceland	1946	Netherlands	1945	Thailand	1946
Burundi	1962	India	1945	New Zealand	1945	Timor-Leste	2002
Cabo Verde	1975	Indonesia[6]	1950	Nicaragua	1945	Togo	1960
Cambodia	1955	Iran	1945	Niger	1960	Tonga	1999
Cameroon	1960	Iraq	1945	Nigeria	1960	Trinidad and Tobago	1962
Canada	1945	Ireland	1955	Norway	1945	Tunisia	1956
Central African Rep.	1960	Israel	1949	Oman	1971	Turkey	1945
Chad	1960	Italy	1955	Pakistan	1947	Turkmenistan	1992
Chile	1945	Jamaica	1962	Palau	1994	Tuvalu	2000
China[1]	1945	Japan	1956	Panama	1945	Uganda	1962
Colombia	1945	Jordan	1955	Papua New Guinea	1975	Ukraine	1945
Comoros	1975	Kazakhstan	1992	Paraguay	1945	United Arab Emirates	1971
Congo, Dem. Rep. of	1960	Kenya	1963	Peru	1945	United Kingdom	1945
Congo Republic	1960	Kiribati	1999	Philippines	1945	United States	1945
Costa Rica	1945	Korea, North	1991	Poland	1945	Uruguay	1945
Côte d'Ivoire	1960	Korea, South	1991	Portugal	1955	Uzbekistan	1992
Croatia[2]	1992	Kuwait	1963	Qatar	1971	Vanuatu	1981
Cuba	1945	Kyrgyzstan	1992	Romania	1955	Venezuela	1945
Cyprus	1960	Laos	1955	Russia[10]	1945	Vietnam	1977
Czech Republic[3]	1993	Latvia	1991	Rwanda	1962	Yemen[14]	1947
Denmark	1945	Lebanon	1945	Saint Kitts and Nevis	1983	Zambia	1964
Djibouti	1977	Lesotho	1966	Saint Lucia	1979	Zimbabwe	1980
		Liberia	1945				

(1) The General Assembly (GA) voted in 1971 to expel the Chinese government in Taiwan and admit the government in Beijing. (2) The Socialist Federal Republic of Yugoslavia was an original UN member. After four of its six republics (Bosnia and Herzegovina, Croatia, Macedonia, and Slovenia) declared independence in 1991-92, the two remaining republics, Montenegro and Serbia, reconstituted as the Federal Republic of Yugoslavia. They sought to take over the former Yugoslavia's UN seat in 1992 but were expelled a few months later by GA vote. The Federal Republic of Yugoslavia was granted membership in 2000. In 2003, the country changed its name to Serbia and Montenegro. In 2006, after Montenegro declared independence, Serbia continued Serbia and Montenegro's UN membership. (3) Czechoslovakia, an original UN member from 1945 to 1992, was succeeded by both the Czech Republic and Slovakia in 1993. (4) Egypt and Syria were original UN members. In 1958, Egypt and Syria established the United Arab Republic and continued under a single UN membership. In 1961, Syria resumed separate membership following independence. (5) The Federal Republic of Germany and the German Democratic Republic became UN members in 1973. In 1990, the two formed one sovereign state. (6) Withdrew from the UN in 1965; rejoined in 1966. (7) Provisionally referred to as the former Yugoslav Republic of Macedonia within the UN pending settlement of Greece's objection to its constitutional name. (8) The Federation of Malaya joined the UN in 1957. In 1963, it changed its name to Malaysia following the accession of Singapore, Sabah, and Sarawak. Singapore became an independent UN member in 1965. (9) After Montenegro declared independence in 2006, the Republic of Serbia continued Serbia and Montenegro's UN membership. Montenegro was admitted to the UN as the Republic of Montenegro the same month. (10) The USSR was an original UN member. After the USSR's dissolution in 1991, Russia informed the UN it would continue the Soviet Union's membership in the Security Council and all other UN organs with the support of the Commonwealth of Independent States (comprising most of the former Soviet republics). (11) Readmitted in 1994. Its delegation had been suspended from participation in 1974 because of apartheid. (12) The Republic of South Sudan seceded from the Republic of the Sudan in 2011 and was admitted to the UN the same year. (13) Tanganyika was a UN member from 1961 and Zanzibar from 1963. The two countries united in 1964 to form the United Republic of Tanganyika and Zanzibar, which continued a single UN membership. It later changed its name to the United Republic of Tanzania. (14) The Yemen Arab Republic was admitted in 1947; the People's Democratic Republic of Yemen in 1967. In 1990, the two nations formed the Republic of Yemen.

U.S. Representatives to the United Nations, 1946-2014

The U.S. Permanent Representative to the United Nations is head of the U.S. Mission to the UN in New York. He or she is appointed by the president and confirmed by the Senate. This individual holds the rank and status of Ambassador Extraordinary and Plenipotentiary. Year given is the year each took office.

Year	Representative	Year	Representative	Year	Representative	Year	Representative
1946	Edward R. Stettinius Jr.	1968	James Russell Wiggins	1985	Vernon A. Walters	2001	John D. Negroponte
1946	Herschel V. Johnson (act.)	1969	Charles W. Yost	1989	Thomas R. Pickering	2004	John C. Danforth
1947	Warren R. Austin	1971	George H. W. Bush	1992	Edward J. Perkins	2005	Anne W. Patterson (act.)
1953	Henry Cabot Lodge Jr.	1973	John A. Scali	1993	Madeleine K. Albright	2005	John R. Bolton
1960	James J. Wadsworth	1975	Daniel P. Moynihan	1997	Bill Richardson	2006	Alejandro D. Wolff (act.)
1961	Adlai E. Stevenson	1976	William W. Scranton	1998	A. Peter Burleigh (act.)	2007	Zalmay M. Khalilzad
1965	Arthur J. Goldberg	1977	Andrew Young	1999	Richard C. Holbrooke	2009	Susan E. Rice
1968	George W. Ball	1979	Donald McHenry	2001	James B. Cunningham (act.)	2013	Samantha Power
		1981	Jeane J. Kirkpatrick				

International Criminal Court

The International Criminal Court (ICC) was created when 120 nations signed the Rome Statute on July 17, 1998. Its mission is to try individuals accused of genocide, war crimes, or other crimes against humanity, which was undertaken in the past by temporary tribunals. The statute came into force on July 1, 2002. As of Aug. 2014, 122 nations were state parties to the Rome Statute of the ICC. China, Russia, and the U.S. have not yet joined.

The ICC, unlike the World Court, is not part of the UN. It is an independent international agency with its own administration and budget, which is made up of funds from member states and voluntary contributions by other institutions, international groups, individuals, and corporations. It consists of 18 judges elected by member nations. An absolute majority of these 18 judges elect three from among themselves to serve as president, first vice president, and second vice president in three-year, renewable terms. A Registry handles the nonjudicial

aspects of administration. The Office of the Prosecutor reviews, investigates, and prosecutes cases referred to it by a state or by the UN Security Council.

As of Aug. 2014, 21 cases in eight situations had been brought before the ICC. These situations were in the Central African Republic; Côte d'Ivoire; Dem. Rep. of the Congo; Kenya; Libya; Mali; Darfur, Sudan; and Uganda. The court issued its first-ever conviction Mar. 14, 2012, when it found the warlord Thomas Lubanga Dyilo guilty of war crimes for his use of child soldiers in the Dem. Rep. of the Congo.

Though jurisdiction is limited to member nations, the ICC is a court of last resort. It may also initiate cases involving non-member nations if it deems the country's authorities have not taken steps to investigate or prosecute a case. The ICC is based in The Hague, Netherlands, though it may sit elsewhere.

Website: icc-cpi.int

Geneva Conventions

The Geneva Conventions are four international treaties governing the protection of civilians in times of war, the treatment of prisoners of war, and the care of the wounded and sick in the armed forces. The first convention, covering the sick and wounded in war, was concluded in Geneva, Switzerland, in 1864, at a conference convened by the Swiss government at the urging of the International Committee of the Red Cross. The convention was amended and expanded in 1906. In 1929, two more conventions covering the wounded and prisoners of war were signed. Outrage at the treatment of prisoners and civilians during WWII by some belligerents, notably Germany and Japan, prompted the conclusion, on Aug. 12, 1949, of four new conventions. Three of these restated and strengthened the previous conventions. The fourth codified general principles of international law governing the treatment of civilians in wartime.

The 1949 convention for civilians provided for special safeguards for wounded persons, children under 15 years of age,

pregnant women, and the elderly. Discrimination on racial, religious, national, or political grounds was forbidden. Torture, collective punishment, reprisals, unwarranted destruction of property, and forced use of civilians for an occupier's armed forces were also prohibited. Also included was a pledge for the humane treatment, adequate feeding, and delivery of supplies to prisoners. They were not to be forced to disclose more than minimal information. Two additional protocols were adopted in June 1977 dealing with the protection of victims, especially civilians, in international and non-international armed conflicts. (A third protocol, adopted in 2005, created the Red Crystal emblem for use along with the Red Cross and Red Crescent.)

Most countries have formally accepted all or most of the humanitarian conventions as binding. However, there is no permanent international machinery in place to enforce these treaties.

Genocide

Source: Convention on the Prevention and Punishment of the Crime of Genocide, United Nations Treaty Series 277; Rome Statute of the International Criminal Court

The term "genocide" (which combines Greek and Latin roots to mean "murder of a race") was coined by Polish-Jewish lawyer Raphael Lemkin in 1944 to describe the intentional destruction or attempted destruction of a national, ethnic, racial, or religious group, whether in wartime or peacetime. Genocide is defined as killing members of a group, causing serious bodily harm to members of a group, or otherwise attempting to bring about a group's destruction, including efforts to prevent births or transfer children away from a group. Although the legal definition of genocide does not extend to political groups, the term is often used colloquially to refer to large-scale political violence.

The prohibition against genocide is part of customary international law and is codified in the Convention on the Prevention and Punishment of the Crime of Genocide, which entered into force on Jan. 12, 1951. As of Aug. 2014, 146 nations, including

the U.S., were parties to it. Genocide is also prohibited by the domestic laws of many nations.

The first modern trials for genocide were conducted by the Allies after WWII. Although the charter of the Nuremberg Tribunal—the international court set up to try Nazi war criminals—did not use the term genocide, its definition of "crimes against humanity" included persecution on racial or religious grounds. More recently, the UN Security Council created ad hoc tribunals to try those responsible for genocide and other serious crimes in the former Yugoslavia and in Rwanda. The International Criminal Court (ICC) also has jurisdiction to try perpetrators of genocide. The ICC issued two arrest warrants for Sudanese Pres. Omar Hassan al-Bashir on multiple counts of genocide, crimes against humanity, and war crimes after the UN Security Council referred the situation in Darfur to the ICC prosecutor.

Examples of Genocides Since 1900

Year	Event	Location	Est. deaths
1915	Extermination of Armenians by the Young Turks	Turkey/Ottoman Empire	1,000,000+
1930s	Intentional infliction of famine on Ukraine	Soviet Union (Ukraine)	6,000,000-7,000,000
1933-45	Attempted destruction of European Jewry (Holocaust)	Europe	6,000,000
1975-79	Khmer Rouge campaign of extermination under Pol Pot[1]	Cambodia	1,500,000-2,000,000
1981-83	Army and paramilitary killings of indigenous Mayan during civil war	Guatemala	200,000+
1988	Anfal Campaign (named by the Iraqi government) against Iraqi Kurds	Iraq	100,000-200,000
1992-95	Ethnic killings during the breakup of Yugoslavia, chiefly Serbs against Bosnian Muslims	Bosnia-Herzegovina, Serbia, Croatia	200,000
1994	Hutu massacre of Tutsis	Rwanda	800,000
2003-present	Rebel group and government-backed Arab militia attacks on non-Arab southern tribes, black population[2]	Darfur region, Sudan	200,000-400,000

Note: Estimates based on historical evidence. The legal definition of "genocide" does not include politically motivated mass killings. Therefore, instances of mass violence against political or class enemies, such as Josef Stalin's purges of some 20 mil Soviets in the 1930s, and Mao Zedong's Cultural Revolution, which killed several million Chinese, are not included. (1) The mass killings during Cambodia's Khmer Rouge regime are often spoken of as genocide, though many of the murders were politically or class motivated. (2) In 2005, a UN commission concluded that although the "international offenses ... that have been committed in Darfur may be no less serious and heinous than genocide," it did not term the situation there a genocide.

As of mid-2014, there were **196 nations** in the world. This number includes three nations that are not United Nations (UN) members—Kosovo, Taiwan, and Vatican City (the Holy See). Certain regions and territories can be found under the entry for their governing nation.

Sources: FAOSTAT, Economic and Social Development Dept., Food and Agric. Org. of the UN (FAO); Joint UN Programme on HIV/AIDS (UNAIDS); Intl. Civil Aviation Org. (ICAO); Intl. Data Base, U.S. Census Bureau; *International Energy Annual*, Energy Information Admin., U.S. Dept. of Energy; *International Financial Statistics*, Intl. Monetary Fund (IMF); ITU World Telecommunication/ICT Indicators Database, Intl. Telecommunication Union; *The Military Balance*, Intl. Inst. for Strategic Studies; *Oil & Gas Journal*, PennWell Corp.; *Statistical Yearbook*, UN Statistics Div.; UN Educational, Scientific, and Cultural Org. (UNESCO); *UNWTO World Tourism Barometer* © World Tourism Org.; U.S. Dept. of State; WardsAuto Group, a div. of Penton; The World Bank; *The World Factbook*, Central Intelligence Agency (CIA); *World Urbanization Prospects*, Dept. of Economic and Social Affairs, UN Population Div.

Note: Because of rounding or incomplete enumeration, percentages may not add up to 100%. FY = Fiscal year. NA = Not available/applicable. **Population, age distrib.**, and **pop. density** are mid-2014 ests. Percent of total pop. living in **urban** areas, as defined by each country, are mid-2014 ests. **Languages** are ranked with those most widely spoken listed first. Pop. of **capitals** and **cities (urban aggl.)** are mid-2014 ests. **Defense budget** is for 2013, **active troops** for 2014. Selected **industries** are ranked by descending value of annual output. **Chief crops** are listed in descending order of importance. **Crude oil reserves** are as of Jan. 1, 2014; countries without this entry lack reserves. **Arable land** is given as percentage of country's land area. **Livestock** are for 2013. **Electricity prod.** indicates net, not gross, generated in 2011. **Labor force** percentages and **unemployment** (percentage of total labor force) are latest available. **GDP** data, for 2013, are based on purchasing power parity calculations; **GDP growth** is year-over-year. **Per capita GDP** is calculated using a country's est. pop. size as of July 1 of given year. Value of **imports** and **exports** are from 2013; trade partners—listed in descending order of importance by percentage of total dollar value—are from 2012 or 2013. **Tourism** is latest available receipts from intl. tourism; data not available for all countries. **Budget** calculated on an exchange rate basis not purchasing power parity terms, is 2013 expenditures. **Total reserves less gold** and **gold** are from 2013. **Inflation** is measured by the percent change in the consumer price index (or avg. consumer cost for certain goods and services) between 2012 and 2013. **Motor vehicle** statistics, for cars and comm. vehicles in operation based on registrations, are for 2013. **Civil aviation** measures the number of passengers carried a certain distance on scheduled flights operated by airlines registered in a country; they are for 2011. The number of **airports** with paved, usable runways are as of 2013. **TV sets** (in businesses and households) and **radios** (receivers for public broadcast) are latest available figures. Number of fixed **telephone lines**; **mobile** cellular telephone subscriptions offering voice communications; and percentage of pop. accessing the **Internet**, regardless of device used, are for 2013. **Life expect.** is in avg. number of years at birth for persons born in 2014. **Natural inc.** measures the difference between the number of **births** and **deaths** in 2014. **Infant mortality** measures the probability of a child dying between birth and exact age 1 in 2014. **HIV** prevalence is the percentage of a country's pop. of 15- to 49-year-olds living with HIV in 2013. **Education** and **literacy** rate ests. are latest available. Literacy measures the percent of the pop. age 15 and older able to read and write simple statements; some countries define as literate those who have completed certain schooling. **Embassy** addresses are for Wash., DC, area code (202).

See pages 457-72 for full-color maps and flags of all nations.

Afghanistan
Islamic Republic of Afghanistan

People: Population: 31,822,848. **Age distrib.:** <15: 42%; 65+: 2.5%. **Pop. density:** 126.4 per sq mi, 48.8 per sq km. **Urban:** 26.3%. **Ethnic groups:** Pashtun 42%, Tajik 27%, Hazara 9%, Uzbek 9%, Aimak 4%, Turkmen 3%, Baloch 2%. **Languages:** Afghan Persian or Dari, Pashto (both official); Turkic langs. (Uzbek, Turkmen); 30 minor langs. (Balochi, Pashai). **Religions:** Sunni Muslim 80%, Shia Muslim 19%.

Geography: Total area: 251,827 sq mi, 652,230 sq km; **Land area:** 251,827 sq mi, 652,230 sq km. **Location:** In SW Asia, NW of the Indian subcontinent. **Neighbors:** Pakistan on E, S; Iran on W; Turkmenistan, Tajikistan, Uzbekistan on N. NE tip touches China. **Topography:** Landlocked and mountainous, much of it over 4,000 ft above sea level. The Hindu Kush Mts. tower 16,000 ft above Kabul and reach a height of 25,000 ft to the E. Trade with Pakistan flows through the 35-mi-long Khyber Pass. Climate is dry, with extreme temperatures; there are large desert regions. **Capital:** Kabul, 4,436,260.

Government: Type: Islamic republic. **Head of state:** Pres. Ashraf Ghani; b. 1949; in office: Sept. 29, 2014. **Head of gov.:** Chief Exec. Abdullah Abdullah; b. Sept. 1960; in office: Sept. 29, 2014. **Local divisions:** 34 provinces. **Defense budget:** $2.9 bil. **Active troops:** 185,800.

Economy: Industries: small-scale prod. of bricks, textiles, soap, furniture, shoes, fertilizer, apparel, food prods. **Chief crops:** opium, wheat, fruits, nuts. **Natural resources:** nat. gas, petroleum, coal, copper, chromite, talc, barites, sulfur, lead, zinc, iron ore, salt, prec. and semiprec. stones. **Arable land:** 11.9%. **Livestock:** cattle: 5.2 mil; chickens: 12.1 mil; goats: 7 mil; sheep: 13.1 mil. **Electricity prod.:** 833.1 mil kWh. **Labor force:** agric. 78.6%, industry 5.7%, services 15.7%. **Unemployment:** 8.6%.

Finance: Monetary unit: Afghani (AFN) (Sept. 2014: 55.50 = $1 U.S.). **GDP:** $45.3 bil; **per capita GDP:** $1,100; **GDP growth:** 3.1%. **Imports** (2012): $6.4 bil; Pakistan 24.3%, U.S. 18%, Russia 8.7%, India 5.8%, China 5.6%, Germany 4.4%. **Exports** (2012): $376 mil (not incl. illicit trade); Pakistan 32.2%, India 27%, Tajikistan 8.5%, U.S. 6.2%. **Tourism:** $56 mil. **Budget** (2012 est.): $4.1 bil. **Total reserves less gold:** $6.4 bil. **Gold:** 703,005 oz t. **Inflation:** 7.6%.

Transport: Motor vehicles: 48 per 1,000 pop. **Civil aviation:** 1.6 bil pass.-mi; 23 airports. **Chief ports:** Kheyrabad, Shir Khan.

Communications: TV sets: 80 per 1,000 pop. **Radios:** 129 per 1,000 pop. **Telephone lines:** 0.3 per 100 pop. **Mobile:** 70 per 100 pop. **Internet:** 5.9%.

Health: Life expect.: 49.2 male; 51.9 female. **Births:** 38.8 per 1,000 pop. **Deaths:** 14.1 per 1,000 pop. **Natural inc.:** 2.47%. **Infant mortality:** 117.2 per 1,000 live births. **HIV:** <0.1%.

Education: Compulsory: ages 7-15. **Literacy:** 38.2%.

Embassy: 2341 Wyoming Ave. NW 20008; 483-6410.

Website: www.president.gov.af

Afghanistan, occupying a favored invasion route since antiquity, has been variously known as Ariana or Bactria (in ancient times) and Khorasan (in the Middle Ages). Foreign empires alternated rule with local emirs and kings until the 18th cent., when a unified kingdom was established. In 1973, a military coup ushered in a republic.

Pro-Soviet leftists took power in a bloody 1978 coup. In Dec. 1979 the USSR began a massive airlift into Kabul and backed a new coup, leading to the installation of a more pro-Soviet leader. Soviet forces fanned out over Afghanistan and waged a protracted guerrilla war with Muslim rebels, in which some 15,000 Soviet troops reportedly died.

A UN-mediated agreement was signed Apr. 14, 1988, providing for withdrawal of Soviet troops, a neutral Afghan state, and repatriation of refugees. Afghan rebels rejected the pact. The Soviets completed their troop withdrawal Feb. 15, 1989; fighting between Afghan rebels and government forces ensued. Communist Pres. Najibullah resigned Apr. 16, 1992, as competing guerrilla forces advanced on Kabul. The rebels achieved power Apr. 28, ending 14 years of Soviet-backed regimes. More than 2 mil Afghans had been killed, and 6 mil had left the country since 1979.

Clashes between moderates and Islamic fundamentalist forces followed the rebel victory. Burhanuddin Rabbani, a guerrilla leader, became president June 28, 1992, but fierce fighting continued around Kabul and elsewhere. The Taliban, an insurgent radical-Islamist faction, captured Kabul in Sept. 1996. The Taliban executed Najibullah and empowered Islamic religious police to enforce strict Islamic codes of dress and behavior. Rabbani and other ousted leaders fled to the north.

Victories in the northern cities of Mazar-e Sharif, Aug. 8, 1998, and Taloqan, Aug. 8-11, gave the Taliban control over more than 90% of the country. On Aug. 20, U.S. cruise missiles struck SE of Kabul, hitting facilities the U.S. said were terrorist training camps run by Osama bin Laden. The UN imposed sanctions Nov. 14, 1999, when Afghanistan refused to turn over bin Laden to the U.S. for prosecution; a UN ban on military aid to the Taliban took effect Jan. 19, 2001.

After the Sept. 11, 2001, attacks on the World Trade Center and Pentagon, the U.S., blaming bin Laden, demanded that the Taliban surrender him and shut down his al-Qaeda terrorist network. When the Taliban refused, the U.S., with British assistance, began bombing Afghanistan Oct. 7, as part of Operation Enduring Freedom (OEF).

Supported by the U.S., the opposition Northern Alliance recaptured Mazar-e Sharif Nov. 9 and took Kabul 4 days later; Taliban forces abandoned Kandahar, their last stronghold, to southern tribal fighters Dec. 7. A power-sharing agreement signed by 4 anti-Taliban factions, including the Northern Alliance, provided for an interim government headed by Hamid Karzai, a Pashtun tribal leader. The UN authorized a multinational security force Dec. 20, 2001.

Meeting June 13, 2002, in Kabul, a traditional council (*loya jirga*) chose Karzai to head a new transitional government. The U.S. announced the end of major combat operations in Afghanistan, May 1, 2003, but resistance continued. NATO officially assumed control of peacekeeping forces (ISAF) Aug. 11. A new constitution took effect Jan. 26, 2004.

The most intense fighting in more than 4 years erupted Mar. 2006 with a new wave of suicide bombings, rocket and mortar attacks, and other strikes by Taliban insurgents against military and civilian targets. Erosion of government authority led to an increase in opium growing; the Taliban, local warlords, and some Karzai associates were accused of profiting from the drug trade.

Operating from sanctuaries across the border in Pakistan, Islamist suicide bombers and Taliban insurgents stepped up their activities, 2007-11. Violence escalated in the run-up to the presidential election Aug. 20, 2009. With Karzai in the lead, a UN-backed commission overseeing the tally ordered a recount, citing "clear and convincing evidence of fraud" at numerous polling stations; a runoff election scheduled for Nov. 7 was canceled when Karzai's lone opponent dropped out of the race. Karzai was sworn in for a second term Nov. 19. Weak turnout, allegations of vote-buying, and Taliban attacks marred parliamentary elections Sept. 18, 2010. After a decade-long manhunt, U.S. commandos killed bin Laden shortly after midnight May 2, 2011, in Abbottabad, Pakistan. Insurgents retaliated Aug. 6 by shooting down a Chinook transport helicopter, killing 30 Americans and 8 Afghans. Other violence included attacks Sept. 13, 2011, on the U.S. embassy, NATO headquarters, and other targets in Kabul, as well as the assassination Sept. 20 of former Pres. Rabbani.

Between Jan. 2009 and June 2011, the number of U.S. troops in Afghanistan rose from about 36,000 to 101,000, while the number of allied foreign forces under ISAF increased from nearly 32,000 to more than 42,000. The U.S., June 22, 2011, outlined a timetable for ending the war. By the end of 2011, 10,000 U.S. troops left and another 23,000 pulled out in 2012; the combined total of 33,000 roughly equaled the "surge" in U.S. troops that Pres. Barack Obama announced in Dec. 2009. Other coalition partners also began troop pullouts. By Sept. 3, 2014, ISAF troop strength in Afghanistan was down to 41,124, including 28,970 U.S., 3,906 UK, and 8,248 from 46 other nations; allied forces killed in OEF since Oct. 2001 exceeded 3,460. U.S. deaths made up more than 2,340 of that total and UK deaths over 450. U.S. Army Maj. Gen. Harold J. Greene was fatally shot by an Afghan soldier, Aug. 5, 2014, the first U.S. general killed in a foreign conflict since the Vietnam War. Pres. Obama announced, May 27, 2014, that by year's end all but about 9,800 U.S. troops would leave Afghanistan with the residual force focusing on combating al-Qaeda and training and advising Afghan troops in 2015-16. As combat between Afghan security forces and insurgents increased, the UN reported 2,959 civilian deaths from conflict in Afghanistan in 2013 (up 7% from 2012), and 1,564 in the first half of 2014 (up 17% from Jan.-June 2013). The first round of elections for a new president was held Apr. 5, 2014. A June 14 runoff between the two top vote-getters—former Foreign Min. Abdullah Abdullah and former Finance Min. Ashraf Ghani Ahmadzai—was marred by allegations of widespread electoral fraud. After an internationally supervised audit of all 8 mil runoff ballots, Ghani was declared the winner Sept. 21. He was sworn in Sept. 29. Under a U.S.-brokered power-sharing agreement, he immediately appointed Abdullah chief executive of the government. Agreements were signed Sept. 30 providing the legal basis for U.S. and other NATO forces to remain in the country after Dec. 31, 2014.

Albania
Republic of Albania

People: Population: 3,020,209. **Age distrib.:** <15: 19.3%; 65+: 11.1%. **Pop. density:** 285.5 per sq mi, 110.2 per sq km. **Urban:** 56.4%. **Ethnic groups:** Albanian 83%, other (Vlach, Roma, Macedonian, Montenegrin, Egyptian) 1%. **Languages:** Albanian (official), Greek, Macedonian, Roma, Vlach, Turkish. **Religions:** Muslim 57%, Roman Catholic 10%, Orthodox 7%, atheist 3%, Bektashi 2%.

Geography: Total area: 11,100 sq mi, 28,748 sq km; **Land area:** 10,578 sq mi, 27,398 sq km. **Location:** SE Europe, on SE coast of Adriatic Sea. **Neighbors:** Greece on S; Montenegro, Kosovo on N; Macedonia on E. **Topography:** Apart from a narrow coastal plain, Albania consists of hills and mountains covered with scrub forest, cut by small E-W rivers. **Capital:** Tirana, 444,580.

Government: Type: Parliamentary democracy. **Head of state:** Pres. Bujar Nishani; b. Sept. 29, 1966; in office: July 24, 2012. **Head of gov.:** Prime Min. Edi Rama; b. July 4, 1964; in office: Sept. 10, 2013. **Local divisions:** 12 counties. **Defense budget:** $182 mil. **Active troops:** 14,250.

Economy: Industries: perfumes and cosmetics, food and tobacco prods., textiles and clothing, lumber. **Chief crops:** wheat, corn, potatoes, vegetables, fruits, sugar beets, grapes. **Natural resources:** petroleum, nat. gas, coal, bauxite, chromite, copper, iron ore, nickel, salt, timber, hydropower. **Crude oil reserves:** 168.3 mil bbls. **Arable land:** 22.6%. **Livestock:** cattle: 498,000; chickens: 6 mil; goats: 810,000; pigs: 158,000; sheep: 1.8 mil. **Electricity prod.:** 3.9 bil kWh. **Labor force:** agric. 54.6%, industry 12.8%, services 32.6%. **Unemployment:** 14.7%.

Finance: Monetary unit: Lek (ALL) (Sept. 2014: 106.20 = $1 U.S.). **GDP:** $28.3 bil; **per capita GDP:** $10,700; **GDP growth:** 0.7%. **Imports:** $4.8 bil; Italy 31.9%, Greece 9.5%, China 6.4%, Germany 6%, Turkey 5.7%. **Exports:** $2.3 bil; Italy 51.1%, Spain 9.2%, Turkey 6.3%, Greece 4.4%. **Tourism:** $1.5 bil. **Budget:** $3.9 bil. **Total reserves less gold:** $2.7 bil. **Gold:** 50,607 oz t. **Inflation:** 1.9%.

Transport: Railways: 211 mi. **Civil aviation:** 965 mil pass.-mi; 4 airports. **Chief ports:** Durres, Sarande, Shengjin, Vlore.

Communications: TV sets: 190 per 1,000 pop. **Radios:** 585 per 1,000 pop. **Telephone lines:** 8.9 per 100 pop. **Mobile:** 116.2 per 100 pop. **Internet:** 60.1%.

Health: Life expect.: 75.3 male; 80.9 female. **Births:** 12.7 per 1,000 pop. **Deaths:** 6.5 per 1,000 pop. **Natural inc.:** 0.63%. **Infant mortality:** 13.2 per 1,000 live births. **HIV:** <0.1%.

Education: Compulsory: ages 6-14. **Literacy:** 97.6%.

Embassy: 2100 S St. NW 20008; 223-4942.

Website: www.km.gov.al

Ancient Illyria was conquered by Romans, Slavs, and Turks (15th cent.); the Turks Islamized the population. Independent Albania was proclaimed in 1912; a republic was formed in 1920. King Zog I ruled 1925-39 until Italy invaded.

Communist partisans took over in 1944 and allied Albania with the USSR but broke with the USSR in 1960 over de-Stalinization. Billions of dollars in Chinese financial assistance was cut off in 1978 when Albania attacked China's policies. Large-scale purges of officials occurred during the 1970s.

Enver Hoxha, the nation's ruler for 4 decades, died Apr. 11, 1985. The new regime introduced some liberalization, including measures in 1990 providing for freedom to travel abroad.

Albania's former Communists were routed in elections Mar. 1992, amid economic collapse and social unrest. Sali Berisha was elected as the first non-Communist president since WWII. Berisha's party claimed a landslide victory in disputed parliamentary elections, May 26 and June 2, 1996. Public protests over the collapse of fraudulent investment schemes in Jan. 1997 led to armed rebellion. The UN Security Council, Mar. 28, authorized a 7,000-member force to restore order. Socialists and their allies won parliamentary elections, June 29 and July 6, and international peacekeepers pulled out by Aug. 11.

During NATO's air war against Yugoslavia, Mar.-June 1999, Albania hosted some 465,000 Kosovar refugees. A pro-Berisha coalition victory in July 3, 2005, elections ended eight years of Socialist rule. Albania became a full member of NATO Apr. 1, 2009; the nation formally applied for EU membership Apr. 28. Socialists won June 23, 2013, parliamentary elections, and Edi Rama became the new prime min. The EU granted Albania official candidate status June 27, 2014. Membership negotiations were expected to include EU requests for reforms to reduce organized crime and political corruption. Pope Francis praised "peaceful and fruitful coexistence" between religious communities in Albania during a trip to Tirana, Sept. 21, 2014, the pope's first visit to a European country outside Italy.

Algeria
People's Democratic Republic of Algeria

People: Population: 38,813,722. **Age distrib.:** <15: 28.4%; 65+: 5.2%. **Pop. density:** 42.2 per sq mi, 16.3 per sq km. **Urban:** 70.1%. **Ethnic groups:** Arab-Berber 99%. **Languages:** Arabic (official), French (lingua franca), Berber dialects. **Religions:** Muslim (official; predom. Sunni) 99%, other (Christian, Jewish) 1%.

Geography: Total area: 919,595 sq mi, 2,381,741 sq km; **Land area:** 919,595 sq mi, 2,381,741 sq km. **Location:** In NW Africa, from Medit. Sea into Sahara. **Neighbors:** Morocco, Western Sahara on W; Mauritania, Mali, Niger on S; Libya, Tunisia on E. **Topography:** The Tell, located on the coast, comprises fertile plains 50-100 mi wide with a moderate climate and adequate rain. Two major chains of Atlas Mts., running roughly E-W and reaching 7,000 ft, enclose a dry plateau region. Below lies the Sahara, mostly desert with major mineral resources. **Capital:** Algiers, 2,559,450. **Cities (urban aggl.):** Oran, 849,797.

Government: Type: Republic. **Head of state:** Pres. Abdelaziz Bouteflika; b. Mar. 2, 1937; in office: Apr. 28, 1999. **Head of gov.:** Prime Min. Abdelmalek Sellal; b. Aug. 1, 1948; in office: Apr. 28, 2014. **Local divisions:** 48 provinces. **Defense budget:** $9.96 bil. **Active troops:** 130,000.

Economy: Industries: petroleum, nat. gas, light industries, mining, electrical, petrochemical, food proc. **Chief crops:** wheat, barley, oats, grapes, olives, citrus, fruits. **Natural resources:** petroleum, nat. gas, iron ore, phosphates, uranium, lead, zinc. **Crude oil reserves:** 12.2 bil bbls. **Arable land:** 3.2%. **Livestock:** cattle: 2 mil; chickens: 130 mil; goats: 4.7 mil; pigs: 5,000; sheep: 25.5 mil. **Electricity prod.** 48.1 bil kWh. **Labor force:** agric. 14%, industry 13.4%, constr. and public works 10%, trade 14.6%, govt. 32%, other 16%. **Unemployment:** 9.8%.

Finance: Monetary unit: Dinar (DZD) (Sept. 2014: 80.46 = $1 U.S.). **GDP:** $284.7 bil; **per capita GDP:** $7,500; **GDP growth:** 3.1%. **Imports:** $55 bil; France 12.8%, China 11.8%, Italy 10.3%, Spain 8.6%, Germany 5.2%. **Exports:** $68.3 bil; Italy 16%, U.S. 15%, Spain 10.9%, France 8.5%, Netherlands 7.3%, Canada 7.1%, UK 5.1%, Brazil 4.7%. **Tourism:** $217 mil. **Budget:** $85.6 bil. **Total reserves less gold:** $194.7 bil. **Gold:** 5.6 mil oz t. **Inflation:** 3.3%. **Transport: Railways:** 2,469 mi. **Motor vehicles:** 1,000 pop. **Civil aviation:** 2.6 bil pass.-mi; 64 airports. **Chief ports:** Algiers, Annaba, Oran.

Communications: TV sets: 190 per 1,000 pop. **Radios:** 229 per 1,000 pop. **Telephone lines:** 8 per 100 pop. **Mobile:** 102 per 100 pop. **Internet:** 16.5%.

Health: Life expect.: 75.1 male; 77.7 female. **Births:** 24.0 per 1,000 pop. **Deaths:** 4.3 per 1,000 pop. **Natural inc.:** 1.97%. **Infant mortality:** 21.8 per 1,000 live births. **HIV:** 0.1%.

Education: Compulsory: ages 6-14. **Literacy:** 80.2%.

Embassy: 2118 Kalorama Rd. NW 20008; 265-2800.

Website: www.premier-ministre.gov.dz or www.algerianembassy.org

Earliest known inhabitants were ancestors of Berbers, followed by Phoenicians, Romans, Vandals, and, finally, Arabs. Turkey rule 1518-1830, when France took control. Large-scale European immigration followed. Arab nationalists launched a guerrilla war, 1954, that more than 400,000 French troops were unable to suppress. After French Pres. Charles de Gaulle came to power, 1958, colonial rule ended, nearly all Europeans left, and Algeria declared independence July 5, 1962. Ahmed Ben Bella ruled until 1965, when an army coup installed Col. Houari Boumedienne, a former guerrilla leader who held power until his death in 1978.

Hundreds died in antigovernment riots protesting economic hardship, Oct. 1988. In 1989, voters approved a new constitution. The government canceled the Jan. 1992 elections and banned all nonreligious activities at Algeria's 10,000 mosques. Pres. Mohammed Boudiaf was assassinated June 29, 1992. Over the next 7 years, Muslim fundamentalists attacked high-ranking officials, security forces, foreigners, and others; pro-government death squads also were active.

Liamine Zeroual won the Nov. 16, 1995, presidential election. A new constitution banning Islamic political parties and increasing the president's powers passed in a Nov. 1996 referendum. Abdelaziz Bouteflika, who became president after a flawed Apr. 15, 1999, election, reconciled with rebels and won approval for an amnesty plan in a referendum, Sept. 16. Some 100 people died and thousands were injured in violent protests Apr.-June 2001, chiefly by Algeria's Berber minority. Bouteflika was reelected Apr. 8, 2004; opponents charged fraud.

Under a reconciliation plan approved by referendum Sept. 2005, the government in Mar. 2006 began freeing Islamists jailed for their role in the 1990s civil war, which left up to 200,000 people dead and 8,000 "disappeared."

Radical Islamists bombed police stations in Oct. 2006 and Feb. 2007. A group known as al-Qaeda in the Islamic Maghreb (AQIM) carried out several suicide bombings throughout 2007, killing more than 100 people. A surge in AQIM violence in Aug. 2008 left more than 100 people dead.

Parliament, Nov. 12, 2008, amended the constitution to abolish presidential term limits, enabling Bouteflika to run for a 3rd term. He claimed more than 90% of the vote in a 2009 election denounced as fraudulent by opposition parties. During Arab Spring uprisings in early 2011, Bouteflika's government suppressed street protests in Algiers, Feb. 12, and used oil revenues to raise salaries of teachers, police, and other discontented civil servants. The country's governing party, the Natl. Liberation Front, strengthened its hold on power in May 10, 2012, parliamentary elections that opposition groups called fraudulent. On Apr. 27, 2013, 76-year-old Bouteflika, who was rarely seen and was suspected of being in poor health, was hospitalized briefly after suffering a transient ischemic attack, or mini-stroke. However, he won a 4th term as president, with 81.5% of the vote, in the Apr. 17, 2014, election, boycotted by some opposition parties.

AQIM members protesting France's involvement in Mali seized the In Amenas gas facility Jan. 16, 2013, holding about 40 foreign workers hostage for 4 days and demanding the release of about 100 Islamist prisoners being held in Algeria. In the end, 37 hostages died, including 3 Americans, as well as some 29 militants at the hands of French-led forces attempting to liberate the facility.

Andorra
Principality of Andorra

People: Population: 85,458. **Age distrib.:** <15: 15.3%; 65+: 14.3%. **Pop. density:** 472.9 per sq mi, 182.6 per sq km. **Urban:** 85.6%. **Ethnic groups:** Spanish 43%, Andorran 33%, Portuguese 11%, French 7%. **Languages:** Catalan (official), French, Castilian, Portuguese. **Religion:** Roman Catholic (predominant).

Geography: Total area: 181 sq mi, 468 sq km; **Land area:** 181 sq mi, 468 sq km. **Location:** SW Europe, in Pyrenees Mts. **Neighbors:** Spain on S, France on N. **Topography:** High mountains and narrow valleys cover the country. **Capital:** Andorra la Vella, 23,449.

Government: Type: Parliamentary democracy. **Heads of state:** President of France and Bishop of Urgel (Spain), as co-princes. **Head of gov.:** Antoni Martí Petit; b. 1963; in office: May 12, 2011. **Local divisions:** 7 parishes. **Defense budget/active troops:** NA.

Economy: Industries: tourism (skiing), banking, tobacco, cattle raising, timber, furniture. **Chief crops:** rye, wheat, barley, oats, vegetables. **Natural resources:** hydropower, mineral water, timber, iron ore, lead. **Arable land:** 5.1%. **Labor force:** agric. 0.4%, industry 4.7%, services 94.9%. **Unemployment:** NA.

Finance: Monetary unit: Euro (EUR) (Sept. 2014: 0.76 = $1 U.S.). **GDP** (2012) $3.2 bil; **per capita GDP** (2011): $37,200; **GDP growth** (2012): −1.6%. **Imports** (2012): $1.4 bil. **Exports** (2012): $70 mil. **Budget** (2012): $1 bil. **Total reserves less gold:** NA. **Inflation:** NA. **Transport:** NA.

Communications: TV sets: 440 per 1,000 pop. **Radios:** 243 per 1,000 pop. **Telephone lines:** 48.7 per 100 pop. **Mobile:** 80.7 per 100 pop. **Internet:** 94%.

Health: Life expect.: 80.5 male; 84.9 female. **Births:** 8.5 per 1,000 pop. **Deaths:** 6.8 per 1,000 pop. **Natural inc.:** 0.17%. **Infant mortality:** 3.7 per 1,000 live births. **HIV:** NA.

Education: Compulsory: ages 6-15. **Literacy:** 100%.
Embassy: 2 UN Plaza, 27th Fl., New York, NY 10017; (212) 750-8064.
Website: www.andorra.ad

France and the bishop of Urgel held joint sovereignty over Andorra from 1278 to 1993. Voters chose to adopt a parliamentary system Mar. 14, 1993, although co-princes remain heads of state. Tourism, especially skiing, is an economic mainstay. Andorra attracts about 10 mil visitors annually. For years, Andorra served as a tax haven, but it began reforms in 2008 and was removed by the OECD from its list of uncooperative tax havens, May 27, 2009. The country's first income tax was scheduled to go into effect in 2015.

Angola
Republic of Angola

People: Population: 19,088,106. **Age distrib.:** <15: 43.2%; 65+: 2.9%. **Pop. density:** 39.7 per sq mi, 15.3 per sq km. **Urban:** 43.3%. **Ethnic groups:** Ovimbundu 37%, Kimbundu 25%, Bakongo 13%, mestico (mixed European and native African) 2%, European 1%. **Languages:** Portuguese (official), Bantu, other African langs. **Religions:** indigenous beliefs 47%, Roman Catholic 38%, Protestant 15%.

Geography: Total area: 481,354 sq mi, 1,246,700 sq km; **Land area:** 481,354 sq mi, 1,246,700 sq km. **Location:** In SW Africa on Atlantic coast. **Neighbors:** Namibia on S, Zambia on E, Dem. Rep. of the Congo on N; Cabinda, an enclave separated from rest of country by short Atlantic coast of Dem. Rep. of the Congo, borders Congo Rep. **Topography:** Mostly plateau 3,000-5,000 ft above sea level, rising from a narrow coastal strip. There is also a temperate highland area in the W-central region, a desert in S, and a tropical rain forest covering Cabinda. **Capital:** Luanda, 5,288,270. **Cities (urban aggl.):** Huambo, 1,204,364.

Government: Type: Republic. **Head of state and gov.:** Pres. José Eduardo dos Santos; b. Aug. 28, 1942; in office: Sept. 21, 1979. **Local divisions:** 18 provinces. **Defense budget:** $6.05 bil. **Active troops:** 107,000.

Economy: Industries: petroleum, diamonds, mining, cement, metal prods., fish and food proc. **Chief crops:** bananas, sugarcane, coffee, sisal, corn, cotton, cassava, tobacco. **Natural resources:** petroleum, diamonds, iron ore, phosphates, copper, feldspar, gold, bauxite, uranium. **Crude oil reserves:** 9.1 bil bbls. **Arable land:** 3.9%. **Livestock:** cattle: 4.7 mil; chickens: 23.5 mil; goats: 4.1 mil; pigs: 2.4 mil; sheep: 1 mil. **Electricity prod.:** 5.5 bil kWh. **Labor force:** agric. 85%, industry and services 15%. **Unemployment:** 7.5%.

Finance: Monetary unit: Kwanza (AOA) (Sept. 2014: 97.63 = $1 U.S.). **GDP:** $131.8 bil; **per capita GDP:** $6,300; **GDP growth:** 5.6%. **Imports:** $26.1 bil; China 20.9%, Portugal 19.5%, U.S. 7.7%, South Africa 7.1%, Brazil 5.9%. **Exports:** $70.8 bil; China 46.3%, U.S. 13.9%, India 10.1%, South Africa 4.2%. **Tourism:** $706 mil. **Budget:** $48.5 bil. **Total reserves less gold:** 32.8 bil. **Inflation:** 8.8%.

Transport: Railways: 1,717 mi. **Motor vehicles:** 7.1 per 1,000 pop. **Civil aviation:** 1.6 bil pass.-mi; 31 airports. **Chief ports:** Cabinda, Lobito, Luanda, Namibe.

Communications: TV sets: 140 per 1,000 pop. **Radios:** 81 per 1,000 pop. **Telephone lines:** 1 per 100 pop. **Mobile:** 61.9 per 100 pop. **Internet:** 19.1%.

Health: Life expect.: 54.2 male; 56.5 female. **Births:** 39.0 per 1,000 pop. **Deaths:** 11.7 per 1,000 pop. **Natural inc.:** 2.73% **Infant mortality:** 80.0 per 1,000 live births. **HIV:** 2.4%.

Education: Compulsory: ages 6-11. **Literacy:** 71.1%.
Embassy: 2100-2108 16th St. NW 20009; 785-1156.
Website: www.governo.gov.ao or www.angola.org

From the early centuries CE to 1500, Bantu tribes penetrated most of the region. Portuguese came in 1583, allied with the Bakongo kingdom in the north, and developed the slave trade. Large-scale colonization began in the 20th cent., when 400,000 Portuguese immigrated.

A guerrilla war, 1961-75, ended when Portugal granted independence. Fighting then erupted among 3 rival rebel groups—the National Front, based in Zaire (now Dem. Rep. of the Congo); the Soviet-backed Popular Movement for the Liberation of Angola (MPLA); and the National Union for the Total Independence of Angola (UNITA), aided by the U.S. and South Africa. Cuban troops and Soviet aid helped the MPLA win control of most of the country by 1976, although fighting continued through the 1980s. The MPLA government and UNITA signed a peace accord May 1, 1991.

Elections were held, Sept. 1992, but fighting again broke out, as UNITA rejected the results. UNITA signed a new peace treaty with the government, Nov. 20, 1994, but the rebels were slow to demobilize. The UN Security Council voted, Aug. 28, 1997, to impose sanctions on UNITA. The UN ended its mission in Angola, Mar. 1999, as the civil war continued.

The UN estimated that the war with UNITA had claimed some 1 mil lives and left another 2.5 mil people homeless by mid-2001. Government troops killed rebel leader Jonas Savimbi Feb. 22, 2002. UNITA agreed to a truce Apr. 4, 2002, ending the 27-year-long civil war but not fighting between government forces and separatists in oil-rich Cabinda; rebels there agreed to a cease-fire July 2006.

With proven petroleum reserves estimated at more than 10 bil barrels, Angola is among Africa's leading oil producers. Due to mismanagement and corruption, up to $4.2 bil in oil revenues went missing, 1997-2002. The ruling MPLA claimed victory in voting Sept. 2008, in Angola's first parliamentary elections in 16 years. Parliament approved Jan. 21, 2010, a new constitution augmenting the power of MPLA leader José Eduardo dos Santos, Angola's president since 1979. The MPLA won flawed elections, Aug 31, 2012, giving Dos Santos another 5-year term.

Antigua and Barbuda

People: Population: 91,295. **Age distrib.:** <15: 24.3%; 65+: 7.3%. **Pop. density:** 533.8 per sq mi, 206.3 per sq km. **Urban:** 24.2%. **Ethnic groups:** black 91%, mixed 4%, white 2%. **Languages:** English (official), local dialects. **Religions:** Protestant 76% (Anglican 26%, Seventh-day Adventist 12%, Pentecostal 11%, Moravian 11%, Methodist 8%, Baptist 5%, Church of God 5%), Roman Catholic 10%, other Christian 5%.

Geography: Total area: 171 sq mi, 443 sq km (Antigua, 108 sq mi, 280 sq km; Barbuda, 62 sq mi, 161 sq km); **Land area:** 171 sq mi, 443 sq km. **Location:** E Caribbean. **Neighbors:** St. Kitts and Nevis to W, Guadeloupe (Fr.) to S. **Topography:** Mostly low-lying and limestone coral islands. Antigua is mostly hilly with an indented coast; Barbuda is a flat island with a large lagoon on W. **Capital:** St. John's, 21,989.

Government: Type: Constitutional monarchy with parliamentary system of govt. **Head of state:** Queen Elizabeth II, rep. by Gov.-Gen. Sir Rodney Williams; in office: Aug. 14, 2014. **Head of gov.:** Prime Min. Gaston Browne; b. Feb. 9, 1967; in office: June 13, 2014. **Local divisions:** 6 parishes, 2 dependencies. **Defense budget:** $26 mil. **Active troops:** 180.

Economy: Industries: tourism, constr., light mfg. **Chief crops:** cotton, fruits, vegetables, bananas, coconuts. **Natural resources:** negligible. **Arable land:** 9.1%. **Livestock:** cattle: 5,000; chickens: 160,000; goats: 27,000; pigs: 5,000; sheep: 14,000. **Electricity prod.:** 310 mil kWh. **Labor force:** agric. 7%, industry 11% services 82%. **Unemployment:** NA.

Finance: Monetary unit: East Caribbean Dollar (XCD) (Sept. 2014: 2.70 = $1 U.S.). **GDP:** $1.6 bil; **per capita GDP:** $18,400; **GDP growth:** 1.7%. **Imports:** $340.8 mil. **Exports:** $55 mil. **Tourism:** $299 mil. **Budget** (2012 est.): $248.7 mil. **Total reserves less gold:** $202.6 mil. **Inflation:** 1.1%.

Transport: Civil aviation: 2 airports. **Chief port:** Saint John's.

Communications: TV sets: 465 per 1,000 pop. **Radios:** 497 per 1,000 pop. **Telephone lines:** 36.8 per 100 pop. **Mobile:** 127.1 per 100 pop. **Internet:** 63.4%.

Health: Life expect.: 74.0 male; 78.3 female. **Births:** 15.9 per 1,000 pop. **Deaths:** 5.7 per 1,000 pop. **Natural inc.:** 1.02%. **Infant mortality:** 13.3 per 1,000 live births. **HIV:** NA.

Education: Compulsory: ages 5-17. **Literacy:** 99%.

Embassy: 3216 New Mexico Ave. NW 20016; 362-5122.

Website: www.ab.gov.ag

Columbus landed on Antigua in 1493. The British colonized it in 1632. The British-associated state of Antigua achieved independence as Antigua and Barbuda on Nov. 1, 1981. Tourism, which accounts for almost 60% of GDP, was hit hard by the worldwide recession in 2008-10. The economy also suffered after Robert Allen Stanford, a Texas businessman, was charged by U.S. authorities Feb. 17, 2009, with employing his Antigua-based Stanford Intl. Bank to conduct a fraudulent $7-bil investment scheme. He was convicted Mar. 6, 2012. With the economy still weak in 2014, the opposition Antigua and Barbuda Labour Party (ABLP) won an overwhelming victory in June 12 elections for the lower house of parliament, and ABLP leader Gaston Browne became prime minister.

Argentina
Argentine Republic

People: Population: 43,024,374. **Age distrib.:** <15: 24.9%; 65+: 11.4%. **Pop. density:** 40.7 per sq mi, 15.7 per sq km. **Urban:** 91.6%. **Ethnic groups:** white (mostly Spanish and Italian) 97%; mestizo (mixed white and Amerindian), Amerindian, other non-white groups 3%. **Languages:** Spanish (official), Italian, English, German, French, indigenous (Mapudungun, Quechua). **Religions:** nominally Roman Catholic 92%, Protestant 2%, Jewish 2%.

Geography: Total area: 1,073,518 sq mi, 2,780,400 sq km; **Land area:** 1,056,642 sq mi, 2,736,690 sq km. **Location:** Occupies most of southern S America. **Neighbors:** Chile on W; Bolivia, Paraguay on N; Brazil, Uruguay on NE. **Topography:** Mountains in W are the Andean, Central, Misiones, and Southern ranges. Aconcagua (22,831 ft) is the highest peak in the Western Hemisphere. E of the Andes are heavily wooded plains, called the Gran Chaco in N, and the fertile, treeless Pampas in the central region. Patagonia, in S, is bleak and arid. Rio de la Plata, an estuary in NE, 170 by 140 mi, is mostly freshwater, from 2,485-mi Parana and 1,000-mi Uruguay Rivers. **Capital:** Buenos Aires, 15,023,800. **Cities (urban aggl.):** Córdoba, 1,503,513; Rosario, 1,366,968.

Government: Type: Republic. **Head of state and gov.:** Pres. Cristina Fernández de Kirchner; b. Feb. 19, 1953; in office:

Dec. 10, 2007. **Local divisions:** 23 provinces, 1 autonomous city. **Defense budget:** $5.1 bil. **Active troops:** 73,100.

Economy: Industries: food proc., motor vehicles, consumer durables, textiles, chemicals and petrochemicals. **Chief crops:** sunflower seeds, lemons, soybeans, grapes, corn. **Natural resources:** lead, zinc, tin, copper, iron ore, manganese, petroleum, uranium. **Crude oil reserves:** 2.8 bil bbls. **Arable land:** 14.4%. **Livestock:** cattle: 51.1 mil; chickens: 107 mil; goats: 4.4 mil; pigs: 2.4 mil; sheep: 14 mil. **Electricity prod.:** 123.2 bil kWh. **Labor force:** agric. 5%, industry 23%, services 72%. **Unemployment:** 7.2%.

Finance: Monetary unit: Peso (ARS) (Sept. 2014: 8.42 = $1 U.S.). **GDP:** $771 bil; **per capita GDP:** $18,600; **GDP growth:** 3.5%. **Imports:** $71.3 bil; Brazil 27.2%, U.S. 15.6%, China 11.9%, Germany 4.5%. **Exports:** $85.1 bil; Brazil 20.4%, China 7.4%, Chile 6%, U.S. 5.2%. **Tourism:** $4.4 bil. **Budget:** $145.3 bil. **Total reserves less gold:** $28.1 bil. **Gold:** 2 mil oz t. **Inflation:** NA.

Transport: Railways: 22,970 mi. **Motor vehicles:** 293.2 per 1,000 pop. **Civil aviation:** 11 bil pass.-mi; 161 airports. **Chief ports:** Bahia Blanca, Buenos Aires, La Plata, Punta Colorado.

Communications: TV sets: 325 per 1,000 pop. **Radios:** 681 per 1,000 pop. **Telephone lines:** 23.3 per 100 pop. **Mobile:** 159 per 100 pop. **Internet:** 59.9%.

Health: Life expect.: 74.3 male; 80.9 female. **Births:** 16.9 per 1,000 pop. **Deaths:** 7.3 per 1,000 pop. **Natural inc.:** 0.95%. **Infant mortality:** 10.0 per 1,000 live births. **HIV:** NA.

Education: Compulsory: ages 5-17. **Literacy:** 98.1%.

Embassy: 1600 New Hampshire Ave. NW 20009; 238-6401.

Website: www.argentina.ar

Nomadic Indians roamed the Pampas when Spaniards arrived, 1515-16, led by Juan Díaz de Solís. Nearly all the Indians were killed by the late 19th cent. The colonists won independence, 1816, and a long period of disorder ended in a strong centralized government.

Large-scale Italian, German, and Spanish immigration in the decades after 1880 spurred modernization. Social reforms were enacted in the 1920s, but military coups prevailed, 1930-46, until Gen. Juan Perón was elected president.

Perón, with his wife, Eva Duarte (d. 1952), introduced labor reforms but suppressed speech and press freedoms, closed religious schools, and ran the country into debt. A 1955 coup exiled Perón. A series of military and civilian regimes followed. Perón returned in 1973 and was again elected president. He died 10 months later. His wife Isabel, who had been elected vice president, succeeded him, becoming the first woman head of state in the Western Hemisphere.

A military junta ousted Perón in 1976 amid charges of corruption. Under a continuing state of siege, the army conducted a "dirty war" against guerrillas and leftists. An estimated 30,000 people "disappeared."

Argentine troops seized control of the British-held Falkland Islands (Islas Malvinas) on Apr. 2, 1982. The British imposed an air and sea blockade around the Falklands. Fighting began May 1. British troops landed on East Falkland May 21. Argentine troops surrendered, June 14.

Democratic rule returned in 1983. On Dec. 9, 1985, 5 former junta members were found guilty of murder and human rights abuses during the "dirty war" period. Buenos Aires Mayor Fernando de la Rúa won the presidential election Oct. 24, 1999, but resigned in 2001 after a prolonged recession resulted in a debt of more than $130 bil.

Congress, Jan. 1, 2002, chose a Peronist, Eduardo Alberto Duhalde, to finish de la Rúa's term after 2 weeks of mass protests. Further economic decline and renewed protests led Duhalde, July 2, to schedule an early presidential election for Mar. 2003; another Peronist, Néstor Kirchner, took office May 25, 2003. A new IMF aid deal, approved Sept. 10, 2003, rescued Argentina from default.

The supreme court, June 14, 2005, overturned amnesty laws that had barred prosecution for "dirty war" crimes committed while the military ruled Argentina. Economic growth, 2004-05, allowed Argentina to repay its $9.57-bil debt to the IMF, Jan. 3, 2006.

Cristina Fernández de Kirchner, ran as the Peronist candidate after her husband and was elected president Oct. 28, 2007. Responding to mass protests by farmers, Argentina's senate voted July 2008 to block Kirchner's proposed tax increase on agricultural exports. A candidate slate led by Néstor Kirchner was defeated in legislative elections June 2009, and the Peronists lost control of both houses of congress. Argentina became the first Latin American country to extend full marriage rights to same-sex couples in July 2010.

Néstor Kirchner died Oct. 27, 2010. Cristina Fernández de Kirchner was reelected Oct. 23, 2011. She was the first woman to win reelection in Latin America. An inflation rate of 22% prompted a general strike by farmers, bank workers, and train operators among others on Nov. 20, 2012. Meanwhile, the nation's Jewish population charged the government with anti-Semitism for attempting to ease relations with Iran in Nov. On May 29, 2013, Argentine special prosecutor Alberto Nisman claimed that Iran was plotting to carry out terrorist attacks throughout Latin America, directly and through the Lebanese militant group Hezbollah.

Former Pres. Carlos Saúl Menem, a senator, was convicted Mar. 8, 2013, of weapons smuggling during his 1989-99 term and was sentenced, June 13, to 7 years in prison. On June 27, 2014, Vice Pres. Amado Boudou was formally charged with bribery and corruption.

Buenos Aires Archbishop Jorge Mario Bergoglio was elected pope Mar. 13, 2013; he was the first Jesuit pope and the first pope from the Americas. He took the name Francis after advocate for the poor St. Francis of Assisi.

Argentina reached the final of the 2014 FIFA men's World Cup, played in Brazil, but lost to Germany 1-0 in extra time in the title game July 13.

Armenia
Republic of Armenia

People: Population: 3,060,927. **Age distrib.:** <15: 19.1%; 65+: 10.5%. **Pop. density:** 281.1 per sq mi, 108.5 per sq km. **Urban:** 62.8%. **Ethnic groups:** Armenian 98%, Yezidi (Kurd) 1%. **Languages:** Armenian (official), Kurdish. **Religions:** Armenian Apostolic 93%.

Geography: Total area: 11,484 sq mi, 29,743 sq km; **Land area:** 10,889 sq mi, 28,203 sq km. **Location:** SW Asia. **Neighbors:** Georgia on N, Azerbaijan on E, Iran on S, Turkey on W. **Topography:** Mountainous with many peaks above 10,000 ft. **Capital:** Yerevan, 1,048,640.

Government: Type: Republic. **Head of state:** Pres. Serzh Sargsyan; b. June 30, 1954; in office: Apr. 9, 2008. **Head of gov.:** Prime Min. Hovik Abrahamyan; b. Jan. 24, 1958; in office: Apr. 13, 2014. **Local divisions:** 11 provinces. **Defense budget:** $447 mil. **Active troops:** 44,800.

Economy: Industries: diamond proc., metal-cutting machine tools, forging-pressing machines, elec. motors, tires, knitted wear. **Chief crops:** fruits (espec. grapes), vegetables. **Natural resources:** gold, copper, molybdenum, zinc, bauxite. **Arable land:** 15.7%. **Livestock:** cattle: 661,003; chickens: 3.8 mil; goats: 29,020; pigs: 145,044; sheep: 645,711. **Electricity prod.:** 7.1 bil kWh. **Labor force:** agric. 44.2%, industry 16.8%, services 39%. **Unemployment:** 18.5%.

Finance: Monetary unit: Dram (AMD) (Sept. 2014: 410.73 = $1 U.S.). **GDP:** $20.6 bil; **per capita GDP:** $6,300; **GDP growth:** 4.6%. **Imports:** $3.5 bil; Russia 20%, Germany 11%, Bulgaria 9%, Belgium 9%, Iran 6.5%, U.S. 6.1%, Canada 5.9%, Netherlands 5.6%, Georgia 5.6%, Switzerland 5.2%. **Exports:** $1.7 bil; Russia 19.6%, Germany 10.7%, Bulgaria 9.1%, Belgium 8.9%, Iran 6.9%, U.S. 6.1%, Canada 6%, Georgia 5.7%, Netherlands 5.6%, Switzerland 5%. **Tourism:** $458 mil. **Budget:** $2.7 bil. **Total reserves less gold:** $2.3 bil. **Inflation:** 5.8%.

Transport: Railways: 540 mi. **Civil aviation:** 10 airports.

Communications: TV sets: 293 per 1,000 pop. **Radios:** 270 per 1,000 pop. **Telephone lines:** 19.4 per 100 pop. **Mobile:** 112.4 per 100 pop. **Internet:** 46.3%.

Health: Life expect.: 70.9 male; 77.8 female. **Births:** 14.0 per 1,000 pop. **Deaths:** 9.3 per 1,000 pop. **Natural inc.:** 0.47%. **Infant mortality:** 14.0 per 1,000 live births. **HIV:** 0.2%.

Education: Compulsory: ages 6-14. **Literacy:** 99.7%.

Embassy: 2225 R St. NW 20008; 319-1976.

Website: www.gov.am

Ancient Armenia extended into parts of what are now Turkey and Iran. Present-day Armenia was set up as a Soviet republic Apr. 2, 1921. It joined Georgian and Azerbaijan SSRs Mar. 12, 1922, to form the Transcaucasian SFSR, which became part of the USSR Dec. 30, 1922. Armenia became a constituent republic of the USSR Dec. 5, 1936. An earthquake struck Armenia Dec. 7, 1988; approximately 25,000 were killed.

Armenia declared independence Sept. 23, 1991, and became an independent state when the USSR disbanded Dec. 26, 1991. Nagorno-Karabakh, an enclave in Azerbaijan with an ethnic Armenian majority, seceded from Azerbaijan in 1988. A 1992-94 war that cost 30,000 lives ended in a cease-fire with Armenian forces in control of the enclave. Voters in the breakaway region approved a pro-independence constitution Dec. 10, 2006, that was rejected by the EU and OSCE.

Voters approved, July 5, 1995, a new constitution increasing presidential powers. Pres. Levon Ter-Petrosian won reelection Sept. 22, 1996, amid claims of fraud; he resigned Feb. 3, 1998, in a conflict over Nagorno-Karabakh. Robert Kocharian, a nationalist born in the disputed region, won the presidency Mar. 30, 1998. Gunmen stormed Parliament Oct. 27, 1999, killing Prime Min. Vazgen Sarkissian and 7 others. Kocharian won a second term Mar. 5, 2003, in a runoff vote that opposition groups and Western observers viewed as flawed.

Prime Min. Andranik Margaryan died of a heart attack Mar. 25, 2007, and was replaced by Def. Min. Serzh Sargsyan. He defeated Ter-Petrosian in a Feb. 19, 2008, presidential election criticized as flawed; opposition protests in Yerevan were forcibly suppressed Mar. 1, and a 20-day state of emergency followed. Sargsyan took office Apr. 9, 2008.

Armenia failed to ratify an Oct. 2009 treaty approved by Armenia and Turkey over the 1915-18 killing of more than 1 mil Armenians by Ottoman Turks due to renewed friction between the 2 countries in 2010. Pres. Sargsyan's party won May 6, 2012, parliamentary elections that the OSCE called "open and peaceful" in spite of lingering shortcomings, and Sargsyan won reelection Feb. 18, 2013, with 59% of the vote.

Australia
Commonwealth of Australia

People: Population: 22,507,617. **Age distrib.:** <15: 18%; 65+: 15.1%. **Pop. density:** 7.6 per sq mi, 2.9 per sq km. **Urban:** 89.3%. **Ethnic groups:** white 92%, Asian 7%, aboriginal and other 1%. **Languages:** English, Chinese, Italian, Arabic, Greek, Vietnamese. **Religions:** Protestant 29% (incl. Anglican 17%, Uniting Church 5%, Presbyterian and Reformed 3%, Baptist 2%), Catholic 25%, Eastern Orthodox 3%, Buddhist 3%, Muslim 2%, none 22%.

Geography: Total area: 2,988,902 sq mi, 7,741,220 sq km; **Land area:** 2,966,153 sq mi, 7,682,300 sq km. **Location:** SE of Asia, Indian O. is W and S, Pacific O. (Coral, Tasman Seas) is E; they meet N of Australia in Timor and Arafura Seas. Tasmania lies 150 mi S of Victoria state, across Bass Strait. **Neighbors:** Nearest are Indonesia, Papua New Guinea on N; Solomons, Fiji, and New Zealand on E. **Topography:** An island continent. The Great Dividing Range along the E coast has Mt. Kosciusko (7,310 ft). The Western Plateau rises to 2,000 ft, with arid areas in the Great Sandy and Great Victoria Deserts. The NW part of Western Australia and Northern Terr. are arid and hot. The NE has heavy rainfall and Cape York Peninsula has jungles. **Capital:** Canberra, 414,684. **Cities (urban aggl.):** Sydney, 4,475,196; Melbourne, 4,151,033; Brisbane, 2,167,014; Perth, 1,827,161; Adelaide, 1,247,392.

Government: Type: Federal parliamentary democracy. **Head of state:** Queen Elizabeth II, rep. by Gov.-Gen. Sir Peter Cosgrove; b. July 28, 1947; in office: Mar. 28, 2014. **Head of gov.:** Prime Min. Anthony John Abbott; b. Nov. 4, 1957; in office: Sept. 18, 2013. **Local divisions:** 6 states, 2 territories. **Defense budget:** $25.97 bil. **Active troops:** 56,200.

Economy: Industries: mining, industrial and transp. equip., food proc., chemicals, steel. **Chief crops:** wheat, barley, sugarcane, fruits. **Natural resources:** bauxite, coal, iron ore, copper, tin, gold, silver, uranium, nickel, tungsten, rare earth elements, mineral sands, lead, zinc, diamonds, nat. gas, petroleum. **Crude oil reserves:** 1.4 bil bbls. **Other resources:** Wool (world's leading producer), beef. **Arable land:** 6.1%. **Livestock:** cattle: 29.3 mil; chickens: 98.7 mil; goats: 3.6 mil; pigs: 2.1 mil; sheep: 75.5 mil. **Electricity prod.** (2012): 239.7 bil kWh. **Labor force:** agric. 3.6%, industry 21.1%, services 75%. **Unemployment:** 5.2%.

Finance: Monetary unit: Dollar (AUD) (Sept. 2014: 1.07 = $1 U.S.). **GDP:** $998.3 bil; **per capita GDP:** $43,000; **GDP growth:** 2.5%. **Imports:** $245.8 bil; China 18.4%, U.S. 11.7%, Japan 7.9%, Singapore 6%, Germany 4.6%, Thailand 4.2%, South Korea 4.1%. **Exports:** $251.7 bil; China 29.5%, Japan 19.3%, South Korea 8%, India 4.9%. **Tourism:** $31 bil. **Budget:** $514.4 bil. **Total reserves less gold:** $49.7 bil. **Gold:** 2.6 mil oz t. **Inflation:** 2.4%.

Transport: Railways: 23,889 mi. **Motor vehicles:** 735.8 per 1,000 pop. **Civil aviation:** 82.2 bil pass.-mi; 349 airports. **Chief ports:** Brisbane, Darwin, Fremantle, Geelong, Gladstone, Melbourne, Newcastle, Sydney.

Communications: TV sets: 659 per 1,000 pop. **Radios:** 1,885 per 1,000 pop. **Telephone lines:** 44.3 per 100 pop. **Mobile:** 106.8 per 100 pop. **Internet:** 83%.

Health: Life expect.: 79.6 male; 84.6 female. **Births:** 12.2 per 1,000 pop. **Deaths:** 7.1 per 1,000 pop. **Natural inc.:** 0.51%. **Infant mortality:** 4.4 per 1,000 live births. **HIV:** 0.2%.

Education: Compulsory: ages 5-15. **Literacy:** 99%.

Embassy: 1601 Massachusetts Ave. NW 20036; 797-3000.

Website: www.australia.gov.au

Australia harbors many plant and animal species not found elsewhere, including kangaroos, koalas, platypuses, dingoes (wild dogs), Tasmanian devils, wombats, and barking and frilled lizards.

Capt. James Cook explored the eastern coast in 1770, when the continent and offshore islands were inhabited by Aborigines and other indigenous peoples. The first European settlers, beginning in 1788, were mostly convicts, soldiers, and government officials. By 1830, Britain had claimed the entire continent, and the immigration of free settlers accelerated. The Commonwealth was proclaimed Jan. 1, 1901. Northern Terr. was granted limited self-rule July 1, 1978.

State/territory, capital	Tot. area (sq mi)	Population (2013 est.)
New South Wales, Sydney	309,130	7,465,500
Victoria, Melbourne	87,806	5,791,000
Queensland, Brisbane	668,207	4,690,900
Western Australia, Perth	976,790	2,550,900
South Australia, Adelaide	379,725	1,677,300
Tasmania, Hobart	26,410	514,000
Australian Capital Terr., Canberra	910	384,100
Northern Terr., Darwin	520,902	242,600

Note: Pop. est. as of Dec. 31. (Source: Australian Bureau of Statistics.)

In a 1967 referendum, Australians voted to change parts of the country's constitution that had discriminated against Aborigines. Racially discriminatory immigration policies ended in 1973, after 3 mil Europeans (half British) had entered since 1945.

Australia is among the top exporters of beef, lamb, wool, and wheat. Major mineral deposits have been developed, largely for export.

The Labor Party won a majority in Feb. 1983 general elections and was reelected in 1984, 1987, 1990, and 1993. Conservatives swept into power in Mar. 2, 1996 after an election that focused mainly on economic issues. Incumbent Prime Min. John Howard retained power in the 1998, 2001, and 2004 elections.

Australia led an international peacekeeping force into Timor in Sept. 1999. In a referendum Nov. 6, voters rejected a proposal that would have made Australia a republic.

Australian troops fought in U.S.-led military operations in Afghanistan (2001) and Iraq (2003). Some 2,000 Australian peacekeepers began arriving in the Solomon Isls., July 24, 2003; nearly all were withdrawn by mid-2005. In race riots in Sydney suburbs, Dec. 11-12, 2005, thousands of youths assaulted people of Middle Eastern ancestry, who then retaliated. Australian troops were dispatched, 2006, to suppress disorder in the Solomon Isls. in Apr. and Timor in May. With the operation finished in Timor, the last Australian troops there returned home on Mar. 27, 2013. The last Australian combat forces in Afghanistan left Dec. 15, 2013. Relations with Indonesia were strained in 2013-14 when documents leaked by former U.S. Natl. Security Agency contractor Edward Snowden revealed that Australia had helped the NSA gather intelligence related to Indonesia and other Asian countries. Australian warplanes, Oct. 1, 2014, joined the U.S.-led air campaign in Iraq against the Sunni extremist group ISIS. The government announced, Oct. 3, plans to send military advisers to assist Iraqi armed forces.

Kevin Rudd led the Labor Party to victory in parliamentary elections Nov. 24, 2007. Quentin Bryce, the nation's first female governor-general, was sworn in Sept. 5, 2008. "Black Saturday" bushfires Feb. 7 in Victoria State claimed 173 lives.

After a series of policy missteps eroded his popularity and alienated his Labor supporters, Rudd was forced out June 24, 2010, by his deputy, Julia Gillard, who became Australia's first female prime minister. Inconclusive parliamentary elections Aug. 21 led to the formation of a minority government headed by Gillard. Downpours from Cyclone Tasha and other storms flooded Queensland in late Dec. 2010 and early Jan. 2011, with three-fourths of the state declared a disaster zone. By late Jan. the flood death toll had reached 35.

Destructive bush fires attributed to a severe heat wave scorched the western and southeastern areas of the country, including populous areas, in the first half of Jan. 2013. They were followed by torrential rainstorms that killed about 6 people and caused some $2.43 bil in damages in the second half of the month.

Prime Min. Gillard, Mar. 20, 2013, officially apologized for Australia's forced adoption policy (in effect late 1950s-70s), in which the state took the babies of single, teenage, or unfit mothers, often under duress, and gave them to childless married couples. Gillard resigned June 26 after being voted out as party leader. Former Prime Min. Rudd, who engineered Gillard's ouster, became premier once again. The conservatives won Sept. 7, 2013, elections, and Tony Abbott, the party leader, became prime min. Sept 16, 2013.

Australian External Territories

Norfolk Isl., area 14 sq mi, pop. (2014 est.) 2,210, was taken over, 1914. The soil is very fertile, suitable for citrus, bananas, and coffee. Many of the inhabitants are descendants of the *Bounty* mutineers, moved to Norfolk 1856 from Pitcairn Isl. Australia offered the island limited home rule in 1978. **Website:** www.info.gov.nf

Coral Sea Isls. territory, area <1.2 sq mi, is administered from Norfolk Isl.

Ashmore and Cartier Isls., area 1.9 sq mi, in the Indian O., came under Australian authority 1934 and are administered as part of Northern Territory. **Heard Isl. and McDonald Isls.**, area 159 sq mi, are administered by the Dept. of Science.

Cocos (Keeling) Isls., 27 small coral islands in the Indian O., 1,750 mi NW of Australia. Area 5.4 sq mi; pop. (2014 est.) 596. The residents voted to become part of Australia, Apr. 1984.

Christmas Isl., area 52 sq mi, pop (2014 est.) 1,530; 230 mi S of Java, was transferred by Britain in 1958. It has phosphate deposits.

Australian Antarctic Territory was claimed by the UK and then transferred to Australian sovereignty in 1933, including 2.3 mil sq mi of territory S of 60th parallel S lat. and between 160th-45th meridians E long. It does not include Adelie Coast.

Austria
Republic of Austria

People: Population: 8,223,062. **Age distrib.:** <15: 13.6%; 65+: 19.2%. **Pop. density:** 258.3 per sq mi, 99.7 per sq km. **Urban:** 65.9%. **Ethnic groups:** Austrian 91%, fmr. Yugoslav (incl. Croatian, Slovene, Serb, Bosniak) 4%, Turk 2%. **Languages:** German (official), Turkish, Serbian, Croatian (official in Burgenland). **Religions:** Roman Catholic 74%, Protestant 5%, Muslim 4%, none 12%.

Geography: Total area: 32,383 sq mi, 83,871 sq km; **Land area:** 31,832 sq mi, 82,445 sq km. **Location:** In S Central Europe. **Neighbors:** Switzerland, Liechtenstein on W; Germany, Czech Rep. on N; Slovakia, Hungary on E; Slovenia, Italy on S. **Topography:** Primarily mountainous, with the Alps and foothills covering the western and southern provinces. The eastern provinces and Vienna are located in the Danube River Basin. **Capital:** Vienna, 1,743,280.

Government: Type: Federal republic. **Head of state:** Pres. Heinz Fischer; b. Oct. 9, 1938; in office: July 8, 2004. **Head of gov.:** Chancellor Werner Faymann; b. May 4, 1960; in office: Dec. 2, 2008. **Local divisions:** 9 states. **Defense budget:** $3.23 bil. **Active troops:** 22,800.

Economy: Industries: constr., machinery, vehicles and parts, food, metals, chemicals, lumber and wood proc., paper and paperboard, communications equip., tourism. **Chief crops:** grains, potatoes, wine, fruit. **Natural resources:** oil, coal, lignite, timber, iron ore, copper, zinc, antimony, magnesite, tungsten, graphite, salt, hydropower. **Crude oil reserves:** 48.5 mil bbls. **Arable land:** 16.4%. **Livestock:** cattle: 2 mil; chickens: 16.3 mil; goats: 73,212; pigs: 3 mil; sheep: 364,645. **Electricity prod.** (2012): 62.9 bil kWh. **Labor force:** agric. 5.5%, industry 26%, services 68.5%. **Unemployment:** 4.3%.

Finance: Monetary unit: Euro (EUR) (Sept. 2014: 0.76 = $1 U.S.). **GDP:** $361 bil; **per capita GDP:** $42,600; **GDP growth:** 0.4%. **Imports:** $167.9 bil; Germany 40.4%, Italy 6.1%, Switzerland 5.4%. **Exports:** $165.6 bil; Germany 29.3%, Italy 6.3%, Switzerland 5.1%, U.S. 5%, France 4.3%. **Tourism:** $20.1 bil. **Budget:** $212.1 bil. **Total reserves less gold:** $12.5 bil. **Gold:** 9 mil oz t. **Inflation:** 2.0%.

Transport: Railways: 3,976 mi. **Motor vehicles:** 617.4 per 1,000 pop. **Civil aviation:** 12.3 bil pass.-mi; 24 airports. **Chief ports:** Enns, Krems, Linz, Vienna.

Communications: TV sets: 656 per 1,000 pop. **Radios:** 752 per 1,000 pop. **Telephone lines:** 39.4 per 100 pop. **Mobile:** 152.2 per 100 pop. **Internet:** 80.6%.

Health: Life expect.: 77.3 male; 83.2 female. **Births:** 8.8 per 1,000 pop. **Deaths:** 10.4 per 1,000 pop. **Natural inc.:** -0.16%. **Infant mortality:** 4.2 per 1,000 live births. **HIV:** NA.

Education: Compulsory: ages 6-14. **Literacy:** 98%.

Embassy: 3524 International Ct. NW 20008; 895-6700.

Website: www.austria.gv.at

Rome conquered Austrian lands from Celtic tribes around 15 BC. In 788 the territory was incorporated into Charlemagne's empire. By 1300, the House of Hapsburg had gained control; they added vast territories in all parts of Europe to their realm in the next few hundred years.

Austrian dominance of Germany was undermined in the 18th cent. and ended by Prussia by 1866. But the Congress of Vienna, 1815, confirmed Austrian control of a large empire in southeast Europe consisting of Germans, Hungarians, Slavs, Italians, and others. The dual Austro-Hungarian monarchy was established in 1867, giving autonomy to Hungary and almost 50 years of peace.

World War I, which started after the June 28, 1914, assassination of Archduke Franz Ferdinand, the Hapsburg heir, by a Serbian nationalist, destroyed the empire. By 1918 Austria was reduced to a small republic, with the borders it has today.

Nazi Germany, ruled by the Austrian-born Adolf Hitler, annexed Austria Mar. 13, 1938. The republic was reestablished in 1945, under Allied occupation. Full independence and neutrality were restored in 1955. Austria joined the EU Jan. 1, 1995.

The rise of the right-wing, anti-immigrant Austrian Freedom Party (FPO) challenged the dominance of the Austrian Social Democratic Party in the late 1990s. When Freedom Party members joined the cabinet, Feb. 4, 2000, the EU imposed political sanctions on Austria for 7 months. Social Democrats won parliamentary elections Oct. 2006. They held onto their plurality in elections Sept. 2008 and Sept. 2013, although the FPO won almost one-fifth of the vote in 2008 and more than 21% in 2013.

Azerbaijan
Republic of Azerbaijan

People: Population: 9,686,210. **Age distrib.:** <15: 22.7%; 65+: 6.3%. **Pop. density:** 303.6 per sq mi, 117.2 per sq km. **Urban:** 54.4%. **Ethnic groups:** Azerbaijani 92%, Lezgian 2%, Russian 1%, Armenian 1%, Talysh 1%. **Languages:** Azerbaijani (Azeri) (official), Russian, Armenian. **Religions:** Muslim 93%, Russian Orthodox 3%, Armenian Orthodox 2%.

Geography: Total area: 33,436 sq mi, 86,600 sq km; **Land area:** 31,903 sq mi, 82,629 sq km. **Location:** SW Asia. **Neighbors:** Russia, Georgia on N; Iran on S; Armenia on W; Caspian Sea on E. **Topography:** The Great Caucasus Mts. in N, Karabakh Upland in W border the Kur-Abas lowland; climate is arid except in the subtropical SE. **Capital:** Baku, 2,317,140.

Government: Type: Republic. **Head of state:** Pres. Ilham Aliyev; b. Dec. 24, 1961; in office: Oct. 31, 2003. **Head of gov.:** Prime Min. Artur Rasizade; b. Feb. 26, 1935; in office: Nov. 4, 2003. **Local division:** 66 rayons, 11 cities. **Defense budget:** $2 bil. **Active troops:** 66,950.

Economy: Industries: petroleum and nat. gas, petroleum prods., oil field equip.; steel, iron ore; cement. **Chief crops:** cotton, grain, rice, grapes. **Natural resources:** petroleum, nat. gas, iron ore, nonferrous metals, bauxite. **Crude oil reserves:** 7 bil bbls. **Arable land:** 22.9%. **Livestock:** cattle: 2.4 mil; chickens: 25.2 mil; goats: 651,115; pigs: 6,495; sheep: 8 mil. **Electricity prod.:** 19.2 bil kWh. **Labor force:** agric. 38.3%, industry 12.1%, services 49.6%. **Unemployment:** 6%.

Finance: Monetary unit: New Manat (AZN) (Sept. 2014: 0.78 = $1 U.S.). **GDP:** $102.7 bil; **per capita GDP:** $10,800; **GDP growth:** 5.8%. **Imports:** $10.7 bil; Russia 14.1%, Turkey 13.7%, UK 12.5%,

Germany 7.7%, Ukraine 5.5%, China 5.3%, France 4%. **Exports:** $34.5 bil; Italy 25%, Indonesia 11.6%, Thailand 7%, Germany 5.7%, Israel 5.3%, France 4.7%, India 4.6%, Russia 4.5%, U.S. 4.1%. **Tourism:** $2.4 bil. **Budget:** $27.2 bil. **Total reserves less gold:** $14.4 bil. **Gold:** 643,515 oz t. **Inflation:** 5.4%.

Transport: Railways: 1,813 mi. **Motor vehicles:** 126.5 per 1,000 pop. **Civil aviation:** 1.3 bil pass.-mi; 30 airports. **Chief port:** Baku.

Communications: TV sets: 216 per 1,000 pop. **Radios:** 214 per 1,000 pop. **Telephone lines:** 18.7 per 100 pop. **Mobile:** 107.6 per 100 pop. **Internet:** 58.7%.

Health: Life expect.: 68.9 male; 75.3 female. **Births:** 17.0 per 1,000 pop. **Deaths:** 7.1 per 1,000 pop. **Natural inc.:** 0.99%. **Infant mortality:** 26.7 per 1,000 live births. **HIV:** 0.2%.

Education: Compulsory: ages 6-16. **Literacy:** 99.8%.

Embassy: 2741 34th St. NW 20008; 337-3500.

Website: www.president.az

Azerbaijan was home to Scythian tribes and part of the Roman Empire. Overrun by Turks in the 11th cent. and conquered by Russia in 1806 and 1813, it joined the USSR Dec. 30, 1922, and became a constituent republic in 1936. Azerbaijan gained independence when the Soviet Union disbanded Dec. 26, 1991.

Nagorno-Karabakh, an enclave with a majority population of eth-nic Armenians, seceded from Azerbaijan in 1988, triggering a war between mostly Muslim Azerbaijan and mostly Christian Armenia, 1992-94, in which 30,000 lives were lost (see Armenia).

Voters approved a new constitution expanding presidential pow-ers, Nov. 12, 1995. Pres. Haydar Aliyev, a pro-Russian former Com-munist, was reelected Oct. 11, 1998, but international monitors called the vote seriously flawed.

The dying Pres. Aliyev named his son Ilham prime min. Aug. 4, 2003. The younger Aliyev won the Oct. 15, 2003, presidential election. International observers called the vote fraudulent. He responded to violent protests Oct. 16 by arresting hundreds of oppo-sition leaders and their supporters. Serious abuses also marred par-liamentary elections, Nov. 6, 2005, won by parties loyal to Aliyev. The opening May 25, 2005, of the Baku-Tbilisi-Ceyhan pipeline, providing an outlet for Azerbaijan's vast Caspian oil reserves, trans-formed the nation's economy.

Pres. Ilham Aliyev won a second term Oct. 15, 2008, but main opposition parties boycotted the election. A constitutional amend-ment abolishing presidential term limits was approved by refer-endum Mar. 18, 2009. Aliyev won a third term Oct. 9, 2013, in an election the OSCE said did not meet international standards.

Riots erupted Jan. 23-24, 2013, in Ismayilli, about 100 mi NW of Baku. Protesters demanded the resignation of the local governor, claiming he was corrupt and unwilling to address the community's income inequality. Police confronted demonstrators Mar. 10, 2013, in Baku over what protesters alleged to be the hazing of noncombat military recruits, 472 of whom had died under suspicious circum-stances, 2003-12.

The Bahamas
Commonwealth of The Bahamas

People: Population: 321,834. **Age distrib.:** <15: 23.2%; 65+: 7%. **Pop. density:** 83.3 per sq mi, 32.2 per sq km. **Urban:** 82.8%. **Ethnic groups:** black 91%, white 5%, black and white 2%. **Lan-guages:** English (official), Creole (among Haitian immigrants). **Religions:** Protestant 70% (incl. Baptist 35%, Anglican 14%, Pen-tecostal 9%, Seventh-day Adventist 4%, Methodist 4%), Roman Catholic 12%.

Geography: Total area: 5,359 sq mi, 13,880 sq km; **Land area:** 3,865 sq mi, 10,010 sq km. **Location:** In Atlantic O., E of Florida. **Neighbors:** Nearest are U.S. on W, Cuba on S. **Topography:** Nearly 700 islands (29 inhabited) and over 2,000 islets in the W Atlantic O. extend 760 mi NW to SE. **Capital:** Nassau, 266,765.

Government: Type: Constitutional parliamentary democracy. **Head of state:** Queen Elizabeth II, rep. by Gov.-Gen. Sir Arthur Foul-kes; b. May 11, 1928; in office: Apr. 14, 2010. **Head of gov.:** Prime Min. Perry Christie; b. Aug. 21, 1943; in office: May 8, 2012. **Local divi-sions:** 31 districts. **Defense budget:** $64 mil. **Active troops:** 860.

Economy: Industries: tourism, banking, cement, oil transship-ment, salt, rum. **Chief crops:** citrus, vegetables. **Natural resources:** salt, aragonite, timber. **Arable land:** 0.8%. **Livestock:** cattle: 750; chickens: 3 mil; goats: 15,000; pigs: 5,000; sheep: 6,600. **Electricity prod.** 2.2 bil kWh. **Labor force:** agric. 3%, industry 11%, tourism 49%, other services 37%. **Unemployment:** 13.6%.

Finance: Monetary unit: Dollar (BSD) (Sept. 2014: 1.00 = $1 U.S.). **GDP:** $11.4 bil; **per capita GDP:** $32,000; **GDP growth:** 1.9%. **Imports:** $3.2 bil; U.S. 30.1%, India 20.3%, Singapore 8.7%, South Korea 6.8%, China 5%, Colombia 4.5%, Canada 4.2%. **Exports:** $960 mil; Singapore 25.1%, U.S. 20.6%, Dominican Republic 12.9%, Ecuador 9.4%, Canada 5.8%, Switzerland 4.1%, China 4.1%. **Tourism:** $2.3 bil. **Budget** (2012 est.): $2.1 bil. **Total reserves less gold:** $807.4 mil. **Inflation:** 0.4%.

Transport: Motor vehicles: 403.7 per 1,000 pop. **Civil aviation:** 24 airports. **Chief ports:** Freeport, Nassau.

Communications: TV sets: 248 per 1,000 pop. **Radios:** 746 per 1,000 pop. **Telephone lines:** 36 per 100 pop. **Mobile:** 76.1 per 100 pop. **Internet:** 72%.

Health: Life expect.: 69.5 male; 74.5 female. **Births:** 15.7 per 1,000 pop. **Deaths:** 7.0 per 1,000 pop. **Natural inc.:** 0.87%. **Infant mortality:** 12.5 per 1,000 live births. **HIV:** 3.2%.

Education: Compulsory: ages 5-16. **Literacy:** NA.

Embassy: 2220 Massachusetts Ave. NW 20008; 319-2660.

Website: www.bahamas.gov.bs

Christopher Columbus first set foot in the New World on San Salvador (Watling Isl.) in 1492, when Arawak Indians inhabited the islands. British settlement began in 1647; the islands became a Brit-ish colony in 1783. Internal self-government was granted in 1964; full independence within the Commonwealth was attained July 10, 1973. International banking and investment management have become major industries alongside tourism. The Progressive Lib-eral Party's Perry Christie, who was prime min. 2002-07, returned to the post after May 7, 2012, parliamentary elections, which saw the defeat of the Free Natl. Movement as the majority party.

Bahrain
Kingdom of Bahrain

People: Population: 1,314,089. **Age distrib.:** <15: 19.7%; 65+: 2.7%. **Pop. density:** 4,478.3 per sq mi, 1,729.1 per sq km. **Urban:** 88.7%. **Ethnic groups:** Bahraini 46%, Asian 46%, other Arabs 5%. **Languages:** Arabic (official), English, Farsi, Urdu. **Religions:** Mus-lim 70%, Christian 15%, Hindu 10%, Buddhist 3%.

Geography: Total area: 293 sq mi, 760 sq km; **Land area:** 293 sq mi, 760 sq km. **Location:** SW Asia, in Persian Gulf. **Neigh-bors:** Nearest are Saudi Arabia on W, Qatar on E. **Topography:** Bahrain Island and several adjacent, smaller islands, are flat, hot, and humid with little rain. **Capital:** Manama, 397,623.

Government: Type: Constitutional monarchy. **Head of state:** King Hamad bin Isa al-Khalifa; b. Jan. 28, 1950; in office: as emir Mar. 6, 1999; as king Feb. 14, 2002. **Head of gov.:** Prime Min. Khalifa bin Salman al-Khalifa; b. Nov. 24, 1936; in office: 1971. **Local divisions:** 5 governorates. **Defense budget:** $1.39 bil. **Active troops:** 8,200.

Economy: Industries: petroleum proc. and refining, aluminum smelting, iron pelletization, fertilizers, Islamic and offshore bank-ing. **Chief crops:** fruit, vegetables. **Natural resources:** oil, nat. gas, fish, pearls. **Crude oil reserves:** 124.6 mil bbls. **Arable land:** 2.1%. **Livestock:** cattle: 10,500; chickens: 550,000; goats: 18,500; sheep: 40,000. **Electricity prod.:** 13 bil kWh. **Labor force:** agric. 1%, industry 79%, services 20%. **Unemployment:** 7.4%.

Finance: Monetary unit: Dinar (BHD) (Sept. 2014: 0.38 = $1 U.S.). **GDP:** $35 bil; **per capita GDP:** $29,800; **GDP growth:** 4.4%. **Imports:** $14.4 bil; Saudi Arabia 27.4%, U.S. 9.6%, China 9.5%, Japan 6.4%, India 4.9%, France 4.7%. **Exports:** $20.7 bil; Saudi Arabia 3.3%, India 2.2%, UAE 2.2%, South Korea 2%. **Tourism:** $1.1 bil. **Budget:** $9.2 bil. **Total reserves less gold:** $5.3 bil. **Gold:** 150,000 oz t. **Inflation:** 3.2%.

Transport: Motor vehicles: 392.3 per 1,000 pop. **Civil aviation:** 7.4 bil pass.-mi; 4 airports. **Chief ports:** Mina Salman, Sitrah.

Communications: TV sets: 414 per 1,000 pop. **Radios:** 544 per 1,000 pop. **Telephone lines:** 21.8 per 100 pop. **Mobile:** 165.9 per 100 pop. **Internet:** 90%.

Health: Life expect.: 76.4 male; 80.8 female. **Births:** 13.9 per 1,000 pop. **Deaths:** 2.7 per 1,000 pop. **Natural inc.:** 1.13%. **Infant mortality:** 9.7 per 1,000 live births. **HIV:** NA.

Education: Compulsory: ages 6-14. **Literacy:** 95.7%.

Embassy: 3502 International Dr. NW 20008; 342-1111.

Website: www.bahrain.bh

Long ruled by the Khalifa family, Bahrain was a British protector-ate from 1861 to Aug. 15, 1971, when it regained independence. Pearls, shrimp, fruits, and vegetables were the mainstays of the economy until oil was discovered in 1932. Crude oil production has declined since the 1970s, but natural gas output has grown, and international banking has thrived. Shiite dissidents have clashed with the Sunni-led government since 1996.

Emir Hamad bin Isa al-Khalifa proclaimed himself king Feb. 14, 2002. Local elections in May 2002 marked the first time Bahraini women were allowed to vote and run for office. The first female judge was appointed June 6, 2006. The monarchy suppressed Arab Spring demonstrations Feb.-Mar. 2011; to bolster security, a Gulf Cooperation Council force of 1,600, led by Saudi Arabia, entered Bahrain Mar. 14, and the government recruited former soldiers and police from Pakistan. Protests, however, continued during 2012-14, largely by members of the country's Shiite majority against the mostly Sunni ruling elite. Forced labor and sexual exploitation of immigrants—many from S and SE Asia and from Africa—has gained international attention. Beginning Sept. 23, 2014, Bahrain took part in U.S.-led airstrikes against Sunni extremist forces in Syria.

Bangladesh
People's Republic of Bangladesh

People: Population: 166,280,712. **Age distrib.:** <15: 32.3%; 65+: 5%. **Pop. density:** 3,308.5 per sq mi, 1,277.4 per sq km. **Urban:** 33.5%. **Ethnic groups:** Bengali 98%. **Languages:** Bangla, or Bengali (official), English. **Religions:** Muslim 89.5%, Hindu 9.6%.

Geography: Total area: 55,598 sq mi, 143,998 sq km; **Land area:** 50,258 sq mi, 130,168 sq km. **Location:** In S Asia, on N bend of Bay of Bengal. **Neighbors:** India nearly surrounds country on W, N, E; Myanmar on SE. **Topography:** Mostly a low plain cut by the Ganges and Brahmaputra Rivers and their delta. The land is alluvial and marshy along the coast, with hills only in the extreme SE and NE. A tropical monsoon climate prevails, among the rainiest in the world. **Capital:** Dhaka, 16,982,400. **Cities (urban aggl.):** Chittagong, 4,446,675; Khulna, 1,034,936.

Government: Type: Parliamentary democracy. **Head of state:** Pres. Abdul Hamid; b. Jan. 1, 1944; in office: Apr. 24, 2013. **Head of gov.:** Prime Min. Sheikh Hasina; b. Sept. 28, 1947; in office: Jan. 6, 2009. **Local divisions:** 7 divisions. **Defense budget:** $1.65 bil. **Active troops:** 157,050.

Economy: Industries: cotton, garments, paper, leather, fertilizer, iron and steel, cement, mineral prods., tobacco, drugs and pharmaceuticals, ceramics. **Chief crops:** rice, jute, tea, wheat, sugarcane, potatoes, tobacco, pulses, oilseeds, spices. **Natural resources:** nat. gas, timber, coal. **Crude oil reserves:** 28 mil bbls. **Arable land:** 59%. **Livestock:** cattle: 24 mil; chickens: 245 mil; goats: 55.6 mil; sheep: 1.9 mil. **Electricity prod.:** 42.4 bil kWh. **Labor force:** agric. 47%, industry 13%, services 40%. **Unemployment:** 4.5%.

Finance: Monetary unit: Taka (BDT) (Sept. 2014: 77.55 = $1 U.S.). **GDP:** $324.6 bil; **per capita GDP:** $2,100; **GDP growth:** 5.8%. **Imports:** $32.9 bil; China 21.7%, India 16.3%, Malaysia 5.2%, South Korea 4.5%, Japan 4.1%. **Exports:** $26.9 bil; U.S. 18.7%, Germany 15.8%, UK 10.2%, France 6.2%, Spain 4.6%, Canada 4.3%, Italy 4%. **Tourism:** $108 mil. **Budget:** $24 bil. **Total reserves less gold:** $17.6 bil. **Gold:** 434,463 oz t. **Inflation:** 7.5%.

Transport: Railways: 1,629 mi. **Motor vehicles:** 3.7 per 1,000 pop. **Civil aviation:** 3.2 bil pass.-mi; 16 airports. **Chief ports:** Chittagong, Mongla Port.

Communications: TV sets: 106 per 1,000 pop. **Radios:** 64 per 1,000 pop. **Telephone lines:** 0.7 per 100 pop. **Mobile:** 67.1 per 100 pop. **Internet:** 6.5%.

Health: Life expect.: 68.8 male; 72.6 female. **Births:** 21.6 per 1,000 pop. **Deaths:** 5.6 per 1,000 pop. **Natural inc.:** 1.60%. **Infant mortality:** 45.7 per 1,000 live births. **HIV:** <0.1%.

Education: Compulsory: ages 6-10. **Literacy:** 61.6%.

Embassy: 3510 International Dr. NW 20008; 244-0183.

Website: www.bangladesh.gov.bd

Muslim invaders conquered the formerly Hindu area in the 12th cent. British rule lasted from the 18th cent. to 1947, when East Bengal became part of Pakistan.

Opposing domination by West Pakistan, the Awami League, based in the East, won control of the National Assembly in 1971. Assembly sessions were postponed; riots broke out. Pakistani troops attacked, Mar. 25; Bangladesh independence was proclaimed the next day. In the ensuing civil war, 1 mil died and 10 mil fled to India. War between India and Pakistan broke out Dec. 3, 1971. Pakistan surrendered in the East on Dec. 16. Mujibur Rahman, known as Sheikh Mujib, became prime min.; he was killed in a coup Aug. 15, 1975.

Army rivals killed Pres. Ziaur Rahman in an unsuccessful coup attempt, May 1981. Vice Pres. Abdus Sattar assumed the presidency but was ousted in a coup led by army chief of staff Gen. H. M. Ershad, Mar. 1982. Ershad declared Bangladesh an Islamic Republic in 1988; a parliamentary system of government was adopted in 1991. A cyclone struck Apr. 1991, killing over 131,000 people.

Political turmoil led to the resignation, Mar. 1996, of Prime Min. Khaleda Zia, the widow of Ziaur Rahman. Sheikh Mujib's daughter, known as Sheikh Hasina, led the country after the June 1996 election. Khaleda Zia returned to power following parliamentary elections, Oct. 1, 2001. Militant Islamists set off more than 400 small bombs in more than 50 cities and towns, Aug. 17, 2005, killing 3. Another wave of jihadist bombings killed 22, Nov. 29-Dec. 8, 2005. Bangladeshi economist Muhammad Yunus won the 2006 Nobel Peace Prize for using very small loans (microcredit) to help alleviate the nation's severe poverty.

Escalating political violence led Pres. Iajuddin Ahmed to declare a state of emergency Jan. 11, 2007. A military-backed caretaker government filed criminal charges against Khaleda Zia and Sheikh Hasina but failed to force the 2 former prime ministers into exile. Cyclone Sidr struck Nov. 15, 2007, damaging more than 1.5 mil homes and leaving about 3,400 dead.

The Awami League triumphed in parliamentary elections Dec. 2008, and Sheikh Hasina was sworn in as prime min. Jan. 6, 2009, ending 2 years of emergency rule. She remained in office when her party won Jan. 5, 2014, elections marred by violence and low turnout.

A fire that raged through a crowded residential area of Dhaka June 3, 2010, killed at least 117. The UN Intl. Tribunal for the Law of the Sea (ITLOS) ruled in favor of Bangladesh in its maritime dispute with Myanmar Mar. 14, 2012, granting its claim to 200 nautical mi in the oil-rich Bay of Bengal and beyond. The online release of an anti-Muslim film made by an American drew days of violent clashes between protesters and police Sept. 2012 in Dhaka. A garment factory fire Nov. 24, 2012, outside Dhaka killed 112 workers and sparked protests at other factories in the region. Rana Plaza, a building that housed 5 garment factories employing 3,000 people, collapsed Apr. 24, 2013, due to poor construction and unsafe practices, killing more than 1,100 workers in the deadliest garment-factory disaster in world history. Inspections and renovations of garment factories proceeded slowly following the Rana Plaza disaster,

amid disputes between Western clothing companies and factory owners over who would bear the costs.

Barbados

People: Population: 289,680. **Age distrib.:** <15: 18.4%; 65+: 10.5%. **Pop. density:** 1,744.8 per sq mi, 673.7 per sq km. **Urban:** 31.6%. **Ethnic groups:** black 92%, white 3%, mixed 3%. **Languages:** English (official), Bajan. **Religions:** Protestant 66% (incl. Anglican 24%, other Pentecostal 20%), Roman Catholic 4%, none 21%.

Geography: Total area: 166 sq mi, 430 sq km; **Land area:** 166 sq mi, 430 sq km. **Location:** In Atlantic O., farthest E of West Indies. **Neighbors:** Nearest are St. Lucia and St. Vincent and the Grenadines to the W. **Topography:** The island lies alone in the Atlantic almost completely surrounded by coral reefs. Highest point is Mt. Hillaby (1,115 ft). **Capital:** Bridgetown, 90,265.

Government: Type: Parliamentary democracy. **Head of state:** Queen Elizabeth II, rep. by Gov.-Gen. Sir Elliot Belgrave; b. Mar. 16, 1931; in office: June 1, 2012. **Head of gov.:** Prime Min. Freundel Stuart; b. Apr. 27, 1951; in office: Oct. 23, 2010. **Local divisions:** 11 parishes, 1 city. **Defense budget:** $33 mil. **Active troops:** 610.

Economy: Industries: tourism, light mfg., component assembly for export. **Chief crops:** sugarcane, vegetables, cotton. **Natural resources:** petroleum, fish, nat. gas. **Crude oil reserves:** 2.8 mil bbls. **Other resources:** Fish. **Arable land:** 25.6%. **Livestock:** cattle: 11,200; chickens: 3.6 mil; goats: 5,500; pigs: 23,000; sheep: 13,200. **Electricity prod.:** 1 bil kWh. **Labor force:** agric. 10%, industry 15%, services 75%. **Unemployment:** 11.6%.

Finance: Monetary unit: Dollar (BBD) (Sept. 2014: 2.00 = $1 U.S.). **GDP:** $7 bil; **per capita GDP:** $25,100; **GDP growth:** –0.8%. **Imports:** $1.7 bil; Trinidad and Tobago 35.9%, U.S. 26.9%, China 5.6%. **Exports:** $1.1 bil; Trinidad and Tobago 20.8%, U.S. 11.9%, St. Lucia 9.7%, St. Vincent and the Grenadines 6%, Jamaica 5.6%, Antigua and Barbuda 4.9%, St. Kitts and Nevis 4.6%, UK 4.4%. **Tourism:** $912 mil. **Budget:** $1.5 bil. **Total reserves less gold:** $681 mil. **Inflation:** 1.8%.

Transport: Motor vehicles: 364.4 per 1,000 pop. **Civil aviation:** 1 airport. **Chief port:** Bridgetown.

Communications: TV sets: 291 per 1,000 pop. **Radios:** 287 per 1,000 pop. **Telephone lines:** 52.3 per 100 pop. **Mobile:** 108.1 per 100 pop. **Internet:** 75%.

Health: Life expect.: 72.6 male; 77.4 female. **Births:** 12.0 per 1,000 pop. **Deaths:** 8.4 per 1,000 pop. **Natural inc.:** 0.36%. **Infant mortality:** 10.9 per 1,000 live births. **HIV:** 0.9%.

Education: Compulsory: ages 5-15. **Literacy:** NA.

Embassy: 2144 Wyoming Ave. NW 20008; 939-9200.

Website: www.gov.bb

Barbados was probably named by Portuguese sailors in reference to bearded fig trees. An English ship visited in 1605, and British settled on the uninhabited island in 1627. Slaves worked the sugar plantations until slavery was abolished in 1834. Self-rule came gradually, with full independence proclaimed Nov. 30, 1966. Tourism, banking, and manufacturing have surpassed the sugar trade in economic importance since the 1990s. The country signed an Economic and Technical Agreement with China Aug. 24, 2012, to strengthen the 2 countries' growing ties.

Airline baggage handler and Barbados native Victor Bourne was convicted and sentenced to life in prison Oct. 2012 after a trial in Brooklyn, NY, for leading a drug-smuggling ring that brought drugs from Barbados to New York in commercial jets.

Belarus
Republic of Belarus

People: Population: 9,608,058. **Age distrib.:** <15: 15.4%; 65+: 14.2%. **Pop. density:** 122.6 per sq mi, 47.4 per sq km. **Urban:** 76.3%. **Ethnic groups:** Belarusian 84%, Russian 8%, Polish 3%, Ukrainian 2%. **Languages:** Belarusian, Russian (both official). **Religions:** Eastern Orthodox 80%, other (incl. Roman Catholic, Protestant, Jewish, Muslim) 20%.

Geography: Total area: 80,155 sq mi, 207,600 sq km; **Land area:** 78,340 sq mi, 202,900 sq km. **Location:** E Europe. **Neighbors:** Poland on W; Latvia, Lithuania on N; Russia on E; Ukraine on S. **Topography:** Landlocked country consisting mostly of hilly lowland with significant marsh areas in S. **Capital:** Minsk, 1,905,250.

Government: Type: Republic. **Head of state:** Pres. Aleksandr Lukashenko; b. Aug. 30, 1954; in office: July 20,1994. **Head of gov.:** Prime Min. Mikhail Myasnikovich; b. May 6, 1950; in office: Dec. 28, 2010. **Local divisions:** 6 provinces, 1 municipality. **Defense budget** (2012): $552 mil. **Active troops:** 48,000.

Economy: Industries: metal-cutting machine tools, tractors, trucks, earthmovers, motorcycles. **Chief crops:** grain, potatoes, vegetables, sugar beets, flax. **Natural resources:** timber, peat, oil, nat. gas, granite, dolomitic limestone, marl, chalk, sand, gravel, clay. **Crude oil reserves:** 198 mil bbls. **Arable land:** 27.2%. **Livestock:** cattle: 4.4 mil; chickens: 39.2 mil; goats: 73,200; pigs: 4.2 mil; sheep: 59,900. **Electricity prod.:** 30.3 bil kWh. **Labor force:** agric. 9.4%, industry 45.9%, services 44.7%. **Unemployment:** 9.7%.

Finance: Monetary unit: Ruble (BYR) (Sept. 2014: 10,440.00 = $1 U.S.). **GDP:** $150.4 bil; **per capita GDP:** $16,100; **GDP growth:** 2.1%. **Imports:** $45.2 bil; Russia 59.4%, Germany 5.9%, China

5.1%, Ukraine 5%. **Exports:** $42.1 bil; Russia 35.4%, Netherlands 16.4%, Ukraine 12.1%, Latvia 7.1%. **Tourism:** $722 mil. **Budget:** $26.8 bil. **Total reserves less gold:** $4.9 bil. **Gold:** 1.4 mil oz t. **Inflation:** 18.3%.

Transport: Railways: 3,441 mi. **Motor vehicles:** 340.6 per 1,000 pop. **Civil aviation:** 33 airports. **Chief port:** Mazyr.

Communications: TV sets: 386 per 1,000 pop. **Radios:** 340 per 1,000 pop. **Telephone lines:** 47.8 per 100 pop. **Mobile:** 118.8 per 100 pop. **Internet:** 54.2%.

Health: Life expect.: 66.5 male; 78.1 female. **Births:** 10.9 per 1,000 pop. **Deaths:** 13.5 per 1,000 pop. **Natural inc.:** −0.27%. **Infant mortality:** 3.6 per 1,000 live births. **HIV:** 0.5%.

Education: Compulsory: ages 6-14. **Literacy:** 99.7%.

Embassy: 1619 New Hampshire Ave. NW 20009; 986-1604.

Website: www.president.gov.by

Belarus became a constituent republic of the USSR in 1922. Overrun by German armies in 1941, Belarus was recaptured by Soviet troops in 1944. Following WWII, Belarus increased in area through Soviet annexation of part of NE Poland. Belarus declared independence Aug. 25, 1991, and became independent when the Soviet Union disbanded Dec. 26, 1991.

After a new constitution was adopted, Mar. 15, 1994, Aleksandr Lukashenko was elected president. Russia and Belarus signed a pact, Apr. 2, 1996, linking their political and economic systems. An authoritarian constitution enacted in Nov. gave Pres. Lukashenko vast new powers. Since then, Lukashenko and his supporters have retained power in elections criticized as seriously flawed by Western observers.

The IMF agreed Jan. 2009 to extend $2.5 bil in credits to help Belarus weather the global economic downturn. Lukashenko crushed protests that followed the Dec. 19, 2010, presidential election in which he claimed nearly 80% of the vote; the U.S. and EU imposed sanctions on Lukashenko and other Belarus officials Jan. 31, 2011. New sanctions imposed Feb. 28, 2012, prompted Lukashenko to expel the EU and Polish ambassadors from Belarus and recall its own envoys. In Sept. 23, 2012, parliamentary elections that many observers considered fraudulent, Lukashenko's supporters won every seat. Belarus, Russia, and Kazakhstan signed an agreement, May 29, 2014, to create a Eurasian Economic Union, effective Jan. 1, 2015.

Belgium
Kingdom of Belgium

People: Population: 10,449,361. **Age distrib.:** <15: 15.6%; 65+: 19%. **Pop. density:** 893.8 per sq mi, 345.1 per sq km. **Urban:** 97.8%. **Ethnic groups:** Fleming 58%, Walloon 31%, mixed or other 11%. **Languages:** Dutch, French, German (all official). **Religions:** Roman Catholic 75%, other (incl. Protestant) 25%.

Geography: Total area: 11,787 sq mi, 30,528 sq km; **Land area:** 11,690 sq mi, 30,278 sq km. **Location:** In W Europe, on North Sea. **Neighbors:** France on W and S, Luxembourg on SE, Germany on E, Netherlands on N. **Topography:** Mostly flat, the country is trisected by the Scheldt and Meuse, major commercial rivers. The land becomes hilly and forested in the SE (Ardennes region). **Capital:** Brussels, 2,028,660 (figure is for urban aggl.). **Cities (urban aggl.):** Antwerp, 989,503.

Government: Type: Federal parliamentary democracy under constitutional monarchy. **Head of state:** King Philippe; b. Apr. 15, 1960; in office: July 21, 2013. **Head of gov.:** Prime Min. Elio Di Rupo; b. July 18, 1951; in office: Dec. 6, 2011. **Local divisions:** 3 regions. **Defense budget:** $5.29 bil. **Active troops:** 30,700.

Economy: Industries: engineering and metal prods., motor vehicle assembly, transp. equip., scientific instruments, processed food and beverages, chemicals, metals, textiles, glass, petroleum. **Chief crops:** sugar beets, vegetables, fruits, grain, tobacco. **Natural resources:** constr. materials, silica sand, carbonates. **Arable land:** 26.5%. **Livestock:** cattle: 2.5 mil; chickens: 36.2 mil; goats: 40,473; pigs: 6.6 mil; sheep: 114,407. **Electricity prod.** (2012): 74.1 bil kWh. **Labor force:** agric. 2%, industry 25%, services 73%. **Unemployment:** 7.5%.

Finance: Monetary unit: Euro (EUR) (Sept. 2014: 0.76 = $1 U.S.). **GDP:** $421.7 bil; **per capita GDP:** $37,800; **GDP growth:** 0.1%. **Imports:** $310.2 bil; Netherlands 20.9%, Germany 14.2%, France 10.6%, U.S. 6.1%, UK 5.5%, Ireland 4.4%. **Exports:** $295.3 bil; Germany 18%, France 16.1%, Netherlands 13%, UK 7.3%, U.S. 5.3%, Italy 4.4%. **Tourism:** $13.5 bil. **Budget:** $258.2 bil. **Total reserves less gold:** $18.1 bil. **Gold:** 7.3 mil oz t. **Inflation:** 1.1%.

Transport: Railways: 2,009 mi. **Motor vehicles:** 603 per 1,000 pop. **Civil aviation:** 5.3 bil pass.-mi; 26 airports. **Chief ports:** Antwerp (one of the world's busiest), Gent, Liege, Zeebrugge.

Communications: TV sets: 585 per 1,000 pop. **Radios:** 791 per 1,000 pop. **Telephone lines:** 41.3 per 100 pop. **Mobile:** 110.9 per 100 pop. **Internet:** 82.2%.

Health: Life expect.: 76.8 male; 83.2 female. **Births:** 10.0 per 1,000 pop. **Deaths:** 10.8 per 1,000 pop. **Natural inc.:** −0.08%. **Infant mortality:** 4.2 per 1,000 live births. **HIV:** NA.

Education: Compulsory: ages 6-17. **Literacy:** 99%.

Embassy: 3330 Garfield St. NW 20008; 333-6900.

Website: www.belgium.be

Belgium derives its name from the Belgae, the first recorded inhabitants, probably Celts. The land was ruled for 1800 years by conquerors, including Rome, the Franks, Burgundy, Spain, Austria, and France. After 1815, Belgium was made a part of the Netherlands but became an independent constitutional monarchy in 1830.

King Leopold III surrendered to Germany, May 28, 1940. After WWII, he was forced to abdicate in favor of his son, King Baudouin. Baudouin was succeeded by his brother, Albert II, Aug. 9, 1993. Albert's son Philippe became king July 21, 2013.

The Flemings of northern Belgium speak Dutch, while the Walloons in the south speak French. The language difference has been a perennial source of controversy between the 2 groups. Parliament has passed measures aimed at transferring power from the central government to 3 regions—Wallonia, Flanders, and Brussels. Constitutional changes in 1993 made Belgium a federal state.

After elections June 2007, rivalries between Flemings and Walloons led to a 9-month political stalemate. June 2010 elections led to a prolonged political deadlock that ended when Elio Di Rupo became prime min. Dec. 2011. After May 25, 2014, elections in which Flemish nationalist parties made gains, negotiations began on the formation of a new coalition government.

A team of thieves Feb. 18, 2013, stole $50 mil in diamonds from a passenger plane at Brussels Airport; 30 people were arrested for the heist in Belgium and Switzerland May 7-8, and its mastermind was arrested in France.

Belize

People: Population: 340,844. **Age distrib.:** <15: 35.3%; 65+: 3.6%. **Pop. density:** 38.7 per sq mi, 14.9 per sq km. **Urban:** 44.1%. **Ethnic groups:** mestizo 49%, Creole 25%, Maya 11%, Garifuna 6%. **Languages:** Spanish, Creole, Mayan dialects, English (official), Garifuna (Carib), German. **Religions:** Roman Catholic 39%, Pentacostal 8%, Seventh-day Adventist 5%, Anglican 5%, Mennonite 4%, Baptist 4%, Methodist 3%, Nazarene 3%, Jehovah's Witnesses 2%, none 15%.

Geography: Total area: 8,867 sq mi, 22,966 sq km; **Land area:** 8,805 sq mi, 22,806 sq km. **Location:** Eastern coast of Central America. **Neighbors:** Mexico on N, Guatemala on W and S. **Topography:** Swampy lowlands in N, Maya Mts. in S, coral reefs and cays near coast. Climate is tropical. **Capital:** Belmopan, 16,921.

Government: Type: Parliamentary democracy. **Head of state:** Queen Elizabeth II, rep. by Gov.-Gen. Sir Colville Young; b. Nov. 20, 1932; in office: Nov. 17, 1993. **Head of gov.:** Prime Min. Dean Barrow; b. Mar. 2, 1951; in office: Feb. 8, 2008. **Local divisions:** 6 districts. **Defense budget:** $18 mil. **Active troops:** 1,050.

Economy: Industries: garment prod., food proc., tourism, constr., oil. **Chief crops:** bananas, cacao, citrus, sugar. **Natural resources:** timber, fish, hydropower. **Crude oil reserves:** 6.7 mil bbls. **Arable land:** 3.4%. **Livestock:** cattle: 91,400; chickens: 1.6 mil; goats: 180; pigs: 22,000; sheep: 13,200. **Electricity prod.:** 452.2 mil kWh. **Labor force:** agric. 10.2%, industry 18.1%, services 71.7%. **Unemployment:** 7.9%.

Finance: Monetary unit: Dollar (BZD) (Sept. 2014: 1.98 = $1 U.S.). **GDP:** $3.1 bil; **per capita GDP:** $8,800; **GDP growth:** 2.5%. **Imports:** $864 mil; U.S. 23.6%, Germany 15%, Mexico 11.5%, Cuba 8.4%, Guatemala 4.8%, China 4.7%, Singapore 4.1%. **Exports:** $633 mil; U.S. 31.8%, UK 21.9%, Nigeria 4.8%, Japan 4.1%, Netherlands 4.1%. **Tourism:** $351 mil. **Budget:** $352.4 mil. **Total reserves less gold:** $402.8 mil. **Inflation:** 0.5%.

Transport: Motor vehicles: 101.4 per 1,000 pop. **Civil aviation:** 6 airports. **Chief ports:** Belize City, Big Creek.

Communications: TV sets: 445 per 1,000 pop. **Radios:** 590 per 1,000 pop. **Telephone lines:** 7.2 per 100 pop. **Mobile:** 52.9 per 100 pop. **Internet:** 31.7%.

Health: Life expect.: 66.9 male; 70.2 female. **Births:** 25.1 per 1,000 pop. **Deaths:** 6.0 per 1,000 pop. **Natural inc.:** 1.92%. **Infant mortality:** 20.3 per 1,000 live births. **HIV:** 1.5%.

Education: Compulsory: ages 5-14. **Literacy:** 70.3%.

Embassy: 2535 Massachusetts Ave. NW 20008; 332-9636.

Website: www.belize.gov.bz

Belize (formerly British Honduras) was Britain's last colony on the American mainland; independence was achieved Sept. 21, 1981. Relations with neighboring Guatemala, which claims the southern half of Belize and its islands as its own territory, have improved in recent years. Belize has become a center for drug trafficking between Colombia and the U.S.

Benin
Republic of Benin

People: Population: 10,160,556. **Age distrib.:** <15: 43.8%; 65+: 2.8%. **Pop. density:** 237.9 per sq mi, 91.8 per sq km. **Urban:** 43.5%. **Ethnic groups:** Fon & related 39%, Adja & related 15%, Yoruba & related 12%, Bariba & related 9%, Peulh & related 7%, Ottamari & related 6%, Yoa-Lokpa & related 4%, Dendi & related 3%. **Languages:** French (official), Fon, Yoruba, tribal langs. **Religions:** Catholic 27%, Muslim 24%, Vodoun 17%, Protestant 10%.

Geography: Total area: 43,484 sq mi, 112,622 sq km; **Land area:** 42,711 sq mi, 110,622 sq km. **Location:** In W Africa on Gulf of Guinea. **Neighbors:** Togo on W; Burkina Faso, Niger on N; Nigeria on E. **Topography:** Most of Benin is flat and covered with dense vegetation. The coast is hot, humid, and rainy. **Capital:** Porto-Novo (constitutional), 268,057; Cotonou (seat), 680,285.

Government: Type: Republic. **Head of state and gov.:** Pres. Boni Yayi; b. July 1, 1952; in office: Apr. 6, 2006. **Local divisions:** 12 departments. **Defense budget:** $86 mil. **Active troops:** 6,950.

Economy: Industries: textiles, food proc., constr. materials, cement. **Chief crops:** cotton, corn, cassava, yams, beans. **Natural resources:** oil, limestone, marble, timber. **Crude oil reserves:** 8 mil bbls. **Arable land:** 23.9%. **Livestock:** cattle: 2.1 mil; chickens: 18.2 mil; goats: 1.7 mil; pigs: 414,000; sheep: 860,000. **Electricity prod.:** 146 mil kWh. **Labor force:** NA. **Unemployment:** 1%.

Finance: Monetary unit: CFA Franc (XOF) (Sept. 2014: 498.91 = $1 U.S.). **GDP:** $16.7 bil; **per capita GDP:** $1,600; **GDP growth:** 5%. **Imports:** $1.8 bil; China 37.2%, U.S. 8.9%, India 6.7%, France 5.6%, Malaysia 5.3%. **Exports:** $1.1 bil; China 25%, India 23.5%, Lebanon 18.7%, Niger 4.3%, Nigeria 4%. **Tourism:** $189 mil. **Budget:** $1.8 bil. **Total reserves less gold:** $694.9 mil. **Inflation:** 1.0%.

Transport: Railways: 272 mi. **Motor vehicles:** 3.3 per 1,000 pop. **Civil aviation:** airport. **Chief port:** Cotonou.

Communications: TV sets: 45 per 1,000 pop. **Radios:** 323 per 1,000 pop. **Telephone lines:** 1.5 per 100 pop. **Mobile:** 93.3 per 100 pop. **Internet:** 4.9%.

Health: Life expect.: 59.8 male; 62.5 female. **Births:** 36.5 per 1,000 pop. **Deaths:** 8.4 per 1,000 pop. **Natural inc.:** 2.81% **Infant mortality:** 57.1 per 1,000 live births. **HIV:** 1.1%.

Education: Compulsory: ages 6-11. **Literacy:** 38.5%.

Embassy: 2124 Kalorama Rd. NW 20008; 232-6656.

Website: www.gouv.bj

The Kingdom of Abomey, rising to power in wars with neighboring kingdoms in the 17th cent., came under French domination in the late 19th cent., and was incorporated into French West Africa by 1904. Under the name Dahomey, the country gained independence Aug. 1, 1960; it became Benin in 1975. In the fifth coup since independence Col. Ahmed Kerekou took power in 1972; 2 years later he declared a socialist state with a Marxist-Leninist philosophy. In Dec. 1989, Kerekou announced Marxism-Leninism would no longer be the state ideology.

In Mar. 1991, Kerekou lost Benin's first free presidential election in 30 years to Nicéphore Soglo. Kerekou defeated Soglo in Mar. 1996 to reclaim the presidency. He won reelection in a runoff Mar. 22, 2001. Boni Yayi, an economist, won a presidential runoff vote, Mar. 19, 2006.

In 2006, Benin signed a 5-year, $307-mil aid deal with the U.S. More than 100,000 people reportedly lost their savings when a fraudulent investment scheme linked to high government officials collapsed in mid-2010. Pres. Yayi won reelection to a second 5-year term Mar. 13, 2011.

Bhutan
Kingdom of Bhutan

People: Population: 733,643. **Age distrib.:** <15: 27.3%; 65+: 6%. **Pop. density:** 49.5 per sq mi, 19.1 per sq km. **Urban:** 37.9%. **Ethnic groups:** Ngalop or Bhote 50%, ethnic Nepalese 35%, indigenous or migrant tribes 15%. **Languages:** Sharchhopka, Dzongkha (official), Lhotshamkha. **Religions:** Lamaistic Buddhist 75%, Indian- and Nepalese-influenced Hinduism 22%.

Geography: Total area: 14,824 sq mi, 38,394 sq km; **Land area:** 14,824 sq mi, 38,394 sq km. **Location:** S Asia, in eastern Himalayan Mts. **Neighbors:** India on W (Sikkim) and S, China on N. **Topography:** Very high mountains in the N, fertile valleys in the center, and thick forests in the Duar Plain in the S. **Capital:** Thimphu, 152,398.

Government: Type: Constitutional monarchy. **Head of state:** King Jigme Khesar Namgyel Wangchuk; b. Feb. 21, 1980; in office: Dec. 14, 2006. **Head of gov.:** Prime Min. Tshering Tobgay; b. Sept. 16, 1965; in office: July 29, 2013. **Local divisions:** 20 districts. **Defense budget/active troops:** NA.

Economy: Industries: cement, wood prods., processed fruits, alcoholic beverages, calcium carbide, tourism. **Chief crops:** rice, corn, root crops, citrus. **Natural resources:** timber, hydropower, gypsum, calcium carbonate. **Arable land:** 2.6%. **Livestock:** cattle: 348,990; chickens: 552,000; goats: 39,264; pigs: 15,373; sheep: 9,917. **Electricity prod.:** 7 bil kWh. **Labor force:** agric. 62%, industry 19%, services 19%. **Unemployment:** 2.1%.

Finance: Monetary unit: Ngultrum (BTN) (Sept. 2014: 60.47 = $1 U.S.). **GDP:** $5.2 bil; **per capita GDP:** $7,000; **GDP growth:** 5.8%. **Imports** (2012): $1.3 bil; India 72.3%, South Korea 6%. **Exports** (2012): $721.8 mil; India 83.8%, Hong Kong 10.8%. **Tourism:** $63 mil. **Budget:** $639.5 mil (nearly one-quarter financed by India's govt.) **Total reserves less gold:** $991.3 mil. **Inflation:** 7.0%.

Transport: Civil aviation: 2 airports.

Communications: TV sets: 12 per 1,000 pop. **Radios:** 118 per 1,000 pop. **Telephone lines:** 3.5 per 100 pop. **Mobile:** 72.2 per 100 pop. **Internet:** 29.9%.

Health: Life expect.: 68.1 male; 70.0 female. **Births:** 18.1 per 1,000 pop. **Deaths:** 6.8 per 1,000 pop. **Natural inc.:** 1.13% **Infant mortality:** 37.9 per 1,000 live births. **HIV:** 0.1%.

Education: Compulsory ages: NA. **Literacy:** 64.9%.

Permanent UN mission: 343 E. 43rd St., New York, NY 10017; (212) 682-2268.

Website: www.bhutan.gov.bt

The region came under Tibetan rule in the 16th cent. British influence grew in the 19th cent. A Buddhist monarchy was set up in 1907. After a 1910 treaty, Britain guided Bhutan's external affairs, while the country remained internally self-governing. Upon independence the treaty was revised, 1949, to allow India to assume Britain's role.

Isolated for much of its history, Bhutan has taken steps toward modernization. King Jigme Singye Wangchuk, in power since 1972, stepped down Dec. 14, 2006, in favor of his son, Jigme Khesar Namgyal Wangchuk. Multiparty parliamentary elections took place Mar. 24, 2008, and a new constitution was ratified July 18, making Bhutan a democratic constitutional monarchy. Namgay Peldon became the first woman elected governor in the Mar. 2008 election, and Tashi Chhozom became the first woman appointed to the country's supreme court Aug. 3, 2012. The ruling party was defeated in July 13, 2013, parliamentary elections, with the opposition People's Democratic Party (PDP) winning 32 out of 47 seats.

Bolivia
Plurinational State of Bolivia

People: Population: 10,631,486. **Age distrib.:** <15: 33.3%; 65+: 4.9%. **Pop. density:** 25.4 per sq mi, 9.8 per sq km. **Urban:** 68.1%. **Ethnic groups:** Quechua 30%, mestizo (mixed white and Amerindian) 30%, Aymara 25%, white 15%. **Languages:** Spanish, Quechua, Aymara, Guarani (all official). **Religions:** Roman Catholic 95%, Protestant (Evangelical Methodist) 5%.

Geography: Total area: 424,164 sq mi, 1,098,581 sq km; **Land area:** 418,265 sq mi, 1,083,301 sq km. **Location:** In W central South America, in the Andes Mts. (one of 2 landlocked countries in South America). **Neighbors:** Peru, Chile on W; Argentina, Paraguay on S; Brazil on E and N. **Topography:** The great central plateau, more than 500 mi long at an elevation of 12,000 ft, lies between 2 great cordilleras having 3 of the highest peaks in S America. Lake Titicaca, on Peruvian border, is world's highest lake (12,500 ft) navigable by large boats. The E central region was semitropical forests; the llanos, or Amazon-Chaco lowlands, are in E. **Capital:** La Paz (admin.), 1,800,310; Sucre (constitutional), 358,337. **Cities (urban aggl.):** Santa Cruz, 2,031,783; Cochabamba, 1,207,821.

Government: Type: Republic. **Head of state and gov.:** Pres. Juan Evo Morales Ayma; b. Oct. 26, 1959; in office: Jan. 22, 2006. **Local divisions:** 9 departments. **Defense budget:** $373 mil. **Active troops:** 46,100.

Economy: Industries: mining, smelting, petroleum, food and beverages, tobacco, handicrafts, clothing. **Chief crops:** soybeans, coffee, coca, cotton, corn, sugarcane, rice, potatoes. **Natural resources:** tin, nat. gas, petroleum, zinc, tungsten, antimony, silver, iron, lead, gold, timber, hydropower. **Crude oil reserves:** 209.8 mil bbls. **Other resources:** Timber. **Arable land:** 4%. **Livestock:** cattle: 8.8 mil; chickens: 200.1 mil; goats: 2.4 mil; pigs: 2.9 mil; sheep: 9.3 mil. **Electricity prod.:** 6.8 bil kWh. **Labor force:** agric. 32%, industry 27.4%, services 40.6%. **Unemployment:** 3.2%.

Finance: Monetary unit: Boliviano (BOB) (Sept. 2014: 6.86 = $1 U.S.). **GDP:** $59.1 bil; **per capita GDP:** $5,500; **GDP growth:** 6.8%. **Imports:** $9.3 bil; Chile 21.3%, Brazil 20.3%, Argentina 10.9%, U.S. 10.1%, Peru 6.5%, Venezuela 6.2%, China 4.9%. **Exports:** $12.2 bil; Brazil 41.8%, U.S. 18.4%, Argentina 7.3%, Peru 4.9%. **Tourism:** $532 mil. **Budget:** $15.1 bil. **Total reserves less gold:** $12.8 bil. **Gold:** 1.4 mil oz t. **Inflation:** 5.7%.

Transport: Railways: 2,269 mi. **Motor vehicles:** 62.6 per 1,000 pop. **Civil aviation:** 1.3 bil pass.-mi; 21 airports. **Chief port:** Puerto Aguirre.

Communications: TV sets: 155 per 1,000 pop. **Radios:** 672 per 1,000 pop. **Telephone lines:** 8.2 per 100 pop. **Mobile:** 97.7 per 100 pop. **Internet:** 39.5%.

Health: Life expect.: 65.8 male; 71.5 female. **Births:** 23.3 per 1,000 pop. **Deaths:** 6.6 per 1,000 pop. **Natural inc.:** 1.67% **Infant mortality:** 38.6 per 1,000 live births. **HIV:** 0.3%.

Education: Compulsory: ages 4-17. **Literacy:** 95.7%.

Embassy: 3014 Massachusetts Ave. NW 20008; 483-4410.

Website: www.bolivia.gob.bo

The Incas conquered the region's earlier Indian inhabitants in the 13th cent. Spanish rule began in the 1530s and lasted until Aug. 6, 1825. The country is named after independence fighter Simón Bolívar. In a series of wars, Bolivia lost its Pacific coast to Chile, the oil-bearing Chaco to Paraguay, and rubber-growing areas to Brazil, 1879-1935.

Economic unrest, especially among militant mine workers, has led to continuing political instability. A reformist government under Victor Paz Estenssoro, 1951-64, nationalized tin mines and attempted to improve conditions for the Indian majority but was overthrown by a military junta. A series of coups and countercoups continued until constitutional government was restored in 1982.

U.S. pressure on the government to reduce coca output, the raw material for cocaine, has led to clashes between police and growers and increased anti-U.S. feeling among Bolivians. Gen. Hugo Banzer Suárez, who ruled as a dictator, 1971-78, later governed as president, 1997-2001.

After an inconclusive presidential election June 2002, Congress chose Gonzalo Sánchez de Lozada, a U.S.-educated mining executive, as head of state. He quit Oct. 17, 2003, after indigenous Bolivians staged a month of antigovernment protests in which over 70 people died. His successor, Vice Pres. Carlos D. Mesa Gisbert, was embroiled in controversies over energy policy.

Juan Evo Morales Ayma, a leftist and coca-farmer advocate, won the presidential election, Dec. 2005. He nationalized the hydrocarbon sector, launched a land-redistribution program to benefit poor farmers, and tightened ties with Venezuela and Cuba. He faced resistance and demands for autonomy from leaders of Bolivia's relatively prosperous lowland provinces. Voters, Jan. 25, 2009, approved a new constitution strengthening the rights of Bolivia's indigenous majority and increasing federal control over the country's natural resources. Morales won a second term Dec. 6, 2009, and his Movement Toward Socialism consolidated its hold over Bolivia's legislature. Morales nationalized a Spanish utility company, May 1, 2012, that served about 74% of the country, and 2 others Dec. 29, 2012.

Bosnia and Herzegovina

People: Population: 3,871,643. **Age distrib.:** <15: 13.7%; 65+: 13.3%. **Pop. density:** 195.9 per sq mi, 75.6 per sq km. **Urban:** 39.6%. **Ethnic groups:** Bosniak 48%, Serb 37%, Croat 14%. **Languages:** Bosnian, Croatian (both official); Serbian. **Religions:** Muslim 40%, Orthodox 31%, Roman Catholic 15%.

Geography: Total area: 19,767 sq mi, 51,197 sq km; **Land area:** 19,763 sq mi, 51,187 sq km. **Location:** On Balkan Peninsula in SE Europe. **Neighbors:** Serbia, Montenegro on E and SE, Croatia on N and W. **Topography:** Hilly with some mountains. About 36% of the land is forested. **Capital:** Sarajevo, 321,714.

Government: Type: Federal democratic republic. **Heads of state:** Collective presidency with rotating leadership every 8 months. **Head of gov.:** Prime Min. Vjekoslav Bevanda; b. May 13, 1956; in office: Jan. 12, 2012. **Local divisions:** 2 first-order admin. divisions, 1 internationally supervised district. **Defense budget** (2012): $231 mil. **Active troops:** 10,500.

Economy: Industries: steel, coal, mining, vehicle assembly, textiles, tobacco prods., wooden furniture, ammunition, domestic appliances, oil refining. **Chief crops:** wheat, corn, fruits, vegetables. **Natural resources:** coal, iron ore, bauxite, copper, lead, zinc, chromite, cobalt, manganese, nickel, clay, gypsum, salt, sand, timber, hydropower. **Arable land:** 19.7%. **Livestock:** cattle: 446,893; chickens: 24.5 mil; goats: 69,369; pigs: 529,644; sheep: 1 mil. **Electricity prod.:** 14.6 bil kWh. **Labor force:** agric. 18.9%, industry 29.8%, services 51.3%. **Unemployment:** 28.2%.

Finance: Monetary unit: Convertible Marka (BAM) (Sept. 2014: 1.49 = $1 U.S.). **GDP:** $32.2 bil; **per capita GDP:** $8,300; **GDP growth:** 0.8%. **Imports:** $10.3 bil; Germany 11.4%, Russian Federation 9.9%, Serbia 9.8%, Italy 9.7%, China 6%, Slovenia 5%, Croatia 12.8%. **Exports:** $5.7 bil; Germany 15.6%, Croatia 14.2%, Italy 12.1%, Serbia 9.1%, Austria 8.2%, Slovenia 8.1%. **Tourism:** $689 mil. **Budget:** $7.5 bil. **Total reserves less gold:** $4.9 bil. **Gold:** 96,000 oz t. **Inflation:** –0.1%.

Transport: Railways: 373 mi. **Civil aviation:** 7 airports. **Chief ports:** Bosanski Samac, Brcko.

Communications: TV sets: 282 per 1,000 pop. **Radios:** 251 per 1,000 pop. **Telephone lines:** 23.2 per 100 pop. **Mobile:** 91.2 per 100 pop. **Internet:** 67.9%.

Health: Life expect.: 73.3 male; 79.6 female. **Births:** 8.9 per 1,000 pop. **Deaths:** 9.6 per 1,000 pop. **Natural inc.:** –0.08%. **Infant mortality:** 5.8 per 1,000 live births. **HIV:** NA.

Education: Compulsory: ages 6-14. **Literacy:** 98.5%.

Embassy: 2109 E St. NW 20037; 337-1500.

Website: www.fbihvlada.gov.ba

Bosnia was ruled by Croatian kings c. 958 CE, and by Hungary 1000-1200. It became organized c. 1200 and later took control of Herzegovina. The kingdom disintegrated after 1391, with the southern part becoming the independent duchy of Herzegovina. It was conquered by Turks in 1463 and made a Turkish province. The area was placed under control of Austria-Hungary in 1878 and made part of the province of Bosnia and Herzegovina, which was formally annexed to Austria-Hungary, 1908. Bosnia became a province of Yugoslavia in 1918. It was reunited with Herzegovina as a federated republic in the 1946 Yugoslav constitution.

Bosnia and Herzegovina declared sovereignty Oct. 15, 1991. A referendum for independence was passed Feb. 29, 1992. Ethnic Serbs' opposition to the referendum spurred violent clashes and bombings. The U.S. and EU recognized the republic Apr. 7. Fierce 3-way fighting continued between Bosnia's Serbs, Muslims, and Croats. Serb forces massacred thousands of Bosnian Muslims and engaged in ethnic cleansing, expelling Muslims and other non-Serbs from areas under Bosnian Serb control. The capital, Sarajevo, was surrounded and besieged by Bosnian Serb forces. Muslims and Croats in Bosnia began a cease-fire Feb. 23, 1994, and signed an accord, Mar. 18, to create a Muslim-Croat confederation in Bosnia. However, by mid-1994, Bosnian Serbs controlled over 70% of the country.

As fighting continued in 1995, the balance of power shifted toward the Muslim-Croat alliance. Massive NATO air strikes at Bosnian Serb targets beginning Aug. 30 triggered a new round of peace talks, and the siege of Sarajevo was lifted Sept. 15. The new talks produced an agreement to create autonomous regions within Bosnia, with the Serb region (Republika Srpska) constituting 49% of the country. A Croat-Muslim offensive in Sept. recaptured significant territory, leaving Bosnian Serbs in control of approximately half that percentage.

A Nov. 1995 peace agreement was signed in Paris, Dec. 14, 1995, by leaders of Bosnia, Croatia, and Serbia. Some 60,000 NATO troops (about 20,000 from the U.S.) moved in to police the accord. Meanwhile, a UN tribunal began bringing charges against suspected war criminals. Elections were held Sept. 14, 1996, for a 3-person collective presidency, for seats in a federal parliament, and for regional offices. In Dec. a revamped NATO Stabilization Force (SFOR) of over 30,000 members (more than 8,000 from the U.S.) received an 18-month mandate, which was later extended.

The UN tribunal found Radislav Krstic, a Bosnian Serb general, guilty Aug. 2, 2001, in connection with the genocide of thousands of Muslims at Srebrenica in 1995. An EU peacekeeping force (EUFOR), with 7,000 members, assumed responsibility from SFOR, Dec. 2, 2004. Accused of complicity in the Sarajevo and Srebrenica atrocities, former Bosnian Serb leader Radovan Karadzic was arrested in Serbia, July 21, 2008, and handed over to the UN tribunal at The Hague, Netherlands. He was charged with 10 counts of genocide, war crimes, and crimes against humanity; the prosecution rested its case in May and Karadzic began his defense Oct. 16, 2012. Also extradited to The Hague was Gen. Ratko Mladic, the former Bosnian Serb military commander accused of directing the Srebrenica massacre, who was arrested in Serbia May 26, 2011. He faced 11 counts of war crimes and crimes against humanity, 2 of them for genocide, in a trial that began May 16, 2012. As the security situation in Bosnia improved, EUFOR strength dropped to about 1,600 troops as of Aug. 2012. On Dec. 12, 2012, Mladic's close associate Zdravko Tolimir was convicted of genocide and sentenced to life in prison.

The government's failure to renew a law allowing it to issue personal ID numbers—for example, to newborns—prompted protests June 5-6, 2013. Violent protests occurred in Feb. 2014 in Sarajevo and other areas, triggered by high unemployment and alleged government corruption and inefficiency.

Botswana
Republic of Botswana

People: Population: 2,155,784. **Age distrib.:** <15: 32.9%; 65+: 4%. **Pop. density:** 9.9 per sq mi, 3.8 per sq km. **Urban:** 57.2%. **Ethnic groups:** Tswana or Setswana 79%, Kalanga 11%, Basarwa 3%, other (incl. Kgalagadi, white) 7%. **Languages:** Setswana, Kalanga, Sekgalagadi, English (official). **Religions:** Christian 72%, Badimo 6%, none 21%.

Geography: Total area: 224,607 sq mi, 581,730 sq km; **Land area:** 218,816 sq mi, 566,730 sq km. **Location:** In southern Africa. **Neighbors:** Namibia on N and W, South Africa on S, Zimbabwe on NE; Botswana claims border with Zambia on N. **Topography:** The Kalahari Desert, supporting nomadic Bushmen and wildlife, spreads over SW; there are swamplands and farming areas in N, and rolling plains in E where livestock are grazed. **Capital:** Gaborone, 246,562.

Government: Type: Parliamentary republic. **Head of state and gov.:** Pres. Seretse Khama Ian Khama; b. Feb. 27, 1953; in office: Apr. 1, 2008. **Local divisions:** 10 districts, 6 town councils. **Defense budget:** $438 mil. **Active troops:** 9,000.

Economy: Industries: diamonds, copper, nickel, salt, soda ash, potash, coal, iron ore, silver. **Chief crops:** sorghum, maize, millet, beans, sunflowers, groundnuts. **Natural resources:** diamonds, copper, nickel, salt, soda ash, potash, coal, iron ore, silver. **Arable land:** 0.5%. **Livestock:** cattle: 2.5 mil; chickens: 5.5 mil; goats: 1.7 mil; pigs: 13,500; sheep: 290,000. **Electricity prod.:** 350 mil kWh. **Labor force:** NA. **Unemployment:** 17.7%.

Finance: Monetary unit: Pula (BWP) (Sept. 2014: 8.93 = $1 U.S.). **GDP:** $34 bil; **per capita GDP:** $16,400; **GDP growth:** 3.9%. **Imports:** $7.4 bil. **Exports:** $7.6 bil. **Tourism:** $34 mil. **Budget:** $5 bil. **Total reserves less gold:** $7.7 bil. **Inflation:** 5.9%.

Transport: Railways: 552 mi. **Motor vehicles:** 179 per 1,000 pop. **Civil aviation:** 10 airports.

Communications: TV sets: 44 per 1,000 pop. **Radios:** 734 per 1,000 pop. **Telephone lines:** 8.6 per 100 pop. **Mobile:** 160.6 per 100 pop. **Internet:** 15%.

Health: Life expect.: 55.8 male; 52.3 female. **Births:** 21.3 per 1,000 pop. **Deaths:** 13.3 per 1,000 pop. **Natural inc.:** 0.80%. **Infant mortality:** 9.4 per 1,000 live births. **HIV:** 21.9%.

Education: Compulsory: ages 6-15. **Literacy:** 88.5%.

Embassy: 1531-1533 New Hampshire Ave. NW 20036; 244-4990.

Website: www.gov.bw

First inhabited by Bushmen, then Bantus, the region became the British protectorate of Bechuanaland in 1886. The country became fully independent Sept. 30, 1966. Cattle raising and mining (diamonds, copper, nickel) have contributed to economic growth. Pres. Festus Mogae transferred power Apr. 1, 2008, to Seretse Khama Ian Khama, son of Botswana's independence leader and first president (1966-80), Sir Seretse Khama. In power since independence, the Botswana Democratic Party dominated national elections Oct. 16, 2009, and Ian Khama was sworn in for a full term Oct. 20. De Beers, the world's largest diamond producer, moved its diamond-sorting operations from London to Botswana in 2012.

Brazil
Federative Republic of Brazil

People: Population: 202,656,788. **Age distrib.:** <15: 23.8%; 65+: 7.6%. **Pop. density:** 62 per sq mi, 24 per sq km. **Urban:** 85.4%. **Ethnic groups:** white 48%, mulatto (mixed white and black) 43%, black 8%. **Languages:** Portuguese (official). **Religions:** Roman Catholic 65%, Protestant 22%, Spiritualist 2%, none 8%.

Geography: Total area: 3,287,612 sq mi, 8,514,877 sq km; **Land area:** 3,266,199 sq mi, 8,459,417 sq km. **Location:** Occupies E half of South America. **Neighbors:** French Guiana, Suriname, Guyana, Venezuela on N; Colombia, Peru, Bolivia, Paraguay, on W; Argentina, Uruguay on S. **Topography:** Brazil's Atlantic coastline stretches 4,603 mi. In N is the heavily wooded Amazon basin covering half the country. Its network of rivers is navigable for 15,814 mi. The Amazon itself flows 2,093 mi in Brazil, all navigable. The NE region is semiarid scrubland, heavily settled and poor. The S central region, favored by climate and resources, has almost half of the pop. The narrow coastal belt includes most of the major cities. Almost the entire country has a tropical or semitropical climate. **Capital:** Brasília, 4,073,720. **Cities (urban aggl.):** São Paulo, 20,830,857; Rio de Janeiro, 12,825,373; Belo Horizonte, 5,667,398.

Government: Type: Federal republic. **Head of state and gov.:** Pres. Dilma Rousseff; b. Dec. 14, 1947; in office: Jan. 1, 2011. **Local divisions:** 26 states, 1 federal district. **Defense budget:** $34.73 bil. **Active troops:** 318,500.

Economy: Industries: textiles, shoes, chemicals, cement, lumber, iron ore, tin, steel, aircraft, motor vehicles and parts. **Chief crops:** coffee, soybeans, wheat, rice, corn, sugarcane, cocoa, citrus. **Natural resources:** bauxite, gold, iron ore, manganese, nickel, phosphates, platinum, tin, rare earth elements, uranium, petroleum hydropower, timber. **Crude oil reserves:** 13.2 bil bbls. **Arable land:** 8.7%. **Livestock:** cattle: 217.4 mil; chickens: 1.3 bil; goats: 8.8 mil; pigs: 39 mil; sheep: 17 mil. **Electricity prod.:** 530.4 bil kWh. **Labor force:** agric. 15.7%, industry 13.3%, services 71%. **Unemployment:** 6.9%.

Finance: Monetary unit: Real (BRL) (Sept. 2014: 2.24 = $1 U.S.). **GDP:** $2.4 tril; **per capita GDP:** $12,100; **GDP growth:** 2.3%. **Imports:** $241.4 bil; China 15.3%, U.S. 14.6%, Argentina 7.4%, Germany 6.4%, South Korea 4.1%. **Exports:** $244.8 bil; China 17%, U.S. 11.1%, Argentina 7.4%, Netherlands 6.2%. **Tourism:** $6.7 bil. **Budget:** $815.6 bil. **Total reserves less gold:** $356.2 bil. **Gold:** 2.2 mil oz t. **Inflation:** 6.2%.

Transport: Railways: 17,733 mi. **Motor vehicles:** 197.5 per 1,000 pop. **Civil aviation:** 65.7 bil pass.-mi; 698 airports. **Chief ports:** Ilha Grande, Paranagua, Rio Grande, Santos, São Sebastião, Tubarão.

Communications: TV sets: 279 per 1,000 pop. **Radios:** 255 per 1,000 pop. **Telephone lines:** 22.3 per 100 pop. **Mobile:** 135.3 per 100 pop. **Internet:** 51.6%.

Health: Life expect.: 69.7 male; 77.0 female. **Births:** 14.7 per 1,000 pop. **Deaths:** 6.5 per 1,000 pop. **Natural inc.:** 0.82%. **Infant mortality:** 19.2 per 1,000 live births. **HIV:** 0.6%.

Education: Compulsory: ages 6-14. **Literacy:** 92.6%.

Embassy: 3006 Massachusetts Ave. NW 20008; 238-2700.

Website: www.brasil.gov.br

Pedro Álvares Cabral, a Portuguese navigator, is generally credited as the first European to reach Brazil, in 1500. The country was thinly settled by various Indian tribes. Only a few survive today, mostly in the Amazon Basin.

In the next centuries, Portuguese colonists gradually pushed inland, bringing along large numbers of African slaves. (Slavery was not abolished until 1888.) The king of Portugal, fleeing Napoleon's army, moved the seat of government to Brazil in 1808. Brazil thereupon became a kingdom under Dom Joao VI. After João VI returned to Portugal, his son Pedro proclaimed Brazil's independence, Sept. 7, 1822, and was crowned emperor. The second emperor, Dom Pedro II, was deposed in 1889, and a republic proclaimed, called the United States of Brazil. It was renamed the Federative Republic of Brazil in 1967.

A military junta took control in 1930; Getulio Vargas assumed dictatorial power. The military forced him out in 1945. A democratic regime prevailed 1945-64, during which time the capital was moved from Rio de Janeiro to Brasília. Military-backed governments ruled Brazil for the next 20 years. Censorship was imposed, and the opposition was suppressed.

Brazil became the leading industrial power of Latin America by the 1970s, while agricultural output soared. By the 1990s, Brazil had one of the world's largest economies; income was poorly distributed, however, and more than one in four Brazilians survived on less than $1 a day. Despite protective environmental legislation, development has destroyed much of the Amazon ecosystem.

Democratic presidential elections held in 1985 brought civilian rule back. Fernando Collor de Mello was elected president, Dec. 1989. In Sept. 1992, Collor was impeached for corruption. He resigned as his trial was beginning, and acting Pres. Itamar Franco was officially sworn in. Fernando Henrique Cardoso won Oct. 1994 and 1998 elections; he guided Brazil through a series of financial crises.

A new civil code guaranteeing legal equality for women was enacted Aug. 15, 2001. With Brazil's debt exceeding $260 bil, the IMF approved a $30-bil loan Aug. 2002. Luiz Inácio Lula da Silva, a union leader and reformer, won a presidential runoff, Oct. 2002. Brazil's space program launched its first rocket into space Oct. 23, 2004.

A top aide to Pres. Lula resigned June 16, 2005, amid allegations the ruling party bribed legislators for votes; he and 2 others involved in the scandal were found guilty and sentenced to upwards of 40 years in prison Oct.-Nov. 2012. Despite this and other scandals, Lula won a second presidential term, Oct. 2006. The nation reported huge offshore oil finds in 2007-08. Lula's former chief of staff, Dilma Rousseff, won a runoff election Oct. 31, 2010, and took office as Brazil's first woman president Jan. 1, 2011. Brazilian police raided Rocinha, Rio de Janeiro's largest slum, Nov. 13, 2011, as part of an effort to bring law to the entire city as it prepared to host the men's soccer World Cup in 2014 and the Olympic Games in 2016. The World Cup tournament took place without major problems June 12-July 13, 2014. Unsafe building conditions and a band's careless use of pyrotechnics caused a deadly fire at the Kiss nightclub in Santa Maria Jan. 27, 2013, that killed more than 230 patrons. Brazil's independent Public Ministry announced Apr. 6, 2013, an investigation into former Pres. Lula for buying votes and for channeling funds into the Workers' Party. After 10 months of sporadic demonstrations over planned increases in the cost of public transportation, fares were raised June 1, 2013, and demonstrations began in São Paulo June 6 and quickly spread to Rio de Janeiro and other cities. Protesters turned their attention to other problems, including a lack of public services and government corruption, and protests continued even after fares were lowered June 20. Demonstrators also targeted the $52-mil price tag of Pope Francis's historic visit the week of July 23, 2013.

Brunei
Brunei Darussalam

People: Population: 422,675. **Age distrib.:** <15: 24.2%; 65+: 4%. **Pop. density:** 207.9 per sq mi, 80.3 per sq km. **Urban:** 76.9%. **Ethnic groups:** Malay 66%, Chinese 10%, other indigenous 3%. **Languages:** Malay (official), English, Chinese. **Religions:** Muslim (official) 79%, Christian 9%, Buddhist 8%, other (incl. indigenous beliefs) 5%.

Geography: Total area: 2,226 sq mi, 5,765 sq km; **Land area:** 2,033 sq mi, 5,265 sq km. **Location:** In SE Asia, on the N coast of the island of Borneo; it is surrounded on its landward side by the Malaysian state of Sarawak. **Topography:** Brunei has a narrow coastal plain, with mountains in E, hilly lowlands in W. There are swamps in W and NE. Climate is tropical. **Capital:** Bandar Seri Begawan, 14,025.

Government: Type: Constitutional sultanate. **Head of state and gov.:** Sultan and Prime Min. Sir Muda Hassanal Bolkiah Mu'izzadin Waddaulah; b. July 15, 1946; in office: Jan. 1, 1984 (sultan since Oct. 5, 1967). **Local divisions:** 4 districts. **Defense budget:** $416 mil. **Active troops:** 7,000.

Economy: Industries: petroleum, petroleum refining, liquefied nat. gas, constr. **Chief crops:** rice, vegetables, fruits. **Natural resources:** petroleum, nat. gas, timber. **Crude oil reserves:** 1.1 bil bbls. **Arable land:** 0.8%. **Livestock:** cattle: 800; chickens: 19 mil; goats: 6,950; pigs: 1,225; sheep: 4,000. **Electricity prod.:** 3.5 bil kWh. **Labor force:** agric. 4.2%, industry 62.8%, services 33%. **Unemployment:** 3.8%.

Finance: Monetary unit: Dollar (BND) (Sept. 2014: 1.25 = $1 U.S.). **GDP:** $22.3 bil; **per capita GDP:** $54,800; **GDP growth:** 1.4%. **Imports** (2011): $3 bil; Singapore 26.3%, China 21.3%, UK 21.3%, Malaysia 11.8%. **Exports** (2011): $12.8 bil; Japan 45.7%, South Korea 15.1%, Australia 9.1%, New Zealand 6.6%, India 5.8%, Vietnam 4.7%. **Tourism:** $191 mil. **Budget:** $5.4 bil. **Total reserves less gold:** $3.4 bil. **Gold:** 146,747 oz t. **Inflation:** 0.4%.

Transport: Motor vehicles: 543.6 per 1,000 pop. **Civil aviation:** 3.1 bil pass.-mi; 1 airport. **Chief ports:** Lumut, Muara, Seria.

Communications: TV sets: 629 per 1,000 pop. **Radios:** 300 per 1,000 pop. **Telephone lines:** 13.6 per 100 pop. **Mobile:** 112.2 per 100 pop. **Internet:** 64.5%.

Health: Life expect.: 74.5 male; 79.2 female. **Births:** 17.5 per 1,000 pop. **Deaths:** 3.5 per 1,000 pop. **Natural inc.:** 1.40%. **Infant mortality:** 10.5 per 1,000 live births. **HIV:** NA.

Education: Compulsory: ages 6-14. **Literacy:** 96%.

Embassy: 3520 International Ct. NW 20008; 237-1838.

Website: www.gov.bn

The Sultanate of Brunei was a powerful state in the early 16th cent., with authority over all of the island of Borneo as well as parts of the Sulu Islands and the Philippines. In 1888, a treaty placed the state under the protection of Great Britain.

Brunei became a fully sovereign and independent state on Jan. 1, 1984. The country fielded female athletes for the first time at the 2012 Summer Olympic Games. Brunei began enacting, May 1, 2014, a new penal code based on Islamic law. If fully implemented in future years, the code will make theft punishable by whipping or limb amputation, and adultery and gay sex will become capital crimes.

Bulgaria
Republic of Bulgaria

People: Population: 6,924,716. **Age distrib.:** <15: 14.2%; 65+: 19.3%. **Pop. density:** 165.3 per sq mi, 63.8 per sq km. **Urban:** 73.6%. **Ethnic groups:** Bulgarian 77%, Turkish 8%, Roma 4%. **Languages:** Bulgarian (official), Turkish, Roma. **Religions:** Eastern Orthodox 60%, Muslim 8%, other (incl. Catholic, Protestant, Armenian Apostolic Orthodox, Judaism) 2%, none 4%.

Geography: Total area: 42,811 sq mi, 110,879 sq km; **Land area:** 41,888 sq mi, 108,489 sq km. **Location:** SE Europe, in E Balkan Peninsula on Black Sea. **Neighbors:** Romania on N; Serbia, Macedonia on W; Greece, Turkey on S. **Topography:** The Stara Planina (Balkan) Mts. stretch E-W across the center of the country, with the Danubian plain on N, the Rhodope Mts. on SW, and Thracian Plain on SE. **Capital:** Sofia, 1,221,930.

Government: Type: Parliamentary democracy. **Head of state:** Pres. Rosen Plevneliev; b. May 14, 1964; in office: Jan. 22, 2012. **Head of gov.:** Prime Min. Plamen Oresharski; b. Feb. 21, 1960; in office: May 29, 2013. **Local divisions:** 28 provinces. **Defense budget:** $751 mil. **Active troops:** 31,300.

Economy: Industries: utilities, food, beverages, tobacco, machinery and equip. **Chief crops:** vegetables, fruits, tobacco, wine, wheat, barley, sunflowers, sugar beets. **Natural resources:** bauxite, copper, lead, zinc, coal, timber. **Crude oil reserves:** 15 mil bbls. **Arable land:** 30.6%. **Livestock:** cattle: 526,112; chickens: 13.8 mil; goats: 293,639; pigs: 530,945; sheep: 1.4 mil. **Electricity prod.:** 46.7 bil kWh. **Labor force:** agric. 7.1%, industry 35.2%, services 57.7%. **Unemployment:** 12.3%.

Finance: Monetary unit: Lev (BGN) (Sept. 2014: 1.49 = $1 U.S.). **GDP:** $104.6 bil; **per capita GDP:** $14,400; **GDP growth:** 0.5%. **Imports:** $32.9 bil; Russia 20.9%, Germany 11.3%, Italy 6.7%, Romania 6.6%, Greece 6.1%, Turkey 4.6%, Spain 4.5%. **Exports:** $27.9 bil; Germany 10.4%, Turkey 9.1%, Italy 8.7%, Romania 8.2%, Greece 7.3%, France 4%. **Tourism:** $4.1 bil. **Budget:** $20.1 bil. **Total reserves less gold:** $18.3 bil. **Gold:** 1.3 mil oz t. **Inflation:** 0.9%.

Transport: Railways: 2,580 mi. **Motor vehicles:** 471.2 per 1,000 pop. **Civil aviation:** 769.9 mil pass.-mi; 57 airports. **Chief ports:** Burgas, Varna.

Communications: TV sets: 429 per 1,000 pop. **Radios:** 553 per 1,000 pop. **Telephone lines:** 26.9 per 100 pop. **Mobile:** 145.2 per 100 pop. **Internet:** 53.1%.

Health: Life expect.: 70.7 male; 78.1 female. **Births:** 8.9 per 1,000 pop. **Deaths:** 14.3 per 1,000 pop. **Natural inc.:** −0.54%. **Infant mortality:** 15.1 per 1,000 live births. **HIV:** NA.

Education: Compulsory: ages 7-14. **Literacy:** 98.4%.
Embassy: 1621 22nd St. NW 20008; 387-0174.
Website: www.government.bg

Bulgaria was settled by Slavs in the 6th cent. Turkic Bulgars arrived in the 7th cent., merged with the Slavs, became Christians by the 9th cent., and set up powerful empires in the 10th and 12th cents. Ottomans took over in 1396 and ruled for nearly 500 years.

An 1876 revolt led to an independent kingdom in 1908. Bulgaria expanded after the first Balkan War but lost its Aegean coastline in WWI, when it sided with Germany. Bulgaria joined the Axis in WWII but withdrew in 1944. Communists took power with Soviet aid; the monarchy was abolished Sept. 8, 1946.

On Nov. 10, 1989, Communist Party leader and head of state Todor Zhivkov, resigned after 35 years. In Jan. 1990, Parliament voted to revoke the constitutionally guaranteed dominant role of the Communist Party. A new constitution took effect July 13, 1991.

Bulgaria became a full member of NATO, Apr. 2, 2004, and entered the EU, Jan. 1, 2007. Restrictions on Bulgarians' right to work in 9 other EU nations ended Jan. 1, 2014.

A terrorist blew up a bus carrying Israeli tourists, July 18, 2012, leaving 5 Israelis, the Bulgarian bus driver, and the bomber dead. An investigation ending Feb. 5, 2013, blamed the attack on the Muslim militant group Hezbollah, which denied involvement. The identity of the bomber, a Lebanese-French citizen, was determined by DNA evidence in July 2014.

Worsening economic conditions during 2012-13 inspired protests, including instances of self-immolation. They began on Jan 28, 2013, in Blagoevgrad and spread to other cities in Feb., leading Prime Min. Boyko Borisov to submit his government's resignation Feb. 20, 2013. No clear winner emerged from May 12 elections. Parliament elected Plamen Oresharski, with no party affiliation, prime min. May 29. Forty days of protests against ineffectual government came to a head July 24, 2013, in Sofia, when police clashed violently with demonstrators outside parliament, injuring about 20 unarmed protesters. Amid a banking crisis that began in June 2014, Oresharski resigned July 23, and elections were scheduled for Oct. 5.

Burkina Faso

People: Population: 18,365,123. **Age distrib.:** <15: 45.4%; 65+: 2.5%. **Pop. density:** 173.7 per sq mi, 67.1 per sq km. **Urban:** 29%. **Ethnic groups:** Mossi 40%+, other (incl. Gurunsi, Senufo, Lobi, Bobo, Mande, Fulani) approx. 60%. **Languages:** French (official), native African Sudanic-family langs. **Religions:** Muslim 61%, Catholic 19%, animist 15%, Protestant 4%.

Geography: Total area: 105,869 sq mi, 274,200 sq km; **Land area:** 105,715 sq mi, 273,800 sq km. **Location:** In W Africa, S of the Sahara. **Neighbors:** Mali on NW; Niger on NE; Benin, Togo, Ghana, Côte d'Ivoire on S. **Topography:** Landlocked in the savanna region of W Africa. The N is arid, hot, and thinly populated. **Capital:** Ouagadougou, 2,565,190.

Government: Type: Parliamentary republic. **Head of state:** Pres. Blaise Compaoré; b. Feb. 3, 1951; in office: Oct. 15, 1987. **Head of gov.:** Prime Min. Luc Adolphe Tiao; b. June 4, 1954; in office: Apr. 18, 2011. **Local divisions:** 13 regions. **Defense budget** $153 mil. **Active troops:** 11,200.

Economy: Industries: cotton lint, beverages, agric. proc., soap, cigarettes, textiles, gold. **Chief crops:** cotton, peanuts, shea nuts, sesame, sorghum, millet. **Natural resources:** manganese, limestone, marble, gold, phosphates, pumice, salt. **Arable land:** 21.9%. **Livestock:** cattle: 8.8 mil; chickens: 42.5 mil; goats: 13.3 mil; pigs: 2.3 mil; sheep: 8.9 mil. **Electricity prod.:** 579 mil kWh. **Labor force:** agric. 90%, industry and services 10%. **Unemployment:** 3.3%.

Finance: Monetary unit: CFA Franc (XOF) (Sept. 2014: 498.91 = $1 U.S.). **GDP:** $26.5 bil; **per capita GDP:** $1,500; **GDP growth:** 6.5%. **Imports:** $2.9 bil; Côte d'Ivoire 17.6%, France 15.2%, Ghana 4.8%, Togo 4.4%. **Exports:** $2.8 bil; China 25.9%, Turkey 24.8%, Belgium 5.2%. **Tourism:** $133 mil. **Budget:** $3.2 bil. **Total reserves less gold:** $628.5 mil. **Inflation:** 0.5%.

Transport: Railways: 386 mi. **Motor vehicles:** 11.1 per 1,000 pop. **Civil aviation:** 2 airports.

Communications: TV sets: 19 per 1,000 pop. **Radios:** 111 per 1,000 pop. **Telephone lines:** 0.8 per 100 pop. **Mobile:** 66.4 per 100 pop. **Internet:** 4.4%.

Health: Life expect.: 52.8 male; 56.9 female. **Births:** 42.4 per 1,000 pop. **Deaths:** 12.0 per 1,000 pop. **Natural inc.:** 3.05% **Infant mortality:** 76.8 per 1,000 live births. **HIV:** 0.9%.

Education: Compulsory: ages 6-15. **Literacy:** 36%.
Embassy: 2340 Massachusetts Ave. NW 20008; 332-5577.
Website: www.primature.gov.bf or burkina-usa.org

The Mossi people entered Burkina Faso in the 11th-13th cents. Their kingdoms ruled until they were defeated by the Mali and Songhai empires.

French control came by 1896, but Upper Volta (renamed Burkina Faso on Aug. 4, 1984) was not established as a separate territory until 1947. Independence came Aug. 5, 1960, and a pro-French government was elected. The military seized power in 1980. A 1987 coup established the current regime, which instituted a multiparty system in the early 1990s. Pres. Blaise Compaoré most recently won reelection, Nov. 21, 2010. The country, among the world's poorest, depends heavily on foreign aid.

Burma
See Myanmar.

Burundi
Republic of Burundi

People: Population: 10,395,931. **Age distrib.:** <15: 45.7%; 65+: 2.5%. **Pop. density:** 1,048.5 per sq mi, 404.8 per sq km. **Urban:** 11.8%. **Ethnic groups:** Hutu (Bantu) 85%, Tutsi (Hamitic) 14%, Twa (Pygmy) 1%. **Languages:** Kirundi, French (both official). **Religions:** Catholic 62%, Protestant 24% (incl. Adventist 2%), Muslim 3%.

Geography: Total area: 10,745 sq mi, 27,830 sq km; **Land area:** 9,915 sq mi, 25,680 sq km. **Location:** In central Africa. **Neighbors:** Rwanda on N, Dem. Rep. of the Congo on W, Tanzania on E and S. **Topography:** Much of the country is grassy highland, with mountains reaching 8,900 ft. The southernmost source of the White Nile is located in Burundi. Lake Tanganyika is the second deepest lake in the world. **Capital:** Bujumbura, 707,191.

Government: Type: Republic. **Head of state and gov.:** Pres. Pierre Nkurunziza; b. Dec. 18, 1963; in office: Aug. 26, 2005. **Local divisions:** 17 provinces. **Defense budget:** $64 mil. **Active troops:** 20,000.

Economy: Industries: light consumer goods, assembly of imported components, public works constr., food proc. **Chief crops:** coffee, cotton, tea, corn; sorghum, sweet potatoes, bananas, cassava. **Natural resources:** nickel, uranium, rare earth oxides, peat, cobalt, copper, platinum, vanadium, hydropower, niobium, tantalum, gold, tin, tungsten, kaolin, limestone. **Arable land:** 42.8%. **Livestock:** cattle: 777,786; chickens: 2.7 mil; goats: 2.5 mil; pigs: 434,204; sheep: 352,722. **Electricity prod.:** 152 mil kWh. **Labor force:** agric. 93.6%, industry 2.3%, services 4.1%. **Unemployment:** 7.7%.

Finance: Monetary unit: Franc (BIF) (Sept. 2014: 1,525.00 = $1 U.S.). **GDP:** $5.8 bil; **per capita GDP:** $600; **GDP growth:** 4.5%. **Imports:** $867.2 mil; Saudi Arabia 11.3%, Belgium 10.1%, China 9.1%, India 7.9%, Tanzania 6.5%, Kenya 6%, Uganda 5.7%, Zambia 4.6%, U.S. 4.1%. **Exports:** $122.8 mil; Switzerland 23.9%, UK 12.9%, Belgium 7.4%, Pakistan 7.4%, Dem. Rep. of the Congo 7.4%, Uganda 5.6%, Germany 5.2%, China 4.9%, Egypt 4.7%. **Tourism:** $2 mil. **Budget:** $855.8 mil. **Total reserves less gold:** $328.2 mil. **Gold:** 961 oz t. **Inflation:** 7.9%.

Transport: Motor vehicles: 5.7 per 1,000 pop. **Civil aviation:** 1 airport. **Chief port:** Bujumbura.

Communications: TV sets: 36 per 1,000 pop. **Radios:** 166 per 1,000 pop. **Telephone lines** 0.2 per 100 pop. **Mobile:** 25 per 100 pop. **Internet:** 1.3%.

Health: Life expect.: 57.9 male; 61.2 female. **Births:** 42.3 per 1,000 pop. **Deaths:** 9.5 per 1,000 pop. **Natural inc.:** 3.28%. **Infant mortality:** 63.4 per 1,000 live births. **HIV:** 1.0%.

Education: Compulsory: ages NA. **Literacy:** 85.6%.

Embassy: 2233 Wisconsin Ave. NW, Ste. 408, 20007; 342-2574. **Website:** www.burundi-gov.bi or www.burundiembassydc-usa.org

The pygmy Twa were the first inhabitants, followed by Bantu Hutus, who were conquered in the 16th cent. by the Tutsi (Watusi), probably from Ethiopia. Germany gained control in 1899. Belgium took over in 1916, successively exercising a League of Nations mandate and UN trusteeship (now the 2 countries of Rwanda and Burundi). Burundi became independent July 1, 1962.

An unsuccessful Hutu rebellion in 1972-73 left 10,000 Tutsi and 150,000 Hutu dead. Over 100,000 Hutu fled to Tanzania and Zaire (now Dem. Rep. of the Congo). In the 1980s, Burundi's Tutsi-dominated regime pledged itself to ethnic reconciliation and democratic reform. In the nation's first democratic presidential election, June 1993, a Hutu, Melchior Ndadaye, was elected. He was killed in an attempted coup, Oct. 21, 1993. At least 150,000 Burundians died in ethnic conflicts over the next 3 years. Pres. Cyprien Ntaryamira, elected Jan. 1994, was killed with the president of Rwanda in a mysterious plane crash, Apr. 6. The incident sparked massive carnage in Rwanda; violence in Burundi, initially far more limited, intensified in 1995. Ethnic strife continued after a military coup, July 25, 1996. Former South African Pres. Nelson Mandela mediated peace talks from Dec. 1999; most warring groups signed a draft peace treaty in Arusha, Tanzania, Aug. 2000. Two coup attempts were suppressed in 2001. A power-sharing government headed by Pierre Buyoya was sworn in Nov. 1, 2001, but clashes with rebels continued.

Domitien Ndayizeye, a Hutu, became president Apr. 2003. The UN Security Council authorized, May 2004, a peacekeeping force (ONUB) for Burundi. Approval of a power-sharing constitution by referendum, Feb. 28, 2005, paved the way for local and parliamentary elections. Pierre Nkurunziza, former leader of a Hutu rebel group, became president Aug. 2005. ONUB was succeeded, Jan. 1, 2007, by the UN Integrated Office in Burundi (BINUB). Under a reconciliation accord reached Dec. 4, 2008, remaining Hutu rebels began to demobilize. Candidates opposing Nkurunziza dropped out of the June 2010, presidential election, claiming the vote was rigged. The government was accused of ordering extrajudicial killings, 2010-11.

Pres. Pierre Nkurunziza signed a controversial law, June 4, 2013, forbidding journalists from reporting on issues of national security. In 2014, group jogging was limited to a few designated locations, because of government concerns that the activity was a pretext for protest demonstrations.

Cabo Verde
Republic of Cabo Verde

People: Population: 538,535. **Age distrib.:** <15: 30.6%; 65+: 5.1%. **Pop. density:** 345.8 per sq mi, 133.5 per sq km. **Urban:** 64.8%. **Ethnic groups:** Creole (mulatto) 71%, African 28%, European 1%. **Languages:** Portuguese (official), Crioulo (blend of Portuguese and W African words). **Religions:** Roman Catholic 77%, Protestant 4%, Muslim 2%, none 11%.

Geography: Total area: 1,557 sq mi, 4,033 sq km; **Land area:** 1,557 sq mi, 4,033 sq km. **Location:** In Atlantic O., off W tip of Africa. **Neighbors:** Nearest are Mauritania, Senegal to E. **Topography:** 15 Cabo Verde islands, volcanic in origin (active crater on Fogo). Landscape is eroded and stark, with vegetation mostly in interior valleys. **Capital:** Praia, 144,648.

Government: Type: Republic. **Head of state:** Pres. Jorge Carlos Fonseca; b. Oct. 20, 1950; in office: Sept. 9, 2011. **Head of gov.:** Prime Min. José Maria Neves; b. Mar. 28, 1960; in office: Feb. 1, 2001. **Local divisions:** 22 municipalities. **Defense budget** $9 mil. **Active troops:** 1,200.

Economy: Industries: food and beverages, fish proc., shoes and garments, salt mining, ship repair. **Chief crops:** bananas, corn, beans, sweet potatoes, sugarcane, coffee, peanuts. **Natural resources:** salt, basalt rock, limestone, kaolin, fish, clay, gypsum. **Arable land:** 11.7%. **Livestock:** cattle: 47,500; chickens: 750,000; goats: 240,000; pigs: 250,000; sheep: 21,000. **Electricity prod.:** 307 mil kWh. **Labor force:** NA. **Unemployment:** 7.6%.

Finance: Monetary unit: Escudo (CVE) (Sept. 2014: 82.62 = $1 U.S.). **GDP:** $2.2 bil; **per capita GDP:** $4,400; **GDP growth:** 1.5%. **Imports:** $796.3 mil; Portugal 38.1%, Netherlands 21.5%, China 7.9%, Spain 7%. **Exports:** $159.9 mil; Spain 66.9%, Portugal 13.9%, U.S. 5%. **Tourism:** $462 mil. **Budget:** $607 mil. **Total reserves less gold:** $475.3 mil. **Inflation:** 1.5%.

Transport: Civil aviation: 9 airports. **Chief port:** Porto Grande. **Communications: TV sets:** 128 per 1,000 pop. **Radios:** 176 per 1,000 pop. **Telephone lines:** 13.3 per 100 pop. **Mobile:** 100.1 per 100 pop. **Internet:** 37.5%.

Health: Life expect.: 69.3 male; 73.9 female. **Births:** 20.7 per 1,000 pop. **Deaths:** 6.2 per 1,000 pop. **Natural inc.:** 1.46%. **Infant mortality:** 24.3 per 1,000 live births. **HIV:** 0.5%.

Education: Compulsory: ages 6-11. **Literacy:** 87.6%.

Embassy: 3415 Massachusetts Ave. NW 20007; 965-6820. **Website:** www.governo.cv

The first Portuguese colonists landed in 1462; African slaves were brought soon after, and most Cabo Verdeans descend from both groups. Cabo Verde independence came July 5, 1975. Antonio Mascarenhas Monteiro won the nation's first free presidential election Feb. 17, 1991; he was reelected without opposition 5 years later. After Pres. Pedro Pires retired after serving two 5-year terms, 2001-11, Jorge Carlos Fonseca won a presidential runoff election Aug. 21, 2011. Remittances from Cabo Verdean emigrants are a major source of income. Japan announced June 3, 2013, that it would help fund the construction of water and energy projects in Cabo Verde. In Oct. 2013, the government announced that the country would no longer be known as Cape Verde.

Cambodia
Kingdom of Cambodia

People: Population: 15,458,332. **Age distrib.:** <15: 31.6%; 65+: 4%. **Pop. density:** 226.8 per sq mi, 87.6 per sq km. **Urban:** 20.5%. **Ethnic groups:** Khmer 90%, Vietnamese 5%, Chinese 1%. **Language:** Khmer (official). **Religions:** Buddhist (official) 97%, Muslim 2%.

Geography: Total area: 69,898 sq mi, 181,035 sq km; **Land area:** 68,153 sq mi, 176,515 sq km. **Location:** SE Asia, on Indochina Peninsula. **Neighbors:** Thailand on W and N, Laos on NE, Vietnam on E. **Topography:** The central area, formed by the Mekong R. basin and Tonle Sap Lake, is level. Hills and mountains are in SE, a long escarpment separates the country from Thailand on NW. 76% of the area is forested. **Capital:** Phnom Penh, 1,684,310.

Government: Type: Multiparty democracy under constitutional monarchy. **Head of state:** King Norodom Sihamoni; b. May 14, 1953; in office: Oct. 29, 2004. **Head of gov.:** Prime Min. Samdech Hun Sen; b. Aug. 5, 1952; in office: Jan. 14, 1985. **Local divisions:** 23 provinces, 1 municipality. **Defense budget** $394 mil. **Active troops:** 124,300.

Economy: Industries: tourism, garments, constr., rice milling, fishing, wood and wood prods., rubber, cement, gem mining, textiles. **Chief crops:** rice, corn, vegetables, cashews, cassava. **Natural resources:** oil and gas, timber, gems, iron ore, manganese, phosphates, hydropower potential. **Arable land:** 23.2%. **Livestock:** cattle: 2.9 mil; chickens: 13 mil; pigs: 2.2 mil. **Electricity prod.:** 991.2 mil kWh. **Labor force:** agric. 55.8%, industry 16.9%, services 27.3%. **Unemployment:** 1.5%.

Finance: Monetary unit: Riel (KHR) (Sept. 2014: 4,060.00 = $1 U.S.). **GDP:** $39.6 bil; **per capita GDP:** $2,600; **GDP growth:** 7%. **Imports:** $8.9 bil; Thailand 27.1%, Vietnam 20.3%, China 19.5%, Singapore 7.1%, Hong Kong 5.8%, South Korea 4.3%. **Exports:** $6.8 bil; U.S. 32.6%, UK 8.3%, Germany 7.7%, Canada 7.7%, Singapore 6.6%, Vietnam 5.7%, Japan 4.7%. **Tourism:** $2.7 bil. **Budget:** $3.1 bil. **Total reserves less gold:** $4.5 bil. **Gold:** 399,832 oz t. **Inflation:** 2.9%.

Transport: Railways: 429 mi (under restoration). **Civil aviation:** 6 airports. **Chief ports:** Phnom Penh, Sihanoukville.

Communications: TV sets: 8 per 1,000 pop. **Radios:** 112 per 1,000 pop. **Telephone lines:** 2.8 per 100 pop. **Mobile:** 133.9 per 100 pop. **Internet:** 6%.

Health: Life expect.: 61.4 male; 66.3 female. **Births:** 24.4 per 1,000 pop. **Deaths:** 7.8 per 1,000 pop. **Natural inc.:** 1.66%. **Infant mortality:** 51.4 per 1,000 live births. **HIV:** 0.7%.

Education: Compulsory: ages NA. **Literacy:** 77.2%.

Embassy: 4530 16th St. NW 20011; 726-7742. **Website:** www.cambodia.gov.kh

Early kingdoms dating from that of Funan in the 1st cent. CE culminated in the great Khmer empire that flourished from the 9th cent. to the 13th, encompassing present-day Thailand, Cambodia, Laos, and southern Vietnam. The peripheral areas were lost to invading Siamese and Vietnamese. France established a protectorate in 1863. Independence came in 1953.

Prince Norodom Sihanouk, king (1941-55) and head of state from 1960, tried to maintain neutrality during the Vietnam War. The U.S. bombed Cambodia, 1969-73, targeting suspected border sanctuaries of Vietnamese insurgents.

In 1970, pro-U.S. Prem. Lon Nol seized power, demanded removal of 40,000 North Vietnamese troops, and abolished the monarchy. Sihanouk formed a government-in-exile in Beijing, and open war began between the government and Communist Khmer Rouge guerrillas. The U.S. provided heavy military and economic aid.

Khmer Rouge forces captured Phnom Penh Apr. 17, 1975. Cities were depopulated and their residents executed or condemned to forced labor. An estimated 1.7 mil people died in "killing fields" or from other hardships under Khmer Rouge rule, 1975-79.

Severe border fighting broke out with Vietnam in 1978 and developed into a full-fledged Vietnamese invasion. Formation of a Vietnamese-backed government was announced, Jan. 8, 1979, one day after the capture of Phnom Penh. Thousands of refugees fled to Thailand, and widespread starvation was reported. Vietnamese troops remained in Cambodia during the 1980s, meeting resistance from Khmer Rouge guerrillas. Vietnam withdrew nearly all its troops by Sept. 1989.

Following 1993 UN-sponsored elections in Cambodia, 2 leading parties agreed to share power in an interim government. On Sept. 21, the National Assembly adopted a constitution reestablishing a monarchy, and Sihanouk became king. The Khmer Rouge boycotted the elections and opposed the new government. The insurgency had weakened and splintered by 1996.

Co-Prime Min. Hun Sen staged a coup July 5, 1997, ousting his rival, Prince Norodom Ranariddh. Pol Pot, the Khmer Rouge leader during the late 1970s, was denounced by his former comrades at a show trial, July 25, 1997, and sentenced to house arrest; he died Apr. 15, 1998. Sihanouk abdicated because of poor health and was succeeded, Oct. 2004, by his son Norodom Sihamoni.

Hun Sen's party retained power through a series of flawed elections. A UN-backed war crimes tribunal convicted a former prison warden known as Duch July 2010 for overseeing the killing and torture of more than 14,000 inmates under the Khmer Rouge. Two Khmer Rouge leaders were convicted of murder, crimes against humanity, and other charges, Aug. 7, 2014, and sentenced to life in prison.

Unsafe working conditions led to 2 factory collapses May 16, 2013, outside of Phnom Penh and in Tream Tbal that killed 4 workers. Large demonstrations in Phnom Penh opposing the Hun Sen government and demanding better pay and working conditions for garment workers were broken up by security forces in Jan. 2014; at least 4 protesters were killed. In June 2014, as many as 200,000 Cambodians working in Thailand repatriated after a Thai military coup raised fears of a crackdown on illegal workers.

Cameroon
Republic of Cameroon

People: Population: 23,130,708. **Age distrib.:** <15: 42.9%; 65+: 3.1%. **Pop. density:** 126.7 per sq mi, 48.9 per sq km. **Urban:** 53.8%. **Ethnic groups:** Cameroon Highlanders 31%, Equatorial Bantu 19%, Kirdi 11%, Fulani 10%, NW Bantu 8%, E Nigritic 7%, other African 13%. **Languages:** 24 major African lang. groups; English, French (both official). **Religions:** indigenous beliefs 40%, Christian 40%, Muslim 20%.

Geography: Total area: 183,568 sq mi, 475,440 sq km; **Land area:** 182,514 sq mi, 472,710 sq km. **Location:** Between W and central Africa. **Neighbors:** Nigeria on NW; Chad, Central African Republic on E; Congo, Gabon, Equatorial Guinea on S. **Topography:** Low coastal plain with rain forests in S; plateaus in center lead to forested mountains in W, including Mt. Cameroon (13,435 ft); grasslands in N lead to marshes around Lake Chad. **Capital:** Yaoundé, 2,930,170. **Cities (urban aggl.):** Douala, 2,838,374.

Government: Type: Republic. **Head of state:** Pres. Paul Biya; b. Feb. 13, 1933; in office: Nov. 6, 1982. **Head of gov.:** Prime Min. Philemon Yang; b. June 14, 1947; in office: June 30, 2009. **Local divisions:** 10 regions. **Defense budget** $393 mil. **Active troops:** 14,200.

Economy: Industries: petroleum prod. and refining, aluminum prod., food proc., light consumer goods, textiles, lumber. **Chief crops:** coffee, cocoa, cotton, rubber, bananas, oilseed, grains, cassava. **Natural resources:** petroleum, bauxite, iron ore, timber, hydropower. **Crude oil reserves:** 200 mil bbls. **Arable land:** 13.1%. **Livestock:** cattle: 5 mil; chickens: 48.5 mil; goats: 4.7 mil; pigs: 1.8 mil; sheep: 4 mil. **Electricity prod.:** 5.9 bil kWh. **Labor force:** agric. 70%, industry 13%, services 17%. **Unemployment:** 3.8%.

Finance: Monetary unit: Central African CFA Franc (XAF) (Sept. 2014: 498.91 = $1 U.S.). **GDP:** $53.2 bil; **per capita GDP:** $2,400; **GDP growth:** 4.6%. **Imports:** $6.8 bil; China 18.7%, France 14.9%, Nigeria 12.3%, Belgium 5.2%, U.S. 4.4%, India 4.2%. **Exports:** $6 bil; China 15.2%, Netherlands 9.7%, Spain 9.1%, India 8.6%, Portugal 8.1%, Italy 6%, U.S. 5.5%, France 4%. **Tourism:** $349 mil. **Budget:** $6.3 bil. **Total reserves less gold** (2012): $3.4 bil. **Inflation:** 1.9%.

Transport: Railways: 774 mi. **Motor vehicles:** 16.3 per 1,000 pop. **Civil aviation:** 11 airports. **Chief ports:** Douala, Limboh Terminal.

Communications: TV sets: 51 per 1,000 pop. **Radios:** 131 per 1,000 pop. **Telephone lines:** 3.6 per 100 pop. **Mobile:** 70.4 per 100 pop. **Internet:** 6.4%.

Health: Life expect.: 56.1 male; 58.7 female. **Births:** 36.6 per 1,000 pop. **Deaths:** 10.4 per 1,000 pop. **Natural inc.:** 2.62%. **Infant mortality:** 55.1 per 1,000 live births. **HIV:** 4.3%.

Education: Compulsory: ages 6-11. **Literacy:** 75%. **Embassy:** 2349 Massachusetts Ave. NW 20008; 265-8790. **Website:** www.spm.gov.cm

Portuguese sailors were the first Europeans to reach Cameroon, in the 15th cent. The European and American slave trade was very active in the area. German control lasted from 1884 to 1916, when France and Britain divided the territory, later receiving League of Nations mandates and UN trusteeships. French Cameroon became independent Jan. 1, 1960; one part of British Cameroon joined Nigeria in 1961 while the other part joined Cameroon. Pres. Paul Biya has retained power since 1982 in a series of elections that were boycotted by opposition parties or disputed as fraudulent. Rising food and fuel costs and discontent with Biya's continued rule sparked antigovernment riots Feb. 23-29, 2008. The legislature, controlled by Biya loyalists, voted Apr. 2008 to abolish presidential term limits introduced in 1996.

More than a dozen French citizens were kidnapped during 2013, allegedly in retaliation for France's intervention in neighboring Mali, and taken to Nigeria by the jihadist group Boko Haram. Kidnappings by Boko Haram of Europeans, other foreigners, and Cameroonian officials and their families continued in 2014.

Canada

People: Population: 34,834,841. **Age distrib.:** <15: 15.5%; 65+: 17.3%. **Pop. density:** 9.9 per sq mi, 3.8 per sq km. **Urban:** 81.6%. **Ethnic groups:** Canadian 32%, English 20%, French 16%, Scottish 14%, Irish 14%, German 10%, Italian 5%, Chinese 5%, N Amer. Indian 4%. **Languages:** English, French (both official). **Religions:** Roman Catholic 39%, Protestant 20%, Muslim 3%, Hindu 2%, none 24%.

Geography: Total area: 3,855,103 sq mi, 9,984,670 sq km; **Land area:** 3,511,023 sq mi, 9,093,507 sq km. The largest country in land size in the Western Hemisphere. **Topography:** Canada stretches 3,426 mi E-W and extends south from the North Pole to the U.S. border. Its seacoast includes 36,356 mi of mainland and 115,133 mi of islands, including the Arctic islands almost from Greenland to near the Alaskan border. **Climate:** While generally temperate, varies from freezing winter cold to blistering summer heat. **Capital:** Ottawa, 1,305,810 (figure is for Ottawa-Gatineau metro area). **Cities (urban aggl.):** Toronto, 5,901,335; Montréal, 3,948,189; Vancouver, 2,446,688; Calgary, 1,308,917; Edmonton, 1,246,286; Québec City, 796,597.

Government: Type: Constitutional monarchy with federal system of parliamentary democracy. **Head of state:** Queen Elizabeth II, rep. by Gov.-Gen. David Johnston; b. June 28, 1941; in office: Oct. 1, 2010. **Head of gov.:** Prime Min. Stephen Harper; b. Apr. 30, 1959; in office: Feb. 6, 2006. **Local divisions:** 10 provinces, 3 territories. **Defense budget:** $16.39 bil. **Active troops:** 66,000.

Economy: Industries: transp. equip., chemicals, minerals, food prods., wood and paper prods., fish prods., petroleum and nat. gas. **Chief crops:** wheat, barley, oilseed, tobacco, fruits, vegetables. **Natural resources:** iron ore, nickel, zinc, copper, gold, lead, rare earth elements, molybdenum, potash, diamonds, silver, fish, timber, wildlife, coal, petroleum, nat. gas, hydropower. **Crude oil reserves:** 173.2 bil bbls. **Arable land:** 5%. **Livestock:** cattle: 12.2 mil; chickens: 166.5 mil; goats: 30,000; pigs: 12.9 mil; sheep: 892,000. **Electricity prod.** (2012): 644.1 bil kWh. **Labor force:** agric. 2%, mfg. 13%, constr. 6%, services 76%, other 3%. **Unemployment:** 7.2%.

Finance: Monetary unit: Dollar (CAD) (Sept. 2014: 1.09 = $1 U.S.). **GDP:** $1.5 tril; **per capita GDP:** $43,100; **GDP growth:** 1.6%. **Imports:** $471 bil; U.S. 50.6%, China 11%, Mexico 5.5%. **Exports:** $458.7 bil; U.S. 74.5%, China 4.3%, UK 4.1%. **Tourism:** $17.7 bil. **Budget:** $740.8 bil. **Total reserves less gold:** $71.8 bil. **Gold:** 96,000 oz t. **Inflation:** 0.9%.

Canada's Provinces and Territories

Provinces/territories	Joined confed.	Tot. area (sq mi)	Population (2013 est.)	Capital	Premier	Party	In office
Alberta	1905	255,541	4,025,074	Edmonton	Alison Redford	Prog. Cons.	2011
British Columbia	1871	364,764	4,581,978	Victoria	Christy Clark	Liberal	2011
Manitoba	1870	250,116	1,265,015	Winnipeg	Greg Selinger	New Democratic	2009
New Brunswick	1867	28,150	756,050	Fredericton	David Alward	Prog. Cons.	2010
Newfoundland and Labrador	1949	156,453	526,702	St. John's	Kathy Dunderdale	Prog. Cons.	2010
Nova Scotia	1867	21,345	940,789	Halifax	Darrell Dexter	New Democratic	2009
Ontario	1867	415,598	13,537,994	Toronto	Kathleen Wynne	Liberal	2013
Prince Edward Island	1873	2,185	145,237	Charlottetown	Robert Ghiz	Liberal	2007
Québec	1867	595,391	8,155,334	Québec	Pauline Marois	Parti Québécois	2012
Saskatchewan	1905	251,366	1,108,303	Regina	Brad Wall	Saskatchewan	2007
Northwest Territories[1]	1871	519,734	43,537	Yellowknife	Bob McLeod	nonpartisan	2011
Nunavut[1,2]	1999	808,185	35,591	Iqaluit	Eva Aariak	nonpartisan	2008
Yukon[1]	1898	186,272	36,700	Whitehorse	Darrell Pasloski	Yukon	2011

Note: Pop. est. as of July 1. (Source: Statistics Canada.) (1) Territories also have federally appointed commissioners to represent federal interests. (2) Territory created in 1999 from eastern portion of Northwest Territories.

Transport: Railways: 28,926 mi. **Motor vehicles:** 646.1 per 1,000 pop. **Civil aviation:** 76.8 bil pass.-mi; 523 airports. **Chief ports:** Fraser River, Halifax, Hamilton, Montréal, Port-Cartier, Québec City, Saint John (New Brunswick), Sept-Isles, Vancouver.

Communications: TV sets: 731 per 1,000 pop. **Radios:** 1,052 per 1,000 pop. **Telephone lines:** 49.7 per 100 pop. **Mobile:** 78.4 per 100 pop. **Internet:** 85.8%.

Health: Life expect.: 79.1 male; 84.4 female. **Births:** 10.3 per 1,000 pop. **Deaths:** 8.3 per 1,000 pop. **Natural inc.:** 0.20%. **Infant mortality:** 4.7 per 1,000 live births. **HIV:** NA.

Education: Compulsory: ages 6-16. **Literacy:** 99%.

Embassy: 501 Pennsylvania Ave. NW 20001; 682-1740.

Website: www.canada.gc.ca

French explorer Jacques Cartier, who reached the Gulf of St. Lawrence in 1534, is generally regarded as Canada's founder. But English seaman John Cabot sighted Newfoundland in 1497, and Vikings are believed to have reached the Atlantic coast centuries before either explorer. The French pioneered Canadian settlement, establishing Quebec City (1608) and Montréal (1642) and declaring New France a colony in 1663.

Britain acquired Acadia (later Nova Scotia) in 1717 and defeated French forces in Canada to gain control of Quebec (1759) and the rest of New France in 1763. The French, through the Quebec Act of 1774, retained rights to their language, religion, and civil law. The British presence in Canada increased during the American Revolution when many colonials, calling themselves United Empire Loyalists, moved north to Canada. Fur traders and explorers led Canadians westward across the continent. Sir Alexander Mackenzie reached the Pacific in 1793 and scrawled on a rock, "From Canada by land."

In Upper and Lower Canada (later called Ontario and Quebec) and in the Maritimes, legislative assemblies were formed in the 18th cent. Upper Canada was involved in the War of 1812, a conflict between Great Britain and the U.S. that ended in a stalemate in 1814.

In 1837 political agitation for more democratic government culminated in rebellions in Upper and Lower Canada and the union of the 2 parts into the colony of Canada in 1839. The union lasted until the 1867 British North America Act (now known as the Constitution Act) launched the Dominion of Canada, consisting of Ontario, Quebec, and the former colonies of Nova Scotia and New Brunswick.

The British North America Act, which was the basis for the country's written constitution, established a federal system of government modeled on the British parliament and cabinet structure under the crown. Canada was proclaimed a self-governing dominion within the British Empire in 1931. The Constitution Act, 1982, gave Canada the right to amend its constitution, thereby severing its last legislative link with Britain.

Failure in 1990 of the so-called Meech Lake Accord, which would have assured constitutional protection for Quebec's efforts to preserve its French language and culture, sparked a separatist revival in Quebec. Subsequently, the Charlottetown agreement, calling for constitutional changes, such as recognition of Quebec as a "distinct society" within the Canadian confederation, was defeated by a national referendum Oct. 1992.

Canada became the first nation to ratify the North American Free Trade Agreement among Canada, Mexico, and the U.S., June 1993. It took effect Jan. 1, 1994. A Quebec referendum on secession held Oct. 1995 was defeated. On Jan. 7, 1998, the government apologized to indigenous peoples for 150 years of mistreatment and pledged to set up a "healing fund." Nunavut ("Our Land"), carved from Northwest Territories as a homeland for the Inuit, was established Apr. 1, 1999.

Victory by the Liberals in national elections Nov. 27, 2000, made Jean Chrétien the first Canadian prime min. in over 50 years to head a third successive majority government. Canada sent troops and warships to aid the U.S.-led coalition in Afghanistan beginning Oct. 2001; 157 Canadian troops led in Afghanistan by the time Canada's combat mission ended July 7, 2011.

Chrétien retired Dec. 12, 2003, and Paul Martin became prime min. Weakened by a scandal involving improper payments to Quebec firms for sponsorship of cultural and sporting events, the Liberals won only 135 of 308 seats in parliamentary elections June 28, 2004. Martin became head of a minority government. Same-sex marriage (already permitted in 8 of 10 provinces) became legal throughout the country July 2005.

Twelve years of Liberal Party rule ended when Conservatives won 124 seats to the Liberals' 103 in parliamentary elections, Jan. 23, 2006. Conservative leader Stephen Harper took office Feb. 6 as head of a minority government. Police and intelligence officials in the Toronto area, June 2-3, 2006, arrested and charged 17 people with plotting terrorist attacks in Canada. The supreme court, Feb. 23, 2007, unanimously struck down a law under which foreign-born terrorism suspects had been indefinitely detained without charge.

Prime Min. Harper remained the head of a minority government after 2008 elections, as Conservatives increased their plurality to 143 seats. A no-confidence vote Mar. 25, 2011, led to federal elections May 2, in which Harper's Conservatives gained a parliamentary majority of 166 seats. The New Democratic Party with 103 seats became the official opposition, as the Liberals had only 34 seats. While the technology for extracting oil from tar sands, large

deposits of which are found in Alberta, has improved, the lack of a pipeline from Alberta to the U.S. has obliged Canada producers to sell oil at discounted prices, thereby losing an estimated $45 mil a day in 2013 and diminishing tax revenue. The figure is disputed by some economists, who argue that Canadian politicians are comparing the price of the oil from the tar sands to higher quality oil produced elsewhere. On June 17, 2014, the Canadian government gave conditional approval for construction of a pipeline from Alberta to a new port in British Columbia.

In a bid to open up the Canadian oil market to international buyers, the government approved Dec. 7, 2012, a $15-bil takeover of the energy company Nexen by China Natl. Offshore Oil and the acquisition of Progress Energy Resources of Canada by the Malaysian state-owned oil and gas company Petronas.

Central African Republic

People: Population: 5,277,959. **Age distrib.:** <15: 40.6%; 65+: 3.6%. **Pop. density:** 21.9 per sq mi, 8.5 per sq km. **Urban:** 39.8%.

Ethnic groups: Baya 33%, Banda 27%, Mandjia 13%, Sara 10%, Mboum 7%, M'Baka 4%, Yakoma 4%. **Languages:** French (official), Sangho (lingua franca and national lang.), tribal langs. **Religions:** indigenous beliefs 35%, Protestant 25%, Roman Catholic 25%, Muslim 15%.

Geography: Total area: 240,535 sq mi, 622,984 sq km; **Land area:** 240,535 sq mi, 622,984 sq km. **Location:** In central Africa. **Neighbors:** Chad on N, Cameroon on W, Congo Republic and Dem. Rep. of the Congo on S, Sudan on E. **Topography:** Mostly rolling plateau, average elevation 2,000 ft, with rivers draining S to the Congo and N to Lake Chad. Open, well-watered savanna covers most of area, with an arid area in NE, and tropical rain forest in SW. **Capital:** Bangui, 780,825.

Government: Type: Republic. **Head of state:** Interim Pres. Catherine Samba-Panza; b. June 26, 1954; in office: Jan. 20, 2014. **Head of gov.:** Interim Prime Min. Mahamat Kamoun; in office: Aug. 10, 2014. **Local divisions:** 14 prefectures, 2 economic prefectures, 1 commune. **Defense budget** (2012): $50 mil. **Active troops:** 7,150.

Economy: Industries: gold and diamond mining, logging, brewing, sugar refining. **Chief crops:** cotton, coffee, tobacco, manioc, yams, millet, corn, bananas. **Natural resources:** diamonds, uranium, timber, gold, oil, hydropower. **Arable land:** 2.9%. **Livestock:** cattle: 4.3 mil; chickens: 6.7 mil; goats: 5.8 mil; pigs: 1 mil; sheep: 400,000. **Electricity prod.:** 175 mil kWh. **Labor force:** NA. **Unemployment:** 7.5%.

Finance: Monetary unit: Central African CFA Franc (XAF) (Sept. 2014: 498.91 = $1 U.S.). **GDP:** $3.3 bil; **per capita GDP:** $700; **GDP growth:** −14.5%. **Imports:** $218.6 mil; Netherlands 20.3%, France 9.7%, Cameroon 9.1%, South Korea 9.1%. **Exports:** $138.9 mil; Belgium 31.7%, China 27.9%, Dem. Rep. of the Congo 7.8%, Indonesia 5.2%, France 4.5%. **Tourism:** $6 mil. **Budget:** $270.7 mil. **Total reserves less gold** (2012): $157.9 mil. **Inflation:** 1.5%.

Transport: Motor vehicles: 0.9 per 1,000 pop. **Civil aviation:** 2 airports. **Chief ports:** Bangui, Nola, Nzinga, Salo.

Communications: TV sets: 10 per 1,000 pop. **Radios:** 111 per 1,000 pop. **Telephone lines:** 0.02 per 100 pop. **Mobile:** 29.5 per 100 pop. **Internet:** 3.5%.

Health: Life expect.: 50.1 male; 52.7 female. **Births:** 35.5 per 1,000 pop. **Deaths:** 14.1 per 1,000 pop. **Natural inc.:** 2.13%. **Infant mortality:** 92.9 per 1,000 live births. **HIV:** 3.8%.

Education: Compulsory: ages 6-11. **Literacy:** 36.8%.

Embassy: 1618 22nd St. NW 20008; 483-7800.

Website: www.centrafricaine.info or www.state.gov/p/af/ci/car/

Various Bantu peoples migrated through the region for centuries before French control was asserted in the late 19th cent., when the region was named Ubangi-Shari. Independence was attained Aug. 13, 1960.

Pres. Jean-Bedel Bokassa, who seized power in a 1965 military coup, proclaimed himself constitutional emperor of the renamed Central African Empire Dec. 1976. Bokassa's rule was characterized by ruthless authoritarianism and human rights violations. He was ousted in a bloodless coup aided by the French government, Sept. 20, 1979. In 1981, Gen. André Kolingba became head of state in another bloodless coup. The government canceled 1992 multiparty legislative and presidential elections because of polling problems. New elections, held in Aug. and Sept. 1993, led to civilian rule under Pres. Ange-Félix Patassé.

Patassé was ousted Mar. 15, 2003, by rebels under former army chief François Bozizé. Bozizé won a presidential runoff election May 8, 2005, but insurgent activity by Patassé loyalists and others continued in the north. A national peace conference, Dec. 8-20, 2008, enabled the establishment of a unity government Jan. 19, 2009. Pres. Bozizé won reelection Jan. 23, 2011, but was ousted 2 years later when the largely Muslim rebel group Seleka, led by Michel Djotodia, seized the capital Mar. 24, 2013. Djotodia declared himself president. Bozizé supporters and Christian militias clashed with pro-Djotodia and Muslim fighters, resulting in about 2,000 deaths and hundreds of thousands of displaced persons by the end of 2013. A National Transitional Council elected Catherine Samba-Panza interim pres. Jan. 20, 2014. Violence continued despite the presence of several thousand African, French, and EU troops. A UN peacekeeping force was authorized Apr. 10, 2014.

Chad
Republic of Chad

People: Population: 11,412,107. **Age distrib.:** <15: 44.7%; 65+: 3%. **Pop. density:** 23.5 per sq mi, 9.1 per sq km. **Urban:** 22.3%. **Ethnic groups:** Sara 28%, Arab 12%, Mayo-Kebbi 12%, Kanem-Bornou 9%, Ouaddai 9%, Hadjarai 7%, Tandjile 7%, Gorane 6%, Fitri-Batha 5%. **Languages:** French, Arabic (both official); Sara; 120+ langs. and dialects. **Religions:** Muslim 53%, Catholic 20%, Protestant 14%, animist 7%, atheist 3%.

Geography: Total area: 495,755, sq mi, 1,284,000 sq km; **Land area:** 486,180 sq mi, 1,259,200 sq km. **Location:** In central N Africa. **Neighbors:** Libya on N; Niger, Nigeria, Cameroon on W; Central African Republic on S; Sudan on E. **Topography:** Wooded savanna, steppe, and desert in the S; part of the Sahara in the N. Southern rivers flow N to Lake Chad, surrounded by marshland. **Capital:** N'Djaména, 1,212,080.

Government: Type: Republic. **Head of state:** Pres. Idriss Déby Itno; b. 1952; in office: Dec. 4, 1990. **Head of gov.:** Prime Min. Kalzeube Pahimi Deubet; in office: Nov. 21, 2013. **Local divisions:** 23 regions. **Defense budget** (2012): $202 mil. **Active troops:** 25,350.

Economy: Industries: oil, cotton textiles, meatpacking, brewing, sodium carbonate, soap, cigarettes, constr. materials. **Chief crops:** cotton, sorghum, millet, peanuts, rice, potatoes, manioc. **Natural resources:** petroleum, uranium, natron, kaolin, fish, gold, limestone, sand and gravel, salt. **Crude oil reserves:** 1.5 bil bbls. **Arable land:** 3.9%. **Livestock:** cattle: 7.8 mil; chickens: 6 mil; goats: 6.8 mil; pigs: 33,000; sheep: 3.2 mil. **Electricity prod.:** 200 mil kWh. **Labor force:** agric. 80%, industry and services 20%. **Unemployment:** 7.8%.

Finance: Monetary unit: Central African CFA Franc (XAF) (Sept. 2014: 498.91 = $1 U.S.). **GDP:** $28 bil; **per capita GDP:** $2,500; **GDP growth:** 3.9%. **Imports:** $2.7 bil; China 20.2%, Cameroon 18.2%, France 16.1%, Saudi Arabia 5.6%, U.S. 4.2%. **Exports:** $3.9 bil; U.S. 81.9%, China 6.7%. **Budget:** $3.6 bil. **Total reserves less gold** (2012): $1.2 bil. **Inflation:** 0.1%.

Transport: Civil aviation: 9 airports.

Communications: TV sets: 9 per 1,000 pop. **Radios:** 103 per 1,000 pop. **Telephone lines:** 0.2 per 100 pop. **Mobile:** 35.6 per 100 pop. **Internet:** 2.3%.

Health: Life expect.: 48.3 male; 50.6 female. **Births:** 37.3 per 1,000 pop. **Deaths:** 14.6 per 1,000 pop. **Natural inc.:** 2.27%. **Infant mortality:** 90.3 per 1,000 live births. **HIV:** 2.5%.

Education: Compulsory: ages 6-15. **Literacy:** 40.2%.

Embassy: 2002 R St. NW 20009; 462-4009.

Website: www.state.gov/p/af/ci/cd/

Chad was the site of Paleolithic and Neolithic cultures before the Sahara Desert formed. A succession of kingdoms and Arab slave traders dominated Chad until France took control around 1900. Independence came Aug. 11, 1960. Northern Muslim rebels have fought animist and Christian southern government and French troops from 1966, despite numerous cease-fires and peace pacts.

Rebel forces, led by Hissène Habré, captured the capital and forced Pres. Goukouni Oueddei to flee the country in June 1982. In Dec. 1990, a Libyan-supported insurgent group, the Patriotic Salvation Movement, overthrew Habré. After approval of a new constitution Mar. 1996, Chad's first multiparty presidential election was held in June and July.

Oil began flowing July 15, 2003, through a 665-mi pipeline that allows landlocked Chad to export via Cameroon. Pres. Idriss Déby Itno won a third term, May 3, 2006, in an election boycotted by major opposition groups. Violence along the Sudan border escalated during the year, as Sudanese *janjaweed* militias and Chadian rebels attacked civilians, and Darfur rebels preyed on refugee camps. Between 140 and 700 civilians died in N'Djamena, Feb. 2-5, 2008, as more than 2,000 Chadian rebels stormed the capital and clashed with government troops in a failed coup attempt.

On Jan. 15, 2010, Chad and Sudan signed an accord aimed at normalizing relations and suppressing cross-border activities by rebel groups. Established in 2007, a UN peacekeeping force (MINURCAT) completed its mandate Dec. 31, 2010. In early 2011, camps in E Chad housed some 262,900 refugees, most from Darfur, and camps in S Chad held about 73,500 refugees, most from the Central African Republic. More than 157,000 Chadians were internally displaced. Pres. Déby won reelection Apr. 25, 2011, in a vote boycotted as fraudulent by major opposition groups.

After Islamist groups took over northern Mali and imposed a repressive regime in late 2012, Chad contributed roughly 2,000 soldiers to aid French, Malian, and other African forces in a military intervention. On Apr. 15, 2013, the Chadian government announced it would begin pulling its troops out of Mali. Former Pres. Hissène Habré, accused of killing and torturing thousands of opponents in the 1980s, was arrested in Senegal June 30, 2013. The Extraordinary African Chambers charged Habré with crimes against humanity, torture, and war crimes July 2, 2013.

Chile
Republic of Chile

People: Population: 17,363,894. **Age distrib.:** <15: 20.7%; 65+: 9.9%. **Pop. density:** 60.5 per sq mi, 23.3 per sq km. **Urban:** 89.4%. **Ethnic groups:** white and non-indigenous 89%, Mapuche 9%. **Languages:** Spanish (official), English, indigenous. **Religions:** Roman Catholic 67%, Evangelical/Protestant 16%, none 12%.

Geography: Total area: 291,933 sq mi, 756,102 sq km; **Land area:** 287,187 sq mi, 743,812 sq km. **Location:** Occupies W coast of southern S America. **Neighbors:** Peru on N, Bolivia on NE, Argentina on E. **Topography:** Andes Mts. on E border incl. some of the world's highest peaks; on W is 2,650-mi Pacific coast. Width varies 100-250 mi. In N is Atacama Desert; in center are agricultural regions; in S, forests and grazing lands. **Capital:** Santiago, 6,471,800. **Cities (urban aggl.):** Valparaíso, 901,624.

Government: Type: Republic. **Head of state and gov.:** Pres. Michelle Bachelet Jeria; b. Sept. 29, 1951; in office: Mar. 11, 2014. **Local divisions:** 15 regions. **Defense budget:** $4.59 bil. **Active troops:** 61,400.

Economy: Industries: copper, lithium, other minerals, foodstuffs, fish proc., iron and steel, wood and wood prods., transp. equip., cement, textiles. **Chief crops:** grapes, apples, pears, onions, wheat, corn, oats, peaches, garlic, asparagus, beans. **Natural resources:** copper, timber, iron ore, nitrates, prec. metals, molybdenum, hydropower. **Crude oil reserves:** 150 mil bbls. **Arable land:** 1.8%. **Livestock:** cattle: 3.3 mil; chickens: 47.6 mil; goats: 730,000; pigs: 2.8 mil; sheep: 3.4 mil. **Electricity prod.:** 61.8 bil kWh. **Labor force:** agric. 13.2%, industry 23%, services 63.9%. **Unemployment:** 6.4%.

Finance: Monetary unit: Peso (CLP) (Sept. 2014: 588.60 = $1 U.S.). **GDP:** $335.4 bil; **per capita GDP:** $19,100; **GDP growth:** 4.4%. **Imports:** $75.7 bil; U.S. 22.9%, China 18.2%, Argentina 6.6%, Brazil 6.5%. **Exports:** $77.9 bil; China 23.3%, U.S. 12.3%, Japan 10.7%, South Korea 5.8%, Brazil 5.5%. **Tourism:** $2.2 bil. **Budget:** $61.3 bil. **Total reserves less gold:** $41.1 bil. **Gold:** 7,900 oz t. **Inflation:** 1.8%.

Transport: Railways: 4,401 mi. **Motor vehicles:** 223.9 per 1,000 pop. **Civil aviation:** 13.5 bil pass.-mi; 90 airports. **Chief ports:** Coronel, Huasco, Lirquen, Puerto Ventanas, San Antonio, San Vicente, Valparaíso.

Communications: TV sets: 313 per 1,000 pop. **Radios:** 783 per 1,000 pop. **Telephone lines:** 18.2 per 100 pop. **Mobile:** 134.3 per 100 pop. **Internet:** 66.5%.

Health: Life expect.: 75.4 male; 81.6 female. **Births:** 14.0 per 1,000 pop. **Deaths:** 5.9 per 1,000 pop. **Natural inc.:** 0.80%. **Infant mortality:** 7.0 per 1,000 live births. **HIV:** 0.3%.

Education: Compulsory: ages 6-17. **Literacy:** 97.5%.

Embassy: 1732 Massachusetts Ave. NW 20036; 785-1746.

Website: www.gob.cl

Northern Chile was under Inca rule before the Spanish conquest, 1536-40. The southern Araucanian Indians resisted until the late 19th cent. Independence was gained 1810-18 under José de San Martin and Bernardo O'Higgins; the latter, as supreme director 1817-23, sought social and economic reforms until deposed. Chile defeated Peru and Bolivia in 1836-39 and 1879-84, gaining mineral-rich northern land.

In 1970, Salvador Allende Gossens, a Marxist, became president with a narrow plurality of the popular vote. His government improved conditions for the poor, but property seizures by left-wing extremists, poorly planned socialist economic programs, and a destabilization campaign backed by the U.S. led to political and financial chaos. A military junta seized power Sept. 11, 1973. With the presidential palace under attack, Allende refused to surrender; a 2011 autopsy confirmed police reports that he killed himself. The junta, headed by Gen. Augusto Pinochet Ugarte, implemented plans to privatize the economy and "exterminate Marxism." Repression continued into the 1980s.

In Dec. 1989 voters elected a civilian president, although Pinochet continued to head the army until Mar. 10, 1998. In Mar. 1994, a Chilean human rights group estimated that human rights violations had claimed more than 3,100 lives during Pinochet's rule. Efforts to prosecute him failed when courts in Britain and Chile declared him mentally unfit to stand trial.

Ricardo Lagos Escobar, Chile's first Socialist president since the 1973 coup, took office Mar. 11, 2000. Chile and the U.S. signed a free trade accord June 6, 2003. Verónica Michelle Bachelet Jeria, also a Socialist, won a runoff election Jan. 2006 and took office in Mar. as Chile's first woman president. Pinochet died Dec. 10, 2006.

Billionaire businessman Sebastián Piñera Echenique, a conservative, won a presidential runoff election Jan. 2010 and took office in Mar. In the interim, a powerful earthquake and the tsunami that followed it Feb. 27, 2010, off the coast of central Chile killed at least 521 people and caused up to $30 bil in property damage. A judge ruled May 16, 2013, that the manslaughter trial of 4 government officials for failing to issue adequate warnings about the approaching tsunami should go forward. Chile successfully rescued 33 miners trapped for 10 weeks 2,300 ft underground after a cave-in at the San José Mine Aug. 5, 2010. A prison fire Dec. 8 in Santiago killed at least 81 inmates. Chile's economy was growing at a 6.6% annual rate in mid-2011, but lagging wages sparked labor protests against the Piñera government that continued into 2012 and spread to the student population. Bachelet won a presidential runoff election Dec. 15, 2013, and returned to office Mar. 11, 2014.

Tierra del Fuego is the largest (18,800 sq mi) island in the archipelago of the same name at the southern tip of S America, an area of majestic mountains, tortuous channels, and high winds. It was visited 1520 by Magellan and named Land of Fire because of its many Indian bonfires. Part of the island is in Chile, part in Argentina. Punta Arenas, on a mainland peninsula, is a center of sheep raising and the world's southernmost city (pop. [2012 census] 130,704); Puerto Williams is the southernmost settlement.

China

People's Republic of China
(Statistical data do not include Hong Kong or Macao.)

People: Population: 1,355,692,576. **Age distrib.:** <15: 17.1%; 65+: 9.6%. **Pop. density:** 366.9 per sq mi, 141.7 per sq km. **Urban:** 54.4%. **Ethnic groups:** Han Chinese 92%; Zhuang 1%, other (incl. Hui, Manchu, Uighur, Miao, Yi, Tujia, Tibetan, Mongol, Dong, Buyei, Yao, Bai, Korean, other nationalities) 7%. **Languages:** Standard Chinese or Mandarin (official; Putonghua, based on Beijing dialect); Yue (Cantonese), Wu (Shanghainese), Minbei (Fuzhou), Minnan (Hokkien-Taiwanese), Xiang, Gan, Hakka dialects, minority langs. **Religions:** officially atheist; Buddhist 18%, Christian 5%, Muslim 2%.

Geography: Total area: 3,705,407 sq mi, 9,596,961 sq km; **Land area:** 3,600,947 sq mi, 9,326,410 sq km. **Location:** Occupies most of the habitable mainland of E Asia. **Neighbors:** Mongolia on N; Russia on NE and NW; Afghanistan, Pakistan, Tajikistan, Kyrgyzstan, Kazakhstan on W; India, Nepal, Bhutan, Myanmar, Laos, Vietnam on S; North Korea on NE. **Topography:** Two-thirds of the vast territory is mountainous or desert; only one-tenth is cultivated. Rolling topography rises to high elevations in the N in the Da Xing'an Ling Mts. separating Manchuria and Mongolia; the Tien Shan in Xinjiang; the Himalayan and Kunlun Mts. in the SW and in Tibet. Length is 1,860 mi from N to S, width E to W is more than 2,000 mi. The eastern half of China is one of the world's best-watered lands. Three great river systems, the Chang (Yangtze), Huang (Yellow), and Xi, provide water for vast farmlands. **Capital:** Beijing, 19,520,300. **Cities (urban aggl.):** Shanghai, 22,991,068; Chongqing, 12,915,712; Guangzhou, Guangdong, 11,842,794; Tianjin, 10,859,761; Shenzhen, 10,680,171; Wuhan, 7,838,127; Dongguan, 7,409,666; Chengdu, 7,288,948; Nanjing, Jiangsu, 7,127,380.

Government: Type: Communist state. **Head of state:** Pres. Xi Jinping; b. June 1953; in office: Mar. 14, 2013 (gen. sec. of Communist Party since Nov. 15, 2012). **Head of gov.:** Prem. Li Keqiang; b. July 1, 1955; in office: Mar. 16, 2013. **Local divisions:** 22 provinces (not incl. Taiwan), 5 autonomous regions, 4 municipalities, plus the special administrative regions of Hong Kong (as of July 1, 1997) and Macao (as of Dec. 20, 1999). **Defense budget:** $112.17 bil. **Active troops:** 2,333,000.

Economy: Industries: world leader in gross value of industrial output; mining and ore proc., iron, steel, aluminum, other metals, coal; machine building; armaments; textiles and apparel; petroleum; cement; chemicals; fertilizers; consumer prods. food proc.; transp. equip.; telecom equip. **Chief crops:** world leader in gross value of agric. output; rice, wheat, potatoes, corn, peanuts, tea, millet, barley, apples, cotton, oilseed. **Natural resources:** coal, iron ore, petroleum, nat. gas, mercury, tin, tungsten, antimony, manganese, molybdenum, vanadium, magnetite, aluminum, lead, zinc, rare earth elements, uranium, hydropower potential (world's largest). **Crude oil reserves:** 24.4 bil bbls. **Arable land:** 11.3%. **Livestock:** cattle: 113.5 mil; chickens: 5.4 bil; goats: 182.7 mil; pigs: 475.9 mil; sheep: 185 mil. **Electricity prod.:** 4.5 tril kWh. **Labor force:** agric. 33.6%, industry 30.3%, services 36.1%. **Unemployment:** 4.5%.

Finance: Monetary unit: Yuan Renminbi (CNY) (Sept. 2014: 6.14 = $1 U.S.). **GDP:** $13.4 tril; **per capita GDP:** $9,800; **GDP growth:** 7.7%. **Imports:** $2 tril; South Korea 9.4%, Japan 8.3%, Taiwan 8%, U.S. 7.8%, Australia 5%, Germany 4.8%. **Exports:** $2.2 tril; Hong Kong 17.4%, U.S. 16.7%, Japan 6.8%, South Korea 4.1%. **Tourism:** $51.7 bil. **Budget:** $2.3 tril. **Total reserves less gold:** $3.8 tril. **Gold:** 33.9 mil oz t. **Inflation:** 2.6%.

Transport: Railways: 53,438 mi. **Motor vehicles:** 88.6 per 1,000 pop. **Civil aviation:** 280.3 bil pass.-mi; 463 airports. **Chief ports:** Dalian, Guangzhou, Ningbo, Qingdao, Qinhuangdao, Shanghai, Shenzhen, Tianjin.

Communications: TV sets: 380 per 1,000 pop. **Radios:** 336 per 1,000 pop. **Telephone lines:** 19.3 per 100 pop. **Mobile:** 88.7 per 100 pop. **Internet:** 45.8%.

Health: Life expect.: 73.1 male; 77.4 female. **Births:** 12.2 per 1,000 pop. **Deaths:** 7.4 per 1,000 pop. **Natural inc.:** 0.47%. **Infant mortality:** 14.8 per 1,000 live births. **HIV:** NA.

Education: Compulsory: ages 6-14. **Literacy:** 96.4%.

Embassy: 2300 Connecticut Ave. NW 20008; 328-2500.

Website: www.gov.cn

Remains of various humanlike creatures who lived as early as several hundred thousand years ago have been found in many parts of China. Neolithic agricultural settlements dotted the Huang (Yellow) R. basin from about 5000 BCE. Their language, religion, and art were the sources of later Chinese civilization.

Bronze metallurgy reached a peak and Chinese pictographic writing, similar to today's, was in use in the more developed culture of the Shang Dynasty (c. 1500 BCE-c. 1000 BCE), which ruled much of North China.

A succession of dynasties and interdynastic warring kingdoms ruled China for the next 3,000 years. They expanded Chinese political and cultural domination to the south and west, and developed a technologically and culturally advanced society that was unaffected by foreign rule (Mongols in the Yuan Dynasty, 1271-1368, and Manchus in the Ch'ing Dynasty, 1644-1911).

Rebellions in the tenth cent. left tens of millions dead. Russia, Japan, Britain, and other powers exercised political and economic control in large parts of the country. China became a republic Jan. 1, 1912, following the Wuchang Uprising inspired by Dr. Sun Yat-sen, founder of the Kuomintang (Nationalist) party. By 1928, the Kuomintang, led by Chiang Kai-shek, succeeded in nominal reunification of China. About the same time, a bloody purge of Communists from the ranks of the Kuomintang fomented hostilities.

For over 50 years, 1894-1945, China was involved in conflicts with Japan. In 1895, China ceded Korea, Taiwan, and other areas. On Sept. 18, 1931, Japan seized the Northeastern Provinces (Manchuria) and set up a puppet state called Manchukuo. Taking advantage of Chinese dissension, Japan invaded China proper July 7, 1937. On Nov. 20 the retreating Nationalist government moved its capital to Chongqing (Chungking) from Nanking (Nanjing), which Japanese troops then ravaged Dec. 13.

From 1939 the Sino-Japanese War (1937-45) became part of the broader world conflict. After its defeat in World War II, Japan relinquished China. Within China, conflicts involving the Kuomintang, Communists, and other factions resumed. China came under the domination of Communist armies, 1949-50. The Kuomintang government fled to Taiwan, Dec. 8, 1949.

The People's Republic of China was proclaimed in Beijing (Peking) Oct. 1, 1949, under Mao Zedong. China and the USSR signed a 30-year treaty of "friendship, alliance, and mutual assistance," Feb. 15, 1950. The U.S. refused to recognize the new regime. On Nov. 26, 1950, the People's Republic sent armies into Korea against U.S. troops and forced a stalemate in the Korean War.

Frequent drastic changes in policy and violent factionalism 1949-52 interfered with economic development. In 1957, Mao admitted an estimated 800,000 people had been executed 1949-54; opponents claimed much higher figures. The Great Leap Forward, 1958-60, tried to accelerate economic development through intensive labor on huge new rural communes, and through emphasis on ideological purity. The program caused resistance and was largely abandoned.

By the 1960s, relations with the USSR deteriorated, with disagreements on borders' ideology, and leadership of world Communism. The USSR canceled aid accords, and China, with Albania, launched anti-Soviet propaganda drives. The Great Proletarian Cultural Revolution, 1965, an attempt to instruct a new generation in revolutionary principles, resulted in massive purges. Millions of urban teenagers were relocated into the countryside. By 1968 the movement had run its course; many purged officials returned to office in subsequent years, and several ideological reforms were gradually weakened.

On Oct. 25, 1971, the UN General Assembly ousted the Taiwan government from the UN and seated the People's Republic in its place. The U.S. had supported the mainland's admission but opposed Taiwan's expulsion.

U.S. Pres. Richard Nixon visited China Feb. 21-28, 1972, on invitation from Prem. Zhou Enlai, ending years of antipathy between the 2 nations. China and the U.S. opened liaison offices in each other's capitals, May-June 1973. The U.S., Dec. 15, 1978, formally recognized the People's Republic of China as the sole legal government of China; diplomatic relations between the 2 nations were established, Jan. 1, 1979.

Mao died Sept. 9, 1976. By 1978, Vice Prem. Deng Xiaoping had consolidated power, succeeding Mao as "paramount leader" of China. The new ruling group modified Maoist policies in education, culture, and industry, and sought better ties with non-Communist countries. By the mid-1980s, China had enacted far-reaching economic reforms, deemphasizing centralized planning and incorporating market-oriented incentives.

Some 100,000 students and workers marched in Beijing to demand political reforms, May 4, 1989. As the unrest spread, martial law was imposed, May 20. Troops entered Beijing, June 3-4, and crushed the pro-democracy protests, as tanks and armored personnel carriers rolled through Tiananmen Square. It is estimated that hundreds died and thousands were injured, and hundreds of students and workers were arrested.

Deng Xiaoping died Feb. 19, 1997, leaving Jiang Zemin in control as president. Hong Kong reverted to Chinese sovereignty July 1, 1997. Portugal returned Macao to China Dec. 20, 1999.

Hu Jintao was named Communist Party general secretary at the 16th party congress, Nov. 2002, and elected president by the 10th National People's Congress, Mar. 2003. With the successful launch and recovery, Oct. 15-16, 2003, of the *Shenzhou 5* spacecraft, China became the third nation (after the U.S. and USSR) to send a person into space. In Dec. 2013, China became the 3rd nation to reach the Moon with a spacecraft that made a soft landing.

China's industries, exports, and oil demand have increased rapidly since the 1990s. Reports in 2007 that China had exported hazardous pet products, toothpaste, tires, and toys resulted in the execution, July 10, of Zheng Xiaoyu, the former head of China's food and drug safety agency.

The National People's Congress Mar. 15-16, 2008, reelected Pres. Hu Jintao and Prem. Wen Jiabao. A powerful earthquake rocked Sichuan prov. May 12, leaving 69,226 people dead and 17,923 missing. China reportedly spent $43 bil preparing for the Summer Olympics, held in Beijing Aug. 8-24, 2008. China's health ministry reported Sept.-Dec. 2008 that 300,000 babies had been sickened by contaminated milk powder.

Western computer security experts Jan.-Feb. 2010 blamed hackers at 2 Chinese schools for Internet attacks on Google and at least 30 other firms. The government reacted angrily when the Nobel Peace Prize was awarded Oct. 8 to Liu Xiaobo, a human rights activist who had received an 11-year prison sentence in 2009.

China has invested heavily in environmental technologies, especially wind and solar power, but illegal mining and ore processing remain major public-health hazards. Rapid growth during 2009-10 made China the world's second-largest economy, ranking behind the U.S. and ahead of Japan.

Xi Jinping was chosen Communist Party general secretary and China's new leader, and Li Keqiang the country's prime min. Nov. 15, 2012. Air quality deteriorated to the most dangerous levels on record in Beijing and N China throughout Jan. 2013. The H7N9 strain of bird flu spread Mar.-Apr., infecting about 130, 44 of whom died. In Lushan County, near Ya'an City in Sichuan prov., a magnitude 7.0 earthquake struck on Apr. 20, killing at least 196 people and injuring about 13,000.

China's economy has slowed in recent years. GDP growth was 7.8% in 2012 and 7.7% in 2013, compared to double-digit gains for most years since the 1980s. China is the largest foreign holder of U.S. debt (more than $1.27 tril as of June 2014).

Autonomous Regions

Guangxi Zhuang is in SE China, bounded on the N by Guizhou and Hunan provinces, E and S by Guangdong, on the SW by Vietnam, and on the W by Yunnan. It produces rice in the river valleys and has valuable forest products. Pop. (2010): 46,026,629.

Inner Mongolia was organized by the People's Republic in 1947. Its boundaries have undergone frequent changes, reaching its greatest extent in 1956 (and restored in 1979), with an area of 454,600 sq mi, allegedly in order to dilute the minority Mongol population. Chinese settlers outnumber the Mongols more than 10 to 1. Pop. (2010) 24,706,321. Capital: Hohhot.

Ningxia Hui, in north-central China, is about 60,000 sq mi. Pop. (2010) 6,301,350. Capital: Yinchuan. The climate is mostly semiarid, with desert areas in the N. The Huang He (Yellow R.) flows across the N, furnishing water for irrigation. Coal is mined in the E. The majority of the population is Han, and the Hui (Chinese Muslims) constitute about one-third of the population. The region experienced a significant population boom, 1950-80, which has now stabilized.

Xinjiang Uighur, in Central Asia, is 635,900 sq mi, pop. (2010) 21,813,334 (75% Uighurs, a Turkic Muslim group, with a heavy Han Chinese increase in recent years). Capital: Urumqi. It is China's richest region in strategic minerals. China has moved to suppress Uighur cultural and religious practices and to crack down on Uighur separatists, whom Beijing regards as terrorists. A protest march July 5, 2009, by Uighurs in Urumqi led to violent clashes with Han Chinese; at least 197 people (mostly Han) were killed in riots. Unrest and terrorist attacks continued, including truck bombings in Urumqi May 22, 2014, that killed more than 40 people. The government's crackdown included the June 16 execution of 13 people convicted of terrorism-related crimes. Violence in Yarkand July 28 left almost 100 people dead.

Tibet, 471,700 sq mi, is a thinly populated region of high plateaus and massive mountains, the Himalayas on the S, the Kunluns on the N. High passes connect with India and Nepal; roads lead into China proper. Capital: Lhasa. Avg. elevation is 15,000 ft. Jiachan, 15,870 ft, is believed to be the highest inhabited town on Earth. Agriculture is primitive. Pop. (2010) 3,002,166 (of whom about 500,000 are Chinese). Another 4 mil Tibetans form the majority of the population of vast adjacent areas that have long been incorporated into China.

China ruled all of Tibet from the 18th cent. Independence came in 1911, but China reasserted control in 1951, and a Communist government was installed in 1953. Serfdom was abolished, but all land remained collectivized.

A Tibetan uprising within China in 1956 spread to Lhasa in 1959. The rebellion was crushed by Chinese troops, and Buddhism was almost totally suppressed. The Dalai Lama and 100,000 Tibetans fled to India. Efforts by Chinese authorities to halt peaceful demonstrations by Tibetan monks led to anti-Chinese riots in Lhasa, Mar. 14, 2008; the Chinese government sent troops into Tibet to crush dissent, sparking international protests. Protests (including self-immolations), and government repression of dissent, continued in subsequent years.

Hong Kong

Hong Kong (Xianggang), located at the mouth of the Zhu Jiang (Pearl R.) in SE China, 90 mi S of Guangzhou, was a British dependency from 1842 until July 1, 1997, when it became a Special Administrative Region of China. Its nucleus is Hong Kong Isl., 31 sq mi, occupied by the British in 1841 and formally ceded to them in 1842, on which was located the seat of government. Opposite is Kowloon Peninsula, 3 sq mi, and Stonecutters Isl., added to the territory in 1860. An additional 355 sq mi known as the New Territories, a mainland area and islands, were leased from China, 1898, for 99 years. Area 426 sq mi (total); 407 sq mi (land); pop. (2014 est.) 7,112,688. **Website:** www.gov.hk

Hong Kong is a major trade and banking center. Per capita GDP, $52,700 (2013 est.), is among the highest in the world. Principal industries are textiles and apparel, tourism, electronics, shipbuilding, iron and steel, fishing, cement, and small manufactures. Tourism receipts in 2013 were $38.9 bil. Hong Kong's spinning mills are among the best in the world. Outside of the public sector, the labor force is engaged in the following sectors: wholesale and retail trade, restaurants, and hotels 53.3%; financing, insurance, and real estate 12.5%; community and social services 17.1%; transport and communications 10.1%; manufacturing 3.8%; and construction 2.8%.

Hong Kong harbor was long an important British naval station and one of the world's great transshipment ports. The colony often provided refuge for exiles from mainland China. It was occupied by Japan during WWII.

From 1949 to 1962, Hong Kong absorbed more than 1 mil refugees fleeing Communist China. Starting in the 1950s, cheap labor led to a boom in light manufacturing, while liberal tax policies attracted foreign investment; Hong Kong became one of the wealthiest, most productive areas in the Far East.

With the end of the 99-year lease on the New Territories drawing near, Britain and China signed an agreement, Dec. 19, 1984, under which all of Hong Kong was to be returned to China in 1997; under this agreement Hong Kong was to be allowed to keep its capitalist system for 50 years. Following the transfer of government, Hong Kong retained its street names and its currency, the Hong Kong dollar, but without the queen's picture. Official languages remained Cantonese (a Chinese dialect) and English.

Hundreds of thousands of Hong Kong residents protested July 1, 2003, a proposed anti-subversion law; the bill was withdrawn Sept. 5. Another mass march, July 1, 2004, protested Beijing's refusal to allow greater freedom. Pro-democracy candidates won a majority of the popular vote in elections, Sept. 12, but failed to gain control of the Legislative Council. After Hong Kong's chief executive, Tung Chee-hwa resigned Mar. 10, 2005, Donald Tsang served the remaining 2 years of Tung's term; he won a full 5-year term Mar. 2007, but left office tarnished by a scandal that involved receiving preferential treatment and favors from wealthy businessmen. Leung Chun-ying, whose close ties to China became an issue during the campaign, was elected Mar. 2012 and took office July 1. Large pro-democracy protests, opposing Chinese plans to limit the openness of 2017 elections, took place July and Sept.-Oct. 2014.

Macao

Macao, area of 11 sq mi, is an enclave, a peninsula and 2 small islands, at the mouth of the Xi (Pearl) R. in China. It was established as a Portuguese trading colony in 1557. In 1849, Portugal claimed sovereignty over the territory; this claim was accepted by China in an 1887 treaty. Portugal granted broad autonomy in 1976. Under a 1987 agreement, Macao reverted to China Dec. 20, 1999. As in the case of Hong Kong, the Chinese government guaranteed Macao it would not interfere in its way of life and capitalist system for a period of 50 years. Tourism is the fastest-growing economic sector. Tourism receipts in 2013 were $51.6 bil. Per capita GDP was $88,700 (2013 est.). The labor force is occupied in the following areas: gambling 25.9%, restaurants and hotels 15%, wholesale and retail trade 12.4%, construction 9.8%, public sector 7.1%, transport and communications 4.4%, manufacturing 2.5%, and financial services 2.6%. Pop. (2014 est.) 587,914. **Website:** www.gov.mo

Colombia
Republic of Colombia

People: Population: 46,245,297. **Age distrib.:** <15: 25.3%; 65+: 6.7%. **Pop. density:** 115.3 per sq mi, 44.5 per sq km. **Urban:** 76.2%. **Ethnic groups:** mestizo 58%, white 20%, mulatto 14%, black 4%, mixed black-Amerindian 3%, Amerindian 1%. **Language:** Spanish (official). **Religion:** Roman Catholic 90%.

Geography: Total area: 439,736 sq mi, 1,138,910 sq km; **Land area:** 401,044 sq mi, 1,038,700 sq km. **Location:** At the NW corner of South America. **Neighbors:** Panama on NW, Ecuador and Peru on S, Brazil and Venezuela on E. **Topography:** Three ranges of Andes—Western, Central, and Eastern Cordilleras—run through the country from N to S. The eastern range consists mostly of high tablelands, densely populated. The Magdalena R. rises in the Andes, flows N to Caribbean, through a rich alluvial plain. Sparsely settled plains in E are drained by Orinoco and Amazon systems. **Capital:** Bogotá, 9,557,600. **Cities (urban aggl.):** Medellín, 3,850,102; Cali, 2,610,387; Barranquilla, 1,974,658.

Government: Type: Republic. **Head of state and gov.:** Pres. Juan Manuel Santos Calderón; b. Aug. 10, 1951; in office: Aug. 7, 2010. **Local divisions:** 32 departments, 1 capital district. **Defense budget:** $7.02 bil. **Active troops:** 281,400.

Economy: Industries: textiles, food proc., oil, clothing and footwear, beverages, chemicals, cement. **Chief crops:** coffee, cut flowers, bananas, rice, tobacco, corn, sugarcane, cocoa beans, oilseed, vegetables. **Natural resources:** petroleum, nat. gas, coal, iron ore, nickel, gold, copper, emeralds, hydropower. **Crude oil reserves:** 2.4 bil bbls. **Arable land:** 1.4%. **Livestock:** cattle: 23.1 mil; chickens: 165 mil; goats: 887,455; pigs: 5.3 mil; sheep: 701,884. **Electricity prod.:** 59.2 bil kWh. **Labor force:** agric. 17%, industry 21%, services 62%. **Unemployment:** 10.4%.

Finance: Monetary unit: Peso (COP) (Sept. 2014: 1,923.80 = $1 U.S.). **GDP:** $526.5 bil; **per capita GDP:** $11,100; **GDP growth:** 4.2%. **Imports:** $53.5 bil; U.S. 24.2%, China 16.3%, Mexico 10.9%, Brazil 4.8%. **Exports:** $58.7 bil; U.S. 36.6%, China 5.5%, Spain 4.8%, Panama 4.7%, Venezuela 4.4%, Netherlands 4.1%. **Tourism:** $2.5 bil. **Budget:** $106 bil. **Total reserves less gold:** $42.8 bil. **Gold:** 332,843 oz t. **Inflation:** 2.0%.

Transport: Railways: 543 mi. **Motor vehicles:** 89.2 per 1,000 pop. **Civil aviation:** 11.1 bil pass.-mi; 121 airports. **Chief ports:** Barranquilla, Buenaventura, Cartagena, Puerto Bolivar, Santa Marta, Turbo.

Communications: TV sets: 291 per 1,000 pop. **Radios:** 543 per 1,000 pop. **Telephone lines:** 14.8 per 100 pop. **Mobile:** 104.1 per 100 pop. **Internet:** 51.7%.

Health: Life expect.: 72.1 male; 78.6 female. **Births:** 16.7 per 1,000 pop. **Deaths:** 5.4 per 1,000 pop. **Natural inc.:** 1.14%. **Infant mortality:** 15.0 per 1,000 live births. **HIV:** 0.5%.

Education: Compulsory: ages 5-14. **Literacy:** 94.7%.

Embassy: 2118 Leroy Pl. NW 20008; 387-8338.

Website: wp.presidencia.gov.co

Spain subdued the local Indian kingdoms (Funza, Tunja) by the 1530s and ruled Colombia and neighboring areas as New Granada for 300 years. Independence was won by 1819. Venezuela and Ecuador broke away in 1829-30, and Panama withdrew in 1903.

Colombia is plagued by rural and urban violence. "La Violencia" of 1948-58 claimed 200,000 lives; since 1989, political killings, kidnappings, and "disappearances" have victimized many thousands of civilians, and the internally displaced population was estimated by UNHCR at more than 5.3 mil as of Jan. 2014. Attempts at land and social reform and progress in industrialization have not reduced massive social problems. Government activity against local drug traffickers has sparked retaliation killings of politicians and judges.

Right-wing paramilitaries launched a campaign Dec. 22, 2000, against suspected left-wing guerrillas. A hardliner, Álvaro Uribe Vélez, whose father had been killed by leftist rebels in 1983, won a presidential election May 2002. A wave of guerrilla violence as he took office led Uribe to declare a state of unrest Aug. 12, and police powers were increased as part of a new government offensive. The constitution was amended, Nov. 2004, to allow the president to seek a second consecutive term; Uribe easily won reelection May 2006. Key political figures, including major allies of Uribe, were arrested in 2007 on charges of colluding with paramilitary death squads. Peace talks with rebel groups began in Norway Oct. 2012 and shifted to Havana, Cuba, where, May 2013, an agreement to provide equal access to rural land for people of all economic levels was reached. Guerrilla violence continued, however.

Former Defense Min. Juan Manuel Santos Calderón, a conservative ally of Uribe, won a presidential runoff election June 2010, and took office Aug. 7. Santos won reelection June 15, 2014, shortly after beginning negotiations with one of the country's rebel groups.

Since 2000, the U.S. has provided billions of dollars to Colombia to combat the drug trade. Cocaine production has fallen substantially, according to U.S. figures disputed by the UN.

Pope Francis, May 12, 2013, canonized Colombia's first saint, Laura of St. Catherine of Siena Montoya y Upegui, a 20th-cent. nun and spiritual adviser for the country's indigenous population.

Comoros
Union of the Comoros

People: Population: 766,865. **Age distrib.:** <15: 41.3%; 65+: 3.8%. **Pop. density:** 888.7 per sq mi, 343.1 per sq km. **Urban:** 28.2%. **Ethnic groups:** Antalote, Cafre, Makoa, Oimatsaha, Sakalava. **Languages:** Arabic, French (both official); Shikomoro (blend of Swahili and Arabic). **Religions:** Sunni Muslim 98%, Roman Catholic 2%.

Geography: Total area: 863 sq mi, 2,235 sq km. **Land area:** 863 sq mi, 2,235 sq km. **Location:** 3 islands—Grande Comore (Njazidja), Anjouan (Nzwani), and Moheli (Mwali)—in the Mozambique Channel between NW Madagascar and SE Africa. **Neighbors:** Nearest are Mozambique on W, Madagascar on E. **Topography:** The islands are of volcanic origin, with an active volcano on Grande Comore. **Capital:** Moroni, 55,872.

Government: Type: Republic. **Head of state and gov.:** Pres. Ikililou Dhoinine; b. Aug. 14, 1962; in office: May 26, 2011. **Local divisions:** 3 islands, 4 municipalities. **Defense budget/active troops:** NA.

Economy: Industries: fishing, tourism, perfume distillation. **Chief crops:** vanilla, cloves, ylang-ylang, copra, coconuts, bananas, cassava. **Natural resources:** negligible. **Arable land:** 47.3%. **Livestock:** cattle: 50,000; chickens: 520,000; goats: 122,000; sheep: 24,000. **Electricity prod.:** 43 mil kWh. **Labor force:** agric. 80%, industry and services 20%. **Unemployment:** 7%.

Finance: Monetary unit: Franc (KMF) (Sept. 2014: 374.18 = $1 U.S.). **GDP:** $911 mil; **per capita GDP:** $1,300; **GDP growth:** 3.5%.

Imports: $208.8 mil; Pakistan 15.7%, France 14.2%, UAE 11.5%, India 8.5%, China 6.7%, Kenya 5.3%, Singapore 5.2%. **Exports:** $19.7 mil; Netherlands 58.6%, Singapore 10.6%, Turkey 9.3%, France 5.6%, India 5%. **Tourism:** $39 mil. **Budget:** $167.4 mil. **Total reserves less gold:** $173.4 mil. **Gold:** 579 oz t. **Inflation:** 2.3%.

Transport: Civil aviation: 4 airports. **Chief ports:** Mayotte, Mutsamudu.

Communications: TV sets: 31 per 1,000 pop. **Radios:** 159 per 1,000 pop. **Telephone lines:** 3.1 per 100 pop. **Mobile:** 47.3 per 100 pop. **Internet:** 6.5%.

Health: Life expect.: 61.2 male; 65.8 female. **Births:** 29.1 per 1,000 pop. **Deaths:** 7.8 per 1,000 pop. **Natural inc.:** 2.13%. **Infant mortality:** 65.3 per 1,000 live births. **HIV:** NA.

Education: Compulsory: ages 6-11. **Literacy:** 77.8%.

Permanent UN Mission: 866 UN Plz., Ste. 418, New York, NY 10017; (212) 750-1637.

Website: www.beit-salam.km

The French acquired the islands from Muslim sultans, 1841-1909. They became a French overseas territory in 1947. In a 1974 referendum, all islands favored independence except Mayotte. The French National Assembly decided to allow each island to decide its own fate. The Comore Chamber of Deputies declared independence July 6, 1975, with Ahmed Abdallah as president. In a 1976 referendum, Mayotte voted to remain French.

A leftist regime that seized power from Abdallah in 1975 was deposed in a pro-French 1978 coup in which he regained the presidency. In Nov. 1989, Pres. Abdallah was assassinated; soon after, a multiparty system was instituted. A Sept. 1995 military coup, assisted by French mercenaries, ousted Pres. Said Mohamed Djohar. French troops invaded, Oct. 4, and forced coup leaders to surrender.

Anjouan and Moheli seceded from the Comoros in 1997. Unrest on Grande Comore culminated in a military coup, Apr. 1999. Anjouans endorsed secession in a disputed vote Jan. 2000. A constitution adopted in a referendum Dec. 2001 that went into effect the following year reunited Anjouan and Moheli with Grande Comore, granting each a semi-autonomous status with their own presidents.

Irregularities marred the Apr. 2002, presidential runoff election, won by Azali Assoumani, who led the 1999 coup. Elections for national and island assemblies took place Mar.-Apr. 2004. Ahmed Abdallah Mohamed Sambi won a presidential runoff vote, May 2006. Each of the 3 islands elected its own president in 2002 and 2007. Col. Mohamed Bacar, who refused to relinquish power after the central government ruled his 2007 election illegal, fled when Comorian and African Union troops took control of the island, Mar. 2008. Sambi's Vice Pres. Ikililou Dhoinine won a presidential runoff election Dec. 2010.

The heaviest rains in decades devastated some of the country's poorest areas Apr. 20-25, 2012, forcing government officials to request $19 mil in aid to facilitate recovery for some 65,000 people who were displaced and affected with waterborne diseases.

Congo
Democratic Republic of the Congo

(Congo, officially Democratic Republic of the Congo, is also known as Congo-Kinshasa. The Republic of the Congo, commonly called Congo Republic, is also known as Congo-Brazzaville.)

People: Population: 77,433,744. **Age distrib.:** <15: 43.1%; 65+: 2.6%. **Pop. density:** 88.5 per sq mi, 34.2 per sq km. **Urban:** 42%. **Ethnic groups:** 200+ groups, majority Bantu. Four largest tribes (Mongo, Luba, Kongo [all Bantu], Mangbetu-Azande [Hamitic]) 45%. **Languages:** French (official), Lingala (lingua franca), Kingwana (Kiswahili or Swahili dialect), Kikongo, Tshiluba. **Religions:** Roman Catholic 50%, Protestant 20%, Kimbanguist 10%, Muslim 10%, other (incl. syncretic sects, indigenous beliefs) 10%.

Geography: Total area: 905,355 sq mi, 2,344,858 sq km; **Land area:** 875,312 sq mi, 2,267,048 sq km. **Location:** In central Africa. **Neighbors:** Congo Republic on W; Central African Republic, Sudan on N; Uganda, Rwanda, Burundi, Tanzania on E; Zambia, Angola on S. **Topography:** Congo includes the bulk of the Congo R. basin. The vast central region is a low-lying plateau covered by rain forest. Mountainous terraces in the W, savannas in the S and SE, grasslands toward the N, and the high Ruwenzori Mts. on the E surround the central region. A short strip of territory borders the Atlantic O. **Capital:** Kinshasa, 11,116,100. **Cities (urban aggl.):** Lubumbashi, 1,935,618; Mbuji-Mayi, 1,918,809.

Government: Type: Republic. **Head of state:** Pres. Joseph Kabila; b. June 24, 1971; in office: Jan. 17, 2001. **Head of gov.:** Prime Min. Augustin Matata Ponyo Mapon; b. June 5, 1964; in office: Apr. 18, 2012. **Local divisions:** 10 provinces, 1 city. **Defense budget:** $416 mil. **Active troops:** 134,250.

Economy: Industries: mining, mineral proc., consumer prods., metal prods., processed foods and beverages, timber, cement. **Chief crops:** coffee, sugar, palm oil, rubber, tea, cotton, cocoa, quinine, cassava, bananas, plantains, peanuts, root crops, corn, fruits. **Natural resources:** cobalt, copper, niobium, tantalum, petroleum, diamonds, gold, silver, zinc, manganese, tin, uranium, coal, hydropower, timber. **Crude oil reserves:** 180 mil bbls. **Arable land:** 3.1%. **Livestock:** cattle: 750,000; chickens: 21 mil; goats: 4.1 mil;

pigs: 1.1 mil; sheep: 910,000. **Electricity prod.:** 7.8 bil kWh. **Labor force:** NA. **Unemployment:** 7.2%.

Finance: Monetary unit: Franc (CDF) (Sept. 2014: 909.00 = $1 U.S.). **GDP:** $29.4 bil; **per capita GDP:** $400; **GDP growth:** 6.2%. **Imports:** $8.9 bil; South Africa 22.3%, China 15.3%, Belgium 8%, Zambia 6.9%, Zimbabwe 5.6%, France 4.9%, Kenya 4.7%. **Exports:** $9.9 bil; China 54.3%, Zambia 22.6%, Belgium 5.7%. **Tourism:** $7 mil. **Budget:** $6.5 bil. **Total reserves less gold:** $1.7 bil. **Inflation:** 1.6%.

Transport: Railways: 2,490 mi. **Motor vehicles:** 23.6 per 1,000 pop. **Civil aviation:** 26 airports. **Chief ports:** Boma, Bukavu, Bumba, Goma, Kinshasa, Kisangani, Matadi, Mbandaka.

Communications: TV sets: 5 per 1,000 pop. **Radios:** 379 per 1,000 pop. **Telephone lines** (2012): 0.09 per 100 pop. **Mobile:** 43.7 per 100 pop. **Internet:** 2.2%.

Health: Life expect.: 55.0 male; 58.1 female. **Births:** 35.6 per 1,000 pop. **Deaths:** 10.3 per 1,000 pop. **Natural inc.:** 2.53%. **Infant mortality:** 73.2 per 1,000 live births. **HIV:** 1.1%.

Education: Compulsory: ages 6-11. **Literacy:** 63.8%.

Embassy: 1726 M St. NW 20036; 234-7690.

Website: www.presidentrdc.cd

The earliest inhabitants of Congo may have been the pygmies, followed by Bantus from the east and Nilotic tribes from the north. The large Bantu Bakongo kingdom ruled much of Congo and Angola when Portuguese explorers visited in the 15th cent.

Leopold II, king of the Belgians, formed an international group to exploit the Congo region in 1876. In 1877, British explorer Henry M. Stanley traveled the Congo, and in 1878 he returned to organize the region and win over the indigenous leaders. The Conference of Berlin, 1884-85, established the Congo Free State with Leopold as king and chief owner. The colony became known as the Belgian Congo in 1908. Millions of Congolese rubber plantation workers were exploited and others died under brutal European rule between 1880 and 1920.

Belgian and Congolese leaders agreed Jan. 27, 1960, that Congo would become independent in June. In the first general elections, May 31, Patrice Lumumba's party won a plurality in the National Assembly. The Republic of the Congo was proclaimed June 30. Europeans and others fled widespread violence. The UN Security Council, Aug. 9, called on Belgium to withdraw its troops and sent a UN contingent. Lumumba was dismissed as premier in Sept. and murdered Jan. 17, 1961. The last UN troops left the Congo June 30, 1964.

In late 1965, Gen. Joseph D. Mobutu was named president. He later changed his name to Mobutu Sese Seko and ruled as a dictator. The country became the Democratic Republic of the Congo (1966) and the Republic of the Congo (1971). Under Mobutu, economic decline and government corruption plagued Zaire. He retained power despite mounting international pressure and internal opposition.

During 1994, Zaire was inundated with refugees from the massive ethnic bloodshed in Rwanda. Ethnic violence spread to eastern Zaire in 1996. In Oct., militant Hutus, who dominated in the refugee camps, fought rebels (mostly Tutsis) in Zaire, precipitating intervention by government troops. As a result of the fighting, Rwandan refugees abandoned the camps; hundreds of thousands returned to Rwanda, while hundreds of thousands more were dispersed throughout eastern Zaire. The rebels, led by Gen. Laurent Kabila—a former Marxist and longtime opponent of Mobutu—began to move west across Zaire. On May 17, 1997, Kabila's troops entered Kinshasa and Mobutu went into exile. The country again became the Dem. Rep. of the Congo. Mobutu died Sept. 7 in Morocco.

Kabila, who ruled by decree, alienated UN officials, international aid donors, and former allies. Rebels assisted by Rwanda and Uganda threatened Kinshasa in Aug. 1998 but were turned back with help from Angola, Namibia, and Zimbabwe. Rebel groups agreed to a cease-fire, Aug. 31, 1999, but the truce was widely violated. Kabila was assassinated Jan. 16, 2001, and was succeeded by his son Joseph.

The estimated death toll from the civil war and related causes was 3.3 mil through Nov. 2002. By then, Rwanda and Uganda had agreed to pull out their remaining troops. A power-sharing accord signed Apr. 2, 2003, led to the installation of a new Congolese government in July. A new constitution won legislative approval May 13, 2005. A UN peacekeeping force (MONUC), established in 1999, oversaw July 2006 elections, the nation's first multiparty vote since 1960. Kabila defeated former rebel leader Jean-Pierre Bemba in a presidential runoff election, Oct. 2006.

Hundreds reportedly died in Kinshasa, Mar. 22-23, 2007, in clashes between security forces and a militia loyal to Bemba, who fled to Europe. He was arrested in Belgium May 24, 2008, on war crimes charges; his trial was ongoing at The Hague in mid-2014. A peace deal with militia groups in eastern Congo, including one led by Tutsi rebel Gen. Laurent Nkunda, was signed Jan. 23, 2008, but Nkunda launched a new offensive Aug. 28; Rwandan authorities arrested him Jan. 2009.

A June 2011 study published by the *American Journal of Public Health* estimated that more than 1,000 women were raped in Congo every day. The Intl. Criminal Court (ICC) convicted Congolese warlord Thomas Lubanga Dyilo Mar. 2012 of war crimes for conscripting child soldiers during the country's civil war. The ICC, May 23, 2014,

sentenced rebel leader Germain Katanga to 12 years in prison in connection with a 2003 massacre of more than 200 villagers.

The MONUC peacekeeping mission, reconstituted and renamed MONUSCO as of July 1, 2010, included about 20,000 military personnel on July 31, 2014. Eleven African nations signed a peace plan Feb. 24, 2013, designed to end the violence in Congo. Rebel leader Bosco Ntaganda turned himself in at the U.S. embassy in Rwanda Mar. 18 to face charges of war crimes and crimes against humanity. A peace agreement with the M23 militia group was reached in Dec. 2013. About 8,000 rebels had lain down their arms by mid-Jan. 2014, but other fighters remained active.

An apparent outbreak of Ebola virus in northern Congo, reported to WHO Aug. 26, 2014, was not related to the Ebola epidemic then occurring in W Africa. By Sept. 28, 2014, there had been 70 cases in Congo and 42 deaths.

Congo Republic
Republic of the Congo

(Congo Republic, officially Republic of the Congo, is also known as Congo-Brazzaville. The Democratic Republic of the Congo [formerly Zaire], now commonly called Congo, is also known as Congo-Kinshasa.)

People: Population: 4,662,446. **Age distrib.:** <15: 41.1%; 65+: 3%. **Pop. density:** 35.4 per sq mi, 13.7 per sq km. **Urban:** 65%. **Ethnic groups:** Kongo 48%, Sangha 20%, Teke 17%, M'Bochi 12%, Europeans and other 3%. **Languages:** French (official), Lingala, Monokutuba (lingua francas); many local langs., dialects (Kikongo most widespread). **Religions:** Roman Catholic 33%, Awakening Churches/Christian Revival 22%, Protestant 20%, Salutiste 2%, none 11%.

Geography: Total area: 132,047 sq mi, 342,000 sq km; **Land area:** 131,854 sq mi, 341,500 sq km. **Location:** In W central Africa. **Neighbors:** Gabon and Cameroon on W, Central African Republic on N, Dem. Rep. of the Congo on E, Angola on SW. **Topography:** Much of country is covered by thick forests. A coastal plain leads to the fertile Niari Valley. The center is a plateau; the Congo R. basin consists of flood plains in the lower and savanna in the upper portion. **Capital:** Brazzaville, 1,826,890.

Government: Type: Republic. **Head of state and gov.:** Pres. Denis Sassou-Nguesso; b. 1943; in office: Oct. 25, 1997. **Local divisions:** 12 departments. **Defense budget** (2012): $325 mil. **Active troops:** 10,000.

Economy: Industries: petroleum extraction, cement, lumber, brewing, soap, palm oil. **Chief crops:** cassava, sugar, rice, corn, peanuts, vegetables, coffee, cocoa. **Natural resources:** petroleum, timber, potash, lead, zinc, uranium, copper, phosphates, gold, magnesium, nat. gas, hydropower. **Crude oil reserves:** 1.6 bil bbls. **Arable land:** 1.6%. **Livestock:** cattle: 337,000; chickens: 2.9 mil; goats: 325,000; pigs: 95,000; sheep: 122,000. **Electricity prod.:** 1.3 bil kWh. **Labor force:** NA. **Unemployment:** 7.1%.

Finance: Monetary unit: Central African CFA Franc (XAF) (Sept. 2014: 498.91 = $1 U.S.). **GDP:** $20.3 bil; **per capita GDP:** $4,800; **GDP growth:** 5.8%. **Imports:** $4.3 bil; France 19.5%, China 13.5%, Brazil 9.1%, U.S. 6.1%, India 5.8%, Italy 4.8%, Belgium 4.4%. **Exports:** $9.9 bil; China 39%, U.S. 13%, France 9.5%, Australia 8.8%, Netherlands 6.8%, Spain 5.3%, India 5.2%. **Budget:** $4.6 bil. **Total reserves less gold** (2012): $5.5 bil. **Inflation:** 6.0%.

Transport: Railways: 551 mi. **Motor vehicles:** 16.2 per 1,000 pop. **Civil aviation:** 8 airports. **Chief ports:** Brazzaville, Djeno, Impfondo, Ouesso, Oyo, Pointe-Noire.

Communications: TV sets: 50 per 1,000 pop. **Radios:** 107 per 1,000 pop. **Telephone lines:** 0.4 per 100 pop. **Mobile:** 104.8 per 100 pop. **Internet:** 6.6%.

Health: Life expect.: 57.4 male; 59.7 female. **Births:** 36.6 per 1,000 pop. **Deaths:** 10.2 per 1,000 pop. **Natural inc.:** 2.64%. **Infant mortality:** 59.3 per 1,000 live births. **HIV:** 2.5%.

Education: Compulsory: ages 6-15. **Literacy:** 79.3%.

Embassy: 4891 Colorado Ave. NW 20011; 726-5500.

Website: www.presidence.cg

The Loango kingdom flourished in the 15th cent., as did the Anzico kingdom of the Batekes; by the late 17th cent. they had weakened. By 1885, France established control of the region, then called the Middle Congo. The Republic of the Congo gained independence Aug. 15, 1960.

After trade unions sparked a 1963 coup, the country adopted a Marxist-Leninist stance, with the USSR and China vying for influence. France remained a dominant trade partner and source of technical assistance, and French-owned private enterprise retained a major economic role. In 1970, the country was renamed People's Republic of the Congo. Since the 1980s, oil has dominated the economy.

In 1990, Marxism was renounced and opposition parties were legalized. In 1991 the country's name was changed back to Rep. of the Congo, and a new constitution was approved. A democratically elected government came into office in 1992. Factional fighting broke out in Brazzaville, June 1997 and intensified during the summer, devastating the capital. Troops loyal to former Marxist dictator Denis Sassou-Nguesso took control of the city Oct. 15, 1997; he claimed lopsided victories in 2002 and 2009 presidential elections. His party won an absolute majority in the country's National Assembly, Aug. 5, 2012.

Costa Rica
Republic of Costa Rica

People: Population: 4,755,234. **Age distrib.:** <15: 23.5%; 65+: 7%. **Pop. density:** 241.2 per sq mi, 93.1 per sq km. **Urban:** 75.9%. **Ethnic groups:** white or mestizo 84%, mulatto 7%, indigenous 2%. **Languages:** Spanish (official), English. **Religions:** Roman Catholic 76%, Evangelical 14%, Jehovah's Witnesses 1%, none 3%.

Geography: Total area: 19,730 sq mi, 51,100 sq km; **Land area:** 19,714 sq mi, 51,060 sq km. **Location:** In Central America. **Neighbors:** Nicaragua on N, Panama on S. **Topography:** Lowlands by the Caribbean are tropical. The interior plateau, at an elevation of about 4,000 ft, is temperate. **Capital:** San José, 1,159,510.

Government: Type: Democratic republic. **Head of state and gov.:** Pres. Luis Guillermo Solís Rivera; b. Apr. 25, 1958; in office: May 8, 2014. **Local divisions:** 7 provinces. **Defense budget:** $397 mil (paramilitary budget). **Active troops:** No armed forces. 9,800 paramilitary only.

Economy: Industries: microprocessors, food proc., medical equip., textiles and clothing, constr. materials, fertilizer, plastic prods. **Chief crops:** bananas, pineapples, coffee, melons, ornamental plants, sugar, corn, rice, beans, potatoes. **Natural resources:** hydropower. **Arable land:** 4.8%. **Livestock:** cattle: 1.3 mil; chickens: 23.2 mil; goats: 5,150; pigs: 434,000; sheep: 2,850. **Electricity prod.:** 9.9 bil kWh. **Labor force:** agric. 14%, industry 22%, services 64%. **Unemployment:** 7.6%.

Finance: Monetary unit: Colon (CRC) (Sept. 2014: 534.25 = $1 U.S.). **GDP:** $61.4 bil; **per capita GDP:** $12,900; **GDP growth:** 3.5%. **Imports:** $17.6 bil; U.S. 49.8%, China 8.2%, Mexico 6.6%. **Exports:** $11.7 bil; U.S. 38.9%, Netherlands 7.5%, Panama 5.1%, Hong Kong 4.6%, Nicaragua 4.4%. **Tourism:** $2.5 bil. **Budget:** $9.6 bil. **Total reserves less gold:** $7.3 bil. **Gold:** 1,909 oz t. **Inflation:** 5.2%.

Transport: Railways: 173 mi (not in current use). **Motor vehicles:** 184.4 per 1,000 pop. **Civil aviation:** 1.8 bil pass.-mi; 47 airports. **Chief ports:** Caldera, Puerto Limon.

Communications: TV sets: 250 per 1,000 pop. **Radios:** 222 per 1,000 pop. **Telephone lines:** 19.9 per 100 pop. **Mobile:** 146 per 100 pop. **Internet:** 46%.

Health: Life expect.: 75.6 male; 81.0 female. **Births:** 16.1 per 1,000 pop. **Deaths:** 4.5 per 1,000 pop. **Natural inc.:** 1.16%. **Infant mortality:** 8.7 per 1,000 live births. **HIV:** 0.2%.

Education: Compulsory: ages 5-14. **Literacy:** 97.8%.

Embassy: 2114 S St. NW 20008; 234-2945.

Website: www.gobiernofacil.go.cr

Guaymi Indians inhabited the area when Spaniards arrived, 1502. Independence came in 1821. Costa Rica seceded from the Central American Federation in 1838. Since the civil war of 1948-49, free political institutions have been preserved.

Costa Rica, still a largely agricultural country, has achieved a relatively high standard of living, and land ownership is widespread. Tourism is an important source of revenue. Nobel Peace Prize-winner Óscar Arias Sánchez, president 1986-90, won a second term in a close election, Feb. 5, 2006. An election victory Feb. 7, 2010, made ruling party candidate Laura Chinchilla Miranda the nation's first female president. Luis Guillermo Solís Rivera of the opposition Citizen Action Party won an Apr. 6, 2014, runoff election and was sworn in as president May 8, 2014.

Côte d'Ivoire
Republic of Côte d'Ivoire

People: Population: 22,848,945. **Age distrib.:** <15: 38.4%; 65+: 3.3%. **Pop. density:** 186.1 per sq mi, 71.9 per sq km. **Urban:** 53.5%. **Ethnic groups:** Akan 42%, Voltaiques or Gur 18%, N Mandes 17%, Krous 11%, S Mandes 10%. **Languages:** French (official), 60 native dialects (Dioula most widely spoken). **Religions:** Muslim 39%, Christian 33%, indigenous 12%, none 17%.

Geography: Total area: 124,504 sq mi, 322,463 sq km; **Land area:** 122,782 sq mi, 318,003 sq km. **Location:** On S coast of W Africa. **Neighbors:** Liberia, Guinea on W; Mali, Burkina Faso on N; Ghana on E. **Topography:** Forests cover the W half of the country, and range from a coastal strip to halfway to the N on the E. A sparse inland plain leads to low mountains in NW. **Capital:** Yamoussoukro, 258,962; Abidjan (admin.), 4,707,560.

Government: Type: Republic. **Head of state:** Pres. Alassane Ouattara; b. Jan. 1, 1942; in office: Apr. 11, 2011 (sworn in Dec. 4, 2010). **Head of gov.:** Prime Min. Daniel Kablan Duncan; b. 1943; in office: Nov. 21, 2012. **Local divisions:** 12 districts, 2 autonomous districts. **Defense budget:** $751 mil. **Active troops:** 40,000 (target).

Economy: Industries: foodstuffs, beverages, wood prods., oil refining, gold mining, truck and bus assembly, textiles, fertilizer. **Chief crops:** coffee, cocoa beans, bananas, palm kernels, corn, rice, cassava, sweet potatoes, sugar, cotton, rubber. **Natural resources:** petroleum, nat. gas, diamonds, manganese, iron ore, cobalt, bauxite, copper, gold, nickel, tantalum, silica sand, clay, cocoa beans, coffee, palm oil, hydropower. **Crude oil reserves:** 100 mil bbls. **Arable land:** 9.1%. **Livestock:** cattle: 1.6 mil; chickens: 58.4 mil; goats:

1.4 mil; pigs: 362,693; sheep: 1.7 mil. **Electricity prod.:** 5.9 bil kWh. **Labor force:** agric. 68%. **Unemployment:** 4%.

Finance: Monetary unit: CFA Franc (XOF) (Sept. 2014: 498.91 = $1 U.S.). **GDP:** $43.7 bil; **per capita GDP:** $1,800; **GDP growth:** 8%. **Imports:** $9.9 bil; Nigeria 25%, France 11%, China 7.2%. **Exports:** $13 bil; Netherlands 8.8%, U.S. 8.1%, Nigeria 8%, Germany 7.5%, France 4.5%, Canada 4.2%. **Tourism:** $141 mil. **Budget:** $6.7 bil. **Total reserves less gold:** $4.2 bil. **Inflation:** 2.6%.

Transport: Railways: 410 mi. **Motor vehicles:** 23.7 per 1,000 pop. **Civil aviation:** 7 airports. **Chief ports:** Abidjan, Espoir, San-Pédro.

Communications: TV sets: 44 per 1,000 pop. **Radios:** 138 per 1,000 pop. **Telephone lines:** 1.3 per 100 pop. **Mobile:** 95.5 per 100 pop. **Internet:** 2.6%.

Health: Life expect.: 56.9 male; 59.2 female. **Births:** 29.3 per 1,000 pop. **Deaths:** 9.7 per 1,000 pop. **Natural inc.:** 1.96%. **Infant mortality:** 60.2 per 1,000 live births. **HIV:** 2.7%.

Education: Compulsory: ages 6-15. **Literacy:** 43.1%.

Embassy: 3421 Massachusetts Ave. NW 20007; 797-0300.

Website: www.gouv.ci

A French protectorate from 1842, Côte d'Ivoire became independent in 1960. The name was officially changed from Ivory Coast, Oct. 1985.

Students and workers protested, Feb. 1990, demanding the ouster of longtime Pres. Félix Houphouët-Boigny. Côte d'Ivoire held its first multiparty presidential election Oct. 1990, which Houphouët-Boigny won. He died Dec. 7, 1993. The National Assembly named as successor Henri Konan Bédié. He was reelected Oct. 1995 but was ousted in a military coup Dec. 24, 1999. The coup leader, Robert Guéi, lost a presidential vote Oct. 2000 but claimed victory anyway. After mass protests, he fled, and Laurent Gbagbo became president. Guéi was killed in Abidjan Sept. 19, 2002.

Agreement on power sharing was reached in Mar. 2003, and Gbagbo and former rebel leaders declared an end to the war July 5. The country remained divided, however. Rebels held the north and government forces controlled the south. Under a new accord reached Mar. 2007, rebel leader Guillaume Soro became prime min.

Both Gbagbo and his main challenger, former Prime Min. Alassane Ouattara, claimed victory after a presidential runoff election Nov. 2010. Gbagbo clung to power, although the UN and much of the international community recognized Ouattara as the legitimate winner. A violent power struggle followed, claiming an estimated 1,500 lives and displacing at least 1 mil people. With support from French and UN forces, Ouattara loyalists captured Gbagbo in Abidjan, Apr. 2011. Human Rights Watch reported June 2 that after taking power, Ouattara's troops killed at least 149 suspected Gbagbo supporters. More than 100 prisoners were freed and 5 people died in a raid at a security post west of Abidjan Aug. 16, 2012, blamed on Gbagbo supporters. In both Feb. 2013 and Feb. 2014 reports, Amnesty Intl. accused the army and its allies of killing and torturing Gbagbo loyalists. A UN peacekeeping mission (UNOCI), authorized since 2004, had almost 9,000 military personnel in Côte d'Ivoire in mid-2014. The ICC, June 12, 2014, ordered Gbagbo to stand trial for crimes against humanity.

Croatia
Republic of Croatia

People: Population: 4,470,534. **Age distrib.:** <15: 14.5%; 65+: 17.8%. **Pop. density:** 206.9 per sq mi, 79.9 per sq km. **Urban:** 58.7%. **Ethnic groups:** Croat 90%, Serb 4%, other (incl. Bosniak, Hungarian, Slovene, Czech, Roma) 4%. **Languages:** Croatian (official), Serbian. **Religions:** Roman Catholic 86%, Orthodox 4%, Muslim 2%, none 4%.

Geography: Total area: 21,851 sq mi, 56,594 sq km; **Land area:** 21,612 sq mi, 55,974 sq km. **Location:** SE Europe, on the Balkan Peninsula. **Neighbors:** Slovenia, Hungary on N; Bosnia and Herzegovina, Serbia, Montenegro on E. **Topography:** Flat plains in NE; highlands, low mts. along Adriatic. **Capital:** Zagreb, 687,007.

Government: Type: Parliamentary democracy. **Head of state:** Pres. Ivo Josipovic; b. Aug. 28, 1957; in office: Feb. 18, 2010. **Head of gov.:** Prime Min. Zoran Milanovic; b. Oct. 30, 1966; in office: Dec. 23, 2011. **Local divisions:** 20 counties, 1 city with special county status. **Defense budget:** $813 mil. **Active troops:** 16,550.

Economy: Industries: chemicals and plastics, machine tools, fabricated metal, electronics. **Chief crops:** wheat, corn, barley, sugar beets, sunflower seeds, rapeseeds, alfalfa, clover, vegetables, fruits. **Natural resources:** oil, coal, bauxite, iron ore, calcium, gypsum, nat. asphalt, silica, mica, clays, salt, hydropower. **Crude oil reserves:** 71 mil bbls. **Arable land:** 16.1%. **Livestock:** cattle: 442,000; chickens: 8.7 mil; goats: 69,000; pigs: 1.1 mil; sheep: 620,000. **Electricity prod.:** 10.2 bil kWh. **Labor force:** agric. 2.1%, industry 29%, services 69%. **Unemployment:** 15.8%.

Finance: Monetary unit: Kuna (HRK) (Sept. 2014: 5.80 = $1 U.S.). **GDP:** $78.9 bil; **per capita GDP:** $17,800; **GDP growth:** –1%. **Imports:** $21.7 bil; Germany 13.7%, Italy 12.5%, Slovenia 11.5%, Austria 9.1%, Hungary 6.2%, Russia 5.4%. **Exports:** $12.4 bil; Italy 14.1%, Bosnia and Herzegovina 13.1%, Germany 11.1%, Slovenia 10.1%, Austria 6.3%. **Tourism:** $9.6 bil. **Budget:** $20.4 bil. **Total reserves less gold:** $17.8 bil. **Inflation:** 2.2%.

Transport: Railways: 1,691 mi. **Motor vehicles:** 343.9 per 1,000 pop. **Civil aviation:** 764.3 mil pass.-mi; 24 airports. **Chief ports:** Omisalj, Ploce, Rijeka, Sibenik, Split, Vukovar.

Communications: TV sets: 550 per 1,000 pop. **Radios:** 327 per 1,000 pop. **Telephone lines:** 36.8 per 100 pop. **Mobile:** 114.5 per 100 pop. **Internet:** 66.8%.

Health: Life expect.: 72.8 male; 80.2 female. **Births:** 9.5 per 1,000 pop. **Deaths:** 12.1 per 1,000 pop. **Natural inc.:** –0.26%. **Infant mortality:** 5.9 per 1,000 live births. **HIV:** NA.

Education: Compulsory: ages 7-14. **Literacy:** 99.3%.

Embassy: 2343 Massachusetts Ave. NW 20008; 588-5899.

Website: www.vlada.hr

From the 7th cent. the area was inhabited by Croats, a south Slavic people. It was formed into a kingdom under Tomislav in 924, and joined with Hungary in 1102. The Croats became westernized and separated from Slavs under Austro-Hungarian influence. Croatia united with other Yugoslav areas to proclaim the Kingdom of Serbs, Croats, and Slovenes in 1918. A nominally independent state between 1941 and 1945, it became a constituent republic of Yugoslavia in the 1946 constitution.

On June 25, 1991, Croatia declared independence from Yugoslavia. Fighting began between ethnic Serbs and Croats. The Serbs gained control of some Croatian territory, but Croatian troops recaptured most of the Serb-held territory Aug. 1995. A peace accord was signed in Paris in Dec. The last Serb-held enclave, E Slavonia, was returned to Croatia in 1998. Indicted in 2001 and arrested in 2005, former Croatian Gen. Ante Gotovina was convicted by a UN tribunal Apr. 2011 and sentenced to 24 years in prison for war crimes committed in the mid-1990s. Croatia became a full NATO member Apr. 1, 2009. Law professor and composer Ivo Josipovic, the nominee of the Social Democratic Party, won a presidential runoff election Jan. 2010 and took office Feb. 18. Croatia joined the EU July 1, 2013.

The convictions of 2 former Croatian generals for war crimes against the Serbs were overturned Nov. 16, 2012. But a UN tribunal convicted 6 other Croats May 29, 2013, for ethnic cleansing of Bosnians during the 1990s, while 2 Serbs were acquitted of war crimes on May 31.

Cuba
Republic of Cuba

People: Population: 11,047,251. **Age distrib.:** <15: 16.3%; 65+: 12.6%. **Pop. density:** 260.5 per sq mi, 100.6 per sq km. **Urban:** 77%. **Ethnic groups:** white 64%, mestizo 27%, black 9%. **Language:** Spanish (official). **Religion:** Roman Catholic (nominally, prior to Castro assuming power) 85%.

Geography: Total area: 42,803 sq mi, 110,860 sq km. **Land area:** 42,402 sq mi, 109,820 sq km. **Location:** In Caribbean, westernmost of West Indies. **Neighbors:** The Bahamas, U.S. to N; Mexico to W; Jamaica to S; Haiti to E. **Topography:** Coastline is about 2,500 mi. The N coast is steep and rocky, the S coast low and marshy. Low hills and fertile valleys cover more than half the country. Sierra Maestra, in E, is the highest of 3 mountain ranges. **Capital:** Havana, 2,146,130.

Government: Type: Communist state. **Head of state and gov.:** Pres. Raúl Castro Ruz; b. June 3, 1931; in office: Feb. 24, 2008 (acting from July 31, 2006). **Local divisions:** 15 provinces, 1 special municipality. **Defense budget** (2011): $96 mil. **Active troops:** 49,000.

Economy: Industries: petroleum, nickel/cobalt, pharmaceuticals, tobacco, constr., steel, cement, agric. machinery. **Chief crops:** sugar, tobacco, citrus, coffee, rice, potatoes, beans. **Natural resources:** cobalt, nickel, iron ore, chromium, copper, salt, timber, silica, petroleum. **Crude oil reserves:** 124 mil bbls. **Arable land:** 30.1%. **Livestock:** cattle: 4.1 mil; chickens: 30 mil; goats: 555,500; pigs: 1.4 mil; sheep: 2 mil. **Electricity prod.:** 16.7 bil kWh. **Labor force:** agric. 19.7%, industry 17.1%, services 63.2%. **Unemployment:** 2.4%.

Finance: Monetary unit: Peso (CUP) (Sept. 2014: 26.50 = $1 U.S.). **GDP** (2012): $121 bil; **per capita GDP** (2010): $10,200; **GDP growth** (2012): 3.1%. **Imports:** $13.6 bil; Venezuela 38.3%, China 10.8%, Spain 8.9%, Brazil 5.2%, U.S. 4.3%. **Exports:** $6.3 bil; Canada 17.7%, China 16.9%, Venezuela 12.5%, Netherlands 9%, Spain 5.9%. **Tourism:** $2.3 bil. **Budget:** $50.3 bil. **Total reserves less gold:** NA. **Inflation:** NA.

Transport: Railways: 5,097 mi. **Motor vehicles:** 41.8 per 1,000 pop. **Civil aviation:** 1.2 bil pass.-mi; 64 airports. **Chief ports:** Cienfuegos, Guantánamo, Havana, Mariel, Matanzas, Santiago de Cuba.

Communications: TV sets: 213 per 1,000 pop. **Radios:** 276 per 1,000 pop. **Telephone lines:** 11 per 100 pop. **Mobile:** 17.7 per 100 pop. **Internet:** 25.7%.

Health: Life expect.: 75.9 male; 80.7 female. **Births:** 9.9 per 1,000 pop. **Deaths:** 7.6 per 1,000 pop. **Natural inc.:** 0.23%. **Infant mortality:** 4.7 per 1,000 live births. **HIV:** 0.2%.

Education: Compulsory: ages 6-14. **Literacy:** 99.9%.

Cuban Interests Section: 2630 16th St. NW 20009; 797-8518.

Website: www.cubagob.cu

Some 50,000 indigenous people lived in Cuba when Columbus reached it in 1492. Its name derives from the Indian Cubanacan.

Except for British occupation of Havana, 1762-63, Cuba remained Spanish until 1898. A slave-based sugar plantation economy developed from the 18th cent. Sugar remains a leading export. Spain failed to deliver on rights guaranteed in 1878, prompting a full-scale liberation movement under Jose Martí in 1895.

The Spanish-American War began Apr. 1898 with the sinking of the USS *Maine* in Havana harbor. Spain lost the war and gave up all claims to Cuba. U.S. troops withdrew in 1902, but under 1903 and 1934 agreements, the U.S. continued to lease a site at Guantánamo Bay in the SE as a naval base. U.S. and other foreign investors dominated the economy. In 1952, former Pres. Fulgencio Batista established a dictatorship, which grew increasingly harsh and corrupt. Fidel Castro began a rebellion in 1956; guerrilla fighting intensified in 1958. Batista fled Jan. 1, 1959, and Castro took power, becoming premier Feb. 16.

Government-instituted economic and social changes failed to restore promised liberties. Opponents were imprisoned or executed. Some 700,000 Cubans emigrated in the first years after Castro's takeover, mostly to the U.S. By 1960, all banks and industrial companies had been nationalized, including over $1 bil worth of U.S.-owned properties, mostly without compensation.

In 1961, some 1,400 Cubans, trained and backed by the U.S. Central Intelligence Agency, unsuccessfully tried to overthrow the regime. On Oct. 22, 1962, U.S. Pres. John F. Kennedy ordered a naval blockade around Cuba and demanded that Soviet-installed nuclear missiles be withdrawn. The crisis ended Oct. 28 when Soviet Prem. Nikita S. Khrushchev agreed to withdraw the missiles; the U.S. ended the blockade, pledged not to invade Cuba, and removed its own missiles from Turkey.

In 1977, Cuba and the U.S. agreed to exchange diplomats, without restoring full ties, and to regulate offshore fishing. In 1978 and 1980, the U.S. agreed to accept political prisoners released by Cuba, some of whom were criminals and mental patients. A 1987 agreement provided for 20,000 Cubans to emigrate to the U.S. each year; Cuba agreed to take back some 2,500 jailed in the U.S. since 1980. Cuba's support for left-wing regimes and liberation movements in Central America, Africa, and the Caribbean contributed to poor relations with the U.S.

Cuba's economy, hobbled by U.S. sanctions and dependent on aid from other Communist countries, was shaken by the collapse of the Communist bloc in the late 1980s. Stiffer trade sanctions enacted by the U.S. in 1992 made things worse. Antigovernment demonstrations in Aug. 1994 prompted Castro to loosen emigration restrictions. A new U.S.-Cuba accord in Sept. ended the exodus of "boat people" after more than 30,000 had left Cuba. The U.S. also announced May 1995 it would admit 20,000 Cuban refugees held at Guantánamo but would return additional refugees to Cuba.

The U.S. imposed additional sanctions after Cuba, Feb. 1996, shot down two aircraft operated by anti-Castro exiles. Cuba blamed exile groups for bombings at Havana tourist hotels, July-Sept. 1997. Pope John Paul II visited Cuba, Jan. 21-25, 1998.

On July 31, 2006, the ailing Fidel Castro yielded power to his 75-year-old brother Raúl, who served as acting president until formally succeeding Feb. 24, 2008.

The U.S. in 2009 eased restrictions on remittances and family travel to the island but retained its trade embargo. The Cuban government announced, Sept. 2010, economic restructuring plans involving cutting more than 500,000 workers from the public payroll. A Communist Party conference, Apr. 2011, confirmed Raúl Castro as first secretary and approved economic reforms, including an expansion of private property rights. Pope Benedict XVI visited Cuba, Mar. 26-28, 2012.

The U.S., Jan. 11, 2002, began using its naval base at Guantánamo Bay to detain prisoners captured in Afghanistan. The indefinite detention and aggressive interrogation of Guantánamo prisoners were criticized by human rights groups. U.S. Pres. Barack Obama signed, Jan. 2009, an executive order calling for the closure of the Guantánamo detention center within a year; as of June 2014, however, 149 detainees were still held there.

Landmark migration rules were enacted Jan. 14, 2013, allowing Cubans to remain overseas—including in the U.S.—longer without forfeiting their Cuban residency. Legislation to encourage foreign investment, in part by lowering taxes and allowing investment in more economic sectors, was adopted in Mar. 2014.

Cyprus
Republic of Cyprus

People: Population: 1,172,458. **Age distrib.:** <15: 15.7%; 65+: 11.2%. **Pop. density:** 328.6 per sq mi, 126.9 per sq km. **Urban:** 67%. **Ethnic groups:** Greek 77%, Turkish 18%. **Languages:** Greek, Turkish (both official); English. **Religions:** Greek Orthodox 78%, Muslim 18%, other (incl. Maronite, Armenian Apostolic) 4%.

Geography: Total area: 3,572 sq mi, 9,251 sq km; **Land area:** 3,568 sq mi, 9,241 sq km. **Location:** In eastern Mediterranean Sea, off Turkish coast. **Neighbors:** Nearest are Turkey on N, Syria and Lebanon on E. **Topography:** Two mountain ranges run E-W, separated by a wide, fertile plain. **Capital:** Nicosia (Lefkosia), 251,142.

Government: Type: Republic. **Head of state and gov.:** Pres. Nicos Anastasiades; b. Sept. 27, 1946; in office: Feb. 28, 2013.

Local divisions: 6 districts. **Defense budget:** $460 mil. **Active troops:** 12,000 (3,500 in territory where govt. does not exercise effective control).

Economy: Industries: tourism, food and beverage proc., cement and gypsum prod., ship repair and refurb., textiles, light chemicals, metal prods. **Chief crops:** citrus, vegetables, barley, grapes, olives, vegetables. **Natural resources:** copper, pyrites, asbestos, gypsum, timber, salt, marble, clay earth pigment. **Arable land:** 9.9%. **Livestock:** cattle: 57,000; chickens: 3.2 mil; goats: 243,130; pigs: 357,900; sheep: 347,000. **Electricity prod.:** 4.6 bil kWh. **Labor force:** agric. 8.5%, industry 20.5%, services 71%. **Unemployment:** 11.8%.

Finance: Monetary unit: Euro (EUR) (Sept. 2014: 0.76 = $1 U.S.). **GDP:** $21.6 bil; **per capita GDP:** $24,500; **GDP growth:** –8.7%. **Imports:** $4.7 bil; Greece 21.6%, Israel 11.9%, Italy 8.3%, UK 7.3%, Germany 7.1%, Netherlands 6.7%, France 6%, China 4.5%. **Exports:** $2.4 bil; Greece 23%, UK 10.1%. **Tourism:** $2.9 bil. **Budget:** $10 bil. **Total reserves less gold:** $379.1 mil. **Gold:** 446,795 oz t. **Inflation:** –0.4%.

Transport: Motor vehicles: 594.3 per 1,000 pop. **Civil aviation:** 1.5 bil pass.-mi; 13 airports. **Chief ports:** Larnaca, Limassol (under govt. control); Famagusta (admin. by Turkish Cypriots).

Communications: TV sets: 358 per 1,000 pop. **Radios:** 505 per 1,000 pop. **Telephone lines:** 30.6 per 100 pop. **Mobile:** 95.2 per 100 pop. **Internet:** 65.5%.

Health: Life expect.: 75.5 male; 81.3 female. **Births:** 11.4 per 1,000 pop. **Deaths:** 6.6 per 1,000 pop. **Natural inc.:** 0.49%. **Infant mortality:** 8.5 per 1,000 live births. **HIV:** <0.1%.

Education: Compulsory: ages 6-14. **Literacy:** 99.1%.

Embassy: 2211 R St. NW 20008; 462-5772.

Website: www.cyprus.gov.cy

The Ottoman Empire held Cyprus, 1571-1878, until it yielded control to Britain. Agitation for *enosis* (union) with Greece increased after WWII, with the Turkish minority opposed, and led to violence in 1955-56. In 1959, Britain, Greece, Turkey, and Cypriot leaders approved a plan for an independent republic, with constitutional guarantees for the Turkish minority and permanent division of offices on an ethnic basis.

Archbishop Makarios III was elected president, and full independence became final Aug. 16, 1960. Communal strife led the UN to send a peacekeeping force (UNFICYP) in 1964; its mandate has been repeatedly renewed.

The Cypriot National Guard, led by officers from the Greek army, seized the government July 15, 1974. On July 20, Turkey invaded the island; Greece mobilized its forces but did not intervene. By Aug. 16, Turkish forces had occupied the northeastern 40% of the island.

Turkish Cyprus opened its border with Greek Cyprus Apr. 23, 2003, for the first time since partition. In separate referendums Apr. 2004, 65% of Turkish Cypriot voters accepted a UN-sponsored reunification plan, but 76% of Greek Cypriots rejected it. Still divided, Cyprus became a full member of the EU on May 1, 2004. It began using the euro as its currency in 2008. Dimitris Christofias won a 2008 runoff election, becoming the country's first Communist president. In a runoff election Feb. 24, 2013, the conservative candidate and head of the Democratic Rally party, Nicos Anastasiades, was voted Cyprus's new president.

In part because Cypriot banks held large amounts of Greek bonds, Cyprus suffered a banking crisis in 2013. The outline of a Cyprus bailout package was agreed upon Mar. 5, 2013, among the Intl. Monetary Fund, the European Central Bank, and eurozone countries. In exchange for $13 bil in IMF and EU assistance, Cyprus agreed to stringent banking reforms and economic austerity measures. Those with deposits of more than 100,000 euros in Cypriot banks lost some or all the money above that amount to help finance the restructuring of the banking system. Cyprus's GDP shrank by 8.7% in 2013, and the unemployment rate passed 17%. The economic recession continued in 2014.

Turkish Republic of Northern Cyprus

A declaration of independence was announced by Turkish-Cypriot leader Rauf Denktash, Nov. 15, 1983. The state is not internationally recognized, but has trade relations with some countries. Denktash was succeeded as president by Mehmet Ali Talat (2005-10) and Dervis Eroglu, who unseated Talat in the Apr. 18, 2010, election. Area 1,295 sq mi; pop. (2010) 287,856, nearly all Turkish. Capital: Nicosia (Lefkosia). Local divisions: 5 districts. Active troops: 3,500. In Apr. 2013, Turkish Prime Min. Tayyip Erdogan expressed an interest in reuniting Northern Cyprus with Cyprus. Antigovernment protests spread from Turkey into Northern Cyprus June 2013.

Czech Republic

People: Population: 10,627,448. **Age distrib.:** <15: 14.9%; 65+: 17.5%. **Pop. density:** 356.3 per sq mi, 137.6 per sq km. **Urban:** 73%. **Ethnic groups:** Czech 64%, Moravian 5%, Slovak 1%. **Languages:** Czech, Slovak. **Religions:** Roman Catholic 10%, Protestant 1%, none 35%.

Geography: Total area: 30,451 sq mi, 78,867 sq km; **Land area:** 29,825 sq mi, 77,247 sq km. **Location:** In E central Europe.

Neighbors: Poland on N, Germany on N and W, Austria on S, Slovakia on E and SE. **Topography:** Bohemia, in W, is a plateau surrounded by mountains; Moravia is hilly. **Capital:** Prague, 1,302,880.

Government: Type: Parliamentary democracy. **Head of state:** Pres. Milos Zeman; b. Sept. 28, 1944; in office: Mar. 8, 2013. **Head of gov.:** Prime Min. Bohuslav Sobotka; b. Oct. 23, 1971; in office: Jan. 29, 2014. **Local divisions:** 13 regions, 1 capital city. **Defense budget:** $2.18 bil. **Active troops:** 23,650.

Economy: Industries: motor vehicles, metallurgy, machinery and equip., glass, armaments. **Chief crops:** wheat, potatoes, sugar beets, hops, fruit. **Natural resources:** coal, kaolin, clay, graphite, timber. **Crude oil reserves:** 15 mil bbls. **Arable land:** 40.9%. **Livestock:** cattle: 1.4 mil; chickens: 23.3 mil; goats: 24,042; pigs: 1.6 mil; sheep: 220,521. **Electricity prod.** (2012): 81.7 bil kWh. **Labor force:** agric. 2.6%, industry 37.4%, services 60%. **Unemployment:** 7%.

Finance: Monetary unit: Koruna (CZK) (Sept. 2014: 21.04 = $1 U.S.). **GDP:** $285.6 bil; **per capita GDP:** $26,300; **GDP growth:** –0.9%. **Imports:** $143.4 bil; Germany 29.5%, Poland 7.7%, Slovakia 7.4%, China 6.3%, Netherlands 5.8%, Russia 5.3%, Austria 4.3%. **Exports:** $161.4 bil; Germany 31.8%, Slovakia 9.1%, Poland 6.1%, France 5.1%, UK 4.9%, Austria 4.7%. **Tourism:** $7.1 bil. **Budget:** $60 bil. **Total reserves less gold:** $55.8 bil. **Gold:** 348,736 oz t. **Inflation:** 1.4%.

Transport: Railways: 5,884 mi. **Motor vehicles:** 540.5 per 1,000 pop. **Civil aviation:** 3.7 bil pass.-mi; 41 airports. **Chief ports:** Decin, Prague, Usti nad Labem.

Communications: TV sets: 457 per 1,000 pop. **Radios:** 802 per 1,000 pop. **Telephone lines:** 18.7 per 100 pop. **Mobile:** 131.3 per 100 pop. **Internet:** 74.1%.

Health: Life expect.: 75.3 male; 81.5 female. **Births:** 9.8 per 1,000 pop. **Deaths:** 10.3 per 1,000 pop. **Natural inc.:** –0.05%. **Infant mortality:** 2.6 per 1,000 live births. **HIV:** <0.1%.

Education: Compulsory: ages 6-14. **Literacy:** 99%.

Embassy: 3900 Spring of Freedom St. NW 20008; 274-9100.

Website: www.czech.cz

Bohemia and Moravia were part of the Great Moravian Empire in the 9th cent. and later became part of the Holy Roman Empire. Under the kings of Bohemia, Prague in the 14th cent. was the cultural center of Central Europe. Bohemia and Hungary became part of Austria-Hungary.

In 1914-18, Thomas G. Masaryk and Eduard Benes formed a provisional government with the support of Slovak leaders, including Milan Stefanik. They proclaimed the Republic of Czechoslovakia Oct. 28, 1918.

By 1938, Nazi Germany had generated disaffection among German-speaking citizens in Sudetenland and demanded its cession. British Prime Min. Neville Chamberlain signed with Hitler at Munich, Sept. 30, 1938, an agreement to the cession, with a guarantee of peace by Hitler and Mussolini. Germany occupied Sudetenland Oct. 1-2. Hitler on Mar. 15, 1939, dissolved Czechoslovakia, made protectorates of Bohemia and Moravia, and supported the autonomy of Slovakia, proclaimed independent Mar. 14, 1939.

Soviet troops with some Czechoslovak contingents entered eastern Czechoslovakia in 1944 and reached Prague in May 1945; Benes returned as president. In May 1946 elections, the Communist Party won 38% of the votes. In Feb. 1948, the Communists seized power in advance of scheduled elections. The country was renamed the Czechoslovak Socialist Republic. A harsh Stalinist period followed; all opposition was suppressed.

In Jan. 1968 a liberalization movement spread through Czechoslovakia. Long-time Stalinist ruler Antonin Novotny was deposed; the democrat Slovak Alexander Dubcek succeeded him. In July, the USSR and 4 Warsaw Pact nations demanded an end to liberalization. On Aug. 20, the Soviet, Polish, East German, Hungarian, and Bulgarian armies invaded Czechoslovakia. Despite demonstrations and riots by students and workers, press censorship was imposed and liberal leaders were ousted. On Apr. 17, 1969, Dubcek resigned as Communist Party leader and was succeeded by Gustav Husak. Censorship was tightened, and the Communist Party expelled a third of its members.

More than 700 leading Czechoslovak intellectuals and former party leaders signed a human rights manifesto in 1977, called Charter 77, prompting a renewed crackdown by the regime.

The police crushed a massive protest in Prague, Nov. 17, 1989. As protesters demanded free elections, the Communist Party leadership resigned Nov. 24; millions went on strike Nov. 27.

On Dec. 10, 1989, the first cabinet in 41 years without a Communist majority took power; Vaclav Havel, playwright and human rights campaigner, was chosen president, Dec. 29. In Mar. 1990 the country was officially renamed the Czech and Slovak Federal Republic. A Slovak-led coalition blocked Havel's bid to win reelection July 1992.

Slovakia declared sovereignty, July 17, 1992. Czech and Slovak leaders agreed, July 23 on a plan for a peaceful division of Czechoslovakia. It split into 2 separate states—the Czech Republic and Slovakia—Jan. 1, 1993. Havel was elected president of the Czech Republic on Jan. 26. The country became a full member of NATO in 1999.

Vaclav Klaus replaced the retiring Havel, 2003. The nation became a full EU member May 1, 2004. Inconclusive parliamentary elections, June 2006, led to a political deadlock, after which a minority center-right government took office Sept. 2006. Center-right parties made a strong showing in May 2010 parliamentary elections. In the country's first direct presidential election, former Social Democrat prime min. Milos Zeman was elected with more than 55% of the vote in a runoff election Jan. 26, 2013.

Heavy rains in early June 2013 caused massive flooding throughout central Europe, crippling Prague, where the Vltava R. overflowed its banks, submerging parts of the city. On June 4, the prime min. declared a state of emergency throughout the country.

A corruption scandal erupted June 13, 2013, with a police raid on government offices and the arrests of 7 parliamentarians, including the prime min.'s closest aide, causing Prime Min. Petr Necas to resign June 17. After Oct. 2013 elections, Social Democrat Bohuslav Sobotka, who had campaigned on increasing government spending to boost the economy, became prime min. Jan. 29, 2014.

Denmark
Kingdom of Denmark

People: Population: 5,569,077. **Age distrib.:** <15: 17%; 65+: 18.4%. **Pop. density:** 339.9 per sq mi, 131.2 per sq km. **Urban:** 87.5%. **Ethnic groups:** Scandinavian, Inuit, Faroese, German, Turkish, Iranian, Somali. **Languages:** Danish, Faroese, Greenlandic, German, English (predominant second lang.). **Religions:** Evangelical Lutheran (official) 80%, Muslim 4%.

Geography: Total area: 16,639 sq mi, 43,094 sq km; **Land area:** 16,384 sq mi, 42,434 sq km. **Location:** In N Europe, separating North and Baltic Seas. **Neighbors:** Germany on S, Norway on NW, Sweden on NE. **Topography:** Consists of the Jutland Peninsula and about 500 islands, 100 inhabited. Land is flat or gently rolling and is almost all in productive use. **Capital:** Copenhagen, 1,254,810 (figure is for urban aggl.).

Government: Type: Constitutional monarchy. **Head of state:** Queen Margrethe II; b. Apr. 16, 1940; in office: Jan. 14, 1972. **Head of gov.:** Prime Min. Helle Thorning-Schmidt; b. Dec. 14, 1966; in office: Oct. 3, 2011. **Local divisions:** 5 regions. **Defense budget:** $4.51 bil. **Active troops:** 17,200.

Economy: Industries: iron, steel, nonferrous metals, chemicals, food proc., machinery and transp. equip., textiles and clothing, electronics, windmills, constr., furniture and other wood prods. **Chief crops:** barley, wheat, potatoes, sugar beets. **Natural resources:** petroleum, nat. gas, fish, salt, limestone, chalk, stone, gravel and sand. **Crude oil reserves:** 805.1 mil bbls. **Arable land:** 57%. **Livestock:** cattle: 1.6 mil; chickens: 14.2 mil; pigs: 12.1 mil; sheep: 151,300. **Electricity prod.** (2012): 29.8 bil kWh. **Labor force:** agric. 2.6%, industry 20.3%, services 77.1%. **Unemployment:** 7.5%.

Finance: Monetary unit: Krone (DKK) (Sept. 2014: 5.66 = $1 U.S.). **GDP:** $211.3 bil; **per capita GDP:** $37,800; **GDP growth:** 0.1%. **Imports:** $98.5 bil; Germany 21.2%, Sweden 13.5%, Netherlands 7.5%, China 6.4%, Norway 6.3%, UK 5.6%. **Exports:** $106 bil; Germany 15.9%, Sweden 13.5%, UK 9.6%, U.S. 5.6%, Norway 6.3%, Netherlands 4.6%. **Tourism:** $7 bil. **Budget:** $189.7 bil. **Total reserves less gold:** $86.1 bil. **Gold** (2012): 2.1 mil oz t. **Inflation:** 0.8%.

Transport: Railways: 1,657 mi. **Motor vehicles:** 492.4 per 1,000 pop. **Civil aviation:** 29.4 bil pass.-mi (incl. Norway, Sweden); 28 airports. **Chief ports:** Aalborg, Aarhus, Copenhagen, Ensted, Esbjerg, Fredericia, Kalundborg.

Communications: TV sets: 975 per 1,000 pop. **Radios:** 1,399 per 1,000 pop. **Telephone lines:** 37.5 per 100 pop. **Mobile:** 127.5 per 100 pop. **Internet:** 94.6%.

Health: Life expect.: 76.7 male; 81.6 female. **Births:** 10.2 per 1,000 pop. **Deaths:** 10.2 per 1,000 pop. **Natural inc.:** 0.00%. **Infant mortality:** 4.1 per 1,000 live births. **HIV:** 0.2%.

Education: Compulsory: ages 6-15. **Literacy:** 99%.

Embassy: 3200 Whitehaven St. NW 20008; 234-4300.

Website: www.denmark.dk

Most of the Viking raiders in the early Middle Ages were Danes. The Danish kingdom was a major power until the 17th cent., when it lost its land in southern Sweden. Norway was separated in 1815, and Schleswig-Holstein in 1864. Northern Schleswig was returned in 1920. Denmark was occupied by Nazi Germany, Apr. 1940-May 1945, but Danes helped more than 7,200 Jews escape to safety in Sweden, Sept. 1943.

Voters ratified the Maastricht Treaty, enabling Denmark to join the EU, in May 1993. In Sept. 2000, Danes voted not to adopt the euro.

The Danish newspaper *Jyllands-Posten* published, Sept. 30, 2005, cartoon images of the prophet Muhammad, offensive to Muslims; the caricatures, republished elsewhere, triggered violent protests and a boycott of Danish products in Islamic countries in early 2006. Danish police raids broke up alleged Islamist bomb plots Sept. 2006 and Sept. 2007. A car bomb blast linked to al-Qaeda killed 8 people outside Denmark's embassy in Islamabad, Pakistan, June 2, 2008.

Ten years of center-right government ended Sept. 2011, as a left-wing coalition won parliamentary elections. Helle Thorning-Schmidt, a Social Democrat, became Denmark's first female prime min. Oct. 3. A bill granting marriage rights to same-sex couples was voted into law, June 7, 2012.

The **Faroe Islands** in the N Atlantic, about 300 mi NW of the Shetlands, and 850 mi from Denmark proper, 18 inhabited, have an area of 540 sq mi and pop. (2014 est.) of 49,947. They are an administrative division of Denmark, self-governing in most matters. Capital: Torshavn; pop. (2014 est.) 20,646. Fish is a primary export (292,519 metric tons in 2006). **Website:** www.us.fo

Greenland (Kalaallit Nunaat)

Greenland, an island between the North Atlantic and the Polar Sea, is separated from the North American continent by Davis Strait and Baffin Bay. Its total area is 836,330 sq mi, about 80% of which is ice-capped. Most of the island is a lofty plateau 9,000-10,000 ft in elevation. The average thickness of the cap is 1,000 ft. Scientists point to accelerated melting of Greenland's ice sheet in recent years as evidence of global warming. The population (2014 est.) is 57,728. Under the 1953 Danish constitution the colony became an integral part of the realm with representatives in the Folketing (Danish legislature). The Danish parliament, 1978, approved home rule for Greenland, effective May 1, 1979. With home rule, Greenlandic place names came into official use. The technically correct name for Greenland is Kalaallit Nunaat. The official name for its capital is Nuuk (2014 est. pop., 16,911), rather than Godthab. Fish is the principal export (about 89% of all exports in 2010). Other natural resources include coal, iron ore, lead, zinc, molybdenum, diamonds, gold, and platinum. **Website:** www.nanoq.gl

Djibouti
Republic of Djibouti

People: Population: 810,179. **Age distrib.:** <15: 32.9%; 65+: 3.5%. **Pop. density:** 90.5 per sq mi, 35 per sq km. **Urban:** 77.3%. **Ethnic groups:** Somali 60%, Afar 35%, other (incl. French, Arab, Ethiopian, Italian) 5%. **Languages:** French, Arabic (both official); Somali; Afar. **Religions:** Muslim 94%, Christian 6%.

Geography: Total area: 8,958 sq mi, 23,200 sq km; **Land area:** 8,950 sq mi, 23,180 sq km. **Location:** On E coast of Africa, separated from Arabian Peninsula by strategically vital strait of Bab el-Mandeb. **Neighbors:** Ethiopia on W and SW, Eritrea on NW, Somalia on SE. **Topography:** The territory, divided into a low coastal plain, mountains behind, and an interior plateau, is arid, sandy, and desolate. Climate is generally hot and dry. **Capital:** Djibouti, 521,840.

Government: Type: Republic. **Head of state:** Pres. Ismail Omar Guelleh; b. Nov. 27, 1947; in office: May 8, 1999. **Head of gov.:** Prime Min. Abdoulkader Kamil Mohamed; b. 1951; in office: Apr. 1, 2013. **Local divisions:** 6 districts. **Defense budget** (2012): $10 mil. **Active troops:** 10,450.

Economy: Industries: constr., agric. proc. **Chief crops:** fruits, vegetables. **Natural resources:** potential geothermal power, gold, clay, granite, limestone, marble, salt, diatomite, gypsum, pumice, petroleum. **Arable land:** 0.1%. **Livestock:** cattle: 298,000; goats: 514,000; sheep: 470,000. **Electricity prod.:** 330 mil kWh. **Labor force:** NA. **Unemployment:** NA.

Finance: Monetary unit: Franc (DJF) (Sept. 2014: 176.20 = $1 U.S.). **GDP:** $2.5 bil; **per capita GDP:** $2,700; **GDP growth:** 5%. **Imports:** $593.3 mil; China 24.4%, Saudi Arabia 16.4%, India 10.6%, Indonesia 7.3%. **Exports:** $90.8 mil; Somalia 80.1%, UAE 4.4%, Yemen 4.1%. **Tourism:** $21 mil. **Budget:** $532.9 mil. **Total reserves less gold:** $425 mil. **Inflation:** 3.5%.

Transport: Railways: 62 mi (part of Addis Ababa-Djibouti railway, under joint control with Ethiopia, but largely inoperable). **Civil aviation:** 3 airports. **Chief port:** Djibouti.

Communications: TV sets: 67 per 1,000 pop. **Radios:** 93 per 1,000 pop. **Telephone lines:** 2.4 per 100 pop. **Mobile:** 28 per 100 pop. **Internet:** 9.5%.

Health: Life expect.: 59.9 male; 64.9 female. **Births:** 24.1 per 1,000 pop. **Deaths:** 7.8 per 1,000 pop. **Natural inc.:** 1.62%. **Infant mortality:** 50.2 per 1,000 live births. **HIV:** 0.9%.

Education: Compulsory: ages 6-16. **Literacy:** NA.

Embassy: 1156 15th St. NW, Ste. 515, 20005; 331-0270.

Website: www.presidence.dj

France gained control of the territory in stages between 1862 and 1900. As French Somaliland, it became an overseas French territory in 1945; in 1967 it was renamed the French Territory of the Afars and the Issas.

Ethiopia and Somalia have renounced their claims to the area, but each has accused the other of trying to gain control. There were clashes between Afars (ethnically related to Ethiopians) and Issas (related to Somalis) in 1976. Immigrants from both countries continued to enter Djibouti until independence on June 27, 1977.

Economic support comes from French aid and Arab countries. A peace accord Dec. 1994 ended a 3-year Afar rebel uprising. Drought in 2007-11 devastated crops and livestock. Protests associated with the Arab Spring broke out in late Jan. 2011 demanding the resignation of Pres. Ismail Omar Guelleh. Authorities suppressed the protests, and Guelleh won a third term in an Apr. 2011 election boycotted by the main opposition. Parliamentary elections, Feb. 22, 2013, in which the ruling coalition won the majority of votes, prompted protests by the opposition Union for National Salvation (USN). The U.S. announced, May 5, 2014, the signing of a new 20-year lease for its military base in Djibouti, used for anti-terrorism and other military operations in the Middle East and Africa.

Dominica
Commonwealth of Dominica

People: Population: 73,449. **Age distrib.:** <15: 22.1%; 65+: 10.5%. **Pop. density:** 253.3 per sq mi, 97.8 per sq km. **Urban:** 69.3%. **Ethnic groups:** black 87%, mixed 9%, Carib Amerindian 3%, white 1%. **Languages:** English (official), French patois. **Religions:** Roman Catholic 61%, Protestant 21% (Seventh-day Adventist 6%, Pentecostal 6%, Baptist 4%, Methodist 4%), none 6%.

Geography: Total area: 290 sq mi, 751 sq km; **Land area:** 290 sq mi, 751 sq km. **Location:** In E Caribbean, most northerly Windward Isl. **Neighbors:** Guadeloupe to N, Martinique to S. **Topography:** Mountainous, a central ridge running from N to S, terminating in cliffs; volcanic in origin, with numerous thermal springs; rich deep topsoil on leeward side, red tropical clay on windward coast. **Capital:** Roseau, 14,994.

Government: Type: Parliamentary democracy. **Head of state:** Pres. Charles A. Savarin; b. Oct. 2, 1943; in office: Oct. 2, 2013. **Head of gov.:** Prime Min. Roosevelt Skerrit; b. June 8, 1972; in office: Jan. 8, 2004. **Local divisions:** 10 parishes. **Defense budget/active troops:** NA.

Economy: Industries: soap, coconut oil, tourism, copra, furniture, cement blocks, shoes. **Chief crops:** bananas, citrus, mangoes, root crops, coconuts, cocoa. **Natural resources:** timber, hydropower. **Arable land:** 8%. **Livestock:** cattle: 14,000; chickens: 200,000; goats: 9,700; pigs: 5,000; sheep: 7,900. **Electricity prod.:** 105.5 mil kWh. **Labor force:** agric. 40%, industry 32%, services 28%. **Unemployment:** NA.

Finance: Monetary unit: East Caribbean Dollar (XCD) (Sept. 2014: 2.70 = $1 U.S.). **GDP:** $1 bil; **per capita GDP:** $14,300; **GDP growth:** 1.1%. **Imports:** $219.6 mil; Japan 39.3%, U.S. 15.6%, Trinidad and Tobago 13.5%, China 5.1%. **Exports:** $40.4 mil; Japan 38.8%, Jamaica 33%, Antigua and Barbuda 7.7%, Guyana 6.5%, Paraguay 5.6%, Trinidad and Tobago 4.2%. **Tourism:** $82 mil. **Budget:** $185.2 mil. **Total reserves less gold:** $87.1 mil. **Inflation:** −0.2%.

Transport: Civil aviation: 2 airports. **Chief ports:** Portsmouth, Roseau.

Communications: TV sets: 230 per 1,000 pop. **Radios:** 602 per 1,000 pop. **Telephone lines** 23.8 per 100 pop. **Mobile:** 130 per 100 pop. **Internet:** 59%.

Health: Life expect.: 73.6 male; 79.7 female. **Births:** 15.5 per 1,000 pop. **Deaths:** 7.9 per 1,000 pop. **Natural inc.:** 0.76%. **Infant mortality:** 11.6 per 1,000 live births. **HIV:** NA.

Education: Compulsory: ages 5-16. **Literacy:** NA.

Embassy: 3216 New Mexico Ave. NW 20016; 364-6781.

Website: www.dominica.gov.dm

A British colony since 1805, Dominica was granted self-government in 1967. Independence was achieved Nov. 3, 1978.

Hurricane David struck, Aug. 30, 1979, devastating the island and destroying the banana plantations, Dominica's economic mainstay. Coups were attempted in 1980 and 1981.

Prime Min. Pierre Charles, 49, died of a heart attack Jan. 6, 2004, and was succeeded by Roosevelt Skerrit. Charles A. Savarin was sworn in as Dominica's 8th pres., Oct. 2, 2013, after being elected by the country's legislature.

Dominican Republic

People: Population: 10,349,741. **Age distrib.:** <15: 28%; 65+: 7%. **Pop. density:** 554.8 per sq mi, 214.2 per sq km. **Urban:** 78.1%. **Ethnic groups:** mixed 73%, white 16%, black 11%. **Language:** Spanish (official). **Religion:** Roman Catholic 95%.

Geography: Total area: 18,792 sq mi, 48,670 sq km; **Land area:** 18,656 sq mi, 48,320 sq km. **Location:** In W Indies, sharing isl. of Hispaniola with Haiti. **Neighbors:** Haiti on W, Puerto Rico (U.S.) to E. **Topography:** The Cordillera Central range crosses center of the country, rising to over 10,000 ft, highest in the Caribbean. The Cibao Valley to N is major agricultural area. **Capital:** Santo Domingo, 2,872,820.

Government: Type: Democratic republic. **Head of state and gov.:** Pres. Danilo Medina Sánchez; b. Nov. 10, 1951; in office: Aug. 16, 2012. **Local divisions:** 10 regions. **Defense budget:** $378 mil. **Active troops:** 46,000.

Economy: Industries: tourism, sugar proc., mining, textiles, cement, tobacco. **Chief crops:** sugarcane, coffee, cotton, cocoa, tobacco, rice, beans, potatoes, corn, bananas. **Natural resources:** nickel, bauxite, gold, silver. **Arable land:** 16.6%. **Livestock:** cattle: 3 mil; chickens: 173 mil; goats: 232,000; pigs: 628,000; sheep: 246,500. **Electricity prod.:** 13.1 bil kWh. **Labor force:** agric. 14.6%, industry 22.3%, services 63.1%. **Unemployment:** 13%.

Finance: Monetary unit: Peso (DOP) (Sept. 2014: 43.15 = $1 U.S.). **GDP:** $101 bil; **per capita GDP:** $9,700; **GDP growth:** 2%. **Imports:** $16.8 bil; U.S. 43.3%, Venezuela 7.7%, China 6.3%, Mexico 5.3%, Colombia 4.1%. **Exports:** $9.8 bil; U.S. 47%, Haiti 16.1%, China 4.3%. **Tourism:** $5.1 bil. **Budget:** $10.8 bil. **Total reserves less gold:** $4.7 bil. **Gold:** 18,296 oz t. **Inflation:** 4.8%.

Transport: Railways: 88 mi. **Motor vehicles:** 145.2 per 1,000 pop. **Civil aviation:** 16 airports. **Chief ports:** Puerto Haina, Puerto Plata, Santo Domingo.

Communications: TV sets: 219 per 1,000 pop. **Radios:** 185 per 1,000 pop. **Telephone lines:** 11.3 per 100 pop. **Mobile:** 88.4 per 100 pop. **Internet:** 45.9%.

Health: Life expect.: 75.6 male; 80.1 female. **Births:** 19.0 per 1,000 pop. **Deaths:** 4.5 per 1,000 pop. **Natural inc.:** 1.45%. **Infant mortality:** 19.6 per 1,000 live births. **HIV:** 0.7%.

Education: Compulsory: ages 5-13. **Literacy:** 91.8%.

Embassy: 1715 22nd St. NW 20008; 332-6280.

Website: www.presidencia.gov.do

Carib and Arawak Indians inhabited the island of Hispaniola when Columbus landed in 1492. The city of Santo Domingo, founded 1496, is the oldest European settlement in the Western Hemisphere.

France took over the western third of the island in 1697 and Santo Domingo in 1795. Haitian leader Toussaint L'Ouverture seized it, 1801. Spain returned intermittently 1803-21, as several native republics came and went. Haiti ruled again, 1822-44; Spanish occupation occurred 1861-63. U.S. Marines occupied the country 1916-24.

In 1930, Gen. Rafael Leonidas Trujillo Molina was elected president. The brutal Trujillo era ended with his assassination in 1961. Pres. Joaquín Balaguer, appointed by Trujillo in 1960, resigned under pressure in 1962.

Juan Bosch, elected president in the first free elections in 38 years, was overthrown in 1963. On Apr. 24, 1965, Bosch's followers and others, including a few Communists, launched a revolt. Four days later U.S. Marines intervened against pro-Bosch forces. Five South American countries later sent token units as a peacekeeping force. A provisional government supervised a June 1966 election in which Balaguer defeated Bosch. Balaguer remained in office for most of the next 28 years, but his May 1994 reelection was widely denounced as fraudulent. He called for new elections but did not run, and Leonel Fernández Reyna was elected June 1996.

The leftist candidate, Hipólito Mejía, won a presidential vote in 2000. With the nation reeling from a banking scandal and soaring inflation, Fernández defeated Mejía in a 2004 election. Fernández was reelected in 2008. Danilo Medina Sánchez, Fernández's ally, was elected May 2012 and sworn into office Aug 16.

The Constitutional Court ruled, Sept. 23, 2013, that people born in the Dominican Rep. after 1929 whose parents were illegal immigrants were not entitled to Dominican citizenship. The decision affected tens of thousands of people, most of Haitian descent. Legislation to provide a path to citizenship for such people was enacted May 2014.

East Timor
See Timor-Leste.

Ecuador
Republic of Ecuador

People: Population: 15,654,411. **Age distrib.:** <15: 28.5%; 65+: 6.9%. **Pop. density:** 146.5 per sq mi, 56.5 per sq km. **Urban:** 63.5%. **Ethnic groups:** mestizo (mixed Amerindian and white) 72%, Montubio 7%, Afroecuadorian 7%, Amerindian 7%, white 6%. **Languages:** Spanish (Castilian, official), indigenous (Quechua, Shuar). **Religion:** Roman Catholic 95%.

Geography: Total area: 109,484 sq mi, 283,561 sq km; **Land area:** 106,889 sq mi, 276,841 sq km. **Location:** In NW S America, on Pacific coast, astride the equator. **Neighbors:** Colombia on N, Peru on E and S. **Topography:** Two ranges of Andes run N and S, splitting country into 3 zones: hot, humid lowlands on coast; temperate highlands between ranges; and rainy, tropical lowlands to E. **Capital:** Quito, 1,699,150. **Cities (urban aggl.):** Guayaquil, 2,663,938.

Government: Type: Republic. **Head of state and gov.:** Pres. Rafael Correa; b. Apr. 6, 1963; in office: Jan. 15, 2007. **Local divisions:** 24 provinces. **Defense budget:** $1.51 bil. **Active troops:** 58,000.

Economy: Industries: petroleum, food proc., textiles, wood prods., chemicals. **Chief crops:** bananas, coffee, cocoa, rice, potatoes, manioc, plantains, sugarcane. **Natural resources:** petroleum, fish, timber, hydropower. **Crude oil reserves:** 8.2 bil bbls. **Arable land:** 4.6%. **Livestock:** cattle: 5.1 mil; chickens: 140 mil; goats: 104,027; pigs: 1.2 mil; sheep: 739,475. **Electricity prod.:** 19.6 bil kWh. **Labor force:** agric. 27.8%, industry 17.8%, services 54.4%. **Unemployment:** 4.5%.

Finance: Monetary unit: U.S. Dollar (USD). **GDP:** $157.6 bil; **per capita GDP:** $10,600; **GDP growth:** 4%. **Imports:** $26.2 bil; U.S. 28.4%, China 11.3%, Colombia 8.8%, Peru 4.5%. **Exports:** $25.5 bil; U.S. 37.3%, Chile 8.1%, Peru 6.5%, Japan 4.5%, Russia 4.5%, Colombia 4%. **Tourism:** $1.2 bil. **Budget:** $39.3 bil. **Total reserves less gold:** $3.3 bil. **Gold:** 845,000 oz t. **Inflation:** 2.7%.

Transport: Railways: 600 mi. **Motor vehicles:** 83.6 per 1,000 pop. **Civil aviation:** 3.6 bil pass.-mi; 104 airports. **Chief ports:** Esmeraldas, Guayaquil, Manta, Puerto Bolivar.

Communications: TV sets: 261 per 1,000 pop. **Radios:** 517 per 1,000 pop. **Telephone lines:** 15.2 per 100 pop. **Mobile:** 111.5 per 100 pop. **Internet:** 40.4%.

Health: Life expect.: 73.4 male; 79.5 female. **Births:** 18.9 per 1,000 pop. **Deaths:** 5.0 per 1,000 pop. **Natural inc.:** 1.38%. **Infant mortality:** 17.9 per 1,000 live births. **HIV:** 0.4%.

Education: Compulsory: ages 3-17. **Literacy:** 94.5%.

Embassy: 2535 15th St. NW 20009; 234-7200.

Website: www.presidencia.gob.ec

The region, which was the northern Inca empire, was conquered by Spain in 1533. Liberation forces defeated the Spanish May 24, 1822, near Quito. Ecuador became part of the Great Colombia Republic but seceded, May 13, 1830.

Ecuadoran indigenous peoples, demanding greater rights, staged protests in the 1990s. A border war with Peru flared Jan. 26-Mar. 1, 1995. Vice Pres. Alberto Dahik resigned and fled Ecuador, Oct. 1995, to avoid arrest on corruption charges. Elected president, July 1996, Abdalá Bucaram—a populist known as El Loco, or "The Crazy One"—imposed stiff price increases and other austerity measures. His rising unpopularity and erratic behavior led the National Congress, Feb. 1997, to dismiss him for "mental incapacity."

Jamil Mahuad Witt won a presidential runoff election July 1998. In Sept. 1998 and Mar. 1999 he imposed emergency measures to cope with a continuing economic crisis. Opposed by Indian groups and military leaders, he was ousted Jan. 2000, and succeeded by Vice Pres. Gustavo Noboa Bejarano. Noboa enacted a plan introduced by Mahuad to replace the sucre with the U.S. dollar as Ecuador's currency. Lucio Gutiérrez Borbúa, a leader in the 2000 coup, won a presidential runoff Nov. 2002. Noboa, under investigation for financial mismanagement, went into exile Aug. 2003.

Gutiérrez imposed economic austerity measures, purged opponents from the supreme court, Dec. 2004, and then dissolved the court, Apr. 15, 2005. With street protests rising, Congress ousted Gutiérrez Apr. 20, and Vice Pres. Alfredo Palacio González became president. The U.S. suspended free-trade talks after Ecuador, May 2006, took over all assets belonging to U.S.-based Occidental Petroleum.

Rafael Correa, a left-wing economist, won a presidential runoff vote Nov. 2006. After a power struggle with the National Congress, Correa won voter approval, Apr. 2007, to convene an assembly to rewrite the constitution. The revised constitution won overwhelming approval in a national referendum Sept. 2008. Early in his term, when oil revenues were high, he boosted development spending and aid to poor families; later, as oil prices dropped, he restricted imports to prevent an outflow of dollars and, Dec. 2008, allowed Ecuador to default on part of its $10 bil foreign debt.

Correa, reelected Apr. 2009, pressured foreign oil companies in 2010 to renegotiate contracts to increase the government's share of mineral revenues. A confrontation Sept. 30, 2010, between Correa and rebellious police officers led to a shootout between government troops and police: 5 people were killed and at least 38 wounded. An Ecuadoran judge Feb. 14, 2011, ordered Chevron (which had absorbed Texaco in 2001) to pay $9.5 bil to clean up oil pollution from Texaco operations in Ecuador, 1965-92; Chevron disputed the ruling and opposed collection efforts in courts in various countries. Ecuador granted asylum, Aug. 16, 2012, to Julian Assange, the founder of WikiLeaks. Assange had been in Ecuador's UK embassy in London since June 19, avoiding extradition to Sweden from Britain. He remained in the embassy as of Oct. 2014.

Correa was reelected Feb. 17, 2013, becoming the longest-serving president in the country's history.

The Galápagos Islands, pop. (2008 est.) 30,000, about 600 mi to the W, are the home of huge tortoises and other unusual animals. The oil tanker *Jessica* ran aground Jan. 16, 2001, off San Cristóbal Isl., spilling some 185,000 gallons of fuel.

Egypt
Arab Republic of Egypt

People: Population: 86,895,099. **Age distrib.:** <15: 32.1%; 65+: 5%. **Pop. density:** 226.1 per sq mi, 87.3 per sq km. **Urban:** 43.1%. **Ethnic groups:** Egyptian 99.6%. **Languages:** Arabic (official), English and French widely understood by educated classes. **Religions:** Muslim (mostly Sunni) 90%, Christian (most Coptic Orthodox) 10%.

Geography: Total area: 386,662 sq mi, 1,001,450 sq km; **Land area:** 384,345 sq mi, 995,450 sq km. **Location:** NE corner of Africa. **Neighbors:** Libya on W; Sudan on S; Israel, Gaza Strip on E. **Topography:** Almost entirely desolate and barren with hills and mountains in E and along Nile. The Nile Valley, where most people live, stretches 550 mi. **Capital:** Cairo, 18,419,100. **Cities (urban aggl.):** Alexandria, 4,694,304.

Government: Type: Republic. **Head of state:** Pres. Abdel Fattah al-Sisi; b. Nov. 19, 1954; in office: June 8, 2014. **Head of gov.:** Prime Min. Ibrahim Mehlab; b. Apr. 12, 1949; in office: Mar. 1, 2014. **Local divisions:** 27 governorates. **Defense budget:** $5.28 bil. **Active troops:** 438,500.

Economy: Industries: textiles, food proc., tourism, chemicals, pharmaceuticals, hydrocarbons, constr., cement, metals, light manufactures. **Chief crops:** cotton, rice, corn, wheat, beans, fruits, vegetables. **Natural resources:** petroleum, nat. gas, iron ore, phosphates, manganese, limestone, gypsum, talc, asbestos, lead, rare earth elements, zinc. **Crude oil reserves:** 4.4 bil bbls. **Arable land:** 2.8%. **Livestock:** cattle: 5 mil; chickens: 126.1 mil; goats: 4.4 mil; pigs:

10,600; sheep: 5.5 mil. **Electricity prod.:** 147.7 bil kWh. **Labor force:** agric. 29%, industry 24%, services 47%. **Unemployment:** 11.9%.

Finance: Monetary unit: Pound (EGP) (Sept. 2014: 7.15 = $1 U.S.). **GDP:** $551.4 bil; **per capita GDP:** $6,600; **GDP growth:** 1.8%. **Imports:** $59.2 bil; China 9.5%, U.S. 7.6%, Germany 6.7%, Russia 5.3%, Ukraine 5.3%, Turkey 5.1%, Italy 5%. **Exports:** $24.8 bil; Italy 7.9%, India 6.9%, U.S. 6.8%, Saudi Arabia 6.2%, Turkey 5.3%, Libya 4.9%. **Tourism:** $6 bil. **Budget:** $80.4 bil. **Total reserves less gold:** $13.6 bil. **Gold:** 2.4 mil oz t. **Inflation:** 9.5%. **Transport: Railways:** 3,158 mi. **Motor vehicles:** 53.3 per 1,000 pop. **Civil aviation:** 8.6 bil pass.-mi; 72 airports. **Chief ports:** Alexandria, Ayn Sukhnah, Damietta, El Dekheila, Port Said, Sidi Kurayr, Suez.

Communications: TV sets: 243 per 1,000 pop. **Radios:** 242 per 1,000 pop. **Telephone lines:** 8.3 per 100 pop. **Mobile:** 121.5 per 100 pop. **Internet:** 49.6%.

Health: Life expect.: 70.8 male; 76.2 female. **Births:** 23.4 per 1,000 pop. **Deaths:** 4.8 per 1,000 pop. **Natural inc.:** 1.86%. **Infant mortality:** 22.4 per 1,000 live births. **HIV:** <0.1%.

Education: Compulsory: ages 6-14. **Literacy:** 73.8%.

Embassy: 3521 International Ct. NW 20008; 895-5400.

Website: www.egypt.gov.eg

Archaeological records of ancient Egyptian civilization date back to 4000 BCE. A unified kingdom arose around 3200 BCE and extended south into Nubia and as far north as Syria. A high culture of rulers and priests was built on an economic base of serfdom, fertile soil, and annual flooding of the Nile.

Imperial decline facilitated conquest by Asian invaders (Hyksos, Assyrians). The last native dynasty fell in 341 BCE to the Persians, who were in turn replaced by Greeks (Alexander and the Ptolemies), Romans, Byzantines, and Arabs, who introduced Islam and the Arabic language. The ancient Egyptian language is preserved only in Coptic Christian liturgy.

Egypt was ruled as part of larger Islamic empires for many centuries. Britain intervened in Egypt in 1882 and ruled the country as a protectorate, 1914-22. A 1936 treaty strengthened Egyptian autonomy, but Britain retained bases in Egypt and a condominium over Sudan. When the state of Israel was proclaimed in 1948, Egypt joined other Arab nations invading Israel and was defeated. In 1951 Egypt abrogated the 1936 treaty; Sudan became independent in 1956.

A July 1952 uprising overthrew King Farouk and established a republic. Lt. Col. Gamal Abdel Nasser rose to power, becoming premier in 1954 and president in 1956. Nasser soon emerged as the most influential leader in the Arab world; he pushed construction of Egypt's Aswan High Dam, completed in 1970.

After guerrilla raids across its border, Israel invaded Egypt's Sinai Peninsula, Oct. 29, 1956. Egypt rejected a cease-fire demand by Britain and France; on Oct. 31 the 2 nations dropped bombs and on Nov. 5-6 landed forces. Egypt and Israel accepted a UN cease-fire; fighting ended Nov. 7. Subsequently, a UN Emergency Force guarded the border. Full-scale war with Israel broke out again, June 5, 1967; before it ended under a UN cease-fire June 10, Israel had captured Gaza and the Sinai Peninsula and taken control of the E bank of the Suez Canal.

Nasser died Sept. 28, 1970, and was replaced by Vice Pres. Anwar Sadat. In a surprise attack Oct. 6, 1973, Egyptian forces crossed the Suez Canal into the Sinai. (At the same time, Syrian forces attacked Israelis on the Golan Heights.) A USSR military airlift supplied Egypt; the U.S. responded with an airlift to Israel. Israel counterattacked, crossed the canal, and surrounded Suez City. A UN cease-fire took effect Oct. 24. Under an agreement signed Jan. 1974, Israeli forces withdrew from the canal's W bank; limited numbers of Egyptian forces occupied a strip along the E bank. A second accord was signed in 1975, with Israel yielding Sinai oil fields.

Pres. Sadat's surprise visit to Jerusalem, Nov. 1977, opened the prospect of peace with Israel. On Mar. 26, 1979, Egypt and Israel signed a formal peace treaty, ending 30 years of war and establishing diplomatic relations. On Oct. 6, 1981, Muslim extremists within the army assassinated Pres. Sadat, who was succeeded by Hosni Mubarak. Israel returned control of the Sinai to Egypt in Apr. 1982.

Egyptian security forces battled Islamist violence in the 1990s, and Pres. Mubarak escaped assassination in Ethiopia, June 26, 1995; Egypt blamed Sudan for the attack. On Nov. 17, 1997, near Luxor, Muslim extremists killed 58 foreign tourists and 4 Egyptians. Bombs Oct. 7, 2004, in and near Taba (a Sinai tourist site popular with Israelis) killed at least 35 people. Another 88 people were killed in bombings July 23, 2005, at Sharm el Sheikh, a Red Sea resort city.

Pressured by the U.S., Mubarak allowed opposition candidates in the Sept. 2005 presidential election, which he easily won. Suicide bombings at the Sinai resort town of Dahab, Apr. 24, 2006, killed at least 18 people; security forces May 9 killed Nasser Khamis al-Mallahi, leader of the group blamed for the Taba, Sharm el Sheikh, and Dahab attacks. Constitutional amendments expanding presidential powers and barring religiously based political parties were approved Mar. 2007.

Following 18 days of mass protests in which at least 846 people died in clashes between Arab Spring dissidents and Mubarak loyalists, Mubarak surrendered power Feb. 11, 2011. While Islamists and pro-democracy secularists contended for influence, the transitional military regime prepared for elections and charged Mubarak and associates with corruption and abuse of power. Mubarak was convicted June 2, 2012, and sentenced to life in prison. The verdict was overturned on appeal Jan. 13, 2013, and a retrial began Apr. 2013. Mubarak was convicted of separate corruption charges, May 21, 2014, and sentenced to 3 years in prison.

Islamist candidate Mohammed Morsi of the Muslim Brotherhood was declared winner of the presidential election, June 2012. Morsi overhauled the country's military leadership Aug. 12 in what some saw as an attempt to reclaim authority assumed by the military after Mubarak left office. On Oct. 8, 2012, he pardoned select political prisoners detained during the Arab Spring uprising. At least 110 people were injured in violent clashes between Morsi supporters and opponents Oct. 12, and additional conflicts erupted Nov. 23 after Morsi announced an edict interpreted as a power-grab. The proposal of a new Islamist constitution prompted demonstrations throughout Dec.; it passed Dec. 23, 2012.

Violent clashes, Jan. 25, 2013, killed 9 demonstrators and injured more than 400. Protesters firebombed the Muslim Brotherhood headquarters June 30 demanding Morsi's ouster. The military forced Morsi out of office July 3. Morsi's supporters protested continuously in Cairo and other cities. The military cracked down violently on these encampments Aug. 14. More than 600 protesters and at least 40 police officers died in confrontations. Vice Pres. Mohamed ElBaradei, a Nobel Peace Prize-winner, resigned Aug. 14 over what he saw as the government's brutality. The military took over the administration of the country. The Muslim Brotherhood was outlawed as a terrorist organization Dec. 25, 2013. Under a new constitution approved in a Jan. 2014 referendum, former Gen. Abdel Fattah al-Sisi, one of the leaders in ousting Morsi, won a May presidential election and was sworn into office June 8. Violence between Morsi supporters and security forces continued, causing hundreds of deaths on both sides. Muslim Brotherhood leader Mohamed Badie was sentenced to death June 21 in connection with July 2013 violence; the sentence was reduced to life in prison Aug. 30. Other courts also sentenced Badie to life in separate cases.

The Suez Canal, 103 mi long, links the Mediterranean and Red Seas. It was built by a French corporation 1859-69, but Britain obtained controlling interest in 1875. The last British troops were removed June 13, 1956. On July 26, Egypt nationalized the canal.

El Salvador
Republic of El Salvador

People: Population: 6,125,512. **Age distrib.:** <15: 28.1%; 65+: 6.9%. **Pop. density:** 765.6 per sq mi, 295.6 per sq km. **Urban:** 66.3%. **Ethnic groups:** mestizo 86%, white 13%, Amerindian 1%. **Languages:** Spanish (official), Nahua. **Religions:** Roman Catholic 57%, Protestant 21%, Jehovah's Witnesses 2%, none 17%.

Geography: Total area: 8,124 sq mi, 21,041 sq km; **Land area:** 8,000 sq mi, 20,721 sq km. **Location:** In Central America. **Neighbors:** Guatemala on W, Honduras on N. **Topography:** A hot Pacific coastal plain in S rises to a cooler plateau and valley region, densely populated. The N is mountainous, including many volcanoes. **Capital:** San Salvador, 1,096,530.

Government: Type: Republic. **Head of state and gov.:** Pres. Salvador Sánchez Cerén; b. June 18, 1944; in office: June 1, 2014. **Local divisions:** 14 departments. **Defense budget:** $154 mil. **Active troops:** 15,300.

Economy: Industries: food proc., beverages, petroleum, chemicals, fertilizer, textiles, furniture, light metals. **Chief crops:** coffee, sugar, corn, rice, beans, oilseed, cotton, sorghum. **Natural resources:** hydropower, geothermal power, petroleum. **Arable land:** 34%. **Livestock:** cattle: 1.1 mil; chickens: 15.5 mil; goats: 15,150; pigs: 445,000; sheep: 5,300. **Electricity prod.:** 6 bil kWh. **Labor force:** agric. 21%, industry 20%, services 58%. **Unemployment:** 6.9%.

Finance: Monetary unit: Colon (SVC) (Sept. 2014: 8.75 = $1 U.S.). **GDP:** $47.5 bil; **per capita GDP:** $7,500; **GDP growth:** 1.6%. **Imports:** $10 bil; U.S. 35.4%, Guatemala 12.7%, Mexico 7%, China 5.6%, Germany 4.2%. **Exports:** $5.1 bil; U.S. 47.3%, Guatemala 13.8%, Honduras 9.6%, Nicaragua 5.4%. **Tourism:** $621 mil. **Budget:** $5.7 bil. **Total reserves less gold:** $2.5 bil. **Gold:** 223,000 oz t. **Inflation:** 0.8%.

Transport: Railways: 176 mi (inoperable because of disuse and costs). **Motor vehicles:** 38.6 per 1,000 pop. **Civil aviation:** 2.6 bil pass.-mi; 5 airports. **Chief ports:** Acajutla, Puerto Cutuco.

Communications: TV sets: 227 per 1,000 pop. **Radios:** 477 per 1,000 pop. **Telephone lines:** 15 per 100 pop. **Mobile:** 136.2 per 100 pop. **Internet:** 23.1%.

Health: Life expect.: 70.9 male; 77.6 female. **Births:** 16.8 per 1,000 pop. **Deaths:** 5.7 per 1,000 pop. **Natural inc.:** 1.11%. **Infant mortality:** 18.4 per 1,000 live births. **HIV:** 0.5%.

Education: Compulsory: ages 7-15. **Literacy:** 88%. **Embassy:** 1400 16th St. NW, Ste. 100, 20036; 265-9671. **Website:** www.presidencia.gob.sv

El Salvador became independent of Spain in 1821, and of the Central American Federation in 1839.

A military coup overthrew the government of Pres. Carlos Humberto Romero in 1979, but the ruling military-civilian junta failed to quell a rebellion by leftist insurgents, armed by Cuba and Nicaragua.

Extreme right-wing death squads organized to eliminate suspected leftists killed thousands in the 1980s. The Reagan administration supported the government with military aid. After taking the lives of some 75,000 people (with thousands more "disappeared"), the 12-year civil war ended Jan. 16, 1992, as the government and leftist rebels signed a formal peace treaty. Rightist legislators in the National Assembly passed a sweeping amnesty Mar. 20, 1993, for civil war atrocities.

Members of the right-wing ARENA party held the presidency from 1989 to 2009. Mauricio Funes, a leftist, won the 2009 presidential election. His vice pres., Salvador Sánchez Cerén, a former rebel commander, narrowly won the 2014 presidential election, with 50.1% of the vote in the runoff. In late 2013 and the first half of 2014, thousands of undocumented immigrants from El Salvador were caught trying to enter the U.S. from Mexico. Most detained were unaccompanied children or children with their mothers, fleeing drug violence and other hardships.

Equatorial Guinea
Republic of Equatorial Guinea

People: Population: 722,254. **Age distrib.:** <15: 40.8%; 65+: 4%. **Pop. density:** 66.7 per sq mi, 25.7 per sq km. **Urban:** 39.8%. **Ethnic groups:** Fang 86%, Bubi 7%, Mdowe 4%, Annobon 2%, Bujeba 1%. **Languages:** Spanish, French (both official); Fang; Bubi. **Religions:** nominally Christian and predominantly Roman Catholic, pagan practices.

Geography: Total area: 10,831 sq mi, 28,051 sq km; **Land area:** 10,831 sq mi, 28,051 sq km. **Location:** Bioko Isl. off W Africa coast in Gulf of Guinea, and Rio Muni, mainland enclave. **Neighbors:** Gabon on S, Cameroon on E and N. **Topography:** Bioko Isl. consists of 2 volcanic mountains and connecting valley. Rio Muni, with over 90% of the area, has coastal plain and low hills beyond. **Capital:** Malabo, 145,077.

Government: Type: Republic. **Head of state:** Pres. Teodoro Obiang Nguema Mbasogo; b. June 5, 1942; in office: Aug. 3, 1979. **Head of gov.:** Prime Min. Vicente Ehate Tomi; b. 1968; in office: May 22, 2012. **Local divisions:** 7 provinces. **Defense budget** (2012): $7 mil. **Active troops:** 1,320.

Economy: Industries: petroleum, nat. gas, sawmilling. **Chief crops:** coffee, cocoa, rice, yams, cassava, bananas, palm oil nuts. **Natural resources:** petroleum, nat. gas, timber, gold, bauxite, diamonds, tantalum, sand and gravel, clay. **Crude oil reserves:** 1.1 bil bbls. **Arable land:** 4.3%. **Livestock:** cattle: 5,300; chickens: 360,000; goats: 9,500; pigs: 6,700; sheep: 40,000. **Electricity prod.:** 97 mil kWh. **Labor force:** NA. **Unemployment:** 7.6%.

Finance: Monetary unit: Central African CFA Franc (XAF) (Sept. 2014: 498.91 = $1 U.S.). **GDP:** $19.7 bil; **per capita GDP:** $25,700; **GDP growth:** –1.5%. **Imports:** $7.9 bil; Spain 18.4%, China 17.4%, U.S. 11.1%, France 8%, Italy 5.9%, Côte d'Ivoire 5.3%, Brazil 4.4%. **Exports:** $15.4 bil; Japan 18.8%, France 16.1%, China 11.7%, U.S. 11.3%, Netherlands 7.2%, Spain 7.1%, Italy 5.1%. **Budget:** $6.8 bil. **Total reserves less gold** (2012): $4.4 bil. **Inflation:** 6.4%.

Transport: Civil aviation: 6 airports. **Chief ports:** Bata, Luba, Malabo.

Communications: TV sets: 116 per 1,000 pop. **Radios:** 431 per 1,000 pop. **Telephone lines** 2 per 100 pop. **Mobile:** 67.5 per 100 pop. **Internet:** 16.4%.

Health: Life expect.: 62.4 male; 64.6 female. **Births:** 33.8 per 1,000 pop. **Deaths:** 8.4 per 1,000 pop. **Natural inc.:** 2.54%. **Infant mortality:** 71.1 per 1,000 live births. **HIV:** NA.

Education: Compulsory: ages 7-12. **Literacy:** 95.3%. **Embassy:** 2020 16th St. NW 20009; 518-5700. **Website:** www.guineaecuatorialpress.com or www.state.gov/p/af/ci/ek/

Fernando Po (now Bioko) Island was reached by Portugal in the late 15th cent. and ceded to Spain in 1778. Independence came Oct. 12, 1968. Riots occurred in 1969 over disputes between the island and the more backward Rio Muni province on the mainland.

Masie Nguema Biyogo, a mainlander, became president for life in 1972. His reign, among the most brutal in Africa, left the nation bankrupt; most of the nation's 7,000 Europeans emigrated. He was ousted in a military coup, Aug. 1979. Teodoro Obiang Nguema Mbasogo, leader of the coup, became president and installed his family members in key government posts. Multiparty presidential elections held in 1996, 2002, and 2009 were seriously flawed.

The economy is heavily dependent on oil exports. There have been allegations of government misuse of oil revenue, and poverty remains widespread. Human Rights Watch (HRW) reported in 2012 that the Obiang regime "regularly tortures and arbitrarily detains" suspected dissidents. A referendum on constitutional reforms was overwhelmingly approved Nov. 2011, but HRW reported voter fraud and intimidation. The government planned to move its capital to a newly built city, Oyala, and finance construction with oil sales.

Eritrea
State of Eritrea

People: Population: 6,380,803. **Age distrib.:** <15: 40.8%; 65+: 3.7%. **Pop. density:** 163.6 per sq mi, 63.2 per sq km. **Urban:** 22.2%.

Ethnic groups: Tigrinya 55%, Tigre 30%, Saho 4%, Kunama 2%, Rashaida 2%, Bilen 2%, other (Afar, Beni Amir, Nera) 5%. **Languages:** Tigrinya, Arabic, English (all official); Tigre; Kunama; Afar; other Cushitic langs. **Religions:** Muslim, Coptic Christian, Roman Catholic, Protestant.

Geography: Total area: 45,406 sq mi, 117,600 sq km; **Land area:** 38,996 sq mi, 101,000 sq km. **Location:** In E Africa, on SW coast of Red Sea. **Neighbors:** Ethiopia on S, Djibouti on SE, Sudan on W. **Topography:** Includes many islands of the Dahlak Archipelago, low coastal plains in S, mountain range with peaks to 9,000 ft in N. **Capital:** Asmara, 774,558.

Government: Type: In transition. **Head of state and gov.:** Pres. Isaias Afworki; b. Feb. 2, 1946; in office: June 8, 1993. **Local divisions:** 6 regions. **Defense budget** (2012): $78 mil. **Active troops:** 201,750.

Economy: Industries: food proc., beverages, clothing and textiles, light mfg. **Chief crops:** sorghum, lentils, vegetables, corn, cotton, tobacco, sisal. **Natural resources:** gold, potash, zinc, copper, salt, poss. oil and nat. gas, fish. **Arable land:** 6.8%. **Livestock:** cattle: 2.1 mil; chickens: 1.4 mil; goats: 1.8 mil; sheep: 2.3 mil. **Electricity prod.:** 317 mil kWh. **Labor force:** agric. 80%, industry and services 20%. **Unemployment:** 7.9%.

Finance: Monetary unit: Nakfa (ERN) (Sept. 2014: 10.47 = $1 U.S.). **GDP:** $4.7 bil; **per capita GDP:** $1,200; **GDP growth:** 7%. **Imports:** $1 bil. **Exports:** $496.2 mil. **Budget:** $1.4 bil. **Total reserves less gold** (2011): $114.8 mil. **Inflation:** NA.

Transport: Railways: 190 mi. **Civil aviation:** 4 airports. **Chief ports:** Assab, Massawa.

Communications: TV sets: 67 per 1,000 pop. **Radios:** 458 per 1,000 pop. **Telephone lines:** 1 per 100 pop. **Mobile:** 5.6 per 100 pop. **Internet:** 0.9%.

Health: Life expect.: 61.4 male; 65.7 female. **Births:** 30.7 per 1,000 pop. **Deaths:** 7.7 per 1,000 pop. **Natural inc.:** 2.30%. **Infant mortality:** 38.4 per 1,000 live births. **HIV:** 0.6%.

Education: Compulsory ages 7-14. **Literacy:** 73.8%.

Embassy: 1708 New Hampshire Ave. NW 20009; 319-1991.

Website: www.shabait.com or www.state.gov/p/af/ci/er/

Eritrea was part of the Ethiopian kingdom of Aksum. It was an Italian colony from 1890 to 1941, when it was captured by the British. Following a period of British and UN supervision, Eritrea was awarded to Ethiopia as part of a federation in 1952. Ethiopia annexed Eritrea as a province in 1962. After a 30-year struggle, Eritrea formally declared its independence May 24, 1993. A constitution was ratified in 1997 but not implemented.

A border war with Ethiopia that erupted in June 1998 intensified in May 2000, as Ethiopian troops plunged into western Eritrea; a cease-fire signed June 18 provided for a UN peacekeeping force (UNMEE) to patrol a buffer zone on Eritrean territory. A peace treaty was signed Dec. 12, 2000.

A 2007 UN report accused Eritrea of aiding an Islamic insurgency in Somalia. Citing Eritrean obstruction of UNMEE activities, the UN Security Council ended the peacekeeping mission July 2008. Many thousands have fled repressive conditions in Eritrea, including defections by the national soccer team during tournaments in Kenya, Dec. 2009, and Uganda, Dec. 2012. Four Eritrean athletes sought asylum in the UK during the 2012 Summer Olympics in London. The Eritrean government is suspected of plotting a failed attack against an African Union summit conference Jan. 30-31, 2011, in Addis Ababa, Ethiopia. A coup attempt against Pres. Isaias Afworki failed Jan. 21, 2013, after about 100 members of the army stormed the Ministry of Information and briefly assumed control of the state-run television service before being stopped, presumably by forces loyal to the president.

Estonia
Republic of Estonia

People: Population: 1,257,921. **Age distrib.:** <15: 15.6%; 65+: 18.6%. **Pop. density:** 76.9 per sq mi, 29.7 per sq km. **Urban:** 67.6%. **Ethnic groups:** Estonian 69%, Russian 25%, Ukrainian 2%. **Languages:** Estonian (official), Russian. **Religions:** Orthodox 16%, Lutheran 10%, none 54%.

Geography: Total area: 17,463 sq mi, 45,228 sq km; **Land area:** 16,366 sq mi, 42,388 sq km. **Location:** E Europe, bordering Baltic Sea and Gulf of Finland. **Neighbors:** Russia on E, Latvia on S. **Topography:** Marshy lowland with numerous lakes and swamps; about 40% forested. Elongated hills show evidence of former glaciation. More than 800 islands on Baltic coast. **Capital:** Tallinn, 391,713.

Government: Type: Parliamentary republic. **Head of state:** Pres. Toomas Hendrik Ilves; b. Dec. 26, 1953; in office: Oct. 9, 2006. **Head of gov.:** Prime Min. Taavi Rõivas; b. Sept. 26, 1979; in office: Mar. 26, 2014. **Local divisions:** 15 counties. **Defense budget:** $480 mil. **Active troops:** 5,750.

Economy: Industries: engineering, electronics, wood and wood prods., textiles, information technology, telecom. **Chief crops:** grain, potatoes, vegetables. **Natural resources:** oil shale, peat, rare earth elements, phosphorite, clay, limestone, sand, dolomite, sea mud. **Arable land:** 14.6%. **Livestock:** cattle: 261,400; chickens: 2.1 mil; goats: 4,900; pigs: 358,700; sheep: 81,900. **Electricity prod.** (2012): 11.7 bil kWh. **Labor force:** agric. 4.2%, industry 20.2%, services 75.6%. **Unemployment:** 10.1%.

Finance: Monetary unit: Euro (EUR) (Sept. 2014: 0.76 = $1 U.S.). **GDP:** $29.9 bil; **per capita GDP:** $22,400; **GDP growth:** 1.5%. **Imports:** $16.4 bil; Finland 15.1%, Germany 10.7%, Sweden 10.7%, Latvia 10%, Lithuania 9%, Poland 6.6%, China 4.4%, Russia 4.1%. **Exports:** $15.1 bil; Sweden 16.8%, Finland 15.3%, Russia 12.7%, Latvia 9.2%, Lithuania 5.7%, Germany 4.8%. **Tourism:** $1.4 bil. **Budget:** $8.6 bil. **Total reserves less gold:** $304.8 mil. **Gold:** 8,000 oz t. **Inflation:** 2.8%.

Transport: Railways: 743 mi. **Civil aviation:** 13 airports. **Chief ports:** Kuivastu, Kunda, Muuga, Sillamae, Tallinn.

Communications: TV sets: 511 per 1,000 pop. **Radios:** 1,200 per 1,000 pop. **Telephone lines:** 33.1 per 100 pop. **Mobile:** 159.7 per 100 pop. **Internet:** 80%.

Health: Life expect.: 68.9 male; 79.6 female. **Births:** 10.3 per 1,000 pop. **Deaths:** 13.7 per 1,000 pop. **Natural inc.:** −0.34%. **Infant mortality:** 6.7 per 1,000 live births. **HIV:** 1.3%.

Education: Compulsory: ages 7-15. **Literacy:** 99.8%.

Embassy: 2131 Massachusetts Ave. NW 20008; 588-0101.

Website: www.eesti.ee

Estonia, a province of imperial Russia before World War I, was independent between World Wars I and II. The USSR conquered it in 1940 and incorporated it as the Estonian SSR. During an abortive Soviet coup, Estonia, Aug. 20, 1991, declared immediate full independence, which the Soviet Union recognized Sept. 1991. The first free elections in over 50 years were held Sept. 20, 1992. The last occupying Russian troops departed Aug. 31, 1994.

Estonia became a full member of the EU and NATO in 2004. The government accused Russia of orchestrating a cyber attack against Estonia's computer network in Apr.-May 2007. Estonia adopted the euro Jan. 1, 2011. On Feb. 20, 2013, it became the first nation to launch a network of fast chargers for electric cars. Amid growing discontent over austerity policies, Prime Min. Andrus Ansip was replaced, Mar. 26, 2014, by Taavi Rõivas, who formed a center-left government.

Ethiopia
Federal Democratic Republic of Ethiopia

People: Population: 96,633,458. **Age distrib.:** <15: 44.2%; 65+: 2.8%. **Pop. density:** 250.3 per sq mi, 96.6 per sq km. **Urban:** 19%. **Ethnic groups:** Oromo 34%, Amhara 27%, Somali 6%, Tigray 6%, Sidama 4%, Gurage 3%, Welaita 2%, Hadiya 2%, Afar 2%, Gamo 2%. **Languages:** Amharic (official nationally); Oromo, Somali, Tigrigna, Afar (all official regionally); Sidamo; Wolaytta; Gurage; Hadiyya; English; Arabic. **Religions:** Ethiopian Orthodox 44%, Muslim 34%, Protestant 19%, traditional 3%.

Geography: Total area: 426,373 sq mi, 1,104,300 sq km; **Land area:** 386,102 sq mi, 1,000,000 sq km. **Location:** In E Africa. **Neighbors:** Sudan on W; Kenya on S; Somalia, Djibouti on E; Eritrea on N. **Topography:** A central plateau, 6,000-10,000 ft high, rises to taller mountains near the Great Rift Valley, cutting in from SW. Blue Nile and other rivers cross the plateau, which descends to plains on W and SE. **Capital:** Addis Ababa, 3,168,040.

Government: Type: Federal republic. **Head of state:** Pres. Mulatu Teshome Wirtu; in office: Oct. 7, 2013. **Head of gov.:** Prime Min. Hailemariam Desalegn; b. July 19, 1965; in office: Sept. 21, 2012. **Local divisions:** 9 states, 2 self-governing administrations. **Defense budget:** $351 mil. **Active troops:** 138,000.

Economy: Industries: food proc., beverages, textiles, leather, chemicals, metals proc., cement. **Chief crops:** cereals, pulses, coffee, oilseed, cotton, sugarcane, potatoes, khat, cut flowers. **Natural resources:** gold, platinum, copper, potash, nat. gas, hydropower. **Crude oil reserves:** 430 bbls. **Arable land:** 15.3%. **Livestock:** cattle: 54 mil; chickens: 51 mil; goats: 25 mil; pigs: 33,000; sheep: 26.5 mil. **Electricity prod.:** 5.1 bil kWh. **Labor force:** agric. 85%, industry 5%, services 10%. **Unemployment:** 5.4%.

Finance: Monetary unit: Birr (ETB) (Sept. 2014: 19.89 = $1 U.S.). **GDP:** $118.2 bil; **per capita GDP:** $1,300; **GDP growth:** 7%. **Imports:** $10.7 bil; China 13.1%, U.S. 11%, Saudi Arabia 8.4%, India 5.4%. **Exports:** $3.2 bil; China 13%, Germany 10.8%, U.S. 8%, Belgium 7.7%, Saudi Arabia 7.6%. **Tourism:** $416 mil. **Budget:** $8 bil. **Total reserves less gold** (2009): $1.8 bil. **Inflation:** 8.1%.

Transport: Railways: 423 mi (part of Addis Ababa-Djibouti railway, under joint control with Djibouti, but largely inoperable). **Motor vehicles:** 1.6 per 1,000 pop. **Civil aviation:** 9.5 bil pass.-mi; 17 airports. **Chief port:** None. Landlocked, Ethiopia uses ports in Djibouti and Somalia.

Communications: TV sets: 7 per 1,000 pop. **Radios:** 171 per 1,000 pop. **Telephone lines:** 8 per 100 pop. **Mobile:** 27.3 per 100 pop. **Internet:** 1.9%.

Health: Life expect.: 58.4 male; 63.2 female. **Births:** 37.7 per 1,000 pop. **Deaths:** 8.5 per 1,000 pop. **Natural inc.:** 2.91%. **Infant mortality:** 55.8 per 1,000 live births. **HIV:** 1.2%.

Education: Compulsory ages: NA. **Literacy:** 49.1%.

Embassy: 3506 International Dr. NW 20008; 364-1200.

Website: www.ethiopia.gov.et

Ethiopian culture was influenced by Egypt and Greece. Italy invaded the region in 1880, but it maintained its independence until the Italian invasion of 1936. British forces freed the country in 1941.

A series of droughts in the 1970s killed hundreds of thousands. An army mutiny, strikes, and student demonstrations led to the 1974 dethronement of Ethiopia's last emperor, Haile Selassie I, ending his 58-year reign; he died a prisoner of the ruling junta, known as the Dergue, 1975. The junta dissolved parliament, abolished the monarchy, established a socialist state, redistributed land, curbed the influence of the Coptic Church, and violently suppressed opposition.

The regime, torn by bloody coups, faced uprisings by tribal and political groups aided in part by Sudan and Somalia. Ties with the U.S., once a major ally, deteriorated, while cooperation accords were signed with the USSR in 1977. In 1978, Soviet advisers and Cuban troops helped defeat Somali forces. Ethiopia and Somalia signed a peace agreement in 1988.

A worldwide relief effort began in 1984, as an extended drought precipitated famine; up to 1 mil people died as a result.

The Ethiopian People's Revolutionary Democratic Front (EPRDF), an umbrella group of 6 rebel armies, launched a major push against government forces in 1991, prompting Pres. Mengistu Haile Mariam's resignation. The EPRDF set up a transitional government. Ethiopia's first multiparty general elections were held in 1995.

Eritrea, a province on the Red Sea, declared its independence May 24, 1993. Fighting along the border with Eritrea, which erupted in 1998, intensified in May 2000, as Ethiopian forces entered Eritrean territory; a cease-fire was signed June 18 and a peace treaty Dec. 12. The war displaced 350,000 Ethiopians and cost the country nearly $3 bil.

The ruling EPRDF won parliamentary elections May 2005, but opposition parties made big gains. Police suppressed antigovernment protesters in Addis Ababa, June and Nov. 2005, leaving more than 80 dead. In July 2006, Ethiopia sent troops into Somalia in response to advances by Islamist militias there. Tried in absentia, former Pres. Mengistu was convicted of genocide Dec. 12, 2006. Drought and other food supply disruptions led Ethiopia June 2008 to appeal for $325 mil in emergency aid in 2008 and $175 mil in 2009. Ethiopia withdrew troops from Somalia Jan. 2009. The EPRDF dominated 2010 parliamentary elections, though the opposition contested the results. When Prime Min. Meles Zenawi died, Aug. 2012, the EPRDF's Hailemariam Desalegn became prime min. Ethiopian troops joined an African Union peacekeeping force in Somalia in Jan. 2014. At that time, Ethiopia housed almost 440,000 refugees, most from Somalia and other nearby nations.

Ethiopia began construction, Apr. 2, 2013, of what will be Africa's largest dam, across the Blue Nile. The project has received sharp criticism from the Egyptian government, which considers the dam a threat to national security.

Fiji
Republic of Fiji

People: Population: 903,207. **Age distrib.:** <15: 28.2%; 65+: 5.8%. **Pop. density:** 128 per sq mi, 49.4 per sq km. **Urban:** 53.4%. **Ethnic groups:** iTaukei 57%, Indian 38%. **Languages:** English, Fijian (both official); Hindustani. **Religions:** Protestant 45% (incl. Methodist 35%, Assembly of God 6%, Seventh-day Adventist 4%), Hindu 28%, Roman Catholic 9%, Muslim 6%.

Geography: Total area: 7,056 sq mi, 18,274 sq km; **Land area:** 7,056 sq mi, 18,274 sq km. **Location:** In western S Pacific O. **Neighbors:** Nearest are Vanuatu to W, Tonga to E. **Topography:** 322 isls. (106 inhabited), many mountainous, with tropical forests and large fertile areas. Viti Levu, the largest isl., has over half the total land area. **Capital:** Suva, 176,397.

Government: Type: Republic. **Head of state:** Pres. Ratu Epeli Nailatikau; b. July 5, 1941; in office: Nov. 5, 2009 (acting from July 30). **Head of gov.:** Prime Min. Voreqe "Frank" Bainimarama; b. Apr. 27, 1954; in office: Jan. 5, 2007. **Local divisions:** 14 provinces, 1 dependency. **Defense budget:** $58 mil. **Active troops:** 3,500.

Economy: Industries: tourism, clothing, copra, gold, silver, lumber. **Chief crops:** sugarcane, coconuts, cassava, rice, sweet potatoes, bananas. **Natural resources:** timber, fish, gold, copper, offshore oil potential, hydropower. **Arable land:** 9%. **Livestock:** cattle: 312,000; chickens: 4.9 mil; goats: 251,500; pigs: 147,000; sheep: 6,450. **Electricity prod.:** 836.1 mil kWh. **Labor force:** agric. 70%, industry and services 30%. **Unemployment:** 8.4%.

Finance: Monetary unit: Dollar (FJD) (Sept. 2014: 1.85 = $1 U.S.). **GDP:** $4.5 bil; **per capita GDP:** $4,900; **GDP growth:** 3%. **Imports:** $2.1 bil; Singapore 32.8%, Australia 15.5%, New Zealand 14.5%, China 10.7%. **Exports:** $1 bil; U.S. 14.6%, Australia 13.2%, Japan 6.9%, Samoa 5.8%, Tonga 5.1%. **Tourism:** $719 mil. **Budget:** $1.2 bil. **Total reserves less gold:** $940.9 mil. **Gold:** 800 oz t. **Inflation:** 2.9%.

Transport: Railways: 371 mi. **Motor vehicles:** 180.2 per 1,000 pop. **Civil aviation:** 2.4 bil pass.-mi; 4 airports. **Chief ports:** Lautoka, Levuka, Suva.

Communications: TV sets: 117 per 1,000 pop. **Radios:** 678 per 1,000 pop. **Telephone lines:** 8.5 per 100 pop. **Mobile:** 101.1 per 100 pop. **Internet:** 37.1%.

Health: Life expect.: 69.5 male; 74.9 female. **Births:** 19.9 per 1,000 pop. **Deaths:** 6.0 per 1,000 pop. **Natural inc.:** 1.39%. **Infant mortality:** 10.2 per 1,000 live births. **HIV:** 0.1%.

Education: Compulsory: ages 6-17. **Literacy:** NA.
Embassy: 2000 M St. NW, Ste. 710, 20036; 466-8320.
Website: www.fiji.gov.fj

A British colony since 1874, Fiji became independent Oct. 10, 1970. Cultural differences between the Indian community (descendants of contract laborers brought to the islands in the 19th cent.) and indigenous Fijians have led to political polarization. More than 100,000 Indians have left Fiji since the mid-1980s.

Military coups have been frequent in recent decades. Fiji's first Indian prime minister, Mahendra Chaudhry, and other government officials were taken captive May 19, 2000, by indigenous Fijian gunmen led by George Speight, culminating in a military takeover, May 29, led by Frank Bainimarama. Release of the last remaining hostages in July 2000 coincided with the installation of an interim military-backed government. Speight was convicted of treason and sentenced to life in prison in 2002. Prime Min. Laisenia Qarase headed an elected civilian government, 2001-06. He retained his office in parliamentary voting, May 2006, but was ousted in a military coup Dec. 5, and Bainimarama took office as interim prime min. After a court ruled in 2009 that the 2006 coup was illegal, Pres. Ratu Josefa Iloilo abrogated the constitution, dissolved the judiciary, and reappointed Interim Prime Min. Bainimarama. In July, Bainimarama promised a new constitution and legislative elections; he also named Vice Pres. Ratu Epeli Nailatikau to replace the retiring Pres. Iloilo. Bainimarama accepted a draft constitution released Mar. 22, 2013, and he retained office in democratic elections Sept. 17, 2014. The Commonwealth, Sept. 26, 2014, reinstated Fiji's membership, which had been suspended since the 2006 coup.

Finland
Republic of Finland

People: Population: 5,268,799. **Age distrib.:** <15: 15.8%; 65+: 19.8%. **Pop. density:** 44.9 per sq mi, 17.3 per sq km. **Urban:** 84.1%. **Ethnic groups:** Finn 93%, Swede 6%. **Languages:** Finnish, Swedish (both official). **Religions:** Lutheran 78%, none 19%.

Geography: Total area: 130,559 sq mi, 338,145 sq km; **Land area:** 117,304 sq mi, 303,815 sq km. **Location:** In N Europe. **Neighbors:** Norway on N, Sweden on W, Russia on E. **Topography:** South and central are generally flat with low hills and many lakes. The N has mountainous areas, 3,000-4,000 ft above sea level. **Capital:** Helsinki, 1,169,900.

Government: Type: Republic. **Head of state:** Pres. Sauli Niinistö; b. Aug. 24, 1948; in office: Mar. 1, 2012. **Head of gov.:** Prime Min. Jyrki Katainen; b. Oct. 14, 1971; in office: June 22, 2011. **Local divisions:** 19 regions. **Defense budget:** $3.81 bil. **Active troops:** 22,200.

Economy: Industries: metals and metal prods., electronics, machinery and scientific instruments, shipbuilding, pulp and paper, foodstuffs, chemicals, textiles, clothing. **Chief crops:** barley, wheat, sugar beets, potatoes. **Natural resources:** timber, iron ore, copper, lead, zinc, chromite, nickel, gold, silver, limestone. **Arable land:** 7.4%. **Livestock:** cattle: 911,847; chickens: 6.9 mil; goats: 4,509; pigs: 1.3 mil; sheep: 135,546. **Electricity prod.** (2012): 67.7 bil kWh. **Labor force:** agric. and forestry 4.4%; industry 15.5%; constr. 7.1%; commerce 21.3%; finance, insurance, and business services 13.3%; transp. and communications 9.9%; public services 28.5%. **Unemployment:** 7.6%.

Finance: Monetary unit: Euro (EUR) (Sept. 2014: 0.76 = $1 U.S.). **GDP:** $195.5 bil; **per capita GDP:** $35,900; **GDP growth:** -0.6%. **Imports:** $70.7 bil; Russia 17.7%, Sweden 14.8%, Germany 13.9%, Netherlands 8.1%, China 4.4%. **Exports:** $75.7 bil; Sweden 11.1%, Russia 9.9%, Germany 9.3%, Netherlands 6.3%, U.S. 6.2%, UK 5.1%, China 4.6%. **Tourism:** $4 bil. **Budget:** $145.3 bil (central govt. budget). **Total reserves less gold:** $9.4 bil. **Gold:** 1.6 mil oz t. **Inflation:** 1.5%.

Transport: Railways: 3,693 mi. **Motor vehicles:** 691.7 per 1,000 pop. **Civil aviation:** 12.7 bil pass.-mi; 74 airports. **Chief ports:** Helsinki, Kotka, Naantali, Porvoo, Raahe, Rauma.

Communications: TV sets: 679 per 1,000 pop. **Radios:** 1,623 per 1,000 pop. **Telephone lines:** 13.9 per 100 pop. **Mobile:** 171.7 per 100 pop. (data-only subscriptions). **Internet:** 91.5%.

Health: Life expect.: 76.2 male; 83.3 female. **Births:** 10.4 per 1,000 pop. **Deaths:** 10.5 per 1,000 pop. **Natural inc.:** -0.02%. **Infant mortality:** 3.4 per 1,000 live births. **HIV:** NA.

Education: Compulsory: ages 7-16. **Literacy:** 100%.
Embassy: 3301 Massachusetts Ave. NW 20008; 298-5800.
Website: www.government.fi

The early Finns probably migrated from the Ural area at about the beginning of the Christian era. Swedish settlers brought the country into Sweden, 1154 to 1809, when Finland became an autonomous grand duchy of the Russian Empire. Russian exactions created a strong national spirit; on Dec. 6, 1917, Finland declared its independence, and in 1919 it became a republic.

On Nov. 30, 1939, the Soviet Union invaded, and the Finns were forced to cede 16,173 sq mi of territory. After World War II, further cessions were exacted. In 1948, Finland signed a treaty of mutual assistance with the USSR that was renegotiated in Jan. 1992.

Following approval by Finnish voters in a 1994 advisory referendum, Finland entered the EU Jan. 1, 1995. Former Pres. Martti Ahtisaari was awarded the Nobel Peace Prize, Oct. 10, 2008, for his efforts in mediating international conflicts. Following 2011 parliamentary elections, Jyrki Katainen, leader of the conservative National Coalition Party, became prime min. The conservative Sauli Niinistö won the 2012 presidential election.

Åland, or Ahvenanmaa, constituting an autonomous province, is a group of small islands, 590 sq mi, in the Gulf of Bothnia, 25 mi from Sweden, 15 mi from Finland. Mariehamn is the chief port. **Website:** www.aland.ax

France
French Republic

People: Population: 66,259,012. **Age distrib.:** <15: 18.7%; 65+: 18.3%. **Pop. density:** 268 per sq mi, 103.5 per sq km. **Urban:** 79.3%. **Ethnic groups:** Celtic and Latin with Teutonic, Slavic, N African, Indochinese, Basque minorities. **Languages:** French (official); rapidly declining regional dialects (Provençal, Breton, Alsatian, Corsican, Catalan, Basque, Flemish). **Religions:** Roman Catholic 83%-88%, Muslim 5%-10%, Protestant 2%, Jewish 1%.

Geography: Total area: 248,573 sq mi, 643,801 sq km; **Land area:** 247,270 sq mi, 640,427 sq km. **Location:** in W Europe, between Atlantic O. and Medit. Sea. **Neighbors:** Spain, Andorra, Monaco on S; Italy, Switzerland, Germany on E; Luxembourg, Belgium on N. **Topography:** A wide plain covers more than half of the country, in N and W, drained to W by Seine, Loire, Garonne Rivers. The Massif Central is a mountainous plateau in center. In E are Alps (Mt. Blanc is tallest in W Europe at 15,781 ft), the lower Jura range, and forested Vosges. The Rhone flows from Lake Geneva to Mediterranean. Pyrenees are in SW, on border with Spain. **Capital:** Paris, 10,764,400. **Cities (urban aggl.):** Lyon, 1,596,704; Marseille-Aix-en-Provence, 1,595,491; Lille, 1,024,995.

Government: Type: Republic. **Head of state:** Pres. François Hollande; b. Aug. 12, 1954; in office: May 15, 2012. **Head of gov.:** Prime Min. Manuel Valls; b. Aug. 13, 1962; in office: Mar. 31, 2014. **Local divisions:** 22 metropolitan regions, 5 overseas regions. **Defense budget:** $52.35 bil. **Active troops:** 222,200.

Economy: Industries: machinery, chemicals, automobiles, metallurgy, aircraft, electronics, textiles, food proc., tourism. **Chief crops:** wheat, cereals, sugar beets, potatoes, wine grapes. **Natural resources:** coal, iron ore, bauxite, zinc, uranium, antimony, arsenic, potash, feldspar, fluorspar, gypsum, timber, fish. **Crude oil reserves:** 89.6 mil bbls. **Other resources:** Timber, dairy. **Arable land:** 33.4%. **Livestock:** cattle: 19.1 mil; chickens: 167.6 mil; goats: 1.3 mil; pigs: 13.5 mil; sheep: 7.2 mil. **Electricity prod.** (2012): 532 bil kWh. **Labor force:** agric. 2.9%, industry 20.6%, services 76.4%. **Unemployment:** 9.9%.

Finance: Monetary unit: Euro (EUR) (Sept. 2014: 0.76 = 1 U.S.). **GDP:** $2.3 tril; **per capita GDP:** $35,700; **GDP growth:** 0.3%. **Imports:** $659.8 bil; Germany 19.5%, Belgium 11.3%, Italy 7.6%, Netherlands 7.4%, Spain 6.6%, UK 5.1%, China 4.9%. **Exports:** $578.6 bil; Germany 16.7%, Belgium 7.5%, Italy 7.5%, Spain 6.9%, UK 6.9%, U.S. 5.6%, Netherlands 4.3%. **Tourism:** $56.1 bil. **Budget:** $1.5 tril. **Total reserves less gold:** $50.8 bil. **Gold:** 78.3 mil oz t. **Inflation:** 0.9%.

Transport: Railways: 18,417 mi. **Motor vehicles:** 579.2 per 1,000 pop. **Civil aviation:** 101.1 bil pass.-mi; 294 airports. **Chief ports:** Calais, Dunkerque, Le Havre, Marseille, Nantes, Paris, Rouen.

Communications: TV sets: 661 per 1,000 pop. **Radios:** 943 per 1,000 pop. **Telephone lines:** 60.8 per 100 pop. **Mobile:** 98.5 per 100 pop. **Internet:** 81.9%.

Health: Life expect.: 78.6 male; 84.9 female. **Births:** 12.5 per 1,000 pop. **Deaths:** 9.1 per 1,000 pop. **Natural inc.:** 0.34%. **Infant mortality:** 3.3 per 1,000 live births. **HIV:** N/A.

Education: Compulsory: ages 6-16. **Literacy:** 99%.

Embassy: 4101 Reservoir Rd. NW 20007; 944-6195.

Website: www.gouvernement.fr

Julius Caesar conquered Celtic Gaul 58-51 BCE; Romans ruled for 500 years. Under Charlemagne, Frankish rule extended over much of Europe. After his death, France emerged as one of the successor kingdoms.

The monarchy was overthrown in the French Revolution (1789-93) and succeeded by the First Republic, followed by the First Empire under Napoleon (1804-15), a monarchy (1814-48), the Second Republic (1848-52), the Second Empire (1852-70), the Third Republic (1871-1946), the Fourth Republic (1946-58), and the Fifth Republic (1958-present).

France suffered severe losses in manpower and wealth in WWI, when it was invaded by Germany. By the Treaty of Versailles, France exacted return of Alsace and Lorraine, provinces seized by Germany in 1871 after it defeated France in the Franco-Prussian War. During WWII, Germany invaded France again in May 1940, and signed an armistice with a government based in Vichy. After the Allies liberated France in 1944, Gen. Charles de Gaulle became head of the provisional government, serving until 1946. De Gaulle

again became premier in 1958, during a crisis over Algeria, and obtained voter approval for a new constitution, ushering in the Fifth Republic. He then became president.

France withdrew from Indochina in 1954 and from Morocco and Tunisia in 1956. Most of its remaining African territories, including Algeria, were freed 1958-62.

In May 1968, rebellious students in Paris and other centers rioted, battled police, and were joined by workers who launched nationwide strikes. The government awarded pay increases to the strikers May 26. De Gaulle resigned from office in Apr. 1969, after losing a nationwide referendum on constitutional reform. Georges Pompidou was elected to succeed him. After Pompidou's death, in 1974, Valery Giscard d'Estaing was elected president; he continued his predecessors' conservative policies.

In 1981, France elected François Mitterrand, a Socialist, president. Under Mitterrand the government nationalized 5 major industries and most private banks. After 1986, however, when rightists won a narrow victory in the National Assembly, Mitterrand chose conservative Jacques Chirac as premier. During a 2-year period of "cohabitation," France pursued a privatization program, selling many state-owned companies. During Mitterrand's second 7-year term starting in 1988, he appointed first a Socialist as premier, then a conservative after the center-right won a large majority in 1993 legislative elections.

Chirac won the 1995 presidency in a runoff election. He cut government spending to meet budgetary goals for the introduction of the euro. With unemployment at nearly 13%, leftist parties won a decisive victory in 1997 legislative elections, resulting in a new period of cohabitation, this time between a conservative president and a Socialist prime min., Lionel Jospin.

Chirac easily won the 2002 presidential election in a runoff, and his center-right allies won parliamentary elections. Parliament gave final approval in 2004 to a law barring the wearing of Islamic head scarves and other religious symbols in public schools.

Displeased with sluggish economic growth, high unemployment, and budget cuts in entitlement programs, voters rejected, 2005, a proposed EU constitution supported by the Chirac government. A state of emergency was declared Nov. 8 after 12 days of riots that began in Paris and spread to some 300 French cities and towns; rioters were mainly young immigrants from N and W Africa. After a wave of mass protests and strikes, Chirac agreed, Apr. 2006, to rescind a law making it easier for employers to fire inexperienced young workers.

The conservative Nicolas Sarkozy won the 2007 presidential runoff election. The French bank Société Générale disclosed Jan. 2008 that it had lost more than $7 bil because of a rogue trader, who in 2010 was sentenced to 3 years in prison and ordered to pay restitution.

Sarkozy responded to the global recession, Dec. 2008, with a $33-bil economic stimulus plan focused on infrastructure development; measures announced Feb. 2009, following labor protests, added $3.3 bil in aid for lower-income people. Sarkozy's policy of shutting Roma (Gypsy) encampments and expelling thousands to Romania and Bulgaria drew public rebukes from EU allies, Sept. 2010.

France, a founding NATO member, formally returned to the alliance's military command structure Apr. 2009 after 43 years. In Dec. 2012, France withdrew its last combat troops deployed with NATO forces in Afghanistan; fewer than 90 other troops remained as of Sept. 2014. France participated in military operations that ousted Libyan leader Muammar al-Qaddafi, Aug. 23, 2011. In Sept. 2014, France joined the U.S.-led campaign of airstrikes in Iraq against the Sunni extremist group ISIS.

Former Pres. Chirac was convicted Dec. 2011 of corruption charges stemming from his tenure (1977-95) as mayor of Paris. With France's economy still struggling, the Socialist François Hollande won a presidential runoff over incumbent Sarkozy in 2012, while the Socialist Party won an absolute majority in parliamentary elections. Hollande's popularity subsequently declined as the economy remained sluggish and the government pursued austerity policies related to EU financial guidelines.

The French entered the conflict between government forces in Mali and Islamist militants Jan. 10, 2013; they quickly overpowered the militants but retained a presence, 2013-14, to prevent a resurgence.

Hollande May 18, 2013, signed a bill that legalized same-sex marriage and allowed gay couples to adopt children. After a weak showing by the Socialists in Mar. 2014 municipal elections, Prime Min. Jean-Marc Ayrault resigned and was replaced by centrist Socialist Manuel Valls. In European Parliament elections May 25, the far-right National Front was the largest vote getter, with 25%.

The island of **Corsica**, in the Mediterranean W of Italy and N of Sardinia, is a territorial collectivity and region of France comprising 2 departments. It elects a total of 2 senators and 3 deputies to the French Parliament. Area 3,369 sq mi; pop. (2006 census) 294,118. The capital is Ajaccio, birthplace of Napoleon I. Violence by Corsican separatist groups has hurt tourism, a leading industry on the island. Corsicans rejected, 51%-49%, a limited autonomy plan in a referendum July 6, 2003.

French Overseas Departments

French Guiana is on the NE coast of South America with Suriname on the W and Brazil on the E and S. Its area is 35,135 sq mi (total); 34,421 sq mi (land); pop. (2012 est.) 245,000. Guiana sends one senator and two deputies to the French Parliament. Guiana is administered by a prefect and has a Council General of 16 elected members; capital is Cayenne.

The famous penal colony, Devil's Island, was phased out between 1938 and 1951. The European Space Agency maintains a satellite-launching center (established by France in 1964) in the city of Kourou.

Immense forests of rich timber cover 88% of the land. Fishing (especially shrimp), forestry, and gold mining are the most important industries. Natural resources include petroleum, kaolin, niobium, tantalum, and clay.

Guadeloupe, in the West Indies' Leeward Islands, consists of 2 large islands, Basse-Terre and Grande-Terre, separated by the Salt R., plus Marie Galante and the Saintes group to the S and, to the N, Desirade. A French possession since 1635, the department is represented in the French Parliament; administration consists of a prefect (governor) as well as an elected general and regional councils. St. Barthélemy and over half of St. Martin (the Netherlands' portion is called St. Maarten), both formerly part of Guadeloupe, voted for secession in 2003 and became separate overseas territorial collectivities in 2007.

Area of the islands is 525 sq mi; pop. (2011 est., incl. St. Barthélemy and St. Martin) 463,000, mainly descendants of slaves; capital is Basse-Terre (2014 est. pop: 55,295) on Basse-Terre Island. The land is fertile; sugar, rum, and bananas are exported. Tourism is an important industry.

Martinique, the northernmost of the Windward Islands, in the West Indies, has been a possession since 1635, and a department since Mar. 1946. It is represented in the French Parliament by 2 senators and 4 deputies. The island was the birthplace of Napoleon's first wife, Empress Josephine.

It has an area of 425 sq mi (total); 409 sq mi (land); pop. (2012 est.) 396,000, mostly descendants of slaves. The capital is Fort-de-France; pop. (2014 est.) 85,817. It is a popular tourist stop. The chief exports are rum, bananas, and petroleum products. **Website:** www.region-martinique.mq

Mayotte, claimed by Comoros and administered by France, voted in 1976 to become a territorial collectivity of France. An island NW of Madagascar, area is 144 sq mi, pop. (2012 est.) 216,000. The capital is Mamoudzou; pop. (2014 est.) 5,715. In a Mar. 29, 2009, referendum, 95% of voters endorsed a plan under which Mayotte became an overseas department of France as of Mar. 31, 2011.

Réunion is a volcanic island in the Indian O. about 420 mi E of Madagascar, and has belonged to France since 1665. Area, 972 sq mi (total); 968 sq mi (land); pop. (2012 est.) 857,000, 30% of French extraction. Capital: Saint-Denis; pop. (2014 est.) 143,617. The chief export is sugar. It elects 5 deputies, 3 senators to the French Parliament. **Website:** www.regionreunion.fr

French Overseas Territorial Collectivities

French Polynesia, comprises 130 islands widely scattered among 5 archipelagos in the S Pacific; administered by a Council of Ministers (headed by a president). Territorial Assembly and the Council have headquarters at Papeete, on Tahiti, one of the Society Islands (which include the Windward Isls. and Leeward Isls.). Two deputies and a senator are elected to the French Parliament.

Other groups are the Marquesas Isls.; the Tuamotu Archipelago; the Gambier Isls.; and the Austral, or Tubuai, Isls.

Total area of the islands administered from Tahiti is 1,609 sq mi (total); 1,478 sq mi (land); pop. (2014 est.) 280,026, more than half on Tahiti. Tahiti is mountainous with a productive coastline bearing coconuts, citrus, pineapples, and vanilla. Cultured pearls are also produced.

Tahiti was visited by Capt. James Cook in 1769 and by Capt. Bligh in the *Bounty*, 1788-89. Its beauty impressed Herman Melville, Paul Gauguin, and Charles Darwin. A coalition favoring independence for French Polynesia within 20 years gained control of the territorial assembly after elections May 23, 2004. An anti-independence party won May 5, 2013, territorial assembly elections. A UN General Assembly resolution May 17, 2013, called on France to grant French Polynesia independence.

St. Pierre and Miquelon became a territorial collectivity in 1985. It consists of 2 groups of rocky islands near the SW coast of Newfoundland, inhabited by fishermen. Fish products are the chief export. The St. Pierre group has an area of 10 sq mi; Miquelon, 83 sq mi. Total pop. (2014 est.) 5,716. Capital: Saint-Pierre; pop. (2014 est.) 5,459. Both Mayotte and St. Pierre and Miquelon elect a deputy and a senator to the French Parliament.

St. Barthélemy and St. Martin became overseas territorial collectivities in 2007, with total pop. (2014 est.) of 7,267 and 31,530 respectively.

The territorial collectivity of **Wallis and Futuna** comprises 2 island groups in the SW Pacific S of Tuvalu, N of Fiji, and W of Western Samoa. It became an overseas territory July 29, 1961. The islands have a total area of 55 sq mi and pop. (2014 est.) of 15,561. Alofi, attached to Futuna, is uninhabited. Capital: Mata-Utu;

pop. (2014 est.) 1,064. Chief products are copra, coconuts, yams, taro, and bananas. A senator and a deputy are elected to the French Parliament.

Overseas Territory and Special Collectivity

The territory of the **French Southern and Antarctic Lands** comprises Adelie Land, on Antarctica, and island groups in the Indian O. Area: 2,991 sq mi (total); 2,960 sq mi (land).

Adelie, reached 1840, has a 185-mi coastline and tapers 1,240 mi inland to the S Pole. (The U.S. does not recognize national claims in Antarctica.) It has a research station. There are 2 glaciers: Ninnis, 22 mi wide, 99 mi long, and Mentz, 11 mi by 140 mi.

The Indian O. groups are as follows: Kerguelen Archipelago, visited 1772, consists of one large and 300 small islands. The chief is 87 mi long, 74 mi wide, and has Mt. Ross (6,429 ft). Principal research station is Port-aux-Français. There are seals, blue whales, coal, peat, semiprecious stones. Crozet Archipelago, reached 1772, covers 136 sq mi. Eastern Island rises to 6,560 ft. Saint Paul, in southern Indian O., has warm springs with earth at places heating to 120° to 390°F. Amsterdam is nearby; both produce cod and rock lobster. Military garrisons and meteorological stations are located on the Scattered Isls.

The special collectivity of **New Caledonia** and Dependencies is a group of islands in the Pacific O. about 1,115 mi E of Australia and approx. the same distance NW of New Zealand. Dependencies are the Loyalty Isls., Isle of Pines, Belep Archipelago, and Huon Isls.

The largest island, New Caledonia, is 6,530 sq mi. Total area of the territory is 7,172 sq mi (total); 7,056 sq mi (land); pop. (2014 est.) 267,840. The group was acquired by France in 1853.

The territory is administered by a High Commissioner. There is a popularly elected Territorial Congress. Two deputies and a senator are elected to the French Parliament. Capital: Nouméa; pop. (2014 est.) 181,002.

Mining is the chief industry. New Caledonia is one of the world's largest nickel producers. Chrome, iron, cobalt, manganese, silver, gold, lead, and copper are also found. Agric. products include yams, sweet potatoes, potatoes, manioc, corn, and coconuts.

In 1987, New Caledonian voters chose by referendum to remain within the Republic. French and Melanesians (Kanaks) clashed in 1988. An agreement Apr. 21, 1998, between France and rival New Caledonian factions specified a 15- to 20-year period of "shared sovereignty" and a referendum on independence no later than 2018. Parties favoring remaining part of France won a majority in May 11, 2014, Territorial Congress elections. **Website:** www.gouv.nc

Gabon
Gabonese Republic

People: Population: 1,672,597. **Age distrib.:** <15: 42.1%; 65+: 3.8%. **Pop. density:** 16.8 per sq mi, 6.5 per sq km. **Urban:** 86.9%. **Ethnic groups:** Bantu tribes (incl. Fang, Bapounou, Nzebi, Obamba). **Languages:** French (official), Fang, Myene, Nzebi, Bapounou/ Eschira, Bandjabi. **Religions:** Christian 55%-75%, animist.

Geography: Total area: 103,347 sq mi, 267,667 sq km; **Land area:** 99,486 sq mi, 257,667 sq km. **Location:** On Atlantic coast of W central Africa. **Neighbors:** Equatorial Guinea, Cameroon on N; Congo on E and S. **Topography:** Heavily forested, consisting of coastal lowlands; plateaus in N, E, and S; mountains in N, SE, and center. The Ogooue R. system covers most of Gabon. **Capital:** Libreville, 694,633.

Government: Type: Republic. **Head of state:** Pres. Ali Bongo Ondimba; b. Feb. 9, 1959; in office: Oct. 16, 2009. **Head of gov.:** Prime Min. Daniel Ona Ondo; b. July 10, 1945; in office: Jan. 27, 2014. **Local divisions:** 9 provinces. **Defense budget** $263 mil. **Active troops:** 4,700.

Economy: Industries: petroleum extraction and refining; manganese, gold; chemicals, ship repair, food and beverages. **Chief crops:** cocoa, coffee, sugar, palm oil, rubber. **Natural resources:** petroleum, nat. gas, diamonds, niobium, manganese, uranium, gold, timber, iron ore, hydropower. **Crude oil reserves:** 2 bil bbls. **Arable land:** 1.3%. **Livestock:** cattle: 38,000; chickens: 3.2 mil; goats: 110,000; pigs: 225,000; sheep: 210,000. **Electricity prod.:** 1.7 bil kWh. **Labor force:** agric. 60%, industry 15%, services 25%. **Unemployment:** 20.3%.

Finance: Monetary unit: Central African CFA Franc (XAF) (Sept. 2014: 498.91 = $1 U.S.). **GDP:** $30.1 bil; **per capita GDP:** $19,200; **GDP growth:** 6.6%. **Imports:** $3.9 bil; France 28.2%, China 12.6%, U.S. 9.4%, Belgium 5.8%, Cameroon 4.3%. **Exports:** $9.8 bil; Japan 24.1%, U.S. 17%, Australia 11.3%, India 7.4%, China 5.4%, Spain 4.1%. **Budget:** $6.6 bil. **Total reserves less gold** (2012): $2.4 bil. **Inflation:** 0.5%.

Transport: Railways: 403 mi. **Civil aviation:** 14 airports. **Chief ports:** Gamba, Libreville, Lucinda, Owendo, Port-Gentil.

Communications: TV sets: 161 per 1,000 pop. **Radios:** 217 per 1,000 pop. **Telephone lines:** 1.2 per 100 pop. **Mobile:** 214.8 per 100 pop. **Internet:** 9.2%.

Health: Life expect.: 51.5 male; 52.6 female. **Births:** 34.6 per 1,000 pop. **Deaths:** 13.1 per 1,000 pop. **Natural inc.:** 2.15%. **Infant mortality:** 47.0 per 1,000 live births. **HIV:** 3.9%.

Education: Compulsory: ages 6-15. **Literacy:** 83.2%.

Embassy: 2034 20th St. NW 20009; 797-1000.
Website: www.gouvernement.ga or www.state.gov/p/af/ci/gb/
France established control over the region in the second half of the 19th cent. Gabon became independent Aug. 17, 1960. Backed by France, Pres. Albert-Bernard Bongo (later Omar Bongo Ondimba) ruled the country 1967-2009, greatly enriching himself and his family. A multiparty political system was introduced in 1990; a new constitution was enacted in 1991. Bongo's reelection victories in 1993, 1998, and 2003 were faulted by international observers. After he died June 8, 2009, his son Ali Bongo Ondimba, Gabon's defense minister 1999-2009, claimed victory in the disputed 2009 presidential election.

Gabon is one of the most prosperous African countries, thanks to abundant natural resources, foreign private investment, and government development programs. Elephant poaching in game reserves, for illegal ivory sales, has become a major problem in recent years.

The Gambia
Republic of The Gambia

People: Population: 1,925,527. Age distrib.: <15: 38.7%; 65+: 3.3%. Pop. density: 498.7 per sq mi, 192.6 per sq km. Urban: 59%. Ethnic groups: Mandinka 42%, Fula 18%, Wolof 16%, Jola 10%, Serahuli 9%. Languages: English (official), Mandinka, Wolof, Fula, other indigenous vernaculars. Religions: Muslim 90%, Christian 8%, indigenous beliefs 2%.

Geography: Total area: 4,361 sq mi, 11,295 sq km. Land area: 3,861 sq mi, 10,000 sq km. Location: On Atlantic coast near W tip of Africa. Neighbors: Surrounded on 3 sides by Senegal. Topography: A narrow strip of land on each side of lower Gambia R. Capital: Banjul, 489,490.

Government: Type: Republic. Head of state and gov.: Pres. Yahya Jammeh; b. May 25, 1965; in office: Oct. 18, 1996. Local divisions: 5 divisions, 1 city. Defense budget (2012): $6 mil. Active troops: 800.

Economy: Industries: peanuts, fish, and hides proc.; tourism; beverages; agric. machinery assembly. Chief crops: rice, millet, sorghum, peanuts, corn, sesame, cassava, palm kernels. Natural resources: fish, clay, silica sand, titanium, tin, zircon. Arable land: 43.5%. Livestock: cattle: 380,000; chickens: 1.3 mil; goats: 320,000; pigs: 7,000; sheep: 150,000. Electricity prod.: 230 mil kWh. Labor force: agric. 75%, industry 19%, services 6%. Unemployment: 7.7%.

Finance: Monetary unit: Dalasi (GMD) (Sept. 2014: 39.30 = $1 U.S.). GDP: $3.7 bil; per capita GDP: $2,000; GDP growth: 6.4%. Imports: $359.7 mil; China 27.6%, Senegal 8.5%, Brazil 8.1%, UK 6.4%, India 6.1%, Indonesia 4.1%. Exports: $113.2 mil; China 57.1%, India 18.6%, France 4.6%, UK 4%. Tourism: $88 mil. Budget: $265.1 mil. Total reserves less gold: $210.6 mil. Inflation: 5.7%.

Transport: Civil aviation: 1 airport. Chief port: Banjul.
Communications: TV Sets: 14 per 1,000 pop. Radios: 147 per 1,000 pop. Telephone lines: 3.5 per 100 pop. Mobile: 100 per 100 pop. Internet: 14%.

Health: Life expect.: 62.0 male; 66.7 female. Births: 31.8 per 1,000 pop. Deaths: 7.3 per 1,000 pop. Natural inc.: 2.45%. Infant mortality: 65.7 per 1,000 live births. HIV: 1.2%.

Education: Compulsory: ages 7-12. Literacy: 55.6%.
Embassy: 1156 15th St. NW 20005; 785-1399.
Website: www.gambia.gm

The peoples of The Gambia were at one time associated with the West African empires of Ghana, Mali, and Songhai. The area became Britain's first African possession in 1588.

Independence came Feb. 18, 1965; republic status within the Commonwealth was achieved in 1970. The country suffered from severe famine in the 1970s. Senegambia, a confederation with Senegal, lasted from 1982 to 1989.

On July 22, 1994, after 24 years in power, Pres. Dawda K. Jawara was deposed in a bloodless coup by a military officer, Yahya Jammeh. Jammeh barred political activity, detained potential opponents, and governed by decree. Despite a nominal return to constitutional government in 1996, Jammeh has retained a tight grip on power. Security forces suppressed an alleged coup plot by army officers Mar. 2006. Pres. Jammeh won a fourth 5-year term in 2011. Jammeh announced Aug. 19, 2012, that the 47 death-row inmates would be executed by the middle of Sept. The announcement drew widespread condemnation by intl. civil rights groups, and Jammeh placed a moratorium on executions on Sept 15. With per capita GDP of $2,000 in 2013, The Gambia is one of the world's poorest countries.

Georgia

People: Population: 4,935,880. Age distrib.: <15: 17.6%; 65+: 15.3%. Pop. density: 183.4 per sq mi, 70.8 per sq km. Urban: 53.5%. Ethnic groups: Georgian 84%, Azeri 7%, Armenian 6%, Russian 2%. Languages: Georgian (official), Russian, Armenian, Azeri, Abkhaz (official in Abkhazia). Religions: Orthodox Christian (official) 84%, Muslim 10%, Armenian-Gregorian 4%.

Geography: Total area: 26,911 sq mi, 69,700 sq km; Land area: 26,911 sq mi, 69,700 sq km. Location: SW Asia, on E coast of

Black Sea. Neighbors: Russia on N and NE, Turkey and Armenia on S, Azerbaijan on SE. Topography: Separated from Russia on NE by main range of Caucasus Mts. Capital: Tbilisi, 1,149,580.

Government: Type: Republic. Head of state: Pres. Giorgi Margvelashvili; b. Sept. 4, 1969; in office: Nov. 17, 2013. Head of gov.: Prime Min. Irakli Garibashvili; b. June 28, 1982; in office: Nov. 20, 2013. Local divisions: 9 regions, 1 city, 2 autonomous republics. Defense budget: $389 mil. Active troops: 20,650.

Economy: Industries: steel, machine tools, elec. appliances, mining, chemicals, wood prods., wine. Chief crops: citrus, grapes, tea, hazelnuts, vegetables. Natural resources: timber, hydropower, manganese, iron ore, copper, minor coal and oil deposits. Crude oil reserves: 35 mil bbls. Arable land: 5.8%. Livestock: cattle: 1.1 mil; chickens: 5.8 mil; goats: 54,400; pigs: 204,300; sheep: 688,200. Electricity prod.: 10 bil kWh. Labor force: agric. 55.6%, industry 8.9%, services 35.5%. Unemployment: 15%.

Finance: Monetary unit: Lari (GEL) (Sept. 2014: 1.74 = $1 U.S.). GDP: $27.3 bil; per capita GDP: $6,100; GDP growth: 2.5%. Imports: $7.1 bil; Turkey 17%, Ukraine 8%, Azerbaijan 8%, Russia 7%, China 7%. Exports: $2.6 bil; Azerbaijan 25%, Armenia 11%, Ukraine 7%, Turkey 6%, Russia 6%. Tourism: $1.7 bil. Budget: $5.3 bil. Total reserves less gold: $2.8 bil. Inflation: −0.5%.

Transport: Railways: 1,002 mi. Civil aviation: 18 airports. Chief ports: Batumi, Poti.

Communications: TV sets: 450 per 1,000 pop. Radios: 542 per 1,000 pop. Telephone lines: 27.7 per 100 pop. Mobile: 115 per 100 pop. Internet: 43.1%.

Health: Life expect.: 71.6 male; 80.2 female. Births: 12.9 per 1,000 pop. Deaths: 10.8 per 1,000 pop. Natural inc.: 0.22%. Infant mortality: 16.7 per 1,000 live births. HIV: 0.3%.

Education: Compulsory: ages 6-14. Literacy: 99.8%.
Embassy: 2209 Massachusetts Ave. NW 20008; 387-2390.
Website: www.government.gov.ge

The region, which contained the ancient kingdoms of Colchis and Iberia, was Christianized in the 4th cent. and conquered by Arabs in the 8th cent. Annexed by Russia in 1801, Georgia was forcibly incorporated into the USSR in 1922.

Georgia declared independence Apr. 9, 1991, and became an independent country when the Soviet Union disbanded Dec. 26. After a power struggle, former Soviet Foreign Min. Eduard A. Shevardnadze became president. He survived several coup attempts and won reelection in 1995 and 2000. Parliamentary elections Nov. 2, 2003, denounced as fraudulent by opposition groups and international observers, sparked massive antigovernment protests, causing Shevardnadze to resign Nov. 23. Opposition leader Mikhail Saakashvili won the 2004 presidential election. He survived an apparent assassination attempt along with U.S. Pres. George W. Bush in Tbilisi May 10, 2005; suppressed an alleged coup plot Sept. 6, 2006; and cracked down violently on antigovernment protests and imposed a state of emergency, Nov. 7-16, 2007. He called early elections, Jan. 2008, which he won. Giorgi Margvelashvili of the recently formed Georgian Dream coalition, which won 2012 parliamentary elections, was elected president Oct. 27, 2013. Irakli Garibashvili of Georgian Dream became prime min., Nov. 20, 2013, a post with greatly increased powers under constitutional revisions. Former Prime Min. Ivane Merabishvili was convicted of corruption Feb. 17, 2014. Saakashvili (then living in the U.S.) was charged, July 28, 2014, with abuse of power in connection the suppression of the Nov. 2007 protests.

Since its independence, secessionist movements in the enclaves of South Ossetia and Abkhazia, supported by Russia, have rejected the Tbilisi government. Open warfare between Georgia and Russia erupted when Saakashvili sent troops Aug. 7, 2008, to suppress insurgent activity in Tskhinvali, the South Ossetian capital. Russia retaliated Aug. 8-9 by dispatching its forces to South Ossetia and Abkhazia and attacking key Georgian cities. A cease-fire signed Aug. 15-16 called for withdrawal of Russian forces from Georgia proper, but allowed thousands of Russian troops to remain in the breakaway regions. On Aug. 26, 2008, Russia formally recognized Ossetia's independence, a step protested by the U.S. and Georgia's other Western allies. Abkahzia's pro-Russian Pres. Sergei Bagapsh died May 2011; his vice pres., Aleksandr Ankvab, was elected to succeed him in Aug. Citing voting irregularities, the supreme court invalidated the results of the South Ossetian Nov. 2011 presidential election. Pro-Russian candidate Leonid Tibilov won a runoff election in Apr. 2012.

Germany
Federal Republic of Germany

People: Population: 80,996,685. Age distrib.: <15: 13%; 65+: 21.1%. Pop. density: 601.7 per sq mi, 232.3 per sq km. Urban: 75.1%. Ethnic groups: German 92%, Turkish 2%, other (incl. Greek, Italian, Polish, Russian, Serbo-Croatian, Spanish) 6%. Language: German. Religions: Protestant 34%, Roman Catholic 34%, Muslim 4%, unaffiliated or other 28%.

Geography: Total area: 137,847 sq mi, 357,022 sq km; Land area: 134,623 sq mi, 348,672 sq km. Location: In central Europe. Neighbors: Denmark on N; Netherlands, Belgium, Luxembourg, France on W; Switzerland, Austria on S; Czech Rep., Poland on E. Topography: Flat in N, hilly in center and W, and mountainous in

Bavaria in the S. Chief rivers are Elbe, Weser, Ems, Rhine, and Main, all flowing toward North Sea, and Danube, flowing toward Black Sea. **Capital:** Berlin, 3,547,290. **Cities (urban aggl.):** Hamburg, 1,822,342; Munich, 1,421,481; Cologne, 1,031,574.

Government: Type: Federal republic. **Head of state:** Pres. Joachim Gauck; b. Jan. 24, 1940; in office: Mar. 23, 2012. **Head of gov.:** Chancellor Angela Merkel; b. July 17, 1954; in office: Nov. 22, 2005. **Local divisions:** 16 states. **Defense budget:** $44.2 bil. **Active troops:** 186,450.

Economy: Industries: among the world's largest and most technologically advanced producers of iron, steel, coal, cement, chemicals, machinery, vehicles, machine tools, electronics, food and beverages, shipbuilding, textiles. **Chief crops:** potatoes, wheat, barley, sugar beets, fruit, cabbages. **Natural resources:** coal, lignite, nat. gas, iron ore, copper, nickel, uranium, potash, salt, constr. materials, timber. **Crude oil reserves:** 232.6 mil bbls. **Arable land:** 34%. **Livestock:** cattle: 12.6 mil; chickens: 122 mil; goats: 165,000; pigs: 27.7 mil; sheep: 1.6 mil. **Electricity prod.** (2012): 575.9 bil kWh. **Labor force:** agric. 1.6%, industry 24.6%, services 73.8%. **Unemployment:** 5.4%.

Finance: Monetary unit: Euro (EUR) (Sept. 2014: 0.76 = $1 U.S.). **GDP:** $3.2 tril; **per capita GDP:** $39,500; **GDP growth:** 0.5%. **Imports:** $1.2 tril; Netherlands 12.9%, France 7.6%, China 6.3%, Belgium 6.1%, Italy 5.3%, UK 4.6%, Austria 4.3%, U.S. 4.2%, Switzerland 4.3%, Austria 4.1%, Poland 4%. **Exports:** $1.5 tril; France 9.2%, U.S. 7.9%, UK 6.5%, Netherlands 6.3%, China 5.9%, Italy 5.1%, Austria 5%, Switzerland 4.3%, Belgium 4%. **Tourism:** $41.2 bil. **Budget:** $1.6 tril. **Total reserves less gold:** $67.4 bil. **Gold:** 108.9 mil oz t. **Inflation:** 1.5%.

Transport: Railways: 26,086 mi. **Motor vehicles:** 579.4 per 1,000 pop. **Civil aviation:** 136.7 bil pass.-mi; 318 airports. **Chief ports:** Bremen, Bremerhaven, Duisburg, Hamburg, Karlsruhe, Lubeck, Neuss-Dusseldorf, Rostock, Wilhemshaven.

Communications: TV sets: 675 per 1,000 pop. **Radios:** 558 per 1,000 pop. **Telephone lines:** 58.9 per 100 pop. **Mobile:** 119 per 100 pop. **Internet:** 84%.

Health: Life expect.: 78.2 male; 82.9 female. **Births:** 8.4 per 1,000 pop. **Deaths:** 11.3 per 1,000 pop. **Natural inc.:** −0.29%. **Infant mortality:** 3.5 per 1,000 live births. **HIV:** NA.

Education: Compulsory: ages 6-18. **Literacy:** 99%.

Embassy: 4645 Reservoir Rd. NW 20007; 298-4000.

Website: www.deutschland.de

Julius Caesar defeated Germanic tribes, 55 and 53 BCE, but Roman expansion north of the Rhine was stopped in 9 CE. Charlemagne, ruler of the Franks, consolidated Saxon, Bavarian, Rhenish, Frankish, and other lands; after him the eastern part became the German Empire. The Thirty Years' War, 1618-48, split Germany into small principalities and kingdoms.

Otto von Bismarck, Prussian chancellor, formed the North German Confederation, 1867. In 1870 Bismarck maneuvered Napoleon III into declaring war. After the quick defeat of France, Bismarck formed the **German Empire** and on Jan. 18, 1871, in Versailles, proclaimed King Wilhelm I of Prussia German emperor (Deutscher kaiser).

The German Empire reached its peak before WWI in 1914, with 208,780 sq mi, plus overseas colonies. After losing the war in 1918, Germany ceded Alsace-Lorraine to France, West Prussia and Posen (Poznan) province to Poland, and part of Schleswig to Denmark. It lost all colonies and the ports of Memel and Danzig.

Republic of Germany, 1919-33, adopted the Weimar constitution; met reparation payments and elected Friedrich Ebert and Gen. Paul von Hindenburg presidents.

Third Reich, 1933-45: Adolf Hitler led the National Socialist German Workers' (Nazi) party after WWI. Pres. von Hindenburg named Hitler chancellor in 1933; on Aug. 3, 1934, the day after Hindenburg's death, the cabinet joined the offices of president and chancellor and made Hitler *fuehrer* (leader). Hitler abolished freedom of speech and assembly, and began a long series of persecutions climaxed by the murder of millions of Jews and others.

He repudiated the Versailles treaty and reparations agreements, remilitarized the Rhineland (1936), and annexed Austria (Anschluss, 1938). At Munich he made an agreement with British Prime Min. Neville Chamberlain, which permitted Germany to annex part of Czechoslovakia. He signed a nonaggression treaty with the USSR, 1939, and declared war on Poland Sept. 1, 1939, precipitating WWII. With total defeat near, Hitler committed suicide in Berlin Apr. 1945. The victorious Allies voided all acts and annexations of Hitler's Reich.

Germany was sectioned into 4 zones of occupation, administered by the Allied Powers (U.S., USSR, UK, and France). The USSR took control of many E German states. The territory E of the so-called Oder-Neisse line was assigned to, and later annexed by, Poland. The USSR annexed Northern East Prussia (now Kaliningrad). Greater Berlin, within but not part of the Soviet zone, was administered by the 4 occupying powers under the Allied Command. In 1948 the USSR withdrew, established its single command in East Berlin, and cut off supplies. The Western Allies utilized a gigantic airlift to bring food to West Berlin, 1948-49.

In 1949, 2 separate German states were established. In May the zones administered by the Western Allies became West Germany; in Oct. the Soviet sector became East Germany. West Berlin was considered a West German enclave, a status the Soviet bloc disputed.

East Germany. The German Democratic Republic (East Germany) was proclaimed in the Soviet sector of Berlin Oct. 7, 1949. It was declared fully sovereign in 1954, but Soviet troops remained.

Coincident with the entrance of West Germany into the European defense community in 1952, the East German government decreed a prohibited zone 3 mi deep along its 600-mi border with West Germany and cut Berlin's telephone system in 2. Berlin was further divided by erection of a fortified wall in 1961, after over 3 mil East Germans had fled to the West. The oppressive Communist regime maintained control through the state security police, known as the Stasi.

By the early 1970s, the economy of East Germany was highly industrialized, and the nation was credited with the highest standard of living among Warsaw Pact countries. Growth slowed in the late 1970s because of shortages of natural resources and labor and huge debt. Comparison with the lifestyle in the West caused many young people to emigrate.

In the late 1980s the government firmly resisted following the USSR's policy of openness (*glasnost*) but was faced with nationwide demonstrations demanding reform. Pres. Erich Honecker, in office since 1976, was forced to resign Oct. 18, 1989. On Nov. 9, the East German government announced its decision to open the border with the West, signaling the end of the Berlin Wall. On Aug. 23, 1990, the East German parliament agreed to reunite with West Germany; this occurred Oct. 3.

West Germany. The Federal Republic of Germany (West Germany) was proclaimed May 23, 1949, in Bonn. The occupying powers, the U.S., Britain, and France, restored civil status, Sept. 21. The Western Allies ended the state of war with Germany in 1951, while the USSR did so in 1955. The powers lifted controls, and the republic became fully independent May 5, 1955.

Dr. Konrad Adenauer, a Christian Democrat, was made chancellor 1949 and was reelected 1953, 1957, 1961. Willy Brandt, heading a coalition of Social Democrats and Free Democrats, became chancellor 1969 and pursued a policy of *Ostpolitik*, or rapprochement with East Germany and the USSR. Brandt resigned May 1974 after a spy scandal. Terrorist acts on German soil in the 1970s included activities of the Baader-Meinhof gang and the murder of Israeli athletes by Palestinian commandos at the Olympic Games in Munich, Sept. 5, 1972.

Helmut Kohl became chancellor in 1982 and led Christian Democrats to victory in 1983 and 1987. In 1990, under Kohl's leadership, West Germany moved rapidly to reunite with East Germany.

Unified Germany. In May 1990, NATO ministers voted to make the united Germany a full member of NATO and barred the new Germany from having its own nuclear, chemical, or biological weapons. The merger of the two Germanys took place Oct. 3, and the first all-German elections since 1932 were held Dec. 2, with West German Chancellor Helmut Kohl confirmed as leader of the unified nation. Eastern Germany received over $1 tril in public and private funds from western Germany between 1990 and 1995. In 1991, Berlin again became Germany's official capital; the Bundestag (parliament) and parts of the federal executive were relocated from Bonn to Berlin in 1999.

Unemployment hit a postwar high of 12.6% in Jan. 1998. The 16-year Kohl era ended with the defeat of the Christian Democrats in parliamentary elections Sept. 27; Gerhard Schröder, of the Social Democratic Party (SPD), became chancellor. The Christian Democrats, led by Angela Merkel, won a razor-thin plurality in 2005 parliamentary elections and she became chancellor Nov. 22, heading a "grand coalition" that included the SPD.

Responding to the global recession, the government passed a 50 bil euro economic stimulus plan in early 2009. Merkel led a center-right coalition to victory in 2009 national elections. After an earthquake and tsunami in Japan caused a nuclear disaster, the Merkel government announced May 2011 that it would close Germany's 17 nuclear power plants by 2022. Merkel and then-French Pres. Nicolas Sarkozy led the international response to the European debt crisis involving Greece in late 2009, followed by Ireland, Portugal, Italy, and Spain; debtor nations were required to adopt stern austerity measures in return for aid. But new recessions in several austerity-bound countries cast doubt on Germany's strategy in resolving the eurozone crisis. Merkel's party performed badly in state parliamentary elections in 2012 and early 2013.

A report released Jan 19, 2013, contained information from more than 1,100 people describing themselves as victims of child sexual abuse perpetrated by German Catholic priests over the course of several years. The Constitutional Court in Karlsruhe, the nation's highest court, affirmed Feb. 19, 2013, gay couples' right to adopt children.

Merkel's Christian Democrats won a clear-cut victory in Sept. 22, 2013, parliamentary elections but fell short of a majority. She formed a new coalition, including the SPD, in Dec. Relations with the U.S. were strained in 2013 and 2014 following revelations of U.S. monitoring of German cell phones and CIA recruiting of German intelligence officials. Germany won the 2014 FIFA men's soccer World Cup, with a 1-0 victory over Argentina in extra time in the final, July 13.

Helgoland, an island of 0.66 sq mi in the North Sea, was taken from Denmark by a British Naval Force in 1807 and later ceded to Germany to become part of Schleswig-Holstein province in return for rights in East Africa. The heavily fortified island was surrendered to UK, May 23, 1945, demilitarized in 1947, and returned to West Germany, Mar. 1, 1952. It is a free port.

Ghana
Republic of Ghana

People: Population: 25,758,108. **Age distrib.:** <15: 38.6%; 65+: 4.1%. **Pop. density:** 293.2 per sq mi, 113.2 per sq km. **Urban:** 53.4%. **Ethnic groups:** Akan 48%, Mole-Dagbon 17%, Ewe 14%, Ga-Dangme 7%, Gurma 6%, Guan 4%, Grusi 3%. **Languages:** Asante, Ewe, Fante, Boron, Dagomba, Dangme, Dagarte, Akyem, Ga, Akuapem, English (official). **Religions:** Christian 71% (incl. Pentecostal/Charismatic 28%, Protestant 18%, Catholic 13%), Muslim 18%, traditional 5%, none 5%.

Geography: Total area: 92,098 sq mi, 238,533 sq km; **Land area:** 87,851 sq mi, 227,533 sq km. **Location:** On S coast of W Africa. **Neighbors:** Côte d'Ivoire on W, Burkina Faso on N, Togo on E. **Topography:** Mostly low fertile plains and scrubland, cut by rivers and by the artificial Lake Volta. **Capital:** Accra, 2,241,690. **Cities (urban aggl.):** Kumasi, 2,481,656.

Government: Type: Constitutional democracy. **Head of state and gov.:** Pres. John Dramani Mahama; b. Nov. 29, 1958; in office: July 24, 2012. **Local divisions:** 10 regions. **Defense budget:** $291 mil. **Active troops:** 15,500.

Economy: Industries: mining, lumbering, light mfg., aluminum smelting, food proc., cement, small comm. shipbuilding. **Chief crops:** cocoa, rice, cassava, peanuts, corn, shea nuts, bananas. **Natural resources:** gold, timber, industrial diamonds, bauxite, manganese, fish, rubber, hydropower, petroleum, silver, salt, limestone. **Crude oil reserves:** 660 mil bbls. **Arable land:** 20.7%. **Livestock:** cattle: 1.6 mil; chickens: 60 mil; goats: 5.5 mil; pigs: 620,000; sheep: 4 mil. **Electricity prod.:** 10.9 bil kWh. **Labor force:** agric. 56%, industry 15%, services 29%. **Unemployment:** 3.6%.

Finance: Monetary unit: Cedi (GHS) (Sept. 2014: 3.75 = $1 U.S.). **GDP:** $90.4 bil; **per capita GDP:** $3,500; **GDP growth:** 7.9%. **Imports:** $18.5 bil; China 25.6%, Nigeria 11%, U.S. 7%, Netherlands 6.2%, Singapore 4.5%, UK 4.1%, India 4%. **Exports:** $13.4 bil; France 13.6%, Italy 12.4%, Netherlands 8.9%, China 7.4%, Germany 4.3%. **Tourism:** $914 mil. **Budget:** $14.9 bil. **Total reserves less gold:** $5.2 bil. **Gold:** 281,000 oz t. **Inflation:** 11.6%.

Transport: Railways: 588 mi. **Motor vehicles:** 7.7 per 1,000 pop. **Civil aviation:** 7 airports. **Chief ports:** Takoradi, Tema.

Communications: TV sets: 52 per 1,000 pop. **Radios:** 133 per 1,000 pop. **Telephone lines:** 1 per 100 pop. **Mobile:** 108.2 per 100 pop. **Internet:** 12.3%.

Health: Life expect.: 63.4 male; 68.2 female. **Births:** 31.4 per 1,000 pop. **Deaths:** 7.4 per 1,000 pop. **Natural inc.:** 2.40%. **Infant mortality:** 38.5 per 1,000 live births. **HIV:** 1.3%.

Education: Compulsory: ages 4-14. **Literacy:** 76.6%.
Embassy: 3512 International Dr. NW 20008; 686-4520.
Website: www.ghana.gov.gh

Named for an African empire along the Niger R., 400-1240 CE, Ghana was ruled by Britain for 113 years as the Gold Coast. The UN in 1956 approved merger with the British Togoland trust territory. Independence came Mar. 6, 1957, and republic status within the Commonwealth in 1960.

Pres. Kwame Nkrumah built hospitals and schools and promoted development projects, including the Volta R. hydroelectric and aluminum plants, but ran the country into debt, jailed opponents, and was accused of corruption. A 1964 referendum gave Nkrumah dictatorial powers and set up a one-party socialist state. A police-army coup overthrew Nkrumah in 1966. Elections were held in 1969, but 4 further coups occurred in 1972, 1978, 1979, and 1981. The 1979 and 1981 coups, led by Flight Lieut. Jerry Rawlings, were followed by suspension of the constitution and banning of political parties. A new constitution, allowing multiparty politics, was approved in Apr. 1992.

In Feb. 1993 more than 1,000 people were killed in ethnic clashes in northern Ghana. Rawlings won the 1996 presidential election. Kofi Annan, a career UN diplomat from Ghana, served as UN sec.-gen., 1997-2006.

Opposition leader John Agyekum Kufuor won a 2000 runoff vote and was sworn in Jan. 7, 2001, marking Ghana's first peaceful transfer of power from one elected president to another. He was reelected in 2004. John Atta Mills, a tax law expert who lost presidential elections in 2000 and 2004, defeated the ruling party candidate, Nana Akufo-Addo, in a 2008 runoff election. A major offshore oil and gas find was announced June 2007; the Jubilee field, estimated to hold recoverable reserves of 1.5 bil barrels, began production Dec. 2010. When Mills died in 2012, Vice Pres. John Dramani Mahama replaced him. Mahama won a full term in Dec. 2012 elections.

Greece
Hellenic Republic

People: Population: 10,775,557. **Age distrib.:** <15: 14.1%; 65+: 20.2%. **Pop. density:** 213.6 per sq mi, 82.5 per sq km. **Urban:**

77.7%. **Ethnic groups:** Greek (citizens) 93%, other (foreign citizens) 7%. **Language:** Greek (official). **Religions:** Greek Orthodox (official) 98%, Muslim 1%.

Geography: Total area: 50,949 sq mi, 131,957 sq km; **Land area:** 50,443 sq mi, 130,647 sq km. **Location:** Occupies S end of Balkan Peninsula in SE Europe. **Neighbors:** Albania, Macedonia, Bulgaria on N; Turkey on E. **Topography:** About three-quarters is non-arable, with mountains in all areas. Pindus Mts. run through the country N-S. The heavily indented coastline is 9,385 mi long. More than 2,000 islands, only 169 inhabited, among them Crete, Rhodes, Milos, Kerkira (Corfu), Chios, Lesbos, Samos, Euboea, Delos, Mykonos. **Capital:** Athens, 3,059,910. **Cities (urban aggl.):** Thessaloniki, 740,482.

Government: Type: Parliamentary republic. **Head of state:** Pres. Karolos Papoulias; b. June 4, 1929; in office: Mar. 12, 2005. **Head of gov.:** Prime Min. Antonis Samaras; b. May 23, 1951; in office: June 20, 2012. **Local divisions:** 13 regions, 1 autonomous monastic state. **Defense budget:** $5.68 bil. **Active troops:** 143,350.

Economy: Industries: tourism, food and tobacco proc., textiles, chemicals, metal prods., mining, petroleum. **Chief crops:** wheat, corn, barley, sugar beets, olives, tomatoes, wine, tobacco, potatoes. **Natural resources:** lignite, petroleum, iron ore, bauxite, lead, zinc, nickel, magnesite, marble, salt, hydropower potential. **Crude oil reserves:** 10 mil bbls. **Arable land:** 19.7%. **Livestock:** cattle: 679,000; chickens: 34 mil; goats: 4.3 mil; pigs: 1.1 mil; sheep: 9.5 mil. **Electricity prod.** (2012): 55 bil kWh. **Labor force:** agric. 12.4%, industry 22.4%, services 65.1%. **Unemployment:** 24.2%.

Finance: Monetary unit: Euro (EUR) (Sept. 2014: 0.76 = $1 U.S.). **GDP:** $267.1 bil; **per capita GDP:** $23,600; **GDP growth:** –3.8%. **Imports:** $50.6 bil; Russia 13.8%, Germany 9.5%, Italy 7.9%, Iraq 7.8%, Netherlands 4.7%, France 4.5%, China 4.5%. **Exports:** $30.4 bil; Turkey 11.6%, Italy 9.9%, Germany 6.5%, Bulgaria 4.9%. **Tourism:** $15.9 bil. **Budget:** $116 bil. **Total reserves less gold:** $1.4 bil. **Gold:** 3.6 mil oz t. **Inflation:** –0.9%.

Transport: Railways: 1,583 mi. **Motor vehicles:** 600.3 per 1,000 pop. **Civil aviation:** 4.5 bil pass.-mi; 68 airports. **Chief ports:** Agioi Theodoroi, Aspropyrgos, Pachi, Piraeus, Thessaloníki.

Communications: TV sets: 556 per 1,000 pop. **Radios:** 464 per 1,000 pop. **Telephone lines:** 47.9 per 100 pop. **Mobile:** 116.8 per 100 pop. **Internet:** 59.9%.

Health: Life expect.: 77.7 male; 83.1 female. **Births:** 8.8 per 1,000 pop. **Deaths:** 11.0 per 1,000 pop. **Natural inc.:** –0.22%. **Infant mortality:** 4.8 per 1,000 live births. **HIV:** NA.

Education: Compulsory: ages 5-14. **Literacy:** 97.7%.
Embassy: 2217 Massachusetts Ave. NW 20008; 939-1306.
Website: www.primeminister.gov.gr

The achievements of ancient Greece in art, architecture, science, mathematics, philosophy, drama, literature, and democracy became legacies for succeeding ages. Greece reached the height of its power, particularly in the Athenian city-state, in the 5th cent. BCE. Greece fell under Roman rule in the 2nd and 1st cents. BCE. In the 4th cent. CE, it became part of the Byzantine Empire and, after the fall of Constantinople to the Turks in 1453, part of the Ottoman Empire.

Greece won its war of independence from Turkey, 1821-29, and became a kingdom. A republic was established 1924; the monarchy was restored, 1935. In Oct. 1940, Greece rejected an ultimatum from Italy, but the country was defeated and occupied by Germans, Italians, and Bulgarians. The end of 1944 the invaders withdrew. Communist resistance forces were overcome by Royalist and British troops. A plebiscite restored the monarchy.

Communists waged guerrilla war 1947-49 against the government but were defeated with the aid of the U.S. A period of reconstruction and rapid development followed, mainly with conservative governments under Prem. Constantine Karamanlis. The Center Union, led by George Papandreou, won elections in 1963 and 1964, but King Constantine forced Papandreou to resign. A period of political maneuvers ended with Col. George Papadopoulos's military takeover Apr. 1967. King Constantine tried to reverse the consolidation of the harsh dictatorship Dec. 1967, but failed and fled to Italy. Papadopoulos was ousted Nov. 1973.

Greek army officers serving in the Cyprus National Guard staged a coup on the island July 15, 1974. Turkey invaded Cyprus a week later, precipitating the collapse of the Greek junta. Democratic government returned, and in 1975 the monarchy was abolished.

The 1981 electoral victory of the Panhellenic Socialist Movement (Pasok) of Andreas Papandreou substantially changed Greece's internal and external policies. A scandal centered on George Kostokas, a banker and publisher, led to the arrest or investigation of leading Socialists, implicated Papandreou, and contributed to the 1989 defeat of the Socialists at the polls. Papandreou, who was acquitted Jan. 1992 of corruption charges, led the Socialists to a comeback victory in 1993 general elections. Costas Simitis replaced the ailing Papandreou as prime minister, Jan. 1996, and led the Socialists to victory in the Sept. 22 election.

An earthquake shook Athens Sept. 7, 1999, killing at least 143 people and leaving more than 60,000 homeless. The Socialists retained power by a narrow margin in the 2000 elections. Police in 2002 cracked down on the November 17 terrorist movement, blamed for 23 killings since the mid-1970s.

The conservative New Democracy Party won the 2004 parliamentary elections, and Konstantinos (Costas) Karamanlis became prime min. Beset by scandals and an ailing economy, Karamanlis called early elections for Oct. 4, 2009, won by Pasok under the leadership of the U.S.-born George A. Papandreou, whose father and grandfather had headed previous Greek governments. The IMF and the 16 eurozone countries agreed in 2010, on a 110 bil euro ($146 bil) loan package to prevent Greece from defaulting; in return, Greek leaders implemented an austerity plan. With default again impending, eurozone leaders agreed July 2011 on another Greek bailout package, for 109 bil euros ($157 bil). The conservative, pro-bailout Antonis Samaras became prime min. of a coalition government, June 2012. The government agreed on a plan for 13.5 bil euro ($23 bil) in budget cuts and austerity measures Sept. 27, touching off a series of often violent protests and nationwide general strikes Oct-Nov. 2012. The measure narrowly survived a vote by the coalition government Nov. 8. The Intl. Monetary Fund, European Central Bank, and eurozone members also agreed to a 43.7 bil euro ($56.7 bil) bailout package Nov. 26. Recession and austerity measures, 2007-13, caused Greece's GDP to shrink by 26%. In 2013, more than 25% of Greek workers were unemployed. In Apr. 2014, Greece was able to sell bonds in international markets for the first time in 4 years.

Grenada

People: Population: 110,152. **Age distrib.:** <15: 24.5%; 65+: 9.4%. **Pop. density:** 829.3 per sq mi, 320.2 per sq km. **Urban:** 35.6%. **Ethnic groups:** black 82%, mixed black and European 13%, European and East Indian 5%. **Languages:** English (official), French patois. **Religions:** Roman Catholic 53%, Anglican 14%, other Protestant 33%.

Geography: Total area: 133 sq mi, 344 sq km; **Land area:** 133 sq mi, 344 sq km. **Location:** In Caribbean, 90 mi N of Venezuela. **Neighbors:** Venezuela, Trinidad and Tobago to S; St. Vincent and the Grenadines to N. **Topography:** Main island is mountainous; country includes Carriacou and Petit Martinique isls. **Capital:** St. George's, 37,822.

Government: Type: Parliamentary democracy. **Head of state:** Queen Elizabeth II, rep. by Gov.-Gen. Cecile La Grenade; b. Dec. 30, 1952; in office: May 7, 2013. **Head of gov.:** Prime Min. Keith Mitchell; b. Nov. 12, 1946; in office: Feb. 20, 2013. **Local divisions:** 6 parishes, 1 dependency. **Defense budget/active troops:** NA.

Economy: Industries: food and beverages, textiles, light assembly operations, tourism, constr. **Chief crops:** bananas, cocoa, nutmeg, mace, citrus, avocados, root crops, sugarcane, corn, vegetables. **Natural resources:** timber, tropical fruit. **Arable land:** 8.8%. **Livestock:** cattle: 4,500; chickens: 270,000; goats: 7,200; pigs: 3,000; sheep: 13,200. **Electricity prod.:** 196 mil kWh. **Labor force:** agric. 11%, industry 20%, services 69%. **Unemployment:** NA.

Finance: Monetary unit: East Caribbean Dollar (XCD) (Sept. 2014: 2.70 = $1 U.S.). **GDP:** $1.5 bil; **per capita GDP:** $13,800; **GDP growth:** 0.8%. **Imports** (2012): $297 mil; Trinidad and Tobago 44.3%, U.S. 16.4%, China 4.6% **Exports** (2012): $40.5 mil; Nigeria 40.2%, St. Lucia 10.7%, Antigua and Barbuda 7.3%, U.S. 6.6%, St. Kitts and Nevis 6.5%, Dominica 6.5%, Switzerland 4.3%. **Tourism:** $120 mil. **Budget** (2012 est.): $196.3 mil. **Total reserves less gold:** $150.6 mil. **Inflation:** 0%.

Transport: Civil aviation: 3 airports. **Chief port:** Saint George's.

Communications: TV sets: 383 per 1,000 pop. **Radios:** 567 per 1,000 pop. **Telephone lines** 27 per 100 pop. **Mobile:** 125.6 per 100 pop. **Internet:** 35%.

Health: Life expect.: 71.2 male; 76.6 female. **Births:** 16.3 per 1,000 pop. **Deaths:** 8.0 per 1,000 pop. **Natural inc.:** 0.83%. **Infant mortality:** 10.5 per 1,000 live births. **HIV:** NA.

Education: Compulsory: ages 5-16. **Literacy:** NA.

Embassy: 1701 New Hampshire Ave. NW 20009; 265-2561.

Website: www.gov.gd

Columbus sighted Grenada in 1498. The first European settlers were French, 1650. The island was held alternately by France and England until final British occupation, 1784. Grenada became fully independent Feb. 7, 1974, during a general strike.

On Oct. 14, 1983, a military coup ousted Prime Min. Maurice Bishop, who was put under house arrest, later freed by supporters, rearrested, and executed Oct. 19. U.S. forces, with a task force from 6 area nations, invaded Grenada, Oct. 25. Resistance from the Grenadian army and Cuban advisors was quickly overcome, and U.S. troops left Grenada in June 1985.

Hurricane Ivan slammed into Grenada, Sept. 7, 2004, killing 39 people and damaging an estimated 90% of the buildings on the island. Tillman Thomas of the National Democratic Congress became prime min. after 2008 parliamentary elections. Thomas survived one no-confidence vote May 15, 2012, and avoided another before dissolving parliament Jan. 9, 2013, and calling for new elections. The opposition New National Party won all 15 seats available in general elections Feb. 19, 2013, and Keith Mitchell was sworn in as prime min. the next day.

Guatemala
Republic of Guatemala

People: Population: 14,647,083. **Age distrib.:** <15: 36.2%; 65+: 4.2%. **Pop. density:** 354 per sq mi, 136.7 per sq km. **Urban:**

51.1%. **Ethnic groups:** mestizo (mixed Amerindian-Spanish) and European 59%, K'iche 9%, Kaqchikel 8%, Mam 8%, Q'eqchi 6%, other Mayan 9%. **Languages:** Spanish (official), Amerindian langs. (23 officially recognized). **Religions:** Roman Catholic, Protestant, indigenous Mayan beliefs.

Geography: Total area: 42,042 sq mi, 108,889 sq km; **Land area:** 41,374 sq mi, 107,159 sq km. **Location:** In Central America. **Neighbors:** Mexico on N and W, El Salvador on S, Honduras and Belize on E. **Topography:** The central highland and mountain areas are bordered by the narrow Pacific coast and lowlands and fertile river valleys on the Caribbean. Numerous volcanoes in S, more than half a dozen over 11,000 ft. **Capital:** Guatemala City, 2,846,890.

Government: Type: Constitutional democratic republic. **Head of state and gov.:** Pres. Otto Fernando Perez Molina; b. Dec. 1, 1950; in office: Jan. 14, 2012. **Local divisions:** 22 departments. **Defense budget:** $256 mil. **Active troops:** 17,300.

Economy: Industries: textiles and clothing, furniture, chemicals, petroleum, metals, rubber, tourism. **Chief crops:** sugarcane, corn, bananas, coffee, beans, cardamom. **Natural resources:** petroleum, nickel, rare woods, fish, chicle, hydropower. **Crude oil reserves:** 83.1 mil bbls. **Arable land:** 14.3%. **Livestock:** cattle: 3.4 mil; chickens: 36 mil; goats: 134,000; pigs: 2.8 mil; sheep: 616,000. **Electricity prod.:** 8.4 bil kWh. **Labor force:** agric. 38%, industry 14%, services 48%. **Unemployment:** 4.2%.

Finance: Monetary unit: Quetzal (GTQ) (Sept. 2014: 7.75 = $1 U.S.). **GDP:** $81.5 bil; **per capita GDP:** $5,300; **GDP growth:** 3.3%. **Imports:** $16.7 bil; U.S. 38%, Mexico 11.3%, China 7.4%, El Salvador 4.6%. **Exports:** $10.3 bil; U.S. 40.2%, El Salvador 11.1%, Honduras 8%, Mexico 5.5%, Nicaragua 4.7%, Costa Rica 4.3%. **Tourism:** $1.5 bil. **Budget:** $7.9 bil. **Total reserves less gold:** $7 bil. **Gold:** 221,600 oz t. **Inflation:** 4.3%.

Transport: Railways: 206 mi. **Motor vehicles:** 117.5 per 1,000 pop. **Civil aviation:** 16 airports. **Chief ports:** Puerto Quetzal, Santo Tomas de Castilla.

Communications: TV sets: 163 per 1,000 pop. **Radios:** 80 per 1,000 pop. **Telephone lines:** 12 per 100 pop. **Mobile:** 140.4 per 100 pop. **Internet:** 19.7%.

Health: Life expect.: 69.8 male; 73.8 female. **Births:** 25.5 per 1,000 pop. **Deaths:** 4.8 per 1,000 pop. **Natural inc.:** 2.06%. **Infant mortality:** 23.5 per 1,000 live births. **HIV:** 0.6%.

Education: Compulsory: ages 6-15. **Literacy:** 81.6%.

Embassy: 2220 R St. NW 20008; 745-4952.

Website: www.guatemala.gob.gt

A Mayan Indian empire flourished in what is today Guatemala for over 1,000 years before Spaniards came. Guatemala was a Spanish colony 1524-1821. A republic was established in 1839.

The U.S. intervened in Guatemala in 1954 when the Central Intelligence Agency engineered the overthrow of elected Pres. Jacobo Arbenz Guzmán, a left-wing reformer. Since then, the country has experienced a variety of military and civilian governments and periods of insurgency, repression, paramilitary violence, and civil war. After military coups in 1982 and 1983, the nation returned to civilian rule in 1986.

On Sept. 19, 1996, the Guatemalan government and leftist rebels approved a peace accord; the final agreement was signed Dec. 29. During more than 35 years of armed conflict, some 200,000 people were killed or "disappeared" (and are presumed dead); most of these casualties were attributed to the government and its paramilitary allies. U.S. Pres. Bill Clinton, on a Mar. 1999 visit to Guatemala, apologized for aid the U.S. had given to forces which he said "engaged in violence and widespread repression."

Drought and weak export prices during 2001-02 worsened the plight of Guatemala's poor, who make up a majority of the population. After a campaign marred by violence, Álvaro Colom Caballeros, a businessman who pledged to fight poverty, took office Jan. 2008. Former Gen. Otto Pérez Molina won a runoff election Nov. 6, 2011, and took office, Jan. 2012. Gen. Efraín Ríos Montt, dictator for 17 months, 1982-83, was found guilty of genocide and sentenced to 80 years in prison May 10, 2013, but the Constitutional Court overturned his conviction May 20 and ruled that part of his trial had to be repeated. Former Pres. Alfonso Portillo was extradited to the U.S. May 24, 2013, to be tried for money laundering; he pleaded guilty and was sentenced May 22, 2014, to nearly 6 years in prison. Drug trafficking, arms smuggling, police corruption, and one of the world's highest homicide rates pose threats to national stability. Apparently seeking safety from drug- and other violence, Guatemalans made up a sizable portion of the tens of thousands of undocumented immigrant children—some with their mothers, many traveling unaccompanied—seized at the U.S.-Mexico border trying to enter the U.S. in late 2013 and 2014.

Guinea
Republic of Guinea

People: Population: 11,474,383. **Age distrib.:** <15: 42%; 65+: 3.6%. **Pop. density:** 120.9 per sq mi, 46.7 per sq km. **Urban:** 36.7%. **Ethnic groups:** Peuhl 40%, Malinke 30%, Soussou 20%, smaller ethnic groups 10%. **Languages:** French (official), ethnic group-specific langs. **Religions:** Muslim 85%, Christian 8%, indigenous beliefs 7%.

Geography: Total area: 94,926 sq mi, 245,857 sq km; **Land area:** 94,872 sq mi, 245,717 sq km. **Location:** On Atlantic coast of W Africa. **Neighbors:** Guinea-Bissau, Senegal, Mali on N; Côte d'Ivoire on E; Liberia, Sierra Leone on S. **Topography:** A narrow coastal belt leads to mountainous middle region, source of the Gambia, Senegal, and Niger rivers. Upper Guinea, farther inland, is cooler upland. The SE is forested. **Capital:** Conakry, 1,885,990.

Government: Type: Republic. **Head of state:** Pres. Alpha Condé; b. Mar. 4, 1938; in office: Dec. 21, 2010. **Head of gov.:** Prime Min. Mohamed Said Fofana; b. 1952; in office: Dec. 24, 2010. **Local divisions:** 7 regions, 1 governate. **Defense budget** (2012): $39 mil. **Active troops:** 9,700.

Economy: Industries: bauxite, gold, diamonds, iron; alumina refining; light mfg.; agric. proc. **Chief crops:** rice, coffee, pineapples, palm kernels, cassava, bananas, sweet potatoes. **Natural resources:** bauxite, iron ore, diamonds, gold, uranium, hydropower, fish, salt. **Arable land:** 12.2%. **Livestock:** cattle: 5 mil; chickens: 15.5 mil; goats: 1.8 mil; pigs: 103,000; sheep: 1.7 mil. **Electricity prod.:** 950 mil kWh. **Labor force:** agric. 76%, industry and services 24%. **Unemployment:** 3.1%.

Finance: Monetary unit: Franc (GNF) (Sept. 2014: 6,780.00 = $1 U.S.). **GDP:** $12.6 bil; **per capita GDP:** $1,100; **GDP growth:** 2.9%. **Imports:** $2.4 bil; China 14.2%, Netherlands 7.6%. **Exports:** $1.3 bil; India 10.6%, Spain 9.6%, Chile 9.4%, U.S. 7.1%, Ireland 6.3%, Germany 6.3%, Ukraine 5.7%, France 5%. **Tourism:** $1 mil. **Budget:** $1.8 bil. **Total reserves less gold** (2011): $103.2 mil. **Gold** (2011): 7,107 oz t. **Inflation:** 11.9%.

Transport: Railways: 736 mi. **Civil aviation:** 4 airports. **Chief ports:** Conakry, Kamsar.

Communications: TV sets: 18 per 1,000 pop. **Radios:** 81 per 1,000 pop. **Telephone lines** (2011): 0.16 per 100 pop. **Mobile:** 63.3 per 100 pop. **Internet:** 1.6%.

Health: Life expect.: 58.1 male; 61.2 female. **Births:** 36.0 per 1,000 pop. **Deaths:** 9.7 per 1,000 pop. **Natural inc.:** 2.63%. **Infant mortality:** 55.2 per 1,000 live births. **HIV:** 1.7%.

Education: Compulsory: ages 7-16. **Literacy:** 30.4%.

Embassy: 2112 Leroy Pl. NW 20008; 906-4300.

Website: www.presidence.gov.gn or www.state.gov/p/af/ci/gv/
Guinea, a French colony, attained independence Oct. 2, 1958. Sékou Touré, Guinea's first president (1958-84), turned to Communist nations for support and set up a one-party state. Thousands of opponents were jailed and tortured, and many were killed in the 1970s after an unsuccessful Portuguese invasion.

The military took control in a bloodless coup after the Mar. 1984 death of Touré. A new constitution was approved in 1991, but movement toward democracy was slow. Gen. Lansana Conté, the incumbent, won a long-awaited presidential election in Dec. 1993, which outside monitors called flawed. Conté suppressed an army mutiny in Conakry, Feb. 2-3, 1996, and won reelection in 1998. Fighting in early 2001 along the border with Liberia and Sierra Leone created a refugee crisis in Guinea; voluntary repatriation of more than 51,000 Liberian refugees was largely completed in 2007.

Major opposition parties boycotted the 2003 presidential election, in which the ailing Conté won 95.6% of the vote. More than 120 died in Jan.-Feb. 2007 strikes and protests that pressured Conté to name a new prime min. from a union-leader approved list; protests followed his ouster by Conté in May 2008. After Conté's death Dec. 22, a military junta took power, calling itself the National Council for Democracy and Development. More than 150 people were reportedly killed Sept. 28, 2009, when Guinean troops fired into a crowd of about 50,000 antigovernment protesters in Conakry. After an assassination attempt Dec. 3, 2009, by a former aide left Pres. Moussa Dadis Camara seriously wounded, Vice Pres. Sékouba Konaté became interim head of state. Presidential elections June-Nov. 2010 brought a civilian government headed by Alpha Condé to power Dec. 21. Postponed legislative elections, held in Sept. 2013, were criticized as flawed. Official results announced Oct. 18 gave a party loyal to Condé a working majority.

The largest known outbreak of Ebola virus disease began in Guinea in Dec. 2013. First identified in Mar. 2014, it spread rapidly to nearby countries. By Sept. 28, 2014, 7,178 cases in 5 African countries, including 1,157 in Guinea, had been reported by WHO; 3,338 victims (710 in Guinea) had died.

Guinea-Bissau
Republic of Guinea-Bissau

People: Population: 1,693,398. **Age distrib.:** <15: 39.8%; 65+: 3.3%. **Pop. density:** 156 per sq mi, 60.2 per sq km. **Urban:** 48.5%. **Ethnic groups:** African 99% (incl. Balanta 30%, Fula 20%, Manjaca 14%, Mandinga 13%, Papel 7%). **Languages:** Portuguese (official), Crioulo, African langs. **Religions:** Muslim 50%, indigenous beliefs 40%, Christian 10%.

Geography: Total area: 13,948 sq mi, 36,125 sq km; **Land area:** 10,857 sq mi, 28,120 sq km. **Location:** On Atlantic coast of W Africa. **Neighbors:** Senegal on N, Guinea on E and S. **Topography:** A swampy coastal plain covers most of country; to E is a low savanna region. **Capital:** Bissau, 473,349.

Government: Type: Republic. **Head of state:** Pres. José Mário Vaz; b. Dec. 10, 1957; in office: June 23, 2014. **Head of gov.:**

Prime Min. Domingos Simoes Pereira; in office: June 26, 2014. **Local divisions:** 9 regions. **Defense budget** (2012): $26 mil. **Active troops:** 4,450.

Economy: Industries: agric. prods. proc., beer, soft drinks. **Chief crops:** rice, corn, beans, cassava, cashew nuts, peanuts, palm kernels, cotton. **Natural resources:** fish, timber, phosphates, bauxite, clay, granite, limestone, unexploited deposits of petroleum. **Arable land:** 10.7%. **Livestock:** cattle: 670,000; chickens: 1.9 mil; goats: 750,000; pigs: 460,000; sheep: 470,000. **Electricity prod.:** 55 mil kWh. **Labor force:** agric. 82%, industry and services 18%. **Unemployment:** 7.5%.

Finance: Monetary unit: CFA Franc (XOF) (Sept. 2014: 498.91 = $1 U.S.). **GDP:** $2 bil; **per capita GDP:** $1,200; **GDP growth:** 3.5%. **Imports:** $206.4 mil; Portugal 28.8%, Senegal 17.5%, U.S. 7.3%, China 5%. **Exports:** $147.6 mil; India 56.5%, Nigeria 27.1%, Togo 5.9%. **Tourism:** $9 mil. **Budget:** $157.7 mil. **Total reserves less gold:** $186.3 mil. **Inflation:** 0.7%.

Transport: Civil aviation: 2 airports. **Chief ports:** Bissau, Buba, Cacheu, Farim.

Communications: TV sets: 39 per 1,000 pop. **Radios:** 41 per 1,000 pop. **Telephone lines** 0.3 per 100 pop. **Mobile:** 74.1 per 100 pop. **Internet:** 3.1%.

Health: Life expect.: 47.9 male; 51.9 female. **Births:** 33.8 per 1,000 pop. **Deaths:** 14.5 per 1,000 pop. **Natural inc.:** 1.93%. **Infant mortality:** 90.9 per 1,000 live births. **HIV:** 3.7%.

Education: Compulsory: ages 6-11. **Literacy:** 59.9%.

Permanent UN Mission: 866 UN Plaza, Ste. 481, New York, NY 10017; (212) 896-8311.

Website: www.state.gov/p/af/ci/pu/
Portuguese mariners explored the area in the mid-15th cent.; the slave trade flourished in the 17th and 18th cents., and colonization began in the 19th. Independence came Sept. 10, 1974, ending 13 years of guerrilla warfare against the Portuguese regime.

A Nov. 1980 coup gave army chief João Bernardo Vieira absolute power. Vieira eventually initiated political liberalization; multiparty elections were held in 1994. A 1998 army uprising triggered a civil war, with Senegal and Guinea aiding the Vieira regime. After a peace accord signed Nov. 2 broke down, rebel troops ousted Vieira on May 7, 1999.

Civilian rule returned with 1999-2000 elections, but top military officers staged a coup Sept. 14, 2003. Vieira won a presidential runoff election, July 24, 2005, and returned to power Oct. 1. A group of soldiers murdered Vieira in his presidential palace Mar. 2, 2009. Political violence continued as the 2009 presidential election approached; the ruling party candidate, Malam Bacai Sanhá, won a runoff vote July 26. He died Jan. 9, 2012. A military coup Apr. 12 derailed a runoff election scheduled for Apr. 29. The military appointed Manuel Serifo Nhamadjo to lead a transitional government. Drug trafficking increased substantially in the country with the support of the military. The U.S. arrested and indicted former navy chief Rear Adm. Jose Americo Bubo Na Tchuto and several others on drug charges Apr. 2013; armed forces head Gen. Antonio Injai was indicted in absentia. Former finance min. Jose Mario Vaz won 61.9% of the vote in a May 18, 2014, presidential runoff.

Guyana
Cooperative Republic of Guyana

People: Population: 735,554. **Age distrib.:** <15: 29%; 65+: 5.3%. **Pop. density:** 9.7 per sq mi, 3.7 per sq km. **Urban:** 28.5%. **Ethnic groups:** East Indian 44%, black (African) 30%, mixed 17%, Amerindian 9%. **Languages:** English, Amerindian dialects, Creole, Caribbean Hindustani, Urdu. **Religions:** Protestant 31% (Pentecostal 17%, Anglican 7%, Seventh-day Adventist 5%, Methodist 2%), Hindu 28%, Roman Catholic 8%, Muslim 7%, other Christian 18%, none 4%.

Geography: Total area: 83,000 sq mi, 214,969 sq km; **Land area:** 76,004 sq mi, 196,849 sq km. **Location:** On N coast of S America. **Neighbors:** Venezuela on W, Brazil on S, Suriname on E. **Topography:** Dense tropical forests cover much of land, although flat coastal area up to 40 mi wide, where 90% of the population lives, provides rich alluvial soil for agriculture. A grassy savanna divides the 2 zones. **Capital:** Georgetown, 123,852.

Government: Type: Republic. **Head of state:** Pres. Donald Rabrindranath Ramotar; b. Oct. 22, 1950; in office: Dec. 3, 2011. **Head of gov.:** Prime Min. Samuel Hinds; b. Dec. 27, 1943; in office: Dec. 19, 1997. **Local divisions:** 10 regions. **Defense budget:** $35 mil. **Active troops:** 1,100.

Economy: Industries: bauxite, rice milling, timber, textiles, gold mining. **Chief crops:** sugarcane, rice, edible oils. **Natural resources:** bauxite, gold, diamonds, timber, shrimp, fish. **Arable land:** 2.1%. **Livestock:** cattle: 112,900; chickens: 25.2 mil; goats: 82,000; pigs: 12,600; sheep: 132,000. **Electricity prod.:** 725 mil kWh. **Labor force:** NA. **Unemployment:** 21.7%.

Finance: Monetary unit: Dollar (GYD) (Sept. 2014: 203.20 = $1 U.S.). **GDP:** $6.6 bil; **per capita GDP:** $8,500; **GDP growth:** 5.3%. **Imports:** $2 bil; U.S. 22.2%, Trinidad and Tobago 21.9%, China 12.3%, Cuba 6.1%, Suriname 4%. **Exports:** $1.3 bil; U.S. 30.8%, Canada 28.9%, UK 6.2%. **Tourism:** $64 mil. **Budget:** $948.5 mil. **Total reserves less gold:** $783.6 mil. **Inflation:** 2.1%.

Transport: Motor vehicles: 75.7 per 1,000 pop. **Civil aviation:** 11 airports. **Chief port:** Georgetown.

Communications: TV sets: 167 per 1,000 pop. **Radios:** 571 per 1,000 pop. **Telephone lines:** 19.6 per 100 pop. **Mobile:** 69.4 per 100 pop. **Internet:** 33%.

Health: Life expect.: 64.8 male; 71.0 female. **Births:** 15.9 per 1,000 pop. **Deaths:** 7.3 per 1,000 pop. **Natural inc.:** 0.86%. **Infant mortality:** 33.6 per 1,000 live births. **HIV:** 1.4%.

Education: Compulsory: ages 6-14. **Literacy:** 88.5%.

Embassy: 2490 Tracy Pl. NW 20008; 265-6900.

Website: www.gina.gov.gy.

Guyana became a Dutch possession in the 17th cent., but sovereignty passed to Britain in 1815. Indentured servants from India soon outnumbered African slaves. Guyana became independent May 26, 1966.

The Port Kaituma ambush of U.S. Rep. Leo J. Ryan and others investigating mistreatment of American followers of the Rev. Jim Jones's People's Temple cult triggered a mass suicide-execution of 911 cultists at Jonestown in the jungle, Nov. 18, 1978.

The People's National Congress, the party in power since Guyana became independent, was voted out of office with the election of Cheddi Jagan in Oct. 1992. When Pres. Jagan died Mar. 6, 1997, Prime Min. Samuel Hinds became prime min. Mar. 17. She won the presidency in a disputed election Dec. 15. She resigned because of ill health Aug. 1999 and was succeeded by Bharrat Jagdeo. He won reelection in 2001 and 2006. Donald Ramotar, the candidate of Jagdeo's party, was elected president in 2011. On June 12, 2013, Guyana was among 38 nations that met a UN challenge to reduce hunger in their countries by half.

Haiti
Republic of Haiti

People: Population: 9,996,731. **Age distrib.:** <15: 34%; 65+: 4.1%. **Pop. density:** 939.5 per sq mi, 362.7 per sq km. **Urban:** 57.4%. **Ethnic groups:** black 95%, mulatto and white 5%. **Languages:** French, Creole (both official). **Religions:** Roman Catholic 80%, Protestant 16% (Baptist 10%, Pentecostal 4%); roughly half of pop. practices voodoo.

Geography: Total area: 10,714 sq mi, 27,750 sq km; **Land area:** 10,641 sq mi, 27,560 sq km. **Location:** In Caribbean, occupies western third of isl. of Hispaniola. **Neighbors:** Dominican Republic on E, Cuba to W. **Topography:** About two-thirds is mountainous. Much of rest is semiarid. Coastal areas are warm and moist. **Capital:** Port-au-Prince, 2,375,910 (urban aggl.).

Government: Type: Republic. **Head of state:** Pres. Michel Martelly; b. Feb. 12, 1961; in office: May 14, 2011. **Head of gov.:** Prime Min. Laurent Lamothe; b. Aug. 14, 1972; in office: May 16, 2012. **Local divisions:** 10 departments. **Defense budget:** NA. **Active troops:** No active armed forces. UN mission MINUSTAH in country since 2004.

Economy: Industries: textiles, sugar refining, flour milling, cement, light assembly of imported parts. **Chief crops:** coffee, mangoes, cocoa, sugarcane, rice, corn, sorghum. **Natural resources:** bauxite, copper, calcium carbonate, gold, marble, hydropower. **Arable land:** 36.3%. **Livestock:** cattle: 1.5 mil; chickens: 5.7 mil; goats: 2 mil; pigs: 1 mil; sheep: 154,000. **Electricity prod.:** 652 mil kWh. **Labor force:** agric. 38.1%, industry 11.5%, services 50.4%. **Unemployment:** 7%.

Finance: Monetary unit: Gourde (HTG) (Sept. 2014: 44.20 = $1 U.S.). **GDP:** $13.4 bil; **per capita GDP:** $1,300; **GDP growth:** 3.4%. **Imports:** $2.7 bil; Dominican Republic 34.5%, U.S. 26.2%, Netherlands Antilles 9.4%, China 7%. **Exports:** $876.8 mil; U.S. 81.7%. **Tourism:** $170 mil. **Budget:** $2.4 bil. **Total reserves less gold:** $1.7 bil. **Gold:** 58,225 oz t. **Inflation:** 5.9%.

Transport: Motor vehicles: 8.2 per 1,000 pop. **Civil aviation:** 4 airports. **Chief ports:** Cap-Haïtien, Gonaïves Jacmel, Port-au-Prince.

Communications: TV sets: 104 per 1,000 pop. **Radios:** 170 per 1,000 pop. **Telephone lines:** 0.4 per 100 pop. **Mobile:** 69.4 per 100 pop. **Internet:** 10.6%.

Health: Life expect.: 61.8 male; 64.6 female. **Births:** 22.8 per 1,000 pop. **Deaths:** 7.9 per 1,000 pop. **Natural inc.:** 1.49%. **Infant mortality:** 49.4 per 1,000 live births. **HIV:** 2.0%.

Education: Compulsory: ages 6-11. **Literacy:** 60.7%.

Embassy: 2311 Massachusetts Ave. NW 20008; 332-4090.

Website: primature.gouv.ht or www.haiti.org

Haiti, visited by Columbus in 1492 and a French colony from 1697, attained its independence, 1804, following a rebellion led by former slave Toussaint L'Ouverture. After a period of political violence, the U.S. occupied the country 1915-34.

François Duvalier, known as Papa Doc, was elected president in 1957; in 1964 he was named president for life. Upon his death in 1971, he was succeeded by his son, Jean Claude Duvalier, known as Baby Doc. Following nearly 15 years Jean Claude fled Haiti aboard a U.S. Air Force jet Feb. 7, 1986. His departure ended the Duvalier family's brutal 28-year dictatorship, but political violence, government corruption, poverty, AIDS and other health problems, and deteriorating environmental quality have continued to plague Haiti.

Jean-Bertrand Aristide was elected president in 1990, but the military arrested and expelled him from the country in Sept. 1991. The U.S. Coast Guard intercepted some 35,000 Haitian refugees as they tried to enter the U.S., 1991-92. Most were returned to Haiti. There was a new upsurge of refugees starting in late 1993.

The UN authorized in 1994 an invasion of Haiti by a multinational force. With U.S. troops already en route, a full-scale invasion was averted, Sept. 18, when military leaders agreed to step down. Aristide returned to Haiti and was restored to office Oct. 15. A UN peacekeeping force exercised responsibility in Haiti from 1995 to 1997. Aristide transferred power to his elected successor, René Préval, in 1996.

At least 140 people died and over 160,000 were left homeless when Hurricane Georges struck Haiti Sept. 22, 1998. Aristide won the 2000 presidency in an election boycotted by opposition groups. An armed uprising in early 2004 brought pressure from France and the U.S. toppled Aristide, who went into exile Feb. 29. A U.S.-led contingent, sent in after the upheaval, yielded authority June 1 to a UN stabilization force (MINUSTAH).

Flooding in late May 2004 killed more than 1,000 people, and more than 2,400 were killed in Tropical Storm Jeanne in Sept. Préval was reelected in 2006. Skyrocketing prices for food imports sparked riots and mass protests in Apr. 2008. A succession of hurricanes and tropical storms (Fay, Gustav, Hanna, Ike), Aug.-Sept. 2008, left more than 550 Haitians dead and up to 1 mil homeless. A school collapse near Port-au-Prince Nov. 7, 2008, killed 91 students and teachers.

An earthquake Jan. 12, 2010, near Port-au-Prince caused cataclysmic damage. More than 220,000 people (including nearly 100 UN peacekeepers) were killed, at least 300,000 were injured, and more than 1.5 mil were left homeless and were given shelter in displacement camps. With the central government paralyzed and the presidential palace and parliament building in ruins, the U.S. and other countries mounted a massive relief effort. Nearly 147,000 Haitians were still living in displacement camps on the 4th anniversary of the quake in 2014. Poor living and sanitation conditions contributed to a cholera epidemic in areas affected by the 2010 earthquake. As of mid-2014, more than 8,500 had died, and over 700,000 had been ill with the disease.

After the first round of presidential balloting Nov. 28, 2010, Michel Martelly, an entertainer popularly known as Sweet Micky, was declared ineligible for the second round. Violent protests by his supporters, allegations of electoral fraud from international observers, and diplomatic pressure from the U.S. and other donor countries gained him a place in the runoff Mar. 20, 2011, which he won. Parliament twice blocked his nominee for prime min. before approving his third choice, Garry Conille, a physician and development expert. Conille resigned Feb. 2012, and was replaced by Laurent Lamothe in May. MINUSTAH uniformed personnel numbered about 7,500 in mid-2014.

Honduras
Republic of Honduras

People: Population: 8,598,561. **Age distrib.:** <15: 34.8%; 65+: 4%. **Pop. density:** 199 per sq mi, 76.8 per sq km. **Urban:** 54.1%. **Ethnic groups:** mestizo (mixed Amerindian and European) 90%, Amerindian 7%, black 2%, white 1%. **Languages:** Spanish (official), Amerindian dialects. **Religions:** Roman Catholic 97%, Protestant 3%.

Geography: Total area: 43,278 sq mi, 112,090 sq km; **Land area:** 43,201 sq mi, 111,890 sq km. **Location:** In Central America. **Neighbors:** Guatemala on W; El Salvador, Nicaragua on S. **Topography:** Caribbean coast is 500 mi long. Pacific coast, on Gulf of Fonseca, is 40 mi long. Country is mountainous, with wide fertile valleys and rich forests. **Capital:** Tegucigalpa, 1,100,590.

Government: Type: Democratic constitutional republic. **Head of state and gov.:** Pres. Juan Orlando Hernandez Alvarado; b. Oct. 28, 1968; in office: Jan. 27, 2014. **Local divisions:** 18 departments. **Defense budget:** $177 mil. **Active troops:** 12,000.

Economy: Industries: sugar, coffee, woven and knit apparel, wood prods., cigars. **Chief crops:** bananas, coffee, citrus, corn, African palm. **Natural resources:** timber, gold, silver, copper, lead, zinc, iron ore, antimony, coal, fish, hydropower. **Arable land:** 9.1%. **Livestock:** cattle: 2.8 mil; chickens: 44.5 mil; goats: 25,000; pigs: 487,000; sheep: 16,000. **Electricity prod.:** 6.7 bil kWh. **Labor force:** agric. 39.2%, industry 20.9%, services 39.8%. **Unemployment:** 4.8%.

Finance: Monetary unit: Lempira (HNL) (Sept. 2014: 21.03 = $1 U.S.). **GDP:** $39.2 bil; **per capita GDP:** $4,800; **GDP growth:** 2.8%. **Imports:** $11.3 bil; U.S. 44.3%, Guatemala 8.5%, El Salvador 5.7%, Mexico 5.6%, China 4.7%, Costa Rica 4.1%. **Exports:** $7.9 bil; U.S. 34.5%, Germany 11.6%, Belgium 6.8%, El Salvador 6.6%, Guatemala 4.9%, Nicaragua 4.6%. **Tourism:** $711 mil. **Budget:** $4.3 bil. **Total reserves less gold:** $3 bil. **Gold:** 22,006 oz t. **Inflation:** 5.2%.

Transport: Railways: 27 mi (2.5 mi in use). **Motor vehicles:** 17.4 per 1,000 pop. **Civil aviation:** 13 airports. **Chief ports:** La Ceiba, Puerto Cortes, San Lorenzo, Tela.

Communications: TV sets: 176 per 1,000 pop. **Radios:** 1,698 per 1,000 pop. **Telephone lines:** 7.7 per 100 pop. **Mobile:** 95.9 per 100 pop. **Internet:** 17.8%.

Health: Life expect.: 69.2 male; 72.7 female. **Births:** 23.7 per 1,000 pop. **Deaths:** 5.1 per 1,000 pop. **Natural inc.:** 1.85%. **Infant mortality:** 18.7 per 1,000 live births. **HIV:** 0.5%.

Education: Compulsory: ages 6-14. **Literacy:** 88.5%.

Embassy: 3007 Tilden St. NW 20008; 966-7702.

Website: www.presidencia.gob.hn

Mayan civilization flourished in Honduras in the 1st millennium CE. Columbus arrived in 1502. Honduras became independent after freeing itself from Spain, 1821, and from the Fed. of Central America, 1838.

The army ousted Gen. Oswaldo Lopez Arellano, president for most of the period 1963-75, in 1975 over charges of pervasive bribery by United Brands Co. of the U.S. An elected civilian government took power in 1982.

Already one of the poorest countries in the Western Hemisphere, Honduras was devastated in late Oct. 1998 by Hurricane Mitch, which killed at least 5,600 people and caused more than $850 mil in damage to crops and livestock.

Ricardo Maduro, a businessman who pledged to crack down on crime, won the 2001 presidency. He was succeeded by Manuel Zelaya Rosales of the opposition Liberal Party, who won the 2005 presidential election. Seeking constitutional changes in his final year in office that may have allowed him to run for a second term, Zelaya lost a political struggle with the Honduran congress and supreme court; the military ousted him June 2009. Porfirio (Pepe) Lobo of the conservative National Party defeated Liberal Party nominee Elvin Santos in the 2009 presidential election, and took office Jan. 27, 2010, resolving the constitutional crisis. National Party candidate Juan Orlando Hernández won the Nov. 2013 presidential election.

Northern Honduras has become a major transshipment point for illegal drugs being smuggled from South America to the U.S. Drug-gang violence and other crime apparently contributed to a significant increase in migration, including thousands of children traveling alone or with their mothers, trying to enter the U.S. along the Mexican border, 2013-14.

Hungary

People: Population: 9,919,128. **Age distrib.:** <15: 14.8%; 65+: 17.8%. **Pop. density:** 286.7 per sq mi, 110.7 per sq km. **Urban:** 70.8%. **Ethnic groups:** Hungarian 92%, Roma 2%. **Language:** Hungarian. **Religions:** Roman Catholic 37%, Calvinist 12%, Lutheran 2%, Greek Catholic 2%, none 18%.

Geography: Total area: 35,918 sq mi, 93,028 sq km; **Land area:** 34,598 sq mi, 89,608 sq km. **Location:** In E central Europe. **Neighbors:** Slovakia, Ukraine on N; Austria on W; Slovenia, Serbia, Croatia on S; Romania on E. **Topography:** Danube R. forms Slovak border in NW, then swings S to bisect the country. Eastern half of Hungary is mainly a great fertile plain, the Alföld; the W and N are hilly. **Capital:** Budapest, 1,717,320.

Government: Type: Parliamentary democracy. **Head of state:** Pres. János Áder; b. May 9, 1959; in office: May 10, 2012. **Head of gov.:** Prime Min. Viktor Orbán; b. May 31, 1963; in office: May 29, 2010. **Local divisions:** 19 counties, 23 urban counties, 1 capital city. **Defense budget:** $1.1 bil. **Active troops:** 26,500.

Economy: Industries: mining, metallurgy, constr. materials, processed foods, textiles, chemicals (spec. pharmaceuticals), motor vehicles. **Chief crops:** wheat, corn, sunflower seeds, potatoes, sugar beets. **Natural resource:** bauxite, coal, nat. gas. **Crude oil reserves:** 27.3 mil bbls. **Arable land:** 48.6%. **Livestock:** cattle: 760,000; chickens: 30.1 mil; goats: 89,000; pigs: 3 mil; sheep: 1.2 mil. **Electricity prod.:** 33.9 bil kWh. **Labor force:** agric. 7.1%, industry 29.7%, services 63.2%. **Unemployment:** 10.9%.

Finance: Monetary unit: Forint (HUF) (Sept. 2014: 238.75 = $1 U.S.). **GDP:** $196.6 bil; **per capita GDP:** $19,800; **GDP growth:** 0.2%. **Imports:** $89.5 bil; Germany 25.1%, Russia 8.8%, China 7.4%, Austria 7.1%, Slovakia 5.6%, Poland 4.8%, Italy 4.5%, Netherlands 4.2%. **Exports:** $93 bil; Germany 25.6%, Romania 6.2%, Slovakia 6.1%, Austria 6%, Italy 4.8%, France 4.8%, UK 4.2%. **Tourism:** $5.1 bil. **Budget:** $66 bil. **Total reserves less gold:** $46.4 bil. **Gold:** 99,000 oz t. **Inflation:** 1.7%.

Transport: Railways: 5,006 mi. **Motor vehicles:** 349.9 per 1,000 pop. **Civil aviation:** 10.6 bil pass.-mi; 20 airports. **Chief ports:** Baja, Budapest, Csepel, Dunaujvaros, Gyor-Gonyu, Mohacs.

Communications: TV sets: 572 per 1,000 pop. **Radios:** 473 per 1,000 pop. **Telephone lines:** 29.9 per 100 pop. **Mobile:** 116.4 per 100 pop. **Internet:** 72.6%.

Health: Life expect.: 71.7 male; 79.4 female. **Births:** 9.3 per 1,000 pop. **Deaths:** 12.7 per 1,000 pop. **Natural inc.:** −0.35%. **Infant mortality:** 5.1 per 1,000 live births. **HIV:** NA.

Education: Compulsory: ages 7-16. **Literacy:** 99.1%.

Embassy: 3910 Shoemaker St. NW 20008; 362-6730.

Website: www.hungary.hu

Earliest settlers, chiefly Slav and Germanic, were overrun by Magyars from the east. Stephen I (997-1038) was made king by Pope Sylvester II in 1000 CE. The country suffered repeated Turkish invasions in the 15th-17th cents. After the Turks were defeated, 1686-97, Austria dominated, but Hungary obtained concessions,

and regained internal independence in 1867 under a dual monarchy with the emperor of Austria. Defeated with the Central Powers in 1918, Hungary lost Transylvania to Romania, Croatia and Bacska to Yugoslavia, and Slovakia and Carpatho-Ruthenia to Czechoslovakia. All had large Hungarian minorities. A republic under Michael Karolyi and a Bolshevist revolt under Bela Kun were followed by a vote for a monarchy in 1920 with Adm. Nicholas Horthy as regent.

Hungary joined Germany in WWII and was allowed to annex most of its lost territories. Russian troops captured the country, 1944-45. By terms of an armistice with the Allied powers Hungary agreed to give up territory acquired by the 1938 dismemberment of Czechoslovakia and to return to its borders of 1937.

A republic was declared Feb. 1, 1946. In 1947 a hard-line Communist, pro-Soviet government was installed. Demonstrations against Communist rule developed into open revolt in 1956. Soviet forces launched a massive attack Nov. 4 against Budapest. About 200,000 persons fled the country. Thousands were arrested and executed.

Major economic reforms were launched early in 1968, switching from a central planning system to one based on market forces and profit. In 1989 Parliament legalized freedom of assembly and association as Hungary shifted away from Communism. In Oct. the Communist Party was formally dissolved. The last Soviet troops left June 19, 1991. Hungary became a full member of NATO in 1999 and of the EU in 2004.

The IMF, EU, and World Bank agreed Oct. 2008 to extend $25.1 bil to rescue Hungary's economy, which was battered by the global financial crisis. With the nation still reeling from recession, the center-right Fidesz party ousted the Socialists in 2010 parliamentary elections. Parliament, dominated by Fidesz, approved Apr. 2011 a fiscally and socially conservative constitution that drew EU criticism; the law went into force Jan. 1, 2012. Fidesz retained its parliamentary majority in Apr. 6, 2014, elections.

Iceland
Republic of Iceland

People: Population: 317,351. **Age distrib.:** <15: 19.7%; 65+: 13.5%. **Pop. density:** 8.2 per sq mi, 3.2 per sq km. **Urban:** 94%. **Ethnic groups:** homogeneous mix of Norse and Celt descendants 94%, pop. of foreign origin 6%. **Languages:** Icelandic, English, Nordic langs., German. **Religions:** Evangelical Lutheran Church of Iceland (official) 76%, Roman Catholic 3%, Reykjavik Free Church 3%, Hafnarfjorour Free Church 2%, none 5%.

Geography: Total area: 39,769 sq mi, 103,000 sq km; **Land area:** 38,707 sq mi, 100,250 sq km. **Location:** Isl. at N end of Atlantic O. **Neighbors:** Nearest is Greenland (Den.) to W. **Topography:** Recent volcanic origin. Three-quarters of surface is wasteland: glaciers, lakes, a lava desert. There are geysers and hot springs, and the climate is moderated by the Gulf Stream. **Capital:** Reykjavík, 184,171.

Government: Type: Constitutional republic. **Head of state:** Pres. Olafur Ragnar Grímsson; b. May 14, 1943; in office: Aug. 1, 1996. **Head of gov.:** Prime Min. Sigmundur David Gunnlaugsson; b. Mar. 12, 1975; in office: May 23, 2013. **Local divisions:** 8 regions. **Defense budget:** $37 mil (Coast Guard budget). **Active troops:** No armed forces. Relies on NATO allies for air policing and defense.

Economy: Industries: fish proc., aluminum smelting, ferrosilicon prod., geothermal power, hydropower, tourism. **Chief crops:** potatoes, green vegetables. **Natural resource:** fish, hydropower, geothermal power, diatomite. **Arable land:** 1.2%. **Livestock:** cattle: 68,014; chickens: 217,000; goats: 877; pigs: 26,033; sheep: 463,807. **Electricity prod.** (2012): 17.2 bil kWh. **Labor force:** agric. 4.8%, industry 22.2%, services 73%. **Unemployment:** 6%.

Finance: Monetary unit: Krona (ISK) (Sept. 2014: 117.20 = $1 U.S.). **GDP:** $13.1 bil; **per capita GDP:** $40,700; **GDP growth:** 1.9%. **Imports:** $4.5 bil; Norway 16.6%, U.S. 10.2%, Germany 9.2%, China 7.2%, Brazil 6.7%, Netherlands 6%, Denmark 5.7%, UK 4.6%. **Exports:** $5.2 bil; Netherlands 30%, Germany 12.9%, UK 9.8%, Norway 5.1%, U.S. 4.5%, France 4.4%. **Tourism:** $1.1 bil. **Budget:** $6.4 bil. **Total reserves less gold:** $4.2 bil. **Gold:** 63,785 oz t. **Inflation:** 3.9%.

Transport: Motor vehicles: 781.8 per 1,000 pop. **Civil aviation:** 3.1 bil pass.-mi; 7 airports. **Chief ports:** Grundartangi, Hafnarfjordur, Reykjavik.

Communications: TV sets: 505 per 1,000 pop. **Radios:** 1,077 per 1,000 pop. **Telephone lines:** 51 per 100 pop. **Mobile:** 108.1 per 100 pop. **Internet:** 96.6%.

Health: Life expect.: 79.0 male; 83.5 female. **Births:** 13.1 per 1,000 pop. **Deaths:** 7.1 per 1,000 pop. **Natural inc.:** 0.60%. **Infant mortality:** 3.2 per 1,000 live births. **HIV:** NA.

Education: Compulsory: ages 6-16. **Literacy:** 99%.

Embassy: 1156 15th St. NW, Ste. 1200, 20005; 265-6653.

Website: www.iceland.is

Iceland was an independent republic from 930 to 1262, when it joined with Norway. Its language has maintained its purity for 1,000 years. The Althing, or assembly, established in 930, is the world's oldest surviving parliament. Danish rule lasted 1380-1918; the last ties with the Danish crown were severed in 1941.

A 55-year U.S. military presence in Iceland ended with the closure of the Keflavík naval air station in Sept. 2006. Iceland's banking system and currency collapsed amid the global financial crisis in Oct. 2008. More than $10 bil in loans from the IMF and European governments restored financial stability; austerity measures were imposed, and the nation entered a deep recession. Political unrest sparked by soaring inflation and unemployment led to the Feb. 2009 installation of a center-left government, which swept to victory in Apr. 25 elections. Parliament July 16 approved a plan for Iceland to seek EU membership. A major eruption Apr. 14, 2010, of the Eyjafjallajökull volcano disrupted European air traffic, affecting about 10 mil passengers and 100,000 flights during the next 6 days. The governing coalition Jan. 14, 2013, tabled discussions about EU membership ahead of Apr. 28, 2013, parliamentary elections, in which the center-left government was voted out in favor of center-right parties.

India
Republic of India

People: Population: 1,236,344,631. **Age distrib.:** <15: 28.5%; 65+: 5.8%. **Pop. density:** 1,077 per sq mi, 415.8 per sq km. **Urban:** 32.4%. **Ethnic groups:** Indo-Aryan 72%, Dravidian 25%, Mongoloid and other 3%. **Languages:** Hindi (most widely spoken and primary tongue); 14 other official langs. (Bengali, Telugu, Marathi, Tamil, Urdu, Gujarati, Malayalam, Kannada, Oriya, Punjabi, Assamese, Kashmiri, Sindhi, Sanskrit); English (crucial for nat'l., political, commercial communication); Hindustani (popular variant of Hindi/Urdu widely spoken throughout N). **Religions:** Hindu 81%, Muslim 13%, Christian 2%, Sikh 2%.

Geography: Total area: 1,269,219 sq mi, 3,287,263 sq km; **Land area:** 1,147,956 sq mi, 2,973,193 sq km. **Location:** Occupies most of Indian subcontinent in S Asia. **Neighbors:** Pakistan on W; China, Nepal, Bhutan on N; Myanmar, Bangladesh on E. **Topography:** The Himalayan Mts., highest in world, stretch across northern borders. Below, the Ganges Plain is wide, fertile, and among the world's most densely populated regions. Area below includes Deccan Peninsula. Close to one quarter of area is forested. The climate varies from tropical heat in S to near-Arctic cold in N. Rajasthan Desert is NW; NE Assam Hills get 400 in. of rain a year. **Capital:** Delhi, 24,953,300. **Cities (urban aggl.):** Mumbai (Bombay), 20,740,815; Kolkata (Calcutta), 14,766,099; Bangalore, 9,717,993; Chennai (Madras), 9,619,579; Hyderabad, 8,670,195; Ahmadabad, 7,115,861.

Government: Type: Federal republic. **Head of state:** Pres. Pranab Mukherjee; b. Dec. 11, 1935; in office: July 22, 2012. **Head of gov.:** Prime Min. Narendra Modi; b. Sept. 17, 1950; in office: May 26, 2014. **Local divisions:** 29 states, 7 union territories. **Defense budget:** $36.3 bil. **Active troops:** 1,325,000.

Economy: Industries: textiles, chemicals, food proc., steel, transp. equip., cement, mining, petroleum, machinery, software, pharmaceuticals. **Chief crops:** rice, wheat, oilseed, cotton, jute, tea, sugarcane, lentils, onions, potatoes. **Natural resources:** coal (world's fourth-largest reserves), iron ore, manganese, mica, bauxite, rare earth elements, titanium ore, chromite, nat. gas, diamonds, petroleum, limestone. **Crude oil reserves:** 5.7 bil bbls. **Arable land:** 52.5%. **Livestock:** cattle: 214.4 mil; chickens: 950 mil; goats: 162 mil; pigs: 9.3 mil; sheep: 75.5 mil. **Electricity prod.:** 974.9 bil kWh. **Labor force:** agric. 49%, industry 20%, services 31%. **Unemployment:** 3.4%.

Finance: Monetary unit: Rupee (INR) (Sept. 2014: 60.47 = $1 U.S.). **GDP:** $5 tril; **per capita GDP:** $4,000; **GDP growth:** 3.2%. **Imports:** $467.5 bil; China 10.7%, UAE 7.8%, Saudi Arabia 6.8%, Switzerland 6.2%, U.S. 5.1%. **Exports:** $313.2 bil; UAE 12.3%, U.S. 12.2%, China 5%, Singapore 4.9%, Hong Kong 4.1%. **Tourism:** $18.4 bil. **Budget:** $281.6 bil. **Total reserves less gold:** $276.5 bil. **Gold:** 17.9 mil oz t. **Inflation:** 10.9%.

Transport: Railways: 39,752 mi. **Motor vehicles:** 26.6 per 1,000 pop. **Civil aviation:** 68.9 bil pass.-mi; 253 airports. **Chief ports:** Chennai, Jawaharal Nehru, Kandla, Kolkata, Mumbai, Sikka, Vishakhapatnam.

Communications: TV sets: 137 per 1,000 pop. **Radios:** 120 per 1,000 pop. **Telephone lines:** 2.3 per 100 pop. **Mobile:** 70.8 per 100 pop. **Internet:** 15.1%.

Health: Life expect.: 66.7 male; 69.1 female. **Births:** 19.9 per 1,000 pop. **Deaths:** 7.4 per 1,000 pop. **Natural inc.:** 1.25%. **Infant mortality:** 43.2 per 1,000 live births. **HIV:** 0.3%.

Education: Compulsory: ages 6-14. **Literacy:** 71.2%.

Embassy: 2107 Massachusetts Ave. NW 20008; 939-7000.

Website: www.india.gov.in

India has one of the oldest civilizations in the world. Excavations trace the Indus Valley civilization back for at least 5,000 years. Paintings in the mountain caves of Ajanta, richly carved temples, the Taj Mahal in Agra, and the Kutab Minar in Delhi are among treasured relics of the past.

Aryan tribes, speaking Sanskrit, invaded from the NW around 1500 BCE. Asoka ruled most of the Indian subcontinent in the 3rd cent. BCE and established Buddhism. But Hinduism revived and eventually predominated. Under the Guptas, 4th-6th cent. CE, science, literature, and the arts enjoyed a golden age. Arab invaders established a Muslim foothold in the west in the 8th cent., and Turkish Muslims gained control of North India by 1200. The Mughal emperors ruled 1526-1857.

Vasco da Gama established Portuguese trading posts 1498-1503. The Dutch followed. The British East India Co. sent Capt. William Hawkins, 1609, to get concessions from the Mughal emperor for spices and textiles. Operating as the East India Co., the British gained control of most of India. The British parliament assumed political direction; under Lord Bentinck, 1828-35, rule by rajahs was curbed. After the Sepoy troops mutinied, 1857-58, the British supported the native rulers.

Nationalism grew after WWI. The Indian National Congress and the Muslim League demanded constitutional reform. A leader emerged in Mohandas K. Gandhi (called Mahatma, or Great Soul) (b. Oct. 2, 1869), who was assassinated Jan. 30, 1948. He advocated self-rule, nonviolence, and an end to caste discrimination against "untouchables." In 1930 he launched a program of civil disobedience, boycotting British goods and rejecting taxes without representation.

In 1935, Britain gave India a constitution providing a bicameral federal congress. Muhammad Ali Jinnah, head of the Muslim League, sought creation of a Muslim nation, Pakistan.

The British government partitioned British India into the dominions of India and Pakistan. India became a member of the UN in 1945, a self-governing member of the Commonwealth in 1947, and a democratic republic, Jan. 26, 1950. More than 12 mil Hindu and Muslim refugees crossed the India-Pakistan borders in 1947; about 200,000 were killed in communal fighting.

After Pakistan troops began attacks on Bengali separatists in East Pakistan, Mar. 25, 1971, some 10 mil refugees fled to India. India and Pakistan went to war Dec. 3, 1971, on both the east and west fronts. Pakistan troops in the east surrendered Dec. 16; Pakistan agreed to a cease-fire in the west Dec. 17.

Indira Gandhi, India's prime minister since Jan. 1966, invoked emergency powers in June 1975. Thousands of opponents were arrested and press censorship imposed. These and other actions, including population control through forced vasectomies, were widely resented. Opposition parties, united in the Janata coalition, won the 1977 elections.

Gandhi became prime minister for the second time in 1980. She was assassinated by 2 of her Sikh bodyguards Oct. 31, 1984, in response to the government suppression in June 1984 of a Sikh uprising in Punjab, which included an assault on the Golden Temple at Amritsar, the holiest Sikh shrine. Widespread rioting followed the assassination; thousands of Sikhs were killed and some 50,000 left homeless. Rajiv, Indira Gandhi's son, replaced her as prime minister. A gas leak at a Union Carbide chemical plant in Bhopal, Dec. 1984, eventually killed some 14,000 people.

Many died in religious, ethnic, and political conflicts during the late 1980s and early '90s. To suppress the Sikh insurgency in Punjab, Indian government troops attacked the Golden Temple again in 1988. Rajiv Gandhi was swept from office in 1989 amid charges of incompetence and corruption and assassinated May 21, 1991, while campaigning to regain power. Nationwide riots followed the destruction of a 16th-cent. mosque by Hindu militants in Dec. 1992. Ethnic clashes in Assam, in NW India, killed thousands in Feb. 1993. Bombs jolted Mumbai and Kolkata, Mar. 12-19, killing over 300.

India's first president from the lowest caste, K. R. Narayanan, took office July 1997. India conducted a series of nuclear tests in mid-May 1998, raising tensions with Pakistan. A cyclone hit the state of Orissa, East India, on Oct. 29, 1999, leaving some 10,000 people dead. A powerful earthquake in Gujarat state, Jan. 26, 2001, claimed more than 20,000 lives.

India blamed Pakistani-sponsored terrorist groups for an Oct. 1, 2001, suicide attack on the state legislature in Jammu and Kashmir (see below), in which at least 40 people died, and a Dec. 13 assault on the Indian parliament in New Delhi that left 13 people dead. Hindu-Muslim clashes in Gujarat Feb.-Mar. 2002 claimed more than 700 lives. A P. J. Abdul Kalam, a Muslim scientist who spearheaded India's nuclear weapons program, became president July 25.

Led by Rajiv Gandhi's Italian-born widow, Sonia, the Congress Party won the most seats in 2004 parliamentary elections. When Hindu nationalists objected to her candidacy, she chose not to become prime minister, and Manmohan Singh, a Sikh economist, took office instead.

The Indian Ocean tsunami of Dec. 26, 2004, left more than 10,700 people dead, some 5,600 missing, and over 647,000 displaced. Islamic extremists were suspected in 7 bombings in Mumbai, July 11, 2006, that killed more than 200 on commuter trains. Pratibha Patil took office July 2007, as India's first female president. Monsoon floods, July-Sept. 2007, killed more than 2,600 people. The next year, monsoon floods killed more than 2,200. At least 224 people died in a stampede Sept. 30, 2008, at a Hindu temple in Jodhpur. The unmanned Chandrayaan-1, India's first lunar survey mission, was launched into space Oct. 22, 2008.

Ten Pakistanis linked to the militant group Lashkar-e-Taiba stormed luxury hotels, a railway station, a Jewish center, and other sites in Mumbai, Nov. 26, 2008; by the time Indian army commandos took control 3 days later, the attackers had slaughtered 163 people. Nine of the terrorists were also killed. Convicted of murder and of waging war against India, the lone surviving gunman, Ajmal Kasab, received a death sentence in 2010, and was executed by hanging Nov. 20, 2012.

In 2009 parliamentary elections, Prime Min. Manmohan Singh's United Progressive Alliance, headed by the Congress party, gained a resounding victory. A triple bombing in Mumbai July 13, 2011, killed 26 people and injured about 140; 11 were killed when a bomb exploded Sept. 7 outside the High Court in New Delhi. Electricity blackouts July 30-31, 2012, left 670 mil people without power.

Several rapes in New Delhi in Nov.-Dec. 2012 prompted outrage and large protests for their mishandling by police and government inaction. Tougher laws against sexual violence were passed Feb. 4, 2013, that included the death penalty for some cases. The Hindu nationalist Bharatiya Janata party won a large majority in Apr.-May 2014 parliamentary elections in which more than 550 mil votes were cast.

Development of high-tech industries has propelled rapid economic growth since the 1990s; nearly 200 mil people have emerged from extreme poverty, although distribution of wealth remains highly uneven.

Sikkim, bordered by Tibet, Bhutan, and Nepal, formerly British protected, became a protectorate of India in 1950. Area 2,740 sq mi; pop. (2011 census) 607,688; capital is Gangtok. In Sept. 1974, India's parliament voted to make Sikkim an associate Indian state, absorbing it into India.

Kashmir is a predominantly Muslim region in the NW that borders India, Pakistan, Afghanistan, and China. Muslim rule of the previously Hindu kingdom began in 1341; after almost 200 years under the Mughals, the area was incorporated into British India in 1846. Fighting broke out in the region between India and Pakistan in 1947 following independence from Britain. A cease-fire was negotiated by the UN Jan. 1, 1949; it gave Pakistan control of one-third of the area as Azad Kashmir, in the W and NW, and India the remaining two-thirds, as the Indian state of Jammu and Kashmir. Area 85,806 sq mi; pop. (2011 census) 12,548,926. Capitals: Srinagar (summer), pop. (2014 est.) 1,393,580 (urban aggl.); Jammu (winter), pop. (2014 est.) 667,261 (urban aggl.). Fighting in the area resumed during the 1965 and 1971 wars with Pakistan. China occupied about 14,000 sq mi in the Ladakh district after a war with India in 1962.

In the 1990s, India's decision to impose central government rule triggered clashes between Indian army troops and separatist fighters. India charged Pakistan with aiding the separatists; fighting was especially heavy in May-June 1999.

A cease-fire between Indian and Pakistani troops along the line of control took effect Nov. 2003. Some breaches have occurred, and fighting between Indian forces and Islamic militants has continued. Estimates of conflict-related deaths since 1989 range from 40,000 to over 80,000. A powerful earthquake Oct. 8, 2005, killed about 80,000 and left up to 3 mil homeless in Pakistani-held Kashmir and northern Pakistan.

France, 1952-54, peacefully yielded to India its 5 colonies, former French India: Pondicherry, Karikal, Mahe, and Yanaon were merged to become Pondicherry, now Puducherry, area 185 sq mi; pop. (2011 census) 1,244,464. The colony of Chandernagor was incorporated into the state of West Bengal.

Indonesia
Republic of Indonesia

People: Population: 253,609,643. **Age distrib.:** <15: 26.2%; 65+: 6.5%. **Pop. density:** 362.6 per sq mi, 140 per sq km. **Urban:** 53%. **Ethnic groups:** Javanese 40%, Sundanese 16%, Malay 4%, Batak 4%, Madurese 3%, Betawi 3%, Minangkabau 3%, Buginese 3%, Bantenese 2%, Banjarese 2%, Balinese 2%. **Languages:** Bahasa Indonesia (official; modified form of Malay), English, Dutch, local dialects (Javanese most widely spoken). **Religions:** Muslim 87%, Christian 7%, Roman Catholic 3%, Hindu 2%.

Geography: Total area: 735,358 sq mi, 1,904,569 sq km; **Land area:** 699,451 sq mi, 1,811,569 sq km. **Location:** Archipelago SE of Asian mainland along the Equator. **Neighbors:** Malaysia on N, Papua New Guinea on E, Timor-Leste on S. **Topography:** Indonesia comprises over 13,500 islands (6,000 inhabited), including Java (one of the most densely populated areas in the world with more than 2,600 persons per sq mi), Sumatra, Kalimantan (most of Borneo), Sulawesi (Celebes), and West Irian (Irian Jaya, the W half of New Guinea). Also Bangka, Billiton, Madura, Bali, Timor. The mountains and plateaus on the major isls. have a cooler climate than the tropical lowlands. **Capital:** Jakarta, 10,176,000 (figure is for functional urban area). **Cities (urban aggl.):** Surabaya, 2,833,913; Bandung, 2,512,791; Medan, 2,181,597; Semarang, 1,613,999; Makassar (Ujung Pandang), 1,456,430.

Government: Type: Republic. **Head of state and gov.:** Pres. Susilo Bambang Yudhoyono; b. Sept. 9, 1949; in office: Oct. 20, 2004. **Local divisions:** 31 provinces, 1 autonomous province, 1 special region, 1 national capital district. **Defense budget:** $8.37 bil. **Active troops:** 395,500.

Economy: Industries: petroleum and nat. gas, textiles, automotive, elec. appliances, apparel, footwear, mining, cement, medical instruments and appliances, handicrafts, chemical fertilizers, plywood, proc. food, jewelry, tourism. **Chief crops:** rubber, palm oil, forest prods., cocoa, coffee, medicinal herbs. **Natural resources:** petroleum, tin, nat. gas, nickel, timber, bauxite, copper, coal, gold, silver. **Crude oil reserves:** 3.6 bil bbls. **Arable land:** 13%. **Livestock:**

cattle: 16.6 mil; chickens: 1.8 bil; goats: 18.6 mil; pigs: 8.2 mil; sheep: 14.6 mil. **Electricity prod.:** 172.7 bil kWh. **Labor force:** agric. 38.9%, industry 13.2%, services 47.9%. **Unemployment:** 6.6%.

Finance: Monetary unit: Rupiah (IDR) (Sept. 2014: 11,765.00 = $1 U.S.). **GDP:** $1.3 tril; **per capita GDP:** $5,200; **GDP growth:** 5.3%. **Imports:** $178.6 bil; China 15.3%, Singapore 13.6%, Japan 11.9%, Malaysia 6.4%, South Korea 6.2%, U.S. 6.1%, Thailand 6%. **Exports:** $178.9 bil; Japan 15.9%, China 11.4%, Singapore 9%, South Korea 7.9%, U.S. 7.8%, India 6.6%, Malaysia 5.9%. **Tourism:** $9.3 bil. **Budget:** $166 bil. **Total reserves less gold:** $96.4 bil. **Gold:** 2.5 mil oz t. **Inflation:** 6.4%.

Transport: Railways: 3,133 mi. **Motor vehicles:** 77.2 per 1,000 pop. **Civil aviation:** 45.4 mil pass.-mi; 186 airports. **Chief ports:** Banjarmasin, Belawan, Kotabaru, Krueg Geukueh, Palembang, Panjang, Sungai Pakning, Tanjung Perak, Tanjung Priok.

Communications: TV sets: 161 per 1,000 pop. **Radios:** 157 per 1,000 pop. **Telephone lines:** 16.1 per 100 pop. **Mobile:** 121.5 per 100 pop. **Internet:** 15.8%.

Health: Life expect.: 69.6 male; 74.9 female. **Births:** 17.0 per 1,000 pop. **Deaths:** 6.3 per 1,000 pop. **Natural inc.:** 1.07%. **Infant mortality:** 25.2 per 1,000 live births. **HIV:** 0.5%.

Education: Compulsory: ages 7-15. **Literacy:** 93.9%.

Embassy: 2020 Massachusetts Ave. NW 20036; 775-5200.

Website: www.indonesia.go.id

Hindu and Buddhist civilization from India reached Indonesia nearly 2,000 years ago, taking root especially in Java. Islam spread along the maritime trade routes in the 15th cent., and became predominant by the 16th cent. The Dutch replaced the Portuguese as the area's most important European trade power in the 17th cent., securing territorial control over Java by 1750. The outer islands were subdued in the early 20th cent.

Following Japanese occupation, 1942-45, nationalists led by Sukarno and Hatta declared independence. The Netherlands ceded sovereignty in 1949. A republic was declared, Aug. 17, 1950, with Sukarno as president. West Irian, on New Guinea, remained under Dutch control but was transferred by the UN to Indonesia in 1963.

Sukarno suspended parliament in 1960 and was named president for life in 1963. He made close alliances with Communist governments. In Sept. 1965 an attempted coup was successfully put down, but Sukarno was forced to cede power to the army, led by Gen. Suharto, who became acting president in 1967 and ruled Indonesia for the next 31 years. The regime blamed the coup on the Communist Party; more than 300,000 alleged Communists were killed in army-initiated massacres.

Parliament reelected Suharto to a seventh consecutive 5-year term in 1998, as a severe economic downturn focused public anger on nepotism, cronyism, and corruption in the Suharto regime. Price increases in May sparked mass protests and then mob violence in Jakarta and other cities, claiming some 500 lives. Suharto resigned May 21 and was succeeded by his vice president, Bacharuddin Jusuf Habibie. Abdurrahman Wahid, leader of Indonesia's largest Muslim organization, was elected president in 1999. In Aug. 2000, under pressure from the legislature, he agreed to share power with Vice Pres. Megawati Sukarnoputri, the daughter of the late Pres. Sukarno. Charging Wahid with incompetence and corruption, the legislature ousted him July 23, 2001, and Megawati became Indonesia's first woman president.

Clashes between Muslims and Christians in the Maluku (Molucca) Isls., 1999-2002, claimed about 5,000 lives. Ethnic violence in Kalimantan, Borneo, killed more than 400 in Feb. 2001. East Timor, a former Portuguese colony that Indonesia invaded in Dec. 1975 and controlled until Oct. 1999, became a fully independent country May 20, 2002, as Timor-Leste. Separatists in Aceh, NW Sumatra, fought against government troops during the 1980s and '90s; peace accords were announced in Dec. 2002. The deal unraveled, July 2005, and the last of 24,000 Indonesian troops pulled out of Aceh, Dec. 29, 2005.

Investigators blamed the Islamic terrorist group Jemaah Islamiyah, an al-Qaeda affiliate, for bombings that killed 202 people, mostly foreign tourists, at nightclubs in Bali, Oct. 12, 2002, and 12 people at a Marriott hotel in Jakarta, Aug. 5, 2003. A car bomb attack outside the Australian embassy in Jakarta, Sept. 9, 2004, killed 9 people. Susilo Bambang Yudhoyono, a retired general, defeated Megawati in a 2004 direct presidential runoff vote.

A massive earthquake off northwest Sumatra, Dec. 26, 2004, triggered tsunamis that wreaked havoc in the Indian Ocean region. The death toll in Indonesia alone exceeded 125,000, not counting almost 40,000 missing. Another large quake off northwest Sumatra, Mar. 28, 2005, left at least 1,300 dead. On Java in 2006, an earthquake May 27 killed 5,800; a tsunami July 17 claimed at least 650 lives.

Faced with falling oil production, Indonesia left OPEC in 2008. Pres. Yudhoyono won a second 5-year term July 8, 2009. Suicide bombings at 2 Jakarta hotels July 17 left 9 people dead. Police confirmed Sept. 17 that Noordin Muhammad Top, suspected of plotting the Jakarta attacks and other terrorist bombings, had been killed in a shootout.

Padang, Sumatra, was hit Sept. 30, 2009, by a powerful earthquake, which also triggered mudslides in the region; at least 1,115 people were killed. On Oct. 25, 2010, a 7.7-magnitude earthquake in the Mentawai Islands, off Sumatra's western coast, triggered a tsunami that killed at least 500 people; that same day, Mt. Merapi, a volcano near Yogyakarta in central Java, began a series of major eruptions that claimed at least 228 lives and displaced 430,500.

The General Elections Commission, July 22, 2014, declared populist Jakarta governor Joko Widodo the presidential election winner, with a 53% to 47% margin over former general Prabowo Subianto.

Iran
Islamic Republic of Iran

People: Population: 80,840,713. **Age distrib.:** <15: 23.7%; 65+: 5.2%. **Pop. density:** 136.7 per sq mi, 52.8 per sq km. **Urban:** 72.9%. **Ethnic groups:** Persian 61%, Azeri 16%, Kurd 10%, Lur 6%, Baloch 2%, Arab 2%, Turkmen and Turkic tribes 2%. **Languages:** Persian (official), Azeri Turkic and Turkic dialects, Kurdich, Gilaki and Mazandarani, Luri, Balochi, Arabic. **Religion:** Muslim (official) 99% (Shia 90%-95%, Sunni 5%-10%).

Geography: Total area: 636,372 sq mi, 1,648,195 sq km; **Land area:** 591,352 sq mi, 1,531,595 sq km. **Location:** Between the Middle East and S Asia. **Neighbors:** Turkey, Iraq on W; Armenia, Azerbaijan, Turkmenistan on N; Afghanistan, Pakistan on E. **Topography:** Interior highlands and plains surrounded by high mountains, up to 18,000 ft. Large salt deserts cover much of area, but there are many oases and forest areas. Most of population inhabits N and NW. **Capital:** Tehran, 8,352,930. **Cities (urban aggl.):** Mashhad, 2,940,341; Esfahan, 1,845,193; Karaj, 1,753,099; Shiraz, 1,604,327; Tabriz, 1,550,006; Ahvaz, 1,186,750; Qom, 1,173,819.

Government: Type: Theocratic republic. **Religious head:** Ayatollah Sayyed Ali Khamenei; b. July 17, 1939; in office: June 4, 1989. **Head of state and gov.:** Pres. Hassan Rouhani; b. Nov. 12, 1948; in office: Aug. 4, 2013. **Local divisions:** 31 provinces. **Defense budget:** $17.75 bil. **Active troops:** 523,000.

Economy: Industries: petroleum, petrochemicals, fertilizers, caustic soda, textiles, cement and other constr. materials, food proc. (sugar refining and vegetable oil prod.), metal fabrication, armaments. **Chief crops:** wheat, rice, other grains, sugar beets, sugarcane, fruits, nuts, cotton. **Natural resources:** petroleum, nat. gas, coal, chromium, copper, iron ore, lead, manganese, zinc, sulfur. **Crude oil reserves:** 157.3 bil bbls. **Arable land:** 10.9%. **Livestock:** cattle: 8.7 mil; chickens: 927 mil; goats: 22.1 mil; sheep: 50.2 mil. **Electricity prod.:** 225.8 bil kWh. **Labor force:** agric. 16.9%, industry 34.4%, services 48.7%. **Unemployment:** 13.1%.

Finance: Monetary unit: Rial (IRR) (Sept. 2014: 26,612.00 = $1 U.S.). **Budget:** $987.1 bil; **per capita GDP:** $12,800; **GDP growth:** –1.5%. **Imports:** $64.4 bil; UAE 33.2%, China 13.8%, Turkey 11.8%, South Korea 7.4%. **Exports:** $61.2 bil; China 22.1%, India 11.9%, Turkey 10.6%, South Korea 7.6%, Japan 7.1%. **Tourism:** $1.1 bil. **Budget:** $66.4 bil. **Total reserves less gold:** NA. **Inflation:** 39.3%.

Transport: Railways: 5,246 mi. **Motor vehicles:** 55.1 per 1,000 pop. **Civil aviation:** 10.3 bil pass.-mi; 140 airports. **Chief ports:** Assaluyeh, Bandar Abbas, Bandar-e-Eman Khomeyni.

Communications: TV sets: 170 per 1,000 pop. **Radios:** 734 per 1,000 pop. **Telephone lines:** 38.3 per 100 pop. **Mobile:** 84.3 per 100 pop. **Internet:** 31.4%.

Health: Life expect.: 69.3 male; 72.5 female. **Births:** 18.2 per 1,000 pop. **Deaths:** 5.9 per 1,000 pop. **Natural inc.:** 1.23%. **Infant mortality:** 39.0 per 1,000 live births. **HIV:** 0.1%.

Education: Compulsory: ages 6-13. **Literacy:** 86.9%.

Permanent UN mission: 622 3rd Ave., 34th Fl., New York, NY 10017; (212) 687-2020.

Website: www.president.ir

Ancestors of inhabitants of Iran, formerly known as Persia, came from the east during the second millennium BCE; they were an Indo-European group related to the Aryans of India. In 549 BCE, Cyrus the Great united the Medes and Persians in the Persian Empire; he conquered Babylonia in 538 BCE, and restored Jerusalem to the Jews. Alexander the Great conquered Persia in 333 BCE, but Persians regained independence in the next century under the Parthians, themselves succeeded by Sassanian Persians in 226 CE. Arabs brought Islam to Persia in the 7th cent., replacing the indigenous Zoroastrian faith. After Persian political and cultural autonomy was reasserted in the 9th cent., arts and sciences flourished.

Turks and Mongols ruled Persia in turn from the 11th cent. to 1502, when Ismael I established the Iranian Safavid dynasty and made Shiite Islam the official religion. The dynasty lasted until 1722. The British and Russian empires vied for influence in the 19th cent.; Britain severed Afghanistan from Iran in 1857.

Reza Khan, a military officer, became prime min., 1923, and shah in 1925. He began modernization, curbed foreign influence, and officially changed the country's name from Persia to Iran in 1935. Fearing the shah's Axis sympathies, British and Soviet troops forced him to abdicate, 1941; he was succeeded by his son, Mohammad Reza Pahlavi. The U.S. Central Intelligence Agency had a major role in the ouster, 1953, of Prime Min. Muhammad Mossadegh, who had nationalized the oil industry.

With U.S. backing, the shah brought economic and social change to Iran (White Revolution), but repression of opposition groups grew severe. Violent protests in 1978 eventually forced the shah to depart, Jan. 16, 1979. Shiite leader Ayatollah Ruhollah Khomeini,

exiled by the shah in 1963, returned to Tehran, Feb. 1. Pro-Khomeini forces defeated government troops, Feb 11. Khomeini established an Islamic theocracy.

Iranian militants seized the U.S. embassy in Tehran Nov. 4, 1979, and took hostages, including 62 Americans. Despite international condemnations and U.S. efforts, including an abortive Apr. 1980 rescue attempt, the crisis continued. The U.S. broke diplomatic relations with Iran, Apr. 7. The shah died in Egypt, July 27. The hostage drama ended Jan. 20, 1981, when an accord, involving the release of frozen Iranian assets, was reached.

A dispute over the Shatt al-Arab waterway between Iran and Iraq led to a long and costly war between the 2 countries, 1980-88, killing hundreds of thousands of people. In Nov. 1986 it became known that the U.S., which had generally sided with Iraq during the war, had secretly shipped arms to Iran to gain that country's help in obtaining the release of U.S. hostages held in Lebanon. The revelation sparked a major scandal in the U.S.A A U.S. Navy warship shot down an Iranian airliner, July 3, 1988, after mistaking it for an F-14 fighter jet; all 290 aboard died.

An earthquake struck northern Iran June 21, 1990, killing more than 45,000 and leaving 400,000 homeless. Some 1 mil Kurdish refugees fled from Iraq to Iran following the Persian Gulf War of 1991. To curb Iran's alleged support for international terrorism, the U.S. in 1996 authorized sanctions on foreign companies that invested there.

Mohammad Khatami, a moderate Shiite Muslim cleric, was elected president in 1997. During the next 3 years, hard-line Islamists clashed, sometimes violently, with reformers, who won a majority in 2000 parliamentary elections. Inviting rapprochement with Iran, the U.S. eased some sanctions Mar. 18. Khatami was reelected in 2001 but continued to face resistance from religious conservatives.

The U.S.-led war in Iraq, beginning Mar. 2003, contributed to a new period of instability in Iran. An earthquake Dec. 26 in Bam, SE Iran, killed about 26,000 people. After the Guardian Council, dominated by religious conservatives, disqualified some 2,400 reformist candidates, hard-liners won legislative elections Feb. 20, 2004.

The religiously conservative mayor of Tehran, Mahmoud Ahmadinejad, defeated former Pres. Hashemi Rafsanjani in a 2005 runoff election. U.S. Pres. George W. Bush's administration accused Iran of seeking to build nuclear weapons, aiding Shiite militias in Iraq, and supplying rockets to Hezbollah fighters in Lebanon for use against Israel.

Seeking to halt Iran's uranium-enrichment program, the UN Security Council imposed sanctions, Dec. 2006, and toughened them, Mar. 2007. After the Guardian Council disqualified about 1,700 reformist candidates, conservative allies of Ahmadinejad won parliamentary elections Mar.-Apr. 2008. Further talks on nuclear enrichment ended in deadlock July 20, and the U.S. imposed additional sanctions Sept. 10.

After a hard-fought campaign, Ahmadinejad won the 2009 presidential election. His main opponent, former Prime Min. Mir Hussein Moussavi claimed the official count, which gave Ahmadinejad more than 62% of the total vote, was fraudulent. Huge protests by Moussavi supporters in Tehran and other major cities were crushed. Tensions with the U.S. and European governments were heightened in late Sept. 2009 by disclosures that Iran had been secretly enriching uranium at an underground site near Qom, and by Iranian tests of medium-range missiles capable of reaching Israel or U.S. and European bases in the Persian Gulf region. Iran agreed in Oct. to allow international inspection of the Qom site and other nuclear safeguards.

The UN and U.S. toughened sanctions, June-July 2010, but did not object when loading of uranium fuel began in Aug. at Iran's Russian-built Bushehr nuclear power plant. Iran blamed Israel, the U.S., and other Western powers for carrying out cyberattacks against the country's nuclear facilities and for assassinating Iranian scientists. In Dec. 2010, the U.S. announced new sanctions targeting companies linked to Iran's nuclear program. The Bushehr plant began generating electricity for the national power grid in Sept. 2011. Iran further advanced its nuclear program, announcing Jan. 2012, that it was enriching uranium at its underground Fordo nuclear facility; more international sanctions followed.

Iran supported the Syrian government with military aid, 2012-14, in its civil war and reportedly provided military assistance to Iraqi forces combating extremist Sunni fighters in northern Iraq in 2014.

The moderate cleric Hassan Rouhani was elected president June 14, 2013, and took office Aug. 4. Rouhani and U.S. Pres. Barack Obama spoke on the telephone Sept. 27—the first time since 1979 that leaders of the two nations directly communicated. An interim agreement was reached Nov. 24, 2013, under which Iran pledged to limit some aspects of its nuclear program and allow wider international inspections in exchange for the temporary lifting of some sanctions. Negotiations toward a longer-term agreement continued in 2014.

Iraq
Republic of Iraq

People: Population: 32,585,692. **Age distrib.:** <15: 36.7%; 65+: 3.2%. **Pop. density:** 193 per sq mi, 74.5 per sq km. **Urban:** 69.4%.

Ethnic groups: Arab 75%-80%; Kurdish 15%-20%; Turkoman, Assyrian, other 5%. **Languages:** Arabic, Kurdish (both official); Turkmen, Assyrian (both official regionally); Armenian. **Religion:** Muslim (official) 99% (Shia 60%-65%, Sunni 32%-37%).

Geography: Total area: 169,235 sq mi, 438,317 sq km; **Land area:** 168,868 sq mi, 437,367 sq km. **Location:** In Middle East, occupying most of historic Mesopotamia. **Neighbors:** Jordan, Syria on W; Turkey on N; Iran on E; Kuwait, Saudi Arabia on S. **Topography:** Mostly an alluvial plain, including the Tigris and Euphrates rivers, descending from mountains in N to desert in SW. Persian Gulf region is marshland. **Capital:** Baghdad, 6,483,210. **Cities (urban aggl.):** Mosul, 1,641,513; Erbil, 1,132,382; Basra, 998,698.

Government: Type: Parliamentary democracy. **Head of state:** Pres. Fuad Masum; b. 1938; in office: July 24, 2014. **Head of gov.:** Prime Min. Haider al-Abadi; b. 1952; in office: Sept. 8, 2014. **Local divisions:** 18 governorates, 1 region (Kurdistan Regional Govt.). **Defense budget:** $16.9 bil. **Active troops:** 271,400.

Economy: Industries: petroleum, chemicals, textiles, leather, constr. materials, food proc., fertilizer, metal fabrication/proc. **Chief crops:** wheat, barley, rice, vegetables, dates, cotton. **Natural resources:** petroleum, nat. gas, phosphates, sulfur. **Arable land:** 7.9%. **Crude oil reserves:** 140.3 bil bbls. **Livestock:** cattle: 2.8 mil; chickens: 38 mil; goats: 1.6 mil; sheep: 8.3 mil. **Electricity prod.:** 51.2 bil kWh. **Labor force:** agric. 21.6%, industry 18.7%, services 59.8%. **Unemployment:** 15.1%.

Finance: Monetary unit: Dinar (IQD) (Sept. 2014: 1,162.00 = $1 U.S.). **GDP:** $249.4 bil; **per capita GDP:** $7,100; **GDP growth:** 4.2%. **Imports:** $66.6 bil; Turkey 27.5%, Syria 16.2%, China 12.5%, U.S. 5.2%, South Korea 4.7%. **Exports:** $92 bil; U.S. 21.1%, India 20.2%, China 13.6%, South Korea 11%, Canada 4.7%, Italy 4.4%, Spain 4.3%. **Tourism:** $1.6 bil. **Budget:** $97.4 bil. **Total reserves less gold:** $76.1 bil. **Gold:** 1.4 mil oz t. **Inflation:** 1.9%.

Transport: Railways: 1,473 mi. **Motor vehicles:** 55.1 per 1,000 pop. **Civil aviation:** 72 airports. **Chief ports:** Al Basrah, Khawr az Zubayr, Umm Qasr.

Communications: TV sets: 82 per 1,000 pop. **Radios:** 211 per 1,000 pop. **Telephone lines:** 5.6 per 100 pop. **Mobile:** 96.1 per 100 pop. **Internet:** 9.2%.

Health: Life expect.: 69.9 male; 73.0 female. **Births:** 26.9 per 1,000 pop. **Deaths:** 4.6 per 1,000 pop. **Natural incr.:** 2.23%. **Infant mortality:** 37.5 per 1,000 live births. **HIV:** NA.

Education: Compulsory: ages 6-11. **Literacy:** 79.7%.

Embassy: 3421 Massachusetts Ave. NW, 20007; 742-1600

Website: www.egov.gov.iq

The Tigris-Euphrates valley, formerly called Mesopotamia, was the site of one of the earliest civilizations in the world. Mesopotamia ceased to be a separate entity after Persian, Greek, and Arab conquests. The Arabs founded Baghdad, from where the caliph ruled a vast Islamic empire in the 8th and 9th cents. Mongol and Turkish conquests led to a decline in the region's population, economy, cultural life, and irrigation system.

Britain secured a League of Nations mandate over Iraq after WWI. Independence under a king came in 1932. Rebellious army officers killed King Faisal II, July 1958, and established a leftist, pan-Arab republic. The Baath Arab Socialist Party increasingly dominated successive regimes. A Baath leader, Saddam Hussein, became president in 1979. He ruled as a dictator for more than 2 decades, repressing Iraq's Kurds and Shiites. Israeli planes destroyed a nuclear reactor near Baghdad in 1981, claiming it could be used to produce nuclear weapons.

After skirmishing intermittently for 10 months over the sovereignty of the disputed Shatt al-Arab waterway dividing the 2 countries, Iraq and Iran entered into open warfare on Sept. 22, 1980. Iran repulsed early Iraqi advances, producing a long and costly stalemate; hundreds of thousands of Iraqis lost their lives during the 8-year conflict. Hussein used poison gas against Iraqi Kurds in 1988, killing more than 5,000 people in Halabja, the first mass use of poison gas against civilians since the Holocaust.

Iraq invaded Kuwait in 1990. Backed by the UN, a U.S.-led coalition launched air and missile attacks on Iraq, Jan. 16, 1991, and began a ground attack to retake Kuwait Feb. 23. Iraqi forces showed little resistance and were defeated in 4 days. Some 175,000 Iraqis were taken prisoner, and Iraqi casualties were estimated at over 85,000. As part of the cease-fire agreement, Iraq agreed to scrap all poison gas and germ weapons and allow UN observers to inspect the sites. UN trade sanctions would remain in effect until Iraq complied with all terms.

Iraqi cooperation with UN weapons inspection teams was intermittent throughout the 1990s. Standoffs over inspections led to diplomatic crises 1997-98, culminating in intensive U.S. and British aerial bombardment of Iraqi military targets, Dec. 16-19, 1998. After 2 years of sporadic activity, U.S. and British warplanes struck sites near Baghdad mid-Feb. 2001.

Despite opposition from some countries, including France, Germany, and Russia, a U.S.-led coalition invaded Iraq Mar. 19, 2003. By Apr. 6 the British controlled Basra and other areas in the south, and the U.S. entered Baghdad Apr. 9. Hussein disappeared, the Iraqi government collapsed, and most of Iraq's armed forces dissolved into the civilian population. On May 1, U.S. Pres. George W. Bush declared the end of major combat. Searches failed to find

chemical, biological, or nuclear weapons that the U.S. and other countries claimed Iraq had stockpiled.

The U.S.-led Coalition Provisional Authority was unable to maintain order in the weeks following Hussein's fall. Reconstruction efforts were hampered by guerrilla attacks from Baath remnants, Islamic extremists, and others. Coalition forces succeeded in neutralizing many leaders of the former regime. U.S. troops killed 2 of Hussein's sons, Uday and Qusay, July 22, 2003, in Mosul. Saddam Hussein was captured in an underground hideout mid-Dec. 2003; tried and convicted for committing crimes against humanity in the 1980s, he was executed Dec. 30, 2006.

Photographs released in Apr. 2004 showed instances of physical abuse and sexual humiliation of Iraqi inmates by U.S. military personnel at Baghdad's Abu Ghraib prison in 2003. The images sparked widespread condemnation and U.S. criminal proceedings against some individuals.

On June 28, 2004, U.S. authorities transferred sovereignty to a transitional Iraqi government. Despite insurgent threats, an estimated 8 mil people in Iraq, mostly Shiites and Kurds, cast ballots Jan. 30, 2005, for a transitional national assembly. The assembly elected Jalal Talabani, a Kurd, as president; Ibrahim al-Jaafari, a Shiite, became prime min. Insurgents launched new waves of attacks. Rumors of a suicide bomber set off a stampede by Shiite pilgrims in northern Baghdad Aug. 31, killing close to 1,000 people. The U.S. blamed Jordanian militant Abu Musab al-Zarqawi, leader of al-Qaeda in Iraq, for directing a series of kidnappings, beheadings, and suicide bombings. He was killed by a U.S. air strike, June 2006.

A new government elected in legislative elections Dec. 15, 2005, was installed May 20, 2006, headed by Shiite leader Nouri Kamel al-Maliki. The Iraqi civilian death toll averaged more than 2,800 per month in 2006.

A 2007 "surge" elevated U.S. troop strength from 132,000 in Jan. to 171,000 in Oct. U.S. troop deaths in 2007 totaled 899 (the highest for any year since the war began), but military and civilian casualties dropped steadily from mid-2007 through 2008. Contributing to the reduction in violence were a cease-fire by Shiite militias and a shift by Sunni clan leaders against al-Qaeda in Iraq.

A Nov. 2008, status-of-forces agreement called for the U.S. to withdraw its troops from Iraqi cities and towns by June 30, 2009, and for all U.S. forces to leave Iraq by Dec. 31, 2011. Legislative elections in 2010 brought gains by the Iraqi coalition headed by former Prime Min. Iyad Allawi, a Shiite who had campaigned as a secularist to win widespread Sunni support. On Aug. 31, Pres. Barack Obama formally declared an end to the U.S. combat role, and Operation Iraqi Freedom was succeeded by Operation New Dawn. More than 9 months of political deadlock ended when Prime Min. Maliki was sworn in for a second term Dec. 21, heading a unity government that included Shiite, Sunni, and Kurdish factions. Civilian casualties declined to about 200 per month during 2010.

U.S. troops completed their withdrawal from Iraq Dec. 15, 2011. From Mar. 2003 through Dec. 2011, more than 4,486 U.S. service members died in operations in Iraq; another 32,000 were wounded. British troop losses totaled 179; other allies, 139. More than 115,000 Iraqi civilians and over 10,000 police and security forces were killed. U.S. budgeted costs of the Iraq war exceeded $820 bil for the 2003-12 period.

Tensions manifested between Sunnis and Shiites after the U.S. departure. The Sunni-backed Iraqiya began a 6-week boycott of parliament Dec. 17, 2011, and accused Prime Min. Maliki of not sharing power. Maliki issued an arrest warrant for Sunni Vice Pres. Tariq al-Hashemi, Dec. 19, for terrorism. The Sunni insurgent group al-Qaeda in Iraq was blamed for ongoing violence; in periodic assaults throughout 2012, 4,573 civilians were killed. Violence accelerated; the UN reported Jan. 1, 2014, that violent attacks killed 8,868 people in Iraq during 2013, including at least 7,818 civilians, the highest annual toll since 2008. In 2014, at least 9,343 civilians were killed Jan.-Sept. according to UN estimates released Oct. 2.

In parliamentary elections Apr. 30, 2014, Maliki's coalition won the largest bloc of seats. Parliament elected, July 24, Kurdish politician Fuad Masum as the country's new president. On Aug. 11, Masum named Shiite Haider al-Abadi, of Maliki's Dawa Party, to be prime min.; parliament approved the appointment and most of Abadi's cabinet Sept. 8.

In Dec. 2013, Sunni extremist fighters of the self-proclaimed Islamic State in Iraq and Syria (ISIS) began crossing from Syria into Iraq and seizing territory. The ISIS offensive intensified beginning in June 2014. The group took control of large areas of northern and central Iraq and imposed Islamic law, including harsh punishments, in areas it controlled while suppressing non-Sunni Muslims and religious minorities. The U.S. (soon joined by other nations) began an airlift, Aug. 7, of food and water to tens of thousands of refugees, many of them members of the Yazidi sect, who had fled to barren Mount Sinjar in northern Iraq and were trapped by ISIS fighters. The U.S. (later joined by European and other allies) began, Aug. 8, airstrikes against ISIS forces, and the U.S. and other nations provided military aid to Kurdish fighters opposing ISIS. The U.S. announced, Aug. 13, that the siege of Mount Sinjar had been broken. A UN effort to aid up to 500,000 refugees from recent fighting in northern Iraq was announced Aug. 19. Pres. Obama stated Sept. 10, 2014, that 475 additional U.S. military advisers would be sent to Iraq, bringing the total to 1,600.

Ireland

People: Population: 4,832,765. **Age distrib.:** <15: 21.4%; 65+: 12.4%. **Pop. density:** 181.7 per sq mi, 70.2 per sq km. **Urban:** 63%. **Ethnic groups:** Irish 85%, other white 10%, Asian 2%. **Languages:** English (official; generally used), Irish (Gaelic or Gaeilge) (official; spoken mainly on W coast). **Religions:** Roman Catholic 85%, Church of Ireland 3%, other Christian 3%, none 6%.

Geography: Total area: 27,133 sq mi, 70,273 sq km; **Land area:** 26,596 sq mi, 68,883 sq km. **Location:** In Atlantic O. just W of Great Britain. **Neighbors:** UK (Northern Ireland) on E. **Topography:** Consists of a central plateau surrounded by isolated groups of hills and mountains. Coastline is heavily indented by the Atlantic O. **Capital:** Dublin, 1,154,900.

Government: Type: Parliamentary republic. **Head of state:** Pres. Michael D. Higgins; b. Apr. 18, 1941; in office: Nov. 11, 2011. **Head of gov.:** Prime Min. Enda Kenny; b. Apr. 24, 1951; in office: Mar. 9, 2011. **Local divisions:** 28 counties, 3 cities. **Defense budget:** $1.2 bil. **Active troops:** 9,350.

Economy: Industries: pharmaceuticals, chemicals, computer hardware and software, food prods., beverages and brewing, medical devices. **Chief crops:** barley, potatoes, wheat. **Natural resources:** nat. gas, peat, copper, lead, zinc, silver, barite, gypsum, limestone, dolomite. **Arable land:** 17%. **Livestock:** cattle: 6.9 mil; chickens: 15 mil; goats: 8,700; pigs: 1.6 mil; sheep: 5.1 mil. **Electricity prod.** (2012): 26.1 bil kWh. **Labor force:** agric. 5%, industry 19%, services 76%. **Unemployment:** 14.7%.

Finance: Monetary unit: Euro (EUR) (Sept. 2014: 0.76 = $1 U.S.). **GDP:** $190.4 bil. **per capita GDP:** $41,300; **GDP growth:** 0.6%. **Imports:** $61.5 bil; UK 39.8%, U.S. 13.2%, Germany 7.6%, Netherlands 5.7%. **Exports:** $113.6 bil; U.S. 17.9%, UK 17.3%, Belgium 15.6%, Germany 8.4%, Switzerland 5.8%, France 5%. **Tourism:** $4.4 bil. **Budget:** $91.3 bil. **Total reserves less gold:** $1.4 bil. **Gold:** 193,000 oz t. **Inflation:** 0.5%.

Transport: Railways: 2,011 mi. **Motor vehicles:** 481.5 per 1,000 pop. **Civil aviation:** 68.3 bil pass.-mi; 16 airports. **Chief ports:** Cork, Dublin, Shannon Foynes, Waterford.

Communications: TV sets: 715 per 1,000 pop. **Radios:** 695 per 1,000 pop. **Telephone lines:** 44 per 100 pop. **Mobile:** 102.8 per 100 pop. **Internet:** 78.3%.

Health: Life expect.: 78.3 male; 83.0 female. **Births:** 15.2 per 1,000 pop. **Deaths:** 6.5 per 1,000 pop. **Natural inc.:** 0.87%. **Infant mortality:** 3.7 per 1,000 live births. **HIV:** NA.

Education: Compulsory: ages 6-15. **Literacy:** 99%.

Embassy: 2234 Massachusetts Ave. NW 20008; 462-3939.

Website: www.gov.ie

Celtic tribes invaded the islands about the 4th cent. BCE; their Gaelic culture and literature flourished in the 5th cent. CE, the same century in which St. Patrick converted the Irish to Christianity. Norse invasions began in the 8th cent., ending with defeat of the Danes by the Irish King Brian Boru in 1014. English invasions started in the 12th cent. For over 700 years the Anglo-Irish struggle continued with bitter rebellions and savage repressions.

The Easter Monday Rebellion in 1916 failed but was followed by guerrilla warfare and harsh reprisals by British troops called the "Black and Tans." The Dail Eireann (Irish parliament) reaffirmed independence in Jan. 1919. The British offered dominion status to Ulster (6 counties) and southern Ireland (26 counties) Dec. 1921. The constitution of the Irish Free State, a British dominion, was adopted Dec. 11, 1922. Northern Ireland remained part of the UK (see United Kingdom—Northern Ireland).

A new constitution adopted by plebiscite came into operation Dec. 29, 1937. It declared the name of the state Eire in the Irish language (Ireland in the English) and declared it a sovereign democratic state. On Dec. 21, 1948, the country was declared a republic rather than a dominion and withdrew from the Commonwealth. The British Parliament recognized both actions, 1949, but the 6 northeastern counties remained in the UK.

Irish governments have favored peaceful unification of all Ireland and cooperated with Britain against terrorist groups. After negotiators in Northern Ireland approved a peace settlement on Good Friday, Apr. 10, 1998, voters in the Irish Republic endorsed the accord, on May 22, and the Irish gave up their constitution's territorial claims on the north.

Expansion of educational opportunities and foreign investment in high-tech industries in the 1990s boosted Ireland's prosperity. Ireland's first woman president, Mary Robinson, resigned Sept. 1997, to become UN high commissioner for human rights, 1997-2002. She was succeeded as president by Mary McAleese, a law professor from Northern Ireland and the first northerner to hold the office.

In an Oct. 2009 referendum, Irish voters approved the Lisbon Treaty, a plan to revamp the EU. Responding to a growing scandal over abusive Catholic clergy, Pope Benedict XVI issued a public apology to victims and their families Mar. 2010 and launched an official church investigation May 31 of Irish dioceses, seminaries, and religious orders.

To aid Ireland's ailing banks and prevent default after a 2008-10 financial crisis, finance ministers from EU member countries approved Nov. 2010 an 85 bil euro ($115 bil) emergency loan package that obligated Ireland to impose unpopular austerity measures. Fianna Fáil, the party that had dominated Irish politics since the 1930s, suffered a crushing defeat in Feb. 2011 elections, and Enda Kenny, leader of the opposition Fine Gael and a critic of the bailout, became prime minister. Ireland voted May 31, 2012, to ratify the 2012 European Fiscal Compact, which 25 of the 27 EU countries that had signed Mar. 2, 2012. Debate erupted over Ireland's abortion ban after an Indian woman having a miscarriage was denied a potentially life-saving abortion and died Oct. 28, 2012, prompting an inquiry. Lawmakers voted July 11, 2013, to legalize abortion when a woman's pregnancy is thought to jeopardize her life.

Israel
State of Israel

People: Population: 7,821,850. **Age distrib.:** <15: 27.1%; 65+: 10.7%. **Pop. density:** 996.5 per sq mi, 384.7 per sq km. **Urban:** 92.1%. **Ethnic groups:** Jewish 75% (Israel-born 74%, Europe/America/Oceania-born 18%, Africa-born 5%, Asia-born 3%), non-Jewish (mostly Arab) 25%. **Languages:** Hebrew, Arabic (both official); English (most common foreign lang.). **Religions:** Jewish 75%, Muslim 17%, Christian 2%, Druze 2%.

Geography: Total area: 8,019 sq mi, 20,770 sq km; **Land area:** 7,849 sq mi, 20,330 sq km. **Location:** Middle East, on E end of Mediterranean Sea. **Neighbors:** Lebanon on N; Syria, West Bank, Jordan on E; Gaza Strip, Egypt on W. **Topography:** The Mediterranean coastal plain is fertile and well-watered. In the center is the Judean Plateau. A triangular-shaped semi-desert region, the Negev, extends from S of Beersheba to an apex at head of Gulf of Aqaba. The E border drops sharply into the Jordan Rift Valley, including Lake Tiberias (Sea of Galilee) and the Dead Sea, which is 1,348 ft below sea level, lowest point in Asia. **Capital:** Jerusalem, 829,396. **Cities (urban aggl.):** Tel Aviv-Jaffa, 3,559,410; Haifa, 1,090,167.

Government: Type: Parliamentary democracy. **Head of state:** Pres. Reuven Rivlin; b. Sept. 9, 1939; in office: July 24, 2014. **Head of gov.:** Prime Min. Benjamin Netanyahu; b. Oct. 21, 1949; in office: Mar. 31, 2009. **Local divisions:** 6 districts. **Defense budget:** $15.16 bil. **Active troops:** 176,500.

Economy: Industries: high-tech prods. (incl. aviation, communications computer-aided design and manufactures, medical electronics, fiber optics), wood and paper prods., potash and phosphates, food, beverages, tobacco. **Chief crops:** citrus, vegetables, cotton. **Natural resources:** timber, potash, copper ore, nat. gas, phosphate rock, magnesium bromide, clays, sand. **Crude oil reserves:** 11.5 mil bbls. **Arable land:** 13.6%. **Livestock:** cattle: 465,000; chickens: 40.2 mil; pigs: 100,000; pigs: 176,900; sheep: 540,000. **Electricity prod.:** 56.1 bil kWh. **Labor force:** agric. 1.6%, industry 18.1%, services 80.3%. **Unemployment:** 6.9%.

Finance: Monetary unit: Shekel (ILS) (Sept. 2014: 3.58 = $1 U.S.). **GDP:** $273.2 bil; **per capita GDP:** $36,200; **GDP growth:** 3.3%. **Imports:** $67 bil; U.S. 12.9%, China 7.3%, Germany 6.3%, Switzerland 5.5%, Belgium 4.8%. **Exports:** $60.7 bil; U.S. 27.8%, Hong Kong 7.7%, UK 5.7%, Belgium 4.6%, China 4.3%. **Tourism:** $5.7 bil. **Budget:** $113.9 bil. **Total reserves less gold:** $81.8 bil. **Inflation:** 1.5%.

Transport: Railways: 606 mi. **Motor vehicles:** 353.5 per 1,000 pop. **Civil aviation:** 11.1 bil pass.-mi; 29 airports. **Chief ports:** Ashdod, Elat, Hadera, Haifa.

Communications: TV sets: 340 per 1,000 pop. **Radios:** 540 per 1,000 pop. **Telephone lines:** 44.8 per 100 pop. **Mobile:** 122.9 per 100 pop. **Internet:** 70.8%.

Health: Life expect.: 79.1 male; 83.6 female. **Births:** 18.4 per 1,000 pop. **Deaths:** 5.5 per 1,000 pop. **Natural inc.:** 1.29%. **Infant mortality:** 4.0 per 1,000 live births. **HIV:** NA.

Education: Compulsory: ages 5-15. **Literacy:** 97.8%.

Embassy: 3514 International Dr. NW 20008; 364-5500.

Website: www.gov.il

Occupying the southwest corner of the ancient Fertile Crescent, Israel contains some of the oldest known evidence of agriculture and of primitive town life. The Hebrews probably arrived early in the 2nd millennium BCE. Under King David and his successors (c. 1000 BCE-597 BCE), Judaism was developed and secured. After conquest by Babylonians, Persians, and Greeks, an independent Jewish kingdom was revived, 168 BCE, but Rome took over in the next century, suppressed Jewish revolts in 70 CE and 135 CE, and renamed Judea Palestine, after the earlier coastal inhabitants, the Philistines.

Arab invaders conquered Palestine in 636. The Arabic language and Islam prevailed within a few centuries, but a Jewish minority remained. The land was ruled from the 11th cent. as a part of non-Arab empires by Seljuks, Mamluks, and Ottomans (with a Crusader interval, 1098-1291).

After 4 centuries of Ottoman rule, the land was taken in 1917 by Britain, which pledged in the Balfour Declaration to support a Jewish homeland there. In 1920 a British Palestine Mandate was recognized; in 1922 the land east of the Jordan was detached.

Jewish immigration, begun in the late 19th cent., swelled in the 1930s with refugees from Nazi Germany; heavy Arab immigration from Syria and Lebanon also occurred. Arab opposition to Jewish immigration turned violent in 1920, 1921, 1929, and 1936. The UN General Assembly voted in 1947 to partition Palestine into an Arab and a Jewish state. Britain withdrew in May 1948.

Israel was declared independent May 14, 1948; Arabs rejected partition. Egypt, Jordan, Syria, Lebanon, Iraq, and Saudi Arabia invaded but failed to destroy the Jewish state, which gained territory. Separate armistices with the Arab nations were signed in 1949; Jordan occupied the West Bank, Egypt occupied Gaza. Neither granted Palestinian autonomy.

After persistent terrorist raids, Israel invaded Egypt's Sinai, Oct. 29, 1956, aided briefly by British and French forces. A UN cease-fire was arranged Nov. 6.

An uneasy truce between Israel and the Arab countries lasted until 1967, when Egypt reoccupied the Gaza Strip and closed the Gulf of Aqaba to Israeli shipping. In a 6-day war that started June 5, the Israelis took the Gaza Strip, occupied the Sinai Peninsula to the Suez Canal, and captured East Jerusalem, Syria's Golan Heights, and Jordan's West Bank. Together, the West Bank and Gaza comprise the Palestinian territories, now represented by the Palestinian Authority.

Egypt and Syria attacked Israel, Oct. 6, 1973 (Yom Kippur, the most solemn day in the Jewish calendar). Israel counterattacked, driving the Syrians back, and crossed the Suez Canal. A cease-fire took effect Oct. 24 and a UN peacekeeping force arrived. Under a 1974 disengagement agreement, Israel withdrew from the canal's west bank. Israeli forces raided Entebbe, Uganda, in 1976 and rescued 103 hostages who had been seized by Arab and German terrorists.

Israel's prime ministers, including David Ben-Gurion, Golda Meir, and Yitzhak Rabin, pursued a moderate socialist program, 1948-77. In 1977, the conservative opposition, led by Menachem Begin, was voted into office for the first time. Egypt's Pres. Anwar al-Sadat visited Jerusalem in 1977, and on Mar. 26, 1979, Egypt and Israel signed a formal peace treaty, ending 30 years of war. Israel returned the Sinai to Egypt in 1982.

Israeli forces invaded Lebanon, June 6, 1982, to destroy Palestine Liberation Organization (PLO) strongholds. After massive Israeli bombing of West Beirut, the PLO agreed to evacuate the city. Israeli troops entered West Beirut after newly elected Lebanese Pres. Bashir Gemayel was assassinated on Sept. 14. Israel drew widespread condemnation when Lebanese Christian forces, Sept. 16, entered 2 West Beirut refugee camps and slaughtered hundreds of Palestinians.

In 1989, violence escalated over the Israeli military occupation of the West Bank and Gaza Strip. In a series of uprisings known as the first intifada, Palestinian protesters defied Israeli troops, who forcibly retaliated. During the Persian Gulf War, 1991, Iraq fired Scud missiles at Israel.

Ongoing peace talks led to historic agreements between Israel and the PLO, Sept. 1993. The PLO recognized Israel's right to exist; Israel recognized the PLO as the Palestinians' representative. The 2 sides then signed, Sept. 13, an agreement for limited Palestinian self-rule in the West Bank and Gaza. Israel and Jordan signed, July 25, 1994, in Washington, DC, a declaration ending their 46-year state of war.

Arab and Jewish extremists repeatedly challenged the peace process. On Nov. 4, 1995, an Orthodox Jewish Israeli assassinated Labor Party Prime Min. Yitzhak Rabin as he left a peace rally in Tel Aviv. Support for Rabin's successor, Shimon Peres, was shaken by a series of suicide bombings and rocket attacks against Israel by Islamic militants. Emphasizing security issues, the candidate of the conservative Likud bloc, Benjamin Netanyahu, was elected prime minister on May 29, 1996.

Under an interim accord brokered by Pres. Bill Clinton and signed by Netanyahu and PLO leader Yasir Arafat at the White House, Oct. 23, 1998, Israel yielded more West Bank territory to the Palestinians, in exchange for new security guarantees. Full implementation did not begin until Sept. 1999. In the interim, Netanyahu lost to the Labor candidate, Ehud Barak, in the May 1999, election.

Israel pulled virtually all its troops out of southern Lebanon in May 2000. Marathon summit talks in the U.S. between Barak and Arafat, July 11-25, failed. A second intifada began in late Sept. in Israel and the Palestinian territories. Barak called new elections for prime minister but lost Feb. 2001 to Ariel Sharon, a hardliner. The bloodshed intensified during the summer, as Palestinian suicide bombers attacked Israeli civilians, and Israel struck at Palestinian-controlled territory attempting to assassinate suspected terrorists.

Israel launched a major West Bank offensive Mar. 29, 2002, 2 days after a suicide bomber killed 26 Israeli Jews at a Passover celebration in Netanya. A U.S.-sponsored "road map" to Middle East peace, unveiled Apr. 2003, made little headway.

Sharon's decision to pull all Israeli settlers and troops out of Gaza, approved by the cabinet Feb. 2005, led Israeli politics to be realigned. When right-wing Likud members opposed the plan, Sharon and Deputy Prime Min. Ehud Olmert broke with them and formed the centrist Kadima Party. Sharon suffered a massive stroke Jan. 4, 2006. With Sharon incapacitated, Olmert became prime minister, led Kadima to victory in Mar. elections, and formed a broad coalition government.

Clashes in mid-2006 along the Gaza and Lebanon borders rapidly escalated into full-scale war. Israeli air and ground forces hit hard in Gaza, but the fiercest fighting raged on the northern

front. By Aug. 14, when a UN-sponsored cease-fire took hold, the estimated death toll from the war included nearly 1,150 Lebanese, almost 200 Gaza Palestinians, and 150 Israelis. Olmert, criticized for leadership failures during the 2006 war and targeted in multiple corruption inquiries, announced his resignation July 30, 2008. (After a 4-year trial, he was acquitted of 2 counts of bribery but convicted of a lesser count of breach of public trust July 10, 2012.) Foreign Min. Tzipi Livni won a hard-fought party primary Sept. 17. Unable to form a stable government, she called early elections for Feb. 2009. After a campaign overshadowed by a 3-week war between Israel and Hamas in Gaza, both Kadima and Likud fell far short of a majority. On Mar. 31, Netanyahu became prime min. for a second time.

Israel's relations with allies were strained when senior Hamas commander Mahmoud al-Mabhouh was killed Jan. 2010 in Dubai, allegedly by agents of the Israeli spy agency Mossad who entered the UAE carrying false European and Australian passports. Further criticism greeted the Israeli government after its Mar. 2010 announcement that it would proceed to build 1,600 homes in Ramat Shlomo (a Jewish settlement in mostly Arab East Jerusalem), and later in the spring, when Israeli commandos killed 9 pro-Palestinian activists in clashes May 31 on board the Mavi Marmara, part of a flotilla that was seeking to break Israel's blockade of Gaza.

Arab Spring uprisings in 2011, which brought to power an Islamist government in neighboring Egypt (until July 2013) and shook other Middle Eastern regimes, unsettled Israeli policy in the region. Egyptian militants Aug. 18, 2011, killed 8 Israelis (6 civilians, 2 soldiers), and Israel killed at least 7 of the attackers, 3 Egyptian security officers, and, according to some reports, several civilians across the border.

Tensions from Iran and Israel have grown over Iran's nuclear program, which Israel sees as an existential threat. Prime Min. Netanyahu met in the U.S. with Pres. Barack Obama Mar. 2012; both nations pledged to use force against Iran if necessary, though the U.S. urged continued diplomacy.

Israel clashed with Palestinians in Gaza Oct.-Nov. 2012. In retaliation for the Gaza attacks, the hacker collective Anonymous launched cyberattacks on Israel before a cease-fire was declared Nov. 21, 2012.

Netanyahu's right-wing Likud-Yisrael Beitenu political bloc narrowly won Jan. 22, 2013, parliamentary elections. Netanyahu assembled a new coalition government Mar. 15.

Conflict between Israel and Hamas escalated in 2014. Rocket attacks from Gaza into Israel increased beginning in June. Israel blamed Hamas for the June 12 kidnapping and killing of 3 Israeli teenagers in the West Bank. Israel launched air and artillery attacks on targets in Gaza, including suspected missile launch sites, and Hamas intensified rocket attacks on Israel. Israeli ground forces entered Gaza July 17, in part to destroy tunnels used to infiltrate fighters into Israel. Israeli ground and air attacks caused high civilian casualties, for which international criticism mounted. It pulled out ground troops Aug. 5. Fighting resumed intermittently (rockets, artillery, air strikes) when a 3-day cease-fire ended Aug. 8. An Israeli airstrike Aug. 21, killed 3 top Hamas commanders. A new cease-fire was agreed Aug. 26. By that time, more than 2,100 Palestinians were estimated to have died in the conflict, and Israel reported 64 soldiers and 5 civilians killed.

Palestinian Territories

The Palestinian territories comprise the Gaza Strip, often called Gaza, and the West Bank, both occupied by Israel in 1967. Since 1996 the Palestinian Authority has been responsible for civil government in the territories. Elected president Jan. 20, 1996, PLO leader Yasir Arafat headed the Palestinian Authority until his death Nov. 11, 2004. Mahmoud Abbas (also called Abu Mazen), who had succeeded Arafat as PLO chairman and leader of the Fatah faction, was elected president Jan. 2005. A victory by Hamas militants in Jan. 2006 legislative elections led to a power struggle with Abbas, who favored a negotiated settlement with Israel. In bitter fighting, Hamas ousted Fatah from Gaza, June 2007, but Abbas retained power in the West Bank. Fatah and Hamas reached a reconciliation agreement Apr. 27, 2011, and announced Feb. 6, 2012, that Abbas would lead an interim unity government. However, Fatah-Hamas tensions increased in 2013. A new reconciliation agreement was completed Apr. 2014 and a unity government sworn in June 2. In a 2011 UN speech, Abbas sought full UN membership of an independent Palestinian state; the U.S. and Israel opposed the request. The General Assembly voted, Nov. 29, 2012, to make Palestine a non-member observer state.

The **Gaza Strip** extends NE from the Sinai Peninsula for 25 mi, with the Mediterranean Sea to the W and Israel to the E. The Palestinian Authority is responsible for civil government. Nearly all the inhabitants are Palestinian Arabs, more than 35% of whom live in refugee camps. Area 139 sq mi; pop. (2014 est.) 1,816,379.

Israel captured Gaza from Egypt in the 1967 war. It remained under Israeli occupation until May 1994, when the Israeli Defense Forces withdrew. Agreements between Israel and the PLO in 1993 and 1994 provided for interim self-rule in Gaza, but Israel retained control over security. Israel forcibly evacuated all 9,000 Jewish settlers from Gaza by Aug. 22, 2005, and the last remaining Israeli soldiers pulled out Sept. 12. Israel established a fortified barrier on its Gaza border to block Palestinian infiltrators.

After the Hamas takeover, Israel declared Gaza a "hostile entity," Sept. 19, 2007, and intensified military and economic pressures. Hamas thwarted an Israeli blockade, Jan. 2008, blowing up part of the border wall between Gaza and Egypt. Retaliating for Hamas rocket and mortar attacks, Israel launched an aerial assault and ground offensive in Gaza, Dec. 2008-Jan. 2009. A UN report issued in 2009 found evidence of war crimes committed by both sides. After the *Mavi Marmara* incident, Israel June 2010 eased some restrictions on the flow of goods to Gaza. Egypt's Islamist govt. lifted the blockade along its Gaza border May 28, 2011; however, Egypt's new government re-closed the border in 2013 and sought to destroy tunnels dug by Hamas to bring military and other equipment into Gaza.

Members of the Israeli Air Force, Oct. 31, 2012, assassinated Hamas's military chief, Ahmed al-Jabari, in the Gaza Strip.

The **West Bank** is located W of the Jordan R. and Dead Sea, bounded by Jordan on the E and by Israel on the N, W, and S. The Palestinian Authority administers several major cities, but Israel retains control over much land, including Jewish settlements. Area 2,263 sq mi; pop. (2014 est.) 2,731,052. The Palestinian Authority's National Security Force is a paramilitary organization of about 56,000 that maintains internal security in the West Bank.

Israel captured the West Bank from Jordan in the 1967 war. An accord between Israel and the PLO expanding Palestinian self-rule in the West Bank was signed Sept. 28, 1995. Later agreements gave Palestinians full or shared control of 40% of West Bank territory.

In June 2002 the Israeli government began building a controversial security barrier in the West Bank to restrict Palestinian access to Israel and reduce infiltration by suicide bombers. In a nonbinding ruling, July 9, 2004, the World Court said the barrier violated international law. Israel has continued to allow the expansion of Jewish settlements on the West Bank, despite U.S. government calls for a settlement freeze; at the beginning of 2014, about 350,000 Jewish settlers were living in the West Bank (not including East Jerusalem, which Israel annexed in 1967).

Italy
Italian Republic

People: Population: 61,680,122. **Age distrib.:** <15: 13.8%; 65+: 21%. **Pop. density:** 543.1 per sq mi, 209.7 per sq km. **Urban:** 68.8%. **Ethnic groups:** Italian (incl. small clusters of German-, French-, and Slovene-Italians in N; Albanian- and Greek-Italians in S). **Languages:** Italian (official), German, French, Slovene. **Religions:** Christian 80% (predominantly Roman Catholic), atheist and agnostic 20%.

Geography: Total area: 116,348 sq mi, 301,340 sq km; **Land area:** 113,568 sq mi, 294,140 sq km. **Location:** In S Europe, jutting into Mediterranean Sea. **Neighbors:** France on W; Switzerland, Austria on N; Slovenia on E; San Marino, Vatican City. **Topography:** Occupies long boot-shaped peninsula, extending SE from the Alps into Mediterranean, with islands of Sicily and Sardinia offshore. The alluvial Po Valley drains most of N. Rest of the country is rugged and mountainous, except for intermittent coastal plains, like the Campania S of Rome. Apennine Mts. run down length of peninsula. **Capital:** Rome, 3,697,150. **Cities (urban aggl.):** Milan, 3,093,844; Naples, 2,206,745; Turin, 1,761,119.

Government: Type: Republic. **Head of state:** Pres. Giorgio Napolitano; b. June 29, 1925; in office: May 15, 2006. **Head of gov.:** Prime Min. Matteo Renzi; b. Jan. 11, 1975; in office: Feb. 22, 2014. **Local divisions:** 20 regions (5 autonomous). **Defense budget:** $25.23 bil. **Active troops:** 176,000.

Economy: Industries: tourism, machinery, iron and steel, chemicals, food proc., textiles, motor vehicles, clothing, footwear, ceramics. **Chief crops:** fruits, vegetables, grapes, potatoes, sugar beets, soybeans, grain, olives. **Natural resources:** coal, mercury, zinc, potash, marble, barite, asbestos, pumice, fluorspar, feldspar, pyrite (sulfur), nat. gas and crude oil reserves, fish. **Crude oil reserves:** 560.5 mil bbls. **Arable land:** 24.2%. **Livestock:** cattle: 6.1 mil; chickens: 136 mil; goats: 891,604; pigs: 8.7 mil; sheep: 7 mil. **Electricity prod.** (2012): 286.2 bil kWh. **Labor force:** agric. 3.9%, industry 28.3%, services 67.8%. **Unemployment:** 10.7%.

Finance: Monetary unit: Euro (EUR) (Sept. 2014: 0.76 = $1 U.S.). **GDP:** $1.8 tril; **per capita GDP:** $29,600; **GDP growth:** −1.8%. **Imports:** $435.8 bil; Germany 14.7%, France 8.4%, China 8.4%, Russia 6.4%, Netherlands 5.9%, Spain 4.5%, Belgium 4.1%. **Exports:** $474 bil; Germany 12.6%, France 11.1%, U.S. 6.8%, Switzerland 5.7%, UK 4.7%, Spain 4.5%. **Tourism:** $43.9 bil. **Budget:** $1.1 tril. **Total reserves less gold:** $50.8 bil. **Gold:** 78.8 mil oz t. **Inflation:** 1.2%.

Transport: Railways: 12,586 mi. **Motor vehicles:** 680.4 per 1,000 pop. **Civil aviation:** 26.7 bil pass.-mi; 98 airports. **Chief ports:** Augusta, Cagliari, Genoa, Livorno, Sarroch, Taranto, Trieste, Venice.

Communications: TV sets: 492 per 1,000 pop. **Radios:** 878 per 1,000 pop. **Telephone lines:** 34.3 per 100 pop. **Mobile:** 158.9 per 100 pop. **Internet:** 58.5%.

Health: Life expect.: 79.4 male; 84.8 female. **Births:** 8.8 per 1,000 pop. **Deaths:** 10.1 per 1,000 pop. **Natural inc.:** −0.13%. **Infant mortality:** 3.3 per 1,000 live births. **HIV:** 0.3%.
Education: Compulsory: ages 6-15. **Literacy:** 99.2%.
Embassy: 3000 Whitehaven St. NW 20008; 612-4400.
Website: www.quirinale.it

Rome emerged as the major power in Italy after 500 BCE, dominating the Etruscans to the north and Greeks to the south. Under the Empire, which lasted until the 5th cent. CE, Rome ruled most of Western Europe, the Balkans, the Middle East, and North Africa. After Rome fell, Italy became a patchwork of kingdoms, principalities, and city-states until reunified, 1870.

The Fascist leader Benito Mussolini came to power, 1922, and aligned Italy with Nazi Germany in WWII. After Fascism was overthrown in 1943, Italy declared war on Germany and Japan and contributed to the Allied victory. It surrendered conquered lands and lost its colonies. Mussolini was killed by partisans Apr. 28, 1945. Victor Emmanuel III abdicated May 9, 1946; his son Humbert II was king until June 10, when Italy became a republic after a referendum, June 2-3. In the postwar decades, Italy had a succession of short-lived governments.

Christian Democratic leader and former prime min. Aldo Moro was abducted and murdered in 1978 by Red Brigade terrorists. The wave of left-wing political violence, including other kidnappings and assassinations, continued into the 1980s.

Political scandals marred the early 1990s, but in Mar. 1994 voting, under reformed election rules, right-wing parties won a majority, dislodging Italy's long-powerful Christian Democratic Party. Italy led a 7,000-member peacekeeping force in Albania, Apr.-Aug. 1997, and contributed 2,000 troops to the NATO-led security force (KFOR) that entered Kosovo in June 1999.

Supporters of Silvio Berlusconi, a multibillionaire media magnate, won the 2001 parliamentary elections. Berlusconi backed American-led military operations in Afghanistan (2001) and Iraq (2003). As of early Sept. 2014, about 1,400 Italian troops were serving with the NATO mission in Afghanistan.

A coalition of center-left parties led by Romano Prodi scored a narrow win over Berlusconi in 2008 parliamentary voting; Berlusconi returned at the head of a center-right coalition. An earthquake in the Abruzzo region of central Italy Apr. 6, 2009, battered the town of L'Aquila, killing more than 300 people. Sluggish economic growth and rising public debt (equal to about 120% of GDP in mid-2011) raised investors' concerns about Italy's financial stability. Berlusconi resigned Nov. 12, 2011, and Mario Monti, an economist, succeeded him Nov. 16. Italy's economic problems worsened, and its public debt reached nearly 2 tril euros ($2.5 tril) by Aug. 30, 2012. Monti announced Dec. 8, 2012, that he would resign the premiership, and elections Feb. 25, 2013, initially produced a deadlock. A coalition government was announced Apr. 27, 2013, with Enrico Letta as prime minister. After leading an intra-party revolt, Matteo Renzi replaced Letta, Feb. 22, 2014, promising political reforms and initiatives to revive the economy.

The luxury cruise ship *Costa Concordia* ran into a reef off the coast of Italy Jan. 13, 2012, killing 32 people. A Milan court found Berlusconi guilty of paying for sex with a teenager and using his office to cover it up, for which he received a 7-year sentence and a lifetime ban from holding public office, June 24, 2013. An appeals court overturned the verdict and sentence, July 18, 2014.

More than 100,000 African and Middle Eastern migrants fleeing violence and economic hardship crossed the Mediterranean to Italy, Jan.-Aug. 2014; almost 3 times the 2013 total; about 1,600 died trying to make the crossing to Europe, often in unseaworthy boats.

Sicily, 9,927 sq mi, pop. (2012 est.) 5,043,000, is an island 180 by 120 mi, seat of an autonomous region that embraces the island of Pantelleria, 32 sq mi, and the Lipari group, 44 sq mi, including 2 active volcanoes: Vulcano (1,637 ft) and Stromboli (3,031 ft). From prehistoric times Sicily has been settled by various peoples; a Greek state had its capital at Syracuse. Rome took Sicily from Carthage 215 BCE. Mt. Etna, a 10,925-ft active volcano, is its tallest peak.

Sardinia, 9,301 sq mi, pop. (2010 est.) 1,675,411, lies in the Mediterranean, 115 mi W of Italy and 7½ mi S of Corsica. It is 160 mi long, 68 mi wide, and mountainous, with mining of coal, zinc, lead, copper. In 1720, Sardinia was added to the possessions of the Dukes of Savoy in Piedmont and Savoy to form the Kingdom of Sardinia. Elba, 86 sq mi, lies 6 mi W of Tuscany. Napoleon I lived in exile on Elba 1814-15.

Jamaica

People: Population: 2,930,050. **Age distrib.:** <15: 28.4%; 65+: 7.8%. **Pop. density:** 700.7 per sq mi, 270.5 per sq km. **Urban:** 54.6%. **Ethnic groups:** black 92%, mixed 6%. **Languages:** English, English patois. **Religions:** Protestant 65% (incl. Seventh-day Adventist 12%, Pentecostal 11%), Roman Catholic 2%, none 21%.

Geography: Total area: 4,244 sq mi, 10,991 sq km; **Land area:** 4,182 sq mi, 10,831 sq km. **Location:** In W Indies. **Neighbors:** Nearest are Cuba to N, Haiti to E. **Topography:** Four-fifths of country covered by mountains. **Capital:** Kingston, 586,702.

Government: Type: Constitutional parliamentary democracy. **Head of state:** Queen Elizabeth II, rep. by Sir Patrick Allen;

b. Feb. 7, 1951; in office: Feb. 26, 2009. **Head of gov.:** Prime Min. Portia Simpson-Miller; b. Dec. 12, 1945; in office: Jan. 5, 2012. **Local divisions:** 14 parishes. **Defense budget:** $129 mil. **Active troops:** 2,830.

Economy: Industries: tourism, bauxite/alumina, agric. proc., light manufactures, rum, cement, metal, paper, chem. prods., telecom. **Chief crops:** sugarcane, bananas, coffee, citrus, yams. **Natural resources:** bauxite, gypsum, limestone. **Arable land:** 11.1%. **Livestock:** cattle: 170,000; chickens: 13.5 mil; goats: 520,000; pigs: 210,000; sheep: 1,350. **Electricity prod.:** 4.7 bil kWh. **Labor force:** agric. 17%, industry 19%, services 64%. **Unemployment:** 13.7%.

Finance: Monetary unit: Dollar (JMD) (Sept. 2014: 112.35 = $1 U.S.). **GDP:** $25.1 bil; **per capita GDP:** $9,000; **GDP growth:** 0.4%. **Imports:** $5.6 bil; U.S. 36.1%, Venezuela 15.6%, Trinidad and Tobago 10.8%, China 4.8%, Mexico 4%. **Exports:** $1.8 bil; U.S. 48%, Canada 7.2%, Slovenia 4.2%, Netherlands 4.1%, UAE 4.1%. **Tourism:** $2 bil. **Budget:** $4.1 bil. **Total reserves less gold:** $1.8 bil. **Inflation:** 9.3%.

Transport: Motor vehicles: 62.1 per 1,000 pop. **Civil aviation:** 11 airports. **Chief ports:** Kingston, Montego Bay, Port Antonio, Port Esquivel, Port Kaiser, Port Rhoades (Discovery Bay), Rocky Point.

Communications: TV sets: 382 per 1,000 pop. **Radios:** 23 per 1,000 pop. **Telephone lines:** 8.9 per 100 pop. **Mobile:** 100.4 per 100 pop. **Internet:** 37.8%.

Health: Life expect.: 71.9 male; 75.2 female. **Births:** 18.4 per 1,000 pop. **Deaths:** 6.7 per 1,000 pop. **Natural inc.:** 1.17%. **Infant mortality:** 13.7 per 1,000 live births. **HIV:** 1.8%.

Education: Compulsory: ages 6-11. **Literacy:** 88.7%.

Embassy: 1520 New Hampshire Ave. NW 20036; 452-0660.

Website: www.jis.gov.jm

Jamaica was visited by Columbus, 1494, and ruled by Spain (under whom Arawak Indians died out) until seized by Britain, 1655. Jamaica won independence Aug. 6, 1962. The island's rich musical innovations include ska and reggae. Rastafarianism is an influential religious movement.

In 1974 Jamaica sought an increase in taxes paid by U.S. and Canadian bauxite mines. The socialist government acquired 50% ownership of the companies' Jamaican interests in 1976. Rudimentary welfare state measures were passed. Relations with the U.S. improved in the 1980s when Jamaican politics entered a more conservative phase.

Portia Simpson-Miller, leader of the People's National Party (PNP), became Jamaica's first female prime min., Mar. 30, 2006. The opposition Jamaica Labour Party (JLP) won the parliamentary elections of Sept. 3, 2007. While trying to arrest an alleged gang leader, Christopher (Dudus) Coke, police and soldiers clashed with residents in the Tivoli Gardens section of Kingston in May 2010, leaving 76 people dead. Coke surrendered June 22, 2010, and was extradited to the U.S.; he pleaded guilty to racketeering charges in 2011. Prime Min. Bruce Golding resigned Oct. 23, 2011. The PNP won a landslide victory in Dec. 2011 elections; Simpson-Miller again became prime min. Jan. 2012.

Japan

People: Population: 127,103,388. **Age distrib.:** <15: 13.2%; 65+: 25.8%. **Pop. density:** 903.2 per sq mi, 348.7 per sq km. **Urban:** 93%. **Ethnic groups:** Japanese 98.5%, Korean 0.5%. **Language:** Japanese. **Religions:** Shintoism 84%, Buddhism 71% (many people observe both); Christian 2%.

Geography: Total area: 145,914 sq mi, 377,915 sq km; **Land area:** 140,728 sq mi, 364,485 sq km. **Location:** Archipelago off E coast of Asia. **Neighbors:** Russia to N, S. Korea to W. **Topography:** Consists of 4 main islands: Honshu ("mainland"), 87,805 sq mi; Hokkaido, 30,144 sq mi; Kyushu, 14,114 sq mi; and Shikoku, 7,049 sq mi. The coast, deeply indented, measures 16,654 mi. The northern islands are continuation of the Sakhalin Mts. The Kunlun range of China continues into southern islands, the ranges meeting in Japanese Alps. In a vast transverse fissure crossing Honshu E-W is a group of volcanoes, mostly extinct or inactive, including Mt. Fuji (Fujiyama) (12,388 ft) near Tokyo. **Capital:** Tokyo, 37,832,900 (figure is for Major Metro area). **Cities (urban aggl.):** Kinki Major Metro Area (MMA) (Osaka), 20,122,692; Chukyo MMA (Nagoya), 9,373,366; Kitakyushu-Fukuoka MMA, 5,527,567; Shizuoka-Hamamatsu MMA, 3,239,303; Sapporo, 2,579,092; Hiroshima, 2,165,736.

Government: Type: Parliamentary govt. with constitutional monarchy. **Head of state:** Emperor Akihito; b. Dec. 23, 1933; in office: Jan. 7, 1989. **Head of gov.:** Prime Min. Shinzo Abe; b. Sept. 21, 1954; in office: Dec. 26, 2012. **Local divisions:** 47 prefectures. **Defense budget:** $50.98 bil. **Active troops:** 247,150.

Economy: Industries: among world's largest and technologically advanced producers of motor vehicles, electronic equip., machine tools, steel and nonferrous metals, ships, chemicals, textiles, processed foods. **Chief crops:** rice, sugar beets, vegetables, fruit. **Natural resources:** negligible mineral resources, fish. **Crude oil reserves:** 44.1 mil bbls. **Arable land:** 11.6%. **Livestock:** cattle: 4.1 mil; chickens: 306.4 mil; goats: 16,700; pigs: 9.7 mil; sheep: 13,000. **Electricity prod.** (2012): 963 bil kWh. **Labor force:** agric. 3.9%, industry 26.2%, services 69.8%. **Unemployment:** 4.3%.

Finance: Monetary unit: Yen (JPY) (Sept. 2014: 104.84 = $1 U.S.). **GDP:** $4.7 tril; **per capita GDP:** $37,100; **GDP growth:** 2%. **Imports:** $766.6 bil; China 21.3%, U.S. 8.8%, Australia 6.4%, Saudi Arabia 6.2%, UAE 5%, South Korea 4.6%, Qatar 4%. **Exports:** $697 bil; China 18.1%, U.S. 17.8%, South Korea 7.7%, Thailand 5.5%, Hong Kong 5.1%. **Tourism:** $14.9 bil. **Budget:** $2.1 tril. **Total reserves less gold:** $1.2 tril. **Gold:** 24.6 mil oz t. **Inflation:** 0.4%.

Transport: Railways: 16,890 mi. **Motor vehicles:** 589.1 per 1,000 pop. **Civil aviation:** 76.2 bil pass.-mi; 142 airports. **Chief ports:** Chiba, Kawasaki, Kobe, Mizushima, Moji, Nagoya, Osaka, Tokyo, Tomakomai, Yokohama.

Communications: TV sets: 842 per 1,000 pop. **Radios:** 955 per 1,000 pop. **Telephone lines:** 50.4 per 100 pop. **Mobile:** 115.2 per 100 pop. **Internet:** 86.3%.

Health: Life expect.: 81.1 male; 88.0 female. **Births:** 8.1 per 1,000 pop. **Deaths:** 9.4 per 1,000 pop. **Natural inc.:** −0.13%. **Infant mortality:** 2.1 per 1,000 live births. **HIV:** NA.

Education: Compulsory: ages 6-14. **Literacy:** 99%.

Embassy: 2520 Massachusetts Ave. NW 20008; 238-6700.

Website: www.kantei.go.jp

According to Japanese legend, the empire was founded by Emperor Jimmu, 660 BCE, but earliest records of a unified Japan date from 1,000 years later. Chinese influence was strong in the formation of Japanese civilization. Buddhism was introduced before the 6th cent. CE.

A feudal system, with locally powerful noble families and their samurai warrior retainers, dominated from 1192. Central power was held by successive families of shoguns (military dictators), 1192-1867, until recovered by Emperor Meiji, 1868. The Portuguese and Dutch had minor trade with Japan in the 16th and 17th cents.; U.S. Commodore Matthew C. Perry opened the country to U.S. trade in a treaty ratified 1854. Industrialization began in the late 19th cent. Military conflicts won Taiwan from China, 1894-95, and the southern half of Sakhalin from Russia, 1904-05. Japan annexed Korea, 1910.

In WWI Japan ousted Germany from Shandong in China and took over German Pacific islands. Japan took Manchuria in 1931 and launched full-scale war in China in 1937. Japan attacked Pearl Harbor Dec. 7, 1941, launching a war with the U.S. The U.S. dropped atomic bombs on Hiroshima, Aug. 6, and Nagasaki, Aug. 9, 1945. Japan surrendered Aug. 14.

In a new constitution adopted May 3, 1947, Japan renounced the right to wage war; the emperor renounced claims to divinity; and the Diet became the sole lawmaking authority. The U.S. and 48 other non-Communist nations signed a peace treaty and the U.S. a bilateral defense agreement with Japan, in San Francisco 1951, restoring Japan's sovereignty as of Apr. 28, 1952.

Rebuilding after WWII, Japan emerged as one of the most powerful economies in the world. Japan's controversial import policies allowed it to accumulate huge trade surpluses.

In 1968, the U.S. returned control of the Bonin Isls., Volcano Isls. (including Iwo Jima), and Marcus Isls to Japan. In 1972, the U.S. returned Okinawa, the other Ryukyu Isls., and the Daito Isls., but the U.S. continued to maintain military bases on Okinawa. An agreement reached in 2012, would reduce the number of U.S. Marines stationed on Okinawa from 19,000 to 10,000.

The Liberal Democratic Party (LDP) governed Japan from the mid-1950s through early 1990s. In 1994, Tomiichi Murayama became Japan's first Socialist premier since 1947-48. An earthquake in the Kobe area in Jan. 1995 claimed more than 5,000 lives. With the country mired in a lengthy recession, the LDP regained power in 1996 and led Japan until 2009.

For the first time since WWII, Japan sent troops to an overseas warzone, when about 600 noncombat troops served in Iraq Feb. 2004-July 2006. In a move likely prompted by China's growing military strength, Japan announced, July 1, 2014, a new constitutional interpretation allowing the military to take offensive action to aid an ally, such as the U.S., under attack.

The 2008-09 global recession hit Japan hard, prompting a series of economic stimulus plans; the largest, unveiled Apr. 2009, called for more than $150 bil in spending and tax measures. The LDP suffered a crushing defeat in 2009 parliamentary elections, and Yukio Hatoyama of the opposition Democratic Party of Japan (DPJ) became prime min. His public support soon plummeted, and he was replaced June 2010 by former finance min. Naoto Kan.

A magnitude 9.0 earthquake and tsunami in the Pacific Ocean off Japan's east coast Mar. 11, 2011, left at least 18,500 people confirmed dead or listed as missing. Inundated by the tsunami, the Fukushima Daiichi nuclear power plant experienced meltdowns at 3 of the plant's 6 nuclear reactors, spewing radiation over a large area. Criticized for his response to the catastrophe, Prime Min. Naoto Kan submitted his resignation Aug. 26, 2011, and was succeeded by Finance Min. Yoshihiko Noda. Following the Fukushima Daiichi meltdowns, Japan began shutting down nuclear reactors for safety tests. Revised nuclear safety guidelines were announced in June 2013.

Prime Min. Noda resigned Dec. 26, 2012, after Dec. 16 elections swept LDP candidates into office, and former Prime Min. Shinzo Abe became prime minister. The ruling Liberal Democrats won upper-house elections July 21, 2013.

Jordan
Hashemite Kingdom of Jordan

People: Population: 6,528,061. **Age distrib.:** <15: 34.5%; 65+: 5.1%. **Pop. density:** 190.4 per sq mi, 73.5 per sq km. **Urban:** 83.4%. **Ethnic groups:** Arab 98%, Circassian 1%, Armenian 1%. **Languages:** Arabic (official), English widely understood among upper and middle classes. **Religions:** Muslim (official; most Sunni) 97%, Christian (most Greek Orthodox) 2%.

Geography: Total area: 34,495 sq mi, 89,342 sq km; **Land area:** 34,287 sq mi, 88,802 sq km. **Location:** In Middle East. **Neighbors:** Israel, West Bank on W; Saudi Arabia on S; Iraq on E; Syria on N. **Topography:** About 88% is arid. Fertile areas are in W. Only port is on short Aqaba Gulf coast. Country shares Dead Sea (1,348 ft below sea level) with Israel. **Capital:** Amman, 1,147,700 (excl. Syrian refugees).

Government: Type: Constitutional monarchy. **Head of state:** King Abdullah II; b. Jan. 30, 1962; in office: Feb. 7, 1999. **Head of gov.:** Prime Min. Abdullah Ensour; b. 1939; in office: Oct. 11, 2012. **Local divisions:** 12 governorates. **Defense budget:** $1.22 bil. **Active troops:** 100,500.

Economy: Industries: clothing, fertilizers, potash, phosphate mining, pharmaceuticals, petroleum refining, cement, inorganic chemicals, light mfg., tourism. **Chief crops:** citrus, tomatoes, cucumbers, olives, strawberries, stone fruits. **Natural resources:** phosphates, potash, shale oil. **Crude oil reserves:** 1 mil bbls. **Arable land:** 2.4%. **Livestock:** cattle: 69,000; chickens: 27 mil; goats: 795,000; sheep: 2.3 mil. **Electricity prod.:** 13.8 bil kWh. **Labor force:** agric. 2.7%, industry 20%, services 77.4%. **Unemployment:** 12.2%.

Finance: Monetary unit: Dinar (JOD) (Sept. 2014: 0.71 = $1 U.S.). **GDP:** $40 bil; **per capita GDP:** $6,100; **GDP growth:** 3.3%. **Imports:** $18.6 bil; Saudi Arabia 23.6%, China 9.4%, U.S. 6.7%, Italy 4.7%, Turkey 4.6%. **Exports:** $7.9 bil; U.S. 16.6%, Iraq 15.1%, Saudi Arabia 11%, India 10.5%, Indonesia 4.2%. **Tourism:** $4.1 bil. **Budget:** $10.7 bil. **Total reserves less gold:** $13.2 bil. **Gold** (2012): 400,000 oz t. **Inflation:** 5.5%.

Transport: Railways: 315 mi. **Motor vehicles:** 170 per 1,000 pop. **Civil aviation:** 5.2 bil pass.-mi; 16 airports. **Chief port:** Al Aqaba.

Communications: TV sets: 207 per 1,000 pop. **Radios:** 361 per 1,000 pop. **Telephone lines:** 5.2 per 100 pop. **Mobile:** 141.8 per 100 pop. **Internet:** 44.2%.

Health: Life expect.: 79.0 male; 81.9 female. **Births:** 25.9 per 1,000 pop. **Deaths:** 2.8 per 1,000 pop. **Natural inc.:** 2.31%. **Infant mortality:** 14.7 per 1,000 live births. **HIV:** NA.

Education: Compulsory: ages 6-15. **Literacy:** 95.4%.

Embassy: 3504 International Dr. NW 20008; 966-2664.

Website: www.kinghussein.gov.jo

From ancient times to 1922 the lands to the east of the Jordan R. were culturally and politically united with the lands to the W. Arabs conquered the area in the 7th cent.; the Ottomans took control in the 16th. Britain's 1920 Palestine Mandate covered both sides of the Jordan. In 1921, Abdullah, son of the ruler of Hejaz in Arabia, was installed by Britain as emir of an autonomous Transjordan, covering two-thirds of Palestine. An independent kingdom was proclaimed, 1946.

During the 1948 Arab-Israeli war, the West Bank and East Jerusalem were added to the kingdom, which changed its name to Jordan. These territories were lost to Israel in 1967, which swelled the number of Arab refugees on the East Bank.

Jordan and Israel officially agreed, July 25, 1994, to end their state of war; a peace treaty was signed Oct. 26. King Hussein died Feb. 7, 1999, ending a nearly 47-year reign; his eldest son assumed the throne as Abdullah II. The king responded to Arab Spring protests, 2011-12, by replacing his prime min. 3 times and somewhat liberalizing election laws in advance of Jan. 2013 parliamentary elections.

According to UNHCR data, more than 600,000 Syrian refugees, fleeing civil war, were living in Jordan in mid-2014. About 29,000 Iraqi refugees in Jordan were registered with the UNHCR, although the total number was believed to be much higher. Jordanian warplanes took part in U.S.-led airstrikes, beginning Sept. 23, 2014, against Sunni extremist forces in Syria.

Kazakhstan
Republic of Kazakhstan

People: Population: 17,948,816. **Age distrib.:** <15: 25.1%; 65+: 7%. **Pop. density:** 17.2 sq mi, 6.6 per sq km. **Urban:** 53.3%. **Ethnic groups:** Kazakh (Qazaq) 63%, Russian 24%, Uzbek 3%, Ukrainian 2%, Uighur 1%, Tatar 1%, German 1%. **Languages:** Kazakh (Qazaq) state lang.), Russian (official; used in everyday business). **Religions:** Muslim 70%, Christian (most Russian Orthodox) 26%, atheist 3%.

Geography: Total area: 1,052,090 sq mi, 2,724,900 sq km; **Land area:** 1,042,360 sq mi, 2,699,700 sq km. **Location:** In Central Asia. **Neighbors:** Russia on N; China on E; Kyrgyzstan, Uzbekistan, Turkmenistan on S; Caspian Sea on W. **Topography:** Extends from lower reaches of Volga in Europe to Altay Mts. on Chinese border. **Capital:** Astana, 740,964. **Cities (urban aggl.):** Almaty, 1,510,486.

Government: Type: Republic. **Head of state:** Pres. Nursultan Nazarbayev; b. July 6, 1940; in office: Apr. 24, 1990. **Head of gov.:** Prime Min. Karim Massimov; b. June 15, 1965; in office: Apr. 2, 2014. **Local divisions:** 14 provinces, 3 cities. **Defense budget:** $2.32 bil. **Active troops:** 39,000.

Economy: Industries: oil, coal, iron ore, manganese, chromite, lead, zinc, copper, titanium, bauxite, gold, silver, phosphates, sulfur, uranium, iron and steel, tractors and other agric. machinery, elec. motors, constr. materials. **Chief crops:** grain (mostly spring wheat, barley), potatoes, vegetables. **Natural resources:** petroleum, nat. gas, coal, iron ore, manganese, chrome ore, nickel, cobalt, copper, molybdenum, lead, zinc, bauxite, gold, uranium. **Crude oil reserves:** 30 bil bbls. **Arable land:** 8.5%. **Livestock:** cattle: 5.9 mil; chickens: 33.2 mil; goats: 2.4 mil; pigs: 922,296; sheep: 15.2 mil. **Electricity prod.:** 81.8 bil kWh. **Labor force:** agric. 25.8%, industry 11.9%, services 62.3%. **Unemployment:** 5.3%.

Finance: Monetary unit: Tenge (KZT) (Sept. 2014: 182.00 = $1 U.S.). **GDP:** $243.6 bil; **per capita GDP:** $14,100; **GDP growth:** 5%. **Imports:** $52 bil; China 28%, Ukraine 10.9%, Germany 8.5%, U.S. 7.9%. **Exports:** $87.2 bil; China 19.3%, Italy 18.1%, Netherlands 8.8%, France 6.6%, Switzerland 5.8%, Austria 5.8%. **Tourism:** $1.5 bil. **Budget:** $49 bil. **Total reserves less gold:** $19.1 bil. **Gold:** 4.6 mil oz t. **Inflation:** 5.8%.

Transport: Railways: 9,527 mi. **Civil aviation:** 4.3 bil pass.-mi; 63 airports. **Chief ports:** Aqtau, Atyrau, Oskemen.

Communications: TV sets: 497 per 1,000 pop. **Radios:** 215 per 1,000 pop. **Telephone lines:** 26.7 per 100 pop. **Mobile:** 180.5 per 100 pop. **Internet:** 54%.

Health: Life expect.: 65.0 male; 75.2 female. **Births:** 19.6 per 1,000 pop. **Deaths:** 8.3 per 1,000 pop. **Natural inc.:** 1.13%. **Infant mortality:** 21.6 per 1,000 live births. **HIV:** NA.

Education: Compulsory: ages 7-17. **Literacy:** 99.8%.

Embassy: 1401 16th St. NW 20036; 232-5488.

Website: www.government.kz

The region came under the Mongols' rule in the 13th cent. and gradually came under Russian rule, 1730-1853. It was admitted to the USSR as a constituent republic in 1936.

Kazakhstan's Dec. 16, 1991, declaration of independence became reality when the Soviet Union dissolved Dec. 26, 1991. The Communist Party chief, Nursultan Nazarbayev, was elected president unopposed. Dissent was suppressed. Nazarbayev encouraged Western investment in the oil industry, boosting the economy. Production began, Sept. 2013, at the Kashagan oil field, the largest outside the Middle East, in the Caspian Sea, though it was suspended in Oct. due to gas leaks.

Kazakhstan agreed, Feb. 1994, to dismantle nuclear missiles. Private land ownership was legalized Dec. 1995. Astana (formerly Akmola) became the nation's new capital, June 9, 1998. Reelected in 1999 and 2005, Pres. Nazarbayev was authorized to run for an unlimited number of terms under a constitutional amendment passed by parliament May 2007; he claimed more than 95% of the vote in the 2011 presidential election, deemed flawed by international election monitors. Nazarbayev's Nur Otan party won 81% of the vote in 2012 parliamentary elections, also faulted despite its introduction of 2 new parties into the formerly one-party parliament. With GDP growth sluggish, Nazarbayev named a new prime min., Karim Massimov, Apr. 2, 2014. An agreement to create a limited economic union of Kazakhstan, Russia, and Belarus was signed May 29, 2014.

Kenya
Republic of Kenya

People: Population: 45,010,056. **Age distrib.:** <15: 42.1%; 65+: 2.8%. **Pop. density:** 204.8 per sq mi, 79.1 per sq km. **Urban:** 25.2%. **Ethnic groups:** Kikuyu 22%, Luhya 14%, Luo 13%, Kalenjin 12%, Kamba 11%, Kisii 6%, Meru 6%, other African 15%, non-African 1%. **Languages:** English, Kiswahili (both official); numerous indigenous langs. **Religions:** Christian 83% (incl. Protestant 47%, Catholic 23%), Muslim 11%, none 2%.

Geography: Total area: 224,081 sq mi, 580,367 sq km; **Land area:** 219,746 sq mi, 569,140 sq km. **Location:** E Africa, on coast of Indian O. **Neighbors:** Uganda on W, Tanzania on S, Somalia on E, Ethiopia on N, Sudan on NW. **Topography:** The northern three-fifths of Kenya is arid. To S, a low coastal area and a plateau varying 3,000-10,000 ft. The Great Rift Valley enters the country N-S, flanked by high mountains. **Capital:** Nairobi, 3,767,650. **Cities (urban aggl.):** Mombasa, 1,068,408.

Government: Type: Republic. **Head of state and gov.:** Pres. Uhuru Kenyatta; b. Oct. 1961; in office: Apr. 9, 2013. **Local divisions:** 47 counties. **Defense budget:** $975 mil. **Active troops:** 24,120.

Economy: Industries: small-scale consumer goods (plastic, furniture, batteries, textiles, clothing, soap, cigarettes, flour), agric. prods., horticulture, oil refining, aluminum, steel, lead, cement. **Chief crops:** tea, coffee, corn, wheat, sugarcane, fruit, vegetables. **Natural resources:** limestone, soda ash, salt, gems, fluorspar, zinc, diatomite, gypsum, wildlife, hydropower. **Arable land:** 9.8%. **Livestock:** cattle: 19.5 mil; chickens: 32.5 mil; goats: 30 mil; pigs: 360,000; sheep: 18.5 mil. **Electricity prod.:** 7.6 bil kWh.

Labor force: agric. 75%, industry and services 25%. **Unemployment:** 9.2%.

Finance: Monetary unit: Shilling (KES) (Sept. 2014: 88.65 = $1 U.S.). **GDP:** $79.9 bil; **per capita GDP:** $1,800; **GDP growth:** 5.1%. **Imports:** $15.9 bil; India 20.9%, China 15.4%, UAE 9.8%, Saudi Arabia 6.9%. **Exports:** $6.6 bil; Uganda 10.3%, Tanzania 10%, Netherlands 7.7%, UK 7.2%, U.S. 6.3%, Egypt 4.8%, Dem. Rep. of the Congo 4.4%. **Tourism:** $935 mil. **Budget:** $9.7 bil. **Total reserves less gold:** $6.6 bil. **Gold:** 600 oz t. **Inflation:** 5.7%.

Transport: Railways: 1,284 mi. **Motor vehicles:** 26.3 per 1,000 pop. **Civil aviation:** 6.2 bil pass.-mi; 16 airports. **Chief ports:** Kisumu, Mombasa.

Communications: TV sets: 46 per 1,000 pop. **Radios:** 89 per 1,000 pop. **Telephone lines:** 0.5 per 100 pop. **Mobile:** 70.6 per 100 pop. **Internet:** 39%.

Health: Life expect.: 62.1 male; 65.0 female. **Births:** 28.3 per 1,000 pop. **Deaths:** 7.0 per 1,000 pop. **Natural inc.:** 2.13%. **Infant mortality:** 40.7 per 1,000 live births. **HIV:** 6.0%.

Education: Compulsory: ages 6-13. **Literacy:** 78%.

Embassy: 2249 R St. NW 20008; 387-6101.

Website: www.statehousekenya.go.ke

Arab colonies exported spices and slaves from the Kenya coast as early as the 8th cent. Britain obtained control in the 19th cent. Kenya won independence Dec. 12, 1963, 4 years after the end of the violent Mau Mau uprising. Jomo Kenyatta, the country's leader since independence, died Aug. 22, 1978. He was succeeded by his vice president, Daniel arap Moi.

During the first half of the 1990s, Kenya suffered widespread unemployment and high inflation. Tribal clashes in the western provinces claimed thousands of lives and left tens of thousands homeless. Pres. Moi won a 3rd term in Dec. 1992 elections, which were marred by violence and fraud. He was reelected Dec. 1997 in an election plagued by irregularities. A truck bomb explosion at the U.S. embassy in Nairobi, Aug. 7, 1998, killed more than 200 people and injured about 5,000. The U.S. blamed the attack and a near-simultaneous embassy bombing in Tanzania on al-Qaeda.

Constitutionally barred from seeking another term, Pres. Moi was succeeded Dec. 2002, by Mwai Kibaki, the candidate of the opposition Democratic Party. After a disputed election Dec. 2007, that drew criticism from European and Kenyan monitors, Kenya's Electoral Commission declared Kibaki the winner over challenger Raila Odinga. Weeks of factional violence followed, leaving some 1,500 people dead and 600,000 displaced. Under a Feb. 28, 2008, power-sharing deal mediated by former UN Sec.-Gen. Kofi Annan, Kibaki remained president and Odinga took the newly created post of prime minister. A new constitution curtailing presidential powers, establishing a senate, and reforming regional government won approval in an Aug. 2010 referendum. The Intl. Criminal Court Jan. 2012, charged 4 with crimes against humanity for their roles in the postelection violence. Two of those charged, Deputy Prime Min. Uhuru Kenyatta and former Education Min. William Ruto, were candidates in the Mar. 4, 2013, presidential election, in which Kenyatta was declared the winner Mar. 10 amid accusations of vote-rigging. After several postponements, his trial was scheduled to begin Oct. 2014. The UNHCR estimated that more than 482,000 Somali refugees were living in Kenya at the beginning of 2014. The Somali Islamist group al-Shabaab carried out a series of deadly terrorist attacks in Kenya, 2013-14.

Kiribati
Republic of Kiribati

People: Population: 104,488. **Age distrib.:** <15: 31.5%; 65+: 4%. **Pop. density:** 333.7 per sq mi, 128.8 per sq km. **Urban:** 44.2%. **Ethnic groups:** I-Kiribati 89.5%, I-Kiribati/mixed 9.7%. **Languages:** I-Kiribati, English (both official). **Religions:** Roman Catholic 56%, Kempsville Presbyterian Church 34%, Mormon 5%, Baha'i 2%, Seventh-day Adventist 2%.

Geography: Total area: 313 sq mi, 811 sq km; **Land area:** 313 sq mi, 811 sq km. **Location:** 33 atolls (the Gilbert, Line, and Phoenix Isls.) in mid-Pacific scattered over an area of about 1.35 mil sq mi around the point where the International Date Line formerly crossed the Equator. The Date Line was moved in 1997 to follow Kiribati's E border. **Neighbors:** Nearest are Nauru to SW, Tuvalu and Tokelau Isls. to S. **Topography:** Except Banaba (Ocean) Isl., all are low-lying, with soil of coral sand and rock fragments, subject to erratic rainfall. **Capital:** Tarawa, 45,915 (figure is for Tarawa Isl.).

Government: Type: Republic. **Head of state and gov.:** Pres. Anote Tong; b. June 11, 1952; in office: July 10, 2003. **Local divisions:** 3 geographical units. **Defense budget/active troops:** NA.

Economy: Industries: fishing, handicrafts. **Chief crops:** copra, taro, breadfruit, sweet potatoes, vegetables. **Natural resources:** phosphate (production discontinued in 1979). **Arable land:** 2.5%. **Livestock:** chickens: 610,000; pigs: 13,500. **Electricity prod.:** 25 mil kWh. **Labor force:** agric. 2.7%, industry 32%, services 65.3%. **Unemployment:** NA.

Finance: Monetary unit: Dollar (AUD) (Sept. 2014: 1.07 = $1 U.S.). **GDP:** $698 mil; **per capita GDP:** $6,400; **GDP growth:** 2.9%. **Imports** (2010): $80.1 mil. **Exports** (2010): $7.1 mil. **Budget** (2010 est.): $107.1 mil. **Total reserves less gold:** NA. **Inflation:** NA.

Transport: Civil aviation: 4 airports. **Chief ports:** Betio, English Harbor.

Communications: TV sets: 41 per 1,000 pop. **Radios:** 830 per 1,000 pop. **Telephone lines:** 8.8 per 100 pop. **Mobile:** 16.6 per 100 pop. **Internet:** 11.5%.

Health: Life expect.: 63.0 male; 68.0 female. **Births:** 21.9 per 1,000 pop. **Deaths:** 7.2 per 1,000 pop. **Natural inc.:** 1.47%. **Infant mortality:** 35.4 per 1,000 live births. **HIV:** NA.

Education: Compulsory: ages 6-14. **Literacy:** NA.

Permanent UN mission: 800 Second Ave., Ste. 400A, New York, NY 10017; (212) 867-3310.

Website: www.parliament.gov.ki

A British protectorate since 1892, the Gilbert and Ellice Islands colony was completed with the inclusion of the Phoenix Islands, 1937. Tarawa Atoll was the scene of some of the bloodiest fighting in the Pacific during WWII.

Self-rule was granted 1971; the Ellice Islands separated from the colony in 1975 and became independent Tuvalu, 1978. Kiribati (pronounced *Kiribass*) independence was attained July 12, 1979. Under a treaty of friendship the U.S. relinquished its claims to several Line and Phoenix islands. Kiribati was admitted to the UN in 1999. Pres. Anote Tong won reelection Oct. 2007. Kiribati's land area is shrinking as a result of rising sea levels, and Tong announced Mar. 7, 2012, negotiations with Fiji to buy 5,000 acres of land on which Kiribati farmers and other people could relocate.

Korea, North
Democratic People's Republic of Korea

People: Population: 24,851,627. **Age distrib.:** <15: 21.5%; 65+: 9.7%. **Pop. density:** 534.6 per sq mi, 206.4 per sq km. **Urban:** 60.7%. **Ethnic group:** mostly homogeneous. **Language:** Korean.

Religions: traditionally Buddhist and Confucianist, some Christian and syncretic Chondogyo; autonomous religious activities almost nonexistent.

Geography: Total area: 46,540 sq mi, 120,538 sq km; **Land area:** 46,490 sq mi, 120,408 sq km. **Location:** In northern E Asia. **Neighbors:** China and Russia on N, S. Korea on S. **Topography:** Mountains and hills cover nearly entire country, with narrow valleys and small plains in between. N and E coasts are most rugged areas. **Capital:** P'yongyang, 2,856,050.

Government: Type: Communist state. **Head of state:** Kim Jong Un; b. Jan. 8, 1983; officially assumed post Dec. 17, 2011. **Head of gov.:** Prem. Pak Pong Ju; b. Oct. 24, 1939; in office: Apr. 2, 2013. **Local divisions:** 9 provinces, 2 municipalities. **Defense budget:** NA. **Active troops:** 1,190,000.

Economy: Industries: military prods.; machine building, elec. power, chemicals; mining, metallurgy; textiles, food proc. **Chief crops:** rice, corn, potatoes, soybeans. **Natural resources:** coal, lead, tungsten, zinc, graphite, magnesite, iron ore, copper, gold, pyrites, salt, fluorspar, hydropower. **Arable land:** 19.5%. **Livestock:** cattle: 590,000; chickens: 18 mil; goats: 3.6 mil; pigs: 2.3 mil; sheep: 170,000. **Electricity prod.:** 21 bil kWh. **Labor force:** agric. 35%, industry and services 65%. **Unemployment:** 4.6%.

Finance: Monetary unit: Won (KPW) (Sept. 2014: 130.38 = $1 U.S.). **GDP** (2012): $40 bil; **per capita GDP** (2011): $1,800; **GDP growth** (2012): 1.3%. **Imports** (2012): $4.8 bil; China 73%, South Korea 19%. **Exports** (2012): $4 bil; China 63%, South Korea 27%. **Budget** (2007 est.): $3.3 bil. **Total reserves less gold:** NA. **Inflation:** NA.

Transport: Railways: 3,257 mi. **Civil aviation:** 39 airports. **Chief ports:** Chongjin, Haeju, Hungnam, Nampo, Senbong, Sonbong, Songnim, Wonsan.

Communications: TV sets: 172 per 1,000 pop. **Radios:** 157 per 1,000 pop. **Telephone lines:** 4.7 per 100 pop. **Mobile:** 9.7 per 100 pop.

Health: Life expect.: 66.0 male; 73.9 female. **Births:** 14.5 per 1,000 pop. **Deaths:** 9.2 per 1,000 pop. **Natural inc.:** 0.53%. **Infant mortality:** 24.5 per 1,000 live births. **HIV:** NA.

Education: Compulsory: ages 6-16. **Literacy:** 100%.

Permanent UN mission: 820 Second Ave., 13th Fl., New York, NY 10017; (212) 972-3105.

Website: www.korea-dpr.com

The Democratic People's Republic of Korea was founded May 1, 1948, in the zone occupied by Russia after WWII. Its armies tried to conquer the south, 1950. After 3 years of fighting, with Chinese and U.S. intervention, a cease-fire was proclaimed.

For the next 4 decades, a hard-line Communist regime headed by Kim Il Sung kept tight control over the nation's political, economic, and cultural life. The nation used its abundant mineral and hydroelectric resources to develop its military strength and heavy industry. By the early 1990s, North Korea was widely believed to be developing nuclear weapons. The U.S. and North Korea signed an agreement, Oct. 21, 1994, providing for phased dismantling of North Korea's nuclear development program in return for U.S. energy aid and improved ties with the U.S.

Kim Il Sung died July 8, 1994. He was succeeded by his son, Kim Jong Il. Defections by high officials, a deteriorating economy, and severe food shortages plagued North Korea in the late 1990s. A first-ever summit conference in P'yongyang between North and

South Korean leaders, June 13-15, 2000, marked an improvement in relations between the 2 nations. North Korea and Japan agreed to normalize relations in a Sept. 2002 summit.

In Oct. 2002, North Korea admitted to pursuing a secret nuclear weapons program, in violation of past agreements. The U.S. insisted that North Korea end its nuclear weapons program, while P'yongyang demanded a nonaggression treaty and economic aid from the U.S. During 2003-09, as 6-nation talks sponsored by China sought to resolve the nuclear dispute, North Korea followed a zigzag course, alternately stopping and resuming its nuclear program in order to win concessions from the U.S.

In Apr.-May 2009, North Korea suspended participation in the 6-nation talks, expelled IAEA inspectors, tested multiple missiles, and exploded a nuclear device underground. The UN Security Council June 12 toughened sanctions on North Korea. Tensions between North and South Korea increased after the Mar. 26, 2010, sinking of the South Korean warship *Cheonan* killed 46 sailors; a South Korean panel including international investigators concluded May 20 that the *Cheonan* had been torpedoed by a North Korean submarine.

Kim Jong Il died Dec. 17, 2011. He was succeeded by his son Kim Jong Un. In an apparent move to consolidate his power, Kim Jong Un ordered the execution, Dec. 2013, of his uncle, Jang Song Thaek, who had been considered one of the most powerful political figures in North Korea.

Kim Jong Un frequently threatened the U.S. and South Korea in rhetoric and action. North Korea launched a satellite into space Dec. 12, 2012, demonstrating its rocket capabilities. It conducted a nuclear test Feb. 10, 2013, and threatened to launch a nuclear strike against the U.S., Mar. 7, after additional sanctions were levied against it in response to its nuclear test. North Korea also negated, Mar. 11, 2013, the cease-fire agreement with the South that ended the Korean War. It conducted numerous short- and long-range missile tests 2013-14, as well as directing artillery fire at South Korea.

Korea, South
Republic of Korea

People: Population: 49,039,986. **Age distrib.:** <15: 14.1%; 65+: 12.7%. **Pop. density:** 1,310.5 per sq mi, 506 per sq km. **Urban:** 82.4%. **Ethnic group:** mostly homogeneous. **Languages:** Korean, English (widely taught in school). **Religions:** Christian 32% (Protestant 24%, Roman Catholic 8%), Buddhist 24%, none 43%.

Geography: Total area: 38,502 sq mi, 99,720 sq km; **Land area:** 37,421 sq mi, 96,920 sq km. **Location:** In northern E Asia. **Neighbors:** North Korea on N. **Topography:** Mountainous, with a rugged E coast. W and S coasts are deeply indented, with many islands and harbors. **Capital:** Seoul, 9,775,380; Sejong City (planned). **Cities (urban aggl.):** Busan, 3,236,750; Incheon, 2,659,489; Daegu, 2,250,061; Daejon, 1,550,082; Gwangju, 1,523,044.

Government: Type: Republic. **Head of state:** Pres. Park Geun Hye; b. Feb. 2, 1952; in office: Feb. 25, 2013. **Head of gov.:** Prime Min. Chung Hongwon; b. Oct. 9, 1944; in office: Feb. 26, 2013. **Local divisions:** 9 provinces, 8 cities. **Defense budget:** $31.85 bil. **Active troops:** 655,000.

Economy: Industries: electronics, telecom, auto prod., chemicals, shipbuilding, steel. **Chief crops:** rice, root crops, barley, vegetables, fruit. **Natural resources:** coal, tungsten, graphite, molybdenum, lead, hydropower potential. **Arable land:** 15.6%. **Livestock:** cattle: 3.3 mil; chickens: 151.3 mil; goats: 260,000; pigs: 9.9 mil; sheep: 3,090. **Electricity prod.** (2012): 494.7 bil kWh. **Labor force:** agric. 6.9%, industry 23.6%, services 69.4%. **Unemployment:** 3.2%.

Finance: Monetary unit: Won (KRW) (Sept. 2014: 1,017.58 = $1 U.S.). **GDP:** $1.7 tril; **per capita GDP:** $33,200; **GDP growth:** 2.8%. **Imports:** $516.6 bil; (2011) China 15.6%, Japan 12.4%, U.S. 8.3%, Saudi Arabia 7.6%, Qatar 4.9%, Australia 4.4%. **Exports:** $557.3 bil; China 24.5%, U.S. 10.7%, Japan 7.1%, Hong Kong 6%, Singapore 4.2%. **Tourism:** $14.3 bil. **Budget:** $287.2 bil. **Total reserves less gold:** $341.6 bil. **Gold:** 3.4 mil oz t. **Inflation:** 1.3%.

Transport: Railways: 2,101 mi. **Motor vehicles:** 396.3 per 1,000 pop. **Civil aviation:** 59.3 bil pass.-mi; 71 airports. **Chief ports:** Busan, Incheon, Pohang, Ulsan, Yeosu.

Communications: TV sets: 424 per 1,000 pop. **Radios:** 1,037 per 1,000 pop. **Telephone lines:** 61.6 per 100 pop. **Mobile:** 111 per 100 pop. **Internet:** 84.8%.

Health: Life expect.: 76.7 male; 83.1 female. **Births:** 8.3 per 1,000 pop. **Deaths:** 6.6 per 1,000 pop. **Natural inc.:** 0.16%. **Infant mortality:** 3.9 per 1,000 live births. **HIV:** NA.

Education: Compulsory: ages 6-14. **Literacy:** NA.

Embassy: 2320 Massachusetts Ave. NW 20008; 939-5663.

Website: www.korea.net

Korea, once called the Hermit Kingdom, has a recorded history since the 1st cent. BCE. It was united in a kingdom under the Silla Dynasty, 668 CE. It was at times associated with the Chinese empire; the treaty that concluded the Sino-Japanese war of 1894-95 recognized Korea's complete independence. In 1910 Japan forcibly annexed Korea as Chosun.

At the Potsdam conference, July 1945, the 38th parallel was designated as the line dividing Soviet and U.S. occupation zones. Russian troops entered Korea Aug. 10, 1945; U.S. troops entered Sept. 8.

The South Koreans formed the Republic of Korea in May 1948 with Seoul as the capital. Dr. Syngman Rhee was chosen president. A separate, Communist regime was formed in the North; its army attacked the south in June 1950, initiating the Korean War. UN troops, under U.S. command, supported South Korea in the war, which ended in an armistice (July 1953) leaving Korea divided by a demilitarized zone (DMZ) along the 38th parallel.

Rhee's authoritarian rule became increasingly unpopular, and a movement spearheaded by college students forced his resignation Apr. 26, 1960. In an army coup May 16, 1961, Gen. Park Chung Hee became chairman of a ruling junta. He was elected president, 1963; a 1972 referendum allowed him to be reelected for an unlimited series of 6-year terms. Park was assassinated by the chief of the Korean CIA, Oct. 26, 1979.

In May 1980, Gen. Chun Doo Hwan, head of military intelligence, ordered the brutal suppression of pro-democracy demonstrations in Kwangju. On July 1, 1987, following weeks of sometimes violent antigovernment protests, Chun agreed to democratic reforms. In Dec., Roh Tae Woo, a longtime ally of Chun's, was elected president. In 1990, the nation's 3 largest political parties merged; some 100,000 students protested the merger as undemocratic.

Pres. Kim Young Sam took office in 1993. Convicted of mutiny, treason, and corruption, Chun was sentenced to death by a Seoul court, Aug. 26, 1996, for his role in the 1979 coup and 1980 Kwangju massacre; Roh received a 225-year prison sentence.

The 1997 collapse of the Hanbo steel firm triggered a series of corruption scandals. With currency and stock values plummeting, the nation averted default by agreeing, Dec. 4, on a $57-bil bailout from the IMF. Kim Dae Jung, a longtime dissident, won the presidential election Dec. 18. Chun and Roh were released and pardoned Dec. 22.

At a summit meeting in P'yongyang, June 13-15, 2000, Pres. Kim Dae Jung and North Korean leader Kim Jong Il agreed to work for reconciliation and eventual reunification of their 2 countries. On Oct. 13, 2000, Kim Dae Jung was named the winner of the Nobel Peace Prize. Roh Moo Hyun won the 2002 presidential election.

The National Assembly, Mar. 12, 2004, impeached Pres. Roh Moo Hyun for violating political neutrality and urging voters to support the Uri Party; the Constitutional Court May 14 restored Roh to office. The IAEA Sept. 2 said South Korea had acknowledged having secretly processed a small amount of uranium to near weapons-grade level in 2000, violating the Nuclear Non-Proliferation Treaty and a bilateral accord with N. Korea.

Ban Ki-Moon, South Korea's foreign minister, 2004-06, became UN sec.-gen. Jan. 1, 2007. Lee Myung Bak, a former construction executive and Seoul mayor, won the presidential election Dec. 19. Former Pres. Roh Moo Hyun, under investigation for corruption, committed suicide May 23, 2009.

Tensions between South Korea and Japan came to the fore after Pres. Lee Myung-bak, Aug. 10, visited Dokdo, a group of small islands that South Korea administers but Japan claims. Conservative Park Geun Hye became South Korea's first female president in Dec. 19, 2012, elections.

On Mar. 11, 2013, North Korea declared a negation of the cease-fire agreement with the South that had ended the Korean War; North Korea asserted, Mar. 29, that a state of war existed between it and the South. The U.S., which had about 28,000 troops in South Korea at the beginning of 2014, announced Jan. 7 it would send an additional 800 soldiers, along with tanks and other equipment. The sinking, Apr. 16, 2014, of the ferry *Sewol* off the South Korean coast caused the deaths of more than 300 people, many of them high school students. Unsafe practices by the ferry company were blamed for the disaster. Pope Francis, Aug. 14, began a 5-day visit to South Korea, the first by a pope in 25 years.

Kosovo
Republic of Kosovo

People: Population: 1,859,203. **Age distrib.:** <15: 26.3%; 65+: 6.9%. **Pop. density:** 442.3 per sq mi, 170.8 per sq km. **Urban:** NA. **Ethnic groups:** Albanian 92%, other (incl. Serb, Bosniak, Gorani, Roma, Turk, Ashkali, Egyptian) 8%. **Languages:** Albanian, Serbian (both official); Bosnian; Turkish; Roma. **Religions:** Muslim, Serbian Orthodox, Roman Catholic.

Geography: Total area: 4,203 sq mi, 10,887 sq km. **Land area:** 4,203 sq mi, 10,887 sq km. **Location:** SE Europe between Serbia and Macedonia. **Neighbors:** Serbia on N, Montenegro on NW, Albania on SW, Macedonia on SE. **Topography:** Low flood basins surrounded by several high mountain ranges. **Capital:** Pristina.

Government: Type: Republic. **Head of state:** Pres. Atifete Jahjaga; b. Apr. 20, 1975; in office: Apr. 7, 2011. **Head of gov.:** Prime Min. Hashim Thaçi; b. Apr. 24, 1968; in office: Jan. 9, 2008. **Local divisions:** 37 municipalities. **Defense budget/active troops:** NA.

Economy: Industries: mineral mining, constr. materials, base metals, leather, machinery, appliances, foodstuffs and beverages, textiles. **Chief crops:** wheat, corn, berries, potatoes, peppers, fruit.

Natural resources: nickel, lead, zinc, magnesium, lignite, kaolin, chrome, bauxite. **Arable land:** NA. **Labor force:** agric. 23.6%. **Unemployment:** NA.
Finance: Monetary unit: Euro (EUR) (Sept. 2014: 0.76 = $1 U.S.). **GDP:** $14.1 bil; **per capita GDP:** $7,600; **GDP growth:** 2.5%. **Imports** $3.4 bil; Germany 11.9%, Macedonia 11.5%, Serbia 11.1%, Italy 8.5%, Turkey 9%, China 6.4%, Albania 4.4%. **Exports:** $408 mil; Italy 25.8%, Albania 14.6%, Macedonia 9.6%, China 5.5%, Germany 5.4%, Switzerland 5.4%, Turkey 4.1%. **Budget:** $2 bil. **Total reserves less gold:** $1.1 bil. **Inflation:** 1.8%.
Transport: Railways: 267 mi. **Civil aviation:** 3 airports.
Communications: NA.
Health: Life expect.: 69.0 male; 73.3 female. **Births:** 17.4 per 1,000 pop. **Deaths:** 7.0 per 1,000 pop. **Natural inc.:** 1.04%. **Infant mortality:** 37.8 per 1,000 live births. **HIV:** NA.
Education: NA. **Literacy:** NA.
Embassy: 900 19th St. NW, Ste. 400, 20006; 380-3581.
Website: www.rks-gov.net

Kosovo was part of the Roman and Byzantine empires before Serbs, a Slavic people, took control in the Middle Ages. After Ottoman Turks defeated Serb forces, 1389, Kosovo's population became predominantly Muslim and Kosovar (ethnic Albanian). Serbia regained control in the First Balkan War (1912-13). Kosovo entered the Kingdom of Serbs, Croats, and Slovenes as part of Serbia after World War I and became an autonomous province of Serbia, a constituent republic of Yugoslavia, after World War II.

Revoking provincial autonomy, Serbia began ruling Kosovo by force in 1989. Albanian secessionists proclaimed an independent Republic of Kosovo in July 1990. As Yugoslavia collapsed, the republics of Serbia (incl. Kosovo) and Montenegro proclaimed a new Federal Republic of Yugoslavia, 1992, under Pres. Slobodan Milosevic. Guerrilla attacks by the Kosovo Liberation Army (KLA) in 1997 brought a ferocious counteroffensive by Serbian authorities.

Fearful that the Serbs were employing "ethnic cleansing" tactics, as they had in Bosnia, the U.S. and its NATO allies pressured the Yugoslav government to end hostilities. When Milosevic refused, NATO launched an air war against Yugoslavia, Mar.-June 1999; the Serbs retaliated by terrorizing the Kosovars. Hundreds of thousands fled, mostly to Albania and Macedonia. A 50,000-member multinational force (KFOR) entered Kosovo in June, and most refugees returned by Sept. 1, 1999.

From June 1999, Kosovo was administered by a UN mission (UNMIK). Kosovo declared independence, Feb. 17, 2008, and the U.S. and most European allies immediately recognized the new country, Serbia and Russia refused. In a nonbinding ruling, the World Court held July 22, 2010, that Kosovo's independence declaration was legal. Kosovo and Serbia, Apr. 19, 2013, completed negotiating a power-sharing agreement between the northern Kosovo regions with a Serb majority and the Kosovo central government led by ethnic Albanians. At the end of 2013, KFOR had almost 5,000 troops in Kosovo. An EU special prosecutor reported, July 29, 2014, evidence of "unlawful killings, abductions, enforced disappearances," and other acts of ethnic cleansing against Serbs by the KLA in the late 1990s. Prime Min. Hashim Thaçi, who headed the KLA at that time, had denied any wrongdoing.

Kuwait
State of Kuwait

People: Population: 2,742,711. **Age distrib.:** <15: 25.4%; 65+: 2.2%. **Pop. density:** 398.7 per sq mi, 153.9 per sq km. **Urban:** 98.3%. **Ethnic groups:** Asian 38%, Kuwaiti 31%, other Arab 28%, African 2%. **Languages:** Arabic (official), English widely spoken. **Religions:** Muslim (official) 77%, Christian 17%.
Geography: Total area: 6,880 sq mi, 17,818 sq km; **Land area:** 6,880 sq mi, 17,818 sq km. **Location:** In Middle East, at N end of Persian Gulf. **Neighbors:** Iraq on N, Saudi Arabia on S. **Topography:** Flat, very dry, and extremely hot. **Capital:** Kuwait City, 2,680,320.
Government: Type: Constitutional emirate. **Head of state:** Emir Sheikh Sabah al-Ahmad al-Jabir al-Sabah; b. June 6, 1929; in office: Jan. 29, 2006. **Head of gov.:** Prime Min. Sheikh Jaber al-Mubarak al-Hamad al-Sabah; b. Jan. 5, 1942; in office: Nov. 30, 2011. **Local divisions:** 6 governorates. **Defense budget:** $4.43 bil. **Active troops:** 15,500.
Economy: Industries: petroleum, petrochemicals, cement, shipbuilding and repair, water desalination, food proc., constr. materials. **Chief crops:** fish. **Natural resources:** petroleum, fish, shrimp, nat. gas. **Crude oil reserves:** 104 bil bbls (incl. half of Neutral Zone reserves). **Arable land:** 0.6%. **Livestock:** cattle: 36,000; chickens: 33 mil; goats: 174,000; sheep: 477,000. **Electricity prod.:** 54 bil kWh. **Labor force:** NA. **Unemployment:** 1.5%.
Finance: Monetary unit: Dinar (KWD) (Sept. 2014: 0.28 = $1 U.S.). **GDP:** $165.8 bil; **per capita GDP:** $42,100; **GDP growth:** 2.3%. **Imports:** $24.4 bil; U.S. 11.8%, China 9.2%, Saudi Arabia 8.6%, Japan 8.2%, South Korea 6.9%, Germany 5.1%, India 4.6%, UAE 4.4%. **Exports:** $112 bil; South Korea 16.1%, India 15.7%, Japan 13.4%, U.S. 11.7%, China 9.2%, Singapore 4.2%. **Tourism:** $298 mil. **Budget:** $61.8 bil. **Total reserves less gold:** $32.2 bil. **Gold:** 2.5 mil oz t. **Inflation:** 2.6%.

Transport: Motor vehicles: 650.8 per 1,000 pop. **Civil aviation:** 5.6 bil pass.-mi; 4 airports. **Chief ports:** Ash Shuaybah, Ash Shuwaykh, Az Zawr, Mina Abd Allah, Mina al Ahmadi.
Communications: TV sets: 399 per 1,000 pop. **Radios:** 572 per 1,000 pop. **Telephone lines** 15.1 per 100 pop. **Mobile:** 190.3 per 100 pop. **Internet:** 75.5%.
Health: Life expect.: 76.4 male; 79.0 female. **Births:** 20.3 per 1,000 pop. **Deaths:** 2.2 per 1,000 pop. **Natural inc.:** 1.81% **Infant mortality:** 7.5 per 1,000 live births. **HIV:** NA.
Education: Compulsory: ages 6-14. **Literacy:** 96.3%.
Embassy: 2940 Tilden St. NW 20008; 966-0702.
Website: www.da.gov.kw

Kuwait is ruled by the Sabah dynasty, founded 1759. Britain ran foreign relations and defense from 1899 until independence in 1961. Nearly half the population is non-Kuwaiti, including many Palestinians, and cannot vote.

Oil is the fiscal mainstay, providing most of Kuwait's income. Oil pays for free medical care, education, and social security. There are no taxes, except customs duties.

Kuwait was attacked and overrun by Iraqi forces Aug. 1990. In Operation Desert Storm a U.S.-led coalition, with authorization from the UN Security Council, began bombing Iraq and Iraqi forces in Kuwait, Jan. 1991, then launched a ground assault Feb. 23. By Feb. 27, Iraqi forces were routed and Kuwait liberated.

Political rights were extended to women, May 16, 2005; the first female cabinet member was appointed June 12. Kuwait enacted a $5.2 bil program Mar. 2009 to bail out banks and investment companies battered by the global financial crisis. The moderate Jaber al-Mubarak al-Hamad al-Sabah was reappointed prime min. July 2012, after resigning in response to a June 2012 ruling of the Constitutional Court that declared unconstitutional the Feb. 2011 elections that had brought him to power. Al-Sabah dissolved parliament Oct. 7, 2012, and called for new elections, but the opposition-led boycott resulted in just a 39% turnout for a Dec. 2 vote. The Constitutional Court dissolved parliament again June 16, 2013, and in elections held July 27 some liberal and marginalized tribal groups won seats, though the majority of seats were won by lawmakers who support Kuwait's ruling family.

Kyrgyzstan
Kyrgyz Republic

People: Population: 5,604,212. **Age distrib.:** <15: 29.8%; 65+: 4.9%. **Pop. density:** 75.7 per sq mi, 29.2 per sq km. **Urban:** 35.6%. **Ethnic groups:** Kyrgyz 65%, Uzbek 14%, Russian 13%, Dungan 1%, Ukrainian 1%, Uighur 1%. **Languages:** Kyrgyz, Russian (both official); Uzbek. **Religions:** Muslim 75%, Russian Orthodox 20%.
Geography: Total area: 77,202 sq mi, 199,951 sq km; **Land area:** 74,055 sq mi, 191,801 sq km. **Location:** In Central Asia. **Neighbors:** Kazakhstan on N, China on E, Uzbekistan on W, Tajikistan on S. **Topography:** Landlocked country nearly covered by Tien Shan and Pamir Mts.; avg. elevation 9,020 ft. A large lake, Issyk-Kul, in NE is 1 mi above sea level. **Capital:** Bishkek, 857,711.
Government: Type: Republic. **Head of state:** Pres. Almazbek Sharshenovich Atambayev; b. Sept. 17, 1956; in office: Dec. 1, 2011. **Head of gov.:** Prime Min. Joomart Otorbaev; b. 1955; in office: Apr. 2, 2014. **Local divisions:** 7 provinces, 2 cities. **Defense budget:** $102 mil. **Active troops:** 10,900.
Economy: Industries: small machinery, textiles, food proc., cement, shoes, sawn logs, refrigerators, furniture, elec. motors. **Chief crops:** tobacco, cotton, potatoes, vegetables, grapes, fruits and berries. **Natural resources:** hydropower, gold, rare earth metals, coal, oil, nat. gas, nepheline, mercury, bismuth, lead, zinc. **Crude oil reserves:** 40 mil bbls. **Arable land:** 6.7%. **Livestock:** cattle: 1.4 mil; chickens: 3.8 mil; goats: 960,391; pigs: 51,777; sheep: 4.7 mil. **Electricity prod.:** 15 bil kWh. **Labor force:** agric. 48%, industry 12.5%, services 39.5%. **Unemployment:** 8.4%.
Finance: Monetary unit: Som (KGS) (Sept. 2014: 52.96 = $1 U.S.). **GDP:** $14.3 bil; **per capita GDP:** $2,500; **GDP growth:** 7.4%. **Imports:** $5.1 bil; China 55.2%, Russia 17.4%, Kazakhstan 7.9%. **Exports:** $1.9 bil; Kazakhstan 26.2%, Uzbekistan 26.1%, Russia 14.6%, China 7%, UAE 6.1%, Afghanistan 5.2%. **Tourism:** $435 mil. **Budget:** $2.5 bil. **Total reserves less gold:** $2.1 bil. **Gold:** 116,065 oz t. **Inflation:** 6.6%.
Transport: Railways: 292 mi. **Civil aviation:** 18 airports. **Chief port:** Balykchy.
Communications: TV sets: 224 per 1,000 pop. **Radios:** 110 per 1,000 pop. **Telephone lines:** 8.3 per 100 pop. **Mobile:** 121.5 per 100 pop. **Internet:** 23.4%.
Health: Life expect.: 65.9 male; 74.5 female. **Births:** 23.3 per 1,000 pop. **Deaths:** 6.7 per 1,000 pop. **Natural inc.:** 1.66%. **Infant mortality:** 28.7 per 1,000 live births. **HIV:** 0.2%.
Education: Compulsory: ages 7-15. **Literacy:** 99.5%.
Embassy: 2360 Massachusetts Ave. NW 20008; 338-5141.
Website: www.president.kg

The region was inhabited around the 13th cent. by the Kyrgyz. It was annexed to Russia, 1864, and became a constituent republic of the USSR in 1936. Kyrgyzstan declared independence Aug. 31, 1991. It became an independent state when the USSR disbanded Dec. 26, 1991.

In power since 1990, Pres. Askar Akayev won a third 5-year term in the 2000 election. Fraud by Akayev loyalists in parliamentary elections Feb.-Mar. 2005 sparked protests. Akayev fled the country, Mar. 24, and formally resigned, Apr. 4. His interim successor, former Prime Min. Kurmanbek Bakiyev, a leader of the "tulip revolution," won the 2005 presidential vote and was reelected 2009, when monitors reported numerous irregularities. He was ousted by opposition parties Apr. 7, 2010, after clashes between protesters and government security forces left at least 77 people dead; he left the country and was sentenced in absentia, July 25, 2014, to life in prison for his role in suppressing the protests.

Fighting in mid-June between majority Kyrgyz and minority Uzbeks in the southern cities of Osh and Jalalabad claimed up to 2,000 lives. A June 2010 referendum on a new constitution received overwhelming approval. Oct. elections brought 5 parties to the parliament, and Omurbek Babanov became prime min. of a coalition government. Almazbek Atambayev won the 2011 presidential election. Babanov's coalition broke up Aug. 2012; a new coalition was formed, and Jantoro Satybaldiev was sworn in as prime min. on Sept. 5. Three members of the opposition were convicted Mar. 30, 2013, of inciting crowds to assault government offices during an Oct. 2012 demonstration supporting the nationalizing of a gold mine. Violent demonstrations to nationalize the country's gold mines continued throughout the spring.

Laos
Lao People's Democratic Republic

People: Population: 6,803,699. **Age distrib.:** <15: 34.8%; 65+: 3.8%. **Pop. density:** 76.3 per sq mi, 29.5 per sq km. **Urban:** 37.6%. **Ethnic groups:** Lao 55%, Khmou 11%, Hmong 8%, other (100+ minor ethnic groups) 26%. **Languages:** Lao (official), French, English, various ethnic langs. **Religions:** Buddhist 67%, Christian 2%.

Geography: Total area: 91,429 sq mi, 236,800 sq km; **Land area:** 89,112 sq mi, 230,800 sq km. **Location:** On Indochina Peninsula in SE Asia. **Neighbors:** Myanmar, China on N; Vietnam on E; Cambodia on S; Thailand on W. **Topography:** Landlocked, dominated by jungle. High mountains along E border are source of the E-W rivers slicing across the country to the Mekong R., which defines most of W border. **Capital:** Vientiane, 945,715.

Government: Type: Communist state. **Head of state:** Pres. Choummaly Sayasone; b. Mar. 6, 1936; in office: June 8, 2006. **Head of gov.:** Prime Min. Thongsing Thammavong; b. 1944; in office: Dec. 24, 2010. **Local divisions:** 16 provinces, 1 capital city. **Defense budget:** $21 mil. **Active troops:** 29,100.

Economy: Industries: mining, timber, elec. power, agric. proc., rubber, constr., garments, cement, tourism. **Chief crops:** sweet potatoes, vegetables, corn, coffee, sugarcane, tobacco, cotton, tea, peanuts, rice, cassava. **Natural resources:** timber, hydropower, gypsum, tin, gold, gems. **Arable land:** 6.3%. **Livestock:** cattle: 1.7 mil; chickens: 30 mil; goats: 450,000; pigs: 2.3 mil. **Electricity prod.:** 12.2 bil kWh. **Labor force:** agric. 73.1%, industry 6.1%, services 20.6%. **Unemployment:** 1.3%.

Finance: Monetary unit: Kip (LAK) (Sept. 2014: 8,020.01 = $1 U.S.). **GDP:** $20.8 bil; **per capita GDP:** $3,100; **GDP growth:** 8.3%. **Imports:** $3.2 bil; Thailand 62.1%, China 16.2%, Vietnam 7.3%. **Exports:** $2.3 bil; Thailand 34%, China 21.5%, Vietnam 12.2%. **Tourism:** $451 mil. **Budget:** $2.6 bil. **Total reserves less gold:** $721.6 mil. **Gold:** 285,000 oz t. **Inflation:** 6.4%.

Transport: Civil aviation: 8 airports.

Communications: TV sets: 57 per 1,000 pop. **Radios:** 148 per 1,000 pop. **Telephone lines:** 10 per 100 pop. **Mobile:** 66.2 per 100 pop. **Internet:** 12.5%.

Health: Life expect.: 61.5 male; 65.6 female. **Births:** 24.8 per 1,000 pop. **Deaths:** 7.7 per 1,000 pop. **Natural inc.:** 1.70%. **Infant mortality:** 54.5 per 1,000 live births. **HIV:** 0.2%.

Education: Compulsory: ages 6-10. **Literacy:** 79.9%.

Embassy: 2222 S St. NW 20008; 332-6416.

Website: www.na.gov.la

Laos became a French protectorate in 1893, but regained independence as a constitutional monarchy July 19, 1949. Conflicts among neutralist, Communist, and conservative factions created a chaotic political situation. Armed conflict increased after 1960.

The 3 factions formed a coalition government in June 1962 with neutralist Prince Souvanna Phouma as premier. A 14-nation conference in Geneva signed agreements, 1962, guaranteeing independence. By 1964 the leftist Pathet Lao had withdrawn from the coalition, and, with aid from North Vietnamese troops, renewed sporadic attacks. U.S. planes bombed the Ho Chi Minh trail, a supply line from North Vietnam to Communist forces in Laos and South Vietnam.

In 1970 the U.S. stepped up air support and military aid. After Pathet Lao military gains, Souvanna Phouma, May 1975, ordered government troops to cease fighting; the Pathet Lao took control. The Lao People's Democratic Republic was proclaimed Dec. 3, 1975.

From the mid-1970s through the 1980s, Laos relied on Vietnam for military and financial aid. After easing its finance laws in 1988, Laos attracted substantial foreign investment from Thailand, China, Vietnam, the U.S., and other nations. Laos was admitted to the Assn. of SE Asian Nations in 1997. The U.S. Congress approved normalization of trade with Laos in 2004. To spur further investment, Laos opened its first stock exchange Jan. 11, 2011, in Vientiane. Ground was broken Nov. 7, 2012, on a controversial hydroelectric dam on the Mekong R., despite environmentalists' concern that it will harm the area's wildlife and natural resources. The government had authorized several more dams to be built on the river in the coming years.

Latvia
Republic of Latvia

People: Population: 2,165,165. **Age distrib.:** <15: 14.2%; 65+: 17.2%. **Pop. density:** 90.1 per sq mi, 34.8 per sq km. **Urban:** 67.4%. **Ethnic groups:** Latvian 61%, Russian 26%, Belarusian 4%, Ukrainian 2%, Polish 2%. **Languages:** Latvian (official), Russian. **Religions:** Lutheran 20%, Orthodox 15%.

Geography: Total area: 24,938 sq mi, 64,589 sq km; **Land area:** 24,034 sq mi, 62,249 sq km. **Location:** E Europe, on Baltic Sea. **Neighbors:** Estonia on N; Lithuania, Belarus on S; Russia on E. **Topography:** Lowland with numerous lakes, marshes, and peat bogs. Principal river, W. Dvina (Daugava), rises in Russia. Glacial hills in E. **Capital:** Riga, 629,370.

Government: Type: Parliamentary democracy. **Head of state:** Pres. Andris Berzins; b. Dec. 10, 1944; in office: July 8, 2011. **Head of gov.:** Prime Min. Laimdota Straujuma; b. Feb. 24, 1951; in office: Jan. 22, 2014. **Local divisions:** 110 municipalities, 9 cities. **Defense budget:** $300 mil. **Active troops:** 5,310.

Economy: Industries: processed foods, processed wood prods., textiles, processed metals, pharmaceuticals, railroad cars, synthetic fibers, electronics. **Chief crops:** grain, rapeseed, potatoes, vegetables. **Natural resources:** peat, limestone, dolomite, amber, hydropower, timber. **Arable land:** 18.9%. **Livestock:** cattle: 393,000; chickens: 4.1 mil; goats: 13,300; pigs: 355,200; sheep: 83,600. **Electricity prod.:** 5.9 bil kWh. **Labor force:** agric. 8.8%, industry 24%, services 67.2%. **Unemployment:** 14.9%.

Finance: Monetary unit: Euro (EUR) (Sept. 2014: 0.76 = $1 U.S.). **GDP:** $38.9 bil; **per capita GDP:** $19,100; **GDP growth:** 4%. **Imports:** $15.6 bil; Lithuania 19.1%, Germany 11.6%, Russia 9.2%, Poland 8.2%, Estonia 7.6%, Italy 4.6%, Finland 4.4%. **Exports:** $12.7 bil; Russia 18.2%, Lithuania 14.9%, Estonia 12.1%, Germany 7.5%, Poland 5.6%, Sweden 4.8%. **Tourism:** $864 mil. **Budget:** $11 bil. **Total reserves less gold:** $7.6 bil. **Gold:** 250,000 oz t. **Inflation:** 0%.

Transport: Railways: 1,391 mi. **Motor vehicles:** 330.3 per 1,000 pop. **Civil aviation:** 2.2 bil pass.-mi; 18 airports. **Chief ports:** Riga, Ventspils.

Communications: TV sets: 855 per 1,000 pop. **Radios:** 700 per 1,000 pop. **Telephone lines:** 23.4 per 100 pop. **Mobile:** 136.6 per 100 pop. **Internet:** 75.2%.

Health: Life expect.: 68.4 male; 78.8 female. **Births:** 9.8 per 1,000 pop. **Deaths:** 13.6 per 1,000 pop. **Natural inc.:** −0.38%. **Infant mortality:** 7.9 per 1,000 live births. **HIV:** NA.

Education: Compulsory: ages 7-15. **Literacy:** 99.9%.

Embassy: 2306 Massachusetts Ave. NW 20008; 328-2840.

Website: www.li.lv

Prior to 1918, Latvia was occupied by the Russians and Germans. It was an independent republic, 1918-39. The Aug. 1939 Soviet-German agreement assigned Latvia to the Soviet sphere of influence. It was officially absorbed by the USSR in 1940. It was overrun by the German army in 1941, but retaken in 1945.

During an abortive Soviet coup, Latvia declared independence, Aug. 21, 1991. The last Russian troops in Latvia withdrew by Aug. 31, 1994. Responding to international pressure, Latvian voters, 1998, eased citizenship laws that had discriminated against some 500,000 ethnic Russians. Latvia joined the EU and NATO in 2004.

Hit hard by recession, Latvia reached agreement Dec. 2008 on a $10.4-bil emergency loan from the EU, IMF, World Bank, and Nordic countries. Angered by the prolonged economic downturn and the growing influence of wealthy oligarchs over Latvian politics, voters in a July 2011 referendum approved a proposal to dissolve parliament. Prime Min. Valdis Dombrovskis's Unity Party came in third in Sept. 2011 elections, but Dombrovskis remained prime min. After more than 50 people died, Nov. 21, 2013, in a Riga supermarket roof collapse blamed on design and construction flaws, Dombrovskis resigned. Laimdota Straujuma became prime min. Jan. 22, 2014. Latvia repaid its IMF loan Dec. 21, 2012. It began using the euro as its currency Jan. 1, 2014.

Lebanon
Lebanese Republic

People: Population: 4,136,895. **Age distrib.:** <15: 21.8%; 65+: 9.5%. **Pop. density:** 1,047.4 per sq mi, 404.4 per sq km. **Urban:** 87.7%. **Ethnic groups:** Arab 95%, Armenian 4%; many Christian Lebanese identify not as Arab but Phoenician. **Languages:** Arabic (official), French, English, Armenian. **Religions:** Muslim 54% (Sunni 27%, Shia 27%), Christian 41%, Druze 6%.

Geography: Total area: 4,015 sq mi, 10,400 sq km; **Land area:** 3,950 sq mi, 10,230 sq km. **Location:** In Middle East, on E end of Mediterranean Sea. **Neighbors:** Syria on E, Israel on S.

Topography: There is a narrow coastal strip, and 2 mountain ranges running N-S enclosing the fertile Beqaa Valley. The Litani R. runs S through the valley, turning W to empty into Mediterranean. **Capital:** Beirut, 2,178,830 (excl. Syrian refugees).

Government: Type: Republic. **Head of state:** vacant. **Head of gov.:** Prime Min. Tammam Salam; b. 1945; in office: Apr. 6, 2013. **Local divisions:** 6 governorates. **Defense budget:** $1.22 bil. **Active troops:** 60,000.

Economy: Industries: banking, tourism, food proc., wine, jewelry, cement, textiles, mineral and chem. prods., wood and furniture prods. **Chief crops:** citrus, grapes, tomatoes, apples, vegetables, potatoes, olives, tobacco. **Natural resources:** limestone, iron ore, salt, water (surplus in a water-deficit region). **Arable land:** 20.2%. **Livestock:** cattle: 80,000; chickens: 65 mil; goats: 553,000; pigs: 7,900; sheep: 452,000. **Electricity prod.:** 15.4 bil kWh. **Labor force:** NA. **Unemployment:** 8.9%.

Finance: Monetary unit: Pound (LBP) (Sept. 2014: 1,511.00 = $1 U.S.). **GDP:** $64.3 bil; **per capita GDP:** $15,800; **GDP growth:** 1.5%. **Imports:** $21 bil; U.S. 11.2%, Italy 8.6%, China 8.3%, France 7.2%, Germany 5.6%, Turkey 4.5%, Greece 4.2%. **Exports:** $5.8 bil; South Africa 19.3%, Switzerland 12.2%, Saudi Arabia 8%, UAE 7.9%, Syria 6.6%, Iraq 4.7%. **Tourism:** $6 bil. **Budget:** $13.6 bil. **Total reserves less gold:** $36.7 bil. **Gold:** 9.2 mil oz t. **Inflation** (2009-10): 4.0%.

Transport: Railways: 249 mi (unusable because of damage from fighting). **Motor vehicles:** 150.8 per 1,000 pop. **Civil aviation:** 2.4 bil pass.-mi; 5 airports. **Chief ports:** Beirut, Tripoli.

Communications: TV sets: 387 per 1,000 pop. **Radios:** 75 per 1,000 pop. **Telephone lines:** 18 per 100 pop. **Mobile:** 80.6 per 100 pop. **Internet:** 70.5%.

Health: Life expect.: 74.1 male; 77.4 female. **Births:** 14.6 per 1,000 pop. **Deaths:** 6.8 per 1,000 pop. **Natural inc.:** 0.78%. **Infant mortality:** 14.3 per 1,000 live births. **HIV:** NA.

Education: Compulsory: ages 6-14. **Literacy:** 93.9%.

Embassy: 2560 28th St. NW 20008; 939-6300.

Website: www.presidency.gov.lb

Formed from 5 former Turkish Empire districts, Lebanon became independent Sept. 1, 1920, administered under French mandate 1920-41. French troops withdrew in 1946.

Under the 1943 National Covenant, all public positions were divided among the various religious communities, with Christians in the majority. By the 1970s, Muslims became the majority and demanded a larger political and economic role.

U.S. Marines intervened, May-Oct. 1958, during a Syrian-aided revolt. Continued raids against Israeli civilians, 1970-75, brought Israeli retaliation in southern Lebanon.

An estimated 60,000 were killed in a 1975-76 civil war. Palestinian units and leftist Muslims fought against Maronite militia (the Phalange) and other Christians. Several Arab countries provided support to various factions, while Israel aided Christian forces. Syria, which intervened in 1976 to fight Palestinian groups, largely policed a cease-fire.

Israeli forces invaded Lebanon June 6, 1982, attacking strongholds of the Palestine Liberation Organization (PLO). Israeli and Syrian forces engaged in the Bekaa Valley. On Aug. 21, the PLO evacuated W Beirut after massive Israeli bombings. Israeli troops entered W Beirut following the Sept. 14 assassination of newly elected Lebanese Pres. Bashir Gemayel. On Sept. 16, 1982, Lebanese Christian troops entered the Sabra and Shatila refugee camps and massacred hundreds of Palestinian civilians. An agreement May 17, 1983, between Lebanon, Israel, and the U.S. (but not Syria) provided for the withdrawal of Israeli troops; at least 30,000 Syrian troops remained in Lebanon, and Israel held onto a "security zone" in the south.

In 1983, some 50 people were killed in an explosion at the U.S. embassy, Apr. 18; 241 U.S. servicemen and 58 French soldiers died in separate Islamist suicide attacks, Oct. 23. The 1980s witnessed kidnappings of U.S., British, French, and Soviet citizens by Islamic militants. All hostages were released by 1992.

A treaty signed May 22, 1991, between Lebanon and Syria recognized Lebanon as a separate state for the first time since 1943.

Israeli forces conducted air raids and artillery strikes against guerrilla bases and villages in southern Lebanon, causing over 200,000 to flee their homes July 25-29, 1993. Some 500,000 civilians fled in Apr. 1996 when Israel struck suspected guerrilla bases in the south. The economy revived in the 1990s, but Syria continued to dominate Lebanon's political affairs. Israel withdrew virtually all its troops from S Lebanon by May 2000, leaving Hezbollah, an Iranian-backed guerrilla group, in control of much of the region.

Rafik al-Hariri, a former prime min. (1992-98, 2000-04), was killed by a truck bomb, Feb. 14, 2005. Many Lebanese blamed Syria. As anti-Syrian protests mounted, Syrian troops left Lebanon (some intelligence agents may have remained). An anti-Syrian bloc won May and June parliamentary elections. A new cabinet, installed July 2005, was headed by Fouad Siniora and included a Hezbollah member.

A Hezbollah rocket attack and border raid, July 2006, in which 3 Israeli soldiers were killed and 2 captured, triggered a massive escalation of hostilities. Hezbollah, led by Sheikh Hassan Nasrallah, bombarded northern Israel with nearly 4,000 rockets, while Israeli air and ground forces assaulted suspected Hezbollah strongholds in southern Lebanon and southern Beirut. By Aug. 14, 2006, when a UN-sponsored cease-fire took hold, the war dead included nearly 1,150 Lebanese. To enforce the truce, thousands of Lebanese troops moved into southern Lebanon, and the small UN force already in Lebanon (UNIFIL) was expanded. As of July 2014, UNIFIL had more than 10,000 uniformed personnel in Lebanon.

At an international conference in Paris, Jan. 2007, donor countries pledged more than $7.6 bil in reconstruction aid. After more than 3 months of fighting in which over 400 people died, Lebanese forces Sept. 2 defeated Islamic militants at the Nahr al-Bared Palestinian refugee camp north of Tripoli. A 2008 power-sharing accord between the Siniora government and Hezbollah eased factional violence and paved the way for Army Chief Gen. Michel Suleiman to become president, ending an 18-month stalemate. A new government headed by Prime Min. Tammam Salam and including representatives of Lebanon's various political and communal factions took office Feb. 15, 2014. However, factional disputes in parliament led to months of delay in electing a successor when Pres. Suleiman's term expired in May 2014.

The Syrian civil war spilled over into Lebanon in 2012, most dramatically in Tripoli, where Sunni Muslims and Alawite Muslims took part in firefights Aug. 21-26, 2012, that left at least 17 dead. A deadly bombing also linked to the Syrian civil war took place in Beirut Oct. 19, killing the anti-Syrian Gen. Wissam al-Hassan. Hezbollah gave military aid to Syria, escalating the conflict on the border and suffering its own casualties. In Apr. 2013, Israel shot down a Hezbollah drone in its airspace. Radical Sunnis fought with the Lebanese Army June 23-24, 2013, in growing sectarian violence. The UNHCR estimated the number of Syrian refugees in Lebanon at more than 1.15 mil as of Sept. 29, 2014. Fighting between Sunni extremists from Syria who seized a border town and Lebanese army units erupted in Aug. 2014.

Lesotho
Kingdom of Lesotho

People: Population: 1,942,008. **Age distrib.:** <15: 32.9%; 65+: 5.4%. **Pop. density:** 165.7 per sq mi, 64 per sq km. **Urban:** 26.8%. **Ethnic groups:** Sotho 99.7%. **Languages:** Sesotho, English (both official); Zulu; Xhosa. **Religions:** Christian 80%, indigenous beliefs 20%.

Geography: Total area: 11,720 sq mi, 30,355 sq km; **Land area:** 11,720 sq mi, 30,355 sq km. **Location:** In southern Africa. **Neighbors:** Completely surrounded by South Africa. **Topography:** Landlocked and mountainous, 5,000 to 11,000 ft in elevation. **Capital:** Maseru, 266,580.

Government: Type: Parliamentary constitutional monarchy. **Head of state:** King Letsie III; b. July 17, 1963; in office: Feb. 7, 1996. **Head of gov.:** Prime Min. Thomas Motsoahae Thabane; b. 1939; in office: June 8, 2012. **Local divisions:** 10 districts. **Defense budget:** $54 mil. **Active troops:** 2,000.

Economy: Industries: food, beverages, textiles, apparel assembly, handicrafts, constr., tourism. **Chief crops:** corn, wheat, pulses, sorghum, barley. **Natural resources:** water, diamonds, sand, clay, building stone. **Arable land:** 9.3%. **Livestock:** cattle: 665,000; chickens: 500,000; goats: 850,000; pigs: 81,000; sheep: 1.2 mil. **Electricity prod.:** 700 mil kWh. **Labor force:** agric. 86% (subsistence), industry and services 14%. Approx. 35% of active male wage earners work in South Africa. **Unemployment:** 26.5%.

Finance: Monetary unit: Loti (LSL) (Sept. 2014: 10.68 = $1 U.S.). **GDP:** $4.3 bil; **per capita GDP:** $2,200; **GDP growth:** 4.1%. **Imports:** $2.1 bil. **Exports:** $941.2 mil. **Tourism:** $46 mil. **Budget:** $1.5 bil. **Total reserves less gold:** $1.1 bil. **Inflation:** 4.9%.

Transport: Civil aviation: 3 airports.

Communications: TV sets: 44 per 1,000 pop. **Radios:** 121 per 1,000 pop. **Telephone lines:** 2.8 per 100 pop. **Mobile:** 86.3 per 100 pop. **Internet:** 0%.

Health: Life expect.: 52.6 male; 52.8 female. **Births:** 25.9 per 1,000 pop. **Deaths:** 14.9 per 1,000 pop. **Natural inc.:** 1.10%. **Infant mortality:** 50.5 per 1,000 live births. **HIV:** 22.9%.

Education: Compulsory ages: NA. **Literacy:** 79.4%.

Embassy: 2511 Massachusetts Ave. NW 20008; 797-5533.

Website: www.gov.ls

Lesotho (once called Basutoland) became a British protectorate in 1868 when Chief Moshesh sought protection against the Boers. Independence came Oct. 4, 1966. Much of Lesotho's GDP is provided by citizens working in South Africa. Livestock raising is a major industry; clothing manufactured for sale abroad and diamonds are leading exports. Cultivation of marijuana for smuggling to South Africa is a significant source of income.

In Mar. 1990, King Moshoeshoe was exiled by the military government. Letsie III became king Nov. 12. In Mar. 1993, Ntsu Mokhehle, a civilian, was elected prime minister, ending 23 years of military rule. After a series of violent disturbances, the king dismissed the Mokhehle government Aug. 17, 1994; constitutional rule was restored Sept. 14.

Letsie abdicated and Moshoeshoe was reinstated Jan. 25, 1995. Moshoeshoe died in an automobile accident, Jan. 15, 1996. Letsie was reinstated Feb. 7. South Africa and Botswana sent troops

Sept. 1998 to help suppress violent antigovernment protests. After parliamentary elections May 26, 2012, the left-leaning Thomas Motsoahae Thabane became the first new prime min. since 1998.

Liberia
Republic of Liberia

People: Population: 4,092,310. **Age distrib.:** <15: 43.2%; 65+: 3.1%. **Pop. density:** 110 per sq mi, 42.5 per sq km. **Urban:** 49.3%. **Ethnic groups:** Kpelle 20%, Bassa 13%, Grebo 10%, Gio 8%, Mano 8%, Kru 6%, Lorma 5%, Kissi 5%, Gola 4%. **Languages:** English (official), about 20 ethnic group langs. **Religions:** Christian 86%, Muslim 12%.

Geography: Total area: 43,000 sq mi, 111,369 sq km; **Land area:** 37,189 sq mi, 96,320 sq km. **Location:** On SW coast of W Africa. **Neighbors:** Sierra Leone on W, Guinea on N, Côte d'Ivoire on E. **Topography:** Marshy Atlantic coastline rises to low mountains and plateaus in forested interior; 6 major rivers flow in parallel courses to the ocean. **Capital:** Monrovia, 1,223,880.

Government: Type: Republic. **Head of state and gov.:** Pres. Ellen Johnson-Sirleaf; b. Oct. 29, 1938; in office: Jan. 16, 2006. **Local divisions:** 15 counties. **Defense budget** (2012): $24 mil. **Active troops:** 2,050.

Economy: Industries: rubber and palm oil proc., timber, diamonds. **Chief crops:** rubber, coffee, cocoa, rice, cassava, palm oil, sugarcane, bananas. **Natural resources:** iron ore, timber, diamonds, gold, hydropower. **Arable land:** 5.2%. **Livestock:** cattle: 42,000; chickens: 7.6 mil; goats: 345,000; pigs: 292,000; sheep: 275,000. **Electricity prod.:** 335 mil kWh. **Labor force:** agric. 70%, industry 8%, services 22%. **Unemployment:** 3.7%.

Finance: Monetary unit: Dollar (LRD) (Sept. 2014: 92.50 = $1 U.S.). **GDP:** $2.9 bil; **per capita GDP:** $700; **GDP growth:** 8.1%. **Imports:** $2.6 bil; South Korea 26.7%, China 24.4%, Singapore 23.2%, Japan 16.1%. **Exports:** $929.8 mil; China 24%, U.S. 15.3%, Spain 11%, Algeria 6.5%, Thailand 4.5%, Malaysia 4.1%, France 4%. **Tourism:** $232 mil. **Budget:** $521.7 mil. **Total reserves less gold:** $493.1 mil. **Inflation:** 7.6%.

Transport: Railways: 267 mi. **Motor vehicles:** 14.6 per 1,000 pop. **Civil aviation:** 2 airports. **Chief ports:** Buchanan, Monrovia.

Communications: TV sets: 26 per 1,000 pop. **Radios:** 318 per 1,000 pop. **Telephone lines** (2011): 0.08 per 100 pop. **Mobile:** 59.5 per 100 pop. **Internet:** 4.6%.

Health: Life expect.: 56.6 male; 59.9 female. **Births:** 35.1 per 1,000 pop. **Deaths:** 9.9 per 1,000 pop. **Natural inc.:** 2.52%. **Infant mortality:** 69.2 per 1,000 live births. **HIV:** 1.1%.

Education: Compulsory ages: 6-11. **Literacy:** 47.6%.

Embassy: 5201 16th St. NW 20011; 723-0437.

Website: www.emansion.gov.lr

Liberia was founded in 1822 by freed black slaves from the U.S. who settled at Monrovia with the aid of colonization societies. It became a republic July 26, 1847, with a constitution modeled on that of the U.S. Descendants of freed slaves dominated politics for much of the 19th and 20th cents.

Under Pres. William V. S. Tubman, Liberia was a founding member of the UN in 1945. Tubman died in 1971 and was succeeded by his vice president, William R. Tolbert Jr. Charging rampant corruption, an Army Redemption Council of enlisted men staged a bloody predawn coup, Apr. 12, 1980, killing Pres. Tolbert and installing Sgt. Samuel Doe, an indigenous African, as head of state. In 1985, Doe was chosen president in a disputed election.

A civil war began Dec. 1989. In Sept. 1990, Pres. Doe was executed. Despite the introduction of a multinational peacekeeping force, the conflict intensified. Factional fighting devastated Monrovia in Apr. 1996. Ruth Perry became modern Africa's first female head of state Sept. 3, 1996, leading a transitional government. By then, the civil war had claimed more than 150,000 lives.

Former rebel leader Charles Taylor was elected president July 1997, in Liberia's first national election in 12 years. The UN imposed sanctions in 2001, to punish Liberia for aiding the Revolutionary United Front (RUF) insurgency in Sierra Leone. Taylor declared a state of emergency Feb. 8, 2002, after Liberian rebels launched raids near Monrovia.

A UN-sponsored war crimes tribunal indicted Taylor June 2003, for his role in the Sierra Leone conflict. With rebels again threatening Monrovia, Taylor resigned Aug. 11 and went into exile. The UN authorized a 15,000-member peacekeeping force (UNMIL) Sept. 19 to help stabilize the nation. A businessman, Charles Gyude Bryant, was sworn in Oct. 14 to head a power-sharing interim government. Ellen Johnson-Sirleaf won presidential elections in 2005 and 2011, and shared the 2011 Nobel Peace Prize with 2 other women. Captured in 2006 while trying to flee Nigeria, Charles Taylor went to trial at The Hague in 2007. After several delays, he was convicted of 11 counts of aiding and abetting war crimes and crimes against humanity in 2012, and sentenced to 50 years in prison May 30.

The UN Security Council passed a resolution Sept. 17, 2012, reducing the UN presence to about 4,000 forces by July 2015. UNMIL had 6,020 uniformed personnel in Liberia as of July 31, 2014. Liberia was seriously affected by an Ebola virus epidemic that began in Guinea in Dec. 2013. By Sept. 28, 2014, 3,696 Liberian cases had been reported, and 1,998 had died; both figures were higher than any other country's.

Libya

People: Population: 6,244,174. **Age distrib.:** <15: 26.9%; 65+: 4%. **Pop. density:** 9.2 per sq mi, 3.5 per sq km. **Urban:** 78.4%. **Ethnic groups:** Berber and Arab 97%, other (incl. Greek, Maltese, Italian, Egyptian, Pakistani, Turk, Indian, Tunisian) 3%. **Languages:** Arabic (official), Italian, English, Berber. **Religions:** Muslim (official; almost all Sunni) 97%, Christian 3%.

Geography: Total area: 679,362 sq mi, 1,759,540 sq km; **Land area:** 679,362 sq mi, 1,759,540 sq km. **Location:** On Mediterranean coast of N Africa. **Neighbors:** Tunisia, Algeria on W; Niger, Chad on S; Sudan, Egypt on E. **Topography:** Desert and semidesert regions cover 92% of land with low mountains in N, higher mountains in S, and a narrow coastal zone. **Capital:** Tarabulus (Tripoli), 1,126,010.

Government: Type: In transition. **Head of state:** General National Congress Pres. Nouri Abusahmain; in office: June 25, 2013. **Head of gov.:** vacant. **Local divisions:** 22 districts. **Defense budget:** $4.77 bil. **Active troops:** 7,000.

Economy: Industries: petroleum, petrochemicals, aluminum, iron and steel, food proc., textiles, handicrafts, cement. **Chief crops:** wheat, barley, olives, dates, citrus, vegetables, peanuts, soybeans. **Natural resources:** petroleum, nat. gas, gypsum. **Crude oil reserves:** 48.5 bil bbls. **Arable land:** 1%. **Livestock:** cattle: 198,500; chickens: 34.9 mil; goats: 2.6 mil; sheep: 7.2 mil. **Electricity prod.:** 26 bil kWh. **Labor force:** agric. 17%, industry 23%, services 59%. **Unemployment:** 8.9%.

Finance: Monetary unit: Dinar (LYD) (Sept. 2014: 1.22 = $1 U.S.). **GDP:** $73.6 bil; **per capita GDP:** $11,300; **GDP growth:** −5.1%. **Imports:** $27.2 bil; China 13%, Turkey 11.6%, Italy 8.2%, Egypt 7.7%, Tunisia 6.6%, South Korea 5.8%, Greece 5.4%, Germany 4.6%. **Exports:** $38.5 bil; Italy 23.3%, Germany 12.4%, China 11.2%, France 9.7%, Spain 7.6%, UK 4.7%, U.S. 4.5%. **Tourism:** $60 mil. **Budget:** $41.9 bil. **Total reserves less gold:** $115.2 bil. **Gold:** 3.8 mil oz t. **Inflation** (2011-12): 6.1%.

Transport: Motor vehicles: 410.2 per 1,000 pop. **Civil aviation:** 1.9 bil pass.-mi; 68 airports. **Chief ports:** Az Zawiyah, Marsa al Burayqah, Ra's Lanuf, Tripoli.

Communications: TV sets: 147 per 1,000 pop. **Radios:** 270 per 1,000 pop. **Telephone lines:** 12.7 per 100 pop. **Mobile:** 165 per 100 pop. **Internet:** 16.5%.

Health: Life expect.: 74.4 male; 77.8 female. **Births:** 18.4 per 1,000 pop. **Deaths:** 3.6 per 1,000 pop. **Natural inc.:** 1.48%. **Infant mortality:** 11.9 per 1,000 live births. **HIV:** NA.

Education: Compulsory: ages 6-14. **Literacy:** 91%.

Embassy: 2600 Virginia Ave. NW, Ste. 705, 20037; 944-9601.

Website: www.pm.gov.ly

First settled by Berbers, Libya was ruled in succession by Carthage, Rome, the Vandals, and the Ottomans. Italy ruled from 1912, and Britain and France after WWII. Libya became an independent constitutional monarchy Jan. 2, 1952. In 1969 a junta led by Col. Muammar al-Qaddafi seized power.

Under Qaddafi's dictatorship, dissent was suppressed and wars were waged with Egypt and Chad. During the 1980s, Libya was accused of promoting terrorism, such as the Apr. 5, 1986, bombing of a West Berlin nightclub, which killed 3, including a U.S. serviceman. The U.S. responded by attacking what it called "terrorist-related targets" in Libya, Apr. 14, including Qaddafi's barracks.

Libyan agents were accused of planting bombs that blew up Pan Am Flight 103 over Lockerbie, Scotland, killing 270 people Dec. 21, 1988, and UTA Flight 772 over Niger, killing 170 people Sept. 19, 1989. The UN imposed sanctions in 1992 for Libya's failure to cooperate in the Lockerbie and UTA cases.

Libya agreed in 2003 to renounce terrorism and settle compensation cases for the families of the Lockerbie and UTA bombing victims. The UN lifted sanctions in Sept., and in Dec., Libya renounced nuclear, chemical, and biological weapons and long-range missiles. The U.S. ended most economic sanctions Apr. 2004 and restored full diplomatic relations May 2006. Abdel Basset Ali al-Megrahi, a former Libyan agent sentenced to life in prison in 2001 for his role in the Lockerbie bombing, was freed by Scottish authorities on humanitarian grounds Aug. 20, 2009; he received a jubilant welcome in Libya.

Arab Spring rebels fought with Qaddafi's forces throughout the spring of 2011. With diplomatic backing from the Arab League and the UN Security Council, NATO forces imposed an arms embargo and no-fly zone against Qaddafi. Aided by NATO, rebels took control of Tripoli Aug. 23, 2011, and began governing. Rebels killed Qaddafi Oct. 20, 2011. Ansar al-Shariah terrorists attacked the U.S. consulate in Benghazi Sept. 11, 2012, killing Ambassador J. Christopher Stephens and 3 others. The U.S. captured, June 15, 2014, the alleged leader of the attack, Ahmed Abu Khattala; he was charged with conspiracy, June 28. The U.S., France, and Britain closed their embassies in Tripoli, July 26, July 30, and Aug. 4, 2014, due to security concerns.

Violence between Islamists and rival militia groups and between Islamists and government forces intensified in 2013 and 2014. A July 2014 battle over control of Tripoli's airport left 47 dead. Parliamentary elections marred by violence and low turnout were held June 25. The new parliament convened Aug. 4; it held its initial meetings, boycotted by some Islamists, in Tobruk because of militia fighting in Tripoli.

Liechtenstein
Principality of Liechtenstein

People: Population: 37,313. **Age distrib.:** <15: 15.7%; 65+: 16%. **Pop. density:** 604 per sq mi, 233.2 per sq km. **Urban:** 14.3%. **Ethnic groups:** Liechtensteiner 66%. **Languages:** German (official). **Religions:** Roman Catholic (official) 76%, Protestant Reformed 7%, Muslim 5%, none 5%.

Geography: Total area: 62 sq mi, 160 sq km; **Land area:** 62 sq mi, 160 sq km. **Location:** Central Europe, in Alps. **Neighbors:** Switzerland on W, Austria on E. **Topography:** Rhine Valley occupies one-third of country, Alps cover the rest. **Capital:** Vaduz, 5,321.

Government: Type: Hereditary constitutional monarchy. **Head of state:** Prince Hans-Adam II; b. Feb. 14, 1945; in office: Nov. 13, 1989. **Head of gov.:** Prime Min. Adrian Hasler; b. Feb. 11, 1964; in office: Mar. 27, 2013. **Local divisions:** 11 communes. **Defense budget/active troops:** NA.

Economy: Industries: electronics, metal mfg., dental prods., ceramics, pharmaceuticals, food prods., precision instruments, tourism, optical instruments. **Chief crops:** wheat, barley, corn, potatoes. **Natural resources:** hydroelectric potential. **Arable land:** 18.8%. **Livestock:** cattle: 6,350; goats: 368; pigs: 1,800; sheep: 4,000. **Labor force:** agric. 0.8%, industry 39.4%, services 59.9%. **Unemployment:** NA.

Finance: Monetary unit: Franc (CHF) (Sept. 2014: 0.92 = $1 U.S.). **GDP (2009):** $3.2 bil; **per capita GDP (2009):** $89,400; **GDP growth (2012):** 1.8%. **Imports (2012):** $2.1 bil. **Exports (2012):** $3.8 bil. (Trade data excl. trade with Switzerland.) **Budget (2011 est.):** $890.4 mil. **Total reserves less gold:** NA. **Inflation:** NA.

Transport: Railways: 6 mi.

Communications: TV sets: 540 per 1,000 pop. **Radios:** 662 per 1,000 pop. **Telephone lines:** 48.8 per 100 pop. **Mobile:** 97.8 per 100 pop. **Internet:** 93.8%.

Health: Life expect.: 79.5 male; 84.4 female. **Births:** 10.5 per 1,000 pop. **Deaths:** 7.0 per 1,000 pop. **Natural inc.:** 0.35%. **Infant mortality:** 4.3 per 1,000 live births. **HIV:** NA.

Education: Compulsory: ages 6-14. **Literacy:** 100%.

Embassy: 2900 K St. NW, Ste. 602B, 20007; 331-0590.

Website: www.liechtenstein.li

Liechtenstein became sovereign in 1806. It is united with Switzerland by a customs and monetary union. Many workers commute daily from Austria, Switzerland, and Germany.

On Aug. 15, 2004, Prince Hans-Adam II assigned day-to-day responsibilities for running the country to his son, Crown Prince Alois. Long regarded as a tax haven, Liechtenstein took steps, 2008-13, to ease banking secrecy laws that had impeded international tax fraud investigations. A referendum to abolish the prince's power to veto referendums was defeated July 1, 2012.

Lithuania
Republic of Lithuania

People: Population: 3,505,738. **Age distrib.:** <15: 13.5%; 65+: 17%. **Pop. density:** 144.9 per sq mi, 55.9 per sq km. **Urban:** 66.5%. **Ethnic groups:** Lithuanian 84%, Polish 7%, Russian 6%. **Languages:** Lithuanian (official), Russian, Polish. **Religions:** Roman Catholic 77%, Russian Orthodox 4%, none 6%.

Geography: Total area: 25,212 sq mi, 65,300 sq km; **Land area:** 24,201 sq mi, 62,680 sq km. **Location:** In E Europe, on SE coast of Baltic. **Neighbors:** Latvia on N; Belarus on E, S; Poland, Russia on W. **Topography:** Lowland with hills in W and S; fertile soil; many small lakes and rivers with marshes espec. in N and W. **Capital:** Vilnius, 518,518.

Government: Type: Parliamentary democracy. **Head of state:** Pres. Dalia Grybauskaite; b. Mar. 1, 1956; in office: July 12, 2009. **Head of gov.:** Prime Min. Algirdas Butkevicius; b. Nov. 19, 1958; in office: Nov. 22, 2012. **Local divisions:** 60 municipalities. **Defense budget:** $355 mil. **Active troops:** 11,800.

Economy: Industries: metal-cutting machine tools, elec. motors, TVs, refrigerators and freezers, petroleum refining, shipbuilding, furniture making, textiles, food proc. **Chief crops:** grain, potatoes, sugar beets, flax, vegetables. **Natural resources:** peat, amber. **Crude oil reserves:** 12 mil bbls. **Arable land:** 36.1%. **Livestock:** cattle: 729,200; chickens: 8.8 mil; goats: 13,600; pigs: 807,500; sheep: 82,800. **Electricity prod.:** 3.4 bil kWh. **Labor force:** agric. 7.9%, industry 19.6%, services 72.5%. **Unemployment:** 13.2%.

Finance: Monetary unit: Litas (LTL) (Sept. 2014: 2.63 = $1 U.S.). **GDP:** $67.4 bil; **per capita GDP:** $22,600; **GDP growth:** 3.4%. **Imports:** $32.5 bil; Russia 29.3%, Germany 10.3%, Poland 9.3%, Latvia 6.1%. **Exports:** $29.3 bil; Russia 19.8%, Latvia 9.9%, Estonia 7.5%, Poland 7.3%, Germany 7.1%, Belarus 5.1%, UK 4.9%, Netherlands 4.3%. **Tourism:** $1.5 bil. **Budget:** $15.4 bil. **Total reserves less gold:** $7.8 bil. **Gold:** 187,000 oz t. **Inflation:** 1.1%.

Transport: Railways: 1,098 mi. **Motor vehicles:** 558.8 per 1,000 pop. **Civil aviation:** 22 airports. **Chief port:** Klaipeda.

Communications: TV sets: 518 per 1,000 pop. **Radios:** 525 per 1,000 pop. **Telephone lines:** 20.7 per 100 pop. **Mobile:** 151.3 per 100 pop. **Internet:** 68.5%.

Health: Life expect.: 71.2 male; 81.0 female. **Births:** 9.4 per 1,000 pop. **Deaths:** 11.6 per 1,000 pop. **Natural inc.:** −0.22%. **Infant mortality:** 6.0 per 1,000 live births. **HIV:** NA.

Education: Compulsory: ages 7-15. **Literacy:** 99.8%.

Embassy: 4590 MacArthur Blvd. NW, Ste. 200, 20007; 234-5860.

Website: www.lrvk.lt

Lithuania, briefly occupied by the German army, 1914-18, was annexed by the Soviet Union until 1919. In 1939 it rejoined the Soviet sphere of influence and was annexed by the USSR Aug. 3, 1940.

Lithuania declared its independence from the Soviet Union Mar. 11, 1990; its independence was ratified by the Soviet Union Sept. 1991. The country became a full member of NATO and the EU in 2004. A plummeting economy spurred popular discontent and brought a rightward shift in parliamentary and presidential elections, 2008-09. The center-left Social Democrats won Oct. 2012 parliamentary elections. Running as an independent and focusing on national security, Pres. Dalia Grybauskaite won reelection in a May 25, 2014, runoff. In July 2014, Lithuania received European Central Bank approval to begin using the euro as of Jan. 1, 2015.

Luxembourg
Grand Duchy of Luxembourg

People: Population: 520,672. **Age distrib.:** <15: 17.9%; 65+: 15.4%. **Pop. density:** 521.5 per sq mi, 201.3 per sq km. **Urban:** 89.9%. **Ethnic groups:** Luxembourger 63%, Portuguese 13%, French 5%, Italian 4%, German 2%, other EU 7%. **Languages:** Luxembourgish (national lang.), German, French (all official admin. langs.). **Religions:** Roman Catholic 87%, other (incl. Protestant, Jewish, Muslim) 13%.

Geography: Total area: 998 sq mi, 2,586 sq km; **Land area:** 998 sq mi, 2,586 sq km. **Location:** In W Europe. **Neighbors:** Belgium on W, France on S, Germany on E. **Topography:** Heavy forests (Ardennes) cover N. S is a low, open plateau. **Capital:** Luxembourg, 106,680.

Government: Type: Constitutional monarchy. **Head of state:** Grand Duke Henri; b. Apr. 16, 1955; in office: Oct. 7, 2000. **Head of gov.:** Prime Min. Xavier Bettel; b. Mar. 3, 1973; in office: Dec. 4, 2013. **Local divisions:** 3 districts. **Defense budget:** $249 mil. **Active troops:** 900.

Economy: Industries: banking and financial services, iron and steel, information tech., telecom, cargo transp., food proc., chemicals, metal prods., engineering, tires, glass, aluminum, tourism. **Chief crops:** grapes, barley, oats, potatoes, wheat, fruits. **Natural resources:** iron ore (no longer exploited). **Arable land:** 24.2%. **Livestock:** cattle: 193,623; chickens: 111,310; goats: 4,456; pigs: 87,518; sheep: 8,582. **Electricity prod.** (2012): 2.2 bil kWh. **Labor force:** agric. 1.2%, industry 19.4%, services 79.4%. **Unemployment:** 5.1%.

Finance: Monetary unit: Euro (EUR) (Sept. 2014: 0.76 = $1 U.S.). **GDP:** $42.7 bil; **per capita GDP:** $77,900; **GDP growth:** 0.5%. **Imports:** $23.1 bil; Belgium 30.6%, Germany 23.6%, France 10.4%, U.S. 8.3%, China 7.2%, Netherlands 5.1%. **Exports:** $15.8 bil; Germany 21.5%, France 15.5%, Belgium 14.5%, UK 5.8%, Italy 5.6%, Switzerland 4.7%. **Tourism:** $4.8 bil. **Budget:** $24.9 bil. **Total reserves less gold:** $876.4 mil. **Gold:** 72,393 oz t. **Inflation:** 1.7%.

Transport: Railways: 171 mi. **Motor vehicles:** 787.6 per 1,000 pop. **Civil aviation:** 288.3 mil pass.-mi; 1 airport. **Chief port:** Mertert.

Communications: TV sets: 605 per 1,000 pop. **Radios:** 683 per 1,000 pop. **Telephone lines:** 50.5 per 100 pop. **Mobile:** 148.6 per 100 pop. **Internet:** 93.8%.

Health: Life expect.: 76.8 male; 83.5 female. **Births:** 11.8 per 1,000 pop. **Deaths:** 8.5 per 1,000 pop. **Natural inc.:** 0.32%. **Infant mortality:** 4.3 per 1,000 live births. **HIV:** NA.

Education: Compulsory: ages 6-15. **Literacy:** 100%.

Embassy: 2200 Massachusetts Ave. NW 20008; 265-4171.

Website: www.gouvernement.lu

Luxembourg, founded about 963, was ruled by Burgundy, Spain, Austria, and France from 1448 to 1815. It left the Germanic Confederation in 1866. Overrun by Germany in 2 world wars, Luxembourg ended its neutrality in 1948, when a customs union with Belgium and the Netherlands was adopted.

Luxembourg was one of the 6 founding members (1951) of what became the European Union. Prime Min. Jean-Claude Juncker, who took office in 1995 and had been the EU's longest-serving head of government, announced July 10, 2013, he would resign, following revelations of abuses by the country's intelligence service. After Oct. 20 elections, Liberal Party leader Xavier Bettel became prime min.

Macedonia
Former Yugoslav Republic of Macedonia

People: Population: 2,091,719. **Age distrib.:** <15: 17.7%; 65+: 12.4%. **Pop. density:** 213 per sq mi, 82.2 per sq km. **Urban:** 57%. **Ethnic groups:** Macedonian 64%, Albanian 25%, Turkish 4%, Roma 3%, Serb 2%. **Languages:** Macedonian, Albanian (both official); Turkish; Roma; Serbian. **Religions:** Macedonian Orthodox 65%, Muslim 33%.

Geography: Total area: 9,928 sq mi, 25,713 sq km; **Land area:** 9,820 sq mi, 25,433 sq km. **Location:** In SE Europe. **Neighbors:** Bulgaria on E, Greece on S, Albania on W, Serbia on N. **Topography:** Landlocked, mostly mountainous country with deep river valleys, 3 large lakes; country is bisected by Vardar R. **Capital:** Skopje, 501,303.

Government: Type: Parliamentary democracy. **Head of state:** Pres. Gjorge Ivanov; b. May 2, 1960; in office: May 12, 2009. **Head of gov.:** Prime Min. Nikola Gruevski; b. Aug. 31, 1970; in office: Aug. 27, 2006. **Local divisions:** 71 municipalities. **Defense budget** (2012): $129 mil. **Active troops:** 8,000.

Economy: Industries: food proc., beverages, textiles, chemicals, iron, steel, cement, energy, pharmaceuticals. **Chief crops:** grapes, tobacco, vegetables, fruits. **Natural resources:** iron ore, copper, lead, zinc, chromite, manganese, nickel, tungsten, gold, silver, asbestos, gypsum, timber. **Arable land:** 16.4%. **Livestock:** cattle: 238,333; chickens: 2.2 mil; goats: 75,028; pigs: 167,492; sheep: 731,828. **Electricity prod.:** 6.5 bil kWh. **Labor force:** agric. 18.8%, industry 27.5%, services 53.7%. **Unemployment:** 31%.

Finance: Monetary unit: Denar (MKD) (Sept. 2014: 46.70 = $1 U.S.). **GDP:** $22.6 bil; **per capita GDP:** $10,800; **GDP growth:** 3.1%. **Imports:** $6.6 bil; Great Britain 11%, Greece 10.6%, Germany 10.5%, Serbia 7.9%, Italy 6.5%, China 5.8%, Bulgaria 5.5%, Turkey 4.8%. **Exports:** $4.3 bil; Germany 36.9%, Bulgaria 7.6%, Italy 6.5%, Kosovo 6.5%, Serbia 6.3%, Greece 5%. **Tourism:** $267 mil. **Budget:** $3.4 bil. **Total reserves less gold:** $2.5 bil. **Gold:** 218,343 oz t. **Inflation:** 2.8%.

Transport: Railways: 434 mi. **Civil aviation:** 8 airports.

Communications: TV sets: 296 per 1,000 pop. **Radios:** 207 per 1,000 pop. **Telephone lines:** 19 per 100 pop. **Mobile:** 106.2 per 100 pop. **Internet:** 61.2%.

Health: Life expect.: 73.2 male; 78.6 female. **Births:** 11.6 per 1,000 pop. **Deaths:** 9.0 per 1,000 pop. **Natural inc.:** 0.26% **Infant mortality:** 7.9 per 1,000 live births. **HIV:** <0.1%.

Education: Compulsory: ages 6-14. **Literacy:** 97.8%.

Embassy: 2129 Wyoming Ave. NW 20008; 667-0501.

Website: www.vlada.mk

Muslim Turks ruled Macedonia from 1389 to 1912. In 1913, the area was incorporated into Serbia, which in 1918 became part of the Kingdom of Serbs, Croats, and Slovenes (later Yugoslavia). In 1946, Macedonia became a constituent republic of Yugoslavia.

Macedonia declared its independence Sept. 8, 1991, and was admitted to the UN in 1993. Greece, which objected to Macedonia's use of what it considered a Hellenic name and symbols, imposed a trade blockade on the landlocked nation; the countries agreed to normalize relations Sept. 13, 1995. However, Greece has blocked Macedonia's bid to join NATO because of the dispute over Macedonia's name.

By the end of NATO's air war against Yugoslavia, Mar.-June 1999, Macedonia had a Kosovar refugee population of more than 250,000; over 90% had been repatriated by Sept. 1.

Ethnic Albanian guerrillas launched an offensive Mar. 2001 in NW Macedonia. An accord signed Aug. 13 paved the way for the introduction of a NATO peacekeeping force. A law broadening the rights of ethnic Albanians was enacted Jan. 2002. A 320-member EU force replaced the NATO peacekeepers, Mar.-Dec. 2003.

Gjorge Ivanov won a presidential runoff vote Apr. 5, 2009, and took office May 12, 2009.

Madagascar
Republic of Madagascar

People: Population: 23,201,926. **Age distrib.:** <15: 40.7%; 65+: 3.2%. **Pop. density:** 103.3 per sq mi, 39.9 per sq km. **Urban:** 34.5%. **Ethnic groups:** Malayo-Indonesian (Merina and related Betsileo), Cotiers (mixed African, Malayo-Indonesian, and Arab ancestry), French, Indian, Creole, Comoran. **Languages:** French, Malagasy (both official); English. **Religions:** indigenous beliefs 52%, Christian 41%, Muslim 7%.

Geography: Total area: 226,658 sq mi, 587,041 sq km; **Land area:** 224,534 sq mi, 581,540 sq km. **Location:** In Indian O., off SE coast of Africa. **Neighbors:** Comoro Isls. to NW, Mozambique to W. **Topography:** Humid coastal strip in E, fertile valleys in mountainous center plateau region, and a wider coastal strip on W. **Capital:** Antananarivo, 2,486,590.

Government: Type: Republic. **Head of state:** Pres. Hery Rajaonarimampianina; b. Nov. 6, 1958; in office: Jan. 25, 2014. **Head of gov.:** Prime Min. Roger Laurent Christophe Kolo; in office: Apr. 11, 2014. **Local divisions:** 6 provinces. **Defense budget:** $72 mil. **Active troops:** 13,500.

Economy: Industries: meat proc., seafood, soap, breweries, tanneries, sugar, textiles, glassware, cement, auto assembly, paper, petroleum, tourism. **Chief crops:** coffee, vanilla, sugarcane, cloves, cocoa, rice, cassava, beans, bananas, peanuts. **Natural resources:** graphite, chromite, coal, bauxite, rare earth elements, salt, quartz, tar sands, semiprec. stones, mica, fish, hydropower. **Arable land:** 6%. **Livestock:** cattle: 10 mil; chickens: 27 mil; goats:

1.5 mil; pigs: 1.5 mil; sheep: 839,000. **Electricity prod.:** 1.3 bil kWh. **Labor force:** NA. **Unemployment:** 3.6%.

Finance: Monetary unit: Ariary (MGA) (Sept. 2014: 2,568.00 = $1 U.S.). **GDP:** $22 bil; **per capita GDP:** $1,000; **GDP growth:** 2.6%. **Imports:** $2.8 bil; China 17.7%, France 12.4%, South Africa 5.3%, India 5.1%, Mauritius 5%, Bahrain 4.7%, Kuwait 4.6%. **Exports:** $644.4 mil; France 23.4%, China 6.6%, U.S. 6.6%, Singapore 5.9%, Canada 5.5%, Germany 5.4%, Indonesia 5.3%, India 5.2%, South Africa 4.5%. **Tourism:** $321 mil. **Budget:** $2.4 bil. **Total reserves less gold:** $776.1 mil. **Inflation:** 5.8%.

Transport: Railways: 531 mi. **Motor vehicles:** 12.1 per 1,000 pop. **Civil aviation:** 680.4 mil pass.-mi; 26 airports. **Chief ports:** Antsiranana, Mahajanga, Toamasina, Toliara.

Communications: TV sets: 37 per 1,000 pop. **Radios:** 268 per 1,000 pop. **Telephone lines:** 1.1 per 100 pop. **Mobile:** 36.1 per 100 pop. **Internet:** 2.2%.

Health: Life expect.: 63.8 male; 66.7 female. **Births:** 33.1 per 1,000 pop. **Deaths:** 7.0 per 1,000 pop. **Natural inc.:** 2.62% **Infant mortality:** 44.9 per 1,000 live births. **HIV:** 0.4%.

Education: Compulsory: ages 6-10. **Literacy:** 64.7%.

Embassy: 2374 Massachusetts Ave. NW 20008; 265-5525.

Website: www.madagascar-presidency.gov.mg

Madagascar was settled 2,000 years ago by Malayan-Indonesian people, whose descendants still predominate. A unified kingdom ruled in the 18th and 19th cent. The island became a French protectorate, 1885, and a colony, 1896. Independence came June 26, 1960.

Discontent with inflation and French domination led to a coup in 1972. The new regime nationalized French-owned financial interests, closed French bases and a U.S. space-tracking station, and obtained Chinese aid. The government conducted a program of arrests, expulsion of foreigners, and repression of strikes in 1979.

In 1990, Madagascar ended a ban on multiparty politics that had existed since 1975. Albert Zafy won the 1993 presidential election, ending the 17-year rule of Adm. Didier Ratsiraka, but was impeached and removed from office in 1996. A cholera epidemic, then cyclones in Feb. and Apr. 2000, claimed 1,600 lives.

Marc Ravalomanana won a contentious presidential election over Ratsiraka Dec. 2001 and was reelected in 2006. A power struggle between Ravalomanana and the military-backed Andry Rajoelina culminated in Rajoelina's installation as head of a transitional regime, Mar. 17, 2009. The African Union suspended Madagascar and pushed for a power-sharing arrangement, but accords signed in Aug. and Nov. 2009 were abrogated by Rajoelina. The transitional government suppressed a coup attempt launched by dissident military officers Nov. 17, 2010. Postponed presidential elections were finally held in late 2013, and won by Hery Rajaonarimampianina, the candidate backed by Rajoelina, although Rajaonarimampianina's runoff opponent disputed the result. Parliamentary elections were also held Dec. 10, 2013.

Malawi
Republic of Malawi

People: Population: 17,241,754. **Age distrib.:** <15: 44.4%; 65+: 2.7%. **Pop. density:** 474.7 per sq mi, 183.3 per sq km. **Urban:** 16.1%. **Ethnic groups:** Chewa 33%, Lomwe 18%, Yao 14%, Ngoni 12%, Tumbuka 9%, Nyanja 6%, Sena 4%, Tonga 2%, Ngonde 1%. **Languages:** English (official), Chichewa (common), Chinyanja, Chiyao, Chitumbuka, Chilomwe, Chinkhonde. **Religions:** Christian 83%, Muslim 13%, none 3%.

Geography: Total area: 45,747 sq mi, 118,484 sq km; **Land area:** 36,324 sq mi, 94,080 sq km. **Location:** In SE Africa. **Neighbors:** Zambia on W, Mozambique on S and E, Tanzania on N. **Topography:** Stretches 560 mi N-S along Lake Nyasa (Lake Malawi), most of which belongs to Malawi. High plateaus and mountains line the Rift Valley the length of the nation. **Capital:** Lilongwe, 867,469.

Government: Type: Multiparty democracy. **Head of state and gov.:** Pres. A. Peter Mutharika; in office: May 31, 2014. **Local divisions:** 28 districts. **Defense budget:** $25 mil. **Active troops:** 5,300.

Economy: Industries: tobacco, tea, sugar, sawmill prods., cement, consumer goods. **Chief crops:** tobacco, sugarcane, cotton, tea, corn, potatoes, cassava, sorghum, pulses, groundnuts. **Natural resources:** limestone, hydropower, uranium, coal, bauxite. **Arable land:** 39.8%. **Livestock:** cattle: 1.2 mil; chickens: 17.2 mil; goats: 5.4 mil; pigs: 2.8 mil; sheep: 255,928. **Electricity prod.:** 2.1 bil kWh. **Labor force:** agric. 90%, industry and services 10%. **Unemployment:** 7.6%.

Finance: Monetary unit: Kwacha (MWK) (Sept. 2014: 385.75 = $1 U.S.). **GDP:** $15 bil; **per capita GDP:** $900; **GDP growth:** 5%. **Imports:** $2.4 bil; South Africa 27%, China 16.6%, India 8.7%, Zambia 8.5%, Tanzania 5.1%, U.S. 4.3%. **Exports:** $1.4 bil; Canada 10.6%, Zimbabwe 9.3%, Germany 7.3%, South Africa 6.6%, Russia 6.5%, U.S. 6.1%, China 4.2%. **Tourism:** $34 mil. **Budget:** $1.4 bil. **Total reserves less gold:** $413.1 mil. **Gold:** 12,837 oz t. **Inflation:** 27.3%.

Transport: Railways: 495 mi. **Motor vehicles:** 2 per 1,000 pop. **Civil aviation:** 7 airports. **Chief ports:** Chilumba, Chipoka, Monkey Bay, Nkhata Bay, Nkhotakota.

Communications: TV sets: 11 per 1,000 pop. **Radios:** 3 per 1,000 pop. **Telephone lines:** 0.2 per 100 pop. **Mobile:** 32.3 per 100 pop. **Internet:** 5.4%.

Health: Life expect.: 52.3 male; 54.0 female. **Births:** 39.5 per 1,000 pop. **Deaths:** 12.3 per 1,000 pop. **Natural inc.:** 2.73%. **Infant mortality:** 74.9 per 1,000 live births. **HIV:** 10.3%.

Education: Compulsory: ages 6-13. **Literacy:** 65.8%.

Embassy: 1029 Vermont Ave. NW, Ste. 1000, 20005; 721-0270.

Website: www.malawi.gov.mw

Bantus came to the land in the 16th cent., Arab slavers in the 19th. The area became the British protectorate Nyasaland in 1891. It became independent July 6, 1964, and a republic in 1966.

After 3 decades as a one-party state under Pres. Hastings Kamuzu Banda, Malawi adopted a new constitution and, in multiparty elections held May 17, 1994, chose a new leader, Bakili Muluzi.

Bingu wa Mutharika, candidate of the ruling United Democratic Front, won a disputed 2004 presidential election. In an ongoing power struggle, an effort by his former political allies to impeach him was halted by Malawi's Constitutional Court, Oct. 2005. Mutharika won reelection May 2009. Clashes between police and anti-government protesters July 2011 left at least 19 people dead. Joyce Banda became Malawi's first female pres. after the death of Bingu wa Mutharika Apr. 5, 2012. Banda finished third in May 20-22, 2014, presidential elections. After her attempt to nullify the result on the basis of voting irregularities was blocked in court, Peter Mutharika was declared the winner.

Malaysia

People: Population: 30,073,353. **Age distrib.:** <15: 28.8%; 65+: 5.5%. **Pop. density:** 237 per sq mi, 91.5 per sq km. **Urban:** 74%. **Ethnic groups:** Malay 50%, Chinese 23%, indigenous 12%, Indian 7%. **Languages:** Bahasa Malaysia (official), English, Chinese, Tamil, Telugu, Malayalam, Panjabi, Thai. **Religions:** Muslim (official) 61%; Buddhist 20%; Christian 9%; Hindu 6%.

Geography: Total area: 127,355 sq mi, 329,847 sq km; **Land area:** 126,895 sq mi, 328,657 sq km. **Location:** On SE tip of Asia, plus N coast of the island of Borneo. **Neighbors:** Thailand, Brunei on N; Indonesia on S. **Topography:** Most of W is covered by tropical jungle, including the central mountain range that runs N-S through the peninsula. W coast is marshy, the E coast, sandy. In E is a wide, swampy coastal plain with interior jungles and mountains. **Capital:** Kuala Lumpur, 6,629,180; Putrajaya (admin.). **Cities (urban aggl.):** Johor Bahru, 890,849.

Government: Type: Constitutional monarchy. **Head of state:** Paramount Ruler Tuanku Abdul Halim Mu'adzam Shah; b. Nov. 28, 1927; in office: Apr. 11, 2012. **Head of gov.:** Prime Min. Najib Razak; b. July 23, 1953; in office: Apr. 3, 2009. **Local divisions:** 13 states, 1 federal territory. **Defense budget:** $5 bil. **Active troops:** 109,000.

Economy: Industries: rubber and palm oil proc., petroleum and nat. gas, light mfg., pharmaceuticals, medical tech., electronics, timber proc., logging. **Chief crops:** palm oil, rubber, cocoa, rice, pepper. **Natural resources:** tin, petroleum, timber, copper, iron ore, nat. gas, bauxite. **Crude oil reserves:** 4 bil bbls. **Arable land:** 2.9%. **Livestock:** cattle: 792,000; chickens: 260 mil; goats: 508,000; pigs: 1.7 mil; sheep: 126,000. **Electricity prod.:** 123.3 bil kWh. **Labor force:** agric. 11.1%, industry 36%, services 53.5%. **Unemployment:** 3.1%.

Finance: Monetary unit: Ringgit (MYR) (Sept. 2014: 3.18 = $1 U.S.). **GDP:** $525 bil; **per capita GDP:** $17,500; **GDP growth:** 4.7%. **Imports:** $192.9 bil; China 15.1%, Singapore 13.3%, Japan 10.3%, U.S. 8.1%, Thailand 6%, Indonesia 5.1%, South Korea 4.1%. **Exports:** $230.7 bil; Singapore 13.6%, China 12.6%, Japan 11.8%, U.S. 8.7%, Thailand 5.4%, Hong Kong 4.3%, India 4.2%, Australia 4.1%. **Tourism:** $21 bil. **Budget:** $79.4 bil. **Total reserves less gold:** $133.4 bil. **Gold:** 1.2 mil oz t. **Inflation:** 2.1%.

Transport: Railways: 1,149 mi. **Motor vehicles:** 415 per 1,000 pop. **Civil aviation:** 46 bil pass.-mi; 39 airports. **Chief ports:** Bintulu, George Town (Penang), Johor Bahru, Port Kelang, Tanjung Pelepas.

Communications: TV sets: 224 per 1,000 pop. **Radios:** 425 per 1,000 pop. **Telephone lines:** 15.3 per 100 pop. **Mobile:** 144.7 per 100 pop. **Internet:** 67%.

Health: Life expect.: 71.7 male; 77.5 female. **Births:** 20.1 per 1,000 pop. **Deaths:** 5 per 1,000 pop. **Natural inc.:** 1.51%. **Infant mortality:** 13.7 per 1,000 live births. **HIV:** 0.4%.

Education: Compulsory: ages 6-11. **Literacy:** 94.6%.

Embassy: 3516 International Ct. NW 20008; 572-9700.

Website: www.malaysia.gov.my

European traders appeared in the 16th cent.; Britain established control in 1867. Malaysia was created Sept. 16, 1963. It included Malaya (which gained independence in 1957 after the suppression of Communist rebels), plus the formerly British Singapore, Sabah (N Borneo) and Sarawak (NW Borneo). Singapore was separated in 1965 in order to end tensions between Chinese—the majority in Singapore—and Malays in control of the Malaysian government.

Malaysia has abundant natural resources, though rainforest destruction has become a major environmental problem. Foreign investment has aided industrialization and trade. Work on a federal administrative center at Putrajaya, south of Kuala Lumpur, was completed in 1999; it is linked by rail with Kuala Lumpur's city center and international airport and with Cyberjaya, a hub for high-tech manufacturing and research.

The Indian Ocean tsunami of Dec. 26, 2004, left at least 68 people dead in Malaysia. Recession and scandals plagued Malaysia as National Front leader Najib Razak took over the premiership in 2009. Tuanku Abdul Halim Mu'adzam Shah was chosen in 2011 to serve as the paramount ruler for a second 5-year term, more than 40 years after his first (1970-75). In a close election May 5, the governing coalition was returned to power, in an election that the opposition deemed fraudulent.

A Malaysia Airlines flight to Beijing, carrying 239 passengers and crew, lost contact with air traffic control Mar. 8, 2014, shortly after takeoff from Kuala Lumpur and was presumed lost in the Indian Ocean. On July 17, a Malaysia Airlines flight from Amsterdam to Kuala Lumpur was shot down by a missile over eastern Ukraine, killing all 298 people onboard; pro-Russian separatists were widely suspected of responsibility for the attack.

Maldives
Republic of Maldives

People: Population: 393,595. **Age distrib.:** <15: 21%; 65+: 4.3%. **Pop. density:** 3,420.8 per sq mi, 1,320.8 per sq km. **Urban:** 44.5%. **Ethnic groups:** South Indian, Sinhalese, Arab. **Languages:** Dhivehi (official), English (spoken by most govt. officials). **Religion:** Sunni Muslim (official).

Geography: Total area: 115 sq mi, 298 sq km; **Land area:** 115 sq mi, 298 sq km. **Location:** In Indian O., SW of India. **Neighbors:** Nearest is India on N. **Topography:** 19 atolls with 1,190 islands, 198 inhabited. None of the islands are over 5 sq mi in area, and all are nearly flat. **Capital:** Male, 156,427.

Government: Type: Republic. **Head of state and gov.:** Pres. Abdulla Yameen Abdul Gayoom; b. May 21, 1959; in office: Nov. 17, 2013. **Local divisions:** 7 provinces, 1 municipality. **Defense budget/active troops:** NA.

Economy: Industries: tourism, fish proc., shipping, boat building, coconut proc., woven mats, rope, handicrafts, coral and sand mining. **Chief crops:** coconuts, corn, sweet potatoes. **Natural resources:** fish. **Arable land:** 10%. **Electricity prod.:** 265.2 mil kWh. **Labor force:** agric. 15%, industry 15%, services 70%. **Unemployment:** 11.3%.

Finance: Monetary unit: Rufiyaa (MVR) (Sept. 2014: 15.27 = $1 U.S.). **GDP:** $3.1 bil; **per capita GDP:** $9,100; **GDP growth:** 3.5%. **Imports** (2012): $1.4 bil; Singapore 21.7%, UAE 20.9%, India 9.6%, Malaysia 7.6%, China 6%, Thailand 5.6%, Sri Lanka 4%. **Exports** (2012): $283 mil; France 18.9%, Thailand 15.8%, UK 11.4%, U.S. 9.4%, Sri Lanka 8.6%, Italy 8.1%, Germany 6.4%. **Tourism:** $2 bil. **Budget** (2012 est.): $917 mil. **Total reserves less gold:** $381.9 mil. **Inflation:** 2.3%.

Transport: Civil aviation: 7 airports. **Chief port:** Male.

Communications: TV sets: 131 per 1,000 pop. **Radios:** 131 per 1,000 pop. **Telephone lines:** 6.5 per 100 pop. **Mobile:** 181.2 per 100 pop. **Internet:** 44.1%.

Health: Life expect.: 72.9 male; 77.6 female. **Births:** 15.6 per 1,000 pop. **Deaths:** 3.8 per 1,000 pop. **Natural inc.:** 1.18%. **Infant mortality:** 24.6 per 1,000 live births. **HIV:** <0.1%.

Education: Compulsory: ages 6-15. **Literacy:** 99.3%.

Embassy: 800 Second Ave., Ste. 400E, New York, NY 10017; (212) 599-6194.

Website: www.presidencymaldives.gov.mv

A British protectorate since 1887, the nation achieved independence July 26, 1965; long a sultanate, the Maldives became a republic in 1968. Tourism and fishing are the most important sectors of the economy. Rising sea levels threaten the country, which comprises at least 1,200 small, low-lying coral islands.

The Indian Ocean tsunami of Dec. 26, 2004, killed at least 82 people and displaced more than 21,600 in the Maldives. Pres. Maumoon Abdul Gayoom, in office 1978-2008, lost a 2008 runoff vote to pro-democracy leader and former political prisoner Mohamed (Anni) Nasheed. Following protests over the arrest of a judge, Nasheed resigned Feb. 2012, and Vice Pres. Mohamed Waheed Hassan Maniku took office. Nasheed later claimed that he resigned at gunpoint, but an international-backed commission ruled, Aug. 29, that it was voluntary. Nasheed ran for president Sept. 7, 2013, and won 45% of the vote, which was not enough to avoid a runoff. The Supreme Court canceled the runoff Sept. 24. In new elections Nov. 9, 2013, Nasheed won 47%. He lost the Nov. 16 runoff to Abdulla Yameen Abdul Gayoom.

Mali
Republic of Mali

People: Population: 16,455,903. **Age distrib.:** <15: 47.6%; 65+: 3%. **Pop. density:** 34.9 per sq mi, 13.5 per sq km. **Urban:** 39.1%. **Ethnic groups:** Mande (Bambara, Malinke, Soninke) 50%, Peul 17%, Voltaic 12%, Songhai 6%, Tuareg and Moor 10%. **Languages:** French (official), Bambara, numerous African langs. **Religions:** Muslim 95%, Christian 2%, animist 2%.

Geography: Total area: 478,841 sq mi, 1,240,192 sq km; **Land area:** 471,118 sq mi, 1,220,190 sq km. **Location:** In interior of W Africa. **Neighbors:** Mauritania, Senegal on W; Guinea, Côte d'Ivoire, Burkina Faso on S; Niger on E; Algeria on N. **Topography:** Landlocked grassy plain in upper basins of the Senegal and Niger Rivers, extending N into the Sahara. **Capital:** Bamako, 2,386,060.

Government: Type: Republic. **Head of state:** Pres. Ibrahim Boubacar Keita; b. Jan. 29, 1945; in office: Sept. 4, 2013. **Head of gov.:** Prime Min. Moussa Mara; b. Mar. 2, 1975; in office: Apr. 9, 2014. **Local divisions:** 8 regions, 1 district. **Defense budget:** $301 mil. **Active troops:** 3,000.

Economy: Industries: food proc., constr., phosphate and gold mining. **Chief crops:** cotton, millet, rice, corn, vegetables, peanuts. **Natural resources:** gold, phosphates, kaolin, salt, limestone, uranium, gypsum, granite, hydropower. **Arable land:** 5.6%. **Livestock:** cattle: 10 mil; chickens: 36.9 mil; goats: 19.1 mil; pigs: 77,594; sheep: 13.7 mil. **Electricity prod.:** 520 mil kWh. **Labor force:** agric. 80%, industry and services 20%. **Unemployment:** 8.1%.

Finance: Monetary unit: CFA Franc (XOF) (Sept. 2014: 498.91 = $1 U.S.). **GDP:** $18.9 bil; **per capita GDP:** $1,100; **GDP growth:** 4.8%. **Imports:** $2.9 bil; France 11.2%, Senegal 9.9%, Côte d'Ivoire 8.7%, China 8.6%. **Exports:** $2.6 bil; China 52.9%, Malaysia 11%, Indonesia 5.3%, India 4.1%. **Tourism:** $267 mil. **Budget:** $2.9 bil. **Total reserves less gold:** $1.3 bil. **Inflation:** −0.6%.

Transport: Railways: 368 mi. **Motor vehicles:** 1.6 per 1,000 pop. **Civil aviation:** 8 airports. **Chief port:** Koulikoro.

Communications: TV sets: 49 per 1,000 pop. **Radios:** 132 per 1,000 pop. **Telephone lines:** 0.8 per 100 pop. **Mobile:** 129.1 per 100 pop. **Internet:** 2.3%.

Health: Life expect.: 53.1 male; 56.8 female. **Births:** 45.5 per 1,000 pop. **Deaths:** 13.2 per 1,000 pop. **Natural inc.:** 3.23%. **Infant mortality:** 104.3 per 1,000 live births. **HIV:** 0.9%.

Education: Compulsory: ages 7-16. **Literacy:** 38.7%.

Embassy: 2130 R St. NW 20008; 332-2249.

Website: www.primature.gov.ml

Until the 15th cent. the area was part of the great Mali Empire. Timbuktu (Tombouctou) was a center of Islamic study. French rule was secured, 1898. The Sudanese Rep. and Senegal became independent as the Mali Federation in 1960, but Senegal withdrew, and the Sudanese Rep. was renamed Mali.

A coup toppled a socialist regime led, 1960-68, by Pres. Modibo Keita. Famine struck in 1973-74, killing as many as 100,000 people. Drought conditions returned in the 1980s.

The military, Mar. 1991, overthrew Pres. Moussa Traoré, who had ruled since 1968. Oumar Konare, a coup leader, was elected president, 1992. The government and a Tuareg rebel group signed a peace accord in 1994, but Tuareg separatists remained active in the north. Twice condemned to death for crimes committed in office, Traoré had his sentences commuted to life imprisonment in 1997 and 1999; he was pardoned in 2002.

Amadou Toumani Touré, who led the 1991 coup, was elected president in 2002 and reelected 2007. Amadou Sanogo, an army captain, staged a coup Mar. 2012 and brokered a deal to transfer power Apr. 12 to an interim government led by Pres. Dioncounda Traoré. The coup enabled Islamist rebels, who had allied themselves with the separatists, to seize control of the country's north. France entered the fight against the Islamists Jan. 10, 2013, and West African regional forces joined them Jan 17. The Islamists were pushed out of most of the territory they had seized. The UN Stabilization Mission in Mali (MINUSMA) was approved Apr. 25, and Taureg rebels signed a peace deal June 18. Ibrahim Boubacar Keita was elected president Aug. 11, 2013. Attacks by Taureg separatists, as well as fighting against Islamists, continued in 2014. A cease-fire agreement with separatist groups was reached in May, and a new accord regarding peace talks was signed in June. France integrated its 1,700 troops in Mali, July 2014, into a regional French counterterrorism force. An Air Algérie plane crashed in Mali, July 24, apparently due to bad weather, killing all 118 aboard.

Malta
Republic of Malta

People: Population: 412,655. **Age distrib.:** <15: 15.1%; 65+: 17.9%. **Pop. density:** 3,382.2 per sq mi, 1,305.9 per sq km. **Urban:** 95.3%. **Ethnic groups:** Maltese (descendants of ancient Carthaginians and Phoenicians with strong Italian, other Mediterranean elements). **Languages:** Maltese, English (both official). **Religion:** Roman Catholic (official) 90%.

Geography: Total area: 122 sq mi, 316 sq km; **Land area:** 122 sq mi, 316 sq km. **Location:** In center of Mediterranean Sea. **Neighbors:** Nearest is Italy on N. **Topography:** Isl. of Malta is 95 sq mi; other islands in the group: Gozo, 26 sq mi; Comino, 1 sq mi. Coastline is heavily indented. Low hills cover the interior. **Capital:** Valletta, 197,447.

Government: Type: Republic. **Head of state:** Pres. Marie-Louise Coleiro Preca; b. Dec. 7, 1958; in office: Apr. 4, 2014. **Head of gov.:** Prime Min. Joseph Muscat; b. Jan. 22, 1974; in office: Mar. 11, 2013. **Local divisions:** 68 localities. **Defense budget:** $60 mil. **Active troops:** 1,950.

Economy: Industries: tourism, electronics, shipbuilding and repair, constr., food and beverages, pharmaceuticals, footwear, clothing, tobacco, aviation services. **Chief crops:** potatoes, cauliflower, grapes, wheat, barley, tomatoes, citrus, cut flowers, green peppers. **Natural resources:** limestone, salt. **Arable land:** 28.1%. **Livestock:** cattle: 15,220; chickens: 1 mil; goats: 4,598; pigs: 49,450; sheep: 10,930. **Electricity prod.:** 2.1 bil kWh. **Labor force:** agric. 1.4%, industry 22.2%, services 76.4%. **Unemployment:** 6.4%.

Finance: Monetary unit: Euro (EUR) (Sept. 2014: 0.76 = $1 U.S.). **GDP:** $11.2 bil; **per capita GDP (2012):** $29,200; **GDP growth:** 2.4%. **Imports:** $7.4 bil; Italy 24.6%, Germany 5.6%, UK 5.4%, Russia 5.1%, France 5%. **Exports:** $5.1 bil; Germany 8.9%, Singapore 7.1%, Libya 6.2%, France 6.2%, U.S. 4.4%. **Tourism:** $1.4 bil. **Budget:** $4.3 bil. **Total reserves less gold:** $584.9 mil. **Gold:** 12,700 oz t. **Inflation:** 1.4%.

Transport: Motor vehicles: 739.9 per 1,000 pop. **Civil aviation:** 1.6 bil pass.-mi; 1 airport. **Chief ports:** Marsaxlokk (Malta Freeport), Valletta.

Communications: TV sets: 554 per 1,000 pop. **Radios:** 664 per 1,000 pop. **Telephone lines:** 53.9 per 100 pop. **Mobile:** 129.8 per 100 pop. **Internet:** 68.9%.

Health: Life expect.: 77.8 male; 82.6 female. **Births:** 10.2 per 1,000 pop. **Deaths:** 9.0 per 1,000 pop. **Natural inc.:** 0.13%. **Infant mortality:** 3.6 per 1,000 live births. **HIV:** Na.

Education: Compulsory: ages 5-15. **Literacy:** 94.4%.

Embassy: 2017 Connecticut Ave. NW 20008; 462-3611.

Website: www.gov.mt

Malta was ruled by Phoenicians, Romans, Arabs, Normans, the Knights of Malta, France, and Britain (since 1814). It became independent Sept. 21, 1964. Malta became a republic in 1974. The last British forces withdrew, Apr. 1, 1979.

From 1971 to 1987 and again from 1996 to 1998, Malta was governed by the socialist Labour Party; the Nationalist Party, which pressed for Malta's entry into the EU, held office 1987-96 and won parliamentary elections in 1998, 2003, and 2008. Malta became a full member of the EU May 1, 2004. The Labour Party returned to power as a result of Mar. 9, 2013, elections.

Marshall Islands
Republic of the Marshall Islands

People: Population: 70,983. **Age distrib.:** <15: 36.6%; 65+: 3.4%. **Pop. density:** 1,015.7 per sq mi, 392.2 per sq km. **Urban:** 72.4%. **Ethnic groups:** Marshallese 92%, mixed Marshallese 6%. **Languages:** Marshallese, English (both official). **Religions:** Protestant 55%, Assembly of God 26%, Roman Catholic 8%, Bukot nan Jesus 3%, Mormon 2%, none 2%.

Geography: Total area: 70 sq mi, 181 sq km; **Land area:** 70 sq mi, 181 sq km. **Location:** In N Pacific O.; composed of two 800-mi-long parallel chains of coral atolls. **Neighbors:** Nearest are Micronesia to W, Nauru and Kiribati to S. **Topography:** Low coral limestone and sand islands. **Capital:** Majuro, 30,861.

Government: Type: Constitutional govt. in free association with U.S. **Head of state and gov.:** Pres. Christopher J. Loeak; b. Nov. 11, 1952; in office: Jan. 17, 2012. **Local divisions:** 24 municipalities. **Defense budget/active troops:** NA.

Economy: Industries: copra, tuna proc., tourism, craft items. **Chief crops:** coconuts, tomatoes, melons, taro, breadfruit, fruits. **Natural resources:** coconut prods., marine prods., deep-seabed minerals. **Arable land:** 11.1%. **Labor force:** agric. 11%, industry 16.3%, services 72.7%. **Unemployment:** NA.

Finance: Monetary unit: U.S. Dollar (USD). **GDP:** $486 mil; **per capita GDP:** $8,700; **GDP growth:** 2.3%. **Imports (2011):** $118.7 mil. **Exports (2011):** $50.1 mil. **Tourism:** $4 mil. **Budget: (FY09 est.)** $104.7 mil. **Total reserves less gold:** NA. **Inflation:** NA.

Transport: Civil aviation: 4 airports. **Chief port:** Majuro.

Communications: Telephone lines (2004): 10.6 per 100 pop. **Mobile (2005):** 1.3 per 100 pop. **Internet:** 11.7%.

Health: Life expect.: 70.4 male; 74.8 female. **Births:** 26.4 per 1,000 pop. **Deaths:** 4.2 per 1,000 pop. **Natural inc.:** 2.21%. **Infant mortality:** 21.4 per 1,000 live births. **HIV:** Na.

Education: Compulsory: ages 6-13. **Literacy:** NA.

Embassy: 2433 Massachusetts Ave. NW 20008; 234-5414.

Website: www.rmi-op.net

The Marshall Islands were a German possession until WWI and were administered by Japan between the World Wars. After WWII, they were administered by the U.S. as part of the UN Trust Territory of the Pacific Islands. During 1946-58, Bikini and Enewetak Atolls were used as test sites for U.S. nuclear weapons.

The Compact of Free Association, ratified by the U.S. in 1986, gave the islands their independence. In the compact, the U.S. agreed to provide financial aid to the islands, maintain their defense, and compensate victims of nuclear testing; it was renewed Dec. 2003. The Marshall Islands joined the UN in 1991. Severe drought conditions in spring 2013 prompted U.S. Pres. Barack Obama to sign a disaster declaration June 21 for the Marshall Islands, making the country eligible for U.S. federal relief funds. Made up of low-lying atolls, the Marshall Islands is considered one of the world's most vulnerable nations to rising sea levels resulting from climate change.

Mauritania
Islamic Republic of Mauritania

People: Population: 3,516,806. **Age distrib.:** <15: 39.5%; 65+: 3.6%. **Pop. density:** 8.8 per sq mi, 3.4 per sq km. **Urban:** 59.3%. **Ethnic groups:** black Moors (Arab-speaking, African origin) 40%, white Moors (of Arab-Berber descent) 30%, black Africans (non-Arabic speaking) 30%. **Languages:** Arabic (official and national); Pulaar, Soninke, Wolof (all national); French; Hassaniya. **Religion:** Muslim (official) 100%.

Geography: Total area: 397,955 sq mi, 1,030,700 sq km; **Land area:** 397,955 sq mi, 1,030,700 sq km. **Location:** In NW Africa. **Neighbors:** Western Sahara on N; Algeria, Mali on E; Senegal on S. **Topography:** Fertile Senegal R. valley in the S gives way to a wide central region of sandy plains and scrub trees. N is arid and extends into the Sahara. **Capital:** Nouakchott, 944,804.

Government: Type: Military junta. **Head of state:** Pres. Mohamed Ould Abdel Aziz; b. Dec. 20, 1956; in office: Aug. 5. 2009. **Head of gov.:** Prime Min. Moulaye Ould Mohamed Laghdaf; b. 1957; in office: Aug. 14, 2008. **Local divisions:** 13 regions. **Defense budget:** NA. **Active troops:** 15,850.

Economy: Industries: fish proc.; oil prod.; iron ore, gold, copper mining. **Chief crops:** dates, millet, sorghum, rice, corn. **Natural resources:** iron ore, gypsum, copper, phosphate, diamonds, gold, oil, fish. **Crude oil reserves:** 20 mil bbls. **Arable land:** 0.4%. **Livestock:** cattle:1.9 mil; chickens: 4.6 mil; goats: 5.7 mil; sheep: 9.1 mil. **Electricity prod.:** 930 mil kWh. **Labor force:** agric. 50%, industry 2%, services 48%. **Unemployment:** 31%.

Finance: Monetary unit: Ouguiya (MRO) (Sept. 2014: 289.00 = $1 U.S.). **GDP:** $8.2 bil; **per capita GDP:** $2,200; **GDP growth:** 6.4%. **Imports:** $3.4 bil; China 12.9%, Netherlands 10.5%, U.S. 7.8%, France 7.8%, Brazil 5.6%, Germany 5.5%, Spain 5.1%, Belgium 4.7%. **Exports:** $2.7 bil; China 50.5%, Italy 7.8%, Japan 7.3%, France 4.9%, Spain 4.2%, Côte d'Ivoire 4.1%, Netherlands 4%. **Budget:** $1.7 bil. **Total reserves less gold** (2012): $949.5 mil. **Gold** (2012): 11,500 oz t. **Inflation:** 4.5%.

Transport: Railways: 452 mi. **Motor vehicles:** 7.4 per 1,000 pop. **Civil aviation:** 9 airports. **Chief ports:** Nouadhibou, Nouakchott.

Communications: TV sets: 46 per 1,000 pop. **Radios:** 384 per 1,000 pop. **Telephone lines:** 1.4 per 100 pop. **Mobile:** 102.5 per 100 pop. **Internet:** 6.2%.

Health: Life expect.: 60.0 male; 64.6 female. **Births:** 31.8 per 1,000 pop. **Deaths:** 8.4 per 1,000 pop. **Natural inc.:** 2.35%. **Infant mortality:** 56.1 per 1,000 live births. **HIV:** NA.

Education: Compulsory: ages 6-15. **Literacy:** 52.1%.

Embassy: 2129 Leroy Pl. NW 20008; 232-5700.

Website: www.mauritania.mr

A French protectorate from 1903, Mauritania became independent Nov. 28, 1960. It annexed the south of former Spanish Sahara (now Western Sahara) in 1976 but renounced its claim to the region after signing a peace treaty with the Saharan guerrillas of the Polisario Front, 1979.

Maaouiya Ould Sid Ahmed Taya took power in a military coup in 1984. Taya, a U.S. ally, was toppled in a bloodless coup in 2005. During Jan.-June 2006, up to 10,000 people tried to emigrate in handmade boats from Mauritania to Spain's Canary Islands; more than 1,700 died. Civilian rule was restored, 2006-07, but a 2008 military coup toppled the elected government. The coup leader, Gen. Mohamed Ould Abdel Aziz, won disputed presidential elections in 2009 and 2014. Security concerns, including a rising threat from al-Qaeda in the Islamic Maghreb, led the U.S. Peace Corps to remove its volunteers from Mauritania in Aug. 2009. Under a program launched in 2013, U.S. Special Operations troops began providing training and equipment to Mauritanian counterterrorism forces, to help combat Islamic extremists.

Major oil finds have recently been developed. Although slavery has been repeatedly abolished, most recently in 1981, and legislation mandating prison terms for slaveholders was enacted in 2007, at least 140,000 Mauritanians continued to live under conditions of servitude according to one 2013 estimate.

Mauritius
Republic of Mauritius

People: Population: 1,331,155. **Age distrib.:** <15: 21%; 65+: 8.4%. **Pop. density:** 1,698.4 per sq mi, 655.7 per sq km. **Urban:** 39.8%. **Ethnic groups:** Indo-Mauritian 68%, Creole 27%, Sino-Mauritian 3%, Franco-Mauritian 2%. **Languages:** Creole, Bhojpuri, French, English (official). **Religions:** Hindu 48%, Roman Catholic 24%, Muslim 17%, other Christian 9%.

Geography: Total area: 788 sq mi, 2,040 sq km; **Land area:** 784 sq mi, 2,030 sq km. **Location:** In Indian O., 500 mi E of Madagascar. **Neighbors:** Nearest is Madagascar to W. **Topography:** A volcanic island nearly surrounded by coral reefs. A central plateau is encircled by mountain peaks. **Capital:** Port Louis, 135,496.

Government: Type: Parliamentary democracy. **Head of state:** Pres. Rajkeswur Kailash Purryag; b. Dec. 12, 1947; in office: July 21, 2012. **Head of gov.:** Prime Min. Navinchandra Ramgoolam; b. July 14, 1947; in office: July 5, 2005. **Local divisions:** 9 districts,

3 dependencies. **Defense budget:** $83 mil. **Active troops:** No standing armed forces; Special Mobile Force and coast guard provide security.

Economy: Industries: food proc. (largely sugar milling), textiles, clothing, mining, chemicals, metal prods. **Chief crops:** sugarcane, tea, corn, potatoes, bananas, pulses. **Natural resources:** fish. **Arable land:** 37.4%. **Livestock:** cattle: 7,000; chickens: 14.5 mil; goats: 27,000; pigs: 14,500; sheep: 16,500. **Electricity prod.:** 2.6 bil kWh. **Labor force:** agric. and fishing 9%; constr. and industry 30%; transp. and communication 7%; trade, restaurants, hotels 22%; finance 6%; other services 25%. **Unemployment:** 7.9%.

Finance: Monetary unit: Rupee (MUR) (Sept. 2014: 31.05 = $1 U.S.). **GDP:** $21 bil; **per capita GDP:** $16,100; **GDP growth:** 3.4%. **Imports:** $5 bil; India 23.1%, China 16%, France 8.5%, South Africa 6.5%. **Exports:** $2.8 bil; UK 19.3%, France 16.4%, U.S. 9.9%, South Africa 9.8%, Spain 7.5%, Italy 6.4%, Madagascar 6.8%. **Tourism:** $1.3 bil. **Budget:** $2.7 bil. **Total reserves less gold:** $3.3 bil. **Gold:** 126,000 oz t. **Inflation:** 3.5%.

Transport: Motor vehicles: 156.4 per 1,000 pop. **Civil aviation:** 4.1 bil pass.-mi; 2 airports. **Chief port:** Port Louis.

Communications: TV sets: 370 per 1,000 pop. **Radios:** 78 per 1,000 pop. **Telephone lines:** 29.2 per 100 pop. **Mobile:** 123.2 per 100 pop. **Internet:** 39%.

Health: Life expect.: 71.7 male; 78.8 female. **Births:** 13.5 per 1,000 pop. **Deaths:** 6.9 per 1,000 pop. **Natural inc.:** 0.66%. **Infant mortality:** 10.6 per 1,000 live births. **HIV:** 1.1%.

Education: Compulsory: ages 5-16. **Literacy:** 90.6%.

Embassy: 4301 Connecticut Ave. NW, Ste. 441, 20008; 244-1491.

Website: www.gov.mu

Mauritius was uninhabited when settled in 1638 by the Dutch, who introduced sugarcane. France took over in 1721, bringing African slaves. Britain ruled from 1810 to Mar. 12, 1968, bringing Indian workers for the sugar plantations.

Mauritius formally severed its association with the British crown Mar. 12, 1992. Since 2006, Mauritius has topped the Ibrahim Index of African Governance as the best-governed African country.

Mexico
United Mexican States

People: Population: 120,286,655. **Age distrib.:** <15: 27.9%; 65+: 6.6%. **Pop. density:** 160.3 per sq mi, 61.9 per sq km. **Urban:** 79%. **Ethnic groups:** mestizo (Amerindian-Spanish) 60%, Amerindian or predom. Amerindian 30%, white 9%. **Languages:** Spanish, indigenous langs. (incl. Mayan, Nahuatl, other regional langs.). **Religions:** Roman Catholic 83%, Pentecostal 2%, none 5%.

Geography: Total area: 758,449 sq mi, 1,964,375 sq km; **Land area:** 750,561 sq mi, 1,943,945 sq km. **Location:** In southern N America. **Neighbors:** U.S. on N, Guatemala and Belize on S. **Topography:** The Sierra Madre Occidental Mts. run NW-SE near the W coast; the Sierra Madre Oriental Mts. run near Gulf of Mexico. They join S of Mexico City. Between the 2 ranges lies the dry central plateau (5,000-8,000 ft) rising toward the S, with temperate vegetation. Coastal lowlands are tropical. About 45% of land is arid. **Capital:** Mexico City, 20,843,500 (figure is for metro area). **Cities (urban aggl.):** Guadalajara, 4,766,004; Monterrey, 4,435,257; Puebla, 2,935,651; Toluca de Lerdo, 2,120,046; Tijuana, 1,940,941; León de los Aldamas, 1,768,664; Ciudad Juárez, 1,379,981.

Government: Type: Federal republic. **Head of state and gov.:** Pres. Enrique Peña Nieto; b. July 20, 1966; in office: Dec. 1, 2012. **Local divisions:** 31 states, 1 federal district. **Defense budget:** $5.78 bil. **Active troops:** 270,250.

Economy: Industries: food and beverages, tobacco, chemicals, iron and steel, petroleum, mining, textiles, clothing, motor vehicles, consumer durables, tourism. **Chief crops:** corn, wheat, soybeans, rice, beans, cotton, coffee, fruit, tomatoes. **Natural resources:** petroleum, silver, copper, gold, lead, zinc, nat. gas, timber. **Crude oil reserves:** 10.1 bil bbls. **Arable land:** 11.9%. **Livestock:** cattle: 32 mil; chickens: 528 mil; goats: 8.7 mil; pigs: 16 mil. **Electricity prod.** (2012): 277.6 bil kWh. **Labor force:** agric. 13.4%, industry 24.1%, services 61.9%. **Unemployment:** 4.9%.

Finance: Monetary unit: Peso (MXN) (Sept. 2014: 13.10 = $1 U.S.). **GDP:** $1.8 tril; **per capita GDP:** $15,600; **GDP growth:** 1.2%. **Imports:** $370.7 bil; U.S. 49.9%, China 15.4%, Japan 4.8%. **Exports:** $370.9 bil; U.S. 78%. **Tourism:** $13.8 bil. **Budget:** $324.1 bil. **Total reserves less gold:** $175.4 bil. **Gold:** 4 mil oz t. **Inflation:** 3.8%.

Transport: Railways: 10,666 mi. **Motor vehicles:** 295.8 per 1,000 pop. **Civil aviation:** 24.6 bil pass.-mi; 243 airports. **Chief ports:** Altamira, Coatzacoalcos, Lazaro Cardenas, Manzanillo, Salina Cruz, Veracruz.

Communications: TV sets: 274 per 1,000 pop. **Radios:** 324 per 1,000 pop. **Telephone lines:** 16.8 per 100 pop. **Mobile:** 85.8 per 100 pop. **Internet:** 43.5%.

Health: Life expect.: 72.7 male; 78.3 female. **Births:** 19.0 per 1,000 pop. **Deaths:** 5.2 per 1,000 pop. **Natural inc.:** 1.38%. **Infant mortality:** 12.6 per 1,000 live births. **HIV:** 0.2%.

Education: Compulsory: ages 4-17. **Literacy:** 95.1%.

Embassy: 1911 Pennsylvania Ave. NW 20006; 728-1600.

Website: www.presidencia.gob.mx

Mexico was the site of advanced civilizations. The Mayans, an agricultural people, moved up from Yucatan, built huge stone pyramids and invented a calendar. The Toltecs were overcome by the Aztecs, who founded Tenochtitlan 1325 CE, now Mexico City. Hernán Cortés, Spanish conquistador, destroyed the Aztec empire, 1519-21. After 3 centuries of Spanish rule the people revolted, under Fr. Miguel Hidalgo y Costilla, 1810, Fr. Morelos y Pavón, 1812, and Gen. Agustín Iturbide, who made himself emperor as Agustín I, 1822. A republic was declared in 1823.

Mexican territory extended into the present American SW and California. Texas established a republic in 1836, and Mexico lost lands north of the Rio Grande during the U.S.-Mexican War, 1846-48.

The French supported an Austrian archduke on the Mexican throne as Maximilian I, 1864-67. He was deposed in an uprising led by Benito Juárez. Dictatorial rule by Porfirio Díaz, president 1877-80, 1884-1911, led to a period of rebellion and factional fighting. A new constitution in 1917 brought reform.

The Institutional Revolutionary Party (PRI) dominated politics from 1929 until the late 1990s. Radical opposition, including some guerrilla activity, was contained by strong measures. Some gains in agriculture, industry, and social services were achieved, but much of the work force remained jobless or underemployed. Although prospects brightened with the discovery of vast oil reserves, inflation and a drop in world oil prices aggravated Mexico's economic problems in the 1980s. Mexico signed the North American Free Trade Agreement (NAFTA) with the U.S. and Canada in 1992; it took effect Jan. 1, 1994.

After guerrillas of the Zapatista National Liberation Army (EZLN) rebelled Jan. 1994, a tentative peace accord was reached Mar. 2. The presidential candidate of the governing PRI, Luis Donaldo Colosio Murrieta, was assassinated at a political rally in Tijuana, Mar. 23. The new PRI candidate, Ernesto Zedillo Ponce de León, won election Aug. 21 and was inaugurated Dec. 1, 1994.

An austerity plan and pledges of aid from the U.S. saved Mexico's currency from collapse in early 1995. Popular Revolutionary Army guerrillas launched coordinated attacks on government targets in Aug. 1996. In 1997 elections, the PRI lost a congressional majority for the first time since 1929.

In the 2000 presidential election, the PRI lost for the first time in over 7 decades; the winner, Vicente Fox Quesada of the National Action Party (PAN), took office Dec. 1, 2000. The PAN candidate, conservative Felipe Calderón Hinojosa, won the 2006 presidential election. Despite a government crackdown on drug cartels, drug-related violence intensified, including an arson attack on a Monterrey casino Aug. 25, 2011, that killed 52 people. The cumulative death toll in the drug war exceeded 47,500, Dec. 2006-Sept. 2012. Enrique Peña Nieto (PRI) won 2012 presidential elections. He continued the policy of using federal troops to combat drug gangs. Peña Nieto passed 2013 constitutional changes intended to bring greater competition to key industries, including oil, telecommunications, and broadcasting. Congress gave final approval to new regulations, Aug. 2014, opening the oil industry (nationalized in 1938) to foreign companies and other private investment. By 2014, Mexico's oil production had declined by 25% from its 2004 level.

Micronesia
Federated States of Micronesia

People: Population: 105,681. **Age distrib.:** <15: 31.9%; 65+: 3.4%. **Pop. density:** 389.9 per sq mi, 150.5 per sq km. **Urban:** 22.4%. **Ethnic groups:** Chuukese/Mortlockese 49%, Pohnpeian 30%, Kosraean 6%, Yapese 6%, Yap outer islands 5%, Polynesian 2%. **Languages:** English (official), Chuukese, Kosrean, Pohnpeian, Yapese, Ulithian, Woleaian, Nukuoro, Kapingamarangi. **Religions:** Roman Catholic 55%, Protestant 41% (incl. Congregational 39%).

Geography: Total area: 271 sq mi, 702 sq km; **Land area:** 271 sq mi, 702 sq km. **Location:** Consists of 607 islands in W Pacific O. **Topography:** Includes both high mountainous islands and low coral atolls; volcanic outcroppings on Pohnpei, Kosrae, and Truk. Climate is tropical. **Capital:** Palikir, 6,821.

Government: Type: Constitutional govt. in free association with U.S. **Head of state and gov.:** Pres. Emanuel (Manny) Mori; b. Dec. 25, 1948; in office: May 11, 2007. **Local divisions:** 4 states. **Defense budget/active troops:** NA.

Economy: Industries: tourism, constr., fish proc., specialized aquaculture, craft items. **Chief crops:** black pepper, tropical fruits and vegetables, coconuts, bananas, cassava, kava, citrus, betel nuts, sweet potatoes. **Natural resources:** timber, marine prods., deep-seabed minerals, phosphate. **Arable land:** 2.9%. **Livestock:** cattle: 14,000; chickens: 190,000; goats: 4,100; pigs: 33,000. **Labor force:** agric. 0.9%, industry 20.6%, services 78.5% (two-thirds of labor force are govt. employees). **Unemployment:** NA.

Finance: Monetary unit: U.S. Dollar (USD). **GDP:** $754 mil; **per capita GDP:** $7,300; **GDP growth:** 0.6%. **Imports** (2004): $132.7 mil. **Exports** (2009): $24.9 mil. **Tourism:** $23 mil. **Budget** (FY10/11 est.): $102 mil. **Total reserves less gold:** $84.3 mil. **Inflation:** NA.

Transport: Civil aviation: 6 airports. **Chief port:** Colonia. **Communications: TV sets:** 27 per 1,000 pop. **Radios:** 47 per 1,000 pop. **Telephone lines** 9.7 per 100 pop. **Mobile:** 30.3 per 100 pop. **Internet:** 27.8%.

Health: Life expect.: 70.3 male; 74.5 female. **Births:** 21.0 per 1,000 pop. **Deaths:** 4.3 per 1,000 pop. **Natural inc.:** 1.67%. **Infant mortality:** 21.9 per 1,000 live births. **HIV:** NA.

Education: Compulsory: ages 6-13. **Literacy:** NA.

Embassy: 1725 N St. NW 20036; 223-4383.

Website: micronesia.fm

Micronesia, formerly known as the Caroline Islands, was ruled successively by Spain, Germany, Japan, and the U.S. The nation gained independence under a compact of free association with the U.S., Nov. 1986, and was admitted to the UN in 1991. Micronesian officials have repeatedly warned of the dangers to their country of rising sea levels linked to global climate change.

Moldova
Republic of Moldova

People: Population: 3,583,288. **Age distrib.:** <15: 17.7%; 65+: 11.1%. **Pop. density:** 282.2 per sq mi, 108.9 per sq km. **Urban:** 44.9%. **Ethnic groups:** Moldovan 76%, Ukrainian 8%, Russian 6%, Gagauz 4%, Bulgarian 2%. **Languages:** Moldovan (official; virtually same as Romanian), Russian, Gagauz. **Religions:** Orthodox 93%.

Geography: Total area: 13,070 sq mi, 33,851 sq km; **Land area:** 12,699 sq mi, 32,891 sq km. **Location:** In E Europe. **Neighbors:** Romania on W; Ukraine on N, E, and S. **Topography:** Country is landlocked; mainly hilly plains with steppelands in S near Black Sea. **Capital:** Chişinău, 720,681.

Government: Type: Republic. **Head of state:** Pres. Nicolae Timofti; b. Dec. 22, 1948; in office: Mar. 23, 2012. **Head of gov.:** Prime Min. Iurie Leancă; b. Oct. 20, 1963; in office: May 31, 2013. **Local divisions:** 32 raions, 3 municipalities, 2 units. **Defense budget:** $24 mil. **Active troops:** 5,350.

Economy: Industries: sugar, vegetable oil, food proc., agric. machinery, foundry equip., refrigerators and freezers. **Chief crops:** vegetables, fruits, grapes, grain, sugar beets, sunflower seeds, tobacco. **Natural resources:** lignite, phosphorites, gypsum, limestone. **Arable land:** 55.2%. **Livestock:** cattle: 191,200; chickens: 26 mil; goats: 128,900; pigs: 410,400; sheep: 695,100. **Electricity prod.:** 5.5 bil kWh. **Labor force:** agric. 26.4%, industry 13.2%, services 60.4%. **Unemployment:** 5.6%.

Finance: Monetary unit: Leu (MDL) (Sept. 2014: 14.07 = $1 U.S.). **GDP:** $13.3 bil; **per capita GDP:** $3,800; **GDP growth:** 8.9%. **Imports:** $5.5 bil; Russia 14.3%, Romania 13.1%, Ukraine 12%, China 8.7%, Germany 7.2%, Turkey 6.9%, Italy 6.3%. **Exports:** $2.4 bil; Russia 26.3%, Romania 17.2%, Italy 7.7%, Ukraine 5.9%, Turkey 5.3%, Germany 4.7%, UK 4.4%. **Tourism:** $226 mil. **Budget:** $3.1 bil. **Total reserves less gold:** $2.8 bil. **Gold:** 2,383 oz t. **Inflation:** 4.6%.

Transport: Railways: 739 mi. **Civil aviation:** 5 airports. **Communications: TV sets:** 310 per 1,000 pop. **Radios:** 39 per 1,000 pop. **Telephone lines:** 35 per 100 pop. **Mobile:** 106 per 100 pop. **Internet:** 48.8%.

Health: Life expect.: 66.3 male; 74.2 female. **Births:** 12.2 per 1,000 pop. **Deaths:** 12.6 per 1,000 pop. **Natural inc.:** –0.04%. **Infant mortality:** 12.9 per 1,000 live births. **HIV:** 0.6%.

Education: Compulsory: ages 7-15. **Literacy:** 99.4%.

Embassy: 2101 S St. NW 20008; 667-1130.

Website: www.moldova.md

In 1918, Romania annexed all of Bessarabia that Russia had acquired from Turkey in 1812 by the Treaty of Bucharest. In 1924, the Soviet Union established the Moldavian Autonomous Soviet Socialist Republic on the eastern bank of the Dniester. It was merged with the Romanian-speaking districts of Bessarabia in 1940 to form the Moldavian SSR.

During WWII, Romania, allied with Germany, occupied the area. It was recaptured by the USSR in 1944. Moldova declared independence Aug. 27, 1991. It became an independent state when the USSR disbanded Dec. 26, 1991.

Fighting erupted Mar. 1992 in the Trans-Dniester region between Moldovan security forces and Slavic separatists—ethnic Russians and ethnic Ukrainians—who feared Moldova's merging with neighboring Romania. In a 1994 plebiscite, voters in Moldova supported independence, without unification with Romania.

Defying the Moldovan government, voters in the breakaway Trans-Dniester region held legislative elections and approved a separatist constitution in 1995. A peace accord with Trans-Dniester separatists was signed in Moscow in 1997. In a 2006 referendum, Trans-Dniester voters overwhelmingly supported independence from Moldova and eventual union with Russia. The Communists gained legislative majorities in 2001 and 2005 but were outpolled by a fragile coalition of pro-Western parties in 2009 and 2010. When a deadlocked parliament failed to agree on a president, a constitutional referendum providing for direct presidential elections was held Sept. 5, 2010. Although 88% of voters supported it, the measure failed to pass because of insufficient turnout. The pro-Western Nicolae Timofti became president in 2012. Parliament passed a no-confidence motion against Prime Min. Vlad Filat Mar. 5, 2013, forcing his resignation. Iurie Leanca was chosen the new prime min. May 31, and June 26 announced that he supported Timofti's plan for EU integration. Moldova and the EU signed an Association Agreement, June 27, 2014.

Monaco
Principality of Monaco

People: Population: 30,508. **Age distrib.:** <15: 11.7%; 65+: 29.5%. **Pop. density:** 39,507.7 per sq mi, 15,254 per sq km. **Urban:** 100%. **Ethnic groups:** French 47%, Monegasque 16%, Italian 16%. **Languages:** French (official), English, Italian, Monegasque. **Religion:** Roman Catholic (official) 90%.

Geography: Total area: 0.77 sq mi, 2 sq km; **Land area:** 0.77 sq mi, 2 sq km. **Location:** On NW Mediterranean coast. **Neighbors:** France to W, N, E. **Topography:** Monaco-Ville sits atop a high promontory; the rest of the principality rises from the port up the hillside. **Capital:** Monaco.

Government: Type: Constitutional monarchy. **Head of state:** Prince Albert II; b. Mar. 14, 1958; in office: Apr. 6, 2005. **Head of gov.:** Min. of State Michel Roger; b. Mar. 9, 1949; in office: Mar. 29, 2010. **Local divisions:** no first-order admin. divisions. **Defense budget/active troops:** NA.

Economy: Industries: tourism, constr., small-scale industrial and consumer prods. **Chief crops:** none. **Natural resources:** none. **Arable land:** NA. **Labor force:** agric. 0%, industry 16.1%, services 83.9%. **Unemployment:** NA.

Finance: Monetary unit: Euro (EUR) (Sept. 2014: 0.76 = $1 U.S.). **GDP** (2012): $6.2 bil; **per capita GDP** (2011): $85,500; **GDP growth** (2012): 0.9%. **Imports** (2011): $1.2 bil; Europe 70.4%, Asia 20.8%, America 4.4%, Africa 4.1%. **Exports** (2011): $1.1 bil; Europe 73.2%, Africa 14.6%, America 5.2%, Asia 4.9%. (Full customs integration with France. Also participates in EU market system through customs union with France.) **Budget** (2011 est.): $1.1 bil. **Total reserves less gold:** NA. **Inflation:** NA.

Transport: Chief port: Monaco.

Communications: TV sets: 758 per 1,000 pop. **Telephone lines:** 123.8 per 100 pop. **Mobile:** 93.7 per 100 pop. **Internet:** 90.7%.

Health: Life expect.: 85.7 male; 93.6 female. **Births:** 6.7 per 1,000 pop. **Deaths:** 9.0 per 1,000 pop. **Natural inc.:** −0.23% **Infant mortality:** 1.8 per 1,000 live births. **HIV:** NA.

Education: Compulsory: ages 6-15. **Literacy:** 99%.

Embassy: 2314 Wyoming Ave. NW 20008; 234-1530.

Website: www.gouv.mc

An independent principality for over 300 years, Monaco has belonged to the House of Grimaldi since 1297, except during the French Revolution. It was placed under the protectorate of Sardinia in 1815, and under France, 1861. The Prince of Monaco was an absolute ruler until the 1911 constitution. Monaco was admitted to the UN in 1993. Monaco is noted for its mild climate, magnificent scenery, elegant casinos, and Formula One Grand Prix auto race. Prince Rainier III, who ruled Monaco from 1949 and turned it into one of Europe's top tourist spots, died in 2005 and was succeeded by his son, Albert II.

Mongolia

People: Population: 2,953,190. **Age distrib.:** <15: 26.8%; 65+: 4.1%. **Pop. density:** 4.9 per sq mi, 1.9 per sq km. **Urban:** 71.2%. **Ethnic groups:** Khalkha 82%, Kazak 4%, Dorvod 3%, Bayad 2%. **Languages:** Khalkha Mongol (official), Turkic, Russian. **Religions:** Buddhist 53%, Muslim 3%, Shamanist 3%, none 39%.

Geography: Total area: 603,909 sq mi, 1,564,116 sq km; **Land area:** 599,831 sq mi, 1,553,556 sq km. **Location:** In E Central Asia. **Neighbors:** Russia on N, China on E, W, and S. **Topography:** Mostly a high plateau with mountains, salt lakes, and vast grasslands. Arid lands in S are part of the Gobi Desert. **Capital:** Ulaanbaatar, 1,333,620.

Government: Type: Parliamentary. **Head of state:** Pres. Tsakhiagiin Elbegdorj; b. Mar. 30, 1963; in office: June 18, 2009. **Head of gov.:** Prime. Min. Norov Altankhuyag; b. Jan. 20, 1958; in office: Aug. 9, 2012. **Local divisions:** 21 provinces, 1 municipality. **Defense budget:** $133 mil. **Active troops:** 10,000.

Economy: Industries: constr. and constr. materials, mining, oil, food and beverages, animal prods. proc., cashmere and natural fiber mfg. **Chief crops:** wheat, barley, vegetables, forage crops. **Natural resources:** oil, coal, copper, molybdenum, tungsten, phosphates, tin, nickel, zinc, fluorspar, gold, silver, iron. **Arable land:** 0.4%. **Livestock:** cattle: 2.6 mil; chickens: 480,000; goats: 18 mil; pigs: 40,000; sheep: 17.5 mil. **Electricity prod.:** 4.5 bil kWh. **Labor force:** agric. 33%, industry 10.6%, services 56.4%. **Unemployment:** 5.2%.

Finance: Monetary unit: Tughrik (MNT) (Sept. 2014: 1,810.00 = $1 U.S.). **GDP:** $17 bil; **per capita GDP:** $5,900; **GDP growth:** 11.8%. **Imports** (2012): $6 bil; China 37.5%, Russia 25.6%, U.S. 9.4%, South Korea 6.1%, Japan 4.9%. **Exports** (2012): $4.3 bil; China 89%, Canada 4.1%. **Tourism:** $369 mil. **Budget:** $4.4 bil. **Total reserves less gold:** $2.1 bil. **Gold:** 126,233 oz t. **Inflation:** 9.2%.

Transport: Railways: 1,186 mi (partly owned by Russian State Railway). **Civil aviation:** 15 airports.

Communications: TV sets: 88 per 1,000 pop. **Radios:** 328 per 1,000 pop. **Telephone lines:** 6.2 per 100 pop. **Mobile:** 124.2 per 100 pop. **Internet:** 17.7%.

Health: Life expect.: 64.7 male; 73.5 female. **Births:** 20.9 per 1,000 pop. **Deaths:** 6.4 per 1,000 pop. **Natural inc.:** 1.45%. **Infant mortality:** 23.2 per 1,000 live births. **HIV:** <0.1%.

Education: Compulsory: ages 6-14. **Literacy:** 98.4%.

Embassy: 2833 M St. NW 20007; 333-7117.

Website: www.pmis.gov.mn

One of the world's oldest countries, Mongolia reached the zenith of its power in the 13th cent. when Genghis Khan and his successors conquered all of China and extended their influence as far west as Hungary and Poland. In later centuries, the empire dissolved and Mongolia became a province of China.

With the advent of the 1911 Chinese revolution, Mongolia, with Russian backing, declared its independence. A Communist regime was established in 1921. In 1990, the Mongolian Communist Party yielded its monopoly on power. A new constitution took effect in 1992.

Mongolia sent more than 100 troops to U.S.-led operations in Afghanistan (2001); as of early Sept. 2014, 40 remained. Riots followed 2008 parliamentary elections, won by the ruling Mongolian People's Revolutionary Party (MPRP). In 2009 presidential voting, former Prime Min. Tsakhiagiin Elbergdorj (1998, 2004-06), the Democratic Party candidate, defeated the MPRP's incumbent Pres. Nambaryn Enkhbayar. A 2012 legislative election gave the Democratic Party the most seats in parliament, and Norov Altankhuyag became prime min. Aug. 9. Elbergdorj was reelected June 27, 2013. Exploitation of vast mineral resources is expected to boost Mongolia's GDP at double-digit annual rates.

Montenegro

People: Population: 650,036. **Age distrib.:** <15: 15.2%; 65+: 14%. **Pop. density:** 125.2 per sq mi, 48.3 per sq km. **Urban:** 63.8%. **Ethnic groups:** Montenegrin 45%, Serbian 29%, Bosniak 9%, Albanian 5%, Muslim 3%. **Languages:** Serbian, Montenegrin (official), Bosnian, Albanian. **Religions:** Orthodox 72%, Muslim 19%, Catholic 3%.

Geography: Total area: 5,333 sq mi, 13,812 sq km; **Land area:** 5,194 sq mi, 13,452 sq km. **Location:** On Balkan Peninsula in SE Europe. **Neighbors:** Bosnia and Herzegovina on N and W; Serbia on E; Albania on SE; Adriatic Sea on SW; Croatia on W. **Topography:** Most terrain is rugged and mountainous, with few arable regions, mostly along the Zeta R.; narrow coastline is highly indented. **Capital:** Podgorica, 164,999.

Government: Type: Republic. **Head of state:** Pres. Filip Vujanovic; b. Sept. 1, 1954; in office: Apr. 6, 2008. **Head of gov.:** Prime. Min. Milo Djukanovic; b. Feb. 15, 1962; in office: Dec. 4, 2012. **Local divisions:** 23 municipalities. **Defense budget:** $54 mil. **Active troops:** 2,080.

Economy: Industries: steelmaking, aluminum, agric. proc., consumer goods, tourism. **Chief crops:** tobacco, potatoes, citrus, olives, grapes. **Natural resources:** bauxite, hydroelectricity. **Arable land:** 12.8%. **Livestock:** cattle: 84,000; chickens: 700,000; pigs: 18,000; sheep: 207,000. **Electricity prod.:** 2.6 bil kWh. **Labor force:** agric. 6.3%, industry 20.9%, services 72.8%. **Unemployment:** 19.6%.

Finance: Monetary unit: Euro (Sept. 2014: 0.76 = $1 U.S.). **GDP:** $7.4 bil; **per capita GDP:** $11,900; **GDP growth:** 1.5%. **Imports** (2012): $2.4 bil; Serbia 29.3%, Greece 8.7%, China 7.1%. **Exports** (2012): $489.2 mil; Croatia 22.7%, Serbia 22.7%, Slovenia 7.8%. **Tourism:** $884 mil. **Budget** (2012 est.): $1.6 bil. **Total reserves less gold:** $584 mil. **Inflation:** 2.1%.

Transport: Railways: 155 mi. **Civil aviation:** 5 airports. **Chief port:** Bar.

Communications: Telephone lines (2010): 26.8 per 100 pop. **Telephone lines:** 27.2 per 100 pop. **Mobile:** 160 per 100 pop. **Internet:** 56.8%.

Health: Life expect.: 75.3 male; 81.4 female. **Births:** 10.6 per 1,000 pop. **Deaths:** 9.3 per 1,000 pop. **Natural inc.:** 0.13%. **Infant mortality:** 8.9 per 1,000 live births. **HIV:** NA.

Education: Compulsory: ages 6-14. **Literacy:** 98.7%.

Embassy: 1610 New Hampshire Ave. NW 20009; 234-6108.

Website: www.gov.me

Part of the medieval Serbian Kingdom, Montenegro preserved its autonomy for centuries because of its mountainous terrain. After WWI, it was part of the Kingdom of Serbs, Croats, and Slovenes, later renamed Yugoslavia. Italian forces occupied parts of Montenegro during WWII. In 1945, with the establishment of a federal Yugoslavia under Communist rule, Montenegro became one of 6 constituent republics.

In Apr. 1992, after 4 other republics had declared independence, Montenegro and Serbia reconstituted themselves as the Federal Republic of Yugoslavia. Because of its ties with Serbia, Montenegro was a target of NATO air strikes during the Kosovo war, Mar.-June 1999. The republic sought closer ties with the West, however, and worked to reduce its political and economic dependence on Serbia. A 2006 referendum on independence passed with barely more than the 55% majority required. Montenegro declared independence June 3, 2006, and was admitted as a UN member June 28. It applied, in 2008, to join the EU.

Morocco
Kingdom of Morocco

People: Population: 32,987,206. **Age distrib.:** <15: 26.7%; 65+: 6.3%. **Pop. density:** 191.4 per sq mi, 73.9 per sq km. **Urban:** 59.7%. **Ethnic groups:** Arab-Berber 99%. **Languages:** Arabic (official), Berber langs., French (lang. of business, govt., diplomacy). **Religion:** Muslim (official; almost all Sunni) 99%.

Geography: Total area: 172,414 sq mi, 446,550 sq km; **Land area:** 172,317 sq mi, 446,300 sq km. **Location:** On NW coast of Africa. **Neighbors:** Western Sahara on S, Algeria on E, Spain on N. **Topography:** Consists of 5 natural regions: mountain ranges (Riff in the N, Middle Atlas, Upper Atlas, and Anti-Atlas); rich plains in W; alluvial plains in SW; well-cultivated plateaus in the center; a pre-Sahara arid zone extending from SE. **Capital:** Rabat, 1,931,620. **Cities (urban aggl.):** Dar-el-Beida (Casablanca), 3,490,568; Fès, 1,148,695; Marrakech, 1,099,920.

Government: Type: Constitutional monarchy. **Head of state:** King Mohammed VI; b. Aug. 21, 1963; in office: July 30, 1999. **Head of gov.:** Prime Min. Abdelilah Benkirane; b. Apr. 4, 1954; in office: Nov. 29, 2011. **Local divisions:** 15 regions (not incl. territory in Western Sahara). **Defense budget:** $3.73 bil. **Active troops:** 195,800.

Economy: Industries: phosphate rock mining and proc., food proc., leather goods, textiles, constr., energy, tourism. **Chief crops:** barley, wheat, citrus, grapes, vegetables, olives. **Natural resources:** phosphates, iron ore, manganese, lead, zinc, fish, salt. **Crude oil reserves:** 680 bbls. **Arable land:** 18%. **Livestock:** cattle: 3.2 mil; chickens: 185 mil; goats: 6.2 mil; pigs: 8,000; sheep: 20 mil. **Electricity prod.:** 23.7 bil kWh. **Labor force:** agric. 44.6%, industry 19.8%, services 35.5%. **Unemployment:** 9%.

Finance: Monetary unit: Dirham (MAD) (Sept. 2014: 8.47 = $1 U.S.). **GDP:** $180 bil; **per capita GDP:** $5,500; **GDP growth:** 5.1%. **Imports:** $38.7 bil; Spain 13.1%, France 12.1%, China 6.9%, U.S. 6.8%, Saudi Arabia 6.2%, Italy 5.1%, Russia 5%, Germany 4.9%. **Exports:** $16.8 bil; France 21%, Spain 17.3%, Brazil 5.4%, India 4.9%, U.S. 4.6%. **Tourism:** $6.9 bil. **Budget:** $34.5 bil. **Total reserves less gold:** $18.4 bil. **Gold** (2012): 708,766 oz t. **Inflation:** 1.9%.

Transport: Railways: 1,284 mi. **Motor vehicles:** 109.4 per 1,000 pop. **Civil aviation:** 9.7 bil pass.-mi; 31 airports. **Chief ports:** Casablanca, Jorf Lasfar, Mohammedia, Safi, Tangier.

Communications: TV sets: 174 per 1,000 pop. **Radios:** 246 per 1,000 pop. **Telephone lines:** 8.9 per 100 pop. **Mobile:** 128.5 per 100 pop. **Internet:** 56%.

Health: Life expect.: 73.4 male; 79.7 female. **Births:** 18.5 per 1,000 pop. **Deaths:** 4.8 per 1,000 pop. **Natural inc.:** 1.37%. **Infant mortality:** 24.5 per 1,000 live births. **HIV:** 0.2%.

Education: Compulsory: ages 6-14. **Literacy:** 68.5%.

Embassy: 1601 21st St. NW 20009; 462-7979.

Website: www.maroc.ma

Berbers were the region's original inhabitants, followed by Carthaginians and Romans. Arabs conquered it in 683. In the 11th and 12th cents., a Berber empire ruled all NW Africa and most of Spain from Morocco.

Part of Morocco came under Spanish rule in the 19th cent.; France controlled the rest in the early 20th. Tribal uprisings lasted from 1911 to 1933. Independence was achieved Mar. 2, 1956. Tangier, an internationalized seaport, was incorporated into Morocco, 1956. Ifni, a Spanish enclave, was ceded in 1969. Morocco annexed the disputed territory of Western Sahara during the second half of the 1970s.

King Hassan II assumed the throne in 1961, reigning until his death in 1999; he was succeeded by his eldest son. A bicameral legislature was established in 1997.

Five terrorist attacks in Casablanca May 16, 2003, left 45 people dead, including 12 suicide bombers; the government blamed Salafia Jihadia, an al-Qaeda-linked group. Following a series of suicide bombings in 2007, the government stepped up its campaign against militant Islamists. Following Arab Spring street demonstrations Feb.-Mar. 2011, the monarchy implemented modest constitutional reforms. Throughout 2011, Moroccans staged protests of what they saw as social injustices, including persistent unemployment, unjust detentions, and lack of free speech. The moderate Islamist Justice and Development Party won a plurality in Nov. 25, 2011 parliamentary elections, and Abdelilah Benkirane was named prime minister.

Western Sahara

Western Sahara, formerly the protectorate of Spanish Sahara, is bounded on the N by Morocco, the NE by Algeria, the E and S by Mauritania, and the W by the Atlantic O. Phosphates are the major resource. Area 102,703 sq mi; pop. (2014 est.) 554,795. Capital is El Aaiún; pop. (2014 est.) 262,360.

Spain withdrew in Feb. 1976. On Apr. 14, 1976, Morocco annexed over 70,000 sq mi, with the remainder annexed by Mauritania. The Polisario Front guerrilla movement, which proclaimed the region independent Feb. 27, launched attacks with Algerian support. After Mauritania signed a treaty with Polisario Aug. 5, 1979, Morocco occupied Mauritania's portion of Western Sahara.

After years of bitter fighting, Morocco controlled the main urban areas, but Polisario guerrillas moved freely in the vast, sparsely populated deserts. The 2 sides implemented a cease-fire in 1991, when a UN peacekeeping force (MINURSO) was established with a mandate to prepare for a referendum on self-determination as early as 1992; as of July 31, 2014, MINURSO had 231 uniformed personnel in Western Sahara, but a referendum had still not been held.

Mozambique
Republic of Mozambique

People: Population: 24,692,144. **Age distrib.:** <15: 45.3%; 65+: 2.9%. **Pop. density:** 81.3 per sq mi, 31.4 per sq km. **Urban:** 31.9%. **Ethnic groups:** African (incl. Makhuwa, Tsonga, Lomwe, Sena) 99.7%. **Languages:** Emakhuwa, Portuguese (official), Xichangana, Cisena, Elomwe, other Mozambican langs. **Religions:** Roman Catholic 28%, Muslim 18%, Zionist Christian 16%, Protestant 12%, none 19%.

Geography: Total area: 308,642 sq mi, 799,380 sq km; **Land area:** 303,623 sq mi, 786,380 sq km. **Location:** On SE coast of Africa. **Neighbors:** Tanzania on N; Malawi, Zambia, Zimbabwe on W; South Africa, Swaziland on S. **Topography:** Coastal lowlands comprise nearly half the country with plateaus rising in steps to the mountains along W border. **Capital:** Maputo, 1,173,990. **Cities (urban aggl.):** Matola, 898,687.

Government: Type: Republic. **Head of state:** Pres. Armando Guebuza; b. Jan. 20, 1943; in office: Feb. 2, 2005. **Head of gov.:** Prime Min. Alberto Clementino Vaquina; in office: Oct. 8, 2012. **Local divisions:** 10 provinces, 1 city. **Defense budget** $75 mil. **Active troops:** 11,200.

Economy: Industries: aluminum, petroleum prods., chemicals, textiles, cement, glass, asbestos, tobacco, food, beverages. **Chief crops:** cotton, cashew nuts, sugarcane, tea, cassava, corn, coconuts, sisal, citrus and tropical fruits, potatoes, sunflowers. **Natural resources:** coal, titanium, nat. gas, hydropower, tantalum, graphite. **Arable land:** 7.2%. **Livestock:** cattle: 1.7 mil; chickens: 19 mil; goats: 4.4 mil; pigs: 1.7 mil; sheep: 250,000. **Electricity prod.:** 16.7 bil kWh. **Labor force:** agric. 81%, industry 6%, services 13%. **Unemployment:** 7.5%.

Finance: Monetary unit: Metical (MZN) (Sept. 2014: 30.20 = $1 U.S.). **GDP:** $28.2 bil; **per capita GDP:** $1,200; **GDP growth:** 7%. **Imports:** $7.1 bil; South Africa 30.5%, China 12.3%, India 11.6%, U.S. 5.1%, Portugal 4.8%, Australia 4.5%. **Exports:** $3.9 bil; South Africa 31.3%, Belgium 12.8%, China 9%, Italy 7.9%, Spain 6.2%, India 5.8%. **Tourism:** $250 mil. **Budget:** $6.1 bil. **Total reserves less gold:** $3.1 bil. **Gold:** 175,189 oz t. **Inflation:** 4.9%.

Transport: Railways: 2,975 mi. **Motor vehicles:** 3.2 per 1,000 pop. **Civil aviation:** 21 airports. **Chief ports:** Beira, Maputo, Nacala.

Communications: TV sets: 21 per 1,000 pop. **Radios:** 63 per 1,000 pop. **Telephone lines:** 0.3 per 100 pop. **Mobile:** 48 per 100 pop. **Internet:** 5.4%.

Health: Life expect.: 51.9 male; 53.4 female. **Births:** 38.8 per 1,000 pop. **Deaths:** 12.3 per 1,000 pop. **Natural inc.:** 2.65%. **Infant mortality:** 72.4 per 1,000 live births. **HIV:** 10.8%.

Education: Compulsory: ages 6-12. **Literacy:** 58.8%.

Embassy: 1525 New Hampshire Ave. NW 20036; 293-7146.

Website: www.mozambique.mz

The first Portuguese post on the Mozambique coast was established in 1505 on the trade route to the East. Mozambique became independent June 25, 1975, after a 10-year war against the Portuguese. The 1974 revolution in Portugal paved the way for an orderly transfer of power to Frelimo (Front for the Liberation of Mozambique).

The Frelimo government, headed by Pres. Samora Machel, a former guerrilla commander, gradually transitioned to a Communist system. Most of the country's whites emigrated. In the 1980s, severe drought and civil war caused famine and heavy loss of life. Pres. Machel was killed in a plane crash just inside the South African border, Oct. 19, 1986. Frelimo formally abandoned Marxist-Leninism in 1989, and a new constitution, effective Nov. 30, 1990, established multiparty elections and a free-market economy.

A 1992 peace agreement ended hostilities between the government and the Mozambique National Resistance (MNR). Repatriation of 1.7 mil Mozambican refugees ended June 1995.

In Mar. 1999 heavy floods left nearly 200,000 people stranded. Worse flooding in Feb.-Mar. 2000 claimed more than 600 lives and devastated the economy. Flooding of the Zambezi River Basin, followed by Cyclone Favio, killed at least 45 people in Feb. 2007. Another flood crisis, Jan.-Mar. 2008, claimed some 700 lives and displaced 650,000 people.

Frelimo retained its hold on power under Pres. Joaquim Chissano (in office 1986-2005) and his successor, Pres. Armando Guebuza, elected in 2004, reelected in 2009. In Mar. 2014, Frelimo nominated Filipe Nyussi as its presidential candidate in elections scheduled for Oct. 15.

Abundant energy resources have the potential to increase economic growth. Natural gas reserves were estimated at 100 tril cu ft (third-largest in Africa) as of Jan. 1, 2014. Oil exploration continued following initial discoveries of onshore and offshore deposits.

Myanmar
(Burma)
Union of Myanmar

People: Population: 55,746,253. **Age distrib.:** <15: 26.4%; 65+: 5.3%. **Pop. density:** 220.9 per sq mi, 85.3 per sq km. **Urban:** 33.6%. **Ethnic groups:** Burman 68%, Shan 9%, Karen 7%, Rakhine 4%, Chinese 3%, Indian 2%, Mon 2%. **Languages:** Burmese (official), ethnic minority langs. **Religions:** Buddhist 89%, Christian 4%, Muslim 4%, animist 1%.

Geography: Total area: 261,228 sq mi, 676,578 sq km; **Land area:** 252,321 sq mi, 653,508 sq km. **Location:** Between S and SE Asia, on Bay of Bengal. **Neighbors:** Bangladesh, India on W; China, Laos, Thailand on E. **Topography:** Mountains surround Myanmar on W, N, and E, and dense forests cover much of the nation. N-S rivers provide habitable valleys, especially the Irrawaddy, navigable for 900 mi. Country has a tropical monsoon climate. **Capital:** Nay Pyi Taw, 1,015,700. **Cities (urban aggl.):** Yangon, 4,705,056; Mandalay, 1,138,675.

Government: Type: Parliamentary govt. took power in Mar. 2011. **Head of state and gov.:** Pres. Thein Sein; b. Apr. 20, 1945; in office: Feb. 3, 2011. **Local divisions:** 7 regions, 7 states. **Defense budget:** $2.4 bil. **Active troops:** 406,000.

Economy: Industries: agric. proc.; wood and wood prods.; copper, tin, tungsten, iron; cement, constr. materials; pharmaceuticals. **Chief crops:** rice, pulses, beans, sesame, groundnuts, sugarcane. **Natural resources:** petroleum, timber, tin, antimony, zinc, copper, tungsten, lead, coal, marble, limestone, prec. stones, nat. gas, hydropower. **Crude oil reserves:** 50 mil bbls. **Arable land:** 16.6%. **Livestock:** cattle: 14.7 mil; chickens: 190 mil; goats: 3.9 mil; pigs: 10.5 mil; sheep: 862,000. **Electricity prod.:** 7.1 bil kWh. **Labor force:** agric. 70%, industry 7%, services 23%. **Unemployment:** 4.1%.

Finance: Monetary unit: Kyat (MMK) (Sept. 2014: 969.00 = $1 U.S.). **GDP:** $111.1 bil; **per capita GDP:** $1,700; **GDP growth:** 6.8%. **Imports:** $10.1 bil; China 36.9%, Thailand 20.2%, Singapore 8.7%, South Korea 8.7%, Japan 8.2%, Malaysia 4.6%. **Exports:** $9 bil; Thailand 40.7%, India 14.8%, China 14.3%, Japan 7.4%. (Import/export figures grossly underestimated due to value of goods smuggled into and out of Thailand, China, Bangladesh, Malaysia, and India). **Tourism:** $281 mil. **Budget:** $4.4 bil. **Total reserves less gold** (2012): $7 bil. **Gold** (2012): 233,700 oz t. **Inflation:** 5.5%.

Transport: Railways: 3,126 mi. **Motor vehicles:** 0.6 per 1,000 pop. **Civil aviation:** 36 airports. **Chief ports:** Moulmein, Rangoon (Yangon), Sittwe.

Communications: TV sets: 7 per 1,000 pop. **Radios:** 203 per 1,000 pop. **Telephone lines:** 1 per 100 pop. **Mobile:** 12.8 per 100 pop. **Internet:** 1.2%.

Health: Life expect.: 63.6 male; 68.5 female. **Births:** 18.7 per 1,000 pop. **Deaths:** 8.0 per 1,000 pop. **Natural inc.:** 1.06%. **Infant mortality:** 44.9 per 1,000 live births. **HIV:** 0.6%.

Education: Compulsory: ages 5-9. **Literacy:** 93.1%.

Embassy: 2300 S St. NW 20008; 332-3344.

Website: www.mofa.gov.mm

The Burmese arrived from Tibet before the 9th cent., displacing earlier cultures, and a Buddhist monarchy was established by the 11th cent. Burma was conquered by China's Mongol dynasty in 1272, then ruled by Shans as a Chinese tributary until the 16th cent. Britain subjugated Burma in three wars, 1824-84, and ruled the country as part of India until 1937, when Burma became self-governing. Full independence was achieved Jan. 4, 1948.

Gen. Ne Win dominated politics from 1962 to 1988, first as military ruler, then as constitutional president, advancing policies that increased economic socialization and international isolation. In 1987, the UN granted Burma, once the richest nation in SE Asia, less-developed status. Ne Win resigned July 1988, following antigovernment riots. In Sept., the military seized power, under Gen. Saw Maung. In 1989 the country's name was changed to Myanmar.

Although the main opposition party won a decisive victory in 1990 multiparty elections, the military refused to surrender power. A key opposition leader, Aung San Suu Kyi, was held under house arrest, 1989-95, 2000-02, and 2003-10. The regime's poor human rights record and continued harassment of Suu Kyi and her supporters led to U.S.-imposed sanctions.

In late Sept. 2007, thousands of Buddhist monks led mass protests in Yangon; security forces cracked down by raiding monasteries, arresting monks, and firing on demonstrators. On Sept. 25, the U.S. announced tougher sanctions. Cyclone Nargis, May 2-3, 2008, left at least 84,537 people dead, with an estimated 53,836 missing.

After the military dominated Nov. 2010 parliamentary elections, the ruling council was dissolved and an initially nominal civilian government returned, Mar. 30, 2011. Suu Kyi's National League for Democracy (NLD) won 43 of 45 parliamentary seats in an Apr. 1, 2012, election, and Suu Kyi traveled to Oslo, Norway, to accept the Nobel Peace Prize, which she was awarded in absentia in 1991. The EU, Apr. 23, and U.S., May 17, suspended most sanctions against Myanmar. Myanmar's government announced Aug. 28, 2012, the removal of more than 2,000 names from the country's notorious blacklist of those banned from entering or leaving the country. More than 1,000 political prisoners were granted amnesty between Sept. 2012 and Apr. 2013. However, 5 journalists received 10-year prison sentences, July 10, 2014, for publishing an article alleging the government was producing chemical weapons.

Violence between Buddhists and Rohingya Muslims in the northwest that began in 2012 had killed about 200 and driven more than 100,000 Muslims from their homes by early 2014. Many Rohingya refugees, who are not recognized as citizens were confined to camps. The UNHCR estimated, Aug. 22, that since 2012 tens of thousands of Rohingya had fled by boat, seeking asylum in other countries. Riots in central Myanmar in Mar. 2013 killed at least 43 and displaced another 13,000 Muslims. Anti-Muslim riots in Mandalay, July 2014, left 2 dead.

Namibia
Republic of Namibia

People: Population: 2,198,406. **Age distrib.:** <15: 31.7%; 65+: 4.4%. **Pop. density:** 6.9 per sq mi, 2.7 per sq km. **Urban:** 45.7%. **Ethnic groups:** black 88%, white 6%, mixed 7%; about 50% of pop. belong to Ovambo tribe. **Languages:** Oshiwambo langs., Nama/Damara, Afrikaans (common), Otjiherero langs., Kavango langs., English (official). **Religions:** Christian 80%-90% (at least 50% Lutheran), indigenous beliefs 10%-20%.

Geography: Total area: 318,261 sq mi, 824,292 sq km; **Land area:** 317,874 sq mi, 823,290 sq km. **Location:** In southern Africa on coast of Atlantic O. **Neighbors:** Angola on N; Botswana, Zambia on E; South Africa on S. **Topography:** Three distinct regions incl. Namib Desert along the Atlantic, a mountainous central plateau with woodland savanna, and Kalahari Desert in E. True forests found in NE. There are 4 rivers but little other surface water. **Capital:** Windhoek, 356,389.

Government: Type: Republic. **Head of state and gov.:** Pres. Hifikepunye Pohamba; b. Aug. 18, 1935; in office: Mar. 21, 2005. **Local divisions:** 14 regions. **Defense budget:** $458 mil. **Active troops:** 9,200.

Economy: Industries: meatpacking, fish proc., dairy prods., pasta and beverages, mining. **Chief crops:** millet, sorghum, peanuts, grapes. **Natural resources:** diamonds, copper, uranium, gold, silver, lead, tin, lithium, cadmium, tungsten, zinc, salt, hydropower, fish. **Arable land:** 1%. **Livestock:** cattle: 2.4 mil; chickens: 5.4 mil; goats: 2.2 mil; pigs: 72,500; sheep: 2.9 mil. **Electricity prod.:** 1.6 bil kWh. **Labor force:** agric. 16.3%, industry 22.4%, services 61.3% (formal sector only). About half of population unemployed. About two-thirds of rural population rely on subsistence agric. **Unemployment:** 16.7%.

Finance: Monetary unit: Dollar (NAD) (Sept. 2014: 10.68 = $1 U.S.). **GDP:** $17.8 bil; **per capita GDP:** $8,200; **GDP growth:** 4.4%. **Imports:** $7.1 bil. **Exports:** $5.1 bil. **Tourism:** $409 mil. **Budget:** $5.1 bil. **Total reserves less gold:** $1.5 bil. **Inflation:** 5.6%.

Transport: Railways: 1,632 mi. **Motor vehicles:** 113.1 per 1,000 pop. **Civil aviation:** 915.3 mil pass.-mi; 19 airports. **Chief ports:** Luderitz, Walvis Bay.

Communications: TV sets: 78 per 1,000 pop. **Radios:** 62 per 1,000 pop. **Telephone lines:** 8 per 100 pop. **Mobile:** 110.2 per 100 pop. **Internet:** 13.9%.

Health: Life expect.: 52.2 male; 51.5 female. **Births:** 20.3 per 1,000 pop. **Deaths:** 13.6 per 1,000 pop. **Natural inc.:** 0.67%. **Infant mortality:** 45.6 per 1,000 live births. **HIV:** 14.3%.

Education: Compulsory: ages 6-16. **Literacy:** 81.9%.

Embassy: 1605 New Hampshire Ave. NW 20009; 986-0540.

Website: www.grnnet.gov.na

Namibia was declared a German protectorate in 1890 and officially called South-West Africa. South Africa seized the territory in 1915 during WWI; the League of Nations gave South Africa a mandate over the territory in 1920. In 1966, the Marxist South-West Africa People's Organization (SWAPO) launched a guerrilla war for independence. The UN General Assembly named the area Namibia in 1968.

After many years of guerrilla warfare, South Africa, Angola, and Cuba signed a U.S.-mediated agreement Dec. 22, 1988, to end South African administration of Namibia and provide for a cease-fire and transition to independence, in accordance with a 1978 UN plan. A separate accord between Cuba and Angola provided for a phased withdrawal of Cuban troops from Namibia. A constitution providing for multiparty government was adopted Feb. 9, 1990, and Namibia gained independence Mar. 21.

Walvis Bay, the principal deepwater port, had been turned over to South African administration in 1922. It remained in South African hands after independence, but South Africa turned control of the port back to Namibia, as of Mar. 1, 1994. Separatist violence flared in the Caprivi Strip in late 1990s. SWAPO, the leading political group since independence, dominated the general election held Nov. 27-28, 2009.

SCIENCE & TECHNOLOGY

Big Bang Proof? A team of scientists announced Mar. 17, 2014, that they had found evidence supporting the theory that the universe dramatically expanded in the moments following its 'Big Bang' origin.

Jumbo Dino Argentinian paleontologists announced May 16, 2014, they had excavated fossils belonging to an 85-ton titanosaur believed to be the largest dinosaur yet discovered.

Security Breaches The Heartbleed bug, a major security vulnerability affecting OpenSSL—a set of widely used encryption tools—was perhaps the most memorably named of a number of high-profile security breaches affecting digital personal information in 2014.

The Heartbleed Bug

The Heartbleed Bug is a serious vulnerability in the popular OpenSSL cryptographic software library. This weakness allows stealing the information protected, under normal conditions, by the SSL/TLS encryption used to secure the Internet. SSL/TLS provides

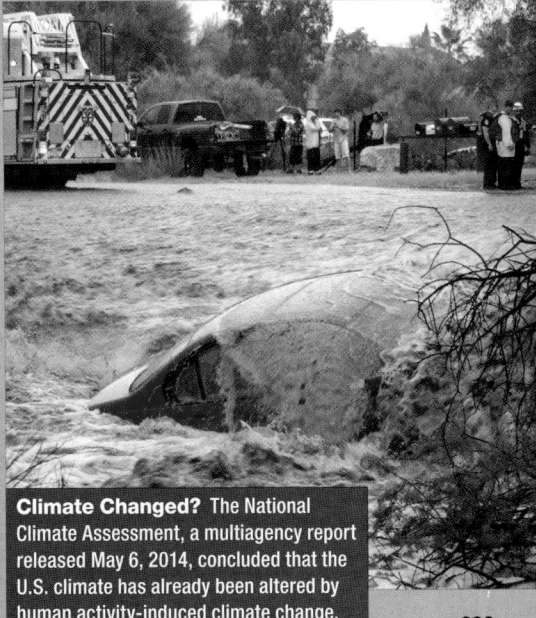

Climate Changed? The National Climate Assessment, a multiagency report released May 6, 2014, concluded that the U.S. climate has already been altered by human activity-induced climate change.

>SPORTS

Auspicious Beginning The dramatic opening ceremony Feb. 7, 2014, at the 2014 Olympic Games in Sochi, Russia, was marred by technical glitches, including an incomplete set of Olympic rings.

FCKC Denies Seattle Reign FC Kansas City won the second National Women's Soccer League championship Aug. 31, 2014, over the Seattle Reign in Tukwila, WA.

Nice Saves U.S. goalie Tim Howard set a record for the most saves in a World Cup match with 16 goals saved in the team's Round of 16 loss to Belgium July 1, 2014.

Break the Ice Meryl Davis and Charlie White became the first U.S. pair to win ice dancing gold Feb. 17, 2014, at the Sochi games.

World Cup Champs Mario Götze scored the deciding (and only) goal in the 2014 FIFA World Cup final July 13, 2014, to give Germany the tournament win in extra time over Argentina.

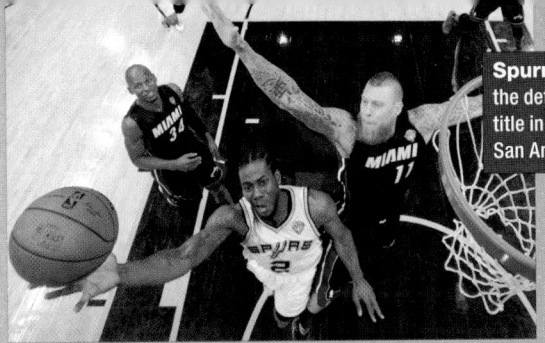

Spurred to Victory The Spurs defeated the defending champion Heat for the NBA title in a decisive Game 5 June 15, 2014, in San Antonio, TX.

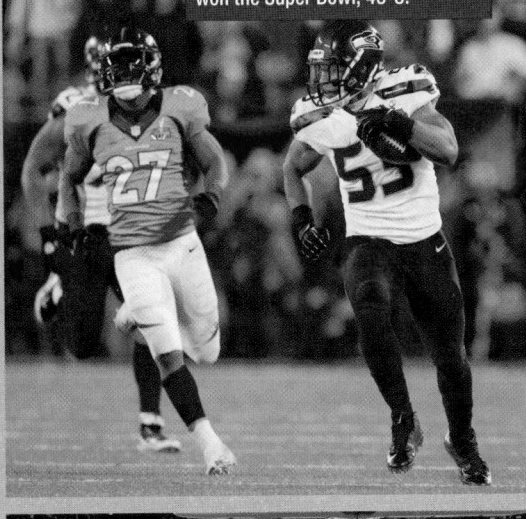

Super Defeat Seahawks linebacker Malcolm Smith returned an interception 69 yards for a touchdown in Super Bowl XLVIII Feb. 2, 2014; Seattle's defense squashed the Denver offense as the team won the Super Bowl, 43-8.

Young Talent Connecticut sophomore Breanna Stewart was named the most outstanding player of the women's Final Four for the second year in a row as UConn defeated Notre Dame in the final Apr. 8, 2014.

Uconn Wins Connecticut guard Shabazz Napier scored 22 points Apr. 7, 2014, as the Huskies defeated Kentucky, 60-54, to win the Division I basketball championship.

Comeback Kids Florida State came from behind to defeat Auburn, 34-31, in the BCS National Championship game Jan. 6, 2014.

>SPORTS

Farewell, Captain After 20 years in pinstripes, Yankee captain Derek Jeter announced Feb. 12, 2014, that the upcoming season would be his last.

In Good Company With his British Open victory in June 2014, Rory McIlroy joined Jack Nicklaus and Tiger Woods as one of only three golfers ever to win three majors by the age of 25; he then won a fourth major, the PGA Championship, Aug. 10, 2014.

Kings Again The L.A. Kings won their second Stanley Cup in three years when Alex Martinez scored on New York goalie Henrik Lundqvist June 13, 2014, to give L.A. the 3-2 win in Game 5.

Homeward Bound Cleveland sports fans anticipated the homecoming of NBA MVP LeBron James, who announced July 11, 2014, that he would return to the Cavaliers after four years with the Miami Heat.

>PEOPLE

Saints in the Making Pontiffs John XXIII and John Paul II were canonized by Pope Francis in St. Peter's Square, Vatican City, Apr. 27, 2014.

Owner Clipped The NBA Apr. 29, 2014, fined L.A. Clippers owner Donald Sterling $2.5 mil and banned him for life, forcing him to sell the franchise, following the release of a recording of Sterling making racist statements to a friend.

New Reign Begins Spain's King Juan Carlos (right) abdicated his throne June 18, 2014, after a 39-year rule; son King Felipe VI replaced him.

Throw Like a Girl Thirteen-year-old Mo'ne Davis pitched a two-hit shutout Aug. 15, 2014, in the Little League World Series.

>ARTS

Second to None Julia Louis-Dreyfus won the Emmy for best actress in a comedy series Aug. 25, 2014, for the third year in a row for *Veep*; it was the third sitcom for which she had won the honor.

(Late) Night Moves Jimmy Fallon took over NBC's *Tonight Show* Feb. 17, 2014; CBS announced Apr. 10, 2014, that Stephen Colbert would take over its *Late Show* from David Letterman in 2015.

Clap Along Pharrell Williams's "Happy" was number one on *Billboard*'s Hot 100 for a 10th consecutive week Apr. 30, 2014.

Ultimate Selfie Academy Awards host Ellen DeGeneres and actor Bradley Cooper were front and center in the viral selfie that collected more than a half-dozen Oscar winners during the show Mar. 2, 2014.

FAREWELLS

MAYA ANGELOU
APR. 4, 1928-MAY 28, 2014

RICHARD ATTENBOROUGH
AUG. 29, 1923-AUG. 24, 2014

LAUREN BACALL
SEPT. 16, 1924-AUG. 12, 2014

AMIRI BARAKA
OCT. 7, 1934-JAN. 9, 2014

JAMES BRADY
AUG. 29, 1940-AUG. 4, 2014

SID CAESAR
SEPT. 8, 1922-FEB. 12, 2014

RUBY DEE
OCT. 27, 1922-JUNE 11, 2014

JOAN FONTAINE
OCT. 22, 1917-DEC. 15, 2013

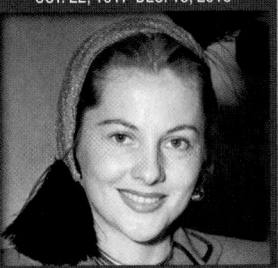

JAMES GARNER
APR. 7, 1928-JULY 19, 2014

TONY GWYNN
MAY 9, 1960-JUNE 16, 2014

PHILIP SEYMOUR HOFFMAN
JULY 23, 1967-FEB. 2, 2014

CASEY KASEM
APR. 27, 1932-JUNE 15, 2014

>FAREWELLS

RALPH KINER
OCT. 27, 1922-FEB. 6, 2014

NELSON MANDELA
JULY 18, 1918-DEC. 5, 2013

GABRIEL GARCÍA MÁRQUEZ
MAR. 6, 1927-APR. 17, 2014

CHUCK NOLL
JAN. 5, 1932-JUNE 13, 2014

PETER O'TOOLE
AUG. 2, 1932-DEC. 14, 2013

JOAN RIVERS
JUNE 8, 1933-SEPT. 4, 2014

MICKEY ROONEY
SEPT. 23, 1920-APR. 6, 2014

PETE SEEGER
MAY 3, 1919-JAN. 27, 2014

ELAINE STRITCH
FEB. 2, 1925-JULY 17, 2014

SHIRLEY TEMPLE BLACK
APR. 23, 1928-FEB. 10, 2014

ELI WALLACH
DEC. 7, 1915-JUNE 24, 2014

ROBIN WILLIAMS
JULY 21, 1951-AUG. 11, 2014

Nauru
Republic of Nauru

People: Population: 9,488. **Age distrib.:** <15: 32.5%; 65+: 1.9%. **Pop. density:** 1,170.2 per sq mi, 451.8 per sq km. **Urban:** 100%. **Ethnic groups:** Nauruan 58%, other Pacific Islander 26%, Chinese 8%, European 8%. **Languages:** Nauruan (official), English (widely understood, used for most govt. and commercial purposes). **Religions:** Protestant 60% (incl. Nauru Congregational 36%, Assembly of God 13%, Nauru Independent Church 10%), Roman Catholic 33%.

Geography: Total area: 8.1 sq mi, 21 sq km; **Land area:** 8.1 sq mi, 21 sq km. **Location:** In W Pacific O. just S of Equator. **Neighbors:** Nearest is Kiribati to E. **Topography:** Mostly a plateau bearing high-grade phosphate deposits, surrounded by a sandy shore and coral reef in concentric rings. **Capital:** Yaren district (admin.).

Government: Type: Republic. **Head of state and gov.:** Pres. Baron Waqa; b. Dec. 31, 1959; in office: June 11, 2013. **Local divisions:** 14 districts. **Defense budget/active troops:** NA.

Economy: Industries: phosphate mining, offshore banking, coconut prods. **Chief crops:** coconuts. **Natural resources:** phosphates, fish. **Arable land:** 0%. **Livestock:** chickens: 5,000; pigs: 3,000. **Electricity prod.:** 25 mil kWh. **Labor force:** phosphate mining, public admin., education, transportation.

Finance: Monetary unit: Australian Dollar (AUD) (Sept. 2014: 1.07 = $1 U.S.). **GDP** (2005): $60 mil; **per capita GDP** (2005): $5,000; **GDP growth:** NA. **Imports** (2005): $64,000. **Budget** (2005): $13.5 mil. **Total reserves less gold:** NA. **Inflation:** NA.

Transport: Civil aviation: 1 airport. **Chief port:** Nauru.

Communications: TV sets: 1 per 1,000 pop. **Radios:** 618 per 1,000 pop. **Telephone lines** (2009): 18.9 per 100 pop. (A public switched telephone network no longer exists in Nauru.) **Mobile** (2012): 67.8 per 100 pop. **Internet** (2011): 54%.

Health: Life expect.: 62.3 male; 69.8 female. **Births:** 25.6 per 1,000 pop. **Deaths:** 5.9 per 1,000 pop. **Natural inc.:** 1.97%. **Infant mortality:** 8.2 per 1,000 live births. **HIV:** NA.

Education: Compulsory: ages 5-18. **Literacy:** NA.

Permanent UN mission: 800 2nd Ave., Ste. 400A, New York, NY 10017; (212) 937-0074.

Website: www.naurugov.nr

The British reached the island in 1798, but it was annexed to the German Empire in 1886. After WWI, Australia administered Nauru under a League of Nations mandate. During WWII the Japanese occupied the island. In 1947 Nauru was made a UN trust territory, administered by Australia. It became an independent republic Jan. 31, 1968, and was admitted to the UN Sept. 14, 1999.

Phosphate exports provided Nauru with per capita revenues that were among the highest in the Third World. Phosphate reserves, however, are nearly depleted, and environmental damage from strip-mining has been severe. Lax banking practices have made Nauru a haven for money laundering. A Nov. 20, 2012, Amnesty Intl. report found inhumane living conditions for the 387 men being kept at Australia's detention center on Nauru. The center held more than 1,100 people in mid-2014, mostly refugees and undocumented immigrants who had sought to enter Australia by boat. Rising sea levels linked to global climate change have eroded Nauru's coastline.

Nepal
Federal Democratic Republic of Nepal

People: Population: 30,986,975. **Age distrib.:** <15: 31.6%; 65+: 4.5%. **Pop. density:** 559.9 per sq mi, 216.2 per sq km. **Urban:** 18.2%. **Ethnic groups:** Chhettri 16%, Brahman-Hill 13%, Magar 7%, Tharu 7%, Tamang 6%, Newar 5%, Kami 5%, Muslim 4%, Yadav 4%. **Languages:** Nepali (official), Maithali, Bhojpuri, Tharu, Tamang, Newar, Magar, Bajjika, Urdu, English (spoken by many in govt. and business). **Religions:** Hindu 81%, Buddhist 9%, Muslim 4%, Kirant 3%.

Geography: Total area: 56,827 sq mi, 147,181 sq km; **Land area:** 55,348 sq mi, 143,351 sq km. **Location:** Astride the Himalaya Mts. **Neighbors:** China on N, India on S. **Topography:** The Himalayas stretch across the N, the hill country with its fertile valleys extends across the center. S border region is part of the flat, subtropical Ganges Plain. **Capital:** Kathmandu, 1,141,730 (figure is for municipality).

Government: Type: Federal democratic republic. **Head of state:** Pres. Ram Baran Yadav; b. Feb. 4, 1948; in office: July 23, 2008. **Head of gov.:** Prime Min. Sushil Koirala; b. Aug. 12, 1939; in office: Feb. 10, 2014. **Local divisions:** 14 zones. **Defense budget:** $238 mil. **Active troops:** 95,750.

Economy: Industries: tourism, carpets, textiles; small rice, jute, sugar, and oilseed mills; cigarettes, cement, and brick prod. **Chief crops:** pulses, rice, corn, wheat, sugarcane, jute, root crops. **Natural resources:** quartz, water, timber, hydropower, lignite, copper, cobalt, iron ore. **Arable land:** 14.8%. **Livestock:** cattle: 7.3 mil; chickens: 48 mil; goats: 9.8 mil; pigs: 1.2 mil; sheep: 809,536. **Electricity prod.:** 3.3 bil kWh. **Labor force:** agric. 75%, industry 7%, services 18%. **Unemployment:** 2.7%.

Finance: Monetary unit: Rupee (NPR) (Sept. 2014: 98.06 = $1 U.S.). **GDP:** $42.1 bil; **per capita GDP:** $1,500; **GDP growth:** 3.6%. **Imports:** $6.3 bil; India 79.4%, South Korea 3.1%, China 2.5%. **Exports:** $1.1 bil; India 93.9%, Bangladesh 4%, Italy 0.4%. **Tourism:** $436 mil. **Budget** (FY12/13): $3.9 bil. **Total reserves less gold:** $5.3 bil. **Gold:** 1.2 mil oz t. **Inflation:** 9.0%.

Transport: Railways: 37 mi. **Civil aviation:** 11 airports. **Communications: TV sets:** 21 per 1,000 pop. **Radios:** 37 per 1,000 pop. **Telephone lines:** 3.1 per 100 pop. **Mobile:** 71.5 per 100 pop. **Internet:** 13.3%.

Health: Life expect.: 65.9 male; 68.6 female. **Births:** 21.1 per 1,000 pop. **Deaths:** 6.6 per 1,000 pop. **Natural inc.:** 1.45%. **Infant mortality:** 40.4 per 1,000 live births. **HIV:** 0.2%.

Education: NA. **Literacy:** 63.9%.

Embassy: 2131 Leroy Pl. NW 20008; 667-4550.

Website: www.nepalgov.gov.np

Nepal was originally a group of principalities, with one, the Gurkhas, becoming dominant about 1769. In 1951 King Tribhubana Bir Bikram, member of the Shah family, ended the system of rule by hereditary premiers of the Ranas family, who had kept the kings virtual prisoners, and established a cabinet system of government. Polygamy, child marriage, and the caste system were officially abolished in 1963. Political parties were legalized in 1990.

Nine members of Nepal's royal family, including King Birendra and Queen Aishwarya, died in a June 1, 2001, massacre. The killings were blamed on a 10th family member, Crown Prince Dipendra, who reportedly shot himself that night and died 3 days later, allowing Birendra's brother Gyanendra Bir Bikram Shah Dev to take the throne.

Citing the government's failure to stop a Maoist insurgency, King Gyanendra assumed absolute authority, Feb. 1, 2005. After weeks of pro-democracy demonstrations, the king agreed, Apr. 24, 2006, to reinstate parliament, which had not met for four years. A new government, led by Prime Min. Girija Prasad Koirala, signed a peace accord with Maoist rebels Nov. 21 ending a decade-long civil war that claimed 13,000 lives.

Under a draft constitution that made Koirala acting head of state, Maoists joined an interim parliament Jan. 2007 and entered the cabinet Apr. 1. A constituent assembly voted May 2008 to abolish the monarchy and make Nepal a republic. Maoist leader Pushpa Kamal Dahal, popularly known as Prachanda, became prime min. Aug. 18. Prachanda resigned May 4, 2009, when Pres. Ram Baran Yadav overruled his firing of the army chief, who refused orders to integrate former Maoist rebels. Maoist Baburam Bhattarai became prime min. Aug. 29, 2011. Bhattarai dissolved the legislature May 27, 2012, when a deadline passed for agreeing on a new constitution. Maoists suffered a defeat in Nov. 19, 2013, elections, in which moderate and pro-India parties won the largest blocs. An avalanche on Mt. Everest killed 16 Nepali guides, Apr. 18, 2014, the largest-ever one-day loss of life on Everest. More than 150 people were believed killed in northern Nepal, Aug. 2, in a landslide triggered by monsoon rains.

Netherlands
Kingdom of the Netherlands

People: Population: 16,877,351. **Age distrib.:** <15: 16.9%; 65+: 17.6%. **Pop. density:** 1,289.7 per sq mi, 498 per sq km. **Urban:** 89.9%. **Ethnic groups:** Dutch 81%, EU 5%, Indonesian 2%, Turkish 2%, Surinamese 2%, Moroccan 2%. **Languages:** Dutch (official). **Religions:** Roman Catholic 28%, Protestant 19% (incl. Dutch Reformed 9%), Muslim 5%, none 42%.

Geography: Total area: 16,040 sq mi, 41,543 sq km; **Land area:** 13,086 sq mi, 33,893 sq km. **Location:** In NW Europe on North Sea. **Neighbors:** Germany on E, Belgium on S. **Topography:** Land is flat, an average alt. of 37 ft above sea level, with much below sea level reclaimed and protected by some 1,500 mi of dikes. Since 1920 the government has been draining the IJsselmeer, formerly the Zuiderzee. **Capital:** Amsterdam, 1,083,570; s-Gravenhage (The Hague) (seat), 646,411. **Cities (urban aggl.):** Rotterdam, 993,346.

Government: Type: Constitutional monarchy. **Head of state:** King Willem-Alexander; b. Apr. 27, 1967; in office: Apr. 30, 2013. **Head of gov.:** Prime Min. Mark Rutte; b. Feb. 14, 1967; in office: Oct. 14, 2010. **Local divisions:** 12 provinces. **Defense budget:** $10.35 bil. **Active troops:** 37,400.

Economy: Industries: agroindustries, metal and engineering prods., elec. machinery and equip., chemicals, petroleum, constr., microelectronics, fishing. **Chief crops:** grains, potatoes, sugar beets, fruits, vegetables. **Natural resources:** nat. gas, petroleum, peat, limestone, salt, sand and gravel. **Crude oil reserves:** 302.6 mil bbls. **Arable land:** 30%. **Livestock:** cattle: 4 mil; chickens: 97.7 mil; goats: 412,550; pigs: 12.2 mil; sheep: 1 mil. **Electricity prod.** (2012): 97.4 bil kWh. **Labor force:** agric. 2.3%, industry 18.8%, services 78.9%. **Unemployment:** 5.3%.

Finance: Monetary unit: Euro (EUR) (Sept. 2014: 0.76 = $1 U.S.). **GDP:** $699.7 bil; **per capita GDP** (2012): $43,300; **GDP growth:** –0.8%. **Imports:** $511 bil; Germany 13.8%, China 12%, Belgium 8.4%, UK 6.7%, Russia 6.4%, U.S. 6.1%. **Exports:** $576.9 bil; Germany 26.5%, Belgium 13.7%, France 8.8%, UK 8%, Italy 4.5%. **Tourism:** $15.6 bil. **Budget** (2014 est.): $339.3 bil. **Total reserves less gold:** $22.6 bil. **Gold:** 19.7 mil oz t. **Inflation:** 2.5%.

Transport: Railways: 1,799 mi. **Motor vehicles:** 547.8 per 1,000 pop. **Civil aviation:** 55.3 bil pass.-mi; 23 airports. **Chief ports:** Amsterdam, Ijmuiden, Moerdijk, Rotterdam, Terneuzen, Vlissingen.

Communications: TV sets: 767 per 1,000 pop. **Radios:** 978 per 1,000 pop. **Telephone lines:** 42.5 per 100 pop. **Mobile:** 113.7 per 100 pop. **Internet:** 94%.

Health: Life expect.: 79.0 male; 83.3 female. **Births:** 10.8 per 1,000 pop. **Deaths:** 8.6 per 1,000 pop. **Natural inc.:** 0.23%. **Infant mortality:** 3.7 per 1,000 live births. **HIV:** NA.

Education: Compulsory: ages 5-17. **Literacy:** 99%.
Embassy: 4200 Linnean Ave. NW 20008; 877-DUTCHHELP.
Website: www.government.nl

Julius Caesar conquered the region in 55 BCE, when it was inhabited by Celtic and Germanic tribes. After the empire of Charlemagne fell apart, the Netherlands (Holland, Belgium, Flanders) split among counts, dukes, and bishops, passed to Burgundy and thence to Spain. William the Silent, prince of Orange, led a confederation of the northern provinces, called Estates, in the Union of Utrecht, 1579; in 1581 they repudiated allegiance to Spain. The rise of the Dutch republic to naval, economic, and artistic eminence came in the 17th cent.

After a period of French hegemony, 1795-1813, the Congress of Vienna in 1815 formed a kingdom of the Netherlands, including Belgium, under William I. In 1830, the Belgians seceded and formed a separate kingdom.

The Netherlands maintained its neutrality in WWI, but during WWII was invaded and occupied by Germany, 1940-45. In 1949, after several years of fighting, the Netherlands granted independence to Indonesia.

The murder May 6, 2002, of right-wing populist leader Pim Fortuyn, 9 days before legislative elections, marked the first political assassination in modern Dutch history. The killing of filmmaker Theo van Gogh, Nov. 2, 2004, by an Islamic extremist shocked many Dutch. On Apr. 30, 2009, the national Queen's Day holiday, an attempted assassination of Queen Beatrix and other royal family members resulted in the deaths of 7 bystanders and the would-be assassin. The anti-Islamic, right-wing Freedom Party, headed by Geert Wilders, gained in parliamentary elections June 2010. Prime Min. Mark Rutte and his cabinet resigned Apr. 23, 2012, after failing to pass a budget in line with EU requirements. Rutte's government nonetheless remained in a caretaker capacity, and his pro-business Liberal party won a majority of seats in parliamentary elections held Sept. 2012. Queen Beatrix, 75, abdicated the throne to her son, Willem-Alexander, Apr. 30, 2013. A Malaysia Airlines flight from Amsterdam to Kuala Lumpur was shot down over eastern Ukraine, July 17, 2014; nearly 200 Dutch passport holders were among the 298 killed.

Dutch Dependencies

The Netherlands Antilles consists of two island groups in the West Indies. **Curaçao** and **Bonaire** are near the coast of Venezuela; **Sint Eustatius, Saba,** and the southern part of **Sint Maarten** are southeast of Puerto Rico. The northern two-thirds of St. Maarten is a French overseas territorial collectivity (Saint Martin). Total area of the two groups is 371 sq mi, incl. Bonaire (111), Curaçao (171), St. Eustatius (8), Saba (5), St. Maarten (13). St. Maarten suffered extensive damage from Hurricane Luis, Sept. 1995. Pop. (2013 est.): Curaçao, 146,836; Sint Maarten, 39,689. Willemstad, on Curaçao, is the capital; pop. (2014 est.) 144,730. The principal industry is the refining of crude oil from Venezuela. Tourism and shipbuilding are other important industries. Constitutional changes effective Oct. 10, 2010, dissolved the Netherlands Antilles as a political entity and elevated Curaçao and St. Maarten to the status of autonomous countries within the Kingdom of the Netherlands. Bonaire, St. Eustatius, and Saba were classified as special municipalities.

Aruba, about 26 mi west of Curaçao, was separated from the Netherlands Antilles on Jan. 1, 1986; it is an autonomous component of the Netherlands, with a status similar to Curaçao and St. Maarten. Area: 69 sq mi; pop. (2013 est.) 109,153. Capital: Oranjestad; pop. (2014 est.) 29,041. Chief industries are oil refining and tourism. **Website:** www.kabga.aw

New Zealand

People: Population: 4,401,916. **Age distrib.:** <15: 20%; 65+: 14.3%. **Pop. density:** 42.6 per sq mi, 16.4 per sq km. **Urban:** 86.3%. **Ethnic groups:** European 71%, Maori 14%, Asian 11%, Pacific peoples 8%. **Languages:** English (de facto official), Maori (de jure official), Samoan, Hindi, French, Northern Chinese, Yue. **Religions:** Christian 44% (Catholic 12%; Anglican 11%; Presbyterian, Congregational 8%; Methodist 2%; Pentecostal 2%; other 10%), Hindu 2%, none 39%.
Geography: Total area: 103,363 sq mi, 267,710 sq km; **Land area:** 103,363 sq mi, 267,710 sq km. **Location:** In SW Pacific O. **Neighbors:** Nearest are Australia on W, Fiji and Tonga on N. **Topography:** The 2 main islands (North and South Isls.) are hilly and mountainous. The E coasts consist of fertile plains, especially the broad Canterbury Plains on South Isl. A volcanic plateau is in center of North Isl. South Isl. has glaciers and 15 peaks over 10,000 ft. **Capital:** Wellington, 380,333. **Cities (urban aggl.):** Auckland, 1,328,793.
Government: Type: Parliamentary democracy. **Head of state:** Queen Elizabeth II, rep. by Gov.-Gen. Sir Jeremiah "Jerry" Mateparae; b. Nov. 14, 1954; in office: Aug. 31, 2011. **Head of gov.:** Prime Min. John Key; b. Aug. 9, 1961; in office: Nov. 19, 2008. **Local divisions:** 16 regions, 1 territory. **Defense budget:** $2.72 bil. **Active troops:** 8,550.
Economy: Industries: food proc., wood and paper prods., textiles, machinery, transp. equip., banking and insurance, tourism, mining. **Chief crops:** dairy prods., wheat, barley, potatoes, pulses, fruits, vegetables. **Natural resources:** nat. gas, iron ore, sand, coal, timber, hydropower, gold, limestone. **Crude oil reserves:** 81.4 mil bbls. **Arable land:** 2.2%. **Livestock:** cattle: 10.2 mil; chickens: 15 mil; goats: 91,500; pigs: 297,724; sheep: 30.8 mil. **Electricity**

prod. (2012): 42.9 bil kWh. **Labor force:** agric. 7%, industry 19%, services 74%. **Unemployment:** 6.9%.
Finance: Monetary unit: Dollar (NZD) (Sept. 2014: 1.20 = $1 U.S). **GDP:** $136 bil; **per capita GDP:** $30,400; **GDP growth:** 2.5%. **Imports:** $37.4 bil; China 16.4%, Australia 15.2%, U.S. 9.3%, Japan 6.5%, Singapore 4.8%, Germany 4.4%. **Exports:** $37.8 bil; Australia 21.1%, China 15%, U.S. 9.2%, Japan 7%. **Tourism:** $7.5 bil. **Budget:** $72.7 bil. **Total reserves less gold:** $16.3 bil. **Inflation:** 0.9%.
Transport: Railways: 2,565 mi. **Motor vehicles:** 740.9 per 1,000 pop. **Civil aviation:** 15.3 bil pass.-mi; 39 airports. **Chief ports:** Auckland, Lyttelton, Manukau Harbor, Marsden Point, Tauranga, Wellington.
Communications: TV sets: 615 per 1,000 pop. **Radios:** 1,006 per 1,000 pop. **Telephone lines:** 41.1 per 100 pop. **Mobile:** 105.8 per 100 pop. **Internet:** 82.8%.
Health: Life expect.: 78.9 male; 83.1 female. **Births:** 13.4 per 1,000 pop. **Deaths:** 7.3 per 1,000 pop. **Natural inc.:** 0.61%. **Infant mortality:** 4.6 per 1,000 live births. **HIV:** NA.
Education: Compulsory: ages 5-16. **Literacy:** 99%.
Embassy: 37 Observatory Cir. NW 20008; 328-4800.
Website: newzealand.govt.nz

New Zealand comprises North Island, 43,911 sq mi; South Island, 58,084 sq mi; Stewart Island, 649 sq mi; Chatham Isls., 373 sq mi; and several groups of smaller islands. The Maori, a Polynesian group from the eastern Pacific, reached New Zealand before and during the 14th cent. The first European to sight New Zealand was Dutch navigator Abel Janszoon Tasman. The Maori refused to allow him to land. British Capt. James Cook explored the coasts, 1769-70.

British sovereignty was proclaimed and Maori land rights were recognized in the Treaty of Waitangi, 1840, with organized settlement beginning in the same year. Representative institutions were granted in 1853. The Maori Wars, or New Zealand Wars, ended in 1870 with British victory. The colony became a dominion in 1907 and gained full independence in 1947.

A progressive tradition in politics dates back to the 19th cent., when New Zealand was known for social experimentation. Much of the nation's economy has been deregulated since the 1980s. Jenny Shipley of the National Party became the nation's first female prime min., Dec. 8, 1997. The Labour Party, led by Helen Clark, won general elections, Nov. 27, 1999, and July 27, 2002. New Zealand supplied small troop contingents to coalition forces in Iraq and Afghanistan.

Prostitution was legalized June 2003. In July, New Zealand contributed troops to the Australian-led force in the Solomon Islands. A measure establishing a supreme court and ending appeals to the UK Privy Council passed Oct. 14. A major settlement of Maori land claims dating from the 19th cent. was signed June 25, 2008.

A South Island earthquake Sept. 3, 2010, caused property damage estimated at $2.7 bil. An explosion Nov. 19 at the Pike River coal mine on South Island killed 29 men. Another Christchurch quake, Feb. 22, 2011, killed 181 people and caused damage estimated at $11 bil to the central business district. Prime Min. John Key's handling of these disasters bolstered the National Party's popularity, and it was returned to power in elections Nov. 26, 2011. New Zealand legalized same-sex marriage in a 77-44 parliamentary vote Apr. 17, 2013.

In 1965, the **Cook Islands** (area: 91 sq mi; 2014 est. pop.: 10,134), halfway between New Zealand and Hawaii, became self-governing. New Zealand retains responsibility for defense and foreign affairs. **Niue** (area: 100 sq mi; 2014 est. pop.: 1,190) attained the same status in 1974; it lies 400 mi W. Cyclone Heta devastated Niue Jan. 6, 2004. **Tokelau** (area: 4 sq mi; 2014 est. pop.: 1,337) comprises three atolls 300 mi N of Samoa. Two referendums on Tokelau self-government, held Feb. 13-15, 2006, and Oct. 20-24, 2007, failed to gain the required two-third majority. **Ross Dependency,** administered by New Zealand since 1923, comprises 160,000 sq mi of Antarctic territory.

Nicaragua
Republic of Nicaragua

People: Population: 5,848,641. **Age distrib.:** <15: 29.3%; 65+: 4.8%. **Pop. density:** 126.2 per sq mi, 48.7 per sq km. **Urban:** 58.5%. **Ethnic groups:** mestizo (mixed Amerindian and white) 69%, white 17%, black 9%, Amerindian 5%. **Languages:** Spanish (official), Miskito, English and indigenous langs. **Religions:** Roman Catholic 59%, Protestant 23% (Evangelical 22%, Moravian 2%), none 16%.
Geography: Total area: 50,336 sq mi, 130,370 sq km; **Land area:** 46,328 sq mi, 119,990 sq km. **Location:** In Central America. **Neighbors:** Honduras on N, Costa Rica on S. **Topography:** Both Caribbean and Pacific coasts are over 200 mi long. Cordillera Mts., with many volcanic peaks, run NW-SE through middle of the country. Between this and a volcanic range to the E lie Lakes Managua and Nicaragua. **Capital:** Managua, 950,736.
Government: Type: Republic. **Head of state and gov.:** Pres. Daniel Ortega Saavedra; b. Nov. 11, 1945; in office: Jan. 10, 2007. **Local divisions:** 15 departments, 2 autonomous regions. **Defense budget:** $85 mil. **Active troops:** 12,000.
Economy: Industries: food proc., chemicals, machinery and metal prods., knit and woven apparel, petroleum refining and distrib., beverages, footwear, wood. **Chief crops:** coffee, bananas, sugarcane, cotton, rice, corn, tobacco, sesame, soya, beans. **Natural**

resources: gold, silver, copper, tungsten, lead, zinc, timber, fish. Arable land: 12.5%. Livestock: cattle: 3.7 mil; chickens: 21.1 mil; goats: 7,400; pigs: 494,000; sheep: 6,300. Electricity prod.: 3.5 bil kWh. Labor force: agric. 31%, industry 18%, services 50%. Unemployment: 7.7%.

Finance: Monetary unit: Cordoba (NIO) (Sept. 2014: 26.17 = $1 U.S.). GDP: $28 bil; per capita GDP: $4,500; GDP growth: 4.6%. Imports: $5.7 bil; Venezuela 18.8%. Exports: $2.4 bil; U.S. 25.2%, Venezuela 16%, Canada 13.1%, El Salvador 8.9%, Costa Rica 5%. Tourism: $417 mil. Budget: $1.7 bil. Total reserves less gold: $2 bil. Inflation: 7.1%.

Transport: Motor vehicles: 50.2 per 1,000 pop. Civil aviation: 12 airports. Chief ports: Bluefields, Corinto.

Communications: TV sets: 129 per 1,000 pop. Radios: 273 per 1,000 pop. Telephone lines: 5.3 per 100 pop. Mobile: 112 per 100 pop. Internet: 15.5%.

Health: Life expect.: 70.6 male; 75.0 female. Births: 18.4 per 1,000 pop. Deaths: 5.1 per 1,000 pop. Natural inc.: 1.33%. Infant mortality: 20.4 per 1,000 live births. HIV: 0.2%.

Education: Compulsory: ages 6-11. Literacy: 82.8%.
Embassy: 1627 New Hampshire Ave. NW 20009; 939-6570.
Website: www.presidencia.gob.ni

Nicaragua, inhabited by various Indian tribes, was conquered by Spain in 1552. After gaining independence from Spain, 1821, Nicaragua was united for a short period with Mexico, then with the United Provinces of Central America, finally becoming an independent republic, 1838. U.S. Marines occupied the country at times in the early 20th cent., the last time from 1926 to 1933.

Gen. Anastasio Somoza Debayle held the presidency 1967-72, 1974-79. Martial law was imposed in Dec. 1974, after officials were kidnapped by Marxist Sandinista guerrillas. Nationwide antigovernment strikes touched off a civil war, 1978, which ended when Somoza fled Nicaragua and the Sandinistas took control of Managua, July 1979. Somoza was assassinated in Paraguay, Sept. 17, 1980.

Relations with the U.S. were strained as a result of Nicaragua's aid to leftist guerrillas in El Salvador and U.S. backing of anti-Sandinista contra guerrilla groups. In 1983 the contras launched a major offensive; the Sandinistas imposed rule by decree. In 1985 the U.S. House rejected Pres. Reagan's request for military aid to the contras. The subsequent diversion of funds to the contras from the proceeds of a secret arms sale to Iran caused a major scandal in the U.S.

In a stunning upset, Violeta Barrios de Chamorro defeated Sandinista leader Daniel Ortega Saavedra in national elections, Feb. 25, 1990. The conservative Arnoldo Alemán Lacayo defeated Ortega in the Oct. 1996 presidential election. Up to 2,000 people died Oct. 30, 1998, in a mudslide caused by rains from Hurricane Mitch.

Drought and a drop in coffee prices precipitated an economic crisis in 2001. Enrique Bolaños Geyer, a conservative businessman, won the presidency that year. Convicted Dec. 7, 2003, on corruption charges, former Pres. Alemán received a $10 mil fine and a 20-year sentence. Ortega won the Nov. 2006 presidential election and cultivated ties with Venezuela and Iran, which offered Nicaragua financial assistance. He was reelected Nov. 6, 2011. The Sandinista-controlled legislature gave final approval, Jan. 28, 2014, to constitutional changes removing presidential term limits. The route of a 173-mi canal to be built across Nicaragua by a Chinese consortium was announced July 7, 2014.

Niger
Republic of Niger

People: Population: 17,466,172. Age distrib.: <15: 49.8%; 65+: 2.6%. Pop. density: 35.7 per sq mi, 13.8 per sq km. Urban: 18.5%. Ethnic groups: Haoussa 55%, Djerma Sonrai 21%, Tuareg 9%, Peuhl 9%, Kanouri Manga 5%. Languages: French (official), Hausa, Djerma. Religions: Muslim 80%, other (incl. indigenous beliefs, Christian) 20%.

Geography: Total area: 489,191 sq mi, 1,267,000 sq km; Land area: 489,076 sq mi, 1,266,700 sq km. Location: In interior of N Africa. Neighbors: Libya, Algeria on N; Mali, Burkina Faso on W; Benin, Nigeria on S; Chad on E. Topography: Mostly arid desert and mountains. A narrow savanna in S and Niger R. basin in the SW contain most of the population. Capital: Niamey, 1,057,560.

Government: Type: Republic. Head of state: Pres. Mahamadou Issoufou; b. 1952; in office: Apr. 7, 2011. Head of gov.: Prime Min. Brigi Rafini; b. Apr. 7, 1953; in office: Apr. 7, 2011. Local divisions: 8 regions, incl. 1 capital district. Defense budget (2012): $70 mil. Active troops: 5,300.

Economy: Industries: uranium mining, cement, brick, soap, textiles, food proc., chemicals, slaughterhouses. Chief crops: cowpeas, cotton, peanuts, millet, sorghum, cassava, rice. Natural resources: uranium, coal, iron ore, tin, phosphates, gold, molybdenum, gypsum, salt, petroleum. Crude oil reserves: 150 mil bbls. Arable land: 12.6%. Livestock: cattle: 10.2 mil; chickens: 17.7 mil; goats: 13.8 mil; pigs: 42,500; sheep: 10.4 mil. Electricity prod.: 300 mil kWh. Labor force: agric. 90%, industry 6%, services 4%. Unemployment: 5.1%.

Finance: Monetary unit: CFA Franc (XOF) (Sept. 2014: 498.91 = $1 U.S.). GDP: $14 bil; per capita GDP: $800; GDP growth: 6.2%. Imports: $2.3 bil; France 14.4%, China 11.3%, Nigeria 10.1%, French Polynesia 9.2%, Togo 5.1%, Côte d'Ivoire 4.5%. Exports: $1.5 bil; Nigeria 40.3%, U.S. 17.2%, India 14.3%, Italy 8.6%, China

7.8%, Ghana 5.3%. Tourism: $96 mil. Budget: $2.1 bil. Total reserves less gold: $1.2 bil. Inflation: 2.3%.

Transport: Motor vehicles: 11.1 per 1,000 pop. Civil aviation: 10 airports.

Communications: TV sets: 12 per 1,000 pop. Radios: 235 per 1,000 pop. Telephone lines: 0.6 per 100 pop. Mobile: 39.3 per 100 pop. Internet: 1.7%.

Health: Life expect.: 53.5 male; 56.0 female. Births: 46.1 per 1,000 pop. Deaths: 12.7 per 1,000 pop. Natural inc.: 3.34%. Infant mortality: 86.3 per 1,000 live births. HIV: 0.4%.

Education: Compulsory: ages 7-15. Literacy: 19.1%.
Embassy: 2204 R St. NW 20008; 483-4224.
Website: www.gouv.ne

Niger was part of ancient and medieval African empires. European explorers reached the area in the late 18th cent. The French colony of Niger was established 1900-22 after the defeat of Tuareg fighters, who had invaded the area from the north a century before. The country became independent Aug. 3, 1960.

In 1993, Niger held its first free and open elections since independence; an opposition leader, Mahamane Ousmane, won the presidency. A peace accord Apr. 24, 1995, ended a Tuareg rebellion that began in 1990. A coup, Jan. 27, 1996, followed by a disputed presidential election in July, left the military in control of Niger. On Apr. 9, 1999, Gen. Ibrahim Bare Mainassara, Niger's president since 1996, was assassinated, apparently by members of his security team. Elections were held Oct. 17 and Nov. 24, 1999, under a new constitution, approved by referendum July 18, that restored civilian rule.

One of the world's poorest countries, Niger experienced severe food shortages in 2005 after locusts and drought ruined the grain harvest. Popularly elected in 1999 and 2004, Pres. Mamadou Tandja invoked emergency powers in 2009, seeking to remain in office for a third 5-year term. He was overthrown by a military junta Feb. 18, 2010. Civilian rule returned following Jan.-Mar. 2011 elections. Increased terrorist activity in countries surrounding Niger led the U.S. and EU to provide training and equipment, beginning in 2012, to help Niger's forces fight Islamic militants. Terrorist attacks in Niger occurred May 23, 2013, as two separate bombings killed 21 soldiers and 5 of the bombers in Agadez and Arlit.

Nigeria
Federal Republic of Nigeria

People: Population: 177,155,754. Age distrib.: <15: 43.2%; 65+: 3.1%. Pop. density: 503.8 per sq mi, 194.5 per sq km. Urban: 46.9%. Ethnic groups: 250+ ethnic groups: Hausa and Fulani 29%, Yoruba 21%, Igbo (Ibo) 18%, Ijaw 10%, Kanuri 4%, Ibibio 4%, and Tiv 3% are most populous, politically influential groups. Languages: English (official), Hausa, Yoruba, Igbo (Ibo), Fulani, 500+ indigenous langs. Religions: Muslim 50%, Christian 40%, indigenous beliefs 10%.

Geography: Total area: 356,669 sq mi, 923,768 sq km; Land area: 351,649 sq mi, 910,768 sq km. Location: On S coast of W Africa. Neighbors: Benin on W, Niger on N, Chad and Cameroon on E. Topography: 4 E-W regions divide Nigeria: a coastal mangrove swamp 10-60 mi wide, a tropical rain forest 50-100 mi wide, a plateau of savanna and open woodland, and semi-desert in N. Capital: Abuja, 2,300,550. Cities (urban aggl.): Lagos, 12,613,579; Kano, 3,507,632; Ibadan, 3,085,293; Port Harcourt, 2,227,133; Benin City, 1,452,599.

Government: Type: Federal republic. Head of state and gov.: Pres. Goodluck Jonathan; b. Nov. 20, 1957; in office: May 6, 2010 (acting from Feb. 9). Local divisions: 36 states, 1 territory. Defense budget: $2.14 bil. Active troops: 80,000.

Economy: Industries: crude oil, coal, tin, columbite; rubber prods., wood; hides and skins, textiles, cement and other constr. materials, food prods. Chief crops: cocoa, peanuts, cotton, palm oil, corn, rice, sorghum, millet, cassava, yams, rubber. Natural resources: nat. gas, petroleum, tin, iron ore, coal, limestone, niobium, lead, zinc. Crude oil reserves: 37.1 bil bbls. Arable land: 38.4%. Livestock: cattle: 20 mil; chickens: 207 mil; goats: 58.3 mil; pigs: 8.1 mil; sheep: 39 mil. Electricity prod.: 25.7 bil kWh. Labor force: agric. 70%, industry 10%, services 20%. Unemployment: 7.5%.

Finance: Monetary unit: Naira (NGN) (Sept. 2014: 162.30 = $1 U.S.). GDP: $478.5 bil; per capita GDP: $2,800; GDP growth: 6.2%. Imports: $56 bil; China 18.3%, U.S. 10.1%, India 5.5%. Exports: $93.6 bil; U.S. 16.8%, India 11.5%, Netherlands 8.6%, Spain 7.8%, Brazil 7.6%, UK 5.1%, Germany 4.9%, Japan 4.1%, France 4.1%. Tourism: $543 mil. Budget: $31.5 bil. Total reserves less gold (2012): $46.4 bil. Gold (2012): 687,000 oz t. Inflation: 8.5%.

Transport: Railways: 2,178 mi. Motor vehicles: 7.9 per 1,000 pop. Civil aviation: 2.2 bil pass.-mi; 40 airports. Chief ports: Calabar, Lagos.

Communications: TV sets: 67 per 1,000 pop. Radios: 602 per 1,000 pop. Telephone lines: 0.2 per 100 pop. Mobile: 73.3 per 100 pop. Internet: 38%.

Health: Life expect.: 51.6 male; 53.7 female. Births: 38.0 per 1,000 pop. Deaths: 13.2 per 1,000 pop. Natural inc.: 2.49%. Infant mortality: 74.1 per 1,000 live births. HIV: 3.2%.

Education: Compulsory: ages 6-14. Literacy: 59.6%.
Embassy: 3519 International Ct. NW 20008; 986-8400.
Website: www.nigeria.gov.ng

Early cultures in Nigeria date back to at least 700 BCE. From the 12th to the 14th cent., more advanced cultures developed in the

Yoruba area, at Ife, and in the north, where Muslim influence prevailed. Portuguese and British slavers appeared in the 15th-16th cent. Britain seized Lagos, 1861, and gradually extended control inland until 1900. Nigeria became independent Oct. 1, 1960, and a republic Oct. 1, 1963.

On May 30, 1967, the Eastern Region seceded, proclaiming itself the Republic of Biafra, plunging the country into civil war. Casualties were estimated at over 1 mil, including many Biafrans (mostly Ibos) who died of starvation despite international relief efforts. The secessionists capitulated Jan. 12, 1970.

Nigeria emerged as one of the world's leading oil exporters in the 1970s, but much of the revenue has been squandered through corruption and mismanagement. Oil spills have polluted much of the Niger Delta region.

After 13 years of military rule, the nation made a peaceful return to civilian government Oct. 1979. Military rule resumed Dec. 31, 1983; a second coup came in 1985. Headed by Gen. Ibrahim Babangida, the military regime held elections June 12, 1993, but annulled the vote June 23 when it appeared that Moshood Abiola would win. Riots followed and many were killed. Babangida resigned and appointed a civilian to head an interim government, Aug. 26, but that government was ousted Nov. 17 in a coup led by Gen. Sani Abacha. On June 11, 1994, Abiola declared himself president; he was jailed June 23.

Abacha's brutal rule ended June 8, 1998, when he died of an apparent heart attack. Abiola died in prison July 7 as Abacha's successor, Gen. Abdulsalam Abubakar, was reportedly preparing to free him. Abiola's death sparked riots in Lagos and other cities; on July 20, Abubakar promised elections and a return to civilian rule. Olusegun Obasanjo won the presidential vote Feb. 27, 1999, Nigeria's first civilian government in 15 years.

An oil pipeline explosion in southern Nigeria, Oct. 17, 1998, killed at least 700 people who were scavenging for fuel. The imposition of strict Islamic law in northern states led to clashes, Jan.-Mar. 2000, in which at least 800 people died. Fighting between Muslims and Christians Sept. 7-12 and Oct. 13-14, 2001, claimed an estimated 600 lives; another 200 people died when soldiers went on a rampage in SE Nigeria Oct. 22-24.

At least 1,000 people were killed Jan. 27, 2002, when an army weapons depot in Lagos exploded. Christian militia members massacred about 630 Muslims at Yelwa, central Nigeria, May 2, 2004. Obasanjo's chosen successor, Umaru Musa YarʼAdua, won a presidential election, Apr. 21, 2007, marred by violence and described as "not credible" by international monitors. After prolonged illness, YarʼAdua died May 5, 2010, and was succeeded by Vice Pres. Goodluck Jonathan, a southern Christian. After he won reelection Apr. 16, 2011, over Muhammadu Buhari, a northern-based Muslim, riots in 12 northern provinces left more than 800 people dead.

Boko Haram, a radical Islamist sect based in NE Nigeria, aims to transform Nigeria into an Islamist state; its terrorist attacks have been blamed for more than 4,000 deaths since 2011. When Islamists gained control of a number of towns, Pres. Jonathan declared a state of emergency in the northeast May 14, 2013. Boko Haram violence escalated in 2014, including the kidnapping of 276 teenage girls from a school, Apr. 14. More than 200 of the girls, and victims of other kidnappings, remained in Boko Haram custody months later. An Ebola outbreak in W. Africa spread to Nigeria in July 2014; as of Sept. 28, 20 Ebola cases had been reported in Nigeria, and 8 people had died.

Norway
Kingdom of Norway

People: Population: 5,147,792. **Age distrib.:** <15: 18.2%; 65+: 16.1%. **Pop. density:** 43.8 per sq mi, 16.9 per sq km. **Urban:** 80.2%. **Ethnic groups:** Norwegian (incl. Sami) 94%, other European 4%. **Languages:** Bokmal Norwegian, Nynorsk Norwegian (both official); Sami (official in 6 municipalities). **Religions:** Church of Norway (Evangelical Lutheran official) 82%, other Christian 4%, Muslim 2%. **Geography: Total area:** 125,021 sq mi, 323,802 sq km; **Land area:** 117,484 sq mi, 304,282 sq km. **Location:** W part of Scandinavian peninsula in NW Europe (extends farther N than any European land). **Neighbors:** Sweden, Finland, Russia on E. **Topography:** Highly indented coast is lined with tens of thousands of islands. Mountains and plateaus cover most of the country, which is only 25% forested. **Capital:** Oslo, 969,862.
Government: Type: Constitutional monarchy. **Head of state:** King Harald V; b. Feb. 21, 1937; in office: Jan. 17, 1991. **Head of gov.:** Prime Min. Erna Solberg; b. Feb. 24, 1961; in office: Oct. 16, 2013. **Local divisions:** 19 counties. **Defense budget:** $7.52 bil. **Active troops:** 25,800.
Economy: Industries: petroleum and gas, food proc., shipbuilding, pulp and paper prods., metals, chemicals, timber, mining, textiles, fishing. **Chief crops:** barley, wheat, potatoes. **Natural resources:** petroleum, nat. gas, iron ore, copper, lead, zinc, titanium, pyrites, nickel, fish, timber, hydropower. **Crude oil reserves:** 5.8 bil bbls. **Arable land:** 2.2%. **Livestock:** cattle: 849,984; chickens: 3.9 mil; goats: 62,800; pigs: 848,063; sheep: 2.2 mil. **Electricity prod.** (2012): 144.7 bil kWh. **Labor force:** agric. 2.2%, industry 20.2%, services 77.6%. **Unemployment:** 3.2%.
Finance: Monetary unit: Krone (NOK) (Sept. 2014: 6.22 = $1 U.S.). **GDP:** $282.2 bil; **per capita GDP:** $55,400; **GDP growth:**

1.6%. **Imports:** $90.1 bil; Sweden 13.6%, Germany 12.4%, China 9.3%, Denmark 6.3%, UK 6.1%, U.S. 5.4%. **Exports:** $154.2 bil; UK 25.6%, Germany 12.6%, Netherlands 12%, France 6.7%, Sweden 6.3%, U.S. 5%. **Tourism:** $5.7 bil. **Budget:** $225 bil. **Total reserves less gold:** $58.3 bil. **Inflation:** 2.1%.
Transport: Railways: 2,590 mi. **Motor vehicles:** 649.2 per 1,000 pop. **Civil aviation:** 29.4 bil pass.-mi (incl. Denmark, Sweden); 67 airports. **Chief ports:** Bergen, Haugesund, Maaloy, Mongstad, Narvik, Sture.
Communications: TV sets: 1,554 per 1,000 pop. **Radios:** 913 per 1,000 pop. **Telephone lines:** 26.2 per 100 pop. **Mobile:** 116.5 per 100 pop. **Internet:** 95.1%.
Health: Life expect.: 79.6 male; 83.7 female. **Births:** 12.1 per 1,000 pop. **Deaths:** 8.2 per 1,000 pop. **Natural inc.:** 0.39%. **Infant mortality:** 2.5 per 1,000 live births. **HIV:** NA.
Education: Compulsory: ages 6-16. **Literacy:** 100%.
Embassy: 2720 34th St. NW 20008; 333-6000.
Website: www.norway.no
The first ruler of Norway was Harald the Fairhaired, who came to power in 872 CE. Between 800 and 1000, Norway's Vikings raided and occupied widely dispersed parts of Europe. The country was united with Denmark, 1381-1814, and with Sweden, 1814-1905. In 1905, the country became independent with Prince Charles of Denmark as king.

Norway remained neutral during WWI. In WWII, Germany attacked Norway Apr. 9, 1940, and held it until liberation May 8, 1945. The country abandoned its neutrality after the war and joined NATO. In a referendum Nov. 28, 1994, Norwegian voters rejected European Union membership.

Abundant hydroelectric resources provide the base for industrialization, giving Norway one of the highest living standards in the world. The country is a leading producer and exporter of crude oil, with extensive reserves in the North Sea.

A center-left bloc headed by Labor Party leader Jens Stoltenberg won parliamentary elections Sept. 2005 and remained in power after elections Sept. 2009. A right-wing extremist, Anders Behring Breivik, confessed to killing 8 people with a car bomb near government buildings in central Oslo and murdering another 69 at an island camp sponsored by the Labor Party's youth wing July 22, 2011. He was declared sane and sentenced Aug. 24, 2012, to 21 years in prison, the maximum sentence in Norway. Parliament voted June 18, 2013, to make military service compulsory for women as well as men; it was the first NATO country to do so. Rightist parties, including the anti-immigration Progress Party, won the most seats in Sept. 9, 2013, elections; Conservative Party leader Erna Solberg became prime min.

Svalbard is a group of mountainous islands in the Arctic O., area 23,956 sq mi, pop. (2013 est.) 2,637. The largest, Spitsbergen (formerly called West Spitsbergen), 15,060 sq mi, seat of the governor, is about 370 mi N of Norway. By a treaty signed in Paris, 1920, major European powers recognized the sovereignty of Norway, which incorporated it in 1925.

Jan Mayen, area 146 sq mi, is a volcanic island located about 565 mi W-NW of Norway; it was annexed in 1929.

Oman
Sultanate of Oman

People: Population: 3,219,775. **Age distrib.:** <15: 30.4%; 65+: 3.3%. **Pop. density:** 26.9 per sq mi, 10.4 per sq km. **Urban:** 77.2%. **Ethnic groups:** Arab, Baluchi, South Asian (Indian, Pakistani, Sri Lankan, Bangladeshi), African. **Languages:** Arabic (official), English, Baluchi, Urdu, Indian dialects. **Religions:** Muslim (official) 86% (70% Ibahi, also Sunni, Shia), Christian 7%, Hindu 6%.
Geography: Total area: 119,499 sq mi, 309,500 sq km; **Land area:** 119,499 sq mi, 309,500 sq km. **Location:** On SE coast of Arabian peninsula. **Neighbors:** United Arab Emirates, Saudi Arabia, Yemen on W. **Topography:** A narrow coastal plain up to 10 mi wide, a range of barren mountains reaching 9,900 ft, and a wide, stony, mostly waterless plateau, avg. alt. 1,000 ft. Also, an exclave at the tip of the Musandam peninsula controls access to the Persian Gulf. **Capital:** Muscat, 812,324.
Government: Type: Monarchy. **Head of state and gov.:** Sultan Qaboos bin Said al-Said; b. Nov. 18, 1940; in office: July 23, 1970 (also prime min. since 1972). **Local divisions:** 11 governorates. **Defense budget:** $9.25 bil. **Active troops:** 42,600.
Economy: Industries: crude oil prod. and refining, nat. and liquefied nat. gas prod., constr., cement, copper, steel, chemicals, optic fiber. **Chief crops:** dates, limes, bananas, alfalfa, vegetables. **Natural resources:** petroleum, copper, asbestos, marble, limestone, chromium, gypsum, nat. gas. **Crude oil reserves:** 5.5 bil bbls. **Arable land:** 0.1%. **Livestock:** cattle: 350,000; chickens: 4.6 mil; goats: 1.8 mil; sheep: 408,000. **Electricity prod.:** 20.1 bil kWh. **Labor force:** NA. **Unemployment:** 8.1%.
Finance: Monetary unit: Rial (OMR) (Sept. 2014: 0.39 = $1 U.S.). **GDP:** $94.9 bil; **per capita GDP:** $29,800; **GDP growth:** 5.1%. **Imports:** $30.8 bil; UAE 24.1%, Japan 12.5%, India 8.5%, China 6.3%, U.S. 6.1%. **Exports:** $56.2 bil; China 31.8%, Japan 12.9%, UAE 10.4%, South Korea 10%, Thailand 4.4%, Singapore 4.4%. **Tourism:** $1.1 bil. **Budget:** $35.5 bil. **Total reserves less gold:** $16 bil. **Gold:** 618 oz t. **Inflation:** 1.2%.

Transport: Motor vehicles: 182.5 per 1,000 pop. **Civil aviation:** 5.3 bil pass.-mi; 13 airports. **Chief ports:** Mina'Qabus, Salalah, Suhar.

Communications: TV sets: 620 per 1,000 pop. **Radios:** 72 per 1,000 pop. **Telephone lines:** 9.7 per 100 pop. **Mobile:** 154.6 per 100 pop. **Internet:** 66.5%.

Health: Life expect.: 73.1 male; 77.0 female. **Births:** 24.5 per 1,000 pop. **Deaths:** 3.4 per 1,000 pop. **Natural inc.:** 2.11%. **Infant mortality:** 14.0 per 1,000 live births. **HIV:** NA.

Education: NA. **Literacy:** 91.1%.

Embassy: 2535 Belmont Rd. NW 20008; 387-1980.

Website: www.oman.om

Oman was originally called Muscat and Oman. A long history of rule by other lands, including Portugal in the 16th cent., ended with the ouster of the Persians in 1744. By the early 19th cent., Muscat and Oman controlled much of the Persian and Pakistan coasts.

British influence was confirmed in a 1951 treaty, and Britain helped suppress an uprising by traditionally rebellious interior tribes against control by Muscat in the 1950s.

On July 23, 1970, Sultan Said bin Taimur was overthrown by his son, Sultan Qabus bin Said, who changed the nation's name to Sultanate of Oman. Petroleum and natural gas are major sources of income. Oman has strong military and economic ties to the U.S. but also has favorable relations with Iran. Sultan Qabus shuffled his cabinet after Arab Spring protests Feb. 2011 and expanded the powers of the Majlis al-Shura, the lower house of parliament, Oct. 20, 2011.

Pakistan
Islamic Republic of Pakistan

People: Population: 196,174,380. **Age distrib.:** <15: 33.3%; 65+: 4.3%. **Pop. density:** 659.1 per sq mi, 254.5 per sq km. **Urban:** 38.3%. **Ethnic groups:** Punjabi 45%, Pashtun (Pathan) 15%, Sindhi 14%, Sariaki 8%, Muhajir 8%, Balochi 4%. **Languages:** Punjabi, Sindhi, Siraiki, Pashtu, Urdu (official), Balochi, Hindko, Brahui, English (official; lingua franca of elite and in most govt. ministries). **Religions:** Muslim (official) 96% (Sunni 85%-90%, Shia 10%-15%), other (incl. Christian, Hindu) 4%.

Geography: Total area: 307,374 sq mi, 796,095 sq km; **Land area:** 297,637 sq mi, 770,875 sq km. **Location:** In W part of South Asia. **Neighbors:** Iran on W, Afghanistan and China on N, India on E. **Topography:** The Indus R. rises in the Hindu Kush and Himalaya Mts. in the N (highest is K2, or Godwin Austen, which at 28,251 ft is the 2nd highest in world), then flows over 1,000 mi through a fertile valley and empties into Arabian Sea. Thar Desert, Eastern Plains flank Indus Valley. **Capital:** Islamabad, 1,296,960. **Cities (urban aggl.):** Karachi, 16,125,936; Lahore, 8,500,347; Faisalabad, 3,460,047; Rawalpindi, 2,432,416; Gujranwala, 2,053,490; Multan, 1,874,053; Hyderabad, 1,734,207; Peshawar, 1,686,581.

Government: Type: Federal republic. **Head of state:** Pres. Mamnoon Hussain; b. Dec. 23, 1940; in office: Sept. 9, 2013. **Head of gov.:** Prime Min. Nawaz Sharif; b. Dec. 25, 1949; in office: June 5, 2013. **Local divisions:** 4 provinces, 1 territory, 1 capital territory; two entities in Pakistani-administered part of Jammu and Kashmir region. **Defense budget:** $5.89 bil. **Active troops:** 643,800.

Economy: Industries: textiles and apparel, food proc., pharmaceuticals, constr. materials, paper prods., fertilizer, shrimp. **Chief crops:** cotton, wheat, rice, sugarcane, fruits, vegetables. **Natural resources:** nat. gas, limited petroleum, poor quality coal, iron ore, copper, salt, limestone. **Crude oil reserves:** 341.9 mil bbls. **Arable land:** 27.5%. **Livestock:** cattle: 38.3 mil; chickens: 413 mil; goats: 64.9 mil; sheep: 28.8 mil. **Electricity prod.:** 89.9 bil kWh. **Labor force:** agric. 45.1%, industry 20.7%, services 34.2%. **Unemployment:** 5.1%.

Finance: Monetary unit: Rupee (PKR) (Sept. 2014: 102.50 = $1 U.S.). **GDP:** $574.1 bil; **per capita GDP:** $3,100; **GDP growth:** 3.6%. **Imports:** $39.3 bil; China 19.7%, Saudi Arabia 12.3%, UAE 12.1%, Kuwait 6.3%. **Exports:** $25.1 bil; U.S. 13.6%, China 11.1%, UAE 8.5%, Afghanistan 7.8%. **Tourism:** $288 mil. **Budget:** $48 bil. **Total reserves less gold:** $5.2 bil. **Gold:** 2.1 mil oz t. **Inflation:** 7.7%.

Transport: Railways: 4,841 mi. **Motor vehicles:** 14.4 per 1,000 pop. **Civil aviation:** 11.7 bil pass.-mi; 108 airports. **Chief ports:** Karachi, Port Muhammad Bin Qasim.

Communications: TV sets: 81 per 1,000 pop. **Radios:** 83 per 1,000 pop. **Telephone lines:** 3.5 per 100 pop. **Mobile:** 70.1 per 100 pop. **Internet:** 10.9%.

Health: Life expect.: 65.2 male; 69.0 female. **Births:** 23.2 per 1,000 pop. **Deaths:** 6.6 per 1,000 pop. **Natural inc.:** 1.66%. **Infant mortality:** 57.5 per 1,000 live births. **HIV:** <0.1%.

Education: Compulsory: ages 5-9. **Literacy:** 57.9%.

Embassy: 3517 International Ct. NW 20008; 243-6500.

Website: www.pakistan.gov.pk

Pakistan shares the 5,000-year history of the India-Pakistan subcontinent. At present-day Harappa and Mohenjo Daro, the Indus Valley civilization, with large cities and elaborate irrigation systems, flourished c. 4,000-2,500 BCE. Aryan invaders from the northwest conquered the region around 1,500 BCE, forging the Vedic civilization that dominated the region for over a thousand years. The first Arab invasion, 712 CE, introduced Islam. Present-day Pakistan and India were part of the Mughal empire from 1526 to 1857. Muslim power faded by the end of the 19th cent. as the British gained control.

Muhammad Ali Jinnah (1876-1948) was the principal architect of Pakistan. When the British withdrew Aug. 14, 1947, India's Islamic majority acquired self-government as Pakistan, with dominion status in the Commonwealth. Pakistan was divided into West Pakistan and East Pakistan, nearly 1,000 mi apart on opposite sides of India. Kashmir, a predominantly Muslim region divided between Pakistan and India, has remained a source of conflict between the two countries.

Rioting and strikes broke out in the East after Pakistan's government, Mar. 1, 1971, postponed the constituent assembly, dominated by supporters of regional autonomy for East Pakistan. Armed conflict between East and West lasted from Mar. to Dec. 1971, with India siding with Easterners, who proclaimed the independent nation of Bangladesh. Thousands were killed and some 10 mil Easterners fled to India. Full-scale war erupted between India and Pakistan, but Pakistan troops in the East surrendered Dec. 16; Pakistan agreed to a ceasefire in the West Dec. 17. On July 3, 1972, Pakistan and India signed a pact agreeing to troop withdrawals and peaceful conflict resolution.

Dec. 1970 elections brought Zulfikar Ali Bhutto to the presidency Dec. 20, 1971. Bhutto was overthrown in a military coup July 1977. Convicted of complicity in a 1974 political murder, he was executed Apr. 4, 1979. Millions of Afghan refugees flooded into Pakistan after the USSR invaded Afghanistan Dec. 1979; during 2002-10, some 3.6 mil refugees were repatriated, but 1.7 mil remained.

Pres. Mohammad Zia ul-Haq was killed when his plane exploded in Aug. 1988. Following Nov. elections, Benazir Bhutto, daughter of Zulfikar Ali Bhutto, was named prime min., becoming the first woman leader of a Muslim nation. She was accused of corruption and dismissed by the president, Aug. 1990. Bhutto returned to power Oct. 1993 but was dismissed Nov. 1996 amid further corruption charges. Responding to India's nuclear weapons tests, Pakistan conducted its own tests in 1998; the U.S. imposed economic sanctions on both countries.

Prime Min. Nawaz Sharif fired, Oct. 1999, army chief Gen. Pervez Musharraf, whose supporters staged a bloodless coup. Musharraf assumed the presidency June 20, 2001. Following the Sept. 11, 2001, terrorist attacks on the U.S., Pres. Musharraf pledged cooperation with the U.S. in fighting Taliban and al-Qaeda militants within Pakistan and in neighboring Afghanistan. In return, the U.S. waived its 1998 sanctions and offered Pakistan financial aid and debt relief. A referendum Apr. 30, 2002, extended Musharraf's rule for 5 years; many observers called the vote rigged. Musharraf Feb. 5, 2004, pardoned Pakistan's top nuclear scientist, Abdul Qadeer Khan, who admitted to selling atomic secrets to Iran, Libya, and North Korea. An earthquake that rocked Pakistan and the Pakistani-held region of Kashmir Oct. 8, 2005, killed about 80,000 people.

Musharraf's grip weakened in 2007, as his efforts to oust Pakistan's chief justice sparked mass pro-democracy demonstrations. He retained the presidency in an electoral-college vote Oct. 6, 2007, after his main opponents boycotted the election. More than 140 people died Oct. 18 when suicide bombers struck a convoy carrying Benazir Bhutto from the Karachi airport after she spent more than eight years in exile. Musharraf imposed emergency rule Nov. 3 and suspended the constitution while Pakistan's supreme court debated the constitutionality of his reelection. Musharraf gave up his army post Nov. 25, was sworn in as civilian president the next day, and lifted emergency rule Dec. 16. Bhutto was assassinated Dec. 27, 2007, after a rally in Rawalpindi.

Headed by Bhutto's widower, Asif Ali Zardari, the Pakistan Peoples Party led in parliamentary elections Feb. 18, 2008. Musharraf resigned Aug. 18 under threat of impeachment, and Zardari became president Sept. 9. Amid deteriorating security, U.S. and Pakistani forces clashed with the Taliban near the Afghan border, and Islamists carried out new suicide attacks. The government announced Feb. 16, 2009, a truce conceding de facto control of the strategic Swat Valley to the Taliban, but in May, government forces launched an offensive that reclaimed most of the region; the fighting displaced nearly 2 mil civilians. Catastrophic floods and monsoon rains, July-Aug. 2010, inundated one-fifth of Pakistan, leaving more than 1,750 people dead and displacing up to 20 mil.

In the 10-yr. period beginning in 2003, terrorist attacks, sectarian clashes, and armed conflict between insurgents and government forces killed more than 17,000 civilians. A decade-long international manhunt came to an end shortly after midnight May 2, 2011, when U.S. commandos killed al-Qaeda leader Osama bin Laden in Abbottabad. The raid, carried out by helicopter from Jalalabad, Afghanistan, was launched without prior warning to Pakistani authorities, escalating tensions between the U.S. and Pakistan.

Volunteers attempting to administer polio vaccine to children were attacked and at least 9 were killed, causing vaccinations to be temporarily halted Dec. 20, 2012. Polio cases increased in 2013-14, especially in Taliban stronghold North Waziristan; the Taliban attacked health workers to protest U.S. drone strikes and the CIA program that had used "vaccination workers" as a cover to gather intelligence.

In the worst industrial accident in Pakistan's history, nearly 300 died in a fire that consumed a factory complex in Karachi Sept. 12, 2012; workers had been trapped by blocked exits. On Oct. 9, 2012, 15-year-old Malala Yousafzai, who advocated for education rights for girls in Pakistan, was shot by the Taliban, sparking worldwide outrage. After treatment at a British hospital, she addressed a UN youth conference July 12, 2013. The Pakistan military announced, Sept. 12, 2014, that 10 people had been arrested in connection with the shooting.

Musharraf returned to Pakistan Mar. 24, 2013, to attempt a political comeback but was arrested Apr. 19. He was permanently barred from Pakistani politics May 1 and indicted for Benazir Bhutto's assassination Aug. 20. Amid accusations of vote rigging, former Prime Min. Nawaz Sharif was returned to office with May 11 elections. Mamnoon Hussain won the presidential election July 30, 2013, and took office Sept. 8. In 2014, terrorist attacks continued, including a Taliban assault on Karachi's international airport June 8, as did conflict between Islamic extremists and Pakistani forces, sometimes supported by U.S. drone strikes. At least 80,000 civilian refugees fled an anti-extremist offensive in North Waziristan beginning in June. Large-scale protests demanding Sharif's resignation began in Lahore, Aug. 14, and reached Islamabad, Aug. 15.

Palau
Republic of Palau

People: Population: 21,186. **Age distrib.:** <15: 20.5%; 65+: 7.1%. **Pop. density:** 119.5 per sq mi, 46.2 per sq km. **Urban:** 86.5%. **Ethnic groups:** Palauan (Micronesian with Malayan and Melanesian) 73%, Filipino 16%, Chinese 2%, Vietnamese 2%. **Languages:** Palauan (official on most islands), English (official), Filipino, Chinese. **Religions:** Roman Catholic 49%, Protestant 31%, Modekngei 9%.

Geography: Total area: 177 sq mi, 459 sq km; **Land area:** 177 sq mi, 459 sq km. **Location:** Archipelago (26 islands, more than 300 islets) in W Pacific O., about 530 mi SE of the Philippines. **Neighbors:** Micronesia to E, Indonesia to S. **Topography:** A mountainous main island and low coral atolls, usually fringed with large barrier reefs. **Capital:** Melekeok.

Government: Type: Constitutional govt. in free association with U.S. **Head of state and gov.:** Pres. Tommy Remengesau; b. Feb. 29, 1956; in office: Jan. 17, 2013. **Local divisions:** 16 states. **Defense budget/active troops:** NA.

Economy: Industries: tourism, craft items, constr., garment making. **Chief crops:** coconuts, copra, cassava, sweet potatoes. **Natural resources:** forests, minerals (espec. gold), marine prods., deep-seabed minerals. **Arable land:** 2.2%. **Labor force:** agric. 20%. **Unemployment:** NA.

Finance: Monetary unit: U.S. Dollar (USD). **GDP:** $245.5 mil; **per capita GDP** (2011): $10,500; **GDP growth** 3.5%. **Imports** (2010): $113.4 mil. **Exports** (2010): $12.3 mil. **Tourism:** $133 mil. **Budget** (2010 est.): $94.3 mil. **Total reserves less gold:** NA. **Inflation:** NA.

Transport: Civil aviation: 1 airport. **Chief port:** Koror.

Communications: TV sets: 98 per 1,000 pop. **Telephone lines:** 33.5 per 100 pop. **Mobile:** 90.4 per 100 pop. **Internet** (2004): 27%.

Health: Life expect.: 69.4 male; 76.0 female. **Births:** 11.0 per 1,000 pop. **Deaths:** 7.9 per 1,000 pop. **Natural inc.:** 0.30%. **Infant mortality:** 11.5 per 1,000 live births. **HIV:** NA.

Education: Compulsory: ages 6-17. **Literacy:** 99.5%.

Embassy: 1700 Pennsylvania Ave. NW, Ste. 400, 20006; 452-6814.

Website: palaugov.org

Spain acquired the Palau Islands, 1886, and sold them to Germany, 1899. Japan seized them in 1914. American forces occupied the islands in 1944; in 1947, they became part of the U.S.-administered UN Trust Territory of the Pacific Islands. In 1981, Palau became an autonomous republic. The republic ratified a compact of free association with the U.S. in 1993 and became an independent nation, Oct. 1, 1994. On Nov. 1, 2009, Palau accepted resettlement of six Uighur (Chinese Muslim) detainees who had been held by the U.S. at Guantánamo Bay, Cuba, since 2001. Palau is threatened by rising sea levels resulting from climate change.

Panama
Republic of Panama

People: Population: 3,608,431. **Age distrib.:** <15: 27.4%; 65+: 7.8%. **Pop. density:** 125.7 per sq mi, 48.5 per sq km. **Urban:** 66.3%. **Ethnic groups:** mestizo (mixed Amerindian and white) 70%, Amerindian and mixed (West Indian) 14%, white 10%, Amerindian 6%. **Languages:** Spanish (official), English. **Religions:** Roman Catholic 85%, Protestant 15%.

Geography: Total area: 29,120 sq mi, 75,420 sq km; **Land area:** 28,703 sq mi, 74,340 sq km. **Location:** In Central America. **Neighbors:** Costa Rica on W, Colombia on E. **Topography:** 2 mountain ranges run the length of the isthmus. Tropical rain forests cover the Caribbean coast and E Panama. **Capital:** Panama City, 1,637,870 (figure is for metro area).

Government: Type: Constitutional democracy. **Head of state and gov.:** Pres. Juan Carlos Varela; b. Dec. 12, 1963; in office: July 1, 2014. **Local divisions:** 10 provinces, 3 indigenous territories. **Defense budget:** $637 mil. **Active troops:** No armed forces. 12,000 paramilitary only.

Economy: Industries: constr., brewing, cement and other constr. materials, sugar milling. **Chief crops:** bananas, rice, corn, coffee, sugarcane, vegetables. **Natural resources:** copper, mahogany forests, shrimp, hydropower. **Arable land:** 7.2%. **Livestock:** cattle: 1.7 mil; chickens: 20.5 mil; goats: 8,450; pigs: 361,000. **Electricity**

prod.: 7.6 bil kWh. **Labor force:** agric. 17%, industry 18.6%, services 64.4%. **Unemployment:** 4.5%.

Finance: Monetary unit: Balboa (PAB) (Sept. 2014: 1.00 = $1 U.S.). **GDP:** $61.5 bil; **per capita GDP:** $16,500; **GDP growth:** 7.5%. **Imports:** $26.6 bil; U.S. 23.6%, China 6.4%, Costa Rica 4.6%, Mexico 4.4%. **Exports:** $18.9 bil; U.S. 20.2%, Canada 14.6%, Costa Rica 6.6%, Netherlands 5.9%, Sweden 4.8%, China 4.1%, Italy 4%. (Import/export figures incl. Colón Free Zone.). **Tourism:** $3.3 bil. **Budget:** $11.4 bil. **Total reserves less gold:** $2.8 bil. **Inflation:** 4.0%.

Transport: Railways: 47 mi. **Motor vehicles:** 178.9 per 1,000 pop. **Civil aviation:** 8.6 bil pass.-mi; 57 airports. **Chief ports:** Balboa, Colon, Cristobal.

Communications: TV sets: 219 per 1,000 pop. **Radios:** 293 per 1,000 pop. **Telephone lines:** 15.2 per 100 pop. **Mobile:** 163 per 100 pop. **Internet:** 42.9%.

Health: Life expect.: 75.5 male; 81.2 female. **Births:** 18.6 per 1,000 pop. **Deaths:** 4.8 per 1,000 pop. **Natural inc.:** 1.38%. **Infant mortality:** 10.7 per 1,000 live births. **HIV:** 0.7%.

Education: Compulsory: ages 6-14. **Literacy:** 95%.

Embassy: 2862 McGill Ter. NW 20008; 483-1407.

Website: www.presidencia.gob.pa

The coast of Panama was sighted by Rodrigo de Bastidas, sailing with Columbus for Spain in 1501, and was visited by Columbus in 1502. Vasco Núñez de Balboa crossed the isthmus and "discovered" the Pacific Ocean, Sept. 13, 1513. Spanish colonies were ravaged by Francis Drake, 1572-95, and Henry Morgan, 1668-71. Morgan destroyed the old city of Panama, which was founded in 1519. Freed from Spain, Panama joined Colombia in 1821.

Panama declared independence from Colombia Nov. 3, 1903, and granted use, occupation, and control of the Canal Zone to the U.S. Feb. 26, 1904. A 1978 treaty provided for a gradual takeover by Panama of the canal. The U.S. handed over control Dec. 31, 1999. A $5.3-bil plan to widen the Panama Canal was approved by national referendum Oct. 22, 2006. Construction was scheduled for completion by the end of 2015.

Pres. Eric Arturo Delvalle was ousted by the National Assembly, Feb. 26, 1988, after he tried to fire Gen. Manuel Antonio Noriega, who was under U.S. federal indictment on drug charges. U.S. troops invaded Panama Dec. 20, 1989, and Noriega surrendered Jan. 3, 1990. Ricardo Martinelli Berrocal, a conservative, was elected president May 3, 2009, and took office July 1. After two decades in a U.S. prison, Noriega was extradited to France Apr. 26, 2010, where he was convicted of money laundering July 7 and received a 7-year sentence. France extradited him to Panama, Dec. 11, 2011, to serve a 20-year sentence for human rights violations he had committed as president. In May 4, 2014, presidential elections, Juan Carols Varela defeated the candidate who had been supported by Martinelli.

Papua New Guinea
Independent State of Papua New Guinea

People: Population: 6,552,730. **Age distrib.:** <15: 35%; 65+: 3.9%. **Pop. density:** 37.5 per sq mi, 14.5 per sq km. **Urban:** 13%. **Ethnic groups:** Melanesian, Papuan, Negrito, Micronesian, Polynesian. **Languages:** Tok Pisin, English, Hiri Motu (all official); some 836 indigenous langs. (most spoken by fewer than 1,000). **Religions:** Protestant 69% (Evangelical Lutheran 20%, United Church 12%, Seventh-day Adventist 10%, Pentecostal 9%, Evangelical Alliance 5%, Anglican 3%, Baptist 3%), Roman Catholic 27%.

Geography: Total area: 178,704 sq mi, 462,840 sq km; **Land area:** 174,850 sq mi, 452,860 sq km. **Location:** SE Asia, occupying E half of island of New Guinea and about 600 nearby islands. **Neighbors:** Indonesia on W, Australia on S. **Topography:** Thickly forested mts. cover much of center of country, with lowlands along the coasts. Included are some islands of Bismarck and Solomon groups, such as Admiralty Isls., New Ireland, New Britain, and Bougainville. **Capital:** Port Moresby, 338,069.

Government: Type: Constitutional parliamentary democracy. **Head of state:** Queen Elizabeth II, rep. by Gov.-Gen. Sir Michael Ogio; b. July 7, 1942; in office: Feb. 25, 2011. **Head of gov.:** Prime Min. Peter O'Neill; b. Feb. 13, 1965; in office: Aug. 2, 2011. **Local divisions:** 20 provinces, 1 autonomous region, 1 district. **Defense budget:** $84 mil. **Active troops:** 1,900.

Economy: Industries: copra crushing, palm oil proc., plywood prod., wood chip prod., mining, crude oil prod., petroleum refining. **Chief crops:** coffee, cocoa, copra, palm kernels, tea, sugar, rubber, sweet potatoes. **Natural resources:** gold, copper, silver, nat. gas, timber, oil, fisheries. **Crude oil reserves:** 185.9 mil bbls. **Arable land:** 0.1%. **Livestock:** cattle: 93,000; chickens: 4.4 mil; goats: 3,000; pigs: 2 mil; sheep: 7,300. **Electricity prod.:** 3.3 bil kWh. **Labor force:** agric. 85%. **Unemployment:** 2.3%.

Finance: Monetary unit: Kina (PGK) (Sept. 2014: 2.52 = $1 U.S.). **GDP:** $20 bil; **per capita GDP:** $2,900; **GDP growth:** 5.4%. **Imports:** $4.6 bil; Australia 36.3%, Singapore 13.8%, Malaysia 8.4%, China 7.9%, Japan 5.8%, U.S. 4.8%. **Exports:** $5.4 bil; Australia 30.1%, Japan 9.9%, China 5%, Germany 4.1%. **Tourism:** $2 mil. **Budget:** $5.1 bil. **Total reserves less gold:** $2.8 bil. **Gold:** 63,000 oz t. **Inflation** (2011-12): 2.2%.

Transport: Motor vehicles: 21.4 per 1,000 pop. **Civil aviation:** 928.9 mil pass.-mi; 21 airports. **Chief ports:** Kimbe, Lae, Madang, Rabaul, Wewak.

Communications: TV sets: 24 per 1,000 pop. **Radios:** 191 per 1,000 pop. **Telephone lines:** 1.9 per 100 pop. **Mobile:** 41 per 100 pop. **Internet:** 6.5%.

Health: Life expect.: 64.6 male; 69.2 female. **Births:** 24.9 per 1,000 pop. **Deaths:** 6.5 per 1,000 pop. **Natural inc.:** 1.84%. **Infant mortality:** 39.7 per 1,000 live births. **HIV:** 0.7%.

Education: NA. **Literacy:** 64.2%.

Embassy: 1779 Massachusetts Ave. NW, Ste. 805, 20036; 745-3680.

Website: www.pm.gov.pg

Human remains have been found in the interior of New Guinea dating back at least 10,000 years and possibly much earlier. European colonization began in the 19th cent., when the Dutch took control of the island's western half (now part of Indonesia). The southern half of eastern New Guinea was claimed by Britain in 1884 and transferred to Australia in 1905. Germany claimed the northern half in 1884, but Australia captured it in WWI, receiving a League of Nations mandate and later a UN trusteeship. The two territories were administered jointly after 1949; gained self-government Dec. 1, 1973; and became independent Sept. 16, 1975.

Secessionist rebels clashed with government forces on Bougainville 1988-97, claiming some 20,000 lives. A tsunami killed at least 3,000 July 17, 1998. A Bougainville autonomy agreement was signed Aug. 30, 2001. Sir Michael Somare, the nation's first prime min. (1975-80, 1982-85), regained the office in 2002 and was reelected by parliament Aug. 13, 2007. Somare took indefinite medical leave Apr. 2011; parliament, Aug. 2, elected Peter O'Neill as permanent replacement. The supreme court ruled that election illegal Dec. 12, 2011, and ordered Somare returned to office. O'Neill refused to step aside. The crisis came to an end after elections Aug. 3, 2012, from which O'Neill emerged as the prime min. The country's Sorcery Act, which had criminalized the practice, was repealed May 29, 2013; to curb vigilante violence against alleged sorcerers and also violence against women, the death penalty was reinstated for rape, robbery, and murder.

The country has extensive energy resources. The initial phase of a project to transport natural gas by pipeline was completed and the first shipments of liquefied natural gas through a new processing and shipping facility near Port Moresby were made in May 2014.

Paraguay
Republic of Paraguay

People: Population: 6,703,860. **Age distrib.:** <15: 26.2%; 65+: 6.6%. **Pop. density:** 43.7 per sq mi, 16.9 per sq km. **Urban:** 59.4%.
Ethnic groups: mestizo (mixed Spanish and Amerindian) 95%.
Languages: Spanish, Guaraní (both official). **Religions:** Roman Catholic 90%, Protestant 6%.
Geography: Total area: 157,048 sq mi, 406,752 sq km; **Land area:** 153,399 sq mi, 397,302 sq km. **Location:** Landlocked country in central S America. **Neighbors:** Bolivia on N, Argentina on S, Brazil on E. **Topography:** Paraguay R. bisects the country. To E are fertile plains, wooded slopes, grasslands. To W is the Gran Chaco plain, with marshes and scrub trees. Extreme W is arid. **Capital:** Asunción, 2,307,330 (figure is for metro area).
Government: Type: Constitutional republic. **Head of state and gov.:** Pres. Horacio Cartes; b. July 5, 1956; in office: Aug. 15, 2013. **Local divisions:** 17 departments, 1 capital city. **Defense budget:** $364 mil. **Active troops:** 10,650.
Economy: Industries: sugar, cement, textiles, beverages, wood prods., steel. **Chief crops:** cotton, sugarcane, soybeans, corn, wheat, tobacco, cassava, fruits, vegetables. **Natural resources:** hydropower, timber, iron ore, manganese, limestone. **Arable land:** 11.1%. **Livestock:** cattle: 13.4 mil; chickens: 25 mil; goats: 140,000; pigs: 1.3 mil; sheep: 417,000. **Electricity prod.:** 57.1 bil kWh. **Labor force:** agric. 26.5%, industry 18.5%, services 55%. **Unemployment:** 6.3%.
Finance: Monetary unit: Guaraní (PYG) (Sept. 2014: 4,263.00 = $1 U.S.). **GDP:** $45.9 bil; **per capita GDP:** $6,800; **GDP growth:** 12%. **Imports:** $12.4 bil; Brazil 24.2%, China 19.5%, Argentina 18.3%, U.S. 11.5%. **Exports:** $14.7 bil; Uruguay 17.7%, Brazil 16.4%, Argentina 15.6%, Russia 12%. **Tourism:** $273 mil. **Budget:** $6.3 bil. **Total reserves less gold:** $5.6 bil. **Gold:** 263,425 oz t. **Inflation:** 2.7%.
Transport: Railways: 22 mi. **Motor vehicles:** 67.5 per 1,000 pop. **Civil aviation:** 15 airports. **Chief ports:** Asunción, Encarnación, San Antonio, Villeta.
Communications: TV sets: 262 per 1,000 pop. **Radios:** 182 per 1,000 pop. **Telephone lines:** 5.9 per 100 pop. **Mobile:** 103.7 per 100 pop. **Internet:** 36.9%.
Health: Life expect.: 74.2 male; 79.6 female. **Births:** 16.7 per 1,000 pop. **Deaths:** 4.6 per 1,000 pop. **Natural inc.:** 1.20%. **Infant mortality:** 20.8 per 1,000 live births. **HIV:** 0.4%.
Education: Compulsory: ages 6-14. **Literacy:** 95.6%.
Embassy: 2400 Massachusetts Ave. NW 20008; 483-6960.
Website: www.embaparusa.gov.py

Guaraní Indians preceded Europeans in Paraguay, which was visited by Sebastian Cabot in 1527 and became a Spanish possession in 1535. Paraguay gained independence from Spain in 1811. It lost its population and much of its territory to Brazil, Uruguay, and Argentina in the War of the Triple Alliance, 1865-70. Large areas were won from Bolivia in the Chaco War, 1932-35. Gen.

Alfredo Stroessner held the presidency 1954-89, until his ouster in a military coup.

Power struggles ensued between civilian and military leaders, 1993-97. The assassination of Vice Pres. Luis María Argaña, Mar. 23, 1999, was widely attributed to Pres. Raúl Cubas Grau and triggered protests and an impeachment vote; Cubas resigned Mar. 28 and was succeeded by Senate leader Luis Angel González Macchi. An attempted military coup was suppressed May 18, 2000.

Mass protests over the depressed economy led to the proclamation of a state of emergency July 15, 2002. Nicanor Duarte Frutos of the conservative Colorado Party won the presidency, Apr. 27, 2003.

Paraguayan authorities blamed a leftist group for the 2004 kidnapping and subsequent murder of Cecilia Cubas, daughter of former Pres. Cubas. Fernando Lugo, a former Catholic cleric known as the "bishop of the poor," won a presidential election Apr. 20, 2008, ending over 6 decades of Colorado rule. On June 22, 2012, Lugo was removed from office after his handling of a dispute between landless peasants and police left 17 dead June 15. Colorado candidate Horacio Cartes, a former tobacco magnate, was elected president Apr. 21, 2013. The leftist Paraguayan People's Army staged a number of attacks during 2013, mostly on security forces in northern Paraguay.

Peru
Republic of Peru

People: Population: 30,147,935. **Age distrib.:** <15: 27.3%; 65+: 6.9%. **Pop. density:** 61 per sq mi, 23.6 per sq km. **Urban:** 78.3%.
Ethnic groups: Amerindian 45%; mestizo (mixed Amerindian and white) 37%; white 15%; black, Japanese, Chinese, and other 3%.
Languages: Spanish, Quechua, Aymara (all official); other native langs. (incl. large number of minor Amazonian langs.). **Religions:** Roman Catholic 81%, Evangelical 13%.
Geography: Total area: 496,225 sq mi, 1,285,216 sq km; **Land area:** 494,209 sq mi, 1,279,996 sq km. **Location:** On Pacific coast of S America. **Neighbors:** Ecuador, Colombia on N; Brazil, Bolivia on E; Chile on S. **Topography:** An arid coastal strip, 10-100 mi wide, supports much of the population thanks to widespread irrigation. The Andes cover 27% of land area. The uplands are well-watered, as are the eastern slopes reaching the Amazon Basin, which covers half the country. **Capital:** Lima, 9,722,070. **Cities (urban aggl.):** Arequipa, 839,388.
Government: Type: Constitutional republic. **Head of state and gov:** Pres. Ollanta Humala Tasso; b. June 27, 1962; in office: July 28, 2011. **Local divisions:** 25 regions, 1 province. **Defense budget:** $2.84 bil. **Active troops:** 115,000.
Economy: Industries: mining and refining of minerals; steel, metal fabrication; petroleum extraction and refining, nat. gas and nat. gas liquefaction; fishing and fish proc., cement, glass, textiles, clothing, food proc. **Chief crops:** asparagus, coffee, cocoa, cotton, sugarcane, rice, potatoes, corn, plantains, grapes, oranges and other fruits, coca, tomatoes, mangoes, barley, medicinal plants. **Natural resources:** copper, silver, gold, petroleum, timber, fish, iron ore, coal, phosphate, potash, hydropower, nat. gas. **Crude oil reserves:** 632.9 mil bbls. **Arable land:** 3.2%. **Livestock:** cattle: 5.6 mil; chickens: 137.7 mil; goats: 1.9 mil; pigs: 3.1 mil; sheep: 12.4 mil. **Electricity prod.:** 38.0 bil kWh. **Labor force:** agric. 25.8%, industry 17.4%, services 56.8%. **Unemployment:** 4%.
Finance: Monetary unit: Nuevo Sol (PEN) (Sept. 2014: 2.85 = $1 U.S.). **GDP:** $344 bil; **per capita GDP:** $11,100; **GDP growth:** 5.1%. **Imports:** $42.1 bil; U.S. 24.6%, China 14%, Brazil 6.4%, Argentina 5%, Chile 4.8%, Colombia 4.2%, Ecuador 4.1%, Mexico 4%. **Exports:** $41.5 bil; China 19.9%, U.S. 15.7%, Canada 9.5%, Japan 6.6%, Spain 5.2%, Chile 4.9%. **Tourism:** $3 bil. **Budget:** $58.9 bil. **Total reserves less gold:** $64.4 bil. **Gold** (2012): 1.1 mil oz t. **Inflation:** 2.8%.
Transport: Railways: 1,185 mi. **Motor vehicles:** 59.9 per 1,000 pop. **Civil aviation:** 8.3 bil pass.-mi; 59 airports. **Chief ports:** Callao, Iquitos, Matarani, Paita, Pucallpa, Yurimaguas.
Communications: TV sets: 201 per 1,000 pop. **Radios:** 269 per 1,000 pop. **Telephone lines:** 11.3 per 100 pop. **Mobile:** 98.1 per 100 pop. **Internet:** 39.2%.
Health: Life expect.: 71.2 male; 75.3 female. **Births:** 18.6 per 1,000 pop. **Deaths:** 6.0 per 1,000 pop. **Natural inc.:** 1.26%. **Infant mortality:** 20.2 per 1,000 live births. **HIV:** 0.4%.
Education: Compulsory: ages 5-16. **Literacy:** 94.5%.
Embassy: 1700 Massachusetts Ave. NW 20036; 833-9860.
Website: www.peru.gob.pe

The powerful Inca Empire had its seat at Cuzco in the Andes and covered much of S America. A civil war had weakened the empire when Spaniard Francisco Pizarro began raiding Peru for its wealth, 1532. In 1533 he executed the Inca ruler, Atahualpa, and enslaved the people.

José de San Martín captured Lima from the Spanish in 1821; Simón Bolívar routed Spanish forces in 1824, and for much of the 19th cent., the country was governed by military leaders. Chile defeated Peru in the War of the Pacific, 1879-83. Right-wing groups allied with the military and the leftist APRA party vied for power in the first half of the 20th cent.

Peru returned to democratic leadership in 1980 but was plagued by economic problems and by leftist Shining Path (Sendero Luminoso) guerrillas. Conflict between guerrillas and government troops, 1980-2000, killed more than 69,000 people, mostly Andean Indians.

Elected president in June 1990, Alberto Fujimori, the son of Japanese immigrants, dissolved the National Congress, suspended parts of the constitution, and initiated press censorship, Apr. 1992. The leader of Shining Path was captured Sept. 12. Fujimori won reelection in 1995 and 2000, but his repressive antiterrorism tactics drew international criticism.

Scandals involving top aide and intelligence chief Vladimiro Montesinos led Fujimori to resign Nov. 20, 2000; instead of accepting his resignation, Congress ousted him as "morally unfit." Montesinos was captured in Venezuela June 23, 2001; extradited to Peru, he was convicted in a series of criminal trials. Fujimori was arrested in Chile, Nov. 7, 2005, and extradited to Peru, Sept. 22, 2007. He was convicted in three separate proceedings, 2007-09, on charges that included complicity in a paramilitary death squad's killing of at least 25 people, 1991-92.

Alan García, whose first term as president, 1985-90, ended with the country facing hyperinflation and guerrilla war, won a presidential runoff election June 4, 2006. In a presidential runoff election June 5, 2011, Ollanta Humala Tasso, a leftist former military officer, defeated Peruvian legislator Keiko Fujimori Higuchi, the daughter of jailed former Pres. Fujimori. A maritime border dispute with Chile (with implications for commercial fishing) was settled largely in Peru's favor by the Intl. Court of Justice, Jan. 27, 2014.

Philippines
Republic of the Philippines

People: Population: 107,668,231. **Age distrib.:** <15: 33.7%; 65+: 4.5%. **Pop. density:** 935.2 per sq mi, 361.1 per sq km. **Urban:** 44.5%. **Ethnic groups:** Tagalog 28%, Cebuano 13%, Ilocano 9%, Bisaya/Binisaya 8%, Hiligaynon Ilonggo 8%, Bikol 6%, Waray 3%. **Languages:** Filipino, English (both official); 8 major dialects. **Religions:** Roman Catholic 81%, Muslim 5%, Evangelical 3%, Iglesia ni Kristo 2%, Aglipayan 2%, other Christian 5%.

Geography: Total area: 115,831 sq mi, 300,000 sq km; **Land area:** 115,124 sq mi, 298,170 sq km. **Location:** An archipelago off SE coast of Asia. **Neighbors:** Nearest are Malaysia, Indonesia on S; Taiwan on N. **Topography:** The country consists of some 7,100 islands stretching 1,100 mi N-S. About 95% of area and population are on 11 largest islands, which are mountainous, except for the heavily indented coastlines and central plain on Luzon. **Capital:** Manila, 12,763,800 (figure is for natl. capital region). **Cities (urban aggl.):** Davao City, 1,597,653; Cebu City, 936,175.

Government: Type: Republic. **Head of state and gov.:** Pres. Benigno "Noynoy" Aquino III; b. Feb. 8, 1960; in office: June 30, 2010. **Local divisions:** 80 provinces, 39 chartered cities. **Defense budget:** $2.21 bil. **Active troops:** 125,000.

Economy: Industries: electronics assembly, garments, footwear, pharmaceuticals, chemicals, wood prods., food proc., petroleum refining, fishing. **Chief crops:** sugarcane, coconuts, rice, corn, bananas, cassava, pineapples, mangoes. **Natural resources:** timber, petroleum, nickel, cobalt, silver, gold, salt, copper. **Crude oil reserves:** 138.5 mil bbls. **Arable land:** 18.6%. **Livestock:** cattle: 2.5 mil; chickens: 163.4 mil; goats: 3.7 mil; pigs: 11.8 mil; sheep: 30,000. **Electricity prod.:** 66.0 bil kWh. **Labor force:** agric. 32%, industry 15%, services 53%. **Unemployment:** 7%.

Finance: Monetary unit: Peso (PHP) (Sept. 2014: 43.56 = $1 U.S.). **GDP:** $454.3 bil; **per capita GDP:** $4,700; **GDP growth:** 6.8%. **Imports:** $63.9 bil; China 11.5%, China 10.8%, Japan 10.4%, South Korea 7.3%, Singapore 7.1%, Thailand 5.6%, Saudi Arabia 5.6%, Indonesia 4.4%, Malaysia 4%. **Exports:** $47.5 bil; Japan 19%, U.S. 14.2%, China 11.8%, Singapore 9.3%, Hong Kong 9.2%, South Korea 5.5%, Thailand 4.7%. **Tourism:** $4.7 bil. **Budget:** $43.9 bil. **Total reserves less gold:** $75.7 bil. **Gold:** 6.2 mil oz t. **Inflation:** 3.0%.

Transport: Railways: 618 mi. **Motor vehicles:** 32.2 per 1,000 pop. **Civil aviation:** 20.3 bil pass.-mi; 89 airports. **Chief ports:** Batangas, Cagayan de Oro, Cebu, Davao, Liman, Manila.

Communications: TV sets: 194 per 1,000 pop. **Radios:** 735 per 1,000 pop. **Telephone lines:** 3.2 per 100 pop. **Mobile:** 104.5 per 100 pop. **Internet:** 37%.

Health: Life expect.: 69.5 male; 75.6 female. **Births:** 24.2 per 1,000 pop. **Deaths:** 4.9 per 1,000 pop. **Natural incr.:** 1.93%. **Infant mortality:** 17.6 per 1,000 live births. **HIV:** NA.

Education: Compulsory: ages 6-11. **Literacy:** 96.3%.

Embassy: 1600 Massachusetts Ave. NW 20036; 467-9300.

Website: www.gov.ph

Originally inhabited by Malay peoples, the archipelago was visited by Magellan, 1521. The Spanish founded Manila, 1571. Spain ceded the islands, named for King Philip II of Spain, to the U.S. for $20 mil, 1898, following the Spanish-American War. U.S. troops suppressed a guerrilla uprising in a brutal war, 1899-1905. Japan attacked the Philippines Dec. 8, 1941, and occupied the islands during WWII. Independence was proclaimed, July 4, 1946. A republic was established.

The repressive and corrupt regime of Pres. Ferdinand Marcos and his wife, Imelda, ruled the Philippines 1965-86. The assassination of prominent opposition leader Benigno S. Aquino Jr., Aug. 21, 1983, sparked calls for Marcos's resignation. Marcos defeated Corazon Aquino, widow of the slain opposition leader, Feb. 16, 1986,

in an allegedly fraudulent election. Mass protests and international pressure forced Marcos to flee the country Feb. 25, and Aquino became president.

Her government was plagued by a weak economy, widespread poverty, Communist and Muslim insurgencies, and lukewarm military support. Rebel troops attempting a coup Dec. 1, 1989, were defeated by government forces and U.S. air support. Fidel Ramos won the May 1992 presidential election. The U.S. vacated the Subic Bay Naval Station in late 1992, ending its long military presence. However, a 2014 agreement gave U.S. forces increased access to Philippines bases. Some Muslim separatist guerrillas refused to abide by a cease-fire agreement signed Jan. 30, 1994, so a new treaty providing for expansion and development of an autonomous Muslim region on Mindanao was signed Sept. 2, 1996; the rebellion had claimed more than 120,000 lives since 1972.

Joseph (Erap) Estrada, a former movie actor, won the presidential election, May 11, 1998, but was impeached on bribery and corruption charges Nov. 13, 2000. Vice Pres. Gloria Macapagal Arroyo became president Jan. 20, 2001.

As part of the post-9/11 war on terror, the U.S. began assisting Filipino troops in combating Abu Sayyaf, an Islamist guerrilla group. The U.S. announced, June 26, 2014, plans to scale back the program. Pres. Arroyo won reelection May 10, 2004. Flooding and mudslides from tropical storms, Nov.-Dec. 2004, killed at least 1,060 people. Former Pres. Estrada was convicted, Sept. 12, 2007, of taking more than $85 mil in bribes and kickbacks while in office; Pres. Arroyo pardoned him Oct. 25. Typhoon Fengshen, June 21-22, 2008, left at least 557 people dead and destroyed more than 90,000 homes; at least 700 more people died when the ferry *Princess of the Stars* capsized and ran aground in the storm. Benigno (NoyNoy) Aquino III, the son of former Pres. Aquino (who died Aug. 1, 2009), defeated Estrada in the May 10, 2010, presidential election.

Former Pres. Arroyo, who was serving in Congress, was arrested Oct. 4, 2012, on corruption charges. The government, Oct. 15, 2012, signed a new peace deal with Muslim rebels on Mindanao; violence had persisted after the 1996 accord. Yet another peace agreement, providing for a large measure of autonomy for Mindanao, was signed between the government and Moro Islamic Liberation Front, Mar. 27, 2014. Abu Sayyaf rejected the accord.

Congress voted, Dec. 17, 2012, to provide contraception to the country's poorest women, despite objections from many of the nation's Catholics; the Supreme Court suspended the law Mar. 19. 2013. Typhoon Haiyan, with winds up to 195 mph, struck the Philippines Nov. 8, 2013; the storm killed more than 6,200 people and displaced over 4 mil.

Poland
Republic of Poland

People: Population: 38,346,279. **Age distrib.:** <15: 14.6%; 65+: 15%. **Pop. density:** 326.4 per sq mi, 126 per sq km. **Urban:** 60.6%. **Ethnic groups:** Polish 97%. **Language:** Polish (official). **Religions:** Roman Catholic 87%.

Geography: Total area: 120,728 sq mi, 312,685 sq km; **Land area:** 117,474 sq mi, 304,255 sq km. **Location:** On Baltic Sea in E central Europe. **Neighbors:** Germany on W; Czech Rep., Slovakia on S; Lithuania, Belarus, Ukraine on E; Russia on N. **Topography:** Mostly lowlands forming part of the Northern European Plain. The Carpathian Mts. along S border rise to 8,200 ft. **Capital:** Warsaw, 1,718,210. **Cities (urban aggl.):** Kraków, 759,292.

Government: Type: Republic. **Head of state:** Pres. Bronisław Komorowski; b. June 4, 1952; in office: Aug. 6, 2010. **Head of gov.:** Prime Min. Ewa Kopacz; b. Dec. 3, 1956; in office: Sept. 22, 2014. **Local divisions:** 16 provinces. **Defense budget:** $9.83 bil. **Active troops:** 99,300.

Economy: Industries: machine building, iron and steel, coal mining, chemicals, shipbuilding, food proc., glass, beverages, textiles. **Chief crops:** potatoes, fruits, vegetables, wheat. **Natural resources:** coal, sulfur, copper, nat. gas, silver, lead, salt, amber. **Crude oil reserves:** 156.5 mil bbls. **Arable land:** 35.7%. **Livestock:** cattle: 5.9 mil; chickens: 123.5 mil; goats: 81,727; pigs: 11.2 mil; sheep: 249,481. **Electricity prod.** (2012): 150.9 bil kWh. **Labor force:** agric. 12.9%, industry 30.2%, services 57%. **Unemployment:** 10.1%.

Finance: Monetary unit: Zloty (PLN) (Sept. 2014: 3.19 = $1 U.S.). **GDP:** $814 bil; **per capita GDP:** $21,100; **GDP growth:** 1.3%. **Imports:** $207.4 bil; Germany 27.3%, Russia 12.2%, Netherlands 5.9%, China 5.4%, Italy 5.2%, Czech Republic 4.3%, France 4.2%. **Exports:** $202.3 bil; Germany 26%, UK 7%, Czech Republic 6.5%, France 6%, Russia 5.2%, Italy 5%, Netherlands 4.6%. **Tourism:** $10.9 bil. **Budget:** $92.5 bil. **Total reserves less gold:** $102.2 bil. **Gold:** 3.3 mil oz t. **Inflation:** 1.2%.

Transport: Railways: 12,072 mi. **Motor vehicles:** 592.3 per 1,000 pop. **Civil aviation:** 4.2 bil pass.-mi; 87 airports. **Chief ports:** Gdansk, Gdynia, Swinoujscie, Szczecin.

Communications: TV sets: 408 per 1,000 pop. **Radios:** 297 per 1,000 pop. **Telephone lines:** 13.9 per 100 pop. **Mobile:** 150 per 100 pop. **Internet:** 62.8%.

Health: Life expect.: 72.7 male; 80.8 female. **Births:** 9.8 per 1,000 pop. **Deaths:** 10.4 per 1,000 pop. **S. Natural incr.:** −0.06%. **Infant mortality:** 6.2 per 1,000 live births. **HIV:** NA.

Education: Compulsory: ages 7-15. **Literacy:** 99.8%.

Embassy: 2640 16th St. NW 20009; 234-3800.
Website: www.poland.gov.pl

Slavic tribes in the area were converted to Latin Christianity in the 10th cent. Poland was a great power from the 14th to the 17th cent. In three partitions (1772, 1793, 1795) it was apportioned among Prussia, Russia, and Austria. Overrun by the Austro-German armies in WWI, it declared its independence on Nov. 11, 1918, and was recognized as independent by the Treaty of Versailles, June 28, 1919. Large territories to the east were taken in a war with Russia, 1921.

Germany and the USSR invaded Poland Sept. 1939 and divided the country. During the war, Nazis killed some 6 mil Polish citizens, half of them Jews. In compensation for territory ceded to the USSR when the war ended, Poland received German territory comprising Silesia, Pomerania, West Prussia, and part of East Prussia. Communists, who aligned themselves with the USSR, dominated the 1947 election.

In 12 years of rule by Stalinists, large estates were abolished, industries nationalized, schools secularized, and Roman Catholic prelates jailed. Farm production fell off. Harsh working conditions caused a riot in Poznan, June 28-29, 1956. A new Politburo, committed to a more independent Polish Communism, was named Oct. 1956, with Wladyslaw Gomulka as first secretary of the party. Collectivization of farms was ended. Gomulka agreed to permit religious liberty and religious publications, provided the church kept out of politics.

In Dec. 1970 workers in port cities rioted because of price rises and new incentive wage rules. On Dec. 20 Gomulka resigned as party leader; he was succeeded by Edward Gierek. The rules were dropped and price rises revoked.

Independent trade union Solidarity grew in popularity and strength throughout the 1980s, organizing strikes and making bold demands. Led by Lech Walesa, who had been arrested along with other Solidarity leaders Dec. 13, 1981, Solidarity helped to win political and economic reforms, including free elections, in an Apr. 5, 1989, accord. Candidates endorsed by Solidarity swept the parliamentary elections, June 4. Lech Walesa became president Dec. 22, 1990.

A radical economic program designed to transform the economy into a free-market system led to inflation, unemployment, and a return to the political left in 1993 parliamentary elections. A former Communist, Aleksander Kwasniewski, defeated Walesa in the 1995 presidential election and was reelected 5 years later. A new constitution was approved by referendum May 25, 1997. Poland became a full member of NATO, Mar. 12, 1999, and entered the European Union May 1, 2004.

Lech Kaczynski, the conservative mayor of Warsaw, won a presidential runoff election Oct. 23, 2005. In July 2006 he appointed his identical twin brother Jaroslaw as prime min. Poland's governing coalition fell apart in 2007, and the center-right Civic Platform party, led by Donald Tusk, won parliamentary elections Oct. 21. Pres. Lech Kaczynski, his wife Maria, and many senior Polish government officials were among the 96 passengers and crew members killed in a plane crash Apr. 10, 2010, near Smolensk, in western Russia. Parliament Speaker Bronislaw Komorowski, an ally of Prime Min. Tusk, became acting president; he won a full term July 4, 2010, by defeating Kaczynski's brother Jaroslaw in a runoff.

U.S. Pres. Barack Obama visited Poland, June 3, 2014, and pledged increased U.S. security support for Eastern Europe. Secretly taped earlier private conversations among Polish officials, made public in June, included remarks by the foreign minister disparaging the value of U.S. security assistance. Parliament Speaker Ewa Kopacz became prime min. Sept. 22, 2014, when Tusk was selected president of the European Council.

Portugal
Portuguese Republic

People: Population: 10,813,834. **Age distrib.:** <15: 15.9%; 65+: 18.6%. **Pop. density:** 306.2 per sq mi, 118.2 per sq km. **Urban:** 62.9%. **Ethnic groups:** homogeneous Mediterranean stock. **Languages:** Portuguese, Mirandese (both official). **Religions:** Roman Catholic 85%, other Christian 2%, none 4%.
Geography: Total area: 35,556 sq mi, 92,090 sq km; **Land area:** 35,317 sq mi, 91,470 sq km. **Location:** At SW extreme of Europe. **Neighbors:** Spain on N, E. **Topography:** Portugal N of Tajus R., which bisects country NE-SW, is mountainous, cool and rainy. To the S there are drier, rolling plains, and a warm climate. **Capital:** Lisbon, 2,868,860. **Cities (urban aggl.):** Porto, 1,296,095.
Government: Type: Republic. **Head of state:** Pres. Aníbal Cavaco Silva; b. July 15, 1939; in office: Mar. 9, 2006. **Head of gov.:** Prime Min. Pedro Passos Coelho; b. July 24,1964; in office: June 21, 2011. **Local divisions:** 18 districts, 2 autonomous regions. **Defense budget:** $2.77 bil. **Active troops:** 42,600.
Economy: Industries: textiles, clothing, footwear, wood and cork, paper, chemicals, auto-parts mfg., base metals, dairy prods., wine and other foods, porcelain and ceramics, glassware, tech., telecom. **Chief crops:** grain, potatoes, tomatoes, olives, grapes. **Natural resources:** fish, forests (cork), iron ore, copper, zinc, tin, tungsten, silver, gold, uranium, marble, clay, gypsum, salt, hydropower. **Arable land:** 11.9%. **Livestock:** cattle: 1.5 mil; chickens: 43 mil; goats: 398,000; pigs: 2 mil; sheep: 2.1 mil. **Electricity prod.** (2012): 44.3 bil kWh. **Labor force:** agric. 11.7%, industry 28.5%, services 59.8%. **Unemployment:** 15.6%.

Finance: Monetary unit: Euro (EUR) (Sept. 2014: 0.76 = $1 U.S.). **GDP:** $243.3 bil; **per capita GDP:** $22,900; **GDP growth:** -1.8%. **Imports:** $59 bil; Spain 32%, Germany 11.5%, France 6.7%, Italy 5.3%, Netherlands 4.9%. **Exports:** $61 bil; Spain 22.7%, Germany 12.4%, France 11.9%, Angola 6.5%, UK 5.3%, Netherlands 4.2%. **Tourism:** $12.3 bil. **Budget:** $106.8 bil. **Total reserves less gold:** $2.8 bil. **Gold:** 12.3 mil oz t. **Inflation:** 0.3%.
Transport: Railways: 2,062 mi. **Motor vehicles:** 532.7 per 1,000 pop. **Civil aviation:** 17.2 bil pass.-mi; 43 airports. **Chief ports:** Leixoes, Lisbon, Setubal, Sines.
Communications: TV sets: 425 per 1,000 pop. **Radios:** 299 per 1,000 pop. **Telephone lines:** 42.7 per 100 pop. **Mobile:** 113 per 100 pop. **Internet:** 62.1%.
Health: Life expect.: 75.8 male; 82.5 female. **Births:** 9.4 per 1,000 pop. **Deaths:** 11.0 per 1,000 pop. **Natural incr.:** -0.16%. **Infant mortality:** 4.5 per 1,000 live births. **HIV:** NA.
Education: Compulsory: ages 6-14. **Literacy:** 95.7%.
Embassy: 2012 Massachusetts Ave. NW 20036; 350-5400.
Website: www.portugal.gov.pt

Portugal, an independent state since the 12th cent., was a kingdom until a 1910 revolution drove out King Manoel II and a republic was proclaimed. Beginning in 1932, Prime Min. Antonio de Oliveira Salazar headed a repressive government. Illness forced his retirement in Sept. 1968.

On Apr. 25, 1974, a military junta led by Gen. Antonio de Spinola seized the government; Spinola became president. The new government granted independence to Guinea-Bissau, Mozambique, Cabo Verde, Angola, and São Tomé and Príncipe. Portugal returned Macao to China on Dec. 20, 1999.

With the economy lagging, Socialists led by Jóse Sócrates, gained a parliamentary majority in 2005 and held onto a plurality in 2009. The conservative Aníbal Cavaco Silva, a former prime min. (1985-95), won the Jan. 2006 presidential election and was reelected 5 years later. After Portugal was given a 78-bil-euro bailout package from international lenders to avert default, the center-right Social Democratic Party, headed by Pedro Passos Coelho, won parliamentary elections June 2011. Austerity cuts caused widespread protests in Nov. 2012; the Constitutional Court ruled Apr. 5, 2013 that many of the cuts were illegal. Portugal completed loan repayments and exited the bailout program in May 2014.

Azores Isls., in the Atlantic, 740 mi W of Portugal, have an area of 868 sq mi and a pop. (2011 est.) of 246,102. A 1951 agreement gave the U.S. rights to use defense facilities in the Azores. The **Madeira Isls.**, 350 mi off the NW coast of Africa, have an area of 306 sq mi and a pop. (2011 est.) of 267,785. Both groups were offered partial autonomy in 1976.

Qatar
State of Qatar

People: Population: 2,123,160. **Age distrib.:** <15: 12.5%; 65+: 0.9%. **Pop. density:** 474.6 per sq mi, 183.2 per sq km. **Urban:** 99.2%. **Ethnic groups:** Arab 40%, Indian 18%, Pakistani 18%, Iranian 10%. **Languages:** Arabic (official), English (commonly used as second lang.). **Religions:** Muslim 78%, Christian 9%.
Geography: Total area: 4,473 sq mi, 11,586 sq km; **Land area:** 4,473 sq mi, 11,586 sq km. **Location:** Middle East, occupying peninsula on W coast of Persian Gulf. **Neighbors:** Saudi Arabia on S. **Topography:** Mostly flat desert with some limestone ridges; vegetation of any kind is scarce. **Capital:** Ad-Dawhah (Doha), 698,535.
Government: Type: Emirate. **Head of state:** Emir Sheikh Tamim bin Hamad al-Thani; b. July 3, 1980; in office: June 25, 2013. **Head of gov.:** Prime Min. Sheikh Abdullah bin Nasser bin Khalifa al-Thani; in office: June 26, 2013. **Local divisions:** 7 municipalities. **Defense budget** (2013): $3.48 bil. **Active troops:** 11,800.
Economy: Industries: liquefied nat. gas, crude oil prod. and refining, ammonia, fertilizers, petrochemicals, steel reinforcing bars, cement, commercial ship repair. **Chief crops:** fruits, vegetables. **Natural resources:** petroleum, nat. gas, fish. **Crude oil reserves:** 25.2 bil bbls. **Arable land:** 1.1%. **Livestock:** cattle: 11,000; chickens: 8.6 mil; goats: 219,500; sheep: 312,000. **Electricity prod.:** 28.9 bil kWh. **Labor force:** NA. **Unemployment:** 0.6%.
Finance: Monetary unit: Riyal (QAR) (Sept. 2014: 3.64 = $1 U.S.). **GDP:** $198.7 bil; **per capita GDP:** $102,100; **GDP growth:** 5.5%. **Imports:** $39.6 bil; U.S. 14.2%, UAE 11.1%, Saudi Arabia 8.6%, UK 6.4%, Japan 6%, China 4.8%, Germany 4.7%, Italy 4.4%, France 4.4%. **Exports:** $12.7 bil; Japan 26.7%, South Korea 19%, India 12.1%, Singapore 5.7%, China 5.4%. **Tourism:** $3.5 bil. **Budget:** $57.3 bil. **Total reserves less gold:** $41.6 bil. **Gold:** 399,100 oz t. **Inflation:** 3.1%.
Transport: Motor vehicles: 166.5 per 1,000 pop. **Civil aviation:** 38.3 bil pass.-mi; 4 airports. **Chief ports:** Doha, Mesaieed, Ra's Laffan.
Communications: TV sets: 405 per 1,000 pop. **Radios:** 468 per 1,000 pop. **Telephone lines:** 19 per 100 pop. **Mobile:** 152.6 per 100 pop. **Internet:** 85.3%.
Health: Life expect.: 76.4 male; 80.4 female. **Births:** 10.0 per 1,000 pop. **Deaths:** 1.5 per 1,000 pop. **Natural incr.:** 0.84%. **Infant mortality:** 6.4 per 1,000 live births. **HIV:** NA.
Education: Compulsory: ages 6-17. **Literacy:** 97.3%.
Embassy: 2555 M St. NW 20037; 274-1600.
Website: portal.www.gov.qa

Qatar was under Bahrain's control until the Ottoman Turks took power, 1872 to 1915. In a treaty signed 1916, Qatar gave Great Britain responsibility for its defense and foreign relations. Qatar declared itself independent, Sept. 1, 1971. Crown Prince Hamad bin Khalifa al-Thani ousted his father, Emir Khalifa bin Hamad al-Thani, June 27, 1995. In municipal elections held Mar. 8, 1999, women participated for the first time as candidates and voters. Sheikh Hamad bin Khalifa al-Thani abdicated in favor of his son, Sheik Tamim bin Hamad al-Thani, June 25, 2013.

Qatar, a major oil producer and one of the world's leading exporters of liquefied natural gas, has experienced rapid economic growth in recent years. Regular flights in and out of Doha's new Hamad Intl. Airport began in May 2014. Military ties with the U.S. have been expanding. Camp As-Sayliyah, a base near Doha, served as a command center for the U.S.-led invasion of Iraq, Mar. 2003. A 10-yr. defense cooperation agreement was signed, Dec. 10, 2013, during a visit to Qatar by U.S. Defense Sec. Chuck Hagel. Qatar provided support for U.S.-led air strikes, beginning Sept. 2014, against Sunni extremists in Syria.

Romania

People: Population: 21,729,871. **Age distrib.:** <15: 14.6%; 65+: 15.4%. **Pop. density:** 244.8 per sq mi, 94.5 per sq km. **Urban:** 54.4%. **Ethnic groups:** Romanian 83%, Hungarian 6%, Roma 3%. **Languages:** Romanian (official), Hungarian, Romany. **Religions:** Eastern Orthodox 82%, Protestant 6%, Roman Catholic 4%.

Geography: Total area: 92,043 sq mi, 238,391 sq km; **Land area:** 88,761 sq mi, 229,891 sq km. **Location:** SE Europe, on the Black Sea. **Neighbors:** Moldova on E, Ukraine on N, Hungary and Serbia on W, Bulgaria on S. **Topography:** The Carpathian Mts. encase the N central Transylvanian plateau. There are wide plains S and E of the mountains, through which flow the lower reaches of the rivers of Danube system. **Capital:** Bucharest, 1,871,520.

Government: Type: Republic. **Head of state:** Pres. Traian Basescu; b. Nov. 4, 1951; in office: Dec. 20, 2004. **Head of gov.:** Prime Min. Victor-Viorel Ponta; b. Sept. 20, 1972; in office: May 7, 2012. **Local divisions:** 41 counties, 1 municipality. **Defense budget:** $2.48 bil. **Active troops:** 71,400.

Economy: Industries: elec. machinery and equip., textiles and footwear, light machinery, auto assembly, mining, timber, constr. materials. **Chief crops:** wheat, corn, barley, sugar beets, sunflower seeds, potatoes, grapes. **Natural resources:** petroleum (reserves declining), timber, nat. gas, coal, iron ore, salt, hydropower. **Crude oil reserves:** 600 mil bbls. **Arable land:** 38.2%. **Livestock:** cattle: 2 mil; chickens: 80.1 mil; goats: 1.3 mil; pigs: 5.2 mil; sheep: 8.8 mil. **Electricity prod.:** 58.8 bil kWh. **Labor force:** agric. 29%, industry 28.6%, services 42.4%. **Unemployment:** 7%.

Finance: Monetary unit: New Leu (RON) (Sept. 2014: 3.35 = $1 U.S.). **GDP:** $288.5 bil; **per capita GDP:** $14,400; **GDP growth:** 3.5%. **Imports:** $73.4 bil; Germany 17.5%, Italy 11%, Hungary 9.1%, France 5.7%, Russia 4.4%, Poland 4.3%, Austria 4.2%, Kazakhstan 4.1%. **Exports:** $65.8 bil; Germany 18.9%, Italy 12.3%, France 7.1%, Turkey 5.5%, Hungary 5.5%. **Tourism:** $1.4 bil. **Budget:** $64.9 bil. **Total reserves less gold:** $44.8 bil. **Gold:** 3.3 mil oz t. **Inflation:** 4.0%.

Transport: Railways: 6,701 mi. **Motor vehicles:** 252.4 per 1,000 pop. **Civil aviation:** 2.8 bil pass.-mi; 26 airports. **Chief ports:** Braila, Constanta, Galati, Mancanului, Midia, Tulcea.

Communications: TV sets: 885 per 1,000 pop. **Radios:** 143 per 1,000 pop. **Telephone lines:** 21.8 per 100 pop. **Mobile:** 105.6 per 100 pop. **Internet:** 49.8%.

Health: Life expect.: 71.2 male; 78.4 female. **Births:** 9.3 per 1,000 pop. **Deaths:** 11.9 per 1,000 pop. **Natural inc.:** −0.26%. **Infant mortality:** 10.2 per 1,000 live births. **HIV:** 0.1%.

Education: Compulsory: ages 7-16. **Literacy:** 98.8%.

Embassy: 1607 23rd St. NW 20008; 332-4846.

Website: www.gov.ro

Romania's earliest known people merged with invading Proto-Thracians, preceding by centuries the Dacians. Rome occupied the Dacian kingdom, 106-271 CE; people and language were Romanized. The Turkey-dominated principalities of Wallachia and Moldavia were united in 1859, became Romania in 1861, and gained recognition as an independent kingdom, 1881.

After WWI, Romania acquired Bessarabia, Bukovina, Transylvania, and Banat. In 1940 it ceded Bessarabia and Northern Bukovina to the USSR, part of southern Dobrudja to Bulgaria, and northern Transylvania to Hungary. In 1941, Prem. Marshal Ion Antonescu led Romania in support of Germany against the USSR. He was overthrown in 1944, and Romania joined the Allies. After occupation by Soviet troops, a People's Republic was proclaimed, Dec. 30, 1947.

On Aug. 22, 1965, a new constitution proclaimed Romania a socialist republic. The domestic policies of Pres. Nicolae Ceausescu were repressive. All industry was state-owned, and state farms and cooperatives owned almost all arable land. Ceausescu's security forces fired on antigovernment demonstrators, Dec. 1989, killing hundreds, but when the army sided with the protesters, his regime fell. Charged with genocide and abuse of power, Ceausescu and his wife were executed Dec. 25, 1989.

A new constitution providing for a multiparty system took effect Dec. 8, 1991. Many of Romania's state-owned companies were privatized in 1996. Romania became a full NATO member in 2004. It entered the European Union Jan. 1, 2007; restrictions on Romanians'

right to work in 9 other EU countries ended Jan. 1, 2014. The IMF and other donors agreed to provide a $27 bil loan Mar. 25, 2009, to rescue the country from the global recession. Romania, a firm U.S. ally, pulled its remaining troops out of Iraq July 2009. Romanian soldiers served with NATO-led forces in Afghanistan; more than 300 remained as of early Sept. 2014. After Victor-Viorel Ponta became prime min. May 7, 2012, he accused Pres. Traian Basescu of abusing his authority, and parliament voted to impeach Basescu July 6. More than 87% of voters called for impeachment in a referendum July 29, 2012. However, the country's Supreme Court overturned the result in Aug., because less than 50% of eligible voters had participated.

Russia
Russian Federation

People: Population: 142,470,272. **Age distrib.:** <15: 16.4%; 65+: 13.3%. **Pop. density:** 22.5 per sq mi, 8.7 per sq km. **Urban:** 73.9%. **Ethnic groups:** Russian 78%, Tatar 4%, Ukrainian 1%, Bashkir 1%, Chuvash 1%, Chechen 1%. **Languages:** Russian (official), Dolgang. **Religions:** Russian Orthodox 15%-20%, Muslim 10%-15%, other Christian 2%.

Geography: Total area: 6,601,668 sq mi, 17,098,242 sq km; **Land area:** 6,323,482 sq mi, 16,377,742 sq km, more than 76% of total area of the former USSR and the largest country in the world. **Location:** Stretches from E Europe across N Asia to the Pacific O. **Neighbors:** Finland, Norway, Estonia, Latvia, Belarus, Ukraine on W; Georgia, Azerbaijan, Kazakhstan, China, Mongolia, N. Korea on S; Kaliningrad exclave bordered by Poland on the S, Lithuania on the N and E. **Topography:** Every type of climate except distinctly tropical. The European portion is a low plain, grassy in S, wooded in N, with Ural Mts. on E, and Caucasus Mts. on S. Urals stretch N-S for 2,500 mi. The Asiatic portion is a vast plain, with mountains on S and in E; tundra covers extreme N with forest belt below; plains, marshes are in W, desert in SW. **Capital:** Moscow, 12,062,700. **Cities (urban aggl.):** Saint Petersburg, 4,984,118; Novosibirsk, 1,496,607; Yekaterinburg, 1,376,907; Nizhniy Novgorod, 1,223,511; Samara, 1,167,748; Omsk, 1,163,602; Kazan, 1,161,692; Chelyabinsk, 1,154,980.

Government: Type: Federation. **Head of state:** Pres. Vladimir Putin; b. Oct. 7, 1952; in office: May 7, 2012. **Head of gov.:** Prime Min. Dmitri Medvedev; b. Sept. 14, 1965; in office: May 8, 2012. **Local divisions:** 46 provinces, 21 republics, 4 autonomous okrugs, 9 krays, 2 federal cities, 1 autonomous oblast. **Defense budget:** $68.16 bil. **Active troops:** 845,000.

Economy: Industries: mining and extractive industries producing coal, oil, gas, chemicals, metals; machine building; defense (incl. radar, missile prod.); transp. equip.; communications equip.; agric. machinery, constr. equip.; elec. power generating and transmitting equip.; medical and scientific instruments; consumer durables, textiles. **Chief crops:** grain, sugar beets, sunflower seeds, vegetables, fruits. **Natural resources:** oil, nat. gas, coal, minerals, rare earth elements, timber (climate, terrain, and distance are obstacles to exploitation of resources). **Crude oil reserves:** 80 bil bbls. **Arable land:** 7.3%. **Livestock:** cattle: 19.9 mil; chickens: 447.6 mil; goats: 2.1 mil; pigs: 18.8 mil; sheep: 22.1 mil. **Electricity prod.:** 996.8 bil kWh. **Labor force:** agric. 9.7%, industry 27.8%, services 62.5%. **Unemployment:** 5.5%.

Finance: Monetary unit: Ruble (RUB) (Sept. 2014: 36.87 = $1 U.S.). **GDP:** $2.6 tril; **per capita GDP:** $18,100; **GDP growth:** 1.3%. **Imports:** $341 bil; China 16.6%, Germany 12.2%, Ukraine 5.7%, Japan 5%, U.S. 4.9%, France 4.4%, Italy 4.3%. **Exports:** $515 bil; Netherlands 14.6%, China 6.8%, Germany 6.8%, Italy 6.2%, Turkey 5.2%, Ukraine 5.2%, Belarus 4.7%. **Tourism:** $12 bil. **Budget:** $450.3 bil. **Total reserves less gold:** $469.6 bil. **Gold:** 33.3 mil oz t. **Inflation:** 6.8%.

Transport: Railways: 54,157 mi. **Motor vehicles:** 331.4 per 1,000 pop. **Civil aviation:** 78.8 bil pass.-mi; 594 airports. **Chief ports:** Kaliningrad, Kavkaz, Nakhodka, Novorossiysk, Primorsk, Saint Petersburg, Vostochny.

Communications: TV sets: 546 per 1,000 pop. **Radios:** 416 per 1,000 pop. **Telephone lines:** 28.5 per 100 pop. **Mobile:** 152.8 per 100 pop. **Internet:** 61.4%.

Health: Life expect.: 64.4 male; 76.3 female. **Births:** 11.9 per 1,000 pop. **Deaths:** 13.8 per 1,000 pop. **Natural inc.:** −0.20%. **Infant mortality:** 7.1 per 1,000 live births. **HIV:** NA.

Education: Compulsory: ages 6-15. **Literacy:** 99.7%.

Embassy: 2650 Wisconsin Ave. NW 20007; 298-5700.

Website: www.government.ru or kremlin.ru

Slavic tribes began migrating into Russia from the W in the 5th cent. The first Russian state, centered in Novgorod and Kiev, was founded by Scandinavian chieftains in the 9th cent. In the 13th cent., Mongols overran the country. It recovered under the grand dukes and princes of Muscovy, or Moscow, and by 1480 freed itself from the Mongols. Ivan the Terrible was proclaimed Tsar, 1547. Peter the Great (1682-1725) extended the domain and, in 1721, founded the Russian empire. Western ideas and the beginnings of modernization spread through the empire in the 19th and early 20th cent.

Military reverses in the 1905 war with Japan and in WWI led to the breakdown of the Tsarist regime. The 1917 Revolution began in Mar. with a series of sporadic strikes for higher wages by factory workers. A provisional democratic government under Prince Georgi Lvov was established but a second provisional government, under

Alexander Kerensky, followed in May. Vladimir Ilyich Lenin, Nov. 7, overthrew the Kerensky government and the freely elected Constituent Assembly in a Communist coup.

Soviet Union. Lenin's death Jan. 21, 1924, led to an internal power struggle won by Joseph Stalin. His brutal tactics, including purge trials, mass executions, and exile of many to work camps, resulted in millions of deaths.

Despite a Germany-USSR non-aggression pact signed in Aug. 1939, Germany invaded the Soviet Union, June 1941. Russian winter counterthrusts, 1941-42 and 1942-43, and resistance to the siege of Leningrad (now St. Petersburg) stopped the German advance. Russians drove the Germans from Eastern Europe and the Balkans in the next two years.

After WWII, Communists took over in countries throughout the region, extending the Soviet sphere of influence. The USSR and the U.S., the world's leading nuclear superpowers, became Cold War rivals. After Stalin died, Mar. 5, 1953, Nikita Khrushchev gained power and denounced Stalin, 1956, beginning "de-Stalinization."

Under Khrushchev the open antagonism of Poles and Hungarians toward Moscow's domination was suppressed in 1956. He aided the Cuban revolution under Fidel Castro but withdrew Soviet missiles from Cuba during a confrontation with U.S. Pres. Kennedy, Sept.-Oct. 1962. Khrushchev was deposed, Oct. 1964, and replaced by Leonid I. Brezhnev. In Aug. 1968, Soviet forces invaded Czechoslovakia, crushing liberalization there.

Massive Soviet military aid to North Vietnam in the late 1960s and early 1970s helped assure Communist victories throughout Indochina. In Dec. 1979, Soviet forces entered Afghanistan to support a pro-Soviet regime against U.S.-supported Muslim resistance fighters. In Apr. 1988, the Soviets agreed to withdraw their troops, ending a futile 8-year war.

Mikhail Gorbachev was chosen Communist Party gen. sec., Mar. 1985. In 1987 he initiated a program of political and economic reforms through openness (*glasnost*) and restructuring (*perestroika*). Gorbachev faced economic problems as well as ethnic and nationalist unrest in the republics. A coup by Communist hardliners Aug. 1991 was foiled with help from Russian Republic Pres. Boris Yeltsin. On Aug. 24, Gorbachev resigned as leader of the Communist Party. Several republics declared their independence, including Russia, Ukraine, and Kazakhstan. On Aug. 29, the Soviet Parliament voted to suspend all activities of the Communist Party. The Soviet Union officially broke up Dec. 26, 1991, ending the 74-year domination of the Communist Party.

Russian Federation. Under Pres. Yeltsin, Russia took steps toward privatization, which caused inflation and a severe economic downturn. In June 1992, Yeltsin and U.S. Pres. George H. W. Bush agreed to massive arms reductions. Yeltsin prevailed in a power struggle with the Congress of People's Deputies, which was dominated by former Communists, and in a referendum Dec. 12, 1993, a new constitution was approved. Russian troops fought rebels in the breakaway republic of Chechnya Dec. 1994-Aug. 1996, when a peace accord temporarily ended the conflict. On May 27, 1997, Yeltsin signed a founding act, increasing cooperation with NATO and paving the way for NATO to admit Eastern European nations.

Russia's economic crisis deepened in the late 1990s, heightening tensions between parliament and Pres. Yeltsin, who had been reelected in 1996. An Aug. 1999 operation to suppress Islamic rebels in Dagestan reignited the war in neighboring Chechnya, where Russia launched a full-scale assault. Yeltsin unexpectedly resigned Dec. 31, 1999, naming Prime Min. Vladimir Putin as his interim successor. Putin won presidential elections Mar. 2000. Putin's allies won legislative elections, Dec. 2003, and the president was reelected Mar. 2004; international election monitors cited flaws on both occasions.

A bomb in Grozny, May 9, 2004, killed Chechnya's pro-Moscow president, Akhmad Kadyrov. In another terrorist act linked to the Chechnya conflict, two passenger planes exploded in midair after taking off from Moscow Aug. 24, killing 90 people. Chechen rebels, Sept. 1, 2004, seized control of a school in Beslan, North Ossetia, taking more than 1,100 hostages. Russian troops stormed the school Sept. 3; more than 330 people died, including 186 children. Putin cited the terrorist threat Sept. 13 in proposing a government overhaul that tightened his control over parliament and regional officeholders. Russian forces killed Chechen rebel leader Aslan Maskhadov, Mar. 8, 2005, and Chechen guerrilla leader Shamil Basayev, organizer of the terrorist attack at Beslan, July 10, 2006.

Constitutionally barred from seeking another term, Pres. Putin backed his protégé Dmitri Medvedev, who won the presidential election Mar. 2, 2008. After taking office May 7 Medvedev named Putin as prime min. A long-simmering conflict with Georgia erupted into open warfare Aug. 7-16. Russia dispatched troops to support secessionists in the enclaves of South Ossetia and Abkhazia and launched assaults on strategic Georgian cities; a cease-fire left thousands of Russian troops in the breakaway regions, which Pres. Medvedev recognized as independent, Aug. 26, 2008.

An economic boom fueled by oil and gas sales stalled in late 2008. The global financial crisis and a drop in oil prices led to turmoil in Russian financial markets, for which the government put together a $130-bil emergency rescue plan. As the crisis deepened, the government loaned banks $37 bil Oct. 7 and began buying shares to prop up the Russian stock exchange.

Russia declared, Apr. 16, 2009, that it had ended counterterrorism operations in Chechnya; from June through Aug., there was an upsurge of insurgent violence in Chechnya and neighboring Dagestan and Ingushetia. Female suicide bombers from Dagestan struck two Moscow subway stations Mar. 29, 2010, killing 40 people. A bombing at a Moscow airport Jan. 24, 2011, killed 37.

With U.S.-Russia relations strained since the 2008 Georgia war, Medvedev and Pres. Barack Obama Apr. 8, 2010, signed a nuclear arms reduction treaty known as New START, which was ratified by the U.S. Senate Dec. 22. Medvedev announced Sept. 24, 2011, that Putin would run for president in elections Mar. 2012, with Medvedev then serving as his prime min. In Dec. 2011 parliamentary elections, Putin's party, United Russia, failed to garner 50% of the vote. In subsequent protests, tens of thousands called for Putin's resignation. Putin nonetheless won 64% of the vote in the Mar. 4, 2012, election, though there were again claims of fraud. Three members of the anti-Putin punk-protest band Pussy Riot were convicted of hooliganism and sentenced to two years in jail Aug. 17, 2012, despite international criticism; the last two women were released in Dec. 2013.

Putin signed a law banning "homosexual propaganda" June 30, 2013, making it illegal to advocate publicly for gay rights. The Putin administration, disregarding U.S. wishes, granted one-year asylum to National Security Agency whistleblower Edward Snowden Aug. 1, 2013—extended for 3 years Aug. 1, 2014.

Sochi, Russia, hosted the 2014 Winter Olympics Feb. 7-23, 2014. Although suicide bombings in Volgograd, for which Dagestan separatists claimed responsibility, killed 34, Dec. 29-30, 2013, there were no major security incidents at the Games.

After Ukraine's pro-Russian president was removed from office Feb. 22, 2014, Russia supported pro-Russian separatists in Ukraine's Crimean Peninsula and sent Russian troops into the region in Mar. Russia annexed Crimea Mar. 18. Russia also apparently provided military equipment and troops to pro-Russian separatists in eastern Ukraine fighting Ukrainian forces beginning in Apr. 2014. The U.S. and EU imposed several rounds of economic sanctions to protest Russia's Ukraine policies; Russia, Aug. 7, banned most food imports from the U.S. and EU.

Rwanda
Republic of Rwanda

People: Population: 12,337,138. **Age distrib.:** <15: 42.1%; 65+: 2.5%. **Pop. density:** 1,295.3 per sq mi, 500.1 per sq km. **Urban:** 27.8%. **Ethnic groups:** Hutu (Bantu) 84%, Tutsi (Hamitic) 15%, Twa (Pygmy) 1%. **Languages:** Kinyarwanda (universal Bantu vernacular), French, English (all official); Swahili (used in commercial centers). **Religions:** Roman Catholic 50%, Protestant 39% (incl. Adventist 12%), Muslim 2%, none 4%.

Geography: Total area: 10,169 sq mi, 26,338 sq km; **Land area:** 9,524 sq mi, 24,668 sq km. **Location:** In E central Africa. **Neighbors:** Uganda on N, Dem. Rep. of the Congo on W, Burundi on S, Tanzania on E. **Topography:** Grassy uplands and hills cover most of country, with chain of volcanoes in the NW. The source of the Nile R. is in headwaters of the Kagera (Akagera) R., SW of Kigali. **Capital:** Kigali, 1,222,570.

Government: Type: Republic. **Head of state:** Pres. Paul Kagame; b. Oct. 23, 1957; in office: Apr. 22, 2000 (de facto from Mar. 24). **Head of gov.:** Prime Min. Pierre Damien Habumuremyi; b. Feb. 21, 1961; in office: Oct. 7, 2011. **Local divisions:** 4 provinces, 1 city. **Defense budget:** $82 mil. **Active troops:** 33,000.

Economy: Industries: cement, agric. prods., small-scale beverages, soap, furniture, shoes, plastic goods, textiles, cigarettes. **Chief crops:** coffee, tea, pyrethrum (insecticide made from chrysanthemums), bananas, beans, sorghum, potatoes. **Natural resources:** gold, tin ore, tungsten ore, methane, hydropower. **Arable land:** 47.9%. **Livestock:** cattle: 1.1 mil; chickens: 4.7 mil; goats: 2.7 mil; pigs: 990,000; sheep: 810,000. **Electricity prod.:** 300.2 mil kWh. **Labor force:** agric. 90%, industry and services 10%. **Unemployment:** 0.6%.

Finance: Monetary unit: Franc (RWF) (Sept. 2014: 685.00 = $1 U.S.). **GDP:** $16.4 bil; **per capita GDP:** $1,500; **GDP growth:** 7.5%. **Imports:** $1.9 bil; Kenya 17.3%, Uganda 15.6%, UAE 8.9%, China 7.2%, India 5.6%, Tanzania 5%, Belgium 4.5%, Canada 4.1%. **Exports:** $538.3 mil; Kenya 30.5%, Dem. Rep. of the Congo 12.2%, China 12.1%, Malaysia 10.7%, U.S. 5.8%, Swaziland 4.9%. **Tourism:** $282 mil. **Budget:** $2.1 bil. **Total reserves less gold:** $1.1 bil. **Inflation:** 4.2%.

Transport: Civil aviation: 4 airports. **Chief ports:** Cyangugu, Gisenyi, Kibuye.

Communications: TV sets: 8 per 1,000 pop. **Radios:** 854 per 1,000 pop. **Telephone lines:** 0.4 per 100 pop. **Mobile:** 56.8 per 100 pop. **Internet:** 8.7%.

Health: Life expect.: 57.7 male; 60.8 female. **Births:** 34.6 per 1,000 pop. **Deaths:** 9.2 per 1,000 pop. **Natural inc.:** 2.54%. **Infant mortality:** 59.6 per 1,000 live births. **HIV:** 2.9%.

Education: Compulsory: ages 7-15. **Literacy:** 70.5%.

Embassy: 1714 New Hampshire Ave. NW 20009; 232-2882.

Website: www.gov.rw

For centuries, the Tutsi dominated the Hutu majority. A civil war broke out in 1959 and Tutsi power was ended. Many Tutsi went into exile. Rwanda, which had been part of the Belgian UN trusteeship of Rwanda-Urundi, became independent July 1, 1962.

A large-scale massacre of Tutsi occurred in 1963. Hutu rivalries led to a bloodless coup July 1973 in which Hutu army officer Juvénal Habyarimana took power. After an invasion and coup attempt by Tutsi exiles in 1990, a multiparty democracy was established.

Renewed ethnic strife led to an Aug. 1993 peace accord between the government and rebels of the Tutsi-led Rwandan Patriotic Front (RPF). But after Habyarimana and Burundi Pres. Cyprien Ntaryamira were killed Apr. 6, 1994, in a suspicious plane crash, violence broke out. More than 1 mil may have died in massacres, mostly of Tutsi by Hutu militias, and in civil warfare as the RPF sought power. About 2 mil Tutsi and Hutu fled to camps in Zaire (now Dem. Rep. of the Congo) and other countries; many died of disease. French troops under a UN mandate moved into SW Rwanda June 23 to establish a safe zone. The RPF claimed victory, installing a government led by a moderate Hutu president in July. French troops pulled out Aug. 22. A UN peacekeeping mission ended Mar. 8, 1996. More than 1 mil refugees, mostly Hutu, returned to Rwanda in Nov.-Dec. 1996.

Firing squads Apr. 24, 1998, executed 22 people convicted of genocide. Former Prime Min. Jean Kambanda pleaded guilty May 1 before the UN-backed Intl. Criminal Tribunal for Rwanda (ICTR) and received a life sentence Sept. 4, 1998. RPF leader Maj. Gen. Paul Kagame became Rwanda's first Tutsi president Apr. 22, 2000.

Rwandans approved a new constitution, May 26, 2003; reelected Pres. Kagame, Aug. 25; and chose a new parliament, Sept. 29-30. Rwanda cut diplomatic ties with France Nov. 24, 2006, after a French judge linked Kagame and his close aides to the 1994 deaths of Habyarimana and Ntaryamira. The country restored relations with France, Nov. 2009, when Rwanda joined the Commonwealth.

Accused of being one of the architects of the 1994 genocide, Col. Theoneste Bagosora was convicted and sentenced by the ICTR, Dec. 18, 2008, to life in prison (later reduced to 35 years). A Rwandan court handed out a life sentence, Jan. 20, 2009, to former Justice Min. Agnes Ntamabyariro for her role in inciting the massacres. Up to 4,000 Rwandan troops fought that month alongside Congolese forces against Hutu militias in E Dem. Rep. of the Congo. After a campaign criticized as repressive by human rights groups, Pres. Kagame won reelection Aug. 9, 2010.

Rwanda's steady economic growth since 2003 has been accompanied by U.S. funding for military training and the control of HIV/AIDS and malaria. An Oct. 17, 2012, UN report found that the Rwanda military was backing M23 rebel troops in the Dem. Rep of the Congo. The U.S. announced in Oct. 2013 that it was sanctioning Rwanda for its continued support of M23 by withholding military funding. After successful offensives by UN troops in the Dem. Rep of the Congo against M23 and the Hutu militia the Democratic Forces for the Liberation of Rwanda (FDLR), some 200 FDLR members laid down their arms in June 2014.

Saint Kitts and Nevis
Federation of Saint Kitts and Nevis

People: Population: 51,538. **Age distrib.:** <15: 21.4%; 65+: 7.9%. **Pop. density:** 511.4 per sq mi, 197.5 per sq km. **Urban:** 32%. **Ethnic group:** predominantly black; some British, Portuguese, Lebanese. **Language:** English (official). **Religions:** Anglican, other Protestant, Roman Catholic.

Geography: Total area: 101 sq mi, 261 sq km; **Land area:** 101 sq mi, 261 sq km. **Location:** In N part of the Leeward group of Lesser Antilles in E Caribbean Sea. **Neighbors:** Antigua and Barbuda to E. **Topography:** St. Kitts has forested volcanic slopes; Nevis rises from beaches to central peak. Climate is tropical moderated by sea breezes. **Capital:** Basseterre, 14,149.

Government: Type: Parliamentary democracy. **Head of state:** Queen Elizabeth II, rep. by Gov.-Gen. Sir Edmund Lawrence; in office: Jan. 2, 2013. **Head of gov.:** Prime Min. Denzil Douglas; b. Jan. 14, 1953; in office: July 6, 1995. **Local divisions:** 14 parishes. **Defense budget/active troops:** NA.

Economy: Industries: tourism, cotton, salt, copra, clothing, footwear, beverages. **Chief crops:** sugarcane, rice, yams, vegetables, bananas. **Arable land:** 19.2%. **Livestock:** cattle: 6,500; chickens: 80,000; goats: 9,100; pigs: 7,000; sheep: 7,100. **Electricity prod.:** 138 mil kWh. **Labor force:** NA. **Unemployment:** NA.

Finance: Monetary unit: East Caribbean Dollar (XCD) (Sept. 2014: 2.70 = $1 U.S.). **GDP:** $952 mil; **per capita GDP:** $16,300; **GDP growth:** 1.9%. **Imports:** $355.4 mil; U.S. 31.7%, Trinidad and Tobago 19.9%, Italy 7%, Germany 6%, Barbados 4.7%. **Exports:** $57.3 mil; U.S. 56%, Canada 9.8%, Bangladesh 6.2%. **Tourism:** $101 mil. **Budget:** $185.2 mil. **Total reserves less gold:** $302 mil. **Inflation:** 0.7%.

Transport: Railways: 31 mi. **Civil aviation:** 2 airports. **Chief ports:** Basseterre, Charlestown.

Communications: TV sets: 312 per 1,000 pop. **Radios:** 697 per 1,000 pop. **Telephone lines:** 35.4 per 100 pop. **Mobile:** 142.1 per 100 pop. **Internet:** 80%.

Health: Life expect.: 72.9 male; 77.8 female. **Births:** 13.6 per 1,000 pop. **Deaths:** 7.1 per 1,000 pop. **Natural inc.:** 0.66%. **Infant mortality:** 9.0 per 1,000 live births. **HIV:** NA.

Education: Compulsory: ages 5-16. **Literacy:** NA.

Embassy: 3216 New Mexico Ave. NW 20016; 686-2636.

Website: www.gov.kn

St. Kitts (formerly St. Christopher; known by indigenous peoples as Liamuiga) and Nevis were reached and named by Columbus in 1493. They were settled by Britain in 1623, but ownership was disputed with France until 1713. They were part of the Leeward Islands Federation, 1871-1956, and the Federation of the West Indies, 1958-62. The colony achieved self-government as an Associated State of the UK in 1967, becoming independent, Sept. 19, 1983. A secession referendum on Nevis, Aug. 10, 1998, fell short of the two-thirds majority required.

Saint Lucia

People: Population: 163,362. **Age distrib.:** <15: 21.2%; 65+: 10.5%. **Pop. density:** 698.2 per sq mi, 269.6 per sq km. **Urban:** 18.5%. **Ethnic groups:** black/African descent 85%, mixed 11%, East Indian 2%. **Languages:** English (official), French patois. **Religions:** Roman Catholic 62%, Protestant 26% (incl. Seventh-day Adventist 10%, Pentecostal 9%, Baptist 2%, Anglican 2%), other Christian 3%, Rastafarian 2%, none 6%.

Geography: Total area: 238 sq mi, 616 sq km; **Land area:** 234 sq mi, 606 sq km. **Location:** In E Caribbean, 2nd largest of Windward Isls. **Neighbors:** Martinique to N, St. Vincent to S. **Topography:** Mountainous, volcanic in origin; Soufrière Volcanic Centre in S. Wooded mountains run N-S to Mt. Gimie (3,145 ft) with streams through fertile valleys. **Capital:** Castries, 22,186.

Government: Type: Parliamentary democracy. **Head of state:** Queen Elizabeth II, rep. by Gov.-Gen. Dame Calliopa Pearlette Louisy; b. June 8, 1946; in office: Sept. 17, 1997. **Head of gov.:** Prime Min. Kenny Davis Anthony; b. Jan. 8, 1951; in office: Nov. 30, 2011. **Local divisions:** 10 districts. **Defense budget/active troops:** NA.

Economy: Industries: tourism, clothing, electronic components assembly, beverages, corrugated cardboard boxes, lime proc., coconut proc. **Chief crops:** bananas, coconuts, vegetables, citrus, root crops, cocoa. **Natural resources:** forests, beaches, pumice, mineral springs, geothermal potential. **Arable land:** 4.9%. **Livestock:** cattle: 11,000; chickens: 450,000; goats: 9,500; pigs: 20,000; sheep: 10,500. **Electricity prod.:** 362 mil kWh. **Labor force:** agric. 21.7%, industry 24.7%, services 53.6%. **Unemployment:** NA.

Finance: Monetary unit: East Caribbean Dollar (XCD) (Sept. 2014: 2.70 = $1 U.S.). **GDP:** $2.2 bil; **per capita GDP:** $13,100; **GDP growth:** 0.2%. **Imports:** $592.7 mil; Brazil 57.4%, U.S. 19%, Trinidad and Tobago 9%. **Exports:** $206.8 mil; U.S. 13.9%, UK 10.3%, Peru 9.7%, Antigua and Barbuda 9.3%, Dominica 9.1%, France 9%, Barbados 8.1%, Trinidad and Tobago 7.6%, Grenada 6.2%. **Tourism:** $354 mil. **Budget** (2011 est.): $222.2 mil. **Total reserves less gold:** $192.2 mil. **Inflation:** 1.5%.

Transport: Civil aviation: 2 airports. **Chief ports:** Castries, Cul-de-Sac, Vieux-Fort.

Communications: TV sets: 341 per 1,000 pop. **Radios:** 193 per 1,000 pop. **Telephone lines:** 18.4 per 100 pop. **Mobile:** 116.3 per 100 pop. **Internet:** 35.2%.

Health: Life expect.: 74.7 male; 80.3 female. **Births:** 13.9 per 1,000 pop. **Deaths:** 7.3 per 1,000 pop. **Natural inc.:** 0.66%. **Infant mortality:** 11.8 per 1,000 live births. **HIV:** NA.

Education: Compulsory: ages 5-14. **Literacy:** NA.

Embassy: 3216 New Mexico Ave. NW 20016; 364-6792.

Website: www.stlucia.gov.lc

St. Lucia was ceded to Britain by France with the Treaty of Paris, 1814. Self-government was granted with the West Indies Act, 1967. Independence was attained Feb. 22, 1979.

Saint Vincent and the Grenadines

People: Population: 102,918. **Age distrib.:** <15: 22.9%; 65+: 8.6%. **Pop. density:** 685.2 per sq mi, 264.6 per sq km. **Urban:** 50.2%. **Ethnic groups:** black 66%, mixed 19%, East Indian 6%, European 4%, Carib Amerindian 2%. **Languages:** English, French patois. **Religions:** Protestant 75% (Anglican 47%, Methodist 28%), Roman Catholic 13%, other (incl. Hindu, Seventh-day Adventist, other Protestant) 12%.

Geography: Total area: 150 sq mi, 389 sq km; **Land area:** 150 sq mi, 389 sq km. **Location:** In E Caribbean; St. Vincent (133 sq mi) and the northern islets of the Grenadines form a part of Windward chain. **Neighbors:** St. Lucia to N, Barbados to E, Grenada to S. **Topography:** St. Vincent is volcanic, with a ridge of thickly wooded mountains running its length. **Capital:** Kingstown, 27,314.

Government: Type: Parliamentary democracy. **Head of state:** Queen Elizabeth II, rep. by Gov.-Gen. Sir Frederick Ballantyne; b. July 5, 1936; in office: Sept. 2, 2002. **Head of gov.:** Prime Min. Ralph Gonsalves; b. Aug. 8, 1946; in office: Mar. 29, 2001. **Local divisions:** 6 parishes. **Defense budget/active troops:** NA.

Economy: Industries: tourism, food proc., cement, furniture, clothing, starch. **Chief crops:** bananas, coconuts, sweet potatoes, spices. **Natural resources:** hydropower. **Arable land:** 12.8%. **Livestock:** cattle: 5,000; chickens: 250,000; goats: 9,300; pigs: 4,800; sheep: 11,300. **Electricity prod.:** 135 mil kWh. **Labor force:** agric. 26%, industry 17%, services 57%. **Unemployment:** NA.

Finance: Monetary unit: East Caribbean Dollar (XCD) (Sept. 2014: 2.70 = $1 U.S.). **GDP:** $1.3 bil; **per capita GDP:** $12,100; **GDP growth:** 2%. **Imports:** $301.5 mil; Singapore 28%, Trinidad and Tobago 22.6%, U.S. 19%, China 5.6%, Barbados 5%. **Exports:** $45.7 mil; Trinidad and Tobago 14.5%, St. Lucia 12.9%, Turkey 12.7%, Barbados 10.7%, Dominica 8.5%, Grenada 8.1%, Antigua and Barbuda 7.3%. **Tourism:** $92 mil. **Budget:** $185.2 mil. **Total reserves less gold:** $135.1 mil. **Inflation:** 0.8%.

Transport: Civil aviation: 5 airports. **Chief port:** Kingstown.
Communications: TV sets: 341 per 1,000 pop. **Radios:** 1,025 per 1,000 pop. **Telephone lines:** 17.4 per 100 pop. **Mobile:** 114.6 per 100 pop. **Internet:** 52%.
Health: Life expect.: 72.9 male; 76.9 female. **Births:** 13.9 per 1,000 pop. **Deaths:** 7.1 per 1,000 pop. **Natural inc.:** 0.67%. **Infant mortality:** 13.1 per 1,000 live births. **HIV:** NA.
Education: Compulsory: ages 5-16. **Literacy:** NA.
Embassy: 3216 New Mexico Ave. NW 20016; 364-6730.
Website: www.gov.vc
Columbus landed on St. Vincent on Jan. 22, 1498 (St. Vincent's Day). Britain and France both laid claim to the island in the 17th and 18th cent.; the Treaty of Versailles, 1783, ceded it to Britain. Associated State status was granted 1969; independence was attained Oct. 27, 1979.

Samoa
Independent State of Samoa

People: Population: 196,628. **Age distrib.:** <15: 33.4%; 65+: 5.4%. **Pop. density:** 180.5 per sq mi, 69.7 per sq km. **Urban:** 19.3%. **Ethnic groups:** Samoan 93%, Euronesians (mixed European, Polynesian) 7%. **Languages:** Samoan (Polynesian) (official), English. **Religions:** Protestant 57% (incl. Congregationalist 32%, Methodist 14%, Assembly of God 8%, Seventh-day Adventist 4%), Roman Catholic 19%, Mormon 15%, other Christian 6%.
Geography: Total area: 1,093 sq mi, 2,831 sq km; **Land area:** 1,089 sq mi, 2,821 sq km. **Location:** In S Pacific O. **Neighbors:** Nearest are Fiji to SW, Tonga to S. **Topography:** Main islands, Savaii (659 sq mi) and Upolu (432 sq mi), both ruggedly mountainous, and small islands Manono and Apolima. **Capital:** Apia, 36,946.
Government: Type: Parliamentary democracy. **Head of state:** Tuiatua Tupua Tamasese Efi; b. Mar. 1, 1938; in office: June 20, 2007. **Head of gov.:** Prime Min. Tuilaepa Sailele Malielegaoi; b. Apr. 14, 1945; in office: Nov. 23, 1998. **Local divisions:** 11 districts. **Defense budget/active troops:** NA.
Economy: Industries: food proc., building materials, auto parts. **Chief crops:** coconuts, bananas, taro, yams, coffee, cocoa. **Natural resources:** hardwood forests, fish, hydropower. **Arable land:** 2.8%. **Livestock:** cattle: 30,000; chickens: 620,000; pigs: 201,000. **Electricity prod.:** 115.2 mil kWh. **Labor force:** agric. 65%. **Unemployment:** NA.
Finance: Monetary unit: Tala (WST) (Sept. 2014: 2.33 = $1 U.S.). **GDP:** $1.1 bil; **per capita GDP:** $6,200; **GDP growth:** 0.1%. **Imports** (2011): $318.7 mil; New Zealand 19.2%, Singapore 18.6%, Fiji 17.6%, China 15.8%, Australia 5.9%, U.S. 5.4%. **Exports** (2011): $11.4 mil; American Samoa 48.4%, Australia 24%. **Tourism:** $136 mil. **Budget:** $258.7 mil. **Total reserves less gold:** $170.9 mil. **Inflation:** 0.6%.
Transport: Civil aviation: 1 airport. **Chief port:** Apia.
Communications: TV sets: 122 per 1,000 pop. **Radios:** 312 per 1,000 pop. **Telephone lines** (2005): 10.8 per 100 pop. **Mobile** (2007): 47.2 per 100 pop. **Internet:** 15.3%.
Health: Life expect.: 70.3 male; 76.2 female. **Births:** 21.3 per 1,000 pop. **Deaths:** 5.3 per 1,000 pop. **Natural inc.:** 1.60%. **Infant mortality:** 20.5 per 1,000 live births. **HIV:** NA.
Education: Compulsory: ages 5-14. **Literacy:** 99%.
Embassy: 800 Second Ave., Ste. 400J, New York, NY 10017; (212) 599-6196.
Website: www.samoagovt.ws
Samoa (formerly known as Western Samoa) was a German colony, 1899 to 1914, when New Zealand landed troops and took over. It became a New Zealand mandate under the League of Nations and, in 1945, a New Zealand UN Trusteeship.
An elected local government took office in Oct. 1959, and the country became fully independent Jan. 1, 1962. Malietoa Tanumafili II, Samoa's head of state since independence, was succeeded by Tuiatua Tupua Tamasese Efi. At the end of the day on Dec. 29, 2011, Samoa moved west of the Intl. Date Line to simplify trade with Australia and New Zealand. Samoa is now 3 hours ahead of eastern Australia rather than 21 hours behind.

San Marino
Republic of San Marino

People: Population: 32,742. **Age distrib.:** <15: 16%; 65+: 18.8%. **Pop. density:** 1,390.2 per sq mi, 536.8 per sq km. **Urban:** 94.2%. **Ethnic groups:** Sammarinese, Italian. **Language:** Italian. **Religion:** Roman Catholic.
Geography: Total area: 24 sq mi, 61 sq km; **Land area:** 24 sq mi, 61 sq km. **Location:** In N central Italy near Adriatic coast. **Neighbors:** Completely surrounded by Italy. **Topography:** The country lies on slopes of Mt. Titano. **Capital:** San Marino, 4,197.
Government: Type: Republic. **Heads of state:** Two captains regent, elected by parliament from among its members, to 6-month term. **Head of gov.:** Sec. of State for Foreign and Political Affairs Pasquale Valentini; b. July 19, 1953; in office: Dec. 5, 2012. **Local divisions:** 9 municipalities. **Defense budget/active troops:** NA.
Economy: Industries: tourism, banking, textiles, electronics, ceramics, cement, wine. **Chief crops:** wheat, grapes, corn, olives. **Natural resources:** building stone. **Arable land:** 16.7%. **Labor**

force: agric. 0.2%, industry 33.5%, services 66.3%. **Unemployment:** NA.
Finance: Monetary unit: Euro (EUR) (Sept. 2014: 0.76 = $1 U.S.). **GDP:** $1.3 bil; **per capita GDP:** NA; **GDP growth:** –3.5%. **Imports** (2011): $2.6 bil; Italy 81.8%. **Exports** (2011): $3.8 bil; Italy 82.3%. **Budget** (2011): $721.8 mil. **Total reserves less gold** (2012): $385 mil. **Inflation:** 1.6%.
Transport: NA.
Communications: TV sets: 792 per 1,000 pop. **Radios:** 1,322 per 1,000 pop. **Telephone lines:** 59.6 per 100 pop. **Mobile:** 117 per 100 pop. **Internet:** 50.8%.
Health: Life expect.: 80.6 male; 85.9 female. **Births:** 8.7 per 1,000 pop. **Deaths:** 8.3 per 1,000 pop. **Natural inc.:** 0.04%. **Infant mortality:** 4.5 per 1,000 live births. **HIV:** NA.
Education: Compulsory: ages 6-15. **Literacy:** 96%.
Embassy: 1711 N St. NW, 2nd Fl., 20036; 223-2418.
Website: www.sanmarino.sm
San Marino claims to be the world's oldest republic, having been founded in the 4th cent. It has had a treaty of friendship with Italy since 1862. A Communist-led coalition ruled 1947-57; a similar coalition ruled 1978-86. The broad-based San Marino Common Good coalition won parliamentary elections Nov. 11, 2012.

São Tomé and Príncipe
Democratic Republic of São Tomé and Príncipe

People: Population: 190,428. **Age distrib.:** <15: 43.5%; 65+: 2.9%. **Pop. density:** 511.6 per sq mi, 197.5 per sq km. **Urban:** 64.5%. **Ethnic groups:** mestico, angolares (descendants of Angolan slaves), forros (descendants of freed slaves), servicais (contract laborers fr. Angola, Mozambique, Cabo Verde), tongas (children of servicais born in country), Europeans (primarily Portuguese). **Language:** Portuguese (official), Forro, Cabo Verdian, French, Angolar, English. **Religions:** Catholic 56%, Adventist 4%, Assembly of God 3%, New Apostolic 3%, none 21%.
Geography: Total area: 372 sq mi, 964 sq km; **Land area:** 372 sq mi, 964 sq km. **Location:** In Gulf of Guinea about 125 mi off W central Africa. **Neighbors:** Gabon, Equatorial Guinea to E. **Topography:** São Tomé and Príncipe Islands, part of an extinct volcano chain, are both covered by lush forests and croplands. **Capital:** São Tomé, 71,294.
Government: Type: Republic. **Head of state:** Pres. Manuel Pinto da Costa; b. Aug. 5, 1937; in office: Sept. 3, 2011. **Head of gov.:** Prime Min. Gabriel Arcanjo Ferreira da Costa; in office: Dec. 12, 2012. **Local divisions:** 2 provinces. **Defense budget/active troops:** NA.
Economy: Industries: light constr., textiles, soap, beer, fish proc., timber. **Chief crops:** cocoa, coconuts, palm kernels, copra, cinnamon, pepper, coffee, bananas, papayas, beans. **Natural resources:** fish, hydropower. **Arable land:** 9.1%. **Livestock:** cattle: 1,141; chickens: 265,000; goats: 5,700; pigs: 33,000; sheep: 3,200. **Electricity prod.:** 60 mil kWh. **Labor force:** Pop. mainly engaged in subsistence agric. and fishing; shortage of skilled workers. **Unemployment:** NA.
Finance: Monetary unit: Dobra (STD) (Sept. 2014: 18,635.00 = $1 U.S.). **GDP:** $421 mil; **per capita GDP:** $2,200; **GDP growth:** 4.5%. **Imports:** $112.8 mil; Portugal 63.1%, Gabon 5.4%. **Exports:** $12.1 mil; Netherlands 33.3%, Belgium 21.8%, Spain 11%, Nigeria 5.6%, U.S. 5.1%. **Tourism:** $14 mil. **Budget:** $120.3 mil. **Total reserves less gold:** $63.8 mil. **Inflation:** 7.1%.
Transport: Civil aviation: 2 airports. **Chief port:** São Tomé.
Communications: TV sets: 127 per 1,000 pop. **Radios:** 106 per 1,000 pop. **Telephone lines:** 3.6 per 100 pop. **Mobile:** 64.9 per 100 pop. **Internet:** 23%.
Health: Life expect.: 62.9 male; 65.5 female. **Births:** 35.1 per 1,000 pop. **Deaths:** 7.5 per 1,000 pop. **Natural inc.:** 2.77%. **Infant mortality:** 49.2 per 1,000 live births. **HIV:** 0.6%.
Education: Compulsory: ages 6-11. **Literacy:** 74.9%.
Permanent UN mission: 675 Third Ave., Ste. 1807, New York, NY 10017; (212) 651-8116.
Website: www.gov.st
The Portuguese discovered the islands in 1471 and brought the first inhabitants—convicts and exiled Jews. Sugarcane planting was replaced by the slave trade as the chief economic activity until coffee and cocoa were introduced in the 19th cent.
Portugal agreed, 1974, to turn the colony over to the Gabon-based Movement for the Liberation of São Tomé and Príncipe; its East German-trained leader, Manuel Pinto da Costa, became the country's first president. Independence came July 12, 1975. Democratic reforms were instituted in 1987. In 1991, Miguel Trovoada won the first free presidential election. A military coup that ousted Trovoada Aug. 15, 1995, was reversed a week later after Angolan mediation. Trovoada defeated Pinto da Costa in a presidential runoff election July 21, 1996.
Fradique de Menezes, a wealthy cocoa exporter, beat Pinto da Costa in July 29, 2001, presidential elections. The government was ousted in a military coup July 16, 2003, but was restored to power a week later and reelected July 30, 2006. After the opposition Independent Democratic Action party won parliamentary elections Aug. 1, 2010, Patrice Trovoada (son of the former president) was chosen to head the new government. Pinto da Costa returned to power after a presidential runoff vote Aug. 7, 2011. The National

Assembly elected Gabriel Arcanjo Ferreira da Costa prime min. Dec. 2012. The country, long one of the world's poorest, has sought to develop oil deposits in the Gulf of Guinea.

Saudi Arabia
Kingdom of Saudi Arabia

People: Population: 27,345,986. **Age distrib.:** <15: 27.6%; 65+: 3.2%. **Pop. density:** 32.9 per sq mi, 12.7 per sq km. **Urban:** 82.9%. **Ethnic groups:** Arab 90%, Afro-Asian 10%. **Language:** Arabic (official). **Religion:** Muslim (official; 85%-90% Sunni, 10%-15% Shia).

Geography: Total area: 830,000 sq mi, 2,149,690 sq km; **Land area:** 830,000 sq mi, 2,149,690 sq km. **Location:** Occupies most of Arabian Peninsula in Mid-East. **Neighbors:** Kuwait, Iraq, Jordan on N; Yemen, Oman on S; United Arab Emirates, Qatar on E. **Topography:** Bordered by Red Sea on W. The highlands in W, up to 9,000 ft, slope as arid, barren desert to the Persian Gulf on E. **Capital:** Riyadh, 6,195,200. **Cities (urban aggl.):** Jiddah, 3,988,490; Mecca, 1,742,147; Medina, 1,257,614.

Government: Type: Monarchy. **Head of state and gov.:** King Abdullah bin Abdul Aziz; b. Aug. 1, 1924; in office: Aug. 1, 2005. **Local divisions:** 13 provinces. **Defense budget:** $59.56 bil. **Active troops:** 233,500.

Economy: Industries: crude oil prod., petroleum refining, basic petrochemicals, ammonia, industrial gases, caustic soda, cement, fertilizer, plastics, metals, commercial ship repair, commercial aircraft repair, constr. **Chief crops:** wheat, barley, tomatoes, melons, dates, citrus. **Natural resources:** petroleum, nat. gas, iron ore, gold, copper. **Crude oil reserves:** 268.4 bil bbls (incl. half of Neutral Zone reserves). **Arable land:** 1.5%. **Livestock:** cattle: 510,000; chickens: 181.5 mil; goats: 3.4 mil; sheep: 11.5 mil. **Electricity prod.:** 235.1 bil kWh. **Labor force:** agric. 6.7%, industry 21.4%, services 71.9%. **Unemployment:** 5.6%.

Finance: Monetary unit: Riyal (SAR) (Sept. 2014: 3.75 = $1 U.S.). **GDP:** $927.8 bil; **per capita GDP:** $31,300; **GDP growth:** 3.6%. **Imports:** $147 bil; China 13.5%, U.S. 13.2%, South Korea 6.6%, Germany 6.5%, India 6.3%, Japan 6%. **Exports:** $376.3 bil; U.S. 14.2%, China 13.6%, Japan 13.6%, South Korea 9.9%, India 8.2%, Singapore 4.3%. **Tourism:** $7.7 bil. **Budget:** $258.4 bil. **Total reserves less gold:** $725.3 bil. **Gold:** 10.4 mil oz t. **Inflation:** 3.5%.

Transport: Railways: 856 mi. **Motor vehicles:** 227.5 per 1,000 pop. **Civil aviation:** 24.1 bil pass.-mi; 82 airports. **Chief ports:** Ad Dammam, Al Jubayl, Jeddah, Yanbu al Bahr.

Communications: TV sets: 275 per 1,000 pop. **Radios:** 317 per 1,000 pop. **Telephone lines:** 16.4 per 100 pop. **Mobile:** 176.5 per 100 pop. **Internet:** 60.5%.

Health: Life expect.: 72.8 male; 76.9 female. **Births:** 18.8 per 1,000 pop. **Deaths:** 3.3 per 1,000 pop. **Natural inc.:** 1.55%. **Infant mortality:** 14.6 per 1,000 live births. **HIV:** NA.

Education: Compulsory: ages 6-14. **Literacy:** 94.7%.

Embassy: 601 New Hampshire Ave. NW 20037; 342-3800.

Website: www.saudi.gov.sa

Before Muhammad, Arabia was divided among numerous warring tribes and small kingdoms. Muhammad united it in the early 7th cent. His successors conquered the entire Near East and North Africa, bringing Islam and the Arabic language. But Arabia soon returned to its former status.

Nejd, in central Arabia, long an independent state and center of the Wahhabi sect, fell under Turkish rule in the 18th cent. Ibn Saud, founder of the Saudi dynasty, overthrew the Turks, 1913. He captured Hasa, a Turkish province in eastern Arabia, also 1913; the Hejaz region in western Arabia, 1925; and most of Asir, in SW Arabia, by 1926. The discovery of oil in the 1930s transformed the nation. The Hejaz contains the holy cities of Islam—Medina and Mecca. About 3 mil Muslims make the *hajj* (pilgrimage) to Mecca annually.

Ibn Saud reigned until his death, Nov. 1953. Subsequent kings have been his sons. The king exercises authority with a Council of Ministers. The Islamic religious code is the law of the land. Alcohol and public entertainments are restricted; women have an inferior legal status.

Saudi Arabia has often allied itself with and purchased arms from the U.S. and other Western nations. Saudi units, nevertheless, fought against Western ally Israel in the 1948 and 1973 Arab-Israeli wars. Beginning with the 1967 Arab-Israeli war, Saudi Arabia gave large annual financial gifts to Egypt, Syria, Jordan, and Palestinian groups. Saudi Arabia played a leading role in the 1973-74 Arab oil embargo against the U.S. and other nations.

After Iraq invaded Kuwait, Aug. 2, 1990, Saudi Arabia accepted the Kuwait royal family and more than 400,000 Kuwaiti refugees. Western and Arab troops also deployed on Saudi soil before and during the 1991 Persian Gulf War.

When 15 of the 19 al-Qaeda hijackers who carried out the Sept. 11, 2001, attacks on the U.S. were found to be Saudi, some in the U.S. blamed the Saudi government for allowing Muslim extremism to flourish in Saudi Arabia. Policy differences over the Israeli-Palestinian dispute and Iraq (where Saudi jihadists supported the Sunni cause) were further irritants. The U.S. completed a pullout of its combat forces from Saudi Arabia, Sept. 2003. Alarmed at guerrilla attacks that killed more than 100 people, mostly foreigners, in Saudi Arabia, 2003-04, the Saudis worked with the U.S. to increase antiterrorist activities.

Islamist candidates on a "golden list" circulated by conservative clerics fared well in Feb.-Apr. 2005, municipal council elections,

the country's first since 1963; women were barred from voting. Just before male-only Sept. 2011 municipal elections, King Abdullah announced that women would be allowed to vote and run for office in future elections, beginning in 2015. In 2012, Saudi women athletes competed in the Olympics for the first time. King Abdullah decreed, Jan. 11, 2013, that women would be permitted to hold 30 of the 150 seats on the government's advisory Shura council.

Cases of Middle East Respiratory Syndrome (MERS), a viral disease first recognized in Saudi Arabia in 2012, increased in 2014. As of July 23, 2014, the Saudi Ministry of Health reported that 721 people had become ill since the outbreak began, of whom 297 had died. MERS had spread to various Middle Eastern, North African, and other countries.

Hoping to contain the wave of 2011 Arab Spring uprisings, a Saudi-led Gulf Cooperation Council force suppressed protests in Bahrain Mar. 14. The Saudis also tried to aid monarchies in Jordan and Morocco, and sent financial assistance to Egypt after the military's 2013 ouster of Islamist Pres. Mohammed Morsi. Saudi Arabia supplied weapons to anti-government rebels in Syria's civil war. Apparently concerned about the growth of Sunni extremist group ISIS, Saudi Arabia gave $100 mil, Aug. 13, 2014, to a UN counterterrorism agency. The U.S. announced, Sept. 10, that Saudi Arabia would provide a base for training Syrian rebel groups fighting both ISIS and government forces. Beginning Sept. 23, Saudi warplanes participated in U.S.-led air strikes against Sunni extremists in Syria.

Senegal
Republic of Senegal

People: Population: 13,635,927. **Age distrib.:** <15: 42.5%; 65+: 2.9%. **Pop. density:** 183.4 per sq mi, 70.8 per sq km. **Urban:** 43.4%. **Ethnic groups:** Wolof 43%, Pular 24%, Serer 15%, Jola 4%, Mandinka 3%, Soninke 1%, European and Lebanese 1%. **Languages:** French (official), Wolof, Pulaar, Jola, Mandinka. **Religions:** Muslim 94%, Christian 5% (mostly Roman Catholic), indigenous beliefs 1%.

Geography: Total area: 75,955 sq mi, 196,722 sq km; **Land area:** 74,336 sq mi, 192,530 sq km. **Location:** At W extreme of Africa. **Neighbors:** Mauritania on N, Mali on E, Guinea and Guinea-Bissau on S; surrounds The Gambia on three sides. **Topography:** Low rolling plains cover most of Senegal, rising somewhat in SE. Swamp and jungles are in SW. **Capital:** Dakar, 3,392,850.

Government: Type: Republic. **Head of state:** Pres. Macky Sall; b. Dec. 11, 1961; in office: Apr. 2, 2012. **Head of gov.:** Prime Min. Aminata Touré; b. Oct. 12, 1962; in office: Sept. 3, 2013. **Local divisions:** 14 regions. **Defense budget** $231 mil. **Active troops:** 13,600.

Economy: Industries: agric. and fish proc., phosphate mining, fertilizer prod., petroleum refining, mining, constr. materials, ship constr. and repair. **Chief crops:** peanuts, millet, corn, sorghum, rice, cotton, tomatoes, green vegetables. **Natural resources:** fish, phosphates, iron ore. **Arable land:** 17.4%. **Livestock:** cattle: 3.4 mil; chickens: 48.9 mil; goats: 5.2 mil; pigs: 386,000; sheep: 6.1 mil. **Electricity prod.:** 2.8 bil kWh. **Labor force:** agric. 77.5%, industry and services 22.5%. **Unemployment:** 9.9%.

Finance: Monetary unit: CFA Franc (XOF) (Sept. 2014: 498.91 = $1 U.S.). **GDP:** $27.7 bil; **per capita GDP:** $2,100; **GDP growth:** 4%. **Imports:** $5.6 bil; France 16.2%, Nigeria 12.9%, India 6.3%, China 6.3%, UK 4.6%. **Exports:** $2.7 bil; Mali 14.4%, Switzerland 14.1%, India 11.9%, France 4.7%, Guinea 4.2%. **Tourism:** $468 mil. **Budget:** $4.4 bil. **Total reserves less gold:** $2.3 bil. **Inflation:** 0.7%.

Transport: Railways: 563 mi. **Civil aviation:** 9 airports. **Chief port:** Dakar.

Communications: TV sets: 44 per 1,000 pop. **Radios:** 536 per 1,000 pop. **Telephone lines:** 2.4 per 100 pop. **Mobile:** 92.9 per 100 pop. **Internet:** 20.9%.

Health: Life expect.: 58.9 male; 63.0 female. **Births:** 35.1 per 1,000 pop. **Deaths:** 8.7 per 1,000 pop. **Natural inc.:** 2.64%. **Infant mortality:** 52.7 per 1,000 live births. **HIV:** 0.5%.

Education: Compulsory: ages 6-15. **Literacy:** 57.7%.

Embassy: 2112 Wyoming Ave. NW 20008; 234-0540.

Website: www.gouv.sn

Portuguese settlers arrived in the 15th cent., but French control grew from the 17th cent. The last independent Muslim state was subdued in 1893. Senegal became an independent republic Aug. 20, 1960, but French political and economic influence remained strong. Senegambia, a loose confederation of Senegal and The Gambia, was established in 1982 but dissolved seven years later.

Forty years of Socialist Party rule ended when Abdoulaye Wade, leader of the Senegalese Democratic Party, won a presidential run-off election, Mar. 19, 2000. A Senegalese ferry capsized off the coast of The Gambia Sept. 26, 2002, killing at least 1,863 people. A peace accord signed Dec. 30, 2004, with separatists in Cassamance Province, S Senegal, sought to end a 22-year insurgency. Pres. Wade was reelected Feb. 25, 2007, but lost his bid for a third term Mar. 26, 2012, to Macky Sall, his former prime min. Former Chad Pres. Hissène Habré, accused of killing and torturing thousands in the 1980s, was arrested June 30, 2013, in Senegal, where authorities planned to try him for genocide and crimes against humanity. An Ebola outbreak in W. Africa spread to Senegal in Aug. 2014 when a person who had become ill in Guinea traveled to Dakar; no further cases had been reported as of late Sept.

Serbia
Republic of Serbia

People: Population: 7,209,764. **Age distrib.:** <15: 14.8%; 65+: 17.2%. **Pop. density:** 241 per sq mi, 93.1 per sq km. **Urban:** 55.5% (incl. Kosovo). **Ethnic groups:** Serb 83%, Hungarian 4%, Romany 2%, Bosniak 2%. **Languages:** Serbian (official), Hungarian, Bosnian, Romany. **Religions:** Serbian Orthodox 85%, Catholic 5%, Muslim 3%, Protestant 1%.

Geography: Total area: 29,913 sq mi, 77,474 sq km; **Land area:** 29,913 sq mi, 77,474 sq km. **Location:** On Balkan Peninsula in SE Europe. **Neighbors:** Croatia, Bosnia and Herzegovina on W; Hungary on N; Romania, Bulgaria on E; Montenegro, Albania, Macedonia on S. **Topography:** Terrain varies widely, with fertile plains drained by Danube and other rivers in N, limestone basins in E, and ancient mountains and hills in SE. **Capital:** Belgrade, 1,180,800.

Government: Type: Republic. **Head of state:** Pres. Tomislav Nikolic; b. Feb. 15, 1952; in office: May 31, 2012. **Head of gov.:** Prime Min. Aleksandar Vucic; b. Mar. 5, 1970; in office: Apr. 22, 2014. **Local divisions:** 122 municipalities, 23 cities. **Defense budget:** $681 mil. **Active troops:** 28,150.

Economy: Industries: base metals, furniture, food proc., machinery, chemicals, sugar, tires, clothes, pharmaceuticals. **Chief crops:** wheat, maize, sugar beets, sunflowers, raspberries. **Natural resources:** oil, gas, coal, iron ore, copper, zinc, antimony, chromite, gold, silver, magnesium, pyrite, limestone, marble, salt. **Crude oil reserves:** 77.5 mil bbls. **Arable land:** 37.5%. **Livestock:** cattle: 913,144; chickens: 23 mil; goats: 225,073; pigs: 3.1 mil; sheep: 1.6 mil. **Electricity prod.:** 35.9 bil kWh. **Labor force:** agric. 23.9%, industry 16.5%, services 59.6%. **Unemployment:** 19.6%.

Finance: Monetary unit: Dinar (RSD) (Sept. 2014: 89.82 = $1 U.S.). **GDP:** $80.5 bil; **per capita GDP:** $11,100; **GDP growth:** 2%. **Imports:** $20.5 bil. **Exports:** $14.6 bil. **Tourism:** $1.1 bil. **Budget:** $19.6 bil. **Total reserves less gold:** $14.8 bil. **Gold:** 522,128 oz t. **Inflation:** 7.7%.

Transport: Railways: 2,100 mi. **Civil aviation:** 728.9 mil pass.-mi; 10 airports.

Communications: TV sets: 248 per 1,000 pop. **Telephone lines:** 39.3 per 100 pop. **Mobile:** 119.4 per 100 pop. **Internet:** 51.5%.

Health: Life expect.: 72.2 male; 78.1 female. **Births:** 9.1 per 1,000 pop. **Deaths:** 13.7 per 1,000 pop. **Natural inc.:** −0.46%. **Infant mortality:** 6.2 per 1,000 live births. **HIV:** <0.1%.

Education: Compulsory: ages 7-14. **Literacy:** 98.1%.

Embassy: 2134 Kalorama Rd. NW 20008; 332-0333.

Website: www.srbija.gov.rs

Serbia was a vassal principality of Turkey from 1389 to 1878, when the Treaty of Berlin established it as an independent kingdom. After the Balkan wars, Serbia annexed Old Serbia and Macedonia, 1913.

When the Austro-Hungarian empire collapsed after WWI, the Kingdom of Serbs, Croats, and Slovenes—Yugoslavia after 1929—was formed from the provinces of Croatia, Dalmatia, Bosnia, Herzegovina, Slovenia, Vojvodina, and the independent state of Montenegro.

After Nazi Germany's occupation 1941-45, Yugoslavia became a federal republic, headed by Josip Broz, a Communist, known as Marshal Tito. He rejected Stalin's dictatorship and accepted economic and military aid from the West. After Tito died in 1980, Yugoslavia held together for a decade before breaking apart. During 1991-95, Serbia, under Pres. Slobodan Milosevic, supported ethnic Serb fighters in Croatia and in Bosnia and Herzegovina, which had declared independence. The republics of Serbia and Montenegro proclaimed a new Federal Republic of Yugoslavia, Apr. 17, 1992. The UN imposed sanctions on the newly reconstituted Yugoslavia to end the bloodshed in Bosnia.

A peace agreement was reached in 1995. A UN-backed war crimes tribunal began in May 1996 to try suspects from the former Yugoslavia. Mass protests erupted when Milosevic refused to accept opposition victories in local elections, Nov. 17; non-Communist governments took office in Belgrade and other cities, Feb. 1997. Barred from running for a third term as Serbian president, Milosevic had himself inaugurated as president of Yugoslavia, July 23, 1997.

Serbian efforts to suppress a secessionist movement in Kosovo led in Mar.-June 1999 to a war with the U.S. and its NATO allies; they accused Milosevic of pursuing a policy of ethnic cleansing against the predominantly Muslim Kosovars (ethnic Albanians). NATO stationed a multinational force in Kosovo, which was placed under UN administration.

Milosevic initially refused to accept defeat to opposition leader Vojislav Kostunica in a 2000 presidential election but resigned Oct. 6 after mass demonstrations. Kostunica was sworn in the next day. Charged with corruption and abuse of power, Milosevic surrendered to Serbian authorities Apr. 1, 2001. He was extradited June 28 to The Hague, Netherlands, where a UN tribunal had indicted him for war crimes. His trial began Feb. 12, 2002. He was found dead in prison Mar. 11, 2006, before a verdict was reached.

A pact to reconstitute Yugoslavia as a new union of Serbia and Montenegro took effect Feb. 4, 2003. Zoran Djindjic, premier of the Republic of Serbia, was assassinated Mar. 12 in Belgrade, triggering a roundup of more than 4,500 people associated with organized crime and the Milosevic regime. Serbia's union with Montenegro

disintegrated in 2006. Montenegrins voted for separation in a referendum May 21, and Montenegro became an independent republic June 3.

Kosovo declared independence from Serbia Feb. 17, 2008, but Serbia refused to recognize the new country. Following parliamentary elections in Serbia May 11, a pro-Western government under Mirko Cvetkovic took office July 7. To meet a requirement for EU membership, Serbia arrested, in 2008, former Bosnian Serb leader Radovan Karadzic, who was extradited to the Intl. Criminal Court in The Hague on charges of genocide and crimes against humanity. Serbia's parliament passed a resolution Mar. 31, 2010, apologizing for the 1995 massacre of thousands of Muslims by Bosnian Serbs at Srebrenica. In a further effort to deal with wartime atrocities, Serbian prosecutors, Sept. 2010, indicted 9 former members of the Jackals paramilitary unit for allegedly killing 43 ethnic Albanian civilians during the 1999 Kosovo conflict. Ratko Mladic, the former Bosnian Serb military commander accused of directing the 1995 massacre of 8,000 Bosnian Muslims in Srebrenica, was arrested in Serbia, May 2011, and sent to The Hague. He was on trial since 2012. Serbia attained EU candidate status, Mar. 1, 2012. Tomislav Nikolic, an advocate for EU membership, was elected president May 20. Zdravko Tolimir, a former commander in the Bosnian Serb Army, was convicted of genocide Dec. 12 for his role in the July 1995 killings of thousands of prisoners near Srebrenica. After reaching an EU-brokered power-sharing deal with Kosovo Apr. 19, 2013, Serbia began accession negotiations for EU membership Jan. 21, 2014. Aleksandar Vucic, who favors EU membership, became prime min. following Mar. 16, 2014, elections.

Vojvodina (8,304 sq mi) is a nominally autonomous province in northern Serbia with a pop. (2011 est.) of 1,916,889, mostly Serbian. The capital is Novi Sad. **Website:** www.vojvodina.gov.rs.

Seychelles
Republic of Seychelles

People: Population: 91,650. **Age distrib.:** <15: 20.9%; 65+: 7.3%. **Pop. density:** 521.7 per sq mi, 201.4 per sq km. **Urban:** 53.6%. **Ethnic groups:** mixed French, African, Indian, Chinese, Arab. **Languages:** Creole, English (official). **Religions:** Roman Catholic 82%, Protestant 8% (Anglican 6%, Seventh-day Adventist 1%), other Christian 3%, Hindu 2%, Muslim 1%.

Geography: Total area: 176 sq mi, 455 sq km; **Land area:** 176 sq mi, 455 sq km. **Location:** In Indian O. 700 mi NE of Madagascar. **Neighbors:** Nearest are Madagascar on SW, Somalia on NW. **Topography:** A group of 86 islands, about half of them composed of coral, the other half granite, the latter predominantly mountainous. **Capital:** Victoria, 26,062.

Government: Type: Republic. **Head of state and gov.:** Pres. James Michel; b. Aug. 18, 1944; in office: Apr. 14, 2004. **Local divisions:** 25 admin. districts. **Defense budget** $12 mil. **Active troops:** 420.

Economy: Industries: fishing, tourism, coconuts and vanilla proc., coir (coconut fiber) rope, boat building, printing, furniture. **Chief crops:** coconuts, cinnamon, vanilla, sweet potatoes, cassava, copra, bananas. **Natural resources:** fish, cinnamon trees. **Arable land:** 2.2%. **Livestock:** cattle: 300; chickens: 450,000; goats: 5,500; pigs: 5,550. **Electricity prod.:** 304 mil kWh. **Labor force:** agric. 3%, industry 23%, services 74%. **Unemployment:** NA.

Finance: Monetary unit: Rupee (SCR) (Sept. 2014: 12.83 = $1 U.S.). **GDP:** $2.4 bil; **per capita GDP:** $25,900; **GDP growth:** 3.3%. **Imports:** $846.4 mil; Saudi Arabia 24%, Spain 12.1%, France 5.9%. **Exports:** $516.7 mil; France 27.7%, UK 17.6%, Japan 15.2%, Italy 10.6%. **Tourism:** $344 mil. **Budget:** $491.7 mil. **Total reserves less gold:** $425.9 mil. **Inflation:** 4.3%.

Transport: Civil aviation: 846.3 mil pass.-mi; 7 airports. **Chief port:** Victoria.

Communications: TV sets: 278 per 1,000 pop. **Radios:** 278 per 1,000 pop. **Telephone lines:** 23.4 per 1,000 pop. **Mobile:** 147.3 per 100 pop. **Internet:** 50.4%.

Health: Life expect.: 69.7 male; 79.0 female. **Births:** 14.5 per 1,000 pop. **Deaths:** 6.9 per 1,000 pop. **Natural inc.:** 0.76%. **Infant mortality:** 10.8 per 1,000 live births. **HIV:** NA.

Education: Compulsory: ages 6-15. **Literacy:** 91.8%.

Embassy: 800 Second Ave., Ste. 400C, New York, NY 10017; (212) 972-1785.

Website: www.egov.sc

The islands were occupied by France in 1768 and seized by Britain in 1794. Ruled as part of Mauritius from 1814, Seychelles became a separate colony in 1903 and declared independence June 29, 1976. The tourism industry, which employs 30% of workers, has been a major driver of rapid economic growth since independence. The country's first president was elected in a 1977 coup by socialist leader France Albert René. A new constitution, approved June 1993, provided for a multiparty state. René resigned Apr. 14, 2004, and Vice Pres. James Michel succeeded him. Michel won 5-year terms in 2006 and 2011 elections.

Sierra Leone
Republic of Sierra Leone

People: Population: 5,743,725. **Age distrib.:** <15: 41.9%; 65+: 3.7%. **Pop. density:** 207.7 per sq mi, 80.2 per sq km. **Urban:** 39.6%.

Ethnic groups: Temne 35%, Mende 31%, Limba 8%, Kono 5%, Kriole (descendants of freed Jamaican slaves) 2%, Mandingo 2%, Loko 2%, other (incl. Liberian refugees and small numbers of Europeans, Lebanese, Pakistanis, Indians) 15%. **Languages:** English (official), Mende (principal vernacular in S), Temne (principal vernacular in N), Krio (English-based Creole, a lingua franca). **Religions:** Muslim 60%, indigenous beliefs 30%, Christian 10%.

Geography: Total area: 27,699 sq mi, 71,740 sq km; **Land area:** 27,653 sq mi, 71,620 sq km. **Location:** On W coast of W Africa. **Neighbors:** Guinea on N and E, Liberia on S. **Topography:** The heavily-indented, 210-mi coastline has mangrove swamps. Behind are wooded hills, rising to a plateau and mountains in E. **Capital:** Freetown, 985,902.

Government: Type: Constitutional democracy. **Head of state and gov.:** Pres. Ernest Bai Koroma; b. Oct. 2, 1953; in office: Sept. 17, 2007. **Local divisions:** 3 provinces, 1 area. **Defense budget:** $4 mil. **Active troops:** 10,500.

Economy: Industries: diamond mining, small-scale mfg. (beverages, textiles), petroleum refining, small commercial ship repair. **Chief crops:** rice, coffee, cocoa, palm kernels, palm oil, peanuts. **Natural resources:** diamonds, titanium ore, bauxite, iron ore, gold, chromite. **Arable land:** 24%. **Livestock:** cattle: 578,000; chickens: 11.5 mil; goats: 896,000; pigs: 55,000; sheep: 757,500. **Electricity prod.:** 145 mil kWh. **Labor force:** NA. **Unemployment:** 3.4%.

Finance: Monetary unit: Leone (SLL) (Sept. 2014: 4,340.00 = $1 U.S.). **GDP:** $9.2 bil; **per capita GDP:** $1,400; **GDP growth:** 13.3%. **Imports:** $1.6 bil; China 16.5%, India 10.2%, South Africa 7.6%, U.S. 6.7%, UK 6.7%, Belgium 4.6%. **Exports:** $1.6 bil; China 51.1%, Belgium 18.2%, Japan 7.7%, Turkey 4.8%. **Tourism:** $59 mil. **Budget:** $754.4 mil. **Total reserves less gold:** $532.5 mil. **Inflation:** 10.3%.

Transport: Motor vehicles: 2.1 per 1,000 pop. **Civil aviation:** 1 airport. **Chief ports:** Freetown, Pepel.

Communications: TV sets: 13 per 1,000 pop. **Radios:** 132 per 1,000 pop. **Telephone lines** 0.3 per 100 pop. **Mobile:** 44.1 per 100 pop. **Internet:** 1.7%.

Health: Life expect.: 54.9 male; 60.0 female. **Births:** 37.4 per 1,000 pop. **Deaths:** 11.0 per 1,000 pop. **Natural inc.:** 2.64%. **Infant mortality:** 73.3 per 1,000 live births. **HIV:** 1.6%.

Education: Compulsory: ages 6-11. **Literacy:** 48.1%.

Embassy: 1701 19th St. NW 20009; 939-9261.

Website: www.statehouse.gov.sl

The British founded Freetown, 1787, as a haven for freed slaves. Full independence arrived Apr. 27, 1961. A one-party state was established by referendum in 1978.

Mutinous soldiers ousted Pres. Joseph Momoh, Apr. 30, 1992. A coup, Jan. 16, 1996, paved the way for multiparty elections and a return to civilian rule. A peace accord, signed Nov. 30 with the Revolutionary United Front (RUF), brought a temporary halt to a civil war that had claimed over 10,000 lives in five years.

A coup on May 25, 1997, was met with international opposition. Nigeria's military restored Pres. Ahmad Tejan Kabbah to power on Mar. 10, 1998, but RUF rebels mounted a guerrilla counteroffensive, killing thousands of civilians and mutilating thousands more. A power-sharing agreement between the Kabbah government and the RUF, July 1999, was maintained by a UN mission (UNAMSIL). The accord collapsed in early May 2000, as RUF guerrillas took more than 500 UN peacekeepers hostage. Rebel leader Foday Sankoh was captured in Freetown, May 17. The hostages were freed by the end of May. A UN-sponsored disarmament program in 2001 reduced the level of violence. The Sierra Leone Special Court was created in 2002 to try war crimes that had occurred after Nov. 1996. Government and rebel leaders declared an official end to the war Jan. 18; more than 50,000 people had died in the conflict. Kabbah won the May 14 presidential election.

Sankoh, an indicted war criminal, died in UN custody, July 29, 2003. Opposition leader Ernest Bai Koroma won a presidential runoff vote, Sept. 8, 2007. Three former RUF leaders were convicted of war crimes, Feb. 25, 2009. A cholera epidemic swept through the country in 2012; more than 19,000 cases were reported in Sierra Leone in the first 9 months of the year, killing at least 274. Koroma won reelection Nov. 17, 2012. An Ebola virus epidemic that began in Guinea in Dec. 2013 caused 2,304 cases of the illness and 622 deaths in Sierra Leone by Sept. 28, 2014.

Singapore
Republic of Singapore

People: Population: 5,567,301. **Age distrib.:** <15: 13.4%; 65+: 8.5%. **Pop. density:** 20,988.7 per sq mi, 8,103.8 per sq km. **Urban:** 100%. **Ethnic groups:** Chinese 74%, Malay 13%, Indian 9%. **Languages:** Mandarin, English, Malay, Tamil (all official); Hokkien; Cantonese; Teochew. **Religions:** Buddhist 34%, Muslim 14%, Taoist 11%, Catholic 7%, Hindu 5%, other Christian 11%, none 16%.

Geography: Total area: 269 sq mi, 697 sq km; **Land area:** 265 sq mi, 687 sq km. **Location:** Off tip of Malayan Peninsula in SE Asia. **Neighbors:** Nearest are Malaysia on N, Indonesia on S. **Topography:** A flat, formerly swampy island with 40 nearby islets. **Capital:** Singapore, 5,517,100.

Government: Type: Parliamentary republic. **Head of state:** Pres. Tony Tan Keng Yam; b. Feb, 7, 1940; in office: Sept. 1, 2011. **Head**

of gov.: Prime Min. Lee Hsien Loong; b. Feb. 10, 1952; in office: Aug. 12, 2004. **Defense budget:** $9.86 bil. **Active troops:** 72,500.

Economy: Industries: electronics, chemicals, financial services, oil drilling equip., petroleum refining, rubber proc. and rubber prods., processed food and beverages, ship repair, offshore platform constr. **Chief crops:** orchids, vegetables. **Natural resources:** fish. **Arable land:** 0.9%. **Livestock:** cattle: 200; chickens: 3.5 mil; goats: 670; pigs: 272,000. **Electricity prod.:** 44.4 bil kWh. **Labor force:** agric. 1.3%, industry 18.6%, services 80.1%. **Unemployment:** 2.8%.

Finance: Monetary unit: Dollar (SGD) (Sept. 2014: 1.25 = $1 U.S.). **GDP:** $339 bil; **per capita GDP:** $62,400; **GDP growth:** 4.1%. **Imports:** $373 bil; Malaysia 10.6%, China 10.3%, U.S. 10.2%, South Korea 6.8%, Japan 6.2%, Indonesia 3.3%, Saudi Arabia 4.5%, UAE 4.1%. **Exports:** $410.3 bil; Malaysia 12.3%, Hong Kong 10.9%, China 10.8%, Indonesia 10.6%, U.S. 5.5%, Japan 4.6%, Australia 4.2%, South Korea 4%. **Tourism:** $19 bil. **Budget:** $41.8 bil (incl. operational and development expenditures). **Total reserves less gold:** $272.9 bil. **Gold:** 4.1 mil oz t. **Inflation:** 2.4%.

Transport: Motor vehicles: 148.9 per 1,000 pop. **Civil aviation:** 63.7 bil pass.-mi; 9 airports. **Chief port:** Singapore.

Communications: TV sets: 213 per 1,000 pop. **Radios:** 689 per 1,000 pop. **Telephone lines** 36.4 per 100 pop. **Mobile:** 155.6 per 100 pop. **Internet:** 73%.

Health: Life expect.: 81.9 male; 87.1 female. **Births:** 8.1 per 1,000 pop. **Deaths:** 3.4 per 1,000 pop. **Natural inc.:** 0.47%. **Infant mortality:** 2.5 per 1,000 live births. **HIV:** NA.

Education: Compulsory: ages 6-11. **Literacy:** 96.8%.

Embassy: 3501 International Pl. NW 20008; 537-3100.

Website: www.gov.sg

Founded in 1819 by Sir Thomas Stamford Raffles, Singapore was a British colony until 1959, when it became autonomous within the Commonwealth. On Sept. 16, 1963, it joined with Malaya, Sarawak, and Sabah to form the Federation of Malaysia. Tensions between Malayans, dominant in the federation, and ethnic Chinese, dominant in Singapore, led to an accord under which Singapore became a separate nation, Aug. 9, 1965.

Singapore is one of the world's largest ports and a major manufacturing, banking, and commerce center with high standards in health, education, and housing. Immigrant workers from elsewhere in Asia hold many low-paying jobs.

Singapore has had only three prime mins.: Lee Kuan Yew, 1959-90; Goh Chok Tong, 1990-2004; and Lee Kuan Yew's son, Lee Hsien Loong, who took office, Aug. 12, 2004. The government, dominated by the People's Action Party (PAP), has taken strong actions to keep order and suppress dissent. Singapore's export-dependent economy was hit hard by the 2008 global downturn; GDP began growing again in 2010.

Slovakia
Slovak Republic

People: Population: 5,492,677. **Age distrib.:** <15: 15.5%; 65+: 13.8%. **Pop. density:** 295.7 per sq mi, 114.2 per sq km. **Urban:** 53.8%. **Ethnic groups:** Slovak 81%, Hungarian 9%, Roma 2%. **Languages:** Slovak (official), Hungarian, Roma. **Religions:** Roman Catholic 62%, Protestant 8%, Greek Catholic 4%, none 13%.

Geography: Total area: 18,933 sq mi, 49,035 sq km; **Land area:** 18,573 sq mi, 48,105 sq km. **Location:** In E central Europe. **Neighbors:** Poland on N, Hungary on S, Austria and Czech Rep. on W, Ukraine on E. **Topography:** Carpathian Mts. in N, fertile Danube plain in S. **Capital:** Bratislava, 403,212.

Government: Type: Parliamentary democracy. **Head of state:** Pres. Andrej Kiska; b. Feb. 2, 1963; in office: June 15, 2014. **Head of gov.:** Prime Min. Robert Fico; b. Sept. 15, 1964; in office: Apr. 4, 2012. **Local divisions:** 8 regions. **Defense budget:** $995 mil. **Active troops:** 15,850.

Economy: Industries: metal and metal prods.; food and beverages; electricity, gas, coke, oil, nuclear fuel; chemicals and manmade fibers; machinery; paper and printing. **Chief crops:** grains, potatoes, sugar beets, hops, fruits. **Natural resources:** brown coal and lignite, iron ore, copper and manganese ore, salt. **Crude oil reserves:** 9 mil bbls. **Arable land:** 29%. **Livestock:** cattle: 471,091; chickens: 11.4 mil; goats: 34,823; pigs: 631,464; sheep: 409,570. **Electricity prod.** (2012): 26.4 mil kWh. **Labor force:** agric. 3.5%, industry 27%, services 69.4%. **Unemployment:** 13.9%.

Finance: Monetary unit: Euro (EUR) (Sept. 2014: 0.76 = $1 U.S.). **GDP:** $133.4 bil; **per capita GDP:** $24,700; **GDP growth:** 0.8%. **Imports:** $78 bil; Germany 18.6%, Czech Republic 18%, Russia 9.9%, Austria 8%, Hungary 6.8%, Poland 6%, South Korea 4.1%. **Exports:** $82.7 bil; Germany 22.3%, Czech Republic 14.9%, Poland 8.8%, Hungary 7.8%, Austria 7%, France 5.6%, Italy 4.9%, UK 4.1%. **Tourism:** $2.6 bil. **Budget:** $35.7 bil. **Total reserves less gold:** $921.9 mil. **Gold** (2012): 1 mil oz t. **Inflation:** 1.4%.

Transport: Railways: 2,251 mi. **Motor vehicles:** 402.1 per 1,000 pop. **Civil aviation:** 21 airports. **Chief ports:** Bratislava, Komarno.

Communications: TV sets: 437 per 1,000 pop. **Radios:** 964 per 1,000 pop. **Telephone lines:** 17.7 per 100 pop. **Mobile:** 113.9 per 100 pop. **Internet:** 77.9%.

Health: Life expect.: 72.6 male; 80.5 female. **Births:** 10.1 per 1,000 pop. **Deaths:** 9.7 per 1,000 pop. **Natural inc.:** 0.04%. **Infant mortality:** 6.2 per 1,000 live births. **HIV:** NA.

Education: Compulsory: ages 6-14. **Literacy:** NA.

Embassy: 3523 International Ct. NW 20008; 237-1054.
Website: www.government.gov.sk

Slovakia was originally settled by Illyrian, Celtic, and Germanic tribes and was incorporated into Great Moravia in the 9th cent. It became part of Hungary in the 11th cent. Overrun by Czech Hussites in the 15th cent., it was restored to Hungarian rule in 1526. The Slovaks disassociated themselves from Hungary after WWI and joined the Czechs of Bohemia to form the Republic of Czechoslovakia, Oct. 28, 1918.

Germany invaded Czechoslovakia, 1939, and declared Slovakia independent. Slovakia rejoined Czechoslovakia in 1945. Czechoslovakia split into two separate states—the Czech Republic and Slovakia—on Jan. 1, 1993.

Slovakia joined the EU and NATO in 2004. The country adopted the euro currency Jan. 1, 2009. Its economy, previously one of Europe's fastest growing, was battered in the global recession 2008-09. Slow growth returned beginning in 2010. In Mar. 10, 2012, legislative elections, Robert Fico's social-democratic party, Smer (Direction), won 83 seats, the first time in Slovakia's post-communist history that a single party held the majority. Fico became prime min. Apr. 4, 2012. He ran for president in 2014 but lost a Mar. 29 runoff election to former businessman Andrej Kiska.

Slovenia
Republic of Slovenia

People: Population: 1,988,292. **Age distrib.:** <15: 13.4%; 65+: 17.9%. **Pop. density:** 255.6 per sq mi, 98.7 per sq km. **Urban:** 49.7%. **Ethnic groups:** Slovene 83%, Serb 2%, Croat 2%, Bosniak 1%. **Languages:** Slovenian (official); Serbo-Croatian; Italian, Hungarian (both official in some municipalities). **Religions:** Catholic 58%, Muslim 2%, Orthodox 2%, none 10%.

Geography: Total area: 7,827 sq mi, 20,273 sq km; **Land area:** 7,780 sq mi, 20,151 sq km. **Location:** In SE Europe. **Neighbors:** Italy on W, Austria on N, Hungary on NE, Croatia on SE, S. **Topography:** Mostly hilly; 42% forested. **Capital:** Ljubljana, 278,903.

Government: Type: Parliamentary republic. **Head of state:** Pres. Borut Pahor; b. Nov. 2, 1963; in office: Dec. 22, 2012. **Head of gov.:** Prime Min. Miro Cerar; b. Aug. 25, 1963; in office: Sept. 18, 2014. **Local divisions:** 200 municipalities, 11 urban municipalities. **Defense budget:** $474 mil. **Active troops:** 7,600.

Economy: Industries: ferrous metallurgy and aluminum prods., lead and zinc smelting, electronics (incl. military), automobiles, elec. power equip., wood prods., textiles, chemicals, machine tools. **Chief crops:** potatoes, hops, wheat, sugar beets, corn, grapes. **Natural resources:** lignite coal, lead, zinc, building stone, hydropower, forests. **Arable land:** 8.5%. **Livestock:** cattle: 460,063; chickens: 3.2 mil; goats: 26,351; pigs: 296,097; sheep: 114,152. **Electricity prod.** (2012): 14.8 bil kWh. **Labor force:** agric. 2.2%, industry 35%, services 62.8%. **Unemployment:** 8.8%.

Finance: Monetary unit: Euro (EUR) (Sept. 2014: 0.76 = $1 U.S.). **GDP:** $57.4 bil; **per capita GDP:** $27,400; **GDP growth:** –1.1%. **Imports:** $29.5 bil; Italy 16.5%, Germany 16.3%, Austria 10.4%, Croatia 4.8%, Hungary 4%. **Exports:** $28.7 bil; Germany 20%, Italy 12%, Austria 7.9%, Croatia 6.2%, France 4.8%, Russia 4.6%. **Tourism:** $2.8 bil. **Budget:** $21.6 bil. **Total reserves less gold:** $799.3 mil. **Gold:** 102,330 oz t. **Inflation:** 1.8%.

Transport: Railways: 763 mi. **Motor vehicles:** 577 per 1,000 pop. **Civil aviation:** 7 airports. **Chief port:** Koper.

Communications: TV sets: 371 per 1,000 pop. **Radios:** 409 per 1,000 pop. **Telephone lines:** 38.2 per 100 pop. **Mobile:** 110.2 per 100 pop. **Internet:** 72.7%.

Health: Life expect.: 74.2 male; 81.7 female. **Births:** 8.5 per 1,000 pop. **Deaths:** 11.3 per 1,000 pop. **Natural inc.:** –0.27%. **Infant mortality:** 4.0 per 1,000 live births. **HIV:** NA.

Education: Compulsory: ages 6-14. **Literacy:** 99.7%.
Embassy: 2410 California St. NW 20008; 386-6601.
Website: e-uprava.gov.si

The Slovenes settled in their current territory during the 6th to the 8th cent. They fell under German domination in the 9th cent. Modern Slovenian political history began after 1848 when the Slovenes, divided among several Austrian provinces, began their struggle for unification. In 1918 a majority of Slovenes became part of the Kingdom of Serbs, Croats, and Slovenes, later renamed Yugoslavia.

Slovenia declared independence June 25, 1991; joined the UN May 22, 1992; attained full membership in the EU and NATO in 2004; and adopted the euro Jan. 1, 2007. The Positive Slovenia party won the largest bloc of seats in Dec. 2011 parliamentary elections and formed a coalition with Janez Jansa as prime min. Jan. 28, 2012. After corruption charges against Jansa, a new coalition with Alenka Bratusek as prime min. took office in 2013. Bratusek resigned May 5, 2014, after losing her party's leadership. In early elections July 13, a new party headed by Miro Cerar won the most seats; Cerar became prime min. Aug. 25.

Solomon Islands

People: Population: 609,883. **Age distrib.:** <15: 36.2%; 65+: 4.1%. **Pop. density:** 56.4 per sq mi, 21.8 per sq km. **Urban:** 21.9%. **Ethnic groups:** Melanesian 95%, Polynesian 3%, Micronesian 1%. **Languages:** Melanesian pidgin (lingua franca in much of country), English (official but spoken by only 1%-2% of pop.), 120 indigenous langs. **Religions:** Protestant 74% (Church of Melanesia 33%, South

Seas Evangelical 17%, Seventh-day Adventist 11%, United Church 10%, Christian Fellowship Church 2%), Roman Catholic 19%, other Christian 4%.

Geography: Total area: 11,157 sq mi, 28,896 sq km; **Land area:** 10,805 sq mi, 27,986 sq km. **Location:** Melanesian Archipelago in W Pacific O. **Neighbors:** Nearest is Papua New Guinea to W. **Topography:** 10 large volcanic, rugged islands; 4 groups of smaller ones. **Capital:** Honiara, 73,302.

Government: Type: Parliamentary democracy. **Head of state:** Queen Elizabeth II, rep. by Gov.-Gen. Sir Frank Ofagioro Kabui; in office: July 7, 2009. **Head of gov.:** Prime Min. Gordon Darcy Lilo; b. Aug. 28, 1965; in office: Nov. 16, 2011. **Local divisions:** 9 provinces, 1 city. **Defense budget/active troops:** NA.

Economy: Industries: fish (tuna), mining, timber. **Chief crops:** cocoa, coconuts, palm kernels, rice, potatoes, vegetables, fruit. **Natural resources:** fish, forests, gold, bauxite, phosphates, lead, zinc, nickel. **Arable land:** 0.7%. **Livestock:** cattle: 10,000; chickens: 240,000; pigs: 54,500. **Electricity prod.:** 85 mil kWh. **Labor force:** agric. 75%, industry 5%, services 20%. **Unemployment:** 4.6%.

Finance: Monetary unit: Dollar (SBD) (Sept. 2014: 7.24 = $1 U.S.). **GDP:** $2 bil; **per capita GDP:** $3,400; **GDP growth:** 4%. **Imports** (2012): $446 mil; Singapore 27.2%, Australia 25.7%, China 7.1%, New Zealand 4.9%, Malaysia 4.8%. **Exports:** $493.1 mil; China 54.8%, Australia 17.5%. **Tourism:** $67 mil. **Budget:** $409.9 mil. **Total reserves less gold:** $491.5 mil. **Gold:** 24,040 oz t. **Inflation:** 6.7%.

Transport: Civil aviation: 1 airport. **Chief ports:** Honiara, Viru Harbor.

Communications: TV sets: 12 per 1,000 pop. **Radios:** 65 per 1,000 pop. **Telephone lines:** 1.4 per 100 pop. **Mobile:** 57.6 per 100 pop. **Internet:** 8%.

Health: Life expect.: 72.3 male; 77.6 female. **Births:** 26.3 per 1,000 pop. **Deaths:** 3.9 per 1,000 pop. **Natural inc.:** 2.25%. **Infant mortality:** 16.2 per 1,000 live births. **HIV:** NA.

Education: 6-11. **Literacy:** NA.

Permanent UN Mission: 800 Second Ave., Ste. 400L, New York, NY 10017; (212) 599-6192.
Website: www.pmc.gov.sb

The Solomon Isls. were sighted 1568 by an expedition from Peru. Britain established a protectorate in the 1890s over most of the group, inhabited by Melanesians. The islands saw major WWII battles. They achieved self-government, Jan. 2, 1976, and formal independence, July 7, 1978.

A coup attempt, June 5, 2000, sparked factional fighting in Honiara. To restore order after 3 years of lawlessness, a 2,225-member intervention force, led by Australia and authorized by the Pacific Isls. Forum, provided security 2003-05.

Following Apr. 2006 elections, parliament's choice of Snyder Rini as prime min. led to two days of rioting in Honiara over alleged influence-buying by the ethnic Chinese business community. Rini resigned Apr. 26, 2006, rather than face a no-confidence vote. Prime Min. Danny Philip, who was elected Aug. 25, 2010, dismissed finance min. Gordon Darcy Lilo and was forced to resign when a number of MPs abandoned the government in protest. The parliament then elected Lilo prime min., Nov. 16, 2011. A tropical storm caused severe flooding in Apr. 2014, leaving 22 dead and more than 50,000 affected.

Somalia
Federal Republic of Somalia

People: Population: 10,428,043. **Age distrib.:** <15: 44%; 65+: 2.3%. **Pop. density:** 43.1 per sq mi, 16.6 per sq km. **Urban:** 39.1%. **Ethnic groups:** Somali 85%, Bantu and other non-Somali 15%. **Languages:** Somali, Arabic (both official); Italian; English. **Religion:** Sunni Muslim (official).

Geography: Total area: 246,201 sq mi, 637,657 sq km; **Land area:** 242,216 sq mi, 627,337 sq km. **Location:** Occupies eastern horn of Africa. **Neighbors:** Djibouti, Ethiopia, Kenya on W. **Topography:** The coastline extends for 1,700 mi. Hills cover the N; center and S are flat. **Capital:** Mogadishu, 2,013,930.

Government: Type: In transition. **Head of state:** Pres. Hassan Sheikh Mohamud; b. Nov. 29, 1955; in office: Sept. 10, 2012. **Head of gov.:** Prime Min. Abdiwelli Sheikh Ahmed; b. 1959; in office: Dec. 21, 2013. **Local divisions:** 18 regions. **Defense budget:** NA. **Active troops:** 20,000.

Economy: Industries: few light industries incl. sugar refining, textiles, wireless communication. **Chief crops:** bananas, sorghum, corn, coconuts, rice, sugarcane, mangoes, sesame seeds, beans. **Natural resources:** uranium, largely unexploited reserves of iron ore, tin, gypsum, bauxite, copper, salt, nat. gas, likely oil reserves. **Arable land:** 1.8%. **Livestock:** cattle: 4.9 mil; chickens: 3.5 mil; goats: 11.6 mil; pigs: 3,700; sheep: 12.3 mil. **Electricity prod.:** 310 mil kWh. **Labor force:** agric. 71%, industry and services 29%. **Unemployment:** 7.6%.

Finance: Monetary unit: Shilling (SOS) (Sept. 2014: 1,198.98 = $1 U.S.). **GDP** (2010): $5.9 bil; **per capita GDP** (2010): $600; **GDP growth** (2010): 2.6%. **Imports** (2010): $1.3 bil; Djibouti 27.3%, India 13.2%, Kenya 7.1%, China 6.7%, Pakistan 6.4%, Oman 5.1%, UAE 5%, Yemen 4.4%. **Exports** (2012): $515.8 mil; UAE 51.7%, Yemen 18.1%, Oman 13%. **Budget:** NA. **Total reserves less gold:** NA. **Inflation:** NA.

Transport: Civil aviation: 6 airports. **Chief ports:** Berbera, Kismaayo.

Communications: TV sets: 26 per 1,000 pop. **Radios:** 242 per 1,000 pop. **Telephone lines:** 0.6 per 100 pop. **Mobile:** 49.4 per 100 pop. **Internet:** 1.5%.

Health: Life expect.: 49.6 male; 53.7 female. **Births:** 40.9 per 1,000 pop. **Deaths:** 13.9 per 1,000 pop. **Natural inc.:** 2.70%. **Infant mortality:** 100.1 per 1,000 live births. **HIV:** 0.5%.

Education: NA. **Literacy:** NA.

Permanent UN mission: 425 E. 61st St., Ste. 702, New York, NY, 10021; (212) 688-9410. (Embassy ceased operation in U.S. in 1991.)

Website: www.state.gov/p/af/ci/so/

British Somaliland (present-day North Somalia) was formed in the 19th cent., as was Italian Somaliland (now central and South Somalia). Italy lost its African colonies in WWII. British Somaliland gained independence, June 26, 1960, and by prearrangement, merged, July 1, with the UN Trust Territory of Somalia to create the independent Somali Republic.

On Oct. 15, 1969, Somalia's first civilian president, Abdirashid Ali Sharmarke, was assassinated. Six days later, Maj. Gen. Muhammad Siad Barre led a military coup. In 1970, he declared the country a socialist state—the Somali Democratic Republic.

Somalia has laid claim to Ogaden, the huge eastern region of Ethiopia, peopled mostly by Somalis. Some 11,000 Cuban troops with Soviet arms defeated Somali army troops and ethnic Somali rebels in Ethiopia, 1978. As many as 1.5 mil refugees entered Somalia. Guerrilla fighting in Ogaden continued until 1988, when a peace agreement was reached with Ethiopia.

Fighting in Mogadishu led Siad Barre to flee the capital, Jan. 1991. Fighting between rival factions caused 40,000 casualties, 1991-92, and by mid-1992 the civil war, drought, and banditry combined to produce a famine that threatened some 1.5 mil people.

U.S. troops and the UN worked to safeguard food delivery, 1991-93, resulting in significant U.S. and other casualties; a failed mission Oct. 3-4, 1993, left 18 U.S. troops and more than 500 Somalis dead. The U.S. withdrew its peacekeeping forces Mar. 25, 1994.

When the last UN troops pulled out, Mar. 3, 1995, armed factions controlled different regions. A joint police force in the capital could not stop the continued violence and food shortages. A peace deal Jan. 29, 2004, led to the Aug. 22 inauguration of a transitional parliament, Somalia's first legislature in 13 years. Meeting in Nairobi, Kenya, the parliament chose Abdullahi Yusuf Ahmed as president; he was sworn in Oct. 14.

Because Mogadishu was held by his rivals, Pres. Yusuf moved, July 26, 2005, to make his transitional capital at Jowhar; an interim parliament convened Feb. 26, 2006, at Baidoa. On June 5, an Islamist militia took over Mogadishu, defeating U.S.-backed secular warlords. The Islamists, calling themselves the Supreme Islamic Courts Council, held much of the central and southern regions. Pres. Yusuf escaped assassination, Sept. 18, 2006.

With aid from Ethiopian troops, transitional govt. forces recaptured Mogadishu in Dec. 2006. The UN Security Council authorized, Feb. 20, 2007, an African Union peacekeeping mission to Somalia (AMISOM). An upsurge of fighting in Mogadishu, Feb.-Apr., killed hundreds of people and caused 350,000 to flee. Bombings and kidnappings escalated in 2007-08; as a series of cease-fires failed, the increasing violence forced international aid workers to pull out, worsening a humanitarian crisis. Many of the attacks on transitional authorities and their allies were blamed on al-Shabaab, an al-Qaeda ally.

After Pres. Yusuf resigned Dec. 29, 2008, the transitional parliament, meeting in Djibouti Jan. 31, 2009, elected a moderate Islamist, Sheikh Sharif Sheikh Ahmed. Meanwhile, pirates carried out more than 200 attacks off the Horn of Africa in 2009. Pirates and Islamist insurgents continued to disrupt famine relief efforts in 2010-11, threatening an estimated 3.7 mil Somalis. Pressured by AMISOM forces, al-Shabaab pulled out of Mogadishu, Aug. 6, 2011, but continued to control much of southern Somalia. Despite continuing violence, Somali leaders met in Feb. 2012 for a second Somali national consultative constitutional conference in Garowe, Somalia, and signed Feb. 18 the Garowe II Principles, which established the conditions to install the caretaker government sworn in Aug. 20. The new parliament elected activist-professor Hassan Sheik Mohamud president Sept. 10. He survived an assassination attempt Sept. 12 and was sworn in Sept. 16, 2012. Bombings and other attacks by al-Shabaab, in Mogadishu and elsewhere, continued in 2013-14. The UN, Nov. 12, 2013, authorized a 4,000-troop increase in the AMISOM force, to more than 22,000. Al-Shabaab attacked the parliament building in Mogadishu in May 2014, briefly took over the presidential palace in July, and assassinated 5 members of parliament by Aug. 1. Al-Shabaab leader Ahmed Abdi Godane was killed by a U.S. airstrike Sept. 1, 2014.

South Africa
Republic of South Africa

People: Population: 48,375,645. **Age distrib.:** <15: 28.3%; 65+: 6.3%. **Pop. density:** 103.2 per sq mi, 39.8 per sq km. **Urban:** 64.3%. **Ethnic groups:** black African 79%, white 10%, colored 9%, Indian/Asian 3%. **Languages:** IsiZulu, IsiXhosa, Afrikaans, Sepedi, English, Setswana, Sesotho, Xitsonga, siSwati,

Tshivenda, isiNdebele (all official). **Religions:** Protestant 37% (Zionist Christian 11%, Pentecostal/Charismatic 8%, Methodist 7%, Dutch Reformed 7%, Anglican 4%), Catholic 7%, Muslim 2%, other Christian 36%, none 15%.

Geography: Total area: 470,693 sq mi, 1,219,090 sq km; **Land area:** 468,909 sq mi, 1,214,470 sq km. **Location:** At southern extreme of Africa. **Neighbors:** Namibia, Botswana, Zimbabwe on N; Mozambique, Swaziland on E; surrounds Lesotho. **Topography:** Large interior plateau reaches close to the country's 1,739-mi coastline. There are few major rivers or lakes. Rainfall is sparse in W, more plentiful in E. **Capital:** Pretoria (admin.), 1,990,690; Cape Town (legis.), 3,623,560; Bloemfontein (judicial), 495,998. **Cities (urban aggl.):** Johannesburg, 9,175,674; Durban, 2,889,916; Port Elizabeth, 1,172,354; Vereeniging, 1,147,295.

Government: Type: Republic. **Head of state and gov.:** Pres. Jacob Zuma; b. Apr. 12, 1942; in office: May 9, 2009. **Local divisions:** 9 provinces. **Defense budget:** $4.85 bil. **Active troops:** 62,100.

Economy: Industries: mining (world's largest producer of platinum, gold, chromium), auto assembly, metalworking, machinery, textiles, iron and steel, chemicals, fertilizer, foodstuffs. **Chief crops:** corn, wheat, sugarcane, fruits, vegetables. **Natural resources:** gold, chromium, antimony, coal, iron ore, manganese, nickel, phosphates, tin, rare earth elements, uranium, gem diamonds, platinum, copper, vanadium, salt, nat. gas. **Crude oil reserves:** 15 mil bbls. **Arable land:** 9.9%. **Livestock:** cattle: 14 mil; chickens: 200 mil; goats: 6.2 mil; pigs: 1.6 mil; sheep: 25 mil. **Electricity prod.:** 243.4 bil kWh. **Labor force:** agric. 9%, industry 26%, services 65%. **Unemployment:** 25%.

Finance: Monetary unit: Rand (ZAR) (Sept. 2014: 10.68 = $1 U.S.). **GDP:** $595.7 bil; **per capita GDP:** $11,500; **GDP growth:** 2%. **Imports:** $99.6 bil; China 14.4%, Germany 10.1%, Saudi Arabia 7.7%, U.S. 7.4%, Japan 4.6%, India 4.5%. **Exports:** $91.1 bil; China 11.8%, U.S. 8.3%, Japan 6%, Germany 5.7%, India 4.2%. **Tourism:** $9.2 bil. **Budget:** $105.5 bil. **Total reserves less gold:** $44.9 bil. **Gold:** 4 mil oz t. **Inflation:** 5.7%.

Transport: Railways: 12,547 mi. **Motor vehicles:** 191.3 per 1,000 pop. **Civil aviation:** 19.1 bil pass.-mi; 144 airports. **Chief ports:** Cape Town, Durban, Port Elizabeth, Richards Bay, Saldanha Bay.

Communications: TV sets: 195 per 1,000 pop. **Radios:** 443 per 1,000 pop. **Telephone lines:** 9.2 per 100 pop. **Mobile:** 147.5 per 100 pop. **Internet:** 48.9%.

Health: Life expect.: 50.5 male; 48.6 female. **Births:** 18.9 per 1,000 pop. **Deaths:** 17.5 per 1,000 pop. **Natural inc.:** 0.15%. **Infant mortality:** 41.6 per 1,000 live births. **HIV:** 19.1%.

Education: Compulsory: ages 7-15. **Literacy:** 94.3%.

Embassy: 3051 Massachusetts Ave. NW 20008; 232-4400.

Website: www.gov.za

Bushmen and KhoiKhoi were the original inhabitants. Bantus, including Zulu, Xhosa, Swazi, and Sotho, occupied the area from northeastern to southern South Africa before the 17th cent.

The Dutch settled the Cape of Good Hope area, beginning in the 17th cent. Britain seized the Cape, 1806. Many Dutch trekked north and founded two republics, Transvaal and Orange Free State. Diamonds were discovered, 1867, and gold, 1886. The Dutch (Boers) resented encroachments by the British and others; the Anglo-Boer War followed, 1899-1902. Britain won and created, May 31, 1910, the Union of South Africa, incorporating two British colonies (Cape and Natal) with Transvaal and Orange Free State. After a referendum, the Union became the Republic of South Africa, May 31, 1961, and withdrew from the Commonwealth.

Daniel Malan's National Party election in 1948 made the policy of separate development of the races, or apartheid, official. Under apartheid, blacks were severely restricted to certain occupations and paid less than whites for similar work. Only whites could vote or run for public office. Persons of Asian Indian ancestry and those of mixed race ("coloureds") had limited political rights.

Protests against apartheid were suppressed. At Sharpeville on Mar. 21, 1960, government troops killed 69 black protesters. At least 600 persons, mostly Bantus, were killed in 1976 anti-apartheid riots. In 1986, Nobel Peace Prize winner Bishop Desmond Tutu called for Western nations to apply sanctions against South Africa to force an end to apartheid. Pres. P. W. Botha offered blacks an advisory role in government starting in Apr. On May 19, South Africa attacked three neighboring countries—Zimbabwe, Botswana, Zambia—striking at guerrilla strongholds of the anti-apartheid African National Congress (ANC).

Some 2 mil South African black workers staged a strike, June 6-8, 1988. Pres. Botha, head of the government since 1978, resigned Aug. 14, 1989, and was replaced by F. W. de Klerk. In 1990 the government lifted its ban on the ANC. Anti-apartheid leader Nelson Mandela was freed Feb. 11 after more than 27 years in prison. In Feb. 1991, Pres. de Klerk pledged to end apartheid laws.

In 1993 negotiators agreed on basic principles for a new democratic constitution. South Africa's partially self-governing black territories, or "homelands," were incorporated into a national system of 9 provinces. The ANC won elections Apr. 26-29, 1994, making Mandela president. The Inkatha Freedom Party won control of the legislature in a mainly Zulu province. By then, fighting between the ANC and Inkatha (aided, during the apartheid era, by South African defense forces) had killed more than 14,000 people in the Zulu region.

A post-apartheid constitution became law Dec. 10, 1996. The ANC won elections, June 2, 1999, and ANC leader Thabo Mbeki became president. South Africa, Nov. 30, 2006, became the first African country to legalize same-sex marriage.

After Mbeki's former deputy president, Jacob Zuma, defeated him in a power struggle for the ANC leadership, Mbeki resigned his presidency, Sept. 21, 2008. Zuma became president after Apr. 22, 2009, elections; despite corruption charges, Zuma was reelected president by the National Assembly, May 21, 2014, following an ANC victory in May 7 parliamentary elections.

Thousands of miners struck for better wages at the Lonmin platinum mine near Marikana, NW of Johannesburg, Aug. 10, 2012, and strikes spread to mines owned by Anglo American Platinum, the world's largest platinum producer, the week of Sept. 10. Protests at the Lonmin mine left at least 10 dead, before police officers opened fire on protesters Aug. 16, killing 34 and wounding 78. A strike-ending wage agreement was reached with Lonmin Sept. 18, but demonstrations continued at Anglo American Platinum. A 5-month strike in 2014 against Lonmin, Anglo American Platinum, and Impala Platinum Holdings ended in June with a wage increase for 70,000 union workers.

Mandela died Dec. 5, 2013; more than 100 past or present heads of state, including U.S. Pres. Barack Obama, attended a memorial service Dec. 10, 2013, in the Johannesburg suburb of Soweto.

South Sudan
Republic of South Sudan

People: Population: 11,562,695. **Age distrib.:** <15: 45.8%; 65+: 2.1%. **Pop. density:** 46.5 per sq mi, 17.9 per sq km. **Urban:** 18.6%. **Ethnic groups:** Dinka, Nuer, Shilluk, Azande, Bari, Kakwa, Kuku, Murle, Mandari, Didinga, Ndogo, Bviri, Lndi, Anuak, Bongo, Lango, Dungotona, Acholi. **Languages:** English (official), Arabic (incl. Juba, Sudanese variants), regional langs. **Religions:** animist, Christian.

Geography: Total area: 248,777 sq mi, 644,329 sq km. **Location:** In NE Africa. **Neighbors:** Sudan on N, Uganda and Kenya on S, Ethiopia on E. **Topography:** The White Nile R. flows N through the center of the country. The river feeds the Sudd, a swampy area occupying more than 15% of the country's center; it is one of the world's largest wetlands. **Capital:** Juba, 306,569.

Government: Type: Republic. **Head of state and gov.:** Pres. Salva Kiir Mayardit; b. 1951; in office: July 9, 2011. **Local divisions:** 10 states. **Defense budget:** $714 mil. **Active troops:** 210,000.

Economy: Chief crops: sorghum, maize, rice, millet, wheat, gum arabic, sugarcane, fruits, sweet potatoes, sunflower, cotton, sesame, cassava, beans, peanuts. **Arable land:** NA. **Natural resources:** hydropower, gold, diamonds, petroleum, hardwoods, limestone, iron ore, copper, chromium ore, zinc, tungsten, mica, silver. **Labor force:** Vast majority of pop. relies on subsistence agriculture. **Unemployment:** NA.

Finance: Monetary unit: Pound (SSP) (Sept. 2014: 3.10 = $1 U.S.). **GDP:** $14.7 bil; **per capita GDP:** $1,400; **GDP growth:** 24.7%. **Budget:** $2.3 bil. **Total reserves less gold:** NA. **Inflation** (2010-11): 47.3%.

Transport: Railways: 154 mi. **Civil aviation:** 3 airports.
Telephone lines: 0.02 per 100 pop. **Mobile:** 25.3 per 100 pop.
Health: Life expect.: 59.0 male; 61.9 female. **Births:** 37.7 per 1,000 pop. **Deaths:** 8.4 per 1,000 pop. **Natural inc.:** 2.93%. **Infant mortality:** 68.2 per 1,000 live births. **HIV:** 2.2%.
Education: Compulsory: ages 6-13. **Literacy:** 27%.
Embassy: 1233 20th St. NW, Ste. 602, 20036; 293-7940.
Website: www.goss.org

South Sudan was a region of the Republic of the Sudan when that country became independent in 1956. Northerners (mostly Arab Muslims) dominated, while southerners (mostly black Africans who practiced Christianity or traditional religions) were marginalized. Southern Anya Nya rebels waged war against the north, 1955-72, until an agreement reached in Addis Ababa, Ethiopia, offered regional self-government for the south. Oil was discovered in the south through the north. South Sudan clashed with Sudanese rebels on its northern border and faced challenges of poverty, underdevelopment, and factional conflict.

Civil war broke out again in 1983, with southern rebels led by the Sudan People's Liberation Movement (SPLM). Fighting and related famine cost an estimated 2 mil lives and displaced millions of southerners. A peace accord was signed in 2005. A power-sharing agreement offered autonomy for southern Sudan and allowed for an independence referendum.

Almost 99% of southern Sudanese who voted in the referendum, Jan 9-15, 2011, supported secession. The UN Security Council, July 8, authorized 7,900 peacekeepers to the area. South Sudan attained full independence July 9, 2011, and was admitted to the UN, July 14. A 4-year interim deal on the division of oil revenues was reached Aug. 4 and another deal Sept. 27 on the transport of oil from the south through the north. South Sudan clashed with Sudanese rebels on its northern border and faced challenges of poverty, underdevelopment, and factional conflict.

Violence within South Sudan continued in 2013-14. Pres. Salva Kiir fired his entire cabinet July 23, 2013, including Vice Pres. Riek Machar. Heavy fighting broke out in Juba in Dec. 2013 between government troops and a rebel group led by Machar. Forces of Kiir and Machar (who belong to different ethnic groups) battled throughout the country in 2014, killing thousands and displacing more than 1 mil; cease-fire agreements in Jan. and May failed to hold.

Spain
Kingdom of Spain

People: Population: 47,737,941. **Age distrib.:** <15: 15.4%; 65+: 17.6%. **Pop. density:** 247.8 per sq mi, 95.7 per sq km. **Urban:** 79.4%. **Ethnic groups:** mixed Mediterranean and Nordic. **Languages:** Castilian Spanish (official), Catalan, Galician, Basque (all official regionally). **Religion:** Roman Catholic 94%.

Geography: Total area: 195,124 sq mi, 505,370 sq km. **Land area:** 192,657 sq mi, 498,980 sq km. **Location:** In SW Europe. **Neighbors:** Portugal on W; France, Andorra on N; Morocco to S. **Topography:** The interior is a high, arid plateau broken by mountain ranges and river valleys. The NW is heavily watered, the S has lowlands and a Medit. climate. **Capital:** Madrid, 6,132,670. **Cities (urban aggl.):** Barcelona, 5,206,828.

Government: Type: Parliamentary monarchy. **Head of state:** King Felipe VI; b. Jan. 30, 1968; in office: June 19, 2014. **Head of gov.:** Prime Min. Mariano Rajoy; b. Mar. 27, 1955; in office: Dec. 20, 2011. **Local divisions:** 17 autonomous communities, 2 autonomous cities. **Defense budget:** $11.59 bil. **Active troops:** 134,900.

Economy: Industries: textiles and apparel (incl. footwear), food and beverages, metals and metal manufactures, chemicals, shipbuilding, automobiles, machine tools, tourism, clay and refractory prods., footwear, pharmaceuticals. **Chief crops:** grain, vegetables, olives, wine grapes, sugar beets, citrus. **Natural resources:** coal, lignite, iron ore, copper, lead, zinc, uranium, tungsten, mercury, pyrites, magnesite, fluorspar, gypsum, sepiolite, kaolin, potash, hydropower. **Crude oil reserves:** 150 mil bbls. **Arable land:** 24.9%. **Livestock:** cattle: 5.7 mil; chickens: 138 mil; goats: 2.6 mil; pigs: 25.5 mil; sheep: 16.1 mil. **Electricity prod.** (2012): 276.5 bil kWh. **Labor force:** agric. 4.2%, industry 24%, services 71.7%. **Unemployment:** 25.2%.

Finance: Monetary unit: Euro (EUR) (Sept. 2014: 0.76 = $1 U.S.). **GDP:** $1.4 tril; **per capita GDP:** $30,100; **GDP growth:** –1.3%. **Imports:** $431 bil; Germany 11.8%, France 11.5%, Italy 6.7%, China 5.6%, Netherlands 5.4%, UK 4.1%. **Exports:** $458 bil; France 16.8%, Germany 10.8%, Italy 7.7%, Portugal 7.1%, UK 6.5%. **Tourism:** $60.4 bil. **Budget:** $597.3 bil. **Total reserves less gold:** $35.4 bil. **Gold:** 9.1 mil oz t. **Inflation:** 1.4%.

Transport: Railways: 9,503 mi. **Motor vehicles:** 573.2 per 1,000 pop. **Civil aviation:** 56.3 bil pass.-mi; 99 airports. **Chief ports:** Algeciras, Barcelona, Bilbao, Cartagena, Huelva, Tarragona, Valencia.

Communications: TV sets: 556 per 1,000 pop. **Radios:** 327 per 1,000 pop. **Telephone lines:** 40.7 per 100 pop. **Mobile:** 106.9 per 100 pop. **Internet:** 71.6%.

Health: Life expect.: 78.5 male; 84.7 female. **Births:** 9.9 per 1,000 pop. **Deaths:** 9.0 per 1,000 pop. **Natural inc.:** 0.09%. **Infant mortality:** 3.3 per 1,000 live births. **HIV:** 0.4%.
Education: Compulsory: ages 6-16. **Literacy:** 98.1%.
Embassy: 2375 Pennsylvania Ave. NW 20037; 452-0100.
Website: www.lamoncloa.gob.es

Settled by Iberians, Basques, and Celts, Spain was successively ruled (wholly or in part) by Carthage, Rome, and the Visigoths. Muslims invaded Iberia from N Africa in 711. Reconquest of the peninsula by Christians from the N laid the foundations of modern Spain. In 1469 the kingdoms of Aragon and Castile were united by the marriage of Ferdinand II and Isabella I. Moorish rule ended with the fall of Granada, 1492, the year Spain's large Jewish community was expelled.

Spain established a colonial empire after Columbus's 1492 "discovery" of America. Cortés conquered Mexico, and Pizarro conquered Peru. Spain also controlled the Netherlands and parts of Italy and Germany. Spain lost its American colonies in the early 19th cent. and Cuba, the Philippines, and Puerto Rico during the Spanish-American War, 1898.

Primo de Rivera became dictator, 1923. King Alfonso XIII revoked the dictatorship, 1930, but was forced into exile in 1931. A republic was proclaimed, which disestablished the church, curtailed its privileges, and secularized education. A Popular Front of socialists, Communists, republicans, and anarchists governed 1936-39.

Army officers under Francisco Franco revolted, 1936. Some 500,000 to 1 mil died before the war's end, Mar. 28, 1939. Franco was named caudillo, leader of the nation. Spain was officially neutral in WWII, but its cordial relations with fascist countries prompted its exclusion from the UN until 1955.

After Franco's death, Nov. 20, 1975, Prince Juan Carlos became king. In free elections, June 1977, moderates and democratic socialists won the most votes. The king thwarted a 1981 coup attempt by right-wing military officers. The Socialist Workers' Party, under Felipe González Márquez, won four consecutive general elections between 1982 and 1993 but lost to a coalition of conservative and regional parties, 1996. Conservative Prime Min. José María Aznar, who won a parliamentary majority in the 2000 election, openly supported the U.S.-led invasion of Iraq, Mar. 2003, against Spanish public opinion.

Islamic extremists bombed four commuter trains in central Madrid, Mar. 11, 2004, killing 191 people. The opposition Socialist Workers' Party won elections three days later, and Socialist leader José Luis Rodríguez Zapatero, who became prime min. Apr. 17, removed all 1,300 Spanish troops from Iraq. Spain legalized same-sex marriage in 2005.

Prime Min. Zapatero won a second term in 2008. Spain's banking, building, and tourism industries suffered during the worldwide financial crisis; in May 2010, as the budget deficit mounted and unemployment surged above 20%, the government introduced austerity measures to reassure international lenders. Mariano Rajoy's conservative Popular Party won elections Nov. 2011, and Rajoy became prime min. Dec. 20. Spain received a 100-bil-euro EU bailout for its ailing banks in 2012. Spain's unemployment rate surpassed 25% in 2012 and 26% in 2013, as GDP declined in both years.

An investigation into Luis Bárcenas, former national treasurer of the Popular Party, widened to include accusations of illegal financing among other party members, including Prime Min. Rajoy, Jan. 15, 2013. Juan Carlos abdicated in favor of his son, who became King Felipe VI, June 19, 2014. Felipe's sister, Princess Cristina, was charged, June 25, with tax fraud and money laundering in connection with an investigation of alleged embezzlement of public funds by her husband.

Catalonia and the Basque country were granted autonomy, Jan. 1980, following overwhelming approval in home-rule referendums. But Basque extremists pushed for independence. The Basque separatist group ETA carried out bombings that killed about 830 since 1968. ETA declared a cease-fire effective Mar. 24, 2006, after which the Spain agreed to formal peace talks. Negotiations broke down after ETA exploded a car bomb at the Madrid airport, Dec. 30, 2006, killing two. ETA declared a new unilateral cease-fire Oct. 20, 2011. In Catalonia, voters approved a plan for expanded home-rule, June 18, 2006. In 2014, Catalonia made preparations for a Nov. 9 referendum on independence, a vote whose legality was disputed by Spain's constitutional court. **Website:** web.gencat.cat.

The **Balearic Isls.** in the W Mediterranean, 1,927 sq mi, are a province of Spain; they include **Majorca** (Mallorca; capital Palma de Mallorca), **Minorca, Cabrera, Ibiza,** and **Formentera.** The **Canary Isls.,** 2,807 sq mi, in the Atlantic W of Morocco, form two provinces, and include the islands of Tenerife, Palma, Gomera, Hierro, Grand Canary, Fuerteventura, and Lanzarote; Las Palmas and Santa Cruz are thriving ports. More than 1,700 people died trying to get from Mauritania to the Canary Isls. in rickety boats, Jan.-June 2006.

Ceuta and **Melilla,** small Spanish enclaves on Morocco's Mediterranean coast, gained limited autonomy in Sept. 1994. In recent years, many undocumented African migrants—tens of thousands in 2014—seeking to reach European-controlled territory have attempted to cross the border between Morocco and the Spanish enclaves.

Spain has sought the return of Gibraltar, in British hands since 1704.

Sri Lanka
Democratic Socialist Republic of Sri Lanka

People: Population: 21,866,445. **Age distrib.:** <15: 24.7%; 65+: 8.7%. **Pop. density:** 876.3 per sq mi, 338.3 per sq km. **Urban:** 18.3%. **Ethnic groups:** Sinhalese 74%, Sri Lankan Moors 7%, Indian Tamil 5%, Sri Lankan Tamil 4%. **Languages:** Sinhala (official and national), Tamil (national), English (commonly used in govt). **Religions:** Buddhist (official) 69%, Muslim 8%, Hindu 7%, Christian 6%.

Geography: Total area: 25,332 sq mi, 65,610 sq km; **Land area:** 24,954 sq mi, 64,630 sq km. **Location:** In Indian O. off SE coast of India. **Neighbors:** India on NW. **Topography:** Coastal area and N half are flat; S central area is hilly and mountainous. **Capital:** Colombo, 704,227; Sri Jayewardenepura Kotte (legis.), 127,534; .

Government: Type: Republic. **Head of state and gov.:** Pres. Mahinda Rajapaksa; b. Nov. 18, 1945; in office: Nov. 19, 2005. **Local divisions:** 9 provinces. **Defense budget:** $1.79 bil. **Active troops:** 160,900.

Economy: Industries: rubber, tea, coconuts, tobacco and other agric. commodities proc.; telecom, insurance, banking; tourism, shipping; clothing, textiles; cement, petroleum refining. **Chief crops:** rice, sugarcane, grains, pulses, oilseed, spices, vegetables, fruit, tea, rubber, coconuts. **Natural resources:** limestone, graphite, mineral sands, gems, phosphates, clay, hydropower. **Arable land:** 19.9%. **Livestock:** cattle: 1.2 mil; chickens: 14.1 mil; goats: 385,000; pigs: 90,000; sheep: 9,300. **Electricity prod.:** 11.0 bil kWh. **Labor force:** agric. 31.8%, industry 25.8%, services 42.4%. **Unemployment:** 4.8%.

Finance: Monetary unit: Rupee (LKR) (Sept. 2014: 130.10 = $1 U.S.). **GDP:** $134.5 bil; **per capita GDP:** $6,500; **GDP growth:** 6.3%. **Imports:** $18 bil; India 22.7%, Singapore 8.8%, UAE 7.7%, China 7%, Iran 6.1%, Malaysia 4.5%. **Exports:** $10.4 bil; U.S. 20.4%, UK 9.9%, India 5.8%, Italy 4.7%, Belgium 4.3%, Germany 4.3%. **Tourism:** $1.7 bil. **Budget:** $12.6 bil. **Total reserves less gold:** $6.6 bil. **Gold:** 737,776 oz t. **Inflation:** 6.9%.

Transport: Railways: 900 mi. **Motor vehicles:** 44.7 per 1,000 pop. **Civil aviation:** 7.2 bil pass.-mi; 15 airports. **Chief port:** Colombo.

Communications: TV lines: 118 per 1,000 pop. **Radios:** 200 per 1,000 pop. **Telephone lines:** 12.7 per 100 pop. **Mobile:** 95.5 per 100 pop. **Internet:** 21.9%.

Health: Life expect.: 72.9 male; 80.0 female. **Births:** 16.2 per 1,000 pop. **Deaths:** 6.1 per 1,000 pop. **Natural inc.:** 1.02%. **Infant mortality:** 9.0 per 1,000 live births. **HIV:** <0.1%.

Education: Compulsory: ages 5-13. **Literacy:** 92.6%.
Embassy: 2148 Wyoming Ave. NW 20008; 483-4025.
Website: www.priu.gov.lk

The island was known to the ancient world as Taprobane (Greek for copper-colored) and later as Serendip (from Arabic). Colonists from N India subdued the indigenous Veddahs about 543 BCE; their descendants, the Buddhist Sinhalese, still form most of the population. Hindu descendants of Tamil immigrants from S India account for about one-fifth of the population.

Parts were occupied by the Portuguese in 1505 and the Dutch in 1658. The British seized the island in 1796. It became an independent member of the Commonwealth as Ceylon in 1948 before changing its name to Sri Lanka May 22, 1972.

Prime Min. Solomon W. R. D. Bandaranaike was assassinated Sept. 25, 1959. His widow, Sirimavo Bandaranaike, served as prime min. 1960-65, 1970-77, 1994-2000. In the 1970s, thousands of ultra-leftists were executed, while massive land reform and nationalization of foreign-owned plantations took place.

Tensions between Sinhalese and Tamil separatists erupted in the early 1980s and turned into a 20-year civil war that killed more than 60,000; another 20,000, mostly young Tamils, "disappeared" while in government custody.

Pres. Ranasinghe Premadasa was assassinated May 1, 1993, by a Tamil rebel. Mrs. Bandaranaike's daughter, Chandrika Bandaranaike Kumaratunga, became prime min. after Aug. 1994 general elections. Elected president Nov. 9, Kumaratunga appointed her mother prime min. Kumaratunga, who was injured in a suicide bomb attack at a campaign rally Dec. 18, 1999, won a second 6-year term three days later. In failing health, Mrs. Bandaranaike resigned Aug. 10 and died Oct. 10, 2000. A truce intended to bring an end to the civil war was signed Feb. 22, 2002. More than 31,000 died in the Dec. 26, 2004, Indian Ocean tsunami.

Prime Min. Mahinda Rajapaksa of the United People's Freedom Alliance won the 2005 presidential election (he was reelected in 2010). Thousands died during three years of fighting among government forces, paramilitary groups, and Tamil rebels beginning in Dec. 2005. About 7,000 noncombatants were killed Jan. 20-May 7, 2009. Tamil leader Vellupillai Prabhakaran was killed May 18-19, 2009, and Pres. Rajapaksa formally declared victory. The UN Human Rights Council, Mar. 27, 2014, voted to begin an investigation of possible war crimes during Sri Lanka's long civil conflict.

Sudan
Republic of the Sudan

(Pre-2012 data and communications statistics include South Sudan, which became independent July 9, 2011.)

People: Population: 35,482,233. **Age distrib.:** <15: 40.8%; 65+: 3.3%. **Pop. density:** 49.4 per sq mi, 19.1 per sq km. **Urban:** 33.6%. **Ethnic groups:** Sudanese Arab 70%, Fur, Beja, Nuba, Fallata. **Languages:** Arabic, English (both official); Nubian; Ta Bedawie; Fur. **Religions:** Sunni Muslim, small Christian minority.

Geography: Total area: 718,723 sq mi, 1,861,484 sq km; **Land area:** NA. **Location:** At E end of Sahara desert zone. **Neighbors:** Egypt on N; Libya, Chad, Central African Republic on W; Dem. Rep. of the Congo, South Sudan, Uganda, Kenya on S; Ethiopia, Eritrea on E. **Topography:** The N consists of Libyan Desert in W, and the mountainous Nubia Desert in E, with narrow Nile Valley between. Center contains large, fertile, rainy areas with fields, pastures, and forests. The S has rich soil, heavy rain. **Capital:** Khartoum, 4,999,790.

Government: Type: Federal republic with strong military influence. **Head of state and gov.:** Pres. Gen. Omar Hassan Ahmad al-Bashir; b. Jan. 1, 1944; in office: Oct. 16, 1993 (de facto since June 30, 1989). **Local divisions:** 17 states. **Defense budget:** $1.52 bil. **Active troops:** 244,300.

Economy: Industries: oil, cotton ginning, textiles, cement, edible oils, sugar, soap distilling, shoes, petroleum refining, pharmaceuticals, armaments. **Chief crops:** cotton, groundnuts, sorghum, millet, wheat, gum arabic, sugarcane, cassava, mangoes, papayas, bananas, sweet potatoes, sesame. **Natural resources:** petroleum; small reserves of iron ore, copper, chromium ore, zinc, tungsten, mica, silver, gold; hydropower. **Crude oil reserves:** 5 bil bbls (incl. South Sudan). **Arable land:** NA. **Livestock:** cattle: 41.9 mil; chickens: 45.6 mil; goats: 44 mil; sheep: 52.5 mil (incl. South Sudan). **Electricity prod.:** 8.9 bil kWh (incl. South Sudan). **Labor force:** agric. 80%, industry 7%, services 13%. **Unemployment:** 14.8%.

Finance: Monetary unit: Pound (SDG) (Sept. 2014: 5.68 = $1 U.S.). **GDP:** $90 bil; **per capita GDP:** $2,600; **GDP growth:** 3.9%. **Imports:** $5.9 bil; Macau 18.1%, India 8.8%, Saudi Arabia 7.9%, Egypt 6.7%, UAE 5.2%. **Exports:** $4.1 bil; UAE 63.2%, Saudi Arabia 9.2%, Ethiopia 5.3%. **Tourism:** $933 mil (incl. South Sudan). **Budget:** $6.8 bil. **Total reserves less gold:** $193 mil. **Inflation:** 37.4%.

Transport: Railways: 3,715 mi. **Motor vehicles:** 2.9 per 1,000 pop. **Civil aviation:** 712.1 mil pass.-mi (incl. South Sudan); 16 airports. **Chief port:** Port Sudan.

Communications: TV lines: 370 per 1,000 pop. **Radios:** 172 per 1,000 pop. **Telephone lines:** 1.1 per 100 pop. **Mobile:** 72.9 per 100 pop. **Internet:** 22.7%.

Health: Life expect.: 61.3 male; 65.5 female. **Births:** 30.0 per 1,000 pop. **Deaths:** 7.9 per 1,000 pop. **Natural inc.:** 2.21%. **Infant mortality:** 52.9 per 1,000 live births. **HIV:** 0.2%.

Education: 6-13. **Literacy:** 75.9%.
Embassy: 2210 Massachusetts Ave. NW 20008; 338-8565.
Website: www.presidency.gov.sd or www.state.gov/p/af/ci/su/
Northern Sudan, ancient Nubia, was settled by Egyptians in antiquity. The population was converted to Coptic Christianity in the 6th cent. Arab conquests brought Islam to the area in the 15th cent. In the 1820s, Egypt took over Sudan, defeating the last of the earlier empires, including the Fung. In the 1880s, Muhammad Ahmad, who called himself the Mahdi (leader of the faithful), and his followers, the dervishes, led a revolution. An Anglo-Egyptian force crushed the Mahdi's successors, 1898.

Sudan gained independence Jan. 1, 1956. In 1969, a Revolutionary Council took power, led by authoritarian Pres. Gaafar al-Nimeiry. He was overthrown, Apr. 6, 1985. Sudan held its first democratic parliamentary elections in 18 years in 1986. Brig. Omar Hassan Ahmad al-Bashir staged a bloodless military coup, toppling the elected government, June 30, 1989. He became president in 1993.

During 1955-72 and 1983-2005, rebels in the south (primarily Christians and followers of traditional religions) rebelled against government domination by mostly Arab-Muslim northern Sudan. War and related famine cost an estimated 2 mil lives. An accord ended the rebellion Jan. 9, 2005.

A rebellion in the Darfur region of western Sudan caused a new crisis, 2003-11. Marauding Arab militias, the *janjaweed*, reportedly acting in collusion with Sudanese government troops, looted and burned homes in Darfur and killed many African villagers. More than 7,000 African Union peacekeepers were ineffectual. Rebel and militia activities in Sudan and Chad led to border clashes and further attacks on civilians. By Sept. 2009, the Darfur war had killed about 300,000 people and displaced another 2.7 mil. A joint UN-African Union force of up to 26,000 peacekeepers (UNMIS) was deployed in Aug. 2007, followed by UNMISS upon South Sudan's independence, July 2011.

The Intl. Criminal Court in The Hague, Netherlands, issued two arrest warrants for Pres. Bashir—one in 2009 for war crimes and other crimes against humanity in Darfur, and another in 2010 for genocide, the first time it had ever accused a head of state of genocide. Bashir defied the calls for his arrest, and in Apr. 2010 won a new 5-year term in elections after his main challengers dropped out, alleging fraud.

After southern Sudanese voted overwhelmingly for secession, Jan. 9-15, 2011, South Sudan attained full independence July 9. Border disputes between Sudan and South Sudan ensued, though a 4-year interim deal on the division of oil revenues was reached Aug. 6, 2012, and an agreement was signed Sept. 27 to ship oil from the south through Sudan. Conflict in Darfur flared up again in 2014, including alleged attacks on civilians by pro-government militias.

Suriname
Republic of Suriname

People: Population: 573,311. **Age distrib.:** <15: 26.2%; 65+: 5.7%. **Pop. density:** 9.5 per sq mi, 3.7 per sq km. **Urban:** 66.1%. **Ethnic groups:** Hindustani (known locally as E Indian) 37%, Creole 31%, Javanese 15%, Maroon (descendants of escaped slaves) 10%, Amerindian 2%, Chinese 2%, white 1%. **Languages:** Dutch (official), English (widely spoken), Sranang Tongo (Surinamese), Caribbean Hindustani, Javanese. **Religions:** Hindu 27%, Protestant 25% (predominantly Moravian), Roman Catholic 23%, Muslim 20%, indigenous beliefs 5%.

Geography: Total area: 63,251 sq mi, 163,820 sq km; **Land area:** 60,232 sq mi, 156,000 sq km. **Location:** On N shore of S America. **Neighbors:** Guyana on W, Brazil on S, French Guiana on E. **Topography:** A flat Atlantic coast, where dikes permit agriculture. Inland is forest belt. To S, largely unexplored hills cover 75% of country. **Capital:** Paramaribo, 234,483 (figure is for district).

Government: Type: Constitutional democracy. **Head of state and gov.:** Pres. Désiré (Dési) Delano Bouterse; b. Oct. 13, 1945; in office: Aug. 12, 2010. **Local divisions:** 10 districts. **Defense budget** (2011): $55 mil. **Active troops:** 1,840.

Economy: Industries: mining, alumina prod., oil, lumber, food proc., fishing. **Chief crops:** rice, bananas, palm kernels, coconuts, plantains, peanuts. **Natural resources:** timber, hydropower, fish, kaolin, shrimp, bauxite, gold; small amounts of nickel, copper, platinum, iron ore. **Crude oil reserves:** 76.7 mil bbls. **Arable land:** 0.4%. **Livestock:** cattle: 58,700; chickens: 6 mil; goats: 4,000; pigs: 32,200; sheep: 5,250. **Electricity prod.:** 1.6 bil kWh. **Labor force:** agric. 8%, industry 14%, services 78%. **Unemployment:** 12.7%.

Finance: Monetary unit: Dollar (SRD) (Sept. 2014: 3.25 = $1 U.S.). **GDP:** $7.1 bil; **per capita GDP:** $12,900; **GDP growth:** 4.7%. **Imports:** $1.8 bil; U.S. 26%, Netherlands 16%, China 9.9%, UAE 8.1%, Antigua and Barbuda 6.7%, Netherlands Antilles 4.9%, Japan 4.3%. **Exports:** $2.5 bil; U.S. 25.7%, Belgium 17.4%, UAE 11.5%, Canada 10.3%, Guyana 5.8%, France 5.5%, Barbados 4.2%. **Tourism:** $84 mil. **Budget** (2010 est.): $939.7 mil. **Total reserves less gold:** $735.1 mil. **Gold:** 33,500 oz t. **Inflation:** 1.9%.

Transport: Motor vehicles: 227.2 per 1,000 pop. **Civil aviation:** 621.4 mil pass.-mi; 6 airports. **Chief ports:** Paramaribo, Wageningen. **Communications: TV sets:** 266 per 1,000 pop. **Radios:** 711 per 1,000 pop. **Telephone lines:** 15.8 per 100 pop. **Mobile:** 127.3 per 100 pop. **Internet:** 37.4%.

Health: Life expect.: 69.3 male; 74.2 female. **Births:** 16.7 per 1,000 pop. **Deaths:** 6.1 per 1,000 pop. **Natural inc.:** 1.06%. **Infant mortality:** 27.1 per 1,000 live births. **HIV:** 0.9%.
Education: Compulsory: ages 7-12. **Literacy:** 95.6%.
Embassy: 4301 Connecticut Ave. NW, Ste. 460, 20008; 244-7488.
Website: www.gov.sr or www.surinameembassy.org
The Netherlands acquired Suriname in 1667 from Britain, in exchange for New Netherland (New York). The 1954 Dutch constitution raised the colony to a level of equality with the Netherlands and the Netherlands Antilles. Independence was granted Nov. 25, 1975. Some 40% of the population (mostly E Indians, who opposed independence) immigrated to the Netherlands in the months before independence.

Désiré (Dési) Bouterse, who masterminded coups in 1982 and 1990, was declared president by parliament, July 19, 2010; as he took office Aug. 12, he was facing trial in Suriname on charges of having executed 15 political opponents in 1982, and he had been convicted in absentia in the Netherlands, 1999, for drug trafficking. The U.S. State Dept. has labeled Suriname a transshipment point for cocaine trafficking. To repair its reputation, Suriname signed the UN-supported Container Control Programme (CCP), Aug. 23, 2012, to ensure better inspection of shipping containers in its ports. Bouterse's son Dino, arrested in Panama in Aug. 2013, was extradited to the U.S. to face drug trafficking and other charges.

Swaziland
Kingdom of Swaziland

People: Population: 1,419,623. **Age distrib.:** <15: 36.5%; 65+: 3.8%. **Pop. density:** 213.7 per sq mi, 82.5 per sq km. **Urban:** 21.3%. **Ethnic groups:** African 97%, European 3%. **Languages:** English (used in govt.), siSwati (both official). **Religions:** Zionist 40%, Roman Catholic 20%, Muslim 10%, other (incl. Anglican, Baha'i, Methodist, Mormon, Jewish) 30%.

Geography: Total area: 6,704 sq mi, 17,364 sq km; **Land area:** 6,643 sq mi, 17,204 sq km. **Location:** In southern Africa, near Indian O. coast. **Neighbors:** South Africa on N, W, S; Mozambique on E. **Topography:** Descends W-E in broad belts, becoming more arid in low veld region, then rising to plateau in E. **Capital:** Mbabane (admin.), 65,990; Lobamba (legis.).

Government: Type: Monarchy. **Head of state:** King Mswati III; b. Apr. 19, 1968; in office: Apr. 25, 1986. **Head of gov.:** Prime Min. Barnabas Sibusiso Dlamini; b. May 15, 1942; in office: Oct. 23, 2008. **Local divisions:** 4 districts. **Defense budget/active troops:** NA.

Economy: Industries: coal, wood pulp, sugar, soft drink concentrates, textiles and apparel. **Chief crops:** sugarcane, cotton, corn, tobacco, rice, citrus, pineapples, sorghum, peanuts. **Natural resources:** asbestos, coal, clay, cassiterite, hydropower, forests, small gold and diamond deposits, quarry stone, talc. **Arable land:** 10.2%. **Livestock:** cattle: 635,000; chickens: 3.7 mil; goats: 270,000; pigs: 35,000; sheep: 36,000. **Electricity prod.:** 415 mil kWh. **Labor force:** agric. 70%. **Unemployment:** 22.5%.

Finance: Monetary unit: Lilangeni (SZL) (Sept. 2014: 10.68 = $1 U.S.). **GDP:** $6.3 bil; **per capita GDP:** $5,700; **GDP growth:** 0%. **Imports:** $1.5 bil. **Exports:** $1.6 bil. **Tourism:** $30 mil. **Budget:** $1.3 bil. **Total reserves less gold:** $841.9 mil. **Inflation:** 5.6%.

Transport: Railways: 187 mi. **Civil aviation:** 2 airports.
Communications: TV sets: 37 per 1,000 pop. **Radios:** 362 per 1,000 pop. **Telephone lines:** 3.7 per 100 pop. **Mobile:** 71.5 per 100 pop. **Internet:** 24.7%.

Health: Life expect.: 51.0 male; 50.0 female. **Births:** 25.2 per 1,000 pop. **Deaths:** 13.8 per 1,000 pop. **Natural inc.:** 1.14%. **Infant mortality:** 54.8 per 1,000 live births. **HIV:** 27.4%.
Education: Compulsory: ages 6-12. **Literacy:** 87.5%.
Embassy: 1712 New Hampshire Ave. NW 20009; 234-5002.
Website: www.gov.sz
The royal house of Swaziland, one of Africa's last ruling dynasties, traces back 400 years. The Zulus drove the Swazis, a Bantu people, to Swaziland from lands to the N, 1820. Britain and Transvaal (later part of South Africa) later guaranteed their autonomy, and Britain assumed control after 1903. Independence came Sept. 6, 1968. In 1973, the king repealed the constitution and assumed full powers.

A new constitution banning political parties took effect Oct. 13, 1978. Under a revised constitution effective Feb. 8, 2006, nonpartisan parliamentary elections were held Sept. 19, 2008. An attempt to unite various Swazi pro-democracy groups under the banner of the People's United Democratic Movement (PUDEMO) in 2012 failed. The AIDS crisis and the huge gap between rich and poor have fueled student and labor unrest in recent years, but the UN reported July 30, 2013, that AIDS-related deaths in Swaziland had fallen drastically due to the use of antiretroviral therapy. Parliamentary elections were again held Sept. 20, 2013, but the monarch retained absolute power.

Sweden
Kingdom of Sweden

People: Population: 9,723,809. **Age distrib.:** <15: 16.9%; 65+: 19.8%. **Pop. density:** 61.4 per sq mi, 23.7 per sq km. **Urban:** 85.7%. **Ethnic groups:** indigenous Swedes, Finns, Sami; foreign-born or immigrant Finns, Yugoslavs, Danes, Norwegians, Greeks, Turks. **Languages:** Swedish (official), small Sami- and Finnish-speaking minorities. **Religions:** Lutheran 87%, other (incl. Roman Catholic, Orthodox, Baptist, Muslim, Jewish, Buddhist) 13%.

Geography: Total area: 173,860 sq mi, 450,295 sq km; **Land area:** 158,431 sq mi, 410,335 sq km. **Location:** On Scandinavian Peninsula in N Europe. **Neighbors:** Norway on W, Denmark on S (across Kattegat), Finland on E. **Topography:** Mountains along NW border cover 25% of Sweden; flat or rolling terrain covers central and southern areas, which include several large lakes. **Capital:** Stockholm, 1,463,750.

Government: Type: Constitutional monarchy. **Head of state:** King Carl XVI Gustaf; b. Apr. 30, 1946; in office: Sept. 19, 1973. **Head of gov.:** Prime Min. Stefan Löfven; b. 1957; in office: Oct. 3, 2014. **Local divisions:** 21 counties. **Defense budget:** $6.63 bil. **Active troops:** 15,300.

Economy: Industries: iron and steel, precision equip. (bearings, radio and phone parts, armaments), wood pulp and paper prods., processed foods, motor vehicles. **Chief crops:** barley, wheat, sugar beets. **Natural resources:** iron ore, copper, lead, zinc, gold, silver, tungsten, uranium, arsenic, feldspar, timber, hydropower. **Arable land:** 6.4%. **Livestock:** cattle: 1.5 mil; chickens: 8.6 mil; pigs: 1.4 mil; sheep: 576,769. **Electricity prod.** (2012): 162.9 bil kWh. **Labor force:** agric. 1.1%, industry 28.2%, services 70.7%. **Unemployment:** 8%.

Finance: Monetary unit: Krona (SEK) (Sept. 2014: 7.01 = $1 U.S.). **GDP:** $393.8 bil; **per capita GDP:** $40,900; **GDP growth:** 0.9%. **Imports:** $158 bil; Germany 17.4%, Denmark 8.5%, Norway 8.4%, UK 6.5%, Netherlands 6.4%, Russia 5.6%, Finland 5.1%, China 4.9%, France 4.2%. **Exports:** $181.5 bil; Norway 10.4%, Germany 10.3%, UK 8.1%, Finland 6.8%, Denmark 6.7%, Netherlands 5.5%, U.S. 5.5%, Belgium 5%, France 4.8%. **Tourism:** $11.5 bil. **Budget:** $294.7 bil. **Total reserves less gold:** $60.5 bil. **Gold:** 4 mil oz t. **Inflation:** 0%.

Transport: Railways: 7,228 mi. **Motor vehicles:** 557.3 per 1,000 pop. **Civil aviation:** 29.4 bil pass.-mi (incl. Denmark, Norway); 149 airports. **Chief ports:** Brofjorden, Göteborg, Helsingborg, Karlshamn, Lulea, Malmö, Stockholm, Trelleborg, Visby.

Communications: TV sets: 551 per 1,000 pop. **Radios:** 931 per 1,000 pop. **Telephone lines:** 40.6 per 100 pop. **Mobile:** 124.4 per 100 pop. **Internet:** 94.8%.

Health: Life expect.: 80.0 male; 83.9 female. **Births:** 11.9 per 1,000 pop. **Deaths:** 9.5 per 1,000 pop. **Natural inc.:** 0.25%. **Infant mortality:** 2.6 per 1,000 live births. **HIV:** NA.

Education: Compulsory: ages 7-16. **Literacy:** 99%.

Embassy: 2900 K St. NW 20007; 467-2600.

Website: www.sweden.se

The Swedes have lived in present-day Sweden for at least 5,000 years, longer than nearly any other European people have lived in their present-day homelands. Gothic tribes from Sweden played a major role in the disintegration of the Roman Empire. Other Swedes helped create the first Russian state in the 9th cent.

The Swedes were Christianized from the 11th cent., and a strong centralized monarchy developed. The Riksdag, the first European parliament to represent all classes of society, was first called in 1435.

A revolt led by Gustavus I in 1521-23 freed Sweden from Danish rule (dating from 1397); he built up the government and military and established the Lutheran Church. In the 17th cent. Sweden was a major European power, gaining most of the Baltic seacoast. The Napoleonic wars, 1799-1815, in which Sweden acquired Norway (it became independent 1905), were the last in which Sweden participated. Armed neutrality was maintained in both world wars.

Social Democrats have governed Sweden for most of the period since World War II. Prime Min. Olof Palme was shot to death in Stockholm, Feb. 28, 1986, and Christer Pettersson was found guilty in 1988. He was sentenced to life in prison, but his conviction was overturned on appeal in 1989 for lack of evidence.

Swedish voters approved EU membership in Nov. 1994, and Sweden entered the EU, Jan. 1, 1995.

A center-right alliance led by Fredrik Reinfeldt defeated the Social Democrats in Sept. 2006 elections. Parliament voted Apr. 1, 2009, to legalize same-sex marriage. The 2008-09 global recession led to a decline in Swedish exports, especially cars and trucks, but the economy began recovering in mid-2009. Reinfeldt's center-right bloc won a renewed mandate in Sept. 2010 parliamentary elections. The Social Democrats won the largest bloc of seats in Sept. 14, 2014, parliamentary elections, and Stefan Löfven became prime minister, heading a center-left government, Oct. 3.

Switzerland
Swiss Confederation

People: Population: 8,061,516. **Age distrib.:** <15: 15.1%; 65+: 17.5%. **Pop. density:** 522 per sq mi, 201.6 per sq km. **Urban:** 73.8%. **Ethnic groups:** German 65%, French 18%, Italian 10%, Romansch 1%. **Languages:** German, French, Italian (all official); Portuguese; Albanian; Serbo-Croatian; Spanish; English; Romansch (official). **Religions:** Roman Catholic 38%, Protestant 27%, Muslim 5%, other Christian 6%, none 21%.

Geography: Total area: 15,937 sq mi, 41,277 sq km; **Land area:** 15,443 sq mi, 39,997 sq km. **Location:** In Alps Mts. in central Europe. **Neighbors:** France on W; Italy on S; Liechtenstein, Austria

on E; Germany on N. **Topography:** The Alps cover 60% of land area; the Jura, near France, 10%. Running in-between, NE-SW, are midlands, 30%. **Capital:** Bern, 357,609. **Cities (urban aggl.):** Zürich, 1,233,760; Geneva, 551,264.

Government: Type: Federal republic in structure (formally a confederation). **Head of state and gov.:** President chosen on rotating basis from among 7-member Federal Council for 1-year term. **Local divisions:** 26 cantons. **Defense budget:** $5.04 bil. **Active troops:** 22,650.

Economy: Industries: machinery, chemicals, watches, textiles, precision instruments, tourism, banking, insurance. **Chief crops:** grains, fruits, vegetables. **Natural resources:** hydropower potential, timber, salt. **Arable land:** 10.2%. **Livestock:** cattle: 1.6 mil; chickens: 10.1 mil; goats: 90,000; pigs: 1.5 mil; sheep: 410,000. **Electricity prod.** (2012): 65.5 bil kWh. **Labor force:** agric. 3.4%, industry 23.4%, services 73.2%. **Unemployment:** 4.2%.

Finance: Monetary unit: Franc (CHF) (Sept. 2014: 0.92 = $1 U.S.). **GDP:** $371.2 bil; **per capita GDP:** $54,800; **GDP growth:** 2%. **Imports:** $200.5 bil; Germany 28.2%, Italy 10.5%, France 8.5%, U.S. 6.1%, China 5.8%, Austria 4.4%. **Exports:** $229.2 bil; Germany 18.5%, U.S. 11.6%, Italy 7.6%, France 7%, UK 5.7%. **Tourism:** $16.5 bil. **Budget:** $208.5 bil (federal, cantonal, and municipal). **Total reserves less gold:** $496 bil. **Gold:** 33.4 mil oz t. **Inflation:** −0.2%.

Transport: Railways: 3,030 mi. **Motor vehicles:** 594.3 per 1,000 pop. **Civil aviation:** 26.9 bil pass.-mi; 40 airports. **Chief port:** Basel.

Communications: TV sets: 594 per 1,000 pop. **Radios:** 1,004 per 1,000 pop. **Telephone lines:** 57.9 per 100 pop. **Mobile:** 133.8 per 100 pop. **Internet:** 86.7%.

Health: Life expect.: 80.1 male; 84.8 female. **Births:** 10.5 per 1,000 pop. **Deaths:** 8.1 per 1,000 pop. **Natural inc.:** 0.24%. **Infant mortality:** 3.7 per 1,000 live births. **HIV:** 0.4%.

Education: Compulsory: ages 7-15. **Literacy:** 99%.

Embassy: 2900 Cathedral Ave. NW 20008; 745-7900.

Website: www.ch.ch

Switzerland, the former Roman province of Helvetia, traces its modern history to 1291, when three cantons created a defensive league. Other cantons were subsequently admitted to the Swiss Confederation, which obtained its independence from the Holy Roman Empire through the Peace of Westphalia (1648). The cantons were joined under a federal constitution in 1848.

Switzerland has maintained an armed neutrality since 1815 and has not been involved in a foreign war since 1515. It is the seat of many UN and other international agencies but only became a full UN member on Sept. 10, 2002.

Switzerland is a world banking center. The government announced, Mar. 1997, a $4.7 bil fund to compensate victims of the Nazi Holocaust and other catastrophes. Swiss banks agreed Aug. 12, 1998, to pay $1.25 bil in reparations. A June 2002 referendum decriminalized abortion. Two more referendums in 2005 harmonized travel, asylum, law enforcement, and labor policies with the EU; more rights for same-sex couples were also endorsed June 5.

The Swiss government bailed out the troubled banking giant UBS during the international financial crisis in Oct. 2008. U.S. tax authorities pressured UBS Jan. 2009 to close some 19,000 hidden offshore accounts and to disclose in Aug. data on accounts for over 4,400 U.S. clients. In a Nov. 2009 referendum reflecting rising anti-Muslim sentiment, voters approved a constitutional ban on construction of new minarets on mosques. Beginning in Sept. 2011, Switzerland essentially pegged its currency at 1.20 Swiss francs per euro to help economic growth by keeping the franc from appreciating in value and making exports too expensive. In a Feb. 9, 2014, referendum, voters narrowly approved a measure requiring government quotas limiting immigration within 3 years.

Syria
Syrian Arab Republic

People: Population: 22,597,531. **Age distrib.:** <15: 33.2%; 65+: 3.9%. **Pop. density:** 318.7 per sq mi, 123.1 per sq km. **Urban:** 57.3%. **Ethnic groups:** Arab 90%; Kurds, Armenians, and other 10%. **Languages:** Arabic (official), Kurdish, Armenian, Aramaic, Circassian (widely understood). **Religions:** Muslim 87% (official; incl. Sunni 74%; and Alawi, Ismaili, Shia 13%), Christian 10%, Druze 3%.

Geography: Total area: 71,498 sq mi, 185,180 sq km; **Land area:** 70,900 sq mi, 183,630 sq km. **Location:** Middle East, at E end of Medit. Sea. **Neighbors:** Lebanon, Israel on W; Jordan on S; Iraq on E; Turkey on N. **Topography:** A short Medit. coastline stretches E and S with fertile lowlands and plains, alternating with mountains and large desert areas. **Capital:** Dimashq (Damascus), 2,573,840 (excl. refugees). **Cities (urban aggl.):** Halab (Aleppo), 3,518,721; Hims (Homs), 1,603,754 (excl. refugees).

Government: Type: Republic under authoritarian regime. **Head of state:** Pres. Bashar al-Assad; b. Sept. 11, 1965; in office: July 17, 2000. **Head of gov.:** Prime Min. Wael al-Halqi; in office: Aug. 9, 2012. **Local divisions:** 14 provinces. **Defense budget:** NA. **Active troops:** 178,000.

Economy: Industries: petroleum, textiles, food proc., beverages, tobacco, phosphate rock mining, cement. **Chief crops:** wheat, barley, cotton, lentils, chickpeas, olives, sugar beets. **Natural resources:** petroleum, phosphates, chrome and manganese ores, asphalt, iron ore, rock salt, marble, gypsum, hydropower. **Crude oil reserves:** 2.5 bil bbls. **Arable land:** 25.4%. **Livestock:** cattle: 830,000; chickens: 20 mil; goats: 2 mil; sheep: 14 mil. **Electricity prod.:** 38.8 bil kWh. **Labor force:** agric. 17%, industry 16%, services 67%. **Unemployment:** 8.3%.

Finance: Monetary unit: Pound (SYP) (Sept. 2014: 154.00 = $1 U.S.). **GDP** (2011): $107.6 bil; **per capita GDP** (2011): $5,100; **GDP growth** (2011): −2.3%. **Imports:** $8.9 bil; Saudi Arabia 22.8%, UAE 11.2%, Iran 8.3%, China 7.3%, Iraq 6.8%. **Exports:** $2.7 bil; Iraq 58.4%, Saudi Arabia 9.7%, Kuwait 6.4%, UAE 5.5%, Libya 4.1%. **Tourism:** $1.8 bil. **Budget:** $7.6 bil. **Total reserves less gold** (2010): $19.5 bil. **Gold** (2010): 830,000 oz t. **Inflation** (2011-12): 36.7%.

Transport: Railways: 1,275 mi. **Motor vehicles:** 84.4 per 1,000 pop. **Civil aviation:** 1.1 bil pass.-mi; 29 airports. **Chief ports:** Baniyas, Latakia, Tartus.

Communications: TV sets: 192 per 1,000 pop. **Radios:** 267 per 1,000 pop. **Telephone lines:** 20.2 per 100 pop. **Mobile:** 56 per 100 pop. **Internet:** 26.2%.

Health: Life expect.: 73.0 male; 77.9 female. **Births:** 22.5 per 1,000 pop. **Deaths:** 3.7 per 1,000 pop. **Natural inc.:** 1.88%. **Infant mortality:** 14.2 per 1,000 live births. **HIV:** NA.

Education: Compulsory: ages 6-14. **Literacy:** 86.4%.

Embassy: 2215 Wyoming Ave. NW 20008; 232-6313.

Website: parliament.sy

Syria was the center of the Seleucid Empire but later was absorbed into the Roman and Arab empires. Ottoman rule prevailed for four cents., until the end of WWI.

The state of Syria was formed from former Turkish districts, separated by the Treaty of Sevres, 1920, and divided into the states of Syria and Greater Lebanon. Both were administered under a French League of Nations mandate, 1920-41. The occupying French proclaimed Syria a republic Sept. 16, 1941; independence came Apr. 17, 1946. Syria joined the Arab invasion of Israel in 1948.

Syria belonged to the United Arab Republic from Feb. 1958 to Sept. 1961. The Socialist Baath party seized power Mar. 1963 and became the only legal party. The Alawite minority has dominated the government.

In the June 1967 Arab-Israeli war, Israel seized and occupied the Golan Heights, from which Syria had shelled Israeli settlements. On Oct. 6, 1973, Syria and Egypt attacked Israel but failed to recapture the Golan Heights. Syrian troops entered Lebanon in 1976, during the Lebanese civil war, and remained a strong presence in the country. They fought Palestinian guerrillas and, later, Christian militiamen. Syria sided with Iran during the Iran-Iraq war, 1980-88.

Thousands died in the city of Hama Feb. 1982 when government forces crushed a Muslim Brotherhood uprising. Following Israel's invasion of Lebanon, June 6, 1982, Israeli planes destroyed 17 Syrian antiaircraft missile batteries in the Bekaa Valley, June 9, and some 25 Syrian planes. Israel and Syria agreed to a cease-fire June 11. Syria condemned the Aug. 1990 Iraqi invasion of Kuwait and sent troops to help Allied forces in the Gulf War.

Hafez al-Assad, president of Syria since 1971, died June 10, 2000, and was succeeded by his son Bashar al-Assad. Following the U.S.-led invasion of Iraq, Mar. 2003, hundreds of thousands of Iraqi refugees flooded into Syria. The U.S. pressured Syria to rein in extremists and deny safe haven to fugitive Iraqi leaders. Israeli planes hit an alleged terrorist camp near Damascus Oct. 4, 2003. The U.S. imposed limited sanctions on Syria, May 11, 2004.

Syria denied responsibility for a truck bomb that killed former Lebanese Prime Min. Rafik al-Hariri in Beirut in Feb. 2005. Syria aided Hezbollah fighters in their conflict with Israel and gave about 180,000 Lebanese temporary refuge when Israeli armed forces targeted Hezbollah in Lebanon, July-Aug. 2006.

On Sept. 6, 2007, Israel bombed a secret site in N Syria where the Israelis believed Syria and North Korea were developing a nuclear facility; both countries denied the claim. The Assad regime used troops and tanks to enforce control during Arab Spring demonstrations in Mar. 2011, but the conflict escalated into outright rebellion. The Intl. Committee of the Red Cross declared the conflict a civil war, July 15, 2012. Various armed opposition groups fought against Assad's forces, and sometimes against each other, for control of territory. The Natl. Coalition for Syrian Revolutionary and Opposition Forces, including a number of opposition groups, was formed Nov. 11, 2012, and gained international support.

On Jan. 30, 2013, Israel bombed a convoy in Damascus allegedly carrying missiles to Hezbollah forces in Lebanon, which backed Assad. Although rebel leaders agreed to peace talks in Feb., they and the Assad regime continued their attacks throughout 2013, killing both armed and unarmed civilians. The U.S. announced Feb. 28 that it would send more than $60 mil in humanitarian aid to Syrian rebels. International intelligence communities announced in May that there was increasing evidence that Assad had already used chemical and biological weapons against his own people during the conflict. The EU May 28 lifted an arms embargo prohibiting weapons shipments to rebel fighters. Findings that Assad was using chemical weapons led to U.S. Pres. Barack Obama's June 13 decision to supply military support to rebel groups, who had been losing ground to the Assad regime. A chemical attack on an opposition-controlled Damascus suburb Aug. 21, 2013, killed more than 1,400. Assad and the rebels accused each other of the attack. In early Sept., Pres.

Obama pressed Congress to approve punitive military strikes but agreed to negotiate with Russia over its Sept. 9, 2013, proposal that Syrian chemical weapons be placed under international control. Russian-U.S. negotiators reached an agreement requiring Syria to relinquish its chemical weapons; the agreement was reinforced by a UN Security Council resolution Sept. 27. Inspectors arrived in Syria Oct. 1 and the last known chemical weapons were believed to have left the country June 23, 2014.

As fighting, including government offensives against rebel-controlled areas, continued in 2014, the death toll in Syria's civil war was estimated by the UN in Aug. 2014 to have passed 191,000 by Apr. The UNHCR reported the number of Syrian refugees at more than 3.2 mil by early Oct.; an estimated 6.5 mil were displaced within Syria in 2014. By summer 2014, the Sunni extremist group ISIS (Islamic State in Iraq and Syria) controlled large areas in eastern and northern Syria. Pres. Obama announced Sept. 10 that the U.S. would train and supply arms to rebel groups fighting both government forces and ISIS. Beginning the night of Sept. 22-23, the U.S., supported by several Middle East countries, began air and cruise missile strikes against ISIS and other Islamist extremist groups in Syria.

Taiwan

People: Population: 23,359,928. **Age distrib.:** <15: 14%; 65+: 12%. **Pop. density:** 1,875.4 per sq mi, 724.1 per sq km. **Urban:** NA. **Ethnic groups:** Taiwanese (incl. Hakka) 84%, mainland Chinese 14%, indigenous 2%. **Languages:** Mandarin Chinese (official), Taiwanese (Min), Hakka dialects. **Religions:** mixture of Buddhist and Taoist 93%, Christian 5%.

Geography: Total area: 13,892 sq mi, 35,980 sq km; **Land area:** 12,456 sq mi, 32,260 sq km. **Location:** Off SE coast of China, between E and S China Seas. **Neighbors:** Nearest is China to NW. **Topography:** A mountain range forms backbone of island. The eastern half is very steep and craggy; western slope is flat, fertile, and well cultivated. **Capital:** Taipei, 2,666,623. **Cities (urban aggl.):** Kaohsiung, 1,522,947; Taichung, 1,209,390.

Government: Type: Multiparty democracy. **Head of state:** Pres. Ma Ying-jeou; b. July 13, 1950; in office: May 20, 2008. **Head of gov.:** Prem. Jiang Yi-huah; b. 1960; in office: Feb. 18, 2013. **Local divisions:** 14 counties, 3 municipalities, 5 special municipalities. **Defense budget:** $10.32 bil. **Active troops:** 290,000.

Economy: Industries: electronics, communications and info. tech. prods., petroleum refining, armaments, chemicals, textiles, iron and steel, machinery, cement, food proc., vehicles, consumer prods., pharmaceuticals. **Chief crops:** rice, vegetables, fruit, tea, flowers. **Natural resources:** small deposits of coal, nat. gas, limestone, marble, asbestos. **Crude oil reserves:** 2.4 mil bbls. **Arable land:** 16.9%. **Livestock:** cattle: 135,000; chickens: 100 mil; goats: 190,000; pigs: 6.2 mil; sheep: 220. **Electricity prod.:** 235.0 bil kWh. **Labor force:** agric. 5%, industry 36.2%, services 58.8%.

Finance: Monetary unit: New Dollar (TWD) (Sept. 2014: 29.90 = $1 U.S.). **GDP:** $926.4 bil; **per capita GDP:** $39,600; **GDP growth:** 2.2%. **Imports:** $268.5 bil; Japan 17.6%, China 16.1%, U.S. 9.5%. **Exports:** $305.8 bil; China 27.1%, Hong Kong 13.2%, U.S. 10.3%, Japan 6.4%, Singapore 4.4%. **Tourism:** $12.7 bil. **Budget:** $90.4 bil. **Total reserves less gold:** NA. **Inflation:** NA.

Transport: Railways: 982 mi. **Motor vehicles:** 313.6 per 1,000 pop. **Civil aviation:** 35 airports. **Chief ports:** Chilung, Hualian, Kaohsiung, Taichung.

Communications: TV sets: 444 per 1,000 pop. **Radios:** 178 per 1,000 pop. **Telephone lines:** 71.2 per 100 pop. **Mobile:** 127.5 per 100 pop. **Internet:** 80%.

Health: Life expect.: 76.7 male; 83.2 female. **Births:** 8.6 per 1,000 pop. **Deaths:** 7.0 per 1,000 pop. **Natural inc.:** 0.16%. **Infant mortality:** 4.5 per 1,000 live births. **HIV:** NA.

Education: Compulsory: ages 6-17. **Literacy:** 96.1%.

Taipei Economic and Cultural Representative Office: 4201 Wisconsin Ave. NW 20016; 895-1800.

Website: www.taiwan.gov.tw

Large-scale Chinese immigration began in the 17th cent. The island came under mainland control after an interval of Dutch rule, 1620-62. Japan ruled Taiwan (also called Formosa), 1895-1945. The Kuomintang (Chinese nationalist govt.) fled to Taiwan in 1949 and established the Republic of China under Chiang Kai-shek, who ruled until his death in 1975. The U.S. provided military aid to deter a Communist invasion.

In 1971, the UN expelled Taiwan from its seat and recognized the mainland government. The U.S. recognized the People's Republic of China, Dec. 15, 1978, and severed ties with Taiwan. However, the U.S. and Taiwan have continued a strong trading relationship and maintain contact via quasi-official agencies.

Land reform, government planning, U.S. aid and investment, and free universal education brought advances in industry, agriculture, and living standards. In 1987 martial law was lifted after 38 years, and in 1991 the 43 years of emergency rule ended. Taiwan held its first direct presidential election Mar. 23, 1996. An earthquake on Sept. 21, 1999, killed more than 2,300 people.

Five decades of Nationalist Party rule ended when Chen Shui-bian, leader of the pro-independence Democratic Progressive Party, won the Mar. 2000 presidential election. Chen was wounded in an apparent assassination attempt Mar. 19, 2004, one day before he won a second term as president. Promising increased cooperation with China, Taipei Mayor Ma Ying-jeou won the presidential election, Mar. 22, 2008, and was reelected Jan. 14, 2012.

Former Pres. Chen was convicted of corruption and sentenced to life in prison, Sept. 11, 2009. Flooding and mudslides from Typhoon Morakot, Aug. 7-9, 2009, left at least 700 people dead or missing. Former Pres. Lee Teng-hui, who introduced democratic reforms 1988-2000, was found not guilty of embezzling $7.8 mil while in office, Nov. 15, 2013.

Since 1949, the People's Republic has considered Taiwan a rebel province of the mainland; until 1991, Taiwan claimed to be the sole government of both. In 2003, China replaced the U.S. as Taiwan's leading trade partner. The first formal talks (focused largely on economic matters) between representatives of Taiwan and China were held Feb. 11, 2014.

The Penghu Isls. (Pescadores), 49 sq mi, pop. (2011 est.) 96,597, lie between Taiwan and the mainland. Kinmen, fmr. Quemoy, pop. (2011 est.) 99,691, and Matsu, pop. (2011 est.) 10,106, lie just off the mainland.

Tajikistan
Republic of Tajikistan

People: Population: 8,051,512. **Age distrib.:** <15: 33%; 65+: 3.2%. **Pop. density:** 147.4 per sq mi, 56.9 per sq km. **Urban:** 26.7%. **Ethnic groups:** Tajik 80%, Uzbek 15%, Russian 1%, Kyrgyz 1%. **Languages:** Tajik (official), Russian (widely used in govt. and business). **Religions:** Sunni Muslim 85%, Shia Muslim 5%.

Geography: Total area: 55,251 sq mi, 143,100 sq km; **Land area:** 54,637 sq mi, 141,510 sq km. **Location:** Central Asia. **Neighbors:** Uzbekistan on N and W, Kyrgyzstan on N, China on E, Afghanistan on S. **Topography:** Mountainous region that contains the Pamirs, Trans-Alai mountain system. **Capital:** Dushanbe, 800,745.

Government: Type: Republic. **Head of state:** Pres. Imomali Rakhmon; b. Oct. 5, 1952; in office: Nov. 6, 1994. **Head of gov.:** Prime Min. Qohir Rasulzoda; b. Mar. 8, 1961; in office: Nov. 23, 2013. **Local divisions:** 2 provinces, 1 autonomous province, 1 capital region, 1 district under republic admin. **Defense budget:** $189 mil. **Active troops:** 8,800.

Economy: Industries: aluminum, cement, vegetable oil. **Chief crops:** cotton, grain, fruits, grapes, vegetables. **Natural resources:** hydropower, petroleum, uranium, mercury, brown coal, lead, zinc, antimony, tungsten, silver, gold. **Crude oil reserves:** 12 mil bbls. **Arable land:** 6.1%. **Livestock:** cattle: 2 mil; chickens: 4.9 mil; goats: 1.8 mil; pigs: 662; sheep: 3 mil. **Electricity prod.:** 16.0 bil kWh. **Labor force:** agric. 46.5%, industry 10.7%, services 42.8%. **Unemployment:** 11.5%.

Finance: Monetary unit: Somoni (TJS) (Sept. 2014: 4.97 = $1 U.S.). **GDP:** $19.2 bil; **per capita GDP:** $2,300; **GDP growth:** 7.4%. **Imports:** $4.1 bil; Russia 22%, Kazakhstan 15.2%, China 14.5%, Lithuania 4.7%, Kyrgyzstan 4.4%, Turkey 4.4%, Iran 4.3%. **Exports:** $1.2 bil; Turkey 40.7%, Russia 10.6%, Iran 9.9%, Afghanistan 8.7%, China 7.4%, Kazakhstan 7.4%, Switzerland 6.6%. **Budget:** $2.4 bil. **Total reserves less gold:** $460.7 mil. **Gold:** 166,530 oz t. **Inflation:** 5.0%.

Transport: Railways: 423 mi. **Civil aviation:** 1.5 bil pass.-mi; 17 airports.

Communications: TV sets: 386 per 1,000 pop. **Radios:** 398 per 1,000 pop. **Telephone lines:** 5.2 per 100 pop. **Mobile:** 91.8 per 100 pop. **Internet:** 16%.

Health: Life expect.: 64.0 male; 70.3 female. **Births:** 25.0 per 1,000 pop. **Deaths:** 6.3 per 1,000 pop. **Natural inc.:** 1.87%. **Infant mortality:** 35.0 per 1,000 live births. **HIV:** 0.3%.

Education: Compulsory: ages 7-15. **Literacy:** 99.8%.

Major International Organizations: UN (FAO, IBRD, ILO, IMF, WHO), CIS, OSCE, WTO (observer).

Embassy: 1005 New Hampshire Ave. NW 20037; 223-6090.

Website: www.parlament.tj

Societies were settled in the region from about 3000 BCE. Invaders have included Iranians, Arabs (who converted the population to Islam), Mongols, Uzbeks, Afghans, and Russians. The USSR gained control 1918-25, making the region a part of the Uzbek SSR until the Tajik SSR was proclaimed, 1929.

Tajikistan declared independence Sept. 9, 1991. Factional fighting led to the installation of a pro-Communist regime, Jan. 1993. A new constitution establishing a presidential system was approved by referendum in 1994.

An estimated 55,000 died in clashes between Muslim rebels and loyalist troops (supported by Russia) by mid-1997, despite a series of peace accords. Constitutional changes including legalization of Islamic political parties were approved by referendum in 1999. Pres. Imomali Rakhmonov, first elected in 1994, won a Nov. 1999 election called a farce by human-rights observers. Voter-approved constitutional changes in 2003 gave Rakhmonov the right to serve as president until 2020. Leading opposition groups boycotted the Nov. 2006 election, again won by Rakhmonov. He changed his name to Rakhmon in 2007 after a decree banned Slavic name endings and other Soviet-era practices. Rakhmon won the Nov. 2013 election with 84% of the vote.

Poverty and corruption are widespread. Much of the nation's income is supplied by international donors and by remittances from young Tajiks working in Russia and Kazakhstan. After rebels

murdered a Tajik general in the semiautonomous province of Gorno-Badakhshan, July 21, 2012, the army attacked and killed about 30 militants July 24; 17 government troops died. A former warlord surrendered Aug. 13, 2012, in exchange for a troop withdrawal from the region.

Tanzania
United Republic of Tanzania

People: Population: 49,639,138. **Age distrib.:** <15: 44.6%; 65+: 2.9%. **Pop. density:** 145.1 per sq mi, 56 per sq km. **Urban:** 30.9%. **Ethnic groups:** African 99% (Bantu 95%). **Languages:** Kiswahili/Swahili, English (primary lang. of commerce, admin., higher ed.) (both official); Arabic (widely spoken in Zanzibar); local langs. **Religions:** Christian 30%, Muslim 35%, indigenous beliefs 35%; 99%+ Muslim on Zanzibar.

Geography: Total area: 365,755 sq mi, 947,300 sq km; **Land area:** 342,009 sq mi, 885,800 sq km. **Location:** On coast of E Africa. **Neighbors:** Kenya, Uganda on N; Rwanda, Burundi, Congo on W; Zambia, Malawi, Mozambique on S. **Topography:** Hot, arid central plateau surrounded by lake region in W, temperate highlands in N and S, the coastal plains. Mt. Kilimanjaro (19,341 ft) is highest in Africa. **Capital:** Dodoma, 227,762 (planned new capital; legis. and National Assembly currently meet here).

Government: Type: Republic. **Head of state and gov.:** Pres. Jakaya Mrisho Kikwete; b. Oct. 7, 1950; in office: Dec. 21, 2005. **Local divisions:** 30 regions. **Defense budget:** $327 mil. **Active troops:** 27,000.

Economy: Industries: agric. proc.; diamond, gold, iron mining; salt, soda ash; cement, oil refining, shoes, apparel. **Chief crops:** coffee, sisal, tea, cotton, pyrethrum (insecticide made from chrysanthemums), cashews, tobacco, cloves, corn, wheat. **Natural resources:** hydropower, tin, phosphates, iron ore, coal, diamonds, gems, gold, nat. gas, nickel. **Arable land:** 16.4%. **Livestock:** cattle: 21.5 mil; chickens: 35.5 mil; goats: 15.4 mil; pigs: 500,000; sheep: 5.9 mil. **Electricity prod.:** 5.1 bil kWh. **Labor force:** agric. 80%, industry and services 20%. **Unemployment:** 3.5%.

Finance: Monetary unit: Shilling (TZS) (Sept. 2014: 1,660.00 = $1 U.S.). **GDP:** $79.3 bil; **per capita GDP:** $1,700; **GDP growth:** 7%. **Imports:** $11.2 bil; China 21.3%, India 16.3%, South Africa 6.4%, Kenya 6%, UAE 5%. **Exports:** $5.9 bil; India 15.2%, China 11.1%, Japan 6.2%, Germany 5.1%, UAE 4.8%. **Tourism:** $1.9 bil. **Budget:** $8.9 bil. **Total reserves less gold:** $4.7 bil. **Inflation:** 7.9%.

Transport: Railways: 2,292 mi. **Motor vehicles:** 1.8 per 1,000 pop. **Civil aviation:** 10 airports. **Chief ports:** Dar es Salaam, Zanzibar.

Communications: TV sets: 41 per 1,000 pop. **Radios:** 352 per 1,000 pop. **Telephone lines:** 0.3 per 100 pop. **Mobile:** 55.7 per 100 pop. **Internet:** 4.4%.

Health: Life expect.: 59.9 male; 62.6 female. **Births:** 36.8 per 1,000 pop. **Deaths:** 8.2 per 1,000 pop. **Natural inc.:** 2.86%. **Infant mortality:** 43.7 per 1,000 live births. **HIV:** 5.0%.

Education: Compulsory: ages 7-13. **Literacy:** 70.6%.

Embassy: 2139 R St. NW 20008; 939-6125.

Website: www.tanzania.go.tz

The Republic of Tanganyika in E Africa and the island Republic of Zanzibar, off Tanganyika's coast, both of which had recently gained independence, joined to form the United Republic of Tanzania, Apr. 26, 1964. Zanzibar retains internal self-government.

Until resigning as president in 1985, Julius K. Nyerere, a former Tanganyikan independence leader, dominated Tanzania's single-party government, which emphasized government planning and economic control. A multiparty system was established in 1992, and the economy was privatized in the 1990s.

A bomb at the U.S. embassy in Dar es Salaam, Aug. 7, 1998, killed 11 people and injured at least 70 others. The U.S. blamed the attack and a near-simultaneous embassy bombing in Kenya on Islamic terrorists associated with Osama bin Laden.

President since 1995, Benjamin Mkapa was reelected in 2000. Jakaya Mrisho Kikwete of the ruling Chama Cha Mapinduzi (Party of the Revolution) won the Dec. 2005, presidential election; he was reelected to a second 5-year term Oct. 2010. Large offshore natural gas deposits have been discovered in recent years; the government estimated total recoverable gas reserves in 2014 at 46.5 tril cubic ft.

Tanganyika. Arab colonization and slaving began in the 8th cent.; Portuguese sailors explored the coast around 1500. Other Europeans followed.

In 1885 Germany established German East Africa, of which Tanganyika formed the bulk. Under Britain, it became a League of Nations mandate and after 1946, a UN trust territory. It became independent, Dec. 9, 1961, and a republic within the Commonwealth a year later.

Zanzibar, the Isle of Cloves, lies 23 mi off mainland Tanzania; area 640 sq mi and pop. (2002) 622,459. The island of **Pemba,** 25 mi to the NE, area 380 sq mi and pop. (2002) 362,166 is included in the administration. Ethnic groups in Zanzibar include Arabs and Africans. Zanzibar and Pemba produce most of the world's supply of cloves and clove oil.

Zanzibar was for centuries the center for Arab slave traders. Portugal ruled the region for two centuries until ousted by Arabs around 1700. Zanzibar became a British Protectorate in 1890;

independence came Dec. 10, 1963. Revolutionary forces overthrew the Sultan, Jan. 12, 1964. The new government ousted Western diplomats and journalists, slaughtered thousands of Arabs, and nationalized farms. Union with Tanganyika followed.

Thailand
Kingdom of Thailand

People: Population: 67,741,401. **Age distrib.:** <15: 17.6%; 65+: 9.5%. **Pop. density:** 343.4 per sq mi, 132.6 per sq km. **Urban:** 49.2%. **Ethnic groups:** Thai 96%, Burmese 2%. **Languages:** Thai (official), English (secondary lang. of elite). **Religions:** Buddhist (official) 94%, Muslim 5%.

Geography: Total area: 198,117 sq mi, 513,120 sq km; **Land area:** 197,256 sq mi, 510,890 sq km. **Location:** On Indochinese and Malayan peninsulas in SE Asia. **Neighbors:** Myanmar on W and N, Laos on N, Cambodia on E, Malaysia on S. **Topography:** A plateau dominates NE third of Thailand, dropping to the fertile alluvial valley of Chao Phraya R. in center. Forested mountains are in N, with narrow fertile valleys. The S peninsula region is covered by rain forests. **Capital:** Krung Thep (Bangkok), 9,097,870. **Cities (urban aggl.):** Samut Prakan, 1,652,145.

Government: Type: Constitutional monarchy. **Head of state:** King Bhumibol Adulyadej; b. Dec. 5, 1927; in office: June 9, 1946. **Head of gov.:** Prime Min. Prayuth Chan-ocha; b. Mar. 21, 1954; in office: Aug. 24, 2014. **Local divisions:** 77 provinces. **Defense budget:** $6.21 bil. **Active troops:** 360,850.

Economy: Industries: tourism, textiles and garments, agric. proc., beverages, tobacco, cement, light mfg. (jewelry, elec. appliances, computers and parts, integrated circuits, furniture); world's second-largest tungsten producer and third-largest tin producer. **Chief crops:** rice, cassava, rubber, corn, sugarcane, coconuts, soybeans. **Natural resources:** tin, rubber, nat. gas, tungsten, tantalum, timber, lead, fish, gypsum, lignite, fluorite. **Crude oil reserves:** 448.8 mil bbls. **Arable land:** 32.4%. **Livestock:** cattle: 5.1 mil; chickens: 252 mil; goats: 455,000; pigs: 7.9 mil; sheep: 55,500. **Electricity prod.:** 140.8 bil kWh. **Labor force:** agric. 38.2%, industry 13.6%, services 48.2%. **Unemployment:** 0.7%.

Finance: Monetary unit: Baht (THB) (Sept. 2014: 32.01 = $1 U.S.). **GDP:** $673 bil; **per capita GDP:** $9,900; **GDP growth:** 2.9%. **Imports:** $219 bil; Japan 20%, China 14.9%, UAE 6.3%, Malaysia 5.3%, U.S. 5.3%. **Exports:** $225.4 bil; China 11.7%, Japan 10.2%, U.S. 9.9%, Hong Kong 5.7%, Malaysia 5.4%, Indonesia 4.9%, Singapore 4.7%, Australia 4.3%. **Tourism:** $42.1 bil. **Budget:** $92.9 bil. **Total reserves less gold:** $161.3 bil. **Gold:** 4.9 mil oz t. **Inflation:** 2.2%.

Transport: Railways: 2,530 mi. **Motor vehicles:** 206.4 per 1,000 pop. **Civil aviation:** 41.9 bil pass.-mi; 63 airports. **Chief ports:** Bangkok, Laem Chabang, Map Ta Phut, Prachuap Port, Si Racha.

Communication: TV sets: 285 per 1,000 pop. **Radios:** 229 per 1,000 pop. **Telephone lines:** 9 per 100 pop. **Mobile:** 138 per 100 pop. **Internet:** 28.9%.

Health: Life expect.: 71.0 male; 77.5 female. **Births:** 11.3 per 1,000 pop. **Deaths:** 7.7 per 1,000 pop. **Natural inc.:** 0.35%. **Infant mortality:** 9.9 per 1,000 live births. **HIV:** 1.1%.

Education: Compulsory: ages 6-14. **Literacy:** 96.7%.

Embassy: 1024 Wisconsin Ave. NW, Ste. 401, 20007; 944-3600. **Website:** www.thaigov.go.th

Thais began migrating from southern China during the 11th cent. and established a unified Thai kingdom, 1350. Known as Siam until 1939, Thailand is the only country in SE Asia never colonized by Europeans. King Mongkut and his son King Chulalongkorn, ruling successively from 1851 to 1910, modernized the country and signed trade treaties with Britain and France. A bloodless revolution in 1932 limited the monarchy. Thailand was an ally of Japan during WWII and of the U.S. during the postwar period. For decades, the military had a dominant role in governing the country.

An economic downturn forced Thailand to seek more than $15 bil in emergency international loans, Aug. 1997. A new constitution won legislative approval Sept. 27. By the end of the 1990s, according to UN estimates, more than 750,000 people in Thailand had HIV/AIDS, with 143,000 new infections in 1991 alone; a nationwide prevention campaign reduced the number of new HIV infections to about 8,800 in 2012.

Following elections in Jan. 2001, Thaksin Shinawatra became prime min. Feb. 2005 elections gave Thaksin's party a huge parliamentary majority. Facing rising opposition and accused of benefiting improperly from the sale of his family's telecom business, Thaksin called snap elections for Apr. 2006; the vote, which major parties boycotted, was later ruled unconstitutional. A military junta took power in a bloodless coup Sept. 19.

Thaksin supporters won Dec. 2007 elections, and Samak Sundaravej became prime min. after civilian rule was restored Jan. 22, 2008. After a series of antigovernment protests paralyzed Bangkok, Prime Min. Samak imposed emergency rule Sept. 2; Thailand's Constitutional Court ousted him a week later, ostensibly for getting paid to host TV cooking shows while he held public office. Thaksin's brother-in-law Somchai Wongsawat became prime min. Sept. 18, but a Constitutional Court ruling, Dec. 2, barred him from politics and dissolved his People Power Party because of electoral fraud.

Mass protests by Thaksin supporters, known as Red Shirts, led the government to declare a state of emergency in Bangkok,

Apr. 12-24, 2009. Meanwhile, about 60,000 security forces in southern Thailand suppressed a Muslim insurgency; from Jan. 2004 to Sept. 2009, more than 3,500 people, mostly civilians, died in the fighting.

On Feb. 26, 2010, Thailand's Supreme Court ordered the seizure of about $1.4 bil of Thaksin's family assets. Thaksin supporters staged mass rallies in Bangkok. After the Red Shirts began to build a fortified compound in the heart of Bangkok's business district, a crackdown by Thai security forces May 14-19, 2010, left more than 90 people dead and some 470 injured. After parliamentary elections July 3, 2011, Thaksin's sister, Yingluck Shinawatra, became Thailand's first female prime min. Monsoon season brought floods beginning July 25, 2011, that covered two-thirds of the country by Oct. 12 and cost the country an estimated $45.7 bil. Insurgents in the southern region continued to attack government forces in 2013. Mass protests against Yingluck Shinawatra began in Nov. 2013. On May 7, 2014, she was removed from office by the Constitutional Court. The military seized power in a May 22 coup. An interim legislature, with a majority of military members, was appointed July 31; it named coup leader Gen. Prayuth Chan-ocha as prime min. Aug. 21.

Timor-Leste
(East Timor)
Democratic Republic of Timor-Leste

People: Population: 1,201,542. **Age distrib.:** <15: 42.4%; 65+: 3.7%. **Pop. density:** 209.2 per sq mi, 80.8 per sq km. **Urban:** 32.1%. **Ethnic groups:** Austronesian (Malayo-Polynesian), Papuan, small Chinese minority. **Languages:** Tetum, Portuguese (both official); Indonesian; English; about 16 indigenous langs. (incl. Tetum, Galole, Mambae, Kemak). **Religions:** Roman Catholic 98%, Muslim 1%, Protestant 1%.

Geography: Total area: 5,743 sq mi, 14,874 sq km. **Land area:** 5,743 sq mi, 14,874 sq km. **Location:** E half of Timor Isl. in SW Pacific O. **Neighbors:** Indonesia (West Timor) on W. **Topography:** Terrain is rugged, rising to 9,721 ft at Mt. Ramelau. **Capital:** Dili, 228,136.

Government: Type: Republic. **Head of state:** Pres. Taur Matan Ruak; b. Oct. 10, 1956; in office: May 20, 2012. **Head of gov.:** Prime Min. Kay Rala Xanana Gusmão; b. June 20, 1946; in office: Aug. 8, 2007. **Local divisions:** 13 admin. districts. **Defense budget:** $67 mil. **Active troops:** 1,330.

Economy: Industries: printing, soap mfg., handicrafts, woven cloth. **Chief crops:** coffee, rice, corn, cassava, sweet potatoes, soybeans. **Natural resources:** gold, petroleum, nat. gas, manganese, marble. **Arable land:** 10.8%. **Livestock:** cattle: 160,000; chickens: 790,000; goats: 153,000; pigs: 360,000; sheep: 46,000. **Electricity prod.:** 0 kWh. **Labor force:** agric. 64%, industry 10%, services 26%. **Unemployment:** 4%.

Finance: Monetary unit: U.S. Dollar (USD). **GDP:** $25.4 mil; **per capita GDP:** $21,400; **GDP growth:** 8.1%. **Imports** (2011): $689 mil. **Exports** (2011): $34.1 mil (excl. oil). **Tourism:** $21 mil. **Budget:** $1.7 bil. **Total reserves less gold:** $687 mil. **Inflation:** 3.3%.

Transport: Civil aviation: 2 airports. **Chief port:** Dili.

Communication: Telephone lines: 0.3 per 100 pop. **Mobile:** 57.4 per 100 pop. **Internet:** 1.1%.

Health: Life expect.: 65.9 male; 69.0 female. **Births:** 34.5 per 1,000 pop. **Deaths:** 6.2 per 1,000 pop. **Natural inc.:** 2.83%. **Infant mortality:** 38.8 per 1,000 live births. **HIV:** NA.

Education: Compulsory: ages 6-14. **Literacy:** 65%.

Embassy: 4201 Connecticut Ave. NW 20008; 966-3202. **Website:** www.timor-leste.gov.tl

The collapse of Portuguese rule in East Timor led to factional fighting, Aug. 1975, and an invasion by Indonesia in Dec. Indonesia annexed East Timor as a 27th province in 1976. In over two decades, some 200,000 Timorese died due to civil war, famine, and persecution by Indonesian authorities. In a referendum held Aug. 1999 under UN auspices, Timorese voted overwhelmingly for independence but were then terrorized by pro-Indonesian militias. An international peacekeeping force entered in Sept.; a UN interim administration formally took command Oct. 26, 1999.

Pro-independence forces won elections for a constituent assembly Aug. 2001. Xanana Gusmão, a former guerrilla leader, won the presidential election Apr. 2002. As Timor-Leste, the territory became independent May 20 and entered the UN Sept. 27. Australia and other nations sent peacekeepers to suppress a wave of gang violence in Dili May 2006.

José Ramos-Horta, a Nobel laureate, won a presidential runoff vote May 2007. After inconclusive parliamentary elections June 30, Ramos-Horta chose Gusmão as prime min. The Gusmão-supported independent candidate, Taur Matan Ruak, became president in a May 2012 runoff election. Gusmão's party won a majority of seats in the July parliamentary election, and he became prime min. of a coalition government in Aug. The UN peacekeeping mission ended Dec. 31, 2012. Beginning in 2005, much of East Timor's budget consisted of revenue from exploitation of offshore petroleum and natural gas deposits. Indications in 2014 that gas reserves could be less than previously estimated, even as the government tapped the energy-revenue fund for infrastructure and other projects, were troubling signs for the country's struggling economy.

Togo
Togolese Republic

People: Population: 7,351,374. **Age distrib.:** <15: 40.7%; 65+: 3.3%. **Pop. density:** 350.1 per sq mi, 135.2 per sq km. **Urban:** 39.5%. **Ethnic groups:** African (37 tribes; Ewe, Mina, Kabre largest) 99%. **Languages:** French (official, lang. of commerce), Ewe and Mina (in S), Kabye and Dagomba (in N). **Religions:** indigenous beliefs 51%, Christian 29%, Muslim 20%.

Geography: Total area: 21,925 sq mi, 56,785 sq km; **Land area:** 20,998 sq mi, 54,385 sq km. **Location:** On S coast of W Africa. **Neighbors:** Ghana on W, Burkina Faso on N, Benin on E. **Topography:** A range of hills running SW-NE splits Togo into 2 savanna plains regions. **Capital:** Lomé, 929,520.

Government: Type: Republic. **Head of state:** Pres. Faure Gnassingbé; b. June 6, 1966; in office: May 4, 2005. **Head of gov.:** Prime Min. Kwesi Ahoomey-Zunu; b. Dec. 1, 1958; in office: July 23, 2012. **Local divisions:** 5 regions. **Defense budget** $72 mil. **Active troops:** 8,550.

Economy: Industries: phosphate mining, agric. proc., cement, handicrafts, textiles, beverages. **Chief crops:** coffee, cocoa, cotton, yams, cassava, corn, beans, rice, millet, sorghum. **Natural resources:** phosphates, limestone, marble. **Arable land:** 48.7%. **Livestock:** cattle: 435,000; chickens: 25 mil; goats: 2.8 mil; pigs: 1 mil; sheep: 220,000. **Electricity prod.:** 136 mil kWh. **Labor force:** agric. 65%, industry 5%, services 30%. **Unemployment:** 7.6%.

Finance: Monetary unit: CFA Franc (XOF) (Sept. 2014: 498.91 = $1 U.S.). **GDP:** $7.3 bil; **per capita GDP:** $1,100; **GDP growth:** 5.5%. **Imports:** $1.7 bil; China 40.4%, Netherlands 7.9%, France 5.4%, UK 5.3%. **Exports:** $982.2 mil; India 14.2%, Lebanon 10.6%, Burkina Faso 7.6%, Benin 7.5%, China 6.1%, Niger 5.8%, Netherlands 5.2%, Ghana 4.4%. **Tourism:** $79 mil. **Budget:** $983 mil. **Total reserves less gold:** $507.1 mil. **Inflation:** 1.8%.

Transport: Railways: 353 mi. **Motor vehicles:** 24.6 per 1,000 pop. **Civil aviation:** 2 airports. **Chief ports:** Kpeme, Lomé.

Communications: TV sets: 26 per 1,000 pop. **Radios:** 669 per 1,000 pop. **Telephone lines:** 0.9 per 100 pop. **Mobile:** 62.5 per 100 pop. **Internet:** 4.5%.

Health: Life expect.: 61.5 male; 66.7 female. **Births:** 34.5 per 1,000 pop. **Deaths:** 7.4 per 1,000 pop. **Natural inc.:** 2.71%. **Infant mortality:** 46.7 per 1,000 live births. **HIV:** 2.3%.

Education: Compulsory: ages 6-15. **Literacy:** 66.5%.

Embassy: 2208 Massachusetts Ave. NW 20008; 234-4212.

Website: www.gouv.tg or www.state.gov/p/af/ci/to/

Togoland was administered by Germany and then by France and Britain. The French sector became the republic of Togo Apr. 27, 1960. In office since 1967, Pres. Gnassingbé Eyadéma was Africa's longest-serving head of state until his death Feb. 5, 2005. His son, Faure Gnassingbé, was installed as president, but African leaders pressured Togo to hold an election, which Gnassingbé won Apr. 24. Opposition parties disputed the result, and protests led to violent clashes in Lomé.

After a shootout at his home Apr. 12, 2009, former Defense Min. Kpatcha Gnassingbé, the president's brother, sought refuge Apr. 15 at the U.S. embassy in Lomé; denied asylum, he was arrested by Togolese authorities and accused of plotting a coup. Pres. Gnassingbé won reelection Mar. 4, 2010, to a second 5-year term. Weeks of antigovernment protest led Prime Min. Gilbert Fossoun Houngbo to resign, July 13, 2012, and a new government was formed under Prime Min. Kwesi Seleagodzi Ahoomey-Zunu. Legislative elections were held July 25, 2013, with the ruling party maintaining its majority and the opposition claiming voting irregularities.

Tonga
Kingdom of Tonga

People: Population: 106,440. **Age distrib.:** <15: 35.6%; 65+: 6.3%. **Pop. density:** 384.5 per sq mi, 148.5 per sq km. **Urban:** 23.6%. **Ethnic groups:** Polynesian, European. **Languages:** Tongan, English (both official). **Religions:** Christian (mostly Free Wesleyan Church).

Geography: Total area: 288 sq mi, 747 sq km; **Land area:** 277 sq mi, 717 sq km. **Location:** In western S Pacific O. **Neighbors:** Nearest are Fiji to W, Samoa to NE. **Topography:** Comprises 170 volcanic and coral islands, 36 inhabited. **Capital:** Nuku'alofa, 24,998.

Government: Type: Constitutional monarchy. **Head of state:** King Tupou VI; b. July 12, 1959; in office: Mar. 18, 2012. **Head of gov.:** Prime Min. Tu'ivakano; b. Jan. 15, 1952; in office: Dec, 22, 2010. **Local divisions:** 5 island divisions. **Defense budget/active troops:** NA.

Economy: Industries: tourism, constr., fishing. **Chief crops:** squash, coconuts, copra, bananas, vanilla beans, cocoa, coffee, ginger, black pepper. **Natural resources:** fish. **Arable land:** 22.2%. **Livestock:** cattle: 11,700; chickens: 330,000; goats: 13,250; pigs: 82,500. **Electricity prod.:** 48 mil kWh. **Labor force:** agric. 31.8%, industry 30.6%, services 37.6%. **Unemployment:** NA.

Finance: Monetary unit: Pa'anga (TOP) (Sept. 2014: 1.88 = $1 U.S.). **GDP:** $846 mil; **per capita GDP:** $8,200; **GDP growth:** 1%. **Imports:** $122.5 mil; Fiji 35.7%, New Zealand 24.4%, U.S. 10.5%, China 10.2%. **Exports:** $9.1 mil; South Korea 18.5%, U.S. 17%, New Zealand 15.6%, Fiji 10.2%, Japan 9.5%, Samoa 8.6%,

American Samoa 5.4%, Australia 5.1%. **Tourism:** $41 mil. **Budget:** $112.4 mil. **Total reserves less gold:** $152.4 mil. **Inflation:** 0.7%.

Transport: Civil aviation: 1 airport. **Chief ports:** Neiafu, Nuku'alofa, Pangai.

Communications: TV sets: 49 per 1,000 pop. **Radios:** 662 per 1,000 pop. **Telephone lines:** 29.4 per 100 pop. **Mobile:** 54.6 per 100 pop. **Internet:** 35%.

Health: Life expect.: 74.4 male; 77.3 female. **Births:** 23.6 per 1,000 pop. **Deaths:** 4.9 per 1,000 pop. **Natural inc.:** 1.87%. **Infant mortality:** 12.4 per 1,000 live births. **HIV:** NA.

Education: Compulsory: ages 6-14. **Literacy:** 99.4%.

Embassy: 250 E. 51st St., New York, NY 10022; (917) 369-1025.

Website: www.tongaportal.gov.to

The Dutch first visited the islands in the early 17th cent. A series of civil wars ended, 1845, with establishment of the Tupou dynasty. In 1900, Tonga became a British protectorate. Tonga gained independence June 1970 and joined the Commonwealth. It joined the UN in 1999. George Tupou VI became king Mar. 18, 2012, following the death of his brother, George Tupou V, who had reigned since 2006 and had introduced democratic reforms. Elections in Nov. 2010 gave the country its first democratically elected parliament, taking the monarch's executive powers and reducing his role to that of an adviser.

Trinidad and Tobago
Republic of Trinidad and Tobago

People: Population: 1,223,916. **Age distrib.:** <15: 19.4%; 65+: 9.5%. **Pop. density:** 618.2 per sq mi, 238.7 per sq km. **Urban:** 8.5%. **Ethnic groups:** Indian (South Asian) 40%, African 38%, mixed 21%. **Languages:** English (official), Caribbean Hindustani, French, Spanish, Chinese. **Religions:** Roman Catholic 26%, Protestant 26% (Anglican 8%, Baptist 7%, Pentecostal 7%, Seventh-day Adventist 4%), Hindu 23%, Muslim 6%, other Christian 6%, none 2%.

Geography: Total area: 1,980 sq mi, 5,128 sq km; **Land area:** 1,980 sq mi, 5,128 sq km. **Location:** In Caribbean, off E coast of Venezuela. **Neighbors:** Nearest is Venezuela to SW. **Topography:** Three low mountain ranges cross Trinidad E-W, with a well-watered plain between N and central ranges. Parts of E and W coasts are swamps. Tobago, 116 sq mi, lies 20 mi NE. **Capital:** Port of Spain, 34,387.

Government: Type: Parliamentary democracy. **Head of state:** Pres. Anthony Carmona; b. Mar. 7, 1953; in office: Mar. 18, 2013. **Head of gov.:** Prime Min. Kamla Persad-Bissessar; b. Apr. 22, 1952; in office: May 26, 2010. **Local divisions:** 9 regions, 3 boroughs, 2 cities, 1 ward. **Defense budget:** $400 mil. **Active troops:** 4,050.

Economy: Industries: petroleum and petroleum prods., liquefied nat. gas, methanol, ammonia, urea, steel prods., beverages, food proc. **Chief crops:** cocoa, rice, citrus, coffee, vegetables. **Natural resources:** petroleum, nat. gas, asphalt. **Crude oil reserves:** 728.3 mil bbls. **Arable land:** 4.9%. **Livestock:** cattle: 34,500; chickens: 35 mil; goats: 18,420; pigs: 35,000; sheep: 21,117. **Electricity prod.:** 8.4 bil kWh. **Labor force:** agric. 3.8%; mfg., mining, and quarrying 12.8%; constr. and utilities 20.4%; services 62.9%. **Unemployment:** 5.8%.

Finance: Monetary unit: Dollar (TTD) (Sept. 2014: 6.32 = $1 U.S.). **GDP:** $27.1 bil; **per capita GDP:** $20,300; **GDP growth:** 1.6%. **Imports:** $9.6 bil; U.S. 33.1%, Brazil 8.1%, Colombia 7.7%, Gabon 5.5%, Canada 4.4%, China 4.2%. **Exports:** $12.9 bil; U.S. 42.1%, Chile 7.1%, Argentina 6.5%, Spain 4.5%. **Tourism:** $472 mil. **Budget:** $8.3 bil. **Total reserves less gold:** $10.6 bil. **Gold:** 61,774 oz t. **Inflation:** 5.2%.

Transport: Motor vehicles: 308.3 per 1,000 pop. **Civil aviation:** 2.8 bil pass.-mi; 2 airports. **Chief ports:** Point Lisas, Port of Spain, Scarborough.

Communications: TV sets: 355 per 1,000 pop. **Radios:** 535 per 1,000 pop. **Telephone lines:** 21.7 per 100 pop. **Mobile:** 144.9 per 100 pop. **Internet:** 63.8%.

Health: Life expect.: 69.4 male; 75.2 female. **Births:** 13.8 per 1,000 pop. **Deaths:** 8.5 per 1,000 pop. **Natural inc.:** 0.53%. **Infant mortality:** 24.8 per 1,000 live births. **HIV:** 1.7%.

Education: Compulsory: ages 6-11. **Literacy:** 99%.

Embassy: 1708 Massachusetts Ave. NW 20036; 467-6490.

Website: www.ttconnect.gov.tt

Columbus sighted Trinidad in 1498. It became a British possession in 1802; in the 1800s tens of thousands of indentured servants and their families were brought from India to work in agriculture. Trinidad and Tobago won independence Aug. 31, 1962. It became a republic in 1976.

The nation, among the most prosperous in the Caribbean, produces oil and natural gas; it also refines and exports Middle Eastern oil.

In July 1990, some 120 Muslim extremists captured the Parliament building and TV station and took about 50 hostages, including Prime Min. Arthur N. R. Robinson, who was beaten, shot in the legs, and tied to explosives. After a 6-day siege, the rebels surrendered.

Basdeo Panday, in office 1995-2001, was the nation's first prime min. of Indian ancestry. The country's first female prime min., Kamla Persad-Bissessar, leader of the People's Partnership coalition, took office May 26, 2010.

Tunisia
Tunisian Republic

People: Population: 10,937,521. **Age distrib.:** <15: 23%; 65+: 7.9%. **Pop. density:** 182.3 per sq mi, 70.4 per sq km. **Urban:** 66.6%. **Ethnic groups:** Arab 98%, European 1%, Jewish and other 1%. **Languages:** Arabic (official), French (used in commerce), Berber (Tamazight). **Religions:** Muslim (official; Sunni) 99%.

Geography: Total area: 63,170 sq mi, 163,610 sq km; **Land area:** 59,985 sq mi, 155,360 sq km. **Location:** On N coast of Africa. **Neighbors:** Algeria on W, Libya on E. **Topography:** The N is wooded and fertile. The central coastal plains are given to grazing and orchards. The S is arid, approaching Sahara Desert. **Capital:** Tunis, 1,978,070.

Government: Type: Republic. **Head of state:** Interim Pres. Moncef Marzouki; b. July 7, 1945; in office: Dec. 12, 2011. **Head of gov.:** Prime Min. Mehdi Jomaa; b. Apr. 21, 1962; in office: Jan. 29, 2014. **Local divisions:** 24 governorates. **Defense budget:** $769 mil. **Active troops:** 35,800.

Economy: Industries: petroleum, mining, tourism, textiles, footwear, agribusiness, beverages. **Chief crops:** olives, olive oil, grain, tomatoes, citrus, sugar beets, dates, almonds. **Natural resources:** petroleum, phosphates, iron ore, lead, zinc, salt. **Crude oil reserves:** 425 mil bbls. **Arable land:** 18.3%. **Livestock:** cattle: 655,000; chickens: 81 mil; goats: 1.3 mil; pigs: 5,500; sheep: 6.8 mil. **Electricity prod.:** 15.2 bil kWh. **Labor force:** agric. 18.3%, industry 31.9%, services 49.8%. **Unemployment:** 12.8%.

Finance: Monetary unit: Dinar (TND) (Sept. 2014: 1.74 = $1 U.S.). **GDP:** $108.4 bil; **per capita GDP:** $9,900; **GDP growth:** 2.8%. **Imports:** $25 bil; France 19.8%, Italy 16.7%, Germany 7.3%, China 6%, Spain 5.3%, Algeria 4.4%. **Exports:** $17.5 bil; France 26.2%, Italy 16%, Germany 9.4%, Libya 7.6%, U.S. 4.3%. **Tourism:** $2.2 bil. **Budget:** $15.8 bil. **Total reserves less gold** $7.3 bil. **Gold** (2012): 216,693 oz t. **Inflation:** 6.1%.

Transport: Railways: 1,345 mi. **Motor vehicles:** 126.3 per 1,000 pop. **Civil aviation:** 2.3 bil pass.-mi; 15 airports. **Chief ports:** Bizerte, Gabes, Rades, Sfax, Skhira.

Communications: TV sets: 225 per 1,000 pop. **Radios:** 158 per 1,000 pop. **Telephone lines:** 9.3 per 100 pop. **Mobile:** 115.6 per 100 pop. **Internet:** 43.8%.

Health: Life expect.: 73.6 male; 77.9 female. **Births:** 16.9 per 1,000 pop. **Deaths:** 5.9 per 1,000 pop. **Natural inc.:** 1.10%. **Infant mortality:** 23.2 per 1,000 live births. **HIV:** <0.1%.

Education: Compulsory: ages 6-16. **Literacy:** 81.8%.

Embassy: 1515 Massachusetts Ave. NW 20005; 862-1850.

Website: www.tunisie.gov.tn

Site of ancient Carthage and a former Barbary state under the suzerainty of Turkey, Tunisia became a protectorate of France, May 12, 1881. The nation became independent Mar. 20, 1956, and ended the monarchy the following year. Habib Bourguiba, an independence leader, served as president until 1987, when he was deposed by his prime min., Zine al-Abidine Ben Ali, who then won five presidential elections, 1989-2009, all tightly controlled.

Arab Spring protests, which began Dec. 2010 in the town of Sidi Bouzid, ousted Ben Ali, Jan. 14, 2011. Subsequent protests also forced the removal of Prime Min. Mohamed Ghannouchi. Moncef Marzouki of the secular center-left Congress for the Republic party was appointed interim president and took office Dec. 13, 2011, but real power lay with Prime Min. Hamadi Jebali, an Islamist leader of the moderate Ennahda party, which won Oct. 2011 elections. Opposition leader Chokri Belaid was shot to death outside his home Feb. 6, 2013, allegedly by a hard-line Islamist, touching off protests across the country. Prime Min. Jebali resigned Feb. 19 after failing to institute promised reforms. The Islamist-dominated Assembly voted Ali Laarayedh his replacement. Another opposition leader, Mohamed Brahmi, was assassinated July 25. On July 29, 65 members of the Assembly withdrew; political parties agreed, Dec. 14, 2013, on the appointment of Mehdi Jomaa as caretaker prime min. to prepare for new elections. A new, largely secular constitution was approved Jan. 26, 2014. Deadly clashes occurred between Islamic extremists and security forces throughout 2014.

Turkey
Republic of Turkey

People: Population: 81,619,392. **Age distrib.:** <15: 25.5%; 65+: 6.7%. **Pop. density:** 274.7 per sq mi, 106 per sq km. **Urban:** 72.9%. **Ethnic groups:** Turkish 70%-75%, Kurdish 18%. **Languages:** Turkish (official), Kurdish, other minority langs. **Religion:** Muslim (mostly Sunni) 99.8%.

Geography: Total area: 302,535 sq mi, 783,562 sq km; **Land area:** 297,157 sq mi, 769,632 sq km. **Location:** Occupies Asia Minor, stretches into continental Europe; borders on Medit. and Black Seas. **Neighbors:** Bulgaria, Greece on W; Georgia, Armenia on N; Iran on E; Iraq, Syria on S. **Topography:** Central Turkey has wide plateaus with hot, dry summers and cold winters. High mountains ring the interior on all but W, with more than 20 peaks over 10,000 ft. Rolling plains are in W; mild, fertile coastal plains are in S, W. **Capital:** Ankara, 4,643,660. **Cities (urban aggl.):** Istanbul, 13,953,703; Izmir, 2,988,886; Bursa, 1,869,377; Adana, 1,778,342; Gaziantep, 1,488,150.

Government: Type: Republican parliamentary democracy. **Head of state:** Pres. Recep Tayyip Erdogan; b. Feb. 26, 1954; in office: Aug. 28, 2014. **Head of gov.:** Prime Min. Ahmet Davutoglu; b. Feb. 26, 1959; in office: Aug. 28, 2014. **Local divisions:** 81 provinces. **Defense budget:** $10.74 bil. **Active troops:** 510,600.

Economy: Industries: textiles, food proc., autos, electronics, mining, steel, petroleum, constr., lumber, paper. **Chief crops:** tobacco, cotton, grain, olives, sugar beets, hazelnuts, pulses, citrus. **Natural resources:** coal, iron ore, copper, chromium, antimony, mercury, gold, barite, borate, strontium, emery, feldspar, limestone, magnesite, marble, perlite, pumice, pyrites (sulfur), clay, hydropower. **Crude oil reserves:** 294.8 mil bbls. **Arable land:** 26.7%. **Livestock:** cattle: 13.9 mil; chickens: 253.7 mil; goats: 8.4 mil; pigs: 2,986; sheep: 27.4 mil. **Electricity prod.** (2012): 228.1 bil kWh. **Labor force:** agric. 25.5%, industry 26.2%, services 48.4%. **Unemployment:** 9.2%.

Finance: Monetary unit: Lira (TRY) (Sept. 2014: 2.16 = $1 U.S.). **GDP:** $1.2 tril; **per capita GDP:** $15,300; **GDP growth:** 3.8%. **Imports:** $242.9 bil; Russia 11.3%, Germany 9%, China 9%, U.S. 6%, Italy 5.6%, Iran 5.1%. **Exports:** $167.6 bil; Germany 8.6%, Iraq 7.1%, Iran 6.5%, UK 5.7%, UAE 5.4%, Russia 4.4%, Italy 4.2%, France 4.1%. **Tourism:** $28 bil. **Budget:** $207.9 bil. **Total reserves less gold:** $110.9 bil. **Gold:** 16.7 mil oz t. **Inflation:** 7.5%.

Transport: Railways: 5,405 mi. **Motor vehicles:** 168.7 per 1,000 pop. **Civil aviation:** 49.4 bil pass.-mi; 91 airports. **Chief ports:** Aliaga, Diliskelesi, Eregli, Izmir, Izmit.

Communications: TV sets: 428 per 1,000 pop. **Radios:** 283 per 1,000 pop. **Telephone lines:** 18.1 per 100 pop. **Mobile:** 93 per 100 pop. **Internet:** 46.3%.

Health: Life expect.: 71.3 male; 75.4 female. **Births:** 16.9 per 1,000 pop. **Deaths:** 6.1 per 1,000 pop. **Natural inc.:** 1.07%. **Infant mortality:** 21.4 per 1,000 live births. **HIV:** NA.

Education: Compulsory: ages 6-13. **Literacy:** 95%.

Embassy: 2525 Massachusetts Ave. NW 20008; 612-6700.

Website: www.tccb.gov.tr

Ancient inhabitants of Turkey were among the world's first agriculturalists. Such civilizations as the Hittite, Phrygian, and Lydian flourished in Asiatic Turkey (Asia Minor), as did much of Greek civilization. After the fall of Rome in the 5th cent., Constantinople (now Istanbul) was the capital of the Byzantine Empire for 1,000 years. It fell in 1453 to Ottoman Turks, who ruled a vast empire for over 400 years.

Just before WWI, Turkey, or the Ottoman Empire, ruled what is now Syria, Lebanon, Iraq, Jordan, Israel, Saudi Arabia, Yemen, and islands in the Aegean Sea. Turkey joined Germany and Austria in WWI, and its defeat resulted in the loss of territory and the fall of the sultanate. A secular republic was established Oct. 29, 1923. The first pres., Mustafa Kemal (later Kemal Ataturk), led Turkey until his death in 1938.

Turkey kept neutral during most of WWII. The country became a full member of NATO in 1952 and remained a Western ally despite domestic political instability. Military coups overthrew civilian governments in 1960 and 1980. Turkey invaded nearby Cyprus July 20, 1974, to prevent that country from uniting with Greece, and Cyprus was divided into Greek and Turkish zones.

In recent decades, Kurdish separatists and Islamic militants have challenged Turkish governments. Turkey joined the U.S.-led force that ousted Iraq from Kuwait, 1991. Millions of Kurdish refugees fled to Turkey's border after the war. Turkish offensives against the Kurds caused heavy casualties among guerrillas and civilians. Kurdish militants raided Turkish diplomatic missions in some 25 Western European cities, June 24, 1993.

Tansu Ciller became Turkey's first woman prime min. July 5, 1993. The Islamic Welfare Party gained strength in the 1990s, and in June 1996, a coalition with Ciller's True Path Party was formed. The pro-Islamic government resigned June 18, 1997, under pressure from the military, which stepped up its campaign against Islamic fundamentalism in 1998.

Kurdish rebel leader Abdullah Öcalan was captured Feb. 15, 1999; convicted of terrorism June 29, he was sentenced to death. His organization, the Kurdistan Workers' Party, announced in 1999 that it would abandon its 14-year-old insurgency.

Earthquakes in Apr. and Nov. 1999 killed over 17,000 people. The death penalty was abolished in 2002, and Öcalan's sentence was commuted to life in prison Oct. 3. The Islamic Justice and Development Party (AKP) led by Recep Tayyip Erdogan won elections Nov. 3. Suicide bombings by Islamic extremists, Nov. 15-20, 2003, killed 58 people and wounded more than 750 in Istanbul. After Erdogan's party scored a landslide win in 2007 national elections, parliament chose an Islamic politician, Abdullah Gül, as president. Secularists failed to ban the ruling AKP in Turkey's Constitutional Court in 2008, but the party's public funding was halved and it was warned against exerting Islamic influence on state institutions. Turkish voters in 2010 gave resounding approval to constitutional changes favored by the Islamic government, including a provision that would expand membership of the Constitutional Court.

The AKP gained a third consecutive general election victory in June 2011, while dozens of military officers were detained for allegedly plotting to seize power. After the nation's four top military commanders resigned en masse, July 29, 2011, Pres. Gül appointed their replacements Aug. 4, breaking with the tradition of the military promoting its own leaders.

Turkey has long sought full membership in the European Union, but the EU has deferred talks on accession until economic, human rights, and immigration issues are resolved. Turkey's ties with Islamic countries have soured relations with Israel, a former ally.

Police tried to suppress May 31, 2013, protests in Istanbul's Taksim Square over plans to replace Gezi Park, but demonstrations spread and became protests against Prime Min. Erdogan. Force was used, June 15, to clear Gezi Park, resulting in scores of injuries. Arrests began June 19 in Istanbul and Ankara, and protests began to die down at the beginning of July. A court order halted the development plan July 4, 2013. A coal mine explosion in Soma, May 13, 2014, killed 301 and prompted protests over mismanagement and a seeming lack of government concern. Erdogan nevertheless won an Aug. 10 election to become Turkey's first popularly elected president. Foreign Min. Ahmet Davutoglu, an Erdogan ally, replaced him as prime min.

During the Syrian civil war that began in 2011, Turkey became a haven for refugees (more than 1 mil as of Sept. 29, 2014, according to UNHCR), as well as Syrian rebel fighters and some opposition groups. Turkey claimed to have found components for Russian weapons on board a Syrian passenger plane that it intercepted Oct. 10, 2012, and banned all Syrian aircraft from flying through Turkish air space Oct. 14. Turkey's NATO allies decided Dec. 4, 2012, to send Patriot anti-aircraft missiles to Turkey for its defense. Attacks beginning in Sept. 2014 by the Sunni extremist group ISIS against Kurdish areas in northern Syria sent tens of thousands of Kurdish refugees across the border into Turkey. Parliament, Oct. 2, authorized the government to send troops into Syria or Iraq if necessary to protect national security.

Turkmenistan

People: Population: 5,171,943. **Age distrib.:** <15: 26.4%; 65+: 4.2%. **Pop. density:** 28.5 per sq mi, 11 per sq km. **Urban:** 49.7%. **Ethnic groups:** Turkmen 85%, Uzbek 5%, Russian 4%. **Languages:** Turkmen (official), Russian, Uzbek. **Religions:** Muslim 89%, Eastern Orthodox 9%.

Geography: Total area: 188,456 sq mi, 488,100 sq km; **Land area:** 181,441 sq mi, 469,930 sq km. **Location:** Central Asia bordering Caspian Sea. **Neighbors:** Kazakhstan on N; Uzbekistan on N and E; Afghanistan, Iran on S. **Topography:** The Kara Kum Desert occupies 80% of the area. Bordered on W by Caspian Sea. **Capital:** Ashgabat, 735,482.

Government: Type: Republic with authoritarian presidential rule. **Head of state and gov.:** Pres. Gurbanguly Berdymukhammedov; b. June 29, 1957; in office: Feb. 14, 2007 (acting from Dec. 21, 2006). **Local divisions:** 5 provinces, 1 independent city. **Defense budget** (2012): $539 mil. **Active troops:** 22,000.

Economy: Industries: nat. gas, oil, petroleum prods., textiles, food proc. **Chief crops:** cotton, grain, melons. **Natural resources:** petroleum, nat. gas, sulfur, salt. **Crude oil reserves:** 600 mil bbls. **Arable land:** 4.1%. **Livestock:** cattle: 2.3 mil; chickens: 16 mil; goats: 2.3 mil; pigs: 29,000; sheep: 14 mil. **Electricity prod.:** 16.2 bil kWh. **Labor force:** agric. 48.2%, industry 14%, services 37.8%. **Unemployment:** 11.3%.

Finance: Monetary unit: Manat (TMT) (Sept. 2014: 2.85 = $1 U.S.). **GDP:** $55.2 bil; **per capita GDP:** $9,700; **GDP growth:** 12.2%. **Imports:** $12.5 bil; China 19.5%, Turkey 17%, Russia 12.6%, UAE 6.8%, Ukraine 6%, Germany 4.7%, UK 4.2%. **Exports:** $17.1 bil; China 69.6%, Italy 4.7%. **Budget:** $5.5 bil. **Total reserves less gold:** NA. **Inflation:** NA.

Transport: Railways: 1,852 mi. **Civil aviation:** 21 airports. **Chief port:** Turkmenbasy.

Communications: TV sets: 190 per 1,000 pop. **Radios:** 155 per 1,000 pop. **Telephone lines:** 11.5 per 100 pop. **Mobile:** 116.9 per 100 pop. **Internet:** 9.6%.

Health: Life expect.: 66.5 male; 72.6 female. **Births:** 19.5 per 1,000 pop. **Deaths:** 6.2 per 1,000 pop. **Natural inc.:** 1.33%. **Infant mortality:** 38.1 per 1,000 live births. **HIV:** NA.

Education: Compulsory: ages 7-16. **Literacy:** 99.7%.

Embassy: 2207 Massachusetts Ave. NW 20008; 588-1500.

Website: www.turkmenistan.gov.tm

The region has been inhabited by Turkic tribes since the 10th cent. It became part of Russian Turkestan in 1881, and a constituent republic of the USSR in 1925. Turkmenistan declared independence Oct. 27, 1991, and became an independent state when the USSR disbanded Dec. 26, 1991.

Extensive oil and gas reserves place Turkmenistan in a favorable economic position. Political power centered around the former Communist Party apparatus and authoritarian leadership. Gurbanguly Berdymukhammedov won the Feb. 2007 presidential election, considered fraudulent by international observers. He was reelected with 97% of the vote, Feb. 12, 2012. In a small gesture toward democracy, the country's one-party system officially ended, Aug. 21, 2012, permitting a second political party, the Party of Industrialists and Entrepreneurs of Turkmenistan, to be founded.

Tuvalu

People: Population: 10,782. **Age distrib.:** <15: 29.6%; 65+: 5.4%. **Pop. density:** 1,074 per sq mi, 414.7 per sq km. **Urban:** 58.8%. **Ethnic groups:** Polynesian 96%, Micronesian 4%. **Languages:** Tuvaluan, English (both official); Samoan; Kiribati.

Religions: Protestant 98% (Church of Tuvalu [Congregationalist] 97%, Seventh-day Adventist 1%), Baha'i 1%.

Geography: Total area: 10 sq mi, 26 sq km; **Land area:** 10 sq mi, 26 sq km. **Location:** 9 islands forming NW-SE chain 360 mi long in SW Pacific O. **Neighbors:** Nearest are Kiribati to N, Fiji to S. **Topography:** The islands are all low-lying atolls, nowhere rising more than 15 ft above sea level, composed of coral reefs. **Capital:** Funafuti, 5,816.

Government: Type: Parliamentary democracy. **Head of state:** Queen Elizabeth II, rep. by Gov.-Gen. Sir Iakoba Taeia Italeli; in office: Apr. 16, 2010. **Head of gov.:** Prime Min. Enele Sopoaga; b. Feb. 10, 1956; in office: Aug. 5, 2013. **Local divisions:** 7 island councils, 1 town council. **Defense budget/active troops:** NA.

Economy: Industries: fishing, tourism, copra. **Chief crops:** coconuts. **Natural resources:** fish. **Arable land:** 0%. **Livestock:** chickens: 45,000; pigs: 13,600. **Labor force:** Pop. makes living mainly through exploitation of the sea, reefs, and atolls and from wages sent home by those abroad (mostly phosphate industry workers and sailors). **Unemployment:** NA.

Finance: Monetary unit: Dollar (TVD) (Sept. 2014: 1.07 = $1 U.S.). **GDP:** $40 mil; **per capita GDP:** $3,500; **GDP growth:** 1.1%. **Imports** (2010): $16.5 mil. **Exports** (2010): $600,000. **Budget** (2006): $23.1 mil. **Total reserves less gold:** NA. **Inflation:** NA.

Transport: Civil aviation: 1 airport (unpaved runway). **Chief port:** Funafuti.

Communications: TV sets: 9 per 1,000 pop. **Telephone lines:** 14.7 per 100 pop. **Mobile:** 34.4 per 100 pop. **Internet:** 37%.

Health: Life expect.: 63.7 male; 68.1 female. **Births:** 23.7 per 1,000 pop. **Deaths:** 8.9 per 1,000 pop. **Natural inc.:** 1.48%. **Infant mortality:** 31.7 per 1,000 live births. **HIV:** NA.

Education: Compulsory: ages 7-14. **Literacy:** NA.

Permanent UN Mission: 800 Second Ave., Ste. 400D, New York, NY 10017; (212) 490-0534.

Website: www.state.gov/p/eap/ci/tv/

The Ellice Islands separated from the British Gilbert and Ellice Islands Colony in 1975 and became Tuvalu; independence came Oct. 1, 1978. In 2000, Tuvalu joined the United Nations. A major drought that began in Nov. 2010 obliged the government to declare a state of emergency Sept. 28, 2011. Rising sea levels due to climate change are threatening to submerge the tiny island nation. Prime Min. Willy Telavi received a no-confidence vote from parliament Aug. 2, 2013, and was ousted in favor of Enele Sopoaga.

Uganda
Republic of Uganda

People: Population: 35,918,915. **Age distrib.:** <15: 48.7%; 65+: 2.1%. **Pop. density:** 472 per sq mi, 182.2 per sq km. **Urban:** 15.8%. **Ethnic groups:** Baganda 17%, Banyakole 10%, Basoga 8%, Bakiga 7%, Iteso 6%, Langi 6%, Acholi 5%, Bagisu 5%, Lugbara 4%, Bunyoro 3%. **Languages:** English (official), Ganda or Luganda, other Niger-Congo langs., Nilo-Saharan langs., Swahili, Arabic. **Religions:** Roman Catholic 42%, Protestant 42% (Anglican 36%, Pentecostal 5%, Seventh-day Adventist 2%), Muslim 12%.

Geography: Total area: 93,065 sq mi, 241,038 sq km; **Land area:** 76,101 sq mi, 197,100 sq km. **Location:** In E Central Africa. **Neighbors:** South Sudan on N, Dem. Rep. of the Congo on W, Rwanda and Tanzania on S, Kenya on E. **Topography:** Most of Uganda is a high plateau 3,000-6,000 ft high, with Ruwenzori Range in W (Mt. Margherita, 16,763 ft), volcanoes in SW; NE is arid, W and SW rainy. Lakes Victoria, Edward, Albert form much of borders. **Capital:** Kampala, 1,862,760.

Government: Type: Republic. **Head of state and gov.:** Pres. Yoweri Kaguta Museveni; b. Aug. 15, 1944; in office: Jan. 26, 1986. **Local divisions:** 111 districts, 1 capital city. **Defense budget:** $342 mil. **Active troops:** 45,000.

Economy: Industries: sugar, brewing, tobacco, cotton textiles, cement, steel prod. **Chief crops:** coffee, tea, cotton, tobacco, cassava, potatoes, corn, millet, pulses, cut flowers. **Natural resources:** copper, cobalt, hydropower, limestone, salt, gold. **Crude oil reserves:** 2.5 bil bbls. **Arable land:** 34.5%. **Livestock:** cattle: 13 mil; chickens: 38 mil; goats: 14.5 mil; pigs: 2.5 mil; sheep: 2 mil. **Electricity prod.:** 2.5 bil kWh. **Labor force:** agric. 82%, industry 5%, services 13%. **Unemployment:** 4.2%.

Finance: Monetary unit: Shilling (UGX) (Sept. 2014: 2,598.00 = $1 U.S.). **GDP:** $54.4 bil; **per capita GDP:** $1,500; **GDP growth:** 5.6%. **Imports:** $4.9 bil; Kenya 15.6%, UAE 15.4%, China 12.8%, India 11.7%, South Africa 4.1%, Japan 4%. **Exports:** $3.2 bil; Kenya 12.3%, Rwanda 10.3%, UAE 10.2%, Dem. Rep. of the Congo 9.4%, Netherlands 6.1%, Germany 5.6%, Italy 4.4%. **Tourism:** $1.2 bil. **Budget:** $3.8 bil. **Total reserves less gold:** $3.3 bil. **Inflation:** 5.5%.

Transport: Railways: 773 mi. **Motor vehicles:** 10.2 per 1,000 pop. **Civil aviation:** 5 airports. **Chief ports:** Entebbe, Jinja, Port Bell.

Communications: TV sets: 22 per 1,000 pop. **Radios:** 888 per 1,000 pop. **Telephone lines:** 0.6 per 100 pop. **Mobile:** 44.1 per 100 pop. **Internet:** 16.2%.

Health: Life expect.: 53.1 male; 55.9 female. **Births:** 44.2 per 1,000 pop. **Deaths:** 11.0 per 1,000 pop. **Natural inc.:** 3.32%. **Infant mortality:** 60.8 per 1,000 live births. **HIV:** 7.4%.

Education: Compulsory: ages 6-12. **Literacy:** 78.4%.
Embassy: 5911 16th St. NW 20011; 726-7100.
Website: www.statehouse.go.ug

Britain obtained a protectorate over Uganda in 1894. The country became independent Oct. 9, 1962, and a republic within the Commonwealth a year later. In 1967, the traditional kingdoms, including the powerful Buganda state, were abolished.

Gen. Idi Amin seized power from Prime Min. Milton Obote in 1971. During his 8-year dictatorship, he was responsible for the deaths of up to 300,000 of his opponents. In 1972 he expelled nearly all of Uganda's 45,000 Asians. Tanzanian troops and Ugandan exiles and rebels ousted Amin, Apr. 11, 1979.

Obote, president from Dec. 1980, was ousted in a military coup July 1985. Guerrilla war and rampant human rights abuses plagued Uganda under Obote's regime.

Conditions improved after Yoweri Museveni took power in Jan. 1986. In 1993 the Buganda and other traditional monarchies were restored for ceremonial purposes. Uganda helped Laurent Kabila seize power in the Dem. Rep. of the Congo (formerly Zaire) in 1997 but sent troops in 1998 to aid insurgents seeking his ouster. A withdrawal accord was signed Sept. 2002.

Pres. Museveni won reelection in 2001 and 2006; opponents disputed the latter result. Museveni won a 2011 presidential election that European observers considered flawed.

An insurgency in N Uganda killed more than 100,000 people and forced about 2 mil to flee. The rebel Lord's Resistance Army (LRA) began fighting the Museveni government in 1986 and abducted some 30,000 children to serve as soldiers and sex slaves. Peace talks brokered by Sudan began July 2006; as talks continued through 2007, the violence diminished. A cease-fire accord was signed Feb. 23, 2008, but Ugandan and Congolese troops (with U.S. aid) launched a new offensive against the LRA in late 2008. Suicide bombings July 11, 2010, killed 76 people watching a World Cup soccer match on outdoor video screens in Kampala. Al-Shabaab, a Somali al-Qaeda-linked Islamist group, claimed responsibility. An Ebola outbreak in summer 2012 took 176 lives before doctors gained control.

An online campaign to capture the LRA's leader, Joseph Kony, was boosted by the film *Kony 2012*, which gained over 100 mil views by Mar. 2012. On Apr. 3, 2013, the U.S. offered a $5 mil reward for information leading to his capture. The UNHCR estimated that more than 172,000 refugees from conflicts in the Dem. Rep. of the Congo were living in Uganda at the beginning of 2014; some later returned home. An Anti-Homosexuality Act, signed by Museveni Feb. 24, 2014, and making some gay behavior punishable by life in prison, was struck down on technical grounds by a Uganda court Aug. 1.

Ukraine

People: Population: 44,291,413. **Age distrib.:** <15: 14%; 65+: 15.9%. **Pop. density:** 198 per sq mi, 76.5 per sq km. **Urban:** 69.5%. **Ethnic groups:** Ukrainian 78%, Russian 17%. **Languages:** Ukrainian (official), Russian. **Religions:** Orthodox, Ukrainian Greek Catholic.

Geography: Total area: 233,032 sq mi, 603,550 sq km; **Land area:** 223,681 sq mi, 579,330 sq km. **Location:** In E Europe. **Neighbors:** Belarus on N; Russia on NE and E; Moldova, Romania on SW; Hungary, Slovakia, Poland on W. **Topography:** Part of the E European plain. Mountainous areas include the Carpathians in the SW and Crimean chain in the S. Arable black soil constitutes a large part of the country. **Capital:** Kiev, 2,916,590. **Cities (urban aggl.):** Kharkiv, 1,444,009; Odesa, 1,010,685.

Government: Type: Republic. **Head of state:** Pres. Petro Poroshenko; b. Sept. 26, 1965; in office: June 7, 2014. **Head of gov.:** Prime Min. Arseniy Yatsenyuk; b. May 22, 1974; in office: Feb. 27, 2014. **Local divisions:** 24 provinces, 2 municipalities, 1 autonomous republic. **Defense budget:** $2.42 bil. **Active troops:** 129,950.

Economy: Industries: coal, elec. power, metals, machinery and transp. equip., chemicals, food proc. **Chief crops:** grain, sugar beets, sunflower seeds, vegetables. **Natural resources:** iron ore, coal, manganese, nat. gas, petroleum, salt, sulfur, graphite, titanium, magnesium, kaolin, nickel, mercury, timber. **Crude oil reserves:** 395 mil bbls. **Arable land:** 56.1%. **Livestock:** cattle: 4.6 mil; chickens: 195.3 mil; goats: 664,800; pigs: 7.6 mil; sheep: 1.1 mil. **Electricity prod.:** 184 bil kWh. **Labor force:** agric. 5.6%, industry 26%, services 68.4%. **Unemployment:** 7.7%.

Finance: Monetary unit: Hryvna (UAH) (Sept. 2014: 12.53 = $1 U.S.). **GDP:** $337.4 bil; **per capita GDP:** $7,400; **GDP growth:** 0.4%. **Imports:** $87.2 bil; Russia 32.4%, China 9.3%, Germany 8%, Belarus 6%, Poland 4.2%. **Exports:** $71.1 bil; Russia 25.6%, Turkey 5.4%, Egypt 4.2%. **Tourism:** $5.1 bil. **Budget:** $66.5 bil (planned and consolidated). **Total reserves less gold:** $18.8 bil. **Gold:** 1.4 mil oz t. **Inflation:** –0.3%.

Transport: Railways: 13,474 mi. **Motor vehicles:** 229.1 per 1,000 pop. **Civil aviation:** 6.2 bil pass.-mi; 108 airports. **Chief ports:** Feodosiya, Illichivsk, Mariupol, Mykolayiv, Odesa, Yuzhnyy.

Communications: TV sets: 433 per 1,000 pop. **Radios:** 283 per 1,000 pop. **Telephone lines:** 26.2 per 100 pop. **Mobile:** 138.1 per 100 pop. **Internet:** 41.8%.

Health: Life expect.: 63.8 male; 74.9 female. **Births:** 9.4 per 1,000 pop. **Deaths:** 15.7 per 1,000 pop. **Natural inc.:** –0.63%. **Infant mortality:** 8.1 per 1,000 live births. **HIV:** 0.8%.

Education: Compulsory: ages 6-16. **Literacy:** 99.8%.
Embassy: 3350 M St. NW 20007; 333-0606.
Website: www.kmu.gov.ua

Ukrainians' Slavic ancestors inhabited the region well before the 1st cent. ᴄᴇ. In the 9th cent., the princes of Kiev established a strong state called Kievan Rus, which included much of present-day Ukraine. Internal conflicts led to the disintegration of the Ukrainian state by the 13th cent. Mongol rule was supplanted by Poland and Lithuania in the 14th and 15th cent. The N Black Sea coast and Crimea came under Turkish control in 1478. Ukrainian Cossacks, starting in the late 16th cent., rebelled against the occupiers of Ukraine: Russia, Poland, and Turkey.

An independent Ukrainian National Republic was proclaimed on Jan. 22, 1918. But in 1921, Ukraine's neighbors occupied and divided Ukrainian territory. In 1922, Ukraine became a constituent republic of the USSR. In 1932-33, the Soviet government engineered a famine in eastern Ukraine, and 6-7 mil Ukrainians died. During WWII the Ukrainian nationalist underground fought Nazi and Soviet forces. Over 5 mil Ukrainians died in the war. The reoccupation of Ukraine by Soviet troops in 1944 brought a renewed wave of repression.

The world's worst nuclear power plant disaster occurred in Chernobyl, Ukraine, in Apr. 1986; many thousands were killed or disabled as a result of the radiation leak.

Ukrainian independence was restored, Dec. 1991, with the Soviet Union's dissolution. Following a 1994 accord with Russia and the U.S., Ukraine's large nuclear arsenal was transferred to Russia for destruction.

President since 1994, Leonid Kuchma attempted to engineer the 2004 election of his handpicked successor, the Russian-backed Prime Min. Viktor Yanukovych. When Yanukovych was declared the winner in Nov., supporters of his main challenger, former Prime Min. Viktor Yushchenko, called the election fraudulent and staged massive protests (the Orange Revolution); the vote was annulled. An election rerun Dec. 26 gave Yushchenko the victory. Yushchenko's party fared poorly in Mar. 2006 parliamentary elections, and Yanukovych returned as prime min. in Aug.

Following Sept. 2007 elections, Yulia Tymoshenko, a former Orange Revolution ally of Yushchenko, became prime min., but she lost the presidential election to Yanukovych in Feb. 2010. Tymoshenko went on trial in June 2011 for abusing her powers as prime min. She was convicted and sentenced to seven years in prison in Oct. She was released in Feb. 2014.

Large anti-Yanukovych protests began in Nov. 2013, following his decision not to sign a free trade pact with the EU. After dozens were killed in violent protests in Kiev, Feb. 18-20, 2014, parliament removed Yanukovych from office, Feb. 22. Pro-EU candidate Petro Poroshenko won a May 25, 2014, presidential election. Signing and ratification of the EU agreement were completed June 27 and Sept. 16, with most implementation delayed until 2016 to appease Russian opposition. Poroshenko, Aug. 25, called new parliamentary elections for Oct. 26, 2014.

Aiding pro-Russian separatists, Russian forces entered Crimea in Mar., and Russia annexed the region Mar. 18, 2014. Fighting began in Apr. in eastern Ukraine between Ukrainian forces and pro-Russian separatists, widely reported to be aided by Russian military equipment and troops. Separatists apparently shot down a Malaysia Airlines commercial flight over eastern Ukraine, July 17, killing all 298 on board. NATO, Aug. 28, released satellite images said to show Russian troops in Ukraine. The UN reported, Aug. 29, more than 2,200 killed in eastern Ukraine fighting since mid-Apr. A ceasefire signed Sept. 5, 2014, reduced the level of fighting.

United Arab Emirates

People: Population: 5,628,805. **Age distrib.:** <15: 20.7%; 65+: 1%. **Pop. density:** 174.4 per sq mi, 67.3 per sq km. **Urban:** 85.3%. **Ethnic groups:** Emirati 19%, other Arab and Iranian 23%, S Asian 50%, other expatriates (incl. Westerners and E Asians) 8%. (Less than 20% are UAE citizens.) **Languages:** Arabic (official), Persian, English, Hindi, Urdu. **Religions:** Muslim (official) 76%, Christian 9%, other (primarily Hindu, Buddhist) 15%.

Geography: Total area: 32,278 sq mi, 83,600 sq km; **Land area:** 32,278 sq mi, 83,600 sq km. **Location:** Middle East, on S shore of the Persian Gulf. **Neighbors:** Saudi Arabia on W and S, Oman on E. **Topography:** A barren, flat coastal plain gives way to uninhabited sand dunes on S. Hajar Mts. in E. **Capital:** Abu Dhabi, 1,113,900. **Cities (urban aggl.):** Dubai, 2,330,499; Sharjah, 1,228,992.

Government: Type: Federation of emirates. **Head of state:** Pres. Sheikh Khalifa ibn Zaid an-Nahayan; b. 1948; in office: Nov. 3, 2004. **Head of gov.:** Prime Min. Sheikh Muhammad ibn Rashid al-Maktum; b. July 15, 1949; in office: Jan. 5, 2006. **Local divisions:** 7 emirates: Abu Dhabi, Ajman, Dubai, Fujaira, Ras al-Khaimah, Sharjah, Umm al-Qaiwain. **Defense budget** (2011): $9.32 bil. **Active troops:** 51,000.

Economy: Industries: petroleum and petrochemicals, fishing, aluminum, cement, fertilizers, commercial ship repair, constr. materials. **Chief crops:** dates, vegetables, watermelons. **Natural resources:** petroleum, nat. gas. **Crude oil reserves:** 97.8 bil bbls. **Arable land:** 0.6%. **Livestock:** cattle: 108,500; chickens: 21.5 mil;

goats: 1.9 mil; sheep: 1.4 mil. **Electricity prod.:** 97.9 bil kWh. **Labor force:** agric. 7%, industry 15%, services 78%. **Unemployment:** 3.8%.

Finance: Monetary unit: Dirham (AED) (Sept. 2014: 3.67 = $1 U.S). **GDP:** $269.8 bil; **per capita GDP:** $29,900; **GDP growth:** 4%. **Imports:** $249.6 bil; India 17%, China 13.7%, U.S. 10.5%, Germany 5.1%, Japan 4.2%. **Exports:** $368.9 bil; Japan 15.4%, India 13.4%, Iran 10.7%, Thailand 5.5%, Singapore 5.5%, South Korea 5.3%. **Tourism:** $10.4 bil. **Budget:** $118.3 bil. **Total reserves less gold:** $68.2 bil. **Inflation** (2010-11): 0.9%.

Transport: Motor vehicles: 405.7 per 1,000 pop. **Civil aviation:** 131.6 bil pass.-mi; 25 airports. **Chief ports:** Al Fujayrah, Mina' Jabal Ali, Khawr Fakkan, Mina' Rashid, Mina' Saqr.

Communications: TV sets: 197 per 1,000 pop. **Radios:** 1,455 per 1,000 pop. **Telephone lines:** 22.3 per 100 pop. **Mobile:** 171.9 per 100 pop. **Internet:** 88%.

Health: Life expect.: 74.5 male; 79.8 female. **Births:** 15.5 per 1,000 pop. **Deaths:** 2.0 per 1,000 pop. **Natural inc.:** 1.36%. **Infant mortality:** 10.9 per 1,000 live births. **HIV:** NA.

Education: Compulsory: ages 6-14. **Literacy:** 93.8%.

Embassy: 3522 International Ct. NW, Ste. 400, 20008; 243-2400.

Website: www.government.ae

The 7 "Trucial Sheikdoms" gave Britain control of defense and foreign relations in the 19th cent. They merged to become an independent state Dec. 2, 1971. Oil revenues have made the UAE one of the world's wealthiest countries. Foreigners make up most of the work force.

International banking, investment, and construction boomed during the late 1990s and early 2000s. But Dubai, hurt by the global recession beginning in 2008, accepted up to $9.5 bil in government loans to help the state-controlled investment company, Dubai World, avoid default. On July 2, 2013, 68 members of the Islamist group Islah were convicted of conspiring to overthrow the government. The UAE and two other Middle Eastern monarchies together donated, July 9-10, $12 bil to Egypt after the country overthrew Islamist Pres. Mohammed Morsi. Beginning in Sept. 2014, UAE warplanes took part in U.S.-led airstrikes against Sunni extremist forces in Syria.

United Kingdom
United Kingdom of Great Britain and Northern Ireland

People: Population: 63,742,977. **Age distrib.:** <15: 17.3%; 65+: 17.5%. **Pop. density:** 682.4 per sq mi, 263.5 per sq km. **Urban:** 82.3%. **Ethnic groups:** white 87%, black 3%, Indian 2%, Pakistani 2%, mixed 2%. **Languages:** English; Scots, Scottish Gaelic, Welsh, Irish, Cornish (all recognized regional langs.). **Religions:** Christian 60%, Muslim 4%, none 26%.

Geography: Total area: 94,058 sq mi, 243,610 sq km; **Land area:** 93,410 sq mi, 241,930 sq km. **Location:** Off NW coast of Europe, across English Channel, Strait of Dover, North Sea. **Neighbors:** Ireland to W, France to SE. **Topography:** England is mostly rolling land, rising to Uplands of southern Scotland. Lowlands are in center of Scotland, granite highlands are in N. Coast is heavily indented, especially on W. British Isles have milder climate than N Europe due to Gulf Stream and ample rainfall. Severn, 220 mi, and Thames, 215 mi, are longest rivers. **Capital:** London, 10,189,300. **Cities (urban aggl.):** Manchester, 2,623,651; Birmingham (West Midlands), 2,497,002; West Yorkshire, 1,880,507.

Government: Type: Constitutional monarchy. **Head of state:** Queen Elizabeth II; b. Apr. 21, 1926; in office: Feb. 6, 1952. **Head of gov.:** Prime Min. David Cameron; b. Oct. 9, 1966; in office: May 11, 2010. **Local divisions:** 232 local authorities (England: 152; Wales: 22; Scotland: 32; Northern Ireland: 26). **Defense budget:** $57.04 bil. **Active troops:** 169,150.

Economy: Industries: machine tools, elec. power equip., automation equip., railroad equip., shipbuilding, aircraft, motor vehicles and parts, electronics and communications equip., metals, chemicals, coal, petroleum, paper and paper prods. **Chief crops:** cereals, oilseed, potatoes, vegetables. **Natural resources:** coal, petroleum, nat. gas, iron ore, lead, zinc, gold, tin, limestone, salt, clay, chalk, gypsum, potash, silica sand, slate. **Crude oil reserves:** 3 bil bbls. **Arable land:** 25.7%. **Livestock:** cattle: 9.8 mil; chickens: 152 mil; goats: 98,000; pigs: 4.9 mil; sheep: 32.9 mil. **Electricity prod.** (2012): 338.9 bil kWh. **Labor force:** agric. 1.4%, industry 18.2%, services 80.4%. **Unemployment:** 7.9%.

Finance: Monetary unit: Pound (GBP) (Sept. 2014: 0.61 = $1 U.S). **GDP:** $2.4 tril; **per capita GDP:** $37,300; **GDP growth:** 1.8%. **Imports:** $782.5 bil; Germany 12.6%, China 8%, Netherlands 7.5%, U.S. 6.7%, France 5.4%, Belgium 4.4%, Norway 4%. **Exports:** $813.2 bil; Germany 11.3%, U.S. 10.5%, Netherlands 8.8%, France 7.4%, Ireland 6.2%, Belgium 5.1%. **Tourism:** $40.6 bil. **Budget:** $1.1 tril. **Total reserves less gold:** $92.4 bil. **Gold:** 10 mil oz t. **Inflation:** 2.6%.

Transport: Railways: 10,224 mi. **Motor vehicles:** 572.3 per 1,000 pop. **Civil aviation:** 151.1 bil pass.-mi; 271 airports. **Chief ports:** Dover, Felixstowe, Immingham, Liverpool, London, Southampton, Teesport.

Communications: TV sets: 1,105 per 1,000 pop. **Radios:** 2,059 per 1,000 pop. **Telephone lines:** 52.9 per 100 pop. **Mobile:** 123.8 per 100 pop. **Internet:** 89.8%.

Health: Life expect.: 78.3 male; 82.7 female. **Births:** 12.2 per 1,000 pop. **Deaths:** 9.3 per 1,000 pop. **Natural inc.:** 0.29%. **Infant mortality:** 4.4 per 1,000 live births. **HIV:** 0.3%.

Education: Compulsory: ages 5-16. **Literacy:** 99%.

Embassy: 3100 Massachusetts Ave. NW 20008; 588-6500.

Website: www.gov.uk

The United Kingdom of Great Britain and Northern Ireland comprises England, Wales, Scotland, and Northern Ireland.

Queen and Royal Family. The ruling sovereign is Elizabeth II of the House of Windsor, elder daughter of King George VI. She succeeded to the throne Feb. 6, 1952, and was crowned June 2, 1953. She was married Nov. 20, 1947, to Lt. Philip Mountbatten (b. June 10, 1921), former Prince of Greece. He was created Duke of Edinburgh, and given the title H.R.H., Nov. 19, 1947; he was named Prince of the United Kingdom and Northern Ireland Feb. 22, 1957. Prince Charles Philip Arthur George (b. Nov. 14, 1948) is the Prince of Wales and heir apparent. His first son, William Philip Arthur Louis (b. June 21, 1982), is second in line to the throne; William's son, George Alexander Louis (b. July 22, 2013) is third in line.

Parliament is the UK's legislative body, with certain powers over dependent units. It consists of two houses. The House of Commons has 650 members, elected by direct ballot and divided as follows: England, 533; Wales, 40; Scotland, 59; Northern Ireland, 18. Following a drastic reduction in 1999 in the number of hereditary peerages, the House of Lords (Jan. 2014) comprised 780 members: 88 hereditary peers, 667 life peers, and 25 archbishops and bishops of the Church of England.

Resources and Industries. Great Britain is a major global trade and financial services center. Service industries account for 78.9% of GDP; industry, 20.5%; agriculture, 0.7%. Domestic agriculture produces about 60% of food needs. Manufacturing, historically important since the Industrial Revolution, has declined in economic significance, while finance, centered in London, has grown in importance. Coal production, also historically important, has declined by more than 90% since 1970. Large oil and gas fields have been found in the North Sea, and commercial oil production began in 1975. However, proved reserves are declining, and the country has been a net energy importer since 2005.

Religion and Education. The Church of England is Protestant Episcopal. The queen is its temporal head, with rights of appointments to archbishoprics, bishoprics, and other offices. There are two provinces, Canterbury and York, each headed by an archbishop. Westminster Abbey (1050-1760) is the site of coronations and the tombs of Elizabeth I, Mary, Queen of Scots, kings, poets, and of the Unknown Warrior. Celebrated British universities Oxford and Cambridge each date to the 13th cent.

History. Recent research indicates that Britain was separated from the European continent at least 200,000 years ago by a catastrophic flood that created the English Channel. Migrants across the Channel included the Celts, who arrived 2,500 to 3,000 years ago. Their language survives in Welsh and Gaelic enclaves.

England was part of the Roman Empire 43-410 CE, after which waves of Jutes, Angles, and Saxons arrived from German lands, followed by Danish raiders from the 8th through 11th cent. French-speaking Normans invaded in 1066, uniting the country with their dominions in France.

Opposition by nobles to royal authority forced King John to agree to the Magna Carta in 1215, a guarantee of rights and the rule of law. In the ensuing decades, the foundations of the parliamentary system were laid.

English dynastic claims to large parts of France led to the Hundred Years War, 1338-1453, an unsuccessful campaign. A long civil war, the War of the Roses, lasted 1455-85, and ended with the establishment of the Tudor monarchy. The economy prospered over long periods of domestic peace unmatched in continental Europe. The Church of England separated from the authority of the pope, 1534.

During the reign of Queen Elizabeth I, 1558-1603, England became a major naval power, leading to the founding of colonies in the New World and the expansion of trade with Europe and Asia. Scotland and England shared a single monarch after James VI of Scotland was crowned James I of England in 1603.

A struggle between Parliament and the Stuart kings led to a civil war, 1642-49, and the establishment of a republic under the Puritan Oliver Cromwell. The monarchy was restored in 1660, but the Glorious Revolution of 1688 confirmed the sovereignty of Parliament: a Bill of Rights was granted 1689. Scotland was united with England after the ratification of the Articles of Union of Scotland and England, May 1707.

Technological and entrepreneurial innovations led to the Industrial Revolution in the 18th cent. The 13 N American colonies were lost but replaced by growing empires in Canada, India, Australia, and elsewhere. Britain's role in the defeat of Napoleon, 1815, strengthened its position as the leading world power.

The limited extension of voting rights in 1832, 1867, and 1884; the formation of trade unions; and the development of universal public education were among the social changes that accompanied the spread of industrialization and urbanization in the 19th cent.

(Men gained full voting rights in 1918 and women in 1928.) Large parts of Africa and Asia were added to the empire during the reign of Queen Victoria, 1837-1901.

Though victorious in WWI, Britain suffered huge casualties and economic dislocation. Ireland became independent in 1921, and independence movements became active in India and other colonies. The country suffered major bombing damage in WWII but rallied behind Prime Min. Winston Churchill and held off Germany until Allied victory was achieved, 1945.

Industrial growth continued in the postwar period, but Britain lost its leadership position to other powers. Labour governments passed socialist programs nationalizing some basic industries and expanding social security. Prime Min. Margaret Thatcher's Conservative governments, 1979-90, fostered private enterprise and began denationalization of key industries. Her Conservative successor, John Major, held power 1990-97. The UK sent military forces to the Persian Gulf War, 1991. The Channel Tunnel linking Britain to the Continent was opened May 6, 1994.

The 1997 victory by the Labour Party made Tony Blair, 43, Britain's youngest prime min. since 1812. Diana, Princess of Wales, died in a car crash in Paris, Aug. 31. Britain played a leading role in the NATO air war against Yugoslavia, Mar.-June 1999, and contributed 12,000 troops to the multinational Kosovo security force.

After the Sept. 11 attacks on the U.S., Britain took an important role in the U.S.-led war against terrorism. The UK participated, beginning in 2001, in the Afghanistan war, maintaining as many as 9,500 troops in the country; more than 3,900 remained as of Sept. 2014, and British troops had suffered more than 450 fatalities since the war started. Blair, who won a landslide election victory June 2001, committed British troops to the U.S.-led invasion of Iraq, Mar.-Apr. 2003, despite dissent within his own cabinet. UK forces, which numbered 46,000 at the height of combat operations, almost entirely pulled out by mid-2009; 179 had died. Following an offensive in Iraq by the Sunni extremist group ISIS, beginning in June 2014, Britain provided humanitarian aid to ISIS victims and military aid to Kurdish forces opposing ISIS fighters. Parliament approved, Sept. 26, British airstrikes against ISIS forces in Iraq.

In May 2005 elections, Blair became the first Labour prime min. to win 3 consecutive terms. Suicide bombings on 3 London underground trains and a bus, July 7, 2005, left 56 people dead and hundreds injured; police identified the bombers as 4 British Muslim men (3 of Pakistani origin).

Blair was succeeded by Gordon Brown, June 2007. Responding Oct. 13, 2008, to the worldwide financial crisis, Prime Min. Brown initiated a plan to partially nationalize three of Britain's largest banks and support them with a capital infusion of up to $63 bil.

In the wake of Britain's deepest recession since WWII, voters rejected Brown and the Labour Party in May 2010 parliamentary elections. Conservatives and Liberal Democrats formed the first coalition government in 70 years, with Conservative leader David Cameron becoming prime min. Cameron responded to the fiscal crisis with austerity measures, including a steep VAT increase, meant to rein in debt. The government reported Oct. 25, 2012, that London's hosting of the Olympics, July 27-Aug. 12, 2012, had helped the economy to recover from its double-dip recession during the third quarter of 2012.

Justin Welby was installed Feb. 4, 2013, as the new Archbishop of Canterbury, the head of the Church of England. Parliament voted in favor of same-sex marriage July 16, 2013, and Queen Elizabeth approved the measure the next day. Prince William's wife, Catherine, gave birth July 22, 2013, to a baby boy, who was third in line to the throne.

Wales

The Principality of Wales in western Britain has an area of 8,019 sq mi and a population (2013 est.) of 3,082,412. Cardiff is the capital, pop. (2010 est., city proper) 341,054.

Less than 20% of Wales residents speak English and Welsh; about 32,000 speak Welsh solely. A 1979 referendum rejected, 4-1, the creation of an elected Welsh assembly; a similar proposal passed by a thin margin on Sept. 18, 1997. Elections for the 60-seat assembly were held in 1999, 2003, 2007, and 2011.

Early Anglo-Saxon invaders drove Celtic peoples into the mountains of Wales, where they developed a distinct nationality. Members of the ruling house of Gwynedd in the 13th cent. fought England but were crushed, 1283. Edward of Caernarvon, son of Edward I of England, was created Prince of Wales, 1301. **Website:** wales.gov.uk

Scotland

Scotland occupies the northern 37% of the main British island, and the Hebrides, Orkney, Shetland, and smaller islands. Length 275 mi, breadth approx. 150 mi, area 30,414 sq mi, pop. (2013 est.) 5,327,700.

The Lowlands, a belt of land approx. 60 mi wide from the Firth of Clyde to the Firth of Forth, divide the farming region of the Southern Uplands from the granite Highlands of the N; they contain 75% of the population and most of the industry. The Highlands, famous for hunting and fishing, have been opened to industry by many hydroelectric power stations.

Edinburgh, pop. (2013 est., city proper) 487,500, is the capital. Glasgow, pop. (2013 est., city proper) 596,550, is Scotland's greatest commercial city. It is a major port and shipbuilding center and has developed a services-based economy in the 21st cent., including financial services, healthcare, and engineering. Aberdeen, pop. (2013 est.) 227,130, NE of Edinburgh, is a major port, center of granite industry, fish-processing, and North Sea oil exploration. Dundee, pop. (2013 est.) 148,170, NE of Edinburgh, is an industrial and fish-processing center. About 90,000 persons speak Gaelic as well as English.

History. Scotland was called Caledonia by the Romans who battled early Celtic tribes and occupied southern areas from the 1st to the 4th cent. Missionaries from Britain introduced Christianity in the 4th cent.; St. Columba, an Irish monk, converted most of Scotland in the 6th cent.

The Kingdom of Scotland was founded in 1018. William Wallace and Robert Bruce both defeated English armies 1297 and 1314, respectively. In 1603, James VI of Scotland, son of Mary, Queen of Scots, succeeded to the English throne as James I, and effected the Union of the Crowns. In 1707 Scotland received representation in the British Parliament, resulting from the union of formerly separate Parliaments. In recent years, the Scottish National Party has urged independence. A 1997 proposal to create a regional legislature with limited taxing authority passed by a landslide. Elections for the 129-seat parliament were held 1999, 2003, 2007, and 2011; in the 2011 vote, Scottish Nationalist candidates won a majority. However, in a referendum on independence Sept. 18, 2014, 55% of Scottish voters opposed separating from the UK.

Memorials of Robert Burns, Sir Walter Scott, John Knox, and Mary, Queen of Scots, draw many tourists, as do the beauties of the Trossachs, Loch Katrine, Loch Lomond, and abbey ruins.

Industries. Engineering products are a key industry, with growing emphasis on office machinery, autos, electronics, and other consumer goods. Oil discoveries offshore in the North Sea stimulated onshore support industries.

Scotland produces fine woolens, worsteds, tweeds, silks, fine linens, and jute. It is known for its special breeds of cattle and sheep. Commercial fishing is an important industry. Whisky is a major export.

The Hebrides are a group of about 500 islands, 100 inhabited, off the W coast. The **Inner Hebrides** include Skye, Mull, and Iona, the last famous for the arrival of St. Columba, 563 CE. The **Outer Hebrides** include Lewis and Harris. Industries include sheep raising and weaving. The **Orkney Isls.**, c. 90, are to the NE. The capital is Kirkwall, on Pomona Isl. Fish curing, sheep raising, and weaving are occupations. NE of the Orkneys are the 200 **Shetland Isls.**, 24 inhabited, home of Shetland ponies. The Orkneys and Shetlands are centers for the North Sea oil industry. **Website:** www.scotland.gov.uk

Northern Ireland

Northern Ireland was constituted in 1920 from 6 of the 9 counties of Ulster, the NE corner of Ireland. Area 5,452 sq mi, pop. (2013 est.) 1,829,725. Capital and chief industrial center, Belfast, pop. (2013 est., city proper) 281,735.

Industries. Shipbuilding, including large tankers, has long been an important industry, centered in Belfast, the largest port. Linen is manufactured, along with apparel, rope, and twine. Growing diversification has added engineering products, synthetic fibers, and electronics. There are large numbers of cattle, hogs, and sheep. Potatoes, poultry, and dairy foods are also produced.

Government and History. An act of the British Parliament, 1920, divided Northern from Southern Ireland, each with a parliament and government. When Ireland became a dominion, 1921, and later a republic, Northern Ireland chose to remain a part of the UK.

During 1968-69, Roman Catholics, a minority comprising about one-third of the population, claimed discrimination against them in voting rights, housing, and employment. Violence and terrorism intensified, involving branches of the Irish Republican Army (IRA; outlawed in the Irish Republic), Protestant groups, police, and British troops. Between 1969 and 2001, more than 3,500 were killed in sectarian violence in Northern Ireland, Ireland, England, and elsewhere. For most of this period, the Northern Ireland parliament was suspended, and Britain imposed direct rule.

A settlement reached on Good Friday, Apr. 10, 1998, and approved May 22 by voters in Northern Ireland and the Irish Republic, restored home rule and election of a 108-member assembly with safeguards for minority rights. Both Ireland and Great Britain agreed to relinquish constitutional claims on Northern Ireland. Elections to the assembly were held June 25. IRA dissidents seeking to derail the agreement detonated a bomb at Omagh Aug. 15 that killed 29 people and injured over 330.

London transferred authority to a Northern Ireland power-sharing government in 1999. Delays in IRA disarmament led to several suspensions of self-government. The IRA July 2005 renounced violence and ordered all units to disarm. The British responded by reducing their military presence in the region. On Sept. 26, an international monitoring group reported that the IRA had apparently scrapped its entire arsenal. The Northern Ireland legislature, suspended for 3½ years, reconvened May 15, 2006. Elections were held in 2007 and 2011. More than 6 weeks of violence erupted after Belfast's city government decided, Dec 3, 2012, to limit the flying of the Union

Jack at the City Council building, provoking pro-British unionists, who clashed with Catholic republicans. More than 100 police and scores of protesters were injured.

Religion and Education. Northern Ireland is about 58% Protestant, 42% Roman Catholic. Education is compulsory between the ages of 5 and 16 years. **Website:** www.northernireland.gov.uk

Channel Islands

The Channel Islands, area 75 sq mi, off the NW coast of France, the only parts of the one-time Dukedom of Normandy belonging to England, are Jersey, Guernsey and the dependencies of Guernsey—Alderney, Brechou, Great Sark, Little Sark, Herm, Jethou, and Lihou. **Jersey,** area 45 sq mi, pop. (2014 est.) 96,513, and **Guernsey,** area 30 sq mi, pop. (2014 est.) 65,849, have separate legal existences and lieutenant governors named by the Crown. The islands were the only British soil occupied by German troops in WWII. **Websites:** www.gov.je (Jersey); www.gov.gg (Guernsey)

Isle of Man

The Isle of Man, area 221 sq mi, pop. (2014 est.) 86,866, is in the Irish Sea, 20 mi from Scotland, 30 mi from Cumberland. It is rich in lead and iron. The island has its own laws and a lieutenant governor appointed by the Crown. The Tynwald (legislature) consists of the Legislative Council, partly elected, and House of Keys, elected. Capital: Douglas; pop. (2014 est.) 28,685. Farming, tourism, and fishing (kippers, scallops) are chief occupations. Man is famous for the Manx tailless cat. **Website:** www.gov.im

Gibraltar

A dependency on the S coast of Spain, Gibraltar guards the entrance to the Mediterranean. The Rock of Gibraltar has been in British possession since 1704. It is 2.5 mi long, 0.75 of a mi wide, and 1,396 ft in height, with a total area of 2.5 sq mi; a narrow isthmus connects it with the mainland. Pop. (2014 est.) 29,185.

Gibraltar has historically been an object of contention between Britain and Spain. In 1967, residents voted almost unanimously to remain under British rule. A new constitution, May 30, 1969, increased Gibraltarian control of domestic affairs (the UK continues to handle defense and internal security matters). The border, closed by Spain in 1969, was fully reopened in Feb. 1985. A UN General Assembly resolution requested Britain to end Gibraltar's colonial status by Oct. 1, 1996. Gibraltar voters rejected a plan for the UK and Spain to share sovereignty, Nov. 7, 2002. Residents approved a new constitution Nov. 30, 2006. Nevertheless, tensions flared again between the two countries in Aug. 2013 over the question of territorial control. **Website:** www.gibraltar.gov.gi

British West Indies

Swinging in a vast arc from the coast of Venezuela NE, then N and NW toward Puerto Rico are the Leeward Isls., forming a coral and volcanic barrier sheltering the Caribbean from the open Atlantic. Many of the islands are self-governing British possessions. Universal suffrage was instituted 1951-54; ministerial systems were set up 1956-60.

The **Leeward Isls.** still associated with the UK are **Montserrat,** area 39 sq mi, pop. (2014 est.) 5,215, capital Plymouth; the **British Virgin Isls.,** 58 sq mi, pop. (2014 est.) 32,680, capital Road Town (2014 est. pop., 13,102); and **Anguilla,** the most northerly of Leeward Isls., 35 sq mi, pop. (2014 est.) 16,086, capital The Valley (2014 est. pop., 1,039). Montserrat has been devastated by the Soufrière Hills volcano, which began erupting July 18, 1995.

The three **Cayman Isls.,** a dependency, lie S of Cuba, NW of Jamaica. Pop. (2014 est.) 54,914, most of it on Grand Cayman. It is a free port; in the 1970s Grand Cayman became a tax-free refuge for foreign funds and branches of many Western banks were opened there. Total area 102 sq mi. Capital: George Town; pop. (2014 est.) 30,603.

The **Turks and Caicos Isls.** are a dependency at the SE end of the Bahama Islands. Of about 40 islands, only 8 are inhabited; area 366 sq mi, pop. (2014 est.) 49,070; capital Grand Turk. Salt, shellfish, and conch shells are the main exports.

Bermuda

Bermuda is a British dependency governed by a royal governor and an assembly, dating from 1620, the oldest legislative body among British dependencies. Capital: Hamilton; pop. (2014 est.) 10,334. It is a group of about 150 small islands of coral formation, 20 inhabited, comprising 21 sq mi in the western Atlantic, 580 mi E of N. Carolina. Pop. (2014 est.) 69,839 (about 54% of African descent). Pop. density is high.

Tourism is the major industry; tourism receipts in 2013 were $437 mil. Bermuda is also a haven for the offshore insurance industry. Exports include petroleum products, medicine. In a referendum Aug. 15, 1995, voters rejected independence by nearly a 3-to-1 majority. Hurricane Fabian, the most potent storm to reach Bermuda in 50 years, struck Sept. 5, 2003; four people were missing and presumed dead, and damage was estimated at over $300 mil. **Website:** www.gov.bm

South Atlantic Territories

The **Falkland Isls.,** a dependency, lie 300 mi E of the Strait of Magellan at the southern end of S America.

The Falklands, or Islas Malvinas, include 2 large islands and about 200 smaller ones, area 4,700 sq mi, pop. (2012) 2,840, capital Stanley. The licensing of foreign fishing vessels has become the major source of revenue. Sheep-grazing is a main industry; wool is the principal export. There are indications of large oil and gas deposits. The islands are also claimed by Argentina, though 97% of inhabitants are of British origin. Argentina invaded the islands Apr. 2, 1982. The British responded by sending a task force to the area, landing their main force on the Falklands, May 21, and forcing an Argentine surrender at Port Stanley, June 14. A pact resuming commercial air service with Argentina was signed July 14, 1999. **Website:** www.falklands.gov.fk

British Antarctic Territory, S of 60° S lat., formerly a dependency of the Falkland Isls., was made a separate colony in 1962 and includes the South Shetland Isls., the South Orkneys, and the Antarctic Peninsula. A chain of meteorological stations is maintained.

South Georgia and the **South Sandwich Isls.,** formerly administered by the Falklands Isls., became a separate dependency in 1985. Total area of 1,507 sq mi. South Georgia, with no permanent population, is about 800 mi SE of the Falklands; the South Sandwich Isls. are uninhabited, about 470 mi SE of South Georgia.

St. Helena, an island 1,200 mi off the W coast of Africa and 1,800 mi E of S America, area 47 sq mi and pop. (2013 est.) 7,754. Flax, lace, and rope-making are the chief industries. After Napoleon Bonaparte was defeated at Waterloo the Allies exiled him to St. Helena, where he lived from Oct. 16, 1815, to his death, May 5, 1821. Capital: Jamestown; pop. (2014 est.) 638. **Website:** www.sainthelena.gov.sh

Tristan da Cunha is the principal island in a group of islands of volcanic origin, total area 38 sq mi, halfway between the Cape of Good Hope and S America. A volcanic peak 6,760 ft high erupted in 1961. The 262 inhabitants were removed to England, but most returned in 1963. The islands are dependencies of St. Helena. Pop. (2010 est.): 265.

Ascension is an island of volcanic origin, 34 sq mi in area, 700 mi NW of St. Helena, through which it is administered. It is a communications relay center for Britain, and has a U.S. satellite tracking center. Pop. (2010) was 884, half of them communications workers. The island is noted for sea turtles. **Website:** www.ascension-island.gov.ac

British Indian Ocean Territory

Formed Nov. 1965, embracing islands formerly dependencies of Mauritius or Seychelles: the Chagos Archipelago (including Diego Garcia), Aldabra, Farquhar, and Des Roches. The latter three were transferred to Seychelles, which became independent in 1976. Total area 21,004 sq mi, land area 23 sq mi. No permanent civilian population remains; the UK and the U.S. maintain a military presence.

Pacific Ocean Territories

Pitcairn Isl. is in the Pacific, halfway between S America and Australia. The island was discovered in 1767 by Philip Carteret but was not inhabited until 23 years later when the mutineers of the *Bounty* landed there. Pop. (2014 est.) 48. It is administered by a British High Commissioner in New Zealand and a local Council. The uninhabited islands of Henderson, Ducie, and Oeno are in the Pitcairn group, area 18 sq mi. **Website:** www.government.pn

United States
United States of America

People: Population: 318,892,103. 50 states and DC. (Note: U.S. pop. figures may differ elsewhere in *The World Almanac*.) **Age distrib.:** <15: 19.4%; 65+: 14.5%. **Pop. density:** 90.3 per sq mi, 34.9 per sq km. **Urban:** 81.4%. **Ethnic groups:** white 80%, black 13%, Asian 4%, Amerindian and Alaska native 1%. (Hispanic, any race 15%.) **Languages:** English, Spanish, other Indo-European, Asian and Pacific island. **Religions:** Protestant 51%, Roman Catholic 24%, Mormon 2%, Jewish 2%, other Christian 2%, unaffiliated 12%, none 4%.

Geography: Total area: 3,794,100 sq mi, 9,826,675 sq km; **Land area:** 3,537,455 sq mi, 9,161,966 sq km. (Area is for 50 states and DC only.) **Topography:** Vast central plain, mountains in W, hills and low mountains in E. **Capital:** Washington, DC, 4,895,970.

Government: Type: Constitution-based federal republic. **Head of state and gov.:** Pres. Barack Obama; b. Aug. 4, 1961; in office: Jan. 20, 2009. **Local divisions:** 50 states, 1 district. **Defense budget:** $600.4 bil. **Active troops:** 1,492,200.

Economy: Industries: second largest industrial output in world; petroleum, steel, motor vehicles, aerospace, telecom, chemicals, electronics, food proc., consumer goods, lumber, mining. **Chief crops:** wheat, corn, other grains, fruits, vegetables, cotton. **Natural resources:** coal, copper, lead, molybdenum, phosphates, rare earth elements, uranium, bauxite, gold, iron, mercury, nickel, potash, silver, tungsten, zinc, petroleum, nat. gas, timber. **Crude oil reserves** (2013): 30.5 bil bbls. **Arable land:** 17%. **Livestock:** cattle: 89.3 mil; chickens: 1.9 bil; goats: 2.8 mil; pigs: 64.8 mil; sheep: 5.3 mil. **Electricity prod.** (2012): 4.0 tril kWh. **Labor force** (excl. unemployed): farming, forestry, fishing 0.7%; mfg., extraction, transp., crafts 20.3%; managerial, professional, technical 37.3%; sales and office 24.2%; other services 17.6%. **Unemployment:** 8.1%.

Finance: Monetary unit: Dollar (USD). **GDP:** $16.7 tril; **per capita GDP:** $52,800; **GDP growth:** 1.6%. **Imports:** $2.3 tril; China 19%, Canada 14.1%, Mexico 12%, Japan 6.4%, Germany 4.7%. **Exports:** $1.6 tril; Canada 18.9%, Mexico 14%, China 7.2%, Japan 4.5%. **Tourism:** $139.6 bil. **Budget:** $3.5 tril (excl. approx. $2.3 tril of social benefits). **Total reserves less gold:** $133.5 bil. **Gold:** 261.5 mil oz t. **Inflation:** 1.5%.

Transport: Railways: 139,679 mi. **Motor vehicles:** 798 per 1,000 pop. **Civil aviation:** 814.3 bil pass.-mi; 5,054 airports.

Communications: TV sets: 844 per 1,000 pop. **Radios:** 145 per 1,000 pop. **Telephone lines:** 42.2 per 100 pop. **Mobile:** 95.5 per 100 pop. **Internet:** 84.2%.

Health: Life expect.: 77.1 male; 81.9 female. **Births:** 13.4 per 1,000 pop. **Deaths:** 8.2 per 1,000 pop. **Natural inc.:** 0.53%. **Infant mortality:** 6.2 per 1,000 live births. **HIV:** NA.

Education: Compulsory: ages 6-17. **Literacy:** 99%.

Website: www.usa.gov
See also U.S. History chapter; Chronology of the Year's Events.

Uruguay
Oriental Republic of Uruguay

People: Population: 3,332,972. **Age distrib.:** <15: 21%; 65+: 13.9%. **Pop. density:** 49.3 per sq mi, 19 per sq km. **Urban:** 95.2%. **Ethnic groups:** white 88%, mestizo 8%, black 4%. **Languages:** Spanish (official), Portunol, Brazilero. **Religions:** Roman Catholic 47%, non-Catholic Christian 11%, nondenominational 23%, atheist or agnostic 17%.

Geography: Total area: 68,037 sq mi, 176,215 sq km; **Land area:** 67,574 sq mi, 175,015 sq km. **Location:** In southern S America, on Atlantic O. **Neighbors:** Argentina on W, Brazil on N. **Topography:** Rolling, grassy plains and hills, well-watered by rivers flowing W to Uruguay R. **Capital:** Montevideo, 1,697,730.

Government: Type: Constitutional republic. **Head of state and gov.:** Pres. José (Pepe) Mujica; b. May 20, 1935; in office: Mar. 1, 2010. **Local divisions:** 19 departments. **Defense budget:** $445 mil. **Active troops:** 24,650.

Economy: Industries: food proc., elec. machinery, transp. equip., petroleum prods., textiles, chemicals, beverages. **Chief crops:** soybeans, rice, wheat. **Natural resources:** hydropower, minor minerals, fish. **Arable land:** 10%. **Livestock:** cattle: 11.5 mil; chickens: 20 mil; goats: 17,500; pigs: 225,000; sheep: 7.5 mil. **Electricity prod.:** 10.2 bil kWh. **Labor force:** agric. 13%, industry 14%, services 73%. **Unemployment:** 6%.

Finance: Monetary unit: Peso (UYU) (Sept. 2014: 23.98 = $1 U.S.). **GDP:** $56.3 bil; **per capita GDP:** $16,600; **GDP growth:** 3.5%. **Imports:** $12.5 bil; China 16.4%, Brazil 14.9%, Argentina 14.6%, U.S. 9.1%, Paraguay 7.3%. **Exports:** $10.5 bil; Brazil 18.6%, China 17.9%, Argentina 6.2%, Germany 4.3%. **Tourism:** $1.9 bil. **Budget:** $18.6 bil. **Total reserves less gold:** $16.3 bil. **Gold:** 10,000 oz t. **Inflation:** 8.6%.

Transport: Railways: 1,020 mi. **Motor vehicles:** 250.9 per 1,000 pop. **Civil aviation:** 11 airports. **Chief port:** Montevideo.

Communications: TV sets: 381 per 1,000 pop. **Radios:** 603 per 1,000 pop. **Telephone lines:** 30.8 per 100 pop. **Mobile:** 154.6 per 100 pop. **Internet:** 58.1%.

Health: Life expect.: 73.7 male; 80.1 female. **Births:** 13.2 per 1,000 pop. **Deaths:** 9.5 per 1,000 pop. **Natural inc.:** 0.37%. **Infant mortality:** 9.0 per 1,000 live births. **HIV:** 0.7%.

Education: Compulsory: ages 4-17. **Literacy:** 98.5%.

Embassy: 1913 I St. NW 20006; 331-1313.

Website: portal.gub.uy

Spanish settlers began to supplant the indigenous Charrua Indians in 1624. Portuguese from Brazil arrived later, but Uruguay was attached to the Spanish Viceroyalty of Rio de la Plata in the 18th cent. Rebels fought against Spain beginning in 1810, with independence declared Aug. 25, 1825. To suppress Tupamaro guerrilla activities, a repressive military regime took power in 1973. Constitutional government was restored in 1985.

Uruguay's standard of living remains one of the highest in S America. José (Pepe) Mujica, a former guerrilla who transformed his Marxist Tupamaro movement into a mainstream political party, won a presidential runoff election Nov. 2009 and took office Mar. 1, 2010. Legislation legalizing same-sex marriage was signed into law May 3, 2013. A law passed in Dec. 2013 made Uruguay the first country to legalize marijuana nationwide.

Uzbekistan
Republic of Uzbekistan

People: Population: 28,929,716. **Age distrib.:** <15: 24.9%; 65+: 4.8%. **Pop. density:** 176.1 per sq mi, 68 per sq km. **Urban:** 36.3%. **Ethnic groups:** Uzbek 80%, Russian 6%, Tajik 5%, Kazakh 3%, Karakalpak 3%, Tatar 2%. **Languages:** Uzbek (official), Russian, Tajik. **Religions:** Muslim (mostly Sunni) 88%, Eastern Orthodox 9%.

Geography: Total area: 172,742 sq mi, 447,400 sq km; **Land area:** 164,248 sq mi, 425,400 sq km. **Location:** Central Asia. **Neighbors:** Kazakhstan on N and W; Kyrgyzstan, Tajikistan on E;

Afghanistan, Turkmenistan on S. **Topography:** Mostly plains and desert. **Capital:** Tashkent, 2,241,460.

Government: Type: Republic with authoritarian presidential rule. **Head of state:** Pres. Islam A. Karimov; b. Jan. 30, 1938; in office: Mar. 24, 1990. **Head of gov.:** Prime Min. Shavkat Mirziyaev; b. 1957; in office: Dec. 11, 2003. **Local divisions:** 12 provinces, 1 autonomous republic, 1 city. **Defense budget** (2011): $1.42 bil. **Active troops:** 48,000.

Economy: Industries: textiles, food proc., machine building, metallurgy, mining, hydrocarbon extraction, chemicals. **Chief crops:** cotton, vegetables, fruits, grain. **Natural resources:** nat. gas, petroleum, coal, gold, uranium, silver, copper, lead, zinc, tungsten, molybdenum. **Crude oil reserves:** 594 mil bbls. **Arable land:** 10.2%. **Livestock:** cattle: 10 mil; chickens: 42 mil; goats: 2.7 mil; pigs: 94,500; sheep: 14.1 mil. **Electricity prod.:** 49.8 bil kWh. **Labor force:** agric. 25.9%, industry 13.2%, services 60.9%. **Unemployment:** 11.3%.

Finance: Monetary unit: Som (UZS) (Sept. 2014: 2,352.94 = $1 U.S.). **GDP:** $112.6 bil; **per capita GDP:** $3,800; **GDP growth:** 7%. **Imports:** $12.6 bil; Russia 20.7%, China 16.6%, South Korea 16.4%, Kazakhstan 12.5%, Germany 4.6%, Turkey 4.2%, Ukraine 4%. **Exports:** $14.9 bil; China 21.2%, Kazakhstan 15.9%, Turkey 15.8%, Russia 14.7%, Bangladesh 9.5%, Kyrgyzstan 4%. **Tourism:** $121 mil. **Budget:** $18.1 bil. **Total reserves less gold:** NA. **Inflation:** NA.

Transport: Railways: 2,265 mi. **Motor vehicles:** 71.6 per 1,000 pop. **Civil aviation:** 3.8 bil pass.-mi; 33 airports. **Chief port:** Termiz.

Communications: TV sets: 226 per 1,000 pop. **Radios:** 456 per 1,000 pop. **Telephone lines:** 6.9 per 100 pop. **Mobile:** 74.3 per 100 pop. **Internet:** 38.2%.

Health: Life expect.: 70.3 male; 76.5 female. **Births:** 17.0 per 1,000 pop. **Deaths:** 5.3 per 1,000 pop. **Natural inc.:** 1.17%. **Infant mortality:** 19.8 per 1,000 live births. **HIV:** 0.2%.

Education: Compulsory: ages 7-18. **Literacy:** 99.6%.

Embassy: 1746 Massachusetts Ave. NW 20036; 887-5300.

Website: www.gov.uz

The region was overrun by the Mongols under Genghis Khan in 1220. In the 14th cent., Uzbekistan became the center of a native Timurid empire. In later centuries Muslim feudal states emerged. Russian military conquest began in the 19th cent. Uzbek SSR became a Soviet republic in 1925.

Uzbekistan gained independence when the Soviet Union disbanded Dec. 26, 1991, and has been led by the authoritarian government of a former Communist, Islam A. Karimov.

Attacks by Islamic militants, Mar.-July 2004, killed more than 50 people. In June 2004, Russia's OAO Lukoil signed a $1 bil deal to develop Uzbekistan's natural gas fields. Militants bombed the U.S. and Israeli embassies in Tashkent, July 30.

After armed dissidents at Andizhan, east Uzbekistan, attacked government buildings and freed hundreds of prisoners, May 2005, Uzbek security forces killed many rebels and unarmed demonstrators. Karimov then launched a general crackdown on human rights activists. Irritated by U.S. human rights pressures, Karimov ordered the U.S. to vacate an airbase used to support operations in Afghanistan; the U.S. pullout was completed Nov. 21. Meeting in Moscow a week earlier, Karimov and Russian Pres. Vladimir Putin signed a military cooperation agreement.

Karimov remained in office following the formal expiration of his presidential term Jan. 22, 2007; despite a 2-term limit under the constitution, he ran for a third term Dec. 23 and won with an 88.1% majority. Sanctions imposed by the EU on Uzbek officials after the 2005 Andizhan shootings were lifted Oct. 13, 2008.

When Pakistan closed its supply route to Afghanistan in Nov. 2011-July 2012, much of the non-lethal cargo that was moved into the warzone through the Northern Distribution Network came through Uzbekistan.

Vanuatu
Republic of Vanuatu

People: Population: 266,937. **Age distrib.:** <15: 37.3%; 65+: 3.7%. **Pop. density:** 56.7 per sq mi, 21.9 per sq km. **Urban:** 25.8%. **Ethnic groups:** Ni-Vanuatu 98%. **Languages:** local langs. (100+); Bislama, English, French (all official). **Religions:** Protestant 70% (incl. Presbyterian 28%, Anglican 15%, Seventh-day Adventist 13%), Roman Catholic 12%, customary beliefs 4%.

Geography: Total area: 4,706 sq mi, 12,189 sq km; **Land area:** 4,706 sq mi, 12,189 sq km. **Location:** SW Pacific, 1,200 mi NE of Brisbane, Australia. **Neighbors:** Fiji to E, Solomon Isls. to NW. **Topography:** Dense forest with narrow coastal strips of cultivated land. **Capital:** Port Vila, 52,542.

Government: Type: Parliamentary republic. **Head of state:** Pres. Baldwin Lonsdale; in office: Sept. 22, 2014. **Head of gov.:** Prime Min. Joe Natuman; b. Nov. 24, 1952; in office: May 14, 2014. **Local divisions:** 6 provinces. **Defense budget/active troops:** NA.

Economy: Industries: food and fish freezing, wood proc., meat canning. **Chief crops:** copra, coconuts, cocoa, coffee, taro, yams, fruits, vegetables. **Natural resources:** manganese, hardwood forests, fish. **Arable land:** 1.6%. **Livestock:** cattle: 173,000; chickens: 750,000; goats: 25,000; pigs: 94,000. **Electricity prod.:** 55 mil kWh. **Labor force:** agric. 65%, industry 5%, services 30%. **Unemployment:** NA.

Finance: Monetary unit: Vatu (VUV) (Sept. 2014: 95.45 = $1 U.S.). **GDP:** $1.3 bil; **per capita GDP:** $4,800; **GDP growth:** 3.3%. **Imports:** $319.4 mil; China 20.2%, Singapore 18.8%, U.S. 15%, Japan 11.6%, Australia 10.4%, Fiji 5.2%, New Zealand 4.8%. **Exports:** $43.1 mil; Thailand 41.9%, Côte d'Ivoire 30.5%, Japan 14.7%. **Tourism:** $261 mil. **Budget:** $201.3 mil. **Total reserves less gold** (2011): $173.8 mil. **Inflation:** 1.4%.

Transport: Motor vehicles: 58.1 per 1,000 pop. **Civil aviation:** 3 airports. **Chief port:** Port-Vila.

Communications: TV sets: 13 per 1,000 pop. **Radios:** 344 per 1,000 pop. **Telephone lines** 2 per 100 pop. **Mobile:** 59.3 per 100 pop. **Internet:** 11.3%.

Health: Life expect.: 71.2 male; 74.4 female. **Births:** 25.7 per 1,000 pop. **Deaths:** 4.1 per 1,000 pop. **Natural inc.:** 2.16%. **Infant mortality:** 16.4 per 1,000 live births. **HIV:** NA.

Education: NA. **Literacy:** 85.2%.

Permanent UN mission: 800 Second Ave., Ste. 400B, New York, NY 10017; (212) 661-4303.

Website: www.governmentofvanuatu.gov.vu

The Anglo-French condominium of the New Hebrides, administered jointly by France and Great Britain since 1906, became the independent Republic of Vanuatu on July 30, 1980. Vanuatu is located in the Ring of Fire, a zone with frequent earthquakes and volcanic eruptions. The nation joined the World Trade Organization Aug. 24, 2012. Joe Natuman, who pledged to curb spending and corruption, became prime min., May 14, 2014, after his predecessor lost a no-confidence vote in parliament.

Vatican City
The Holy See (Vatican City State)

People: Population: 842. **Pop. density:** 4,956.3 per sq mi, 1,913.6 per sq km. **Urban:** 100%. **Ethnic groups:** Italian, Swiss, other. **Languages:** Italian, Latin, French, various others. **Religion:** Roman Catholic.

Geography: Total area: 0.17 sq mi, 0.44 sq km; **Land area:** 0.17 sq mi, 0.44 sq km. **Location:** In Rome, Italy. **Neighbors:** Completely surrounded by Italy.

Defense budget/active troops: NA.

Economy: Industries: printing; coins, medals, postage stamps prod.; mosaics and staff uniforms; worldwide banking and financial activities. **Labor force:** Essentially services with small amount of industry; nearly all dignitaries, priests, nuns, guards, and approx. 3,000 lay workers live outside the Vatican.

Finance: Monetary unit: Euro (EUR) (Sept. 2014: 0.76 = $1 U.S.). **Budget** (2011): $326.4 mil. **Total reserves less gold:** NA. **Inflation:** NA.

Apostolic Nunciature: 3339 Massachusetts Ave. NW 20008; 333-7121.

Website: www.vatican.va

The popes for many centuries, with brief interruptions, held temporal sovereignty over mid-Italy (the so-called Papal States), comprising an area of some 16,000 sq mi, with a population in the 19th cent. of more than 3 mil. This territory was incorporated in the new Kingdom of Italy (1861), the sovereignty of the pope being confined to the palaces of the Vatican and the Lateran in Rome and the villa of Castel Gandolfo, by an Italian law, May 13, 1871.

A Treaty of Conciliation, a concordat, and a financial convention were signed Feb. 11, 1929, by Cardinal Gasparri and Prem. Mussolini. The documents established the independent state of Vatican City and gave the Roman Catholic Church special status in Italy. The treaty (Lateran Agreement) was incorporated into Italy's Constitution (Article 7) in 1947. Italy and the Vatican signed an agreement in 1984 eliminating Roman Catholicism as the state religion and ending required religious education in Italian schools.

Vatican City includes the Basilica of Saint Peter, the Vatican Palace and Museum covering over 13 acres, the Vatican gardens, and neighboring buildings between Viale Vaticano and the church. Thirteen buildings in Rome, outside the boundaries, which house congregations or officers necessary for the administration of the Holy See, enjoy extraterritorial rights.

The legal system is based on the code of canon law, the apostolic constitutions, and laws especially promulgated for Vatican City by the pope. The Secretariat of State represents the Holy See in its diplomatic relations.

Citing health problems, Pope Benedict XVI, elected Apr. 19, 2005, announced he would resign Feb. 11, 2013, the first pontiff to do so since 1415. He became Pope Emeritus Feb. 28. Cardinal Jorge Mario Bergoglio, from Argentina, was elected Mar. 13, taking the name of Francis. Pope Francis became the first Latin American and the first Jesuit pope. Francis named, July 9, 2014, a new head of the Vatican Bank, Jean-Baptiste de Franssu, as part of an ongoing effort to improve financial management at the scandal-tainted bank.

Venezuela
Bolivarian Republic of Venezuela

People: Population: 28,868,486. **Age distrib.:** <15: 28.2%; 65+: 5.9%. **Pop. density:** 84.8 per sq mi, 32.7 per sq km. **Urban:** 88.9%.

Ethnic groups: Spanish, Italian, Portuguese, Arab, German, African, indigenous. **Languages:** Spanish (official), many indigenous dialects. **Religions:** Roman Catholic (nominally) 96%, Protestant 2%.

Geography: Total area: 352,144 sq mi, 912,050 sq km; **Land area:** 340,561 sq mi, 882,050 sq km. **Location:** On Carib. coast of S America. **Neighbors:** Colombia on W, Brazil on S, Guyana on E. **Topography:** Flat coastal plain and Orinoco Delta are bordered by Andes Mts. and hills. Plains, called llanos, extend between mountains and Orinoco. Guiana Highlands and plains are S of Orinoco, which stretches 1,600 mi and drains 80% of country. **Capital:** Caracas, 2,912,070 (incl. pop. of some other municipalities). **Cities (urban aggl.):** Maracaibo, 2,163,837; Valencia, 1,710,601; Maracay, 1,145,785; Barquisimeto, 1,033,603.

Government: Type: Federal republic. **Head of state and gov.:** Pres. Nicolás Maduro Moros; b. Nov. 23, 1962; in office: Apr. 19, 2013. **Local divisions:** 23 states, 1 capital district, 1 federal dependency (11 federally controlled island groups). **Defense budget:** $5.24 bil. **Active troops:** 115,000.

Economy: Industries: petroleum, constr. materials, food proc., textiles, iron ore mining, steel, aluminum, motor vehicle assembly, chem. prods. **Chief crops:** corn, sorghum, sugarcane, rice, bananas, vegetables, coffee. **Natural resources:** petroleum, nat. gas, iron ore, gold, bauxite, hydropower, diamonds. **Crude oil reserves:** 297.7 bil bbls. **Arable land:** 3.1%. **Livestock:** cattle: 14.5 mil; chickens: 122 mil; goats: 1.5 mil; pigs: 3.9 mil; sheep: 600,000. **Electricity prod.:** 118.9 bil kWh. **Labor force:** agric. 7.3%, industry 21.8%, services 70.9%. **Unemployment:** 7.8%.

Finance: Monetary unit: Bolivar (VEF) (Sept. 2014: 6.29 = $1 U.S.). **GDP:** $407.4 bil; **per capita GDP:** $13,600; **GDP growth:** 1.6%. **Imports:** $59.3 bil; U.S. 31.7%, China 16.8%, Brazil 9.1%, Colombia 4.8%. **Exports:** $91.8 bil; U.S. 39.1%, China 14.3%, India 12%, Netherlands Antilles 7.8%, Cuba 4.6%. **Tourism:** $844 mil. **Budget:** $139.4 bil. **Total reserves less gold:** $6 bil. **Gold:** 11.8 mil oz t. **Inflation:** 40.6%.

Transport: Railways: 501 mi. **Motor vehicles:** 118.1 per 1,000 pop. **Civil aviation:** 3.1 bil pass.-mi; 127 airports. **Chief ports:** La Guaira, Maracaibo, Puerto Cabello, Punta Cardon.

Communications: TV sets: 208 per 1,000 pop. **Radios:** 291 per 1,000 pop. **Telephone lines:** 25.6 per 100 pop. **Mobile:** 101.6 per 100 pop. **Internet:** 54.9%.

Health: Life expect.: 71.3 male; 77.7 female. **Births:** 19.4 per 1,000 pop. **Deaths:** 5.3 per 1,000 pop. **Natural inc.:** 1.42%. **Infant mortality:** 19.3 per 1,000 live births. **HIV:** 0.6%.

Education: Compulsory: ages 3-16. **Literacy:** 96.3%.

Embassy: 1099 30th St. NW 20007; 342-2214.

Website: www.presidencia.gob.ve or venezuela-us.org

Columbus first set foot on the South American continent on the peninsula of Paria, Aug. 1498. Alonso de Ojeda, 1499, called the land Venezuela, or Little Venice, because the Indians had houses on stilts. Spanish colonialists dominated Venezuela until Simón Bolívar's victory near Carabobo in June 1821. The republic was formed after secession from the Colombian Federation in 1830. Military strongmen ruled Venezuela for much of its history. Since 1959, the country has had democratically elected governments.

Venezuela has the world's largest crude oil reserves, and oil accounts for more than 95% of export earnings and almost half of government revenues. The government, Jan. 1, 1976, nationalized the oil industry. Attempts to reduce dependence on the hydrocarbon sector have had limited success. The country has large reserves of natural gas.

Two attempted coups were thwarted by loyalist troops in Feb. and Nov. 1992. Pres. Carlos Andrés Pérez was removed from office on corruption charges, May 1993, and convicted, May 1996, of mismanaging a $17 mil secret government fund.

A 1992 coup leader, Hugo Chávez, who ran as a populist, was elected president Dec. 1998. That month, voters approved a new constitution greatly increasing his powers.

Popular among the poor, Chávez alienated middle- and upper-class Venezuelans with economic and political reforms, and his foreign policy antagonized the U.S. Gunfire erupted at a mass protest Apr. 11, 2002, in Caracas, killing at least 17 people. Chávez was forced to relinquish power, but when an interim government suspended democratic institutions, Chávez loyalists rebelled; the coup fell apart, and the president reclaimed his office Apr. 14. Chávez opponents organized strikes and recall efforts, 2003-04, but failed to oust him.

Chávez countered U.S. attempts to isolate him diplomatically and militarily by solidifying ties with Latin American leftist leaders and with Iran and Russia. With the economy surging, he won the Dec. 2006 presidential election. On Jan. 31, 2007, the legislature granted him the power to rule by decree. Venezuelan voters approved constitutional changes abolishing presidential term limits Feb. 15, 2009. Chávez traveled repeatedly to Cuba for cancer treatments 2011-12 and won a tough reelection challenge Oct. 7, 2012. He died Mar. 5, 2013, before he could be sworn in. Vice Pres. Nicolás Maduro Moros became interim president Mar. 8. He won a narrow victory in Apr. 14, 2013, elections; 7 people died in violence that erupted as supporters of the opposition candidate, Henrique Capriles Radonski, demonstrated in Caracas. The economy was plagued by high inflation (56% in 2013) and shortages of electricity, food, and other goods. Large-scale anti-Maduro protests began in Feb. 2014 and were met with a harsh crackdown by security forces; by early June, more than 40 people, mostly protesters, had been killed in the unrest.

Vietnam
Socialist Republic of Vietnam

People: Population: 93,421,835. **Age distrib.:** <15: 24.3%; 65+: 5.7%. **Pop. density:** 780.3 per sq mi, 301.3 per sq km. **Urban:** 33%. **Ethnic groups:** Kinh (Viet) 86%, Tay 2%, Thai 2%, Muong 2%, Khmer 2%, Mong 1%, Nung 1%. **Languages:** Vietnamese (official), English (increasingly favored as second lang.), French, Chinese, Khmer, mountain area langs. (Mon-Khmer, Malayo-Polynesian). **Religions:** Buddhist 9%, Catholic 7%, Hoa Hao 2%, Cao Dai 1%, none 81%.

Geography: Total area: 127,881 sq mi, 331,210 sq km; **Land area:** 119,719 sq mi, 310,070 sq km. **Location:** SE Asia, on E coast of Indochinese Peninsula. **Neighbors:** China on N; Laos, Cambodia on W. **Topography:** Long and narrow, with 1,400-mi coast. About 22% of country is readily arable, including densely settled Red R. Valley in N, narrow coastal plains in center, and the wide, often marshy Mekong R. Delta in S. The rest consists of semi-arid plateaus and barren mountains, with some stretches of tropical rain forest. **Capital:** Hà Noi, 3,469,710. **Cities (urban aggl.):** Ho Chi Minh City, 7,100,328; Can Tho, 1,108,429; Hai Phòng, 1,041,158.

Government: Type: Communist state. **Head of state:** Pres. Truong Tan Sang; b. Jan. 21, 1949; in office: July 25, 2011. **Head of gov.:** Prime Min. Nguyen Tan Dung; b. Nov. 17, 1949; in office: June 27, 2006. **Local divisions:** 58 provinces, 5 municipalities. **Defense budget:** $3.8 bil. **Active troops:** 482,000.

Economy: Industries: food proc., garments, shoes, machine-building, mining, coal, steel, cement, chemical fertilizer. **Chief crops:** paddy rice, coffee, rubber, cotton, tea, pepper, soybeans, cashews, sugarcane, peanuts, bananas. **Natural resources:** phosphates, coal, manganese, rare earth elements, bauxite, chromate, offshore oil and gas deposits, timber, hydropower. **Crude oil reserves:** 4.4 bil bbls. **Arable land:** 20.6%. **Livestock:** cattle: 5.2 mil; chickens: 220.3 mil; goats: 1.4 mil; pigs: 26.3 mil. **Electricity prod.:** 105.7 bil kWh. **Labor force:** agric. 48%, industry 21%, services 31%. **Unemployment:** 2%.

Finance: Monetary unit: Dong (VND) (Sept. 2014: 21,185.00 = $1 U.S.). **GDP:** $358.9 bil; **per capita GDP:** $4,000; **GDP growth:** 5.3%. **Imports:** $121.4 bil; China 25.8%, South Korea 13.9%, Japan 10.4%, Singapore 6%, Thailand 5.2%, U.S. 4.3%. **Exports:** $128.9 bil; U.S. 17.8%, Japan 11.8%, China 11.2%, South Korea 5%, Malaysia 4.1%. **Tourism:** $7.5 bil. **Budget:** $50 bil. **Total reserves less gold:** $25.9 bil. **Inflation:** 6.6%.

Transport: Railways: 1,635 mi. **Motor vehicles:** 4.2 per 1,000 pop. **Civil aviation:** 14.8 bil pass.-mi; 38 airports. **Chief ports:** Cam Pha Port, Da Nang, Hai Phong, Ho Chi Minh City, Phu My, Quy Nhon.

Communications: TV sets: 208 per 1,000 pop. **Radios:** 109 per 1,000 pop. **Telephone lines:** 10.1 per 100 pop. **Mobile:** 130.9 per 100 pop. **Internet:** 43.9%.

Health: Life expect.: 70.4 male; 75.7 female. **Births:** 16.3 per 1,000 pop. **Deaths:** 5.9 per 1,000 pop. **Natural inc.:** 1.03%. **Infant mortality:** 19.0 per 1,000 live births. **HIV:** 0.4%.

Education: Compulsory: ages 6-14. **Literacy:** 94.5%. **Embassy:** 1233 20th St. NW, Ste. 400, 20036; 861-0737. **Website:** www.na.gov.vn

Settled by Viets from central China, Vietnam was held by China, 111 BCE-939 CE, and was a vassal state during subsequent periods. Conquest by France began in 1858 and ended in 1884 with the protectorates of Tonkin and Annam in the N and the colony of Cochin-China in the S.

Japan occupied Vietnam in 1940. Several groups formed the Vietminh (Independence) League, headed by Communist guerrilla leader Ho Chi Minh. In Aug. 1945, the Vietminh forced out Bao Dai, former emperor of Annam and head of a Japan-sponsored regime. France, seeking to reestablish colonial control, unsuccessfully battled Communist and nationalist forces, 1946-54.

Separate states formed in N. and S. Vietnam, with Communists under Ho Chi Minh (backed by Russia and China) controlling N. Vietnam and a non-Communist government (backed by the U.S.) controlling S. Vietnam. N. Vietnam aided Vietcong guerrillas who sought to take over S. Vietnam. U.S. troops and the S. Vietnamese army fought N. Vietnamese and Vietcong forces, including in border areas of Laos and Cambodia. Casualties of the war were as follows—combat deaths: U.S. 47,434 (Aug. 4, 1964-Jan. 27, 1973); S. Vietnam more than 200,000; other allied forces 5,225. Total U.S. fatalities numbered more than 58,000. Vietnamese civilian casualties were more than 1 mil. The war displaced more than 6.5 mil in S. Vietnam.

A never-implemented cease-fire agreement was signed in Paris Jan. 27, 1973, by the U.S., N. and S. Vietnam, and the Vietcong. The last U.S. troops left Vietnam Mar. 27, 1973. S. Vietnam surrendered Apr. 30, 1975. N. Vietnam assumed control. The country was officially reunited July 2, 1976.

Among the unstable conditions that persisted in the region, heavy fighting with Cambodia took place, 1977-80. China cut off economic aid when 140,000 ethnic Chinese fled discrimination in Vietnam. Reacting to Vietnam's 1979 invasion of Cambodia, China attacked four Vietnamese border provinces, Feb. 1979.

Vietnam announced reforms aimed at reducing central control of the economy in 1987. Citing Hanoi's cooperation in returning remains of U.S. soldiers killed in the Vietnam War, the U.S. ended, Feb. 1994, a 19-year U.S. embargo on trade with Vietnam. The U.S. extended full diplomatic recognition to Vietnam July 11, 1995. In Aug. 2012, the U.S. began cleaning up the herbicide Agent Orange, which it had used to clear forests during the Vietnam War. U.S. Gen. Martin E. Dempsey, chair of the Joint Chiefs of Staff, visited Vietnam, Aug. 2014, for talks on military cooperation, apparently aimed at countering China's growing power in the South China Sea region. On Oct. 2, 2014, the U.S. eased its embargo on lethal arms sales to allow Vietnam to obtain naval matériel.

Yemen
Republic of Yemen

People: Population: 26,052,966. **Age distrib.:** <15: 41.7%; 65+: 2.6%. **Pop. density:** 127.8 per sq mi, 49.3 per sq km. **Urban:** 34%. **Ethnic groups:** predominantly Arab; Afro-Arab, S Asian, European. **Language:** Arabic (official). **Religion:** Muslim 99% (official; 65% Sunni, 35% Shia).

Geography: Total area: 203,850 sq mi, 527,968 sq km; **Land area:** 203,850 sq mi, 527,968 sq km. **Location:** Middle East, on S coast of the Arabian Peninsula. **Neighbors:** Saudi Arabia on N, Oman on E. **Topography:** A sandy coastal strip leads to well-watered fertile mountains in interior. **Capital:** Sana'a, 2,833,200. **Cities (urban aggl.):** Aden, 854,655.

Government: Type: Republic. **Head of state:** Pres. Abd Rabbuh Mansur Hadi; b. Sept. 9, 1950; in office: Feb. 25, 2012. **Head of gov.:** Prime Min. Khaled Bahah; b. 1965; in office: Oct. 13, 2014. **Local divisions:** 20 governorates, 1 municipality. **Defense budget:** $1.81 bil. **Active troops:** 66,700.

Economy: Industries: crude oil prod. and petroleum refining, small-scale prod. of cotton textiles and leather goods, food proc., handicrafts. **Chief crops:** grains, fruits, vegetables, pulses, khat, coffee, cotton. **Natural resources:** petroleum; fish; rock salt; marble; small deposits of coal, gold, lead, nickel, copper. **Crude oil reserves:** 3 bil bbls. **Arable land:** 2.4%. **Livestock:** cattle: 1.7 mil; chickens: 63 mil; goats: 9.2 mil; sheep: 9.5 mil. **Electricity prod.:** 5.8 bil kWh. **Labor force:** Most people employed in agric. and herding; services, constr., industry, and commerce account for less than one-fourth of labor force. **Unemployment:** 17.6%.

Finance: Monetary unit: Rial (YER) (Sept. 2014: 214.85 = $1 U.S.). **GDP:** $61.6 bil; **per capita GDP:** $2,500; **GDP growth:** 3.8%. **Imports:** $11 bil; EU 48.8%, UAE 9.8%, Switzerland 8.8%, China 7.4%, India 5.8%. **Exports:** $6.7 bil; China 41%, Thailand 19.2%, India 11.4%, South Korea 4.4%. **Tourism:** $940 mil. **Budget:** $12.3 bil. **Total reserves less gold:** $5.3 bil. **Gold:** 50,000 oz t. **Inflation** (2011-12): 17.3%.

Transport: Motor vehicles: 28.2 per 1,000 pop. **Civil aviation:** 1.2 pass.-mi; 17 airports. **Chief ports:** Aden, Al Hudaydah, Al Mukalla.

Communications: TV sets: 344 per 1,000 pop. **Radios:** 64 per 1,000 pop. **Telephone lines:** 4.7 per 100 pop. **Mobile:** 69 per 100 pop. **Internet:** 20%.

Health: Life expect.: 62.7 male; 67.0 female. **Births:** 31.0 per 1,000 pop. **Deaths:** 6.5 per 1,000 pop. **Natural inc.:** 2.46%. **Infant mortality:** 50.4 per 1,000 live births. **HIV:** <0.1%.

Education: Compulsory: ages 6-14. **Literacy:** 70.1%. **Embassy:** 2319 Wyoming Ave. NW 20008; 965-4760. **Website:** www.yemen.gov.ye or www.yemenembassy.org

Yemen's territory once was part of the ancient biblical Kingdom of Sheba, or Saba. Yemen became independent in 1918, after centuries of Ottoman Turkish rule.

Imam Yahya ibn Muhammad ruled, 1904-48, and after his assassination was succeeded by his son, Imam Ahmed, 1948-62. Army officers headed by Brig. Gen. Abdullah al-Salal declared the country the Yemen Arab Republic, Sept. 1962. Ahmed's heir, the Imam Mohamad al-Badr, fled to the mountains where tribesmen joined royalist forces, aided by the Saudi monarchy. Fighting between royalists and republicans killed about 150,000 people until hostilities ended in 1970.

South Yemen, formed from the British colony of Aden and the British protectorate of South Arabia, became independent Nov. 1967. A Marxist state and a Soviet ally, it took the name People's Democratic Republic of Yemen in 1970. More than 300,000 Yemenis fled from the S to the N after independence, contributing to two decades of hostility between the two states.

The two countries were formally united May 21, 1990, but regional clan-based rivalries led to full-scale civil war in 1994. Secessionists declared a breakaway state in South Yemen, May 21, 1994, but northern troops captured the former southern capital of Aden in July. A new constitution was approved Sept. 28.

Yemen, the ancestral home of Osama bin Laden, has been caught in a crossfire between the U.S. and Islamic extremists. While on a refueling stop in Aden, Oct. 12, 2000, the destroyer U.S.S. Cole was bombed, killing 17 Americans and injuring more than three dozen; the U.S. government blamed the attack on terrorists associated with bin Laden.

Clashes beginning in June 2004 between Yemeni government forces and Shiite rebels led by an anti-U.S. cleric, Hussein al-Houthi, left more than 200 people dead. The government announced Sept. 10 that Yemeni troops had killed al-Houthi.

During 2007-10, Shiite rebels in the northwest, secessionists in the south, al-Qaeda militants in the east, and pirates in coastal waters challenged Yemeni government authority. Emboldened by the success of Arab Spring protests in Tunisia and Egypt in early 2011, mass demonstrations in Yemeni cities demanded Pres. Ali Abdullah Saleh's resignation. The U.S. and Gulf Arab nations also pressed him to depart. Saleh was severely wounded June 3 in a rocket attack on the presidential compound in Sana'a'. Vice Pres. Abd Rabbuh Mansur Hadi served as acting president June 4-Sept. 23, 2011, while Saleh received extended medical treatment in Saudi Arabia. After a 2-year manhunt, Anwar al-Awlaki, an American citizen and radical Muslim cleric linked to several plots against the U.S., was killed Sept. 30, 2011, by a U.S. missile in northern Yemen. Saleh ceded power Nov. 23, 2011, remaining in office in name only. Hadi served as acting president. He officially became president in uncontested Feb. 2012 elections but subsequently failed to stabilize the country. Islamic militants and separatists staged terrorist bombings and other attacks, 2012-14. The U.S. continued drone strikes and other attacks against al-Qaeda operatives and key leaders. After heavy fighting, Shiite rebels in the north captured the city of Omran, July 8, 2014. Shiite rebels known as Houthis took over most of Sana'a' Sept. 21; an agreement signed by Pres. Hadi provided for a new prime minister and devolution of government power.

Zambia
Republic of Zambia

People: Population: 14,638,505. **Age distrib.:** <15: 46.2%; 65+: 2.4%. **Pop. density:** 51 per sq mi, 19.7 per sq km. **Urban:** 40.5%. **Ethnic groups:** Bemba 21%, Tonga 14%, Chewa 7%, Lozi 6%, Nsenga 5%, Tumbuka 4%, Ngoni 4%, Lala 3%, Kaonde 3%, Namwanga 3%, Lunda 3%. **Languages:** Bantu langs. (incl. Bemba, Nyanja, Tonga, Lozi, Chewa, Nsenga, Tumbuka); English (official). **Religions:** Protestant 75%, Roman Catholic 20%.

Geography: Total area: 290,587 sq mi, 752,618 sq km; **Land area:** 287,028 sq mi, 743,398 sq km. **Location:** In S central Africa. **Neighbors:** Congo on N; Tanzania, Malawi, Mozambique on E; Zimbabwe, Namibia on S; Angola on W. **Topography:** Mostly high plateau covered with thick forests and drained by several important rivers, including the Zambezi. **Capital:** Lusaka, 2,078,430.

Government: Type: Republic. **Head of state and gov.:** Pres. Michael Sata; b. 1937; in office: Sept. 23, 2011. **Local divisions:** 10 provinces. **Defense budget:** $390 mil. **Active troops:** 15,100.

Economy: Industries: copper mining and proc., constr., foodstuffs, beverages, chemicals, textiles, fertilizer, horticulture. **Chief crops:** corn, sorghum, rice, peanuts, sunflower seeds, vegetables, flowers, tobacco, cotton, sugarcane, cassava, coffee. **Natural resources:** copper, cobalt, zinc, lead, coal, emeralds, gold, silver, uranium, hydropower. **Arable land:** 5.1%. **Livestock:** cattle: 3.1 mil; chickens: 38 mil; goats: 2.5 mil; pigs: 730,000; sheep: 240,000. **Electricity prod.:** 11.3 bil kWh. **Labor force:** agric. 85%, industry 6%, services 9%. **Unemployment:** 13.1%.

Finance: Monetary unit: Kwacha (ZMW) (Sept. 2014: 6.02 = $1 U.S.). **GDP:** $25.5 bil; **per capita GDP:** $1,800; **GDP growth:** 6%. **Imports:** $8.2 bil; South Africa 36.7%, Dem. Rep. of the Congo 19.8%, China 10.4%, Kuwait 6%. **Exports:** $8.5 bil; China 33.4%, South Africa 7.2%, Dem. Rep. of the Congo 6.7%, South Korea 5.4%, India 4.7%, UAE 4.3%, Egypt 4.1%. **Tourism:** $155 mil. **Budget:** $6.7 bil. **Total reserves less gold:** $2.7 bil. **Inflation:** 7.0%.

Transport: Railways: 1,816 mi (incl. part of Tanzania-Zambia Railway Authority). **Motor vehicles:** 21.5 per 1,000 pop. **Civil aviation:** 8 airports. **Chief port:** Mpulungu.

Communications: TV sets: 64 per 1,000 pop. **Radios:** 145 per 1,000 pop. **Telephone lines:** 0.8 per 100 pop. **Mobile:** 71.5 per 100 pop. **Internet:** 15.4%.

Health: Life expect.: 50.2 male; 53.5 female. **Births:** 42.5 per 1,000 pop. **Deaths:** 12.9 per 1,000 pop. **Natural inc.:** 2.95%. **Infant mortality:** 66.6 per 1,000 live births. **HIV:** 12.5%.

Education: Compulsory: ages 7-13. **Literacy:** 63.4%.

Embassy: 2419 Massachusetts Ave. NW 20008; 265-9717.

Website: www.zambia.gov.zm

Ruled by the British as Northern Rhodesia, the country became the independent republic of Zambia within the Commonwealth Oct. 24, 1964. Independence leader Kenneth Kaunda governed as president, 1964-91. A Zambian government corporation in 1970 took over 51% of two foreign-owned copper-mining companies. Privately held land and other enterprises were nationalized in 1975. In the 1980s and 1990s, lowered copper prices hurt the economy and severe drought caused famine.

Food riots erupted in June 1990. Oct. 1991 elections brought an end to Kaunda's one-party rule. The new government sought to sell state enterprises, including the copper industry. Pres. Frederick Chiluba won reelection Nov. 1996. A coup attempt was suppressed Oct. 1997.

Unable to change the constitution to allow himself a third term, Chiluba endorsed Levy Patrick Mwanawasa, who won a disputed election Dec. 2001. Food shortages threatened more than 2 mil Zambians in 2002; the government refused to distribute shipments of U.S. grain because it was genetically modified. In a hard-fought 2006 election, Mwanawasa won a second term. Accused of embezzling state funds as president, Chiluba was ordered to pay

$58 mil by a British court, June 2007; he was acquitted by a Zambian court, Aug. 2009, of misusing $500,000 in public money.

Pres. Mwanawasa suffered a stroke June 29, 2008, and died Aug. 19. Vice Pres. Rupiah Banda became acting pres. He won the presidency by a narrow margin in the Oct. 2008 election but lost to opposition leader Michael Sata Sept. 2011.

The country has made progress in treating HIV/AIDS, which afflicted more than 1.1 mil Zambians as of 2013. However, progress has been compromised by periodic shortages of antiretroviral drugs to treat the disease.

Zimbabwe
Republic of Zimbabwe

People: Population: 13,771,721. **Age distrib.:** <15: 38.4%; 65+: 3.5%. **Pop. density:** 92.2 per sq mi, 35.6 per sq km. **Urban:** 32.5%. **Ethnic groups:** African 98% (Shona 82%, Ndebele 14%), mixed and Asian 1%. **Languages:** English (official), Shona, Sindebele, minor tribal dialects. **Religions:** syncretic (Christian and indigenous beliefs) 50%, Christian 25%, indigenous beliefs 24%, Muslim and other 1%.

Geography: Total area: 150,872 sq mi, 390,757 sq km; **Land area:** 149,362 sq mi, 386,847 sq km. **Location:** In southern Africa. **Neighbors:** Zambia on N, Botswana on W, South Africa on S, Mozambique on E. **Topography:** High plateau country, rising to mountains on E border, sloping down on other borders. **Capital:** Harare, 1,494,660.

Government: Type: Parliamentary democracy. **Head of state and gov.:** Pres. Robert Gabriel Mugabe; b. Feb. 21, 1924; in office: Dec. 31, 1987. **Local divisions:** 8 provinces, 2 cities with provincial status. **Defense budget:** $356 mil. **Active troops:** 29,000.

Economy: Industries: mining, steel, wood prods., cement, chemicals, fertilizer, clothing and footwear, foodstuffs. **Chief crops:** corn, cotton, tobacco, wheat, coffee, sugarcane, peanuts. **Natural resources:** coal, chromium ore, asbestos, gold, nickel, copper, iron ore, vanadium, lithium, tin, platinum group metals. **Arable land:** 10.3%. **Livestock:** cattle: 5.2 mil; chickens: 36 mil; goats: 2.8 mil; pigs: 500,000; sheep: 375,000. **Electricity prod.:** 7.3 bil kWh. **Labor force:** agric. 66%, industry 10%, services 24%. **Unemployment:** 4%.

Finance: Monetary unit: Dollar (ZWD) (Sept. 2014: 361.90 = $1 U.S.). **GDP:** $7.5 bil; **per capita GDP:** $600; **GDP growth:** 3.2%. **Imports:** $4.6 bil; South Africa 51.9%, China 10%. **Exports:** $3.1 bil; China 21.1%, South Africa 15.1%, Dem. Rep. of the Congo 12.1%, Botswana 10.8%, Italy 4.6%. **Tourism:** $851 mil. **Budget:** NA. **Total reserves less gold (2008):** $75.5 mil. **Gold:** 404 oz t. **Inflation:** NA.

Transport: Railways: 2,129 mi. **Motor vehicles:** 39.9 per 1,000 pop. **Civil aviation:** 17 airports. **Chief ports:** Binga, Kariba.

Communications: TV sets: 71 per 1,000 pop. **Radios:** 135 per 1,000 pop. **Telephone lines:** 2.1 per 100 pop. **Mobile:** 96.3 per 100 pop. **Internet:** 18.5%.

Health: Life expect.: 55.4 male; 56.0 female. **Births:** 32.5 per 1,000 pop. **Deaths:** 10.6 per 1,000 pop. **Natural inc.:** 2.19%. **Infant mortality:** 26.6 per 1,000 live births. **HIV:** 15.0%.

Education: Compulsory: ages 6-12. **Literacy:** 86.5%.

Embassy: 1608 New Hampshire Ave. NW 20009; 332-7100.

Website: www.zim.gov.zw

Britain took over the area as Southern Rhodesia in 1923 from the British South Africa Co. (which, under Cecil Rhodes, had conquered it by 1897) and granted internal self-government. A 1961 constitution restricted voting to keep whites in power.

On Nov. 11, 1965, Prime Min. Ian D. Smith unilaterally declared independence. Britain termed the act illegal and demanded that the country (known as Rhodesia until 1980) enfranchise the black African majority. The UN imposed sanctions and, in May 1968, a trade embargo, as black nationalists launched guerrilla attacks.

After the country held its first universal-franchise election, Apr. 21, 1979, all parties accepted a cease-fire, Dec. 5. The country changed its name to Zimbabwe upon independence, Apr. 18, 1980. Robert Mugabe, the nation's first prime min., became executive president in 1987.

From the late 1990s, Mugabe's rule became increasingly repressive. A land redistribution campaign triggered violent attacks in Apr. 2000 against some white farmers. (Whites made up less than 1% of the population but had held 70% of the land.) Production of corn, the nation's food staple, subsequently declined sharply. Mugabe, relying on fraud and intimidation, international observers claimed, won the Mar. 9-11, 2002, presidential election. The EU, U.S., and Commonwealth imposed sanctions. In May 2005, Mugabe launched Operation Murambatsvina ("Drive out rubbish"), razing shanty dwellings and illegal street markets in urban areas and leaving some 700,000 people homeless. During 2006-08, inflation soared to a yearly rate of more than 100,000%.

Mugabe clung to power after a widely discredited 2008 presidential election and runoff. A power-sharing deal was reached Sept. 2008, and opposition leader Morgan Tsvangirai was sworn in as prime min., Feb. 2009. Opposition groups, Jan. 18, 2013, condemned an increasing crackdown on Mugabe's critics. A referendum on a new constitution that technically curbs presidential powers but eliminated the prime min. passed overwhelmingly, Mar. 16, 2013. In the July 31 presidential elections, Mugabe was once again declared the winner.

SPORTS

Sports Highlights, 2014

Some of the biggest headlines in sports in 2014 were generated off the field. The issues of violence against women and child abuse pushed star players to the sidelines in the NFL, and the NCAA saw the first successful legal challenge to its amateurism policies.

The Bowl Championship Series (BCS) will use a four-team playoff to decide its national champion beginning in 2015. In the last **BCS National Championship** game Jan. 6, 2014, at the Rose Bowl in Pasadena, CA, Florida State rallied to defeat Auburn, 34-31, in the final minute. The Seminoles' freshman Heisman Trophy-winning quarterback Jameis Winston threw a 2-yard pass for the winning touchdown. Thirteen months earlier, a fellow Florida State student reported being sexually assaulted by Winston, but authorities had declined to press charges.

The Seattle Seahawks trounced the Denver Broncos, 43-8, in **Super Bowl XLVIII**, Feb. 2, at MetLife Stadium in East Rutherford, NJ. A botched Denver snap resulted in a Seattle safety for the quickest score in Super Bowl history; the Broncos didn't score until the second half. Seahawks linebacker Malcolm Smith, who recovered a fumble and returned an interception for a touchdown, was the game's MVP. Despite the one-sided score, the game drew a record 111.5 mil viewers.

Less appealing to fans was the NFL's handling of a Feb. 15 incident in which Baltimore Ravens running back Ray Rice assaulted his then-fiancée in a casino elevator. NFL Commissioner Roger Goodell initially suspended Rice for two games, but website TMZ Sept. 8 made public surveillance video of the assault. The Ravens released Rice, and Goodell suspended him indefinitely. Minnesota Vikings running back Adrian Peterson was indicted Sept. 12 in Houston, TX, for abusing his four-year-old son, after the boy's mother took him to the hospital with lacerations and bruises. Several advertisers withdrew their sponsorship of the Vikings or Peterson. The Vikings deactivated Peterson, preventing his participation in team activities.

A record 88 nations (including Togo, Tonga, and Zimbabwe for the first time) participated in the **2014 Winter Olympics** in Sochi, Russia, Feb. 7-23. The host country led the medal count with 33 and also won the most gold medals (13). The U.S. finished second with 28 overall medals, including 9 gold. Norway was third with 26 medals (11 gold).

The Univ. of Connecticut won both the **NCAA men's and women's basketball championships**, only the second time one school has won both Division I titles (UConn achieved the feat in 2004 as well). The Huskies defeated Kentucky's five freshmen starters, 60-54, at AT&T Stadium in Arlington, TX, Apr. 7. UConn guard Shabazz Napier won the most outstanding player award with 22 points. The following night, the undefeated Lady Huskies took down the previously unbeaten Notre Dame, 79-58, at Bridgestone Arena in Nashville, TN. Before the men's final, Napier spoke about how he had sometimes gone hungry due to the NCAA's amateurism restrictions, and the NCAA revised its rules, Apr. 24, to allow unlimited food for student athletes. A day later, scholarship football players at Northwestern Univ. cast a historic vote on whether to unionize after the Natl. Labor Relations Board ruled that players were university employees. The NCAA's principles of amateurism took a blow Aug. 8 when a U.S. District Court struck down the league's rules against compensating college athletes. The full implications of the decision were still being sorted out in the fall of 2014.

Bubba Watson won his second **Masters Championship** in three years in Augusta, GA, Apr. 13, defeating fellow American Jordan Spieth and Sweden's Jonas Blixt, who tied for second place. Germany's Martin Kaymer shot 65 in the first two rounds and went on to win the **U.S. Open** June 15 at Pinehurst Resort, NC. Northern Ireland's Rory McIlroy won the **British Open**, July 20, at Royal Liverpool Golf Club in Hoylake, England. McIlroy also held off three competitors—and the rain—in the final holes of the **PGA Championship**, Aug. 10, at Valhalla Golf Club in Louisville, KY.

For the 36th year, no horse won racing's Triple Crown. California Chrome, the 5-2 favorite, breezed to victory in the **Kentucky Derby** at Churchill Downs in Louisville, KY, May 3, and followed it up with a win in the **Preakness Stakes** at Pimlico Race Course in Baltimore, MD, May 17. But the colt ran out of gas in the **Belmont Stakes** at Belmont Park in Elmont, NY, June 7, finishing out of the money behind the 12-1 winner Tonalist, Commissioner, and Medal Count.

The L.A. Kings vanquished the New York Rangers in five games to take the **Stanley Cup**, June 13, at Staples Center in Los Angeles. Three games in the finals went beyond regulation, including the clincher, which L.A. won in double overtime. Kings right wing Justin Williams had 9 goals and 16 assists to snag the Conn Smythe Trophy as playoff MVP.

The FIFA men's World Cup soccer tournament was held June 12-July 13 at a dozen stadiums across Brazil. After the host nation's star forward, Neymar, fractured a vertebra in his spine during the quarterfinals, Brazil suffered a 7-1 defeat by Germany in the semifinals. Germany July 13 defeated Argentina 1-0 in the World Cup final. It was Germany's fourth championship and the first since the country's reunification.

The San Antonio Spurs avenged their 2013 loss to the Miami Heat in the **NBA Championship** June 15, winning the rematch in five games. Twenty-two-year-old Kawhi Leonard was named Finals MVP. Oklahoma City's Kevin Durant took the regular season MVP, averaging 32.0 points per game. Earlier rounds of the NBA playoffs were overshadowed by the release of a recording of L.A. Clippers owner Donald Sterling making racist comments. New NBA Commissioner Adam Silver banned the 80-year-old Sterling for life. Sterling's estranged wife and Clippers co-owner Rochelle Sterling sold the team for $2 bil to former Microsoft CEO Steve Ballmer.

Vincenzo Nibali became the first Italian in 16 years to win the Tour de France, which ended in Paris July 27.

In tennis, Switzerland's Stanislas Wawrinka upset Rafael Nadal of Spain to win his first **Australian Open** title in Melbourne, Jan. 26. A day earlier, Li Na of China took the women's title over Slovakia's Dominika Cibulkova. At Roland Garros, Nadal and Serbia's Novak Djokovic squared off in the final June 8; Nadal won to take his record ninth **French Open**. Russia's Maria Sharapova defeated Romania's Simona Halep for the women's crown June 7. Djokovic outlasted Switzerland's Roger Federer in a five-set thriller at **Wimbledon**, July 6 at the All England Club in London. Sixth-seeded Czech Petra Kvitova dispensed with Canada's Eugenie Bouchard, the 13th seed, in straight sets July 5 for her second Wimbledon championship. Croatia's Marin Cilic won a straight-set victory in the **U.S. Open** in Flushing Meadows, NY, Sept. 8, downing Japan's Kei Nishikori, who was the first Asian male to play in a Grand Slam final. Serena Williams routed Denmark's Caroline Wozniacki Sept. 7 for her third straight U.S. Open win and 18th Grand Slam title.

Major League Baseball team owners Aug. 14 chose MLB chief operating officer Rob Manfred to succeed longtime commissioner Bud Selig. Manfred took over a league that has had two decades of labor peace and healthy revenues and attendance league-wide. The playoffs included small-market teams from Pittsburgh, Oakland, Baltimore, Kansas City, and Washington, DC, as well as from larger markets. The defending champion Boston Red Sox became the first team ever to go from worst (2012) to first (2013) back to worst (2014). San Francisco defeated Kansas City Oct. 29 to claim its third World Series title in five years.

WORLD ALMANAC EDITORS' PICKS: CONTROVERSIAL SPORTS FRANCHISE OWNERS

Owners of sports franchises usually prefer to stay out of the limelight that players seek on the field—but not always. The brash actions of these colorful owners have at times overshadowed the successes and failures of their teams.

Bill Veeck
Cleveland Indians, 1946-49; St. Louis Browns, 1951-53; Chicago White Sox, 1959-61, 1975-80

The son of the Chicago Cubs president, Bill Veeck advised the team to plant ivy on the outfield walls of Wrigley Field. Upon purchasing the Cleveland Indians, he introduced fan-friendly promotions like fireworks and giveaways. Attendance topped 1 mil for the first time in 1946, and the Indians won the World Series in 1948.

Veeck pulled his most famous stunt in 1951 when he gave a Browns contract to Eddie Gaedel, who was 3 ft, 7 in. tall, and put him in the lineup as a pinch hitter with a miniscule strike zone (Gaedel walked). But his comeuppance came in 1979, when fans were encouraged to bring loathed disco recordings to the park for a Disco Demolition Night. The anti-disco furor left the field unplayable and forced Veeck's White Sox to forfeit.

Walter O'Malley
Brooklyn/Los Angeles Dodgers, 1950-79

The man revered in Los Angeles for bringing major league baseball to California is still vilified in New York for taking away its beloved Bums. Dodgers owner Walter O'Malley moved the team after the 1957 season, ending a long standoff with Robert Moses, New York City's planning czar, over plans for a new stadium in Brooklyn. O'Malley persuaded NY Giants owner Horace Stoneham to move his team to San Francisco so the two teams could continue their rivalry on the West Coast. New York went from hosting three baseball teams to just one overnight, and major league baseball grabbed its first footholds west of Kansas City. Once in Los Angeles, O'Malley privately financed and built Dodger Stadium, which the team continues to occupy.

Robert Irsay
Baltimore/Indianapolis Colts, 1972-97

Robert Irsay's Colts made three straight playoff appearances (1975-77), then played nine consecutive losing seasons. In the 1983 draft, the Colts selected quarterback John Elway, who threatened to sign with the NY Yankees rather than play for Irsay. The city of Baltimore refused Irsay's demands to fund a new stadium and made moves to take over the team. In response, Irsay made a Mar. 1984 deal with Indianapolis and departed with the franchise's property less than 24 hours after a deal was finalized. The team's woes followed it to Indianapolis: the Colts were 4-12 that first season. Irsay did not live to see his son draft Peyton Manning, who would become the face of the franchise and win Super Bowl XLI in 2007.

Al Davis
Oakland/Los Angeles Raiders, 1972-2011

The only man in pro football history to serve as coach, general manager, team owner, and league commissioner, Al Davis ran the Raiders as a true iconoclast. As commissioner of the upstart American Football League, he strategically used big contracts to lure star players. After the NFL-AFL merger, he bought the Oakland Raiders and hired the modern NFL's first black head coach and its first female chief executive. He moved the Raiders to Los Angeles in 1982, back to Oakland in 1995, and repeatedly sued the NFL for blocking attempts at relocation. In 1967-85, the Raiders won three Super Bowls and one AFL championship. But the team's playoff droughts—1994-99 and 2003-13—tarnished Davis's legacy.

George Steinbrenner
New York Yankees, 1973-2010

Known simply as "The Boss," the mercurial George Steinbrenner changed managers 20 times in his first 23 seasons, hiring Billy Martin five separate times. Major League Baseball suspended him in 1974 after he pleaded guilty to making illegal contributions to Pres. Richard Nixon's reelection campaign, and again in 1990 from day-to-day operations for paying a gambler to dig up dirt on one of his players. But Steinbrenner was one of the first owners to master free agency, signing Catfish Hunter, Reggie Jackson, and Dave Winfield to some of the day's most expensive contracts, leading to World Series titles in 1977 and 1978. Steinbrenner's impatience for developing young players led to a 17-year championship drought until a nucleus of farm system talent—developed during Steinbrenner's second suspension—led to Series victories in 1996 and 1998-2000.

Donald Sterling
San Diego/Los Angeles Clippers, 1981-2014

The ultralitigious Donald Sterling was a headache for the NBA from the start. The league fined him $10,000 in 1982 for admitting that he wouldn't mind if his team finished last so that he could have the no. 1 draft pick. Then, in 1984, he moved the team from San Diego to Los Angeles without NBA approval. Sterling's departure was no less troubled. The NBA suspended him for life and fined him $2.5 mil Apr. 29, 2014, after learning of racist remarks he made during a secretly recorded conversation with a paramour. Sterling's estranged wife and team co-owner, Shelly, had him declared mentally incompetent, then quickly agreed to sell the franchise for $2 bil.

Marge Schott
Cincinnati Reds, 1984-99

Even in an era before the Internet and social media would have exposed her to wider scrutiny and censure, Marge Schott was infamous for making offensive statements. A 1992 lawsuit by a former employee unearthed documents in which she referred to Reds outfielders Eric Davis and Dave Parker as "million-dollar n-----s." An investigation into those comments earned her a year-long suspension from Major League Baseball in 1993. Schott also consistently discriminated against minorities and women in the Reds' front office, and pinched pennies everywhere, making an injured Davis pay his own way home from Oakland to Cincinnati following the team's World Series victory in 1990. MLB suspended Schott a second time in 1996, after she defended a swastika she kept in her home with the statement, "Hitler was good in the beginning, but he went too far." She was forced to sell the franchise in 1999.

Jerry Jones
Dallas Cowboys, 1989-present

Jerry Jones bought "America's Team" in 1989 and immediately alienated fans by firing legendary coach Tom Landry. He replaced Landry with Jimmy Johnson, with whom he'd played college football, then fired general manager Tex Schramm and took over his duties. Jones traded Heisman-winning running back Herschel Walker for five players and multiple draft choices—including future Hall of Famer Emmitt Smith. Johnson and Smith helped the Cowboys win back-to-back Super Bowls in 1993 and 1994, but Jones fired Johnson in 1994 and replaced him with Barry Switzer, with whom the Cowboys won another Super Bowl in 1996. But since then, the Cowboys' fortunes have been more checkered. The team has had five different head coaches in 16 seasons (1998-2013) and has won just one playoff game.

Daniel Snyder
Washington Redskins, 1999-present

Regardless of how they feel about their team's exceedingly controversial nickname, most Washington football fans haven't been rushing to cheer for owner Daniel Snyder. From 1999 to 2013, Snyder burned through seven head coaches who owned a combined record of 104-136. He also developed a reputation for acquiring expensive free agents past their primes. Despite his willingness to overpay for expired talent, Snyder has earned a reputation as a miser. In 2000, the billionaire charged fans $10 to attend Redskins' training camp—and another $10 to park. He also sued more than 100 season-ticket owners who had signed 10-year renewal agreements but could no longer afford their seats during the recession in 2009.

Mark Cuban
Dallas Mavericks, 2000-present

Internet tycoon Mark Cuban bought the Dallas Mavericks in 2000 for $285 mil. A longtime fan of the perennially losing team, Cuban sat in regular seats and heckled referees and opposing players. In 2011, the Mavericks defeated the Miami Heat for their first NBA championship. But the NBA has fined Cuban almost $2 mil for public statements such as calling sexual assault charges against Lakers star Kobe Bryant in 2003-04 "great for the NBA . . . people love train-wreck television" and saying he "wouldn't hire [former NBA director of officiating Ed Rush] to manage a Dairy Queen." Cuban dismissed critics who question his outspokenness, saying, "The more people think I'm crazy and out of my mind, typically, the better I do."

OLYMPIC GAMES

General Olympic Information

The modern Olympic Games, first held in Athens, Greece, in 1896, were the result of efforts by Baron Pierre de Coubertin, a French educator, to promote interest in education and culture and to foster better international understanding through love of athletics. His inspiration was the ancient Greek Olympic Games, most notable of the four Panhellenic celebrations. The games were combined patriotic, religious, and athletic festivals held every four years. The first such recorded festival was held in 776 BCE, when the Greeks began to keep their calendar by "Olympiads," or four-year spans between the games.

Coubertin enlisted 14 nations to send athletes to the first modern Olympics. Now athletes from more than 200 nations and territories compete in the Summer Olympics. The Winter Olympic Games, started in 1924, draws competitors from about 80 countries and territories.

Symbol: Five rings or circles, linked to represent the sporting friendship of all peoples. They also symbolize five geographic areas—Africa, America, Asia, Australia, and Europe. Each ring is a different color—blue, yellow, black, green, and red—which, with the color white, represent the colors of the world's flags.

Flag: The five-ring symbol on a plain white background.

Creed: "The most important thing in the Olympic Games is not to win but to take part, just as the most important thing in life is not the triumph but the struggle. The essential thing is not to have conquered but to have fought well."

Motto: Citius, Altius, Fortius. ("Faster, higher, stronger" in Latin).

Oath: "In the name of all the competitors I promise that we shall take part in these Olympic Games, respecting and abiding by the rules which govern them, committing ourselves to a sport without doping and without drugs, in the true spirit of sportsmanship, for the glory of sport and the honor of our teams."

Flame: The modern version of the flame was adopted in 1936. The torch used to kindle it is first lit by the sun's rays in Olympia, Greece, then carried to the site of the Games by relays of runners. Ships and planes are used when necessary.

Winter Olympic Games Sites, 1924-2018

1924 Chamonix, France	1956 Cortina d'Ampezzo, Italy	1980 Lake Placid, NY, U.S.	2006 Turin, Italy
1928 St. Moritz, Switzerland	1960 Squaw Valley, CA, U.S.	1984 Sarajevo, Yugoslavia	2010 Vancouver, BC, Canada
1932 Lake Placid, NY, U.S.	1964 Innsbruck, Austria	1988 Calgary, AB, Canada	2014 Sochi, Russia
1936 Garmisch-Partenkirchen, Germany	1968 Grenoble, France	1992 Albertville, France	2018 PyeongChang, South Korea
1948 St. Moritz, Switzerland	1972 Sapporo, Japan	1994 Lillehammer, Norway	
1952 Oslo, Norway	1976 Innsbruck, Austria	1998 Nagano, Japan	
		2002 Salt Lake City, UT, U.S.	

Summer Olympic Games Sites, 1896-2020

1896 Athens, Greece	1928 Amsterdam, Netherlands	1968 Mexico City, Mexico	1996 Atlanta, GA, U.S.
1900 Paris, France	1932 Los Angeles, CA, U.S.	1972 Munich, W. Germany	2000 Sydney, Australia
1904 St. Louis, MO, U.S.	1936 Berlin, Germany	1976 Montreal, QC, Canada	2004 Athens, Greece
1906 Athens, Greece*	1948 London, England, UK	1980 Moscow, USSR	2008 Beijing, China
1908 London, England, UK	1952 Helsinki, Finland	1984 Los Angeles, CA, U.S.	2012 London, England, UK
1912 Stockholm, Sweden	1956 Melbourne, Australia	1988 Seoul, South Korea	2016 Rio de Janeiro, Brazil
1920 Antwerp, Belgium	1960 Rome, Italy	1992 Barcelona, Spain	2020 Tokyo, Japan
1924 Paris, France	1964 Tokyo, Japan		

*Games not recognized by International Olympic Committee. **Note:** Games VI (1916), XII (1940), and XIII (1944) were not celebrated.

2014 Winter Olympic Games

Sochi, Russia, Feb. 7-23, 2014

More than 2,800 athletes from 88 nations met in Sochi, Russia, to compete in a record 98 events in the XXII Olympic Winter Games Feb. 7-23, 2014. Host nation Russia won 33 medals, including 13 gold, to top the final medal count, followed by the United States, Norway, and Canada.

Meryl Davis and Charlie White became the first Americans ever to win gold in ice dancing, but the figure skating events were mostly dominated by Russia, which claimed gold in the women's, pairs, and team events. Russia's former Olympic champion Yevgeny Plushenko bowed out of the men's competition just before the short program, citing a back injury, and Yuzuru Hanyu of Japan won men's gold.

Eighteen-year-old American Mikaela Shiffrin became the youngest ever to win a gold medal in slalom. Canada won both ice hockey events, with the Canadian women defeating the U.S. in dramatic overtime fashion for the gold.

Twelve new medal events debuted at the Sochi Games, including a figure skating mixed team event, women's ski jumping, ski slopestyle and halfpipe, and snowboard slopestyle and parallel slalom.

2014 Winter Olympic Games: Final Medal Standings

Country	Gold	Silver	Bronze	Total	Country	Gold	Silver	Bronze	Total
Russia	13	11	9	33	Japan	1	4	3	8
United States	9	7	12	28	Italy	0	2	6	8
Norway	11	5	10	26	Belarus	5	0	1	6
Canada	10	10	5	25	Poland	4	1	1	6
Netherlands	8	7	9	24	Finland	1	3	1	5
Germany	8	6	5	19	Great Britain	1	1	2	4
Austria	4	8	5	17	Latvia	0	2	2	4
France	4	4	7	15	Australia	0	2	1	3
Sweden	2	7	6	15	Ukraine	1	0	1	2
Switzerland	6	3	2	11	Slovakia	1	0	0	1
China	3	4	2	9	Croatia	0	1	0	1
South Korea	3	3	2	8	Kazakhstan	0	0	1	1
Czech Republic	2	4	2	8	**Total**	**99**	**97**	**99**	**295**
Slovenia	2	2	4	8					

2014 Winter Olympic Games: Medal Winners

(G = Gold, S = Silver, B = Bronze)

Alpine Skiing

Men

Downhill: G–Matthias Mayer, Austria; S–Christof Innerhofer, Italy; B–Kjetil Jansrud, Norway

Giant Slalom: G–Ted Ligety, United States; S–Steve Missillier, France; B–Alexis Pinturault, France

Slalom: G–Mario Matt, Austria; S–Marcel Hirscher, Austria; B–Henrik Kristoffersen, Norway

Super Combined: G–Sandro Viletta, Switzerland; S–Ivica Kostelic, Croatia; B–Christof Innerhofer, Italy

Super-G: G–Kjetil Jansrud, Norway; S–Andrew Weibrecht, United States; B–Jan Hudec, Canada, and Bode Miller, United States

Women

Downhill: G–Tina Maze, Slovenia, and Dominique Gisin, Switzerland; B–Lara Gut, Switzerland
Giant Slalom: G–Tina Maze, Slovenia; S–Anna Fenninger, Austria; B–Viktoria Rebensburg, Germany
Slalom: G–Mikaela Shiffrin, United States; S–Marlies Schild, Austria; B–Kathrin Zettel, Austria
Super Combined: G–Maria Hoefl-Riesch, Germany; S–Nicole Hosp, Austria; B–Julia Mancuso, United States
Super-G: G–Anna Fenninger, Austria; S–Maria Hoefl-Riesch, Germany; B–Nicole Hosp, Austria

Biathlon

Mixed 2x6-km and 2x7.5-km Relay: G–Norway (Berger, Bjoerndalen, Eckhoff, Svendsen); S–Czech Republic (Moravec, Soukalova, Soukup, Vitkova); B–Italy (Hofer, Oberhofer, Wierer, Windisch)

Men

10-km Sprint: G–Ole Einar Bjoerndalen, Norway; S–Dominik Landertinger, Austria; B–Jaroslav Soukup, Czech Republic
12.5-km Pursuit: G–Martin Fourcade, France; S–Ondrej Moravec, Czech Republic; B–Jean Guillaume Beatrix, France
15-km Mass Start: G–Emil Hegle Svendsen, Norway; S–Martin Fourcade, France; B–Ondrej Moravec, Czech Republic
20-km Individual: G–Martin Fourcade, France; S–Erik Lesser, Germany; B–Evgeniy Garanichev, Russia
4x7.5-km Relay: G–Russia (Malyshko, Shipulin, Ustyugov, Volkov); S–Germany (Boehm, Lesser, Peiffer, Schempp); B–Austria (Eder, Landertinger, Mesotitsch, Sumann)

Women

7.5-km Sprint: G–Anastasiya Kuzmina, Slovakia; S–Olga Vilukhina, Russia; B–Vita Semerenko, Ukraine
10-km Pursuit: G–Darya Domracheva, Belarus; S–Tora Berger, Norway; B–Teja Gregorin, Slovenia
12.5-km Mass Start: G–Darya Domracheva, Belarus; S–Gabriela Soukalova, Czech Republic; B–Tiril Eckhoff, Norway
15-km Individual: G–Darya Domracheva, Belarus; S–Selina Gasparin, Switzerland; B–Nadezhda Skardino, Belarus
4x6-km Relay: G–Ukraine (Dzhyma, Pidhrushna, Semerenko, Semerenko); S–Russia (Romanova, Shumilova, Vilukhina, Zaitseva); B–Norway (Berger, Eckhoff, Flatland, Horn)

Bobsledding

Two-Man: G–Alexey Voevoda and Alexander Zubkov, Russia; S–Alex Baumann and Beat Hefti, Switzerland; B–Steven Holcomb and Steven Langton, United States
Four-Man: G–Russia (Negodaylo, Trunenkov, Voevoda, Zubkov); S–Latvia (Dreishkens, Melbardis, Strenga, Vilkaste); B–United States (Fogt, Holcomb, Langton, Tomasevicz)
Women: G–Kaillie Humphries and Heather Moyse, Canada; S–Elana Meyers and Lauryn Williams, United States; B–Aja Evans and Jamie Greubel, United States

Cross-Country Skiing

Men

Individual Sprint: G–Ola Vigen Hattestad, Norway; S–Teodor Peterson, Sweden; B–Emil Joensson, Sweden
15 km: G–Dario Cologna, Switzerland; S–Johan Olsson, Sweden; B–Daniel Richardsson, Sweden
Skiathlon (15-km Classic + 15-km Free): G–Dario Cologna, Switzerland; S–Marcus Hellner, Sweden; B–Martin Johnsrud Sundby, Norway
50-km Mass Start: G–Alexander Legkov, Russia; S–Maxim Vylegzhanin, Russia; B–Ilia Chernousov, Russia
Team Sprint: G–Sami Jauhojaervi and Iivo Niskanen, Finland; S–Nikita Kriukov and Maxim Vylegzhanin, Russia; B–Emil Joensson and Teodor Peterson, Sweden
4x10-km Relay: G–Sweden (Hellner, Nelson, Olsson, Richardsson); S–Russia (Bessmertnykh, Japarov, Legkov, Vylegzhanin); B–France (Duvillard, Gaillard, Manificat, Perrillat Boiteux)

Women

Individual Sprint: G–Maiken Caspersen Falla, Norway; S–Ingvild Flugstad Oestberg, Norway; B–Vesna Fabjan, Slovenia
10 km: G–Justyna Kowalczyk, Poland; S–Charlotte Kalla, Sweden; B–Therese Johaug, Norway
Skiathlon (7.5-km Classic + 7.5-km Free): G–Marit Bjoergen, Norway; S–Charlotte Kalla, Sweden; B–Heidi Weng, Norway
30-km Mass Start: G–Marit Bjoergen, Norway; S–Therese Johaug, Norway; B–Kristin Stoermer Steira, Norway
Team Sprint: G–Marit Bjoergen and Ingvild Flugstad Oestberg, Norway; S–Kerttu Niskanen and Aino-Kaisa Saarinen, Finland; B–Ida Ingemarsdotter and Stina Nilsson, Sweden
4x5-km Relay: G–Sweden (Haag, Ingemarsdotter, Kalla, Wiken); S–Finland (Kylloenen, Lahteenmaki, Niskanen, Saarinen); B–Germany (Boehler, Fessel, Herrmann, Nystad)

Curling

Men: G–Canada; S–Great Britain; B–Sweden
Women: G–Canada; S–Sweden; B–Great Britain

Figure Skating

Men: G–Yuzuru Hanyu, Japan; S–Patrick Chan, Canada; B–Denis Ten, Kazakhstan
Women: G–Adelina Sotnikova, Russia; S–Kim Yu-Na, South Korea; B–Carolina Kostner, Italy
Ice Dancing: G–Meryl Davis and Charlie White, United States; S–Scott Moir and Tessa Virtue, Canada; B–Elena Ilinykh and Nikita Katsalapov, Russia
Pairs: G–Maxim Trankov and Tatiana Volosozhar, Russia; S–Fedor Klimov and Ksenia Stolbova, Russia; B–Aliona Savchenko and Robin Szolkowy, Germany
Mixed Team: G–Russia; S–Canada; B–United States

Freestyle Skiing

Men

Aerials: G–Anton Kushnir, Belarus; S–David Morris, Australia; B–Jia Zongyang, China
Moguls: G–Alex Bilodeau, Canada; S–Mikael Kingsbury, Canada; B–Alexandr Smyshlyaev, Russia
Ski Cross: G–Jean Frederic Chapuis, France; S–Arnaud Bovolenta, France; B–Jonathan Midol, France
Ski Halfpipe: G–David Wise, United States; S–Mike Riddle, Canada; B–Kevin Rolland, France
Ski Slopestyle: G–Joss Christensen, United States; S–Gus Kenworthy, United States; B–Nicholas Goepper, United States

Women

Aerials: G–Alla Tsuper, Belarus; S–Xu Mengtao, China; B–Lydia Lassila, Australia
Moguls: G–Justine Dufour-Lapointe, Canada; S–Chloe Dufour-Lapointe, Canada; B–Hannah Kearney, United States
Ski Cross: G–Marielle Thompson, Canada; S–Kelsey Serwa, Canada; B–Anna Holmlund, Sweden
Ski Halfpipe: G–Maddie Bowman, United States; S–Marie Martinod, France; B–Ayana Onozuka, Japan
Ski Slopestyle: G–Dara Howell, Canada; S–Devin Logan, United States; B–Kim Lamarre, Canada

Ice Hockey

Men: G–Canada; S–Sweden; B–Finland
Women: G–Canada; S–United States; B–Switzerland

Luge

Men's Singles: G–Felix Loch, Germany; S–Albert Demchenko, Russia; B–Armin Zoeggeler, Italy
Men's Doubles: G–Tobias Arlt and Tobias Wendl, Germany; S–Andreas Linger and Wolfgang Linger, Austria; B–Andris Sics and Juris Sics, Latvia
Women's Singles: G–Natalie Geisenberger, Germany; S–Tatjana Huefner, Germany; B–Erin Hamlin, United States
Mixed Team Relay: G–Germany (Arlt, Geisenberger, Loch, Wendl); S–Russia (Antonov, Demchenko, Denisyev, Ivanova); B–Latvia (Rubenis, Sics, Sics, Tiruma)

Nordic Combined

Large Hill/10 km: G–Joergen Graabak, Norway; S–Magnus Hovdal Moan, Norway; B–Fabian Riessle, Germany
Normal Hill/10 km: G–Eric Frenzel, Germany; S–Akito Watabe, Japan; B–Magnus Krog, Norway
Team 4x5-km Relay: G–Norway (Graabak, Klemetsen, Krog, Moan); S–Germany (Frenzel, Kircheisen, Riessle, Rydzek); B–Austria (Bieler, Gruber, Klapfer, Stecher)

Skeleton

Men: G–Alexander Tretiakov, Russia; S–Martins Dukurs, Latvia; B–Matthew Antoine, United States
Women: G–Elizabeth Yarnold, Great Britain; S–Noelle Pikus-Pace, United States; B–Elena Nikitina, Russia

Ski Jumping

Men

Large Hill: G–Kamil Stoch, Poland; S–Noriaki Kasai, Japan; B–Peter Prevc, Slovenia
Normal Hill: G–Kamil Stoch, Poland; S–Peter Prevc, Slovenia; B–Anders Bardal, Norway
Team: G–Germany (Freund, Kraus, Wank, Wellinger); S–Austria (Diethart, Hayboeck, Morgenstern, Schlierenzauer); B–Japan (Ito, Kasai, Shimizu, Takeuchi)

Women

Normal Hill: G–Carina Vogt, Germany; S–Daniela Iraschko-Stolz, Austria; B–Coline Mattel, France

Snowboarding
Men

Halfpipe: G–Iouri Podladtchikov, Switzerland; S–Ayumu Hirano, Japan; B–Taku Hiraoka, Japan
Parallel Giant Slalom: G–Vic Wild, Russia; S–Nevin Galmarini, Switzerland; B–Zan Kosir, Slovenia
Parallel Slalom: G–Vic Wild, Russia; S–Zan Kosir, Slovenia; B–Benjamin Karl, Austria
Slopestyle: G–Sage Kotsenburg, United States; S–Staale Sandbech, Norway; B–Mark McMorris, Canada
Snowboard Cross: G–Pierre Vaultier, France; S–Nikolay Olyunin, Russia; B–Alex Deibold, United States

Women

Halfpipe: G–Kaitlyn Farrington, United States; S–Torah Bright, Australia; B–Kelly Clark, United States
Parallel Giant Slalom: G–Patrizia Kummer, Switzerland; S–Tomoka Takeuchi, Japan; B–Alena Zavarzina, Russia
Parallel Slalom: G–Julia Dujmovits, Austria; S–Anke Karstens, Germany; B–Amelie Kober, Germany
Slopestyle: G–Jamie Anderson, United States; S–Enni Rukajarvi, Finland; B–Jenny Jones, Great Britain
Snowboard Cross: G–Eva Samkova, Czech Republic; S–Dominique Maltais, Canada; B–Chloe Trespeuch, France

Speed Skating
Men

500 m: G–Michel Mulder, Netherlands; S–Jan Smeekens, Netherlands; B–Ronald Mulder, Netherlands
1,000 m: G–Stefan Groothuis, Netherlands; S–Denny Morrison, Canada; B–Michel Mulder, Netherlands
1,500 m: G–Zbigniew Brodka, Poland; S–Koen Verweij, Netherlands; B–Denny Morrison, Canada
5,000 m: G–Sven Kramer, Netherlands; S–Jan Blokhuijsen, Netherlands; B–Jorrit Bergsma, Netherlands
10,000 m: G–Jorrit Bergsma, Netherlands; S–Sven Kramer, Netherlands; B–Bob de Jong, Netherlands
Team Pursuit: G–Netherlands (Blokhuijsen, Kramer, Verweij); S–South Korea (Joo, Kim, Lee); B–Poland (Brodka, Niedzwiedzki, Szymanski)

Women

500 m: G–Lee Sang-Hwa, South Korea; S–Olga Fatkulina, Russia; B–Margot Boer, Netherlands
1,000 m: G–Zhang Hong, China; S–Ireen Wust, Netherlands; B–Margot Boer, Netherlands
1,500 m: G–Jorien Ter Mors, Netherlands; S–Ireen Wust, Netherlands; B–Lotte van Beek, Netherlands
3,000 m: G–Ireen Wust, Netherlands; S–Martina Sablikova, Czech Republic; B–Olga Graf, Russia
5,000 m: G–Martina Sablikova, Czech Republic; S–Ireen Wust, Netherlands; B–Carien Kleibeuker, Netherlands
Team Pursuit: G–Netherlands (Leenstra, Ter Mors, Van Beek, Wust); S–Poland (Bachleda-Curus, Czerwonka, Wozniak, Zlotkowska); B–Russia (Graf, Lobysheva, Shikhova, Skokova)

Speed Skating (Short Track)
Men

500 m: G–Victor An, Russia; S–Wu Dajing, China; B–Charle Cournoyer, Canada
1,000 m: G–Victor An, Russia; S–Vladimir Grigorev, Russia; B–Sjinkie Knegt, Netherlands
1,500 m: G–Charles Hamelin, Canada; S–Han Tianyu, China; B–Victor An, Russia
5,000-m Relay: G–Russia (An, Elistratov, Grigorev, Zakharov); S–United States (Alvarez, Celski, Creveling, Malone); B–China (Chen, Han, Shi, Wu)

Women

500 m: G–Li Jianrou, China; S–Arianna Fontana, Italy; B–Park Seung-Hi, South Korea
1,000 m: G–Park Seung-Hi, South Korea; S–Fan Kexin, China; B–Shim Suk Hee, South Korea
1,500 m: G–Zhou Yang, China; S–Shim Suk Hee, South Korea; B–Arianna Fontana, Italy
3,000-m Relay: G–South Korea (Cho, Kim, Kong, Park, Shim); S–Canada (Drolet, Hewitt, Maltais, St-Gelais); B–Italy (Fontana, Peretti, Valcepina, Viviani)

Winter Olympic Games Champions, 1924-2014

In 1992, the Unified Team represented the former Soviet republics of Russia, Ukraine, Belarus, Kazakhstan, and Uzbekistan. Times are shown in hour:minute:sec.

Alpine Skiing

	Men's Downhill	Time
1948	Henri Oreiller, France	2:55.0
1952	Zeno Colo, Italy	2:30.8
1956	Toni Sailer, Austria	2:52.2
1960	Jean Vuarnet, France	2:06.0
1964	Egon Zimmermann, Austria	2:18.16
1968	Jean-Claude Killy, France	1:59.85
1972	Bernhard Russi, Switzerland	1:51.43
1976	Franz Klammer, Austria	1:45.73
1980	Leonhard Stock, Austria	1:45.50
1984	Bill Johnson, United States	1:45.49
1988	Pirmin Zurbriggen, Switzerland	1:59.63
1992	Patrick Ortlieb, Austria	1:50.37
1994	Tommy Moe, United States	1:45.75
1998	Jean-Luc Cretier, France	1:50.11
2002	Fritz Strobl, Austria	1:39.13
2006	Antoine Deneriaz, France	1:48.80
2010	Didier Defago, Switzerland	1:54.31
2014	Matthias Mayer, Austria	2:06.23

	Men's Giant Slalom	Time
1952	Stein Eriksen, Norway	2:25.0
1956	Toni Sailer, Austria	3:00.1
1960	Roger Staub, Switzerland	1:48.3
1964	Francois Bonlieu, France	1:46.71
1968	Jean-Claude Killy, France	3:29.28
1972	Gustavo Thoeni, Italy	3:09.62
1976	Heini Hemmi, Switzerland	3:26.97
1980	Ingemar Stenmark, Sweden	2:40.74
1984	Max Julen, Switzerland	2:41.18
1988	Alberto Tomba, Italy	2:06.37
1992	Alberto Tomba, Italy	2:06.98
1994	Markus Wasmeier, Germany	2:52.46
1998	Hermann Maier, Austria	2:38.51
2002	Stephan Eberharter, Austria	2:23.28
2006	Benjamin Raich, Austria	2:35.00
2010	Carlo Janka, Switzerland	2:37.83
2014	Ted Ligety, United States	2:45.29

	Men's Slalom	Time
1948	Edi Reinalter, Switzerland	2:10.3
1952	Othmar Schneider, Austria	2:00.0
1956	Toni Sailer, Austria	3:14.7
1960	Ernst Hinterseer, Austria	2:08.9
1964	Josef Stiegler, Austria	2:11.13
1968	Jean-Claude Killy, France	1:39.73
1972	Francisco Fernandez-Ochoa, Spain	1:49.27
1976	Piero Gros, Italy	2:03.29
1980	Ingemar Stenmark, Sweden	1:44.26
1984	Phil Mahre, United States	1:39.41
1988	Alberto Tomba, Italy	1:39.47
1992	Finn Christian Jagge, Norway	1:44.39
1994	Thomas Stangassinger, Austria	2:02.02
1998	Hans-Petter Buraas, Norway	1:49.31
2002	Jean-Pierre Vidal, France	1:41.06
2006	Benjamin Raich, Austria	1:43.14
2010	Giuliano Razzoli, Italy	1:39.32
2014	Mario Matt, Austria	1:41.84

	Men's Super Combined	Time
1936	Franz-Pfnuer, Germany	99.25 (pts.)
1948	Henri Oreiller, France	3.27 (pts.)
1988	Hubert Strolz, Austria	36.55 (pts.)
1992	Josef Polig, Italy	14.58 (pts.)
1994	Lasse Kjus, Norway	3:17.53
1998	Mario Reiter, Austria	3:08.06
2002	Kjetil Andre Aamodt, Norway	3:17.56
2006	Ted Ligety, United States	3:09.35
2010	Bode Miller, United States	2:44.92
2014	Sandro Viletta, Switzerland	2:45.20

Note: In 2010, a one-day super combined event replaced the traditional two-day combined event.

	Men's Super Giant Slalom	Time
1988	Franck Piccard, France	1:39.66
1992	Kjetil Andre Aamodt, Norway	1:13.04
1994	Markus Wasmeier, Germany	1:32.53
1998	Hermann Maier, Austria	1:34.82
2002	Kjetil Andre Aamodt, Norway	1:21.58
2006	Kjetil Andre Aamodt, Norway	1:30.65
2010	Aksel Lund Svindal, Norway	1:30.34
2014	Kjetil Jansrud, Norway	1:18.14

Women's Downhill

Year	Champion	Time
1948	Hedi Schlunegger, Switzerland	2:28.3
1952	Trude Beiser-Jochum, Austria	1:47.1
1956	Madeleine Berthod, Switzerland	1:40.7
1960	Heidi Biebl, Germany	1:37.6
1964	Christl Haas, Austria	1:55.39
1968	Olga Pall, Austria	1:40.87
1972	Marie-Theres Nadig, Switzerland	1:36.68
1976	Rosi Mittermaier, W. Germany	1:46.16
1980	Annemarie Moser-Proell, Austria	1:37.52
1984	Michela Figini, Switzerland	1:13.36
1988	Marina Kiehl, W. Germany	1:25.86
1992	Kerrin Lee-Gartner, Canada	1:52.55
1994	Katja Seizinger, Germany	1:35.93
1998	Katja Seizinger, Germany	1:28.89
2002	Carole Montillet, France	1:39.56
2006	Michaela Dorfmeister, Austria	1:56.49
2010	Lindsey Vonn, United States	1:44.19
2014	Tina Maze, Slovenia	1:41.57
	Dominique Gisin, Switzerland (tie)	1:41.57

Women's Giant Slalom[1]

Year	Champion	Time
1952	Andrea Mead Lawrence, United States	2:06.8
1956	Ossi Reichert, Germany	1:56.5
1960	Yvonne Ruegg, Switzerland	1:39.9
1964	Marielle Goitschel, France	1:52.24
1968	Nancy Greene, Canada	1:51.97
1972	Marie-Theres Nadig, Switzerland	1:29.90
1976	Kathy Kreiner, Canada	1:29.13
1980	Hanni Wenzel, Liechtenstein	2:41.66
1984	Debbie Armstrong, United States	2:20.98
1988	Vreni Schneider, Switzerland	2:06.49
1992	Pernilla Wiberg, Sweden	2:12.74
1994	Deborah Compagnoni, Italy	2:30.97
1998	Deborah Compagnoni, Italy	2:50.59
2002	Janica Kostelic, Croatia	2:30.01
2006	Julia Mancuso, United States	2:09.19
2010	Viktoria Rebensburg, Germany	2:27.11
2014	Tina Maze, Slovenia	2:36.87

(1) Beginning in 1980, the event time combined two runs.

Women's Slalom

Year	Champion	Time
1948	Gretchen Fraser, United States	1:57.2
1952	Andrea Mead Lawrence, United States	2:10.6
1956	Renee Colliard, Switzerland	1:52.3
1960	Anne Heggtveit, Canada	1:49.6
1964	Christine Goitschel, France	1:29.86
1968	Marielle Goitschel, France	1:25.86
1972	Barbara Ann Cochran, United States	1:31.24
1976	Rosi Mittermaier, W. Germany	1:30.54
1980	Hanni Wenzel, Liechtenstein	1:25.09
1984	Paoletta Magoni, Italy	1:36.47
1988	Vreni Schneider, Switzerland	1:36.69
1992	Petra Kronberger, Austria	1:32.68
1994	Vreni Schneider, Switzerland	1:56.01
1998	Hilde Gerg, Germany	1:32.40
2002	Janica Kostelic, Croatia	1:46.10
2006	Anja Paerson, Sweden	1:29.04
2010	Maria Riesch, Germany	1:42.89
2014	Mikaela Shiffrin, United States	1:44.54

Women's Super Combined

Year	Champion	Time
1936	Christl Cranz, Germany	97.06 (pts.)
1948	Trude Beiser-Jochum, Austria	6.58 (pts.)
1988	Anita Wachter, Austria	29.25 (pts.)
1992	Petra Kronberger, Austria	2.55 (pts.)
1994	Pernilla Wiberg, Sweden	3:05.16
1998	Katja Seizinger, Germany	2:40.74
2002	Janica Kostelic, Croatia	2:43.28
2006	Janica Kostelic, Croatia	2:51.08
2010	Maria Riesch, Germany	2:09.14
2014	Maria Hoefl-Riesch, Germany	2:34.62

Note: In 2010, a one-day super combined event replaced the traditional two-day combined event.

Women's Super Giant Slalom

Year	Champion	Time
1988	Sigrid Wolf, Austria	1:19.03
1992	Deborah Compagnoni, Italy	1:21.22
1994	Diann Roffe (Steinrotter), United States	1:22.15
1998	Picabo Street, United States	1:18.02
2002	Daniela Ceccarelli, Italy	1:13.59
2006	Michaela Dorfmeister, Austria	1:32.47
2010	Andrea Fischbacher, Austria	1:20.14
2014	Anna Fenninger, Austria	1:25.52

Biathlon

Mixed 2x6-Kilometer and 2x7.5-Kilometer Relay

Year	Champion	Time
2014	Norway, Czech Republic, Italy	1:09:17.0

Men's 10-Kilometer Sprint

Year	Champion	Time
1980	Frank Ullrich, E. Germany	32:10.69
1984	Eirik Kvalfoss, Norway	30:53.80
1988	Frank-Peter Roetsch, E. Germany	25:08.10
1992	Mark Kirchner, Germany	26:02.30
1994	Serguei Tchepikov, Russia	28:07.00
1998	Ole Einar Bjoerndalen, Norway	27:16.20
2002	Ole Einar Bjoerndalen, Norway	24:51.30
2006	Sven Fischer, Germany	26:11.6
2010	Vincent Jay, France	24:07.8
2014	Ole Einar Bjoerndalen, Norway	24:33.5

Men's 12.5-Kilometer Pursuit

Year	Champion	Time
2002	Ole Einar Bjoerndalen, Norway	32:34.6
2006	Vincent Defrasne, France	35:20.2
2010	Bjorn Ferry, Sweden	33:38.4
2014	Martin Fourcade, France	33:48.6

Men's 15-Kilometer Mass Start

Year	Champion	Time
2006	Michael Greis, Germany	47:20.0
2010	Evgeny Ustyugov, Russia	35:35.7
2014	Emil Hegle Svendsen, Norway	42:29.1

Men's 20-Kilometer Individual

Year	Champion	Time
1960	Klas Lestander, Sweden	1:33:21.6
1964	Vladimir Melanin, USSR	1:20:26.8
1968	Magnar Solberg, Norway	1:13:45.9
1972	Magnar Solberg, Norway	1:15:55.50
1976	Nikolai Kruglov, USSR	1:14:12.26
1980	Anatoli Aljabiev, USSR	1:08:16.31
1984	Peter Angerer, W. Germany	1:11:52.7
1988	Frank-Peter Roetsch, E. Germany	0:56:33.33
1992	Yevgeny Redkine, Unified Team	0:57:34.4
1994	Serguei Tarasov, Russia	0:57:25.3
1998	Halvard Hanevold, Norway	0:56:16.4
2002	Ole Einar Bjoerndalen, Norway	0:51:03.03
2006	Michael Greis, Germany	0:54:23.0
2010	Emil Hegle Svendsen, Norway	0:48:22.5
2014	Martin Fourcade, France	0:49:31.7

Men's 4x7.5-Kilometer Relay

Year	Champion	Time
1968	USSR, Norway, Sweden (40 km)	2:13:02.4
1972	USSR, Finland, E. Germany (40 km)	1:51:44.92
1976	USSR, Finland, E. Germany (40 km)	1:57:55.64
1980	USSR, E. Germany, W. Germany	1:34:03.27
1984	USSR, Norway, W. Germany	1:38:51.70
1988	USSR, W. Germany, Italy	1:22:30.00
1992	Germany, Unified Team, Sweden	1:24:43.50
1994	Germany, Russia, France	1:30:22.1
1998	Germany, Norway, Russia	1:19:43.3
2002	Norway, Germany, France	1:23:42.3
2006	Germany, Russia, France	1:21:51.5
2010	Norway, Austria, Russia	1:21:38.1
2014	Russia, Germany, Austria	1:12:15.9

Women's 7.5-Kilometer Sprint

Year	Champion	Time
1992	Anfissa Restsova, Unified Team	24:29.2
1994	Myriam Bedard, Canada	26:08.8
1998	Galina Koukleva, Russia	23:08.0
2002	Kati Wilhelm, Germany	20:41.4
2006	Florence Baverel-Robert, France	22:31.4
2010	Anastasiya Kuzmina, Slovakia	19:55.6
2014	Anastasiya Kuzmina, Slovakia	21:06.8

Women's 10-Kilometer Pursuit

Year	Champion	Time
2002	Olga Pyleva, Russia	31:07.7
2006	Kati Wilhelm, Germany	36:43.6
2010	Magdalena Neuner, Germany	30:16.0
2014	Darya Domracheva, Belarus	29:30.7

Women's 12.5-Kilometer Mass Start

Year	Champion	Time
2006	Anna Carin Olofsson, Sweden	40:36.5
2010	Magdalena Neuner, Germany	35:19.6
2014	Darya Domracheva, Belarus	35:25.6

Women's 15-Kilometer Individual

Year	Champion	Time
1992	Antje Misersky, Germany	51:47.2
1994	Myriam Bedard, Canada	52:06.6
1998	Ekaterina Dafovska, Bulgaria	54:52.0
2002	Andrea Henkel, Germany	47:30.0
2006	Svetlana Ishmouratova, Russia	49:24.1
2010	Tora Berger, Norway	40:52.8
2014	Darya Domracheva, Belarus	43:19.6

Women's 4x6-Kilometer Relay

Year	Champion	Time
1992	France, Germany, Unified Team (22.5 km)	1:15:55.6
1994	Russia, Germany, France (30 km)	1:47:19.5
1998	Germany, Russia, Norway (30 km)	1:40:13.6
2002	Germany, Norway, Russia (30 km)	1:27:55.0
2006	Russia, Germany, France	1:16:12.5
2010	Russia, France, Germany	1:09:36.3
2014	Ukraine, Russia, Norway	1:10:02.5

Bobsledding
(Driver in parentheses.)

2-Man Bobsled

Year	Team	Time
1932	United States (Hubert Stevens)	8:14.74
1936	United States (Ivan Brown)	5:29.29
1948	Switzerland (Felix Endrich)	5:29.20
1952	Germany (Andreas Ostler)	5:24.54
1956	Italy (Dalla Costa)	5:30.14
1964	Great Britain (Anthony Nash)	4:21.90
1968	Italy (Eugenio Monti)	4:41.54
1972	W. Germany (Wolfgang Zimmerer)	4:57.07
1976	E. Germany (Meinhard Nehmer)	3:44.42
1980	Switzerland (Erich Schaerer)	4:09.36
1984	E. Germany (Wolfgang Hoppe)	3:25.56
1988	USSR (Janis Kipours)	3:54.19
1992	Switzerland (Gustav Weber)	4:03.26
1994	Switzerland (Gustav Weber)	3:30.81
1998	Canada (Pierre Lueders)	3:37.24
	Italy (Guenther Huber) (tie)	3:37.24
2002	Germany II (Christoph Langen)	3:10.11
2006	Germany (Andre Lange)	3:43.38
2010	Germany (Andre Lange)	3:26.65
2014	Russia (Alexander Zubkov)	3:45.39

4-Man Bobsled

Year	Team	Time
1924	Switzerland (Eduard Scherrer)	5:45.54
1928	United States (William Fiske) (5-man)	3:20.50
1932	United States (William Fiske)	7:53.68
1936	Switzerland (Pierre Musy)	5:19.85
1948	United States (Francis Tyler)	5:20.10
1952	Germany (Andreas Ostler)	5:07.84
1956	Switzerland (Franz Kapus)	5:10.44
1964	Canada (Victor Emery)	4:14.46
1968	Italy (Eugenio Monti) (2 heats)	2:17.39
1972	Switzerland (Jean Wicki)	4:43.07
1976	E. Germany (Meinhard Nehmer)	3:40.43
1980	E. Germany (Meinhard Nehmer)	3:59.92
1984	E. Germany (Wolfgang Hoppe)	3:20.22
1988	Switzerland (Ekkehard Fasser)	3:47.51
1992	Austria (Ingo Appelt)	3:53.90
1994	Germany (Wolfgang Hoppe)	3:27.28
1998	Germany II (Christoph Langen)	2:39.41
2002	Germany II (Andre Lange)	3:07.51
2006	Germany (Andre Lange)	3:40.42
2010	United States (Steven Holcomb)	3:24.46
2014	Russia (Alexander Zubkov)	3:40.60

2-Woman Bobsled

Year	Team	Time
2002	United States II (Jill Bakken)	1:37.76
2006	Germany (Sandra Kiriasis)	3:49.98
2010	Canada (Kaillie Humphries)	3:32.28
2014	Canada (Kaillie Humphries)	3:50.61

Cross-Country Skiing

Men's Individual Sprint

Year	Athlete	Time
2002	Tor Arne Hetland, Norway (1.5 km)	2:56.9
2006	Bjoern Lind, Sweden (1.3 km)	2:26.5
2010	Nikita Kriukov, Russia	3:36.3
2014	Ola Vigen Hattestad, Norway	3:38.39

Men's 10 Kilometers

Year	Athlete	Time
1992	Vegard Ulvang, Norway	27:36.0
1994	Bjoern Daehlie, Norway	24:20.1
1998	Bjoern Daehlie, Norway	27:24.5
2002	Thomas Alsgaard, Norway	49:48.9
	Frode Estil, Norway (tie)[1]	49:48.9

(1) Both awarded gold after Johann Muehlegg of Spain was stripped of gold for a drug offense.

Men's 15 Kilometers

Year	Athlete	Time
1924	Thorleif Haug, Norway	1:14:31
1928	Johan Grottumsbraaten, Norway	1:37:01
1932	Sven Utterstrom, Sweden	1:23:07
1936	Erik-August Larsson, Sweden	1:14:38
1948	Martin Lundstrom, Sweden	1:13:50
1952	Hallgeir Brenden, Norway	1:01:34
1956	Hallgeir Brenden, Norway	0:49:39.0
1960	Haakon Brusveen, Norway	0:51:55.5
1964	Eero Maentyranta, Finland	0:50:54.1
1968	Harald Groenningen, Norway	0:47:54.2
1972	Sven-Ake Lundback, Sweden	0:45:28.24
1976	Nikolai Balukov, USSR	0:43:58.47
1980	Thomas Wassberg, Sweden	0:41:57.63
1984	Gunde Svan, Sweden	0:41:25.6
1988	Mikhail Deviatiarov, USSR	0:41:18.9
1992	Bjoern Daehlie, Norway	0:38:01.9
1994	Bjoern Daehlie, Norway	0:35:48.8
1998	Thomas Alsgaard, Norway	1:07:01.7
2002	Andrus Veerpalu, Estonia	0:37:07.4

Men's 15 Kilometers

Year	Athlete	Time
2006	Andrus Veerpalu, Estonia	0:38:01.3
2010	Dario Cologna, Switzerland	0:33:36.3
2014	Dario Cologna, Switzerland	0:38:29.7

Note: Approx. 18-km course 1924-52.

Men's 30-Kilometer Pursuit

Year	Athlete	Time
1956	Veikko Hakulinen, Finland	1:44:06.0
1964	Eero Maentyranta, Finland	1:30:50.7
1968	Franco Nones, Italy	1:35:39.2
1972	Vyacheslav Vedenine, USSR	1:36:31.15
1976	Sergei Saveliev, USSR	1:30:29.38
1980	Nikolai Zimyatov, USSR	1:27:02.80
1984	Nikolai Zimyatov, USSR	1:28:56.3
1988	Aleksei Prokourorov, USSR	1:24:26.3
1992	Vegard Ulvang, Norway	1:22:27.8
1994	Thomas Alsgaard, Norway	1:12:26.4
1998	Mika Myllylae, Finland	1:33:55.8
2002	Christian Hoffmann, Austria[1]	1:11:31.0
2006	Eugeni Dementiev, Russia	1:17:00.8
2010	Marcus Hellner, Sweden	1:15:11.4

(1) Awarded gold after Johann Muehlegg of Spain was stripped of gold for a drug offense.

Men's Skiathlon

Year	Athlete	Time
2014	Dario Cologna, Switzerland	1:08:15.4

Men's 50-Kilometer Mass Start

Year	Athlete	Time
1924	Thorleif Haug, Norway	3:44:32.0
1928	Per Erik Hedlund, Sweden	4:52:03.0
1932	Veli Saarinen, Finland	4:28:00.0
1936	Elis Wiklund, Sweden	3:30:11.0
1948	Nils Karlsson, Sweden	3:47:48.0
1952	Veikko Hakulinen, Finland	3:33:33.0
1956	Sixten Jernberg, Sweden	2:50:27.0
1960	Kalevi Hamalainen, Finland	2:59:06.3
1964	Sixten Jernberg, Sweden	2:43:52.6
1968	Ole Ellefsaeter, Norway	2:28:45.8
1972	Paal Tyldum, Norway	2:43:14.75
1976	Ivar Formo, Norway	2:37:30.05
1980	Nikolai Zimyatov, USSR	2:27:24.60
1984	Thomas Wassberg, Sweden	2:15:55.8
1988	Gunde Svan, Sweden	2:04:30.9
1992	Bjoern Daehlie, Norway	2:03:41.5
1994	Vladimir Smirnov, Kazakhstan	2:07:20.3
1998	Bjoern Daehlie, Norway	2:05:08.2
2002	Mikhail Ivanov, Russia	2:06:20.8
2006	Giorgio di Centa, Italy	2:06:11.8
2010	Petter Northug, Norway	2:05:35.5
2014	Alexander Legkov, Russia	1:46:55.2

Men's 4x10-Kilometer Relay

Year	Team	Time
1936	Finland, Norway, Sweden	2:41:33.0
1948	Sweden, Finland, Norway	2:32:08.0
1952	Finland, Norway, Sweden	2:20:16.0
1956	USSR, Finland, Sweden	2:15:30.0
1960	Finland, Norway, USSR	2:18:45.6
1964	Sweden, Finland, USSR	2:18:34.6
1968	Norway, Sweden, Finland	2:08:33.5
1972	USSR, Norway, Switzerland	2:04:47.94
1976	Finland, Norway, USSR	2:07:59.72
1980	USSR, Norway, Finland	1:57:03.46
1984	Sweden, USSR, Finland	1:55:06.30
1988	Sweden, USSR, Czechoslovakia	1:43:58.60
1992	Norway, Italy, Finland	1:39:26.00
1994	Italy, Norway, Finland	1:41:15.00
1998	Norway, Italy, Finland	1:40:55.70
2002	Norway, Italy, Germany	1:32:45.5
2006	Italy, Germany, Sweden	1:43:45.7
2010	Sweden, Norway, Czech Republic	1:45:05.4
2014	Sweden, Russia, France	1:28:42.0

Men's Team Sprint

Year	Team	Time
2006	Bjoern Lind & Thobias Fredriksson, Sweden	17:02.9
2010	Oeystein Pettersen & Petter Northug, Norway	19:01.0
2014	Sami Jauhojaervi & Iivo Niskanen, Finland	23:14.89

Women's Individual Sprint

Year	Athlete	Time
2002	Julia Tchepalova, Russia (1.5 km)	3:10.6
2006	Chandra Crawford, Canada (1.1 km)	2:12.3
2010	Marit Bjoergen, Norway	3:39.2
2014	Maiken Caspersen Falla, Norway	2:35.49

Women's 5 Kilometers

Year	Athlete	Time
1964	Claudia Boyarskikh, USSR	17:50.5
1968	Toini Gustafsson, Sweden	16:45.2
1972	Galina Koulacova, USSR	17:00.50
1976	Helena Takalo, Finland	15:48.69
1980	Raisa Smetanina, USSR	15:06.92
1984	Marja-Liisa Haemaelainen, Finland	17:04.0
1988	Marjo Matikainen, Finland	15:04.0
1992	Marjut Lukkarinen, Finland	14:13.8

Women's 5 Kilometers	Time
1994	Ljubov Egorova, Russia 14:08.8
1998	Larissa Lazutina, Russia. 17:37.9
2002	Beckie Scott, Canada[1] 25:09.9

(1) Awarded gold after Olga Danilova of Russia was stripped of gold and Larissa Lazutina of Russia was stripped of silver for drug offenses.

Women's 10 Kilometers	Time
1952	Lydia Wideman, Finland. 41:40.0
1956	Lyubov Kosyreva, USSR 38:11.0
1960	Maria Gusakova, USSR 39:46.6
1964	Claudia Boyarskikh, USSR. 40:24.3
1968	Toini Gustafsson, Sweden 36:46.5
1972	Galina Koulacova, USSR 34:17.82
1976	Raisa Smetanina, USSR 30:13.41
1980	Barbara Petzold, E. Germany. 30:31.54
1984	Marja-Liisa Haemaelainen, Finland 31:44.2
1988	Vida Ventsene, USSR 30:08.3
1992	Lyubov Egorova, Unified Team 25:53.7
1994	Lyubov Egorova, Russia. 27:30.1
1998	Larissa Lazutina, Russia. 46.06.9
2002	Bente Skari, Norway. 28:05.6
2006	Kristina Smigun, Estonia. 27:51.4
2010	Charlotte Kalla, Sweden. 24:58.4
2014	Justyna Kowalczyk, Poland 28:17.8

Women's 15-Kilometer Pursuit	Time
1992	Lyubov Egorova, Unified Team 42:20.8
1994	Manuela Di Centa, Italy. 39:44.5
1998	Olga Danilova, Russia 46:55.4
2002	Stefania Belmondo, Italy. 39:54.4
2006	Kristina Smigun, Estonia. 42:48.7
2010	Marit Bjoergen, Norway 39:58.1

Women's Skiathlon	Time
2014	Marit Bjoergen, Norway. 38:33.6

Women's 30-Kilometer Mass Start	Time
1992	Stefania Belmondo, Italy. 1:22:30.1
1994	Manuela Di Centa, Italy 1:25:41.6
1998	Julija Tchepalova, Russia. 1:22:01.5
2002	Gabriella Paruzzi, Italy 1:30:57.1
2006	Katerina Neumannova, Czech Republic. 1:22:25.4
2010	Justyna Kowalczyk, Poland 1:30:33.7
2014	Marit Bjoergen, Norway 1:11:05.2

Women's 4x5-Kilometer Relay	Time
1956	Finland, USSR, Sweden (15 km) 1:09:01.0
1960	Sweden, USSR, Finland (15 km) 1:04:21.4
1964	USSR, Sweden, Finland (15 km) 0:59:20.2
1968	Norway, Sweden, USSR (15 km) 0:57:30.0
1972	USSR, Finland, Norway (15 km) 0:48:46.15
1976	USSR, Finland, E. Germany 1:07:49.75
1980	E. Germany, USSR, Norway 1:02:11.1
1984	Norway, Czechoslovakia, Finland 1:06:49.7
1988	USSR, Norway, Finland 0:59:51.1
1992	United Team, Norway, Italy 0:59:34.8
1994	Russia, Norway, Italy 0:57:12.5
1998	Russia, Norway, Italy 0:55:13.5
2002	Germany, Norway, Switzerland 0:49:30.6
2006	Russia, Germany, Italy. 0:54:47.7
2010	Norway, Germany, Finland. 0:55:19.5
2014	Sweden, Finland, Germany 0:53:02.7

Women's Team Sprint	Time
2006	Lina Andersson & Anna Dahlberg, Sweden . . . 16:36.9
2010	Evi Sachenbacher-Stehle & Claudia Nystad, Germany 18:03.7
2014	Marit Bjoergen & Ingvild Flugstad Oestberg, Norway 16:04.05

Curling

Men
1998	Switzerland, Canada, Norway
2002	Norway, Canada, Switzerland
2006	Canada, Finland, United States
2010	Canada, Norway, Switzerland
2014	Canada, Great Britain, Sweden

Women
1998	Canada, Denmark, Sweden
2002	Britain, Switzerland, Canada
2006	Sweden, Switzerland, Canada
2010	Sweden, Canada, China
2014	Canada, Sweden, Great Britain

Figure Skating

Men's Singles
1908[1]	Ulrich Salchow, Sweden
1920[1]	Gillis Grafstrom, Sweden

Men's Singles
1924	Gillis Grafstrom, Sweden
1928	Gillis Grafstrom, Sweden
1932	Karl Schaefer, Austria
1936	Karl Schaefer, Austria
1948	Richard Button, United States
1952	Richard Button, United States
1956	Hayes Alan Jenkins, United States
1960	David W. Jenkins, United States
1964	Manfred Schnelldorfer, Germany
1968	Wolfgang Schwartz, Austria
1972	Ondrej Nepela, Czechoslovakia
1976	John Curry, Great Britain
1980	Robin Cousins, Great Britain
1984	Scott Hamilton, United States
1988	Brian Boitano, United States
1992	Viktor Petrenko, Unified Team
1994	Aleksei Urmanov, Russia
1998	Ilya Kulik, Russia
2002	Alexei Yagudin, Russia
2006	Yevgeny Plushenko, Russia
2010	Evan Lysacek, United States
2014	Yuzuru Hanyu, Japan

(1) Event held during Summer Olympic Games.

Women's Singles
1908[1]	Madge Syers, Great Britain
1920[1]	Magda Julin-Mauroy, Sweden
1924	Herma von Szabo-Planck, Austria
1928	Sonja Henie, Norway
1932	Sonja Henie, Norway
1936	Sonja Henie, Norway
1948	Barbara Ann Scott, Canada
1952	Jeanette Altwegg, Great Britain
1956	Tenley Albright, United States
1960	Carol Heiss, United States
1964	Sjoukje Dijkstra, Netherlands
1968	Peggy Fleming, United States
1972	Beatrix Schuba, Austria
1976	Dorothy Hamill, United States
1980	Anett Poetzsch, E. Germany
1984	Katarina Witt, E. Germany
1988	Katarina Witt, E. Germany
1992	Kristi Yamaguchi, United States
1994	Oksana Baiul, Ukraine
1998	Tara Lipinski, United States
2002	Sarah Hughes, United States
2006	Shizuka Arakawa, Japan
2010	Kim Yu-Na, South Korea
2014	Adelina Sotnikova, Russia

(1) Event held during Summer Olympic Games.

Pairs
1908[1]	Anna Hubler & Heinrich Burger, Germany
1920[1]	Ludovika Jakobsson & Walter Jakobsson, Finland
1924	Helene Engelman & Alfred Berger, Austria
1928	Andree Joly & Pierre Brunet, France
1932	Andree Joly & Pierre Brunet, France
1936	Maxi Herber & Ernst Baier, Germany
1948	Micheline Lannoy & Pierre Baugniet, Belgium
1952	Ria Falk & Paul Falk, Germany
1956	Elisabeth Schwartz & Kurt Oppelt, Austria
1964	Ludmila Beloussova & Oleg Protopopov, USSR
1968	Ludmila Beloussova & Oleg Protopopov, USSR
1972	Irina Rodnina & Alexei Ulanov, USSR
1976	Irina Rodnina & Aleksandr Zaitzev, USSR
1980	Irina Rodnina & Aleksandr Zaitzev, USSR
1984	Elena Valova & Oleg Vassiliev, USSR
1988	Ekaterina Gordeeva & Sergei Grinkov, USSR
1992	Natalia Mishkutienok & Artur Dimitriev, Unified Team
1994	Ekaterina Gordeeva & Sergei Grinkov, Russia
1998	Oksana Kazakova & Artur Dmitriev, Russia
2002	Elena Berezhnaya & Anton Sikharulidze, Russia; Jamie Sale & David Pelletier, Canada (tie)
2006	Tatyana Totmianina & Maxim Marinin, Russia
2010	Shen Xue & Zhao Hongbo, China
2014	Tatiana Volosozhar & Maxim Trankov, Russia

(1) Event held during Summer Olympic Games.

Ice Dancing
1976	Ludmila Pakhomova & Aleksandr Gorschkov, USSR
1980	Natalya Linichuk & Gennadi Karponosov, USSR
1984	Jayne Torvill & Christopher Dean, Great Britain
1988	Natalia Bestemianova & Andrei Bukin, USSR
1992	Marina Klimova & Sergei Ponomarenko, Unified Team
1994	Pasha Grishuk & Evgeny Platov, Russia
1998	Pasha Grishuk & Evgeny Platov, Russia
2002	Marina Anissina & Gwendal Peizerat, France
2006	Tatyana Navka & Roman Kostomarov, Russia
2010	Tessa Virtue & Scott Moir, Canada
2014	Meryl Davis & Charlie White, United States

Mixed Team

2014	Russia, Canada, United States

Freestyle Skiing

Men's Aerials

		Points
1994	Andreas Schoenbaechler, Switzerland	234.67
1998	Eric Bergoust, United States	255.64
2002	Ales Valenta, Czech Republic	257.02
2006	Xiaopeng Han, China	250.77
2010	Alexei Grishin, Belarus	248.41
2014	Anton Kushnir, Belarus	134.50

Men's Moguls

		Points
1992	Edgar Grospiron, France	25.81
1994	Jean-Luc Brassard, Canada	27.24
1998	Jonny Moseley, United States	26.93
2002	Janne Lahtela, Finland	27.97
2006	Dale Begg-Smith, Australia	26.77
2010	Alex Bilodeau, Canada	26.75
2014	Alex Bilodeau, Canada	26.31

Men's Ski Cross

2010	Michael Schmid, Switzerland
2014	Jean Frederic Chapuis, France

Men's Ski Halfpipe

		Points
2014	David Wise, United States	92.00

Men's Ski Slopestyle

		Points
2014	Joss Christensen, United States	95.80

Women's Aerials

		Points
1994	Lina Tcherjazova, Uzbekistan	166.84
1998	Nikki Stone, United States	193.00
2002	Alisa Camplin, Australia	193.47
2006	Evelyne Leu, Switzerland	202.55
2010	Lydia Lassila, Australia	214.74
2014	Alla Tsuper, Belarus	98.01

Women's Moguls

		Points
1992	Donna Weinbrecht, United States	23.69
1994	Stine Lise Hattestad, Norway	25.97
1998	Tae Satoya, Japan	25.06
2002	Kari Traa, Norway	25.94
2006	Jennifer Heil, Canada	26.50
2010	Hannah Kearney, United States	26.63
2014	Justine Dufour-Lapointe, Canada	22.44

Women's Ski Cross

2010	Ashleigh McIvor, Canada
2014	Marielle Thompson, Canada

Women's Ski Halfpipe

		Points
2014	Maddie Bowman, United States	89.00

Women's Ski Slopestyle

		Points
2014	Dara Howell, Canada	94.20

Ice Hockey

Men

1920[1]	Canada, United States, Czechoslovakia
1924	Canada, United States, Great Britain
1928	Canada, Sweden, Switzerland
1932	Canada, United States, Germany
1936	Great Britain, Canada, United States
1948	Canada, Czechoslovakia, Switzerland
1952	Canada, United States, Sweden
1956	USSR, United States, Canada
1960	United States, Canada, USSR
1964	USSR, Sweden, Czechoslovakia
1968	USSR, Czechoslovakia, Canada
1972	USSR, United States, Czechoslovakia
1976	USSR, Czechoslovakia, W. Germany
1980	United States, USSR, Sweden
1984	USSR, Czechoslovakia, Sweden
1988	USSR, Finland, Sweden
1992	Unified Team, Canada, Czechoslovakia
1994	Sweden, Canada, Finland
1998	Czech Republic, Russia, Finland
2002	Canada, United States, Russia
2006	Sweden, Finland, Czech Republic
2010	Canada, United States, Finland
2014	Canada, Sweden, Finland

(1) Event held during Summer Olympic Games.

Women

1998	United States, Canada, Finland
2002	Canada, United States, Sweden
2006	Canada, Sweden, United States
2010	Canada, United States, Finland
2014	Canada, United States, Switzerland

Luge

Men's Singles

		Time
1964	Thomas Keohler, E. Germany	3:27.77
1968	Manfred Schmid, Austria	2:52.48
1972	Wolfgang Scheidel, E. Germany	3:27.58
1976	Detlef Guenther, E. Germany	3:27.688
1980	Bernhard Glass, E. Germany	2:54.796
1984	Paul Hildgartner, Italy	3:04.258
1988	Jens Mueller, E. Germany	3:05.548
1992	Georg Hackl, Germany	3:02.363
1994	Georg Hackl, Germany	3:21.571
1998	Georg Hackl, Germany	3:18.436
2002	Armin Zoeggeler, Italy	2:57.941
2006	Armin Zoeggeler, Italy	3:26.088
2010	Felix Loch, Germany	3:13.085
2014	Felix Loch, Germany	3:27.526

Men's Doubles

		Time
1964	Austria	1:41.62
1968	E. Germany	1:35.85
1972	Italy, E. Germany (tie)	1:28.35
1976	E. Germany	1:25.604
1980	E. Germany	1:19.331
1984	W. Germany	1:23.620
1988	E. Germany	1:31.940
1992	Germany	1:32.053
1994	Italy	1:36.720
1998	Germany	1:41.105
2002	Germany	1:26.082
2006	Austria	1:34.497
2010	Austria	1:22.705
2014	Germany	1:38.933

Women's Singles

		Time
1964	Ortun Enderlein, Germany	3:24.67
1968	Erica Lechner, Italy	2:28.66
1972	Anna M. Muller, E. Germany	2:59.18
1976	Margit Schumann, E. Germany	2:50.621
1980	Vera Zozulya, USSR	2:36.537
1984	Steffi Martin, E. Germany	2:46.570
1988	Steffi Walter, E. Germany	3:03.973
1992	Doris Neuner, Austria	3:06.696
1994	Gerda Weissensteiner, Italy	3:15.517
1998	Silke Kraushaar, Germany	3:23.779
2002	Sylke Otto, Germany	2:52.464
2006	Sylke Otto, Germany	3:07.979
2010	Tatjana Huefner, Germany	2:46.524
2014	Natalie Geisenberger, Germany	3:19.768

Mixed Team Relay

		Time
2014	Germany, Russia, Latvia	2:45.649

Nordic Combined

Men's Individual

1924	Thorleif Haug, Norway
1928	Johan Grottumsbraaten, Norway
1932	Johan Grottumsbraaten, Norway
1936	Oddbjorn Hagen, Norway
1948	Heikki Hasu, Finland
1952	Simon Slattvik, Norway
1956	Sverre Stenersen, Norway
1960	Georg Thoma, W. Germany
1964	Tormod Knutsen, Norway
1968	Franz Keller, W. Germany
1972	Ulrich Wehling, E. Germany
1976	Ulrich Wehling, E. Germany
1980	Ulrich Wehling, E. Germany
1984	Tom Sandberg, Norway
1988	Hippolyt Kempf, Switzerland
1992	Fabrice Guy, France
1994	Fred Barre Lundberg, Norway
1998	Bjarte Engen Vik, Norway
2002	Samppa Lajunen, Finland
2006	Georg Hettich, Germany

Men's 10-Kilometer Large Hill

2010	Bill Demong, United States
2014	Joergen Graabak, Norway

Men's 10-Kilometer Normal Hill

2010	Jason Lamy Chappuis, France
2014	Eric Frenzel, Germany

Men's Team 4x5-Kilometer Relay

1988	W. Germany, Switzerland, Austria
1992	Japan, Norway, Austria
1994	Japan, Norway, Switzerland

Men's Team 4x5-Kilometer Relay

1998	Norway, Finland, France
2002	Finland, Germany, Austria
2006	Austria, Germany, Finland
2010	Austria, United States, Germany
2014	Norway, Germany, Austria

Skeleton

	Men	Time
1928	Jennison Heaton, United States	3:01.8
1948	Nino Bibbia, Italy	5:23.2
2002	Jim Shea, United States	1:41.96
2006	Duff Gibson, Canada	1:55.88
2010	Jon Montgomery, Canada	3:29.73
2014	Alexander Tretiakov, Russia	3:44.29

	Women	Time
2002	Tristan Gale, United States	1:45.11
2006	Maya Pedersen, Switzerland	1:59.83
2010	Amy Williams, Great Britain	3:35.64
2014	Elizabeth Yarnold, Great Britain	3:52.89

Ski Jumping

	Men's Normal Hill	Points
1964	Veikko Kankkonen, Finland	229.9
1968	Jiri Raska, Czechoslovakia	216.5
1972	Yukio Kasaya, Japan	244.2
1976	Hans-Georg Aschenbach, E. Germany	252.0
1980	Toni Innauer, Austria	266.3
1984	Jens Weissflog, E. Germany	215.2
1988	Matti Nykaenen, Finland	230.5
1992	Ernst Vettori, Austria	222.8
1994	Espen Bredesen, Norway	282.0
1998	Jani Soininen, Finland	234.5
2002	Simon Ammann, Switzerland	269.0
2006	Lars Bystoel, Norway	266.5
2010	Simon Ammann, Switzerland	276.5
2014	Kamil Stoch, Poland	278.0

	Men's Large Hill	Points
1924	Jacob Tullin Thams, Norway	18.960
1928	Alfred Andersen, Norway	19.208
1932	Birger Ruud, Norway	228.1
1936	Birger Ruud, Norway	232.0
1948	Petter Hugsted, Norway	228.1
1952	Arnfinn Bergmann, Norway	226.0
1956	Antti Hyvarinen, Finland	227.0
1960	Helmut Recknagel, E. Germany	227.2
1964	Toralf Engan, Norway	230.7
1968	Vladimir Beloussov, USSR	231.3
1972	Wojciech Fortuna, Poland	219.9
1976	Karl Schnabl, Austria	234.8
1980	Jouko Tormanen, Finland	271.0
1984	Matti Nykaenen, Finland	231.2
1988	Matti Nykaenen, Finland	224.0
1992	Toni Nieminen, Finland	239.5
1994	Jens Weissflog, Germany	274.5
1998	Kazuyoshi Funaki, Japan	272.3
2002	Simon Ammann, Switzerland	281.4
2006	Thomas Morgenstern, Austria	276.9
2010	Simon Ammann, Switzerland	283.6
2014	Kamil Stoch, Poland	278.7

	Men's Team	Points
1988	Finland, Yugoslavia, Norway	634.4
1992	Finland, Austria, Czechoslovakia	644.4
1994	Germany, Japan, Austria	970.1
1998	Japan, Germany, Austria	933.0
2002	Germany, Finland, Slovenia	974.1
2006	Austria, Finland, Norway	984.0
2010	Austria, Germany, Norway	1,107.9
2014	Germany, Austria, Japan	1,041.1

	Women's Normal Hill	Points
2014	Carina Vogt, Germany	247.4

Snowboarding

	Men's Halfpipe	Points
1998	Gian Simmen, Switzerland	85.2
2002	Ross Powers, United States	46.1
2006	Shaun White, United States	46.8
2010	Shaun White, United States	48.4
2014	Iouri Podladtchikov, Switzerland	94.75

Men's Parallel Giant Slalom

1998	Ross Rebagliati, Canada
2002	Philipp Schoch, Switzerland
2006	Philipp Schoch, Switzerland
2010	Jasey Jay Anderson, Canada
2014	Vic Wild, Russia

Note: In 2002, the Giant Slalom became the Parallel Giant Slalom.

Men's Parallel Slalom

2014	Vic Wild, Russia

	Men's Slopestyle	Points
2014	Sage Kotsenburg, United States	93.50

Men's Snowboard Cross

2006	Seth Wescott, United States
2010	Seth Wescott, United States
2014	Pierre Vaultier, France

	Women's Halfpipe	Points
1998	Nicola Thost, Germany	74.6
2002	Kelly Clark, United States	47.9
2006	Hannah Teter, United States	46.4
2010	Torah Bright, Australia	45.0
2014	Kaitlyn Farrington, United States	91.75

Women's Parallel Giant Slalom

1998	Karine Ruby, France
2002	Isabelle Blanc, France
2006	Daniela Meuli, Switzerland
2010	Nicolien Sauerbreij, Netherlands
2014	Patrizia Kummer, Switzerland

Note: In 2002, the Giant Slalom became the Parallel Giant Slalom.

Women's Parallel Slalom

2014	Julia Dujmovits, Austria

	Women's Slopestyle	Points
2014	Jamie Anderson, United States	95.25

Women's Snowboard Cross

2006	Tanja Frieden, Switzerland
2010	Maelle Ricker, Canada
2014	Eva Samkova, Czech Republic

Speed Skating

*Olympic record

	Men's 500 Meters	Time
1924	Charles Jewtraw, United States	0:44.0
1928	C. Thunberg, Finland; B. Evensen, Norway (tie)	0:43.4
1932	John A. Shea, United States	0:43.4
1936	Ivar Ballangrud, Norway	0:43.4
1948	Finn Helgesen, Norway	0:43.1
1952	Kenneth Henry, United States	0:43.2
1956	Evgeniy Grishin, USSR	0:40.2
1960	Evgeniy Grishin, USSR	0:40.2
1964	Terry McDermott, United States	0:40.1
1968	Erhard Keller, W. Germany	0:40.3
1972	Erhard Keller, W. Germany	0:39.44
1976	Evgeny Kulikov, USSR	0:39.17
1980	Eric Heiden, United States	0:38.03
1984	Sergei Fokichev, USSR	0:38.19
1988	Uwe-Jens Mey, E. Germany	0:36.45
1992	Uwe-Jens Mey, Germany	0:37.14
1994	Aleksandr Golubev, Russia	0:36.33
1998	Hiroyasu Shimizu, Japan	0:35.59
2002	Casey FitzRandolph, United States	0:34.42*
2006	Joey Cheek, United States	0:34.82
2010	Mo Tae-Bum, S. Korea	0:34.906
2014	Michel Mulder, Netherlands	0:69.312

Note: In 2014, results include the total of two 500-km race times.

	Men's 1,000 Meters	Time
1976	Peter Mueller, United States	1:19.32
1980	Eric Heiden, United States	1:15.18
1984	Gaetan Boucher, Canada	1:15.80
1988	Nikolai Guliaev, USSR	1:13.03
1992	Olaf Zinke, Germany	1:14.85
1994	Dan Jansen, United States	1:12.43
1998	Ids Postma, Netherlands	1:10.64
2002	Gerard van Velde, Netherlands	1:07.18*
2006	Shani Davis, United States	1:08.89
2010	Shani Davis, United States	1:08.94
2014	Stefan Groothuis, Netherlands	1:08.39

	Men's 1,500 Meters	Time
1924	Clas Thunberg, Finland	2:20.8
1928	Clas Thunberg, Finland	2:21.1
1932	John A. Shea, United States	2:57.5
1936	Charles Mathiesen, Norway	2:19.2
1948	Sverre Farstad, Norway	2:17.6
1952	Hjalmar Andersen, Norway	2:20.4

Men's 1,500 Meters	Time
1956 Y. Grishin, USSR; Y. Mikhailov, USSR (tie) . . .	2:08.6
1960 R. Aas, Norway; Y. Grishin, USSR (tie)	2:10.4
1964 Ants Anston, USSR	2:10.3
1968 Cornetis Verkerk, Netherlands	2:03.4
1972 Ard Schenk, Netherlands	2:02.96
1976 Jan Egil Storholt, Norway	1:59.38
1980 Eric Heiden, United States	1:55.44
1984 Gaetan Boucher, Canada	1:58.36
1988 Andre Hoffmann, E. Germany	1:52.06
1992 Johann Koss, Norway	1:54.81
1994 Johann Koss, Norway	1:51.29
1998 Aadne Sondral, Norway	1:47.87
2002 Derek Parra, United States	1:43.95*
2006 Enrico Fabris, Italy	1:45.97
2010 Mark Tuitert, Netherlands	1:45.57
2014 Zbigniew Brodka, Poland	1:45.006

Men's 5,000 Meters	Time
1924 Clas Thunberg, Finland	8:39.0
1928 Ivar Ballangrud, Norway	8:50.5
1932 Irving Jaffee, United States	9:40.8
1936 Ivar Ballangrud, Norway	8:19.6
1948 Reidar Liaklev, Norway	8:29.4
1952 Hjalmar Andersen, Norway	8:10.6
1956 Boris Shilkov, USSR	7:48.7
1960 Viktor Kosichkin, USSR	7:51.3
1964 Knut Johannesen, Norway	7:38.4
1968 F. Anton Maier, Norway	7:22.4
1972 Ard Schenk, Netherlands	7:23.61
1976 Sten Stensen, Norway	7:24.48
1980 Eric Heiden, United States	7:02.29
1984 Tomas Gustafson, Sweden	7:12.28
1988 Tomas Gustafson, Sweden	6:44.63
1992 Geir Karlstad, Norway.	6:59.97
1994 Johann Koss, Norway.	6:34.96
1998 Gianni Romme, Netherlands	6:22.20
2002 Jochem Uytdehaage, Netherlands	6:14.66
2006 Chad Hedrick, United States	6:14.68
2010 Sven Kramer, Netherlands	6:14.60
2014 Sven Kramer, Netherlands	6:10.76*

Men's 10,000 Meters	Time
1924 Julius Skutnabb, Finland	18:04.8
1928 Event not held because of thawing of ice	
1932 Irving Jaffee, United States	19:13.6
1936 Ivar Ballangrud, Norway	17:24.3
1948 Ake Seyffarth, Sweden	17:26.3
1952 Hjalmar Andersen, Norway	16:45.8
1956 Sigvard Ericsson, Sweden	16:35.9
1960 Knut Johannesen, Norway	15:46.6
1964 Jonny Nilsson, Sweden	15:50.1
1968 Jonny Hoeglin, Sweden	15:23.6
1972 Ard Schenk, Netherlands	15:01.35
1976 Piet Kleine, Netherlands	14:50.59
1980 Eric Heiden, United States	14:28.13
1984 Igor Malkov, USSR.	14:39.90
1988 Tomas Gustafson, Sweden	13:48.20
1992 Bart Veldkamp, Netherlands.	14:12.12
1994 Johann Koss, Norway.	13:30.55
1998 Gianni Romme, Netherlands	13:15.33
2002 Jochem Uytdehaage, Netherlands.	12:58.92
2006 Bob de Jong, Netherlands	13:01.57
2010 Lee Seung-Hoon, S. Korea	12:58.55
2014 Jorrit Bergsma, Netherlands.	12:44.45*

Men's Team Pursuit	Time
2006 Italy, Canada, Netherlands	3:44.46
2010 Canada, United States, Netherlands	3:41.37
2014 Netherlands, South Korea, Poland	3:37.71*

Women's 500 Meters	Time
1960 Helga Haase, Germany	0:45.9
1964 Lydia Skoblikova, USSR.	0:45.0
1968 Ludmila Titova, USSR	0:46.1
1972 Anne Henning, United States	0:43.33
1976 Sheila Young, United States	0:42.76
1980 Karin Enke, E. Germany	0:41.78
1984 Christa Rothenburger, E. Germany	0:41.02
1988 Bonnie Blair, United States.	0:39.10
1992 Bonnie Blair, United States.	0:40.33
1994 Bonnie Blair, United States.	0:39.25
1998 Catriona Le May-Doan, Canada	0:38.21
2002 Catriona Le May Doan, Canada	0:37.30
2006 Svetlana Zhurova, Russia.	0:38.23
2010 Lee Sang-Hwa, S. Korea	0:37.850
2014 Lee Sang-Hwa, S. Korea	0:74.70*
Note: In 2014, results include the total of two 500-km race times.	

Women's 1,000 Meters	Time
1960 Klara Guseva, USSR	1:34.1
1964 Lydia Skoblikova, USSR	1:33.2
1968 Carolina Geijssen, Netherlands	1:32.6
1972 Monika Pflug, W. Germany	1:31.40
1976 Tatiana Averina, USSR	1:28.43
1980 Natalya Petruseva, USSR	1:24.10
1984 Karin Enke, E. Germany.	1:21.61
1988 Christa Rothenburger, E. Germany	1:17.65
1992 Bonnie Blair, United States	1:21.90
1994 Bonnie Blair, United States	1:18.74
1998 Marianne Timmer, Netherlands	1:16.51
2002 Chris Witty, United States	1:13.83*
2006 Marianne Timmer, Netherlands	1:16.05
2010 Christine Nesbitt, Canada	1:16.56
2014 Zhang Hong, China	1:14.02

Women's 1,500 Meters	Time
1960 Lydia Skoblikova, USSR	2:52.2
1964 Lydia Skoblikova, USSR	2:22.6
1968 Kaija Mustonen, Finland.	2:22.4
1972 Dianne Holum, United States	2:20.85
1976 Galina Stepanskaya, USSR	2:16.58
1980 Anne Borckink, Netherlands	2:10.95
1984 Karin Enke, E. Germany.	2:03.42
1988 Yvonne van Gennip, Netherlands	2:00.68
1992 Jacqueline Boerner, Germany	2:05.87
1994 Emese Hunyady, Austria	2:02.19
1998 Marianne Timmer, Netherlands	1:57.58
2002 Anni Friesinger, Germany	1:54.02
2006 Cindy Klassen, Canada	1:55.27
2010 Ireen Wust, Netherlands.	1:56.89
2014 Jorien Ter Mors, Netherlands.	1:53.51*

Women's 3,000 Meters	Time
1960 Lydia Skoblikova, USSR	5:14.3
1964 Lydia Skoblikova, USSR	5:14.9
1968 Johanna Schut, Netherlands	4:56.2
1972 Christina Baas-Kaiser, Netherlands	4:52.14
1976 Tatiana Averina, USSR	4:45.19
1980 Bjoerg Eva Jensen, Norway	4:32.13
1984 Andrea Schoene, E. Germany	4:24.79
1988 Yvonne van Gennip, Netherlands	4:11.94
1992 Gunda Niemann, Germany	4:19.90
1994 Svetlana Bazhanova, Russia	4:17.43
1998 Gunda Niemann-Stirnemann, Germany	4:07.29
2002 Claudia Pechstein, Germany	3:57.70*
2006 Ireen Wust, Netherlands.	4:02.43
2010 Martina Sablikova, Czech Republic	4:02.53
2014 Ireen Wust, Netherlands.	4:00.34

Women's 5,000 Meters	Time
1988 Yvonne van Gennip, Netherlands	7:14.13
1992 Gunda Niemann, Germany	7:31.57
1994 Claudia Pechstein, Germany	7:14.37
1998 Claudia Pechstein, Germany	6:59.61
2002 Claudia Pechstein, Germany	6:46.91*
2006 Clara Hughes, Canada.	6:59.07
2010 Martina Sablikova, Czech Republic	6:50.91
2014 Martina Sablikova, Czech Republic	6:51.54

Women's Team Pursuit	Time
2006 Germany, Canada, Russia.	3:01.25
2010 Germany, Japan, Poland	3:02.82
2014 Netherlands, Poland, Russia	2:58.05*

Speed Skating (Short Track)

*Olympic record

Men's 500 Meters	Time
1998 Takafumi Nishitani, Japan	0:42.862
2002 Marc Gagnon, Canada.	0:41.802
2006 Apolo Anton Ohno, United States	0:41.935
2010 Charles Hamelin, Canada	0:40.981
2014 Victor An, Russia	0:41.312

Men's 1,000 Meters	Time
1992 Kim Ki-Hoon, S. Korea	1:30.76
1994 Kim Ki-Hoon, S. Korea	1:34.57
1998 Kim Dong-Sung, S. Korea	1:32.375
2002 Steven Bradbury, Australia.	1:29.109
2006 Ahn Hyun-Soo, S. Korea	1:26.739
2010 Lee Jung-Su, S. Korea.	1:23.747*
2014 Victor An, Russia	1:25.325

Men's 1,500 Meters	Time
2002 Apolo Anton Ohno, United States	2:18.541
2006 Ahn Hyun-Soo, S. Korea	2:25.341

Men's 1,500 Meters	Time
2010 Lee Jung-Su, S. Korea	2:17.611
2014 Charles Hamelin, Canada	2:14.985

Men's 5,000-Meter Relay	Time
1992 S. Korea, Canada, Japan	7:14.02
1994 Italy, United States, Australia	7:11.74
1998 Canada, S. Korea, China	7:06.075
2002 Canada, Italy, China	6:51.579
2006 S. Korea, Canada, United States	6:43.376*
2010 Canada, S. Korea, United States	6:44.224
2014 Russia, United States, China	6:42.100*

Women's 500 Meters	Time
1992 Cathy Turner, United States	0:47.04
1994 Cathy Turner, United States	0:45.98
1998 Annie Perreault, Canada	0:46.568
2002 Yang Yang (A), China	0:44.187
2006 Wang Meng, China	0:44.345
2010 Wang Meng, China	0:43.048
2014 Li Jianrou, China	0:45.263

Women's 1,000 Meters	Time
1998 Chun Lee-Kyung, S. Korea	1:42.776
2002 Yang Yang (A), China	1:36.391
2006 Jin Sun-Yu, S. Korea	1:32.859
2010 Wang Meng, China	1:29.213
2014 Park Seung-Hi, S. Korea	1:30.761

Women's 1,500 Meters	Time
2002 Ko Gi-Hyun, S. Korea	2:31.581
2006 Jin Sun-Yu, S. Korea	2:23.494
2010 Zhou Yang, China	2:16.993*
2014 Zhou Yang, China	2:19.140

Women's 3,000-Meter Relay	Time
1992 Canada, United States, Unified Team	4:36.62
1994 S. Korea, Canada, United States	4:26.64
1998 S. Korea, China, Canada	4:16.26
2002 S. Korea, China, Canada	4:12.793
2006 S. Korea, Canada, Italy	4:17.040
2010 China, Canada, United States	4:06.610*
2014 S. Korea, Canada, Italy	4:09.498

2012 Summer Olympic Games

London, England, UK, July 27-Aug. 12, 2012

London welcomed more than 11,000 athletes from 204 nations and territories at the Summer Olympic Games, July 27-Aug. 12, 2012. The XXX Summer Olympiad marked the first time in history that each nation or territory's delegation included women athletes. The U.S. was ahead of all countries with 46 gold medals and 104 overall. Michael Phelps topped all athletes at the Summer Games with six medals and became the all-time most decorated Olympian with 22 career medals. Fellow U.S. swimmers Missy Franklin, Ryan Lochte, and Allison Schmitt each collected five medals. For the first time since 1996, the U.S. women won the gymnastics team all-around gold, and American gymnasts Gabby Douglas and Aly Raisman captured individual gold medals.

London hosted the Olympic Games for the third time and Britain's athletes recorded the country's best performance in over a century, winning 65 medals. Among the British gold medalists were track-and-field stars Mo Farah (men's 5,000-m and 10,000-m) and Jessica Ennis (heptathlon), while Andy Murray earned tennis gold when he defeated Switzerland's Roger Federer in the final in straight sets. Jamaica's Usain Bolt won gold in both the men's 100-m and 200-m sprints, as he did in Beijing, and was part of the team that won the 4x100-m relay in world-record time (36.84 sec.). South African sprinter Oscar Pistorius became the first double-amputee to compete in the Olympics, reaching the semifinals in the men's 400-m race and running in the 4x400-m relay.

2012 Summer Olympic Games: Final Medal Standings

Country	G	S	B	T	Country	G	S	B	T	Country	G	S	B	T
United States	46	29	29	104	Colombia	1	3	4	8	Estonia	0	1	1	2
China	38	27	23	88	Ethiopia	3	1	3	7	Indonesia	0	1	1	2
Russia	24	26	32	82	Georgia	1	3	3	7	Malaysia	0	1	1	2
Great Britain	29	17	19	65	Mexico	1	3	3	7	Puerto Rico	0	1	1	2
Germany	11	19	14	44	North Korea	4	0	2	6	Taiwan	0	1	1	2
Japan	7	14	17	38	South Africa	3	2	1	6	Greece	0	0	2	2
Australia	7	16	12	35	Croatia	3	1	2	6	Moldova	0	0	2	2
France	11	11	12	34	India	0	2	4	6	Qatar	0	0	2	2
South Korea	13	8	7	28	Turkey	2	2	1	5	Singapore	0	0	2	2
Italy	8	9	11	28	Lithuania	2	1	2	5	Algeria	1	0	0	1
Netherlands	6	6	8	20	Ireland	1	1	3	5	The Bahamas	1	0	0	1
Ukraine	6	5	9	20	Mongolia	0	2	3	5	Grenada	1	0	0	1
Canada	1	5	12	18	Switzerland	2	2	0	4	Uganda	1	0	0	1
Hungary	8	4	5	17	Norway	2	1	1	4	Venezuela	1	0	0	1
Spain	3	10	4	17	Argentina	1	1	2	4	Botswana	0	1	0	1
Brazil	3	5	9	17	Serbia	1	1	2	4	Cyprus	0	1	0	1
Cuba	5	3	6	14	Slovenia	1	1	2	4	Gabon	0	1	0	1
Kazakhstan	7	1	5	13	Trinidad and Tobago	1	0	3	4	Guatemala	0	1	0	1
New Zealand	6	2	5	13	Uzbekistan	1	0	3	4	Montenegro	0	1	0	1
Iran	4	5	3	12	Slovakia	0	1	3	4	Portugal	0	1	0	1
Jamaica	4	4	4	12	Tunisia	1	1	1	3	Afghanistan	0	0	1	1
Belarus	2	5	5	12	Thailand	0	2	1	3	Bahrain	0	0	1	1
Kenya	2	4	5	11	Armenia	0	1	2	3	Hong Kong	0	0	1	1
Czech Republic	4	3	3	10	Belgium	0	1	2	3	Kuwait	0	0	1	1
Azerbaijan	2	2	6	10	Finland	0	1	2	3	Morocco	0	0	1	1
Poland	2	2	6	10	Dominican Republic	1	1	0	2	Saudi Arabia	0	0	1	1
Romania	2	5	2	9	Latvia	1	0	1	2	Tajikistan	0	0	1	1
Denmark	2	4	3	9	Egypt	0	2	0	2	Total	302	304	356	962
Sweden	1	4	3	8	Bulgaria	0	1	1	2					

Summer Olympic Games Champions, 1896-2012

* = Olympic record; (w) wind-aided; times are shown in hour:minute:sec.

The 1980 games were boycotted by 62 nations, including the U.S. The 1984 games were boycotted by the USSR and most Eastern bloc nations. East and West Germany competed separately, 1968-88. The 1992 Unified Team consisted of 12 former Soviet republics. The 1992 Independent Olympic Participants (IOP) were from Serbia, Montenegro, and Macedonia.

Not all sports are listed here, and many events are omitted, even within listed sports, particularly if the event has not been held in more recent Games. Point systems for scoring events have changed many times. Points shown are those under the point system in use at the time.

Boxing—Men

Weight class limits have changed many times since the first Olympic boxing events were held in 1904. The limits shown were used in the 2012 Olympic Games. The Super Heavyweight class was known as Heavyweight 1904-80.

Lt. Flyweight (49 kg/108 lbs)

1968	Francisco Rodriguez, Venezuela
1972	Gyorgy Gedo, Hungary
1976	Jorge Hernandez, Cuba
1980	Shamil Sabyrov, USSR
1984	Paul Gonzalez, United States
1988	Ivailo Hristov, Bulgaria
1992	Rogelio Marcelo, Cuba
1996	Daniel Petrov, Bulgaria
2000	Brahim Asloum, France
2004	Yan Bhartelemy Varela, Cuba
2008	Zou Shiming, China
2012	Zou Shiming, China

Flyweight (52 kg/114 lbs)

1904	George Finnegan, United States
1920	Frank Di Gennara, United States
1924	Fidel LaBarba, United States
1928	Antal Kocsis, Hungary
1932	Istvan Enekes, Hungary
1936	Willi Kaiser, Germany
1948	Pascual Perez, Argentina
1952	Nathan Brooks, United States
1956	Terence Spinks, Great Britain
1960	Gyula Török, Hungary
1964	Fernando Atzori, Italy
1968	Ricardo Delgado, Mexico
1972	Georgi Kostadinov, Bulgaria
1976	Leo Randolph, United States
1980	Peter Lesov, Bulgaria
1984	Steve McCrory, United States
1988	Kim Kwang Sun, S. Korea
1992	Choi Chol-Su, N. Korea
1996	Maikro Romero, Cuba
2000	Wijan Ponlid, Thailand
2004	Yuriorkis Gamboa Toledano, Cuba
2008	Somjit Jongjohor, Thailand
2012	Robeisy Ramírez, Cuba

Bantamweight (56 kg/123 lbs)

1904	Oliver Kirk, United States
1908	A. Henry Thomas, Great Britain
1920	Clarence Walker, South Africa
1924	William Smith, South Africa
1928	Vittorio Tamagnini, Italy
1932	Horace Gwynne, Canada
1936	Ulderico Sergo, Italy
1948	Tibor Csik, Hungary
1952	Pentti Hamalainen, Finland
1956	Wolfgang Behrendt, E. Germany
1960	Oleg Grigoryev, USSR
1964	Takao Sakurai, Japan
1968	Valery Sokolov, USSR
1972	Orlando Martinez, Cuba
1976	Yong-Jo Gu, N. Korea
1980	Juan Hernandez, Cuba
1984	Maurizio Stecca, Italy
1988	Kennedy McKinney, United States
1992	Joel Casamayor, Cuba
1996	Istvan Kovacs, Hungary
2000	Guillermo Rigondeaux, Cuba
2004	Guillermo Rigondeaux, Cuba
2008	Badar-Uugan Enkhbat, Mongolia
2012	Luke Campbell, Great Britain

Featherweight (57 kg/125 lbs)

1904	Oliver Kirk, United States
1908	Richard Gunn, Great Britain
1920	Paul Fritsch, France
1924	John Fields, United States
1928	Lambertus van Klaveren, Netherlands
1932	Carmelo Robledo, Argentina
1936	Oscar Casanovas, Argentina
1948	Ernesto Formenti, Italy
1952	Jan Zachara, Czechoslovakia
1956	Vladimir Safronov, USSR
1960	Francesco Musso, Italy
1964	Stanislav Stephashkin, USSR
1968	Antonio Roldan, Mexico
1972	Boris Kousnetsov, USSR
1976	Angel Herrera, Cuba
1980	Rudi Fink, E. Germany
1984	Meldrick Taylor, United States
1988	Giovanni Parisi, Italy
1992	Andreas Tews, Germany
1996	Somluck Kamsing, Thailand

Featherweight (57 kg/125 lbs)

2000	Bekzat Sattarkhanov, Kazakhstan
2004	Alexei Tichtchenko, Russia
2008	Vasyl Lomachenko, Ukraine

Lightweight (60 kg/132 lbs)

1904	Harry Spanger, United States
1908	Frederick Grace, Great Britain
1920	Samuel Mosberg, United States
1924	Hans Nielsen, Denmark
1928	Carlo Orlandi, Italy
1932	Lawrence Stevens, South Africa
1936	Imre Harangi, Hungary
1948	Gerald Dreyer, South Africa
1952	Aureliano Bolognesi, Italy
1956	Richard McTaggart, Great Britain
1960	Kazimierz Pazdzior, Poland
1964	Jozef Grudzien, Poland
1968	Ronald Harris, United States
1972	Jan Szczepanski, Poland
1976	Howard Davis, United States
1980	Angel Herrera, Cuba
1984	Pernell Whitaker, United States
1988	Andreas Zülow, E. Germany
1992	Oscar De La Hoya, United States
1996	Hocine Soltani, Algeria
2000	Mario Kindelan, Cuba
2004	Mario Kindelan, Cuba
2008	Alexey Tishchenko, Russia
2012	Vasyl Lomachenko, Ukraine

Lt. Welterweight (64 kg/141 lbs)

1952	Charles Adkins, United States
1956	Vladimir Yengibaryan, USSR
1960	Bohumil Nemecek, Czechoslovakia
1964	Jerzy Kulej, Poland
1968	Jerzy Kulej, Poland
1972	Ray Seales, United States
1976	Ray Leonard, United States
1980	Patrizio Oliva, Italy
1984	Jerry Page, United States
1988	Viatcheslav Janovski, USSR
1992	Hector Vinent, Cuba
1996	Hector Vinent, Cuba
2000	Mahamadkadyz Abdullaev, Uzbekistan
2004	Manus Boonjumnong, Thailand
2008	Felix Diaz, Dominican Republic
2012	Rosniel Iglesias, Cuba

Welterweight (69 kg/152 lbs)

1904	Albert Young, United States
1920	Albert Schneider, Canada
1924	Jean Delarge, Belgium
1928	Edward Morgan, New Zealand
1932	Edward Flynn, United States
1936	Sten Suvio, Finland
1948	Julius Torma, Czechoslovakia
1952	Zygmunt Chychia, Poland
1956	Nicolae Linca, Romania
1960	Giovanni Benvenuti, Italy
1964	Marian Kasprzyk, Poland
1968	Manfred Wolke, E. Germany
1972	Emilio Correa, Cuba
1976	Jochen Bachfeld, E. Germany
1980	Andres Aldama, Cuba
1984	Mark Breland, United States
1988	Robert Wangila, Kenya
1992	Michael Carruth, Ireland
1996	Oleg Saitov, Russia
2000	Oleg Saitov, Russia
2004	Artayev Bakhtiyar, Kazakhstan
2008	Bakhyt Sarsekbayev, Kazakhstan
2012	Serik Sapiyev, Kazakhstan

Lt. Middleweight (71 kg/156 lbs)

1952	Laszlo Papp, Hungary
1956	Laszlo Papp, Hungary
1960	Wilbert McClure, United States
1964	Boris Lagutin, USSR
1968	Boris Lagutin, USSR
1972	Dieter Kottysch, W. Germany
1976	Jerzy Rybicki, Poland
1980	Armando Martinez, Cuba
1984	Frank Tate, United States
1988	Park Si Hun, S. Korea
1992	Juan Lemus, Cuba
1996	David Reid, United States
2000	Yermakhan Ibraimov, Kazakhstan

Middleweight (75 kg/165 lbs)

1904	Charles Mayer, United States
1908	John Douglas, Great Britain
1920	Harry Mallin, Great Britain
1924	Harry Mallin, Great Britain
1928	Piero Toscani, Italy
1932	Carmen Barth, United States
1936	Jean Despeaux, France
1948	Laszlo Papp, Hungary
1952	Floyd Patterson, United States
1956	Gennady Schatkov, USSR
1960	Edward Crook, United States
1964	Valery Popenchenko, USSR
1968	Christopher Finnegan, Great Britain
1972	Vyacheslav Lemechev, USSR
1976	Michael Spinks, United States
1980	Jose Gomez, Cuba
1984	Joon-Sup Shin, S. Korea
1988	Henry Maske, E. Germany
1992	Ariel Hernandez, Cuba
1996	Ariel Hernandez, Cuba
2000	Jorge Gutierrez, Cuba
2004	Gaydarbek Gaydarbekov, Russia
2008	James Degale, Great Britain
2012	Ryota Murata, Japan

Lt. Heavyweight (81 kg/178 lbs)

1920	Edward Eagan, United States
1924	Harry Mitchell, Great Britain
1928	Victor Avendaño, Argentina
1932	David Carstens, South Africa
1936	Roger Michelot, France
1948	George Hunter, South Africa
1952	Norvel Lee, United States
1956	James Boyd, United States
1960	Cassius Clay, United States
1964	Cosimo Pinto, Italy
1968	Dan Poznyak, USSR
1972	Mate Parlov, Yugoslavia
1976	Leon Spinks, United States
1980	Slobodan Kacar, Yugoslavia
1984	Anton Josipovic, Yugoslavia
1988	Andrew Maynard, United States
1992	Torsten May, Germany
1996	Vassili Jirov, Kazakhstan
2000	Alexander Lebziak, Russia
2004	Andre Ward, United States
2008	Zhang Xiaoping, China
2012	Yegor Mekhontsev, Russia

Heavyweight (91 kg/201 lbs)

1984	Henry Tillman, United States
1988	Ray Mercer, United States
1992	Felix Savon, Cuba
1996	Felix Savon, Cuba
2000	Felix Savon, Cuba
2004	Odlanier Solis Fonte, Cuba
2008	Rakhim Chakhkiev, Russia
2012	Oleksandr Usik, Ukraine

Super Heavyweight (91+ kg/201+ lbs)

1904	Samuel Berger, United States
1908	Albert Oldham, Great Britain
1920	Ronald Rawson, Great Britain
1924	Otto von Porat, Norway
1928	Arturo Rodriguez Jurado, Argentina
1932	Santiago Lovell, Argentina
1936	Herbert Runge, Germany
1948	Rafael Iglesias, Argentina
1952	H. Edward Sanders, United States
1956	T. Peter Rademacher, United States
1960	Franco De Piccoli, Italy
1964	Joe Frazier, United States
1968	George Foreman, United States
1972	Teofilo Stevenson, Cuba
1976	Teofilo Stevenson, Cuba
1980	Teofilo Stevenson, Cuba
1984	Tyrell Biggs, United States
1988	Lennox Lewis, Canada
1992	Roberto Balado, Cuba
1996	Vladimir Klitchko, Ukraine
2000	Audley Harrison, Great Britain
2004	Alexander Povetkin, Russia
2008	Roberto Cammarelle, Italy
2012	Anthony Joshua, Great Britain

Boxing—Women

Flyweight (51 kg/112 lbs)	Lightweight (60 kg/132 lbs)	Middleweight (75 kg/165 lbs)
2012 Nicola Adams, Great Britain	2012 Katie Taylor, Ireland	2012 Claressa Shields, United States

Gymnastics—Men

Floor Exercise
1932	István Pelle, Hungary
1936	Georges Miez, Switzerland
1948	Ferenc Pataki, Hungary
1952	William Thoresson, Sweden
1956	Valentin Muratov, USSR
1960	Nobuyuki Aihara, Japan
1964	Franco Menichelli, Italy
1968	Sawao Kato, Japan
1972	Nikolay Andrianov, USSR
1976	Nikolay Andrianov, USSR
1980	Roland Brückner, E. Germany
1984	Li Ning, China
1988	Serguei Kharikov, USSR
1992	Li Xiaoshuang, China
1996	Ioannis Melissanidis, Greece
2000	Igors Vihrovs, Latvia
2004	Kyle Shewfelt, Canada
2008	Zou Kai, China
2012	Zou Kai, China

Horizontal Bar
1896	Hermann Weingärtner, Germany
1904	Anton Heida, United States; Edward Hennig, United States (tie)
1924	Leon Stukelj, Yugoslavia
1928	Georges Miez, Switzerland
1932	Dallas Denver Bixler, United States
1936	Aleksanteri Saarvala, Finland
1948	Josef Stadler, Switzerland
1952	Jakob "Jack" Günthard, Switzerland
1956	Takashi Ono, Japan
1960	Takashi Ono, Japan
1964	Boris Shakhlin, USSR
1968	Mikhail Voronin, USSR; Akinori Nakayama, Japan (tie)
1972	Mitsuo Tsukahara, Japan
1976	Mitsuo Tsukahara, Japan
1980	Stoyan Deltchev, Bulgaria
1984	Shinji Morisue, Japan
1988	Valeri Lioukine, USSR; Vladimir Artemov, USSR (tie)
1992	Trent Dimas, United States
1996	Andreas Wecker, Germany
2000	Alexei Nemov, Russia
2004	Igor Cassina, Italy
2008	Zou Kai, China
2012	Epke Zonderland, Netherlands

Individual All-Around
1900	Gustave Sandras, France
1904	Julius Lenhart, United States
1908	G. Alberto Braglia, Italy
1912	G. Alberto Braglia, Italy
1920	Giorgio Zampori, Italy
1924	Leon Stukelj, Yugoslavia
1928	Georges Miez, Switzerland
1932	Romeo Neri, Italy
1936	Karl-Alfred Schwarzmann, Germany
1948	Veikko Huhtanen, Finland
1952	Viktor Ivanovich Chukarin, USSR
1956	Viktor Ivanovich Chukarin, USSR
1960	Boris Shakhlin, USSR
1964	Yukio Endo, Japan
1968	Sawao Kato, Japan
1972	Sawao Kato, Japan
1976	Nikolay Andrianov, USSR
1980	Aleksandr Dityatin, USSR
1984	Koji Gushiken, Japan
1988	Vladimir Artemov, USSR
1992	Vitaly Scherbo, Unified Team (Belarus)
1996	Li Xiaoshuang, China
2000	Alexei Nemov, Russia
2004	Paul Hamm, United States
2008	Yang Wei, China
2012	Kohei Uchimura, Japan

Parallel Bars
1896	Alfred Flatow, Germany
1904	George Eyser, United States
1924	August Güttinger, Switzerland
1928	Ladislav Vacha, Czechoslovakia
1932	Romeo Neri, Italy
1936	Konrad Frey, Germany
1948	Michael Reusch, Switzerland
1952	Hans Eugster, Switzerland
1956	Viktor Ivanovich Chukarin, USSR
1960	Boris Shakhlin, USSR
1964	Yukio Endo, Japan
1968	Akinori Nakayama, Japan
1972	Sawao Kato, Japan
1976	Sawao Kato, Japan
1980	Aleksandr Tkachev, USSR
1984	Bart Conner, United States
1988	Vladimir Artemov, USSR
1992	Vitaly Scherbo, Unified Team (Belarus)
1996	Roustam Sharipov, Ukraine
2000	Li Xiaopeng, China
2004	Valeri Goncharov, Ukraine
2008	Li Xiaopeng, China
2012	Feng Zhe, China

Pommel Horse
1896	Louis Zutter, Switzerland
1904	Anton Heida, United States
1924	Josef Wilhelm, Switzerland
1928	Hermann Hänggi, Switzerland
1932	István Pelle, Hungary
1936	Konrad Frey, Germany
1948	Heikki Savolainen, Finland; Paavo Johannes Aaltonen, Finland; Veikko Huhtanen, Finland (tie)
1952	Viktor Ivanovich Chukarin, USSR
1956	Boris Shakhlin, USSR
1960	Eugen Georg Oskar Ekman, Finland; Boris Shakhlin, USSR (tie)
1964	Miroslav Cerar, Yugoslavia
1968	Miroslav Cerar, Yugoslavia
1972	Viktor Klimenko, USSR
1976	Zoltan Magyar, Hungary
1980	Zoltan Magyar, Hungary
1984	Li Ning, China; Peter Glen Vidmar, United States (tie)
1988	Zsolt Borkai, Hungary; Dmitri Bilozerchev, USSR; Lubomir Geraskov, Bulgaria (tie)
1992	Pae Gil-Su, N. Korea; Vitaly Scherbo, Unified Team (Belarus) (tie)
1996	Li Donghua, Switzerland
2000	Marius Daniel Urzica, Romania
2004	Teng Haibin, China
2008	Xiao Qin, China
2012	Krisztián Berki, Hungary

Rings
1896	Ioannis Mitropoulos, Greece
1904	Hermann Glass, United States
1924	Francesco Martino, Italy
1928	Leon Stukelj, Yugoslavia
1932	George Julius Gulack, United States
1936	Alois Hudec, Czechoslovakia
1948	Karl Frei, Switzerland
1952	Grant Shaginyan, USSR
1956	Albert Azaryan, USSR
1960	Albert Azaryan, USSR
1964	Takuji Hayata, Japan
1968	Akinori Nakayama, Japan
1972	Akinori Nakayama, Japan
1976	Nikolay Andrianov, USSR
1980	Aleksandr Dityatin, USSR

Rings
1984	Li Ning, China; Koji Gushiken, Japan (tie)
1988	Holger Behrendt, E. Germany; Dmitri Bilozerchev, USSR (tie)
1992	Vitaly Scherbo, Unified Team (Belarus)
1996	Juri Chechi, Italy
2000	Szilveszter Csollany, Hungary
2004	Dimosthenis Tampakos, Greece
2008	Chen Yibing, China
2012	Arthur Zanetti, Brazil

Team Competition
1904	United States, United States, United States
1908	Sweden, Norway, Finland
1912	Italy, Hungary, Great Britain
1920	Italy, Belgium, France
1924	Italy, France, Switzerland
1928	Switzerland, Czechoslovakia, Yugoslavia
1932	Italy, United States, Finland
1936	Germany, Switzerland, Finland
1948	Finland, Switzerland, Hungary
1952	USSR, Switzerland, Finland
1956	USSR, Japan, Finland
1960	Japan, USSR, Italy
1964	Japan, USSR, Unified Team of Germany
1968	Japan, USSR, E. Germany
1972	Japan, USSR, E. Germany
1976	Japan, USSR, E. Germany
1980	USSR, E. Germany, Hungary
1984	United States, China, Japan
1988	USSR, E. Germany, Japan
1992	Unified Team, China, Japan
1996	Russia, China, Ukraine
2000	China, Ukraine, Russia
2004	Japan, United States, Romania
2008	China, Japan, United States
2012	China, Japan, Great Britain

Vault
1896	Carl Schumann, Germany
1904	George Eyser, United States; Anton Heida, United States (tie)
1924	Frank Kriz, United States
1928	Eugen Mack, Switzerland
1932	Savino Guglielmetti, Italy
1936	Karl-Alfred Schwarzmann, Germany
1948	Paavo Johannes Aaltonen, Finland
1952	Viktor Ivanovich Chukarin, USSR
1956	Helmut Bantz, Unified Team of Germany; Valentin Muratov, USSR (tie)
1960	Takashi Ono, Japan; Boris Shakhlin, USSR (tie)
1964	Haruhiro Yamashita, Japan
1968	Mikhail Voronin, USSR
1972	Klaus Köste, E. Germany
1976	Nikolay Andrianov, USSR
1980	Nikolay Andrianov, USSR
1984	Lou Yun, China
1988	Lou Yun, China
1992	Vitaly Scherbo, Unified Team (Belarus)
1996	Alexei Nemov, Russia
2000	Gervasio Deferr, Spain
2004	Gervasio Deferr, Spain
2008	Leszek Blanik, Poland
2012	Yang Hak-Seon, South Korea

Gymnastics—Women

Balance Beam
1952	Nina Bocharova, USSR
1956	Agnes Keleti, Hungary
1960	Eva Vechtova-Bosakova, Czechoslovakia
1964	Vera Caslavska, Czechoslovakia
1968	Natalya Kuchinskaya, USSR
1972	Olga Korbut, USSR
1976	Nadia Comaneci, Romania
1980	Nadia Comaneci, Romania
1984	Ecaterina Szabo, Romania; Simona Pauca, Romania (tie)
1988	Daniela Silivas, Romania
1992	Tatiana Lyssenko, Unified Team (Ukraine)
1996	Shannon Miller, United States
2000	Liu Xuan, China
2004	Catalina Ponor, Romania
2008	Shawn Johnson, United States
2012	Deng Linlin, China

Floor Exercise
1952	Agnes Keleti, Hungary
1956	Agnes Keleti, Hungary; Larisa Latynina, USSR (tie)
1960	Larisa Latynina, USSR
1964	Larisa Latynina, USSR
1968	Vera Caslavska, Czechoslovakia; Larisa Petrik, USSR (tie)
1972	Olga Korbut, USSR
1976	Nelli Kim, USSR
1980	Nelli Kim, USSR; Nadia Comaneci, Romania (tie)
1984	Ecaterina Szabo, Romania
1988	Daniela Silivas, Romania
1992	Lavinia Corina Milosovici, Romania
1996	Lilia Podkopayeva, Ukraine
2000	Elena Zamolodchikova, Russia
2004	Catalina Ponor, Romania
2008	Sandra Izbasa, Romania

Floor Exercise
2012	Aly Raisman, United States

Individual All-Around
1952	Mariya Gorokhovskaya, USSR
1956	Larisa Latynina, USSR
1960	Larisa Latynina, USSR
1964	Vera Caslavska, Czechoslovakia
1968	Vera Caslavska, Czechoslovakia
1972	Lyudmila Turischeva, USSR
1976	Nadia Comaneci, Romania
1980	Elena Davydova, USSR
1984	Mary-Lou Retton, United States
1988	Elena Shushunova, USSR
1992	Tatiana Goutsou, Unified Team (Ukraine)
1996	Lilia Podkopayeva, Ukraine
2000	Simona Amanar, Romania
2004	Carly Patterson, United States
2008	Nastia Liukin, United States
2012	Gabby Douglas, United States

Team Competition
1928	Netherlands, Italy, Great Britain
1936	Germany, Czechoslovakia, Hungary
1948	Czechoslovakia, Hungary, United States
1952	USSR, Hungary, Czechoslovakia
1956	USSR, Hungary, Romania
1960	USSR, Czechoslovakia, Romania
1964	USSR, Czechoslovakia, Japan
1968	USSR, Czechoslovakia, E. Germany
1972	USSR, E. Germany, Hungary
1976	USSR, Romania, E. Germany
1980	USSR, Romania, E. Germany
1984	Romania, United States, China
1988	USSR, Romania, E. Germany
1992	Unified Team, Romania, United States
1996	United States, Russia, Romania
2000	Romania, Russia, United States

Team Competition
2004	Romania, United States, Russia
2008	China, United States, Romania
2012	United States, Russia, Romania

Uneven Bars
1952	Margit Korondi, Hungary
1956	Agnes Keleti, Hungary
1960	Polina Astakhova, USSR
1964	Polina Astakhova, USSR
1968	Vera Caslavska, Czechoslovakia
1972	Karin Janz, E. Germany
1976	Nadia Comaneci, Romania
1980	Maxi Gnauck, E. Germany
1984	Julianne McNamara, United States; Yan-Hong Ma, China (tie)
1988	Daniela Silivas, Romania
1992	Lu Li, China
1996	Svetlana Khorkina, Russia
2000	Svetlana Khorkina, Russia
2004	Emilie LePennec, France
2008	He Kexin, China
2012	Aliya Mustafina, Russia

Vault
1952	Ekaterina Kalinchuk, USSR
1956	Larisa Latynina, USSR
1960	Margarita Nikolaeva, USSR
1964	Vera Caslavska, Czechoslovakia
1968	Vera Caslavska, Czechoslovakia
1972	Karin Janz, E. Germany
1976	Nelli Kim, USSR
1980	Natalia Shaposhnikova, USSR
1984	Ecaterina Szabo, Romania
1988	Svetlana Boginskaya, USSR
1992	Henrietta Onodi, Hungary; Lavinia Milosovici, Romania (tie)
1996	Simona Amanar, Romania
2000	Elena Zamolodchikova, Russia
2004	Monica Rosu, Romania
2008	Hong Un Jong, N. Korea
2012	Sandra Izbaşa, Romania

Soccer

Men
1900	Great Britain, France, Belgium
1904	Canada, United States, United States
1908	Great Britain, Denmark, Netherlands
1912	Great Britain, Denmark, Netherlands
1920	Belgium, Spain, Netherlands
1924	Uruguay, Switzerland, Sweden
1928	Uruguay, Argentina, Italy
1936	Italy, Austria, Norway
1948	Sweden, Yugoslavia, Denmark
1952	Hungary, Yugoslavia, Sweden
1956	USSR, Yugoslavia, Bulgaria

Men
1960	Yugoslavia, Denmark, Hungary
1964	Hungary, Czechoslovakia, Unified Team of Germany
1968	Hungary, Bulgaria, Japan
1972	Poland; Hungary; USSR, E. Germany (tie for bronze)
1976	E. Germany, Poland, USSR
1980	Czechoslovakia, E. Germany, USSR
1984	France, Brazil, Yugoslavia
1988	USSR, Brazil, W. Germany
1992	Spain, Poland, Ghana

Men
1996	Nigeria, Argentina, Brazil
2000	Cameroon, Spain, Chile
2004	Argentina, Paraguay, Italy
2008	Argentina, Nigeria, Brazil
2012	Mexico, Brazil, South Korea

Women
1996	United States, China, Norway
2000	Norway, United States, Germany
2004	United States, Brazil, Germany
2008	United States, Brazil, Germany
2012	United States, Japan, Canada

Swimming and Diving—Men

50-Meter Freestyle		Time
1988	Matt Biondi, United States	0:22.14
1992	Aleksandr Popov, Unified Team	0:21.91
1996	Aleksandr Popov, Russia	0:22.13
2000	Anthony Ervin, United States	0:21.98
	Gary Hall Jr., United States (tie)	0:21.98
2004	Gary Hall Jr., United States	0:21.93
2008	Cesar Cielo Filho, Brazil	0:21.30*
2012	Florent Manaudou, France	0:21.34

100-Meter Freestyle		Time
1896	Alfred Hajos, Hungary	1:22.2
1904	Zoltan de Halmay, Hungary (100 yds)	1:02.8
1908	Charles Daniels, United States	1:05.6
1912	Duke P. Kahanamoku, United States	1:03.4
1920	Duke P. Kahanamoku, United States	1:01.4
1924	Johnny Weissmuller, United States	0:59.0
1928	Johnny Weissmuller, United States	0:58.6
1932	Yasuji Miyazaki, Japan	0:58.2
1936	Ferenc Csik, Hungary	0:57.6
1948	Wally Ris, United States	0:57.3
1952	Clark Scholes, United States	0:57.4
1956	Jon Henricks, Australia	0:55.4
1960	John Devitt, Australia	0:55.2
1964	Don Schollander, United States	0:53.4
1968	Mike Wenden, Australia	0:52.2
1972	Mark Spitz, United States	0:51.22
1976	Jim Montgomery, United States	0:49.99

100-Meter Freestyle		Time
1980	Jorg Woithe, E. Germany	0:50.40
1984	Ambrose "Rowdy" Gaines, United States	0:49.80
1988	Matt Biondi, United States	0:48.63
1992	Aleksandr Popov, Unified Team	0:49.02
1996	Aleksandr Popov, Russia	0:48.74
2000	Pieter van den Hoogenband, Netherlands	0:48.30
2004	Pieter van den Hoogenband, Netherlands	0:48.17
2008	Alain Bernard, France	0:47.21
2012	Nathan Adrian, United States	0:47.52

200-Meter Freestyle		Time
1968	Mike Wenden, Australia	1:55.2
1972	Mark Spitz, United States	1:52.78
1976	Bruce Furniss, United States	1:50.29
1980	Sergei Kopliakov, USSR	1:49.81
1984	Michael Gross, W. Germany	1:47.44
1988	Duncan Armstrong, Australia	1:47.25
1992	Yevgeny Sadovyi, Unified Team	1:46.70
1996	Danyon Loader, New Zealand	1:47.63
2000	Pieter van den Hoogenband, Netherlands	1:45.35
2004	Ian Thorpe, Australia	1:44.71
2008	Michael Phelps, United States	1:42.96*
2012	Yannick Agnel, France	1:43.14

400-Meter Freestyle		Time
1904	C. M. Daniels, United States (440 yds)	6:16.2
1908	Henry Taylor, Great Britain	5:36.8

400-Meter Freestyle	Time
1912 George Hodgson, Canada	5:24.4
1920 Norman Ross, United States	5:26.8
1924 Johnny Weissmuller, United States	5:04.2
1928 Albert Zorilla, Argentina	5:01.6
1932 Clarence Crabbe, United States	4:48.4
1936 Jack Medica, United States	4:44.5
1948 William Smith, United States	4:41.0
1952 Jean Boiteux, France	4:30.7
1956 Murray Rose, Australia	4:27.3
1960 Murray Rose, Australia	4:18.3
1964 Don Schollander, United States	4:12.2
1968 Mike Burton, United States	4:09.0
1972 Brad Cooper, Australia	4:00.27
1976 Brian Goodell, United States	3:51.93
1980 Vladimir Salnikov, USSR	3:51.31
1984 George DiCarlo, United States	3:51.23
1988 Ewe Dassler, E. Germany	3:46.95
1992 Yevgeny Sadovyi, Unified Team	3:45.00
1996 Danyon Loader, New Zealand	3:47.97
2000 Ian Thorpe, Australia	3:40.59
2004 Ian Thorpe, Australia	3:43.10
2008 Park Taehwan, S. Korea	3:41.86
2012 Sun Yang, China	3:40.14*

1,500-Meter Freestyle	Time
1908 Henry Taylor, Great Britain	22:48.4
1912 George Hodgson, Canada	22:00.0
1920 Norman Ross, United States	22:23.2
1924 Johnny Charlton, Australia	20:06.6
1928 Arne Borg, Sweden	19:51.8
1932 Kusuo Kitamura, Japan	19:12.4
1936 Noboru Terada, Japan	19:13.7
1948 James McLane, United States	19:18.5
1952 Ford Konno, United States	18:30.3
1956 Murray Rose, Australia	17:58.9
1960 Jon Konrads, Australia	17:19.6
1964 Robert Windle, Australia	17:01.7
1968 Mike Burton, United States	16:38.9
1972 Mike Burton, United States	15:52.58
1976 Brian Goodell, United States	15:02.40
1980 Vladimir Salnikov, USSR	14:58.27
1984 Michael O'Brien, United States	15:05.20
1988 Vladimir Salnikov, USSR	15:00.40
1992 Kieren Perkins, Australia	14:43.48
1996 Kieren Perkins, Australia	14:56.40
2000 Grant Hackett, Australia	14:48.33
2004 Grant Hackett, Australia	14:43.40
2008 Oussama Mellouli, Tunisia	14:40.84
2012 Sun Yang, China	14:31.02*

100-Meter Backstroke	Time
1904 Walter Brack, Germany (100 yds)	1:16.8
1908 Arno Bieberstein, Germany	1:24.6
1912 Harry Hebner, United States	1:21.2
1920 Warren Kealoha, United States	1:15.2
1924 Warren Kealoha, United States	1:13.2
1928 George Kojac, United States	1:08.2
1932 Masaji Kiyokawa, Japan	1:08.6
1936 Adolph Kiefer, United States	1:05.9
1948 Allen Stack, United States	1:06.4
1952 Yoshi Oyakawa, United States	1:05.4
1956 David Thiele, Australia	1:02.2
1960 David Thiele, Australia	1:01.9
1968 Roland Matthes, E. Germany	0:58.7
1972 Roland Matthes, E. Germany	0:56.58
1976 John Naber, United States	0:55.49
1980 Bengt Baron, Sweden	0:56.33
1984 Rick Carey, United States	0:55.79
1988 Daichi Suzuki, Japan	0:55.05
1992 Mark Tewksbury, Canada	0:53.98
1996 Jeff Rouse, United States	0:54.10
2000 Lenny Krayzelburg, United States	0:53.72
2004 Aaron Peirsol, United States	0:54.06
2008 Aaron Peirsol, United States	0:52.54
2012 Matt Grevers, United States	0:52.16*

200-Meter Backstroke	Time
1964 Jed Graef, United States	2:10.3
1968 Roland Matthes, E. Germany	2:09.6
1972 Roland Matthes, E. Germany	2:02.82
1976 John Naber, United States	1:59.19
1980 Sandor Wladar, Hungary	2:01.93
1984 Rick Carey, United States	2:00.23
1988 Igor Polianski, USSR	1:59.37
1992 Martin Lopez-Zubero, Spain	1:58.47
1996 Brad Bridgewater, United States	1:58.54
2000 Lenny Krayzelburg, United States	1:56.76
2004 Aaron Peirsol, United States	1:54.95
2008 Ryan Lochte, United States	1:53.94
2012 Tyler Clary, United States	1:53.41*

100-Meter Breaststroke	Time
1968 Don McKenzie, United States	1:07.79
1972 Nobutaka Taguchi, Japan	1:04.94
1976 John Hencken, United States	1:03.11
1980 Duncan Goodhew, Great Britain	1:03.44
1984 Steve Lundquist, United States	1:01.65
1988 Adrian Moorhouse, Great Britain	1:02.04
1992 Nelson Diebel, United States	1:01.50
1996 Fred Deburghgraeve, Belgium	1:00.60
2000 Domenico Fioravanti, Italy	1:00.46
2004 Kosuke Kitajima, Japan	1:00.08
2008 Kosuke Kitajima, Japan	0:58.91
2012 Cameron van der Burgh, South Africa	0:58.46*

200-Meter Breaststroke	Time
1908 Frederick Holman, Great Britain	3:09.2
1912 Walter Bathe, Germany	3:01.8
1920 Haken Malmroth, Sweden	3:04.4
1924 Robert Skelton, United States	2:56.6
1928 Yoshiyuki Tsuruta, Japan	2:48.8
1932 Yoshiyuki Tsuruta, Japan	2:45.4
1936 Tetsuo Hamuro, Japan	2:41.5
1948 Joseph Verdeur, United States	2:39.3
1952 John Davies, Australia	2:34.4
1956 Masura Furukawa, Japan	2:34.7
1960 William Mulliken, United States	2:37.4
1964 Ian O'Brien, Australia	2:27.8
1968 Felipe Munoz, Mexico	2:28.7
1972 John Hencken, United States	2:21.55
1976 David Wilkie, Great Britain	2:15.11
1980 Robertas Zhulpa, USSR	2:15.85
1984 Victor Davis, Canada	2:13.34
1988 Jozsef Szabo, Hungary	2:13.52
1992 Mike Barrowman, United States	2:10.16
1996 Norbert Rozsa, Hungary	2:12.57
2000 Domenico Fioravanti, Italy	2:10.87
2004 Kosuke Kitajima, Japan	2:09.44
2008 Kosuke Kitajima, Japan	2:07.64
2012 Dániel Gyurta, Hungary	2:07.28*

100-Meter Butterfly	Time
1968 Doug Russell, United States	0:55.9
1972 Mark Spitz, United States	0:54.27
1976 Matt Vogel, United States	0:54.35
1980 Par Arvidsson, Sweden	0:54.92
1984 Michael Gross, W. Germany	0:53.08
1988 Anthony Nesty, Suriname	0:53.00
1992 Pablo Morales, United States	0:53.32
1996 Denis Pankratov, Russia	0:52.27
2000 Lars Froelander, Sweden	0:52.00
2004 Michael Phelps, United States	0:51.25
2008 Michael Phelps, United States	0:50.58*
2012 Michael Phelps, United States	0:51.21

200-Meter Butterfly	Time
1956 William Yorzyk, United States	2:19.3
1960 Michael Troy, United States	2:12.8
1964 Kevin J. Berry, Australia	2:06.6
1968 Carl Robie, United States	2:08.7
1972 Mark Spitz, United States	2:00.70
1976 Mike Bruner, United States	1:59.23
1980 Sergei Fesenko, USSR	1:59.76
1984 Jon Sieben, Australia	1:57.04
1988 Michael Gross, W. Germany	1:56.94
1992 Mel Stewart, United States	1:56.26
1996 Denis Pankratov, Russia	1:56.51
2000 Tom Malchow, United States	1:55.35
2004 Michael Phelps, United States	1:54.04
2008 Michael Phelps, United States	1:52.03*
2012 Chad le Clos, South Africa	1:52.96

200-Meter Individual Medley	Time
1968 Charles Hickcox, United States	2:12.0
1972 Gunnar Larsson, Sweden	2:07.17
1984 Alex Baumann, Canada	2:01.42
1988 Tamas Darnyi, Hungary	2:00.17
1992 Tamas Darnyi, Hungary	2:00.76
1996 Attila Czene, Hungary	1:59.91
2000 Massimiliano Rosolino, Italy	1:58.98
2004 Michael Phelps, United States	1:57.14
2008 Michael Phelps, United States	1:54.23*
2012 Michael Phelps, United States	1:54.27

400-Meter Individual Medley	Time
1964 Dick Roth, United States	4:45.4
1968 Charles Hickcox, United States	4:48.4
1972 Gunnar Larsson, Sweden	4:31.98
1976 Rod Strachan, United States	4:23.68
1980 Aleksandr Sidorenko, USSR	4:22.89
1984 Alex Baumann, Canada	4:17.41
1988 Tamas Darnyi, Hungary	4:14.75
1992 Tamas Darnyi, Hungary	4:14.23

400-Meter Individual Medley	Time
1996 Tom Dolan, United States	4:14.90
2000 Tom Dolan, United States	4:11.76
2004 Michael Phelps, United States	4:08.26
2008 Michael Phelps, United States	4:03.84*
2012 Ryan Lochte, United States	4:05.18

4x100-Meter Freestyle Relay	Time
1964 United States	3:31.2
1968 United States	3:31.7
1972 United States	3:26.42
1984 United States	3:19.03
1988 United States	3:16.53
1992 United States	3:16.74
1996 United States	3:15.41
2000 Australia	3:13.67
2004 South Africa	3:13.17
2008 United States	3:08.24*
2012 France	3:09.93

4x200-Meter Freestyle Relay	Time
1908 Great Britain	10:55.6
1912 Australasia	10:11.6
1920 United States	10:04.4
1924 United States	9:53.4
1928 United States	9:36.2
1932 Japan	8:58.4
1936 Japan	8:51.5
1948 United States	8:46.0
1952 United States	8:31.1
1956 Australia	8:23.6
1960 United States	8:10.2
1964 United States	7:52.1
1968 United States	7:52.33
1972 United States	7:35.78
1976 United States	7:23.22
1980 USSR	7:23.50
1984 United States	7:15.69
1988 United States	7:12.51
1992 Unified Team	7:11.95
1996 United States	7:14.84
2000 Australia	7:07.05
2004 United States	7:07.33
2008 United States	6:58.56*
2012 United States	6:59.70

4x100-Meter Medley Relay	Time
1960 United States	4:05.4
1964 United States	3:58.4
1968 United States	3:54.9
1972 United States	3:48.16
1976 United States	3:42.22
1980 Australia	3:45.70
1984 United States	3:39.30
1988 United States	3:36.93
1992 United States	3:36.93
1996 United States	3:34.84
2000 United States	3:33.73
2004 United States	3:30.68
2008 United States	3:29.34*
2012 United States	3:29.35

10-Kilometer Marathon	Time
2008 Maarten van der Weijden, Netherlands	1:51:51.6
2012 Oussama Mellouli, Tunisia	1:49:55.1

Platform Diving	Points
1904 Dr. G. E. Sheldon, United States	112.75
1908 Hjalmar Johansson, Sweden	183.75
1912 Erik Adlerz, Sweden	73.94
1920 Clarence Pinkston, United States	100.67
1924 Albert White, United States	97.46
1928 Pete Desjardins, United States	98.74
1932 Harold Smith, United States	124.80
1936 Marshall Wayne, United States	113.58
1948 Sammy Lee, United States	130.05
1952 Sammy Lee, United States	156.28
1956 Joaquin Capilla, Mexico	152.44
1960 Robert Webster, United States	165.56
1964 Robert Webster, United States	148.58
1968 Klaus Dibiasi, Italy	164.18
1972 Klaus Dibiasi, Italy	504.12
1976 Klaus Dibiasi, Italy	600.51
1980 Falk Hoffmann, E. Germany	835.65
1984 Greg Louganis, United States	710.91
1988 Greg Louganis, United States	638.61
1992 Sun Shuwei, China	677.31
1996 Dmitri Sautin, Russia	692.34
2000 Tian Liang, China	724.53
2004 Hu Jia, China	748.08
2008 Matthew Mitcham, Australia	537.95
2012 David Boudia, United States	568.65

Springboard Diving	Points
1908 Albert Zurner, Germany	85.50
1912 Paul Guenther, Germany	79.23
1920 Louis Kuehn, United States	675.40
1924 Albert White, United States	97.46
1928 Pete Desjardins, United States	185.04
1932 Michael Galitzen, United States	161.38
1936 Richard Degener, United States	163.57
1948 Bruce Harlan, United States	163.64
1952 David Browning, United States	205.29
1956 Robert Clotworthy, United States	159.56
1960 Gary Tobian, United States	170.00
1964 Kenneth Sitzberger, United States	159.90
1968 Bernie Wrightson, United States	170.15
1972 Vladimir Vasin, USSR	594.09
1976 Phil Boggs, United States	619.52
1980 Aleksandr Portnov, USSR	905.02
1984 Greg Louganis, United States	754.41
1988 Greg Louganis, United States	730.80
1992 Mark Lenzi, United States	676.53
1996 Xiong Ni, China	701.46
2000 Xiong Ni, China	708.72
2004 Peng Bo, China	787.30
2008 He Chong, China	572.90
2012 Ilya Zakharov, Russia	555.90

Synchronized Platform Diving	Points
2004 Tian Liang and Yang Jinghui, China	383.88
2008 Lin Yue and Huo Liang, China	468.18
2012 Cao Yuan and Zhang Yanquan, China	486.78

Synchronized Springboard Diving	Points
2004 Nikolaos Siranidis and Thomas Bimis, Greece	353.34
2008 Wang Feng and Qin Kai, China	469.08
2012 Luo Yutong and Qin Kai, China	477.00

Swimming and Diving—Women

50-Meter Freestyle	Time
1988 Kristin Otto, E. Germany	0:25.49
1992 Yang Wenyi, China	0:24.76
1996 Amy Van Dyken, United States	0:24.87
2000 Inge de Bruijn, Netherlands	0:24.32
2004 Inge de Bruijn, Netherlands	0:24.58
2008 Britta Steffen, Germany	0:24.06
2012 Ranomi Kromowidjojo, Netherlands	0:24.05*

100-Meter Freestyle	Time
1912 Fanny Durack, Australia	1:22.2
1920 Ethelda Bleibtrey, United States	1:13.6
1924 Ethel Lackie, United States	1:12.4
1928 Albina Osipowich, United States	1:11.0
1932 Helene Madison, United States	1:06.8
1936 Hendrika Mastenbroek, Holland	1:05.9
1948 Greta Andersen, Denmark	1:06.3
1952 Katalin Szoke, Hungary	1:06.8
1956 Dawn Fraser, Australia	1:02.0
1960 Dawn Fraser, Australia	1:01.2
1964 Dawn Fraser, Australia	0:59.5
1968 Jan Henne, United States	1:00.0
1972 Sandra Neilson, United States	0:58.59
1976 Kornelia Ender, E. Germany	0:55.65
1980 Barbara Krause, E. Germany	0:54.79

100-Meter Freestyle	Time
1984 Carrie Steinseifer, United States	0:55.92
Nancy Hogshead, United States (tie)	0:55.92
1988 Kristin Otto, E. Germany	0:54.93
1992 Zhuang Yong, China	0:54.64
1996 Li Jingyi, China	0:54.50
2000 Inge de Bruijn, Netherlands	0:53.83
2004 Jodie Henry, Australia	0:53.84
2008 Britta Steffen, Germany	0:53.12
2012 Ranomi Kromowidjojo, Netherlands	0:53.00*

200-Meter Freestyle	Time
1968 Debbie Meyer, United States	2:10.5
1972 Shane Gould, Australia	2:03.56
1976 Kornelia Ender, E. Germany	1:59.26
1980 Barbara Krause, E. Germany	1:58.33
1984 Mary Wayte, United States	1:59.23
1988 Heike Friedrich, E. Germany	1:57.65
1992 Nicole Haislett, United States	1:57.90
1996 Claudia Poll, Costa Rica	1:58.16
2000 Susan O'Neill, Australia	1:58.24
2004 Camelia Potec, Romania	1:58.03
2008 Federica Pellegrini, Italy	1:54.82
2012 Allison Schmitt, United States	1:53.61*

400-Meter Freestyle	Time
1924 Martha Norelius, United States	6:02.2
1928 Martha Norelius, United States	5:42.8
1932 Helene Madison, United States	5:28.5
1936 Hendrika Mastenbroek, Netherlands	5:26.4
1948 Ann Curtis, United States	5:17.8
1952 Valerie Gyenge, Hungary	5:12.1
1956 Lorraine Crapp, Australia	4:54.6
1960 Chris von Saltza, United States	4:50.6
1964 Virginia Duenkel, United States	4:43.3
1968 Debbie Meyer, United States	4:31.8
1972 Shane Gould, Australia	4:19.44
1976 Petra Thuemer, E. Germany	4:09.89
1980 Ines Diers, E. Germany	4:08.76
1984 Tiffany Cohen, United States	4:07.10
1988 Janet Evans, United States	4:03.85
1992 Dagmar Hase, Germany	4:07.18
1996 Michelle Smith, Ireland	4:07.25
2000 Brooke Bennett, United States	4:05.80
2004 Laure Manaudou, France	4:05.34
2008 Rebecca Adlington, Great Britain	4:03.22
2012 Camille Muffat, France	4:01.45*

800-Meter Freestyle	Time
1968 Debbie Meyer, United States	9:24.0
1972 Keena Rothhammer, United States	8:53.68
1976 Petra Thuemer, E. Germany	8:37.14
1980 Michelle Ford, Australia	8:28.90
1984 Tiffany Cohen, United States	8:24.95
1988 Janet Evans, United States	8:20.20
1992 Janet Evans, United States	8:25.52
1996 Brooke Bennett, United States	8:27.89
2000 Brooke Bennett, United States	8:19.67
2004 Ai Shibata, Japan	8:24.54
2008 Rebecca Adlington, Great Britain	8:14.10*
2012 Katie Ledecky, United States	8:14.63

100-Meter Backstroke	Time
1924 Sybil Bauer, United States	1:23.2
1928 Marie Braun, Netherlands	1:22.0
1932 Eleanor Holm, United States	1:19.4
1936 Dina Senff, Netherlands	1:18.9
1948 Karen Harup, Denmark	1:14.4
1952 Joan Harrison, South Africa	1:14.3
1956 Judy Grinham, Great Britain	1:12.9
1960 Lynn Burke, United States	1:09.3
1964 Cathy Ferguson, United States	1:07.7
1968 Kaye Hall, United States	1:06.2
1972 Melissa Belote, United States	1:05.78
1976 Ulrike Richter, E. Germany	1:01.83
1980 Rica Reinisch, E. Germany	1:00.86
1984 Theresa Andrews, United States	1:02.55
1988 Kristin Otto, E. Germany	1:00.89
1992 Krisztina Egerszegi, Hungary	1:00.68
1996 Beth Botsford, United States	1:01.19
2000 Diana Mocanu, Romania	1:00.21
2004 Natalie Coughlin, United States	1:00.37
2008 Natalie Coughlin, United States	0:58.96
2012 Missy Franklin, United States	0:58.33

200-Meter Backstroke	Time
1968 Pokey Watson, United States	2:24.8
1972 Melissa Belote, United States	2:19.19
1976 Ulrike Richter, E. Germany	2:13.43
1980 Rica Reinisch, E. Germany	2:11.77
1984 Jolanda De Rover, Netherlands	2:12.38
1988 Krisztina Egerszegi, Hungary	2:09.29
1992 Krisztina Egerszegi, Hungary	2:07.06
1996 Krisztina Egerszegi, Hungary	2:07.83
2000 Diana Mocanu, Romania	2:08.16
2004 Kirsty Coventry, Zimbabwe	2:09.19
2008 Kirsty Coventry, Zimbabwe	2:05.24
2012 Missy Franklin, United States	2:04.06*

100-Meter Breaststroke	Time
1968 Djurdjica Bjedov, Yugoslavia	1:15.8
1972 Cathy Carr, United States	1:13.58
1976 Hannelore Anke, E. Germany	1:11.16
1980 Ute Geweniger, E. Germany	1:10.22
1984 Petra Van Staveren, Netherlands	1:09.88
1988 Tania Dangalakova, Bulgaria	1:07.95
1992 Yelena Rudkovskaya, Unified Team	1:08.00
1996 Penny Heyns, South Africa	1:07.73
2000 Megan Quann, United States	1:07.05
2004 Luo Xuejuan, China	1:06.64
2008 Leisel Jones, Australia	1:05.17*
2012 Rūta Meilutytė, Lithuania	1:05.47

200-Meter Breaststroke	Time
1924 Lucy Morton, Great Britain	3:33.2
1928 Hilde Schrader, Germany	3:12.6

200-Meter Breaststroke	Time
1932 Clare Dennis, Australia	3:06.3
1936 Hideko Maehata, Japan	3:03.6
1948 Nelly Van Vliet, Netherlands	2:57.2
1952 Eva Szekely, Hungary	2:51.7
1956 Ursula Happe, Germany	2:53.1
1960 Anita Lonsbrough, Great Britain	2:49.5
1964 Galina Prozumenschikova, USSR	2:46.4
1968 Sharon Wichman, United States	2:44.4
1972 Beverly Whitfield, Australia	2:41.71
1976 Marina Koshevaia, USSR	2:33.35
1980 Lina Kachushite, USSR	2:29.54
1984 Anne Ottenbrite, Canada	2:30.38
1988 Silke Hoerner, E. Germany	2:26.71
1992 Kyoko Iwasaki, Japan	2:26.65
1996 Penny Heyns, South Africa	2:25.41
2000 Agnes Kovacs, Hungary	2:24.35
2004 Amanda Beard, United States	2:23.37
2008 Rebecca Soni, United States	2:20.22
2012 Rebecca Soni, United States	2:19.59*

100-Meter Butterfly	Time
1956 Shelley Mann, United States	1:11.0
1960 Carolyn Schuler, United States	1:09.5
1964 Sharon Stouder, United States	1:04.7
1968 Lynn McClements, Australia	1:05.5
1972 Mayumi Aoki, Japan	1:03.34
1976 Kornelia Ender, E. Germany	1:00.13
1980 Caren Metschuck, E. Germany	1:00.42
1984 Mary T. Meagher, United States	0:59.26
1988 Kristin Otto, E. Germany	0:59.00
1992 Qian Hong, China	0:58.62
1996 Amy Van Dyken, United States	0:59.13
2000 Inge de Bruijn, Netherlands	0:56.61
2004 Petria Thomas, Australia	0:57.72
2008 Lisbeth Trickett, Australia	0:56.73
2012 Dana Vollmer, United States	0:55.98*

200-Meter Butterfly	Time
1968 Ada Kok, Netherlands	2:24.7
1972 Karen Moe, United States	2:15.57
1976 Andrea Pollack, E. Germany	2:11.41
1980 Ines Geissler, E. Germany	2:10.44
1984 Mary T. Meagher, United States	2:06.90
1988 Kathleen Nord, E. Germany	2:09.51
1992 Summer Sanders, United States	2:08.67
1996 Susan O'Neill, Australia	2:07.76
2000 Misty Hyman, United States	2:05.88
2004 Otylia Jedrzejczak, Poland	2:06.05
2008 Liu Zige, China	2:04.18
2012 Jiao Liuyang, China	2:04.06*

200-Meter Individual Medley	Time
1968 Claudia Kolb, United States	2:24.7
1972 Shane Gould, Australia	2:23.07
1984 Tracy Caulkins, United States	2:12.64
1988 Daniela Hunger, E. Germany	2:12.59
1992 Lin Li, China	2:11.65
1996 Michelle Smith, Ireland	2:13.93
2000 Yana Klochkova, Ukraine	2:10.68
2004 Yana Klochkova, Ukraine	2:11.14
2008 Stephanie Rice, Australia	2:08.45
2012 Ye Shiwen, China	2:07.57*

400-Meter Individual Medley	Time
1964 Donna de Varona, United States	5:18.7
1968 Claudia Kolb, United States	5:08.5
1972 Gail Neall, Australia	5:02.97
1976 Ulrike Tauber, E. Germany	4:42.77
1980 Petra Schneider, E. Germany	4:36.29
1984 Tracy Caulkins, United States	4:39.24
1988 Janet Evans, United States	4:37.76
1992 Krisztina Egerszegi, Hungary	4:36.54
1996 Michelle Smith, Ireland	4:39.18
2000 Yana Klochkova, Ukraine	4:33.59
2004 Yana Klochkova, Ukraine	4:34.83
2008 Stephanie Rice, Australia	4:29.45
2012 Ye Shiwen, China	4:28.43*

4x100-Meter Freestyle Relay	Time
1912 Great Britain	5:52.8
1920 United States	5:11.6
1924 United States	4:58.8
1928 United States	4:47.6
1932 United States	4:38.0
1936 Netherlands	4:36.0
1948 United States	4:29.2
1952 Hungary	4:24.4
1956 Australia	4:17.1
1960 United States	4:08.9

4x100-Meter Freestyle Relay

		Time
1964	United States	4:03.8
1968	United States	4:02.5
1972	United States	3:55.19
1976	United States	3:44.82
1980	East Germany	3:42.71
1984	United States	3:43.43
1988	East Germany	3:40.63
1992	United States	3:39.46
1996	United States	3:39.29
2000	United States	3:36.61
2004	Australia	3:35.94
2008	Netherlands	3:33.76
2012	Australia	3:33.15*

4x200-Meter Freestyle Relay

		Time
1996	United States	7:59.87
2000	United States	7:57.80
2004	United States	7:53.42
2008	Australia	7:44.31
2012	United States	7:42.92*

4x100-Meter Medley Relay

		Time
1960	United States	4:41.1
1964	United States	4:33.9
1968	United States	4:28.3
1972	United States	4:20.75
1976	East Germany	4:07.95
1980	East Germany	4:06.67
1984	United States	4:08.34
1988	East Germany	4:03.74
1992	United States	4:02.54
1996	United States	4:02.88
2000	United States	3:58.30
2004	Australia	3:57.32
2008	Australia	3:52.69
2012	United States	3:52.05*

10-Kilometer Marathon

		Time
2008	Larisa Ilchenko, Russia	1:59:27.7
2012	Éva Risztov, Hungary	1:57:38.2

Platform Diving

		Points
1912	Greta Johansson, Sweden	39.90
1920	Stefani Fryland-Clausen, Denmark	34.60
1924	Caroline Smith, United States	33.20
1928	Elizabeth B. Pinkston, United States	31.60
1932	Dorothy Poynton, United States	40.26
1936	Dorothy Poynton Hill, United States	33.93
1948	Victoria M. Draves, United States	68.87
1952	Patricia McCormick, United States	79.37

Platform Diving

		Points
1956	Patricia McCormick, United States	84.85
1960	Ingrid Kramer, Germany	91.28
1964	Lesley Bush, United States	99.80
1968	Milena Duchkova, Czechoslovakia	109.59
1972	Ulrika Knape, Sweden	390.00
1976	Elena Vaytsekhouskaya, USSR	406.59
1980	Martina Jaschke, E. Germany	596.25
1984	Zhou Jihong, China	435.51
1988	Xu Yanmei, China	445.20
1992	Fu Mingxia, China	461.43
1996	Fu Mingxia, China	521.58
2000	Laura Wilkinson, United States	543.75
2004	Chantelle Newbery, Australia	590.31
2008	Chen Ruolin, China	447.70
2012	Chen Ruolin, China	422.30

Springboard Diving

		Points
1920	Aileen Riggin, United States	539.90
1924	Elizabeth Becker, United States	474.50
1928	Helen Meany, United States	78.62
1932	Georgia Coleman United States	87.52
1936	Marjorie Gestring, United States	89.27
1948	Victoria M. Draves, United States	108.74
1952	Patricia McCormick, United States	147.30
1956	Patricia McCormick, United States	142.36
1960	Ingrid Kramer, Germany	155.81
1964	Ingrid Engel-Kramer, Germany	145.00
1968	Sue Gossick, United States	150.77
1972	Micki King, United States	450.03
1976	Jenni Chandler, United States	506.19
1980	Irina Kalinina, USSR	725.91
1984	Sylvie Bernier, Canada	530.70
1988	Gao Min, China	580.23
1992	Gao Min, China	572.40
1996	Fu Mingxia, China	547.68
2000	Fu Mingxia, China	609.42
2004	Guo Jingjing, China	633.15
2008	Guo Jingjing, China	415.35
2012	Wu Minxia, China	414.00

Synchronized Platform Diving

		Points
2004	Lao Lishi and Li Ting, China	352.14
2008	Wang Xin and Chen Ruolin, China	363.54
2012	Chen Ruolin and Wang Hao, China	368.40

Synchronized Springboard Diving

		Points
2004	Wu Minxia and Guo Jingjing, China	336.90
2008	Guo Jingjing and Wu Minxia, China	343.50
2012	He Zi and Wu Minxia, China	346.20

Tennis

Men's Singles

1896	John Boland, Great Britain
1900	Hugh Lawrence Doherty, Great Britain
1904	Beals Coleman Wright, United States
1908	Josiah George Ritchie, Great Britain
1912	Charles Lyndhurst Winslow, South Africa
1920	Louis Raymond, South Africa
1924	Vincent Richards, United States
1988	Miloslav Mecir, Czechoslovakia
1992	Marc Rosset, Switzerland
1996	Andre Agassi, United States
2000	Eugueni Kafelnikov, Russia
2004	Nicolas Massu, Chile
2008	Rafael Nadal, Spain
2012	Andy Murray, Great Britain

Men's Doubles

1896	John Boland, Great Britain & Friedrick Traun, Germany
1900	Hugh Lawrence Doherty & Reginald Frank Doherty, Great Britain
1904	Edgar Welch Leonard & Beals Coleman Wright, U.S.
1908	George Whiteside Hillyard & Reginald Frank Doherty, Great Britain
1912	Harry Austin Kitson & Charles Lyndhurst Winslow, South Africa
1920	Oswald Graham Noel Turnbull & Maxwell Woosnam, Great Britain
1924	Vincent Richards & Francis Townsend Hunter, U.S.
1988	Kenneth Flach & Robert A. Seguso, United States
1992	Boris Becker & Michael Stich, Germany
1996	Mark Woodforde & Todd Woodbridge, Australia
2000	Sebastien Lareau & Daniel Nestor, Canada

Men's Doubles

2004	Fernando Gonzales & Nicolas Massu, Chile
2008	Roger Federer & Stanislas Wawrinka, Switzerland
2012	Mike Bryan & Bob Bryan, United States

Women's Singles

1900	Charlotte Cooper, Great Britain
1908	Dorothy Katherine Chambers, Great Britain
1912	Marguerite Broquedis, France
1920	Suzanne Lenglen, France
1924	Helen Wills, United States
1988	Steffi Graf, W. Germany
1992	Jennifer Capriati, United States
1996	Lindsay Davenport, United States
2000	Venus Williams, United States
2004	Justine Henin-Hardenne, Belgium
2008	Elena Dementieva, Russia
2012	Serena Williams, United States

Women's Doubles

1920	Winifred Margaret McNair & Kathleen McKane, Great Britain
1924	Hazel Virginia Wightman & Helen Wills, United States
1988	Pam Shriver & Zina Garrison, United States
1992	Gigi Fernandez & Mary Joe Fernandez, United States
1996	Gigi Fernandez & Mary Joe Fernandez, United States
2000	Venus Williams & Serena Williams, United States
2004	Ting Li & Tian Tian Sun, China
2008	Serena Williams & Venus Williams, United States
2012	Serena Williams & Venus Williams, United States

Mixed Doubles

2012	Victoria Azarenka & Max Mirnyi, Belarus

Track and Field—Men

100-Meter Run	Time	800-Meter Run	Time
1896 Thomas Burke, United States	0:12.0	**1896** Edwin Flack, Australia	2:11.0
1900 Francis Jarvis, United States	0:11.0	**1900** Alfred Tysoe, Great Britain	2:01.2
1904 Archie Hahn, United States	0:11.0	**1904** James Lightbody, United States	1:56.0
1908 Reginald Walker, South Africa	0:10.8	**1908** Mel Sheppard, United States	1:52.8
1912 Ralph Craig, United States	0:10.8	**1912** James "Ted" Meredith, United States	1:51.9
1920 Charles Paddock, United States	0:10.8	**1920** Albert Hill, Great Britain	1:53.4
1924 Harold Abrahams, Great Britain	0:10.6	**1924** Douglas Lowe, Great Britain	1:52.4
1928 Percy Williams, Canada	0:10.8	**1928** Douglas Lowe, Great Britain	1:51.8
1932 Eddie Tolan, United States	0:10.3	**1932** Thomas Hampson, Great Britain	1:49.8
1936 Jesse Owens, United States	0:10.3	**1936** John Woodruff, United States	1:52.9
1948 Harrison Dillard, United States	0:10.3	**1948** Mal Whitfield, United States	1:49.2
1952 Lindy Remigino, United States	0:10.4	**1952** Mal Whitfield, United States	1:49.2
1956 Bobby Morrow, United States	0:10.5	**1956** Tom Courtney, United States	1:47.7
1960 Armin Hary, Germany	0:10.2	**1960** Peter Snell, New Zealand	1:46.3
1964 Bob Hayes, United States	0:10.0	**1964** Peter Snell, New Zealand	1:45.1
1968 Jim Hines, United States	0:09.95	**1968** Ralph Doubell, Australia	1:44.3
1972 Valery Borzov, USSR	0:10.14	**1972** Dave Wottle, United States	1:45.9
1976 Hasely Crawford, Trinidad	0:10.06	**1976** Alberto Juantorena, Cuba	1:43.50
1980 Allan Wells, Great Britain	0:10.25	**1980** Steve Ovett, Great Britain	1:45.40
1984 Carl Lewis, United States	0:09.99	**1984** Joaquim Cruz, Brazil	1:43.00
1988 Carl Lewis, United States	0:09.92	**1988** Paul Ereng, Kenya	1:43.45
1992 Linford Christie, Great Britain	0:09.96	**1992** William Tanui, Kenya	1:43.66
1996 Donovan Bailey, Canada	0:09.84	**1996** Vebjørn Rodal, Norway	1:42.58
2000 Maurice Greene, United States	0:09.87	**2000** Nils Schumann, Germany	1:45.08
2004 Justin Gatlin, United States	0:09.85	**2004** Yuriy Borzakovskiy, Russia	1:44.45
2008 Usain Bolt, Jamaica	0:09.69	**2008** Wilfred Bungei, Kenya	1:44.65
2012 Usain Bolt, Jamaica	0:09.63*	**2012** David Lekuta Rudisha, Kenya	1:40.91*

200-Meter Run	Time	1,500-Meter Run	Time
1900 Walter Tewksbury, United States	0:22.2	**1896** Edwin Flack, Australia	4:33.2
1904 Archie Hahn, United States	0:21.6	**1900** Charles Bennett, Great Britain	4:06.2
1908 Robert Kerr, Canada	0:22.6	**1904** James Lightbody, United States	4:05.4
1912 Ralph Craig, United States	0:21.7	**1908** Mel Sheppard, United States	4:03.4
1920 Allan Woodring, United States	0:22.0	**1912** Arnold Jackson, Great Britain	3:56.8
1924 Jackson Scholz, United States	0:21.6	**1920** Albert Hill, Great Britain	4:01.8
1928 Percy Williams, Canada	0:21.8	**1924** Paavo Nurmi, Finland	3:53.6
1932 Eddie Tolan, United States	0:21.2	**1928** Harry Larva, Finland	3:53.2
1936 Jesse Owens, United States	0:20.7	**1932** Luigi Beccali, Italy	3:51.2
1948 Mel Patton, United States	0:21.1	**1936** Jack Lovelock, New Zealand	3:47.8
1952 Andrew Stanfield, United States	0:20.7	**1948** Henry Eriksson, Sweden	3:49.8
1956 Bobby Morrow, United States	0:20.6	**1952** Joseph Barthel, Luxembourg	3:45.2
1960 Livio Berruti, Italy	0:20.5	**1956** Ron Delany, Ireland	3:41.2
1964 Henry Carr, United States	0:20.3	**1960** Herb Elliott, Australia	3:35.6
1968 Tommie Smith, United States	0:19.83	**1964** Peter Snell, New Zealand	3:38.1
1972 Valery Borzov, USSR	0:20.00	**1968** Kipchoge Keino, Kenya	3:34.91
1976 Donald Quarrie, Jamaica	0:20.23	**1972** Pekka Vasala, Finland	3:36.33
1980 Pietro Mennea, Italy	0:20.19	**1976** John Walker, New Zealand	3:39.17
1984 Carl Lewis, United States	0:19.80	**1980** Sebastian Coe, Great Britain	3:38.4
1988 Joe DeLoach, United States	0:19.75	**1984** Sebastian Coe, Great Britain	3:32.53
1992 Mike Marsh, United States	0:20.01	**1988** Peter Rono, Kenya	3:35.96
1996 Michael Johnson, United States	0:19.32	**1992** Fermin Cacho Ruiz, Spain	3:40.12
2000 Konstantinos Kenteris, Greece	0:20.09	**1996** Noureddine Morceli, Algeria	3:35.78
2004 Shawn Crawford, United States	0:19.79	**2000** Noah Ngeny, Kenya	3:32.07*
2008 Usain Bolt, Jamaica	0:19.30*	**2004** Hicham El Guerrouj, Morocco	3:34.18
2012 Usain Bolt, Jamaica	0:19.32	**2008** Asbel Kiprop, Kenya[1]	3:33.11
		2012 Taoufik Makhloufi, Algeria	3:34.08

(1) Originally won by Rashid Ramzi, Bahrain, who was stripped of the gold in 2009 due to doping.

400-Meter Run	Time	3,000-Meter Steeplechase	Time
1896 Thomas Burke, United States	0:54.2		
1900 Maxwell Long, United States	0:49.4	**1920** Percy Hodge, Great Britain	10:00.4
1904 Harry Hillman, United States	0:49.2	**1924** Ville Ritola, Finland	9:33.6
1908 Wyndham Halswelle, Gr. Brit. (walkover)	0:50.0	**1928** Toivo Loukola, Finland	9:21.8
1912 Charles Reidpath, United States	0:48.2	**1932** Volmari Iso-Hollo, Finland	
1920 Bevil Rudd, South Africa	0:49.6	(about 3,450 m; extra lap by error)	10:33.4
1924 Eric Liddell, Great Britain	0:47.6	**1936** Volmari Iso-Hollo, Finland	9:03.8
1928 Ray Barbuti, United States	0:47.8	**1948** Tore Sjöstrand, Sweden	9:04.6
1932 William Carr, United States	0:46.2	**1952** Horace Ashenfelter, United States	8:45.4
1936 Archie Williams, United States	0:46.5	**1956** Chris Brasher, Great Britain	8:41.2
1948 Arthur Wint, Jamaica	0:46.2	**1960** Zdzislaw Krzyszkowiak, Poland	8:34.2
1952 George Rhoden, Jamaica	0:45.9	**1964** Gaston Roelants, Belgium	8:30.8
1956 Charles Jenkins, United States	0:46.7	**1968** Amos Biwott, Kenya	8:51.0
1960 Otis Davis, United States	0:44.9	**1972** Kipchoge Keino, Kenya	8:23.64
1964 Michael Larrabee, United States	0:45.1	**1976** Anders Garderud, Sweden	8:08.02
1968 Lee Evans, United States	0:43.86	**1980** Bronislaw Malinowski, Poland	8:09.7
1972 Vincent Matthews, United States	0:44.66	**1984** Julius Korir, Kenya	8:11.80
1976 Alberto Juantorena, Cuba	0:44.26	**1988** Julius Kariuki, Kenya	8:05.51*
1980 Viktor Markin, USSR	0:44.60	**1992** Matthew Birir, Kenya	8:08.84
1984 Alonzo Babers, United States	0:44.27	**1996** Joseph Keter, Kenya	8:07.12
1988 Steve Lewis, United States	0:43.87	**2000** Reuben Kosgei, Kenya	8:21.43
1992 Quincy Watts, United States	0:43.50	**2004** Ezekiel Kemboi, Kenya	8:05.81
1996 Michael Johnson, United States	0:43.49*	**2008** Brimin Kiprop Kirpruto, Kenya	8:10.34
2000 Michael Johnson, United States	0:43.84	**2012** Ezekiel Kemboi, Kenya	8:18.56
2004 Jeremy Wariner, United States	0:44.00		
2008 LaShawn Merritt, United States	0:43.75		
2012 Kirani James, Grenada	0:43.94		

5,000-Meter Run	Time
1912 Hannes Kolehmainen, Finland	14:36.6
1920 Joseph Guillemot, France	14:55.6
1924 Paavo Nurmi, Finland	14:31.2
1928 Ville Ritola, Finland	14:38.0
1932 Lauri Lehtinen, Finland	14:30.0
1936 Gunnar Höckert, Finland	14:22.2
1948 Gaston Reiff, Belgium	14:17.6
1952 Emil Zatopek, Czechoslovakia	14:06.6
1956 Vladimir Kuts, USSR	13:39.6
1960 Murray Halberg, New Zealand	13:43.4
1964 Bob Schul, United States	13:48.8
1968 Mohamed Gammoudi, Tunisia	14:05.0
1972 Lasse Viren, Finland	13:26.4
1976 Lasse Viren, Finland	13:24.76
1980 Miruts Yifter, Ethiopia	13:20.91
1984 Said Aouita, Morocco	13:05.59
1988 John Ngugi, Kenya	13:11.70
1992 Dieter Baumann, Germany	13:12.52
1996 Venuste Niyongabo, Burundi	13:07.96
2000 Millon Wolde, Ethiopia	13:35.49
2004 Hicham El Guerrouj, Morocco	13:14.39
2008 Kenenisa Bekele, Ethiopia	12:57.82*
2012 Mo Farah, Great Britain	13:41.66

10,000-Meter Run	Time
1912 Hannes Kolehmainen, Finland	31:20.8
1920 Paavo Nurmi, Finland	31:45.8
1924 Ville Ritola, Finland	30:23.2
1928 Paavo Nurmi, Finland	30:18.8
1932 Janusz Kusocinski, Poland	30:11.4
1936 Ilmari Salminen, Finland	30:15.4
1948 Emil Zatopek, Czechoslovakia	29:59.6
1952 Emil Zatopek, Czechoslovakia	29:17.0
1956 Vladimir Kuts, USSR	28:45.6
1960 Pyotr Bolotnikov, USSR	28:32.2
1964 Billy Mills, United States	28:24.4
1968 Naftali Temu, Kenya	29:27.4
1972 Lasse Viren, Finland	27:38.4
1976 Lasse Viren, Finland	27:40.38
1980 Miruts Yifter, Ethiopia	27:42.7
1984 Alberto Cova, Italy	27:47.54
1988 Brahim Boutayeb, Morocco	27:21.46
1992 Khalid Skah, Morocco	27:46.70
1996 Haile Gebrselassie, Ethiopia	27:07.34
2000 Haile Gebrselassie, Ethiopia	27:18.20
2004 Kenenisa Bekele, Ethiopia	27:05.10
2008 Kenenisa Bekele, Ethiopia	27:01.17*
2012 Mo Farah, Great Britain	27:30.42

Marathon	Time
1896 Spyridon Louis, Greece	2:58:50
1900 Michel Theato, France	2:59:45.0
1904 Thomas Hicks, United States	3:28:53.0
1908 John Hayes, United States	2:55:18.4
1912 Kenneth McArthur, South Africa	2:36:54.8
1920 Hannes Kolehmainen, Finland	2:32:35.8
1924 Albin Stenroos, Finland	2:41:22.6
1928 Boughera El Ouafi, France	2:32.57
1932 Juan Zabala, Argentina	2:31:36
1936 Kee-chung Sohn, Japan[1]	2:29:19.2
1948 Delfo Cabrera, Argentina	2:34:51.6
1952 Emil Zatopek, Czechoslovakia	2:23:03.2
1956 Alain Mimoun, France	2:25:00.0
1960 Abebe Bikila, Ethiopia	2:15:16.2
1964 Abebe Bikila, Ethiopia	2:12:11.2
1968 Mamo Wolde, Ethiopia	2:20:26.4
1972 Frank Shorter, United States	2:12:19.8
1976 Waldemar Cierpinski, E. Germany	2:09:55.0
1980 Waldemar Cierpinski, E. Germany	2:11:03.0
1984 Carlos Lopes, Portugal	2:09:21
1988 Gelindo Bordin, Italy	2:10:32
1992 Hwang Young-Cho, S. Korea	2:13:23
1996 Josia Thugwane, South Africa	2:12:36
2000 Gezahegne Abera, Ethiopia	2:10:11
2004 Stefano Baldini, Italy	2:10:55
2008 Samuel Kamau Wansiru, Kenya	2:06:32*
2012 Stephen Kiprotich, Uganda	2:08:01

(1) Korean runner who competed under Japanese name Kitei Son.

4x100-Meter Relay	Time
1912 Great Britain	0:42.4
1920 United States	0:42.2
1924 United States	0:41.0
1928 United States	0:41.0
1932 United States	0:40.0

4x100-Meter Relay	Time
1936 United States	0:39.8
1948 United States	0:40.6
1952 United States	0:40.1
1956 United States	0:39.5
1960 Germany (U.S. disqualified)	0:39.5
1964 United States	0:39.0
1968 United States	0:38.24
1972 United States	0:38.19
1976 United States	0:38.33
1980 USSR	0:38.26
1984 United States	0:37.83
1988 USSR (U.S. disqualified)	0:38.19
1992 United States	0:37.40
1996 Canada	0:37.69
2000 United States	0:37.61
2004 Great Britain	0:38.07
2008 Jamaica	0:37.10
2012 Jamaica	0:36.84*

4x400-Meter Relay	Time
1908 United States	3:29.4
1912 United States	3:16.6
1920 Great Britain	3:22.2
1924 United States	3:16.0
1928 United States	3:14.2
1932 United States	3:08.2
1936 Great Britain	3:09.0
1948 United States	3:10.4
1952 Jamaica	3:03.9
1956 United States	3:04.8
1960 United States	3:02.2
1964 United States	3:00.7
1968 United States	2:56.16
1972 Kenya	2:59.8
1976 United States	2:58.65
1980 USSR	3:01.1
1984 United States	2:57.91
1988 United States	2:56.16
1992 United States	2:55.74
1996 United States	2:55.99
2000 Nigeria[1]	2:58.68
2004 United States	2:55.91
2008 United States	2:55.39*
2012 The Bahamas	2:56.72

(1) Originally won by the U.S. but awarded to Nigeria in 2012 after U.S. team member Antonio Pettigrew admitted to doping.

20-Kilometer Walk	Time
1956 Leonid Spirin, USSR	1:31:27.4
1960 Vladimir Golubnichy, USSR	1:34:07.2
1964 Kenneth Matthews, Great Britain	1:29:34.0
1968 Vladimir Golubnichy, USSR	1:33:58.4
1972 Peter Frenkel, E. Germany	1:26:42.4
1976 Daniel Bautista, Mexico	1:24:40.6
1980 Maurizio Damilano, Italy	1:23:35.5
1984 Ernesto Canto, Mexico	1:23:13
1988 Jozef Pribilinec, Czechoslovakia	1:19:57
1992 Daniel Plaza Montero, Spain	1:21:45
1996 Jefferson Perez, Ecuador	1:20:07
2000 Robert Korzeniowski, Poland	1:18:59
2004 Ivano Brugnetti, Italy	1:19:40
2008 Valeriy Borchin, Russia	1:19:01
2012 Chen Ding, China	1:18.46*

50-Kilometer Walk	Time
1932 Thomas "Tommy" Green, Great Britain	4:50.10
1936 Harold Whitlock, Great Britain	4:30:41.4
1948 John Ljunggren, Sweden	4:41:52
1952 Giuseppe Dordoni, Italy	4:28:07.8
1956 Norman Read, New Zealand	4:30:42.8
1960 Donald Thompson, Great Britain	4:25:30
1964 Abdon Pamich, Italy	4:11:12.4
1968 Christoph Höhne, E. Germany	4:20:13.6
1972 Bernd Kannenberg, W. Germany	3:56:11.6
1980 Hartwig Gauder, E. Germany	3:49:24.0
1984 Raul Gonzalez, Mexico	3:47:26
1988 Vyacheslav Ivanenko, USSR	3:38.29
1992 Andrey Perlov, Unified Team	3:50:13
1996 Robert Korzeniowski, Poland	3:43:30
2000 Robert Korzeniowski, Poland	3:42:22
2004 Robert Korzeniowski, Poland	3:38:46
2008 Alex Schwazer, Italy	3:37:09
2012 Sergey Kirdyapkin, Russia	3:35:59*

110-Meter Hurdles	Time
1896 Thomas Curtis, United States	0:17.6
1900 Alvin Kraenzlein, United States	0:15.4

110-Meter Hurdles	Time
1904 Frederick Schule, United States	0:16.0
1908 Forrest Smithson, United States	0:15.0
1912 Frederick Kelly, United States	0:15.1
1920 Earl Thomson, Canada	0:14.8
1924 Daniel Kinsey, United States	0:15.0
1928 Sydney Atkinson, South Africa	0:14.8
1932 George Saling, United States	0:14.6
1936 Forrest Towns, United States	0:14.2
1948 William Porter, United States	0:13.9
1952 Harrison Dillard, United States	0:13.7
1956 Lee Calhoun, United States	0:13.5
1960 Lee Calhoun, United States	0:13.8
1964 Hayes Jones, United States	0:13.6
1968 Willie Davenport, United States	0:13.33
1972 Rod Milburn, United States	0:13.24
1976 Guy Drut, France	0:13:30
1980 Thomas Munkelt, E. Germany	0:13.39
1984 Roger Kingdom, United States	0:13.20
1988 Roger Kingdom, United States	0:12.98
1992 Mark McKoy, Canada	0:13.12
1996 Allen Johnson, United States	0:12.95
2000 Anier Garcia, Cuba	0:13.00
2004 Liu Xiang, China	0:12.91*
2008 Dayron Robles, Cuba	0:12.93
2012 Aries Merritt, United States	0:12.92

400-Meter Hurdles	Time
1900 Walter Tewksbury, United States	0:57.6
1904 Harry Hillman, United States	0:53.0
1908 Charles Bacon, United States	0:55.0
1920 Frank Loomis, United States	0:54.0
1924 F. Morgan Taylor, United States	0:52.6
1928 Lord Burghley, Great Britain	0:53.4
1932 Bob Tisdall, Ireland	0:51.7
1936 Glenn Hardin, United States	0:52.4
1948 Roy Cochran, United States	0:51.1
1952 Charles Moore, United States	0:50.8
1956 Glenn Davis, United States	0:50.1
1960 Glenn Davis, United States	0:49.3
1964 Rex Cawley, United States	0:49.6
1968 David Hemery, Great Britain	0:48.12
1972 John Akii-Bua, Uganda	0:47.82
1976 Edwin Moses, United States	0:47.64
1980 Volker Beck, E. Germany	0:48.70
1984 Edwin Moses, United States	0:47.75
1988 Andre Phillips, United States	0:47.19
1992 Kevin Young, United States	0:46.78
1996 Derrick Adkins, United States	0:47.54
2000 Angelo Taylor, United States	0:47.50
2004 Félix Sánchez, Dominican Republic	0:47.63
2008 Angelo Taylor, United States	0:47.25
2012 Félix Sánchez, Dominican Republic	0:47.63

Note: Event not held in 1912.

Discus Throw	Dist.
1896 Robert Garrett, United States	29.15m (95' 7")
1900 Rudolf Bauer, Hungary	36.04m (118' 3")
1904 Martin Sheridan, United States	39.28m (128' 10")
1908 Martin Sheridan, United States	40.89m (134' 1")
1912 Armas Taipale, Finland	45.21m (148' 3")
1920 Elmer Niklander, Finland	44.68m (146' 7")
1924 Clarence "Bud" Houser, U.S.	46.15m (151' 4")
1928 Clarence "Bud" Houser, U.S.	47.32m (155' 3")
1932 John Anderson, United States	49.49m (162' 4")
1936 Ken Carpenter, United States	50.48m (165' 7")
1948 Adolfo Consolini, Italy	52.78m (173' 2")
1952 Sim Iness, United States	55.03m (180' 6")
1956 Al Oerter, United States	56.36m (184' 11")
1960 Al Oerter, United States	59.18m (194' 2")
1964 Al Oerter, United States	61.00m (200' 1")
1968 Al Oerter, United States	64.78m (212' 6")
1972 Ludvik Danek, Czechoslovakia	64.40m (211' 3")
1976 Mac Wilkins, United States	67.50m (221' 5")
1980 Viktor Rashchupkin, USSR	66.64m (218' 8")
1984 Rolf Dannenberg, W. Germany	66.60m (218' 6")
1988 Jürgen Schult, E. Germany	68.82m (225' 9")
1992 Romas Ubartas, Lithuania	65.12m (213' 8")
1996 Lars Riedel, Germany	69.40m (227' 8")
2000 Virgilijus Alekna, Lithuania	69.30m (227' 4")
2004 Virgilijus Alekna, Lithuania	69.89m (228' 9¾")*
2008 Gerd Kanter, Estonia	68.82m (225' 9½")
2012 Robert Harting, Germany	68.27m (224')

Hammer Throw	Dist.
1900 John Flanagan, United States	49.73m (163' 1")

Hammer Throw	Dist.
1904 John Flanagan, United States	51.23m (168' 1")
1908 John Flanagan, United States	51.92m (170' 4")
1912 Matt McGrath, United States	54.74m (179' 7")
1920 Pat Ryan, United States	52.875m (173' 5¾")
1924 Fred Tootell, United States	53.295m (174' 10")
1928 Patrick O'Callaghan, Ireland	51.39m (168' 7")
1932 Patrick O'Callaghan, Ireland	53.92m (176' 11")
1936 Karl Hein, Germany	56.49m (185' 4")
1948 Imre Németh, Hungary	56.07m (183' 11½")
1952 József Csérmák, Hungary	60.34m (197' 11")
1956 Harold Connolly, United States	63.19m (207' 3")
1960 Vasily Rudenkov, USSR	67.10m (202' 0")
1964 Romuald Klim, USSR	69.74m (228' 10")
1968 Gyula Zsivótzky, Hungary	73.36m (240' 8")
1972 Anatoly Bondarchuk, USSR	75.50m (247' 8")
1976 Yuri Sedykh, USSR	77.52m (254' 4")
1980 Yuri Sedykh, USSR	81.80m (268' 4")
1984 Juha Tiainen, Finland	78.08m (256' 2")
1988 Sergei Litvinov, USSR	84.80m (278' 2")*
1992 Andrey Abduvaliyev, Unified Team	82.54m (270' 9")
1996 Balázs Kiss, Hungary	81.24m (266' 6")
2000 Szymon Ziolkowski, Poland	80.02m (262' 6")
2004 Koji Murofushi, Japan	82.91m (272')
2008 Primoz Kozmus, Slovenia	82.02m (269' 1")
2012 Krisztián Pars, Hungary	80.59m (264' 5")

High Jump	Height
1896 Ellery Clark, United States	1.81m (5' 11¼")
1900 Irving Baxter, United States	1.90m (6' 2¾")
1904 Samuel Jones, United States	1.80m (5' 11")
1908 Harry Porter, United States	1.90m (6' 2¾")
1912 Alma Richards, United States	1.93m (6' 4")
1920 Richmond Landon, United States	1.94m (6' 4¼")
1924 Harold Osborn, United States	1.98m (6' 6")
1928 Robert "Bob" King, United States	1.94m (6' 4¼")
1932 Duncan McNaughton, Canada	1.97m (6' 5½")
1936 Cornelius Johnson, United States	2.03m (6' 8")
1948 John Winter, Australia	1.98m (6' 6")
1952 Walter Davis, United States	2.04m (6' 8¼")
1956 Charles Dumas, United States	2.12m (6' 11½")
1960 Robert Shavlakadze, USSR	2.16m (7' 1")
1964 Valery Brumel, USSR	2.18m (7' 1¾")
1968 Dick Fosbury, United States	2.24m (7' 4¼")
1972 Jüri Tarmak, USSR	2.23m (7' 3¾")
1976 Jacek Wszola, Poland	2.25m (7' 4½")
1980 Gerd Wessig, E. Germany	2.36m (7' 8¾")
1984 Dietmar Mögenburg, W. Germany	2.35m (7' 8½")
1988 Gennadi Avdeyenko, USSR	2.38m (7' 9¾")
1992 Javier Sotomayor, Cuba	2.34m (7' 8")
1996 Charles Austin, United States	2.39m (7' 10")*
2000 Sergey Kliugin, Russia	2.35m (7' 8½")
2004 Stefan Holm, Sweden	2.36m (7' 8¾")
2008 Andrey Silnov, Russia	2.36m (7' 8¾")
2012 Ivan Ukhov, Russia	2.38m (7' 9¾")

Javelin Throw	Dist.
1908 Eric Lemming, Sweden	54.82m (179' 10")
1912 Eric Lemming, Sweden	60.64m (198' 11")
1920 Jonni Myyrä, Finland	65.78m (215' 9¾")
1924 Jonni Myyrä, Finland	62.96m (206' 7")
1928 Erik Lundkvist, Sweden	66.60m (218' 6")
1932 Matti Järvinen, Finland	72.71m (238' 6½")
1936 Gerhard Stöck, Germany	71.84m (235' 8")
1948 Kaj Tapio Rautavaara, Finland	69.77m (228' 11")
1952 Cy Young, United States	73.78m (242' 1")
1956 Egil Danielsen, Norway	85.71m (281' 2½")
1960 Viktor Tsybulenko, USSR	84.64m (277' 8")
1964 Pauli Nevala, Finland	82.66m (271' 2")
1968 Janis Lusis, USSR	90.10m (295' 7")
1972 Klaus Wolfermann, W. Germany	90.48m (296' 10")
1976 Miklós Németh, Hungary	94.58m (310' 4")
1980 Dainis Kula, USSR	91.20m (299' 2")
1984 Arto Härkönen, Finland	86.76m (284' 8")
1988 Tapio Korjus, Finland	84.28m (276' 6")
1992 Jan Zelezny, Czechoslovakia	89.66m (294' 2")
1996 Jan Zelezny, Czech Republic	88.16m (289' 3")
2000 Jan Zelezny, Czech Republic	90.17m (295' 9½")
2004 Andreas Thorkildsen, Norway	86.50m (283' 10")
2008 Andreas Thorkildsen, Norway	90.57m (297' 1¾")
2012 Keshorn Walcott, Trinidad & Tobago	84.58m (277' 6")

Long Jump	Dist.
1896 Ellery Clark, United States	6.35m (20' 10")
1900 Alvin Kraenzlein, United States	7.18m (23' 6¾")

Long Jump	Dist.	
1904 Meyer Prinstein, United States	7.34m	(24' 1")
1908 Frank Irons, United States	7.48m	(24' 6½")
1912 Albert Gutterson, United States	7.60m	(24' 11¼")
1920 William Petersson, Sweden	7.15m	(23' 5½")
1924 William DeHart Hubbard, U.S.	7.45m	(24' 5¼")
1928 Ed Hamm, United States	7.73m	(25' 4¾")
1932 Edward Gordon, United States	7.64m	(25' ¾")
1936 Jesse Owens, United States	8.06m	(26' 5½")
1948 Willie Steele, United States	7.82m	(25' 8")
1952 Jerome Biffle, United States	7.57m	(24' 10")
1956 Gregory Bell, United States	7.83m	(25' 8¼")
1960 Ralph Boston, United States	8.12m	(26' 7¾")
1964 Lynn Davies, Great Britain	8.07m	(26' 5¾")
1968 Bob Beamon, United States	8.90m	(29' 2½")*
1972 Randy Williams, United States	8.24m	(27' ½")
1976 Arnie Robinson, United States	8.35m	(27' 4¾")
1980 Lutz Dombrowski, E. Germany	8.54m	(28' ¼")
1984 Carl Lewis, United States	8.54m	(28' ¼")
1988 Carl Lewis, United States	8.72m	(28' 7½")
1992 Carl Lewis, United States	8.67m	(28' 5½")
1996 Carl Lewis, United States	8.50m	(27' 10¾")
2000 Ivan Pedroso, Cuba	8.55m	(28' ¾")
2004 Dwight Phillips, United States	8.59m	(28' 2¼")
2008 Irving Jahir Saladino Aranda, Panama	8.34m	(27' 4¼")
2012 Greg Rutherford, Great Britain	8.31m	(27' 3¼")

Pole Vault	Height	
1896 William Welles Hoyt, United States	3.30m	(10' 10")
1900 Irving Baxter, United States	3.30m	(10' 10")
1904 Charles Dvorak, United States	3.50m	(11' 6")
1908 Edward Cooke, United States	3.71m	(12' 2")
Alfred Gilbert, United States (tie)	3.71m	(12' 2")
1912 Harry Stoddard Babcock, U.S.	3.95m	(12' 11½")
1920 Frank Foss, United States	4.09m	(13' 5")
1924 Lee Barnes, United States	3.95m	(12' 11½")
1928 Sabin Carr, United States	4.20m	(13' 9¼")
1932 Bill Miller, United States	4.31m	(14' 1¾")
1936 Earle Meadows, United States	4.35m	(14' 3¼")
1948 Guinn Smith, United States	4.30m	(14' 1¼")
1952 Robert Richards, United States	4.55m	(14' 11¼")
1956 Robert Richards, United States	4.56m	(14' 11½")
1960 Don Bragg, United States	4.70m	(15' 5")
1964 Fred Hansen, United States	5.10m	(16' 8¾")
1968 Bob Seagren, United States	5.40m	(17' 8½")
1972 Wolfgang Nordwig, E. Germany	5.50m	(18' ½")
1976 Tadeusz Slusarski, Poland	5.50m	(18' ½")
1980 Wladyslaw Kozakiewicz, Poland	5.78m	(18' 11½")
1984 Pierre Quinon, France	5.75m	(18' 10¼")
1988 Sergei Bubka, USSR	5.90m	(19' 4¼")
1992 Maksim Tarasov, Unified Team	5.80m	(19' ¼")
1996 Jean Galfione, France	5.92m	(19' 5")
2000 Nick Hysong, United States	5.90m	(19' 4¼")
2004 Timothy Mack, United States	5.95m	(19' 6¼")
2008 Steve Hooker, Australia	5.96m	(19' 6¾")
2012 Renaud Lavillenie, France	5.97m	(19' 7")*

Shot Put	Dist.	
1896 Robert Garrett, United States	11.22m	(36' 9¾")
1900 Richard Sheldon, United States	14.10m	(46' 3¼")
1904 Ralph Rose, United States	14.81m	(48' 7")
1908 Ralph Rose, United States	14.21m	(46' 7½")
1912 Pat McDonald, United States	15.34m	(50' 4")
1920 Ville Pörhölä, Finland	14.81m	(48' 7¼")
1924 Clarence "Bud" Houser, United States	14.99m	(49' 2¼")
1928 John Kuck, United States	15.87m	(52' ¾")
1932 Leo Sexton, United States	16.00m	(52' 6")
1936 Hans Woellke, Germany	16.20m	(53' 1¾")
1948 Wilbur Thompson, United States	17.12m	(56' 2")
1952 W. Parry O'Brien, United States	17.41m	(57' 1½")
1956 W. Parry O'Brien, United States	18.57m	(60' 11¼")
1960 Bill Nieder, United States	19.68m	(64' 6¾")
1964 Dallas Long, United States	20.33m	(66' 8½")

Shot Put	Dist.	
1968 Randy Matson, United States	20.54m	(67' 4¾")
1972 Wladyslaw Komar, Poland	21.18m	(69' 6")
1976 Udo Beyer, E. Germany	21.05m	(69' ¾")
1980 Vladimir Kiselyov, USSR	21.35m	(70' ½")
1984 Alessandro Andrei, Italy	21.26m	(69' 9")
1988 Ulf Timmermann, E. Germany	22.47m	(73' 8¾")*
1992 Michael Stulce, United States	21.70m	(71' 2½")
1996 Randy Barnes, United States	21.62m	(70' 11¼")
2000 Arsi Harju, Finland	21.29m	(69' 10¼")
2004 Adam Nelson, United States[1]	21.16m	(69' 5¼")
2008 Tomasz Majewski, Poland	21.51m	(70' 6¾")
2012 Tomasz Majewski, Poland	21.89m	(71' 9¾")

(1) Originally won by Yuriy Bilonog, Ukraine, who was stripped of the gold in 2012 due to doping.

Triple Jump	Dist.	
1896 James Connolly, United States	13.71m	(44' 11¾")
1900 Meyer Prinstein, United States	14.47m	(47' 5¾")
1904 Meyer Prinstein, United States	14.35m	(47' 1")
1908 Tim Ahearne, Gr. Brit.-Ireland	14.92m	(48' 11½")
1912 Gustaf Lindblom, Sweden	14.76m	(48' 5")
1920 Vilho Tuulos, Finland	14.505m	(47' 7")
1924 Anthony Winter, Australia	15.525m	(50' 11¼")
1928 Mikio Oda, Japan	15.21m	(49' 11")
1932 Chuhei Nambu, Japan	15.72m	(51' 7")
1936 Naoto Tajima, Japan	16.00m	(52' 6")
1948 Arne Ahman, Sweden	15.40m	(50' 6¼")
1952 Adhemar Ferreira da Silva, Brazil	16.22m	(53' 2¾")
1956 Adhemar Ferreira da Silva, Brazil	16.35m	(53' 7¾")
1960 Jozef Schmidt, Poland	16.81m	(55' 1½")
1964 Jozef Schmidt, Poland	16.85m	(55' 3½")
1968 Viktor Saneyev, USSR	17.39m	(57' ¾")
1972 Viktor Saneyev, USSR	17.35m	(56' 11¼")
1976 Viktor Saneyev, USSR	17.29m	(56' 8¾")
1980 Jaak Uudmäe, USSR	17.35m	(56' 11")
1984 Al Joyner, United States	17.26m	(56' 7½")
1988 Khristo Markov, Bulgaria	17.61m	(57' 9½")
1992 Mike Conley, United States	18.17m	(59' 7½")(w)
1996 Kenny Harrison, United States	18.09m	(59' 4¼")*
2000 Jonathan Edwards, Britain	17.71m	(58' 1¼")
2004 Christian Olsson, Sweden	17.79m	(58' 4½")
2008 Nelson Evora, Portugal	17.67m	(57' 11¾")
2012 Christian Taylor, United States	17.81m	(58' 5¼")

Decathlon	Points
1904 Thomas F. Kiely, Ireland	6,036
1912 Jim Thorpe, United States[1]	8,412.995
1920 Helge Lovland, Norway	6,804.355
1924 Harold Osborn, United States	7,710.775
1928 Paavo Yrjölä, Finland	8,053.29
1932 James Bausch, United States	8,462.23
1936 Glenn Morris, United States	7,900
1948 Robert Mathias, United States	7,139
1952 Robert Mathias, United States	7,887
1956 Milton Campbell, United States	7,937
1960 Rafer Johnson, United States	8,392
1964 Willi Holdorf, Germany	7,887
1968 Bill Toomey, United States	8,193
1972 Nikolai Avilov, USSR	8,454
1976 Bruce Jenner, United States	8,618
1980 Daley Thompson, Great Britain	8,495
1984 Daley Thompson, Great Britain	8,797
1988 Christian Schenk, E. Germany	8,488
1992 Robert Zmelik, Czechoslovakia	8,611
1996 Dan O'Brien, United States	8,824
2000 Erki Nool, Estonia	8,641
2004 Roman Sebrle, Czech Republic	8,893*
2008 Bryan Clay, United States	8,791
2012 Ashton Eaton, United States	8,869

Note: Event not held in 1908. (1) Thorpe had been stripped of his medal for playing pro baseball prior to the Olympics. The Intl. Olympic Committee in 1982 posthumously restored his decathlon and pentathlon gold medals.

Track and Field—Women

100-Meter Run	Time		100-Meter Run	Time
1928 Elizabeth Robinson, United States	0:12.2		1960 Wilma Rudolph, United States	0:11.0
1932 Stella Walsh, Poland[1]	0:11.9		1964 Wyomia Tyus, United States	0:11.4
1936 Helen Stephens, United States	0:11.5		1968 Wyomia Tyus, United States	0:11.08
1948 Fanny Blankers-Koen, Netherlands	0:11.9		1972 Renate Stecher, E. Germany	0:11.07
1952 Marjorie Jackson, Australia	0:11.5		1976 Annegret Richter, W. Germany	0:11.08
1956 Betty Cuthbert, Australia	0:11.5		1980 Lyudmila Kondratyeva, USSR	0:11.06

100-Meter Run

		Time
1984	Evelyn Ashford, United States	0:10:97
1988	Florence Griffith-Joyner, United States	0:10.54*
1992	Gail Devers, United States	0:10.82
1996	Gail Devers, United States	0:10.94
2000	No winner[2]	NA
2004	Yuliya Nesterenko, Belarus	0:10.93
2008	Shelly-Ann Fraser, Jamaica	0:10.78
2012	Shelly-Ann Fraser-Pryce, Jamaica	0:10.75

(1) Born Stanislawa Walasiewicz. Postmortem testing revealed Walsh possessed both male and female chromosomes. (2) Marion Jones, U.S., was stripped of her gold medal in 2007 due to doping; the Intl. Olympic Committee declined to award the medal to the runner-up, who was also suspected of doping.

200-Meter Run

		Time
1948	Fanny Blankers-Koen, Netherlands	0:24.4
1952	Marjorie Jackson, Australia	0:23.7
1956	Betty Cuthbert, Australia	0:23.4
1960	Wilma Rudolph, United States	0:24.0
1964	Edith McGuire, United States	0:23.0
1968	Irena Szewinska, Poland	0:22.5
1972	Renate Stecher, E. Germany	0:22.40
1976	Bärbel Eckert, E. Germany	0:22.37
1980	Bärbel Wöckel, E. Germany	0:22.03
1984	Valerie Brisco-Hooks, United States	0:21.81
1988	Florence Griffith-Joyner, United States	0:21.34*
1992	Gwen Torrence, United States	0:21.81
1996	Marie-Jose Perec, France	0:22.12
2000	Pauline Davis-Thompson, The Bahamas[1]	0:22.27
2004	Veronica Campbell, Jamaica	0:22.05
2008	Veronica Campbell-Brown, Jamaica	0:21.74
2012	Allyson Felix, United States	0:21.88

(1) Originally won by Marion Jones, U.S., who was stripped of the gold in 2007 due to doping.

400-Meter Run

		Time
1964	Betty Cuthbert, Australia	0:52.0
1968	Colette Besson, France	0:52.0
1972	Monika Zehrt, E. Germany	0:51.08
1976	Irena Szewinska, Poland	0:49.29
1980	Marita Koch, E. Germany	0:48.88
1984	Valerie Brisco-Hooks, United States	0:48.83
1988	Olga Bryzgina, USSR	0:48.65
1992	Marie-Jose Perec, France	0:48.83
1996	Marie-Jose Perec, France	0:48.25*
2000	Cathy Freeman, Australia	0:49.11
2004	Tonique Williams-Darling, The Bahamas	0:49.41
2008	Christine Ohuruogu, Great Britain	0:49.62
2012	Sanya Richards-Ross, United States	0:49.55

800-Meter Run

		Time
1928	Lina Radke, Germany	2:16.8
1960	Lyudmila Shevtsova, USSR	2:04.3
1964	Ann Packer, Great Britain	2:01.1
1968	Madeline Manning, United States	2:00.9
1972	Hildegard Falck, W. Germany	1:58.55
1976	Tatyana Kazankina, USSR	1:54.94
1980	Nadezhda Olizarenko, USSR	1:53.43*
1984	Doina Melinte, Romania	1:57.60
1988	Sigrun Wodars, E. Germany	1:56.10
1992	Ellen Van Langen, Netherlands	1:55.54
1996	Svetlana Masterkova, Russia	1:57.73
2000	Maria Mutola, Mozambique	1:56.15
2004	Kelly Holmes, Great Britain	1:56.38
2008	Pamela Jelimo, Kenya	1:54.87
2012	Mariya Savinova, Russia	1:56.19

1,500-Meter Run

		Time
1972	Lyudmila Bragina, USSR	4:01.04
1976	Tatyana Kazankina, USSR	4:05.48
1980	Tatyana Kazankina, USSR	3:56.06
1984	Gabriella Dorio, Italy	4:03.25
1988	Paula Ivan, Romania	3:53.96*
1992	Hassiba Boulmerka, Algeria	3:55.30
1996	Svetlana Masterkova, Russia	4:00.83
2000	Nouria Merah-Benida, Algeria	4:05.10
2004	Kelly Holmes, Great Britain	3:57.90
2008	Nancy Jebet Langat, Kenya	4:00.23
2012	Asli Cakir Alptekin, Turkey	4:10.23

3,000-Meter Run

		Time
1984	Maricica Puica, Romania	8:35.96
1988	Tatyana Samolenko, USSR	8:26.53*
1992	Elena Romanova, Unified Team	8:46.04

3,000-Meter Steeplechase

		Time
2008	Gulnara Galkina-Samitova, Russia	8:58.81*
2012	Yuliya Zaripova, Russia	9:06.72

5,000-Meter Run

		Time
1996	Wang Junxia, China	14:59.88
2000	Gabriela Szabo, Romania	14:40.79*
2004	Meseret Defar, Ethiopia	14:45.65
2008	Tirunesh Dibaba, Ethiopia	15:41.40
2012	Meseret Defar, Ethiopia	15:04.25

10,000-Meter Run

		Time
1988	Olga Boldarenko, USSR	31:05.21
1992	Derartu Tulu, Ethiopia	31:06.02
1996	Fernanda Ribeiro, Portugal	31:01.63
2000	Derartu Tulu, Ethiopia	30:17.49
2004	Xing Huina, China	30:24.36
2008	Tirunesh Dibaba, Ethiopia	29:54.66*
2012	Tirunesh Dibaba, Ethiopia	30:20.75

Marathon

		Time
1984	Joan Benoit, United States	2:24:52
1988	Rosa Mota, Portugal	2:25:40
1992	Valentina Yegorova, Unified Team	2:32:41
1996	Fatuma Roba, Ethiopia	2:26:05
2000	Naoko Takahashi, Japan	2:23:14
2004	Mizuki Noguchi, Japan	2:26:20
2008	Constantina Tomescu, Romania	2:26:44
2012	Tiki Gelana, Ethiopia	2:23:07*

4x100-Meter Relay

		Time
1928	Canada	0:48.4
1932	United States	0:46.9
1936	United States	0:46.9
1948	Netherlands	0:47.5
1952	United States	0:45.9
1956	Australia	0:44.5
1960	United States	0:44.5
1964	Poland	0:43.6
1968	United States	0:42.8
1972	West Germany	0:42.81
1976	East Germany	0:42.55
1980	East Germany	0:41.60
1984	United States	0:41.65
1988	United States	0:41.98
1992	United States	0:42.11
1996	United States	0:41.95
2000	The Bahamas	0:41.95
2004	Jamaica	0:41.73
2008	Russia	0:42.31
2012	United States	0:40.82*

4x400-Meter Relay

		Time
1972	East Germany	3:23.0
1976	East Germany	3:19.23
1980	USSR	3:20.2
1984	United States	3:18.29
1988	USSR	3:15.18*
1992	Unified Team	3:20.20
1996	United States	3:20.91
2000	United States[1]	3:22.62
2004	United States[2]	3:19.01
2008	United States	3:18.54
2012	United States	3:16.87

(1) Due to team member Marion Jones's doping, the U.S. was stripped of the victory in 2008, but Jones's teammates won an appeal in 2010 to have their medals restored. (2) Team member Crystal Cox was stripped of her gold medal due to doping.

20-Kilometer Walk

		Time
2000	Wang Liping, China	1:29:05
2004	Athanasia Tsoumeleka, Greece	1:29:12
2008	Olga Kaniskina, Russia	1:26:31
2012	Elena Lashmanova, Russia	1:25:02*

100-Meter Hurdles

		Time
1972	Annelie Ehrhardt, E. Germany	0:12.59
1976	Johanna Schaller, E. Germany	0:12.77
1980	Vera Komisova, USSR	0:12.56
1984	Benita Fitzgerald-Brown, United States	0:12.84
1988	Yordanka Donkova, Bulgaria	0:12.38
1992	Paraskevi Patoulidou, Greece	0:12.64
1996	Ludmila Engquist, Sweden	0:12.58
2000	Olga Shishigina, Kazakhstan	0:12.65
2004	Joanna Hayes, United States	0:12.37
2008	Dawn Harper, United States	0:12.54
2012	Sally Pearson, Australia	0:12.35*

400-Meter Hurdles

		Time
1984	Nawal El Moutawakel, Morocco	0:54.61
1988	Debra Flintoff-King, Australia	0:53.17
1992	Sally Gunnell, Great Britain	0:53.23

400-Meter Hurdles

		Time
1996	Deon Hemmings, Jamaica	0:52.82
2000	Irina Privalova, Russia	0:53.02
2004	Faní Halkia, Greece	0:52.82
2008	Melaine Walker, Jamaica	0:52.64*
2012	Natalya Antyukh, Russia	0:52.70

Discus Throw

		Dist.	
1928	Halina Konopacka, Poland	39.62m	(130' 0")
1932	Lillian Copeland, United States	40.58m	(133' 2")
1936	Gisela Mauermayer, Germany	47.63m	(156' 3")
1948	Micheline Ostermeyer, France	41.92m	(137' 6")
1952	Nina Ponomareva, USSR	51.42m	(168' 8")
1956	Olga Fikotová, Czechoslovakia	53.69m	(176' 1¾")
1960	Nina Ponomareva, USSR	55.10m	(180' 9")
1964	Tamara Press, USSR	57.27m	(187' 10¾")
1968	Lia Manoliu, Romania	58.28m	(191' 2")
1972	Faina Melnik, USSR	66.62m	(218' 7")
1976	Evelin Jahl, E. Germany	69.00m	(226' 4")
1980	Evelin Jahl, E. Germany	69.96m	(229' 6")
1984	Ria Stalman, Netherlands	65.36m	(214' 5")
1988	Martina Hellmann, E. Germany	72.30m	(237' 2")*
1992	Maritza Martén, Cuba	70.06m	(229' 10")
1996	Ilke Wyludda, Germany	69.66m	(228' 6")
2000	Ellina Zvereva, Belarus	68.40m	(224' 5")
2004	Natalya Sadova, Russia	67.02m	(219' 8¾")
2008	Stephanie Brown Trafton, U.S.	64.74m	(212' 4¾")
2012	Sandra Perkovič, Croatia	69.11m	(226' 9")

Hammer Throw

		Dist.	
2000	Kamila Skolimowska, Poland	71.16m	(233' 5¾")
2004	Olga Kuzenkova, Russia	75.02m	(246' 1")
2008	Aksana Miankova, Belarus	76.34m	(250' 5½")
2012	Tatyana Lysenko, Russia	78.18m	(256' 6")*

High Jump

		Height	
1928	Ethel Catherwood, Canada	1.59m	(5' 2½")
1932	Jean Shiley, United States	1.67m	(5' 5½")
1936	Ibolya Csák, Hungary	1.60m	(5' 3")
1948	Alice Coachman, United States	1.68m	(5' 6")
1952	Esther Brand, South Africa	1.67m	(5' 5¾")
1956	Mildred McDaniel, United States	1.76m	(5' 9¼")
1960	Iolanda Balas, Romania	1.85m	(6' ¾")
1964	Iolanda Balas, Romania	1.90m	(6' 2¾")
1968	Miloslava Rezková, Czech.	1.82m	(5' 11½")
1972	Ulrike Meyfarth, W. Germany	1.92m	(6' 3½")
1976	Rosemarie Ackermann, E. Germany	1.93m	(6' 4")
1980	Sara Simeoni, Italy	1.97m	(6' 5½")
1984	Ulrike Meyfarth, W. Germany	2.02m	(6' 7½")
1988	Louise Ritter, United States	2.03m	(6' 8")
1992	Heike Henkel, Germany	2.02m	(6' 7½")
1996	Stefka Kostadinova, Bulgaria	2.05m	(6' 8¾")
2000	Yelena Yelesina, Russia	2.01m	(6' 7")
2004	Yelena Slesarenko, Russia	2.06m	(6' 9")*
2008	Tia Hellebaut, Belgium	2.05m	(6' 8¾")
2012	Anna Chicherova, Russia	2.05m	(6' 8¾")

Javelin Throw

		Dist.	
1932	"Babe" Didrikson, United States	43.68m	(143' 4")
1936	Tilly Fleischer, Germany	45.18m	(148' 3")
1948	Herma Bauma, Austria	45.57m	(149' 6")
1952	Dana Zátopková, Czechoslovakia	50.47m	(165' 7")
1956	Inese Jaunzeme, USSR	53.86m	(176' 8")
1960	Elvira Ozolina, USSR	55.98m	(183' 8")
1964	Mihaela Penes, Romania	60.54m	(198' 7")
1968	Angéla Németh, Hungary	60.36m	(198' 0")
1972	Ruth Fuchs, E. Germany	63.88m	(209' 7")
1976	Ruth Fuchs, E. Germany	65.94m	(216' 4")
1980	Maria Colón, Cuba	68.40m	(224' 5")
1984	Tessa Sanderson, Great Britain	69.56m	(228' 2")
1988	Petra Felke, E. Germany	74.68m	(245' 0")

Javelin Throw

		Dist.	
1992	Silke Renk, Germany	68.34m	(224' 2")
1996	Heli Rantanen, Finland	67.94m	(222' 11")
2000	Trine Hattestad, Norway	68.91m	(226' 1")
2004	Osleidys Menendez, Cuba	71.53m	(234' 8")*
2008	Barbora Špotáková, Czech Republic	71.42m	(234' ¾")
2012	Barbora Špotáková, Czech Republic	69.55m	(228' 2¼")

Note: New records were kept after javelin was modified in 1999.

Long Jump

		Dist.	
1948	Olga Gyarmati, Hungary	5.69m	(18' 8")
1952	Yvette Williams, New Zealand	6.24m	(20' 5¼")
1956	Elzbieta Krzesinska, Poland	6.35m	(20' 10")
1960	Vera Krepkina, USSR	6.37m	(20' 10¾")
1964	Mary Rand, Great Britain	6.76m	(22' 2¼")
1968	Viorica Viscopoleanu, Romania	6.82m	(22' 4½")
1972	Heidemarie Rosendahl, W. Ger.	6.78m	(22' 3")
1976	Angela Voigt, E. Germany	6.72m	(22' ¾")
1980	Tatyana Kolpakova, USSR	7.06m	(23' 2")
1984	Anisoara Cusmir-Stanciu, Rom.	6.96m	(22' 10")
1988	Jackie Joyner-Kersee, United States	7.40m	(24' 3½")*
1992	Heike Drechsler, Germany	7.14m	(23' 5¼")
1996	Chioma Ajunwa, Nigeria	7.12m	(23' 4¼")
2000	Heike Drechsler, Germany	6.99m	(22' 11¼")
2004	Tatyana Lebedeva, Russia	7.07m	(23' 2½")
2008	Maurren Higa Maggi, Brazil	7.04m	(23' 1¼")
2012	Brittney Reese, United States	7.12m	(23' 4¼")

Pole Vault

		Height	
2000	Stacy Dragila, United States	4.60m	(15' 1")
2004	Elena Isinbaeva, Russia	4.91m	(16' 1¼')
2008	Elena Isinbaeva, Russia	5.05m	(16' 6¾")
2012	Jennifer Suhr, United States	4.75m	(15' 7")

Shot Put

		Dist.	
1948	Micheline Ostermeyer, France	13.75m	(45' 1½")
1952	Galina Zybina, USSR	15.28m	(50' 1½")
1956	Tamara Tyshkevich, USSR	16.59m	(54' 5¼")
1960	Tamara Press, USSR	17.32m	(56' 10")
1964	Tamara Press, USSR	18.14m	(59' 6¼")
1968	Margitta Gummel, E. Germany	19.61m	(64' 4")
1972	Nadezhda Chizhova, USSR	21.03m	(69' 0")
1976	Ivanka Khristova, Bulgaria	21.16m	(69' 5¼")
1980	Ilona Slupianek, E. Germany	22.41m	(73' 6¼")*
1984	Claudia Losch, W. Germany	20.48m	(67' 2")
1988	Natalya Lisovskaya, USSR	22.24m	(72' 11¼")
1992	Svetlana Krivelyova, Unified Team	21.06m	(69' 1¼")
1996	Astrid Kumbernuss, Germany	20.56m	(67' 5½")
2000	Yanina Karolchik, Belarus	20.56m	(67' 5½")
2004	Yumileidi Cumbá, Cuba	19.59m	(64' 3¼")
2008	Valerie Vili, New Zealand	20.56m	(67' 5½")
2012	Valerie Adams, New Zealand	20.70m	(67' 11")

Triple Jump

		Dist.	
1996	Inessa Kravets, Ukraine	15.33m	(50' 3½")
2000	Tereza Marinova, Bulgaria	15.20m	(49' 10½")
2004	Francoise Mbango Etone, Cameroon	15.30m	(50' 2¼")
2008	Francoise Mbango Etone, Cameroon	15.39m	(50' 6")*
2012	Olga Rypakova, Kazakhstan	14.98m	(49' 1¾")

Heptathlon

		Points
1984	Glynis Nunn, Australia	6,390
1988	Jackie Joyner-Kersee, United States	7,291*
1992	Jackie Joyner-Kersee, United States	7,044
1996	Ghada Shouaa, Syria	6,780
2000	Denise Lewis, Great Britain	6,584
2004	Carolina Kluft, Sweden	6,952
2008	Nataliia Dobrynska, Ukraine	6,733
2012	Jessica Ennis, Great Britain	6,955

Paralympic Games

The first Olympic Games for athletes with disabilities were held in Rome after the 1960 Summer Olympics; use of the name "paralympic" began with the 1964 games in Tokyo. The Paralympics are held by the Olympic host country in the same year and usually the same city and venue or venues. A goal of the Paralympics is to provide elite competition for athletes with functional disabilities that prevent their involvement in the Olympics. In 1976, the first Winter Paralympics were held in Ornskoldsvik, Sweden.

The XI Paralympic Winter Games were held Mar. 7-16, 2014, in Sochi, Russia. More than 500 athletes from 45 nations competed in five sports. Russia dominated the total medal count with 80, followed by Ukraine, with 25 medals, and the U.S., with 18. More than 4,250 athletes from a record 164 countries met at the XIV Paralympic Summer Games, held Aug. 29-Sept. 9, 2012, in London, England, UK. A total of 503 gold medals were awarded in 20 sports. China claimed 231 medals, nearly twice as many as host country Great Britain, which collected 120 medals. Russia finished third with 102 medals, just ahead of the U.S., in fourth with 98.

COLLEGE SPORTS

COLLEGE BASKETBALL

2014 Men's NCAA Tournament: UConn Beats Kentucky

The Univ. of Connecticut Huskies defeated the Univ. of Kentucky Wildcats, 60-54, in Arlington, TX, to claim the NCAA Men's Division I national basketball title Apr. 7, 2014. The championship game was the lowest-seed matchup in NCAA history, with seventh-seed UConn, coached by Kevin Ollie, facing off against eighth-seed Kentucky, coached by John Calipari. Shabazz Napier, who had played on UConn's 2011 championship team as a freshman, led the Huskies with 22 points and was named the Final Four's most outstanding player.

NCAA Men's Basketball Division I Champions, 1943-2014

Year	Champion	Winning coach	Final opponent	Score	Most outstanding player	Site
1943	Wyoming	Everett Shelton	Georgetown	46-34	Ken Sailors, Wyoming	New York, NY
1944	Utah	Vadal Peterson	Dartmouth	42-40[1]	Arnold Ferrin, Utah	New York, NY
1945	Oklahoma St.[2]	Henry Iba	NYU	49-45	Bob Kurland, Oklahoma St.	New York, NY
1946	Oklahoma St.[2]	Henry Iba	North Carolina	43-40	Bob Kurland, Oklahoma St.	New York, NY
1947	Holy Cross	Alvin Julian	Oklahoma	58-47	George Kaftan, Holy Cross	New York, NY
1948	Kentucky	Adolph Rupp	Baylor	58-42	Alex Groza, Kentucky	New York, NY
1949	Kentucky	Adolph Rupp	Oklahoma St.	46-36	Alex Groza, Kentucky	Seattle, WA
1950	CCNY	Nat Holman	Bradley	71-68	Irwin Dambrot, CCNY	New York, NY
1951	Kentucky	Adolph Rupp	Kansas St.	68-58	Bill Spivey, Kentucky	Minneapolis, MN
1952	Kansas	Forrest Allen	St. John's (NY)	80-63	Clyde Lovellette, Kansas	Seattle, WA
1953	Indiana	Branch McCracken	Kansas	69-68	B. H. Born, Kansas	Kansas City, MO
1954	La Salle	Kenneth Loeffler	Bradley	92-76	Tom Gola, La Salle	Kansas City, MO
1955	San Francisco	Phil Woolpert	La Salle	77-63	Bill Russell, San Francisco	Kansas City, MO
1956	San Francisco	Phil Woolpert	Iowa	83-71	Hal Lear, Temple	Evanston, IL
1957	North Carolina	Frank McGuire	Kansas	54-53[1]	Wilt Chamberlain, Kansas	Kansas City, MO
1958	Kentucky	Adolph Rupp	Seattle	84-72	Elgin Baylor, Seattle	Louisville, KY
1959	California	Pete Newell	West Virginia	71-70	Jerry West, West Virginia	Louisville, KY
1960	Ohio St.	Fred Taylor	California	75-55	Jerry Lucas, Ohio St.	San Francisco, CA
1961	Cincinnati	Edwin Jucker	Ohio St.	70-65[1]	Jerry Lucas, Ohio St.	Kansas City, MO
1962	Cincinnati	Edwin Jucker	Ohio St.	71-59	Paul Hogue, Cincinnati	Louisville, KY
1963	Loyola (IL)	George Ireland	Cincinnati	60-58[1]	Art Heyman, Duke	Louisville, KY
1964	UCLA	John Wooden	Duke	98-83	Walt Hazzard, UCLA	Kansas City, MO
1965	UCLA	John Wooden	Michigan	91-80	Bill Bradley, Princeton	Portland, OR
1966	Texas-El Paso[3]	Don Haskins	Kentucky	72-65	Jerry Chambers, Utah	College Park, MD
1967	UCLA	John Wooden	Dayton	79-64	Lew Alcindor[4], UCLA	Louisville, KY
1968	UCLA	John Wooden	North Carolina	78-55	Lew Alcindor[4], UCLA	Los Angeles, CA
1969	UCLA	John Wooden	Purdue	92-72	Lew Alcindor[4], UCLA	Louisville, KY
1970	UCLA	John Wooden	Jacksonville	80-69	Sidney Wicks, UCLA	College Park, MD
1971	UCLA	John Wooden	Villanova*	68-62	Howard Porter, Villanova*	Houston, TX
1972	UCLA	John Wooden	Florida St.	81-76	Bill Walton, UCLA	Los Angeles, CA
1973	UCLA	John Wooden	Memphis[5]	87-66	Bill Walton, UCLA	St. Louis, MO
1974	North Carolina St.	Norm Sloan	Marquette	76-64	David Thompson, NC State	Greensboro, NC
1975	UCLA	John Wooden	Kentucky	92-85	Richard Washington, UCLA	San Diego, CA
1976	Indiana	Bob Knight	Michigan	86-68	Kent Benson, Indiana	Philadelphia, PA
1977	Marquette	Al McGuire	North Carolina	67-59	Butch Lee, Marquette	Atlanta, GA
1978	Kentucky	Joe Hall	Duke	94-88	Jack Givens, Kentucky	St. Louis, MO
1979	Michigan St.	Jud Heathcote	Indiana St.	75-64	Magic Johnson, Michigan St.	Salt Lake City, UT
1980	Louisville	Denny Crum	UCLA*	59-54	Darrell Griffith, Louisville	Indianapolis, IN
1981	Indiana	Bob Knight	North Carolina	63-50	Isiah Thomas, Indiana	Philadelphia, PA
1982	North Carolina	Dean Smith	Georgetown	63-62	James Worthy, N. Carolina	New Orleans, LA
1983	North Carolina St.	Jim Valvano	Houston	54-52	Hakeem Olajuwon, Houston	Albuquerque, NM
1984	Georgetown	John Thompson	Houston	84-75	Patrick Ewing, Georgetown	Seattle, WA
1985	Villanova	Rollie Massimino	Georgetown	66-64	Ed Pinckney, Villanova	Lexington, KY
1986	Louisville	Denny Crum	Duke	72-69	Pervis Ellison, Louisville	Dallas, TX
1987	Indiana	Bob Knight	Syracuse	74-73	Keith Smart, Indiana	New Orleans, LA
1988	Kansas	Larry Brown	Oklahoma	83-79	Danny Manning, Kansas	Kansas City, MO
1989	Michigan	Steve Fisher	Seton Hall	80-79[1]	Glen Rice, Michigan	Seattle, WA
1990	UNLV	Jerry Tarkanian	Duke	103-73	Anderson Hunt, UNLV	Denver, CO
1991	Duke	Mike Krzyzewski	Kansas	72-65	Christian Laettner, Duke	Indianapolis, IN
1992	Duke	Mike Krzyzewski	Michigan	71-51	Bobby Hurley, Duke	Minneapolis, MN
1993	North Carolina	Dean Smith	Michigan	77-71	Donald Williams, N. Carolina	New Orleans, LA
1994	Arkansas	Nolan Richardson	Duke	76-72	Corliss Williamson, Arkansas	Charlotte, NC
1995	UCLA	Jim Harrick	Arkansas	89-78	Ed O'Bannon, UCLA	Seattle, WA
1996	Kentucky	Rick Pitino	Syracuse	76-67	Tony Delk, Kentucky	E. Rutherford, NJ
1997	Arizona	Lute Olson	Kentucky	84-79[1]	Miles Simon, Arizona	Indianapolis, IN
1998	Kentucky	Tubby Smith	Utah	78-69	Jeff Sheppard, Kentucky	San Antonio, TX
1999	Connecticut	Jim Calhoun	Duke	77-74	Richard Hamilton, Connecticut	St. Petersburg, FL
2000	Michigan St.	Tom Izzo	Florida	89-76	Mateen Cleaves, Michigan St.	Indianapolis, IN
2001	Duke	Mike Krzyzewski	Arizona	82-72	Shane Battier, Duke	Minneapolis, MN
2002	Maryland	Gary Williams	Indiana	64-52	Juan Dixon, Maryland	Atlanta, GA
2003	Syracuse	Jim Boeheim	Kansas	81-78	Carmelo Anthony, Syracuse	New Orleans, LA
2004	Connecticut	Jim Calhoun	Georgia Tech	82-73	Emeka Okafor, Connecticut	San Antonio, TX
2005	North Carolina	Roy Williams	Illinois	75-70	Sean May, N. Carolina	St. Louis, MO
2006	Florida	Billy Donovan	UCLA	73-57	Joakim Noah, Florida	Indianapolis, IN
2007	Florida	Billy Donovan	Ohio St.	84-75	Corey Brewer, Florida	Atlanta, GA
2008	Kansas	Bill Self	Memphis	75-68[1]	Mario Chalmers, Kansas	San Antonio, TX
2009	North Carolina	Roy Williams	Michigan St.	89-72	Wayne Ellington, N. Carolina	Detroit, MI
2010	Duke	Mike Krzyzewski	Butler	61-59	Kyle Singler, Duke	Indianapolis, IN
2011	Connecticut	Jim Calhoun	Butler	53-41	Kemba Walker, Connecticut	Houston, TX
2012	Kentucky	John Calipari	Kansas	67-59	Anthony Davis, Kentucky	New Orleans, LA
2013	Louisville	Rick Pitino	Michigan	82-76	Luke Hancock, Louisville	Atlanta, GA
2014	Connecticut	Kevin Ollie	Kentucky	60-54	Shabazz Napier, Connecticut	Arlington, TX

*Declared ineligible after the tournament. (1) Overtime. (2) Then known as Oklahoma A&M. (3) Then known as Texas Western. (4) Changed name to Kareem Abdul-Jabbar in 1971. (5) Then known as Memphis State.

2014 Men's NCAA Basketball Tournament

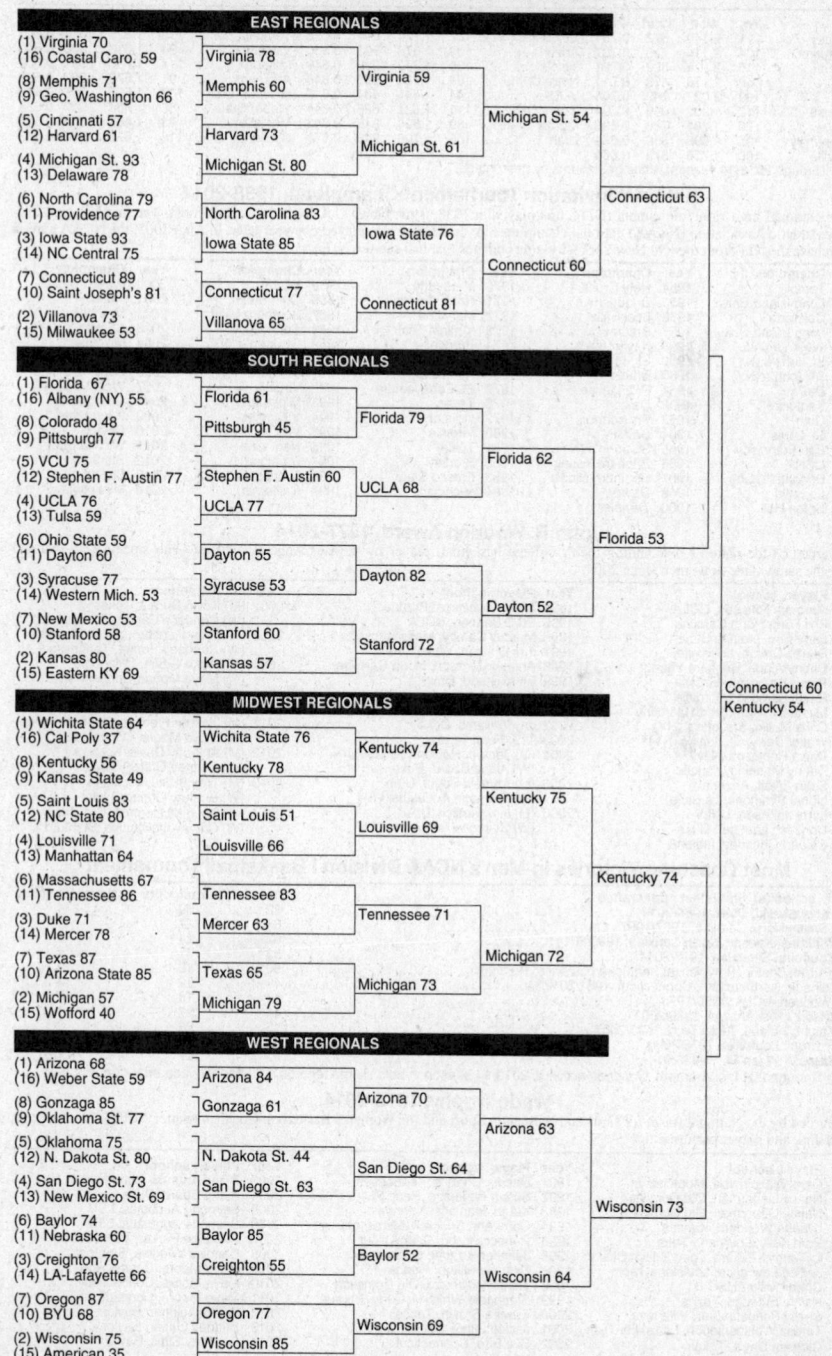

EAST REGIONALS

(1) Virginia 70
(16) Coastal Caro. 59
— Virginia 78

(8) Memphis 71
(9) Geo. Washington 66
— Memphis 60

Virginia 59

(5) Cincinnati 57
(12) Harvard 61
— Harvard 73

(4) Michigan St. 93
(13) Delaware 78
— Michigan St. 80

Michigan St. 61

Michigan St. 54

(6) North Carolina 79
(11) Providence 77
— North Carolina 83

(3) Iowa State 93
(14) NC Central 75
— Iowa State 85

Iowa State 76

Connecticut 63

(7) Connecticut 89
(10) Saint Joseph's 81
— Connecticut 77

(2) Villanova 73
(15) Milwaukee 53
— Villanova 65

Connecticut 81

Connecticut 60

SOUTH REGIONALS

(1) Florida 67
(16) Albany (NY) 55
— Florida 61

(8) Colorado 48
(9) Pittsburgh 77
— Pittsburgh 45

Florida 79

(5) VCU 75
(12) Stephen F. Austin 77
— Stephen F. Austin 60

(4) UCLA 76
(13) Tulsa 59
— UCLA 77

UCLA 68

Florida 62

(6) Ohio State 59
(11) Dayton 60
— Dayton 55

(3) Syracuse 77
(14) Western Mich. 53
— Syracuse 53

Dayton 82

Florida 53

(7) New Mexico 53
(10) Stanford 58
— Stanford 60

(2) Kansas 80
(15) Eastern KY 69
— Kansas 57

Stanford 72

Dayton 52

MIDWEST REGIONALS

(1) Wichita State 64
(16) Cal Poly 37
— Wichita State 76

(8) Kentucky 56
(9) Kansas State 49
— Kentucky 78

Kentucky 74

(5) Saint Louis 83
(12) NC State 80
— Saint Louis 51

(4) Louisville 71
(13) Manhattan 64
— Louisville 66

Louisville 69

Kentucky 75

(6) Massachusetts 67
(11) Tennessee 86
— Tennessee 83

(3) Duke 71
(14) Mercer 78
— Mercer 63

Tennessee 71

Kentucky 74

(7) Texas 87
(10) Arizona State 85
— Texas 65

(2) Michigan 57
(15) Wofford 40
— Michigan 79

Michigan 73

Michigan 72

WEST REGIONALS

(1) Arizona 68
(16) Weber State 59
— Arizona 84

(8) Gonzaga 85
(9) Oklahoma St. 77
— Gonzaga 61

Arizona 70

(5) Oklahoma 75
(12) N. Dakota St. 80
— N. Dakota St. 44

(4) San Diego St. 73
(13) New Mexico St. 69
— San Diego St. 63

San Diego St. 64

Arizona 63

(6) Baylor 74
(11) Nebraska 60
— Baylor 85

(3) Creighton 76
(14) LA-Lafayette 66
— Creighton 55

Baylor 52

Wisconsin 73

(7) Oregon 87
(10) BYU 68
— Oregon 77

(2) Wisconsin 75
(15) American 35
— Wisconsin 85

Wisconsin 69

Wisconsin 64

Connecticut 60
Kentucky 54

All-Time Winningest Men's NCAA Division I Basketball Teams

Team	Yrs	Won	Lost	Pct.	Team	Yrs	Won	Lost	Pct.	Team	Yrs	Won	Lost	Pct.
Kentucky	111	2,140	672	0.761	St. John's (NY)	107	1,774	944	0.653	Temple	118	1,823	1,014	0.643
N. Carolina	104	2,114	755	0.737	Arizona	109	1,678	905	0.650	Villanova	94	1,613	908	0.640
Kansas	116	2,126	822	0.721	Illinois	109	1,710	925	0.649	Indiana	114	1,736	981	0.639
UNLV	56	1,178	479	0.711	Notre Dame	109	1,763	966	0.646	Arkansas	91	1,578	892	0.639
Duke	109	2,027	849	0.705	VCU	44	844	464	0.645	Missouri State	102	1,595	905	0.638
Syracuse	113	1,902	838	0.694	Connecticut	111	1,621	896	0.644	Weber State	52	964	547	0.638
UCLA	95	1,781	788	0.693	Murray State	89	1,524	846	0.643	Memphis	93	1,465	848	0.633
W. Kentucky	95	1,695	856	0.664	Utah	106	1,706	948	0.643	Cincinnati	113	1,673	970	0.633
Louisville	100	1,728	875	0.664										

Note: Through 2013-14 season; winningest teams by percentage.

National Invitation Tournament Champions, 1938-2014

The National Invitation Tournament (NIT), first played in 1938, is the oldest U.S. basketball tournament. The first National Collegiate Athletic Association (NCAA) national championship tournament was played one year later. In Aug. 2005, the NCAA agreed to purchase the NIT from the five New York City-area colleges that had run the NIT.

Year	Champion	Year	Champion	Year	Champion	Year	Champion	Year	Champion
1938	Temple	1954	Holy Cross	1970	Marquette	1985	UCLA	2000	Wake Forest
1939	Long Island Univ.	1955	Duquesne	1971	North Carolina	1986	Ohio State	2001	Tulsa
1940	Colorado	1956	Louisville	1972	Maryland	1987	Southern Miss	2002	Memphis
1941	Long Island Univ.	1957	Bradley	1973	Virginia Tech	1988	Connecticut	2003	St. John's (NY)
1942	West Virginia	1958	Xavier (OH)	1974	Purdue	1989	St. John's (NY)	2004	Michigan
1943	St. John's (NY)	1959	St. John's (NY)	1975	Princeton	1990	Vanderbilt	2005	South Carolina
1944	St. John's (NY)	1960	Bradley	1976	Kentucky	1991	Stanford	2006	South Carolina
1945	DePaul	1961	Providence	1977	St. Bonaventure	1992	Virginia	2007	West Virginia
1946	Kentucky	1962	Dayton	1978	Texas	1993	Minnesota	2008	Ohio State
1947	Utah	1963	Providence	1979	Indiana	1994	Villanova	2009	Penn State
1948	St. Louis	1964	Bradley	1980	Virginia	1995	Virginia Tech	2010	Dayton
1949	San Francisco	1965	St. John's (NY)	1981	Tulsa	1996	Nebraska	2011	Wichita State
1950	CCNY	1966	Brigham Young	1982	Bradley	1997	Michigan	2012	Stanford
1951	Brigham Young	1967	Southern Illinois	1983	Fresno State	1998	Minnesota	2013	Baylor
1952	La Salle	1968	Dayton	1984	Michigan	1999	California	2014	Minnesota
1953	Seton Hall	1969	Temple						

John R. Wooden Award, 1977-2014

Awarded to the nation's outstanding men's college basketball player by the Los Angeles Athletic Club since 1977; awarded under the same name to women since 2004.

Year	Player, school	Year	Player, school	Year	Player, school
1977	Marques Johnson, UCLA	1994	Glenn Robinson, Purdue	2007	(M) Kevin Durant, Texas
1978	Phil Ford, North Carolina	1995	Ed O'Bannon, UCLA		(W) Candace Parker, Tennessee
1979	Larry Bird, Indiana State	1996	Marcus Camby, Massachusetts	2008	(M) Tyler Hansbrough, N. Carolina
1980	Darrell Griffith, Louisville	1997	Tim Duncan, Wake Forest		(W) Candace Parker, Tennessee
1981	Danny Ainge, Brigham Young	1998	Antawn Jamison, North Carolina	2009	(M) Blake Griffin, Oklahoma
1982	Ralph Sampson, Virginia	1999	Elton Brand, Duke		(W) Maya Moore, Connecticut
1983	Ralph Sampson, Virginia	2000	Kenyon Martin, Cincinnati	2010	(M) Evan Turner, Ohio State
1984	Michael Jordan, North Carolina	2001	Shane Battier, Duke		(W) Tina Charles, Connecticut
1985	Chris Mullin, St. John's (NY)	2002	Jay Williams, Duke	2011	(M) Jimmer Fredette, Brigham Young
1986	Walter Berry, St. John's (NY)	2003	T. J. Ford, Texas		(W) Maya Moore, Connecticut
1987	David Robinson, Navy	2004	(M) Jameer Nelson, St. Joseph's	2012	(M) Anthony Davis, Kentucky
1988	Danny Manning, Kansas		(W) Alana Beard, Duke		(W) Brittney Griner, Baylor
1989	Sean Elliott, Arizona	2005	(M) Andrew Bogut, Utah	2013	(M) Trey Burke, Michigan
1990	Lionel Simmons, La Salle		(W) Seimone Augustus, LSU		(W) Brittney Griner, Baylor
1991	Larry Johnson, UNLV	2006	(M) J. J. Redick, Duke	2014	(M) Doug McDermott, Creighton
1992	Christian Laettner, Duke		(W) Seimone Augustus, LSU		(W) Chiney Ogwumike, Stanford
1993	Calbert Cheaney, Indiana				

Most Coaching Victories in Men's NCAA Division I Basketball Tournament

Coach, school(s), first/latest appearance	Wins	Tournaments	Championships
Mike Krzyzewski; Duke, 1984/2014	82	30	4
Dean Smith, North Carolina, 1967/1997	65	27	2
Roy Williams; Kansas, North Carolina; 1990/2014	63	24	2
Jim Boeheim, Syracuse, 1977/2014	53	31	1
Rick Pitino; Boston, Providence, Kentucky, Louisville; 1983/2014	50	19	2
Jim Calhoun; Northeastern, Connecticut; 1981/2012	49	22	3
John Wooden, UCLA, 1950/1975	47	16	10
Lute Olson; Iowa, Arizona; 1979/2007	46	27	1
Bob Knight; Indiana, Texas Tech; 1973/2007	45	28	3
Denny Crum, Louisville, 1972/2000	42	23	2
Tom Izzo, Michigan St., 1998/2014	42	17	1

Note: Through 2014 tournament. Coaches active in 2013-14 season in bold. Some records adjusted for vacated victories.

Wade Trophy, 1978-2014

Awarded by the National Assn. for Girls and Women in Sport and the Women's Basketball Coaches Assn. (WBCA) for character, leadership, and player performance.

Year	Player, school	Year	Player, school	Year	Player, school
1978	Carol Blazejowski, Montclair St.	1991	Daedra Charles, Tennessee	2003	Diana Taurasi, Connecticut
1979	Nancy Lieberman, Old Dominion	1992	Susan Robinson, Penn St.	2004	Alana Beard, Duke
1980	Nancy Lieberman, Old Dominion	1993	Karen Jennings, Nebraska	2005	Seimone Augustus, LSU
1981	Lynette Woodard, Kansas	1994	Carol Ann Shudlick, Minnesota	2006	Seimone Augustus, LSU
1982	Pam Kelly, Louisiana Tech	1995	Rebecca Lobo, Connecticut	2007	Candace Parker, Tennessee
1983	LaTaunya Pollard, Long Beach St.	1996	Jennifer Rizzotti, Connecticut	2008	Candice Wiggins, Stanford
1984	Janice Lawrence, Louisiana Tech	1997	DeLisha Milton, Florida	2009	Maya Moore, Connecticut
1985	Cheryl Miller, USC	1998	Ticha Penicheiro, Old Dominion	2010	Maya Moore, Connecticut
1986	Kamie Ethridge, Texas	1999	Stephanie White-McCarty, Purdue	2011	Maya Moore, Connecticut
1987	Shelly Pennefeather, Villanova	2000	Edwina Brown, Texas	2012	Brittney Griner, Baylor
1988	Teresa Weatherspoon, Louisiana Tech	2001	Jackie Stiles, SW Missouri St.	2013	Brittney Griner, Baylor
1989	Clarissa Davis, Texas	2002	Sue Bird, Connecticut	2014	Odyssey Sims, Baylor
1990	Jennifer Azzi, Stanford				

2014 Women's NCAA Basketball Tournament

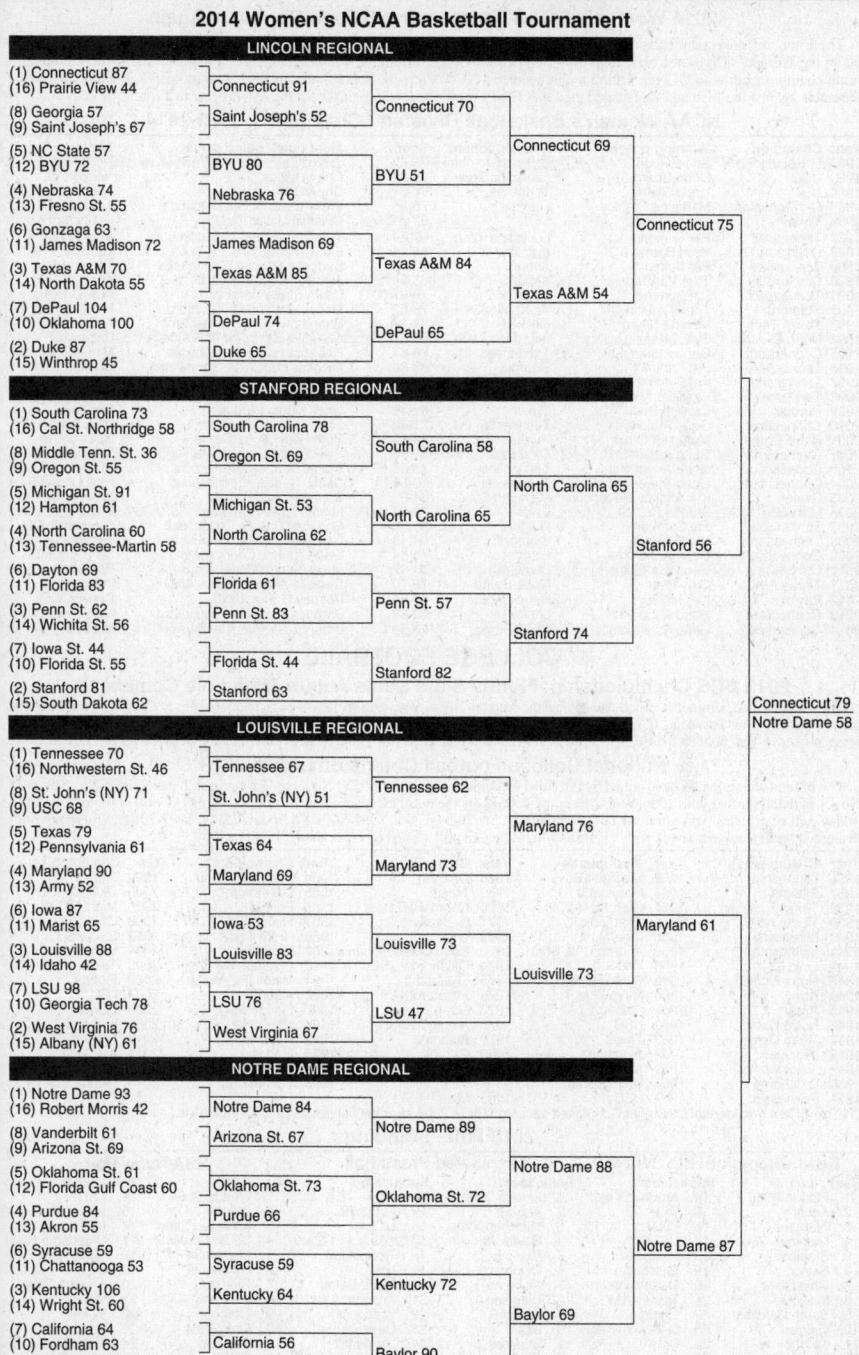

LINCOLN REGIONAL

(1) Connecticut 87
(16) Prairie View 44
Connecticut 91

(8) Georgia 57
(9) Saint Joseph's 67
Saint Joseph's 52
Connecticut 70

Connecticut 69

(5) NC State 57
(12) BYU 72
BYU 80

(4) Nebraska 74
(13) Fresno St. 55
Nebraska 76
BYU 51

Connecticut 75

(6) Gonzaga 63
(11) James Madison 72
James Madison 69

(3) Texas A&M 70
(14) North Dakota 55
Texas A&M 85
Texas A&M 84

Texas A&M 54

(7) DePaul 104
(10) Oklahoma 100
DePaul 74

(2) Duke 87
(15) Winthrop 45
Duke 65
DePaul 65

STANFORD REGIONAL

(1) South Carolina 73
(16) Cal St. Northridge 58
South Carolina 78

(8) Middle Tenn. St. 36
(9) Oregon St. 55
Oregon St. 69
South Carolina 58

North Carolina 65

(5) Michigan St. 91
(12) Hampton 61
Michigan St. 53

(4) North Carolina 60
(13) Tennessee-Martin 58
North Carolina 62
North Carolina 65

Stanford 56

(6) Dayton 69
(11) Florida 83
Florida 61

(3) Penn St. 62
(14) Wichita St. 56
Penn St. 83
Penn St. 57

Stanford 74

(7) Iowa St. 44
(10) Florida St. 55
Florida St. 44

(2) Stanford 81
(15) South Dakota 62
Stanford 63
Stanford 82

Connecticut 79
Notre Dame 58

LOUISVILLE REGIONAL

(1) Tennessee 70
(16) Northwestern St. 46
Tennessee 67

(8) St. John's (NY) 71
(9) USC 68
St. John's (NY) 51
Tennessee 62

Maryland 76

(5) Texas 79
(12) Pennsylvania 61
Texas 64

(4) Maryland 90
(13) Army 52
Maryland 69
Maryland 73

Maryland 61

(6) Iowa 87
(11) Marist 65
Iowa 53

(3) Louisville 88
(14) Idaho 42
Louisville 83
Louisville 73

Louisville 73

(7) LSU 98
(10) Georgia Tech 78
LSU 76

(2) West Virginia 76
(15) Albany (NY) 61
West Virginia 67
LSU 47

NOTRE DAME REGIONAL

(1) Notre Dame 93
(16) Robert Morris 42
Notre Dame 84

(8) Vanderbilt 61
(9) Arizona St. 69
Arizona St. 67
Notre Dame 89

Notre Dame 88

(5) Oklahoma St. 61
(12) Florida Gulf Coast 60
Oklahoma St. 73

(4) Purdue 84
(13) Akron 55
Purdue 66
Oklahoma St. 72

Notre Dame 87

(6) Syracuse 59
(11) Chattanooga 53
Syracuse 59

(3) Kentucky 106
(14) Wright St. 60
Kentucky 64
Kentucky 72

Baylor 69

(7) California 64
(10) Fordham 63
California 56

(2) Baylor 87
(15) Western Kentucky 74
Baylor 75
Baylor 90

2014 Women's NCAA Tournament: UConn Conquers Again

The Univ. of Connecticut Huskies Apr. 8, 2014, dominated the Notre Dame Fighting Irish in a 79-58 victory in Nashville, TN, to claim the Women's Division I basketball title. Head coach Geno Auriemma, who has never lost a national title game, claimed his ninth championship with UConn, setting a new women's NCAA record. Sophomore Breanna Stewart scored 21 points with nine rebounds against the Irish and was named the Final Four's most outstanding player for the second year in a row.

NCAA Women's Basketball Division I Champions, 1982-2014

Year	Champion	Winning coach	Final opponent	Score	Most outstanding player	Site
1982	Louisiana Tech	Sonja Hogg	Cheyney	76-62	Janice Lawrence, LA Tech	Norfolk, VA
1983	USC	Linda Sharp	Louisiana Tech	69-67	Cheryl Miller, USC	Norfolk, VA
1984	USC	Linda Sharp	Tennessee	72-61	Cheryl Miller, USC	Los Angeles, CA
1985	Old Dominion	Marianne Stanley	Georgia	70-65	Tracy Claxton, Old Dominion	Austin, TX
1986	Texas	Jody Conradt	USC	97-81	Clarissa Davis, Texas	Lexington, KY
1987	Tennessee	Pat Summitt	Louisiana Tech	67-44	Tonya Edwards, Tennessee	Austin, TX
1988	Louisiana Tech	Leon Barmore	Auburn	56-54	Erica Westbrooks, LA Tech	Tacoma, WA
1989	Tennessee	Pat Summitt	Auburn	76-60	Bridgette Gordon, Tennessee	Tacoma, WA
1990	Stanford	Tara VanDerveer	Auburn	88-81	Jennifer Azzi, Stanford	Knoxville, TN
1991	Tennessee	Pat Summitt	Virginia	70-67 (OT)	Dawn Staley, Virginia	New Orleans, LA
1992	Stanford	Tara VanDerveer	W. Kentucky	78-62	Molly Goodenbour, Stanford	Los Angeles, CA
1993	Texas Tech	Marsha Sharp	Ohio St.	84-82	Sheryl Swoopes, Texas Tech	Atlanta, GA
1994	North Carolina	Sylvia Hatchell	Louisiana Tech	60-59	Charlotte Smith, North Carolina	Richmond, VA
1995	Connecticut	Geno Auriemma	Tennessee	70-64	Rebecca Lobo, Connecticut	Minneapolis, MN
1996	Tennessee	Pat Summitt	Georgia	83-65	Michelle Marciniak, Tennessee	Charlotte, NC
1997	Tennessee	Pat Summitt	Old Dominion	68-59	Chamique Holdsclaw, Tennessee	Cincinnati, OH
1998	Tennessee	Pat Summitt	Louisiana Tech	93-75	Chamique Holdsclaw, Tennessee	Kansas City, MO
1999	Purdue	Carolyn Peck	Duke	62-45	Ukari Figgs, Purdue	San Jose, CA
2000	Connecticut	Geno Auriemma	Tennessee	71-52	Shea Ralph, Connecticut	Philadelphia, PA
2001	Notre Dame	Muffet McGraw	Purdue	68-66	Ruth Riley, Notre Dame	St. Louis, MO
2002	Connecticut	Geno Auriemma	Oklahoma	82-70	Swin Cash, Connecticut	San Antonio, TX
2003	Connecticut	Geno Auriemma	Tennessee	73-68	Diana Taurasi, Connecticut	Atlanta, GA
2004	Connecticut	Geno Auriemma	Tennessee	70-61	Diana Taurasi, Connecticut	New Orleans, LA
2005	Baylor	Kim Mulkey-Robertson	Michigan State	84-62	Sophia Young, Baylor	Indianapolis, IN
2006	Maryland	Brenda Frese	Duke	78-75 (OT)	Laura Harper, Maryland	Boston, MA
2007	Tennessee	Pat Summitt	Rutgers	59-46	Candace Parker, Tennessee	Cleveland, OH
2008	Tennessee	Pat Summitt	Stanford	64-48	Candace Parker, Tennessee	Tampa Bay, FL
2009	Connecticut	Geno Auriemma	Louisville	76-54	Tina Charles, Connecticut	St. Louis, MO
2010	Connecticut	Geno Auriemma	Stanford	53-47	Maya Moore, Connecticut	San Antonio, TX
2011	Texas A&M	Gary Blair	Notre Dame	76-70	Danielle Adams, Texas A&M	Indianapolis, IN
2012	Baylor	Kim Mulkey	Notre Dame	80-61	Brittney Griner, Baylor	Denver, CO
2013	Connecticut	Geno Auriemma	Louisville	93-60	Breanna Stewart, Connecticut	New Orleans, LA
2014	Connecticut	Geno Auriemma	Notre Dame	79-58	Breanna Stewart, Connecticut	Nashville, TN

COLLEGE FOOTBALL

2013 BCS Championship: Florida State Stuns Auburn With Late Comeback

The Florida State Seminoles rallied late against the Auburn Tigers, 34-31, to win the Bowl Championship Series (BCS) national title game Jan. 6, 2014, in Pasadena, CA. With the comeback win, the Atlantic Coast Conference's Florida State ended the Southeastern Conference's seven-year hold on the BCS title. It was the 16th and final BCS title game (to be replaced by a four-game playoff next season).

National College Football Champions, 1936-2013

The official champion, as determined by the Bowl Championship Series (BCS) National Championship game (BCS No. 1 vs. BCS No. 2), is listed starting with 2006. Years preceding 2006 show the unofficial champion, as selected by the AP poll of writers and USA Today poll of coaches (sponsored by UPI until 1990; USA Today/CNN, 1991-96; USA Today/ESPN, 1997-2004). Where the polls disagreed, both teams are listed with AP winner first. The AP poll started in 1936, the UPI poll in 1950.

Year	Champion(s)	Year	Champion(s)	Year	Champion(s)	Year	Champion(s)	Year	Champion(s)
1936	Minnesota	1952	Michigan St.	1968	Ohio St.	1984	Brigham Young	1999	Florida St.
1937	Pittsburgh	1953	Maryland	1969	Texas	1985	Oklahoma	2000	Oklahoma
1938	Texas Christian	1954	Ohio St./UCLA	1970	Nebraska/Texas	1986	Penn St.	2001	Miami (FL)
1939	Texas A&M	1955	Oklahoma	1971	Nebraska	1987	Miami (FL)	2002	Ohio St.
1940	Minnesota	1956	Oklahoma	1972	USC	1988	Notre Dame	2003	LSU/USC
1941	Minnesota	1957	Auburn/Ohio St.	1973	Notre Dame/Alabama	1989	Miami (FL)	2004	Vacated[1]
1942	Ohio St.	1958	LSU	1974	Oklahoma/USC	1990	Colorado/GA Tech	2005	Texas
1943	Notre Dame	1959	Syracuse	1975	Oklahoma	1991	Miami (FL)/Wash.	2006	Florida
1944	Army	1960	Minnesota	1976	Pittsburgh	1992	Alabama	2007	LSU
1945	Army	1961	Alabama	1977	Notre Dame	1993	Florida St.	2008	Florida
1946	Notre Dame	1962	USC	1978	Alabama/USC	1994	Nebraska	2009	Alabama
1947	Notre Dame	1963	Texas	1979	Alabama	1995	Nebraska	2010	Auburn
1948	Michigan	1964	Alabama	1980	Georgia	1996	Florida	2011	Alabama
1949	Notre Dame	1965	Alabama/Mich. St.	1981	Clemson	1997	Mich./Nebraska	2012	Alabama
1950	Oklahoma	1966	Notre Dame	1982	Penn St.	1998	Tennessee	2013	Florida St.
1951	Tennessee	1967	USC	1983	Miami (FL)				

(1) The BCS's Presidential Oversight Committee vacated USC's 2004 championship due to rules violations.

2013 Final Standings

Bowl Championship Series

Rank, team		Rank, team	
1. Florida State		14. Arizona State	
2. Auburn		15. UCF	
3. Alabama		16. LSU	
4. Michigan State		17. UCLA	
5. Stanford		18. Louisville	
6. Baylor		19. Wisconsin	
7. Ohio State		20. Fresno State	
8. Missouri		21. Texas A&M	
9. South Carolina		22. Georgia	
10. Oregon		23. Northern Illinois	
11. Oklahoma		24. Duke	
12. Clemson		25. USC	
13. Oklahoma State			

Associated Press Poll

Rank, team	Rank, team
1. Florida State	14. LSU
2. Auburn	15. Louisville
3. Michigan State	16. UCLA
4. South Carolina	17. Oklahoma State
5. Missouri	18. Texas A&M
6. Oklahoma	19. USC
7. Alabama	20. Notre Dame
8. Clemson	21. Arizona State
9. Oregon	22. Wisconsin
10. UCF	23. Duke
11. Stanford	24. Vanderbilt
12. Ohio State	25. Washington
13. Baylor	

USA Today Poll

Rank, team	Rank, team
1. Florida State	14. LSU
2. Auburn	15. Louisville
3. Michigan State	16. UCLA
4. South Carolina	17. Oklahoma State
5. Missouri	18. Texas A&M
6. Oklahoma	19. USC
7. Clemson	20. Arizona State
8. Alabama	21. Wisconsin
9. Oregon	22. Duke
10. Ohio State	23. Vanderbilt
11. Stanford	24. Notre Dame
12. UCF	25. Nebraska
13. Baylor	

Note: BCS ranking is as of Dec. 8, 2013, prior to bowl games. Final AP and USA Today polls are as of Jan. 7, 2014 (after all bowl games).

Annual Results of Major Bowl Games

Date indicates year the game was played; bowl games are generally played in late Dec. or early Jan.

Rose Bowl Results, 1935-2014

Year	Result	Year	Result	Year	Result
1935	Alabama 29, Stanford 13	1962	Minnesota 21, UCLA 3	1989	Michigan 22, USC 14
1936	Stanford 7, SMU 0	1963	USC 42, Wisconsin 37	1990	USC 17, Michigan 10
1937	Pittsburgh 21, Washington 0	1964	Illinois 17, Washington 7	1991	Washington 46, Iowa 34
1938	California 13, Alabama 0	1965	Michigan 34, Oregon St. 7	1992	Washington 34, Michigan 14
1939	USC 7, Duke 3	1966	UCLA 14, Michigan St. 12	1993	Michigan 38, Washington 31
1940	USC 14, Tennessee 0	1967	Purdue 14, USC 13	1994	Wisconsin 21, UCLA 16
1941	Stanford 21, Nebraska 13	1968	USC 14, Indiana 3	1995	Penn St. 38, Oregon 20
1942	Oregon St. 20, Duke 16	1969	Ohio St. 27, USC 16	1996	USC 41, Northwestern 32
1943	Georgia 9, UCLA 0	1970	USC 10, Michigan 3	1997	Ohio St. 20, Arizona St. 17
1944	USC 29, Washington 0	1971	Stanford 27, Ohio St. 17	1998	Michigan 21, Washington St. 16
1945	USC 25, Tennessee 0	1972	Stanford 13, Michigan 12	1999	Wisconsin 38, UCLA 31
1946	Alabama 34, USC 14	1973	USC 42, Ohio St. 17	2000	Wisconsin 17, Stanford 9
1947	Illinois 45, UCLA 14	1974	Ohio St. 42, USC 21	2001	Washington 34, Purdue 24
1948	Michigan 49, USC 0	1975	USC 18, Ohio St. 17	2002	Miami (FL) 37, Nebraska 14
1949	Northwestern 20, California 14	1976	UCLA 23, Ohio St. 10	2003	Oklahoma 34, Washington St. 14
1950	Ohio St. 17, California 14	1977	USC 14, Michigan 6	2004	USC 28, Michigan 14
1951	Michigan 14, California 6	1978	Washington 27, Michigan 20	2005	Texas 38, Michigan 37
1952	Illinois 40, Stanford 7	1979	USC 17, Michigan 10	2006	Texas 41, USC 38
1953	USC 7, Wisconsin 0	1980	USC 17, Ohio St. 16	2007	USC 32, Michigan 18
1954	Michigan St. 28, UCLA 20	1981	Michigan 23, Washington 6	2008	USC 49, Illinois 17
1955	Ohio St. 20, USC 7	1982	Washington 28, Iowa 0	2009	USC 38, Penn St. 24
1956	Michigan St. 17, UCLA 14	1983	UCLA 24, Michigan 14	2010	Ohio St. 26, Oregon 17
1957	Iowa 35, Oregon St. 19	1984	UCLA 45, Illinois 9	2011	TCU 21, Wisconsin 19
1958	Ohio St. 10, Oregon 7	1985	USC 20, Ohio St. 17	2012	Oregon 45, Wisconsin 38
1959	Iowa 38, California 12	1986	UCLA 45, Iowa 28	2013	Stanford 20, Wisconsin 14
1960	Washington 44, Wisconsin 8	1987	Arizona St. 22, Michigan 15	2014	Michigan St. 24, Stanford 20
1961	Washington 17, Minnesota 7	1988	Michigan St. 20, USC 17		

Orange Bowl Results, 1935-2014

Year	Result	Year	Result	Year	Result
1935	(Jan.) Bucknell 26, Miami (FL) 0	1962	LSU 25, Colorado 7	1989	Miami (FL) 23, Nebraska 3
1936	Catholic U. 20, Mississippi 19	1963	Alabama 17, Oklahoma 0	1990	Notre Dame 21, Colorado 6
1937	Duquesne 13, Mississippi St. 12	1964	Nebraska 13, Auburn 7	1991	Colorado 10, Notre Dame 9
1938	Auburn 6, Michigan St. 0	1965	Texas 21, Alabama 17	1992	Miami (FL) 22, Nebraska 0
1939	Tennessee 17, Oklahoma 0	1966	Alabama 39, Nebraska 28	1993	Florida St. 27, Nebraska 14
1940	Georgia Tech 21, Missouri 7	1967	Florida 27, Georgia Tech 12	1994	Florida St. 18, Nebraska 16
1941	Mississippi St. 14, Georgetown 7	1968	Oklahoma 26, Tennessee 24	1995	Nebraska 24, Miami (FL) 17
1942	Georgia 40, TCU 26	1969	Penn St. 15, Kansas 14	1996	Florida St. 31, Notre Dame 26
1943	Alabama 37, Boston College 21	1970	Penn St. 10, Missouri 3	1996	(Dec.) Nebraska 41, Virginia Tech 21
1944	LSU 19, Texas A&M 14	1971	Nebraska 17, LSU 12	1998	Nebraska 42, Tennessee 17
1945	Tulsa 26, Georgia Tech 12	1972	Nebraska 38, Alabama 6	1999	Florida 31, Syracuse 10
1946	Miami (FL) 13, Holy Cross 6	1973	Nebraska 40, Notre Dame 6	2000	Michigan 35, Alabama 34 (OT)
1947	Rice 8, Tennessee 0	1974	Penn St. 16, LSU 9	2001	Oklahoma 13, Florida St. 2
1948	Georgia Tech 20, Kansas 14	1975	Notre Dame 13, Alabama 11	2002	Florida 56, Maryland 23
1949	Texas 41, Georgia 28	1976	Oklahoma 14, Michigan 6	2003	USC 38, Iowa 17
1950	Santa Clara 21, Kentucky 13	1977	Ohio St. 27, Colorado 10	2004	Miami (FL) 16, Florida St. 14
1951	Clemson 15, Miami (FL) 14	1978	Arkansas 31, Oklahoma 6	2005	USC 55, Oklahoma 19
1952	Georgia Tech 17, Baylor 14	1979	Oklahoma 31, Nebraska 24	2006	Penn St. 26, Florida St. 23 (3 OT)[1]
1953	Alabama 61, Syracuse 6	1980	Oklahoma 24, Florida St. 7	2007	Louisville 24, Wake Forest 13
1954	Oklahoma 7, Maryland 0	1981	Oklahoma 18, Florida St. 17	2008	Kansas 24, Virginia Tech 21
1955	Duke 34, Nebraska 7	1982	Clemson 22, Nebraska 15	2009	Virginia Tech 20, Cincinnati 7
1956	Oklahoma 20, Maryland 6	1983	Nebraska 21, LSU 20	2010	Iowa 24, Georgia Tech 14
1957	Colorado 27, Clemson 21	1984	Miami (FL) 31, Nebraska 30	2011	Stanford 40, Virginia Tech 12
1958	Oklahoma 48, Duke 21	1985	Washington 28, Oklahoma 17	2012	West Virginia 70, Clemson 33
1959	Oklahoma 21, Syracuse 6	1986	Oklahoma 25, Penn St. 10	2013	Florida St. 31, Northern Illinois 10
1960	Georgia 14, Missouri 0	1987	Oklahoma 42, Arkansas 8	2014	Clemson 40, Ohio St. 35
1961	Missouri 21, Navy 14	1988	Miami (FL) 20, Oklahoma 14		

(1) The NCAA vacated all of Penn State's 1998-2011 victories July 23, 2012, due to a child sexual abuse scandal at the school.

Sugar Bowl Results, 1935-2014

Year	Result	Year	Result	Year	Result
1935	(Jan.) Tulane 20, Temple 14	1962	Alabama 10, Arkansas 3	1989	Florida St. 13, Auburn 7
1936	TCU 3, LSU 2	1963	Mississippi 17, Arkansas 13	1990	Miami (FL) 33, Alabama 25
1937	Santa Clara 21, LSU 14	1964	Alabama 12, Mississippi 7	1991	Tennessee 23, Virginia 22
1938	Santa Clara 6, LSU 0	1965	LSU 13, Syracuse 10	1992	Notre Dame 39, Florida 28
1939	TCU 15, Carnegie Tech 7	1966	Missouri 20, Florida 18	1993	Alabama 34, Miami (FL) 13
1940	Texas A&M 14, Tulane 13	1967	Alabama 34, Nebraska 7	1994	Florida 41, West Virginia 7
1941	Boston College 19, Tennessee 13	1968	LSU 20, Wyoming 13	1995	Florida St. 23, Florida 17
1942	Fordham 2, Missouri 0	1969	Arkansas 16, Georgia 2	1995	(Dec.) Virginia Tech 28, Texas 10
1943	Tennessee 14, Tulsa 7	1970	Mississippi 27, Arkansas 22	1997	Florida 52, Florida St. 20
1944	Georgia Tech 20, Tulsa 18	1971	Tennessee 34, Air Force 13	1998	Florida St. 31, Ohio St. 14
1945	Duke 29, Alabama 26	1972	Oklahoma 40, Auburn 22	1999	Ohio St. 24, Texas A&M 14
1946	Oklahoma A&M 33, St. Mary's (CA) 13	1972	(Dec.) Oklahoma 14, Penn St. 0	2000	Florida St. 46, Virginia Tech 29
1947	Georgia 20, N. Carolina 10	1973	(Dec.) Notre Dame 24, Alabama 23	2001	Miami (FL) 37, Florida 20
1948	Texas 27, Alabama 7	1974	(Dec.) Nebraska 13, Florida 10	2002	LSU 47, Illinois 34
1949	Oklahoma 14, N. Carolina 6	1975	(Dec.) Alabama 13, Penn St. 6	2003	Georgia 26, Florida St. 13
1950	Oklahoma 35, LSU 0	1977	Pittsburgh 27, Georgia 3	2004	LSU 21, Oklahoma 14
1951	Kentucky 13, Oklahoma 7	1978	Alabama 35, Ohio St. 6	2005	Auburn 16, Virginia Tech 13
1952	Maryland 28, Tennessee 13	1979	Alabama 14, Penn St. 7	2006	West Virginia 38, Georgia 35
1953	Georgia Tech 24, Mississippi 7	1980	Alabama 24, Arkansas 9	2007	LSU 41, Notre Dame 14
1954	Georgia Tech 42, West Virginia 19	1981	Georgia 17, Notre Dame 10	2008	Georgia 41, Hawaii 10
1955	Navy 21, Mississippi 0	1982	Pittsburgh 24, Georgia 20	2009	Utah 31, Alabama 17
1956	Georgia Tech 7, Pittsburgh 0	1983	Penn St. 27, Georgia 23	2010	Florida 51, Cincinnati 24
1957	Baylor 13, Tennessee 7	1984	Auburn 9, Michigan 7	2011	Ohio St. 31, Arkansas 26
1958	Mississippi 39, Texas 7	1985	Nebraska 28, LSU 10	2012	Michigan 23, Virginia Tech 20
1959	LSU 7, Clemson 0	1986	Tennessee 35, Miami (FL) 7	2013	Louisville 33, Florida 23
1960	Mississippi 21, LSU 0	1987	Nebraska 30, LSU 15	2014	Oklahoma 45, Alabama 31
1961	Mississippi 14, Rice 6	1988	Syracuse 16, Auburn 16		

Other Bowl Results, Dec. 2013-Jan. 2014

Alamo Bowl, San Antonio, TX: Oregon 30, Texas 7
Armed Forces Bowl, Ft. Worth, TX: Navy 24, Middle Tennessee State 6
BBVA Compass Bowl, Birmingham, AL: Vanderbilt 41, Houston 24
Beef 'O' Brady's Bowl, St. Petersburg, FL: East Carolina 37, Ohio 20
Belk Bowl, Charlotte, NC: North Carolina 39, Cincinnati 17
Buffalo Wild Wings Bowl, Tempe, AZ: Kansas State 31, Michigan 14
Capital One Bowl, Orlando, FL: South Carolina 34, Wisconsin 24
Chick-fil-A Bowl, Atlanta, GA: Texas A&M 52, Duke 48
Cotton Bowl, Arlington, TX: Missouri 41, Oklahoma State 31
Famous Idaho Potato Bowl, Boise, ID: San Diego State 49, Buffalo 24
Fiesta Bowl, Glendale, AZ: UCF 52, Baylor 42

Fight Hunger Bowl, San Francisco, CA: Washington 31, Brigham Young 16
Gator Bowl, Jacksonville, FL: Nebraska 24, Georgia 19
GoDaddy.com Bowl, Mobile, AL: Arkansas State 23, Ball State 20
Hawaii Bowl, Honolulu, HI: Oregon State 38, Boise State 23
Heart of Dallas Bowl, Dallas, TX: North Texas 36, UNLV 14
Holiday Bowl, San Diego, CA: Texas Tech 37, Arizona State 23
Independence Bowl, Shreveport, LA: Arizona 42, Boston College 19
Las Vegas Bowl, Las Vegas, NV: USC 45, Fresno State 20
Liberty Bowl, Memphis, TN: Mississippi State 44, Rice 7
Little Caesars Bowl, Detroit, MI: Pittsburgh 30, Bowling Green 27

Military Bowl, Annapolis, MD: Marshall 31, Maryland 20
Music City Bowl, Nashville, TN: Mississippi 25, Georgia Tech 17
New Mexico Bowl, Albuquerque, NM: Colorado State 48, Washington State 45
New Orleans Bowl, New Orleans, LA: LA-Lafayette 24, Tulane 21
Outback Bowl, Tampa, FL: LSU 21, Iowa 14
Pinstripe Bowl, Bronx, NY: Notre Dame 29, Rutgers 16
Poinsettia Bowl, San Diego, CA: Utah State 21, Northern Illinois 14
Russell Athletic Bowl, Orlando, FL: Louisville 36, Miami (FL) 9
Sun Bowl, El Paso, TX: UCLA 42, Virginia Tech 12
Texas Bowl, Houston, TX: Syracuse 21, Minnesota 17

All-Time NCAA Bowl Subdivision (FBS) Statistical Leaders

Career Rushing Yards

Player, team	Yrs	Carries	Yds	Avg
Ron Dayne, Wisconsin	1996-99	1,115	6,397	5.74
Ricky Williams, Texas	1995-98	1,011	6,279	6.21
Tony Dorsett, Pittsburgh	1973-76	1,074	6,082	5.66
DeAngelo Williams, Memphis	2002-05	969	6,026	6.22
Charles White, USC	1976-79	1,023	5,598	5.47

Career Passing Yards

Player, team	Yrs	Comp/att	Yds
Case Keenum, Houston	2007-11	1,546/2,229	19,217
Timmy Chang, Hawaii	2000-04	1,388/2,436	17,072
Landry Jones, Oklahoma	2009-12	1,388/2,183	16,646
Graham Harrell, Texas Tech	2005-08	1,403/2,010	15,793
Ty Detmer, BYU	1988-91	958/1,530	15,031

Career Rushing Yards/Game (min. 2,500 yds)

Player, team	Yrs	Carries	Yds	Avg/game
Ed Marinaro, Cornell	1969-71	918	4,715	174.6
O. J. Simpson, USC	1967-68	621	3,214	164.4
Herschel Walker, Georgia	1980-82	994	5,259	159.4
Garrett Wolfe, N. Illinois	2004-06	807	5,164	156.5
LeShon Johnson, N. Illinois	1992-93	592	3,314	150.6

Career Receiving Yards

Player, team	Yrs	Rec	Yds	Avg
Trevor Insley, Nevada	1996-99	298	5,005	16.8
Ryan Broyles, Oklahoma	2008-11	349	4,586	13.1
Marcus Harris, Wyoming	1993-96	259	4,518	17.4
Rashaun Woods, Oklahoma St.	2000-03	293	4,414	15.1
Ryan Yarborough, Wyoming	1990-93	229	4,357	19.0

Note: As of end of 2013 season. Prior to 2002, postseason games were not included in NCAA final football statistics or records. All postseason games were included for the 2002 season and thereafter. Career rushing yards per game rankings do not include active players.

All-Time NCAA Bowl Subdivision (FBS) Team Won-Lost Records

Team	Yrs	W	L	T	Games	Pct.	Team	Yrs	W	L	T	Games	Pct.
Notre Dame	125	874	305	42	1,221	0.733	Penn St.[2]	127	730	370	41	1,141	0.658
Michigan	134	910	321	36	1,267	0.732	LSU	120	753	396	47	1,196	0.649
Boise St. (1996)	46	396	153	2	551	0.721	Georgia	120	767	407	54	1,228	0.647
Oklahoma	119	842	312	53	1,207	0.720	Miami (FL)	88	590	335	19	944	0.635
Ohio St.[1]	124	849	318	53	1,220	0.718	Auburn	121	726	416	47	1,189	0.630
Texas	121	875	339	33	1,247	0.715	Florida	107	684	395	40	1,119	0.629
Alabama[1]	119	838	323	43	1,204	0.714	Washington	124	688	428	50	1,166	0.611
USC[1]	121	796	323	54	1,173	0.702	Arizona St.	101	579	365	24	968	0.611
Nebraska	124	865	357	40	1,262	0.701	Miami (OH)	125	668	422	44	1,134	0.608
Tennessee	117	804	361	53	1,218	0.682	Virginia Tech	120	704	446	46	1,196	0.608
Florida St.[1]	67	499	237	17	753	0.674							

Note: As of end of 2013 season. Includes records as senior college only. Bowl and playoff games are included, and each tie game is computed as half won and half lost. Team listed with year in parentheses indicates reclassification to Bowl Subdivision (FBS), formerly Division I-A. The year in parentheses is the first year of FBS membership. Tiebreaker rule began with 1996 season. (1) Record adjusted by action of the NCAA Committee on Infractions. (2) Does not include 111 Penn St. 1998-2011 victories, which the NCAA vacated July 23, 2012.

Heisman Trophy Winners, 1935-2013

Awarded annually to the nation's outstanding college football player by the Downtown Athletic Club.

Year	Winner, school, position	Year	Winner, school, position	Year	Winner, school, position
1935	Jay Berwanger, Chicago, HB	1962	Terry Baker, Oregon St., QB	1988	Barry Sanders, Oklahoma St., RB
1936	Larry Kelley, Yale, E	1963	Roger Staubach, Navy, QB	1989	Andre Ware, Houston, QB
1937	Clinton Frank, Yale, HB	1964	John Huarte, Notre Dame, QB	1990	Ty Detmer, BYU, QB
1938	David O'Brien, Texas Christian, QB	1965	Mike Garrett, USC, HB	1991	Desmond Howard, Michigan, WR
1939	Nile Kinnick, Iowa, HB	1966	Steve Spurrier, Florida, QB	1992	Gino Torretta, Miami (FL), QB
1940	Tom Harmon, Michigan, HB	1967	Gary Beban, UCLA, QB	1993	Charlie Ward, Florida St., QB
1941	Bruce Smith, Minnesota, HB	1968	O. J. Simpson, USC, RB	1994	Rashaan Salaam, Colorado, RB
1942	Frank Sinkwich, Georgia, HB	1969	Steve Owens, Oklahoma, RB	1995	Eddie George, Ohio St., RB
1943	Angelo Bertelli, Notre Dame, QB	1970	Jim Plunkett, Stanford, QB	1996	Danny Wuerffel, Florida, QB
1944	Leslie Horvath, Ohio St., QB	1971	Pat Sullivan, Auburn, QB	1997	Charles Woodson, Michigan, CB
1945	Felix Blanchard, Army, FB	1972	Johnny Rodgers, Nebraska, RB-WR	1998	Ricky Williams, Texas, RB
1946	Glenn Davis, Army, HB	1973	John Cappelletti, Penn St., RB	1999	Ron Dayne, Wisconsin, RB
1947	John Lujack, Notre Dame, QB	1974	Archie Griffin, Ohio St., RB	2000	Chris Weinke, Florida St., QB
1948	Doak Walker, SMU, HB	1975	Archie Griffin, Ohio St., RB	2001	Eric Crouch, Nebraska, QB
1949	Leon Hart, Notre Dame, E	1976	Tony Dorsett, Pittsburgh, RB	2002	Carson Palmer, USC, QB
1950	Vic Janowicz, Ohio St., HB	1977	Earl Campbell, Texas, RB	2003	Jason White, Oklahoma, QB
1951	Richard Kazmaier, Princeton, HB	1978	Billy Sims, Oklahoma, RB	2004	Matt Leinart, USC, QB
1952	Billy Vessels, Oklahoma, HB	1979	Charles White, USC, RB	2005	Reggie Bush, USC, RB[1]
1953	John Lattner, Notre Dame, HB	1980	George Rogers, S. Carolina, RB	2006	Troy Smith, Ohio State, QB
1954	Alan Ameche, Wisconsin, FB	1981	Marcus Allen, USC, RB	2007	Tim Tebow, Florida, QB
1955	Howard Cassady, Ohio St., HB	1982	Herschel Walker, Georgia, RB	2008	Sam Bradford, Oklahoma, QB
1956	Paul Hornung, Notre Dame, QB	1983	Mike Rozier, Nebraska, RB	2009	Mark Ingram, Alabama, RB
1957	John Crow, Texas A&M, HB	1984	Doug Flutie, Boston College, QB	2010	Cam Newton, Auburn, QB
1958	Pete Dawkins, Army, HB	1985	Bo Jackson, Auburn, RB	2011	Robert Griffin III, Baylor, QB
1959	Billy Cannon, LSU, HB	1986	Vinny Testaverde, Miami (FL), QB	2012	Johnny Manziel, Texas A&M, QB
1960	Joe Bellino, Navy, HB	1987	Tim Brown, Notre Dame, WR	2013	Jameis Winston, Florida State, QB
1961	Ernest Davis, Syracuse, HB				

(1) Bush forfeited the trophy voluntarily Sept. 14, 2010, following revelations of NCAA rules violations while Bush was at USC.

All-Time Bowl Subdivision (FBS) Coaching Victories

Bobby Bowden	377	Bo Schembechler	234	Jim Sweeney	200	Darrell Royal	184
Glenn "Pop" Warner	336	**Chris Ault**	233	Dana X. Bible	198	Dick Tomey	183
Paul "Bear" Bryant	323	Hayden Fry	232	Fielding Yost	198	Gil Dobie	181
Amos Alonzo Stagg	314	Jim Tressel	229	Dan McGugin	197	Jackie Sherrill	180
Joe Paterno	298[1]	**Steve Spurrier**	219	Howard Jones	194	Carl Snavely	180
Frank Beamer	266	Jess Neely	207	John Cooper	192	Jerry Claiborne	179
LaVell Edwards	257	**Dennis Franchione**	203	John Vaught	190	Carmen Cozza	179
Tom Osborne	255	Warren Woodson	203	George Welsh	189	Dennis Erickson	179
Lou Holtz	249	Don Nehlen	202	John Heisman	186	Ben Schwartzwalder	178
Mack Brown	244	Eddie Anderson	201	Johnny Majors	185	**Bill Snyder**	178
Woody Hayes	238	Vince Dooley	201				

Note: Coaches active in 2013 shown in bold. Total victories through Jan. 6, 2014, including bowl games; coaches must have at least 10 seasons coaching Bowl Championship Series (BCS) schools to be eligible. (1) Does not include Paterno's 111 victories at Penn St., 1998-2011, which were vacated by the NCAA July 23, 2012.

College Football Coach of the Year, 1935-2013

The Coach of the Year has been selected by the American Football Coaches Assn. (AFCA) since 1935 as well as the Football Writers Assn. of America (FWAA) since 1957. When polls disagree, both winners are indicated.

1935 Lynn Waldorf, Northwestern
1936 Dick Harlow, Harvard
1937 Edward Mylin, Lafayette
1938 Bill Kern, Carnegie Tech
1939 Eddie Anderson, Iowa
1940 Clark Shaughnessy, Stanford
1941 Frank Leahy, Notre Dame
1942 Bill Alexander, Georgia Tech
1943 Amos Alonzo Stagg, Pacific (CA)
1944 Carroll Widdoes, Ohio St.
1945 Bo McMillin, Indiana
1946 Earl "Red" Blaik, Army
1947 Fritz Crisler, Michigan
1948 Bennie Oosterbaan, Michigan
1949 Bud Wilkinson, Oklahoma
1950 Charlie Caldwell, Princeton
1951 Chuck Taylor, Stanford
1952 Biggie Munn, Michigan St.
1953 Jim Tatum, Maryland
1954 Henry "Red" Sanders, UCLA
1955 Duffy Daugherty, Michigan St.
1956 Bowden Wyatt, Tennessee
1957 Woody Hayes, Ohio St.
1958 Paul Dietzel, LSU
1959 Ben Schwartzwalder, Syracuse
1960 Murray Warmath, Minnesota
1961 Paul "Bear" Bryant, Alabama (AFCA);
    Darrell Royal, Texas (FWAA)
1962 John McKay, USC
1963 Darrell Royal, Texas
1964 Ara Parseghian, Notre Dame &
    Frank Broyles, Arkansas (AFCA);
    Ara Parseghian, Notre Dame
    (FWAA)
1965 Tommy Prothro, UCLA (AFCA);
    Duffy Daugherty, Mich. St. (FWAA)

1966 Tom Cahill, Army
1967 John Pont, Indiana
1968 Joe Paterno, Penn St. (AFCA);
    Woody Hayes, Ohio St. (FWAA)
1969 Bo Schembechler, Michigan
1970 Charles McClendon, LSU &
    Darrell Royal, Texas (AFCA);
    Alex Agase, Northwestern (FWAA)
1971 Paul "Bear" Bryant, Alabama (AFCA);
    Bob Devaney, Nebraska (FWAA)
1972 John McKay, USC
1973 Paul "Bear" Bryant, Alabama (AFCA);
    Johnny Majors, Pittsburgh (FWAA)
1974 Grant Teaff, Baylor
1975 Frank Kush, Arizona St. (AFCA);
    Woody Hayes, Ohio St. (FWAA)
1976 Johnny Majors, Pittsburgh
1977 Don James, Washington (AFCA);
    Lou Holtz, Arkansas (FWAA)
1978 Joe Paterno, Penn St.
1979 Earle Bruce, Ohio St.
1980 Vince Dooley, Georgia
1981 Danny Ford, Clemson
1982 Joe Paterno, Penn St.
1983 Ken Hatfield, Air Force (AFCA);
    Howard Schnellenberger,
    Miami (FL) (FWAA)
1984 LaVell Edwards, Brigham Young
1985 Fisher De Berry, Air Force
1986 Joe Paterno, Penn St.
1987 Dick MacPherson, Syracuse
1988 Don Nehlen, W. Virginia (AFCA);
    Lou Holtz, Notre Dame (FWAA)
1989 Bill McCartney, Colorado
1990 Bobby Ross, Georgia Tech

1991 Don James, Washington
1992 Gene Stallings, Alabama
1993 Barry Alvarez, Wisconsin (AFCA);
    Terry Bowden, Auburn (FWAA)
1994 Tom Osborne, Nebraska (AFCA);
    Rich Brooks, Oregon (FWAA)
1995 Gary Barnett, Northwestern
1996 Bruce Snyder, Arizona St.
1997 Mike Price, Washington St.
1998 Phillip Fulmer, Tennessee
1999 Frank Beamer, Virginia Tech
2000 Bob Stoops, Oklahoma
2001 Larry Coker, Miami (FL) &
    Ralph Friedgen, Maryland (AFCA);
    Ralph Friedgen, Maryland (FWAA)
2002 Jim Tressel, Ohio St.
2003 Pete Carroll, USC (AFCA);
    Nick Saban, LSU (FWAA)
2004 Tommy Tuberville, Auburn (AFCA);
    Urban Meyer, Utah (FWAA)
2005 Joe Paterno, Penn St. (AFCA);
    Charlie Weis, Notre Dame (FWAA)
2006 Jim Grobe, Wake Forest (AFCA);
    Greg Schiano, Rutgers (FWAA)
2007 Mark Mangino, Kansas
2008 Kyle Whittingham, Utah (AFCA);
    Nick Saban, Alabama (FWAA)
2009 Gary Patterson, TCU
2010 Chip Kelly, Oregon
2011 Les Miles, LSU (AFCA);
    Mike Gundy, Oklahoma St. (FWAA)
2012 Brian Kelly, Notre Dame
2013 David Cutcliffe, Duke (AFCA);
    Gus Malzahn, Auburn (FWAA)

NCAA Div. I-A (FBS) Football Conference Champions, 1990-2013

American Athletic
2013 Central Florida

Atlantic Coast
1990 Georgia Tech
1991 Clemson
1992 Florida St.
1993 Florida St.
1994 Florida St.
1995 Virginia, Florida St.
1996 Florida St.
1997 Florida St.
1998 Florida St.,
    Georgia Tech
1999 Florida St.
2000 Florida St.
2001 Maryland
2002 Florida St.
2003 Florida St.
2004 Virginia Tech
2005 Florida St.
2006 Wake Forest
2007 Virginia Tech
2008 Virginia Tech
2009 Georgia Tech
2010 Virginia Tech
2011 Clemson
2012 Florida St.
2013 Florida St.

Big Ten
1990 Iowa, Illinois, Mich.,
    Michigan St.
1991 Michigan
1992 Michigan

1993 Ohio St., Wisconsin
1994 Penn St.
1995 Northwestern
1996 Northwestern,
    Ohio St.
1997 Michigan
1998 Michigan, Ohio St.,
    Wisconsin
1999 Wisconsin
2000 Michigan,
    Northwestern,
    Purdue
2001 Illinois
2002 Iowa, Ohio St.
2003 Michigan
2004 Iowa, Michigan
2005 Ohio St., Penn St.[1]
2006 Ohio St.
2007 Ohio St.
2008 Ohio St., Penn St.[1]
2009 Ohio St.
2010 Michigan St.,
    Ohio St., Wisconsin
2011 Wisconsin
2012 Wisconsin
2013 Michigan St.

Big 12
1996 Texas
1997 Nebraska
1998 Texas A&M
1999 Nebraska
2000 Oklahoma
2001 Colorado

2002 Oklahoma
2003 Kansas St.
2004 Oklahoma
2005 Texas
2006 Oklahoma
2007 Oklahoma
2008 Oklahoma
2009 Texas
2010 Oklahoma
2011 Oklahoma St.
2012 Kansas St.
2013 Baylor

Conference USA
1996 Houston,
    Southern Miss
1997 Southern Miss
1998 Tulane
1999 Southern Miss
2000 Louisville
2001 Louisville
2002 Cincinnati, TCU
2003 Southern Miss
2004 Louisville
2005 Tulsa
2006 Houston
2007 Central Florida
2008 East Carolina
2009 East Carolina
2010 Central Florida
2011 Southern Miss
2012 Tulsa
2013 Rice

Mid-American
1990 Central Michigan
1991 Bowling Green
1992 Bowling Green
1993 Ball St.
1994 Central Michigan
1995 Toledo
1996 Ball St.
1997 Marshall
1998 Marshall
1999 Marshall
2000 Marshall
2001 Toledo
2002 Marshall
2003 Miami (OH)
2004 Toledo
2005 Akron
2006 Central Michigan
2007 Central Michigan
2008 Buffalo
2009 Central Michigan
2010 Miami (OH)
2011 Northern Illinois
2012 Northern Illinois
2013 Bowling Green

Mountain West
1999 BYU, Colorado St.,
    Utah
2000 Colorado St.
2001 BYU
2002 Colorado St.
2003 Utah
2004 Utah

2005 TCU
2006 BYU, TCU
2007 BYU
2008 Utah
2009 TCU
2010 TCU
2011 TCU
2012 Boise St., Fresno
    St., San Diego St.
2013 Fresno St.

Pac-12
1990 Washington
1991 Washington
1992 Stanford,
    Washington
1993 Arizona, UCLA,
    USC
1994 Oregon
1995 USC, Washington
1996 Arizona St.
1997 UCLA,
    Washington St.
1998 UCLA
1999 Stanford
2000 Oregon, Oregon St.,
    Washington
2001 Oregon
2002 USC, Washington St.
2003 USC
2004 USC
2005 USC
2006 California, USC
2007 Arizona St., USC

2008 USC	1993 Florida	2004 Auburn	**Sun Belt**	2007 Florida Atlantic, Troy
2009 Oregon	1994 Florida	2005 Georgia	2001 Mid. Tenn. St., North Texas	2008 Troy
2010 Oregon	1995 Florida	2006 Florida	2002 North Texas	2009 Troy
2011 Oregon	1996 Florida	2007 LSU	2003 North Texas	2010 Florida Intl., Troy
2012 Stanford	1997 Tennessee	2008 Florida	2004 North Texas	2011 Arkansas St.
2013 Stanford	1998 Tennessee	2009 Alabama	2005 Arkansas St., LA-Lafayette, LA-Monroe	2012 Arkansas St.
Southeastern	1999 Alabama	2010 Auburn		2013 Arkansas St., LA-Lafayette
1990 Tennessee	2000 Florida	2011 LSU	2006 Mid. Tenn. St., Troy	
1991 Florida	2001 LSU	2012 Alabama		
1992 Alabama	2002 Georgia	2013 Auburn		
	2003 LSU			

Note: Includes conferences active in 2013. (1) On July 23, 2012, the NCAA vacated all of Penn State's football victories between 1998 and 2011.

NCAA Div. I-AA (FCS) Football Conference Champions, 1990-2013

Big Sky
1990	Nevada
1991	Nevada
1992	Eastern Wash., Idaho
1993	Montana
1994	Boise St.
1995	Montana
1996	Montana
1997	Eastern Wash.
1998	Montana
1999	Montana
2000	Montana
2001	Montana
2002	Idaho St., Montana, Montana St.
2003	Montana, Montana St., N. Arizona
2004	Eastern Wash., Montana
2005	Eastern Wash., Montana, Montana St.
2006	Montana
2007	Montana
2008	Montana, Weber St.
2009	Montana
2010	Eastern Wash., Montana St.
2011	Montana, Montana St.
2012	Eastern Wash., Montana St., Cal Poly
2013	Eastern Wash.

Big South
2002	Gardner-Webb
2003	Gardner-Webb
2004	Coastal Carolina
2005	Charleston Southern, Coastal Carolina
2006	Coastal Carolina
2007	Liberty
2008	Liberty
2009	Liberty, Stony Brook
2010	Coastal Carolina, Liberty, Stony Brook
2011	Stony Brook
2012	Coastal Carolina, Liberty, Stony Brook
2013	Coastal Carolina, Liberty

Ivy League
1990	Cornell, Dartmouth
1991	Dartmouth
1992	Dartmouth, Princeton
1993	Pennsylvania
1994	Pennsylvania
1995	Princeton
1996	Dartmouth
1997	Harvard
1998	Pennsylvania
1999	Brown, Yale
2000	Pennsylvania
2001	Harvard
2002	Pennsylvania
2003	Pennsylvania
2004	Harvard
2005	Brown
2006	Princeton, Yale
2007	Harvard
2008	Harvard, Brown
2009	Pennsylvania
2010	Pennsylvania
2011	Harvard
2012	Pennsylvania
2013	Harvard, Princeton

Mid-Eastern Athletic
1990	Florida A&M
1991	North Carolina A&T
1992	North Carolina A&T
1993	Howard
1994	South Carolina St.
1995	Florida A&M
1996	Florida A&M
1997	Hampton
1998	Florida A&M, Hampton
1999	North Carolina A&T
2000	Florida A&M
2001	Florida A&M
2002	Bethune-Cookman
2003	North Carolina A&T
2004	Hampton, South Carolina St.
2005	Hampton
2006	Hampton
2007	Delaware St.
2008	South Carolina St.
2009	South Carolina St.
2010	Bethune-Cookman, Florida A&M, South Carolina St.
2011	Norfolk St.
2012	Bethune-Cookman
2013	Bethune-Cookman, South Carolina St.

Missouri Valley
1990	Northern Iowa
1991	Northern Iowa
1992	Northern Iowa
1993	Northern Iowa
1994	Northern Iowa
1995	Eastern Illinois, Northern Iowa
1996	Northern Iowa
1997	Western Illinois
1998	Western Illinois
1999	Illinois St.
2000	Western Illinois
2001	Northern Iowa
2002	W. Illinois, W. Kentucky
2003	N. Iowa, S. Illinois
2004	Southern Illinois
2005	N. Iowa, S. Illinois, Youngstown St.
2006	Youngstown St.
2007	Northern Iowa
2008	N. Iowa, S. Illinois
2009	Southern Illinois
2010	Northern Iowa
2011	North Dakota St., Northern Iowa
2012	North Dakota St.
2013	North Dakota St.

Northeast
1996	Monmouth, Robert Morris
1997	Robert Morris
1998	Monmouth, Robert Morris
1999	Robert Morris
2000	Robert Morris
2001	Sacred Heart
2002	Albany
2003	Albany, Monmouth
2004	Central Conn. St., Monmouth
2005	Central Conn. St., Stony Brook
2006	Monmouth
2007	Albany
2008	Albany
2009	Central Conn. St.
2010	Central Conn. St., Robert Morris
2011	Albany, Duquesne
2012	Albany, Wagner
2013	Duquesne, Sacred Heart

Ohio Valley
1990	Eastern Kentucky, Mid. Tenn. St.
1991	Eastern Kentucky
1992	Mid. Tenn. St.
1993	Eastern Kentucky
1994	Eastern Kentucky
1995	Murray St.
1996	Murray St.
1997	Eastern Kentucky
1998	Tennessee St.
1999	Tennessee St.
2000	Western Kentucky
2001	Eastern Illinois
2002	Eastern Illinois, Murray St.
2003	Jacksonville St.
2004	Jacksonville St.
2005	Eastern Illinois
2006	Eastern Illinois, Tenn.-Martin
2007	Eastern Kentucky
2008	Eastern Kentucky
2009	Eastern Illinois
2010	SE Missouri St.
2011	Eastern Kentucky, Jacksonville St., Tennessee Tech
2012	Eastern Illinois
2013	Eastern Illinois

Patriot
1990	Holy Cross
1991	Holy Cross
1992	Lafayette
1993	Lehigh
1994	Lafayette
1995	Lehigh
1996	Bucknell
1997	Colgate
1998	Lehigh
1999	Colgate, Lehigh
2000	Lehigh
2001	Lehigh
2002	Colgate, Fordham
2003	Colgate
2004	Lafayette, Lehigh
2005	Colgate, Lafayette
2006	Colgate, Lafayette, Lehigh
2007	Fordham
2008	Colgate
2009	Holy Cross
2010	Lehigh
2011	Lehigh
2012	Colgate
2013	Lafayette

Pioneer
1993	Dayton
1994	Butler, Dayton
1995	Drake
1996	Dayton
1997	Dayton
1998	Drake
1999	Dayton
2000	Dayton, Drake, Valparaiso
2001	Dayton
2002	Dayton
2003	Valparaiso
2004	Drake
2005	San Diego
2006	San Diego
2007	Dayton, San Diego
2008	Jacksonville
2009	Butler, Dayton
2010	Dayton, Jacksonville
2011	Drake, San Diego
2012	Butler, Drake, San Diego
2013	Butler, Marist

Southern
1990	Furman
1991	Appalachian St.
1992	Citadel
1993	Georgia Southern
1994	Marshall
1995	Appalachian St.
1996	Marshall
1997	Georgia Southern
1998	Georgia Southern
1999	Appalachian St., Furman, Georgia Southern
2000	Georgia Southern
2001	Furman, Georgia Southern
2002	Georgia Southern
2003	Wofford
2004	Furman, Georgia Southern
2005	Appalachian St.
2006	Appalachian St.
2007	Appalachian St., Wofford
2008	Appalachian St.
2009	Appalachian St.
2010	Appalachian St., Wofford
2011	Georgia Southern
2012	Appalachian St., Georgia Southern, Wofford
2013	Chattanooga, Furman, Samford

Southland
1990	LA-Monroe
1991	McNeese St.
1992	LA-Monroe
1993	McNeese St.
1994	North Texas
1995	McNeese St.
1996	Troy St.
1997	McNeese St., Northwestern St.
1998	Northwestern St.
1999	Stephen F. Austin, Troy
2000	Troy
2001	McNeese St.
2002	McNeese St.
2003	McNeese St.
2004	Northwestern St., Sam Houston St.
2005	Nicholls St., Texas St.
2006	McNeese St.
2007	McNeese St.
2008	Texas St.
2009	McNeese St., Stephen F. Austin
2010	Stephen F. Austin
2011	Sam Houston St.
2012	Central Arkansas, Sam Houston St.
2013	Southeastern LA

Southwestern Athletic
1990	Jackson St.
1991	Alabama St.
1992	Alcorn St.
1993	Southern
1994	Alcorn St., Southern
1995	Jackson St.
1996	Jackson St.
1997	Southern
1998	Southern
1999	Southern
2000	Grambling St.
2001	Grambling St.
2002	Grambling St.
2003	Southern
2004	Alabama St.
2005	Grambling St.
2006	Alabama A&M
2007	Jackson St.
2008	Grambling St.
2009	Prairie View A&M
2010	Texas Southern
2011	Grambling St.
2012	Arkansas-Pine Bluff
2013	Southern

Colonial Athletic
2007	Massachusetts, Richmond
2008	James Madison
2009	Richmond, Villanova
2010	Delaware, William & Mary
2011	Towson
2012	New Hampshire, Richmond, Villanova, Towson
2013	Maine

Note: Missouri Valley Conference was known as Gateway Football Conference, 1992-2007, and as Gateway Collegiate Athletic Conference, 1985-91.

Selected NCAA Division I Teams
(Conferences and coaches listed are as of Aug. 2013.)

Team	Nickname	Team colors	Conference	Basketball coach	Football coach
Air Force	Falcons	Blue & silver	Mountain West	Dave Pilipovich	Troy Calhoun
Akron	Zips	Blue & gold	Mid-American	Keith Dambrot	Terry Bowden
Alabama	Crimson Tide	Crimson & white	Southeastern	Anthony Grant	Nick Saban
Appalachian State	Mountaineers	Black & gold	Southern	Jim Fox	Scott Satterfield
Arizona	Wildcats	Cardinal & navy	Pac-12	Sean Miller	Rich Rodriguez
Arizona State	Sun Devils	Maroon & gold	Pac-12	Herb Sendek	Todd Graham
Arkansas	Razorbacks	Cardinal & white	Southeastern	Mike Anderson	Bret Bielema
Arkansas State	Red Wolves	Scarlet & black	Sun Belt	John Brady	Blake Anderson
Army	Black Knights	Black, gold, & gray	Independent#	Zach Spiker	Jeff Monken
Auburn	Tigers	Burnt orange & navy blue	Southeastern	Bruce Pearl	Gus Malzahn
Ball State	Cardinals	Cardinal & white	Mid-American	James Whitford	Pete Lembo
Baylor	Bears	Green & gold	Big 12	Scott Drew	Art Briles
Boise State	Broncos	Blue & orange	Mountain West	Leon Rice	Bryan Harsin
Boston College	Eagles	Maroon & gold	Atlantic Coast	Jim Christian	Steve Addazio
Bowling Green	Falcons	Orange & brown	Mid-American	Chris Jans	Dino Babers
Brigham Young (BYU)	Cougars	Dark blue & white	Independent#	Dave Rose	Bronco Mendenhall
Brown*	Bears	Brown, red, & white	Ivy League	Mike Martin	Phil Estes
California	Golden Bears	Blue & gold	Pac-12	Cuonzo Martin	Sonny Dykes
Central Michigan	Chippewas	Maroon & gold	Mid-American	Keno Davis	Dan Enos
Cincinnati	Bearcats	Red & black	American Athletic	Mick Cronin	Tommy Tuberville
Citadel*	Bulldogs	Citadel blue & white	Southern	Chuck Driesell	Mike Houston
Clemson	Tigers	Clemson orange & regalia	Atlantic Coast	Brad Brownell	Dabo Swinney
Colgate*	Raiders	Maroon & white	Patriot League	Matt Langel	Dan Hunt
Colorado	Buffaloes	Silver, gold, & black	Pac-12	Tad Boyle	Mike MacIntyre
Colorado State	Rams	Green & gold	Mountain West	Larry Eustachy	Jim McElwain
Columbia*	Lions	Columbia blue & white	Ivy League	Kyle Smith	Pete Mangurian
Connecticut	Huskies	National flag blue & white	American Athletic	Kevin Ollie	Bob Diaco
Cornell*	Big Red	Carnelian red & white	Ivy League	Bill Courtney	David Archer
Dartmouth*	Big Green	Dartmouth green & white	Ivy League	Paul Cormier	Buddy Teevens
Delaware*	Fightin' Blue Hens	Blue & gold	Colonial Athletic	Monté Ross	Dave Brock
Duke	Blue Devils	Duke blue & white	Atlantic Coast	Mike Krzyzewski	David Cutcliffe
East Carolina	Pirates	Purple & gold	Conference USA	Jeff Lebo	Ruffin McNeill
Eastern Illinois*	Panthers	Blue & gray	Ohio Valley	Jay Spoonhour	Kim Dameron
Eastern Kentucky*	Colonels	Maroon & white	Ohio Valley	Jeff Neubauer	Dean Hood
Eastern Michigan	Eagles	Green & white	Mid-American	Rob Murphy	Chris Creighton
Eastern Washington*	Eagles	Red & white	Big Sky	Jim Hayford	Beau Baldwin
Florida	Gators	Orange & blue	Southeastern	Billy Donovan	Will Muschamp
Florida A&M*	Rattlers	Orange & green	Mid-Eastern Athletic	Byron Samuels	Earl Holmes
Florida State	Seminoles	Garnet & gold	Atlantic Coast	Leonard Hamilton	Jimbo Fisher
Fresno State	Bulldogs	Red & blue	Mountain West	Rodney Terry	Tim DeRuyter
Furman*	Paladins	Purple & white	Southern	Niko Medved	Bruce Fowler
Georgia	Bulldogs	Red & black	Southeastern	Mark Fox	Mark Richt
Georgia Southern	Eagles	Blue & white	Southern	Mark Byington	Willie Fritz
Georgia Tech	Yellow Jackets	Old gold & white	Atlantic Coast	Brian Gregory	Paul Johnson
Harvard*	Crimson	Crimson, black, & white	Ivy League	Tommy Amaker	Tim Murphy
Hawaii	Rainbow Warriors	Green, black, white, silver	Mountain West#	Gib Arnold	Norm Chow
Holy Cross*	Crusaders	Royal purple	Patriot League	Milan Brown	Tom Gilmore
Houston	Cougars	Scarlet & white	American Athletic	Kelvin Samson	Tony Levine
Howard*	Bison	Blue & white	Mid-Eastern Athletic	Kevin Nickelberry	Gary Harrell
Idaho	Vandals	Silver & vandal gold	Western Athletic	Don Verlin	Paul Petrino
Illinois	Fighting Illini	Orange & blue	Big Ten	John Groce	Tim Beckman
Illinois State*	Redbirds	Red & white	Missouri Valley	Dan Muller	Brock Spack
Indiana	Hoosiers	Cream & crimson	Big Ten	Tom Crean	Kevin Wilson
Indiana State*	Sycamores	Royal blue & white	Missouri Valley	Greg Lansing	Mike Sanford
Iowa	Hawkeyes	Black & gold	Big Ten	Fran McCaffery	Kirk Ferentz
Iowa State	Cyclones	Cardinal & gold	Big 12	Fred Hoiberg	Paul Rhoads
Jackson State*	Tigers	Blue & white	Southwestern Athletic	Wayne Brent	Harold Jackson
James Madison*	Dukes	Purple & gold	Colonial Athletic	Matt Brady	Everett Withers
Kansas	Jayhawks	Crimson & blue	Big 12	Bill Self	Charlie Weis
Kansas State	Wildcats	Purple & white	Big 12	Bruce Weber	Bill Snyder
Kent State	Golden Flashes	Navy blue & gold	Mid-American	Rob Senderoff	Paul Haynes
Kentucky	Wildcats	Blue & white	Southeastern	John Calipari	Mark Stoops
Lafayette*	Leopards	Maroon & white	Patriot League	Fran O'Hanlon	Frank Tavani
Lehigh*	Mountain Hawks	Brown & white	Patriot League	Brett Reed	Andy Coen
Liberty*	Flames	Red, white, & blue	Big South	Dale Layer	Turner Gill
Louisiana State (LSU)	Fighting Tigers	Purple & gold	Southeastern	Johnny Jones	Les Miles
Louisiana Tech	Bulldogs	Red & blue	Conference USA	Michael White	Skip Holtz
Louisiana-Lafayette	Ragin' Cajuns	Vermilion & white	Sun Belt	Bob Marlin	Mark Hudspeth
Louisiana-Monroe	Warhawks	Maroon & gold	Sun Belt	Keith Richard	Todd Berry
Louisville	Cardinals	Red & black	American Athletic	Rick Pitino	Bobby Petrino
Maine*	Black Bears	Blue & white	Colonial Athletic#	Bob Walsh	Jack Cosgrove
Marshall	Thundering Herd	Green & white	Conference USA	Dan D'Antoni	Doc Holliday
Maryland	Terrapins	Red, white, black, gold	Atlantic Coast	Mark Turgeon	Randy Edsall
Massachusetts	Minutemen	Maroon & white	Mid-American#	Derek Kellogg	Mark Whipple
Memphis	Tigers	Blue & gray	American Athletic	Josh Pastner	Justin Fuente
Miami (Florida)	Hurricanes	Orange & green	Atlantic Coast	Jim Larranaga	Al Golden
Miami (Ohio)	RedHawks	Red & white	Mid-American	John Cooper	Chuck Martin
Michigan	Wolverines	Maize & blue	Big Ten	John Beilein	Brady Hoke
Michigan State	Spartans	Green & white	Big Ten	Tom Izzo	Mark Dantonio
Mid. Tennessee State	Blue Raiders	Royal blue & white	Conference USA	Kermit Davis	Rick Stockstill
Minnesota	Golden Gophers	Maroon & gold	Big Ten	Richard Pitino	Jerry Kill
Mississippi	Rebels	Cardinal red & navy blue	Southeastern	Andy Kennedy	Hugh Freeze
Mississippi State	Bulldogs	Maroon & white	Southeastern	Rick Ray	Dan Mullen
Missouri	Tigers	Old gold & black	Southeastern	Kim Anderson	Gary Pinkel

Team	Nickname	Team colors	Conference	Basketball coach	Football coach
Montana*	Grizzlies	Maroon & silver	Big Sky	Travis DeCuire	Mick Delaney
Montana State*	Bobcats	Blue & gold	Big Sky	Brian Fish	Rob Ash
Morgan State*	Bears	Blue & orange	Mid-Eastern Athletic	Todd Bozeman	Lee Hull
Murray State*	Racers	Navy & gold	Ohio Valley	Steve Prohm	Chris Hatcher
Navy	Midshipmen	Navy blue & gold	Independent#	Ed DeChellis	Ken Niumatalolo
Nebraska	Cornhuskers	Scarlet & cream	Big Ten	Tim Miles	Bo Pelini
Nevada	Wolf Pack	Silver & blue	Mountain West	David Carter	Brian Polian
Nevada-Las Vegas (UNLV)	Rebels	Scarlet & gray	Mountain West	Dave Rice	Bobby Hauck
New Hampshire*	Wildcats	Blue & white	Colonial Athletic#	Bill Herrion	Sean McDonnell
New Mexico	Lobos	Cherry & silver	Mountain West	Craig Neal	Bob Davie
New Mexico State	Aggies	Crimson & white	Western Athletic	Marvin Menzies	Doug Martin
Nicholls State*	Colonels	Red & gray	Southland	J. P. Piper	Charlie Stubbs
North Carolina	Tar Heels	Carolina blue & white	Atlantic Coast	Roy Williams	Larry Fedora
North Carolina State	Wolfpack	Red & white	Atlantic Coast	Mark Gottfried	Dave Doeren
North Texas	Mean Green	Green & white	Conference USA	Tony Benford	Dan McCarney
Northern Illinois	Huskies	Cardinal & black	Mid-American	Mark Montgomery	Rod Carey
Northern Iowa*	Panthers	Purple & old gold	Missouri Valley	Ben Jacobson	Mark Farley
Northwestern	Wildcats	Purple & white	Big Ten	Chris Collins	Pat Fitzgerald
Northwestern State*	Demons	Purple, white, & orange	Southland	Mike McConathy	Jay Thomas
Notre Dame	Fighting Irish	Blue & gold	Independent#	Mike Brey	Brian Kelly
Ohio	Bobcats	Hunter green & white	Mid-American	Saul Phillips	Frank Solich
Ohio State	Buckeyes	Scarlet & gray	Big Ten	Thad Matta	Urban Meyer
Oklahoma	Sooners	Crimson & cream	Big 12	Lon Kruger	Bob Stoops
Oklahoma State	Cowboys	Orange & black	Big 12	Travis Ford	Mike Gundy
Oregon	Ducks	Green & yellow	Pac-12	Dana Altman	Mark Helfrich
Oregon State	Beavers	Orange & black	Pac-12	Wayne Tinkle	Mike Riley
Penn State	Nittany Lions	Blue & white	Big Ten	Patrick Chambers	James Franklin
Pennsylvania*	Quakers	Red & blue	Ivy League	Jerome Allen	Al Bagnoli
Pittsburgh	Panthers	Gold & blue	Atlantic Coast	Jamie Dixon	Paul Chryst
Princeton*	Tigers	Orange & black	Ivy League	Mitch Henderson	Bob Surace
Purdue	Boilermakers	Old gold & black	Big Ten	Matt Painter	Darrell Hazell
Rhode Island*	Rams	Keaney blue, dark blue, white	Colonial Athletic#	Dan Hurley	Jim Fleming
Rice	Owls	Blue & gray	Conference USA	Mike Rhoades	David Bailiff
Richmond*	Spiders	Red & blue	Colonial Athletic#	Chris Mooney	Danny Rocco
Rutgers	Scarlet Knights	Scarlet	American Athletic	Eddie Jordan	Kyle Flood
Sam Houston State*	Bearkats	Orange & white	Southland	Jason Hooten	K. C. Keeler
San Diego State	Aztecs	Scarlet & black	Mountain West	Steve Fisher	Rocky Long
San Jose State	Spartans	Gold, white, & blue	Mountain West	Dave Wojcik	Ron Caragher
South Carolina	Gamecocks	Garnet & black	Southeastern	Frank Martin	Steve Spurrier
South Carolina State*	Bulldogs	Garnet & blue	Mid-Eastern Athletic	Murray Garvin	Oliver Pough
South Florida	Bulls	Green & gold	American Athletic	Orlando Antigua	Willie Taggart
Southeast Missouri State*	Redhawks	Red, black, & white	Ohio Valley	Dickey Nutt	Tom Matukewicz
Southern California (USC)	Trojans	Cardinal & gold	Pac-12	Andy Enfield	Steve Sarkisian
Southern Illinois*	Salukis	Maroon & white	Missouri Valley	Barry Hinson	Dale Lennon
Southern Methodist (SMU)	Mustangs	Red & blue	American Athletic	Larry Brown	June Jones
Southern Mississippi	Golden Eagles	Black & gold	Conference USA	Doc Sadler	Todd Monken
Stanford	Cardinal	Cardinal & white	Pac-12	Johnny Dawkins	David Shaw
Stephen F. Austin*	Lumberjacks	Purple & white	Southland	Brad Underwood	Clint Conque
Syracuse	Orange	Orange	Atlantic Coast	Jim Boeheim	Scott Shafer
Temple	Owls	Cherry & white	American Athletic	Fran Dunphy	Matt Rhule
Tennessee	Volunteers	Orange & white	Southeastern	Donnie Tyndall	Butch Jones
Tennessee State*	Tigers	Reflex blue & white	Ohio Valley	Dana Ford	Rod Reed
Tennessee Tech*	Golden Eagles	Purple & gold	Ohio Valley	Steve Payne	Watson Brown
Texas	Longhorns	Burnt orange & white	Big 12	Rick Barnes	Charlie Strong
Texas A&M	Aggies	Maroon & white	Southeastern	Billy Kennedy	Kevin Sumlin
Texas Christian (TCU)	Horned Frogs	Purple & white	Big 12	Trent Johnson	Gary Patterson
Texas Southern*	Tigers	Maroon & gray	Southwestern Athletic	Mike Davis	Darrell Asberry
Texas State*	Bobcats	Maroon & gold	Sun Belt	Danny Kaspar	Dennis Franchione
Texas Tech	Red Raiders	Scarlet & black	Big 12	Tubby Smith	Kliff Kingsbury
Toledo	Rockets	Midnight blue & gold	Mid-American	Tod Kowalczyk	Matt Campbell
Troy	Trojans	Cardinal, silver, & black	Sun Belt	Phil Cunningham	Larry Blakeney
Tulane	Green Wave	Olive green & sky blue	Conference USA	Ed Conroy	Curtis Johnson
Tulsa	Golden Hurricane	Old gold, royal blue, & crimson	Conference USA	Frank Haith	Bill Blankenship
UCLA	Bruins	Blue & gold	Pac-12	Steve Alford	Jim Mora
Utah	Utes	Crimson & white	Pac-12	Larry Krystkowiak	Kyle Whittingham
Utah State	Aggies	Navy blue & white	Mountain West	Stew Morrill	Matt Wells
UTEP (Texas-El Paso)	Miners	Dark blue, orange, & silver	Conference USA	Tim Floyd	Sean Kugler
Vanderbilt	Commodores	Black & gold	Southeastern	Kevin Stallings	Derek Mason
Villanova*	Wildcats	Blue & white	Colonial Athletic#	Jay Wright	Andy Talley
Virginia	Cavaliers	Orange & blue	Atlantic Coast	Tony Bennett	Mike London
Virginia Tech	Hokies	Burnt orange & Chicago maroon	Atlantic Coast	Buzz Williams	Frank Beamer
Wake Forest	Demon Deacons	Old gold & black	Atlantic Coast	Danny Manning	Dave Clawson
Washington	Huskies	Purple & gold	Pac-12	Lorenzo Romar	Chris Peterson
Washington State	Cougars	Crimson & gray	Pac-12	Ernie Kent	Mike Leach
Weber State*	Wildcats	Royal purple & white	Big Sky	Randy Rahe	Jay Hill
West Virginia	Mountaineers	Old gold & blue	Big 12	Bob Huggins	Dana Holgorsen
Western Illinois*	Leathernecks	Purple & gold	Missouri Valley#	Billy Wright	Bob Nielson
Western Kentucky	Hilltoppers	Red & white	Sun Belt	Ray Harper	Jeff Brohm
Western Michigan	Broncos	Brown & gold	Mid-American	Steve Hawkins	P. J. Fleck
William & Mary*	Tribe	Green, gold, & silver	Colonial Athletic	Tony Shaver	Jimmye Laycock
Wisconsin	Badgers	Cardinal & white	Big Ten	Bo Ryan	Gary Andersen
Wyoming	Cowboys	Brown & gold	Mountain West	Larry Shyatt	Craig Bohl
Yale*	Bulldogs, Elis	Yale blue & white	Ivy League	James Jones	Tony Reno
Youngstown State*	Penguins	Red & white	Missouri Valley#	Jerry Slocum	Eric Wolford

* = Football Championship Subdivision (FCS) team (formerly known as I-AA). # = Team competes in conference listed in football but not in basketball.

NCAA Men's Baseball Division I Champions, 1947-2014

Year	Champion	Year	Champion	Year	Champion	Year	Champion	Year	Champion
1947	California	1961	USC	1975	Texas	1989	Wichita St.	2002	Texas
1948	USC	1962	Michigan	1976	Arizona	1990	Georgia	2003	Rice
1949	Texas	1963	USC	1977	Arizona St.	1991	LSU	2004	Cal St. Fullerton
1950	Texas	1964	Minnesota	1978	USC	1992	Pepperdine	2005	Texas
1951	Oklahoma	1965	Arizona St.	1979	Cal St. Fullerton	1993	LSU	2006	Oregon St.
1952	Holy Cross	1966	Ohio St.	1980	Arizona	1994	Oklahoma	2007	Oregon St.
1953	Michigan	1967	Arizona St.	1981	Arizona St.	1995	Cal St. Fullerton	2008	Fresno St.
1954	Missouri	1968	USC	1982	Miami (FL)	1996	LSU	2009	LSU
1955	Wake Forest	1969	Arizona St.	1983	Texas	1997	LSU	2010	South Carolina
1956	Minnesota	1970	USC	1984	Cal St. Fullerton	1998	USC	2011	South Carolina
1957	California	1971	USC	1985	Miami (FL)	1999	Miami (FL)	2012	Arizona
1958	USC	1972	USC	1986	Arizona	2000	LSU	2013	UCLA
1959	Oklahoma St.	1973	USC	1987	Stanford	2001	Miami (FL)	2014	Vanderbilt
1960	Minnesota	1974	USC	1988	Stanford				

NCAA Women's Softball Division I Champions, 1982-2014

Year	Champion	Year	Champion	Year	Champion	Year	Champion	Year	Champion
1982	UCLA	1989	UCLA	1996	Arizona	2003	UCLA	2009	Washington
1983	Texas A&M	1990	UCLA	1997	Arizona	2004	UCLA	2010	UCLA
1984	UCLA	1991	Arizona	1998	Fresno St.	2005	Michigan	2011	Arizona St.
1985	UCLA	1992	UCLA	1999	UCLA	2006	Arizona	2012	Alabama
1986	Cal St. Fullerton	1993	Arizona	2000	Oklahoma	2007	Arizona	2013	Oklahoma
1987	Texas A&M	1994	Arizona	2001	Arizona	2008	Arizona St.	2014	Florida
1988	UCLA	1995	UCLA	2002	California				

NCAA Men's Hockey Division I Champions, 1948-2014

Year	Champion	Year	Champion	Year	Champion	Year	Champion	Year	Champion
1948	Michigan	1962	Michigan Tech	1976	Minnesota	1989	Harvard	2002	Minnesota
1949	Boston College	1963	North Dakota	1977	Wisconsin	1990	Wisconsin	2003	Minnesota
1950	Colorado College	1964	Michigan	1978	Boston Univ.	1991	North Michigan	2004	Denver
1951	Michigan	1965	Michigan Tech	1979	Minnesota	1992	Lake Superior St.	2005	Denver
1952	Michigan	1966	Michigan St.	1980	North Dakota	1993	Maine	2006	Wisconsin
1953	Michigan	1967	Cornell	1981	Wisconsin	1994	Lake Superior St.	2007	Michigan St.
1954	Rensselaer	1968	Denver	1982	North Dakota	1995	Boston Univ.	2008	Boston College
1955	Michigan	1969	Denver	1983	Wisconsin	1996	Michigan	2009	Boston Univ.
1956	Michigan	1970	Cornell	1984	Bowling Green	1997	North Dakota	2010	Boston College
1957	Colorado College	1971	Boston Univ.	1985	Rensselaer	1998	Michigan	2011	Minnesota-Duluth
1958	Denver	1972	Boston Univ.	1986	Michigan St.	1999	Maine	2012	Boston College
1959	North Dakota	1973	Wisconsin	1987	North Dakota	2000	North Dakota	2013	Yale
1960	Denver	1974	Minnesota	1988	Lake Superior St.	2001	Boston College	2014	Union College
1961	Denver	1975	Michigan Tech						

NCAA Women's Hockey Champions, 2001-14

Year	Champion	Year	Champion	Year	Champion	Year	Champion	Year	Champion
2001	Minnesota-Duluth	2004	Minnesota	2007	Wisconsin	2010	Minnesota-Duluth	2013	Minnesota
2002	Minnesota-Duluth	2005	Minnesota	2008	Minnesota-Duluth	2011	Wisconsin	2014	Clarkson Univ.
2003	Minnesota-Duluth	2006	Wisconsin	2009	Wisconsin	2012	Minnesota		

NCAA Division I Lacrosse Champions, 1982-2014

Year[1]	Men	Women	Year[1]	Men	Women	Year[1]	Men	Women
1982	North Carolina	Massachusetts	1993	Syracuse	Virginia	2004	Syracuse	Virginia
1983	Syracuse	Delaware	1994	Princeton	Princeton	2005	Johns Hopkins	Northwestern
1984	Johns Hopkins	Temple	1995	Syracuse	Maryland	2006	Virginia	Northwestern
1985	Johns Hopkins	New Hampshire	1996	Princeton	Maryland	2007	Johns Hopkins	Northwestern
1986	North Carolina	Maryland	1997	Princeton	Maryland	2008	Syracuse	Northwestern
1987	Johns Hopkins	Penn St.	1998	Princeton	Maryland	2009	Syracuse	Northwestern
1988	Syracuse	Temple	1999	Virginia	Maryland	2010	Duke	Maryland
1989	Syracuse	Penn St.	2000	Syracuse	Maryland	2011	Virginia	Northwestern
1990	Vacated	Harvard	2001	Princeton	Maryland	2012	Loyola (MD)	Northwestern
1991	North Carolina	Virginia	2002	Syracuse	Princeton	2013	Duke	North Carolina
1992	Princeton	Maryland	2003	Virginia	Princeton	2014	Duke	Maryland

(1) NCAA Championships began in 1971 for men, in 1982 for women.

NCAA Division I Soccer Champions, 1982-2013

Year[1]	Men	Women	Year[1]	Men	Women	Year[1]	Men	Women
1982	Indiana	North Carolina	1992	Virginia	North Carolina	2003	Indiana	North Carolina
1983	Indiana	North Carolina	1993	Virginia	North Carolina	2004	Indiana	Notre Dame
1984	Clemson	North Carolina	1994	Virginia	North Carolina	2005	Maryland	Portland
1985	UCLA	George Mason	1995	Wisconsin	Notre Dame	2006	UC Santa Barbara	North Carolina
1986	Duke	North Carolina	1996	St. John's (NY)	North Carolina	2007	Wake Forest	USC
1987	Clemson	North Carolina	1997	UCLA	North Carolina	2008	Maryland	North Carolina
1988	Indiana	North Carolina	1998	Indiana	Florida	2009	Virginia	North Carolina
1989	Santa Clara;	North Carolina	1999	Indiana	North Carolina	2010	Akron	Notre Dame
	Virginia (tie)		2000	Connecticut	North Carolina	2011	North Carolina	Stanford
1990	UCLA	North Carolina	2001	North Carolina	Santa Clara	2012	Indiana	North Carolina
1991	Virginia	North Carolina	2002	UCLA	Portland	2013	Notre Dame	UCLA

(1) NCAA Championships began in 1959 for men, in 1982 for women.

NCAA Division I Wrestling Champions, 1964-2014

Year	Champion	Year	Champion	Year	Champion	Year	Champion	Year	Champion
1964	Oklahoma St.	1975	Iowa	1985	Iowa	1995	Iowa	2005	Oklahoma St.
1965	Iowa St.	1976	Iowa	1986	Iowa	1996	Iowa	2006	Oklahoma St.
1966	Oklahoma St.	1977	Iowa St.	1987	Iowa St.	1997	Iowa	2007	Minnesota
1967	Michigan St.	1978	Iowa	1988	Arizona St.	1998	Iowa	2008	Iowa
1968	Oklahoma St.	1979	Iowa	1989	Oklahoma St.	1999	Iowa	2009	Iowa
1969	Iowa St.	1980	Iowa	1990	Oklahoma St.	2000	Iowa	2010	Iowa
1970	Iowa St.	1981	Iowa	1991	Iowa	2001	Minnesota	2011	Penn St.
1971	Oklahoma St.	1982	Iowa	1992	Iowa	2002	Minnesota	2012	Penn St.
1972	Iowa St.	1983	Iowa	1993	Iowa	2003	Oklahoma St.	2013	Penn St.
1973	Iowa St.	1984	Iowa	1994	Oklahoma St.	2004	Oklahoma St.	2014	Penn St.
1974	Oklahoma								

FOOTBALL

NFL 2013: Peyton Shines, But Seattle Prevails

The Denver Broncos set new records during the 2013 NFL season, but the Seattle Seahawks took home the ultimate prize. Seattle stopped Peyton Manning's Denver offense with a resounding 43-8 victory in Super Bowl XLVIII on Feb. 2, 2014, at MetLife Stadium in East Rutherford, NJ.

Peyton Manning set NFL records for most passing yards (5,477) and touchdown passes (55) in a season while leading the Broncos to the AFC West title. Manning tied the NFL single-game record with seven touchdown passes in a 49-27 Week 1 victory over the defending Super Bowl champion Baltimore Ravens Sept. 5, 2013. The Broncos set the league's single-season record with 606 points and became the first team in NFL history to have five players score at least 10 touchdowns in the same season. Manning outdueled Tom Brady and the New England Patriots in Denver in the AFC title game Jan. 19, 2014, passing for 400 yards and two TDs in a 26-16 victory. Brady (4,343 passing yards) surpassed the 4,000-yard season mark for the sixth time in his career; he was one of nine quarterbacks with more than 4,000 passing yards in 2013.

Seattle and its dominating defense allowed a league-low 273.6 yards per game in 2013, and its cornerback Richard Sherman led the league with eight interceptions. The Seahawks forced three turnovers in the fourth quarter for a 23-17 win over the San Francisco 49ers in the NFC Championship game on Jan. 19, 2014, at Seattle's CenturyLink Field. (Post-game comments made by Sherman during a TV interview went viral and became the talk of Super Bowl week.)

Quarterback Nick Foles and running back LeSean McCoy led the Philadelphia Eagles to the NFC East division title. Foles passed for 27 touchdowns with only two interceptions and his 119.2 passer rating was the third-highest single-season rating in NFL history. McCoy led the NFL with 1,607 rushing yards and 2,146 scrimmage yards. Green Bay quarterback Aaron Rodgers missed seven games due to a broken collarbone suffered against Chicago on Nov. 4, but running back Eddie Lacy did his part to lift the Packers to the NFC North crown. Lacy led all NFL rookies in rushing yards (1,178), rushing touchdowns (11), and scrimmage yards (1,435).

Veteran head coach Andy Reid joined Kansas City in 2013 after 14 years in Philadelphia and guided the Chiefs to an AFC wild card berth, one year after the team finished 2-14. Three Wild Card Weekend games were decided by three points or less, including the Chiefs' 45-44 loss in Indianapolis Jan. 4, 2014, at Lucas Oil Stadium, in which the Colts erased a 31-10 deficit at the half.

NFL Final Standings, 2013
(playoff seeding in parentheses)

AMERICAN FOOTBALL CONFERENCE

	W	L	T	Pct	PF	PA	Div
East Division							
New England (2)...	12	4	0	.750	444	338	4-2
NY Jets	8	8	0	.500	290	387	3-3
Miami	8	8	0	.500	317	335	2-4
Buffalo..........	6	10	0	.375	339	388	3-3
North Division							
Cincinnati (3)	11	5	0	.688	430	305	3-3
Pittsburgh	8	8	0	.500	379	370	4-2
Baltimore	8	8	0	.500	320	352	3-3
Cleveland	4	12	0	.250	308	406	2-4
South Division							
Indianapolis (4)...	11	5	0	.688	391	336	6-0
Tennessee	7	9	0	.438	362	381	2-4
Jacksonville	4	12	0	.250	247	449	3-3
Houston	2	14	0	.125	276	428	1-5
West Division							
Denver (1).......	13	3	0	.813	606	399	5-1
*Kansas City (5)...	11	5	0	.688	430	305	2-4
*San Diego (6)	9	7	0	.563	396	348	4-2
Oakland	4	12	0	.250	322	453	1-5

* = Wild card qualifier for playoffs. **Note:** Cincinnati finished ahead of Indianapolis based on head-to-head win percentage.

NATIONAL FOOTBALL CONFERENCE

	W	L	T	Pct	PF	PA	Div
East Division							
Philadelphia (3)....	10	6	0	.625	442	382	4-2
Dallas	8	8	0	.500	439	432	5-1
NY Giants........	7	9	0	.438	294	383	3-3
Washington.......	3	13	0	.188	334	478	0-6
North Division							
Green Bay (4).....	8	7	1	.531	417	428	3-2-1
Chicago	8	8	0	.500	445	478	2-4
Detroit..........	7	9	0	.438	395	376	4-2
Minnesota........	5	10	1	.344	391	480	2-3-1
South Division							
Carolina (2)......	12	4	0	.750	366	241	5-1
*New Orleans (6) ..	11	5	0	.688	414	304	5-1
Atlanta	4	12	0	.250	353	443	1-5
Tampa Bay	4	12	0	.250	288	389	1-5
West Division							
Seattle (1)........	13	3	0	.813	417	231	4-2
*San Francisco (5)	12	4	0	.750	406	272	5-1
Arizona	10	6	0	.625	379	324	2-4
St. Louis	7	9	0	.438	348	364	1-5

* = Wild card qualifier for playoffs.

2013 Playoffs

AFC Wild Card Games: Indianapolis 45, Kansas City 44; San Diego 27, Cincinnati 10
NFC Wild Card Games: New Orleans 26, Philadelphia 24; San Francisco 23, Green Bay 20
AFC Divisional Playoff Games: New England 43, Indianapolis 22; Denver 24, San Diego 17

NFC Divisional Playoff Games: Seattle 23, New Orleans 15; San Francisco 23, Carolina 10
AFC Championship Game: Denver 26, New England 16
NFC Championship Game: Seattle 23, San Francisco 17
Super Bowl XLVIII: Seattle 43, Denver 8

NFL Individual Leaders: American Football Conference, 2013
(* = rookie)

PASSING

Player, team	Att	Comp	Pct comp	Yds	Yds/Att	Long	TD	Pct TD	Int	Rating
Peyton Manning, Denver...............	659	450	68.3	5,477	8.3	78T	55	8.3	10	115.1
Philip Rivers, San Diego..............	544	378	69.5	4,478	8.2	60T	32	5.9	11	105.5
Ben Roethlisberger, Pittsburgh..........	584	375	64.2	4,261	7.3	67	28	4.8	14	92.0
Alex Smith, Kansas City...............	508	308	60.6	3,313	6.5	71T	23	4.5	7	89.1
Andy Dalton, Cincinnati...............	586	363	61.9	4,293	7.3	82T	33	5.6	20	88.8
Tom Brady, New England..............	628	380	60.5	4,343	6.9	81T	25	4.0	11	87.3
Andrew Luck, Indianapolis.............	570	343	60.2	3,822	6.7	73T	23	4.0	9	87.0
Ryan Fitzpatrick, Tennessee...........	350	217	62.0	2,454	7.0	77T	14	4.0	12	82.0
Ryan Tannehill, Miami................	588	355	60.4	3,913	6.7	67	24	4.1	17	81.7
*Case Keenum, Houston	253	137	54.2	1,760	7.0	66	9	3.6	6	78.2
*EJ Manuel, Buffalo	306	180	58.8	1,972	6.4	45	11	3.6	9	77.7
Jason Campbell, Cleveland	317	180	56.8	2,015	6.4	80T	11	3.5	8	76.9
Chad Henne, Jacksonville	503	305	60.6	3,241	6.4	62T	13	2.6	14	76.5

RUSHING YARDS

Player, team	Yds	Att	Avg	Long	TD
Jamaal Charles, Kansas City ...	1,287	259	5.0	46	12
Ryan Mathews, San Diego	1,255	285	4.4	51	6
Chris Johnson, Tennessee	1,077	279	3.9	30T	6
Knowshon Moreno, Denver	1,038	241	4.3	31	10
C.J. Spiller, Buffalo	933	202	4.6	77	2
Fred Jackson, Buffalo	890	206	4.3	59	9
*Le'Veon Bell, Pittsburgh.......	860	244	3.5	43	8
Chris Ivory, NY Jets	833	182	4.6	69	3
Maurice Jones-Drew, Jacksonville	803	234	3.4	48	5
Stevan Ridley, New England....	773	178	4.3	29	7

RECEPTIONS

Player, team	Rec	Yds	Avg	Long	TD
Antonio Brown, Pittsburgh	110	1,499	13.6	56	8
Andre Johnson, Houston	109	1,407	12.9	62T	5
Julian Edelman, New England ..	105	1,056	10.1	44	6
A.J. Green, Cincinnati.........	98	1,426	14.6	82T	11
Kendall Wright, Tennessee	94	1,079	11.5	45	2
Demaryius Thomas, Denver....	92	1,430	15.5	78T	14
Eric Decker, Denver	87	1,288	14.8	61	11
Josh Gordon, Cleveland	87	1,646	18.9	95T	9
T.Y. Hilton, Indianapolis.......	82	1,083	13.2	73T	5
Jordan Cameron, Cleveland....	80	917	11.5	53	7

INTERCEPTIONS

Player, team	No.	Yds	Avg	Long	TD
Alterraun Verner, Tennessee.....	5	68	13.6	34	1
Tashaun Gipson, Cleveland	5	143	28.6	44T	1
*Logan Ryan, New England	5	82	16.4	79T	1
Jim Leonhard, Buffalo..........	4	72	18.0	41	0
Dimitri Patterson, Miami	4	7	1.8	3	0
Corey Graham, Baltimore.......	4	28	7.0	28	0
Brent Grimes, Miami...........	4	102	25.5	94T	1
Aqib Talib, New England	4	12	3.0	14	0
Quintin Demps, Kansas City.....	4	61	15.3	35	0
Darius Butler, Indianapolis	4	79	19.8	41T	1
Jairus Byrd, Buffalo...........	4	85	21.3	57	0
Joe Haden, Cleveland	4	57	14.3	29T	1
Aaron Williams, Buffalo........	4	43	10.8	34	0
*Kiko Alonso, Buffalo..........	4	38	9.5	32	0

SCORING—KICKERS

Player, team	PAT	FG	Long	Pts
Stephen Gostkowski, New England	44/44	38/41	54	158
Matt Prater, Denver............	75/75	25/26	64	150
Nick Novak, San Diego.........	42/42	34/37	50	144
Justin Tucker, Baltimore........	26/26	38/41	61	140
Adam Vinatieri, Indianapolis.....	34/34	35/40	52	139
Dan Carpenter, Buffalo	32/32	33/36	55	131

SCORING—NON-KICKERS

Player, team (position)	TD	Rush	Rec	2-Pt	Pts
Jamaal Charles, Kansas City (RB)..	19	12	7	0	114
Demaryius Thomas, Denver (WR)..	14	0	14	0	84
Knowshon Moreno, Denver (RB)...	13	10	3	0	78
Julius Thomas, Denver (TE).......	12	0	12	0	72
Eric Decker, Denver (WR)	11	0	11	0	66
A.J. Green, Cincinnati (WR)	11	0	11	0	66

KICKOFF RETURNS

Player, team	No.	Yds	Avg	Long	TD
Quintin Demps, Kansas City...	33	992	30.1	95T	1
Jacoby Jones, Baltimore......	31	892	28.8	77T	1
Trindon Holliday, Denver......	28	775	27.7	105T	1
Jordan Todman, Jacksonville ..	26	712	27.4	59	0
Keshawn Martin, Houston......	36	947	26.3	50	0
Brandon Tate, Cincinnati......	35	914	26.1	71	0

PUNTING

Player, team	No.	Yds	Long	Avg
Marquette King, Oakland	84	4,107	66	48.9
Brandon Fields, Miami	85	4,150	74	48.8
Shane Lechler, Houston	88	4,189	65	47.6
Pat McAfee, Indianapolis	76	3,499	65	46.0
Dustin Colquitt, Kansas City....	87	4,005	65	46.0
Sam Koch, Baltimore	90	4,138	69	46.0
*Ryan Allen, New England	76	3,491	65	45.9

PUNT RETURNS

Player, team	No.	Yds	Avg	Long	TD
Tandon Doss, Baltimore	23	359	15.6	82T	1
Antonio Brown, Pittsburgh	32	409	12.8	67T	1
Dexter McCluster, Kansas City .	58	686	11.8	89T	2
Travis Benjamin, Cleveland....	22	257	11.7	79T	1
Julian Edelman, New England	35	374	10.7	43	0
Brandon Tate, Cincinnati......	36	336	9.3	43	0
Keshawn Martin, Houston.....	39	345	8.8	87T	1

SACKS

Player, team	No.
Robert Mathis, Indianapolis	19.5
Mario Williams, Buffalo	13.0
Chandler Jones, New England..................	11.5
Olivier Vernon, Miami	11.5
Tamba Hali, Kansas City	11.0
Justin Houston, Kansas City....................	11.0
Jurrell Casey, Tennessee	10.5
J.J. Watt, Houston...........................	10.5
Muhammad Wilkerson, NY Jets	10.5
Kyle Williams, Buffalo	10.5

NFL Individual Leaders: National Football Conference, 2013

(* = rookie)

PASSING

Player, team	Att	Comp	Pct comp	Yds	Yds/Att	Long	TD	Pct TD	Int	Rating
Nick Foles, Philadelphia	317	203	64.0	2,891	9.1	63T	27	8.5	2	119.2
Josh McCown, Chicago	224	149	66.5	1,829	8.2	80T	13	5.8	1	109.0
Aaron Rodgers, Green Bay.............	290	193	66.6	2,536	8.7	83T	17	5.9	6	104.9
Drew Brees, New Orleans	650	446	68.6	5,162	7.9	76T	39	6.0	12	104.7
Russell Wilson, Seattle................	407	257	63.1	3,357	8.3	80T	26	6.4	9	101.2
Tony Romo, Dallas	535	342	63.9	3,828	7.2	82T	31	5.8	10	96.7
Colin Kaepernick, San Francisco	416	243	58.4	3,197	7.7	64T	21	5.0	8	91.6
Sam Bradford, St. Louis	262	159	60.7	1,687	6.4	73	14	5.3	4	90.9
Matt Ryan, Atlanta	651	439	67.4	4,515	6.9	81T	26	4.0	17	89.6
Jay Cutler, Chicago...................	355	224	63.1	2,621	7.4	67	19	5.4	12	89.2
Cam Newton, Carolina	473	292	61.7	3,379	7.1	79T	24	5.1	13	88.8
Matthew Stafford, Detroit	634	371	58.5	4,650	7.3	87	29	4.6	19	84.2
Carson Palmer, Arizona	572	362	63.3	4,274	7.5	91T	24	4.2	22	83.9
*Mike Glennon, Tampa Bay	416	247	59.4	2,608	6.3	85T	19	4.6	9	83.9

RUSHING YARDS

Player, team	Yds	Att	Avg	Long	TD		Player, team	Yds	Att	Avg	Long	TD
LeSean McCoy, Philadelphia ..	1,607	314	5.1	57T	9		*Eddie Lacy, Green Bay	1,178	284	4.1	60	11
Matt Forte, Chicago	1,339	289	4.6	55	9		Frank Gore, San Francisco....	1,128	276	4.1	51	9
Alfred Morris, Washington....	1,275	276	4.6	45T	7		DeMarco Murray, Dallas	1,121	217	5.2	43	9
Adrian Peterson, Minnesota...	1,266	279	4.5	78T	10		Reggie Bush, Detroit	1,006	223	4.5	39	4
Marshawn Lynch, Seattle.....	1,257	301	4.2	43	12		*Zac Stacy, St. Louis.........	973	250	3.9	40T	7

RECEPTIONS

Player, team	Rec	Yds	Avg	Long	TD
Pierre Garcon, Washington.....	113	1,346	11.9	53T	5
Brandon Marshall, Chicago	100	1,295	13.0	44	12
Dez Bryant, Dallas	93	1,233	13.3	79	13
Alshon Jeffery, Chicago	89	1,421	16.0	80T	7
Jimmy Graham, New Orleans ..	86	1,215	14.1	56T	16
Anquan Boldin, San Francisco ..	85	1,179	13.9	63	7
Harry Douglas, Atlanta	85	1,067	12.6	80T	2
Jordy Nelson, Green Bay	85	1,314	15.5	76T	8
Calvin Johnson, Detroit........	84	1,492	17.8	87	12
Tony Gonzalez, Atlanta........	83	859	10.3	25	8

INTERCEPTIONS

Player, team	No.	Yds	Avg	Long	TD
Richard Sherman, Seattle	8	125	15.6	58T	1
Brandon Boykin, Philadelphia...	6	136	22.7	76	1
DeAndre Levy, Detroit.........	6	76	12.7	66T	1
Antrel Rolle, NY Giants	6	23	3.8	25	0
Tramaine Brock, San Francisco .	5	82	16.4	41	1
Lavonte David, Tampa Bay	5	87	17.4	32	0
Earl Thomas, Seattle	5	9	1.8	11	0
10 players tied with...........	4				

SCORING—KICKERS

Player, team	PAT	FG	Long	Pts
Steven Hauschka, Seattle......	44/44	33/35	53	143
Mason Crosby, Green Bay	42/42	33/37	57	141
Phil Dawson, San Francisco....	44/44	32/36	56	140
Dan Bailey, Dallas............	47/47	28/30	53	131
Jay Feely, Arizona............	37/37	30/36	52	127
Robbie Gould, Chicago	45/46	26/29	58	123

SCORING—NON-KICKERS

Player, team (position)	TD	Rush	Rec	2-Pt	Pts
Jimmy Graham, New Orleans (TE)	16	0	16	0	96
Marshawn Lynch, Seattle (RB)....	14	12	2	0	84
Dez Bryant, Dallas (WR)	13	0	13	0	78
Vernon Davis, San Francisco (TE)	13	0	13	0	78
Brandon Marshall, Chicago (WR)..	12	0	12	2	76
Matt Forte, Chicago (RB)	12	9	3	1	74

KICKOFF RETURNS

Player, team	No.	Yds	Avg	Long	TD
*Cordarrelle Patterson, Minnesota..................	43	1,393	32.4	109T	2
Dwayne Harris, Dallas	28	857	30.6	90	0
Devin Hester, Chicago	52	1,436	27.6	80	0
*Eric Page, Tampa Bay..........	22	548	24.9	44	0
Jeremy Ross, Detroit/Green Bay	21	514	24.5	98T	1
*Micah Hyde, Green Bay	22	531	24.1	70	0

PUNTING

Player, team	No.	Yds	Long	Avg
Andy Lee, San Francisco	79	3,804	62	48.2
Brad Nortman, Carolina	70	3,344	72	47.8
*Sam Martin, Detroit............	72	3,399	72	47.2
Thomas Morstead, New Orleans ..	61	2,859	61	46.9
Steve Weatherford, NY Giants ...	91	4,271	68	46.9
Matt Bosher, Atlanta	68	3,166	63	46.6
Johnny Hekker, St. Louis	78	3,609	64	46.3

PUNT RETURNS

Player, team	No.	Yds	Avg	Long	TD
Marcus Sherels, Minnesota	22	335	15.2	86T	1
Dwayne Harris, Dallas	20	256	12.8	86T	1
*Micah Hyde, Green Bay	24	296	12.3	93T	1
Ted Ginn, Carolina	26	316	12.2	41	0
Golden Tate, Seattle	51	585	11.5	71	0
LaMichael James, San Francisco..	23	251	10.9	40	0
*Eric Page, Tampa Bay	23	251	10.9	52	0

SACKS

Player, team	No.
Robert Quinn, St. Louis	19.0
Greg Hardy, Carolina	15.0
Cameron Jordan, New Orleans	12.5
Junior Galette, New Orleans.....................	12.0
John Abraham, Arizona	11.5
Jared Allen, Minnesota	11.5
Jason Hatcher, Dallas..........................	11.0
Charles Johnson, Carolina	11.0
Justin Tuck, NY Giants	11.0
Brian Orakpo, Washington	10.0

Super Bowl XLVIII: Seattle 43, Denver 8

The Seattle Seahawks won the franchise's first-ever Super Bowl title with a dominating 43-8 victory over the Denver Broncos in Super Bowl XLVIII on Feb. 2, 2014, at MetLife Stadium in East Rutherford, NJ. It was the first Super Bowl to be played outdoors in a cold-weather state, though game-time temperature was 49°F.

Seattle quarterback Russell Wilson passed for 206 yards and two touchdowns while the Seahawks defense smothered QB Peyton Manning and the Denver offense. Manning passed for 280 yards, but the Denver rushing game managed just 27 net yards against the Seahawks. Seattle built a 36-0 lead before the Broncos scored their first and only touchdown late in the third quarter.

Denver's troubles began on the first play from scrimmage when Seattle recorded a safety following a bad snap. The veteran Manning threw a pair of interceptions in the game, including one snagged by Seattle linebacker Malcolm Smith, who returned it 69 yards for a touchdown that made the score 22-0 in the second quarter. Smith earned Super Bowl MVP; he was the first defensive player to win the award since Tampa Bay's Dexter Jackson in Super Bowl XXXVII in 2003.

Quarters

Team	1	2	3	4	Final
Seattle	8	14	14	7	43
Denver	0	0	8	0	8

Total attendance: 82,529
Game length: 3:23

Scoring

Seattle: Moreno tackled in end zone by Cliff Avril for a safety
Seattle: Hauschka, 31-yard field goal
Seattle: Hauschka, 33-yard field goal
Seattle: Lynch, 1-yard run (Steven Hauschka PAT)
Seattle: Smith, 69-yard interception return (Hauschka PAT)
Seattle: Harvin, 87-yard kickoff return (Hauschka PAT)
Seattle: Kearse, 23-yard pass from Wilson (Hauschka PAT)
Denver: Thomas, 14-yard pass from Manning (Welker pass from Manning for 2-point conversion)
Seattle: Baldwin, 10-yard pass from Wilson (Hauschka PAT)

Team statistics

	Seahawks	Broncos
First downs	17	18
Total net yards	341	306
Rushes-yards	29-135	14-27
Passing yards, net	206	279
Punt returns-yards	0-0	1-9
Kickoff returns-yards...........	2-107	5-105
Interception returns-yards.......	2-71	0-0
Field goals made-attempts	2-2	0-0
Att-comp-int	26-18-0	49-34-2
Sacked-yards lost	0-0	1-1
Punts-average	1-45.0	2-30.0
Fumbles-lost	0-0	4-2
Penalties-yards	10-104	5-44
Time of possession	31:53	28:07

Super Bowl Sites, 2015-18

No.	Site	Date	No.	Site	Date
XLIX	Univ. of Phoenix Stadium, Glendale, AZ...	Feb. 1, 2015	LI	NRG Stadium, Houston, TX	Feb. 2017
L (50)	Levi's Stadium, Santa Clara, CA..........	Feb. 2016	LII	Vikings Stadium, Minneapolis, MN.......	Feb. 2018

Super Bowl Results, 1967-2014

No.	Year	Winner	Opponent	Winning coach	Site
I	1967	*Green Bay Packers, 35	Kansas City Chiefs, 10	Vince Lombardi	Memorial Coliseum, Los Angeles, CA
II	1968	Green Bay Packers, 33	*Oakland Raiders, 14	Vince Lombardi	Orange Bowl, Miami, FL
III	1969	*NY Jets, 16	Baltimore Colts, 7	Weeb Ewbank	Orange Bowl, Miami, FL
IV	1970	Kansas City Chiefs, 23	*Minnesota Vikings, 7	Hank Stram	Tulane Stadium, New Orleans, LA
V	1971	Baltimore Colts, 16	*Dallas Cowboys, 13	Don McCafferty	Orange Bowl, Miami, FL
VI	1972	Dallas Cowboys, 24	*Miami Dolphins, 3	Tom Landry	Tulane Stadium, New Orleans, LA
VII	1973	*Miami Dolphins, 14	Washington Redskins, 7	Don Shula	Memorial Coliseum, Los Angeles, CA
VIII	1974	*Miami Dolphins, 24	Minnesota Vikings, 7	Don Shula	Rice Stadium, Houston, TX
IX	1975	*Pittsburgh Steelers, 16	Minnesota Vikings, 6	Chuck Noll	Tulane Stadium, New Orleans, LA
X	1976	Pittsburgh Steelers, 21	*Dallas Cowboys, 17	Chuck Noll	Orange Bowl, Miami, FL
XI	1977	*Oakland Raiders, 32	Minnesota Vikings, 14	John Madden	Rose Bowl, Pasadena, CA
XII	1978	*Dallas Cowboys, 27	Denver Broncos, 10	Tom Landry	Superdome, New Orleans, LA
XIII	1979	Pittsburgh Steelers, 35	*Dallas Cowboys, 31	Chuck Noll	Orange Bowl, Miami, FL
XIV	1980	Pittsburgh Steelers, 31	*L.A. Rams, 19	Chuck Noll	Rose Bowl, Pasadena, CA
XV	1981	Oakland Raiders, 27	*Philadelphia Eagles, 10	Tom Flores	Superdome, New Orleans, LA
XVI	1982	*San Francisco 49ers, 26	Cincinnati Bengals, 21	Bill Walsh	Silverdome, Pontiac, MI
XVII	1983	Washington Redskins, 27	*Miami Dolphins, 17	Joe Gibbs	Rose Bowl, Pasadena, CA
XVIII	1984	*L.A. Raiders, 38	Washington Redskins, 9	Tom Flores	Tampa Stadium, Tampa, FL
XIX	1985	*San Francisco 49ers, 38	Miami Dolphins, 16	Bill Walsh	Stanford Stadium, Stanford, CA
XX	1986	*Chicago Bears, 46	New England Patriots, 10	Mike Ditka	Superdome, New Orleans, LA
XXI	1987	NY Giants, 39	*Denver Broncos, 20	Bill Parcells	Rose Bowl, Pasadena, CA
XXII	1988	*Washington Redskins, 42	Denver Broncos, 10	Joe Gibbs	Jack Murphy Stadium, San Diego, CA
XXIII	1989	*San Francisco 49ers, 20	Cincinnati Bengals, 16	Bill Walsh	Joe Robbie Stadium, Miami, FL
XXIV	1990	San Francisco 49ers, 55	*Denver Broncos, 10	George Seifert	Superdome, New Orleans, LA
XXV	1991	NY Giants, 20	*Buffalo Bills, 19	Bill Parcells	Tampa Stadium, Tampa, FL
XXVI	1992	*Washington Redskins, 37	Buffalo Bills, 24	Joe Gibbs	Metrodome, Minneapolis, MN
XXVII	1993	Dallas Cowboys, 52	*Buffalo Bills, 17	Jimmy Johnson	Rose Bowl, Pasadena, CA
XXVIII	1994	*Dallas Cowboys, 30	Buffalo Bills, 13	Jimmy Johnson	Georgia Dome, Atlanta, GA
XXIX	1995	*San Francisco 49ers, 49	San Diego Chargers, 26	George Seifert	Joe Robbie Stadium, Miami, FL
XXX	1996	Dallas Cowboys, 27	Pittsburgh Steelers, 17	Barry Switzer	Sun Devil Stadium, Tempe, AZ
XXXI	1997	Green Bay Packers, 35	*New England Patriots, 21	Mike Holmgren	Superdome, New Orleans, LA
XXXII	1998	Denver Broncos, 31	*Green Bay Packers, 24	Mike Shanahan	Qualcomm Stadium, San Diego, CA
XXXIII	1999	Denver Broncos, 34	*Atlanta Falcons, 19	Mike Shanahan	Pro Player Stadium, Miami, FL
XXXIV	2000	*St. Louis Rams, 23	Tennessee Titans, 16	Dick Vermeil	Georgia Dome, Atlanta, GA
XXXV	2001	Baltimore Ravens, 34	*NY Giants, 7	Brian Billick	Raymond James Stadium, Tampa, FL
XXXVI	2002	New England Patriots, 20	*St. Louis Rams, 17	Bill Belichick	Superdome, New Orleans, LA
XXXVII	2003	*Tampa Bay Buccaneers, 48	Oakland Raiders, 21	Jon Gruden	Qualcomm Stadium, San Diego, CA
XXXVIII	2004	New England Patriots, 32	*Carolina Panthers, 29	Bill Belichick	Reliant Stadium, Houston, TX
XXXIX	2005	New England Patriots, 24	*Philadelphia Eagles, 21	Bill Belichick	Alltel Stadium, Jacksonville, FL
XL	2006	Pittsburgh Steelers, 21	*Seattle Seahawks, 10	Bill Cowher	Ford Field, Detroit, MI
XLI	2007	Indianapolis Colts, 29	*Chicago Bears, 17	Tony Dungy	Dolphin Stadium, Miami Gardens, FL
XLII	2008	*NY Giants, 17	New England Patriots, 14	Tom Coughlin	Univ. of Phoenix Stadium, Glendale, AZ
XLIII	2009	Pittsburgh Steelers, 27	*Arizona Cardinals, 23	Mike Tomlin	Raymond James Stadium, Tampa, FL
XLIV	2010	*New Orleans Saints, 31	Indianapolis Colts, 17	Sean Payton	Sun Life Stadium, Miami Gardens, FL
XLV	2011	*Green Bay Packers, 31	Pittsburgh Steelers, 25	Mike McCarthy	Cowboys Stadium, Arlington, TX
XLVI	2012	NY Giants, 21	*New England Patriots, 17	Tom Coughlin	Lucas Oil Stadium, Indianapolis, IN
XLVII	2013	*Baltimore Ravens, 34	San Francisco 49ers, 31	John Harbaugh	Mercedes-Benz Superdome, New Orleans, LA
XLVIII	2014	*Seattle Seahawks, 43	Denver Broncos, 8	Pete Carroll	MetLife Stadium, East Rutherford, NJ

*Team that won the coin toss. All teams that won the toss elected to receive, except the 2009 Cardinals, 2011 Packers, 2012 Patriots, 2013 Ravens, and 2014 Seahawks, who deferred their choice to receive in the second half.

Super Bowl MVPs, 1967-2014

Year	Most valuable player, team	Year	Most valuable player, team	Year	Most valuable player, team
1967	Bart Starr, Green Bay	1983	John Riggins, Washington	1999	John Elway, Denver
1968	Bart Starr, Green Bay	1984	Marcus Allen, L.A. Raiders	2000	Kurt Warner, St. Louis
1969	Joe Namath, NY Jets	1985	Joe Montana, San Francisco	2001	Ray Lewis, Baltimore
1970	Len Dawson, Kansas City	1986	Richard Dent, Chicago	2002	Tom Brady, New England
1971	Chuck Howley, Dallas	1987	Phil Simms, NY Giants	2003	Dexter Jackson, Tampa Bay
1972	Roger Staubach, Dallas	1988	Doug Williams, Washington	2004	Tom Brady, New England
1973	Jake Scott, Miami	1989	Jerry Rice, San Francisco	2005	Deion Branch, New England
1974	Larry Csonka, Miami	1990	Joe Montana, San Francisco	2006	Hines Ward, Pittsburgh
1975	Franco Harris, Pittsburgh	1991	Ottis Anderson, NY Giants	2007	Peyton Manning, Indianapolis
1976	Lynn Swann, Pittsburgh	1992	Mark Rypien, Washington	2008	Eli Manning, NY Giants
1977	Fred Biletnikoff, Oakland	1993	Troy Aikman, Dallas	2009	Santonio Holmes, Pittsburgh
1978	Randy White, Harvey Martin; Dallas	1994	Emmitt Smith, Dallas	2010	Drew Brees, New Orleans
1979	Terry Bradshaw, Pittsburgh	1995	Steve Young, San Francisco	2011	Aaron Rodgers, Green Bay
1980	Terry Bradshaw, Pittsburgh	1996	Larry Brown, Dallas	2012	Eli Manning, NY Giants
1981	Jim Plunkett, Oakland	1997	Desmond Howard, Green Bay	2013	Joe Flacco, Baltimore
1982	Joe Montana, San Francisco	1998	Terrell Davis, Denver	2014	Malcolm Smith, Seattle

Super Bowl Single-Game Statistical Leaders

Passing Yards

Player, team	Year	Att/comp	Yds	TD
Kurt Warner, St. Louis	2000	45/24	414	2
Kurt Warner, Arizona	2009	43/31	377	3
Kurt Warner, St. Louis	2002	44/28	365	1
Donovan McNabb, Philadelphia	2005	51/30	357	3
Joe Montana, San Francisco	1989	36/23	357	2

Passing Touchdowns

Player, team	Year	Att/comp	Yds	TD
Steve Young, San Francisco	1995	36/24	325	6
Joe Montana, San Francisco	1990	29/22	297	5
Troy Aikman, Dallas	1993	30/22	273	4
Doug Williams, Washington	1988	29/18	340	4
Terry Bradshaw, Pittsburgh	1979	30/17	318	4

Receiving Yards

Player, team	Year	Rec	Yds	TD
Jerry Rice, San Francisco	1989	11	215	1
Ricky Sanders, Washington	1988	9	193	2
Isaac Bruce, St. Louis	2000	6	162	1

Scoring

Player, team	Year	Pts	
Terrell Davis, Denver	1998	18	(3 TDs)
Jerry Rice, San Francisco	1995	18	(3 TDs)
Ricky Watters, San Francisco	1995	18	(3 TDs)
Jerry Rice, San Francisco	1990	18	(3 TDs)
Roger Craig, San Francisco	1985	18	(3 TDs)

Rushing Yards

Player, team	Year	Att	Yds	TD
Timmy Smith, Washington	1988	22	204	2
Marcus Allen, L.A. Raiders	1984	20	191	2
John Riggins, Washington	1983	38	166	1

Player, team	Year			
Don Chandler, Green Bay	1968	15	(4 FGs, 3 PATs)	
Kevin Butler, Chicago Bears	1986	14	(3 FGs, 5 PATs)	
Ray Wersching, San Francisco	1982	14	(4 FGs, 2 PATs)	

First-Round Selections in the 2014 NFL Draft

Held May 8-10, 2014.

Team	Player	Pos.	College
1. Houston	Jadeveon Clowney	DE	S. Carolina
2. St. Louis[1]	Greg Robinson	OT	Auburn
3. Jacksonville	Blake Bortles	QB	UCF
4. Buffalo[2]	Sammy Watkins	WR	Clemson
5. Oakland	Khalil Mack	LB	Buffalo
6. Atlanta	Jake Matthews	OT	Texas A&M
7. Tampa Bay	Mike Evans	WR	Texas A&M
8. Cleveland[3]	Justin Gilbert	CB	Oklahoma St.
9. Minnesota[4]	Anthony Barr	LB	UCLA
10. Detroit	Eric Ebron	TE	N. Carolina
11. Tennessee	Taylor Lewan	OT	Michigan
12. NY Giants	Odell Beckham Jr.	WR	LSU
13. St. Louis	Aaron Donald	DT	Pittsburgh
14. Chicago	Kyle Fuller	CB	Virginia Tech
15. Pittsburgh	Ryan Shazier	LB	Ohio St.
16. Dallas	Zack Martin	OT	Notre Dame
17. Baltimore	C.J. Mosley	LB	Alabama
18. NY Jets	Calvin Pryor	S	Louisville
19. Miami	Ja'Wuan James	OT	Tennessee
20. New Orleans[5]	Brandin Cooks	WR	Oregon St.
21. Green Bay	Ha Ha Clinton-Dix	S	Alabama
22. Cleveland[6]	Johnny Manziel	QB	Texas A&M
23. Kansas City	Dee Ford	DE	Auburn
24. Cincinnati	Darqueze Dennard	CB	Michigan St.
25. San Diego	Jason Verrett	CB	TCU
26. Philadelphia[7]	Marcus Smith	DE	Louisville
27. Arizona[8]	Deone Bucannon	S	Wash. St.
28. Carolina	Kelvin Benjamin	WR	Florida St.
29. New England	Dominique Easley	DT	Florida
30. San Francisco	Jimmie Ward	S	No. Illinois
31. Denver	Bradley Roby	CB	Ohio St.
32. Minnesota[9]	Teddy Bridgewater	QB	Louisville

(1) From Washington. (2) From Cleveland. (3) From Minnesota. (4) From Buffalo through Cleveland. (5) From Arizona. (6) From Philadelphia. (7) From Indianapolis through Cleveland. (8) From New Orleans. (9) From Seattle.

Number One NFL Draft Choices, 1960-2014

Year	Team	Player, pos., college
1960	L.A. Rams	Billy Cannon, HB, LSU
1961	Minnesota	Tommy Mason, HB, Tulane
1962	Washington	Ernie Davis, HB, Syracuse
1963	L.A. Rams	Terry Baker, QB, Oregon St.
1964	San Francisco	Dave Parks, E, Texas Tech
1965	NY Giants	Tucker Frederickson, RB, Auburn
1966	Atlanta	Tommy Nobis, LB, Texas
1967	Baltimore Colts	Bubba Smith, DE, Michigan St.
1968	Minnesota	Ron Yary, OT, USC
1969	Buffalo	O. J. Simpson, RB, USC
1970	Pittsburgh	Terry Bradshaw, QB, LA Tech
1971	New England	Jim Plunkett, QB, Stanford
1972	Buffalo	Walt Patulski, DE, Notre Dame
1973	Houston	John Matuszak, DE, Tampa
1974	Dallas	Ed "Too Tall" Jones, DE, Tenn. St.
1975	Atlanta	Steve Bartkowski, QB, California
1976	Tampa Bay	Lee Roy Selmon, DE, Oklahoma
1977	Tampa Bay	Ricky Bell, RB, USC
1978	Houston	Earl Campbell, RB, Texas
1979	Buffalo	Tom Cousineau, LB, Ohio St.
1980	Detroit	Billy Sims, RB, Oklahoma
1981	New Orleans	George Rogers, RB, S. Carolina
1982	New England	Kenneth Sims, DT, Texas
1983	Baltimore Colts	John Elway, QB, Stanford
1984	New England	Irving Fryar, WR, Nebraska
1985	Buffalo	Bruce Smith, DE, Virginia Tech
1986	Tampa Bay	Bo Jackson, RB, Auburn
1987	Tampa Bay	Vinny Testaverde, QB, Miami (FL)
1988	Atlanta	Aundray Bruce, LB, Auburn
1989	Dallas	Troy Aikman, QB, UCLA
1990	Indianapolis	Jeff George, QB, Illinois
1991	Dallas	Russell Maryland, DL, Miami (FL)
1992	Indianapolis	Steve Emtman, DL, Washington
1993	New England	Drew Bledsoe, QB, Washington St.
1994	Cincinnati	Dan Wilkinson, DT, Ohio St.
1995	Cincinnati	Ki-Jana Carter, RB, Penn State
1996	NY Jets	Keyshawn Johnson, WR, USC
1997	St. Louis	Orlando Pace, OT, Ohio St.
1998	Indianapolis	Peyton Manning, QB, Tennessee
1999	Cleveland	Tim Couch, QB, Kentucky
2000	Cleveland	Courtney Brown, DE, Penn State
2001	Atlanta	Michael Vick, QB, Virginia Tech
2002	Houston	David Carr, QB, Fresno St.
2003	Cincinnati	Carson Palmer, QB, USC
2004	San Diego	Eli Manning, QB, Mississippi
2005	San Francisco	Alex D. Smith, QB, Utah
2006	Houston	Mario Williams, DE, NC State
2007	Oakland	JaMarcus Russell, QB, LSU
2008	Miami	Jake Long, OT, Michigan
2009	Detroit	Matthew Stafford, QB, Georgia
2010	St. Louis	Sam Bradford, QB, Oklahoma
2011	Carolina	Cam Newton, QB, Auburn
2012	Indianapolis	Andrew Luck, QB, Stanford
2013	Kansas City	Eric Fisher, OT, Central Michigan
2014	Houston	Jadeveon Clowney, DE, S. Carolina

American Football League Champions, 1960-69

Year	Eastern (W-L-T)	Western (W-L-T)	Championship
1960	Houston Oilers (10-4-0)	L.A. Chargers (10-4-0)	Houston 24, L.A. 16
1961	Houston Oilers (10-3-1)	San Diego Chargers (12-2-0)	Houston 10, San Diego 3
1962	Houston Oilers (11-3-0)	Dallas Texans (11-3-0)	Dallas 20, Houston 17 (2 OT)
1963	Boston Patriots (7-6-1)[1]	San Diego Chargers (11-3-0)	San Diego 51, Boston 10
1964	Buffalo Bills (12-2-0)	San Diego Chargers (8-5-1)	Buffalo 20, San Diego 7
1965	Buffalo Bills (10-3-1)	San Diego Chargers (9-2-3)	Buffalo 23, San Diego 0
1966	Buffalo Bills (9-4-1)	Kansas City Chiefs (11-2-1)	Kansas City 31, Buffalo 7
1967	Houston Oilers (9-4-1)	Oakland Raiders (13-1-0)	Oakland 40, Houston 7
1968	NY Jets (11-3-0)	Oakland Raiders (12-2-0)[2]	NY Jets 27, Oakland 23
1969	NY Jets (10-4-0)	Oakland Raiders (12-1-1)	Kansas City 17, Oakland 7[3]

(1) Defeated conference champion Buffalo Bills in divisional playoff. (2) Defeated conference champion Kansas City Chiefs in divisional playoff. (3) Kansas City Chiefs defeated NY Jets, and Oakland Raiders defeated Houston Oilers in divisional playoffs.

National Football League Champions, 1933-69

Year	Eastern (W-L-T)	Western (W-L-T)	Championship
1933	NY Giants (11-3-0)	Chicago Bears (10-2-1)	Chicago Bears 23, NY Giants 21
1934	NY Giants (8-5-0)	Chicago Bears (13-0-0)	NY Giants 30, Chicago Bears 13
1935	NY Giants (9-3-0)	Detroit Lions (7-3-2)	Detroit 26, NY Giants 7
1936	Boston Redskins (7-5-0)	Green Bay Packers (10-1-1)	Green Bay 21, Boston 6
1937	Washington Redskins (8-3-0)	Chicago Bears (9-1-1)	Washington 28, Chicago Bears 21
1938	NY Giants (8-2-1)	Green Bay Packers (8-3-0)	NY Giants 23, Green Bay 17
1939	NY Giants (9-1-1)	Green Bay Packers (9-2-0)	Green Bay 27, NY Giants 0
1940	Washington Redskins (9-2-0)	Chicago Bears (8-3-0)	Chicago Bears 73, Washington 0
1941	NY Giants (8-3-0)	Chicago Bears (10-1-0)[1]	Chicago Bears 37, NY Giants 9
1942	Washington Redskins (10-1-0)	Chicago Bears (11-0-0)	Washington 14, Chicago Bears 6
1943	Washington Redskins (6-3-1)[1]	Chicago Bears (8-1-1)	Chicago Bears, 41, Washington 21
1944	NY Giants (8-1-1)	Green Bay Packers (8-2-0)	Green Bay 14, NY Giants 7
1945	Washington Redskins (8-2-0)	Cleveland Rams (9-1-0)	Cleveland Rams 15, Washington 14
1946	NY Giants (7-3-1)	Chicago Bears (8-2-1)	Chicago Bears 24, NY Giants 14
1947	Philadelphia Eagles (8-4-0)[1]	Chicago Cardinals (9-3-0)	Chicago Cardinals 28, Philadelphia 21
1948	Philadelphia Eagles (9-2-1)	Chicago Cardinals (11-1-0)	Philadelphia 7, Chicago Cardinals 0
1949	Philadelphia Eagles (11-1-0)	L.A. Rams (8-2-2)	Philadelphia 14, L.A. Rams 0
1950	Cleveland Browns (10-2-0)[1]	L.A. Rams (9-3-0)[1]	Cleveland 30, L.A. Rams 28
1951	Cleveland Browns (11-1-0)	L.A. Rams (8-4-0)	L.A. Rams 24, Cleveland Browns 17
1952	Cleveland Browns (8-4-0)	Detroit Lions (9-3-0)[1]	Detroit 17, Cleveland Browns 7
1953	Cleveland Browns (11-1-0)	Detroit Lions (10-2-0)	Detroit 17, Cleveland Browns 16
1954	Cleveland Browns (9-3-0)	Detroit Lions (9-2-1)	Cleveland Browns 56, Detroit 10
1955	Cleveland Browns (9-2-1)	L.A. Rams (8-3-1)	Cleveland Browns 38, L.A. Rams 14
1956	NY Giants (8-3-1)	Chicago Bears (9-2-1)	NY Giants 47, Chicago Bears 7
1957	Cleveland Browns (9-2-1)	Detroit Lions (8-4-0)[1]	Detroit 59, Cleveland Browns 14
1958	NY Giants (9-3-0)[1]	Baltimore Colts (9-3-0)	Baltimore 23, NY Giants 17[2]
1959	NY Giants (10-2-0)	Baltimore Colts (9-3-0)	Baltimore 31, NY Giants 16
1960	Philadelphia Eagles (10-2-0)	Green Bay Packers (8-4-0)	Philadelphia 17, Green Bay 13
1961	NY Giants (10-3-1)	Green Bay Packers (11-3-0)	Green Bay 37, NY Giants 0
1962	NY Giants (12-2-0)	Green Bay Packers (13-1-0)	Green Bay 16, NY Giants 7
1963	NY Giants (11-3-0)	Chicago Bears (11-1-2)	Chicago 14, NY Giants 10
1964	Cleveland Browns (10-3-1)	Baltimore Colts (12-2-0)	Cleveland Browns 27, Baltimore 0
1965	Cleveland Browns (11-3-0)	Green Bay Packers (10-3-1)[1]	Green Bay 23, Cleveland Browns 12
1966	Dallas Cowboys (10-3-1)	Green Bay Packers (12-2-0)	Green Bay 34, Dallas 27
1967	Dallas Cowboys (9-5-0)	Green Bay Packers (9-4-1)	Green Bay 21, Dallas 17
1968	Cleveland Browns (10-4-0)	Baltimore Colts (13-1-0)	Baltimore 34, Cleveland Browns 0
1969	Cleveland Browns (10-3-1)	Minnesota Vikings (12-2-0)	Minnesota 27, Cleveland Browns 7

Note: Conference title games preceded NFL Championship from 1967-69. (1) Won divisional or conference playoff. (2) Won at 8:15 of sudden death overtime period.

NFL Divisional Champions and Wild Cards, 1970-95

The American Football League and National Football League officially merged in 1966. At the beginning of the 1970 season, the two leagues became the AFC and NFC conferences in the new NFL. Regular-season (W-L-T) records are in parentheses.

	AMERICAN FOOTBALL CONFERENCE			
Year	Eastern	Central	Western	Wild card
1970	Baltimore Colts (11-2-1)	Cincinnati Bengals (8-6-0)	Oakland Raiders (8-4-2)	Miami Dolphins (10-4-0)
1971	Miami Dolphins (10-3-1)	Cleveland Browns (9-5-0)	Kansas City Chiefs (10-3-1)	Baltimore Colts (10-4-0)
1972	Miami Dolphins (14-0-0)	Pittsburgh Steelers (11-3-0)	Oakland Raiders (10-3-1)	Cleveland Browns (10-4-0)
1973	Miami Dolphins (12-2-0)	Cincinnati Bengals (10-4-0)	Oakland Raiders (9-4-1)	Pittsburgh Steelers (10-4-0)
1974	Miami Dolphins (11-3-0)	Pittsburgh Steelers (10-3-1)	Oakland Raiders (12-2-0)	Buffalo Bills (9-5-0)
1975	Baltimore Colts (10-4-0)	Pittsburgh Steelers (12-2-0)	Oakland Raiders (11-3-0)	Cincinnati Bengals (11-3-0)
1976	Baltimore Colts (11-3-0)	Pittsburgh Steelers (10-4-0)	Oakland Raiders (13-1-0)	New England Patriots (11-3-0)
1977	Baltimore Colts (10-4-0)	Pittsburgh Steelers (9-5-0)	Denver Broncos (12-2-0)	Oakland Raiders (11-3-0)
1978	New England Patriots (11-5-0)	Pittsburgh Steelers (14-2-0)	Denver Broncos (10-6-0)	Houston Oilers (10-6-0) Miami Dolphins (11-5-0)
1979	Miami Dolphins (10-6-0)	Pittsburgh Steelers (12-4-0)	San Diego Chargers (12-4-0)	Houston Oilers (11-5-0) Denver Broncos (10-6-0)
1980	Buffalo Bills (11-5-0)	Cleveland Browns (11-5-0)	San Diego Chargers (11-5-0)	Houston Oilers (11-5-0) Oakland Raiders (11-5-0)
1981	Miami Dolphins (11-4-1)	Cincinnati Bengals (12-4-0)	San Diego Chargers (10-6-0)	Buffalo Bills (10-6-0) NY Jets (10-5-1)
1982	Strike abbreviated season. See note.			
1983	Miami Dolphins (12-4-0)	Pittsburgh Steelers (10-6-0)	L.A. Raiders (12-4-0)	Denver Broncos (9-7-0) Seattle Seahawks (9-7-0)
1984	Miami Dolphins (14-2-0)	Pittsburgh Steelers (9-7-0)	Denver Broncos (13-3-0)	L.A. Raiders (11-5-0) Seattle Seahawks (12-4-0)
1985	Miami Dolphins (12-4-0)	Cleveland Browns (8-8-0)	L.A. Raiders (12-4-0)	New England Patriots (11-5-0) NY Jets (11-5-0)
1986	New England Patriots (11-5-0)	Cleveland Browns (12-4-0)	Denver Broncos (11-5-0)	Kansas City Chiefs (10-6-0) NY Jets (10-6-0)
1987	Indianapolis Colts (9-6-0)	Cleveland Browns (10-5-0)	Denver Broncos (10-4-1)	Houston Oilers (9-6-0) Seattle Seahawks (9-6-0)
1988	Buffalo Bills (12-4-0)	Cincinnati Bengals (12-4-0)	Seattle Seahawks (9-7-0)	Cleveland Browns (10-6-0) Houston Oilers (10-6-0)
1989	Buffalo Bills (9-7-0)	Cleveland Browns (9-6-1)	Denver Broncos (11-5-0)	Houston Oilers (9-7-0) Pittsburgh Steelers (9-7-0)
1990	Buffalo Bills (13-3-0)	Cincinnati Bengals (9-7-0)	L.A. Raiders (12-4-0)	Houston Oilers (9-7-0) Kansas City Chiefs (10-6-0) Miami Dolphins (12-4-0)

AMERICAN FOOTBALL CONFERENCE

Year	Eastern	Central	Western	Wild card
1991	Buffalo Bills (13-3-0)	Houston Oilers (11-5-0)	Denver Broncos (12-4-0)	Kansas City Chiefs (10-6-0) L.A. Raiders (9-7-0) NY Jets (8-8-0)
1992	Miami Dolphins (11-5-0)	Pittsburgh Steelers (11-5-0)	San Diego Chargers (11-5-0)	Buffalo Bills (11-5-0) Houston Oilers (10-6-0) Kansas City Chiefs (10-6-0)
1993	Buffalo Bills (12-4-0)	Houston Oilers (12-4-0)	Kansas City Chiefs (11-5-0)	Denver Broncos (9-7-0) L.A. Raiders (10-6-0) Pittsburgh Steelers (9-7-0)
1994	Miami Dolphins (10-6-0)	Pittsburgh Steelers (12-4-0)	San Diego Chargers (11-5-0)	Cleveland Browns (11-5-0) Kansas City Chiefs (9-7-0) New England Patriots (10-6-0)
1995	Buffalo Bills (10-6-0)	Pittsburgh Steelers (11-5-0)	Kansas City Chiefs (13-3-0)	Miami Dolphins (9-7-0) Indianapolis Colts (9-7-0) San Diego Chargers (9-7-0)

NATIONAL FOOTBALL CONFERENCE

Year	Eastern	Central	Western	Wild card
1970	Dallas Cowboys (10-4-0)	Minnesota Vikings (12-2-0)	San Francisco 49ers (10-3-1)	Detroit Lions (10-4-0)
1971	Dallas Cowboys (11-3-0)	Minnesota Vikings (11-3-0)	San Francisco 49ers (9-5-0)	Washington Redskins (9-4-1)
1972	Washington Redskins (11-3-0)	Green Bay Packers (10-4-0)	San Francisco 49ers (8-5-1)	Dallas Cowboys (10-4-0)
1973	Dallas Cowboys (10-4-0)	Minnesota Vikings (12-2-0)	L.A. Rams (12-2-0)	Washington Redskins (10-4-0)
1974	St. Louis Cardinals (10-4-0)	Minnesota Vikings (10-4-0)	L.A. Rams (10-4-0)	Washington Redskins (10-4-0)
1975	St. Louis Cardinals (11-3-0)	Minnesota Vikings (12-2-0)	L.A. Rams (12-2-0)	Dallas Cowboys (10-4-0)
1976	Dallas Cowboys (11-3-0)	Minnesota Vikings (11-2-1)	L.A. Rams (10-3-1)	Washington Redskins (10-4-0)
1977	Dallas Cowboys (12-2-0)	Minnesota Vikings (9-5-0)	L.A. Rams (10-4-0)	Chicago Bears (9-5-0)
1978	Dallas Cowboys (12-4-0)	Minnesota Vikings (8-7-1)	L.A. Rams (12-4-0)	Atlanta Falcons (9-7-0) Philadelphia Eagles (9-7-0)
1979	Dallas Cowboys (11-5-0)	Tampa Bay Buccaneers (10-6-0)	L.A. Rams (9-7-0)	Chicago Bears (10-6-0) Philadelphia Eagles (11-5-0)
1980	Philadelphia Eagles (12-4-0)	Minnesota Vikings (9-7-0)	Atlanta Falcons (12-4-0)	Dallas Cowboys (12-4-0) L.A. Rams (11-5-0)
1981	Dallas Cowboys (12-4-0)	Tampa Bay Buccaneers (9-7-0)	San Francisco 49ers (13-3-0)	NY Giants (9-7-0) Philadelphia Eagles (10-6-0)
1982	Strike abbreviated season. See note.			
1983	Washington Redskins (14-2-0)	Detroit Lions (9-7-0)	San Francisco 49ers (10-6-0)	Dallas Cowboys (12-4-0) L.A. Rams (9-7-0)
1984	Washington Redskins (11-5-0)	Chicago Bears (10-6-0)	San Francisco 49ers (15-1-0)	L.A. Rams (10-6-0) NY Giants (9-7-0)
1985	Dallas Cowboys (10-6-0)	Chicago Bears (15-1-0)	L.A. Rams (11-5-0)	NY Giants (10-6-0) San Francisco 49ers (10-6-0)
1986	NY Giants (14-2-0)	Chicago Bears (14-2-0)	San Francisco 49ers (10-5-1)	L.A. Rams (10-6-0) Washington Redskins (12-4-0)
1987	Washington Redskins (11-4-0)	Chicago Bears (11-4-0)	San Francisco 49ers (13-2-0)	Minnesota Vikings (8-7-0) New Orleans Saints (12-3-0)
1988	Philadelphia Eagles (10-6-0)	Chicago Bears (12-4-0)	San Francisco 49ers (10-6-0)	L.A. Rams (10-6-0) Minnesota Vikings (11-5-0)
1989	NY Giants (12-4-0)	Minnesota Vikings (10-6-0)	San Francisco 49ers (14-2-0)	L.A. Rams (11-5-0) Philadelphia Eagles (11-5-0)
1990	NY Giants (13-3-0)	Chicago Bears (11-5-0)	San Francisco 49ers (14-2-0)	New Orleans Saints (8-8-0) Philadelphia Eagles (10-6-0) Washington Redskins (10-6-0)
1991	Washington Redskins (14-2-0)	Detroit Lions (12-4-0)	New Orleans Saints (11-5-0)	Atlanta Falcons (10-6-0) Chicago Bears (11-5-0) Dallas Cowboys (11-5-0)
1992	Dallas Cowboys (13-3-0)	Minnesota Vikings (11-5-0)	San Francisco 49ers (14-2-0)	New Orleans Saints (12-4-0) Philadelphia Eagles (11-5-0) Washington Redskins (9-7-0)
1993	Dallas Cowboys (12-4-0)	Detroit Lions (10-6-0)	San Francisco 49ers (10-6-0)	Green Bay Packers (9-7-0) Minnesota Vikings (9-7-0) NY Giants (11-5-0)
1994	Dallas Cowboys (12-4-0)	Minnesota Vikings (10-6-0)	San Francisco 49ers (13-3-0)	Chicago Bears (9-7-0) Detroit Lions (9-7-0) Green Bay Packers (9-7-0)
1995	Dallas Cowboys (12-4-0)	Green Bay Packers (11-5-0)	San Francisco 49ers (11-5-0)	Philadelphia Eagles (10-6-0) Detroit Lions (10-6-0) Atlanta Falcons (9-7-0)

Note: A strike shortened the 1982 season from 16 to 9 games. The top eight teams in each conference played in a tournament to determine the conference champion.

NFL Playoff Results, 1996-2013

Year	Conference	Division	Winner (W-L-T)	Playoffs[1]	Year
1996	American	Eastern	New England Patriots (11-5-0)	Jacksonville* 30, Denver 27	1996
		Central	Pittsburgh Steelers (10-6-0)	New England 28, Pittsburgh 3	
		Western	Denver Broncos (13-3-0)	New England 20, Jacksonville* 6	
	National	Eastern	Dallas Cowboys (10-6-0)	Green Bay 35, San Francisco* 14	
		Central	Green Bay Packers (13-3-0)	Carolina 26, Dallas 17	
		Western	Carolina Panthers (12-4-0)	Green Bay 30, Carolina 13	

Year	Conference	Division	Winner (W-L-T)	Playoffs[1]	Year
1997	American	Eastern	New England Patriots (10-6-0)	Pittsburgh 7, New England 6	1997
		Central	Pittsburgh Steelers (11-5-0)	Denver* 14, Kansas City 10	
		Western	Kansas City Chiefs (13-3-0)	Denver* 24, Pittsburgh 21	
	National	Eastern	NY Giants (10-5-1)	San Francisco 38, Minnesota* 22	
		Central	Green Bay Packers (13-3-0)	Green Bay 21, Tampa Bay* 7	
		Western	San Francisco 49ers (13-3-0)	Green Bay 23, San Francisco 10	
1998	American	Eastern	NY Jets (12-4-0)	Denver 38, Miami* 3	1998
		Central	Jacksonville Jaguars (11-5-0)	NY Jets 34, Jacksonville 24	
		Western	Denver Broncos (14-2-0)	Denver 23, NY Jets 10	
	National	Eastern	Dallas Cowboys (10-6-0)	Atlanta 20, San Francisco* 18	
		Central	Minnesota Vikings (15-1-0)	Minnesota 41, Arizona* 21	
		Western	Atlanta Falcons (14-2-0)	Atlanta 30, Minnesota 27 (OT)	
1999	American	Eastern	Indianapolis Colts (13-3-0)	Jacksonville 62, Miami* 7	1999
		Central	Jacksonville Jaguars (14-2-0)	Tennessee* 19, Indianapolis 16	
		Western	Seattle Seahawks (9-7-0)	Tennessee* 33, Jacksonville 14	
	National	Eastern	Washington Redskins (10-6-0)	Tampa Bay 14, Washington 13	
		Central	Tampa Bay Buccaneers (11-5-0)	St. Louis 49, Minnesota* 37	
		Western	St. Louis Rams (13-3-0)	St. Louis 11, Tampa Bay 6	
2000	American	Eastern	Miami Dolphins (11-5-0)	Oakland 27, Miami 0	2000
		Central	Tennessee Titans (13-3-0)	Baltimore* 24, Tennessee 10	
		Western	Oakland Raiders (12-4-0)	Baltimore* 16, Oakland 3	
	National	Eastern	NY Giants (12-4-0)	Minnesota 34, New Orleans 16	
		Central	Minnesota Vikings (11-5-0)	NY Giants 20, Philadelphia* 10	
		Western	New Orleans Saints (10-6-0)	NY Giants 41, Minnesota 0	
2001	American	Eastern	New England Patriots (11-5-0)	New England 16, Oakland 13 (OT)	2001
		Central	Pittsburgh Steelers (13-3-0)	Pittsburgh 27, Baltimore* 10	
		Western	Oakland Raiders (10-6-0)	New England 24, Pittsburgh 17	
	National	Eastern	Philadelphia Eagles (11-5-0)	Philadelphia 33, Chicago 19	
		Central	Chicago Bears (13-3-0)	St. Louis 45, Green Bay* 17	
		Western	St. Louis Rams (14-2-0)	St. Louis 29, Philadelphia 24	
2002	American	East	NY Jets (9-7-0)		2002
		North	Pittsburgh Steelers (10-5-1)	Oakland 30, NY Jets 10	
		South	Tennessee Titans (11-5-0)	Tennessee 34, Pittsburgh 31 (OT)	
		West	Oakland Raiders (11-5-0)	Oakland 41, Tennessee 24	
	National	East	Philadelphia Eagles (12-4-0)		
		North	Green Bay Packers (12-4-0)	Philadelphia 20, Atlanta* 6	
		South	Tampa Bay Buccaneers (12-4-0)	Tampa Bay 31, San Francisco 6	
		West	San Francisco 49ers (10-6-0)	Tampa Bay 27, Philadelphia 10	
2003	American	East	New England Patriots (14-2-0)		2003
		North	Baltimore Ravens (10-6-0)	Indianapolis 38, Kansas City 31	
		South	Indianapolis Colts (12-4-0)	New England 17, Tennessee* 14	
		West	Kansas City Chiefs (13-3-0)	New England 24, Indianapolis 14	
	National	East	Philadelphia Eagles (12-4-0)		
		North	Green Bay Packers (10-6-0)	Carolina 29, St. Louis 23 (2 OT)	
		South	Carolina Panthers (11-5-0)	Philadelphia 20, Green Bay 17 (OT)	
		West	St. Louis Rams (12-4-0)	Carolina 14, Philadelphia 3	
2004	American	East	New England Patriots (14-2-0)		2004
		North	Pittsburgh Steelers (15-1-0)	Pittsburgh 20, NY Jets* 17 (OT)	
		South	Indianapolis Colts (12-4-0)	New England 20, Indianapolis 3	
		West	San Diego Chargers (12-4-0)	New England 41, Pittsburgh 27	
	National	East	Philadelphia Eagles (13-3-0)		
		North	Green Bay Packers (10-6-0)	Atlanta 47, St. Louis* 17	
		South	Atlanta Falcons (11-5-0)	Philadelphia 27, Minnesota* 14	
		West	Seattle Seahawks (9-7-0)	Philadelphia 27, Atlanta 10	
2005	American	East	New England Patriots (10-6-0)		2005
		North	Cincinnati Bengals (11-5-0)	Denver 27, New England 13	
		South	Indianapolis Colts (14-2-0)	Pittsburgh* 21, Indianapolis 18	
		West	Denver Broncos (13-3-0)	Pittsburgh* 34, Denver 17	
	National	East	NY Giants (11-5-0)		
		North	Chicago Bears (11-5-0)	Seattle 20, Washington* 10	
		South	Tampa Bay Buccaneers (11-5-0)	Carolina* 29, Chicago 21	
		West	Seattle Seahawks (13-3-0)	Seattle 34, Carolina* 14	
2006	American	East	New England Patriots (12-4-0)		2006
		North	Baltimore Ravens (13-3-0)	Indianapolis 15, Baltimore 6	
		South	Indianapolis Colts (12-4-0)	New England 24, San Diego 21	
		West	San Diego Chargers (14-2-0)	Indianapolis 38, New England 34	
	National	East	Philadelphia Eagles (10-6-0)		
		North	Chicago Bears (13-3-0)	New Orleans 27, Philadelphia 24	
		South	New Orleans Saints (10-6-0)	Chicago 27, Seattle 24 (OT)	
		West	Seattle Seahawks (9-7-0)	Chicago 39, New Orleans 14	

Year	Conference	Division	Winner (W-L-T)	Playoffs[1]	Year
2007	American	East	New England Patriots (16-0-0)		2007
		North	Pittsburgh Steelers (10-6-0)	New England 31, Jacksonville* 20	
		South	Indianapolis Colts (13-3-0)	San Diego 28, Indianapolis 24	
		West	San Diego Chargers (11-5-0)	New England 21, San Diego 12	
	National	East	Dallas Cowboys (13-3-0)		
		North	Green Bay Packers (13-3-0)	Green Bay 42, Seattle 20	
		South	Tampa Bay Buccaneers (9-7-0)	NY Giants* 21, Dallas 17	
		West	Seattle Seahawks (10-6-0)	NY Giants* 23, Green Bay 20 (OT)	
2008	American	East	Miami Dolphins (11-5-0)		2008
		North	Pittsburgh Steelers (12-4-0)	Baltimore* 13, Tennessee 10	
		South	Tennessee Titans (13-3-0)	Pittsburgh 35, San Diego 24	
		West	San Diego Chargers (8-8-0)	Pittsburgh 23, Baltimore* 14	
	National	East	NY Giants (12-4-0)		
		North	Minnesota Vikings (10-6-0)	Arizona 33, Carolina 13	
		South	Carolina Panthers (12-4-0)	Philadelphia* 23, NY Giants 11	
		West	Arizona Cardinals (9-7-0)	Arizona 32, Philadelphia* 25	
2009	American	East	New England Patriots (10-6-0)		2009
		North	Cincinnati Bengals (10-6-0)	Indianapolis 20, Baltimore* 3	
		South	Indianapolis Colts (14-2-0)	NY Jets* 17, San Diego 14	
		West	San Diego Chargers (13-3-0)	Indianapolis 30, NY Jets* 17	
	National	East	Dallas Cowboys (11-5-0)		
		North	Minnesota Vikings (12-4-0)	New Orleans 45, Arizona 14	
		South	New Orleans Saints (13-3-0)	Minnesota 34, Dallas 3	
		West	Arizona Cardinals (10-6-0)	New Orleans 31, Minnesota 28 (OT)	
2010	American	East	New England Patriots (14-2-0)		2010
		North	Pittsburgh Steelers (12-4-0)	Pittsburgh 31, Baltimore* 24	
		South	Indianapolis Colts (10-6-0)	NY Jets* 28, New England 21	
		West	Kansas City Chiefs (10-6-0)	Pittsburgh 24, NY Jets* 19	
	National	East	Philadelphia Eagles (10-6-0)		
		North	Chicago Bears (11-5-0)	Green Bay* 48, Atlanta 21	
		South	Atlanta Falcons (13-3-0)	Chicago 35, Seattle 24	
		West	Seattle Seahawks (7-9-0)	Green Bay* 21, Chicago 14	
2011	American	East	New England Patriots (13-3-0)		2011
		North	Baltimore Ravens (12-4-0)	New England 45, Denver 10	
		South	Houston Texans (10-6-0)	Baltimore 20, Houston 13	
		West	Denver Broncos (8-8-0)	New England 23, Baltimore 20	
	National	East	NY Giants (9-7-0)		
		North	Green Bay Packers (15-1-0)	San Francisco 36, New Orleans 32	
		South	New Orleans (13-3-0)	NY Giants 37, Green Bay 20	
		West	San Francisco (13-3-0)	NY Giants 20, San Francisco 17 (OT)	
2012	American	East	New England Patriots (12-4-0)		2012
		North	Baltimore Ravens (10-6-0)	Baltimore 38, Denver 35 (2 OT)	
		South	Houston Texans (12-4-0)	New England 41, Houston 28	
		West	Denver Broncos (13-3-0)	Baltimore 28, New England 13	
	National	East	Washington Redskins (10-6-0)		
		North	Green Bay Packers (11-5-0)	San Francisco 45, Green Bay 31	
		South	Atlanta Falcons (13-3-0)	Atlanta 30, Seattle* 28	
		West	San Francisco 49ers (11-4-1)	San Francisco 28, Atlanta 24	
2013	American	East	New England Patriots (12-4-0)		2013
		North	Cincinnati Bengals (11-5-0)	New England 43, Indianapolis 22	
		South	Indianapolis Colts (11-5-0)	Denver 24, San Diego* 17	
		West	Denver Broncos (13-3-0)	Denver 26, New England 16	
	National	East	Philadelphia Eagles (10-6-0)		
		North	Green Bay Packers (8-7-1)	Seattle 23, New Orleans* 15	
		South	Carolina Panthers (12-4-0)	San Francisco* 23, Carolina 10	
		West	Seattle Seahawks (13-3-0)	Seattle 23, San Francisco* 17	

*Wild card team. (1) Only the final two conference playoff rounds are shown.

American Football Conference Leaders, 1960-2013

(American Football League, 1960-69)

Passing (based on QB rating points)							Receptions			
Player, team	Rating	Att	Comp	Yds	TD	Year	Player, team	Rec	Yds	TD
Jack Kemp, L.A. Chargers	NA	406	211	3,018	20	1960	Lionel Taylor, Denver	92	1,235	12
George Blanda, Houston	NA	362	187	3,330	36	1961	Lionel Taylor, Denver	100	1,176	4
Len Dawson, Dallas Texans	NA	310	189	2,759	29	1962	Lionel Taylor, Denver	77	908	4
Tobin Rote, San Diego	NA	286	170	2,510	20	1963	Lionel Taylor, Denver	78	1,101	10
Len Dawson, Kansas City	NA	354	199	2,879	30	1964	Charley Hennigan, Houston	101	1,546	8
John Hadl, San Diego	NA	348	174	2,798	20	1965	Lionel Taylor, Denver	85	1,131	6
Len Dawson, Kansas City	NA	284	159	2,527	26	1966	Lance Alworth, San Diego	73	1,383	13
Daryle Lamonica, Oakland	NA	425	220	3,228	30	1967	George Sauer, NY Jets	75	1,189	6
Len Dawson, Kansas City	NA	224	131	2,109	17	1968	Lance Alworth, San Diego	68	1,312	10
Greg Cook, Cincinnati	NA	197	106	1,854	15	1969	Lance Alworth, San Diego	64	1,003	4
Daryle Lamonica, Oakland	NA	356	179	2,516	22	1970	Marlin Briscoe, Buffalo	57	1,036	8
Bob Griese, Miami	NA	263	145	2,089	19	1971	Fred Biletnikoff, Oakland	61	929	9
Earl Morrall, Miami	NA	150	83	1,360	11	1972	Fred Biletnikoff, Oakland	58	802	7
Ken Stabler, Oakland	88.3	260	163	1,997	14	1973	Fred Willis, Houston	57	371	1
Ken Anderson, Cincinnati	95.7	328	213	2,667	18	1974	Lydell Mitchell, Baltimore Colts	72	544	2
Ken Anderson, Cincinnati	93.9	377	228	3,169	21	1975	Reggie Rucker, Cleveland	60	770	3
							Lydell Mitchell, Baltimore Colts	60	554	4
Ken Stabler, Oakland	103.4	291	194	2,737	27	1976	MacArthur Lane, Kansas City	66	686	1

Passing (based on QB rating points)

Player, team	Rating	Att	Comp	Yds	TD	Year
Bob Griese, Miami	87.8	307	180	2,252	22	1977
Terry Bradshaw, Pittsburgh	84.7	368	207	2,915	28	1978
Dan Fouts, San Diego	82.6	530	332	4,082	24	1979
Brian Sipe, Cleveland	91.4	554	337	4,132	30	1980
Ken Anderson, Cincinnati	98.4	479	300	3,754	29	1981
Ken Anderson, Cincinnati	95.3	309	218	2,495	12	1982
Dan Marino, Miami	96.0	296	173	2,210	20	1983
Dan Marino, Miami	108.9	564	362	5,084	48	1984
Ken O'Brien, NY Jets	96.2	488	297	3,888	25	1985
Dan Marino, Miami	92.5	623	378	4,746	44	1986
Bernie Kosar, Cleveland	95.4	389	241	3,033	22	1987
Boomer Esiason, Cincinnati	97.4	388	223	3,572	28	1988
Boomer Esiason, Cincinnati	92.1	455	258	3,525	28	1989
Jim Kelly, Buffalo	101.2	346	219	2,829	24	1990
Jim Kelly, Buffalo	97.6	474	304	3,844	33	1991
Warren Moon, Houston	89.3	346	224	2,521	18	1992
John Elway, Denver	92.8	551	348	4,030	25	1993
Dan Marino, Miami	89.2	615	385	4,453	30	1994
Jim Harbaugh, Indianapolis	100.7	314	200	2,575	17	1995
John Elway, Denver	89.2	466	287	3,328	26	1996
Mark Brunell, Jacksonville	91.2	435	264	3,281	18	1997
Vinny Testaverde, NY Jets	101.6	421	259	3,256	29	1998
Peyton Manning, Indianapolis	90.7	533	331	4,135	26	1999
Brian Griese, Denver	102.9	336	216	2,688	19	2000
Rich Gannon, Oakland	95.5	549	361	3,828	27	2001
Chad Pennington, NY Jets	104.2	399	275	3,120	22	2002
Steve McNair, Tennessee	100.4	400	250	3,215	24	2003
Peyton Manning, Indianapolis	121.1	497	336	4,557	49	2004
Peyton Manning, Indianapolis	104.1	453	305	3,747	28	2005
Peyton Manning, Indianapolis	101.0	557	362	4,397	31	2006
Tom Brady, New England	117.2	578	398	4,806	50	2007
Philip Rivers, San Diego	105.5	478	312	4,009	34	2008
Philip Rivers, San Diego	104.4	486	317	4,254	28	2009
Tom Brady, New England	111.0	492	324	3,900	36	2010
Tom Brady, New England	105.6	611	401	5,235	39	2011
Peyton Manning, Denver	105.8	583	400	4,659	37	2012
Peyton Manning, Denver	115.1	659	450	5,477	55	2013

Receptions

Year	Player, team	Rec	Yds	TD
1977	Lydell Mitchell, Baltimore Colts	71	620	4
1978	Steve Largent, Seattle	71	1,168	8
1979	Joe Washington, Baltimore Colts	82	750	3
1980	Kellen Winslow, San Diego	89	1,290	9
1981	Kellen Winslow, San Diego	88	1,075	10
1982	Kellen Winslow, San Diego	54	721	6
1983	Todd Christensen, L.A. Raiders	92	1,247	12
1984	Ozzie Newsome, Cleveland	89	1,001	5
1985	Lionel James, San Diego	86	1,027	6
1986	Todd Christensen, L.A. Raiders	95	1,153	8
1987	Al Toon, NY Jets	68	976	5
1988	Al Toon, NY Jets	93	1,067	5
1989	Andre Reed, Buffalo	88	1,312	9
1990	Haywood Jeffires, Houston	74	1,048	8
	Drew Hill, Houston	74	1,019	5
1991	Haywood Jeffires, Houston	100	1,181	7
1992	Haywood Jeffires, Houston	90	913	9
1993	Reggie Langhorne, Indianapolis	85	1,038	3
1994	Ben Coates, New England	96	1,174	7
1995	Carl Pickens, Cincinnati	99	1,234	17
1996	Carl Pickens, Cincinnati	100	1,180	12
1997	Tim Brown, Oakland	104	1,408	5
1998	O. J. McDuffie, Miami	90	1,050	7
1999	Jimmy Smith, Jacksonville	116	1,636	6
2000	Marvin Harrison, Indianapolis	102	1,413	14
2001	Rod Smith, Denver	113	1,343	11
2002	Marvin Harrison, Indianapolis	143	1,722	11
2003	LaDainian Tomlinson, San Diego	100	725	4
2004	Tony Gonzalez, Kansas City	102	1,258	7
2005	Chad Johnson, Cincinnati	97	1,432	9
2006	Andre Johnson, Houston	103	1,147	5
2007	Wes Welker, New England	112	1,175	8
	T.J. Houshmandzadeh, Cincinnati	112	1,143	12
2008	Andre Johnson, Houston	115	1,575	8
2009	Wes Walker, New England	123	1,348	4
2010	Reggie Wayne, Indianapolis	111	1,355	6
2011	Wes Welker, New England	122	1,569	9
2012	Wes Welker, New England	118	1,354	6
2013	Antonio Brown, Pittsburgh	110	1,499	8

Scoring

Player, team	TD	XPM	FGM	Pts	Year
Gene Mingo, Denver	6	33	18	123	1960
Gino Cappelletti, Boston	8	48	17	147	1961
Gene Mingo, Denver	4	32	27	137	1962
Gino Cappelletti, Boston	2	35	22	113	1963
Gino Cappelletti, Boston	7	36	25	155	1964
Gino Cappelletti, Boston	9	27	17	132	1965
Gino Cappelletti, Boston	6	35	16	119	1966
George Blanda, Oakland	0	56	20	116	1967
Jim Turner, NY Jets	0	43	34	145	1968
Jim Turner, NY Jets	0	33	32	129	1969
Jan Stenerud, Kansas City	0	26	30	116	1970
Garo Yepremian, Miami	0	33	28	117	1971
Bobby Howfield, NY Jets	0	40	27	121	1972
Roy Gerela, Pittsburgh	0	36	29	123	1973
Roy Gerela, Pittsburgh	0	33	20	93	1974
O. J. Simpson, Buffalo	23	0	0	138	1975
Toni Linhart, Baltimore Colts	0	49	20	109	1976
Errol Mann, Oakland	0	39	20	99	1977
Pat Leahy, NY Jets	0	41	22	107	1978
John Smith, New England	0	46	23	115	1979
John Smith, New England	0	51	26	129	1980
Jim Breech, Cincinnati	0	49	22	115	1981
Nick Lowery, Kansas City	0	37	26	115	
Marcus Allen, L.A. Raiders	14	0	0	84	1982
Gary Anderson, Pittsburgh	0	38	27	119	1983
Gary Anderson, Pittsburgh	0	45	24	117	1984
Gary Anderson, Pittsburgh	0	40	33	139	1985
Tony Franklin, New England	0	44	32	140	1986
Jim Breech, Cincinnati	0	25	24	97	1987
Scott Norwood, Buffalo	0	33	32	129	1988
David Treadwell, Denver	0	39	27	120	1989
Nick Lowery, Kansas City	0	37	34	139	1990
Pete Stoyanovich, Miami	0	28	31	121	1991
Pete Stoyanovich, Miami	0	34	30	124	1992
Jeff Jaeger, L.A. Raiders	0	27	35	132	1993
John Carney, San Diego	0	33	34	135	1994
Norm Johnson, Pittsburgh	0	39	34	141	1995
Cary Blanchard, Indianapolis	0	27	36	135	1996
Mike Hollis, Jacksonville	0	41	31	134	1997
Steve Christie, Buffalo	0	41	33	140	1998
Mike Vanderjagt, Indianapolis	0	43	34	145	1999
Matt Stover, Baltimore	0	30	35	135	2000
Mike Vanderjagt, Indianapolis	0	41	28	125	2001

Rushing Yards

Year	Player, team	Yds	Att	TD
1960	Abner Haynes, Dallas Texans	875	156	9
1961	Billy Cannon, Houston	948	200	6
1962	Cookie Gilchrist, Buffalo	1,096	214	13
1963	Clem Daniels, Oakland	1,099	215	3
1964	Cookie Gilchrist, Buffalo	981	230	6
1965	Paul Lowe, San Diego	1,121	222	7
1966	Jim Nance, Boston	1,458	299	11
1967	Jim Nance, Boston	1,216	269	7
1968	Paul Robinson, Cincinnati	1,023	238	8
1969	Dickie Post, San Diego	873	182	6
1970	Floyd Little, Denver	901	209	3
1971	Floyd Little, Denver	1,133	284	6
1972	O. J. Simpson, Buffalo	1,251	292	6
1973	O. J. Simpson, Buffalo	2,003	332	12
1974	Otis Armstrong, Denver	1,407	263	9
1975	O. J. Simpson, Buffalo	1,817	329	16
1976	O. J. Simpson, Buffalo	1,503	290	8
1977	Mark van Eeghen, Oakland	1,273	324	7
1978	Earl Campbell, Houston	1,450	302	13
1979	Earl Campbell, Houston	1,697	368	19
1980	Earl Campbell, Houston	1,934	373	13
1981	Earl Campbell, Houston	1,376	361	10
1982	Freeman McNeil, NY Jets	786	151	6
1983	Curt Warner, Seattle	1,449	335	13
1984	Earnest Jackson, San Diego	1,179	296	8
1985	Marcus Allen, L.A. Raiders	1,759	380	11
1986	Curt Warner, Seattle	1,481	319	13
1987	Eric Dickerson, L.A. Rams-Ind.	1,288*	283	6
1988	Eric Dickerson, Indianapolis	1,659	388	14
1989	Christian Okoye, Kansas City	1,480	370	12
1990	Thurman Thomas, Buffalo	1,297	271	11
1991	Thurman Thomas, Buffalo	1,407	288	7
1992	Barry Foster, Pittsburgh	1,690	390	11
1993	Thurman Thomas, Buffalo	1,315	355	6
1994	Chris Warren, Seattle	1,545	333	9
1995	Curtis Martin, New England	1,487	368	14
1996	Terrell Davis, Denver	1,538	345	13
1997	Terrell Davis, Denver	1,750	369	15
1998	Terrell Davis, Denver	2,008	392	21
1999	Edgerrin James, Indianapolis	1,553	369	13
2000	Edgerrin James, Indianapolis	1,709	387	13
2001	Priest Holmes, Kansas City	1,555	327	8

Scoring / Rushing Yards

Player, team	TD	XPM	FGM	Pts	Year	Player, team	Yds	Att	TD
Priest Holmes, Kansas City	24	0	0	144	2002	Ricky Williams, Miami	1,853	383	16
Priest Holmes, Kansas City	27	0	0	162	2003	Jamal Lewis, Baltimore	2,066	387	14
Adam Vinatieri, New England	0	48	31	141	2004	Curtis Martin, NY Jets	1,697	371	12
Shayne Graham, Cincinnati	0	47	28	131	2005	Larry Johnson, Kansas City	1,750	336	20
LaDainian Tomlinson, San Diego	31	0	0	186	2006	LaDainian Tomlinson, San Diego	1,815	348	28
Randy Moss, New England	23	0	0	138	2007	LaDainian Tomlinson, San Diego	1,474	315	15
Stephen Gostkowski, New England	0	40	36	148	2008	Thomas Jones, NY Jets	1,312	290	13
Nate Kaeding, San Diego	0	50	32	146	2009	Chris Johnson, Tennessee	2,006	358	14
Sebastian Janikowski, Oakland	0	43	33	142	2010	Arian Foster, Houston	1,616	327	16
Stephen Gostkowski, New England	0	59	28	143	2011	Maurice Jones-Drew, Jacksonville	1,606	343	8
Stephen Gostkowski, New England	0	66	29	153	2012	Jamaal Charles, Kansas City	1,509	285	5
Stephen Gostkowski, New England	0	44	38	158	2013	Jamaal Charles, Kansas City	1,287	259	12

*Includes 277 yards after being traded to NFC; 1,011 yards led AFC. NA = Not applicable/available. **Note:** Passer ratings for years prior to 1973 were determined by different measures and are not directly comparable to current passer ratings.

National Football Conference Leaders, 1960-2013
(National Football League, 1960-69)

Passing (based on QB rating points) / Receptions

Player, team	Rating	Att	Comp	Yds	TD	Year	Player, team	Rec	Yds	TD
Milt Plum, Cleveland	NA	250	151	2,297	21	1960	Raymond Berry, Baltimore Colts	74	1,298	10
Milt Plum, Cleveland	NA	302	177	2,416	18	1961	Jim Phillips, L.A. Rams	78	1,092	5
Bart Starr, Green Bay	NA	285	178	2,438	12	1962	Bobby Mitchell, Washington	72	1,384	11
Y. A. Tittle, NY Giants	NA	367	221	3,145	36	1963	Bobby Joe Conrad, St. Louis Cardinals	73	967	10
Bart Starr, Green Bay	NA	272	163	2,144	15	1964	Johnny Morris, Chicago	93	1,200	10
Rudy Bukich, Chicago	NA	312	176	2,641	20	1965	Dave Parks, San Francisco	80	1,344	12
Bart Starr, Green Bay	NA	251	156	2,257	14	1966	Charley Taylor, Washington	72	1,119	12
Sonny Jurgensen, Washington	NA	508	288	3,747	31	1967	Charley Taylor, Washington	70	990	9
Earl Morrall, Baltimore Colts	NA	317	182	2,909	26	1968	Clifton McNeil, San Francisco	71	994	7
Sonny Jurgensen, Washington	NA	442	274	3,102	22	1969	Dan Abramowicz, New Orleans	73	1,015	7
John Brodie, San Francisco	NA	378	223	2,941	24	1970	Dick Gordon, Chicago	71	1,026	13
Roger Staubach, Dallas	NA	211	126	1,882	15	1971	Bob Tucker, NY Giants	59	791	4
Norm Snead, NY Giants	NA	325	196	2,307	17	1972	Harold Jackson, Philadelphia	62	1,048	4
Roger Staubach, Dallas	94.6	286	179	2,428	23	1973	Harold Carmichael, Philadelphia	67	1,116	9
Sonny Jurgensen, Washington	94.5	167	107	1,185	11	1974	Charles Young, Philadelphia	63	696	3
Fran Tarkenton, Minnesota	91.8	425	273	2,994	25	1975	Chuck Foreman, Minnesota	73	691	9
James Harris, L.A. Rams	89.6	158	91	1,460	8	1976	Drew Pearson, Dallas	58	806	6
Roger Staubach, Dallas	87.0	361	210	2,620	18	1977	Ahmad Rashad, Minnesota	51	681	2
Roger Staubach, Dallas	84.9	413	231	3,190	25	1978	Rickey Young, Minnesota	88	704	5
Roger Staubach, Dallas	92.3	461	267	3,586	27	1979	Ahmad Rashad, Minnesota	80	1,156	9
Ron Jaworski, Philadelphia	91.0	451	257	3,529	27	1980	Earl Cooper, San Francisco	83	567	4
Joe Montana, San Francisco	88.4	488	311	3,565	19	1981	Dwight Clark, San Francisco	85	1,105	4
Joe Theismann, Washington	91.3	252	161	2,033	13	1982	Dwight Clark, San Francisco	60	913	5
Steve Bartkowski, Atlanta	97.6	432	274	3,167	22	1983	Roy Green, St. Louis Cardinals	78	1,227	14
							Charlie Brown, Washington	78	1,225	8
							Earnest Gray, NY Giants	78	1,139	5
Joe Montana, San Francisco	102.9	432	279	3,630	28	1984	Art Monk, Washington	106	1,372	7
Joe Montana, San Francisco	91.3	494	303	3,653	27	1985	Roger Craig, San Francisco	92	1,016	6
Tommy Kramer, Minnesota	92.6	372	208	3,000	24	1986	Jerry Rice, San Francisco	86	1,570	15
Joe Montana, San Francisco	102.1	398	266	3,054	31	1987	J. T. Smith, St. Louis Cardinals	91	1,117	8
Wade Wilson, Minnesota	91.5	332	204	2,746	15	1988	Henry Ellard, L.A. Rams	86	1,414	10
Joe Montana, San Francisco	112.4	386	271	3,521	26	1989	Sterling Sharpe, Green Bay	90	1,423	12
Phil Simms, NY Giants	92.7	311	184	2,284	15	1990	Jerry Rice, San Francisco	100	1,502	13
Steve Young, San Francisco	101.8	279	180	2,517	17	1991	Michael Irvin, Dallas	93	1,523	8
Steve Young, San Francisco	107.0	402	268	3,465	25	1992	Sterling Sharpe, Green Bay	108	1,461	13
Steve Young, San Francisco	101.5	314	314	4,023	29	1993	Sterling Sharpe, Green Bay	112	1,274	11
Steve Young, San Francisco	112.8	461	324	3,969	35	1994	Cris Carter, Minnesota	122	1,256	7
Brett Favre, Green Bay	99.5	570	359	4,413	38	1995	Herman Moore, Detroit	123	1,686	14
Steve Young, San Francisco	97.2	316	214	2,410	14	1996	Jerry Rice, San Francisco	108	1,254	8
Steve Young, San Francisco	104.7	356	241	3,029	19	1997	Herman Moore, Detroit	104	1,293	8
Randall Cunningham, Minnesota	106.0	425	259	3,704	34	1998	Frank Sanders, Arizona	89	1,145	3
Kurt Warner, St. Louis	109.2	499	325	4,353	41	1999	Muhsin Muhammad, Carolina	96	1,253	8
Trent Green, St. Louis	101.8	240	145	2,063	16	2000	Muhsin Muhammad, Carolina	102	1,183	6
Kurt Warner, St. Louis	101.4	546	375	4,830	36	2001	Keyshawn Johnson, Tampa Bay	106	1,266	1
Brad Johnson, Tampa Bay	92.9	451	281	3,049	22	2002	Randy Moss, Minnesota	106	1,347	7
Daunte Culpepper, Minnesota	96.4	454	295	3,479	25	2003	Torry Holt, St. Louis	117	1,696	12
Daunte Culpepper, Minnesota	110.9	548	379	4,717	39	2004	Joe Horn, New Orleans	94	1,399	11
							Torry Holt, St. Louis	94	1,372	10
Matt Hasselbeck, Seattle	98.2	449	294	3,459	24	2005	Steve Smith, Carolina	103	1,563	12
							Larry Fitzgerald, Arizona	103	1,409	10
Drew Brees, New Orleans	96.2	554	356	4,418	26	2006	Mike Furrey, Detroit	98	1,086	6
Tony Romo, Dallas	97.4	520	335	4,211	36	2007	Larry Fitzgerald, Arizona	100	1,409	10
Kurt Warner, Arizona	96.9	598	401	4,583	30	2008	Larry Fitzgerald, Arizona	96	1,431	12
Drew Brees, New Orleans	109.6	514	363	4,388	34	2009	Steve Smith, NY Giants	107	1,220	7
Aaron Rodgers, Green Bay	101.2	475	312	3,922	28	2010	Roddy White, Atlanta	115	1,389	10
Aaron Rodgers, Green Bay	122.5	502	343	4,643	45	2011	Roddy White, Atlanta	100	1,296	8
Aaron Rodgers, Green Bay	108.0	552	371	4,295	39	2012	Calvin Johnson, Detroit	122	1,964	5
Nick Foles, Philadelphia	119.2	317	203	2,891	27	2013	Pierre Garcon, Washington	113	1,346	5

Scoring Player, team	TD	XPM	FGM	Pts	Year	Rushing Yards Player, team	Yds	Att	TD
Paul Hornung, Green Bay	15	41	15	176	1960	Jim Brown, Cleveland	1,257	215	9
Paul Hornung, Green Bay	10	41	15	146	1961	Jim Brown, Cleveland	1,408	305	8
Jim Taylor, Green Bay	19	0	0	114	1962	Jim Taylor, Green Bay	1,474	272	19
Don Chandler, NY Giants	0	52	18	106	1963	Jim Brown, Cleveland	1,863	291	12
Lenny Moore, Baltimore Colts	20	0	0	120	1964	Jim Brown, Cleveland	1,446	280	7
Gale Sayers, Chicago	22	0	0	132	1965	Jim Brown, Cleveland	1,544	289	17
Bruce Gossett, L.A. Rams	0	29	28	113	1966	Gale Sayers, Chicago	1,231	229	8
Jim Bakken, St. Louis Cardinals	0	36	27	117	1967	Leroy Kelly, Cleveland	1,205	235	11
Leroy Kelly, Cleveland	20	0	0	120	1968	Leroy Kelly, Cleveland	1,239	248	16
Fred Cox, Minnesota	0	43	26	121	1969	Gale Sayers, Chicago	1,032	236	8
Fred Cox, Minnesota	0	35	30	125	1970	Larry Brown, Washington	1,125	237	5
Curt Knight, Washington	0	27	29	114	1971	John Brockington, Green Bay	1,105	216	4
Chester Marcol, Green Bay	0	29	33	128	1972	Larry Brown, Washington	1,216	285	8
David Ray, L.A. Rams	0	40	30	130	1973	John Brockington, Green Bay	1,144	265	3
Chester Marcol, Green Bay	0	19	25	94	1974	Lawrence McCutcheon, L.A. Rams	1,109	236	3
Chuck Foreman, Minnesota	22	0	0	132	1975	Jim Otis, St. Louis Cardinals	1,076	269	5
Mark Moseley, Washington	0	31	22	97	1976	Walter Payton, Chicago	1,390	311	13
Walter Payton, Chicago	16	0	0	96	1977	Walter Payton, Chicago	1,852	339	14
Frank Corral, L.A. Rams	0	31	29	118	1978	Walter Payton, Chicago	1,395	333	11
Mark Moseley, Washington	0	39	25	114	1979	Walter Payton, Chicago	1,610	369	14
Ed Murray, Detroit	0	35	27	116	1980	Walter Payton, Chicago	1,460	317	6
Ed Murray, Detroit	0	46	25	121	1981	George Rogers, New Orleans	1,674	378	13
Rafael Septien, Dallas	0	40	27	121					
Wendell Tyler, L.A. Rams	13	0	0	78	1982	Tony Dorsett, Dallas	745	177	5
Mark Moseley, Washington	0	62	33	161	1983	Eric Dickerson, L.A. Rams	1,808	390	18
Ray Wersching, San Francisco	0	56	25	131	1984	Eric Dickerson, L.A. Rams	2,105	379	14
Kevin Butler, Chicago	0	51	31	144	1985	Gerald Riggs, Atlanta	1,719	397	10
Kevin Butler, Chicago	0	36	28	120	1986	Eric Dickerson, L.A. Rams	1,821	404	11
Jerry Rice, San Francisco	23	0	0	138	1987	Charles White, L.A. Rams	1,374	324	11
Mike Cofer, San Francisco	0	40	27	121	1988	Herschel Walker, Dallas	1,514	361	5
Mike Cofer, San Francisco	0	49	29	136	1989	Barry Sanders, Detroit	1,470	280	14
Chip Lohmiller, Washington	0	41	30	131	1990	Barry Sanders, Detroit	1,304	255	13
Chip Lohmiller, Washington	0	56	31	149	1991	Emmitt Smith, Dallas	1,563	365	12
Morten Andersen, New Orleans	0	33	29	120	1992	Emmitt Smith, Dallas	1,713	373	18
Chip Lohmiller, Washington	0	30	30	120					
Jason Hanson, Detroit	0	28	34	130	1993	Emmitt Smith, Dallas	1,486	283	9
Fuad Reveiz, Minnesota	0	30	34	132	1994	Barry Sanders, Detroit	1,883	331	7
Emmitt Smith, Dallas	22	0	0	132					
Emmitt Smith, Dallas	25	0	0	150	1995	Emmitt Smith, Dallas	1,773	377	25
John Kasay, Carolina	0	34	37	145	1996	Barry Sanders, Detroit	1,553	307	11
Richie Cunningham, Dallas	0	24	34	126	1997	Barry Sanders, Detroit	2,053	335	11
Gary Anderson, Minnesota	0	59	35	164	1998	Jamal Anderson, Atlanta	1,846	410	14
Jeff Wilkins, St. Louis	0	64	20	124	1999	Stephen Davis, Washington	1,405	290	17
Marshall Faulk, St. Louis	26	0	0	160	2000	Robert Smith, Minnesota	1,521	295	7
Marshall Faulk, St. Louis	21	0	0	128	2001	Stephen Davis, Washington	1,432	356	5
Jay Feely, Atlanta	0	42	32	138	2002	Deuce McAllister, New Orleans	1,388	325	13
Jeff Wilkins, St. Louis	0	46	39	163	2003	Ahman Green, Green Bay	1,883	355	15
David Akers, Philadelphia	0	41	27	122	2004	Shaun Alexander, Seattle	1,696	353	16
Shaun Alexander, Seattle	28	0	0	168	2005	Shaun Alexander, Seattle	1,880	370	27
Robbie Gould, Chicago	0	47	32	143	2006	Frank Gore, San Francisco	1,695	312	8
Mason Crosby, Green Bay	0	48	31	141	2007	Adrian Peterson, Minnesota	1,341	238	12
David Akers, Philadelphia	0	45	33	144	2008	Adrian Peterson, Minnesota	1,760	363	10
David Akers, Philadelphia	0	43	32	139	2009	Steven Jackson, St. Louis	1,416	324	4
David Akers, Philadelphia	0	47	32	143	2010	Michael Turner, Atlanta	1,371	334	12
David Akers, San Francisco	0	34	44	166	2011	Michael Turner, Atlanta	1,340	301	11
Lawrence Tynes, NY Giants	0	46	33	145	2012	Adrian Peterson, Minnesota	2,097	348	12
Steven Hauschka, Seattle	0	44	33	143	2013	LeSean McCoy, Philadelphia	1,607	314	9

Note: Passer ratings for years prior to 1973 were determined by different measures and are not directly comparable to current passer ratings.

NFL MVP and Rookies of the Year, 1957-2013

The Most Valuable Player, Offensive Rookie of the Year, and Defensive Rookie of the Year are a few of the many awards given out annually by the Associated Press according to the results of balloting by a nationwide panel of media. Many other organizations give out annual awards honoring the NFL's best players.

Year	NFL Most Valuable Player Award	Offensive Rookie of the Year	Defensive Rookie of the Year
1957	Jim Brown, Cleveland	NA	NA
1958	Jim Brown, Cleveland	NA	NA
1959	Charley Conerly, NY Giants	NA	NA
1960	Norm Van Brocklin, Philadelphia	NA	NA
1961	Paul Hornung, Green Bay	NA	NA
1962	Jim Taylor, Green Bay	NA	NA
1963	Y. A. Tittle, NY Giants	NA	NA
1964	Johnny Unitas, Baltimore	NA	NA
1965	Jim Brown, Cleveland	NA	NA

Year	NFL Most Valuable Player Award	Offensive Rookie of the Year	Defensive Rookie of the Year
1966	Bart Starr, Green Bay	NA	NA
1967	Johnny Unitas, Baltimore	Mel Farr, Detroit	Lem Barney, Detroit
1968	Earl Morrall, Baltimore	Earl McCullouch, Detroit	Claude Humphrey, Atlanta
1969	Roman Gabriel, Los Angeles	Calvin Hill, Dallas	Joe Greene, Pittsburgh
1970	John Brodie, San Francisco	Dennis Shaw, Buffalo	Bruce Taylor, San Francisco
1971	Alan Page, Minnesota	John Brockington, Green Bay	Isiah Robertson, Los Angeles
1972	Larry Brown, Washington	Franco Harris, Pittsburgh	Willie Buchanon, Green Bay
1973	O. J. Simpson, Buffalo	Chuck Foreman, Minnesota	Wally Chambers, Chicago
1974	Ken Stabler, Oakland	Don Woods, San Diego	Jack Lambert, Pittsburgh
1975	Fran Tarkenton, Minnesota	Mike Thomas, Washington	Robert Brazile, Houston
1976	Bert Jones, Baltimore	Sammy White, Minnesota	Mike Haynes, New England
1977	Walter Payton, Chicago	Tony Dorsett, Dallas	A. J. Duhe, Miami
1978	Terry Bradshaw, Pittsburgh	Earl Campbell, Houston	Al Baker, Detroit
1979	Earl Campbell, Houston	Ottis Anderson, St. Louis	Jim Haslett, Buffalo
1980	Brian Sipe, Cleveland	Billy Sims, Detroit	Buddy Curry, Atlanta; Al Richardson, Atlanta
1981	Ken Anderson, Cincinnati	George Rogers, New Orleans	Lawrence Taylor, NY Giants
1982	Mark Moseley, Washington	Marcus Allen, Los Angeles	Chip Banks, Cleveland
1983	Joe Theismann, Washington	Eric Dickerson, Los Angeles	Vernon Maxwell, Baltimore
1984	Dan Marino, Miami	Louis Lipps, Pittsburgh	Bill Maas, Kansas City
1985	Marcus Allen, Los Angeles	Eddie Brown, Cincinnati	Duane Bickett, Indianapolis
1986	Lawrence Taylor, NY Giants	Rueben Mayes, New Orleans	Leslie O'Neal, San Diego
1987	John Elway, Denver	Troy Stradford, Miami	Shane Conlan, Buffalo
1988	Boomer Esiason, Cincinnati	John Stephens, New England	Erik McMillan, NY Jets
1989	Joe Montana, San Francisco	Barry Sanders, Detroit	Derrick Thomas, Kansas City
1990	Joe Montana, San Francisco	Emmitt Smith, Dallas	Mark Carrier, Chicago
1991	Thurman Thomas, Buffalo	Leonard Russell, New England	Mike Croel, Denver
1992	Steve Young, San Francisco	Carl Pickens, Cincinnati	Dale Carter, Kansas City
1993	Emmitt Smith, Dallas	Jerome Bettis, Los Angeles	Dana Stubblefield, San Francisco
1994	Steve Young, San Francisco	Marshall Faulk, Indianapolis	Tim Bowens, Miami
1995	Brett Favre, Green Bay	Curtis Martin, New England	Hugh Douglas, NY Jets
1996	Brett Favre, Green Bay	Eddie George, Houston	Simeon Rice, Arizona
1997	Brett Favre, Green Bay; Barry Sanders, Detroit	Warrick Dunn, Tampa Bay	Peter Boulware, Baltimore
1998	Terrell Davis, Denver	Randy Moss, Minnesota	Charles Woodson, Oakland
1999	Kurt Warner, St. Louis	Edgerrin James, Indianapolis	Jevon Kearse, Tennessee
2000	Marshall Faulk, St. Louis	Mike Anderson, Denver	Brian Urlacher, Chicago
2001	Kurt Warner, St. Louis	Anthony Thomas, Chicago	Kendrell Bell, Pittsburgh
2002	Rich Gannon, Oakland	Clinton Portis, Denver	Julius Peppers, Carolina
2003	Peyton Manning, Indianapolis; Steve McNair, Tennessee	Anquan Boldin, Arizona	Terrell Suggs, Baltimore
2004	Peyton Manning, Indianapolis	Ben Roethlisberger, Pittsburgh	Jonathan Vilma, NY Jets
2005	Shaun Alexander, Seattle	Cadillac Williams, Tampa Bay	Shawne Merriman, San Diego
2006	LaDainian Tomlinson, San Diego	Vince Young, Tennessee	DeMeco Ryans, Houston
2007	Tom Brady, New England	Adrian Peterson, Minnesota	Patrick Willis, San Francisco
2008	Peyton Manning, Indianapolis	Matt Ryan, Atlanta	Jerod Mayo, New England
2009	Peyton Manning, Indianapolis	Percy Harvin, Minnesota	Brian Cushing, Houston
2010	Tom Brady, New England	Sam Bradford, St. Louis	Ndamukong Suh, Detroit
2011	Aaron Rodgers, Green Bay	Cam Newton, Carolina	Von Miller, Denver
2012	Adrian Peterson, Minnesota	Robert Griffin III, Washington	Luke Kuechly, Carolina
2013	Peyton Manning, Denver	Eddie Lacy, Green Bay Packers	Sheldon Richardson, NY Jets

All-Time Professional (NFL and AFL) Football Records

(at end of 2013 season; * = active in 2013; (a) includes AFL statistics; ** = 2-pt conversions scored)

Leading Lifetime Scorers

Player	Yrs	TD	PAT	FG	Total
Morten Andersen	25	0	849	565	2,544
Gary Anderson	23	0	820	538	2,434
Jason Hanson	21	0	665	495	2,150
John Carney	23	0	628	478	2,062
Adam Vinatieri*	18	0	660**	448	2,006
Matt Stover	19	0	591	471	2,004
George Blanda (a) . . .	26	9	943	335	2,002
Jason Elam	17	0	675	436	1,983
John Kasay	20	0	587	461	1,970
Norm Johnson	18	0	638	366	1,736
David Akers*	16	0	563	386	1,721
Nick Lowery	18	0	562	383	1,711
Jan Stenerud (a)	19	0	580	373	1,699
Ryan Longwell	15	0	604	361	1,687
Eddie Murray	19	0	538	352	1,594
Al Del Greco	17	0	543	347	1,584

Leading Lifetime Touchdown Scorers

Player	Yrs	Rush	Rec	Ret	TD
Jerry Rice	20	10	197	1	208
Emmitt Smith	15	164	11	0	175
LaDainian Tomlinson . .	11	145	17	0	162
Randy Moss	14	0	156	1	157
Terrell Owens	15	3	153	0	156
Marcus Allen	16	123	21	1	145
Marshall Faulk	12	100	36	0	136
Cris Carter	16	0	130	1	131
Marvin Harrison	13	0	128	0	128
Jim Brown	9	106	20	0	126
Walter Payton	13	110	15	0	125
John Riggins	14	104	12	0	116
Lenny Moore	12	63	48	2	113
Shaun Alexander	9	100	12	0	112
Tony Gonzalez	17	0	111	0	111
Barry Sanders	10	99	10	0	109

Points, season: 186, LaDainian Tomlinson, San Diego, 2006 (31 TDs).
Points, game: 40, Ernie Nevers, Chicago Cardinals vs. Chicago Bears, Nov. 28, 1929 (6 TDs, 4 PATs).
Touchdowns, season: 31, LaDainian Tomlinson, San Diego, 2006.
Touchdowns, game: 6; Ernie Nevers, Chicago Cardinals vs. Chicago Bears, Nov. 28, 1929 (6 rushing);
Dub Jones, Cleveland Browns vs. Chicago Bears, Nov. 25, 1951 (4 rushing, 2 pass receptions);
Gale Sayers, Chicago Bears vs. San Francisco, Dec. 12, 1965 (4 rushing, 1 pass reception, 1 punt return).
Points after TD, season: 75, Matt Prater, Denver, 2013.
Consecutive points after TD: 422, Matt Stover, Baltimore Ravens-Indianapolis, 1996-2009.
Field goals, career: 565, Morten Andersen, New Orleans-Atlanta-NY Giants-Kansas City-Minnesota-Atlanta, 1982-2007.
Field goals, season: 44, David Akers, San Francisco, 2011.
Field goals, game: 8, Rob Bironas, Tennessee vs. Houston, Oct. 21, 2007.
Longest field goal: 64 yards, Matt Prater, Denver vs. Tennesee, Dec. 8, 2013.

Defensive Records

Interceptions, career: 81, Paul Krause, Washington-Minnesota, 1964-79.
Interceptions, season: 14, Dick "Night Train" Lane, L.A. Rams, 1952.
Interception touchdowns, career: 12, Rod Woodson, Pittsburgh-San Francisco-Baltimore Ravens-Oakland, 1987-2003.
Interception touchdowns, season: 4; Ken Houston, Houston, 1971; Jim Kearney, Kansas City, 1972; Eric Allen, Philadelphia, 1993.
Sacks, career (since 1982): 200.0, Bruce Smith, Buffalo-Washington, 1985-2003.
Sacks, season (since 1982): 22.5, Michael Strahan, NY Giants, 2001.

Leading Lifetime Rushers

(ranked by rushing yards; * = active in 2013)

Player	Yrs	Att	Yds	Avg	Long	TD	Player	Yrs	Att	Yds	Avg	Long	TD
Emmitt Smith	15	4,409	18,355	4.2	75T	164	Edgerrin James	11	3,028	12,246	4.0	72	80
Walter Payton	13	3,838	16,726	4.4	76	110	Marcus Allen	16	3,022	12,243	4.1	61T	123
Barry Sanders	10	3,062	15,269	5.0	85	99	Franco Harris	13	2,949	12,120	4.1	75T	91
Curtis Martin	11	3,518	14,101	4.0	70T	90	Thurman Thomas	13	2,877	12,074	4.2	80T	65
LaDainian Tomlinson	11	3,174	13,684	4.3	85T	145	Fred Taylor	13	2,534	11,695	4.6	80T	66
Jerome Bettis	13	3,479	13,662	3.9	71T	91	John Riggins	14	2,916	11,352	3.9	66T	104
Eric Dickerson	11	2,996	13,259	4.4	85T	90	Corey Dillon	10	2,618	11,241	4.3	96T	82
Tony Dorsett	12	2,936	12,739	4.3	99T	77	O. J. Simpson	11	2,404	11,236	4.7	94T	61
Jim Brown	9	2,359	12,312	5.2	80T	106	Warrick Dunn	12	2,669	10,967	4.1	90T	49
Marshall Faulk	12	2,836	12,279	4.3	71T	100	Steven Jackson*	10	2,553	10,681	4.2	59T	62

Yards gained, season: 2,105, Eric Dickerson, L.A. Rams, 1984.
Yards gained, game: 296, Adrian Peterson, Minnesota vs. San Diego, Nov. 4, 2007.
Rushing TDs, career: 164, Emmitt Smith, Dallas-Arizona, 1990-2004.
Rushing TDs, season: 28, LaDainian Tomlinson, San Diego, 2006.
Rushing TDs, game: 6, Ernie Nevers, Chicago Cardinals vs. Chicago Bears, Nov. 28, 1929.
Rushing attempts, game: 45, Jamie Morris, Washington vs. Cincinnati, Dec. 17, 1988 (OT).
Longest run from scrimmage: 99 yards (TD), Tony Dorsett, Dallas vs. Minnesota, Jan. 3, 1983.

Leading Lifetime Receivers

(ranked by number of receptions; * = active in 2013)

Player	Yrs	No.	Yds	Avg	Long	TD	Player	Yrs	No.	Yds	Avg	Long	TD
Jerry Rice	20	1,549	22,895	14.8	96T	197	Andre Reed	16	951	13,198	13.9	83T	87
Tony Gonzalez*	17	1,325	15,127	11.4	73T	111	Derrick Mason	15	943	12,061	12.8	79T	66
Marvin Harrison	13	1,102	14,580	13.2	80T	128	Art Monk	16	940	12,721	13.5	79T	68
Cris Carter	16	1,101	13,899	12.6	80T	130	Andre Johnson*	11	927	12,661	13.7	77T	61
Tim Brown	17	1,094	14,934	13.7	80T	100	Torry Holt	11	920	13,382	14.5	85T	74
Terrell Owens	15	1,078	15,934	14.8	98T	153	Keenan McCardell	16	883	11,373	12.9	76T	63
Isaac Bruce	16	1,024	15,208	14.9	80T	91	Jason Witten*	11	879	9,799	11.1	69	52
Reggie Wayne*	13	1,006	13,566	13.5	71T	80	Jimmy Smith	12	862	12,287	14.3	75	67
Hines Ward	14	1,000	12,083	12.1	85T	85	Muhsin Muhammad	14	860	11,438	13.3	72T	62
Randy Moss	14	982	15,292	15.6	82T	156	Anquan Boldin*	11	857	11,344	13.2	79T	65

Yards gained, career: 22,895, Jerry Rice, San Francisco-Oakland-Seattle, 1985-2004.
Yards gained, season: 1,964, Calvin Johnson, Detroit, 2012.
Yards gained, game: 336, Willie "Flipper" Anderson, L.A. Rams vs. New Orleans, Nov. 26, 1989 (OT).
Pass receptions, season: 143, Marvin Harrison, Indianapolis, 2002.
Pass receptions, game: 21, Brandon Marshall, Denver vs. Indianapolis, Dec. 13, 2009.
Touchdown receptions, career: 197, Jerry Rice, San Francisco-Oakland-Seattle, 1985-2004.
Touchdown receptions, season: 23, Randy Moss, New England, 2007.
Touchdown receptions, game: 5; Bob Shaw, Chicago Cardinals vs. Baltimore Colts, Oct. 2, 1950; Kellen Winslow, San Diego vs. Oakland, Nov. 22, 1981; Jerry Rice, San Francisco vs. Atlanta, Oct. 14, 1990.

Leading Lifetime Passers

(minimum 1,500 attempts; ranked by quarterback rating points; * = active in 2013)

Player	Yrs	Att	Comp	Yds	TD	Int	Pts[1]	Player	Yrs	Att	Comp	Yds	TD	Int	Pts[1]
Aaron Rodgers*	9	2,955	1,945	24,197	188	52	104.9	Matt Ryan*	6	3,288	2,093	23,472	153	77	90.6
Peyton Manning*	15	8,452	5,532	64,964	491	219	97.2	Chad Pennington	11	2,471	1,632	17,823	102	64	90.1
Steve Young	15	4,149	2,667	33,124	232	107	96.8	Matt Schaub*	10	3,181	2,035	24,254	130	84	89.8
Philip Rivers*	10	4,108	2,646	32,369	221	104	96.0	Daunte Culpepper	11	3,199	2,016	24,153	149	106	87.8
Tony Romo*	10	3,775	2,439	29,565	208	101	95.8	Jeff Garcia	11	3,676	2,264	25,537	161	83	87.5
Tom Brady*	14	6,586	4,178	49,149	359	134	95.7	Dan Marino	17	8,358	4,967	61,361	420	252	86.4
Drew Brees*	13	6,799	4,481	51,081	363	177	95.3	Trent Green	11	3,740	2,266	28,475	162	114	86.0
Kurt Warner	12	4,070	2,666	32,344	208	128	93.7	Brett Favre	20	10,169	6,300	71,838	508	336	86.0
Ben Roethlisberger*	10	4,346	2,749	34,105	219	122	92.6	Carson Palmer*	10	4,682	2,930	33,739	213	152	85.9
Joe Montana	15	5,391	3,409	40,551	273	139	92.3	David Garrard*	10	2,281	1,406	16,003	89	54	85.8

(1) Rating points based on performances in the following categories: percentage of completions, percentage of touchdown passes, percentage of interceptions, and average gain per pass attempt.

Yards gained, career: 71,838, Brett Favre, Atlanta-Green Bay-NY Jets-Minnesota, 1991-2010.
Yards gained, season: 5,477, Peyton Manning, Denver, 2013.
Yards gained, game: 554, Norm Van Brocklin, L.A. Rams vs. NY Yanks, Sept. 28, 1951 (27 completions in 41 attempts).
Passing touchdowns, career: 508, Brett Favre, Atlanta-Green Bay-NY Jets-Minnesota, 1991-2010.
Passing touchdowns, season: 55, Peyton Manning, Denver, 2013.
Passing touchdowns, game: 7; Sid Luckman, Chicago Bears vs. NY Giants, Nov. 14, 1943; Adrian Burk, Philadelphia vs. Washington, Oct. 17, 1954; George Blanda, Houston vs. NY Titans, Nov. 19, 1961; Y. A. Tittle, NY Giants vs. Washington, Oct. 28, 1962; Joe Kapp, Minnesota vs. Baltimore Colts, Sept. 28, 1969; Peyton Manning, Denver vs. Baltimore, Sept. 5, 2013; Nick Foles, Philadelphia vs. Oakland, Nov. 3, 2013.
Passes completed, career: 6,300, Brett Favre, Atlanta-Green Bay-NY Jets-Minnesota, 1991-2010.
Passes completed, season: 468, Drew Brees, New Orleans, 2011.
Passes completed, game: 45, Drew Bledsoe, New England vs. Minnesota, Nov. 13, 1994 (OT).

National Football League Franchise Origins

(Team: founding year, league. Home stadium location; subsequent history.)

Arizona Cardinals: 1920, American Professional Football Association (APFA)[1]. Chicago, 1920-59; St. Louis, 1960-87; Tempe, AZ, 1988-2005; Glendale, AZ, 2006-present.
Atlanta Falcons: 1966, NFL. Atlanta, 1966-present.
Baltimore Ravens: 1996, NFL. Baltimore, 1996-present.
Buffalo Bills: 1960, American Football League (AFL)[2]. Buffalo, 1960-72; Orchard Park, NY, 1973-present.
Carolina Panthers: 1995, NFL. Clemson, SC, 1995; Charlotte, NC, 1996-present.
Chicago Bears: 1920, APFA. Decatur, IL, 1920; Chicago, 1921-present.
Cincinnati Bengals: 1968, AFL. Cincinnati, 1968-present.
Cleveland Browns: 1946, All-America Football Conference (AAFC)[3]. Cleveland, 1946-95; 1999-present.
Dallas Cowboys: 1960, NFL. Dallas, 1960-70; Irving, TX, 1971-2008; Arlington, TX, 2009-present.
Denver Broncos: 1960, AFL. Denver, 1960-present.
Detroit Lions: 1930, NFL. Portsmouth, OH, 1930-33; Detroit, 1934-74; Pontiac, MI, 1975-2001; Detroit, 2002-present.
Green Bay Packers: 1921, APFA. Green Bay, WI, 1921-present.
Houston Texans: 2002, NFL. Houston, 2002-present.
Indianapolis Colts: 1953, NFL[3]. Baltimore, 1953-83; Indianapolis, 1984-present.
Jacksonville Jaguars: 1995, NFL. Jacksonville, FL, 1995-present.
Kansas City Chiefs: 1960, AFL. Dallas, 1960-62; Kansas City, MO, 1963-present.
Miami Dolphins: 1966, AFL. Miami, 1966-2002; Miami Gardens, FL, 2003-present.

Minnesota Vikings: 1961, NFL. Bloomington, MN, 1961-81; Minneapolis, 1982-present.
New England Patriots: 1960, AFL. Boston, 1960-70; Foxborough, MA, 1971-present.
New Orleans Saints: 1967, NFL. New Orleans, 1967-2004; Baton Rouge and San Antonio, 2005; New Orleans, 2006-present.
NY Giants: 1925, NFL. New York, NY, 1925-73; 1975; New Haven, CT, 1973-74; E. Rutherford, NJ, 1976-present.
NY Jets: 1960, AFL. New York, NY, 1960-83; E. Rutherford, NJ, 1984-present.
Oakland Raiders: 1960, AFL. San Francisco, 1960-61; Oakland, CA, 1962-81; Los Angeles, 1982-94; Oakland, CA, 1995-present.
Philadelphia Eagles: 1933, NFL. Philadelphia, 1933-present.
Pittsburgh Steelers: 1933, NFL. Pittsburgh, 1933-present.
St. Louis Rams: 1937, NFL. Cleveland, 1936-45; Los Angeles, 1946-79; Anaheim, CA, 1980-94; St. Louis, 1995-present.
San Diego Chargers: 1960, AFL. Los Angeles, 1960; San Diego, 1961-present.
San Francisco 49ers: 1946, AAFC. San Francisco, 1946-present.
Seattle Seahawks: 1976, NFL. Seattle, 1976-present.
Tampa Bay Buccaneers: 1976, NFL. Tampa, 1976-present.
Tennessee Titans: 1960, AFL. Houston, 1960-96; Memphis, 1997; Nashville, 1998-present.
Washington Redskins: 1932, NFL. Boston, 1932-36; Washington, DC, 1937-96; Landover, MD, 1997-present.

(1) The American Professional Football Association (APFA) was formed in 1920 to standardize the rules of professional football. In 1922, the name was changed to the National Football League (NFL). (2) The most successful of four leagues called the American Football League, or AFL (1926; 1936-37; 1940-41; 1960-69). Congress approved an NFL/AFL merger in 1966. Baltimore, Cleveland, and Pittsburgh agreed to join the 10 incoming AFL teams to form the American Football Conference. The NFL began play in 1970 with 26 teams. (3) The All-America Football Conference (AAFC), 1946-49. In 1950, three of its teams joined the NFL (Baltimore, Cleveland, and San Francisco). The Baltimore franchise failed, but the NFL awarded the city a second one, also called the Colts, in 1953.

NFL Stadiums, 2013

(**A** = A-Turf Titan, **D** = DD Grassmaster (grass), **F** = FieldTurf, **G** = Grass, **N** = Natural grass,
S = Synthetic, **SM** = Sportexe Momentum, **SS** = Sportfield Softtop)

Team: stadium, location, surface (year built)	Capacity[1]
Bears: Soldier Field[2], Chicago, IL, N (1924)	61,500
Bengals: Paul Brown Stadium, Cincinnati, OH, S (2000)	65,515
Bills: Ralph Wilson Stadium, Orchard Park, NY, A (1973)	73,079
Broncos: Sports Authority Field at Mile High[3], Denver, CO, D (2001)	76,125
Browns: FirstEnergy Stadium[4], Cleveland, OH, G (1999)	73,200
Buccaneers: Raymond James Stadium, Tampa, FL, G (1998)	65,908
Cardinals: University of Phoenix Stadium, Glendale, AZ, G (2006)	65,000
Chargers: Qualcomm Stadium[5], San Diego, CA, G (1967)	70,000
Chiefs: Arrowhead Stadium, Kansas City, MO, G (1972; fully renovated 2010)	76,416
Colts: Lucas Oil Stadium, Indianapolis, IN, F (2008)	63,000
Cowboys: AT&T Stadium[6], Arlington, TX, SS (2009)	100,000
Dolphins: Sun Life Stadium[7], Miami Gardens, FL, G (1987)	75,192
Eagles: Lincoln Financial Field, Philadelphia, PA, N (2003)	69,144
Falcons: Georgia Dome, Atlanta, GA, F (1992)	71,228
49ers: Candlestick Park[8], San Francisco, CA, N (1960)	69,732

Team: stadium, location, surface (year built)	Capacity[1]
Giants: MetLife Stadium[9], E. Rutherford, NJ, F (2010)	82,500
Jaguars: EverBank Field[10], Jacksonville, FL, G (1995)	67,246
Jets: MetLife Stadium[9], E. Rutherford, NJ, F (2010)	82,500
Lions: Ford Field, Detroit, MI, F (2002)	64,500
Packers: Lambeau Field[11], Green Bay, WI, D (1957)	80,750
Panthers: Bank of America Stadium[12], Charlotte, NC, G (1996)	74,455
Patriots: Gillette Stadium, Foxborough, MA, F (2002)	68,756
Raiders: O.co Coliseum[13], Oakland, CA, G (1966)	53,286
Rams: Edward Jones Dome[14], St. Louis, MO, F (1995)	66,000
Ravens: M&T Bank Stadium[15], Baltimore, MD, SM (1998)	71,008
Redskins: FedExField[16], Landover, MD, N (1997)	79,000
Saints: Mercedes-Benz Superdome[17], New Orleans, LA, S (1975)	73,000
Seahawks: CenturyLink Field[18], Seattle, WA, F (2002)	67,000
Steelers: Heinz Field, Pittsburgh, PA, N (2001)	65,500
Texans: NRG Stadium[19], Houston, TX, G (2002)	71,054
Titans: LP Field[20], Nashville, TN, N (1999)	69,149
Vikings: Mall of America Field at Hubert H. Humphrey Metrodome[21], Minneapolis, MN, SM (1982)	64,126

(1) As of the start of the 2013 season. (2) Renovation in 2002 replaced interior of stadium. (3) Formerly INVESCO Field at Mile High (2001-11). (4) Formerly Cleveland Browns Stadium (1999-2012). (5) Formerly San Diego Stadium (1967-80); San Diego Jack Murphy Stadium (1981-97). (6) Formerly Cowboys Stadium (2009-12). (7) Formerly Joe Robbie Stadium (1987-96); Pro Player Stadium (1996-2005); Land Shark Stadium (2009). (8) Formerly Candlestick Park (1960-94); 3Com Park at Candlestick Point (1995-2004). (9) Formerly New Meadowlands Stadium (2010-11). (10) Formerly ALLTEL Stadium (1997-2007); Jacksonville Municipal Stadium (1946-97, 2007-09). (11) Formerly City Stadium (1957-65). Renovation completed in 2003 added 11,625 seats. (12) Formerly Ericsson Stadium (1996-2003). (13) Formerly Oakland-Alameda County Coliseum (1966-98); Network Associates Coliseum (1998-2004); McAfee Stadium (2004-08); Oakland Coliseum (2008-11). (14) Formerly Trans World Dome (1995-2001). (15) Formerly PSINet Stadium (1998-2002); Ravens Stadium (2002-03). (16) Formerly Jack Kent Cooke Stadium (1997-99). (17) Formerly Louisiana Superdome (1975-2011). (18) Formerly Seahawks Stadium (2002-04); Qwest Field (2004-11). (19) Formerly Reliant Stadium (2002-14). (20) Formerly Adelphia Coliseum (1999-2002). (21) Formerly Hubert H. Humphrey Metrodome (1982-2009). Demolished in Apr. 2014; new stadium set to open for the 2016 season.

Pro Football Hall of Fame, Canton, OH

(Asterisk indicates member elected in Feb. 2014 and inducted Aug. 2, 2014.)

Herb Adderley
Troy Aikman
George Allen
Larry Allen
Marcus Allen
Lance Alworth
Doug Atkins
Morris "Red" Badgro
Lem Barney
Cliff Battles
Sammy Baugh
Chuck Bednarik
Bert Bell
Bobby Bell
Raymond Berry
Elvin Bethea
Charles Bidwill
Fred Biletnikoff
George Blanda
Mel Blount
Terry Bradshaw
*Derrick Brooks
Bob Brown
Jim Brown
Paul Brown
Roosevelt Brown
Willie Brown
Junious "Buck" Buchanan
Nick Buoniconti
Dick Butkus
Jack Butler
Earl Campbell
Tony Canadeo
Joe Carr
Harry Carson
Cris Carter
Dave Casper
Guy Chamberlin
Jack Christiansen
Earl "Dutch" Clark
George Connor
Jim Conzelman
Lou Creekmur
Larry Csonka
Curley Culp
Al Davis
Willie Davis
Dermontti Dawson
Len Dawson
Fred Dean
Joe DeLamielleure
Richard Dent
Eric Dickerson
Dan Dierdorf
Mike Ditka
Chris Doleman
Art Donovan

Tony Dorsett
John "Paddy" Driscoll
Bill Dudley
Glen "Turk" Edwards
Carl Eller
John Elway
Weeb Ewbank
Marshall Faulk
Tom Fears
Jim Finks
Ray Flaherty
Len Ford
Dr. Daniel Fortmann
Dan Fouts
Benny Friedman
Frank Gatski
Bill George
Joe Gibbs
Frank Gifford
Sid Gillman
Otto Graham
Harold "Red" Grange
Bud Grant
Darrell Green
Joe Greene
Forrest Gregg
Bob Griese
Russ Grimm
Lou Groza
*Ray Guy
Joe Guyon
George Halas
Jack Ham
Dan Hampton
Chris Hanburger
John Hannah
Bob Hayes
Mike Haynes
Mel Hein
Ted Hendricks
Wilbur "Pete" Henry
Arnold Herber
Bill Hewitt
Gene Hickerson
Clarke Hinkle
Elroy "Crazylegs" Hirsch
Paul Hornung
Ken Houston
Robert "Cal" Hubbard
Sam Huff
*Claude Humphrey
Lamar Hunt
Don Hutson
Michael Irvin
Rickey Jackson
Jimmy Johnson
John Henry Johnson
Charlie Joiner

David "Deacon" Jones
Stan Jones
*Walter Jones
Henry Jordan
Sonny Jurgensen
Jim Kelly
Leroy Kelly
Cortez Kennedy
Walt Kiesling
Frank "Bruiser" Kinard
Paul Krause
Earl "Curly" Lambeau
Jack Lambert
Tom Landry
Dick "Night Train" Lane
Jim Langer
Willie Lanier
Steve Largent
Yale Lary
Dante Lavelli
Bobby Layne
Dick LeBeau
Alphonse "Tuffy" Leemans
Marv Levy
Bob Lilly
Floyd Little
Larry Little
James Lofton
Vince Lombardi
Howie Long
Ronnie Lott
Sid Luckman
Roy "Link" Lyman
Tom Mack
John Mackey
John Madden
Tim Mara
Wellington Mara
Gino Marchetti
Dan Marino
George Preston Marshall
Curtis Martin
Bruce Mathews
Ollie Matson
Don Maynard
George McAfee
Mike McCormack
Randall McDaniel
Tommy McDonald
Hugh McElhenny
Johnny "Blood" McNally
Mike Michalske
Wayne Millner
Bobby Mitchell
Ron Mix
Art Monk

Joe Montana
Warren Moon
Lenny Moore
Marion Motley
Mike Munchak
Anthony Muñoz
George Musso
Bronko Nagurski
Joe Namath
Earle "Greasy" Neale
Ernie Nevers
Ozzie Newsome
Ray Nitschke
Chuck Noll
Leo Nomellini
Jonathan Ogden
Merlin Olsen
Jim Otto
Steve Owen
Alan Page
Bill Parcells
Clarence "Ace" Parker
Jim Parker
Walter Payton
Joe Perry
Pete Pihos
Fritz Pollard
John Randle
Hugh "Shorty" Ray
*Andre Reed
Dan Reeves
Mel Renfro
Jerry Rice
Les Richter
John Riggins
Jim Ringo
Willie Roaf
Dave Robinson
Andy Robustelli
Art Rooney
Dan Rooney
Pete Rozelle
Ed Sabol
Bob St. Clair
Barry Sanders
Charlie Sanders
Deion Sanders
Warren Sapp
Gale Sayers
Joe Schmidt
Tex Schramm
Lee Roy Selmon
Shannon Sharpe
Billy Shaw
Art Shell
Don Shula
O. J. Simpson
Mike Singletary

Jackie Slater
Bruce Smith
Emmitt Smith
Jackie Smith
John Stallworth
Bart Starr
Roger Staubach
Ernie Stautner
Jan Stenerud
Dwight Stephenson
*Michael Strahan
Hank Stram
Ken Strong
Joe Stydahar
Lynn Swann
Fran Tarkenton
Charley Taylor
Jim Taylor
Lawrence "LT" Taylor
Derrick Thomas
Emmitt Thomas
Thurman Thomas
Jim Thorpe
Andre Tippett
Y. A. Tittle
George Trafton
Charley Trippi
Emlen Tunnell
Clyde "Bulldog" Turner
Johnny Unitas
Gene Upshaw
Norm Van Brocklin
Steve Van Buren
Doak Walker
Bill Walsh
Paul Warfield
Bob Waterfield
Mike Webster
Randy White
Reggie White
Dave Wilcox
*Aeneas Williams
Bill Willis
Larry Wilson
Ralph Wilson Jr.
Kellen Winslow
Alex Wojciechowicz
Willie Wood
Rod Woodson
Rayfield Wright
Ron Yary
Steve Young
Jack Youngblood
Gary Zimmerman

All-Time NFL Coaching Victories

(at end of 2013 season; ranked by overall career wins; * = active in 2013)

Coach	Team	Yrs	Regular Season				Overall			
			W	L	T	Pct	W	L	T	Pct
Don Shula	Colts, Dolphins	33	328	156	6	.677	347	173	6	.666
George Halas	Bears	40	318	148	31	.682	324	151	31	.682
Tom Landry	Cowboys	29	250	162	6	.607	270	178	6	.603
Earl "Curly" Lambeau	Packers, Chicago Cardinals, Redskins	33	226	132	22	.631	229	134	22	.631
Bill Belichick*	Browns, Patriots	19	199	105	0	.655	218	114	0	.657
Chuck Noll	Steelers	23	193	148	1	.566	209	156	1	.572
Marty Schottenheimer	Browns, Chiefs, Redskins, Chargers	21	200	126	1	.613	205	139	1	.596
Dan Reeves	Broncos, Giants, Falcons	23	190	165	2	.535	201	174	2	.536
Chuck Knox	Rams, Bills, Seahawks	22	186	147	1	.558	193	158	1	.550
Bill Parcells	Giants, Patriots, Jets, Cowboys	19	172	130	1	.569	183	138	1	.570
Mike Shanahan*	Raiders, Broncos, Redskins	20	170	138	0	.552	178	144	0	.553
Mike Holmgren	Packers, Seahawks	17	161	111	0	.592	174	122	0	.588
Joe Gibbs	Redskins	16	154	94	0	.621	171	101	0	.629
Paul Brown	Browns, Bengals	25	166	100	6	.624	170	108	6	.612
Tom Coughlin*	Jaguars, Giants	18	158	130	0	.549	170	137	0	.554
Bud Grant	Vikings	18	158	96	5	.621	168	108	5	.608
Bill Cowher	Steelers	15	149	90	1	.623	161	99	1	.619
Jeff Fisher*	Oilers, Titans, Rams	19	156	137	1	.532	161	143	1	.530
Marv Levy	Chiefs, Bills	17	143	112	0	.561	154	120	0	.562
Steve Owen	Giants	23	151	100	17	.602	153	108	17	.586

BASEBALL

Playoff Results, 2014

American League

American League Wild Card Game: Kansas City defeated Oakland, 9-8 (12 innings).

American League Division Series (ALDS): Baltimore defeated Detroit, 3 games to 0; Kansas City defeated L.A. Angels, 3 games to 0.

American League Championship Series (ALCS): Kansas City defeated Baltimore, 4 games to 0.

National League

National League Wild Card Game: San Francisco defeated Pittsburgh, 8-0.

National League Division Series (NLDS): San Francisco defeated Washington, 3 games to 1; St. Louis defeated L.A. Dodgers, 3 games to 1.

National League Championship Series (NLCS): San Francisco defeated St. Louis, 4 games to 1.

World Series, 2014
San Francisco Defeats Kansas City, 4 Games to 3

The San Francisco Giants defeated the Kansas City Royals, 3-2, in an exciting Game 7 on Oct. 29, 2014, at Kauffman Stadium in Kansas City for their third World Series victory in five years. On short rest, starting pitcher Madison Bumgarner entered the game in relief and threw five scoreless innings, getting the final out with the tying run at third base. Bumgarner earned the save and was voted World Series MVP. The 25-year-old left-hander had ended the Royals' eight-game postseason winning streak as the Giants took the Series opener, 7-1, Oct. 21, 2014, at Kauffman Stadium. Bumgarner shut down the Royals offense again in a 5-0 Game 5 win Oct. 26 at AT&T Park in San Francisco, allowing four hits and striking out eight to record the first World Series shutout since 2003. Giants outfielder Hunter Pence, who batted .444 over the course of the series, and Pablo Sandoval (.429) tied for a new Giants franchise-record with 12 hits in the 2014 World Series.

Kansas City forced a seventh game with a 10-0 victory in Game 6 at Kauffman Stadium Oct. 28. The Royals exploded for seven runs in the bottom of the second, highlighted by a two-run single from Lorenzo Cain and Eric Hosmer's two-run double. Mike Moustakas added a home run and two RBI in KC's 15-hit barrage. Royals right-hander Yordano Ventura allowed just three hits in seven innings against a Giants offense that had totaled 28 hits in Games 4 and 5.

Game 1
Oct. 21 at Kauffman Stadium, Kansas City, MO

	1	2	3	4	5	6	7	8	9	R	H	E
San Francisco Giants	3	0	0	2	0	0	2	0	0	7	11	1
Kansas City Royals	0	0	0	0	0	0	1	0	0	1	4	0

Winning pitcher: Madison Bumgarner
Losing pitcher: James Shields
Attendance: 40,459

Game 2
Oct. 22 at Kauffman Stadium, Kansas City, MO

	1	2	3	4	5	6	7	8	9	R	H	E
San Francisco Giants	1	0	0	1	0	0	0	0	0	2	9	0
Kansas City Royals	1	1	0	0	0	5	0	0	X	7	10	0

Winning pitcher: Kelvin Herrera
Losing pitcher: Jake Peavy
Attendance: 40,446

Game 3
Oct. 24 at AT&T Park, San Francisco, CA

	1	2	3	4	5	6	7	8	9	R	H	E
Kansas City Royals	1	0	0	0	0	2	0	0	0	3	6	0
San Francisco Giants	0	0	0	0	0	2	0	0	0	2	4	0

Winning pitcher: Jeremy Guthrie
Losing pitcher: Tim Hudson
Save: Greg Holland
Attendance: 43,020

Game 4
Oct. 25 at AT&T Park, San Francisco, CA

	1	2	3	4	5	6	7	8	9	R	H	E
Kansas City Royals	0	0	4	0	0	0	0	0	0	4	12	1
San Francisco Giants	1	0	1	0	2	3	4	0	X	11	16	0

Winning pitcher: Yusmeiro Petit
Losing pitcher: Brandon Finnegan
Attendance: 43,066

Game 5
Oct. 26 at AT&T Park, San Francisco, CA

	1	2	3	4	5	6	7	8	9	R	H	E
Kansas City Royals	0	0	0	0	0	0	0	0	0	4	1	
San Francisco Giants	0	1	0	1	0	0	0	3	X	5	12	0

Winning pitcher: Madison Bumgarner
Losing pitcher: James Shields
Attendance: 43,087

Game 6
Oct. 28 at Kauffman Stadium, Kansas City, MO

	1	2	3	4	5	6	7	8	9	R	H	E
San Francisco Giants	0	0	0	0	0	0	0	0	0	0	6	0
Kansas City Royals	0	7	1	0	1	0	1	0	X	10	15	0

Winning pitcher: Yordano Ventura
Losing pitcher: Jake Peavy
Attendance: 40,372

Game 7
Oct. 29 at Kauffman Stadium, Kansas City, MO

	1	2	3	4	5	6	7	8	9	R	H	E
San Francisco Giants	0	2	0	1	0	0	0	0	0	3	8	1
Kansas City Royals	0	2	0	0	0	0	0	0	2	6	0	

Winning pitcher: Jeremy Affeldt
Losing pitcher: Jeremy Guthrie
Save: Madison Bumgarner
Attendance: 40,535

Major League Baseball, 2014: Video Replay Expands; Jeter, Selig Retire

Perennial American League powers took a backseat in 2014 to the Kansas City Royals, who reached the postseason for the first time in nearly three decades and won eight straight playoff games. The Wild Card-winning Kansas City swept the AL Championship Series against the Baltimore Orioles (96-66), who had won the AL East for the first time since 1997. The Orioles were 12 games ahead of the NY Yankees, and the defending champion Boston Red Sox (71-91) faded to last place. Baltimore hit a Major League-high 211 home runs and its top three sluggers alone—Nelson Cruz (MLB-leading 40 homers), Adam Jones (29), and Chris Davis (26)—matched the Royals league-low team total of 95 home runs. (Davis was suspended for 25 games on Sept. 12, 2014, after testing positive for a banned substance.) Baltimore swept the AL Division Series against the Detroit Tigers, who had earned their fourth straight AL Central crown. Kansas City also completed a sweep against the L.A. Angels in the ALDS with an 8-3 victory Oct. 5. The Angels had the best record in baseball (98-64) and Angels first baseman Albert Pujols became the 26th player to reach 500 career home runs Apr. 22, 2014.

San Francisco advanced to the NL Championship Series against St. Louis, which reached the NLCS for the fourth straight year. But the Cardinals' season ended Oct. 16, 2014, at AT&T Park when San Francisco outfielder Travis Ishikawa hit a three-run homer in the bottom of the ninth in Game 5 that propelled the Giants toward their third World Series in five seasons. The Giants topped the NL East-champion Washington Nationals in four games in the NL Division Series, which included an 18-inning, 2-1 Giants victory Oct. 4, 2014, at Nationals Park in a game that lasted 6 hr., 23 min.; it was the longest postseason game in MLB history. The L.A. Dodgers won the NL West, but All-Star left-hander Clayton Kershaw (21-3, 1.77 ERA) lost both of his NL Division Series starts as St. Louis beat the Dodgers in four games. Kershaw became the first pitcher in history to lead the majors in earned run average four straight years; he also threw his first no-hitter in an 8-0 victory over Colorado June 18, 2014, at Dodger Stadium.

Kershaw's gem was one of five no-hitters in the National League in 2014, including one by Dodger teammate Josh Beckett (May 25, 8-0 win at Philadelphia). Tim Lincecum threw his second career no-hitter (June 25, Giants' 4-0 win over San Diego), and Cole Hamels combined with three Phillies' relievers on Sept. 1 in a 7-0 win in Atlanta. On the final day of the regular season Sept. 28, Washington's Jordan Zimmermann struck out 10 in his first no-hitter, a 1-0 triumph over visiting Miami.

The Yanks said farewell to veteran shortstop Derek Jeter, who retired after a 20-year career and finished sixth in MLB history with 3,465 career hits. Major League owners voted unanimously Aug. 14, 2014, to elect Rob Manfred to succeed Bud Selig as MLB commissioner. MLB's chief operating officer since Sept. 2013, Manfred will formally take the reins Jan. 25, 2015. During Selig's 22 seasons as commissioner, he oversaw PED (performance-enhancing drugs) scandals, the 1994 player strike, and the introduction of interleague play, divisional playoffs, the wild card, and, in the last season, expanded video replay reviews of umpire calls. The video replay option resulted in 1,275 total reviews during the 2014 regular season (47% of those calls were overturned).

National League Final Standings, 2014

(* = wild card)

Eastern Division

Team	W	L	PCT	GB	Home	Road	vs. East	vs. Central	vs. West	vs. AL
Washington	96	66	.593	—	51-30	45-36	45-31	17-16	24-9	10-10
NY Mets	79	83	.488	17	40-41	39-42	38-38	16-18	14-18	11-9
Atlanta	79	83	.488	17	42-39	37-44	40-36	20-13	12-21	7-13
Miami	77	85	.475	19	42-39	35-46	33-43	14-18	17-17	13-7
Philadelphia	73	89	.451	23	37-44	36-45	34-42	15-18	17-16	7-13

Central Division

Team	W	L	PCT	GB	Home	Road	vs. East	vs. Central	vs. West	vs. AL
St. Louis	90	72	.556	—	51-30	39-42	17-16	45-31	20-13	8-12
Pittsburgh*	88	74	.543	2	51-30	37-44	21-13	36-40	20-12	11-9
Milwaukee	82	80	.506	8	42-39	40-41	15-19	36-40	20-12	11-9
Cincinnati	76	86	.469	14	44-37	32-49	14-18	40-36	16-18	6-14
Chicago Cubs	73	89	.451	17	41-40	32-49	16-16	33-43	15-19	9-11

Western Division

Team	W	L	PCT	GB	Home	Road	vs. East	vs. Central	vs. West	vs. AL
L.A. Dodgers	94	68	.580	—	45-36	49-32	18-14	15-19	50-26	11-9
San Francisco*	88	74	.543	6	45-36	43-38	22-12	16-16	40-36	10-10
San Diego	77	85	.475	17	48-33	29-52	17-17	18-14	33-43	9-11
Colorado	66	96	.407	28	45-36	21-60	13-20	10-23	36-40	7-13
Arizona	64	98	.395	30	33-48	31-50	11-21	15-19	31-45	7-13

American League Final Standings, 2014

(* = wild card)

Eastern Division

Team	W	L	PCT	GB	Home	Road	vs. East	vs. Central	vs. West	vs. NL
Baltimore	96	66	.593	—	50-31	46-35	47-29	16-17	21-12	12-8
NY Yankees	84	78	.519	12	43-38	41-40	37-39	19-16	15-16	13-7
Toronto	83	79	.512	13	46-35	37-44	39-37	16-16	15-19	13-7
Tampa Bay	77	85	.475	19	36-45	41-40	36-40	14-18	17-17	10-10
Boston	71	91	.438	25	34-47	37-44	31-45	17-16	14-19	9-11

Central Division

Team	W	L	PCT	GB	Home	Road	vs. East	vs. Central	vs. West	vs. NL
Detroit	90	72	.556	—	45-36	45-36	17-15	43-33	18-16	12-8
Kansas City*	89	73	.549	1	42-39	47-34	17-17	39-37	18-14	15-5
Cleveland	85	77	.525	5	48-33	37-44	19-14	39-37	17-16	10-10
Chicago White Sox	73	89	.451	17	40-41	33-48	16-18	33-43	13-19	11-9
Minnesota	70	92	.432	20	35-46	35-46	14-18	36-40	11-23	9-11

Western Division

Team	W	L	PCT	GB	Home	Road	vs. East	vs. Central	vs. West	vs. NL
L.A. Angels	98	64	.605	—	52-29	46-35	19-14	24-9	43-33	12-8
Oakland*	88	74	.543	10	48-33	40-41	20-12	17-17	38-38	13-7
Seattle	87	75	.537	11	41-40	46-35	18-15	19-14	41-35	9-11
Houston	70	92	.432	28	38-43	32-49	16-18	14-18	35-41	5-15
Texas	67	95	.414	31	33-48	34-47	10-23	14-19	33-43	10-10

National League Statistics, 2014

Individual statistics. Players recording fewer than 150 at-bats (batters) or fewer than 70 innings or 10 saves (pitchers) are not listed here. * = Changed teams within NL during season; entry includes statistics for more than one team. # = Changed teams to or from AL during season; entry includes only NL statistics. Team Batting and Team Pitching include players not shown separately.

Team Batting

Team	AVG	AB	R	H	HR	RBI
Colorado Rockies	.276	5,612	755	1,551	186	721
Los Angeles Dodgers	.265	5,560	718	1,476	134	686
Pittsburgh Pirates	.259	5,536	682	1,436	156	659
San Francisco Giants	.255	5,523	665	1,407	132	636
Washington Nationals	.253	5,542	686	1,403	152	635
St. Louis Cardinals	.253	5,426	619	1,371	105	585
Miami Marlins	.253	5,538	645	1,399	122	614
Milwaukee Brewers	.250	5,462	650	1,366	150	617
Arizona Diamondbacks	.248	5,552	615	1,379	118	573
Philadelphia Phillies	.242	5,603	619	1,356	125	584
Atlanta Braves	.241	5,468	573	1,316	123	545
Chicago Cubs	.239	5,508	614	1,315	157	590
New York Mets	.239	5,472	629	1,306	125	602
Cincinnati Reds	.238	5,395	595	1,282	131	562
San Diego Padres	.226	5,294	535	1,199	109	500

Team Pitching

Team	ERA	IP	H	BB	SO	SV
Washington Nationals	3.03	1,470.2	1,351	352	1,288	45
San Diego Padres	3.27	1,438.2	1,300	462	1,284	41
Atlanta Braves	3.38	1,455.0	1,369	472	1,301	54
Los Angeles Dodgers	3.40	1,464.2	1,338	429	1,373	47
Pittsburgh Pirates	3.47	1,456.1	1,341	499	1,228	48
New York Mets	3.49	1,463.2	1,370	509	1,303	42
San Francisco Giants	3.50	1,449.0	1,305	389	1,211	46
St. Louis Cardinals	3.50	1,448.2	1,321	470	1,221	55
Cincinnati Reds	3.59	1,446.0	1,282	507	1,290	44
Milwaukee Brewers	3.67	1,457.2	1,386	431	1,246	45
Miami Marlins	3.78	1,457.2	1,481	468	1,190	42
Philadelphia Phillies	3.79	1,468.1	1,396	521	1,255	40
Chicago Cubs	3.91	1,463.1	1,398	504	1,311	37
Arizona Diamondbacks	4.26	1,444.1	1,467	469	1,278	35
Colorado Rockies	4.84	1,431.0	1,528	531	1,074	24

Arizona Diamondbacks

Batters	AVG	AB	R	H	HR	RBI	SO	SB
A. J. Pollock	.302	265	41	80	7	24	46	14
Paul Goldschmidt	.300	406	75	122	19	69	110	9
David Peralta	.286	329	40	94	8	36	60	6
Ender Inciarte	.278	418	54	116	4	27	53	19
Martin Prado#	.270	403	44	109	5	42	57	2
Chris Owings	.261	310	34	81	6	26	67	8
Gerardo Parra*	.261	529	64	138	9	40	100	9
Jordan Pacheco*	.255	153	10	39	0	16	27	0
Cliff Pennington	.254	177	21	45	2	10	36	6
Cody Ross	.252	202	15	51	2	15	44	0
Aaron Hill	.244	501	52	122	10	60	92	4
Miguel Montero	.243	489	40	119	13	72	97	0
Mark Trumbo	.235	328	37	77	14	61	89	2
Didi Gregorius	.226	270	35	61	6	27	52	3

Pitchers	ERA	W	L	IP	H	BB	SO	SV
Josh Collmenter	3.46	11	9	179.1	163	39	115	1
Vidal Nuno#	3.76	0	7	83.2	71	20	69	0
Chase Anderson	4.01	9	7	114.1	117	40	105	0
Bronson Arroyo	4.08	7	4	86.0	92	19	47	0
Addison Reed	4.25	1	7	59.1	57	15	69	32
Wade Miley	4.34	8	12	201.1	207	75	183	0
Randall Delgado	4.87	4	4	77.2	71	35	86	0
Brandon McCarthy#	5.01	3	10	109.2	131	20	93	0
Trevor Cahill	5.61	3	12	110.2	123	55	105	1

Managers: Kirk Gibson, Alan Trammell

Atlanta Braves

Batters	AVG	AB	R	H	HR	RBI	SO	SB
Freddie Freeman	.288	607	93	175	18	78	145	3
Jason Heyward	.271	573	74	155	11	58	98	20
Justin Upton	.270	566	77	153	29	102	171	8
Chris Johnson	.263	582	43	153	10	58	159	6
Evan Gattis	.263	369	41	97	22	52	97	0
Emilio Bonifacio*	.259	394	47	102	3	24	85	26
Tommy La Stella	.251	319	22	80	1	31	40	2
Andrelton Simmons	.244	540	44	132	7	46	60	4
B. J. Upton	.208	519	67	108	12	35	173	20
Gerald Laird	.204	152	12	31	0	10	33	0
Ryan Doumit	.197	157	11	31	5	17	49	1

Pitchers	ERA	W	L	IP	H	BB	SO	SV
Craig Kimbrel	1.61	0	3	61.2	30	26	95	47
Alex Wood	2.78	11	11	171.2	151	45	170	0
Julio Teheran	2.89	14	13	221.0	188	51	186	0
David Hale	3.30	4	5	87.1	89	39	44	0
Aaron Harang	3.57	12	12	204.1	215	71	161	0
Ervin Santana	3.95	14	10	196.0	193	63	179	0
Mike Minor	4.77	6	12	145.1	165	44	120	0

Manager: Fredi González

Chicago Cubs

Batters	AVG	AB	R	H	HR	RBI	SO	SB
Starlin Castro	.292	528	58	154	14	65	100	4
Anthony Rizzo	.286	524	89	150	32	78	116	5
Chris Coghlan	.283	385	50	109	9	41	81	7
Justin Ruggiano	.281	224	29	63	6	28	70	2
Emilio Bonifacio*	.259	394	47	102	3	24	85	26
Ryan Sweeney	.251	207	22	52	3	20	33	0
Luis Valbuena	.249	478	68	119	16	51	113	1
Darwin Barney*	.241	237	24	57	3	23	34	1
Welington Castillo	.237	380	28	90	13	46	102	0
Junior Lake	.211	308	30	65	9	25	110	7
Arismendy Alcantara	.205	278	31	57	10	29	93	8
Nate Schierholtz*	.195	353	32	69	7	37	84	4
John Baker	.192	182	9	35	0	15	58	0
Javier Baez	.169	213	25	36	9	20	95	5
Mike Olt	.160	225	23	36	12	33	100	0

Pitchers	ERA	W	L	IP	H	BB	SO	SV
Hector Rondon	2.42	4	4	63.1	52	15	63	29
Kyle Hendricks	2.46	7	2	80.1	72	15	47	0
Jake Arrieta	2.53	10	5	156.2	114	41	167	0
Jeff Samardzija#	2.83	2	7	108.0	99	31	103	0
Jason Hammel#	2.98	8	5	108.2	88	23	104	0
Carlos Villanueva	4.64	5	7	77.2	89	19	72	2
Travis Wood	5.03	8	13	173.2	190	76	146	0
Jacob Turner*	6.13	6	11	113.0	148	33	71	0
Edwin Jackson	6.33	6	15	140.2	168	63	123	0

Manager: Rick Renteria

Cincinnati Reds

Batters	AVG	AB	R	H	HR	RBI	SO	SB
Devin Mesoraco	.273	384	54	105	25	80	103	1
Todd Frazier	.273	597	88	163	29	80	139	20
Brandon Phillips	.266	462	44	123	8	51	74	2
Joey Votto	.255	220	32	56	6	23	49	1
Brayan Pena	.253	348	23	88	5	26	42	2
Billy Hamilton	.250	563	72	141	6	48	117	56
Ramon Santiago	.246	179	20	44	2	17	38	2
Ryan Ludwick	.244	357	28	87	9	45	94	0
Skip Schumaker	.235	247	22	58	2	22	50	2
Chris Heisey	.222	275	34	61	8	22	64	9
Zack Cozart	.221	506	48	112	4	38	79	7
Jay Bruce	.217	493	71	107	18	66	149	12

Pitchers	ERA	W	L	IP	H	BB	SO	SV
Aroldis Chapman	2.00	0	3	54.0	21	24	106	36
Johnny Cueto	2.25	20	9	243.2	169	65	242	0
Mat Latos	3.25	5	5	102.1	92	26	74	0
Alfredo Simon	3.44	15	10	196.1	181	56	127	0
Mike Leake	3.70	11	13	214.1	217	50	164	0
Homer Bailey	3.71	9	5	145.2	134	45	124	0

Manager: Bryan Price

Colorado Rockies

Batters	AVG	AB	R	H	HR	RBI	SO	SB
Troy Tulowitzki	.340	315	71	107	21	52	57	1
Michael Cuddyer	.332	190	32	63	10	31	30	3
Justin Morneau	.319	502	62	160	17	82	60	0
Michael McKenry	.315	168	23	53	8	22	42	0
Corey Dickerson	.312	436	74	136	24	76	101	8
Drew Stubbs	.289	388	67	112	15	43	136	20
Charlie Blackmon	.288	593	82	171	19	72	96	28
Nolan Arenado	.287	432	58	124	18	61	58	2
Josh Rutledge	.269	309	44	83	4	33	83	2
DJ LeMahieu	.267	494	59	132	5	42	97	10
Wilin Rosario	.267	382	46	102	13	54	70	1
Brandon Barnes	.257	292	37	75	8	27	100	5
Jordan Pacheco*	.255	153	10	39	0	16	27	0
Carlos Gonzalez	.238	260	35	62	11	38	70	3
Charlie Culberson	.195	210	17	41	3	24	62	2

Pitchers	ERA	W	L	IP	H	BB	SO	SV
LaTroy Hawkins	3.31	4	3	54.1	52	13	32	23
Tyler Matzek	4.05	6	11	117.2	120	44	91	0
Jorge De La Rosa	4.10	14	11	184.1	161	67	139	0
Jordan Lyles	4.33	7	4	126.2	127	46	90	0
Franklin Morales	5.37	6	9	142.1	166	65	100	0
Juan Nicasio	5.38	6	6	93.2	107	31	63	0

Manager: Walt Weiss

Los Angeles Dodgers

Batters	AVG	AB	R	H	HR	RBI	SO	SB
Justin Turner	.340	288	46	98	7	43	58	6
Juan Uribe	.311	386	36	120	9	54	77	0
Carl Crawford	.300	343	56	103	8	46	55	23
Scott Van Slyke	.297	212	32	63	11	29	71	4
Yasiel Puig	.296	558	92	165	16	69	124	11
Dee Gordon	.289	609	92	176	2	34	107	64
Matt Kemp	.287	541	77	155	25	89	145	8
Hanley Ramirez	.283	449	64	127	13	71	84	14
Adrian Gonzalez	.276	591	83	163	27	116	112	1
Andre Ethier	.249	341	29	85	4	42	74	2
Darwin Barney*	.241	237	24	57	3	23	34	1
A. J. Ellis	.191	283	21	54	3	25	57	0
Drew Butera	.188	170	16	32	3	14	41	0

Pitchers	ERA	W	L	IP	H	BB	SO	SV
Clayton Kershaw	1.77	21	3	198.1	139	31	239	0
Zack Greinke	2.71	17	8	202.1	190	43	207	0
Kenley Jansen	2.76	2	3	65.1	55	19	101	44
Josh Beckett	2.88	6	6	115.2	96	39	107	0
Hyun-Jin Ryu	3.38	14	7	152.0	152	29	139	0
Dan Haren	4.02	13	11	186.0	183	36	145	0
Roberto Hernandez*	4.10	8	11	164.2	156	73	105	0
Jamey Wright	4.35	5	4	70.1	72	27	54	1
Paul Maholm	4.84	1	5	70.2	82	28	34	0

Manager: Don Mattingly

Miami Marlins

Batters	AVG	AB	R	H	HR	RBI	SO	SB
Giancarlo Stanton	.288	539	89	155	37	105	170	13
Casey McGehee	.287	616	56	177	4	76	102	4
Christian Yelich	.284	582	94	165	9	54	137	21
Adeiny Hechavarria	.276	536	53	148	1	34	86	7
Marcell Ozuna	.269	565	72	152	23	85	164	3
Jeff Baker	.264	208	27	55	3	28	51	1
Donovan Solano	.252	310	26	78	3	28	61	1
Ed Lucas	.251	179	19	45	1	9	48	1
Garrett Jones	.246	496	59	122	15	53	116	0
Reed Johnson	.235	187	24	44	2	25	37	0
Derek Dietrich	.228	158	31	36	5	17	38	1
Jarrod Saltalamacchia	.220	373	43	82	11	44	143	0
Jeff Mathis	.200	175	12	35	2	12	64	0

Milwaukee Brewers

Pitchers	ERA	W	L	IP	H	BB	SO	SV
Henderson Alvarez	2.65	12	7	187.0	198	33	111	0
Steve Cishek	3.17	4	5	65.1	58	21	84	39
Tom Koehler	3.81	10	10	191.1	177	71	153	0
Nathan Eovaldi	4.37	6	14	199.2	223	43	142	0
Brad Hand	4.38	3	8	111.0	112	39	67	1
Jacob Turner*	6.13	6	11	113.0	148	33	71	0

Manager: Mike Redmond

Milwaukee Brewers

Batters	AVG	AB	R	H	HR	RBI	SO	SB
Jonathan Lucroy	.301	585	73	176	13	69	71	4
Scooter Gennett	.289	440	55	127	9	54	67	6
Aramis Ramirez	.285	494	47	141	15	66	75	3
Carlos Gomez	.284	574	95	163	23	73	141	34
Rickie Weeks	.274	252	36	69	8	29	73	3
Ryan Braun	.266	530	68	141	19	81	113	11
Gerardo Parra*	.261	529	64	138	9	40	100	9
Jean Segura	.246	513	61	126	5	31	70	20
Khris Davis	.244	501	70	122	22	69	122	4
Lyle Overbay	.233	258	24	60	4	35	60	2
Mark Reynolds	.196	387	47	74	22	45	122	5

Pitchers	ERA	W	L	IP	H	BB	SO	SV
Mike Fiers	2.13	6	5	71.2	46	17	76	0
Francisco Rodriguez	3.04	5	5	68.0	49	18	73	44
Yovani Gallardo	3.51	8	11	192.1	195	54	146	0
Wily Peralta	3.53	17	11	198.2	198	61	154	0
Kyle Lohse	3.54	13	9	198.1	183	45	141	0
Matt Garza	3.64	8	8	163.1	143	50	126	0
Marco Estrada	4.36	7	6	150.2	137	44	127	0

Manager: Ron Roenicke

New York Mets

Batters	AVG	AB	R	H	HR	RBI	SO	SB
Daniel Murphy	.289	596	79	172	9	57	86	13
Juan Lagares	.281	416	46	117	4	47	87	13
David Wright	.269	535	54	144	8	63	113	8
Eric Campbell	.263	190	16	50	3	16	55	3
Lucas Duda	.253	514	74	130	30	92	135	3
Wilmer Flores	.251	259	28	65	6	29	31	1
Matt den Dekker	.250	152	23	38	0	7	34	7
Travis d'Arnaud	.242	385	48	93	13	41	64	1
Ruben Tejada	.237	355	30	84	5	34	73	1
Ike Davis*	.233	360	43	84	11	51	78	0
Eric Young Jr.	.229	280	48	64	1	17	60	30
Curtis Granderson	.227	564	73	128	20	66	141	8
Chris Young#	.205	254	31	52	8	28	54	7
Anthony Recker	.201	174	18	35	7	27	64	1

Pitchers	ERA	W	L	IP	H	BB	SO	SV
Jeurys Familia	2.21	2	5	77.1	59	32	73	5
Jacob deGrom	2.69	9	6	140.1	117	43	144	0
Carlos Torres	3.06	8	6	97.0	89	38	96	2
Jonathon Niese	3.40	9	11	187.2	193	45	138	0
Zack Wheeler	3.54	11	11	185.1	167	79	187	0
Jenrry Mejia	3.65	6	6	93.2	98	41	98	28
Daisuke Matsuzaka	3.89	3	3	83.1	62	50	78	1
Dillon Gee	4.00	7	8	137.1	128	43	94	0
Bartolo Colon	4.09	15	13	202.1	218	30	151	0

Manager: Terry Collins

Philadelphia Phillies

Batters	AVG	AB	R	H	HR	RBI	SO	SB
Ben Revere	.306	601	71	184	2	28	49	49
Chase Utley	.270	589	74	159	11	78	85	10
Marlon Byrd	.264	591	71	156	25	85	185	3
Grady Sizemore#	.253	162	21	41	3	12	35	1
Carlos Ruiz	.252	381	43	96	6	31	60	4
Cody Asche	.252	397	43	100	10	46	102	0
Jimmy Rollins	.243	538	78	131	17	55	100	28
Domonic Brown	.235	473	47	111	10	63	91	7
Ryan Howard	.223	569	65	127	23	95	190	0

Pitchers	ERA	W	L	IP	H	BB	SO	SV
Jonathan Papelbon..	2.04	2	3	66.1	45	15	63	39
Cole Hamels.......	2.46	9	9	204.2	176	59	198	0
Cliff Lee	3.65	4	5	81.1	100	12	72	0
David Buchanan....	3.75	6	8	117.2	120	32	71	0
Jake Diekman......	3.80	5	5	71.0	66	35	100	0
Roberto Hernandez*	4.10	8	11	164.2	156	73	105	0
A. J. Burnett......	4.59	8	18	213.2	205	96	190	0
Kyle Kendrick	4.61	10	13	199.0	214	57	121	0
Manager: Ryne Sandberg								

Pittsburgh Pirates

Batters	AVG	AB	R	H	HR	RBI	SO	SB
Josh Harrison	.315	520	77	164	13	52	81	18
Andrew McCutchen ..	.314	548	89	172	25	83	115	18
Starling Marte	.291	495	73	144	13	56	131	30
Russell Martin.....	.290	379	45	110	11	67	78	4
Jose Tabata	.282	174	14	49	0	17	26	1
Neil Walker	.271	512	74	139	23	76	88	2
Travis Snider.......	.264	322	37	85	13	38	67	1
Jordy Mercer.......	.255	506	56	129	12	55	89	4
Gregory Polanco....	.235	277	50	65	7	33	59	14
Ike Davis*	.233	360	43	84	11	51	78	0
Pedro Alvarez	.231	398	46	92	18	56	113	8
Gaby Sanchez	.229	262	31	60	7	33	58	2

Pitchers	ERA	W	L	IP	H	BB	SO	SV
Tony Watson	1.63	10	2	77.1	64	15	81	2
Mark Melancon.....	1.90	3	5	71.0	51	11	71	33
Vance Worley	2.85	8	4	110.2	112	22	79	0
Edinson Volquez....	3.04	13	7	192.2	166	71	140	0
Francisco Liriano ...	3.38	7	10	162.1	130	81	175	0
Gerrit Cole	3.65	11	5	138.0	127	40	138	0
Charlie Morton.....	3.72	6	12	157.1	143	57	126	0
Jeff Locke.........	3.91	7	6	131.1	127	40	89	0
Jason Grilli#	4.87	0	2	20.1	22	11	21	11
Brandon Cumpton ...	4.89	3	4	70.0	82	18	46	0
Manager: Clint Hurdle								

St. Louis Cardinals

Batters	AVG	AB	R	H	HR	RBI	SO	SB
Jon Jay	.303	413	52	125	3	46	78	6
Matt Adams........	.288	527	55	152	15	68	114	3
Yadier Molina	.282	404	40	114	7	38	55	1
Matt Carpenter	.272	595	99	162	8	59	111	5
Matt Holliday.......	.272	574	83	156	20	90	100	4
Jhonny Peralta	.263	560	61	147	21	75	112	3
Kolten Wong	.249	402	52	100	12	42	71	20
Daniel Descalso ...	.242	161	20	39	0	10	33	1
Oscar Taveras	.239	234	18	56	3	22	37	0
Allen Craig#	.237	367	34	87	7	44	77	1
Peter Bourjos	.231	264	32	61	4	24	78	9
Mark Ellis	.180	178	15	32	0	12	38	4

Pitchers	ERA	W	L	IP	H	BB	SO	SV
Adam Wainwright ...	2.38	20	9	227.0	184	50	179	0
Lance Lynn........	2.74	15	10	203.2	185	72	181	0
Seth Maness	2.91	6	4	80.1	77	11	55	3
Michael Wacha.....	3.20	5	6	107.0	95	33	94	0
Trevor Rosenthal....	3.20	2	6	70.1	57	42	87	45
Shelby Miller	3.74	10	9	183.0	160	73	127	0
Carlos Martinez	4.03	2	4	89.1	90	36	84	1
Manager: Mike Matheny								

San Diego Padres

Batters	AVG	AB	R	H	HR	RBI	SO	SB
Yangervis Solarte#..	.267	217	30	58	4	17	24	0
Seth Smith	.266	443	55	118	12	48	87	1
Rene Rivera	.252	294	27	74	11	44	76	0
Chris Denorfia#.....	.242	248	25	60	1	16	51	8
Yonder Alonso	.240	267	27	64	7	27	36	6
Alexi Amarista......	.239	423	39	101	5	40	69	12
Cameron Maybin ...	.235	251	24	59	1	15	56	4

Batters	AVG	AB	R	H	HR	RBI	SO	SB
Tommy Medica	.233	240	31	56	9	27	75	6
Everth Cabrera ...	.232	357	36	83	3	20	86	18
Chase Headley#...	.229	279	27	64	7	32	73	4
Yasmani Grandal ..	.225	377	47	85	15	49	115	3
Will Venable	.224	406	47	91	8	33	107	11
Jedd Gyorko	.210	400	37	84	10	51	100	3

Pitchers	ERA	W	L	IP	H	BB	SO	SV
Huston Street#	1.09	1	0	33.0	18	7	34	24
Joaquin Benoit	1.49	4	2	54.1	28	14	64	11
Andrew Cashner...	2.55	5	7	123.1	110	29	93	0
Tyson Ross.......	2.81	13	14	195.2	165	72	195	0
Jesse Hahn.......	3.07	7	4	73.1	57	32	70	0
Odrisamer Despaigne......	3.36	4	7	96.1	85	32	65	0
Ian Kennedy	3.63	13	13	201.0	189	70	207	0
Eric Stults	4.30	8	17	176.0	197	45	111	0
Manager: Bud Black								

San Francisco Giants

Batters	AVG	AB	R	H	HR	RBI	SO	SB
Buster Posey	.311	547	72	170	22	89	69	0
Joe Panik	.305	269	31	82	1	18	33	0
Angel Pagan	.300	383	56	115	3	27	53	16
Pablo Sandoval....	.279	588	68	164	16	73	85	0
Michael Morse	.279	438	48	122	16	61	121	0
Hunter Pence	.277	650	106	180	20	74	130	13
Gregor Blanco	.260	393	51	102	5	38	77	16
Joaquin Arias	.254	193	18	49	0	15	23	1
Brandon Crawford..	.246	491	54	121	10	69	129	5
Brandon Belt......	.243	214	30	52	12	27	64	3
Hector Sanchez ...	.196	163	8	32	3	28	55	0
Brandon Hicks	.162	204	27	33	8	22	77	0

Pitchers	ERA	W	L	IP	H	BB	SO	SV
Santiago Casilla ...	1.70	3	3	58.1	35	15	45	19
Jake Peavy#......	2.17	6	4	78.2	65	17	58	0
Madison Bumgarner	2.98	18	10	217.1	194	43	219	0
Tim Hudson	3.57	9	13	189.1	199	34	120	0
Yusmeiro Petit.....	3.69	5	5	117.0	97	22	133	0
Sergio Romo	3.72	6	4	58.0	43	12	59	23
Ryan Vogelsong ...	4.00	8	13	184.2	178	58	151	0
Matt Cain	4.18	2	7	90.1	81	32	70	0
Tim Lincecum	4.74	12	9	155.2	154	63	134	1
Manager: Bruce Bochy								

Washington Nationals

Batters	AVG	AB	R	H	HR	RBI	SO	SB
Denard Span	.302	610	94	184	5	37	65	31
Jayson Werth	.292	534	85	156	16	82	113	9
Anthony Rendon..	.287	613	111	176	21	83	104	17
Ryan Zimmerman..	.280	214	26	60	5	38	37	0
Bryce Harper	.273	352	41	96	13	32	104	2
Wilson Ramos	.267	341	32	91	11	47	57	0
Adam LaRoche....	.259	494	73	128	26	92	108	3
Kevin Frandsen...	.259	220	17	57	1	17	26	0
Ian Desmond	.255	593	73	151	24	91	183	24
Jose Lobaton	.234	214	18	50	2	12	61	0
Asdrubal Cabrera#	.229	175	20	40	5	21	29	3
Danny Espinosa ...	.219	333	31	73	8	27	122	8
Nate Schierholtz* ..	.195	353	32	69	7	37	84	4

Pitchers	ERA	W	L	IP	H	BB	SO	SV
Drew Storen	1.12	2	1	56.1	44	11	46	11
Tyler Clippard.....	2.18	7	4	70.1	47	23	82	1
Doug Fister.......	2.41	16	6	164.0	153	24	98	0
Jordan Zimmermann	2.66	14	5	199.2	185	29	182	0
Tanner Roark.....	2.85	15	10	198.2	178	39	138	0
Stephen Strasburg	3.14	14	11	215.0	198	43	242	0
Rafael Soriano ...	3.19	4	1	62.0	51	19	59	32
Gio Gonzalez	3.57	10	10	158.2	134	56	162	0
Craig Stammen....	3.84	4	5	72.2	78	14	56	0
Manager: Matt Williams								

American League Statistics, 2014

Individual statistics. Players recording fewer than 150 at-bats (batters) or fewer than 70 innings or 10 saves (pitchers) are not listed here. * = Changed teams within AL during season; entry includes statistics for more than one team. # = Changed teams to or from NL during season; entry includes only AL statistics. Team Batting and Team Pitching include players not shown separately.

Team Batting

Team	AVG	AB	R	H	HR	RBI
Detroit Tigers	.277	5,630	757	1,557	155	731
Kansas City Royals	.263	5,545	651	1,456	95	604
Los Angeles Angels	.259	5,652	773	1,464	155	729
Toronto Blue Jays	.259	5,549	723	1,435	177	690
Texas Rangers	.256	5,460	637	1,400	111	597
Baltimore Orioles	.256	5,596	705	1,434	211	681
Minnesota Twins	.254	5,567	715	1,412	128	675
Cleveland Indians	.253	5,575	669	1,411	142	644
Chicago White Sox	.253	5,543	660	1,400	155	625
Tampa Bay Rays	.247	5,516	612	1,361	117	586
New York Yankees	.245	5,497	633	1,349	147	591
Oakland Athletics	.244	5,545	729	1,354	146	686
Boston Red Sox	.244	5,551	634	1,355	123	601
Seattle Mariners	.244	5,450	634	1,328	136	600
Houston Astros	.242	5,447	629	1,317	163	596

Team Pitching

Team	ERA	IP	H	BB	SO	SV
Seattle Mariners	3.17	1,452.0	1,240	463	1,317	51
Oakland Athletics	3.22	1,463.1	1,269	406	1,244	31
Baltimore Orioles	3.43	1,461.1	1,342	472	1,174	53
Kansas City Royals	3.51	1,450.2	1,386	440	1,168	53
Tampa Bay Rays	3.56	1,463.2	1,292	482	1,437	37
Cleveland Indians	3.56	1,468.1	1,398	464	1,450	40
Los Angeles Angels	3.58	1,482.2	1,307	504	1,343	46
New York Yankees	3.75	1,453.0	1,392	398	1,370	48
Toronto Blue Jays	4.00	1,443.0	1,400	490	1,199	45
Boston Red Sox	4.01	1,465.2	1,458	482	1,213	36
Detroit Tigers	4.01	1,454.0	1,475	462	1,244	41
Houston Astros	4.11	1,438.2	1,437	484	1,137	31
Chicago White Sox	4.29	1,441.0	1,468	557	1,152	36
Texas Rangers	4.49	1,426.1	1,510	505	1,110	33
Minnesota Twins	4.57	1,435.0	1,588	408	1,031	38

Baltimore Orioles

Batters	AVG	AB	R	H	HR	RBI	SO	SB
Delmon Young	.302	242	27	73	7	30	51	2
Steve Pearce	.293	338	51	99	21	49	76	5
Adam Jones	.281	644	88	181	29	96	133	7
Manny Machado	.278	327	38	91	12	32	68	2
Nick Markakis	.276	642	81	177	14	50	84	4
Nelson Cruz	.271	613	87	166	40	108	140	4
J.J. Hardy	.268	529	56	142	9	52	104	0
Alejandro De Aza*	.252	477	56	120	8	41	119	17
David Lough	.247	174	31	43	4	16	33	8
Nick Hundley#	.233	159	17	37	5	19	50	1
Ryan Flaherty	.221	281	33	62	7	32	68	1
Kelly Johnson*	.215	265	29	57	7	27	71	2
Jonathan Schoop	.209	455	48	95	16	45	122	2
Caleb Joseph	.207	246	22	51	9	28	69	0
Chris Davis	.196	450	65	88	26	72	173	2

Pitchers	ERA	W	L	IP	H	BB	SO	SV
Zach Britton	1.65	3	2	76.1	46	23	62	37
Tommy Hunter	2.97	3	2	60.2	55	12	45	11
Miguel Gonzalez	3.23	10	9	159.0	155	51	111	0
Chris Tillman	3.34	13	6	207.1	189	66	150	0
Wei-Yin Chen	3.54	16	6	185.2	193	35	136	0
Kevin Gausman	3.57	7	7	113.1	111	38	88	0
Bud Norris	3.65	15	8	165.1	149	52	139	0
Ubaldo Jimenez	4.81	6	9	125.1	113	77	116	0

Manager: Buck Showalter

Boston Red Sox

Batters	AVG	AB	R	H	HR	RBI	SO	SB
Mookie Betts	.291	189	34	55	5	18	31	7
Brock Holt	.281	449	68	126	4	29	98	12
Dustin Pedroia	.278	551	72	153	7	53	75	6
Daniel Nava	.270	363	41	98	4	37	81	4
David Ortiz	.263	518	59	136	35	104	95	0
Yoenis Cespedes*	.260	600	89	156	22	100	128	7
A.J. Pierzynski#	.254	256	19	65	4	31	40	0
Mike Napoli	.248	415	49	103	17	55	133	3
Christian Vazquez	.240	175	15	42	1	20	33	0
Xander Bogaerts	.240	538	60	129	12	46	138	2
Jonny Gomes*	.234	273	28	64	6	37	88	0
Grady Sizemore*	.216	185	14	40	2	15	41	5
Kelly Johnson*	.215	265	29	57	7	27	71	2
Jackie Bradley Jr.	.198	384	45	76	1	30	121	8
Will Middlebrooks	.191	215	14	41	2	19	70	1
David Ross	.184	152	16	28	7	15	58	0
Stephen Drew*	.162	271	18	44	7	26	75	1

Pitchers	ERA	W	L	IP	H	BB	SO	SV
Burke Badenhop	2.29	0	3	70.2	70	19	40	1
Jon Lester*	2.46	16	11	219.2	194	48	220	0
Koji Uehara	2.52	6	5	64.1	51	8	80	26
John Lackey*	3.60	11	7	137.1	137	32	116	0
Rubby De La Rosa	4.43	4	8	101.2	116	35	74	0
Chris Capuano*	4.35	3	4	97.1	101	34	84	0

Pitchers	ERA	W	L	IP	H	BB	SO	SV
Jake Peavy#	4.72	1	9	124.0	131	46	100	0
Brandon Workman	5.17	1	10	87.0	88	36	70	0
Clay Buchholz	5.34	8	11	170.1	182	54	132	0

Manager: John Farrell

Chicago White Sox

Batters	AVG	AB	R	H	HR	RBI	SO	SB
Jose Abreu	.317	556	80	176	36	107	131	3
Adam Eaton	.300	486	76	146	1	35	83	15
Conor Gillaspie	.282	464	50	131	7	57	78	0
Alexei Ramirez	.273	622	82	170	15	74	81	21
Alejandro De Aza*	.252	477	56	120	8	41	119	17
Avisail Garcia	.244	172	19	42	7	29	44	4
Tyler Flowers	.241	407	42	98	15	50	159	0
Marcus Semien	.234	231	30	54	6	28	70	3
Dayan Viciedo	.231	523	65	121	21	58	122	0
Moises Sierra*	.230	161	22	37	2	9	43	3
Gordon Beckham*	.226	446	53	101	9	44	81	3
Adam Dunn*	.219	429	49	94	22	64	159	1
Paul Konerko	.207	208	15	43	5	22	51	0

Pitchers	ERA	W	L	IP	H	BB	SO	SV
Chris Sale	2.17	12	4	174.0	129	39	208	0
Jake Petricka	2.96	1	6	73.0	67	33	55	14
Jose Quintana	3.32	9	11	200.1	197	52	178	0
John Danks	4.74	11	11	193.2	205	74	129	0
Hector Noesi*	4.75	8	12	172.1	180	56	123	0
Scott Carroll	4.80	5	10	129.1	147	45	64	0

Manager: Robin Ventura

Cleveland Indians

Batters	AVG	AB	R	H	HR	RBI	SO	SB
Michael Brantley	.327	611	94	200	20	97	56	23
Lonnie Chisenhall	.280	478	62	134	13	59	99	3
Yan Gomes	.278	485	61	135	21	74	120	0
David Murphy	.262	416	40	109	8	58	61	2
Jose Ramirez	.262	237	27	62	2	17	35	10
Michael Bourn	.257	444	57	114	3	28	114	10
Mike Aviles	.247	344	38	85	5	39	49	14
Asdrubal Cabrera#	.246	378	54	93	9	40	79	7
Jason Kipnis	.240	500	61	120	6	41	100	22
Carlos Santana	.231	541	68	125	27	85	124	5
Nick Swisher	.208	360	33	75	8	42	111	0
Ryan Raburn	.200	195	18	39	4	22	51	0

Pitchers	ERA	W	L	IP	H	BB	SO	SV
Cody Allen	2.07	6	4	69.2	48	26	91	24
Corey Kluber	2.44	18	9	235.2	207	51	269	0
Carlos Carrasco	2.55	8	7	134.0	103	29	140	1
Bryan Shaw	2.59	5	5	76.1	61	22	64	2
Scott Atchison	2.75	6	0	72.0	60	14	49	2
T. J. House	3.35	5	3	102.0	113	22	80	0
John Axford#	3.92	2	3	43.2	34	30	51	10
Trevor Bauer	4.18	5	8	153.0	151	60	143	0
Danny Salazar	4.25	6	8	110.0	117	35	120	0

Pitchers	ERA	W	L	IP	H	BB	SO	SV
Josh Tomlin	4.76	6	9	104.0	120	14	94	0
Zach McAllister	5.23	4	7	86.0	96	28	74	0
Justin Masterson#	5.51	4	6	98.0	106	56	93	0

Manager: Terry Francona

Detroit Tigers

Batters	AVG	AB	R	H	HR	RBI	SO	SB
Victor Martinez	.335	561	87	188	32	103	42	3
J. D. Martinez	.315	441	57	139	23	76	126	6
Miguel Cabrera	.313	611	101	191	25	109	117	1
Torii Hunter	.286	549	71	157	17	83	89	4
Rajai Davis	.282	461	64	130	8	51	75	36
Ian Kinsler	.275	684	100	188	17	92	79	15
Nick Castellanos	.259	533	50	138	11	66	140	2
Austin Jackson*	.256	597	71	153	4	47	144	20
Don Kelly	.245	163	24	40	0	7	29	6
Eugenio Suarez	.242	244	33	59	4	23	67	3
Bryan Holaday	.231	156	14	36	0	15	37	1
Andrew Romine	.227	251	30	57	2	12	60	12
Alex Avila	.218	390	44	85	11	47	151	0

Pitchers	ERA	W	L	IP	H	BB	SO	SV
Max Scherzer	3.15	18	5	220.1	196	63	252	0
Drew Smyly*	3.24	9	10	153.0	136	42	133	0
Joakim Soria*	3.25	2	4	44.1	38	6	48	18
David Price*	3.26	15	12	248.1	230	38	271	0
Anibal Sanchez	3.43	8	5	126.0	108	30	102	0
Rick Porcello	3.43	15	13	204.2	211	41	129	0
Justin Verlander	4.54	15	12	206.0	223	65	159	0
Joe Nathan	4.81	5	4	58.0	60	29	54	35

Manager: Brad Ausmus

Houston Astros

Batters	AVG	AB	R	H	HR	RBI	SO	SB
Jose Altuve	.341	660	85	225	7	59	53	56
Marwin Gonzalez	.277	285	33	79	6	23	58	2
Dexter Fowler	.276	434	61	120	8	35	108	11
Jake Marisnick#	.272	173	18	47	3	19	48	6
Alex Presley	.244	254	22	62	6	19	44	5
Carlos Corporan	.235	170	22	40	6	19	37	0
Robbie Grossman	.233	360	42	84	6	37	105	9
George Springer	.231	295	45	68	20	51	114	5
Chris Carter	.227	507	68	115	37	88	182	5
Jason Castro	.222	465	43	103	14	56	151	1
Matt Dominguez	.215	564	51	121	16	57	125	0
Jonathan Villar	.209	263	31	55	7	27	80	17
Marc Krauss	.194	186	16	36	6	21	54	0
Jesus Guzman	.188	165	10	31	2	9	52	3
Jon Singleton	.168	310	42	52	13	44	134	2

Pitchers	ERA	W	L	IP	H	BB	SO	SV
Collin McHugh	2.73	11	9	154.2	117	41	157	0
Dallas Keuchel	2.93	12	9	200.0	187	48	146	0
Chad Qualls	3.33	1	5	51.1	54	5	43	19
Scott Feldman	3.74	8	12	180.1	185	50	107	0
Brett Oberholtzer	4.39	5	13	143.2	170	28	94	0
Jarred Cosart#	4.41	9	7	116.1	119	51	75	0
Samuel Deduno	4.47	2	6	100.2	97	46	83	0
Brad Peacock	4.72	4	9	131.2	136	70	119	0

Managers: Bo Porter, Tom Lawless

Kansas City Royals

Batters	AVG	AB	R	H	HR	RBI	SO	SB
Lorenzo Cain	.301	471	55	142	5	53	108	28
Norichika Aoki*	.285	491	63	140	1	43	49	17
Alcides Escobar	.285	578	74	165	3	50	83	31
Billy Butler	.271	549	57	149	9	66	96	0
Eric Hosmer	.270	503	54	136	9	58	93	4
Jarrod Dyson	.269	260	33	70	1	24	52	36
Alex Gordon	.266	563	87	150	19	74	126	12
Salvador Perez	.260	578	57	150	17	70	85	1
Danny Valencia*	.258	264	20	68	4	30	62	1
Omar Infante	.252	528	50	133	6	66	68	9
Josh Willingham*	.215	297	48	64	14	40	102	2
Mike Moustakas	.212	457	45	97	15	54	74	1
Raul Ibanez*	.167	246	23	41	5	26	59	3

Pitchers	ERA	W	L	IP	H	BB	SO	SV
Wade Davis	1.00	9	2	72.0	38	23	109	3
Kelvin Herrera	1.41	4	3	70.0	54	26	59	0
Greg Holland	1.44	1	3	62.1	37	20	90	46
Danny Duffy	2.53	9	12	149.1	113	53	113	0

Pitchers	ERA	W	L	IP	H	BB	SO	SV
Yordano Ventura	3.20	14	10	183.0	168	69	159	0
James Shields	3.21	14	8	227.0	224	44	180	0
Jason Vargas	3.71	11	10	187.0	197	41	128	0
Jeremy Guthrie	4.13	13	11	202.2	215	49	124	0

Manager: Ned Yost

Los Angeles Angels

Batters	AVG	AB	R	H	HR	RBI	SO	SB
Howie Kendrick	.293	617	85	181	7	75	110	14
Mike Trout	.287	602	115	173	36	111	184	16
Erick Aybar	.278	589	77	164	7	68	62	16
Kole Calhoun	.272	493	90	134	17	58	104	5
Albert Pujols	.272	633	89	172	28	105	71	5
Josh Hamilton	.263	338	43	89	10	44	108	3
David Freese	.260	462	53	120	10	55	124	1
C. J. Cron	.256	242	28	62	11	37	61	0
Chris Iannetta	.252	306	41	77	7	43	91	3
Collin Cowgill	.250	260	37	65	5	21	74	4
Efren Navarro	.245	159	17	39	1	14	27	1
Gordon Beckham*	.226	446	53	101	9	44	81	3
Hank Conger	.221	231	24	51	4	25	57	0
Raul Ibanez*	.167	246	23	41	5	26	59	3

Pitchers	ERA	W	L	IP	H	BB	SO	SV
Huston Street#	1.71	1	2	26.1	24	7	23	17
Joe Smith	1.81	7	2	74.2	45	15	68	15
Garrett Richards	2.61	13	4	168.2	124	51	164	0
Matt Shoemaker	3.04	16	4	136.0	122	24	124	0
Jered Weaver	3.59	18	9	213.1	193	65	169	0
Hector Santiago	3.75	6	9	127.1	120	53	108	0
Tyler Skaggs	4.30	5	5	113.0	107	30	86	0
C. J. Wilson	4.51	13	10	175.2	169	85	151	0
Ernesto Frieri#	6.39	0	3	31.0	33	9	38	11

Manager: Mike Scioscia

Minnesota Twins

Batters	AVG	AB	R	H	HR	RBI	SO	SB
Danny Santana	.319	405	70	129	7	40	98	20
Kurt Suzuki	.288	452	37	130	3	61	46	0
Joe Mauer	.277	455	60	126	4	55	96	3
Eduardo Escobar	.275	433	52	119	6	37	93	1
Kennys Vargas	.274	215	26	59	9	38	63	0
Trevor Plouffe	.258	520	69	134	14	80	109	2
Chris Parmelee	.256	250	27	64	7	28	64	0
Eduardo Nunez	.250	204	26	51	4	24	31	9
Brian Dozier	.242	598	112	145	23	71	129	21
Sam Fuld*	.239	351	40	84	4	36	63	21
Oswaldo Arcia*	.231	372	46	86	20	57	127	1
Chris Colabello	.229	205	17	47	6	39	66	0
Jason Kubel*	.224	156	12	35	1	13	59	1
Josmil Pinto	.219	169	25	37	7	18	50	0
Kendrys Morales*	.218	367	28	80	8	42	68	0
Aaron Hicks	.215	186	22	40	1	18	56	4
Josh Willingham*	.215	297	48	64	14	40	102	2

Pitchers	ERA	W	L	IP	H	BB	SO	SV
Phil Hughes	3.52	16	10	209.2	221	16	186	0
Glen Perkins	3.65	4	3	61.2	62	11	66	34
Tommy Milone*	4.19	6	4	118.0	128	37	75	0
Kyle Gibson	4.47	13	12	179.1	178	57	107	0
Samuel Deduno*	4.47	2	6	100.2	97	46	83	0
Anthony Swarzak	4.60	3	2	86.0	100	28	47	0
Kevin Correia#	4.94	5	13	129.1	157	32	61	0
Ricky Nolasco*	5.38	6	12	159.0	203	38	115	0

Manager: Ron Gardenhire

New York Yankees

Batters	AVG	AB	R	H	HR	RBI	SO	SB
Ichiro Suzuki	.284	359	42	102	1	22	68	15
Jacoby Ellsbury	.271	575	71	156	16	70	93	39
Chase Headley#	.262	191	28	50	6	17	49	3
Derek Jeter	.256	581	47	149	4	50	87	10
Brett Gardner	.256	555	87	142	17	58	134	21
Yangervis Solarte#	.254	252	26	64	6	31	34	0
Brian Roberts	.237	317	40	75	5	21	53	7
Carlos Beltran	.233	403	46	94	15	49	80	3
Brian McCann	.232	495	57	115	23	75	77	0
Alfonso Soriano	.221	226	22	50	6	23	71	1
Mark Teixeira	.216	440	56	95	22	62	109	1
Kelly Johnson*	.215	265	29	57	7	27	71	2
Stephen Drew*	.162	271	18	44	7	26	75	1

Pitchers	ERA	W	L	IP	H	BB	SO	SV
Dellin Betances	1.40	5	0	90.0	46	24	135	1
Michael Pineda	1.89	5	5	76.1	56	7	59	0
Masahiro Tanaka	2.77	13	5	136.1	123	21	141	0
Brandon McCarthy#	2.89	7	5	90.1	91	13	82	0
Adam Warren	2.97	3	6	78.2	63	24	76	3
David Robertson	3.08	4	5	64.1	45	23	96	39
Hiroki Kuroda	3.71	11	9	199.0	191	35	146	0
Shane Greene	3.78	5	4	78.2	81	29	81	0
Chris Capuano*	4.35	3	4	97.1	101	34	84	0
David Phelps	4.38	5	5	113.0	115	46	92	1
Chase Whitley	5.23	4	3	75.2	94	18	60	0
Vidal Nuno#	5.42	2	5	78.0	86	26	60	0

Manager: Joe Girardi

Oakland Athletics

Batters	AVG	AB	R	H	HR	RBI	SO	SB
Stephen Vogt	.279	269	26	75	9	35	39	1
Derek Norris	.270	385	46	104	10	55	86	2
Josh Reddick	.264	363	53	96	12	54	63	1
John Jaso	.264	307	42	81	9	40	60	2
Yoenis Cespedes*	.260	600	89	156	22	100	128	7
Josh Donaldson	.255	608	93	155	29	98	130	8
Craig Gentry	.254	232	38	59	0	12	44	20
Jed Lowrie	.249	502	59	125	6	50	79	0
Coco Crisp	.246	463	68	114	9	47	66	19
Sam Fuld*	.239	351	40	84	4	36	63	21
Jonny Gomes*	.234	273	28	64	6	37	88	0
Brandon Moss	.234	500	70	117	25	81	153	1
Eric Sogard	.223	291	38	65	1	22	37	11
Alberto Callaspo	.223	404	37	90	4	39	50	0
Adam Dunn*	.219	429	49	94	22	64	159	1
Nick Punto	.207	198	21	41	2	14	56	3

Pitchers	ERA	W	L	IP	H	BB	SO	SV
Luke Gregerson	2.12	5	5	72.1	58	15	59	3
Dan Otero	2.28	8	2	86.2	80	15	45	1
Jon Lester*	2.46	16	11	219.2	194	48	220	0
Sean Doolittle	2.73	2	4	62.2	38	8	89	22
Sonny Gray	3.08	14	10	219.0	187	74	183	0
Jeff Samardzija#	3.14	5	6	111.2	92	12	99	0
Jesse Chavez	3.45	8	8	146.0	142	49	136	0
Scott Kazmir	3.55	15	9	190.1	171	50	164	0
Tommy Milone*	4.19	6	4	118.0	128	37	75	0

Manager: Bob Melvin

Seattle Mariners

Batters	AVG	AB	R	H	HR	RBI	SO	SB
Robinson Cano	.314	595	77	187	14	82	68	10
Endy Chavez	.276	232	22	64	2	23	30	5
Michael Saunders	.273	231	38	63	8	34	59	4
Kyle Seager	.268	590	71	158	25	96	118	7
Logan Morrison	.262	336	41	88	11	38	59	5
Austin Jackson*	.256	597	71	153	4	47	144	20
James Jones	.250	312	46	78	0	9	67	27
Dustin Ackley	.245	502	64	123	14	65	90	8
Brad Miller	.221	367	47	81	10	36	95	4
Kendrys Morales*	.218	367	28	80	8	42	68	0
Corey Hart	.203	232	17	47	6	21	59	2
Justin Smoak	.202	248	28	50	7	30	66	0
Mike Zunino	.199	438	51	87	22	60	158	0
Stefen Romero	.192	177	19	34	3	11	48	0

Pitchers	ERA	W	L	IP	H	BB	SO	SV
Felix Hernandez	2.14	15	6	236.0	170	46	248	0
Tom Wilhelmsen	2.27	3	2	79.1	47	36	72	1
Danny Farquhar	2.66	3	1	71.0	58	22	81	1
Fernando Rodney	2.85	1	6	66.1	61	28	76	48
James Paxton	3.04	6	4	74.0	60	29	59	0
Hisashi Iwakuma	3.52	15	9	179.0	167	21	154	0
Chris Young	3.65	12	9	165.0	143	60	108	0
Roenis Elias	3.85	10	12	163.2	151	64	143	0
Hector Noesi*	4.75	8	12	172.1	180	56	123	0
Erasmo Ramirez	5.26	1	6	75.1	82	34	60	0

Manager: Lloyd McClendon

Tampa Bay Rays

Batters	AVG	AB	R	H	HR	RBI	SO	SB
James Loney	.290	600	59	174	9	69	80	4
Ben Zobrist	.272	570	83	155	10	52	84	10
Brandon Guyer	.266	259	37	69	3	26	52	6
Kevin Kiermaier	.263	331	35	87	10	35	71	5
Yunel Escobar	.258	476	33	123	7	39	60	1
Matt Joyce	.254	418	51	106	9	52	111	2
Evan Longoria	.253	624	83	158	22	91	133	5
David DeJesus	.248	238	24	59	6	19	43	0
Desmond Jennings	.244	479	64	117	10	36	108	15
Logan Forsythe	.223	301	32	67	6	26	71	2
Wil Myers	.222	325	37	72	6	35	90	6
Ryan Hanigan	.218	225	18	49	5	34	39	1
Sean Rodriguez	.211	237	30	50	12	41	66	2
Jose Molina	.178	225	4	40	0	10	55	3

Pitchers	ERA	W	L	IP	H	BB	SO	SV
Jake McGee	1.89	5	2	71.1	48	16	90	19
Alex Cobb	2.87	10	9	166.1	142	47	149	0
Drew Smyly*	3.24	9	10	153.0	136	42	133	0
David Price*	3.26	15	12	248.1	230	38	271	0
Chris Archer	3.33	10	9	194.2	177	72	173	0
Cesar Ramos	3.70	2	6	82.2	73	39	66	0
Jake Odorizzi	4.13	11	13	168.0	156	59	174	0
Erik Bedard	4.76	4	6	75.2	84	29	64	0
Grant Balfour	4.91	2	6	62.1	49	41	57	12

Manager: Joe Maddon

Texas Rangers

Batters	AVG	AB	R	H	HR	RBI	SO	SB
Adrian Beltre	.324	549	79	178	19	77	74	1
Alex Rios	.280	492	54	138	4	54	93	17
Leonys Martin	.274	533	68	146	7	40	114	31
Daniel Robertson	.271	177	23	48	0	21	28	6
Elvis Andrus	.263	619	72	163	2	41	96	27
Adam Rosales	.262	164	20	43	4	19	42	4
Rougned Odor	.259	386	39	100	9	48	71	4
Prince Fielder	.247	150	19	37	3	16	24	0
Mitch Moreland	.246	167	18	41	2	23	43	0
Shin-Soo Choo	.242	455	58	110	13	40	131	3
Robinson Chirinos	.239	306	36	73	13	40	71	0
Michael Choice	.182	253	20	46	9	36	69	1
J.P. Arencibia	.177	203	20	36	10	35	62	0

Pitchers	ERA	W	L	IP	H	BB	SO	SV
Neftali Feliz	1.99	2	1	31.2	20	11	21	13
Shawn Tolleson	2.76	3	1	71.2	56	28	69	0
Yu Darvish	3.06	10	7	144.1	133	49	182	0
Joakim Soria*	3.25	2	4	44.1	38	6	48	18
Nick Tepesch	4.36	5	11	126.0	128	44	56	0
Nick Martinez	4.55	5	12	140.1	150	55	77	0
Hector Noesi*	4.75	8	12	172.1	180	56	123	0
Colby Lewis	5.18	10	14	170.1	211	48	133	0
Scott Baker	5.47	3	4	80.2	82	14	55	0
Robbie Ross	6.20	3	6	78.1	103	30	51	0

Managers: Ron Washington, Tim Bogar

Toronto Blue Jays

Batters	AVG	AB	R	H	HR	RBI	SO	SB
Adam Lind	.321	290	38	93	6	40	48	0
Melky Cabrera	.301	568	81	171	16	73	67	6
Jose Reyes	.287	610	94	175	9	51	73	30
Jose Bautista	.286	553	101	158	35	103	96	6
Dioner Navarro	.274	481	40	132	12	69	76	3
Edwin Encarnacion	.268	477	75	128	34	98	82	2
Munenori Kawasaki	.258	240	31	62	0	17	49	1
Danny Valencia*	.258	264	20	68	4	30	62	1
Steve Tolleson	.253	170	21	43	3	16	49	3
Brett Lawrie	.247	259	27	64	12	38	49	0
Moises Sierra*	.230	161	22	37	2	9	43	3
Anthony Gose	.226	239	31	54	2	13	74	15
Colby Rasmus	.225	346	45	78	18	40	124	4
Juan Francisco	.220	287	40	63	16	43	116	0
Ryan Goins	.188	181	14	34	1	15	42	0

Pitchers	ERA	W	L	IP	H	BB	SO	SV
Todd Redmond	3.24	1	4	75.0	73	27	60	1
Mark Buehrle	3.39	13	10	202.0	228	46	119	0
Marcus Stroman	3.65	11	6	130.2	125	28	111	1
R.A. Dickey	3.71	14	13	215.2	191	74	173	0
Casey Janssen	3.94	3	3	45.2	47	7	28	25
Dustin McGowan	4.17	5	3	82.0	80	33	61	1
J.A. Happ	4.22	11	11	158.0	160	51	133	0
Drew Hutchison	4.48	11	13	184.2	173	60	184	0

Manager: John Gibbons

Major League Leaders, 2014
National League

Batting Average: Justin Morneau, Colorado, .319; Josh Harrison, Pittsburgh, .315; Andrew McCutchen, Pittsburgh, .314; Buster Posey, San Francisco, .311; Ben Revere, Philadelphia, .306.

Runs Scored: Anthony Rendon, Washington, 111; Hunter Pence, San Francisco, 106; Matt Carpenter, St. Louis, 99; Carlos Gomez, Milwaukee, 95; Denard Span, Washington, 94; Christian Yelich, Miami, 94.

Runs Batted In: Adrian Gonzalez, L.A. Dodgers, 116; Giancarlo Stanton, Miami, 105; Justin Upton, Atlanta, 102; Ryan Howard, Philadelphia, 95; Lucas Duda, NY Mets, 92; Adam LaRoche, Washington, 92.

Hits: Ben Revere, Philadelphia, 184; Denard Span, Washington, 184; Hunter Pence, San Francisco, 180; Casey McGehee, Miami, 177; Dee Gordon, L.A. Dodgers, 176; Jonathan Lucroy, Milwaukee, 176; Anthony Rendon, Washington, 176.

Doubles: Jonathan Lucroy, Milwaukee, 53; Freddie Freeman, Atlanta, 43; Adrian Gonzalez, L.A. Dodgers, 41; Paul Goldschmidt, Arizona, 39; Anthony Rendon, Washington, 39; Denard Span, Washington, 39.

Triples: Dee Gordon, L.A. Dodgers, 12; Brandon Crawford, San Francisco, 10; Adeiny Hechavarria, Miami, 10; Hunter Pence, San Francisco, 10; David Peralta, Arizona, 9; Yasiel Puig, L.A. Dodgers, 9.

Home Runs: Giancarlo Stanton, Miami, 37; Anthony Rizzo, Chicago Cubs, 32; Lucas Duda, NY Mets, 30; Todd Frazier, Cincinnati, 29; Justin Upton, Atlanta, 29.

Stolen Bases: Dee Gordon, L.A. Dodgers, 64; Billy Hamilton, Cincinnati, 56; Ben Revere, Philadelphia, 49; Carlos Gomez, Milwaukee, 34; Denard Span, Washington, 31.

Pitching wins: Clayton Kershaw, L.A. Dodgers, 21; Johnny Cueto, Cincinnati, 20; Adam Wainwright, St. Louis, 20; Madison Bumgarner, San Francisco, 18; Zack Greinke, L.A. Dodgers, 17; Wily Peralta, Milwaukee, 17.

Earned Run Average: Clayton Kershaw, L.A. Dodgers, 1.77; Johnny Cueto, Cincinnati, 2.25; Adam Wainwright, St. Louis, 2.38; Doug Fister, Washington, 2.41; Cole Hamels, Philadelphia, 2.46.

Strikeouts: Johnny Cueto, Cincinnati, 242; Stephen Strasburg, Washington, 242; Clayton Kershaw, L.A. Dodgers, 239; Madison Bumgarner, San Francisco, 219; Zack Greinke, L.A. Dodgers, 207; Ian Kennedy, San Diego, 207.

Saves: Craig Kimbrel, Atlanta, 47; Trevor Rosenthal, St. Louis, 45; Kenley Jansen, L.A. Dodgers, 44; Francisco Rodriguez, Milwaukee, 44; Steve Cishek, Miami, 39; Jonathan Papelbon, Philadelphia, 39.

American League

Batting Average: Jose Altuve, Houston, .341; Victor Martinez, Detroit, .335; Michael Brantley, Cleveland, .327; Adrian Beltre, Texas, .324; Jose Abreu, Chicago White Sox, .317.

Runs Scored: Mike Trout, L.A. Angels, 115; Brian Dozier, Minnesota, 112; Jose Bautista, Toronto, 101; Miguel Cabrera, Detroit, 101; Ian Kinsler, Detroit, 100.

Runs Batted In: Mike Trout, L.A. Angels, 111; Miguel Cabrera, Detroit, 109; Nelson Cruz, Baltimore, 108; Jose Abreu, Chicago White Sox, 107; Albert Pujols, L.A. Angels, 105.

Hits: Jose Altuve, Houston, 225; Michael Brantley, Cleveland, 200; Miguel Cabrera, Detroit, 191; Ian Kinsler, Detroit, 188; Victor Martinez, Detroit, 188.

Doubles: Miguel Cabrera, Detroit, 52; Jose Altuve, Houston, 47; Michael Brantley, Cleveland, 45; Ian Kinsler, Detroit, 40; Trevor Plouffe, Minnesota, 40.

Triples: Michael Bourn, Cleveland, 10; Adam Eaton, Chicago White Sox, 10; Mike Trout, L.A. Angels, 9; Alejandro De Aza, Baltimore/Chicago White Sox, 8; Brett Gardner, NY Yankees, 8; Kevin Kiermaier, Tampa Bay, 8; Alex Rios, Texas, 8.

Home Runs: Nelson Cruz, Baltimore, 40; Chris Carter, Houston, 37; Jose Abreu, Chicago White Sox, 36; Mike Trout, L.A. Angels, 36; Jose Bautista, Toronto, 35; David Ortiz, Boston, 35.

Stolen Bases: Jose Altuve, Houston, 56; Jacoby Ellsbury, NY Yankees, 39; Rajai Davis, Detroit, 36; Jarrod Dyson, Kansas City, 36; Alcides Escobar, Kansas City, 31; Leonys Martin, Texas, 31.

Pitching wins: Corey Kluber, Cleveland, 18; Max Scherzer, Detroit, 18; Jered Weaver, L.A. Angels, 18; Wei-Yin Chen, Baltimore, 16; Phil Hughes, Minnesota, 16; Jon Lester, Boston/Oakland, 16; Matt Shoemaker, L.A. Angels, 16.

Earned Run Average: Felix Hernandez, Seattle, 2.14; Chris Sale, Chicago White Sox, 2.17; Corey Kluber, Cleveland, 2.44; Jon Lester, Boston/Oakland, 2.46; Garrett Richards, L.A. Angels, 2.61.

Strikeouts: David Price, Tampa Bay/Detroit, 271; Corey Kluber, Cleveland, 269; Max Scherzer, Detroit, 252; Felix Hernandez, Seattle, 248; Jon Lester, Boston/Oakland, 220.

Saves: Fernando Rodney, Seattle, 48; Greg Holland, Kansas City, 46; David Robertson, NY Yankees, 39; Zach Britton, Baltimore, 37; Joe Nathan, Detroit, 35.

All-Time Major League Single-Season Leaders

Source: www.mlb.com; * = Active in 2014 season; records for "modern" era beginning in 1901.

Home Runs

Barry Bonds (2001)	73
Mark McGwire (1998)	70
Sammy Sosa (1998)	66
Mark McGwire (1999)	65
Sammy Sosa (2001)	64

Runs Scored

Babe Ruth (1921)	177
Lou Gehrig (1936)	167
Lou Gehrig (1931)	163
Babe Ruth (1928)	163
Chuck Klein (1930)	158
Babe Ruth (1920, 1927)	158

Hits

Ichiro Suzuki* (2004)	262
George Sisler (1920)	257
Lefty O'Doul (1929)	254
Bill Terry (1930)	254
Al Simmons (1925)	253
Rogers Hornsby (1922)	250
Chuck Klein (1930)	250

Runs Batted In

Hack Wilson (1930)	191
Lou Gehrig (1931)	184
Hank Greenberg (1937)	183
Jimmie Foxx (1938)	175
Lou Gehrig (1927)	175

Batting Average

Rogers Hornsby (1924)	.424
Napoleon Lajoie (1901)	.421
George Sisler (1922)	.420
Ty Cobb (1911)	.420
Ty Cobb (1912)	.410

Stolen Bases

Rickey Henderson (1982)	130
Lou Brock (1974)	118
Vince Coleman (1985)	110
Vince Coleman (1987)	109
Rickey Henderson (1983)	108

Walks (Batter)

Barry Bonds (2004)	232
Barry Bonds (2002)	198
Barry Bonds (2001)	177
Babe Ruth (1923)	170
Mark McGwire (1998)	162
Ted Williams (1947, 1949)	162

Strikeouts (Batter)

Mark Reynolds* (2009)	223
Adam Dunn* (2012)	222
Chris Carter* (2013)	212
Mark Reynolds* (2010)	211
Drew Stubbs* (2011)	205

Earned Run Average

Dutch Leonard (1914)	0.96
Mordecai "Three Finger" Brown (1906)	1.04
Bob Gibson (1968)	1.12
Christy Mathewson (1909)	1.14
Walter Johnson (1913)	1.14

Wins

Jack Chesbro (1904)	41
Ed Walsh (1908)	40
Christy Mathewson (1908)	37
Walter Johnson (1913)	36
Joe McGinnity (1904)	35

Strikeouts

Nolan Ryan (1973)	383
Sandy Koufax (1965)	382
Randy Johnson (2001)	372
Nolan Ryan (1974)	367
Randy Johnson (1999)	364

Saves

Francisco Rodriguez* (2008)	62
Bobby Thigpen (1990)	57
Eric Gagne (2003)	55
John Smoltz (2002)	55
Trevor Hoffman (1998)	53
Randy Myers (1993)	53
Mariano Rivera (2004)	53

All-Time Major League Leaders

Source: www.mlb.com; * = Active in 2014 season; career records for players in "modern" era beginning in 1901 may include statistics from preceding years.

Games		At Bats		Runs Batted In		Runs	
Pete Rose	3,562	Pete Rose	14,053	Hank Aaron	2,297	Rickey Henderson	2,295
Carl Yastrzemski	3,308	Hank Aaron	12,364	Babe Ruth	2,213	Ty Cobb	2,246
Hank Aaron	3,298	Carl Yastrzemski	11,988	Barry Bonds	1,996	Barry Bonds	2,227
Rickey Henderson	3,081	Cal Ripken Jr.	11,551	Lou Gehrig	1,995	Hank Aaron	2,174
Ty Cobb	3,035	Ty Cobb	11,429	Alex Rodriguez	1,969	Babe Ruth	2,174
Eddie Murray	3,026	Eddie Murray	11,336	Stan Musial	1,951	Pete Rose	2,165
Stan Musial	3,026	Derek Jeter*	11,195	Ty Cobb	1,938	Willie Mays	2,062
Cal Ripken Jr.	3,001	Robin Yount	11,008	Jimmie Foxx	1,922	Stan Musial	1,949
Willie Mays	2,992	Dave Winfield	11,003	Eddie Murray	1,917	Derek Jeter*	1,923
Barry Bonds	2,986	Stan Musial	10,972	Willie Mays	1,903	Alex Rodriguez	1,919

Stolen Bases		Triples		Batting Average		Walks (Batter)	
Rickey Henderson	1,406	Sam Crawford	309	Ty Cobb	.367	Barry Bonds	2,558
Lou Brock	938	Ty Cobb	297	Rogers Hornsby	.358	Rickey Henderson	2,190
Billy Hamilton	912	Honus Wagner	252	Joe Jackson	.356	Babe Ruth	2,062
Ty Cobb	892	Jake Beckley	243	Ed Delahanty	.346	Ted Williams	2,019
Tim Raines	808	Roger Connor	233	Tris Speaker	.345	Joe Morgan	1,865
Vince Coleman	752	Tris Speaker	222	Ted Williams	.344	Carl Yastrzemski	1,845
Eddie Collins	745	Fred Clarke	220	Billy Hamilton	.344	Jim Thome	1,747
Arlie Latham	739	Dan Brouthers	205	Dan Brouthers	.342	Mickey Mantle	1,733
Max Carey	738	Joe Kelley	194	Babe Ruth	.342	Mel Ott	1,708
Honus Wagner	722	Paul Waner	191	Harry Heilmann	.342	Frank Thomas	1,667

Strikeouts		Saves		Shutouts		Losses	
Nolan Ryan	5,714	Mariano Rivera	652	Walter Johnson	110	Cy Young	316
Randy Johnson	4,875	Trevor Hoffman	601	Grover Alexander	90	Nolan Ryan	292
Roger Clemens	4,672	Lee Smith	478	Christy Mathewson	79	Walter Johnson	279
Steve Carlton	4,136	John Franco	424	Cy Young	76	Phil Niekro	274
Bert Blyleven	3,701	Billy Wagner	422	Eddie Plank	69	Gaylord Perry	265
Tom Seaver	3,640	Dennis Eckersley	390	Warren Spahn	63	Don Sutton	256
Don Sutton	3,574	Joe Nathan*	376	Nolan Ryan	61	Jack Powell	254
Gaylord Perry	3,534	Jeff Reardon	367	Tom Seaver	61	Eppa Rixey	251
Walter Johnson	3,508	Troy Percival	358	Bert Blyleven	60	Bert Blyleven	250
Greg Maddux	3,371	Francisco Rodriguez*	348	Don Sutton	58	Robin Roberts	245
						Warren Spahn	245

All-Time Home Run Leaders

Source: www.mlb.com; * = Active in 2014 season.

Player	HR	Player	HR	Player	HR	Player	HR
Barry Bonds	762	Mike Schmidt	548	Stan Musial	475	Andre Dawson	438
Hank Aaron	755	Mickey Mantle	536	Willie Stargell	475	Juan Gonzalez	434
Babe Ruth	714	Jimmie Foxx	534	Carlos Delgado	473	Andruw Jones	434
Willie Mays	660	Willie McCovey	521	Chipper Jones	468	Cal Ripken Jr.	431
Alex Rodriguez	654	Frank Thomas	521	David Ortiz*	466	Mike Piazza	427
Ken Griffey Jr.	630	Ted Williams	521	Dave Winfield	465	Billy Williams	426
Jim Thome	612	Albert Pujols*	520	Jose Canseco	462	Darrell Evans	414
Sammy Sosa	609	Ernie Banks	512	Adam Dunn*	462	Alfonso Soriano*	412
Frank Robinson	586	Eddie Mathews	512	Carl Yastrzemski	452	Duke Snider	407
Mark McGwire	583	Mel Ott	511	Jeff Bagwell	449	Andres Galarraga	399
Harmon Killebrew	573	Gary Sheffield	509	Vladimir Guerrero	449	Al Kaline	399
Rafael Palmeiro	569	Eddie Murray	504	Dave Kingman	442	Dale Murphy	398
Reggie Jackson	563	Lou Gehrig	493	Jason Giambi*	440	Joe Carter	396
Manny Ramirez	555	Fred McGriff	493	Paul Konerko*	439	Adrian Beltre*	395

Players With 3,000 Major League Hits

Source: www.mlb.com; * = Active in 2014 season.

Player	Hits	Player	Hits	Player	Hits	Player	Hits
Pete Rose	4,256	Carl Yastrzemski	3,419	George Brett	3,154	Rod Carew	3,053
Ty Cobb	4,191	Paul Molitor	3,319	Paul Waner	3,152	Lou Brock	3,023
Hank Aaron	3,771	Eddie Collins	3,314	Robin Yount	3,142	Rafael Palmeiro	3,020
Stan Musial	3,630	Willie Mays	3,283	Tony Gwynn	3,141	Cap Anson	3,011
Tris Speaker	3,515	Eddie Murray	3,255	Dave Winfield	3,110	Wade Boggs	3,010
Derek Jeter	3,465	Napoleon Lajoie	3,252	Craig Biggio	3,060	Al Kaline	3,007
Honus Wagner	3,430	Cal Ripken Jr.	3,184	Rickey Henderson	3,055	Roberto Clemente	3,000

50 Home Run Club

Only Barry Bonds and Mark McGwire hit 70 or more home runs in a season. Five players—including Babe Ruth and Roger Maris—hit 60 or more, a feat Sammy Sosa accomplished for the third time in 2001.

HR	Player, team	Year	HR	Player, team	Year
73	Barry Bonds, San Francisco Giants	2001	54	Alex Rodriguez, NY Yankees	2007
70	Mark McGwire, St. Louis Cardinals	1998	54	Babe Ruth, NY Yankees	1920
66	Sammy Sosa, Chicago Cubs	1998	54	Babe Ruth, NY Yankees	1928
65	Mark McGwire, St. Louis Cardinals	1999	53	Chris Davis, Baltimore Orioles	2013
64	Sammy Sosa, Chicago Cubs	2001	52	George Foster, Cincinnati Reds	1977
63	Sammy Sosa, Chicago Cubs	1999	52	Mickey Mantle, NY Yankees	1956
61	Roger Maris, NY Yankees	1961	52	Willie Mays, San Francisco Giants	1965
60	Babe Ruth, NY Yankees	1927	52	Mark McGwire, Oakland A's	1996
59	Babe Ruth, NY Yankees	1921	52	Alex Rodriguez, Texas Rangers	2001
58	Jimmie Foxx, Philadelphia Athletics	1932	52	Jim Thome, Cleveland Indians	2002
58	Hank Greenberg, Detroit Tigers	1938	51	Cecil Fielder, Detroit Tigers	1990
58	Ryan Howard, Philadelphia Phillies	2006	51	Andruw Jones, Atlanta Braves	2005
58	Mark McGwire, Oakland A's/St. Louis Cardinals	1997	51	Ralph Kiner, Pittsburgh Pirates	1947
57	Luis Gonzalez, Arizona Diamondbacks	2001	51	Willie Mays, NY Giants	1955
57	Alex Rodriguez, Texas Rangers	2002	51	Johnny Mize, NY Giants	1947
56	Ken Griffey Jr., Seattle Mariners	1997	50	Brady Anderson, Baltimore Orioles	1996
56	Ken Griffey Jr., Seattle Mariners	1998	50	Albert Belle, Cleveland Indians	1995
56	Hack Wilson, Chicago Cubs	1930	50	Prince Fielder, Milwaukee Brewers	2007
54	Jose Bautista, Toronto Blue Jays	2010	50	Jimmie Foxx, Boston Red Sox	1938
54	Ralph Kiner, Pittsburgh Pirates	1949	50	Sammy Sosa, Chicago Cubs	2000
54	Mickey Mantle, NY Yankees	1961	50	Greg Vaughn, San Diego Padres	1998
54	David Ortiz, Boston Red Sox	2006			

Pitchers With 300 Major League Wins

Source: www.mlb.com

Pitcher	Wins	Pitcher	Wins	Pitcher	Wins	Pitcher	Wins
Cy Young	511	Charles "Kid" Nichols	361	Eddie Plank	326	Charley Radbourn	309
Walter Johnson	417	Greg Maddux	355	Nolan Ryan	324	Mickey Welch	307
Grover Alexander	373	Roger Clemens	354	Don Sutton	324	Tom Glavine	305
Christy Mathewson	373	Tim Keefe	342	Phil Niekro	318	Randy Johnson	303
Warren Spahn	363	Steve Carlton	329	Gaylord Perry	314	Robert "Lefty" Grove	300
James "Pud" Galvin	361	John Clarkson	328	Tom Seaver	311	Early "Gus" Wynn	300

Official Major League Perfect Games Since 1901

Date	Pitcher	Teams	Date	Pitcher	Teams
5/5/1904	Cy Young	Boston 3 vs. Phil. 0 (AL)	7/28/1994	Kenny Rogers	Texas 4 vs. California 0 (AL)
10/2/1908	Addie Joss	Clev. 1 vs. Chicago 0 (AL)	5/17/1998	David Wells	NY 4 vs. Minn. 0 (AL)
4/30/1922	Charlie Robertson	Chicago 2 vs. Detroit 0 (AL)	7/18/1999	David Cone	NY 6 vs. Montréal 0 (AL)
10/8/1956	Don Larsen	NY 2 (AL) vs. Brooklyn 0* (NL)	5/18/2004	Randy Johnson	Arizona 2 vs. Atlanta 0 (NL)
6/21/1964	Jim Bunning	Phil. 6 vs. NY 0 (NL)	7/23/2009	Mark Buehrle	Chicago 5 vs. Tampa Bay 0 (AL)
9/9/1965	Sandy Koufax	L.A. 1 vs. Chicago 0 (NL)	5/9/2010	Dallas Braden	Oakland 4 vs. Tampa Bay 0 (AL)
5/8/1968	Jim "Catfish" Hunter	Oakland 4 vs. Minn. 0 (AL)	5/29/2010	Roy Halladay	Phil. 1 vs. Florida 0 (NL)
5/15/1981	Len Barker	Clev. 3 vs. Toronto 0 (AL)	4/21/2012	Philip Humber	Chicago 4 vs. Seattle 0 (AL)
9/30/1984	Mike Witt	California 1 vs. Texas 0 (AL)	6/13/2012	Matt Cain	S.F. 10 vs. Houston 0 (NL)
9/16/1988	Tom Browning	Cincinnati 1 vs. L.A. 0 (NL)	8/15/2012	Felix Hernandez	Seattle 1 vs. Tampa Bay 0 (AL)
7/28/1991	Dennis Martinez	Montréal 2 vs. L.A. 0 (NL)			

* = World Series game. **Note:** Two pre-1901 National League pitchers are also credited with perfect games. Within one week in 1880, Lee Richmond (June 12, Worcester 1, Cleveland 0) and John "Monte" Ward (June 17, Providence 5, Buffalo 0) each threw a perfect game.

Most Career Major League No-Hitters

No.	Pitcher	No.	Pitcher
7	Nolan Ryan	2	Homer Bailey, Mark Buehrle, Jim Bunning, Steve Busby, Carl Erskine, Bob Forsch,
4	Sandy Koufax		Pud Galvin, Roy Halladay, Ken Holtzman, Randy Johnson, Addie Joss, Dutch Leonard,
3	Larry Corcoran,		Tim Lincecum, Jim Maloney, Christy Mathewson, Hideo Nomo, Allie Reynolds, Frank
	Bob Feller,		Smith, Warren Spahn, Bill Stoneman, Virgil Trucks, Johnny Vander Meer, Justin
	Cy Young		Verlander, Ed Walsh, Don Wilson

Home Run Leaders, by Season, 1901-2014

* = All-time single-season record for league since beginning of "modern" era in 1901.

	National League			American League	
Year	Player, team	HR	Year	Player, team	HR
1901	Sam Crawford, Cincinnati	16	1901	Napoleon Lajoie, Philadelphia	14
1902	Thomas Leach, Pittsburgh	6	1902	Socks Seybold, Philadelphia	16
1903	James Sheckard, Brooklyn	9	1903	Buck Freeman, Boston	13
1904	Harry Lumley, Brooklyn	9	1904	Harry Davis, Philadelphia	10
1905	Fred Odwell, Cincinnati	9	1905	Harry Davis, Philadelphia	8
1906	Timothy Jordan, Brooklyn	12	1906	Harry Davis, Philadelphia	12
1907	David Brain, Boston	10	1907	Harry Davis, Philadelphia	8
1908	Timothy Jordan, Brooklyn	12	1908	Sam Crawford, Detroit	7
1909	Red Murray, New York	7	1909	Ty Cobb, Detroit	9
1910	Fred Beck, Boston; Frank Schulte, Chicago	10	1910	Jake Stahl, Boston	10
1911	Frank Schulte, Chicago	21	1911	J. Franklin Baker, Philadelphia	11
1912	Henry Zimmerman, Chicago	14	1912	J. Franklin Baker, Phil.; Tris Speaker, Boston	10
1913	Gavvy Cravath, Philadelphia	19	1913	J. Franklin Baker, Philadelphia	12
1914	Gavvy Cravath, Philadelphia	19	1914	J. Franklin Baker, Philadelphia	9
1915	Gavvy Cravath, Philadelphia	24	1915	Robert Roth, Chicago-Cleveland	7
1916	Dave Robertson, NY; Fred "Cy" Williams, Chi.	12	1916	Wally Pipp, New York	12
1917	Gavvy Cravath, Phil.; Dave Robertson, NY	12	1917	Wally Pipp, New York	9

	National League			American League	
Year	Player, team	HR	Year	Player, team	HR
1918	Gavvy Cravath, Philadelphia	8	1918	Babe Ruth, Boston; Tilly Walker, Philadelphia	11
1919	Gavvy Cravath, Philadelphia	12	1919	Babe Ruth, Boston	29
1920	Cy Williams, Philadelphia	15	1920	Babe Ruth, New York	54
1921	George Kelly, New York	23	1921	Babe Ruth, New York	59
1922	Rogers Hornsby, St. Louis	42	1922	Ken Williams, St. Louis	39
1923	Cy Williams, Philadelphia	41	1923	Babe Ruth, New York	41
1924	Jacques Fournier, Brooklyn	27	1924	Babe Ruth, New York	46
1925	Rogers Hornsby, St. Louis	39	1925	Bob Meusel, New York	33
1926	Hack Wilson, Chicago	21	1926	Babe Ruth, New York	47
1927	Hack Wilson, Chicago; Cy Williams, Philadelphia	30	1927	Babe Ruth, New York	60
1928	Hack Wilson, Chicago; Jim Bottomley, St. Louis	31	1928	Babe Ruth, New York	54
1929	Chuck Klein, Philadelphia	43	1929	Babe Ruth, New York	46
1930	Hack Wilson, Chicago	56	1930	Babe Ruth, New York	49
1931	Chuck Klein, Philadelphia	31	1931	Lou Gehrig, New York; Babe Ruth, New York	46
1932	Chuck Klein, Philadelphia; Mel Ott, New York	38	1932	Jimmie Foxx, Philadelphia	58
1933	Chuck Klein, Philadelphia	28	1933	Jimmie Foxx, Philadelphia	48
1934	Rip Collins, St. Louis; Mel Ott, New York	35	1934	Lou Gehrig, New York	49
1935	Walter Berger, Boston	34	1935	Jimmie Foxx, Phil.; Hank Greenberg, Detroit	36
1936	Mel Ott, New York	33	1936	Lou Gehrig, New York	49
1937	Joe Medwick, St. Louis; Mel Ott, New York	31	1937	Joe DiMaggio, New York	46
1938	Mel Ott, New York	36	1938	Hank Greenberg, Detroit	58
1939	John Mize, St. Louis	28	1939	Jimmie Foxx, Boston	35
1940	John Mize, St. Louis	43	1940	Hank Greenberg, Detroit	41
1941	Dolph Camilli, Brooklyn	34	1941	Ted Williams, Boston	37
1942	Mel Ott, New York	30	1942	Ted Williams, Boston	36
1943	Bill Nicholson, Chicago	29	1943	Rudy York, Detroit	34
1944	Bill Nicholson, Chicago	33	1944	Nick Etten, New York	22
1945	Tommy Holmes, Boston	28	1945	Vern Stephens, St. Louis	24
1946	Ralph Kiner, Pittsburgh	23	1946	Hank Greenberg, Detroit	44
1947	Ralph Kiner, Pittsburgh; John Mize, New York	51	1947	Ted Williams, Boston	32
1948	Ralph Kiner, Pittsburgh; John Mize, New York	40	1948	Joe DiMaggio, New York	39
1949	Ralph Kiner, Pittsburgh	54	1949	Ted Williams, Boston	43
1950	Ralph Kiner, Pittsburgh	47	1950	Al Rosen, Cleveland	37
1951	Ralph Kiner, Pittsburgh	42	1951	Gus Zernial, Chicago-Philadelphia	33
1952	Ralph Kiner, Pittsburgh; Hank Sauer, Chicago	37	1952	Larry Doby, Cleveland	32
1953	Ed Mathews, Milwaukee	47	1953	Al Rosen, Cleveland	43
1954	Ted Kluszewski, Cincinnati	49	1954	Larry Doby, Cleveland	32
1955	Willie Mays, New York	51	1955	Mickey Mantle, New York	37
1956	Duke Snider, Brooklyn	43	1956	Mickey Mantle, New York	52
1957	Hank Aaron, Milwaukee	44	1957	Roy Sievers, Washington	42
1958	Ernie Banks, Chicago	47	1958	Mickey Mantle, New York	42
1959	Ed Mathews, Milwaukee	46	1959	Rocky Colavito, Clev.; Harmon Killebrew, Wash.	42
1960	Ernie Banks, Chicago	41	1960	Mickey Mantle, New York	40
1961	Orlando Cepeda, San Francisco	46	1961	Roger Maris, New York	61*
1962	Willie Mays, San Francisco	49	1962	Harmon Killebrew, Minnesota	48
1963	Hank Aaron, Milwaukee; Willie McCovey, S.F.	44	1963	Harmon Killebrew, Minnesota	45
1964	Willie Mays, San Francisco	47	1964	Harmon Killebrew, Minnesota	49
1965	Willie Mays, San Francisco	52	1965	Tony Conigliaro, Boston	32
1966	Hank Aaron, Atlanta	44	1966	Frank Robinson, Baltimore	49
1967	Hank Aaron, Atlanta	39	1967	Harmon Killebrew, Minn.; Carl Yastrzemski, Boston	44
1968	Willie McCovey, San Francisco	36	1968	Frank Howard, Washington	44
1969	Willie McCovey, San Francisco	45	1969	Harmon Killebrew, Minnesota	49
1970	Johnny Bench, Cincinnati	45	1970	Frank Howard, Washington	44
1971	Willie Stargell, Pittsburgh	48	1971	Bill Melton, Chicago	33
1972	Johnny Bench, Cincinnati	40	1972	Dick Allen, Chicago	37
1973	Willie Stargell, Pittsburgh	44	1973	Reggie Jackson, Oakland	32
1974	Mike Schmidt, Philadelphia	36	1974	Dick Allen, Chicago	32
1975	Mike Schmidt, Philadelphia	38	1975	Reggie Jackson, Oak.; George Scott, Milw.	36
1976	Mike Schmidt, Philadelphia	38	1976	Graig Nettles, New York	32
1977	George Foster, Cincinnati	52	1977	Jim Rice, Boston	39
1978	George Foster, Cincinnati	40	1978	Jim Rice, Boston	46
1979	Dave Kingman, Chicago	48	1979	Gorman Thomas, Milwaukee	45
1980	Mike Schmidt, Philadelphia	48	1980	Reggie Jackson, New York; Ben Oglivie, Milw.	41
1981	Mike Schmidt, Philadelphia	31	1981	Tony Armas, Oakland; Dwight Evans, Boston; Bobby Grich, Cal.; Eddie Murray, Baltimore	22
1982	Dave Kingman, New York	37	1982	Gorman Thomas, Milw.; Reggie Jackson, Cal.	39
1983	Mike Schmidt, Philadelphia	40	1983	Jim Rice, Boston	39
1984	Dale Murphy, Atlanta; Mike Schmidt, Philadelphia	36	1984	Tony Armas, Boston	43
1985	Dale Murphy, Atlanta	37	1985	Darrell Evans, Detroit	40
1986	Mike Schmidt, Philadelphia	37	1986	Jesse Barfield, Toronto	40
1987	Andre Dawson, Chicago	49	1987	Mark McGwire, Oakland	49
1988	Darryl Strawberry, New York	39	1988	Jose Canseco, Oakland	42
1989	Kevin Mitchell, San Francisco	47	1989	Fred McGriff, Toronto	36
1990	Ryne Sandberg, Chicago	40	1990	Cecil Fielder, Detroit	51
1991	Howard Johnson, New York	38	1991	Jose Canseco, Oakland; Cecil Fielder, Detroit	44
1992	Fred McGriff, San Diego	35	1992	Juan Gonzalez, Texas	43
1993	Barry Bonds, San Francisco	46	1993	Juan Gonzalez, Texas	46
1994	Matt Williams, San Francisco	43	1994	Ken Griffey Jr., Seattle	40
1995	Dante Bichette, Colorado	40	1995	Albert Belle, Cleveland	50
1996	Andres Galarraga, Colorado	47	1996	Mark McGwire, Oakland	52
1997[1]	Larry Walker, Colorado	49	1997[1]	Ken Griffey Jr., Seattle	56
1998	Mark McGwire, St. Louis	70	1998	Ken Griffey Jr., Seattle	56
1999	Mark McGwire, St. Louis	65	1999	Ken Griffey Jr., Seattle	48
2000	Sammy Sosa, Chicago	50	2000	Troy Glaus, Anaheim	47
2001	Barry Bonds, San Francisco	73*	2001	Alex Rodriguez, Texas	52
2002	Sammy Sosa, Chicago	49	2002	Alex Rodriguez, Texas	57
2003	Jim Thome, Philadelphia	47	2003	Alex Rodriguez, Texas	47
2004	Adrian Beltre, Los Angeles	48	2004	Manny Ramirez, Boston	43

Year	National League Player, team	HR	Year	American League Player, team	HR
2005	Andruw Jones, Atlanta	51	2005	Alex Rodriguez, New York	48
2006	Ryan Howard, Philadelphia	58	2006	David Ortiz, Boston	54
2007	Prince Fielder, Milwaukee	50	2007	Alex Rodriguez, New York	54
2008	Ryan Howard, Philadelphia	48	2008	Miguel Cabrera, Detroit	37
2009	Albert Pujols, St. Louis	47	2009	Carlos Pena, Tampa Bay; Mark Teixeira, New York	39
2010	Albert Pujols, St. Louis	42	2010	Jose Bautista, Toronto	54
2011	Matt Kemp, Los Angeles	39	2011	Jose Bautista, Toronto	43
2012	Ryan Braun, Milwaukee	41	2012	Miguel Cabrera, Detroit	44
2013	Pedro Alvarez, Pitt.; Paul Goldschmidt, Arizona	36	2013	Chris Davis, Baltimore	53
2014	Giancarlo Stanton, Miami	37	2014	Nelson Cruz, Baltimore	40

(1) In 1997, Mark McGwire hit 58 home runs, 34 with the Oakland Athletics (AL) and 24 with the St. Louis Cardinals (NL).

Batting Champions, by Season, 1901-2014

* = All-time single-season record for league since beginning of "modern" era in 1901.

Year	National League Player, team	AVG	Year	American League Player, team	AVG
1901	Jesse C. Burkett, St. Louis	.376	1901[1]	Napoleon Lajoie, Philadelphia	.426*
1902	Clarence Beaumont, Pittsburgh	.357	1902	Ed Delahanty, Washington	.376
1903	Honus Wagner, Pittsburgh	.355	1903	Napoleon Lajoie, Cleveland	.357
1904	Honus Wagner, Pittsburgh	.349	1904	Napoleon Lajoie, Cleveland	.382
1905	James Seymour, Cincinnati	.377	1905	Elmer Flick, Cleveland	.306
1906	Honus Wagner, Pittsburgh	.339	1906	George Stone, St. Louis	.358
1907	Honus Wagner, Pittsburgh	.350	1907	Ty Cobb, Detroit	.350
1908	Honus Wagner, Pittsburgh	.354	1908	Ty Cobb, Detroit	.324
1909	Honus Wagner, Pittsburgh	.339	1909	Ty Cobb, Detroit	.377
1910	Sherwood Magee, Philadelphia	.331	1910[2]	Ty Cobb, Detroit	.385
1911	Honus Wagner, Pittsburgh	.334	1911	Ty Cobb, Detroit	.420
1912	Henry Zimmerman, Chicago	.372	1912	Ty Cobb, Detroit	.410
1913	Jacob Daubert, Brooklyn	.350	1913	Ty Cobb, Detroit	.390
1914	Jacob Daubert, Brooklyn	.329	1914	Ty Cobb, Detroit	.368
1915	Larry Doyle, New York	.320	1915	Ty Cobb, Detroit	.369
1916	Hal Chase, Cincinnati	.339	1916	Tris Speaker, Cleveland	.386
1917	Edd Roush, Cincinnati	.341	1917	Ty Cobb, Detroit	.383
1918	Zach Wheat, Brooklyn	.335	1918	Ty Cobb, Detroit	.382
1919	Edd Roush, Cincinnati	.321	1919	Ty Cobb, Detroit	.384
1920	Rogers Hornsby, St. Louis	.370	1920	George Sisler, St. Louis	.407
1921	Rogers Hornsby, St. Louis	.397	1921	Harry Heilmann, Detroit	.394
1922	Rogers Hornsby, St. Louis	.401	1922	George Sisler, St. Louis	.420
1923	Rogers Hornsby, St. Louis	.384	1923	Harry Heilmann, Detroit	.403
1924	Rogers Hornsby, St. Louis	.424*	1924	Babe Ruth, New York	.378
1925	Rogers Hornsby, St. Louis	.403	1925	Harry Heilmann, Detroit	.393
1926	Eugene Hargrave, Cincinnati	.353	1926	Henry Manush, Detroit	.378
1927	Paul Waner, Pittsburgh	.380	1927	Harry Heilmann, Detroit	.398
1928	Rogers Hornsby, Boston	.387	1928	Goose Goslin, Washington	.379
1929	Lefty O'Doul, Philadelphia	.398	1929	Lew Fonseca, Cleveland	.369
1930	Bill Terry, New York	.401	1930	Al Simmons, Philadelphia	.381
1931	Chick Hafey, St. Louis	.349	1931	Al Simmons, Philadelphia	.390
1932	Lefty O'Doul, Brooklyn	.368	1932	Dale Alexander, Detroit-Boston	.367
1933	Chuck Klein, Philadelphia	.368	1933	Jimmie Foxx, Philadelphia	.356
1934	Paul Waner, Pittsburgh	.362	1934	Lou Gehrig, New York	.363
1935	Arky Vaughan, Pittsburgh	.385	1935	Buddy Myer, Washington	.349
1936	Paul Waner, Pittsburgh	.373	1936	Luke Appling, Chicago	.388
1937	Joe Medwick, St. Louis	.374	1937	Charlie Gehringer, Detroit	.371
1938	Ernie Lombardi, Cincinnati	.342	1938	Jimmie Foxx, Boston	.349
1939	Johnny Mize, St. Louis	.349	1939	Joe DiMaggio, New York	.381
1940	Debs Garms, Pittsburgh	.355	1940	Joe DiMaggio, New York	.352
1941	Pete Reiser, Brooklyn	.343	1941	Ted Williams, Boston	.406
1942	Ernie Lombardi, Boston	.330	1942	Ted Williams, Boston	.356
1943	Stan Musial, St. Louis	.357	1943	Luke Appling, Chicago	.328
1944	Dixie Walker, Brooklyn	.357	1944	Lou Boudreau, Cleveland	.327
1945	Phil Cavarretta, Chicago	.355	1945	George Stirnweiss, New York	.309
1946	Stan Musial, St. Louis	.365	1946	Mickey Vernon, Washington	.353
1947	Harry Walker, St. Louis-Phil.	.363	1947	Ted Williams, Boston	.343
1948	Stan Musial, St. Louis	.376	1948	Ted Williams, Boston	.369
1949	Jackie Robinson, Brooklyn	.342	1949	George Kell, Detroit	.343
1950	Stan Musial, St. Louis	.346	1950	Billy Goodman, Boston	.354
1951	Stan Musial, St. Louis	.355	1951	Ferris Fain, Philadelphia	.344
1952	Stan Musial, St. Louis	.336	1952	Ferris Fain, Philadelphia	.327
1953	Carl Furillo, Brooklyn	.344	1953	Mickey Vernon, Washington	.337
1954	Willie Mays, New York	.345	1954	Roberto Avila, Cleveland	.341
1955	Richie Ashburn, Philadelphia	.338	1955	Al Kaline, Detroit	.340
1956	Hank Aaron, Milwaukee	.328	1956	Mickey Mantle, New York	.353
1957	Stan Musial, St. Louis	.351	1957	Ted Williams, Boston	.388
1958	Richie Ashburn, Philadelphia	.350	1958	Ted Williams, Boston	.328
1959	Hank Aaron, Milwaukee	.355	1959	Harvey Kuenn, Detroit	.353
1960	Dick Groat, Pittsburgh	.325	1960	Pete Runnels, Boston	.320
1961	Roberto Clemente, Pittsburgh	.351	1961	Norm Cash, Detroit	.361
1962	Tommy Davis, Los Angeles	.346	1962	Pete Runnels, Boston	.326
1963	Tommy Davis, Los Angeles	.326	1963	Carl Yastrzemski, Boston	.321
1964	Roberto Clemente, Pittsburgh	.339	1964	Tony Oliva, Minnesota	.323
1965	Roberto Clemente, Pittsburgh	.329	1965	Tony Oliva, Minnesota	.321
1966	Matty Alou, Pittsburgh	.342	1966	Frank Robinson, Baltimore	.316
1967	Roberto Clemente, Pittsburgh	.357	1967	Carl Yastrzemski, Boston	.326
1968	Pete Rose, Cincinnati	.335	1968	Carl Yastrzemski, Boston	.301
1969	Pete Rose, Cincinnati	.348	1969	Rod Carew, Minnesota	.332
1970	Rico Carty, Atlanta	.366	1970	Alex Johnson, California	.329
1971	Joe Torre, St. Louis	.363	1971	Tony Oliva, Minnesota	.337

National League			American League	
Year	Player, team	AVG	Year	Player, team	AVG
1972	Billy Williams, Chicago	.333	1972	Rod Carew, Minnesota	.318
1973	Pete Rose, Cincinnati	.338	1973	Rod Carew, Minnesota	.350
1974	Ralph Garr, Atlanta	.353	1974	Rod Carew, Minnesota	.364
1975	Bill Madlock, Chicago	.354	1975	Rod Carew, Minnesota	.359
1976	Bill Madlock, Chicago	.339	1976	George Brett, Kansas City	.333
1977	Dave Parker, Pittsburgh	.338	1977	Rod Carew, Minnesota	.388
1978	Dave Parker, Pittsburgh	.334	1978	Rod Carew, Minnesota	.333
1979	Keith Hernandez, St. Louis	.344	1979	Fred Lynn, Boston	.333
1980	Bill Buckner, Chicago	.324	1980	George Brett, Kansas City	.390
1981	Bill Madlock, Pittsburgh	.341	1981	Carney Lansford, Boston	.336
1982	Al Oliver, Montréal	.331	1982	Willie Wilson, Kansas City	.332
1983	Bill Madlock, Pittsburgh	.323	1983	Wade Boggs, Boston	.361
1984	Tony Gwynn, San Diego	.351	1984	Don Mattingly, New York	.343
1985	Willie McGee, St. Louis	.353	1985	Wade Boggs, Boston	.368
1986	Tim Raines, Montréal	.334	1986	Wade Boggs, Boston	.357
1987	Tony Gwynn, San Diego	.370	1987	Wade Boggs, Boston	.363
1988	Tony Gwynn, San Diego	.313	1988	Wade Boggs, Boston	.366
1989	Tony Gwynn, San Diego	.336	1989	Kirby Puckett, Minnesota	.339
1990	Willie McGee, St. Louis	.335	1990	George Brett, Kansas City	.329
1991	Terry Pendleton, Atlanta	.319	1991	Julio Franco, Texas	.341
1992	Gary Sheffield, San Diego	.330	1992	Edgar Martinez, Seattle	.343
1993	Andres Galarraga, Colorado	.370	1993	John Olerud, Toronto	.363
1994	Tony Gwynn, San Diego	.394	1994	Paul O'Neill, New York	.359
1995	Tony Gwynn, San Diego	.368	1995	Edgar Martinez, Seattle	.356
1996	Tony Gwynn, San Diego	.353	1996	Alex Rodriguez, Seattle	.358
1997	Tony Gwynn, San Diego	.372	1997	Frank Thomas, Chicago	.347
1998	Larry Walker, Colorado	.363	1998	Bernie Williams, New York	.339
1999	Larry Walker, Colorado	.379	1999	Nomar Garciaparra, Boston	.357
2000	Todd Helton, Colorado	.372	2000	Nomar Garciaparra, Boston	.372
2001	Larry Walker, Colorado	.350	2001	Ichiro Suzuki, Seattle	.350
2002	Barry Bonds, San Francisco	.370	2002	Manny Ramirez, Boston	.349
2003	Albert Pujols, St. Louis	.359	2003	Bill Mueller, Boston	.326
2004	Barry Bonds, San Francisco	.362	2004	Ichiro Suzuki, Seattle	.372
2005	Derrek Lee, Chicago	.335	2005	Michael Young, Texas	.331
2006	Freddy Sanchez, Pittsburgh	.344	2006	Joe Mauer, Minnesota	.347
2007	Matt Holliday, Colorado	.340	2007	Magglio Ordonez, Detroit	.363
2008	Chipper Jones, Atlanta	.364	2008	Joe Mauer, Minnesota	.328
2009	Hanley Ramirez, Florida	.342	2009	Joe Mauer, Minnesota	.365
2010	Carlos Gonzalez, Colorado	.336	2010	Josh Hamilton, Texas	.359
2011	Jose Reyes, New York	.377	2011	Miguel Cabrera, Detroit	.344
2012	Buster Posey, San Francisco	.336	2012	Miguel Cabrera, Detroit	.330
2013	Michael Cuddyer, Colorado	.331	2013	Miguel Cabrera, Detroit	.348
2014	Justin Morneau, Colorado	.319	2014	Jose Altuve, Houston	.341

(1) Napoleon Lajoie's 1901 batting average varies in historical records from .421 to .426. (2) Some baseball researchers have concluded that Ty Cobb actually hit .382 in 1910 while Napoleon Lajoie, Cleveland, hit .383.

Earned Run Average Leaders, by Season, 1977-2014

National League					American League			
Year	Pitcher, team	G	IP	ERA	Year	Pitcher, team	G	IP	ERA
1977	John Candelaria, Pittsburgh	33	230.2	2.34	1977	Frank Tanana, California	31	241.1	2.54
1978	Craig Swan, New York	29	207.1	2.43	1978	Ron Guidry, New York	35	273.2	1.74
1979	J. R. Richard, Houston	38	292.1	2.71	1979	Ron Guidry, New York	33	236.1	2.78
1980	Don Sutton, Los Angeles	32	212.1	2.20	1980	Rudy May, New York	41	175.1	2.46
1981	Nolan Ryan, Houston	21	149.0	1.69	1981	Sammy Stewart, Baltimore	29	112.1	2.32
1982	Steve Rogers, Montréal	35	277.0	2.40	1982	Rick Sutcliffe, Cleveland	34	216.0	2.96
1983	Atlee Hammaker, San Francisco	23	172.1	2.25	1983	Rick Honeycutt, Texas	25	174.2	2.42
1984	Alejandro Pena, Los Angeles	28	199.1	2.48	1984	Mike Boddicker, Baltimore	34	261.1	2.79
1985	Dwight Gooden, New York	35	276.2	1.53	1985	Dave Stieb, Toronto	36	265.0	2.48
1986	Mike Scott, Houston	37	275.1	2.22	1986	Roger Clemens, Boston	33	254.0	2.48
1987	Nolan Ryan, Houston	34	211.2	2.76	1987	Jimmy Key, Toronto	36	261.0	2.76
1988	Joe Magrane, St. Louis	24	165.1	2.18	1988	Allan Anderson, Minnesota	30	202.1	2.45
1989	Scott Garrelts, San Francisco	30	193.1	2.28	1989	Bret Saberhagen, Kansas City	36	262.1	2.16
1990	Danny Darwin, Houston	48	162.2	2.21	1990	Roger Clemens, Boston	31	228.1	1.93
1991	Dennis Martinez, Montréal	31	222.0	2.39	1991	Roger Clemens, Boston	35	271.1	2.62
1992	Bill Swift, San Francisco	30	164.2	2.08	1992	Roger Clemens, Boston	32	246.2	2.41
1993	Greg Maddux, Atlanta	36	267.0	2.36	1993	Kevin Appier, Kansas City	34	238.2	2.56
1994	Greg Maddux, Atlanta	25	202.0	1.56	1994	Steve Ontiveros, Oakland	27	115.1	2.65
1995	Greg Maddux, Atlanta	28	209.2	1.63	1995	Randy Johnson, Seattle	30	214.1	2.48
1996	Kevin Brown, Florida	32	233.0	1.89	1996	Juan Guzman, Toronto	27	187.2	2.93
1997	Pedro Martinez, Montréal	31	241.1	1.90	1997	Roger Clemens, Toronto	34	264.0	2.05
1998	Greg Maddux, Atlanta	34	251.0	2.22	1998	Roger Clemens, Toronto	33	234.2	2.65
1999	Randy Johnson, Arizona	35	271.2	2.48	1999	Pedro Martinez, Boston	31	213.1	2.07
2000	Kevin Brown, Los Angeles	33	230.0	2.58	2000	Pedro Martinez, Boston	29	217.0	1.74
2001	Randy Johnson, Arizona	35	249.2	2.49	2001	Freddy Garcia, Seattle	34	238.2	3.05
2002	Randy Johnson, Arizona	35	260.0	2.32	2002	Pedro Martinez, Boston	30	199.1	2.26
2003	Jason Schmidt, San Francisco	29	207.2	2.34	2003	Pedro Martinez, Boston	29	186.2	2.22
2004	Jake Peavy, San Diego	27	166.1	2.27	2004	Johan Santana, Minnesota	34	228.0	2.61
2005	Roger Clemens, Houston	32	211.1	1.87	2005	Kevin Millwood, Cleveland	30	192.0	2.86
2006	Roy Oswalt, Houston	33	220.2	2.98	2006	Johan Santana, Minnesota	34	233.2	2.77
2007	Jake Peavy, San Diego	34	223.1	2.54	2007	John Lackey, Los Angeles	33	224.0	3.01
2008	Johan Santana, New York	34	234.1	2.53	2008	Cliff Lee, Cleveland	31	223.1	2.54
2009	Chris Carpenter, St. Louis	28	192.2	2.24	2009	Zack Greinke, Kansas City	33	229.1	2.16
2010	Josh Johnson, Florida	28	183.2	2.30	2010	Felix Hernandez, Seattle	34	249.2	2.27
2011	Clayton Kershaw, Los Angeles	33	233.1	2.28	2011	Justin Verlander, Detroit	34	251.0	2.40
2012	Clayton Kershaw, Los Angeles	33	227.2	2.53	2012	David Price, Tampa Bay	31	211.0	2.56
2013	Clayton Kershaw, Los Angeles	33	236.0	1.83	2013	Anibal Sanchez, Detroit	29	182.0	2.57
2014	Clayton Kershaw, Los Angeles	27	198.1	1.77	2014	Felix Hernandez, Seattle	34	236.0	2.14

Note: ERA is computed by multiplying earned runs allowed by 9, then dividing by innings pitched.

Strikeout Leaders, by Season, 1901-2014

* = All-time single-season record for league since beginning of "modern" era in 1901.

	National League			American League	
Year	Pitcher, team	SO	Year	Pitcher, team	SO
1901	Noodles Hahn, Cincinnati	239	1901	Cy Young, Boston	158
1902	Vic Willis, Boston	225	1902	Rube Waddell, Philadelphia	210
1903	Christy Mathewson, New York	267	1903	Rube Waddell, Philadelphia	302
1904	Christy Mathewson, New York	212	1904	Rube Waddell, Philadelphia	349
1905	Christy Mathewson, New York	206	1905	Rube Waddell, Philadelphia	287
1906	Fred Beebe, Chicago-St. Louis	171	1906	Rube Waddell, Philadelphia	196
1907	Christy Mathewson, New York	178	1907	Rube Waddell, Philadelphia	232
1908	Christy Mathewson, New York	259	1908	Ed Walsh, Chicago	269
1909	Orval Overall, Chicago	205	1909	Frank Smith, Chicago	177
1910	Earl Moore, Philadelphia	185	1910	Walter Johnson, Washington	313
1911	Rube Marquard, New York	237	1911	Ed Walsh, Chicago	255
1912	Grover Alexander, Philadelphia	195	1912	Walter Johnson, Washington	303
1913	Tom Seaton, Philadelphia	168	1913	Walter Johnson, Washington	243
1914	Grover Alexander, Philadelphia	214	1914	Walter Johnson, Washington	225
1915	Grover Alexander, Philadelphia	241	1915	Walter Johnson, Washington	203
1916	Grover Alexander, Philadelphia	167	1916	Walter Johnson, Washington	228
1917	Grover Alexander, Philadelphia	200	1917	Walter Johnson, Washington	188
1918	Hippo Vaughn, Chicago	148	1918	Walter Johnson, Washington	162
1919	Hippo Vaughn, Chicago	141	1919	Walter Johnson, Washington	147
1920	Grover Alexander, Chicago	173	1920	Stan Coveleski, Cleveland	133
1921	Burleigh Grimes, Brooklyn	136	1921	Walter Johnson, Washington	143
1922	Dazzy Vance, Brooklyn	134	1922	Urban Shocker, St. Louis	149
1923	Dazzy Vance, Brooklyn	197	1923	Walter Johnson, Washington	130
1924	Dazzy Vance, Brooklyn	262	1924	Walter Johnson, Washington	158
1925	Dazzy Vance, Brooklyn	221	1925	Lefty Grove, Philadelphia	116
1926	Dazzy Vance, Brooklyn	140	1926	Lefty Grove, Philadelphia	194
1927	Dazzy Vance, Brooklyn	184	1927	Lefty Grove, Philadelphia	174
1928	Dazzy Vance, Brooklyn	200	1928	Lefty Grove, Philadelphia	183
1929	Pat Malone, Chicago	166	1929	Lefty Grove, Philadelphia	170
1930	Bill Hallahan, St. Louis	177	1930	Lefty Grove, Philadelphia	209
1931	Bill Hallahan, St. Louis	159	1931	Lefty Grove, Philadelphia	175
1932	Dizzy Dean, St. Louis	191	1932	Red Ruffing, New York	190
1933	Dizzy Dean, St. Louis	199	1933	Lefty Gomez, New York	163
1934	Dizzy Dean, St. Louis	195	1934	Lefty Gomez, New York	158
1935	Dizzy Dean, St. Louis	190	1935	Tommy Bridges, Detroit	163
1936	Van Lingle Mungo, Brooklyn	238	1936	Tommy Bridges, Detroit	175
1937	Carl Hubbell, New York	159	1937	Lefty Gomez, New York	194
1938	Clay Bryant, Chicago	135	1938	Bob Feller, Cleveland	240
1939	Claude Passeau, Philadelphia-Chicago; Bucky Walters, Cincinnati	137	1939	Bob Feller, Cleveland	246
1940	Kirby Higbe, Philadelphia	137	1940	Bob Feller, Cleveland	261
1941	John Vander Meer, Cincinnati	202	1941	Bob Feller, Cleveland	260
1942	John Vander Meer, Cincinnati	186	1942	Tex Hughson, Boston; Bobo Newsom, Washington	113
1943	John Vander Meer, Cincinnati	174	1943	Allie Reynolds, Cleveland	151
1944	Bill Voiselle, New York	161	1944	Hal Newhouser, Detroit	187
1945	Preacher Roe, Pittsburgh	148	1945	Hal Newhouser, Detroit	212
1946	Johnny Schmitz, Cincinnati	135	1946	Bob Feller, Cleveland	348
1947	Ewell Blackwell, Cincinnati	193	1947	Bob Feller, Cleveland	196
1948	Harry Brecheen, St. Louis	149	1948	Bob Feller, Cleveland	164
1949	Warren Spahn, Boston	151	1949	Virgil Trucks, Detroit	153
1950	Warren Spahn, Boston	191	1950	Bob Lemon, Cleveland	170
1951	Warren Spahn, Boston; Don Newcombe, Brooklyn	164	1951	Vic Raschi, New York	164
1952	Warren Spahn, Boston	183	1952	Allie Reynolds, New York	160
1953	Robin Roberts, Philadelphia	198	1953	Billy Pierce, Chicago	186
1954	Robin Roberts, Philadelphia	185	1954	Bob Turley, Baltimore	185
1955	Sam Jones, Chicago	198	1955	Herb Score, Cleveland	245
1956	Sam Jones, Chicago	176	1956	Herb Score, Cleveland	263
1957	Jack Sanford, Philadelphia	188	1957	Early Wynn, Cleveland	184
1958	Sam Jones, St. Louis	225	1958	Early Wynn, Chicago	179
1959	Don Drysdale, Los Angeles	242	1959	Jim Bunning, Detroit	201
1960	Don Drysdale, Los Angeles	246	1960	Jim Bunning, Detroit	201
1961	Sandy Koufax, Los Angeles	269	1961	Camilo Pascual, Minnesota	221
1962	Don Drysdale, Los Angeles	232	1962	Camilo Pascual, Minnesota	206
1963	Sandy Koufax, Los Angeles	306	1963	Camilo Pascual, Minnesota	202
1964	Bob Veale, Pittsburgh	250	1964	Al Downing, New York	217
1965	Sandy Koufax, Los Angeles	382*	1965	Sam McDowell, Cleveland	325
1966	Sandy Koufax, Los Angeles	317	1966	Sam McDowell, Cleveland	225
1967	Jim Bunning, Philadelphia	253	1967	Jim Lonborg, Boston	246
1968	Bob Gibson, St. Louis	268	1968	Sam McDowell, Cleveland	283
1969	Ferguson Jenkins, Chicago	273	1969	Sam McDowell, Cleveland	279
1970	Tom Seaver, New York	283	1970	Sam McDowell, Cleveland	304
1971	Tom Seaver, New York	289	1971	Mickey Lolich, Detroit	308
1972	Steve Carlton, Philadelphia	310	1972	Nolan Ryan, California	329
1973	Tom Seaver, New York	251	1973	Nolan Ryan, California	383*
1974	Steve Carlton, Philadelphia	240	1974	Nolan Ryan, California	367
1975	Tom Seaver, New York	243	1975	Frank Tanana, California	269
1976	Tom Seaver, New York	235	1976	Nolan Ryan, California	327
1977	Phil Niekro, Atlanta	262	1977	Nolan Ryan, California	341
1978	J. R. Richard, Houston	303	1978	Nolan Ryan, California	260

Year	National League — Pitcher, team	SO	Year	American League — Pitcher, team	SO
1979	J. R. Richard, Houston	313	1979	Nolan Ryan, California	223
1980	Steve Carlton, Philadelphia	286	1980	Len Barker, Cleveland	187
1981	Fernando Valenzuela, Los Angeles	180	1981	Len Barker, Cleveland	127
1982	Steve Carlton, Philadelphia	286	1982	Floyd Bannister, Seattle	209
1983	Steve Carlton, Philadelphia	275	1983	Jack Morris, Detroit	232
1984	Dwight Gooden, New York	276	1984	Mark Langston, Seattle	204
1985	Dwight Gooden, New York	268	1985	Bert Blyleven, Cleveland-Minnesota	206
1986	Mike Scott, Houston	306	1986	Mark Langston, Seattle	245
1987	Nolan Ryan, Houston	270	1987	Mark Langston, Seattle	262
1988	Nolan Ryan, Houston	228	1988	Roger Clemens, Boston	291
1989	Jose DeLeon, St. Louis	201	1989	Nolan Ryan, Texas	301
1990	David Cone, New York	233	1990	Nolan Ryan, Texas	232
1991	David Cone, New York	241	1991	Roger Clemens, Boston	241
1992	John Smoltz, Atlanta	215	1992	Randy Johnson, Seattle	241
1993	Jose Rijo, Cincinnati	227	1993	Randy Johnson, Seattle	308
1994	Andy Benes, San Diego	189	1994	Randy Johnson, Seattle	204
1995	Hideo Nomo, Los Angeles	236	1995	Randy Johnson, Seattle	294
1996	John Smoltz, Atlanta	276	1996	Roger Clemens, Boston	257
1997	Curt Schilling, Philadelphia	319	1997	Roger Clemens, Toronto	292
1998	Curt Schilling, Philadelphia	300	1998	Roger Clemens, Toronto	271
1999	Randy Johnson, Arizona	364	1999	Pedro Martinez, Boston	313
2000	Randy Johnson, Arizona	347	2000	Pedro Martinez, Boston	284
2001	Randy Johnson, Arizona	372	2001	Hideo Nomo, Boston	220
2002	Randy Johnson, Arizona	334	2002	Pedro Martinez, Boston	239
2003	Kerry Wood, Chicago	266	2003	Esteban Loaiza, Chicago	207
2004	Randy Johnson, Arizona	290	2004	Johan Santana, Minnesota	265
2005	Jake Peavy, San Diego	216	2005	Johan Santana, Minnesota	238
2006	Aaron Harang, Cincinnati	216	2006	Johan Santana, Minnesota	245
2007	Jake Peavy, San Diego	240	2007	Scott Kazmir, Tampa Bay	239
2008	Tim Lincecum, San Francisco	265	2008	A. J. Burnett, Toronto	231
2009	Tim Lincecum, San Francisco	261	2009	Justin Verlander, Detroit	269
2010	Tim Lincecum, San Francisco	231	2010	Jered Weaver, Los Angeles	233
2011	Clayton Kershaw, Los Angeles	248	2011	Justin Verlander, Detroit	250
2012	R. A. Dickey, New York	230	2012	Justin Verlander, Detroit	239
2013	Clayton Kershaw, Los Angeles	232	2013	Yu Darvish, Texas	277
2014	Johnny Cueto, Cincinnati; Stephen Strasburg, Washington	242	2014	David Price, Tampa Bay-Detroit	271

Victory Leaders, by Season, 1901-2014

* = All-time single-season record for league since beginning of "modern" era in 1901.

Year	National League — Pitcher, team	Wins	Year	American League — Pitcher, team	Wins
1901	Bill Donovan, Brooklyn	25	1901	Cy Young, Boston	33
1902	Jack Chesbro, Pittsburgh	28	1902	Cy Young, Boston	32
1903	Joe McGinnity, New York	31	1903	Cy Young, Boston	28
1904	Joe McGinnity, New York	35	1904	Jack Chesbro, New York	41*
1905	Christy Mathewson, New York	31	1905	Rube Waddell, Philadelphia	27
1906	Joe McGinnity, New York	27	1906	Al Orth, New York	27
1907	Christy Mathewson, New York	24	1907	Addie Joss, Cleveland; Doc White, Chicago	27
1908	Christy Mathewson, New York	37*	1908	Ed Walsh, Chicago	40
1909	Mordecai Brown, Chicago	27	1909	George Mullin, Detroit	29
1910	Christy Mathewson, New York	27	1910	Jack Coombs, Philadelphia	31
1911	Grover Alexander, Chicago	28	1911	Jack Coombs, Philadelphia	28
1912	Larry Cheney, Chicago; Rube Marquard, New York	26	1912	Joe Wood, Boston	34
1913	Tom Seaton, Philadelphia	27	1913	Walter Johnson, Washington	36
1914	Grover Alexander, Philadelphia	27	1914	Walter Johnson, Washington	28
1915	Grover Alexander, Philadelphia	31	1915	Walter Johnson, Washington	27
1916	Grover Alexander, Philadelphia	33	1916	Walter Johnson, Washington	25
1917	Grover Alexander, Philadelphia	30	1917	Eddie Cicotte, Chicago	28
1918	Hippo Vaughn, Chicago	22	1918	Walter Johnson, Washington	23
1919	Jesse Barnes, New York	25	1919	Eddie Cicotte, Chicago	29
1920	Grover Alexander, Philadelphia	27	1920	Jim Bagby, Cleveland	31
1921	Wilbur Cooper, Pitt.; Burleigh Grimes, Brooklyn	22	1921	Carl Mays, New York; Urban Shocker, St. Louis	27
1922	Eppa Rixey, Cincinnati	25	1922	Eddie Rommel, Philadelphia	27
1923	Dolf Luque, Cincinnati	27	1923	George Uhle, Cleveland	26
1924	Dazzy Vance, Brooklyn	28	1924	Walter Johnson, Washington	23
1925	Dazzy Vance, Brooklyn	22	1925	Ted Lyons, Chicago; Eddie Rommel, Philadelphia	21
1926	Pete Donohue, Cincinnati; Remy Kremer, Pitt.; Lee Meadows, Pitt.; Flint Rhem, St. Louis	20	1926	George Uhle, Cleveland	27
1927	Charlie Root, Chicago	26	1927	Waite Hoyt, New York; Ted Lyons, Chicago	22
1928	Burleigh Grimes, Pittsburgh; Larry Benton, NY	25	1928	Lefty Grove, Philadelphia; George Pipgras, NY	24
1929	Pat Malone, Chicago	22	1929	George Earnshaw, Philadelphia	24
1930	Pat Malone, Chicago; Remy Kremer, Pitt.	20	1930	Lefty Grove, Philadelphia	28
1931	Jumbo Elliott, Phil.; Bill Hallahan, St. Louis; Heinie Meine, Pittsburgh	19	1931	Lefty Grove, Philadelphia	31
1932	Lon Warneke, Chicago	22	1932	Alvin Crowder, Washington	26
1933	Carl Hubbell, New York	23	1933	Alvin Crowder, Wash.; Lefty Grove, Phila.	24
1934	Dizzy Dean, St. Louis	30	1934	Lefty Gomez, New York	26
1935	Dizzy Dean, St. Louis	28	1935	Wes Ferrell, Boston	25
1936	Carl Hubbell, New York	26	1936	Tommy Bridges, Detroit	23
1937	Carl Hubbell, New York	22	1937	Lefty Gomez, New York	21
1938	Bill Lee, Chicago	22	1938	Red Ruffing, New York	21
1939	Bucky Walters, Cincinnati	27	1939	Bob Feller, Cleveland	24
1940	Bucky Walters, Cincinnati	22	1940	Bob Feller, Cleveland	27

Year	National League Pitcher, team	Wins	Year	American League Pitcher, team	Wins
1941	Kirby Higbe, Brooklyn; Whit Wyatt, Brooklyn	22	1941	Bob Feller, Cleveland	25
1942	Mort Cooper, St. Louis	22	1942	Tex Hughson, Boston	22
1943	Mort Cooper, St. Louis; Elmer Riddle, Cincinnati; Rip Sewell, Pittsburgh	21	1943	Spurgeon "Spud" Chandler, New York; Dizzy Trout, Detroit	20
1944	Bucky Walters, Cincinnati	23	1944	Hal Newhouser, Detroit	29
1945	Red Barrett, Boston-St. Louis	23	1945	Hal Newhouser, Detroit	25
1946	Howie Pollet, St. Louis	21	1946	Bob Feller, Cleveland; Hal Newhouser, Detroit	26
1947	Ewell Blackwell, Cincinnati	22	1947	Bob Feller, Cleveland	20
1948	Johnny Sain, Boston	24	1948	Hal Newhouser, Detroit	21
1949	Warren Spahn, Boston	21	1949	Mel Parnell, Boston	25
1950	Warren Spahn, Boston	21	1950	Bob Lemon, Cleveland	23
1951	Larry Jansen, New York; Sal Maglie, New York	23	1951	Bob Feller, Cleveland	22
1952	Robin Roberts, Philadelphia	28	1952	Bobby Shantz, Philadelphia	24
1953	Robin Roberts, Phil.; Warren Spahn, Milwaukee	23	1953	Bob Porterfield, Washington	22
1954	Robin Roberts, Philadelphia	23	1954	Bob Lemon, Cleveland; Early Wynn, Cleveland	23
1955	Robin Roberts, Philadelphia	23	1955	Whitey Ford, New York; Bob Lemon, Cleveland; Frank Sullivan, Boston	18
1956	Don Newcombe, Brooklyn	27	1956	Frank Lary, Detroit	21
1957	Warren Spahn, Milwaukee	21	1957	Jim Bunning, Detroit; Billy Pierce, Chicago	20
1958	Bob Friend, Pitt.; Warren Spahn, Milwaukee	22	1958	Bob Turley, New York	21
1959	Lew Burdette, Warren Spahn, Milwaukee; Sam Jones, NY Giants	21	1959	Early Wynn, Chicago	22
1960	Ernie Broglio, St. Louis; Warren Spahn, Milwaukee	21	1960	Chuck Estrada, Baltimore; Jim Perry, Cleveland	18
1961	Joey Jay, Cincinnati; Warren Spahn, Milwaukee	21	1961	Whitey Ford, New York	25
1962	Don Drysdale, Los Angeles	25	1962	Ralph Terry, New York	23
1963	Sandy Koufax, L.A.; Juan Marichal, San Francisco	25	1963	Whitey Ford, New York	24
1964	Larry Jackson, Chicago	24	1964	Dean Chance, Los Angeles; Gary Peters, Chicago	20
1965	Sandy Koufax, Los Angeles	26	1965	Jim "Mudcat" Grant, Minnesota	21
1966	Sandy Koufax, Los Angeles	27	1966	Jim Kaat, Minnesota	25
1967	Mike McCormick, San Francisco	22	1967	Jim Lonborg, Boston; Earl Wilson, Detroit	22
1968	Juan Marichal, San Francisco	26	1968	Denny McLain, Detroit	31
1969	Tom Seaver, New York	25	1969	Denny McLain, Detroit	24
1970	Bob Gibson, St. Louis; Gaylord Perry, San Francisco	23	1970	Mike Cuellar, Dave McNally, Baltimore; Jim Perry, Minnesota	24
1971	Ferguson Jenkins, Chicago	24	1971	Mickey Lolich, Detroit	25
1972	Steve Carlton, Philadelphia	27	1972	Gaylord Perry, Cleveland; Wilbur Wood, Chicago	24
1973	Ron Bryant, San Francisco	24	1973	Wilbur Wood, Chicago	24
1974	Andy Messersmith, L.A.; Phil Niekro, Atlanta	20	1974	Jim "Catfish" Hunter, Oak.; Ferguson Jenkins, Tex.	25
1975	Tom Seaver, New York	22	1975	Jim "Catfish" Hunter, NY; Jim Palmer, Baltimore	23
1976	Randy Jones, San Diego	22	1976	Jim Palmer, Baltimore	22
1977	Steve Carlton, Philadelphia	23	1977	Dave Goltz, Minnesota; Dennis Leonard, Kansas City; Jim Palmer, Baltimore	20
1978	Gaylord Perry, San Diego	21	1978	Ron Guidry, New York	25
1979	Joe Niekro, Houston; Phil Niekro, Atlanta	21	1979	Mike Flanagan, Baltimore	23
1980	Steve Carlton, Philadelphia	24	1980	Steve Stone, Baltimore	25
1981	Tom Seaver, Cincinnati	14	1981	Dennis Martinez, Balt.; Steve McCatty, Oakland; Jack Morris, Detroit; Pete Vuckovich, Milwaukee	14
1982	Steve Carlton, Philadelphia	23	1982	LaMarr Hoyt, Chicago	19
1983	John Denny, Philadelphia	19	1983	LaMarr Hoyt, Chicago	24
1984	Joaquin Andujar, St. Louis	20	1984	Mike Boddicker, Baltimore	20
1985	Dwight Gooden, New York	24	1985	Ron Guidry, New York	22
1986	Fernando Valenzuela, Los Angeles	21	1986	Roger Clemens, Boston	24
1987	Rick Sutcliffe, Chicago	18	1987	Roger Clemens, Boston; Dave Stewart, Oakland	20
1988	Orel Hershiser, L.A.; Danny Jackson, Cincinnati	23	1988	Frank Viola, Minnesota	24
1989	Mike Scott, Houston	20	1989	Bret Saberhagen, Kansas City	23
1990	Doug Drabek, Pittsburgh	22	1990	Bob Welch, Oakland	27
1991	Tom Glavine, Atlanta; John Smiley, Pittsburgh	20	1991	Scott Erickson, Minnesota; Bill Gullickson, Detroit	20
1992	Tom Glavine, Atlanta; Greg Maddux, Chicago	20	1992	Kevin Brown, Texas; Jack Morris, Toronto	21
1993	John Burkett, San Francisco; Tom Glavine, Atlanta	22	1993	Jack McDowell, Chicago	22
1994	Ken Hill, Montréal; Greg Maddux, Atlanta	16	1994	Jimmy Key, New York	17
1995	Greg Maddux, Atlanta	19	1995	Mike Mussina, Baltimore	19
1996	John Smoltz, Atlanta	24	1996	Andy Pettitte, New York	21
1997	Denny Neagle, Atlanta	20	1997	Roger Clemens, Toronto	21
1998	Tom Glavine, Atlanta	20	1998	Roger Clemens, Toronto; David Cone, New York; Rick Helling, Texas	20
1999	Mike Hampton, Houston	22	1999	Pedro Martinez, Boston	23
2000	Tom Glavine, Atlanta	21	2000	Tim Hudson, Oakland; David Wells, Toronto	20
2001	Matt Morris, St. Louis; Curt Schilling, Arizona	22	2001	Mark Mulder, Oakland	21
2002	Randy Johnson, Arizona	24	2002	Barry Zito, Oakland	23
2003	Russ Ortiz, Atlanta	21	2003	Roy Halladay, Toronto	22
2004	Roy Oswalt, Houston	20	2004	Curt Schilling, Boston	21
2005	Dontrelle Willis, Florida	22	2005	Bartolo Colon, Los Angeles	21
2006	Aaron Harang, Cincinnati; Derek Lowe, L.A.; Brad Penny, L.A.; John Smoltz, Atlanta; Brandon Webb, Arizona; Carlos Zambrano, Chicago	16	2006	Johan Santana, Minnesota; Chien-Ming Wang, New York	19
2007	Jake Peavy, San Diego	19	2007	Josh Beckett, Boston	20
2008	Brandon Webb, Arizona	22	2008	Cliff Lee, Cleveland	22
2009	Adam Wainwright, St. Louis	19	2009	Felix Hernandez, Seattle; CC Sabathia, New York; Justin Verlander, Detroit	19
2010	Roy Halladay, Philadelphia	21	2010	CC Sabathia, New York	21
2011	Ian Kennedy, Arizona; Clayton Kershaw, L.A.	21	2011	Justin Verlander, Detroit	24
2012	Gio Gonzalez, Washington	21	2012	David Price, Tampa Bay; Jered Weaver, L.A.	20
2013	Adam Wainwright, St. Louis; Jordan Zimmermann, Washington	19	2013	Max Scherzer, Detroit	21
2014	Clayton Kershaw, Los Angeles	21	2014	Corey Kluber, Cleveland; Max Scherzer, Detroit; Jered Weaver, Los Angeles	18

Cy Young Award Winners, 1956-2013

Year	Pitcher, team	Year	Pitcher, team	Year	Pitcher, team
1956	Don Newcombe, Brooklyn	1979	(NL) Bruce Sutter, Chicago	1996	(NL) John Smoltz, Atlanta
1957	Warren Spahn, Milwaukee		(AL) Mike Flanagan, Baltimore		(AL) Pat Hentgen, Toronto
1958	Bob Turley, NY	1980	(NL) Steve Carlton, Philadelphia	1997	(NL) Pedro Martinez, Montréal
1959	Early Wynn, Chicago		(AL) Steve Stone, Baltimore		(AL) Roger Clemens, Toronto
1960	Vernon Law, Pittsburgh	1981	(NL) Fernando Valenzuela, L.A.	1998	(NL) Tom Glavine, Atlanta
1961	Whitey Ford, NY		(AL) Rollie Fingers, Milwaukee		(AL) Roger Clemens, Toronto
1962	Don Drysdale, L.A.	1982	(NL) Steve Carlton, Philadelphia	1999	(NL) Randy Johnson, Arizona
1963	Sandy Koufax, L.A.		(AL) Pete Vuckovich, Milwaukee		(AL) Pedro Martinez, Boston
1964	Dean Chance, L.A.	1983	(NL) John Denny, Philadelphia	2000	(NL) Randy Johnson, Arizona
1965	Sandy Koufax, L.A.		(AL) LaMarr Hoyt, Chicago		(AL) Pedro Martinez, Boston
1966	Sandy Koufax, L.A.	1984	(NL) Rick Sutcliffe, Chicago	2001	(NL) Randy Johnson, Arizona
1967	(NL) Mike McCormick, S.F.		(AL) Willie Hernandez, Detroit		(AL) Roger Clemens, NY
	(AL) Jim Lonborg, Boston	1985	(NL) Dwight Gooden, NY	2002	(NL) Randy Johnson, Arizona
1968	(NL) Bob Gibson, St. Louis		(AL) Bret Saberhagen,		(AL) Barry Zito, Oakland
	(AL) Denny McLain, Detroit		Kansas City	2003	(NL) Eric Gagne, L.A.
1969	(NL) Tom Seaver, NY	1986	(NL) Mike Scott, Houston		(AL) Roy Halladay, Toronto
	(AL) (tie) Denny McLain, Detroit;		(AL) Roger Clemens, Boston	2004	(NL) Roger Clemens, Houston
	Mike Cuellar, Baltimore	1987	(NL) Steve Bedrosian,		(AL) Johan Santana, Minnesota
1970	(NL) Bob Gibson, St. Louis		Philadelphia	2005	(NL) Chris Carpenter, St. Louis
	(AL) Jim Perry, Minnesota		(AL) Roger Clemens, Boston		(AL) Bartolo Colon, L.A.
1971	(NL) Ferguson Jenkins, Chicago	1988	(NL) Orel Hershiser, L.A.	2006	(NL) Brandon Webb, Arizona
	(AL) Vida Blue, Oakland		(AL) Frank Viola, Minnesota		(AL) Johan Santana, Minnesota
1972	(NL) Steve Carlton, Philadelphia	1989	(NL) Mark Davis, San Diego	2007	(NL) Jake Peavy, San Diego
	(AL) Gaylord Perry, Cleveland		(AL) Bret Saberhagen,		(AL) CC Sabathia, Cleveland
1973	(NL) Tom Seaver, NY		Kansas City	2008	(NL) Tim Lincecum, S.F.
	(AL) Jim Palmer, Baltimore	1990	(NL) Doug Drabek, Pittsburgh		(AL) Cliff Lee, Cleveland
1974	(NL) Mike Marshall, L.A.		(AL) Bob Welch, Oakland	2009	(NL) Tim Lincecum, S.F.
	(AL) Jim "Catfish" Hunter,	1991	(NL) Tom Glavine, Atlanta		(AL) Zack Greinke, Kansas City
	Oakland		(AL) Roger Clemens, Boston	2010	(NL) Roy Halladay, Philadelphia
1975	(NL) Tom Seaver, NY	1992	(NL) Greg Maddux, Chicago		(AL) Felix Hernandez, Seattle
	(AL) Jim Palmer, Baltimore		(AL) Dennis Eckersley, Oakland	2011	(NL) Clayton Kershaw, L.A.
1976	(NL) Randy Jones, San Diego	1993	(NL) Greg Maddux, Atlanta		(AL) Justin Verlander, Detroit
	(AL) Jim Palmer, Baltimore		(AL) Jack McDowell, Chicago	2012	(NL) R. A. Dickey, NY
1977	(NL) Steve Carlton, Philadelphia	1994	(NL) Greg Maddux, Atlanta		(AL) David Price, Tampa Bay
	(AL) Sparky Lyle, NY		(AL) David Cone, Kansas City	2013	(NL) Clayton Kershaw, L.A.
1978	(NL) Gaylord Perry, San Diego	1995	(NL) Greg Maddux, Atlanta		(AL) Max Scherzer, Detroit
	(AL) Ron Guidry, NY		(AL) Randy Johnson, Seattle		

Most Valuable Players, 1931-2013

As selected by the Baseball Writers' Assn. of America. Prior to 1931, MVP honors were named by various sources.

National League

Year	Player, team	Year	Player, team	Year	Player, team
1931	Frank Frisch, St. Louis	1960	Dick Groat, Pittsburgh	1987	Andre Dawson, Chicago
1932	Chuck Klein, Philadelphia	1961	Frank Robinson, Cincinnati	1988	Kirk Gibson, Los Angeles
1933	Carl Hubbell, New York	1962	Maury Wills, Los Angeles	1989	Kevin Mitchell, San Francisco
1934	Dizzy Dean, St. Louis	1963	Sandy Koufax, Los Angeles	1990	Barry Bonds, Pittsburgh
1935	Gabby Hartnett, Chicago	1964	Ken Boyer, St. Louis	1991	Terry Pendleton, Atlanta
1936	Carl Hubbell, New York	1965	Willie Mays, San Francisco	1992	Barry Bonds, Pittsburgh
1937	Joe Medwick, St. Louis	1966	Roberto Clemente, Pittsburgh	1993	Barry Bonds, San Francisco
1938	Ernie Lombardi, Cincinnati	1967	Orlando Cepeda, St. Louis	1994	Jeff Bagwell, Houston
1939	Bucky Walters, Cincinnati	1968	Bob Gibson, St. Louis	1995	Barry Larkin, Cincinnati
1940	Frank McCormick, Cincinnati	1969	Willie McCovey, San Francisco	1996	Ken Caminiti, San Diego
1941	Dolph Camilli, Brooklyn	1970	Johnny Bench, Cincinnati	1997	Larry Walker, Colorado
1942	Mort Cooper, St. Louis	1971	Joe Torre, St. Louis	1998	Sammy Sosa, Chicago
1943	Stan Musial, St. Louis	1972	Johnny Bench, Cincinnati	1999	Chipper Jones, Atlanta
1944	Martin Marion, St. Louis	1973	Pete Rose, Cincinnati	2000	Jeff Kent, San Francisco
1945	Phil Cavarretta, Chicago	1974	Steve Garvey, Los Angeles	2001	Barry Bonds, San Francisco
1946	Stan Musial, St. Louis	1975	Joe Morgan, Cincinnati	2002	Barry Bonds, San Francisco
1947	Bob Elliott, Boston	1976	Joe Morgan, Cincinnati	2003	Barry Bonds, San Francisco
1948	Stan Musial, St. Louis	1977	George Foster, Cincinnati	2004	Barry Bonds, San Francisco
1949	Jackie Robinson, Brooklyn	1978	Dave Parker, Pittsburgh	2005	Albert Pujols, St. Louis
1950	Jim Konstanty, Philadelphia	1979	(tie) Keith Hernandez, St. Louis;	2006	Ryan Howard, Philadelphia
1951	Roy Campanella, Brooklyn		Willie Stargell, Pittsburgh	2007	Jimmy Rollins, Philadelphia
1952	Hank Sauer, Chicago	1980	Mike Schmidt, Philadelphia	2008	Albert Pujols, St. Louis
1953	Roy Campanella, Brooklyn	1981	Mike Schmidt, Philadelphia	2009	Albert Pujols, St. Louis
1954	Willie Mays, New York	1982	Dale Murphy, Atlanta	2010	Joey Votto, Cincinnati
1955	Roy Campanella, Brooklyn	1983	Dale Murphy, Atlanta	2011	Ryan Braun, Milwaukee
1956	Don Newcombe, Brooklyn	1984	Ryne Sandberg, Chicago	2012	Buster Posey, San Francisco
1957	Hank Aaron, Milwaukee	1985	Willie McGee, St. Louis	2013	Andrew McCutchen,
1958	Ernie Banks, Chicago	1986	Mike Schmidt, Philadelphia		Pittsburgh
1959	Ernie Banks, Chicago				

American League

Year	Player, team	Year	Player, team	Year	Player, team
1931	Lefty Grove, Philadelphia	1934	Mickey Cochrane, Detroit	1937	Charlie Gehringer, Detroit
1932	Jimmie Foxx, Philadelphia	1935	Hank Greenberg, Detroit	1938	Jimmie Foxx, Boston
1933	Jimmie Foxx, Philadelphia	1936	Lou Gehrig, New York	1939	Joe DiMaggio, New York

Year	Player, team	Year	Player, team	Year	Player, team
1940	Hank Greenberg, Detroit	1964	Brooks Robinson, Baltimore	1989	Robin Yount, Milwaukee
1941	Joe DiMaggio, New York	1965	Zoilo Versalles, Minnesota	1990	Rickey Henderson, Oakland
1942	Joe Gordon, New York	1966	Frank Robinson, Baltimore	1991	Cal Ripken Jr., Baltimore
1943	Spurgeon "Spud" Chandler, New York	1967	Carl Yastrzemski, Boston	1992	Dennis Eckersley, Oakland
1944	Hal Newhouser, Detroit	1968	Denny McLain, Detroit	1993	Frank Thomas, Chicago
1945	Hal Newhouser, Detroit	1969	Harmon Killebrew, Minnesota	1994	Frank Thomas, Chicago
1946	Ted Williams, Boston	1970	John "Boog" Powell, Baltimore	1995	Mo Vaughn, Boston
1947	Joe DiMaggio, New York	1971	Vida Blue, Oakland	1996	Juan Gonzalez, Texas
1948	Lou Boudreau, Cleveland	1972	Dick Allen, Chicago	1997	Ken Griffey Jr., Seattle
1949	Ted Williams, Boston	1973	Reggie Jackson, Oakland	1998	Juan Gonzalez, Texas
1950	Phil Rizzuto, New York	1974	Jeff Burroughs, Texas	1999	Ivan Rodriguez, Texas
1951	Yogi Berra, New York	1975	Fred Lynn, Boston	2000	Jason Giambi, Oakland
1952	Bobby Shantz, Philadelphia	1976	Thurman Munson, New York	2001	Ichiro Suzuki, Seattle
1953	Al Rosen, Cleveland	1977	Rod Carew, Minnesota	2002	Miguel Tejada, Oakland
1954	Yogi Berra, New York	1978	Jim Rice, Boston	2003	Alex Rodriguez, Texas
1955	Yogi Berra, New York	1979	Don Baylor, California	2004	Vladimir Guerrero, Anaheim
1956	Mickey Mantle, New York	1980	George Brett, Kansas City	2005	Alex Rodriguez, New York
1957	Mickey Mantle, New York	1981	Rollie Fingers, Milwaukee	2006	Justin Morneau, Minnesota
1958	Jackie Jensen, Boston	1982	Robin Yount, Milwaukee	2007	Alex Rodriguez, New York
1959	Nellie Fox, Chicago	1983	Cal Ripken Jr., Baltimore	2008	Dustin Pedroia, Boston
1960	Roger Maris, New York	1984	Willie Hernandez, Detroit	2009	Joe Mauer, Minnesota
1961	Roger Maris, New York	1985	Don Mattingly, New York	2010	Josh Hamilton, Texas
1962	Mickey Mantle, New York	1986	Roger Clemens, Boston	2011	Justin Verlander, Detroit
1963	Elston Howard, New York	1987	George Bell, Toronto	2012	Miguel Cabrera, Detroit
		1988	Jose Canseco, Oakland	2013	Miguel Cabrera, Detroit

Rookie of the Year, 1949-2013

(as selected by the Baseball Writers' Assn. of America)

1947: Jackie Robinson, Brooklyn, 1B (combined selection); 1948: Alvin Dark, Boston (NL), SS (combined selection).

National League

Year	Player, team, position	Year	Player, team, position	Year	Player, team, position
1949	Don Newcombe, Brooklyn, P	1971	Earl Williams, Atlanta, C	1992	Eric Karros, L.A., 1B
1950	Sam Jethroe, Boston, OF	1972	Jon Matlack, NY, P	1993	Mike Piazza, L.A., C
1951	Willie Mays, NY, OF	1973	Gary Matthews, San Francisco, OF	1994	Raul Mondesi, L.A., OF
1952	Joe Black, Brooklyn, P	1974	Bake McBride, St. Louis, OF	1995	Hideo Nomo, L.A., P
1953	Jim Gilliam, Brooklyn, 2B	1975	John Montefusco, San Francisco, P	1996	Todd Hollandsworth, L.A., OF
1954	Wally Moon, St. Louis, OF	1976	(tie) Butch Metzger, San Diego, P;	1997	Scott Rolen, Philadelphia, 3B
1955	Bill Virdon, St. Louis, OF		Pat Zachry, Cincinnati, P	1998	Kerry Wood, Chicago, P
1956	Frank Robinson, Cincinnati, OF	1977	Andre Dawson, Montréal, OF	1999	Scott Williamson, Cincinnati, P
1957	Jack Sanford, Philadelphia, P	1978	Bob Horner, Atlanta, 3B	2000	Rafael Furcal, Atlanta, SS
1958	Orlando Cepeda, San Francisco, 1B	1979	Rick Sutcliffe, L.A., P	2001	Albert Pujols, St. Louis, OF
1959	Willie McCovey, San Francisco, 1B	1980	Steve Howe, L.A., P	2002	Jason Jennings, Colorado, P
1960	Frank Howard, L.A., OF	1981	Fernando Valenzuela, L.A., P	2003	Dontrelle Willis, Florida, P
1961	Billy Williams, Chicago, OF	1982	Steve Sax, L.A., 2B	2004	Jason Bay, Pittsburgh, OF
1962	Ken Hubbs, Chicago, 2B	1983	Darryl Strawberry, NY, OF	2005	Ryan Howard, Philadelphia, 1B
1963	Pete Rose, Cincinnati, 2B	1984	Dwight Gooden, NY, P	2006	Hanley Ramirez, Florida, SS
1964	Richie Allen, Philadelphia, 3B	1985	Vince Coleman, St. Louis, OF	2007	Ryan Braun, Milwaukee, OF
1965	Jim Lefebvre, L.A., 2B	1986	Todd Worrell, St. Louis, P	2008	Geovany Soto, Chicago, C
1966	Tommy Helms, Cincinnati, 2B	1987	Benito Santiago, San Diego, C	2009	Chris Coghlan, Florida, OF
1967	Tom Seaver, NY, P	1988	Chris Sabo, Cincinnati, 3B	2010	Buster Posey, San Francisco, C
1968	Johnny Bench, Cincinnati, C	1989	Jerome Walton, Chicago, OF	2011	Craig Kimbrel, Atlanta, P
1969	Ted Sizemore, L.A., 2B	1990	Dave Justice, Atlanta, 1B	2012	Bryce Harper, Washington, OF
1970	Carl Morton, Montréal, P	1991	Jeff Bagwell, Houston, 1B	2013	Jose Fernandez, Miami, P

American League

Year	Player, team, position	Year	Player, team, position	Year	Player, team, position
1949	Roy Sievers, St. Louis, OF	1971	Chris Chambliss, Cleveland, 1B	1992	Pat Listach, Milwaukee, SS
1950	Walt Dropo, Boston, 1B	1972	Carlton Fisk, Boston, C	1993	Tim Salmon, California, OF
1951	Gil McDougald, NY, 3B	1973	Al Bumbry, Baltimore, OF	1994	Bob Hamelin, Kansas City, DH
1952	Harry Byrd, Philadelphia, P	1974	Mike Hargrove, Texas, 1B	1995	Marty Cordova, Minnesota, OF
1953	Harvey Kuenn, Detroit, SS	1975	Fred Lynn, Boston, OF	1996	Derek Jeter, NY, SS
1954	Bob Grim, NY, P	1976	Mark Fidrych, Detroit, P	1997	Nomar Garciaparra, Boston, SS
1955	Herb Score, Cleveland, P	1977	Eddie Murray, Baltimore, DH	1998	Ben Grieve, Oakland, OF
1956	Luis Aparicio, Chicago, SS	1978	Lou Whitaker, Detroit, 2B	1999	Carlos Beltran, Kansas City, OF
1957	Tony Kubek, NY, IF-OF	1979	(tie) John Castino, Minnesota, 3B;	2000	Kazuhiro Sasaki, Seattle, P
1958	Albie Pearson, Washington, OF		Alfredo Griffin, Toronto, SS	2001	Ichiro Suzuki, Seattle, OF
1959	Bob Allison, Washington, OF	1980	Joe Charboneau, Cleveland, OF	2002	Eric Hinske, Toronto, 3B
1960	Ron Hansen, Baltimore, SS	1981	Dave Righetti, NY, P	2003	Angel Berroa, Kansas City, SS
1961	Don Schwall, Boston, P	1982	Cal Ripken Jr., Baltimore, SS	2004	Bobby Crosby, Oakland, SS
1962	Tom Tresh, NY, IF-OF	1983	Ron Kittle, Chicago, OF	2005	Huston Street, Oakland, P
1963	Gary Peters, Chicago, P	1984	Alvin Davis, Seattle, 1B	2006	Justin Verlander, Detroit, P
1964	Tony Oliva, Minnesota, OF	1985	Ozzie Guillen, Chicago, SS	2007	Dustin Pedroia, Boston, 2B
1965	Curt Blefary, Baltimore, OF	1986	Jose Canseco, Oakland, OF	2008	Evan Longoria, Tampa Bay, 3B
1966	Tommie Agee, Chicago, OF	1987	Mark McGwire, Oakland, 1B	2009	Andrew Bailey, Oakland, P
1967	Rod Carew, Minnesota, 2B	1988	Walt Weiss, Oakland, SS	2010	Neftali Feliz, Texas, P
1968	Stan Bahnsen, NY, P	1989	Gregg Olson, Baltimore, P	2011	Jeremy Hellickson, Tampa Bay, P
1969	Lou Piniella, Kansas City, OF	1990	Sandy Alomar Jr., Cleveland, C	2012	Mike Trout, L.A., OF
1970	Thurman Munson, NY, C	1991	Chuck Knoblauch, Minnesota, 2B	2013	Wil Myers, Tampa Bay, OF

Major League Pennant Winners, 1901-75

	National League					American League			
Year	Winner	W	L	PCT	Manager	Year	Winner	W	L	PCT	Manager
1901	Pittsburgh	90	49	.647	Clarke	1901	Chicago	83	53	.610	Griffith
1902	Pittsburgh	103	36	.741	Clarke	1902	Philadelphia	83	53	.610	Mack
1903	Pittsburgh	91	49	.650	Clarke	1903	Boston	91	47	.659	Collins
1904	New York	106	47	.693	McGraw	1904	Boston	95	59	.617	Collins
1905	New York	105	48	.686	McGraw	1905	Philadelphia	92	56	.622	Mack
1906	Chicago	116	36	.763	Chance	1906	Chicago	93	58	.616	Jones
1907	Chicago	107	45	.704	Chance	1907	Detroit	92	58	.613	Jennings
1908	Chicago	99	55	.643	Chance	1908	Detroit	90	63	.588	Jennings
1909	Pittsburgh	110	42	.724	Clarke	1909	Detroit	98	54	.645	Jennings
1910	Chicago	104	50	.675	Chance	1910	Philadelphia	102	48	.680	Mack
1911	New York	99	54	.647	McGraw	1911	Philadelphia	101	50	.669	Mack
1912	New York	103	48	.682	McGraw	1912	Boston	105	47	.691	Stahl
1913	New York	101	51	.664	McGraw	1913	Philadelphia	96	57	.627	Mack
1914	Boston	94	59	.614	Stallings	1914	Philadelphia	99	53	.651	Mack
1915	Philadelphia	90	62	.592	Moran	1915	Boston	101	50	.669	Carrigan
1916	Brooklyn	94	60	.610	Robinson	1916	Boston	91	63	.591	Carrigan
1917	New York	98	56	.636	McGraw	1917	Chicago	100	54	.649	Rowland
1918	Chicago	84	45	.651	Mitchell	1918	Boston	75	51	.595	Barrow
1919	Cincinnati	96	44	.686	Moran	1919	Chicago	88	52	.629	Gleason
1920	Brooklyn	93	61	.604	Robinson	1920	Cleveland	98	56	.636	Speaker
1921	New York	94	59	.614	McGraw	1921	New York	98	55	.641	Huggins
1922	New York	93	61	.604	McGraw	1922	New York	94	60	.610	Huggins
1923	New York	95	58	.621	McGraw	1923	New York	98	54	.645	Huggins
1924	New York	93	60	.608	McGraw	1924	Washington	92	62	.597	Harris
1925	Pittsburgh	95	58	.621	McKechnie	1925	Washington	96	55	.636	Harris
1926	St. Louis	89	65	.578	Hornsby	1926	New York	91	63	.591	Huggins
1927	Pittsburgh	94	60	.610	Bush	1927	New York	110	44	.714	Huggins
1928	St. Louis	95	59	.617	McKechnie	1928	New York	101	53	.656	Huggins
1929	Chicago	98	54	.645	McCarthy	1929	Philadelphia	104	46	.693	Mack
1930	St. Louis	92	62	.597	Street	1930	Philadelphia	102	52	.662	Mack
1931	St. Louis	101	53	.656	Street	1931	Philadelphia	107	45	.704	Mack
1932	Chicago	90	64	.584	Hornsby, Grimm	1932	New York	107	47	.695	McCarthy
1933	New York	91	61	.599	Terry	1933	Washington	99	53	.651	Cronin
1934	St. Louis	95	58	.621	Frisch	1934	Detroit	101	53	.656	Cochrane
1935	Chicago	100	54	.649	Grimm	1935	Detroit	93	58	.616	Cochrane
1936	New York	92	62	.597	Terry	1936	New York	102	51	.667	McCarthy
1937	New York	95	57	.625	Terry	1937	New York	102	52	.662	McCarthy
1938	Chicago	89	63	.586	Grimm, Hartnett	1938	New York	99	53	.651	McCarthy
1939	Cincinnati	97	57	.630	McKechnie	1939	New York	106	45	.702	McCarthy
1940	Cincinnati	100	53	.654	McKechnie	1940	Detroit	90	64	.584	Baker
1941	Brooklyn	100	54	.649	Durocher	1941	New York	101	53	.656	McCarthy
1942	St. Louis	106	48	.688	Southworth	1942	New York	103	51	.669	McCarthy
1943	St. Louis	105	49	.682	Southworth	1943	New York	98	56	.636	McCarthy
1944	St. Louis	105	49	.682	Southworth	1944	St. Louis	89	65	.578	Sewell
1945	Chicago	98	56	.636	Grimm	1945	Detroit	88	65	.575	O'Neill
1946	St. Louis	98	58	.628	Dyer	1946	Boston	104	50	.675	Cronin
1947	Brooklyn	94	60	.610	Shotton	1947	New York	97	57	.630	Harris
1948	Boston	91	62	.595	Southworth	1948	Cleveland	97	58	.626	Boudreau
1949	Brooklyn	97	57	.630	Shotton	1949	New York	97	57	.630	Stengel
1950	Philadelphia	91	63	.591	Sawyer	1950	New York	98	56	.636	Stengel
1951	New York	98	59	.624	Durocher	1951	New York	98	56	.636	Stengel
1952	Brooklyn	96	57	.627	Dressen	1952	New York	95	59	.617	Stengel
1953	Brooklyn	105	49	.682	Dressen	1953	New York	99	52	.656	Stengel
1954	New York	97	57	.630	Durocher	1954	Cleveland	111	43	.721	Lopez
1955	Brooklyn	98	55	.641	Alston	1955	New York	96	58	.623	Stengel
1956	Brooklyn	93	61	.604	Alston	1956	New York	97	57	.630	Stengel
1957	Milwaukee	95	59	.617	Haney	1957	New York	98	56	.636	Stengel
1958	Milwaukee	92	62	.597	Haney	1958	New York	92	62	.597	Stengel
1959	Los Angeles	88	68	.564	Alston	1959	Chicago	94	60	.610	Lopez
1960	Pittsburgh	95	59	.617	Murtaugh	1960	New York	97	57	.630	Stengel
1961	Cincinnati	93	61	.604	Hutchinson	1961	New York	109	53	.673	Houk
1962	San Francisco	103	62	.624	Dark	1962	New York	96	66	.593	Houk
1963	Los Angeles	99	63	.611	Alston	1963	New York	104	57	.646	Houk
1964	St. Louis	93	69	.574	Keane	1964	New York	99	63	.611	Berra
1965	Los Angeles	97	65	.599	Alston	1965	Minnesota	102	60	.630	Mele
1966	Los Angeles	95	67	.586	Alston	1966	Baltimore	97	63	.606	Bauer
1967	St. Louis	101	60	.627	Schoendienst	1967	Boston	92	70	.568	Williams
1968	St. Louis	97	65	.599	Schoendienst	1968	Detroit	103	59	.636	Smith
1969	NY Mets	100	62	.617	Hodges	1969	Baltimore	109	53	.673	Weaver
1970	Cincinnati	102	60	.630	Anderson	1970	Baltimore	108	54	.667	Weaver
1971	Pittsburgh	97	65	.599	Murtaugh	1971	Baltimore	101	57	.639	Weaver
1972	Cincinnati	95	59	.617	Anderson	1972	Oakland	93	62	.600	Williams
1973	NY Mets	82	79	.509	Berra	1973	Oakland	94	68	.580	Williams
1974	Los Angeles	102	60	.630	Alston	1974	Oakland	90	72	.556	Dark
1975	Cincinnati	108	54	.667	Anderson	1975	Boston	95	65	.594	Johnson

Major League Pennant Winners, 1976-2014

National League

	East				West				Pennant
Year	Winner	W	L	PCT	Manager	Winner	W	L	PCT	Manager	winner
1976	Philadelphia	101	61	.623	Ozark	Cincinnati	102	60	.630	Anderson	Cincinnati
1977	Philadelphia	101	61	.623	Ozark	Los Angeles	98	64	.605	Lasorda	Los Angeles
1978	Philadelphia	90	72	.556	Ozark	Los Angeles	95	67	.586	Lasorda	Los Angeles
1979	Pittsburgh	98	64	.605	Tanner	Cincinnati	90	71	.559	McNamara	Pittsburgh

National League

Year	Winner (East)	W	L	PCT	Manager	Winner (West)	W	L	PCT	Manager	Pennant winner
1980	Philadelphia	91	71	.562	Green	Houston	93	70	.571	Virdon	Philadelphia
1981(a)	Philadelphia	34	21	.618	Green	Los Angeles	36	21	.632	Lasorda	(c)
1981(b)	Montréal	30	23	.566	Williams, Fanning	Houston	33	20	.623	Virdon	Los Angeles
1982	St. Louis	92	70	.568	Herzog	Atlanta	89	73	.549	Torre	St. Louis
1983	Philadelphia	90	72	.556	Corrales, Owens	Los Angeles	91	71	.562	Lasorda	Philadelphia
1984	Chicago	96	65	.596	Frey	San Diego	92	70	.568	Williams	San Diego
1985	St. Louis	101	61	.623	Herzog	Los Angeles	95	67	.586	Lasorda	St. Louis
1986	NY Mets	108	54	.667	Johnson	Houston	96	66	.593	Lanier	New York
1987	St. Louis	95	67	.586	Herzog	San Francisco	90	72	.556	Craig	St. Louis
1988	NY Mets	100	60	.625	Johnson	Los Angeles	94	67	.584	Lasorda	Los Angeles
1989	Chicago	93	69	.571	Zimmer	San Francisco	92	70	.568	Craig	San Francisco
1990	Pittsburgh	95	67	.586	Leyland	Cincinnati	91	71	.562	Piniella	Cincinnati
1991	Pittsburgh	98	64	.605	Leyland	Atlanta	94	68	.580	Cox	Atlanta
1992	Pittsburgh	96	66	.593	Leyland	Atlanta	98	64	.605	Cox	Atlanta
1993	Philadelphia	97	65	.599	Fregosi	Atlanta	104	58	.642	Cox	Philadelphia

Year	Division	Winner	W	L	PCT	Manager	Playoffs	Pennant winner
1994(d)	East	Montréal	74	40	.649	Alou	—	—
	Central	Cincinnati	66	48	.579	Johnson		
	West	Los Angeles	58	56	.509	Lasorda		
1995	East	Atlanta	90	54	.625	Cox	Atlanta 3, Colorado* 1	Atlanta
	Central	Cincinnati	85	59	.590	Johnson	Cincinnati 3, Los Angeles 0	
	West	Los Angeles	78	66	.542	Lasorda	Atlanta 4, Cincinnati 0	
1996	East	Atlanta	96	66	.593	Cox	Atlanta 3, Los Angeles* 0	Atlanta
	Central	St. Louis	88	74	.543	La Russa	St. Louis 3, San Diego 0	
	West	San Diego	91	71	.562	Bochy	Atlanta 4, St. Louis 3	
1997	East	Atlanta	101	61	.623	Cox	Atlanta 3, Houston 0	Florida*
	Central	Houston	84	78	.519	Dierker	Florida* 3, San Francisco 0	(Leyland)
	West	San Francisco	90	72	.556	Baker	Florida* 4, Atlanta 2	
1998	East	Atlanta	106	56	.654	Cox	Atlanta 3, Chicago* 0	San Diego
	Central	Houston	102	60	.630	Dierker	San Diego 3, Houston 1	
	West	San Diego	98	64	.605	Bochy	San Diego 4, Atlanta 2	
1999	East	Atlanta	103	59	.636	Cox	Atlanta 3, Houston 1	Atlanta
	Central	Houston	97	65	.599	Dierker, Galante	New York* 3, Arizona 1	
	West	Arizona	100	62	.617	Showalter	Atlanta 4, New York* 2	
2000	East	Atlanta	95	67	.586	Cox	St. Louis 3, Atlanta 0	New York*
	Central	St. Louis	95	67	.586	La Russa	New York* 3, San Francisco 1	(Valentine)
	West	San Francisco	97	65	.599	Baker	New York* 4, St. Louis 1	
2001	East	Atlanta	88	74	.543	Cox	Atlanta 3, Houston 0	Arizona
	Central	Houston	93	69	.574	Dierker	Arizona 3, St. Louis* 2	
	West	Arizona	92	70	.568	Brenly	Arizona 4, Atlanta 1	
2002	East	Atlanta	101	59	.631	Cox	St. Louis 3, Arizona 0	San Francisco*
	Central	St. Louis	97	65	.599	La Russa	San Francisco* 3, Atlanta 2	(Baker)
	West	Arizona	98	64	.605	Brenly	San Francisco* 4, St. Louis 1	
2003	East	Atlanta	101	61	.623	Cox	Chicago 3, Atlanta 2	Florida*
	Central	Chicago	88	74	.543	Baker	Florida* 3, San Francisco 1	(McKeon)
	West	San Francisco	100	61	.621	Alou	Florida* 4, Chicago 3	
2004	East	Atlanta	96	66	.593	Cox	Houston* 3, Atlanta 2	St. Louis
	Central	St. Louis	105	57	.648	La Russa	St. Louis 3, Los Angeles 1	
	West	Los Angeles	93	69	.574	Tracy	St. Louis 4, Houston* 3	
2005	East	Atlanta	90	72	.556	Cox	St. Louis 3, San Diego 0	Houston*
	Central	St. Louis	100	62	.617	La Russa	Houston* 3, Atlanta 1	(Garner)
	West	San Diego	82	80	.506	Bochy	Houston* 4, St. Louis 2	
2006	East	New York	97	65	.599	Randolph	New York 3, Los Angeles* 0	St. Louis
	Central	St. Louis	83	78	.516	La Russa	St. Louis 3, San Diego 1	
	West	San Diego	88	74	.543	Bochy	St. Louis 4, New York 3	
2007	East	Philadelphia	89	73	.549	Manuel	Colorado* 3, Philadelphia 0	Colorado*
	Central	Chicago	85	77	.525	Piniella	Arizona 3, Chicago 0	(Hurdle)
	West	Arizona	90	72	.556	Melvin	Colorado* 4, Arizona 0	
2008	East	Philadelphia	92	70	.568	Manuel	Philadelphia 3, Milwaukee* 1	Philadelphia
	Central	Chicago	97	64	.602	Piniella	Los Angeles 3, Chicago 0	
	West	Los Angeles	84	78	.519	Torre	Philadelphia 4, Los Angeles 1	
2009	East	Philadelphia	93	69	.574	Manuel	Philadelphia 3, Colorado* 1	Philadelphia
	Central	St. Louis	91	71	.562	La Russa	Los Angeles 3, St. Louis 0	
	West	Los Angeles	95	67	.586	Torre	Philadelphia 4, Los Angeles 1	
2010	East	Philadelphia	97	65	.599	Manuel	San Francisco 3, Atlanta* 1	San Francisco
	Central	Cincinnati	91	71	.562	Baker	Philadelphia 3, Cincinnati 0	
	West	San Francisco	92	70	.568	Bochy	San Francisco 4, Philadelphia 2	
2011	East	Philadelphia	102	60	.630	Manuel	Milwaukee 3, Arizona 2	St. Louis*
	Central	Milwaukee	96	66	.593	Roenicke	St. Louis* 3, Philadelphia 2	(La Russa)
	West	Arizona	94	68	.580	Gibson	St. Louis* 4, Milwaukee 2	
2012	East	Washington	98	64	.605	Johnson	#St. Louis* 6, Atlanta* 3	San Francisco
	Central	Cincinnati	97	65	.599	Baker	*St. Louis* 3, Washington 2	
	West	San Francisco	94	68	.580	Bochy	San Francisco 3, Cincinnati 2	
							San Francisco 4, St. Louis* 3	
2013	East	Atlanta	96	66	.593	González	#Pittsburgh* 6, Cincinnati* 2	St. Louis
	Central	St. Louis	97	65	.599	Matheny	St. Louis 3, Pittsburgh* 2	
	West	Los Angeles	92	70	.568	Mattingly	Los Angeles 3, Atlanta 1	
							St. Louis 4, Los Angeles 2	
2014	East	Washington	96	66	.593	Williams	#San Francisco* 8, Pittsburgh* 0	San Francisco*
	Central	St. Louis	90	72	.556	Matheny	San Francisco* 3, Washington 1	(Bochy)
	West	Los Angeles	94	68	.580	Mattingly	St. Louis 3, Los Angeles 1	
							San Francisco* 4, St. Louis 1	

American League

Year	Winner (East)	W	L	PCT	Manager	Winner (West)	W	L	PCT	Manager	Pennant winner
1976	New York	97	62	.610	Martin	Kansas City	90	72	.556	Herzog	New York
1977	New York	100	62	.617	Martin	Kansas City	102	60	.630	Herzog	New York
1978	New York	100	63	.613	Martin, Lemon	Kansas City	92	70	.568	Herzog	New York
1979	Baltimore	102	57	.642	Weaver	California	88	74	.543	Fregosi	Baltimore

Year	East Winner	W	L	PCT	Manager	West Winner	W	L	PCT	Manager	Pennant winner
1980	New York	103	59	.636	Howser	Kansas City	97	65	.599	Frey	Kansas City
1981(a)	New York	34	22	.607	Michael	Oakland	37	23	.617	Martin	(c)
1981(b)	Milwaukee	31	22	.585	Rodgers	Kansas City	30	23	.566	Frey, Howser	New York
1982	Milwaukee	95	67	.586	Rodgers, Kuenn	California	93	69	.574	Mauch	Milwaukee
1983	Baltimore	98	64	.605	Altobelli	Chicago	99	63	.611	La Russa	Baltimore
1984	Detroit	104	58	.642	Anderson	Kansas City	84	78	.519	Howser	Detroit
1985	Toronto	99	62	.615	Cox	Kansas City	91	71	.562	Howser	Kansas City
1986	Boston	95	66	.590	McNamara	California	92	70	.568	Mauch	Boston
1987	Detroit	98	64	.605	Anderson	Minnesota	85	77	.525	Kelly	Minnesota
1988	Boston	89	73	.549	McNamara, Morgan	Oakland	104	58	.642	La Russa	Oakland
1989	Toronto	89	73	.549	Williams, Gaston	Oakland	99	63	.611	La Russa	Oakland
1990	Boston	88	74	.543	Morgan	Oakland	103	59	.636	La Russa	Oakland
1991	Toronto	91	71	.562	Gaston, Tenace	Minnesota	95	67	.586	Kelly	Minnesota
1992	Toronto	96	66	.593	Gaston	Oakland	96	66	.593	La Russa	Toronto
1993	Toronto	95	67	.586	Gaston	Chicago	94	68	.580	Lamont	Toronto

Year	Division	Winner	W	L	PCT	Manager	Playoffs	Pennant winner
1994(d)	East	New York	70	43	.619	Showalter	—	—
	Central	Chicago	67	46	.593	Lamont		
	West	Texas	52	62	.456	Kennedy		
1995	East	Boston	86	58	.597	Kennedy	Cleveland 3, Boston 0	Cleveland
	Central	Cleveland	100	44	.694	Hargrove	Seattle 3, New York* 2	
	West	Seattle	79	66	.545	Piniella	Cleveland 4, Seattle 2	
1996	East	New York	92	70	.568	Torre	Baltimore* 3, Cleveland 1	New York
	Central	Cleveland	99	62	.615	Hargrove	New York 3, Texas 1	
	West	Texas	90	72	.556	Oates	New York 4, Baltimore* 1	
1997	East	Baltimore	98	64	.605	Johnson	Baltimore 3, Seattle 1	Cleveland
	Central	Cleveland	86	75	.534	Hargrove	Cleveland 3, New York* 2	
	West	Seattle	90	72	.556	Piniella	Cleveland 4, Baltimore 2	
1998	East	New York	114	48	.704	Torre	New York 3, Texas 0	New York
	Central	Cleveland	89	73	.549	Hargrove	Cleveland 3, Boston* 1	
	West	Texas	88	74	.543	Oates	New York 4, Cleveland 2	
1999	East	New York	98	64	.605	Torre	New York 3, Texas 0	New York
	Central	Cleveland	97	65	.599	Hargrove	Boston* 3, Cleveland 2	
	West	Texas	95	67	.586	Oates	New York 4, Boston* 1	
2000	East	New York	87	74	.540	Torre	New York 3, Oakland 2	New York
	Central	Chicago	95	67	.586	Manuel	Seattle* 3, Chicago 0	
	West	Oakland	91	70	.565	Howe	New York 4, Seattle* 2	
2001	East	New York	95	65	.594	Torre	Seattle 3, Cleveland 2	New York
	Central	Cleveland	91	71	.562	Manuel	New York 3, Oakland* 2	
	West	Seattle	116	46	.716	Piniella	New York 4, Seattle 1	
2002	East	New York	103	58	.640	Torre	Anaheim* 3, New York 1	Anaheim*
	Central	Minnesota	94	67	.584	Gardenhire	Minnesota 3, Oakland 2	(Scioscia)
	West	Oakland	103	59	.636	Howe	Anaheim* 4, Minnesota 1	
2003	East	New York	101	61	.623	Torre	New York 3, Minnesota 1	New York
	Central	Minnesota	90	72	.556	Gardenhire	Boston* 3, Oakland 2	
	West	Oakland	96	66	.593	Macha	New York 4, Boston* 3	
2004	East	New York	101	61	.623	Torre	New York 3, Minnesota 1	Boston*
	Central	Minnesota	92	70	.568	Gardenhire	Boston* 3, Anaheim 0	(Francona)
	West	Anaheim	92	70	.568	Scioscia	Boston* 4, New York 3	
2005	East	New York	95	67	.586	Torre	Chicago 3, Boston* 0	Chicago
	Central	Chicago	99	63	.611	Guillen	Los Angeles 3, New York 2	
	West	Los Angeles	95	67	.586	Scioscia	Chicago 4, Los Angeles 1	
2006	East	New York	97	65	.599	Torre	Oakland 3, Minnesota 0	Detroit*
	Central	Minnesota	96	66	.593	Gardenhire	Detroit* 3, New York 1	(Leyland)
	West	Oakland	93	69	.574	Macha	Detroit* 4, Oakland 0	
2007	East	Boston	96	66	.593	Francona	Boston 3, Los Angeles 0	Boston
	Central	Cleveland	96	66	.593	Wedge	Cleveland 3, New York* 1	
	West	Los Angeles	94	68	.580	Scioscia	Boston 4, Cleveland 3	
2008	East	Tampa Bay	97	65	.599	Maddon	Tampa Bay 3, Chicago 1	Tampa Bay
	Central	Chicago	89	74	.546	Guillen	Boston* 3, Los Angeles 1	
	West	Los Angeles	100	62	.617	Scioscia	Tampa Bay 4, Boston* 3	
2009	East	New York	103	59	.636	Girardi	New York 3, Minnesota 0	New York
	Central	Minnesota	87	76	.534	Gardenhire	Los Angeles 3, Boston* 0	
	West	Los Angeles	97	65	.599	Scioscia	New York 4, Los Angeles 2	
2010	East	Tampa Bay	96	66	.593	Maddon	New York* 3, Minnesota 0	Texas
	Central	Minnesota	94	68	.580	Gardenhire	Texas 3, Tampa Bay 2	
	West	Texas	90	72	.556	Washington	Texas 4, New York* 2	
2011	East	New York	97	65	.599	Girardi	Detroit 3, New York 2	Texas
	Central	Detroit	95	67	.586	Leyland	Texas 3, Tampa Bay* 1	
	West	Texas	96	66	.593	Washington	Texas 4, Detroit 2	
2012	East	New York	95	67	.586	Girardi	#Baltimore* 5, Texas* 1	Detroit
	Central	Detroit	88	74	.543	Leyland	New York 3, Baltimore* 2	
	West	Oakland	94	68	.580	Melvin	Detroit 3, Oakland 2 / Detroit 4, New York 0	
2013	East	Boston	97	65	.599	Farrell	#Tampa Bay* 4, Cleveland* 0	Boston
	Central	Detroit	93	69	.574	Leyland	Boston 3, Tampa Bay* 1	
	West	Oakland	96	66	.593	Melvin	Detroit 3, Oakland 2 / Boston 4, Detroit 2	
2014	East	Baltimore	96	66	.593	Showalter	#Kansas City* 9, Oakland* 8	Kansas City
	Central	Detroit	90	72	.556	Ausmus	Kansas City* 3, Los Angeles 0	(Yost)
	West	Los Angeles	98	64	.605	Scioscia	Baltimore 3, Detroit 0 / Kansas City* 4, Baltimore 0	

* = Wild card team. If pennant winner is wild card team, manager's name is given in parentheses. # = Single-game wild card playoff (debuted in 2012). (a) First half. (b) Second half. (c) Montréal, L.A., NY Yankees, and Oakland won the divisional playoffs. (d) In Aug. 1994, a players' strike began that caused the cancellation of the remainder of the season, the playoffs, and the World Series. Teams listed as division "winners" for 1994 were leading their divisions at the time of the strike.

World Series Results, 1903-2014

Year	Result	Year	Result	Year	Result
1903	Boston AL 5, Pittsburgh NL 3	1941	New York AL 4, Brooklyn NL 1	1978	New York AL 4, Los Angeles NL 2
1904	No series	1942	St. Louis NL 4, New York AL 1	1979	Pittsburgh NL 4, Baltimore AL 3
1905	New York NL 4, Philadelphia AL 1	1943	New York AL 4, St. Louis NL 1	1980	Philadelphia NL 4, Kansas City AL 2
1906	Chicago AL 4, Chicago NL 2	1944	St. Louis NL 4, St. Louis AL 2	1981	Los Angeles NL 4, New York AL 2
1907	Chicago NL 4, Detroit AL 0, 1 tie	1945	Detroit AL 4, Chicago NL 3	1982	St. Louis NL 4, Milwaukee AL 3
1908	Chicago NL 4, Detroit AL 1	1946	St. Louis NL 4, Boston AL 3	1983	Baltimore AL 4, Philadelphia NL 1
1909	Pittsburgh NL 4, Detroit AL 3	1947	New York AL 4, Brooklyn NL 3	1984	Detroit AL 4, San Diego NL 1
1910	Philadelphia AL 4, Chicago NL 1	1948	Cleveland AL 4, Boston NL 2	1985	Kansas City AL 4, St. Louis NL 3
1911	Philadelphia AL 4, New York NL 2	1949	New York AL 4, Brooklyn NL 1	1986	New York NL 4, Boston AL 3
1912	Boston AL 4, New York NL 3, 1 tie	1950	New York AL 4, Philadelphia NL 0	1987	Minnesota AL 4, St. Louis NL 3
1913	Philadelphia AL 4, New York NL 1	1951	New York AL 4, New York NL 2	1988	Los Angeles NL 4, Oakland AL 1
1914	Boston NL 4, Philadelphia AL 0	1952	New York AL 4, Brooklyn NL 3	1989	Oakland AL 4, San Francisco NL 0
1915	Boston AL 4, Philadelphia NL 1	1953	New York AL 4, Brooklyn NL 2	1990	Cincinnati NL 4, Oakland AL 0
1916	Boston AL 4, Brooklyn NL 1	1954	New York NL 4, Cleveland AL 0	1991	Minnesota AL 4, Atlanta NL 3
1917	Chicago AL 4, New York NL 2	1955	Brooklyn NL 4, New York AL 3	1992	Toronto AL 4, Atlanta NL 2
1918	Boston AL 4, Chicago NL 2	1956	New York AL 4, Brooklyn NL 3	1993	Toronto AL 4, Philadelphia NL 2
1919	Cincinnati NL 5, Chicago AL 3	1957	Milwaukee NL 4, New York AL 3	1994	No series due to strike
1920	Cleveland AL 5, Brooklyn NL 2	1958	New York AL 4, Milwaukee NL 3	1995	Atlanta NL 4, Cleveland AL 2
1921	New York NL 5, New York AL 3	1959	Los Angeles NL 4, Chicago AL 2	1996	New York AL 4, Atlanta NL 2
1922	New York NL 4, New York AL 0, 1 tie	1960	Pittsburgh NL 4, New York AL 3	1997	Florida NL 4, Cleveland AL 3
1923	New York AL 4, New York NL 2	1961	New York AL 4, Cincinnati NL 1	1998	New York AL 4, San Diego NL 0
1924	Washington AL 4, New York NL 3	1962	New York AL 4, San Francisco NL 3	1999	New York AL 4, Atlanta NL 0
1925	Pittsburgh NL 4, Washington AL 3	1963	Los Angeles NL 4, New York AL 0	2000	New York AL 4, New York NL 1
1926	St. Louis NL 4, New York AL 3	1964	St. Louis NL 4, New York AL 3	2001	Arizona NL 4, New York AL 3
1927	New York AL 4, Pittsburgh NL 0	1965	Los Angeles NL 4, Minnesota AL 3	2002	Anaheim AL 4, San Francisco NL 3
1928	New York AL 4, St. Louis NL 0	1966	Baltimore AL 4, Los Angeles NL 0	2003	Florida NL 4, New York AL 2
1929	Philadelphia AL 4, Chicago NL 1	1967	St. Louis NL 4, Boston AL 3	2004	Boston AL 4, St. Louis NL 0
1930	Philadelphia AL 4, St. Louis NL 2	1968	Detroit AL 4, St. Louis NL 3	2005	Chicago AL 4, Houston NL 0
1931	St. Louis NL 4, Philadelphia AL 3	1969	New York NL 4, Baltimore AL 1	2006	St. Louis NL 4, Detroit AL 1
1932	New York AL 4, Chicago NL 0	1970	Baltimore AL 4, Cincinnati NL 1	2007	Boston AL 4, Colorado NL 0
1933	New York NL 4, Washington AL 1	1971	Pittsburgh NL 4, Baltimore AL 3	2008	Philadelphia NL 4, Tampa Bay AL 1
1934	St. Louis NL 4, Detroit AL 3	1972	Oakland AL 4, Cincinnati NL 3	2009	New York AL 4, Philadelphia NL 2
1935	Detroit AL 4, Chicago NL 2	1973	Oakland AL 4, New York NL 3	2010	San Francisco NL 4, Texas AL 1
1936	New York AL 4, New York NL 2	1974	Oakland AL 4, Los Angeles NL 1	2011	St. Louis NL 4, Texas AL 3
1937	New York AL 4, New York NL 1	1975	Cincinnati NL 4, Boston AL 3	2012	San Francisco NL 4, Detroit AL 0
1938	New York AL 4, Chicago NL 0	1976	Cincinnati NL 4, New York AL 0	2013	Boston AL 4, St. Louis NL 2
1939	New York AL 4, Cincinnati NL 0	1977	New York AL 4, Los Angeles NL 2	2014	San Fran. NL 4, Kansas City AL 3
1940	Cincinnati NL 4, Detroit AL 3				

World Series Most Valuable Player, 1955-2014

Year	Player, position, team	Year	Player, position, team	Year	Player, position, team
1955	Johnny Podres, P, Brooklyn	1977	Reggie Jackson, OF, NY (AL)	1996	John Wetteland, P, NY (AL)
1956	Don Larsen, P, NY (AL)	1978	Bucky Dent, SS, NY (AL)	1997	Livan Hernandez, P, Florida
1957	Lew Burdette, P, Milwaukee (NL)	1979	Willie Stargell, 1B, Pittsburgh	1998	Scott Brosius, 3B, NY (AL)
1958	Bob Turley, P, NY (AL)	1980	Mike Schmidt, 3B, Philadelphia	1999	Mariano Rivera, P, NY (AL)
1959	Larry Sherry, P, Los Angeles (NL)	1981	Ron Cey, 3B, Los Angeles (NL);	2000	Derek Jeter, SS, NY (AL)
1960[1]	Bobby Richardson, 2B, NY (AL)		Pedro Guerrero, OF, Los Angeles;	2001	Curt Schilling, P, Arizona;
1961	Whitey Ford, P, NY (AL)		Steve Yeager, C, Los Angeles		Randy Johnson, P, Arizona
1962	Ralph Terry, P, NY (AL)	1982	Darrell Porter, C, St. Louis	2002	Troy Glaus, 3B, Anaheim
1963	Sandy Koufax, P, Los Angeles (NL)	1983	Rick Dempsey, C, Baltimore	2003	Josh Beckett, P, Florida
1964	Bob Gibson, P, St. Louis	1984	Alan Trammell, SS, Detroit	2004	Manny Ramirez, OF, Boston
1965	Sandy Koufax, P, Los Angeles (NL)	1985	Bret Saberhagen, P, Kansas City	2005	Jermaine Dye, OF, Chicago (AL)
1966	Frank Robinson, OF, Baltimore	1986	Ray Knight, 3B, NY (NL)	2006	David Eckstein, SS, St. Louis
1967	Bob Gibson, P, St. Louis	1987	Frank Viola, P, Minnesota	2007	Mike Lowell, 3B, Boston
1968	Mickey Lolich, P, Detroit	1988	Orel Hershiser, P, Los Angeles (NL)	2008	Cole Hamels, P, Philadelphia
1969	Donn Clendenon, 1B, NY (NL)	1989	Dave Stewart, P, Oakland	2009	Hideki Matsui, DH, NY (AL)
1970	Brooks Robinson, 3B, Baltimore	1990	Jose Rijo, P, Cincinnati	2010	Edgar Renteria, SS, San Francisco
1971	Roberto Clemente, OF, Pittsburgh	1991	Jack Morris, P, Minnesota	2011	David Freese, 3B, St. Louis
1972	Gene Tenace, C, Oakland	1992	Pat Borders, C, Toronto	2012	Pablo Sandoval, 3B, San Francisco
1973	Reggie Jackson, OF, Oakland	1993	Paul Molitor, DH, Toronto	2013	David Ortiz, DH, Boston
1974	Rollie Fingers, P, Oakland	1994	No series due to strike	2014	Madison Bumgarner, P, San Francisco
1975	Pete Rose, 3B, Cincinnati	1995	Tom Glavine, P, Atlanta		
1976	Johnny Bench, C, Cincinnati				

(1) Richardson won the MVP although Pittsburgh beat New York.

World Series Won-Lost Records, by Franchise

Since beginning of "modern" era in 1901. Figures represent overall Series wins, not individual games.

Team	Wins	Losses	Team	Wins	Losses
New York Yankees	27	13	Toronto Blue Jays	2	0
St. Louis Cardinals	11	8	New York Mets	2	3
Philadelphia/Kansas City/Oakland A's	9	5	Cleveland Indians	2	3
Boston Red Sox	8	4	Philadelphia Phillies	2	5
New York/San Francisco Giants	8	12	Chicago Cubs	2	8
Brooklyn/Los Angeles Dodgers	6	12	L.A./California/Anaheim/L.A. Angels	1	0
Pittsburgh Pirates	5	2	Arizona Diamondbacks	1	0
Cincinnati Reds	5	4	Kansas City Royals	1	2
Detroit Tigers	4	7	Houston Astros	0	1
Chicago White Sox	3	2	Seattle Pilots/Milwaukee Brewers	0	1
Washington Senators/Minnesota Twins	3	3	Tampa Bay Rays	0	1
St. Louis Browns/Baltimore Orioles	3	4	Colorado Rockies	0	1
Boston/Milwaukee/Atlanta Braves	3	6	San Diego Padres	0	2
Florida Marlins	2	0	Texas Rangers	0	2

All-Time World Series Career Leaders
(through 2014)

Batting Leaders

Batter (min. 50 PA)	H	AB	AVG	Batter (min. 50 PA)	H	AB	AVG
1. David Ortiz	20	44	.455	6. Hal McRae	18	45	.400
2. Pablo Sandoval	20	47	.426	7. Lou Brock	34	87	.391
3. Johnny "Pepper" Martin	23	55	.418	8. Marquis Grissom	30	77	.390
4. Paul Molitor	23	55	.418	9. Thurman Munson	25	67	.373
5. Lance Berkman	16	39	.410	10. George Brett	19	51	.373

Games Played		Hits		Runs	
Yogi Berra	75	Yogi Berra	71	Mickey Mantle	42
Mickey Mantle	65	Mickey Mantle	59	Yogi Berra	41
Elston Howard	54	Frankie Frisch	58	Babe Ruth	37
Hank Bauer	53	Joe DiMaggio	54	Derek Jeter	32
Gil McDougald	53	Derek Jeter	50	Lou Gehrig	30
Phil Rizzuto	52	Hank Bauer	46	Joe DiMaggio	27
Joe DiMaggio	51	Pee Wee Reese	46	Roger Maris	26
Frankie Frisch	50	Gil McDougald	45	Elston Howard	25
Pee Wee Reese	44	Phil Rizzuto	45	Gil McDougald	23
Roger Maris	41	Lou Gehrig	43	Jackie Robinson	22
Babe Ruth	41				

Runs Batted In		Home Runs		Stolen Bases	
Mickey Mantle	40	Mickey Mantle	18	Lou Brock	14
Yogi Berra	39	Babe Ruth	15	Eddie Collins	14
Lou Gehrig	35	Yogi Berra	12	Frank Chance	10
Babe Ruth	33	Duke Snider	11	Dave Lopes	10
Joe DiMaggio	30	Lou Gehrig	10	Phil Rizzuto	10
Bill Skowron	29	Reggie Jackson	10	Frankie Frisch	9
Duke Snider	26	Joe DiMaggio	8	Kenny Lofton	9
		Frank Robinson	8	Honus Wagner	9
		Bill Skowron	8	Johnny Evers	8

Pitching Leaders

Games Pitched		Wins		Strikeouts		Saves	
Mariano Rivera	24	Whitey Ford	10	Whitey Ford	94	Mariano Rivera	11
Whitey Ford	22	Bob Gibson	7	Bob Gibson	92	Rollie Fingers	6
Mike Stanton	20	Allie Reynolds	7	Allie Reynolds	62	Johnny Murphy	4
Rollie Fingers	16	Red Ruffing	7	Sandy Koufax	61	Robb Nen	4
Jeff Nelson	16	Chief Bender	6	Red Ruffing	61	Allie Reynolds	4
Allie Reynolds	15	Lefty Gomez	6	Chief Bender	59	John Wetteland	4
Bob Turley	15	Waite Hoyt	6	George Earnshaw	56	Roy Face	3
Clay Carroll	14	Three Finger Brown	5	Andy Pettitte	56	Neftali Feliz	3
Clem Labine	13	Jack Coombs	5	John Smoltz	52	Firpo Marberry	3
Andy Pettitte	13	Catfish Hunter	5	Roger Clemens	49	Will McEnaney	3
Mark Wohlers	13	Christy Mathewson	5	Waite Hoyt	49	Tug McGraw	3
Jeremy Affeldt	12	Herb Pennock	5	Christy Mathewson	48	Jonathan Papelbon	3
Waite Hoyt	12	Andy Pettitte	5	Bob Turley	46	Herb Pennock	3
Catfish Hunter	12	Vic Raschi	5			Troy Percival	3
Art Nehf	12					Sergio Romo	3
						Kent Tekulve	3
						Todd Worrell	3

All-Star Baseball Games, 1933-2014

Year	Winner, score	Host team	Year	Winner, score	Host team	Year	Winner, score	Host team
1933*	American, 4-2	Chicago (AL)	1960*	National, 6-0	New York (AL)	1987	National, 2-0[5]	Oakland
1934*	American, 9-7	New York (NL)	1961*	National, 5-4[3]	San Francisco	1988	American, 2-1	Cincinnati
1935*	American, 4-1	Cleveland	1961	Called-rain, 1-1	Boston	1989	American, 5-3	California
1936*	National, 4-3	Boston (NL)	1962*	National, 3-1[3]	Washington	1990	American, 2-0	Chicago (NL)
1937*	American, 8-3	Washington	1962	American, 9-4	Chicago (NL)	1991	American, 4-2	Toronto
1938*	National, 4-1	Cincinnati	1963*	National, 5-3	Cleveland	1992	American, 13-6	San Diego
1939*	American, 3-1	New York (AL)	1964*	National, 7-4	New York (NL)	1993	American, 9-3	Baltimore
1940*	National, 4-0	St. Louis (NL)	1965*	National, 6-5	Minnesota	1994	National, 8-7[3]	Pittsburgh
1941*	American, 7-5	Detroit	1966*	National, 2-1[3]	St. Louis	1995	National, 3-2	Texas
1942	American, 3-1	New York (NL)	1967*	National, 2-1[4]	California	1996	National, 6-0	Philadelphia
1943	American, 5-3	Philadelphia (AL)	1968	National, 1-0	Houston	1997	American, 3-1	Cleveland
1944	National, 7-1	Pittsburgh	1969*	National, 9-3	Washington	1998	American, 13-8	Colorado
1945	Not played		1970*	National, 5-4[2]	Cincinnati	1999	American, 4-1	Boston
1946*	American, 12-0	Boston (AL)	1971	American, 6-4	Detroit	2000	American, 6-3	Atlanta
1947*	American, 2-1	Chicago (NL)	1972	National, 4-3[3]	Atlanta	2001	American, 4-1	Seattle
1948*	American, 5-2	St. Louis (AL)	1973	National, 7-1	Kansas City	2002	Tie, 7-7[6]	Milwaukee
1949*	American, 11-7	Brooklyn	1974	National, 7-2	Pittsburgh	2003	American, 7-6[7]	Chicago (AL)
1950*	National, 4-3[1]	Chicago (AL)	1975	National, 6-3	Milwaukee	2004	American, 9-4	Houston
1951*	National, 8-3	Detroit	1976	National, 7-1	Philadelphia	2005	American, 7-5	Detroit
1952*	National, 3-2	Philadelphia (NL)	1977	National, 7-5	New York (AL)	2006	American, 3-2	Pittsburgh
1953*	National, 5-1	Cincinnati	1978	National, 7-3	San Diego	2007	American, 5-4	San Francisco
1954*	American, 11-9	Cleveland	1979	National, 7-6	Seattle	2008	American, 4-3[4]	New York (AL)
1955*	National, 6-5[2]	Milwaukee	1980	National, 4-2	Los Angeles (NL)	2009	American, 4-3	St. Louis
1956*	National, 7-3	Washington	1981	National, 5-4	Cleveland	2010	National, 3-1	Los Angeles (AL)
1957*	American, 6-5	St. Louis	1982	National, 4-1	Montréal	2011	National, 5-1	Arizona
1958*	American, 4-3	Baltimore	1983	American, 13-3	Chicago (AL)	2012	National, 8-0	Kansas City
1959*	National, 5-4	Pittsburgh	1984	National, 3-1	San Francisco	2013	American, 3-0	New York (NL)
1959*	National, 5-3	Los Angeles (NL)	1985	National, 6-1	Minnesota	2014	American, 5-3	Minnesota
1960*	National, 5-3	Kansas City	1986	American, 3-2	Houston			

* = Day game. **Note:** Two all-star games played 1959-62 to help increase players' pension fund. (1) 14 innings. (2) 12 innings. (3) 10 innings. (4) 15 innings. (5) 13 innings. (6) Commissioner's decision—game called in 11th inning when both teams ran out of pitchers. (7) Under rule change beginning in 2003, league winning All-Star game earned World Series home-field advantage.

MLB Stadiums, 2014

Team	Stadium (year opened)	Surface	Distances (ft) LF	Center	RF	Seating capacity[1]
Arizona Diamondbacks	Chase Field (1998)	Grass	330	407	335	48,635
Atlanta Braves	Turner Field (1997)	Grass	335	400	330	49,377
Chicago Cubs	Wrigley Field (1914)	Grass	355	400	353	41,072
Cincinnati Reds	Great American Ball Park (2003)	Grass	328	404	325	42,319
Colorado Rockies	Coors Field (1995)	Grass	347	415	350	50,480
Los Angeles Dodgers	Dodger Stadium (1962)	Grass	330	395	330	56,000
Miami Marlins	Marlins Park (2012)	Grass	344	422	335	37,442
Milwaukee Brewers	Miller Park (2001)	Grass	344	400	345	41,900
New York Mets	Citi Field (2009)	Grass	335	408	330	41,922
Philadelphia Phillies	Citizens Bank Park (2004)	Grass	329	401	330	43,651
Pittsburgh Pirates	PNC Park at North Shore (2001)	Grass	325	399	320	38,362
St. Louis Cardinals	Busch Stadium (2006)	Grass	336	400	335	43,975
San Diego Padres	Petco Park (2004)	Grass	336	396	322	42,524
San Francisco Giants	AT&T Park (2000)	Grass	339	399	309	41,915
Washington Nationals	Nationals Park (2008)	Grass	336	402	335	41,408
Baltimore Orioles	Oriole Park at Camden Yards (1992)	Grass	333	400	318	45,971
Boston Red Sox	Fenway Park (1912)	Grass	310	390	302	37,071[2]
Chicago White Sox	U.S. Cellular Field (1991)	Grass	330	400	335	40,615
Cleveland Indians	Progressive Field (1994)	Grass	325	405	325	42,404
Detroit Tigers	Comerica Park (2000)	Grass	345	420	330	41,681
Houston Astros	Minute Maid Park (2000)	Grass	315	435	326	42,060
Kansas City Royals	Kauffman Stadium (1973)	Grass	330	410	330	37,903
Los Angeles Angels	Angel Stadium of Anaheim (1966)	Grass	347	396	348	45,483
Minnesota Twins	Target Field (2010)	Grass	339	404	328	39,021
New York Yankees	Yankee Stadium (2009)	Grass	318	408	314	49,642
Oakland Athletics	O.co Coliseum (1968)	Grass	330	400	330	35,067
Seattle Mariners	Safeco Field (1999)	Grass	331	401	326	47,476
Tampa Bay Rays	Tropicana Field (1990)	Astroturf	315	404	322	31,042
Texas Rangers	Globe Life Park in Arlington (1994)	Grass	332	400	325	48,114
Toronto Blue Jays	Rogers Centre (1989)	Astroturf	328	400	328	49,286

(1) As of 2014 season. (2) For day games; night game capacity is 37,499.

Major League Franchise Shifts and Additions

1953: Boston Braves (NL) became Milwaukee Braves.
1954: St. Louis Browns (AL) became Baltimore Orioles.
1955: Philadelphia Athletics (AL) became Kansas City Athletics.
1958: New York Giants (NL) became San Francisco Giants.
1958: Brooklyn Dodgers (NL) became L.A. Dodgers.
1961: Washington Senators (AL) became Minnesota Twins.
1961: L.A. Angels enfranchised by the AL.
1961: Washington Senators enfranchised by the AL, replacing the former Washington club, whose franchise moved to Minneapolis-St. Paul.
1962: Houston Colt .45's enfranchised by the NL.
1962: New York Mets enfranchised by the NL.
1966: Milwaukee Braves (NL) became Atlanta Braves.
1968: Kansas City Athletics (AL) became Oakland Athletics.

1969: Kansas City Royals and Seattle Pilots enfranchised by the AL; Montréal Expos and San Diego Padres enfranchised by the NL.
1970: Seattle Pilots (AL) became Milwaukee Brewers.
1971: Washington Senators (AL) became Texas Rangers (Dallas-Fort Worth area).
1977: Toronto Blue Jays and Seattle Mariners enfranchised by the AL.
1993: Colorado Rockies (Denver) and Florida Marlins (Miami) enfranchised by the NL.
1998: Tampa Bay Devil Rays began play in the AL; Arizona Diamondbacks (Phoenix) began play in the NL (both teams enfranchised in 1995). Milwaukee Brewers moved from the AL to the NL.
2005: Montréal Expos (NL) became Washington Nationals.
2013: Houston Astros moved from the NL to the AL.

Little League World Series, 1947-2014

The Little League World Series is played annually in Williamsport, PA.

Year	Winning team; opponent	Score
1947	Williamsport, PA; Lock Haven, PA	16-7
1948	Lock Haven, PA; St. Petersburg, FL	6-5
1949	Hammonton, NJ; Pensacola, FL	5-0
1950	Houston, TX; Bridgeport, CT	2-1
1951	Stamford, CT; Austin, TX	3-0
1952	Norwalk, CT; Monongahela, PA	4-3
1953	Birmingham, AL; Schenectady, NY	1-0
1954	Schenectady, NY; Colton, CA	7-5
1955	Morrisville, PA; Merchantville, NJ	4-3
1956	Roswell, NM; Delaware, NJ	3-1
1957	Mexico; La Mesa, CA	4-0
1958	Mexico; Kankakee, IL	10-1
1959	Hamtramck, MI; Auburn, CA	12-0
1960	Levittown, PA; Ft. Worth, TX	5-0
1961	El Cajon, CA; El Campo, TX	4-2
1962	San Jose, CA; Kankakee, IL	3-0
1963	Granada Hills, CA; Stratford, CT	2-1
1964	Staten Island, NY; Mexico	4-0
1965	Windsor Locks, CT; Ontario, Canada	3-1
1966	Houston, TX; W. New York, NJ	8-2
1967	Tokyo, Japan; Chicago, IL	4-1
1968	Osaka, Japan; Richmond, VA	1-0
1969	Taiwan; Santa Clara, CA	5-0
1970	Wayne, NJ; Campbell, CA	2-0
1971	Taiwan; Gary, IN	12-3
1972	Taiwan; Hammond, IN	6-0
1973	Taiwan; Tucson, AZ	12-0
1974	Taiwan; Red Bluff, CA	12-1
1975	Lakewood, NJ; Tampa, FL	4-3
1976	Tokyo, Japan; Campbell, CA	10-3
1977	Taiwan; El Cajon, CA	7-2
1978	Taiwan; Danville, CA	11-1
1979	Taiwan; Campbell, CA	2-1
1980	Taiwan; Tampa, FL	4-3
1981	Taiwan; Tampa, FL	4-2
1982	Kirkland, WA; Taiwan	6-0
1983	Marietta, GA; Dominican Republic	3-1
1984	South Korea; Altamonte Springs, FL	6-2
1985	South Korea; Mexico	7-1
1986	Taiwan; Tucson, AZ	12-0
1987	Taiwan; Irvine, CA	21-1
1988	Taiwan; Pearl City, HI	10-0
1989	Trumbull, CT; Chinese Taipei	5-2
1990	Taiwan; Shippensburg, PA	9-0
1991	Taiwan; Danville, CA	11-0
1992	Long Beach, CA; Philippines	6-0[1]
1993	Long Beach, CA; Panama	3-2
1994	Venezuela; Northridge, CA	4-3
1995	Taiwan; Spring, TX	17-3
1996	Taiwan; Cranston, RI	13-3
1997	Mexico; Mission Viejo, CA	5-0
1998	Toms River, NJ; Japan	12-9
1999	Japan; Phenix City, AL	5-0
2000	Venezuela; Bellaire, TX	3-2
2001	Japan; Apopka, FL	2-1
2002	Louisville, KY; Japan	1-0
2003	Tokyo, Japan; East Boynton Beach, FL	10-1
2004	Curaçao; Conejo Valley of Thousand Oaks, CA	5-2
2005	Ewa Beach, HI; Curaçao, Neth. Antilles	7-6
2006	Columbus, GA; Kawaguchi City, Japan	2-1
2007	Macon, GA; Tokyo, Japan	3-2
2008	Waipahu, HI; Mexico	12-3
2009	Chula Vista, CA; Taiwan	6-3
2010	Tokyo, Japan; Waipahu, HI	4-1
2011	Huntington Beach, CA; Hamamatsu, Japan	2-1
2012	Tokyo, Japan; Goodlettsville, TN	12-2
2013	Tokyo, Japan; Chula Vista, CA	6-4
2014	Seoul, South Korea; Chicago, IL	8-4

(1) Philippines won 15-4 but was disqualified for using ineligible players. Long Beach was awarded title by forfeit 6-0 (1 run per inning).

Manager of the Year, 1983-2013

1983	(NL) Tommy Lasorda, L.A.		1994	(NL) Felipe Alou, Montréal		2004	(NL) Bobby Cox, Atlanta
	(AL) Tony La Russa, Chicago			(AL) Buck Showalter, NY			(AL) Buck Showalter, Texas
1984	(NL) Jim Frey, Chicago		1995	(NL) Don Baylor, Colorado		2005	(NL) Bobby Cox, Atlanta
	(AL) Sparky Anderson, Detroit			(AL) Lou Piniella, Seattle			(AL) Ozzie Guillen, Chicago
1985	(NL) Whitey Herzog, St. Louis		1996	(NL) Bruce Bochy, San Diego		2006	(NL) Joe Girardi, Florida
	(AL) Bobby Cox, Toronto			(AL) (tie) Joe Torre, NY;			(AL) Jim Leyland, Detroit
1986	(NL) Hal Lanier, Houston			Johnny Oates, Texas		2007	(NL) Bob Melvin, Arizona
	(AL) John McNamara, Boston		1997	(NL) Dusty Baker, San Francisco			(AL) Eric Wedge, Cleveland
1987	(NL) Buck Rodgers, Montréal			(AL) Davey Johnson, Baltimore		2008	(NL) Lou Piniella, Chicago
	(AL) Sparky Anderson, Detroit		1998	(NL) Larry Dierker, Houston			(AL) Joe Maddon, Tampa Bay
1988	(NL) Tommy Lasorda, L.A.			(AL) Joe Torre, NY		2009	(NL) Jim Tracy, Colorado
	(AL) Tony La Russa, Oakland		1999	(NL) Jack McKeon, Cincinnati			(AL) Mike Scioscia, L.A.
1989	(NL) Don Zimmer, Chicago			(AL) Jimy Williams, Boston		2010	(NL) Bud Black, San Diego
	(AL) Frank Robinson, Baltimore		2000	(NL) Dusty Baker, San Francisco			(AL) Ron Gardenhire, Minnesota
1990	(NL) Jim Leyland, Pittsburgh			(AL) Jerry Manuel, Chicago		2011	(NL) Kirk Gibson, Arizona
	(AL) Jeff Torborg, Chicago		2001	(NL) Larry Bowa, Philadelphia			(AL) Joe Maddon, Tampa Bay
1991	(NL) Bobby Cox, Atlanta			(AL) Lou Piniella, Seattle		2012	(NL) Davey Johnson, Washington
	(AL) Tom Kelly, Minnesota		2002	(NL) Tony La Russa, St. Louis			(AL) Bob Melvin, Oakland
1992	(NL) Jim Leyland, Pittsburgh			(AL) Mike Scioscia, Anaheim		2013	(NL) Clint Hurdle, Pittsburgh
	(AL) Tony La Russa, Oakland		2003	(NL) Jack McKeon, Florida			(AL) Terry Francona, Cleveland
1993	(NL) Dusty Baker, San Francisco			(AL) Tony Pena, Kansas City			
	(AL) Gene Lamont, Chicago						

National Baseball Hall of Fame and Museum, Cooperstown, NY

Player must generally be retired for five seasons before eligibility. Babe Ruth (1936), Lou Gehrig (1939), Joe DiMaggio (1955), and Roberto Clemente (1973) were inducted in fewer than five years. # = Players chosen in first year of eligibility or earlier. * = 2014 inductee.

#Aaron, Hank	Crawford, Sam	Heilmann, Harry	Mathewson, Christy[1]	Selee, Frank
Alexander, Grover	Cronin, Joe	#Henderson, Rickey	#Mays, Willie	Sewell, Joe
Alomar, Roberto	Cummings, W. A.	Herman, Billy	Mazeroski, Bill	Simmons, Al
Alston, Walt	Cuyler, Hazen "Kiki"	Herzog, Whitey	McCarthy, Joe	Sisler, George
Anderson, George	Dandridge, Ray	Hill, Pete	McCarthy, Thomas	Slaughter, Enos
Anson, Cap	Davis, George	Hooper, Harry	#McCovey, Willie	Smith, Hilton
Aparicio, Luis	Dawson, Andre	Hornsby, Rogers	McGinnity, Joe	#Smith, Ozzie
Appling, Luke	Day, Leon	Hoyt, Waite	McGowan, Bill	Snider, Duke
Ashburn, Richie	Dean, Jay Hanna "Dizzy"	Hubbard, Cal	McGraw, John	Southworth, Billy
Averill, Earl	Delahanty, Ed	Hubbell, Carl	McKechnie, Bill	#Spahn, Warren
Baker, Frank "Home Run"	Dickey, Bill	Huggins, Miller	McPhee, John "Bid"	Spalding, Albert
Bancroft, Dave	Dihigo, Martín	Hulbert, William	Medwick, Joe	Speaker, Tris
#Banks, Ernie	#DiMaggio, Joe	Hunter, James "Catfish"	Mendez, Jose	#Stargell, Willie
Barlick, Al	#Doby, Larry	Irvin, Monte	Mize, Johnny	Stearnes, Norman
Barrow, Edward G.	Doerr, Bobby	#Jackson, Reggie	#Molitor, Paul	Stengel, Casey
Beckley, Jake	Dreyfuss, Barney	Jackson, Travis	#Morgan, Joe	Sutter, Bruce
Bell, James "Cool Papa"	Drysdale, Don	Jenkins, Ferguson	#Murray, Eddie	Suttles, George "Mule"
#Bench, Johnny	Duffy, Hugh	Jennings, Hugh	#Musial, Stan	Sutton, Don
Bender, Charles "Chief"	Durocher, Leo	Johnson, Byron "Ban"	Newhouser, Hal	Taylor, Ben
Berra, Lawrence "Yogi"	#Eckersley, Dennis	Johnson, Walter[1]	Nichols, Kid	Terry, Bill
Blyleven, Bert	Evans, Billy	Johnson, William "Judy"	Niekro, Phil	*#Thomas, Frank
#Boggs, Wade	Evers, John	Joss, Addie	O'Day, Hank	Thompson, Sam
Bottomley, Jim	Ewing, Buck	#Kaline, Al	O'Malley, Walter	Tinker, Joe
Boudreau, Lou	Faber, Urban "Red"	Keefe, Timothy	O'Rourke, James	*Torre, Joe
Bresnahan, Roger	#Feller, Bob	Keeler, William	Ott, Mel	Torriente, Cristobal
#Brett, George	Ferrell, Rick	Kell, George	Paige, Satchel	Traynor, Harold J. "Pie"
#Brock, Lou	Fingers, Rollie	Kelley, Joe	#Palmer, Jim	Vance, Arthur "Dazzy"
Brouthers, Dan	Fisk, Carlton	Kelly, George	Pennock, Herb	Vaughan, Joseph "Arky"
Brown, Mordecai	Flick, Elmer H.	Kelly, King	Perez, Tony	Veeck, Bill
Brown, Ray	Ford, Whitey	Killebrew, Harmon	Perry, Gaylord	Waddell, Rube
Brown, Willard	Foster, Andrew "Rube"	Kiner, Ralph	Plank, Ed	Wagner, Honus[1]
Bulkeley, Morgan C.	Foster, Bill	Klein, Chuck	Pompez, Alex	Wallace, Roderick
Bunning, Jim	Fox, Nellie	Klem, Bill	Posey, Cum(berland)	Walsh, Ed
Burkett, Jesse C.	Foxx, Jimmie	#Koufax, Sandy	#Puckett, Kirby	Waner, Lloyd
Campanella, Roy	Frick, Ford	Kubek, Tony	Radbourn, Charlie	Waner, Paul
#Carew, Rod	Frisch, Frank	Kuhn, Bowie	Reese, Pee Wee	Ward, John
Carey, Max	Galvin, James "Pud"	Lajoie, Napoleon	Rice, Jim	Weaver, Earl
#Carlton, Steve	*#Gehrig, Lou	Landis, Kenesaw M.	Rice, Sam	Weiss, George
Carter, Gary	Gehringer, Charles	Larkin, Barry	Rickey, Branch	Welch, Mickey
Cartwright, Alexander	#Gibson, Bob	Lasorda, Tom	#Ripken, Cal, Jr.	Wells, Willie
Cepeda, Orlando	Gibson, Josh	Lazzeri, Tony	Rixey, Eppa	Wheat, Zach
Chadwick, Henry	Giles, Warren	Lemon, Bob	Rizzuto, Phil "Scooter"	White, Deacon
Chance, Frank	Gillick, Pat	Leonard, Buck	Roberts, Robin	White, Sol
Chandler, Albert "Happy"	*#Glavine, Tom	Lindstrom, Fred	#Robinson, Brooks	Wilhelm, Hoyt
Charleston, Oscar	Gomez, Lefty	Lloyd, Pop	#Robinson, Frank	Wilkinson, J. L.
Chesbro, John	Gordon, Joe	Lombardi, Ernie	#Robinson, Jackie	Williams, Billy
Chylak, Nestor	Goslin, Leon "Goose"	Lopez, Al	Robinson, Wilbert	Williams, Dick
Clarke, Fred	Gossage, Rich	Lyons, Ted	Rogan, Joe "Bullet"	Williams, Joe
Clarkson, John	Grant, Frank	Mack, Connie	Roush, Edd	#Williams, Ted
#Clemente, Roberto	Greenberg, Hank	Mackey, James "Biz"	Ruffing, Red	Willis, Vic
Cobb, Ty[1]	Griffith, Clark	MacPhail, Larry	Ruppert, Jacob	Wilson, Hack
Cochrane, Mickey	Grimes, Burleigh	MacPhail, Lee	Rusie, Amos	Wilson, Jud
Collins, Eddie	Grove, Lefty	Madden, Bill	#Ruth, Babe[1]	#Winfield, Dave
Collins, James	#Gwynn, Tony	*#Maddux, Greg	#Ryan, Nolan	Wright, George
Combs, Earle	Hafey, Charles "Chick"	Manley, Effa	Sandberg, Ryne	Wright, Harry
Comiskey, Charles A.	Haines, Jesee	#Mantle, Mickey	Santo, Ron	Wynn, Early
Conlan, John "Jocko"	Hamilton, Bill	Manush, Henry	Santop, Louis	#Yastrzemski, Carl
Connolly, Thomas H.	Hanlon, Ned	Maranville, Walter	Schalk, Ray	Yawkey, Tom
Connor, Roger	Harridge, Will	Marichal, Juan	#Schmidt, Mike	Young, Cy
Cooper, Andy	Harris, Bucky	Marquard, Rube	Schoendienst, Red	Youngs, Ross
Coveleski, Stan	Hartnett, Gabby	Mathews, Eddie	#Seaver, Tom	#Yount, Robin
*Cox, Bobby	Harvey, Doug			

(1) Player inducted in 1936, the year the Hall of Fame began.

BASKETBALL

San Antonio Defeats Heat to Claim 2014 NBA Title

The San Antonio Spurs toppled the two-time defending champion Miami Heat, four games to one, in the 2014 NBA Finals to win their fifth NBA title since 1999. The Spurs dominated Miami throughout the series, claiming each of their victories by at least 15 points, including a 104-87 title-clinching Game 5 June 15, 2014, at the AT&T Center in San Antonio. Spurs small forward Kawhi Leonard scored 71 points in the final three games of the series, including 22 in the final game, and was voted NBA Finals MVP. San Antonio head coach Gregg Popovich and veteran forward Tim Duncan led the Spurs to all five titles. Miami's LeBron James averaged 28.2 points per game in the Finals and had 35 points in the Heat's lone win, 98-96, in Game 2 in San Antonio June 8. On June 5, the Spurs won Game 1 in San Antonio, 110-95, despite playing the game without air conditioning due to an electrical malfunction.

San Antonio's league-best 62-win season included a franchise-record 19-game winning streak that began at home over Detroit Feb. 26, 2014, and ended in a 106-94 loss at Oklahoma City Apr. 3. The Thunder's Kevin Durant averaged 32 points per game and was the NBA's leading scorer for the fourth time in five years. Durant's 2013-14 season included a streak of 41 games with at least 25 points, third-longest in NBA history behind Wilt Chamberlain (80 games) and Oscar Robertson (46). The Thunder lost to the Spurs in six games in the Western Conference finals. The Indiana Pacers (56-26) earned top seed in the Eastern Conference playoffs but fell to Miami for the second year in a row in the conference finals.

Adam Silver took over as NBA commissioner from David Stern on Feb. 1, 2014, and was forced to address a major incident during the playoffs involving L.A. Clippers owner Donald Sterling and offensive racial comments he had made, which were recorded and made public. Silver announced Apr. 29, 2014, that Sterling was banned for life from any association with the Clippers or the NBA. Former Microsoft executive Steve Ballmer bought the team Aug. 12 for a record $2 bil from Shelly Sterling, Sterling's estranged wife, though Sterling unsuccessfully sued to prevent the sale.

NBA Final Standings, 2013-14

(playoff seeding in parentheses)

Eastern Conference	W	L	PCT	GB	Western Conference	W	L	PCT	GB
Atlantic Division					**Northwest Division**				
Toronto Raptors (3)	48	34	.585	—	Oklahoma City Thunder (2)	59	23	.720	—
Brooklyn Nets (6)	44	38	.537	4	Portland Trail Blazers (5)	54	28	.659	5
New York Knicks	37	45	.451	11	Minnesota Timberwolves	40	42	.488	19
Boston Celtics	25	57	.305	23	Denver Nuggets	36	46	.439	23
Philadelphia 76ers	19	63	.232	29	Utah Jazz	25	57	.305	34
Central Division	W	L	PCT	GB	**Pacific Division**	W	L	PCT	GB
Indiana Pacers (1)	56	26	.683	—	L.A. Clippers (3)	57	25	.695	—
Chicago Bulls (4)	48	34	.585	8	Golden State Warriors (6)	51	31	.622	6
Cleveland Cavaliers	33	49	.402	23	Phoenix Suns	48	34	.585	9
Detroit Pistons	29	53	.354	27	Sacramento Kings	28	54	.341	29
Milwaukee Bucks	15	67	.183	41	L.A. Lakers	27	55	.329	30
Southeast Division	W	L	PCT	GB	**Southwest Division**	W	L	PCT	GB
Miami Heat (2)	54	28	.659	—	San Antonio Spurs (1)	62	20	.756	—
Washington Wizards (5)	44	38	.537	10	Houston Rockets (4)	54	28	.659	8
Charlotte Bobcats (7)	43	39	.524	11	Memphis Grizzlies (7)	50	32	.610	12
Atlanta Hawks (8)	38	44	.463	16	Dallas Mavericks (8)	49	33	.598	13
Orlando Magic	23	59	.280	31	New Orleans Pelicans	34	48	.415	28

Note: The Washington Wizards earned the no. 5 seed over Brooklyn in the East due to a better head-to-head record (3-0); the Houston Rockets earned the no. 4 seed over Portland in the West due to a better head-to-head record (3-1).

NBA Playoff Results, 2014

Eastern Conference
Indiana defeated Atlanta, 4 games to 3
Miami defeated Charlotte, 4 games to 0
Brooklyn defeated Toronto, 4 games to 3
Washington defeated Chicago, 4 games to 1
Indiana defeated Washington, 4 games to 2
Miami defeated Brooklyn, 4 games to 1
Miami defeated Indiana, 4 games to 2

Western Conference
San Antonio defeated Dallas, 4 games to 3
Oklahoma City defeated Memphis, 4 games to 3
L.A. Clippers defeated Golden State, 4 games to 3
Portland defeated Houston, 4 games to 2
San Antonio defeated Portland, 4 games to 1
Oklahoma City defeated the L.A. Clippers, 4 games to 2
San Antonio defeated Oklahoma City, 4 games to 2

Championship
San Antonio defeated Miami, 4 games to 1 (110-95, 96-98, 111-92, 107-86, 104-87)

NBA Regular Season Individual Highs, 2013-14

Minutes, game: 60, Jimmy Butler, Chicago v. Orlando, Jan. 15 (3 OT)
Points, game: 62, Carmelo Anthony, New York v. Charlotte, Jan. 24
Field goals, game: 23, Carmelo Anthony, New York v. Charlotte, Jan. 24
Field goal attempts, game: 37, Rudy Gay, Toronto v. Houston, Nov. 11 (2 OT)
3-pointers, game: 10, Joe Johnson, Brooklyn v. Philadelphia, Dec. 16; C. J. Miles, Cleveland v. Philadelphia, Jan. 7; Chandler Parsons, Houston v. Memphis, Jan. 24; Terrence Ross, Toronto v. L.A. Clippers, Jan. 25; Trevor Ariza, Washington v. Houston, Feb. 12; J.R. Smith, New York v. Miami, Apr. 6
3-pt attempts, game: 22, J.R. Smith, New York v. Miami, Apr. 6
Free throws, game: 22, Kevin Durant, Oklahoma City v. Utah, Oct. 30; James Harden, Houston v. Memphis, Dec. 26

Free throw attempts, game: 25, James Harden, Houston v. Memphis, Dec. 26; Dwight Howard, Houston v. San Antonio, Jan. 28
Rebounds, game: 29, Timofey Mozgov, Denver v. Golden State, Apr. 10
Assists, game: 18, Brandon Jennings, Detroit v. Phoenix, Jan. 1; Rajon Rondo, Boston v. Detroit, Mar. 9
Steals, game: 9, Michael Carter-Williams, Philadelphia v. Miami, Oct. 30
Blocked shots, game: 9, Anthony Davis, New Orleans v. Philadelphia, Nov. 16; DeAndre Jordan, L.A. Clippers v. Sacramento, Nov. 29
Minutes played, season: 3,122, Kevin Durant, Oklahoma City
Off. rebounds, season: 440, Andre Drummond, Detroit
Def. rebounds, season: 783, DeAndre Jordan, L.A. Clippers
Personal fouls, season: 273, Andre Drummond, Detroit

NBA Finals MVP, 1969-2014

Year	Player, team	Year	Player, team	Year	Player, team
1969	Jerry West, L.A. Lakers	1984	Larry Bird, Boston	1999	Tim Duncan, San Antonio
1970	Willis Reed, New York	1985	Kareem Abdul-Jabbar,	2000	Shaquille O'Neal, L.A. Lakers
1971	Lew Alcindor (Kareem Abdul-		L.A. Lakers	2001	Shaquille O'Neal, L.A. Lakers
	Jabbar), Milwaukee	1986	Larry Bird, Boston	2002	Shaquille O'Neal, L.A. Lakers
1972	Wilt Chamberlain, L.A. Lakers	1987	Magic Johnson, L.A. Lakers	2003	Tim Duncan, San Antonio
1973	Willis Reed, New York	1988	James Worthy, L.A. Lakers	2004	Chauncey Billups, Detroit
1974	John Havlicek, Boston	1989	Joe Dumars, Detroit	2005	Tim Duncan, San Antonio
1975	Rick Barry, Golden State	1990	Isiah Thomas, Detroit	2006	Dwyane Wade, Miami
1976	JoJo White, Boston	1991	Michael Jordan, Chicago	2007	Tony Parker, San Antonio
1977	Bill Walton, Portland	1992	Michael Jordan, Chicago	2008	Paul Pierce, Boston
1978	Wes Unseld, Washington	1993	Michael Jordan, Chicago	2009	Kobe Bryant, L.A. Lakers
1979	Dennis Johnson, Seattle	1994	Hakeem Olajuwon, Houston	2010	Kobe Bryant, L.A. Lakers
1980	Magic Johnson, L.A. Lakers	1995	Hakeem Olajuwon, Houston	2011	Dirk Nowitzki, Dallas
1981	Cedric Maxwell, Boston	1996	Michael Jordan, Chicago	2012	LeBron James, Miami
1982	Magic Johnson, L.A. Lakers	1997	Michael Jordan, Chicago	2013	LeBron James, Miami
1983	Moses Malone, Philadelphia	1998	Michael Jordan, Chicago	2014	Kawhi Leonard, San Antonio

NBA Finals All-Time Statistical Leaders

(At the end of the 2014 NBA Finals. * = Active in 2013-14 season. Minimum 10 games played.)

Scoring average leader	GP	FG	FT	PTS	AVG	Scoring average leader	GP	FG	FT	PTS	AVG
Rick Barry	10	138	87	363	36.3	Hakeem Olajuwon	17	187	91	467	27.5
Michael Jordan	35	438	258	1,176	33.6	Elgin Baylor	44	442	227	1,161	26.4
Jerry West	55	612	455	1,679	30.5	Julius Erving	22	216	128	561	25.5
Shaquille O'Neal	30	340	185	865	28.8	*Kobe Bryant	37	333	223	937	25.3
Bob Pettit	25	241	227	709	28.4	Joe Fulks	11	84	104	272	24.7

Games Played		Rebounds		Assists	
Bill Russell	70	Bill Russell	1,718	Magic Johnson	584
Sam Jones	64	Wilt Chamberlain	862	Bob Cousy	400
Kareem Abdul-Jabbar	56	Elgin Baylor	593	Bill Russell	315
Jerry West	55	Kareem Abdul-Jabbar	507	Jerry West	306
Tom Heinsohn	52	Tom Heinsohn	473	Dennis Johnson	228

NBA Scoring Leaders, 1947-2014

(Average points per game; 58 games minimum in 2013-14; prior season minimums vary.)

Year	Player, team	PTS	AVG	Year	Player, team	PTS	AVG
1947	Joe Fulks, Philadelphia	1,389	23.2	1981	Adrian Dantley, Utah	2,452	30.7
1948	Max Zaslofsky, Chicago	1,007	21.0	1982	George Gervin, San Antonio	2,551	32.3
1949	George Mikan, Minneapolis	1,698	28.3	1983	Alex English, Denver	2,326	28.4
1950	George Mikan, Minneapolis	1,865	27.4	1984	Adrian Dantley, Utah	2,418	30.6
1951	George Mikan, Minneapolis	1,932	28.4	1985	Bernard King, New York	1,809	32.9
1952	Paul Arizin, Philadelphia	1,674	25.4	1986	Dominique Wilkins, Atlanta	2,366	30.3
1953	Neil Johnston, Philadelphia	1,564	22.3	1987	Michael Jordan, Chicago	3,041	37.1
1954	Neil Johnston, Philadelphia	1,759	24.4	1988	Michael Jordan, Chicago	2,868	35.0
1955	Neil Johnston, Philadelphia	1,631	22.7	1989	Michael Jordan, Chicago	2,633	32.5
1956	Bob Pettit, St. Louis	1,849	25.7	1990	Michael Jordan, Chicago	2,753	33.6
1957	Paul Arizin, Philadelphia	1,817	25.6	1991	Michael Jordan, Chicago	2,580	31.5
1958	George Yardley, Detroit	2,001	27.8	1992	Michael Jordan, Chicago	2,404	30.1
1959	Bob Pettit, St. Louis	2,105	29.2	1993	Michael Jordan, Chicago	2,541	32.6
1960	Wilt Chamberlain, Philadelphia	2,707	37.6	1994	David Robinson, San Antonio	2,383	29.8
1961	Wilt Chamberlain, Philadelphia	3,033	38.4	1995	Shaquille O'Neal, Orlando	2,315	29.3
1962	Wilt Chamberlain, Philadelphia	4,029	50.4	1996	Michael Jordan, Chicago	2,491	30.4
1963	Wilt Chamberlain, San Francisco	3,586	44.8	1997	Michael Jordan, Chicago	2,431	29.6
1964	Wilt Chamberlain, San Francisco	2,948	36.9	1998	Michael Jordan, Chicago	2,357	28.7
1965	Wilt Chamberlain, San Francisco-Phil.	2,534	34.7	1999	Allen Iverson, Philadelphia	1,284	26.8
1966	Wilt Chamberlain, Philadelphia	2,649	33.5	2000	Shaquille O'Neal, L.A. Lakers	2,344	29.7
1967	Rick Barry, San Francisco	2,775	35.6	2001	Allen Iverson, Philadelphia	2,207	31.1
1968	Dave Bing, Detroit	2,142	27.1	2002	Allen Iverson, Philadelphia	1,883	31.4
1969	Elvin Hayes, San Diego	2,327	28.4	2003	Tracy McGrady, Orlando	2,407	32.1
1970	Jerry West, L.A. Lakers	2,309	31.2	2004	Tracy McGrady, Orlando	1,878	28.0
1971	Lew Alcindor (Kareem Abdul-Jabbar), Milw.	2,596	31.7	2005	Allen Iverson, Philadelphia	2,302	30.7
1972	Kareem Abdul-Jabbar, Milwaukee	2,822	34.8	2006	Kobe Bryant, L.A. Lakers	2,832	35.4
1973	Nate Archibald, Kansas City-Omaha	2,719	34.0	2007	Kobe Bryant, L.A. Lakers	2,430	31.6
1974	Bob McAdoo, Buffalo	2,261	30.6	2008	LeBron James, Cleveland	2,250	30.0
1975	Bob McAdoo, Buffalo	2,831	34.5	2009	Dwyane Wade, Miami	2,386	30.2
1976	Bob McAdoo, Buffalo	2,427	31.1	2010	Kevin Durant, Oklahoma City	2,472	30.1
1977	Pete Maravich, New Orleans	2,273	31.1	2011	Kevin Durant, Oklahoma City	2,161	27.7
1978	George Gervin, San Antonio	2,232	27.2	2012	Kevin Durant, Oklahoma City	1,850	28.0
1979	George Gervin, San Antonio	2,365	29.6	2013	Carmelo Anthony, New York	1,920	28.7
1980	George Gervin, San Antonio	2,585	33.1	2014	Kevin Durant, Oklahoma City	2,593	32.0

NBA Most Valuable Player, 1956-2014

Year	Player, team	Year	Player, team	Year	Player, team
1956	Bob Pettit, St. Louis	1963	Bill Russell, Boston	1970	Willis Reed, New York
1957	Bob Cousy, Boston	1964	Oscar Robertson, Cincinnati	1971	Lew Alcindor (Abdul-Jabbar), Milw.
1958	Bill Russell, Boston	1965	Bill Russell, Boston	1972	Kareem Abdul-Jabbar, Milwaukee
1959	Bob Pettit, St. Louis	1966	Wilt Chamberlain, Philadelphia	1973	Dave Cowens, Boston
1960	Wilt Chamberlain, Philadelphia	1967	Wilt Chamberlain, Philadelphia	1974	Kareem Abdul-Jabbar, Milwaukee
1961	Bill Russell, Boston	1968	Wilt Chamberlain, Philadelphia	1975	Bob McAdoo, Buffalo
1962	Bill Russell, Boston	1969	Wes Unseld, Baltimore	1976	Kareem Abdul-Jabbar, L.A. Lakers

Year	Player, team	Year	Player, team	Year	Player, team
1977	Kareem Abdul-Jabbar, L.A. Lakers	1990	Magic Johnson, L.A. Lakers	2003	Tim Duncan, San Antonio
1978	Bill Walton, Portland	1991	Michael Jordan, Chicago	2004	Kevin Garnett, Minnesota
1979	Moses Malone, Houston	1992	Michael Jordan, Chicago	2005	Steve Nash, Phoenix
1980	Kareem Abdul-Jabbar, L.A. Lakers	1993	Charles Barkley, Phoenix	2006	Steve Nash, Phoenix
1981	Julius Erving, Philadelphia	1994	Hakeem Olajuwon, Houston	2007	Dirk Nowitzki, Dallas
1982	Moses Malone, Houston	1995	David Robinson, San Antonio	2008	Kobe Bryant, L.A. Lakers
1983	Moses Malone, Philadelphia	1996	Michael Jordan, Chicago	2009	LeBron James, Cleveland
1984	Larry Bird, Boston	1997	Karl Malone, Utah	2010	LeBron James, Cleveland
1985	Larry Bird, Boston	1998	Michael Jordan, Chicago	2011	Derrick Rose, Chicago
1986	Larry Bird, Boston	1999	Karl Malone, Utah	2012	LeBron James, Miami
1987	Magic Johnson, L.A. Lakers	2000	Shaquille O'Neal, L.A. Lakers	2013	LeBron James, Miami
1988	Michael Jordan, Chicago	2001	Allen Iverson, Philadelphia	2014	Kevin Durant, Oklahoma City
1989	Magic Johnson, L.A. Lakers	2002	Tim Duncan, San Antonio		

NBA Champions, 1947-2014

	Regular season			Playoffs	
Year	Eastern champion	Western champion	Champion	Winning coach	Opponent
1947	Washington Capitols	Chicago Stags	Philadelphia	Ed Gottlieb	Chicago
1948	Philadelphia Warriors	St. Louis Bombers	Baltimore	Buddy Jeannette	Philadelphia
1949	Washington Capitols	Rochester	Minneapolis	John Kundla	Washington
1950[1]	Syracuse	Indianapolis	Minneapolis	John Kundla	Syracuse
1951	Philadelphia Warriors	Minneapolis	Rochester	Lester Harrison	New York
1952	Syracuse	Rochester	Minneapolis	John Kundla	New York
1953	New York	Minneapolis	Minneapolis	John Kundla	New York
1954	New York	Minneapolis	Minneapolis	John Kundla	Syracuse
1955	Syracuse	Ft. Wayne	Syracuse	Al Cervi	Ft. Wayne
1956	Philadelphia Warriors	Ft. Wayne	Philadelphia	George Senesky	Ft. Wayne
1957	Boston	St. Louis	Boston	Red Auerbach	St. Louis
1958	Boston	St. Louis	St. Louis	Alex Hannum	Boston
1959	Boston	St. Louis	Boston	Red Auerbach	Minneapolis
1960	Boston	St. Louis	Boston	Red Auerbach	St. Louis
1961	Boston	St. Louis	Boston	Red Auerbach	St. Louis
1962	Boston	L.A. Lakers	Boston	Red Auerbach	L.A. Lakers
1963	Boston	L.A. Lakers	Boston	Red Auerbach	L.A. Lakers
1964	Boston	San Francisco	Boston	Red Auerbach	San Francisco
1965	Boston	L.A. Lakers	Boston	Red Auerbach	L.A. Lakers
1966	Philadelphia	L.A. Lakers	Boston	Red Auerbach	L.A. Lakers
1967	Philadelphia	San Francisco	Philadelphia	Alex Hannum	San Francisco
1968	Philadelphia	St. Louis	Boston	Bill Russell	L.A. Lakers
1969	Baltimore	L.A. Lakers	Boston	Bill Russell	L.A. Lakers
1970	New York	Atlanta	New York	Red Holzman	L.A. Lakers

Year	Atlantic	Central	Midwest	Pacific	Champion	Winning coach	Opponent
1971	New York	Baltimore	Milwaukee	L.A. Lakers	Milwaukee	Larry Costello	Baltimore
1972	Boston	Baltimore	Milwaukee	L.A. Lakers	L.A. Lakers	Bill Sharman	New York
1973	Boston	Baltimore	Milwaukee	L.A. Lakers	New York	Red Holzman	L.A. Lakers
1974	Boston	Capital	Milwaukee	L.A. Lakers	Boston	Tom Heinsohn	Milwaukee
1975	Boston	Washington	Chicago	Golden State	Golden State	Al Attles	Washington
1976	Boston	Cleveland	Milwaukee	Golden State	Boston	Tom Heinsohn	Phoenix
1977	Philadelphia	Houston	Denver	L.A. Lakers	Portland	Jack Ramsay	Philadelphia
1978	Philadelphia	San Antonio	Denver	Portland	Washington	Dick Motta	Seattle
1979	Washington	San Antonio	Kansas City	Seattle	Seattle	Len Wilkens	Washington
1980	Boston	Atlanta	Milwaukee	L.A. Lakers	L.A. Lakers	Paul Westhead	Philadelphia
1981	Boston	Milwaukee	San Antonio	Phoenix	Boston	Bill Fitch	Houston
1982	Boston	Milwaukee	San Antonio	L.A. Lakers	L.A. Lakers	Pat Riley	Philadelphia
1983	Philadelphia	Milwaukee	San Antonio	L.A. Lakers	Philadelphia	Billy Cunningham	L.A. Lakers
1984	Boston	Milwaukee	Utah	L.A. Lakers	Boston	K. C. Jones	L.A. Lakers
1985	Boston	Milwaukee	Denver	L.A. Lakers	L.A. Lakers	Pat Riley	Boston
1986	Boston	Milwaukee	Houston	L.A. Lakers	Boston	K. C. Jones	Houston
1987	Boston	Atlanta	Dallas	L.A. Lakers	L.A. Lakers	Pat Riley	Boston
1988	Boston	Detroit	Denver	L.A. Lakers	L.A. Lakers	Pat Riley	Detroit
1989	New York	Detroit	Utah	L.A. Lakers	Detroit	Chuck Daly	L.A. Lakers
1990	Philadelphia	Detroit	San Antonio	L.A. Lakers	Detroit	Chuck Daly	Portland
1991	Boston	Chicago	San Antonio	Portland	Chicago	Phil Jackson	L.A. Lakers
1992	Boston	Chicago	Utah	Portland	Chicago	Phil Jackson	Portland
1993	New York	Chicago	Houston	Phoenix	Chicago	Phil Jackson	Phoenix
1994	New York	Atlanta	Houston	Seattle	Houston	Rudy Tomjanovich	New York
1995	Orlando	Indiana	San Antonio	Phoenix	Houston	Rudy Tomjanovich	Orlando
1996	Orlando	Chicago	San Antonio	Seattle	Chicago	Phil Jackson	Seattle
1997	Miami	Chicago	Utah	Seattle	Chicago	Phil Jackson	Utah
1998	Miami	Chicago	Utah	L.A. Lakers	Chicago	Phil Jackson	Utah
1999	Miami	Indiana	San Antonio	Portland	San Antonio	Gregg Popovich	New York
2000	Miami	Indiana	Utah	L.A. Lakers	L.A. Lakers	Phil Jackson	Indiana
2001	Philadelphia	Milwaukee	San Antonio	L.A. Lakers	L.A. Lakers	Phil Jackson	Philadelphia
2002	New Jersey	Detroit	San Antonio	Sacramento	L.A. Lakers	Phil Jackson	New Jersey
2003	New Jersey	Detroit	San Antonio	Sacramento	San Antonio	Gregg Popovich	New Jersey
2004	New Jersey	Indiana	Minnesota	L.A. Lakers	Detroit	Larry Brown	L.A. Lakers

Year	Atlantic	Central	Southeast	Northwest	Pacific	Southwest	Champion	Winning coach	Opponent
2005	Boston	Detroit	Miami	Seattle	Phoenix	San Antonio	San Antonio	Gregg Popovich	Detroit
2006	New Jersey	Detroit	Miami	Denver	Phoenix	San Antonio	Miami	Pat Riley	Dallas
2007	Toronto	Detroit	Miami	Utah	Phoenix	Dallas	San Antonio	Gregg Popovich	Cleveland
2008	Boston	Detroit	Orlando	Utah	L.A. Lakers	New Orleans	Boston	Glenn "Doc" Rivers	L.A. Lakers
2009	Boston	Cleveland	Orlando	Denver	L.A. Lakers	San Antonio	L.A. Lakers	Phil Jackson	Orlando
2010	Boston	Cleveland	Orlando	Denver	L.A. Lakers	Dallas	L.A. Lakers	Phil Jackson	Boston
2011	Boston	Chicago	Miami	OK City	L.A. Lakers	San Antonio	Dallas	Rick Carlisle	Miami
2012	Boston	Chicago	Miami	OK City	L.A. Lakers	San Antonio	Miami	Erik Spoelstra	OK City
2013	New York	Indiana	Miami	OK City	L.A. Clippers	San Antonio	Miami	Erik Spoelstra	San Antonio
2014	Toronto	Indiana	Miami	OK City	L.A. Clippers	San Antonio	San Antonio	Gregg Popovich	Miami

(1) The newly formed NBA combined the 11-team BAA (Basketball Assn. of Amer.) and six NBL (Natl. Basketball League) teams in the 1949-50 season and had three divisions for one year. The Minneapolis Lakers were co-champions of the soon-defunct Central Division.

All-NBA and All-Defensive Teams, 2013-14

All-NBA Team

First Team	Second Team	Position	First Team	Second Team
Kevin Durant, Oklahoma City	Blake Griffin, L.A. Clippers	**Forward**	Paul George, Indiana	LeBron James, Miami
LeBron James, Miami	Kevin Love, Minnesota	**Forward**	Serge Ibaka, Oklahoma City	Kawhi Leonard, San Antonio
Joakim Noah, Chicago	Dwight Howard, Houston	**Center**	Joakim Noah, Chicago	Roy Hibbert, Indiana
James Harden, Houston	Stephen Curry, Golden State	**Guard**	Chris Paul, L.A. Clippers	Patrick Beverley, Houston
Chris Paul, L.A. Clippers	Tony Parker, San Antonio	**Guard**	Andre Iguodala, Golden State	Jimmy Butler, Chicago

The middle columns are labeled "All-Defensive Team" for the right side.

NBA Statistical Leaders, 2013-14

Scoring Average
(Minimum 58 games)

Player, team	GP	FG	FT	PTS	AVG
Kevin Durant, Oklahoma City	81	849	703	2,593	32.0
Carmelo Anthony, New York	77	743	459	2,112	27.4
LeBron James, Miami	77	767	439	2,089	27.1
Kevin Love, Minnesota	77	650	520	2,010	26.1
James Harden, Houston	73	549	576	1,851	25.4
Blake Griffin, L.A. Clippers	80	718	482	1,930	24.1
Stephen Curry, Golden State	78	652	308	1,873	24.0
LaMarcus Aldridge, Portland	69	652	296	1,603	23.2
DeMarcus Cousins, Sacramento	71	591	432	1,614	22.7
DeMar DeRozan, Toronto	79	604	519	1,791	22.7

Rebounds per Game
(Minimum 58 games)

Player, team	GP	OFF	DEF	TOT	AVG
DeAndre Jordan, L.A. Clippers	82	331	783	1,114	13.6
Andre Drummond, Detroit	81	440	631	1,071	13.2
Kevin Love, Minnesota	77	224	739	963	12.5
Dwight Howard, Houston	71	231	635	866	12.2
DeMarcus Cousins, Sacramento	71	218	613	831	11.7
Joakim Noah, Chicago	80	282	618	900	11.3
LaMarcus Aldridge, Portland	69	166	599	765	11.1
Al Jefferson, Charlotte	73	156	636	792	10.8
Zach Randolph, Memphis	79	265	530	795	10.1
Anthony Davis, New Orleans	67	207	466	673	10.0
Andrew Bogut, Golden State	67	182	489	671	10.0

3-Point Field Goal Percentage
(Minimum 82 3-point field goals made)

Player, team	3-FGM	3-FGA	PCT
Kyle Korver, Atlanta	185	392	.472
Mike Miller, Memphis	107	233	.459
Anthony Morrow, New Orleans	88	195	.451
Jose Calderon, Dallas	191	425	.449
Marco Belinelli, San Antonio	126	293	.430
Arron Afflalo, Orlando	128	300	.427
Patty Mills, San Antonio	135	318	.425
Stephen Curry, Golden State	261	615	.424
Klay Thompson, Golden State	223	535	.417
Spencer Hawes, Cleveland/Philadelphia	128	308	.416

Assists per Game
(Minimum 58 games)

Player, team	GP	AST	APG
Chris Paul, L.A. Clippers	62	663	10.7
John Wall, Washington	82	721	8.8
Ty Lawson, Denver	62	543	8.8
Ricky Rubio, Minnesota	82	704	8.6
Stephen Curry, Golden State	78	666	8.5
Brandon Jennings, Detroit	80	609	7.6
Kyle Lowry, Toronto	79	586	7.4
Jameer Nelson, Orlando	68	476	7.0
Jeff Teague, Atlanta	79	528	6.7
LeBron James, Miami	77	488	6.3
Isaiah Thomas, Sacramento	72	454	6.3
Michael Carter-Williams, Philadelphia	70	441	6.3

Field Goal Percentage
(Minimum 300 field goals made)

Player, team	FGM	FGA	PCT
DeAndre Jordan, L.A. Clippers	348	515	.676
Andre Drummond, Detroit	479	769	.623
Dwight Howard, Houston	473	800	.591
LeBron James, Miami	767	1,353	.567
Amir Johnson, Toronto	344	612	.562
Amar'e Stoudemire, New York	311	558	.557
Robin Lopez, Portland	355	644	.551
Dwyane Wade, Miami	415	761	.545
Kenneth Faried, Denver	447	820	.545
Terrence Jones, Houston	386	712	.542
Marcin Gortat, Washington	455	840	.542

Steals per Game
(Minimum 58 games)

Player, team	GP	STL	AVG
Chris Paul, L.A. Clippers	62	154	2.5
Ricky Rubio, Minnesota	82	191	2.3
Thaddeus Young, Philadelphia	79	167	2.1
Jimmy Butler, Chicago	67	127	1.9
Paul George, Indiana	80	151	1.9
Corey Brewer, Minnesota	81	151	1.9
Michael Carter-Williams, Philadelphia	70	130	1.9
John Wall, Washington	82	149	1.8
Paul Millsap, Atlanta	74	129	1.7
Kawhi Leonard, San Antonio	66	114	1.7
Monta Ellis, Dallas	82	141	1.7

Free Throw Percentage
(Minimum 125 free throws made)

Player, team	FTM	FTA	PCT
Brian Roberts, New Orleans	125	133	.940
Dirk Nowitzki, Dallas	338	376	.899
Reggie Jackson, Oklahoma City	158	177	.893
Kevin Martin, Minnesota	303	340	.891
D.J. Augustin, Chicago/Toronto	201	227	.885
Stephen Curry, Golden State	308	348	.885
Kevin Durant, Oklahoma City	703	805	.873
Damian Lillard, Portland	371	426	.871
Jamal Crawford, L.A. Clippers	279	322	.866
James Harden, Houston	576	665	.866

Blocked Shots per Game
(Minimum 58 games)

Player, team	GP	BLK	AVG
Anthony Davis, New Orleans	67	189	2.82
Serge Ibaka, Oklahoma City	81	219	2.70
DeAndre Jordan, L.A. Clippers	82	203	2.48
Roy Hibbert, Indiana	81	182	2.25
Tim Duncan, San Antonio	74	139	1.88
Andrew Bogut, Golden State	67	121	1.81
Dwight Howard, Houston	71	128	1.80
Robin Lopez, Portland	82	139	1.70
John Henson, Milwaukee	70	116	1.66
Andre Drummond, Detroit	81	131	1.62

NBA Defensive Player of the Year, 1983-2014

Year	Player, team	Year	Player, team	Year	Player, team
1983	Sidney Moncrief, Milwaukee	1994	Hakeem Olajuwon, Houston	2004	Ron Artest, Indiana
1984	Sidney Moncrief, Milwaukee	1995	Dikembe Mutombo, Denver	2005	Ben Wallace, Detroit
1985	Mark Eaton, Utah	1996	Gary Payton, Seattle	2006	Ben Wallace, Detroit
1986	Alvin Robertson, San Antonio	1997	Dikembe Mutombo, Atlanta	2007	Marcus Camby, Denver
1987	Michael Cooper, L.A. Lakers	1998	Dikembe Mutombo, Atlanta	2008	Kevin Garnett, Boston
1988	Michael Jordan, Chicago	1999	Alonzo Mourning, Miami	2009	Dwight Howard, Orlando
1989	Mark Eaton, Utah	2000	Alonzo Mourning, Miami	2010	Dwight Howard, Orlando
1990	Dennis Rodman, Detroit	2001	Dikembe Mutombo, Philadelphia/ Atlanta	2011	Dwight Howard, Orlando
1991	Dennis Rodman, Detroit			2012	Tyson Chandler, New York
1992	David Robinson, San Antonio	2002	Ben Wallace, Detroit	2013	Marc Gasol, Memphis
1993	Hakeem Olajuwon, Houston	2003	Ben Wallace, Detroit	2014	Joakim Noah, Chicago

NBA Rookie of the Year, 1953-2014

Year	Player, team	Year	Player, team	Year	Player, team
1953	Don Meineke, Ft. Wayne	1974	Ernie DiGregorio, Buffalo	1996	Damon Stoudamire, Toronto
1954	Ray Felix, Baltimore	1975	Keith Wilkes, Golden State	1997	Allen Iverson, Philadelphia
1955	Bob Pettit, Milwaukee	1976	Alvan Adams, Phoenix	1998	Tim Duncan, San Antonio
1956	Maurice Stokes, Rochester	1977	Adrian Dantley, Buffalo	1999	Vince Carter, Toronto
1957	Tom Heinsohn, Boston	1978	Walter Davis, Phoenix	2000	Elton Brand, Chicago;
1958	Woody Sauldsberry, Philadelphia	1979	Phil Ford, Kansas City		Steve Francis, Houston
1959	Elgin Baylor, Minneapolis	1980	Larry Bird, Boston	2001	Mike Miller, Orlando
1960	Wilt Chamberlain, Philadelphia	1981	Darrell Griffith, Utah	2002	Pau Gasol, Memphis
1961	Oscar Robertson, Cincinnati	1982	Buck Williams, New Jersey	2003	Amar'e Stoudemire, Phoenix
1962	Walt Bellamy, Chicago	1983	Terry Cummings, San Diego	2004	LeBron James, Cleveland
1963	Terry Dischinger, Chicago	1984	Ralph Sampson, Houston	2005	Emeka Okafor, Charlotte
1964	Jerry Lucas, Cincinnati	1985	Michael Jordan, Chicago	2006	Chris Paul, New Orl./OK City
1965	Willis Reed, New York	1986	Patrick Ewing, New York	2007	Brandon Roy, Portland
1966	Rick Barry, San Francisco	1987	Chuck Person, Indiana	2008	Kevin Durant, Seattle
1967	Dave Bing, Detroit	1988	Mark Jackson, New York	2009	Derrick Rose, Chicago
1968	Earl Monroe, Baltimore	1989	Mitch Richmond, Golden State	2010	Tyreke Evans, Sacramento
1969	Wes Unseld, Baltimore	1990	David Robinson, San Antonio	2011	Blake Griffin, L.A. Clippers
1970	Lew Alcindor (Abdul-Jabbar),	1991	Derrick Coleman, New Jersey	2012	Kyrie Irving, Cleveland
	Milwaukee	1992	Larry Johnson, Charlotte	2013	Damian Lillard, Portland
1971	Dave Cowens, Boston;	1993	Shaquille O'Neal, Orlando	2014	Michael Carter-Williams,
	Geoff Petrie, Portland	1994	Chris Webber, Golden State		Philadelphia
1972	Sidney Wicks, Portland	1995	Grant Hill, Detroit;		
1973	Bob McAdoo, Buffalo		Jason Kidd, Dallas		

NBA Sixth Man Award, 1983-2014

Year	Player, team	Year	Player, team	Year	Player, team
1983	Bobby Jones, Philadelphia	1994	Dell Curry, Charlotte	2005	Ben Gordon, Chicago
1984	Kevin McHale, Boston	1995	Anthony Mason, New York	2006	Mike Miller, Memphis
1985	Kevin McHale, Boston	1996	Toni Kukoc, Chicago	2007	Leandro Barbosa, Phoenix
1986	Bill Walton, Boston	1997	John Starks, New York	2008	Manu Ginobili, San Antonio
1987	Ricky Pierce, Milwaukee	1998	Danny Manning, Phoenix	2009	Jason Terry, Dallas
1988	Roy Tarpley, Dallas	1999	Darrell Armstrong, Orlando	2010	Jamal Crawford, Atlanta
1989	Eddie Johnson, Phoenix	2000	Rodney Rogers, Phoenix	2011	Lamar Odom, L.A. Lakers
1990	Ricky Pierce, Milwaukee	2001	Aaron McKie, Philadelphia	2012	James Harden, Oklahoma City
1991	Detlef Schrempf, Indiana	2002	Corliss Williamson, Detroit	2013	J.R. Smith, New York
1992	Detlef Schrempf, Indiana	2003	Bobby Jackson, Sacramento	2014	Jamal Crawford, L.A. Clippers
1993	Clifford Robinson, Portland	2004	Antawn Jamison, Dallas		

NBA Player Draft First-Round Picks, 2014
(June 26, 2014)

	Team	Player, position, school/team		Team	Player, position, school/team
1.	Cleveland	Andrew Wiggins, Guard, Kansas	17.	Boston[9]	James Young, Guard, Kentucky
2.	Milwaukee.	Jabari Parker, Forward, Duke	18.	Phoenix[10]	Tyler Ennis, Guard, Syracuse
3.	Philadelphia . . .	Joel Embiid, Center, Kansas	19.	Chicago	Gary Harris, Guard, Michigan State[11]
4.	Orlando	Aaron Gordon, Forward, Arizona	20.	Toronto	Bruno Caboclo, Forward, Pinheiros (Brazil)
5.	Utah	Dante Exum, Guard, Australian Inst. of Sport	21.	Oklahoma City[12]	Mitch McGary, Forward, Michigan
6.	Boston	Marcus Smart, Guard, Oklahoma State	22.	Memphis	Jordan Adams, Guard, UCLA
7.	L.A. Lakers	Julius Randle, Forward, Kentucky	23.	Utah[13]	Rodney Hood, Forward, Duke
8.	Sacramento	Nik Stauskas, Guard, Michigan	24.	Charlotte[14]	Shabazz Napier, Guard, Connecticut[15]
9.	Charlotte[1]	Noah Vonleh, Forward, Indiana	25.	Houston	Clint Capela, Forward, Chalon (France)
10.	Philadelphia[2] . .	Elfrid Payton, Guard, Louisiana-Lafayette[3]	26.	Miami	P.J. Hairston, Guard, North Carolina/
11.	Denver	Doug McDermott, Forward, Creighton[4]			Texas Legends (NBA D-League)[16]
12.	Orlando[5]	Dario Saric, Forward, Cibona (Croatia)[6]	27.	Phoenix[17]	Bogdan Bogdanovic, Guard, Partizan
13.	Minnesota	Zach LaVine, Guard, UCLA			(Serbia)
14.	Phoenix.	T.J. Warren, Forward, NC State	28.	L.A. Clippers . . .	C.J. Wilcox, Guard, Washington
15.	Atlanta	Adreian Payne, Forward, Michigan State	29.	Oklahoma City	Josh Huestis, Forward, Stanford
16.	Chicago[7]	Jusuf Nurkic, Center, Cedevita (Croatia)[8]	30.	San Antonio	Kyle Anderson, Forward, UCLA

(1) From Detroit. (2) From New Orleans. (3) Rights traded to Orlando. (4) Rights traded to Chicago. (5) From New York via Denver. (6) Rights traded to Philadelphia. (7) From Charlotte. (8) Rights traded to Denver. (9) From Brooklyn. (10) From Washington. (11) Rights traded to Denver. (12) From Dallas via Houston and L.A. Lakers. (13) From Golden State. (14) From Portland. (15) Rights traded to Miami. (16) Rights traded to Charlotte. (17) From Indiana.

Number-One First-Round NBA Draft Picks, 1966-2014

Year	Team	Player, school/team	Year	Team	Player, school/team
1966	New York	Cazzie Russell, Michigan	1984	Houston	Hakeem Olajuwon, Houston
1967	Detroit	Jimmy Walker, Providence	1985	New York	Patrick Ewing, Georgetown
1968	San Diego	Elvin Hayes, Houston	1986	Cleveland	Brad Daugherty, North Carolina
1969	Milwaukee	Lew Alcindor (Kareem Abdul-Jabbar),	1987	San Antonio	David Robinson, Navy
		UCLA	1988	L.A. Clippers	Danny Manning, Kansas
1970	Detroit	Bob Lanier, St. Bonaventure	1989	Sacramento	Pervis Ellison, Louisville
1971	Cleveland	Austin Carr, Notre Dame	1990	New Jersey	Derrick Coleman, Syracuse
1972	Portland	LaRue Martin, Loyola-Chicago	1991	Charlotte	Larry Johnson, UNLV
1973	Philadelphia	Doug Collins, Illinois State	1992	Orlando	Shaquille O'Neal, LSU
1974	Portland	Bill Walton, UCLA	1993	Orlando	Chris Webber[2], Michigan
1975	Atlanta	David Thompson[1], NC State	1994	Milwaukee	Glenn Robinson, Purdue
1976	Houston	John Lucas, Maryland	1995	Golden State	Joe Smith, Maryland
1977	Milwaukee	Kent Benson, Indiana	1996	Philadelphia	Allen Iverson, Georgetown
1978	Portland	Mychal Thompson, Minnesota	1997	San Antonio	Tim Duncan, Wake Forest
1979	L.A. Lakers	Earvin "Magic" Johnson, Michigan State	1998	L.A. Clippers	Michael Olowokandi, Pacific (CA)
1980	Golden State	Joe Barry Carroll, Purdue	1999	Chicago	Elton Brand, Duke
1981	Dallas	Mark Aguirre, DePaul	2000	New Jersey	Kenyon Martin, Cincinnati
1982	L.A. Lakers	James Worthy, North Carolina	2001	Washington	Kwame Brown, Glynn Academy (HS)
1983	Houston	Ralph Sampson, Virginia	2002	Houston	Yao Ming, Shanghai Sharks (China)

Year	Team	Player, school/team	Year	Team	Player, school/team
2003	Cleveland	LeBron James, St. Vincent-St. Mary (HS)	2009	L.A. Clippers	Blake Griffin, Oklahoma
2004	Orlando	Dwight Howard, Southwest Atlanta Christian Academy (HS)	2010	Washington	John Wall, Kentucky
			2011	Cleveland	Kyrie Irving, Duke
2005	Milwaukee	Andrew Bogut, Utah	2012	New Orleans	Anthony Davis, Kentucky
2006	Toronto	Andrea Bargnani, Benetton Treviso (Italy)	2013	Cleveland	Anthony Bennett, UNLV
2007	Portland	Greg Oden, Ohio State	2014	Cleveland	Andrew Wiggins, Kansas
2008	Chicago	Derrick Rose, Memphis			

HS = High school. (1) Signed with Denver of the American Basketball Association (ABA). (2) Traded to Golden State for rights to Anfernee Hardaway and three future first-round choices.

All-Time NBA Statistical Leaders

(At the end of the 2013-14 season. * = Active in 2013-14 season.)

Scoring Average
(Minimum 400 games or 10,000 points)

	GP	PTS	AVG
Michael Jordan	1,072	32,292	30.1
Wilt Chamberlain	1,045	31,419	30.1
*LeBron James	842	23,170	27.5
Elgin Baylor	846	23,149	27.4
*Kevin Durant	542	14,851	27.4
Jerry West	932	25,192	27.0
Allen Iverson	914	24,368	26.7
Bob Pettit	792	20,880	26.4
George Gervin	791	20,708	26.2
Oscar Robertson	1,040	26,710	25.7

Field Goal Percentage
(Minimum 2,000 field goals made)

	FGM	FGA	PCT
Artis Gilmore	5,732	9,570	.599
*Tyson Chandler	2,733	4,678	.584
Shaquille O'Neal	11,330	19,457	.582
Mark West	2,528	4,356	.580
*Dwight Howard	4,977	8,601	.579
Darryl Dawkins	3,477	6,079	.572
Steve Johnson	2,841	4,965	.572
James Donaldson	3,105	5,442	.571
Bo Outlaw	2,005	3,534	.567
Jeff Ruland	2,105	3,734	.564

Free Throw Percentage
(Minimum 1,200 free throws made)

	FTM	FTA	PCT
*Steve Nash	3,060	3,384	.904
Mark Price	2,135	2,362	.904
Rick Barry	3,818	4,243	.900
Peja Stojakovic	2,237	2,500	.895
*Ray Allen	4,398	4,920	.894
*Chauncey Billups	4,496	5,029	.894
Calvin Murphy	3,445	3,864	.892
Scott Skiles	1,548	1,741	.889
Reggie Miller	6,237	7,026	.888
Larry Bird	3,960	4,471	.886

3-Point Field Goal Percentage
(Minimum 250 3-point field goals made)

	3-FGM	3-FGA	PCT
Steve Kerr	726	1,599	.454
Hubert Davis	728	1,651	.441
*Stephen Curry	905	2,058	.440
Drazen Petrovic	255	583	.437
Jason Kapono	457	1,054	.434
*Steve Novak	548	1,268	.432
Tim Legler	260	603	.431
*Steve Nash	1,685	3,939	.428
*Anthony Morrow	546	1,275	.428
B.J. Armstrong	436	1,026	.425
*Kyle Korver	1,508	3,549	.425

Minutes Played

Kareem Abdul-Jabbar	57,446
Karl Malone	54,852
Jason Kidd	50,111
Elvin Hayes	50,000
*Kevin Garnett	48,910
Wilt Chamberlain	47,859
John Stockton	47,764
Reggie Miller	47,619
Gary Payton	47,117
John Havlicek	46,471

Field Goals Attempted

Kareem Abdul-Jabbar	28,307
Karl Malone	26,210
Michael Jordan	24,537
*Kobe Bryant	24,374
Elvin Hayes	24,272
John Havlicek	23,930
Wilt Chamberlain	23,497
Dominique Wilkins	21,589
Alex English	21,036
Hakeem Olajuwon	20,991

Points

Kareem Abdul-Jabbar	38,387
Karl Malone	36,928
Michael Jordan	32,292
*Kobe Bryant	31,700
Wilt Chamberlain	31,419
Shaquille O'Neal	28,596
Moses Malone	27,409
Elvin Hayes	27,313
Hakeem Olajuwon	26,946
*Dirk Nowitzki	26,786

Games Played

Robert Parish	1,611
Kareem Abdul-Jabbar	1,560
John Stockton	1,504
Karl Malone	1,476
Kevin Willis	1,424
Jason Kidd	1,391
Reggie Miller	1,389
Clifford Robinson	1,380
*Kevin Garnett	1,377
Gary Payton	1,335

Field Goals Made

Kareem Abdul-Jabbar	15,837
Karl Malone	13,528
Wilt Chamberlain	12,681
Michael Jordan	12,192
Shaquille O'Neal	11,330
*Kobe Bryant	11,055
Elvin Hayes	10,976
Hakeem Olajuwon	10,749
Alex English	10,659
John Havlicek	10,513

Rebounds

Wilt Chamberlain	23,924
Bill Russell	21,620
Kareem Abdul-Jabbar	17,440
Elvin Hayes	16,279
Moses Malone	16,212
Karl Malone	14,968
Robert Parish	14,715
Nate Thurmond	14,464
Walt Bellamy	14,241
*Kevin Garnett	14,201

Personal Fouls

Kareem Abdul-Jabbar	4,657
Karl Malone	4,578
Robert Parish	4,443
Charles Oakley	4,421
Hakeem Olajuwon	4,383
Buck Williams	4,267
Elvin Hayes	4,193
Clifford Robinson	4,175
Kevin Willis	4,172
Shaquille O'Neal	4,146
Otis Thorpe	4,146

3-Point Field Goals Attempted

*Ray Allen	7,429
Reggie Miller	6,486
Jason Kidd	5,701
*Paul Pierce	5,228
*Jason Terry	5,140
*Kobe Bryant	4,895
*Jamal Crawford	4,831
*Vince Carter	4,788
*Chauncey Billups	4,725
*Rashard Lewis	4,625

Assists

John Stockton	15,806
Jason Kidd	12,091
*Steve Nash	10,335
Mark Jackson	10,334
Magic Johnson	10,141
Oscar Robertson	9,887
Isiah Thomas	9,061
Gary Payton	8,966
*Andre Miller	8,153
Rod Strickland	7,987

Blocked Shots

Hakeem Olajuwon	3,830
Dikembe Mutombo	3,289
Kareem Abdul-Jabbar	3,189
Mark Eaton	3,064
David Robinson	2,954
Patrick Ewing	2,894
*Tim Duncan	2,791
Shaquille O'Neal	2,732
Tree Rollins	2,542
Robert Parish	2,361

3-Point Field Goals Made

*Ray Allen	2,973
Reggie Miller	2,560
Jason Kidd	1,988
*Jason Terry	1,950
*Paul Pierce	1,935
*Chauncey Billups	1,830
*Vince Carter	1,809
*Rashard Lewis	1,787
Peja Stojakovic	1,760
Dale Ellis	1,719

Steals

John Stockton	3,265
Jason Kidd	2,684
Michael Jordan	2,514
Gary Payton	2,445
Maurice Cheeks	2,310
Scottie Pippen	2,307
Clyde Drexler	2,207
Hakeem Olajuwon	2,162
Alvin Robertson	2,112
Karl Malone	2,085

NBA Coach of the Year, 1963-2014

Year	Coach, team	Year	Coach, team	Year	Coach, team
1963	Harry Gallatin, St. Louis	1981	Jack McKinney, Indiana	1998	Larry Bird, Indiana
1964	Alex Hannum, San Francisco	1982	Gene Shue, Washington	1999	Mike Dunleavy, Portland
1965	Red Auerbach, Boston	1983	Don Nelson, Milwaukee	2000	Glenn "Doc" Rivers, Orlando
1966	Dolph Schayes, Philadelphia	1984	Frank Layden, Utah	2001	Larry Brown, Philadelphia
1967	Johnny Kerr, Chicago	1985	Don Nelson, Milwaukee	2002	Rick Carlisle, Detroit
1968	Richie Guerin, St. Louis	1986	Mike Fratello, Atlanta	2003	Gregg Popovich, San Antonio
1969	Gene Shue, Baltimore	1987	Mike Schuler, Portland	2004	Hubie Brown, Memphis
1970	Red Holzman, New York	1988	Doug Moe, Denver	2005	Mike D'Antoni, Phoenix
1971	Dick Motta, Chicago	1989	Cotton Fitzsimmons, Phoenix	2006	Avery Johnson, Dallas
1972	Bill Sharman, L.A. Lakers	1990	Pat Riley, L.A. Lakers	2007	Sam Mitchell, Toronto
1973	Tom Heinsohn, Boston	1991	Don Chaney, Houston	2008	Byron Scott, New Orleans
1974	Ray Scott, Detroit	1992	Don Nelson, Golden State	2009	Mike Brown, Cleveland
1975	Phil Johnson, Kansas City-Omaha	1993	Pat Riley, New York	2010	Scott Brooks, Oklahoma City
1976	Bill Fitch, Cleveland	1994	Lenny Wilkens, Atlanta	2011	Tom Thibodeau, Chicago
1977	Tom Nissalke, Houston	1995	Del Harris, L.A. Lakers	2012	Gregg Popovich, San Antonio
1978	Hubie Brown, Atlanta	1996	Phil Jackson, Chicago	2013	George Karl, Denver
1979	Cotton Fitzsimmons, Kansas City	1997	Pat Riley, Miami	2014	Gregg Popovich, San Antonio
1980	Bill Fitch, Boston				

National Basketball Association Franchise Origins

Team, founding year (in NBA, BAA, or ABA), location, and subsequent history. Neutral sites and arena sites in the same metropolitan area not listed separately.

Atlanta Hawks: 1949, NBA, as Tri-Cities Blackhawks, 1949-51, Moline, IL. Milwaukee Hawks, 1951-55; St. Louis Hawks, 1955-68; Atlanta Hawks, 1968-present.

Boston Celtics: 1946, BAA, Boston, 1946-present.

Brooklyn Nets: 1967, ABA, as New Jersey Americans, 1967-68, Teaneck, NJ. New York Nets, 1968-77; New Jersey Nets, 1977-2012; Brooklyn Nets, 2012-present.

Charlotte Bobcats: 2004, NBA, Charlotte, NC, 2004-present.

Chicago Bulls: 1966, NBA, Chicago, 1966-present.

Cleveland Cavaliers: 1970, NBA, Cleveland, OH, 1970-present.

Dallas Mavericks: 1980, NBA, Dallas, TX, 1980-present.

Denver Nuggets: 1967, ABA, as Denver Rockets, 1967-74, Denver, CO. Denver Nuggets, 1974-present.

Detroit Pistons: 1948, BAA, as Ft. Wayne Pistons, 1948-57, Ft. Wayne, IN. Detroit Pistons, 1957-present.

Golden State Warriors: 1946, BAA, as Philadelphia Warriors, 1946-62, Philadelphia, PA. San Francisco Warriors, 1962-71; Golden State Warriors, 1971-present.

Houston Rockets: 1967, NBA, as San Diego Rockets, 1967-71, San Diego, CA. Houston Rockets, 1971-present.

Indiana Pacers: 1967, ABA, Indianapolis, IN, 1974-present.

L.A. Clippers: 1970, NBA, as Buffalo Braves, 1970-78, Buffalo, NY. San Diego Clippers, 1978-84; L.A. Clippers, 1984-present.

L.A. Lakers: 1948, BAA, as Minneapolis Lakers, 1948-60, Minneapolis, MN. L.A. Lakers, 1960-present.

Memphis Grizzlies: 1995, NBA, as Vancouver Grizzlies, 1995-2001, Vancouver, BC, Canada. Memphis Grizzlies, 2001-present.

Miami Heat: 1988, NBA, Miami, FL, 1988-present.

Milwaukee Bucks: 1968, NBA, Milwaukee, WI, 1968-present.

Minnesota Timberwolves: 1989, NBA, Minneapolis, MN, 1989-present.

New Orleans Pelicans: 1988, NBA, as Charlotte Hornets, 1988-2002, Charlotte, NC. New Orleans Hornets, 2002-13 (Hornets played most home games in Oklahoma City, 2005-07, as city repaired Hurricane Katrina damage); New Orleans Pelicans, 2013-present.

New York Knicks: 1946, BAA, New York, 1946-present.

Oklahoma City Thunder: 1967, NBA, as Seattle SuperSonics, 1967-2008, Seattle, WA. Oklahoma City Thunder, 2008-present.

Orlando Magic: 1989, NBA, Orlando, FL, 1989-present.

Philadelphia 76ers: 1949, NBA, as Syracuse Nationals, 1949-63, Syracuse, NY. Philadelphia 76ers, 1963-present.

Phoenix Suns: 1968, NBA, Phoenix, AZ, 1968-present.

Portland Trail Blazers: 1970, NBA, Portland, OR, 1970-present.

Sacramento Kings: 1948, BAA, as Rochester Royals, 1948-57, Rochester, NY. Cincinnati Royals, 1957-72; Kansas City-Omaha Kings, 1972-75; Kansas City Kings, 1975-85; Sacramento Kings, 1985-present.

San Antonio Spurs: ABA, as Dallas Chaparrals, 1967-73, Dallas, TX. San Antonio Spurs, 1973-present.

Toronto Raptors: 1995, NBA, Toronto, ON, Canada, 1995-present.

Utah Jazz: 1974, NBA, as New Orleans Jazz, 1974-79, New Orleans, LA. Utah Jazz, 1979-present.

Washington Wizards: 1961, NBA, as Chicago Packers, 1961-62, Chicago, IL. Chicago Zephyrs, 1962-63; Baltimore Bullets, 1963-73; Capital Bullets, 1973-74, Landover, MD; Washington Bullets, 1974-97; Washington Wizards, 1997-present.

NBA Home Courts

Team	Name (year built)	Capacity[1]	Team	Name (year built)	Capacity[1]
Atlanta	Philips Arena (1999)	18,118	Miami	AmericanAirlines Arena (1999)	19,600
Boston	TD Garden[2] (1995)	18,624	Milwaukee	BMO Harris Bradley Center[6] (1988)	18,717
Brooklyn	Barclays Center[3] (2012)	17,732	Minnesota	Target Center (1990)	19,356
Charlotte	Time Warner Cable Arena (2005)	19,077	New Orleans	Smoothie King Center[7] (1999)	17,003
Chicago	United Center (1994)	20,917	New York	Madison Square Garden (IV) (1968)	19,033
Cleveland	Quicken Loans Arena (1994)	20,562	Oklahoma City	Chesapeake Energy Arena[8] (2002)	18,203
Dallas	American Airlines Center (2001)	19,200	Orlando	Amway Center (2010)	18,846
Denver	Pepsi Center (1999)	19,155	Philadelphia	Wells Fargo Center[9] (1996)	20,328
Detroit	The Palace of Auburn Hills (1988)	22,076	Phoenix	US Airways Center[10] (1992)	18,422
Golden State	ORACLE Arena[4] (1966)	19,596	Portland	Moda Center[11] (1995)	19,980
Houston	Toyota Center (2003)	18,023	Sacramento	Sleep Train Arena[12] (1988)	17,317
Indiana	Bankers Life Fieldhouse[5] (1999)	18,165	San Antonio	AT&T Center[13] (2002)	18,581
L.A. Clippers	STAPLES Center (1999)	19,060	Toronto	Air Canada Centre (1999)	19,800
L.A. Lakers	STAPLES Center (1999)	18,997	Utah	EnergySolutions Arena[14] (1991)	19,911
Memphis	FedExForum (2004)	18,119	Washington	Verizon Center[15] (1997)	20,290

(1) At the end of the 2013-14 season. (2) FleetCenter, 1995-2005; TD Banknorth Garden, 2005-09. (3) The New Jersey Nets relocated to Brooklyn prior to the 2012-13 season. (4) Oakland Coliseum Arena, 1966-96; Arena in Oakland, 1997-2006. (5) Conseco Fieldhouse, 1999-2011. (6) Bradley Center, 1988-2012. (7) New Orleans Arena, 1999-2014; because of damage to New Orleans Arena due to Hurricane Katrina, the Hornets played 35 games in the Ford Center in Oklahoma City, OK, 3 games in New Orleans Arena, and 3 games at other locations during the 2005-06 season; in 2006-07, the Hornets played 35 games at the Ford Center and 6 games in New Orleans Arena. (8) Ford Center (2008-11); the Seattle SuperSonics relocated to Oklahoma City prior to the 2008-09 season. (9) CoreStates Center, 1996-98; First Union Center, 1998-2003; Wachovia Center, 2003-10. (10) America West Arena, 1992-2006. (11) The Rose Garden, 1995-2013. (12) ARCO Arena, 1988-2011; Power Balance Pavilion, 2011-12. (13) SBC Center, 2002-06. (14) Delta Center, 1991-2006. (15) MCI Center, 1997-2006.

All-Time NBA Regular Season Coaching Victories

(At the end of the 2013-14 season, ranked by wins. * = Active in 2013-14 season.)

Coach	W	L	PCT	Coach	W	L	PCT	Coach	W	L	PCT
Don Nelson	1,335	1,063	.557	*Gregg Popovich	967	443	.686	Red Holzman	696	604	.535
Lenny Wilkens	1,332	1,155	.536	Bill Fitch	944	1,106	.460	Mike Fratello	667	548	.549
Jerry Sloan	1,221	803	.603	Red Auerbach	938	479	.662	*Glenn "Doc" Rivers	644	498	.564
Pat Riley	1,210	694	.636	Dick Motta	935	1,017	.479	Chuck Daly	638	437	.593
Phil Jackson	1,155	485	.704	Jack Ramsay	864	783	.525	Flip Saunders	638	526	.548
George Karl	1,131	756	.599	Cotton Fitzsimmons	832	775	.518	Doug Moe	628	529	.543
Larry Brown	1,098	904	.548	Gene Shue	784	861	.477	Mike Dunleavy	613	716	.461
*Rick Adelman	1,042	749	.582	John MacLeod	707	657	.518				

Naismith Memorial Basketball Hall of Fame

(Located in Springfield, MA. * = 2014 inductee. ** = Enshrined as both a player and coach.)

Players

Abdul-Jabbar, Kareem
Archibald, Nate
Arizin, Paul
Barkley, Charles
Barlow, Thomas
Barry, Rick
Baylor, Elgin
Beckman, John "Buddy"
Bellamy, Walt
Belov, Sergei
Bing, Dave
Bird, Larry
Blazejowski, Carol
Borgmann, Bennie
Bradley, Bill
Brennan, Joseph
Brown, Roger
Cervi, Al
Chamberlain, Wilt
Cooper, Charles
Cooper, Cynthia
Cosic, Kresimir
Cousy, Bob
Cowens, Dave
Crawford, Joan
Cunningham, Billy
Curry, Denise
Dalipagic, Drazen
Daniels, Mel
Dantley, Adrian
Davies, Bob
DeBernardi, Forrest
DeBusschere, Dave
Dehnert, Henry "Dutch"
Donovan, Anne
Drexler, Clyde
Dumars, Joe
Edwards, Teresa
English, Alex
Erving, Julius
Ewing, Patrick
Foster, Bud
Frazier, Walt
Friedman, Max
Fulks, Joe
Gale, Lauren
Gallatin, Harry
Gates, William "Pop"
Gervin, George
Gilmore, Artis
Gola, Tom
Goodrich, Gail
Greer, Hal
Gruenig, Robert "Ace"
Guerin, Richard
Hagan, Cliff
Hanson, Victor
Harris-Stewart, Lusia
Havlicek, John
Hawkins, Cornelius "Connie"

Hayes, Elvin
Haynes, Marques
Heinsohn, Tom
Holman, Nat
Houbregs, Bob
Howell, Bailey
Hyatt, Chuck
Issel, Dan
Jeannette, Harry "Buddy"
Johnson, Dennis
Johnson, Earvin "Magic"
Johnson, Gus
Johnson, William
Johnston, Neil
Jones, K. C.
Jones, Sam "Satch"
Jordan, Michael
King, Bernard
Krause, Ed "Moose"
Kurland, Bob
Lanier, Bob
Lapchick, Joe
Lieberman, Nancy
Lovellette, Clyde
Lucas, Jerry
Luisetti, Angelo "Hank"
Macauley, Ed
Malone, Karl
Malone, Moses
Maravich, Pete
Marcari, Hortencia
*Marciulionis, Sarunas
Martin, Slater
McAdoo, Bob
McClain, Katrina
McCracken, Emmett "Branch"
McCracken, Jack
McDermott, Bobby
McGuire, Dick
McHale, Kevin
Meneghin, Dino
Meyers, Ann
Mikan, George
Mikkelsen, Vern
Miller, Cheryl
Miller, Reggie
Monroe, Earl
*Mourning, Alonzo
Mullin, Chris
Murphy, Calvin
Murphy, Charles "Stretch"
Olajuwon, Hakeem
Page, Harlan "Pat"
Parish, Robert
Payton, Gary
Pereira, Maciel "Ubiratan"
Petrovic, Drazen
Pettit, Bob
Phillip, Andy

Pippen, Scottie
Pollard, Jim
Ramsey, Frank
Reed, Willis
*Richmond, Mitch
Risen, Arnie
Robertson, Oscar
Robinson, David
*Rodgers, Guy
Rodman, Dennis
Roosma, John
Russell, Bill
Russell, John "Honey"
Sabonis, Arvydas
Sampson, Ralph
Sanders, Tom "Satch"
Schayes, Adolph
Schmidt, Ernest
Schmidt, Oscar
Schommer, John
Sedran, Barney
Semjonova, Uljana
**Sharman, Bill
Staley, Dawn
Steinmetz, Chris
Stockton, John
Stokes, Maurice
Tatum, Reece "Goose"
Thomas, Isiah
Thompson, David
Thompson, John
Thurmond, Nate
Twyman, Jack
Unseld, Wes
Vandivier, Robert "Fuzzy"
Wachter, Ed
Walker, Chet
Walton, Bill
Wanzer, Bobby
West, Jerry
White, Nera
*Wilkens, Lenny
Wilkes, Jamaal
Wilkins, Dominique
Woodard, Lynette
**Wooden, John
Worthy, James
Yardley, George

Coaches

Alexeeva, Lidia
Allen, Forrest C. "Phog"
Anderson, Harold
Auerbach, Arnold "Red"
Auriemma, Geno
Barmore, Leon
Barry, Justin "Sam"
Blood, Ernest
Boeheim, Jim
Brown, Larry
Calhoun, Jim

Cann, Howard
Carlson, Clifford
Carnesecca, Lou
Carnevale, Ben
Carril, Pete
Case, Everett
Chancellor, Van
Chaney, John
Conradt, Jody
Crum, Denzil
Daly, Chuck
Dean, Everett
Diaz-Miguel, Antonio
Diddle, Edgar
Drake, Bruce
Ferrandiz, Pedro
Gaines, Clarence
Gamba, Sandro
Gardner, James "Jack"
Gill, Amory "Slats"
Gomelsky, Aleksandr
Gunter, Sue
Hannum, Alex
Harshman, Marv
Haskins, Don
Hatchell, Sylvia
Hickey, Edgar
Hobson, Howard
Holzman, William "Red"
Hurley, Bob, Sr.
Iba, Hank
Jackson, Phil
Julian, Alvin
Keaney, Frank
Keogan, George
Knight, Bob
Krzyzewski, Mike
Kundla, John
Lambert, Ward
*Leonard, Bob
Lewis, Guy V.
Litwack, Harry
Loeffler, Kenneth
Lonborg, Arthur "Dutch"
Magee, Herb
McCutchan, Arad
McGuire, Al
McGuire, Frank
McLendon, John
Meanwell, Dr. Walter
Meyer, Ray
Miller, Ralph
Moore, Billie
Nelson, Don
Newell, Pete
Nikolic, Aleksandar
Novosel, Mirko
Olson, Robert "Lute"
Pitino, Rick

Ramsay, John "Jack"
*Richardson, Nolan
Riley, Pat
Rubini, Cesare
Rupp, Adolph
Rush, Cathy
Sachs, Leonard
Shelton, Everett
Sloan, Jerry
Smith, Dean
Stringer, C. Vivian
Summitt, Pat
Tarkanian, Jerry
Taylor, Fred
Thompson, John R.
VanDerveer, Tara
Wade, Margaret
Watts, Stan
**Wilkens, Lenny
*Williams, Gary
Williams, Roy
Winter, Tex
**Wooden, John
Woolpert, Phil
Wootten, Morgan
Yow, Kay

Teams

1960 USA Men's Olympic Team
1992 USA Men's Olympic "Dream Team"
All American Red Heads
Buffalo Germans First Team
Harlem Globetrotters
*Immaculata University
New York Renaissance
Original Celtics
Texas Western

Referees

Enright, James
Hepbron, George
Hoyt, George
Kennedy, Matthew
Leith, Lloyd
Mihalik, Zigmund "Red"
Nichols, Hank
Nucatola, John
Quigley, Ernest
Rudolph, Marvin "Mendy"
Shirley, J. Dallas
Strom, Earl
Tobey, David
Walsh, David

Contributors

Abbott, Senda
Berenson
Barksdale, Don

Bee, Clair
Biasone, Danny
Brown, Hubert "Hubie"
Brown, Walter
Bunn, John
Buss, Jerry
*Clifton, Nat
Colangelo, Jerry
Davidson, Bill
Douglas, Bob
Duer, Al
Embry, Wayne
Fagan, Cliff
Fisher, Harry
Fleisher, Larry
Gavitt, David
Gottlieb, Edward
Granik, Russ
Gulick, Dr. Luther
Harrison, Lester
Hearn, Francis "Chick"
Henderson, E. B.
Hepp, Dr. Ferenc
Hickox, Edward
Hinkle, Tony
Irish, Edward "Ned"
Jones, R. William
Kennedy, Walter
Knight, Phil
Lemon, Meadowlark
Liston, Emil
Lloyd, Earl
Mokray, Bill
Morgan, Ralph
Morgenweck, Frank
Naismith, Dr. James
Newton, C. M.
O'Brien, John
O'Brien, Larry
Olsen, Harold
Podoloff, Maurice
Porter, Henry V.
Reid, William
Ripley, Elmer
St. John, Lynn
Saperstein, Abe
Schabinger, Arthur
Stagg, Alonzo
Stankovic, Boris
Steitz, Edward
*Stern, David
Taylor, Chuck
Teague, Bertha
Tower, Oswald
Trester, Arthur
Wells, Clifford
Wilke, Lou
Zollner, Fred

Phoenix Sets League Record En Route to 2014 WNBA Title

The Phoenix Mercury capped a record-setting 2014 regular season by sweeping the Chicago Sky in the WNBA Finals for their third league title. Veteran guard Diana Taurasi and forward Candice Dupree each scored 24 points in Phoenix's 87-82 win over the Sky in Game 3 Sept. 12, 2014, at UIC Pavilion in Chicago. Taurasi averaged 20.3 points in the Finals and was voted WNBA Finals MVP.

Chicago reached its first-ever WNBA final by upsetting Atlanta and Indiana in the Eastern Conference playoffs. Phoenix set a WNBA regular-season record with 29 wins, four games ahead of Minnesota, and beat the Lynx in the Western Conference finals. Lynx forward Maya Moore scored 30 or more points in 12 regular season games and won the league's Most Valuable Player Award.

San Antonio Stars' veteran guard Becky Hammon retired after 16 WNBA seasons. Hammon was hired by the NBA's San Antonio Spurs in Aug. 2014, becoming the league's first full-time female assistant coach.

WNBA Final Standings, 2014

(playoff seeding in parentheses; conference winner automatically gets top seed)

Eastern Conference	W	L	PCT	GB	Western Conference	W	L	PCT	GB
Atlanta Dream (1)	19	15	.559	—	Phoenix Mercury (1)	29	5	.853	—
Indiana Fever (2)	16	18	.471	3	Minnesota Lynx (2)	25	9	.735	4
Washington Mystics (3)	16	18	.471	3	San Antonio Stars (3)	16	18	.471	13
Chicago Sky (4)	15	19	.441	4	Los Angeles Sparks (4)	16	18	.471	13
New York Liberty	15	19	.441	4	Seattle Storm	12	22	.353	17
Connecticut Sun	13	21	.382	6	Tulsa Shock	12	22	.353	17

Note: Indiana earned the no. 2 playoff seed in the East over Washington due to a better conference record; Chicago earned the no. 4 seed over New York by sweeping the season series. San Antonio earned the no. 3 seed in the West over L.A. by winning three of four regular season games.

WNBA Playoff Results, 2014

Eastern Conference
(4) Chicago defeated (1) Atlanta, 2 games to 1
(2) Indiana defeated (3) Washington, 2 games to 0
(4) Chicago defeated (2) Indiana, 2 games to 1

Western Conference
(1) Phoenix defeated (4) Los Angeles, 2 games to 0
(2) Minnesota defeated (3) San Antonio, 2 games to 0
(1) Phoenix defeated (2) Minnesota, 2 games to 1

WNBA Championship, 2014

Phoenix defeated Chicago, 3 games to 0 (83-62, 97-68, 87-82), in the best-of-five series.

All-WNBA Teams, 2014

First team	Position	Second team	Position
Maya Moore, Minnesota	Forward	Angel McCoughtry, Atlanta	Forward
Candace Parker, Los Angeles	Forward	Nneka Ogwumike, Los Angeles	Forward
Brittney Griner, Phoenix	Center	Tina Charles, New York	Center
Diana Taurasi, Phoenix	Guard	Lindsay Whalen, Minnesota	Guard
Skylar Diggins, Tulsa	Guard	Danielle Robinson, San Antonio (tie)	Guard
		Seimone Augustus, Minnesota (tie)	Guard

WNBA Statistical Leaders, 2014

Minutes played: 1,192, Skylar Diggins, Tulsa
Total points: 812, Maya Moore, Minnesota
Points per game: 23.9, Maya Moore, Minnesota
Field goal pct.: .599, Erlana Larkins, Indiana
3-point field goal pct.: .449, Erin Phillips, Phoenix

Free throw pct.: .941, Danielle Robinson, San Antonio
Rebounds: 347, Courtney Paris, Tulsa
Assists: 189, Lindsay Whalen, Minnesota
Steals: 75, Sancho Lyttle, Atlanta
Blocked shots: 129, Brittney Griner, Phoenix

WNBA Champions, 1997-2014

	Regular Season		Playoffs		
Year	Eastern champion	Western champion	Champion	Winning coach	Opponent
1997	Houston Comets	Phoenix Mercury	Houston	Van Chancellor	New York
1998	Cleveland Rockers	Houston Comets	Houston	Van Chancellor	Phoenix
1999	New York Liberty	Houston Comets	Houston	Van Chancellor	New York
2000	New York Liberty	Los Angeles Sparks	Houston	Van Chancellor	New York
2001	Cleveland Rockers	Los Angeles Sparks	Los Angeles	Michael Cooper	Charlotte
2002	New York Liberty	Los Angeles Sparks	Los Angeles	Michael Cooper	New York
2003	Detroit Shock	Los Angeles Sparks	Detroit	Bill Laimbeer	Los Angeles
2004	Connecticut Sun	Los Angeles Sparks	Seattle	Anne Donovan	Connecticut
2005	Connecticut Sun	Sacramento Monarchs	Sacramento	John Whisenant	Connecticut
2006	Connecticut Sun	Los Angeles Sparks	Detroit	Bill Laimbeer	Sacramento
2007	Detroit Shock	Phoenix Mercury	Phoenix	Paul Westhead	Detroit
2008	Detroit Shock	San Antonio Silver Stars	Detroit	Bill Laimbeer	San Antonio
2009	Indiana Fever	Phoenix Mercury	Phoenix	Corey Gaines	Indiana
2010	Washington Mystics	Seattle Storm	Seattle	Brian Agler	Atlanta
2011	Indiana Fever	Minnesota Lynx	Minnesota	Cheryl Reeve	Atlanta
2012	Connecticut Sun	Minnesota Lynx	Indiana	Lin Dunn	Minnesota
2013	Chicago Sky	Minnesota Lynx	Minnesota	Cheryl Reeve	Atlanta
2014	Atlanta Dream	Phoenix Mercury	Phoenix	Sandy Brondello	Chicago

WNBA Finals MVP, 1997-2014

Year	Player, team	Year	Player, team	Year	Player, team
1997	Cynthia Cooper, Houston	2003	Ruth Riley, Detroit	2009	Diana Taurasi, Phoenix
1998	Cynthia Cooper, Houston	2004	Betty Lennox, Seattle	2010	Lauren Jackson, Seattle
1999	Cynthia Cooper, Houston	2005	Yolanda Griffith, Sacramento	2011	Seimone Augustus, Minnesota
2000	Cynthia Cooper, Houston	2006	Deanna Nolan, Detroit	2012	Tamika Catchings, Indiana
2001	Lisa Leslie, Los Angeles	2007	Cappie Pondexter, Phoenix	2013	Maya Moore, Minnesota
2002	Lisa Leslie, Los Angeles	2008	Katie Smith, Detroit	2014	Diana Taurasi, Phoenix

WNBA Most Valuable Player, 1997-2014

Year	Player, team	Year	Player, team	Year	Player, team
1997	Cynthia Cooper, Houston	2003	Lauren Jackson, Seattle	2009	Diana Taurasi, Phoenix
1998	Cynthia Cooper, Houston	2004	Lisa Leslie, Los Angeles	2010	Lauren Jackson, Seattle
1999	Yolanda Griffith, Sacramento	2005	Sheryl Swoopes, Houston	2011	Tamika Catchings, Indiana
2000	Sheryl Swoopes, Houston	2006	Lisa Leslie, Los Angeles	2012	Tina Charles, Connecticut
2001	Lisa Leslie, Los Angeles	2007	Lauren Jackson, Seattle	2013	Candace Parker, Los Angeles
2002	Sheryl Swoopes, Houston	2008	Candace Parker, Los Angeles	2014	Maya Moore, Minnesota

WNBA Rookie of the Year, 1997-2014

Year	Player, team	Year	Player, team	Year	Player, team
1997	No award	2003	Cheryl Ford, Detroit	2009	Angel McCoughtry, Atlanta
1998	Tracy Reid, Charlotte	2004	Diana Taurasi, Phoenix	2010	Tina Charles, Connecticut
1999	Chamique Holdsclaw, Washington	2005	Temeka Johnson, Washington	2011	Maya Moore, Minnesota
2000	Betty Lennox, Minnesota	2006	Seimone Augustus, Minnesota	2012	Nneka Ogwumike, Los Angeles
2001	Jackie Stiles, Portland	2007	Armintie Price, Chicago	2013	Elena Delle Donne, Chicago
2002	Tamika Catchings, Indiana	2008	Candace Parker, Los Angeles	2014	Chiney Ogwumike, Connecticut

WNBA Scoring Leaders, 1997-2014

(Average points per game; 24 games or 480 point minimum in 2014; prior season minimums vary.)

Year	Player, team	PTS	AVG	Year	Player, team	PTS	AVG
1997	Cynthia Cooper, Houston	621	22.2	2006	Diana Taurasi, Phoenix	860	25.3
1998	Cynthia Cooper, Houston	680	22.7	2007	Lauren Jackson, Seattle	739	23.8
1999	Cynthia Cooper, Houston	686	22.1	2008	Diana Taurasi, Phoenix	820	24.1
2000	Sheryl Swoopes, Houston	643	20.7	2009	Diana Taurasi, Phoenix	631	20.4
2001	Katie Smith, Minnesota	739	23.1	2010	Diana Taurasi, Phoenix	702	22.6
2002	Chamique Holdsclaw, Washington	397	19.9	2011	Diana Taurasi, Phoenix	692	21.6
2003	Lauren Jackson, Seattle	698	21.2	2012	Angel McCoughtry, Atlanta	514	21.4
2004	Lauren Jackson, Seattle	634	20.5	2013	Angel McCoughtry, Atlanta	711	21.5
2005	Sheryl Swoopes, Houston	614	18.6	2014	Maya Moore, Minnesota	812	23.9

WNBA Rebounding Leaders, 1997-2014

(Average rebounds per game; 24 games minimum in 2014; prior season minimums vary.)

Year	Player, team	REB	RPG	Year	Player, team	REB	RPG
1997	Lisa Leslie, Los Angeles	266	9.5	2006	Cheryl Ford, Detroit	363	11.3
1998	Lisa Leslie, Los Angeles	285	10.2	2007	Lauren Jackson, Seattle	300	9.7
1999	Yolanda Griffith, Sacramento	329	11.3	2008	Candace Parker, Los Angeles	313	9.5
2000	Natalie Williams, Utah	336	11.6	2009	Candace Parker, Los Angeles	244	9.8
2001	Yolanda Griffith, Sacramento	357	11.2	2010	Tina Charles, Connecticut	398	11.7
2002	Chamique Holdsclaw, Washington	232	11.6	2011	Tina Charles, Connecticut	374	11.0
2003	Chamique Holdsclaw, Washington	294	10.9	2012	Tina Charles, Connecticut	345	10.5
2004	Lisa Leslie, Los Angeles	336	9.9	2013	Sylvia Fowles, Chicago	369	11.5
2005	Cheryl Ford, Detroit	322	9.8	2014	Courtney Paris, Tulsa	347	10.2

WNBA Assist Leaders, 1997-2014

(Average assists per game; 24 games minimum in 2014; prior season minimums vary.)

Year	Player, team	AST	APG	Year	Player, team	AST	APG
1997	Teresa Weatherspoon, New York	172	6.1	2006	Nikki Teasley, Washington	183	5.4
1998	Ticha Penicheiro, Sacramento	224	7.5	2007	Becky Hammon, San Antonio	140	5.0
1999	Ticha Penicheiro, Sacramento	226	7.1	2008	Lindsay Whalen, Connecticut	166	5.4
2000	Ticha Penicheiro, Sacramento	236	7.9	2009	Sue Bird, Seattle	179	5.8
2001	Ticha Penicheiro, Sacramento	172	7.5	2010	Ticha Penicheiro, Los Angeles	220	6.9
2002	Ticha Penicheiro, Sacramento	192	8.0	2011	Lindsay Whalen, Minnesota	199	5.9
2003	Ticha Penicheiro, Sacramento	229	6.7	2012	Lindsay Whalen, Minnesota	178	5.4
2004	Nikki Teasley, Los Angeles	207	6.1	2013	Danielle Robinson, San Antonio	168	6.7
2005	Sue Bird, Seattle	176	5.9	2014	Lindsay Whalen, Minnesota	189	5.6

All-Time WNBA Statistical Leaders

(At the end of the 2014 season. * = Active in 2014 season.)

Scoring Average
(minimum 100 games)

Player	G	PTS	AVG	Player	G	PTS	AVG
Cynthia Cooper	124	2,601	21.0	*Cappie Pondexter	295	5,453	18.5
*Diana Taurasi	334	6,722	20.1	*Maya Moore	136	2,447	18.0
*Angel McCoughtry	189	3,662	19.4	*Candace Parker	179	3,170	17.7
Lauren Jackson	317	6,007	18.9	Lisa Leslie	363	6,263	17.3
*Seimone Augustus	248	4,584	18.5	*Tina Charles	164	2,833	17.3

Points		Rebounds		Assists	
Tina Thompson	7,488	Lisa Leslie	3,307	Ticha Penicheiro	2,599
*Diana Taurasi	6,722	Tina Thompson	3,070	*Sue Bird	2,068
*Tamika Catchings	6,554	Taj McWilliams-Franklin	3,013	*Lindsay Whalen	1,911
Katie Smith	6,452	*Tamika Catchings	2,940	*Becky Hammon	1,708
Lisa Leslie	6,263	*DeLisha Milton-Jones	2,541	*Diana Taurasi	1,448
Lauren Jackson	6,007	Michelle Snow	2,479	Shannon Johnson	1,424
*Becky Hammon	5,841	*Rebekkah Brunson	2,470	*Tamika Catchings	1,355
*Katie Douglas	5,563	Lauren Jackson	2,447	Teresa Weatherspoon	1,338
*DeLisha Milton-Jones	5,533	Yolanda Griffith	2,444	Dawn Staley	1,337
*Cappie Pondexter	5,453	Tangela Smith	2,335	*Temeka Johnson	1,260

3-Point Field Goals Made		Steals		Blocked Shots	
Katie Smith	906	*Tamika Catchings	957	Margo Dydek	877
*Becky Hammon	829	Ticha Penicheiro	764	Lisa Leslie	822
*Diana Taurasi	811	Sheryl Swoopes	657	Lauren Jackson	586
Tina Thompson	748	*Katie Douglas	623	Tangela Smith	557
*Katie Douglas	727	*DeLisha Milton-Jones	612	Tammy Sutton-Brown	555
*Sue Bird	639	Taj McWilliams-Franklin	580	Ruth Riley	505
*Nicole Powell	580	Tully Bevilaqua	573	Taj McWilliams-Franklin	443
*Kara Lawson	558	*Jia Perkins	529	Michelle Snow	403
*Tamika Catchings	553	Yolanda Griffith	529	*Sylvia Fowles	376
Lauren Jackson	436	*Sue Bird	523	Tina Thompson	372

HOCKEY

L.A. Prevails Over New York in Bicoastal 2014 Stanley Cup

The Los Angeles Kings won their second NHL title in three seasons by defeating the New York Rangers, four games to one, in the 2014 Stanley Cup Finals. The Cup-clinching win came in Game 5 June 13, 2014, at Staples Center in Los Angeles, when Alec Martinez scored at 14:43 of the second overtime to lift the Kings to a 3-2 victory. Kings right winger Justin Williams won the Conn Smythe Trophy as playoff MVP, totaling 25 points in 26 playoff games, including 7 points in the Finals.

The Boston Bruins (54-19-9) won the Presidents' Trophy with a league-best 117 points at the end of the regular season in the newly realigned Atlantic Division. Pittsburgh Penguins captain Sidney Crosby won his second Hart Trophy as league MVP.

A frosty Michigan Stadium was the setting for the NHL Winter Classic as the Toronto Maple Leafs beat the Detroit Red Wings 3-2 in a shootout Jan. 1, 2014, in Ann Arbor, MI, before a crowd of 105,491. The Winter Classic was one of six outdoor regular-season games; the others were held at New York's Yankee Stadium (two games), Dodger Stadium in Los Angeles, Chicago's Soldier Field, and BC Place in Vancouver. The NHL season paused for close to three weeks so that 147 players could participate in the Winter Olympic Games in Sochi, Russia.

Final NHL Standings, 2013-14

(* = clinched playoff berth)

Standings are determined by total points, then by the greater number of games won, excluding games won in a shootout. This figure is reflected in the ROW column. Teams tied at the end of regulation time are each awarded one point. An additional point is awarded to the overtime or shootout winner.

The top three finishers in each division qualify for the first 12 playoff seeds. Two additional wild card playoff spots are awarded in each conference, to the next two highest-placed finishers, regardless of division.

Eastern Conference

Atlantic Division	W	L	OT	GF	GA	PTS	ROW
*Boston Bruins	54	19	9	261	177	117	51
*Tampa Bay Lightning	46	27	9	240	215	101	38
*Montréal Canadiens	46	28	8	215	204	100	40
*Detroit Red Wings	39	28	15	222	230	93	34
Ottawa Senators	37	31	14	236	265	88	30
Toronto Maple Leafs	38	36	8	231	256	84	29
Florida Panthers	29	45	8	196	268	66	21
Buffalo Sabres	21	51	10	157	248	52	14

Metropolitan Division	W	L	OT	GF	GA	PTS	ROW
*Pittsburgh Penguins	51	24	7	249	207	109	44
*New York Rangers	45	31	6	218	193	96	41
*Philadelphia Flyers	42	30	10	236	235	94	39
*Columbus Blue Jackets	43	32	7	231	216	93	38
Washington Capitals	38	30	14	235	240	90	28
New Jersey Devils	35	29	18	197	208	88	35
Carolina Hurricanes	36	35	11	207	230	83	34
New York Islanders	34	37	11	225	267	79	25

Western Conference

Central Division	W	L	OT	GF	GA	PTS	ROW
*Colorado Avalanche	52	22	8	250	220	112	47
*St. Louis Blues	52	23	7	248	191	111	43
*Chicago Blackhawks	46	21	15	267	220	107	40
*Minnesota Wild	43	27	12	207	206	98	35
*Dallas Stars	40	31	11	235	228	91	36
Nashville Predators	38	32	12	216	242	88	36
Winnipeg Jets	37	35	10	227	237	84	29

Pacific Division	W	L	OT	GF	GA	PTS	ROW
*Anaheim Ducks	54	20	8	266	209	116	51
*San Jose Sharks	51	22	9	249	200	111	41
*Los Angeles Kings	46	28	8	206	174	100	38
Phoenix Coyotes	37	30	15	216	231	89	31
Vancouver Canucks	36	35	11	196	223	83	31
Calgary Flames	35	40	7	209	241	77	28
Edmonton Oilers	29	44	9	203	270	67	25

Stanley Cup Playoff Results, 2014

Eastern Conference

Boston defeated Detroit, 4 games to 1
Montréal defeated Tampa Bay, 4 games to 0
Pittsburgh defeated Columbus, 4 games to 2
NY Rangers defeated Philadelphia, 4 games to 3
Montréal defeated Boston, 4 games to 3
NY Rangers defeated Pittsburgh, 4 games to 3
NY Rangers defeated Montréal, 4 games to 2

Western Conference

Minnesota defeated Colorado, 4 games to 3
Chicago defeated St. Louis, 4 games to 2
Anaheim defeated Dallas, 4 games to 2
Los Angeles defeated San Jose, 4 games to 3
Chicago defeated Minnesota, 4 games to 2
Los Angeles defeated Anaheim, 4 games to 3
Los Angeles defeated Chicago, 4 games to 3

Stanley Cup Final

Los Angeles defeated NY Rangers, 4 games to 1 (3-2 [OT], 5-4 [2 OT], 3-0, 1-2, 3-2 [2 OT])

Stanley Cup Champions, 1927-2014

Year	Champion	Coach	Final opponent	Year	Champion	Coach	Final opponent
1927	Ottawa	Dave Gill	Boston	1956	Montréal	Toe Blake	Detroit
1928	NY Rangers	Lester Patrick	Montréal Maroons	1957	Montréal	Toe Blake	Boston
				1958	Montréal	Toe Blake	Boston
1929	Boston	Cy Denneny	NY Rangers	1959	Montréal	Toe Blake	Toronto
1930	Montréal Canadiens	Cecil Hart	Boston	1960	Montréal	Toe Blake	Toronto
1931	Montréal Canadiens	Cecil Hart	Chicago	1961	Chicago	Rudy Pilous	Detroit
1932	Toronto	Dick Irvin	NY Rangers	1962	Toronto	Punch Imlach	Chicago
1933	NY Rangers	Lester Patrick	Toronto	1963	Toronto	Punch Imlach	Detroit
1934	Chicago	Tommy Gorman	Detroit	1964	Toronto	Punch Imlach	Detroit
1935	Montréal Maroons	Tommy Gorman	Toronto	1965	Montréal	Toe Blake	Chicago
1936	Detroit	Jack Adams	Toronto	1966	Montréal	Toe Blake	Detroit
1937	Detroit	Jack Adams	NY Rangers	1967	Toronto	Punch Imlach	Montréal
1938	Chicago	Bill Stewart	Toronto	1968	Montréal	Toe Blake	St. Louis
1939	Boston	Art Ross	Toronto	1969	Montréal	Claude Ruel	St. Louis
1940	NY Rangers	Frank Boucher	Toronto	1970	Boston	Harry Sinden	St. Louis
1941	Boston	Cooney Weiland	Detroit	1971	Montréal	Al MacNeil	Chicago
1942	Toronto	Hap Day	Detroit	1972	Boston	Tom Johnson	NY Rangers
1943	Detroit	Jack Adams	Boston	1973	Montréal	Scotty Bowman	Chicago
1944	Montréal	Dick Irvin	Chicago	1974	Philadelphia	Fred Shero	Boston
1945	Toronto	Hap Day	Detroit	1975	Philadelphia	Fred Shero	Buffalo
1946	Montréal	Dick Irvin	Boston	1976	Montréal	Scotty Bowman	Philadelphia
1947	Toronto	Hap Day	Montréal	1977	Montréal	Scotty Bowman	Boston
1948	Toronto	Hap Day	Detroit	1978	Montréal	Scotty Bowman	Boston
1949	Toronto	Hap Day	Detroit	1979	Montréal	Scotty Bowman	NY Rangers
1950	Detroit	Tommy Ivan	NY Rangers	1980	NY Islanders	Al Arbour	Philadelphia
1951	Toronto	Joe Primeau	Montréal	1981	NY Islanders	Al Arbour	Minnesota
1952	Detroit	Tommy Ivan	Montréal	1982	NY Islanders	Al Arbour	Vancouver
1953	Montréal	Dick Irvin	Boston	1983	NY Islanders	Al Arbour	Edmonton
1954	Detroit	Tommy Ivan	Montréal	1984	Edmonton	Glen Sather	NY Islanders
1955	Detroit	Jimmy Skinner	Montréal	1985	Edmonton	Glen Sather	Philadelphia

Year	Champion	Coach	Final opponent	Year	Champion	Coach	Final opponent
1986	Montréal	Jean Perron	Calgary	2001	Colorado	Bob Hartley	New Jersey
1987	Edmonton	Glen Sather	Philadelphia	2002	Detroit	Scotty Bowman	Carolina
1988	Edmonton	Glen Sather	Boston	2003	New Jersey	Pat Burns	Anaheim
1989	Calgary	Terry Crisp	Montréal	2004	Tampa Bay	John Tortorella	Calgary
1990	Edmonton	John Muckler	Boston	2005	No competition (labor dispute; season cancelled)		
1991	Pittsburgh	Bob Johnson	Minnesota	2006	Carolina	Peter Laviolette	Edmonton
1992	Pittsburgh	Scotty Bowman	Chicago	2007	Anaheim	Randy Carlyle	Ottawa
1993	Montréal	Jacques Demers	Los Angeles	2008	Detroit	Mike Babcock	Pittsburgh
1994	NY Rangers	Mike Keenan	Vancouver	2009	Pittsburgh	Dan Bylsma	Detroit
1995	New Jersey	Jacques Lemaire	Detroit	2010	Chicago	Joel Quenneville	Philadelphia
1996	Colorado	Marc Crawford	Florida	2011	Boston	Claude Julien	Vancouver
1997	Detroit	Scotty Bowman	Philadelphia	2012	Los Angeles	Darryl Sutter	New Jersey
1998	Detroit	Scotty Bowman	Washington	2013	Chicago	Joel Quenneville	Boston
1999	Dallas	Ken Hitchcock	Buffalo	2014	Los Angeles	Darryl Sutter	NY Rangers
2000	New Jersey	Larry Robinson	Dallas				

Most NHL Goals in a Season

Player	Team	Season	Goals	Player	Team	Season	Goals
Wayne Gretzky	Edmonton	1981-82	92	Jari Kurri	Edmonton	1984-85	71
Wayne Gretzky	Edmonton	1983-84	87	Mario Lemieux	Pittsburgh	1987-88	70
Brett Hull	St. Louis	1990-91	86	Bernie Nicholls	Los Angeles	1988-89	70
Mario Lemieux	Pittsburgh	1988-89	85	Brett Hull	St. Louis	1991-92	70
Phil Esposito	Boston	1970-71	76	Mike Bossy	NY Islanders	1978-79	69
Alexander Mogilny	Buffalo	1992-93	76	Mario Lemieux	Pittsburgh	1992-93	69
Teemu Selanne	Winnipeg	1992-93	76	Mario Lemieux	Pittsburgh	1995-96	69
Wayne Gretzky	Edmonton	1984-85	73	Phil Esposito	Boston	1973-74	68
Brett Hull	St. Louis	1989-90	72	Mike Bossy	NY Islanders	1980-81	68
Wayne Gretzky	Edmonton	1982-83	71	Jari Kurri	Edmonton	1985-86	68

All-Time Regular Season Leading Scorers
(Through end of 2013-14 season. * = active in 2013-14 season.)

Player	Goals	Assists	Points	Player	Goals	Assists	Points	Player	Goals	Assists	Points
Wayne Gretzky	894	1,963	2,857	Mario Lemieux	690	1,033	1,723	*Teemu Selanne	684	773	1,457
Mark Messier	694	1,193	1,887	Joe Sakic	625	1,016	1,641	Bryan Trottier	524	901	1,425
Gordie Howe	801	1,049	1,850	Phil Esposito	717	873	1,590	Adam Oates	341	1,079	1,420
Ron Francis	549	1,249	1,798	Ray Bourque	410	1,169	1,579	Doug Gilmour	450	964	1,414
Marcel Dionne	731	1,040	1,771	Mark Recchi	577	956	1,533	Dale Hawerchuk	518	891	1,409
*Jaromir Jagr	705	1,050	1,755	Paul Coffey	396	1,135	1,531	Jari Kurri	601	797	1,398
Steve Yzerman	692	1,063	1,755	Stan Mikita	541	926	1,467	Luc Robitaille	668	726	1,394

Hart Memorial Trophy (MVP), 1927-2014

Year	Player, team	Year	Player, team	Year	Player, team
1927	Herb Gardiner, Montréal Canadiens	1957	Gordie Howe, Detroit	1985	Wayne Gretzky, Edmonton
1928	Howie Morenz, Montréal Canadiens	1958	Gordie Howe, Detroit	1986	Wayne Gretzky, Edmonton
1929	Roy Worters, NY Americans	1959	Andy Bathgate, NY Rangers	1987	Wayne Gretzky, Edmonton
1930	Nels Stewart, Montréal Maroons	1960	Gordie Howe, Detroit	1988	Mario Lemieux, Pittsburgh
1931	Howie Morenz, Montréal Canadiens	1961	Bernie Geoffrion, Montréal	1989	Wayne Gretzky, Los Angeles
1932	Howie Morenz, Montréal Canadiens	1962	Jacques Plante, Montréal	1990	Mark Messier, Edmonton
1933	Eddie Shore, Boston	1963	Gordie Howe, Detroit	1991	Brett Hull, St. Louis
1934	Aurel Joliat, Montréal Canadiens	1964	Jean Beliveau, Montréal	1992	Mark Messier, NY Rangers
1935	Eddie Shore, Boston	1965	Bobby Hull, Chicago	1993	Mario Lemieux, Pittsburgh
1936	Eddie Shore, Boston	1966	Bobby Hull, Chicago	1994	Sergei Fedorov, Detroit
1937	Babe Siebert, Montréal Canadiens	1967	Stan Mikita, Chicago	1995	Eric Lindros, Philadelphia
1938	Sid Abel, Detroit	1968	Stan Mikita, Chicago	1996	Mario Lemieux, Pittsburgh
1939	Toe Blake, Montréal	1969	Phil Esposito, Boston	1997	Dominik Hasek, Buffalo
1940	Ebbie Goodfellow, Detroit	1970	Bobby Orr, Boston	1998	Dominik Hasek, Buffalo
1941	Bill Cowley, Boston	1971	Bobby Orr, Boston	1999	Jaromir Jagr, Pittsburgh
1942	Tom Anderson, Brooklyn Americans	1972	Bobby Orr, Boston	2000	Chris Pronger, St. Louis
1943	Bill Cowley, Boston	1973	Bobby Clarke, Philadelphia	2001	Joe Sakic, Colorado
1944	Babe Pratt, Toronto	1974	Phil Esposito, Boston	2002	Jose Theodore, Montréal
1945	Elmer Lach, Montréal	1975	Bobby Clarke, Philadelphia	2003	Peter Forsberg, Colorado
1946	Max Bentley, Chicago	1976	Bobby Clarke, Philadelphia	2004	Martin St. Louis, Tampa Bay
1947	Maurice Richard, Montréal	1977	Guy Lafleur, Montréal	2006	Joe Thornton, San Jose
1948	Buddy O'Connor, NY Rangers	1978	Guy Lafleur, Montréal	2007	Sidney Crosby, Pittsburgh
1949	Sid Abel, Detroit	1979	Bryan Trottier, NY Islanders	2008	Alexander Ovechkin, Washington
1950	Chuck Rayner, NY Rangers	1980	Wayne Gretzky, Edmonton	2009	Alexander Ovechkin, Washington
1951	Milt Schmidt, Boston	1981	Wayne Gretzky, Edmonton	2010	Henrik Sedin, Vancouver
1952	Gordie Howe, Detroit	1982	Wayne Gretzky, Edmonton	2011	Corey Perry, Anaheim
1953	Gordie Howe, Detroit	1983	Wayne Gretzky, Edmonton	2012	Evgeni Malkin, Pittsburgh
1954	Al Rollins, Chicago	1984	Wayne Gretzky, Edmonton	2013	Alexander Ovechkin, Washington
1955	Ted Kennedy, Toronto			2014	Sidney Crosby, Pittsburgh
1956	Jean Beliveau, Montréal				

Conn Smythe Trophy (MVP in Playoffs), 1965-2014

Year	Player, team	Year	Player, team	Year	Player, team
1965	Jean Beliveau, Montréal	1977	Guy Lafleur, Montréal	1989	Al MacInnis, Calgary
1966	Roger Crozier, Detroit	1978	Larry Robinson, Montréal	1990	Bill Ranford, Edmonton
1967	Dave Keon, Toronto	1979	Bob Gainey, Montréal	1991	Mario Lemieux, Pittsburgh
1968	Glenn Hall, St. Louis	1980	Bryan Trottier, NY Islanders	1992	Mario Lemieux, Pittsburgh
1969	Serge Savard, Montréal	1981	Butch Goring, NY Islanders	1993	Patrick Roy, Montréal
1970	Bobby Orr, Boston	1982	Mike Bossy, NY Islanders	1994	Brian Leetch, NY Rangers
1971	Ken Dryden, Montréal	1983	Billy Smith, NY Islanders	1995	Claude Lemieux, New Jersey
1972	Bobby Orr, Boston	1984	Mark Messier, Edmonton	1996	Joe Sakic, Colorado
1973	Yvan Cournoyer, Montréal	1985	Wayne Gretzky, Edmonton	1997	Mike Vernon, Detroit
1974	Bernie Parent, Philadelphia	1986	Patrick Roy, Montréal	1998	Steve Yzerman, Detroit
1975	Bernie Parent, Philadelphia	1987	Ron Hextall, Philadelphia	1999	Joe Nieuwendyk, Dallas
1976	Reggie Leach, Philadelphia	1988	Wayne Gretzky, Edmonton	2000	Scott Stevens, New Jersey

Year	Player, team	Year	Player, team	Year	Player, team
2001	Patrick Roy, Colorado	2007	Scott Niedermayer, Anaheim	2011	Tim Thomas, Boston
2002	Nicklas Lidstrom, Detroit	2008	Henrik Zetterberg, Detroit	2012	Jonathan Quick, Los Angeles
2003	Jean-Sebastien Giguere, Anaheim	2009	Evgeni Malkin, Pittsburgh	2013	Patrick Kane, Chicago
2004	Brad Richards, Tampa Bay	2010	Jonathan Toews, Chicago	2014	Justin Williams, Los Angeles
2006	Cam Ward, Carolina				

Calder Memorial Trophy (Rookie of the Year), 1933-2014

Year	Player, team	Year	Player, team	Year	Player, team
1933	Carl Voss, Detroit	1960	Bill Hay, Chicago	1987	Luc Robitaille, Los Angeles
1934	Russ Blinco, Montréal Maroons	1961	Dave Keon, Toronto	1988	Joe Nieuwendyk, Calgary
1935	Dave Schriner, NY Americans	1962	Bobby Rousseau, Montréal	1989	Brian Leetch, NY Rangers
1936	Mike Karakas, Chicago	1963	Kent Douglas, Toronto	1990	Sergei Makarov, Calgary
1937	Syl Apps, Toronto	1964	Jacques Laperrière, Montréal	1991	Ed Belfour, Chicago
1938	Cully Dahlstrom, Chicago	1965	Roger Crozier, Detroit	1992	Pavel Bure, Vancouver
1939	Frank Brimsek, Boston	1966	Brit Selby, Toronto	1993	Teemu Selanne, Winnipeg
1940	Kilby MacDonald, NY Rangers	1967	Bobby Orr, Boston	1994	Martin Brodeur, New Jersey
1941	John Quilty, Montréal	1968	Derek Sanderson, Boston	1995	Peter Forsberg, Quebec
1942	Grant Warwick, NY Rangers	1969	Danny Grant, Minnesota	1996	Daniel Alfredsson, Ottawa
1943	Gaye Stewart, Toronto	1970	Tony Esposito, Chicago	1997	Bryan Berard, NY Islanders
1944	Gus Bodnar, Toronto	1971	Gilbert Perreault, Buffalo	1998	Sergei Samsonov, Boston
1945	Frank McCool, Toronto	1972	Ken Dryden, Montréal	1999	Chris Drury, Colorado
1946	Edgar Laprade, NY Rangers	1973	Steve Vickers, NY Rangers	2000	Scott Gomez, New Jersey
1947	Howie Meeker, Toronto	1974	Denis Potvin, NY Islanders	2001	Evgeni Nabokov, San Jose
1948	Jim McFadden, Detroit	1975	Eric Vail, Atlanta	2002	Dany Heatley, Atlanta
1949	Pentti Lund, NY Rangers	1976	Bryan Trottier, NY Islanders	2003	Barret Jackman, St. Louis
1950	Jack Gelineau, Boston	1977	Willi Plett, Atlanta	2004	Andrew Raycroft, Boston
1951	Terry Sawchuk, Detroit	1978	Mike Bossy, NY Islanders	2006	Alexander Ovechkin, Washington
1952	Bernie Geoffrion, Montréal	1979	Bobby Smith, Minnesota	2007	Evgeni Malkin, Pittsburgh
1953	Gump Worsley, NY Rangers	1980	Ray Bourque, Boston	2008	Patrick Kane, Chicago
1954	Camille Henry, NY Rangers	1981	Peter Stastny, Quebec	2009	Steve Mason, Columbus
1955	Ed Litzenberger, Chicago	1982	Dale Hawerchuk, Winnipeg	2010	Tyler Myers, Buffalo
1956	Glenn Hall, Detroit	1983	Steve Larmer, Chicago	2011	Jeff Skinner, Carolina
1957	Larry Regan, Boston	1984	Tom Barrasso, Buffalo	2012	Gabriel Landeskog, Colorado
1958	Frank Mahovlich, Toronto	1985	Mario Lemieux, Pittsburgh	2013	Jonathan Huberdeau, Florida
1959	Ralph Backstrom, Montréal	1986	Gary Suter, Calgary	2014	Nathan MacKinnon, Colorado

Lady Byng Memorial Trophy (Most Gentlemanly Player), 1925-2014

Year	Player, team	Year	Player, team	Year	Player, team
1925	Frank Nighbor, Ottawa	1955	Sid Smith, Toronto	1985	Jari Kurri, Edmonton
1926	Frank Nighbor, Ottawa	1956	Earl Reibel, Detroit	1986	Mike Bossy, NY Islanders
1927	Billy Burch, NY Americans	1957	Andy Hebenton, NY Rangers	1987	Joe Mullen, Calgary
1928	Frank Boucher, NY Rangers	1958	Camille Henry, NY Rangers	1988	Mats Naslund, Montréal
1929	Frank Boucher, NY Rangers	1959	Alex Delvecchio, Detroit	1989	Joe Mullen, Calgary
1930	Frank Boucher, NY Rangers	1960	Don McKenney, Boston	1990	Brett Hull, St. Louis
1931	Frank Boucher, NY Rangers	1961	Red Kelly, Toronto	1991	Wayne Gretzky, Los Angeles
1932	Joe Primeau, Toronto	1962	Dave Keon, Toronto	1992	Wayne Gretzky, Los Angeles
1933	Frank Boucher, NY Rangers	1963	Dave Keon, Toronto	1993	Pierre Turgeon, NY Islanders
1934	Frank Boucher, NY Rangers	1964	Ken Wharram, Chicago	1994	Wayne Gretzky, Los Angeles
1935	Frank Boucher, NY Rangers	1965	Bobby Hull, Chicago	1995	Ron Francis, Pittsburgh
1936	Doc Romnes, Chicago	1966	Alex Delvecchio, Detroit	1996	Paul Kariya, Anaheim
1937	Marty Barry, Detroit	1967	Stan Mikita, Chicago	1997	Paul Kariya, Anaheim
1938	Gordie Drillon, Toronto	1968	Stan Mikita, Chicago	1998	Ron Francis, Pittsburgh
1939	Clint Smith, NY Rangers	1969	Alex Delvecchio, Detroit	1999	Wayne Gretzky, NY Rangers
1940	Bobby Bauer, Boston	1970	Phil Goyette, St. Louis	2000	Pavol Demitra, St. Louis
1941	Bobby Bauer, Boston	1971	John Bucyk, Boston	2001	Joe Sakic, Colorado
1942	Syl Apps, Toronto	1972	Jean Ratelle, NY Rangers	2002	Ron Francis, Carolina
1943	Max Bentley, Chicago	1973	Gil Perreault, Buffalo	2003	Alexander Mogilny, Toronto
1944	Clint Smith, Chicago	1974	John Bucyk, Boston	2004	Brad Richards, Tampa Bay
1945	Bill Mosienko, Chicago	1975	Marcel Dionne, Detroit	2006	Pavel Datsyuk, Detroit
1946	Toe Blake, Montréal	1976	Jean Ratelle, NYR-Boston	2007	Pavel Datsyuk, Detroit
1947	Bobby Bauer, Boston	1977	Marcel Dionne, Los Angeles	2008	Pavel Datsyuk, Detroit
1948	Buddy O'Connor, NY Rangers	1978	Butch Goring, Los Angeles	2009	Pavel Datsyuk, Detroit
1949	Bill Quackenbush, Boston	1979	Bob MacMillan, Atlanta	2010	Martin St. Louis, Tampa Bay
1950	Edgar Laprade, NY Rangers	1980	Wayne Gretzky, Edmonton	2011	Martin St. Louis, Tampa Bay
1951	Red Kelly, Detroit	1981	Rick Kehoe, Pittsburgh	2012	Brian Campbell, Florida
1952	Sid Smith, Toronto	1982	Rick Middleton, Boston	2013	Martin St. Louis, Tampa Bay
1953	Red Kelly, Detroit	1983	Mike Bossy, NY Islanders	2014	Ryan O'Reilly, Colorado
1954	Red Kelly, Detroit	1984	Mike Bossy, NY Islanders		

James Norris Memorial Trophy (Outstanding Defenseman), 1954-2014

Year	Player, team	Year	Player, team	Year	Player, team
1954	Red Kelly, Detroit	1974	Bobby Orr, Boston	1994	Ray Bourque, Boston
1955	Doug Harvey, Montréal	1975	Bobby Orr, Boston	1995	Paul Coffey, Detroit
1956	Doug Harvey, Montréal	1976	Denis Potvin, NY Islanders	1996	Chris Chelios, Chicago
1957	Doug Harvey, Montréal	1977	Larry Robinson, Montréal	1997	Brian Leetch, NY Rangers
1958	Doug Harvey, Montréal	1978	Denis Potvin, NY Islanders	1998	Rob Blake, Los Angeles
1959	Tom Johnson, Montréal	1979	Denis Potvin, NY Islanders	1999	Al MacInnis, St. Louis
1960	Doug Harvey, Montréal	1980	Larry Robinson, Montréal	2000	Chris Pronger, St. Louis
1961	Doug Harvey, Montréal	1981	Randy Carlyle, Pittsburgh	2001	Nicklas Lidstrom, Detroit
1962	Doug Harvey, NY Rangers	1982	Doug Wilson, Chicago	2002	Nicklas Lidstrom, Detroit
1963	Pierre Pilote, Chicago	1983	Rod Langway, Washington	2003	Nicklas Lidstrom, Detroit
1964	Pierre Pilote, Chicago	1984	Rod Langway, Washington	2004	Scott Niedermayer, New Jersey
1965	Pierre Pilote, Chicago	1985	Paul Coffey, Edmonton	2006	Nicklas Lidstrom, Detroit
1966	Jacques Laperrière, Montréal	1986	Paul Coffey, Edmonton	2007	Nicklas Lidstrom, Detroit
1967	Harry Howell, NY Rangers	1987	Ray Bourque, Boston	2008	Nicklas Lidstrom, Detroit
1968	Bobby Orr, Boston	1988	Ray Bourque, Boston	2009	Zdeno Chara, Boston
1969	Bobby Orr, Boston	1989	Chris Chelios, Montréal	2010	Duncan Keith, Chicago
1970	Bobby Orr, Boston	1990	Ray Bourque, Boston	2011	Nicklas Lidstrom, Detroit
1971	Bobby Orr, Boston	1991	Ray Bourque, Boston	2012	Erik Karlsson, Ottawa
1972	Bobby Orr, Boston	1992	Brian Leetch, NY Rangers	2013	P. K. Subban, Montréal
1973	Bobby Orr, Boston	1993	Chris Chelios, Chicago	2014	Duncan Keith, Chicago

Art Ross Trophy (Leading Points Scorer), 1947-2014

Year	Player, team	Year	Player, team	Year	Player, team
1947	Max Bentley, Chicago	1970	Bobby Orr, Boston	1992	Mario Lemieux, Pittsburgh
1948	Elmer Lach, Montréal	1971	Phil Esposito, Boston	1993	Mario Lemieux, Pittsburgh
1949	Roy Conacher, Chicago	1972	Phil Esposito, Boston	1994	Wayne Gretzky, Los Angeles
1950	Ted Lindsay, Detroit	1973	Phil Esposito, Boston	1995	Jaromir Jagr, Pittsburgh
1951	Gordie Howe, Detroit	1974	Phil Esposito, Boston	1996	Mario Lemieux, Pittsburgh
1952	Gordie Howe, Detroit	1975	Bobby Orr, Boston	1997	Mario Lemieux, Pittsburgh
1953	Gordie Howe, Detroit	1976	Guy Lafleur, Montréal	1998	Jaromir Jagr, Pittsburgh
1954	Gordie Howe, Detroit	1977	Guy Lafleur, Montréal	1999	Jaromir Jagr, Pittsburgh
1955	Bernie Geoffrion, Montréal	1978	Guy Lafleur, Montréal	2000	Jaromir Jagr, Pittsburgh
1956	Jean Beliveau, Montréal	1979	Bryan Trottier, NY Islanders	2001	Jaromir Jagr, Pittsburgh
1957	Gordie Howe, Detroit	1980	Marcel Dionne, Los Angeles	2002	Jarome Iginla, Calgary
1958	Dickie Moore, Montréal	1981	Wayne Gretzky, Edmonton	2003	Peter Forsberg, Colorado
1959	Dickie Moore, Montréal	1982	Wayne Gretzky, Edmonton	2004	Martin St. Louis, Tampa Bay
1960	Bobby Hull, Chicago	1983	Wayne Gretzky, Edmonton	2006	Joe Thornton, San Jose
1961	Bernie Geoffrion, Montréal	1984	Wayne Gretzky, Edmonton	2007	Sidney Crosby, Pittsburgh
1962	Bobby Hull, Chicago	1985	Wayne Gretzky, Edmonton	2008	Alexander Ovechkin, Washington
1963	Gordie Howe, Detroit	1986	Wayne Gretzky, Edmonton	2009	Evgeni Malkin, Pittsburgh
1964	Stan Mikita, Chicago	1987	Wayne Gretzky, Edmonton	2010	Henrik Sedin, Vancouver
1965	Stan Mikita, Chicago	1988	Mario Lemieux, Pittsburgh	2011	Daniel Sedin, Vancouver
1966	Bobby Hull, Chicago	1989	Mario Lemieux, Pittsburgh	2012	Evgeni Malkin, Pittsburgh
1967	Stan Mikita, Chicago	1990	Wayne Gretzky, Los Angeles	2013	Martin St. Louis, Tampa Bay
1968	Stan Mikita, Chicago	1991	Wayne Gretzky, Los Angeles	2014	Sidney Crosby, Pittsburgh
1969	Phil Esposito, Boston				

Vezina Trophy (Outstanding Goalie), 1927-2014

Before 1982, awarded to the goalie or goalies who played a minimum of 25 games for the team that allowed the fewest goals; since 1982, awarded to the most outstanding goalie, as determined by a vote of NHL general managers.

Year	Player, team	Year	Player, team	Year	Player, team
1927	George Hainsworth, Montréal Canadiens	1955	Terry Sawchuk, Detroit	1984	Tom Barrasso, Buffalo
1928	George Hainsworth, Montréal Canadiens	1956	Jacques Plante, Montréal	1985	Pelle Lindbergh, Philadelphia
		1957	Jacques Plante, Montréal	1986	John Vanbiesbrouck, NY Rangers
1929	George Hainsworth, Montréal Canadiens	1958	Jacques Plante, Montréal	1987	Ron Hextall, Philadelphia
		1959	Jacques Plante, Montréal	1988	Grant Fuhr, Edmonton
1930	Tiny Thompson, Boston	1960	Jacques Plante, Montréal	1989	Patrick Roy, Montréal
1931	Roy Worters, NY Americans	1961	Johnny Bower, Toronto	1990	Patrick Roy, Montréal
1932	Charlie Gardiner, Chicago	1962	Jacques Plante, Montréal	1991	Ed Belfour, Chicago
1933	Tiny Thompson, Boston	1963	Glenn Hall, Chicago	1992	Patrick Roy, Montréal
1934	Charlie Gardiner, Chicago	1964	Charlie Hodge, Montréal	1993	Ed Belfour, Chicago
1935	Lorne Chabot, Chicago	1965	Sawchuk, Bower; Toronto	1994	Dominik Hasek, Buffalo
1936	Tiny Thompson, Boston	1966	Worsley, Hodge; Montréal	1995	Dominik Hasek, Buffalo
1937	Normie Smith, Detroit	1967	Hall, DeJordy; Chicago	1996	Jim Carey, Washington
1938	Tiny Thompson, Boston	1968	Worsley, Vachon; Montréal	1997	Dominik Hasek, Buffalo
1939	Frank Brimsek, Boston	1969	Hall, Plante; St. Louis	1998	Dominik Hasek, Buffalo
1940	Dave Kerr, NY Rangers	1970	Tony Esposito, Chicago	1999	Dominik Hasek, Buffalo
1941	Turk Broda, Toronto	1971	Giacomin, Villemure; NY Rangers	2000	Olaf Kolzig, Washington
1942	Frank Brimsek, Boston	1972	Esposito, Smith; Chicago	2001	Dominik Hasek, Buffalo
1943	Johnny Mowers, Detroit	1973	Ken Dryden, Montréal	2002	Jose Theodore, Montréal
1944	Bill Durnan, Montréal	1974	Bernie Parent, Philadelphia; Tony Esposito, Chicago	2003	Martin Brodeur, New Jersey
1945	Bill Durnan, Montréal			2004	Martin Brodeur, New Jersey
1946	Bill Durnan, Montréal	1975	Bernie Parent, Philadelphia	2006	Miikka Kiprusoff, Calgary
1947	Bill Durnan, Montréal	1976	Ken Dryden, Montréal	2007	Martin Brodeur, New Jersey
1948	Turk Broda, Toronto	1977	Dryden, Larocque; Montréal	2008	Martin Brodeur, New Jersey
1949	Bill Durnan, Montréal	1978	Dryden, Larocque; Montréal	2009	Tim Thomas, Boston
1950	Bill Durnan, Montréal	1979	Dryden, Larocque; Montréal	2010	Ryan Miller, Buffalo
1951	Al Rollins, Toronto	1980	Sauve, Edwards; Buffalo	2011	Tim Thomas, Boston
1952	Terry Sawchuk, Detroit	1981	Sevigny, Larocque, Herron; Montréal	2012	Henrik Lundqvist, NY Rangers
1953	Terry Sawchuk, Detroit	1982	Bill Smith, NY Islanders	2013	Sergei Bobrovsky, Columbus
1954	Harry Lumley, Toronto	1983	Pete Peeters, Boston	2014	Tuukka Rask, Boston

NHL Home Ice

Team	Name (year built)	Capacity[1]	Team	Name (year built)	Capacity[1]
Anaheim	Honda Center[2] (1993)	17,174	New Jersey	Prudential Center (2007)	17,625
Boston	TD Garden[3] (1995)	17,565	NY Islanders	Nassau Veterans Memorial Coliseum (1972)	16,170
Buffalo	First Niagara Center[4] (1996)	19,070	NY Rangers	Madison Square Garden (1968)	18,200
Calgary	Scotiabank Saddledome[5] (1983)	19,289	Ottawa	Canadian Tire Centre[11] (1996)	19,153
Carolina	PNC Arena[6] (1999)	18,680	Philadelphia	Wells Fargo Center[12] (1996)	19,541
Chicago	United Center (1994)	19,717	Phoenix	Jobing.com Arena[13] (2003)	17,125
Colorado	Pepsi Center (1999)	18,007	Pittsburgh	CONSOL Energy Center (2010)	18,387
Columbus	Nationwide Arena (2000)	18,144	St. Louis	Scottrade Center[14] (1994)	19,150
Dallas	American Airlines Center (2001)	18,532	San Jose	SAP Center at San Jose[15] (1993)	17,562
Detroit	Joe Louis Arena (1979)	20,066	Tampa Bay	Tampa Bay Times Forum[16] (1996)	19,204
Edmonton	Rexall Place[7] (1974)	16,839	Toronto	Air Canada Centre (1999)	18,819
Florida	BB&T Center[8] (1998)	17,040	Vancouver	Rogers Arena[17] (1995)	18,910
Los Angeles	STAPLES Center (1999)	18,118	Washington	Verizon Center[18] (1997)	18,506
Minnesota	Xcel Energy Center (2000)	17,954	Winnipeg	MTS Centre (2004)	15,004
Montréal	Le Centre Bell[9] (1996)	21,273			
Nashville	Bridgestone Arena[10] (1997)	17,113			

(1) At the end of the 2013-14 season. (2) Arrowhead Pond of Anaheim, 1993-2006. (3) FleetCenter, 1995-2005; TD Banknorth Garden, 2005-09. (4) Marine Midland Arena, 1996-99; HSBC Arena, 1999-2011. (5) Olympic Saddledome, 1983-96; Canadian Airlines Saddledome, 1996-2000; Pengrowth Saddledome, 2000-10. (6) Raleigh Entertainment and Sports Arena, 1999-2002; RBC Center, 2002-11. (7) Northlands Coliseum, 1974-79; Edmonton Col., 1979-98; Skyreach Centre, 1998-2003. (8) National Car Rental Center, 1998-2002; Office Depot Ctr., 2002-05; BankAtlantic Ctr., 2005-12. (9) Le Centre Molson, 1996-2002. (10) Nashville Arena, 1997-99; Gaylord Entertainment Center, 1999-2007; Sommet Center, 2007-10. (11) Corel Centre, 1996-2006; Scotiabank Place, 2006-13. (12) CoreStates Center, 1996-98; First Union Center, 1998-2003; Wachovia Center, 2003-10. (13) Glendale Arena, 2003-06. (14) Kiel Center, 1994-2000; Savvis Center, 2000-06. (15) San Jose Arena, 1993-2001; Compaq Center, 2001-02; HP Pavilion at San Jose, 2002-13. (16) Ice Palace, 1996-2002; St. Pete Times Forum, 2002-12. (17) General Motors Place, 1995-2010. (18) MCI Center, 1997-2006.

Hockey Hall of Fame
(Located in Toronto, ON, Canada. * = 2014 inductee.)

Players

Abel, Sid
Adams, Jack
Anderson, Glenn
Apps, Syl
Armstrong, George
Bailey, Irvine "Ace"
Bain, Dan
Baker, Hobey
Barber, Bill
Barry, Marty
Bathgate, Andy
Bauer, Bobby
Belfour, Ed
Beliveau, Jean
Benedict, Clint
Bentley, Doug
Bentley, Max
Blake, Hector "Toe"
*Blake, Rob
Boivin, Leo
Boon, Dickie
Bossy, Mike
Bouchard, Butch
Boucher, Frank
Boucher, George
Bourque, Ray
Bower, Johnny
Bowie, Russell "Dubbie"
Brimsek, Frank
Broadbent, Harry L.
   "Punch"
Broda, Turk
Bucyk, John
Burch, Billy
Bure, Pavel
Cameron, Harry
Cheevers, Gerry
Chelios, Chris
Ciccarelli, Dino
Clancy, King
Clapper, Aubrey "Dit"
Clarke, Bobby
Cleghorn, Sprague
Coffey, Paul
Colville, Neil
Conacher, Charlie
Conacher, Lionel
Conacher, Roy
Connell, Alex
Cook, Bill
Cook, Frederick "Bun"
Coulter, Art
Cournoyer, Yvan
Cowley, Bill
Crawford, Rusty
Darragh, Jack
Davidson, Scotty
Day, Clarence "Hap"
Delvecchio, Alex
Denneny, Cy
Dionne, Marcel
Drillon, Gordie
Drinkwater, Graham
Dryden, Ken
Duff, Terrance "Dick"
Dumart, Woody
Dunderdale, Tommy
Durnan, Bill
Dutton, Mervyn "Red"
Dye, Babe
Esposito, Phil
Esposito, Tony
Farrel, Arthur
Federko, Bernie
Fetisov, Viacheslav
Flaman, Fernie
*Forsberg, Peter

Foyston, Frank
Francis, Ron
Fredrickson, Frank
Fuhr, Grant
Gadsby, Bill
Gainey, Bob
Gardiner, Chuck
Gardiner, Herb
Gardiner, Jimmy
Gartner, Mike
Geoffrion, Bernie
Gerard, Eddie
Giacomin, Eddie
Gilbert, Rod
Gillies, Clark
Gilmour, Billy
Gilmour, Doug
Goheen, Frank "Moose"
Goodfellow, Ebbie
Goulet, Michel
Granato, Cammi
Grant, Mike
Green, Wilfred "Shorty"
Gretzky, Wayne
Griffis, Si
Hainsworth, George
Hall, Glenn
Hall, Joe
Harvey, Doug
*Hasek, Dominik
Hawerchuk, Dale
Hay, George
Heaney, Geraldine
Hern, Riley
Hextall, Bryan
Holmes, Hap
Hooper, Tom
Horner, Red
Horton, Tim
Howe, Gordie
Howe, Mark
Howe, Syd
Howell, Harry
Hull, Bobby
Hull, Brett
Hutton, John "Bouse"
Hyland, Harry
Irvin, Dick
Jackson, Harvey "Busher"
James, Angela
Johnson, Ching
Johnson, Ernie
Johnson, Tom
Joliat, Aurel
Keats, Duke
Kelly, Red
Kennedy, Ted
Keon, Dave
Kharlamov, Valeri
Kurri, Jari
Lach, Elmer
Lafleur, Guy
LaFontaine, Pat
Lalonde, Newsy
Langway, Rod
Laperrière, Jacques
Lapointe, Guy
Laprade, Edgar
Larionov, Igor
Laviolette, Jack
Leetch, Brian
Lehman, Hughie
Lemaire, Jacques
Lemieux, Mario
LeSueur, Percy
Lewis, Herbie
Lindsay, Ted
Lumley, Harry
MacInnis, Al

MacKay, Mickey
Mahovlich, Frank
Malone, Joe
Mantha, Sylvio
Marshall, Jack
Maxwell, Fred
McDonald, Lanny
McGee, Frank
McGimsie, Billy
McNamara, George
Messier, Mark
Mikita, Stan
*Modano, Mike
Moore, Dickie
Moran, Paddy
Morenz, Howie
Mosienko, Bill
Mullen, Joe
Murphy, Larry
Neely, Cam
Niedermayer, Scott
Nieuwendyk, Joe
Nighbor, Frank
Noble, Reg
Oates, Adam
O'Connor, Buddy
Oliver, Harry
Olmstead, Bert
Orr, Bobby
Parent, Bernie
Park, Brad
Patrick, Lester
Patrick, Lynn
Perreault, Gilbert
Phillips, Tom
Pilote, Pierre
Pitre, Didier
Plante, Jacques
Potvin, Denis
Pratt, Babe
Primeau, Joe
Pronovost, Marcel
Pulford, Bob
Pulford, Harvey
Quackenbush, Bill
Rankin, Frank
Ratelle, Jean
Rayner, Chuck
Reardon, Kenny
Richard, Henri
Richard, Maurice
Richardson, George
Roberts, Gordie
Robinson, Larry
Robitaille, Luc
Ross, Art
Roy, Patrick
Russel, Blair
Russell, Ernie
Ruttan, Jack
Sakic, Joe
Salming, Börje
Savard, Denis
Savard, Serge
Sawchuk, Terry
Scanlan, Fred
Schmidt, Milt
Schriner, Sweeney
Seibert, Earl
Seibert, Oliver
Shanahan, Brendan
Shore, Eddie
Shutt, Steve
Siebert, Babe
Simpson, Joe "Bullet"
Sittler, Darryl
Smith, Alf
Smith, Billy
Smith, Clint

Smith, Hooley
Smith, Tommy
Stanley, Allan
Stanley, Barney
Stastny, Peter
Stevens, Ronald Scott
Stewart, Jack
Stewart, Nels
Stuart, Bruce
Stuart, Hod
Sundin, Mats
Taylor, Frederick "Cyclone"
Thompson, Cecil "Tiny"
Tretiak, Vladislav
Trihey, Harry
Trottier, Bryan
Ullman, Norm
Vezina, Georges
Walker, Jack
Walsh, Marty
Watson, Harry "Moose"
Watson, Harry Percival
Weiland, Cooney
Westwick, Harry
Whitcroft, Fred
Wilson, Gordon Allan
   "Phat"
Worsley, Gump
Worters, Roy
Yzerman, Steve

Builders

Adams, Charles
Adams, Weston
Ahearn, Frank
Ahearn, John "Bunny"
Allan, Sir Montagu
Allen, Keith
Arbour, Al
Ballard, Harold
Bauer, Father David
Bickell, J. P.
Bowman, Scotty
Brooks, Herbert
Brown, George
Brown, Walter
Buckland, Frank
*Burns, Pat
Bush, Walter, Jr.
Butterfield, Jack
Calder, Frank
Campbell, Angus
Campbell, Clarence
Cattarinich, Joseph
Chynoweth, Ed
Costello, Murray
Dandurand, Leo
Devellano, Jim
Dilio, Frank
Dudley, George
Dunn, James
Fletcher, Cliff
Francis, Emile
Gibson, Jack
Gorman, Tommy
Gregory, Jim
Griffiths, Frank
Hanley, Bill
Hay, Charles
Hendy, Jim
Hewitt, Foster
Hewitt, William
Hotchkiss, Harley
Hume, Fred
Ilitch, Mike
Imlach, Harry "Punch"
Ivan, Tommy
Jennings, William

Johnson, Bob
Juckes, Gordon
Kilpatrick, John
Kilrea, Brian
Knox, Seymour
Lamoriello, Lou
Leader, Al
LeBel, Robert
Lockhart, Thomas
Loicq, Paul
Mariucci, John
Mathers, Frank
McLaughlin, Frederic
Milford, Jake
Molson, Sen. Hartland
Morrison, Ian "Scotty"
Murray, Athol "Père"
Neilson, Roger
Nelson, Francis
Norris, Bruce
Norris, James
Norris, James, Sr.
Northey, William
O'Brien, J. Ambrose
O'Neill, Brian Francis
Page, Frederick
Patrick, Craig
Patrick, Frank
Pickard, Allan
Pilous, Rudy
Poile, Bud
Pollock, Sam
Raymond, Sen. Donat
Robertson, John Ross
Robinson, Claude
Ross, Philip
Sabetzki, Gunther
Sather, Glen
Seaman, Daryl "Doc"
Selke, Frank
Shero, Fred
Sinden, Harry
Smith, Frank
Smythe, Conn
Snider, Ed
Stanley, Lord
   (of Preston)
Sutherland, Capt.
   James T.
Tarasov, Anatoli
Torrey, Bill
Turner, Lloyd
Tutt, William
Voss, Carl
Waghorne, Fred
Wirtz, Arthur
Wirtz, Bill
Ziegler, John A., Jr.

**Referees
and Linesmen**

Armstrong, Neil
Ashley, John
Chadwick, Bill
D'Amico, John
Elliott, Edwin "Chaucer"
Hayes, George
Hewiston, Bobby
Ion, Mickey
*McCreary, Bill
Pavelich, Matt
Rodden, Mike
Scapinello, Ray
Smeaton, Cooper
Storey, Red
Udvari, Frank
Van Hellemond, Andy

SOCCER

Germany Defeats Argentina for 2014 Men's World Cup Title

Germany won its fourth FIFA World Cup title July 13, 2014, with a dramatic goal in extra time, defeating Argentina, 1-0, at the Estádio do Maracanã in Rio de Janeiro, Brazil. Mario Götze, who entered the match as a substitute for Germany in the 88th minute, sent the ball into the right side of the goal in the 113th minute. Thomas Müller led Germany with five goals in the tournament, and teammate Manuel Neuer won the Golden Glove award as the tournament's top goalkeeper. Argentina's Lionel Messi earned the FIFA Golden Ball award as the competition's best player, and James Rodriguez of Colombia won the Golden Boot as top scorer with six goals in five games.

The German squad reached the final with a record-setting 7-1 victory over host country Brazil in their semifinal match July 8 at Estádio Mineirão in Belo Horizonte. Germany's victory, by the largest margin of any World Cup semifinal, included a record 16th World Cup goal by veteran Miroslav Klose, who was playing in his fourth tournament. Brazil played the match without its superstar, Neymar, who had suffered a broken vertebra in Brazil's quarterfinal victory against Colombia. After its semifinal loss, Brazil's misfortune continued in the third-place match, which it lost, 3-0, to the Netherlands July 12, 2014, at Estádio Nacional in Brasília.

The most infamous moment of the 2014 tournament occurred during Uruguay's Group D match victory over Italy June 24, when Uruguay striker Luis Suárez appeared to bite Italy's Giorgio Chiellini on the shoulder late in the second half. Two days later, Suárez was suspended by FIFA for nine games and banned from soccer-related activity for four months. Without Suárez, who had been disciplined for biting twice before in other leagues, Uruguay lost its Round of 16 match to Colombia June 28.

After exceeding expectations somewhat in the so-called "Group of Death," the U.S. team fell July 1, 2-1, to Belgium in the Round of 16.

World Cup Group Standings, 2014
* = advanced to Round of 16.

Group A	W	L	T	GF	GA	PTS		Group E	W	L	T	GF	GA	PTS
Brazil*	2	0	1	7	2	7		France*	2	0	1	8	2	7
Mexico*	2	0	1	4	1	7		Switzerland*	2	1	0	7	6	6
Croatia	1	2	0	6	6	3		Ecuador	1	1	1	3	3	4
Cameroon	0	3	0	1	9	0		Honduras	0	3	0	1	8	0
Group B								**Group F**						
Netherlands*	3	0	0	10	3	9		Argentina*	3	0	0	6	3	9
Chile*	2	1	0	5	3	6		Nigeria*	1	1	1	3	3	4
Spain	1	2	0	4	7	3		Bosnia-						
Australia	0	3	0	3	9	0		Herzegovina	1	2	0	4	4	3
Group C								Iran	0	2	1	1	4	1
Colombia*	3	0	0	9	2	9		**Group G**						
Greece*	1	1	1	2	4	4		Germany*	2	0	1	7	2	7
Côte d'Ivoire	1	2	0	4	5	3		United States*	1	1	1	4	4	4
Japan	0	2	1	2	6	1		Portugal	1	1	1	4	7	4
Group D								Ghana	0	2	1	4	6	1
Costa Rica*	2	0	1	4	1	7		**Group H**						
Uruguay*	2	1	0	4	4	6		Belgium*	3	0	0	4	1	9
Italy	1	2	0	2	3	3		Algeria*	1	1	1	6	5	4
England	0	2	1	2	4	1		Russia	0	1	2	2	3	2
								South Korea	0	2	1	3	6	1

World Cup Results, 2014

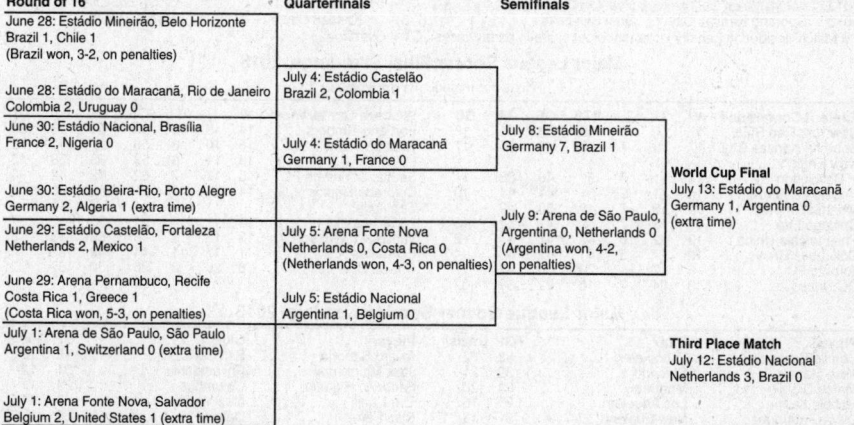

Round of 16

June 28: Estádio Mineirão, Belo Horizonte
Brazil 1, Chile 1
(Brazil won, 3-2, on penalties)

June 28: Estádio do Maracanã, Rio de Janeiro
Colombia 2, Uruguay 0

June 30: Estádio Nacional, Brasília
France 2, Nigeria 0

June 30: Estádio Beira-Rio, Porto Alegre
Germany 2, Algeria 1 (extra time)

June 29: Estádio Castelão, Fortaleza
Netherlands 2, Mexico 1

June 29: Arena Pernambuco, Recife
Costa Rica 1, Greece 1
(Costa Rica won, 5-3, on penalties)

July 1: Arena de São Paulo, São Paulo
Argentina 1, Switzerland 0 (extra time)

July 1: Arena Fonte Nova, Salvador
Belgium 2, United States 1 (extra time)

Quarterfinals

July 4: Estádio Castelão
Brazil 2, Colombia 1

July 4: Estádio do Maracanã
Germany 1, France 0

July 5: Arena Fonte Nova
Netherlands 0, Costa Rica 0
(Netherlands won, 4-3, on penalties)

July 5: Estádio Nacional
Argentina 1, Belgium 0

Semifinals

July 8: Estádio Mineirão
Germany 7, Brazil 1

July 9: Arena de São Paulo,
Argentina 0, Netherlands 0
(Argentina won, 4-2,
on penalties)

World Cup Final
July 13: Estádio do Maracanã
Germany 1, Argentina 0
(extra time)

Third Place Match
July 12: Estádio Nacional
Netherlands 3, Brazil 0

Men's World Cup Results, 1930-2014

Year	Winner	Final opponent	Score	Site	Year	Winner	Final opponent	Score	Site
1930	Uruguay	Argentina	4-2	Uruguay	1978	Argentina	Netherlands	3-1#	Argentina
1934	Italy	Czechoslovakia	2-1#	Italy	1982	Italy	W. Germany	3-1	Spain
1938	Italy	Hungary	4-2	France	1986	Argentina	W. Germany	3-2	Mexico
1950	Uruguay	Brazil	2-1	Brazil	1990	W. Germany	Argentina	1-0	Italy
1954	W. Germany	Hungary	3-2	Switzerland	1994	Brazil	Italy	0-0 (3-2)*	U.S.
1958	Brazil	Sweden	5-2	Sweden	1998	France	Brazil	3-0	France
1962	Brazil	Czechoslovakia	3-1	Chile	2002	Brazil	Germany	2-0	Japan/S. Korea
1966	England	W. Germany	4-2#	England	2006	Italy	France	1-1 (5-3)*	Germany
1970	Brazil	Italy	4-1	Mexico	2010	Spain	Netherlands	1-0#	South Africa
1974	W. Germany	Netherlands	2-1	W. Germany	2014	Germany	Argentina	1-0#	Brazil

* = Match decided in penalty kicks (shootout score in parentheses). # = Match decided in extra time.

Women's World Cup Results, 1991-2011

The 2015 Women's World Cup was scheduled to be held June 6-July 5, 2015, in Vancouver, BC, Canada.

Year	Winner	Final opponent	Score	Site	Year	Winner	Final opponent	Score	Site
1991	U.S.	Norway	2-1	China	2003	Germany	Sweden	2-1#	Carson, CA, U.S.
1995	Norway	Germany	2-0	Sweden	2007	Germany	Brazil	2-0	China
1999	U.S.	China	0-0 (5-4)*	Pasadena, CA, U.S.	2011	Japan	U.S.	2-2 (3-1)*	Germany

* = Match decided in penalty kicks (shootout score in parentheses). # = Match decided in extra time.

Sporting Kansas City Wins 2013 MLS Cup in Record Shootout

Sporting Kansas City won their second Major League Soccer (MLS) Cup Dec. 7, 2013, 1-1 (7-6), over Real Salt Lake at Sporting Park in Kansas City, KS. SKC defender Aurelien Collin tied the game at 1-1 in the 76th minute, then scored the seventh and winning goal in the longest shootout in MLS history; he was voted match MVP.

SKC advanced to the MLS Cup final after a 2-1 home win over the Houston Dynamo in the second leg of the Eastern Conference championship Nov. 23, 2013, after the two clubs played to a scoreless draw in Houston Nov. 9. In the Western Conference final, Real Salt Lake celebrated a 5-2 aggregate victory over the Portland Timbers, who topped the West during the season with 57 points (14-5-15).

The MLS All-Stars were defeated, 3-1, by AS Roma of Italy's Serie A at the MLS All-Star Game at Sporting Park July 31, 2013. Undefeated in the last eight regular season matches, the New York Red Bulls won their first Supporters' Shield with the league's best record (17-9-8 and 59 points). Mike Magee, who was traded midseason from the L.A. Galaxy to his hometown Chicago Fire, won the 2013 MLS Most Valuable Player award.

Major League Soccer (MLS) Cup Results, 1996-2013

Year	Winner	Final opponent	Score	Site	MVP
1996	DC United	Los Angeles Galaxy	3-2 (OT)	Foxborough, MA	Marco Etcheverry
1997	DC United	Colorado Rapids	2-1	Washington, DC	Jaime Moreno
1998	Chicago Fire	DC United	2-0	Pasadena, CA	Peter Nowak
1999	DC United	Los Angeles Galaxy	2-0	Foxborough, MA	Ben Olsen
2000	Kansas City Wizards	Chicago Fire	1-0	Washington, DC	Tony Meola
2001	San Jose Earthquakes	Los Angeles Galaxy	2-1 (OT)	Columbus, OH	Dwayne De Rosario
2002	Los Angeles Galaxy	New England Revolution	1-0 (OT)	Foxborough, MA	Carlos Ruiz
2003	San Jose Earthquakes	Chicago Fire	4-2	Carson, CA	Landon Donovan
2004	DC United	Kansas City Wizards	3-2	Carson, CA	Alecko Eskandarian
2005	Los Angeles Galaxy	New England Revolution	1-0 (OT)	Frisco, TX	Guillermo Ramírez
2006	Houston Dynamo	New England Revolution	1-1 (4-3)	Frisco, TX	Brian Ching
2007	Houston Dynamo	New England Revolution	2-1	Washington, DC	Dwayne De Rosario
2008	Columbus Crew	New York Red Bulls	3-1	Carson, CA	Guillermo Barros Schelotto
2009	Real Salt Lake	Los Angeles Galaxy	1-1 (5-4)*	Seattle, WA	Nick Rimando
2010	Colorado Rapids	FC Dallas	2-1 (OT)	Toronto, ON, Canada	Conor Casey
2011	Los Angeles Galaxy	Houston Dynamo	1-0	Carson, CA	Landon Donovan
2012	Los Angeles Galaxy	Houston Dynamo	3-1	Carson, CA	Omar Gonzalez
2013	Sporting Kansas City	Real Salt Lake	1-1 (7-6)*	Kansas City, KS	Aurelien Collin

* = Match decided in penalty kicks (shootout score in parentheses). OT = Overtime.

Major League Soccer Final Standings, 2013

(Does not include playoff games.)

Eastern Conference	W	L	T	PTS	GF	GA	GD	Western Conference	W	L	T	PTS	GF	GA	GD
New York Red Bulls	17	9	8	59	58	41	17	Portland Timbers	14	5	15	57	54	33	21
Sporting Kansas City	17	10	7	58	47	30	17	Real Salt Lake	16	10	8	56	57	41	16
New England Revolution	14	11	9	51	49	38	11	L.A. Galaxy	15	11	8	53	53	38	15
Houston Dynamo	14	11	9	51	41	41	0	Seattle Sounders FC	15	12	7	52	42	42	0
Montréal Impact	14	13	7	49	50	49	1	Colorado Rapids	14	11	9	51	45	38	7
Chicago Fire	14	13	7	49	47	52	-5	San Jose Earthquakes	14	11	9	51	35	42	-7
Philadelphia Union	12	12	10	46	42	44	-2	Vancouver Whitecaps	13	12	9	48	53	45	8
Columbus Crew	12	17	5	41	42	46	-4	FC Dallas	11	12	11	44	48	52	-4
Toronto FC	6	17	11	29	30	47	-17	Chivas USA	6	20	8	26	30	67	-37
DC United	3	24	7	16	22	59	-37								

Major League Soccer Scoring Leaders, 2013

Player	Club	GP	Goals	Player	Club	GP	Goals
Camilo Sanvezzo	Vancouver	32	22	Alvaro Saborio	Salt Lake	16	12
Mike Magee	Chicago	32	21	Jack McInerney	Philadelphia	31	12
Marco Di Vaio	Montréal	33	20	Federico Higuain	Columbus	29	11
Robbie Keane	Los Angeles	23	16	Tim Cahill	New York	27	11
Diego Fagundez	New England	31	13	Blas Perez	Dallas	25	11
Dominic Oduro	Columbus	34	13	Chris Wondolowski	San Jose	29	11

Selected European Soccer League Champions, 1950-2014

Season	England: Premier League[1]	Spain: La Liga	Italy: Serie A	Germany: Bundesliga[2]
1949-50	Portsmouth FC	Atlético Madrid	Juventus	VfB Stuttgart
1950-51	Tottenham Hotspur	Atlético Madrid	AC Milan	Kaiserslautern
1951-52	Manchester United	FC Barcelona	Juventus	VfB Stuttgart
1952-53	Arsenal	FC Barcelona	Inter Milan	Kaiserslautern
1953-54	Wolverhampton Wanderers	Real Madrid	Inter Milan	Hannoverscher SV 96
1954-55	Chelsea	Real Madrid	AC Milan	Rot-Weiss Essen
1955-56	Manchester United	Athletic Bilbao	Fiorentina	Borussia Dortmund
1956-57	Manchester United	Real Madrid	AC Milan	Borussia Dortmund
1957-58	Wolverhampton Wanderers	Real Madrid	Juventus	Schalke 04
1958-59	Wolverhampton Wanderers	FC Barcelona	AC Milan	Eintracht Frankfurt
1959-60	Burnley FC	FC Barcelona	Juventus	Hamburg SV
1960-61	Tottenham Hotspur	Real Madrid	Juventus	FC Nuremberg
1961-62	Ipswich Town	Real Madrid	AC Milan	FC Cologne
1962-63	Everton	Real Madrid	Inter Milan	Borussia Dortmund
1963-64	Liverpool	Real Madrid	Bologna	FC Cologne
1964-65	Manchester United	Real Madrid	Inter Milan	Werder Bremen
1965-66	Liverpool	Atlético Madrid	Inter Milan	TSV 1860 Munich
1966-67	Manchester United	Real Madrid	Juventus	Eintracht Braunschweig
1967-68	Manchester City	Real Madrid	AC Milan	FC Nuremberg
1968-69	Leeds United	Real Madrid	Fiorentina	Bayern Munich
1969-70	Everton	Atlético Madrid	Cagliari	Borussia Mönchengladbach
1970-71	Arsenal	Valencia	Inter Milan	Borussia Mönchengladbach
1971-72	Derby County	Real Madrid	Juventus	Bayern Munich
1972-73	Liverpool	Atlético Madrid	Juventus	Bayern Munich
1973-74	Leeds United	FC Barcelona	Lazio	Bayern Munich
1974-75	Derby County	Real Madrid	Juventus	Borussia Mönchengladbach
1975-76	Liverpool	Real Madrid	Torino	Borussia Mönchengladbach
1976-77	Liverpool	Atlético Madrid	Juventus	Borussia Mönchengladbach
1977-78	Nottingham Forest	Real Madrid	Juventus	FC Cologne
1978-79	Liverpool	Real Madrid	AC Milan	Hamburg SV
1979-80	Liverpool	Real Madrid	Inter Milan	Bayern Munich
1980-81	Aston Villa	Real Sociedad	Juventus	Bayern Munich
1981-82	Liverpool	Real Sociedad	Juventus	Hamburg SV
1982-83	Liverpool	Athletic Bilbao	AS Roma	Hamburg SV
1983-84	Liverpool	Athletic Bilbao	Juventus	VfB Stuttgart
1984-85	Everton	FC Barcelona	Verona	Bayern Munich
1985-86	Liverpool	Real Madrid	Juventus	Bayern Munich
1986-87	Everton	Real Madrid	Napoli	Bayern Munich
1987-88	Liverpool	Real Madrid	AC Milan	Werder Bremen
1988-89	Arsenal	Real Madrid	Inter Milan	Bayern Munich
1989-90	Liverpool	Real Madrid	Napoli	Bayern Munich
1990-91	Arsenal	FC Barcelona	Sampdoria	FC Kaiserslautern
1991-92	Leeds United	FC Barcelona	AC Milan	VfB Stuttgart
1992-93	Manchester United	FC Barcelona	AC Milan	Werder Bremen
1993-94	Manchester United	FC Barcelona	AC Milan	Bayern Munich
1994-95	Blackburn Rovers	Real Madrid	Juventus	Borussia Dortmund
1995-96	Manchester United	Atlético Madrid	AC Milan	Borussia Dortmund
1996-97	Manchester United	Real Madrid	Juventus	Bayern Munich
1997-98	Arsenal	FC Barcelona	Juventus	FC Kaiserslautern
1998-99	Manchester United	FC Barcelona	AC Milan	Bayern Munich
1999-2000	Manchester United	Deportivo Coruña	Lazio	Bayern Munich
2000-01	Manchester United	Real Madrid	AS Roma	Bayern Munich
2001-02	Arsenal	Valencia	Juventus	Borussia Dortmund
2002-03	Manchester United	Real Madrid	Juventus	Bayern Munich
2003-04	Arsenal	Valencia	AC Milan	Werder Bremen
2004-05	Chelsea	FC Barcelona	None[3]	Bayern Munich
2005-06	Chelsea	FC Barcelona	Inter Milan[3]	Bayern Munich
2006-07	Manchester United	Real Madrid	Inter Milan	VfB Stuttgart
2007-08	Manchester United	Real Madrid	Inter Milan	Bayern Munich
2008-09	Manchester United	FC Barcelona	Inter Milan	VfL Wolfsburg
2009-10	Chelsea	FC Barcelona	Inter Milan	Bayern Munich
2010-11	Manchester United	FC Barcelona	AC Milan	Borussia Dortmund
2011-12	Manchester City	Real Madrid	Juventus	Borussia Dortmund
2012-13	Manchester United	FC Barcelona	Juventus	Bayern Munich
2013-14	Manchester City	Atlético Madrid	Juventus	Bayern Munich

(1) Football League champions are listed prior to 1992-93 season, when the Premier League formed. (2) Regional champions are listed prior to 1963-64 season, when National Bundesliga formed. (3) Juventus was stripped of two titles in 2006 because of match-fixing.

UEFA Champions League Results, 1956-2014

Year	Winner	Final opponent	Score	Year	Winner	Final opponent	Score
1956	Real Madrid	Reims	4-3	1971	Ajax	Panathinaikos	2-0
1957	Real Madrid	Fiorentina	2-0	1972	Ajax	Inter Milan	2-0
1958	Real Madrid	AC Milan	3-2#	1973	Ajax	Juventus	1-0
1959	Real Madrid	Reims	2-0	1974	Bayern Munich	Atlético Madrid	5-1[1]
1960	Real Madrid	Eintracht Frankfurt	7-3	1975	Bayern Munich	Leeds United	2-0
1961	Benfica	FC Barcelona	3-2	1976	Bayern Munich	St-Étienne	1-0
1962	Benfica	Real Madrid	5-3	1977	Liverpool	Borussia Mönchengladbach	3-1
1963	AC Milan	Benfica	2-1				
1964	Inter Milan	Real Madrid	3-1	1978	Liverpool	Club Brugge	1-0
1965	Inter Milan	Benfica	1-0	1979	Nottingham Forest	Malmö	1-0
1966	Real Madrid	Partizan	2-1	1980	Nottingham Forest	Hamburg SV	1-0
1967	Celtic	Inter Milan	2-1	1981	Liverpool	Real Madrid	1-0
1968	Manchester United	Benfica	4-1#	1982	Aston Villa	Bayern Munich	1-0
1969	AC Milan	Ajax	4-1	1983	Hamburg SV	Juventus	1-0
1970	Feyenoord	Celtic	2-1#	1984	Liverpool	AS Roma	1-1 (4-2)*

Year	Winner	Final opponent	Score	Year	Winner	Final opponent	Score
1985	Juventus	Liverpool	1-0	2000	Real Madrid	Valencia	3-0
1986	Steaua	FC Barcelona	0-0 (2-0)*	2001	Bayern Munich	Valencia	1-1 (5-4)*
1987	Porto	Bayern Munich	2-1	2002	Real Madrid	Leverkusen	2-1
1988	PSV	Benfica	0-0 (6-5)*	2003	AC Milan	Juventus	0-0 (3-2)*
1989	AC Milan	Steaua	4-0	2004	Porto	Monaco	3-0
1990	AC Milan	Benfica	1-0	2005	Liverpool	AC Milan	3-3 (3-2)*
1991	Crvena Zvezda	Marseille	0-0 (5-3)*	2006	FC Barcelona	Arsenal	2-1
1992	FC Barcelona	Sampdoria	1-0#	2007	AC Milan	Liverpool	2-1
1993	Marseille	AC Milan	1-0	2008	Manchester United	Chelsea	1-1 (6-5)*
1994	AC Milan	FC Barcelona	4-0	2009	FC Barcelona	Manchester United	2-0
1995	Ajax	AC Milan	1-0	2010	Inter Milan	Bayern Munich	2-0
1996	Juventus	Ajax	1-1 (4-2)*	2011	FC Barcelona	Manchester United	3-1
1997	Borussia Dortmund	Juventus	3-1	2012	Chelsea	Bayern Munich	1-1 (4-3)*
1998	Real Madrid	Juventus	1-0	2013	Bayern Munich	Borussia Dortmund	2-1
1999	Manchester United	Bayern Munich	2-1	2014	Real Madrid	Atlético Madrid	4-1#

* = Match decided in penalty kicks (shootout score in parentheses). # = Match decided in extra time. (1) Aggregate score. First game 1-1; second, 4-0.

UEFA European Football Championships, 1960-2012

The final rounds of the 2012 UEFA European Championships were jointly hosted by Poland and Ukraine and opened June 8, 2012, in Warsaw and Wroclawa, Poland, with the final match at Olympic Stadium in Kiev, Ukraine, on July 1, 2012.

Year	Winner	Final opponent	Score	Site	Year	Winner	Final opponent	Score	Site
1960	USSR	Yugoslavia	2-1#	France	1988	Netherlands	USSR	2-0	W. Germany
1964	Spain	USSR	2-1	Spain	1992	Denmark	Germany	2-0	Sweden
1968	Italy	Yugoslavia	2-0	Italy	1996	Germany	Czech Rep.	2-1#	England
1972	W. Germany	USSR	3-0	Belgium	2000	France	Italy	2-1#	Belgium/Neth.
1976	Czechoslovakia	W. Germany	2-2 (5-3)*	Yugoslavia	2004	Greece	Portugal	1-0	Portugal
1980	W. Germany	Belgium	2-1	Italy	2008	Spain	Germany	1-0	Austria/Switz.
1984	France	Spain	2-0	France	2012	Spain	Italy	4-0	Poland/Ukr.

* = Match decided in penalty kicks (shootout score in parentheses). # = Match decided in extra time.

FIFA Confederations Cup, 2013

Brazil won its third straight Confederations Cup title with a 3-0 victory over Spain June 30, 2013, at Maracanã Stadium in Rio de Janeiro, Brazil. Fred scored twice in the championship and Neymar, who won the Golden Ball as the tournament's top player, added his fourth goal of the tournament in the 44th minute. Throughout the tournament, anti-government protesters battled with police near many of the host stadiums, but the tournament schedule was not affected. Brazil advanced to the championship game with a 2-1 victory over Uruguay June 26 on a goal by Paulinho in the 86th minute at Mineirão Stadium in Belo Horizonte. Spain and Italy played to a 0-0 draw in the semifinals June 27 at Castelão Stadium in Fortaleza, but Spain advanced with a 7-6 win in penalty kicks.

FIFA Confederations Cup Results, 1997-2013

Year	Winner	Final opponent	Score	Third place	Fourth place	Site
1997	Brazil	Australia	6-0	Czech Republic	Uruguay	Saudi Arabia
1999	Mexico	Brazil	4-3	U.S.	Saudi Arabia	Mexico
2001	France	Japan	1-0	Australia	Brazil	S. Korea/Japan
2003	France	Cameroon	1-0	Turkey	Colombia	France
2005	Brazil	Argentina	4-1	Germany	Mexico	Germany
2009	Brazil	U.S.	3-2	Spain	South Africa	South Africa
2013	Brazil	Spain	3-0	Italy	Uruguay	Brazil

FC Kansas City Claims 2014 National Women's Soccer League Championship

FC Kansas City captured the 2014 National Women's Soccer League championship Aug. 31, 2014, over Seattle Reign FC at Starfire Stadium in Tukwila, WA. Amy Rodriguez scored twice on a pair of assists from Lauren Holiday to lead KC to a 2-1 victory; Holiday was named the 2014 NWSL Championship MVP. The Reign had only lost 2 of 24 regular season games and advanced to the title game with a 2-1 win over the Washington Spirit in a playoff semifinal Aug. 24. Kansas City advanced to the final after a 2-0 victory at home over 2013 champion Portland Aug. 23.

Women's Professional Soccer Champions

Year	Winner	Final opponent	Score	Site	MVP
		Women's United Soccer Association champions			
2001	Bay Area CyberRays	Atlanta Beat	3-3 (4-2)*	Foxborough, MA	Julie Murray
2002	Carolina Courage	Washington Freedom	3-2	Atlanta, GA	Birgit Prinz
2003	Washington Freedom	Atlanta Beat	2-1	San Diego, CA	Abby Wambach
		Women's Professional Soccer champions			
2009	Sky Blue FC	Los Angeles Sol	1-0	Carson, CA	Heather O'Reilly
2010	FC Gold Pride	Philadelphia Independence	4-0	Hayward, CA	Marta
2011	Western New York Flash	Philadelphia Independence	1-1 (5-4)*	Rochester, NY	Christine Sinclair
		National Women's Soccer League champions			
2013	Portland Thorns FC	Western New York Flash	2-0	Rochester, NY	Tobin Heath
2014	FC Kansas City	Seattle Reign FC	2-1	Tukwila, WA	Lauren Holiday

* = Match decided on penalty kicks (shootout score in parentheses). **Note:** The Women's United Soccer Association (WUSA) folded in 2003. Women's Professional Soccer (WPS) began play in 2009 but stopped operating in 2012, suspending its fourth season. In Apr. 2013, the new National Women's Soccer League (NWSL) began play with eight teams competing: Boston Breakers, Chicago Red Stars, FC Kansas City, Portland Thorns FC, Seattle Reign FC, Sky Blue FC (New York/New Jersey), Washington Spirit, and Western New York Flash. Houston Dash began play as an expansion team in the 2014 season.

GOLF

Men's All-Time Major Professional Championship Leaders

Through Sept. 2014. * = Active PGA player in 2014. (a) = Amateur.

Player	Masters	U.S. Open	British Open	PGA	Total
Jack Nicklaus	1963, '65-'66, '72, '75, '86	1962, '67, '72, '80	1966, '70, '78	1963, '71, '73, '75, '80	18
Tiger Woods*	1997, 2001-02, '05	2000, '02, '08	2000, '05-'06	1999-2000, '06-'07	14
Walter Hagen	—	1914, '19	1922, '24, '28-'29	1921, '24-'27	11
Ben Hogan	1951, '53	1948, '50-'51, '53	1953	1946, '48	9
Gary Player	1961, '74, '78	1965	1959, '68, '74	1962, '72	9
Tom Watson	1977, '81	1982	1975, '77, '80, '82-'83	—	8
Bobby Jones (a)	—	1923, '26, '29-'30	1926-27, '30	—	7
Arnold Palmer	1958, '60, '62, '64	1960	1961-62	—	7
Gene Sarazen	1935	1922, '32	1932	1922-23, '33	7
Sam Snead	1949, '52, '54	—	1946	1942, '49, '51	7
Harry Vardon	—	1900	1896, '98-'99, 1903, '11, '14	—	7
Nick Faldo	1989-90, '96	—	1987, '90, '92	—	6
Lee Trevino	—	1968, '71	1971-72	1974, '84	6

Professional Golfers' Association Leading Money Winners, 1946-2014

Year	Player	Earnings	Year	Player	Earnings	Year	Player	Earnings
1946	Ben Hogan	$42,556	1969	Frank Beard	$164,707	1992	Fred Couples	$1,344,188
1947	Jimmy Demaret	27,936	1970	Lee Trevino	157,037	1993	Nick Price	1,478,557
1948	Ben Hogan	32,112	1971	Jack Nicklaus	244,490	1994	Nick Price	1,499,927
1949	Sam Snead	31,593	1972	Jack Nicklaus	320,542	1995	Greg Norman	1,654,959
1950	Sam Snead	35,758	1973	Jack Nicklaus	308,362	1996	Tom Lehman	1,780,159
1951	Lloyd Mangrum	26,088	1974	Johnny Miller	353,201	1997	Tiger Woods	2,066,833
1952	Julius Boros	37,032	1975	Jack Nicklaus	298,149	1998	David Duval	2,591,031
1953	Lew Worsham	34,002	1976	Jack Nicklaus	266,438	1999	Tiger Woods	6,616,585
1954	Bob Toski	65,819	1977	Tom Watson	310,653	2000	Tiger Woods	9,188,321
1955	Julius Boros	63,121	1978	Tom Watson	362,429	2001	Tiger Woods	5,687,777
1956	Ted Kroll	72,835	1979	Tom Watson	462,636	2002	Tiger Woods	6,912,625
1957	Dick Mayer	65,835	1980	Tom Watson	530,808	2003	Vijay Singh	7,573,907
1958	Arnold Palmer	42,607	1981	Tom Kite	375,699	2004	Vijay Singh	10,905,166
1959	Art Wall Jr.	53,167	1982	Craig Stadler	446,462	2005	Tiger Woods	10,628,024
1960	Arnold Palmer	75,262	1983	Hal Sutton	426,668	2006	Tiger Woods	9,941,563
1961	Gary Player	64,540	1984	Tom Watson	476,260	2007	Tiger Woods	10,867,052
1962	Arnold Palmer	81,448	1985	Curtis Strange	542,321	2008	Vijay Singh	6,601,094
1963	Arnold Palmer	128,230	1986	Greg Norman	653,296	2009	Tiger Woods	10,508,163
1964	Jack Nicklaus	113,284	1987	Curtis Strange	925,941	2010	Matt Kuchar	4,910,477
1965	Jack Nicklaus	140,752	1988	Curtis Strange	1,147,644	2011	Luke Donald	6,683,214
1966	Billy Casper	121,944	1989	Tom Kite	1,395,278	2012	Rory McIlroy	8,047,952
1967	Jack Nicklaus	188,998	1990	Greg Norman	1,165,477	2013	Tiger Woods	8,553,439
1968	Billy Casper	205,168	1991	Corey Pavin	979,430	2014	Rory McIlroy	8,280,096

Note: The PGA tour introduced a new split season format in Oct. 2013, which concluded with the FedEx Cup in Sept. 2014. From 2014 on, year shown is year season ended.

Masters Golf Tournament Winners, 1940-2014

First contested in 1934 as Augusta National Invitation Tournament (name changed in 1939); not played, 1943-45.

Year	Winner	Year	Winner	Year	Winner	Year	Winner	Year	Winner
1940	Jimmy Demaret	1958	Arnold Palmer	1973	Tommy Aaron	1988	Sandy Lyle	2001	Tiger Woods
1941	Craig Wood	1959	Art Wall Jr.	1974	Gary Player	1989	Nick Faldo	2002	Tiger Woods
1942	Byron Nelson	1960	Arnold Palmer	1975	Jack Nicklaus	1990	Nick Faldo	2003	Mike Weir
1946	Herman Keiser	1961	Gary Player	1976	Ray Floyd	1991	Ian Woosnam	2004	Phil Mickelson
1947	Jimmy Demaret	1962	Arnold Palmer	1977	Tom Watson	1992	Fred Couples	2005	Tiger Woods
1948	Claude Harmon	1963	Jack Nicklaus	1978	Gary Player	1993	Bernhard Langer	2006	Phil Mickelson
1949	Sam Snead	1964	Arnold Palmer	1979	Fuzzy Zoeller	1994	José María Olazábal	2007	Zach Johnson
1950	Jimmy Demaret	1965	Jack Nicklaus	1980	Seve Ballesteros	1995	Ben Crenshaw	2008	Trevor Immelman
1951	Ben Hogan	1966	Jack Nicklaus	1981	Tom Watson	1996	Nick Faldo	2009	Angel Cabrera
1952	Sam Snead	1967	Gay Brewer Jr.	1982	Craig Stadler	1997	Tiger Woods	2010	Phil Mickelson
1953	Ben Hogan	1968	Bob Goalby	1983	Seve Ballesteros	1998	Mark O'Meara	2011	Charl Schwartzel
1954	Sam Snead	1969	George Archer	1984	Ben Crenshaw	1999	José María Olazábal	2012	Bubba Watson
1955	Cary Middlecoff	1970	Billy Casper	1985	Bernhard Langer	2000	Vijay Singh	2013	Adam Scott
1956	Jack Burke	1971	Charles Coody	1986	Jack Nicklaus			2014	Bubba Watson
1957	Doug Ford	1972	Jack Nicklaus	1987	Larry Mize				

U.S. Open Winners, 1940-2014

First contested in 1895; not played, 1942-45.

Year	Winner	Year	Winner	Year	Winner	Year	Winner	Year	Winner
1940	Lawson Little	1959	Billy Casper	1973	Johnny Miller	1987	Scott Simpson	2001	Retief Goosen
1941	Craig Wood	1960	Arnold Palmer	1974	Hale Irwin	1988	Curtis Strange	2002	Tiger Woods
1946	Lloyd Mangrum	1961	Gene Littler	1975	Lou Graham	1989	Curtis Strange	2003	Jim Furyk
1947	Lew Worsham	1962	Jack Nicklaus	1976	Jerry Pate	1990	Hale Irwin	2004	Retief Goosen
1948	Ben Hogan	1963	Julius Boros	1977	Hubert Green	1991	Payne Stewart	2005	Michael Campbell
1949	Cary Middlecoff	1964	Ken Venturi	1978	Andy North	1992	Tom Kite	2006	Geoff Ogilvy
1950	Ben Hogan	1965	Gary Player	1979	Hale Irwin	1993	Lee Janzen	2007	Angel Cabrera
1951	Ben Hogan	1966	Billy Casper	1980	Jack Nicklaus	1994	Ernie Els	2008	Tiger Woods
1952	Julius Boros	1967	Jack Nicklaus	1981	David Graham	1995	Corey Pavin	2009	Lucas Glover
1953	Ben Hogan	1968	Lee Trevino	1982	Tom Watson	1996	Steve Jones	2010	Graeme McDowell
1954	Ed Furgol	1969	Orville Moody	1983	Larry Nelson	1997	Ernie Els	2011	Rory McIlroy
1955	Jack Fleck	1970	Tony Jacklin	1984	Fuzzy Zoeller	1998	Lee Janzen	2012	Webb Simpson
1956	Cary Middlecoff	1971	Lee Trevino	1985	Andy North	1999	Payne Stewart	2013	Justin Rose
1957	Dick Mayer	1972	Jack Nicklaus	1986	Ray Floyd	2000	Tiger Woods	2014	Martin Kaymer
1958	Tommy Bolt								

British Open Winners, 1946-2014

First contested in 1860; not played, 1940-45.

Year	Winner	Year	Winner	Year	Winner	Year	Winner	Year	Winner
1946	Sam Snead	1960	Kel Nagle	1973	Tom Weiskopf	1987	Nick Faldo	2001	David Duval
1947	Fred Daly	1961	Arnold Palmer	1974	Gary Player	1988	Seve Ballesteros	2002	Ernie Els
1948	Henry Cotton	1962	Arnold Palmer	1975	Tom Watson	1989	Mark Calcavecchia	2003	Ben Curtis
1949	Bobby Locke	1963	Bob Charles	1976	Johnny Miller	1990	Nick Faldo	2004	Todd Hamilton
1950	Bobby Locke	1964	Tony Lema	1977	Tom Watson	1991	Ian Baker-Finch	2005	Tiger Woods
1951	Max Faulkner	1965	Peter Thomson	1978	Jack Nicklaus	1992	Nick Faldo	2006	Tiger Woods
1952	Bobby Locke	1966	Jack Nicklaus	1979	Seve Ballesteros	1993	Greg Norman	2007	Padraig Harrington
1953	Ben Hogan	1967	Roberto de	1980	Tom Watson	1994	Nick Price	2008	Padraig Harrington
1954	Peter Thomson		Vicenzo	1981	Bill Rogers	1995	John Daly	2009	Stewart Cink
1955	Peter Thomson	1968	Gary Player	1982	Tom Watson	1996	Tom Lehman	2010	Louis Oosthuizen
1956	Peter Thomson	1969	Tony Jacklin	1983	Tom Watson	1997	Justin Leonard	2011	Darren Clarke
1957	Bobby Locke	1970	Jack Nicklaus	1984	Seve Ballesteros	1998	Mark O'Meara	2012	Ernie Els
1958	Peter Thomson	1971	Lee Trevino	1985	Sandy Lyle	1999	Paul Lawrie	2013	Phil Mickelson
1959	Gary Player	1972	Lee Trevino	1986	Greg Norman	2000	Tiger Woods	2014	Rory McIlroy

PGA Championship Winners, 1940-2014

First contested in 1916; not played, 1943.

Year	Winner	Year	Winner	Year	Winner	Year	Winner	Year	Winner
1940	Byron Nelson	1956	Jack Burke	1971	Jack Nicklaus	1986	Bob Tway	2001	David Toms
1941	Victor Ghezzi	1957	Lionel Hebert	1972	Gary Player	1987	Larry Nelson	2002	Rich Beem
1942	Sam Snead	1958	Dow Finsterwald	1973	Jack Nicklaus	1988	Jeff Sluman	2003	Shaun Micheel
1944	Bob Hamilton	1959	Bob Rosburg	1974	Lee Trevino	1989	Payne Stewart	2004	Vijay Singh
1945	Byron Nelson	1960	Jay Hebert	1975	Jack Nicklaus	1990	Wayne Grady	2005	Phil Mickelson
1946	Ben Hogan	1961	Jerry Barber	1976	Dave Stockton	1991	John Daly	2006	Tiger Woods
1947	Jim Ferrier	1962	Gary Player	1977	Lanny Wadkins	1992	Nick Price	2007	Tiger Woods
1948	Ben Hogan	1963	Jack Nicklaus	1978	Jon Mahaffey	1993	Paul Azinger	2008	Padraig Harrington
1949	Sam Snead	1964	Bob Nichols	1979	David Graham	1994	Nick Price	2009	Y.E.Yang
1950	Chandler Harper	1965	Dave Marr	1980	Jack Nicklaus	1995	Steve Elkington	2010	Martin Kaymer
1951	Sam Snead	1966	Al Geiberger	1981	Larry Nelson	1996	Mark Brooks	2011	Keegan Bradley
1952	James Turnesa	1967	Don January	1982	Ray Floyd	1997	Davis Love III	2012	Rory McIlroy
1953	Walter Burkemo	1968	Julius Boros	1983	Hal Sutton	1998	Vijay Singh	2013	Jason Dufner
1954	Melvin Harbert	1969	Ray Floyd	1984	Lee Trevino	1999	Tiger Woods	2014	Rory McIlroy
1955	Doug Ford	1970	Dave Stockton	1985	Hubert Green	2000	Tiger Woods		

FedEx Cup, 2007-14

The FedEx Cup, a season-long, $10-mil competition with points awarded by finishing rank in each tournament, divides the PGA Tour into a regular season consisting of 43 events, combined with a 4-event playoff that ends with the Tour Championship.

Year	Winner	Year	Winner	Year	Winner	Year	Winner	Year	Winner
2007	Tiger Woods	2009	Tiger Woods	2011	Bill Haas	2013	Henrik Stenson	2014	Billy Horschel
2008	Vijay Singh	2010	Jim Furyk	2012	Brandt Snedeker				

Women's All-Time Major Professional Championship Leaders

Through Oct. 2014. * = Active in 2014 LPGA season.

Player	Kraft Nabisco[1]	LPGA	U.S. Women's Open	Women's British Open[2]	Titleholders[3]	Western Open[4]	Total
Patty Berg	—		1946		1937-39, '48, '53, '55, '57	1941, '43, '48, '51, '55, '57-'58	15
Mickey Wright	—	1958, '60-'61, '63	1958-59, '61, '64		1961-62	1962-63, '66	13
Louise Suggs	—	1957	1949, '52		1946, '54, '56, '59	1946-47, '49, '53	11
Annika Sorenstam	2001-02, '05	2003-05	1995-96, 2006	2003	—	—	10
Babe Zaharias	—		1948, '50, '54		1947, '50, '52	1940, '44-'45, '50	10
Betsy Rawls	—	1959, '69	1951, '53, '57, '60		—	1952, '59	8
Juli Inkster*	1984, '89	1999-2000	1999, 2002	1984	—	—	7
Karrie Webb*	2000, '06	2001	2000-01	1999, 2002	—	—	7
Pat Bradley	1986	1986	1981	1980, '85-'86	—	—	6
Betsy King	1987, '90, '97	1992	1989-90	—	—	—	6
Patty Sheehan	1996	1983-84, '93	1992, '94	—	—	—	6
Kathy Whitworth	—	1967, '71, '75	—	—	1965-66	1967	6

(1) Formerly the Nabisco Dinah Shore (1982-99) and the Nabisco Championship (2000-01); designated major in 1983. (2) In 2001, the British Open replaced the du Maurier Classic as the LPGA's fourth major; wins in column prior to 2001 are for the Peter Jackson (1979-82) or du Maurier (1983-2000) Classic. (3) Titleholders Championship was a major, 1937-72. (4) Western Open was a major, 1930-67.

Ladies Professional Golf Association Leading Money Winners, 1954-2013

Year	Player	Earnings	Year	Player	Earnings	Year	Player	Earnings
1954	Patty Berg	$16,011	1974	JoAnne Carner	$87,094	1994	Laura Davies	$687,201
1955	Patty Berg	16,492	1975	Sandra Palmer	76,374	1995	Annika Sorenstam	666,533
1956	Marlene Hagge	20,235	1976	Judy Rankin	150,734	1996	Karrie Webb	1,002,000
1957	Patty Berg	16,272	1977	Judy Rankin	122,890	1997	Annika Sorenstam	1,236,789
1958	Beverly Hanson	12,639	1978	Nancy Lopez	189,814	1998	Annika Sorenstam	1,092,748
1959	Betsy Rawls	26,774	1979	Nancy Lopez	197,489	1999	Karrie Webb	1,591,959
1960	Louise Suggs	16,892	1980	Beth Daniel	231,000	2000	Karrie Webb	1,876,853
1961	Mickey Wright	22,236	1981	Beth Daniel	206,998	2001	Annika Sorenstam	2,105,868
1962	Mickey Wright	21,641	1982	JoAnne Carner	310,400	2002	Annika Sorenstam	2,863,904
1963	Mickey Wright	31,269	1983	JoAnne Carner	291,404	2003	Annika Sorenstam	2,029,506
1964	Mickey Wright	29,800	1984	Betsy King	266,771	2004	Annika Sorenstam	2,544,707
1965	Kathy Whitworth	28,658	1985	Nancy Lopez	416,472	2005	Annika Sorenstam	2,588,240
1966	Kathy Whitworth	33,517	1986	Pat Bradley	492,021	2006	Lorena Ochoa	2,592,872
1967	Kathy Whitworth	32,937	1987	Ayako Okamoto	466,034	2007	Lorena Ochoa	4,364,994
1968	Kathy Whitworth	48,379	1988	Sherri Turner	350,851	2008	Lorena Ochoa	2,763,193
1969	Carol Mann	49,152	1989	Betsy King	654,132	2009	Jiyai Shin	1,807,334
1970	Kathy Whitworth	30,235	1990	Beth Daniel	863,578	2010	Na Yeon Choi	1,871,166
1971	Kathy Whitworth	41,181	1991	Pat Bradley	763,118	2011	Yani Tseng	2,921,713
1972	Kathy Whitworth	65,063	1992	Dottie Mochrie	693,335	2012	Inbee Park	2,287,080
1973	Kathy Whitworth	82,864	1993	Betsy King	595,992	2013	Inbee Park	2,456,619

Kraft Nabisco Championship Winners, 1983-2014

Formerly the Colgate Dinah Shore (1972-81), the Nabisco Dinah Shore (1982-99), and the Nabisco Championship (2000-01). Designated as a major championship in 1983.

Year	Winner	Year	Winner	Year	Winner	Year	Winner	Year	Winner
1983	Amy Alcott	1990	Betsy King	1997	Betsy King	2003	P. Meunier-Lebouc	2009	Brittany Lincicome
1984	Juli Inkster	1991	Amy Alcott	1998	Pat Hurst	2004	Grace Park	2010	Yani Tseng
1985	Alice Miller	1992	Dottie Pepper	1999	Dottie Pepper	2005	Annika Sorenstam	2011	Stacy Lewis
1986	Pat Bradley	1993	Helen Alfredsson	2000	Karrie Webb	2006	Karrie Webb	2012	Sun Young Yoo
1987	Betsy King	1994	Donna Andrews	2001	Annika Sorenstam	2007	Morgan Pressel	2013	Inbee Park
1988	Amy Alcott	1995	Nanci Bowen	2002	Annika Sorenstam	2008	Lorena Ochoa	2014	Lexi Thompson
1989	Juli Inkster	1996	Patty Sheehan						

LPGA Championship Winners, 1955-2014

Year	Winner	Year	Winner	Year	Winner	Year	Winner	Year	Winner
1955	Beverly Hanson	1967	Kathy Whitworth	1979	Donna Caponi	1991	Meg Mallon	2003	Annika Sorenstam
1956	Marlene Hagge	1968	Sandra Post	1980	Sally Little	1992	Betsy King	2004	Annika Sorenstam
1957	Louise Suggs	1969	Betsy Rawls	1981	Donna Caponi	1993	Patty Sheehan	2005	Annika Sorenstam
1958	Mickey Wright	1970	Shirley Englehorn	1982	Jan Stephenson	1994	Laura Davies	2006	Se Ri Pak
1959	Betsy Rawls	1971	Kathy Whitworth	1983	Patty Sheehan	1995	Kelly Robbins	2007	Suzann Pettersen
1960	Mickey Wright	1972	Kathy Ahern	1984	Patty Sheehan	1996	Laura Davies	2008	Yani Tseng
1961	Mickey Wright	1973	Mary Mills	1985	Nancy Lopez	1997	Christa Johnson	2009	Anna Nordqvist
1962	Judy Kimball	1974	Sandra Haynie	1986	Pat Bradley	1998	Se Ri Pak	2010	Cristie Kerr
1963	Mickey Wright	1975	Kathy Whitworth	1987	Jane Geddes	1999	Juli Inkster	2011	Yani Tseng
1964	Mary Mills	1976	Betty Burfeindt	1988	Sherri Turner	2000	Juli Inkster	2012	Shanshan Feng
1965	Sandra Haynie	1977	Chako Higuchi	1989	Nancy Lopez	2001	Karrie Webb	2013	Inbee Park
1966	Gloria Ehret	1978	Nancy Lopez	1990	Beth Daniel	2002	Se Ri Pak	2014	Inbee Park

U.S. Women's Open Winners, 1946-2014

Year	Winner	Year	Winner	Year	Winner	Year	Winner	Year	Winner
1946	Patty Berg	1960	Betsy Rawls	1974	Sandra Haynie	1988	Liselotte Neumann	2002	Juli Inkster
1947	Betty Jameson	1961	Mickey Wright	1975	Sandra Palmer	1989	Betsy King	2003	Hilary Lunke
1948	Babe Zaharias	1962	Murle Lindstrom	1976	JoAnne Carner	1990	Betsy King	2004	Meg Mallon
1949	Louise Suggs	1963	Mary Mills	1977	Hollis Stacy	1991	Meg Mallon	2005	Birdie Kim
1950	Babe Zaharias	1964	Mickey Wright	1978	Hollis Stacy	1992	Patty Sheehan	2006	Annika Sorenstam
1951	Betsy Rawls	1965	Carol Mann	1979	Jerilyn Britz	1993	Lauri Merten	2007	Cristie Kerr
1952	Louise Suggs	1966	Sandra Spuzich	1980	Amy Alcott	1994	Patty Sheehan	2008	Inbee Park
1953	Betsy Rawls	1967	Catherine Lacoste	1981	Pat Bradley	1995	Annika Sorenstam	2009	Eun-Hee Ji
1954	Babe Zaharias	1968	Susie Berning	1982	Janet Alex	1996	Annika Sorenstam	2010	Paula Creamer
1955	Fay Crocker	1969	Donna Caponi	1983	Jan Stephenson	1997	Alison Nicholas	2011	So Yeon Ryu
1956	Kathy Cornelius	1970	Donna Caponi	1984	Hollis Stacy	1998	Se Ri Pak	2012	Na Yeon Choi
1957	Betsy Rawls	1971	JoAnne Carner	1985	Kathy Baker	1999	Juli Inkster	2013	Inbee Park
1958	Mickey Wright	1972	Susie Berning	1986	Jane Geddes	2000	Karrie Webb	2014	Michelle Wie
1959	Mickey Wright	1973	Susie Berning	1987	Laura Davies	2001	Karrie Webb		

Women's British Open Winners, 1979-2014

First contested as the Ladies' British Open in 1976; became the LPGA's fourth major championship in 2001, replacing the du Maurier Classic. Winners listed are for the Peter Jackson (1979-82) and du Maurier (1983-2000) Classic.

Year	Winner	Year	Winner	Year	Winner	Year	Winner	Year	Winner
1979	Amy Alcott	1987	Jody Rosenthal	1994	Martha Nause	2001	Se Ri Pak	2008	Jiyai Shin
1980	Pat Bradley	1988	Sally Little	1995	Jenny Lidback	2002	Karrie Webb	2009	Catriona Matthew
1981	Jan Stephenson	1989	Tammie Green	1996	Laura Davies	2003	Annika Sorenstam	2010	Yani Tseng
1982	Sandra Haynie	1990	Cathy Johnston	1997	Colleen Walker	2004	Karen Stupples	2011	Yani Tseng
1983	Hollis Stacy	1991	Nancy Scranton	1998	Brandie Burton	2005	Jeong Jang	2012	Jiyai Shin
1984	Juli Inkster	1992	Sherri Steinhauer	1999	Karrie Webb	2006	Sherri Steinhauer	2013	Stacy Lewis
1985	Pat Bradley	1993	Brandie Burton	2000	Meg Mallon	2007	Lorena Ochoa	2014	Mo Martin
1986	Pat Bradley								

Evian Championship

The Evian Championship began in 1994 as the Evian Masters on the Ladies European Tour, and the LPGA Tour has co-sanctioned it since 2000. It became an LPGA major tournament in 2013, when it was won by Suzann Pettersen; Hyo Joo Kim won in 2014.

Ryder Cup, 1927-2014

The Ryder Cup began in 1927 as a biennial team competition between pro male golfers from the U.S. and Great Britain. The British team was expanded in 1973 to include players from Ireland and in 1979 to golfers from the rest of Europe. The Ryder Cup moved to even years after it was postponed following the terrorist attacks of Sept. 11, 2001. Not played, 1939-45.

Year	Winner, score	Year	Winner, score	Year	Winner, score	Year	Winner, score
1927	U.S., 9½-2½	1955	U.S., 8-4	1975	U.S., 21-11	1995	Europe, 14½-13½
1929	Britain-Ireland, 7-5	1957	Britain-Ireland, 7½-4½	1977	U.S., 12½-7½	1997	Europe, 14½-13½
1931	U.S., 9-3	1959	U.S., 8½-3½	1979	U.S., 17-11	1999	U.S., 14½-13½
1933	Britain, 6½-5½	1961	U.S., 14½-9½	1981	U.S., 18½-9½	2002	Europe, 15½-12½
1935	U.S., 9-3	1963	U.S., 23-9	1983	U.S., 14½-13½	2004	Europe, 18½-9½
1937	U.S., 8-4	1965	U.S., 19½-12½	1985	Europe, 16½-11½	2006	Europe, 18½-9½
1947	U.S., 11-1	1967	U.S., 23½-8½	1987	Europe, 15-13	2008	U.S., 16½-11½
1949	U.S., 7-5	1969	Draw, 16-16	1989	Draw, 14-14	2010	Europe, 14½-13½
1951	U.S., 9½-2½	1971	U.S., 18½-13½	1991	U.S., 14½-13½	2012	Europe, 14½-13½
1953	U.S., 6½-5½	1973	U.S., 19-13	1993	U.S., 15-13	2014	Europe, 16½-11½

Solheim Cup, 1990-2013

The Solheim Cup began in 1990 as a biennial team competition between pro women golfers from the U.S. and Europe. Competition moved to odd years beginning in 2003 to alternate with the Ryder Cup.

Year	Winner, score	Year	Winner, score	Year	Winner, score	Year	Winner, score
1990	U.S., 11½-4½	1998	U.S., 16-12	2003	Europe, 17½-10½	2009	U.S., 16-12
1992	Europe, 11½-6½	2000	Europe, 14½-11½	2005	U.S., 15½-12½	2011	Europe, 15-13
1994	U.S., 13-7	2002	U.S., 15½-12½	2007	U.S., 16-12	2013	Europe, 18-10
1996	U.S., 17-11						

TENNIS

Australian Open Champions, 1969-2014

First contested 1905 for men, 1922 for women. Became an open championship in 1969. Two tournaments held in 1977, in Jan. and Dec. No tournament held in 1986.

Men's Singles / Women's Singles

Year	Champion	Final opponent	Year	Champion	Final opponent
1969	Rod Laver	Andrés Gimeno	1969	Margaret Smith Court	Billie Jean King
1970	Arthur Ashe	Dick Crealy	1970	Margaret Smith Court	Kerry Melville Reid
1971	Ken Rosewall	Arthur Ashe	1971	Margaret Smith Court	Evonne Goolagong
1972	Ken Rosewall	Mal Anderson	1972	Virginia Wade	Evonne Goolagong
1973	John Newcombe	Onny Parun	1973	Margaret Smith Court	Evonne Goolagong
1974	Jimmy Connors	Phil Dent	1974	Evonne Goolagong	Chris Evert
1975	John Newcombe	Jimmy Connors	1975	Evonne Goolagong	Martina Navratilova
1976	Mark Edmondson	John Newcombe	1976	Evonne Goolagong Cawley	Renata Tomanova
1977	Roscoe Tanner	Guillermo Vilas	1977	Kerry Reid	Dianne Balestrat
	Vitas Gerulaitis	John Lloyd		Evonne Goolagong Cawley	Helen Gourlay
1978	Guillermo Vilas	John Marks	1978	Chris O'Neil	Betsy Nagelsen
1979	Guillermo Vilas	John Sadri	1979	Barbara Jordan	Sharon Walsh
1980	Brian Teacher	Kim Warwick	1980	Hana Mandlikova	Wendy Turnbull
1981	Johan Kriek	Steve Denton	1981	Martina Navratilova	Chris Evert Lloyd
1982	Johan Kriek	Steve Denton	1982	Chris Evert Lloyd	Martina Navratilova
1983	Mats Wilander	Ivan Lendl	1983	Martina Navratilova	Kathy Jordan
1984	Mats Wilander	Kevin Curren	1984	Chris Evert Lloyd	Helena Sukova
1985	Stefan Edberg	Mats Wilander	1985	Martina Navratilova	Chris Evert Lloyd
1987	Stefan Edberg	Pat Cash	1987	Hana Mandlikova	Martina Navratilova
1988	Mats Wilander	Pat Cash	1988	Steffi Graf	Chris Evert
1989	Ivan Lendl	Miloslav Mecir	1989	Steffi Graf	Helena Sukova
1990	Ivan Lendl	Stefan Edberg	1990	Steffi Graf	Mary Joe Fernandez
1991	Boris Becker	Ivan Lendl	1991	Monica Seles	Jana Novotna
1992	Jim Courier	Stefan Edberg	1992	Monica Seles	Mary Joe Fernandez
1993	Jim Courier	Stefan Edberg	1993	Monica Seles	Steffi Graf
1994	Pete Sampras	Todd Martin	1994	Steffi Graf	Arantxa Sánchez Vicario
1995	Andre Agassi	Pete Sampras	1995	Mary Pierce	Arantxa Sánchez Vicario
1996	Boris Becker	Michael Chang	1996	Monica Seles	Anke Huber
1997	Pete Sampras	Carlos Moya	1997	Martina Hingis	Mary Pierce
1998	Petr Korda	Marcelo Rios	1998	Martina Hingis	Conchita Martínez
1999	Yevgeny Kafelnikov	Thomas Enqvist	1999	Martina Hingis	Amélie Mauresmo
2000	Andre Agassi	Yevgeny Kafelnikov	2000	Lindsay Davenport	Martina Hingis
2001	Andre Agassi	Arnaud Clement	2001	Jennifer Capriati	Martina Hingis
2002	Thomas Johansson	Marat Safin	2002	Jennifer Capriati	Martina Hingis
2003	Andre Agassi	Rainer Schuettler	2003	Serena Williams	Venus Williams
2004	Roger Federer	Marat Safin	2004	Justine Henin-Hardenne	Kim Clijsters
2005	Marat Safin	Lleyton Hewitt	2005	Serena Williams	Lindsay Davenport
2006	Roger Federer	Marcos Baghdatis	2006	Amélie Mauresmo	Justine Henin-Hardenne
2007	Roger Federer	Fernando Gonzalez	2007	Serena Williams	Maria Sharapova
2008	Novak Djokovic	Jo-Wilfried Tsonga	2008	Maria Sharapova	Ana Ivanovic
2009	Rafael Nadal	Roger Federer	2009	Serena Williams	Dinara Safina
2010	Roger Federer	Andy Murray	2010	Serena Williams	Justine Henin
2011	Novak Djokovic	Andy Murray	2011	Kim Clijsters	Li Na
2012	Novak Djokovic	Rafael Nadal	2012	Victoria Azarenka	Maria Sharapova
2013	Novak Djokovic	Andy Murray	2013	Victoria Azarenka	Li Na
2014	Stanislas Wawrinka	Rafael Nadal	2014	Li Na	Dominika Cibulkova

French Open (Roland Garros) Champions, 1968-2014

First contested 1891 for men, 1897 for women. Became an open championship in 1968.

Men's Singles

Year	Champion	Final opponent
1968	Ken Rosewall	Rod Laver
1969	Rod Laver	Ken Rosewall
1970	Jan Kodes	Zeljko Franulovic
1971	Jan Kodes	Ilie Nastase
1972	Andrés Gimeno	Patrick Proisy
1973	Ilie Nastase	Nikki Pilic
1974	Björn Borg	Manuel Orantes
1975	Björn Borg	Guillermo Vilas
1976	Adriano Panatta	Harold Solomon
1977	Guillermo Vilas	Brian Gottfried
1978	Björn Borg	Guillermo Vilas
1979	Björn Borg	Victor Pecci
1980	Björn Borg	Vitas Gerulaitis
1981	Björn Borg	Ivan Lendl
1982	Mats Wilander	Guillermo Vilas
1983	Yannick Noah	Mats Wilander
1984	Ivan Lendl	John McEnroe
1985	Mats Wilander	Ivan Lendl
1986	Ivan Lendl	Mikael Pernfors
1987	Ivan Lendl	Mats Wilander
1988	Mats Wilander	Henri Leconte
1989	Michael Chang	Stefan Edberg
1990	Andres Gomez	Andre Agassi
1991	Jim Courier	Andre Agassi
1992	Jim Courier	Petr Korda
1993	Sergei Bruguera	Jim Courier
1994	Sergei Bruguera	Alberto Berasategui
1995	Thomas Muster	Michael Chang
1996	Yevgeny Kafelnikov	Michael Stich
1997	Gustavo Kuerten	Sergi Bruguera
1998	Carlos Moya	Alex Corretja
1999	Andre Agassi	Andrei Medvedev
2000	Gustavo Kuerten	Magnus Norman
2001	Gustavo Kuerten	Alex Corretja
2002	Albert Costa	Juan Carlos Ferrero
2003	Juan Carlos Ferrero	Martin Verkerk
2004	Gaston Gaudio	Guillermo Coria
2005	Rafael Nadal	Mariano Puerta
2006	Rafael Nadal	Roger Federer
2007	Rafael Nadal	Roger Federer
2008	Rafael Nadal	Roger Federer
2009	Roger Federer	Robin Soderling
2010	Rafael Nadal	Robin Soderling
2011	Rafael Nadal	Roger Federer
2012	Rafael Nadal	Novak Djokovic
2013	Rafael Nadal	David Ferrer
2014	Rafael Nadal	Novak Djokovic

Women's Singles

Year	Champion	Final opponent
1968	Nancy Richey	Ann Jones
1969	Margaret Smith Court	Ann Jones
1970	Margaret Smith Court	Helga Niessen
1971	Evonne Goolagong	Helen Gourlay
1972	Billie Jean King	Evonne Goolagong
1973	Margaret Smith Court	Chris Evert
1974	Chris Evert	Olga Morozova
1975	Chris Evert	Martina Navratilova
1976	Sue Barker	Renata Tomanova
1977	Mima Jausovec	Florenta Mihai
1978	Virginia Ruzici	Mima Jausovec
1979	Chris Evert Lloyd	Wendy Turnbull
1980	Chris Evert Lloyd	Virginia Ruzici

Year	Champion	Final opponent	Year	Champion	Final opponent
1981	Hana Mandlikova	Sylvia Hanika	1998	Arantxa Sánchez Vicario	Monica Seles
1982	Martina Navratilova	Andrea Jaeger	1999	Steffi Graf	Martina Hingis
1983	Chris Evert Lloyd	Mima Jausovec	2000	Mary Pierce	Conchita Martínez
1984	Martina Navratilova	Chris Evert Lloyd	2001	Jennifer Capriati	Kim Clijsters
1985	Chris Evert Lloyd	Martina Navratilova	2002	Serena Williams	Venus Williams
1986	Chris Evert Lloyd	Martina Navratilova	2003	Justine Henin-Hardenne	Kim Clijsters
1987	Steffi Graf	Martina Navratilova	2004	Anastasia Myskina	Elena Dementieva
1988	Steffi Graf	Natalia Zvereva	2005	Justine Henin-Hardenne	Mary Pierce
1989	Arantxa Sánchez Vicario	Steffi Graf	2006	Justine Henin-Hardenne	Svetlana Kuznetsova
1990	Monica Seles	Steffi Graf	2007	Justine Henin	Ana Ivanovic
1991	Monica Seles	Arantxa Sánchez Vicario	2008	Ana Ivanovic	Dinara Safina
1992	Monica Seles	Steffi Graf	2009	Svetlana Kuznetsova	Dinara Safina
1993	Steffi Graf	Mary Joe Fernandez	2010	Francesca Schiavone	Samantha Stosur
1994	Arantxa Sánchez Vicario	Mary Pierce	2011	Li Na	Francesca Schiavone
1995	Steffi Graf	Arantxa Sánchez Vicario	2012	Maria Sharapova	Sara Errani
1996	Steffi Graf	Arantxa Sánchez Vicario	2013	Serena Williams	Maria Sharapova
1997	Iva Majoli	Martina Hingis	2014	Maria Sharapova	Simona Halep

Wimbledon Champions, 1925-2014

First contested 1877 for men, 1884 for women. Became an open championship in 1968. Not held 1940-45.

Men's Singles

Year	Champion	Final opponent	Year	Champion	Final opponent
			1997	Pete Sampras	Cedric Pioline
1925	René Lacoste	Jean Borotra	1998	Pete Sampras	Goran Ivanisevic
1926	Jean Borotra	Howard Kinsey	1999	Pete Sampras	Andre Agassi
1927	Henri Cochet	Jean Borotra	2000	Pete Sampras	Patrick Rafter
1928	René Lacoste	Henri Cochet	2001	Goran Ivanisevic	Patrick Rafter
1929	Henri Cochet	Jean Borotra	2002	Lleyton Hewitt	David Nalbandian
1930	Bill Tilden	Wilmer Allison	2003	Roger Federer	Mark Philippoussis
1931	Sidney B. Wood	Francis X. Shields	2004	Roger Federer	Andy Roddick
1932	Ellsworth Vines	Henry Austin	2005	Roger Federer	Andy Roddick
1933	Jack Crawford	Ellsworth Vines	2006	Roger Federer	Rafael Nadal
1934	Fred Perry	Jack Crawford	2007	Roger Federer	Rafael Nadal
1935	Fred Perry	Gottfried von Cramm	2008	Rafael Nadal	Roger Federer
1936	Fred Perry	Gottfried von Cramm	2009	Roger Federer	Andy Roddick
1937	Donald Budge	Gottfried von Cramm	2010	Rafael Nadal	Tomas Berdych
1938	Donald Budge	Henry Austin	2011	Novak Djokovic	Rafael Nadal
1939	Bobby Riggs	Elwood Cooke	2012	Roger Federer	Andy Murray
1946	Yvon Petra	Geoff E. Brown	2013	Andy Murray	Novak Djokovic
1947	Jack Kramer	Tom P. Brown	2014	Novak Djokovic	Roger Federer
1948	Bob Falkenburg	John Bromwich			
1949	Ted Schroeder	Jaroslav Drobny			
1950	Budge Patty	Frank Sedgman			
1951	Dick Savitt	Ken McGregor			
1952	Frank Sedgman	Jaroslav Drobny			
1953	Vic Seixas	Kurt Nielsen		### Women's Singles	
1954	Jaroslav Drobny	Ken Rosewall			
1955	Tony Trabert	Kurt Nielsen	Year	Champion	Final opponent
1956	Lew Hoad	Ken Rosewall	1925	Suzanne Lenglen	Joan Fry
1957	Lew Hoad	Ashley Cooper	1926	Kathleen McKane Godfree	Lili de Alvarez
1958	Ashley Cooper	Neale Fraser	1927	Helen Wills	Lili de Alvarez
1959	Alex Olmedo	Rod Laver	1928	Helen Wills	Lili de Alvarez
1960	Neale Fraser	Rod Laver	1929	Helen Wills	Helen H. Jacobs
1961	Rod Laver	Chuck McKinley	1930	Helen Wills Moody	Elizabeth Ryan
1962	Rod Laver	Martin Mulligan	1931	Cilly Aussem	Hilde Krahwinkel
1963	Chuck McKinley	Fred Stolle	1932	Helen Wills Moody	Helen H. Jacobs
1964	Roy Emerson	Fred Stolle	1933	Helen Wills Moody	Dorothy Round
1965	Roy Emerson	Fred Stolle	1934	Dorothy Round	Helen H. Jacobs
1966	Manuel Santana	Dennis Ralston	1935	Helen Wills Moody	Helen H. Jacobs
1967	John Newcombe	Wilhelm Bungert	1936	Helen H. Jacobs	Hilde Krahwinkel Sperling
1968	Rod Laver	Tony Roche	1937	Dorothy Round	Jadwiga Jedrzejowska
1969	Rod Laver	John Newcombe	1938	Helen Wills Moody	Helen H. Jacobs
1970	John Newcombe	Ken Rosewall	1939	Alice Marble	Kay Stammers
1971	John Newcombe	Stan Smith	1946	Pauline Betz	Louise Brough
1972	Stan Smith	Ilie Nastase	1947	Margaret Osborne	Doris Hart
1973	Jan Kodes	Alex Metreveli	1948	Louise Brough	Doris Hart
1974	Jimmy Connors	Ken Rosewall	1949	Louise Brough	Margaret Osborne duPont
1975	Arthur Ashe	Jimmy Connors	1950	Louise Brough	Margaret Osborne duPont
1976	Björn Borg	Ilie Nastase	1951	Doris Hart	Shirley Fry
1977	Björn Borg	Jimmy Connors	1952	Maureen Connolly	Louise Brough
1978	Björn Borg	Jimmy Connors	1953	Maureen Connolly	Doris Hart
1979	Björn Borg	Roscoe Tanner	1954	Maureen Connolly	Louise Brough
1980	Björn Borg	John McEnroe	1955	Louise Brough	Beverly Fleitz
1981	John McEnroe	Björn Borg	1956	Shirley Fry	Angela Buxton
1982	Jimmy Connors	John McEnroe	1957	Althea Gibson	Darlene Hard
1983	John McEnroe	Chris Lewis	1958	Althea Gibson	Angela Mortimer
1984	John McEnroe	Jimmy Connors	1959	Maria Bueno	Darlene Hard
1985	Boris Becker	Kevin Curren	1960	Maria Bueno	Sandra Reynolds
1986	Boris Becker	Ivan Lendl	1961	Angela Mortimer	Christine Truman
1987	Pat Cash	Ivan Lendl	1962	Karen Hantze-Susman	Vera Sukova
1988	Stefan Edberg	Boris Becker	1963	Margaret Smith	Billie Jean Moffitt
1989	Boris Becker	Stefan Edberg	1964	Maria Bueno	Margaret Smith
1990	Stefan Edberg	Boris Becker	1965	Margaret Smith	Maria Bueno
1991	Michael Stich	Boris Becker	1966	Billie Jean King	Maria Bueno
1992	Andre Agassi	Goran Ivanisevic	1967	Billie Jean King	Ann Haydon Jones
1993	Pete Sampras	Jim Courier	1968	Billie Jean King	Judy Tegart
1994	Pete Sampras	Goran Ivanisevic	1969	Ann Haydon Jones	Billie Jean King
1995	Pete Sampras	Boris Becker	1970	Margaret Smith Court	Billie Jean King
1996	Richard Krajicek	MaliVai "Mai" Washington	1971	Evonne Goolagong	Margaret Smith Court
			1972	Billie Jean King	Evonne Goolagong
			1973	Billie Jean King	Chris Evert
			1974	Chris Evert	Olga Morozova
			1975	Billie Jean King	Evonne Goolagong Cawley

Year	Champion	Final opponent	Year	Champion	Final opponent
1976	Chris Evert	Evonne Goolagong Cawley	1995	Steffi Graf	Arantxa Sánchez Vicario
1977	Virginia Wade	Betty Stove	1996	Steffi Graf	Arantxa Sánchez Vicario
1978	Martina Navratilova	Chris Evert	1997	Martina Hingis	Jana Novotna
1979	Martina Navratilova	Chris Evert Lloyd	1998	Jana Novotna	Nathalie Tauziat
1980	Evonne Goolagong Cawley	Chris Evert Lloyd	1999	Lindsay Davenport	Steffi Graf
1981	Chris Evert Lloyd	Hana Mandlikova	2000	Venus Williams	Lindsay Davenport
1982	Martina Navratilova	Chris Evert Lloyd	2001	Venus Williams	Justine Henin
1983	Martina Navratilova	Andrea Jaeger	2002	Serena Williams	Venus Williams
1984	Martina Navratilova	Chris Evert Lloyd	2003	Serena Williams	Venus Williams
1985	Martina Navratilova	Chris Evert Lloyd	2004	Maria Sharapova	Serena Williams
1986	Martina Navratilova	Hana Mandlikova	2005	Venus Williams	Lindsay Davenport
1987	Martina Navratilova	Steffi Graf	2006	Amélie Mauresmo	Justine Henin-Hardenne
1988	Steffi Graf	Martina Navratilova	2007	Venus Williams	Marion Bartoli
1989	Steffi Graf	Martina Navratilova	2008	Venus Williams	Serena Williams
1990	Martina Navratilova	Zina Garrison	2009	Serena Williams	Venus Williams
1991	Steffi Graf	Gabriela Sabatini	2010	Serena Williams	Vera Zvonareva
1992	Steffi Graf	Monica Seles	2011	Petra Kvitova	Maria Sharapova
1993	Steffi Graf	Jana Novotna	2012	Serena Williams	Agnieszka Radwanska
1994	Conchita Martínez	Martina Navratilova	2013	Marion Bartoli	Sabine Lisicki
			2014	Petra Kvitova	Eugenie Bouchard

U.S. Open Champions, 1925-2014

First contested 1881 for men, 1887 for women. The former U.S. National Championship became an open championship in 1968.

Men's Singles

Year	Champion	Final opponent	Year	Champion	Final opponent
1925	Bill Tilden	William Johnston	1986	Ivan Lendl	Miloslav Mecir
1926	René Lacoste	Jean Borotra	1987	Ivan Lendl	Mats Wilander
1927	René Lacoste	Bill Tilden	1988	Mats Wilander	Ivan Lendl
1928	Henri Cochet	Francis Hunter	1989	Boris Becker	Ivan Lendl
1929	Bill Tilden	Francis Hunter	1990	Pete Sampras	Andre Agassi
1930	John Doeg	Francis X. Shields	1991	Stefan Edberg	Jim Courier
1931	Ellsworth Vines	George Lott	1992	Stefan Edberg	Pete Sampras
1932	Ellsworth Vines	Henri Cochet	1993	Pete Sampras	Cedric Pioline
1933	Fred Perry	John Crawford	1994	Andre Agassi	Michael Stich
1934	Fred Perry	Wilmer Allison	1995	Pete Sampras	Andre Agassi
1935	Wilmer Allison	Sidney Wood	1996	Pete Sampras	Michael Chang
1936	Fred Perry	Don Budge	1997	Patrick Rafter	Greg Rusedski
1937	Don Budge	Gottfried von Cramm	1998	Patrick Rafter	Mark Philippoussis
1938	Don Budge	C. Gene Mako	1999	Andre Agassi	Todd Martin
1939	Bobby Riggs	S. Welby Van Horn	2000	Marat Safin	Pete Sampras
1940	Don McNeill	Bobby Riggs	2001	Lleyton Hewitt	Pete Sampras
1941	Bobby Riggs	F. L. Kovacs	2002	Pete Sampras	Andre Agassi
1942	F. R. Schroeder Jr.	Frank Parker	2003	Andy Roddick	Juan Carlos Ferrero
1943	Joseph Hunt	Jack Kramer	2004	Roger Federer	Lleyton Hewitt
1944	Frank Parker	Bill Talbert	2005	Roger Federer	Andre Agassi
1945	Frank Parker	Bill Talbert	2006	Roger Federer	Andy Roddick
1946	Jack Kramer	Tom Brown Jr.	2007	Roger Federer	Novak Djokovic
1947	Jack Kramer	Frank Parker	2008	Roger Federer	Andy Murray
1948	Pancho Gonzales	Eric Sturgess	2009	Juan Martin del Potro	Roger Federer
1949	Pancho Gonzales	F. R. Schroeder Jr.	2010	Rafael Nadal	Novak Djokovic
1950	Arthur Larsen	Herbert Flam	2011	Novak Djokovic	Rafael Nadal
1951	Frank Sedgman	E. Victor Seixas Jr.	2012	Andy Murray	Novak Djokovic
1952	Frank Sedgman	Gardnar Mulloy	2013	Rafael Nadal	Novak Djokovic
1953	Tony Trabert	E. Victor Seixas Jr.	2014	Marin Cilic	Kei Nishikori
1954	E. Victor Seixas Jr.	Rex Hartwig			
1955	Tony Trabert	Ken Rosewall			
1956	Ken Rosewall	Lewis Hoad			
1957	Malcolm Anderson	Ashley Cooper			
1958	Ashley Cooper	Malcolm Anderson			
1959	Neale A. Fraser	Alejandro Olmedo			
1960	Neale A. Fraser	Rod Laver			
1961	Roy Emerson	Rod Laver			
1962	Rod Laver	Roy Emerson			
1963	Rafael Osuna	F. A. Froehling III			
1964	Roy Emerson	Fred Stolle			
1965	Manuel Santana	Cliff Drysdale			
1966	Fred Stolle	John Newcombe			
1967	John Newcombe	Clark Graebner			
1968	Arthur Ashe	Tom Okker			
1969	Rod Laver	Tony Roche			
1970	Ken Rosewall	Tony Roche			
1971	Stan Smith	Jan Kodes			
1972	Ilie Nastase	Arthur Ashe			
1973	John Newcombe	Jan Kodes			
1974	Jimmy Connors	Ken Rosewall			
1975	Manuel Orantes	Jimmy Connors			
1976	Jimmy Connors	Björn Borg			
1977	Guillermo Vilas	Jimmy Connors			
1978	Jimmy Connors	Björn Borg			
1979	John McEnroe	Vitas Gerulaitis			
1980	John McEnroe	Björn Borg			
1981	John McEnroe	Björn Borg			
1982	Jimmy Connors	Ivan Lendl			
1983	Jimmy Connors	Ivan Lendl			
1984	John McEnroe	Ivan Lendl			
1985	Ivan Lendl	John McEnroe			

Women's Singles

Year	Champion	Final opponent
1925	Helen Wills	Kathleen McKane
1926	Molla B. Mallory	Elizabeth Ryan
1927	Helen Wills	Betty Nuthall
1928	Helen Wills	Helen H. Jacobs
1929	Helen Wills	Phoebe Holcroft-Watson
1930	Betty Nuthall	Anna McCune Harper
1931	Helen Wills Moody	E. B. Whittingstall
1932	Helen H. Jacobs	Carolin A. Babcock
1933	Helen H. Jacobs	Helen Wills Moody
1934	Helen H. Jacobs	Sarah H. Palfrey
1935	Helen H. Jacobs	Sarah Palfrey Fabyan
1936	Alice Marble	Helen H. Jacobs
1937	Anita Lizana	Jadwiga Jedrzejowska
1938	Alice Marble	Nancye Wynne
1939	Alice Marble	Helen H. Jacobs
1940	Alice Marble	Helen H. Jacobs
1941	Sarah Palfrey Cooke	Pauline Betz
1942	Pauline Betz	Louise Brough
1943	Pauline Betz	Louise Brough
1944	Pauline Betz	Margaret Osborne
1945	Sarah Palfrey Cooke	Pauline Betz
1946	Pauline Betz	Patricia Canning
1947	Louise Brough	Margaret Osborne
1948	Margaret Osborne duPont	Louise Brough
1949	Margaret Osborne duPont	Doris Hart
1950	Margaret Osborne duPont	Doris Hart
1951	Maureen Connolly	Shirley Fry
1952	Maureen Connolly	Doris Hart
1953	Maureen Connolly	Doris Hart
1954	Doris Hart	Louise Brough

Year	Champion	Final opponent	Year	Champion	Final opponent
1955	Doris Hart	Patricia Ward	1984	Martina Navratilova	Chris Evert Lloyd
1956	Shirley Fry	Althea Gibson	1985	Hana Mandlikova	Martina Navratilova
1957	Althea Gibson	Louise Brough	1986	Martina Navratilova	Helena Sukova
1958	Althea Gibson	Darlene Hard	1987	Martina Navratilova	Steffi Graf
1959	Maria Bueno	Christine Truman	1988	Steffi Graf	Gabriela Sabatini
1960	Darlene Hard	Maria Bueno	1989	Steffi Graf	Martina Navratilova
1961	Darlene Hard	Ann Haydon	1990	Gabriela Sabatini	Steffi Graf
1962	Margaret Smith	Darlene Hard	1991	Monica Seles	Martina Navratilova
1963	Maria Bueno	Margaret Smith	1992	Monica Seles	Arantxa Sánchez Vicario
1964	Maria Bueno	Carole Graebner	1993	Steffi Graf	Helena Sukova
1965	Margaret Smith	Billie Jean Moffitt	1994	Arantxa Sánchez Vicario	Steffi Graf
1966	Maria Bueno	Nancy Richey	1995	Steffi Graf	Monica Seles
1967	Billie Jean King	Ann Haydon Jones	1996	Steffi Graf	Monica Seles
1968	Virginia Wade	Billie Jean King	1997	Martina Hingis	Venus Williams
1969	Margaret Smith Court	Nancy Richey	1998	Lindsay Davenport	Martina Hingis
1970	Margaret Smith Court	Rosemary Casals	1999	Serena Williams	Martina Hingis
1971	Billie Jean King	Rosemary Casals	2000	Venus Williams	Lindsay Davenport
1972	Billie Jean King	Kerry Melville	2001	Venus Williams	Serena Williams
1973	Margaret Smith Court	Evonne Goolagong	2002	Serena Williams	Venus Williams
1974	Billie Jean King	Evonne Goolagong	2003	Justine Henin-Hardenne	Kim Clijsters
1975	Chris Evert	Evonne Goolagong Cawley	2004	Svetlana Kuznetsova	Elena Dementieva
			2005	Kim Clijsters	Mary Pierce
1976	Chris Evert	Evonne Goolagong Cawley	2006	Maria Sharapova	Justine Henin-Hardenne
			2007	Justine Henin	Svetlana Kuznetsova
1977	Chris Evert	Wendy Turnbull	2008	Serena Williams	Jelena Jankovic
1978	Chris Evert	Pam Shriver	2009	Kim Clijsters	Caroline Wozniacki
1979	Tracy Austin	Chris Evert Lloyd	2010	Kim Clijsters	Vera Zvonareva
1980	Chris Evert Lloyd	Hana Mandlikova	2011	Samantha Stosur	Serena Williams
1981	Tracy Austin	Martina Navratilova	2012	Serena Williams	Victoria Azarenka
1982	Chris Evert Lloyd	Hana Mandlikova	2013	Serena Williams	Victoria Azarenka
1983	Martina Navratilova	Chris Evert Lloyd	2014	Serena Williams	Caroline Wozniacki

Davis Cup, 1950-2013

The Davis Cup began in 1900 as a competition between the U.S. and Great Britain and later expanded to include other countries.

Year	Result	Year	Result	Year	Result
1950	Australia 4, U.S. 1	1972	U.S. 3, Romania 2	1993	Germany 4, Australia 1
1951	Australia 3, U.S. 2	1973	Australia 5, U.S. 0	1994	Sweden 4, Russia 1
1952	Australia 4, U.S. 1	1974	South Africa (default by India)	1995	U.S. 3, Russia 2
1953	Australia 3, U.S. 2	1975	Sweden 3, Czechoslovakia 2	1996	France 3, Sweden 2
1954	U.S. 3, Australia 2	1976	Italy 4, Chile 1	1997	Sweden 5, U.S. 0
1955	Australia 5, U.S. 0	1977	Australia 3, Italy 1	1998	Sweden 4, Italy 1
1956	Australia 5, U.S. 0	1978	U.S. 4, Great Britain 1	1999	Australia 3, France 2
1957	Australia 3, U.S. 2	1979	U.S. 5, Italy 0	2000	Spain 3, Australia 1
1958	U.S. 3, Australia 2	1980	Czechoslovakia 4, Italy 1	2001	France 3, Australia 2
1959	Australia 3, U.S. 2	1981	U.S. 3, Argentina 1	2002	Russia 3, France 2
1960	Australia 4, Italy 1	1982	U.S. 4, France, 1	2003	Australia 3, Spain 1
1961	Australia 5, Italy 0	1983	Australia 3, Sweden 2	2004	Spain 3, U.S. 2
1962	Australia 5, Mexico 0	1984	Sweden 4, U.S. 1	2005	Croatia 3, Slovakia 2
1963	U.S. 3, Australia 2	1985	Sweden 3, W. Germany 2	2006	Russia 3, Argentina 2
1964	Australia 3, U.S. 2	1986	Australia 3, Sweden 2	2007	U.S. 4, Russia 1
1965	Australia 4, Spain 1	1987	Sweden 5, India 0	2008	Spain 3, Argentina 1
1966	Australia 4, India 1	1988	W. Germany 4, Sweden 1	2009	Spain 5, Czech Republic 0
1967	Australia 4, Spain 1	1989	W. Germany 3, Sweden 2	2010	Serbia 3, France 2
1968	U.S. 4, Australia 1	1990	U.S. 3, Australia 2	2011	Spain 3, Argentina 1
1969	U.S. 5, Romania 0	1991	France 3, U.S. 1	2012	Czech Republic 3, Spain 2
1970	U.S. 5, W. Germany 0	1992	U.S. 3, Switzerland 1	2013	Czech Republic 3, Serbia 2
1971	U.S. 3, Romania 2				

Note: The challenge round format, which guaranteed the previous year's winner a spot in the finals at home, was eliminated in 1972.

All-Time Grand Slam Singles Titles Leaders

Men	Australian Open	French Open[1]	Wimbledon	U.S. Open	Total
Roger Federer	2004, '06-'07, '10	2009	2003-07, '09, '12	2004-08	17
Rafael Nadal	2009	2005-08, '10-'14	2008, '10	2010, '13	14
Pete Sampras	1994, '97	—	1993-95, 1997-2000	1990, '93, '95-'96, 2002	14
Roy Emerson	1961, '63-'67	1963, '67	1964-65	1961, '64	12
Björn Borg	—	1974-75, '78-'81	1976-80	—	11
Rod Laver	1960, '62, '69	1962, '69	1961-62, '68-'69	1962, '69	11
Bill Tilden	—	—	1920-21, '30	1920-25, '29	10
Andre Agassi	1995, 2000, '01, '03	1999	1992	1994, '99	8
Jimmy Connors	1974	—	1974, '82	1974, '76, '78, '82-'83	8
Ivan Lendl	1989-90	1984, '86-'87	—	1985-87	8
Fred Perry	1934	1935	1934-36	1933-34, '36	8
Ken Rosewall	1953, '55, '71-'72	1953, '68	—	1956, '70	8

Women	Australian Open	French Open[1]	Wimbledon	U.S. Open	Total
Margaret Smith Court	1960-66, '69-'71, '73	1962, '64, '69-'70, '73	1963, '65, '70	1962, '65, '69-'70, '73	24
Steffi Graf	1988-90, '94	1987-88, '93, '95-'96, '99	1988-89, '91-'93, '95-'96	1988-89, '93, '95-'96	22
Helen Wills Moody	—	1928-30, '32	1927-30, '32-'33, '35, '38	1923-25, '27-'29, '31	19
Chris Evert	1982, '84	1974-75, '79-'80, '83, '85-'86	1974, '76, '81	1975-78, '80, '82	18
Martina Navratilova	1981, '83, '85	1982, '84	1978-79, '82-'87, '90	1983-84, '86-'87	18
Serena Williams	2003, '05, '07, '09-'10	2002, '13	2002-03, '09-'10, '12	1999, 2002, '08, '12-'14	18
Billie Jean King	1968	1972	1966-68, '72-'73, '75	1967, '71-'72, '74	12
Suzanne Lenglen	—	1920-23, '25-'26	1919-23, '25	—	12
Maureen Connolly	1953	1953-54	1952-54	1951-53	9
Monica Seles	1991-93, '96	1990-92	—	1991-92	9

Note: Players active in 2014 are in bold. (1) Prior to 1925, French Open entry was limited to members of French clubs.

AUTO RACING

Indianapolis 500 Winners, 1911-2014

At Indianapolis Motor Speedway in Indianapolis, IN. Not held 1917-18, 1942-45. * = Race record.

Year	Driver(s), car[1]	Avg. mph	Year	Driver(s), car[1]	Avg. mph
1911	Ray Harroun, Marmon	74.602	1966	Graham Hill, Lola-Ford	144.317
1912	Joe Dawson, National	78.719	1967	A. J. Foyt, Coyote-Ford	151.207
1913	Jules Goux, Peugeot	75.933	1968	Bobby Unser, Eagle-Offy	152.882
1914	Rene Thomas, Delage	82.474	1969	Mario Andretti, Hawk-Ford	156.867
1915	Ralph DePalma, Mercedes	89.840	1970	Al Unser, P.J. Colt-Ford	155.749
1916	Dario Resta, Peugeot	84.001	1971	Al Unser, P.J. Colt-Ford	157.735
1919	Howdy Wilcox, Peugeot	88.050	1972	Mark Donohue, McLaren-Offy	162.962
1920	Gaston Chevrolet, Frontenac	88.618	1973	Gordon Johncock, Eagle-Offy	159.036
1921	Tommy Milton, Frontenac	89.621	1974	Johnny Rutherford, McLaren-Offy	158.589
1922	Jimmy Murphy, Duesenberg-Miller	94.484	1975	Bobby Unser, Eagle-Offy	149.213
1923	Tommy Milton, Miller	90.954	1976	Johnny Rutherford, McLaren-Offy	148.725
1924	L. L. Corum/Joe Boyer, Duesenberg	98.234	1977	A. J. Foyt, Coyote-Foyt	161.331
1925	Peter DePaolo, Duesenberg	101.127	1978	Al Unser, Lola-Cosworth	161.363
1926	Frank Lockhart, Miller	95.904	1979	Rick Mears, Penske-Cosworth	158.899
1927	George Souders, Duesenberg	97.545	1980	Johnny Rutherford, Chaparral-Cosworth	142.862
1928	Louie Meyer, Miller	99.482	1981	Bobby Unser, Penske-Cosworth	139.084
1929	Ray Keech, Miller	97.585	1982	Gordon Johncock, Wildcat-Cosworth	162.029
1930	Billy Arnold, Summers-Miller	100.448	1983	Tom Sneva, March-Cosworth	162.117
1931	Louis Schneider, Stevens-Miller	96.629	1984	Rick Mears, March-Cosworth	163.612
1932	Fred Frame, Wetteroth-Miller	104.144	1985	Danny Sullivan, March-Cosworth	152.982
1933	Louie Meyer, Miller	104.162	1986	Bobby Rahal, March-Cosworth	170.722
1934	Bill Cummings, Miller	104.863	1987	Al Unser, March-Cosworth	162.175
1935	Kelly Petillo, Wetteroth-Offy	106.240	1988	Rick Mears, Penske-Chevy Indy V8	144.809
1936	Louie Meyer, Stevens-Miller	109.069	1989	Emerson Fittipaldi, Penske-Chevy Indy V8	167.581
1937	Wilbur Shaw, Shaw-Offy	113.580	1990	Arie Luyendyk, Lola-Chevy Indy V8	185.981
1938	Floyd Roberts, Wetteroth-Miller	117.200	1991	Rick Mears, Penske-Chevy Indy V8	176.457
1939	Wilbur Shaw, Maserati	115.035	1992	Al Unser Jr., Galmer-Chevy Indy V8A	134.477
1940	Wilbur Shaw, Maserati	114.277	1993	Emerson Fittipaldi, Penske-Chevy Indy V8C	157.207
1941	Floyd Davis/Mauri Rose, Wetteroth-Offy	115.117	1994	Al Unser Jr., Penske-Mercedes Benz	160.872
1946	George Robson, Adams-Sparks	114.820	1995	Jacques Villeneuve, Reynard-Ford Cosworth XB	153.616
1947	Mauri Rose, Deidt-Offy	116.338	1996	Buddy Lazier, Reynard-Ford Cosworth XB	147.956
1948	Mauri Rose, Deidt-Offy	119.814	1997	Arie Luyendyk, G Force-Aurora	145.827
1949	Bill Holland, Deidt-Offy	121.327	1998	Eddie Cheever, Dallara-Aurora	145.155
1950	Johnnie Parsons, Kurtis-Offy	124.002	1999	Kenny Brack, Dallara-Aurora	153.176
1951	Lee Wallard, Kurtis-Offy	126.244	2000	Juan Montoya, G Force-Oldsmobile	167.607
1952	Troy Ruttman, Kuzma-Offy	128.922	2001	Helio Castroneves, Dallara-Oldsmobile	141.574
1953	Bill Vukovich, KK500A-Offy	127.740	2002	Helio Castroneves, Dallara-Chevrolet	166.499
1954	Bill Vukovich, KK500A-Offy	130.840	2003	Gil de Ferran, G Force-Toyota	156.291
1955	Bob Sweikert, KK500C-Offy	128.213	2004	Buddy Rice, G Force-Honda	138.518
1956	Pat Flaherty, Watson-Offy	128.490	2005	Dan Wheldon, Dallara-Honda	157.603
1957	Sam Hanks, Salih-Offy	135.601	2006	Sam Hornish Jr., Dallara-Honda	157.085
1958	Jimmy Bryan, Salih-Offy	133.791	2007	Dario Franchitti, Dallara-Honda	151.774
1959	Rodger Ward, Watson-Offy	135.857	2008	Scott Dixon, Dallara-Honda	143.567
1960	Jim Rathmann, Watson-Offy	138.767	2009	Helio Castroneves, Dallara-Honda	150.318
1961	A. J. Foyt, Trevis-Offy	139.130	2010	Dario Franchitti, Dallara-Honda	161.623
1962	Rodger Ward, Watson-Offy	140.293	2011	Dan Wheldon, Dallara-Honda	170.265
1963	Parnelli Jones, Watson-Offy	143.137	2012	Dario Franchitti, Dallara-Honda	167.734
1964	A. J. Foyt, Watson-Offy	147.350	2013	Tony Kanaan, Dallara-Chevrolet	187.433*
1965	Jim Clark, Lotus-Ford	150.686	2014	Ryan Hunter-Reay, Dallara-Honda	186.563

Note: The race was less than 500 mi in the following years: 1916 (300 mi), 1926 (400 mi), 1950 (345 mi), 1973 (332.5 mi), 1975 (435 mi), 1976 (255 mi), 2004 (450 mi), and 2007 (415 mi). (1) Chassis-engine.

IndyCar Series Champions, 1996-2014

A breakaway group of Championship Auto Racing Teams (CART) drivers began the Indy Racing League (IRL) in 1994; it awarded its first championship in 1996. Known as the IndyCar Series in 2003-11, and as IndyCar from 2011 on. Merged with Champ Car World Series, 2008.

Year	Driver	Year	Driver	Year	Driver	Year	Driver	Year	Driver
1996	Scott Sharp; Buzz Calkins (tie)	1999	Greg Ray	2003	Scott Dixon	2007	Dario Franchitti	2011	Dario Franchitti
		2000	Buddy Lazier	2004	Tony Kanaan	2008	Scott Dixon	2012	Ryan Hunter-Reay
1997	Tony Stewart	2001	Sam Hornish Jr.	2005	Dan Wheldon	2009	Dario Franchitti	2013	Scott Dixon
1998	Kenny Brack	2002	Sam Hornish Jr.	2006	Sam Hornish Jr.	2010	Dario Franchitti	2014	Will Power

Champ Car World Series Winners, 1959-2007

Known as U.S. Auto Club, 1959-78; Championship Auto Racing Teams (CART), 1979-2003; Champ Car World Series, 2004-07. The Vanderbilt Cup became the series championship trophy in 2000. Merged with Indy Racing League (now IndyCar) in 2008.

Year	Driver	Year	Driver	Year	Driver	Year	Driver	Year	Driver
1959	Rodger Ward	1969	Mario Andretti	1979	Rick Mears	1989	Emerson Fittipaldi	1999	Juan Montoya
1960	A. J. Foyt	1970	Al Unser	1980	Johnny Rutherford	1990	Al Unser Jr.	2000	Gil de Ferran
1961	A. J. Foyt	1971	Joe Leonard	1981	Rick Mears	1991	Michael Andretti	2001	Gil de Ferran
1962	Rodger Ward	1972	Joe Leonard	1982	Rick Mears	1992	Bobby Rahal	2002	Cristiano da Matta
1963	A. J. Foyt	1973	Roger McCluskey	1983	Al Unser	1993	Nigel Mansell	2003	Paul Tracy
1964	A. J. Foyt	1974	Bobby Unser	1984	Mario Andretti	1994	Al Unser Jr.	2004	Sébastien Bourdais
1965	Mario Andretti	1975	A. J. Foyt	1985	Al Unser	1995	Jacques Villeneuve	2005	Sébastien Bourdais
1966	Mario Andretti	1976	Gordon Johncock	1986	Bobby Rahal	1996	Jimmy Vasser	2006	Sébastien Bourdais
1967	A. J. Foyt	1977	Tom Sneva	1987	Bobby Rahal	1997	Alex Zanardi	2007	Sébastien Bourdais
1968	Bobby Unser	1978	Tom Sneva	1988	Danny Sullivan	1998	Alex Zanardi		

NASCAR Sprint Cup Series Champions, 1949-2013

Known as Strictly Stock, 1949; Grand National, 1950-70; Winston Cup, 1971-2003; and Sprint Cup, 2004-present.

Year	Driver	Year	Driver	Year	Driver	Year	Driver	Year	Driver
1949	Red Byron	1962	Joe Weatherly	1975	Richard Petty	1988	Bill Elliott	2001	Jeff Gordon
1950	Bill Rexford	1963	Joe Weatherly	1976	Cale Yarborough	1989	Rusty Wallace	2002	Tony Stewart
1951	Herb Thomas	1964	Richard Petty	1977	Cale Yarborough	1990	Dale Earnhardt	2003	Matt Kenseth
1952	Tim Flock	1965	Ned Jarrett	1978	Cale Yarborough	1991	Dale Earnhardt	2004	Kurt Busch
1953	Herb Thomas	1966	David Pearson	1979	Richard Petty	1992	Alan Kulwicki	2005	Tony Stewart
1954	Lee Petty	1967	Richard Petty	1980	Dale Earnhardt	1993	Dale Earnhardt	2006	Jimmie Johnson
1955	Tim Flock	1968	David Pearson	1981	Darrell Waltrip	1994	Dale Earnhardt	2007	Jimmie Johnson
1956	Buck Baker	1969	David Pearson	1982	Darrell Waltrip	1995	Jeff Gordon	2008	Jimmie Johnson
1957	Buck Baker	1970	Bobby Isaac	1983	Bobby Allison	1996	Terry Labonte	2009	Jimmie Johnson
1958	Lee Petty	1971	Richard Petty	1984	Terry Labonte	1997	Jeff Gordon	2010	Jimmie Johnson
1959	Lee Petty	1972	Richard Petty	1985	Darrell Waltrip	1998	Jeff Gordon	2011	Tony Stewart
1960	Rex White	1973	Benny Parsons	1986	Dale Earnhardt	1999	Dale Jarrett	2012	Brad Keselowski
1961	Ned Jarrett	1974	Richard Petty	1987	Dale Earnhardt	2000	Bobby Labonte	2013	Jimmie Johnson

NASCAR Sprint Cup Series Rookie of the Year, 1958-2013

Year	Driver	Year	Driver	Year	Driver	Year	Driver	Year	Driver
1958	Shorty Rollins	1970	Bill Dennis	1981	Ron Bouchard	1992	Jimmy Hensley	2003	Jamie McMurray
1959	Richard Petty	1971	Walter Ballard	1982	Geoff Bodine	1993	Jeff Gordon	2004	Kasey Kahne
1960	David Pearson	1972	Larry Smith	1983	Sterling Marlin	1994	Jeff Burton	2005	Kyle Busch
1961	Woodie Wilson	1973	Lennie Pond	1984	Rusty Wallace	1995	Ricky Craven	2006	Denny Hamlin
1962	Tom Cox	1974	Earl Ross	1985	Ken Schrader	1996	Johnny Benson	2007	Juan Montoya
1963	Billy Wade	1975	Bruce Hill	1986	Alan Kulwicki	1997	Mike Skinner	2008	Regan Smith
1964	Doug Cooper	1976	Skip Manning	1987	Davey Allison	1998	Kenny Irwin	2009	Joey Logano
1965	Sam McQuagg	1977	Ricky Rudd	1988	Ken Bouchard	1999	Tony Stewart	2010	Kevin Conway
1966	James Hylton	1978	Ronnie Thomas	1989	Dick Trickle	2000	Matt Kenseth	2011	Andy Lally
1967	Donnie Allison	1979	Dale Earnhardt	1990	Rob Moroso	2001	Kevin Harvick	2012	Stephen Leicht
1968	Pete Hamilton	1980	Jody Riley	1991	Bobby Hamilton	2002	Ryan Newman	2013	Ricky Stenhouse Jr.
1969	Dick Brooks								

Daytona 500 Winners, 1959-2014

At Daytona International Speedway in Daytona Beach, FL.

Year	Driver, car	Avg. mph	Year	Driver, car	Avg. mph	Year	Driver, car	Avg. mph
1959	Lee Petty, Oldsmobile	135.521	1979	Richard Petty, Oldsmobile	143.977	1999	Jeff Gordon, Chevrolet	161.551
1960	Junior Johnson, Chevrolet	124.740	1980	Buddy Baker, Oldsmobile	177.602	2000	Dale Jarrett, Ford	155.669
1961	Marvin Panch, Pontiac	149.601	1981	Richard Petty, Buick	169.651	2001	Michael Waltrip, Chevrolet	161.783
1962	Fireball Roberts, Pontiac	152.529	1982	Bobby Allison, Buick	153.991	2002	Ward Burton, Dodge	142.971
1963	Tiny Lund, Ford	151.566	1983	Cale Yarborough, Pontiac	155.979	2003	Michael Waltrip, Chevrolet	133.870
1964	Richard Petty, Plymouth	154.334	1984	Cale Yarborough,		2004	Dale Earnhardt Jr.,	
1965	Fred Lorenzen, Ford	141.539		Chevrolet	150.994		Chevrolet	156.345
1966	Richard Petty, Plymouth	160.627	1985	Bill Elliott, Ford	172.265	2005	Jeff Gordon, Chevrolet	135.173
1967	Mario Andretti, Ford	146.926	1986	Geoff Bodine, Chevrolet	148.124	2006	Jimmie Johnson, Chevrolet	142.667
1968	Cale Yarborough, Mercury	143.251	1987	Bill Elliott, Ford	176.263	2007	Kevin Harvick, Chevrolet	149.335
1969	LeeRoy Yarbrough, Ford	157.950	1988	Bobby Allison, Buick	137.531	2008	Ryan Newman, Dodge	152.672
1970	Pete Hamilton, Plymouth	149.601	1989	Darrell Waltrip, Chevrolet	148.466	2009	Matt Kenseth, Ford	132.816
1971	Richard Petty, Plymouth	144.462	1990	Derrike Cope, Chevrolet	165.761	2010	Jamie McMurray,	
1972	A. J. Foyt, Mercury	161.550	1991	Ernie Irvan, Chevrolet	148.148		Chevrolet	137.284
1973	Richard Petty, Dodge	157.205	1992	Davey Allison, Ford	160.256	2011	Trevor Bayne, Ford	130.326
1974	Richard Petty, Dodge	140.894	1993	Dale Jarrett, Chevrolet	154.972	2012	Matt Kenseth, Ford	140.256
1975	Benny Parsons, Chevrolet	153.649	1994	Sterling Marlin, Chevrolet	156.931	2013	Jimmie Johnson,	
1976	David Pearson, Mercury	152.181	1995	Sterling Marlin, Chevrolet	141.710		Chevrolet	159.250
1977	Cale Yarborough,		1996	Dale Jarrett, Ford	154.308	2014	Dale Earnhardt Jr.,	
	Chevrolet	153.218	1997	Jeff Gordon, Chevrolet	148.295		Chevrolet	145.290
1978	Bobby Allison, Ford	159.730	1998	Dale Earnhardt, Chevrolet	172.712			

Note: The race was less than 500 mi in the following years: 1965 (322.5 mi), 1966 (495 mi), 1974 (450 mi), 2003 (272.5 mi).

Coca-Cola 600 Winners, 1960-2014

At Charlotte Motor Speedway in Concord, NC. Known as the World 600, 1960-85. * = Rain-shortened.

Year	Driver, car	Avg. mph	Year	Driver, car	Avg. mph	Year	Driver, car	Avg. mph
1960	Joe Lee Johnson,		1978	Darrell Waltrip, Chevrolet	138.355	1996	Dale Jarrett, Ford	147.581
	Chevrolet	107.735	1979	Darrell Waltrip, Chevrolet	136.674	1997	Jeff Gordon, Chevrolet	136.745*
1961	David Pearson, Pontiac	111.633	1980	Benny Parsons,		1998	Jeff Gordon, Chevrolet	136.424
1962	Nelson Stacy, Ford	125.552		Chevrolet	119.265	1999	Jeff Burton, Ford	151.367
1963	Fred Lorenzen, Ford	132.418	1981	Bobby Allison, Buick	129.326	2000	Matt Kenseth, Ford	142.640
1964	Jim Paschal, Plymouth	125.772	1982	Neil Bonnett, Ford	130.058	2001	Jeff Burton, Ford	138.107
1965	Fred Lorenzen, Ford	121.772	1983	Neil Bonnett, Chevrolet	140.707	2002	Mark Martin, Ford	137.729
1966	Marvin Panch, Plymouth	135.042	1984	Bobby Allison, Buick	129.233	2003	Jimmie Johnson, Chevrolet	126.198*
1967	Jim Paschal, Plymouth	135.832	1985	Darrell Waltrip, Chevrolet	141.807	2004	Jimmie Johnson, Chevrolet	142.763
1968	Buddy Baker, Dodge	104.207*	1986	Dale Earnhardt, Chevrolet	140.406	2005	Jimmie Johnson, Chevrolet	114.698
1969	LeeRoy Yarbrough,		1987	Kyle Petty, Ford	131.483	2006	Kasey Kahne, Dodge	128.840
	Mercury	134.361	1988	Darrell Waltrip, Chevrolet	124.460	2007	Casey Mears, Chevrolet	130.222
1970	Donnie Allison, Ford	129.680	1989	Darrell Waltrip, Chevrolet	144.077	2008	Kasey Kahne, Dodge	135.772
1971	Bobby Allison, Mercury	140.422	1990	Rusty Wallace, Pontiac	137.650	2009	David Reutimann, Toyota	120.899*
1972	Buddy Baker, Dodge	142.255	1991	Davey Allison, Ford	138.951	2010	Kurt Busch, Dodge	144.966
1973	Buddy Baker, Dodge	134.890	1992	Dale Earnhardt, Chevrolet	132.980	2011	Kevin Harvick, Chevrolet	132.414
1974	David Pearson, Mercury	135.720	1993	Dale Earnhardt, Chevrolet	145.504	2012	Kasey Kahne, Chevrolet	155.687
1975	Richard Petty, Dodge	145.327	1994	Jeff Gordon, Chevrolet	139.445	2013	Kevin Harvick, Chevrolet	130.521
1976	David Pearson, Mercury	137.352	1995	Bobby Labonte, Chevrolet	151.952	2014	Jimmie Johnson, Chevrolet	145.484
1977	Richard Petty, Dodge	137.676						

Brickyard 400 Winners, 1994-2014

At Indianapolis Motor Speedway in Indianapolis, IN.

Year	Driver, car	Avg. mph	Year	Driver, car	Avg. mph	Year	Driver, car	Avg. mph
1994	Jeff Gordon, Chevrolet	131.977	2001	Jeff Gordon, Chevrolet	130.790	2008	Jimmie Johnson, Chevrolet	115.117
1995	Dale Earnhardt, Chevrolet	155.206	2002	Bill Elliott, Dodge	125.033	2009	Jimmie Johnson, Chevrolet	145.882
1996	Dale Jarrett, Ford	139.508	2003	Kevin Harvick, Chevrolet	134.554	2010	Jamie McMurray, Chevrolet	136.054
1997	Ricky Rudd, Ford	130.814	2004	Jeff Gordon, Chevrolet	115.037	2011	Paul Menard, Chevrolet	140.762
1998	Jeff Gordon, Chevrolet	126.772	2005	Tony Stewart, Chevrolet	118.782	2012	Jimmie Johnson, Chevrolet	137.680
1999	Dale Jarrett, Ford	148.194	2006	Jimmie Johnson, Chevrolet	137.182	2013	Ryan Newman, Chevrolet	153.485
2000	Bobby Labonte, Pontiac	155.912	2007	Tony Stewart, Chevrolet	117.379	2014	Jeff Gordon, Chevrolet	150.297

Irwin Tools Night Race Winners, 1961-2014

At Bristol Motor Speedway in Bristol, TN. Known as the Volunteer 500, 1961-75, '78-'79; Volunteer 400, 1976-77; Busch 500, 1980-90; Bud 500, 1991-93; Goody's 500, 1994-99; goracing.com 500, 2000; Sharpie 500, 2001-09. * = Rain-shortened.

Year	Driver, car	Avg. mph	Year	Driver, car	Avg. mph	Year	Driver, car	Avg. mph
1961	Jack Smith, Pontiac	68.373	1979	Darrell Waltrip, Chevrolet	91.493	1998	Mark Martin, Ford	86.949
1962	Bobby Johns, Pontiac	73.320	1980	Cale Yarborough, Chevrolet	86.973	1999	Dale Earnhardt, Chevrolet	91.276
1963	Fred Lorenzen, Ford	74.844	1981	Darrell Waltrip, Buick	84.723	2000	Rusty Wallace, Ford	85.394
1964	Fred Lorenzen, Ford	78.044	1982	Darrell Waltrip, Buick	94.318	2001	Tony Stewart, Pontiac	85.106
1965	Ned Jarrett, Ford	61.826	1983	Darrell Waltrip, Chevrolet	89.430*	2002	Jeff Gordon, Chevrolet	77.097
1966	Paul Goldsmith, Plymouth	77.963	1984	Terry Labonte, Chevrolet	85.365	2003	Kurt Busch, Ford	77.421
1967	Richard Petty, Plymouth	78.705	1985	Dale Earnhardt, Chevrolet	81.388	2004	Dale Earnhardt Jr.,	
1968	David Pearson, Ford	76.310	1986	Darrell Waltrip, Chevrolet	86.934		Chevrolet	88.538
1969	David Pearson, Ford	79.737	1987	Dale Earnhardt, Chevrolet	90.373	2005	Matt Kenseth, Ford	84.678
1970	Bobby Allison, Dodge	84.880	1988	Dale Earnhardt, Chevrolet	78.775	2006	Matt Kenseth, Ford	90.025
1971	Charlie Glotzbach,		1989	Darrell Waltrip, Chevrolet	85.554	2007	Carl Edwards, Ford	89.006
	Chevrolet	101.074	1990	Ernie Irvan, Chevrolet	91.782	2008	Carl Edwards, Ford	91.581
1972	Bobby Allison, Chevrolet	92.735	1991	Alan Kulwicki, Ford	82.028	2009	Kyle Busch, Toyota	84.820
1973	Benny Parsons, Chevrolet	91.342	1992	Darrell Waltrip, Chevrolet	91.198	2010	Kyle Busch, Toyota	99.071
1974	Cale Yarborough, Chevrolet	75.430	1993	Mark Martin, Ford	88.172	2011	Brad Keselowski, Dodge	96.753
1975	Richard Petty, Dodge	97.016	1994	Rusty Wallace, Ford	91.363	2012	Denny Hamlin, Toyota	84.402
1976	Cale Yarborough, Chevrolet	99.175	1995	Terry Labonte, Chevrolet	81.979	2013	Matt Kenseth, Toyota	90.279
1977	Cale Yarborough, Chevrolet	79.726	1996	Rusty Wallace, Ford	91.267	2014	Joey Logano, Ford	92.965
1978	Cale Yarborough, Olds.	88.628	1997	Dale Jarrett, Ford	80.013			

NASCAR Sprint All-Star Race Winners, 1985-2014

At Charlotte Motor Speedway in Concord, NC. Known as The Winston, 1985-93, 1997-2003; The Winston Select, 1994-96; and Nextel All-Star Challenge, 2004-07.

Year	Driver, car	Year	Driver, car	Year	Driver, car
1985	Darrell Waltrip, Chevrolet	1995	Jeff Gordon, Chevrolet	2005	Mark Martin, Ford
1986	Bill Elliott, Ford	1996	Michael Waltrip, Ford	2006	Jimmie Johnson, Chevrolet
1987	Dale Earnhardt, Chevrolet	1997	Jeff Gordon, Chevrolet	2007	Kevin Harvick, Chevrolet
1988	Terry Labonte, Chevrolet	1998	Mark Martin, Ford	2008	Kasey Kahne, Dodge
1989	Rusty Wallace, Pontiac	1999	Terry Labonte, Chevrolet	2009	Tony Stewart, Chevrolet
1990	Dale Earnhardt, Chevrolet	2000	Dale Earnhardt Jr., Chevrolet	2010	Kurt Busch, Dodge
1991	Davey Allison, Ford	2001	Jeff Gordon, Chevrolet	2011	Carl Edwards, Ford
1992	Davey Allison, Ford	2002	Ryan Newman, Ford	2012	Jimmie Johnson, Chevrolet
1993	Dale Earnhardt, Chevrolet	2003	Jimmie Johnson, Chevrolet	2013	Jimmie Johnson, Chevrolet
1994	Geoffrey Bodine, Ford	2004	Matt Kenseth, Ford	2014	Jamie McMurray, Chevrolet

Formula One World Drivers' Champions, 1950-2013

Awarded by the Fédération Internationale de l'Automobile (FIA); champions determined through a series of Grand Prix races.

Year	Driver, country	Year	Driver, country	Year	Driver, country
1950	Giuseppe "Nino" Farina, Italy	1972	Emerson Fittipaldi, Brazil	1993	Alain Prost, France
1951	Juan Manuel Fangio, Argentina	1973	Jackie Stewart, Scotland, UK	1994	Michael Schumacher, Germany
1952	Alberto Ascari, Italy	1974	Emerson Fittipaldi, Brazil	1995	Michael Schumacher, Germany
1953	Alberto Ascari, Italy	1975	Niki Lauda, Austria	1996	Damon Hill, England, UK
1954	Juan Manuel Fangio, Argentina	1976	James Hunt, England, UK	1997	Jacques Villeneuve, Canada
1955	Juan Manuel Fangio, Argentina	1977	Niki Lauda, Austria	1998	Mika Hakkinen, Finland
1956	Juan Manuel Fangio, Argentina	1978	Mario Andretti, United States	1999	Mika Hakkinen, Finland
1957	Juan Manuel Fangio, Argentina	1979	Jody Scheckter, South Africa	2000	Michael Schumacher, Germany
1958	Mike Hawthorn, England, UK	1980	Alan Jones, Australia	2001	Michael Schumacher, Germany
1959	Jack Brabham, Australia	1981	Nelson Piquet, Brazil	2002	Michael Schumacher, Germany
1960	Jack Brabham, Australia	1982	Keke Rosberg, Finland	2003	Michael Schumacher, Germany
1961	Phil Hill, United States	1983	Nelson Piquet, Brazil	2004	Michael Schumacher, Germany
1962	Graham Hill, England, UK	1984	Niki Lauda, Austria	2005	Fernando Alonso, Spain
1963	Jim Clark, Scotland, UK	1985	Alain Prost, France	2006	Fernando Alonso, Spain
1964	John Surtees, England, UK	1986	Alain Prost, France	2007	Kimi Raikkonen, Finland
1965	Jim Clark, Scotland, UK	1987	Nelson Piquet, Brazil	2008	Lewis Hamilton, England, UK
1966	Jack Brabham, Australia	1988	Ayrton Senna, Brazil	2009	Jenson Button, England, UK
1967	Denis Hulme, New Zealand	1989	Alain Prost, France	2010	Sebastian Vettel, Germany
1968	Graham Hill, England, UK	1990	Ayrton Senna, Brazil	2011	Sebastian Vettel, Germany
1969	Jackie Stewart, Scotland, UK	1991	Ayrton Senna, Brazil	2012	Sebastian Vettel, Germany
1970	Jochen Rindt, Austria	1992	Nigel Mansell, England, UK	2013	Sebastian Vettel, Germany
1971	Jackie Stewart, Scotland, UK				

24 Hours of Le Mans Race, 2014

Audi was victorious for the fifth consecutive year at the 24 Hours of Le Mans June 14-15, 2014. Marcel Fassler of Switzerland, Andre Lotterer of Germany, and France's Benoit Treluyer completed 379 laps in the No. 2 Audi R18 e-tron quattro for the trio's third victory in four years at Circuit de la Sarthe in Le Mans, France. The team finished three laps ahead of Lucas di Grassi of Brazil, Spain's Marc Gene, and Tom Kristensen of Denmark in the No. 1 Audi. Only 36 cars of 54 cars finished the 82nd edition of the endurance race. Audi has won Le Mans 13 times in the last 15 years. With 16 wins, Porsche remains atop the all-time list but last won the race in 1998.

BOXING

There are many boxing governing bodies, including the World Boxing Assn. (WBA; known as the National Boxing Assn. [NBA] until 1962), World Boxing Council (WBC), International Boxing Fed. (IBF), World Boxing Org., U.S. Boxing Assn., N. American Boxing Fed., and European Boxing Union. All have their own champions and divisions.

Boxing Champions by Class

Class (weight limit)	WBA Champion	WBC Champion	IBF Champion
Heavyweight (none)	Wladimir Klitschko, Ukraine[1] Ruslan Chagaev, Uzbekistan[2]	Bermane Stiverne, Haiti	Wladimir Klitschko, Ukraine
Cruiserweight (200 lbs)	Denis Lebedev, Russia	Grigory Drozd, Russia	Yoan Pablo Hernandez, Germany
Light Heavyweight (175 lbs)	Bernard Hopkins, U.S. Juergen Braehmer, Germany[2]	Adonis Stevenson, Canada	Bernard Hopkins, U.S.
Super Middleweight (168 lbs)	Andre Ward, U.S.[1] Carl Froch, UK[2]	Anthony Dirrell, U.S.	Carl Froch, UK
Middleweight (160 lbs)	Gennady Golovkin, Kazakhstan[1] Daniel Jacobs, U.S.[2]	Miguel Cotto, Puerto Rico Marco Antonio Rubio, Mexico[2]	Jermain Taylor, U.S.
Super Welterweight/ Jr. Middleweight (154 lbs)	Floyd Mayweather Jr., U.S.[1] Erislandy Lara, Cuba[2]	Floyd Mayweather Jr., U.S.	Cornelius Brundage, U.S.
Welterweight (147 lbs)	Floyd Mayweather Jr., U.S.	Floyd Mayweather Jr., U.S.	Kell Brook, UK
Super Lightweight/ Jr. Welterweight (140 lbs)	Danny Garcia, U.S.[1] Jesse Vargas, U.S.[2]	Danny Garcia, U.S.	Lamont Peterson, U.S.
Lightweight (135 lbs)	Richard Abril, Cuba	Omar Figueroa, U.S.	Mickey Bey, U.S.
Super Featherweight/ Jr. Lightweight (130 lbs)	Takashi Uchiyama, Japan	Takashi Miura, Japan	Rances Barthelemy, Cuba
Featherweight (126 lbs)	Nonito Donaire, Philippines Nicholas Walters, Jamaica[2]	Jhonny Gonzalez, Mexico	Evgeny Gradovich, Russia
Super Bantamweight/ Jr. Featherweight (122 lbs)	Guillermo Rigondeaux, Cuba Scott Quigg, UK[2]	Leo Santa Cruz, Mexico	Carl Frampton, N. Ireland, UK
Bantamweight (118 lbs)	Juan Carlos Payano, Dominican Republic Jamie McDonnell, UK[2]	Shinsuke Yamanaka, Japan	Vacant
Super Flyweight/ Jr. Bantamweight (115 lbs)	Kohei Kono, Japan	Carlos Cuadras, Mexico	Zolani Tete, South Africa
Flyweight (112 lbs)	Juan Francisco Estrada, Mexico Juan Carlos Reveco, Argentina[2]	Roman Gonzalez, Nicaragua	Amnat Ruenroeng, Thailand
Jr. Flyweight (108 lbs)	Vacant	Naoya Inoue, Japan	Javier Mendoza, Mexico
Strawweight/ Mini Flyweight (105 lbs)	Hekkie Budler, South Africa	Oswaldo Novoa, Mexico	Francisco Rodriguez Jr., Mexico

Note: As of Oct. 13, 2014. Interim champions not shown. (1) Super champion. (2) Regular champion.

Ring Champions by Years

* = Abandoned/relinquished the title or was stripped of it. IBF champions listed only for heavyweight division. International Boxing Hall of Fame inductees in *italics*.

Heavyweights

1882-92	*John L. Sullivan*[1]	1978-79	*Muhammad Ali* (WBA*)[5]	1995-96	Bruce Seldon (WBA);
1892-97	*James J. Corbett*[2]	1978-83	*Larry Holmes* (WBC*)[6]		Frank Bruno (WBC)
1897-99	*Bob Fitzsimmons*	1979-80	John Tate (WBA)	1996	*Mike Tyson* (WBA/WBC*)
1899-1905	*James J. Jeffries**[3]	1980-82	Mike Weaver (WBA)	1996-97	Michael Moorer (IBF)
1905-06	Marvin Hart	1982-83	Michael Dokes (WBA)	1996-99	*Evander Holyfield* (WBA/IBF)
1906-08	Tommy Burns	1983-84	Gerrie Coetzee (WBA)	1997-99	*Lennox Lewis* (WBC)
1908-15	*Jack Johnson*	1983-85	*Larry Holmes* (IBF)[6]	1999-2001	*Lennox Lewis* (WBA*/WBC/IBF)
1915-19	Jess Willard	1984	Tim Witherspoon (WBC)	2000-01	Evander Holyfield (WBA)
1919-26	*Jack Dempsey*	1984-85	Greg Page (WBA)	2001	Hasim Rahman (WBC/IBF)
1926-28	*Gene Tunney**	1984-86	Pinklon Thomas (WBC)	2001-02	*Lennox Lewis* (IBF*)
1928-30	Vacant	1985-86	Tony Tubbs (WBA)	2001-03	John Ruiz (WBA)
1930-32	Max Schmeling	1985-87	*Michael Spinks* (IBF*)	2001-04	*Lennox Lewis* (WBC)
1932-33	Jack Sharkey	1986	Tim Witherspoon (WBA);	2002-06	Chris Byrd (IBF)
1933-34	Primo Carnera		Trevor Berbick (WBC)	2003	Roy Jones Jr. (WBA*)
1934-35	Max Baer	1986-87	*Mike Tyson* (WBC); James	2004-05	John Ruiz (WBA)[7];
1935-37	James J. Braddock		"Bonecrusher" Smith (WBA)		Vitali Klitschko (WBC*)
1937-49	*Joe Louis**	1987	Tony Tucker (IBF)	2005-06	Hasim Rahman (WBC)
1949-51	*Ezzard Charles*	1987-90	*Mike Tyson* (WBA/WBC/IBF)	2005-07	Nicolai Valuev (WBA)
1951-52	*Joe Walcott*	1990	James "Buster" Douglas	2006-08	Oleg Maskaev (WBC)
1952-56	*Rocky Marciano**		(WBA/WBC/IBF)	2006-	Wladimir Klitschko (IBF)
1956-59	*Floyd Patterson*	1990-92	Evander Holyfield	2007-08	Ruslan Chagaev (WBA)
1959-60	*Ingemar Johansson*		(WBA/WBC/IBF)	2008	Samuel Peter (WBC)
1960-62	*Floyd Patterson*	1992-93	Riddick Bowe (WBA/WBC*/IBF)	2008-09	Nikolai Valuev (WBA)
1962-64	Sonny Liston	1992-94	*Lennox Lewis* (WBC)	2008-13	Vitali Klitschko (WBC)
1964-67	*Cassius Clay*	1993-94	Evander Holyfield (WBA/IBF)	2009-11	David Haye (WBA)
	(*Muhammad Ali*)[4]	1994	Michael Moorer (WBA/IBF)	2011-	Wladimir Klitschko (WBA)
1970-73	*Joe Frazier*[4]	1994-95	Oliver McCall (WBC);	2014	Bermane Stiverne (WBC)
1973-74	*George Foreman*		*George Foreman* (WBA*/IBF*)		
1974-78	*Muhammad Ali*	1995	Frans Botha (IBF*)		
1978	Leon Spinks (WBA/WBC*)[5];				
	Ken Norton (WBC)				

(1) London Prize Ring (bare-knuckle champion). (2) First Marquis of Queensberry champion. (3) Jeffries vacated title (1905) and designated Marvin Hart and Jack Root as logical contenders. Hart def. Root in 12 rounds (1905); in turn was def. by Tommy Burns (1906), who claimed the title. Jack Johnson def. Burns (1908) and was recognized as champ. Johnson won the title by defeating Jeffries in the latter's attempted comeback (1910). (4) Title declared vacant by the WBA and others in 1967 after Ali refused military induction for religious reasons during the Vietnam War. Joe Frazier recognized as champ by six states, Mexico, and S. America. Jimmy Ellis declared champ by the WBA. Frazier KOd Ellis, Feb. 16, 1970. (5) After Spinks def. Ali, the WBC recognized Ken Norton as champ. Ali def. Spinks in 1978 rematch for WBA title and retired in 1979. (6) Relinquished WBC title in Dec. 1983 to fight as champ of the new IBF. (7) James Toney def. Ruiz Apr. 30, 2005, to claim the title, but it was rescinded when Toney tested positive for steroids.

Light Heavyweights

1903	Jack Root; George Gardner	1977-78	Miguel Cuello (WBC)	1992-97	Virgil Hill (WBA)

1903	Jack Root; George Gardner	1977-78 Miguel Cuello (WBC)	1992-97 Virgil Hill (WBA)
1903-05	Bob Fitzsimmons	1978 Mate Parlov (WBC)	1994-95 Mike McCallum (WBC)
1905-12	Philadelphia Jack O'Brien*	1978-79 Mike Rossman (WBA);	1995-96 Fabrice Tiozzo (WBC*)
1912-16	Jack Dillon	Marvin Johnson (WBC)	1996-97 Roy Jones Jr. (WBC)
1916-20	Battling Levinsky	1979 Victor Galindez (WBA)	1997 Montell Griffin (WBC);
1920-22	Georges Carpentier	1979-81 Matthew Saad Muhammad	Roy Jones Jr. (WBC);
1922-23	Battling Siki	(WBC)	Darius Michalczewski (WBA*)
1923-25	Mike McTigue	1979-80 Marvin Johnson (WBA)	1997-98 Lou Del Valle (WBA)
1925-26	Paul Berlenbach	1980-81 Eddie Mustafa Muhammad	1998-2003 Roy Jones Jr. (WBA*/WBC*)
1926-27	Jack Delaney*	(WBA)	2003 Mehdi Sahnoune (WBA);
1927-29	Tommy Loughran*	1981-85 Michael Spinks (WBA)	Antonio Tarver (WBC)
1930-34	Maxie Rosenbloom	1981-83 Dwight Muhammed-Qawi	2003-04 Roy Jones Jr. (WBA/WBC*)
1934-35	Bob Olin	Braxton (WBC)	2004 Antonio Tarver (WBA/WBC*)
1935-39	John Henry Lewis*	1983-85 Michael Spinks (WBC*)	2004-06 Fabrice Tiozzo (WBA)
1939	Melio Bettina	1985-86 J. B. Williamson (WBC)	2005-07 Tomasz Adamek (WBC)
1939-41	Billy Conn*	1986-87 Marvin Johnson (WBA);	2006-07 Silvio Branco (WBA)
1941	Anton Christoforidis (NBA)	Dennis Andries (WBC)	2007-08 Chad Dawson (WBC)
1941-48	Gus Lesnevich	1987 Leslie Stewart (WBA)	2007 Stipe Drews (WBA);
1948-50	Freddie Mills	1987-91 Virgil Hill (WBA)	Danny Green (WBA)
1950-52	Joey Maxim	1987 Thomas Hearns (WBC*)	2008 Hugo Hernan Garay (WBA);
1952-62	Archie Moore	1987-88 Don Lalonde (WBC)	Adrian Diaconu (WBC)
1962-63	Harold Johnson	1988 Sugar Ray Leonard (WBC*)	2009-10 Gabriel Campillo (WBA)
1963-65	Willie Pastrano	1989 Dennis Andries (WBC)	2009-11 Jean Pascal (WBC)
1965-66	Jose Torres	1989-90 Jeff Harding (WBC)	2010-14 Beibut Shumenov (WBA)
1966-68	Dick Tiger	1990-91 Dennis Andries (WBC)	2011-12 Bernard Hopkins (WBC)
1968-74	Bob Foster*	1991-94 Jeff Harding (WBC)	2012-13 Chad Dawson (WBC)
1974-77	John Conteh (WBC)	1991-92 Thomas Hearns (WBC)	2013- Adonis Stevenson (WBC)
1974-78	Victor Galindez (WBA)	1992 Iran Barkley (WBA*)	2014 Bernard Hopkins (WBA)

Middleweights

1884-91	Jack "Nonpareil" Dempsey	1957-58 Carmen Basilio	1989-91 Mike McCallum (WBA)
1891-97	Bob Fitzsimmons*	1958 "Sugar" Ray Robinson	1990-93 Julian Jackson (WBC)
1897-1907	Tommy Ryan*	1959 Gene Fullmer (NBA);	1992-93 Reggie Johnson (WBA)
1907-08	Stanley Ketchel; Billy Papke	"Sugar" Ray Robinson (NY)	1993-95 Gerald McClellan (WBC*)
1908-10	Stanley Ketchel	1960 Gene Fullmer (NBA);	1993-94 John David Jackson (WBA)
1911-13	Vacant	Paul Pender (NY/MA)	1994-97 Jorge Castro (WBA)
1913	Frank Klaus; George Chip	1961 Frank Klaus (NBA);	1995 Julian Jackson (WBC)
1914-17	Al McCoy	Terry Downes (NY/MA/Europe)	1995-96 Quincy Taylor (WBC);
1917-20	Mike O'Dowd	1962 Gene Fullmer;	Shinji Takehara (WBA)
1920-23	Johnny Wilson	Dick Tiger (NBA);	1996-98 Keith Holmes (WBC)
1923-26	Harry Greb	Paul Pender (NY/MA*)	1996-97 William Joppy (WBA)
1926	Theodore "Tiger" Flowers	1963 Dick Tiger (universal)	1997 Julio Cesar Green (WBA)
1926-31	Mickey Walker	1963-65 Joey Giardello	1998-2001 William Joppy (WBA)
1931-32	William "Gorilla" Jones (NBA)	1965-66 Dick Tiger	1998-99 Hassine Cherifi (WBC)
1932-37	Marcel Thil	1966-67 Emile Griffith	1999-2001 Keith Holmes (WBC)
1938	Al Hostak (NBA);	1967 Nino Benvenuti	2001 Felix Trinidad (WBA)
	Solly Krieger (NBA)	1967-68 Emile Griffith	2001-05 Bernard Hopkins (WBC/WBA)
1939-40	Al Hostak (NBA)	1968-70 Nino Benvenuti	2005-06 Jermain Taylor (WBA)
1940-47	Tony Zale	1970-77 Carlos Monzon*	2005-07 Jermain Taylor (WBC)
1947-48	Rocky Graziano	1977-78 Rodrigo Valdez	2006-07 Javier Castillejo (WBA)[1]
1948	Tony Zale; Marcel Cerdan	1978-79 Hugo Corro	2007-12 Felix Sturm (WBA)
1949-51	Jake LaMotta	1979-80 Vito Antuofermo	2007-10 Kelly Pavlik (WBC)
1951	"Sugar" Ray Robinson;	1980 Alan Minter	2009-11 Sebastian Zbik (WBC)
	Randy Turpin;	1980-87 "Marvelous" Marvin Hagler	2010 Sergio Martinez (WBC)
	"Sugar" Ray Robinson*	1987 Sugar Ray Leonard (WBC*)	2011-12 Julio Cesar Chavez Jr. (WBC)
1953-55	Carl "Bobo" Olson	1987-89 Sumbu Kalambay (WBA)	2012 Daniel Geale (WBA*)
1955-57	"Sugar" Ray Robinson	1987-88 Thomas Hearns (WBC)	2012-14 Sergio Martinez (WBC)
1957	Gene Fullmer;	1988-89 Iran Barkley (WBC)	2012- Gennady Golovkin (WBA)
	"Sugar" Ray Robinson	1989-90 Roberto Duran (WBC*)	2014 Miguel Cotto (WBC)

(1) Castillejo lost title to Mariano Carrera Dec. 2, 2006, but regained it Feb. 23, 2007, after Carrera tested positive for steroids.

Welterweights

1892-94	"Mysterious" Billy Smith	1934 Barney Ross;	1966-69 Curtis Cokes
1894-96	Tommy Ryan	Jimmy McLarnin	1969-70 Jose Napoles
1896	Kid McCoy*	1935-38 Barney Ross	1970-71 Billy Backus
1900	Rube Ferns; Matty Matthews	1938-40 Henry Armstrong	1971-75 Jose Napoles
1901	Rube Ferns	1940-41 Fritzie Zivic	1975-76 John Stracey (WBC);
1901-04	Joe Walcott	1941-46 Fred Cochrane	Angel Espada (WBA)
1904-06	Dixie Kid; Joe Walcott	1946 Marty Servo*	1976-79 Carlos Palomino (WBC)
1906	William "Honey" Mellody	1946-51 Ray Robinson*[1]	1976-80 Jose "Pipino" Cuevas (WBA)
1907-11	Mike Sullivan	1951 Johnny Bratton (NBA)	1979 Wilfred Benitez (WBC)
1911-15	Vacant	1951-54 Kid Gavilan	1979-80 Sugar Ray Leonard (WBC)
1915-19	Ted Lewis	1954-55 Johnny Saxton	1980 Roberto Duran (WBC)
1919-22	Jack Britton	1955 Tony De Marco	1980-81 Thomas Hearns (WBA)
1922-26	Mickey Walker	1955-56 Carmen Basilio	1980-82 Sugar Ray Leonard*
1926	Pete Latzo	1956 Johnny Saxton	1983-85 Donald Curry (WBA)
1927-29	Joe Dundee	1956-57 Carmen Basilio*	1985-86 Donald Curry (WBC)
1929	Jackie Fields	1958 Virgil Akins	1986-87 Lloyd Honeyghan (WBC)
1930	Jack Thompson;	1958-60 Don Jordan	1987 Mark Breland (WBA)
	Tommy Freeman	1960-61 Benny Paret	1987-88 Marlon Starling (WBA);
1931	Tommy Freeman;	1961 Emile Griffith	Jorge Vaca (WBC)
	Jack Thompson;	1961-62 Benny Paret	1988-89 Thomas Hearns (WBA);
	Lou Brouillard	1962-63 Emile Griffith	Lloyd Honeyghan (WBC)
1932	Jackie Fields	1963 Luis Rodriguez	1989-90 Marlon Starling (WBC);
1933	Young Corbett III;	1963-66 Emile Griffith*	Mark Breland (WBA)
	Jimmy McLarnin		

1990-91	Maurice Blocker (WBC);	2000-02	Shane Mosley (WBC)	2008	Antonio Margarito (WBA)
	Aaron Davis (WBA)	2001-02	Andrew Lewis (WBA)	2008-11	Andre Berto (WBC)
1991	Simon Brown (WBC)	2002	Ricardo Mayorga (WBA)	2009	Shane Mosley (WBA)
1991-92	Meldrick Taylor (WBA)	2002-03	Vernon Forrest (WBC)	2009-12	Vyacheslav Senchenko (WBA)
1991-93	Buddy McGirt (WBC)	2003	Ricardo Mayorga (WBA/WBC)	2011	Victor Ortiz (WBC)
1992-94	Crisanto Espana (WBA)	2003-05	Cory Spinks (WBA/WBC)	2011-	Floyd Mayweather Jr. (WBC)
1993-97	Pernell Whitaker (WBC)	2005-06	Zab Judah (WBA/WBC)	2012-13	Paulie Malignaggi (WBA)
1994-98	Ike Quartey (WBA*)	2006	Ricky Hatton (WBA);	2013	Adrien Broner (WBA);
1997-99	Oscar De La Hoya (WBC*)		Carlos Baldomir (WBC)		Marcos Maidana (WBA)
1998	James Page (WBA*)	2006-08	Floyd Mayweather Jr. (WBC);	2014	Floyd Mayweather Jr.
1999-00	Felix Trinidad (WBC*)		Miguel Cotto (WBA)		(WBA)
2000	Oscar De La Hoya (WBC*)				

(1) Robinson gained the title by defeating Tommy Bell in an elimination agreed to by the New York Commission and the National Boxing Association. Both claimed Robinson waived his title when he won the middleweight crown from LaMotta in 1951.

Lightweights

1896-99	Kid Lavigne	1968-69	Teo Cruz	1992-96	Miguel Angel Gonzalez (WBC*)
1899-1902	Frank Erne	1969-70	Mando Ramos	1992-93	Tony Lopez (WBA)
1902-08	Joe Gans	1970	Ismael Laguna	1993	Dingaan Thobela (WBA)
1908-10	Oscar "Battling" Nelson	1970-72	Ken Buchanan (WBA)	1993-98	Orzubek Nazarov (WBA)
1910-12	Ad Wolgast	1971-72	Pedro Carrasco (WBC)	1996-97	Jean-Baptiste Mendy (WBC)
1912-14	Willie Ritchie	1972-79	Roberto Duran (WBA*)	1997-98	Steve Johnston (WBC)
1914-17	Freddie Welsh	1972	Mando Ramos (WBC);	1998-99	Jean-Baptiste Mendy (WBA);
1917-25	Benny Leonard*		Chango Carmona (WBC)		Cesar Bazan (WBC)
1925	Jimmy Goodrich;	1972-74	Rodolfo Gonzalez (WBC)	1999	Julian Lorcy (WBA);
	Rocky Kansas	1974-76	Ishimatsu Suzuki (WBC)		Stefano Zoff (WBA)
1926-30	Sammy Mandell	1976-78	Esteban De Jesus (WBC)	1999-2000	Gilberto Serrano (WBA);
1930	Al Singer; Tony Canzoneri	1979-81	Jim Watt (WBC)		Steve Johnston (WBC)
1930-33	Tony Canzoneri	1979-80	Ernesto Espana (WBA)	2000-01	Takanori Hatakeyama (WBA)
1933-35	Barney Ross*	1980-81	Hilmer Kenty (WBA)	2000-02	Jose Luis Castillo (WBC)
1935-36	Tony Canzoneri	1981	Sean O'Grady (WBA);	2001	Julien Lorcy (WBA)
1936-38	Lou Ambers		Claude Noel (WBA)	2001-02	Raul Balbi (WBA)
1938	Henry Armstrong	1981-83	Alexis Arguello (WBC*)	2002-03	Leonard Dorin (WBA)
1939	Lou Ambers	1981-82	Arturo Frias (WBA)	2002-04	Floyd Mayweather Jr. (WBC)
1940	Lew Jenkins	1982-84	Ray Mancini (WBA)	2004	Lakva Sim (WBA)
1941-43	Sammy Angott	1983-84	Edwin Rosario (WBC)	2004-05	Jose Luis Castillo (WBC)
1944	Sammy Angott (NBA);	1984-86	Livingstone Bramble (WBA)	2004-08	Juan Diaz (WBA)
	Juan Zurita (NBA)	1984-85	Jose Luis Ramirez (WBC)	2005-06	Diego Corrales (WBC)
1945-51	Ike Williams	1985-86	Hector "Macho" Camacho	2006	Joel Casamayor (WBC)
	(NBA; later universal)		(WBC)	2006-08	David Diaz (WBC)
1951-52	James Carter	1986-87	Edwin Rosario (WBA)	2008	Nate Campbell (WBA);
1952	Lauro Salas; James Carter	1987-88	Julio Cesar Chavez (WBA);		Manny Pacquiao (WBC)
1953-54	James Carter		Jose Luis Ramirez (WBC)	2009-12	Juan Manuel Marquez
1954	Paddy De Marco; James Carter	1988-89	Julio Cesar Chavez		(WBA*)
1955	James Carter; Bud Smith		(WBA/WBC)	2009-10	Edwin Valero (WBC)
1956	Bud Smith; Joe Brown	1989-90	Edwin Rosario (WBA);	2010-11	Humberto Soto (WBC*)
1956-62	Joe Brown		Pernell Whitaker (WBC)	2011-12	Antonio DeMarco (WBC)
1962-65	Carlos Ortiz	1990	Juan Nazario (WBA)	2012-14	Adrien Broner (WBC*)
1965	Ismael Laguna	1990-92	Pernell Whitaker*	2013-	Richard Abril (WBA)
1965-68	Carlos Ortiz	1992	Joey Gamache (WBA)	2014	Omar Figueroa (WBC)

Featherweights

1892-1900	George Dixon (disputed)	1970-72	Kuniaki Shibata (WBC)	1995	Alejandro Gonzalez (WBC);
1900-01	Terry McGovern;	1971-72	Antonio Gomez (WBA)		Manuel Medina (WBC)
	Young Corbett II*	1972	Clemente Sanchez (WBC*)	1995-99	Luisito Espinosa (WBC)
1901-12	Abe Attell	1972-74	Ernesto Marcel (WBA*)	1996-97	Wilfredo Vasquez (WBA*)
1912-23	Johnny Kilbane	1972-73	Jose Legra (WBC)	1998	Freddie Norwood (WBA)
1923	Eugene Criqui	1973-74	Eder Jofre (WBC*)	1998-99	Antonio Cermeno (WBA)
1923-25	Johnny Dundee*	1974	Ruben Olivares (WBA)	1999	Cesar Soto (WBC);
1925-27	Kid Kaplan*	1974-75	Bobby Chacon (WBC)		Naseem Hamed (WBC*);
1927-28	Benny Bass; Tony Canzoneri	1974-76	Alexis Arguello (WBA*)	1999-2000	Freddie Norwood (WBA)
1928-29	Andre Routis	1975	Ruben Olivares (WBC)	2000-01	Guty Espadas (WBC)
1929-32	Battling Battalino*	1975-76	David Kotey (WBC)	2000-03	Derrick Gainer (WBA)
1932-34	Tommy Paul (NBA)	1976-80	Danny "Little Red"	2001-04	Erik Morales (WBC)[1]
1933-36	Freddie Miller		Lopez (WBC)	2003-06	Juan Manuel Marquez (WBA)
1936-37	Petey Sarron	1977	Rafael Ortega (WBA)	2004-06	In-Jin Chi (WBC)
1937-38	Henry Armstrong*	1977-78	Cecilio Lastra (WBA)	2006-13	Chris John (WBA)
1938-40	Joey Archibald	1978-85	Eusebio Pedroza (WBA)	2006	Takashi Koshimoto (WBC);
1940-41	Harry Jeffra	1980-82	Salvador Sanchez (WBC)		Rodolfo Lopez (WBC)
1942-48	Willie Pep	1982-84	Juan LaPorte (WBC)	2006-07	In-Jin Chi (WBC)
1948-49	Sandy Saddler	1984	Wilfredo Gomez (WBC)	2007-08	Jorge Linares (WBC)
1949-50	Willie Pep	1984-88	Azumah Nelson (WBC)	2008	Oscar Larios (WBC)
1950-57	Sandy Saddler*	1985-86	Barry McGuigan (WBA)	2009	Takahiro Ao (WBC)
1957-59	Hogan "Kid" Bassey	1986-87	Steve Cruz (WBA)	2009-10	Elio Rojas (WBC)
1959-63	Davey Moore	1987-91	Antonio Esparragoza (WBA)	2010-11	Hozumi Hasegawa (WBC)
1963-64	Ultiminio "Sugar" Ramos	1988-90	Jeff Fenech (WBC)	2011-12	Jhonny Gonzalez (WBC)
1964-67	Vicente Saldivar*	1990-91	Marcos Villasana (WBC)	2012-13	Daniel Ponce de León (WBC)
1968	Raul Rojas (WBA)	1991-93	Park Yung Kyun (WBA);	2013	Abner Mares (WBC)
1968-69	Jose Legra (WBC)		Paul Hodkinson (WBC)	2013-	Jhonny Gonzalez (WBC)
1968-71	Shozo Saijyo (WBA)	1993	Goyo Vargas (WBC)	2013	Simpiwe Vetyeka (WBA)
1969-70	Johnny Famechon (WBC)	1993-95	Kevin Kelley (WBC)	2014	Nonito Donaire (WBA)
1970	Vicente Salvidar (WBC)	1993-96	Eloy Rojas (WBA)		

(1) Marco Antonio Barrera won unanimous decision over Morales, June 22, 2002, but refused WBC title. Morales regained WBC title with unanimous decision over Paulie Ayala, Nov. 16, 2002. Morales moved up to Jr. Lightweight div. in 2004.

International Boxing Hall of Fame Inductees, 2014

Source: International Boxing Hall of Fame, 1 Hall of Fame Dr., Canastota, NY 13032. www.ibhof.com

Modern	Joe Calzaghe, 46-0 (32 KO)	Oscar De La Hoya, 39-6 (30 KO)	Felix Trinidad, 42-3 (35 KO)
Old-Timer	George "K.O." Chaney, 101-21-3 (78 KO)	Charles Ledoux, 98-29-6 (80 KO)	Mike O'Dowd, 51-7-3 (39 KO)
Pioneer	Tom Allen		
Non-participant	Barry Hearn, promoter	Richard Steele, referee	Eugene Corri, referee
Observer	Graham Houston, journalist	Neil Leifer, photographer	

Title-Changing Heavyweight Championship Bouts, 1889-2014

1889: July 8, John L. Sullivan def. Jake Kilrain, 75, Richburg, MS.

1892: Sept. 7, James J. Corbett def. John L. Sullivan, 21, New Orleans.

1897: Mar. 17, Bob Fitzsimmons def. James J. Corbett, 14, Carson City, NV.

1899: June 9, James J. Jeffries def. Bob Fitzsimmons, 11, Coney Island, NY. (Jeffries retired as champion in 1905.)

1905: July 3, Marvin Hart KOd Jack Root, 12, Reno, NV. (James J. Jeffries refereed, gave title to Hart. Jack O'Brien also claimed the title.)

1906: Feb. 23, Tommy Burns def. Marvin Hart, 20, Los Angeles.

1908: Dec. 26, Jack Johnson KOd Tommy Burns, 14, Sydney, Australia. (Police halted contest.)

1915: Apr. 5, Jess Willard KOd Jack Johnson, 26, Havana, Cuba.

1919: July 4, Jack Dempsey KOd Jess Willard, Toledo, OH (Willard failed to answer bell for 4th round).

1926: Sept. 23, Gene Tunney def. Jack Dempsey, 10, Philadelphia. (Tunney retired as champion in 1928.)

1930: June 12, Max Schmeling def. Jack Sharkey on a foul, 4, New York City. (Resulted in the election of a successor to Gene Tunney.)

1932: June 21, Jack Sharkey def. Max Schmeling, 15, NYC.

1933: June 29, Primo Carnera KOd Jack Sharkey, 6, NYC.

1934: June 14, Max Baer KOd Primo Carnera, 11, NYC.

1935: June 13, James J. Braddock def. Max Baer, 15, NYC.

1937: June 22, Joe Louis KOd James J. Braddock, 8, Chicago. (Louis retired as champion in 1949.)

1949: June 22, Ezzard Charles def. Joe Walcott, 15, Chicago; NBA recognition only.

1951: July 18, Joe Walcott KOd Ezzard Charles, 7, Pittsburgh.

1952: Sept. 23, Rocky Marciano KOd Joe Walcott, 13, Philadelphia. (Marciano retired as champion in 1956.)

1956: Nov. 30, Floyd Patterson KOd Archie Moore, 5, Chicago.

1959: June 26, Ingemar Johansson KOd Floyd Patterson, 3, NYC.

1960: June 20, Floyd Patterson KOd Ingemar Johansson, 5, NYC.

1962: Sept. 25, Sonny Liston KOd Floyd Patterson, 1, Chicago.

1964: Feb. 25, Cassius Clay (Muhammad Ali) KOd Sonny Liston, 7, Miami Beach, FL. (In 1967, Ali was stripped of his title by the WBA and others for refusing military service.)

1970: Feb. 16, Joe Frazier KOd Jimmy Ellis, 5, NYC. (Frazier def. Ali, 15, NYC, on Mar. 8, 1971, in "Fight of the Century.")

1973: Jan. 22, George Foreman KOd Joe Frazier, 2, Jamaica.

1974: Oct. 30, Muhammad Ali KOd George Foreman, 8, Kinshasa, Zaire (billed as the "Rumble in the Jungle").

1978: Feb. 15, Leon Spinks def. Muhammad Ali, 15, Las Vegas (WBC recognized Ken Norton as champion after Spinks refused to fight him before his rematch with Ali); June 9, (WBC) Larry Holmes def. Ken Norton, 15, Las Vegas; Sept. 15, (WBA) Muhammad Ali def. Leon Spinks, 15, New Orleans. (Ali retired as champion in 1979.)

1979: Oct. 20, (WBA) John Tate def. Gerrie Coetzee, 15, Pretoria, South Africa.

1980: Mar. 31, (WBA) Mike Weaver KOd John Tate, 15, Knoxville, TN.

1982: Dec. 10, (WBA) Michael Dokes KOd Mike Weaver, 1, Las Vegas.

1983: Sept. 23, (WBA) Gerrie Coetzee KOd Michael Dokes, 10, Richfield, OH; in Dec., Larry Holmes relinquished the WBC title and was named champion of the newly formed IBF.

1984: Mar. 9, (WBC) Tim Witherspoon def. Greg Page, 12, Las Vegas; Aug. 31, (WBC) Pinklon Thomas def. Tim Witherspoon, 12, Las Vegas; Dec. 1, (WBA) Greg Page KOd Gerrie Coetzee, 8, Sun City, Bophuthatswana, South Africa.

1985: Apr. 29, (WBA) Tony Tubbs def. Greg Page, 15, Buffalo, NY; Sept. 21, (IBF) Michael Spinks def. Larry Holmes, 15, Las Vegas (Spinks relinquished title in Feb. 1987).

1986: Jan. 17, (WBA) Tim Witherspoon def. Tony Tubbs, 15, Atlanta, GA; Mar. 22, (WBC) Trevor Berbick def. Pinklon Thomas, 12, Miami; Nov. 22, (WBC) Mike Tyson KOd Trevor Berbick, 2, Las Vegas; Dec. 12, (WBA) James "Bonecrusher"

Smith KOd Tim Witherspoon, 1, NYC.

1987: Mar. 7, (WBA) Mike Tyson def. James "Bonecrusher" Smith, 12, Las Vegas; May 30, (IBF) Tony Tucker KOd James "Buster" Douglas, 10, Las Vegas; Aug. 1, (IBF) Mike Tyson def. Tony Tucker, 12, Las Vegas. (Tyson became undisputed champion.)

1990: Feb. 11, (WBA/WBC/IBF) James "Buster" Douglas KOd Mike Tyson, 10, Tokyo, Japan; Oct. 25, (WBA/WBC/IBF) Evander Holyfield KOd James "Buster" Douglas, 3, Las Vegas.

1992: Nov. 13, (WBA/WBC/IBF) Riddick Bowe def. Evander Holyfield, 12, Las Vegas; in Dec., Lennox Lewis was named WBC champion after Bowe relinquished the WBC title rather than fight Lewis.

1993: Nov. 6, (WBA/IBF) Evander Holyfield def. Riddick Bowe, 12, Las Vegas.

1994: Apr. 22, (WBA/IBF) Michael Moorer def. Evander Holyfield, 12, Las Vegas; Sept. 24, (WBC) Oliver McCall KOd Lennox Lewis, 2, London, Eng.; Nov. 5, (WBA/IBF) George Foreman KOd Michael Moorer, 10, Las Vegas.

1995: In Mar., George Foreman was stripped of his WBA title for refusing to fight challenger Tony Tucker; in June, Foreman relinquished his IBF title rather than submit to a rematch with Axel Schulz; Sept. 2, (WBC) Frank Bruno def. Oliver McCall, 12, London, Eng.; Dec. 9, (IBF) Frans Botha def. Axel Schulz, 12, Stuttgart, Germany (Botha was subsequently stripped of title after testing positive for a steroid).

1996: Mar. 16, (WBC) Mike Tyson KOd Frank Bruno, 3, Las Vegas; June 22, (IBF) Michael Moorer def. Axel Schulz, 12, Dortmund, Germany; Sept. 7, (WBA) Mike Tyson KOd Bruce Seldon, 1, Las Vegas (Tyson was subsequently stripped of WBC title after refusing to fight Lennox Lewis); Nov. 9, (WBA) Evander Holyfield KOd Mike Tyson, 11, Las Vegas.

1997: Feb. 7, (WBC) Lennox Lewis TKOd Oliver McCall, 5, Las Vegas; Nov. 8, (IBF) Evander Holyfield def. Michael Moorer, 8, Las Vegas.

1999: Nov. 13, (IBF) Lennox Lewis def. Evander Holyfield, 12, Las Vegas. (Lewis became undisputed champion.)

2000: In Apr., Lennox Lewis was stripped of his WBA title after refusing to fight challenger John Ruiz; Aug. 12, (WBA) Evander Holyfield def. John Ruiz, 12, Las Vegas.

2001: Mar. 3, (WBA) John Ruiz def. Evander Holyfield, 12, Las Vegas; Apr. 21, (WBC/IBF) Hasim Rahman KOd Lennox Lewis, 5, Brakpan, South Africa; Nov. 17, (WBC/IBF) Lennox Lewis KOd Hasim Rahman, 4, Las Vegas.

2002: In Sept., Lennox Lewis relinquished his IBF title; Dec. 14, (IBF) Chris Byrd def. Evander Holyfield, 12, Atlantic City, NJ.

2003: Mar. 1, (WBA) Roy Jones Jr. def. John Ruiz, 12, Las Vegas.

2004: Feb. 20, (WBA) John Ruiz gained title when Roy Jones Jr. relinquished it; Apr. 24, (WBC) Vitali Klitschko TKOd Corrie Sanders, 8, Los Angeles, to win title vacated by retirement of Lennox Lewis in Feb.

2005: Apr. 30, (WBA) James Toney def. John Ruiz, 12, NYC (title was returned to Ruiz after Toney tested positive for steroids); Nov. 9, (WBC) Hasim Rahman gained title when Vitali Klitschko retired due to an injury; Dec. 17, (WBA) Nikolai Valuev def. John Ruiz, 12, Berlin, Germany.

2006: Apr. 22, (IBF) Wladimir Klitschko TKOd Chris Byrd, 7, Mannheim, Germany; Aug. 12, (WBA) Oleg Maskaev TKOd Hasim Rahman, 12, Las Vegas.

2007: Apr. 14, (WBA) Ruslan Chagaev def. Nikolai Valuev, 12, Stuttgart, Ger (an injured Chagaev named champion in recess, July 2008).

2008: Mar. 8, (WBC) Samuel Peter TKOd Oleg Maskaev, 6, Cancun, Mexico; Aug. 30, (WBA) Nikolai Valuev def. John Ruiz, 12, Berlin, Germany; Oct. 11, (WBC) Vitali Klitschko TKOd Samuel Peter, 8, Berlin, Germany.

2009: Nov. 7, (WBA) David Haye def. Nikolai Valuev, 12, Nuremberg, Germany.

2011: July 2, (WBA) Wladimir Klitschko def. David Haye, 12, Hamburg, Germany.

2014: May 10, (WBC) Bermane Stiverne TKOd Chris Arreola, 6, Los Angeles, to win title vacated by Vitali Klitschko in Dec. 2013.

THOROUGHBRED RACING

Triple Crown Winners

The Kentucky Derby, Preakness Stakes, and Belmont Stakes make up the Triple Crown. Since 1920, colts have carried 126 lbs in Triple Crown events; fillies, 121 lbs.

Year	Horse	Jockey	Trainer	Year	Horse	Jockey	Trainer
1919	Sir Barton	J. Loftus	H. G. Bedwell	1946	Assault	W. Mehrtens	M. Hirsch
1930	Gallant Fox	E. Sande	J. Fitzsimmons	1948	Citation	E. Arcaro	H. A. Jones
1935	Omaha	W. Sanders	J. Fitzsimmons	1973	Secretariat	R. Turcotte	L. Laurin
1937	War Admiral	C. Kurtsinger	G. Conway	1977	Seattle Slew	J. Cruguet	W. H. Turner Jr.
1941	Whirlaway	E. Arcaro	B. A. Jones	1978	Affirmed	S. Cauthen	L. S. Barrera
1943	Count Fleet	J. Longden	G. D. Cameron				

Kentucky Derby Winners, 1875-2014

Churchill Downs, Louisville, KY; inaug. 1875. Distance: 1-1/4 mi; 1-1/2 mi until 1896. 3-year-olds. Best time: 1:59 2/5, Secretariat (1973); 2014 time: 2:03.66. (Until 2001, times were measured in fifths of a second.)

Year	Horse	Jockey	Year	Horse	Jockey	Year	Horse	Jockey
1875	Aristides	O. Lewis	1922	Morvich	A. Johnson	1969	Majestic Prince	W. Hartack
1876	Vagrant	R. Swim	1923	Zev	E. Sande	1970	Dust Commander	M. Manganello
1877	Baden Baden	W. Walker	1924	Black Gold	J. D. Mooney	1971	Canonero II	G. Avila
1878	Day Star	J. Carter	1925	Flying Ebony	E. Sande	1972	Riva Ridge	R. Turcotte
1879	Lord Murphy	C. Schauer	1926	Bubbling Over	A. Johnson	1973	Secretariat	R. Turcotte
1880	Fonso	G. Lewis	1927	Whiskery	L. McAtee	1974	Cannonade	A. Cordero
1881	Hindoo	J. McLaughlin	1928	Reigh Count	C. Lang	1975	Foolish Pleasure	J. Vasquez
1882	Apollo	B. Hurd	1929	Clyde Van Dusen	L. McAtee	1976	Bold Forbes	A. Cordero
1883	Leonatus	W. Donohue	1930	Gallant Fox	E. Sande	1977	Seattle Slew	J. Cruguet
1884	Buchanan	I. Murphy	1931	Twenty Grand	C. Kurtsinger	1978	Affirmed	S. Cauthen
1885	Joe Cotton	E. Henderson	1932	Burgoo King	E. James	1979	Spectacular Bid	R. Franklin
1886	Ben Ali	P. Duffy	1933	Brokers Tip	D. Meade	1980	Genuine Risk[1]	J. Vasquez
1887	Montrose	I. Lewis	1934	Cavalcade	M. Garner	1981	Pleasant Colony	J. Velasquez
1888	Macbeth II	G. Covington	1935	Omaha	W. Saunders	1982	Gato del Sol	E. Delahoussaye
1889	Spokane	T. Kiley	1936	Bold Venture	I. Hanford	1983	Sunny's Halo	E. Delahoussaye
1890	Riley	I. Murphy	1937	War Admiral	C. Kurtsinger	1984	Swale	L. Pincay
1891	Kingman	I. Murphy	1938	Lawrin	E. Arcaro	1985	Spend a Buck	A. Cordero
1892	Azra	A. Clayton	1939	Johnstown	J. Stout	1986	Ferdinand	W. Shoemaker
1893	Lookout	E. Kunze	1940	Gallahadion	C. Bierman	1987	Alysheba	C. McCarron
1894	Chant	F. Goodale	1941	Whirlaway	E. Arcaro	1988	Winning Colors[1]	G. Stevens
1895	Halma	J. Perkins	1942	Shut Out	W. Wright	1989	Sunday Silence	P. Valenzuela
1896	Ben Brush	W. Simms	1943	Count Fleet	J. Longden	1990	Unbridled	C. Perret
1897	Typhoon II	F. Garner	1944	Pensive	C. McCreary	1991	Strike the Gold	C. Antley
1898	Plaudit	W. Simms	1945	Hoop Jr.	E. Arcaro	1992	Lil E. Tee	P. Day
1899	Manuel	F. Taral	1946	Assault	W. Mehrtens	1993	Sea Hero	J. Bailey
1900	Lieut. Gibson	J. Boland	1947	Jet Pilot	E. Guerin	1994	Go for Gin	C. McCarron
1901	His Eminence	J. Winkfield	1948	Citation	E. Arcaro	1995	Thunder Gulch	G. Stevens
1902	Alan-a-Dale	J. Winkfield	1949	Ponder	S. Brooks	1996	Grindstone	J. Bailey
1903	Judge Himes	H. Booker	1950	Middleground	W. Boland	1997	Silver Charm	G. Stevens
1904	Elwood	F. Prior	1951	Count Turf	C. McCreary	1998	Real Quiet	K. Desormeaux
1905	Agile	J. Martin	1952	Hill Gail	E. Arcaro	1999	Charismatic	C. Antley
1906	Sir Huon	R. Troxler	1953	Dark Star	H. Moreno	2000	Fusaichi Pegasus	K. Desormeaux
1907	Pink Star	A. Minder	1954	Determine	R. York	2001	Monarchos	J. Chavez
1908	Stone Street	A. Pickens	1955	Swaps	W. Shoemaker	2002	War Emblem	V. Espinoza
1909	Wintergreen	V. Powers	1956	Needles	D. Erb	2003	Funny Cide	J. Santos
1910	Donau	F. Herbert	1957	Iron Liege	W. Hartack	2004	Smarty Jones	S. Elliot
1911	Meridian	G. Archibald	1958	Tim Tam	I. Valenzuela	2005	Giacomo	M. Smith
1912	Worth	C. Shilling	1959	Tomy Lee	W. Shoemaker	2006	Barbaro	E. Prado
1913	Donerail	R. Goose	1960	Venetian Way	W. Hartack	2007	Street Sense	C. Borel
1914	Old Rosebud	J. McCabe	1961	Carry Back	J. Sellers	2008	Big Brown	K. Desormeaux
1915	Regret[1]	J. Notter	1962	Decidedly	W. Hartack	2009	Mine That Bird	C. Borel
1916	George Smith	J. Loftus	1963	Chateaugay	B. Baeza	2010	Super Saver	C. Borel
1917	Omar Khayyam	C. Borel	1964	Northern Dancer	W. Hartack	2011	Animal Kingdom	J. Velazquez
1918	Exterminator	W. Knapp	1965	Lucky Debonair	W. Shoemaker	2012	I'll Have Another	M. Gutierrez
1919	Sir Barton	J. Loftus	1966	Kauai King	D. Brumfield	2013	Orb	J. Rosario
1920	Paul Jones	T. Rice	1967	Proud Clarion	R. Ussery	2014	California Chrome	V. Espinoza
1921	Behave Yourself	C. Thompson	1968	Forward Pass[2]	I. Valenzuela			

Only two jockeys have won the Kentucky Derby five times: Eddie Arcaro (1938, 1941, 1945, 1948, 1952) and Bill Hartack (1957, 1960, 1962, 1964, 1969). Willie Shoemaker won four times (1955, 1959, 1965, 1986). Six jockeys won three times: Isaac Murphy (1884, 1890, 1891); Earle Sande (1923, 1925, 1930); Angel Cordero (1974, 1976, 1985); Gary Stevens (1988, 1995, 1997); Kent Desormeaux (1998, 2000, 2008); and Calvin Borel (2007, 2009, 2010). (1) Regret, Genuine Risk, and Winning Colors are the only fillies to have won the Derby. (2) Dancer's Image came in first but was disqualified after tests disclosed that the horse had run with a prohibited painkilling drug in his system. All wagers were paid on Dancer's Image, but Forward Pass was awarded the first-place money.

Fastest Winning Times for the Kentucky Derby

Until 2001, Kentucky Derby times were measured in fifths of a second.

Time	Horse	Jockey	Year	Time	Horse	Jockey	Year
1 min., 59 2/5 s.	Secretariat	Ron Turcotte	1973	2 min., 1.19 s.	Funny Cide	Jose Santos	2003
1 min., 59.97 s.	Monarchos	Jorge Chavez	2001	2 min., 1 1/5 s.	Thunder Gulch	Gary Stevens	1995
2 min.	Northern Dancer	Bill Hartack	1964		Affirmed	Steve Cauthen	1978
2 min., 1/5 s.	Spend a Buck	Angel Cordero Jr.	1985		Lucky Debonair	Bill Shoemaker	1965
2 min., 2/5 s.	Decidedly	Bill Hartack	1962	2 min., 1 2/5 s.	Barbaro	Edgar Prado	2006
2 min., 3/5 s.	Proud Clarion	Robert Ussery	1967		Whirlaway	Eddie Arcaro	1941
2 min., 1 s.	Fusaichi Pegasus	Kent Desormeaux	2000	2 min., 1 3/5 s.	Bold Forbes	Angel Cordero Jr.	1976
	Grindstone	Jerry Bailey	1996		Hill Gail	Eddie Arcaro	1952
2 min., 1.13 s.	War Emblem	Victor Espinoza	2002		Middleground	William Boland	1950

Preakness Stakes Winners, 1873-2014

Pimlico Race Course, Baltimore, MD; inaug. 1873. Distance: 1-3/16 mi. 3-year-olds. * = Horses ran in two divisions. Best time: 1:53, Secretariat (1973); 2014 time: 1:54.84.

Year	Horse	Jockey	Year	Horse	Jockey	Year	Horse	Jockey
1873	Survivor	G. Barbee	1922	Pillory	L. Morris	1969	Majestic Prince	W. Hartack
1874	Culpepper	M. Donohue	1923	Vigil	B. Marinelli	1970	Personality	E. Belmonte
1875	Tom Ochiltree	L. Hughes	1924	Nellie Morse	J. Merimee	1971	Canonero II	G. Avila
1876	Shirley	G. Barbee	1925	Coventry	C. Kummer	1972	Bee Bee Bee	E. Nelson
1877	Cloverbrook	C. Holloway	1926	Display	J. Malben	1973	Secretariat	R. Turcotte
1878	Duke of Magenta	C. Holloway	1927	Bostonian	A. Abel	1974	Little Current	M. Rivera
1879	Harold	L. Hughes	1928	Victorian	R. Workman	1975	Master Derby	D. McHargue
1880	Grenada	L. Hughes	1929	Dr. Freeland	L. Schaefer	1976	Elocutionist	J. Lively
1881	Saunterer	W. Costello	1930	Gallant Fox	E. Sande	1977	Seattle Slew	J. Cruguet
1882	Vanguard	W. Costello	1931	Mate	G. Ellis	1978	Affirmed	S. Cauthen
1883	Jacobus	G. Barbee	1932	Burgoo King	E. James	1979	Spectacular Bid	R. Franklin
1884	Knight of Ellerslie	S. Fisher	1933	Head Play	C. Kurtsinger	1980	Codex	A. Cordero
1885	Tecumseh	J. McLaughlin	1934	High Quest	R. Jones	1981	Pleasant Colony	J. Velasquez
1886	The Bard	S. Fisher	1935	Omaha	W. Saunders	1982	Aloma's Ruler	J. Kaenel
1887	Dunboyne	W. Donohue	1936	Bold Venture	G. Woolf	1983	Deputed	
1888	Refund	F. Littlefield	1937	War Admiral	C. Kurtsinger		Testamony	D. Miller
1889	Buddhist	G. Anderson	1938	Dauber	M. Peters	1984	Gate Dancer	A. Cordero
1890	Montague	W. Martin	1939	Challedon	G. Seabo	1985	Tank's Prospect	P. Day
1894	Assignee	F. Taral	1940	Bimelech	F. A. Smith	1986	Snow Chief	A. Solis
1895	Belmar	F. Taral	1941	Whirlaway	E. Arcaro	1987	Alysheba	C. McCarron
1896	Margrave	H. Griffin	1942	Alsab	B. James	1988	Risen Star	E. Delahoussaye
1897	Paul Kauvar	C. Thorpe	1943	Count Fleet	J. Longden	1989	Sunday Silence	P. Valenzuela
1898	Sly Fox	W. Simms	1944	Pensive	C. McCreary	1990	Summer Squall	P. Day
1899	Half Time	R. Clawson	1945	Polynesian	W. D. Wright	1991	Hansel	J. Bailey
1900	Hindus	H. Spencer	1946	Assault	W. Mehrtens	1992	Pine Bluff	C. McCarron
1901	The Parader	F. Landry	1947	Faultless	D. Dodson	1993	Prairie Bayou	M. Smith
1902	Old England	L. Jackson	1948	Citation	E. Arcaro	1994	Tabasco Cat	P. Day
1903	Flocarline	W. Gannon	1949	Capot	T. Atkinson	1995	Timber Country	P. Day
1904	Bryn Mawr	E. Hildebrand	1950	Hill Prince	E. Arcaro	1996	Louis Quatorze	P. Day
1905	Cairngorm	W. Davis	1951	Bold	E. Arcaro	1997	Silver Charm	G. Stevens
1906	Whimsical	W. Miller	1952	Blue Man	C. McCreary	1998	Real Quiet	K. Desormeaux
1907	Don Enrique	G. Mountain	1953	Native Dancer	E. Guerin	1999	Charismatic	C. Antley
1908	Royal Tourist	E. Dugan	1954	Hasty Road	J. Adams	2000	Red Bullet	J. Bailey
1909	Effendi	W. Doyle	1955	Nashua	E. Arcaro	2001	Point Given	G. Stevens
1910	Layminster	R. Estep	1956	Fabius	W. Hartack	2002	War Emblem	V. Espinoza
1911	Watervale	E. Dugan	1957	Bold Ruler	E. Arcaro	2003	Funny Cide	J. Santos
1912	Colonel Holloway	C. Turner	1958	Tim Tam	I. Valenzuela	2004	Smarty Jones	S. Elliot
1913	Buskin	J. Butwell	1959	Royal Orbit	W. Harmatz	2005	Afleet Alex	J. Rose
1914	Holiday	A. Schuttinger	1960	Bally Ache	R. Ussery	2006	Bernardini	J. Castellano
1915	Rhine Maiden	D. Hoffman	1961	Carry Back	J. Sellers	2007	Curlin	R. Albarado
1916	Damrosch	L. McAtee	1962	Greek Money	J. L. Rotz	2008	Big Brown	K. Desormeaux
1917	Kalitan	E. Haynes	1963	Candy Spots	W. Shoemaker	2009	Rachel Alexandra	C. Borel
1918*	War Cloud	J. Loftus	1964	Northern Dancer	W. Hartack	2010	Lookin At Lucky	M. Garcia
	Jack Hare Jr.	C. Peak	1965	Tom Rolfe	R. Turcotte	2011	Shackleford	J. Castanon
1919	Sir Barton	J. Loftus	1966	Kauai King	D. Brumfield	2012	I'll Have Another	M. Gutierrez
1920	Man o' War	C. Kummer	1967	Damascus	W. Shoemaker	2013	Oxbow	G. Stevens
1921	Broomspun	F. Coltiletti	1968	Forward Pass	I. Valenzuela	2014	California Chrome	V. Espinoza

Belmont Stakes Winners, 1867-2014

Belmont Park, Elmont, NY; inaug. 1867. Distance: 1-1/2 mi. 3-year-olds. Best time: 2:24, Secretariat (1973); 2014 time: 2:28.52.

Year	Horse	Jockey	Year	Horse	Jockey	Year	Horse	Jockey
1867	Ruthless	J. Gilpatrick	1900	Ildrim	N. Turner	1935	Omaha	W. Saunders
1868	General Duke	R. Swim	1901	Commando	H. Spencer	1936	Granville	J. Stout
1869	Fenian	C. Miller	1902	Masterman	J. Bullman	1937	War Admiral	C. Kurtsinger
1870	Kingfisher	W. Dick	1903	Africander	J. Bullman	1938	Pasteurized	J. Stout
1871	Harry Bassett	W. Miller	1904	Delhi	G. Odom	1939	Johnstown	J. Stout
1872	Joe Daniels	J. Rowe	1905	Tanya	E. Hildebrand	1940	Bimelech	F. A. Smith
1873	Springbok	J. Rowe	1906	Burgomaster	L. Lyne	1941	Whirlaway	E. Arcaro
1874	Saxon	G. Barbee	1907	Peter Pan	G. Mountain	1942	Shut Out	E. Arcaro
1875	Calvin	R. Swim	1908	Colin	J. Notter	1943	Count Fleet	J. Longden
1876	Algerine	W. Donohue	1909	Joe Madden	E. Dugan	1944	Bounding Home	G. L. Smith
1877	Cloverbrook	C. Holloway	1910	Sweep	J. Butwell	1945	Pavot	E. Arcaro
1878	Duke of Magenta	L. Hughes	1913	Prince Eugene	R. Troxler	1946	Assault	W. Mehrtens
1879	Spendthrift	S. Evans	1914	Luke McLuke	M. Buxton	1947	Phalanx	R. Donoso
1880	Grenada	L. Hughes	1915	The Finn	G. Byrne	1948	Citation	E. Arcaro
1881	Saunterer	T. Costello	1916	Friar Rock	E. Haynes	1949	Capot	T. Atkinson
1882	Forester	J. McLaughlin	1917	Hourless	J. Butwell	1950	Middleground	W. Boland
1883	George Kinney	J. McLaughlin	1918	Johren	F. Robinson	1951	Counterpoint	D. Gorman
1884	Panique	J. McLaughlin	1919	Sir Barton	J. Loftus	1952	One Count	E. Arcaro
1885	Tyrant	P. Duffy	1920	Man o' War	C. Kummer	1953	Native Dancer	E. Guerin
1886	Inspector B.	J. McLaughlin	1921	Grey Lag	E. Sande	1954	High Gun	E. Guerin
1887	Hanover	J. McLaughlin	1922	Pillory	C. H. Miller	1955	Nashua	E. Arcaro
1888	Sir Dixon	J. McLaughlin	1923	Zev	E. Sande	1956	Needles	D. Erb
1889	Eric	W. Hayward	1924	Mad Play	E. Sande	1957	Gallant Man	W. Shoemaker
1890	Burlington	S. Barnes	1925	American Flag	A. Johnson	1958	Cavan	P. Anderson
1891	Foxford	E. Garrison	1926	Crusader	A. Johnson	1959	Sword Dancer	W. Shoemaker
1892	Patron	W. Hayward	1927	Chance Shot	E. Sande	1960	Celtic Ash	W. Hartack
1893	Comanche	W. Simms	1928	Vito	C. Kummer	1961	Sherluck	B. Baeza
1894	Henry of Navarre	W. Simms	1929	Blue Larkspur	M. Garner	1962	Jaipur	W. Shoemaker
1895	Belmar	F. Taral	1930	Gallant Fox	E. Sande	1963	Chateaugay	B. Baeza
1896	Hastings	H. Griffin	1931	Twenty Grand	C. Kurtsinger	1964	Quadrangle	M. Ycaza
1897	Scottish Chieftain	J. Scherrer	1932	Faireno	T. Malley	1965	Hail to All	J. Sellers
1898	Bowling Brook	F. Littlefield	1933	Hurryoff	M. Garner	1966	Amberoid	W. Boland
1899	Jean Bereaud	R. R. Clawson	1934	Peace Chance	W. D. Wright	1967	Damascus	W. Shoemaker

Year	Horse	Jockey	Year	Horse	Jockey	Year	Horse	Jockey
1968	Stage Door Johnny	H. Gustines	1984	Swale	L. Pincay	2000	Commendable	P. Day
1969	Arts and Letters	B. Baeza	1985	Creme Fraiche	E. Maple	2001	Point Given	G. Stevens
1970	High Echelon	J. L. Rotz	1986	Danzig Connection	C. McCarron	2002	Sarava	E. Prado
1971	Pass Catcher	W. Blum	1987	Bet Twice	C. Perret	2003	Empire Maker	J. Bailey
1972	Riva Ridge	R. Turcotte	1988	Risen Star	E. Delahoussaye	2004	Birdstone	E. Prado
1973	Secretariat	R. Turcotte	1989	Easy Goer	P. Day	2005	Afleet Alex	J. Rose
1974	Little Current	M. Rivera	1990	Go and Go	M. Kinane	2006	Jazil	F. Jara
1975	Avatar	W. Shoemaker	1991	Hansel	J. Bailey	2007	Rags to Riches	J. Velazquez
1976	Bold Forbes	A. Cordero	1992	A.P. Indy	E. Delahoussaye	2008	Da' Tara	A. Garcia
1977	Seattle Slew	J. Cruguet	1993	Colonial Affair	J. Krone	2009	Summer Bird	K. Desormeaux
1978	Affirmed	S. Cauthen	1994	Tabasco Cat	P. Day	2010	Drosselmeyer	M. Smith
1979	Coastal	R. Hernandez	1995	Thunder Gulch	G. Stevens	2011	Ruler On Ice	J. Valdivia Jr.
1980	Temperence Hill	E. Maple	1996	Editor's Note	R. Douglas	2012	Union Rags	J. Velazquez
1981	Summing	G. Martens	1997	Touch Gold	C. McCarron	2013	Palace Malice	M. Smith
1982	Conquistador Cielo	L. Pincay	1998	Victory Gallop	G. Stevens	2014	Tonalist	J. Rosario
1983	Caveat	L. Pincay	1999	Lemon Drop Kid	J. Santos			

Annual Leading Jockey by Earnings, 1957-2013

Total purses earned by all horses that jockey raced in year listed; does not reflect what jockey earned.

Year	Jockey	Earnings	Year	Jockey	Earnings	Year	Jockey	Earnings
1957	Bill Hartack	$3,060,501	1976	Angel Cordero Jr.	$4,709,500	1995	Jerry D. Bailey	$16,311,876
1958	Willie Shoemaker	2,961,693	1977	Steve Cauthen	6,151,750	1996	Jerry D. Bailey	19,465,376
1959	Willie Shoemaker	2,843,133	1978	Darrel McHargue	6,029,885	1997	Jerry D. Bailey	18,320,743
1960	Willie Shoemaker	2,123,961	1979	Laffit Pincay Jr.	8,193,535	1998	Gary Stevens	19,622,855
1961	Willie Shoemaker	2,690,819	1980	Chris McCarron	7,663,300	1999	Pat Day	18,092,845
1962	Willie Shoemaker	2,916,844	1981	Chris McCarron	8,397,604	2000	Pat Day	17,479,838
1963	Willie Shoemaker	2,526,925	1982	Angel Cordero Jr.	9,483,590	2001	Jerry D. Bailey	22,597,720
1964	Willie Shoemaker	2,649,553	1983	Angel Cordero Jr.	10,116,697	2002	Jerry D. Bailey	19,271,814
1965	Braulio Baeza	2,582,702	1984	Chris McCarron	12,045,813	2003	Jerry D. Bailey	23,354,960
1966	Braulio Baeza	2,951,022	1985	Laffit Pincay Jr.	13,353,299	2004	John R. Velazquez	22,220,261
1967	Braulio Baeza	3,088,888	1986	Jose Santos	11,329,297	2005	John R. Velazquez	20,799,923
1968	Braulio Baeza	2,835,108	1987	Jose Santos	12,375,433	2006	Garrett K. Gomez	20,122,592
1969	Jorge Velasquez	2,542,315	1988	Jose Santos	14,877,298	2007	Garrett K. Gomez	22,800,074
1970	Laffit Pincay Jr.	2,626,526	1989	Jose Santos	13,838,389	2008	Garrett K. Gomez	23,344,351
1971	Laffit Pincay Jr.	3,784,377	1990	Gary Stevens	13,881,198	2009	Garrett K. Gomez	18,536,105
1972	Laffit Pincay Jr.	3,225,827	1991	Chris McCarron	14,441,083	2010	Ramon A. Dominguez	16,911,880
1973	Laffit Pincay Jr.	4,093,492	1992	Kent Desormeaux	14,193,006	2011	Ramon A. Dominguez	20,267,032
1974	Laffit Pincay Jr.	4,251,060	1993	Mike Smith	14,024,815	2012	Ramon A. Dominguez	25,584,852
1975	Braulio Baeza	3,695,198	1994	Mike Smith	15,979,820	2013	Javier Castellano	26,214,007

Breeders' Cup World Thoroughbred Championships, 1984-2014

The Breeders' Cup began in 1984 and through 2006, consisted of seven races all on one track on one day. In 2007, it expanded to two days, and three new races debuted: Filly and Mare Sprint, Juvenile Turf, and Dirt. In 2008, a "Ladies' Day" for fillies and several more races debuted: Turf Sprint, Marathon (eliminated in 2014), and Juvenile Fillies Turf. In 2011, the Juvenile Sprint debuted; it was eliminated in 2013.

Classic
Distance: 1-1/4 mi.

Year	Horse	Jockey	Year	Horse	Jockey	Year	Horse	Jockey
1984	Wild Again	P. Day	1995	Cigar	J. Bailey	2005	Saint Liam	J. Bailey
1985	Proud Truth	J. Velasquez	1996	Alphabet Soup	C. McCarron	2006	Invasor	F. Jara
1986	Skywalker	L. Pincay Jr.	1997	Skip Away	M. Smith	2007	Curlin	R. Albarado
1987	Ferdinand	W. Shoemaker	1998	Awesome Again	P. Day	2008	Raven's Pass	F. Dettori
1988	Alysheba	C. McCarron	1999	Cat Thief	P. Day	2009	Zenyatta	M. Smith
1989	Sunday Silence	C. McCarron	2000	Tiznow	C. McCarron	2010	Blame	G. Gomez
1990	Unbridled	P. Day	2001	Tiznow	C. McCarron	2011	Drosselmeyer	M. Smith
1991	Black Tie Affair	J. Bailey	2002	Volponi	J. Santos	2012	Fort Larned	B. Hernandez
1992	A.P. Indy	E. Delahoussaye	2003	Pleasantly Perfect	A. Solis	2013	Mucho Macho Man	G. Stevens
1993	Arcangues	J. Bailey	2004	Ghostzapper	J. Castellano	2014	Bayern	M. Garcia
1994	Concern	J. Bailey						

Juvenile
Distance: 1 mi, 1984-85, 1987; 1-1/16 mi, 1986 and since 1988.

Year	Horse	Jockey	Year	Horse	Jockey	Year	Horse	Jockey
1984	Chief's Crown	D. MacBeth	1995	Unbridled's Song	M. Smith	2005	Stevie Wonderboy	G. Gomez
1985	Tasso	L. Pincay Jr.	1996	Boston Harbor	J. Bailey	2006	Street Sense	C. Borel
1986	Capote	L. Pincay Jr.	1997	Favorite Trick	P. Day	2007	War Pass	C. Velasquez
1987	Success Express	J. Santos	1998	Answer Lively	J. Bailey	2008	Midshipman	G. Gomez
1988	Is It True	L. Pincay Jr.	1999	Anees	G. Stevens	2009	Vale of York	A. Ajtebi
1989	Rhythm	C. Perret	2000	Macho Uno	J. Bailey	2010	Uncle Mo	J. Velazquez
1990	Fly So Free	J. Santos	2001	Johannesburg	M. Kinane	2011	Hansen	R. Dominguez
1991	Arazi	P. Valenzuela	2002	Vindication	M. Smith	2012	Shanghai Bobby	R. Napravnik
1992	Gilded Time	C. McCarron	2003	Action This Day	D. Flores	2013	New Year's Day	M. Garcia
1993	Brocco	G. Stevens	2004	Wilko	F. Dettori	2014	Texas Red	K. Desormeaux
1994	Timber Country	P. Day						

Juvenile Fillies
Distance: 1 mi, 1984-85, 1987; 1-1/16 mi, 1986 and since 1988. Outstandingly won the 1984 race by disqualification.

Year	Horse	Jockey	Year	Horse	Jockey	Year	Horse	Jockey
1984	Outstandingly	W. Guerra	1995	My Flag	J. Bailey	2006	Dreaming of Anna	R. Douglas
1985	Twilight Ridge	J. Velasquez	1996	Storm Song	C. Perret	2007	Indian Blessing	G. Gomez
1986	Brave Raj	P. Valenzuela	1997	Countess Diana	S. Sellers	2008	Stardom Bound	M. Smith
1987	Epitome	P. Day	1998	Silverbulletday	G. Stevens	2009	She Be Wild	J. Leparoux
1988	Open Mind	A. Cordero Jr.	1999	Cash Run	J. Bailey	2010	Awesome Feather	J. Sanchez
1989	Go for Wand	R. Romero	2000	Caressing	J. Velazquez	2011	My Miss Aurelia	C. Nakatani
1990	Meadow Star	J. Santos	2001	Tempera	D. Flores	2012	Beholder	G. Gomez
1991	Pleasant Stage	E. Delahoussaye	2002	Storm Flag Flying	J. Velazquez	2013	Ria Antonia	J. Castellano
1992	Eliza	P. Valenzuela	2003	Halfbridled	J. Krone	2014	Take Charge Brandi	V. Espinoza
1993	Phone Chatter	L. Pincay Jr.	2004	Sweet Catomine	C. Nakatani			
1994	Flanders	P. Day	2005	Folklore	E. Prado			

Sprint
Distance: 6 furlongs.

Year	Horse	Jockey	Year	Horse	Jockey	Year	Horse	Jockey
1984	Eillo	C. Perret	1995	Desert Stormer	K. Desormeaux	2005	Silver Train	E. Prado
1985	Precisionist	C. McCarron	1996	Lit de Justice	C. Nakatani	2006	Thor's Echo	C. Nakatani
1986	Smile	J. Vasquez	1997	Elmhurst	C. Nakatani	2007	Midnight Lute	G. Gomez
1987	Very Subtle	P. Valenzuela	1998	Reraise	C. Nakatani	2008	Midnight Lute	G. Gomez
1988	Gulch	A. Cordero Jr.	1999	Artax	J. Chaves	2009	Dancing in Silks	J. Rosario
1989	Dancing Spree	A. Cordero Jr.	2000	Kona Gold	A. Solis	2010	Big Drama	E. Coa
1990	Safely Kept	C. Perret	2001	Squirtle Squirt	J. Bailey	2011	Amazombie	M. Smith
1991	Sheikh Albadou	P. Eddery	2002	Orientate	J. Bailey	2012	Trinniberg	W. Martinez
1992	Thirty Slews	E. Delahoussaye	2003	Cajun Beat	C. Velasquez	2013	Secret Circle	M. Garcia
1993	Cardmania	E. Delahoussaye	2004	Speightstown	J. Velazquez	2014	Work All Week	F. Geroux
1994	Cherokee Run	M. Smith						

Mile

Year	Horse	Jockey	Year	Horse	Jockey	Year	Horse	Jockey
1984	Royal Heroine	F. Toro	1995	Ridgewood Pearl	J. Murtagh	2005	Artie Schiller	G. Gomez
1985	Cozzene	W. Guerra	1996	Da Hoss	G. Stevens	2006	Miesque's Approval	E. Castro
1986	Last Tycoon	Y. St.-Martin	1997	Spinning World	C. Asmussen	2007	Kip Deville	C. Velasquez
1987	Miesque	F. Head	1998	Da Hoss	J. Velazquez	2008	Goldikova	O. Peslier
1988	Miesque	F. Head	1999	Silic	C. Nakatani	2009	Goldikova	O. Peslier
1989	Steinlen	J. Santos	2000	War Chant	G. Stevens	2010	Goldikova	O. Peslier
1990	Royal Academy	L. Piggott	2001	Val Royal	J. Valdivia Jr.	2011	Court Vision	R. Albarado
1991	Opening Verse	P. Valenzuela	2002	Domedriver	T. Thulliez	2012	Wise Dan	J. Velazquez
1992	Lure	M. Smith	2003	Six Perfections	J. Bailey	2013	Wise Dan	J. Lezcano
1993	Lure	M. Smith	2004	Singletary	D. Flores	2014	Karakatonie	S. Pasquier
1994	Barathea	F. Dettori						

Filly and Mare Turf
Distance: 1-3/8 mi, 1999-2000, 2004, 2006-07; 1-1/4 mi, 2001-03, 2005, and since 2008.

Year	Horse	Jockey	Year	Horse	Jockey	Year	Horse	Jockey
1999	Soaring Softly	J. Bailey	2005	Intercontinental	R. Bejarano	2010	Shared Account	E. Prado
2000	Perfect Sting	J. Bailey	2006	Ouija Board	F. Dettori	2011	Perfect Shirl	J. Velazquez
2001	Banks Hill	O. Peslier	2007	Lahudood	A. Garcia	2012	Zagora	J. Castellano
2002	Starine	J. Velazquez	2008	Forever Together	J. Leparoux	2013	Dank	R. Moore
2003	Islington	K. Fallon	2009	Midday	T. Queally	2014	Dayatthespa	J. Castellano
2004	Ouija Board	K. Fallon						

Distaff
Distance: 1-1/4 mi, 1984-87; 1-1/8 mi since 1988. Race known as Ladies' Classic, 2008-12.

Year	Horse	Jockey	Year	Horse	Jockey	Year	Horse	Jockey
1984	Princess Rooney	E. Delahoussaye	1995	Inside Information	M. Smith	2005	Pleasant Home	C. Velasquez
1985	Life's Magic	A. Cordero Jr.	1996	Jewel Princess	C. Nakatani	2006	Round Pond	E. Prado
1986	Lady's Secret	P. Day	1997	Ajina	M. Smith	2007	Ginger Punch	R. Bejarano
1987	Sacahuista	R. Romero	1998	Escena	G. Stevens	2008	Zenyatta	M. Smith
1988	Personal Ensign	R. Romero	1999	Beautiful Pleasure	J. Chavez	2009	Life Is Sweet	G. Gomez
1989	Bayakoa	L. Pincay Jr.	2000	Spain	V. Espinoza	2010	Unrivaled Belle	K. Desormeaux
1990	Bayakoa	L. Pincay Jr.	2001	Unbridled Elaine	P. Day	2011	Royal Delta	J. Lezcano
1991	Dance Smartly	P. Day	2002	Azeri	M. Smith	2012	Royal Delta	M. Smith
1992	Paseana	C. McCarron	2003	Adoration	P. Valenzuela	2013	Beholder	G. Stevens
1993	Hollywood Wildcat	E. Delahoussaye	2004	Ashado	J. Velazquez	2014	Untapable	R. Napravnik
1994	One Dreamer	G. Stevens						

Turf
Distance: 1-1/2 mi.

Year	Horse	Jockey	Year	Horse	Jockey	Year	Horse	Jockey
1984	Lashkari	Y. St.-Martin	1994	Tikkanen	M. Smith	2004	Better Talk Now	R. Dominguez
1985	Pebbles	P. Eddery	1995	Northern Spur	C. McCarron	2005	Shirocco	C. Soumillon
1986	Manila	J. Santos	1996	Pilsudski	W. Swinburn	2006	Red Rocks	F. Dettori
1987	Theatrical	P. Day	1997	Chief Bearhart	J. Santos	2007	English Channel	J. Velasquez
1988	Great Communicator	R. Sibille	1998	Buck's Boy	S. Sellers	2008	Conduit	R. Moore
1989	Prized	E. Delahoussaye	1999	Daylami	F. Dettori	2009	Conduit	R. Moore
1990	In the Wings	G. Stevens	2000	Kalanisi	J. Murtagh	2010	Dangerous Midge	F. Dettori
1991	Miss Alleged	E. Legrix	2001	Fantastic Light	F. Dettori	2011	St Nicholas Abbey	J. O'Brien
1992	Fraise	P. Valenzuela	2002	High Chaparral	M. Kinane	2012	Little Mike	R. Dominguez
1993	Kotashaan	K. Desormeaux	2003	(tie) High Chaparral	M. Kinane	2013	Magician	R. Moore
				Johar	A. Solis	2014	Main Sequence	J. Velazquez

Filly and Mare Sprint
Distance: 6 furlongs, 2007; 7 furlongs since 2008.

Year	Horse	Jockey	Year	Horse	Jockey	Year	Horse	Jockey
2007	Maryfield	E. Trujillo	2010	Dubai Majesty	J. Theriot	2013	Groupie Doll	R. Maragh
2008	Ventura	G. Gomez	2011	Musical Romance	J. Leyva	2014	Judy the Beauty	M. Smith
2009	Informed Decision	J. Leparoux	2012	Groupie Doll	R. Maragh			

Juvenile Turf
Distance: 1 mi.

Year	Horse	Jockey	Year	Horse	Jockey	Year	Horse	Jockey
2007	Nownownow	J. Leparoux	2010	Pluck	G. Gomez	2013	Outstrip	M. Smith
2008	Donativum	F. Dettori	2011	Wrote	R. Moore	2014	Hootenanny	F. Dettori
2009	Pounced	F. Dettori	2012	George Vancouver	R. Moore			

Dirt Mile

Year	Horse	Jockey	Year	Horse	Jockey	Year	Horse	Jockey
2007	Corinthian	K. Desormeaux	2010	Dakota Phone	J. Rosario	2013	Goldencents	R. Bejarano
2008	Albertus Maximus	G. Gomez	2011	Caleb's Posse	R. Maragh	2014	Goldencents	R. Bejarano
2009	Furthest Land	J. Leparoux	2012	Tapizar	C. Nakatani			

Turf Sprint

Distance: 6-1/2 furlongs, 2008-09, and since 2012; 5 furlongs, 2010-11.

Year	Horse	Jockey	Year	Horse	Jockey	Year	Horse	Jockey
2008	Desert Code	R. Migliore	2011	Regally Ready	C. Nakatani	2013	Mizdirection	M. Smith
2009	California Flag	J. Talamo	2012	Mizdirection	M. Smith	2014	Bobby's Kitten	J. Rosario
2010	Chamberlain Bridge	J. Theriot						

Juvenile Fillies Turf

Distance: 1 mi.

Year	Horse	Jockey	Year	Horse	Jockey	Year	Horse	Jockey
2008	Maram	J. Lezcano	2011	Stephanie's Kitten	J. Velazquez	2013	Chriselliam	R. Hughes
2009	Tapitsfly	R. Albarado	2012	Flotilla	C. Lemaire	2014	Lady Eli	I. Ortiz Jr.
2010	More Than Real	G. Gomez						

Eclipse Awards

The Eclipse Awards, honoring the Horse of the Year and other champions of thoroughbred racing, began in 1971 and are sponsored by the *Daily Racing Form*, the National Thoroughbred Racing Association, and the National Turf Writers Assn. Prior to 1971, the *DRF* (1936-70) and the NTRA (1950-70) issued separate selections for Horse of the Year.

Eclipse Awards, 2013

Horse of the Year: Wise Dan
2-year-old male: Shared Belief
2-year-old female: She's a Tiger
3-year-old male: Will Take Charge
3-year-old female: Beholder
Older male (4+ years old): Wise Dan

Older female (4+ years old): Royal Delta
Male sprinter: Points Offthebench
Female sprinter: Groupie Doll
Male turf horse: Wise Dan
Female turf horse: Dank

Steeplechase horse: Divine Fortune
Trainer: Todd Pletcher
Jockey: Javier Castellano
Apprentice jockey: Victor Carrasco
Breeder: Kenneth and Sarah Ramsey
Owner: Kenneth and Sarah Ramsey

Horse of the Year, 1936-2013

Year	Horse	Year	Horse	Year	Horse	Year	Horse
1936	Granville	1956	Swaps	1974	Forego	1994	Holy Bull
1937	War Admiral	1957	Bold Ruler (DRF);	1975	Forego	1995	Cigar
1938	Seabiscuit		Dedicate (NTRA)	1976	Forego	1996	Cigar
1939	Challedon	1958	Round Table	1977	Seattle Slew	1997	Favorite Trick
1940	Challedon	1959	Sword Dancer	1978	Affirmed	1998	Skip Away
1941	Whirlaway	1960	Kelso	1979	Affirmed	1999	Charismatic
1942	Whirlaway	1961	Kelso	1980	Spectacular Bid	2000	Tiznow
1943	Count Fleet	1962	Kelso	1981	John Henry	2001	Point Given
1944	Twilight Tear	1963	Kelso	1982	Conquistador Cielo	2002	Azeri
1945	Busher	1964	Kelso	1983	All Along	2003	Mineshaft
1946	Assault	1965	Roman Brother (DRF);	1984	John Henry	2004	Ghostzapper
1947	Armed		Moccasin (NTRA)	1985	Spend a Buck	2005	Saint Liam
1948	Citation	1966	Buckpasser	1986	Lady's Secret	2006	Invasor
1949	Capot	1967	Damascus	1987	Ferdinand	2007	Curlin
1950	Hill Prince	1968	Dr. Fager	1988	Alysheba	2008	Curlin
1951	Counterpoint	1969	Arts and Letters	1989	Sunday Silence	2009	Rachel Alexandra
1952	One Count (DRF);	1970	Fort Marcy (DRF);	1990	Criminal Type	2010	Zenyatta
	Native Dancer (NTRA)		Personality (NTRA)	1991	Black Tie Affair	2011	Havre de Grace
1953	Tom Fool	1971	Ack Ack	1992	A.P. Indy	2012	Wise Dan
1954	Native Dancer	1972	Secretariat	1993	Kotashaan	2013	Wise Dan
1955	Nashua	1973	Secretariat				

HARNESS RACING

Harness Horse of the Year, 1947-2013

Chosen by the U.S. Trotting Assn. and the U.S. Harness Writers Assn.

Year	Horse	Year	Horse	Year	Horse	Year	Horse
1947	Victory Song	1964	Bret Hanover	1981	Fan Hanover	1998	Moni Maker
1948	Rodney	1965	Bret Hanover	1982	Cam Fella	1999	Moni Maker
1949	Good Time	1966	Bret Hanover	1983	Cam Fella	2000	Gallo Blue Chip
1950	Proximity	1967	Nevele Pride	1984	Fancy Crown	2001	Bunny Lake
1951	Pronto Don	1968	Nevele Pride	1985	Nihilator	2002	Real Desire
1952	Good Time	1969	Nevele Pride	1986	Forrest Skipper	2003	No Pan Intended
1953	Hi Lo's Forbes	1970	Fresh Yankee	1987	Mack Lobell	2004	Rainbow Blue
1954	Stenographer	1971	Albatross	1988	Mack Lobell	2005	Rocknroll Hanover
1955	Scott Frost	1972	Albatross	1989	Matt's Scooter	2006	Glidemaster
1956	Scott Frost	1973	Sir Dalrae	1990	Beach Towel	2007	Donato Hanover
1957	Torpid	1974	Delmonica Hanover	1991	Precious Bunny	2008	Somebeachsomewhere
1958	Emily's Pride	1975	Savoir	1992	Artsplace	2009	Muscle Hill
1959	Bye Bye Byrd	1976	Keystone Ore	1993	Staying Together	2010	Rock N Roll Heaven
1960	Adios Butler	1977	Green Speed	1994	Cam's Card Shark	2011	San Pail
1961	Adios Butler	1978	Abercrombie	1995	CR Kay Suzie	2012	Chapter Seven
1962	Su Mac Lad	1979	Niatross	1996	Continental Victory	2013	Bee a Magician
1963	Speedy Scot	1980	Niatross	1997	Malabar Man		

The Hambletonian Winners (3-year-old trotters), 1965-2014

Year	Horse	Driver	Year	Horse	Driver
1965	Egyptian Candor	Del Cameron	1977	Green Speed	Bill Haughton
1966	Kerry Way	Frank Ervin	1978	Speedy Somolli	Howard Beissinger
1967	Speedy Streak	Del Cameron	1979	Legend Hanover	George Sholty
1968	Nevele Pride	Stanley Dancer	1980	Burgomeister	Bill Haughton
1969	Lindy's Pride	Howard Beissinger	1981	Shiaway St. Pat	Ray Remmen
1970	Timothy T	John Simpson Sr.	1982	Speed Bowl	Tommy Haughton
1971	Speedy Crown	Howard Beissinger	1983	Duenna	Stanley Dancer
1972	Super Bowl	Stanley Dancer	1984	Historic Freight	Ben Webster
1973	Flirth	Ralph Baldwin	1985	Prakas	Bill O'Donnell
1974	Christopher T	Bill Haughton	1986	Nuclear Kosmos	Ulf Thoresen
1975	Bonefish	Stanley Dancer	1987	Mack Lobell	John Campbell
1976	Steve Lobell	Bill Haughton	1988	Armbro Goal	John Campbell

Year	Horse	Driver	Year	Horse	Driver
1989	Park Avenue Joe	Ron Waples	2002	Chip Chip Hooray	Eric Ledford
1990	Harmonious	John Campbell	2003	Amigo Hall	Mike Lachance
1991	Giant Victory	Jack Moiseyev	2004	Windsong's Legacy	Trond Smedshammer
1992	Alf Palema	Mickey McNicholl	2005	Vivid Photo	Roger Hammer
1993	American Winner	Ron Pierce	2006	Glidemaster	John Campbell
1994	Victory Dream	Michel Lachance	2007	Donato Hanover	Ron Pierce
1995	Tagliabue	John Campbell	2008	Deweycheatumnhowe	Ray Schnittker
1996	Continental Victory	Michel Lachance	2009	Muscle Hill	Brian Sears
1997	Malabar Man	Malvern Burroughs	2010	Muscle Massive	Ron Pierce
1998	Muscles Yankee	John Campbell	2011	Broad Bahn	George Brennan
1999	Self Possessed	Mike Lachance	2012	Market Share	Tim Tetrick
2000	Yankee Paco	Trevor Ritchie	2013	Royalty For Life	Brian Sears
2001	Scarlet Knight	Stefan Melander	2014	Trixton	Jimmy Takter

BOWLING

Professional Bowlers Association Tournament of Champions, 1965-2014

Year	Winner	Year	Winner	Year	Winner	Year	Winner
1965	Billy Hardwick	1977	Mike Berlin	1989	Del Ballard Jr.	2003	Patrick Healey Jr.
1966	Wayne Zahn	1978	Earl Anthony	1990	Dave Ferraro	2005	Steve Jaros
1967	Jim Stefanich	1979	George Pappas	1991	David Ozio	2006	Chris Barnes
1968	Dave Davis	1980	Wayne Webb	1992	Marc McDowell	2007	Tommy Jones
1969	Jim Godman	1981	Steve Cook	1993	George Branham III	2008	Michael Haugen Jr.
1970	Don Johnson	1982	Mike Durbin	1994	Norm Duke	2009	Patrick Allen
1971	Johnny Petraglia	1983	Joe Berardi	1996	Dave D'Entremont	2010	Kelly Kulick
1972	Mike Durbin	1984	Mike Durbin	1997	John Gant	2011	Mika Koivuniemi
1973	Jim Godman	1985	Mark Williams	1998	Bryan Goebel	2012	Sean Rash
1974	Earl Anthony	1986	Marshall Holman	1999	Jason Couch	2013	Pete Weber
1975	Dave Davis	1987	Pete Weber	2000	Jason Couch	2014	Jason Belmonte
1976	Marshall Holman	1988	Mark Williams	2002	Jason Couch		

Note: No tournament held in 2001 or 2004.

Professional Bowlers Association Leading Money Winners, 1962-2014

Total winnings from tournaments only. For 2000-13, year shown is year the PBA season ended. As of Aug. 27, 2014.

Year	Bowler	Earnings	Year	Bowler	Earnings	Year	Bowler	Earnings
1962	Don Carter	$49,972	1980	Wayne Webb	$116,700	1997	Walter Ray Williams Jr.	$240,544
1963	Dick Weber	46,333	1981	Earl Anthony	164,735	1998	Walter Ray Williams Jr.	238,225
1964	Bob Strampe	33,592	1982	Earl Anthony	134,760	1999	Parker Bohn III	240,912
1965	Dick Weber	47,674	1983	Earl Anthony	135,605	2000	Norm Duke	143,325
1966	Wayne Zahn	54,720	1984	Mark Roth	158,712	2002	Parker Bohn III	245,200
1967	Dave Davis	54,165	1985	Mike Aulby	201,200	2003	Walter Ray Williams Jr.	419,700
1968	Jim Stefanich	67,377	1986	Walter Ray Williams Jr.	145,550	2004	Mika Koivuniemi	238,590
1969	Billy Hardwick	64,160	1987	Pete Weber	175,491	2005	Patrick Allen	350,740
1970	Mike McGrath	52,049	1988	Brian Voss	225,485	2006	Tommy Jones	301,700
1971	Johnny Petraglia	85,065	1989	Mike Aulby	298,237	2007	Doug Kent	200,530
1972	Don Johnson	56,648	1990	Amleto Monacelli	204,775	2008	Norm Duke	176,855
1973	Don McCune	69,000	1991	David Ozio	225,585	2009	Norm Duke	199,130
1974	Earl Anthony	99,585	1992	Marc McDowell	174,215	2010	Walter Ray Williams Jr.	152,670
1975	Earl Anthony	107,585	1993	Walter Ray Williams Jr.	296,370	2011	Mika Koivuniemi	333,040
1976	Earl Anthony	110,833	1994	Norm Duke	273,753	2012	Sean Rash	140,250
1977	Mark Roth	105,583	1995	Mike Aulby	219,792	2013	Sean Rash	248,317
1978	Mark Roth	134,500	1996	Walter Ray Williams Jr.	241,330	2014	Jason Belmonte	134,500
1979	Mark Roth	124,517						

World Chess Champions, 1886-2013

Source: U.S. Chess Federation, International Chess Federation (FIDE)
Official world champions since the title was first used.

Years	Champion, country	Years	Champion, country
1886-94	Wilhelm Steinitz, Austria	1972-75	Bobby Fischer, U.S.[2]
1894-1921	Emanuel Lasker, Germany	1975-85	Anatoly Karpov, USSR
1921-27	Jose R. Capablanca, Cuba	1985-2000	Garry Kasparov, USSR/Russia[3]
1927-35	Alexander Alekhine, France	1993-99	Anatoly Karpov, Russia (FIDE)[3]
1935-37	Max Euwe, Netherlands	1999-2000	Alexander Khalifman, Russia (FIDE)
1937-46	Alexander Alekhine, France[1]	2000-02	Viswanathan Anand, India (FIDE)
1948-57	Mikhail Botvinnik, USSR	2000-06	Vladimir Kramnik, Russia (classical)[4]
1957-58	Vassily Smyslov, USSR	2002-04	Ruslan Ponomariov, Ukraine (FIDE)
1958-59	Mikhail Botvinnik, USSR	2004-05	Rustam Kasimdzhanov, Uzbekistan (FIDE)
1960-61	Mikhail Tal, USSR	2005-06	Veselin Topalov, Bulgaria (FIDE)
1961-63	Mikhail Botvinnik, USSR	2006-07	Vladimir Kramnik, Russia[5]
1963-69	Tigran Petrosian, USSR	2007-13	Viswanathan Anand, India
1969-72	Boris Spassky, USSR	2013-	Magnus Carlsen, Norway

(1) After Alekhine died in 1946, the title was vacant until 1948, when Botvinnik won the first world championship event sanctioned by FIDE. (2) Defaulted championship after refusing to accept FIDE rules for a championship match, Apr. 1975. (3) Kasparov broke with FIDE, Feb. 26, 1993. FIDE stripped Kasparov of his FIDE title Mar. 23. Kasparov defeated Nigel Short (UK) in a world championship match played Sept.-Oct. 1993 under the auspices of the Professional Chess Association (PCA), a new organization the two had founded. FIDE held a championship match between Anatoly Karpov (Russia) and Jan Timman (Netherlands), which Karpov won in Nov. 1993. The PCA folded in 1995, but Kasparov was still considered the "classical" world champion. (That is, he defended his title against challengers; FIDE matches are arranged differently.) (4) In Nov. 2000, Kramnik defeated Garry Kasparov (Russia) for the classical world championship title. (5) Kramnik, the classical world champion since 2000, unified the chess titles by defeating Veselin Topalov, FIDE champion since 2005, on Oct. 13, 2006, at a world championship match.

U.S. and World Figure Skating Championships, 1952-2014

U.S. Champions			World Champions	
Men's winner	**Women's winner**	**Year**	**Men's winner, country**	**Women's winner, country**
Dick Button	Tenley Albright	1952	Dick Button, U.S.	Jacqueline du Bief, France
Hayes Jenkins	Tenley Albright	1953	Hayes Jenkins, U.S.	Tenley Albright, U.S.
Hayes Jenkins	Tenley Albright	1954	Hayes Jenkins, U.S.	Gundi Busch, W. Germany
Hayes Jenkins	Tenley Albright	1955	Hayes Jenkins, U.S.	Tenley Albright, U.S.
Hayes Jenkins	Tenley Albright	1956	Hayes Jenkins, U.S.	Carol Heiss, U.S.
David Jenkins	Carol Heiss	1957	David Jenkins, U.S.	Carol Heiss, U.S.
David Jenkins	Carol Heiss	1958	David Jenkins, U.S.	Carol Heiss, U.S.
David Jenkins	Carol Heiss	1959	David Jenkins, U.S.	Carol Heiss, U.S.
David Jenkins	Carol Heiss	1960	Alain Giletti, France	Carol Heiss, U.S.
Bradley Lord	Laurence Owen	1961	Competition canceled[1]	Competition canceled[1]
Monty Hoyt	Barbara Roles Pursley	1962	Don Jackson, Canada	Sjoukje Dijkstra, Netherlands
Tommy Litz	Lorraine Hanlon	1963	Don McPherson, Canada	Sjoukje Dijkstra, Netherlands
Scott Allen	Peggy Fleming	1964	Manfred Schnelldorfer, W. Germany	Sjoukje Dijkstra, Netherlands
Gary Visconti	Peggy Fleming	1965	Alain Calmat, France	Petra Burka, Canada
Scott Allen	Peggy Fleming	1966	Emmerich Danzer, Austria	Peggy Fleming, U.S.
Gary Visconti	Peggy Fleming	1967	Emmerich Danzer, Austria	Peggy Fleming, U.S.
Tim Wood	Peggy Fleming	1968	Emmerich Danzer, Austria	Peggy Fleming, U.S.
Tim Wood	Janet Lynn	1969	Tim Wood, U.S.	Gabriele Seyfert, E. Germany
Tim Wood	Janet Lynn	1970	Tim Wood, U.S.	Gabriele Seyfert, E. Germany
John Misha Petkevich	Janet Lynn	1971	Ondrej Nepela, Czechoslovakia	Beatrix Schuba, Austria
Ken Shelley	Janet Lynn	1972	Ondrej Nepela, Czechoslovakia	Beatrix Schuba, Austria
Gordon McKellen Jr.	Janet Lynn	1973	Ondrej Nepela, Czechoslovakia	Karen Magnussen, Canada
Gordon McKellen Jr.	Dorothy Hamill	1974	Jan Hoffmann, E. Germany	Christine Errath, E. Germany
Gordon McKellen Jr.	Dorothy Hamill	1975	Sergei Volkov, USSR	Dianne de Leeuw, Neth.
Terry Kubicka	Dorothy Hamill	1976	John Curry, UK	Dorothy Hamill, U.S.
Charles Tickner	Linda Fratianne	1977	Vladimir Kovalev, USSR	Linda Fratianne, U.S.
Charles Tickner	Linda Fratianne	1978	Charles Tickner, U.S.	Anett Poetzsch, E. Germany
Charles Tickner	Linda Fratianne	1979	Vladimir Kovalev, USSR	Linda Fratianne, U.S.
Charles Tickner	Linda Fratianne	1980	Jan Hoffmann, E. Germany	Anett Poetzsch, E. Germany
Scott Hamilton	Elaine Zayak	1981	Scott Hamilton, U.S.	Denise Biellmann, Switzerland
Scott Hamilton	Rosalynn Sumners	1982	Scott Hamilton, U.S.	Elaine Zayak, U.S.
Scott Hamilton	Rosalynn Sumners	1983	Scott Hamilton, U.S.	Rosalynn Sumners, U.S.
Scott Hamilton	Rosalynn Sumners	1984	Scott Hamilton, U.S.	Katarina Witt, E. Germany
Brian Boitano	Tiffany Chin	1985	Aleksandr Fadeev, USSR	Katarina Witt, E. Germany
Brian Boitano	Debi Thomas	1986	Brian Boitano, U.S.	Debi Thomas, U.S.
Brian Boitano	Jill Trenary	1987	Brian Orser, Canada	Katarina Witt, E. Germany
Brian Boitano	Debi Thomas	1988	Brian Boitano, U.S.	Katarina Witt, E. Germany
Christopher Bowman	Jill Trenary	1989	Kurt Browning, Canada	Midori Ito, Japan
Todd Eldredge	Jill Trenary	1990	Kurt Browning, Canada	Jill Trenary, U.S.
Todd Eldredge	Tonya Harding	1991	Kurt Browning, Canada	Kristi Yamaguchi, U.S.
Christopher Bowman	Kristi Yamaguchi	1992	Viktor Petrenko, Ukraine	Kristi Yamaguchi, U.S.
Scott Davis	Nancy Kerrigan	1993	Kurt Browning, Canada	Oksana Baiul, Ukraine
Scott Davis	Vacant[2]	1994	Elvis Stojko, Canada	Yuka Sato, Japan
Todd Eldredge	Nicole Bobek	1995	Elvis Stojko, Canada	Chen Lu, China
Rudy Galindo	Michelle Kwan	1996	Todd Eldredge, U.S.	Michelle Kwan, U.S.
Todd Eldredge	Tara Lipinski	1997	Elvis Stojko, Canada	Tara Lipinski, U.S.
Todd Eldredge	Michelle Kwan	1998	Alexei Yagudin, Russia	Michelle Kwan, U.S.
Michael Weiss	Michelle Kwan	1999	Alexei Yagudin, Russia	Maria Butyrskaya, Russia
Michael Weiss	Michelle Kwan	2000	Alexei Yagudin, Russia	Michelle Kwan, U.S.
Timothy Goebel	Michelle Kwan	2001	Yevgeny Plushenko, Russia	Michelle Kwan, U.S.
Todd Eldredge	Michelle Kwan	2002	Alexei Yagudin, Russia	Irina Slutskaya, Russia
Michael Weiss	Michelle Kwan	2003	Yevgeny Plushenko, Russia	Michelle Kwan, U.S.
Johnny Weir	Michelle Kwan	2004	Yevgeny Plushenko, Russia	Shizuka Arakawa, Japan
Johnny Weir	Michelle Kwan	2005	Stephane Lambiel, Switzerland	Irina Slutskaya, Russia
Johnny Weir	Sasha Cohen	2006	Stephane Lambiel, Switzerland	Kimmie Meissner, U.S.
Evan Lysacek	Kimmie Meissner	2007	Brian Joubert, France	Miki Ando, Japan
Evan Lysacek	Mirai Nagasu	2008	Jeffrey Buttle, Canada	Mao Asada, Japan
Jeremy Abbott	Alissa Czisny	2009	Evan Lysacek, U.S.	Yuna Kim, South Korea
Jeremy Abbott	Rachael Flatt	2010	Daisuke Takahashi, Japan	Mao Asada, Japan
Ryan Bradley	Alissa Czisny	2011	Patrick Chan, Canada	Miki Ando, Japan
Jeremy Abbott	Ashley Wagner	2012	Patrick Chan, Canada	Carolina Kostner, Italy
Max Aaron	Ashley Wagner	2013	Patrick Chan, Canada	Yuna Kim, South Korea
Jeremy Abbott	Gracie Gold	2014	Yuzuru Hanyu, Japan	Mao Asada, Japan

(1) Competition canceled after 18-member U.S. team died in plane crash en route. (2) Tonya Harding was stripped of the title for her involvement in an attack on rival Nancy Kerrigan.

Alpine Skiing Men's World Cup Champions, 1967-2014

Year	Champion, country	Year	Champion, country	Year	Champion, country
1967	Jean Claude Killy, France	1983	Phil Mahre, U.S.	1999	Lasse Kjus, Norway
1968	Jean Claude Killy, France	1984	Pirmin Zurbriggen, Switzerland	2000	Hermann Maier, Austria
1969	Karl Schranz, Austria	1985	Marc Girardelli, Luxembourg	2001	Hermann Maier, Austria
1970	Karl Schranz, Austria	1986	Marc Girardelli, Luxembourg	2002	Stephan Eberharter, Austria
1971	Gustavo Thoeni, Italy	1987	Pirmin Zurbriggen, Switzerland	2003	Stephan Eberharter, Austria
1972	Gustavo Thoeni, Italy	1988	Pirmin Zurbriggen, Switzerland	2004	Hermann Maier, Austria
1973	Gustavo Thoeni, Italy	1989	Marc Girardelli, Luxembourg	2005	Bode Miller, U.S.
1974	Piero Gros, Italy	1990	Pirmin Zurbriggen, Switzerland	2006	Benjamin Raich, Austria
1975	Gustavo Thoeni, Italy	1991	Marc Girardelli, Luxembourg	2007	Aksel Lund Svindal, Norway
1976	Ingemar Stenmark, Sweden	1992	Paul Accola, Switzerland	2008	Bode Miller, U.S.
1977	Ingemar Stenmark, Sweden	1993	Marc Girardelli, Luxembourg	2009	Aksel Lund Svindal, Norway
1978	Ingemar Stenmark, Sweden	1994	Kjetil Andre Aamodt, Norway	2010	Carlo Janka, Switzerland
1979	Peter Luescher, Switzerland	1995	Alberto Tomba, Italy	2011	Ivica Kostelic, Croatia
1980	Andreas Wenzel, Liechtenstein	1996	Lasse Kjus, Norway	2012	Marcel Hirscher, Austria
1981	Phil Mahre, U.S.	1997	Luc Alphand, France	2013	Marcel Hirscher, Austria
1982	Phil Mahre, U.S.	1998	Hermann Maier, Austria	2014	Marcel Hirscher, Austria

Alpine Skiing Women's World Cup Champions, 1967-2014

Year	Champion, country	Year	Champion, country	Year	Champion, country
1967	Nancy Greene, Canada	1983	Tamara McKinney, U.S.	1999	Alexandra Meissnitzer, Austria
1968	Nancy Greene, Canada	1984	Erika Hess, Switzerland	2000	Renate Goetschl, Austria
1969	Gertrud Gabl, Austria	1985	Michela Figini, Switzerland	2001	Janica Kostelic, Croatia
1970	Michele Jacot, France	1986	Maria Walliser, Switzerland	2002	Michaela Dorfmeister, Austria
1971	Annemarie Proell, Austria	1987	Maria Walliser, Switzerland	2003	Janica Kostelic, Croatia
1972	Annemarie Proell, Austria	1988	Michela Figini, Switzerland	2004	Anja Paerson, Sweden
1973	Annemarie Proell, Austria	1989	Vreni Schneider, Switzerland	2005	Anja Paerson, Sweden
1974	Annemarie Proell, Austria	1990	Petra Kronberger, Austria	2006	Janica Kostelic, Croatia
1975	Annemarie Proell, Austria	1991	Petra Kronberger, Austria	2007	Nicole Hosp, Austria
1976	Rose Mittermaier, W. Germany	1992	Petra Kronberger, Austria	2008	Lindsey Vonn, U.S.
1977	Lise-Marie Morerod, Switzerland	1993	Anita Wachter, Austria	2009	Lindsey Vonn, U.S.
1978	Hanni Wenzel, Liechtenstein	1994	Vreni Schneider, Switzerland	2010	Lindsey Vonn, U.S.
1979	Annemarie Proell Moser, Austria	1995	Vreni Schneider, Switzerland	2011	Maria Höfl-Riesch, Germany
1980	Hanni Wenzel, Liechtenstein	1996	Katja Seizinger, Germany	2012	Lindsey Vonn, U.S.
1981	Marie-Theres Nadig, Switzerland	1997	Pernilla Wiberg, Sweden	2013	Tina Maze, Slovenia
1982	Erika Hess, Switzerland	1998	Katja Seizinger, Germany	2014	Anna Fenninger, Austria

Tour de France, 2014

Vincenzo Nibali became the first Italian rider in 16 years to win the Tour de France in the 101st edition of cycling's premier race July 27, 2014. The first stage of the 2,277-mi (3,664-km) Tour de France began July 5 in Leeds, England, UK. The final and 21st stage concluded on the streets of Paris, where Nibali claimed victory in 89 hr., 59 min., 6 sec., followed by two French cyclists: Jean-Christophe Péraud, 7 min., 37 sec. behind, and Thibaut Pinot, 8 min., 15 sec. behind. Pinot won the white jersey as the best rider under age 25 in the Tour de France, and Rafal Majka of Russia won the polka dot jersey as the best climber. Slovakian Peter Sagan won the green jersey as the points leader for the second straight year.

The 2015 Tour de France is scheduled to be held July 4-26. Its route will take cyclists from Utrecht, Netherlands, to Paris.

Tour de France Winners, 1903-2014

The Tour de France was first held in 1903. Sixty cyclists began the 1,509-mi (2,428-km) race at Montgeron, a suburb of Paris, and 21 cyclists finished the six-stage race 17 days later in Paris. The race route changes every year. Race not held, 1915-18; 1940-46.

Year	Winner, country	Year	Winner, country	Year	Winner, country
1903	Maurice Garin, France	1948	Gino Bartali, Italy	1982	Bernard Hinault, France
1904	Henri Cornet, France	1949	Fausto Coppi, Italy	1983	Laurent Fignon, France
1905	Louis Trousselier, France	1950	Ferdi Kübler, Switzerland	1984	Laurent Fignon, France
1906	René Pottier, France	1951	Hugo Koblet, Switzerland	1985	Bernard Hinault, France
1907	Lucien Petit-Breton, France	1952	Fausto Coppi, Italy	1986	Greg LeMond, U.S.
1908	Lucien Petit-Breton, France	1953	Louison Bobet, France	1987	Stephen Roche, Ireland
1909	François Faber, Luxembourg	1954	Louison Bobet, France	1988	Pedro Delgado, Spain
1910	Octave Lapize, France	1955	Louison Bobet, France	1989	Greg LeMond, U.S.
1911	Gustave Garrigou, France	1956	Roger Walkowiak, France	1990	Greg LeMond, U.S.
1912	Odile Defraye, Belgium	1957	Jacques Anquetil, France	1991	Miguel Indurain, Spain
1913	Philippe Thys, Belgium	1958	Charly Gaul, Luxembourg	1992	Miguel Indurain, Spain
1914	Philippe Thys, Belgium	1959	Federico Bahamontes, Spain	1993	Miguel Indurain, Spain
1919	Firmin Lambot, Belgium	1960	Gastone Nencini, Italy	1994	Miguel Indurain, Spain
1920	Philippe Thys, Belgium	1961	Jacques Anquetil, France	1995	Miguel Indurain, Spain
1921	Léon Scieur, Belgium	1962	Jacques Anquetil, France	1996	Bjarne Riis, Denmark
1922	Firmin Lambot, Belgium	1963	Jacques Anquetil, France	1997	Jan Ullrich, Germany
1923	Henri Pélissier, France	1964	Jacques Anquetil, France	1998	Marco Pantani, Italy
1924	Ottavio Bottecchia, Italy	1965	Felice Gimondi, Italy	1999	Vacant[1]
1925	Ottavio Bottecchia, Italy	1966	Lucien Aimar, France	2000	Vacant[1]
1926	Lucien Buysse, Belgium	1967	Roger Pingeon, France	2001	Vacant[1]
1927	Nicolas Frantz, Luxembourg	1968	Jan Janssen, Netherlands	2002	Vacant[1]
1928	Nicolas Frantz, Luxembourg	1969	Eddy Merckx, Belgium	2003	Vacant[1]
1929	Maurice Dewaele, Belgium	1970	Eddy Merckx, Belgium	2004	Vacant[1]
1930	André Leducq, France	1971	Eddy Merckx, Belgium	2005	Vacant[1]
1931	Antonin Magne, France	1972	Eddy Merckx, Belgium	2006	Óscar Pereiro, Spain[2]
1932	André Leducq, France	1973	Luis Ocana, Spain	2007	Alberto Contador, Spain
1933	Georges Speicher, France	1974	Eddy Merckx, Belgium	2008	Carlos Sastre, Spain
1934	Antonin Magne, France	1975	Bernard Thévenet, France	2009	Alberto Contador, Spain
1935	Romain Maes, Belgium	1976	Lucien Van Impe, Belgium	2010	Andy Schleck, Luxembourg[3]
1936	Sylvère Maes, Belgium	1977	Bernard Thévenet, France	2011	Cadel Evans, Australia
1937	Roger Lapépie, France	1978	Bernard Hinault, France	2012	Bradley Wiggins, UK
1938	Gino Bartali, Italy	1979	Bernard Hinault, France	2013	Chris Froome, UK
1939	Sylvère Maes, Belgium	1980	Joop Zoetemelk, Netherlands	2014	Vincenzo Nibali, Italy
1947	Jean Robic, France	1981	Bernard Hinault, France		

(1) Lance Armstrong, U.S., was stripped of his seven Tour titles Oct. 22, 2012, in accordance with World Anti-Doping Code; Armstrong had dropped his fight against doping charges Aug. 23, 2012. (2) Floyd Landis, U.S., was stripped of the 2006 title, Sept. 20, 2007, for doping. Landis lost a final appeal of the ruling June 30, 2008. (3) Alberto Contador, Spain, was stripped of the 2010 title, Feb. 6, 2012, for doping.

Swimming World Records

Long course (50-m pools only) records, as of Sept. 2014. All times in minutes:seconds. * = Record pending ratification.

Men's Records

Freestyle

Distance	Record	Holder	Nationality	Location	Date
50 meters	0:20.91	César Cielo Filho	Brazil	São Paulo, Brazil	Dec. 18, 2009
100 meters	0:46.91	César Cielo Filho	Brazil	Rome, Italy	July 30, 2009
200 meters	1:42.00	Paul Biedermann	Germany	Rome, Italy	July 28, 2009
400 meters	3:40.07	Paul Biedermann	Germany	Rome, Italy	July 26, 2009
800 meters	7:32.12	Zhang Lin	China	Rome, Italy	July 29, 2009
1,500 meters	14:31.02	Yang Sun	China	London, England, UK	Aug. 4, 2012

Backstroke

50 meters	0:24.04	Liam Tancock	UK	Rome, Italy	Aug. 2, 2009
100 meters	0:51.94	Aaron Peirsol	U.S.	Indianapolis, IN	July 8, 2009
200 meters	1:51.92	Aaron Peirsol	U.S.	Rome, Italy	July 31, 2009

Breaststroke

50 meters	0:26.67	Cameron van der Burgh	South Africa	Rome, Italy	July 29, 2009
100 meters	0:58.46	Cameron van der Burgh	South Africa	London, England, UK	July 29, 2012
200 meters	2:07.01	Akihiro Yamaguchi	Japan	Gifu, Japan	Sept. 15, 2012

Butterfly

50 meters	0:22.43	Rafael Muñoz	Spain	Malaga, Spain	Apr. 5, 2009
100 meters	0:49.82	Michael Phelps	U.S.	Rome, Italy	Aug. 1, 2009
200 meters	1:51.51	Michael Phelps	U.S.	Rome, Italy	July 29, 2009

Individual medley

200 meters	1:54.00	Ryan Lochte	U.S.	Shanghai, China	July 28, 2011
400 meters	4:03.84	Michael Phelps	U.S.	Beijing, China	Aug. 10, 2008

Freestyle relay

400 m (4×100)	3:08.24	Phelps, Weber-Gale, Jones, Lezak	U.S.	Beijing, China	Aug. 11, 2008
800 m (4×200)	6:58.55	Phelps, Berens, Walters, Lochte	U.S.	Rome, Italy	July 31, 2009

Medley relay

400 m (4×100)	3:27.28	Peirsol, Shanteau, Phelps, Walters	U.S.	Rome, Italy	Aug. 2, 2009

Women's Records

Freestyle

Distance	Record	Holder	Nationality	Location	Date
50 meters	0:23.73	Britta Steffen	Germany	Rome, Italy	Aug. 2, 2009
100 meters	0:52.07	Britta Steffen	Germany	Rome, Italy	July 31, 2009
200 meters	1:52.98	Federica Pellegrini	Italy	Rome, Italy	July 29, 2009
400 meters	3:58.37*	Katie Ledecky	U.S.	Irvine, CA	Aug. 9, 2014
800 meters	8:11.00	Katie Ledecky	U.S.	Shenandoah, TX	June 22, 2014
1,500 meters	15:22.69*	Lauren Boyle	New Zealand	Wellington, New Zealand	Aug. 10, 2014

Backstroke

50 meters	0:24.43*	Sarah Sjostrom	Sweden	Boras, Sweden	July 15, 2014
100 meters	0:58.12	Gemma Spofforth	UK	Rome, Italy	July 28, 2009
200 meters	2:04.06	Missy Franklin	U.S.	London, England, UK	Aug. 3, 2012

Breaststroke

50 meters	0:29.48	Ruta Meilutyte	Lithuania	Barcelona, Spain	Aug. 3, 2013
100 meters	1:04.35	Ruta Meilutyte	Lithuania	Barcelona, Spain	July 29, 2013
200 meters	2:19.11	Rikke Moller Pedersen	Denmark	Barcelona, Spain	Aug. 1, 2013

Butterfly

50 meters	0:25.07	Therese Alshammar	Sweden	Rome, Italy	July 31, 2009
100 meters	0:55.98	Dana Vollmer	U.S.	London, England, UK	July 29, 2012
200 meters	2:01.81	Liu Zige	China	Jinan, China	Oct. 21, 2009

Individual medley

200 meters	2:06.15	Ariana Kukors	U.S.	Rome, Italy	July 27, 2009
400 meters	4:28.43	Ye Shiwen	China	London, England, UK	July 28, 2012

Freestyle relay

400 m (4×100)	3:30.98*	Campbell, Schlanger, McKeon, Campbell	Australia	Glasgow, Scotland, UK	July 24, 2014
800 m (4×200)	7:42.08	Yang, Zhu, Liu, Pang	China	Rome, Italy	July 30, 2009

Medley relay

400 m (4×100)	3:52.05	Franklin, Soni, Vollmer, Schmitt	U.S.	London, England, UK	Aug. 4, 2012

World Track and Field Outdoor Records

The International Association of Athletics Federations (IAAF), the world body of track and field, recognizes only records in metric distances, except for the mile. * = Record pending ratification. As of Sept. 2014.

Men's Records

Running

Event	Record	Holder	Nationality	Location	Date
100 meters	9.58 s.	Usain Bolt	Jamaica	Berlin, Germany	Aug. 16, 2009
200 meters	19.19 s.	Usain Bolt	Jamaica	Berlin, Germany	Aug. 20, 2009
400 meters	43.18 s.	Michael Johnson	U.S.	Seville, Spain	Aug. 26, 1999
800 meters	1 min., 40.91 s.	David Lekuta Rudisha	Kenya	London, England, UK	Aug. 9, 2012
1,000 meters	2 min., 11.96 s.	Noah Ngeny	Kenya	Rieti, Italy	Sept. 5, 1999
1,500 meters	3 min., 26.00 s.	Hicham El Guerrouj	Morocco	Rome, Italy	July 14, 1998
1 mile	3 min., 43.13 s.	Hicham El Guerrouj	Morocco	Rome, Italy	July 7, 1999
2,000 meters	4 min., 44.79 s.	Hicham El Guerrouj	Morocco	Berlin, Germany	Sept. 7, 1999
3,000 meters	7 min., 20.67 s.	Daniel Komen	Kenya	Rieti, Italy	Sept. 1, 1996
3,000-meter stpl.	7 min., 53.63 s.	Saif Saaeed Shaheen	Qatar	Brussels, Belgium	Sept. 3, 2004
5,000 meters	12 min., 37.35 s.	Kenenisa Bekele	Ethiopia	Hengelo, Netherlands	May 31, 2004
10,000 meters	26 min., 17.53 s.	Kenenisa Bekele	Ethiopia	Brussels, Belgium	Aug. 26, 2005
20,000 meters	56 min., 26.00 s.	Haile Gebrselassie	Ethiopia	Ostrava, Czech Rep.	June 27, 2007
25,000 meters	1 hr., 12 min., 25.4 s.	Moses Cheruiyot Mosop	Kenya	Eugene, OR	June 3, 2011
Marathon	2 hr., 2 min., 57 s.	Dennis Kimetto	Kenya	Berlin, Germany	Sept. 28, 2014
110-meter hurdles	12.80 s.	Aries Merritt	U.S.	Brussels, Belgium	Sept. 7, 2012
400-meter hurdles	46.78 s.	Kevin Young	U.S.	Barcelona, Spain	Aug. 6, 1992
400 (4×100)	36.84 s.	Carter, Frater, Blake, Bolt	Jamaica	London, England, UK	Aug. 11, 2012
800 m (4×200)	1 min., 18.63 s.	Ashmeade, Weir, Brown, Blake	Jamaica	Nassau, The Bahamas	May 24, 2014
1,600 m (4×400)	2 min., 54.29 s.[1]	Valmon, Watts, Reynolds, Johnson	U.S.	Stuttgart, Germany	Aug. 22, 1993
3,200 m (4×800)	7 min., 2.43 s.	Mutua, Yiampoy, Kombich, Bungei	Kenya	Brussels, Belgium	Aug. 25, 2006

(1) IAAF voted in Aug. 2008 to revoke a world record set by the U.S. team in 1998; one of the team's members, Antonio Pettigrew, admitted to doping in May 2008.

Field Events

Event	Record	Holder	Nationality	Location	Date
High jump	2.45 m (8' ½")	Javier Sotomayor	Cuba	Salamanca, Spain	July 27, 1993
Long jump	8.95 m (29' 4½")	Mike Powell	U.S.	Tokyo, Japan	Aug. 30, 1991
Triple jump	18.29 m (60' ¼")	Jonathan Edwards	UK	Gothenburg, Sweden	Aug. 7, 1995
Pole vault	6.16 m (20' 2½")	Renaud Lavillenie	France	Donetsk, Ukraine	Feb. 15, 2014
Discus	74.08 m (243' 0")	Jürgen Schult	E. Germany	Neubrandenburg, E. Germany	June 6, 1986
Hammer	86.74 m (284' 7")	Yuriy Sedykh	USSR	Stuttgart, W. Germany	Aug. 30, 1986
Javelin	98.48 m (323' 1")	Jan Zelezný	Czech Rep.	Jena, W. Germany	May 25, 1996
Shot put	23.12 m (75' 10¼")	Randy Barnes	U.S.	Westwood, CA	May 20, 1990
Decathlon	9,039 pts.	Ashton Eaton	U.S.	Eugene, OR	June 23, 2012

Women's Records

Running

Event	Record	Holder	Nationality	Location	Date
100 meters	10.49 s.	Florence Griffith-Joyner	U.S.	Indianapolis, IN	July 16, 1988
200 meters	21.34 s.	Florence Griffith-Joyner	U.S.	Seoul, S. Korea	Sept. 29, 1988
400 meters	47.60 s.	Marita Koch	E. Germany	Canberra, Australia	Oct. 6, 1985
800 meters	1 min., 53.28 s.	Jarmila Kratochvílová	Czechoslovakia	Munich, W. Germany	July 26, 1983
1,000 meters	2 min., 28.98 s.	Svetlana Masterkova	Russia	Brussels, Belgium	Aug. 23, 1996
1,500 meters	3 min., 50.46 s.	Qu Yunxia	China	Beijing, China	Sept. 11, 1993
1 mile	4 min., 12.56 s.	Svetlana Masterkova	Russia	Zürich, Switzerland	Aug. 14, 1996
2,000 meters	5 min., 25.36 s.	Sonia O'Sullivan	Ireland	Edinburgh, Scotland, UK	July 8, 1994
3,000 meters	8 min., 6.11 s.	Wang Junxia	China	Beijing, China	Sept. 13, 1993
3,000-meter stpl.	8 min., 58.81 s.	Gulnara Galkina-Samitova	Russia	Beijing, China	Aug. 17, 2008
5,000 meters	14 min., 11.15 s.	Tirunesh Dibaba	Ethiopia	Oslo, Norway	June 6, 2008
10,000 meters	29 min., 31.78 s.	Wang Junxia	China	Beijing, China	Sept. 8, 1993
20,000 meters	1 hr., 5 min., 26.6 s.	Tegla Loroupe	Kenya	Borgholzhausen, Germany	Sept. 3, 2000
30,000 meters	1 hr., 45 min., 50.0 s.	Tegla Loroupe	Kenya	Warstein, Germany	June 6, 2003
Marathon	2 hr., 15 min., 25.0 s.	Paula Radcliffe	UK	London, England, UK	Apr. 13, 2003
100-meter hurdles	12.21 s.	Yordanka Donkova	Bulgaria	Stara Zagora, Bulgaria	Aug. 20, 1988
400-meter hurdles	52.34 s.	Yuliya Pechenkina	Russia	Tula, Russia	Aug. 8, 2003
400 m (4×100)	40.82 s.	Madison, Felix, Knight, Jeter	U.S.	London, England, UK	Aug. 10, 2012
800 m (4×200)	1 min., 27.46 s.	Jenkins, Colander, Perry, Jones	U.S.	Philadelphia, PA	Apr. 29, 2000
1,600 m (4×400)	3 min., 15.17 s.	Ledovskaya, Nazarova, Pinigina, Bryzgina	USSR	Seoul, S. Korea	Oct. 1, 1988
3,200 m (4×800)	7 min., 50.17 s.	Olizarenko, Gurina, Borisova, Podyalovskaya	USSR	Moscow, USSR	Aug. 5, 1984

Field Events

Event	Record	Holder	Nationality	Location	Date
High jump	2.09 m (6' 10¼")	Stefka Kostadinova	Bulgaria	Rome, Italy	Aug. 30, 1987
Long jump	7.52 m (24' 8¼")	Galina Chistyakova	USSR	Leningrad, Russia	June 11, 1988
Triple jump	15.50 m (50' 10¼")	Inessa Kravets	Ukraine	Gothenburg, Sweden	Aug. 10, 1995
Pole vault	5.06 m (16' 7¾")	Yelena Isinbaeva	Russia	Zürich, Switzerland	Aug. 28, 2009
Discus	76.80 m (252' 0")	Gabriele Reinsch	E. Germany	Neubrandenburg, E. Germany	July 9, 1988
Hammer	79.58 m (261' 1")	Anita Włodarczyk	Poland	Berlin, Germany	Aug. 31, 2014
Javelin	72.28 m (237' 1¾")	Barbora Špotáková	Czech Rep.	Stuttgart, Germany	Sept. 13, 2008
Shot put	22.63 m (74' 3")	Natalya Lisovskaya	USSR	Moscow, Russia	June 7, 1987
Heptathlon	7,291 pts.	Jackie Joyner-Kersee	U.S.	Seoul, S. Korea	Sept. 24, 1988

Iditarod Trail Sled Dog Race, 2014

Dallas Seavey won the 42nd annual Iditarod Trail Sled Dog Race from Anchorage to Nome, AK, Mar. 11, 2014. The 27-year-old Seavey (who was 26 when the race commenced Mar. 1) finished the 975-mi course along the northern route to Nome in a record-setting 8 days, 13 hr., 4 min., and 19 sec.—less than 2½ min. ahead of Aliy Zirkle—to win the second closest race in Iditarod history. The 2015 race is scheduled to begin Mar. 7 in Anchorage and follow the 998-mi southern route to Nome.

Westminster Kennel Club Best-In-Show Dogs, 1980-2014

Year	Best-in-Show winner, breed	Year	Best-in-Show winner, breed
1980	Ch. Innisfree's Sierra Cinnar, Siberian Husky	1998	Ch. Fairewood Frolic, Norwich Terrier
1981	Ch. Dhandys Favorite Woodchuck, Pug	1999	Ch. Loteki Supernatural Being, Papillon
1982	Ch. St. Aubrey Dragonora of Elsdon, Pekingese	2000	Ch. Salilyn 'N Erin's Shameless, Spaniel (English Springer)
1983	Ch. Kabiks The Challenger, Afghan Hound	2001	Ch. Special Times Just Right, Bichon Frise
1984	Ch. Seaward's Blackbeard, Newfoundland	2002	Ch. Surrey Spice Girl, Poodle (Miniature)
1985	Ch. Braeburn's Close Encounter, Scottish Terrier	2003	Ch. Torums Scarf Michael, Kerry Blue Terrier
1986	Ch. Marjetta's National Acclaim, Pointer	2004	Ch. Darbydale's All Rise PouCh. Cove, Newfoundland
1987	Ch. Covy Tucker Hill's Manhattan, German Shepherd Dog	2005	Ch. Kan-Point's VJK Autumn Roses, Pointer (German
1988	Ch. Great Elms Prince Charming II, Pomeranian		Shorthaired)
1989	Ch. Royal Tudor's Wild As The Wind, Doberman Pinscher	2006	Ch. Rocky Top's Sundance Kid, Bull Terrier (Colored)
1990	Ch. Wendessa Crown Prince, Pekingese	2007	Ch. Felicity's Diamond Jim, Spaniel (English Springer)
1991	Ch. Whisperwind On A Carousel, Poodle (Standard)	2008	Ch. K-Run's Park Me In First, Beagle (15 Inch)
1992	Ch. Registry's Lonesome Dove, Fox Terrier (Wire)	2009	Ch. Clussexx Three D Grinchy Glee, Spaniel (Sussex)
1993	Ch. Salilyn's Condor, Spaniel (English Springer)	2010	Ch. Roundtown Mercedes Of Maryscot, Scottish Terrier
1994	Ch. Chidley Willum The Conqueror, Norwich Terrier	2011	GCh. Foxcliffe Hickory Wind, Scottish Deerhound
1995	Ch. Gaelforce Post Script, Scottish Terrier	2012	GCh. Palacegarden Malachy, Pekingese
1996	Ch. Clussexx Country Sunrise, Spaniel (Clumber)	2013	GCh. Banana Joe V Tani Kazari, Affenpinscher
1997	Ch. Parsifal Di Casa Netzer, Standard Schnauzer	2014	GCh. Afterall Painting The Sky, Fox Terrier (Wire)

MARATHONS

World Marathon Majors, 2006-13

Five of the world's leading marathons (Berlin, Boston, Chicago, London, and New York) agreed Jan. 23, 2006, to form a series called the World Marathon Majors. Tokyo joined the series in 2013. Marathon runners are awarded points relative to their finish in each race in the series and in Olympic and the Intl. Assn. of Athletics Federations World Championships marathons. The male and female runners with the most points at the end of each two-year cycle win $500,000.

Cycle	Men's winner, country	Women's winner, country	Cycle	Men's winner, country	Women's winner, country
2006-07	Robert Kipkoech Cheruiyot, Kenya	Gete Wami, Ethiopia	2009-10	Samuel Wanjiru, Kenya	Liliya Shobukhova, Russia
			2010-11	Emmanuel Mutai, Kenya	Liliya Shobukhova, Russia
2007-08	Martin Lel, Kenya	Gete Wami, Ethiopia	2011-12	Geoffrey Mutai, Kenya	Mary Keitany, Kenya
2008-09	Samuel Wanjiru, Kenya	Irina Mikitenko, Germany	2012-13	Tsegaye Kebede, Ethiopia	Priscah Jeptoo, Kenya

Boston Marathon Winners, 1972-2014

All times in hour:minute:second format. * = Course record.

Men's winner, country	Time	Year	Women's winner, country	Time
Olavi Suomalainen, Finland	2:15:39	1972	Nina Kuscsik, U.S.	3:10:26
Jon Anderson, U.S.	2:16:03	1973	Jacqueline Hansen, U.S.	3:05:59
Neil Cusack, Ireland	2:13:39	1974	Michiko Gorman, U.S.	2:47:11
Bill Rodgers, U.S.	2:09:55	1975	Liane Winter, West Germany	2:42:24
Jack Fultz, U.S.	2:20:19	1976	Kim Merritt, U.S.	2:47:10
Jerome Drayton, Canada	2:14:46	1977	Michiko Gorman, U.S.	2:48:33
Bill Rodgers, U.S.	2:10:13	1978	Gayle S. Barron, U.S.	2:44:52
Bill Rodgers, U.S.	2:09:27	1979	Joan Benoit, U.S.	2:35:15
Bill Rodgers, U.S.	2:12:11	1980	Jacqueline Gareau, Canada	2:34:28
Toshihiko Seko, Japan	2:09:26	1981	Allison Roe, New Zealand	2:26:46
Alberto Salazar, U.S.	2:08:52	1982	Charlotte Teske, West Germany	2:29:33
Greg Meyer, U.S.	2:09:00	1983	Joan Benoit, U.S.	2:22:43
Geoff Smith, England, UK	2:10:34	1984	Lorraine Moller, New Zealand	2:29:28
Geoff Smith, England, UK	2:14:05	1985	Lisa Larsen Weidenbach, U.S.	2:34:06
Robert de Castella, Australia	2:07:51	1986	Ingrid Kristiansen, Norway	2:24:55
Toshihiko Seko, Japan	2:11:50	1987	Rosa Mota, Portugal	2:25:21
Ibrahim Hussein, Kenya	2:08:43	1988	Rosa Mota, Portugal	2:24:30
Abebe Mekonnen, Ethiopia	2:09:06	1989	Ingrid Kristiansen, Norway	2:24:33
Gelindo Bordin, Italy	2:08:19	1990	Rosa Mota, Portugal	2:25:24
Ibrahim Hussein, Kenya	2:11:06	1991	Wanda Panfil, Poland	2:24:18
Ibrahim Hussein, Kenya	2:08:14	1992	Olga Markova, Russia	2:23:43
Cosmas Ndeti, Kenya	2:09:33	1993	Olga Markova, Russia	2:25:27
Cosmas Ndeti, Kenya	2:07:15	1994	Uta Pippig, Germany	2:21:45
Cosmas Ndeti, Kenya	2:09:22	1995	Uta Pippig, Germany	2:25:11
Moses Tanui, Kenya	2:09:15	1996	Uta Pippig, Germany	2:27:12
Lameck Aguta, Kenya	2:10:34	1997	Fatuma Roba, Ethiopia	2:26:23
Moses Tanui, Kenya	2:07:34	1998	Fatuma Roba, Ethiopia	2:23:21
Joseh Chebet, Kenya	2:09:52	1999	Fatuma Roba, Ethiopia	2:23:25
Elijah Lagat, Kenya	2:09:47	2000	Catherine Ndereba, Kenya	2:26:11
Lee Bong-ju, South Korea	2:09:43	2001	Catherine Ndereba, Kenya	2:23:53
Rodgers Rop, Kenya	2:09:02	2002	Margaret Okayo, Kenya	2:20:43
Robert Kipkoech Cheruiyot, Kenya	2:10:11	2003	Svetlana Zakharova, Russia	2:25:20
Timothy Cherigat, Kenya	2:10:37	2004	Catherine Ndereba, Kenya	2:24:27
Hailu Negussie, Ethiopia	2:11:45	2005	Catherine Ndereba, Kenya	2:25:13
Robert Kipkoech Cheruiyot, Kenya	2:07:14	2006	Rita Jeptoo, Kenya	2:23:38
Robert Kipkoech Cheruiyot, Kenya	2:14:13	2007	Lidiya Grigoryeva, Russia	2:29:18
Robert Kipkoech Cheruiyot, Kenya	2:07:46	2008	Dire Tune, Ethiopia	2:25:25
Deriba Merga, Ethiopia	2:08:42	2009	Salina Kosgei, Kenya	2:32:16
Robert Kiprono Cheruiyot, Kenya	2:05:52	2010	Teyba Erkesso, Ethiopia	2:26:11
Geoffrey Mutai, Kenya	2:03:02*	2011	Caroline Kilel, Kenya	2:22:36
Wesley Korir, Kenya	2:12:40	2012	Sharon Cherop, Kenya	2:31:50
Lelisa Desisa, Ethiopia	2:10:22	2013	Rita Jeptoo, Kenya	2:26:25
Meb Keflezighi, U.S.	2:08:37	2014	Rita Jeptoo, Kenya	2:18:57*

Boston Marathon Winners, 1897-1971

The first Boston Marathon was held in 1897. Women were officially accepted into the race in 1972. Times in hr:min.:sec. format.

Year	Winner, state/country	Time	Year	Winner, state/country	Time
1897	John J. McDermott, New York	2:55:10	1935	John A. Kelley, Massachusetts	2:32:07
1898	Ronald J. MacDonald, Canada	2:42:00	1936	Ellison M. Brown, Rhode Island	2:33:40
1899	Lawrence Brignolia, Massachusetts	2:54:38	1937	Walter Young, Canada	2:33:20
1900	John Caffery, Canada	2:39:44	1938	Leslie S. Pawson, Rhode Island	2:35:34
1901	John Caffery, Canada	2:29:23	1939	Ellison M. Brown, Rhode Island	2:28:51
1902	Sammy Mellor, New York	2:43:12	1940	Gerard Cote, Canada	2:28:28
1903	John Lorden, Massachusetts	2:41:29	1941	Leslie S. Pawson, Rhode Island	2:30:38
1904	Michael Spring, New York	2:38:04	1942	Joe Smith, Massachusetts	2:26:51
1905	Frederick Lorz, New York	2:38:25	1943	Gerard Cote, Canada	2:28:25
1906	Tim Ford, Massachusetts	2:45:45	1944	Gerard Cote, Canada	2:31:50
1907	Thomas Longboat, Canada	2:24:24	1945	John A. Kelley, Massachusetts	2:30:40
1908	Thomas Morrissey, New York	2:25:43	1946	Stylianos Kyriakides, Greece	2:29:27
1909	Henri Renaud, New Hampshire	2:53:36	1947	Yun Bok Suh, Korea	2:25:39
1910	Fred Cameron, Canada	2:28:52	1948	Gerard Cote, Canada	2:31:02
1911	Clarence DeMar, Massachusetts	2:21:39	1949	Karl Leandersson, Sweden	2:31:50
1912	Michael Ryan, New York	2:21:18	1950	Kee Yong Ham, Korea	2:32:39
1913	Fritz Carlson, Minnesota	2:25:14	1951	Shigeki Tanaka, Japan	2:27:45
1914	James Duffy, Canada	2:25:14	1952	Doroteo Flores, Guatamela	2:31:53
1915	Edouard Fabre, Canada	2:31:41	1953	Keizo Yamada, Japan	2:18:51
1916	Arthur Roth, Massachusetts	2:27:16	1954	Veikko Karvonen, Finland	2:20:39
1917	Bill Kennedy, New York	2:28:37	1955	Hideo Hamamura, Japan	2:18:22
1918	Military relay, Camp Devens	2:29:53	1956	Antti Viskari, Finland	2:14:14
1919	Carl Linder, Massachusetts	2:29:13	1957	John J. Kelley, Connecticut	2:20:05
1920	Peter Trivoulides, New York	2:29:31	1958	Franjo Mihalic, Yugoslavia	2:25:54
1921	Frank Zuna, New York	2:18:57	1959	Eino Oksanen, Finland	2:22:42
1922	Clarence DeMar, Massachusetts	2:18:10	1960	Paavo Kotila, Finland	2:20:54
1923	Clarence DeMar, Massachusetts	2:23:47	1961	Eino Oksanen, Finland	2:23:39
1924	Clarence DeMar, Massachusetts	2:29:40	1962	Eino Oksanen, Finland	2:23:48
1925	Charles Mellor, Illinois	2:33:00	1963	Aurele Vandendriessche, Belgium	2:18:58
1926	John C. Miles, Canada	2:25:40	1964	Aurele Vandendriessche, Belgium	2:19:59
1927	Clarence DeMar, Massachusetts	2:40:22	1965	Morio Shigematsu, Japan	2:16:33
1928	Clarence DeMar, Massachusetts	2:37:07	1966	Kenji Kemihara, Japan	2:17:11
1929	John C. Miles, Canada	2:33:08	1967	David McKenzie, New Zealand	2:15:45
1930	Clarence DeMar, Massachusetts	2:34:48	1968	Amby Burfoot, Connecticut	2:22:17
1931	James P. Henigan, Massachusetts	2:46:45	1969	Yoshiaki Unetani, Japan	2:13:49
1932	Paul DeBruyn, Germany	2:33:36	1970	Ron Hill, England, UK	2:10:30
1933	Leslie S. Pawson, Rhode Island	2:31:01	1971	Alvaro Mejia, Colombia	2:18:45
1934	Dave Komonen, Canada	2:32:53			

New York City Marathon Winners, 1970-2014

All times in hour:minute:second format. * = Course record. Race not held, 2012.

Men's winner, country	Time	Year	Women's winner, country	Time
Gary Muhrcke, U.S.	2:31:38	1970	No finisher	—
Norman Higgins, U.S.	2:22:54	1971	Beth Bonner, U.S.	2:55:22
Sheldon Karlin, U.S.	2:27:52	1972	Nina Kuscsik, U.S.	3:08:41
Tom Fleming, U.S.	2:19:25	1973	Nina Kuscsik, U.S.	2:57:07
Norbert Sander, U.S.	2:26:30	1974	Katherine Switzer, U.S.	3:07:29
Tom Fleming, U.S.	2:19:27	1975	Kim Merritt, U.S.	2:46:14
Bill Rodgers, U.S.	2:10:10	1976	Miki Gorman, U.S.	2:39:11
Bill Rodgers, U.S.	2:11:28	1977	Miki Gorman, U.S.	2:43:10
Bill Rodgers, U.S.	2:12:12	1978	Grete Waitz, Norway	2:32:30
Bill Rodgers, U.S.	2:11:42	1979	Grete Waitz, Norway	2:27:33
Alberto Salazar, U.S.	2:09:41	1980	Grete Waitz, Norway	2:25:42
Alberto Salazar, U.S.	2:08:13	1981	Allison Roe, New Zealand	2:25:29
Alberto Salazar, U.S.	2:09:29	1982	Grete Waitz, Norway	2:27:14
Rod Dixon, New Zealand	2:08:59	1983	Grete Waitz, Norway	2:27:00
Orlando Pizzolato, Italy	2:14:53	1984	Grete Waitz, Norway	2:29:30
Orlando Pizzolato, Italy	2:11:34	1985	Grete Waitz, Norway	2:28:34
Gianni Poli, Italy	2:11:06	1986	Grete Waitz, Norway	2:28:06
Ibrahim Hussein, Kenya	2:11:01	1987	Priscilla Welch, England, UK	2:30:17
Steve Jones, Wales, UK	2:08:20	1988	Grete Waitz, Norway	2:28:07
Juma Ikangaa, Tanzania	2:08:01	1989	Ingrid Kristiansen, Norway	2:25:30
Douglas Wakiihuri, Kenya	2:12:39	1990	Wanda Panfil, Poland	2:30:45
Salvador Garcia, Mexico	2:09:28	1991	Liz McColgan, Scotland, UK	2:27:32
Willie Mtolo, South Africa	2:09:29	1992	Lisa Ondieki, Australia	2:24:40
Andres Espinosa, Mexico	2:10:04	1993	Uta Pippig, Germany	2:26:24
German Silva, Mexico	2:11:21	1994	Tegla Loroupe, Kenya	2:27:37
German Silva, Mexico	2:11:00	1995	Tegla Loroupe, Kenya	2:28:06
Giacomo Leone, Italy	2:09:54	1996	Anuta Catuna, Romania	2:28:43
John Kagwe, Kenya	2:08:12	1997	F. Rochat-Moser, Switzerland	2:28:43
John Kagwe, Kenya	2:08:45	1998	Franca Fiacconi, Italy	2:25:17
Joseph Chebet, Kenya	2:09:14	1999	Adriana Fernandez, Mexico	2:25:06
Abdelkader El Mouaziz, Morocco	2:10:09	2000	Ludmila Petrova, Russia	2:25:45
Tesfaye Jifar, Ethiopia	2:07:43	2001	Margaret Okayo, Kenya	2:24:21
Rodgers Rop, Kenya	2:08:07	2002	Joyce Chepchumba, Kenya	2:25:56
Martin Lel, Kenya	2:10:30	2003	Margaret Okayo, Kenya	2:22:31*
Hendrik Ramaala, South Africa	2:09:28	2004	Paula Radcliffe, England, UK	2:23:10
Paul Tergat, Kenya	2:09:30	2005	Jelena Prokopcuka, Latvia	2:24:41
Marilson Gomes dos Santos, Brazil	2:09:58	2006	Jelena Prokopcuka, Latvia	2:25:05
Martin Lel, Kenya	2:09:04	2007	Paula Radcliffe, England, UK	2:23:09
Marilson Gomes dos Santos, Brazil	2:08:43	2008	Paula Radcliffe, England, UK	2:23:56
Meb Keflezighi, U.S.	2:09:15	2009	Derartu Tulu, Ethiopia	2:28:52
Gebre Gebrmariam, Ethiopia	2:08:14	2010	Edna Kiplagat, Kenya	2:28:20
Geoffrey Mutai, Kenya	2:05:06*	2011	Firehiwot Dado, Ethiopia	2:23:15
Geoffrey Mutai, Kenya	2:08:24	2013	Priscah Jeptoo, Kenya	2:25:07
Wilson Kipsang, Kenya	2:10:59	2014	Mary Keitany, Kenya	2:25:07

Other Marathon Results, 2014

Tokyo Marathon: Feb. 23. Men: Dickson Chumba, Kenya, 2:05:42. Women: Tirfi Tsegaye, Ethiopia, 2:22:23.
Los Angeles Marathon: Mar. 9. Men: Gebo Burka, Ethiopia, 2:10:37. Women: Amane Gobena, Ethiopia, 2:27:37.
Paris Marathon: Apr. 6. Men: Kenenisa Bekele, Ethiopia, 2:05:04. Women: Flomena Cheyech, Kenya, 2:22:44.
Rotterdam Marathon: Apr. 13. Men: Eliud Kipchoge, Kenya, 2:05:00. Women: Abebech Afework, Ethiopia, 2:27:50.

London Marathon: Apr. 13. Men: Wilson Kipsang, Kenya, 2:04:29. Women: Edna Kiplagat, Kenya, 2:20:21.
Berlin Marathon: Sept. 28. Men: Dennis Kimetto, Kenya, 2:02:57. Women: Tirfi Tsegaye, Ethiopia, 2:20:18.
Chicago Marathon: Oct. 12. Men: Eliud Kipchoge, Kenya, 2:04:11. Women: Rita Jeptoo, Kenya, 2:24:35.

Ironman Triathlon World Championships, 1978-2014

The Ironman Triathlon World Championship—a 2.4-mi ocean swim, 112-mi bike ride, and 26.2-mi run—is held annually in Kailua-Kona, HI. All times in hour:minute:second format. * = Course record.

Men's winner, country	Time	Year	Women's winner, country	Time
Gordon Haller, U.S.	11:46:58	1978	No finisher	—
Tom Warren, U.S.	11:15:56	1979	Lyn Lemaire, U.S.	12:55:00
Dave Scott, U.S.	9:24:33	1980	Robin Beck, U.S.	11:21:24
John Howard, U.S.	9:38:29	1981	Linda Sweeney, U.S.	12:00:32
Dave Scott, U.S.	9:08:23	1982	Julie Leach, U.S.	10:54:08
Dave Scott, U.S.	9:05:57	1983	Sylviane Puntous, Canada	10:43:36
Dave Scott, U.S.	8:54:20	1984	Sylviane Puntous, Canada	10:25:13
Scott Tinley, U.S.	8:50:54	1985	Joanne Ernst, U.S.	10:25:22
Dave Scott, U.S.	8:28:37	1986	Paula Newby-Fraser, Zimbabwe	9:49:14
Dave Scott, U.S.	8:34:13	1987	Erin Baker, New Zealand	9:35:25
Scott Molina, U.S.	8:31:00	1988	Paula Newby-Fraser, Zimbabwe	9:01:01
Mark Allen, U.S.	8:09:15	1989	Paula Newby-Fraser, Zimbabwe	9:00:56
Mark Allen, U.S.	8:28:17	1990	Erin Baker, New Zealand	9:13:42
Mark Allen, U.S.	8:18:32	1991	Paula Newby-Fraser, Zimbabwe	9:07:52
Mark Allen, U.S.	8:09:08	1992	Paula Newby-Fraser, Zimbabwe	8:55:28
Mark Allen, U.S.	8:07:45	1993	Paula Newby-Fraser, Zimbabwe	8:58:23
Greg Welch, Australia	8:20:27	1994	Paula Newby-Fraser, Zimbabwe	9:20:14
Mark Allen, U.S.	8:20:34	1995	Karen Smyers, U.S.	9:16:46
Luc Van Lierde, Belgium	8:04:08	1996	Paula Newby-Fraser, Zimbabwe	9:06:49
Thomas Hellriegel, Germany	8:33:01	1997	Heather Fuhr, Canada	9:31:43
Peter Reid, Canada	8:24:20	1998	Natascha Badmann, Switzerland	9:24:16
Luc Van Lierde, Belgium	8:17:17	1999	Lori Bowden, U.S.	9:13:02
Peter Reid, Canada	8:21:01	2000	Natascha Badmann, Switzerland	9:26:16
Timothy Deboom, U.S.	8:31:18	2001	Natascha Badmann, Switzerland	9:28:37
Timothy Deboom, U.S.	8:29:56	2002	Natascha Badmann, Switzerland	9:07:54
Peter Reid, Canada	8:22:35	2003	Lori Bowden, Canada	9:11:55
Normann Stadler, Germany	8:33:29	2004	Natascha Badmann, Switzerland[1]	9:50:04
Faris al-Sultan, Germany	8:14:17	2005	Natascha Badmann, Switzerland	9:09:30
Normann Stadler, Germany	8:11:56	2006	Michellie Jones, Australia	9:18:31
Chris McCormack, Australia	8:15:34	2007	Chrissie Wellington, UK	9:08:45
Craig Alexander, Australia	8:17:45	2008	Chrissie Wellington, UK	9:06:23
Craig Alexander, Australia	8:20:21	2009	Chrissie Wellington, UK	8:54:02
Chris McCormack, Australia	8:10:37	2010	Mirinda Carfrae, Australia	8:58:36
Craig Alexander, Australia	8:03:56*	2011	Chrissie Wellington, UK	8:55:08
Pete Jacobs, Australia	8:18:37	2012	Leanda Cave, U.S.	9:15:54
Frederik Van Lierde, Belgium	8:12:29	2013	Mirinda Carfrae, Australia	8:52:14*
Sebastian Kienle, Germany	8:14:18	2014	Mirinda Carfrae, Australia	9:00:55

(1) First-place finisher Nina Kraft, Germany, admitted to using performance-enhancing drugs and was disqualified, Nov. 15, 2004.

James E. Sullivan Award Winners, 1930-2013

The James E. Sullivan Award, named after the former president of the Amateur Athletic Union (AAU), is given annually by the AAU to the American athlete who "by his or her performance, example, and influence as an amateur, has done the most during the year to advance the cause of sportsmanship."

Year Winner	Sport	Year Winner	Sport	Year Winner	Sport
1930 Bobby Jones	Golf	1962 James Beatty	Track	1992 Bonnie Blair	Speed skating
1931 Barney Berlinger	Track	1963 John Pennel	Track	1993 Charlie Ward	Football, basketball
1932 Jim Bausch	Track	1964 Don Schollander	Swimming	1994 Dan Jansen	Speed skating
1933 Glenn Cunningham	Track	1965 Bill Bradley	Basketball	1995 Bruce Baumgartner	Wrestling
1934 Bill Bonthron	Track	1966 Jim Ryun	Track	1996 Michael Johnson	Track
1935 Lawson Little	Golf	1967 Randy Matson	Track	1997 Peyton Manning	Football
1936 Glenn Morris	Track	1968 Debbie Meyer	Swimming	1998 Chamique Holdsclaw	Basketball
1937 Don Budge	Tennis	1969 Bill Toomey	Track	1999 Coco Miller & Kelly Miller	Basketball
1938 Don Lash	Track	1970 John Kinsella	Swimming	2000 Rulon Gardner	Wrestling
1939 Joe Burk	Rowing	1971 Mark Spitz	Swimming	2001 Michelle Kwan	Figure skating
1940 Greg Rice	Track	1972 Frank Shorter	Track	2002 Sarah Hughes	Figure skating
1941 Leslie MacMitchell	Track	1973 Bill Walton	Basketball	2003 Michael Phelps	Swimming
1942 Cornelius Warmerdam	Track	1974 Rick Wohlhutter	Track	2004 Paul Hamm	Gymnastics
1943 Gilbert Dodds	Track	1975 Tim Shaw	Swimming	2005 J. J. Redick	Basketball
1944 Ann Curtis	Swimming	1976 Bruce Jenner	Track	2006 Jessica Long	Swimming (paralympics)
1945 Doc Blanchard	Football	1977 John Naber	Swimming	2007 Tim Tebow	Football
1946 Arnold Tucker	Football	1978 Tracy Caulkins	Swimming	2008 Shawn Johnson	Gymnastics
1947 John Kelly Jr.	Rowing	1979 Kurt Thomas	Gymnastics	2009 Amy Palmiero-Winters	Ultra-marathon
1948 Robert Mathias	Track	1980 Eric Heiden	Speed skating	2010 Evan Lysacek	Figure skating
1949 Dick Button	Skating	1981 Carl Lewis	Track	2011 Andrew Rodriguez	Football
1950 Fred Wilt	Track	1982 Mary Decker	Track	2012 Missy Franklin	Swimming
1951 Rev. Robert Richards	Track	1983 Edwin Moses	Track	2013 John Urschel	Football
1952 Horace Ashenfelter	Track	1984 Greg Louganis	Diving		
1953 Dr. Sammy Lee	Diving	1985 Joan Benoit Samuelson	Marathon		
1954 Mal Whitfield	Track	1986 Jackie Joyner-Kersee	Track		
1955 Harrison Dillard	Track	1987 Jim Abbott	Baseball		
1956 Patricia McCormick	Diving	1988 Florence Griffith Joyner	Track		
1957 Bobby Joe Morrow	Track	1989 Janet Evans	Swimming		
1958 Glenn Davis	Track	1990 John Smith	Wrestling		
1959 Parry O'Brien	Track	1991 Mike Powell	Track		
1960 Rafer Johnson	Track				
1961 Wilma Rudolph Ward	Track				

America's Cup Yacht Race, 1851-2013

Competition for the America's Cup grew out of a yachting race during the London Exposition of 1851. The race covered an approximately 60-mi course around the Isle of Wight. The prize was a cup donated by the Royal Yacht Squadron of England. It became known as the America's Cup after the New York Yacht Club won the race with the ship *America*. Prior to 1983, all yachts are American unless otherwise noted.

Year	Result	Year	Result
1851	America	1962	Weatherly defeated Gretel, Australia (4-1)
1870	Magic defeated Cambria, England (1-0)	1964	Constellation defeated Sovereign, England (4-0)
1871	Columbia (first three races) and Sappho (last two races) defeated Livonia, England (4-1)	1967	Intrepid defeated Dame Pattie, Australia (4-0)
1876	Madeline defeated Countess of Dufferin, Canada (2-0)	1970	Intrepid defeated Gretel II, Australia (4-1)
1881	Mischief defeated Atalanta, Canada (2-0)	1974	Courageous defeated Southern Cross, Australia (4-0)
1885	Puritan defeated Genesta, England (2-0)	1977	Courageous defeated Australia, Australia (4-0)
1886	Mayflower defeated Galatea, England (2-0)	1980	Freedom defeated Australia, Australia (4-1)
1887	Volunteer defeated Thistle, Scotland (2-0)	1983	Australia II, Australia, defeated Liberty, U.S. (4-3)
1893	Vigilant defeated Valkyrie II, England (3-0)	1987	Stars & Stripes, U.S., defeated Kookaburra III, Aust. (4-0)
1895	Defender defeated Valkyrie III, England (3-0)	1988	Stars & Stripes, U.S., defeated New Zealand, NZ (2-0)
1899	Columbia defeated Shamrock, England (3-0)	1992	America[3], U.S., defeated Il Moro di Venezia, Italy (4-1)
1901	Columbia defeated Shamrock II, England (3-0)	1995	Black Magic 1, NZ, defeated Young America, U.S. (5-0)
1903	Reliance defeated Shamrock III, England (3-0)	2000	New Zealand, NZ, defeated Luna Rossa, Italy (5-0)
1920	Resolute defeated Shamrock IV, England (3-2)	2003	Alinghi, Switzerland, defeated Team New Zealand, NZ (5-0)
1930	Enterprise defeated Shamrock V, England (4-0)	2007	Alinghi, Switzerland, defeated Emirates Team New Zealand, NZ (5-2)
1934	Rainbow defeated Endeavour, England (4-2)		
1937	Ranger defeated Endeavour II, England (4-0)	2010	USA-17, U.S., defeated Alinghi 5, Switzerland (2-0)
1958	Columbia defeated Sceptre, England (4-0)	2013	Oracle, U.S., defeated Emirates Team New Zealand, NZ (9-8)

Rifle and Pistol Championships, 2014

Source: National Rifle Association (NRA)

NRA Bianchi Cup National Action Pistol Championship

Action Pistol: Kevin Angstadt, Rural Retreat, VA, 1920-17183X

Woman Action Pistol: Jessie Duff, Horn Lake, MS, 1893-135X

Junior Action Pistol: Louis Surgi, Web City, MO, 1838-111X

National Outdoor Rifle and Pistol Championships

Pistol: SSG Patrick W. Franks, USA, Phenix City, AL, 2649-147X

Civilian Pistol: John S. Zurek, Tucson, AZ, 2639-117X

Woman Pistol: Brenda Silva, Snowflake, AZ, 2567-82X

Smallbore Rifle Prone: Kevin Nevius, Gibsonburg, OH, 4799

Civilian Smallbore Rifle Prone: Morgan Dietrich, Oliva, MN, 4794

Woman Smallbore Rifle Prone: Michelle Bohren, Taylor, MI, 4792

Smallbore Rifle Metric Position: Dan P. Lowe, Ft. Benning, GA, 2300

Woman Smallbore Rifle Metric Position: Sarah Beard, Danville, IN, 2277

High Power Rifle: Joseph W. Hendricks, Wexford, PA, 1789-76X

Civilian High Power Rifle: Joseph W. Hendricks, Wexford, PA, 1789-76X

Woman High Power Rifle: MSG Julia L. Carlson, USMC Res., Provo, UT, 1773-84X

High Power Rifle Long Range: Michelle M. Gallagher, Phoenix, AZ, 1096-66X

Woman High Power Rifle Long Range: Michelle M. Gallagher, Phoenix, AZ, 1096-66X

National Indoor Rifle and Pistol Championships

Smallbore Rifle Conventional Position: Lisette Grunwell-Lacey, Old Lyme, CT, 798-77X

Woman Smallbore Rifle Conventional Position: Molly Hensley, Kennerdall, PA, 792-49X

Smallbore Rifle NRA Metric Position: Alec Patajo, Puyallup, WA, 1156

Woman Smallbore Rifle NRA Metric Position: Lisette Grunwell-Lacey, Old Lyme, CT, 1152

International Smallbore Rifle: Hanna Carr, Versailles, KY, 1155

Woman International Smallbore Rifle: Abi Winegarden, Pittsboro, NC, 1127

Air Rifle: Michael Steinel, Lowell, OH, 589

Woman Air Rifle: Ethel Alves, New Castle, DE, 584

Conventional Pistol: John Zurek, Tucson, AZ, 893-43X

Woman Conventional Pistol: Brenda Martin Silva, Snowflake, AZ, 876-36X

International Free Pistol: James Henderson, Midland, GA, 563

Woman International Free Pistol: Helen Oh, Walnut, CA, 506

International Standard Pistol: Greg Markowski, Columbus, GA, 574

Woman International Standard Pistol: Kathy Chatterton, Glen Rock, NJ, 540

Air Pistol: Will Brown, Twin Falls, ID, 588

Woman Air Pistol: Alana Townsend, Kalispell, MT, 558

Pro Rodeo Cowboys Association All-Around Champions, 1977-2013

Year	Winner, hometown	Earnings	Year	Winner, hometown	Earnings
1977	Tom Ferguson, Miami, OK	$76,730	1996	Joe Beaver, Huntsville, TX	$166,103
1978	Tom Ferguson, Miami, OK	103,734	1997	Dan Mortensen, Manhattan, MT	184,559
1979	Tom Ferguson, Miami, OK	96,272	1998	Ty Murray, Stephenville, TX	264,673
1980	Paul Tierney, Rapid City, SD	105,568	1999	Fred Whitfield, Hockley, TX	217,819
1981	Jimmie Cooper, Monument, NM	105,862	2000	Joe Beaver, Huntsville, TX	225,396
1982	Chris Lybbert, Coyote, CA	123,709	2001	Cody Ohl, Stephensville, TX	296,419
1983	Roy Cooper, Durant, OK	153,391	2002	Trevor Brazile, Anson, TX	273,997
1984	Dee Pickett, Caldwell, ID	122,618	2003	Trevor Brazile, Anson, TX	294,839
1985	Lewis Feild, Elk Ridge, UT	130,347	2004	Trevor Brazile, Decatur, TX	253,170
1986	Lewis Feild, Elk Ridge, UT	166,042	2005	Ryan Jarrett, Summerville, GA	263,665
1987	Lewis Feild, Elk Ridge, UT	144,335	2006	Trevor Brazile, Decatur, TX	329,924
1988	Dave Appleton, Arlington, TX	121,546	2007	Trevor Brazile, Decatur, TX	425,115
1989	Ty Murray, Odessa, TX	134,806	2008	Trevor Brazile, Decatur, TX	419,868
1990	Ty Murray, Stephenville, TX	213,772	2009	Trevor Brazile, Decatur, TX	346,779
1991	Ty Murray, Stephenville, TX	244,230	2010	Trevor Brazile, Decatur, TX	507,921
1992	Ty Murray, Stephenville, TX	225,992	2011	Trevor Brazile, Decatur, TX	337,601
1993	Ty Murray, Stephenville, TX	297,896	2012	Trevor Brazile, Decatur, TX	298,626
1994	Ty Murray, Stephenville, TX	246,170	2013	Trevor Brazile, Decatur, TX	426,010
1995	Joe Beaver, Huntsville, TX	141,753			

GENERAL INDEX

Note: Page numbers in boldface indicate key reference. Page numbers in italics indicate photo or illustration captions.

QUICK REFERENCE INDEX

For complete index, see pages 979-1007.